ICFA Continuing Education
Deregulation of the Electric Utility Industry

Proceedings of the AIMR seminar *Deregulation of the Electric Utility Industry*

January 28, 1997
New York, New York

Leonard S. Hyman, CFA, *Moderator*
Kit Konolige, CFA
Ellen Lapson, CFA
Terran A. Miller, CFA

Philip R. O'Connor
Michael Sayers
William I. Tilles

To obtain the *AIMR Publications Catalog*, contact:
AIMR, P.O. Box 3668, Charlottesville, Virginia 22903, U.S.A.
Phone 804-980-3668; Fax 804-980-9755; E-mail info@aimr.org
or
visit AIMR's World Wide Web site at **www.aimr.org**
to view the AIMR publications list.

©1997, Association for Investment Management and Research

All rights reserved. No part of this publication may be reproduced, stored in a retrieval system, or transmitted, in any form or by any means, electronic, mechanical, photocopying, recording, or otherwise, without prior written permission of the copyright holder.

ICFA Continuing Education is published monthly seven times a year in March, April, May, May, July, September, and November by the Association for Investment Management and Research, P.O. Box 3668, Charlottesville, Virginia 22903, U.S.A. This publication is designed to provide accurate and authoritative information with regard to the subject matter covered. It is sold with the understanding that the publisher is not engaged in rendering legal, accounting, or other professional services. If legal advice or other expert assistance is required, the services of a competent professional should be sought. Periodicals postage paid at the post office in Richmond, Virginia, and additional mailing offices.

Copies are mailed as a benefit of membership to CFA® charterholders. Subscriptions also are available at US$100 for one year. Address all circulation communications to ICFA Continuing Education, P.O. Box 3668, Charlottesville, Virginia 22903, U.S.A.; Phone 804-980-3668; Fax 804-980-9755. For change of address, send mailing label and new address six weeks in advance.

Postmaster: Send address changes to the Association for Investment Management and Research, P.O. Box 3668, Charlottesville, Virginia 22903.

ISBN 1-879087-85-5
Printed in the United States of America
July 1997

Editorial Staff

Terence E. Burns, CFA
Vice President

Maryann Dupes
Editor

Jaynee M. Dudley
Production Manager

Roger Mitchell
Assistant Editor

Diane B. Hamshar
Typesetting/Layout

Contents

Foreword v
    Katrina F. Sherrerd, CFA

Biographies of Speakers vi

Deregulation of the Electric Utility Industry: An Overview 1

U.S. Electric Industry: Understanding the Basics 5
    Ellen Lapson, CFA

Deregulation and Its Repercussions 15
    Philip R. O'Connor

Electric Utilities M&A: What, Why, and How 24
    Kit Konolige, CFA

Interpreting Electric Utilities' Numbers and Equity Valuation 33
    William I. Tilles

Implications of Industry Restructuring on the Valuation of Debt Securities 41
    Terran A. Miller, CFA

Analyzing Non-U.S.-Based Electric Utilities 53
    Michael Sayers

Fearless Forecast: Electric Utilities in 2007 63
    Leonard S. Hyman, CFA

Self-Evaluation Examination
    Questions 71
    Answers 73

Selected Publications 75

ICFA Board of Trustees, 1996–97

Frank K. Reilly, CFA, *Chair*
Notre Dame, Indiana

Fred H. Speece, Jr., CFA, *Vice Chair*
Minneapolis, Minnesota

I. Rossa O'Reilly, CFA, *AIMR Chair*
Toronto, Ontario, Canada

Abby Joseph Cohen, CFA, *AIMR Vice Chair*
New York, New York

Thomas A. Bowman, CFA, *AIMR President and CEO*
Charlottesville, Virginia

Edmund D. Kellogg, CFA
Boston, Massachusetts

George W. Long, CFA
Hong Kong

Thomas P. Moore, Jr., CFA
Boston, Massachusetts

George W. Noyes, CFA*
Boston, Massachusetts

Lee N. Price, CFA
San Francisco, California

Philippe A. Sarasin, CFA
Geneva, Switzerland

Brian F. Wruble, CFA
New York, New York

ex officio

AIMR Education Committee, 1996–97

Frank K. Reilly, CFA, *Chair*
Notre Dame, Indiana

Fred H. Speece, Jr., CFA, *Vice Chair*
Minneapolis, Minnesota

Terry L. Arndt, CFA
Mount Pleasant, Michigan

Thomas A. Bowman, CFA
Charlottesville, Virginia

Keith C. Brown, CFA
Austin, Texas

Abby Joseph Cohen, CFA
New York, New York

Scott L. Lummer, CFA
Chicago, Illinois

Charles F. O'Connell, CFA
Chicago, Illinois

I. Rossa O'Reilly, CFA
Toronto, Ontario, Canada

Katrina F. Sherrerd, CFA
Charlottesville, Virginia

J. Clay Singleton, CFA
Charlottesville, Virginia

R. Charles Tschampion, CFA
New York, New York

AIMR Senior Education Staff

Thomas A. Bowman, CFA
President and CEO

Katrina F. Sherrerd, CFA
Senior Vice President

J. Clay Singleton, CFA
Senior Vice President

Terence E. Burns, CFA
Vice President

Julia S. Hammond, CFA
Vice President

Robert R. Johnson, CFA
Vice President

Robert M. Luck, Jr., CFA
Vice President

Aaron L. Shackelford, CFA
Vice President

Donald L. Tuttle, CFA
Vice President

Barbara L. Higgins
Director

Paul W. Turner
Director

Foreword

We have seen it happen to the airline industry, we have seen it happen to the telephone industry, and now we are seeing it happen to the electric utilities industry. Deregulation is again changing the way investors, analysts, and consumers will operate in the future. As a result of the restructuring of the industry, investors will have to rethink their debt and equity positions in electric utilities. Electric companies will no longer be the steady dividend-producing companies that they were, but for those investors who are looking for companies with good cash-flow positions, many electric utilities will fit the bill. As the traditional electric company disaggregates its generation, transmission, and distribution functions, analysts will have to come up with new tools for analyzing these companies. Even the terminology that analysts have used for years will have to change; for example, the focus will no longer be on cents per kilowatt hour but on dollars per megawatt hour. And finally, consumers will be free to choose who produces their electricity, although not who transmits and distributes it.

Providing consumers with choice is the focal point of restructuring the electric utility industry. Regulations on the state and federal levels are moving the electric utilities in that direction. And the electric companies are positioning themselves for this inevitability by reconsidering their business strategies: to merge or not to merge, to divest generating assets or not to divest, to close unprofitable nuclear plants or not to close. As a consequence of this goal to provide choice, the electric industry is changing at a remarkable pace, bringing numerous challenges. The authors of this proceedings draw on their expertise as industry participants to explain the challenges that lie ahead. With their skillful explanations, they cover the industry from a discussion of the industry basics through security and industry analysis to a projection of the industry in the future.

Special thanks go to Leonard S. Hyman, CFA, Smith Barney, for serving as both moderator and speaker at this seminar. We also wish to thank the seminar's speakers for their valuable participation: Kit Konolige, CFA, Morgan Stanley & Co., Inc.; Ellen Lapson, CFA, Fitch Investors Service; Terran A. Miller, CFA, Donaldson, Lufkin & Jenrette; Philip R. O'Connor, Coopers and Lybrand Consulting; Michael Sayers, Morgan Stanley International; and William I. Tilles, Smith Barney.

What started with a key and a kite has become a firmly established multibillion dollar industry. But with deregulation that firm foundation is shifting. We hope this proceedings provides you with the background, explanations, and forecasts that you need to participate in the industry yourself, whether as an investor, analyst, or consumer.

Katrina F. Sherrerd, CFA
Senior Vice President
Educational Products

Biographies of Speakers

Leonard S. Hyman, CFA, serves as senior industry advisor to Smith Barney. Previously, he was managing director of Fulcrum International, a consultant in the economics and finances of energy and telecommunication utilities, head of the Utility Research Group, and first vice president at Merrill Lynch. Mr. Hyman has also served on advisory panels for the Congressional Office of Technology Assessment and the National Science Foundation. He serves on the advisory boards for the Electric Power Research Institute and EXNET and on the editorial board of the *Forum for Applied Research and Public Policy*. Mr. Hyman is the author of *America's Electric Utilities* and numerous articles, co-author of *The New Telecommunications Industry*, and editor of *The Privatization of Public Utilities*. He holds a B.A. from New York University and an M.A. in economics from Cornell University.

Kit Konolige, CFA, is a principal at Morgan Stanley & Company and the firm's equity research analyst for electric utilities. Prior to joining Morgan Stanley, he performed a similar role at CS First Boston. Mr. Konolige is the author of two books and numerous magazine articles. He holds an undergraduate degree in English and history from Haverford College and an M.B.A. from the Wharton School of the University of Pennsylvania.

Ellen Lapson, CFA, is senior director of Fitch Investors Service's global power group and the manager of credit ratings for investor-owned electric utilities and energy markets. She also participates in rating project finance transactions, structured finance based on utility tariffs or contracts, and international utility privatizations and energy projects. Prior to joining Fitch, Ms. Lapson was an officer of Chemical Securities Inc. and Chemical Bank and also served as an equity analyst for the electric, gas, and telephone industries at Argus Research Corporation. Ms. Lapson holds a B.A. from Barnard College and an M.B.A. from New York University.

Terran A. Miller, CFA, is vice president and senior utility analyst focusing on high-grade and high-yield electric utilities and independent power producers for Donaldson, Lufkin & Jenrette, where he also oversees the firm's research in the telecommunications and cable areas. Prior to joining DLJ, Mr. Miller spent four years in utility research at Merrill Lynch and six years in bond analysis at Drexel Burnham Lambert. He holds a B.S.B.A. in business administration from Georgetown University.

Philip R. O'Connor is a principal of Coopers & Lybrand Consulting/Palmer Bellevue, the national utility strategic consulting group of Coopers & Lybrand L.L.P. Prior to forming Palmer Bellevue in 1985, he served as chief utility regulator of Illinois, the chair of the Illinois Commerce Commission, director of the Illinois Department of Insurance, deputy director of the Illinois Insurance Department, and administrative assistant to Congressman George Miller (D, CA) and former Illinois Governor Richard B. Ogilvie. Mr. O'Connor is a graduate of Loyola University in Chicago and holds master's and doctoral degrees in political science from Northwestern University.

Michael Sayers is a vice president with Morgan Stanley International, where he is responsible for research coverage of the European utilities sector. He was previously the European utilities analyst for Salomon Brothers. He holds a B.A. in industrial economics from the University of Nottingham.

William I. Tilles is vice president and senior electric utilities analyst at Smith Barney. Before joining Smith Barney, he was associated with Dean Witter Reynolds, Standard & Poor's Corporation, and Regulatory Research Associates. Mr. Tilles has also lectured in political science at the University of Notre Dame. He holds a B.A. in political science from Queens College (CUNY) and a master's degree in political science from the University of Chicago.

Deregulation of the Electric Utility Industry: An Overview

The electric utility industry has historically been viewed as a highly mature and heavily regulated natural monopoly. With more than $200 billion in annual revenues and about $585 billion in assets, it is the biggest industry ever to be deregulated. The consensus growing among U.S. state and federal regulators and industry participants is that the industry needs to be deregulated. In many parts of the world, electric utilities have already been deregulated or are closer than the United States is to achieving deregulation. In the United States, several states are in the process of phasing in deregulation, and at the federal level, several bills pending in Congress would further deregulate the industry.

Investing in the electric utility industry has been viewed as a safe haven—a place to invest in stable companies providing secure, although slow-growing, dividends. As the industry is moving from a market with completely administered prices to a competitive open market for electric power generation, the industry is experiencing a major restructuring and can no longer be described as a safe haven—it is an industry with increased risk and return opportunities.

Everything about the electric utility industry is undergoing a transformation. The basics of this industry are no longer valid, which means new analytical tools are needed to understand and to analyze electric utilities. Deregulation is redefining the environment in which the industry operates and creating new challenges for industry participants. Industry restructuring is affecting the valuation of electric utility securities, making investing in these securities more challenging today than ever before. Dividends are no longer secure, which is creating a rotation in the shareholder base. Average credit ratings are trending downward because of increasing business and event risks, and this downward trend is requiring more-active management of electric utility bond investments. Internationalization is creating additional opportunities for investors interested in non-U.S.-based electric utilities. And finally, restructuring is transforming the industry from traditional electric companies, with a "rate payer" mindset, to integrated energy companies, with a customer service focus.

This proceedings is the product of an AIMR seminar intended to give participants an understanding of this exciting, evolving industry. The authors draw on their extensive experiences as industry participants to provide an overview of the *new* basics of this evolving industry, an evaluation of the rampant merger and acquisition activity, an analysis of how industry restructuring affects the valuation of electric utility securities, an assessment of non-U.S.-based electric utility opportunities, and finally, a forecast of where the industry will be in 2007.

INDUSTRY BASICS

Having a firm grasp of the industry basics is critical in analyzing how deregulation, mergers and acquisitions, and competition affect the outlook for electric utility companies. Ellen Lapson discusses the current status of the industry, the various industry participants and their roles, the major characteristics that affect market participants, the regulatory framework in which the industry currently operates, and the long-term outlook for the industry.

Because of the changing structure of the industry, analysts, investors, and portfolio managers must anticipate change to survive the challenges facing the industry and to profit from the myriad of opportunities. Industry participants include investor-owned electric utilities (IOUs), governmental entities, cooperatives, power marketers, and independent power producers (IPPs). IOUs are regulated by the Federal Energy Regulatory Commission, the Securities and Exchange Commission, the Nuclear Regulatory Commission, and by state legislatures. Over the next 5–10 years, the number of IOUs will decline as a result of merger and acquisition activity, wholesale and retail power marketers will experience rapid growth, IPPs will be combined into large consolidated power-generation companies, and new categories of participants will emerge, such as independent system operators.

The important characteristics of this industry include wholesale and retail distribution; cost-of-service pricing, which will be replaced by commodity market pricing; a fuel mix dominated by coal and nuclear energy but affected by gas at the margin; and volatile spot prices. Although generation currently dominates the financial statements of electric utilities, asset and revenue concentration will change as managers determine the new strategic directions of their companies.

With so much change occurring in this industry, it is a time for investors and analysts to develop new analytical tools and a different set of skills from those demanded in the past—it is a time for all participants to learn.

DEREGULATION AND ITS REPERCUSSIONS

Electric utilities can learn valuable lessons from other industries that have already experienced deregulation. Philip O'Connor explains that, even though complete deregulation never occurs, competition certainly develops. Various forces can drive deregulation, but the key drivers for deregulation in the electric utility industry are surplus capacity, new low-cost generation technology, and customers—not rate payers—who want choice. Thus, electric utilities must learn from the experiences of other deregulated industries how surplus prices and new technology quickly drive prices to marginal costs, how important understanding customer satisfaction is in a competitive environment, and how crucial financial depth is in a transitional business.

Successful electric utilities will understand how the industry environment has changed and adapt their policies and strategies to successfully compete in the *new electric paradigm*. Potential strategies include disaggregating and separately managing the generation, transmission, and distribution functions; divesting one or more business segments in which the utility lacks a distinct competence; or merging with a neighboring utility to survive. Successful electric utilities will realize that *today's* public policy debates—recovery methods for stranded costs, retail access, and the repeal of anachronistic laws—are *yesterday's* issues and focus on proactive solutions to *tomorrow's* challenges—creating growth strategies, achieving better asset utilization, and assuring power quality and reliability for the electronic age. The stranded-cost problem, estimated to be in the range of $70–135 billion, provokes debate as to whether this problem is the result of poor business decisions or is grounded in the context of explicit federal and state policies. Regardless of who is to blame, successful companies will realize that full recovery of stranded costs may not be possible and recognize these costs as a price for a smooth transition to a competitive market. Finally, the biggest challenge facing electric utilities will be understanding customer satisfaction in a competitive market and adopting a corporate culture that fosters this understanding within the new *electricom* company—an integrated energy company with a customer service focus.

MERGERS AND ACQUISITIONS

In anticipation of deregulation, many managers of U.S. electric utilities view mergers and acquisitions as a strategy to prepare for competition. Kit Konolige explains that M&A activity can best be understood by asking what is happening, why is it happening, and how should it be analyzed? He believes that the present and future implications of this M&A activity affect investors and industry participants alike.

M&A strategies can be divided into two categories: a defensive approach, which is a strategic alliance of neighboring utilities formed to cut costs, and an offensive approach, in which the overall idea is for large local companies to become national companies. The offensive approach includes *electric/gas mergers*, a strategy that reflects the industry's desire to be an integrated energy industry; *geographical mergers*, a strategy designed to establish a national presence; *acquisitions of generation assets*, a strategy based on the idea that integrated energy companies of the future will need assets in different regions; and *international mergers*, a strategy based on growth and geographical extension.

Electric utilities pursue M&A strategies to spread costs over a larger service area, to realize higher growth prospects, and to reallocate capital to better risk–reward opportunities in order to position themselves as deregulation progresses. These strategies would not be achievable if excess cash flows were not available. In order to analyze M&A deals, investors must ask tough questions. Does the merger enhance scale, strength, and skill? Are the risk–reward trade-offs appropriate? Does it earn at least 10 percent, taking into consideration the cost of carry? Is it appropriately priced? Are the managers, and the strategic direction in which they are moving the company, trustworthy? A major issue for investors is whether they trust management to navigate the upcoming minefield on the way to deregulation.

The implications of M&A activity for investors and electric utility managers include potential dilution for utilities with low earnings multiples, pressure to reduce dividends, and cost of carry—a merger can take up to two years to complete—which can completely offset the average 25 percent premium of an electric/electric merger.

SECURITY ANALYSIS AND VALUATION

Industry restructuring provides significant near-term opportunities for equity investors but requires careful consideration of the positives and negatives of alternative investments. William Tilles discusses how an abundance of free cash flow, which can be used to repurchase stock, retire outstanding debt, or diversify into other business ventures, underscores the important role of managers and the strategic direction in which they take their electric companies. A solid free cash flow position and a positive valuation implication, at least for the generation and distribution segments, are tempered by the quickening pace of industry change and the increasing business risk of the power-generation segment.

The disaggregation of electric utilities into a non-regulated power-generation business segment, a regulated transmission and distribution business, and a lightly regulated energy services business will have important valuation implications for investors. The power-generation business will become a commodity business with substantial business risk and volatile earnings—guaranteed returns on capital will be a thing of the past. Transmission and distribution assets are likely to remain more or less rate-of-return regulated with relatively low business risk and stable earnings.

Equity valuation must also deal with the risks of recovering stranded costs and the problem of nuclear power plant ownership. Investors can analyze potential investments in a variety of ways, including dividend yield, total return, relative yield, yield spread, and special high-risk, superior-return opportunities.

Recognizing that investing in debt securities of electric utilities is more challenging today than ever before, Terran Miller explains that investors must have more than just a good understanding of the standard factors that go into valuing debt securities, and he notes that the changing landscape of the electric utility industry requires more-active management of electric utility bonds. Held-for-trading strategies are replacing buy-and-hold strategies, as total return players seek to enhance performance. Security structures are becoming more complex, requiring thorough analysis of bonds with embedded options, asset-backed securities, and bond covenants. Investors with minimum credit rating requirements face an absence of supply because A-rated and AA-rated electric utilities are not issuing much new paper and are repurchasing outstanding debt with available free cash flow. Security modifiers now include "credit watch" or "outlook change," and bond yields can change significantly on an outlook change.

Industry restructuring has created new event risks—M&A activity, disaggregation, and changes in company structure—that can significantly affect the credit ratings and valuation of electric utility bonds. As the homogeneity of the industry breaks down, the business risk profiles of integrated energy companies will be vastly different from utilities that focus on a specific business segment, thus requiring the creation of peer groups with similar business risk profiles. The risks affect sector attractiveness, credit spreads, and the supply of electric utility bonds.

NON-U.S.-BASED ELECTRIC UTILITIES

Deregulation of electric utilities is not isolated to the United States. Michael Sayers provides an analysis of the United Kingdom's experience with liberalization, examines the developments in the rest of Europe, and takes a look at Spain, a country that is addressing many of the challenges associated with moving from a regulated industry to a competitive market.

Competition in the United Kingdom substantially reduced market share for the two dominant generators and forced them to improve generation plant efficiency and drastically reduce costs, which was accomplished in a variety of ways—closing older, less efficient plants; investing in gas-fired stations, reducing headcount by about 70 percent; and renegotiating high-cost coal contracts. The primary motivation for competition among European electric utilities comes from the wide range of prices for industrial power. Liberalization of electric utilities in Europe has forced firms to shift their focus from security of supply under the traditional monopoly structure to a focus on security of demand in an open and competitive market. Spain has realized that competition will be a benefit, but it may be a long-term benefit.

Investors seeking to increase returns and diversify their portfolios may look to the non-U.S. electric utilities, many of which have better growth prospects than their U.S. counterparts. Investors analyzing non-U.S. electric utilities should focus on firms with cost-cutting potential, positive after-tax cash flow, fuel mix improvements, a coherent competitive strategy, and a focus on enhancing shareholder value.

ELECTRIC UTILITIES IN 2007

In 10 years, much of the deregulation and industry restructuring that is only now beginning is likely to be fully accomplished. The electric utility industry will look nothing like it does today. Leonard Hyman gives a historical perspective of what brought the industry to deregulation, where the industry stands now, and where the industry will be in 2007. Technological change forces electric utilities to address tough questions. What is the right financial policy for a competitive utility? How does the industry define the rules of operation and design the means of payment for system services that are required to keep the network system running? What regulatory techniques will produce the right incentives for investment and efficiency and also send correct price signals to consumers and network users?

The energy supply industry will emerge over the next 10 years as firms choose their strategic direction. Some firms will act as virtual utilities, some will be integrated energy companies, and some will provide only one function because of disaggregating the generation, transmission, and distribution functions along the road to deregulation. Firms will separate the regulated from the unregulated aspects of their business and develop appropriate financial policies out of necessity. Ownership patterns will shift, and the industry will become internationalized. As a result of this incredible amount of change, picking the winners in 2007 will be quite a challenge.

CONCLUSION

In almost 100 years, this industry will have gone from the discovery of the electron through the evolution of the energy supply industry. Constant technological change has been the key driver for deregulation and the movement toward a competitive market for electricity. This change will benefit consumers and force investors, analysts, and portfolio managers to develop new analytical tools to analyze this industry. In this proceedings, the authors' experience, intellect, and foresight help us understand a rapidly changing industry and benefit from the fundamental analysis of the new energy supply industry.

U.S. Electric Industry: Understanding the Basics

Ellen Lapson, CFA
Senior Director
Fitch Investors Service, L.P.

> The electric utility industry is experiencing exciting, challenging, and troubling times because of rapid industry restructuring. In this environment, industry participants must anticipate change to survive and profit. This is a time of rapid industry transformation, a time for electric utility managers to redeploy capital and shrink their balance sheets, and a time for investors and analysts to develop new analytical ratios and tools for a changing industry—a time for all participants to learn.

The U.S. electric industry is a highly mature industry that has perfected the transmission, generation, and distribution of electricity but is going through a profound transformation. During the transition, the industry will move from a market with completely administered prices to a competitive, open market for electric power generation, and the distribution and transmission of electricity will continue as a regulated utility function with administered prices.

During this transformational period from now through the year 2003 or 2005, analysts, investors, and portfolio managers must anticipate change—expect the unimaginable. Whatever people thought would never happen in this staid industry could happen, will happen, or may have already happened. New industry analysts will have an advantage over seasoned analysts in that they will not be burdened by preconceptions and the "old" way of looking at the industry.

In order to understand the basics of U.S. electric utilities, one needs to know the current status of this evolving industry, the various industry participants and their roles, the major characteristics that affect market participants (such as the different market segments, pricing methods, fuel mix, and production costs), the regulatory framework in which the industry operates, and the long-term industry outlook.

CURRENT STATUS OF THE INDUSTRY

The U.S. electricity market is more highly saturated than the markets in many other countries. **Figure 1** shows that U.S. electricity production per capita is among the highest in the world. Although per capita consumption of electricity in the United States is at the high end of the spectrum, Canada's per capita production is 42 percent higher than the United States's, and some of the Scandinavian countries have per capita production comparable to Canada's. These high numbers are typical of developed countries with significant exports and industrial use of low-cost hydroelectric production. European consumption is typically lower than that of the United States; the majority of the European nations have relatively high energy prices, use less air conditioning than the United States, and have smaller residences.

The highest growth rates in production and consumption of electricity are in less-developed countries, such as India, China, and Argentina, where annual growth rates in production and demand may exceed 10–12 percent; the lowest growth rates are in the most developed nations. But even in developed countries such as the United States, electricity consumption is still growing 1–2 percent a year, which is impressive for such a highly developed market. Elasticity of demand also affects growth in electricity consumption—low prices increase demand, high prices diminish demand growth.

INDUSTRY PARTICIPANTS

Participants in the U.S. electric industry include investor-owned electric utilities (IOUs), governmental entities, cooperatives, power marketers, and independent power producers (IPPs). The restructuring

Figure 1. Worldwide Electric Production per Capita, 1992

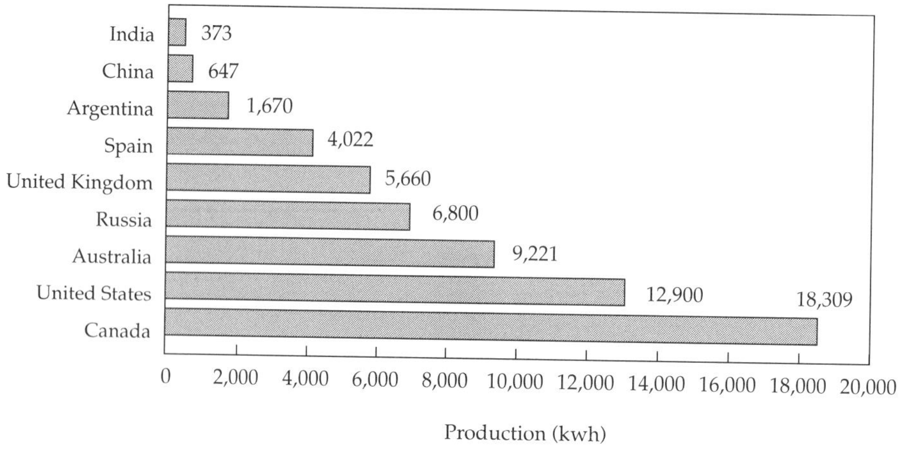

Country	Production (kwh)
India	373
China	647
Argentina	1,670
Spain	4,022
United Kingdom	5,660
Russia	6,800
Australia	9,221
United States	12,900
Canada	18,309

Source: Data from the World Bank.

of the industry will give rise to new categories of participants, such as independent system operators (ISOs).

■ *Investor-owned utilities.* IOUs are currently the largest sector of the electric market. Roughly 120–140 IOUs exist in the United States, accounting for about 80 percent of the U.S. market in production of electricity, revenue, and sales. They are represented in the securities markets as issuers of common and preferred stock as well as substantial amounts of public debt.

■ *Governmental entities.* These roughly 2,000 entities include municipal utilities and joint-action agencies (typically formed to provide generation or transmission to groups of municipals); federal power marketers, such as Bonneville Power Administration; and large federal agencies, such as the Tennessee Valley Authority. Municipals and joint-action agencies are usually represented in capital markets through tax-exempt debt financing. Governmental entities and cooperatives combined represent about 20 percent of U.S. electricity sales.

■ *Cooperatives.* These entities were formed to provide electricity distribution in less-developed parts of the United States; today, they serve a mixture of rural areas and some rapidly growing exurbs or suburbs. In the United States, about 1,000 small distribution cooperatives serve very small communities. These cooperatives are financed almost entirely by the Federal Finance Bank and the Cooperative Finance Corporation and do not have traded equities. Getting information about public ratings on their debt is difficult. Small distribution cooperatives have banded together to form large cooperatives called generation and transmission (G&T) cooperatives. The majority of their financing needs have been met by the Rural Utility Service, the Federal Finance Bank, the Bank for Cooperatives, and the Cooperative Finance Corporation. G&T co-ops have issued relatively small amounts of taxable debt in the public markets up to now, but the issuance of taxable public debt by G&T co-ops could become more prevalent in the future.

■ *Power marketers.* This is a relatively new type of entity that is experiencing rapid growth and change in the unregulated wholesale power market. Power marketers are licensed by the Federal Energy Regulatory Commission (FERC) to transact business in the wholesale electric market at market-based prices. FERC's regulatory supervision of power marketers does not include any role in price setting nor any supervision of power marketers' capital adequacy. They must prove that they do not control market power in the region in which they transact electric business. Currently, relatively little capital is invested in this segment of the market; power marketers are either subsidiaries of larger corporations or are privately owned, and so few or no securities are in the marketplace. Wholesale and retail marketers, however, are a likely growth area as the industry restructuring progresses.

■ *Independent power producers.* IPPs were formed to generate and sell electricity. In the past, they sold electricity to utilities under long-term contracts. In the future, they may evolve into competitors in open wholesale power markets. Over the next 5–10 years, many of these entities may become combined into large consolidated power-generation companies.

■ *Independent system operators* (ISOs). FERC has suggested that the formation of independent third-party operators, ISOs, to operate and control regional transmission networks will be an acceptable mechanism for assuring all generators open and nondiscriminatory access to the transmission system.

MARKET SHARE ANALYSIS

Interesting observations can be drawn from looking at **Table 1,** which provides sales and revenue comparisons for the different industry participants. Although IOU sales volume and revenues dominate the industry with 80 percent market share, IOUs have a higher average price per kilowatt hour than governmental entities and cooperatives. Some governmental entities are the beneficiaries of low-cost federally owned or licensed hydroelectric production. Municipal utilities and joint-action agencies are typically financed with tax-exempt debt and have no required return on equity, which lowers their overall cost of capital.

Table 1. U.S. Electric Industry Sales and Revenues, 1995

	IOUs	Governmental Entities and Co-Ops
Sales (millions of mwh)	2,340	654
Revenues ($billions)	$163.00	$44.00
Average price (cents per kwh)	7.14	6.60

Source: Data from Edison Electric Institute.

The integrated electric utility model presented in **Table 2** is prevalent for IOUs with integrated generation, distribution, and transmission of electricity. A single company traditionally generates electricity, transmits it over some distance, and distributes it through a distribution network to homes, businesses, and manufacturers. Today, generation dominates in these integrated utilities because generation is highly capital and fuel intensive. Generation predominates on the balance sheets, income statements, and cash flows of these utilities and demands the largest share of management attention. Generation currently represents about 59 percent of the book value of IOUs' assets and about 70 percent of the revenues. The difference between the asset concentration and the revenue concentration reflects the fuel intensity of the generation sector of the industry. The wire business, which refers to both the transmission and distribution of electricity, represents about 30 percent of revenues and about 40 percent of the book value of IOU assets.

Table 2. Integrated Electric Utility Model, 1995

	Assets	Revenues
Generation	59%	70%
Transmission	10	7
Distribution	30	23
Total	100	100

Note: Numbers may not total because of rounding error.
Source: Data from Resource Data International.

INDUSTRY CHARACTERISTICS

The different market segments for electricity (retail versus wholesale), current and future pricing methods, the fuel mix that helps to meet peak and off-peak loads, and changes in production costs—all have a significant impact on market participants.

Retail versus Wholesale

The most confusing words in the electric utility industry are "retail" and "wholesale." Retail refers to the sale of electricity to the ultimate users. Wholesale refers to sales for resale, for example, sales from one utility to another or sales from a generating company to a distribution utility. Large-scale industrial users of electricity believe they are wholesale users and should be able to get wholesale pricing and buy electricity in the competitive market, but under the Federal Power Act, they are considered retail users, or end users, of electricity.

Bypass occurs when an electric consumer can buy electricity directly from a competing generator, eluding the monopoly of the franchised utility. Most aggressive utility consumers, including industrial and large commercial customers, would like direct retail access—the ability to buy electricity directly from competitively priced producers in the market. Restructuring of the industry, which is taking place on a state-by-state basis—currently in such states as California, Pennsylvania, and Massachusetts—will give retail consumers of electricity the right to purchase electric power directly from competing power producers or marketers, but currently, the restructuring initiatives prohibit customers from bypassing the incumbent utility for distribution service.

Pricing Methods

In the United States, the current system for pricing electricity in the retail market is a cost-of-service approach—that is, cost plus return of capital and return on capital. Utilities that generate and distribute electricity are compensated for their production costs plus the return of capital used in the business, usually on a historical cost basis, and a return on capital.

Commodity market pricing, which is the opposite of cost-of-service pricing, is currently being used in the wholesale market for trading electricity among generators and power marketers. Variants on cost-of-service pricing include performance-based incentive pricing and cap-rate pricing; these pricing mechanisms provide additional incentives to utilities for operating efficiently.

Fuel Mix

Coal and nuclear dominate the base load for U.S. electricity generation, as shown by the breakdown of fuel sources in **Figure 2**. Nuclear and coal production combined represent about 80 percent of the production base-load capacity; gas is used to meet peak or seasonal loads. Although gas provides only 10 percent of the energy used for generating electricity, it is a driving factor affecting wholesale market prices, which are often determined by the marginal cost of gas production.

Figure 2. U.S. Electric Generation by Fuel Source

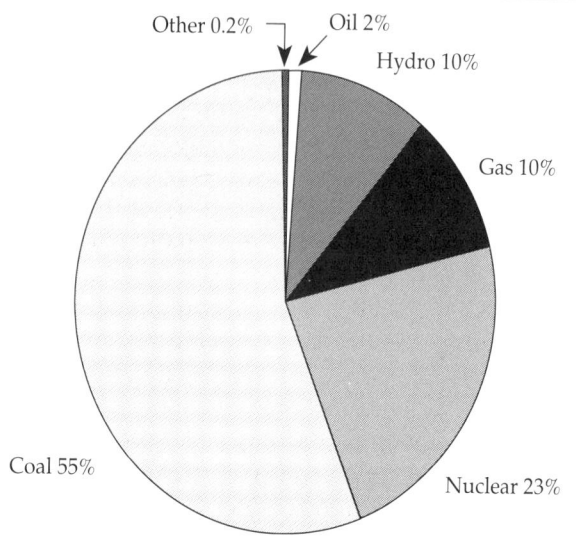

Note: Numbers do not total 100 because of rounding error.
Source: Data from Edison Electric Institute.

Production Costs

A comparison of production costs and spot electricity prices in the mid-Atlantic and western regions is provided in **Figure 3**. The bars represent the total embedded costs of production and generation and break out the fixed costs and variable costs, reflecting the last authorized return on equity for each IOU in the region. Because of regional weather and consumption patterns, one would expect slightly different cost structures in each region of the United States. Very cold weather in the mid-Atlantic region during the week shown in Figure 3 (January 21, 1997) increased spot prices, especially on-peak spot prices. For example, a utility in the mid-Atlantic region with embedded costs equal to 3.5 cents per kwh recovered only about 80 percent of its fixed costs on peak and only about 20 percent of its fixed costs off peak. Although market prices during that week exceeded variable costs in the mid-Atlantic region, they were lower than the cost that would have been recovered under traditional cost-of-service pricing. "Native load" customers, the ultimate customers in a utility's franchise territory, would have been paying rates incorporating a power price of about 3.5 cents per kwh under cost-of-service pricing. To the extent that utilities were selling any power in the wholesale market at competitive spot prices during that week, they were losing 0.7 cents per on-peak kwh and about 1.8 cents per off-peak kwh sold relative to their all-in cost, including fixed costs and the cost of capital.

In the western region in the same week, tremendous precipitation and flooding reduced demand slightly and increased hydroelectric production. During January, increased hydroelectric production decreased prices in the western power pool. Off-peak prices during this week were equal, on average, to variable costs of production; however, utilities in the West recovered no fixed costs for wholesale power sold at off-peak spot prices. Off-peak prices the following week fell so low that they were down to 0.6 to 0.8 cents per kwh, well below average variable costs of production but presumably higher than the variable cost of the marginal unit of production.

Volatility in spot prices resulting from competitive pricing and regional weather and consumption patterns is the real dilemma challenging electric utilities' embedded cost structure, including fixed costs such as the principal and interest on bonds, return on capital, and equity returns. Transition to a full market-pricing system prompts the questions: Are these wholesale market prices indicative of the future price curve for the electric power market? If all electricity is priced through a competitive market mechanism, will power prices throughout the market fall to this level?

Figure 3. Cost of Production Relative to Spot Market Prices for the Week Ending January 21, 1997

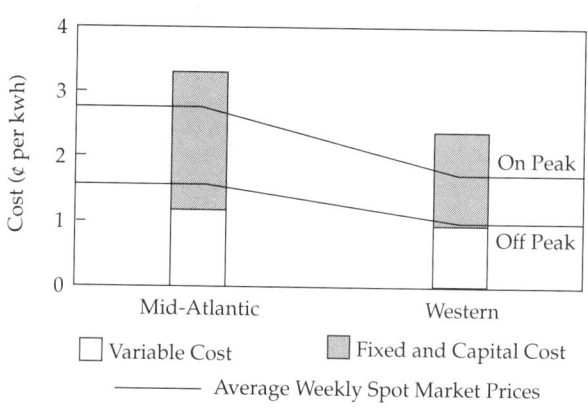

Note: Fixed costs include depreciation, interest expense, return on capital, and fixed operating and maintenance expenses. Variable costs include fuel, operations, and variable maintenance expenses.
Source: 1995 embedded-cost data from Resource Data International and market price data from Telerate.

If the answers are "yes," revenues from generation could decline by 50 percent or more, and net income from utility generation would drop by a far greater percentage.

REGULATORY FRAMEWORK

Investor-owned electric utilities are regulated at the federal level by the FERC, the Securities and Exchange Commission (SEC), the Nuclear Regulatory Commission (NRC), and state legislatures.

FERC plays an important role in the regulation of electric power through its jurisdiction over interstate transmission of electricity and interstate wholesale electricity sales. But FERC's role in regulating the electric utility industry is not as dominant as it is in the natural gas industry, which FERC single-handedly deregulated in the 1980s to create a competitive market environment and a transformed industry structure. Because electricity is often generated and transmitted within the same state, FERC's jurisdiction extends at most to the wholesale transmission of electricity and not to retail sales within a state.

In 1996, FERC enacted new rules (Order 888) mandating open access for transmission to comply with the legislative mandate of the Energy Policy Act of 1992. How can third-party users of the transmission network be assured of fair, open, nondiscriminatory access that does not favor the generation or the distribution of a company that also happens to own the transmission system? The mechanism FERC and many companies in the industry have currently settled on to resolve this problem is the formation of ISOs, along with unbundled transmission pricing and the elimination of exclusive regional power pools.

In addition to regulating the public issuance and trading of securities, the SEC administers the Public Utility Holding Company Act of 1935 (PUHCA), which governs the operations of any utility that qualifies as a public utility holding company. This act is of particular interest because of the impact it currently has on many merger and acquisition transactions. PUHCA is a considerable barrier to many types of mergers and corporate organizational structures within the industry. PUHCA has several unusual features. No other industry in the United States is subject to such heavy regulation of capital structure and ownership. First, the companies must have a simple capital structure, which eliminates the use of any unusual or creative forms of equity or debt structures. Second, their utility holdings must be contiguous and interconnected, so a company cannot own one electric utility in California and one in Massachusetts. Third, PUHCA mandates limits on equity investments in other industries. For example, if General Electric were to acquire a public utility, it would have to divest most of its other businesses in accordance with PUHCA requirements. These features significantly limit the freedom of electric companies to acquire other companies, be acquired by other companies, or to form holding companies. Regulation of holding companies by the SEC relates to the excesses committed in the pyramid schemes of the 1920s for the ownership of electric utilities, although no evidence indicates that these excesses would occur today if PUHCA were eliminated. At Fitch, we predict the industry will be transformed over the next two-to-five years and PUHCA will be repealed or eviscerated.

The NRC exercises a significant degree of authority over the operators of nuclear power plants. The NRC has placed some power plants on its watch list, which indicates a stringent review of nuclear safety issues and which can potentially affect utilities' operating expenses, credit ratings, and stock and bond prices. The NRC also has very broad powers that affect the operating licenses of nuclear plants and could, therefore, have a profound impact on those companies that own and operate nuclear facilities.

Finally, state legislatures have the ultimate authority over retail sales of electricity. Typically, the states delegate that authority to public utility commissions, to boards of municipal electric companies, or to independent boards of joint-action agencies. State legislatures are the definitive source of authority for most of the retail distribution of electricity. The transformation now occurring in the industry is primarily at the state level, and the time frame for a transformed electric utility industry in the United States will be determined by state legislatures.

Timeline for Transformation

Fitch's projected time line for industry transformation, as shown in **Figure 4,** begins with Congress passing the Energy Policy Act in 1992, which gave the FERC the responsibility to provide for open-access transmission of electricity. Prior to 1992, transmission networks were owned by electric utilities, which treated this function as a monopoly and sold the rights to send electricity over the transmission network. In 1996, based on the Energy Policy Act and additional mandates from Congress, the FERC enforced open-access transmission and ordered utilities to implement fair and transparent transmission pricing and policies so that any power producer could transmit electricity on a nondiscriminatory basis. These federal mandates did not automatically result in direct retail market access to electric transmission because control of retail markets can be regulated only on the state level.

Figure 4. Time Line for Industry Transformation

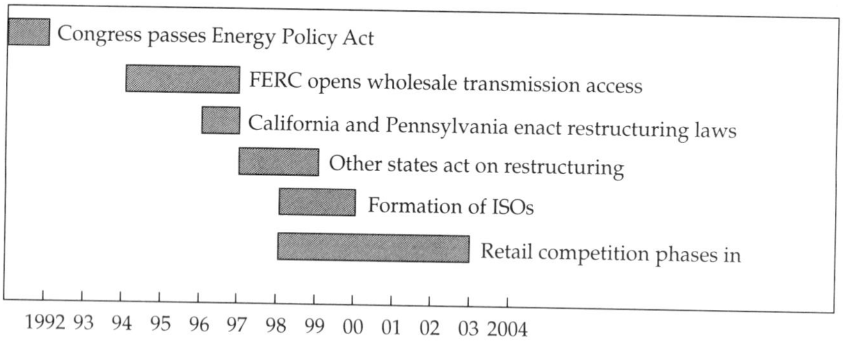

Congress passes Energy Policy Act	1992–93
FERC opens wholesale transmission access	1994–96
California and Pennsylvania enact restructuring laws	1994–96
Other states act on restructuring	1995–98
Formation of ISOs	1996–99
Retail competition phases in	1997–2004

The California and Pennsylvania Experiences

In 1996, California and Pennsylvania enacted legislation that restructures the sale of electricity in their states and sets a time frame for opening direct retail access. In other states, activities such as public utility commission recommendations, legislative forums, and other types of proposed legislation are occurring. Fitch predicts that other states will act on restructuring during the next two years. If the states do not act promptly, we believe that in 1998 or 1999 growing pressures will force Congress to enact some form of national deregulation that will require state legislatures to implement open-access legislation by a certain time. Keep in mind, however, that there are many local issues and several reasons why it may not happen as fast as some of the proponents of direct access would like.

At Fitch, we predict that the ISO role will become a problem and that we will eventually see the sale of transmission facilities to regional transmission companies that will be third-party entities with ownership of transmission networks.

Fitch's 1998–2003 time line for open direct-market access is similar to that already enacted by the legislatures in several states, including California (1998 to 2003) and Pennsylvania (1999 to 2001). Some states will lag and some states will lead, but an increasing percentage of the U.S. population will be served by utilities that offer direct access to competitively priced electric power generation. In most cases, the distribution franchises that are now in effect will remain as a regulated utility function. Complete deregulation will not occur because in this period of transformation, regulators and legislators are calling the shots, but the supply of electricity as a commodity will be subject to open-market competition.

Common Themes

The California and Pennsylvania laws enacted in 1996 provide some common themes that will be repeated in other states. Although these laws do not stipulate any changes in the distribution franchises, they do open up a competitive market for electric generation that will be phased in over several years. Both states call for the formation of ISOs or other mechanisms to ensure fair and nondiscriminatory access to transmission. Retail customers will become eligible to purchase electricity over a period of years, typically starting with large-scale industrial and commercial accounts and eventually phasing in full access for residential consumers.

Both of these statutes recognize that companies have made substantial investments and entered into long-term contracts under the assumption that those investments would be recovered through cost-of-service pricing and state-administered tariffs. As the industry moves to open-market competition, some of these costs will prove to be uneconomic and are typically referred to as stranded costs. Examples of stranded costs include expensive generating units that were built based on prior expectations of fuel costs, high-priced purchase power contracts, and above-market labor contracts. Both the California and Pennsylvania laws recognize that in order to transform the market environment, some or all of these stranded costs must be passed on to consumers through access charges imposed on the distribution of electricity and borne via non-bypassable tariffs, which are mandated in the laws. Beginning in 1997, the responsibility to enact the tariffs and regulations that enforce these laws belongs to the public utility commissions (PUCs) of California and Pennsylvania.

Finally, both of these laws permit the securitization of those non-bypassable charges or tariffs levied on the wire or distribution services for the recovery of stranded costs. This new class of securities will come into existence in late 1997 or early 1998. California law authorizes initial securitization of approximately $5 billion, and Pennsylvania has no statutory limit on the securitizations of stranded costs. The first filing, which was made by PECO Energy, asked for authorization to sell about $3.6 billion of bonds backed by stranded-cost recovery rights.[1]

1997–2001 INDUSTRY OUTLOOK

From now until the year 2003 or 2005, a significant industry transformation will take place. In the near term, the 1997–2001 period, the full impact of the transformation will be felt by IOUs and will be expressed in their balance sheets, specifically in the accounting methodology applied to the companies in the form of price regulation and in the absolute level of revenues or composition of revenues. Securitization will effectively accelerate the liquidation of uneconomic costs embedded in the balance sheets of IOUs. Given this outlook, utilities must meet the challenge to redeploy capital and shrink their balance sheets. The current consensus is that utility asset values are overstated, especially generation assets, which average about 60 percent of the balance sheet for IOUs. For example, PECO Energy's generation assets represent about 80 percent of the book value of its electricity plant and equipment, which reflects high original cost valuations. The challenge to management is to recover as much as possible of the debt and equity that was invested in these assets, to unbundle prices and products, and to prepare to sell products at competitive market prices.

Prices and products must be unbundled in such a way that prices reflect the cost of entry for new entrants into each business segment, especially on the generation side of the business. Depending on how aggressive some of the states get, a deeper disaggregation and unbundling of products and prices may occur because some states are seeing an increasing demand to unbundle the distribution function and to disaggregate distribution into competitively provided services for meter reading, billing and collecting customer accounts, and maintaining customer service.

During the next five years, utilities are likely to disaggregate through either (1) spin-offs of distribution and transmission properties into different subsidiaries under the same ownership or (2) the actual divestiture of generation or distribution assets. ISOs will be an ineffective solution for transmission in the long run, and owners of transmission properties will not be satisfied seeing their transmission assets managed by a third party that has no financial stake at risk in the industry. Thus, we expect to see transmission divested at some point in the future.

[1] In May 1997, the Pennsylvania PUC authorized PECO to securitize $1.1 billion of stranded costs.

Asset divestitures are likely to occur. The California Public Utility Commission has called for the two largest utilities in the state, Southern California Edison and Pacific Gas & Electric, to divest at least 50 percent of their non-nuclear generating assets. Those utilities are planning to commence sales of generation assets in 1997 and expect to complete the transactions by 1998. New England Electric System has already announced the sale of its non-nuclear generation assets to commence in 1997. We expect to see the development of a much broader market in generation facilities, which will establish merger and acquisition values and transaction comparables. Some companies may begin buying up divested properties, and we may see the formation of some wholesale generating companies as subsidiaries of large utility holding companies, as arms of diversified gas or energy companies, or as affiliates of power marketers. As transformation progresses, the industry will break apart and many new entities will form from these divestitures and spin-offs of existing electric utilities.

At the same time, we expect substantial industry consolidation, which is already happening with numerous mergers. As some of these business units—generation, transmission, and distribution—are sold off from the utilities, they will be combined with other entities. The merger and acquisition trend will continue throughout the entire transition period and will bring a continual change and resorting of the industry.

Finally, utilities are feeling tremendous pressure to reinvest the receipts of the recovered stranded assets, either in related businesses or new businesses, or to distribute these funds to their shareholders and bondholders. Companies will be transformed by merger and acquisition activities, by the liquidation of capital in the form of recovered stranded assets, by reinvesting capital, and by the return of capital to investors.

CONCLUSION

These are exciting, challenging, and troubling times for electric utility investors and analysts because of the rapid restructuring under way. Everything that was learned in the past about electric utilities must be relearned. New industry segments, new marketing entities, and new types of generation companies will emerge. Power marketers will grow from fairly small activities into larger integrated energy service companies that provide both wholesale and retail products and services, including gas, electricity, and maybe other products. Current industry participants and power marketers in the energy marketing sector may not be the survivors after the industry is completely transformed.

In the future, power marketing may be dominated by entities that today have no presence in this market segment, which calls for new analytical tools for investors and portfolio managers. Experienced industry analysts will have to forget all the acronyms learned in the past and develop new analytical ratios and tools that are more suited to understanding the new electric utility industry. If 60 percent of assets and 70 percent of the cash flow of current integrated utilities are related to generation, you can bet that experienced analysts know more about analytical methodologies for understanding power production than they know about the efficient distribution of electricity or how to analyze the profitability of the distribution or transmission businesses.

Analysts will learn new things about the industry as the market segments are unbundled. Analyses that had focused on bundled services on an average-cost basis must now focus on unbundled services on a marginal-cost basis. Those of us who learned to understand regulated rates of return and the technology of rate cases will have to learn about profit margins and commodity markets. Those of us who talk about electricity prices in terms of cents per kilowatt hour will have to learn to talk about dollars per megawatt hour, the prevailing terminology in the wholesale market and commodity arena. This is a time of significant growth and development in our intellectual skills, a time of rapid industry transformation, and a time to learn. Those who are brand new in the industry and those who are veterans are learning at the same time.

Question and Answer Session

Ellen Lapson, CFA

Question: Do you think we will see complete recovery of stranded costs, and how might these costs be recovered?

Lapson: Fitch believes that a significant amount of electric utility stranded costs will be recovered, but utilities will only recover 100 percent if their stranded costs are relatively modest. The larger the burden of stranded costs, the more difficult complete recovery will be. We see a time frame stretching out to a maximum of perhaps 10 years during which the recovery of stranded costs will be considered to benefit public policy. But only a very few states will allow higher prices in order to recover stranded costs.

Many IOUs' cost curves are declining. If you freeze prices or allow a modest price reduction to certain customers and then freeze prices for several years, you can recover as much as possible under that flat price trend. This mechanism provides an incentive to utilities to lower their variable costs of production, to cut their fixed costs, and to recover as much as they can. But for the high-cost utilities, the amount of costs that can be recovered will be limited under this system. Higher-cost utilities will have to write off unrecovered costs.

Question: Please comment on how the elasticity of demand for electricity may change as the electric utility industry moves toward a competitive market?

Lapson: We believe that the demand for electricity is elastic: At lower prices, more electric power will be demanded. Over the next five-to-seven years, the aggregate of the cost of distribution, transmission, and generation of electricity will probably be constant or only slightly declining. Power users will be paying a fixed access fee for the recovery of stranded costs along with a competitive market price for the actual commodity use of electricity, but large consumers of power may achieve price reductions as users find cheaper sources to replace the electric commodity. We could see some increasing demand as a result of access to competitively priced power on the margin.

In 10 years, when you get beyond the recovery of stranded costs, the all-in cost of electricity should drop. The aggregate cost of generation, distribution, and transmission of power will be lower, and you may see the elasticity of demand result in more significant demand growth. Once electricity prices drop by 20 percent or more, other energy sources could be challenged by electricity.

Question: What is the future of public power?

Lapson: Public power will have to adapt to the changes in the power market, but changes will be slower than those affecting the IOUs. For example, the restructuring law in California (AB 1890), for example, applies only to IOUs that are subject to the California Public Utility Commission and does not apply to public power entities in the state. The Los Angeles Department of Water and Power is the largest municipal electric company in California; the management of the Los Angeles Department of Water believes that even though the act does not apply to them, the political environment will make it difficult for them to deny comparable direct access to their customers. They are studying options to reduce their costs, to unbundle their services, and to meet the competitive environment in the state.

Some municipal and governmental entities are extremely low-cost producers and distributors of electricity. Some are high cost and inefficient. At Fitch, we have reviewed and, in some cases, we have reduced the bond ratings of some of the higher-cost generators and distributors of electricity in the public power sector. In other cases, we have reaffirmed our ratings. Over all, public power is still several years behind the IOUs in preparing for the industry transformation. An important issue that must be solved is whether governmental entities financed with tax-exempt debt can open access to their transmission and distribution systems without risking the loss of their tax-exempt funding status resulting from the private use of their facilities.

Question: What functions do you think IOUs will outsource? Is it possible that deregulation or the industry transformation might create a big industry for outsourcing of services?

Lapson: That is quite possible. In some states, the distribution function will become a common-carrier function and everything will be outsourced. The common-carrier function would be to distribute electricity to households and businesses, while competitors would be permitted to come in and read meters, administer customer accounts, and provide customer service. A vast outsourcing of all of these services or unbundling of all of these services could take place. Utilities might outsource everything, except the maintenance of a wired network and system reliability functions.

Question: How does securitization reduce costs and for whom?

Lapson: Securitization accelerates the collection of revenues and allows utilities to benefit from accelerating their recognition of revenues that they would be entitled to collect from customers over a period of years. To the extent utilities use that money to reduce their fixed costs, to retire debt, and to repurchase stock, for example, we would expect to see a significant reduction in their cost of service. In the case of a utility such as Niagara Mohawk Power, we could see an application of stranded-cost recovery debt being used to pay down uneconomic power contracts with above-market fixed costs. But in some cases, proving a savings will be tough. Most of our model results show that using the funds to reduce debt will not necessarily produce significant savings. The overall after-tax cost of capital can be reduced if the utility uses the proceeds of securitization to buy back a blend of debt and equity.

In this industry, balance sheets are extremely inflated. Utilities with large power plants financed by debt and equity have overstated their assets. Although it will be necessary to retain more equity on the generation side of the business—substantially more equity for generation than currently held—the distribution function may be able to be more leveraged. Electricity may become a low-volatility, low-risk business that could be more leveraged than currently.

Question: For an analyst new to the electric utility industry, please comment on sources for industry data and information.

Lapson: I use data from the Edison Electric Institute for information on IOUs, the National Rural Utilities Cooperative Association for co-ops, and the American Public Power Association for municipal and government-owned utilities. I also rely on information from the Department of Energy, the Energy Information Agency, and the FERC for many numbers. I use the Resource Data International (RDI) database for information on FERC and Energy Information Agency filings; Utility Data Institute (UDI) is a competing vendor of similar data. George Pugh and other vendors such as Compustat supply IOU accounting data. The World Bank is an excellent source for data on worldwide electric utility consumption and production, and it is preeminent with regard to data on less-developed nations. With regard to developed economies, the Organization of Economic Cooperation and Development is a very impressive supplier of consistent statistical information about consumption and production. Also, a forthcoming book by Shimon Awerbuch and Alistair Preston called *The Virtual Utility*, published by Kluwer Academic, should be a great help to new analysts. Although it is very technical, you should be able to understand most of it.

Question: Frequently, utilities are expected to subsidize low-income customers, and in some cases, they are required to do so by law. What entities will pick up this burden in a new paradigm?

Lapson: Restructuring bills that have been introduced in a number of states indicate a tendency for states to mandate that electricity distributors continue to provide universal service subsidies or carry out other social mandates, such as conservation; however, in the restructured and open-access environment, the costs of these social welfare benefits will have to be recovered from all electricity users regardless of their choice of power supplier via non-bypassable access fees (a "wires charge"). My own preference would be for the state to fund such social welfare activities through direct taxation rather than hide the subsidies in the electricity bill.

Deregulation and Its Repercussions

Philip R. O'Connor[1]
Principal
Coopers and Lybrand Consulting

> Electric utilities can learn from other deregulated industries how surplus prices and new technology quickly drive prices to marginal cost, how important customer satisfaction is in a competitive environment, and how crucial financial depth is in a transitional business. Successful electric utilities in the *new electric paradigm* will learn from these experiences and effectively address tomorrow's challenges today. Prepare to say goodbye to the traditional electric utility and hello to the new *electricom* company—an integrated energy company with a customer service focus.

To a social scientist, the historical pattern of deregulation is seen as a transition in which regulated industries move from a monopoly or shared market with intense regulation to a great deal of competition and a mix of regulation. This pattern—as demonstrated by deregulation in the banking, transportation, telecommunications, and natural gas industries—suggests that complete deregulation never occurs but competition certainly develops.

Although various forces can drive deregulation, the key drivers for deregulation of the electric utility industry are surplus capacity, new low-cost generation technology, and customers who want choice. Thus, deregulation is actually a subset of broader, more profound developments.

This presentation discusses the lessons of deregulation applicable to electric utilities, the new electric paradigm, current issues in public policy debates, the live-wire topic of stranded costs, the implications for equity investors, and finally, the future challenges industry participants must address to be successful in this dynamic industry.

LESSONS OF DEREGULATION

When the experiences of other deregulated industries are boiled down, three lessons can be applied to electric utilities. First, surplus capacity and new technology drive prices to marginal cost. A fundamental problem right now is that the embedded costs of production, the sunk investment, are so high that they are not totally recoverable in a completely open and competitive market—that is, the regulated prices are above the marginal cost of production. Second, customers start to demand choice not only because of price increases in the regulated business but also because of lower perceived service quality. The creative use of information then moves competition to all customer classes. The third lesson is that the keys to success in these transitional businesses are financial depth at the outset, the ability to identify and control costs, and the ability to shape both policy and the culture inside the company.

Several patterns in the electric business validate these lessons right now.

■ *Price pressures.* When new technology or improvements in production methods become available, particularly concerning the core product, marginal production costs decline in industries that already have surplus capacity. For example, General Electric recently developed a new gas turbine with a thermal efficiency (amount of electricity extracted from fuel) of 60 percent. This turbine could save utilities up to $100 million in fuel costs over the life of the turbine compared with the most efficient plants now in operation. Although production costs are declining, regulation is driving up the cost of performing the traditional function.

In the wholesale power market, contract prices will range between 1.5 cents and 3 cents per kilowatt hour (kwh), depending on the region of the country, and the retail regulated price for only the generation component will be up in the range of 4, 5, or even 6 cents. In comparison, average 1995 U.S. wholesale market rates ranged from 2.8 cents per kwh in the

---

[1] This written presentation was prepared with the help of John Domagalski, Senior Associate, Coopers and Lybrand Consulting.

Midwest to almost 4.8 cents per kwh in the Northeast. Average 1995 retail rates ranged from a low of 3.9 cents per kwh (Idaho Power) to 15.4 cents per kwh (LILCO).

In the electric utility industry, surplus generating capacity is currently a good deal higher than demand warrants, particularly in some parts of the country. For example, 1995 capacity margins (available capacity resources minus peak demand, adjusted for direct load control and interruptible demand, divided by available capacity resources) indicate that excess generating capacity ranged from a low of 16 percent in the Southeast to a high of 23 percent in the Northeast. In the old days, regulation would smooth out excess supply, but increasingly, regulation makes it a rougher ride.

■ *Customer choice.* In almost every state, organized industrial and commercial customer groups are lobbying state legislators for retail access. In an attempt to change the rules of the game, active efforts to reshape regulation have begun in more than half the states, in either the regulatory arena, state legislatures, or both.

Information appeals to all types of customers. Although much of the discussion currently focuses on industrial and large commercial customers having a choice of a power provider, this trend will not stop at the commercial level but will continue down to the retail level. When price and product competition starts in an industry, it tends to be a high-end phenomenon concerning only sophisticated customers who want choices—the big dogs—but the little dogs, the small customers, do eat eventually. So, electric utilities will have to provide extensive product choices at the residential and small commercial levels.

■ *Keys to success.* The utility industry is involved in a massive effort to control costs. As most utility managers pat themselves on the back for having reduced head count by 10–15 percent over the past four or five years, they must realize that this cost cutting is only the beginning. Cost control has also been accomplished by outsourcing, as Ellen Lapson discussed.[2] Nationwide, the average cost of production per kilowatt hour and the system lambda, which is the marginal cost of generating the very last kilowatt hour, have been declining for the past few years, falling from $17.42 per megawatt hour in 1993 to $15.14 per megawatt hour in 1995.

Electric utilities are trying to reconfigure themselves in various ways. They are starting new businesses, or creating "functional" businesses, in which they separate or unbundle the distribution, generation, and transmission functions. Some utilities are creating retailing operations, and others are creating energy-trading businesses. Consolidation through mergers and acquisitions is another phenomenon characteristic of industries undergoing deregulation, as Kit Konolige discussed.[3] In 1996, electric utilities was the number one industry for initiating merger and acquisition activity, although completing the mergers may take two years or longer.

A real generational struggle has arisen in the electric utility industry with respect to how companies relate to customers. Some companies are adapting very well by changing their corporate culture; others are stuck in the past. Some are reaching out and trying to hire people from other industries that have been through this process or people who possess skills different from the skills of traditional utility managers. Changing a corporate culture and deciding how to view customers are interrelated topics. As management struggles to change corporate culture, it attempts to answer a tough question: Does the utility dictate the fundamental level of service provided, or does it ask customers the level of service and products they desire?

NEW ELECTRIC PARADIGM

To understand the new electric paradigm, one must know the major characteristics, or dimensions, that define the environment of the electric utility industry and how these characteristics change with deregulation. **Exhibit 1** provides a template for assessing where a particular market, regulatory regime, or company might be in this process. For instance, utility companies are moving from monopoly to competition, from distorted prices to accurate prices.

Companies cannot afford to withhold information in a competitive arrangement. As competition increases, information becomes very inexpensive and widely available. Customers will find another provider if they cannot freely receive information from their current provider. Therefore, information must flow freely between customers and providers in order for companies to remain competitive. Moving from information control to information flow is an interesting transition. A regulated enterprise has tight control of information. The information is closely held among regulated parties, regulators, and the interveners, and they all speak a language that is understandable to only a relatively small number of people besides themselves, such as utility analysts.

To avoid problems, symmetry is necessary across the different dimensions shown in Exhibit 1. As any company or market moves from left to right in the exhibit, it must progress at a fairly even pace

---

[2]See Ms. Lapson's presentation, pp. 5–14.

[3]See Mr. Konolige's presentation, pp. 24–32.

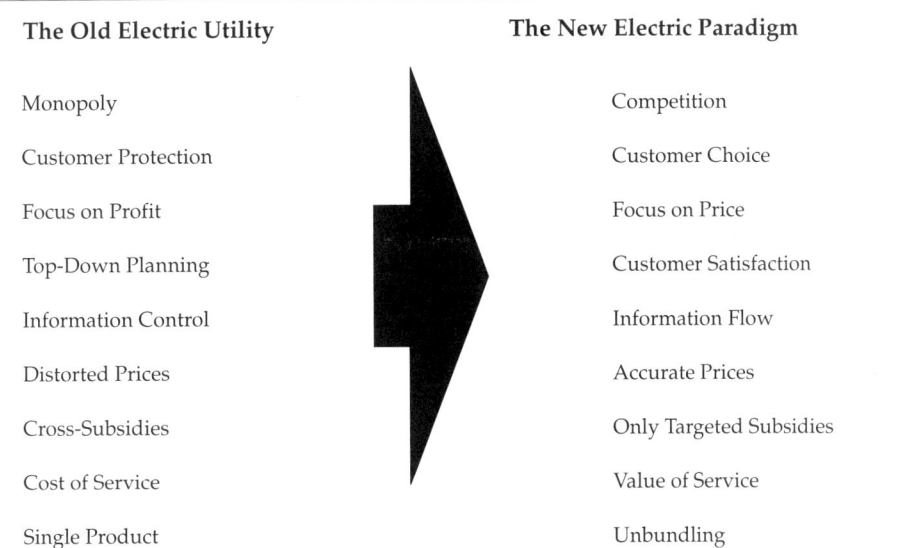

Exhibit 1. New Electric Paradigm

along all dimensions. Moving along one dimension much more quickly than another can cause trouble. For example, assume the idea in a particular state is to move from the position of customer protection to customer choice—that is, giving customers choices rather than only one supplier. But at the same time, the utility commission continues to insist on distorting prices to provide cross-subsidies to certain customers. Such an asymmetrical situation will cause problems and certainly unintended consequences.

CURRENT ISSUES

The dominant themes in *today's* public policy debates are *yesterday's* issues, essentially problems of the past. Although these issues are important, they have been around for a while and still have not been resolved. The issues that invoke the strongest debate are

- retail access by industrial/large customers,
- recovery methods for higher-than-market embedded costs,
- pricing the use of remaining "monopoly" facilities,
- repeal of anachronistic laws, and
- the federal role in electric production.

Retail access by industrial and commercial customers is going to happen, so the real issues are how long will retail access take to become a reality and to what extent and how quickly will other kinds of customers get access?

Another hot topic for debate is whether to provide recovery for stranded costs. If recovery is provided, how exactly will it be handled over some extended period of time when the industry is changing? Regulators are in the business of creating a sustainable method for the recovery of these costs, but this process is uncertain.

No one knows how to price the use of the remaining monopoly facilities, assuming these facilities—such as transmission wires and distribution wires—can even be defined. Whether their use will be priced on a flat basis or if congestion pricing is the solution is still under consideration.

Movement is underway to repeal or substantially modify some anachronistic laws, such as the Public Utility Holding Company Act (PUHCA), which governs how a public utility holding company operates, or the Public Utility Regulatory Policy Act (PURPA), which requires the purchase of power from third-party providers at an administered cost. PURPA is essentially a defunct law, but it is not entirely defunct until it is actually repealed.

A major question is how the federal government will participate as a producer of power. The federal government is an extraordinarily large player in the market, whether the subject is the Tennessee Valley Authority, Bonneville Power Administration, the power-marketing agencies, or the way the federal government provides certain advantages to municipal utilities. As the industry moves to competition, two major questions are (1) will municipal utilities be allowed to compete outside their service territories and (2) if so, will the rules be changed so that these utilities can use the tax-exempt status of their securities to finance expansion of their competitive efforts outside their own territories?

These themes are dominant right now, but they will ultimately take second place to concern over other challenges facing electric utilities, such as stranded costs.

STRANDED COSTS

This discussion focuses on how the problem of

stranded costs relates to some of the broader issues facing the industry. As William Tilles discussed, everyone involved with electric utilities is interested in what stranded costs will do to the value of utility securities.[4]

Definition

Stranded costs are the costs that cannot, or are very unlikely to be, recovered in a purely free market. Electric utilities have numerous types of potentially stranded costs, including the following:
- nuclear plants with high sunk investment,
- nuclear plants with high fixed-operating costs,
- partially unfunded nuclear decommissioning accounts,
- fossil-fuel plants with high variable-operating costs,
- high-cost independent power provider and qualifying facilities contracts,
- uneconomic demand-side management investments,
- the recovery of deferred costs,
- future tax payments or deferred tax liabilities,
- high general overhead,
- above-market labor agreements, and
- substantial state and local tax burdens.

The obvious items on the list are sunk investments in nuclear power plants and above-market, long-term contracts with independent power providers. Some stranded costs are cultural or institutional, such as high general overhead and expectations about the role of the utility as a surrogate for government—as a provider of cross-subsidies, as a tax collector, or as a standard for dealings with organized labor, because electric utilities generally employ organized labor, often at above-market rates.

The challenge is how to deal with stranded costs, which currently contribute to regulated above-market prices. One complicating factor is that many of these costs are not reflected in today's price for electricity because in various ways, they have been deferred for recovery—the fiction being that companies could somehow incur costs today and because of the durability of regulation, fold them into the price at a later date. This fiction is becoming increasingly unsustainable, particularly as the market price drops and the magnitude of the remaining stranded costs has never been reflected in the price.

History of Stranded Costs

Discussions of stranded costs provoke vigorous debates as to whether or not these costs are the function of a series of bad business decisions. Some people contend that around the same time, a lot of electric utility managers made a lot of bad decisions and that the consequences are their problem and the problem of their shareholders. This argument has some integrity, but overall, the history of the electric business suggests that these decisions were primarily taken in the context of fairly explicit policies at the federal and state levels, most of which were very forceful. For example, less than a year after the atomic bombs were dropped on Japan, President Harry Truman announced a concerted national policy of converting nuclear power to peaceful use. The memoirs of Harry Truman and Dwight Eisenhower express the moral imperative of making sure this terrible thing—the atomic bomb—could be somehow turned into a major benefit for humanity.

This development was very profound. A review of the history on this issue reveals that the process of bringing nuclear power into the electric business for use on a commercial basis was generally a very rocky road. For almost 10 years, the plan met with intense skepticism from the electric industry. Every time the electric industry came up with a reason not to begin using nuclear power, a political choice was made to solve that problem, whether it was liability, availability of enriched uranium for civilian ownership, or solving a variety of technical problems.

This concerted effort in national and state policy was reflected in a number of other areas, some of which were very closely related to the nuclear decision and some of which were not. For instance, from the mid-1970s to mid-1980s, a mania existed for national energy independence. President Jimmy Carter declared in the much-maligned MEOW (moral equivalent of war) speech that energy independence should be a top national priority. National policies were predicated on these ideas, some of which now seem laughable. The goal of $100 per barrel of oil was not simply a guess somebody made but an integral part of the laws that were passed and public policies that were pursued. Government policy had a concerted effect on business decisions for a long list of issues. As Congress and the states attempt to cope with the problem of stranded costs, they will have to discuss what responsibility government has for helping to manage the transition costs.

In other industries, such as natural gas and telecommunications, government has provided explicit and implicit transitional mechanisms. All the mechanisms have meant money changing hands to smooth over the problem of the incumbent meeting competition and coping with costs that the incumbent had incurred in a prior regulatory regime.

Magnitude of Stranded Costs

The magnitude of stranded costs is an open

---
[4]See Mr. Tilles' presentation, pp. 33–40.

question that will depend on three key developments *beyond* regulatory control—growth in demand for electric power, the rate of increase in generation efficiency and installation costs of new generation facilities, and future prices of uranium and coal. First, how much growth in demand will electric power experience? The difference between 2 and 3 percent growth is 50 percent, which makes a big difference in eating up margin. Second, no one knows how much generation efficiency is going to increase as a result of the enormous amount of development in new turbines. Finally, the future of fuel prices and resource availability is also uncertain.

The magnitude of the problem of stranded costs will also depend on three key developments largely *under* regulatory control—the pace of retail access, the period of uncertainty in the financing of new independent power plants, and the degree of flexibility to adjust prices and to respond to customers with alternatives. Some of these issues are highly dependent on specific public policies, for example, how quickly different classes of customers have access to choices for their power supply.

Government could also induce sufficient uncertainty in the market, thereby severely limiting investment in third-party independent power plants. In this environment, entering into long-term contracts for a large amount of power with the idea of reselling it in the future does not make sense. The future customer may not be around. The industry could be entering a period when the financing of third-party power plants, particularly highly leveraged transactions, is simply not feasible because of low margins.

On the other hand, if enough certainty developed, a lot of new, efficient generation might be brought online. The answer is unclear as to how states will provide utilities with the flexibility to adjust their prices and service alternatives during the transition in order to meet competition. Prices are currently set at average cost with relatively little variation, and a lot of effort is necessary to get permission to begin moving down the demand line of customers to give them more choices, time-oriented choices, and so forth. A lot of utilities are quite hamstrung in trying to price to the market.

Estimates of the magnitude of stranded costs vary. Moody's Investors Service and Standard & Poor's Corporation have done a terrific job in trying to estimate stranded costs. Moody's estimates the amount for investor-owned utilities (IOUs) at approximately $135 billion, 45 percent of which is concentrated in the Northeast and the West, and research completed at Oak Ridge National Laboratory estimates IOU stranded costs between $70 billion and $100 billion.[5] The Oak Ridge research provides two alarming statistics illustrating the potential impact of stranded costs on equity prices. They estimate that 20 utilities have potential stranded costs of at least $1 billion apiece and that these costs exceed 50 percent of total equity in 13 states.

The mix of stranded costs differs according to geographical region. Moody's analysis estimates approximately $31 billion in the Northeast with $8 billion in owned generation (most of which is nuclear), $12 billion in purchased power, and $11 billion in deferred assets, about one-third of which belongs to Long Island Lighting Company. Although a fair amount of stranded costs is in owned generation, about 50 percent more is in purchased power. In the Northeast, $11 billion in stranded costs is not even reflected in current prices, and no one is promising that these utilities will recover these costs, which has alarming implications for their equity prices.

The West has a different situation from the Northeast concerning stranded costs: $11 billion is in owned generation, $17 billion is in purchased power, and only $1 billion is in deferred assets. Because almost nothing is in deferred assets, most of these costs are already reflected in current prices. The same relationship exists in the West as in the Northeast between owned generation and purchased power: About 50 percent more of stranded costs is in purchased power. These costs are involved with power plants that the utilities do not even own. These contracts could be renegotiated and long-term exposure reduced, making the collection of such costs in a transition more tolerable. Natural gas companies used a similar approach to solve the problem of high-cost gas contracts by negotiating buyouts, thus providing for collection at the retail level by pipelines.

Transition and Resolution

The keys to a smooth transition and resolution of the issue of stranded costs involve recognizing the difficulty of full recovery of costs and deconcentrating stranded costs—that is, "sharing the pain," shifting some costs to the power grid and treating stranded costs as a price for transition to competition. As for methods by which stranded costs might be recovered, the big issue that must be confronted in terms of a collection mechanism is that stranded costs are highly concentrated in particular companies and in particular regions, which is one factor that drives competition. If in the transition to competition this fact is ignored and nothing is done to deconcentrate stranded costs, the intended result of a transitional

---

[5] Lester Baxter and Eric Hirst, "Estimating Potential Stranded Commitments for U.S. Investor-Owned Electric Utilities," Oak Ridge National Laboratory, January 1995.

mechanism may not happen. In telephone, for instance, the pain was shared: When people in Illinois or New Jersey made a long-distance phone call, part of what they paid was promptly shipped to Florida or Arizona or California to pay for somebody else's phone bill. This arrangement was true 10 years ago, and it is true today.

IMPLICATIONS FOR EQUITY INVESTORS

Deregulation will probably not have a positive effect on dividend policies, such as payout, dividend growth, and dividend safety. Equity investors are beginning to consider new criteria for evaluating electric utility stocks, especially those investors seeking explanations for the variation in stock prices. These criteria may include changes in state regulation of company-specific data that track competitive indicators, such as stranded costs, production costs, asset mix, price advantage, or customer profile. Market-to-book ratios (M/Bs) provide a comparative measure of the effects of stranded costs.

At Coopers and Lybrand Consulting, we performed two analyses that provided us with interesting results. Our 1995 study found that using return on equity (ROE) and estimates of stranded costs explained about 55 percent of the variance in M/B as of December 1995.[6]

When we used Moody's estimates of stranded costs, our latest results explained about three-fourths of the differences in M/B for 73 utility stocks.[7] The amount of variance explained by the estimates of stranded costs almost doubled, from about 6 percent of the variance to 11.4 percent.

ROE explained 48.4 percent of the variance, and the next variable, the industrial price, explained 15 percent of the variance. Industrial price represents what a utility generally charges an industrial customer for electricity; therefore, the higher the price, the lower the M/B on average.

Embedded generation capacity cost, measured in dollars per kilowatt installed less accumulated depreciation—an easily accessible surrogate variable for stranded costs—explained another 7.7 percent of the variance. The higher the embedded cost of generation, the lower the M/B.

The degree of state regulatory restructuring explained 3.7 percent of the variance. The more a state had accomplished to restructure regulation, the lower the M/B. Curiously, no readily available explanation can be found for this negative relationship. One might think that the more a state had done to restructure and get with the program on competition, the more investors would have liked the state's approach. This negative relationship, however, may indicate that politicians were moved to make these changes only to the extent that the situation was desperate enough to warrant the changes.

This finding warns investors that a rough road lies ahead. As the power industry moves to retail competition, factors indicating competitive position—the industrial price of electricity and the embedded generation costs—are likely to account for a great deal of the difference in the equity price performance of electric utilities.

FUTURE CHALLENGES

Although *yesterday's* issues continue to invoke strong debate *today*, the focus now has to be on proactive, forward-looking solutions. *Tomorrow's* challenges that utilities must currently address are

- achieving cost parity within the market,
- creating growth strategies,
- achieving markedly better asset utilization,
- understanding customer satisfaction in a competitive market,
- decoupling earnings from hard assets,
- diversifying the utility product mix,
- addressing traditional social obligations in the new electric paradigm, and
- ensuring power quality and reliability for the electronic age.

Cost parity has to occur. Companies are not going to be able to survive unless their underlying costs are at least similar to those of the market. Growth strategies have to be created. A 2–3 percent growth rate is expected in a mature business, but 2–3 percent may not be enough because the electric industry is going through a second childhood. The winners will find a way to grow at 4–7 percent.

Higher growth rates will involve new products, new ways of dealing with customers, and expansion outside current service areas—all while companies rely on their core strengths. A hard question for management to answer is, "What are our core strengths and distinct competencies?" Many utilities are looking at certain activities in the telecommunications field, and some are involved with infrastructure issues. Utilities may well know about these areas, but they simply lack experience.

Successful utilities must understand customer satisfaction in a competitive market and adopt a corporate culture that enhances this understanding. Most electric utilities do not have a clue as to what their customers actually think of them, because they

---

[6]Augustin Ros, John L. Domagalski, and Philip R. O'Connor, "Stranded Costs: Is the Market Paying Attention?" *Public Utilities Fortnightly* (May 15, 1996):18–21.

[7]John L. Domagalski, Augustin Ros, and Philip R. O'Connor, "Another Look at What's Driving Utility Stock Prices," *Public Utilities Fortnightly* (January 15, 1997):42–44.

never ask. Utilities need to ask for customers' opinions and obtain a comparison that offers a real measure of customer satisfaction and sense of quality. Current comparisons are usually made to the customer's cable TV company or a similar service. Comparisons need to be made with companies and products that are known, admired, and valued by the public.

Another big challenge is to find some way during the transition to decouple earnings from hard assets. Utilities must have an extended period when they can have some freedom about making the decision to retain savings, to reinvest those savings, to pass those savings on to investors as higher dividends, or to decrease prices. They must have some degree of flexibility to make these decisions, and in order to do so, regulators must decouple the earnings regulation from the calculation of the hard assets in the company. The traditional social obligations will also have to be addressed by asking what the role of the incumbent utility should be—tax collector or conveyor of cross-subsidies?

Finally, an interesting challenge that applies to investment and customer satisfaction is how does a company make customers happy from a quality and reliability standpoint in the computer era? In terms of traditional measures of reliability, the utility industry is better today than it has ever been. But the need for reliability may well have surpassed the classic definition of reliability. The solution may require utilities' involvement in a lot of end-user, customer-type equipment, such as on-site reliability, interactive-metering, and equipment-monitoring systems. Companies can never invest enough money on the delivery side to ensure the level of quality that people expect in the electronic age.

CONCLUSION

By the year 2000, a "new-style" electric utility will emerge and dominate the industry. The winners will be the companies that organize themselves totally from the perspective of the customer—the companies that wake up every morning thinking about customers and how exactly to make them happy. Such an approach gets back to the roots of the electric business (i.e., providing a brand new product with a lot of sex appeal). The last time electric utilities had such an opportunity was about 40 years ago.

Another characteristic of the new-style electric utility is a commitment to enhancing the lifetime value of the relationship with the customer. Today, customers are still called rate payers and are thought of in terms of an annual revenue figure. More than any other provider of any kind of service, electric utilities continually provide a service to customers.

Every microsecond of the day, they are providing service in multiple places—at home, at the office, at any number of places—all at the same time. But what do they do? They send the customer a bill once a month. Just like the life insurance industry, electric utilities must think beyond selling that one policy, getting a commission, and moving on to the next customer. They must change how they view their customers. Electric utilities must think about how to make customers happy every day, how to let them know they are happy, how to sell them new products, and how to keep them buying new products.

Finally, the new-style utility will be predicated on an electronic communications interface for an ongoing dialogue with the customer. Again, this change is generational. People in their 40s and older may struggle to think of communicating with their electricity provider, but for people in their 30s and younger, this method of communication will become increasingly the way that they deal with providers of power.

This electronic communications interface suggests that an "electricom" company is coming down the road. The challenge is interesting because a number of competitors will arise. The pathways into the home or the business today are separate from one another. Consumers know who does what and whose pipe belongs to whom, and the homeowner or the customer is the one who mediates everything. Although the question has recurred over the years about whether somebody can provide an interface or can bundle the services together, the task has never been fully accomplished and the question remains open. Will somebody create an energy and information interface that provides convenient, cheap, and high-quality bundled services?

The challenge for the electric utility industry is determining what role it will play in the future. Some companies have already decided that they would like to be that interface company or at least be aligned with whoever has some capability of being that interface company. This decision will be a central question for utility managers who design and construct business strategies. This interface-company concept is one of the roles a company can assume, and managements will have to make pragmatic choices as to whether or not this role is suitable for them. If the question is stranded costs, then these companies must be able to grow their business because policy makers are unlikely to say, "Here is the 100 percent number. Here is a check. Now go on about your business." It is not going to work that way.

In the future competitive environment, traditional providers will vie for control of the customer, and kilowatts will be a commodity.

Question and Answer Session

Philip R. O'Connor

Question: Should we think about other forms of deregulation and wonder whether service to higher-cost areas will be decreased (we have matters of urban policy to consider), whether reliability will actually increase, and whether such matters as environmental regulations might be pushed aside in an effort to control costs?

O'Connor: First of all, I wouldn't expect the environmental requirements to be set aside. All the players will probably be brought in more equitably to deal with the environmental question, but issues about service to high-cost areas and so forth have traditionally been dealt with by cross-subsidies that regulators try their best to avoid identifying. What will be required in a more competitive business is a more explicit identification of these cross-subsidies.

The National Rural Electric Cooperative Association is grappling with these problems. If all the rural cooperatives in the country were combined as one utility, they would be about twice the size of the largest investor-owned electric utility. Rural co-ops account for maybe 8–9 percent of the meters and 7 percent of the demand. They have explicitly said that without certain kinds of transitional policies, the result will be a combination of generating and transmission co-op bankruptcies. Some bankruptcies have already occurred, but more will occur without the correct transitional policies.

Second, in sparsely populated areas, we can expect at least the delivery service cost of electric power to rise. The other problem is that those enterprises have nowhere else to go for the money besides their own customers—their owners—or the federal government. In effect, they have no outside shareholders. In most places, the amount of transfer through the utility system to low-income customers is fairly modest and is primarily in the form of forgiveness of bad debt, with very little in the way of explicit identification of low-income people and a subsidy to pay for their electric power.

Implicit subsidies will become unsustainable unless they are all loaded up somehow on the wire companies or unless electric utilities emulate the insurance business—establishing pools with high-risk people who need to be subsidized and then sharing the subsidy among all of the players. In this case, all generators would take a proportional burden of providing that subsidy. We currently do not have explicit subsidy mechanisms; they are highly implicit. Actually, the situation is fairly inequitable. The problem that develops when we move away from the ease of sustaining subsidies in a regulated monopoly is that some kind of substitute—or at least an answer to the question of whether or not we are going to have a substitute—will be required. The public goes along with these implicit arrangements all the time and pays huge amounts to these implicit subsidy systems. The minute that the subsidy gets identified, the public goes haywire.

A few years ago, the Illinois Commerce Commission allowed approximately 15 cents a month to be identified on the phone bill as state money to get federal matching money for a low-income subsidy program for basic telephone service. First the *Chicago Sun Times* and then the legislature went absolutely crazy; the legislature actually passed a law prohibiting such subsidies. Today, Illinois is the only state that does not participate in that program, largely because other states did not put it explicitly on the bills.

Question: How can we be assured that we do not have the same inefficiencies built into whatever new regulatory system comes along as we had in the old system, and how are we going to assure that these new entities actually invest the necessary funds to keep the system going?

O'Connor: The answers to those two things are somewhat opposed to each other. Efficiencies will probably come in some form of price-cap regulation that sets a fair price in the beginning but allows the distribution company or the monopoly company to benefit from savings that it makes over some sustained period and share the savings with its shareholders. On the other hand, part of the history of price caps is the tendency to set them a little bit low at the outset, meaning that in order to make these savings and achieve the better earnings, the tendency will be to make only those investments that are absolutely necessary for basic service. This problem has developed to some extent in some of the Baby Bells. Unfortunately, the only adequate answer is a price-cap system that starts out high enough to encourage reinvestment and that has a sustained period of time during which savings can be realized to encourage management to go for the long-term savings.

Question: Wouldn't the magnitude of stranded costs be more dependent on the price of natural gas than the price of coal and uranium?

O'Connor: Not necessarily. The more that coal prices can be reduced, the less gas will be a baseload fuel. And if uranium prices fall, the fixed nuclear operating costs can likely be compensated in a competitive market.

Question: If transmission is still going to be a monopoly run by an independent system operator (ISO), what incentives will there be for ISOs to maintain transmission assets adequately? What incentives will there be to extend or upgrade transmission grids?

O'Connor: This is where some combination of price caps, incentive regulation, functional focus, and marginal cost of congestion pricing will play a role. The economy can afford whatever it costs for conveyance reliability and quality because the downside risk of failure is so great.

Question: Do you see the repeal of PUHCA laws triggering a massive consolidation in the industry?

O'Connor: The consolidation is well under way. The EPA Act of 1992 already allows consolidation in generation, and PUHCA already accommodates distribution and transmission consolidation. PUHCA will be repealed in response to its own obsolescence.

Question: Are there significant privatization pressures in the public power area (federal, municipal)?

O'Connor: The first phase of the process will be alliances between munis, co-ops, and such for-profit firms as energy marketers.

Question: How much degradation of power quality and reliability do you expect because of deregulation, and how much do you think customers will accept before they demand re-regulation?

O'Connor: None to speak of, although I expect that every normal perturbation will be blamed on competition.

Electric Utilities M&A: What, Why, and How

Kit Konolige, CFA
Principal
Morgan Stanley & Co., Inc.

> The electric utility industry is experiencing significant changes as a result of rampant merger and acquisition activity. This M&A activity can best be understood by asking what is happening, why is it happening, and how should the deals be analyzed? The present and future implications of M&A activity affect investors and industry participants alike.

An enormous amount of merger and acquisition activity is taking place in the electric utility industry, as **Table 1** shows. International merger activity would add an additional $23 billion in M&A activity. Notice that several of the deals listed in Table 1 are almost two years old, reflecting the painfully slow approval process at state regulatory commissions and the Federal Energy Regulatory Commission (FERC). This lengthy approval process is a key impediment to progress in the restructuring of the industry.

This presentation describes the M&A activity in terms of what is going on, why it is happening, and how investors can analyze and, ideally, profit from this activity.

WHAT IS TAKING PLACE

M&A strategies can be divided into two categories: defensive and offensive strategies. The defensive strategy is relatively straightforward; the offensive strategy warrants a more detailed discussion.

Defense

A defensive strategy describes the traditional utility merger—a strategic alliance in which neighboring utilities combine to cut costs. The utilities know each other, and the merger creates an opportunity to spread costs over a larger service territory. The combined regional company focuses on the distribution business and on control of the customer.

Offense

In the offensive approach, the overall idea is for large local companies to become national companies. The corporate focus shifts from the customer to the commodity; therefore, the company becomes more involved in trading and marketing and less involved in production and delivery.

■ *Electric/gas company mergers.* An electric company buying a gas company (or vice versa) was unheard of a year and a half ago, but since then, seven such mergers have been announced, as shown in Panel B of Table 1.

The Duke Power Company/PanEnergy Corporation merger (included in Panel B of Table 1) is a watershed event in a traditionally uneventful industry. The electric industry is no longer simply electric companies; it is now an integrated energy industry. The combined assets of Duke Power and PanEnergy will be worth about $20 billion, with a market capitalization of approximately $17 billion, making it the largest company in this group. The premium paid, 18 percent, was not huge, but PanEnergy's stock price rose substantially before the announced merger. Premiums tend to be larger for this type of merger than for the pure electric-on-electric mergers. For example, Enron Corporation is buying Portland General Corporation for a 48 percent premium, and Texas Utilities Company is paying a 51 percent premium for ENSERCH Corporation.

Companies are willing to pay high premiums for gas companies because gas companies have higher growth rates than electric companies. The expected time to complete electric/gas company mergers is shorter than the expected time to complete electric/electric mergers, so managers' time commitments are reduced in these electric/gas deals. The fact that electric-on-electric mergers take so long to complete contributes to the rush to merge with gas companies.

Table 1. Pending Electric Utility Mergers and Acquisitions

Acquirer Target	Date Announced	Expected Closing Date	Market Cap (billions)	Exchange Ratio	Premium to Market	Discount to Deal Price	Offer Price to Book Value	Offer Price to Earnings[a]
A. Electric/Electric								
Northern States Power Company	05/01/95	3Q97	$3.2	1.626				
Wisconsin Energy Corporation			3.1	—	1%	18%	1.6x	13.5x
Union Electric	08/14/95	4Q97	3.9	—				
CIPSCO Inc.			1.2	1.030	23	7	1.9	18.5
Public Service Company of Colorado	08/23/95	2Q97	2.5	—				
Southwestern Public Service			1.5	0.950	2	2	1.7	12.0
Baltimore Gas & Electric Company	09/25/95	2Q97	4.0	—				
Potomac Electric Power Company			3.0	0.997	21	8	1.6	16.6
WPL Holdings	11/13/95	3Q97	0.9	—				
Interstate Power			0.3	1.110	15	3	1.6	13.6
IES Industries			0.9	1.140	29	8	1.7	13.8
Delmarva Power and Light Company	08/09/96	1Q98	1.2	—				
Atlantic Energy			0.9	0.75 plus 0.125 of new Class A shares	6	(1)	1.2	11.2
Ohio Edison Company	08/16/96	1Q98	3.5	—				
Centerior Energy Corporation			1.6	0.525	43	8	0.8	9.9
Western Resources	04/15/96	1Q98	2.0	—				
Kansas City Power and Light Company			2.4	$31.00	10	15	2.2	16.2
B. Electric/Gas								
Puget Sound Power and Light Company	10/19/95	closed on 2/7/97	1.6	—				
Washington Energy Company			0.5	0.860	20	2	2.3	19.5
Enova Corporation	10/11/96	4Q97	2.6	—				
Pacific Enterprises			2.6	1.504	7	8	2.2	14.9
Texas Utilities Company	04/15/96	2Q97	9.3	—				
ENSERCH Corporation			1.6	1.529 times EEX plus $8.00	51	18	2.2	29.5
Enron Corporation	07/22/96	3Q97	10.4	—				
Portland General Corporation			2.1	1.000	48	7	2.2	22.3
Houston Industries	08/09/96	2Q97	5.7	—				
NorAm Energy Corporation			2.0	$16.00	38	10	2.6	31.6
Duke Power Company	11/25/96	3Q97	9.6	—				
PanEnergy Corporation			7.1	1.044	18	6	3.1	21.8
Brooklyn Union Gas Company	12/30/96	1Q98	1.5	—				
Long Island Lighting Company			2.8	0.803	29	(7)	1.2	11.6

[a]Equity value divided by trailing 12-months' earnings. Washington Energy multiple based on year-ahead earnings as a result of operating loss in prior period.

Electric companies, probably including several in Table 1, are going to end up buying other electric companies, other gas companies, and other individual properties over the next few years on their way to becoming $50 billion companies. The best place to start this acquisition process is to buy a gas company, because at least the deal should be done by late 1997. For investors, the ultimate success of the Duke/PanEnergy merger will be critical not only because it is the largest but also because Duke has historically been considered one of the best utility companies, if not the best, in the industry. By merging with PanEnergy, Duke retains that reputation. This transaction may be a real bellwether, because if Duke cannot make this merger work and make money doing it, nobody can.

■ *Geographical mergers.* Among offensive mergers, geographical extension is still relatively rare, but I believe it will become an important trend. Extension means specifically jumping well outside the company's service territory or outside the power grid, as opposed to the defensive next-door-neighbor approach to enlarging the service territory. Extension is a strategy to establish national presence. Houston Industries Incorporated's acquisition of NorAm Energy Corporation is an electric/gas merger, but with this purchase, Houston gets gas local distribution companies (LDCs) as far afield as Minnesota. UtiliCorp United, a small company, has been working on this strategy for some time.

Increasingly, many of the large-capitalization, aggressive electric companies, such as Duke and Southern Company, are saying, on record, that they want to be nationwide electric and gas providers. They will either own electric companies or electric assets, or at least have some type of joint-venture participation, in the five or six power grids currently outside their U.S. service areas. The drive for expansion in the United States necessitates geographical extension. Consensus holds that companies need to be located close to the customers. If a company wants to be the national provider of gas and electricity to IBM, McDonald's, or Intel, it will probably need to have gas and electric assets in five to seven regions of the country because of the way the electricity grid is designed.

■ *Generation assets*. Buying generating assets is a separate offensive strategy. In 1997, California utilities and New England Electric System in Massachusetts plan to sell their non-nuclear power plants. They have agreed with regulators, who no longer want these companies vertically integrated, that they should formally divest their power plants. Domestic utilities such as Cinergy Corporation and Southern Company, British companies such as National Power and PowerGen, and nonutility power firms such as AES Corporation will bid for these assets with the idea that national, integrated energy companies of the future will need assets in different regions. Companies cannot afford to ignore the California market because it is the largest market, and beginning in 1998, it will be the first state with a fairly open trading regime in electricity. The competition for the California market should be interesting in late 1997.

■ *International mergers.* Many U.S. companies and non-U.S. companies are actively scouring the globe for growth opportunities. International acquisitions, as shown in **Table 2,** are essentially focused on geographical extension. U.S. companies have acquired about $12 billion worth of British companies and about $10 billion worth of Australian utilities. Houston Industries, in partnership with AES Corporation and Electricité de France (EDF), recently made a $1.7 billion investment in Light of Brazil. Table 2 lists only one Latin American acquisition because individual deals have been small, but in aggregate, billions of dollars have already been put into Argentina, Chile, Peru, and Venezuela. Companies have also invested in Kazakhstan, Hungary, Morocco, China, and Pakistan, among other developing countries.

WHY M&A ACTIVITY?

Electric companies are pursuing M&A strategies to spread costs over larger service areas, to realize higher growth prospects, and to reallocate capital to better position themselves as deregulation progresses. Declining production costs, declining core revenues, and deregulation provide the ammunition and catalysts for merger activity. But none of this M&A activity would be taking place if these companies did not currently have available financial resources.

Table 2. Major Overseas Transactions

Target	Date Announced	Acquirer	Value (US$ billions)
A. United Kingdom			
Midlands Electricity	May 1996	Cinergy Corporation/GPU Inc. (formerly General Public Utilities)	$2.6
East Midlands Electricity	November 1996	Dominion Resources	2.2
London Electricity	December 1996	Entergy Corporation	2.1
South Western Electricity	September 1995	Southern Company	1.7
Northern Electric	December 1996	CalEnergy	1.3
SEEBOARD	November 1995	Central and South West Corporation	1.2
B. Asia and Australia			
Consolidated Electric Power Asia (CEPA)	October 1996	Southern Company	2.7
Hazelwood Power	August 1996	National Power/Destec Energy/PacifiCorp	1.9
Powercor	December 1995	PacifiCorp	1.6
Eastern Energy	November 1995	Texas Utilities Company	1.6
CitiPower	January 1996	Entergy Corporation	1.2
United Energy	August 1995	Utilicorp United/AMP Investments	1.2
C. Latin America			
Light (Brazil)	May 1996	Houston Industries Energy/AES Corporation/Electricité de France	1.7
Total			23.0

Cost Control

A deregulated commodity industry forces participants to maintain tight cost control. If a company wants to merge with the electric utility next door or acquire the gas LDC that overlays its electric service territory, its primary interest is cost reduction. This defensive strategy enables the company to remain financially strong during ensuing price and market-share wars.

Higher Growth

The ultimate goal for many companies is higher growth. The farther afield an acquisition is, geographically and outside the core electric business, the more the acquisition can clearly be seen as part of a growth strategy. For example, the Duke/PanEnergy merger involved virtually no cost savings and little overlap of services. If the deal is going to succeed at all, it will succeed because the combined companies will have a higher growth rate than they would have as stand-alone companies. Of course, investors are keenly interested in the sum of the parts, and only time will provide the ultimate answer as to whether these electric/gas mergers result in higher growth.

This hypothesis for higher growth is unproven, but it makes a certain amount of sense. Gas companies are growing at 10 percent or more a year and have price–earnings multiples considerably higher than those of electric companies. Indeed, electric utility managers are thinking aloud how nice it would be for their companies to be the next Enron or the next PanEnergy. Electric utility managers and investors take hope from gas companies' performance because gas companies have already been through this experience.

The electric and gas industries are both slow-growth commodity businesses; both were heavily regulated as monopolies and then partially deregulated. To think of electricity as the next gas business, in terms of ultimate investment results, is not a far-fetched idea. The picture is fairly promising, with the only caveat being that the gas companies took 10 years to get where they are and were pretty poor stocks for the first 8 years. Electric deregulation may be moving faster, but at any rate, we are now in about Year 3 or 4 of the electric deregulation story and have another 3–5 years left in the transition period, with the remnants of flat rates for generation, before the full open market arrives.

Capital Allocation

During the next five years, as the electric industry completes the transition to a deregulated environment, a large-scale recapitalization will take place—a reallocation of capital to more appropriate risk–reward trade-offs. Deregulation forces utilities to rethink how to allocate precious capital because core revenues are no longer as secure as they once were. One can broadly think of the U.S. electric industry as withdrawing massive amounts of capital from areas where it has been overinvested—in generating plants, especially nuclear ones—and redirecting it to more efficient uses. So-called stranded costs represent too much capital invested in a generating plant, and to the extent the company can extract any of this capital, it needs to redeploy its excess capital efficiently. Utilities can pay down debt and improve leverage ratios, or they can repurchase stock and improve return ratios. Most companies, including growth companies, are following these financial engineering strategies, but even after retiring large amounts of debt and equity, in aggregate, billions of dollars in excess cash flow remain in the industry.

Electric companies are undertaking these M&A strategies because excess cash flows are available and potential acquisition targets exist domestically and internationally. Understanding why electric companies are pursuing M&A strategies will help to understand how to analyze these mergers.

HOW TO ANALYZE ELECTRIC MERGERS

Investors need to focus on the following questions when analyzing electric utility M&A deals and making appropriate investment selections:

- Does the merger enhance scale, strength, and skill?
- Are the dilution–growth and risk–reward trade-offs appropriate?
- Does it boost growth?
- Does it earn 10 percent?
- Is it appropriately priced?
- Do you trust the management?

Does the merger enhance scale, strength, and skill? Any M&A activity will have to enhance these three critical elements. The drive for size is not only to increase the number of power plants and the length of distribution pipeline (i.e., achieve economies of scale) but also to increase financial strength. Because this industry is so capital intensive, a low cost of capital and critical balance sheet size are necessary for competitive success.

In a deregulated commodity market, the core business of utilities will be risk management, not how good they are at finding gas in the ground or how good they are at running nuclear plants, although these skills are also important. What will also matter is how smart companies are at trading gas and electricity and how persuasive they are in signing up customers. Given their portfolio of available energy, managers need to assess how good a portfolio they have, how good a price they can get for that portfolio, and most important, how well they manage risk. When economic variables change, it is crucial to ensure that commitments to buy and sell move together so that the company does not get financially crushed.

Although some interesting technological developments are underway, technology will produce limited cost reductions in the future. The best way to lower costs of electricity coming out of power plants is to renegotiate coal contracts, which overwhelms any possible achievement from, say, replacing the boiler or installing a new control panel. I also do not believe that most power plants will see very large payroll savings.

■ *Are the dilution–growth and risk–reward trade-offs appropriate?* When Western Resources made a bid to buy Kansas City Power and Light, analysts did not need to do a whole lot of work. They are very similar companies with similar multiples, and the result is likely to be a moderate, predictable amount of cost savings. But when Southern Company bid to buy Consolidated Electric Power Asia (CEPA), which has a collection of finished and half-finished power plants in politically volatile places, nobody could estimate the level of risk involved. Given how this industry trades and who trades it, this level of risk is hard to swallow. When people shoot first and ask questions later, stocks sell off. Likewise, Southern Company took on dilution of about 5 percent in return for an enhancement of perhaps 1–2 percent in the growth rate at its parent company. Was this the appropriate amount? When and if companies show that they are receiving important results from their deals, investors will bid the stocks up again.

In this context, consider AES Corporation, which now trades at about 30 times earnings on the strength of an expansion strategy that has brought it into Kazakhstan, Hungary, and Brazil. A certain audience believes that an aggressive international growth strategy in somewhat obscure electric markets can produce big gains for investors. Such investor support does not currently exist for the companies I follow, such as Southern Company. If support does not develop, Southern Company, Edison International, and CMS Energy Corporation are going to start selling off their non-U.S. power operations or doing initial public offerings for them.

■ *Does it boost growth?* This issue can be fairly straightforward. Arithmetic suggests that Duke/PanEnergy will be a higher growth company than stand-alone Duke because PanEnergy's growth rate is higher than Duke's. But it is uncertain whether the combination of PanEnergy's trading and marketing skills with Duke's operational skills will make the combined company more productive and thus boost growth beyond the arithmetic. What has happened in the gas industry is a promising indicator, but a fully traded electricity commodity market is not yet a reality. No one can determine whether having gas traders and marketers working on electricity will add value, but it is a good bet.

■ *Does it earn 10 percent?* The rule of thumb for electric utilities is a 10 percent risk-adjusted cost of equity capital. The good news is that 10 percent is not very high, so investors who trust a company's management may be able to make a case for success. A number of companies are earning rather low returns, and investments that are not necessarily brilliant could significantly enhance their outlooks. (Of course, such companies generally have only very low-priced stocks to use as currency.)

■ *Is it appropriately priced?* Recent merger bids, offer-price–earnings multiples, and premiums for deals that have already been announced in the industry are shown in Table 1. Typical premiums range from roughly 20–50 percent for electric/gas and some electric/electric mergers. Premiums of 1–3 percent are the fly in the ointment because these premiums indicate mergers of equals, poison pill mergers, or defensive mergers. The companies get something out of the deal, such as lower costs or a larger service area, but current investors do not benefit. For example, investors in Southwestern Public Service Company would have been better off if the company had auctioned itself off rather than sell itself to Public Service Company of Colorado for a 2 percent premium. Although this particular deal was great for Public Service Company of Colorado shareholders, one can understand the difficulty of investing in these small stocks in an industry with an M&A focus. Price-to-book ratios (P/B) are still relevant, especially with electric utilities; the ratios have not been too high. Any transaction done at a P/B below two times is questionable for the target, because many electric utilities trade in the open market at two times. Exorbitant P/B multiples have not been paid. On P/Es, the good news is that some pretty low P/E multiples exist, but the bad news is that even pretty low multiples are above the P/Es of the likely bidders, thus making a transaction more difficult because it would cause dilution.

Utilities are sometimes sacrificing diluted earnings for potentially higher growth rates. Earnings dilution is very important to management and shareholders; it comes into play especially in mergers for gas companies. Duke Power, which has about the highest earnings multiple in the industry at 14–15 times, was barely able to buy out PanEnergy, which trades at about 20 times earnings and took a moderate dilution hit in the process. The earnings dilution for companies with undervalued stocks in electricity that acquire another company would be even greater than for companies with appropriately priced stocks. On the other hand, these companies have a lot of cash flow. I believe that companies with high cash flow and a desire for growth will eventually make acquisitions, perhaps using a lot of leverage to help overcome dilution.

■ *Do you trust them?* The final criterion for investors is whether they trust what management is doing as industry restructuring continues. Utility managers are buying and sometimes selling assets and companies to prepare for an industry that does not exist yet. For example, they are buying power plants to sell power in an unregulated market, without knowing what the unregulated price will be and without having a history on which to base an estimated price. Investors who own large-capitalization electric stocks today have to think hard about what management is thinking and whether it can dance through the upcoming mine field. The winning strategy is not yet obvious, but the goal is clear: To be a well-managed national energy provider with higher growth prospects than currently exist. For electric utility managers, exactly how to organize all the possible assets is a mystery. But for investors, the issue clearly comes down to trusting management to do the right thing given the array of possibilities.

IMPLICATIONS FOR INVESTORS AND THE INDUSTRY

The M&A activity taking place now is in preparation for a full open market. How much benefit an investor will get from M&A activity during the next few years is difficult to determine. Five years from now, some company will be the Enron of electricity, and half a dozen companies could be significant winners. This M&A activity has both near-term and long-term implications for electric utility managers and investors.

Present Implications

The road to this wonderful deregulated future passes through the present, which is not quite as wonderful. The near-term investment implication of doing M&A deals with utilities having earnings multiples of 12 is dilution. Lower dividend growth is an inevitable outcome of deregulation, and the more aggressively one wants to grow in the near term, the greater the pressure to reduce dividends, which will make traditional utility investors very unhappy.

M&A activity will inevitably result in higher-risk companies, although the question is, higher risk compared with what? On the spectrum from Treasury bills to Netscape Communications, electric utilities, even with a more ambitious growth strategy, will be closer to the Treasury bill end of the spectrum. Electric utilities will not radically change to a Netscape-type risk level, even if they acquire two gas companies and three non-U.S. companies. But shareholder rotation will certainly occur, as happened in the Duke transaction—Duke stock sold off heavily for about two weeks following the merger announcement. The initial reaction in the market is to sell utility stocks involved in acquisitions, because people focus on the risk of earnings dilution.

Although dilution is a potential problem of investing in acquiring companies, investing in target companies also has problems. Assembling a portfolio of target companies is difficult because it is like waiting for lightning to strike. The lower the P/E and P/B multiples, the more attractive a company looks, but lower multiples also indicate a lower quality company. By investing in potential target companies, investors may wait too long and end up with poor returns before anybody comes along and buys these companies. For example, companies have bid for Centerior and Long Island Lighting—both of which are in financially weak situations with difficult outlooks—and these offers may indicate a floor value on how far down a stock can go before it becomes an attractive acquisition target.

The biggest problem with any strategy of investing in potential takeover targets is the FERC. A deal can take two years to complete, and an electric/electric merger in general provides about a 25 percent premium, which is about the cost of carry for this time period. Consequently, after the investor has done all this careful analysis and picked the right stock, the stock does not go anywhere when the bid is announced.

Future Implications

In about five years, the industry will be dominated by the integrated giants, which will almost inevitably be combined gas and electric companies. Gas is too important and too closely related to electricity not to be part of the picture. Anyone trading in electricity cannot be without gas to trade, because arbitrage opportunities arise to make profits.

Electricity production will increasingly come from gas-fired power plants. Any company with a national ambition or even a substantial regional ambition will have to get into gas, either by following an acquisition strategy or by participating in gas storage, marketing, or joint ventures. One clear implication of this M&A activity is that no pure gas companies will remain; they will all be part of an integrated energy company, especially for the larger gas companies. A few LDCs may remain that are not part of a larger company, but only for political reasons. Six to 10 national giants will form, and several regional players will emerge. Strong regional companies might be found in areas lacking a strong electrical connection to the rest of the country. For example, Public Service Company of Colorado, which is a low-cost producer in a high-growth area but is not close to any competing electricity sources, can dominate its regional market. Although no one has an obvious strategic reason to acquire such a utility, it may be acquired simply because it is a good company.

The local winners in gas LDCs and probably electric distribution companies will be the companies that have sold off their power plants in the deregulated generation market and have retained the poles and wires—the regulated monopoly function of delivering the electricity to end customers. If local utilities want to remain independent, they will have to get the local politicians on their side. The regulated-return effect of a monopoly also limits the interest of potential acquirers. With limited upside potential and a difficult road to travel, acquirers tend to leave local utilities alone if they want to be left alone, and that trend may continue.

CONCLUSION

The electric utility industry is undergoing a tremendous amount of domestic and international M&A activity. Defensive mergers seek to reduce costs and to focus on control of the customer; offensive mergers that are executed with the goal of becoming a national company focus on the commodity side of the business. While trying to understand what electric utilities are doing, why they are doing it, and how to analyze M&A activity, investors and managers must keep an eye on deregulation and the FERC—two powerful forces shaping the new utility industry—and they must understand the present and future implications of these deals.

Question and Answer Session

Kit Konolige, CFA

Question: Although you spoke about several types of mergers, you did not talk about the related diversification model—for example, Western Resources going after ADT. How does that model fit into the picture?

Konolige: Frankly, it doesn't fit very well. It is a bells-and-whistles reinvestment strategy. A lot of theories have been created to explain what types of businesses might be related to electricity. Western believes that ADT's home security fits with an electric company because it is a constant monitoring business, a monthly billing business, and a business that depends on customers' absolute trust in the employees. Although those connections exist, for the most part, I do not think of those as two complementary industries.

In general, these companies are looking to expand into unregulated businesses on the periphery of the regulated businesses and to reinvest the regulated cash flows. Not everyone will agree on what the related businesses are, other than gas.

Question: How does an electric company get higher growth rates by merging with a gas company?

Konolige: Gas companies have been able to take a slow-growth business and find its higher-growth business segments. Overall, I don't think gas is growing any faster than it used to, but when gas was deregulated and unbundled, parts of the gas business—marketing, trading, exploration and production, and storage—earned higher returns and achieved faster growth than when they were part of a bundled, fully regulated business.

In the past three years, major gas companies have managed to achieve more than a 10 percent growth rate in a slow-growth industry. Ultimately, that is the electric industry's hope. These companies will achieve higher growth rates by efficiently reallocating capital and resources, investing in growing subsectors, and disinvesting in the commodity businesses.

Question: Is the risk premium for investing outside the United States, especially in the emerging markets, declining, and are shareholders being properly rewarded for taking the higher risk?

Konolige: Most of the companies that are investing outside the United States will tell you that their non-risk-adjusted returns at the parent level, after the effects of significant leverage, range from the high teens to the low 30s. They also tell you that in many cases, they are able to obtain some kind of business risk insurance from the Overseas Private Investment Corporation, for example, and that they may hedge the currencies. Frankly, I do not think that we have a long enough track record to evaluate whether those are the correct risk-adjusted returns. The returns are high enough that companies can afford to lose out occasionally on one of these investments, but how frequently they can afford to lose is a good question.

Duke and some other companies have already taken write-downs for power plant investments in Argentina, but the pool price of the power has been consistently too low for anybody to make any money. If that investment had been bigger, it would have been a big hit, but fortunately, it was a small investment. A lot of these investments have been fairly small to date. Developing-country investments are still basically at a startup stage.

For investments in the United Kingdom and Australia—and now Southern Company in Asia with CEPA—real money is at stake, so the return needs to be higher. Investors are finally entering the period in which they will find out whether or not they are being appropriately rewarded for the risks. The British investments, which have been the largest ones in aggregate so far, would be described as fairly low risk. Those investments were typically bought at 9–11 times earnings and then leveraged up. Frankly, it is hard to analyze these individual projects unless the companies let you see their books, and they don't. They tend to pat you on the back and say, "Don't worry. We are getting all our cash out in three years." But who knows?

Question: The FERC is talking about streamlining the process for approving mergers. Could you comment on what you think it is doing and whether that will speed up the process?

Konolige: FERC recently announced that its 18–24 month approval period is a little long, so they now have a new set of guidelines, including the standard market power analysis used in other industries, that should result in merger completions from 5–15 months, still longer than any other industry. Of course, we will believe that improvement when we see it. One unfortunate early indication is that companies already in the approval pipeline at about the 12–18 month time frame now have to refile. Thus, the situation is a little bit of a Catch-22 for them.

When you filter out all the noise, the FERC does want to streamline the process. It has been overwhelmed and is struggling to cope with how quickly the industry is changing and how many companies want to merge at the same time. It will eventually reorganize the process sufficiently, and we will end up with a standard one-year period to complete a merger, which will certainly be better than it has been. When managers have some conviction that they will be able to complete a merger in a year, we will see a lot more electric-on-electric mergers. The mergers are currently stacked up over LaGuardia airport waiting to land.

Question: You didn't mention mergers between investor-owned companies and government entities. Is this something that we should also be thinking about?

Konolige: I don't see those type of mergers as being a big movement anytime soon, because the role of the government in the whole industry needs to be determined. I expect to see joint venture, leasing, or service agreement types of arrangements. The government power operations want to preserve their sinecures, but I think they recognize that to do that effectively or for a long time, they have to become more efficient.

One of the obvious approaches is to bring in investor-owned utilities that will give the government utilities back some cut of the savings, or the profits from reselling, or whatever their area of concern is, which lends itself to a joint-venture type of arrangement. I have heard a number of companies talking about going in and reorganizing these inefficient government organizations and then running them—the power plant, the distribution system—as a potential profit center, which may create some benefits for everybody. I do not, however, see them being sold to private investors in the current climate. The local politicians will fight to preserve their subsidized power.

Question: If an investor purchased electric utility stocks for the dividend payments, should that investor keep or sell those stocks?

Konolige: One problem is, what are the alternatives? Risk tolerance is a key issue here. My own feeling is that quality companies are out there, such as FPL Group or Southern Company, that are not going to mess around with the dividend a whole lot. The dividend growth profile going forward is lower than it has been in the past, which is true of a lot of companies in a lot of industries. If dividend growth is the sole criterion, then that investor should look around or, alternatively, look at a select few of these companies that are already focused on a distribution-only strategy and want to remain a utility. A number of companies will continue to pay that 75 percent payout ratio and try to grow the dividend.

But for most investors, who are not solely concerned with the exact level of their dividend, now is a worthwhile time to stay invested with a quality company and quality management. If those investors have a long time horizon and they own an electric utility fund, the aggregate value of the industry will have increased substantially 10 years from now.

Interpreting Electric Utilities' Numbers and Equity Valuation

William I. Tilles
Vice President and Senior Analyst
Smith Barney Inc.

> Industry restructuring provides significant near-term opportunities for equity investors but requires careful consideration of the positives and negatives of alternative investments. An abundance of free cash flow—which can be used to repurchase stock, retire outstanding debt, or diversify into other business ventures—underscores the important role of managers and the strategic direction in which they take electric utilities. Investors can analyze potential opportunities in a variety of ways, including current yield, total return, relative yield, and special situations.

Industry restructuring has a significant impact on the equity valuation of electric utilities, and it has important implications for utility investors. This presentation addresses the positive and negative elements of industry changes; assesses the increasing importance of management in determining the strategic direction of electric utilities; discusses the fundamental importance of free cash flow; identifies opportunities involved with the disaggregation of generation, transmission, and distribution functions; and evaluates the impact of risk and return on the equity valuation of electric utilities.[1]

POSITIVES AND NEGATIVES

The restructuring of the electric utility industry has at least two distinctly positive dimensions for investors. The first relates to the relatively solid free cash flow position of the industry as it enters the brave new world of competition. This free cash flow position should provide management with the financial flexibility to pursue share repurchase programs, retire debt, and invest in other nonregulated, earnings-enhancing businesses. The second positive dimension relates to the positive valuation implications, at least for the generation and distribution business segments of the electric industry. The electric distribution business may be poised to get a valuation boost as investors recognize a disparity versus other distribution entities. And on the generation side, regulatory guarantees appear to ensure accelerated recovery of high-cost nuclear assets in return for a lowering of permitted earnings levels on these assets.

These positive dimensions are offset by two disadvantages. First, the quickening pace of industry change exceeds what industry participants had previously expected, thus requiring managers to evaluate new business opportunities against a backdrop of increasing earnings volatility and potential dividend uncertainty. Second, the business risk in the power-generation segment is also increasing in the face of a competitive domestic wholesale electric power market, which is expected within the next several years.

IMPORTANCE OF MANAGEMENT

As electric utilities contemplate focusing on one specific part of the business versus another (e.g., generation versus distribution), management's importance increases dramatically because utilities are seeking new strategic directions. During the past decade, a transition has taken place from using engineers as senior managers to using personnel with a background in finance and accounting, and the next set of relevant managerial skills is in strategic planning. For the first time not only in my career but also probably in the lifetimes of most people, the kind of business an electric company is, or will be, is not obvious. Will management sell generation assets and

---

[1] This presentation draws heavily from "Investment Implications of Electric Utility Restructuring" by William Tilles, Paul Fremont, Roy Ericsson, and Raymond Niles in *Electric Utility Monthly* (January 1997), published by Smith Barney.

focus on distribution or vice versa? This question pertains only to the formerly regulated parts of the business. Meaningful participation in nonregulated ventures involves an entirely different set of decisions. All of these questions about the role of managers and the decisions they will have to make stem from a common concern about growth rates because the core growth rate for the average electric utility in my universe of coverage is a fairly modest 3 percent, with little opportunity for reinvestment in the core utility business. In other words, standing still and doing nothing strategically will not be viewed as a viable option, even by the most stodgy and traditional utility managers.

FREE CASH FLOW

The industry's free cash flow position also underscores the important role of management. The first positive dimension of restructuring the electric utility industry is free cash flow. Although utility earnings power will become more volatile in a deregulated environment, cash flow generation is expected to remain robust for at least the next several years. The bulk of the industry has been spending freely on power-generation assets and transmission and distribution upgrades. Suddenly, with the looming prospect of competition in the generation market, capital spending for new power plant construction has all but dried up, thus providing the majority of participants in the electric utility industry with free cash flow—free cash after capital expenditures and even after the payment of common stock dividends.

At Smith Barney, we expect utility managers to deploy this cash primarily in three ways: common stock buybacks (the preferred method), the retirement of debt (reducing financial leverage), and diversification into either regulated or nonregulated business ventures, with a focus on accelerating an otherwise anemic earnings growth outlook. Over time, stock buybacks may replace dividend growth as a way of enhancing shareholder value because this approach provides management greater financial flexibility than the traditional dividend policy—fixed dividends with periodic increases. But management's track record with respect to redeployment of free cash flow into higher growth areas will be closely scrutinized by investors.

DISAGGREGATION

At some point in the future, the bulk of electric utilities will be disaggregated into at least three components: a nonregulated electric-power-generation business segment, a regulated transmission and distribution business, and a lightly regulated energy services business that sells new products and services, such as telecommunications and security services, both within and outside historical franchise areas. For those companies that do not legally separate along functional business lines, we would expect these business units to be managed as if they were stand-alone operations.

Power Generation

The power-generation business is the business segment that will be most affected by the transition to a competitive market. Of the three major business segments of a traditional utility, power generation is the principal business segment that is likely to be operating in a completely deregulated market in the near future. Power generation will involve the sale of a commodity product, kilowatt hours of electricity, into a competitive regional wholesale market. As a result, guaranteed returns on invested capital are likely to become a regulatory relic. A reasonable assumption, given the existence of significant excess capacity on a national basis, is considerable earnings volatility and declining margins on power sales. Because of the potential earnings volatility and the fact that about 50 percent of an electric company's assets are invested in the power-generation business segment, the largest segment of a typical electric company's asset base has little or no ability to pay dividends. At the same time, the equity capitalization of generation should be much higher and, given the business risk, much less capable of supporting large amounts of debt leverage.

The only positive news about the power-generation aspect is the regulatory response. The regulators have shown extreme willingness to encourage the sale of regulated assets and at the same time guarantee recouping at least the book value of the investment in these assets. As a result of this fairly generous offer, several companies—such as Pacific Gas and Electric, Edison International, and New England Electric System—are in the process of practically exiting the generation business. These companies are only the first group. If the regulators continue to guarantee recouping the book value of generation assets, more companies will follow suit and attempt to exit the generation business altogether.

From a valuation perspective, generating assets should be valued the same as deep cyclicals—such as steel or pulp and paper—with earnings multiples possibly in the high single digits. Valuing the power-generation business as a deep cyclical is valid in light of the substantial business risks and the relatively high capital costs involved in these new long-lead-time power-generation projects. In addition, utility managers need to accurately gauge the prospective acceleration in demand for electricity—a skill that has evaded most electric utility managers. Other likely features of this business segment are the need for a strong balance sheet and a relatively low payout ratio, given the elevated business risk for this segment in a competitive environment.

Any company that is going to continue to own significant power-generation assets will need to be involved in power marketing and foreign independent power producers (IPPs). Foreign IPPs will help maintain engineering expertise for new power plant construction, which is not occurring in the United States at this time. Foreign IPPs go hand in hand with power generation because they are the only way to offset the cost of maintaining engineering staffs. And because electric companies are not building new power plants in the United States, a company that wants to stay involved with state-of-the-art technology will probably have to have a foreign IPP arm.

An important dilemma for management is whether to sell or retain generating assets. The downside of selling generating assets is the acceptance of a modest diminution in earnings power associated with those assets. For example, in California, the return on equity (ROE) associated with generation was equal to the utility's embedded cost of debt, or about 7–8 percent, and in Massachusetts, ROEs associated with power generation were about 9 percent. But, as a fully competitive market for wholesale power develops, the guaranteed ROEs in these recent regulatory settlements are likely to exceed what generating-owning utilities could earn on those assets in a fully competitive wholesale power market. As a result, generating-owning utilities may be inclined to sell fossil-fired generation rather than assume the risk associated with those assets.

Transmission and Distribution

Electric utility transmission and distribution assets are likely to get a valuation benefit from industry disaggregation. From an earnings perspective, the transmission and distribution business should emerge relatively unscathed in the transition to competition. These business segments are likely to remain more or less rate based and rate-of-return regulated, primarily by current state public utility commissions. As a result, earnings growth trends—modest though they may be—should remain in line with prior expectations. The upside potential from an earnings-per-share viewpoint comes mostly from expense reductions and, to a lesser extent, customer growth and new product and services offerings. Overall, because of the high level of capital required and regulatory barriers to entry, the transmission and distribution segment should continue to be characterized by relatively low business risk. As a result, this business segment should still enjoy the earnings stability that investors have come to expect from the entire electric utility business in general and could sustain greater leverage and a higher payout ratio than the integrated utility overall.

The valuation of the transmission and distribution segment is likely to resemble earnings multiples of other pure distribution entities, such as water companies, which currently enjoy very high payouts and very low rates of growth, and gas distribution entities, which have lower dividend payouts and somewhat more robust growth rates than electric utilities. In terms of P/E multiples, a pure distribution entity on the electric side could trade at a P/E around 13–14 times forward earnings, which is in line with gas and water multiples and compares with the average electric earnings multiple for 1998—between 11 and 11.5 times earnings. This analysis implies an approximate 20 percent potential P/E expansion for the portion of earnings derived from this business segment.

EQUITY VALUATION: RISK AND RETURN

Equity valuation of electric utilities must address the inherent risks within the industry (i.e., stranded costs and nuclear plants) and potential return opportunities. Investors may evaluate return opportunities in terms of dividend yield, total return, special higher-risk superior-return opportunities, relative yield, and yield spread.

Stranded-Cost Recovery

Stranded assets are those relatively high-cost electric-power-generating facilities and above-market purchased power contracts whose fixed costs plus a return on capital could not be recovered in a competitive wholesale power market. The new regulatory agreement involves the recovery of stranded assets in return for breaking the electric industry's monopoly hold on generation. This new agreement stems in part from state and federal regulators' desire to bring about competition in the wholesale electric-generating market. Although both groups of regulators probably agree on the ultimate outcome—competition in the wholesale power-generation market—they often disagree on the time frame in which to accomplish this task. In return for the present franchise-owning utility's surrender of its monopoly position in generation, regulators have tended to guarantee stranded-asset recovery via a non-bypassable competitive transition charge.

The probability of recouping stranded assets opens two separate cans of worms. The first issue pertains more to the nuclear-exposed utilities and the complication caused by a political agenda. The exposure for the companies is that the review process prior to finding a resolution of stranded assets might turn into a nightmare. If so, then the outcome will be another haircut of nuclear assets or any other potentially high-cost assets that the regulators or the politicians did not like before. This first problem of recouping assets is not a huge issue, but an investor must be cognizant of it.

The second issue is much more difficult to get a handle on and pertains to the mechanism of recovery. If these stranded assets are deemed certified for recovery, the utilities are going to add some kind of extra charge that the distribution entity will be able to collect from anyone who wants to use its wires, which is the so-called competitive transition charge (CTC). Utilities must assess whether anybody will figure out a way around paying the CTC. The higher the amount of stranded assets that need to be recovered, the longer the utility is going to try to charge that CTC. My feeling is the longer the tail on CTC recovery, the higher the probability that people will find a way around it. Loopholes in the CTC are where utilities get into trouble, because the longer they think they are going to collect the CTC and the more vibrant the competitive market that opens up, the greater the risk for the continued recouping of assets.

Nuclear Power Plant Ownership Risks

Recent regulatory restructuring measures and proposals appear to reduce the investor risk of nuclear power plant ownership, albeit at the expense of a modest earnings erosion. For example, in California, managers have chosen to accept a lower return on equity associated with nuclear investments in return for a five-year recovery of nuclear asset costs—that is, accelerated depreciation—and guaranteed recovery of nuclear decommissioning costs. In addition, we are also seeing nuclear operating incentive plans that may render the company indifferent as to whether nuclear plants run or not, except with respect to operating efficiency. This relatively constructive regulatory response to the dilemmas posed by nuclear power plant ownership may hasten other premature nuclear plant retirement decisions. On the operating side, however, problem plants continue to be exposed to extended plant outages, with a potentially adverse impact on earnings.

Equity Return Implications

Because of the industry restructuring, yield-oriented investors will be forced to rethink their commitment to electric utilities. The coming deregulation of the electric-power-generation segment implies the potential for significant earnings volatility. This part of the industry, which typically involves more than half of an average company's assets, cannot be expected to contribute to a dividend policy that compares with the 70–80 percent payout ratio currently enjoyed by investors. As a result, the math is very simple. If half of the business can contribute zero dividends and the other half has an 80 percent payout ratio potential, the target payout ratio probably trends toward 40 percent.

Although regulators have taken steps to diminish the risk profile of the generation segment, especially with respect to treatment of high-cost nuclear assets, these steps—accelerated depreciation and a lower authorized return on stranded assets including nuclear-related equity—have nevertheless contributed to modest earnings erosion. As a consequence, we believe that the electric industry's dividend policy will continue to be revised downward. Currently, the average payout ratio of my universe of companies is between 70 and 75 percent, which obviously is not good for yield-oriented investors.

Total Return

Total-return-oriented investors will continue to find attractive investment opportunities. For example, Duke Power typifies the potentially attractive restructuring opportunities in the industry. As a consequence of its pending merger with faster-growing PanEnergy Corporation, Duke will have the potential to double its earnings growth rate from about 4 percent to 8 percent. If these numbers materialize, considerable P/E expansion is possible: The 12-month potential return could well exceed 20 percent with 15 percent price appreciation plus about 4–5 percent current yield.

Utilities with the bulk of their assets invested in the lower-risk distribution segment will also benefit from industry restructuring. Examples include Puget Sound Energy (formed from the merger of Puget Sound Power & Light and Washington Energy Company), Consolidated Edison, and GPU (formerly General Public Utilities). Such stocks could experience an upward revaluation as investors recognize the relatively modest asset exposure of these companies compared with power-generation companies. The flip side is that distribution companies have greater reliance on purchased power contracts.

Special Situations

Special-situation electric utilities, such as Niagara Mohawk Power Corporation, Eastern Utilities Associates, TNP Enterprises, Centerior Energy Corporation, and Pinnacle West Capital Corporation, continue to offer superior total return potential. The compelling return potential, given the relatively higher risks, would keep investors focused on these types of companies.

Relative Yield

Electric utilities continue to look attractive versus the broad market on a relative yield basis. The relative yield relationship between the S&P electric utilities and the S&P 400 Industrials currently stands at 324 percent, which means that as of December 31, 1996, the yield of S&P electric utilities was 3.24 times the yield of the S&P 400 Industrials—the S&P electric utilities yielded 5.99 percent, but the S&P 400 yielded only 1.85 percent. This yield remains at the upper boundary of relative yields during the past 10 years, suggesting the continued relative yield attraction of electric utilities vis-à-vis the broad market.

Yield Spread

Electric utilities seem more or less fairly valued versus long-term U.S. Treasury bonds. The yield spread of the S&P electric utilities versus 30-year U.S. Treasury bonds at the end of December 1996 stood at 64 basis points, with electric utilities yielding less than U.S. Treasury bonds, which is a modest increase from the late November 1996 49 basis point yield spread. Electric utilities' yield spread has continued to remain at about the midpoint of yield spreads during the past several years. For example, during the past three years, the yield relationship between the electric utilities and the long bond has ranged from virtual parity to 122 basis points—electric utilities under bonds.

CONCLUSION

Investors must consider the positives and negatives of investing in electric utility equities and recognize that the key drivers of common stock value going forward will be the strategic direction in which management leads utilities and the free cash flow situation. Although disaggregation of generation, transmission, and distribution functions challenges electric utility managers, it provides interesting opportunities for equity investors. After looking at the inherent risks of electric utilities, investors can select appropriate equities by evaluating utilities in terms of current yield, total return, special situations, relative yield, and yield spread. Given the industry restructuring, significant investment opportunities can be found in the near term.

Question and Answer Session

William I. Tilles

Question: You said Duke Power is going to double its growth, to about 8 percent. But if the gas business is essentially a slow-growing business, how do you get that number?

Tilles: First, what makes PanEnergy different from other gas companies is its growth. It has some growth potential, perhaps 3–4 percent, in its core gas utility business. PanEnergy also has modest growth potential in its power-marketing subsidiary, and that growth will probably ramp up over time. Second, you have to look at PanEnergy historically. It made excellent midstream acquisitions of gas processors that have generated returns significantly above its other businesses. PanEnergy has basically shown a real ability to make acquisitions in the range of $250 to $500 million, to run those businesses well, and to crank out very high returns. So, the bet on whether it can maintain such performance is: Can this management continue to deploy capital wisely (i.e., in further acquisitions)? If you net that out of the equation, you can make the numbers work.

Question: To be successful, it seems Duke will have to meld the two management groups (Duke and PanEnergy) together and not let anybody escape. Is this observation correct, or does some overlap exist?

Tilles: Melding the two groups is certainly the correct strategy, and I would take it a step further. Duke's management will also have to provide the proper incentives to personnel in the form of significant amounts of common equity, but I think they are planning to do that.

Question: When are we going to stop looking at the dividends and start looking at electric utility companies as real businesses?

Tilles: We will start sometime later in 1997, and I do not say that to put off the question. At Smith Barney, we are in the process of doing the quantitative research to put some meat on that proposition. In terms of the data, we have analyzed about 50 companies out of the 65-company universe, and the midpoint multiple is about four times earnings before interest, taxes, depreciation, and amoritization (EBITDA).

I think the better question is, "Why do we have to stop using P/E-based analysis and start using EBITDA?" The reason we have to use cash flow is because earnings are no longer comparable. Two obvious companies—Texas Utilities Company and Pacific Gas and Electric—serve as examples. Both have significant nuclear exposures. Pacific Gas and Electric has decided to rapidly amortize its nuclear plant in five years, trashing its earnings power but removing the assets from the books in an expedited fashion. Texas Utilities is taking the "What, me worry?" approach. So, how do you compare the earnings of Texas Utilities and Pacific Gas? They have similar fundamental risks, but the EPS potential looks rather disparate. People have to move to an analysis of cash flow because it eliminates the management piece of the earnings equation.

Question: What role will bankruptcy play in the industry's reorganization?

Tilles: The honest answer is some bankruptcies will occur. In the extreme, some companies will always get into trouble. The reason I am spending a lot less time thinking about it now than I was, say, six months ago is because what has continued to surprise me is the relatively responsive and constructive approach of the regulators, especially to the most nuclear-troubled companies. So, if a company is financially risky and has a business that is not in good shape and it does something stupid, it will find itself over the precipice. The company that comes to mind near term is Northeast Utilities, which is doing a terrible job of running its nuclear plants. Except for the extreme cases like Northeast, I am optimistic about the bankruptcy issue simply because the regulators seem inclined to put so much money into managements' hands in a relatively near-term fashion.

Question: A rapid consolidation is already occurring in the power-marketing sector. Will these new power-generating companies actually find they can get into power marketing?

Tilles: The simple answer is that power marketing is not an asset-intensive business. It is a people-intensive business. Power marketing has two aspects. One aspect is the soft assets, which is simply people and infrastructure, and the other is that if a company wants to do power marketing well and stop being simply a financial intermediary providing intellectual expertise, it will have to put its money where its mouth is and start to own generating assets.

If the question is whether anyone can get into the game, the answer is yes. But if you want to pay the salaries, your assets go up and down on the elevator every night. What will separate serious from unserious contenders will be the managements that realize the only way they can make money in this business is to start owning generation assets in the various regions in which they are operating so that they can back up these contracts with physical supply. My guess is that the next shakeout will occur in power marketing, because the consolidation is very easy. Anyone with enough cash can take over one of these companies, and in that sense, no barrier to entry exists. The key will be who feels smart enough to start buying some of the assets of, say, the California companies or the New England companies that are likely to come up for sale in the very near term.

Question: What prices are utilities going to get for the sale of generating assets (e.g., book value, one-third of book value), and what drives the valuation?

Tilles: No one knows because no sales have transpired. All that can be said for certain is that a lot of capacity appears to be ready to come up for sale very quickly. The impact of that situation is making the potential buyers more reticent, because if a lot of capacity is coming on the market and if you think even more is coming on, say, in a second tranche, you have absolutely no incentive to be the first one out the door unless such a gem of a property becomes available that it is a "must own." My suspicion is that very few gems are around. To make matters worse, companies entering the generation market from the other side—the fuel suppliers who think they can build a better mousetrap—are contemplating building gas-fired merchant plants, which would further scare the potential buyers because it makes the competitive landscape even that much more unattractive.

Question: If I were selling power plants, should I be a little nervous about the price I am going to get?

Tilles: You should not care. If the regulators are going to indemnify you for the book value of your assets, no negative consequence exists. So, if you get $1, that's fine. The rest goes into your CTC.

Question: Niagara Mohawk has had problems with its nuclear plant and a huge problem with purchased power. (I think they purchased all the power that could ever be produced in the United States, and they signed contracts for it.) In light of this problem, can you comment on the impact of a potential write-off on the income statement and company valuation?

Tilles: From an income statement perspective, we see the settlement of the non-utility-generation contract problem as a huge positive. The problem, however, is the earnings power that results is somewhat lackluster, because if you think about the income statement, two principal changes are involved. First, you have a problem that you are trying to monetize; second, you are basically trying to reach a number to get your nonutility generators to accept a lump-sum cash payment that represents some discount to their future value. If you get that result and they agree to that number, two things happen. The fuel and purchase power line on your income statement declines precipitously, which is wonderful. Your interest expense, however, goes up dramatically because you are going to have to issue huge amounts of incremental debt—in the range of $3.5 billion to $4 billion—to make these people go away. The net effect of those two adjustments is positive for shareholders, and you are left with a highly leveraged utility.

The fact of the write-off is you are not going to have any equity at the end of the day anyway, so whether you write off some or none is the least of my problems. The income statement will be relatively fixed, if you will, and then you will just be left with whatever service area trends you want to postulate and so forth. I would think about it from the equity perspective in terms of those two adjustments, and merely to complete the loop, we think they would come up with $1.20 of earnings power. In the best case, you will pay between 10 and 10.5 times. The price target is obviously about $12.00 to $13.00 per share, probably 20 percent or more than the stock is currently worth.

Question: Please comment on the potential nightmare of a whole series of additional regulatory hearings, with everyone debating what constitutes justified stranded assets, and how we may be back in the regulatory mode in a big way.

Tilles: Certain managers have already described the forthcoming regulatory proceedings as the mother of all rate cases. I do not think they take these lightly. The ones that we have seen have not been disastrous, but such precedents do not mean that the next one will not be a shareholder debacle. Thus far, California seems to be reasonably constructive. New York does not seem to want to put all the companies into bankruptcy. Massachusetts would appear to be fairly constructive. The ones that we have seen do not seem to be terrible from the point of view of shareholder value.

Question: We have heard a lot about rotating the shareholder base. That is, you have the old shareholder base, the retirees aged 65 and older who depend on the dividend, and new people looking at the business. Because individuals own approximately two-thirds of the electric utility stocks, do you get a sense now of a change in the shareholder base?

Tilles: The question is obviously multifaceted. Does the average individual retail investor know something is going on? The answer is yes. The problem is that investors are no different from the public at large, and when they see bad things happening, their first reaction is denial. After they get over denial, they probably will move to action, so utility investors are someplace in the denial–action continuum.

The brokers also are aware that something is going on, and they seem more inclined to start to move people around, but the problem for the retail investor is no new paradigm has emerged. Where they should go is not clear. Some people are telling you to buy low-cost producers. Some people are telling you to buy good cash flow companies. Where should you be? The shareholder base will rotate, probably slowly; the worst case is to have the wrong people holding the wrong stocks. As a result, they will just sell them at the wrong time, and that result would be terrible.

At the same time, new participants, people who have never played utilities before and could care less what business they are in, see these companies popping up on cash flow screens and say, "I don't care. Give me the smartest managements with the most free cash flow." The fact that they happen to sell kilowatts is a matter of supreme indifference to the newer breed of investors.

Implications of Industry Restructuring on the Valuation of Debt Securities

Terran A. Miller, CFA
Vice President
Donaldson, Lufkin & Jenrette

> Investing in debt securities of electric utilities is more challenging today than ever before because industry restructuring is altering the landscape of the industry—changing the types of investors, security modifiers, and security structures. More debt securities are now held for trading; security modifiers now include "credit watch" or "outlook change"; and security structures now include asset-backed securities. Industry restructuring has a significant impact on event risks—M&A activity, disaggregation, and changes in company structures—and business risk profiles. These risks affect sector attractiveness, credit spreads, and the supply of electric utility bonds.

In order to evaluate electric utility debt securities effectively, investors must have a good understanding of the standard factors that go into valuing debt securities, such as analysis of cash flow, fixed-charge coverages, and capital structure. But because of the restructuring occurring within the electric utility industry, debt investors must also analyze the impact of industry restructuring on the valuation of debt securities. This presentation identifies potential electric utility debt investors and the various security structures, assesses the impact of restructuring initiatives on valuation, discusses how the increasing event risk from merger and acquisition (M&A) activity and disaggregation affects bondholders, and analyzes how changing business risk profiles affect sector weighting and selection decisions in the wake of deregulation.

INVESTING IN ELECTRIC UTILITIES

The times are certainly changing in the electric utilities industry, bringing changes in investment patterns and a restructuring of investors. The changes primarily focus on who is and who is not currently investing in electric utilities debt securities, how the various debt securities are described, and the structure of the securities.

The Investors

Electric utilities are seeing a difference, although some overlap exists, between traditional investors in electric utility bonds versus current investors. Traditional investors have been insurance companies following a buy-and-hold strategy, opportunistic money managers, and state pension funds. Insurance companies continue to have significant investments in electric utility bonds, but in addition to following a buy-and-hold strategy, they now have more portfolio investments designated as held for sale or held for trading, which requires a large portion of their portfolio to be marked to market.

Total return players, or opportunistic players, have participated in the past and continue to participate today. They are looking to enhance short-term performance or outperform their benchmark index in order to receive additional compensation or bonuses.

State pension funds that have played a role in the past will continue to play a role in the future. But because many of them have A-rated or AA-rated investment requirements, the biggest problem they face today is the absence of supply, because A-rated and AA-rated electric utilities are not issuing much new paper.

Asset-backed securities (ABS), such as securitization of stranded costs within the industry, will attract a whole new set of investors and raise a whole new set of questions that utilities must answer.

Security Modifiers

Being a fixed-income money manager used to be easier. In the past, if you looked at a credit trend and thought it was going to be upgraded, you told your clients to get in on the early part of the curve and they generally made money. If you thought something was going to be downgraded, you made the same call and told people to sell. Today, however, the valuation considerations and modifiers have been extended. Bond analysts no longer simply issue "buy" and "sell" recommendations for companies; companies can now be placed on "credit watch" and have their "outlooks" changed. These new modifiers are not trivial additions. A company's bond spread can change significantly on an outlook change, and analysts no longer have to say that a company is going to be included on credit watch or that it will even see an upgrade or a downgrade. Essentially, what investors try to anticipate has changed substantially.

Security Structures

Fifteen years ago, the traditional electric utility bond had two flavors—either a 30-year nonrefundable 5-year bond or a 10-year nonrefundable 5-year bond. Today, there are putable, callable, and bullet securities with significantly different performance characteristics—duration and convexity—and maturities than traditional utility bonds. Driven by option-adjusted-spread (OAS) analysis, the "traditional" electric utility bond today is a 30-year noncallable 10-year security, offering investors additional call protection. Bond issuers and investors are taking advantage of sophisticated valuation techniques, such as OAS analysis, to value bonds with embedded put and call options in order to minimize the average cost of capital or maximize returns.

Electric utility bond investors are also seeing new seniority structures. The traditional electric utility paper is the first-mortgage bond. Today, electric utility paper comes in firsts, seconds, senior unsecured, unsecured, trust preferred, and straight preferred structures. So, a much wider array of potential investment opportunities exists, each with a different risk profile.

Investors will also see a lot of different ABS structures. Smaller companies that may issue only $150 million or $200 million worth of securitized debt might issue a single-tranche amortizing bond, a very traditional structure, but multibillion-dollar deals will certainly be more complex. For example, the bigger issues, such as PECO Energy Company's proposed $3.6 billion issue, probably would not do a single-asset tranche, because it would not minimize its effective cost of capital. As in every other asset-backed model, once you have the cash flows, analysts will use computer optimization models to minimize the cost to the issuer.

Covenant packages are also more important in the analysis of indentures, especially with the potential to disaggregate companies into their business segments. Some companies may limit the segmentation to a functional rather than legal reorganization. The ultimate goal is for companies to restructure their debt in order to more effectively match the business risk profile of those changing business units.

RESTRUCTURING INITIATIVES

At Donaldson, Lufkin & Jenrette (DLJ), the biggest topic we talk about with clients today is restructuring at the individual state level. We see restructuring taking place in three phases, as shown in **Figure 1**. The first phase is the debate phase. Most states are at least in this phase. The second phase is implementation. Four states have passed restructuring initiatives—California, Pennsylvania, Rhode Island, and New Hampshire—and are beginning to move into the implementation phase. The third phase is the competition phase, which will start in 1998 in the most aggressive states.

Figure 2 indicates when customers in the contiguous states are going to get choice, showing the states in which (1) initiatives have been enacted, (2) advanced discussions are taking place, (3) proposals have been introduced, and (4) no action is being pursued. Notice that tremendous activity is taking place in the Northeast, Midwest, and California; those are the areas with the highest electric rates.

At DLJ, we have analyzed extensively the indi-

Figure 1. Timeline for Restructuring Phases

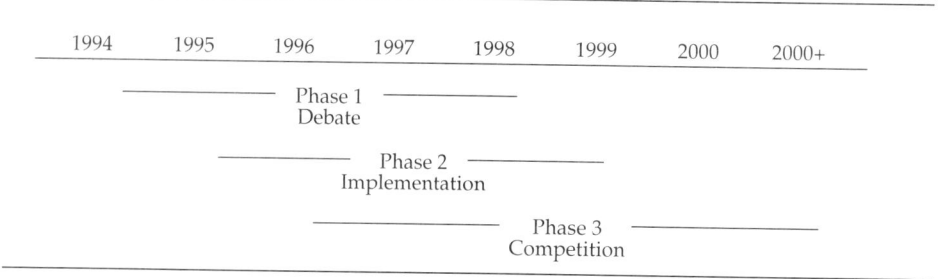

Figure 2. Progress of Restructuring Initiatives by State

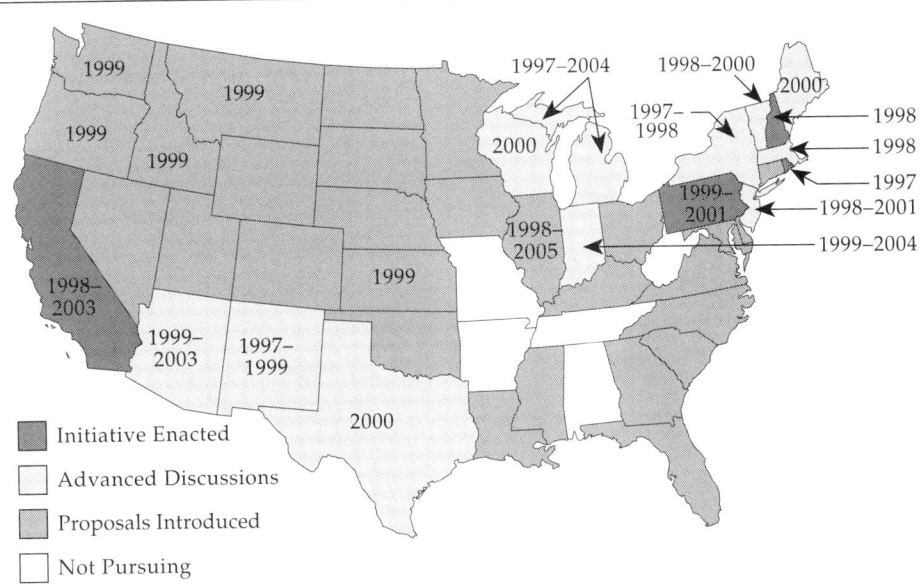

vidual production costs of the companies, because their competitive positions are extremely important in our evaluation of potential investments. **Figure 3** shows the organization of the regional power pools in the United States, and **Figure 4** summarizes the production costs for the regional power pools. NEPOOL, which is the New England region, and NYPP, which covers New York, have the highest costs, followed by MAAC, the mid-Atlantic pool, which includes Pennsylvania, New Jersey, and Maryland.

The Proposals

To date, the states have made fairly similar decisions with reference to electric restructuring in terms of a core set of discoveries or a core set of findings. Transition periods are generally ranging between 5 and 12 years, and customers will be allowed to either participate in a pool or conduct a bilateral transaction, which is a direct buy-and-sell decision between customer and generator. "Verified," "prudent," and "nonmitigatable" are the three words that regulators use in characterizing how much stranded assets the companies will be able to recover.

In order to protect end users, discussion has focused on functionally separating generation, transmission, and distribution. Although many regulators do not believe they have the legal authority to order disaggregation, they have decided to provide incentives for disaggregation. For example, in Massachusetts, New England Electric System and the other Massachusetts companies decided to voluntarily divest their generation portfolios of assets in exchange for a 100 percent recovery of stranded assets. In California, electric utilities were asked to divest 50 percent of fossil-fuel generation, with the idea of securing higher recovery of stranded assets. So, although the regulators do not have the stick, they have figured out how to use the carrot.

Transmission is often seen as the bottleneck in the new competitive marketplace. Therefore, many postulate that transmission needs to get out of the hands of the vertically integrated electric utility, at least in terms of operation but not in terms of ownership, so that it cannot be used as a weapon to defer the end user from getting the best price from the generator. So, the concept of an independent system operator has been developed.

Stranded Assets

The big question that needs to be resolved as part of this restructuring process is how to handle the problem of stranded assets. At DLJ, our conclusion is that all stranded assets are not created equally. We believe three phases, or three risks, are associated with stranded assets. First is the regulatory and legislative risk and how stranded assets are defined and measured. To date, no utility has gone through the administrative or market-based pricing mechanism to quantify stranded investments, although Pennsylvania and California will lead the way in that regard. Second is collection risk: Will 100 percent of the stranded assets be collected? And third is redeployment risk: What will utilities do with the money?

■ *Regulatory risk.* The two big questions in the regulatory/legislative area are (1) how the states individually will deal with the stranded investment issue and (2) whether Congress will link changes in the Public Utility Holding Company Act (PUHCA)

Figure 3. U.S. Regional Power Pools

ECAR
East Central Area Reliability Coordination Agreement

ERCOT
Electric Reliability Council of Texas

MAAC
Mid-America Area Council

MAIN
Mid-Atlantic Interconnected Network

MAPP
Mid-Continent Area Power Pool

NPCC
Northeast Power Coordinating Council

SERC
Southeastern Electric Reliability Council

SPP
Southwest Power Pool

WSCC
Western Systems Coordinating Council

Source: Based on data from North American Electric Reliability Council.

and changes in the Public Utility Regulatory Policy Act (PURPA) of 1978 to the restructuring of the entire industry and to customer choice. Senator Dale Bumpers (D, AR), the ranking minority member of the Committee on Energy and Natural Resources, would like all customers to be able to choose their power provider by the year 2003, and he would allow states to individually decide on how much stranded assets customers should pay. A number of initiatives are going to be introduced, but we do not think Congress will get to restructuring of the electric utility industry in 1997. If it chooses to tie together the relegislation of these three issues—PUHCA, PURPA, and stranded assets—more than likely it would be 1998 or 1999 before significant changes take place.

■ *Collection risk.* The risk of collecting stranded assets increases with time because people may figure out how to bypass the competitive transition charges (CTCs)—the charges established to recover the stranded assets—forcing companies to discount their CTCs in order to maintain market share. We think that a state with a longer transition period—such as Massachusetts with a 12-year transition period versus California with a 5-year transition period—potentially has more collection risk. But we would also argue that because Massachusetts companies are getting out of generation, the pressure on these companies to discount CTCs in order to maintain market share will be minimized because they will no longer be in the generation/commodity business.

In addition, the ability of California companies to collect their stranded assets within the five-year transition period is partly a function of their ability to create headroom, or reduce expenses, such that they will have the room under their rate freeze to accelerate the recovery of the stranded assets and still maintain margins. Failure to create that headroom will result in write-offs if they cannot collect all the

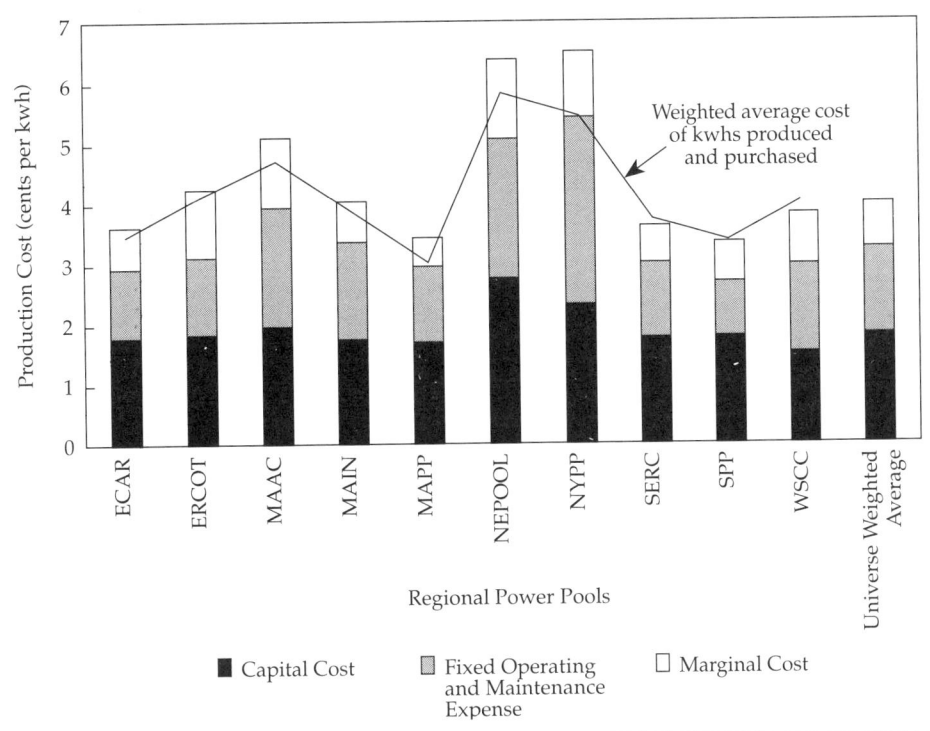

Figure 4. 1995 Average Regional Production and Capital Cost Components

stranded assets. So, some risk exists that these companies will not collect all their stranded assets.

Redeployment risk. The last issue is the redeployment of cash: what to do with the proceeds. In cases of asset securitization, in which the proceeds are received up front, the problem of redeploying the assets is more significant. Generally, we expect the companies to repurchase their capital with the proceeds. Expectations remain that the companies will repurchase their capital proportionately to their current capital structure. For holding companies, an added level of analysis must take place because the proceeds for an electric utility that repurchases its common stock end up at the holding company for a completely separate decision of how to redeploy the cash at that level. Among a number of options, holding companies may end up buying back their own common stock or using the cash to fund diversification.

From the bondholders' standpoint, the repurchase of outstanding debt in proportion to the current capital structure will both reduce the float outstanding in a given name and create circumstances in which companies will have to tender for bonds that are currently call protected. Also, the act of securitizing stranded investments helps reduce the business risk profile of the underlying electric utility and thus could lead to credit upgrades.

One indenture covenant that would cause bondholders problems is whether the transfer to the trust of the assets that are to be securitized results in a release of property under the indenture. If the transfer qualifies as a release of property, then existing extraordinary release of property calls could be triggered. The answer to this complex legal question resides in the analysis of each company's indenture. At this time, we do not believe that there will be widespread extraordinary calls triggered by the aforementioned transfer.

EVENT RISK

The electric utility industry has traditionally not had to deal with event risk, but it is now relevant in light of industry restructuring. The primary events that must be analyzed are M&A deals—global versus domestic acquisitions, vertical versus horizontal mergers, and acquisitions versus joint ventures—and the disaggregation of the business into individually managed generation, transmission, and distribution business segments or companies.

M&A Activity

At this point, approximately 16 mergers are pending before the Federal Energy Regulatory Commission (FERC), including both electric/electric mergers and electric/gas mergers. Although the concept of merging an electric and gas company makes long-term strategic sense for management and can be a tremendous positive in the short term for equity investors, it generally causes heartburn for electric utility bondholders, who are frequently looking at downgrades because of these transactions. For example, the average gas company's bond rating is mid-BBB and the average electric utility rating is a weak A-rating. So, when the companies are combined, the weak A-rated electric utility is generally looking at a downgrade and the mid-BBB-rated gas company is generally looking at an upgrade.

M&A activity could result in global and domestic acquisitions of energy-related businesses, nonenergy businesses, or separate distribution versus generation operations. Other mergers could result in vertically or horizontally diversified companies. For example, horizontal mergers may involve home security, such as Western Resources' interest in ADT, telecommunications, or cable businesses. Keep in mind that diversification can also be achieved through joint venture arrangements and that M&A activity can significantly affect the value of electric utilities' debt securities.

Repeal of PUHCA would result in another wave of consolidation, or another wave of event risk, for the electric utilities. Once PUHCA goes away, you will start to see super-regionals, similar to the banks. Companies will control assets in different regions of the United States, especially if they want to be a national power marketer.

If PUHCA does go away, then such a company as the Southern Company will no longer be limited, on the domestic acquisition front, to acquiring only southeastern companies, and American Electric Power will not have to look only at midwestern companies. This change will, however, raise concerns over the market power issue included in the new FERC guidelines and may result in divestiture of generation.

Disaggregation

Although disaggregation has yet to occur, at DLJ, we think it is coming. We think these companies will have to break themselves up strategically in order to manage the individual businesses, because significantly different risk profiles become more prevalent for generation, transmission, and distribution businesses. A company's management has to ask itself whether it is good at everything or good at select elements. Is it good in the customer service business, or is it better in the generation business? If it does not have a competitive strength in customer service, then maybe the answer is to divest its distribution assets. If it does not have a distinct competence in generation, or does not have anything to differentiate itself from other generation businesses, it may be best to sell the generation business and concentrate core strengths in distribution.

Another issue becomes the relative size of a company's investments. Some companies are 100 percent generation; some are 95 percent distribution. Even though they are largely vertically integrated, the generation, transmission, and distribution business segments will have substantially different business risk profiles when they disaggregate.

Companies can also disaggregate with the idea of concentrating on a specific business domestically and/or internationally. For example, PG&E Corporation decided to reduce its exposure to the generation business and concentrate on the distribution business, domestically and internationally. Under this strategy, the business risk profile of PG&E is likely to decrease dramatically over time, especially as it accelerates the recovery of its Diablo Canyon nuclear power plant investment.

Stakeholder Considerations

Bondholders and stockholders have very different stakeholder considerations, as shown in **Exhibit 1**. Although stockholders consider earnings power, dividend requirements, and tax treatment, bondholders' number one concern is special calls. Investors must consider whether they will get special calls at par under a release of property and whether they can be assigned to a specific business, rather than having the company extinguish the current bonds and then recapitalize the new company. Although stockholders will get benefits from disaggregation, we believe that companies and management are currently thinking of further ways to enhance shareholder value.

Exhibit 1. Stakeholder Considerations

Bondholders	Stockholders
Special calls	Tax treatment
Release of property	Spin-off versus sale
Ratings	Earnings power
Generation versus distribution companies	Dividend requirements
Exchangeable versus assignable	Multiple valuations
Future covenant provisions	Unregulated businesses
Collateralization	Risk versus reward

Changes in Company Structure

One of the most important things to look at today is how an electric utility is structured. Where is the electric utility? Is it within a holding-company structure? If it diversifies, are bondholders legally separated from some of the additional risk? If the utility is in a holding company situation, is the electric utility on top, such as with PacifiCorp? Consider what is going to happen with Houston Industries Incorporated when it collapses the holding company in order to complete the NorAm Energy Corporation deal. Those bondholders are going to have a much different risk profile than if they were at an operating electric company level, such as at Southern Company, which although it is diversifying geographically from the business line standpoint, less of the risk is attributable to investors at the individual operating subsidiaries.

Rating agencies and bondholders constantly debate regulatory separation. Bondholders must consider if regulators will step in to protect the customers and effectively protect the bondholders should something go awry with a diversification effort.

If regulatory separation exists, then bondholders can derive comfort from the fact that the regulators will provide some protection against the electric utility weakening its own credit quality to support the declining credit quality of the parent, resulting from a bad diversification decision. The other way that bondholders can be protected is if the diversified operations are funded with nonrecourse debt, limiting the parent's exposure to its equity investment. A number of the recent global diversification efforts have used nonrecourse debt to fund a large portion of the acquisition, thereby, providing protection for the investors in the domestic electric utility subsidiaries.

BUSINESS RISK

The homogeneity of this industry is breaking down. Making a presentation on *the* electric utility industry is almost a misnomer because several industries are developing. Bondholders must analyze the company's strategic direction, which determines what business it will be in, and how the future business risk profile will change as a result of management's strategies. The business risk profiles of integrated energy companies will be significantly different from utilities that chose to focus on a specific business segment. For example, Duke Power Company (with its merger of PanEnergy to become Duke Energy, an integrated energy company), Enron Corporation (with its merger with Portland General Corporation), and Southern Company are clearly positioning themselves to be national marketers. Their business risk profile will in no way compare with that of Puget Sound Energy, which is largely getting out of the generation business to become a local distribution company. It will at best be a regional player selling ancillary customer and distribution services. As management's strategies begin to play out, peer groups will have to be created to look at business risk profiles in order to determine future credit quality. Potential peer groups may have the following broad groupings with subgroups for international and domestic concerns: vertically integrated energy providers, horizontal service providers, aggregate distribution businesses, and aggregate generation businesses.

Sector Attractiveness

At DLJ, we have recently moved to a market-weighted position from an underweighted position. For about the past 6–12 months, we have been in an underweighted position, largely based on our fear that we were not sure of the extent to which companies were going to be able to recover stranded assets. Recent developments with regard to stranded assets are more reassuring. Although specific situations are still questionable, the vast majority of the states appear ready to allow 100 percent recovery. Furthermore, if a company is able to securitize 100 percent of its stranded assets, not only does it recover them, but it also gets them up front in one fell swoop.

Even with an improvement in the stranded assets situation, we still see a general negative trend in terms of credit ratings, as shown in **Figure 5**. Electric utilities, on average, currently have a weak A rating. Many people have speculated that electric utilities are heading toward a mid-BBB rating, which is probably an overstatement at this point, although they will probably edge down toward a strong BBB rating in the next 24–36 months.

At DLJ, we track Standard & Poor's Corporation's outlook distribution, as shown in **Figure 6**. Outlooks generally reflect the anticipated credit trend over the upcoming one-to-three year period. The current distribution indicates about 60 percent stable outlooks and about 24 percent negative outlooks—a big change from October 1993, when S&P re-evaluated the electric utility industry and indicated about 50 percent negative outlooks. This outlook distribution has certainly stabilized during the past 12–18 months; with positive outlooks also on the rise, some companies might see upgrades, which has not happened that much in the recent past.

Technical Situation

The industry has seen an absence of construction spending, because most companies are able to internally fund their capital spending. A trend toward delevering also exists among the electric utilities as companies actively pay down debt. The biggest change over the past 12 months is the issue of the role of asset securitization. The estimates for stranded assets range from $100 billion to $200 billion. Some companies will be able to securitize those assets and sell ABS, and our best estimate at this point is that the securitization market will be in the $30–$50 billion range. The total debt for the electric utility industry is currently about $200 billion. If you believe that the companies will use 50 percent of the proceeds from $50 billion of ABS, the debt portion of their capital structure will shrink dramatically—a $25 billion potential debt retirement. When you compare that

Figure 5. S&P Electric Utility Industry Average Credit Rating

Figure 6. S&P Electric Outlook Distribution

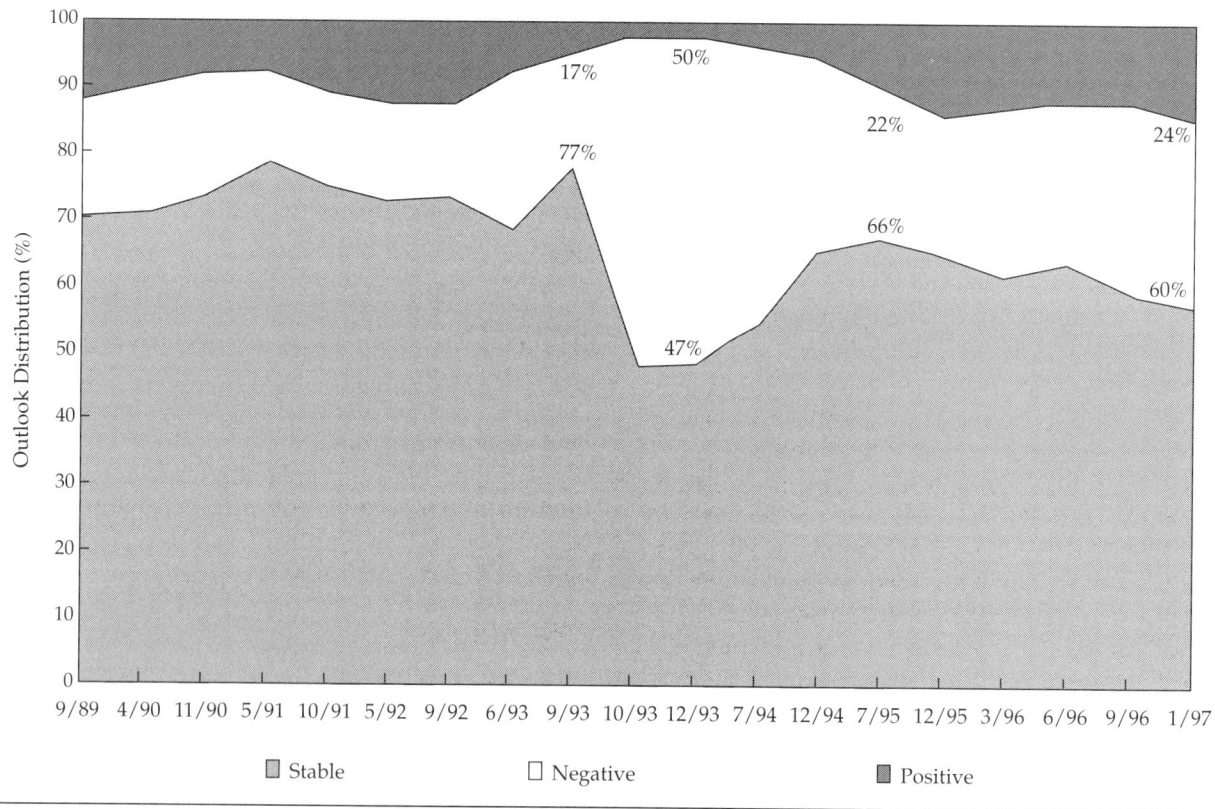

figure with the $200 billion worth of debt outstanding for the industry, extremely strong technicals will get even stronger. For people who have had underweighted positions in this industry in the past 12–24 months, getting back to a market-weighted position will be difficult because of absence of supply.

Figure 7 shows generally tight spreads between AA-rated, A-rated, and BBB-rated electric utility bonds during the past six years. Recent improvement in credit spreads is largely driven by what has

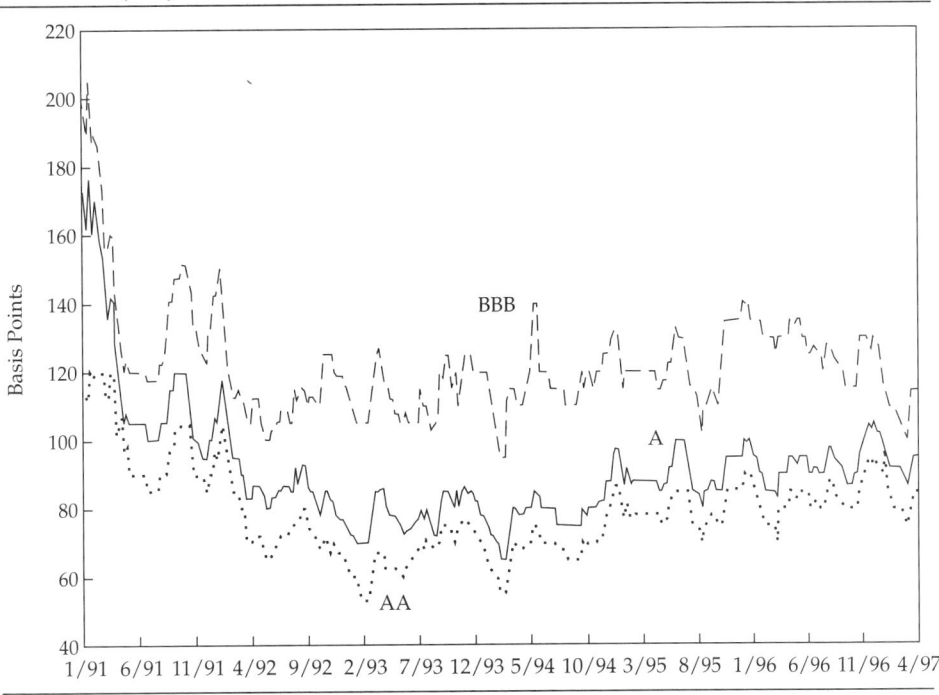

Figure 7. Generic Utility New Issue Spreads
(30-year noncall 10)

happened in Pennsylvania and the fact that PECO is now talking about potentially securitizing up to $6.8 billion of stranded investment. If it is able to sell all of this debt, it will retire 65 percent of its outstanding fixed-income float—a huge number—removing one of the major trading vehicles from the market.

Selectivity

In this industry, it still pays to be highly selective about the companies to invest in, because a general, negative credit quality trend still exists. Investors must first concentrate on a company's business risk profile: What is management doing? What businesses will it be in in the future? Does the company have a strong competitive position? Competitive position is very important. PECO is a perfect example. If PECO can securitize $6.8 billion of stranded investment and significantly reduce the capital it has invested in the generation portion of its business, then it could dramatically improve its competitive position in Pennsylvania. We expect this change in competitive position will be fully reflected in an improved business risk assessment by the rating agencies and result in an upgrade for PECO Energy, probably from strong BBB into either the weak or mid-A range.

Investors must also follow the asset securitization trend, which seems to be a fairly golden trail. Before asset securitization was discussed in California and Pennsylvania, bonds of the major electric utilities in those states traded at fairly wide spreads. Following discussion of securitization, we have seen from 15–30 basis points of credit spread tightening, based almost exclusively on asset securitization.

Managing event risk is very important, and investors have to be very cognizant of a company's business strategy and what it does to fulfill that strategy. For example, PacifiCorp is an extremely well-positioned company and probably an excellent long-term fixed-income investment, but in the short term, we think it is going to make an acquisition that will likely be detrimental to its credit quality. Therefore, our call on a name such as PacifiCorp is buy it on the weakness after the announced deal. Special situations in the high-yield area also provide potential investment opportunities despite recent allusions to bankruptcy, such as North Atlantic Energy or Public Service of New Hampshire.

CONCLUSION

Investors must carefully assess the implications of industry restructuring on the valuation of electric utility debt securities. The changing landscape of the electric utility industry requires more active management of electric utility bonds. Portfolio strategies are changing from buy and hold to held for trading and total return, and security structures are more complex, including ABS. Restructuring initiatives require careful analysis of regulatory and legislative risk, collection risk, and redeployment risk associated with stranded assets. Investors must recognize the impact of event risks, such as M&A activity and disaggregation, which are influenced by the strategic direction in which managers take electric utilities and which affect changes in credit ratings. As the homogeneity of the industry breaks down, business risk increases and creates the need for peer group profiles to evaluate the different business risks of integrated energy companies versus distribution companies. Although industry restructuring has increased the risk in electric utilities, it has created opportunities for enhanced returns after careful analysis of available debt investments.

Question and Answer Session

Terran A. Miller, CFA

Question: What are the important criteria for evaluating generation and transmission cooperatives, and how will restructuring affect them?

Miller: The most important criterion is going to be competitive position. A lot of people believe that a number of the cooperatives will have to consolidate either with investor-owned utilities (IOUs) or among themselves in order to improve their competitive position. Failing to do that, they are going to be in a very difficult situation, and investors will have to differentiate in that regard between the generation and transmission and the distribution cooperatives.

Depending on the makeup of the distribution cooperatives' service territories and who their neighbors are, they might be fairly well insulated, unless they have a very aggressive IOU neighbor who is going to go after their customers in order to sell them enhanced services. Generation and transmission cooperatives are going to have a tough road, unless they have very competitively priced power. And to the extent that they have borrowed at tax-exempt rates, they should be in pretty good stead, except for the obvious ones who have gotten into trouble in the past.

Question: How does a company disaggregate without refunding its bonds?

Miller: The first place we start is with management intent: Who do we think is going to disaggregate? The next place we look is how that company handled, or how it dealt with, bondholders in the past. If a company has aggressively used special calls in the past and we believe it has a strong intention to disaggregate, then we go into the legal work of what options that company has under its indenture to begin to spin off assets, what its asset mix is, how it can substitute property, and whether it has unpledged property that could be substituted. So, it gets into a fairly complex analysis rather quickly.

Question: A lot of rather weak companies are thinking of disaggregation because of regulatory or other rules. Are these companies in a much more difficult position than the strong companies?

Miller: My guess is that for a lot of the weaker companies that have nuclear power, disaggregation might very well be limited by the Nuclear Regulatory Commission's (NRC) stepped-up review on how these plants are being run. A correlation exists between weaker companies and nuclear owners, but you also have to divide the weaker players into those that own nuclear power plants and operate them and those that have what we will call a more passive investment—they are not the actual operators. We think the nuclear owners can be segmented into four groups: strong players that operate, strong players that have a passive investment, weak players that operate, and weak players that have a passive investment.

Certainly, the strongest players with a passive investment are not going to present a problem for the NRC. But the weakest players that are operators are going to have a very difficult time getting the NRC to sign off on putting that nuclear investment in a specific generating company, especially if the NRC is uncertain what the financial profile of that company will be. The NRC is supposed to issue some pronouncement in the future, so we are going to have to stay tuned on that subject.

Question: Can I as a bondholder be assigned to a particular segment of the disaggregated company?

Miller: The lawyer's answer is, it depends on the indenture. It also depends, in my mind, on what the asset mix is. Let's use an extreme example. If you have a company that is 80 percent distribution and 20 percent generation, it is likely that under its indenture, the easiest way for it to disaggregate would be to spin off the generation side, because it is a smaller portion of the assets under the indenture.

Most people have the greatest concern about the nuclear-dominated companies because they generally have more of their assets in generation; therefore, it is likely that if they are going to do anything, they will spin off distribution. So, the remaining company that you lent to could end up being the generation company, but again, you have to deal with what the NRC might allow, which is still a huge question mark.

Question: Has your view of the timeline for competition changed any in the past year or two?

Miller: My view of what competition will mean has changed. In April 1994, when California came out with its draft "Blue Book," and even before that when New Mexico started to talk about competition in a meaningful fashion, most people started with the concept of how much of the stranded assets companies would be able to recover. Most people started someplace south of 100 percent. Certainly at this point, the pendulum has swung very dramatically in the other direction to where not only do we talk about 100 percent, but if a company is able to securitize, it also gets 100 percent of its stranded assets almost on Day 1.

The other very subtle change with competition's three phases—the debate phase, the implementation phase, and the competition phase—is that the companies and the market continue to move faster than the regulators. Although Figure 1 showed three nice lines, the competition phase starts well after the debate phase ends, but in reality, the competition phase has already started. So, the competition phase is being collapsed into the back end of the debate and implementation phases.

In the case of California, it took more than two years for the process to result in a signed legislative initiative. The governor finally signed AB 1890 in September 1996, completing a process that commenced in earnest with the publishing of the infamous "Blue Book" in April 1994. In contrast, the governor of Pennsylvania signed HB 1509 in December 1996 following a relatively short legislative debate. The Pennsylvania Public Utility Commission (PUC) had commenced some generic hearings on the subject in 1994, but the process in Pennsylvania was largely completed within the 1996 time frame.

The simple answer at this point is that it is better to borrow than to recreate the wheel. Because we have some fundamental understandings on the key issues, the time frame for each state to get from the debate phase to the implementation phase is going to shrink even further. Competition is going to happen faster than we originally thought.

Question: When the businesses are split up, what sort of returns do you expect on the different parts of the business and where would a debt investor perhaps be happiest?

Miller: Where debt investors will be the happiest will be a function of their appetite for risk. The generation piece of the business is going to be the riskiest, and it is also the piece in which we expect to have the least amount of debt. Simply put, the debt structure of generation-only companies cannot support anything close to a 50 percent debt component to the capital structure. We would be surprised to see much more than 20 percent. The highest rated generation-only company very well might be A, but that company would be the exception to the rule. Most people believe that the average generation-only company is going to be someplace in the BBB or BB range, depending on what type of debt structure the company chooses. We could end up having transmission-only and distribution-only companies with substantially higher ratings than generation-only companies. Transmission companies might end up being the AA companies of the future. Distribution companies are likely to be high- to mid-A companies.

Figure 5 showed that the average electric utility rating is heading toward strong BBB. In the future, my ability to make that statement is going to be very limited, because I will have to differentiate among the average rating for generation, transmission, and distribution companies.

Question: Is bankruptcy going to play a role in restructuring of the industry, and if so, how significant will mergers be in the reorganizations?

Miller: In the immediate past, we have seen several mergers in which strong companies have purchased much weaker companies, which has eliminated some of the bankruptcy risk in the industry. A perfect example is Ohio Edison's decision to merge with much weaker Centerior Energy. Bankruptcy risk is not zero, but it has decreased.

With companies that have significant stranded assets, the risk of bankruptcy is certainly not zero because so much of their cash flow is tied up in what we will call either current rates or what will become competitive transition charges. So, a detrimental decision on how much of the stranded assets they will get to recover could result in a bankruptcy, but bankruptcy risks today are probably lower than they were in 1993, when industry restructuring first started. Also, as PUHCA breaks down, stronger companies will be in an even better position to buy weaker companies. In certain instances, a number of weak companies are all sitting next to each other; the best example of that is the southwestern region. Their ability to merge with each other and get a significant benefit is not as great as if someone outside that region, after the breakdown of PUHCA, comes in and refinances the capital structure of those companies.

Analyzing Non-U.S.-Based Electric Utilities

Michael Sayers
Vice President, Equity Research
Morgan Stanley International

> Competition among European electric utilities is the result of the wide range of prices—more than 5 pence per kilowatt hour—for industrial power in Europe. Liberalization of electric utilities in Europe forces firms to shift their focus from security of supply under the traditional monopoly structure to a focus on security of demand in an open and competitive market. Investors analyzing non-U.S. electric utilities should focus on firms with cost-cutting potential, positive after-tax cash flow, fuel mix improvements, a coherent competitive strategy, and a focus on enhancing shareholder value.

Competition is the key issue facing the European electric industry. This presentation focuses on competition from four angles. First, it analyzes the U.K. experience because the United Kingdom was the first market in Europe to liberalize and because it has adopted perhaps the most radical liberalization to date. Second, I will consider developments in the rest of Europe in terms of liberalization. The third angle is to take a look at Spain, which is addressing many of the challenges associated with moving from a regulated industry to a competitive industry. Finally, this presentation will look at some stock selection issues and identify some European companies that may be unfamiliar to U.S. investors but that have attractive fundamental and valuation stories.

THE U.K. EXPERIENCE

The U.K. electric industry today is unrecognizable from the industry five years ago. Previously, one company, the Central Electricity Generating Board (CEGB), operated 100 percent of the country's generation assets and transmission business. As part of the liberalization process, the CEGB was broken into three competing generators, and to promote further competition, the transmission business was spun off and the National Grid Company was created.

The introduction of competition in generation and transmission resulted in open access to the transmission business, generators remunerated on the basis of a competitive pool, and a host of new entrants. Competition was concurrently introduced in the supply of electricity to final consumers on a phased-in basis, starting with the largest industrial customers and extending to all customers, including the smallest residential customers, by March 1998.

Transmission and distribution remain monopoly businesses, even in the liberalized competitive environment. Charges are regulated in recognition of this monopoly, and the pricing method chosen in the United Kingdom has been on an RPI (retail price index) basis—in other words, price cap with a built-in efficiency factor. Finally, an independent regulatory body known as OFFER (Office of Electricity Regulation) has been created.

Consequences of Competition

The first and most powerful result of this competitive market is that the two dominant generators in the United Kingdom—National Power and PowerGen—have lost substantial market share, as shown in **Figure 1**. Before liberalization, the incumbent generators had about 75 percent of the total market, but they are now down to a 55 percent market share, which is expected to continue to decline according to most estimates.

Enron, which is already a player in the United States, built the first major station intended to take market share away from National Power, PowerGen, and British Energy. Other stations were built by small-scale distribution consortiums. In most cases, the consortium included a regional electric company, which used its franchise over the residential customer base through 1998 to become involved and finance some of these stations. The challengers have basically been the distribution businesses looking to exert competitive pressure on the major generators, which have an imbalance in their relative market power. Although

Figure 1. PowerGen and National Power's Market Share, 1990–96

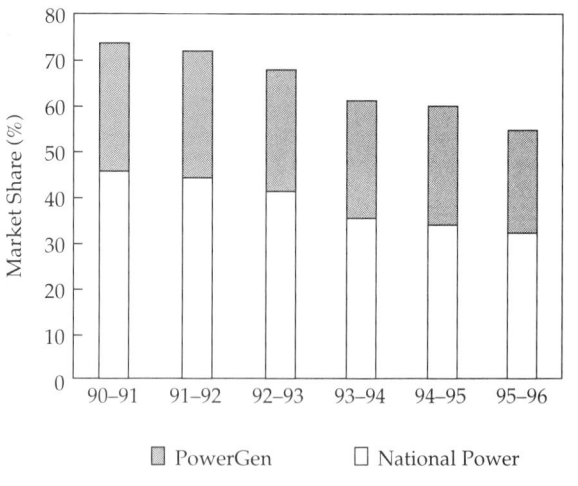

National Power and PowerGen dominated 75 percent of the market between them, British Energy—or Nuclear Electric, as it was known then—controlled 20 percent. Three companies were the only sellers of electricity in the market, with 12 fragmented competing buyers. So, the consortiums were an effort to redress some of the market power issues.

The second U.K. issue is that gas has taken a substantial share of the electricity-generation market, as shown in **Figure 2**. Before liberalization, almost no combined-cycle gas turbine (CCGT) stations were operating in the United Kingdom, but within five years, the CCGT stations have taken approximately 20 percent of the total market at the expense of the existing traditional coal and oil stations. This percentage is expected to grow substantially, and many people estimate that gas may have up to 40 percent of the total electricity market within two or three years.

Customers and generators have had to live with price volatility in the United Kingdom as a result of the move to a pool-based method of pricing generation. Initially, the market was incredibly volatile, partly reflecting the market distortion put in place by the U.K. government to smooth the path toward liberalization, although in recent years, price volatility has been declining.

Trying to forecast the direction of pool prices is an incredibly difficult exercise. Existing generators currently have sufficient market share to ensure that pool prices exceed short-run marginal costs, but pool prices are still below long-run marginal costs of an average plant needed to encourage new entrants into the generation business.

National Power and PowerGen Experiences

Faced with declining market share, National

Figure 2. U.K. Electricity Output by Generating Source, 1991 and 1996

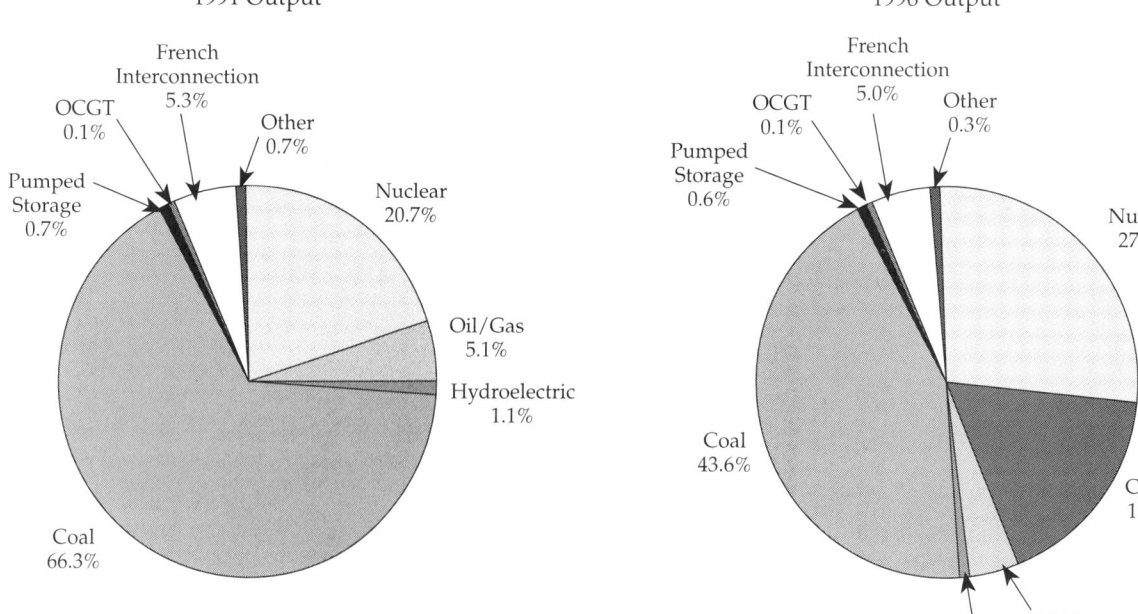

Note: 1996 output totals do not add because of rounding.
Source: Data from British Energy.

Power and PowerGen have had to improve generation plant efficiency and cut their costs, and they have done so in a number of ways. They have increased efficiency of operations by closing down older, less efficient coal-fired capacity—closing about 20 percent of their total generating base—and by investing in gas-fired stations, which is roughly 20 percent of their current generating base. To reduce costs, they have put pressure on upstream fuel suppliers, renegotiated the original higher-cost coal contracts, and started importing low-cost coal rather than using high-cost U.K. coal.

The most dramatic impact of cost cutting has been felt on the headcount of these two companies. Over the past five years in moving from a monopoly to a liberalized environment, the combined headcount of the two major companies has fallen by about 70 percent. These reductions are genuine efficiency improvements. For example, National Power had close to 15,000 employees in 1991 and now has less than 5,000. Historically, a 1,000 megawatt station operating when it was a monopoly might have had about 500 employees; now, the number is down to 180. These companies have closed some capacity and replaced it with low-workforce gas capacity, which is certainly a genuine reduction.

Aside from slashing and burning their cost base, these two companies have expanded their businesses outside the traditional electric generation arena by looking at combined heat and power and investing in gas. They have also grasped the opportunity to expand overseas, and they have bought back their own shares on a number of occasions. National Power has returned a substantial amount of value, by U.K. standards, to shareholders in the form of a special dividend. Following the decision not to allow Southern Company's acquisition to go ahead, they returned close to £1 billion in value.

As a result of these shareholder value-enhancing strategies, both companies have been able to show extremely attractive earnings and dividend growth, as shown in **Figure 3**, despite the substantial market share loss. Typically, earnings have been growing at an annual rate of 15 percent. Dividend growth initially kept up with that pace but has exceeded it in recent years as the companies have increased their payout ratios.

LIBERALIZATION IN EUROPE

Competition is not simply a U.K. phenomenon; it is also happening throughout the rest of Europe. Because the question of competition has been debated for nine years in the European Union (EU), the United Kingdom and some of the Scandinavian countries have had to go it alone. But in the middle of 1996, the countries in the EU finally agreed to open up their electric markets to competition on a Pan-European basis. Similar to the United Kingdom, competition will be phased in starting in 1999, and by 2003, roughly one-third of the total EU market will be open to competition. I would not rule out the extension of that goal to include all retail customers, including the smallest residential customers.

The Motivation for Competition

The primary motivation for competition in Europe is coming from the industrial customers. **Figure 4** shows the electricity prices paid by major industrial customers across Europe. Note that these prices vary widely; for example, typically, a German industrial customer is paying close to three times what a customer in Norway pays and roughly 1.5

Figure 3. National Power and PowerGen's Growth in Earnings per Share and Dividend per Share, 1991–96

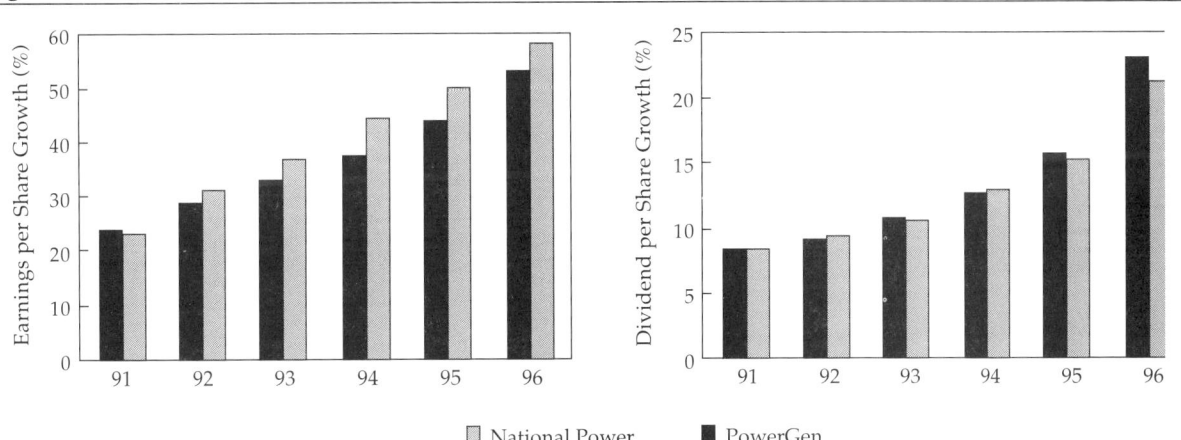

Source: Data from National Power and PowerGen.

Figure 4. Industrial Electricity Prices as of January 1996

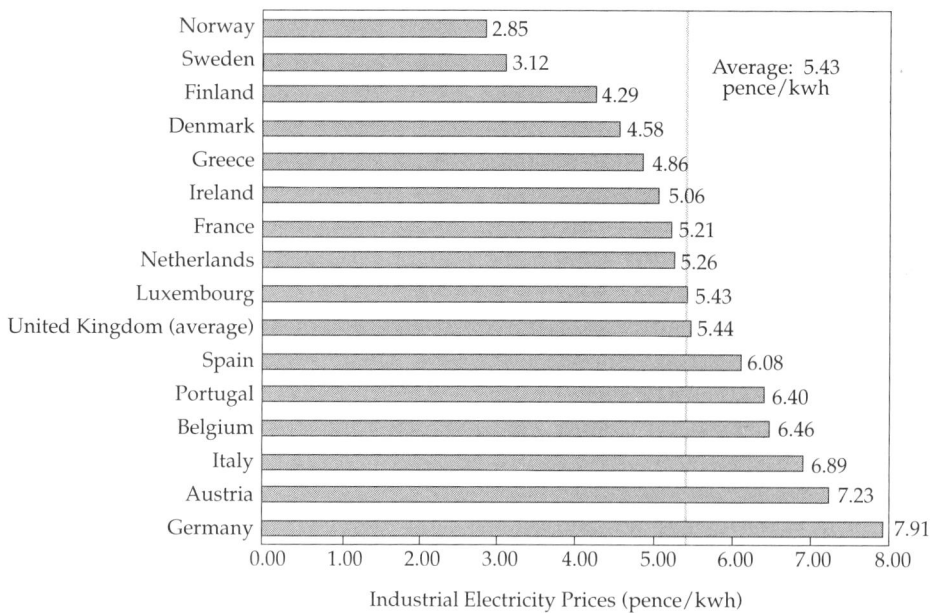

Note: Annual maximum demand 2,500 kw; 40 percent load factor.
Source: Data from the Electricity Association.

times the average price being paid by customers in the rest of Europe. At this moment, the pressure for liberalization is felt acutely in Germany. Competition will materially narrow these differentials, largely by pressuring the high-cost countries to reduce their electricity prices.

The high-cost countries can reduce their prices in two ways. The first is to use cross-border transmission. The physical links among the markets in Europe are in place but underused. At the moment, only about 7 percent of electric supply in Europe takes place across borders. This link is underused largely because most countries in Europe have dominant monopoly suppliers and dominant generators; they use these cross-border links only to counter short-term imbalances in supply and demand. As industrial customers acquire access to these links, competition should substantially boost the amount of cross-border flows. For example, the link between two noncompetitive countries, such as France and Germany, is running at about 20 percent of capacity. The link between the United Kingdom, a competitive market, and France is running at close to 100 percent. Finally, the links among the countries are actually increasing, which will increase the use of cross-border transmission and will put downward pressure on prices.

The second way to reduce costs is with natural gas. As natural gas availability improves in Europe, gas should take a substantial market share within the generation market. In the United Kingdom, gas generation has gone from virtually 0 to 20 percent of the total market within five years and is still increasing. **Table 1** shows that building a modern combined-cycle

Table 1. Operating Costs for Various Sources of Electric Generation
(pence/kwh)

Costs	Hydroelectric	Nuclear	Coal	Oil	CCGT
Fuel	0.00	0.40	1.12	1.40	1.09
Nonfuel	0.15	0.70	0.91	0.96	0.20
Depreciation	—	—	—	—	0.27
Interest	—	—	—	—	0.60
Total	**0.15**	**1.10**	**2.03**	**2.36**	**2.16**
Adjustments					
Transport cost for fuel	—	—	0.20	—	—
Environmental	—	—	0.82	—	—
Total	—	—	3.05	—	—

gas turbine plant in Europe is cheaper, in many cases, than operating existing coal- and oil-fired capacity at the margin.

As a result of competition and an increasing use of gas generation, electricity prices in Europe are expected to decline dramatically over the next five years, which is consistent with the U.K. experience. To achieve this price reduction, some disaggregation of electricity prices in Europe will be necessary. Although current electricity prices from nongas generation are substantially higher in Europe than the price of electricity from gas generation, this premium will not be sustainable in a competitive market.

Table 2 shows the final selling revenues for eight European companies. Verbund is the largest generator in Austria; Electrabel, the dominant player in Belgium; RWE, Veba, and Viag, the three biggest companies in Germany; and ENDESA, Iberdrola, and Unión Eléctrica Fenosa (UEF) represent approximately 95 percent of the Spanish market. At Morgan Stanley International, we calculated how much of those revenues are from transmission and distribution, and from those calculations, we derived an implied generation price. We have adjusted that price to a base load, reflecting current industrial demand and have estimated the "sterling equivalent" generation price. Thus, each company is charging substantially more for generation than would a competing company using a gas-fired station, which Table 1 indicated at about 2.2 pence per unit.

The impact on cash flow from this pricing pressure will be substantial. **Table 3** shows an estimate of the impact of moving to CCGT prices for generation. Based on current generating prices and competing generating prices from CCGT stations, we assessed the impact on cash flow from the downward cost pressure. If generation prices in the competitive arena alone fall to the level of a competing gas-fired station, cash flows could fall by as much as 60 percent across the board, forcing very difficult decisions.

Implications of Competition

For European companies to survive in this new competitive environment, they will have to reduce costs, as the U.K. companies did. They will have to invest in gas, put pressure on their coal suppliers, reduce inefficient capacity, and most importantly, reduce headcount.

Although the U.K. companies may not have an absolutely optimal cost base, five years of competition and tough regulation should have pushed the cost base down to a reasonable level. If U.K. productivity numbers for generation, distribution, and transmission are applied to the European companies, as shown in **Table 4,** the European companies appear capable of operating with headcounts as much as 50 percent below current numbers. Although other European markets differ from the United Kingdom, these companies have substantial scope to cut costs to meet the threat of competition.

The European electric industry has been dominated by monopolies, so the key theme historically has been to maintain *security of supply*. But the issue in a competitive market is ensuring *security of demand*. In other words, how do they make sure that they can sell what they generate? One way of ensuring security of demand is to increase the scope of investment in the distribution business. Other opportunities include share buybacks, business expansion, and restructuring of the portfolios. The final message coming out of Europe is that governments have basically ceded control of the pricing of electricity and the strategic direction of the industry, thus allowing these two issues to be market determined. The logical extension is that the governments should cede ownership of the industry, and we should expect a major wave of further privatization within Europe.

Investors in Europe have historically relied on yield to value electric utilities, a practice that makes less sense in a competitive market. Investors must focus increasingly on underlying cash flow generation. Our equity-valuation approach takes current cash flows, adjusts them downward for the potential pricing pressure, and then adjusts them back upward for the potential cost savings. Investors in European utilities face a number of issues, and the move to competition means that European governments also have a number of important issues to consider as they move from monopoly to liberalization on a national basis.

SPAIN ADDRESSES THE CHALLENGES

Spain may be doing more than any other European country to introduce competition. The Spanish government is trying to achieve a number of objectives by introducing competition to the electricity sector. The first goal is to reduce prices in order to improve competitiveness for its own industrial base. Second, a doctrine of competition is gaining influence within Europe, and the situation in Spain is certainly an example of this movement. Third, it is trying to prepare for the expected Europewide liberalization. Fourth, Spain is trying to maintain the strength of the domestic sector, which is faced with this competitive threat. Finally, it is trying to do all of these things while maintaining the value of the two-thirds of ENDESA that it has not sold but will be looking to sell in the next two or three years.

Spain has realized that competition will be a benefit, but it may be a long-term benefit; therefore,

Table 2. Generating Prices
(currency in local denominations)

	Verbund	Electrabel	RWE	Veba	Viag	ENDESA	Iberdrola	UEF
Units sold (gigawatts per hour)	28,834	66,167	136,043	98,543	52,100	43,329	54,163	21,532
Electric sales revenues (in millions)	Sch19,635	BFr127,793	DM19,323	DM13,692	DM8,258	PTA468,060	PTA809,177	PTA346,916
Unit sales price	0.681	1.931	0.142	0.139	0.158	10.802	14.940	16.112
Less:								
Assumed transmission	(0.017)	(0.049)	(0.002)	(0.002)	(0.002)	(0.201)	(0.201)	(0.201)
Assumed distribution	0.000	0.000	−0.006	−0.004	−0.004	0.000	−1.313	−1.362
Implied generation price	0.664	1.883	0.134	0.132	0.152	10.601	13.425	14.548
Adjustment to baseload	Sch0.626	BFr1.774	DM0.126	DM0.125	DM0.143	PTA9.990	PTA12.651	PTA13.709
Sterling equivalent (pence/kwh)	3.9	3.8	5.4	5.3	6.1	5.1	6.5	7.0
Sterling exchange rate	16.1	47.1	2.35	2.35	2.35	194.5	194.5	194.5

Table 3. CCGT Prices for Generation
(currency in local denominations)

	Verbund	Electrabel	RWE	Veba	Viag	ENDESA[a]	Iberdrola	UEF
Sold to competitive market (gigawatts per hour)	11,534	33,084	61,219	44,344	23,445	17,479	15,166	6,029
Generation price per kwh	Sch0.626	BFr1.774	DM0.126	DM0.125	DM0.143	PTA9.990	PTA12.651	PTA13.709
Equivalent CCGT price per kwh[b]	0.361	1.055	0.053	0.053	0.053	4.357	4.357	4.357
Impact of convergence	3,060	23,786	4,490	3,198	2,114	98,453	125,782	56,382
1995 cash flow	Sch6,143	BFr61,229	DM8,643	DM8,570	DM4,422	PTA303,279	PTA269,440	PTA93,326
Cash flow impact	50%	39%	52%	37%	48%	32	47	60
Sterling exchange rate	16.1	47.1	2.35	2.35	2.35	194.5	194.5	194.5

[a]Group sales and cash-flow data.
[b]Based on 2.24 pence per kwh.

Table 4. Estimated Headcount for Selected European Utilities

	Verbund	Electrabel	RWE	Veba	Viag	ENDESA	Iberdrola	UEF
Generation (gigawatts per hour)	25,000	70,605	145,437	61,653	41,770	62,424	41,947	19,838
Implied headcount	1,337	3,776	7,777	3,297	2,234	3,338	2,243	1,061
Transmission (gigawatts per hour)	56,030	64,062	136,043	98,543	52,100	0	0	0
Implied headcount	794	908	1,928	1,397	738	0	0	0
Distribution (gigawatts per hour)	2,643	25,426	85,950	39,816	22,400	28,769	54,163	23,165
Implied headcount	400	3,852	13,023	6,033	3,394	4,359	8,207	3,510
Total implied headcount	2,531	8,536	22,728	10,726	6,366	7,697	10,450	4,571
Current headcount	4,704	15,359	37,176	24,113	13,888	13,558	14,366	4,914
Implied reduction (%)	46	44	39	56	54	43	27	7
Operating cash flow savings (local currency)	Sch2,621	BFr26,863	DM1,329	DM1,182	DM580	PTA42,342	PTA28,510	PTA3,436

it has reduced the electricity tariffs by about 3 percent for 1997, which is the first ever tariff reduction in Spain. Given the impact of competition over the next four or five years, further price reductions will occur.

To introduce competition in the electric industry, Spain has set a deadline of January 1, 1998, for complete competition in the generation market. It will have a separately owned and operated transmission system that will be handled by a company called Red Eléctrica, or REE. This company will provide access to all generators on an open and nondiscriminatory basis, and plants will be called to operate and sell into the pool in ascending order of costs until demand is actually satisfied. Marginal plants will effectively set the price for the rest of the system. The problem Spain faces is that the prices, which I think will be set in the pool, will simply not cover the existing cost base, and several reasons exist for these stranded costs. Certainly, surplus capacity and inefficient operations contribute to the problem of stranded costs.

To calculate stranded costs, the Spanish government took the expected trend in revenues per unit under the current system through 2007 and compared this trend with expected competitively determined pool prices. The net present value of the difference was then used to estimate the total stranded costs—about 2 trillion pesetas (PTA).

Table 5 illustrates the allocation of the stranded costs. Roughly 80 percent of the stranded costs will be predetermined in terms of their allocation, with the final 20 percent to be allocated on an *ad hoc* basis, effectively after the fact. Stranded costs will be recovered over 10 years in Spain. After 2007, prices will simply be determined by the market. In the meantime, the combination of pool prices, capacity payments, distribution revenues (which will remain outside the competitive arena), stranded costs, and pool revenues will leave the companies with the same revenues as before the introduction of competition, so a timing issue is involved. Spain has until 2007 to use the umbrella of stranded-cost recovery to get its cost base down to a competitive level.

Table 5. Allocation of Revenues for Stranded Costs

Company	Stranded Costs (PTA billions)	Percentage of Total Stranded Costs
ENDESA	830	42%
Iberdrola	432	22
Unión Eléctrica Fenosa	205	10
Cantabrico	91	5
Other	32	2
Unallocated	398	20
Total	1,988	—

Note: Totals may not add because of rounding.

STOCK SELECTION

Successful stock selection of non-U.S. utilities should focus on identifying companies with fundamental strengths so that they will be well positioned for a liberalized environment. These success factors include cost-cutting potential, positive after-tax cash flow, improvements in the fuel mix, a coherent competitive strategy, and a focus on shareholder value.

ENDESA should be reasonably familiar to U.S. investors; it was the worst-performing stock of the Spanish utilities in 1996. It lagged behind because the market took the view that ENDESA had more to fear from the introduction of competition than did the other Spanish utilities, but that fear is unwarranted.

The company has great cost-cutting potential and strong cash flow. Its recent acquisitions of two small utilities in Spain have substantially rebalanced the company's operations away from generation and toward distribution, enhanced the cost-saving potential of the distribution side of the business, and substantially improved the company's fuel mix and thus its competitive position within the generation market. In any event, the company has until 2007 before investors need to worry about the impact of competition.

Although Verbund may be less familiar than ENDESA, it is Austria's largest utility. Of all the utilities in Europe, this one has the most favorable fuel mix; approximately 90 percent of total production is hydroelectric. Given its fuel mix, the company should still have lower operating costs, but it is aggressively cutting costs by reducing mining levels by about 15 percent over the past couple of years, with potential for substantial further progress. The company has positive cash flow after tax, after dividends, and after capital expenditures from 1997. Decreasing financial leverage will be one source of substantial earnings growth. Investors are getting Verbund for less than four times cash flow. The outperformance of the company's share price over the past five years indicates that its strengths are recognized by the market, but given its valuation, substantial upside potential still remains.

The direction of European bond markets has been the subject of a lot of talk in Europe. At Morgan Stanley, we expect bond markets in Europe to go into reverse, as happened in 1994. On that basis, the important consideration is which companies can outperform against the background of rising bond yields.

Veba, one of the major German electric companies, is one of these companies that can outperform a bearish bond market. In 1994, Veba recorded substantial outperformance, and many of the factors contributing to its success in 1994 remain in place for 1997. This company has the most coherent strategy for meeting the threat of competition by forming strategic alliances with Scandinavian low-cost generators, and by using hydroelectric power, it has increased some of its low-cost nuclear capacity exposure. Veba has a track record second to none in terms of cost cutting. It has identified DM1.5 billion of further cost saving over the next five years. Industry discussions have focused on how utilities will be offering the full range of utility services in the medium term, and Veba is well advanced in terms of its telecom business. This company has a strong focus on shareholder value, and although such a focus may not be a unique concept in the United States, it is fairly revolutionary in Germany. The company has delivered in terms of its dividend policy. This year, when the German authorities finally allow share buybacks to take place in Germany, Veba will come through very strongly and may be the first company to start aggressively repurchasing its shares.

CONCLUSION

Competition is coming and will exert substantial pressure on all European utilities' prices and cash flow, but the companies have substantial cost-cutting strategies and other options in place to meet this threat. The share price performance of National Power and PowerGen provides a good indication that shareholder value can continue to be improved against the background of market share loss through competition.

Motivation for competition from industrial customers in response to a wide variation in electricity prices throughout Europe and the increased use of gas generation will decrease prices over the next five years. For European utilities to be successful in this competitive environment, they must invest in gas, pressure coal suppliers, improve plant efficiency, and reduce costs and headcount.

As the industry moves from monopoly to competition, utilities must shift their focus from ensuring security of supply to ensuring security of demand by increasing the scope of investment in the distribution business. As the market mechanism begins to determine prices and the strategic direction of the industry, further privatization within Europe is expected.

Investors looking for attractive non-U.S. utilities in which to invest must identify those utilities that focus on value-enhancing strategies and that have effectively positioned themselves to succeed in this changing industry environment.

Question and Answer Session

Michael Sayers

Question: Will European companies have problems reducing staff and achieving cost efficiencies?

Sayers: In Continental Europe, achieving the cost savings necessary to compete in the market will be more difficult than in the United Kingdom, but not impossible. In 1995, the Spanish company Iberdrola, which has some of the more arcane working practices in Europe, reduced its headcount by 10 percent in one year. Verbund has reduced personnel by close to 15 percent in two years. To get to one-third of the market being competitive by 2003, the companies effectively have a grace period during which to cut their costs. A company faced with a target of a 50 percent headcount reduction must reduce personnel by about 7 percent a year, and a lot of that trimming can be done simply through attrition, as was the experience in the United Kingdom.

Question: Do you think labor could upset the plans to open markets in such places as France, which seems to be having that difficulty now with the banking industry?

Sayers: In the United Kingdom, labor can upset plans in many different ways, but I see no reason why it would want to upset the plan to introduce competition in 1998. After all, this change would be the first opportunity for the small people, the residential consumers, to begin benefiting from low-price electricity. Although it did not invent the issue of competition in the electric industry, I see no reason why it would want to prevent residential customers from getting the benefit. After all, in the United Kingdom, these jobs are gone. Headcount at National Power is 30 percent of what it was.

In France, labor very clearly can upset the liberalization process. In fact, if you look at how the European Union set up different models for establishing a competitive market, you will see that it has given two options. One is a form of negotiated third-party access, a much weaker version of the full third-party access than in the United Kingdom. The other is the single-buyer principle, whereby one entity in each country could—if there is a competing generator—buy the power and sell it to its final customer base and continue to control the import of power from the rest of Europe. France will be the country that makes best use of that option.

Question: How do you account for the fact that nuclear generation's market share has increased rather substantially in the past five years?

Sayers: The increase in market share is relatively easy to explain. One nuclear generating company's management team decided not to buy the off-the-shelf pressurized water reactor technology that most other companies were investing in at the time and decided to develop a second generation of gas-cooled reactor known as the advanced gas-cooled reactor. The basic problem was this company could not get it to work, so average availability was running in the 30–40 percent range. With time, many of the problems have been ironed out, and the result is that availability is now in the 70–80 percent range. One station maintained 90 percent availability during the course of 1996. The solution is a matter of getting the technology to work.

Question: Are some of the gains that these companies have shown the result of rapid growth and not "actual" gains?

Sayers: Volume growth in the United Kingdom is running at about 1 or 1.5 percent a year and has been driven by a number of factors. Cost cutting is the clearest example. Prices have not fallen by as much as one would expect given the degree of market power exerted by the companies. They were privatized with very strong balance sheets, and they have certainly used those balance sheets to good effect. A lot of the assets were written down before privatization, so the recovery of stranded costs was not much of an issue. The lesson is that to introduce a liberalized market, the best starting point is if the government owns the assets in the first place.

Question: How have cash flows and capital expenditures changed in the United Kingdom since privatization?

Sayers: Instead of a one-step adjustment to cash flows, companies have derived continual growth from their cost-cutting strategies. In terms of capital expenditures, all of the companies are running at substantially lower levels of annual spending than they were when the government owned them. In those days, the name of the game was simply to spend money, because the companies were run by engineers who had no shareholders to keep happy. In effect, management said, "Give us some money, and we will improve the system even further." That mentality has changed radically with privatization and competition, and capital-spending figures are running at probably less than two-thirds of where they were running before privatization.

Question: What do you think about the availability of gas in Europe, and what is the minimum price of electricity if gas keeps coming along and the price of gas remains constant?

Sayers: Gas availability was an issue, but not any longer. A map of Europe showing the major new pipelines that have been either recently constructed or about to be constructed would reveal substantial progress. The U.K. market, which has excess gas, is being connected to the rest of Europe in 1998. Gas is coming from Algeria and Morocco through the Maghreb pipeline into Portugal and Spain. Gas is coming from Gazprom in a joint venture with Edison into Italy to compete with SNAM, an existing Italian gas company. Gas is coming into Poland, also from Gazprom. Gas is coming from Norway into France. Gas availability will not be an issue.

As for how low electricity prices could fall given the amount of gas coming in, all of my cost estimates on gas are based on 15 pence per therm, and on that basis, the answer is 2.2 pence per unit for new gas-fired stations. If gas prices go even lower, electricity prices are going to follow them down. In the United Kingdom during the summer of 1996, gas was trading at around 9 pence per therm, but that was a spot price rather than a contract price.

Question: Where do you think these companies are going to make the best profits—generation, transmission, or distribution?

Sayers: At the moment, they are making the most money from generation. If they are smart, before they have to disaggregate the numbers and use them for transmission and distribution to justify the tariffs in a regulated environment, they should be loading as much of their costs into those two businesses as possible. This process is already starting to happen in Spain. That is the message in terms of the trend in profitability.

A lot of people are talking about how generation profits will be incredibly volatile, but the U.K. experience shows such volatility is not necessarily the case. National Power and PowerGen have done a terrific job of managing volatility by contracting their output three-to-five years ahead or one year ahead to iron out the volatility in prices and, therefore, in profitability. Although distribution and transmission will continue to be relatively stable by virtue of the regulation, generation does not necessarily have to be as volatile as some people might say.

Question: Because ENDESA's costs already show up pretty low on Table 4, how can it get costs lower, and can Iberdrola keep pace?

Sayers: Although ENDESA may have low costs, its costs can go substantially lower if it starts putting its staffing levels in line with the U.K. numbers. The cost in Table 4 was a pure generation cost. ENDESA can make further savings in distribution and transmission. Like all vertically integrated monopolies, the companies in Spain have tended to view transmission and distribution as being the poor relations of the generation business and, therefore, have not spent as much time managing the cost base or developing some of the value-added services, which will be critical in the competitive market.

Can Iberdrola keep up? It has less cost-cutting potential than ENDESA, but on the other hand, it is probably starting from the basis of a more favorable generation mix in terms of exposure to hydroelectric and nuclear, which are low-cost production methods at the margin.

Question: Why are Spanish companies investing in Latin America when they still have some challenges for restructuring at home, and do shareholders perceive some value from these investments?

Sayers: Their investments in Latin America are more talk than achievement. ENDESA was talking about some very major acquisitions of businesses in Latin America, but those plans seem to have been shelved because the market is moving toward liberalization. At the end of December 1996, ENDESA acquired two Spanish electric companies—FECSA and Sevillana. As a result of those acquisitions, ENDESA is more heavily indebted, which for such a financially conservative company, does not give as much scope for overseas expansion as it had talked about in the past. So, Spanish companies' Latin American acquisitions are on the back burner.

Question: What is more important in reducing prices, the competition in generation or the competition in supply (the distribution or transmission end)?

Sayers: In the United Kingdom, the rule of thumb has always been that generation is 50 percent of the final price of electricity, transmission is about 15–20 percent, distribution is 25 percent, and then the final add-on for having bought the electricity, transmitted and distributed it—in other words, supply—is about 5 percent. In the U.K. experience, a critical issue with the biggest influence on prices has been to get the cost of generation down.

Fearless Forecast: Electric Utilities in 2007

Leonard S. Hyman, CFA
Senior Industry Advisor
Smith Barney, Inc.

> After almost a century of regulation, the electric utility industry faces deregulation brought about by technological change. The pace of industry change makes picking the winners in 2007 all the more challenging, because a competitive energy supply industry will replace today's electric utility industry.

A century ago, Thomson discovered the electron. In Chicago, that same year, street railway tycoon Charles Tyson Yerkes, fed up with paying off a corrupt board of aldermen, lobbied the Illinois state legislature to create 50-year franchises and state regulation. Unfortunately, a reporter discovered that Yerkes had set up a fund to buy legislative votes, and the scandal killed the legislation. Ten years later, in 1907, electricity output had septupled, Spangler invented the electric vacuum cleaner and Fisher the electric washing machine, and the states of Massachusetts, New York, and Wisconsin inaugurated utility regulation.[1]

Will 1997 to 2007 produce like revolutionary changes? My answer is yes and no. The industry will undergo an operating, organizational, and regulatory revolution. The changes will occur in a period of slow domestic sales growth and internationalization of activities, giving less margin for error than does a period of robust growth close to home.

HISTORY FIRST, VERDICT LATER

For eight decades, the electric supply industry moved in one direction, thanks to economies of scale. In almost every year, the industry installed larger, more efficient plants. The larger the unit, the lower the cost of production, but in order to reach the maximum economy of scale, the largest possible generator had to serve customers in any one place. To assure that outcome, the government had to require that all customers take the output of the one largest generator, to the exclusion of the other generators. The state, therefore, granted one generating company the exclusive right to serve an area so that the generator could attain maximum economies of scale. Then, to protect consumers from the monopolist and to assure that customers would benefit from economies of scale, the state regulated the monopolist's profits.

The government had two reasons for permitting only one carrier to distribute in the area: to prevent numerous firms from digging up streets or crisscrossing the air with wires and because duplicate systems serving only some of the population had higher costs per customer than one system serving all. The generator and the wires need not have belonged to the same owner—and did not in some places for many years. In the United States, the electric magnates wanted to control all aspects of the business, so they joined generation and wires under one roof.

The system of regulated monopoly, which exploited economies of scale, not only produced reliable service but also declining prices (down 75 percent in real terms from the onset of regulation in 1907 to 1960) as the industry enjoyed increasing economies in its operations.

In the 1960s, two seemingly unrelated events changed the picture. First, new steam units ceased showing increasing economies of scale, because they had reached the physical limits imposed by the Rankine Cycle, as illustrated in **Figure 1**. That fact, by itself, did not invalidate the utilities' claim to a natural monopoly justified by economies of scale. The utilities' plants still generated at lower costs than anything else around. They had simply stopped getting more efficient.

The second event, however, began a process that undermined the utility's claim to a natural monopoly. In 1961, a utility installed the first stationary gas

---

[1] For a discussion of industry development, see Leonard S. Hyman, *America's Electric Utilities: Past, Present and Future*, 6th ed. (Vienna, VA: Public Utilities Reports, 1997).

Figure 1. Generating Efficiencies

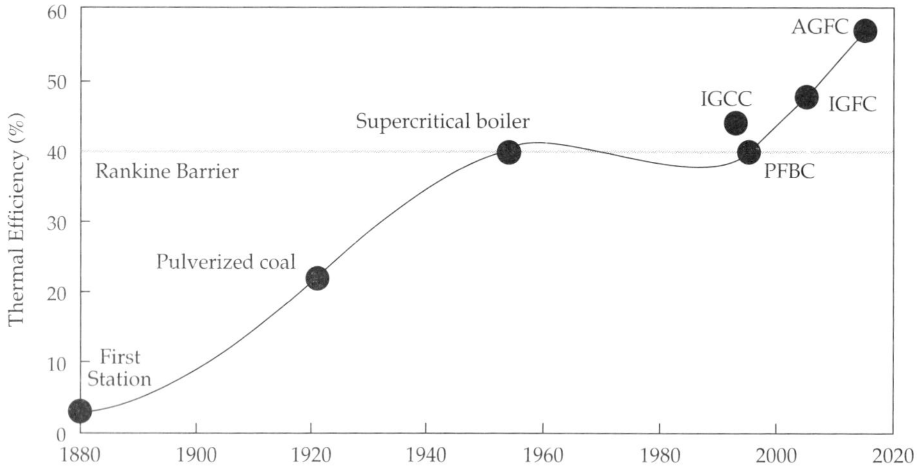

Note: AGFC = advanced gasification fuel cell; IGCC = integrated gasification-combined cycle; IGFC = integrated gasification fuel cell; PFBC = pressurized fluidized-bed combustion.
Source: Based on EPRI data.

turbine, a small generator derived from the jet engine. Just as the dinosaurs might have ignored the insignificant, furry mammals that succeeded them, the utilities did not realize that the gas turbine represented a significant shift in generation technology. Power equipment manufacturers then turned the gas turbine into an increasingly efficient device, while the productivity of larger power stations stagnated. In effect, this technological shift demolished the rationale for a natural monopoly in generation. Small generators could produce electricity for less than the big utility-owned generators. Regulation of generation no longer protected the consumer from a monopolist; it protected the monopolist from competition.

In the 1970s, as a result of the energy crisis, the nation sought to encourage more efficient production and use of energy. Congress did not view electric utilities as progressive firms ready to embrace new technologies, because the utilities seemed intent on solving the problem through the continued construction of unpopular and expensive nuclear power plants. In 1978, Congress enacted a law, the Public Utility Regulatory Policies Act (PURPA), that opened up electric generation to nonutilities and forced the utilities to buy from the upstarts. PURPA favored small producers and environmentally friendly operations and generators that used waste heat (co-generators). The law demonstrated that nonutilities could build and run power plants at least as well as utilities and created a healthy market for the new generating technologies. From the inception of PURPA to the present, the U.S. nonutility generators, including self-generating industrial firms, not only have raised their share of production from 3.5 percent to more than 11 percent and provided one-third of incremental generation in the period, but they also produce more power than the entire electric industries of the United Kingdom, Italy, or Brazil.

In 1992, Congress passed the Energy Policy Act, which created a new class of electric generation freed of PURPA restrictions, opened the way to electricity marketing, allowed utilities to invest abroad, and directed that utilities open their transmission lines to use by others. Since then, energy marketers have proliferated, electric utility affiliates have invested billions of dollars in foreign ventures, and in 1996, the Federal Energy Regulatory Commission (FERC) issued Rule 888, which laid the groundwork for a more competitive industry structure.

The industry, and some in Congress, desire more legislation. They want to repeal the Public Utility Holding Company Act of 1935 (PUHCA) because it limits the activities of those firms that fall under it and forces others to adopt strange organizational structures in order not to fall under it. They also want to repeal PURPA, a law that confers artificial advantages on certain classes of generators. Large industrial consumers of electricity and procompetitive forces in Congress, buoyed by the telecommunications legislation in 1996, want to push the pace of deregulation and force the states to accept electricity competition at the retail level on a schedule set by the federal government.

CURRENT PICTURE

The investor-owned electric utility industry, which accounts for 76 percent of electricity sales in the United States and has revenues of $163 billion and assets of $585 billion, stands at the proverbial crossroads, with its millions of owners perhaps as perplexed as many of its managers. The utilities face competition for wholesale customers now and will face competition for their retail customers within a few years. In order to choose the right road, the utilities must answer the following questions:

- Should we merge with other utilities in order to attain a critical mass of customers and economies of scale in operation, which will reduce our costs?
- Should we merge with gas companies in order to create a full-service energy firm with competitive market skills?
- How can we recover costs we incurred during the regulated era when attempting to do so through high prices would drive away customers?
- Should we continue to invest in regulated generating assets when generation could turn into an unregulated business?
- Should we maintain an integrated utility that operates in the generation, transmission, and distribution areas, or should we divest operations in which we cannot excel competitively?
- Should we encourage the rapid development of a competitive market (because we benefit from it) or oppose the development of competition (because we will lose out to competitors)?
- What is the right financial policy for a competitive utility?
- In which business should we invest our excess cash flow?
- If the electricity market in the United States grows slowly and competition holds down profitability, should we invest abroad?

At present, no industry consensus exists for any of those questions. That lack of consensus should surprise no one. Despite the fact that they all produce or sell the same commodity, the industry participants do so with an enormous range of cost structures and customer mixes. What surprises me, though, is how little attention the industry has paid to three basic issues:

- financial policies wholly unsuited for a competitive industry,
- definition of the rules of operation and design of the means of payment for system services that are required to keep the network running reliably, and
- regulatory techniques that produce incentives for investment and efficiency and also send correct price signals to consumers and network users.

Dealing with those three questions could contribute more to the health of the average utility than the fad-of-the-month strategies so prevalent today.

Financial Policies

The financial policies of the industry were fashioned in another time to meet the requirements of an industry that had no competitors in providing a necessary service. The industry had to raise capital on a regular basis to meet a growing demand that it had an obligation to serve. The regulators also had a say in formulating this financial policy, and they believed that leverage produced a lower cost of capital and that a utility plant had a long life. Bankers who had to sell huge amounts of utility stock to millions of stockholders encouraged policies that they believed would help the utilities raise money.

The industry, as a result of those influences, developed the following characteristics:

- heavy reliance on senior securities,
- low depreciation rate,
- external financing of capital needs, and
- high dividend payout ratios.

The industry's financial ratios in 1995, after years of correcting for past excesses, remained uncomfortably out of line with those of competitive industries, as shown in **Table 1**. Why should investors care about policies that have persisted for more than 80 years? The conditions that allowed those policies no longer prevail. More than half of the industry's assets are tied up in generation, a business rapidly turning competitive. Whether utilities retain generating assets or not, they own them now. They require financial policies that meld regulated and competitive elements.

Table 1 shows that depreciation expense as a percentage of net plant and equipment is 5 percent for investor-owned electric utilities (IOUs) versus 14.3 percent, on average, for the 400 industrials within the S&P 500 Index. Dividend payout as a percentage of reported net income for IOUs is almost twice as much as the S&P 400 Industrials—78 percent versus 44 percent.

Table 1 further shows that the utility industry cannot maintain current prices or net income and meet all ratios required to bring its finances in line with its composite risk levels. This projection assumes that 55 percent of the industry (generation) must bring its practices in line with competitive industries and that the balance of the utility industry keeps utility-type ratios. The problem appears to be inadequate depreciation expense. Raising depreciation to 4.5 percent, for example, would reduce pretax coverage to 2.4 times and would increase the dividend payout to 177 percent. In order to raise pretax coverage to 4.5

Table 1. Industry Financial Ratios for 1995

	S&P 400 Industrials	Investor-Owned Electric Utilities	Required Utility Ratios Adjusted for Deregulation	Comment
All senior securities (as percentage of capitalization)[a]	45%	55%	50%	Requires $17 billion in new common equity or similar reduction in debt and preferred stock.
Current ratio[b]	1.0	0.8	0.9	Requires $6 billion additional working capital.
Pretax interest coverage[c]	5.4x	3.0x	4.5x	Need $23 billion more pretax income or must reduce interest costs by $10 billion.
Depreciation expense (as percentage of net plant)[d]	14.3%	5.0%	10.0%	Depreciation expense should be $20 billion higher.
Depreciation expense (as percentage of gross plant of generating companies)[e]	6.0%	3.0%	4.5%	Depreciation expense should be $10 billion higher.
Dividend payout (as percentage of reported net income)[f]	44%	78%	59%	Cut dividends by $4 billion or raise net income $6 billion.
Dividend payout (as percentage of net income from operations)[g]	39%	81%	58%	Cut dividends by $4 billion or raise net income $6 billion.
Internal funds (as percentage of capital expenditures)[h]	117%	107%	113%	Raise internal funds by $1.5 billion or cut expenditures by $1.5 billion.

[a] Includes preferred stock and long-term debt in current liabilities.
[b] All current assets divided by all current liabilities.
[c] Excludes nonoperating items, including allowance for funds used during construction.
[d] Net plant was used because of availability of data; see next note.
[e] A more realistic number than net plant, based on the experience of U.K. generating companies.
[f] Dividend paid to common stock as percentage of reported net income.
[g] Excludes from net income special charges that reduced industrial income and excludes allowance for funds and extraordinary items from utility income.
[h] Internal funds calculated after deducting dividend payments from internal cash flow.

times without raising prices, utilities need to lower their debt ratio to 26 percent, in which case all senior securities would make up only 35 percent of capitalization. But dividend payout would exceed 100 percent under this scenario because the interest savings would not offset the higher depreciation rate. In the old utility framework, a 10–15 percent price increase would have solved all problems for the average utility, but this solution is not possible in the current climate. A 20 percent reduction in operating costs, other than depreciation and taxes, would solve this problem. Other deregulated industries have implemented equally large expense reductions.

The industry, as a whole, cannot reach a reasonable financial structure by maintaining current financial policies, even if it suffers no losses in the transition to competition. It certainly cannot support foreign expansion and domestic acquisitions with its present structure. Therefore, despite cash flow in excess of capital expenditure needs, I believe that the only way for the electric industry to get into shape financially, without making drastic reductions in expenses or dividends or raising prices to customers, is by selling new issues of common stock—not a popular forecast.

Network System Operations

Wall Streeters have paid no attention to the systems operations of the industry in a competitive framework and have ignored the implications of the creation of an independent system operator (ISO), which involves handing over 15 percent of profitable assets to a committee. Worse, they have failed to note that the reliable operation of a system requires a complex series of services, and at present, only utilities can provide the full range of such services. The big question for investors is whether they will collect adequate, market-based payments for such services. Such payments could mitigate stranded-cost problems as well, because some supposedly stranded plants play a vital role in supporting the network and, if paid for that role, would have a greater value than indicated by calculations of stranding that are based on ability to sell into a competitive bulk power market. Providing services might prove more profitable than fighting in the bulk power market. Furthermore, from a public policy standpoint, creating market-based pricing for systems services would help to create a more efficient electricity system than we have today. But those concepts could easily be lost in the rush to deregulate generation as an end in itself.[2]

Regulation

Neither the states nor the federal government seem eager to retreat from regulation. They will regulate anything that they consider a natural monopoly, and so far, that means transmission, distribution, and generation in those areas where competition is nonexistent or unlikely.

At present, regulation works on a cost-of-service basis, which means return on assets plus operating costs. The system discourages incentive and efficient operation, because all cost reductions flow to consumers. The British, as an antidote, applied to utilities a regulatory system that they had developed to regulate the price of condoms. They raised prices annually in line with the cost of living, less a fixed factor to encourage productivity. U.S. regulators have applied that system to the telephone industry here. The price-cap system, as it is called, does wonders for productivity, but it has two major drawbacks. First, if the initial bargaining to set up the formula goes badly for consumers, the utilities can earn truly obscene profits in a safe, regulated business. Second, the price-cap scheme encourages the cutting of corners in providing service, as U.S. telephone companies have demonstrated. I expect the states to move toward hybrid, productivity-sharing schemes that keep regulated operating profits within a rate of return range. Such a system, however, does not send price signals to consumers in a way that would encourage societal efficiency. A functioning, competitive market requires price signals in order to work well. Otherwise, electric utilities will mislocate power plants, not make needed investments in transmission, and encourage utilities to close down facilities required to provide reliable service. I am not sanguine about the willingness of regulators to send such signals, if somebody stands to make a bigger than normal profit, every so often, as a result of those signals.

2007: THE FEARLESS FORECAST

No more history lessons. No more complaints about regulators. What will the industry look like in a decade?

The energy supply industry—not the electric or gas utility industries—will sell energy and related services. Some companies will act as virtual utilities, assembling packages of services for customers from a variety of sources. Other firms will furnish only part of the package, which they will do for virtual utilities, for the grid, or for customers. Although people talk about the convergence of the electric and gas industries, the real convergence is between the three "C" technologies (computers, communications, and controls) and the energy business. Without the three-C technologies, the new market will not operate.[3]

Energy firms will separate the regulated from the unregulated aspects of their businesses, either by setting up subsidiaries or by spinning off or selling assets. Initially, they will resist doing so, as the movement to create ISOs has shown, but eventually, they will see the virtue of operating unencumbered by regulatory conflicts.

Ownership patterns will shift. With the demise of PUHCA and PURPA, restrictions on ownership of energy assets and companies will end. Foreign and nonutility firms will take control of assets and of companies. I also expect a major shift in ownership as companies split off noncompatible activities. The traditional utility shareholders will gravitate to the companies that emphasize stable transmission and distribution activities.

The distinction between utility generation and nonutility generation will evaporate. Independent producers will require deep pockets to operate without the old long-term power contracts on which they depended for so long. They will require a savvy knowledge of the market, they will use sophisticated futures market schemes to limit risks, they will build

---

[2]This topic has received little attention in nontechnical publications. See Marija Ilic and Leonard Hyman, "Getting It Right the First Time: The Value of Transmission and High Technologies," *Electricity Journal* (November 1996).

[3]The most comprehensive review of the technological and economic issues involved in the formation of the virtual utility appears in *The Virtual Utility*, edited by Shimon Awerbuch and Alistair Preston (Boston: Kluwer, 1997).

plants that easily fit into the market, and they will have deep pockets.

The component parts of the industry will adopt appropriate financial policies for no other reason than they could not finance any other way. The industry cannot get from its current financial structure to a target structure within five years without raising prices or dropping dividends. Sale of assets and payment of debt, however, might aid the process.

Annual reports of energy suppliers in 2007 will feature maps of the world, color-coded like the globes of the colonial era. Utilities previously diversified by investing in businesses that they knew nothing about but that were in a familiar country, the United States. This time around, they will invest in businesses they understand, but do they have the other requirements for success? If the utility business is not good here, how long will it take to get not good there? Utilities probably gain no strategic advantage through scattered investments, but they feel compelled to make those purchases for fear of missing the boat altogether. By 2007, the companies will have completed a process of swapping properties in order to create cohesive regional entities, few of which will produce risk-adjusted returns superior to those available in the United States or Canada.[4]

CONCLUSION

By 2007, electricity supply will constitute a large component of the energy supply and services industry and the customer service function will overlap into a services function that could include electricity, gas, water, and telecommunications among services rendered. Big players could resemble financial institutions rather than converters of energy. Heavy industrial consumers who self-generate will turn that function over to energy industry specialists capable of milking the fuel of all its useful energy. A properly incentivized network will produce and distribute energy more efficiently and reliably than the current system.

Deregulation, however, tends to benefit consumers rather than industry participants, especially incumbents carrying all the baggage of incumbency. According to a survey conducted by Jim Doudiet, an industry consultant, 75 percent of the companies in the electric industry expect to be in the top quartile. Obviously, some people have exaggerated hopes. Picking the winners out of today's crowd will not be easy.

[4] For a review of privatization and international investment, see *The Privatization of Public Utilities*, edited by Leonard S. Hyman (Vienna, VA: Public Utilities Reports, 1995)

Question and Answer Session

Leonard S. Hyman, CFA

Question: Does California law AB 1890 mandate the sale of generating assets for the California utilities or merely recommend that they do so?

Hyman: As I understand it, nothing has been mandated, but the regulators have given some rather strong hints that if the utilities did certain things, such as selling their generating assets, the regulators would look more favorably on them.

Question: If ISOs prove inadequate, will we see a number of national-grid-type companies develop in the United States?

Hyman: We will see transmission companies develop. I cannot see the ISOs as being anything more than an interim solution, because people are going to get tired of dealing with an organization that does not have any reason to exist and that cannot make a lot of the capital decisions necessary to strengthen the power grid. Yes, we are going to have a number of national-grid-type companies, some of which may well be government owned, but they will be transmission companies.

Question: How long do you think it will take before foreign returns revert to U.S. levels?

Hyman: I am not sure what foreign returns are right now. Everyone says they are fine, but try to get some real numbers. I do not think people are really thinking through what the risks and returns are and whether the foreign returns are actually doing something for investors. I would like to investigate exactly what some of these foreign acquisitions have done for the shareholders.

In 5–10 years, getting better risk-adjusted returns than the ones found in the United States will be difficult.

Question: Please elaborate on your comment that the United States does not have the equipment in place for retail competition.

Hyman: If you want a good retail market, you must have a system of metering that is responsive to all the price changes occurring in a competitive market, which means you have to have meters that tell you not only how much electricity was used but when it was used. You have to have meters that tell customers what they are being charged at a particular moment so they can make decisions. We do not have any of those things right now.

Question: What percentage of revenues do utilities currently invest in R&D (new technologies), and where do you think that figure should be in a competitive environment?

Hyman: The total budget for the Electric Power Research Institute (EPRI), which is the industry's R&D arm, is approximately $500 million, although not all that money comes from the industry. The total industry revenue, including government companies that belong to EPRI, is about $200 billion. So, roughly one-quarter of 1 percent of the industry revenue goes to R&D. I cannot imagine any company that plans to keep up with technological change spending such a small amount of money. I don't know what the correct number is, but one-quarter of 1 percent is not the right number.

Question: Are high-efficiency microturbines, fuel cells, and other distributed-generation technologies the gas turbines of the stranded-cost-recovery world?

Hyman: Distributed generation means having a little plant located near the customer, even in the customer's basement. This plant might not be attached to the electric system at all—that is, it might not have wires coming in to provide backup. It is a power plant that could use gas and be connected to the gas pipeline. These new, small generating facilities are becoming more and more efficient.

If the local electric company decides to charge its customers everything it possibly can to recover stranded costs and pushes prices high enough, customers might switch to distributed generation and disconnect from the power system. I don't know how many customers are actually going to take this action, but a local electric company had better know ahead of time what the technology is capable of doing, what the price of providing distributed generation will be in its area, and whether it has some large customers out there who can go to distributed generation when it decides to charge 7 cents per kilowatt hour.

Question: Have the technological improvements of the past 10 years or so come out of the electric utility industry or from other R&D sources?

Hyman: The reason that the gas turbine has improved so much is because it is essentially a jet engine,

Deregulation of the Electric Utility Industry

so it has benefited from federal government military R&D. A lot of additional R&D that has taken place was partially funded by the industry. EPRI is working on more efficient turbines and on making the old clunkers work better. So, technological innovations are coming from different sources.

Question: Given that electricity cannot be physically identified by a producer, how do the producers determine which production units are kept online at any given time and how do the producers match the units with the contracts to sell power?

Hyman: In essence, you have to separate the physical from the financial. The producer does not decide which unit will be kept running. In each area, a power pool organization—a market for electricity—will have to exist. In effect, the individual power plants will go to this market or this power exchange and say, "We are willing to run our plant if the price of electricity is 5 cents." Someone else says, "We will run our power plant if the price of electricity is 6 cents," and someone else says, "We cannot afford to do anything for less than 7 cents." This power exchange will look at all the bids and, for example, say it can fill all the demand it expects by purchasing electricity from all these plants that are willing to provide electricity at a price ranging from 5 to 7 cents. So, the power exchange tells them to get their plants ready to run. Each of these power plants puts its electricity into the power grid, and that electricity goes to consumers.

Under the U.K. system, the contract is simple. All the electricity goes into the same pot. You do not know where the electron comes from. All you know is you made a deal with somebody to assure that you will pay 5 cents, because that seller of electricity figures that, over time, 5 cents is a good price. So, the seller is now insured and knows that whatever the pool price does, the seller gets 5 cents and you know that whatever the pool price does, you pay 5 cents. Although this answer is a gross oversimplification, the contracts will work this way in essence.

Question: To what extent will transmission bottlenecks, particularly to the Northeast, mitigate risks to bondholders and stockholders in the intermediate term (5–10 years)?

Hyman: Getting the electricity into some areas is difficult. New England is a perfect example. Look at the line to Canada, a big line. The problem is that the whole system works in such a way that if one big event happens—for instance, the line from Canada goes down—all of this electricity that was supposed to go to New England bounces all around. It will go into Pennsylvania and mess up the system there. The line from Canada has a limited load not because the line cannot carry more but because other problems will be created if it goes down.

New England has all this supposedly high-cost capacity, which is really needed. New England escaped from very severe blackouts in the summer of 1996 only because it was a mild summer. This could be an area where a supposedly stranded plant is really not stranded. The plant provides an important service in keeping the network going. A simulation of the entire eastern interconnection would help determine whether a supposedly stranded plant is stranded or is needed.

Question: What is your philosophy on investing in electric utility stocks?

Hyman: Although I don't give stock picks any more, let me give you my philosophy instead, for what it is worth. Telling which companies are going to be the bigger losers is hard to do. Stick with companies with the right assets and the right management team—that is, a company that will be around and should be successful in the future. You may want to look at the really competitive and well-organized utilities. If I were focusing on stocks, I would look at the ones that have the ability to succeed as opposed to the ones that might make it if they do not trip over themselves—by doing things like spending too much money in Afghanistan.

Self-Evaluation Examination

1. Which of the following characteristics describes the electric utility industry?
   I. Large-scale industrial electricity users are considered wholesale users.
   II. Gas dominates the base load for U.S. electricity generation.
   III. Competitive pricing, regional weather patterns, and consumption affect electricity spot prices.
   IV. Transmission and distribution assets dominate the balance sheet of investor-owned utilities.
   a. I, III, and IV.
   b. III.
   c. I, II, and III.
   d. II, III, and IV.

2. Investor-owned utilities have lower average prices per kilowatt hour than governmental and municipal entities.
   a. True.
   b. False.

3. According to O'Connor, which of the following lessons from other deregulated industries can be applied to electric utilities?
   a. Surplus capacity and new technology drive prices to marginal cost.
   b. Customers start to demand choice because of lower perceived quality and higher prices.
   c. The key to success in a transitional business is financial depth at the outset.
   d. All of the above.

4. Which of the following best characterizes stranded costs?
   I. Stranded costs include nuclear power plants with high sunk investments.
   II. Stranded costs are not reflected in today's price of electricity.
   III. Electric utilities will recover any remaining stranded costs from the Federal Energy Regulatory Commission in 2005.
   IV. Stranded costs are a function of good and bad business decisions made in the context of explicit federal and state policies.
   a. I, II, and III.
   b. III.
   c. II, III, and IV.
   d. I, II, and IV.

5. According to O'Connor, the "new style" electric utility will be characterized by companies that organize themselves totally from the perspective of the customer.
   a. True.
   b. False.

6. Which of the following is the primary objective for electric utilities pursuing a defensive merger strategy?
   a. To achieve higher growth rates.
   b. To reallocate excess capital.
   c. To combine in order to cut costs.
   d. To shift their focus from the customer to the commodity.

7. According to Konolige, which of the following is not an example of an offensive M&A strategy?
   a. An electric/electric merger.
   b. A geographical merger.
   c. An electric/gas merger.
   d. The purchase of generation assets.

8. According to Konolige, which of the following implications of M&A deals affect electric utility investors?
   a. Potential earnings dilution.
   b. Pressure to reduce dividends.
   c. Cost of carry.
   d. All of the above.

9. Which business function will be most affected by disaggregation and the transition to a competitive market?
   a. Power generation.
   b. Transmission.
   c. Distribution.
   d. All functions will be equally affected.

10. According to Tilles, which of the following apply to the valuation of electric utilities?
    I. Generating assets will have high earnings multiples and volatile earnings.
    II. Transmission and distribution assets will have stable earnings and high dividend payouts.
    III. Regulators have tended to guarantee the recovery of stranded assets via non-bypassable competitive transition charges.
    IV. Free cash flow underscores the important role of management.
    a. I and IV.
    b. II, III, and IV.
    c. I, II, and III.
    d. I and III.

11. The relative yield of electric utilities is higher than the S&P 400 Industrials.
    a. True.
    b. False.

12. Which of the following describes the "traditional" electric utility bond structure issued today?
    a. A 30-year nonrefundable 5-year bond.
    b. A 10-year nonrefundable 5-year bond.
    c. A 30-year noncallable 10-year security.
    d. Commercial paper.

13. According to Miller, which of the following risks is not associated with the recovery of stranded assets?
    a. How stranded assets will be defined and measured.
    b. Whether 100 percent of stranded assets will be collected.
    c. How securitization of stranded costs will affect capital structure and financial ratios.
    d. What to do with the money.

14. In the event of an electric/gas merger, which of the following apply to the credit ratings of the two companies' bonds?
    a. The average electric company's bonds will be upgraded, and the average gas company's bonds will be downgraded.
    b. The average electric company's bonds will be downgraded, and the average gas company's bonds will be upgraded.
    c. Both companies' bonds will be upgraded.
    d. Both companies' bonds will be downgraded.

15. According to Miller, disaggregation has no effect on bondholders because each business segment has a similar risk profile.
    a. True.
    b. False.

16. According to Sayers, which of the following cost-cutting initiatives has had the most dramatic impact on the major U.K. power generators?
    a. Using low-cost imported coal rather than high-priced domestic coal.
    b. Closing down less efficient coal-fired capacity.
    c. Reducing headcount.
    d. Investing in gas-fired stations.

17. When considering stocks of non-U.S.-based electric utilities, investors should focus on companies with which of the following attribute(s).
    a. Cost-cutting potential.
    b. Positive after-tax cash flow.
    c. A coherent competitive strategy.
    d. All of the above.

18. Liberalization of European electric utilities is primarily the result of high retail electricity prices.
    a. True.
    b. False.

19. According to Hyman, which of the following undermined the electric utility's claim to a natural monopoly?
    a. The physical limits of the Rankine Cycle.
    b. The stationary gas turbine.
    c. The energy crisis.
    d. The Energy Policy Act of 1992.

20. According to Hyman, which of the following financial situations characterizes the electric utility industry before competition?
    a. Use of subordinated debt.
    b. Low depreciation rates.
    c. Use of retained earnings to finance capital expenditures.
    d. Declining dividend payout ratios.

Self-Evaluation Answers

1. b. Under the Federal Power Act, large-scale industrial customers are defined as end users and thus considered retail users; wholesale refers to sales for resale, for example, sales from one utility to another. Coal and nuclear dominate the base load; gas is used to meet peak or seasonal demand. Although gas provides only 10 percent of the energy used for generating electricity, it is a driving factor affecting wholesale market prices. Generation dominates the balance sheet of IOUs, with about 59 percent of the book value.

2. b. IOUs have higher average prices per kilowatt hour than both governmental and municipal entities. Governmental agencies are the beneficiaries of low-cost federally owned or licensed hydroelectric production. Municipal utilities are financed with tax-exempt debt and have no required return on equity, which lowers their overall cost of capital.

3. d.

4. d. According to O'Connor, the FERC does not guarantee the recovery of any stranded assets.

5. a. Successful utilities in the new electric paradigm will be companies that are committed to enhancing the lifetime value of the relationship with the customer.

6. c. According to Konolige, a defensive strategy describes the traditional electric/electric utility merger, a strategic alliance in which neighboring utilities combine to cut costs. The combined regional company focuses on the distribution business and on control of the customer.

7. a. An electric/electric merger is a defensive strategy designed to cut costs by spreading them over a larger service area.

8. d.

9. a. According to Tilles, the power-generation business is the business segment that will be most affected by the transition to a competitive market. Power generation is the principal business segment that is likely to be operating in a completely deregulated environment in the near future. Power generation will involve the sale of a commodity product and kilowatt hours of electricity. The guaranteed returns on invested capital will be a thing of the past.

10. b. Generating assets will be valued like deep cyclicals with upper single-digit earnings multiples and volatile earnings.

11. a. According to Tilles, the relative yield of electric utilities continues to be higher than the dividend yield of the S&P 400 Industrials—324 percent higher. The relative yield has been at the upper boundary of relative yields during the past 10 years.

12. c. According to Miller, the traditional electric utility bond 15 years ago had two flavors—either a 30-year nonrefundable 5-year bond or a 10-year nonrefundable 5-year bond. Short-term debt would not be an appropriate strategy for funding capital expenditures of a utility.

13. c. Regulatory risk, collection risk, and redeployment risk are associated with the recovery of stranded assets. Securitizing stranded investments will help reduce the business risk profile of the underlying electric utility and, therefore, could lead to credit upgrades. Management may elect to maintain the existing capital structure or retire a substantial portion of its outstanding debt with the proceeds from securitized assets, substantially improving leverage ratios.

14. b. According to Miller, although an electric/gas merger may make strategic sense for management, it generally causes heartburn for electric utility bondholders. For example, the average gas company's bond rating is mid-BBB, and the average electric utility rating has a weak A rating. So, when the two companies are combined, the weak A-rated electric utility is generally looking at a downgrade and the mid-BBB-rated gas company is generally looking at an upgrade.

15. b. Even though they are largely vertically integrated, the generation, transmission, and distribution business segments will have substantially different business risk profiles when they disaggregate. Generation will have higher business risk than the transmission and distribution segments, which will have lower but stable earnings.

16. c. Although using low-cost imported coal, closing down less efficient coal-fired capacity, and investing in gas-fired stations does reduce costs and improve efficiency, the most dramatic impact of cost cutting has been on the headcount of National Power and PowerGen. Over the past five years in moving from a monopoly to a liberalized environment, the combined headcount of the two companies has fallen about 70 percent.

17. d.

18. b. According to Sayers, the primary motivation for the liberalization of European electric utilities is the wide range of power prices for industrial users.

19. b. In 1961, a utility installed the first stationary gas turbine, a small generator derived from the jet engine. The gas turbine could produce electricity for less than the big utility-owned generators. This technological shift demolished the rationale for a natural monopoly for generation. As a result, regulation of generation no longer protected the consumer from the monopolist, it protected the monopolist from competition.

20. b. Utilities did not rely heavily on subordinated debt but did rely heavily on senior securities. Bankers who had to sell huge amounts of utility stock to millions of stockholders encouraged various policies—reliance on external debt financing to finance capital expenditures, high dividend payout ratios, and low depreciation rates—that they believed would help the utilities raise money. Low depreciation rates were used because plants were believed to have very long lives.

Selected Publications

AIMR

AIMR Performance Presentation Standards Handbook, 2nd edition, 1997

Economic Analysis for Investment Professionals, 1997

Finding Reality in Reported Earnings, 1997

Global Equity Investing, 1996

Global Portfolio Management, 1996
Jan R. Squires, CFA, *Editor*

Implementing Global Equity Strategy: Spotlight on Asia, 1997

Investing in Small-Cap and Microcap Securities, 1997

Managing Endowment and Foundation Funds, 1996

Managing Investment Firms: People and Culture, 1996
Jan R. Squires, CFA, *Editor*

The Media Industry, 1996

Merck & Company: A Comprehensive Equity Valuation Analysis, 1996
Randall S. Billingsley, CFA

Risk Management, 1996

Standards of Practice Casebook, 1996

Standards of Practice Handbook, 7th edition, 1996

Research Foundation

Company Performance and Measures of Value Added, 1996
by Pamela P. Peterson, CFA, and David R. Peterson

Currency Management: Concepts and Practices, 1996
by Roger G. Clarke and Mark P. Kritzman, CFA

Emerging Stock Markets: Risk, Return, and Performance, 1997
Christopher B. Barry, John W. Peavy III, CFA, and Mauricio Rodriguez

Information Trading, Volatility, and Liquidity in Option Markets, 1997
by Joseph A. Cherian and Anne Fremault Vila

Initial Dividends and Implications for Investors, 1997
by James W. Wansley, CFA, William R. Lane, CFA, and Phillip R. Daves

Interest Rate and Currency Swaps: A Tutorial, 1995
by Keith C. Brown, CFA, and Donald J. Smith

Interest Rate Modeling and the Risk Premiums in Interest Rate Swaps, 1997
Robert Brooks, CFA

TELEVISION & CABLE FACTBOOK
VOLUME 85

Albert Warren
Editor & Publisher 1961-2006

Paul L. Warren, Chairman & Publisher
Daniel Y. Warren, President & Editor

EDITORIAL & BUSINESS HEADQUARTERS
2115 Ward Court, N.W., Washington, DC 20037
Phones: 202-872-9200; 800-771-9202
Fax: 202-318-8350
E-mail: factbook-info@warren-news.com
Web site: http://www.warren-news.com

Editorial-Factbook/Directories
Michael C. Taliaferro, Managing Editor & Assistant Publisher—Directories
Kari M. Osel, Senior Editor & Editorial Supvr.
Colleen M. Crosby, Sr. Editor & Editorial Supvr.
Robert T. Dwyer, Senior Research Editor

Advertising – Factbook/Directories
Richard Nordin, Director of Advertising
Phone: 703-819-7976
Fax: 202-478-5135

Editorial-News
Jonathan Make, Executive Editor
Paul Gluckman, Executive Senior Editor
Howard Buskirk, Executive Senior Editor
Rebecca Day, Senior Editor
David Kaut, Senior Editor
Matt Daneman, Senior Editor
Dibya Sarkar, Senior Editor
Monty Tayloe, Associate Editor
John Hendel, Associate Editor
Adam Bender, Associate Editor
Jimm Phillips, Assistant Editor
R. Michael Feazel, Consulting Editor

Business
Brig Easley, Executive Vice President & Controller
Sheran Fernando, Chief Operating Officer
Annette Munroe, Director, Marketing & Circulation
Katrina McCray, Senior Sales & Marketing Support Specialist
Loraine Taylor, Sales & Marketing Support Assistant

Information Systems
Deborah Jacobs, Information Systems Manager
Gregory E. Jones, Database/Network Manager

Sales
William R. Benton, Sales Director
Agnes Mannarelli, National Accounts Manager
Jim Sharp, Account Manager
Bruce Ryan, Account Manager
Matt Long, Account Manager

Publications & Services of Warren Communications News

TELEVISION & CABLE FACTBOOK: ONLINE

CABLE & STATION COVERAGE ATLAS
Published Annually

COMMUNICATIONS DAILY

CONSUMER ELECTRONICS DAILY

INTERNATIONAL TRADE TODAY

WARREN'S WASHINGTON INTERNET DAILY

Copyright © 2017 by Warren Communications News.
All Rights Reserved
ISBN: 978-1-57696-010-3
ISSN: 0732-8648

It is against the law to make a copy of this publication or any portion of its content without our explicit permission. Federal copyright law (17 USC 504) makes it illegal, punishable with fines up to $100,000 per violation plus attorney's fees. It is also illegal to input any of this publication into any computer or data retrieval system without our permission. Warren Communications News frequently has taken action against individuals and firms that violated our copyright, or other rights, and we will continue to do so. We request that subscribers advise their staffs of the law and the financial penalties that will result from the copying or improper use of this publication. We welcome inquiries about additional subscriptions and we are prepared to grant authorization for certain occasional reproduction of portions of this publication, but only upon formal request to the publisher. For additional subscriptions, please contact our Sales Dept. at 800-771-9202.

Index to Sections
Television & Cable Factbook No. 85

TV STATIONS VOLUME

Section A

Call Letters of U.S. Television Stations A-9

Ownership of U.S. Commercial Television Stations A-1560

Television Market Rankings (Nielsen) A-1

Television Stations, Commercial A-20

Television Stations, Public/Educational. A-1489

Section B

Low Power Television/Translator Stations B-1

Low Power Television/Translator Station Ownership B-189

Section C – Charts

Nielsen Geographic Regions Summary C-9

Nielsen TV Household Estimates ranked by DMA C-10

Nielsen TV Households by States and Counties C-12

Parent/Satellite Television Stations C-3

Total Television Stations On Air C-1

TV Station Affiliations by Market C-5

CABLE SYSTEMS VOLUME

Section D

Call Letters of U.S. Television Stations D-1

Cable Systems D-14

Cable Community Index . . . . (Back of Cable Volume 2)

Cable Owners D-887

Section E

Brokerage & Financing Services E-133

Management & Technical Consulting Services E-139

Pay TV & Satellite Services E-1

Program Sources & Services E-105

Section F – Charts

Abbreviations F-8

Cable Penetration by State F-7

Estimated Growth of the Cable Industry F-1

Glossary of Cable Terms F-13

Largest U.S. Cable Systems F-2

Nielsen Cable TV Household Estimates Alphabetical by DMA F-4

Nielsen Cable TV Household Estimates by State F-6

Index to Contents
Television & Cable Factbook No. 85

A

@Radical Media Inc.	E-105
@Max	E-5
@Max (See also Max Latino)	E-57
1-World LLC	E-105
3ABN	E-5
3ABN Latino (See also 3ABN)	E-5
3 Ball Entertainment	E-105
3DGO!	E-5
4SD	E-5
4SD (See also Channel 4 San Diego)	E-19
5 News	E-5
5 Star Max	E-5
5 Star Max (See also Cinemax)	E-20
6 News	E-6
10 News 2	E-6
10 News Channel	E-6
24/7 News Channel	E-6
52MX	E-6
54 Broadcasting Inc.	A-1560
62nd Street Productions	E-105
89 Edit	E-105
101 Network	E-6
101 Network (See also Audience Network)	E-11
A&E	E-6
Aapka Colors	E-6
AARP TV	E-105
AAT Television	E-6
Abbreviations	1
ABC Family Channel	E-6
ABC Family Channel (See also Freeform)	E-40
ABC News	E-105
ABC News/Univision Network	E-6
ABC News/Univision Network (See also Fusion)	E-41
ABC Studios	E-105
ABI Research	E-139
ABP Ananda	E-6
ABP Ananda (See also ABP News)	E-6
ABP News	E-6
David Abraham & Co. LLC	E-133
ACC Digital Network	E-6
Accenthealth	E-105
Accent Media	E-105
ACC Network	E-7
AccuWeather Inc.	E-105
AccuWeather Network	E-7
Action Max	E-7
Action Max (See also Cinemax)	E-20
ActiveVideo	E-139
Adell Broadcasting Corp.	A-1560
Admiralty Properties LLC	A-1560
Adult Swim	E-7
Adventist Television Network	E-7
Adventist Television Network (See also Hope Channel)	E-48
Aerco Broadcasting Corp.	A-1560
The Africa Channel	E-7
African Box Office	E-7
African Box Office (See also Afrotainment Plus)	E-7
African TV Network (ATVN)	E-7
Afrique Music Television	E-7
Afrotainment Music	E-7
Afrotainment Plus	E-7
Afrotainment Music (See also Afrotainment Plus)	E-7
Agency for Instructional Technology	E-105
Aircraft Music Library	E-105
The Aker Partners Inc.	E-139
Alden Films/Films Of The Nations	E-105
Aliento Vision	E-7
Al Karma TV	E-7
Allegro Productions Inc.	E-106
The Allen Broadcasting Corp.	A-1560
Alliance for Christian Media	E-106
Allied Vaughn	E-106
Allison Payment Systems LLC	E-139
All Mobile Video	E-106
Almavision	E-7
Alpha Broadcasting Corp.	A-1560
Alta Communications	E-133
Alterna'TV	E-106
Altitude Sports & Entertainment	E-7
Amazon Inc.	E-106
AmberWatch TV	E-8
AMC	E-8
Amdocs, Broadband Cable & Satellite Division	E-139
America One Television	E-8
America One Television (See also Youtoo America)	E-103
America teve	E-8
America CV Network LLC	E-106
America-CV Station Group Inc.	A-1560
American Christian Television Services Inc.	A-1560
American Desi	E-8
American ED TV	E-8
American European Consulting Co. Inc.	E-139
American Heroes Channel	E-8
American Heroes Channel (See also Discovery Channel)	E-27
American ICN TV Network	E-8
American Jewish Committee	E-106
AmericanLife TV Network	E-8
AmericanLife TV Network (See also Youtoo America)	E-103
American Movie Classics	E-9
American Movie Classics (See also AMC)	E-8
American Public Television (APTV)	E-106
American Religious Town Hall Meeting Inc.	E-106
American Sports Network	E-9
America's Auction Network	E-9
AMGTV	E-9
AMIT	E-106
Amrita TV	E-9
ANA Television Network	E-9
Anchor Pacific Corp.	E-139
Angel One	E-9
Angel Two	E-9
Angel Two (See also Angel One)	E-9

2017 Edition   iii

Index to Contents

Anhui TV International . . . E-9
Animal Planet . . . E-9
Animal Planet (See also Discovery Channel) . . . E-27
Animal Planet HD . . . E-9
Animal Planet HD (See also Animal Planet) . . . E-9
Anime Network . . . E-9
Annenberg Channel . . . E-106
Another Country . . . E-106
Antena 3 Internacional . . . E-9
Antenna Satellite TV . . . E-9
Antenna TV . . . E-9
APA International Film Distributors Inc. . . . E-106
AP ENPS . . . E-106
Aperio Communications LLC . . . A-1560
Aplauso TV . . . E-10
AP Radio Network (APRN) . . . E-106
AP Television News . . . E-107
Aptinet Inc. . . . E-107
Arabic Channel . . . E-10
Arabic Channel (See also TAC TV) . . . E-84
Archdiocese of Baltimore . . . E-107
Neal Ardman . . . A-1560
ARENAS . . . E-107
Ariana Afghanistan TV . . . E-10
Ariana TV . . . E-10
Arirang DTV . . . E-10
Arizona News Channel . . . E-10
ARCTEK Satellite Productions . . . E-107
Armenian Film Foundation . . . E-107
Armenian Public Channel . . . E-10
Armenian Russian Television Network (ARTN) . . . E-10
Army & Air Force Hometown News Service . . . E-107
Army & Air Force Hometown News Service (See also Joint Hometown News Service) . . . E-118
Philip A Arno . . . A-1560
ART America . . . E-10
Artbeats Software Inc. . . . E-107
Ascent Media Group . . . E-107, E-139
ASC-TV . . . E-10
Asianet . . . E-10
Asianet Movies . . . E-10
Asianet Movies (See also Asianet) . . . E-10
Asianet News . . . E-10
Asianet News (See also Asianet) . . . E-10
Asianet Plus . . . E-10
Asianet Plus (See also Asianet) . . . E-10
Asia Travel TV . . . E-10
Asia TV USA Ltd. . . . E-107
Asociacion Evangelistica Cristo Viene Inc. . . . A-1560
Aspire . . . E-10
Associated Christian Television System Inc. . . . A-1560
Associated Press . . . E-107
Associated Television International . . . E-107
AssyriaSat . . . E-11
Atlanta Interfaith Broadcasters . . . E-11
ATLX (Athletics Training Lifestyle) . . . E-11
Atres Series . . . E-11
ATV Broadcast LLC . . . E-139
ATV Home Channel (America) . . . E-11
Audience Network . . . E-11
Audience Research & Development LLC . . . E-139
AUS Consultants . . . E-133
The Austin Co. . . . E-139
The Auto Channel . . . E-11
Automotive.TV . . . E-11
Aviva TV . . . E-11
AWE . . . E-11
Awesomeness Films . . . E-107
AwesomenessTV . . . E-107
AXA Equitable . . . E-133
AXS TV . . . E-11
AYM Sports . . . E-11
AZ Clic . . . E-11
AZCAR USA Inc. . . . E-139
AZ Corazon . . . E-11
Azteca . . . E-12
AZ TV . . . E-12

B

B4U Movies . . . E-13
B4U Music . . . E-13
B4U Music (See B4U Movies) . . . E-13
BabyFirst Americas . . . E-12
BabyFirstTV . . . E-12
Baby TV . . . E-12
Backchannelmedia Inc. . . . E-139
Bahakel Communications Ltd. . . . A-1560
Bruce R Baker . . . A-1561
Baker Scott & Co. . . . E-140
Balboa Capital . . . E-133
Bandamax . . . E-12
Bandamax (See also Univision) . . . E-96
Band Internacional . . . E-12
Bang U . . . E-12
Bank of America . . . E-133
BNY Mellon, Media & Technology Division . . . E-133
Barbary Post . . . E-107
Barca TV . . . E-12
Barclays Capital . . . E-133
Barger Broadcast Services Inc. . . . E-133
Barker Capital LLC . . . E-133
Baron Services Inc. . . . E-107
Batjac Productions Inc. . . . E-107
Bay News 9 . . . E-12
Bay News 9 en Espanol . . . E-12
Bay News 9 en Espanol (See also InfoMas) . . . E-50
Bayou City Broadcasting Evansville Inc. . . . A-1561
BBC America . . . E-12
BBC America On Demand . . . E-13
BBC America On Demand (See also BBC America) . . . E-12
BBC Arabic . . . E-13
BBC Arabic (See also BBC World News) . . . E-13
BBC World News . . . E-13
BBC Worldwide Ltd. . . . E-107
BeachTV . . . E-13
Beach TV Properties Inc. . . . A-1561
Beamly . . . E-108
Beast . . . E-108
Beauty & Fashion Channel . . . E-13
Beijing TV . . . E-13
beIN SPORT . . . E-13
beIN SPORT En Espanol . . . E-13
beIN SPORT En Espanol (See also BeIN Sport) . . . E-13
Dave Bell Associates Inc. . . . E-108

Index to Contents

Bellum Entertainment	E-108
Thomas Benson Jr.	A-1561
BET	E-13
BET Gospel	E-13
BET Gospel (See also BET)	E-13
BET Hip Hop	E-13
BET Hip Hop (See also BET)	E-13
BET J	E-13
BET J (See also Centric)	E-19
BET Play	E-13
BET Play (See also BET)	E-13
BET Soul	E-13
BET Soul (See also BET)	E-13
Better Life Media	E-108
Better Life Television Inc.	A-1561
BIA Capital Strategies LLC	E-133
BIA Digital Partnership LP	E-133
The BIA Kelsey Group	E-133, E-140
Big Shoulders Digital Video Productions	E-108
Big Sky Edit	E-108
Big Ten Network	E-13
Big Ten Network (See also BTN)	E-16
Bikini Edit	E-108
BIO	E-13
BIO (See also FYI)	E-42
BitCentral	E-140
BiteSizeTV	E-108
Biz TV	E-13
Blackburn & Co. Inc.	E-134
Blackhawk Broadcasting LLC	A-1561
Black Heritage Network	E-14
Blackmagic Design USA	E-140
Black Network Television	E-14
Black Television News Channel	E-14
Blast Digital	E-108
Blockbuster On Demand	E-14
Block Communications Inc.	A-1561
Bloomberg Television	E-14
BlueHighways TV	E-14
Blue Ocean Network	E-14
BlueRock	E-108
BMO Capital Markets, Media & Communications Group	E-134
Boerner Communications Inc.	E-140
Boise Telecasters LP	A-1561
Bolivia TV	E-14
Bollywood Hits On Demand	E-14
Bond & Pecaro Inc.	E-134, E-140
Bonded Services	E-108
Bonjour America TV	E-14
Bonneville International	E-108
Bonneville International Corp.	A-1561
Bonten Media Group LLC	A-1561
Book TV	E-14
Boomerang	E-14
Boosey & Hawkes Music Publishers Ltd.	E-108
Booz, Allen & Hamilton Inc.	E-140
Bortz Media & Sports Group	E-140
Bosco Productions	E-108
BosTel	E-15
Boston Catholic Television	E-15
Boston Catholic Television (See also CatholicTV)	E-18
Boston Kids & Family	E-15
Bounce TV	E-15
Bowman Valuation Services LLC	E-134
Box	E-15
BoxTV: The Boxing Channel	E-15
Frank Boyle & Co. LLC	E-134
Bravo	E-15
Brazzers TV	E-15
Brean Murray, Carret & Co. LLC	E-134
Breathe Editing Inc.	E-108
Bridges TV	E-15
Bright House Sports Network	E-15
Bright House Travel Weather Now	E-16
Bright House Travel Weather Now (See also Bay News 9)	E-12
Stephen C Brissette	A-1561
Bristlecone Broadcasting LLC	A-1562
Broadcasting Licenses LP	A-1562
Broadcast Media Group Inc.	E-108
Broadcast Music Inc. (BMI)	E-108
Broadcast Services Inc.	E-140
Broadcast Trust	A-1562
Broad Green Pictures	E-109
BroadView Software Inc.	E-140
Broadway Television Network	E-109
Broadway Video Entertainment	E-109
Brokerage & Financing Services	E-133
Stuart N. Brotman Communications	E-140
Eugene J. Brown	A-1562
BTN	E-16
BTN2Go	E-16
BTN2Go (See also BTN)	E-16
Buckalew Media Inc.	A-1562
BuenaVision TV	E-16
Bug Editorial Inc.	E-109
Bulkley Capital LP	E-134
Bunim-Murray Productions	E-109
Burrud Productions Inc.	E-109
Buzzco Associates Inc.	E-109
BuzzFeed Motion Pictures	E-109
BUZZR TV	E-16
Buzztime	E-16
Buzztime (See also NTN Buzztime)	E-67
BV Investment Partners LLC	E-134
Byrne Acquisition Group LLC	A-1562
BYUtv	E-16

C

C7 Jalisco	E-16
C13 de Chile	E-26
C13 de Chile (See also Canal 13 de Chile)	E-16
Cable Systems	D-14
Cable Community Index	(Back of Cable Volume 2)
Cable Ownership	D-887
Alabama	D-15
Alaska	D-37
Arizona	D-44
Arkansas	D-54
California	D-82
Colorado	D-111
Connecticut	D-127
Delaware	D-132
District of Columbia	D-133
Florida	D-134
Georgia	D-151

2017 Edition

Index to Contents

Communications Daily
Warren Communications News

Get the industry standard FREE —
For a no-obligation trial call 800-771-9202 or visit www.warren-news.com

Hawaii	D-177
Idaho	D-179
Illinois	D-186
Indiana	D-225
Iowa	D-240
Kansas	D-278
Kentucky	D-306
Louisiana	D-333
Maine	D-353
Maryland	D-359
Massachusetts	D-365
Michigan	D-370
Minnesota	D-391
Mississippi	D-426
Missouri	D-440
Montana	D-464
Nebraska	D-479
Nevada	D-500
New Hampshire	D-506
New Jersey	D-510
New Mexico	D-519
New York	D-529
North Carolina	D-550
North Dakota	D-568
Ohio	D-577
Oklahoma	D-607
Oregon	D-637
Pennsylvania	D-648
Puerto Rico	D-884
Rhode Island	D-683
South Carolina	D-684
South Dakota	D-694
Tennessee	D-705
Texas	D-718
Utah	D-790
Vermont	D-797
Virginia	D-801
Washington	D-814
West Virginia	D-833
Wisconsin	D-848
Wyoming	D-871
Cuba	D-881
Guam	D-882
Mariana Islands	D-883
Virgin Islands	D-886
Cable Audit Associates Inc.	E-140
Cable Noticias	E-16
Cable Ownership	D-887
Cable Penetration by State	F-1
Cable System Services	E-140
Cable TV Network of New Jersey	E-16
CAD Drafting Services Inc.	E-140
Cadent Network	E-140
Cadillac Telecasting Co.	A-1562
Cala Broadcast Partners LLC	A-1562
California Channel	E-16
California-Oregon Broadcasting Inc.	A-1562
Call Letters (U.S.)	A-9, D-1
Campus Group Companies	E-109
Camrac Studios	E-109
Canal 10 de Cancun	E-16
Canal 10 de Honduras	E-16
Canal 13 de Chile	E-16
Canal 22 Internacional	E-16
Canal 24 Horas	E-17
Canal 24 Horas (See also TVE International)	E-93
Canal 44 (XHIJ-TV)	E-16
Canal Once	E-17
Canal Sur	E-17
Canal Sur (See also Sur)	E-83
Candid Camera Inc.	E-109
Cannell Studios	E-109
CAN TV	E-17
Capgemini, Telecom, Media & Entertainment Group	E-140
Capital News 9	E-17
Capital Off Track Betting Television Network	E-17
Capitol Broadcasting Co. Inc.	A-1562
Caption Colorado	E-109
CaptionMax	E-109
Caracol TV	E-17
Career Entertainment Television	E-17
Caribbean Broadcasting Network LLC	A-1562
Carolina Christian Broadcasting Inc.	A-1562
Carousel	E-17
William B. Carr & Associates Inc.	E-141
Cars.TV	E-17
Cartoon Network	E-17
Cartoon Network en Espanol (See also Cartoon Network)	E-17
Cartoon Network en Espanol	E-17
Casa Club TV	E-17
Casa Club TV (See also MasChic)	E-56
Casa en Denver, Debtor-in-Possession	A-1562
Castle Rock Entertainment	E-109
Catch 47	E-18
Catch 47 (See also Bright House Sports Network)	E-15
The Catholic, Apostolic & Roman Church In Puerto Rico	A-1562
Catholic Communication Campaign	E-109
Catholic Television Network	E-18
CatholicTV	E-18
CB24	E-18
CB Communications Inc.	E-141
CBC/Radio-Canada	E-18, E-109
C.B. Distribution Co.	E-110
C.B. Distribution Co. (See also listing for Jess S. Morgan & Co)	E-121
CBeebies	E-18
CBS All Access	E-18
CBS Sports Network	E-18
CBS Corp.	A-1562
CBS News Inc.	E-110
CBS Television Distribution	E-110
CBS Television Studios	E-110
CB Tu Television Michoacan	E-18
CCI Systems	E-141
CCTV-4	E-18
CCTV-4 (See also CCTV America)	E-18
CCTV-6	E-18
CCTV-6 (See also China Movie Channel)	E-19
CCTV-9	E-18
CCTV-9 (See also CCTV-Documentary)	E-18
CCTV-11	E-18
CCTV-11 (See also CCTV-Opera)	E-18
CCTV-13	E-18
CCTV-13 (See also CCTV-News)	E-18
CCTV America	E-18
CCTV-Documentary	E-18
CCTV-Entertainment	E-18

Index to Contents

CCTV-Entertainment (See also CCTV-Documentary)	E-18
CCTV-News	E-18
CCTV-News (See also CCTV-Documentary)	E-18
CCTV-Opera	E-18
CCTV-Opera (See also CCTV-Documentary)	E-18
Celebrity Shopping Network	E-18
Central Florida News 13	E-18
Centric	E-19
Centric (See also BET)	E-13
Centroamerica TV	E-19
CET: Comcast Entertainment Television	E-19
CGNTV USA	E-19
Chadbourn Marcath Inc.	E-141
Chaisson & Co. Inc.	E-134
Jeff Chang	A-1563
Channel 3 TV Co LLC	A-1563
Channel 4 San Diego	E-19
Channel One Russia	E-19
Channel Z Edit.	E-110
Chapman/Leonard Studio Equipment Inc.	E-110
Chase	E-134
Chena Broadcasting LLC	A-1563
Chernin Entertainment	E-110
Chicago Access Network Television	E-19
Chicago Access Network Television (See also CAN TV)	E-17
Chiller	E-19
China Movie Channel	E-19
China Movie Channel (See also CCTV-Documentary)	E-18
Chinese Entertainment Television (CETV)	E-19
Chinese Television Network	E-19
Chinese Television Network (See also CTI-Zhong Tian)	E-26
Christian Church (Disciples of Christ), Communication Ministries	E-110
Christian Faith Broadcast Inc.	A-1563
Christian Television Network	E-19, E-110
Christian Television Network Inc.	A-1563
The Christophers	E-110
CHR Solutions Inc.	E-141
Church Channel	E-19
Church Federation of Greater Indianapolis Inc.	E-110
The Church of Jesus Christ of Latter-Day Saints	E-110
Church World Service	E-110
Cine Mexicano	E-20
Cine Nostalgia	E-20
Cine Sony Television	E-20
Cine Clasico	E-20
Cinecraft Productions Inc.	E-110
Cinedigm	E-110
Cine Estelar	E-20
CineGroupe	E-110
Cinelan	E-110
Cinelatino	E-20
Cinema Arts Inc.	E-111
Cine Magnetics Digital & Video Laboratories	E-111
Cinemax	E-20
Cinemax On Demand	E-20
Cinemax On Demand (See also Cinemax)	E-20
Cinemoi North America	E-20
Cisneros Media Distribution	E-111
Citadel Communications LLC	A-1563
Citibank N.A.	E-134
Dick Clark Productions Inc.	E-111
Clasico TV	E-20
Classic Arts Showcase	E-20
Cloo	E-21
CLTV	E-21
Club Jenna	E-21
Club Jenna (See also Reality Kings TV (RKTV))	E-74

Advanced TV Factbook
FULLY SEARCHABLE • CONTINUOUSLY UPDATED • DISCOUNT RATES FOR PRINT PURCHASERS
For more information call 800-771-9202 or visit www.warren-news.com

CMS Station Brokerage	E-134
CMT	E-21
CMT Loaded	E-21
CMT Loaded (See also CMT)	E-21
CMT Pure Country	E-21
CMT Pure Country (See also CMT)	E-21
cn/2	E-21
CN8	E-21
CN8 (See also Comcast Network Philadelphia)	E-22
CN100	E-21
CNBC	E-21
CNBC Pro	E-21
CNBC Pro (See also CNBC)	E-21
CNBC World	E-21
CNBC World (See also CNBC)	E-21
CNET Networks Inc.	E-111
CNN	E-21
CNN en Espanol	E-22
CNN en Espanol (See also CNN)	E-21
CNNGo	E-22
CNNGo (See also CNN)	E-21
CNN International	E-22
CNN International (See also CNN)	E-21
CNN Newsource Sales Inc.	E-111, E-141
CNZ Communications SE LLC	A-1563
Coastal Television Network	E-22
Coastal Television Broadcasting Co. LLC	A-1564
Coastline Community College Center	E-111
CobbCorp LLC	E-134
Cocola Broadcasting Companies LLC	A-1564
College & School Network	E-111
College Bowl Co.	E-111
College Sports Television	E-22
College Sports Television (See also CBS Sports Network)	E-18
Colors Kannada	E-22
Colors Marathi	E-22
Colors Marathi (See also Colors Kannada)	E-22
Colours	E-22
Columbia Telecommunications Corp./CTC Technology & Energy	E-141
Columbia Tristar Television Group	E-111
Columbia Tristar Television Group (See also listing for Sony Pictures Television)	E-126
Comcast/Charter Sports Southeast (CSS)	E-22
Comcast Entertainment Television	E-22
Comcast Entertainment Television (See also CET: Comcast Entertainment Television)	E-19
Comcast Hometown Network	E-22
Comcast Network Philadelphia	E-22
Comcast SportsNet Bay Area	E-23
Comcast SportsNet California	E-23
Comcast SportsNet Chicago	E-23
Comcast SportsNet Houston	E-23
Comcast SportsNet Houston (See also Root Sports Southwest)	E-76
Comcast SportsNet Mid-Atlantic	E-23
Comcast SportsNet New England	E-23
Comcast SportsNet Northwest	E-23
Comcast SportsNet Philadelphia	E-23
Comcast SportsNet Washington	E-24
Comcast SportsNet West	E-24
Comcast SportsNet West (See also Comcast SportsNet California)	E-23

2017 Edition

Index to Contents

Comcast Sports Southwest (CSS)	E-24
Comcast Sports Southwest (CSS) (See also Root Sports Southwest)	E-76
Comcast Television 2	E-24
Comcast Television 2 (See also Comcast Television (Michigan))	E-24
Comcast Television (Michigan)	E-24
Comedy Central	E-24
Comedy Time	E-24
Comedy.TV	E-24
Comet	E-24
Communications Engineering Inc.	E-141
Communications Equity Associates	E-134, E-141
Compro Productions Inc.	E-111
Comsearch	E-141
Comsonics Inc.	E-141
Comtel Video Services Inc.	E-111, E-141
Concert TV	E-24
Concordia Publishing House	E-111
Conde Nast Entertainment	E-111
Conley & Associates LLC	E-134, E-141
Connecticut Network	E-24
Connecticut Network (See also CT-N)	E-26
Connecticut Public Broadcasting Inc.	E-111
Consulate	E-111
Contec	E-141
Content Media Corp. Ltd.	E-111
Continental Film Productions Corp.	E-112
Contradiction Films	E-112
Cookie Jar Entertainment Inc.	E-112
Cooking Channel	E-24
Corgan Media Lab.	E-112
Cornerstone Television	E-24
Cornerstone Television Inc.	A-1564
Cornwall Associates	E-141
Corridor Television LLP	A-1564
Cosmo Street	E-112
Costa de Oro Television Inc.	A-1564
Country Music Television	E-24
Country Music Television (See also CMT)	E-21
The Country Network	E-24
County Television Network San Diego	E-25
Court TV	E-25
Court TV (See also truTV)	E-92
Cowles Co.	A-1564
Cox & Cox LLC	E-134
Cox Enterprises Inc.	A-1564
Cox Sports Television	E-25
COZI TV	E-25
Crackle	E-25, E-112
Cranston Acquisition LLC	A-1564
Craven Film.	E-112
Create TV	E-25
CreaTV San Jose	E-25
Credit Protection Association Inc.	E-142
Credit Suisse	E-134
Crew Cuts	E-112
CrewStar Inc.	E-142
Crime & Investigation Network	E-25
Crime & Investigation Network (See also A&E)	E-6
Crime Channel	E-25
Critical Mention Inc. (Clip Syndicate)	E-142
Critical Content	E-112
CRN Digital Talk Radio	E-112
Cross Hill Communications LLC	A-1565
Crossings TV	E-25
Crosspoint	E-112
Crossroads Christian Communications Inc.	E-112
Crown International Pictures Inc.	E-112
Crystal Cathedral Ministries	E-112
Crystal Computer Corp.	E-142
Crystal Pictures Inc.	E-112
CSG Systems Inc.	E-142
CSN+	E-25
CSN+ (See also regional Comcast SportsNet listings)	E-23
C-SPAN	E-25
C-SPAN 2	E-26
C-SPAN 2 (See also C-SPAN)	E-25
C-SPAN 3	E-26
C-SPAN 3 (See also C-SPAN)	E-25
C-SPAN Extra	E-26
C-SPAN Extra (See also C-SPAN 3)	E-26
CTC International	E-26
CTI-Zhong Tian	E-26
CT-N	E-26
CTNi	E-26
CTNi (See also Christian Television Network)	E-19, E-110
CTV Inc.	E-112
Cubamax TV	E-26
CubaNetwork	E-26
CubaPlay Television	E-26
Cumbia Entertainment LLC	A-1565
Cunningham Broadcasting Corp.	A-1565
Cut & Run	E-112
Cutters	E-112
CVC Capital Corp.	E-135
CW11 New York	E-26
CW11 New York (See also PIX11)	E-72
CWK Network Inc.	E-112
CW PLUS	E-26
Cyclones.tv	E-26
CYR TV (Chinese Yellow River TV)	E-26

D

Damas TV	E-26
dapTV associates	E-112
Dare to Dream Network	E-26
Dare to Dream Network (See also 3ABN)	E-5
Dataworld	E-142
Dennis J Davis	A-1565
Day 1	E-113
Day of Discovery (RBC Ministries)	E-113
Daystar TV Network	E-27
Debmar-Mercury	E-113
Decades	E-27
Deep Dish TV	E-113
Defense Media Activity	E-113
DeLaHoyaTV	E-27
Deloitte & Touche LLP	E-135
Deluxe Advertising Services	E-113
Deluxe Laboratories Inc.	E-113
De Pelicula	E-27
De Pelicula (See also Univision)	E-96
De Pelicula Clasico	E-27
De Pelicula Clasico (See also De Pelicula)	E-27
Destination America	E-27

Index to Contents

ADVANCED TV Factbook
FULLY SEARCHABLE • CONTINUOUSLY UPDATED • DISCOUNT RATES FOR PRINT PURCHASERS
For more information call **800-771-9202** or visit **www.warren-news.com**

Destination America (See also Discovery Channel)	E-27
Destination Education	E-113
Deutsche Welle TV	E-27
DeWolfe Music	E-113
DG FastChannel Inc.	E-142
DG FastChannel Inc. (See also Extreme Reach Inc)	E-142
Digimation Inc.	E-113
Digital Force	E-113
Digital Juice Inc.	E-113
Digital Post Services	E-113
Diligent Systems Inc.	E-113
DIRECTV Cinema	E-27
Discovery Channel	E-27
Discovery Digital Networks	E-113
Discovery Education	E-113
Discovery en Espanol	E-28
Discovery en Espanol (See also Discovery Channel)	E-27
Discovery Familia	E-28
Discovery Familia (See also Discovery Channel)	E-27
Discovery Family	E-28
Discovery Fit & Health (See also Discovery Life Channel)	E-28
Discovery Fit & Health	E-28
Discovery Health Channel	E-28
Discovery Health Channel (See also OWN: Oprah Winfrey Network)	E-70
Discovery Home Channel	E-28
Discovery Home Channel (See also Destination America)	E-27
Discovery Kids Channel	E-28
Discovery Kids Channel (See also Discovery Family)	E-28
Discovery Kids en Espanol	E-28
Discovery Kids en Espanol (See also Discovery Familia)	E-28
Discovery Life Channel	E-28
Discovery Life Channel (See also Discovery Channel)	E-27
Discovery Times Channel	E-28
Discovery Times Channel (See also Investigation Discovery)	E-51
Discovery Travel & Living (Viajar y Vivir)	E-28
Discovery Travel & Living (Viajar y Vivir) (See also Discovery Familia)	E-28
Disney Channel	E-28
Disney Enterprises Inc.	A-1565
Disney Family Movies	E-29
Disney Family Movies (See also Disney Channel)	E-28
Disney Junior	E-29
Disney Junior (See also Disney Channel)	E-28
Disney XD	E-29
Disney XD (See also Disney XD)	E-29
Disney XD en Espanol	E-29
Disney XD en Espanol (See also Disney Channel)	E-28
Dispatch Broadcast Group	A-1565
Diversified Communications	A-1565
Diversified Systems Inc.	E-142
Diya TV	E-29
DIY Network	E-29
DJM Films Inc.	E-113
DLT Entertainment Ltd.	E-113
DMTV7	E-29
DMX Music	E-29, E-113
Doctor Television Channel (DrTV)	E-30
Documentary Channel	E-30
Documentary Channel (See also Pivot)	E-72
Docurama Films	E-114
Docu TVE	E-30
Docu TVE (See also TVE Internacional)	E-93
Dodgers On Demand	E-30
DogTV	E-30
Dolphins Television Network	E-30
Dom Kino	E-30
Dominican View	E-30
Dominican View (See also ULTRA HDPlex)	E-95
Dominion Broadcasting Inc.	A-1565
Dominion Sky Angel	E-30
Dominion Sky Angel (See also Angel One)	E-9
Dove Broadcasting Inc.	A-1565, E-114
Dow Jones Newswires	E-114
DragonTV	E-30
Draper Holdings Business Trust	A-1565
Dreamcatcher Broadcasting LLC	A-1566
DreamWorks Animation SKG	E-114
DreamWorks Studios SKG	E-114
Drew Associates Inc.	E-114
Driver	E-114
DriverTV	E-30
DuArt Film & Video	E-114
Dubai TV	E-30
Paul H. Dujardin	A-1566

E

E!	E-30
Eastern Television Corp.	A-1566
Ebenezer Broadcasting Group Inc.	A-1566
EBRU TV	E-30
EBS International (Entertainment Business Services)	E-142
Ecology Cable Service	E-31
ECTV	E-31
Ecuador TV	E-31
Ecuador TV (See also ECTV)	E-31
Ecuavisa Internacional	E-31
Ecumenical TV Channel	E-31
Editbar	E-114
Ralph Edwards Productions	E-114
EDX Wireless LLC	E-142
E! Entertainment Television	E-31
E! Entertainment Television (See also E!)	E-30
Effros Communications	E-142
EJTV	E-31
El Garage TV USA	E-31
elgourmet	E-31
Bert Elliott Sound	E-114
Ellis Communications Group LLC	A-1566
Ellis Entertainment Corp.	E-114
El Rey	E-31
Emirates Dubai Television	E-31
Emirates Dubai Television (See also Dubai TV)	E-30
Employment & Career Channel	E-31
Encore	E-31
Encore (See also Starz Encore)	E-82
Encore Action	E-31
Encore Action (See also Starz Encore Action)	E-82
Encore Black	E-31
Encore Black (See also Starz Encore Black)	E-82
Encore Classic	E-31
Encore Classic (See also Starz Encore Classic)	E-82
Encore Drama	E-31
Encore Drama (See also Starz Encore Black)	E-82
Encore Espanol	E-31
Encore Espanol (See also Starz Encore Espanol)	E-82
Encore Family	E-31

2017 Edition ix

Index to Contents

CABLE & TV STATION COVERAGE
Atlas 2017
The perfect companion to the Television & Cable Factbook
To order call 800-771-9202 or visit www.warren-news.com

Encore Family (See also Starz Encore Family)	E-83
Encore Love	E-31
Encore Love (See also Starz Encore Classic)	E-82
Encore Mystery	E-31
Encore Mystery (See also Starz Encore Suspense)	E-83
Encore Play	E-31
Encore Play (See also Starz Encore)	E-82
Encore Suspense	E-31
Encore Suspense (See also Starz Encore Suspense)	E-83
Encore Wam	E-31
Encore Wam (See also Starz Encore Family)	E-83
Encore Westerns	E-31
Encore Westerns (See also Starz Encore Westerns)	E-83
Encuentro Christian Network Corp.	A-1566
Encyclopaedia Britannica Inc.	E-114
Endemol Shine North America	E-114
English Club	E-31
English On Demand	E-32
Enlace Juvenil	E-32
Enlace Juvenil (See also EJTV)	E-31
Enlace USA	E-32
Enoki Films USA Inc.	E-115
Entravision Communications Corp.	A-1566
EnVest Media LLC	E-135
Envision TV	E-32
Envoy Productions	E-115
EPI Group LLC	A-1566
EPIX	E-32
EPIX 2	E-32
EPIX 2 (See also EPIX)	E-32
EPIX 3	E-32
EPIX 3 (See also EPIX Hits)	E-32
EPIX Drive-In	E-32
EPIX Drive-In (See also EPIX)	E-32
EPIX Hits	E-32
EPIX Hits (See also EPIX)	E-32
Equidata	E-142
The Erotic Network	E-32
Escape	E-32
eScapes Network	E-32
Espiritu Santo y Fuego Network	E-32
ESPN	E-32
ESPN2	E-33
ESPN2 (See also ESPN)	E-32
ESPN3	E-33
ESPN3 (See also WATCH ESPN)	E-100
ESPN360.com	E-33
ESPN360.com (See also ESPN3)	E-33
ESPN Bases Loaded	E-33
ESPN Bases Loaded (See also ESPN)	E-32
ESPN Buzzer Beater	E-33
ESPN Buzzer Beater (See also ESPN)	E-32
ESPN Classic	E-33
ESPN Classic (See also ESPN)	E-32
ESPN College Extra	E-33
ESPN College Extra (See also ESPN)	E-32
ESPN Deportes	E-33
ESPN Deportes (See also ESPN)	E-32
ESPN Deportes + por ESPN3	E-33
ESPN Deportes + por ESPN3 (See also ESPN Deportes)	E-33
ESPNews	E-33
ESPNews (See also ESPN)	E-32
ESPN Full Court	E-33
ESPN Full Court (See also ESPN College Extra)	E-33
ESPN Game Plan	E-33
ESPN Game Plan (See also ESPN College Extra)	E-33
ESPN Goal Line	E-33
ESPN Goal Line (See also ESPN)	E-32
ESPN Now	E-33
ESPN Now (See also WATCH ESPN)	E-100
ESPNU	E-33
ESPNU (See also ESPN)	E-32
Esquire Network	E-33
Esquire TV Now	E-33
Esquire TV Now (See also Esquire Network)	E-33
Esteem Broadcasting LLC	A-1566
Estimated Growth of the Cable Industry	F-1
Estrella TV	E-33
estudio5	E-34
ES.TV	E-34
ETC	E-115
Eternal Word TV Network	E-34
Eternal Word TV Network (See also EWTN Global Catholic Network)	E-34
ET-Global	E-34
ET-News	E-34
ET-News (See also ET-GLOBAL)	E-34
ETV Kannada	E-34
ETV Kannada (See also Colors Kannada)	E-22
ETV Marathi	E-34
ETV Marathi (See also Colors Marathi)	E-22
EUE/Screen Gems Studios	E-115
Eurochannel	E-34
Eurocinema	E-34
EuroNews	E-34
Evangelistic Alaska Missionary Fellowship	A-1567
EVINE Live	E-34
EWTN en Espanol	E-34
EWTN en Espanol (See also EWTN Global Catholic Network)	E-34
EWTN Global Catholic Network	E-34
EXFO	E-142
The Exline Co.	E-135, E-142
Expo TV	E-34
Extreme Reach Inc.	E-142
Exxxotica	E-34

F

Faith Broadcasting Network Inc.	A-1567
Faith For Today	E-115
Faith Television Network	E-35
Faith Television Network (See also The Family Channel)	E-35
Familia TV	E-35
The Family Channel	E-35
Family Friendly Entertainment	E-35
FamilyNet	E-35
Family Theater Productions	E-115
Farm Journal Media	E-115
Fashion One 4K	E-35
Fashion One Television Ltd.	E-35
FashionTV	E-35
Fast Cuts	E-115
FBR Capital Markets, Technology, Media & Telecommunications Group	E-135
Festival Direct	E-35
Festival Direct (See also Independent Film Channel)	E-50
FidoTV	E-35

Index to Contents

The Field	E-115
Fight Network	E-35
Fight Now TV	E-35
Fil Am TV	E-35
Gregory P. Filandrinos	A-1567
The Filipino Channel	E-36
Filmack Studios	E-115
FilmCore	E-115
FilmCore (See also Deluxe Advertising Services)	E-113
Film Festival Channel	E-36
FilmRise	E-115
Films Around the World Inc.	E-115
Films of India	E-115
Films of India (See also listing for 1-World LLC)	E-105
Final Cut Ltd.	E-115
Find it on Demand	E-36
Fine Art Productions, Richie Suraci Pictures MultiMedia, InterActive	E-115
Fine Living Network	E-36
Fine Living Network (See also Cooking Channel)	E-24
Michael Fiore Films	E-115
FiOS1 Dallas	E-36
FiOS1 High School Sports Widget	E-36
FiOS1 Long Island	E-36
FiOS1 New Jersey	E-36
FiOS1 New Jersey (See also FiOS Long Island)	E-36
FiOS1 Potomac	E-36
FiOS1 Potomac (See also FiOS Long Island)	E-36
Firestone Communications Inc.	E-115
Fireworks International	E-115
First Assembly of God of West Monroe	A-1567
First Light Video Publishing	E-115
Fischer Edit	E-116
FitTV	E-36
FitTV (See also Discovery Life Channel)	E-28
Fix & Foxi	E-36
Flatiron Film Co.	E-116
Flinn Broadcasting Corp.	A-1567
George S. Flinn III	A-1567
George S. Flinn Jr.	A-1567
Flix	E-36
Florida Channel	E-36
Fluid	E-116
FMX Cable FM System	E-36
FNTSY Sports Network	E-36
Follow Productions	E-116
Food Network	E-36
Paul Dean Ford	E-142
Richard A. Foreman Associates Inc.	E-135
FOROtv	E-37
FOROtv (See also Univision)	E-96
Forrester Research Inc.	E-143
Fort Myers Broadcasting Co.	A-1567
Forum Communications Co.	A-1567
Foundation	E-116
Fox 21 Television Studios	E-116
Fox Business Go	E-37
Fox Business Go (See also Fox Business Network)	E-37
Fox Business Network	E-37
FOX College Sports Atlantic	E-37
FOX College Sports Central	E-37
FOX College Sports Central (See also FOX College Sports Atlantic)	E-37
FOX College Sports Pacific	E-37
FOX College Sports Pacific (See also FOX College Sports Atlantic)	E-37
Fox Deportes	E-37
Fox Life	E-37
Fox Movie Channel	E-37
Fox Movie Channel (See also FXM)	E-42
Fox News Channel	E-37
Fox News Go	E-37
Fox News Go (See also Fox News Channel)	E-37
Fox Reality Channel	F-37
Fox Reality Channel (See also Nat Geo WILD)	E-62
Fox Soccer	E-38
Fox Soccer (See also Fox Soccer Plus)	E-38
Fox Soccer 2Go	E-38
Fox Soccer 2Go (See also Fox Soccer Plus)	E-38
Fox Soccer Plus	E-38
FOX Sports 1	E-38
FOX Sports 2	E-38
FOX Sports 2 (See also FOX Sports 1)	E-38
FOX Sports Arizona	E-38
FOX Sports Arizona Plus	E-38
FOX Sports Arizona Plus (See also FOX Sports Arizona)	E-38
FOX Sports Carolinas	E-38
FOX Sports Detroit	E-38
FOX Sports Detroit Plus	E-38
FOX Sports Detroit Plus (See also FOX Sports Detroit)	E-38
FOX Sports Florida/Sun Sports	E-38
FOX Sports Florida Plus	E-38
FOX Sports Florida Plus (See also FOX Sports Florida/Sun Sports)	E-38
FOX Sports Go	E-38
FOX Sports Go (See also Fox Sports Networks)	E-39
FOX Sports Houston	E-38
FOX Sports Indiana	E-39
FOX Sports Indiana Plus	E-39
FOX Sports Indiana Plus (See also FOX Sports Indiana)	E-39
FOX Sports Kansas City	E-39
FOX Sports Kansas City (See also FOX Sports Midwest)	E-39
FOX Sports Kansas City Plus	E-39
FOX Sports Kansas City Plus (See also FOX Sports Kansas City)	E-39
FOX Sports Midwest	E-39
FOX Sports Midwest Plus	E-39
FOX Sports Midwest Plus (See also FOX Sports Midwest)	E-39
FOX Sports Net New York	E-39
FOX Sports Net New York (See also MSG Plus)	E-60
FOX Sports Net Northwest	E-39
FOX Sports Net Northwest (See also Root Sports Northwest)	E-76
FOX Sports Net Pittsburgh	E-39
FOX Sports Net Pittsburgh (See also Root Sports Pittsburgh)	E-76
FOX Sports Net Rocky Mountain	E-39
FOX Sports Net Rocky Mountain (See also Root Sports Rocky Mountain)	E-76
FOX Sports Net Utah	E-39
FOX Sports Net Utah (See also Root Sports Rocky Mountain)	E-76
FOX Sports Net West 2	E-39
FOX Sports Net West 2 (See also FOX Sports West/Prime Ticket)	E-40
FOX Sports Networks	E-39
FOX Sports Networks (See also regional FOX Sports Networks)	E-39
FOX Sports New Orleans	E-39
FOX Sports New Orleans (See also FOX Sports Southwest)	E-40
FOX Sports North	E-39
FOX Sports North Plus	E-39
FOX Sports North Plus (See also FOX Sports North)	E-39
FOX Sports Ohio/Sports Time Ohio	E-39
FOX Sports Ohio Plus	E-39
FOX Sports Ohio Plus (See also FOX Sports Ohio/Sports Time Ohio)	E-39
FOX Sports Oklahoma	E-40
FOX Sports Oklahoma (See also FOX Sports Southwest)	E-40

2017 Edition — xi

Index to Contents

Get the industry standard FREE —
For a no-obligation trial call 800-771-9202 or visit www.warren-news.com

FOX Sports Oklahoma Plus	E-40
FOX Sports Oklahoma Plus (See also FOX Sports Oklahoma)	E-40
FOX Sports San Diego	E-40
FOX Sports South/SportSouth	E-40
FOX Sports South Plus	E-40
FOX Sports South Plus (See also FOX Sports South/SportSouth)	E-40
FOX Sports Southwest	E-40
FOX Sports Southwest Plus	E-40
FOX Sports Southwest Plus (See also FOX Sports Southwest)	E-40
FOX Sports Tennessee	E-40
FOX Sports Tennessee (See also FOX Sports South/SportSouth)	E-40
FOX Sports West/Prime Ticket	E-40
FOX Sports West Plus	E-40
FOX Sports West Plus (See also FOX Sports West/Prime Ticket)	E-40
FOX Sports Wisconsin	E-40
FOX Sports Wisconsin (See also FOX Sports North)	E-39
FOX Sports Wisconsin Plus	E-40
FOX Sports Wisconsin Plus (See also FOX Sports Wisconsin)	E-40
FOX Sports World	E-40
FOX Sports World (See also FOX Soccer PLUS)	E-38
Fox Studios Australia	E-116
Fox Studios Australia (See also listing for Granada Media)	E-117
Fox Television Holdings LLC	A-1567
France 24	E-40
Sandy Frank Entertainment Inc.	E-116
Frederator Studios	E-116
Freeform	E-40
Freeman Corp.	E-143
Free Speech TV	E-41
Free To Choose Network	E-41
Fremantle Corp.	E-116
FremantleMedia Ltd.	E-116
Jim French Design Shop	E-143
Fresh	E-41
Fresh (See also Brazzers TV)	E-15
Chuck Fries Productions	E-116
Peter Froehlich & Co.	E-143
Frost Great Outdoors	E-41
FSZ TV (Fantasy Sports Zone TV)	E-41
Fuel TV	E-41
Fuel TV (See also Fox Sports 2)	E-38
Fujian Straits TV	E-41
FUMC Television Ministries	E-116
FUNimation Channel	E-41
Funny or Die	E-116
Fuse	E-41
Fusion	E-41
Future is Now (FIN)	E-116
FX	E-42
FXM	E-42
FXM (See also FX)	E-42
FXNOW	E-42
FXNOW (See also FX)	E-42
FXX	E-42
FXX (See also FX)	E-42
FYI	E-42

G

Gabba Media LLC	E-116
Gaiam TV Fit & Yoga	E-42
GalaVision	E-42
GalaVision (See also Univision)	E-96
GameHD	E-42
GameHD (See also iN DEMAND)	E-50
Game Show Network	E-42
Game Show Network (See also GSN)	E-44
Gammon Miller LLC	E-135
Clifton Gardiner & Co. LLC	E-135
Gari Media Group	E-116
GAS	E-42
GAS (See also TeenNick)	E-85
Gateway Films/Vision Video	E-116
Gavel to Gavel Alaska	E-42
GBTV	E-42
GBTV (See also TheBlaze)	E-87
GCN	E-42
GEB America	E-42
GE Capital Solutions	E-135
Geller Media International	E-143
Gem Shopping Network	E-43
GemsTV	E-43
General Communication Inc.	A-1568
GeoMart	E-143
Georgia Highlands Television (GHTV)	E-43
Georgia Public Broadcasting	E-43
Georgia U.S. Data Services Inc.	E-143
Gerren Entertainment Productions	E-116
getTV	E-43
G.I.G. of North Dakota LLC	A-1568
GLC	E-43
Glendive Broadcasting Corp.	A-1568
Global Christian Network	E-43
Global Christian Network (See also GCN)	E-42
GlobeCast America	E-116
Globo International NY Ltd.	E-117
Glossary of Cable Terms	F-13
GMA Life TV	E-43
GMA Life TV (See also GMA Pinoy TV)	E-43
GMA Pinoy TV	E-43
gmc	E-43
gmc (See also UP)	E-97
gMovies	E-43
GOCOM Media of Illinois LLC	A-1568
God TV	E-43
Golf Channel	E-43
GolTV	E-43
Gabriela Gomez	A-1568
Good Life Broadcasting Inc.	E-117
Mark Gordon Co	E-117
Gorman & Associates	E-143
GoScout Homes	E-44
Gospel Music Channel	E-44
Gospel Music Channel (See also UP)	E-97
Gospel Music TV	E-44
Gospel Music TV (See also Family Friendly Entertainment)	E-35
Gracenote	E-117
Graham Brock Inc.	E-143
Graham Media Group Inc.	A-1568
Granada Media	E-117
Gran Cine	E-44
Granite Broadcasting LLC	A-1568
Sherry Grant Enterprises Inc.	E-117
Gray Television Inc.	A-1568

Index to Contents

GRB Entertainment	E-117
Great American Country	E-44
Great Lakes Data Systems Inc.	E-143
Greek Channel	E-44
Greek Channel (See also New Greek TV)	E-62
Ross Greenburg Productions	E-117
Griffin Communications LLC	A-1569
W.B. Grimes & Co.	E-135
Grit	E-44
GSN	E-44
GTN	E-44
GTN (See also Guardian Television Network)	E-44
Guangdong Southern Television (TVS)	E-44
Guardian Television Network	E-44

H

H2	E-44
H2 (See also Viceland)	E-98
Alfred Haber Distribution Inc.	E-117
Hadden & Associates	E-135
Hallmark Channel	E-44
Hallmark Movies & Mysteries	E-45
Hallmark Movies & Mysteries (See also Hallmark Channel)	E-44
Halogen TV	E-45
Halogen TV (See also Pivot)	E-72
Harmony Gold USA Inc.	E-117
Harpo Productions Inc.	E-117
Hartley Film Foundation Inc.	E-117
Havoc TV	E-45
Hawaii Catholic TV Inc.	A-1569
Hawkeye Network	E-45
Hazardous	E-45
Hazardous (See also NBCSN)	E-63
HBO	E-45
HBO 2	E-45
HBO 2 (See also HBO)	E-45
HBO Comedy	E-45
HBO Comedy (See also HBO)	E-45
HBO en Espanol	E-45
HBO en Espanol (See also HBO Latino)	E-45
HBO Enterprises	E-117
HBO Family	E-45
HBO Family (See also HBO)	E-45
HBO GO	E-45
HBO GO (See also HBO)	E-45
HBO Latino	E-45
HBO Latino (See also HBO)	E-45
HBO Now	E-45
HBO Now (See also HBO)	E-45
HBO on Broadband	E-45
HBO Signature	E-46
HBO Signature (See also HBO)	E-45
HBO Studio Productions	E-117
HBO Zone	E-46
HBO Zone (See also HBO)	E-45
HDNet	E-46
HDNet (See also AXS TV)	E-11
HDNet Movies	E-46
HDNet Movies (See also AXS TV)	E-11
HD Theater	E-46
HD Theater (See also Velocity)	E-98
Headline News	E-46
Headline News (See also HLN)	E-47
Health & Wellness Channel	E-46
HealthiNation	E-46
Health on Demand	E-46
F.P. Healy & Co. Inc.	E-143
Hearst Entertainment Inc.	E-117
Hearst Television Inc.	A-1569, E-117
Hearst Television Inc. (See also Hearst Entertainment Inc)	E-117
Heartland	E-46
Heartland Media LLC	A-1569
Norman Hecht Research Inc.	E-143
Helena Civic Television (HCT)	E-46
Hellerstein & Associates	E-143
Hemisphere Media Holdings LLC	A-1569
Henninger Media Services	E-117
Henson Media Inc.	E-135
Thomas B Henson	A-1569
here! TV	E-46
Heritage Broadcasting Group	A-1569
HERO Broadcasting LLC	A-1569
Heroes & Icons	E-46
HGTV	E-46
R. Miller Hicks & Co.	E-135, E-143
High 4K TV	E-47
High Noon Entertainment	E-117
H. Dean Hinson	A-1569
Hispanic Pay TV Channel	E-47
History	E-47
History en Espanol	E-47
History en Espanol (See also History)	E-47
History International	E-47
History International (See also Viceland)	E-98
The HistoryMakers	E-118
HITN	E-47
HITS (Headend In The Sky)	E-47
HITV Operating Co. Inc.	A-1569
HLN	E-47
HLW International LLP	E-143
Hmong TV Network	E-47
HmongUSA TV	E-47
HMX, El Canal del Hombre	E-47
Hoffman Communications Inc.	E-118
Hoffman-Schutz Media Capital	E-135
Hola! TV	E-47
Hollywood Vaults Inc.	E-118
Holston Valley Broadcasting Corp.	A-1570
Holt Media Group	E-135
Home & Garden Television	E-48
Home & Garden Television (See also HGTV)	E-46
Home Box Office	E-48
Home Box Office (See also HBO)	E-45
Home Shopping Network	E-48
Home Shopping Network (See also HSN)	E-48
Home Shopping Network 2	E-48
Home Shopping Network 2 (See also HSN2)	E-48
Homestead Editorial Inc.	E-118
Homestead Films	E-118
Hope Channel	E-48
Horizon Media Inc.	E-143
Horseshoe Curve Communications LLC	A-1570
HorseTV Channel	E-48
Hot Choice	E-48

2017 Edition

Index to Contents

CABLE & TV STATION COVERAGE
Atlas 2017
The perfect companion to the Television & Cable Factbook
To order call 800-771-9202 or visit www.warren-news.com

HOT TV (History of Television)	E-48
Hour of Harvest Inc.	A-1570
HPC Puckett & Co.	E-135
HRTV	E-48
HSN	E-48
HSN2	E-48
HSN2 (See also HSN)	E-48
HTV	E-48
Hubbard Broadcasting Inc.	A-1570
Hub Network	E-48
Hub Network (See also Discovery Family)	E-28
Hulu	E-48
Hulu Latino	E-48
Hulu Latino (See also Hulu)	E-48
J.C. Humke & Associates Inc.	E-144
Hunan Satellite TV (HTV)	E-48
Hunt Channel	E-49
Hunt Channel (See also Angel Two)	E-9
Hurricane Vision	E-49
Hustler TV	E-49
Hwazan TV	E-49
Hyena Editorial Inc.	E-118

I

IAVC	E-49
ICTV	E-49
ICTV (See also ActiveVideo)	E-139
i-cubed HYPERMEDIA	E-118
IDC Services Inc.	E-144
Idea Channel	E-49
Idea Channel (See also Free To Choose Network)	E-41
iDriveTV	E-49
IFC	E-49
IFC Films	E-118
Iglesia JEMIR	E-49
i-Health	E-49
i-Health (See also ION Life)	E-51
i-Lifetv	E-49
i-Lifetv (See also Pivot)	E-72
Illinois Channel	E-49
iMetro	E-49
iMetro (See also ION Television)	E-51
IMG World	E-118
Impact	E-49
The Impact Network	E-49
Impact Productions	E-118
iN DEMAND	E-50
Independent Communications Inc.	A-1570
Independent Film Channel	E-50
Independent Film Channel (See also IFC)	E-49
Independent Music Network	E-50
Indianapolis Community Television Inc.	A-1570
IndiePlex	E-50
iND PPV en Espanol	E-50
iND PPV en Espanol (See also iN DEMAND)	E-50
Infinito	E-50
InfoMas	E-50
Infonetics Research	E-144

Informa Telecoms & Media	E-144
Infosys Technologies Ltd.	E-144
ING Investment Management	E-135
Initiative Media Worldwide Inc.	E-144
Inmigrante TV	E-50
Insight Research Corp.	E-144
INSP	E-50
Integrated Alliance LP	E-144
Intellicast	E-50
Intellicast (See also The Weather Channel)	E-100
Intermountain West Communications LLC	A-1570
International Contact Inc.	E-118
International Creative Management Inc.	E-144
International Family Television	E-50
International Media Distribution (IMD)	E-118
International Program Consultants Inc.	E-118
International Technology & Trade Associates Inc.	E-144
International Tele-Film	E-118
International Television (ITV)	E-50
IntiNetwork	E-50
Investigation Discovery	E-51
Investigation Discovery (See also Discovery Channel)	E-27
ION Life	E-51
ION Life (See also ION Television)	E-51
ION Media Stations LLC	A-1570
ION Television	E-51
Iowa Communications Network	E-51
I-Play	E-51
I Square Media LLC	A-1571
The Israeli Network	E-51
iSuppli	E-144
Italianation	E-51
It Is Written International Television	E-118
Ivanhoe Broadcast News Inc.	E-118

J

Jade Channel	E-51
Jane.TV	E-51
Janus Films Co.	E-118
JB Broadcasting Inc.	A-1571
JCTV	E-51
JCTV (See also JUCE TV)	E-52
Jewelry Television	E-51
Jewish Broadcasting Service	E-52
The Jewish Channel	E-52
Jewish Life TV	E-52
Jiangsu International Channel	E-52
Jia Yu Channel	E-52
The Jim Henson Company	E-118
JK Investments LLC	A-1571
Johnson Publishing Co. Inc.	E-118
Joint Hometown News Service	E-118
Jones Group Ltd.	E-135
Jones/NCTI	E-144
Jones/NCTI (See also NCTI)	E-146
Jorgenson Broadcast Brokerage Inc.	E-135
David J Joseph	A-1571
JTV	E-52
JTV Direct	E-52
JTV Direct (See also Jewelry Television)	E-51
JUCE TV	E-52
Juicy	E-52
Jump TV	E-119
Jupiter Entertainment	E-119

Index to Contents

Justice Central.TV ... E-52
Justice Network ... E-52

K

Kabillion ... E-52
Kabillion Girls Rule ... E-52
Kabillion Girls Rule (See also Kabillion) ... E-52
kaBOOM! Entertainment Inc. ... E-119
Kalba International Inc. ... E-144
Kalil & Co. Inc. ... E-136
Kamen Entertainment Group Inc. ... E-119
Kane Reece Associates Inc. ... E-136, E-144
Kansas Now 22 ... E-52
Karaoke Channel ... E-52
KAZT LLC ... A-1571
KBS America ... E-53
Kelso Longview Television ... E-53
KEMS ... E-53
Kentucky Educational Television (KET) ... E-53
Kepper, Tupper & Co. ... E-136
KET2 ... E-53
KET2 (See also Kentucky Educational Television (KET)) ... E-53
Ketchikan TV LLC ... A-1571
KETKY ... E-53
KETKY (See also Kentucky Educational Television (KET)) ... E-53
KeyCorp. ... E-136
Killer Tracks: Network Music ... E-119
Kinetic Content ... E-119
King World Productions Inc. ... E-119
King World Productions Inc. (See also listing for CBS Television Distribution) ... E-110
KITV Inc. ... A-1571
Klavo ... E-53
Klein & ... E-119
KLRU Create ... E-53
KLRU Create (See also KLRU-Q) ... E-53
KLRU Q ... E-53
KLRU-TOO ... E-53
KLRU-TOO (See also KLRU Q) ... E-53
KLTV ... E-53
KLTV (See also Kelso Longview Television) ... E-53
KM Communications Inc. ... A-1571
K-MTN Television ... E-53
Knowles Media Brokerage Services ... E-136
Knoxville TV LLC ... A-1571
Edward J. Koplar ... A-1571
Paul H. Koplin ... A-1571
Korean EverRock Multi-Media Service ... E-53
Korean Channel ... E-53
Korean EverRock Multi-Media Service (See also KEMS) ... E-53
Korea One: Chicagoland Korean TV ... E-53
Korea One: Chicagoland Korean TV (See also Washington Korean TV) ... E-99
Kozacko Media Services ... E-136
KSQA LLC ... A-1571
KStateHD.TV ... E-53
KTBS LLC ... A-1571
KTGF License Corp. ... A-1571
KTLA Los Angeles ... E-53
KTV - Kids & Teens Television ... E-54
Kultur International Films Inc. ... E-119
Lara Kunkler ... A-1571
Kunlun Drama ... E-54
KUSA Productions ... E-119
Kushner Locke Co. Inc. ... E-119
KyLinTV ... E-119

Communications Daily
Warren Communications News

Get the industry standard FREE —
For a no-obligation trial call 800-771-9202 or visit www.warren-news.com

L

LA1 ... E-54
La Cadena del Milagro Inc. ... A-1571
La Familia Cosmovision ... E-54
LAFF ... E-54
Lake Superior Community Broadcasting Corp. ... A-1571
Largest U.S. Cable Systems (chart) ... F-2
Latele Novela Network ... E-54
Latham Foundation ... E-119
Latin American Sports ... E-54
Latinoamerica Television ... E-54
Latin World Entertainment ... E-145
LATV ... E-54
Lazard ... E-136
Leftfield Pictures ... E-119
Legacy Broadcasting LLC ... A-1571
Legendary Entertainment ... E-119
Legislative Counsel Bureau - Broadcast and Production Services ... E-54
Lehmann Strobel PC ... E-145
Lyle Leimkuhler ... A-1572
H. Chase Lenfest ... A-1572
LeSEA Broadcasting Corp. ... A-1572
LeSEA Broadcasting Network ... E-54, E-119
LeSEA Broadcasting Network (See also World Harvest Television) ... E-102
Lear Levin Productions Inc. ... E-119
Liberman Broadcasting Inc. ... A-1572
Liberty U. ... A-1572
Life Design TV ... E-54
Life OK ... E-54
Lifestyle Family Television ... E-54
Lifestyle Magazine ... E-119
Lifestyle Network ... E-54
Lifetime ... E-54
Lifetime Movie Network ... E-55
Lifetime Movie Network (See also LMN) ... E-55
Lifetime Real Women ... E-55
Lifetime Real Women (See also LRW) ... E-56
Lilly Broadcasting Holdings LLC ... A-1572
Kevin T. Lilly ... A-1572
Lincoln Broadcasting Co. ... A-1572
Lincoln Square Productions ... E-119
Link TV ... E-55
Linsman Film ... E-119
Lionsgate Entertainment ... E-119
Liquidation Channel ... E-55
Arthur D. Little Inc. ... E-145
Litton Entertainment ... E-120
Live Well Network ... E-55
Living Faith Ministries Inc. ... A-1572
Living Faith Television ... E-55
LMN ... E-55
LMN (See also Lifetime) ... E-54
LNS Captioning ... E-120
Local Cable Weather ... E-55
James L. Lockwood Jr. ... A-1572
LocusPoint Networks LLC ... A-1572
Logic General Inc. ... E-120

2017 Edition xv

Index to Contents

LOGO	E-55
Lo Mejor On Demand	E-55
London Broadcasting Co. LP.	A-1572
Long Communications LLC	A-1572
Longhorn Network	E-55
Look & Co.	E-120
Lottery Channel	E-56
Loud TV	E-120
Louisiana Legislative Network	E-56
Louisiana Television Broadcasting LLC.	A-1572
Low Power Television Stations	B-1
Low Power Television Stations Ownership	B-189
LRW	E-56
LRW (See also Lifetime)	E-54
Paul Lucci	A-1573
Luxe.TV	E-56
LVES-TV	E-56
LWS Local Weather Station	E-56
LX.TV	E-120
Lynx Images Inc.	E-120

M

Macau Asia Satellite TV (MASTV)	E-56
MAC TV	E-56
Madison Dearborn Partners LLC	E-136
Madison Square Garden Network	E-56
Madison Square Garden Network (See also MSG)	E-60
Frank N. Magid Associates Inc.	E-145
Maginglia Media	E-120
Magnetic Image Video	E-145
Mag Rack	E-56
The Mahlman Co.	E-136
Major Market Broadcasting of North Dakota Inc.	A-1573
Maker Studios Inc.	E-120
Malibu Broadcasting LLC	A-1573
Management & Technical Consulting Services	E-139
Manavision3	E-56
Manhan Media Inc.	A-1573
Maranatha Broadcasting Co. Inc.	A-1573
M/A/R/C Research	E-145
Mariavision	E-56
Market Strategies	E-145
Guenter Marksteiner	A-1573
Mark III Media Inc.	A-1573
Marquee Broadcasting Inc.	A-1573
Pluria Marshall Jr.	A-1573
Marsh & McLennan Cos. (MMC)	E-145
Lynn M Martin	A-1573
Maryknoll World Productions	E-120
MasChic	E-56
MasMusica TeVe Network	E-56
Massachusetts Spanish TV Network (MASTV)	E-56
Mauck & Associates Inc.	E-145
Mauna Kea Broadcasting Co Inc.	A-1573
MavTV	E-56
Max GO	E-56
Max GO (See also Cinemax)	E-20
Max Latino	E-57

Max Latino (See also Cinemax)	E-20
Max Media X LLC	A-1573
MaxxSouth Sports	E-57
Maysles Films Inc.	E-120
MBC Action	E-57
MBC Action (See also MBC TV)	E-57
MBC America	E-57
MBCD	E-57
MBC Drama	E-57
MBC Drama (See also MBC America)	E-57
MBC Drama (See also MBC TV)	E-57
MBC Kids	E-57
MBC Kids (See also MBC TV)	E-57
MBC Masr	E-57
MBC Masr (See also MBC TV)	E-57
MBC TV	E-57
MB Revolution LLC	A-1573
MC	E-57
MC-TV	E-57
MCG Capital Corp.	E-136
McGuane Studio Inc.	E-120
MCH Enterprises Inc.	E-136
B.K. McIntyre & Associates	E-145
MC Play	E-57
MC Play (See also MC)	E-57
M/C Venture Partners	E-136
MDTV: Medical News Now	E-57
R.E. Meador & Associates Inc.	E-136
Meadowlane Enterprises Inc.	E-120
Meadows Racing Network	E-57
Meadows Racing Network (See also HRTV)	E-48
Media General Inc.	A-1573
Medialink Worldwide Inc.	E-120
Media Services Group Inc.	E-136
Mediaset Italia	E-57
MediaSpan Online Services	E-145
Media Venture Partners LLC	E-136
Medstar Television Inc.	E-120
Mega TV	E-57
Melli TV	E-58
Melli TV (See also MTC Persian Television)	E-60
Lee Mendelson Film Productions Inc.	E-120
Mercury Broadcasting Co. Inc.	A-1574
Meredith Corp.	A-1574
Meridian Design Associates Architects	E-145
Meruelo Media Holdings	A-1574
MetroChannels	E-58
MetroChannels (See also News 12 Interactive)	E-64
Metro Sports	E-58
Metro Sports (See also Time Warner Cable SportsChannel (Kansas City))	E-90
Metro Sports 2	E-58
Metro Sports 2 (See also Time Warner Cable SportsChannel 2 (Kansas City))	E-89
MeTV	E-58
Mexicanal	E-58
Mexico TV	E-58
MGM Channel	E-58
MGM Television Entertainment Inc.	E-120
MHz Networks	E-58
MHz Worldview	E-58
MHz Worldview (See also MHz Networks)	E-58
Mi Musica	E-58
Miami Station Split Co.	A-1574
Miami TeVe	E-58
Mi Cine	E-58
Micronesia Broadcasting LLC	A-1574
Mid-Atlantic Sports Network (MASN)	E-58
Midco Sports Network	E-58

Index to Contents

Midhudsonmedia	E-145
Mid-State Television Inc.	A-1574
Midwest Christian Television	E-58
Midwest Christian Television (See also MC-TV)	E-57
Midwest Television Inc.	A-1574
Milenio Television	E-58
Milestone Communications Inc.	E-137
Military Channel	E-59
Military Channel (See also American Heroes Channel)	E-8
Military History	E-59
Military History (See also History)	E-47
Warren Miller Entertainment	E-121
Milner-Fenwick Inc.	E-121
Milwaukee Media LLC	A-1574
Minnesota House & Senate Television	E-59
Miramax	E-121
Mira TV	E-59
Mission TV.	E-59
Mission Broadcasting Inc.	A-1575
Mississippi TV LLC	A-1575
The Curators of the U. of Missouri	A-1575
Mitts Telecasting Co. LLC	A-1575
MLB Extra Innings	E-59
MLB Extra Innings (See also MLB Network)	E-59
MLB Network	E-59
MLB Network Strike Zone	E-59
MLB Network Strike Zone (See also MLB Network)	E-59
MLS Direct Kick	E-59
MMMRC LLC	A-1575
MMTC Media & Telecom Brokers	E-137
Mnet	E-59
Mobile Video Tapes Inc.	A-1575
MobiTV Inc.	E-145
Modern Sound Pictures Inc.	E-121
Dan Modisett	A-1575
Moffitt-Lee Productions	E-121
MOFOS	E-59
Mojo HD	E-59
Mojo HD (See also iN DEMAND)	E-50
Mokupuni Television Co. Inc.	A-1575
Momentum	E-59
Monkeyland Audio Inc.	E-121
More MAX	E-59
More MAX (See also Cinemax)	E-20
Jess S. Morgan & Co.	E-121
Morgan Murphy Media	A-1575
Morris Multimedia Inc.	A-1575
Motors TV	E-59
Mountain Broadcasting Corp.	A-1575
Mountain Licenses LP	A-1575
Mount Mansfield Television Inc.	A-1575
The Movie Channel	E-59
The Movie Channel Xtra	E-59
Moviecraft Inc.	E-121
Movie Max	E-59
Movie Max (See also Cinemax)	E-20
MoviePlex	E-60
Movies!	E-60
Movies! Carolina	E-60
MSG	E-60
MSG 3D	E-60
MSG 3D (See also MSG)	E-60
MSG Plus	E-60
MSNBC	E-60
MTC Persian Television	E-60
MTV	E-60
MTV2	E-61
MTV2 (See also MTV)	E-60
MTV Classic	E-61
MTV Classic (See also MTV)	E-60
MTV Hits	E-61
MTV Hits (See also NickMusic)	E-67
MTV Jams	E-61
MTV Jams (See also MTV)	E-60
MTV Live	E-61
MTV Live (See also MTV)	E-60
mtvU	E-61
mtvU (See also MTV)	E-60
Multicom Entertainment Group Inc.	E-121
Multicomm Sciences International Inc.	E-146
Multimedios Television	E-61
Stephen P Mumblow	A-1575
mun2	E-61
mun2 (See also NBC Universo)	E-63
MundoFOX	E-61
MundoFOX (See also MundoMax)	E-61
MundoMax	E-61
Muscular Dystrophy Association	E-121
Music Choice	E-61
Music Choice (See also MC)	E-57
Muzika Pervogo	E-61
My Combat Channel	E-61
My Damn Channel	E-121
MyDestination.TV	E-61
My Family TV	E-61
My Family TV (See also The Family Channel)	E-35
MyFootage.com	E-121
MyMediaBroker.com	E-137
MyNetworkTV	E-61
MYX TV	E-61

N

Nacion TV	E-61
Narrative Television Network	E-61
NASA TV	E-61
NASA TV UHD	E-62
Nat Geo Mundo	E-62
Nat Geo WILD	E-62
Nathan Associates Inc.	E-146
National Captioning Institute	E-121
National City Corp.	E-137
National Council of Churches USA (NCC)	E-121
National Economic Research Associates Inc. (NERA)	E-146
National Film Board of Canada	E-121
National Geographic Channel	E-62
National Geographic Television	E-121
New Greek TV	E-62
National Iranian Television	E-62
National Jewish TV (NJT)	E-62
National Lampoon College Television	E-62
National Technical Information Service	E-121
National TeleConsultants Inc.	E-146
Native American Television	E-146
Navy Office of Information (OI-03)	E-122
NBA League Pass	E-62

Index to Contents

Communications Daily
Warren Communications News

Get the industry standard FREE —
For a no-obligation trial call 800-771-9202 or visit www.warren-news.com

NBA League Pass (See also NBA TV)	E-63
NBA TV	E-63
NBC Deportes	E-63
NBC Deportes (See also Telemundo Deportes)	E-86
NBC News	E-122
NBCSN	E-63
NBC Sports Network	E-63
NBC Sports Network (See also NBCSN)	E-63
NBCUniversal LLC	A-1575
NBC Universo	E-63
NBI Holdings LLC	A-1576
NCTI	E-146
NEO Cricket	E-63
NEON	E-63
NEON (See also Time Warner Cable SportsChannel Ohio)	E-90
NESN	E-63
NESN (See also New England Sports Network)	E-63
NESN National	E-63
NESN National (See also New England Sports Network)	E-63
NESNPlus	E-63
NESNPlus (See also New England Sports Network)	E-63
Netflix	E-63, E-122
Netherlands Consulate General	E-122
New Age Media	A-1576
New Commerce Communications (NCC)	E-137
New England Cable News	E-63
New England Sports Network	E-63
New Evangelization TV	E-64
New Form Digital	E-122
New Life Evangelistic Center Inc.	A-1577
News 8 Austin	E-64
News 8 Austin (See also Time Warner Cable News (Austin))	E-88
News 10 Now	E-64
News 10 Now (See also Time Warner Cable News (Central NY))	E-88
News 12 Bronx	E-64
News 12 Bronx (See also News 12 Interactive)	E-64
News 12 Brooklyn	E-64
News 12 Brooklyn (See also News 12 Interactive)	E-64
News 12 Connecticut	E-64
News 12 Connecticut (See also News 12 Interactive)	E-64
News 12 Hudson Valley	E-64
News 12 Hudson Valley (See also News 12 Interactive)	E-64
News 12 Interactive	E-64
News 12 Long Island	E-64
News 12 New Jersey	E-64
News 12 New Jersey (See also News 12 Interactive)	E-64
News 12 New Jersey en Espanol	E-64
News 12 New Jersey en Espanol (See also News 12 New Jersey)	E-64
News 12 the Bronx en Espanol	E-64
News 12 the Bronx en Espanol (See also News 12 Bronx)	E-64
News 12 Traffic & Weather	E-64
News 12 Traffic & Weather (See also News 12 Interactive)	E-64
News 12 Westchester	E-64
News 12 Westchester (See also News 12 Interactive)	E-64
News 14 Carolina	E-64
News Broadcast Network	E-122
News Channel 3 Anytime	E-64

News Channel 5+	E-65
NewsChannel 8	E-65
Newsday TV	E-65
Newsmax TV	E-65
NewsON	E-65
News on One - WOWT	E-65
News on One - WOWT (See also WOWT 6 News)	E-102
News Plus	E-65
News-Press & Gazette Co.	A-1577
Newswatch 15	E-65
Newsy	E-65
New Tang Dynasty TV	E-65
Newton Media Associates Inc.	E-122
New Visions Syndication	E-122
New York 1 Noticias	E-65
New York 1 Noticias (See also Time Warner Cable News NY1)	E-89
New York Network	E-65
New York Racing Channel	E-65
New York State Assembly Radio Television	E-65
Nexstar Broadcasting Group Inc.	A-1577
NFL Films Inc.	E-122
NFL Network	E-66
NFL RedZone	E-66
NFL RedZone (See also NFL Network)	E-66
NHK World Premium	E-66
NHK World Premium (See also NHK World TV)	E-66
NHK World TV	E-66
NHL Center Ice	E-66
NHL Center Ice (See also NHL Network)	E-66
NHL Network	E-66
Nick 2	E-66
Nick 2 (See also Nickelodeon)	E-66
Nick At Nite	E-66
Nick At Nite (See also Nickelodeon)	E-66
Nickelodeon	E-66
Nick en Espanol	E-67
Nick en Espanol (See also Nickelodeon)	E-66
Nick Jr.	E-67
Nick Jr. (See also Nickelodeon)	E-66
NickMusic	E-67
NickMusic (See also Nickelodeon)	E-66
Nicktoons	E-67
Nicktoons (See also Nickelodeon)	E-66
NickToons en Espanol	E-67
NickToons en Espanol (See also Nicktoons)	E-67
Nielsen Cable TV Household Estimates (chart)	C-10, F-4
Nielsen Geographic Regions Summary (chart)	C-9
Nippon Golden Network	E-67
Nippon Golden Network 2	E-67
Nippon Golden Network 2 (See also Nippon Golden Network)	E-67
Nippon Golden Network 3	E-67
Nippon Golden Network 3 (See also Nippon Golden Network)	E-67
NJTV	E-67
Noggin	E-67
Noggin (See also Nick Jr)	E-67
NoireTV Africa	E-67
Nonstop Network	E-67
Nonstop Network (See also COZI TV)	E-25
Norflicks Productions Ltd.	E-122
Norman Fischer & Associates Inc. (NFA Inc.)	E-137, E-146
Northeast Ohio Network	E-67
Northeast Ohio Network (See also Time Warner Cable SportsChannel (Northeast Ohio))	E-90
Northeast Video Productions	E-122
North Shore-LIJ Health TV	E-67
Northstar Media LLC	A-1577
NorthStar Telesolutions	E-146

xviii   TV & Cable Factbook No. 85

Index to Contents

Northwest Broadcasting Inc.	A-1577
Northwest Cable News	E-67
Norwell Television LLC	A-1577
The NOW Network	E-67
NPM Inc.	A-1578
NRB Network	E-67
NRJ Holdings LLC	A-1578
NRT Communications Group LLC	A-1578
N.S. Bienstock Inc.	E-146
NTDTV	E-67
NTDTV (See also New Tang Dynasty TV)	E-65
NTN24	E-67
NTN Buzztime	E-67
NTV America	E-68
NTV International Corp.	E-122
NUVOtv	E-68
NUVOtv (See also Fuse)	E-41
NW Media	E-122
NY1	E-68
NY1 (See also Time Warner Cable News NY1)	E-89
NY1 Noticias	E-68
NY1 Noticias (See also Time Warner Cable News NY1 Noticias)	E-89
NY1 Rail & Road	E-68

O

Oasis TV	E-68
OC 16	E-68
Ocean Park Pictures Inc.	E-122
Ocean State Networks	E-68
OC Sports	E-68
ODU-TV	E-68
The Office of Communication of The Episcopal Church	E-122
Ogletree Productions	E-122
OGM Production Music	E-122
Ohio Channel	E-68
OKState.TV	E-68
Olelo	E-68
Ole TV	E-68
Olympusat Inc.	E-122
Once TV Mexico	E-68
Once TV Mexico (See also Canal Once)	E-17
One America News Network	E-68
One Caribbean Television	E-68
OneSportsPLUS	E-68
One World Sports	E-69
On The Air Studios	E-122
Open Student Television Network (OSTN)	E-123
Oppenheimer & Co. Inc.	E-137
Opus1 Music Library	E-123
Oral Roberts University	A-1578
Orbita TV	E-69
ORC International	E-146
Oregon Public Affairs Network	E-69
Oregon TV LLC	A-1578
Orion Television	E-123
Orion Television (See also listing for MGM Television Entertainment Inc)	E-120
OTA Broadcasting LLC	A-1578
Oui TV	E-69
Oui TV (See also Afrotainment Plus)	E-7
Outdoor Channel	E-69
Outer Max	E-69
Outer Max (See also Cinemax)	E-20
Outpost Entertainment	E-123
Outside Television	E-69
OUTV	E-69

ADVANCED TV Factbook

FULLY SEARCHABLE • CONTINUOUSLY UPDATED • DISCOUNT RATES FOR PRINT PURCHASERS
For more information call **800-771-9202** or visit **www.warren-news.com**

Ovation	E-69
Ovation Data Services Inc.	E-146
Earl Owensby Studios	E-123
Jim Owens Entertainment Inc.	E-123
Ownership of U.S. Commercial Television Stations	A-1560
OWN: Oprah Winfrey Network	E-70
Oxford Media Group Inc.	A-1578
Oxygen	E-70

P

PAC-12 Arizona	E-70
PAC-12 Arizona (See also PAC-12 Networks)	E-70
PAC-12 Bay Area	E-70
PAC-12 Bay Area (See also PAC-12 Networks)	E-70
PAC-12 Los Angeles	E-70
PAC-12 Los Angeles (See also PAC-12 Networks)	E-70
PAC-12 Mountain	E-70
PAC-12 Mountain (See also PAC-12 Networks)	E-70
PAC-12 Networks	E-70
PAC-12 Now	E-70
PAC-12 Now (See also PAC-12 Networks)	E-70
PAC-12 Oregon	E-70
PAC-12 Oregon (See also PAC-12 Networks)	E-70
PAC-12 Washington	E-70
PAC-12 Washington (See also PAC-12 Networks)	E-70
Pacvia TV	E-70
Raul & Consuelo Palazuelos	A-1578
Palladia	E-70
Palladia (See also MTV Live)	E-61
Pantomime Pictures Inc.	E-123
Parables Television Network	E-70
Paramount Licensing	E-123
Paramount Studios Group	E-123
Paramount Studios Group (See also listing for The Studios at Paramount)	E-127
Paramount Television Group	E-123
Paramount Television Group (See also listing for CBS Television Studios)	E-110
Parent & Satellite TV Stations	C-3
Parker Broadcasting of Colorado Holdco LLC	A-1578
Pasiones	E-70
Pathe News Inc.	E-123
Patrick Communications LLC	E-137, E-146
Patriots On Demand	E-70
Patterson Studios Inc.	E-123
Paulist Productions	E-123
Paxton Media Group Inc.	A-1578
Pay TV & Satellite Services	E-1
PBJ	E-70
PBS HD	E-71
PBS International	E-123
PBS Kids	E-71
PCTV	E-71
PDI Construction	E-146
PeaceTV	E-71
Peacock Productions	E-123
Peckham Productions Inc.	E-123
PegasusTV	E-71
Pennebaker Associates Inc.	E-123
Penn National Racing Alive	E-71

2017 Edition   xix

Index to Contents

Pennsylvania Cable Network	E-71
Penthouse TV	E-71
Peregrine Communications	E-146
Perennial Pictures Film Corp.	E-123
Peru Magico	E-71
Pets.TV	E-71
PFC - O Canal do Futebol	E-71
Phoenix Communications Group Inc.	E-123
Phoenix Entertainment Group	E-123
Phoenix Films & Video	E-123
Phoenix InfoNews	E-71
Phoenix Movies Channel	E-71
Phoenix Movies Channel (See also Phoenix Infonews)	E-71
Phoenix North America Chinese Channel	E-71
Phoenix North America Chinese Channel (See also Phoenix Infonews)	E-71
John Pierce & Co. LLC	E-137
Pikes Peak Community College	E-71
Pilot Productions Inc.	E-123
Pinnacle Media Worldwide	E-147
Pittsburgh Cable News Channel	E-71
Pivot	E-72
PIX11	E-72
Pixar Animation Studios	E-123
Planet Green	E-72
Planet Green (See also Destination America)	E-27
Playboy en Espanol	E-72
Playboy en Espanol (See also Playboy TV)	E-72
Playboy Entertainment Group Inc.	E-123
Playboy TV	E-72
Players Network (PNTV)	E-72
Playgirl TV	E-72
Play-It Productions	E-124
PlayOn! Sports	E-124
Pleasure	E-72
PMCM TV LLC	A-1578
PNC Financial Services Group	E-137
Pohly Co.	E-147
Point of View Productions	E-124, E-147
Poker Central	E-72
PokerTV Network	E-72
Kenneth D. Polin	A-1578
Pollack/Belz Broadcasting Co. LLC	A-1578
Pop	E-72
Popcornflix.com	E-73
Portuguese Channel	E-73
Pottstown Community TV	E-73
Pottstown Community TV (See also PCTV)	E-71
Power Television International LLC	A-1579
PPV En Espanol	E-73
PPV En Espanol (See also iN DEMAND)	E-50
Praise Television	E-73
Presbyterian Church (U.S.A.)	E-124
PriceWaterhouseCoopers (PWC)	E-147
PrideVision TV	E-73
PrideVision TV (See also OutTV)	E-69
Prime Ticket	E-73
Prime Ticket (See also FOX Sports West)	E-40
Prime Time Christian Broadcasting Inc.	A-1579
Production Studio Inc.	E-124
Program Sources & Services	E-105
Promark Television Inc.	E-124
Providence Equity Partners Inc.	E-137
PSSI Global Services/Strategic Television	E-124
Public Interest Video Network	E-73
Puerto Rico Network	E-73
Pulse Films	E-124
Punch TV Network	E-73
Pursuit Channel	E-73
PX TV	E-73
Pyramid Media	E-124

Q

The Quad	E-73
Quality Cable Services Inc.	E-147
Quartet International Inc.	E-124
Qubo	E-73
Que Huong	E-73
Quincy Newspapers Inc.	A-1579
QVC	E-73
QVC Plus	E-74
QVC Plus (See also QVC)	E-73

R

Radar Channel	E-74
Radiant Life Ministries Inc.	A-1579
RAI Italia	E-74
Raleigh Studios	E-124
Ramar Communications Inc.	A-1579
Rancho Palos Verde Broadcasters Inc.	A-1579
R & F Broadcasting	A-1579
Rang-A-Rang Television	E-74
Rapid Broadcasting Co.	A-1579
Raycom Sports Inc.	E-124
Raycom Media Inc.	A-1579
Dana Christian Raymant	A-1579
Stan Raymond & Associates Inc.	E-137
RBC Daniels	E-137
RCH Cable	E-147
RCN Novelas	E-74
RCN Nuestra Tele	E-74
RCN TV	E-74
RCTV International	E-124
RCW Associates	E-147
ReacTV	E-74
Real	E-74
Real Hip-Hop Network	E-74
Reality Kings TV (RKTV)	E-74
Realtor.com Channel	E-74
Recipe.TV	E-74
Red ADvenir	E-74
Red Ryder Enterprises Inc.	E-124
Red River Broadcast Co. LLC	A-1580
Michael Reed	A-1580
Reel Media International	E-124
Reeltime Distributing Corp.	E-124
Reelz	E-75
Regional Music Television	E-75
Regional News Network	E-75
Register Communications Inc., Debtor in Possession	A-1580
Reino Unido TV	E-75
Relativity Media	E-124
Rembrandt Films	E-124
Renegade	E-124

Index to Contents

RetroPlex	E-75
Retro TV Network	E-75
Retro TV Network (See also RTV)	E-77
Revelations Entertainment	E-125
Rev'n	E-75
Revolt TV	E-75
REZN8	E-125
RFD-TV	E-75
RFK Engineering Solutions LLC	E-147
Rhode Island News Channel	E-75
Rhode Island Statewide Interconnect	E-75
Ride TV	E-76
RingSide Creative	E-125
Riot Creative	E-125
Ritmoson	E-76
Ritmoson (See also Univision)	E-96
RKO Pictures	E-125
RLTV	E-76
R News	E-76
R News (See also Time Warner Cable News (Rochester))	E-89
RNL	E-147
Roberts Media LLC	A-1580
Robinson/Jeffrey Associates Inc.	E-137
Rockfleet Broadcasting LP	A-1580
Peter Rodgers Organization	E-125
Roku Channel Store	E-125
Roland Company Inc.	E-125
Root Sports Northwest	E-76
Root Sports Pittsburgh	E-76
Root Sports Rocky Mountain	E-76
Root Sports Southwest	E-76
Root Sports Utah	E-76
Root Sports Utah (See also Root Sports Rocky Mountain)	E-76
Robert Rosenheim Associates	E-125
RSN Resort TV	E-76
RSN Resort TV (See also Outside Television)	E-69
RT America	E-76
RTN	E-76
RTN+	E-76
RTN+ (See also RTN)	E-76
RTP Internacional	E-77
RTP-USA	E-125
RTR Planeta	E-77
RTV	E-77
RTVI	E-77
Rumba TV	E-77
Rumbaut & Company	E-137
Rural TV	E-77
Russian Kino	E-77
Russian Kino (See also TV 1000 Russian Kino)	E-94
Russian Media Group LLC	E-125
Russia Today	E-77
Thomas D. Rutherford	A-1580
RW Productions Inc.	E-125

S

S2One Inc.	E-148
SAB TV	E-77
Safe TV	E-77
Saga Communications Inc.	A-1580
SagamoreHill Broadcasting LLC	A-1580
SagamoreHill Midwest LLC	A-1580
SagamoreHill of Columbus GA LLC	A-1580
Saigon Broadcasting Television Network (SBTN)	E-77
Saigon TV	E-77
Saint Cloud State University Channel	E-77
Saint Johns County Government Television	E-77
Salaam TV	E-77
San Diego News Channel 10	E-78
San Diego News Channel 10 (See also 10 News Channel)	E-6
Sandler Capital Management	E-137
Santiago ROI	E-147
Satterfield & Perry Inc.	E-137
SATV 10 LLC	A-1580
SaudiTV	E-78
SBTN	E-78
SBTN (See also Saigon Broadcasting Television Network)	E-77
Scenic Cable Network & Production	E-125
Schurz Communications Inc.	A-1580
Ernesto Schweikert III	A-1580
Science Channel	E-78
Sci-Fi Channel	E-78
Sci-Fi Channel (See also Syfy)	E-84
Scream Factory	E-125
The E. W. Scripps Co.	A-1580
Seal Rock Broadcasters LLC	A-1581
Seals Entertainment Co. Inc.	E-125
Sear Sound	E-125
SEC Network	E-78
SEC Network+	E-78
SEC Network+ (See also SEC Network)	E-78
Second Generation of Iowa Ltd.	A-1581
Seeso	E-78
Semillitas	E-78
Senal de Vida	E-78
Senal de Vida (See also ULTRA HDPlex)	E-95
SendtoNews	E-125
September Productions	E-125
Serestar Communications Corp.	A-1581
Sesame Workshop	E-125
Setanta Sports USA	E-78
Seventh-Day Adventist Church, Communications Department	E-126
SexSee	E-78
SFM Entertainment	E-126
Shalom TV	E-78
Shalom TV (See also Jewish Broadcasting Service)	E-52
Shanghai Dragon TV	E-78
Shanghai Dragon TV (See also DragonTV)	E-30
SharjahTV	E-78
Timothy G. Sheehan	A-1581
Shenzhen Satellite TV	E-78
Shepherd's Chapel Network	E-78
Burt Sherwood & Associates Inc.	E-138
Shield Media LLC	A-1581
SHO2	E-78
SHO2 (See also Showtime)	E-79
SHO Beyond	E-78
SHO Beyond (See also Showtime)	E-79
SHO Extreme	E-78
SHO Extreme (See also Showtime)	E-79
SHO Next	E-78
SHO Next (See also Showtime)	E-79
Shop at Home	E-78
ShopHQ	E-78

2017 Edition xxi

Index to Contents

ShopHQ (See also EVINE Live)	E-34
ShopNBC	E-78
ShopNBC (See also EVINE Live)	E-34
ShopTV	E-78
Shorteez	E-78
Shorteez (See also Bang U)	E-12
ShortsHD	E-78
Showcase Productions Inc.	E-126
Showcase Productions Inc. (See also Films Around the World Inc)	E-115
SHO Women	E-79
SHO Women (See also Showtime)	E-79
Showplace Television Syndication	E-126
Showtime	E-79
Showtime 2	E-78
Showtime 2 (See also SHO2)	E-78
Showtime Beyond	E-79
Showtime Beyond (See also SHO Beyond)	E-78
Showtime en Espanol	E-79
Showtime en Espanol (See also Showtime)	E-79
Showtime Extreme	E-79
Showtime Extreme (See also SHO Extreme)	E-78
Showtime FamilyZone	E-79
Showtime FamilyZone (See also Showtime)	E-79
Showtime Next	E-79
Showtime Next (See also SHO Next)	E-78
Showtime Showcase	E-79
Showtime Showcase (See also Showtime)	E-79
Showtime Women	E-79
Showtime Women (See also SHO Women)	E-79
Si TV	E-79
Siemens Power Technologies Intl.	E-147
Silverton Broadcasting Co. LLC	A-1581
James F. Simpson	A-1581
Sinclair Broadcast Group Inc.	A-1581
SignaSys Inc.	E-147
Sino TV	E-79
SinoVision	E-79
Sirens Media	E-126
Si TV (See also Fuse)	E-41
Six News Now	E-79
Six News Now (See also SNN: Suncoast News Network)	E-80
SJL of Pennsylvania Inc.	A-1582
The Ski Channel	E-79
Skotleski Productions	E-126
Sky Angel US LLC	E-126
Sky Link TV	E-79
Sky Television LLC	A-1582
Sleuth	E-79
Sleuth (See also cloo)	E-21
Slice	E-79
Smile of a Child TV	E-79
Smith	E-126
Smith & Fisher	E-147
Smithsonian Channel	E-79
Sneak Prevue (See also Pop)	E-72
Sneak Prevue	E-79
SNJ Today	E-79
SNL Financial	E-138
SNN Local News	E-80
SNN Local News (See also SNN: Suncoast News Network)	E-80
SNN: Suncoast News Network	E-80
Snowden Associates	E-138
Softwright LLC	E-147
Somat Publishing Ltd.	E-126
Son Broadcasting	E-80
Son Broadcasting Inc.	A-1582
SonLife Broadcasting Network	E-80
Sonshine Family TV Inc.	A-1582
Sony BMG Music Entertainment	E-126
Sony Entertainment Television Asia	E-80
Sony Movie Channel	E-80
Sony Movie Channel Everywhere	E-80
Sony Movie Channel Everywhere (See also Sony Movie Channel)	E-80
Sony Pictures Television	E-126
SoonerVision	E-80
Sorpresa!	E-80
Sorensen Media Group Inc.	A-1582
Soul of the South Network	E-80
Soundtrack Channel	E-80
The South Carolina Channel	E-80
Southeastern Channel	E-80
Southeastern Ohio Television System	A-1583
Southern Broadcast Corp. of Sarasota	A-1583
Southern TV Corp.	A-1583
Spanish Independent Broadcast Network	E-80
Spanish Broadcasting System (SBS)	E-126
Spanish Broadcasting System Inc.	A-1583
SpanPro Inc.	E-147
Speed	E-80
Speed (See also Fox Sports 1)	E-38
Spice 2	E-80
Spice 2 (See also Bang U)	E-12
Spice	E-80
Spice (See also Brazzers TV)	E-15
Spice Hot	E-81
Spice Hot (See also Reality Kings TV (RKTV))	E-74
Spice: Xcess	E-81
Spice: Xcess (See also MOFOS)	E-59
Spike TV	E-81
Sporting Channel	E-81
SportsChoice	E-81
Sportskool	E-81
The Sportsman Channel	E-81
SportsNet New York	E-81
SportSouth	E-81
SportSouth (See also FOX Sports South)	E-40
Sports PPV	E-81
SportsTime Ohio	E-81
SportsTime Ohio (See also FOX Sports Ohio)	E-39
Sports View Plus	E-81
Sprout	E-81
STAR One	E-82
STAR Chinese Channel	E-82
STAR Gold	E-82
STAR Gold (See also STAR Plus)	E-82
STAR India NEWS	E-82
STAR India NEWS (See also ABP News)	E-6
Star News	E-82
Star News (See also ABP News)	E-6
STAR One (See also Life OK)	E-54
STAR Plus	E-82
Starz	E-82
Starz Cinema	E-82
Starz Cinema (See also Starz)	E-82
Starz Comedy	E-82
Starz Comedy (See also Starz)	E-82

Index to Contents

Starz Edge	E-82
Starz Edge (See also Starz)	E-82
Starz Encore	E-82
Starz Encore Action	E-82
Starz Encore Action (See also Starz Encore)	E-82
Starz Encore Black	E-82
Starz Encore Black (See also Starz Encore)	E-82
Starz Encore Classic	E-82
Starz Encore Classic (See also Starz Encore)	E-82
Starz Encore Espanol	E-82
Starz Encore Espanol (See also Starz Encore)	E-82
Starz Encore Family	E-83
Starz Encore Family (See also Starz Encore)	E-82
Starz Encore Suspense	E-83
Starz Encore Suspense (See also Starz Encore)	E-82
Starz Encore Westerns	E-83
Starz Encore Westerns (See also Starz Encore)	E-82
Starz In Black	E-83
Starz In Black (See also Starz)	E-82
Starz Kids & Family	E-83
Starz Kids & Family (See also Starz)	E-82
Starz Play	E-83
Starz Play (See also Starz)	E-82
State Street Corp.	E-138
Sterling Institute Inc.	E-147
James A. Stern	A-1583
Stevens Design & Animation LLC	E-126
Howard Stirk Holdings LLC	A-1583
Stonegate Capital Group LLC	E-138
Marty Stouffer Productions Ltd.	E-126
Strata Marketing Inc.	E-147
Streampix	E-83
Structural Systems Technology Inc.	E-148
The Studios at Paramount	E-127
STX Entertainment	E-127
Style Network	E-83
Style Network (See also Esquire Network)	E-33
Suddenlink2GO	E-83
Sunbeam Television Corp.	A-1583
Sunbelt-South Telecommunications Ltd.	A-1583
Sunbelt Television Inc.	A-1583
Sun Broadcasting Inc.	A-1583
Sun Channel	E-83
Sundance Select	E-127
Sundance TV	E-83
Sunrise Media LLC	E-127
Sun Sports	E-83
Sun Sports (See also FOX Sports Florida/Sun Sports)	E-38
Super Canal	E-83
Super Canal (See also ULTRA HDPlex)	E-95
Superene	E-83
Superstation WGN	E-83
Superstation WGN (See also WGN America)	E-101
Sur	E-83
The Surf Channel	E-83
Sur Peru	E-83
Sur Peru (See also Sur)	E-83
Swain Film & Video Inc.	E-127
SWRV TV	E-84
SWRV TV (See also MC)	E-57
Syfy	E-84
Syntellect Inc.	E-148
The Syzygy Network	E-84
Szabo Associates Inc.	E-148

T

TAC TV	E-84
TACH-TV	E-84
Taiwan Macroview TV	E-84
Taiwan Macroview TV (See also MAC TV)	E-56
Talkline Communications TV Network	E-84
Tamer Media LLC	A-1583
Tanana Valley Television Co.	A-1583
Tango Traffic	E-84
Tapesh TV	E-84
Sarkes Tarzian Inc.	A-1583
Tavsir Iran	E-84
TBN Enlace USA	E-84
TBN Enlace USA (See also Enlace USA)	E-32
TBN Salsa	E-84
TBS	E-84
TC Specialties	E-148
TCT	E-85
TCT Family	E-85
TCT Family (See also TCT)	E-85
TCT La Fuente	E-85
TCT La Fuente (See also TCT)	E-85
TCT of Michigan Inc.	A-1584
TD Bank	E-138
TeamHD	E-85
TeamHD (See also iN DEMAND)	E-50
Technicolor Inc./CFI	E-127
TeenNick	E-85
TEGNA Inc.	A-1584
Tele Vida Abudante	E-85
Teleadoracion Christian Network Inc.	A-1584
Teleamazonas	E-85
Telecafe	E-85
Telecare	E-85
TeleCentro	E-85
TeleCentro (See also ULTRA HDPlex)	E-95
Telecinco Inc.	A-1584
TeleCom Productions	E-127
Tele El Salvador	E-85
Tele El Salvador (See also ULTRA HDPlex)	E-95
Telefe Internacional	E-85
Telefilm Canada	E-127
TeleFormula	E-85
TeleFutura	E-85
TeleFutura (See also UniMas)	E-96
Telegenic Programs Inc.	E-127
Telehit	E-85
Telehit (See also Univision)	E-96
Telekaribe	E-85
Telemiami	E-85
Telemicro Internacional	E-86
Telemundo	E-86
Telemundo Deportes	E-86
Telemundo Internacional	E-86
Telemundo Internacional (See also Telemundo)	E-86
Telemundo Network Group	E-127
Telemundo Puerto Rico	E-86

2017 Edition   xxiii

Index to Contents

CABLE & TV STATION COVERAGE
Atlas 2017
The perfect companion to the Television & Cable Factbook
To order call 800-771-9202 or visit www.warren-news.com

Telemundo Puerto Rico (See also Telemundo)	E-86
Tele N	E-86
Telenostalgia	E-86
Telephone and Data Systems	A-1584
Telepictures Productions	E-127
TeleRitmo	E-86
Tele-Romantica	E-86
Telestrategies Inc.	E-148
Teletech Communications	E-127
Teletech Inc.	E-148
Televen America	E-86
Televisa	E-127
Television Stations (Commercial)	A-20
Television Station Owners	A-1560
Alabama	A-21
Alaska	A-57
Arizona	A-71
Arkansas	A-99
California	A-122
Colorado	A-215
Connecticut	A-244
Delaware	A-254
District of Columbia	A-258
Florida	A-265
Georgia	A-342
Hawaii	A-380
Idaho	A-404
Illinois	A-419
Indiana	A-458
Iowa	A-492
Kansas	A-517
Kentucky	A-542
Louisiana	A-564
Maine	A-597
Maryland	A-608
Massachusetts	A-619
Michigan	A-638
Minnesota	A-681
Mississippi	A-707
Missouri	A-731
Montana	A-764
Nebraska	A-783
Nevada	A-802
New Hampshire	A-819
New Jersey	A-824
New Mexico	A-837
New York	A-857
North Carolina	A-908
North Dakota	A-948
Ohio	A-969
Oklahoma	A-1011
Oregon	A-1037
Pennsylvania	A-1066
Puerto Rico	A-1456
Rhode Island	A-1107
South Carolina	A-1112
South Dakota	A-1136
Tennessee	A-1154
Texas	A-1190
Utah	A-1310
Vermont	A-1324
Virginia	A-1329
Washington	A-1358
West Virginia	A-1387
Wisconsin	A-1404
Wyoming	A-1441
Guam	A-1454
Virgin Islands	A-1484
Television Korea 24	E-86
Television Market Rankings (Nielsen)	A-1
Television Representatives Inc.	E-127
Television Station Owners	A-1560
Television Stations on Air (Chart)	C-1
Television Stations Public & Educational	A-1492
The Television Syndication Co. Inc.	E-127
TeleXitos	E-87
Telvue Corp.	E-148
Tempo	E-87
TEN	E-87
Ten Cricket	E-87
Tennessee Broadcasting LLC	A-1584
Tennis Channel	E-87
Tennis Channel Plus	E-87
Tennis Channel Plus (See also Tennis Channel)	E-87
TERRITORY	E-127
Texas Channel	E-87
Texas House of Representatives Video/Audio Services	E-87
Texas Television Inc.	A-1584
TFC	E-87
TFC (See also The Filipino Channel)	E-36
The Auto Channel (See also TACH-TV)	E-84
TheBlaze	E-87
TheCoolTV	E-87
The Erotic Network (See also TEN)	E-87
The Learning Channel	E-87
The Learning Channel (See also TLC)	E-90
The Movie Channel (See also Showtime)	E-79
The Movie Channel Xtra (See also The Movie Channel)	E-59
The N	E-87
The N (See also TeenNick)	E-85
The New Encore	E-63
The New Encore (See also Starz Encore)	E-82
Thirteen/WNET	E-127
This TV	E-87
Thomas Broadcasting Co.	A-1584
Thomson Reuters Corp.	E-127
Three Angels Broadcasting Network	E-88
Three Angels Broadcasting Network (See also 3ABN)	E-5
Three Thousand Eight	E-128
Thriller Max	E-88
Thriller Max (See also Cinemax)	E-20
Thunder Bay Broadcasting Corp.	A-1584
TiBA Solutions	E-148
Tigervision	E-88
Timeless Media Group	E-128
Time Warner Cable Community (Socal)	E-88
Time Warner Cable Deportes	E-88
Time Warner Cable News (Antelope Valley)	E-88
Time Warner Cable News (Austin)	E-88
Time Warner Cable News (Brooklyn)	E-88
Time Warner Cable News (Brooklyn) (See also Time Warner Cable News NY1)	E-89
Time Warner Cable News (Buffalo)	E-88
Time Warner Cable News (Capital Region NY)	E-88
Time Warner Cable News (Central NC)	E-88
Time Warner Cable News (Central NY)	E-88
Time Warner Cable News (Charlotte)	E-88

xxiv   TV & Cable Factbook No. 85

Index to Contents

Time Warner Cable News (Coastal NC)	E-88
Time Warner Cable News (Hudson Valley)	E-88
Time Warner Cable News (Hudson Valley) (See also Time Warner Cable News (Capital Region NY))	E-88
Time Warner Cable News (Jamestown)	E-88
Time Warner Cable News (Manhattan)	E-89
Time Warner Cable News (Manhattan) (See also Time Warner Cable News NY1)	E-89
Time Warner Cable News (Northern NY)	E-89
Time Warner Cable News (Northern NY) (See also Time Warner Cable News (Central NY))	E-88
Time Warner Cable News (Queens)	E-89
Time Warner Cable News (Queens) (See also Time Warner Cable News NY1)	E-89
Time Warner Cable News (Rochester)	E-89
Time Warner Cable News (San Antonio)	E-89
Time Warner Cable News (Southern Tier NY)	E-89
Time Warner Cable News (Southern Tier NY) (See also Time Warner Cable News (Central NY))	E-88
Time Warner Cable News (Staten Island)	E-89
Time Warner Cable News (Staten Island) (See also Time Warner Cable News NY1)	E-89
Time Warner Cable News (The Bronx)	E-88
Time Warner Cable News (The Bronx) (See also Time Warner Cable News NY1)	E-89
Time Warner Cable News (Triad NC)	E-89
Time Warner Cable News NY1 Noticias	E-89
Time Warner Cable News NY1 Noticias (See also Time Warner Cable News NY1)	E-89
Time Warner Cable News NY1	E-89
Time Warner Cable Sports 3 Albany	E-89
Time Warner Cable Sports 3 Albany (See also Time Warner Cable SportsChannel (Albany))	E-89
Time Warner Cable Sports Central New York	E-89
Time Warner Cable Sports Central New York (See also Time Warner Cable SportsChannel (Syracuse))	E-90
Time Warner Cable SportsChannel (Albany)	E-89
Time Warner Cable SportsChannel (Austin)	E-89
Time Warner Cable SportsChannel (Buffalo)	E-89
Time Warner Cable SportsChannel (Columbia)	E-89
Time Warner Cable SportsChannel (Columbia) (See also Time Warner Cable SportsChannel (Eastern North Carolina))	E-89
Time Warner Cable SportsChannel (Dallas)	E-89
Time Warner Cable SportsChannel (Eastern North Carolina)	E-89
Time Warner Cable SportsChannel (Green Bay)	E-89
Time Warner Cable SportsChannel (Green Bay) (See also Time Warner Cable SportsChannel (Milwaukee))	E-90
Time Warner Cable SportsChannel (Kansas City)	E-90
Time Warner Cable SportsChannel (Lincoln)	E-90
Time Warner Cable SportsChannel (Mid Ohio)	E-90
Time Warner Cable SportsChannel (Mid Ohio) (See also Time Warner Cable SportsChannel (Northeast Ohio))	E-90
Time Warner Cable SportsChannel (Milwaukee)	E-90
Time Warner Cable SportsChannel (Northeast Ohio)	E-90
Time Warner Cable SportsChannel (Rochester)	E-90
Time Warner Cable SportsChannel (Southwest Ohio)	E-90
Time Warner Cable SportsChannel (Southwest Ohio) (See also Time Warner Cable SportsChannel (Northeast Ohio))	E-90
Time Warner Cable SportsChannel (Syracuse)	E-90
Time Warner Cable SportsChannel (Western North Carolina)	E-90
Time Warner Cable SportsChannel (Western North Carolina) (See also Time Warner Cable SportsChannel (Eastern North Carolina))	E-89
Time Warner Cable SportsChannel Wisconsin	E-90
Time Warner Cable SportsChannel Wisconsin (See also Time Warner Cable SportsChannel (Milwaukee))	E-90
Time Warner Cable SportsChannel 2 (Kansas City)	E-89
Time Warner Cable SportsNet	E-90
Time Warner Cable SportsNet Buffalo	E-90
Time Warner Cable SportsNet Buffalo (See also Time Warner Cable SportsChannel (Buffalo))	E-89
Time Warner Cable SportsNet LA	E-90
Time Warner Cable SportsNet Rochester	E-90
Time Warner Cable SportsNet Rochester (See also Time Warner Cable SportsChannel (Rochester))	E-90
Time Warner Inc.	A-1584
Tivi5MONDE	E-90
TKMI Broadcasting	E-90
TLC	E-90
Total Living Network	E-91
TMC	E-91
TMC (See also The Movie Channel)	E-59
TMC Xtra	E-91
TMC Xtra (See also The Movie Channel Xtra)	E-59
TM Studios	E-128
TNN (The Nashville Network)	E-91
TNN (The Nashville Network) (See also Heartland)	E-46
Turner Network Television	E-91
Today Video	E-128
Tokyo TV	E-91
Too Much for TV On Demand	E-91
Too Much for TV On Demand (See also iN DEMAND)	E-50
Toon Disney	E-91
Toon Disney (See also Disney XD)	E-29
TOP Channel TV	E-91
Top Kopy	E-128
Torstar Media Group Television (Toronto Star TV)	E-91
Touchstone Pictures/Walt Disney	E-128
Touchstone Television	E-128
Touchstone Television (See also listing for ABC Studios)	E-105
Tougaloo College	A-1585
Towers Watson	E-148
Tr3s	E-91
Tr3s (See also MTV)	E-60
Trace Sport Stars	E-91
Transcomm Inc.	E-148
Trans World International	E-128
Trans World International (See also listing for IMG World)	E-118
Travel Channel	E-91
Travel Channel Beyond	E-91
Travel Channel Beyond (See also Travel Channel)	E-91
Travel on Demand	E-91
Travelview International	E-128
Travel Weather Now	E-91
Travel Weather Now (See also Bright House Travel Weather Now)	E-16
Triangle Inc.	E-128
Tribeca Film Center	E-128
Tribune Broadcasting Co.	A-1585
Tribune Media Services Inc.	E-128
Tribune Media Services Inc. (See also Gracenote)	E-117
Trimark Television	E-128
Trimark Television (See also listing for Lionsgate Entertainment)	E-119
Trinity Broadcasting Network (TBN)	E-91
Trinity Broadcasting Network Inc.	A-1585
Tristar Television	E-128
Tristar Television (See also listing for Sony Pictures Television)	E-126
Tri-State Christian Television	E-92
Tri-State Christian Television (See also TCT)	E-85
Tri-State Christian TV Inc.	A-1585
Tri-State Family Broadcasting Inc.	A-1585
Trojan Vision	E-92
Troma Entertainment Inc.	E-128
True Blue	E-92
truTV	E-92

Index to Contents

FULLY SEARCHABLE • CONTINUOUSLY UPDATED • DISCOUNT RATES FOR PRINT PURCHASERS
For more information call 800-771-9202 or visit www.warren-news.com

TTV Capital	E-138
Benjamin A Tucker	A-1585
TUFF TV	E-92
Tu Ingles TV	E-92
John B Tupper	A-1585
Turner Broadcasting System Inc.	E-128
Turner Classic Movies	E-92
Turner Network Television (See also TNT)	E-92
TNT	E-92
Turner South	E-93
Turner South (See also SportSouth)	E-81
Turner Sports	E-128
TV2	E-93
TV5, La Television International	E-93
TV5MONDE USA	E-93
TV 1000 Russian Kino	E-94
TV Agro	E-93
TV Asia	E-93
TVC+ Latino	E-93
TV Chile	E-93
TV Chile (See also ULTRA HDPlex)	E-95
TV Colombia	E-93
TV Colombia (See also RCN Nuestra Tele)	E-74
Television Dominicana	E-93
TVE Internacional	E-93
TV Globo Internacional	E-93
TVGN	E-93
TVGN (See also Pop)	E-72
TVG Network	E-93
TV Guide Interactive Inc.	E-93
TV Guide Network	E-93
TV Guide Network (See also Pop)	E-72
TV Households by State and County (chart)	C-12
TVHS	E-93
Tvidavision	E-94
TV Japan	E-94
TVK2	E-94
TVK2 (See also TVK (Korean)	E-94
TVK (Korean)	E-94
TVK Pop on Demand	E-94
TVK Pop on Demand (See also TVK (Korean)	E-94
TV Land	E-94
TV Mex	E-94
TVO	E-128
TV One	E-94
TV Orient	E-95
TVP Info	E-95
TVP Info (See also TV Polonia)	E-95
TV Polonia	E-95
TV Record	E-95
TV Romania International	E-95
TV Venezuela	E-95
TVW	E-95
TW3	E-95
TW3 (See also Time Warner Cable Sports 3 Albany)	E-89
TWC TV New England	E-95
Twentieth Century Fox Film Corp.	E-128
Twentieth Century Fox Home Entertainment	E-129
Twentieth Century Fox Television	E-129
Twentieth Television	E-129
TyC Sports	E-95
Tyler Media LLC	A-1585

U

UBC-TV Network	E-95
UCTV	E-95
UHD-1	E-95
Ronald Ulloa	A-1585
Ultra Cine	E-95
Ultra Cine (See also ULTRA HDPlex)	E-95
Ultra Clasico	E-95
Ultra Clasico (See also ULTRA HDPlex)	E-95
Ultra Docu	E-95
Ultra Docu (See also ULTRA HDPlex)	E-95
Ultra Familia	E-95
Ultra Familia (See also ULTRA HDPlex)	E-95
Ultra Fiesta	E-95
Ultra Fiesta (See also ULTRA HDPlex)	E-95
Ultra Film	E-95
Ultra Film (See also ULTRA HDPlex)	E-95
ULTRA HDPlex	E-95
Ultra Kidz	E-95
Ultra Kidz (See also ULTRA HDPlex)	E-95
Ultra Luna	E-95
Ultra Luna (See also ULTRA HDPlex)	E-95
Ultra Macho	E-96
Ultra Macho (See also ULTRA HDPlex)	E-95
Ultra Mex	E-96
Ultra Mex (See also ULTRA HDPlex)	E-95
Ultra Tainment	E-96
Ultra Tainment (See also ULTRA HDPlex)	E-95
UniMas	E-96
UniMas (See also Univision)	E-96
Unique Business News	E-96
Unique Satellite TV	E-96
United Church of Christ, Office of Communications	E-129
United Communications Corp.	A-1585
United Film Enterprises Inc.	E-129
United Methodist Communications	E-129
United Nations	E-129
United Nations (See also listing for UN Multimedia)	E-130
United Press International	E-129
United Recovery Systems	E-148
Universal Cable Productions	E-129
Universal HD	E-96
Universal Music Publishing Group (UMPG)	E-129
Universal Television	E-129
Board of Trustees, U. of Alabama	A-1586
University of California TV (UCTV)	E-96
University of Southern California: Hugh M. Hefner Moving Image Archive	E-129
Univision	E-96
Univision Communications Inc.	A-1586
Univision Deportes	E-96
Univision Deportes (See also Univision)	E-96
Univision Deportes Dos	E-96
Univision Deportes Dos (See also Univision Deportes)	E-96
Univision Story House	E-130
Univision Studios	E-130
Univision tdn	E-96
Univision tdn (See also Univision Deportes)	E-96
Univision tlnovelas	E-96
Univision tlnovelas (See also Univision)	E-96
UN Multimedia	E-130
Untamed Sports TV	E-96

Index to Contents

Unum Provident Corp.	E-138
Unusual Films	E-130
UP	E-97
UPA Productions of America	E-130
Upliftv	E-97
Urban Movie Channel	E-97
USA 800 Inc.	E-148
USA Network	E-97
USA Now	E-97
USA Now (See also USA Network)	E-97
USA Television Holdings LLC	A-1587
U.S. Department of Agriculture, Office of Communications	E-130
U.S. Department of Commerce	E-148
U.S. Military TV Network	E-97
Utilisima	E-97
Utilisima (See also Fox Life)	E-37
UVideos	E-97
Valuation Research Corp.	E-138
VAN-TV	E-97
Varvid Inc.	E-148
VasalloVision Network	E-98

V

Thomas J Vaughan	A-1587
T.J. Vaughan & Associates	E-148
VaVoom	E-98
VCY America Inc.	A-1587
Velocity	E-98
VeneMovies	E-98
VeneMovies (See also ViendoMovies)	E-98
Venevision International Inc.	E-130
Venevision International Inc. (See also Cisneros Media Distribution)	E-111
Venevision Productions	E-130
Venture Technologies Group LLC	A-1587
Veria Living	E-98
Veria Living (See also Z Living)	E-104
Veritas Productions Inc.	E-130
Veronis Suhler Stevenson	E-138
Versus	E-98
Versus (See also NBCSN)	E-63
Vertigo Productions	E-130
VH1	E-98
VH1 Classic	E-98
VH1 Classic (See also MTV)	E-60
VH1 Country	E-98
VH1 Country (See also CMT Pure Country)	E-21
VH1 Soul	E-98
VH1 Soul (See also BET)	E-13
Viacom Inc.	E-130
Vice	E-130
Viceland	E-98
Victory Studios	E-130
Victory Television Network Inc.	A-1587
Vida Vision	E-98
VidCAD	E-148
Video Mix TV	E-98
Video Zona TV	E-98
Video-Cinema Films Inc.	E-130
Video Enterprises Inc.	E-130
Video Express Productions	E-130
Video/Fashion Network	E-130
Video Music Club	E-98
Video Music Club (See also VMC)	E-99
VideoRola	E-98
ViendoMovies	E-98

Communications Daily
Warren Communications News

Get the industry standard FREE —
For a no-obligation trial call 800-771-9202 or visit www.warren-news.com

Vietnamese American Network Television	E-98
Vietnamese American Network Television (See also VAN-TV)	E-97
VIP 2000	E-130
Viratech.org	E-130
Vision Communications LLC (New York)	A-1587
VisLink Services	E-148
Vista Street Entertainment	E-130
VITAC	E-130
Viva Television Network	E-98
Viva Television Network (See also Vme TV)	E-99
VividTV	E-98
VMC	E-99
Vme Kids	E-99
Vme TV	E-99
Vozzcom Inc.	E-149
Vremya	E-99
VRV	E-99
V-Soft Communications	E-149
VStv	E-99
Vubiquity Inc.	E-130
VUDU	E-99
VU Television Network	E-99

W

Wachovia Corp.	E-138
Waitt Broadcasting Inc.	A-1587
TheWalktv	E-99
Wallach Entertainment	E-131
Waller Capital Partners	E-138
WALN Cable Radio	E-99
Walt Disney Animation Studios	E-131
Walt Disney Pictures	E-131
Walt Disney Studios	E-131
Walters-Storyk Design Group Inc.	E-149
WAM! America's Kidz Network	E-99
WAM! America's Kidz Network (See also Starz Encore Family)	E-83
WAPA America	E-99
Warner Bros. Animation Inc.	E-131
Warner Bros. Digital Networks	E-131
Warner Bros. Domestic Television Distribution	E-131
Warner Bros. International Television Distribution	E-131
Warner Bros. Pictures	E-131
Warner Bros. Pictures Domestic Distribution	E-131
Warner Bros. Pictures International	E-131
Warner Bros. Television Group	E-131
Warner Home Video	E-131
Warner Independent Pictures	E-131
Warren & Morris Ltd.	E-149
Frank Washington	A-1587
Washington Korean TV	E-99
WATCH ABC Family	E-99
WATCH ABC Family (See also WATCH Freeform)	E-100
WATCH Disney Channel	E-99
WATCH Disney Channel (See also Disney Channel)	E-28
WATCH Disney Junior	E-99
WATCH Disney Junior (See also Disney Channel)	E-28
WATCH Disney XD	E-100
WATCH Disney XD (See also Disney Channel)	E-28

2017 Edition xxvii

Index to Contents

CABLE & TV STATION COVERAGE
Atlas 2017
The perfect companion to the Television & Cable Factbook
To order call 800-771-9202 or visit www.warren-news.com

WATCH ESPN	E-100
WATCH ESPN (See also ESPN)	E-32
WATCH Food Network	E-100
WATCH Food Network (See also Food Network)	E-36
WATCH Freeform	E-100
WATCH Freeform (See also Freeform)	E-40
WATCH TBS	E-100
WATCH TBS (See also TBS)	E-84
WATCH TCM	E-100
WATCH TCM (See also Turner Classic Movies)	E-92
WATCH TNT	E-100
WATCH TNT (See also TNT)	E-92
WATCH truTV	E-100
WATCH truTV (See also truTV)	E-92
Waterman Broadcasting Corp.	A-1587
Waypoint Media	A-1587
WBHQ Columbia LLC	A-1587
WBIN Inc.	A-1587
WCTY Channel 16	E-100
The Weather Channel	E-100
WeatherNation	E-100
Weather Network	E-100
Weathernews Inc.	E-131
Weatherscan	E-100
WeatherVision	E-131
Weber Shandwick	E-149
Weigel Broadcasting Co.	A-1587
Evan Weiner Productions	E-131
Wells Fargo Securities LLC	E-138
West American Finance Corp.	A-1587
Westchester Films	E-132
Western Broadcasting Corp. of Puerto Rico	A-1587
Western New Life Inc.	A-1588
Western Pacific Broadcast LLC	A-1588
Weston Woods Studios Inc.	E-132
West Virginia Media Holdings LLC	A-1588
WETA UK	E-101
WE tv	E-101
WGN	E-101
WGN America	E-101
WGN (See also WGN America)	E-101
WHDH LLC	A-1588
Wheeler Broadcasting LLC.	A-1588
WheelsTV	E-101
White Knight Holdings Inc.	A-1588
Wicked On Demand	E-101
WideOrbit	E-149
Wilderness Communications LLC	A-1588
Wild TV	E-101
William Morris Endeavor Entertainment	E-149
Williams Communications Inc.	E-149
Willow	E-101
WINK News Now 24/7	E-101
Winston Broadcasting Network Inc.	A-1588
WisconsinEye	E-101
Dana R. Withers	A-1588
WizeBuys TV	E-101
WKTV	E-102
WKYT-TV	E-102

Jason Wolff	A-1588
Woods Communications Corp.	A-1588
Word Broadcasting Network Inc.	A-1588
The Word Network	E-102
Word of God Fellowship Inc.	A-1588
The Works	E-102
World	E-102
World Class Video	E-132
World Fishing Network	E-102
World Harvest Television	E-102
World of Wonder Productions	E-132
World Picks On Demand (Hindi, Latino, Mandarin, Russian)	E-102
World Property Channel	E-132
Worldwide Entertainment Corp.	E-132
World Wrestling Entertainment Inc.	E-132
Worship Network	E-102
WOWT 6 News	E-102
WPA Film Library	E-132
WQED Multimedia	E-132
WRNN-TV Associates LP	A-1589
WRS Motion Picture & Video Laboratory	E-132
WSI Corp.	E-149
WTTW Local Productions	E-132
WTTW National Productions	E-132
WWE Network	E-102
Wyomedia Corp.	A-1589

X

Xfinity on Demand	E-102
XHIJ-TV	E-102
XHIJ-TV (See also Canal 44 (XHIJ-TV)	E-16
Xiamen TV	E-102
XTSY	E-103
XTV	E-103

Y

Yangtse River Drama	E-103
Yankees Entertainment & Sports	E-103
Yankees Entertainment & Sports (See also YES Network)	E-103
YES2	E-103
YES2 (See also YES Network)	E-103
YES Network	E-103
Yesterday USA	E-103
YNN (Capital Region & Hudson Valley, NY) (See also Time Warner Cable News (Capital Region) & Time Warner Cable News (Hudson Valley)	E-88
YNN (Central, Northern & Southern Tier, NY) (See also Time Warner Cable News (Central NY), (Northern NY) & (Southern Tier NY)	E-88
YNN Austin	E-103
YNN Austin (See also Time Warner Cable News (Austin)	E-88
YNN (Capital Region & Hudson Valley, NY)	E-103
YNN (Central, Northern & Southern Tier, NY)	E-103
YNN Rochester	E-103
YNN Rochester (See also Time Warner Cable News (Rochester)	E-89
Jim Young & Associates Inc.	E-149
Youtoo America	E-103
YouTube	E-132
Yuma 77	E-103

Z

Zeebox	E-132
Zeebox (See also Beamly)	E-108
Zee Business	E-103
Zee Business (See also Zee TV)	E-103

Index to Contents

Zee Cinema.	E-103
Zee Cinema (See also Zee TV)	E-103
Zee Kannada	E-103
Zee Marathi.	E-103
Zee Marathi (See also Zee TV)	E-103
Zee Punjabi.	E-103
Zee Smile.	E-103
Zee Smile (See also Zee TV)	E-103
Zee TV.	E-103
ZGS Broadcasting Holdings Inc.	A-1589
Zhejiang TV.	E-104
Zhong Tian Channel.	E-104
Zhong Tian Channel (See also CTI-Zhong Tian)	E-26
Zing Networks Ltd.	E-104
Z Living.	E-104
Z Living Go	E-104
Z Living Go (See also Z Living)	E-104
ZoneTV.	E-104
ZUUS Country	E-104
ZUUS Country (See also The Country Network)	E-24

Communications Daily

Warren Communications News

Get the industry standard FREE —
For a no-obligation trial call 800-771-9202 or visit www.warren-news.com

Subscription pays for itself in just a few searches

Now you can access the entire contents of the Television & Cable Factbook instantly on your desktop or any Internet connection.

Your subscription to the *Advanced TV Factbook* online will provide you with access to over 1 million detailed records. Best of all, the database is continuously updated to ensure you always have the most current industry intelligence.

Save enormous amounts of time, effort & money

The user-friendly query interface allows you to perform fully customized data searches—so you can retrieve data in a number of ways, tailored to your precise needs. The search options are extensive and flexible, and will save you hours and hours of cumbersome research time.

You'll <u>recover your subscription cost after just a few searches</u> and continue to save enormous amounts of time, money and effort with every search.

See for yourself— take a risk free 7-day trial

Take a FREE 7-day trial —
See for yourself why the *Advanced TV Factbook* online is referred to as "an invaluable reference tool."

Sign up at **www.warren-news.com/factbookonline.htm**
You have **nothing to lose** and lots of time and money to save.

Continuously Updated • Easy Internet Access • Fully Searchable

U.S. Television Stations by Call Letters
As of October 1, 2016

Operating stations only. Dagger (†) indicates Non-Commercial/Educational station.
Asterisk (*) indicates operating construction permit.
Please refer to the Advanced TV & Cable Factbook ONLINE (www.advancedtvfactbook.com) for the most current information.

K

KAAH-TV (27) — Honolulu, HI		p. A-386
KAAL (36) — Austin, MN		p. A-685
KAAS-TV (17) — Salina, KS		p. A-533
KABB (30) — San Antonio, TX		p. A-1287
KABC-TV (7) — Los Angeles, CA		p. A-151
KABY-TV (9) — Aberdeen, SD		p. A-1137
† KACV-TV (9) — Amarillo, TX		p. A-1549
KADN-TV (16) — Lafayette, LA		p. A-575
KAEF-TV (22) — Arcata, CA		p. A-125
† KAET (8) — Phoenix, AZ		p. A-1494
† KAFT (9) — Fayetteville, AR		p. A-1495
† KAID (21) — Boise, ID		p. A-1507
KAII-TV (7) — Wailuku, HI		p. A-398
KAIL (7) — Fresno, CA		p. A-145
KAIT (8) — Jonesboro, AR		p. A-111
KAJB (36) — Calipatria, CA		p. A-133
KAKE (10) — Wichita, KS		p. A-538
† KAKM (8) — Anchorage, AK		p. A-1493
KAKW-DT (13) — Killeen, TX		p. A-1259
KALB-TV (35) — Alexandria, LA		p. A-566
† KALO (38) — Honolulu, HI		p. A-1506
KAMC (27) — Lubbock, TX		p. A-1266
KAME-TV (20) — Reno, NV		p. A-813
KAMR-TV (19) — Amarillo, TX		p. A-1196
† KAMU-TV (12) — College Station, TX		p. A-1550
KAPP (14) — Yakima, WA		p. A-1384
KARD (36) — West Monroe, LA		p. A-595
KARE (11) — Minneapolis, MN		p. A-694
KARK-TV (32) — Little Rock, AR		p. A-113
KARZ-TV (44) — Little Rock, AR		p. A-114
KASA-TV (27) — Santa Fe, NM		p. A-854
KASN (39) — Pine Bluff, AR		p. A-118
KASW (49) — Phoenix, AZ		p. A-79
KASY-TV (45) — Albuquerque, NM		p. A-838
KATC (28) — Lafayette, LA		p. A-576
KATN (18) — Fairbanks, AK		p. A-64
KATU (43) — Portland, OR		p. A-1056
KATV (22) — Little Rock, AR		p. A-115
KAUT-TV (40) — Oklahoma City, OK		p. A-1018
KAUZ-TV (22) — Wichita Falls, TX		p. A-1306
KAVU-TV (15) — Victoria, TX		p. A-1300
† KAWB (28) — Brainerd, MN		p. A-1523
† KAWE (9) — Bemidji, MN		p. A-1523
KAYU-TV (28) — Spokane, WA		p. A-1374
KAZA-TV (47) — Avalon, CA		p. A-126
KAZD (39) — Lake Dallas, TX		p. A-1260
† KAZQ (17) — Albuquerque, NM		p. A-1531
KAZT-TV (7) — Phoenix, AZ		p. A-80
KBAK-TV (33) — Bakersfield, CA		p. A-127
KBCA (41) — Alexandria, LA		p. A-567
KBCB (19) — Bellingham, WA		p. A-1362
KBCW (45) — San Francisco, CA		p. A-188
† KBDI-TV (13) — Broomfield, CO		p. A-1498
KBEH (24) — Oxnard, CA		p. A-167
KBFD-DT (33) — Honolulu, HI		p. A-387
† KBGS-TV (16) — Billings, MT		p. A-1526
† KBHE-TV (26) — Rapid City, SD		p. A-1547
KBIM-TV (10) — Roswell, NM		p. A-850
† KBIN-TV (33) — Council Bluffs, IA		p. A-1511
KBJR-TV (19) — Superior, WI		p. A-1437
KBLN-TV (30) — Grants Pass, OR		p. A-1047
KBLR (40) — Paradise, NV		p. A-812
† KBME-TV (22) — Bismarck, ND		p. A-1536
KBMT (12) — Beaumont, TX		p. A-1207
KBMY (17) — Bismarck, ND		p. A-949
KBOI-TV (9) — Boise, ID		p. A-405
KBRR (10) — Thief River Falls, MN		p. A-705
KBSD-DT (6) — Ensign, KS		p. A-521
KBSH-DT (7) — Hays, KS		p. A-526
KBSI (22) — Cape Girardeau, MO		p. A-733
KBSL-DT (10) — Goodland, KS		p. A-524
† KBSV (15) — Ceres, CA		p. A-1496
† KBTC-TV (27) — Tacoma, WA		p. A-1556
KBTV-TV (40) — Port Arthur, TX		p. A-1281
KBTX-TV (50) — Bryan, TX		p. A-1213
KBVO (27) — Llano, TX		p. A-1263
KBVU (28) — Eureka, CA		p. A-141
† KBYU-TV (44) — Provo, UT		p. A-1552
KBZK (13) — Bozeman, MT		p. A-768
KCAL-TV (9) — Los Angeles, CA		p. A-152
KCAU-TV (9) — Sioux City, IA		p. A-512
KCBA (13) — Salinas, CA		p. A-180
KCBD (11) — Lubbock, TX		p. A-1267
KCBS-TV (43) — Los Angeles, CA		p. A-153
KCBY-TV (11) — Coos Bay, OR		p. A-1041
KCCI (8) — Des Moines, IA		p. A-503
KCCO-TV (7) — Alexandria, MN		p. A-683
KCCW-TV (12) — Walker, MN		p. A-706
KCDO-TV (23) — Sterling, CO		p. A-243
† KCDT (45) — Coeur d'Alene, ID		p. A-1507
KCEB (26) — Longview, TX		p. A-1264
KCEC (26) — Denver, CO		p. A-222
KCEN-TV (9) — Temple, TX		p. A-1296
† KCET (28) — Los Angeles, CA		p. A-1496
KCFW-TV (9) — Kalispell, MT		p. A-778
† KCGE-DT (16) — Crookston, MN		p. A-1523
KCHF (10) — Santa Fe, NM		p. A-855
KCIT (15) — Amarillo, TX		p. A-1197
† KCKA (19) — Centralia, WA		p. A-1555
KCLO-TV (15) — Rapid City, SD		p. A-1144
KCNC-TV (35) — Denver, CO		p. A-223
KCNS (39) — San Francisco, CA		p. A-189
KCOP-TV (13) — Los Angeles, CA		p. A-154
† KCOS (13) — El Paso, TX		p. A-1550
KCOY-TV (19) — Santa Maria, CA		p. A-206
KCPM (27) — Grand Forks, ND		p. A-959
KCPQ (13) — Tacoma, WA		p. A-1380
† KCPT (18) — Kansas City, MO		p. A-1526
KCRA-TV (35) — Sacramento, CA		p. A-175
KCRG-TV (9) — Cedar Rapids, IA		p. A-497
† KCSD-TV (24) — Sioux Falls, SD		p. A-1547
KCSG (14) — Cedar City, UT		p. A-1311
† KCSM-TV (43) — San Mateo, CA		p. A-1498
† KCTS-TV (9) — Seattle, WA		p. A-1556
KCTV (24) — Kansas City, MO		p. A-742
KCVU (20) — Paradise, CA		p. A-170
† KCWC-DT (8) — Lander, WY		p. A-1558
KCWE (31) — Kansas City, MO		p. A-743
KCWI-TV (23) — Ames, IA		p. A-494
KCWV (27) — Duluth, MN		p. A-688
KCWX (5) — Fredericksburg, TX		p. A-1242
KCWY-DT (12) — Casper, WY		p. A-1442
KCWY-DT (12) — Casper, WY		p. A-1442
KDAF (32) — Dallas, TX		p. A-1222
KDBC-TV (18) — El Paso, TX		p. A-1231
† KDCK (21) — Dodge City, KS		p. A-1512
KDCU-DT (31) — Derby, KS		p. A-520
KDEN-TV (29) — Longmont, CO		p. A-239
KDFI (36) — Dallas, TX		p. A-1223
KDFW (35) — Dallas, TX		p. A-1224
† KDIN-TV (11) — Des Moines, IA		p. A-1511
KDKA-TV (25) — Pittsburgh, PA		p. A-1092
KDKF (29) — Klamath Falls, OR		p. A-1048
KDLH (33) — Duluth, MN		p. A-689
KDLO-TV (3) — Florence, SD		p. A-1138
KDLT-TV (47) — Sioux Falls, SD		p. A-1149
KDLV-TV (26) — Mitchell, SD		p. A-1142
KDMD (33) — Anchorage, AK		p. A-58
KDMI (19) — Des Moines, IA		p. A-504
KDNL-TV (31) — St. Louis, MO		p. A-758
KDOC-TV (32) — Anaheim, CA		p. A-124
KDOR-TV (17) — Bartlesville, OK		p. A-1014
KDRV (12) — Medford, OR		p. A-1051
† KDSD-TV (17) — Aberdeen, SD		p. A-1546
† KDSE (9) — Dickinson, ND		p. A-1536
KDSM-TV (16) — Des Moines, IA		p. A-505
† KDTN (43) — Denton, TX		p. A-1550
† KDTP (11) — Holbrook, AZ		p. A-1494
KDTV-DT (51) — San Francisco, CA		p. A-190
KDTX-TV (45) — Dallas, TX		p. A-1225
KDVR (32) — Denver, CO		p. A-224
KECI-TV (13) — Missoula, MT		p. A-780
KECY-TV (9) — El Centro, CA		p. A-139
† KEDT (23) — Corpus Christi, TX		p. A-1550
KEET (11) — Eureka, CA		p. A-1496
† KEFB (34) — Ames, IA		p. A-1511

2017 Edition   D-1

U.S. Television Stations by Call Letters

KEJB (43)	El Dorado, AR	p. A-102
KELO-TV (11)	Sioux Falls, SD	p. A-1150
KEMO-TV (32)	Santa Rosa, CA	p. A-207
† KEMV (13)	Mountain View, AR	p. A-1495
KENS (39)	San Antonio, TX	p. A-1288
KENV-DT (10)	Elko, NV	p. A-803
† KENW (32)	Portales, NM	p. A-1531
† KEPB-TV (29)	Eugene, OR	p. A-1540
KEPR-TV (18)	Pasco, WA	p. A-1366
† KERA-TV (14)	Dallas, TX	p. A-1550
KERO-TV (10)	Bakersfield, CA	p. A-128
† KESD-TV (8)	Brookings, SD	p. A-1546
KESQ-TV (42)	Palm Springs, CA	p. A-168
† KETA-TV (48)	Oklahoma City, OK	p. A-1540
† KETC (39)	St. Louis, MO	p. A-1526
KETD (45)	Castle Rock, CO	p. A-218
† KETG (13)	Arkadelphia, AR	p. A-1494
† KETH-TV (24)	Houston, TX	p. A-1551
KETK-TV (22)	Jacksonville, TX	p. A-1256
† KETS (7)	Little Rock, AR	p. A-1495
KETV (20)	Omaha, NE	p. A-794
† KETZ (10)	El Dorado, AR	p. A-1494
KEYC-TV (12)	Mankato, MN	p. A-693
KEYE-TV (43)	Austin, TX	p. A-1201
KEYT-TV (27)	Santa Barbara, CA	p. A-204
KEYU (31)	Borger, TX	p. A-1211
KEZI (9)	Eugene, OR	p. A-1043
KFBB-TV (8)	Great Falls, MT	p. A-773
KFCT (21)	Fort Collins, CO	p. A-232
KFDA-TV (10)	Amarillo, TX	p. A-1198
KFDM (25)	Beaumont, TX	p. A-1208
KFDX-TV (28)	Wichita Falls, TX	p. A-1307
KFFV (44)	Seattle, WA	p. A-1369
KFFX-TV (11)	Pendleton, OR	p. A-1055
KFJX (13)	Pittsburg, KS	p. A-531
KFMB-TV (8)	San Diego, CA	p. A-183
† KFME (13)	Fargo, ND	p. A-1536
KFNB (20)	Casper, WY	p. A-1443
KFNE (10)	Riverton, WY	p. A-1451
KFNR (9)	Rawlins, WY	p. A-1450
KFOR-TV (27)	Oklahoma City, OK	p. A-1019
KFOX-TV (15)	El Paso, TX	p. A-1232
KFPH-DT (13)	Flagstaff, AZ	p. A-74
KFPX-TV (39)	Newton, IA	p. A-510
KFQX (15)	Grand Junction, CO	p. A-234
KFRE-TV (36)	Sanger, CA	p. A-202
KFSF-DT (34)	Vallejo, CA	p. A-212
KFSM-TV (18)	Fort Smith, AR	p. A-106
KFSN-TV (30)	Fresno, CA	p. A-146
KFTA-TV (27)	Fort Smith, AR	p. A-107
KFTC (26)	Bemidji, MN	p. A-686
KFTH-DT (36)	Alvin, TX	p. A-1195
KFTR-DT (29)	Ontario, CA	p. A-166
† KFTS (33)	Klamath Falls, OR	p. A-1541
KFTU-DT (36)	Douglas, AZ	p. A-73
KFTV-DT (20)	Hanford, CA	p. A-149
KFVE (22)	Honolulu, HI	p. A-388
KFVS-TV (12)	Cape Girardeau, MO	p. A-734
KFWD (9)	Fort Worth, TX	p. A-1238
KFXA (27)	Cedar Rapids, IA	p. A-498
KFXB-TV (43)	Dubuque, IA	p. A-507
KFXF (7)	Fairbanks, AK	p. A-65
KFXK-TV (31)	Longview, TX	p. A-1265
KFXL-TV (15)	Lincoln, NE	p. A-789
KFYR-TV (31)	Bismarck, ND	p. A-950
KGAN (29)	Cedar Rapids, IA	p. A-499
KGBT-TV (31)	Harlingen, TX	p. A-1246
KGBY (7)	Grand Junction, CO	p. A-235
KGCW (41)	Burlington, IA	p. A-496
KGEB (49)	Tulsa, OK	p. A-1029
KGET-TV (25)	Bakersfield, CA	p. A-129
† KGFE (15)	Grand Forks, ND	p. A-1537
KGIN (11)	Grand Island, NE	p. A-785
KGLA-DT (42)	Hammond, LA	p. A-574
KGMB (23)	Honolulu, HI	p. A-389
KGMC (43)	Clovis, CA	p. A-136
KGMD-TV (9)	Hilo, HI	p. A-381
KGMV (24)	Wailuku, HI	p. A-399
KGNS-TV (8)	Laredo, TX	p. A-1261
KGO-TV (7)	San Francisco, CA	p. A-191
KGPE (34)	Fresno, CA	p. A-147
KGPX-TV (34)	Spokane, WA	p. A-1375
† KGTF (12)	Agana, GU	p. A-1559
KGTV (10)	San Diego, CA	p. A-184
KGUN-TV (9)	Tucson, AZ	p. A-91
KGW (8)	Portland, OR	p. A-1057
KGWC-TV (14)	Casper, WY	p. A-1444
KGWL-TV (7)	Lander, WY	p. A-1449
KGWN-TV (30)	Cheyenne, WY	p. A-1446
KGWR-TV (13)	Rock Springs, WY	p. A-1452
KHAW-TV (11)	Hilo, HI	p. A-382
KHBC-TV (22)	Hilo, HI	p. A-383
KHBS (21)	Fort Smith, AR	p. A-108
† KHCE-TV (23)	San Antonio, TX	p. A-1551
† KHET (11)	Honolulu, HI	p. A-1506
KHGI-TV (13)	Kearney, NE	p. A-788
† KHIN (35)	Red Oak, IA	p. A-1512
KHME (2)	Rapid City, SD	p. A-1145
KHMT (22)	Hardin, MT	p. A-776
† KHNE-TV (14)	Hastings, NE	p. A-1527
KHNL (35)	Honolulu, HI	p. A-390
KHOG-TV (15)	Fayetteville, AR	p. A-105
KHON-TV (8)	Honolulu, HI	p. A-391
KHOU (11)	Houston, TX	p. A-1248
KHQA-TV (7)	Hannibal, MO	p. A-737
KHQ-TV (15)	Spokane, WA	p. A-1376
KHRR (40)	Tucson, AZ	p. A-92
KHSD-TV (5)	Lead, SD	p. A-1140
KHSL-TV (43)	Chico, CA	p. A-134
KHSV (2)	Las Vegas, NV	p. A-805
KHVO (13)	Hilo, HI	p. A-384
KIAH (38)	Houston, TX	p. A-1249
KICU-TV (36)	San Jose, CA	p. A-196
KIDK (36)	Idaho Falls, ID	p. A-409
KIDY (19)	San Angelo, TX	p. A-1284
KIEM-TV (3)	Eureka, CA	p. A-142
KIFI-TV (8)	Idaho Falls, ID	p. A-410
KIII (8)	Corpus Christi, TX	p. A-1217
† KIIN (12)	Iowa City, IA	p. A-1511
KIKU (19)	Honolulu, HI	p. A-392
KILM (44)	Barstow, CA	p. A-131
KIMA-TV (33)	Yakima, WA	p. A-1385
KIMT (42)	Mason City, IA	p. A-509
KINC (16)	Las Vegas, NV	p. A-806
KING-TV (48)	Seattle, WA	p. A-1370
KINT-TV (25)	El Paso, TX	p. A-1233
KION-TV (32)	Monterey, CA	p. A-162
† KIPT (22)	Twin Falls, ID	p. A-1507
KIRO-TV (39)	Seattle, WA	p. A-1371
† KISU-TV (17)	Pocatello, ID	p. A-1507
† KITU-TV (33)	Beaumont, TX	p. A-1549
KITV (40)	Honolulu, HI	p. A-393
KIVI-TV (24)	Nampa, ID	p. A-412
† KIXE-TV (9)	Redding, CA	p. A-1497
KJLA (49)	Ventura, CA	p. A-213
KJNP-TV (20)	North Pole, AK	p. A-69
† KJRE (20)	Ellendale, ND	p. A-1536
KJRH-TV (8)	Tulsa, OK	p. A-1030
KJRR (7)	Jamestown, ND	p. A-960
KJTL (15)	Wichita Falls, TX	p. A-1308
KJTV-TV (35)	Lubbock, TX	p. A-1268
KJUD (11)	Juneau, AK	p. A-67
KJWP (2)	Wilmington, DE	p. A-256
KJZZ-TV (46)	Salt Lake City, UT	p. A-1317
KKAI (50)	Kailua, HI	p. A-395
† KKAP (36)	Little Rock, AR	p. A-1495
KKCO (12)	Grand Junction, CO	p. A-236
KKJB (39)	Boise, ID	p. A-406
KKPX-TV (41)	San Jose, CA	p. A-197
KKTV (49)	Colorado Springs, CO	p. A-219
KLAS-TV (7)	Las Vegas, NV	p. A-807
KLAX-TV (31)	Alexandria, LA	p. A-568
KLBK-TV (40)	Lubbock, TX	p. A-1269
KLBY (17)	Colby, KS	p. A-519
† KLCS (41)	Los Angeles, CA	p. A-1496
KLCW-TV (43)	Wolfforth, TX	p. A-1309
KLDO-TV (19)	Laredo, TX	p. A-1262
KLEI-TV (25)	Kailua Kona, HI	p. A-396
KLEW-TV (32)	Lewiston, ID	p. A-411
KLFY-TV (10)	Lafayette, LA	p. A-577
KLJB (49)	Davenport, IA	p. A-501
KLKN (8)	Lincoln, NE	p. A-790
† KLNE-TV (26)	Lexington, NE	p. A-1528
† KLPA-TV (26)	Alexandria, LA	p. A-1516
† KLPB-TV (23)	Lafayette, LA	p. A-1517
† KLRN (9)	San Antonio, TX	p. A-1552
KLRT-TV (30)	Little Rock, AR	p. A-116
† KLRU (22)	Austin, TX	p. A-1549
KLSR-TV (31)	Eugene, OR	p. A-1044
KLST (11)	San Angelo, TX	p. A-1285
† KLTJ (23)	Galveston, TX	p. A-1551
† KLTL-TV (20)	Lake Charles, LA	p. A-1517
† KLTM-TV (13)	Monroe, LA	p. A-1517
† KLTS-TV (24)	Shreveport, LA	p. A-1517
KLTV (7)	Tyler, TX	p. A-1298
† KLUJ-TV (34)	Harlingen, TX	p. A-1551
KLUZ-TV (42)	Albuquerque, NM	p. A-839
† KLVX (11)	Las Vegas, NV	p. A-1529
KLWB (50)	New Iberia, LA	p. A-582
KLWY (27)	Cheyenne, WY	p. A-1447
KMAU (12)	Wailuku, HI	p. A-400
KMAX-TV (21)	Sacramento, CA	p. A-176
KMBC-TV (29)	Kansas City, MO	p. A-744
KMBH (38)	Harlingen, TX	p. A-1247
KMCB (22)	Coos Bay, OR	p. A-1042
KMCC (32)	Laughlin, NV	p. A-811
KMCI-TV (41)	Lawrence, KS	p. A-530
KMCT-TV (38)	West Monroe, LA	p. A-596
KMCY (14)	Minot, ND	p. A-961
† KMDE (25)	Devils Lake, ND	p. A-1536
† KMEB (10)	Wailuku, HI	p. A-1506
KMEG (39)	Sioux City, IA	p. A-513
KMEX-DT (34)	Los Angeles, CA	p. A-155
KMGH-TV (7)	Denver, CO	p. A-225
KMID (26)	Midland, TX	p. A-1273
KMIR-TV (46)	Palm Springs, CA	p. A-169
KMIZ (17)	Columbia, MO	p. A-735
KMLM-DT (42)	Odessa, TX	p. A-1276
KMLU (11)	Columbia, LA	p. A-573
† KMNE-TV (7)	Bassett, NE	p. A-1527
KMOH-TV (19)	Kingman, AZ	p. A-77
† KMOS-TV (15)	Sedalia, MO	p. A-1526
KMOT (10)	Minot, ND	p. A-962
KMOV (4)	St. Louis, MO	p. A-759
KMPH-TV (28)	Visalia, CA	p. A-214
KMPX (30)	Decatur, TX	p. A-1228
KMSB (25)	Tucson, AZ	p. A-93
KMSP-TV (9)	Minneapolis, MN	p. A-695

U.S. Television Stations by Call Letters

KMSS-TV (34) — Shreveport, LA		p. A-590
† KMTP-TV (33) — San Francisco, CA		p. A-1497
KMTR (17) — Eugene, OR		p. A-1045
KMTV (45) — Omaha, NE		p. A-795
KMTW (35) — Hutchinson, KS		p. A-528
KMVT (11) — Twin Falls, ID		p. A-417
KMVU-DT (26) — Medford, OR		p. A-1052
KMYA-DT (49) — Camden, AR		p. A-101
KMYS (32) — Kerrville, TX		p. A-1258
KMYT-TV (42) — Tulsa, OK		p. A-1031
KMYU (9) — St. George, UT		p. A-1323
KNAT-TV (24) — Albuquerque, NM		p. A-840
KNAZ-TV (22) — Flagstaff, AZ		p. A-75
KNBC (36) — Los Angeles, CA		p. A-156
KNBN (21) — Rapid City, SD		p. A-1146
† KNCT (46) — Belton, TX		p. A-1549
KNDB (26) — Bismarck, ND		p. A-951
KNDM (24) — Minot, ND		p. A-963
KNDO (16) — Yakima, WA		p. A-1386
KNDU (26) — Richland, WA		p. A-1368
KNEP (7) — Scottsbluff, NE		p. A-799
KNHL (5) — Hastings, NE		p. A-786
KNIC-DT (18) — Blanco, TX		p. A-1210
KNIN-TV (10) — Caldwell, ID		p. A-408
KNLC (14) — St. Louis, MO		p. A-760
KNLJ (20) — Jefferson City, MO		p. A-738
† KNMD-TV (8) — Santa Fe, NM		p. A-1531
† KNME-TV (35) — Albuquerque, NM		p. A-1531
KNMT (45) — Portland, OR		p. A-1058
KNOE-TV (8) — Monroe, LA		p. A-581
KNOP-TV (2) — North Platte, NE		p. A-793
† KNPB (15) — Reno, NV		p. A-1529
KNRR (12) — Pembina, ND		p. A-965
KNSD (40) — San Diego, CA		p. A-185
KNSO (11) — Merced, CA		p. A-160
KNTV (12) — San Jose, CA		p. A-198
KNVA (49) — Austin, TX		p. A-1202
KNVN (24) — Chico, CA		p. A-135
KNVO (49) — McAllen, TX		p. A-1272
KNWA-TV (50) — Rogers, AR		p. A-120
† KNXT (50) — Visalia, CA		p. A-1498
KNXV-TV (15) — Phoenix, AZ		p. A-81
KOAA-TV (42) — Pueblo, CO		p. A-241
† KOAB-TV (11) — Bend, OR		p. A-1540
† KOAC-TV (7) — Corvallis, OR		p. A-1540
KOAM-TV (7) — Pittsburg, KS		p. A-532
KOAT-TV (7) — Albuquerque, NM		p. A-841
KOB (26) — Albuquerque, NM		p. A-842
KOBF (12) — Farmington, NM		p. A-847
KOBI (5) — Medford, OR		p. A-1053
KOBR (8) — Roswell, NM		p. A-851
KOCB (33) — Oklahoma City, OK		p. A-1020
† KOCE-TV (48) — Huntington Beach, CA		p. A-1496
KOCM (46) — Norman, OK		p. A-1017
KOCO-TV (7) — Oklahoma City, OK		p. A-1021
KOCW (14) — Hoisington, KS		p. A-527
KODE-TV (43) — Joplin, MO		p. A-740
† KOED-TV (11) — Tulsa, OK		p. A-1540
† KOET (31) — Eufaula, OK		p. A-1540
KOFY-TV (19) — San Francisco, CA		p. A-192
KOGG (16) — Wailuku, HI		p. A-401
KOHD (18) — Bend, OR		p. A-1039
KOIN (40) — Portland, OR		p. A-1059
KOKH-TV (24) — Oklahoma City, OK		p. A-1022
KOKI-TV (22) — Tulsa, OK		p. A-1032
KOLD-TV (32) — Tucson, AZ		p. A-94
KOLN (10) — Lincoln, NE		p. A-791
KOLO-TV (8) — Reno, NV		p. A-814
KOLR (10) — Springfield, MO		p. A-752
KOMO-TV (38) — Seattle, WA		p. A-1372
KOMU-TV (8) — Columbia, MO		p. A-736
KONG (31) — Everett, WA		p. A-1364
† KOOD (16) — Hays, KS		p. A-1513
† KOPB-TV (10) — Portland, OR		p. A-1541
KOPX-TV (50) — Oklahoma City, OK		p. A-1023
KORO (27) — Corpus Christi, TX		p. A-1218
KOSA-TV (7) — Odessa, TX		p. A-1277
KOTA-TV (7) — Rapid City, SD		p. A-1147
KOTI (13) — Klamath Falls, OR		p. A-1049
KOTV-DT (45) — Tulsa, OK		p. A-1033
KOVR (25) — Stockton, CA		p. A-208
† KOZJ (25) — Joplin, MO		p. A-1525
† KOZK (23) — Springfield, MO		p. A-1526
KOZL-TV (28) — Springfield, MO		p. A-753
KPAX-TV (7) — Missoula, MT		p. A-781
KPAZ-TV (20) — Phoenix, AZ		p. A-82
† KPBS (30) — San Diego, CA		p. A-1497
† KPBT-TV (38) — Odessa, TX		p. A-1551
KPCB-DT (17) — Snyder, TX		p. A-1294
KPDX (30) — Vancouver, WA		p. A-1383
KPEJ-TV (23) — Odessa, TX		p. A-1278
KPHO-TV (17) — Phoenix, AZ		p. A-83
KPIC (19) — Roseburg, OR		p. A-1061
KPIF (15) — Pocatello, ID		p. A-414
KPIX-TV (29) — San Francisco, CA		p. A-193
KPJR-TV (38) — Greeley, CO		p. A-238
KPLC (7) — Lake Charles, LA		p. A-578
KPLO-TV (13) — Reliance, SD		p. A-1148
KPLR-TV (26) — St. Louis, MO		p. A-761
KPMR (21) — Santa Barbara, CA		p. A-205
† KPNE-TV (9) — North Platte, NE		p. A-1528
KPNX (12) — Mesa, AZ		p. A-78
KPNZ (24) — Ogden, UT		p. A-1313
KPOB-TV (15) — Poplar Bluff, MO		p. A-751
KPPX-TV (51) — Tolleson, AZ		p. A-90
KPRC-TV (35) — Houston, TX		p. A-1250
KPRY-TV (19) — Pierre, SD		p. A-1143
† KPSD-TV (13) — Eagle Butte, SD		p. A-1546
KPTB-DT (16) — Lubbock, TX		p. A-1270
KPTF-DT (18) — Farwell, TX		p. A-1237
KPTH (49) — Sioux City, IA		p. A-514
KPTM (43) — Omaha, NE		p. A-796
† KPTS (8) — Hutchinson, KS		p. A-1513
KPTV (12) — Portland, OR		p. A-1060
† KPTW (8) — Casper, WY		p. A-1558
KPVI-DT (23) — Pocatello, ID		p. A-415
KPXB-TV (32) — Conroe, TX		p. A-1215
KPXC-TV (43) — Denver, CO		p. A-226
KPXD-TV (42) — Arlington, TX		p. A-1200
KPXE-TV (30) — Kansas City, MO		p. A-745
KPXG-TV (22) — Salem, OR		p. A-1064
KPXJ (21) — Minden, LA		p. A-580
KPXL-TV (26) — Uvalde, TX		p. A-1299
KPXM-TV (40) — St. Cloud, MN		p. A-703
KPXN-TV (38) — San Bernardino, CA		p. A-182
KPXO-TV (41) — Kaneohe, HI		p. A-397
KPXR-TV (47) — Cedar Rapids, IA		p. A-500
KQCA (46) — Stockton, CA		p. A-209
KQCD-TV (7) — Dickinson, ND		p. A-954
KQCK (11) — Cheyenne, WY		p. A-1448
KQCW-DT (20) — Muskogee, OK		p. A-1016
KQDS-TV (17) — Duluth, MN		p. A-690
† KQED (30) — San Francisco, CA		p. A-1497
† KQEH (50) — San Jose, CA		p. A-1498
† KQET (25) — Watsonville, CA		p. A-1498
† KQIN (34) — Davenport, IA		p. A-1511
KQME (10) — Lead, SD		p. A-1141
† KQSD-TV (11) — Lowry, SD		p. A-1546
KQSL (8) — Fort Bragg, CA		p. A-144
KQTV (7) — St. Joseph, MO		p. A-756
KQUP (24) — Pullman, WA		p. A-1367
KRBC-TV (29) — Abilene, TX		p. A-1192
KRBK (49) — Osage Beach, MO		p. A-750
KRCA (35) — Riverside, CA		p. A-174
† KRCB (23) — Cotati, CA		p. A-1496
KRCG (12) — Jefferson City, MO		p. A-739
KRCR-TV (7) — Redding, CA		p. A-173
KRCW-TV (33) — Salem, OR		p. A-1065
KRDK-TV (38) — Valley City, ND		p. A-966
KRDO-TV (24) — Colorado Springs, CO		p. A-220
KREG-TV (23) — Glenwood Springs, CO		p. A-233
KREM (20) — Spokane, WA		p. A-1377
KREN-TV (26) — Reno, NV		p. A-815
KREX-TV (2) — Grand Junction, CO		p. A-237
KREY-TV (13) — Montrose, CO		p. A-240
KREZ-TV (15) — Durango, CO		p. A-230
KRGV-TV (13) — Weslaco, TX		p. A-1305
KRII (11) — Chisholm, MN		p. A-687
† KRIN (35) — Waterloo, IA		p. A-1512
KRIS-TV (13) — Corpus Christi, TX		p. A-1219
KRIV (26) — Houston, TX		p. A-1251
† KRMA-TV (18) — Denver, CO		p. A-1498
† KRMJ (18) — Grand Junction, CO		p. A-1499
† KRMT (40) — Denver, CO		p. A-1499
† KRMU (20) — Durango, CO		p. A-1499
† KRMZ (10) — Steamboat Springs, CO		p. A-1499
† KRNE-TV (12) — Merriman, NE		p. A-1528
KRNV-DT (7) — Reno, NV		p. A-816
KRON-TV (38) — San Francisco, CA		p. A-194
KRPV-DT (27) — Roswell, NM		p. A-852
KRQE (13) — Albuquerque, NM		p. A-843
† KRSU-TV (36) — Claremore, OK		p. A-1539
KRTN (33) — Durango, CO		p. A-231
KRTV (7) — Great Falls, MT		p. A-774
KRWB-TV (21) — Roswell, NM		p. A-853
KRWF (27) — Redwood Falls, MN		p. A-700
† KRWG-TV (23) — Las Cruces, NM		p. A-1531
KRXI-TV (44) — Reno, NV		p. A-817
KSAN-TV (16) — San Angelo, TX		p. A-1286
KSAS-TV (26) — Wichita, KS		p. A-539
KSAT-TV (12) — San Antonio, TX		p. A-1289
KSAX (42) — Alexandria, MN		p. A-684
KSAZ-TV (10) — Phoenix, AZ		p. A-84
KSBI (23) — Oklahoma City, OK		p. A-1024
KSBW (8) — Salinas, CA		p. A-181
KSBY (15) — San Luis Obispo, CA		p. A-200
† KSCE (39) — El Paso, TX		p. A-1550
KSCI (18) — Long Beach, CA		p. A-150
KSCW-DT (12) — Wichita, KS		p. A-540
KSDK (35) — St. Louis, MO		p. A-762
KSEE (38) — Fresno, CA		p. A-148
KSFY-TV (13) — Sioux Falls, SD		p. A-1151
KSGW-TV (13) — Sheridan, WY		p. A-1453
KSHB-TV (42) — Kansas City, MO		p. A-746
KSHV-TV (44) — Shreveport, LA		p. A-591
† KSIN-TV (28) — Sioux City, IA		p. A-1512
KSKN (36) — Spokane, WA		p. A-1378
KSLA (17) — Shreveport, LA		p. A-592
KSL-TV (38) — Salt Lake City, UT		p. A-1318
† KSMN (15) — Worthington, MN		p. A-1524
KSMO-TV (47) — Kansas City, MO		p. A-747
† KSMQ-TV (20) — Austin, MN		p. A-1522
KSMS-TV (31) — Monterey, CA		p. A-163
KSNB-TV (4) — Superior, NE		p. A-801
KSNC (22) — Great Bend, KS		p. A-525
KSNF (46) — Joplin, MO		p. A-741
KSNG (11) — Garden City, KS		p. A-522
KSNK (12) — McCook, NE		p. A-792
KSNT (27) — Topeka, KS		p. A-534
KSNV (22) — Las Vegas, NV		p. A-808

2017 Edition D-3

U.S. Television Stations by Call Letters

KSNW (45)	Wichita, KS	p. A-541
KSPR (19)	Springfield, MO	p. A-754
†KSPS-TV (7)	Spokane, WA	p. A-1556
KSPX-TV (48)	Sacramento, CA	p. A-177
KSQA (12)	Topeka, KS	p. A-535
†KSRE (40)	Minot, ND	p. A-1537
KSTC-TV (45)	Minneapolis, MN	p. A-696
KSTF (29)	Scottsbluff, NE	p. A-800
KSTP-TV (35)	St. Paul, MN	p. A-704
KSTR-DT (48)	Irving, TX	p. A-1255
KSTS (49)	San Jose, CA	p. A-199
KSTU (28)	Salt Lake City, UT	p. A-1319
KSTW (11)	Tacoma, WA	p. A-1381
KSVI (18)	Billings, MT	p. A-765
KSWB-TV (19)	San Diego, CA	p. A-186
†KSWK (8)	Lakin, KS	p. A-1513
KSWO-TV (11)	Lawton, OK	p. A-1015
KSWT (13)	Yuma, AZ	p. A-97
†KSYS (8)	Medford, OR	p. A-1541
KTAB-TV (24)	Abilene, TX	p. A-1193
KTAJ-TV (21)	St. Joseph, MO	p. A-757
KTAL-TV (15)	Texarkana, TX	p. A-1297
KTAS (34)	San Luis Obispo, CA	p. A-201
KTAZ (39)	Phoenix, AZ	p. A-85
KTBC (7)	Austin, TX	p. A-1203
KTBN-TV (33)	Santa Ana, CA	p. A-203
KTBO-TV (15)	Oklahoma City, OK	p. A-1025
KTBS-TV (28)	Shreveport, LA	p. A-593
KTBU (42)	Conroe, TX	p. A-1216
KTBW-TV (14)	Tacoma, WA	p. A-1382
KTBY (20)	Anchorage, AK	p. A-59
†KTCA-TV (34)	St. Paul, MN	p. A-1523
†KTCI-TV (23)	St. Paul, MN	p. A-1523
KTCW (45)	Roseburg, OR	p. A-1062
KTDO (47)	Las Cruces, NM	p. A-849
†KTEJ (20)	Jonesboro, AR	p. A-1495
KTEL-TV (25)	Carlsbad, NM	p. A-845
KTEN (26)	Ada, OK	p. A-1013
KTFD-DT (15)	Boulder, CO	p. A-217
KTFF-DT (48)	Porterville, CA	p. A-171
KTFK-DT (26)	Stockton, CA	p. A-210
KTFN (51)	El Paso, TX	p. A-1234
KTFQ-DT (22)	Albuquerque, NM	p. A-844
KTGF (45)	Great Falls, MT	p. A-775
KTHV (12)	Little Rock, AR	p. A-117
†KTIN (25)	Fort Dodge, IA	p. A-1511
KTIV (41)	Sioux City, IA	p. A-515
KTKA-TV (49)	Topeka, KS	p. A-536
KTLA (31)	Los Angeles, CA	p. A-157
KTLM (40)	Rio Grande City, TX	p. A-1282
KTLN-TV (47)	Novato, CA	p. A-164
KTMD (48)	Galveston, TX	p. A-1243
KTMF (23)	Missoula, MT	p. A-782
KTMW (20)	Salt Lake City, UT	p. A-1320
KTNC-TV (14)	Concord, CA	p. A-137
†KTNE-TV (13)	Alliance, NE	p. A-1527
KTNL-TV (7)	Sitka, AK	p. A-70
KTNV-TV (13)	Las Vegas, NV	p. A-809
†KTNW (38)	Richland, WA	p. A-1555
†KTOO-TV (10)	Juneau, AK	p. A-1494
KTPX-TV (28)	Okmulgee, OK	p. A-1027
KTRE (9)	Lufkin, TX	p. A-1271
KTRK-TV (13)	Houston, TX	p. A-1252
KTRV-TV (13)	Nampa, ID	p. A-413
†KTSC (8)	Pueblo, CO	p. A-1499
†KTSD-TV (10)	Pierre, SD	p. A-1547
KTSF (27)	San Francisco, CA	p. A-195
KTSM-TV (16)	El Paso, TX	p. A-1235
KTTC (10)	Rochester, MN	p. A-701
KTTM (12)	Huron, SD	p. A-1139
KTTU (19)	Tucson, AZ	p. A-95
KTTV (11)	Los Angeles, CA	p. A-158
KTTW (7)	Sioux Falls, SD	p. A-1152
†KTTZ-TV (39)	Lubbock, TX	p. A-1551
KTUL (10)	Tulsa, OK	p. A-1034
KTUU-TV (10)	Anchorage, AK	p. A-60
KTUZ-TV (29)	Shawnee, OK	p. A-1028
KTVA (28)	Anchorage, AK	p. A-61
KTVB (7)	Boise, ID	p. A-407
KTVC (18)	Roseburg, OR	p. A-1063
KTVD (19)	Denver, CO	p. A-227
KTVE (27)	El Dorado, AR	p. A-103
KTVF (26)	Fairbanks, AK	p. A-66
KTVH-DT (12)	Helena, MT	p. A-777
KTVI (43)	St. Louis, MO	p. A-763
KTVK (24)	Phoenix, AZ	p. A-86
KTVL (10)	Medford, OR	p. A-1054
KTVM-TV (6)	Butte, MT	p. A-769
KTVN (13)	Reno, NV	p. A-818
KTVO (33)	Kirksville, MO	p. A-749
KTVQ (10)	Billings, MT	p. A-766
†KTVR (13)	La Grande, OR	p. A-1541
KTVT (19)	Fort Worth, TX	p. A-1239
KTVU (44)	Oakland, CA	p. A-165
KTVW-DT (33)	Phoenix, AZ	p. A-87
KTVX (40)	Salt Lake City, UT	p. A-1321
KTVZ (21)	Bend, OR	p. A-1040
KTWO-TV (17)	Casper, WY	p. A-1445
†KTWU (11)	Topeka, KS	p. A-1513
KTXA (29)	Fort Worth, TX	p. A-1240
KTXD-TV (46)	Greenville, TX	p. A-1245
KTXH (19)	Houston, TX	p. A-1253
KTXL (40)	Sacramento, CA	p. A-178
KTXS-TV (20)	Sweetwater, TX	p. A-1295
†KUAC-TV (9)	Fairbanks, AK	p. A-1493
†KUAS-TV (28)	Tucson, AZ	p. A-1494
†KUAT-TV (30)	Tucson, AZ	p. A-1494
KUBD (13)	Ketchikan, AK	p. A-68
KUBE-TV (41)	Baytown, TX	p. A-1206
KUCW (48)	Ogden, UT	p. A-1314
†KUED (42)	Salt Lake City, UT	p. A-1552
†KUEN (36)	Ogden, UT	p. A-1552
†KUES (19)	Richfield, UT	p. A-1552
†KUEW (18)	St. George, UT	p. A-1552
†KUFM-TV (11)	Missoula, MT	p. A-1527
†KUGF (21)	Great Falls, MT	p. A-1527
†KUHM-TV (29)	Helena, MT	p. A-1527
†KUHT (8)	Houston, TX	p. A-1551
†KUID-TV (12)	Moscow, ID	p. A-1507
†KUKL-TV (46)	Kalispell, MT	p. A-1527
KULR-TV (11)	Billings, MT	p. A-767
KUMV-TV (8)	Williston, ND	p. A-967
KUNP (16)	La Grande, OR	p. A-1050
KUNS-TV (50)	Bellevue, WA	p. A-1360
KUOK (35)	Woodward, OK	p. A-1036
†KUON-TV (12)	Lincoln, NE	p. A-1528
KUPB (18)	Midland, TX	p. A-1274
KUPK (13)	Garden City, KS	p. A-523
KUPT (29)	Hobbs, NM	p. A-848
KUPU (15)	Waimanalo, HI	p. A-403
KUPX-TV (29)	Provo, UT	p. A-1315
KUQI (38)	Corpus Christi, TX	p. A-1220
KUSA (9)	Denver, CO	p. A-228
†KUSD-TV (34)	Vermillion, SD	p. A-1547
KUSI-TV (18)	San Diego, CA	p. A-187
†KUSM-TV (8)	Bozeman, MT	p. A-1526
KUTF (12)	Logan, UT	p. A-1312
KUTH-DT (32)	Provo, UT	p. A-1316
KUTP (26)	Phoenix, AZ	p. A-88
KUTV (34)	Salt Lake City, UT	p. A-1322
KUVE-DT (46)	Green Valley, AZ	p. A-76
KUVI-DT (45)	Bakersfield, CA	p. A-130
KUVN-DT (23)	Garland, TX	p. A-1244
KUVS-DT (18)	Modesto, CA	p. A-161
KVAL-TV (13)	Eugene, OR	p. A-1046
KVAW (18)	Eagle Pass, TX	p. A-1230
†KVCR-DT (26)	San Bernardino, CA	p. A-1497
KVCT (11)	Victoria, TX	p. A-1301
KVCW (29)	Las Vegas, NV	p. A-810
KVDA (38)	San Antonio, TX	p. A-1290
KVEA (39)	Corona, CA	p. A-138
KVEO-TV (24)	Brownsville, TX	p. A-1212
KVEW (44)	Kennewick, WA	p. A-1365
KVHP (30)	Lake Charles, LA	p. A-579
KVIA-TV (7)	El Paso, TX	p. A-1236
†KVIE (9)	Sacramento, CA	p. A-1497
KVIH-TV (12)	Clovis, NM	p. A-846
KVII-TV (7)	Amarillo, TX	p. A-1199
KVIQ (17)	Eureka, CA	p. A-143
KVLY-TV (44)	Fargo, ND	p. A-956
KVMD (23)	Twentynine Palms, CA	p. A-211
KVME-TV (20)	Bishop, CA	p. A-132
KVOA (23)	Tucson, AZ	p. A-96
KVOS-TV (35)	Bellingham, WA	p. A-1363
†KVPT (40)	Fresno, CA	p. A-1496
KVRR (19)	Fargo, ND	p. A-957
KVSN-DT (48)	Pueblo, CO	p. A-242
KVTH-DT (26)	Hot Springs, AR	p. A-110
KVTJ-DT (48)	Jonesboro, AR	p. A-112
KVTN-DT (24)	Pine Bluff, AR	p. A-119
KVUE (33)	Austin, TX	p. A-1204
KVUI (31)	Pocatello, ID	p. A-416
KVVU-TV (24)	Henderson, NV	p. A-804
KVYE (22)	El Centro, CA	p. A-140
KWAB-TV (33)	Big Spring, TX	p. A-1209
KWBA-TV (44)	Sierra Vista, AZ	p. A-89
KWBM (31)	Harrison, AR	p. A-109
†KWBN (43)	Honolulu, HI	p. A-1506
KWBQ (29)	Santa Fe, NM	p. A-856
KWCH-DT (19)	Hutchinson, KS	p. A-529
†KWCM-TV (10)	Appleton, MN	p. A-1522
†KWDK (42)	Tacoma, WA	p. A-1556
KWES-TV (9)	Odessa, TX	p. A-1279
†KWET (8)	Cheyenne, OK	p. A-1539
KWEX-DT (41)	San Antonio, TX	p. A-1291
KWGN-TV (34)	Denver, CO	p. A-229
KWHB (47)	Tulsa, OK	p. A-1035
KWHD (23)	Hilo, HI	p. A-385
KWHE (31)	Honolulu, HI	p. A-394
KWHM (21)	Wailuku, HI	p. A-402
KWHY-TV (42)	Los Angeles, CA	p. A-159
KWKB (25)	Iowa City, IA	p. A-508
†KWKS (19)	Colby, KS	p. A-1512
KWKT-TV (44)	Waco, TX	p. A-1302
KWNB-TV (6)	Hayes Center, NE	p. A-787
KWOG (39)	Springdale, AR	p. A-121
KWPX-TV (33)	Bellevue, WA	p. A-1361
KWQC-TV (36)	Davenport, IA	p. A-502
KWSD (36)	Sioux Falls, SD	p. A-1153
†KWSE (11)	Williston, ND	p. A-1537
†KWSU-TV (10)	Pullman, WA	p. A-1555
KWTV-DT (39)	Oklahoma City, OK	p. A-1026
KWTX-TV (10)	Waco, TX	p. A-1303
KWWL (7)	Waterloo, IA	p. A-516
KWWT (30)	Odessa, TX	p. A-1280
KWYB (19)	Butte, MT	p. A-770
†KWYP-DT (8)	Laramie, WY	p. A-1559
KXAN-TV (21)	Austin, TX	p. A-1205
KXAS-TV (41)	Fort Worth, TX	p. A-1241
KXGN-TV (5)	Glendive, MT	p. A-772
KXII (12)	Sherman, TX	p. A-1293

U.S. Television Stations by Call Letters

Call (Ch)	City	Page
KXLA (51)	Rancho Palos Verdes, CA	p. A-172
KXLF-TV (5)	Butte, MT	p. A-771
KXLN-DT (45)	Rosenberg, TX	p. A-1283
KXLT-TV (46)	Rochester, MN	p. A-702
KXLY-TV (13)	Spokane, WA	p. A-1379
KXMA-TV (19)	Dickinson, ND	p. A-955
KXMB-TV (12)	Bismarck, ND	p. A-952
KXMC-TV (13)	Minot, ND	p. A-964
KXMD-TV (14)	Williston, ND	p. A-968
† KXNE-TV (19)	Norfolk, NE	p. A-1528
KXNW (34)	Eureka Springs, AR	p. A-104
KXRM-TV (22)	Colorado Springs, CO	p. A-221
KXTF (34)	Twin Falls, ID	p. A-418
KXTV (10)	Sacramento, CA	p. A-179
KXTX-TV (40)	Dallas, TX	p. A-1226
KXVA (15)	Abilene, TX	p. A-1194
KXVO (38)	Omaha, NE	p. A-797
KXXV (26)	Waco, TX	p. A-1304
KYAZ (47)	Katy, TX	p. A-1257
KYES-TV (5)	Anchorage, AK	p. A-62
† KYIN (18)	Mason City, IA	p. A-1512
KYLE-TV (28)	Bryan, TX	p. A-1214
KYMA-DT (11)	Yuma, AZ	p. A-98
† KYNE-TV (17)	Omaha, NE	p. A-1529
KYOU-TV (15)	Ottumwa, IA	p. A-511
KYTV (44)	Springfield, MO	p. A-755
KYTX (18)	Nacogdoches, TX	p. A-1275
KYUR (12)	Anchorage, AK	p. A-63
KYUS-TV (3)	Miles City, MT	p. A-779
† KYVE (21)	Yakima, WA	p. A-1556
KYVV-TV (28)	Del Rio, TX	p. A-1229
KYW-TV (26)	Philadelphia, PA	p. A-1086
KZJL (44)	Houston, TX	p. A-1254
KZJO (25)	Seattle, WA	p. A-1373
† KZSD-TV (8)	Martin, SD	p. A-1546
KZTV (10)	Corpus Christi, TX	p. A-1221

W

Call (Ch)	City	Page
WAAY-TV (32)	Huntsville, AL	p. A-36
WABC-TV (7)	New York, NY	p. A-880
WABG-TV (32)	Greenwood, MS	p. A-712
WABI-TV (13)	Bangor, ME	p. A-598
WABM (36)	Birmingham, AL	p. A-25
† WABW-TV (6)	Pelham, GA	p. A-1505
WACH (48)	Columbia, SC	p. A-1119
WACP (4)	Atlantic City, NJ	p. A-825
† WACS-TV (8)	Dawson, GA	p. A-1505
WACX (40)	Leesburg, FL	p. A-294
WACY-TV (27)	Appleton, WI	p. A-1407
WADL (39)	Mount Clemens, MI	p. A-671
WAFB (9)	Baton Rouge, LA	p. A-569
WAFF (48)	Huntsville, AL	p. A-37
WAGA-TV (27)	Atlanta, GA	p. A-347
WAGM-TV (8)	Presque Isle, ME	p. A-606
WAGT (30)	Augusta, GA	p. A-354
WAGV (51)	Harlan, KY	p. A-550
† WAIQ (27)	Montgomery, AL	p. A-1493
WAKA (42)	Selma, AL	p. A-51
WALA-TV (9)	Mobile, AL	p. A-40
WALB (10)	Albany, GA	p. A-344
WAMI-DT (47)	Hollywood, FL	p. A-284
WAND (17)	Decatur, IL	p. A-433
WANE-TV (31)	Fort Wayne, IN	p. A-469
WAOE (39)	Peoria, IL	p. A-444
WAOW (51)	Wausau, WI	p. A-1439
WAPA-TV (27)	San Juan, PR	p. A-1477
WAPT (21)	Jackson, MS	p. A-716
WAQP (48)	Saginaw, MI	p. A-674
† WATC-DT (41)	Atlanta, GA	p. A-1504
WATE-TV (26)	Knoxville, TN	p. A-1170
WATL (25)	Atlanta, GA	p. A-348
WATM-TV (24)	Altoona, PA	p. A-1069
WATN-TV (25)	Memphis, TN	p. A-1176
WAVE (47)	Louisville, KY	p. A-555
WAVY-TV (31)	Portsmouth, VA	p. A-1347
WAWD (49)	Fort Walton Beach, FL	p. A-279
WAWV-TV (39)	Terre Haute, IN	p. A-489
WAXN-TV (50)	Kannapolis, NC	p. A-932
WBAL-TV (11)	Baltimore, MD	p. A-609
WBAY-TV (23)	Green Bay, WI	p. A-1414
WBBH-TV (15)	Fort Myers, FL	p. A-276
WBBJ-TV (43)	Jackson, TN	p. A-1165
WBBM-TV (12)	Chicago, IL	p. A-425
WBBZ-TV (7)	Springville, NY	p. A-897
WBDT (26)	Springfield, OH	p. A-1000
† WBEC-TV (40)	Boca Raton, FL	p. A-1501
WBFF (46)	Baltimore, MD	p. A-610
WBFS-TV (32)	Miami, FL	p. A-298
† WBGU-TV (27)	Bowling Green, OH	p. A-1538
WBIF (51)	Marianna, FL	p. A-295
WBIH (29)	Selma, AL	p. A-52
WBIN (35)	Derry, NH	p. A-821
† WBIQ (10)	Birmingham, AL	p. A-1492
WBIR-TV (10)	Knoxville, TN	p. A-1171
WBKB-TV (11)	Alpena, MI	p. A-640
WBKI-TV (19)	Campbellsville, KY	p. A-548
WBKO (13)	Bowling Green, KY	p. A-546
WBKP (5)	Calumet, MI	p. A-648
WBMM (22)	Tuskegee, AL	p. A-56
WBNA (8)	Louisville, KY	p. A-556
WBNG-TV (7)	Binghamton, NY	p. A-864
WBNS-TV (21)	Columbus, OH	p. A-984
WBNX-TV (30)	Akron, OH	p. A-971
WBOC-TV (21)	Salisbury, MD	p. A-617
WBOY-TV (12)	Clarksburg, WV	p. A-1394
WBPH-TV (9)	Bethlehem, PA	p. A-1072
WBPX-TV (32)	Boston, MA	p. A-621
† WBRA-TV (3)	Roanoke, VA	p. A-1555
WBRC (50)	Birmingham, AL	p. A-26
WBRE-TV (11)	Wilkes-Barre, PA	p. A-1104
WBRZ-TV (13)	Baton Rouge, LA	p. A-570
WBSF (46)	Bay City, MI	p. A-644
WBTV (23)	Charlotte, NC	p. A-914
WBTW (13)	Florence, SC	p. A-1124
WBUI (22)	Decatur, IL	p. A-434
WBUP (10)	Ishpeming, MI	p. A-662
WBUW (32)	Janesville, WI	p. A-1418
WBUY-TV (41)	Holly Springs, MS	p. A-715
WBXX-TV (20)	Crossville, TN	p. A-1162
WBZ-TV (30)	Boston, MA	p. A-622
WCAU (34)	Philadelphia, PA	p. A-1087
WCAV (19)	Charlottesville, VA	p. A-1334
WCAX-TV (22)	Burlington, VT	p. A-1325
† WCBB (10)	Augusta, ME	p. A-1518
WCBD-TV (50)	Charleston, SC	p. A-1114
WCBI-TV (35)	Columbus, MS	p. A-710
WCBS-TV (33)	New York, NY	p. A-881
WCCB (27)	Charlotte, NC	p. A-915
WCCO-TV (32)	Minneapolis, MN	p. A-697
WCCT-TV (20)	Waterbury, CT	p. A-253
WCCU (26)	Urbana, IL	p. A-457
WCCV-TV (46)	Arecibo, PR	p. A-1459
WCDC-TV (36)	Adams, MA	p. A-620
† WCES-TV (6)	Wrens, GA	p. A-1506
† WCET (22)	Cincinnati, OH	p. A-1538
† WCFE-TV (38)	Plattsburgh, NY	p. A-1533
WCGV-TV (25)	Milwaukee, WI	p. A-1428
WCHS-TV (41)	Charleston, WV	p. A-1391
WCIA (48)	Champaign, IL	p. A-423
† WCIQ (7)	Mount Cheaha State Park, AL	p. A-1493
WCIU-TV (27)	Chicago, IL	p. A-426
WCIV (36)	Charleston, SC	p. A-1115
WCIX (13)	Springfield, IL	p. A-454
WCJB-TV (16)	Gainesville, FL	p. A-281
WCLF (21)	Clearwater, FL	p. A-269
WCLJ-TV (42)	Bloomington, IN	p. A-461
WCMH-TV (14)	Columbus, OH	p. A-985
† WCML (24)	Alpena, MI	p. A-1520
† WCMU-TV (26)	Mount Pleasant, MI	p. A-1522
† WCMV (17)	Cadillac, MI	p. A-1521
† WCMW (21)	Manistee, MI	p. A-1522
† WCMZ-TV (28)	Flint, MI	p. A-1521
WCNC-TV (22)	Charlotte, NC	p. A-916
† WCNY-TV (25)	Syracuse, NY	p. A-1533
WCOV-TV (20)	Montgomery, AL	p. A-45
† WCPB (28)	Salisbury, MD	p. A-1519
WCPO-TV (22)	Cincinnati, OH	p. A-976
WCPX-TV (43)	Chicago, IL	p. A-427
WCSC-TV (47)	Charleston, SC	p. A-1116
WCSH (44)	Portland, ME	p. A-603
† WCTE (22)	Cookeville, TN	p. A-1548
WCTI-TV (12)	New Bern, NC	p. A-936
WCTV (46)	Thomasville, GA	p. A-377
WCTX (39)	New Haven, CT	p. A-250
WCVB-TV (20)	Boston, MA	p. A-623
† WCVE-TV (42)	Richmond, VA	p. A-1554
WCVI-TV (23)	Christiansted, VI	p. A-1486
† WCVN-TV (24)	Covington, KY	p. A-1514
† WCVW (44)	Richmond, VA	p. A-1555
WCWF (21)	Suring, WI	p. A-1438
WCWG (19)	Lexington, NC	p. A-933
WCWJ (34)	Jacksonville, FL	p. A-285
WCWN (43)	Schenectady, NY	p. A-894
WCYB-TV (5)	Bristol, VA	p. A-1333
WDAF-TV (34)	Kansas City, MO	p. A-748
WDAM-TV (7)	Laurel, MS	p. A-721
WDAY-TV (21)	Fargo, ND	p. A-958
WDAZ-TV (8)	Devils Lake, ND	p. A-953
WDBB (18)	Bessemer, AL	p. A-24
WDBD (40)	Jackson, MS	p. A-717
WDBJ (18)	Roanoke, VA	p. A-1352
WDCA (35)	Washington, DC	p. A-259
† WDCQ-TV (15)	Bad Axe, MI	p. A-1521
WDCW (50)	Washington, DC	p. A-260
WDEF-TV (12)	Chattanooga, TN	p. A-1156
WDFX-TV (33)	Ozark, AL	p. A-50
WDHN (21)	Dothan, AL	p. A-29
WDIO-DT (10)	Duluth, MN	p. A-691
† WDIQ (10)	Dozier, AL	p. A-1492
WDIV-TV (45)	Detroit, MI	p. A-650
WDJT-TV (46)	Milwaukee, WI	p. A-1429
WDKA (49)	Paducah, KY	p. A-562
WDKY-TV (31)	Danville, KY	p. A-549
WDLI-TV (49)	Canton, OH	p. A-973
† WDPB (44)	Seaford, DE	p. A-1500
WDPM-DT (23)	Mobile, AL	p. A-41
WDPX-TV (40)	Vineyard Haven, MA	p. A-636
WDRB (49)	Louisville, KY	p. A-557
† WDSC-TV (33)	New Smyrna Beach, FL	p. A-1503
† WDSE (8)	Duluth, MN	p. A-1523
WDSI-TV (40)	Chattanooga, TN	p. A-1157
WDSU (43)	New Orleans, LA	p. A-583
WDTI (44)	Indianapolis, IN	p. A-475
WDTN (50)	Dayton, OH	p. A-988
WDTV (5)	Weston, WV	p. A-1402
WDWL (30)	Bayamon, PR	p. A-1461
† WEAO (50)	Akron, OH	p. A-1537
WEAR-TV (17)	Pensacola, FL	p. A-321

2017 Edition — D-5

U.S. Television Stations by Call Letters

WEAU (38) — Eau Claire, WI . . . p. A-1411
† WEBA-TV (33) — Allendale, SC . . . p. A-1544
WECN (18) — Naranjito, PR . . . p. A-1471
WECT (44) — Wilmington, NC . . . p. A-942
† WEDH (45) — Hartford, CT . . . p. A-1500
† WEDN (9) — Norwich, CT . . . p. A-1500
† WEDU (13) — Tampa, FL . . . p. A-1503
† WEDW (49) — Bridgeport, CT . . . p. A-1499
† WEDY (41) — New Haven, CT . . . p. A-1500
WEEK-TV (25) — Peoria, IL . . . p. A-445
† WEFS (30) — Cocoa, FL . . . p. A-1501
WEHT (7) — Evansville, IN . . . p. A-465
† WEIQ (41) — Mobile, AL . . . p. A-1493
† WEIU-TV (50) — Charleston, IL . . . p. A-1508
† WEKW-TV (49) — Keene, NH . . . p. A-1529
WELF-TV (16) — Dalton, GA . . . p. A-366
† WELU (34) — Aguadilla, PR . . . p. A-1542
WEMT (38) — Greeneville, TN . . . p. A-1163
† WENH-TV (11) — Durham, NH . . . p. A-1529
WENY-TV (36) — Elmira, NY . . . p. A-875
WEPH (49) — Tupelo, MS . . . p. A-727
WEPX-TV (26) — Greenville, NC . . . p. A-926
WESH (11) — Daytona Beach, FL . . . p. A-272
† WETA-TV (27) — Washington, DC . . . p. A-1501
† WETK (32) — Burlington, VT . . . p. A-1553
WETM-TV (18) — Elmira, NY . . . p. A-876
† WETP-TV (41) — Sneedville, TN . . . p. A-1549
WEUX (49) — Chippewa Falls, WI . . . p. A-1408
WEVV-TV (45) — Evansville, IN . . . p. A-466
WEWS-TV (15) — Cleveland, OH . . . p. A-980
WEYI-TV (30) — Saginaw, MI . . . p. A-675

WFAA (8) — Dallas, TX . . . p. A-1227
WFBD (48) — Destin, FL . . . p. A-274
WFDC-DT (15) — Arlington, VA . . . p. A-1331
WFFF-TV (43) — Burlington, VT . . . p. A-1326
WFFP-TV (24) — Danville, VA . . . p. A-1336
WFFT-TV (36) — Fort Wayne, IN . . . p. A-470
WFGC (49) — Palm Beach, FL . . . p. A-316
WFGX (50) — Fort Walton Beach, FL . . . p. A-280
WFIE (46) — Evansville, IN . . . p. A-467
† WFIQ (22) — Florence, AL . . . p. A-1492
WFLA-TV (7) — Tampa, FL . . . p. A-332
WFLD (31) — Chicago, IL . . . p. A-428
WFLI-TV (42) — Cleveland, TN . . . p. A-1160
WFLX (28) — West Palm Beach, FL . . . p. A-339
WFMJ-TV (20) — Youngstown, OH . . . p. A-1007
WFMY-TV (51) — Greensboro, NC . . . p. A-923
WFMZ-TV (46) — Allentown, PA . . . p. A-1068
WFNA (25) — Gulf Shores, AL . . . p. A-34
WFOR-TV (22) — Miami, FL . . . p. A-299
WFOX-TV (32) — Jacksonville, FL . . . p. A-286
† WFPT (28) — Frederick, MD . . . p. A-1519
WFPX-TV (36) — Fayetteville, NC . . . p. A-920
WFQX-TV (32) — Cadillac, MI . . . p. A-646
WFRV-TV (39) — Green Bay, WI . . . p. A-1415
WFSB (33) — Hartford, CT . . . p. A-246
† WFSG (38) — Panama City, FL . . . p. A-1503
† WFSU-TV (32) — Tallahassee, FL . . . p. A-1503
WFTC (29) — Minneapolis, MN . . . p. A-698
WFTS-TV (29) — Tampa, FL . . . p. A-333
WFTT-DT (47) — Tampa, FL . . . p. A-334
WFTV (39) — Orlando, FL . . . p. A-311
WFTX-TV (35) — Cape Coral, FL . . . p. A-268
WFTY-DT (23) — Smithtown, NY . . . p. A-896
WFUP (45) — Vanderbilt, MI . . . p. A-680
WFUT-DT (30) — Newark, NJ . . . p. A-831
† WFWA (40) — Fort Wayne, IN . . . p. A-1510
WFXB (18) — Myrtle Beach, SC . . . p. A-1131
WFXG (31) — Augusta, GA . . . p. A-355
WFXI (8) — Morehead City, NC . . . p. A-935
WFXL (12) — Albany, GA . . . p. A-345
WFXP (22) — Erie, PA . . . p. A-1073
WFXR (17) — Roanoke, VA . . . p. A-1353
WFXT (31) — Boston, MA . . . p. A-624
WFXV (27) — Utica, NY . . . p. A-904
† WFYI (21) — Indianapolis, IN . . . p. A-1510

WGAL (8) — Lancaster, PA . . . p. A-1084
WGBA-TV (41) — Green Bay, WI . . . p. A-1416
WGBC (31) — Meridian, MS . . . p. A-723
† WGBH-TV (19) — Boston, MA . . . p. A-1520
WGBO-DT (38) — Joliet, IL . . . p. A-439
† WGBX-TV (43) — Boston, MA . . . p. A-1520
† WGBY-TV (22) — Springfield, MA . . . p. A-1520
WGCB-TV (30) — Red Lion, PA . . . p. A-1099
WGCL-TV (19) — Atlanta, GA . . . p. A-349
† WGCU (31) — Fort Myers, FL . . . p. A-1501
WGEM-TV (10) — Quincy, IL . . . p. A-448
WGEN-TV (8) — Key West, FL . . . p. A-290
WGFL (28) — High Springs, FL . . . p. A-283
WGGB-TV (40) — Springfield, MA . . . p. A-634
WGGN-TV (42) — Sandusky, OH . . . p. A-998
WGGS-TV (16) — Greenville, SC . . . p. A-1127
WGHP (35) — High Point, NC . . . p. A-930
† WGIQ (44) — Louisville, AL . . . p. A-1493
WGMB-TV (45) — Baton Rouge, LA . . . p. A-571
WGME-TV (38) — Portland, ME . . . p. A-604
WGNM (45) — Macon, GA . . . p. A-367
WGNO (26) — New Orleans, LA . . . p. A-584
WGNT (50) — Portsmouth, VA . . . p. A-1348
WGN-TV (19) — Chicago, IL . . . p. A-429
† WGPT (36) — Oakland, MD . . . p. A-1519
WGPX-TV (14) — Burlington, NC . . . p. A-913
WGRZ (33) — Buffalo, NY . . . p. A-867
WGSA (35) — Baxley, GA . . . p. A-359
WGTA (24) — Toccoa, GA . . . p. A-378
† WGTE-TV (29) — Toledo, OH . . . p. A-1539
WGTQ (8) — Sault Ste. Marie, MI . . . p. A-676
WGTU (29) — Traverse City, MI . . . p. A-678
† WGTV (8) — Athens, GA . . . p. A-1504
WGTW-TV (27) — Burlington, NJ . . . p. A-828
† WGVK (5) — Kalamazoo, MI . . . p. A-1522
† WGVU-TV (11) — Grand Rapids, MI . . . p. A-1521
WGWG (34) — Charleston, SC . . . p. A-1117
WGWW (9) — Anniston, AL . . . p. A-23
WGXA (16) — Macon, GA . . . p. A-368

WHAG-TV (26) — Hagerstown, MD . . . p. A-615
WHAM-TV (13) — Rochester, NY . . . p. A-889
WHAS-TV (11) — Louisville, KY . . . p. A-558
† WHA-TV (20) — Madison, WI . . . p. A-1557
WHBF-TV (4) — Rock Island, IL . . . p. A-450
WHBQ-TV (13) — Memphis, TN . . . p. A-1177
WHBR (34) — Pensacola, FL . . . p. A-322
WHDF (14) — Florence, AL . . . p. A-31
WHDH (42) — Boston, MA . . . p. A-625
WHDT (42) — Stuart, FL . . . p. A-328
WHEC-TV (10) — Rochester, NY . . . p. A-890
WHFT-TV (46) — Miami, FL . . . p. A-300
WHIO-TV (41) — Dayton, OH . . . p. A-989
† WHIQ (24) — Huntsville, AL . . . p. A-1492
WHIZ-TV (40) — Zanesville, OH . . . p. A-1010
WHKY-TV (40) — Hickory, NC . . . p. A-929
† WHLA-TV (30) — La Crosse, WI . . . p. A-1557
WHLT (22) — Hattiesburg, MS . . . p. A-714
WHLV-TV (51) — Cocoa, FL . . . p. A-271
WHMB-TV (20) — Indianapolis, IN . . . p. A-476
† WHMC (9) — Conway, SC . . . p. A-1544
WHME-TV (48) — South Bend, IN . . . p. A-486
WHNO (21) — New Orleans, LA . . . p. A-585
WHNS (21) — Greenville, SC . . . p. A-1128
WHNT-TV (19) — Huntsville, AL . . . p. A-38
WHO-DT (13) — Des Moines, IA . . . p. A-506
WHOI (19) — Peoria, IL . . . p. A-446
WHP-TV (21) — Harrisburg, PA . . . p. A-1078
WHPX-TV (26) — New London, CT . . . p. A-252
† WHRM-TV (24) — Wausau, WI . . . p. A-1558
† WHRO-TV (16) — Hampton-Norfolk, VA . . . p. A-1554
WHSG-TV (44) — Monroe, GA . . . p. A-371
WHSV-TV (49) — Harrisonburg, VA . . . p. A-1339
† WHTJ (46) — Charlottesville, VA . . . p. A-1553
WHTM-TV (10) — Harrisburg, PA . . . p. A-1079
WHTN (38) — Murfreesboro, TN . . . p. A-1182
WHTV (34) — Jackson, MI . . . p. A-663
† WHUT-TV (33) — Washington, DC . . . p. A-1501
† WHWC-TV (27) — Menomonie, WI . . . p. A-1557
† WHYY-TV (12) — Wilmington, DE . . . p. A-1500

WIAT (30) — Birmingham, AL . . . p. A-27
WIBW-TV (13) — Topeka, KS . . . p. A-537
WICD (41) — Champaign, IL . . . p. A-424
WICS (42) — Springfield, IL . . . p. A-455
WICU-TV (12) — Erie, PA . . . p. A-1074
WICZ-TV (8) — Binghamton, NY . . . p. A-865
WIDP (45) — Guayama, PR . . . p. A-1466
WIFR (41) — Freeport, IL . . . p. A-436
† WIIQ (19) — Demopolis, AL . . . p. A-1492
† WILL-TV (9) — Urbana, IL . . . p. A-1509
WILX-TV (10) — Onondaga, MI . . . p. A-673
WINK-TV (50) — Fort Myers, FL . . . p. A-277
WINM (12) — Angola, IN . . . p. A-460
WINP-TV (38) — Pittsburgh, PA . . . p. A-1093
† WIPB (23) — Muncie, IN . . . p. A-1510
† WIPM-TV (35) — Mayaguez, PR . . . p. A-1543
† WIPR-TV (43) — San Juan, PR . . . p. A-1543
WIPX-TV (27) — Bloomington, IN . . . p. A-462
WIRS (41) — Yauco, PR . . . p. A-1483
WIRT-DT (13) — Hibbing, MN . . . p. A-692
WIS (10) — Columbia, SC . . . p. A-1120
WISC-TV (50) — Madison, WI . . . p. A-1423
WISE-TV (18) — Fort Wayne, IN . . . p. A-471
WISH-TV (9) — Indianapolis, IN . . . p. A-477
WISN-TV (34) — Milwaukee, WI . . . p. A-1430
† WITF-TV (36) — Harrisburg, PA . . . p. A-1542
WITI (33) — Milwaukee, WI . . . p. A-1431
WITN-TV (32) — Washington, NC . . . p. A-941
† WITV (7) — Charleston, SC . . . p. A-1544
WIVB-TV (39) — Buffalo, NY . . . p. A-868
WIVT (34) — Binghamton, NY . . . p. A-866
WIWN (5) — Fond du Lac, WI . . . p. A-1413
WIYC (48) — Troy, AL . . . p. A-53

WJAC-TV (34) — Johnstown, PA . . . p. A-1082
WJAL (39) — Hagerstown, MD . . . p. A-616
WJAR (50) — Providence, RI . . . p. A-1109
WJAX-TV (19) — Jacksonville, FL . . . p. A-287
WJBF (42) — Augusta, GA . . . p. A-356
WJBK (7) — Detroit, MI . . . p. A-651
WJCL (22) — Savannah, GA . . . p. A-374
† WJCT (7) — Jacksonville, FL . . . p. A-1502
† WJEB-TV (44) — Jacksonville, FL . . . p. A-1502
WJET-TV (24) — Erie, PA . . . p. A-1075
WJFB (44) — Lebanon, TN . . . p. A-1175
WJFW-TV (16) — Rhinelander, WI . . . p. A-1436
WJHG-TV (18) — Panama City, FL . . . p. A-317
WJHL-TV (11) — Johnson City, TN . . . p. A-1168
WJKT (39) — Jackson, TN . . . p. A-1166
WJLA-TV (7) — Washington, DC . . . p. A-261
WJLP (3) — Middletown Township, NJ . . . p. A-830
WJMN-TV (48) — Escanaba, MI . . . p. A-656
† WJPM-TV (45) — Florence, SC . . . p. A-1544
WJPX (21) — San Juan, PR . . . p. A-1478
WJRT-TV (12) — Flint, MI . . . p. A-657
† WJSP-TV (23) — Columbus, GA . . . p. A-1505
WJTC (45) — Pensacola, FL . . . p. A-323

D-6

TV & Cable Factbook No. 85

U.S. Television Stations by Call Letters

WJTV (12) — Jackson, MS		p. A-718
WJW (8) — Cleveland, OH		p. A-981
†WJWJ-TV (44) — Beaufort, SC		p. A-1544
WJWN-TV (39) — San Sebastian, PR		p. A-1482
WJXT (42) — Jacksonville, FL		p. A-288
WJXX (10) — Orange Park, FL		p. A-310
WJYS (36) — Hammond, IN		p. A-474
WJZ-TV (13) — Baltimore, MD		p. A-611
WJZY (47) — Belmont, NC		p. A-912
WKAQ-TV (28) — San Juan, PR		p. A-1479
†WKAR-TV (40) — East Lansing, MI		p. A-1521
†WKAS (26) — Ashland, KY		p. A-1513
WKBD-TV (14) — Detroit, MI		p. A-652
WKBN-TV (41) — Youngstown, OH		p. A-1008
WKBS-TV (46) — Altoona, PA		p. A-1070
WKBT-DT (8) — La Crosse, WI		p. A-1420
WKBW-TV (38) — Buffalo, NY		p. A-869
WKCF (17) — Clermont, FL		p. A-270
WKEF (18) — Dayton, OH		p. A-990
†WKGB-TV (48) — Bowling Green, KY		p. A-1513
†WKHA (16) — Hazard, KY		p. A-1514
†WKLE (42) — Lexington, KY		p. A-1514
†WKMA-TV (42) — Madisonville, KY		p. A-1515
WKMG-TV (26) — Orlando, FL		p. A-312
†WKMJ-TV (38) — Louisville, KY		p. A-1514
†WKMR (15) — Morehead, KY		p. A-1514
†WKMU (36) — Murray, KY		p. A-1515
†WKNO (29) — Memphis, TN		p. A-1548
WKNX-TV (7) — Knoxville, TN		p. A-1172
†WKOH (30) — Owensboro, KY		p. A-1515
WKOI-TV (39) — Richmond, IN		p. A-484
†WKON (44) — Owenton, KY		p. A-1515
†WKOP-TV (17) — Knoxville, TN		p. A-1548
WKOW (26) — Madison, WI		p. A-1424
†WKPC-TV (17) — Louisville, KY		p. A-1515
†WKPD (41) — Paducah, KY		p. A-1516
†WKPI-TV (24) — Pikeville, KY		p. A-1516
WKPT-TV (27) — Kingsport, TN		p. A-1169
WKPV (19) — Ponce, PR		p. A-1472
WKRC-TV (12) — Cincinnati, OH		p. A-977
WKRG-TV (27) — Mobile, AL		p. A-42
WKRN-TV (27) — Nashville, TN		p. A-1183
†WKSO-TV (14) — Somerset, KY		p. A-1516
WKTC (39) — Sumter, SC		p. A-1135
WKTV (29) — Utica, NY		p. A-905
WKYC (17) — Cleveland, OH		p. A-982
WKYT-TV (36) — Lexington, KY		p. A-552
†WKYU-TV (18) — Bowling Green, KY		p. A-1514
†WKZT-TV (43) — Elizabethtown, KY		p. A-1514
†WLAE-TV (31) — New Orleans, LA		p. A-1517
WLAJ (25) — Lansing, MI		p. A-666
WLAX (17) — La Crosse, WI		p. A-1421
WLBT (30) — Jackson, MS		p. A-719
WLBZ (2) — Bangor, ME		p. A-599
†WLED-TV (48) — Littleton, NH		p. A-1529
†WLEF-TV (36) — Park Falls, WI		p. A-1558
WLEX-TV (39) — Lexington, KY		p. A-553
WLFB (40) — Bluefield, WV		p. A-1389
WLFG (49) — Grundy, VA		p. A-1337
WLFI-TV (11) — Lafayette, IN		p. A-482
WLFL (27) — Raleigh, NC		p. A-937
WLGA (30) — Opelika, AL		p. A-49
WLII-DT (11) — Caguas, PR		p. A-1462
WLIO (8) — Lima, OH		p. A-992
†WLIW (21) — Garden City, NY		p. A-1532
WLJC-TV (7) — Beattyville, KY		p. A-545
†WLJT-DT (47) — Lexington, TN		p. A-1548
WLKY (26) — Louisville, KY		p. A-559
WLLA (45) — Kalamazoo, MI		p. A-664
WLMB (5) — Toledo, OH		p. A-1002
WLMT (31) — Memphis, TN		p. A-1178
WLNE-TV (49) — New Bedford, MA		p. A-630
WLNS-TV (36) — Lansing, MI		p. A-667
WLNY-TV (47) — Riverhead, NY		p. A-888
WLOO (41) — Vicksburg, MS		p. A-729
WLOS (13) — Asheville, NC		p. A-910
WLOV-TV (16) — West Point, MS		p. A-730
WLOX (39) — Biloxi, MS		p. A-709
†WLPB-TV (25) — Baton Rouge, LA		p. A-1516
WLPX-TV (39) — Charleston, WV		p. A-1392
†WLRN-TV (20) — Miami, FL		p. A-1502
WLS-TV (44) — Chicago, IL		p. A-430
WLTV-DT (23) — Miami, FL		p. A-301
WLTX (17) — Columbia, SC		p. A-1121
WLTZ (35) — Columbus, GA		p. A-361
WLUC-TV (35) — Marquette, MI		p. A-669
WLUK-TV (11) — Green Bay, WI		p. A-1417
WLVI (41) — Cambridge, MA		p. A-627
†WLVT-TV (39) — Allentown, PA		p. A-1541
WLWC (22) — New Bedford, MA		p. A-631
WLWT (35) — Cincinnati, OH		p. A-978
WLXI (43) — Greensboro, NC		p. A-924
†WMAB-TV (10) — Mississippi State, MS		p. A-1525
†WMAE-TV (12) — Booneville, MS		p. A-1524
†WMAH-TV (19) — Biloxi, MS		p. A-1524
†WMAO-TV (25) — Greenwood, MS		p. A-1524
WMAQ-TV (29) — Chicago, IL		p. A-431
WMAR-TV (38) — Baltimore, MD		p. A-612
†WMAU-TV (18) — Bude, MS		p. A-1524
†WMAV-TV (36) — Oxford, MS		p. A-1525
†WMAW-TV (44) — Meridian, MS		p. A-1525
WMAZ-TV (13) — Macon, GA		p. A-369
WMBB (13) — Panama City, FL		p. A-318
WMBC-TV (18) — Newton, NJ		p. A-832
WMBD-TV (30) — Peoria, IL		p. A-447
WMBF-TV (32) — Myrtle Beach, SC		p. A-1132
WMCF-TV (46) — Montgomery, AL		p. A-46
WMCN-TV (44) — Atlantic City, NJ		p. A-826
WMC-TV (5) — Memphis, TN		p. A-1179
WMDE (5) — Dover, DE		p. A-255
WMDN (24) — Meridian, MS		p. A-724
WMDT (47) — Salisbury, MD		p. A-618
†WMEA-TV (45) — Biddeford, ME		p. A-1518
†WMEB-TV (9) — Orono, ME		p. A-1518
†WMEC (21) — Macomb, IL		p. A-1508
†WMED-TV (10) — Calais, ME		p. A-1518
WMEI (14) — Arecibo, PR		p. A-1460
†WMEM-TV (10) — Presque Isle, ME		p. A-1518
WMFD-TV (12) — Mansfield, OH		p. A-995
WMFP (18) — Lawrence, MA		p. A-628
WMGM-TV (36) — Wildwood, NJ		p. A-836
WMGT-TV (40) — Macon, GA		p. A-370
†WMHT (34) — Schenectady, NY		p. A-1533
WMLW-TV (48) — Racine, WI		p. A-1435
WMOR-TV (19) — Lakeland, FL		p. A-293
WMOW (12) — Crandon, WI		p. A-1409
†WMPB (29) — Baltimore, MD		p. A-1519
†WMPN-TV (20) — Jackson, MS		p. A-1525
†WMPT (42) — Annapolis, MD		p. A-1518
WMPV-TV (20) — Mobile, AL		p. A-43
WMSN-TV (49) — Madison, WI		p. A-1425
†WMSY-TV (42) — Marion, VA		p. A-1554
†WMTJ (16) — Fajardo, PR		p. A-1543
WMTV (19) — Madison, WI		p. A-1426
WMTW (8) — Poland Spring, ME		p. A-602
†WMUM-TV (7) — Cochran, GA		p. A-1505
WMUR-TV (9) — Manchester, NH		p. A-822
†WMVS (8) — Milwaukee, WI		p. A-1558
†WMVT (35) — Milwaukee, WI		p. A-1558
WMWC-TV (8) — Galesburg, IL		p. A-437
WMYA-TV (14) — Anderson, SC		p. A-1113
WMYD (21) — Detroit, MI		p. A-653
WMYO (51) — Salem, IN		p. A-485
WMYT-TV (39) — Rock Hill, SC		p. A-1133
WMYV (33) — Greensboro, NC		p. A-925
WNAB (23) — Nashville, TN		p. A-1184
WNAC-TV (12) — Providence, RI		p. A-1110
WNBC (28) — New York, NY		p. A-882
WNBW-DT (9) — Gainesville, FL		p. A-282
WNCF (31) — Montgomery, AL		p. A-47
WNCN (17) — Goldsboro, NC		p. A-922
WNCT-TV (10) — Greenville, NC		p. A-927
WNDU-TV (42) — South Bend, IN		p. A-487
WNDY-TV (32) — Marion, IN		p. A-483
†WNED-TV (43) — Buffalo, NY		p. A-1532
†WNEH (18) — Greenwood, SC		p. A-1545
WNEM-TV (22) — Bay City, MI		p. A-645
†WNEO (45) — Alliance, OH		p. A-1537
WNEP-TV (50) — Scranton, PA		p. A-1100
†WNET (13) — Newark, NJ		p. A-1530
WNEU (34) — Merrimack, NH		p. A-823
†WNGH-TV (33) — Chatsworth, GA		p. A-1505
†WNIN (9) — Evansville, IN		p. A-1509
†WNIT (35) — South Bend, IN		p. A-1510
†WNJB (8) — New Brunswick, NJ		p. A-1530
†WNJN (51) — Montclair, NJ		p. A-1530
†WNJS (22) — Camden, NJ		p. A-1530
†WNJT (43) — Trenton, NJ		p. A-1530
WNJU (36) — Linden, NJ		p. A-829
WNJX-TV (23) — Mayaguez, PR		p. A-1468
WNKY (16) — Bowling Green, KY		p. A-547
WNLO (32) — Buffalo, NY		p. A-870
†WNMU (13) — Marquette, MI		p. A-1522
WNNE (25) — Hartford, VT		p. A-1328
WNOL-TV (15) — New Orleans, LA		p. A-586
†WNPB-TV (33) — Morgantown, WV		p. A-1557
†WNPI-DT (23) — Norwood, NY		p. A-1532
†WNPT (8) — Nashville, TN		p. A-1549
WNPX-TV (36) — Cookeville, TN		p. A-1161
†WNSC-TV (15) — Rock Hill, SC		p. A-1545
†WNTV (9) — Greenville, SC		p. A-1545
WNTZ-TV (49) — Natchez, MS		p. A-726
WNUV (40) — Baltimore, MD		p. A-613
†WNVC (24) — Fairfax, VA		p. A-1553
†WNVT (30) — Goldvein, VA		p. A-1554
WNWO-TV (49) — Toledo, OH		p. A-1003
WNYA (13) — Pittsfield, MA		p. A-633
WNYB (26) — Jamestown, NY		p. A-878
†WNYE-TV (24) — New York, NY		p. A-1532
WNYI (20) — Ithaca, NY		p. A-877
†WNYJ-TV (29) — West Milford, NJ		p. A-1531
WNYO-TV (49) — Buffalo, NY		p. A-871
WNYS-TV (44) — Syracuse, NY		p. A-898
WNYT (12) — Albany, NY		p. A-859
WNYW (44) — New York, NY		p. A-883
WOAI-TV (48) — San Antonio, TX		p. A-1292
WOAY-TV (50) — Oak Hill, WV		p. A-1400
WOFL (22) — Orlando, FL		p. A-313
WOGX (31) — Ocala, FL		p. A-309
WOI-DT (5) — Ames, IA		p. A-495
WOIO (10) — Shaker Heights, OH		p. A-999
WOLE-DT (12) — Aguadilla, PR		p. A-1457
WOLF-TV (45) — Hazleton, PA		p. A-1080
WOLO-TV (8) — Columbia, SC		p. A-1122
WOOD-TV (7) — Grand Rapids, MI		p. A-659
WOPX-TV (48) — Melbourne, FL		p. A-296
WORA-TV (29) — Mayaguez, PR		p. A-1469
WORO-DT (13) — Fajardo, PR		p. A-1464
WOST (22) — Mayaguez, PR		p. A-1470
†WOSU-TV (38) — Columbus, OH		p. A-1538
WOTF-DT (43) — Melbourne, FL		p. A-297

2017 Edition

D-7

U.S. Television Stations by Call Letters

WOTV (20) — Battle Creek, MI		p. A-642
† WOUB-TV (27) — Athens, OH		p. A-1537
† WOUC-TV (35) — Cambridge, OH		p. A-1538
WOWK-TV (13) — Huntington, WV		p. A-1396
WOWT (22) — Omaha, NE		p. A-798
† WPBA (21) — Atlanta, GA		p. A-1504
WPBF (16) — Tequesta, FL		p. A-336
WPBN-TV (47) — Traverse City, MI		p. A-679
† WPBO (43) — Portsmouth, OH		p. A-1539
† WPBS-DT (41) — Watertown, NY		p. A-1533
† WPBT (18) — Miami, FL		p. A-1502
WPCB-TV (50) — Greensburg, PA		p. A-1077
WPCH-TV (20) — Atlanta, GA		p. A-350
WPCT (47) — Panama City Beach, FL		p. A-320
WPCW (11) — Jeannette, PA		p. A-1081
WPDE-TV (16) — Florence, SC		p. A-1125
WPEC (13) — West Palm Beach, FL		p. A-340
WPFO (23) — Waterville, ME		p. A-607
WPGA-TV (32) — Perry, GA		p. A-372
WPGD-TV (33) — Hendersonville, TN		p. A-1164
WPGH-TV (43) — Pittsburgh, PA		p. A-1094
WPGX (9) — Panama City, FL		p. A-319
WPHL-TV (17) — Philadelphia, PA		p. A-1088
WPIX (11) — New York, NY		p. A-884
WPLG (10) — Miami, FL		p. A-302
WPME (35) — Lewiston, ME		p. A-601
WPMI-TV (15) — Mobile, AL		p. A-44
WPMT (47) — York, PA		p. A-1106
† WPNE-TV (42) — Green Bay, WI		p. A-1557
WPNT (42) — Pittsburgh, PA		p. A-1095
WPPX-TV (31) — Wilmington, DE		p. A-257
WPRI-TV (13) — Providence, RI		p. A-1111
WPSD-TV (32) — Paducah, KY		p. A-563
WPSG (32) — Philadelphia, PA		p. A-1089
† WPSU-TV (15) — Clearfield, PA		p. A-1541
WPTA (24) — Fort Wayne, IN		p. A-472
† WPTD (16) — Dayton, OH		p. A-1538
† WPTO (28) — Oxford, OH		p. A-1539
WPTV-TV (12) — West Palm Beach, FL		p. A-341
WPTZ (14) — Plattsburgh, NY		p. A-886
WPVI-TV (6) — Philadelphia, PA		p. A-1090
WPWR-TV (51) — Gary, IN		p. A-473
WPXA-TV (31) — Rome, GA		p. A-373
WPXC-TV (24) — Brunswick, GA		p. A-360
WPXD-TV (50) — Ann Arbor, MI		p. A-641
WPXE-TV (40) — Kenosha, WI		p. A-1419
WPXG-TV (33) — Concord, NH		p. A-820
WPXH-TV (45) — Gadsden, AL		p. A-32
WPXI (48) — Pittsburgh, PA		p. A-1096
WPXJ-TV (23) — Batavia, NY		p. A-863
WPXK-TV (23) — Jellico, TN		p. A-1167
WPXL-TV (50) — New Orleans, LA		p. A-587
WPXM-TV (35) — Miami, FL		p. A-303
WPXN-TV (31) — New York, NY		p. A-885
WPXP-TV (36) — Lake Worth, FL		p. A-292
WPXQ-TV (17) — Block Island, RI		p. A-1108
WPXR-TV (36) — Roanoke, VA		p. A-1354
WPXS (11) — Mount Vernon, IL		p. A-443
WPXT (43) — Portland, ME		p. A-605
WPXU-TV (34) — Jacksonville, NC		p. A-931
WPXV-TV (46) — Norfolk, VA		p. A-1343
WPXW-TV (34) — Manassas, VA		p. A-1342
WPXX-TV (51) — Memphis, TN		p. A-1180
WQAD-TV (38) — Moline, IL		p. A-442
WQCW (17) — Portsmouth, OH		p. A-997
† WQEC (34) — Quincy, IL		p. A-1509
† WQED (13) — Pittsburgh, PA		p. A-1542
WQHA (50) — Aguada, PR		p. A-1456
WQHS-DT (34) — Cleveland, OH		p. A-983
† WQLN (50) — Erie, PA		p. A-1542
WQMY (29) — Williamsport, PA		p. A-1105
WQOW (15) — Eau Claire, WI		p. A-1412
† WQPT-TV (23) — Moline, IL		p. A-1508
WQPX-TV (32) — Scranton, PA		p. A-1101
WQRF-TV (42) — Rockford, IL		p. A-451
† WQTO (25) — Ponce, PR		p. A-1543
WRAL-TV (48) — Raleigh, NC		p. A-938
WRAY-TV (42) — Wilson, NC		p. A-945
WRAZ (49) — Raleigh, NC		p. A-939
WRBJ-TV (34) — Magee, MS		p. A-722
WRBL (15) — Columbus, GA		p. A-362
WRBU (47) — East St. Louis, IL		p. A-435
WRBW (41) — Orlando, FL		p. A-314
WRCB (13) — Chattanooga, TN		p. A-1158
WRC-TV (48) — Washington, DC		p. A-262
WRDC (28) — Durham, NC		p. A-918
WRDQ (27) — Orlando, FL		p. A-315
WRDW-TV (12) — Augusta, GA		p. A-357
WREG-TV (28) — Memphis, TN		p. A-1181
† WRET-TV (43) — Spartanburg, SC		p. A-1545
WREX (13) — Rockford, IL		p. A-452
WRFB (51) — Carolina, PR		p. A-1463
WRGB (6) — Schenectady, NY		p. A-895
WRGT (30) — Dayton, OH		p. A-991
WRIC-TV (22) — Petersburg, VA		p. A-1346
† WRJA-TV (28) — Sumter, SC		p. A-1545
WRLH-TV (26) — Richmond, VA		p. A-1349
† WRLK-TV (32) — Columbia, SC		p. A-1544
WRLM (47) — Canton, OH		p. A-974
WRNN-TV (48) — Kingston, NY		p. A-879
WROC-TV (45) — Rochester, NY		p. A-891
† WRPT-DT (31) — Hibbing, MN		p. A-1523
WRPX-TV (15) — Rocky Mount, NC		p. A-940
WRSP-TV (44) — Springfield, IL		p. A-456
WRTV (25) — Indianapolis, IN		p. A-478
WRUA (33) — Fajardo, PR		p. A-1465
WRXY-TV (33) — Tice, FL		p. A-337
WSAV-TV (39) — Savannah, GA		p. A-375
WSAW-TV (7) — Wausau, WI		p. A-1440
WSAZ-TV (23) — Huntington, WV		p. A-1397
† WSBE-TV (21) — Providence, RI		p. A-1543
WSBK-TV (39) — Boston, MA		p. A-626
† WSBN-TV (32) — Norton, VA		p. A-1554
WSBS-TV (3) — Key West, FL		p. A-291
WSBT (22) — South Bend, IN		p. A-488
WSB-TV (39) — Atlanta, GA		p. A-351
WSCV (30) — Fort Lauderdale, FL		p. A-275
† WSEC (15) — Jacksonville, IL		p. A-1508
WSEE-TV (16) — Erie, PA		p. A-1076
WSES (33) — Tuscaloosa, AL		p. A-54
WSET-TV (13) — Lynchburg, VA		p. A-1340
WSFA (12) — Montgomery, AL		p. A-48
WSFJ-TV (24) — Newark, OH		p. A-996
WSFL-TV (19) — Miami, FL		p. A-304
WSFX-TV (30) — Wilmington, NC		p. A-943
WSIL-TV (34) — Harrisburg, IL		p. A-438
† WSIU-TV (8) — Carbondale, IL		p. A-1507
WSJU-TV (31) — San Juan, PR		p. A-1480
WSJV (28) — Elkhart, IN		p. A-464
† WSKA (30) — Corning, NY		p. A-1532
† WSKG-TV (42) — Binghamton, NY		p. A-1532
WSKY-TV (9) — Manteo, NC		p. A-934
WSLS-TV (30) — Roanoke, VA		p. A-1355
WSMH (16) — Flint, MI		p. A-658
WSMV-TV (10) — Nashville, TN		p. A-1185
WSNS-TV (45) — Chicago, IL		p. A-432
WSOC-TV (34) — Charlotte, NC		p. A-917
WSPA-TV (7) — Spartanburg, SC		p. A-1134
WSPX-TV (15) — Syracuse, NY		p. A-899
† WSRE (31) — Pensacola, FL		p. A-1503
WSST-TV (22) — Cordele, GA		p. A-365
WSTE-DT (7) — Ponce, PR		p. A-1473
WSTM-TV (24) — Syracuse, NY		p. A-900
WSTR-TV (33) — Cincinnati, OH		p. A-979
WSUR-DT (9) — Ponce, PR		p. A-1474
WSVI (20) — Christiansted, VI		p. A-1487
WSVN (7) — Miami, FL		p. A-305
WSWB (31) — Scranton, PA		p. A-1102
WSWG (43) — Valdosta, GA		p. A-379
† WSWP-TV (10) — Grandview, WV		p. A-1556
WSYM-TV (38) — Lansing, MI		p. A-668
WSYR-TV (17) — Syracuse, NY		p. A-901
WSYT (19) — Syracuse, NY		p. A-902
WSYX (48) — Columbus, OH		p. A-986
WTAE-TV (51) — Pittsburgh, PA		p. A-1097
WTAJ-TV (32) — Altoona, PA		p. A-1071
WTAP-TV (49) — Parkersburg, WV		p. A-1401
WTAT-TV (24) — Charleston, SC		p. A-1118
WTBY-TV (27) — Poughkeepsie, NY		p. A-887
† WTCE-TV (38) — Fort Pierce, FL		p. A-1501
† WTCI (29) — Chattanooga, TN		p. A-1547
WTCT (17) — Marion, IL		p. A-441
WTCV (32) — San Juan, PR		p. A-1481
WTEN (26) — Albany, NY		p. A-860
† WTGL (46) — Leesburg, FL		p. A-1502
WTGS (28) — Hardeeville, SC		p. A-1130
WTHI-TV (10) — Terre Haute, IN		p. A-490
WTHR (13) — Indianapolis, IN		p. A-479
WTIC-TV (31) — Hartford, CT		p. A-247
WTIN-TV (15) — Ponce, PR		p. A-1475
† WTIU (14) — Bloomington, IN		p. A-1509
WTJP-TV (26) — Gadsden, AL		p. A-33
WTJR (32) — Quincy, IL		p. A-449
† WTJX-TV (44) — Charlotte Amalie, VI		p. A-1559
WTKR (40) — Norfolk, VA		p. A-1344
WTLF (47) — Tallahassee, FL		p. A-329
WTLH (50) — Bainbridge, GA		p. A-358
WTLJ (24) — Muskegon, MI		p. A-672
WTLV (13) — Jacksonville, FL		p. A-289
WTLW (44) — Lima, OH		p. A-993
WTMJ-TV (28) — Milwaukee, WI		p. A-1432
WTNH (10) — New Haven, CT		p. A-251
WTNZ (34) — Knoxville, TN		p. A-1173
WTOC-TV (11) — Savannah, GA		p. A-376
WTOG (44) — St. Petersburg, FL		p. A-325
WTOK-TV (11) — Meridian, MS		p. A-725
WTOL (11) — Toledo, OH		p. A-1004
WTOM-TV (35) — Cheboygan, MI		p. A-649
WTOV-TV (9) — Steubenville, OH		p. A-1001
WTPC-TV (7) — Virginia Beach, VA		p. A-1356
WTPX-TV (46) — Antigo, WI		p. A-1406
WTRF-TV (7) — Wheeling, WV		p. A-1403
WTSF (44) — Ashland, KY		p. A-544
WTSP (10) — St. Petersburg, FL		p. A-326
WTTA (32) — St. Petersburg, FL		p. A-327
WTTE (36) — Columbus, OH		p. A-987
WTTG (36) — Washington, DC		p. A-263
WTTK (29) — Kokomo, IN		p. A-481
WTTO (28) — Homewood, AL		p. A-35
WTTV (48) — Bloomington, IN		p. A-463
† WTTW (47) — Chicago, IL		p. A-1508
WTVA (8) — Tupelo, MS		p. A-728
WTVC (9) — Chattanooga, TN		p. A-1159
WTVD (11) — Durham, NC		p. A-919
WTVE (25) — Reading, PA		p. A-1098
WTVF (25) — Nashville, TN		p. A-1186
WTVG (13) — Toledo, OH		p. A-1005
WTVH (47) — Syracuse, NY		p. A-901
† WTVI (11) — Charlotte, NC		p. A-1534
WTVJ (31) — Miami, FL		p. A-306
WTVM (11) — Columbus, GA		p. A-363

U.S. Television Stations by Call Letters

WTVO (16) — Rockford, IL	p. A-453	
†WTVP (46) — Peoria, IL	p. A-1509	
WTVQ-DT (40) — Lexington, KY	p. A-554	
WTVR-TV (25) — Richmond, VA	p. A-1350	
†WTVS (43) — Detroit, MI	p. A-1521	
WTVT (12) — Tampa, FL	p. A-335	
WTVW (28) — Evansville, IN	p. A-468	
WTVX (34) — Fort Pierce, FL	p. A-278	
WTVY (36) — Dothan, AL	p. A-30	
WTVZ-TV (33) — Norfolk, VA	p. A-1345	
WTWC-TV (40) — Tallahassee, FL	p. A-330	
WTWO (36) — Terre Haute, IN	p. A-491	
†WTWV (23) — Memphis, TN	p. A-1548	
WTXF-TV (42) — Philadelphia, PA	p. A-1091	
WTXL-TV (27) — Tallahassee, FL	p. A-331	
WUAB (28) — Lorain, OH	p. A-994	
†WUCF-TV (23) — Orlando, FL	p. A-1503	
WUCW (22) — Minneapolis, MN	p. A-699	
†WUFT (36) — Gainesville, FL	p. A-1502	
WUHF (28) — Rochester, NY	p. A-892	
†WUJA (48) — Caguas, PR	p. A-1543	
†WUNC-TV (25) — Chapel Hill, NC	p. A-1534	
†WUND-TV (20) — Edenton, NC	p. A-1534	
†WUNE-TV (17) — Linville, NC	p. A-1535	
†WUNF-TV (25) — Asheville, NC	p. A-1533	
†WUNG-TV (44) — Concord, NC	p. A-1534	
WUNI (29) — Worcester, MA	p. A-637	
†WUNJ-TV (29) — Wilmington, NC	p. A-1535	
†WUNK-TV (23) — Greenville, NC	p. A-1535	
†WUNL-TV (32) — Winston-Salem, NC	p. A-1536	
†WUNM-TV (19) — Jacksonville, NC	p. A-1535	
†WUNP-TV (36) — Roanoke Rapids, NC	p. A-1535	
†WUNU (31) — Lumberton, NC	p. A-1535	
†WUNW (27) — Canton, NC	p. A-1534	
WUPA (43) — Atlanta, GA	p. A-352	
WUPL (24) — Slidell, LA	p. A-594	
WUPV (47) — Ashland, VA	p. A-1332	
WUPW (46) — Toledo, OH	p. A-1006	
WUPX-TV (21) — Morehead, KY	p. A-560	
WUSA (9) — Washington, DC	p. A-264	
†WUSF-TV (34) — Tampa, FL	p. A-1504	
†WUSI-TV (19) — Olney, IL	p. A-1509	
WUTB (41) — Baltimore, MD	p. A-614	
WUTF-DT (27) — Marlborough, MA	p. A-629	
WUTR (30) — Utica, NY	p. A-906	
WUTV (14) — Buffalo, NY	p. A-872	
WUVC-DT (38) — Fayetteville, NC	p. A-921	
WUVG-DT (48) — Athens, GA	p. A-346	
WUVN (46) — Hartford, CT	p. A-248	
WUVP-DT (29) — Vineland, NJ	p. A-835	
WUXP-TV (21) — Nashville, TN	p. A-1187	
WVAH-TV (19) — Charleston, WV	p. A-1393	

†WVAN-TV (9) — Savannah, GA	p. A-1505
WVBT (29) — Virginia Beach, VA	p. A-1357
WVCY-TV (22) — Milwaukee, WI	p. A-1433
WVEA-TV (25) — Venice, FL	p. A-338
WVEC (13) — Hampton, VA	p. A-1338
WVEN-TV (49) — Daytona Beach, FL	p. A-273
WVEO (17) — Aguadilla, PR	p. A-1458
†WVER (9) — Rutland, VT	p. A-1553
WVFX (10) — Clarksburg, WV	p. A-1395
†WVIA-TV (41) — Scranton, PA	p. A-1542
WVII-TV (7) — Bangor, ME	p. A-600
WVIR-TV (32) — Charlottesville, VA	p. A-1335
WVIT (35) — New Britain, CT	p. A-249
†WVIZ (26) — Cleveland, OH	p. A-1538
WVLA-TV (34) — Baton Rouge, LA	p. A-572
WVLR (48) — Tazewell, TN	p. A-1189
WVLT-TV (30) — Knoxville, TN	p. A-1174
WVNS-TV (8) — Lewisburg, WV	p. A-1398
WVNY (13) — Burlington, VT	p. A-1327
WVOZ-TV (47) — Ponce, PR	p. A-1476
†WVPB-TV (34) — Huntington, WV	p. A-1556
†WVPT (11) — Staunton, VA	p. A-1555
WVPX-TV (23) — Akron, OH	p. A-972
†WVPY (21) — Front Royal, VA	p. A-1554
WVSN (49) — Humacao, PR	p. A-1467
†WVTA (24) — Windsor, VT	p. A-1553
†WVTB (18) — St. Johnsbury, VT	p. A-1553
WVTM-TV (13) — Birmingham, AL	p. A-28
WVTV (18) — Milwaukee, WI	p. A-1434
WVUA (6) — Tuscaloosa, AL	p. A-55
WVUE-DT (29) — New Orleans, LA	p. A-588
†WVUT (22) — Vincennes, IN	p. A-1510
WVVA (46) — Bluefield, WV	p. A-1390
WVXF (17) — Charlotte Amalie, VI	p. A-1484
WWAY (46) — Wilmington, NC	p. A-944
WWBT (12) — Richmond, VA	p. A-1351
WWCP-TV (8) — Johnstown, PA	p. A-1083
WWCW (20) — Lynchburg, VA	p. A-1341
WWDP (10) — Norwell, MA	p. A-632
WWHO (46) — Chillicothe, OH	p. A-975
WWJ-TV (44) — Detroit, MI	p. A-654
WWJX (23) — Jackson, MS	p. A-720
WWLP (11) — Springfield, MA	p. A-635
WWL-TV (36) — New Orleans, LA	p. A-589
WWMB (21) — Florence, SC	p. A-1126
WWMT (8) — Kalamazoo, MI	p. A-665
WWNY-TV (7) — Carthage, NY	p. A-873
WWOR-TV (38) — Secaucus, NJ	p. A-834
†WWPB (44) — Hagerstown, MD	p. A-1519
WWPX-TV (12) — Martinsburg, WV	p. A-1399
WWRS-TV (43) — Mayville, WI	p. A-1427
WWSB (24) — Sarasota, FL	p. A-324
WWSI (49) — Atlantic City, NJ	p. A-827

WWTI (21) — Watertown, NY	p. A-907
WWTO-TV (10) — La Salle, IL	p. A-440
WWTV (9) — Cadillac, MI	p. A-647
†WWTW (34) — Senatobia, MS	p. A-1525
WWUP-TV (10) — Sault Ste. Marie, MI	p. A-677
WXBU (23) — Lancaster, PA	p. A-1085
WXCW (45) — Naples, FL	p. A-307
†WXEL-TV (27) — West Palm Beach, FL	p. A-1504
WXFT-DT (50) — Aurora, IL	p. A-421
†WXGA-TV (8) — Waycross, GA	p. A-1506
WXIA-TV (10) — Atlanta, GA	p. A-353
WXII-TV (31) — Winston-Salem, NC	p. A-946
WXIN (45) — Indianapolis, IN	p. A-480
WXIX-TV (29) — Newport, KY	p. A-561
WXLV-TV (29) — Winston-Salem, NC	p. A-947
WXMI (19) — Grand Rapids, MI	p. A-660
WXOW (48) — La Crosse, WI	p. A-1422
WXPX-TV (42) — Bradenton, FL	p. A-267
WXTV-DT (40) — Paterson, NJ	p. A-833
WXTX (49) — Columbus, GA	p. A-364
WXVT (15) — Greenville, MS	p. A-711
WXXA-TV (7) — Albany, NY	p. A-861
†WXXI-TV (16) — Rochester, NY	p. A-1533
WXXV-TV (48) — Gulfport, MS	p. A-713
WXYZ-TV (41) — Detroit, MI	p. A-655
†WYBE (35) — Philadelphia, PA	p. A-1542
†WYCC (21) — Chicago, IL	p. A-1508
WYCI (40) — Saranac Lake, NY	p. A-893
WYCW (45) — Asheville, NC	p. A-911
WYDC (48) — Corning, NY	p. A-874
†WYDN (47) — Worcester, MA	p. A-1520
WYDO (47) — Greenville, NC	p. A-928
†WYES-TV (11) — New Orleans, LA	p. A-1517
WYFF (36) — Greenville, SC	p. A-1129
†WYIN (17) — Gary, IN	p. A-1510
WYMT-TV (12) — Hazard, KY	p. A-551
WYOU (13) — Scranton, PA	p. A-1103
WYOW (28) — Eagle River, WI	p. A-1410
WYPX-TV (50) — Amsterdam, NY	p. A-862
WYTV (36) — Youngstown, OH	p. A-1009
WYZZ-TV (28) — Bloomington, IL	p. A-422
WZDX (41) — Huntsville, AL	p. A-39
WZME (42) — Bridgeport, CT	p. A-245
WZMQ (19) — Marquette, MI	p. A-670
WZPX-TV (44) — Battle Creek, MI	p. A-643
WZRB (47) — Columbia, SC	p. A-1123
WZTV (15) — Nashville, TN	p. A-1188
WZVI (43) — Charlotte Amalie, VI	p. A-1485
WZVN-TV (41) — Naples, FL	p. A-308
WZZM (13) — Grand Rapids, MI	p. A-661

Keep your key players on top of breaking telecom and media news.

Get them their own daily dose...

Take advantage of our **highly affordable multi-copy subscription** discounts and ensure all your key players are up to speed on business-critical regulatory activity, legislation, industry developments and competitive intelligence — **first thing, every business morning.**

No more waiting to receive a routed copy after the news cycle is over.

Now you can provide your team with breaking telecom news and analysis while the process can still be influenced.

Contact us today and eliminate the hassles of forwarding/routing while maintaining copyright compliance. Your account manager will help define a distribution package that **meets your intelligence needs and budget.**

Put your whole team in the know.

Communications Daily

Warren Communications News

Call **800-771-9202** today so we can help you find an affordable way to get Communications Daily on eveyone's desk tomorrow morning!

ICARUS ™

Integrated Cable Areas – U.S.
Television & Cable Factbook's Cable Systems Database

Integrated Cable Area (ICA) Definition

Warren Communications News defines as one cable system a community or group of communities which receive essentially the same service at the same price from the same company, regardless of the number of headends or hubs used to deliver this service. *Television & Cable Factbook* has designated each system as an **I**ntegrated **C**able **A**rea and assigned it a unique identifier, the ICA. The ICA also is the unique record number used to relate data in clients' computerized applications that use the ICARUS ™ cable system database.

General Description

A cable television system is defined by the FCC (Sec. 76.5 of the Rules) as follows: "A facility consisting of a set of closed transmission paths and associated signal generation, reception, and control equipment that is designed to provide cable service which includes video programming and which is provided to multiple subscribers within a community, but such term does not include (1) a facility that serves only to retransmit the television signals of one or more television broadcast stations; (2) a facility that serves only subscribers in one or more multiple unit dwellings under common ownership, control or management, unless such facility or facilities uses any public right-of-way; (3) a facility of a common carrier which is subject, in whole or in part, to the provisions of Title II of the Communications Act of 1934, as amended, except that such facility shall be considered a cable system to the extent such facility is used in the transmission of video programming directly to subscribers; or (4) any facilities of any electric utility used solely for operating its electric utility systems."

*Indicates a franchise awarded but not yet operating.

†Indicates application for franchise is pending.

N.A. means information is not available.

All communities with cable service are listed in the index following the cable listings, with a reference to the appropriate cable system.

Information/Data

NOTE: All data is as reported by cable operators or individual cable systems. Not all cable systems report complete data.

Subscriber Counts

Subscriber count is as reported by cable operators or individual cable systems or Factbook editorial research. Basic Subscribers, Expanded Basic Subscribers, and Pay Unit totals at the beginning of each state include a total of analog and digital subscribers. Not all cable systems report complete data.

NOTE: Reports from systems are of varying dates. Total basic subscribers listed in this edition of the Factbook is 58,743,965. Including subscribers not reported to the *Factbook* or to the government, we estimated total basic subscribers as of January 1, 2017 at 48,750,000.

TV Market Ranking

Indicates whether a system lies within 35-mile radius of commercial TV market as defined by FCC Rules & Regulations Governing Cable. If a system lies within the 35-mile radius of more than one Top-100 TV Market, both market numbers are shown. These market rankings are as of September 2016.

Began

Date service started.

Signals

Call letters and affiliations are as of October 1, 2016.

A cable network program is any program furnished to the system by a cable network (national, regional or special) or by a series of interconnected cable systems. Delayed telecasts of programs originated by cable networks or by a series of interconnected cable systems are classified as a network.

Subscriber Fee

Charges for installation and monthly service are shown as well as converter charges when separately stated by the system operator.

Pay Service

A special program service, for which the subscriber pays an extra fee, is listed under "Pay Service" for each system providing such service. Data include number of units using the pay-cable service, programming, transmission method (via local tape, microwave or satellite) and charges to subscribers.

Pay-Per-View

The number of addressable homes; services offered; fee.

Interactive Services

Subscribers; services offered; fee.

Personnel

The five types listed are: Manager; chief technician; program director; marketing director; customer service manager.

Ownership

Officers, titles and percentages listed are as reported by system operators to *Television & Cable Factbook* or to the FCC.

All cable system owners are listed in Ownership of Cable Systems in U.S. following the cable system listings.

Interests in broadcasting, telephone, publishing, etc., are noted.

Cable Directory Description

Recent sales of systems are reported on individual systems as well as in ownership sections.

Information is obtained through system operators, the FCC, franchise holders, applicants, city officials and other sources. Though data may be incomplete, it is the best obtainable through diligent inquiry.

For statistical tables of cable industry development, largest systems, etc., consult the Index at beginning of this volume.

WARREN COMMUNICATIONS NEWS
2115 Ward Court NW
Washington, DC 20037

Phone: 202-872-9200
Fax: 202-318-8350
Email: info@warren-news.com
web site: www.warren-news.com

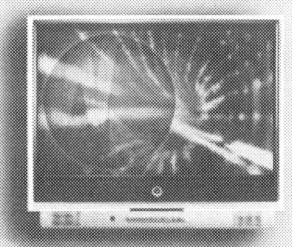

ADVANCED TVFactbook
TELCO/IPTV • CABLE TV • TV STATIONS

Subscription pays for itself in just a few searches

Now you can access the entire contents of the Television & Cable Factbook instantly on your desktop or any Internet connection.

Your subscription to the *Advanced TV Factbook* online will provide you with access to over 1 million detailed records. Best of all, the database is continuously updated to ensure you always have the most current industry intelligence.

Save enormous amounts of time, effort & money

The user-friendly query interface allows you to perform fully customized data searches—so you can retrieve data in a number of ways, tailored to your precise needs. The search options are extensive and flexible, and will save you hours and hours of cumbersome research time.

You'll recover your subscription cost after just a few searches and continue to save enormous amounts of time, money and effort with every search.

See for yourself— take a risk free 7-day trial

Take a FREE 7-day trial —
See for yourself why the *Advanced TV Factbook* online is referred to as "an invaluable reference tool."

Sign up at **www.warren-news.com/factbookonline.htm**
You have **nothing to lose** and lots of time and money to save.

Continuously Updated • Easy Internet Access • Fully Searchable

Cable Systems State Index

Alabama	D-15
Alaska	D-37
Arizona	D-44
Arkansas	D-54
California	D-82
Colorado	D-111
Connecticut	D-127
Delaware	D-132
District of Columbia	D-133
Florida	D-134
Georgia	D-151
Hawaii	D-177
Idaho	D-179
Illinois	D-186
Indiana	D-225
Iowa	D-240
Kansas	D-278
Kentucky	D-306
Louisiana	D-333
Maine	D-353
Maryland	D-359
Massachusetts	D-365
Michigan	D-370
Minnesota	D-391
Mississippi	D-426
Missouri	D-440
Montana	D-464
Nebraska	D-479
Nevada	D-500
New Hampshire	D-506
New Jersey	D-510
New Mexico	D-519
New York	D-529
North Carolina	D-550
North Dakota	D-568
Ohio	D-577
Oklahoma	D-607
Oregon	D-637
Pennsylvania	D-648
Rhode Island	D-683
South Carolina	D-684
South Dakota	D-694
Tennessee	D-705
Texas	D-718
Utah	D-790
Vermont	D-797
Virginia	D-801
Washington	D-814
West Virginia	D-833
Wisconsin	D-848
Wyoming	D-871
Other U.S. Territories and Possessions	D-881
Cable Owners	D-887
Cable Community Index	(end of Cable Volume 2)

ALABAMA

Total Systems: 90	Communities with Applications: 0
Total Communities Served: 535	Number of Basic Subscribers: 802,478
Franchises Not Yet Operating: 0	Number of Expanded Basic Subscribers: 957
Applications Pending: 0	Number of Pay Units: 4,120

Top 100 Markets Represented: Atlanta-Rome, GA (18); Birmingham (40); Mobile, AL-Pensacola, FL (59); Chattanooga, TN (78); Columbus, GA (94); Huntsville-Decatur (96).

For a list of cable communities in this section, see the Cable Community Index located in the back of Cable Volume 2.
For explanation of terms used in cable system listings, see p. D-11.

ABBEVILLE—Comcast Cable. Now served by TALLAHASSEE, FL [FL0283]. ICA: AL0161.

ABERNANT—Formerly served by Comcast Cable. No longer in operation. ICA: AL0113.

ADDISON—Charter Communications. Now served by PELHAM, AL [AL0192]. ICA: AL0162.

AKRON (town)—Formerly served by CableSouth Inc. No longer in operation. ICA: AL0163.

ALBERTVILLE—Charter Communications. Now served by DECATUR, AL [AL0184]. ICA: AL0014.

ALEXANDER CITY—Charter Communications. Now served by PELHAM, AL [AL0192]. ICA: AL0164.

ALICEVILLE—Northland Cable Television, 307 1st St South, PO Box 1269, Reform, AL 35481. Phones: 205-375-2275; 800-828-8019. Fax: 205-375-2298. E-mail: aliceville@northlandcabletv.com. Web Site: http://www.yournorthland.com. Also serves Carrollton, Gordo, Kennedy, Lamar County (southern portion), Millport, Pickens County, Pickensville & Reform. ICA: AL0055.
TV Market Ranking: Below 100 (ALICEVILLE, Carrollton, Gordo, Kennedy, Lamar County (southern portion), Pickens County (portions), Pickensville, Reform, Millport, Outside TV Markets (Pickens County (portions)). Franchise award date: N.A. Franchise expiration date: N.A. Began: May 1, 1971.
Channel capacity: 55 (operating 2-way). Channels available but not in use: N.A.
Basic Service
Subscribers: 1,331.
Programming (received off-air): WBIQ (PBS) Birmingham; WBRC (Bounce TV, FOX) Birmingham; WCBI-TV (CBS, CW, MNT) Columbus; WDBB (CW) Bessemer; WLOV-TV (FOX, MeTV, This TV) West Point; WSES (ABC, TNN) Tuscaloosa; WTVA (ABC, NBC) Tupelo; WVTM-TV (MeTV, NBC) Birmingham.
Programming (via satellite): A&E; AMC; BET; Cartoon Network; CNN; C-SPAN; Discovery Channel; ESPN; ESPN2; Freeform; Great American Country; HGTV; HLN; Nickelodeon; QVC; Spike TV; TBS; The Weather Channel; TNT; Trinity Broadcasting Network (TBN); Turner Classic Movies; USA Network; WGN America.
Fee: $60.00 installation; $47.64 monthly.
Pay Service 1
Pay Units: N.A.
Programming (via satellite): Cinemax; HBO; Showtime; Starz Encore.

Fee: $20.95 monthly.
Video-On-Demand: Yes
Internet Service
Operational: Yes.
Broadband Service: Northland Express.
Telephone Service
None
Miles of Plant: 237.0 (coaxial); 130.0 (fiber optic).
Executive Vice President: Richard I. Clark. Regional Manager: Ricky Moneyham. Chief Technician: Bart Hudgins. Marketing Director: Lee Beck.
Ownership: Northland Communications Corp. (MSO).

ALLGOOD—Formerly served by SouthTel Communications LP. No longer in operation. ICA: AL0165.

ALTOONA—Formerly served by Charter Communications. No longer in operation. ICA: AL0231.

ANDALUSIA—TV Cable Company of Andalusia, 213 Dunson St, PO Box 34, Andalusia, AL 36420. Phone: 334-222-6464. Fax: 334-222-7226. E-mail: support@andycable.com. Web Site: http://www.andycable.com. ICA: AL0043.
TV Market Ranking: Outside TV Markets (ANDALUSIA). Franchise award date: January 1, 1963. Franchise expiration date: N.A. Began: March 1, 1965.
Channel capacity: N.A. Channels available but not in use: N.A.
Basic Service
Subscribers: 5,902.
Programming (received off-air): WAKA (CBS, MeTV) Selma; WCOV-TV (Antenna TV, FOX, This TV) Montgomery; WDIQ (PBS) Dozier; WEAR-TV (ABC, The Country Network) Pensacola; WIYC (WeatherNation) Troy; WKRG-TV (CBS, MeTV) Mobile; WNCF (ABC) Montgomery; WPMI-TV (NBC) Mobile; WSFA (Bounce TV, NBC) Montgomery; WTVY (CBS, CW, MeTV, MNT, This TV) Dothan; 1 FM.
Programming (via satellite): A&E; AMC; Animal Planet; BET; CMT; CNBC; CNN; C-SPAN; Discovery Channel; Disney Channel; Disney XD; ESPN; ESPN2; Fox News Channel; Fox Sports 1; Freeform; FX; Golf Channel; Hallmark Channel; HGTV; History; HLN; Lifetime; MSNBC; MTV; Nickelodeon; Outdoor Channel; Pop; QVC; Spike TV; Syfy; TBS; The Weather Channel; TLC; TNT; Trinity Broadcasting Network (TBN); Turner Classic Movies; TV Land; USA Network; VH1; WGN America.
Fee: $30.00 installation; $25.00 monthly.
Pay Service 1
Pay Units: 1,181.
Programming (via satellite): Cinemax; HBO; Showtime.

Fee: $15.00 installation; $8.00 monthly.
Video-On-Demand: No
Internet Service
Operational: Yes. Began: May 1, 2003.
Subscribers: 2,070.
Broadband Service: In-house.
Fee: $45.00 installation; $39.00 monthly.
Telephone Service
Analog: Not Operational
Digital: Operational
Subscribers: 549.
Fee: $39.95 monthly
Miles of Plant: 180.0 (coaxial); 60.0 (fiber optic).
General Manager: Ivan Bishop. Chief Technician: Darrell Mitchell. Senior Internet Administrator: Wayne E. Alday.
Ownership: TV Cable Co. of Andalusia Inc.

ANNISTON—Cable One, 620 Noble St, Anniston, AL 36201-5622. Phone: 256-236-7034. Fax: 256-236-4475. Web Site: http://www.cableone.net. Also serves Anniston Army Depot, Calhoun County (unincorporated areas), Hobson City, Jacksonville, Munford, Ohatchee, Oxford, Talladega County (unincorporated areas) & Weaver. ICA: AL0008.
TV Market Ranking: Below 100 (ANNISTON, Anniston Army Depot, Calhoun County (unincorporated areas), Hobson City, Jacksonville, Munford, Ohatchee, Oxford, Talladega County (unincorporated areas), Weaver). Franchise award date: May 5, 2009. Franchise expiration date: N.A. Began: May 2, 1961.
Channel capacity: 58 (operating 2-way). Channels available but not in use: N.A.
Basic Service
Subscribers: 15,585.
Programming (received off-air): WABM (MNT) Birmingham; WBMA-LD (ABC, TNN) Birmingham; WBRC (Bounce TV, FOX) Birmingham; WCIQ (PBS) Mount Cheaha State Park; WEAC-CD Jacksonville; WIAT (CBS, Untamed Sports TV) Birmingham; WPXH-TV (ION) Gadsden; WTJP-TV (TBN) Gadsden; WTTO (Antenna TV, CW, The Country Network) Homewood; WVTM-TV (MeTV, NBC) Birmingham.
Fee: $90.00 installation; $35.00 monthly.
Expanded Basic Service 1
Subscribers: N.A.
Programming (via satellite): A&E; AMC; Animal Planet; BET; Cartoon Network; CMT; CNBC; CNN; Comedy Central; C-SPAN; C-SPAN 2; Discovery Channel; Disney Channel; E!; ESPN; ESPN2; Food Network; Fox News Channel; Freeform; FX; FXM; HGTV; History; HLN; Lifetime; MSNBC; MTV; Nickelodeon; Pop; QVC; Spike TV; Syfy; TBS; The Weather Channel; TLC; TNT; Turner Classic Movies; TV Land; USA Network; VH1.

Digital Basic Service
Subscribers: N.A.
Programming (via satellite): 3ABN; A&E HD; Boomerang; BYUtv; Cine Mexicano; CNN en Espanol; Discovery Channel HD; Discovery Kids Channel; Disney Channel HD; Disney XD; ESPN Classic; ESPN Deportes; ESPN HD; ESPN2 HD; ESPNews; FamilyNet; Food Network HD; FOX College Sports Central; FOX College Sports Pacific; Fox Deportes; Fox HD; Fox Sports 1; Fox Sports 2; Freeform HD; FYI; Golf Channel; Great American Country; GSN; Hallmark Channel; HD Theater; HGTV HD; History HD; History International; INSP; La Familia Cosmovision; MC; National Geographic Channel; National Geographic Channel HD; NBC Universo; Outdoor Channel; OWN; Oprah Winfrey Network; PBS HD; Science Channel; TBS HD; Telemundo; TLC HD; TNT HD; Toon Disney en Espanol; Trinity Broadcasting Network (TBN); TVG Network; Universal HD; WE tv.
Digital Pay Service 1
Pay Units: N.A.
Programming (via satellite): Cinemax (multiplexed); Flix; HBO (multiplexed); HBO HD; HBO Latino; Showtime (multiplexed); Showtime HD; Starz (multiplexed); Starz Encore (multiplexed); Sundance TV; The Movie Channel.
Fee: $15.00 monthly (each).
Video-On-Demand: No
Pay-Per-View
Pleasure (delivered digitally); SexSee (delivered digitally); Juicy (delivered digitally); VaVoom (delivered digitally).
Internet Service
Operational: Yes. Began: July 1, 2000.
Subscribers: 19,485.
Broadband Service: CableONE.net.
Fee: $75.00 installation; $43.00 monthly; $5.00 modem lease.
Telephone Service
Digital: Operational
Subscribers: 11,019.
Fee: $39.95 monthly
Miles of Plant: 2,092.0 (coaxial); 451.0 (fiber optic). Homes passed: 48,172.
Vice President: Patrick A. Dolohanty. General Manager: Terry Womack. Plant Manager: Tim Thompson. Marketing Manager: Mike Huey.
Ownership: Cable ONE Inc. (MSO).

APPLETON—Formerly served by Trust Cable. No longer in operation. ICA: AL0166.

ARDMORE—Mediacom, 123 Ware Dr NE, Huntsville, AL 35811-1061. Phones: 800-479-2082; 850-934-7700 (Gulf Breeze regional office); 256-852-7427. Fax: 256-851-7708. Web Site: http://www.mediacomcable.com. Also serves Limestone County, AL; Braceville (village), East Brooklyn

Alabama—Cable Systems

(village), Essex (village) & Godley (village), IL; Ardmore, Elkton, Giles County, Lincoln County & Prospect, TN. ICA: AL0095.
TV Market Ranking: 96 (Ardmore, ARDMORE, Elkton, Giles County (portions), Limestone County, Lincoln County (portions), Prospect; Below 100 (Braceville (village), East Brooklyn (village), Essex (village), Godley (village)); Outside TV Markets (Giles County (portions), Lincoln County (portions)). Franchise award date: November 3, 1980. Franchise expiration date: N.A. Began: August 15, 1982.
Channel capacity: N.A. Channels available but not in use: N.A.

Basic Service
Subscribers: 1,776.
Programming (received off-air): WAAY-TV (ABC) Huntsville; WAFF (Bounce TV, NBC, This TV) Huntsville; WHDF (CW) Florence; WHIQ (PBS) Huntsville; WHNT-TV (Antenna TV, CBS) Huntsville; WSMV-TV (COZI TV, NBC, TNN) Nashville; WZDX (FOX, MeTV, MNT) Huntsville.
Programming (via satellite): A&E; AMC; Animal Planet; BET; Bravo; Cartoon Network; CMT; CNBC; CNN; Comedy Central; C-SPAN; C-SPAN 2; Discovery Channel; Discovery Life Channel; Disney Channel; Disney XD; E! HD; ESPN; ESPN2; EWTN Global Catholic Network; Food Network; Fox News Channel; Fox Sports 1; FOX Sports South/SportSouth; Freeform; FX; FXM; Golf Channel; Hallmark Channel; HGTV; History; HLN; INSP; ION Television; Lifetime; MSNBC; MTV; NASA TV; Nickelodeon; Outdoor Channel; Oxygen; Pop; QVC; Spike TV; Syfy; TBS; The Weather Channel; TLC; TNT; Travel Channel; Trinity Broadcasting Network (TBN); truTV; Turner Classic Movies; TV Land; USA Network; VH1; WE tv; WGN America.
Fee: $21.50 installation; $72.95 monthly; $1.00 converter.

Digital Basic Service
Subscribers: N.A.
Programming (via satellite): BBC America; Bloomberg Television; Discovery Digital Networks; Fuse; FYI; GSN; History International; IFC; LMN; MC; National Geographic Channel; NBCSN.

Digital Pay Service 1
Pay Units: N.A.
Programming (via satellite): Cinemax (multiplexed); Flix; HBO (multiplexed); Showtime (multiplexed); Starz (multiplexed); Starz Encore; Sundance TV; The Movie Channel (multiplexed).
Video-On-Demand: Yes
Pay-Per-View
ESPN Now (delivered digitally); Pleasure (delivered digitally); Vubiquity Inc.; Vubiquity Inc. (delivered digitally).
Internet Service
Operational: Yes. Began: September 1, 2002.
Broadband Service: Mediacom High Speed Internet.
Fee: $106.00 installation; $40.95 monthly.
Telephone Service
None
Miles of Plant: 1,200.0 (coaxial); None (fiber optic). Homes passed: 11,944.
Vice President: David Servies. General Manager: Tommy Hill. Chief Technician: Harold Balch. Sales & Marketing Manager: Joey Nagem. Customer Service Supervisor: Sandy Acklin.
Ownership: Mediacom LLC (MSO).

ARLEY—Formerly served by Zoom Media. No longer in operation. ICA: AL0128.

ASHVILLE—Charter Communications. Now served by PELHAM, AL [AL0192]. ICA: AL0168.

ATHENS—Charter Communications. Now served by DECATUR, AL [AL0184]. ICA: AL0169.

ATHENS—Formerly served by Madison Communications. No longer in operation. ICA: AL0256.

ATHENS—Formerly served by WOW! Internet, Cable & Phone. No longer in operation. ICA: AL0257.

ATMORE—Mediacom. Now served by GULF BREEZE, FL [FL0070]. ICA: AL0064.

ATTALLA—Comcast Cable. Now served by TUPELO, MS [MS0009]. ICA: AL0170.

AUBURN—Auburn University Campus Cable System, OIT Dept., 300 Lem Morrison Dr, Auburn, AL 36849. Phone: 334-844-4000. Web Site: http://www.auburn.edu. ICA: AL0279.
TV Market Ranking: 94 (AUBURN).
Channel capacity: N.A. Channels available but not in use: N.A.
Basic Service
Subscribers: 4,800.
Fee: $8.80 monthly.
Information Technology Manager: John W. Gober.
Ownership: Auburn U.

AUBURN—Charter Communications. Now served by PELHAM, AL [AL0192]. ICA: AL0009.

AUTAUGAVILLE—Formerly served by NewWave Communications. No longer in operation. ICA: AL0141.

BAILEYTON—Zito Media, 102 S Main St, PO Box 665, Coudersport, PA 16915. Phones: 814-260-9055; 800-365-6988. E-mail: info@zitomedia.com. Web Site: http://www.zitomedia.com. Also serves Arab, Cullman County (portions), Eva, Hog Jaw, Hulaco, Joppa, Marshall County (portions), Morgan City, Morgan County (portions) & Ruth. ICA: AL0053.
TV Market Ranking: 96 (Arab, BAILEYTON, Cullman County (portions), Eva, Hog Jaw, Hulaco, Joppa, Marshall County (portions), Morgan City, Morgan County (portions), Ruth). Franchise award date: January 20, 1989. Franchise expiration date: N.A. Began: January 1, 1989.
Channel capacity: N.A. Channels available but not in use: N.A.
Basic Service
Subscribers: 85. Commercial subscribers: 3.
Programming (received off-air): WAAY-TV (ABC) Huntsville; WAFF (Bounce TV, NBC, This TV) Huntsville; WBRC (Bounce TV, FOX) Birmingham; WHDF (CW) Florence; WHIQ (PBS) Huntsville; WHNT-TV (Antenna TV, CBS) Huntsville; WIAT (CBS, Untamed Sports TV) Birmingham; WTJP-TV (TBN) Gadsden; WTTO (Antenna TV, CW, The Country Network) Homewood; WVTM-TV (MeTV, NBC) Birmingham; WZDX (FOX, MeTV, MNT) Huntsville.
Programming (via satellite): WGN America.
Fee: $49.95 installation; $22.58 monthly.

Expanded Basic Service 1
Subscribers: N.A.
Programming (via satellite): A&E; AMC; Animal Planet; Cartoon Network; CMT; CNBC; CNN; Comcast/Charter Sports Southeast (CSS); Comedy Central; C-SPAN; Discovery Channel; Disney Channel; ESPN; ESPN2; Fox News Channel; Fox Sports 1; FOX Sports South/SportSouth; Freeform; FX; HGTV; History; HLN; ION Television; Lifetime; MTV; Nickelodeon; Pop; QVC; Spike TV; Syfy; TBS; The Weather Channel; TLC; TNT; Turner Classic Movies; TV Land; Univision Studios; USA Network; VH1; WE tv.
Fee: $32.00 monthly.
Digital Basic Service
Subscribers: N.A.
Programming (via satellite): BBC America; Discovery Digital Networks; DIY Network; FYI; Great American Country; History International; IFC; LMN; MC; NBCSN; Sundance TV; Univision.
Pay Service 1
Pay Units: N.A.
Programming (via satellite): Cinemax (multiplexed).
Planned programming (via satellite): Flix.
Programming (via satellite): HBO (multiplexed); Starz (multiplexed); Starz Encore; The Movie Channel (multiplexed).
Fee: $4.95 installation; $14.00 monthly (Cinemax/HBO, Showtime/TMC/Flix or Starz/Encore).
Video-On-Demand: No
Pay-Per-View
iN DEMAND (delivered digitally); Playboy TV (delivered digitally); Pleasure (delivered digitally); Fresh (delivered digitally); Shorteez (delivered digitally).
Internet Service
Operational: No.
Telephone Service
None
Miles of Plant: 356.0 (coaxial); 83.0 (fiber optic). Homes passed: 6,476.
President: James Rigas.
Ownership: Zito Media (MSO).

BALDWIN COUNTY (northwestern portion)—Formerly served by Baldwin County Cable. No longer in operation. ICA: AL0237.

BALDWIN COUNTY (portions)—Mediacom. Now served by FAIRHOPE, AL [AL0124]. ICA: AL0121.

BARNWELL—Mediacom. Now served by FAIRHOPE, AL [AL0124]. ICA: AL0234.

BAY MINETTE—Mediacom. Now served by FAIRHOPE, AL [AL0124]. ICA: AL0057.

BEATRICE—TV Cable Company of Andalusia, 213 Dunson St, PO Box 34, Andalusia, AL 36420. Phone: 334-222-6464. Fax: 334-222-7226. E-mail: Support@andycable.com. Web Site: http://www.andycable.com. ICA: AL0156.
TV Market Ranking: Outside TV Markets (BEATRICE). Franchise award date: May 17, 1989. Franchise expiration date: N.A. Began: November 1, 1989.
Channel capacity: N.A. Channels available but not in use: N.A.
Basic Service
Subscribers: 61.
Programming (received off-air): WAKA (CBS, MeTV) Selma; WALA-TV (FOX) Mobile; WEAR-TV (ABC, The Country Network) Pensacola; WHBR (Christian TV Network) Pensacola; WSFA (Bounce TV, NBC) Montgomery.
Programming (via satellite): AMC; Animal Planet; BET; Cartoon Network; CMT; CNBC; CNN; Discovery Channel; Disney Channel; ESPN; Fox News Channel; Freeform; Lifetime; Nickelodeon; Spike TV; TBS; TNT; Travel Channel; USA Network; WGN America.
Fee: $29.95 installation; $30.00 monthly.
Pay Service 1
Pay Units: N.A. Included in Heath
Programming (via satellite): Cinemax; HBO.
Fee: $10.95 monthly.
Video-On-Demand: No
Internet Service
Operational: No.
Telephone Service
None
Miles of Plant: 11.0 (coaxial); None (fiber optic). Homes passed: 200.
Ownership: TV Cable Co. of Andalusia Inc. (MSO).

BELLAMY—Community Cable & Broadband LLC, 1309 Roebuck Dr, PO Box 65, Meridian, MS 39301. Phone: 601-485-6980. ICA: AL0157.
TV Market Ranking: Below 100 (BELLAMY). Franchise award date: N.A. Franchise expiration date: N.A. Began: September 1, 1990.
Channel capacity: N.A. Channels available but not in use: N.A.
Basic Service
Subscribers: 52.
Programming (received off-air): WAKA (CBS, MeTV) Selma; WDBB (CW) Bessemer; WIIQ (PBS) Demopolis; WSFA (Bounce TV, NBC) Montgomery; WTOK-TV (ABC, CW, FOX, MNT) Meridian.
Programming (via satellite): CNN; Discovery Channel; Disney Channel; ESPN; Freeform; TBS; TNT; USA Network; WGN America.
Fee: $20.00 installation; $39.00 monthly.
Pay Service 1
Pay Units: N.A.
Programming (via satellite): HBO.
Fee: $11.00 monthly.
Internet Service
Operational: Yes.
Telephone Service
None
Miles of Plant: 9.0 (coaxial); None (fiber optic). Homes passed: 220.
General Manager & Chief Technician: Berry Ward.
Ownership: Community Cable & Broadband LLC (MSO).

BERRY—Formerly served by Almega Cable. No longer in operation. ICA: AL0240.

BEULAH—Charter Communications. Now served by NEWNAN, GA [GA0042]. ICA: AL0171.

BIG COVE—Formerly served by Mediacom. No longer in operation. ICA: AL0172.

BIRMINGHAM—AT&T U-verse. This is the regional video hub for the BIRMINGHAM area, 208 South Akard St, Dallas, TX 75202. Phone: 800-288-2020. Web Site: http://www.att.com. Also serves Adamsville, Addison, Alabaster, Albertville, Alexandria, Anniston, Arley, Athens, Attalia, Baileyton, Bessemer, Bibb County (unincorporated areas), Blount County (unincorporated areas), Boaz, Brighton, Brookwood, Calera, Calhoun County (unincorporated areas), Carrollton, Center

Cable Systems—Alabama

Point, Chalkville, Chelsea, Chilton County (unincorporated areas), Choccolocco, Clanton, Clay, Clerburne County (unincorporated areas), Coaling, Coker, Colbert County (unincorporated areas), Columbiana, Concord, Cullman, Cullman County (unincorporated areas), Decatur, Dora, Douglas, Edgewater, Elkmont, Etowah County (unincorporated areas), Eva, Fairfield, Fairview, Falkville, Florence, Forestdale, Fultondale, Gadsden, Gardendale, Glenco, Good Hope, Graysville, Guntersville, Harpersville, Hartselle, Harvest, Hayden, Hazel Green, Helena, Holly Pond, Holt, Homewood, Hoover, Hueytown, Huntsville, Indian Springs, Irondale, Jacksonville, Jasper, Jefferson County (unincorporated areas), Jemison, Killen, Kimberly, Lake Purdy, Lakeview, Lauderdale County (unincorporated areas), Lawrence County (unincorporated areas), Limestone County (unincorporated areas), Lipscomb, Locust Fork, Madison, Madison County (unincorporated areas), Maytown, Meadowbrook, Meridianville, Midfield, Minor, Montevallo, Moores Mill, Morgan County (unincorporated areas), Morris, Moulton, Mount Olive, Mountain Brook, Muscle Shoals, New Market, Northport, Oxford, Pelham, Petersville, Pickens County (unincorporated areas), Pickensville, Pinson, Pleasant Grove, Priceville, Rainbow City, Sheffield, Shelby, Shelby County (unincorporated areas), Smoke Rise, South Vinemont, Southside, St. Florian, Steele, Sumiton, Sylvan Springs, Talladega County (unincorporated areas), Tarrant, Triana, Trinity, Trussville, Tuscaloosa, Tuscaloosa County (unincorporated areas), Tuscumbia, Underwood, Vance, Vestavia Hills, Walker County (unincorporated areas), Warrior, Waterloo, Weaver, West Blocton, West End Cobb, West Point, Westover, Wilsonville, Wilton, Winston County (unincorporated areas) & Woodstock, AL; Fayetteville & Lincoln County (unincorporated areas), TN. ICA: AL5004.

TV Market Ranking: Franchise award date: July 8, 2008. Franchise expiration date: N.A. Began: December 22, 2008.

Channel capacity: N.A. Channels available but not in use: N.A.

U-basic
Subscribers: 88,069 Subscriber counts include all areas in the BIRMINGHAM regional video hub.. Commercial subscribers: 123.
Fee: $199.00 installation; $19.00 monthly. Includes only local channels.

U-family
Subscribers: N.A.
Fee: $67.00 monthly. Up to 130 channels, including 38 music channels & 1 DVR.

U200
Subscribers: N.A.
Fee: $83.00 monthly. Up to 290 channels, including 46 music channels & 1 DVR.

U200 Latino
Subscribers: N.A.
Fee: $93.00 monthly. Up to 350 channels, including 46 music channels & 1 DVR.

U300
Subscribers: N.A.
Fee: $99.00 monthly. Up to 390 channels, including 46 music channels, The Movie Package & 1 DVR.

U300 Latino
Subscribers: N.A.
Fee: $109.00 monthly. Up to 440 channels, including 46 music channels, 60 Spanish language channels, The Movie Package & 1 DVR.

U450
Subscribers: N.A.
Fee: $131.00 monthly. Up to 460 channels, including 46 music channels, The Movie Package, HBO/Cinemax, The Sports Package, HD Tech Fee & 1 DVR.

U450 Latino
Subscribers: N.A.
Fee: $141.00 monthly. Up to 510 channels, including 46 music channels, 60 Spanish language channels, The Movie Package, HBO/Cinemax, The Sports Package, HD Tech Fee & 1 DVR.

HD
Subscribers: N.A.
Fee: $10.00 monthly. Includes up to 205 channels in HD.

Premium HD
Subscribers: N.A.
Fee: $7.00 monthly. Includes 31 additional channels in HD.

Cinemax
Subscribers: N.A.
Fee: $14.00 monthly. Includes 24 channels.

HBO
Subscribers: N.A.
Fee: $16.00 monthly. Includes 28 channels.

Cinemax/HBO
Subscribers: N.A.
Fee: $26.00 monthly. Includes 52 channels.

Encore
Subscribers: N.A.
Fee: $14.00 monthly. Includes 10 channels.

Showtime Unlimited
Subscribers: N.A.
Fee: $14.00 monthly. Includes 29 channels of Showtime, TMC & Flix.

Starz/Encore
Subscribers: N.A.
Fee: $14.00 monthly. Includes 14 channels.

Movie Package
Subscribers: N.A.
Fee: $20.00 monthly. Includes 55 channels of Showtime, TMC, Starz, Encore & Flix.

Sports Package
Subscribers: N.A.
Fee: $10.00 monthly. Includes 28 channels.

International Channels
Subscribers: N.A.
Fee: $5.00 -$35.00.

Video-On-Demand: Yes

Internet Service
Operational: Yes.
Fee: $29.95-$64.95 monthly.

Telephone Service
Digital: Operational
Fee: $30.00 monthly
Ownership: AT&T Inc.

BIRMINGHAM—Bright House Networks, 2251 Lucien Way, Ste 200B, Maitland, FL 32751. Phones: 407-667-5200; 205-591-6880 (Customer service); 205-290-1300. Web Site: http://brighthouse.com. Also serves Bessemer (portions), Brighton, Center Point, Fairfield (portions), Helena, Hoover, Hueytown (portions), Irondale, Jefferson County (portions), Lakeview, Lipscomb & Roosevelt City. ICA: AL0001.

TV Market Ranking: 40 (Bessemer (portions), BIRMINGHAM, Brighton, Center Point, Fairfield (portions), Helena, Hoover, Hueytown (portions), Irondale, Jefferson County (portions), Lipscomb, Roosevelt City); Below 100 (Lakeview). Franchise award date: January 1, 1973. Franchise expiration date: N.A. Began: September 30, 1976.

Channel capacity: 72 (operating 2-way). Channels available but not in use: N.A.

Basic Service
Subscribers: 46,298. Commercial subscribers: 2,692.
Programming (received off-air): WABM (MNT) Birmingham; WBIQ (PBS) Birmingham; WBRC (Bounce TV, FOX) Birmingham; WGWW (ABC, TNN) Anniston; WIAT (CBS, Untamed Sports TV) Birmingham; WLTZ (CW, NBC) Columbus; WPXH-TV (ION) Gadsden; WRBL (CBS, MeTV) Columbus; WTJP-TV (TBN) Gadsden; WTTO (Antenna TV, CW, The Country Network) Homewood; WTVM (ABC, Bounce TV) Columbus; WVTM-TV (MeTV, NBC) Birmingham; WXTX (FOX, Movies!, This TV) Columbus.
Programming (via satellite): C-SPAN; C-SPAN 2; Pop; QVC; WGN America.
Fee: $38.45 installation; $27.00 monthly; $.65 converter.

Expanded Basic Service 1
Subscribers: N.A.
Programming (via satellite): A&E; AMC; Animal Planet; BET; Cartoon Network; CNBC; CNN; Comedy Central; Discovery Channel; Disney Channel; E! HD; ESPN; ESPN Classic; ESPN2; EVINE Live; EWTN Global Catholic Network; Food Network; Fox News Channel; FOX Sports South/SportSouth; Freeform; Fuse; FX; Golf Channel; Great American Country; Hallmark Channel; HGTV; History; HLN; Lifetime; LMN; MoviePlex; MSNBC; MTV; National Geographic Channel; NBCSN; Nickelodeon; Oxygen; Spike TV; Syfy; TBS; The Weather Channel; TLC; TNT; Travel Channel; truTV; Turner Classic Movies; TV Land; Univision Studios; USA Network; VH1; WE tv.
Fee: $49.45 monthly.

Digital Basic Service
Subscribers: 22,000.
Programming (via satellite): BBC America; Bloomberg Television; CBS Sports Network; Church Channel; Cloo; Daystar TV Network; Destination America; Discovery Kids Channel; Discovery Life Channel; Disney XD; ESPNews; Fox Business Network; FOX College Sports Central; FOX College Sports Pacific; Fox Sports 1; FXM; FYI; GSN; Hallmark Movies & Mysteries; History International; IFC; Investigation Discovery; LMN; MC; Nick Jr.; Nicktoons; OWN; Oprah Winfrey Network; RFD-TV; Science Channel; TeenNick; UP; WE tv.
Fee: $11.00 monthly.

Digital Expanded Basic Service
Subscribers: N.A.
Programming (via satellite): A&E HD; ESPN HD; ESPN2 HD; HD Theater; National Geographic Channel HD; TNT HD; Universal HD.

Digital Expanded Basic Service 2
Subscribers: N.A.
Programming (via satellite): CMT; Fuse; MTV Classic; MTV Hits; MTV Jams; MTV2; Tr3s; VH1 Soul.

Digital Expanded Basic Service 3
Subscribers: N.A.
Programming (via satellite): 52MX; Cinelatino; CNN en Espanol; ESPN Deportes; Fuse; History International; ViendoMovies.

Digital Pay Service 1
Pay Units: N.A.
Programming (via satellite): Cinemax (multiplexed); HBO (multiplexed); HBO HD; Showtime (multiplexed); Showtime HD; Starz (multiplexed); The Movie Channel (multiplexed).
Fee: $10.50 monthly (each).

Video-On-Demand: Yes

Pay-Per-View
iN DEMAND (delivered digitally); NBA League Pass (delivered digitally); Playboy TV (delivered digitally); Fresh (delivered digitally); Pleasure (delivered digitally); Hot Choice (delivered digitally); ESPN (delivered digitally); MLB Extra Innings (delivered digitally); NHL Center Ice (delivered digitally).

Internet Service
Operational: Yes.
Subscribers: 37,301.
Broadband Service: Road Runner; AOL for Broadband; EarthLink.
Fee: $24.95 installation; $29.95 monthly.

Telephone Service
Digital: Operational
Subscribers: 19,637.
Fee: $29.95 monthly.

Miles of Plant: 3,183.0 (coaxial); 1,071.0 (fiber optic). Homes passed: 164,051.

Division President: Karen Broach. Vice President & General Manager: Scott Horne. Chief Financial Officer: William Futera. Vice President, Engineering: Garland Thomas. Marketing Director: Tammy Strong. Program Director: Tim Stout. Customer Service Director: Jimmy Robinson.

Ownership: Bright House Networks LLC (MSO).

BLOUNT COUNTY—Formerly served by Alabama Broadband LLC. Now served by Charter Communications, ASHVILLE, AL [AL0168]. ICA: AL0198.

BLOUNTSVILLE—Formerly served by Time Warner Cable. Now served by Charter Communications, CULLMAN, AL [AL0034]. ICA: AL0142.

BOLIGEE—Sky Cablevision, 1309 Roebuck Dr, PO Box 65, Meridian, MS 39301. Phone: 601-485-6980. Fax: 601-483-0103. ICA: AL0173.

TV Market Ranking: Outside TV Markets (BOLIGEE). Franchise award date: N.A. Franchise expiration date: N.A. Began: August 1, 1989.

Channel capacity: N.A. Channels available but not in use: N.A.

Basic Service
Subscribers: 441.
Programming (received off-air): WGBC (FOX, NBC) Meridian; WIIQ (PBS) Demopolis; WMDN (CBS) Meridian; WTOK-TV (ABC, CW, FOX, MNT) Meridian.
Programming (via satellite): A&E; CNN; Discovery Channel; Disney Channel; ESPN; Freeform; TBS; TNT; USA Network; WGN America.
Fee: $44.00 monthly.

Pay Service 1
Pay Units: N.A.
Programming (via satellite): HBO.
Fee: $11.00 monthly.

Internet Service
Operational: No.

Telephone Service
None

General Manager: Berry Ward.
Ownership: Community Cable & Broadband LLC (MSO).

BOOTH—Formerly served by Zito Media. No longer in operation. ICA: AL0277.

BREWTON—Mediacom. Now served by GULF BREEZE, FL [FL0070]. ICA: AL0051.

BRIDGEPORT—Charter Communications. Now served by JASPER, TN [TN0070]. ICA: AL0266.

Alabama—Cable Systems

BROOKWOOD—Charter Communications. Now served by PELHAM, AL [AL0192]. ICA: AL0059.

BUTLER—Pine Belt Broadband, 3984 County Rd 32, PO Box 279, Arlington, AL 36722. Phones: 888-810-4638; 334-385-2106. Fax: 334-385-2103. E-mail: contact@pinebelttalk.com. Web Site: http://www.pinebelt.net. Also serves Lisman. ICA: AL0174.
TV Market Ranking: Below 100 (BUTLER, Lisman). Franchise award date: January 1, 1968. Franchise expiration date: N.A. Began: December 12, 1968.
Channel capacity: N.A. Channels available but not in use: N.A.
Basic Service
Subscribers: 322.
Programming (received off-air): WAKA (CBS, MeTV) Selma; WALA-TV (FOX) Mobile; WGBC (FOX, NBC) Meridian; WIIQ (PBS) Demopolis; WMDN (CBS) Meridian; WTOK-TV (ABC, CW, FOX, MNT) Meridian. Programming (via satellite): A&E; AMC; BET; Cartoon Network; CNBC; CNN; Discovery Channel; Disney Channel; Disney XD; E! HD; ESPN; ESPN2; Fox News Channel; Fox Sports 1; FOX Sports South/SportSouth; Freeform; Fuse; FX; Great American Country; Hallmark Channel; HGTV; History; HLN; Lifetime; Outdoor Channel; QVC; TBS; The Weather Channel; TLC; TNT; Trinity Broadcasting Network (TBN); truTV; USA Network; WGN America.
Fee: $24.99 installation; $19.99 monthly.
Digital Basic Service
Subscribers: N.A.
Programming (via satellite): BBC America; Bloomberg Television; Cloo; Destination America; Discovery Kids Channel; Discovery Life Channel; ESPN Classic; ESPNews; FOX College Sports Central; FOX College Sports Pacific; FXM; FYI; Golf Channel; GSN; History International; IFC; Investigation Discovery; LMN; National Geographic Channel; OWN; Oprah Winfrey Network; RFD-TV; Science Channel; Sprout; WE tv.
Pay Service 1
Pay Units: N.A.
Programming (via satellite): HBO; Showtime.
Fee: $25.00 installation; $11.00 monthly (HBO).
Digital Pay Service 1
Pay Units: N.A.
Programming (via satellite): Cinemax (multiplexed); Flix; HBO (multiplexed); Showtime (multiplexed); Starz (multiplexed); Starz Encore (multiplexed); The Movie Channel (multiplexed).
Pay-Per-View
iN DEMAND (delivered digitally); Playboy TV (delivered digitally); Club Jenna (delivered digitally).
Internet Service
Operational: Yes.
Broadband Service: Galaxy Cable Internet.
Fee: $49.95 installation; $35.00 monthly.
Telephone Service
Digital: Operational
Miles of Plant: 55.0 (coaxial); None (fiber optic). Homes passed: 1,532.
General Manager: John C. Nettles.
Ownership: Pine Belt Telephone Co.

CASTLEBERRY—TV Cable Company of Andalusia, 213 Dunson St, PO Box 34, Andalusia, AL 36420. Phone: 334-222-6464. Fax: 334-222-7226. E-mail: support@andycable.com. Web Site: http://www.andycable.com. ICA: AL0149.

TV Market Ranking: Outside TV Markets (CASTLEBERRY). Franchise award date: N.A. Franchise expiration date: N.A. Began: January 1, 1989.
Channel capacity: 40 (not 2-way capable). Channels available but not in use: N.A.
Basic Service
Subscribers: 50.
Programming (received off-air): WALA-TV (FOX) Mobile; WDIQ (PBS) Dozier; WEAR-TV (ABC, The Country Network) Pensacola; WHBR (Christian TV Network) Pensacola; WKRG-TV (CBS, MeTV) Mobile; WMPV-TV (TBN) Mobile; WPMI-TV (NBC) Mobile; WSFA (Bounce TV, NBC) Montgomery. Programming (via satellite): A&E; BET; CNBC; CNN; Disney Channel; ESPN; Fox News Channel; Freeform; HLN; Spike TV; Syfy; TBS; TNT; USA Network; WGN America.
Fee: $29.95 installation; $30.00 monthly.
Pay Service 1
Pay Units: N.A. Included in Heath
Programming (via satellite): Cinemax; HBO.
Fee: $10.95 monthly (each).
Video-On-Demand: No
Internet Service
Operational: No.
Telephone Service
None
Miles of Plant: 10.0 (coaxial); None (fiber optic). Homes passed: 250.
Ownership: TV Cable Co. of Andalusia Inc. (MSO).

CEDAR BLUFF—Formerly served by Ridge Networks. No longer in operation. ICA: AL0175.

CENTER POINT—Charter Communications. Now served by PELHAM, AL [AL0192]. ICA: AL0029.

CENTRE—Charter Communications. Now served by PIEDMONT, AL [AL0065]. ICA: AL0085.

CENTREVILLE—Community Cable & Broadband LLC, 1309 Roebuck Dr, PO Box 65, Meridian, MS 39301. Phone: 601-485-6980. Fax: 601-483-0103. Also serves Bibb County (portions), Brent, Jefferson County (portions), Tuscaloosa County (portions), West Blocton & Woodstock. ICA: AL0069.
TV Market Ranking: Below 100 (Brent, CENTREVILLE, Jefferson County (portions), Tuscaloosa County (portions), West Blocton, Woodstock). Franchise award date: January 10, 1980. Franchise expiration date: N.A. Began: December 1, 1980.
Channel capacity: N.A. Channels available but not in use: N.A.
Basic Service
Subscribers: N.A.
Programming (received off-air): WBIQ (PBS) Birmingham; WBRC (Bounce TV, FOX) Birmingham; WIAT (CBS, Untamed Sports TV) Birmingham; WSES (ABC, TNN) Tuscaloosa; WTTO (Antenna TV, CW, The Country Network) Homewood; WVTM-TV (MeTV, NBC) Birmingham.
Programming (via satellite): C-SPAN; Trinity Broadcasting Network (TBN); WGN America.
Fee: $29.95 installation; $43.00 monthly.
Expanded Basic Service 1
Subscribers: N.A.
Programming (via satellite): A&E; AMC; Animal Planet; Bravo; Cartoon Network; CMT; CNBC; CNN; Comedy Central; Discovery Channel; Disney Channel; Disney XD; E! HD; ESPN; ESPN2; Fox News Channel; Fox Sports 1; Freeform; FX; Golf Channel; HGTV; History; HLN; Lifetime; MSNBC; MTV; Nickelodeon; Oxygen; Spike TV; Syfy; TBS; The Weather Channel; TLC; TNT; Turner Classic Movies; TV Land; USA Network; VH1.
Fee: $20.00 monthly.
Digital Basic Service
Subscribers: N.A.
Programming (via satellite): BBC America; Bloomberg Television; Discovery Life Channel; ESPN Classic; Fuse; FXM; FYI; GSN; History International; IFC; LMN; MC; Nick 2; Nick Jr.; Nicktoons; Sundance TV; TeenNick; WE tv.
Digital Pay Service 1
Pay Units: N.A.
Programming (via satellite): Cinemax (multiplexed); Flix; HBO (multiplexed); Starz (multiplexed); Starz Encore (multiplexed); The Movie Channel (multiplexed).
Video-On-Demand: No
Pay-Per-View
ESPN Now (delivered digitally); iN DEMAND (delivered digitally); Playboy TV (delivered digitally); Fresh (delivered digitally).
Internet Service
Operational: No.
Telephone Service
None
Miles of Plant: 53.0 (coaxial); None (fiber optic). Homes passed: 2,682.
General Manager & Chief Technician: Berry Ward.
Ownership: Community Cable & Broadband LLC (MSO).

CHAMBERS COUNTY (portions)—WOW! Internet, Cable & Phone, 7887 East Belleview Ave, Ste 1000, Englewood, CO 80111. Phones: 720-479-3500; 706-642-2246 (Customer service); 706-645-8630. Fax: 720-479-3585. E-mail: wow_general@wideopenwest.com. Web Site: http://www.wowway.com. Also serves Lanett & Valley, AL; West Point, GA. ICA: AL0259.
Note: This system is an overbuild.
TV Market Ranking: 94 (CHAMBERS COUNTY (PORTIONS), Lanett, Valley, West Point).
Channel capacity: 71 (operating 2-way). Channels available but not in use: N.A.
Basic Service
Subscribers: 3,331.
Programming (received off-air): WCIQ (PBS) Mount Cheaha State Park; WJCN-LD LaGrange; WJSP-TV (PBS) Columbus; WLGA (WeatherNation) Opelika; WLTZ (CW, NBC) Columbus; WRBL (CBS, MeTV) Columbus; WSB-TV (ABC, MeTV) Atlanta; WSFA (Bounce TV, NBC) Montgomery; WTVM (ABC, Bounce TV) Columbus; WXTX (FOX, Movies!, This TV) Columbus.
Programming (via satellite): A&E; AMC; Animal Planet; BET; Bravo; Cartoon Network; CMT; CNBC; CNN; Comcast/Charter Sports Southeast (CSS); Comedy Central; C-SPAN; C-SPAN 2; Discovery Channel; Disney Channel; Disney XD; E! HD; ESPN; ESPN Classic; ESPN2; EVINE Live; Food Network; Fox News Channel; Fox Sports 1; FOX Sports South/SportSouth; Freeform; FX; Golf Channel; Great American Country; GSN; Hallmark Channel; HGTV; History; HLN; Lifetime; LMN; MTV; Nick At Nite; Nickelodeon; Outdoor Channel; Oxygen; Pop; QVC; Spike TV; Syfy; TBS; The Weather Channel; TLC; TNT; Travel Channel; Trinity Broadcasting Network (TBN); truTV; Turner Classic Movies; TV Land; UP; USA Network; VH1; WGN America.
Fee: $41.00 monthly.

Digital Basic Service
Subscribers: N.A.
Programming (via satellite): AXS TV; BBC America; Bloomberg Television; Boomerang; Church Channel; CMT; C-SPAN 3; Destination America; Discovery Channel HD; Discovery Kids Channel; Discovery Life Channel; ESPN HD; ESPN2 HD; ESPNU; FSN HD; Hallmark Movies & Mysteries; HD Theater; IFC; INSP; Investigation Discovery; Jewelry Television; JUCE TV; MC; MTV Classic; MTV Hits; MTV Jams; MTV2; mtvU; National Geographic Channel; NBCSN; NFL Network; Nick 2; Nick Jr.; Nicktoons; OWN; Oprah Winfrey Network; QVC HD; Science Channel; TBS HD; TeenNick; TLC HD; TNT HD; Tr3s; Universal HD; Versus HD; VH1 Soul; WE tv.
Digital Expanded Basic Service
Subscribers: N.A.
Programming (via satellite): CBS Sports Network; ESPNews; FOX College Sports Central; FOX College Sports Pacific; Fox Sports 2; Tennis Channel.
Digital Pay Service 1
Pay Units: N.A.
Programming (via satellite): Cinemax (multiplexed); Cinemax HD; Cinemax On Demand; Flix; Flix On Demand; HBO (multiplexed); HBO HD; HBO on Demand; Showtime (multiplexed); Showtime HD; Showtime On Demand; Starz (multiplexed); Starz Encore (multiplexed); Starz HD; Sundance TV; The Movie Channel (multiplexed); The Movie Channel On Demand.
Fee: $56.35 monthly.
Video-On-Demand: Yes
Pay-Per-View
iN DEMAND (delivered digitally); Hot Choice (delivered digitally); Spice: Xcess (delivered digitally); Playboy TV (delivered digitally); Fresh (delivered digitally); Shorteez (delivered digitally); Club Jenna (delivered digitally); ESPN Now (delivered digitally).
Internet Service
Operational: Yes.
Broadband Service: Knology.Net.
Fee: $29.95 installation; $57.95 monthly.
Telephone Service
Analog: Not Operational
Digital: Operational
Fee: $23.15 monthly
Miles of Plant: 4,899.0 (coaxial); 1,127.0 (fiber optic). Homes passed: 136,596.
Chief Executive Officer: Colleen Abdoulah. President: Steven Cochran. Chief Financial Officer: Rich Fish.
Ownership: WideOpenWest LLC (MSO).

CHANCELLOR—Formerly served by TV Cable Company of Andalusia. No longer in operation. ICA: AL0105.

CHATOM—Formerly served by Community Cable & Broadband LLC. No longer in operation. ICA: AL0176.

CHEROKEE—Formerly served by Ramco Broadband Services. No longer in operation. ICA: AL0177.

CLANTON—Zito Media, 102 S Main St, PO Box 665, Coudersport, PA 16915. Phones: 814-260-9055; 800-365-6988. E-mail: info@zitomedia.com. Web Site: http://www.zitomedia.com. Also serves Chilton County (portions). ICA: AL0056.
TV Market Ranking: Below 100 (Chilton County (portions)); Outside TV Markets (CLANTON, Chilton County (portions)). Franchise award date: N.A. Franchise

D-18

TV & Cable Factbook No. 85

Cable Systems—Alabama

expiration date: N.A. Began: March 16, 1979.
Channel capacity: N.A. Channels available but not in use: N.A.
Basic Service
Subscribers: 363. Commercial subscribers: 119.
Programming (received off-air): WAKA (CBS, MeTV) Selma; WBIQ (PBS) Birmingham; WBRC (Bounce TV, FOX) Birmingham; WIAT (CBS, Untamed Sports TV) Birmingham; WPXH-TV (ION) Gadsden; WSES (ABC, TNN) Tuscaloosa; WSFA (Bounce TV, NBC) Montgomery; WTTO (Antenna TV, CW, The Country Network) Homewood; WVTM-TV (MeTV, NBC) Birmingham; allband FM.
Programming (via satellite): C-SPAN; INSP; Trinity Broadcasting Network (TBN).
Fee: $49.95 installation; $24.91 monthly.
Expanded Basic Service 1
Subscribers: N.A.
Programming (via satellite): A&E; AMC; Animal Planet; BET; Cartoon Network; CMT; CNN; Comedy Central; C-SPAN 2; Discovery Channel; Disney Channel; ESPN; ESPN2; Fox News Channel; Fox Sports 1; FOX Sports South/SportSouth; Freeform; FX; HGTV; HLN; HSN; INSP; Lifetime; MSNBC; MTV; Nickelodeon; Oxygen; QVC; Spike TV; TBS; The Weather Channel; TLC; TNT; truTV; TV Land; USA Network.
Fee: $32.00 monthly.
Digital Basic Service
Subscribers: N.A.
Programming (via satellite): BBC America; Bloomberg Television; Bravo; Discovery Life Channel; Disney XD; DMX Music; ESPN Classic; ESPNews; Fuse; FXM; FYI; Golf Channel; Great American Country; GSN; History; History International; IFC; LMN; National Geographic Channel; NBCSN; Nick Jr.; Outdoor Channel; Sundance TV; Syfy; TeenNick; Turner Classic Movies; TV Guide Interactive Inc.; WE tv.
Pay Service 1
Pay Units: N.A.
Programming (via satellite): Cinemax (multiplexed); Flix; HBO (multiplexed); Showtime (multiplexed); Starz (multiplexed); Starz Encore; The Movie Channel (multiplexed).
Fee: $14.00 monthly (Cinemax/HBO, Showtime/TMC/Flix or Starz/Encore).
Video-On-Demand: No
Pay-Per-View
iN DEMAND (delivered digitally); Playboy TV (delivered digitally); Fresh (delivered digitally); Shorteez (delivered digitally).
Internet Service
Operational: Yes.
Fee: $39.95 monthly.
Telephone Service
Digital: Operational
Fee: $30.00 monthly
Miles of Plant: 80.0 (coaxial); None (fiber optic). Homes passed: 5,170.
President: James Rigas.
Ownership: Zito Media (MSO).

CLAYTON (town)—Comcast Cable, One Comcast Center, Philadelphia, PA 19103. Phones: 850-769-0392; 850-769-2929. Web Site: http://www.comcast.com. ICA: AL0134.
TV Market Ranking: Below 100 (CLAYTON (TOWN)). Franchise award date: N.A. Franchise expiration date: N.A. Began: November 1, 1982.
Channel capacity: N.A. Channels available but not in use: N.A.

Basic Service
Subscribers: 140.
Programming (received off-air): WDHN (ABC) Dothan; WGIQ (PBS) Louisville; WLTZ (CW, NBC) Columbus; WRBL (CBS, MeTV) Columbus; WSFA (Bounce TV, NBC) Montgomery; WTVM (ABC, Bounce TV) Columbus; WTVY (CBS, CW, MeTV, MNT, This TV) Dothan.
Programming (via satellite): A&E; AMC; Animal Planet; BET; CMT; CNN; Comedy Central; C-SPAN; Discovery Channel; Disney Channel; E! HD; ESPN; ESPN2; Food Network; Fox News Channel; Freeform; FX; Golf Channel; Great American Country; HGTV; HLN; Lifetime; MSNBC; MTV; Nickelodeon; QVC; Spike TV; TBS; The Weather Channel; TLC; TNT; Trinity Broadcasting Network (TBN); TV Land; USA Network.
Fee: $45.20 monthly.
Pay Service 1
Pay Units: N.A.
Programming (via satellite): HBO; Showtime.
Video-On-Demand: No
Internet Service
Operational: Yes.
Telephone Service
Digital: Operational
Fee: $39.95 monthly
Homes passed: 736.
Vice President, Accounting: Joan Ritchie. General Manager: Fritz Hoehne. Technical Operations Manager: Tim Denton. Marketing Manager: Kevin Canel.
Ownership: Comcast Cable Communications Inc. (MSO).

CLIO—Bright House Networks, 2251 Lucien Way, Ste 200B, Maitland, FL 32751. Phones: 407-667-5200; 334-687-5555. Web Site: http://brighthouse.com. Also serves Ariton, Dale County & Louisville. ICA: AL0123.
TV Market Ranking: Below 100 (Ariton, CLIO, Louisville). Franchise award date: N.A. Franchise expiration date: N.A. Began: December 1, 1981.
Channel capacity: N.A. Channels available but not in use: N.A.
Basic Service
Subscribers: 285. Commercial subscribers: 6.
Programming (received off-air): WDFX-TV (Bounce TV, FOX) Ozark; WDHN (ABC) Dothan; WGIQ (PBS) Louisville; WSFA (Bounce TV, NBC) Montgomery; WTVM (ABC, Bounce TV) Columbus; WTVY (CBS, CW, MeTV, MNT, This TV) Dothan.
Programming (via satellite): CNN; TBS; WGN America.
Fee: $27.00 monthly.
Expanded Basic Service 1
Subscribers: N.A.
Programming (via satellite): A&E; AMC; Animal Planet; BET; Cartoon Network; CMT; CNBC; Comedy Central; C-SPAN; C-SPAN 2; Discovery Channel; Disney Channel; E! HD; ESPN; ESPN2; EVINE Live; Food Network; Fox News Channel; FOX Sports South/SportSouth; Freeform; Fuse; FX; Hallmark Channel; HGTV; History; HLN; INSP; Lifetime; LMN; MSNBC; MTV; National Geographic Channel; NBCSN; Nickelodeon; Oxygen; QVC; Spike TV; Syfy; The Weather Channel; The Word Network; TLC; TNT; Travel Channel; Trinity Broadcasting Network (TBN); truTV; Turner Classic Movies; TV Land; USA Network; VH1; WE tv.
Fee: $44.35 monthly.

Digital Basic Service
Subscribers: N.A.
Programming (via satellite): BBC America; Bloomberg Television; Discovery Digital Networks; Disney XD; ESPN Classic; ESPN Now; ESPNews; Fox Sports 1; FXM; Golf Channel; GSN; MC; Nick Jr.; Outdoor Channel; Ovation; TeenNick.
Digital Pay Service 1
Pay Units: N.A.
Programming (via satellite): Cinemax (multiplexed); HBO (multiplexed); IFC; Showtime (multiplexed); Starz (multiplexed); Starz Encore; Sundance TV; The Movie Channel (multiplexed).
Fee: $10.50 monthly (each).
Video-On-Demand: No
Pay-Per-View
iN DEMAND (delivered digitally); Hot Choice (delivered digitally); Fresh (delivered digitally); Shorteez (delivered digitally); Sports PPV (delivered digitally).
Internet Service
Operational: Yes.
Broadband Service: Road Runner.
Fee: $32.95-$57.95 monthly.
Telephone Service
Analog: Operational
Miles of Plant: 51.0 (coaxial); None (fiber optic).
General Manager: Jim Smith. Chief Technician: Jeff Clark. Office Manager: Lisa Taylor.
Ownership: Bright House Networks LLC (MSO).

CLOVERDALE—Comcast Cable. Now served by TUPELO, MS [MS0009]. ICA: AL0178.

CODEN—Formerly served by Mediacom. No longer in operation. ICA: AL0179.

COFFEEVILLE—Formerly served by Sky Cablevision. No longer in operation. ICA: AL0265.

COLLINSVILLE—Formerly served by Collinsville TV Cable. No longer in operation. ICA: AL0138.

COLUMBIANA—Zito Media, 102 S Main St, PO Box 665, Coudersport, PA 16915. Phones: 814-260-9055; 800-365-6988. E-mail: info@zitomedia.com. Web Site: http://www.zitomedia.com. Also serves Lay Lake, Shelby County (portions), Shelby Lake & Wilsonville. ICA: AL0180.
TV Market Ranking: 40 (COLUMBIANA, Lay Lake, Shelby County (portions), Shelby Lake, Wilsonville). Franchise award date: January 1, 1981. Franchise expiration date: N.A. Began: January 1, 1982.
Channel capacity: N.A. Channels available but not in use: N.A.
Basic Service
Subscribers: 144. Commercial subscribers: 7.
Programming (received off-air): WABM (MNT) Birmingham; WBIQ (PBS) Birmingham; WBRC (Bounce TV, FOX) Birmingham; WIAT (CBS, Untamed Sports TV) Birmingham; WPXH-TV (ION) Gadsden; WSES (ABC, TNN) Tuscaloosa; WTTO (Antenna TV, CW, The Country Network) Homewood; WVTM-TV (MeTV, NBC) Birmingham.
Programming (via satellite): C-SPAN; Trinity Broadcasting Network (TBN); WGN America.
Fee: $49.95 installation; $24.99 monthly.

Expanded Basic Service 1
Subscribers: N.A.
Programming (via satellite): A&E; AMC; Bravo; Cartoon Network; CMT; CNBC; CNN; Comedy Central; Discovery Channel; Disney Channel; E! HD; ESPN; ESPN2; Fox News Channel; Fox Sports 1; FOX Sports South/SportSouth; Freeform; FX; Golf Channel; HGTV; History; HLN; Lifetime; MSNBC; MTV; Nickelodeon; Oxygen; Spike TV; Syfy; TBS; The Weather Channel; TLC; TNT; Turner Classic Movies; TV Land; USA Network; VH1; WE tv.
Fee: $24.00 monthly.
Digital Basic Service
Subscribers: N.A.
Programming (via satellite): BBC America; Bloomberg Television; Discovery Life Channel; Disney XD; ESPN Classic; Fuse; FXM; FYI; GSN; History International; IFC; LMN; MC; Nick 2; Nick Jr.; Nicktoons; Sundance TV; TeenNick.
Pay Service 1
Pay Units: N.A.
Planned programming (via satellite): Cinemax (multiplexed).
Programming (via satellite): Flix; HBO (multiplexed); Showtime (multiplexed); Starz (multiplexed); Starz Encore; The Movie Channel (multiplexed).
Fee: $14.00 monthly (Cinemax/HBO, Showtime/TMC/Flix or Starz/Encore).
Video-On-Demand: No
Pay-Per-View
ESPN Now (delivered digitally); iN DEMAND (delivered digitally); Playboy TV (delivered digitally); Fresh (delivered digitally).
Internet Service
Operational: No.
Telephone Service
None
Miles of Plant: 69.0 (coaxial); None (fiber optic). Homes passed: 2,775.
President: James Rigas.
Ownership: Zito Media (MSO).

CUBA—Formerly served by Zoom Media. No longer in operation. ICA: AL0181.

CULLMAN—Charter Communications, 256 US Hwy 276 E, Cullman, AL 35055. Phones: 314-543-2236; 636-207-5100 (Corporate office); 888-438-2427. Web Site: http://www.charter.com. Also serves Blount County (northwestern portion), Blountsville, Cullman County (portions), Fairview, Garden City, Hanceville, Holly Pond, Jefferson County (portions), Kimberly, Morris, Vinemont, Warrior & West Point. ICA: AL0034.
TV Market Ranking: 40 (Jefferson County (portions), Kimberly, Morris, Warrior); 96 (CULLMAN, Fairview, Garden City, Hanceville, Holly Pond, Vinemont, West Point); Below 100 (Blount County (northwestern portion), Blountsville). Franchise award date: May 1, 1967. Franchise expiration date: N.A. Began: May 1, 1967.
Channel capacity: 63 (operating 2-way). Channels available but not in use: N.A.
Digital Basic Service
Subscribers: 7,715.
Programming (via satellite): BBC America; Bloomberg Television; Bravo; Discovery Digital Networks; Disney XD; ESPN Classic; ESPNews; Fox Sports 1; Fuse; FXM; FYI; Golf Channel; GSN; History International; IFC; INSP; MC; National Geographic Channel; NBCSN; Nick Jr.; Nicktoons; Outdoor Channel; TeenNick; Trinity Broadcasting Network (TBN); Turner Classic Movies; WE tv.
Fee: $49.99 installation; $26.99 monthly.

Alabama—Cable Systems

Digital Pay Service 1
Pay Units: N.A.
Programming (via satellite): Cinemax (multiplexed); HBO (multiplexed); Showtime (multiplexed); Starz (multiplexed); Starz Encore (multiplexed); The Movie Channel (multiplexed).
Fee: $13.00 monthly (each).
Video-On-Demand: Planned
Pay-Per-View
Fresh (delivered digitally); Playboy TV (delivered digitally).
Internet Service
Operational: Yes.
Subscribers: 6,468.
Broadband Service: Charter Internet.
Fee: $20.99-$49.99 installation; $44.95 monthly.
Telephone Service
Digital: Operational
Subscribers: 3,031.
Fee: $49.95 monthly
Miles of Plant: 1,391.0 (coaxial); 263.0 (fiber optic). Homes passed: 28,400.
Accounting Director: David Sovanski.
Ownership: Charter Communications Inc. (MSO).

CULLMAN—Formerly served by Alabama Broadband LLC. Now served by Charter Communications, CULLMAN, AL [AL0034]. ICA: AL0193.

CURRY—Charter Communications, 12405 Powerscourt Dr, St. Louis, MO 63131. Phones: 636-207-5100 (Corporate office); 205-824-1051; 205-824-5400. Fax: 205-824-5490. Web Site: http://www.charter.com. ICA: AL0182.
TV Market Ranking: Outside TV Markets (CURRY).
Channel capacity: 60 (not 2-way capable). Channels available but not in use: N.A.
Basic Service
Subscribers: 125,753.
Programming (received off-air): WABM (MNT) Birmingham; WBIQ (PBS) Birmingham; WBRC (Bounce TV, FOX) Birmingham; WIAT (CBS, Untamed Sports TV) Birmingham; WPXH-TV (ION) Gadsden; WSES (ABC, TNN) Tuscaloosa; WTTO (Antenna TV, CW, The Country Network) Homewood; WVTM-TV (MeTV, NBC) Birmingham.
Programming (via satellite): C-SPAN; WGN America.
Fee: $29.99 installation.
Digital Basic Service
Subscribers: N.A.
Programming (via satellite): BBC America; Bloomberg Television; Discovery Digital Networks; DMX Music; ESPN Classic; ESPNews; Fuse; FXM; FYI; GSN; History International; IFC; LMN; Nick 2; Nick Jr.; Nicktoons; Sundance TV; TeenNick.
Fee: $16.99 monthly.
Digital Expanded Basic Service
Subscribers: N.A.
Programming (via satellite): A&E; AMC; Animal Planet; Bravo; Cartoon Network; CMT; CNBC; CNN; Comedy Central; Discovery Channel; Disney Channel; Disney XD; E! HD; ESPN; ESPN2; Fox News Channel; Fox Sports 1; Freeform; FX; Golf Channel; HGTV; History; HLN; MTV; Nickelodeon; Oxygen; Spike TV; Syfy; TBS; The Weather Channel; TLC; TNT; Turner Classic Movies; TV Land; USA Network; VH1; WE tv.
Fee: $43.00 monthly.

Pay Service 1
Pay Units: N.A.
Programming (via satellite): Flix; Showtime (multiplexed); The Movie Channel (multiplexed).
Fee: $9.95 monthly (each).
Digital Pay Service 1
Pay Units: N.A.
Programming (via satellite): Cinemax (multiplexed); HBO (multiplexed); Starz (multiplexed); Starz Encore (multiplexed).
Video-On-Demand: No
Pay-Per-View
iN DEMAND (delivered digitally); ESPN Now (delivered digitally); Hot Choice (delivered digitally); Urban Xtra (delivered digitally); Playboy TV (delivered digitally); Fresh (delivered digitally); Shorteez (delivered digitally).
Internet Service
Operational: Yes.
Subscribers: 99,406.
Broadband Service: Charter Internet.
Telephone Service
Digital: Operational
Subscribers: 50,899.
Miles of Plant: 9,844.0 (coaxial); 3,563.0 (fiber optic). Homes passed: 306,757.
Vice President & General Manager: Don Karell. Technical Operations Manager: Greg Prim. Marketing Director: David Redmond. Marketing Manager: Jeff Hatcher. Accounting Director: David Sovanski.
Ownership: Charter Communications Inc. (MSO).

DADEVILLE—Charter Communications, 3164 Hwy 431, Ste 8, Roanoke, AL 36274. Phones: 636-207-5100 (Corporate office); 334-863-8112; 314-543-2236. Web Site: http://www.charter.com. ICA: AL0183.
TV Market Ranking: Below 100 (DADEVILLE). Franchise award date: N.A. Franchise expiration date: N.A. Began: December 1, 1982.
Channel capacity: 60 (operating 2-way). Channels available but not in use: N.A.
Digital Basic Service
Subscribers: 482.
Programming (via satellite): BBC America; Bloomberg Television; Cloo; Destination America; Discovery Kids Channel; Discovery Life Channel; Disney XD; DMX Music; Fox Sports 1; Golf Channel; GSN; IFC; Investigation Discovery; NBCSN; OWN; Oprah Winfrey Network; Science Channel; Turner Classic Movies.
Fee: $49.99 installation; $26.99 monthly.
Digital Expanded Basic Service
Subscribers: N.A.
Programming (via satellite): A&E; AMC; Animal Planet; BET; Bravo; Cartoon Network; CMT; CNBC; CNN; Comcast/Charter Sports Southeast (CSS); Comedy Central; C-SPAN; C-SPAN 2; Disney Channel; E! HD; ESPN Classic; ESPN2; EVINE Live; Food Network; Fox News Channel; Freeform; FX; FXM; Great American Country; Hallmark Channel; HGTV; History; HLN; ION Television; Lifetime; LMN; MSNBC; Nick Jr.; Outdoor Channel; QVC; Spike TV; SportSouth; Syfy; The Weather Channel; TLC; Travel Channel; Trinity Broadcasting Network (TBN); truTV; TV Land; USA Network; VH1; WE tv.
Digital Pay Service 1
Pay Units: 173.
Programming (via satellite): Cinemax (multiplexed); HBO (multiplexed); Showtime (multiplexed); Starz (multiplexed); Starz Encore (multiplexed).
Video-On-Demand: No

Pay-Per-View
iN DEMAND (delivered digitally); Playboy TV (delivered digitally); Fresh (delivered digitally).
Internet Service
Operational: Yes.
Broadband Service: Charter Internet.
Fee: $39.95 installation; $51.95 monthly.
Telephone Service
None
Miles of Plant: 9,627.0 (coaxial); 3,524.0 (fiber optic). Homes passed: 302,752.
President & Chief Executive Officer: Tom Rutledge. General Manager: Brian Chase. Chief Technician: William Boyd. Accounting Director: David Sovanski.
Ownership: Charter Communications Inc. (MSO).

DALEVILLE—Time Warner Cable, 104 South Woodburn Dr, Dothan, AL 36305-1020. Phones: 334-836-0680; 334-793-3383. Fax: 334-793-5667. Web Site: http://www.timewarnercable.com. Also serves Clayhatchee, Dothan, Fort Rucker, Geneva County, Grimes, Houston County, Level Plains, Malvern, Midland City, Napier Field, Newton, Pinckard, Rehobeth & Taylor. ICA: AL0012.
TV Market Ranking: Below 100 (Clayhatchee, Fort Rucker, Geneva County (portions), Grimes, Houston County, Level Plains, Malvern, Midland City, Napier Field, Newton, Pinckard, Rehobeth, Taylor, DALEVILLE, Dothan); Outside TV Markets (Geneva County (portions)). Franchise award date: February 18, 1966. Franchise expiration date: N.A. Began: August 1, 1966.
Channel capacity: 68 (operating 2-way). Channels available but not in use: N.A.
Basic Service
Subscribers: 14,429.
Programming (received off-air): WDFX-TV (Bounce TV, FOX) Ozark; WDHN (ABC) Dothan; WGIQ (PBS) Louisville; WJHG-TV (CW, MNT, NBC) Panama City; WSFA (Bounce TV, NBC) Montgomery; WTVY (CBS, CW, MeTV, MNT, This TV) Dothan; 1 FM.
Programming (via satellite): C-SPAN; C-SPAN 2; Pop.
Fee: $42.50 installation; $11.99 monthly.
Expanded Basic Service 1
Subscribers: N.A.
Programming (via satellite): A&E; AMC; Animal Planet; BET; Bravo; Cartoon Network; CMT; CNBC; CNN; Comedy Central; Discovery Channel; Disney Channel; E! HD; ESPN; ESPN Classic; ESPN2; EWTN Global Catholic Network; Food Network; Fox News Channel; Fox Sports 1; FOX Sports South/SportSouth; Freeform; FX; Golf Channel; Hallmark Channel; HGTV; History; HLN; ION Television; Lifetime; MSNBC; MTV; National Geographic Channel; Nickelodeon; Ovation; Oxygen; QVC; Spike TV; Syfy; TBS; The Weather Channel; TLC; TNT; Travel Channel; Trinity Broadcasting Network (TBN); truTV; Turner Classic Movies; TV Land; Univision Studios; USA Network; VH1; WE tv.
Fee: $22.79 monthly.
Digital Basic Service
Subscribers: N.A.
Programming (via satellite): BBC America; Bloomberg Television; Discovery Life Channel; Disney XD; ESPNews; Fuse; GSN; LMN; MC; MTV2; NBCSN; Nick Jr.; Outdoor Channel; TeenNick.
Fee: $4.00 monthly (digital access), $6.00 monthly (each tier).

Digital Pay Service 1
Pay Units: N.A.
Programming (via satellite): Cinemax (multiplexed); HBO (multiplexed); IFC; Showtime (multiplexed); Starz (multiplexed); Starz Encore (multiplexed); Sundance TV; The Movie Channel (multiplexed).
Fee: $14.00 monthly (each).
Video-On-Demand: Yes
Pay-Per-View
NBA TV (delivered digitally); NHL (delivered digitally); Fresh (delivered digitally); Shorteez (delivered digitally); Hot Choice (delivered digitally); iN DEMAND (delivered digitally).
Internet Service
Operational: Yes.
Subscribers: 8,724.
Broadband Service: Road Runner.
Fee: $99.95 installation; $44.95 monthly.
Telephone Service
Digital: Operational
Subscribers: 3,221.
Fee: $44.95 monthly
Miles of Plant: 1,099.0 (coaxial); 48.0 (fiber optic). Homes passed: 28,864. Homes passed includes Enterprise.
President, Residential Services: Brian Kelly. General Manager: Ramona Byrd. Technical Operations Supervisor: John Carr. Marketing Manager: Judi Gates.
Ownership: Time Warner Cable (MSO).

DALEVILLE—Troy Cable, 1006 Brundidge St, Troy, AL 36081-3121. Phones: 334-566-3310; 800-735-9546. Fax: 334-598-1200. E-mail: sales@troycable.net. Web Site: http://www.troycable.net. ICA: AL0068. **Note:** This system is an overbuild.
TV Market Ranking: Below 100 (DALEVILLE). Franchise award date: N.A. Franchise expiration date: N.A. Began: February 1, 1993.
Channel capacity: N.A. Channels available but not in use: N.A.
Basic Service
Subscribers: 808.
Programming (received off-air): WDFX-TV (Bounce TV, FOX) Ozark; WDHN (ABC) Dothan; WGIQ (PBS) Louisville; WJHG-TV (CW, MNT, NBC) Panama City; WSFA (Bounce TV, NBC) Montgomery; WTVY (CBS, CW, MeTV, MNT, This TV) Dothan.
Programming (via satellite): Animal Planet; INSP; QVC; TBS; WGN America.
Fee: $25.00 installation; $17.95 monthly.
Expanded Basic Service 1
Subscribers: N.A.
Programming (via satellite): A&E; AMC; BET; Cartoon Network; CMT; CNBC; CNN; Comedy Central; C-SPAN; C-SPAN 2; Discovery Channel; Disney Channel; Disney XD; E! HD; ESPN; ESPN2; Fox News Channel; Freeform; FX; HGTV; History; HLN; Lifetime; MTV; Nickelodeon; Spike TV; Syfy; The Weather Channel; TLC; TNT; Travel Channel; Trinity Broadcasting Network (TBN); truTV; Univision Studios; USA Network; VH1.
Fee: $28.95 monthly.
Pay Service 1
Pay Units: 122.
Programming (via satellite): Cinemax (multiplexed).
Fee: $8.50 monthly.
Pay Service 2
Pay Units: 264.
Programming (via satellite): HBO (multiplexed).
Fee: $8.50 monthly.

Cable Systems—Alabama

Pay Service 3
Pay Units: 92.
Programming (via satellite): The Movie Channel.
Fee: $8.50 monthly.
Pay Service 4
Pay Units: 142.
Programming (via satellite): Showtime (multiplexed).
Fee: $8.50 monthly.
Video-On-Demand: No
Internet Service
Operational: No, DSL & dial-up.
Telephone Service
Analog: Operational
Miles of Plant: 27.0 (coaxial); None (fiber optic). Homes passed: 2,700.
General Manager: William Freeman. Chief Technician: Ken Jordan.
Ownership: Troy Cablevision (MSO).

DAPHNE—Mediacom. Now served by FAIRHOPE, AL [AL0124]. ICA: AL0148.

DAUPHIN ISLAND—Comcast Cable. Now served by MOBILE, AL [AL0002]. ICA: AL0247.

DECATUR—Charter Communications, 1622 5th Ave SE, Decatur, AL 35601. Phones: 636-207-5100 (Corporate office); 888-438-2427; 205-824-1051; 205-824-5400. Web Site: http://www.charter.com. Also serves Albertville, Arab, Athens, Boaz, Colbert County, Cotaco, Crossville, Danville, Douglas, Elkmont, Etowah County (portions), Falkville, Five Points, Flint, Franklin County, Geraldine, Guntersville, Gurley, Hartselle, Hollywood, Horton, Jackson County, Laceys Spring, Lakeview, Lawrence County (portions), Limestone County (portions), Littleville, Madison County, Marshall County, Morgan City (portions), Morgan County, Moulton, Mountainboro, Oakville, Oleander, Paint Rock, Priceville, Russellville, Sardis City, Scottsboro, Section, Somerville, Union Grove, Union Hill & Valhermoso Springs. ICA: AL0184.
TV Market Ranking: 78 (Jackson County (portions)); 96 (Arab, Athens, Colbert County (portions), Cotaco, Danville, DECATUR, Elkmont, Falkville, Flint, Guntersville, Gurley, Hartselle, Hollywood, Horton, Laceys Spring, Lawrence County (portions), Limestone County (portions), Madison County, Morgan City (portions), Morgan County, Moulton, Oakville, Oleander, Paint Rock, Priceville, Priceville, Scottsboro, Somerville, Union Grove, Union Hill, Valhermoso Springs); Below 100 (Boaz, Crossville, Douglas, Etowah County (portions), Franklin County, Geraldine, Lakeview, Littleville, Marshall County, Mountainboro, Sardis City, Albertville, Russellville, Section, Colbert County (portions), Morgan City (portions)); Outside TV Markets (Five Points, Jackson County (portions)). Franchise award date: N.A. Franchise expiration date: N.A. Began: August 20, 1964.
Channel capacity: 68 (operating 2-way). Channels available but not in use: N.A.
Digital Basic Service
Subscribers: 49,055.
Programming (via satellite): BBC America; Bloomberg Television; CBS Sports Network; CMT; Discovery Digital Networks; DIY Network; DIY Network On Demand; ESPN Classic; ESPN HD; ESPN2 HD; ESPNews; ESPNU; Food Network On Demand; FOX College Sports Central; FOX College Sports Pacific; Fox Sports 2; Fuse; FXM;

FYI; Great American Country; HBO HD; HD Theater; HGTV On Demand; History International; HITS (Headend In The Sky); IFC; Jewelry Television; LMN; LOGO; MC; Nick 2; Nick Jr.; Nicktoons; Sundance TV; TeenNick; Telemundo; Tennis Channel; TNT HD; Universal HD; Univision; UP; WE tv.
Fee: $49.99 installation; $26.99 monthly.
Digital Pay Service 1
Pay Units: N.A.
Programming (via satellite): Cinemax (multiplexed); Cinemax HD; Cinemax On Demand; Flix; HBO (multiplexed); HBO on Demand; Showtime (multiplexed); Showtime HD; Showtime On Demand; Starz (multiplexed); Starz Encore (multiplexed); Starz HD; Starz On Demand; The Movie Channel (multiplexed).
Fee: $19.99 monthly (each).
Video-On-Demand: Yes
Pay-Per-View
iN DEMAND (delivered digitally); NHL Center Ice (delivered digitally); MLB Extra Innings (delivered digitally); Juicy (delivered digitally); SexSee (delivered digitally); Playboy TV (delivered digitally).
Internet Service
Operational: Yes.
Subscribers: 60,450.
Broadband Service: Charter Internet.
Fee: $29.99 monthly.
Telephone Service
Digital: Operational
Subscribers: 30,682.
Miles of Plant: 6,866.0 (coaxial); 2,113.0 (fiber optic). Homes passed: 184,147.
Vice President & General Manager: Don Karell. Technical Operations Director: Greg Prim. Marketing Director: David Redmond. Marketing Manager: Jeff Hatcher. Accounting Director: Steve Lottmann.
Ownership: Charter Communications Inc. (MSO).

DEMOPOLIS—Demopolis CATV Co, 105 South Cedar St., PO Box 477, Demopolis, AL 36732. Phone: 334-289-0727. Fax: 334-289-2707. Web Site: http://www.demopoliscatv.com. ICA: AL0071.
TV Market Ranking: Outside TV Markets (DEMOPOLIS). Franchise award date: N.A. Franchise expiration date: N.A. Began: October 1, 1963.
Channel capacity: N.A. Channels available but not in use: N.A.
Basic Service
Subscribers: 875.
Programming (received off-air): WBIQ (PBS) Birmingham; WBRC (Bounce TV, FOX) Birmingham; WDBB (CW) Bessemer; WIIQ (PBS) Demopolis; WMAW-TV (PBS) Meridian; WNCF (ABC) Montgomery; WSES (ABC, TNN) Tuscaloosa; WSFA (Bounce TV, NBC) Montgomery; WTOK-TV (ABC, CW, FOX, MNT) Meridian; 1 FM.
Programming (via satellite): A&E; AMC; Animal Planet; BET; Cartoon Network; CMT; CNBC; CNN; Comcast/Charter Sports Southeast (CSS); Comedy Central; C-SPAN; C-SPAN 2; Discovery Channel; Disney Channel; E! HD; ESPN; ESPN Classic; ESPN2; EVINE Live; EWTN Global Catholic Network; Food Network; Fox News Channel; Fox Sports 1; FOX Sports South/SportSouth; Freeform; FX; Golf Channel; Great American Country; Hallmark Channel; HGTV; History; HLN; INSP; Lifetime; MTV; Nickelodeon; Outdoor Channel; OWN: Oprah Winfrey Network; Pop; QVC; Spike TV; Syfy; TBS; The Weather Channel; TLC; TNT; Travel Channel; Trinity Broadcasting Network (TBN); truTV; Turner

Access the most current data instantly
FREE TRIAL @ ADVANCED **TVFactbook**
TELCO/IPTV • CABLE TV • TV STATIONS
www.warren-news.com/factbook.htm

Classic Movies; TV Land; USA Network; VH1; WGN America.
Fee: $25.00 installation; $54.00 monthly.
Pay Service 1
Pay Units: 221.
Programming (via satellite): Cinemax; HBO; Showtime.
Fee: $20.00 installation; $9.00 monthly (each).
Video-On-Demand: No
Internet Service
Operational: Yes.
Broadband Service: In-house.
Fee: $30.00-$60.00 monthly.
Telephone Service
None
Miles of Plant: 75.0 (coaxial); None (fiber optic).
President & General Manager: Lynn Goldman. Chief Technician: David Johnson.
Ownership: Demopolis CATV Co.

DOTHAN—Comcast Cable. Now served by TALLAHASSEE, FL [FL0283]. ICA: AL0185.

DOTHAN—WOW! Internet, Cable & Phone, 7887 East Belleview Ave, Ste 1000, Englewood, CO 80111. Phones: 720-479-3500; 706-645-8553; 334-699-3333. Fax: 720-479-3585. E-mail: wow_general@wideopenwest.com. Web Site: http://www.wowway.com. Also serves Ashford, Avon, Cowarts, Kinsey & Webb. ICA: AL0267. **Note:** This system is an overbuild.
TV Market Ranking: Below 100 (Ashford, Avon, Cowarts, DOTHAN, Kinsey, Webb).
Channel capacity: 71 (not 2-way capable). Channels available but not in use: N.A.
Basic Service
Subscribers: 6,385.
Programming (received off-air): WDFX-TV (Bounce TV, FOX) Ozark; WDHN (ABC) Dothan; WGIQ (PBS) Louisville; WJHG-TV (CW, MNT, NBC) Panama City; WSFA (Bounce TV, NBC) Montgomery; WTVY (CBS, CW, MeTV, MNT, This TV) Dothan.
Programming (via satellite): CW PLUS; INSP; Pop; WGN America.
Fee: $50.00 installation; $28.10 monthly.
Expanded Basic Service 1
Subscribers: N.A.
Programming (via satellite): A&E; AMC; Animal Planet; BET; Cartoon Network; CMT; CNBC; CNN; Comedy Central; C-SPAN; C-SPAN 2; Discovery Channel; Disney Channel; E! HD; ESPN; ESPN Classic; ESPN2; ESPNU; Food Network; Fox News Channel; Fox Sports 1; FOX Sports South/SportSouth; Freeform; FX; Golf Channel; Hallmark Channel; HGTV; History; HLN; ION Television; Lifetime; MSNBC; MTV; MyNetworkTV; National Geographic Channel; Nickelodeon; Outdoor Channel; OWN: Oprah Winfrey Network; QVC; Spike TV; Syfy; TBS; The Weather Channel; TLC; TNT; Travel Channel; Trinity Broadcasting Network (TBN); truTV; Turner Classic Movies; TV Land; UP; USA Network; VH1.
Digital Basic Service
Subscribers: N.A. Included in Valley Twp.
Programming (via satellite): BBC America; Bloomberg Television; CMT; Destina-

tion America; Discovery Channel HD; Discovery Kids Channel; Disney XD; DMX Music; ESPN HD; ESPN2 HD; ESPNews; FXM; FYI; GSN; History International; Investigation Discovery; LMN; MTV Classic; MTV Hits; MTV2; NBCSN; Nick Jr.; Nicktoons; PBS HD; Science Channel; TeenNick; Universal HD; VH1 Soul; WAM! America's Kidz Network; WE tv.
Digital Pay Service 1
Pay Units: N.A.
Programming (via satellite): Cinemax (multiplexed); Cinemax HD; HBO (multiplexed); HBO HD; Showtime (multiplexed); Starz (multiplexed); Starz Encore (multiplexed); Sundance TV; The Movie Channel (multiplexed).
Video-On-Demand: No
Pay-Per-View
iN DEMAND (delivered digitally); Spice (delivered digitally); Spice: Xcess (delivered digitally).
Internet Service
Operational: Yes.
Subscribers: 7,374.
Broadband Service: Knology.Net.
Fee: $57.95 monthly.
Telephone Service
Digital: Operational
Subscribers: 9,412.
Miles of Plant: 770.0 (coaxial); 39.0 (fiber optic). Homes passed: 26,134.
Chief Executive Officer: Colleen Abdoulah. President: Steven Cochran. Chief Financial Officer: Rich Fish.
Ownership: WideOpenWest LLC (MSO).

DOUBLE SPRINGS—Zito Media. Now served by HALEYVILLE, AL [AL0047]. ICA: AL0241.

ELBA—Formerly served by Charter Communications. Now served by Troy Cablevision. This cable system has converted to IPTV. See TROY, AL [AL5091]. ICA: AL0086.

ENTERPRISE—Time Warner Cable, 7800 Crescent Executive Dr, Charlotte, NC 28217. Phones: 334-393-9720; 866-744-1678. Web Site: http://www.timewarnercable.com. Also serves Coffee County (portions), Dale County & New Brockton. ICA: AL0022.
TV Market Ranking: Below 100 (Coffee County (portions), Dale County, ENTERPRISE, New Brockton). Franchise award date: N.A. Franchise expiration date: N.A. Began: September 1, 1966.
Channel capacity: 68 (operating 2-way). Channels available but not in use: N.A.
Basic Service
Subscribers: 7,103.
Programming (received off-air): WDFX-TV (Bounce TV, FOX) Ozark; WDHN (ABC) Dothan; WGIQ (PBS) Louisville; WIYC (WeatherNation) Troy; WSFA (Bounce TV, NBC) Montgomery; WTVY (CBS, CW, MeTV, MNT, This TV) Dothan.
Programming (via satellite): AMC; Bravo; C-SPAN; C-SPAN 2; EVINE Live; Family Friendly Entertainment; INSP; ION Televi-

2017 Edition   D-21

Alabama—Cable Systems

sion; Pop; QVC; Trinity Broadcasting Network (TBN); WGN America.
Fee: $47.99 installation; $11.99 monthly.

Expanded Basic Service 1
Subscribers: N.A.
Programming (via satellite): A&E; Animal Planet; BET; Cartoon Network; CMT; CNBC; CNN; Comedy Central; Discovery Channel; Disney Channel; E! HD; ESPN; ESPN2; EWTN Global Catholic Network; Food Network; Fox News Channel; Freeform; FX; Golf Channel; Hallmark Channel; HGTV; History; HLN; Lifetime; MSNBC; MTV; Nickelodeon; Oxygen; Spike TV; SportSouth; Syfy; TBS; The Weather Channel; TLC; TNT; Travel Channel; truTV; Turner Classic Movies; TV Land; Univision Studios; USA Network; VH1; WE tv.
Fee: $41.51 monthly.

Digital Basic Service
Subscribers: N.A.
Programming (via satellite): BBC America; Bloomberg Television; Discovery Digital Networks; Disney XD; DIY Network; ESPN Classic; ESPNews; Fox Sports 1; Fuse; FXM; FYI; Great American Country; History International; IFC; MC; National Geographic Channel; NBCSN; Nick 2; Nick Jr.; Outdoor Channel; Sundance TV; TeenNick.

Digital Pay Service 1
Pay Units: N.A.
Programming (via satellite): Cinemax (multiplexed); HBO (multiplexed); Showtime (multiplexed); Starz (multiplexed); Starz Encore (multiplexed); The Movie Channel (multiplexed).
Fee: $14.00 monthly (each).

Video-On-Demand: Yes

Pay-Per-View
Hot Choice (delivered digitally); Fresh (delivered digitally); Shorteez (delivered digitally); Playboy TV (delivered digitally).

Internet Service
Operational: Yes.
Subscribers: 7,870.
Broadband Service: Road Runner.
Fee: $99.95 installation; $44.95 monthly.

Telephone Service
Digital: Operational
Subscribers: 2,877.
Fee: $44.95 monthly
Miles of Plant: 722.0 (coaxial); 9.0 (fiber optic). Homes passed: 19,794. Homes passed included in Daleville.
President, Residential Services: Brian Kelly. Senior Accounting Director: Karen Goodfellow. General Manager: Ramona Byrd. Technical Operations Supervisor: Don Baker. Marketing Manager: Judi Gates.
Ownership: Time Warner Cable (MSO).

EUFAULA—Bright House Networks, 2251 Lucien Way, Ste 200B, Maitland, FL 32751. Phones: 407-667-5200; 334-687-5555. Web Site: http://brighthouse.com. Also serves Barbour County (unincorporated areas) & Henry County (unincorporated areas), AL; Georgetown & Quitman County, GA. ICA: AL0036.
TV Market Ranking: 94 (Barbour County (unincorporated areas) (portions)); Below 100 (Henry County (unincorporated areas), Barbour County (unincorporated areas) (portions)); Outside TV Markets (EUFAULA, Georgetown, Quitman County, Barbour County (unincorporated areas) (portions)). Franchise award date: January 1, 1970. Franchise expiration date: N.A. Began: October 2, 1971.
Channel capacity: N.A. Channels available but not in use: N.A.

Basic Service
Subscribers: 3,528. Commercial subscribers: 151.
Programming (received off-air): WACS-TV (PBS) Dawson; WGIQ (PBS) Louisville; WLTZ (CW, NBC) Columbus; WRBL (CBS, MeTV) Columbus; WSFA (Bounce TV, NBC) Montgomery; WTVM (ABC, Bounce TV) Columbus; WXTX (FOX, Movies!, This TV) Columbus.
Programming (via satellite): WGN America.
Fee: $38.35 installation; $27.00 monthly.

Expanded Basic Service 1
Subscribers: N.A.
Programming (via satellite): A&E; AMC; Animal Planet; BET; Bravo; Cartoon Network; CMT; CNBC; CNN; Comedy Central; C-SPAN; C-SPAN 2; Discovery Channel; Disney Channel; E! HD; ESPN; ESPN Classic; ESPN Now; ESPN2; EVINE Live; Food Network; Fox News Channel; FOX Sports South/SportSouth; Freeform; Fuse; FX; Hallmark Channel; HGTV; History; HLN; ION Television; Lifetime; LMN; MSNBC; MTV; National Geographic Channel; NBCSN; Nickelodeon; Oxygen; QVC; Spike TV; Syfy; TBS; The Weather Channel; The Word Network; TLC; TNT; Travel Channel; Trinity Broadcasting Network (TBN); truTV; Turner Classic Movies; TV Land; USA Network; VH1; WE tv.
Fee: $44.35 monthly.

Digital Basic Service
Subscribers: N.A.
Programming (via satellite): BBC America; Bloomberg Television; Discovery Life Channel; Disney XD; DMX Music; ESPNews; Fox Sports 1; FXM; Golf Channel; GSN; MTV Classic; MTV2; Nick Jr.; Outdoor Channel; Ovation; TeenNick.

Digital Pay Service 1
Pay Units: N.A.
Programming (via satellite): Cinemax (multiplexed); HBO (multiplexed); Showtime (multiplexed); Starz (multiplexed); The Movie Channel (multiplexed).
Fee: $15.00 monthly (each).

Video-On-Demand: No

Pay-Per-View
Concert TV (delivered digitally); iN DEMAND (delivered digitally); ESPN Now (delivered digitally); Fresh (delivered digitally); Shorteez (delivered digitally); Sports PPV (delivered digitally).

Internet Service
Operational: Yes. Began: June 1, 2003.
Broadband Service: RoadRunner.
Fee: $29.95 monthly.

Telephone Service
Digital: Operational
Fee: $39.95 monthly
Miles of Plant: 365.0 (coaxial); 62.0 (fiber optic). Homes passed: 7,663.
Chief Financial Officer: William Futera. General Manager: Bruce Burgess. Chief Technician: Jeff Clark. Office Manager: Lisa Taylor.
Ownership: Bright House Networks LLC (MSO).

EUTAW—Community Cable & Broadband LLC, 1309 Roebuck Dr, PO Box 65, Meridian, MS 39301. Phone: 601-485-6980. Fax: 601-483-0103. Also serves Greene County (unincorporated areas). ICA: AL0186.
TV Market Ranking: Below 100 (EUTAW, Greene County (unincorporated areas)). Franchise award date: N.A. Franchise expiration date: N.A. Began: September 1, 1972.
Channel capacity: N.A. Channels available but not in use: N.A.

Basic Service
Subscribers: N.A. Includes Marion
Programming (received off-air): WBIQ (PBS) Birmingham; WBRC (Bounce TV, FOX) Birmingham; WCBI-TV (CBS, MNT) Columbus; WIAT (CBS, Untamed Sports TV) Birmingham; WSES (ABC, TNN) Tuscaloosa; WTOK-TV (ABC, CW, FOX, MNT) Meridian; WTTO (Antenna TV, CW, The Country Network) Homewood; WTVA (ABC, NBC) Tupelo; WVTM-TV (MeTV, NBC) Birmingham; WVUA-CD (This TV) Tuscaloosa.
Programming (via satellite): A&E; AMC; Animal Planet; BET; Cartoon Network; CMT; CNN; Comedy Central; C-SPAN; Discovery Channel; Disney Channel; E! HD; ESPN; ESPN Classic; ESPN2; Flix; Food Network; Fox News Channel; Fox Sports 1; FOX Sports South/SportSouth; FX; FXM; Golf Channel; Great American Country; Hallmark Channel; HGTV; History; HLN; INSP; Lifetime; MTV; Nickelodeon; Outdoor Channel; Pop; QVC; Spike TV; Syfy; TBS; The Weather Channel; TLC; TNT; Trinity Broadcasting Network (TBN); truTV; Turner Classic Movies; TV Land; USA Network; VH1; WE tv; WGN America.
Fee: $25.00 installation; $3.00 converter.

Pay Service 1
Pay Units: N.A.
Programming (via satellite): Cinemax; HBO; Showtime; Starz Encore (multiplexed).
Fee: $7.00 monthly (Cinemax or HBO).

Internet Service
Operational: No.

Telephone Service
None

Miles of Plant: 61.0 (coaxial); 24.0 (fiber optic). Homes passed: 1,500.
General Manager & Chief Technician: Berry Ward.
Ownership: Community Cable & Broadband LLC (MSO).

FAIRFIELD—Charter Communications, 12405 Powerscourt Dr, St. Louis, MO 63131. Phones: 636-207-5100 (Corporate office); 205-824-1051; 205-824-5400. Fax: 205-824-5490. Web Site: http://www.charter.com. Also serves Hueytown, Midfield & Pleasant Grove. ICA: AL0013.
TV Market Ranking: 40 (FAIRFIELD, Hueytown, Midfield, Pleasant Grove). Franchise award date: N.A. Franchise expiration date: N.A. Began: December 1, 1970.
Channel capacity: 60 (operating 2-way). Channels available but not in use: N.A.

Basic Service
Subscribers: N.A.
Programming (received off-air): WABM (MNT) Birmingham; WBIQ (PBS) Birmingham; WBRC (Bounce TV, FOX) Birmingham; WIAT (CBS, Untamed Sports TV) Birmingham; WOTM-LD Montevallo; WPXH-TV (ION) Gadsden; WSES (ABC, TNN) Tuscaloosa; WTTO (Antenna TV, CW, The Country Network) Homewood; WVTM-TV (MeTV, NBC) Birmingham.
Programming (via satellite): INSP; Trinity Broadcasting Network (TBN); WGN America.
Fee: $11.53 installation; $11.53 monthly.

Digital Basic Service
Subscribers: N.A.
Programming (via satellite): BBC America; Bloomberg Television; Bravo; Disney XD; DMX Music; ESPNews; FXM; FYI; Great American Country; GSN; History International; HITS (Headend In The Sky); IFC; LMN; NBCSN; Nick Jr.; Outdoor Channel; OWN: Oprah Winfrey Network; Sundance TV; TeenNick; TV Guide Interactive Inc.
Fee: $16.99 monthly.

Digital Expanded Basic Service
Subscribers: N.A.
Programming (via satellite): A&E; AMC; Animal Planet; BET; Cartoon Network; CMT; CNBC; CNN; Comcast/Charter Sports Southeast (CSS); Comedy Central; C-SPAN; C-SPAN 2; Discovery Channel; Disney Channel; E! HD; ESPN; ESPN Classic; ESPN2; EWTN Global Catholic Network; Food Network; Fox News Channel; Fox Sports 1; FOX Sports South/SportSouth; Freeform; FX; Golf Channel; Hallmark Channel; HGTV; History; HLN; Lifetime; MSNBC; MTV; National Geographic Channel; Nickelodeon; Oxygen; QVC; Spike TV; Syfy; TBS; The Weather Channel; TLC; TNT; Travel Channel; truTV; Turner Classic Movies; TV Land; USA Network; VH1; WE tv.
Fee: $43.00 monthly.

Digital Pay Service 1
Pay Units: N.A.
Programming (via satellite): Cinemax (multiplexed); HBO (multiplexed); Showtime (multiplexed); Starz (multiplexed); Starz Encore (multiplexed); The Movie Channel (multiplexed).

Video-On-Demand: Yes

Pay-Per-View
iN DEMAND (delivered digitally); Playboy TV (delivered digitally); Fresh (delivered digitally); Shorteez (delivered digitally).

Internet Service
Operational: Yes.
Subscribers: 99,406.
Broadband Service: Charter Internet.
Fee: $29.99 monthly; $10.00 modem lease.

Telephone Service
Digital: Operational
Subscribers: 50,899.
Miles of Plant: 9,844.0 (coaxial); 3,563.0 (fiber optic). Homes passed: 306,757.
Vice President & General Manager: Don Karell. Technical Operations Director: Greg Prim. Marketing Manager: Jeff Hatcher. Marketing Director: David Redmond. Accounting Director: David Sovanski.
Ownership: Charter Communications Inc. (MSO).

FAIRHOPE—Mediacom, 760 Middle St, PO Box 1009, Fairhope, AL 36532. Phones: 800-479-2082; 251-928-0374. Fax: 251-928-3804. Web Site: http://www.mediacomcable.com. Also serves Baldwin County (portions), Barnwell, Bay Minette, Daphne, Fish River, Lillian, Marlow, Montrose, Point Clear, Spanish Cove, Spanish Fort & Stapleton. ICA: AL0124.
TV Market Ranking: 59 (Baldwin County (portions), Barnwell, Bay Minette, Daphne, FAIRHOPE, Fish River, Lillian, Marlow, Montrose, Point Clear, Spanish Cove, Spanish Fort, Stapleton). Franchise award date: May 18, 1982. Franchise expiration date: N.A. Began: January 1, 1988.
Channel capacity: 66 (operating 2-way). Channels available but not in use: N.A.

Basic Service
Subscribers: 8,594.
Programming (received off-air): WALA-TV (FOX) Mobile; WEAR-TV (ABC, The Country Network) Pensacola; WEIQ (PBS) Mobile; WFNA (Bounce TV, CW) Gulf Shores; WHBR (Christian TV Network) Pensacola; WJTC (IND) Pensacola; WKRG-TV (CBS, MeTV) Mobile; WMPV-TV (TBN) Mobile; WPMI-TV (NBC) Mobile.

Programming (via satellite): A&E; AMC; Animal Planet; BET; Bravo; Cartoon Network; CMT; CNBC; CNN; Comedy Central; C-SPAN; C-SPAN 2; Discovery Channel; Disney Channel; E! HD; ESPN; ESPN2; EWTN Global Catholic Network; Food Network; Fox News Channel; FOX Sports South/SportSouth; Freeform; FX; Golf Channel; Hallmark Channel; HGTV; History; HLN; INSP; ION Television; Lifetime; MoviePlex; MSNBC; MTV; Nickelodeon; Oxygen; Pop; QVC; Spike TV; Syfy; TBS; The Weather Channel; TLC; TNT; Travel Channel; truTV; TV Land; USA Network; VH1; WE tv; WGN America.
Fee: $34.95 installation; $41.00 monthly.

Digital Basic Service
Subscribers: N.A.
Programming (via satellite): BBC America; Bloomberg Television; Discovery Digital Networks; ESPNews; Fox Sports 1; Fuse; FXM; FYI; GSN; History International; IFC; LMN; MC; National Geographic Channel; NBCSN; Outdoor Channel; Trinity Broadcasting Network (TBN); Turner Classic Movies.

Digital Pay Service 1
Pay Units: N.A.
Programming (via satellite): Cinemax (multiplexed); Flix; HBO (multiplexed); Showtime (multiplexed); Starz (multiplexed); Starz Encore (multiplexed); Sundance TV; The Movie Channel (multiplexed).
Fee: $10.95 monthly (Cinemax, HBO, Showtime, Flix/Sundance/TMC, or Starz/Encore).
Video-On-Demand: Yes
Pay-Per-View
ESPN Now (delivered digitally); Playboy TV (delivered digitally); Pleasure (delivered digitally); Fresh (delivered digitally); Vubiquity Inc. (delivered digitally).
Internet Service
Operational: Yes.
Subscribers: 6,389.
Broadband Service: Mediacom High Speed Internet.
Telephone Service
Digital: Operational
Subscribers: 3,661.
Miles of Plant: 1,260.0 (coaxial); 289.0 (fiber optic). Homes passed: 39,020.
General Manager: Jeff Walker. Technical Operations Manager: Bobby Hollifield. Chief Technician: Billy Brooks.
Ownership: Mediacom LLC (MSO).

FAYETTE—West Alabama TV Cable Co. Inc, 213 2nd Ave NE, PO Box 930, Fayette, AL 35555-0930. Phones: 205-921-3800; 205-487-2884; 205-932-4700 (Fayette office). Fax: 205-932-3585. E-mail: cable@watvc.com. Web Site: http://www.watvc.com. Also serves Belk. ICA: AL0072.
TV Market Ranking: Below 100 (Belk); Outside TV Markets (FAYETTE). Franchise award date: N.A. Franchise expiration date: N.A. Began: February 1, 1966.
Channel capacity: 60 (operating 2-way). Channels available but not in use: N.A.
Basic Service
Subscribers: N.A.
Programming (received off-air): WABM (MNT) Birmingham; WBIQ (PBS) Birmingham; WBRC (Bounce TV, FOX) Birmingham; WIAT (CBS, Untamed Sports TV) Birmingham; WSES (ABC, TNN) Tuscaloosa; WTTO (Antenna TV, CW, The Country Network) Homewood; WTVA (ABC, NBC) Tupelo; WVTM-TV (MeTV, NBC) Birmingham; allband FM.

Programming (via satellite): A&E; AMC; BET; Cartoon Network; CMT; CNBC; CNN; C-SPAN; Discovery Channel; Disney Channel; E! HD; ESPN; ESPN2; Family Friendly Entertainment; Food Network; Fox News Channel; FOX Sports South/SportSouth; Freeform; FX; Golf Channel; Hallmark Channel; HGTV; History; HLN; Lifetime; MTV; Nickelodeon; Pop; QVC; TBS; The Weather Channel; TLC; TNT; Travel Channel; Trinity Broadcasting Network (TBN); Turner Classic Movies; TV Land; USA Network; VH1; WGN America.
Fee: $35.00 installation; $34.75 monthly.
Digital Basic Service
Subscribers: N.A.
Programming (via satellite): BBC America; Bloomberg Television; Cloo; Destination America; Discovery Kids Channel; Disney XD; DMX Music; ESPN Classic; ESPN Now; ESPNews; Fox Sports 1; FXM; FYI; History International; IFC; INSP; Investigation Discovery; LMN; National Geographic Channel; NBCSN; Outdoor Channel; OWN; Oprah Winfrey Network; Science Channel; WE tv.
Pay Service 1
Pay Units: N.A.
Programming (via satellite): Cinemax; HBO.
Fee: $15.00 installation; $10.95 (Cinemax), $11.95 monthly (HBO).
Digital Pay Service 1
Pay Units: N.A.
Programming (via satellite): Cinemax (multiplexed); HBO (multiplexed); Showtime (multiplexed); Starz (multiplexed); Starz Encore (multiplexed); The Movie Channel (multiplexed).
Fee: $10.95 monthly (Cinemax or Starz/Encore/TMC), $12.95 monthly (HBO or Showtime).
Video-On-Demand: No
Pay-Per-View
iN DEMAND (delivered digitally); Hot Choice (delivered digitally); Spice (delivered digitally); ESPN Now (delivered digitally); Sports PPV (delivered digitally).
Internet Service
Operational: Yes.
Broadband Service: In-house.
Fee: $24.95 monthly.
Telephone Service
Analog: Operational
Miles of Plant: 150.0 (coaxial); None (fiber optic). Homes passed: 8,000.
General Manager: Kyle South.
Ownership: West Alabama TV Cable Co. Inc. (MSO).

FLORALA—Bright House Networks. Now served by DE FUNIAK SPRINGS, FL [FL0111]. ICA: AL0092.

FLORENCE—Comcast Cable. Now served by TUPELO, MS [MS0009]. ICA: AL0187.

FOLEY—Riviera Utilities Cable TV, 413 East Laurel Ave, PO Box 2050, Foley, AL 36535-2619. Phone: 251-943-5001. Fax: 251-943-5275. Web Site: http://www.rivierautilities.com. Also serves Bon Secour, Elberta, Magnolia Springs, Miflin & Summerdale. ICA: AL0046.
TV Market Ranking: 59 (Bon Secour, Elberta, FOLEY, Magnolia Springs, Miflin, Summerdale). Franchise award date: June 2, 1980. Franchise expiration date: N.A. Began: March 2, 1982.
Channel capacity: 75 (operating 2-way). Channels available but not in use: N.A.

Basic Service
Subscribers: 3,836.
Programming (received off-air): WALA-TV (FOX) Mobile; WEAR-TV (ABC, The Country Network) Pensacola; WEIQ (PBS) Mobile; WHBR (Christian TV Network) Pensacola; WJTC (IND) Pensacola; WKRG-TV (CBS, MeTV) Mobile; WMPV-TV (TBN) Mobile; WPAN (Soul of the South) Fort Walton Beach [LICENSED & SILENT]; WPMI-TV (NBC) Mobile; WSRE (PBS) Pensacola.
Programming (via satellite): QVC; The Weather Channel; WPIX (Antenna TV, CW, This TV) New York.
Fee: $35.00 installation; $25.50 monthly.
Expanded Basic Service 1
Subscribers: N.A.
Programming (via satellite): A&E; AMC; Animal Planet; BET; Bravo; Cartoon Network; CMT; CNBC; CNN; Comedy Central; C-SPAN; C-SPAN 2; Discovery Channel; Disney Channel; Disney XD; E! HD; ESPN; ESPN Classic; ESPN2; EWTN Global Catholic Network; Food Network; Freeform; FX; FXM; Great American Country; Hallmark Channel; HGTV; History; HLN; Lifetime; MSNBC; MTV; National Geographic Channel; Nickelodeon; Outdoor Channel; Oxygen; Spike TV; SportSouth; Syfy; TBS; TLC; TNT; Travel Channel; truTV; TV Land; USA Network; VH1; WGN America.
Fee: $28.95 monthly.
Digital Basic Service
Subscribers: N.A.
Programming (via satellite): A&E HD; BBC America; Bloomberg Television; Destination America; Discovery Kids Channel; Discovery Life Channel; DMX Music; ESPN HD; ESPN2 HD; ESPNews; Food Network HD; Fox Sports 1; FXM; FYI; Golf Channel; GSN; HGTV HD; History International; Investigation Discovery; Lifetime; MTV Classic; MTV2; National Geographic Channel HD; NBCSN; Nick Jr.; Nicktoons; OWN: Oprah Winfrey Network; Science Channel; TeenNick; Turner Classic Movies; Universal HD; VH1 Country; WE tv.
Fee: $35.00 installation.
Pay Service 1
Pay Units: 383.
Programming (via satellite): Cinemax.
Fee: $13.95 monthly.
Pay Service 2
Pay Units: 866.
Programming (via satellite): HBO.
Fee: $13.95 monthly.
Digital Pay Service 1
Pay Units: N.A.
Programming (via satellite): Cinemax (multiplexed); Flix; HBO (multiplexed); Showtime (multiplexed); Starz (multiplexed); Starz Encore (multiplexed); Starz HD; The Movie Channel (multiplexed).
Video-On-Demand: No
Pay-Per-View
iN DEMAND (delivered digitally); Fresh (delivered digitally); Playboy TV (delivered digitally).
Internet Service
Operational: No.

Telephone Service
None
Miles of Plant: 495.0 (coaxial); 493.0 (fiber optic). Homes passed: 10,965.
Chief Executive Officer & General Manager: Michael Dugger. Assistant Manager: Brad Pitt. CATV & Public Affairs Manager: David A. Horton. Office Manager: Tina Sanders. Consumer Services Superintendent: Chris Bonner. CATV Superintendent: Robert Clark. Chief Engineer: Mike Replogle.
Ownership: Riviera Utilities Cable TV.

FORKLAND—Sky Cablevision, 1309 Roebuck Dr, PO Box 65, Meridian, MS 39301. Phone: 601-485-6980. Fax: 601-483-0103. ICA: AL0189.
TV Market Ranking: Outside TV Markets (FORKLAND). Franchise award date: N.A. Franchise expiration date: N.A. Began: February 1, 1990.
Channel capacity: N.A. Channels available but not in use: N.A.
Basic Service
Subscribers: N.A.
Programming (received off-air): WGBC (FOX, NBC) Meridian; WIIQ (PBS) Demopolis; WMDN (CBS) Meridian; WTOK-TV (ABC, CW, FOX, MNT) Meridian.
Programming (via satellite): A&E; CNN; Discovery Channel; Disney Channel; ESPN; Freeform; TBS; TNT; USA Network; WGN America.
Fee: $44.00 monthly.
Pay Service 1
Pay Units: N.A.
Programming (via satellite): HBO.
Fee: $11.00 monthly.
Internet Service
Operational: No.
Telephone Service
None
General Manager & Chief Technician: Berry Ward.
Ownership: Community Cable & Broadband LLC (MSO).

FORT PAYNE—Charter Communications, 302 Godfrey Ave NE, Fort Payne, AL 35967. Phones: 636-207-5100 (Corporate office); 314-288-3125; 888-438-2427; 314-965-0555. Web Site: http://www.charter.com. Also serves DeKalb County, Hammondville, Pine Ridge & Valley Head. ICA: AL0040.
TV Market Ranking: 18 (DeKalb County, FORT PAYNE, Pine Ridge, Valley Head); 78 (Hammondville). Franchise award date: N.A. Franchise expiration date: N.A. Began: August 19, 1968.
Channel capacity: 68 (operating 2-way). Channels available but not in use: N.A.
Digital Basic Service
Subscribers: 2,627.
Programming (via satellite): BBC America; Bloomberg Television; Discovery Digital Networks; Disney XD; DIY Network; ESPNews; FOX College Sports Central; FOX College Sports Pacific; Fuse; FXM; FYI; Golf Channel; Great American Country; GSN; History International; HITS (Headend In The Sky); IFC; MC; National Geographic Channel; NBCSN; Nick 2; Nick Jr.; Nicktoons;

Alabama—Cable Systems

Outdoor Channel; Sundance TV; TeenNick; Trinity Broadcasting Network (TBN); Turner Classic Movies; WE tv.
Fee: $49.99 installation; $26.99 monthly.
Digital Pay Service 1
Pay Units: N.A.
Programming (via satellite): Cinemax (multiplexed); Flix; HBO (multiplexed); Showtime (multiplexed); Starz (multiplexed); Starz Encore (multiplexed); The Movie Channel (multiplexed).
Fee: $12.00 monthly (HBO, Cinemax, Showtime/TMC or Starz), $19.95 monthly (Playboy).
Video-On-Demand: Planned
Pay-Per-View
Hot Choice (delivered digitally); Fresh (delivered digitally); Playboy TV (delivered digitally).
Internet Service
Operational: Yes.
Broadband Service: Charter Internet.
Fee: $20.99-$49.99 installation; $44.95 monthly.
Telephone Service
Digital: Operational
Fee: $49.95 monthly
Miles of Plant: 6,294.0 (coaxial); 1,929.0 (fiber optic). Homes passed: 173,474.
Accounting Director: David Sovanski.
Ownership: Charter Communications Inc. (MSO).

FREEMANVILLE—Formerly served by CableSouth Inc. No longer in operation. ICA: AL0190.

GADSDEN—Comcast Cable. Now served by TUPELO, MS [MS0009]. ICA: AL0191.

GENEVA—Bright House Networks. Now served by CHIPLEY, FL [FL0126]. ICA: AL0081.

GORDON—Formerly served by Gordon Cable TV. No longer in operation. ICA: AL0242.

GRANT—New Hope Telephone Cooperative. Now served by NEW HOPE, AL [AL0070]. ICA: AL0195.

GREENSBORO—Mediacom, 760 Middle St, PO Box 1009, Fairhope, AL 36532. Phones: 800-479-2082; 850-934-7700 (Gulf Breeze regional office); 251-928-0374. Fax: 251-928-3804. Web Site: http://www.mediacomcable.com. Also serves Hale County (portions) & Linden. ICA: AL0110.
TV Market Ranking: Below 100 (Hale County (portions)); Outside TV Markets (GREENSBORO, Linden, Hale County (portions)). Franchise award date: August 27, 1970. Franchise expiration date: N.A. Began: October 1, 1970.
Channel capacity: N.A. Channels available but not in use: N.A.
Basic Service
Subscribers: 852.
Programming (received off-air): WAKA (CBS, MeTV) Selma; WBIH (IND) Selma; WBRC (Bounce TV, FOX) Birmingham; WDBB (CW) Bessemer; WDVZ-CD (This TV) Greensboro; WIIQ (PBS) Demopolis; WNCF (ABC) Montgomery; WSES (ABC, TNN) Tuscaloosa; WSFA (Bounce TV, NBC) Montgomery; WTOK-TV (ABC, CW, FOX, MNT) Meridian; WVTM-TV (MeTV, NBC) Birmingham.
Programming (via satellite): A&E; AMC; Animal Planet; BET; Bravo; Cartoon Network; CMT; CNBC; CNN; Comedy Central; C-SPAN; C-SPAN 2; Discovery Channel; Discovery Life Channel; E! HD; ESPN; ESPN2; Food Network; Fox News Channel; Fox Sports 1; FOX Sports South/SportSouth; Freeform; FX; Hallmark Channel; HGTV; History; HLN; INSP; Lifetime; MSNBC; MTV; Nickelodeon; Outdoor Channel; QVC; Spike TV; Syfy; TBS; The Weather Channel; TLC; TNT; Travel Channel; Trinity Broadcasting Network (TBN); truTV; Turner Classic Movies; TV Land; USA Network; VH1; WE tv; WGN America.
Fee: $49.95 installation; $41.00 monthly; $2.95 converter.
Digital Basic Service
Subscribers: N.A.
Programming (via satellite): BBC America; Bloomberg Television; Discovery Digital Networks; DMX Music; FXM; FYI; GSN; History International; IFC; INSP; LMN; Outdoor Channel.
Digital Pay Service 1
Pay Units: N.A.
Programming (via satellite): Cinemax (multiplexed); Flix (multiplexed); HBO (multiplexed); Showtime (multiplexed); Starz Encore (multiplexed); Sundance TV (multiplexed); The Movie Channel (multiplexed).
Video-On-Demand: No
Pay-Per-View
Special events (delivered digitally).
Internet Service
Operational: Yes.
Subscribers: 286.
Broadband Service: Mediacom High Speed Internet.
Fee: $45.95 monthly.
Telephone Service
Digital: Operational
Subscribers: 9.
Miles of Plant: 100.0 (coaxial); 123.0 (fiber optic). Homes passed: 3,270.
Vice President: David Servies. Operations Director: Gene Wuchner. Technical Operations Manager: Mike Sneary. Sales & Marketing Manager: Joey Nagem.
Ownership: Mediacom LLC (MSO).

GREENVILLE—Bright House Networks, 2251 Lucien Way, Ste 200B, Maitland, FL 32751. Phones: 407-667-5200; 334-567-4344 (Office); 205-290-1300; 800-822-0060 (Customer service). Web Site: http://brighthouse.com. Also serves Butler County (portions), Fort Deposit & Georgiana. ICA: AL0058.
TV Market Ranking: Below 100 (Fort Deposit); Outside TV Markets (Georgiana, GREENVILLE). Franchise award date: January 1, 1965. Franchise expiration date: N.A. Began: February 1, 1965.
Channel capacity: N.A. Channels available but not in use: N.A.
Basic Service
Subscribers: 2,059. Commercial subscribers: 54.
Programming (received off-air): WAIQ (PBS) Montgomery; WAKA (CBS, MeTV) Selma; WBIH (IND) Selma; WBMM (CW, TNN) Tuskegee; WCOV-TV (Antenna TV, FOX, This TV) Montgomery; WIYC (WeatherNation) Troy; WMCF-TV (TBN) Montgomery; WNCF (ABC) Montgomery; WSFA (Bounce TV, NBC) Montgomery.
Programming (via satellite): Pop; TBS; WGN America.
Fee: $38.35 installation; $27.00 monthly.
Digital Basic Service
Subscribers: N.A.
Programming (via satellite): BBC America; Bloomberg Television; Boomerang; CNN International; Cooking Channel; Discovery Digital Networks; Disney XD; DIY Network; Discovery Life Channel; E! HD; ESPN; ESPN2; Food Network; Fox News Channel; Fox Sports 1; FOX Sports South/SportSouth; Freeform; FX; Hallmark Channel; HGTV; History; HLN; INSP; Lifetime; MSNBC; MTV; Nickelodeon; Outdoor Channel; QVC; Spike TV; Syfy; TBS; The Weather Channel; TLC; TNT; Travel Channel; Trinity Broadcasting Network (TBN); truTV; Turner Classic Movies; TV Land; USA Network; VH1; WE tv; WGN America.
Fee: $49.95 installation; $41.00 monthly; $2.95 converter.
Digital Basic Service
Subscribers: N.A.
Programming (via satellite): BBC America; Bloomberg Television; Discovery Digital Networks; DMX Music; FXM; FYI; GSN; History International; IFC; INSP; LMN; Outdoor Channel.
Digital Pay Service 1
Pay Units: N.A.
Programming (via satellite): Cinemax (multiplexed); Flix (multiplexed); HBO (multiplexed); Showtime (multiplexed); Starz Encore (multiplexed); Sundance TV (multiplexed); The Movie Channel (multiplexed).
Video-On-Demand: No
Pay-Per-View
Special events (delivered digitally).
ESPN Classic; ESPNews; Fox Sports 1; FXM; FYI; Great American Country; GSN; HD Theater; History International; MC; Nick Jr.; Nicktoons; Ovation; TeenNick; TNT.
Digital Expanded Basic Service
Subscribers: N.A.
Programming (via satellite): CBS Sports Network; FOX College Sports Central; FOX College Sports Pacific; Fox Sports 2; NBA TV; Outdoor Channel; Tennis Channel; The Movie Channel (multiplexed).
Fee: $3.95 monthly.
Digital Expanded Basic Service 2
Subscribers: N.A.
Programming (via satellite): IFC; Starz Encore (multiplexed); Sundance TV.
Fee: $4.95 monthly.
Digital Pay Service 1
Pay Units: N.A.
Programming (via satellite): Cinemax (multiplexed); HBO (multiplexed); HBO HD; Showtime (multiplexed); Showtime HD; Starz (multiplexed).
Fee: $15.00 monthly (each).
Video-On-Demand: No
Pay-Per-View
Hot Choice (delivered digitally); iN DEMAND (delivered digitally); Shorteez (delivered digitally); Pleasure (delivered digitally); Fresh (delivered digitally); NBA TV (delivered digitally).
Internet Service
Operational: Yes.
Broadband Service: RoadRunner.
Fee: $29.95 monthly.
Telephone Service
Digital: Operational
Fee: $39.95 monthly
Miles of Plant: 52.0 (coaxial); None (fiber optic). Homes passed: 4,425.
Chief Financial Officer: William Futera. General Manager: Bruce Burgess. Marketing Director: Dennis Burns. Technical Operations Manager: Mike Truelove.
Ownership: Bright House Networks LLC (MSO).

GROVE HILL—Pine Belt Broadband, 3984 County Rd 32, PO Box 279, Arlington, AL 36722. Phones: 888-810-4638; 334-385-2106. Fax: 334-385-2103. E-mail: contact@pinebelttalk.com. Web Site: http://www.pinebelt.net. Also serves Clarke County (portions) & Whatley. ICA: AL0117.
TV Market Ranking: Outside TV Markets (Clarke County (portions), GROVE HILL, Whatley). Franchise award date: July 18, 1980. Franchise expiration date: N.A. Began: December 10, 1980.
Channel capacity: N.A. Channels available but not in use: N.A.
Basic Service
Subscribers: 342.
Programming (received off-air): WAKA (CBS, MeTV) Selma; WALA-TV (FOX) Mobile; WEAR-TV (ABC, The Country Network) Pensacola; WIIQ (PBS) Demopolis; WJTC (IND) Pensacola; WKRG-TV (CBS, MeTV) Mobile; WPMI-TV (NBC) Mobile; WSFA (Bounce TV, NBC) Montgomery; WTOK-TV (ABC, CW, FOX, MNT) Meridian; allband FM.
Programming (via satellite): A&E; BET; Cartoon Network; CNBC; CNN; Comedy Central; Discovery Channel; Disney Channel; ESPN; ESPN2; Fox News Channel; Freeform; Great American Country; Hallmark Channel; HGTV; HLN; Lifetime; Outdoor Channel; QVC; Syfy; TBS; The Weather Channel; TNT; Trinity Broadcasting Network (TBN); USA Network; WGN America.
Fee: $24.99 installation; $19.99 monthly.
Digital Basic Service
Subscribers: N.A.
Programming (via satellite): BBC America; Bloomberg Television; Discovery Life Channel; Disney XD; DMX Music; ESPN Classic; ESPNews; FOX College Sports Central; FOX College Sports Pacific; FXM; FYI; Golf Channel; GSN; History International; INSP; LMN; National Geographic Channel; Starz Encore; Turner Classic Movies; WE tv.
Pay Service 1
Pay Units: N.A.
Programming (via satellite): HBO; Showtime.
Fee: $10.00 monthly (each).
Digital Pay Service 1
Pay Units: 82.
Programming (via satellite): Cinemax (multiplexed); Flix; HBO (multiplexed); Showtime (multiplexed); The Movie Channel (multiplexed).
Fee: $10.00 monthly (each).
Pay-Per-View
ESPN Now (delivered digitally); Hot Choice (delivered digitally); Playboy TV (delivered digitally); Fresh (delivered digitally); Shorteez (delivered digitally); Urban Xtra (delivered digitally).
Internet Service
Operational: Yes.
Broadband Service: Galaxy Cable Internet.
Fee: $49.95 installation; $44.95 monthly.
Telephone Service
None
Miles of Plant: 42.0 (coaxial); None (fiber optic). Homes passed: 1,147.
General Manager: John C. Nettles.
Ownership: Pine Belt Telephone Co. (MSO).

GUIN—Charter Communications. Now served by SULLIGENT, AL [AL0084]. ICA: AL0109.

GULF SHORES—Formerly served by Beyond Communications. No longer in operation. ICA: AL5080.

GUNTERSVILLE—Charter Communications. Now served by DECATUR, AL [AL0184]. ICA: AL0033.

GURLEY—Charter Communications. Now served by DECATUR, AL [AL0184]. ICA: AL0130.

HACKLEBURG—Formerly served by Mediastream. No longer in operation. ICA: AL0137.

HALEYVILLE—Zito Media, 102 S Main St, PO Box 665, Coudersport, PA 16915. Phones: 814-260-9055; 800-365-6988. E-mail: info@zitomedia.com. Web Site: http://www.zitomedia.com. Also serves Bear Creek, Double Springs, Marion County (portions) & Winston County (portions). ICA: AL0047.
TV Market Ranking: Outside TV Markets (Bear Creek, HALEYVILLE, Marion County (portions), Winston County (portions), Double Springs). Franchise award date: N.A. Franchise expiration date: N.A. Began: April 1, 1969.
Channel capacity: N.A. Channels available but not in use: N.A.
Basic Service
Subscribers: 286. Commercial subscribers: 63.
Programming (received off-air): WBIQ (PBS) Birmingham; WBRC (Bounce TV, FOX) Birmingham; WHNT-TV (Antenna TV, CBS) Huntsville; WIAT (CBS, Untamed Sports TV) Birmingham; WPXH-TV (ION) Gadsden; WSES (ABC, TNN) Tuscaloosa;

Cable Systems—Alabama

WTTO (Antenna TV, CW, The Country Network) Homewood; WVTM-TV (MeTV, NBC) Birmingham.
Programming (via satellite): C-SPAN; The Weather Channel; Trinity Broadcasting Network (TBN); WGN America.
Fee: $49.99 installation; $21.11 monthly.

Expanded Basic Service 1
Subscribers: N.A.
Programming (via satellite): A&E; AMC; Animal Planet; Cartoon Network; CMT; CNBC; CNN; Comedy Central; Discovery Channel; Disney Channel; E! HD; ESPN; ESPN2; Fox News Channel; Fox Sports 1; FOX Sports South/SportSouth; Freeform; FX; HGTV; History; HLN; Lifetime; MTV; Nickelodeon; Oxygen; Spike TV; Syfy; TBS; TLC; TNT; Travel Channel; TV Land; USA Network; VH1.
Fee: $23.00 monthly.

Digital Basic Service
Subscribers: N.A.
Programming (via satellite): BBC America; Bloomberg Television; Discovery Life Channel; Disney XD; ESPN Classic; ESPNews; Fuse; FXM; FYI; GSN; History International; IFC; LMN; MC; Nick 2; Nick Jr.; Nicktoons; Sundance TV; TeenNick; WE tv.

Pay Service 1
Pay Units: N.A.
Programming (via satellite): Cinemax (multiplexed); Flix; HBO (multiplexed); Showtime (multiplexed); Starz (multiplexed); Starz Encore; The Movie Channel (multiplexed).

Video-On-Demand: No

Pay-Per-View
ESPN Now (delivered digitally); iN DEMAND (delivered digitally); Playboy TV (delivered digitally); Fresh (delivered digitally).

Internet Service
Operational: Yes.
Fee: $39.95 monthly.

Telephone Service
Digital: Operational
Fee: $30.00 monthly
Miles of Plant: 84.0 (coaxial); None (fiber optic). Homes passed: 4,691.
President: James Rigas.
Ownership: Zito Media (MSO).

HAMILTON—West Alabama TV Cable Co. Inc, 213 2nd Ave NE, PO Box 930, Fayette, AL 35555-0930. Phones: 205-487-2884; 205-921-3800; 205-932-4700 (Fayette office). Fax: 205-932-3585. E-mail: cable@watvc.com. Web Site: http://www.watvc.com. ICA: AL0073.
TV Market Ranking: Outside TV Markets (HAMILTON). Franchise award date: N.A. Franchise expiration date: N.A. Began: June 1, 1965.
Channel capacity: N.A. Channels available but not in use: N.A.

Basic Service
Subscribers: N.A.
Programming (received off-air): WABM (MNT) Birmingham; WBIQ (PBS) Birmingham; WBRC (Bounce TV, FOX) Birmingham; WIAT (CBS, Untamed Sports TV) Birmingham; WSES (ABC, TNN) Tuscaloosa; WTTO (Antenna TV, CW, The Country Network) Homewood; WTVA (ABC, NBC) Tupelo; WVTM-TV (MeTV, NBC) Birmingham; allband FM.
Programming (via satellite): A&E; AMC; BET; Cartoon Network; CMT; CNBC; CNN; C-SPAN; Discovery Channel; Disney Channel; E! HD; ESPN; ESPN2; Family Friendly Entertainment; Food Network; Fox News Channel; FOX Sports South/SportSouth; Freeform; FX; Golf Channel; Hallmark Channel; HGTV; History; HLN; Lifetime; MTV; Nickelodeon; Pop; QVC; TBS; The Weather Channel; TLC; TNT; Travel Channel; Trinity Broadcasting Network (TBN); Turner Classic Movies; TV Land; USA Network; VH1; WGN America.
Fee: $35.00 installation; $34.75 monthly.

Digital Basic Service
Subscribers: N.A.
Programming (via satellite): BBC America; Bloomberg Television; Cloo; Destination America; Discovery Kids Channel; Disney XD; DMX Music; ESPN Classic; ESPNews; Fox Sports 1; FXM; FYI; History International; IFC; INSP; Investigation Discovery; LMN; National Geographic Channel; NBCSN; Outdoor Channel; OWN: Oprah Winfrey Network; Science Channel; WE tv.

Pay Service 1
Pay Units: N.A.
Programming (via satellite): Cinemax; HBO.
Fee: $15.00 installation; $10.95 monthly (Cinemax), $11.95 monthly (HBO).

Digital Pay Service 1
Pay Units: N.A.
Programming (via satellite): Cinemax (multiplexed); HBO (multiplexed); Showtime (multiplexed); Starz (multiplexed); Starz Encore (multiplexed); The Movie Channel (multiplexed).
Fee: $10.95 monthly (Cinemax or Starz/Encore/TMC), $12.95 monthly (HBO or Showtime).

Video-On-Demand: No

Pay-Per-View
iN DEMAND (delivered digitally); Hot Choice (delivered digitally); Spice (delivered digitally); ESPN Now (delivered digitally); Sports PPV (delivered digitally).

Internet Service
Operational: Yes.
Broadband Service: In-house.
Fee: $24.95 monthly.

Telephone Service
Analog: Operational
Miles of Plant: 150.0 (coaxial); None (fiber optic). Homes passed: 8,000.
General Manager: Kyle South.
Ownership: West Alabama TV Cable Co. Inc. (MSO).

HARTSELLE—Charter Communications. Now served by DECATUR, AL [AL0184]. ICA: AL0020.

HAYNEVILLE—Formerly served by Alabama Broadband LLC. No longer in operation. ICA: AL0143.

HEATH—TV Cable Company of Andalusia, 213 Dunson St, PO Box 34, Andalusia, AL 36420. Phone: 334-222-6464. Fax: 334-222-7226. E-mail: support@andycable.com. Web Site: http://www.andycable.com. Also serves Antioch, Babbie, Dozier, Gantt, Harmony, Red Level, River Falls, Sanford & Straughn. ICA: AL0078.
TV Market Ranking: Below 100 (Dozier); Outside TV Markets (Antioch, Babbie, Gantt, Harmony, HEATH, Red Level, River Falls, Sanford, Straughn). Franchise award date: June 1, 1986. Franchise expiration date: N.A. Began: October 1, 1987.
Channel capacity: N.A. Channels available but not in use: N.A.

Basic Service
Subscribers: 1,637.
Programming (received off-air): WAKA (CBS, MeTV) Selma; WCOV-TV (Antenna TV, FOX, This TV) Montgomery; WDIQ (PBS) Dozier; WIYC (WeatherNation) Troy; WNCF (ABC) Montgomery; WSFA (Bounce TV, NBC) Montgomery.
Programming (via satellite): A&E; AMC; Animal Planet; BET; Cartoon Network; CMT; CNN; Discovery Channel; Disney Channel; E! HD; ESPN; ESPN2; Fox News Channel; Freeform; HGTV; Lifetime; National Geographic Channel; NBCSN; Nickelodeon; QVC; Spike TV; Syfy; TBS; The Weather Channel; TLC; TNT; Trinity Broadcasting Network (TBN); USA Network; WGN America.
Fee: $29.95 installation; $25.00 monthly.

Pay Service 1
Pay Units: 235 Includes Beatrice, Castleberry & McKenzie.
Programming (via satellite): Cinemax; HBO.
Fee: $10.00 installation; $10.95 monthly (each).

Video-On-Demand: No

Internet Service
Operational: Yes.
Broadband Service: In-house.
Fee: $45.00 installation; $19.00 monthly.

Telephone Service
None
Miles of Plant: 180.0 (coaxial); 60.0 (fiber optic). Homes passed: 4,374.
Ownership: TV Cable Co. of Andalusia Inc. (MSO).

HEFLIN—Zito Media, 102 S Main St, PO Box 665, Coudersport, PA 16915. Phones: 814-260-9055; 800-365-6988. E-mail: info@zitomedia.com. Web Site: http://www.zitomedia.com. Also serves Cleburne County (western portion), Edwardsville & Fruithurst. ICA: AL0087.
TV Market Ranking: Below 100 (Cleburne County (western portion), Edwardsville, Fruithurst, HEFLIN). Franchise award date: N.A. Franchise expiration date: N.A. Began: May 1, 1984.
Channel capacity: N.A. Channels available but not in use: N.A.

Basic Service
Subscribers: 200. Commercial subscribers: 16.
Programming (received off-air): WBRC (Bounce TV, FOX) Birmingham; WCIQ (PBS) Mount Cheaha State Park; WGCL-TV (CBS, COZI TV, Grit) Atlanta; WGWW (ABC, TNN) Anniston; WTJP-TV (TBN) Gadsden; WTTO (Antenna TV, CW, The Country Network) Homewood; WVTM-TV (MeTV, NBC) Birmingham; WXIA-TV (NBC) Atlanta.
Programming (via satellite): ION Television; WGN America.
Fee: $49.95 installation; $24.99 monthly.

Expanded Basic Service 1
Subscribers: N.A.
Programming (via satellite): A&E; AMC; Animal Planet; Cartoon Network; CMT; CNBC; CNN; Comcast/Charter Sports Southeast (CSS); Comedy Central; C-SPAN; C-SPAN 2; Discovery Channel; Disney Channel; Disney XD; E! HD; ESPN; ESPN2; Food Network; Fox News Channel; FOX Sports South/SportSouth; Freeform; FX; HGTV; History; HLN; Lifetime; MSNBC; MTV; National Geographic Channel; Nickelodeon; Pop; Spike TV; Syfy; TBS; The Weather Channel; TLC; TNT; Travel Channel; TV Land; USA Network; VH1.
Fee: $27.00 monthly.

Digital Basic Service
Subscribers: N.A.
Programming (via satellite): BBC America; Bloomberg Television; Bravo; Discovery Digital Networks; ESPN Classic; EVINE Live; Fox Sports 1; FXM; FYI; Golf Channel; GSN; History International; IFC; LMN; MC; NBCSN; Nick Jr.; Outdoor Channel; TeenNick; Turner Classic Movies; TV Guide Interactive Inc.; WE tv.

Pay Service 1
Pay Units: N.A.
Programming (via satellite): Cinemax (multiplexed); Flix; HBO (multiplexed); Showtime (multiplexed); Starz (multiplexed); Starz Encore (multiplexed); The Movie Channel (multiplexed).
Fee: $14.00 monthly (Cinemax/HBO, Showtime/TMC/Flix or Starz/Encore).

Video-On-Demand: No

Pay-Per-View
ESPN Now (delivered digitally); Hot Choice (delivered digitally); iN DEMAND (delivered digitally); Playboy TV; Playboy TV (delivered digitally); Spice (delivered digitally); Spice 2 (delivered digitally).

Internet Service
Operational: No.

Telephone Service
None
Miles of Plant: 214.0 (coaxial); 16.0 (fiber optic). Homes passed: 2,053.
President: James Rigas.
Ownership: Zito Media (MSO).

HENAGAR—Zito Media, 102 S Main St, PO Box 665, Coudersport, PA 16915. Phones: 814-260-9055; 800-365-6988. E-mail: info@zitomedia.com. Web Site: http://www.zitomedia.com. Also serves DeKalb County (portions), Ider, Jackson County (portions), Pisgah & Sylvania. ICA: AL0045.
TV Market Ranking: 78 (Ider); Outside TV Markets (HENAGAR, Pisgah, Sylvania). Franchise award date: N.A. Franchise expiration date: N.A. Began: N.A.
Channel capacity: N.A. Channels available but not in use: N.A.

Basic Service
Subscribers: 306. Commercial subscribers: 4.
Programming (received off-air): WAAY-TV (ABC) Huntsville; WAFF (Bounce TV, NBC, This TV) Huntsville; WDEF-TV (Bounce TV, CBS, Escape) Chattanooga; WHIQ (PBS) Huntsville; WHNT-TV (Antenna TV, CBS) Huntsville; WRCB (Antenna TV, NBC) Chattanooga; WTVC (ABC, This TV, WeatherNation) Chattanooga; WZDX (FOX, MeTV, MNT) Huntsville.
Programming (via satellite): INSP; ION Television.
Fee: $29.99 installation; $24.49 monthly.

Expanded Basic Service 1
Subscribers: N.A.
Programming (via satellite): A&E; AMC; Animal Planet; Bravo; Cartoon Network; CMT; CNBC; CNN; Comedy Central; C-

2017 Edition D-25

Alabama—Cable Systems

SPAN; Discovery Channel; Disney Channel; Disney XD; E! HD; ESPN; ESPN2; Food Network; Fox News Channel; Fox Sports 1; FOX Sports South/SportSouth; Freeform; FX; Golf Channel; Hallmark Channel; HGTV; History; HLN; Lifetime; MSNBC; MTV; Nickelodeon; Oxygen; Spike TV; Syfy; TBS; Telemundo; The Weather Channel; TLC; TNT; Travel Channel; truTV; Turner Classic Movies; TV Land; Univision; Univision Studios; USA Network; VH1; WE tv.
Fee: $27.00 monthly.

Digital Basic Service
Subscribers: N.A.
Programming (via satellite): BBC America; Discovery Digital Networks; Fuse; FXM; FYI; GSN; History International; IFC; LMN; MC; Nick 2; Nick Jr.; Nicktoons; TeenNick.

Pay Service 1
Pay Units: N.A.
Programming (via satellite): Cinemax (multiplexed); Flix; HBO (multiplexed); Showtime (multiplexed); Starz (multiplexed); Starz Encore; The Movie Channel (multiplexed).
Fee: $14.00 monthly (Cinemax/HBO, Showtime/TMC/Flix or Starz/Encore).

Video-On-Demand: No

Pay-Per-View
ESPN Now (delivered digitally); iN DEMAND (delivered digitally); Playboy TV (delivered digitally); Fresh (delivered digitally); Shorteez (delivered digitally).

Internet Service
Operational: No.

Telephone Service
None
Miles of Plant: 237.0 (coaxial); 16.0 (fiber optic). Homes passed: 3,724.
President: James Rigas.
Ownership: Zito Media (MSO).

HILLSBORO—Formerly served by Shoals Cable TV Inc. No longer in operation. ICA: AL0140.

HOLLIS CROSSROADS—Formerly served by Mediastream. No longer in operation. ICA: AL0199.

HOOVER—Charter Communications. Now served by PELHAM, AL [AL0192]. ICA: AL0007.

HUNTSVILLE—Comcast Cable. Now served by TUPELO, MS [MS0009]. ICA: AL0004.

HUNTSVILLE—WOW! Internet, Cable & Phone, 7887 East Belleview Ave, Ste 1000, Englewood, CO 80111. Phones: 720-479-3500; 706-645-8553 (Corporate office). 256-533-5359; 256-533-5353 (Customer service). Fax: 720-479-3585. E-mail: wow_general@wideopenwest.com. Web Site: http://www.wowway.com. Also serves Athens, Limestone County (eastern portion), Madison, Madison County (portions) & Redstone Arsenal. ICA: AL0006.
Note: This system is an overbuild.
TV Market Ranking: 96 (Athens, HUNTSVILLE, Limestone County (eastern portion), Madison, Madison County (portions), Redstone Arsenal). Franchise award date: March 1, 1986. Franchise expiration date: N.A. Began: April 1, 1986.
Channel capacity: 80 (operating 2-way). Channels available but not in use: N.A.

Basic Service
Subscribers: 29,569.
Programming (received off-air): WAAY-TV (ABC) Huntsville; WAFF (Bounce TV, NBC, This TV) Huntsville; WHDF (CW) Florence;

WHIQ (PBS) Huntsville; WHNT-TV (Antenna TV, CBS) Huntsville; WZDX (FOX, MeTV, MNT) Huntsville.
Programming (via satellite): A&E; AMC; Animal Planet; BET; Bravo; Cartoon Network; CMT; CNBC; CNN; Comedy Central; C-SPAN; C-SPAN 2; Discovery Channel; Disney Channel; Disney XD; E! HD; ESPN; ESPN Classic; ESPN2; EVINE Live; EWTN Global Catholic Network; Food Network; Fox News Channel; Fox Sports 1; FOX Sports South/SportSouth; Freeform; FX; Golf Channel; Great American Country; Hallmark Channel; HGTV; History; HLN; INSP; Lifetime; LMN; MSNBC; MTV; MyNetworkTV; NASA TV; National Geographic Channel; Nick At Nite; Nickelodeon; Outdoor Channel; OWN: Oprah Winfrey Network; Oxygen; Pop; QVC; Spike TV; Syfy; TBS; The Weather Channel; TLC; TNT; Travel Channel; Trinity Broadcasting Network (TBN); truTV; Turner Classic Movies; TV Land; Univision Studios; USA Network; VH1; WE tv; WGN America.
Fee: $50.00 installation; $33.00 monthly; $1.45 converter.

Digital Basic Service
Subscribers: N.A.
Programming (via satellite): AXS TV; BBC America; Bloomberg Television; Boomerang; CBS Sports Network; Church Channel; CMT; Cooking Channel; C-SPAN 3; Destination America; Discovery Kids Channel; DIY Network; ESPN HD; ESPN2 HD; ESPNews; ESPNU; FOX College Sports Central; FOX College Sports Pacific; Fox Sports 2; FSN HD; Fuse; FYI; GSN; Hallmark Movies & Mysteries; HD Theater; History International; IFC; Investigation Discovery; Jewelry Television; JUCE TV; MC; MTV Classic; MTV Hits; MTV Jams; MTV2; mtvU; National Geographic Channel HD; NBCSN; NFL Network; Nick Jr.; Nicktoons; QVC HD; Science Channel; TBS HD; TeenNick; Tennis Channel; TNT HD; Tr3s; Universal HD; UP; Versus HD; VH1 Soul.

Pay Service 1
Pay Units: N.A.
Programming (via satellite): HBO; Showtime.
Fee: $10.95 monthly (each).

Digital Pay Service 1
Pay Units: N.A.
Programming (via satellite): Cinemax (multiplexed); Cinemax HD; Cinemax On Demand; Flix; Flix On Demand; HBO (multiplexed); HBO HD; HBO on Demand; Showtime (multiplexed); Showtime HD; Showtime On Demand; Starz (multiplexed); Starz Encore (multiplexed); Starz HD; Sundance TV; The Movie Channel (multiplexed); The Movie Channel On Demand.

Video-On-Demand: Yes

Pay-Per-View
iN DEMAND (delivered digitally); Hot Choice (delivered digitally); Spice: Xcess (delivered digitally); Shorteez (delivered digitally); Playboy TV (delivered digitally); Fresh (delivered digitally); Club Jenna (delivered digitally); ESPN Now (delivered digitally).

Internet Service
Operational: Yes.
Subscribers: 42,854.
Broadband Service: Knology.Net.
Fee: $29.95 installation; $57.95 monthly.

Telephone Service
Analog: Operational
Subscribers: 33,277.
Digital: Operational
Fee: $23.15 monthly
Miles of Plant: 2,793.0 (coaxial); 535.0 (fiber optic). Homes passed: 115,576.

Chief Executive Officer: Colleen Abdoulah. President: Steven Cochran. Chief Financial Officer: Rich Fish.
Ownership: WideOpenWest LLC (MSO).

JACKSON—Mediacom. Now served by THOMASVILLE, AL [AL0080]. ICA: AL0083.

JASPER—Charter Communications. Now served by PELHAM, AL [AL0192]. ICA: AL0026.

JASPER—Formerly served by Zoom Media. No longer in operation. ICA: AL0262.

LAFAYETTE—Charter Communications, 12405 Powerscourt Dr, St. Louis, MO 63131. Phones: 636-207-5100 (Corporate office); 334-863-8112; 334-863-7080. Fax: 334-863-2027. Web Site: http://www.charter.com. ICA: AL0097.
TV Market Ranking: Outside TV Markets (LAFAYETTE). Franchise award date: N.A. Franchise expiration date: N.A. Began: July 1, 1981.
Channel capacity: 71 (operating 2-way). Channels available but not in use: N.A.

Digital Basic Service
Subscribers: 11,864.
Programming (via satellite): BBC America; Destination America; Discovery Kids Channel; DMX Music; ESPN Classic; Fox Sports 1; Golf Channel; GSN; IFC; Investigation Discovery; NBCSN; OWN: Oprah Winfrey Network; Science Channel; Turner Classic Movies; WE tv.
Fee: $29.95 monthly.

Digital Pay Service 1
Pay Units: 80.
Programming (via satellite): Cinemax (multiplexed); HBO (multiplexed); Showtime; Starz (multiplexed); Starz Encore (multiplexed).
Fee: $13.95 monthly (Cinemax, HBO, Showtime, Starz or Encore).

Video-On-Demand: No

Pay-Per-View
iN DEMAND (delivered digitally); Playboy TV (delivered digitally).

Internet Service
Operational: Yes.
Subscribers: 8,180.
Broadband Service: Charter Internet.

Telephone Service
Digital: Operational
Subscribers: 6,047.
Miles of Plant: 5,363.0 (coaxial); 1,184.0 (fiber optic). Homes passed: 144,317.
President & Chief Executive Officer: Tom Rutledge. General Manager: Brian Chase. Chief Technician: William Boyd. Accounting Director: David Sovanski.
Ownership: Charter Communications Inc. (MSO).

LAKE MARTIN RESORT—Com-Link Inc, 206 Hardaway Ave East, PO Box 272, Union Springs, AL 36089. Phones: 800-722-2805; 334-738-2204. Fax: 334-738-5555. E-mail: ustc@ustconline.net. Web Site: http://www.ustconline.net. ICA: AL0090.
TV Market Ranking: Below 100 (LAKE MARTIN RESORT). Franchise award date: November 13, 1989. Franchise expiration date: N.A. Began: January 17, 1990.
Channel capacity: N.A. Channels available but not in use: N.A.

Basic Service
Subscribers: 1,400.
Programming (received off-air): WAIQ (PBS) Montgomery; WAKA (CBS, MeTV) Selma; WAXC-LD (IND) Alexander City;

WCOV-TV (Antenna TV, FOX, This TV) Montgomery; WNCF (ABC) Montgomery; WSFA (Bounce TV, NBC) Montgomery.
Programming (via satellite): A&E; AMC; BET; Cartoon Network; CMT; CNBC; CNN; C-SPAN; C-SPAN 2; Discovery Channel; E! HD; ESPN; Freeform; Hallmark Channel; HLN; Lifetime; MTV; Nickelodeon; QVC; Spike TV; Syfy; TBS; The Weather Channel; TLC; TNT; Travel Channel; truTV; Turner Classic Movies; USA Network; VH1; WGN America.
Fee: $35.00 installation; $41.70 monthly.

Pay Service 1
Pay Units: N.A.
Programming (via satellite): Cinemax; HBO; Showtime; The Movie Channel.
Fee: $8.50 monthly (each).

Video-On-Demand: No

Pay-Per-View
Special events, Addressable: No.

Internet Service
Operational: Yes.
Broadband Service: In-house.
Fee: $42.50 installation; $34.95-$59.95 monthly.

Telephone Service
Analog: Operational
Miles of Plant: 165.0 (coaxial); None (fiber optic). Homes passed: 2,486.
Executive Vice President: Larry Grogan. Vice President, Technical Services: Lynn Rotton.
Ownership: Com-Link Inc. (MSO).

LAY LAKE—Zito Media. Now served by COLUMBIANA, AL [AL0180]. ICA: AL0278.

LEESBURG—Formerly served by Ridge Networks. No longer in operation. ICA: AL0264.

LEIGHTON—Zito Media, 102 S Main St, PO Box 665, Coudersport, PA 16915. Phones: 814-260-9055; 800-365-6988. E-mail: info@zitomedia.com. Web Site: http://www.zitomedia.com. Also serves Colbert County (portions), Courtland, Lawrence County (portions), North Courtland, Spring Valley & Town Creek. ICA: AL0203.
TV Market Ranking: 96 (Colbert County (portions), Courtland, Lawrence County (portions), LEIGHTON, North Courtland, Town Creek; Below 100 (Spring Valley, Colbert County (portions)). Franchise award date: N.A. Franchise expiration date: N.A. Began: March 1, 1982.
Channel capacity: N.A. Channels available but not in use: N.A.

Basic Service
Subscribers: 70. Commercial subscribers: 2.
Programming (received off-air): WAAY-TV (ABC) Huntsville; WAFF (Bounce TV, NBC, This TV) Huntsville; WFIQ (PBS) Florence; WHDF (CW) Florence; WHNT-TV (Antenna TV, CBS) Huntsville; WZDX (FOX, MeTV, MNT) Huntsville.
Programming (via satellite): BET; C-SPAN; INSP; QVC; Trinity Broadcasting Network (TBN); WGN America.
Fee: $49.95 installation; $23.84 monthly.

Digital Basic Service
Subscribers: N.A.
Programming (via satellite): BBC America; Bloomberg Television; Discovery Life Channel; ESPN Classic; Fuse; FXM; FYI; GSN; History International; IFC; LMN; MC; Nick 2; Nick Jr.; Nicktoons; Sundance TV; TeenNick.

Pay Service 1
Pay Units: N.A.
Programming (via satellite): Cinemax (multiplexed); Flix; HBO (multiplexed);

Cable Systems—Alabama

Access the most current data instantly
FREE TRIAL @ ADVANCED TVFactbook
TELCO/IPTV • CABLE TV • TV STATIONS
www.warren-news.com/factbook.htm

Showtime (multiplexed); Starz (multiplexed); Starz Encore (multiplexed); The Movie Channel (multiplexed).
Fee: $14.00 monthly (Cinemax/HBO, Showtime/TMC/Flix or Starz/Encore).
Video-On-Demand: No
Pay-Per-View
iN DEMAND (delivered digitally); Playboy TV (delivered digitally); Shorteez (delivered digitally); Shorteez (delivered digitally).
Internet Service
Operational: No.
Telephone Service
None
Miles of Plant: 116.0 (coaxial); None (fiber optic). Homes passed: 4,372.
President: James Rigas.
Ownership: Zito Media (MSO).

LIMESTONE COUNTY (portions)—Charter Communications. Now served by DECATUR, AL [AL0184]. ICA: AL0120.

LINCOLN—USA Communications, 1701 Coggswell Ave, Pell City, AL 35125-1646. Phones: 800-234-0102; 800-824-4773; 205-884-4545. E-mail: csr@usacommunications.tv. Web Site: http://usacommunications.tv. ICA: AL0098.
Channel capacity: N.A. Channels available but not in use: N.A.
Basic Service
Subscribers: 723.
Fee: $42.00 installation; $37.50 monthly.
Internet Service
Operational: Yes.
Fee: $18.50-$45.45 monthly.
Telephone Service
Digital: Operational
Fee: $36.61 monthly
President: Jeffrey T. Smith.
Ownership: USA Companies LP (MSO).

LINDEN—Mediacom. Now served by GREENSBORO, AL [AL0110]. ICA: AL0106.

LINEVILLE—Charter Communications, 3164 Hwy 431, Ste 8, Roanoke, AL 36274. Phones: 636-207-5100 (Corporate office); 314-543-2236; 334-863-7080. Web Site: http://www.charter.com. Also serves Ashland. ICA: AL0096.
TV Market Ranking: Below 100 (Ashland, LINEVILLE). Franchise award date: January 1, 1984. Franchise expiration date: N.A. Began: April 1, 1987.
Channel capacity: 60 (operating 2-way). Channels available but not in use: N.A.
Digital Basic Service
Subscribers: 400.
Programming (via satellite): BBC America; Bloomberg Television; Cloo; Destination America; Discovery Kids Channel; Discovery Life Channel; Disney XD; DMX Music; Fox Sports 1; Golf Channel; GSN; IFC; Investigation Discovery; NBCSN; OWN; Oprah Winfrey Network; Science Channel; Turner Classic Movies.
Fee: $49.99 installation; $26.99 monthly.
Digital Expanded Basic Service
Subscribers: N.A.
Programming (via satellite): A&E; AMC; Animal Planet; BET; Bravo; Cartoon Network; CMT; CNBC; CNN; Comcast/Charter Sports Southeast (CSS); Comedy Central; C-SPAN; C-SPAN 2; Discovery Channel; Disney Channel; E! HD; ESPN; ESPN Classic; ESPN2; EVINE Live; Food Network; Fox News Channel; Freeform; FX; FXM; Great American Country; Hallmark Channel; HGTV; History; HLN; ION Television; Lifetime; LMN; MSNBC; MTV; Nick Jr.; Outdoor Channel; QVC; Spike TV; SportSouth; Syfy; The Weather Channel; TLC; TNT; Travel Channel; Trinity Broadcasting Network (TBN); truTV; TV Land; USA Network; VH1; WE tv.
Digital Pay Service 1
Pay Units: 137.
Programming (via satellite): Cinemax (multiplexed); HBO (multiplexed); Showtime (multiplexed); Starz (multiplexed); Starz Encore (multiplexed).
Video-On-Demand: No
Pay-Per-View
iN DEMAND (delivered digitally); Hot Choice (delivered digitally); Playboy TV (delivered digitally); Fresh (delivered digitally).
Internet Service
Operational: Yes.
Broadband Service: Charter Internet.
Telephone Service
None
Miles of Plant: 9,627.0 (coaxial); 3,524.0 (fiber optic). Homes passed: 302,752.
President & Chief Executive Officer: Tom Rutledge. General Manager: Brian Chase. Chief Technician: William Boyd. Accounting Director: David Sovanski.
Ownership: Charter Communications Inc. (MSO).

LOCUST FORK—Formerly served by Almega Cable. No longer in operation. ICA: AL0204.

LOWNDES COUNTY—Formerly served by Alabama Broadband LLC. No longer in operation. ICA: AL0102.

LUVERNE—Crenshaw Cable, 90 South Forest Ave, Luverne, AL 36049-1501. Phones: 800-735-9546; 334-335-3435. Fax: 334-335-3177. E-mail: sales@troycable.net. Web Site: http://www.troycable.net. Also serves Brantley, Glenwood & Rutledge. ICA: AL0103.
TV Market Ranking: Below 100 (Brantley, Glenwood, LUVERNE, Rutledge). Franchise award date: January 1, 1965. Franchise expiration date: N.A. Began: December 1, 1967.
Channel capacity: N.A. Channels available but not in use: N.A.
Basic Service
Subscribers: 10,416.
Programming (received off-air): WAKA (CBS, MeTV) Selma; WBMM (CW, TNN) Tuskegee; WCIQ (PBS) Mount Cheaha State Park; WCOV-TV (Antenna TV, FOX, This TV) Montgomery; WIYC (WeatherNation) Troy; WLTZ (CW, NBC) Columbus; WNCF (ABC) Montgomery; WSFA (Bounce TV, NBC) Montgomery; WTVM (ABC, Bounce TV) Columbus; WTVY (CBS, CW, MeTV, MNT, This TV) Dothan.
Programming (via satellite): A&E; AMC; Animal Planet; BET; Bravo; Cartoon Network; CMT; CNBC; CNN; Comcast/Charter Sports Southeast (CSS); Comedy Central; C-SPAN; C-SPAN 2; Discovery Channel; Disney Channel; E! HD; ESPN; ESPN Classic; ESPN2; Food Network; Fox News Channel; Fox Sports 1; FOX Sports South/SportSouth; Freeform; FX; Golf Channel; GSN; Hallmark Channel; HGTV; History; HLN; INSP; Lifetime; MSNBC; MTV; National Geographic Channel; Nickelodeon; Pop; QVC; Spike TV; Syfy; TBS; The Weather Channel; TLC; TNT; Travel Channel; truTV; Turner Classic Movies; TV Land; USA Network; VH1; WGN America.
Fee: $29.95 installation; $23.95 monthly.

Digital Basic Service
Subscribers: N.A.
Programming (via satellite): AXS TV; BBC America; Bloomberg Television; Cloo; Discovery Life Channel; Disney XD; ESPN; ESPNews; FOX College Sports Central; FOX College Sports Pacific; Fox Deportes; Fuse; FXM; FYI; HD Theater; History International; LMN; MC; Nick 2; Nick Jr.; Nicktoons; Outdoor Channel; TeenNick; Trinity Broadcasting Network (TBN).
Digital Pay Service 1
Pay Units: N.A.
Programming (via satellite): Cinemax (multiplexed); Flix; HBO (multiplexed); Showtime (multiplexed); Starz (multiplexed); Starz Encore (multiplexed); Sundance TV; The Movie Channel (multiplexed).
Fee: $7.95 monthly (Cinemax or Starz), $8.95 monthly (Encore), $10.95 monthly (Showtime/TMC), $11.95 monthly (HBO).
Video-On-Demand: No
Pay-Per-View
iN DEMAND (delivered digitally); Hot Choice (delivered digitally); Pleasure (delivered digitally); College Football (delivered digitally).
Internet Service
Operational: Yes.
Broadband Service: In-house.
Fee: $39.95 monthly.
Telephone Service
Digital: Operational
Miles of Plant: 45.0 (coaxial); 9.0 (fiber optic).
General Manager: William Freeman. Chief Technician: Ken Jordan.
Ownership: Troy Cablevision (MSO).

MADISON COUNTY—Mediacom, 123 Ware Dr NE, Huntsville, AL 35811-1061. Phones: 256-852-7427; 850-934-7700 (Gulf Breeze regional office). Fax: 256-851-7708. Web Site: http://www.mediacomcable.com. Also serves Capshaw & Harvest. ICA: AL0285.
TV Market Ranking: 96 (Capshaw, Harvest, MADISON COUNTY). Franchise award date: January 1, 1980. Franchise expiration date: N.A. Began: August 1, 1982.
Channel capacity: N.A. Channels available but not in use: N.A.
Basic Service
Subscribers: 9,224. Commercial subscribers: 90.
Programming (received off-air): WAAY-TV (ABC) Huntsville; WAFF (Bounce TV, NBC, This TV) Huntsville; WHDF (CW) Florence; WHIQ (PBS) Huntsville; WHNT-TV (Antenna TV, CBS) Huntsville; WTZT-CD (America One, Retro TV, TNN) Athens; WZDX (FOX, MeTV, MNT) Huntsville.
Programming (via satellite): A&E; AMC; Animal Planet; BET; Bravo; Cartoon Network; CMT; CNBC; CNN; Comedy Central; C-SPAN; C-SPAN 2; Discovery Channel; Disney XD; E! HD; ESPN; ESPN2; EWTN Global Catholic Network; Food Network; Fox News Channel; Fox Sports 1; FOX Sports South/SportSouth; Freeform; FX; Golf Channel; Hallmark Channel; HGTV; History; HLN; INSP; Lifetime; MSNBC; MTV; NASA TV; Nickelodeon; Outdoor Channel; QVC; Spike TV; Syfy; TBS; The Weather Channel; TLC; TNT; Travel Channel; Trinity Broadcasting Network (TBN); truTV; Turner Classic Movies; TV Land; USA Network; VH1; WE tv; WGN America.
Fee: $44.25 installation; $41.95 monthly.
Digital Basic Service
Subscribers: N.A.
Programming (via satellite): BBC America; Discovery Digital Networks; GSN; IFC; MC.
Digital Pay Service 1
Pay Units: N.A.
Programming (via satellite): Cinemax; Flix; HBO; Showtime; Starz; Starz Encore; Sundance TV; The Movie Channel.
Fee: $2.95 monthly (Flix), $9.95 monthly (Cinemax, HBO, Showtime or TMC).
Video-On-Demand: Yes
Pay-Per-View
ESPN Now (delivered digitally); Hot Choice (delivered digitally); iN DEMAND (delivered digitally); Fresh (delivered digitally); Sports PPV (delivered digitally).
Internet Service
Operational: Yes.
Broadband Service: Mediacom High Speed Internet.
Fee: $29.95 monthly; $10.00 modem lease.
Telephone Service
Digital: Operational
Miles of Plant: None (coaxial); 25.0 (fiber optic).
Vice President: David Servies. Operations Manager: Tommy Hill. Chief Technician: Harold Balch. Technical Operations Supervisor: Mark Darwin. Sales & Marketing Manager: Joey Nagem. Customer Service Supervisor: Sandy Acklin.
Ownership: Mediacom LLC (MSO).

MARGARET—Formerly served by Alabama Broadband LLC. Now served by Charter, ASHVILLE, AL [AL0168]. ICA: AL0205.

MARION—Community Cable & Broadband LLC, 1309 Roebuck Dr, PO Box 65, Meridian, MS 39301. Phone: 601-485-6980. Fax: 601-483-0103. Also serves Perry County (unincorporated areas). ICA: AL0091.
TV Market Ranking: Below 100 (MARION, Perry County (unincorporated areas)). Franchise award date: N.A. Franchise expiration date: N.A. Began: January 1, 1982.
Channel capacity: N.A. Channels available but not in use: N.A.
Basic Service
Subscribers: N.A.
Programming (received off-air): WAKA (CBS, MeTV) Selma; WBIQ (PBS) Birmingham; WBRC (Bounce TV, FOX) Birmingham; WCOV-TV (Antenna TV, FOX, This TV) Montgomery; WNCF (ABC) Montgomery; WSES (ABC, TNN) Tuscaloosa; WSFA (Bounce TV, NBC) Montgomery; WTTO (Antenna TV, CW, The Country Network) Homewood; WVTM-TV (MeTV, NBC) Birmingham.

2017 Edition   D-27

Alabama—Cable Systems

Programming (via satellite): A&E; AMC; Animal Planet; BET; Cartoon Network; CMT; CNN; Comedy Central; C-SPAN; Discovery Channel; Disney Channel; E! HD; ESPN; ESPN Classic; ESPN2; Flix; Food Network; Fox News Channel; Fox Sports 1; FOX Sports South/SportSouth; FX; FXM; Golf Channel; Great American Country; Hallmark Channel; HGTV; History; HLN; INSP; Lifetime; MTV; Nickelodeon; Outdoor Channel; Pop; QVC; Spike TV; Syfy; TBS; The Weather Channel; TLC; TNT; Trinity Broadcasting Network (TBN); truTV; Turner Classic Movies; TV Land; USA Network; VH1; WE tv; WGN America.
Fee: $25.00 installation; $3.00 converter.

Pay Service 1
Pay Units: N.A.
Programming (via satellite): Cinemax; HBO; Showtime; Starz Encore (multiplexed).
Fee: $7.00 monthly (Cinemax or HBO).

Internet Service
Operational: No.

Telephone Service
None
Miles of Plant: 64.0 (coaxial); 24.0 (fiber optic). Homes passed: 1,600.
General Manager & Chief Technician: Berry Ward.
Ownership: Community Cable & Broadband LLC (MSO).

McKENZIE—TV Cable Company of Andalusia, 213 Dunson St, PO Box 34, Andalusia, AL 36420. Phone: 334-222-6464. Fax: 334-222-7226. E-mail: support@andycable.com. Web Site: http://www.andycable.com. ICA: AL0144.
TV Market Ranking: Outside TV Markets (MCKENZIE). Franchise award date: June 1, 1986. Franchise expiration date: N.A. Began: December 23, 1987.
Channel capacity: N.A. Channels available but not in use: N.A.

Basic Service
Subscribers: 76.
Programming (received off-air): WAKA (CBS, MeTV) Selma; WCOV-TV (Antenna TV, FOX, This TV) Montgomery; WDIQ (PBS) Dozier; WIYC (WeatherNation) Troy; WNCF (ABC) Montgomery; WSFA (Bounce TV, NBC) Montgomery.
Programming (via satellite): Animal Planet; BET; CMT; CNBC; CNN; Discovery Channel; ESPN; Fox News Channel; Freeform; Lifetime; Nickelodeon; Spike TV; Syfy; TBS; TNT; Travel Channel; USA Network; WGN America.
Fee: $29.95 installation; $25.00 monthly.

Pay Service 1
Pay Units: N.A. Included in Heath.
Programming (via satellite): Cinemax; HBO.
Fee: $10.00 installation; $10.95 monthly (each).

Video-On-Demand: No

Internet Service
Operational: No.

Telephone Service
None
Miles of Plant: 180.0 (coaxial); 60.0 (fiber optic). Homes passed: 4,374.
Ownership: TV Cable Co. of Andalusia Inc. (MSO).

MENTONE—Charter Communications, 12405 Powerscourt Dr, St. Louis, MO 63131. Phones: 636-207-5100 (Corporate office); 877-581-3485. Web Site: http://www.charter.com. ICA: AL0243.
TV Market Ranking: 18 (MENTONE).
Channel capacity: 70 (operating 2-way). Channels available but not in use: N.A.

Digital Basic Service
Subscribers: 196.
Programming (via satellite): A&E; AMC; Animal Planet; BBC America; BET; Bravo; Cartoon Network; CMT; CNBC; CNN; Comcast/Charter Sports Southeast (CSS); Comedy Central; Discovery Channel; Discovery Digital Networks; Disney Channel; Disney XD; DIY Network; E! HD; ESPN; ESPN2; EWTN Global Catholic Network; Food Network; Fox News Channel; Fox Sports 1; FOX Sports South/SportSouth; Freeform; FX; FXM; FYI; Golf Channel; Great American Country; Hallmark Channel; HGTV; History; History International; HLN; IFC; Jewelry Television; Lifetime; LMN; MC; MSNBC; MTV; National Geographic Channel; NBCSN; Nick 2; Nick Jr.; Nickelodeon; Nicktoons; Oxygen; Pop; Spike TV; Sundance TV; Syfy; TBS; TeenNick; Telemundo; The Weather Channel; TLC; TNT; Travel Channel; truTV; Turner Classic Movies; TV Land; Univision; USA Network; VH1; WE tv.
Fee: $26.99 monthly.

Digital Expanded Basic Service
Subscribers: N.A.
Programming (via satellite): ESPN Classic; ESPNews; FOX College Sports Central; FOX College Sports Pacific; Fox Sports 2; Jewelry Television; NFL Network.

Digital Pay Service 1
Pay Units: N.A.
Programming (via satellite): Cinemax (multiplexed); HBO (multiplexed); Starz (multiplexed).
Fee: $24.99 monthly (each).

Video-On-Demand: No

Internet Service
Operational: Yes.
Broadband Service: Charter Internet.
Fee: $29.99 monthly.

Telephone Service
Digital: Operational
Miles of Plant: 3,485.0 (coaxial); 628.0 (fiber optic). Homes passed: 75,894.
Vice President & General Manager: Don Karell. Technical Operations Director: Greg Prim. Marketing Director: David Redmond. Marketing Manager: Jeff Hatcher. Accounting Director: David Sovanski.
Ownership: Charter Communications Inc. (MSO).

MEXIA—Formerly served by Galaxy Cablevision. No longer in operation. ICA: AL0261.

MILLPORT—Northland Cable Television. Now served by ALICEVILLE, AL [AL0055]. ICA: AL0125.

MILLRY—Formerly served by Sky Cablevision. No longer in operation. ICA: AL0207.

MOBILE—Bristers Cable TV, 107 Sleepy Oaks Rd, Fort Walton Beach, FL 32548. Phone: 251-367-4243. ICA: AL0282.
TV Market Ranking: 59 (MOBILE).
Channel capacity: N.A. Channels available but not in use: N.A.

Basic Service
Subscribers: 96.
Fee: $62.00 monthly.
General Manager: Terry Brister. Bookkeeper: Cheryl Brister.
Ownership: Bristers Cable TV.

MOBILE—Comcast Cable, 3248 Springhill Ave, Mobile, AL 36607-1831. Phones: 251-476-7600; 251-665-2217; 251-476-2190. Fax: 251-665-6670. Web Site: http://www.comcast.com. Also serves Chickasaw, Dauphin Island, Mobile County (portions), Prichard, Saraland & Satusma, AL; Edgard, Garyville, Gray, Houma, La Place, Lafourche Parish (portions), Mount Airy, Reserve, Schriever, Thibodaux, Vacherie & Wallace, LA. ICA: AL0002.
TV Market Ranking: 31 (La Place, Lafourche Parish (portions)); 59 (Chickasaw, Dauphin Island, MOBILE, Mobile County (portions), Prichard, Saraland, Satusma); Below 100 (Edgard, Garyville, Mount Airy, Reserve, Wallace); Outside TV Markets (Gray, Schriever, Thibodaux, Vacherie, Houma, Lafourche Parish (portions)). Franchise award date: N.A. Franchise expiration date: N.A. Began: July 1, 1971.
Channel capacity: 15 (operating 2-way). Channels available but not in use: N.A.

Basic Service
Subscribers: 58,206. Commercial subscribers: 2,779.
Programming (received off-air): WALA-TV (FOX) Mobile; WEAR-TV (ABC, The Country Network) Pensacola; WEIQ (PBS) Mobile; WHBR (Christian TV Network) Pensacola; WJTC (IND) Pensacola; WKRG-TV (CBS, MeTV) Mobile; WMPV-TV (TBN) Mobile; WPMI-TV (NBC) Mobile.
Programming (via satellite): HLN.
Fee: $52.95-$67.95 installation; $52.20 monthly.

Expanded Basic Service 1
Subscribers: N.A.
Programming (via satellite): A&E; AMC; Animal Planet; BET; Bravo; Cartoon Network; CMT; CNBC; CNN; Comcast/Charter Sports Southeast (CSS); Comedy Central; C-SPAN; C-SPAN 2; Discovery Channel; E! HD; ESPN; ESPN Classic; ESPN2; EWTN Global Catholic Network; Food Network; Fox News Channel; Fox Sports 1; FOX Sports South/SportSouth; Freeform; FX; Golf Channel; Great American Country; GSN; Hallmark Channel; HGTV; History; MSNBC; MTV; Nickelodeon; Outdoor Channel; OWN: Oprah Winfrey Network; Pop; QVC; Spike TV; Syfy; TBS; The Weather Channel; TLC; TNT; Travel Channel; truTV; Turner Classic Movies; TV Land; TV One; UP; USA Network; VH1; WGN America.
Fee: $40.89 monthly.

Digital Basic Service
Subscribers: N.A.
Programming (via satellite): BBC America; CMT; Cooking Channel; C-SPAN 3; Destination America; Discovery Channel HD; Discovery Kids Channel; Disney Channel; Disney XD; DIY Network; DMX Music; ESPN HD; ESPNews; Flix; FSN HD; FYI; History International; Investigation Discovery; LMN; MoviePlex; MTV Classic; MTV Hits; MTV2; National Geographic Channel; NFL Network; Nick 2; Nick Jr.; Nicktoons; RTV; Science Channel; Sprout; Starz Encore (multiplexed); Sundance TV; TeenNick; TNT HD; Tr3s; VH1 Soul.

Pay Service 1
Pay Units: N.A.
Programming (via satellite): Cinemax; HBO (multiplexed); Showtime.
Fee: $10.95 monthly (each).

Digital Pay Service 1
Pay Units: N.A.
Programming (via satellite): Cinemax (multiplexed); Cinemax HD; HBO (multiplexed); HBO HD; Showtime (multiplexed); Showtime HD; Starz (multiplexed); Starz HD; The Movie Channel (multiplexed).
Fee: $14.05 monthly (each).

Video-On-Demand: Yes

Pay-Per-View
iN DEMAND; iN DEMAND (delivered digitally); Hot Choice (delivered digitally); Playboy TV (delivered digitally); Pleasure (delivered digitally).

Internet Service
Operational: Yes.
Subscribers: 47,547.
Broadband Service: Comcast High Speed Internet.
Fee: $42.95 monthly; $7.00 modem lease.

Telephone Service
Digital: Operational
Subscribers: 23,502.
Miles of Plant: 3,466.0 (coaxial); 885.0 (fiber optic). Homes passed: 181,628.
General Manager: Ray Kistler. Technical Operations Manager: Jan Murray.
Ownership: Comcast Cable Communications Inc. (MSO).

MOBILE COUNTY—Formerly served by Charter Communications. No longer in operation. ICA: AL0037.

MOBILE COUNTY—Mediacom, 7325 Theodore Dawes Rd, Ste 7, Theodore, AL 36582-4029. Phones: 800-479-2082; 800-239-8411 (Customer service); 850-934-7700. Fax: 850-932-9237. Web Site: http://www.mediacomcable.com. Also serves Axis, Bayou la Batre, Citronelle, Creola, Grand Bay, Irvington, McIntosh, Mobile (portions), Mount Vernon, Saraland (portions), Satsuma, Semmes, Theodore, Tillman's Corner & Washington County (unincorporated areas). ICA: AL0017.
TV Market Ranking: 59 (Axis, Bayou la Batre, Citronelle, Creola, Grand Bay, Irvington, Mobile (portions), MOBILE COUNTY, Mount Vernon, Saraland (portions), Satsuma, Semmes, Theodore, Tillman's Corner); Outside TV Markets (McIntosh, Washington County (unincorporated areas)). Franchise award date: January 27, 1981. Franchise expiration date: N.A. Began: October 21, 1981.
Channel capacity: 80 (operating 2-way). Channels available but not in use: N.A.

Basic Service
Subscribers: 8,565.
Programming (received off-air): WALA-TV (FOX) Mobile; WEAR-TV (ABC, The Country Network) Pensacola; WEIQ (PBS) Mobile; WFNA (Bounce TV, CW) Gulf Shores; WHBR (Christian TV Network) Pensacola; WJTC (IND) Pensacola; WKRG-TV (CBS, MeTV) Mobile; WMPV-TV (TBN) Mobile; WPMI-TV (NBC) Mobile.
Programming (via satellite): A&E; AMC; Animal Planet; BET; Cartoon Network; CMT; CNBC; CNN; Comedy Central; C-SPAN; Discovery Channel; Disney Channel; Disney XD; E! HD; ESPN; ESPN2; EWTN Global Catholic Network; Fox News Channel; Fox Sports 1; FOX Sports South/SportSouth; Freeform; FX; Golf Channel; Hallmark Channel; HGTV; History; HLN; INSP; ION Television; Lifetime; LMN; MSNBC; MTV; Nickelodeon; Outdoor Channel; Pop; QVC; Spike TV; Syfy; TBS; The Weather Channel; TLC; TNT; Travel Channel; truTV; Turner Classic Movies; USA Network; VH1; WE tv; WGN America.
Fee: $32.00 installation; $59.08 monthly.

Digital Basic Service
Subscribers: N.A.
Programming (via satellite): American Heroes Channel; AmericanLife TV Network; AXS TV; BBC America; Bloomberg Television; CCTV-Documentary; Cloo; CNN HD; Discovery Family; ESPN HD; ESP-

Cable Systems—Alabama

News; Fuse; FXM; FYI; Great American Country; GSN; HD Theater; History International; IFC; Investigation Discovery; ION Television; LMN; MTV Classic; MTV Hits; MTV2; Music Choice; National Geographic Channel; Nick Jr.; Nicktoons; Outdoor Channel; OWN: Oprah Winfrey Network; Planet Green; Qubo; Reelz; Science Channel; TBS HD; TeenNick; TNT HD; TVG Network; Universal HD; Weatherscan.

Digital Pay Service 1
Pay Units: N.A.
Programming (via satellite): Cinemax (multiplexed); Flix; HBO; HBO HD; Showtime; Showtime HD; Starz (multiplexed); Starz Encore (multiplexed); The Movie Channel (multiplexed).
Fee: $10.45 monthly (Showtime HD/HBO HD/Cinemax, Showtime, Flix/TMC/Sundance, or Starz/Encore).
Video-On-Demand: Planned

Pay-Per-View
ESPN Now (delivered digitally); Pleasure (delivered digitally); iN DEMAND (delivered digitally); Playboy TV (delivered digitally).

Internet Service
Operational: Yes.
Subscribers: 9,393.
Broadband Service: Mediacom High Speed Internet.
Fee: $40.95 monthly; $5.00 modem lease.

Telephone Service
Analog: Not Operational
Digital: Operational
Subscribers: 4,087.
Fee: $29.95 monthly
Miles of Plant: 1,588.0 (coaxial); 499.0 (fiber optic). Homes passed: 46,831.
General Manager: David Fyffe. Marketing Director: Steve Purcell. Chief Technician: Garry Evans. Customer Service Manager: Judy Smythe.
Ownership: Mediacom LLC (MSO).

MONROEVILLE—Mediacom, 760 Middle St, PO Box 1009, Fairhope, AL 36532. Phones: 800-479-2082; 850-934-7700 (Gulf Breeze regional office); 251-928-0374. Fax: 251-928-3804. Web Site: http://www.mediacomcable.com. Also serves Camden, Conecuh County (portions), Evergreen, Excel, Frisco City, Monroe County (portions), Repton & Wilcox County (portions). ICA: AL0112.
TV Market Ranking: Below 100 (Camden, Wilcox County (portions)); Outside TV Markets (Conecuh County (portions), Evergreen, Excel, Frisco City, Monroe County (portions), Repton, MONROEVILLE). Franchise award date: December 9, 1975. Franchise expiration date: N.A. Began: July 1, 1970.
Channel capacity: N.A. Channels available but not in use: N.A.

Basic Service
Subscribers: 1,783.
Programming (received off-air): WAKA (CBS, MeTV) Selma; WALA-TV (FOX) Mobile; WBIH (IND) Selma; WCOV-TV (Antenna TV, FOX, This TV) Montgomery; WEAR-TV (ABC, The Country Network) Pensacola; WEIQ (PBS) Mobile; WKRG-TV (CBS, MeTV) Mobile; WNCF (ABC) Montgomery; WPMI-TV (NBC) Mobile; WSFA (Bounce TV, NBC) Montgomery.
Programming (via satellite): A&E; AMC; Animal Planet; BET; Bravo; Cartoon Network; CMT; CNBC; CNN; Comedy Central; C-SPAN; C-SPAN 2; Discovery Channel; Discovery Life Channel; Disney Channel; E! HD; ESPN; ESPN2; EWTN Global Catholic Network; Food Network; Fox News Channel; Fox Sports 1; FOX Sports South/ SportSouth; Freeform; FX; Hallmark Channel; HGTV; History; HLN; INSP; Lifetime; MSNBC; MTV; Nickelodeon; Outdoor Channel; QVC; Spike TV; Syfy; TBS; The Weather Channel; TLC; TNT; Travel Channel; Trinity Broadcasting Network (TBN); truTV; Turner Classic Movies; TV Land; USA Network; VH1; WE tv; WGN America.
Fee: $41.95 monthly.

Digital Basic Service
Subscribers: N.A.
Programming (via satellite): BBC America; Bloomberg Television; Cloo; Discovery Digital Networks; ESPNews; FXM; FYI; Golf Channel; GSN; History International; LMN; MC; National Geographic Channel; NBCSN; Nick Jr.; Nicktoons; TVG Network; Weatherscan.

Digital Pay Service 1
Pay Units: N.A.
Programming (via satellite): Cinemax (multiplexed); Flix (multiplexed); HBO (multiplexed); Starz (multiplexed); Starz Encore (multiplexed); Sundance TV (multiplexed); The Movie Channel (multiplexed).
Video-On-Demand: No

Internet Service
Operational: Yes.
Broadband Service: Mediacom High Speed Internet.
Fee: $45.95 monthly.

Telephone Service
Digital: Planned
Miles of Plant: 800.0 (coaxial); None (fiber optic). Miles of plant (coax) includes miles of plant (fiber).
Vice President: David Servies. Operations Director: Gene Wuchner. Technical Operations Manager: Mike Sneary. Sales & Marketing Manager: Joey Nagen.
Ownership: Mediacom LLC (MSO).

MONROEVILLE—Mediacom. Now served by MONROEVILLE, AL [AL0112]. ICA: AL0052.

MONTGOMERY—Charter Communications, 12405 Powerscourt Dr, St. Louis, MO 63131. Phones: 636-207-5100 (Corporate office); 205-824-5400. Fax: 205-824-5490. Web Site: http://www.charter.com. Also serves Autauga County, Dallas County, Elmore County, Montgomery County, Pike Road, Prattville, Selma & Valley Grande. ICA: AL0003.
TV Market Ranking: Below 100 (Autauga County, Dallas County, Elmore County, MONTGOMERY, Montgomery County, Pike Road, Prattville, Valley Grande, Selma). Franchise award date: January 1, 1969. Franchise expiration date: N.A. Began: July 1, 1977.
Channel capacity: 53 (operating 2-way). Channels available but not in use: N.A.

Digital Basic Service
Subscribers: 49,448.
Programming (via satellite): BBC America; Bloomberg Television; Discovery Digital Networks; Disney XD; DMX Music; ESPN Classic; ESPNews; FXM; FYI; Great American Country; GSN; History; History International; HITS (Headend In The Sky); IFC; LMN; NBCSN; Nick Jr; Outdoor Channel; Sundance TV; TeenNick; Trinity Broadcasting Network (TBN); Turner Classic Movies; TV Guide Interactive Inc.
Fee: $26.99 monthly.

Digital Expanded Basic Service
Subscribers: N.A.
Programming (via satellite): A&E; AMC; Animal Planet; BET; Bravo; Cartoon Network; CMT; CNBC; CNN; Comcast/Charter Sports Southeast (CSS); Comedy Central; C-SPAN; C-SPAN 2; Discovery Channel; Disney Channel; E! HD; ESPN; ESPN2; EWTN Global Catholic Network; Food Network; Fox News Channel; Fox Sports 1; FOX Sports South/SportSouth; Freeform; FX; Golf Channel; Hallmark Channel; HGTV; History; HLN; Lifetime; MSNBC; MTV; National Geographic Channel; Nickelodeon; Oxygen; Pop; QVC; Spike TV; Syfy; TBS; TLC; TNT; Travel Channel; truTV; TV Land; Univision Studios; USA Network; VH1; WE tv.
Fee: $43.00 monthly.

Digital Pay Service 1
Pay Units: N.A.
Programming (via satellite): Cinemax (multiplexed); HBO (multiplexed); Showtime (multiplexed); Starz (multiplexed); The Movie Channel (multiplexed).
Fee: $21.99 monthly (each).
Video-On-Demand: Yes

Pay-Per-View
iN DEMAND (delivered digitally); Playboy TV (delivered digitally); Fresh (delivered digitally); Shorteez (delivered digitally); Urban Xtra (delivered digitally).

Internet Service
Operational: Yes.
Subscribers: 35,869.
Broadband Service: Charter Internet.
Fee: $29.99 monthly; $10.00 modem lease.

Telephone Service
Digital: Operational
Subscribers: 24,762.
Miles of Plant: 2,941.0 (coaxial); 1,164.0 (fiber optic). Homes passed: 138,406.
Vice President & General Manager: Don Karell. Technical Operations Director: Greg Prim. Marketing Manager: Jeff Hatcher. Marketing Director: David Redmond. Accounting Director: David Sovanski.
Ownership: Charter Communications Inc. (MSO).

MONTGOMERY—WOW! Internet, Cable & Phone, 7887 East Belleview Ave, Ste 1000, Englewood, CO 80111. Phones: 720-479-3500; 706-645-8553 (Corporate office); 334-356-1000 (Customer service). Fax: 720-479-3585. E-mail: wow_general@wideopenwest.com. Web Site: http://www.wowway.com. Also serves Autauga County (portions), Maxwell AFB & Prattville. ICA: AL0015. **Note:** This system is an overbuild.
TV Market Ranking: Below 100 (Autauga County (portions), Maxwell AFB, MONTGOMERY, Prattville). Franchise award date: April 5, 1990. Franchise expiration date: N.A. Began: September 28, 1990.
Channel capacity: 80 (operating 2-way). Channels available but not in use: N.A.

Basic Service
Subscribers: 20,433.
Programming (received off-air): WAIQ (PBS) Montgomery; WAKA (CBS, MeTV) Selma; WBIH (IND) Selma; WBMM (CW, TNN) Tuskegee; WCOV-TV (Antenna TV, FOX, This TV) Montgomery; WIYC (WeatherNation) Troy; WMCF-TV (TBN) Montgomery; WNCF (ABC) Montgomery; WSFA (Bounce TV, NBC) Montgomery.
Programming (via satellite): A&E; AMC; Animal Planet; BET; Bravo; Cartoon Network; CMT; CNBC; CNN; Comedy Central; C-SPAN; C-SPAN 2; Discovery Channel; Disney Channel; Disney XD; E! HD; ESPN; ESPN Classic; ESPN2; EVINE Live; Food Network; Fox News Channel; FOX Sports South/SportSouth; Freeform; FX; Golf Channel; Hallmark Channel; HGTV; History; HLN; Lifetime; LMN; MSNBC; MTV; Nick At Nite; Nickelodeon; Outdoor Channel; OWN: Oprah Winfrey Network; Oxygen; Pop; QVC; Spike TV; Syfy; TBS; The Weather Channel; TLC; TNT; Travel Channel; truTV; Turner Classic Movies; TV Land; Univision Studios; USA Network; VH1; WGN America.
Fee: $50.00 installation; $33.00 monthly; $3.50 converter.

Digital Basic Service
Subscribers: N.A. Included in Valley Twp.
Programming (via satellite): AXS TV; BBC America; Bloomberg Television; Boomerang; Church Channel; CMT; C-SPAN 3; Destination America; Discovery Channel HD; Discovery Kids Channel; Discovery Life Channel; ESPN HD; ESPN2 HD; ESPNU; EWTN Global Catholic Network; Fox Sports 1; FSN HD; GSN; Hallmark Movies & Mysteries; HD Theater; IFC; INSP; Investigation Discovery; Jewelry Television; JUCE TV; MBC America; MC; MTV Classic; MTV Hits; MTV Jams; MTV2; mtvU; NASA TV; National Geographic Channel; National Geographic Channel HD; NBCSN; NFL Network; Nick 2; Nick Jr.; Nicktoons; PBS HD; RTV; Science Channel; Science HD; TBS HD; TeenNick; TLC HD; TNT HD; Tr3s; Universal HD; UP; Versus HD; VH1 Soul; WE tv.
Programming (vis atellite): QVC HD.

Digital Expanded Basic Service
Subscribers: N.A.
Programming (via satellite): CBS Sports Network; ESPNews; FOX College Sports Central; FOX College Sports Pacific; Fox Sports 2; Tennis Channel.

Pay Service 1
Pay Units: N.A.
Programming (via satellite): HBO; Showtime.
Fee: $6.95 monthly (Showtime), $10.95 monthly (HBO).

Digital Pay Service 1
Pay Units: N.A.
Programming (via satellite): Cinemax (multiplexed); Cinemax HD; Flix; HBO (multiplexed); HBO HD; Showtime (multiplexed); Showtime HD; Starz (multiplexed); Starz Encore (multiplexed); Starz HD; Sundance TV; The Movie Channel (multiplexed).
Video-On-Demand: Yes

Pay-Per-View
iN DEMAND (delivered digitally); Hot Choice (delivered digitally); Pleasure (delivered digitally); Playboy TV (delivered digitally); Fresh (delivered digitally); Shorteez (delivered digitally); Spice: Xcess (delivered digitally); Club Jenna (delivered digitally); ESPN Now (delivered digitally).

Alabama—Cable Systems

Internet Service
Operational: Yes.
Subscribers: 25,274.
Broadband Service: Knology.Net.
Fee: $29.95 installation; $59.95 monthly.
Telephone Service
Digital: Operational
Subscribers: 22,939.
Fee: $24.15 monthly
Miles of Plant: 1,996.0 (coaxial); 420.0 (fiber optic). Homes passed: 101,192.
Chief Executive Officer: Colleen Abdoulah. President: Steven Cochran. Chief Financial Officer: Rich Fish.
Ownership: WideOpenWest LLC (MSO).

MORGAN CITY (portions)—Charter Communications. Now served by DECATUR, AL [AL0184]. ICA: AL0093.

MOULTON—Charter Communications. Now served by DECATUR, AL [AL0184]. ICA: AL0252.

NAUVOO—Formerly served by Zoom Media. No longer in operation. ICA: AL0210.

NEW HOPE—New Hope Telephone Cooperative, 5415 Main Dr, PO Box 452, New Hope, AL 35760. Phones: 877-474-4211; 256-723-4211. Fax: 256-723-2800. E-mail: support@nehp.net. Web Site: http://nhtc.coop. Also serves Grant, Madison County (portions), Marshall County (portions) & Owens Cross Roads. ICA: AL0070.
TV Market Ranking: 96 (Grant, Madison County (portions), Marshall County (portions), NEW HOPE, Owens Cross Roads). Franchise award date: N.A. Franchise expiration date: N.A. Began: October 1, 1966.
Channel capacity: N.A. Channels available but not in use: N.A.
Basic Service
Subscribers: 2,634.
Programming (received off-air): WAAY-TV (ABC) Huntsville; WAFF (Bounce TV, NBC, This TV) Huntsville; WHIQ (PBS) Huntsville; WHNT-TV (Antenna TV, CBS) Huntsville; WZDX (FOX, MeTV, MNT) Huntsville.
Programming (via satellite): A&E; AMC; Animal Planet; Bravo; Cartoon Network; CMT; CNN; Comedy Central; C-SPAN; C-SPAN 2; Discovery Channel; Disney Channel; E! HD; ESPN; ESPN2; Food Network; Fox News Channel; Fox Sports 1; Freeform; FX; Hallmark Channel; HGTV; History; HLN; Lifetime; MTV; Nickelodeon; Outdoor Channel; Oxygen; Pop; Spike TV; SportSouth; Syfy; TBS; The Weather Channel; TLC; TNT; Travel Channel; Trinity Broadcasting Network (TBN); truTV; Turner Classic Movies; TV Land; USA Network; VH1; WE tv; WGN America.
Fee: $30.00 installation; $48.00 monthly.
Video-On-Demand: No
Internet Service
Operational: No, DSL & dial-up.
Telephone Service
Analog: Operational
Subscribers: 4,504.
Miles of Plant: 483.0 (coaxial); 388.0 (fiber optic). Homes passed: 4,504.
General Manager: Tom Wing. Engineer: Robert Patterson. Marketing Manager: Misty Williams. Office Manager: Tammy Weeks.
Ownership: New Hope Telephone Cooperative.

NORTH BREWTON—Formerly served by CableSouth Inc. No longer in operation. ICA: AL0238.

NOTASULGA—Formerly served by Com-Link Inc. No longer in operation. ICA: AL0135.

OAKMAN—Formerly served by Almega Cable. No longer in operation. ICA: AL0239.

ODENVILLE—Cablevision Services Inc., 1701 Cogswell Ave, Pell City, AL 35125-1646. Phones: 800-824-4773; 205-884-4545. Fax: 205-525-1585. E-mail: coosacable@coosahs.net. Also serves Branchville & St. Clair County (portions). ICA: AL0283.
TV Market Ranking: 40 (Branchville, ODENVILLE, St. Clair County (portions)).
Channel capacity: N.A. Channels available but not in use: N.A.
Basic Service
Subscribers: 526.
Programming (via satellite): Cinemax (multiplexed); HBO (multiplexed); Showtime (multiplexed); Starz (multiplexed).
Fee: $45.00 installation; $37.50 monthly.
Digital Basic Service
Subscribers: 424.
Fee: $2.50 monthly.
Digital Expanded Basic Service
Subscribers: 21.
Fee: $14.25 monthly.
Digital Pay Service 1
Pay Units: N.A.
Fee: $7.15 monthly (Starz), $9.55 monthly (Cinemax), $13.50 monthly (HBO), $14.50 monthly (Showtime).
Internet Service
Operational: Yes.
Fee: $18.50 monthly.
Telephone Service
Digital: Operational
Fee: $34.67-$46.95 monthly
Miles of Plant: 45.0 (coaxial); 20.0 (fiber optic). Homes passed: 2,700.
President: Jeffrey T. Smith.
Ownership: Cablevision Services Inc.

ODENVILLE—Formerly served by Coosa Cable. No longer in operation. ICA: AL0104.

ONEONTA—Otelco, 505 Third Ave East, Oneonta, AL 35121-1557. Phones: 205-625-3574; 205-625-3591. Fax: 205-625-3523. E-mail: support@otelco.net. Web Site: http://www.otelco.net. Also serves Allgood, Altoona, Blount County (portions), Cleveland, Lacey's Springs, Nectar, Rosa, Snead, Susan Moore, Union Grove & Walnut Grove. ICA: AL0049.
TV Market Ranking: 40 (ONEONTA). Franchise award date: January 1, 1972. Franchise expiration date: N.A. Began: January 1, 1975.
Channel capacity: 40 (operating 2-way). Channels available but not in use: N.A.
Basic Service
Subscribers: 2,497.
Programming (received off-air): WABM (MNT) Birmingham; WBIQ (PBS) Birmingham; WBRC (Bounce TV, FOX) Birmingham; WIAT (CBS, Untamed Sports TV) Birmingham; WTJP-TV (TBN) Gadsden; WTTO (Antenna TV, CW, The Country Network) Homewood; WVTM-TV (MeTV, NBC) Birmingham; WZDX (FOX, MeTV, MNT) Huntsville; 1 FM.
Programming (via satellite): A&E; Animal Planet; Bravo; Cartoon Network; CMT; CNBC; CNN; Comedy Central; C-SPAN; C-SPAN 2; Discovery Channel; Discovery Life Channel; Disney Channel; Disney XD; DIY Network; E! HD; ESPN; ESPN Classic; ESPN2; Food Network; Fox News Channel; FOX Sports Networks; FOX Sports South/SportSouth; Freeform; FX; Golf Channel; GSN; Hallmark Channel; HGTV; History; HLN; Lifetime; MSNBC; MTV; National Geographic Channel; Nickelodeon; OWN: Oprah Winfrey Network; QVC; Spike TV; Syfy; TBS; The Weather Channel; TLC; TNT; Travel Channel; truTV; Turner Classic Movies; TV Land; Univision Studios; USA Network; VH1; WGN America.
Fee: $40.00 installation; $53.95 monthly.
Digital Basic Service
Subscribers: N.A.
Programming (via satellite): BBC America; Bloomberg Television; CBS Sports Network; Discovery Digital Networks; DMX Music; ESPNews; FOX College Sports Central; FOX College Sports Pacific; Fox Sports 1; Fuse; FXM; FYI; Great American Country; History International; LMN; NBCSN; Nick Jr.; Nicktoons; Outdoor Channel; Sundance TV; TeenNick; WE tv.
Digital Expanded Basic Service
Subscribers: N.A.
Programming (via satellite): HITS (Headend In The Sky).
Fee: $9.95 monthly.
Pay Service 1
Pay Units: N.A.
Programming (via satellite): HBO.
Fee: $13.95 monthly.
Digital Pay Service 1
Pay Units: N.A.
Programming (via satellite): Cinemax (multiplexed); HBO (multiplexed); Showtime; Starz; Starz Encore; The Movie Channel.
Fee: $10.00 monthly (Starz/Encore), $15.95 monthly (Showtime/TMC), $16.95 monthly (Cinemax/HBO).
Video-On-Demand: No
Pay-Per-View
iN DEMAND (delivered digitally).
Internet Service
Operational: Yes.
Broadband Service: Otelco.
Fee: $39.95 monthly.
Telephone Service
Analog: Operational
Miles of Plant: 150.0 (coaxial); None (fiber optic). Homes passed: 8,227.
President & Chief Executive Officer: Robert J. Souza. Chief Financial Officer: Curtis L. Garner Jr.
Ownership: Otelco (MSO).

OPELIKA—Opelika Power Services, 600 Fox Run Pkwy, Opelika, AL 36801. Phone: 334-705-5170. Web Site: http://www.opelikapower.com. ICA: AL2084.
Channel capacity: N.A. Channels available but not in use: N.A.
Basic Service
Subscribers: N.A.
Fee: $49.95 monthly.
Internet Service
Operational: Yes.
Fee: $34.95-$499.95 monthly.
Telephone Service
Digital: Operational
Fee: $19.95 monthly
Ownership: Opelika Power Services.

OPP—Opp Cablevision, 213 Dunson St., PO Box 34, Andalusia, AL 36420. Phone: 334-493-4571. Fax: 334-222-7226. E-mail: support@andycable.com. Web Site: http://www.oppcatv.com. Also serves Horn Hill & Kinston. ICA: AL0050.
TV Market Ranking: Below 100 (Kinston); Outside TV Markets (Horn Hill, OPP). Franchise award date: N.A. Franchise expiration date: N.A. Began: August 1, 1967.
Channel capacity: N.A. Channels available but not in use: N.A.
Basic Service
Subscribers: 2,916.
Programming (received off-air): WAAO-LD Andalusia; WAKA (CBS, MeTV) Selma; WBMM (CW, TNN) Tuskegee; WCOV-TV (Antenna TV, FOX, This TV) Montgomery; WDHN (ABC) Dothan; WDIQ (PBS) Dozier; WKNI-LP (America One, My Family TV, Punch TV) Andalusia; WNCF (ABC) Montgomery; WSFA (Bounce TV, NBC) Montgomery; WTVY (CBS, CW, MeTV, MNT, This TV) Dothan.
Programming (via satellite): A&E; AMC; Animal Planet; BET; Bravo; Cartoon Network; CMT; CNBC; CNN; Comcast/Charter Sports Southeast (CSS); C-SPAN; Discovery Channel; Disney Channel; E! HD; ESPN; ESPN Classic; ESPN2; Food Network; Fox News Channel; Fox Sports 1; FOX Sports Networks; FOX Sports South/SportSouth; Freeform; FX; Golf Channel; Great American Country; Hallmark Channel; HGTV; History; HLN; HSN; INSP; Lifetime; MSNBC; MTV; National Geographic Channel; Nickelodeon; Outdoor Channel; Pop; QVC; RFD-TV; Science Channel; Spike TV; Syfy; TBS; The Weather Channel; TLC; TNT; Travel Channel; Trinity Broadcasting Network (TBN); truTV; Turner Classic Movies; TV Land; USA Network; VH1; WGN America.
Fee: $15.00 installation; $19.00 monthly.
Digital Basic Service
Subscribers: N.A.
Programming (via satellite): A&E HD; AXS TV; BBC America; Bloomberg Television; CMT; Destination America; Discovery Kids Channel; Disney Channel HD; Disney XD; ESPN HD; ESPN2 HD; ESPNews; ESPNU; Food Network HD; FOX College Sports Central; FOX College Sports Pacific; Fox News HD; Freeform HD; Fuse; FX HD; FXM; FYI; GSN; HD Theater; HGTV HD; History HD; History International; Investigation Discovery; LMN; MTV Classic; MTV Hits; MTV Jams; MTV2; Nick Jr.; Nicktoons; Outdoor Channel HD; OWN: Oprah Winfrey Network; Pursuit Channel; TeenNick; The Weather Channel HD; Tr3s; Travel Channel HD; VH1 Soul.
Digital Pay Service 1
Pay Units: N.A.
Programming (via satellite): Cinemax (multiplexed); HBO (multiplexed); Showtime (multiplexed); Starz (multiplexed); Starz Encore (multiplexed); Starz HD; The Movie Channel (multiplexed).
Video-On-Demand: No
Pay-Per-View
iN DEMAND (delivered digitally).
Internet Service
Operational: Yes. Began: January 1, 2000.
Broadband Service: Gill Blue.
Fee: $45.00 installation; $24.95-$49.95 monthly; $125.00 modem purchase.
Telephone Service
None
Miles of Plant: 180.0 (coaxial); 60.0 (fiber optic). Homes passed: 4,374.
General Manager: Jerome Rogers.
Ownership: Opp Cablevision.

ORANGE BEACH—Formerly served by Beyond Communications. No longer in operation. ICA: AL5081.

ORRVILLE—Formerly served by Zoom Media. No longer in operation. ICA: AL0158.

OWENS CROSS ROADS—New Hope Telephone Cooperative. Now served by NEW HOPE, AL [AL0070]. ICA: AL0263.

Cable Systems—Alabama

OZARK—Formerly served by Charter Communications. Now served by Troy Cablevision. This cable system has converted to IPTV. See TROY, AL [AL5091]. ICA: AL0211.

PELHAM—Charter Communications, 12405 Powerscourt Dr, St. Louis, MO 63131. Phones: 636-207-5100 (Corporate office); 205-824-1051; 205-824-5400. Fax: 205-824-5490. Web Site: http://www.charter.com. Also serves Adamsville, Addison, Alabaster, Alexander City, Argo, Ashville, Auburn, Bessemer, Birmingham (portions), Bluff Park, Bon Air, Brookside, Brookwood, Buhl, Cahaba Heights, Calera, Camp Hill, Carbon Hill, Cardiff, Center Point, Chambers County (portions), Chelsea, Childersburg, Chilton County (portions), Clay County (portions), Coaling, Coker, Coosa County (portions), Cordova, Cottondale, Dora, Duncanville, Eldridge, Elrod, Forestdale, Fultondale, Gardendale, Goodwater, Grayson Valley, Graysville, Harpersville, Helena, Homewood, Hoover, Indian Springs Village, Irondale, Jacksons' Gap, Jasper, Jefferson County, Kansas, Kellyton, Lee County (portions), Leeds, Margaret, Maytown, Montevallo, Moody, Moundville, Mount Olive, Mountain Brook, Mulga, New Site, Northport, Oak Grove, Odenville, Opelika, Parish, Parrish, Peterson, Pinson, Riverchase, Rockford, Shelby County (portions), Sipsey, Springville, St. Clair County (portions), Sumiton, Sycamore, Sylacauga, Sylvan Springs, Talladega, Talladega County (portions), Tallapoosa County (portions), Tarrant City, Taylorville, Trussville, Tuscaloosa, Tuscaloosa County (portions), Tuskegee, Vance, Vestavia Hills, Vincent, Walker County (portions), West End, West Jefferson, Westover, Whites Chapel, Wilton & Winston County (portions). ICA: AL0192.

TV Market Ranking: 40 (Adamsville, Alabaster, Argo, Ashville, Bessemer, Birmingham (portions), Bluff Park, Bon Air, Brookside, Brookwood, Cahaba Heights, Calera, Cardiff, Center Point, Chelsea, Childersburg, Cordova, Dora, Forestdale, Fultondale, Gardendale, Grayson Valley, Graysville, Harpersville, Helena, Homewood, Hoover, Indian Springs Village, Irondale, Jefferson County, Leeds, Margaret, Maytown, Montevallo, Moody, Mount Olive, Mountain Brook, Mulga, Odenville, Parish, PELHAM, Pinson, Riverchase, Shelby County (portions), Sipsey, Springville, St. Clair County (portions), Sumiton, Sylvan Springs, Talladega County (portions), Tarrant City, Trussville, Tuscaloosa County (portions), Vance, Vestavia Hills, Vincent, West Jefferson, Westover, Whites Chapel, Wilton); 94 (Auburn, Chambers County (portions), Lee County (portions), Opelika); 96 (Addison, Winston County (portions)); Below 100 (Buhl, Camp Hill, Clay County (portions), Coaling, Coker, Cottondale, Duncanville, Elrod, Jacksons' Gap, Moundville, Northport, Peterson, Tallapoosa County (portions), Taylorville, Tuscaloosa, Tuskegee, West End, Chilton County (portions), Coosa County (portions), Talladega County (portions), Tuscaloosa County (portions), Auburn, Chambers County (portions), Lee County (portions)); Outside TV Markets (Alexander City, Carbon Hill, Clay County (portions), Eldridge, Goodwater, Kansas, New Site, Oak Grove, Parrish, Rockford, Sycamore, Sylacauga, Tallapoosa County (portions), Chilton County (portions), Coosa County (portions), Jasper, Birmingham (portions)). Franchise award date: N.A. Franchise expiration date: N.A. Began: October 1, 1979.

Channel capacity: 60 (operating 2-way). Channels available but not in use: N.A.

Digital Basic Service
Subscribers: 120,593.
Programming (via satellite): A&E HD; BabyFirstTV; BBC America; Bloomberg Television; CBS Sports Network; Cinelatino; CMT; Cooking Channel; C-SPAN 2; Destination America; Discovery Kids Channel; Discovery Life Channel; DIY Network; ESPN Classic; ESPN Deportes; ESPN HD; ESPN2 HD; ESPNews; ESPNU; Fox Business Network; FOX College Sports Central; FOX College Sports Pacific; Fox Deportes; Fox Sports 2; Fuse; FXM; FYI; Great American Country; HD Theater; History HD; History International; IFC; Investigation Discovery; Jewelry Television; La Familia Cosmovision; LMN; MC; MTV Classic; MTV Hits; MTV Jams; MTV Live; NHL Network; Nick 2; Nick Jr.; Nicktoons; Outdoor Channel; OWN; Oprah Winfrey Network; Science Channel; Sundance TV; TeenNick; Telemundo; Tennis Channel; TNT HD; Tr3s; TV One; Universal HD; UP; VH1 Soul; Vubiquity Inc.; WE tv.
Fee: $26.99 monthly.

Digital Expanded Basic Service
Subscribers: N.A.
Programming (via satellite): A&E; AMC; Animal Planet; BET; Bravo; Cartoon Network; CMT; CNBC; CNN; Comcast/Charter Sports Southeast (CSS); Comedy Central; C-SPAN; C-SPAN 2; Discovery Channel; Disney Channel; Disney XD; E! HD; ESPN; ESPN2; EWTN Global Catholic Network; Food Network; Fox News Channel; Fox Sports 1; FOX Sports South/SportSouth; Freeform; FX; Golf Channel; GSN; Hallmark Channel; HGTV; History; HLN; Lifetime; MSNBC; MTV; MTV2; National Geographic Channel; NBCSN; Nickelodeon; Oxygen; Pop; QVC; Spike TV; Syfy; TBS; The Weather Channel; TLC; TNT; Travel Channel; truTV; TV Land; Univision Studios; USA Network; VH1.
Fee: $43.00 monthly.

Digital Pay Service 1
Pay Units: N.A.
Programming (via satellite): Cinemax (multiplexed); Cinemax HD; Flix; HBO (multiplexed); HBO HD; Showtime (multiplexed); Showtime HD; Starz (multiplexed); Starz Encore (multiplexed); Starz HD; The Movie Channel (multiplexed); The Movie Channel HD.
Fee: $9.95 monthly (each).

Video-On-Demand: Yes
Pay-Per-View
iN DEMAND (delivered digitally); Playboy TV (delivered digitally); Pleasure (delivered digitally); Fresh (delivered digitally); Shorteez (delivered digitally); Video On Demand (delivered digitally).

Internet Service
Operational: Yes.
Subscribers: 127,389.
Broadband Service: Charter Internet.
Fee: $29.99 monthly.

Telephone Service
Digital: Operational
Subscribers: 64,842.
Fee: $29.99 monthly
Miles of Plant: 16,468.0 (coaxial); 5,216.0 (fiber optic). Homes passed: 511,305.
Vice President & General Manager: Don Karell. Technical Operations Director: Greg Prim. Marketing Manager: Jeff Hatcher. Marketing Director: David Redmond. Accounting Director: David Sovanski.
Ownership: Charter Communications Inc. (MSO)

PELL CITY—USA Communications, 1701 Coggswell Ave, Pell City, AL 35125-1646. Phones: 800-560-7707 (Talladega office); 800-824-4773 (Ogenville office); 800-234-0102. Fax: 205-884-4510. Web Site: http://usacommunications.tv. Also serves Riverside & St. Clair County (portions). ICA: AL0212.
TV Market Ranking: 40 (PELL CITY, Riverside, St. Clair County (portions)). Franchise award date: October 1, 1968. Franchise expiration date: N.A. Began: September 11, 1971.
Channel capacity: N.A. Channels available but not in use: N.A.

Basic Service
Subscribers: 3,380.
Programming (received off-air): WABM (MNT) Birmingham; WBIQ (PBS) Birmingham; WBRC (Bounce TV, FOX) Birmingham; WGWW (ABC, TNN) Anniston; WIAT (CBS, Untamed Sports TV) Birmingham; WPXH-TV (ION) Gadsden; WTJP-TV (TBN) Gadsden; WTTO (Antenna TV, CW, The Country Network) Homewood; WVTM-TV (MeTV, NBC) Birmingham.
Programming (via satellite): A&E; AMC; Animal Planet; BET; Cartoon Network; CMT; CNBC; CNN; Comedy Central; Discovery Channel; Discovery Life Channel; Disney Channel; E! HD; ESPN; ESPN2; Fox News Network; FOX Sports South/SportSouth; Freeform; FX; Great American Country; Hallmark Channel; HGTV; History; Lifetime; MSNBC; MTV; National Geographic Channel; Nickelodeon; Pop; QVC; Spike TV; Syfy; TBS; The Weather Channel; TLC; TNT; Travel Channel; TV Land; USA Network; VH1; WGN America.
Fee: $42.00 installation; $37.50 monthly; $1.80 converter.

Digital Basic Service
Subscribers: N.A.
Programming (via satellite): 3ABN; BBC America; Bloomberg Television; BYUtv; Church Channel; Cloo; Daystar TV Network; Destination America; Discovery Kids Channel; DIY Network; EWTN Global Catholic Network; Family Friendly Entertainment; FamilyNet; Food Network; FXM; FYI; GEB America; GSN; History International; IFC; Investigation Discovery; JUCE TV; LMN; MTV Classic; MTV2; National Geographic Channel; Nick Jr.; OWN; Oprah Winfrey Network; Science Channel; Starz Encore (multiplexed); TeenNick; Trinity Broadcasting Network (TBN); truTV; Turner Classic Movies; VH1 Country; WE tv.

Digital Expanded Basic Service
Subscribers: N.A.
Programming (via satellite): CBS Sports Network; ESPN Classic; ESPNews; FOX College Sports Central; FOX College Sports Pacific; Fox Sports 1; Fox Sports 2; Golf Channel; NBCSN; Outdoor Channel; RFD-TV.
Fee: $7.95 monthly.

Digital Pay Service 1
Pay Units: N.A.
Programming (via satellite): Cinemax (multiplexed); Flix; HBO (multiplexed); Showtime (multiplexed); Starz (multiplexed); The Movie Channel (multiplexed).
Fee: $5.95 monthly (Starz), $9.50 monthly (Cinemax), $12.00 monthly (HBO), $13.50 monthly (Showtime/TMC/Flix).

Video-On-Demand: No
Pay-Per-View
iN DEMAND (delivered digitally).

Internet Service
Operational: Yes.
Broadband Service: In-house.
Fee: $40.00 installation; $18.50-$45.95 monthly; $5.00 modem lease; $65.40 modem purchase.

Telephone Service
Analog: Not Operational
Digital: Operational
Fee: $36.61 monthly
Miles of Plant: 300.0 (coaxial); 17.0 (fiber optic).
President & Chief Technician: Jeff Smith. Chief Executive Officer: Arthur M. Smith.
Ownership: USA Companies L.P.

PENNINGTON—Formerly served by Zoom Media. No longer in operation. ICA: AL0160.

PERDIDO BEACH—Mediacom. Now served by ROBERTSDALE, AL [AL0019]. ICA: AL0236.

PHENIX CITY—Phenix Cable TV, PO Box 130, Phenix City, AL 36867. Phone: 334-298-7000. Fax: 334-298-0833. Web Site: http://ctvea.net. Also serves Fort Mitchell, Hatchechubbee, Hurtsboro, Lee County, Russell County, Salem, Seale & Smiths. ICA: AL0011.
TV Market Ranking: 94 (Fort Mitchell, Hatchechubbee, Hurtsboro, Lee County, PHENIX CITY, Russell County, Salem, Seale, Smiths). Franchise award date: N.A. Franchise expiration date: N.A. Began: May 1, 1965.
Channel capacity: 83 (operating 2-way). Channels available but not in use: N.A.

Basic Service
Subscribers: 11,507.
Programming (received off-air): WCIQ (PBS) Mount Cheaha State Park; WIYC (WeatherNation) Troy; WJSP-TV (PBS) Columbus; WLGA (WeatherNation) Opelika; WLTZ (CW, NBC) Columbus; WRBL (CBS, MeTV) Columbus; WTVM (ABC, Bounce TV) Columbus; WXTX (FOX, Movies!, This TV) Columbus; WYBU-CD (Christian TV Network) Columbus.
Programming (via satellite): A&E; AMC; Animal Planet; BET; Cartoon Network; CMT; CNBC; CNN; Comedy Central; C-SPAN; C-SPAN 2; Discovery Channel; Disney Channel; E! HD; ESPN; ESPN Classic; ESPN2; Food Network; Fox News Channel; FOX Sports Networks; FOX Sports South/SportSouth; Freeform; FX; Golf Channel; Great American Country; Hallmark Channel; HGTV; History; HLN; INSP; ION Television; Lifetime; MSNBC; MTV; National Geographic Channel; NBCSN; Nickelodeon; Outdoor Channel; Pop; QVC; Radar Channel; Spike TV; Syfy; TBS; The Weather Channel; TLC; TNT; Travel Chan-

Alabama—Cable Systems

nel); Trinity Broadcasting Network (TBN); truTV; Turner Classic Movies; TV Land; USA Network; VH1; WGN America.
Fee: $25.00 installation; $24.75 monthly; $3.00 converter.
Digital Basic Service
Subscribers: N.A.
Programming (via satellite): BBC America; Bloomberg Television; Bravo; Discovery Digital Networks; Disney XD; ESPN Classic; Fox Sports 1; FYI; GSN; History International; IFC; LMN; MC; Sundance TV; VH1; WE tv.
Digital Pay Service 1
Pay Units: N.A.
Programming (via satellite): Cinemax (multiplexed); Flix; HBO (multiplexed); Showtime (multiplexed); Starz (multiplexed); Starz Encore (multiplexed); Starz HD; Sundance TV; The Movie Channel (multiplexed).
Fee: $4.00 monthly (Encore), $7.50 monthly (Starz), $12.95 monthly (Cinemax or Showtime/Sundance/TMC), $13.95 monthly (HBO).
Video-On-Demand: Yes
Pay-Per-View
ESPN Now (delivered digitally); Hot Choice (delivered digitally); iN DEMAND (delivered digitally); iN DEMAND (delivered digitally).
Internet Service
Operational: Yes. Began: March 1, 2000.
Subscribers: 7,234.
Broadband Service: In-house.
Fee: $80.00 installation; $29.95-$69.95 monthly.
Telephone Service
Digital: Operational
Subscribers: 981.
Fee: $34.95-$39.95 monthly
Miles of Plant: 1,091.0 (coaxial); 250.0 (fiber optic). Homes passed: 36,987.
General Manager: Lynne Frakes. Chief Technician: Jerry Burrell. Administration: Myra Boatwell.
Ownership: R. M. Greene Inc. (MSO).

PHIL CAMPBELL—Charter Communications, 12405 Powerscourt Dr, St. Louis, MO 63131. Phones: 636-207-5100 (Corporate office); 334-863-8112; 334-863-7080. Fax: 334-863-2027. Web Site: http://www.charter.com. Also serves Franklin County (portions). ICA: AL0136.
TV Market Ranking: Below 100 (Franklin County (portions), PHIL CAMPBELL).
Channel capacity: 68 (operating 2-way). Channels available but not in use: N.A.
Digital Basic Service
Subscribers: 56,250.
Programming (via satellite): BBC America; Bloomberg Television; Bravo; Cloo; CMT; Destination America; Discovery Kids Channel; Discovery Life Channel; DMX Music; ESPN Classic; ESPNews; Fox Sports 1; Fuse; FXM; FYI; Golf Channel; GSN; History; History International; IFC; Investigation Discovery; LMN; MTV Classic; MTV Hits; MTV2; NBCSN; Nick Jr.; Outdoor Channel; Ovation; OWN; Oprah Winfrey Network; Science Channel; TeenNick; Turner Classic Movies; VH1 Soul; WE tv.
Fee: $29.95 monthly.
Digital Expanded Basic Service
Subscribers: N.A.
Programming (via satellite): A&E; AMC; Cartoon Network; CMT; CNN; Comcast/Charter Sports Southeast (CSS); C-SPAN; Discovery Channel; ESPN; ESPN2; Freeform; HGTV; History; HLN; Lifetime; Nick Jr.; Nickelodeon; QVC; Spike TV; The

Weather Channel; TLC; TNT; Trinity Broadcasting Network (TBN); Turner Classic Movies; USA Network; VH1.
Pay Service 1
Pay Units: N.A.
Programming (via satellite): Cinemax; HBO.
Fee: $9.95 monthly (Cinemax), $10.95 monthly (HBO).
Digital Pay Service 1
Pay Units: N.A.
Programming (via satellite): Cinemax (multiplexed); HBO (multiplexed); Starz (multiplexed); Starz Encore (multiplexed).
Video-On-Demand: No
Pay-Per-View
iN DEMAND (delivered digitally); Club Jenna (delivered digitally); Playboy TV (delivered digitally); Fresh (delivered digitally).
Internet Service
Operational: Yes.
Subscribers: 60,450.
Broadband Service: Charter Internet.
Telephone Service
Digital: Operational
Subscribers: 30,682.
Miles of Plant: 6,866.0 (coaxial); 2,113.0 (fiber optic). Homes passed: 184,147.
President & Chief Executive Officer: Tom Rutledge. General Manager: Brian Chase. Chief Technician: William Boyd. Accounting Director: David Sovanski.
Ownership: Charter Communications Inc. (MSO).

PIEDMONT—Charter Communications, 303 Main St, Cedartown, GA 30125. Phones: 314-543-2236; 636-207-5100 (Corporate office); 877-581-3485. Web Site: http://www.charter.com. Also serves Centre, Cherokee County (portions), Etowah, Etowah County (portions), Hokes Bluff & Southside. ICA: AL0065.
TV Market Ranking: 18 (Centre, Cherokee County (portions), PIEDMONT); Below 100 (Etowah, Etowah County (portions), Hokes Bluff, Southside). Franchise award date: N.A. Franchise expiration date: N.A. Began: August 1, 1966.
Channel capacity: 68 (not 2-way capable). Channels available but not in use: N.A.
Digital Basic Service
Subscribers: 3,489.
Programming (via satellite): BBC America; Bloomberg Television; Discovery Digital Networks; GSN; MC; Nick 2; Nick Jr.; Nicktoons; Sundance TV.
Fee: $49.99 installation; $26.99 monthly.
Digital Expanded Basic Service
Subscribers: N.A.
Programming (via satellite): A&E; AMC; Animal Planet; BET; Bravo; Cartoon Network; CMT; CNBC; CNN; Comcast/Charter Sports Southeast (CSS); Comedy Central; Discovery Channel; Disney Channel; Disney XD; E! HD; ESPN; ESPN Classic; ESPN2; Food Network; Fox News Channel; Fox Sports 1; FOX Sports South/SportSouth; Freeform; FX; Golf Channel; Hallmark Channel; HGTV; History; HLN; Lifetime; MSNBC; MTV; National Geographic Channel; NBCSN; Nickelodeon; Outdoor Channel; Oxygen; Spike TV; Syfy; TBS; TLC; TNT; Travel Channel; TV Land; Univision Studios; USA Network; VH1; WE tv.
Fee: $43.00 monthly.
Digital Pay Service 1
Pay Units: N.A.
Programming (via satellite): Cinemax (multiplexed); HBO (multiplexed); Starz (multiplexed).
Fee: $14.00 monthly (each).
Video-On-Demand: No

Pay-Per-View
iN DEMAND (delivered digitally); Playboy TV (delivered digitally); Fresh (delivered digitally); Shorteez (delivered digitally).
Internet Service
Operational: Yes.
Broadband Service: Charter Internet.
Telephone Service
Digital: Operational
Fee: $29.99 monthly
Miles of Plant: 6,294.0 (coaxial); 1,929.0 (fiber optic). Homes passed: 173,474.
Vice President & General Manager: Don Karell. Technical Operations Director: Greg Prim. Marketing Manager: Jeff Hatcher. Marketing Director: David Redmond. Accounting Director: David Sovanski.
Ownership: Charter Communications Inc. (MSO).

PINE HILL—Formerly served by Zoom Media. No longer in operation. ICA: AL0145.

POLLARD—Formerly served by CableSouth Inc. No longer in operation. ICA: AL0214.

PROVIDENCE—Formerly served by Community Cable & Broadband LLC. No longer in operation. ICA: AL0151.

RAGLAND—Ragland Telephone Co, 630 Main St., PO Box 577, Ragland, AL 35131. Phone: 205-472-2141. Fax: 205-472-2145. E-mail: support@ragland.net. Web Site: http://www.ragland.net. ICA: AL0216.
TV Market Ranking: Below 100 (RAGLAND). Franchise award date: N.A. Franchise expiration date: N.A. Began: March 1, 1984.
Channel capacity: N.A. Channels available but not in use: N.A.
Basic Service
Subscribers: 367.
Programming (received off-air): WABM (MNT) Birmingham; WBIQ (PBS) Birmingham; WBRC (Bounce TV, FOX) Birmingham; WDBB (CW) Bessemer; WGWW (ABC, TNN) Anniston; WTTO (Antenna TV, CW, The Country Network) Homewood; WVTM-TV (MeTV, NBC) Birmingham.
Programming (via satellite): CNN; Discovery Channel; Disney Channel; ESPN; Freeform; Spike TV; TBS; TNT; Trinity Broadcasting Network (TBN); USA Network; WGN America.
Fee: $40.00 installation; $43.50 monthly.
Pay Service 1
Pay Units: N.A.
Programming (via satellite): HBO.
Fee: $10.00 monthly.
Video-On-Demand: No
Telephone Service
None
Miles of Plant: 47.0 (coaxial); None (fiber optic).
Vice President: Stephanie Jackson. General Manager & Chief Technician: Stanley Bean. Financial Director: Susan Williams.
Ownership: Cablestar Inc.

RAINSVILLE—Zito Media, 102 S Main St, PO Box 665, Coudersport, PA 16915. Phones: 814-260-9055; 800-365-6988. E-mail: info@zitomedia.com. Web Site: http://www.zitomedia.com. Also serves DeKalb County (portions), Dutton & Fyffe. ICA: AL0220.
TV Market Ranking: 78,18 (DeKalb County (portions)); 96 (Dutton, RAINSVILLE); Below 100 (Fyffe, DeKalb County (portions)); Outside TV Markets (DeKalb County (portions), RAINSVILLE). Franchise award

date: N.A. Franchise expiration date: N.A. Began: March 1, 1981.
Channel capacity: N.A. Channels available but not in use: N.A.
Basic Service
Subscribers: 325. Commercial subscribers: 7.
Programming (received off-air): WAAY-TV (ABC) Huntsville; WAFF (Bounce TV, NBC, This TV) Huntsville; WDEF-TV (Bounce TV, CBS, Escape) Chattanooga; WHIQ (PBS) Huntsville; WHNT-TV (Antenna TV, CBS) Huntsville; WRCB (Antenna TV, NBC) Chattanooga; WTVC (ABC, This TV, Weather-Nation) Chattanooga; WZDX (FOX, MeTV, MNT) Huntsville.
Programming (via satellite): AMC; CMT; CNN; ESPN; ESPN2; HLN; MTV; QVC; Syfy; The Weather Channel; TLC; TNT; Travel Channel; Trinity Broadcasting Network (TBN); TV Land; USA Network.
Fee: $29.99 installation; $26.49 monthly.
Digital Basic Service
Subscribers: N.A.
Programming (via satellite): BBC America; Bloomberg Television; Bravo; Discovery Digital Networks; Disney XD; ESPN Classic; EVINE Live; Fox Sports 1; FXM; FYI; Golf Channel; GSN; History; History International; IFC; LMN; MC; NBCSN; Nick Jr.; Outdoor Channel; TeenNick; Turner Classic Movies; TV Guide Interactive Inc.
Pay Service 1
Pay Units: N.A.
Programming (via satellite): Cinemax (multiplexed); Flix; HBO (multiplexed); Showtime (multiplexed); Starz (multiplexed); Starz Encore (multiplexed); The Movie Channel (multiplexed).
Fee: $14.00 monthly (Cinemax/HBO, Showtime/TMC/Flix or Starz/Encore).
Video-On-Demand: No
Pay-Per-View
ESPN Now (delivered digitally); iN DEMAND (delivered digitally); Playboy TV (delivered digitally); Fresh (delivered digitally); Shorteez (delivered digitally).
Internet Service
Operational: No.
Telephone Service
None
Miles of Plant: 237.0 (coaxial); 16.0 (fiber optic). Homes passed: 3,724.
President: James Rigas.
Ownership: Zito Media (MSO).

RANBURNE—Formerly served by Ranburne Cable. No longer in operation. ICA: AL0217.

RED BAY—MetroCast Communications. Now served by PONTOTOC, MS [MS0045]. ICA: AL0218.

ROANOKE—Charter Communications, 3164 Hwy 431, Ste 8, Roanoke, AL 36274. Phones: 314-543-2236; 636-207-5100 (Corporate office); 334-644-2121; 888-438-2427. Web Site: http://www.charter.com. Also serves Randolph County & Wadley. ICA: AL0023.
TV Market Ranking: Outside TV Markets (Randolph County, ROANOKE, Wadley). Franchise award date: January 1, 1970. Franchise expiration date: N.A. Began: April 1, 1970.
Channel capacity: 71 (operating 2-way). Channels available but not in use: N.A.
Digital Basic Service
Subscribers: 1,311.
Programming (via satellite): BBC America; Bloomberg Television; Cloo; Destination America; Discovery Kids Channel; Dis-

Cable Systems—Alabama

ney XD; DMX Music; Fox Sports 1; Fuse; FYI; Golf Channel; GSN; History International; IFC; Investigation Discovery; National Geographic Channel; NBCSN; OWN; Oprah Winfrey Network; Science Channel.
Fee: $49.99 installation; $26.99 monthly.

Digital Expanded Basic Service
Subscribers: N.A.
Programming (via satellite): A&E; AMC; Animal Planet; BET; Bravo; Cartoon Network; CMT; CNBC; CNN; Comcast/Charter Sports Southeast (CSS); Comedy Central; C-SPAN; C-SPAN 2; Discovery Channel; Disney Channel; E! HD; ESPN; ESPN Classic; ESPN2; EVINE Live; Food Network; Fox News Network; Freeform; FX; FXM; Great American Country; Hallmark Channel; HGTV; History; HLN; ION Television; Lifetime; LMN; MSNBC; MTV; Nick Jr.; Nickelodeon; Outdoor Channel; Pop; Spike TV; SportSouth; Syfy; The Weather Channel; TLC; TNT; Travel Channel; Trinity Broadcasting Network (TBN); truTV; Turner Classic Movies; TV Land; USA Network; VH1; WE tv.
Fee: $15.00 installation; $5.00 monthly.

Pay Service 1
Pay Units: N.A.
Programming (via satellite): Cinemax (multiplexed); HBO (multiplexed); MoviePlex; Starz (multiplexed); Starz Encore.
Fee: $15.00 installation; $10.00 monthly (each).

Digital Pay Service 1
Pay Units: N.A.
Programming (via satellite): Cinemax (multiplexed); HBO (multiplexed); Showtime (multiplexed); Starz (multiplexed); Starz Encore.

Video-On-Demand: No
Pay-Per-View
iN DEMAND (delivered digitally); Hot Choice (delivered digitally); Playboy TV (delivered digitally); Fresh (delivered digitally).

Internet Service
Operational: Yes.
Broadband Service: Charter Internet.
Fee: $39.95 installation; $51.95 monthly.

Telephone Service
None
Miles of Plant: 4,899.0 (coaxial); 1,127.0 (fiber optic). Homes passed: 136,596.
Vice President & General Manager: Matt Favre.
Accounting Director: David Sovanski.
Ownership: Charter Communications Inc. (MSO).

ROBERTSDALE—Mediacom, 760 Middle St, PO Box 1009, Fairhope, AL 36532. Phones: 800-479-2082; 800-239-8411 (Customer service); 251-928-3804. Fax: 251-928-3804. Web Site: http://www.mediacomcable.com. Also serves Baldwin County (portions), Foley, Fort Morgan, Gulf Shores, Loxley, Orange Beach, Perdido Beach & Silver Hill. ICA: AL0019.
TV Market Ranking: 59 (Baldwin County (portions), Foley, Fort Morgan, Gulf Shores, Loxley, Orange Beach, Perdido Beach, ROBERTSDALE, Silver Hill). Franchise award date: April 23, 1980. Franchise expiration date: N.A. Began: September 1, 1981.
Channel capacity: 66 (operating 2-way). Channels available but not in use: N.A.

Basic Service
Subscribers: 4,061.
Programming (received off-air): WALA-TV (FOX) Mobile; WEAR-TV (ABC, The Country Network) Pensacola; WEIQ (PBS) Mobile; WFNA (Bounce TV, CW) Gulf Shores; WHBR (Christian TV Network) Pensacola; WJTC (IND) Pensacola; WKRG-TV (CBS, MeTV) Mobile; WMPV-TV (TBN) Mobile; WPAN (Soul of the South) Fort Walton Beach [LICENSED & SILENT]; WPMI-TV (NBC) Mobile; WSRE (PBS) Pensacola.
Programming (via satellite): A&E; AMC; Animal Planet; BET; Bravo; Cartoon Network; CMT; CNBC; CNN; Comedy Central; C-SPAN; C-SPAN 2; Discovery Channel; Disney Channel; E! HD; ESPN; ESPN2; EWTN Global Catholic Network; Food Network; Fox News Channel; Fox Sports 1; FOX Sports South/SportSouth; Freeform; FX; Golf Channel; Hallmark Channel; HGTV; History; HLN; INSP; ION Television; Lifetime; MSNBC; MTV; Nickelodeon; Outdoor Channel; Oxygen; Pop; QVC; Spike TV; Syfy; TBS; The Weather Channel; TLC; TNT; Travel Channel; truTV; TV Land; USA Network; VH1; WE tv; WGN America.
Fee: $21.50 installation; $77.17 monthly.

Digital Basic Service
Subscribers: N.A.
Programming (via satellite): BBC America; Bloomberg Television; Discovery Digital Networks; Fuse; FXM; FYI; GSN; History International; IFC; LMN; MC; Trinity Broadcasting Network (TBN); Turner Classic Movies.

Pay Service 1
Pay Units: N.A.
Programming (via satellite): Cinemax; Flix; HBO; Showtime.
Fee: $3.95 monthly (Flix), $10.45 monthly (Cinemax, HBO or Showtime).

Digital Pay Service 1
Pay Units: N.A.
Programming (via satellite): Cinemax (multiplexed); Flix; HBO (multiplexed); Showtime (multiplexed); Starz (multiplexed); Starz Encore (multiplexed); Sundance TV; The Movie Channel (multiplexed).
Fee: $10.95 monthly (Cinemax, HBO, Showtime, Flix/Sundance/TMC, or Starz/Encore).

Video-On-Demand: Planned
Pay-Per-View
ESPN Now (delivered digitally); Pleasure (delivered digitally); Vubiquity Inc. (delivered digitally).

Internet Service
Operational: Yes.
Subscribers: 4,435.
Broadband Service: Mediacom High Speed Internet.
Fee: $45.95 monthly.

Telephone Service
Digital: Operational
Subscribers: 2,220.
Miles of Plant: 720.0 (coaxial); 255.0 (fiber optic). Homes passed: 29,685.
General Manager: Joe Tetro. Chief Technician: Billy Brooks. Technical Operations Manager: Bobby Hollifield.
Ownership: Mediacom LLC (MSO).

ROGERSVILLE—Zito Media, 102 S Main St, PO Box 665, Coudersport, PA 16915. Phones: 814-260-9055; 800-365-6988. E-mail: info@zitomedia.com. Web Site: http://www.zitomedia.com. Also serves Anderson, Center Star, Elgin, Killen, Lauderdale County (portions), Lexington, North Rogersville & West Killen. ICA: AL0039.
TV Market Ranking: 96 (Anderson, Center Star, Elgin, Lauderdale County (portions), ROGERSVILLE); Below 100 (Killen, Lexington, North Rogersville, West Killen, Lauderdale County (portions)). Franchise

Access the most current data instantly
www.warren-news.com/factbook.htm

award date: N.A. Franchise expiration date: N.A. Began: May 1, 1981.
Channel capacity: N.A. Channels available but not in use: N.A.

Basic Service
Subscribers: 241. Commercial subscribers: 18.
Programming (received off-air): WAAY-TV (ABC) Huntsville; WAFF (Bounce TV, NBC, This TV) Huntsville; WFIQ (PBS) Florence; WHDF (CW) Florence; WHNT-TV (Antenna TV, CBS) Huntsville; WZDX (FOX, MeTV, MNT) Huntsville.
Programming (via satellite): A&E; AMC; Animal Planet; CMT; CNN; C-SPAN; Discovery Channel; E! HD; ESPN; ESPN2; HLN; MTV; QVC; Syfy; The Weather Channel; TLC; TNT; USA Network; VH1.
Fee: $49.95 installation; $27.74 monthly.

Expanded Basic Service 1
Subscribers: N.A.
Programming (via satellite): Comedy Central; Disney Channel; Fox News Channel; Freeform; Golf Channel; HGTV; Lifetime; Nickelodeon; Spike TV; TBS; TV Land; WGN America.
Fee: $19.00 monthly.

Pay Service 1
Pay Units: N.A.
Programming (via satellite): Cinemax (multiplexed); HBO (multiplexed); Showtime (multiplexed); The Movie Channel (multiplexed).
Fee: $14.00 monthly (Cinemax/HBO or Showtime/TMC).

Video-On-Demand: No
Pay-Per-View
ESPN Now (delivered digitally); Hot Choice (delivered digitally); iN DEMAND (delivered digitally); Playboy TV (delivered digitally); Spice (delivered digitally); Spice 2 (delivered digitally); Urban Xtra (delivered digitally).

Internet Service
Operational: Yes.
Fee: $39.95 monthly.

Telephone Service
Digital: Operational
Fee: $30.00 monthly
Miles of Plant: 136.0 (coaxial); 19.0 (fiber optic). Homes passed: 5,578.
President: James Rigas.
Ownership: Zito Media (MSO).

RUSSELLVILLE—Charter Communications. Now served by DECATUR, AL [AL0184]. ICA: AL0028.

SAMSON—Bright House Networks. Now served by CHIPLEY, FL [FL0126]. ICA: AL0115.

SCOTTSBORO—Charter Communications. Now served by DECATUR, AL [AL0184]. ICA: AL0219.

SCOTTSBORO—Scottsboro Electric Power Board, 404 East Willow St, PO Box 550, Scottsboro, AL 35768-0550. Phones: 256-574-2682; 256-574-2682. Fax: 256-574-5085. E-mail: feedback@scottsboropower.com. Web Site: http://www.scottsboropower.com. ICA: AL0260.
Note: This system is an overbuild.
TV Market Ranking: 96 (SCOTTSBORO).
Channel capacity: N.A. Channels available but not in use: N.A.

Basic Service
Subscribers: 5,611.
Programming (received off-air): WAAY-TV (ABC) Huntsville; WAFF (Bounce TV, NBC, This TV) Huntsville; WDEF-TV (Bounce TV, CBS, Escape) Chattanooga; WHDF (CW) Florence; WHIQ (PBS) Huntsville; WHNT-TV (Antenna TV, CBS) Huntsville; WRCB (Antenna TV, NBC) Chattanooga; WTVC (ABC, This TV, WeatherNation) Chattanooga; WZDX (FOX, MeTV, MNT) Huntsville.
Programming (via satellite): C-SPAN 2; CW PLUS; HLN; INSP; Pop; Radar Channel; TBS; The Weather Channel; WGN America.
Fee: $15.24 monthly.

Expanded Basic Service 1
Subscribers: N.A.
Programming (via satellite): A&E; AMC; Animal Planet; BET; Bravo; Cartoon Network; CMT; CNBC; CNN; Comcast/Charter Sports Southeast (CSS); Comedy Central; C-SPAN; Discovery Channel; Discovery Life Channel; Disney Channel; Disney XD; E! HD; ESPN; ESPN Classic; ESPN2; ESPNews; EWTN Global Catholic Network; Food Network; Fox News Channel; Fox Sports 1; Freeform; FX; Golf Channel; Great American Country; HGTV; History; ION Television; Lifetime; MTV; National Geographic Channel; Nickelodeon; Outdoor Channel; QVC; Spike TV; SportSouth; Syfy; TLC; TNT; Travel Channel; Trinity Broadcasting Network (TBN); Turner Classic Movies; TV Land; USA Network; VH1.
Fee: $22.00 monthly.

Digital Basic Service
Subscribers: 1,500.
Programming (via satellite): AXS TV; BBC America; CBS Sports Network; Discovery Digital Networks; DIY Network; FOX College Sports Central; FOX College Sports Pacific; FXM; FYI; GSN; Hallmark Channel; HD Theater; History International; IFC; WE tv.
Fee: $13.00 monthly; $5.00 converter.

Pay Service 1
Pay Units: N.A.
Programming (via satellite): Cinemax; HBO (multiplexed); Showtime; Starz; Starz Encore; The Movie Channel.
Fee: $14.00 monthly (Cinemax, Showtime, TMC or Starz/Encore), $10.00 monthly (HBO).

Digital Pay Service 1
Pay Units: N.A.
Programming (via satellite): Cinemax (multiplexed); Flix; HBO (multiplexed); HITS (Headend In The Sky); Showtime (multiplexed); Starz (multiplexed); Starz Encore (multiplexed); Sundance TV; The Movie Channel (multiplexed).
Fee: $6.00 monthly (Canales N), $12.00 monthly (Cinemax or Starz/Encore), $14.00 monthly (Showtime/TMC/Flix), $16.00 monthly (HBO).

Video-On-Demand: No

2017 Edition · D-33

Alabama—Cable Systems

Pay-Per-View
iN DEMAND (delivered digitally); Hot Choice (delivered digitally); Fresh (delivered digitally).
Internet Service
Operational: Yes.
Subscribers: 3,600.
Broadband Service: In-house.
Fee: $33.00-$60.00 monthly; $8.00 modem lease; $370.00 modem purchase.
Telephone Service
Digital: Operational
Subscribers: 1,938.
Fee: $28.00-$54.98 monthly
Miles of Plant: 200.0 (coaxial); None (fiber optic). Homes passed: 6,300.
General Manager: Jimmy Sandlin. Chief Technician: Philip Chaney.
Ownership: Scottsboro Electric Power Board.

SELBROOK—Formerly served by Alabama Broadband LLC. No longer in operation. ICA: AL0139.

SELMA—Charter Communications. Now served by MONTGOMERY, AL [AL0003]. ICA: AL0018.

SHELBY LAKE—Zito Media. Now served by COLUMBIANA, AL [AL0180]. ICA: AL0222.

SKYLINE—Formerly served by Almega Cable. No longer in operation. ICA: AL0223.

SOUTHSIDE—Charter Communications. Now served by PIEDMONT, AL [AL0065]. ICA: AL0076.

SPANISH COVE—Mediacom. Now served by FAIRHOPE, AL [AL0124]. ICA: AL0119.

STAPLETON—Mediacom. Now served by FAIRHOPE, AL [AL0124]. ICA: AL0235.

SULLIGENT—Charter Communications, 12405 Powerscourt Dr, St. Louis, MO 63131. Phones: 636-207-5100 (Corporate office); 888-438-2427. Web Site: http://www.charter.com. Also serves Beaverton, Guin, Marion County (portions) & Vernon. ICA: AL0084.
TV Market Ranking: Below 100 (Beaverton, SULLIGENT, Vernon); Outside TV Markets (Marion County (portions), Guin). Franchise award date: N.A. Franchise expiration date: N.A. Began: December 1, 1964.
Channel capacity: 60 (operating 2-way). Channels available but not in use: N.A.
Digital Basic Service
Subscribers: 490.
Programming (via satellite): BBC America; Bloomberg Television; Church Channel; Cloo; CMT; Destination America; Discovery Life Channel; Disney XD; DMX Music; Fuse; FXM; FYI; Golf Channel; Great American Country; GSN; History International; Investigation Discovery; JUCE TV; LMN; MTV Classic; MTV Hits; MTV Jams; National Geographic Channel; NBCSN; Ovation; OWN; Oprah Winfrey Network; Science Channel; Sundance TV; TeenNick; The Word Network; UP; VH1 Soul.
Fee: $24.99 monthly.
Digital Expanded Basic Service
Subscribers: N.A.
Programming (via satellite): A&E; AMC; Animal Planet; BET; Bravo; Cartoon Network; CMT; CNBC; CNN; Comcast/Charter Sports Southeast (CSS); Comedy Central; C-SPAN; C-SPAN 2; Discovery Channel; Disney Channel; E! HD; ESPN; ESPN Clas-

sic; ESPN2; ESPNews; EVINE Live; Food Network; Fox News Channel; Fox Sports 1; Freeform; FX; HGTV; History; HLN; Lifetime; MSNBC; MTV; Nick Jr.; Nickelodeon; Outdoor Channel; QVC; RFD-TV; Spike TV; Syfy; TBS; The Weather Channel; TLC; TNT; Travel Channel; Trinity Broadcasting Network (TBN); truTV; Turner Classic Movies; TV Land; USA Network; VH1; WE tv.
Digital Pay Service 1
Pay Units: 93.
Programming (via satellite): Cinemax (multiplexed); Flix; HBO (multiplexed); Showtime (multiplexed); Starz (multiplexed); Starz Encore (multiplexed); The Movie Channel.
Video-On-Demand: No
Pay-Per-View
iN DEMAND (delivered digitally); Hot Choice (delivered digitally); Playboy TV (delivered digitally); Fresh (delivered digitally); Spice Xcess (delivered digitally).
Internet Service
Operational: Yes.
Broadband Service: Charter Internet.
Fee: $39.95 installation; $51.95 monthly.
Telephone Service
None
Miles of Plant: 9,627.0 (coaxial); 3,524.0 (fiber optic). Homes passed: 302,752.
Accounting Director: David Sovanski.
Ownership: Charter Communications Inc. (MSO).

SWEET WATER—Community Cable & Broadband LLC, 1309 Roebuck Dr, PO Box 65, Meridian, MS 39301. Phone: 601-485-6980. Fax: 601-483-0103. ICA: AL0227.
TV Market Ranking: Outside TV Markets (SWEET WATER). Franchise award date: N.A. Franchise expiration date: N.A. Began: September 9, 1989.
Channel capacity: N.A. Channels available but not in use: N.A.
Basic Service
Subscribers: 177.
Programming (received off-air): WGBC (FOX, NBC) Meridian; WIIQ (PBS) Demopolis; WMDN (CBS) Meridian; WTOK-TV (ABC, CW, FOX, MNT) Meridian.
Programming (via satellite): A&E; CNN; Discovery Channel; Disney Channel; ESPN; Freeform; TBS; TNT; USA Network; WGN America.
Fee: $39.00 monthly.
Pay Service 1
Pay Units: N.A.
Programming (via satellite): HBO.
Fee: $11.00 monthly.
Internet Service
Operational: No.
Telephone Service
None
General Manager & Chief Technician: Berry Ward.
Ownership: Community Cable & Broadband LLC (MSO).

SYLACAUGA—Charter Communications. Now served by PELHAM, AL [AL0192]. ICA: AL0031.

TALLADEGA—Charter Communications. Now served by PELHAM, AL [AL0192]. ICA: AL0024.

TALLADEGA COUNTY (portions)—USA Communications, 1701 Coggswell Ave, Pell City, AL 35125-1646. Phones: 800-234-0102; 205-884-4545; 800-824-4773. E-mail: csr@usacommunications.tv.

Web Site: http://usacommunications.tv. ICA: AL0280.
TV Market Ranking: 40 (TALLADEGA COUNTY (portions)); Below 100 (TALLADEGA COUNTY (portions)).
Channel capacity: N.A. Channels available but not in use: N.A.
Basic Service
Subscribers: 307.
Fee: $42.00 installation; $39.50 monthly.
Internet Service
Operational: Yes.
Fee: $35.95 monthly.
Telephone Service
Digital: Operational
Fee: $46.95 monthly
President: Jeffrey T. Smith.
Ownership: USA Companies LP (MSO).

THOMASTON—Formerly served by Zoom Media. No longer in operation. ICA: AL0146.

THOMASVILLE—Mediacom, 760 Middle St, PO Box 1009, Fairhope, AL 36532. Phones: 800-479-2082; 850-934-7700 (Gulf Breeze regional office); 251-928-0374. Fax: 251-928-3804. Web Site: http://www.mediacomcable.com. Also serves Clarke County (portions) & Jackson. ICA: AL0080.
TV Market Ranking: Outside TV Markets (Clarke County (portions), Jackson, THOMASVILLE). Franchise award date: February 23, 1976. Franchise expiration date: N.A. Began: February 1, 1976.
Channel capacity: N.A. Channels available but not in use: N.A.
Basic Service
Subscribers: 962.
Programming (received off-air): WAKA (CBS, MeTV) Selma; WALA-TV (FOX) Mobile; WBIH (IND) Selma; WEAR-TV (ABC, The Country Network) Pensacola; WIIQ (PBS) Demopolis; WKRG-TV (CBS, MeTV) Mobile; WMAH-TV (PBS) Biloxi; WPMI-TV (NBC) Mobile; WSFA (Bounce TV, NBC) Montgomery; WTOK-TV (ABC, CW, FOX, MNT) Meridian; 1 FM.
Programming (via satellite): A&E; AMC; Animal Planet; BET; Bravo; Cartoon Network; CMT; CNBC; CNN; Comedy Central; C-SPAN; C-SPAN 2; Discovery Channel; Discovery Life Channel; Disney Channel; E! HD; ESPN; ESPN2; EWTN Global Catholic Network; Food Network; Fox News Channel; Fox Sports 1; FOX Sports South/SportSouth; Freeform; FX; Hallmark Channel; HGTV; History; HLN; INSP; ION Television; Lifetime; MSNBC; MTV; Nickelodeon; Outdoor Channel; QVC; Spike TV; Syfy; TBS; The Weather Channel; TLC; TNT; Travel Channel; Trinity Broadcasting Network (TBN); truTV; Turner Classic Movies; TV Land; USA Network; VH1; WE tv; WGN America.
Fee: $41.00 monthly.
Digital Basic Service
Subscribers: N.A.
Programming (via satellite): BBC America; Bloomberg Television; Discovery Digital Networks; Fuse; FXM; FYI; GSN; History International; IFC; LMN; MC; NBCSN.
Digital Pay Service 1
Pay Units: N.A.
Programming (via satellite): Cinemax (multiplexed); Flix; HBO (multiplexed); Showtime (multiplexed); Starz (multiplexed); Starz Encore (multiplexed); Sundance TV; The Movie Channel (multiplexed).
Fee: $10.45 monthly (Cinemax, HBO, Showtime, Flix/TMC/Sundance or Starz/Encore).
Video-On-Demand: No

Pay-Per-View
ESPN Now (delivered digitally); ETC (delivered digitally); Pleasure (delivered digitally); Vubiquity Inc. (delivered digitally).
Internet Service
Operational: Yes.
Telephone Service
Digital: Planned
Miles of Plant: 179.0 (coaxial); 134.0 (fiber optic). Homes passed: 6,444.
Vice President: David Servies. Operations Director: Gene Wuchner. Technical Operations Manager: Mike Sneary. Sales & Marketing Manager: Joey Nagem.
Ownership: Mediacom LLC (MSO).

THORSBY—Zito Media, 102 S Main St, PO Box 665, Coudersport, PA 16915. Phones: 814-260-9055; 800-365-6988. E-mail: info@zitomedia.com. Web Site: http://www.zitomedia.com. Also serves Chilton County (portions) & Jemison. ICA: AL0200.
TV Market Ranking: Below 100 (Chilton County (portions), Jemison, THORSBY). Franchise award date: N.A. Franchise expiration date: N.A. Began: June 1, 1984.
Channel capacity: N.A. Channels available but not in use: N.A.
Basic Service
Subscribers: 47. Commercial subscribers: 44.
Programming (received off-air): WABM (MNT) Birmingham; WBIQ (PBS) Birmingham; WBRC (Bounce TV, FOX) Birmingham; WIAT (CBS, Untamed Sports TV) Birmingham; WPXH-TV (ION) Gadsden; WSES (ABC, TNN) Tuscaloosa; WTTO (Antenna TV, CW, The Country Network) Homewood; WVTM-TV (MeTV, NBC) Birmingham.
Programming (via satellite): C-SPAN; WGN America.
Fee: $49.95 installation; $21.11 monthly.
Expanded Basic Service 1
Subscribers: N.A.
Programming (via satellite): A&E; AMC; Animal Planet; Bravo; Cartoon Network; CMT; CNBC; CNN; Comedy Central; Discovery Channel; Disney Channel; Disney XD; E! HD; ESPN; ESPN2; Fox News Channel; Fox Sports 1; FOX Sports South/SportSouth; Freeform; FX; Golf Channel; HGTV; History; HLN; MTV; Nickelodeon; Oxygen; Spike TV; Syfy; TBS; The Weather Channel; TLC; TNT; Travel Channel; Turner Classic Movies; TV Land; USA Network; VH1; WE tv.
Fee: $24.00 monthly.
Digital Basic Service
Subscribers: N.A.
Programming (via satellite): BBC America; Bloomberg Television; Discovery Digital Networks; ESPN Classic; ESPNews; Fuse; FXM; FYI; GSN; History International; IFC; LMN; MC; Nick 2; Nick Jr.; Nicktoons; Sundance TV; TeenNick.
Pay Service 1
Pay Units: N.A.
Programming (via satellite): Cinemax (multiplexed); Flix (multiplexed); HBO (multiplexed); Showtime (multiplexed); Starz (multiplexed); Starz Encore; The Movie Channel (multiplexed).
Fee: $14.00 monthly (Cinemax/HBO, Showtime/TMC/Flix or Starz/Encore).
Video-On-Demand: No
Pay-Per-View
ESPN Now (delivered digitally); iN DEMAND (delivered digitally); Playboy TV (delivered digitally); Fresh (delivered digitally).
Internet Service
Operational: No.

Cable Systems—Alabama

Telephone Service
None
Miles of Plant: 53.0 (coaxial); None (fiber optic). Homes passed: 1,819.
President: James Rigas.
Ownership: Zito Media (MSO).

TRAFFORD—Formerly served by Almega Cable. No longer in operation. ICA: AL0228.

TRINITY—Charter Communications, 12405 Powerscourt Dr, St. Louis, MO 63131. Phone: 636-207-5100 (Corporate office). Web Site: http://www.charter.com. ICA: AL0281.
TV Market Ranking: 96 (TRINITY).
Channel capacity: 68 (not 2-way capable). Channels available but not in use: N.A.
Digital Basic Service
Subscribers: 317.
Fee: $18.95 monthly.
Miles of Plant: 6,294.0 (coaxial); 1,929.0 (fiber optic). Homes passed: 173,474.
Vice President, Operations & General Manager: Tom Early. Accounting Director: David Sovanski.
Ownership: Charter Communications Inc. (MSO).

TRINITY—Formerly served by Coosa Cable. No longer in operation. ICA: AL0108.

TROY—Formerly served by Knology. Now served by Troy Cablevision. This cable system has converted to IPTV. See TROY, AL [AL5091]. ICA: AL0027.

TROY—Troy Cablevision. Formerly [AL0032]. This cable system has converted to IPTV, 1006 S Brundidge St, Troy, AL 36081-3121. Phones: 800-735-9546; 334-566-3310. Fax: 334-566-3304. E-mail: sales@troycable.net. Web Site: http://www.troycable.net. Also serves Banks, Brundidge, Clayhatchee, Daleville, Elba, Enterprise, Glenwood, Goshen, Level Plains, Luverne, Midland, Napier Field, New Brockton, Newton, Ozark, Petrey, Pinckard & Rutledge. ICA: AL5091.
TV Market Ranking: Below 100 (Brundidge, Elba, Ozark, TROY). Franchise award date: May 6, 1985. Franchise expiration date: N.A. Began: July 15, 1986.
Channel capacity: N.A. Channels available but not in use: N.A.
Basic
Subscribers: 10,416.
Programming (received off-air): WAKA (CBS, MeTV) Selma; WBMM (CW, TNN) Tuskegee; WCIQ (PBS) Mount Cheaha State Park; WCOV-TV (Antenna TV, FOX, This TV) Montgomery; WIYC (WeatherNation) Troy; WLTZ (CW, NBC) Columbus; WNCF (ABC) Montgomery; WSFA (Bounce TV, NBC) Montgomery; WTVM (ABC, Bounce TV) Columbus; WTVY (CBS, CW, MeTV, MNT, This TV) Dothan.
Programming (via satellite): A&E; AMC; Animal Planet; BET; Bravo; CMT; CNBC; CNN; Comcast/Charter Sports Southeast (CSS); Comedy Central; C-SPAN; C-SPAN 2; Discovery Channel; Disney Channel; Disney XD; E! HD; ESPN; ESPN Classic; ESPN2; Food Network; Fox News Channel; Fox Sports 1; FOX Sports South/SportSouth; Freeform; FX; Golf Channel; GSN; Hallmark Channel; HGTV; History; HLN; INSP; Lifetime; MSNBC; MTV; National Geographic Channel; Nickelodeon; Pop; QVC; Spike TV; Syfy; TBS; The Weather Channel; TLC; TNT; Travel Channel; Turner Classic Movies; TV Land; USA Network; VH1; WGN America.

Fee: $23.95 monthly.
Video-On-Demand: No
Pay-Per-View
iN DEMAND (delivered digitally); Hot Choice (delivered digitally); Pleasure (delivered digitally); College Football (delivered digitally).
Internet Service
Operational: Yes. Began: June 1, 2000.
Broadband Service: In-house.
Fee: $49.95 installation; $41.95-$54.95 monthly.
Telephone Service
Digital: Operational
General Manager: William Freeman. Head Engineer: Ken Jordan.
Ownership: Troy Cablevision (MSO).

TROY—Troy Cablevision. This cable system has converted to IPTV. See TROY, AL [AL5091]. ICA: AL0032.

TUSCALOOSA—Comcast Cable. Now served by TUPELO, MS [MS0009]. ICA: AL0230.

TUSCALOOSA COUNTY—Charter Communications. Now served by PELHAM, AL [AL0192]. ICA: AL0060.

TUSKEGEE—Charter Communications. Now served by PELHAM, AL [AL0192]. ICA: AL0041.

UNION SPRINGS—Union Springs Telephone Co, 206 Hardaway Ave East, PO Box 272, Union Springs, AL 36089. Phones: 800-722-2805; 334-738-4400. Fax: 334-738-5555. E-mail: ustc@ustconline.net. Web Site: http://www.ustconline.net. Also serves Midway. ICA: AL0088.
TV Market Ranking: Below 100 (Midway, UNION SPRINGS). Franchise award date: October 1, 1980. Franchise expiration date: N.A. Began: April 1, 1981.
Channel capacity: N.A. Channels available but not in use: N.A.
Basic Service
Subscribers: 1,090.
Programming (received off-air): WAIQ (PBS) Montgomery; WAKA (CBS, MeTV) Selma; WBIH (IND) Selma; WCOV-TV (Antenna TV, FOX, This TV) Montgomery; WMCF-TV (TBN) Montgomery; WNCF (ABC) Montgomery; WPCH-TV (IND) Atlanta; WSFA (Bounce TV, NBC) Montgomery; WTVM (ABC, Bounce TV) Columbus.
Programming (via satellite): CNN; Discovery Channel; ESPN; HLN; Lifetime; QVC; TBS.
Fee: $42.50 installation; $36.95 monthly.
Expanded Basic Service 1
Subscribers: 936.
Programming (via satellite): A&E; AMC; BET; Bravo; Cartoon Network; CMT; CNBC; C-SPAN; C-SPAN 2; Disney Channel; ESPN2; ESPNU; Food Network; Fox News Channel; FOX Sports South/SportSouth; Freeform; Hallmark Channel; History; LMN; MTV; National Geographic Channel; Nickelodeon; Outdoor Channel; Spike TV; Syfy; The Weather Channel; TLC; TNT; truTV; Turner Classic Movies; TV Land; USA Network; VH1; WGN America.
Fee: $30.00 monthly.
Digital Basic Service
Subscribers: 101.
Programming (via satellite): BBC America; Bloomberg Television; Centric; Cooking Channel; Destination America; Discovery Kids Channel; Discovery Life Channel; Disney XD; DMX Music; ESPN Classic; ESPNews; Fox Sports 1; FXM; FYI; Golf Channel; GSN; History International; Investigation Discovery; MTV Classic; MTV Hits; MTV2; National Geographic Channel; Nick Jr.; Nicktoons; Outdoor Channel; OWN: Oprah Winfrey Network; Pivot; Science Channel; TeenNick; Trinity Broadcasting Network (TBN); VH1 Soul; WE tv.
Fee: $8.00 monthly.
Pay Service 1
Pay Units: N.A.
Programming (via satellite): Cinemax; HBO; Showtime; The Movie Channel.
Digital Pay Service 1
Pay Units: N.A.
Programming (via satellite): Cinemax (multiplexed); HBO (multiplexed); Showtime (multiplexed); Starz (multiplexed); Starz Encore (multiplexed); The Movie Channel (multiplexed).
Video-On-Demand: No
Internet Service
Operational: Yes.
Broadband Service: In-house.
Fee: $42.50 installation; $34.95-$59.95 monthly.
Telephone Service
Analog: Operational
Miles of Plant: 30.0 (coaxial); 50.0 (fiber optic). Homes passed: 2,227.
President: Larry Grogan. Vice President, Technical Services: Lynn Rotton.
Ownership: Com-Link Inc. (MSO).

UNIONTOWN—Alliance Communications, PO Box 9090, Tyler, TX 75711. Phones: 903-561-4411; 800-842-8160; 501-679-6619 (Greenbrier, AR office). Fax: 501-679-5694. Web Site: http://www.alliancecable.net. Also serves Perry County. ICA: AL0118.
TV Market Ranking: Below 100 (Perry County, UNIONTOWN).
Channel capacity: N.A. Channels available but not in use: N.A.
Basic Service
Subscribers: 105.
Programming (received off-air): WAKA (CBS, MeTV) Selma; WCOV-TV (Antenna TV, FOX, This TV) Montgomery; WIIQ (PBS) Demopolis; WNCF (ABC) Montgomery; WSES (ABC, TNN) Tuscaloosa; WSFA (Bounce TV, NBC) Montgomery.
Programming (via satellite): A&E; BET; Cartoon Network; CNN; C-SPAN; Discovery Channel; Disney Channel; Disney XD; ESPN; ESPN2; Fox News Channel; Freeform; FX; Great American Country; History; HLN; Outdoor Channel; QVC; Syfy; TBS; The Weather Channel; TNT; Trinity Broadcasting Network (TBN); Turner Classic Movies; USA Network; WGN America.
Fee: $35.00 installation; $25.45 monthly.
Pay Service 1
Pay Units: N.A.
Programming (via satellite): HBO; Starz (multiplexed); Starz Encore.
Fee: $25.00 installation; $8.50 monthly.
Internet Service
Operational: No.

Telephone Service
None
Miles of Plant: 22.0 (coaxial); None (fiber optic). Homes passed: 962.
Chief Financial Officer: David Starrett. Vice President & General Manager: John Brinker. Vice President, Programming: Julie Newman.
Ownership: Buford Media Group LLC (MSO).

VESTAVIA HILLS—AT&T U-verse. This cable system has converted to IPTV. See BIRMINGHAM, AL [AL5004]. ICA: AL0258.

WADLEY—Charter Communications. Now served by ROANOKE, AL [AL0023]. ICA: AL0155.

WARRIOR—Formerly served by Time Warner Cable. Now served by Charter Communications, CULLMAN, AL [AL0034]. ICA: AL0082.

WATERLOO—Formerly served by North Crossroads Communications Inc. No longer in operation. ICA: AL0233.

WEDOWEE—Charter Communications, 3164 Hwy 431, Ste 8, Roanoke, AL 36274. Phones: 636-207-5100 (Corporate office); 314-543-2236; 334-863-7080. Web Site: http://www.charter.com. ICA: AL0147.
TV Market Ranking: Below 100 (WEDOWEE). Franchise award date: April 20, 1983. Franchise expiration date: N.A. Began: December 1, 1983.
Channel capacity: 71 (operating 2-way). Channels available but not in use: N.A.
Digital Basic Service
Subscribers: 11,864.
Programming (via satellite): BBC America; Bloomberg Television; Cloo; Destination America; Discovery Kids Channel; Discovery Life Channel; Disney XD; DMX Music; Fox Sports 1; Golf Channel; GSN; IFC; Investigation Discovery; NBCSN; OWN: Oprah Winfrey Network; Science Channel; Turner Classic Movies.
Fee: $49.99 installation; $26.99 monthly.
Digital Expanded Basic Service
Subscribers: N.A.
Programming (via satellite): A&E; AMC; Animal Planet; BET; Bravo; Cartoon Network; CMT; CNBC; CNN; Comcast/Charter Sports Southeast (CSS); Comedy Central; C-SPAN; C-SPAN 2; Discovery Channel; Disney Channel; E! HD; ESPN; ESPN Classic; ESPN2; EVINE Live; Food Network; Fox News Channel; Freeform; FX; FXM; Great American Country; HGTV; History; HLN; ION Television; Lifetime; LMN; MSNBC; MTV; Nick Jr.; Nickelodeon; Outdoor Channel; QVC; Spike TV; SportSouth; Syfy; The Weather Channel; TLC; TNT; Travel Channel; Trinity Broadcasting Network (TBN); truTV; TV Land; USA Network; VH1; WE tv.
Digital Pay Service 1
Pay Units: 49.
Programming (via satellite): Cinemax (multiplexed); HBO (multiplexed); Showtime

2017 Edition D-35

Alabama—Cable Systems

(multiplexed); Starz (multiplexed); Starz Encore (multiplexed).
Video-On-Demand: No
Pay-Per-View
iN DEMAND (delivered digitally); Fresh (delivered digitally); Playboy TV (delivered digitally).
Internet Service
Operational: Yes.
Subscribers: 8,180.
Broadband Service: Charter Internet.
Fee: $39.95 installation; $51.95 monthly.
Telephone Service
Digital: Operational
Subscribers: 6,047.
Miles of Plant: 5,363.0 (coaxial); 1,184.0 (fiber optic). Homes passed: 144,317.
President & Chief Executive Officer: Tom Rutledge. General Manager: Brian Chase. Chief Technician: William Boyd. Accounting Director: David Sovanski.
Ownership: Charter Communications Inc. (MSO).

WEST BLOCTON—Formerly served by Almega Cable. No longer in operation. ICA: AL0061.

WESTOVER—Charter Communications. Now served by PELHAM, AL [AL0192]. ICA: AL0196.

WETUMPKA—Bright House Networks, 2251 Lucien Way, Ste 200B, Maitland, FL 32751. Phones: 407-667-5200; 334-567-4344; 205-290-1300; 800-822-0060. Web Site: http://brighthouse.com. Also serves Coosada (town), Deatsville (town), Eclectic (town), Elmore (town), Elmore County (portions), Maxwell-Gunter AFB, Millbrook, Montgomery County, Prattville, Tallapoosa County (southern portion) & Tallassee. ICA: AL0016.
TV Market Ranking: Below 100 (Coosada (town), Deatsville (town), Eclectic (town), Elmore (town), Elmore County (portions), Maxwell-Gunter AFB, Millbrook, Montgomery County (southern portion), Tallassee, WETUMPKA). Franchise award date: January 1, 1977. Franchise expiration date: N.A. Began: December 1, 1977.
Channel capacity: 72 (operating 2-way). Channels available but not in use: N.A.
Basic Service
Subscribers: 15,646. Commercial subscribers: 419.
Programming (received off-air): WABM (MNT) Birmingham; WBIQ (PBS) Birmingham; WBRC (Bounce TV, FOX) Birmingham; WIAT (CBS, Untamed Sports TV) Birmingham; WPXH-TV (ION) Gadsden; WTJP-TV (TBN) Gadsden; WTTO (Antenna TV, CW, The Country Network) Homewood; WTVM (ABC, Bounce TV) Columbus; WVTM-TV (MeTV, NBC) Birmingham.
Programming (via satellite): Concert TV; C-SPAN; C-SPAN 2; Pop; QVC; WGN America.
Fee: $38.35 installation; $27.00 monthly; $1.00 converter.
Expanded Basic Service 1
Subscribers: N.A.
Programming (via satellite): A&E; AMC; Animal Planet; BET; Cartoon Network; CNBC; CNN; Comedy Central; Discovery Channel; Disney Channel; E! HD; ESPN; ESPN Classic; ESPN2; EVINE Live; EWTN Global Catholic Network; Food Network; Fox News Channel; FOX Sports South/SportSouth; Freeform; Fuse; FX; Golf Channel; Great American Country; Hallmark Channel; HGTV; History; HLN; Lifetime; LMN; MSNBC; MTV; National Geographic Channel; NBCSN; Nickelodeon; Oxygen; Spike TV; Starz Encore; Syfy; TBS; The Weather Channel; TLC; TNT; Travel Channel; truTV; Turner Classic Movies; TV Land; Univision Studios; USA Network; VH1; WE tv.
Fee: $49.45 monthly.
Digital Basic Service
Subscribers: N.A.
Programming (via satellite): AXS TV; BBC America; Boomerang; Bravo; CNN International; Cooking Channel; C-SPAN 3; Discovery Life Channel; Disney XD; DIY Network; ESPN; ESPNews; FamilyNet; Fox Sports 1; FYI; GSN; HD Theater; History International; iN DEMAND; MC; MTV Classic; MTV2; NBA TV; Nick Jr.; Nicktoons; Outdoor Channel; Ovation; TeenNick; TNT.
Digital Expanded Basic Service
Subscribers: N.A.
Programming (via satellite): CBS Sports Network; Flix; FOX College Sports Central; FOX College Sports Pacific; Fox Sports 2; FXM; HITS (Headend In The Sky); IFC; NBA TV; Outdoor Channel; Starz Encore (multiplexed); Sundance TV; Tennis Channel; WAM! America's Kidz Network.
Digital Pay Service 1
Pay Units: N.A.
Programming (via satellite): Cinemax (multiplexed); HBO (multiplexed); Playboy TV; Showtime (multiplexed); Starz (multiplexed); The Movie Channel (multiplexed).
Fee: $10.50 monthly (each).
Video-On-Demand: No
Pay-Per-View
Movies/Events (delivered digitally); Fresh (delivered digitally); Playboy TV (delivered digitally); Hot Choice (delivered digitally); NBA TV (delivered digitally); Ten Clips (delivered digitally); Pleasure (delivered digitally); ESPN (delivered digitally); MLB Extra Innings (delivered digitally); NHL Center Ice (delivered digitally).
Internet Service
Operational: Yes.
Subscribers: 15,383.
Broadband Service: Road Runner.
Fee: $49.95 installation; $29.95 monthly.
Telephone Service
Digital: Operational
Subscribers: 10,393.
Fee: $39.95 monthly
Miles of Plant: 1,442.0 (coaxial); 410.0 (fiber optic). Homes passed: 32,489.
Chief Financial Officer: William Futera. General Manager: Bruce Burgess. Marketing Director: Dennis Burns. Chief Technician: Mike Truelove.
Ownership: Bright House Networks LLC (MSO).

WINFIELD—West Alabama TV Cable Co. Inc, 213 2nd Ave NE, PO Box 930, Fayette, AL 35555-0930. Phones: 205-921-3800; 205-487-2884; 205-932-4700 (Fayette office). Fax: 205-932-3585. E-mail: cable@watvc.com. Web Site: http://www.watvc.com. Also serves Brilliant. ICA: AL0074.
TV Market Ranking: Outside TV Markets (Brilliant, WINFIELD). Franchise award date: N.A. Franchise expiration date: N.A. Began: May 10, 1965.
Channel capacity: N.A. Channels available but not in use: N.A.
Basic Service
Subscribers: N.A.
Programming (received off-air): WABM (MNT) Birmingham; WBIQ (PBS) Birmingham; WBRC (Bounce TV, FOX) Birmingham; WIAT (CBS, Untamed Sports TV) Birmingham; WSES (ABC, TNN) Tuscaloosa; WTTO (Antenna TV, CW, The Country Network) Homewood; WTVA (ABC, NBC) Tupelo; WVTM-TV (MeTV, NBC) Birmingham.
Programming (via satellite): A&E; AMC; BET; Cartoon Network; CMT; CNBC; CNN; C-SPAN; Discovery Channel; Disney Channel; E! HD; ESPN; ESPN2; Family Friendly Entertainment; Food Network; Fox News Channel; FOX Sports South/SportSouth; Freeform; FX; Golf Channel; Hallmark Channel; HGTV; History; HLN; Lifetime; MTV; Nickelodeon; Pop; QVC; TBS; The Weather Channel; TLC; TNT; Travel Channel; Trinity Broadcasting Network (TBN); Turner Classic Movies; TV Land; USA Network; VH1; WGN America.
Fee: $35.00 installation; $20.40 monthly.
Digital Basic Service
Subscribers: N.A.
Programming (via satellite): BBC America; Bloomberg Television; Cloo; Destination America; Discovery Kids Channel; Disney XD; DMX Music; ESPN Classic; ESPNews; Fox Sports 1; FXM; FYI; History International; IFC; INSP; Investigation Discovery; LMN; National Geographic Channel; NBCSN; Outdoor Channel; OWN; Oprah Winfrey Network; Science Channel; WE tv.
Pay Service 1
Pay Units: N.A.
Programming (via satellite): Cinemax; HBO.
Fee: $15.00 installation; $10.95 - $11.95 monthly (each).
Digital Pay Service 1
Pay Units: N.A.
Programming (via satellite): Cinemax (multiplexed); HBO (multiplexed); Showtime (multiplexed); Starz (multiplexed); Starz Encore (multiplexed); The Movie Channel (multiplexed).
Fee: $10.95 monthly (Cinemax or Starz/Encore/TMC), $12.95 monthly (HBO or Showtime).
Video-On-Demand: No
Pay-Per-View
iN DEMAND (delivered digitally); Hot Choice (delivered digitally); Spice (delivered digitally); ESPN Now (delivered digitally); Sports PPV (delivered digitally).
Internet Service
Operational: Yes.
Broadband Service: In-house.
Fee: $24.95 installation.
Telephone Service
Analog: Operational
Miles of Plant: 205.0 (coaxial); 75.0 (fiber optic). Homes passed: 7,000.
General Manager: Kyle South.
Ownership: West Alabama TV Cable Co. Inc. (MSO).

YORK—Mediacom, 760 Middle St, PO Box 1009, Fairhope, AL 36532. Phones: 800-479-2082; 251-928-0374. Fax: 251-928-3804. Web Site: http://www.mediacomcable.com. Also serves Livingston (town). ICA: AL0067.
TV Market Ranking: Below 100 (Livingston (town), YORK). Franchise award date: July 27, 1970. Franchise expiration date: N.A. Began: July 1, 1970.
Channel capacity: N.A. Channels available but not in use: N.A.
Basic Service
Subscribers: 1,017.
Programming (received off-air): WBIH (IND) Selma; WCOV-TV (Antenna TV, FOX, This TV) Montgomery; WDBB (CW) Bessemer; WEIQ (PBS) Mobile; WGBC (FOX, NBC) Meridian; WMDN (CBS) Meridian; WSES (ABC, TNN) Tuscaloosa; WTOK-TV (ABC, CW, FOX, MNT) Meridian; WVTM-TV (MeTV, NBC) Birmingham.
Programming (via satellite): A&E; AMC; Animal Planet; BET; Bravo; Cartoon Network; CMT; CNBC; CNN; Comedy Central; C-SPAN; C-SPAN 2; Discovery Channel; Discovery Life Channel; Disney Channel; E! HD; ESPN; ESPN2; EVINE Live; EWTN Global Catholic Network; Food Network; Fox News Channel; Fox Sports 1; FOX Sports South/SportSouth; Freeform; FX; Great American Country; Hallmark Channel; HGTV; History; HLN; INSP; Lifetime; MSNBC; MTV; Nickelodeon; Outdoor Channel; QVC; Spike TV; Syfy; TBS; The Weather Channel; TLC; TNT; Travel Channel; Trinity Broadcasting Network (TBN); truTV; Turner Classic Movies; TV Land; USA Network; VH1; WE tv; WGN America.
Fee: $49.95 installation; $55.56 monthly; $1.75 converter.
Digital Basic Service
Subscribers: N.A.
Programming (via satellite): BBC America; Bloomberg Television; Cloo; Discovery Digital Networks; ESPNews; Fuse; FXM; FYI; Golf Channel; GSN; History International; IFC; LMN; National Geographic Channel; NBCSN; Nick Jr.; Nicktoons; TVG Network; Weatherscan.
Digital Pay Service 1
Pay Units: N.A.
Programming (via satellite): Cinemax (multiplexed); Flix (multiplexed); HBO (multiplexed); MC; Showtime (multiplexed); Starz (multiplexed); Starz Encore (multiplexed); Sundance TV (multiplexed); The Movie Channel (multiplexed).
Video-On-Demand: No
Internet Service
Operational: Yes.
Broadband Service: Mediacom High Speed Internet.
Fee: $45.95 monthly.
Telephone Service
Digital: Planned
Homes passed: 2,343.
Vice President: David Servies. Operations Director: Gene Wuchner. Technical Operations Manager: Mike Sneary. Sales & Marketing Manager: Joey Nagem.
Ownership: Mediacom LLC (MSO).

ALASKA

Total Systems: 30	Communities with Applications: 0
Total Communities Served: 55	Number of Basic Subscribers: 88,922
Franchises Not Yet Operating: 0	Number of Expanded Basic Subscribers: 6,780
Applications Pending: 0	Number of Pay Units: 35,487

Top 100 Markets Represented: N.A.

For a list of cable communities in this section, see the Cable Community Index located in the back of Cable Volume 2.
For explanation of terms used in cable system listings, see p. D-11.

ADAK—Adak Cablevision. Formerly [AK0044]. This cable system has converted to IPTV, 1410 Rudakof Cir, Anchorage, AK 99508. Phones: 888-328-4222; 907-222-0844. Fax: 907-222-0845. E-mail: aeeservices@adaktu.com. Web Site: http://www.adaktu.com. ICA: AK5003.
Channel capacity: N.A. Channels available but not in use: N.A.
Local Basic Expanded
Subscribers: N.A.
Programming (via satellite): AMC; Boomerang; Cartoon Network; CNN; CNN en Espanol; CNN International; Fuse; IFC Free; Sundance TV; Syfy; TBS; TBS HD; TNT; TNT HD; truTV; Turner Classic Movies; Turner Classic Movies HD; USA Network; WGN America.
Programming (via translator): KTBY (FOX) Anchorage; KTUU-TV (NBC) Anchorage; KTVA (CBS) Anchorage; KYES-TV (MNT) Anchorage.
Fee: $125.00 installation; $185.00 monthly. Includes 29 channels, 1 STB & remote.
Local Basic Encore Plex
Subscribers: N.A.
Fee: $220.00 monthly. Includes Local Basic Expanded, 10 Encore/Plex channels, 1 STB & remote.
Local Basic Encore Plex Starz
Subscribers: N.A.
Fee: $270.00 monthly. Includes Local Basic Encore Plex plus 6 Starz channels, 1 STB & remote.
Video-On-Demand: No
Internet Service
Operational: Yes.
Fee: $125.00 installation; $75.00-$150.00 monthly.
Telephone Service
Digital: Operational
Fee: $40.60 monthly
Ownership: Adak Eagle Enterprises LLC.

ADAK—Adak Cablevision. This cable system has converted to IPTV. See ADAK, AK [AK5003]. ICA: AK0044.

ANCHORAGE—Formerly served by ACS Television. No longer in operation. ICA: AK0047.

ANCHORAGE—Formerly served by Sprint Corp. No longer in operation. ICA: AK0045.

ANCHORAGE—GCI Cable Inc, 2550 Denali St, Ste 1000, PO Box 99016, Anchorage, AK 99503-3910. Phones: 907-265-5600 (Corporate office); 800-800-4800; 907-265-5400. Fax: 907-868-8570. E-mail: support@gci.net. Web Site: http://www.gci.com. Also serves Chugiak, Eagle River, Elmendorf AFB, Fort Richardson & Peters Creek. ICA: AK0001.
TV Market Ranking: Below 100 (ANCHORAGE, Chugiak, Eagle River, Elmendorf AFB, Fort Richardson, Peters Creek). Franchise award date: N.A. Franchise expiration date: N.A. Began: October 1, 1980.
Channel capacity: N.A. Channels available but not in use: N.A.
Basic Service
Subscribers: 47,574.
Programming (received off-air): KAKM (PBS) Anchorage; KCFT-CD Anchorage; KDMD (ION, TMO) Anchorage; KTBY (FOX) Anchorage; KTUU-TV (NBC) Anchorage; KTVA (CBS) Anchorage; KYUR (ABC, CW) Anchorage; 6 FMs.
Programming (via satellite): C-SPAN; C-SPAN 2; CW PLUS; Pop; WGN America.
Fee: $25.50 installation; $33.95 monthly; $5.99 converter.
Expanded Basic Service 1
Subscribers: N.A.
Programming (via satellite): A&E; AMC; Animal Planet; BET; Bravo; Cartoon Network; CMT; CNBC; CNN; Comedy Central; C-SPAN 2; Discovery Channel; Disney Channel; Disney XD; E! HD; ESPN; ESPN Classic; ESPN2; EVINE Live; Food Network; Fox News Channel; Freeform; Fuse; FX; HGTV; History; HLN; Lifetime; LMN; MSNBC; MTV; National Geographic Channel; NBCSN; NFL Network; Nickelodeon; Outdoor Channel; Oxygen; QVC; Spike TV; Syfy; TBS; The Weather Channel; TLC; TNT; Travel Channel; truTV; Turner Classic Movies; TV Land; Univision Studios; USA Network; VH1; WE tv.
Fee: $35.79 monthly.
Digital Basic Service
Subscribers: N.A.
Programming (via satellite): 3ABN; AWE; AXS TV; BBC America; Bloomberg Television; Boomerang; BYUtv; Church Channel; CNN International; Daystar TV Network; Discovery Digital Networks; DIY Network; ESPN HD; ESPNews; EWTN Global Catholic Network; FamilyNet; FOX College Sports Central; FOX College Sports Pacific; Fox Sports 1; Fox Sports 2; FYI; Golf Channel; Great American Country; GSN; HD Theater; History; History International; IFC; INSP; MC; NFL Network; Nick Jr.; Nicktoons; TeenNick; Tennis Channel; TNT HD; Trinity Broadcasting Network (TBN); TVG Network; Universal HD; UP.
Pay Service 1
Pay Units: N.A.
Programming (via satellite): Cinemax (multiplexed); HBO (multiplexed); Showtime (multiplexed); The Movie Channel (multiplexed).
Fee: $10.95 monthly (Cinemax), $13.95 monthly (HBO or Showtime/TMC).
Digital Pay Service 1
Pay Units: N.A.
Programming (via satellite): Cinemax (multiplexed); Cinemax HD; Flix; HBO (multiplexed); HBO HD; Korean Channel; Showtime (multiplexed); Showtime HD; Starz (multiplexed); Starz Encore (multiplexed); Starz HD; Sundance TV; The Filipino Channel; The Movie Channel (multiplexed); The Movie Channel HD.
Fee: $10.95 monthly (Cinemax), $12.95 monthly (Starz/Encore), $13.95 monthly (HBO or Showtime), $13.99 (Filipino Channel or Korean Channel).
Video-On-Demand: No
Pay-Per-View
ESPN (delivered digitally); iN DEMAND (delivered digitally).
Internet Service
Operational: Yes.
Subscribers: 77,167.
Broadband Service: GCI Hypernet.
Fee: $24.99 monthly.
Telephone Service
Digital: Operational
Subscribers: 46,135.
Miles of Plant: 2,939.0 (coaxial); 1,278.0 (fiber optic). Homes passed: 152,476.
Executive Vice President & General Manager: Gregory F. Chapados. Vice President, Content Product Management: Robert W. Ormberg. Marketing Manager: David Fox.
Ownership: GCI Cable Inc. (MSO).

ANGOON—GCI Cable Inc, 8390 Airport Blvd, Ste 101, Juneau, AK 99801. Phone: 800-800-4800. E-mail: support@gci.net. Web Site: http://www.gci.com. ICA: AK0033.
TV Market Ranking: Outside TV Markets (ANGOON). Franchise award date: N.A. Franchise expiration date: N.A. Began: January 1, 1986.
Channel capacity: 33 (not 2-way capable). Channels available but not in use: N.A.
Basic Service
Subscribers: 51.
Programming (via satellite): CNN; Discovery Channel; Disney Channel; ESPN; Freeform; HBO; KCNC-TV (CBS, Decades) Denver; KUSA (NBC, WeatherNation) Denver; Showtime; Spike TV; TBS; TNT; USA Network; WGN America.
Fee: $25.50 installation; $32.45 monthly.
Video-On-Demand: No
Internet Service
Operational: No.
Telephone Service
None
Homes passed: 135.
Executive Vice President & General Manager: Gregory F. Chapados. Vice President, Content & Product Management: Robert W. Ormberg.
Ownership: GCI Cable Inc. (MSO).

BARROW—GCI Cable Inc, 1230 Agvik St, PO Box 489, Barrow, AK 99723. Phone: 907-852-5511. Fax: 907-852-5510. E-mail: support@gci.net. Web Site: http://www.gci.com. ICA: AK0013.
TV Market Ranking: Outside TV Markets (BARROW). Franchise award date: N.A. Franchise expiration date: N.A. Began: January 1, 1968.
Channel capacity: N.A. Channels available but not in use: N.A.
Basic Service
Subscribers: 1,044. Commercial subscribers: 44.
Programming (via microwave): KTBY (FOX) Anchorage; KTOO-TV (PBS) Juneau; KTUU-TV (NBC) Anchorage; KTVA (CBS) Anchorage; KYUR (ABC, CW) Anchorage.
Programming (via satellite): C-SPAN; C-SPAN 2; Pop; QVC; WGN America.
Fee: $25.50 installation; $33.95 monthly.
Expanded Basic Service 1
Subscribers: N.A.
Programming (via satellite): A&E; AMC; Animal Planet; BET; Cartoon Network; CMT; CNBC; CNN; Comedy Central; Discovery Channel; Disney Channel; Disney XD; E! HD; ESPN; ESPN2; Food Network; Freeform; Hallmark Channel; HGTV; History; HLN; Lifetime; MSNBC; MTV; Nickelodeon; Outdoor Channel; Spike TV; Syfy; TBS; TLC; TNT; Travel Channel; Trinity Broadcasting Network (TBN); truTV; Turner Classic Movies; TV Land; USA Network; VH1.
Fee: $66.00 monthly.
Digital Pay Service 1
Pay Units: 220.
Programming (via satellite): Cinemax (multiplexed).
Fee: $10.95 monthly.
Digital Pay Service 2
Pay Units: 407.
Programming (via satellite): HBO (multiplexed).
Fee: $13.95 monthly.
Digital Pay Service 3
Pay Units: 199.
Programming (via satellite): Starz (multiplexed); Starz Encore (multiplexed).
Fee: $12.95 monthly.
Digital Pay Service 4
Pay Units: 329.
Programming (via satellite): Flix; Showtime (multiplexed); Sundance TV; The Movie Channel (multiplexed).
Fee: $12.95 monthly.
Video-On-Demand: No
Pay-Per-View
iN DEMAND (delivered digitally); Adult Swim (delivered digitally).
Internet Service
Operational: Yes.
Fee: $49.99 monthly.
Telephone Service
Digital: Operational
Miles of Plant: 30.0 (coaxial); None (fiber optic). Homes passed: 1,540.
Executive Vice President & General Manager: Gregory F. Chapados. Vice President, Content & Product Management: Robert W. Ormberg. Chief Technician: Robert David.
Ownership: GCI Cable Inc.

Alaska—Cable Systems

BETHEL—GCI Cable Inc, 210 3rd St, PO Box 247, Bethel, AK 99559. Phones: 907-265-5600 (Anchorage office); 907-543-3226. Fax: 907-543-5127. E-mail: support@gci.net. Web Site: http://www.gci.com. ICA: AK0050.
TV Market Ranking: Outside TV Markets (BETHEL).
Channel capacity: N.A. Channels available but not in use: N.A.

Basic Service
Subscribers: 923. Commercial subscribers: 15.
Programming (via microwave): KAKM (PBS) Anchorage; KTBY (FOX) Anchorage; KTUU-TV (NBC) Anchorage; KTVA (CBS) Anchorage; KYUR (ABC, CW) Anchorage.
Programming (via satellite): C-SPAN; C-SPAN 2; Pop; QVC; WGN America.
Fee: $25.50 installation; $33.95 monthly.

Expanded Basic Service 1
Subscribers: N.A.
Programming (via satellite): A&E; AMC; Animal Planet; Cartoon Network; CMT; CNBC; CNN; Comedy Central; Discovery Channel; Disney Channel; Disney XD; ESPN; ESPN2; Food Network; Freeform; HGTV; History; HLN; Lifetime; MSNBC; MTV; Nickelodeon; Outdoor Channel; Spike TV; Syfy; TBS; The Weather Channel; TLC; TNT; Travel Channel; Trinity Broadcasting Network (TBN); truTV; Turner Classic Movies; TV Land; USA Network; VH1.
Fee: $66.40 monthly.

Digital Pay Service 1
Pay Units: N.A.
Programming (via satellite): Cinemax (multiplexed); Flix; HBO (multiplexed); Showtime (multiplexed); Starz (multiplexed); Starz Encore (multiplexed); Sundance TV; The Movie Channel (multiplexed).
Fee: $10.95 - $13.95 monthly (each).

Video-On-Demand: No

Pay-Per-View
iN DEMAND (delivered digitally); Adult Swim (delivered digitally).

Internet Service
Operational: Yes.
Broadband Service: GCI Hypernet.
Fee: $24.99 monthly.

Telephone Service
Digital: Operational
Miles of Plant: 23.0 (coaxial); None (fiber optic). Homes passed: 2,388.
Executive Vice President & General Manager: Gregory F. Chapados. Vice President, Content Product Management: Robert W. Ormberg.
Ownership: GCI Cable Inc. (MSO).

CORDOVA—GCI Cable Inc, PO Box 828, Cordova, AK 99574. Phone: 907-424-7317. Fax: 907-424-5138. E-mail: support@gci.net. Web Site: http://www.gci.com. ICA: AK0012.
TV Market Ranking: Outside TV Markets (CORDOVA). Franchise award date: N.A. Franchise expiration date: N.A. Began: April 1, 1968.
Channel capacity: 40 (operating 2-way). Channels available but not in use: N.A.

Basic Service
Subscribers: 516. Commercial subscribers: 11.
Programming (received off-air): KTBY (FOX) Anchorage; KTOO-TV (PBS) Juneau; KTUU-TV (NBC) Anchorage; KTVA (CBS) Anchorage; KYUR (ABC, CW) Anchorage; 8 FMs.
Programming (via satellite): C-SPAN; C-SPAN 2; Pop; QVC; WGN America.
Fee: $25.50 installation; $33.95 monthly; $1.00 converter.

Expanded Basic Service 1
Subscribers: N.A.
Programming (via satellite): A&E; AMC; Animal Planet; CMT; CNBC; CNN; Comedy Central; Discovery Channel; Disney Channel; Disney XD; ESPN; ESPN2; Food Network; Fox News Channel; Freeform; HGTV; History; HLN; Lifetime; MSNBC; MTV; Nickelodeon; Northwest Cable News; Outdoor Channel; Spike TV; Syfy; TBS; The Weather Channel; TLC; TNT; Travel Channel; Trinity Broadcasting Network (TBN); USA Network; VH1.
Fee: $36.84 installation; $69.07 monthly.

Digital Pay Service 1
Pay Units: 79.
Programming (via satellite): Cinemax (multiplexed).
Fee: $10.95 monthly.

Digital Pay Service 2
Pay Units: 153.
Programming (via satellite): HBO (multiplexed).
Fee: $13.95 monthly.

Digital Pay Service 3
Pay Units: 56.
Programming (via satellite): Flix; Showtime (multiplexed); Sundance TV; The Movie Channel (multiplexed).
Fee: $12.95 monthly.

Digital Pay Service 4
Pay Units: 55.
Programming (via satellite): Starz (multiplexed); Starz Encore (multiplexed).
Fee: $12.95 monthly.

Video-On-Demand: No

Pay-Per-View
iN DEMAND (delivered digitally); Adult Swim (delivered digitally).

Internet Service
Operational: Yes. Began: July 1, 2002.
Broadband Service: GCI Hypernet.
Fee: $24.99 monthly.

Telephone Service
Digital: Operational
Miles of Plant: 24.0 (coaxial); None (fiber optic). Homes passed: 1,193.
Executive Vice President & General Manager: Gregory F. Chapados. Vice President, Content Product Management: Robert W. Ormberg. Chief Technician: Jesse Carter.
Ownership: GCI Cable Inc. (MSO).

CRAIG—Craig Cable TV Inc, 1301 Water Tower Rd, PO Box 131, Craig, AK 99921-0131. Phone: 907-826-3470. Fax: 907-826-3469. E-mail: office@craigcabletv.com. Web Site: http://www.craigcabletv.com. ICA: AK0034.
TV Market Ranking: Outside TV Markets (CRAIG).
Channel capacity: N.A. Channels available but not in use: N.A.

Basic Service
Subscribers: N.A.
Programming (received off-air): KAKM (PBS) Anchorage; KTBY (FOX) Anchorage; KYUR (ABC, CW) Anchorage.
Programming (via microwave): KING-TV (NBC) Seattle; KIRO-TV (CBS, getTV, Retro TV) Seattle.
Programming (via satellite): Alaska Rural Communications Service (ARCS); CMT; CNN; Discovery Channel; Disney Channel; ESPN; Freeform; HLN; Lifetime; MTV; NASA TV; Nickelodeon; Pop; Showtime; Spike TV; Syfy; TBS; The Movie Channel; TLC; TNT; USA Network; VH1; WGN America.
Fee: $45.00 installation; $45.00 monthly.

Pay Service 1
Pay Units: N.A.
Programming (via satellite): Cinemax (multiplexed); Showtime; The Movie Channel.
Fee: $10.00 monthly (HBO/Cinemax or Showtime/TMC).

Video-On-Demand: No

Internet Service
Operational: Yes.
Fee: $45.00-$125.00 monthly.

Telephone Service
None
Miles of Plant: 10.0 (coaxial); None (fiber optic).
General Manager: Bob McNamara.
Ownership: Craig Cable TV Inc.

DILLINGHAM—Nushagak Cooperative Inc, 557 Kenny Wren Rd, PO Box 350, Dillingham, AK 99576-0350. Phones: 907-842-5295; 800-478-5296; 907-842-5251. Fax: 907-842-2799. E-mail: nushtel@nushtel.com. Web Site: http://www.nushtel.com. ICA: AK0017.
TV Market Ranking: Outside TV Markets (DILLINGHAM). Franchise award date: N.A. Franchise expiration date: N.A. Began: November 1, 1994.
Channel capacity: N.A. Channels available but not in use: N.A.

Basic Service
Subscribers: 332.
Programming (via satellite): Alaska Rural Communications Service (ARCS).
Programming (via translator): KTVA (CBS) Anchorage; KUAC-TV (PBS) Fairbanks.
Fee: $38.05 installation; $85.00 monthly.

Video-On-Demand: No

Internet Service
Operational: Yes.
Fee: $38.05 installation; $54.95-$144.95 monthly.

Telephone Service
Analog: Operational
Miles of Plant: 27.0 (coaxial); None (fiber optic). Homes passed: 635.
President: Pete Andrews. Customer Service Manager: Nancy Favors.
Ownership: Nushagak Cooperative Inc.

FAIRBANKS—GCI Cable Inc, 510 Mehar Ave, Ste A, Fairbanks, AK 99701. Phones: 800-800-4800; 907-452-7191. Fax: 907-374-4673. E-mail: support@gci.net. Web Site: http://www.gci.com. Also serves Eielson AFB, Fairbanks County (unincorporated areas), Fort Wainwright, North Pole & North Star Borough. ICA: AK0002.
TV Market Ranking: Below 100 (Eielson AFB, FAIRBANKS, Fairbanks County (unincorporated areas) (portions), Fort Wainwright, North Pole, North Star Borough); Outside TV Markets (Fairbanks County (unincorporated areas) (portions)). Franchise award date: N.A. Franchise expiration date: N.A. Began: September 15, 1979.
Channel capacity: N.A. Channels available but not in use: N.A.

Basic Service
Subscribers: 11,261.
Programming (received off-air): K13XD-D (CBS) Fairbanks; KATN (ABC, CW) Fairbanks; KFXF (FOX) Fairbanks; KJNP-TV (IND) North Pole; KTVF (NBC) Fairbanks; KUAC (PBS) Fairbanks.
Programming (via satellite): C-SPAN; C-SPAN 2; CW PLUS; Pop; WGN America.
Fee: $25.50 installation; $33.95 monthly.

Expanded Basic Service 1
Subscribers: N.A.
Programming (via satellite): A&E; AMC; Animal Planet; BET; Bravo; Cartoon Network; CMT; CNBC; CNN; Comedy Central; Discovery Channel; Disney Channel; Disney XD; E! HD; ESPN; ESPN2; EVINE Live; Food Network; Fox News Channel; Freeform; Fuse; FX; HGTV; History; HLN; Lifetime; LMN; MSNBC; MTV; National Geographic Channel; NBCSN; NFL Network; Nickelodeon; Outdoor Channel; Oxygen; QVC; Spike TV; Syfy; TBS; The Weather Channel; TLC; TNT; Travel Channel; truTV; Turner Classic Movies; TV Land; Univision Studios; USA Network; VH1; WE tv.
Fee: $9.11 installation; $57.75 monthly; $2.82 converter.

Digital Basic Service
Subscribers: N.A.
Programming (via satellite): 3ABN; AWE; AXS TV; BBC America; Bloomberg Television; Boomerang; BYUtv; Church Channel; CNN International; Daystar TV Network; Discovery Digital Networks; DIY Network; ESPN HD; ESPNews; EWTN Global Catholic Network; FamilyNet; FOX College Sports Central; FOX College Sports Pacific; Fox Sports 1; Fox Sports 2; FYI; Golf Channel; Great American Country; GSN; HD Theater; History; History International; IFC; INSP; MC; NFL Network; Nick Jr.; Nicktoons; TeenNick; Tennis Channel; TNT HD; Trinity Broadcasting Network (TBN); TVG Network; Universal HD; UP.

Digital Pay Service 1
Pay Units: 2,024.
Programming (via satellite): Cinemax (multiplexed); Cinemax HD.
Fee: $10.95 monthly.

Digital Pay Service 2
Pay Units: 2,597.
Programming (via satellite): Flix; Showtime (multiplexed); Showtime HD; The Movie Channel (multiplexed); The Movie Channel HD.
Fee: $12.95 monthly.

Digital Pay Service 3
Pay Units: 8,093.
Programming (via satellite): HBO (multiplexed); HBO HD.
Fee: $13.95 monthly.

Digital Pay Service 4
Pay Units: 2,155.
Programming (via satellite): Starz (multiplexed); Starz Encore (multiplexed); Starz HD.
Fee: $12.95 monthly.

Video-On-Demand: No

Pay-Per-View
Hot Choice (delivered digitally); ESPN (delivered digitally); iN DEMAND (delivered digitally); Fresh (delivered digitally).

Internet Service
Operational: Yes.
Subscribers: 15,814.
Broadband Service: GCI Hypernet.
Fee: $24.99 monthly.

Telephone Service
Digital: Operational
Subscribers: 7,974.
Miles of Plant: 887.0 (coaxial); 249.0 (fiber optic). Homes passed: 38,126.
Executive Vice President & General Manager: Gregory F. Chapados. Vice President, Content Product Management: Robert W. Ormberg. Interior Operations Director: Marven E Smith. Regional Technical Manager: David Schram.
Ownership: GCI Cable Inc. (MSO).

FORT GREELY—GCI Cable Inc, 510 Mehar Ave, Ste A, Fairbanks, AK 99701. Phone: 800-800-4800. E-mail: support@gci.net. Web Site: http://www.gci.com. ICA: AK0052.

Cable Systems—Alaska

TV Market Ranking: Outside TV Markets (FORT GREELY).
Channel capacity: N.A. Channels available but not in use: N.A.
Basic Service
Subscribers: 31. Commercial subscribers: 2.
Fee: $25.50 installation; $33.95 monthly.
Internet Service
Operational: Yes.
Subscribers: 35.
Broadband Service: GCI Hypernet.
Miles of Plant: 4.0 (coaxial); 3.0 (fiber optic). Homes passed: 811.
Executive Vice President & General Manager: Gregory F. Chapados. Vice President, Content Product Management: Robert W. Ormberg.
Ownership: GCI Cable Inc. (MSO).

GALENA—Eyecom Cable, 201 East 56th Ave, Anchorage, AK 99518-1283. Phones: 907-563-2003; 907-563-2074. Fax: 907-565-5539. E-mail: customerservice@telalaska.com. Web Site: http://www.telalaska.com. ICA: AK0035.
TV Market Ranking: Outside TV Markets (GALENA). Franchise award date: N.A. Franchise expiration date: N.A. Began: April 1, 1984.
Channel capacity: 60 (2-way capable). Channels available but not in use: N.A.
Basic Service
Subscribers: N.A.
Programming (via satellite): A&E; Animal Planet; Cartoon Network; CMT; CNBC; CNN; Discovery Channel; Disney Channel; ESPN; ESPN2; Freeform; History; HLN; Pop; Spike TV; Syfy; TBS; TLC; TNT; Turner Classic Movies; USA Network; WGN America.
Programming (via translator): KTBY (FOX) Anchorage; KTUU-TV (NBC) Anchorage; KTVA (CBS) Anchorage; KUAC-TV (PBS) Fairbanks; KYUR (ABC, CW) Anchorage.
Fee: $41.05 monthly.
Pay Service 1
Pay Units: N.A.
Programming (via satellite): Cinemax; HBO.
Fee: $10.95 - $13.95 monthly (each).
Video-On-Demand: No
Internet Service
Operational: No, DSL.
Telephone Service
Analog: Operational
Miles of Plant: 13.0 (coaxial); None (fiber optic).
President & Chief Executive Officer: Patrick Eudy. Vice President, Operations: Dave Goggins. Vice President, Marketing: Marnie Brennan. Chief Technician: Dan Christensen.
Ownership: Eyecom Inc. (MSO).

GAMBELL—Formerly served by Frontier Cable Inc. No longer in operation. ICA: AK0036.

GIRDWOOD—GCI Cable Inc, 2550 Denali St, Ste 5000, Anchorage, AK 99503. Phone: 800-800-4800. E-mail: support@gci.net. Web Site: http://www.gci.com. ICA: AK0018.
TV Market Ranking: Below 100 (GIRDWOOD). Franchise award date: May 1, 1986. Franchise expiration date: N.A. Began: April 1, 1987.
Channel capacity: N.A. Channels available but not in use: N.A.
Basic Service
Subscribers: 583. Commercial subscribers: 6.
Programming (received off-air): KAKM (PBS) Anchorage; KTBY (FOX) Anchorage; KTUU-TV (NBC) Anchorage; KTVA (CBS) Anchorage; KYUR (ABC, CW) Anchorage.
Programming (via satellite): A&E; AMC; Animal Planet; Bravo; Cartoon Network; CMT; CNBC; CNN; Comedy Central; Discovery Channel; Disney Channel; ESPN; ESPN2; Food Network; Freeform; HGTV; History; HLN; Lifetime; MSNBC; MTV; Nickelodeon; Spike TV; Syfy; TBS; TLC; TNT; Travel Channel; Turner Classic Movies; TV Land; USA Network; VH1; WGN America.
Fee: $25.50 installation; $33.95 monthly.
Pay Service 1
Pay Units: 37.
Programming (via satellite): Cinemax.
Fee: $10.95 monthly.
Pay Service 2
Pay Units: 91.
Programming (via satellite): HBO (multiplexed).
Fee: $13.95 monthly.
Video-On-Demand: No
Internet Service
Operational: No.
Telephone Service
None
Miles of Plant: 2,802.0 (coaxial); 567.0 (fiber optic). Homes passed: 150,404.
Executive Vice President & General Manager: Gregory F. Chapados. Vice President, Content Product Management: Robert W. Ormberg.
Ownership: GCI Cable Inc. (MSO).

HAINES—Haines Cable TV, 715 Main St, PO Box 1229, Haines, AK 99827-1229. Phones: 907-983-2205; 907-766-2337. Fax: 907-766-2345. E-mail: pcampbell99827@yahoo.com. Web Site: http://hainescable.com. ICA: AK0019.
TV Market Ranking: Outside TV Markets (HAINES). Franchise award date: April 1, 1967. Franchise expiration date: N.A. Began: August 1, 1972.
Channel capacity: N.A. Channels available but not in use: N.A.
Basic Service
Subscribers: N.A.
Programming (via microwave): KING-TV (NBC) Seattle.
Programming (via satellite): Alaska Rural Communications Service (ARCS); CNN; Disney Channel; ESPN; Freeform; FX; KCNC-TV (CBS, Decades) Denver; KUSA (NBC, WeatherNation) Denver; KWGN-TV (CW, This TV) Denver; QVC; Spike TV; Syfy; TLC; TNT; Trinity Broadcasting Network (TBN); USA Network; VH1; WGN America.
Programming (via translator): KYUR (ABC, CW) Anchorage.
Fee: $55.00 installation; $50.68 monthly.
Pay Service 1
Pay Units: N.A.
Programming (via satellite): Showtime.
Fee: $15.75 installation; $12.95 monthly.
Video-On-Demand: No
Pay-Per-View
iN DEMAND.
Internet Service
Operational: No.
Telephone Service
None
Miles of Plant: 42.0 (coaxial); None (fiber optic). Homes passed: 800.
General Manager: Patty Campbell. Chief Engineer: Andrew Glackin. Advertising Manager: Daniel Glackin.
Ownership: Haines & Skagway Cable TV (MSO).

HOMER—GCI Cable Inc, 3541 Greatland St, Homer, AK 99603. Phones: 800-800-4800; 907-235-6366. Fax: 907-235-6625. E-mail: support@gci.net. Web Site: http://www.gci.com. Also serves Kachemak City. ICA: AK0046.
TV Market Ranking: Outside TV Markets (HOMER, Kachemak City).
Channel capacity: 60 (operating 2-way). Channels available but not in use: N.A.
Basic Service
Subscribers: 487. Commercial subscribers: 7.
Programming (received off-air): KAKM (PBS) Anchorage; KTBY (FOX) Anchorage; KTUU-TV (NBC) Anchorage; KTVA (CBS) Anchorage; KYUR (ABC, CW) Anchorage.
Programming (via satellite): C-SPAN; C-SPAN 2; Pop; QVC.
Fee: $25.50 installation; $33.95 monthly.
Expanded Basic Service 1
Subscribers: N.A.
Programming (via satellite): A&E; AMC; Animal Planet; Bravo; Cartoon Network; CMT; CNBC; CNN; Comedy Central; Discovery Channel; Disney Channel; Disney XD; ESPN; ESPN2; Food Network; Fox News Channel; Freeform; HGTV; History; HLN; Lifetime; MSNBC; MTV; NBCSN; Nickelodeon; Northwest Cable News; Spike TV; Syfy; TBS; The Weather Channel; TLC; TNT; Travel Channel; Trinity Broadcasting Network (TBN); USA Network; VH1.
Fee: $39.47 monthly.
Digital Basic Service
Subscribers: N.A.
Programming (via satellite): MC.
Digital Pay Service 1
Pay Units: 75.
Programming (via satellite): Cinemax (multiplexed).
Fee: $10.95 monthly.
Digital Pay Service 2
Pay Units: 204.
Programming (via satellite): HBO (multiplexed).
Fee: $13.95 monthly.
Digital Pay Service 3
Pay Units: 75.
Programming (via satellite): Flix; Showtime (multiplexed); Sundance TV; The Movie Channel (multiplexed).
Fee: $12.95 monthly.
Digital Pay Service 4
Pay Units: 54.
Programming (via satellite): Starz (multiplexed); Starz Encore (multiplexed).
Fee: $12.95 monthly.
Video-On-Demand: No
Pay-Per-View
Adult Swim (delivered digitally); special events (delivered digitally).
Internet Service
Operational: Yes. Began: September 1, 2002.
Broadband Service: GCI Hypernet.
Fee: $24.99 monthly.
Telephone Service
Digital: Operational
Miles of Plant: 49.0 (coaxial); None (fiber optic). Homes passed: 2,092.
Executive Vice President & General Manager: Gregory F. Chapados. Vice President, Content Product Management: Robert W. Ormberg. Chief Technician: Charles D. Smith.
Ownership: GCI Cable Inc. (MSO).

HOONAH—Formerly served by Hoonah Community TV. No longer in operation. ICA: AK0037.

HOOPER BAY—Formerly served by Frontier Cable Inc. No longer in operation. ICA: AK0023.

JUNEAU—GCI Cable Inc, 8390 Airport Blvd, Ste 101, Juneau, AK 99801. Phones: 800-800-4800; 907-265-5600 (Administrative office); 907-586-3320. Fax: 907-463-3880. E-mail: support@gci.net. Web Site: http://www.gci.com. Also serves Auke Bay & Douglas. ICA: AK0003.
TV Market Ranking: Below 100 (Auke Bay, Douglas, JUNEAU). Franchise award date: January 1, 1966. Franchise expiration date: N.A. Began: January 1, 1966.
Channel capacity: N.A. Channels available but not in use: N.A.
Basic Service
Subscribers: 6,302.
Programming (received off-air): KJUD (ABC, CW, FOX) Juneau; KTBY (FOX) Anchorage; KTOO-TV (PBS) Juneau; 14 FMs.
Programming (via microwave): KTNL-TV (CBS, ION) Sitka.
Programming (via satellite): C-SPAN; C-SPAN 2; CW PLUS; Pop; Trinity Broadcasting Network (TBN); WGN America.
Fee: $25.50 installation; $19.70 monthly; $3.95 converter.
Expanded Basic Service 1
Subscribers: N.A.
Programming (via satellite): A&E; AMC; Animal Planet; Bravo; Cartoon Network; CMT; CNBC; CNN; Comedy Central; Discovery Channel; Disney Channel; Disney XD; E! HD; ESPN; ESPN2; EVINE Live; Food Network; Fox News Channel; Freeform; Fuse; FX; Hallmark Channel; HGTV; History; HLN; Lifetime; LMN; MSNBC; MTV; National Geographic Channel; NBCSN; NFL Network; Nickelodeon; Northwest Cable News; Outdoor Channel; Oxygen; QVC; Spike TV; Syfy; TBS; The Weather Channel; TLC; TNT; Travel Channel; truTV; Turner Classic Movies; TV Land; Univision Studios; USA Network; VH1; WE tv.
Fee: $24.09 monthly.
Digital Basic Service
Subscribers: N.A.
Programming (via satellite): 3ABN; AWE; AXS TV; BBC America; Bloomberg Television; Boomerang; BYUtv; Church Channel; CNN International; Daystar TV Network; Discovery Digital Networks; DIY Network; ESPN HD; ESPNews; EWTN Global Catholic Network; FamilyNet; FOX College Sports Central; FOX College Sports Pacific; Fox Sports 1; Fox Sports 2; FYI; Golf Channel; Great American Country; GSN; HD Theater; History; History International; IFC; INSP;

Alaska—Cable Systems

Access the most current data instantly
FREE TRIAL @ Advanced TVFactbook
TELCO/IPTV • CABLE TV • TV STATIONS
www.warren-news.com/factbook.htm

MavTV; MC; NFL Network; Nick Jr.; Nicktoons; TeenNick; Tennis Channel; TNT HD; TVG Network; Universal HD; UP.
Digital Pay Service 1
Pay Units: 631.
Programming (via satellite): Cinemax (multiplexed); Cinemax HD.
Fee: $10.95 monthly.
Digital Pay Service 2
Pay Units: 2,260.
Programming (via satellite): HBO (multiplexed); HBO HD.
Fee: $13.95 monthly.
Digital Pay Service 3
Pay Units: 737.
Programming (via satellite): Flix; Showtime (multiplexed); Showtime HD; The Movie Channel (multiplexed); The Movie Channel HD.
Fee: $12.95 monthly.
Digital Pay Service 4
Pay Units: 669.
Programming (via satellite): Starz (multiplexed); Starz Encore (multiplexed); Starz HD.
Fee: $12.95 monthly.
Digital Pay Service 5
Pay Units: 218.
Programming (via satellite): The Filipino Channel.
Fee: $13.99 monthly.
Video-On-Demand: No
Pay-Per-View
ESPN (delivered digitally); special events (delivered digitally); Adult Swim (delivered digitally).
Internet Service
Operational: Yes. Began: December 1, 1999.
Subscribers: 7,605.
Broadband Service: GCI Hypernet.
Fee: $24.99 monthly.
Telephone Service
Digital: Operational
Subscribers: 4,701.
Miles of Plant: 292.0 (coaxial); 112.0 (fiber optic). Homes passed: 15,230.
Executive Vice President & General Manager: Gregory F. Chapados. Vice President, Content Product Management: Robert W. Ormberg. Plant Manager: Rob Knorr.
Ownership: GCI Cable Inc. (MSO).

KENAI—GCI Cable Inc, 44661 Sterling Hwy, Ste E, Soldotna, AK 99669. Phones: 800-800-4800; 907-262-3266. E-mail: support@gci.net. Web Site: http://www.gci.com. Also serves Ridgeway & Soldotna. ICA: AK0051.
TV Market Ranking: Outside TV Markets (Ridgeway, KENAI, Soldotna).
Channel capacity: N.A. Channels available but not in use: N.A.
Basic Service
Subscribers: 2,236. Commercial subscribers: 37.
Programming (via microwave): KAKM (PBS) Anchorage; KTBY (FOX) Anchorage; KTUU-TV (NBC) Anchorage; KTVA (CBS) Anchorage; KYUR (ABC, CW) Anchorage.
Programming (via satellite): C-SPAN; C-SPAN 2; Pop; QVC; WGN America.
Fee: $25.50 installation; $33.95 monthly.
Expanded Basic Service 1
Subscribers: N.A.
Programming (via satellite): A&E; AMC; Animal Planet; Bravo; Cartoon Network; CMT; CNBC; CNN; Comedy Central; Discovery Channel; Disney Channel; Disney XD; E! HD; ESPN; ESPN2; Food Network; Fox News Channel; Freeform; FX; HGTV; History; HLN; Lifetime; LMN; MSNBC; MTV; Nickelodeon; Northwest Cable News; Outdoor Channel; Spike TV; Syfy; TBS; TLC; TNT; Travel Channel; truTV; Turner Classic Movies; USA Network; VH1.
Fee: $33.79 monthly.
Digital Basic Service
Subscribers: N.A.
Programming (via satellite): BBC America; Boomerang; Discovery Digital Networks; ESPNews; FOX College Sports Central; FOX College Sports Pacific; Fox Sports 1; GSN; History; IFC; MC.
Digital Pay Service 1
Pay Units: 1,878.
Programming (via satellite): Cinemax (multiplexed); Flix; HBO (multiplexed); Showtime (multiplexed); Starz (multiplexed); Starz Encore (multiplexed); The Movie Channel (multiplexed).
Fee: $10.95 monthly (Cinemax), $12.95 monthly (Showtime or Starz), $13.95 monthly (HBO).
Video-On-Demand: No
Pay-Per-View
Adult Swim (delivered digitally); special events (delivered digitally).
Internet Service
Operational: Yes.
Broadband Service: GCI Hypernet.
Fee: $54.99 monthly.
Telephone Service
Digital: Operational
Miles of Plant: 121.0 (coaxial); 18.0 (fiber optic). Homes passed: 6,251.
Executive Vice President & General Manager: Gregory F. Chapados. Vice President, Content Product Management: Robert W. Ormberg. Office Manager: Denise Daley. Chief Technician: Walt Zuck.
Ownership: GCI Cable Inc. (MSO).

KETCHIKAN—GCI Cable Inc, 2417 North Tongass, Ste 104, Ketchikan, AK 99901. Phone: 907-225-2191. Fax: 907-225-4943. E-mail: support@gci.net. Web Site: http://www.gci.com. Also serves Ketchikan Gateway Borough, Saxman & Ward Cove. ICA: AK0005.
TV Market Ranking: Below 100 (KETCHIKAN, Ketchikan Gateway Borough, Ward Cove, Saxman). Franchise award date: N.A. Franchise expiration date: N.A. Began: November 11, 1953.
Channel capacity: 57 (operating 2-way). Channels available but not in use: N.A.
Basic Service
Subscribers: 1,759. Commercial subscribers: 51.
Programming (received off-air): KJUD (ABC, CW, FOX) Juneau; KUBD (CBS, ION) Ketchikan.
Programming (via microwave): KING-TV (NBC) Seattle; KTBY (FOX) Anchorage.
Programming (via satellite): C-SPAN; C-SPAN 2; CW PLUS; Pop; QVC; Trinity Broadcasting Network (TBN); WGN America.
Fee: $25.50 installation; $28.75 monthly; $2.74 converter.
Expanded Basic Service 1
Subscribers: N.A.
Programming (via satellite): A&E; AMC; Animal Planet; Bravo; Cartoon Network; CMT; CNBC; CNN; Comedy Central; Discovery Channel; Disney Channel; Disney XD; E! HD; ESPN; ESPN2; Food Network; Fox News Channel; Freeform; FX; Hallmark Channel; HGTV; History; HLN; Lifetime; LMN; MSNBC; MTV; National Geographic Channel; NBCSN; NFL Network; Nickelodeon; Northwest Cable News; Outdoor Channel; Spike TV; Syfy; TBS; The Weather Channel; TLC; TNT; Travel Channel; truTV; Turner Classic Movies; TV Land; USA Network; VH1; WE tv.
Fee: $37.55 monthly.
Digital Basic Service
Subscribers: N.A.
Programming (via satellite): 3ABN; AXS TV; BBC America; Boomerang; BYUtv; Church Channel; Daystar TV Network; DIY Network; ESPN HD; ESPNews; EWTN Global Catholic Network; FamilyNet; FOX College Sports Central; Fox College Sports Pacific; Fox Sports 1; Fox Sports 2; FXM; GSN; HD Theater; History; IFC; INSP; MC; NFL Network; Nick Jr.; Nicktoons; TeenNick; TNT HD; TVG Network; Universal HD.
Digital Pay Service 1
Pay Units: 316.
Programming (via satellite): Cinemax (multiplexed); Cinemax HD.
Fee: $10.95 monthly.
Digital Pay Service 2
Pay Units: 657.
Programming (via satellite): HBO (multiplexed); HBO HD.
Fee: $13.95 monthly.
Digital Pay Service 3
Pay Units: 298.
Programming (via satellite): Flix; Showtime (multiplexed); Showtime HD; Sundance TV; The Movie Channel (multiplexed); The Movie Channel HD.
Fee: $12.95 monthly.
Digital Pay Service 4
Pay Units: 274.
Programming (via satellite): Starz (multiplexed); Starz Encore (multiplexed); Starz HD.
Fee: $12.95 monthly.
Digital Pay Service 5
Pay Units: 88.
Programming (via satellite): The Filipino Channel.
Fee: $13.99 monthly.
Video-On-Demand: No
Pay-Per-View
Adult Swim (delivered digitally); special events (delivered digitally).
Internet Service
Operational: Yes.
Broadband Service: GCI Hypernet.
Fee: $24.99 monthly.
Telephone Service
Digital: Operational
Miles of Plant: 74.0 (coaxial); 18.0 (fiber optic). Homes passed: 6,924.
Executive Vice President & General Manager: Gregory F. Chapados. Vice President, Content Product Management: Robert W. Ormberg. Chief Technician: Russell Tramell.
Ownership: GCI Cable Inc. (MSO).

KING COVE—Formerly served by Mount Dutton Cable Corp. No longer in operation. ICA: AK0024.

KING SALMON—Bay Cablevision, 1 Main St, PO Box 259, King Salmon, AK 99613. Phones: 907-246-3403; 907-246-3300; 800-478-9100. Fax: 907-246-1115. E-mail: bbtccsr@bristolbay.com. Web Site: http://www.bristolbay.com. Also serves Naknek. ICA: AK0015.
TV Market Ranking: Outside TV Markets (KING SALMON, Naknek). Franchise award date: N.A. Franchise expiration date: N.A. Began: January 1, 1986.
Channel capacity: N.A. Channels available but not in use: N.A.
Basic Service
Subscribers: N.A.
Programming (via satellite): A&E; Alaska Rural Communications Service (ARCS); AMC; Animal Planet; CMT; CNN; Discovery Channel; Disney Channel; ESPN; ESPN2; Food Network; Freeform; HGTV; History; MTV; Nickelodeon; Spike TV; Syfy; TBS; TLC; TNT; Trinity Broadcasting Network (TBN); Turner Classic Movies; TV Land; USA Network; VH1; WGN America.
Programming (via translator): KTVA (CBS) Anchorage; KUAC-TV (PBS) Fairbanks; KYUR (ABC, CW) Anchorage.
Fee: $40.00 installation; $50.00 monthly.
Pay Service 1
Pay Units: N.A.
Programming (via satellite): Cinemax; HBO.
Fee: $17.50 monthly (each).
Video-On-Demand: No
Internet Service
Operational: Yes.
Telephone Service
Analog: Operational
Miles of Plant: 15.0 (coaxial); None (fiber optic). Homes passed: 700.
General Manager: Todd Hoppe. Plant Supervisor: Earl Hubb. Chief Technician: Robert Hadfield.
Ownership: Bristol Bay Telephone Cooperative Inc.

KIPNUK—Formerly served by Frontier Cable Inc. No longer in operation. ICA: AK0027.

KODIAK—GCI Cable Inc, 2011 Mill Bay Rd, Kodiak, AK 99615-6991. Phone: 907-486-3334. Fax: 907-486-5160. E-mail: support@gci.net. Web Site: http://www.gci.com. Also serves Kodiak Island Borough. ICA: AK0006.
TV Market Ranking: Outside TV Markets (KODIAK, Kodiak Island Borough). Franchise award date: N.A. Franchise expiration date: N.A. Began: July 1, 1969.
Channel capacity: N.A. Channels available but not in use: N.A.
Basic Service
Subscribers: 2,224. Commercial subscribers: 40.
Programming (via satellite): C-SPAN; C-SPAN 2; CW PLUS; Pop; WGN America.
Programming (via translator): KTBY (FOX) Anchorage; KTUU-TV (NBC) Anchorage; KTVA (CBS) Anchorage; KYUR (ABC, CW) Anchorage.
Fee: $35.50 installation; $33.95 monthly.
Expanded Basic Service 1
Subscribers: N.A.
Programming (via satellite): A&E; AMC; Animal Planet; BET; Bravo; Cartoon Net-

Cable Systems—Alaska

work; CMT; CNBC; CNN; Comedy Central; Discovery Channel; Disney Channel; Disney XD; E! HD; ESPN; ESPN2; EVINE Live; Food Network; Fox News Channel; Freeform; Fuse; FX; HGTV; History; HLN; Lifetime; LMN; MSNBC; MTV; National Geographic Channel; NBCSN; NFL Network; Nickelodeon; Northwest Cable News; Outdoor Channel; Oxygen; QVC; Spike TV; Syfy; TBS; The Weather Channel; TLC; TNT; Travel Channel; truTV; Turner Classic Movies; TV Land; Univision Studios; USA Network; VH1; WE tv.
Fee: $43.79 monthly.

Digital Basic Service
Subscribers: N.A.
Programming (via satellite): 3ABN; AWE; AXS TV; BBC America; Bloomberg Television; Boomerang; BYUtv; Church Channel; CNN International; Daystar TV Network; Discovery Digital Networks; DIY Network; ESPN HD; ESPNews; EWTN Global Catholic Network; FamilyNet; FOX College Sports Central; FOX College Sports Pacific; Fox Sports 1; Fox Sports 2; FYI; Golf Channel; Great American Country; GSN; HD Theater; History; History International; IFC; INSP; MavTV; MC; NFL Network; Nick Jr.; Nicktoons; TeenNick; Tennis Channel; TNT HD; Trinity Broadcasting Network (TBN); TVG Network; Universal HD; UP.

Digital Pay Service 1
Pay Units: 365.
Programming (via satellite): Cinemax (multiplexed); Cinemax HD.
Fee: $10.95 monthly.

Digital Pay Service 2
Pay Units: 829.
Programming (via satellite): HBO (multiplexed); HBO HD.
Fee: $13.95 monthly.

Digital Pay Service 3
Pay Units: 250.
Programming (via satellite): Flix; Showtime (multiplexed); Showtime HD; The Movie Channel (multiplexed); The Movie Channel HD.
Fee: $12.95 monthly.

Digital Pay Service 4
Pay Units: 256.
Programming (via satellite): Starz (multiplexed); Starz Encore (multiplexed); Starz HD.
Fee: $12.95 monthly.

Digital Pay Service 5
Pay Units: 439.
Programming (via satellite): The Filipino Channel.
Fee: $12.95 monthly.

Video-On-Demand: No

Pay-Per-View
Adult Swim (delivered digitally); special events (delivered digitally).

Internet Service
Operational: Yes. Began: October 17, 2002.
Broadband Service: GCI Hypernet.
Fee: $24.99 monthly.

Telephone Service
Digital: Operational
Miles of Plant: 113.0 (coaxial); 38.0 (fiber optic). Homes passed: 5,661.
Executive Vice President & General Manager: Gregory F. Chapados. Vice President, Content Product Management: Robert W. Ormberg.
Ownership: GCI Cable Inc. (MSO).

KOTZEBUE—GCI Cable Inc, 606 Bison St, PO Box 750, Kotzebue, AK 99752. Phone: 907-442-2620. Fax: 907-442-3732. E-mail: support@gci.net. Web Site: http://www.gci.com. ICA: AK0016.

TV Market Ranking: Outside TV Markets (KOTZEBUE). Franchise award date: N.A. Franchise expiration date: N.A. Began: January 1, 1973.
Channel capacity: 63 (2-way capable). Channels available but not in use: N.A.

Basic Service
Subscribers: 517. Commercial subscribers: 8.
Programming (via microwave): KAKM (PBS) Anchorage; KTBY (FOX) Anchorage; KTUU-TV (NBC) Anchorage; KTVA (CBS) Anchorage; KYUR (ABC, CW) Anchorage.
Programming (via satellite): Alaska Rural Communications Service (ARCS); C-SPAN; C-SPAN 2; Pop; QVC; WGN America.
Fee: $35.50 installation; $33.95 monthly.

Expanded Basic Service 1
Subscribers: N.A.
Programming (via satellite): A&E; AMC; Animal Planet; Cartoon Network; CMT; CNBC; CNN; Comedy Central; Discovery Channel; Disney Channel; Disney XD; ESPN; ESPN2; Food Network; Freeform; HGTV; History; HLN; Lifetime; MSNBC; MTV; Nickelodeon; Outdoor Channel; Spike TV; Syfy; TBS; The Weather Channel; TLC; TNT; Travel Channel; Trinity Broadcasting Network (TBN); Turner Classic Movies; TV Land; USA Network; VH1.
Fee: $42.86 monthly.

Digital Basic Service
Subscribers: N.A.
Programming (via satellite): MC.

Digital Pay Service 1
Pay Units: 196.
Programming (via satellite): Cinemax (multiplexed).
Fee: $10.95 monthly.

Digital Pay Service 2
Pay Units: 242.
Programming (via satellite): HBO (multiplexed).
Fee: $13.95 monthly.

Digital Pay Service 3
Pay Units: 219.
Programming (via satellite): Flix; Showtime (multiplexed); Sundance TV; The Movie Channel (multiplexed).
Fee: $12.95 monthly.

Digital Pay Service 4
Pay Units: 148.
Programming (via satellite): Starz (multiplexed); Starz Encore (multiplexed).
Fee: $12.95 monthly.

Video-On-Demand: No

Pay-Per-View
iN DEMAND (delivered digitally); Adult Swim (delivered digitally).

Internet Service
Operational: No.

Telephone Service
None
Miles of Plant: 7.0 (coaxial); None (fiber optic). Homes passed: 1,144.
Executive Vice President & General Manager: Gregory F. Chapados. Vice President, Content Product Management: Robert W. Ormberg. Marketing Director: Taryl Gebhardt.
Ownership: GCI Cable Inc. (MSO).

MOUNTAIN VILLAGE—Formerly served by Village Cable Co. No longer in operation. ICA: AK0022.

NOME—GCI Cable Inc, PO Box 274, Nome, AK 99762. Phones: 800-800-4800; 907-265-5600 (Administrative office); 907-443-2550. Fax: 907-443-5845. E-mail: support@gci.net. Web Site: http://www.gci.com. ICA: AK0038.

TV Market Ranking: Outside TV Markets (NOME). Franchise award date: N.A. Franchise expiration date: N.A. Began: February 1, 1971.
Channel capacity: 67 (operating 2-way). Channels available but not in use: N.A.

Basic Service
Subscribers: 795. Commercial subscribers: 13.
Programming (via microwave): KAKM (PBS) Anchorage; KTBY (FOX) Anchorage; KTUU-TV (NBC) Anchorage; KTVA (CBS) Anchorage; KYUR (ABC, CW) Anchorage.
Programming (via satellite): C-SPAN; C-SPAN 2; Pop; WGN America.
Fee: $25.50 installation; $33.95 monthly.

Expanded Basic Service 1
Subscribers: N.A.
Programming (via satellite): A&E; AMC; Animal Planet; BET; Bravo; Cartoon Network; CMT; CNBC; CNN; Comedy Central; Discovery Channel; Disney Channel; Disney XD; E! HD; ESPN; ESPN2; EVINE Live; Food Network; Freeform; HGTV; History; HLN; Lifetime; LMN; MSNBC; MTV; Nickelodeon; Outdoor Channel; QVC; Spike TV; Syfy; TBS; The Weather Channel; TLC; TNT; Travel Channel; truTV; Turner Classic Movies; TV Land; Univision Studios; USA Network; VH1; WE tv.
Fee: $47.29 monthly.

Digital Basic Service
Subscribers: N.A.
Programming (via satellite): 3ABN; AWE; AXS TV; BBC America; Bloomberg Television; Boomerang; BYUtv; Church Channel; CNN International; Daystar TV Network; Destination America; Discovery Kids Channel; DIY Network; ESPN HD; ESPNews; FamilyNet; FYI; Great American Country; GSN; HD Theater; History International; IFC; INSP; Investigation Discovery; MC; MTV Classic; MTV Hits; MTV2; Nick Jr.; Nicktoons; OWN: Oprah Winfrey Network; Science Channel; TeenNick; TNT HD; Trinity Broadcasting Network (TBN); Universal HD.

Digital Pay Service 1
Pay Units: 193.
Programming (via satellite): Cinemax (multiplexed); Cinemax HD; HBO HD; Showtime HD; Starz HD; The Movie Channel HD.
Fee: $10.95 monthly.

Digital Pay Service 2
Pay Units: 325.
Programming (via satellite): HBO (multiplexed).
Fee: $13.95 monthly.

Digital Pay Service 3
Pay Units: 137.
Programming (via satellite): Flix; Showtime (multiplexed); The Movie Channel (multiplexed).
Fee: $12.95 monthly.

Digital Pay Service 4
Pay Units: 152.
Programming (via satellite): Starz (multiplexed); Starz Encore (multiplexed).
Fee: $12.95 monthly.

Video-On-Demand: No

Pay-Per-View
iN DEMAND (delivered digitally); Adult Swim (delivered digitally).

Internet Service
Operational: Yes.
Broadband Service: GCI Hypernet.
Fee: $24.99 monthly.

Telephone Service
Digital: Operational
Miles of Plant: 21.0 (coaxial); 1.0 (fiber optic). Homes passed: 1,625.
Executive Vice President & General Manager: Gregory F. Chapados. Vice President, Content & Product Management: Robert W. Ormberg. Chief Technician: Earl Merchant.
Ownership: GCI Cable Inc. (MSO).

PETERSBURG—GCI Cable Inc, PO Box 1167, Anchorage, AK 99833. Phones: 907-265-5600 (Corporate office); 907-772-3292. Fax: 907-772-3942. E-mail: support@gci.net. Web Site: http://www.gci.com. ICA: AK0011.

TV Market Ranking: Outside TV Markets (PETERSBURG). Franchise award date: December 1, 1980. Franchise expiration date: N.A. Began: September 1, 1968.
Channel capacity: 40 (operating 2-way). Channels available but not in use: N.A.

Basic Service
Subscribers: 738. Commercial subscribers: 11.
Programming (via microwave): KING-TV (NBC) Seattle; KJUD (ABC, CW, FOX) Juneau; KTBY (FOX) Anchorage; KTOO-TV (PBS) Juneau; KTVA (CBS) Anchorage.
Programming (via satellite): C-SPAN; C-SPAN 2; Pop; QVC; WGN America.
Fee: $25.50 installation; $33.95 monthly.

Expanded Basic Service 1
Subscribers: N.A.
Programming (via satellite): A&E; AMC; Animal Planet; Cartoon Network; CMT; CNBC; CNN; Comedy Central; Discovery Channel; Disney Channel; Disney XD; ESPN; ESPN2; Food Network; Fox News Channel; Freeform; Hallmark Channel; HGTV; History; HLN; Lifetime; MSNBC; MTV; NBCSN; Nickelodeon; Northwest Cable News; Outdoor Channel; Spike TV; Syfy; TBS; The Weather Channel; TLC; TNT; Travel Channel; Trinity Broadcasting Network (TBN); truTV; TV Land; USA Network; VH1.
Fee: $26.50 installation; $35.29 monthly.

Digital Basic Service
Subscribers: N.A.
Programming (via satellite): DMX Music.

Digital Pay Service 1
Pay Units: 139.
Programming (via satellite): Cinemax (multiplexed); Showtime (multiplexed).
Fee: $10.95 monthly.

Digital Pay Service 2
Pay Units: 213.
Programming (via satellite): HBO (multiplexed).
Fee: $13.95 monthly.

Digital Pay Service 3
Pay Units: 117.
Programming (via satellite): Flix; Sundance TV; The Movie Channel (multiplexed).
Fee: $12.95 monthly.

Alaska—Cable Systems

Digital Pay Service 4
Pay Units: 80.
Programming (via satellite): Starz (multiplexed); Starz Encore (multiplexed).
Fee: $12.95 monthly.
Video-On-Demand: No
Pay-Per-View
Adult Swim (delivered digitally); special events (delivered digitally).
Internet Service
Operational: Yes. Began: July 1, 2002.
Broadband Service: GCI Hypernet.
Fee: $99.99 installation; $24.99 monthly.
Telephone Service
Digital: Operational
Miles of Plant: 25.0 (coaxial); None (fiber optic). Homes passed: 1,583.
Executive Vice President & General Manager: Gregory F. Chapados. Vice President, Content & Product Management: Robert W. Ormberg. Chief Technician: Perry Allen.
Ownership: GCI Cable Inc. (MSO).

PORT LIONS—Formerly served by Eyecom Cable. No longer in operation. ICA: AK0026.

QUINHAGAK—Formerly served by Frontier Cable Inc. No longer in operation. ICA: AK0039.

SAVOONGA—Formerly served by Frontier Cable Inc. No longer in operation. ICA: AK0040.

SEWARD—GCI Cable Inc, PO Box 929, Seward, AK 99664. Phones: 800-800-4800; 907-224-8912. Fax: 907-224-7318. E-mail: support@gci.net. Web Site: http://www.gci.com. Also serves Kenai Peninsula. ICA: AK0009.
TV Market Ranking: Outside TV Markets (Kenai Peninsula, SEWARD). Franchise award date: December 1, 1986. Franchise expiration date: N.A. Began: June 5, 1987.
Channel capacity: N.A. Channels available but not in use: N.A.
Basic Service
Subscribers: 867. Commercial subscribers: 16.
Programming (via microwave): KTBY (FOX) Anchorage; KTOO-TV (PBS) Juneau; KTUU-TV (NBC) Anchorage; KTVA (CBS) Anchorage; KYUR (ABC, CW) Anchorage.
Programming (via satellite): Alaska Rural Communications Service (ARCS); C-SPAN; C-SPAN 2; CW PLUS; Pop; WGN America.
Fee: $25.50 installation; $33.95 monthly.
Expanded Basic Service 1
Subscribers: N.A.
Programming (via satellite): A&E; AMC; Animal Planet; BET; Bravo; Cartoon Network; CMT; CNBC; CNN; Comedy Central; Discovery Channel; Disney Channel; Disney XD; E! HD; ESPN; ESPN2; EVINE Live; Food Network; Fox News Channel; Fox Sports 1; Freeform; Fuse; FX; HGTV; History; HLN; Lifetime; LMN; MSNBC; MTV; National Geographic Channel; NBCSN; NFL Network; Nickelodeon; Outdoor Channel; Oxygen; QVC; Spike TV; Syfy; TBS; The Weather Channel; TLC; TNT; Travel Channel; truTV; Turner Classic Movies; TV Land; Univision Studios; USA Network; VH1; WE tv.
Fee: $40.28 monthly.
Digital Basic Service
Subscribers: N.A.
Programming (via satellite): 3ABN; AWE; BBC America; Bloomberg Television; Boomerang; BYUtv; Church Channel; CNN International; Daystar TV Network; Destination America; Discovery Kids Channel; DIY Network; ESPNews; EWTN Global Catholic Network; FamilyNet; FOX College Sports Central; FOX College Sports Pacific; Fox Sports 2; FYI; Golf Channel; Great American Country; GSN; History International; HRTV; IFC; INSP; International Television (ITV); Investigation Discovery; MC; MTV Classic; MTV Hits; MTV2; Nick Jr.; Nicktoons; OWN: Oprah Winfrey Network; Science Channel; TeenNick; Tennis Channel; Trinity Broadcasting Network (TBN); UP.
Digital Pay Service 1
Pay Units: 111.
Programming (via satellite): Cinemax (multiplexed).
Fee: $10.95 monthly.
Digital Pay Service 2
Pay Units: 386.
Programming (via satellite): HBO (multiplexed).
Fee: $13.95 monthly.
Digital Pay Service 3
Pay Units: 115.
Programming (via satellite): Flix; Showtime (multiplexed); The Movie Channel (multiplexed).
Fee: $12.95 monthly.
Digital Pay Service 4
Pay Units: 81.
Programming (via satellite): Starz (multiplexed); Starz Encore (multiplexed).
Fee: $12.95 monthly.
Video-On-Demand: No
Pay-Per-View
Adult Swim (delivered digitally); special events (delivered digitally).
Internet Service
Operational: Yes. Began: December 1, 2001.
Broadband Service: GCI Hypernet.
Fee: $24.99 monthly.
Telephone Service
Digital: Operational
Miles of Plant: 43.0 (coaxial); None (fiber optic). Homes passed: 1,923.
Executive Vice President & General Manager: Gregory F. Chapados. Vice President, Content Product Management: Robert W. Ormberg. Office Manager: Jeannette Kimes. Chief Technician: Gary Lindquist.
Ownership: GCI Cable Inc. (MSO).

SITKA—GCI Cable Inc, PO Box 274, Nome, AK 99762. Phone: 907-747-3535. Fax: 907-747-4929. E-mail: support@gci.net. Web Site: http://www.gci.com. Also serves Sitka County. ICA: AK0007.
TV Market Ranking: Below 100 (SITKA, Sitka County (portions)); Outside TV Markets (Sitka County (portions)). Franchise award date: N.A. Franchise expiration date: N.A. Began: November 15, 1959.
Channel capacity: 58 (operating 2-way). Channels available but not in use: N.A.
Basic Service
Subscribers: 1,721. Commercial subscribers: 31.
Programming (received off-air): KSCT-LP (NBC) Sitka; KTNL-TV (CBS, ION) Sitka.
Programming (via microwave): KING-TV (NBC) Seattle; KJUD (ABC, CW, FOX) Juneau; KTBY (FOX) Anchorage; KTOO-TV (PBS) Juneau.
Programming (via satellite): C-SPAN; C-SPAN 2; CW PLUS; Pop; WGN America.
Fee: $25.50 installation; $32.45 monthly; $1.59 converter.
Expanded Basic Service 1
Subscribers: N.A.
Programming (via satellite): A&E; AMC; Animal Planet; BET; Bravo; Cartoon Network; CMT; CNBC; CNN; Comedy Central; Discovery Channel; Disney Channel; Disney XD; E! HD; ESPN; ESPN2; EVINE Live; Food Network; Fox News Channel; Freeform; Fuse; FX; HGTV; History; HLN; Lifetime; LMN; MSNBC; MTV; National Geographic Channel; NBCSN; NFL Network; Nickelodeon; Northwest Cable News; Outdoor Channel; Oxygen; QVC; Spike TV; Syfy; TBS; The Weather Channel; TLC; TNT; Travel Channel; truTV; Turner Classic Movies; TV Land; Univision Studios; USA Network; VH1; WE tv.
Fee: $12.08 installation; $41.29 monthly.
Digital Basic Service
Subscribers: N.A.
Programming (via satellite): 3ABN; AWE; AXS TV; BBC America; Bloomberg Television; Boomerang; BYUtv; Church Channel; CNN International; Daystar TV Network; Discovery Digital Networks; DIY Network; ESPN HD; ESPNews; EWTN Global Catholic Network; FamilyNet; FOX College Sports Central; FOX College Sports Pacific; Fox Sports 1; Fox Sports 2; FYI; Golf Channel; Great American Country; GSN; HD Theater; History International; IFC; INSP; MC; Nick Jr.; Nicktoons; TeenNick; Tennis Channel; The Movie Channel HD; TNT HD; Trinity Broadcasting Network (TBN); TVG Network; Universal HD; UP.
Digital Pay Service 1
Pay Units: 199.
Programming (via satellite): Cinemax (multiplexed); Cinemax HD; Flix.
Fee: $10.95 monthly.
Digital Pay Service 2
Pay Units: 377.
Programming (via satellite): HBO (multiplexed); HBO HD.
Fee: $13.95 monthly.
Digital Pay Service 3
Pay Units: 210.
Programming (via satellite): Showtime (multiplexed); Showtime HD; Sundance TV; The Movie Channel (multiplexed).
Fee: $12.95 monthly.
Digital Pay Service 4
Pay Units: 67.
Programming (via satellite): Starz (multiplexed); Starz Encore (multiplexed); Starz HD.
Fee: $12.95 monthly.
Digital Pay Service 5
Pay Units: 66.
Programming (via satellite): The Filipino Channel.
Fee: $13.99 monthly.
Video-On-Demand: No
Pay-Per-View
Adult Swim (delivered digitally); special events (delivered digitally).
Internet Service
Operational: Yes.
Broadband Service: GCI Hypernet.
Fee: $24.99 monthly.
Telephone Service
Digital: Operational
Miles of Plant: 42.0 (coaxial); 1.0 (fiber optic). Homes passed: 4,461.
Executive Vice President & General Manager: Gregory F. Chapados. Vice President, Content Product Management: Robert W. Ormberg. Marketing Director: Tricia Wurtz.
Ownership: GCI Cable Inc. (MSO).

SKAGWAY—Skagway Cable TV, 715 Main St, PO Box 1229, Haines, AK 99827-1229. Phones: 907-983-2205; 907-766-2137. Fax: 907-766-2345. E-mail: pcampbell99827@yahoo.com. Web Site: http://hainescable.com. ICA: AK0020.
TV Market Ranking: Outside TV Markets (SKAGWAY). Franchise award date: April 1, 1962. Franchise expiration date: N.A. Began: January 1, 1965.
Channel capacity: N.A. Channels available but not in use: N.A.
Basic Service
Subscribers: N.A.
Programming (via microwave): KYUR (ABC, CW) Anchorage.
Programming (via satellite): Alaska Rural Communications Service (ARCS); CNN; Discovery Channel; Disney Channel; ESPN; Freeform; KCNC-TV (CBS, Decades) Denver; KUSA (NBC, WeatherNation) Denver; Spike TV; Syfy; TBS; TLC; TNT; USA Network; WGN America.
Fee: $55.00 installation; $53.00 monthly.
Pay Service 1
Pay Units: N.A.
Programming (via satellite): Showtime; The Movie Channel.
Video-On-Demand: No
Internet Service
Operational: No.
Telephone Service
None
Miles of Plant: 7.0 (coaxial); None (fiber optic). Homes passed: 277.
General Manager: Patty Campbell. Marketing Manager: Daniel Glackin. Lineman: Andrew Glackin.
Ownership: Haines & Skagway Cable TV (MSO).

ST. MARY'S—Formerly served by Frontier Cable Inc. No longer in operation. ICA: AK0030.

TANANA—Supervision Inc, 6270 East Beechcraft Rd, Wasilla, AK 99654. Phone: 907-745-5363. Fax: 907-745-5362. E-mail: csr@yukontel.com. Web Site: http://www.uui-alaska.com. Also serves Whittier. ICA: AK0031.
TV Market Ranking: Below 100 (Whittier); Outside TV Markets (TANANA). Franchise award date: N.A. Franchise expiration date: N.A. Began: December 1, 1986.
Channel capacity: N.A. Channels available but not in use: N.A.
Basic Service
Subscribers: 179.
Programming (via microwave): KAKM (PBS) Anchorage; KYUR (ABC, CW) Anchorage.
Programming (via satellite): CNN; Discovery Channel; Disney Channel; ESPN; Fox News Channel; HLN; KCNC-TV (CBS, Decades) Denver; KUSA (NBC, WeatherNation) Denver; MTV2; Spike TV; TBS; TLC; TNT; TV Land; USA Network; VH1; WGN America.
Fee: $40.00 installation; $40.00 monthly.
Pay Service 1
Pay Units: N.A.
Programming (via satellite): HBO; Showtime (multiplexed).
Fee: $10.00 monthly.
Video-On-Demand: No
Internet Service
Operational: Yes.
Broadband Service: In-house.
Fee: $30.00 installation; $50.00 monthly.
Telephone Service
Analog: Operational
President: Don Eller. General Manager: Chelle Sommerville. Project Manager: Katy Henson.
Ownership: Supervision Inc. (MSO).

Cable Systems—Alaska

THORNE BAY—Formerly served by Thorne Bay Community TV Inc. No longer in operation. ICA: AK0041.

TOGIAK—Formerly served by Frontier Cable Inc. No longer in operation. ICA: AK0025.

TOKSOOK BAY—Formerly served by Frontier Cable Inc. No longer in operation. ICA: AK0029.

TUNUNAK—Formerly served by Frontier Cable Inc. No longer in operation. ICA: AK0028.

UNALAKLEET—Formerly served by Frontier Cable Inc. No longer in operation. ICA: AK0021.

UNALASKA—Eyecom Cable, 201 East 56th Ave, Anchorage, AK 99518-1283. Phones: 907-563-2003; 907-563-2074. Fax: 907-565-5539. E-mail: customerservice@telalaska.com. Web Site: http://www.telalaska.com. ICA: AK0042.
  TV Market Ranking: Outside TV Markets (UNALASKA). Franchise award date: N.A. Franchise expiration date: N.A. Began: December 1, 1984.
  Channel capacity: N.A. Channels available but not in use: N.A.
  Basic Service
    Subscribers: N.A.
    Programming (via microwave): KTUU-TV (NBC) Anchorage; KTVA (CBS) Anchorage; KUAC-TV (PBS) Fairbanks; KYUR (ABC, CW) Anchorage.
    Programming (via satellite): A&E; Alaska Rural Communications Service (ARCS); AMC; Animal Planet; Bravo; Cartoon Network; CMT; CNN; Comedy Central; Cooking Channel; Discovery Channel; Disney Channel; ESPN; ESPN2; Freeform; History; HLN; Lifetime; MTV; Nickelodeon; Spike TV; Syfy; TBS; TLC; TNT; Trinity Broadcasting Network (TBN); TV Land; Univision; USA Network; VH1; WGN America.
    Fee: $35.00 installation; $76.95 monthly.
  Digital Basic Service
    Subscribers: N.A.
    Programming (via satellite): MC.
    Fee: $8.95 monthly.
  Digital Pay Service 1
    Pay Units: N.A.
    Programming (via satellite): Cinemax; HBO; Playboy TV.
    Fee: $10.95 - $13.95 monthly (each).
  Video-On-Demand: No
  Internet Service
    Operational: Yes.
    Broadband Service: arctic.net.
    Fee: $79.90 monthly.
  Telephone Service
    Analog: Operational
  Miles of Plant: 26.0 (coaxial); None (fiber optic).
  President & Chief Executive Officer: Patrick Eudy. Chief Executive Officer: Brenda Shepard. Vice President, Operations: Dave Goggins. Vice President, Marketing: Marnie Brennan. Chief Technician: Dan Christensen.
  Ownership: Eyecom Inc. (MSO).

VALDEZ—GCI Cable Inc, PO Box 1047, Valdez, AK 99686. Phones: 907-265-5600 (Administrative office); 907-835-4930. Fax: 907-835-4257. E-mail: support@gci.net. Web Site: http://www.gci.com. ICA: AK0010.
  TV Market Ranking: Outside TV Markets (VALDEZ). Franchise award date: N.A. Franchise expiration date: N.A. Began: September 1, 1974.
  Channel capacity: 36 (operating 2-way). Channels available but not in use: N.A.
  Basic Service
    Subscribers: 478. Commercial subscribers: 20.
    Programming (via microwave): KAKM (PBS) Anchorage; KTBY (FOX) Anchorage; KTUU-TV (NBC) Anchorage; KTVA (CBS) Anchorage; KYUR (ABC, CW) Anchorage.
    Programming (via satellite): Alaska Rural Communications Service (ARCS); C-SPAN; C-SPAN 2; Pop; QVC; WGN America.
    Fee: $25.50 installation; $33.95 monthly.
  Expanded Basic Service 1
    Subscribers: N.A.
    Programming (via satellite): A&E; AMC; Animal Planet; CMT; CNBC; CNN; Comedy Central; Discovery Channel; Disney Channel; Disney XD; ESPN; ESPN2; Food Network; Fox News Channel; Freeform; HGTV; History; HLN; Lifetime; MSNBC; MTV; NBCSN; Nickelodeon; Northwest Cable News; Outdoor Channel; Spike TV; Syfy; TBS; The Weather Channel; TLC; TNT; Travel Channel; TV Land; USA Network; VH1.
    Fee: $40.26 monthly.
  Digital Basic Service
    Subscribers: N.A.
    Programming (via satellite): MC.
  Digital Pay Service 1
    Pay Units: 455.
    Programming (via satellite): HBO (multiplexed).
    Fee: $13.95 monthly.
  Digital Pay Service 2
    Pay Units: 120.
    Programming (via satellite): Cinemax (multiplexed).
    Fee: $10.95 monthly.
  Digital Pay Service 3
    Pay Units: 74.
    Programming (via satellite): Starz (multiplexed); Starz Encore (multiplexed).
    Fee: $12.95 monthly.
  Digital Pay Service 4
    Pay Units: 119.
    Programming (via satellite): Flix; Showtime (multiplexed); Sundance TV; The Movie Channel (multiplexed).
    Fee: $12.95 monthly.
  Video-On-Demand: No
  Pay-Per-View
    iN DEMAND (delivered digitally); Adult Swim (delivered digitally).
  Internet Service
    Operational: Yes. Began: January 1, 2000.
    Broadband Service: GCI Hypernet.
    Fee: $24.99 monthly.
  Telephone Service
    Digital: Operational
  Miles of Plant: 33.0 (coaxial); 10.0 (fiber optic). Homes passed: 2,032.
  Executive Vice President & General Manager: Gregory F. Chapados. Vice President, Content Product Management: Robert W. Ormberg.
  Ownership: GCI Cable Inc. (MSO).

WASILLA—GCI Cable Inc, 501 North Main St, Ste 130, Wasilla, AK 99654-7023. Phones: 800-800-4800; 907-373-2288. Fax: 907-376-8888. E-mail: support@gci.net. Web Site: http://www.gci.com. Also serves Matanuska Valley & Palmer. ICA: AK0004.
  TV Market Ranking: Below 100 (Matanuska Valley, Palmer, WASILLA). Franchise award date: N.A. Franchise expiration date: N.A. Began: October 1, 1982.
  Channel capacity: 57 (operating 2-way). Channels available but not in use: N.A.
  Basic Service
    Subscribers: 7,813.
    Programming (received off-air): KAKM (PBS) Anchorage; KCFT-CD Anchorage; KDMD (ION, TMO) Anchorage; KTBY (FOX) Anchorage; KTUU-TV (NBC) Anchorage; KTVA (CBS) Anchorage; KYUR (ABC, CW) Anchorage.
    Programming (via satellite): C-SPAN; C-SPAN 2; CW PLUS; Pop; WGN America.
    Fee: $25.50 installation; $33.95 monthly.
  Expanded Basic Service 1
    Subscribers: 6,780.
    Programming (via satellite): A&E; AMC; Animal Planet; BET; Bravo; Cartoon Network; CMT; CNBC; CNN; Comedy Central; Discovery Channel; Disney Channel; Disney XD; E!; ESPN; ESPN Classic; ESPN2; EVINE Live; Food Network; Fox News Channel; Freeform; Fuse; FX; HGTV; History; HLN; Lifetime; LMN; MSNBC; MTV; National Geographic Channel; NBCSN; NFL Network; Nickelodeon; Outdoor Channel; Oxygen; QVC; Spike TV; Syfy; TBS; The Weather Channel; TLC; TNT; Travel Channel; truTV; Turner Classic Movies; TV Land; Univision Studios; USA Network; VH1; WE tv.
    Fee: $35.79 monthly.
  Digital Basic Service
    Subscribers: N.A.
    Programming (via satellite): 3ABN; AWE; AXS TV; BBC America; Bloomberg Television; Boomerang; BYUtv; Church Channel; CNN International; Daystar TV Network; Discovery Digital Networks; DIY Network; ESPN HD; ESPNews; EWTN Global Catholic Network; FamilyNet; FOX College Sports Central; FOX College Sports Pacific; Fox Sports 1; Fox Sports 2; FYI; Golf Channel; Great American Country; GSN; HD Theater; History; History International; IFC; INSP; MC; NFL Network; Nick Jr.; Nicktoons; TeenNick; Tennis Channel; TNT HD; Trinity Broadcasting Network (TBN); TVG Network; Universal HD; UP.
  Digital Pay Service 1
    Pay Units: 3,564.
    Programming (via satellite): Cinemax (multiplexed); Cinemax HD; HBO (multiplexed); Korean Channel; Showtime (multiplexed); Starz (multiplexed); The Filipino Channel.
    Fee: $10.95 monthly (Cinemax), $12.95 monthly (Starz), $13.95 monthly (Showtime or HBO), $13.99 monthly (Korean Channel or Filipino Channel).
  Video-On-Demand: No
  Pay-Per-View
    Hot Choice (delivered digitally); iN DEMAND (delivered digitally); ESPN (delivered digitally).
  Internet Service
    Operational: Yes.
    Broadband Service: GCI Hypernet.
    Fee: $24.99 monthly.
  Telephone Service
    Digital: Operational
  Miles of Plant: 371.0 (coaxial); 27.0 (fiber optic). Homes passed: 16,778.
  Executive Vice President & General Manager: Gregory F. Chapados. Vice President, Content Product Management: Robert W. Ormberg.
  Ownership: GCI Cable Inc. (MSO).

WHITTIER—Supervision Inc. Now served by TANANA, AK [AK0031]. ICA: AK0032.

WRANGELL—GCI Cable Inc, 325 Front St, PO Box 909, Wrangell, AK 99929. Phone: 907-874-2392. E-mail: support@gci.net. Web Site: http://www.gci.com. ICA: AK0014.
  TV Market Ranking: Outside TV Markets (WRANGELL). Franchise award date: N.A. Franchise expiration date: N.A. Began: September 1, 1968.
  Channel capacity: N.A. Channels available but not in use: N.A.
  Basic Service
    Subscribers: 491.
    Programming (via microwave): KING-TV (NBC) Seattle; KJUD (ABC, CW, FOX) Juneau; KTBY (FOX) Anchorage; KTVA (CBS) Anchorage.
    Programming (via satellite): C-SPAN; C-SPAN 2; Pop; QVC; WGN America.
    Fee: $25.50 installation; $33.95 monthly.
  Expanded Basic Service 1
    Subscribers: N.A.
    Programming (via satellite): A&E; AMC; Animal Planet; Cartoon Network; CMT; CNBC; CNN; Comedy Central; Discovery Channel; Disney Channel; Disney XD; ESPN; ESPN2; Food Network; Fox News Channel; Freeform; Hallmark Channel; HGTV; History; HLN; Lifetime; MSNBC; MTV; NBCSN; Nickelodeon; Northwest Cable News; Spike TV; Syfy; TBS; The Weather Channel; TLC; TNT; Travel Channel; Trinity Broadcasting Network (TBN); truTV; TV Land; USA Network; VH1.
    Fee: $35.29 monthly.
  Digital Basic Service
    Subscribers: N.A.
    Programming (via satellite): MC.
  Digital Pay Service 1
    Pay Units: 72.
    Programming (via satellite): Cinemax (multiplexed).
    Fee: $10.95 monthly.
  Digital Pay Service 2
    Pay Units: 109.
    Programming (via satellite): HBO (multiplexed).
    Fee: $13.95 monthly.
  Digital Pay Service 3
    Pay Units: 84.
    Programming (via satellite): Flix; Showtime (multiplexed); Sundance TV; The Movie Channel (multiplexed).
    Fee: $12.95 monthly.
  Digital Pay Service 4
    Pay Units: 49.
    Programming (via satellite): Starz (multiplexed); Starz Encore (multiplexed).
    Fee: $12.95 monthly.
  Video-On-Demand: No
  Pay-Per-View
    Adult Swim (delivered digitally); special events (delivered digitally).
  Internet Service
    Operational: Yes.
    Broadband Service: GCI Hypernet.
    Fee: $49.99 monthly.
  Telephone Service
    Digital: Operational
  Miles of Plant: 27.0 (coaxial); None (fiber optic). Homes passed: 1,223.
  Executive Vice President & General Manager: Gregory F. Chapados. Vice President, Content Product Management: Robert W. Ormberg. Chief Technician: Don McConachie.
  Ownership: GCI Cable Inc. (MSO).

ARIZONA

Total Systems: 34	Communities with Applications: 0
Total Communities Served: 163	Number of Basic Subscribers: 841,021
Franchises Not Yet Operating: 0	Number of Expanded Basic Subscribers: 0
Applications Pending: 0	Number of Pay Units: 52,006

Top 100 Markets Represented: Phoenix-Mesa (43).

For a list of cable communities in this section, see the Cable Community Index located in the back of Cable Volume 2.
For explanation of terms used in cable system listings, see p. D-11.

AJO—Mediacom, 1 West Pajaro St, Ajo, AZ 85321. Phones: 800-332-0245; 520-387-3798. Web Site: http://www.mediacomcable.com. ICA: AZ0037.
 TV Market Ranking: Outside TV Markets (AJO). Franchise award date: N.A. Franchise expiration date: N.A. Began: February 1, 1952.
 Channel capacity: N.A. Channels available but not in use: N.A.
 Basic Service
  Subscribers: 72.
  Programming (via microwave): KAET (PBS) Phoenix; KGUN-TV (ABC, IND) Tucson; KOLD-TV (CBS, MeTV) Tucson; KPAZ-TV (TBN) Phoenix; KPHO-TV (CBS, COZI TV) Phoenix; KPNX (NBC) Mesa; KTVK (This TV) Phoenix; KUAT-TV (PBS) Tucson; KVOA (Escape, NBC) Tucson.
  Programming (via satellite): A&E; AMC; CMT; CNN; Discovery Channel; Disney Channel; ESPN; EWTN Global Catholic Network; Freeform; HLN; KTLA (Antenna TV, CW, This TV) Los Angeles; Lifetime; Nickelodeon; TBS; Telemundo; TNT; Trinity Broadcasting Network (TBN); USA Network; WGN America.
  Fee: $29.50 installation; $64.95 monthly; $2.00 converter.
 Pay Service 1
  Pay Units: N.A.
  Programming (via satellite): HBO; Showtime; Starz Encore; The Movie Channel.
  Fee: $5.95 monthly (Encore), $12.95 monthly (HBO or Showtime/TMC).
 Video-On-Demand: No
 Internet Service
  Operational: No.
 Telephone Service
  None
 Homes passed: 2,000. Miles of plant (coax) included in Apache Junction.
 General Manager: Steven Lamb.
 Ownership: Mediacom LLC (MSO).

ALPINE—Formerly served by Eagle West Communications Inc. No longer in operation. ICA: AZ0083.

APACHE JUNCTION—Mediacom, 672 S Ironwood St, Apache Junction, AZ 85120. Phones: 800-479-2082; 480-474-2078. Web Site: http://www.mediacomcable.com. Also serves Gold Canyon, Pinal County (portions), Queen Creek, Queen Valley & Rock Shadows. ICA: AZ0008.
 TV Market Ranking: 43 (APACHE JUNCTION, Gold Canyon, Pinal County (portions), Queen Creek, Queen Valley, Rock Shadows); Below 100 (Pinal County (portions)); Outside TV Markets (Pinal County (portions)). Franchise award date: N.A. Franchise expiration date: N.A. Began: March 1, 1985.
 Channel capacity: N.A. Channels available but not in use: N.A.
 Basic Service
  Subscribers: 4,780.
  Programming (received off-air): KAET (PBS) Phoenix; KASW (CW) Phoenix; KAZT-TV (MeTV, Retro TV) Phoenix; KDTP (Daystar TV, ETV) Holbrook; KNXV-TV (ABC) Phoenix; KPAZ-TV (TBN) Phoenix; KPHO-TV (CBS, COZI TV) Phoenix; KPNX (NBC) Mesa; KPPX-TV (ION) Tolleson; KSAZ-TV (Bounce TV, FOX, Heroes & Icons) Phoenix; KTVK (This TV) Phoenix; KTVW-DT (UNV) Phoenix; KUTP (Buzzr, MNT, Movies!) Phoenix.
  Programming (via satellite): A&E; AMC; Animal Planet; Cartoon Network; CMT; CNBC; CNN; Comedy Central; C-SPAN; Discovery Channel; Disney Channel; E! HD; ESPN; ESPN2; Food Network; Fox News Channel; FOX Sports Arizona; Freeform; FX; Hallmark Channel; HGTV; History; HLN; Lifetime; MSNBC; MTV; Nickelodeon; Pop; QVC; Spike TV; Syfy; TBS; The Weather Channel; TLC; TNT; Travel Channel; TV Land; USA Network; VH1; WGN America.
  Fee: $44.25 installation; $57.23 monthly.
 Digital Basic Service
  Subscribers: N.A.
  Programming (via satellite): BBC America; Bloomberg Television; Discovery Digital Networks; DMX Music; ESPN Classic; FXM; Golf Channel; GSN; IFC; INSP; NBCSN; Outdoor Channel; Turner Classic Movies; WE tv; Weatherscan.
 Pay Service 1
  Pay Units: N.A.
  Programming (via satellite): Cinemax; HBO; Starz; Starz Encore.
  Fee: $25.00 installation; $6.95 monthly (Starz/Encore), $7.95 monthly (Cinemax), $11.95 monthly (HBO).
 Digital Pay Service 1
  Pay Units: N.A.
  Programming (via satellite): Cinemax (multiplexed); HBO (multiplexed); Showtime (multiplexed); Starz (multiplexed); Starz Encore (multiplexed); The Movie Channel (multiplexed).
  Fee: $8.00 monthly (Starz/Encore), $9.95 (Cinemax or Showtime), $13.95 monthly (HBO).
 Video-On-Demand: Yes
 Pay-Per-View
  Hot Choice (delivered digitally); iN DEMAND (delivered digitally); Playboy TV (delivered digitally); Fresh (delivered digitally); Sports PPV (delivered digitally).
 Internet Service
  Operational: Yes.
  Subscribers: 5,834.
  Broadband Service: Mediacom High Speed Internet.
  Fee: $59.95 installation; $42.95 monthly; $3.00 modem lease; $239.95 modem purchase.
 Telephone Service
  Analog: Not Operational
  Digital: Operational
  Subscribers: 3,666.
 Miles of Plant: 972.0 (coaxial); 89.0 (fiber optic). Homes passed: 45,169. Miles of plant (coax) includes Ajo & Nogales.
 Vice President, Financial Reporting: Kenneth J. Kohrs. General Manager: Steven Lamb.
 Ownership: Mediacom LLC (MSO).

AVONDALE—Cox Communications. Now served by PHOENIX, AZ [AZ0001]. ICA: AZ0020.

BAGDAD—Formerly served by Eagle West Communications Inc. No longer in operation. ICA: AZ0048.

BENSON—Cox Communications. Now served by TUCSON, AZ [AZ0002]. ICA: AZ0138.

BISBEE—Cable One, 99 Bisbee Rd, Bisbee, AZ 85603-1118. Phone: 520-432-5397. Fax: 520-432-7981. Web Site: http://www.cableone.net. Also serves Cochise County (portions) & Naco. ICA: AZ0029.
 TV Market Ranking: Below 100 (BISBEE, Cochise County (portions), Naco). Franchise award date: N.A. Franchise expiration date: N.A. Began: April 1, 1952.
 Channel capacity: N.A. Channels available but not in use: N.A.
 Basic Service
  Subscribers: 1,603.
  Programming (received off-air): KGUN-TV (ABC, IND) Tucson; KMSB (FOX, Movies!, This TV) Tucson; KOLD-TV (CBS, MeTV) Tucson; KTTU (Estrella TV, MNT) Tucson; KUAT-TV (PBS) Tucson; KVOA (Escape, NBC) Tucson.
  Programming (via satellite): A&E; Animal Planet; Cartoon Network; CMT; CNBC; CNN; Comedy Central; C-SPAN; Discovery Channel; Disney Channel; ESPN; ESPN2; Fox News Channel; FOX Sports Arizona; Freeform; FX; History; HLN; Lifetime; MTV; Nickelodeon; Ovation; Pop; QVC; Spike TV; Syfy; TBS; Telemundo; The Weather Channel; TLC; TNT; Turner Classic Movies; TV Land; Univision Studios; USA Network; VH1; WGN America.
  Fee: $76.00 installation; $24.00 monthly.
 Digital Basic Service
  Subscribers: N.A.
  Programming (via satellite): Boomerang; Discovery Digital Networks; Disney XD; DMX Music; ESPN Classic; ESPNews; Fox Sports 1; FXM; FYI; Golf Channel; GSN; History International; HITS (Headend In The Sky); National Geographic Channel; NBCSN; Outdoor Channel; Trinity Broadcasting Network (TBN).
 Digital Pay Service 1
  Pay Units: N.A.
  Programming (via satellite): Cinemax (multiplexed); Flix; HBO (multiplexed); Showtime (multiplexed); Starz (multiplexed); Starz Encore (multiplexed); The Movie Channel.
  Fee: $15.00 monthly (each).
 Video-On-Demand: No
 Pay-Per-View
  iN DEMAND (delivered digitally).
 Internet Service
  Operational: Yes.
  Broadband Service: CableONE.net.
  Fee: $75.00 installation; $43.00 monthly.
 Telephone Service
  Digital: Operational
 Miles of Plant: 67.0 (coaxial); None (fiber optic). Homes passed: 3,949.
 Vice President: Patrick A. Dolohanty. General Manager: Steve Brideau. Technical Operations Manager: Chuck Dunlap.
 Ownership: Cable ONE Inc. (MSO).

BLACK CANYON CITY—Formerly served by RealStar Communications. No longer in operation. ICA: AZ0127.

BULLHEAD CITY—Suddenlink Communications, 520 Maryville Centre Dr, Ste 300, St. Louis, MO 63141. Phones: 314-315-9400; 800-999-6845 (Customer service). Web Site: http://www.suddenlink.com. Also serves Fort Mohave, Mohave County (portions), Mohave Valley & Willow Valley. ICA: AZ0009.
 TV Market Ranking: Below 100 (BULLHEAD CITY, Fort Mohave, Mohave Valley, Willow Valley, Mohave County (portions)); Outside TV Markets (Mohave County (portions)). Franchise award date: November 1, 1974. Franchise expiration date: N.A. Began: November 1, 1974.
 Channel capacity: 70 (operating 2-way). Channels available but not in use: N.A.
 Basic Service
  Subscribers: 7,409.
  Programming (received off-air): KAZT-TV (MeTV, Retro TV) Phoenix; KMOH-TV (MundoMax) Kingman.
  Programming (via microwave): KAET (PBS) Phoenix; KASW (CW) Phoenix; KNXV-TV (ABC) Phoenix; KPHO-TV (CBS, COZI TV) Phoenix; KPNX (NBC) Mesa; KSAZ-TV (Bounce TV, FOX, Heroes & Icons) Phoenix; KTAZ (TMO) Phoenix; KTVK (This TV) Phoenix; KTVW-DT (UNV) Phoenix; KUTP (Buzzr, MNT, Movies!) Phoenix.
  Programming (via satellite): A&E; AMC; Animal Planet; Bravo; Cartoon Network; CMT; CNBC; CNN; Comedy Central; C-SPAN; C-SPAN 2; Discovery Channel; Disney Channel; E! HD; ESPN; ESPN Classic; ESPN2; Food Network; Fox News Channel; Fox Sports 1; FOX Sports Arizona; Freeform; FX; Great American Country; HGTV; History; HLN; ION Television; KTLA Los Angeles; Lifetime; LMN; MSNBC; MTV; National Geographic Channel; Nickelodeon; OWN: Oprah Winfrey

Cable Systems—Arizona

Network; Pop; QVC; Spike TV; Syfy; TBS; The Weather Channel; TLC; TNT; Travel Channel; Trinity Broadcasting Network (TBN); truTV; Turner Classic Movies; TV Land; USA Network; VH1; WGN America.
Fee: $40.00 installation; $60.99 monthly.

Digital Basic Service
Subscribers: N.A.
Programming (via satellite): AXS TV; BBC America; Chiller; Cooking Channel; Destination America; Discovery Channel HD; Discovery Kids Channel; Disney XD; DIY Network; DMX Music; ESPN HD; ESPN2 HD; ESPNews; ESPNU; Food Network HD; Fox Deportes; Fox Sports 1; Fox Sports 2; FSN Digital Atlantic; FSN Digital Central; FSN Digital Pacific; FSN HD; FX HD; FYI; Golf Channel; GSN; Hallmark Channel; HGTV HD; History International; IFC; Investigation Discovery; MTV Classic; MTV2; NBCSN; Nick Jr.; Nicktoons; Oxygen; Science Channel; Syfy HD; TeenNick; TNT HD; Universal HD; USA Network HD; VH1 Country; WE tv.

Digital Pay Service 1
Pay Units: N.A.
Programming (via satellite): Cinemax (multiplexed); HBO (multiplexed); Showtime (multiplexed); Starz (multiplexed); Starz Encore (multiplexed); The Movie Channel (multiplexed).
Fee: $6.95 monthly (Cinemax), $9.95 monthly (Starz/Encore), $11.95 monthly (Showtime/TMC), $12.00 monthly (HBO).

Video-On-Demand: Planned

Pay-Per-View
iN DEMAND (delivered digitally); Club Jenna (delivered digitally); Fresh (delivered digitally); Spice: Xcess (delivered digitally).

Internet Service
Operational: Yes. Began: May 1, 1999.
Subscribers: 5,546.
Broadband Service: Suddenlink High Speed Internet.
Fee: $59.95 installation; $24.95 monthly; $5.00 modem lease.

Telephone Service
Analog: Not Operational
Digital: Operational
Subscribers: 2,273.
Fee: $39.95 monthly
Miles of Plant: 724.0 (coaxial); 129.0 (fiber optic). Homes passed: 40,507.
Senior Vice President, Corporate Finance: Michael Pflantz. Chief Executive Officer: Jerald L. Kent. Executive Vice President & Chief Operating Officer: Thomas P. McMillin. Senior Vice President, Marketing: Mary R. Meier. Vice President, Accounting: Sabrina Warr.
Ownership: Cequel Communications Holdings I LLC (MSO).

BYLAS—San Carlos Apache Telecom. Now served by SAN CARLOS, AZ [AZ0046]. ICA: AZ0134.

CAREFREE—Cox Communications. Now served by PHOENIX, AZ [AZ0001]. ICA: AZ0030.

CASA GRANDE—Cox Communications. Now served by PHOENIX, AZ [AZ0001]. ICA: AZ0019.

CASA GRANDE (northern portion)—Formerly served by RealStar Communications. No longer in operation. ICA: AZ0126.

CAVE CREEK—Formerly served by RealStar Communications. No longer in operation. ICA: AZ0060.

CHINLE—Formerly served by Frontier Communications. No longer in operation. ICA: AZ0038.

CLIFTON—Cable One. Now served by SAFFORD, AZ [AZ0021]. ICA: AZ0034.

CONCHO VALLEY—Formerly served by Eagle West Communications Inc. No longer in operation. ICA: AZ0111.

COOLIDGE—Formerly served by Cable America Corp. Now served by Cox Communications, PHOENIX, AZ [AZ0001]. ICA: AZ0032.

CORDES LAKES—Formerly served by Cordes Lakes Cablevision. No longer in operation. ICA: AZ0065.

COTTONWOOD—Cable One, 235 South 6th St, Cottonwood, AZ 86326-4241. Phone: 928-634-9677. Fax: 928-634-5394. Web Site: http://www.cableone.net. Also serves Clarkdale, Cornville, Page Springs, Yavapai County (northeastern portion) & Yavapai-Apache-Clarksdale Reservation. ICA: AZ0129.
TV Market Ranking: Below 100 (Page Springs, Yavapai County (northeastern portion)); Outside TV Markets (Clarkdale, Cornville, COTTONWOOD, Yavapai-Apache-Clarksdale Reservation, Yavapai County (northeastern portion)).
Channel capacity: N.A. Channels available but not in use: N.A.

Basic Service
Subscribers: 1,374.
Programming (received off-air): KFPH-DT (getTV, UniMas) Flagstaff; KNAZ-TV (NBC) Flagstaff.
Programming (via microwave): KAET (PBS) Phoenix; KASW (CW) Phoenix; KNXV-TV (ABC) Phoenix; KPHO-TV (CBS, COZI TV) Phoenix; KPNX (NBC) Mesa; KSAZ-TV (Bounce TV, FOX, Heroes & Icons) Phoenix; KTAZ (TMO) Phoenix; KTVK (This TV) Phoenix; KUTP (Buzzr, MNT, Movies!) Phoenix.
Programming (via satellite): C-SPAN; C-SPAN 2; QVC; WGN America.
Fee: $90.00 installation; $35.00 monthly.

Expanded Basic Service 1
Subscribers: N.A.
Programming (via satellite): A&E; AMC; Animal Planet; Cartoon Network; CMT; CNBC; CNN; Comedy Central; Discovery Channel; Disney Channel; ESPN; ESPN2; Food Network; Fox News Channel; FOX Sports Arizona; Freeform; FX; HGTV; History; HLN; Lifetime; MSNBC; MTV; Nickelodeon; Pop; Spike TV; Syfy; TBS; The Weather Channel; TLC; TNT; Travel Channel; Trinity Broadcasting Network (TBN); Turner Classic Movies; TV Land; USA Network; VH1.

Digital Basic Service
Subscribers: N.A.
Programming (via satellite): 3ABN; A&E HD; Boomerang; BYUtv; Cine Mexicano; CNN en Espanol; Discovery Channel HD; Discovery Kids Channel; Disney XD; ESPN Classic; ESPN Deportes; ESPN HD; ESPN2 HD; ESPNews; FamilyNet; Food Network HD; FOX College Sports Central; FOX College Sports Pacific; Fox Deportes; Fox Sports 1; Fox Sports 2; FXM; FYI; Golf Channel; Great American Country; GSN; Hallmark Channel; HD Theater; HGTV HD; History HD; History International; INSP; La Familia Cosmovision; MC; National Geographic Channel; National Geographic Channel HD; NBC Universo; Outdoor Channel; OWN: Oprah Winfrey Network; Science Channel; TBS HD; Telemundo; TLC HD; TNT HD; Toon Disney en Espanol; Trinity Broadcasting Network (TBN); TVG Network; Universal HD; WE tv.

Digital Pay Service 1
Pay Units: N.A.
Programming (via satellite): Cinemax (multiplexed); Flix; HBO (multiplexed); HBO HD; HBO Latino; Showtime (multiplexed); Showtime HD; Starz (multiplexed); Starz Encore (multiplexed); Sundance TV; The Movie Channel (multiplexed); The Movie Channel HD.
Fee: $15.15 monthly (HBO/HBO HD/HBO Latino or (Flix/Showtime/Showtime HD/Sundance/TMC/TMC HD).

Video-On-Demand: No

Pay-Per-View
iN DEMAND (delivered digitally); SexSee (delivered digitally); Juicy (delivered digitally); VaVoom (delivered digitally).

Internet Service
Operational: Yes.
Broadband Service: CableONE.net.
Fee: $75.00 installation; $33.00 monthly.

Telephone Service
Digital: Operational
Fee: $39.95 monthly
Homes passed: 7,948.
Vice President: Patrick A. Dolohanty. General Manager: Dennis Edwards. Marketing Director: J. J. McCormick. Office Manager: Mindy Gray.
Ownership: Cable ONE Inc. (MSO).

DOUGLAS—Cox Communications. Now served by SIERRA VISTA, AZ [AZ0005]. ICA: AZ0023.

DUDLEYVILLE—Formerly served by RealStar Communications. No longer in operation. ICA: AZ0075.

EAGAR—Formerly served by RealStar Communications. No longer in operation. ICA: AZ0086.

EAST MESA—Formerly served by Eagle West Communications Inc. No longer in operation. ICA: AZ0022.

ELOY—Formerly served by RealStar Communications. No longer in operation. ICA: AZ0043.

FLAGSTAFF—Formerly served by Microwave Communication Services. No longer in operation. ICA: AZ0116.

FLAGSTAFF—Suddenlink Communications, 520 Maryville Centre Dr, Ste 300, St. Louis, MO 63141. Phones: 800-999-6845 (Customer service); 314-315-9400. Web Site: http://www.suddenlink.com. Also serves Coconino County. ICA: AZ0012.
TV Market Ranking: Below 100 (Coconino County (portions), FLAGSTAFF); Outside TV Markets (Coconino County (portions)).
Franchise award date: May 1, 1954. Franchise expiration date: N.A. Began: May 1, 1954.
Channel capacity: N.A. Channels available but not in use: N.A.

Basic Service
Subscribers: 8,914. Commercial subscribers: 1,551.
Programming (received off-air): KFPH-DT (getTV, UniMas) Flagstaff; KMOH-TV (MundoMax) Kingman; KNAZ-TV (NBC) Flagstaff; 10 FMs.
Programming (via microwave): KAET (PBS) Phoenix; KASW (CW) Phoenix; KAZT-TV (MeTV, Retro TV) Phoenix; KNXV-TV (ABC) Phoenix; KPHO-TV (CBS, COZI TV) Phoenix; KPNX (NBC) Mesa; KSAZ-TV (Bounce TV, FOX, Heroes & Icons) Phoenix; KTVK (This TV) Phoenix; KTVW-DT (UNV) Phoenix; KUTP (Buzzr, MNT, Movies!) Phoenix.
Programming (via satellite): A&E; AMC; Animal Planet; Cartoon Network; CMT; CNBC; CNN; Comedy Central; C-SPAN; C-SPAN 2; Discovery Channel; Disney Channel; E! HD; ESPN; ESPN Classic; ESPN2; Food Network; Fox News Channel; FOX Sports Arizona; Freeform; FX; Great American Country; HGTV; History; HLN; ION Television; KTLA (Antenna TV, CW, This TV) Los Angeles; Lifetime; LMN; MSNBC; MTV; National Geographic Channel; Nickelodeon; OWN: Oprah Winfrey Network; Pop; QVC; Spike TV; Syfy; TBS; The Weather Channel; TLC; TNT; Travel Channel; Trinity Broadcasting Network (TBN); truTV; Turner Classic Movies; TV Land; USA Network; VH1.
Fee: $40.00 installation; $60.99 monthly; $2.50 converter.

Digital Basic Service
Subscribers: N.A.
Programming (via satellite): AXS TV; BBC America; Bloomberg Television; CMT; Cooking Channel; Discovery Digital Networks; Disney XD; DIY Network; DMX Music; ESPN HD; ESPN2 HD; ESPNews; ESPNU; Food Network HD; Fox Deportes; Fox Sports 1; Fox Sports 2; FSN Digital Atlantic; FSN Digital Central; FSN Digital Pacific; FXM; FYI; Golf Channel; GSN; HD Theater; HGTV HD; History International; IFC; LMN; NBCSN; Nick Jr.; Nicktoons; TeenNick; WE tv.

Digital Pay Service 1
Pay Units: N.A.
Programming (via satellite): Cinemax (multiplexed); HBO (multiplexed); Showtime (multiplexed); Starz (multiplexed); Starz Encore (multiplexed); The Movie Channel (multiplexed).
Fee: $6.95 monthly (Cinemax), $9.95 monthly (Starz/Encore), $11.95 monthly (Showtime/TMC), $12.00 monthly (HBO).

Video-On-Demand: Planned

Pay-Per-View
iN DEMAND (delivered digitally); Fresh (delivered digitally).

Internet Service
Operational: Yes.
Subscribers: 11,817.
Broadband Service: Suddenlink High Speed Internet.
Fee: $59.95 installation; $24.95 monthly.

Telephone Service
Digital: Operational
Subscribers: 2,640.
Fee: $39.95 monthly
Miles of Plant: 710.0 (coaxial); 95.0 (fiber optic). Homes passed: 43,116.
Senior Vice President, Corporate Finance: Michael Pflantz. Chief Executive Officer: Jerald L. Kent. Executive Vice President & Chief Operating Officer: Thomas P. McMillin. Senior Vice President, Marketing: Mary R. Meier. Vice President, Accounting: Sabrina Warr.
Ownership: Cequel Communications Holdings I LLC (MSO).

Arizona—Cable Systems

FLORENCE GARDEN MOBILE HOME PARK—Formerly served by Eagle West Communications Inc. No longer in operation. ICA: AZ0035.

FORT MOHAVE MESA—Formerly served by Americable International Arizona Inc. No longer in operation. ICA: AZ0041.

FREDONIA—South Central Communications. Now served by PANGUITCH, UT [UT0043]. ICA: AZ0072.

GILA BEND—CableAmerica (formerly Cox Communications). This cable system has converted to IPTV, 350 East 10th St, Mesa, AZ 85210. Phones: 800-338-1808; 866-871-4492. Web Site: http://www.cableamerica.com. ICA: AZ5021.
Channel capacity: N.A. Channels available but not in use: N.A.
Basic Entertainment
Subscribers: 119.
Fee: $9.95 installation; $20.00 monthly. Includes 12 channels.
Digital Intro
Subscribers: N.A.
Fee: $45.40 monthly. Includes 63 channels plus music channels.
Digital Choice
Subscribers: N.A.
Fee: $65.40 monthly. Includes 96 channels plus music channels.
HD
Subscribers: N.A.
Espanol
Subscribers: N.A.
Movie Pack
Subscribers: N.A.
Fee: $4.95 monthly. Includes 10 channels.
Sports
Subscribers: N.A.
Fee: $3.95 monthly. Includes 7 channels.
Premium Channels
Subscribers: N.A.
Fee: $15.95 monthly/one movie package, $28.90/two movie packages, $38.85/three movie packages, $51.80/four movie packages, $64.94/five movie packages. Packages include Cinemax, Flix, HBO, Showtime & TMC.
Video-On-Demand: No
Internet Service
Operational: Yes.
Fee: $24.95-$54.94 monthly.
Telephone Service
Digital: Operational
Fee: $19.99 monthly
Ownership: CableAmerica Corp.

GILA BEND—CableAmerica (formerly Cox Communications). This cable system has converted to IPTV. See GILA BEND, AZ [AZ5021]. ICA: AZ0055.

GILA COUNTY—San Carlos Apache Telecom. Now served by SAN CARLOS, AZ [AZ0046]. ICA: AZ0135.

GILBERT—Cox Communications. Now served by PHOENIX, AZ [AZ0001]. ICA: AZ0090.

GISELA—Formerly served by Indevideo Co. Inc. No longer in operation. ICA: AZ0076.

GLENDALE (portions)—Formerly served by Qwest Choice TV. IPTV service has been discontinued. ICA: AZ5014.

GLOBE-MIAMI—Cable One, 727 Paxton Ave, PO Box 30, Globe, AZ 85502-0030. Phones: 928-425-3161; 928-425-6351. Fax: 928-425-5404. E-mail: joni.maldonado@cableone.net. Web Site: http://www.cableone.net. Also serves Gila County. ICA: AZ0018.
TV Market Ranking: Outside TV Markets (Gila County, GLOBE-MIAMI). Franchise award date: November 12, 1972. Franchise expiration date: N.A. Began: October 1, 1953.
Channel capacity: N.A. Channels available but not in use: N.A.
Basic Service
Subscribers: 1,736.
Programming (via microwave): KAET (PBS) Phoenix; KGUN-TV (ABC, IND) Tucson; KNXV-TV (ABC) Phoenix; KPHO-TV (CBS, COZI TV) Phoenix; KPNX (NBC) Mesa; KSAZ-TV (Bounce TV, FOX, Heroes & Icons) Phoenix; KTVK (This TV) Phoenix.
Programming (via satellite): A&E; Animal Planet; Cartoon Network; CMT; CNBC; CNN; C-SPAN; C-SPAN 2; Discovery Channel; Disney Channel; E! HD; ESPN; ESPN2; Food Network; Fox Deportes; Fox News Channel; FOX Sports Arizona; Freeform; FX; HGTV; History; HLN; ION Television; Lifetime; MSNBC; MTV; Nickelodeon; Pop; QVC; Spike TV; Syfy; TBS; The Weather Channel; TLC; TNT; Trinity Broadcasting Network (TBN); Turner Classic Movies; TV Land; USA Network; VH1; WGN America.
Fee: $90.00 installation; $35.00 monthly.
Digital Basic Service
Subscribers: N.A.
Programming (via satellite): Boomerang; Discovery Digital Networks; Disney XD; DMX Music; ESPN Classic; ESPNews; FOX College Sports Central; FOX College Sports Pacific; Fox Sports 1; Fox Sports 2; FXM; FYI; Golf Channel; Great American Country; Hallmark Channel; History; History International; HITS (Headend In The Sky) (multiplexed); INSP; National Geographic Channel; Outdoor Channel; Trinity Broadcasting Network (TBN); truTV; TVG Network.
Fee: $10.00 converter.
Digital Pay Service 1
Pay Units: 500.
Programming (via satellite): Cinemax (multiplexed); Flix (multiplexed); HBO (multiplexed); Showtime (multiplexed); Starz (multiplexed); Starz Encore (multiplexed); Sundance TV (multiplexed); The Movie Channel.
Fee: $7.00 monthly (each); $10.00 converter.
Video-On-Demand: No
Internet Service
Operational: Yes. Began: April 1, 2001.
Broadband Service: CableONE.net.
Fee: $75.00 installation; $43.00 monthly; $6.00 modem lease.
Telephone Service
Digital: Operational
Fee: $39.95 monthly
Miles of Plant: 141.0 (coaxial); None (fiber optic). Homes passed: 7,500.
Vice President: Patrick A. Dolohanty. General Manager: Joni Maldonado. Chief Technician: Brian Johns.
Ownership: Cable ONE Inc. (MSO).

GOLDEN SHORES—Golden Valley Cable, 4206 US Hwy 68, Golden Valley, AZ 86413. Phone: 928-565-4190. E-mail: cs@goldenvalleycable.com. Web Site: http://goldenvalleycable.com. Also serves Topock. ICA: AZ0050.
TV Market Ranking: Below 100 (GOLDEN SHORES, Topock).
Channel capacity: 54 (not 2-way capable). Channels available but not in use: N.A.
Basic Service
Subscribers: 49.
Programming (received off-air): KLAS-TV (CBS, MeTV, Movies!) Las Vegas; KTNV-TV (ABC, Grit, Laff) Las Vegas.
Programming (via microwave): KAET (PBS) Phoenix; KAZT-TV (MeTV, Retro TV) Phoenix; KPHO-TV (CBS, COZI TV) Phoenix; KPNX (NBC) Mesa; KSAZ-TV (Bounce TV, FOX, Heroes & Icons) Phoenix; KTVK (This TV) Phoenix; KUTP (Buzzr, MNT, Movies!) Phoenix.
Programming (via satellite): A&E; AMC; CMT; CNN; Comedy Central; C-SPAN 2; Discovery Channel; Disney Channel; ESPN; ESPN2; Fox News Channel; Fox Sports 1; Freeform; FX; History; HLN; KTLA (Antenna TV, CW, This TV) Los Angeles; Lifetime; MSNBC; MTV; Nickelodeon; Pop; QVC; Spike TV; Syfy; TBS; TNT; Trinity Broadcasting Network (TBN); truTV; Turner Classic Movies; TV Land; USA Network; VH1; WGN America.
Fee: $29.95 installation; $43.00 monthly.
Pay Service 1
Pay Units: N.A.
Programming (via satellite): HBO; Showtime; Starz Encore; The Movie Channel.
Internet Service
Operational: No.
Fee: $24.95 monthly.
Telephone Service
None
Miles of Plant: 35.0 (coaxial); None (fiber optic). Homes passed: 1,367.
Ownership: Golden Valley Cable & Communications Inc. (MSO).

GOLDEN VALLEY—Golden Valley Cable & Communications, 4225 West Hwy 68, Unit A, Golden Valley, AZ 86413. Phones: 928-565-3355; 928-565-4190. E-mail: cs@goldenvalleycable.com. Web Site: http://www.goldenvalleycable.com. ICA: AZ0051.
TV Market Ranking: Below 100 (GOLDEN VALLEY).
Channel capacity: N.A. Channels available but not in use: N.A.
Basic Service
Subscribers: 412.
Programming (received off-air): KLAS-TV (CBS, MeTV, Movies!) Las Vegas; KTNV-TV (ABC, Grit, Laff) Las Vegas.
Programming (via microwave): KAET (PBS) Phoenix; KASW (CW) Phoenix; KAZT-TV (MeTV, Retro TV) Phoenix; KMOH-TV (MundoMax) Kingman; KPHO-TV (CBS, COZI TV) Phoenix; KPNX (NBC) Mesa; KSAZ-TV (Bounce TV, FOX, Heroes & Icons) Phoenix; KTVK (This TV) Phoenix.
Programming (via satellite): A&E; AMC; Animal Planet; AZ TV; Bloomberg Television; Cartoon Network; CMT; CNN; Comedy Central; Crime & Investigation Network; C-SPAN; C-SPAN 2; Discovery Channel; ESPN; ESPN2; Food Network; Fox News Channel; Fox Sports 1; FOX Sports West/Prime Ticket; Freeform; FX; FXM; FYI; HGTV; History; History International; HLN; HRTV; Lifetime; MSNBC; MTV; National Geographic Channel; Nickelodeon; Pop; QVC; Spike TV; Syfy; TBS; The Weather Channel; TNT; Trinity Broadcasting Network (TBN); truTV; TV Land; USA Network; VH1; WGN America.
Fee: $39.00 monthly.
Expanded Basic Service 1
Subscribers: N.A.
Programming (via satellite): Hallmark Channel; Hallmark Movies & Mysteries.
Fee: $5.95 monthly.
Pay Service 1
Pay Units: N.A.
Programming (via satellite): HBO; Showtime; Starz Encore; The Movie Channel.
Fee: $3.00 monthly (Encore), $11.95 monthly (Showtime/TMC), $12.95 monthly (HBO), $14.95 monthly (Showtime/TMC/Encore).
Internet Service
Operational: Yes.
Fee: $29.95-$49.95 monthly.
Telephone Service
None
Miles of Plant: 100.0 (coaxial); None (fiber optic). Homes passed: 2,000.
General Manager: D. J. Huffman. Chief Technical Officer: Dan Foote.
Ownership: Golden Valley Cable & Communications Inc.

GRAND CANYON—Formerly served by Indevideo Co. Inc. No longer in operation. ICA: AZ0058.

GRAND MISSOURI MOBILE HOME PARK—Formerly served by Sun Valley Cable Inc. No longer in operation. ICA: AZ0122.

HEBER—Formerly served by RealStar Communications. No longer in operation. ICA: AZ0061.

HOLBROOK—Cable One. Now served by SHOW LOW, AZ [AZ0014]. ICA: AZ0040.

KAYENTA—Formerly served by Frontier Communications. No longer in operation. ICA: AZ0123.

KEARNY—Formerly served by RealStar Communications. No longer in operation. ICA: AZ0052.

KINGMAN—Suddenlink Communications, 520 Maryville Centre Dr, Ste 300, St. Louis, MO 63141. Phones: 800-999-6845 (Customer service); 314-965-2020. Web Site: http://www.suddenlink.com. Also serves Mohave County (portions). ICA: AZ0015.
TV Market Ranking: Below 100 (KINGMAN, Mohave County (portions); Outside TV Markets (Mohave County (portions)). Franchise award date: N.A. Franchise expiration date: N.A. Began: June 1, 1980.
Channel capacity: 70 (operating 2-way). Channels available but not in use: N.A.
Basic Service
Subscribers: 5,912. Commercial subscribers: 569.
Programming (received off-air): KMOH-TV (MundoMax) Kingman; 7 FMs.
Programming (via microwave): KAET (PBS) Phoenix; KASW (CW) Phoenix; KAZT-TV (MeTV, Retro TV) Phoenix; KNXV-TV (ABC) Phoenix; KPHO-TV (CBS, COZI TV) Phoenix; KPNX (NBC) Mesa; KSAZ-TV (Bounce TV, FOX, Heroes & Icons) Phoenix; KTVK (This TV) Phoenix; KUTP (Buzzr, MNT, Movies!) Phoenix.
Programming (via satellite): A&E; AMC; Animal Planet; Cartoon Network; CMT; CNBC; CNN; Comedy Central; C-SPAN; Discovery Channel; Disney Channel; E! HD; ESPN; ESPN Classic; ESPN2; Food Network; Fox News Channel; FOX Sports Arizona; Freeform; FX; Great American Country; HGTV; History; HLN; Lifetime; MSNBC; MTV; Nickelodeon; OWN: Oprah Winfrey Network; Pop; QVC; Spike TV; Syfy; TBS; The Weather Channel; TLC; TNT; Travel Channel; truTV; Turner Classic

Cable Systems—Arizona

Movies; TV Land; Univision Studios; USA Network; VH1; WGN America.
Fee: $40.00 installation; $60.99 monthly; $5.00 converter.

Digital Basic Service
Subscribers: N.A.
Programming (via satellite): AXS TV; BBC America; Chiller; CMT; Cooking Channel; Destination America; Discovery Channel HD; Discovery Kids Channel; Disney XD; DIY Network; DMX Music; ESPN HD; ESPN2 HD; ESPNews; Food Network HD; Fox Deportes; Fox Sports 1; Fox Sports 2; FSN Digital Atlantic; FSN Digital Central; FSN Digital Pacific; FYI; Golf Channel; GSN; Hallmark Channel; HGTV HD; History International; IFC; Investigation Discovery; ION Television; LMN; MTV Classic; MTV2; National Geographic Channel; NBCSN; Nick Jr.; Nicktoons; Oxygen; Science Channel; Syfy HD; TeenNick; TNT HD; Universal HD; USA Network HD; WE tv.

Digital Pay Service 1
Pay Units: N.A.
Programming (via satellite): Cinemax (multiplexed); HBO (multiplexed); Showtime (multiplexed); Starz (multiplexed); Starz Encore (multiplexed); The Movie Channel (multiplexed).
Fee: $6.95 monthly (Cinemax), $9.95 monthly (Starz/Encore), $11.95 monthly (Showtime/TMC), $12.00 monthly (HBO).

Video-On-Demand: Planned

Pay-Per-View
Hot Choice (delivered digitally); iN DEMAND; iN DEMAND (delivered digitally); Spice.

Internet Service
Operational: Yes.
Subscribers: 5,546.
Broadband Service: Suddenlink High Speed Internet.
Fee: $59.95 installation; $24.95 monthly; $5.00 modem lease.

Telephone Service
Digital: Operational
Subscribers: 2,273.
Fee: $39.95 monthly
Miles of Plant: 459.0 (coaxial); 42.0 (fiber optic). Homes passed: 24,186.
Chief Executive Officer: Jerald L. Kent. Executive Vice President & Chief Operating Officer: Thomas P. McMillin. Senior Vice President, Marketing: Mary R. Meier. Senior Vice President, Corporate Finance: Michael Pflantz. Vice President, Accounting: Sabrina Warr.
Ownership: Cequel Communications Holdings I LLC (MSO).

LAKE HAVASU CITY—Suddenlink Communications, 520 Maryville Centre Dr, Ste 300, St. Louis, MO 63141. Phones: 314-315-9400; 800-999-6845 (Customer service). Web Site: http://www.suddenlink.com. Also serves Desert Hills & Mohave County (portions). ICA: AZ0010.
TV Market Ranking: Outside TV Markets (Desert Hills, LAKE HAVASU CITY, Mohave County (portions)). Franchise award date: October 16, 1973. Franchise expiration date: N.A. Began: October 16, 1973.
Channel capacity: 70 (operating 2-way). Channels available but not in use: N.A.

Basic Service
Subscribers: 11,117. Commercial subscribers: 705.
Programming (received off-air): KLHU-CD (IND, The Family Channel) Lake Havasu City; KMOH-TV (MundoMax) Kingman.
Programming (via microwave): KAET (PBS) Phoenix; KASW (CW) Phoenix; KAZT-CD Phoenix; KNXV-TV (ABC) Phoenix; KPHO-TV (CBS, COZI TV) Phoenix; KPNX (NBC) Mesa; KSAZ-TV (Bounce TV, FOX, Heroes & Icons) Phoenix; KTAZ (TMO) Phoenix; KTVK (This TV) Phoenix; KTVW-DT (UNV) Phoenix; KUTP (Buzzr, MNT, Movies!) Phoenix.
Programming (via satellite): A&E; AMC; Animal Planet; Bravo; Cartoon Network; CMT; CNBC; CNN; Comedy Central; C-SPAN; Discovery Channel; Disney Channel; E! HD; ESPN; ESPN Classic; ESPN2; Food Network; Fox News Channel; Fox Sports 1; FOX Sports Arizona; Freeform; FX; HGTV; History; HLN; ION Television; KTLA (Antenna TV, CW, This TV) Los Angeles; Lifetime; LMN; MSNBC; MTV; National Geographic Channel; Nickelodeon; Outdoor Channel; OWN: Oprah Winfrey Network; Pop; QVC; Spike TV; Syfy; TBS; The Weather Channel; TLC; TNT; Travel Channel; Trinity Broadcasting Network (TBN); truTV; TV Land; USA Network; VH1; WGN America.
Fee: $40.00 installation; $60.99 monthly.

Digital Basic Service
Subscribers: N.A.
Programming (via satellite): Discovery Kids Channel; Disney XD; MC; Nick Jr.; Nicktoons; Science Channel; TeenNick.

Digital Pay Service 1
Pay Units: N.A.
Programming (via satellite): Cinemax; HBO; Showtime; Starz; Starz Encore (multiplexed); The Movie Channel.
Fee: $6.95 monthly (Cinemax), $9.95 monthly (Starz/Encore), $11.95 monthly (Showtime/TMC), $12.00 monthly (HBO).

Video-On-Demand: Yes

Pay-Per-View
Hot Choice (delivered digitally); Fresh (delivered digitally); iN DEMAND; iN DEMAND (delivered digitally).

Internet Service
Operational: Yes. Began: May 1, 1998.
Subscribers: 10,377.
Broadband Service: Suddenlink High Speed Internet.
Fee: $59.95 installation; $24.95 monthly; $5.00 modem lease.

Telephone Service
Digital: Operational
Subscribers: 3,879.
Fee: $39.95 monthly
Miles of Plant: 772.0 (coaxial); 172.0 (fiber optic). Homes passed: 43,538.
Chief Executive Officer: Jerald L. Kent. Executive Vice President & Chief Operating Officer: Thomas P. McMillin. Senior Vice President, Corporate Finance: Michael Pflantz. Senior Vice President, Marketing: Mary R. Meier. Vice President, Accounting: Sabrina Warr.
Ownership: Cequel Communications Holdings I LLC (MSO).

LEUPP—Formerly served by Indevideo Co. Inc. No longer in operation. ICA: AZ0115.

LUKE AFB—Cox Communications. Now served by PHOENIX, AZ [AZ0001]. ICA: AZ0092.

MAMMOTH—Formerly served by RealStar Communications. No longer in operation. ICA: AZ0125.

MARICOPA—Orbitel Communications, 9666 East Riggs Rd, Ste 108, Sun Lakes, AZ 85248. Phones: 800-998-8084; 520-568-8890. Fax: 480-895-3150. E-mail: sales@orbitelcom.com. Web Site: http://www.orbitelcom.com. ICA: AZ0142.
TV Market Ranking: 43 (MARICOPA). Franchise award date: N.A. Franchise expiration date: N.A. Began: January 1, 2002.
Channel capacity: N.A. Channels available but not in use: N.A.

Basic Service
Subscribers: 8,790. Commercial subscribers: 537.
Programming (received off-air): KAET (PBS) Phoenix; KASW (CW) Phoenix; KAZT-TV (MeTV, Retro TV) Phoenix; KNXV-TV (ABC) Phoenix; KPAZ-TV (TBN) Phoenix; KPHO-TV (CBS, COZI TV) Phoenix; KPNX (NBC) Mesa; KPPX-TV (ION) Tolleson; KSAZ-TV (Bounce TV, FOX, Heroes & Icons) Phoenix; KTVK (This TV) Phoenix; KTVW-DT (UNV) Phoenix; KUTP (Buzzr, MNT, Movies!) Phoenix.
Programming (via satellite): C-SPAN; EWTN Global Catholic Network; Pop; QVC; TBS; UniMas.
Fee: $49.95 installation; $28.95 monthly.

Expanded Basic Service 1
Subscribers: N.A.
Programming (via satellite): A&E; AMC; Animal Planet; BET; Boomerang; Bravo; Cartoon Network; CMT; CNBC; CNN; CNN en Espanol; Comedy Central; C-SPAN 2; C-SPAN 3; Discovery Channel; Disney Channel; E! HD; ESPN; ESPN2; Food Network; Fox News Channel; FOX Sports Arizona; Freeform; FX; Great American Country; Hallmark Channel; HGTV; History; HLN; Lifetime; MSNBC; MTV; NFL Network; Nickelodeon; Oxygen; Spike TV; The Weather Channel; TLC; TNT; Travel Channel; truTV; TV Land; Univision; USA Network; VH1.
Fee: $29.95 monthly.

Digital Basic Service
Subscribers: N.A.
Programming (via satellite): AXS TV; BBC America; Cloo; Discovery Channel; Disney XD; DMX Music; ESPN Classic; ESPN HD; ESPNews; FOX College Sports Central; FOX College Sports Pacific; Fox Sports 1; Fuse; FXM; FYI; Golf Channel; GSN; HD Theater; History International; IFC; LMN; National Geographic Channel; NBCSN; Nick Jr.; Nicktoons; Outdoor Channel; Syfy; TeenNick; TNT HD; Turner Classic Movies; WE tv; WGN America.

Digital Pay Service 1
Pay Units: N.A.
Programming (via satellite): Cinemax (multiplexed); Cinemax HD; HBO (multiplexed); HBO HD; Outdoor Channel 2 HD; Showtime (multiplexed); Showtime HD; Starz (multiplexed); Starz Encore (multiplexed); Starz HD (multiplexed); The Movie Channel.
Fee: $9.95 monthly (Cinemax or TMC), $11.95 monthly (HBO, Showtime or Starz/Encore).

Internet Service
Operational: Yes.
Fee: $40.95-$55.95 monthly.

Telephone Service
Digital: Operational
Fee: $34.95 monthly
President & Chief Executive Officer: Tom Basinger. Marketing & Programming Director: Bryan Johnson. Technical Operations Manager: Jerry Scullawl. Customer Service Manager: Linda Taylor.
Ownership: Schurz Communications Inc. (MSO).

MESA—Cox Communications. Now served by PHOENIX, AZ [AZ0001]. ICA: AZ0006.

MUNDS PARK—Suddenlink Communications. Now served by SEDONA, AZ [AZ0025]. ICA: AZ0096.

NOGALES—Mediacom, 181 North Arroyo Blvd, Nogales, AZ 85621. Phones: 800-239-8411; 480-474-2087. Fax: 480-474-2084. Web Site: http://www.mediacomcable.com. Also serves Rio Rico & Santa Cruz County (portions). ICA: AZ0017.
TV Market Ranking: Below 100 (NOGALES, Rio Rico, Santa Cruz County (portions)); Outside TV Markets (Santa Cruz County (portions)). Franchise award date: N.A. Franchise expiration date: N.A. Began: May 15, 1978.
Channel capacity: N.A. Channels available but not in use: N.A.

Basic Service
Subscribers: 2,061.
Programming (received off-air): KHRR (TMO) Tucson; KMSB (FOX, Movies!, This TV) Tucson; KWBA-TV (CW, LATV) Sierra Vista; allband FM.
Programming (via microwave): KGUN-TV (ABC, IND) Tucson; KOLD-TV (CBS, MeTV) Tucson; KVOA (Escape, NBC) Tucson.
Programming (via satellite): A&E; AMC; Animal Planet; Cartoon Network; CNBC; CNN; Comedy Central; C-SPAN; Discovery Channel; Disney Channel; Disney XD; E! HD; ESPN; ESPN2; EWTN Global Catholic Network; Food Network; Fox News Channel; Fox Sports 1; Freeform; FX; HGTV; History; HLN; KTTV (FOX) Los Angeles; Lifetime; MSNBC; MTV; Nickelodeon; Outdoor Channel; Pop; QVC; Spike TV; Syfy; TBS; Televisa; The Weather Channel; TLC; TNT; Travel Channel; Trinity Broadcasting Network (TBN); truTV; TV Land; UniMas; Univision; Univision Studios; USA Network; VH1; WGN America.
Fee: $34.95 installation; $68.95 monthly.

Digital Basic Service
Subscribers: N.A.
Programming (via satellite): BBC America; Discovery Digital Networks; ESPNews; GSN; IFC; MTV Classic; National Geographic Channel; NBCSN; Nick Jr.; Starz Encore (multiplexed); Turner Classic Movies.

Digital Pay Service 1
Pay Units: N.A.
Programming (via satellite): Cinemax; Flix; HBO (multiplexed); Showtime; The Movie Channel (multiplexed).
Fee: $8.00 monthly (Starz/Encore), $11.95 monthly (Cinemax or Showtime), $12.95 monthly (HBO).

Video-On-Demand: No

Pay-Per-View
iN DEMAND.

Internet Service
Operational: Yes.
Broadband Service: Mediacom High Speed Internet.
Fee: $59.95 installation; $42.95 monthly; $3.00 modem lease.

Telephone Service
None
Homes passed: 7,495. Miles of plant (coax) included in Apache Junction.
General Manager: Peter Quam. Technical Operations Manager: Pete Purvis. Sales & Marketing Manager: Paul Tremblay.
Ownership: Mediacom LLC (MSO).

ORACLE—Formerly served by RealStar Communications. No longer in operation. ICA: AZ0068.

Arizona—Cable Systems

PAGE—Cable One, 155 5th Ave, PO Box 3049, Page, AZ 86040. Phone: 928-645-2132. Fax: 928-645-3087. E-mail: webmaster@cableone.net. Web Site: http://www.cableone.net. Also serves Coconino County. ICA: AZ0033.
TV Market Ranking: Below 100 (Coconino County (portions)); Outside TV Markets (Coconino County (portions), PAGE). Franchise award date: N.A. Franchise expiration date: N.A. Began: April 1, 1960.
Channel capacity: N.A. Channels available but not in use: N.A.
Basic Service
Subscribers: 641.
Programming (via microwave): KAET (PBS) Phoenix; KASW (CW) Phoenix; KNXV-TV (ABC) Phoenix; KPHO-TV (CBS, COZI TV) Phoenix; KPNX (NBC) Mesa; KSAZ-TV (Bounce TV, FOX, Heroes & Icons) Phoenix; KTVK (This TV) Phoenix.
Programming (via satellite): A&E; AMC; Animal Planet; BYUtv; Cartoon Network; CMT; CNBC; CNN; Comedy Central; C-SPAN; C-SPAN 2; Discovery Channel; Disney Channel; ESPN; ESPN2; Food Network; Fox News Channel; FOX Sports Arizona; Freeform; FX; Hallmark Channel; HGTV; History; HLN; Lifetime; MSNBC; MTV; Nickelodeon; QVC; Spike TV; Syfy; TBS; The Weather Channel; TLC; TNT; Trinity Broadcasting Network (TBN); Turner Classic Movies; TV Land; TVG Network; USA Network; VH1.
Fee: $90.00 installation; $35.00 monthly.
Digital Basic Service
Subscribers: N.A.
Programming (via satellite): Bloomberg Television; Discovery Digital Networks; Disney XD; DMX Music; ESPN Classic; ESPNews; FOX College Sports Central; FOX College Sports Pacific; Fox Sports 1; FXM; FYI; Golf Channel; Great American Country; GSN; History International; National Geographic Channel; NBCSN; Outdoor Channel; TNT HD; Trinity Broadcasting Network (TBN); Universal HD.
Digital Pay Service 1
Pay Units: N.A.
Programming (via satellite): Cinemax (multiplexed); Flix; HBO (multiplexed); Showtime (multiplexed); The Movie Channel (multiplexed).
Fee: $15.00 monthly (each).
Video-On-Demand: No
Pay-Per-View
Hot Network (delivered digitally); movies (delivered digitally); Special Events (delivered digitally).
Internet Service
Operational: Yes.
Broadband Service: CableONE.net.
Fee: $75.00 installation; $43.00 monthly.
Telephone Service
Digital: Operational
Miles of Plant: 56.0 (coaxial); 14.0 (fiber optic). Homes passed: 2,992.
Vice President: Patrick A. Dolohanty. General Manager: John Giattino.
Ownership: Cable ONE Inc. (MSO).

PARADISE VALLEY (portions)—Formerly served by Qwest Choice TV. IPTV service has been discontinued. ICA: AZ5016.

PARKER—Suddenlink Communications, 520 Maryville Centre Dr, Ste 300, St. Louis, MO 63141. Phones: 314-315-9400; 828-855-9855. Web Site: http://www.suddenlink.com. Also serves Colorado River Indian Tribes & La Paz County (portions), AZ; Colorado River Indian Reservation & San Bernardino County (portions), CA. ICA: AZ0016.
TV Market Ranking: Outside TV Markets (Colorado River Indian Reservation, Colorado River Indian Tribes, La Paz County (portions), PARKER, San Bernardino County (portions)). Franchise award date: N.A. Franchise expiration date: N.A. Began: April 1, 1970.
Channel capacity: N.A. Channels available but not in use: N.A.
Basic Service
Subscribers: 2,046.
Programming (received off-air): KYMA-DT (NBC, This TV) Yuma; allband FM.
Programming (via microwave): KAET (PBS) Phoenix; KASW (CW) Phoenix; KMOH-TV (MundoMax) Kingman; KNXV-TV (ABC) Phoenix; KPHO-TV (CBS, COZI TV) Phoenix; KPNX (NBC) Mesa; KSAZ-TV (Bounce TV, FOX, Heroes & Icons) Phoenix; KTVK (This TV) Phoenix; KTVW-DT (UNV) Phoenix; KUTP (Buzzr, MNT, Movies!) Phoenix.
Programming (via satellite): A&E; AMC; Animal Planet; Cartoon Network; CMT; CNBC; CNN; Comedy Central; C-SPAN; Discovery Channel; Disney Channel; E! HD; ESPN; ESPN Classic; ESPN2; Food Network; Fox News Channel; FOX Sports Arizona; Freeform; FX; Great American Country; GSN; HGTV; History; HLN; ION Television; KTLA (Antenna TV, CW, This TV) Los Angeles; Lifetime; MSNBC; MTV; Nickelodeon; OWN: Oprah Winfrey Network; Pop; QVC; Spike TV; Syfy; TBS; Telemundo; The Weather Channel; TLC; TNT; Travel Channel; Trinity Broadcasting Network (TBN); truTV; Turner Classic Movies; TV Land; USA Network; VH1; WE tv; WGN America.
Fee: $24.95 installation; $60.99 monthly; $2.50 converter.
Digital Basic Service
Subscribers: N.A.
Programming (via satellite): BBC America; CMT; Cooking Channel; Discovery Digital Networks; Disney XD; DIY Network; DMX Music; ESPNews; Fox Deportes; Fox Sports 1; Fox Sports 2; FSN Digital Atlantic; FSN Digital Central; FSN Digital Pacific; FYI; Golf Channel; Hallmark Channel; History International; IFC; National Geographic Channel; NBCSN; Nick Jr.; Nicktoons; Outdoor Channel; TeenNick.
Digital Pay Service 1
Pay Units: N.A.
Programming (via satellite): Cinemax (multiplexed); HBO (multiplexed); Showtime (multiplexed); Starz (multiplexed); Starz Encore (multiplexed); The Movie Channel (multiplexed).
Fee: $6.95 monthly (Cinemax), $9.95 monthly (Starz/Encore), $11.95 monthly (Showtime/TMC), $12.00 monthly (HBO).
Video-On-Demand: No
Pay-Per-View
iN DEMAND (delivered digitally); Hot Network; Fresh (delivered digitally).
Internet Service
Operational: Yes.
Broadband Service: Suddenlink High Speed Internet.
Fee: $59.95 installation; $24.95 monthly; $5.00 modem lease.
Telephone Service
Digital: Operational
Fee: $39.95 monthly
Miles of Plant: 172.0 (coaxial); 51.0 (fiber optic). Homes passed: 9,600.
Chief Executive Officer: Jerald L. Kent. Executive Vice President & Chief Operating Officer: Thomas P. McMillin. Senior Vice President, Marketing: Mary R. Meier. Senior Vice President, Corporate Finance: Michael Pflantz.
Ownership: Cequel Communications Holdings I LLC (MSO).

PATAGONIA—Cox Communications. Now served by SIERRA VISTA, AZ [AZ0005]. ICA: AZ0064.

PAYSON (town)—Suddenlink Communications, 520 Maryville Centre Dr, Ste 300, St. Louis, MO 63141. Phones: 800-999-6845 (Customer service); 314-315-9400. Web Site: http://www.suddenlink.com. Also serves Gila County (portions) & Star Valley. ICA: AZ0024.
TV Market Ranking: Outside TV Markets (Gila County (portions), PAYSON (TOWN), Star Valley). Franchise award date: October 1, 1981. Franchise expiration date: N.A. Began: January 1, 1955.
Channel capacity: N.A. Channels available but not in use: N.A.
Basic Service
Subscribers: 3,220. Commercial subscribers: 281.
Programming (received off-air): KAZT-TV (MeTV, Retro TV) Phoenix; KSAZ-TV (Bounce TV, FOX, Heroes & Icons) Phoenix; KTVK (This TV) Phoenix; 12 FMs.
Programming (via microwave): KAET (PBS) Phoenix; KASW (CW) Phoenix; KMOH-TV (MundoMax) Kingman; KNXV-TV (ABC) Phoenix; KPHO-TV (CBS, COZI TV) Phoenix; KPNX (NBC) Mesa; KTVW-DT (UNV) Phoenix; KUTP (Buzzr, MNT, Movies!) Phoenix.
Programming (via satellite): A&E; AMC; Animal Planet; BYUtv; Cartoon Network; CMT; CNBC; CNN; Comedy Central; C-SPAN; Discovery Channel; Disney Channel; E! HD; ESPN; ESPN Classic; ESPN2; ESPNews; EVINE Live; EWTN Global Catholic Network; Food Network; Fox News Channel; Fox Sports 1; FOX Sports Arizona; Freeform; Great American Country; HGTV; History; HLN; ION Television; Lifetime; MSNBC; MTV; Nickelodeon; OWN: Oprah Winfrey Network; Pop; QVC; Spike TV; Syfy; TBS; The Weather Channel; TLC; TNT; Travel Channel; Trinity Broadcasting Network (TBN); Turner Classic Movies; TV Land; USA Network; VH1; WGN America.
Fee: $39.95 installation; $60.99 monthly; $2.50 converter.
Digital Basic Service
Subscribers: N.A.
Programming (via satellite): BBC America; CMT; Cooking Channel; Discovery Digital Networks; Disney XD; DIY Network; DMX Music; Fox Deportes; Fox Sports 2; FSN Digital Atlantic; FSN Digital Central; FSN Digital Pacific; FX; FYI; Golf Channel; GSN; History International; IFC; National Geographic Channel; NBCSN; Nick Jr.; Nicktoons; TeenNick; WE tv.
Digital Pay Service 1
Pay Units: N.A.
Programming (via satellite): Cinemax (multiplexed); HBO (multiplexed); Showtime (multiplexed); Starz; Starz Encore (multiplexed); The Movie Channel (multiplexed).
Fee: $6.95 monthly (Cinemax), $9.95 monthly (Starz/Encore), $11.95 monthly (Showtime/TMC), $12.00 monthly (HBO).
Video-On-Demand: No
Pay-Per-View
iN DEMAND (delivered digitally).
Internet Service
Operational: Yes.
Subscribers: 3,319.
Broadband Service: Suddenlink High Speed Internet.
Fee: $59.95 installation; $24.95 monthly.
Telephone Service
Digital: Operational
Subscribers: 1,385.
Fee: $39.95 monthly
Miles of Plant: 386.0 (coaxial); 34.0 (fiber optic). Homes passed: 12,932. Homes passed includes Pine.
Chief Executive Officer: Jerald L. Kent. Executive Vice President & Chief Operating Officer: Thomas P. McMillin. Senior Vice President, Marketing: Mary R. Meier. Senior Vice President, Corporate Finance: Michael Pflantz.
Ownership: Cequel Communications Holdings I LLC (MSO).

PEACH SPRINGS—Formerly served by Eagle West Communications Inc. No longer in operation. ICA: AZ0071.

PEORIA (portions)—Formerly served by Qwest Choice TV. Now served by CenturyLink Prism, SCOTTSDALE, AZ [AZ5019]. This cable system has converted to IPTV. ICA: AZ5017.

PERRYVILLE—Formerly served by Eagle West Communications Inc. No longer in operation. ICA: AZ0078.

PHOENIX—Cox Communications, 6205 Peachtree Dunwoody Rd, 12th Floor, Atlanta, GA 30328. Phones: 623-594-1000 (Customer service); 404-269-6590. Web Site: http://www.cox.com. Also serves Avondale, Buckeye, Carefree, Casa Grande, Cashion, Cave Creek, Chandler, Coolidge, El Mirage, Florence, Fountain Hills, Gilbert, Glendale, Goodyear, Guadalupe, Litchfield Park, Luke AFB, Maricopa County (portions), Mesa, Paradise Valley, Peoria, Pinal County, Queen Creek, Rio Verde, Scottsdale, Sun City, Sun City West, Sun Lakes, Surprise, Tempe, Tolleson, Wickenburg & Youngtown. ICA: AZ0001.
TV Market Ranking: 43 (Avondale, Buckeye, Carefree, Casa Grande, Cashion, Cave Creek, Chandler, Coolidge, El Mirage, Florence, Fountain Hills, Gilbert, Glendale, Goodyear, Guadalupe, Litchfield Park, Luke AFB, Mesa, Paradise Valley, Peoria, PHOENIX, Pinal County (portions), Queen Creek, Rio Verde, Scottsdale, Sun City, Sun City West, Sun Lakes, Surprise, Tempe, Tolleson, Youngtown); Below 100 (Pinal County (portions)); Outside TV Markets (Wickenburg, Casa Grande, Pinal County (portions)). Franchise award date: N.A. Franchise expiration date: N.A. Began: January 1, 1960.
Channel capacity: 66 (operating 2-way). Channels available but not in use: N.A.
Basic Service
Subscribers: 560,627. Commercial subscribers: 62,027.
Programming (received off-air): KAET (PBS) Phoenix; KASW (CW) Phoenix; KAZT-TV (MeTV, Retro TV) Phoenix; KNXV-TV (ABC) Phoenix; KPAZ-TV (TBN) Phoenix; KPHO-TV (CBS, COZI TV) Phoenix; KPNX (NBC) Mesa; KPPX-TV (ION) Tolleson; KSAZ-TV (Bounce TV, FOX, Heroes & Icons) Phoenix; KTVK (This TV) Phoenix; KTVW-DT (UNV) Phoenix; KUTP (Buzzr, MNT, Movies!) Phoenix; allband FM.

Cable Systems—Arizona

Programming (via satellite): QVC; TBS; WGN America.
Fee: $34.95 installation; $24.99 monthly; $2.65 converter.

Expanded Basic Service 1
Subscribers: N.A.
Programming (via satellite): A&E; Animal Planet; BET; Bravo; Cartoon Network; CMT; CNBC; CNN; Comedy Central; C-SPAN; C-SPAN 2; Disney Channel; E! HD; ESPN; ESPN Classic; ESPN2; Food Network; Fox Sports 1; FOX Sports West/Prime Ticket; Freeform; FX; Golf Channel; Hallmark Channel; HGTV; History; HLN; IFC; Lifetime; MSNBC; MTV; NBC Universo; NBCSN; Nickelodeon; Pop; Syfy; Telemundo; The Weather Channel; TLC; Travel Channel; Turner Classic Movies; TV Land; USA Network; VH1.
Fee: $22.00 monthly.

Expanded Basic Service 2
Subscribers: N.A.
Programming (via satellite): AMC; CMT; Discovery Channel; Spike TV; TNT.
Fee: $3.35 monthly.

Digital Basic Service
Subscribers: N.A.
Programming (via satellite): BBC America; Bloomberg Television; Discovery Digital Networks; Flix; Fuse; GSN; MC; Ovation; Sundance TV.
Fee: $9.95 installation; $2.82 converter.

Pay Service 1
Pay Units: N.A.
Programming (via satellite): Cinemax (multiplexed); HBO (multiplexed); Showtime; Starz (multiplexed); The Movie Channel (multiplexed).
Fee: $7.95 monthly (Cinemax, Starz or TMC), $9.95 monthly (HBO or Showtime).

Digital Pay Service 1
Pay Units: N.A.
Programming (via satellite): Cinemax (multiplexed); HBO (multiplexed); Showtime; Starz (multiplexed); The Movie Channel (multiplexed).
Fee: $10.00 monthly (each).

Video-On-Demand: No

Pay-Per-View
Hot Choice (delivered digitally); iN DEMAND; Fresh; special events (delivered digitally).

Internet Service
Operational: Yes.
Subscribers: 806,174.
Broadband Service: Cox High Speed Internet.
Fee: $99.00 installation; $39.95 monthly; $15.00 modem lease; $399.00 modem purchase.

Telephone Service
Digital: Operational
Subscribers: 446,351.
Fee: $13.00 monthly
Miles of Plant: 24,211.0 (coaxial); 5,264.0 (fiber optic). Homes passed: 1,828,072.
Vice President & Regional Manager: Steve Rizley. Vice President, Ad Sales: Fran Mallace. Vice President, Marketing: Anthony Maldonado. Vice President, Network Operations: Herb Dougall. Vice President, Tax: Mary Vickers. Media Relations Director: David Grabert. Studio Production/Rental Manager: Jonathan Snider.
Ownership: Cox Communications Inc. (MSO).

PHOENIX—Formerly served by Sprint Corp. No longer in operation. ICA: AZ0120.

PHOENIX—Formerly served by TV Max. No longer in operation. ICA: AZ0136.

PHOENIX (portions)—CenturyLink (formerly Qwest). This cable system has converted to IPTV. See SCOTTSDALE, AZ [AZ5019]. ICA: AZ0130.

PINE—Suddenlink Communications, 520 Maryville Centre Dr, Ste 300, St. Louis, MO 63141. Phones: 800-999-6845 (Customer service); 314-315-9400. Web Site: http://www.suddenlink.com. Also serves Gila County (portions) & Strawberry. ICA: AZ0027.
TV Market Ranking: Outside TV Markets (Gila County (portions), PINE, Strawberry). Franchise award date: N.A. Franchise expiration date: N.A. Began: October 1, 1978.
Channel capacity: N.A. Channels available but not in use: N.A.

Basic Service
Subscribers: 527.
Programming (via microwave): KAET (PBS) Phoenix; KASW (CW) Phoenix; KNXV-TV (ABC) Phoenix; KPHO-TV (CBS, COZI TV) Phoenix; KPNX (NBC) Mesa; KSAZ-TV (Bounce TV, FOX, Heroes & Icons) Phoenix; KTVK (This TV) Phoenix; KTVW-DT (UNV) Phoenix; KUTP (Buzzr, MNT, Movies!) Phoenix.
Programming (via satellite): A&E; AMC; Animal Planet; Cartoon Network; CNN; Comedy Central; C-SPAN; Discovery Channel; ESPN; ESPN Classic; ESPN2; EVINE Live; Food Network; Fox News Channel; FOX Sports Arizona; Freeform; FX; Great American Country; HGTV; History; HLN; Lifetime; MTV; Nickelodeon; OWN: Oprah Winfrey Network; QVC; Spike TV; Syfy; TBS; The Weather Channel; TLC; TNT; Travel Channel; Trinity Broadcasting Network (TBN); Turner Classic Movies; TV Land; USA Network; VH1; WGN America.
Fee: $40.00 installation; $60.99 monthly; $5.00 converter.

Pay Service 1
Pay Units: N.A.
Programming (via satellite): Cinemax; HBO.
Fee: $6.95 monthly (Cinemax), $12.00 monthly (HBO).

Video-On-Demand: No

Internet Service
Operational: Yes.
Broadband Service: Suddenlink High Speed Internet.
Fee: $59.95 installation; $24.95 monthly.

Telephone Service
None
Homes passed included in Payson.
Chief Executive Officer: Jerald L. Kent. Executive Vice President & Chief Operating Officer: Thomas P. McMillin. Senior Vice President, Marketing: Mary R. Meier. Vice President, Accounting: Sabrina Warr.
Ownership: Cequel Communications Holdings I LLC (MSO).

POMERENE—Formerly served by Midvale Telephone Exchange Inc. No longer in operation. ICA: AZ0133.

PRESCOTT—Cable One, 3201 Tower Rd, Prescott, AZ 86305-3734. Phone: 928-445-4511. Fax: 928-443-3303. Web Site: http://www.cableone.net. Also serves Chino Valley, Dewey, Humboldt, Mayer, Paulden, Prescott Valley & Yavapai County (portions). ICA: AZ0007.
TV Market Ranking: Outside TV Markets (Chino Valley, Dewey, Humboldt, Mayer, Paulden, PRESCOTT, Prescott Valley, Yavapai County (portions)). Franchise award date: December 1, 1953. Franchise expiration date: N.A. Began: July 1, 1953.
Channel capacity: 54 (operating 2-way). Channels available but not in use: N.A.

Basic Service
Subscribers: 15,368.
Programming (received off-air): KAZT-TV (MeTV, Retro TV) Phoenix; 17 FMs.
Programming (via microwave): KAET (PBS) Phoenix; KASW (CW) Phoenix; KFPH-DT (getTV, UniMas) Flagstaff; KNAZ-TV (NBC) Flagstaff; KNXV-TV (ABC) Phoenix; KPHO-TV (CBS, COZI TV) Phoenix; KPNX (NBC) Mesa; KSAZ-TV (Bounce TV, FOX, Heroes & Icons) Phoenix; KTVK (This TV) Phoenix; KUTP (Buzzr, MNT, Movies!) Phoenix.
Programming (via satellite): A&E; AMC; Animal Planet; Bravo; Cartoon Network; CMT; CNBC; CNN; Comedy Central; C-SPAN; C-SPAN 2; Discovery Channel; Disney Channel; ESPN; ESPN2; Fox News Channel; FOX Sports Arizona; Freeform; FX; HGTV; History; HLN; ION Television; Lifetime; MSNBC; MTV; Nickelodeon; Pop; QVC; Spike TV; Syfy; TBS; The Weather Channel; TLC; TNT; Trinity Broadcasting Network (TBN); Turner Classic Movies; TV Land; USA Network; VH1; WGN America.
Fee: $90.00 installation; $35.00 monthly; $.90 converter.

Digital Basic Service
Subscribers: N.A.
Programming (via satellite): Boomerang; Discovery Digital Networks; Disney XD; ESPN Classic; ESPNews; Fox Sports 1; FYI; Hallmark Channel; History International; National Geographic Channel; truTV.

Digital Pay Service 1
Pay Units: N.A.
Programming (via satellite): Cinemax (multiplexed); DMX Music; Flix (multiplexed); HBO (multiplexed); Showtime (multiplexed); Sundance TV (multiplexed); The Movie Channel (multiplexed).

Video-On-Demand: No

Pay-Per-View
ESPN Sports 1-6 (delivered digitally); ETC (delivered digitally); Playboy TV (delivered digitally); Pleasure (delivered digitally); Fresh (delivered digitally); Shorteez (delivered digitally).

Internet Service
Operational: Yes.
Subscribers: 25,687.
Broadband Service: CableONE.net.
Fee: $75.00 installation; $43.00 monthly.

Telephone Service
Digital: Operational
Subscribers: 10,323.
Fee: $39.95 monthly
Miles of Plant: 2,056.0 (coaxial); 298.0 (fiber optic). Homes passed: 64,887.
Vice President: Patrick A. Dolohanty. General Manager: Dennis Edwards. Marketing Director: J. J. McCormick. Customer Service Manager: Trudy Szabo.
Ownership: Cable ONE Inc. (MSO).

Access the most current data instantly
FREE TRIAL @ ADVANCED TVFactbook
TELCO/IPTV • CABLE TV • TV STATIONS
www.warren-news.com/factbook.htm

QUARTZSITE—Formerly served by Americable International Arizona Inc. No longer in operation. ICA: AZ0036.

RIO VERDE—Cox Communications. Now served by PHOENIX, AZ [AZ0001]. ICA: AZ0100.

ROBSON RANCH—Orbitel Communications, 9666 East Riggs Rd, Ste 108, Sun Lakes, AZ 85248. Phones: 480-895-8084; 800-998-8084. Fax: 480-895-3150. E-mail: sales@orbitelcom.com. Web Site: http://www.orbitelcom.com. ICA: AZ0141.
TV Market Ranking: Outside TV Markets (ROBSON RANCH).
Channel capacity: N.A. Channels available but not in use: N.A.

Basic Service
Subscribers: 124.
Programming (received off-air): KAET (PBS) Phoenix; KASW (CW) Phoenix; KAZT-TV (MeTV, Retro TV) Phoenix; KNXV-TV (ABC) Phoenix; KPAZ-TV (TBN) Phoenix; KPHO-TV (CBS, COZI TV) Phoenix; KPNX (NBC) Mesa; KPPX-TV (ION) Tolleson; KSAZ-TV (Bounce TV, FOX, Heroes & Icons) Phoenix; KTVK (This TV) Phoenix; KTVW-DT (UNV) Phoenix; KUTP (Buzzr, MNT, Movies!) Phoenix.
Programming (via satellite): EVINE Live; INSP; Pop; QVC; WGN America.
Fee: $40.00 installation; $32.55 monthly.

Expanded Basic Service 1
Subscribers: N.A.
Programming (via satellite): A&E; AMC; Animal Planet; AWE; Bravo; CMT; CNBC; CNN; Comedy Central; C-SPAN; C-SPAN 2; Discovery Channel; Disney Channel; E! HD; ESPN; ESPN Classic; ESPN2; Food Network; Fox News Channel; Fox Sports 1; FOX Sports Arizona; Freeform; FX; Golf Channel; GSN; Hallmark Channel; HGTV; History; HLN; Lifetime; MSNBC; MTV; National Geographic Channel; NBCSN; Nickelodeon; Spike TV; Syfy; TBS; Tennis Channel; The Weather Channel; TLC; TNT; Travel Channel; truTV; Turner Classic Movies; TV Land; USA Network; VH1; WE tv.
Fee: $27.00 monthly.

Digital Basic Service
Subscribers: N.A.
Programming (via satellite): BBC America; Bloomberg Television; Cloo; Cooking Channel; Discovery Digital Networks; DMX Music; ESPNews; FOX College Sports Central; FOX College Sports Pacific; FXM; FYI; Great American Country; History International; LMN; Nick Jr.; Nicktoons; Outdoor Channel; TeenNick; Trinity Broadcasting Network (TBN).

Digital Pay Service 1
Pay Units: 5.
Programming (via satellite): Cinemax (multiplexed); HBO (multiplexed); Showtime (multiplexed); Starz (multiplexed); Starz Encore (multiplexed); The Movie Channel (multiplexed).
Fee: $13.00 monthly (Cinemax, HBO, Showtime/TMC or Starz/Encore).

Video-On-Demand: No

2017 Edition

Arizona—Cable Systems

Pay-Per-View
iN DEMAND (delivered digitally); Hot Choice (delivered digitally).
Internet Service
Operational: Yes.
Broadband Service: In-house.
Fee: $99.00 installation; $41.95-$73.45 monthly.
Telephone Service
Digital: Operational
Fee: $39.95 monthly
Miles of Plant: 13.0 (coaxial); None (fiber optic). Homes passed: 388. Miles of plant (coaxial) includes fiber miles.
President & Chief Executive Officer: Tom Basinger. Marketing & Programming Director: Bryan Johnson. Technical Operations Manager: Jerry Scullawl. Customer Service Manager: Linda Taylor.
Ownership: Schurz Communications Inc. (MSO).

ROOSEVELT TWP.—Formerly served by Salt River Cablevision. No longer in operation. ICA: AZ0131.

SADDLE MOUNTAIN—Formerly served by Eagle West Communications Inc. No longer in operation. ICA: AZ0109.

SADDLEBROOKE—Orbitel Communications, 9666 East Riggs Rd, Ste 108, Sun Lakes, AZ 85248. Phones: 480-895-8084; 800-998-8084. Fax: 480-895-3150. E-mail: sales@orbitelcom.com. Web Site: http://www.orbitelcom.com. ICA: AZ0140.
TV Market Ranking: Below 100 (SADDLEBROOKE).
Channel capacity: N.A. Channels available but not in use: N.A.
Basic Service
Subscribers: 1,569.
Programming (received off-air): KGUN-TV (ABC, IND) Tucson; KMSB (FOX, Movies!, This TV) Tucson; KOLD-TV (CBS, MeTV) Tucson; KTTU (Estrella TV, MNT) Tucson; KUAT-TV (PBS) Tucson; KVOA (Escape, NBC) Tucson; KWBA-TV (CW, LATV) Sierra Vista.
Programming (via satellite): C-SPAN; C-SPAN 2; EVINE Live; KUSA (NBC, WeatherNation) Denver; QVC; TBS; Telemundo; Trinity Broadcasting Network (TBN); WGN America.
Fee: $32.55 monthly.
Expanded Basic Service 1
Subscribers: N.A.
Programming (via satellite): A&E; AMC; Animal Planet; AWE; Bravo; CMT; CNBC; CNN; Comedy Central; Discovery Channel; Disney Channel; E! HD; ESPN; ESPN Classic; ESPN2; Food Network; Fox News Channel; Fox Sports 1; FOX Sports Arizona; Freeform; FX; Golf Channel; GSN; Hallmark Channel; HGTV; History; HLN; Lifetime; MSNBC; MTV; National Geographic Channel; NBCSN; Nickelodeon; Pop; Spike TV; Syfy; Tennis Channel; The Weather Channel; TLC; TNT; Travel Channel; truTV; Turner Classic Movies; TV Land; USA Network; VH1; WE tv.
Fee: $27.00 monthly.
Digital Basic Service
Subscribers: N.A.
Programming (via satellite): AXS TV; BBC America; Bloomberg Television; Cloo; Cooking Channel; Discovery Digital Networks; DMX Music; ESPNews; FOX College Sports Central; FOX College Sports Pacific; FXM; FYI; Great American Country; HD Theater; History International; LMN; Nick Jr.; Nicktoons; Outdoor Channel; TeenNick; Trinity Broadcasting Network (TBN); Universal HD.
Digital Pay Service 1
Pay Units: 464.
Programming (via satellite): Cinemax (multiplexed); HBO (multiplexed); Showtime (multiplexed); Starz (multiplexed); Starz Encore (multiplexed); The Movie Channel (multiplexed).
Fee: $13.00 monthly (Cinemax, HBO, Starz/Encore or Showtime/TMC).
Video-On-Demand: No
Pay-Per-View
iN DEMAND (delivered digitally); Hot Choice (delivered digitally).
Internet Service
Operational: Yes.
Broadband Service: In-house.
Fee: $99.00 installation; $41.95-$73.45 monthly.
Telephone Service
Digital: Operational
Miles of Plant: 93.0 (coaxial); None (fiber optic). Homes passed: 4,549. Miles of plant (coax) includes miles of plant (fiber).
President & Chief Executive Officer: Tom Basinger. Marketing & Programming Director: Bryan Johnson. Technical Operations Manager: Jerry Scullawl. Customer Service Manager: Linda Taylor.
Ownership: Schurz Communications Inc. (MSO).

SAFFORD—Cable One, 1996 Thatcher Blvd, Safford, AZ 85546-3318. Phone: 928-428-1850. Fax: 928-428-0774. E-mail: sbrideau@cableone.net. Web Site: http://www.cableone.net. Also serves Clifton, Graham County, Morenci, Pima, Solomon, Swift Trail & Thatcher. ICA: AZ0021.
TV Market Ranking: Outside TV Markets (Graham County, Morenci, Pima, SAFFORD, Solomon, Swift Trail, Thatcher, Clifton). Franchise award date: N.A. Franchise expiration date: N.A. Began: April 1, 1962.
Channel capacity: N.A. Channels available but not in use: N.A.
Basic Service
Subscribers: 2,590.
Programming (via microwave): KAET (PBS) Phoenix; KGUN-TV (ABC, IND) Tucson; KNXV-TV (ABC) Phoenix; KPHO-TV (CBS, COZI TV) Phoenix; KPNX (NBC) Mesa; KSAZ-TV (Bounce TV, FOX, Heroes & Icons) Phoenix; KTVK (This TV) Phoenix; KUTP (Buzzr, MNT, Movies!) Phoenix.
Programming (via satellite): A&E; Animal Planet; BYUtv; Cartoon Network; CMT; CNBC; CNN; Comedy Central; C-SPAN; C-SPAN 2; Discovery Channel; Disney Channel; ESPN; ESPN2; Food Network; Fox Deportes; Fox News Channel; FOX Sports Arizona; FX; HGTV; History; HLN; Lifetime; MSNBC; MTV; Nickelodeon; Pop; QVC; Syfy; TBS; The Weather Channel; TLC; Trinity Broadcasting Network (TBN); Turner Classic Movies; TV Land; USA Network; VH1; WGN America.
Fee: $15.47 installation; $35.00 monthly.
Digital Basic Service
Subscribers: N.A.
Programming (via satellite): Boomerang; BYUtv; Discovery Digital Networks; Disney XD; ESPN Classic; ESPNews; FamilyNet; FOX College Sports Central; FOX College Sports Pacific; Fox Sports 1; Fox Sports 2; FXM; FYI; Golf Channel; Great American Country; Hallmark Channel; History; History International; INSP; MC; National Geographic Channel; Outdoor Channel; Trinity Broadcasting Network (TBN); truTV; TVG Network.
Digital Pay Service 1
Pay Units: N.A.
Programming (via satellite): Cinemax (multiplexed); HBO (multiplexed); Showtime; Starz; Starz Encore; The Movie Channel.
Fee: $7.00 monthly (each).
Video-On-Demand: No
Pay-Per-View
Shorteez (delivered digitally); ESPN Now (delivered digitally); Pleasure (delivered digitally); ETC (delivered digitally); Playboy TV (delivered digitally); Fresh (delivered digitally).
Internet Service
Operational: Yes. Began: October 2, 2002.
Broadband Service: CableONE.net.
Fee: $75.00 installation; $43.00 monthly; $5.00 modem lease.
Telephone Service
Digital: Operational
Fee: $39.95 monthly
Miles of Plant: 224.0 (coaxial); 43.0 (fiber optic). Homes passed: 9,900.
General Manager: Stephen Brideau. Chief Technician: Chuck Dunlap.
Ownership: Cable ONE Inc. (MSO).

SALOME—Formerly served by San Carlos Cablevision. No longer in operation. ICA: AZ0128.

SAN CARLOS—San Carlos Apache Telecom, 10 Telecom Ln, PO Box 1000, Peridot, AZ 85542. Phone: 928-475-2433. Fax: 928-475-7047. Web Site: http://www.scatui.net. Also serves Bylas, Gila County (portions) & Peridot. ICA: AZ0046.
TV Market Ranking: Outside TV Markets (Gila County (portions), Peridot, SAN CARLOS, Bylas). Franchise award date: N.A. Franchise expiration date: N.A. Began: April 1, 1983.
Channel capacity: N.A. Channels available but not in use: N.A.
Basic Service
Subscribers: 526.
Programming (received off-air): KAET (PBS) Phoenix; KGUN-TV (ABC, IND) Tucson; KNXV-TV (ABC) Phoenix; KPHO-TV (CBS, COZI TV) Phoenix; KPNX (NBC) Mesa; KSAZ-TV (Bounce TV, FOX, Heroes & Icons) Phoenix; KTVK (This TV) Phoenix; KUTP (Buzzr, MNT, Movies!) Phoenix; allband FM.
Fee: $44.00 installation; $49.95 monthly.
Digital Basic Service
Subscribers: 187.
Programming (via satellite): A&E; AMC; CNN; Comedy Central; C-SPAN; Discovery Channel; Discovery Life Channel; Disney Channel; Disney XD; ESPN; ESPN2; FOX Sports Arizona; Freeform; Great American Country; Hallmark Channel; HGTV; History; HLN; MTV; Nickelodeon; Outdoor Channel; Spike TV; Syfy; TBS; The Weather Channel; TLC; TNT; Trinity Broadcasting Network (TBN); Turner Classic Movies; TV Land; USA Network; VH1.
Fee: $44.00 installation; $49.95 monthly.
Pay Service 1
Pay Units: N.A.
Programming (via satellite): HBO; Showtime; The Movie Channel.
Fee: $8.00 monthly (Showtime or TMC), $10.95 monthly (Showtime/TMC), $10.00 monthly (HBO).
Digital Pay Service 1
Pay Units: N.A.
Programming (via satellite): Flix; HBO (multiplexed); Showtime (multiplexed); Starz (multiplexed); Starz Encore (multiplexed); The Movie Channel (multiplexed).
Fee: $15.00 monthly (each).
Internet Service
Operational: Yes.
Fee: $99.00 installation; $29.95 monthly.
Telephone Service
Digital: Operational
Fee: $15.00 monthly
Miles of Plant: 64.0 (coaxial); 6.0 (fiber optic). Homes passed: 1,200.
Chief Executive Officer & General Manager: Shirley Ortiz. Operations Manager: Gary Uhles. Sales & Marketing: Marion Case.
Ownership: San Carlos Apache Telecommunications Utility Inc. (MSO).

SAN JUAN—Formerly served by RealStar Communications. No longer in operation. ICA: AZ0044.

SANTA RITA BEL AIRE—Cox Communications. Now served by TUCSON, AZ [AZ0002]. ICA: AZ0137.

SCOTTSDALE—CenturyLink Prism, 135 West Orion St, Tempe, AZ 85283. Phones: 888-723-8010; 888-273-5968; 800-244-1111. E-mail: prismtveverywhere@centurylink.net. Web Site: http://www.centurylink.com/prismtv. Also serves Apache Junction, Buckeye, Casa Grande, Chandler, Gilbert, Glendale, Goodyear, Maricopa City, Maricopa County (unincorporated areas), Mesa, Paradise Valley, Peoria, Phoenix, Pinal County (unincorporated areas), Queen Creek, Surprise & Tempe. ICA: AZ5019.
Channel capacity: N.A. Channels available but not in use: N.A.
Prism Essential
Subscribers: 50,241.
Fee: $39.99 monthly. Includes 150+ channels including music channels.
Prism Complete
Subscribers: N.A.
Fee: $44.99 monthly. Includes 200+ channels including music channels.
Prism Preferred
Subscribers: N.A.
Fee: $54.99 monthly. Includes 310+ channels including Showtime/TMC & Starz/Encore.
Prism Premium
Subscribers: N.A.
Fee: $84.99 monthly. Includes 340+ channels including all premium movie channels.
HD
Subscribers: N.A.
Fee: $11.99 monthly.
Prism Paquette Latino
Subscribers: N.A.
Fee: $8.49 monthly.
Prism Sports
Subscribers: N.A.
Fee: $8.99 monthly.
Cinemax
Subscribers: N.A.
Fee: $17.49 monthly.
HBO
Subscribers: N.A.
Fee: $18.99 monthly.
Showtime/TMC
Subscribers: N.A.
Fee: $14.49 monthly.
Starz/Encore
Subscribers: N.A.
Fee: $17.49 monthly.
Video-On-Demand: Yes
Internet Service
Operational: Yes.
Fee: $29.95 monthly.
Telephone Service
Digital: Operational
Fee: $16.47 monthly

Cable Systems—Arizona

Vice President, Operations: Guy Gunther. Ownership: CenturyLink.

SEDONA—Suddenlink Communications, 520 Maryville Centre Dr, Ste 300, St. Louis, MO 63141. Phones: 800-999-6845 (Customer service); 314-315-9400. Web Site: http://www.suddenlink.com. Also serves Camp Verde, Cottonwood (southeastern portions), Lake Montezuma, Munds Park, Oak Creek (village), Pinewood & Verde Village. ICA: AZ0025.

TV Market Ranking: Below 100 (Munds Park, Oak Creek (village), Pinewood, SEDONA); Outside TV Markets (Camp Verde, Cottonwood (southeastern portions), Lake Montezuma, Verde Village). Franchise award date: November 1, 1959. Franchise expiration date: N.A. Began: November 1, 1959. Channel capacity: 5 (operating 2-way). Channels available but not in use: N.A.

Basic Service
Subscribers: 4,746. Commercial subscribers: 539.
Programming (received off-air): KMOH-TV (MundoMax) Kingman; allband FM.
Programming (via microwave): KAET (PBS) Phoenix; KASW (CW) Phoenix; KAZT-TV (MeTV, Retro TV) Phoenix; KFPH-DT (getTV, UniMas) Flagstaff; KNAZ-TV (NBC) Flagstaff; KNXV-TV (ABC) Phoenix; KPHO-TV (CBS, COZI TV) Phoenix; KPNX (NBC) Mesa; KSAZ-TV (Bounce TV, FOX, Heroes & Icons) Phoenix; KTVK (This TV) Phoenix; KTVW-DT (UNV) Phoenix; KUTP (Buzzr, MNT, Movies!) Phoenix.
Programming (via satellite): A&E; AMC; Animal Planet; Cartoon Network; CMT; CNBC; CNN; Comedy Central; C-SPAN; C-SPAN 2; Discovery Channel; E! HD; ESPN; ESPN Classic; ESPN2; EWTN Global Catholic Network; Food Network; Fox News Channel; FOX Sports Arizona; Freeform; FX; Golf Channel; Great American Country; HGTV; History; HLN; Lifetime; MSNBC; MTV; Nickelodeon; OWN: Oprah Winfrey Network; Pop; QVC; Spike TV; Syfy; TBS; The Weather Channel; TLC; TNT; Travel Channel; Trinity Broadcasting Network (TBN); truTV; Turner Classic Movies; TV Land; USA Network; VH1; WGN America.
Fee: $39.95 installation; $60.99 monthly.

Digital Basic Service
Subscribers: N.A.
Programming (via satellite): BBC America; Cooking Channel; Discovery Digital Networks; DIY Network; DMX Music; ESPNews; FOX College Sports Central; FOX College Sports Pacific; Fox Deportes; Fox Sports 1; Fox Sports 2; FYI; GSN; History International; IFC; LMN; National Geographic Channel; NBCSN; Nick Jr.; Nicktoons; TeenNick; WE tv.

Digital Pay Service 1
Pay Units: N.A.
Programming (via satellite): Cinemax (multiplexed); HBO (multiplexed); Showtime (multiplexed); Starz (multiplexed); Starz Encore (multiplexed); The Movie Channel (multiplexed).
Fee: $6.95 monthly (Cinemax), $9.95 monthly (Starz/Encore), $11.95 monthly (Showtime/TMC), $12.00 monthly (HBO).

Video-On-Demand: No

Pay-Per-View
iN DEMAND (delivered digitally).

Internet Service
Operational: Yes.
Subscribers: 3,965.

Broadband Service: Suddenlink High Speed Internet.
Fee: $59.95 installation; $24.95 monthly; $5.00 modem lease.

Telephone Service
Analog: Not Operational
Digital: Operational
Subscribers: 1,424.
Fee: $39.95 monthly

Miles of Plant: 607.0 (coaxial); 36.0 (fiber optic). Homes passed: 25,768.
Chief Executive Officer: Jerald L. Kent. Executive Vice President & Chief Operating Officer: Thomas P. McMillin. Senior Vice President, Marketing: Mary R. Meier. Senior Vice President, Corporate Finance: Michael Pflantz.
Ownership: Cequel Communications Holdings I LLC (MSO).

SELLS—Formerly served by Red Hawk Cable. No longer in operation. ICA: AZ0053.

SHOW LOW—Cable One, 1341 East Thornton St, Show Low, AZ 85901. Phones: 602-364-6000 (Phoenix office); 800-742-4524; 928-537-2279. Fax: 928-537-0607. E-mail: bdorsey@cableone.net. Web Site: http://www.cableone.net. Also serves Bushman Acres, Holbrook, Joseph City, Lakeside, Navajo County (portions), Pinetop, Pineview, Snowflake, Taylor & Winslow. ICA: AZ0014.
TV Market Ranking: Below 100 (Bushman Acres, Holbrook, Joseph City, Pineview, Snowflake, Taylor, Winslow, Navajo County (portions)); Outside TV Markets (Lakeside, Pinetop, SHOW LOW, Navajo County (portions)). Franchise award date: September 1, 1968. Franchise expiration date: N.A. Began: April 1, 1962.
Channel capacity: N.A. Channels available but not in use: N.A.

Basic Service
Subscribers: 11,301.
Programming (via microwave): KAET (PBS) Phoenix; KNXV-TV (ABC) Phoenix; KPHO-TV (CBS, COZI TV) Phoenix; KPNX (NBC) Mesa; KSAZ-TV (Bounce TV, FOX, Heroes & Icons) Phoenix; KTVK (This TV) Phoenix.
Programming (via satellite): Telemundo; Univision Studios; WGN America.
Fee: $90.00 installation; $24.00 monthly.

Expanded Basic Service 1
Subscribers: N.A.
Programming (via satellite): A&E; AMC; Animal Planet; Cartoon Network; CMT; CNBC; CNN; C-SPAN; Discovery Channel; Disney Channel; ESPN; ESPN2; Food Network; Fox News Channel; FOX Sports Arizona; Freeform; FX; HGTV; History; HLN; MSNBC; MTV; Nickelodeon; Pop; QVC; Spike TV; Syfy; TBS; The Weather Channel; TLC; TNT; Travel Channel; Turner Classic Movies; TV Land; USA Network; VH1.
Fee: $42.50 monthly.

Digital Basic Service
Subscribers: N.A.
Programming (via satellite): 3ABN; Boomerang; BYUtv; Discovery Digital Networks; Disney XD; ESPN Classic; FamilyNet; FOX College Sports Central; FOX College Sports Pacific; Fox Sports 1; Fox Sports 2; FXM; FYI; Golf Channel; Great American Country; GSN; Hallmark Channel; History International; HITS (Headend In The Sky); INSP; MC; National Geographic Channel; Outdoor Channel; TNT HD; Trinity Broadcasting Network (TBN); truTV; TVG Network; Universal HD; WE tv.

Digital Pay Service 1
Pay Units: N.A.
Programming (via satellite): Cinemax (multiplexed); HBO (multiplexed); Showtime; Showtime HD; Starz In Black; Sundance TV; The Movie Channel (multiplexed); The Movie Channel HD.
Fee: $7.00 monthly (each).

Video-On-Demand: No

Pay-Per-View
Pleasure (delivered digitally); SexSee (delivered digitally); Juicy (delivered digitally); VaVoom (delivered digitally).

Internet Service
Operational: Yes. Began: June 1, 2002.
Subscribers: 7,998.
Broadband Service: CableONE.net.
Fee: $75.00 installation; $43.00 monthly; $5.00 modem lease.

Telephone Service
Digital: Operational
Subscribers: 3,485.
Fee: $39.95 monthly

Miles of Plant: 1,104.0 (coaxial); 245.0 (fiber optic). Homes passed: 26,999.
Vice President: Patrick A. Dolohanty. General Manager: Brad Dorsey. Chief Technician: Lyle Sumic. Marketing Director: Glen Erickson.
Ownership: Cable ONE Inc. (MSO).

SIERRA VISTA—Cox Communications, 6205 Peachtree Dunwoody Rd, 12th Floor, Atlanta, GA 30328. Phones: 623-328-3121 (Phoenix office); 404-269-6590. Web Site: http://www.cox.com. Also serves Douglas, Fort Huachuca, Huachuca City, Miller Canyon (unincorporated area), Nicksville, Patagonia, Pirtleville, Ramsey Canyon (unincorporated area), Sonoita, St. David, Stump Canyon (unincorporated area), Sunsites, Tombstone & Whetstone. ICA: AZ0005.
TV Market Ranking: Below 100 (Fort Huachuca, Huachuca City, Miller Canyon (unincorporated area), Nicksville, Ramsey Canyon (unincorporated area), SIERRA VISTA, Sonoita, St. David, Stump Canyon (unincorporated area), Tombstone, Whetstone, Patagonia); Outside TV Markets (Pirtleville, Sunsites, Douglas). Franchise award date: June 1, 1967. Franchise expiration date: N.A. Began: January 1, 1967.
Channel capacity: N.A. Channels available but not in use: N.A.

Basic Service
Subscribers: 10,697. Commercial subscribers: 370.
Programming (received off-air): KGUN-TV (ABC, IND) Tucson; KMSB (FOX, Movies!, This TV) Tucson; KOLD-TV (CBS, MeTV) Tucson; KTTU (Estrella TV, MNT) Tucson; KUAT-TV (PBS) Tucson; KVOA (Escape, NBC) Tucson; KWBA-TV (CW, LATV) Sierra Vista; 20 FMs.
Programming (via satellite): Discovery Channel; HLN; TBS; WGN America.
Fee: $50.21 installation; $24.99 monthly.

Expanded Basic Service 1
Subscribers: N.A.
Programming (via satellite): A&E; AMC; Animal Planet; BET; Cartoon Network; CMT; CNBC; CNN; Comedy Central; C-SPAN; Disney Channel; E! HD; ESPN; ESPN2; Food Network; Fox News Channel; FOX Sports Southwest; Freeform; Hallmark Channel; HGTV; History; Lifetime; MoviePlex; MTV; Nickelodeon; Pop; Spike TV; Syfy; The Weather Channel; TLC; TNT; Travel Channel; Turner Classic Movies; USA Network; VH1.
Fee: $27.52 monthly.

Digital Basic Service
Subscribers: N.A.
Programming (via satellite): BBC America; Bravo; Discovery Digital Networks; ESPN Classic; Golf Channel; GSN; HGTV; IFC; NBCSN; WE tv.

Pay Service 1
Pay Units: N.A.
Programming (via satellite): Cinemax; HBO; Showtime; Starz; Starz Encore; The Movie Channel.
Fee: $20.00 installation; $10.95 monthly (Cinemax/HBO/Showtime/TMC or Starz/Encore).

Digital Pay Service 1
Pay Units: N.A.
Programming (via satellite): Cinemax (multiplexed); HBO (multiplexed); Showtime (multiplexed); Starz (multiplexed); Starz Encore (multiplexed); The Movie Channel.
Fee: $10.95 monthly (Cinemax, HBO, Showtime/TMC or Starz/Encore).

Video-On-Demand: Planned

Pay-Per-View
ESPN Now (delivered digitally); iN DEMAND (delivered digitally); Fresh (delivered digitally).

Internet Service
Operational: Yes.
Subscribers: 16,242.
Broadband Service: Cox High Speed Internet.
Fee: $49.95 monthly.

Telephone Service
Digital: Operational
Subscribers: 4,165.

Miles of Plant: 862.0 (coaxial); 304.0 (fiber optic). Homes passed: 52,056. Miles of plant (coax & fiber) included in Phoenix.
Vice President & Regional Manager: Steve Rizley. Vice President, Marketing: Anthony Maldonado. Vice President & Systems Manager: Anne Doris. Vice President, Tax: Mary Vickers. Media Relations Director: David Grabert.
Ownership: Cox Communications Inc. (MSO).

ST. JOHNS—Formerly served by RealStar Communications. No longer in operation. ICA: AZ0045.

SUN LAKES—Orbitel Communications, 9666 East Riggs Rd, Ste 108, Sun Lakes, AZ 85248. Phones: 480-895-8084; 800-998-8084. Fax: 480-895-3150. E-mail: sales@orbitelcom.com. Web Site: http://www.orbitelcom.com. Also serves Sunbird. ICA: AZ0139.
TV Market Ranking: 43 (SUN LAKES).
Channel capacity: N.A. Channels available but not in use: N.A.

Arizona—Cable Systems

Basic Service
Subscribers: 2,618.
Programming (received off-air): KAET (PBS) Phoenix; KASW (CW) Phoenix; KAZT-TV (MeTV, Retro TV) Phoenix; KDPH-LP (Daystar TV, TMO) Phoenix; KNXV-TV (ABC) Phoenix; KPAZ-TV (TBN) Phoenix; KPHO-TV (CBS, COZI TV) Phoenix; KPNX (NBC) Mesa; KPPX-TV (ION) Tolleson; KSAZ-TV (Bounce TV, FOX, Heroes & Icons) Phoenix; KTVK (This TV) Phoenix; KTVW-DT (UNV) Phoenix; KUTP (Buzzr, MNT, Movies!) Phoenix.
Programming (via satellite): EVINE Live; QVC; TBS; WGN America.
Fee: $40.00 installation; $32.55 monthly.

Expanded Basic Service 1
Subscribers: N.A.
Programming (via satellite): A&E; AMC; Animal Planet; AWE; Bravo; CMT; CNBC; CNN; Comedy Central; C-SPAN; C-SPAN 2; Discovery Channel; Disney Channel; E! HD; ESPN; ESPN Classic; ESPN2; Food Network; Fox News Channel; Fox Sports 1; FOX Sports Arizona; Freeform; FX; Golf Channel; GSN; Hallmark Channel; HGTV; History; HLN; INSP; Jewelry Television; Lifetime; MSNBC; MTV; National Geographic Channel; NBCSN; Nickelodeon; Pop; Spike TV; Syfy; Tennis Channel; The Weather Channel; TLC; TNT; Travel Channel; truTV; Turner Classic Movies; TV Land; USA Network; VH1; WE tv.
Fee: $27.95 monthly.

Digital Basic Service
Subscribers: N.A.
Programming (via satellite): AXS TV; BBC America; Bloomberg Television; Cloo; Cooking Channel; Discovery Digital Networks; DIY Network; DMX Music; ESPNews; FOX College Sports Central; FOX College Sports Pacific; FXM; FYI; Great American Country; HD Theater; History International; LMN; Nick Jr.; Nicktoons; Outdoor Channel; TeenNick; Trinity Broadcasting Network (TBN); Universal HD.

Digital Pay Service 1
Pay Units: 796.
Programming (via satellite): Cinemax (multiplexed); HBO (multiplexed); Showtime (multiplexed); Starz (multiplexed); Starz Encore (multiplexed); The Movie Channel (multiplexed).
Fee: $13.00 monthly (Cinemax, HBO, Starz/Encore or Showtime/TMC).

Video-On-Demand: No

Pay-Per-View
iN DEMAND (delivered digitally); Hot Choice (delivered digitally).

Internet Service
Operational: Yes.
Broadband Service: In-house.
Fee: $99.00 installation; $41.95-$73.45 monthly.

Telephone Service
Digital: Operational
Miles of Plant: None (coaxial); 105.0 (fiber optic). Homes passed: 11,677.
President & Chief Executive Officer: Tom Basinger. Marketing & Programming Director: Bryan Johnson. Technical Operations Manager: Jerry Scullawl. Customer Service Manager: Linda Taylor.
Ownership: Schurz Communications Inc. (MSO).

SUPERIOR—Formerly served by RealStar Communications. No longer in operation. ICA: AZ0042.

TSAILE—Formerly served by Frontier Communications. No longer in operation. ICA: AZ0124.

TUBA CITY—Formerly served by Indevideo Co. Inc. No longer in operation. ICA: AZ0039.

TUCSON—Comcast Cable, 8251 North Cortaro Rd, Tucson, AZ 85743-9393. Phones: 520-744-1900; 520-744-2653. Fax: 520-744-4737. E-mail: lori_green@cable.comcast.com. Web Site: http://www.comcast.com. Also serves Marana, Oro Valley, Pima County & Tortolita. ICA: AZ0003.
TV Market Ranking: Below 100 (Marana, Oro Valley, Tortolita, Pima County, TUCSON). Franchise award date: August 1, 1979. Franchise expiration date: N.A. Began: July 1, 1982.
Channel capacity: 27 (operating 2-way). Channels available but not in use: N.A.

Basic Service
Subscribers: 63,519.
Programming (received off-air): KGUN-TV (ABC, IND) Tucson; KHRR (TMO) Tucson; KMSB (FOX, Movies!, This TV) Tucson; KOLD-TV (CBS, MeTV) Tucson; KTTU (Estrella TV, MNT) Tucson; KUAT-TV (PBS) Tucson; KUVE-DT (getTV, UNV) Green Valley; KVOA (Escape, NBC) Tucson; KWBA-TV (CW, LATV) Sierra Vista.
Programming (via satellite): ESPN; WGN America.
Fee: $50.00 installation; $30.51 monthly.

Expanded Basic Service 1
Subscribers: N.A.
Programming (via satellite): A&E; AMC; Animal Planet; BET; Bravo; Cartoon Network; CMT; CNBC; CNN; Comedy Central; C-SPAN; C-SPAN 2; Discovery Channel; Disney Channel; E! HD; ESPN Classic; ESPN2; Food Network; Fox News Channel; Fox Sports 1; FOX Sports Networks; Freeform; FX; Golf Channel; Great American Country; GSN; HGTV; History; HLN; INSP; Lifetime; MSNBC; MTV; MTV Classic; NBCSN; Nickelodeon; Pop; QVC; Spike TV; Syfy; TBS; The Weather Channel; TLC; TNT; Travel Channel; Trinity Broadcasting Network (TBN); truTV; Turner Classic Movies; TV Land; Univision; USA Network; VH1.
Fee: $36.00 monthly.

Digital Basic Service
Subscribers: N.A.
Programming (via satellite): BBC America; Bravo; Cooking Channel; C-SPAN 3; Discovery Digital Networks; Disney XD; DIY Network; DMX Music; ESPNews; Flix; FOX Sports West/Prime Ticket; National Geographic Channel; Nick 2; Nicktoons; Starz Encore (multiplexed); Syfy; TeenNick; WAM! America's Kidz Network.

Digital Expanded Basic Service
Subscribers: N.A.
Programming (via satellite): Nick Jr.
Fee: $4.00 monthly.

Digital Pay Service 1
Pay Units: N.A.
Programming (via satellite): Cinemax; HBO; Showtime; Starz (multiplexed); The Movie Channel.
Fee: $17.95 monthly (each).

Video-On-Demand: Yes

Pay-Per-View
Hot Network; Spice.

Internet Service
Operational: Yes.
Subscribers: 33,798.
Broadband Service: Comcast High Speed Internet.
Fee: $42.95 monthly.

Telephone Service
Digital: Operational
Subscribers: 31,542.
Miles of Plant: 4,028.0 (coaxial); 605.0 (fiber optic). Homes passed: 157,203.
General Manager: Paul Pecora. Chief Technician: Scott Anderson. Marketing Manager: Hans Rhey. Community & Government Affairs Director: Kelle Maslyn.
Ownership: Comcast Cable Communications Inc. (MSO).

TUCSON—Cox Communications, 6205 Peachtree Dunwoody Rd, 12th Floor, Atlanta, GA 30328. Phones: 623-328-3121 (Phoenix office); 404-269-6590. Web Site: http://www.cox.com. Also serves Benson, Davis-Monthan AFB, Green Valley, Pima County, Sahuarita, Santa Rita Bel Aire & South Tucson. ICA: AZ0002.
TV Market Ranking: Below 100 (Davis-Monthan AFB, Green Valley, Pima County (portions), Sahuarita, South Tucson, TUCSON, Santa Rita Bel Aire); Outside TV Markets (Pima County (portions), Benson). Franchise award date: December 7, 1981. Franchise expiration date: N.A. Began: September 7, 1982.
Channel capacity: 74 (operating 2-way). Channels available but not in use: N.A.

Basic Service
Subscribers: 88,002.
Programming (received off-air): KGUN-TV (ABC, IND) Tucson; KHRR (TMO) Tucson; KMSB (FOX, Movies!, This TV) Tucson; KOLD-TV (CBS, MeTV) Tucson; KTTU (Estrella TV, MNT) Tucson; KUAT-TV (PBS) Tucson; KVOA (Escape, NBC) Tucson; KWBA-TV (CW, LATV) Sierra Vista; 30 FMs.
Programming (via satellite): C-SPAN; Hallmark Channel; Pop; QVC; The Weather Channel; WGN America.
Programming (via translator): KTVW-DT (UNV) Phoenix.
Fee: $50.21 installation; $24.99 monthly.

Expanded Basic Service 1
Subscribers: N.A.
Programming (via satellite): A&E; AMC; Animal Planet; BET; Bravo; Cartoon Network; CMT; CNBC; CNN; Comedy Central; Discovery Channel; Disney Channel; E! HD; ESPN; ESPN2; Food Network; Fox News Channel; Fox Sports 1; FOX Sports Arizona; Freeform; FX; Golf Channel; HGTV; History; HLN; Lifetime; MSNBC; MTV; NBCSN; Nickelodeon; Oxygen; Spike TV; TBS; TLC; TNT; Travel Channel; Turner Classic Movies; TV Land; USA Network; VH1.
Fee: $22.72 monthly.

Digital Basic Service
Subscribers: N.A.
Programming (via satellite): BBC America; Bloomberg Television; Cartoon Network en Espanol; Discovery Digital Networks; Disney XD; ESPN Classic; Fox Deportes; GSN; IFC; INSP; LMN; MC; Sundance TV; Syfy; truTV; WE tv.

Pay Service 1
Pay Units: N.A.
Programming (via satellite): Cinemax; HBO (multiplexed); Showtime; Starz; Starz Encore; The Movie Channel.
Fee: $20.45 installation; $10.95 monthly (Cinemax, HBO, Showtime/TMC or Starz/Encore).

Digital Pay Service 1
Pay Units: N.A.
Programming (via satellite): Cinemax (multiplexed); HBO (multiplexed); Showtime (multiplexed); Starz (multiplexed); Starz Encore; The Movie Channel (multiplexed).
Fee: $10.95 monthly (Cinemax, HBO, Showtime/TMC or Starz/Encore).

Video-On-Demand: No

Pay-Per-View
ESPN Extra (delivered digitally); ESPN Full Court (delivered digitally); ESPN Game Plan (delivered digitally); ESPN Now (delivered digitally); iN DEMAND (delivered digitally); Playboy TV (delivered digitally); Spice (delivered digitally); Spice2 (delivered digitally); The Hot Network (delivered digitally); The Hot Zone.

Internet Service
Operational: Yes.
Subscribers: 124,924.
Broadband Service: Cox High Speed Internet.
Fee: $149.95 installation; $49.95 monthly; $15.00 modem lease.

Telephone Service
Digital: Operational
Subscribers: 65,085.
Miles of Plant: 4,348.0 (coaxial); 889.0 (fiber optic). Homes passed: 298,392.
Vice President & Regional Manager: Steve Rizley. Vice President & Systems Manager: Anne Doris. Vice President, Marketing: Anthony Maldonado. Vice President, Tax: Mary Vickers. Marketing Director: Nancy Duckett. Media Relations Director: David Grabert. Media Relations Manager: Monica Contreras.
Ownership: Cox Communications Inc. (MSO).

TUCSON—Formerly served by Sprint Corp. No longer in operation. ICA: AZ0118.

TUCSON ESTATES—Formerly served by Comcast Cable. No longer in operation. ICA: AZ0105.

TUSAYAN—Formerly served by Indevideo Co. Inc. No longer in operation. ICA: AZ0063.

WELLTON—Beamspeed LLC, 2481 East Palo Verde St, Yuma, AZ 85365-3619. Phones: 760-556-9000; 928-343-0300. Fax: 928-726-8238. Web Site: http://www.beamspeed.net. ICA: AZ0062.
TV Market Ranking: Below 100 (WELLTON). Franchise award date: N.A. Franchise expiration date: N.A. Began: October 8, 1987.
Channel capacity: 35 (not 2-way capable). Channels available but not in use: N.A.

Basic Service
Subscribers: N.A.
Programming (received off-air): KECY-TV (ABC, FOX, MNT, TMO) El Centro; KSWT (CBS, Estrella TV, Tuff TV) Yuma; KVYE (LATV, UNV) El Centro; KYMA-DT (NBC, This TV) Yuma.
Programming (via microwave): KAET (PBS) Phoenix; KASW (CW) Phoenix; KNXV-TV (ABC) Phoenix; KTVK (This TV) Phoenix.
Programming (via satellite): A&E; AMC; Animal Planet; Bravo; CMT; CNBC; CNN; Comedy Central; C-SPAN; Discovery Channel; Disney Channel; E! HD; ESPN; ESPN2; Fox News Channel; Freeform; HGTV; History; HLN; INSP; Lifetime; MTV; Nickelodeon; QVC; Spike TV; Syfy; TBS; TLC; TNT; Travel Channel; Turner Classic Movies; TV Land; Univision; USA Network; VH1; WE tv; WGN America.
Fee: $60.00 installation; $29.95 monthly; $2.10 converter.

Pay Service 1
Pay Units: N.A.
Programming (via satellite): Cinemax; HBO.
Fee: $25.00 installation; $12.95 monthly (each).

Cable Systems—Arizona

Internet Service
Operational: Yes.
Fee: $39.95-$69.95 monthly.
Telephone Service
None
Miles of Plant: 9.0 (coaxial); None (fiber optic). Homes passed: 525.
General Manager: Harold Hendrick. Chief Technician: Hughie Williams. Marketing Director: Christi Weber.
Ownership: Beamspeed LLC (MSO).

WICKENBURG—Cox Communications. Now served by PHOENIX, AZ [AZ0001]. ICA: AZ0132.

WILLCOX—Formerly served by Cox Communications. Now served by Valley Telecom Group. This cable system has converted to IPTV. See WILLCOX, AZ [AZ5009]. ICA: AZ0108.

WILLCOX—Valley Connections. Formerly [AZ0108]. This cable system has converted to IPTV., 752 East Maley, PO Box 970, Willcox, AZ 85644. Phones: 520-384-2231; 800-421-5711. E-mail: customer.service@vtc.net. Web Site: http://www.vtc.net. Also serves Bonita, Bowie, Clifton, Cochise County (portions), Duncan, Elfrida, Graham County (portions), Greenlee County (portions), McNeal, Morenci, Pearce, Portal, Safford, San Simeon, Sunizona, Sunsites, Thatcher & York Valley, AZ; Animas, Columbus, Hachita, Luna County (portions), Playas, Rodeo & Virden, NM. ICA: AZ5009.
Channel capacity: N.A. Channels available but not in use: N.A.
Basic
Subscribers: 1,265.
Fee: $55.95 monthly. Includes 60+ channels plus 50 music channels.
Expanded Basic
Subscribers: N.A.
Fee: $72.95 monthly. Includes 100+ channels plus 50 music channels.
HD
Subscribers: N.A.
Fee: $9.95 monthly.
Premium
Subscribers: N.A.
Fee: $17.95 monthly (one movie package), $30.95 monthly (two movie packages), $42.95 (three movie packages), $48.95 (four movie packages). Packages include Cinemax, Flix, HBO, Showtime & TMC.
Internet Service
Operational: Yes.
Fee: $39.95-$59.95 monthly.
Telephone Service
Digital: Operational
Fee: $18.00 monthly
Chief Executive Officer: Steve Metts. Chief Financial Officer: Troy Judd. Chief Information Officer: Kristi Lee. Marketing Supervisor: Bob Dahlstrom.
Ownership: Valley Telecom Group.

WILLIAMS—Formerly served by New Day Broadband. No longer in operation. ICA: AZ0106.

WINSLOW—Cable One. Now served by SHOW LOW, AZ [AZ0014]. ICA: AZ0026.

YARNELL—Formerly served by RealStar Communications. No longer in operation. ICA: AZ0069.

YUMA (portions)—Time Warner Cable, 1289 South 2nd Ave, Yuma, AZ 85364-4715. Phones: 928-782-0022 (Local office); 888-683-1000 (Customer service). Fax: 928-783-0242. Web Site: http://www.timewarnercable.com. Also serves Marine Corps Air Station, San Luis, Somerton, Somerton Indian Reservation, Yuma County (portions) & Yuma Proving Ground, AZ; Winterhaven, CA. ICA: AZ0004.
TV Market Ranking: Below 100 (Marine Corps Air Station, San Luis, Somerton, Somerton Indian Reservation, Winterhaven, YUMA (PORTIONS), Yuma County (portions), Yuma Proving Ground). Franchise award date: N.A. Franchise expiration date: N.A. Began: August 1, 1961.
Channel capacity: 77 (operating 2-way). Channels available but not in use: N.A.
Basic Service
Subscribers: 17,100.
Programming (received off-air): KECY-TV (ABC, FOX, MNT, TMO) El Centro; KSWT (CBS, Estrella TV, Tuff TV) Yuma; KVYE (LATV, UNV) El Centro; KYMA-DT (NBC, This TV) Yuma; 13 FMs.
Programming (via microwave): KAET (PBS) Phoenix; KAZT-TV (MeTV, Retro TV) Phoenix; KCOP-TV (Bounce TV, Buzzr, Heroes & Icons, MNT, Movies!) Los Angeles; KNXV-TV (ABC) Phoenix; KTVK (This TV) Phoenix.
Programming (via satellite): A&E; AMC; Animal Planet; BET; Cartoon Network; CMT; CNBC; CNN; C-SPAN; C-SPAN 2; Discovery Channel; E! HD; ESPN; ESPN2; EVINE Live; Food Network; Fox Deportes; Freeform; FX; Hallmark Channel; HGTV; History; HLN; INSP; ION Television; Lifetime; MSNBC; MTV; Nickelodeon; Pop; QVC; Syfy; Telemundo; The Weather Channel; TLC; Travel Channel; truTV; TV Land; UniMas; Univision; USA Network; VH1.
Fee: $32.99 installation; $.26 converter.
Expanded Basic Service 1
Subscribers: N.A.
Programming (via satellite): Bravo; Comedy Central; Disney Channel; Fox News Channel; Fox Sports 1; FOX Sports Arizona; Oxygen; Spike TV; TBS; TNT.
Fee: $10.98 monthly.
Digital Basic Service
Subscribers: N.A.
Programming (via satellite): BBC America; Bloomberg Television; Concert TV; Discovery Life Channel; DIY Network; ESPN Classic; ESPNews; Fuse; FYI; Golf Channel; Great American Country; GSN; History International; INSP; MC; National Geographic Channel; Nick 2; Nick Jr.; Nicktoons; TeenNick; Trinity Broadcasting Network (TBN); WE tv.
Digital Expanded Basic Service
Subscribers: N.A.
Programming (via satellite): ART America; Disney XD; FOX College Sports Central; FOX College Sports Pacific; FXM; HITS (Headend In The Sky); IFC; LMN; NBCSN; Outdoor Channel; RAI Italia; RTN; The Filipino Channel; Turner Classic Movies; TV Asia; TV5, La Television International; Zee TV.
Digital Pay Service 1
Pay Units: N.A.
Programming (via satellite): Cinemax (multiplexed); Flix; HBO (multiplexed); Showtime (multiplexed); Starz (multiplexed); Starz Encore (multiplexed); Sundance TV; The Movie Channel (multiplexed).
Fee: $14.00 monthly (Cinemax, HBO, Showtime/TMC or Starz).
Video-On-Demand: Planned
Pay-Per-View
HITS PPV (delivered digitally); Hot Choice (delivered digitally); Playboy TV (delivered digitally); Fresh (delivered digitally); Shorteez (delivered digitally).
Internet Service
Operational: Yes.
Subscribers: 27,241.
Broadband Service: Road Runner.
Fee: $44.95 monthly; $5.00 modem lease.
Telephone Service
Digital: Operational
Subscribers: 8,672.
Fee: $49.95 monthly
Miles of Plant: 1,076.0 (coaxial); 355.0 (fiber optic). Homes passed: 94,658. Homes passed & miles of plant (coax & fiber combined) includes El Centro, CA.
General Manager: Ricky Rinehart. Operations Manager: Hughie Williams. Marketing Manager: Shayne Abney. Business Manager: Jessica Haggard.
Ownership: Time Warner Cable (MSO).

ARKANSAS

Total Systems: 114	Communities with Applications: 0
Total Communities Served: 405	Number of Basic Subscribers: 312,570
Franchises Not Yet Operating: 0	Number of Expanded Basic Subscribers: 20,025
Applications Pending: 0	Number of Pay Units: 5,809

Top 100 Markets Represented: Memphis, TN (26); Little Rock-Pine Bluff (50); Texarkana, TX-Shreveport, LA (58); Monroe, LA-El Dorado, AR (99).

For a list of cable communities in this section, see the Cable Community Index located in the back of Cable Volume 2.
For explanation of terms used in cable system listings, see p. D-11.

ALMYRA—Formerly served by Cebridge Connections. No longer in operation. ICA: AR0299.

ALPENA—Ritter Communications. Now served by WESTERN GROVE, AR [AR0183]. ICA: AR0197.

ALTHEIMER—Formerly served by Almega Cable. No longer in operation. ICA: AR0130.

AMITY—Formerly served by Cablevision of Amity. No longer in operation. ICA: AR0158.

ARKADELPHIA—Suddenlink Communications, PO Box 709, Arkadelphia, AR 71923. Phones: 888-592-3861; 314-315-9400. Fax: 870-246-4356. E-mail: gene.regan@suddenlink.com. Web Site: http://www.suddenlink.com. Also serves Caddo Valley & Gum Springs. ICA: AR0216.
TV Market Ranking: Below 100 (ARKADELPHIA, Caddo Valley, Gum Springs). Franchise award date: February 1, 1989. Franchise expiration date: N.A. Began: November 1, 1976.
Channel capacity: 70 (not 2-way capable). Channels available but not in use: N.A.
Basic Service
Subscribers: 1,884. Commercial subscribers: 479.
Programming (received off-air): KARK-TV (NBC) Little Rock; KARZ-TV (Bounce TV, MNT) Little Rock; KASN (CW, The Country Network) Pine Bluff; KATV (ABC, Retro TV) Little Rock; KETG (PBS) Arkadelphia; KKAP (Daystar TV, ETV) Little Rock; KLRT-TV (FOX, This TV) Little Rock; KMYA-DT (MeTV, WeatherNation) Camden; KTHV (Antenna TV, CBS) Little Rock; KVTH-DT (IND) Hot Springs; allband FM.
Programming (via satellite): C-SPAN; FamilyNet; LWS Local Weather Station; Pop; QVC; TBS; WGN America.
Fee: $40.00 installation; $34.50 monthly.
Expanded Basic Service 1
Subscribers: N.A.
Programming (via satellite): A&E; AMC; Animal Planet; BET; Cartoon Network; CMT; CNBC; CNN; Comedy Central; C-SPAN 2; Discovery Channel; Disney Channel; E! HD; ESPN; ESPN2; EWTN Global Catholic Network; Food Network; Fox News Channel; Fox Sports 1; FOX Sports Southwest; Freeform; FX; Great American Country; HGTV; History; HLN; INSP; Lifetime; LMN; MSNBC; MTV; NBCSN; Nickelodeon; Outdoor Channel; Spike TV; Syfy; The Weather Channel; TLC; TNT; Travel Channel; Trinity Broadcasting Network (TBN); truTV; Turner Classic Movies; TV Land; USA Network; VH1.
Fee: $28.05 monthly.
Digital Basic Service
Subscribers: N.A.
Programming (via satellite): A&E HD; Animal Planet HD; AXS TV; BBC America; Bloomberg Television; Boomerang; CBS Sports Network; Chiller; CMT; Cooking Channel; Cox Sports Television; Destination America; Discovery Channel HD; Discovery Kids Channel; Disney XD; DIY Network; ESPN Classic; ESPN HD; ESPN2 HD; ESPNews; ESPNU; FamilyNet; Food Network HD; Fox Sports 2; FSN HD; Fuse; FX HD; FYI; Golf Channel; GSN; Hallmark Channel; HD Theater; HGTV HD; History HD; History International; IFC; Investigation Discovery; MC; MTV Classic; MTV Hits; MTV2; Nat Geo WILD; National Geographic Channel; National Geographic Channel HD; Nick Jr.; Nicktoons; OWN: Oprah Winfrey Network; Oxygen; Science Channel; Starz Encore (multiplexed); Sundance TV; Syfy HD; TBS HD; TeenNick; Tennis Channel; TLC HD; TNT HD; TV One; Universal HD; UP; USA Network HD; VH1 Soul; WE tv; Weatherscan.
Digital Pay Service 1
Pay Units: N.A.
Programming (via satellite): Cinemax (multiplexed); HBO (multiplexed); HBO HD; Showtime (multiplexed); Showtime HD; Starz (multiplexed); The Movie Channel (multiplexed).
Fee: $11.99 monthly (Cinemax, HBO, Showtime/TMC or Starz).
Video-On-Demand: No
Pay-Per-View
iN DEMAND (delivered digitally); Shorteez (delivered digitally); Fresh (delivered digitally); Playboy TV (delivered digitally); Club Jenna (delivered digitally); Spice: Xcess (delivered digitally).
Internet Service
Operational: Yes.
Subscribers: 1,870.
Broadband Service: Suddenlink High Speed Internet.
Fee: $49.95 monthly.
Telephone Service
Digital: Operational
Subscribers: 861.
Miles of Plant: 249.0 (coaxial); 66.0 (fiber optic). Homes passed: 8,836.
Senior Vice President, Corporate Finance: Michael Pflantz. Vice President, Accounting: Sabrina Warr. General Manager: Robbie Lee. Chief Technician: Chris Echols. Marketing Director: Kathy Wyrick.
Ownership: Cequel Communications Holdings I LLC (MSO).

ARKANSAS CITY—Formerly served by Cablevision of Arkansas City. No longer in operation. ICA: AR0174.

ASH FLAT—Crystal Broadband Networks, PO Box 180336, Chicago, IL 60618. Phones: 877-319-0328; 817-685-9588. E-mail: helpdesk@crystalbn.com. Web Site: http://crystalbn.com. ICA: AR0175.
TV Market Ranking: Outside TV Markets (ASH FLAT). Franchise award date: April 1, 1986. Franchise expiration date: N.A. Began: August 1, 1975.
Channel capacity: 36 (not 2-way capable). Channels available but not in use: N.A.
Basic Service
Subscribers: 25.
Programming (received off-air): KAIT (ABC, NBC) Jonesboro; KEMV (PBS) Mountain View; KOLR (CBS) Springfield; KTHV (Antenna TV, CBS) Little Rock; KVTJ-DT (IND) Jonesboro; KYTV (CW, NBC, WeatherNation) Springfield.
Programming (via satellite): A&E; AMC; CNBC; CNN; Discovery Channel; Disney Channel; ESPN; ESPN2; Fox News Channel; FOX Sports Southwest; Freeform; Great American Country; History; Lifetime; Nickelodeon; Spike TV; TBS; The Weather Channel; TNT; Trinity Broadcasting Network (TBN); TV Land; USA Network; WGN America; WNBC (COZI TV, NBC) New York.
Fee: $29.95 installation; $43.76 monthly.
Pay Service 1
Pay Units: N.A.
Programming (via satellite): Cinemax; HBO.
Fee: $8.99 monthly (Cinemax), $12.99 monthly (HBO).
Video-On-Demand: No
Internet Service
Operational: Yes.
Telephone Service
Digital: Operational
Miles of Plant: 12.0 (coaxial); None (fiber optic). Homes passed: 303.
General Manager: Nidhin Johnson. Program Manager: Shawn Smith.
Ownership: Crystal Broadband Networks (MSO).

ASHDOWN—NewWave Communications, One Montgomery Plaza, 4th Floor, Sikeston, MO 63801. Phone: 888-863-9928 (Customer service). Fax: 573-614-4802. E-mail: info@newwavecom.com. Web Site: http://www.newwavecom.com. Also serves Little River County (portions). ICA: AR0033.
TV Market Ranking: 58 (ASHDOWN, Little River County (portions)). Franchise award date: May 1, 1977. Franchise expiration date: N.A. Began: May 31, 1977.
Channel capacity: N.A. Channels available but not in use: N.A.
Basic Service
Subscribers: 321. Commercial subscribers: 41.
Programming (received off-air): KARK-TV (NBC) Little Rock; KATV (ABC, Retro TV) Little Rock; KETG (PBS) Arkadelphia; KMSS-TV (FOX) Shreveport; KPXJ (Antenna TV, CW, MeTV, Movies!) Minden; KSLA (Bounce TV, CBS, Grit, This TV) Shreveport; KTAL-TV (NBC) Texarkana; KTBS-TV (ABC) Shreveport; KTSS-LP Hope; allband FM.
Programming (via satellite): C-SPAN; C-SPAN 2; INSP; QVC; Trinity Broadcasting Network (TBN); WGN America.
Programming (via translator): KJEP-LP Nashville.
Fee: $40.00 installation; $34.78 monthly.
Expanded Basic Service 1
Subscribers: N.A.
Programming (via satellite): A&E; AMC; Animal Planet; BET; Bravo; Cartoon Network; CMT; CNBC; CNN; Comedy Central; Discovery Channel; Disney Channel; E! HD; ESPN; ESPN Classic; ESPN2; Food Network; Fox News Channel; Fox Sports 1; Freeform; FX; Golf Channel; Hallmark Channel; HGTV; History; HLN; Lifetime; MSNBC; MTV; Nickelodeon; Outdoor Channel; Spike TV; Syfy; TBS; The Weather Channel; TLC; TNT; Travel Channel; truTV; TV Land; USA Network; VH1.
Fee: $40.95 monthly.
Digital Basic Service
Subscribers: N.A.
Programming (via satellite): BBC America; Bloomberg Television; Cloo; Discovery Life Channel; Disney XD; DMX Music; ESPNews; EVINE Live; FXM; FYI; Great American Country; GSN; History International; IFC; LMN; NBCSN; Nick Jr.; Nicktoons; TeenNick; The Word Network; Turner Classic Movies.
Digital Pay Service 1
Pay Units: 171.
Programming (via satellite): Cinemax (multiplexed); Flix; HBO (multiplexed); Showtime (multiplexed); Starz (multiplexed); Starz Encore (multiplexed); The Movie Channel (multiplexed).
Pay-Per-View
Hot Choice (delivered digitally); Playboy TV (delivered digitally); Fresh (delivered digitally); Shorteez (delivered digitally); iN DEMAND (delivered digitally).
Internet Service
Operational: Yes.
Subscribers: 194.
Broadband Service: SpeedNet.
Fee: $31.99 monthly.
Telephone Service
Digital: Operational
Subscribers: 86.
Fee: $34.99 monthly
Miles of Plant: 572.0 (coaxial); None (fiber optic). Homes passed: 28,024.
Chief Financial Officer: Rod Siemers. General Manager: John Helmers.
Ownership: NewWave Communications LLC (MSO).

ATKINS—Suddenlink Communications, 520 Maryville Centre Dr, Ste 300, St. Louis, MO 63141. Phones: 314-315-9400; 888-822-5151. E-mail: gene.regan@suddenlink.com. Web Site: http://www.suddenlink.com. Also serves Pope County (portions). ICA: AR0079.

Cable Systems—Arkansas

TV Market Ranking: Outside TV Markets (ATKINS, Pope County (portions)). Franchise award date: N.A. Franchise expiration date: N.A. Began: December 1, 1982.
Channel capacity: N.A. Channels available but not in use: N.A.

Basic Service
Subscribers: 375.
Programming (received off-air): KARK-TV (NBC) Little Rock; KARZ-TV (Bounce TV, MNT) Little Rock; KASN (CW, The Country Network) Pine Bluff; KATV (ABC, Retro TV) Little Rock; KETS (PBS) Little Rock; KKAP (Daystar TV, ETV) Little Rock; KLRT-TV (FOX, This TV) Little Rock; KMYA-DT (MeTV, WeatherNation) Camden; KTHV (Antenna TV, CBS) Little Rock; KVTN-DT (IND) Pine Bluff.
Programming (via satellite): C-SPAN; Jewelry Television; Trinity Broadcasting Network (TBN); WGN America.
Fee: $40.00 installation; $38.50 monthly.

Expanded Basic Service 1
Subscribers: N.A.
Programming (via satellite): A&E; AMC; Animal Planet; BET; Cartoon Network; CNBC; CNN; Comedy Central; Discovery Channel; Disney Channel; E! HD; ESPN; ESPN2; Food Network; Fox News Channel; Fox Sports 1; FOX Sports Southwest; Freeform; FX; Great American Country; Hallmark Channel; HGTV; History; HLN; Lifetime; MSNBC; MTV; National Geographic Channel; Nickelodeon; Outdoor Channel; Spike TV; Syfy; TBS; The Weather Channel; TLC; TNT; Travel Channel; Turner Classic Movies; TV Land; USA Network; VH1.
Fee: $22.04 monthly.

Pay Service 1
Pay Units: N.A.
Programming (via satellite): HBO; Showtime; The Movie Channel.
Fee: $10.95 monthly (each).

Video-On-Demand: No

Internet Service
Operational: Yes. Began: May 27, 2003.
Broadband Service: Suddenlink High Speed Internet.
Fee: $33.00 monthly.

Telephone Service
Digital: Operational
Fee: $29.95 monthly
Miles of Plant: 37.0 (coaxial); None (fiber optic). Homes passed: 1,278.
Senior Vice President, Corporate Finance: Michael Pflantz. Vice President, Accounting: Sabrina Warr. Regional Manager: Todd Cruthird. Plant Manager: Danny Keith. Marketing Director: Beverly Gambell.
Ownership: Cequel Communications Holdings I LLC (MSO).

AUBREY—Media3, PO Box 650, Milan, TN 38358. Phone: 866-257-2044. E-mail: customerservice@mymedia3.com. Web Site: http://www.mymedia3.com. Also serves LaGrange, Lee County (southern portion) & Rondo. ICA: AR0208.
TV Market Ranking: Outside TV Markets (LaGrange, Rondo, AUBREY, Lee County (southern portion)). Franchise award date: N.A. Franchise expiration date: N.A. Began: April 24, 1990.
Channel capacity: N.A. Channels available but not in use: N.A.

Basic Service
Subscribers: 94.
Programming (received off-air): KASN (CW, The Country Network) Pine Bluff; KATV (ABC, Retro TV) Little Rock; KTHV (Antenna TV, CBS) Little Rock; WATN-TV (ABC) Memphis; WHBQ-TV (Decades, FOX, Movies!) Memphis; WKNO (PBS) Memphis; WLMT (CW, MeTV, MNT) Memphis; WMC-TV (Bounce TV, NBC, This TV) Memphis; WREG-TV (Antenna TV, CBS) Memphis.
Programming (via satellite): A&E; Animal Planet; BET; Cartoon Network; CMT; CNN; C-SPAN; Discovery Channel; ESPN; ESPN2; Freeform; GSN; HGTV; History; HLN; Lifetime; MTV; Nickelodeon; Outdoor Channel; Spike TV; Syfy; TBS; The Weather Channel; TLC; TNT; Trinity Broadcasting Network (TBN); truTV; Turner Classic Movies; TV Land; USA Network; VH1; WGN America.
Fee: $24.95 installation; $22.45 monthly.

Digital Basic Service
Subscribers: N.A.
Programming (via satellite): BBC America; Bloomberg Television; Discovery Digital Networks; DMX Music; ESPN Classic; ESPNews; Fox Sports 1; Fuse; FXM; FYI; Golf Channel; History International; IFC; National Geographic Channel; NBCSN; Nick Jr.; Nicktoons; Ovation; Sundance TV; TeenNick; WE tv.

Pay Service 1
Pay Units: N.A.
Programming (via satellite): Cinemax; HBO.

Digital Pay Service 1
Pay Units: N.A.
Programming (via satellite): Cinemax (multiplexed); Flix; HBO (multiplexed); Showtime (multiplexed); Starz (multiplexed); Starz Encore (multiplexed); The Movie Channel (multiplexed).
Fee: $11.95 monthly (each).

Video-On-Demand: No

Pay-Per-View
iN DEMAND (delivered digitally); Hot Choice (delivered digitally); Playboy TV (delivered digitally); Fresh (delivered digitally); Shorteez (delivered digitally).

Internet Service
Operational: Yes.

Telephone Service
None
Miles of Plant: 30.0 (coaxial); None (fiber optic). Homes passed: 740.
Chief Financial Officer: Thomas Pate.
Ownership: CableSouth Media3 LLC (MSO).

AUGUSTA—Augusta Video Inc, PO Box 2221, Little Rock, AR 72203. Phone: 501-378-3400. Web Site: http://m.wehco.com. ICA: AR0068.
TV Market Ranking: Outside TV Markets (AUGUSTA).
Channel capacity: N.A. Channels available but not in use: N.A.

Basic Service
Subscribers: 141.
Fee: $79.95 installation; $66.90 monthly.
Vice President, Administration: Charlotte A. Dial.
Ownership: Augusta Video Inc.

BATESVILLE—Suddenlink Communications, 2490 Harrison St, Batesville, AR 72501-7421. Phone: 314-315-9400. Fax: 870-793-6185. E-mail: Gene.Regan@suddenlink.com. Web Site: http://www.suddenlink.com. Also serves Desha, Independence County (portions), Moorefield, South Side & Sulphur Rock. ICA: AR0218.
TV Market Ranking: Outside TV Markets (BATESVILLE, Desha, Independence County (portions), Moorefield, South Side, Sulphur Rock). Franchise award date: N.A. Franchise expiration date: N.A. Began: September 3, 1951.
Channel capacity: 78 (operating 2-way). Channels available but not in use: N.A.

Basic Service
Subscribers: 4,045.
Programming (received off-air): KAIT (ABC, NBC) Jonesboro; KARK-TV (NBC) Little Rock; KARZ-TV (Bounce TV, MNT) Little Rock; KASN (CW, The Country Network) Pine Bluff; KATV (ABC, Retro TV) Little Rock; KKAP (Daystar TV, ETV) Little Rock; KLRT-TV (FOX, This TV) Little Rock; KMYA-DT (MeTV, WeatherNation) Camden; KTEJ (PBS) Jonesboro; KTHV (Antenna TV, CBS) Little Rock; allband FM.
Programming (via satellite): C-SPAN; C-SPAN 2; ESPN; HLN; INSP; Jewelry Television; QVC; TBS; The Weather Channel; Trinity Broadcasting Network (TBN); Univision; WGN America.
Fee: $40.00 installation; $34.50 monthly.

Expanded Basic Service 1
Subscribers: N.A.
Programming (via satellite): A&E; AMC; Animal Planet; BET; Bravo; Cartoon Network; CMT; CNBC; CNN; Comedy Central; Discovery Channel; Disney Channel; E! HD; ESPN2; Food Network; Fox News Channel; Fox Sports 1; FOX Sports Southwest; Freeform; FX; Great American Country; HGTV; History; Lifetime; LMN; MSNBC; MTV; NBCSN; Nickelodeon; Outdoor Channel; Oxygen; Spike TV; Syfy; TLC; TNT; Travel Channel; truTV; TV Land; USA Network; VH1.
Fee: $13.14 monthly.

Digital Basic Service
Subscribers: N.A.
Programming (via satellite): A&E HD; Animal Planet HD; AXS TV; BBC America; Bloomberg Television; Boomerang; CBS Sports Network; Chiller; CMT; Cooking Channel; Cox Sports Television; Destination America; Discovery Channel HD; Discovery Kids Channel; Disney XD; DIY Network; ESPN Classic; ESPN HD; ESPN2 HD; ESPNews; ESPNU; Food Network HD; Fox Sports 2; FSN HD; Fuse; FX HD; FYI; Golf Channel; GSN; Hallmark Channel; HD Theater; HGTV HD; History HD; History International; IFC; Investigation Discovery; MC; MTV Classic; MTV Hits; MTV2; Nat Geo WILD; National Geographic Channel; National Geographic Channel HD; Nick Jr.; Nicktoons; OWN: Oprah Winfrey Network; RFD-TV; Science Channel; Starz Encore (multiplexed); Sundance TV; Syfy HD; TBS HD; TeenNick; TLC HD; TNT HD; Turner Classic Movies; Universal HD; USA Network HD.

Digital Pay Service 1
Pay Units: N.A.
Programming (via satellite): Cinemax (multiplexed); HBO (multiplexed); HBO HD; Showtime (multiplexed); Showtime HD; Starz (multiplexed); The Movie Channel (multiplexed).
Fee: $12.95 monthly (Cinemax, HBO, Showtime/TMC or Starz).

Video-On-Demand: No

Pay-Per-View
iN DEMAND (delivered digitally); Fresh (delivered digitally); Spice: Xcess (delivered digitally); Playboy TV (delivered digitally).

Internet Service
Operational: Yes.
Subscribers: 3,876.
Broadband Service: Suddenlink High Speed Internet.
Fee: $49.95 installation; $33.00 monthly.

Telephone Service
Digital: Operational
Subscribers: 1,976.
Fee: $33.00 monthly
Miles of Plant: 426.0 (coaxial); 64.0 (fiber optic). Homes passed: 10,202.
Senior Vice President, Corporate Finance: Michael Pflantz. General Manager: Dwayne Millikin. Chief Technician: Don Province. Marketing Director: Kathy Wyrick.
Ownership: Cequel Communications Holdings I LLC (MSO).

BAXTER COUNTY (unincorporated areas)—Formerly served by Almega Cable. No longer in operation. ICA: AR0119.

BEARDEN—Formerly served by Zoom Media. No longer in operation. ICA: AR0107.

BEAVER LAKE—Cox Communications. Now served by SPRINGDALE, AR [AR0220]. ICA: AR0092.

BEEBE—Fidelity Communications, 64 North Clark St, Sullivan, MO 63080. Phones: 800-392-8070; 501-859-0384 (Maumelle office); 501-315-4405 (Benton office); 855-262-7434. E-mail: fidelityinfo@fidelitycommunications.com. Web Site: http://www.fidelitycommunications.com. Also serves White County (portions). ICA: AR0059.
TV Market Ranking: 50 (BEEBE, White County (portions)); Outside TV Markets (White County (portions)). Franchise award date: January 1, 1984. Franchise expiration date: N.A. Began: December 1, 1984.
Channel capacity: 116 (not 2-way capable). Channels available but not in use: N.A.

Basic Service
Subscribers: 540. Commercial subscribers: 10.
Programming (received off-air): KARK-TV (NBC) Little Rock; KARZ-TV (Bounce TV, MNT) Little Rock; KASN (CW, The Country Network) Pine Bluff; KATV (ABC, Retro TV) Little Rock; KETS (PBS) Little Rock; KLRT-TV (FOX, This TV) Little Rock; KTHV (Antenna TV, CBS) Little Rock; KVTN-DT (IND) Pine Bluff.
Programming (via satellite): A&E; CMT; CNN; Comedy Central; C-SPAN; E! HD; ESPN; FOX Sports Southwest; Freeform; HLN; Lifetime; MTV; Nickelodeon; QVC; Syfy; TLC; WGN America.
Fee: 33.39/hr installation; $28.99 monthly; $3.48 converter.

Expanded Basic Service 1
Subscribers: N.A.
Programming (via satellite): AMC; Animal Planet; Bravo; Cartoon Network; CNBC; Discovery Channel; Discovery Life Channel; Disney Channel; Disney XD; ESPN2; Food Network; Fox News Channel; Fox Sports 1; FX; FXM; Hallmark Channel; HGTV; History; MSNBC; NBCSN; Pop; Spike TV; TBS; The Weather Channel; TNT; Travel Channel; truTV; Turner Classic Movies; TV Land; USA Network; VH1; WE tv.
Fee: $49.99 monthly.

Pay Service 1
Pay Units: 58.
Programming (via satellite): HBO (multiplexed).
Fee: $10.00 monthly.

Pay Service 2
Pay Units: 38.
Programming (via satellite): Showtime (multiplexed).
Fee: $10.00 monthly.

Pay Service 3
Pay Units: N.A.
Programming (via satellite): Starz.

Arkansas—Cable Systems

Fee: $10.00 monthly.
Video-On-Demand: No
Pay-Per-View
 Urban Xtra (delivered digitally).
Internet Service
 Operational: Yes.
 Subscribers: 309.
Telephone Service
 Digital: Operational
 Subscribers: 74.
 Miles of Plant: 102.0 (coaxial); 20.0 (fiber optic). Homes passed: 3,675.
 General Manager, AR/MO/LA/TX: Andy Davis.
 Ownership: Fidelity Communications Co. (MSO).

BENTON—Fidelity Communications, 64 North Clark St, Sullivan, MO 63080. Phones: 800-392-8070; 855-262-7434; 501-859-0384 (Benton office). E-mail: fidelityinfo@fidelitycommunications.com. Web Site: http://www.fidelitycommunications.com. Also serves Alexander, Bauxite, Bryant, Haskell, Hensley, Landmark, Little Rock, Mabelvale, Pulaski County (portions), Saline County (portions), Shannon Hills, Tull & Wrightsville. ICA: AR0005.
 TV Market Ranking: 50 (Alexander, Bauxite, BENTON, Bryant, Haskell, Landmark, Little Rock, Mabelvale, Saline County (portions), Shannon Hills, Tull, Wrightsville). Franchise award date: May 1, 1980. Franchise expiration date: N.A. Began: October 15, 1980.
 Channel capacity: N.A. Channels available but not in use: N.A.
Basic Service
 Subscribers: 4,199. Commercial subscribers: 261.
 Programming (received off-air): KARK-TV (NBC) Little Rock; KARZ-TV (Bounce TV, MNT) Little Rock; KASN (CW, The Country Network) Pine Bluff; KATV (ABC, Retro TV) Little Rock; KETS (PBS) Little Rock; KLRT-TV (FOX, This TV) Little Rock; KMYA-DT (MeTV, WeatherNation) Camden; KTHV (Antenna TV, CBS) Little Rock; KVTN-DT (IND) Pine Bluff; allband FM.
 Programming (via satellite): A&E; CNN; Comedy Central; C-SPAN; E! HD; ESPN; ESPN2; FOX Sports Southwest; Freeform; Jewelry Television; Lifetime; MTV; Nickelodeon; QVC; Syfy; The Weather Channel; TLC; VH1; WGN America.
 Fee: $29.99 installation; $28.99 monthly; $3.48 converter.
Expanded Basic Service 1
 Subscribers: N.A.
 Programming (via satellite): AMC; Animal Planet; Bravo; Cartoon Network; CMT; CNBC; Discovery Channel; Disney Channel; Disney XD; Flix; Food Network; Fox News Channel; Fox Sports 1; FX; FXM; Golf Channel; Great American Country; GSN; Hallmark Channel; HGTV; History; HLN; MSNBC; National Geographic Channel; NBCSN; Oxygen; Pop; Spike TV; TBS; TNT; Travel Channel; truTV; Turner Classic Movies; TV Land; USA Network; WE tv.
 Fee: $49.99 monthly.
Digital Basic Service
 Subscribers: N.A.
 Programming (via satellite): BBC America; Bloomberg Television; Discovery Life Channel; DIY Network; FOX College Sports Central; FOX College Sports Pacific; Fox Sports 2; FYI; History International; LMN; MC; Sundance TV; WE tv.
Digital Pay Service 1
 Pay Units: N.A.
 Programming (via satellite): Cinemax (multiplexed); Flix; HBO (multiplexed); Showtime (multiplexed); Starz (multiplexed); Starz Encore (multiplexed); The Movie Channel (multiplexed).
Video-On-Demand: No
Pay-Per-View
 ETC (delivered digitally); Hot Choice (delivered digitally); iN DEMAND (delivered digitally); Pleasure (delivered digitally); Sports PPV (delivered digitally).
Internet Service
 Operational: Yes.
 Subscribers: 3,360.
Telephone Service
 Digital: Operational
 Subscribers: 131.
 Miles of Plant: 1,714.0 (coaxial); 241.0 (fiber optic). Homes passed: 35,658.
 Vice President: Dave Beier. General Manager: Andy Davis.
 Ownership: Fidelity Communications Co. (MSO).

BENTON COUNTY—Cox Communications. Now served by SPRINGDALE, AR [AR0220]. ICA: AR0039.

BERRYVILLE—Cox Communications, 6205 Peachtree Dunwoody Rd, 12th Floor, Atlanta, GA 30328. Phones: 316-262-4270 (Wichita office); 404-269-6590. Web Site: http://www.cox.com. Also serves Beaver, Carroll County (portions), Eureka Springs, Green Forest & Holiday Island. ICA: AR0221.
 TV Market Ranking: Below 100 (Beaver, BERRYVILLE, Eureka Springs, Green Forest, Holiday Island). Franchise award date: N.A. Franchise expiration date: N.A. Began: January 1, 1963.
 Channel capacity: N.A. Channels available but not in use: N.A.
Basic Service
 Subscribers: 2,584. Commercial subscribers: 201.
 Programming (received off-air): KAFT (PBS) Fayetteville; KARK-TV (NBC) Little Rock; KATV (ABC, Retro TV) Fayetteville; KHOG-TV (ABC, CW) Fayetteville; KOLR (CBS) Springfield; KOZL (IND) Springfield; KSPR (ABC) Springfield; KTHV (Antenna TV, CBS) Little Rock; KYTV (CW, NBC, WeatherNation) Springfield; allband FM.
 Programming (via satellite): A&E; CNN; C-SPAN; C-SPAN 2; Discovery Channel; Disney Channel; ESPN; Freeform; Great American Country; ION Television; Lifetime; Nickelodeon; Pop; TBS; The Weather Channel; TNT; Trinity Broadcasting Network (TBN); WGN America.
 Fee: $35.00 installation; $21.99 monthly; $1.50 converter.
Expanded Basic Service 1
 Subscribers: N.A.
 Programming (via satellite): AMC; Animal Planet; CNBC; Comedy Central; ESPN2; Fox News Channel; Fox Sports 1; FOX Sports Southwest; FX; HGTV; History; HLN; MSNBC; NBCSN; Outdoor Channel; Oxygen; Spike TV; Syfy; TLC; Trinity Broadcasting Network (TBN); Turner Classic Movies; TV Land; Univision; USA Network; VH1; WE tv.
 Fee: $43.15 monthly.
Digital Basic Service
 Subscribers: N.A.
 Programming (via satellite): BBC America; Bloomberg Television; Discovery Digital Networks; Disney XD; DMX Music; ESPNews; Fuse; Golf Channel; GSN; LMN; truTV.
Pay Service 1
 Pay Units: N.A.
 Programming (via satellite): HBO (multiplexed); Showtime (multiplexed); Starz; Starz Encore; The Movie Channel.
 Fee: $35.00 installation; $9.00 monthly (Encore, HBO, Showtime or Starz), $9.50 monthly (TMC).
Digital Pay Service 1
 Pay Units: N.A.
 Programming (via satellite): Cinemax (multiplexed); HBO (multiplexed); Showtime (multiplexed); Starz (multiplexed); The Movie Channel.
Video-On-Demand: No
Pay-Per-View
 ESPN Now (delivered digitally); iN DEMAND; iN DEMAND (delivered digitally).
Internet Service
 Operational: Yes.
 Broadband Service: Cox High Speed Internet.
 Fee: $19.99-$59.99 monthly.
Telephone Service
 Digital: Operational
 Fee: $15.95 monthly
 Miles of Plant: 313.0 (coaxial); 66.0 (fiber optic). Homes passed: 7,671.
 Vice President & General Manager: Kimberly Edmunds. Vice President, Operations: Nelson Mower. Vice President, Marketing: Tony Matthews. Vice President, Tax: Mary Vickers. Marketing Director: Tina Gabbard. Media Relations Director: David Grabert. Community Relations Manager: Kelly Zaga.
 Ownership: Cox Communications Inc.

BIGGERS—Formerly served by Boycom Cablevision Inc. No longer in operation. ICA: AR0109.

BISCOE—Formerly served by Cebridge Connections. No longer in operation. ICA: AR0194.

BISMARCK—Formerly served by Cablevision of Bismarck. No longer in operation. ICA: AR0135.

BLACK ROCK—Indco Cable TV, 2700 North Saint Louis, PO Box 3799, Batesville, AR 72503-3799. Phones: 800-364-0831; 870-793-4175; 870-793-4174. Fax: 870-793-7439. Web Site: http://www.indco.net. Also serves Imboden, Portia, Powhatan & Ravenden. ICA: AR0114.
 TV Market Ranking: Below 100 (BLACK ROCK, Portia, Powhatan); Outside TV Markets (Imboden, Ravenden). Franchise award date: N.A. Franchise expiration date: N.A. Began: January 1, 1979.
 Channel capacity: N.A. Channels available but not in use: N.A.
Basic Service
 Subscribers: 197.
 Programming (received off-air): KAIT (ABC, NBC) Jonesboro; KATV (ABC, Retro TV) Little Rock; KTEJ (PBS) Jonesboro; WHBQ-TV (Decades, FOX, Movies!) Memphis; WMC-TV (Bounce TV, NBC, This TV) Memphis; WREG-TV (Antenna TV, CBS) Memphis.
 Programming (via satellite): AMC; Cartoon Network; CNN; C-SPAN; Discovery Channel; Disney Channel; ESPN; ESPN2; Fox News Channel; FOX Sports Networks; Freeform; Great American Country; HGTV; History; Lifetime; Nickelodeon; Outdoor Channel; QVC; Spike TV; TBS; The Weather Channel; TNT; Trinity Broadcasting Network (TBN); TV Land; USA Network; VH1; WGN America.
 Fee: $40.00 installation; $66.95 monthly.

Pay Service 1
 Pay Units: 9.
 Programming (via satellite): Cinemax.
 Fee: $8.00 monthly.
Pay Service 2
 Pay Units: 8.
 Programming (via satellite): HBO.
 Fee: $10.00 monthly.
Pay Service 3
 Pay Units: N.A.
 Programming (via satellite): Showtime; The Movie Channel.
 Fee: $9.00 monthly (each).
Video-On-Demand: Planned
Internet Service
 Operational: Yes.
Telephone Service
 Digital: Operational
 Miles of Plant: 10.0 (coaxial); None (fiber optic).
 President & General Manager: J.D. Pierce. Chief Technician: Tommy Barnett. Marketing Director: Connie Barnett.
 Ownership: Indco Cable TV (MSO).

BLYTHEVILLE—Ritter Communications. Now served by MARKED TREE, AR [AR0072]. ICA: AR0018.

BONO—Ritter Communications. Now served by MARKED TREE, AR [AR0072]. ICA: AR0105.

BOONEVILLE—Suddenlink Communications, PO Box 10010, Russellville, AR 72812. Phones: 888-592-3861; 314-315-9400; 800-582-9577. Fax: 479-968-2223. E-mail: Gene.Regan@suddenlink.com. Web Site: http://www.suddenlink.com. ICA: AR0053.
 TV Market Ranking: Below 100 (BOONEVILLE). Franchise award date: November 1, 1963. Franchise expiration date: N.A. Began: November 1, 1963.
 Channel capacity: 62 (operating 2-way). Channels available but not in use: N.A.
Basic Service
 Subscribers: 322.
 Programming (received off-air): KAFT (PBS) Fayetteville; KARK-TV (NBC) Little Rock; KFSM-TV (CBS, MNT) Fort Smith; KFTA-TV (FOX, NBC) Fort Smith; KHBS (ABC, CW) Fort Smith; KTHV (Antenna TV, CBS) Little Rock; allband FM.
 Programming (via satellite): C-SPAN; Pop; QVC; TBS; The Weather Channel; Trinity Broadcasting Network (TBN); TV Land; WGN America.
 Fee: $40.00 installation; $32.50 monthly.
Expanded Basic Service 1
 Subscribers: N.A.
 Programming (via satellite): A&E; AMC; Animal Planet; Cartoon Network; CNBC; CNN; Discovery Channel; Disney Channel; E! HD; ESPN; ESPN2; Fox News Channel; Fox Sports 1; FOX Sports Southwest; Freeform; Great American Country; HGTV; History; HLN; Lifetime; NBCSN; Nickelodeon; Spike TV; Syfy; TLC; TNT; Trinity Broadcasting Network (TBN); USA Network; VH1.
 Fee: $18.00 monthly.
Digital Basic Service
 Subscribers: N.A.
 Programming (via satellite): BBC America; Bloomberg Television; Destination America; Discovery Kids Channel; Disney XD; DMX Music; ESPN Classic; ESPNews; Fuse; FYI; Golf Channel; GSN; IFC; Investigation Discovery; LMN; OWN: Oprah Winfrey Network; Science Channel; Sundance TV.

Cable Systems—Arkansas

Access the most current data instantly
www.warren-news.com/factbook.htm

Digital Pay Service 1
Pay Units: N.A.
Programming (via satellite): Cinemax (multiplexed); HBO (multiplexed); Showtime (multiplexed); Starz (multiplexed); Starz Encore (multiplexed); The Movie Channel (multiplexed).
Fee: $12.95 monthly (Cinemax, HBO, Showtime/TMC or Starz/Encore).
Video-On-Demand: No
Pay-Per-View
iN DEMAND (delivered digitally); ESPN Now (delivered digitally); Shorteez (delivered digitally); Fresh (delivered digitally); Playboy TV (delivered digitally); Spice: Xcess (delivered digitally).
Internet Service
Operational: Yes.
Broadband Service: Suddenlink High Speed Internet.
Fee: $29.95 monthly.
Telephone Service
Digital: Operational
Miles of Plant: 31.0 (coaxial); None (fiber optic). Homes passed: 1,792.
Senior Vice President, Corporate Finance: Michael Pflantz. General Manager: Mike Ederington. Plant Manager: Wayne Ollis. Chief Technician: Clint Petty. Marketing Director: Kathy Wyrick.
Ownership: Cequel Communications Holdings I LLC (MSO).

BOONEVILLE HUMAN DEVELOPMENT CENTER—Formerly served by Eagle Media. No longer in operation. ICA: AR0313.

BRADFORD—Indco Cable TV, 2700 North Saint Louis, PO Box 3799, Batesville, AR 72503-3799. Phones: 800-364-0831; 870-793-4175; 501-793-4174. Fax: 501-793-7439. Web Site: http://www.indco.net. ICA: AR0131.
TV Market Ranking: Outside TV Markets (BRADFORD).
Channel capacity: N.A. Channels available but not in use: N.A.
Basic Service
Subscribers: 62.
Programming (received off-air): KAIT (ABC, NBC) Jonesboro; KARK-TV (NBC) Little Rock; KASN (CW, The Country Network) Pine Bluff; KATV (ABC, Retro TV) Little Rock; KLRT-TV (FOX, This TV) Little Rock; KTEJ (PBS) Jonesboro; KTHV (Antenna TV, CBS) Little Rock.
Programming (via satellite): A&E; CMT; CNN; Discovery Channel; Disney Channel; ESPN; ESPN2; FOX Sports Southwest; Freeform; FX; Nickelodeon; Outdoor Channel; QVC; Spike TV; Syfy; TBS; The Weather Channel; TNT; Trinity Broadcasting Network (TBN); Turner Classic Movies; USA Network; WGN America.
Fee: $40.00 installation; $63.95 monthly.
Pay Service 1
Pay Units: 17.
Programming (via satellite): HBO.
Fee: $10.00 monthly.
Pay Service 2
Pay Units: 4.
Programming (via satellite): Cinemax.
Fee: $8.00 monthly.
Video-On-Demand: Planned
Internet Service
Operational: Yes.
Fee: $29.95 monthly.
Telephone Service
None
Miles of Plant: 10.0 (coaxial); None (fiber optic). Homes passed: 425.

President & General Manager: J.D. Pierce. Chief Technician: Tommy Barnett. Marketing Director: Connie Barnett.
Ownership: Indco Cable TV (MSO).

BRADLEY—Formerly served by Cebridge Connections. No longer in operation. ICA: AR0152.

BRIARCLIFF—Formerly served by Almega Cable. No longer in operation. ICA: AR0090.

BRINKLEY—East Arkansas Video Inc, 4804 N Washington St, Forrest City, AR 72335. Phones: 870-633-8934; 870-633-1079 (Headend); 870-633-8932. Fax: 870-633-8898. E-mail: eastarkansasvideocs@cablelynx.com. Web Site: http://www.eastarkansasvideo.com. ICA: AR0055.
TV Market Ranking: Outside TV Markets (BRINKLEY). Franchise award date: August 1, 1969. Franchise expiration date: N.A. Began: August 1, 1969.
Channel capacity: 35 (operating 2-way). Channels available but not in use: N.A.
Basic Service
Subscribers: 168.
Programming (received off-air): KAIT (ABC, NBC) Jonesboro; KARK-TV (NBC) Little Rock; KATV (ABC, Retro TV) Little Rock; KTEJ (PBS) Jonesboro; KTHV (Antenna TV, CBS) Little Rock; KVTN-DT (IND) Pine Bluff; WATN-TV (ABC) Memphis; WHBQ-TV (Decades, FOX, Movies!) Memphis; WKNO (PBS) Memphis; WLMT (CW, MeTV, MNT) Memphis; WMC-TV (Bounce TV, NBC, This TV) Memphis; WPXX-TV (ION, MNT) Memphis; WREG-TV (Antenna TV, CBS) Memphis; 1 FM.
Programming (via satellite): A&E; AMC; Animal Planet; BET; CMT; CNBC; CNN; Comedy Central; Concert TV; C-SPAN; C-SPAN 2; Discovery Channel; Disney Channel; Disney XD; ESPN; ESPN2; EVINE Live; Food Network; Fox News Channel; FOX Sports Southwest; Freeform; FX; HGTV; History; HLN; Lifetime; MTV; Nickelodeon; Pop; Spike TV; Syfy; TBS; The Weather Channel; TLC; TNT; Trinity Broadcasting Network (TBN); Turner Classic Movies; TV Land; Univision Studios; USA Network; VH1; WGN America.
Fee: $79.00 installation; $71.90 monthly; $3.17 converter.
Digital Basic Service
Subscribers: N.A.
Programming (via satellite): BBC America; CMT; Destination America; Discovery Kids Channel; Discovery Life Channel; Disney XD; DMX Music; ESPNews; Fox Sports 1; FSN Digital Atlantic; FSN Digital Central; FSN Digital Pacific; FYI; Golf Channel; Great American Country; GSN; History International; Investigation Discovery; LMN; MTV Classic; MTV Hits; MTV Jams; MTV2; National Geographic Channel; Nick 2; Nick Jr.; Nicktoons; Outdoor Channel; OWN: Oprah Winfrey Network; Science Channel; TeenNick; Tr3s; VH1 Soul; WE tv.
Digital Expanded Basic Service
Subscribers: N.A.
Programming (via satellite): AXS TV; CNN HD; Discovery Channel HD; ESPN HD; Outdoor Channel 2 HD; TBS HD; TNT HD.
Fee: $5.00 monthly.
Digital Pay Service 1
Pay Units: N.A.
Programming (via satellite): Cinemax (multiplexed); Cinemax HD; HBO (multiplexed); HBO HD; Starz (multiplexed); Starz Encore; Starz HD.
Fee: $12.95 monthly (Cinemax, HBO or Starz/Encore).

Internet Service
Operational: Yes. Began: June 1, 2003.
Broadband Service: Cablelynx.
Fee: $24.95-$44.95 monthly.
Telephone Service
Digital: Operational
Fee: $45.70 monthly
Miles of Plant: 33.0 (coaxial); None (fiber optic). Homes passed: 1,765.
Vice President, Administration: Charlotte A. Dial. General Manager: Laurie Ringler. Chief Technician: Chris Heard. Marketing Director: Lori Haight.
Ownership: WEHCO Video Inc. (MSO).

CABOT—Suddenlink Communications, 520 Maryville Centre Dr, Ste 300, St. Louis, MO 63141. Phones: 501-843-9122; 314-315-9400; 888-588-4711. Web Site: http://www.suddenlink.com. Also serves Austin, Faulkner County (portions), Little Rock AFB, Lonoke County (portions), Macon, Pulaski County (portions), South Bend & Ward. ICA: AR0023.
TV Market Ranking: 50 (Austin, CABOT, Faulkner County (portions), Little Rock AFB, Lonoke County (portions), Macon, Pulaski County (portions), South Bend, Ward); Outside TV Markets (Faulkner County (portions)). Franchise award date: N.A. Franchise expiration date: N.A. Began: January 1, 1983.
Channel capacity: 49 (operating 2-way). Channels available but not in use: N.A.
Basic Service
Subscribers: 7,569. Commercial subscribers: 198.
Programming (received off-air): KARK-TV (NBC) Little Rock; KARZ-TV (Bounce TV, MNT) Little Rock; KASN (CW, The Country Network) Pine Bluff; KATV (ABC, Retro TV) Little Rock; KETS (PBS) Little Rock; KKAP (Daystar TV, ETV) Little Rock; KLRT-TV (FOX, This TV) Little Rock; KMYA-DT (MeTV, WeatherNation) Camden; KTHV (Antenna TV, CBS) Little Rock; KTWN-LD (IND) Searcy; KVTN-DT (IND) Pine Bluff.
Programming (via satellite): C-SPAN; Hallmark Channel; QVC.
Fee: $28.45 monthly.
Expanded Basic Service 1
Subscribers: N.A.
Programming (via satellite): A&E; AMC; Animal Planet; Cartoon Network; CNBC; CNN; Comedy Central; Discovery Channel; Disney Channel; E! HD; ESPN; ESPN2; Food Network; Fox News Channel; FOX Sports Southwest; Freeform; FX; Great American Country; Hallmark Channel; HGTV; History; HLN; INSP; Lifetime; MTV; National Geographic Channel; Nickelodeon; Spike TV; Syfy; TBS; The Weather Channel; TLC; TNT; Turner Classic Movies; TV Land; USA Network; VH1.
Fee: $22.04 monthly.
Digital Basic Service
Subscribers: N.A.
Programming (via satellite): AXS TV; BBC America; Bloomberg Television; Cloo; CMT; Destination America; Discovery Kids Channel; Disney XD; DMX Music; ESPN Classic; ESPN HD; ESPNews; Fox Sports 1; Fuse;

FYI; Golf Channel; GSN; HD Theater; History International; IFC; Investigation Discovery; LMN; MTV Classic; MTV2; National Geographic Channel HD; NBCSN; Nick Jr.; Nicktoons; Outdoor Channel; OWN: Oprah Winfrey Network; Science Channel; Sundance TV; TeenNick; TNT HD; WE tv.
Pay Service 1
Pay Units: N.A.
Programming (via satellite): HBO; Showtime.
Fee: $12.95 monthly (each).
Digital Pay Service 1
Pay Units: N.A.
Programming (via satellite): Cinemax (multiplexed); HBO (multiplexed); Showtime (multiplexed); Starz (multiplexed); Starz Encore (multiplexed); The Movie Channel (multiplexed).
Fee: $12.95 monthly (Cinemax, HBO, Showtime/TMC or Starz/Encore).
Video-On-Demand: No
Pay-Per-View
iN DEMAND (delivered digitally); Playboy TV (delivered digitally); Fresh (delivered digitally); Club Jenna (delivered digitally).
Internet Service
Operational: Yes. Began: September 1, 2002.
Subscribers: 10,730.
Broadband Service: Suddenlink High Speed Internet.
Fee: $21.95 monthly; $9.95 modem lease.
Telephone Service
Digital: Operational
Subscribers: 2,472.
Fee: $33.00 monthly
Miles of Plant: 1,632.0 (coaxial); 197.0 (fiber optic). Homes passed: 27,456.
Senior Vice President, Corporate Finance: Michael Pflantz. Regional Manager: Todd Cruthird. Chief Technician: Randy Oliger.
Ownership: Cequel Communications Holdings I LLC (MSO).

CALDWELL—Indco Cable TV, 2700 North Saint Louis, PO Box 3799, Batesville, AR 72503-3799. Phones: 800-364-0831; 870-793-4175; 870-793-4174. Fax: 870-793-7439. Web Site: http://www.indco.net. Also serves Colt & St. Francis County. ICA: AR0222.
TV Market Ranking: 26 (St. Francis County (portions)); Outside TV Markets (CALDWELL, Colt, St. Francis County (portions)). Franchise award date: N.A. Franchise expiration date: N.A. Began: December 1, 1988.
Channel capacity: N.A. Channels available but not in use: N.A.
Basic Service
Subscribers: 357.
Programming (received off-air): KAIT (ABC, NBC) Jonesboro; KATV (ABC, Retro TV) Little Rock; KMYA-DT (MeTV, WeatherNation) Camden; KTHV (Antenna TV, CBS) Little Rock; WATN-TV (ABC) Memphis; WHBQ-TV (Decades, FOX, Movies!) Memphis; WKNO (PBS) Memphis; WLMT (CW, MeTV, MNT) Memphis; WMC-TV (Bounce TV, NBC, This TV) Memphis; WREG-TV (Antenna TV, CBS) Memphis.

2017 Edition   D-57

Arkansas—Cable Systems

Programming (via satellite): A&E; BET; CMT; CNN; Discovery Channel; Disney Channel; ESPN; ESPN2; Fox News Channel; FOX Sports Southwest; Freeform; FX; HGTV; History; HLN; Lifetime; Nickelodeon; Outdoor Channel; QVC; Spike TV; Syfy; TBS; The Weather Channel; TNT; Trinity Broadcasting Network (TBN); Turner Classic Movies; USA Network; WGN America.
Fee: $40.00 installation; $66.95 monthly.
Pay Service 1
Pay Units: 28.
Programming (via satellite): Cinemax.
Fee: $8.00 monthly.
Pay Service 2
Pay Units: 38.
Programming (via satellite): HBO.
Fee: $10.00 monthly.
Pay Service 3
Pay Units: 48.
Programming (via satellite): Cinemax; HBO.
Fee: $16.00 monthly.
Internet Service
Operational: Yes.
Telephone Service
Digital: Operational
Miles of Plant: 21.0 (coaxial); None (fiber optic). Homes passed: 1,050.
President & General Manager: J.D. Pierce. Chief Technician: Tom Barnett. Marketing Director: Connie Barnett.
Ownership: Indco Cable TV (MSO).

CALICO ROCK—Yelcot Communications, 225 North Mill St, Yellville, AR 72687. Phone: 800-270-1198. Web Site: http://www.yelcot.com. Also serves Pineville. ICA: AR0223.
TV Market Ranking: Outside TV Markets (CALICO ROCK, Pineville). Franchise award date: N.A. Franchise expiration date: N.A. Began: January 1, 1970.
Channel capacity: N.A. Channels available but not in use: N.A.
Basic Service
Subscribers: 228.
Programming (received off-air): KAIT (ABC, NBC) Jonesboro; KARK-TV (NBC) Little Rock; KATV (ABC, Retro TV) Little Rock; KEMV (PBS) Mountain View; KOLR (CBS) Springfield; KTHV (Antenna TV, CBS) Little Rock; KYTV (CW, NBC, WeatherNation) Springfield.
Programming (via satellite): CMT; CNN; Discovery Channel; Disney Channel; ESPN; ESPN2; FOX Sports Networks; Freeform; FX; HGTV; History; HLN; Lifetime; Nickelodeon; Outdoor Channel; QVC; Spike TV; Syfy; TBS; The Weather Channel; TLC; TNT; Trinity Broadcasting Network (TBN); Turner Classic Movies; USA Network; WGN America.
Fee: $41.00 monthly.
Pay Service 1
Pay Units: 8.
Programming (via satellite): Cinemax.
Fee: $8.00 monthly.
Pay Service 2
Pay Units: 7.
Programming (via satellite): HBO.
Fee: $10.00 monthly.
Video-On-Demand: Planned
Internet Service
Operational: Yes.
Fee: $29.95 monthly.
Telephone Service
None
Miles of Plant: 17.0 (coaxial); 7.0 (fiber optic). Homes passed: 550.
Ownership: Yelcot Communications (MSO).

CAMDEN—Cam-Tel Co, 113 Madison Ave NE, PO Box 835, Camden, AR 71701-3514. Phones: 800-903-0508; 870-836-8112; 870-836-5969 (Headend); 870-836-8111. Fax: 870-836-2109. E-mail: camdencabletvcs@cablelynx.com. Web Site: http://www.camdencabletv.com. ICA: AR0019.
TV Market Ranking: 99 (CAMDEN). Franchise award date: N.A. Franchise expiration date: N.A. Began: March 1, 1964.
Channel capacity: 76 (operating 2-way). Channels available but not in use: N.A.
Basic Service
Subscribers: 1,593. Commercial subscribers: 6.
Programming (received off-air): KARK-TV (NBC) Little Rock; KARZ-TV (Bounce TV, MNT) Little Rock; KASN (CW, The Country Network) Pine Bluff; KATV (ABC, Retro TV) Little Rock; KETS (PBS) Little Rock; KKAP (Daystar TV, ETV) Little Rock; KKYK-CD (IND, WeatherNation) Little Rock; KLRT-TV (FOX, This TV) Little Rock; KTHV (Antenna TV, CBS) Little Rock; KTVE (NBC) El Dorado; KVTN-DT (IND) Pine Bluff.
Programming (via satellite): A&E; AMC; Animal Planet; BET; Cartoon Network; CMT; CNBC; CNN; C-SPAN; C-SPAN 2; Discovery Channel; Disney Channel; ESPN; ESPN2; EVINE Live; Food Network; Fox News Channel; FOX Sports Southwest; Freeform; FX; Hallmark Channel; HGTV; History; HLN; Lifetime; MTV; Nickelodeon; Pop; Spike TV; Syfy; TBS; The Weather Channel; TLC; TNT; Turner Classic Movies; TV Land; USA Network; VH1; WGN America.
Fee: $79.95 installation; $31.90 monthly.
Digital Basic Service
Subscribers: N.A.
Programming (via satellite): BBC America; CMT; Destination America; Discovery Kids Channel; Discovery Life Channel; Disney XD; DMX Music; ESPNews; Fox Sports 1; FSN Digital Atlantic; FSN Digital Central; FSN Digital Pacific; FYI; Golf Channel; Great American Country; GSN; History International; Investigation Discovery; LMN; MTV Classic; MTV Hits; MTV Jams; MTV2; National Geographic Channel; Nick 2; Nick Jr.; Nicktoons; Outdoor Channel; OWN: Oprah Winfrey Network; Science Channel; TeenNick; Tr3s; VH1 Soul; WE tv.
Digital Pay Service 1
Pay Units: N.A.
Programming (via satellite): Cinemax (multiplexed); HBO (multiplexed); Starz (multiplexed); Starz Encore.
Fee: $12.95 monthly (Cinemax, HBO or Starz/Encore).
Video-On-Demand: No
Pay-Per-View
iN DEMAND (delivered digitally).
Internet Service
Operational: Yes. Began: August 10, 2001.
Broadband Service: Cablelynx.
Fee: $24.95-$74.95 monthly; $10.00 modem lease.
Telephone Service
Analog: Not Operational
Digital: Operational
Fee: $45.70 monthly
Miles of Plant: 189.0 (coaxial); 99.0 (fiber optic). Homes passed: 7,570.
Vice President, Administration: Charlotte A. Dial. General Manager: Stacy Eads. Technical Operations & Plant Manager: Billy Bechtel.
Ownership: WEHCO Video Inc. (MSO).; Walter E. Hussman Jr.

CARPENTER DAM—Formerly served by Cablevision of Carpenter Dam. No longer in operation. ICA: AR0293.

CARTHAGE—Formerly served by Almega Cable. No longer in operation. ICA: AR0185.

CARTHAGE—Formerly served by Almega Cable. No longer in operation. ICA: AR0182.

CASA—Formerly served by Eagle Media. No longer in operation. ICA: AR0308.

CEDARVILLE—Cox Communications. Now served by FORT SMITH, AR [AR0003]. ICA: AR0060.

CHARLESTON—Suddenlink Communications, 520 Maryville Centre Dr, Ste 300, St. Louis, MO 63141. Phones: 314-315-9400; 888-822-5151. E-mail: Gene.Regan@suddenlink.com. Web Site: http://www.suddenlink.com. ICA: AR0225.
TV Market Ranking: Below 100 (CHARLESTON). Franchise award date: December 1, 1970. Franchise expiration date: N.A. Began: January 1, 1972.
Channel capacity: N.A. Channels available but not in use: N.A.
Basic Service
Subscribers: 165.
Programming (received off-air): KAFT (PBS) Fayetteville; KFSM-TV (CBS, MNT) Fort Smith; KFTA-TV (FOX, NBC) Fort Smith; KHBS (ABC, CW) Fort Smith; KNWA-TV (FOX, NBC) Rogers.
Programming (via satellite): C-SPAN; CW PLUS; INSP.
Fee: $28.45 monthly.
Expanded Basic Service 1
Subscribers: N.A.
Programming (via satellite): A&E; AMC; Animal Planet; BET; Cartoon Network; CNBC; CNN; Comedy Central; Discovery Channel; Disney Channel; E! HD; ESPN; ESPN2; Food Network; Fox News Channel; Fox Sports 1; FOX Sports Southwest; Freeform; FX; Great American Country; Hallmark Channel; HGTV; History; HLN; Lifetime; MSNBC; MTV; National Geographic Channel; Nickelodeon; Outdoor Channel; Spike TV; Syfy; TBS; The Weather Channel; TLC; TNT; Travel Channel; truTV; Turner Classic Movies; TV Land; USA Network; VH1.
Fee: $22.04 monthly.
Pay Service 1
Pay Units: N.A.
Programming (via satellite): HBO; Showtime; The Movie Channel.
Fee: $12.95 monthly (each).
Video-On-Demand: No
Internet Service
Operational: Yes. Began: November 12, 2003.
Broadband Service: Suddenlink High Speed Internet.
Fee: $19.95 monthly.
Telephone Service
None
Miles of Plant: 21.0 (coaxial); None (fiber optic). Homes passed: 1,050.
Senior Vice President, Corporate Finance: Michael Pflantz. Regional Manager: Todd Cruthird. Plant Manager: Danny Keith. Marketing Director: Beverly Gambell.
Ownership: Cequel Communications Holdings I LLC (MSO).

CHIDESTER—Formerly served by Almega Cable. No longer in operation. ICA: AR0138.

CLARENDON—Formerly served by Zoom Media. No longer in operation. ICA: AR0084.

CLARKSVILLE—Suddenlink Communications, PO Box 10010, Russellville, AR 72812. Phones: 888-592-3861; 314-315-9400; 800-582-9577. Web Site: http://www.suddenlink.com. Also serves Lamar. ICA: AR0043.
TV Market Ranking: Outside TV Markets (CLARKSVILLE, Lamar). Franchise award date: N.A. Franchise expiration date: N.A. Began: September 1, 1964.
Channel capacity: N.A. Channels available but not in use: N.A.
Basic Service
Subscribers: 1,677. Commercial subscribers: 256.
Programming (received off-air): KAFT (PBS) Fayetteville; KARK-TV (NBC) Little Rock; KATV (ABC, Retro TV) Little Rock; KFSM-TV (CBS, MNT) Fort Smith; KFTA-TV (FOX, NBC) Fort Smith; KHBS (ABC, CW) Fort Smith; KTHV (Antenna TV, CBS) Little Rock; KXUN-LD (UNV) Fort Smith; allband FM.
Programming (via satellite): C-SPAN; QVC; TBS; The Weather Channel; UniMas; WGN America.
Fee: $40.00 installation; $31.50 monthly; $2.25 converter.
Expanded Basic Service 1
Subscribers: N.A.
Programming (via satellite): A&E; AMC; Animal Planet; BET; Bravo; Cartoon Network; CMT; CNBC; CNN; Comedy Central; C-SPAN 2; Discovery Channel; Disney Channel; E! HD; ESPN; ESPN2; EWTN Global Catholic Network; Food Network; Fox News Channel; Fox Sports 1; FOX Sports Southwest; Freeform; FX; Great American Country; HGTV; History; HLN; INSP; Jewelry Television; Lifetime; LMN; MSNBC; MTV; NBCSN; Nickelodeon; Outdoor Channel; Pop; Spike TV; Syfy; TLC; TNT; Travel Channel; Trinity Broadcasting Network (TBN); truTV; Turner Classic Movies; TV Land; Univision; USA Network; VH1.
Fee: $23.75 monthly.
Digital Basic Service
Subscribers: N.A.
Programming (via satellite): A&E HD; Animal Planet HD; AXS TV; Bandamax; BBC America; Bloomberg Television; Boomerang; CBS Sports Network; Chiller; Cine Mexicano; Cinelatino; CMT; CNN en Espanol; Cooking Channel; Cox Sports Television; De Pelicula; De Pelicula Clasico; Destination America; Discovery Channel HD; Discovery Kids Channel; Disney XD; DIY Network; Enlace USA; ESPN Classic; ESPN Deportes; ESPN HD; ESPN2 HD; ESPNews; ESPNU; FamilyNet; Food Network HD; Fox Deportes; Fox Sports 2; FSN HD; Fuse; FX HD; FYI; Golf Channel; GSN; Hallmark Channel; HD Theater; HGTV HD; History en Espanol; History HD; History International; IFC; Investigation Discovery; MC; MTV Classic; MTV Hits; MTV Live; MTV2; mtvU; Nat Geo WILD; National Geographic Channel; National Geographic Channel HD; NBC Universo; Nick Jr.; Nicktoons; NickToons en Espanol; OWN: Oprah Winfrey Network; Oxygen; RFD-TV; Science Channel; Starz Encore (multiplexed); Sundance TV; Sur; Syfy HD; TBS HD; TeenNick; Telehit; Telemundo; Tennis Channel; TLC HD; TNT HD; Toon Disney en Espanol; Tr3s; TV One; ULTRA HDPlex; Universal HD; Univision; UP; USA Network HD; VideoRola; WE tv; Weatherscan.

Cable Systems—Arkansas

Digital Pay Service 1
Pay Units: N.A.
Programming (via satellite): Cinemax (multiplexed); HBO (multiplexed); HBO HD; HBO Latino; Showtime (multiplexed); Showtime HD; Starz (multiplexed); The Movie Channel (multiplexed).
Fee: $12.95 monthly (Cinemax, HBO, Showtime/TMC or Starz).
Video-On-Demand: No
Pay-Per-View
iN DEMAND (delivered digitally); Fresh (delivered digitally); Playboy TV (delivered digitally); Shorteez (delivered digitally); Club Jenna (delivered digitally); Spice: Xcess (delivered digitally); Playboy en Espanol (delivered digitally).
Internet Service
Operational: Yes.
Broadband Service: Suddenlink High Speed Internet.
Fee: $33.00 monthly.
Telephone Service
Digital: Operational
Fee: $33.00 monthly
Miles of Plant: 53.0 (coaxial); None (fiber optic).
Senior Vice President, Corporate Finance: Michael Pflantz. Vice President, Accounting: Sabrina Warr. General Manager: Mike Ederington. Chief Engineer: Wayne Ollis. Customer Service Manager: Jane Ollis.
Ownership: Cequel Communications Holdings I LLC (MSO).

CLINTON—Clinton Cablevision Inc, 114 Richard Rd, PO Box 900, Clinton, AR 72031-0900. Phones: 877-383-8257; 501-745-4040. Fax: 501-745-4663. E-mail: clintoncable@clintoncable.net. Web Site: http://www.clintoncable.net. Also serves Van Buren County (portions). ICA: AR0226.
TV Market Ranking: Outside TV Markets (CLINTON, Van Buren County (portions)). Franchise award date: N.A. Franchise expiration date: N.A. Began: November 1, 1976.
Channel capacity: N.A. Channels available but not in use: N.A.
Basic Service
Subscribers: N.A.
Programming (received off-air): KARK-TV (NBC) Little Rock; KASN (CW, The Country Network) Pine Bluff; KATV (ABC, Retro TV) Little Rock; KEMV (PBS) Mountain View; KKYK-CD (IND, WeatherNation) Little Rock; KLRT-TV (FOX, This TV) Little Rock; KTHV (Antenna TV, CBS) Little Rock.
Programming (via satellite): Bloomberg Television; Cartoon Network; CMT; CNN; C-SPAN; Daystar TV Network; Discovery Channel; Disney Channel; ESPN; Family Friendly Entertainment; Food Network; Fox News Channel; FX; Great American Country; HGTV; HLN; Lifetime; Nickelodeon; Outdoor Channel; QVC; RFD-TV; Spike TV; TBS; The Weather Channel; TLC; TNT; Trinity Broadcasting Network (TBN); Turner Classic Movies; TV Land; USA Network; WGN America.
Fee: $25.00 installation.
Expanded Basic Service 1
Subscribers: 301.
Fee: $16.95 monthly.
Digital Basic Service
Subscribers: 598.
Programming (via satellite): BBC America; Cloo; Discovery Life Channel; Disney XD; DMX Music; ESPN Classic; ESPN2; ESPNews; Fox Sports 1; Fuse; Golf Channel; GSN; History; LMN; NBCSN; Nick Jr.; Nicktoons; Syfy; TeenNick; WE tv.
Fee: $43.95 monthly.
Digital Pay Service 1
Pay Units: N.A.
Programming (via satellite): Cinemax (multiplexed); HBO (multiplexed); Showtime (multiplexed); Starz (multiplexed); Starz Encore (multiplexed); The Movie Channel (multiplexed).
Fee: $8.95 monthly (Cinemax or Starz/Encore), $11.95 monthly (HBO), $12.95 monthly (Showtime/TMC).
Video-On-Demand: No; No
Pay-Per-View
Sports PPV (delivered digitally); Special events (delivered digitally); Adult Channels (delivered digitally).
Internet Service
Operational: Yes. Began: July 1, 2002.
Broadband Service: In-house.
Fee: $50.00 installation; $39.95 monthly.
Telephone Service
None
Miles of Plant: 30.0 (coaxial); 12.0 (fiber optic). Homes passed: 1,300.
Chief Executive Officer: John Hastings.
Ownership: Clinton Cable Inc.

CLINTON—Media3, PO Box 650, Milan, TN 38358. Phone: 866-257-2044. E-mail: customerservice@mymedia3.com. Web Site: http://www.mymedia3.com. Also serves Damascus, Guy & Quitman. ICA: AR0328.
TV Market Ranking: Outside TV Markets (Damascus, Guy, Quitman, CLINTON).
Channel capacity: N.A. Channels available but not in use: N.A.
Basic Service
Subscribers: 721.
Fee: $24.95 installation; $22.95 monthly.
Chief Financial Officer: Thomas Pate.
Ownership: CableSouth Media3 LLC (MSO).

COAL HILL—Formerly served by Suddenlink Communications. No longer in operation. ICA: AR0101.

CONWAY—Buford Media. Now served by GREENBRIER, AR [AR0077]. ICA: AR0325.

CONWAY—Conway Corp. C.T.S., 1307 Prairie St, Conway, AR 72034. Phones: 501-450-6040 (Customer service); 501-450-6020; 501-450-6000. Fax: 501-450-6099. E-mail: comments@conwaycorp.net. Web Site: http://www.conwaycorp.com. ICA: AR0011.
TV Market Ranking: 50 (CONWAY). Franchise award date: May 22, 1979. Franchise expiration date: N.A. Began: June 1, 1980.
Channel capacity: 72 (operating 2-way). Channels available but not in use: N.A.
Basic Service
Subscribers: 14,691.
Programming (received off-air): KARK-TV (NBC) Little Rock; KARZ-TV (Bounce TV, MNT) Little Rock; KASN (CW, The Country Network) Pine Bluff; KATV (ABC, Retro TV) Little Rock; KETS (PBS) Little Rock; KKAP (Daystar TV, ETV) Little Rock; KLRT-TV (FOX, This TV) Little Rock; KMYA-DT (MeTV, WeatherNation) Camden; KTHV (Antenna TV, CBS) Little Rock; KVTN-DT (IND) Pine Bluff.
Programming (via satellite): A&E; CNN; C-SPAN; Discovery Channel; Disney XD; E! HD; ESPN; ESPN2; EWTN Global Catholic Network; Fox News Channel; FOX Sports Southwest; Freeform; FX; HGTV; HLN; Lifetime; MSNBC; Nickelodeon; Pop; QVC; Spike TV; TBS; The Weather Channel; TLC; Trinity Broadcasting Network (TBN); TV Land; USA Network; VH1; WGN America.
Fee: $50.00 installation; $50.50 monthly; $4.00 converter.
Expanded Basic Service 1
Subscribers: 12,704.
Programming (via satellite): AMC; Animal Planet; BET; Bravo; Cartoon Network; CMT; CNBC; Comedy Central; Discovery Life Channel; Disney Channel; ESPNews; Food Network; Golf Channel; History; MTV; National Geographic Channel; NBCSN; Outdoor Channel; Syfy; Telemundo; Travel Channel; truTV; Turner Classic Movies.
Fee: $12.00 monthly.
Digital Basic Service
Subscribers: N.A.
Programming (via satellite): BBC America; Boomerang; Discovery Digital Networks; DIY Network; ESPN Classic; Fox Sports 1; FXM; FYI; Great American Country; Hallmark Channel; History International; LMN; Nick 2; Nick Jr.; TeenNick; Trinity Broadcasting Network (TBN); WE tv.
Fee: $4.00 converter.
Digital Pay Service 1
Pay Units: 1,024.
Programming (via satellite): Cinemax (multiplexed).
Fee: $5.00 installation; $9.45 monthly.
Digital Pay Service 2
Pay Units: 2,389.
Programming (via satellite): HBO (multiplexed).
Fee: $5.00 installation; $12.95 monthly.
Digital Pay Service 3
Pay Units: 1,214.
Programming (via satellite): Showtime (multiplexed).
Fee: $5.00 installation; $11.95 monthly.
Digital Pay Service 4
Pay Units: 304.
Programming (via satellite): Starz.
Fee: $8.45 monthly.
Video-On-Demand: No
Pay-Per-View
iN DEMAND.
Internet Service
Operational: Yes.
Subscribers: 15,649.
Fee: $38.50 installation; $29.95-$84.95 monthly.
Telephone Service
Digital: Operational
Subscribers: 3,778.
Miles of Plant: 795.0 (coaxial); 265.0 (fiber optic). Homes passed: 26,124.
Chief Executive Officer: Richard Arnold. Chief Operating Officer: Tommy Shackelford. Chief Financial Officer: Bret A. Carroll. Marketing Manager: Crystal Kemp.
Ownership: Conway Corp.

CONWAY—Formerly served by Alliance Communications. Now served by Media3, MAYFLOWER, AR [AR0049]. ICA: AR0104.

CORNING—Vyve Broadband, 4 International Dr, Ste 330, Rye Brook, NY 10573. Phones: 800-937-1397; 405-395-1131; 405-275-6923. Web Site: http://www.vyvebroadband.com. Also serves Clay County (portions). ICA: AR0227.
TV Market Ranking: Below 100 (Clay County (portions), CORNING). Franchise award date: N.A. Franchise expiration date: N.A. Began: January 1, 1966.
Channel capacity: N.A. Channels available but not in use: N.A.
Basic Service
Subscribers: 281. Commercial subscribers: 23.
Programming (received off-air): KAIT (ABC, NBC) Jonesboro; KARK-TV (NBC) Little Rock; KATV (ABC, Retro TV) Little Rock; KBSI (FOX) Cape Girardeau; KFVS-TV (CBS, CW, MeTV) Cape Girardeau; KTEJ (PBS) Jonesboro; KVTJ-DT (IND) Jonesboro; WMC-TV (Bounce TV, NBC, This TV) Memphis; allband FM.
Programming (via satellite): CNN; C-SPAN; CW PLUS; Pop; QVC; The Weather Channel; Trinity Broadcasting Network (TBN); WGN America.
Fee: $64.95 installation; $25.00 monthly.
Expanded Basic Service 1
Subscribers: 275.
Programming (via satellite): A&E; Cartoon Network; Comedy Central; Discovery Channel; Disney Channel; ESPN; ESPN Classic; ESPN2; Fox News Channel; FOX Sports Southwest; Freeform; HGTV; History; INSP; Lifetime; NFL Network; Nickelodeon; Spike TV; Syfy; TBS; TLC; TNT; Travel Channel; Turner Classic Movies; TV Land; USA Network; VH1.
Fee: $35.76 monthly.
Digital Basic Service
Subscribers: N.A.
Programming (via satellite): BBC America; Bloomberg Television; Bravo; Cine Mexicano; Cinelatino; Cloo; CMT; CNN en Espanol; Destination America; Discovery Kids Channel; Discovery Life Channel; Disney XD; DMX Music; ESPN Classic; ESPN Deportes; ESPN2; ESPNews; EVINE Live; Flix; FOX College Sports Central; FOX College Sports Pacific; Fox Deportes; Fox Sports 1; Fuse; FXM; FYI; Golf Channel; Great American Country; GSN; HGTV; History; History en Espanol; History International; IFC; Investigation Discovery; LMN; MTV Classic; MTV Hits; MTV2; National Geographic Channel; NBC Universo; NBCSN; Nick Jr.; Nicktoons; Outdoor Channel; OWN: Oprah Winfrey Network; Science Channel; Starz Encore (multiplexed); Sundance TV; Syfy; TeenNick; The Word Network; Tr3s; Trinity Broadcasting Network (TBN); Turner Classic Movies; UP; VH1 Soul; ViendoMovies; WE tv.
Pay Service 1
Pay Units: N.A.
Programming (via satellite): Cinemax; HBO; Showtime.
Digital Pay Service 1
Pay Units: N.A.
Programming (via satellite): Cinemax (multiplexed); HBO (multiplexed); HBO Latino; Showtime (multiplexed); Starz (multiplexed); The Movie Channel (multiplexed).
Video-On-Demand: No

Arkansas—Cable Systems

Pay-Per-View
iN DEMAND (delivered digitally); Playboy TV (delivered digitally); Fresh (delivered digitally); Shorteez (delivered digitally).
Internet Service
Operational: Yes.
Fee: $24.95 installation; $39.95 monthly.
Telephone Service
Digital: Operational
Miles of Plant: 40.0 (coaxial); 7.0 (fiber optic). Homes passed: 1,985.
Chief Executive Officer: Bill Haggarty. Regional Vice President: Andrew Dearth. Senior Vice President, Financial Planning: Daniel White. Vice President, Marketing: Tracy Bass.
Ownership: Vyve Broadband LLC (MSO).

CRAWFORDSVILLE (portions)—Formerly served by Ritter Communications. No longer in operation. ICA: AR0166.

CROSSETT—Media3, PO Box 620, Milan, TN 38358. Phone: 866-257-2044. E-mail: customerservice@mymedia3.com. Web Site: http://www.mymedia3.com. Also serves Ashley County (portions), North Crossett & West Crossett. ICA: AR0028.
TV Market Ranking: 99 (West Crossett); Outside TV Markets (Ashley County (portions), CROSSETT, North Crossett, West Crossett). Franchise award date: N.A. Franchise expiration date: N.A. Began: November 1, 1966.
Channel capacity: N.A. Channels available but not in use: N.A.
Basic Service
Subscribers: 1,026.
Programming (received off-air): KARD (Bounce TV, FOX) West Monroe; KATV (ABC, Retro TV) Little Rock; KETS (PBS) Little Rock; KLTM-TV (PBS) Monroe; KMLU (MeTV) Columbia; KNOE-TV (ABC, CBS, CW) Monroe; KTVE (NBC) El Dorado.
Programming (via satellite): ION Television; Pop; QVC; WGN America.
Fee: $24.95 installation; $22.45 monthly; $1.37 converter.
Expanded Basic Service 1
Subscribers: N.A.
Programming (via satellite): A&E; AMC; Animal Planet; BET; Bravo; Cartoon Network; CMT; CNBC; CNN; Comedy Central; C-SPAN; Discovery Channel; Disney Channel; E! HD; ESPN; ESPN2; Food Network; Fox News Channel; Fox Sports 1; FOX Sports Southwest; Freeform; FX; Golf Channel; GSN; Hallmark Channel; HGTV; History; HLN; INSP; Lifetime; MSNBC; MTV; National Geographic Channel; NBCSN; Nickelodeon; Outdoor Channel; Oxygen; Spike TV; Syfy; TBS; The Weather Channel; TLC; TNT; Travel Channel; Trinity Broadcasting Network (TBN); truTV; Turner Classic Movies; TV Land; USA Network; VH1; WE tv.
Fee: $29.25 monthly.
Digital Basic Service
Subscribers: N.A.
Programming (via satellite): BBC America; Bloomberg Television; Discovery Digital Networks; DIY Network; FYI; History International; IFC; MC; Nick Jr.; Nicktoons; Sundance TV; TV Guide Interactive Inc.
Pay Service 1
Pay Units: N.A.
Programming (via satellite): The Movie Channel.
Fee: $8.00 monthly.
Digital Pay Service 1
Pay Units: N.A.
Programming (via satellite): Cinemax (multiplexed); Flix; HBO (multiplexed); Showtime (multiplexed); Starz (multiplexed); Starz Encore (multiplexed); The Movie Channel (multiplexed).
Video-On-Demand: No
Pay-Per-View
iN DEMAND (delivered digitally); NBA TV (delivered digitally); NHL Center Ice/MLB Extra Innings (delivered digitally); Playboy TV (delivered digitally); Pleasure (delivered digitally); Fresh (delivered digitally); Shorteez (delivered digitally).
Internet Service
Operational: Yes.
Fee: $45.00 monthly.
Telephone Service
Digital: Operational
Fee: $50.00 monthly
Miles of Plant: 81.0 (coaxial); 88.0 (fiber optic). Homes passed: 4,574.
President: G. Alan Taylor. Chief Financial Officer: Thomas Pate.
Ownership: CableSouth Media3 LLC (MSO).

CURTIS—Formerly served by Community Communications Co. No longer in operation. ICA: AR0147.

CUSHMAN—Indco Cable TV, 2700 North Saint Louis, PO Box 3799, Batesville, AR 72503-3799. Phones: 800-364-0831; 870-793-4175; 870-793-4174. Fax: 870-793-7439. Web Site: http://www.indco.net. ICA: AR0228.
TV Market Ranking: Outside TV Markets (CUSHMAN).
Channel capacity: N.A. Channels available but not in use: N.A.
Basic Service
Subscribers: 32.
Programming (received off-air): KAIT (ABC, NBC) Jonesboro; KARK-TV (NBC) Little Rock; KEMV (PBS) Mountain View; KLRT-TV (FOX, This TV) Little Rock; KTHV (Antenna TV, CBS) Little Rock.
Programming (via satellite): CMT; CNN; Discovery Channel; Disney Channel; ESPN; ESPN2; Freeform; HGTV; Lifetime; Nickelodeon; Outdoor Channel; QVC; Spike TV; Syfy; TBS; The Weather Channel; TNT; Trinity Broadcasting Network (TBN); Turner Classic Movies; USA Network; VH1; WGN America.
Fee: $40.00 installation; $63.95 monthly.
Video-On-Demand: Planned
Internet Service
Operational: Yes.
Fee: $29.95 monthly.
Telephone Service
None
President & General Manager: J.D. Pierce. Chief Technician: Tommy Barnett. Marketing Director: Connie Barnett.
Ownership: Indco Cable TV (MSO).

DANVILLE—Formerly served by Suddenlink Communications. No longer in operation. ICA: AR0046.

DE QUEEN—Vyve Broadband, 4 International Dr, Ste 330, Rye Brook, NY 10573. Phones: 800-937-1397; 405-275-6923; 405-395-1131. Web Site: http://vyvebroadband.com. Also serves Horatio & Sevier County. ICA: AR0045.
TV Market Ranking: 58 (Sevier County (portions)); Outside TV Markets (DE QUEEN, Horatio, Sevier County (portions)). Franchise award date: February 1, 1994. Franchise expiration date: N.A. Began: December 1, 1965.
Channel capacity: 35 (operating 2-way). Channels available but not in use: N.A.
Basic Service
Subscribers: 320. Commercial subscribers: 28.
Programming (received off-air): KARK-TV (NBC) Little Rock; KATV (ABC, Retro TV) Little Rock; KETG (PBS) Arkadelphia; KMSS-TV (FOX) Shreveport; KSLA (Bounce TV, CBS, Grit, This TV) Shreveport; KTAL-TV (NBC) Texarkana; KTBS-TV (ABC) Shreveport; KTHV (Antenna TV, CBS) Little Rock; allband FM.
Programming (via satellite): CNN; QVC; Telemundo; The Weather Channel; Univision Studios.
Fee: $64.95 installation; $25.00 monthly.
Expanded Basic Service 1
Subscribers: N.A.
Programming (via satellite): A&E; AMC; Animal Planet; BET; CMT; CNBC; Discovery Channel; Disney Channel; ESPN; ESPN Classic; ESPN2; Food Network; Fox News Channel; FOX Sports Southwest; Freeform; FX; Hallmark Channel; HGTV; History; HLN; Lifetime; NFL Network; Nickelodeon; Spike TV; Syfy; TBS; TLC; TNT; truTV; Turner Classic Movies; TV Land; USA Network; VH1.
Fee: $32.56 monthly.
Digital Basic Service
Subscribers: N.A.
Programming (via satellite): 3ABN; BBC America; Bloomberg Television; Bravo; BYUtv; Church Channel; Cine Mexicano; Cinelatino; CNN en Espanol; Daystar TV Network; Destination America; Discovery Kids Channel; Discovery Life Channel; Disney XD; DMX Music; Enlace USA; ESPN Classic; ESPNews; EVINE Live; Family Friendly Entertainment; FamilyNet; Flix; FOX College Sports Central; FOX College Sports Pacific; Fox Deportes; Fox Sports 1; Fuse; FXM; FYI; GEB America; Golf Channel; Great American Country; GSN; History; History en Espanol; History International; IFC; Investigation Discovery; JUCE TV; La Familia Cosmovision; LMN; MTV Classic; MTV Hits; MTV2; National Geographic Channel; NBCSN; Nick Jr.; Nicktoons; Outdoor Channel; OWN: Oprah Winfrey Network; Science Channel; Starz Encore (multiplexed); Sundance TV; Syfy; TeenNick; The Word Network; Toon Disney en Espanol; Tr3s; Trinity Broadcasting Network (TBN); Turner Classic Movies; ULTRA HDPlex; VH1 Country; WE tv.
Pay Service 1
Pay Units: N.A.
Programming (via satellite): Cinemax; HBO; Showtime; Starz; Starz Encore.
Fee: $9.95 monthly (Cinemax/Starz or Encore), $10.95 monthly (HBO).
Digital Pay Service 1
Pay Units: N.A.
Programming (via satellite): Cinemax (multiplexed); HBO (multiplexed); HBO Latino; Showtime (multiplexed); Starz (multiplexed); The Movie Channel (multiplexed).
Pay-Per-View
iN DEMAND (delivered digitally); Hot Choice (delivered digitally); Playboy TV (delivered digitally); Fresh (delivered digitally); Shorteez (delivered digitally).
Internet Service
Operational: Yes.
Fee: $24.95 installation; $39.95 monthly.
Telephone Service
Digital: Operational
Miles of Plant: 48.0 (coaxial); None (fiber optic). Homes passed: 2,499.
Chief Executive Officer: Bill Haggarty. Regional Vice President: Andrew Dearth. Vice President, Marketing: Tracy Bass. Senior Vice President, Financial Planning: Daniel White.
Ownership: Vyve Broadband LLC (MSO).

DE WITT—Suddenlink Communications, 520 Maryville Centre Dr, Ste 300, St. Louis, MO 63141. Phones: 314-315-9400; 888-822-5151. Web Site: http://www.suddenlink.com. ICA: AR0064.
TV Market Ranking: Below 100 (DE WITT). Franchise award date: April 11, 1979. Franchise expiration date: N.A. Began: November 15, 1980.
Channel capacity: N.A. Channels available but not in use: N.A.
Basic Service
Subscribers: 217.
Programming (received off-air): KARK-TV (NBC) Little Rock; KARZ-TV (Bounce TV, MNT) Little Rock; KASN (CW, The Country Network) Pine Bluff; KATV (ABC, Retro TV) Little Rock; KETS (PBS) Little Rock; KKAP (Daystar TV, ETV) Little Rock; KLRT-TV (FOX, This TV) Little Rock; KTHV (Antenna TV, CBS) Little Rock; KVTN-DT (IND) Pine Bluff.
Fee: $28.45 monthly.
Expanded Basic Service 1
Subscribers: N.A.
Programming (via satellite): A&E; AMC; Animal Planet; BET; Cartoon Network; CNBC; CNN; Comedy Central; C-SPAN; Discovery Channel; Disney Channel; E! HD; ESPN; ESPN2; Food Network; Fox News Channel; FOX Sports Southwest; Freeform; FX; Great American Country; Hallmark Channel; HGTV; History; HLN; Jewelry Television; Lifetime; MSNBC; MTV; National Geographic Channel; Nickelodeon; Outdoor Channel; QVC; Spike TV; Syfy; TBS; The Weather Channel; TLC; TNT; Travel Channel; Turner Classic Movies; TV Land; USA Network; VH1.
Fee: $31.00 monthly.
Digital Basic Service
Subscribers: N.A.
Programming (via satellite): BBC America; Bloomberg Television; Cloo; Destination America; Discovery Kids Channel; Disney XD; DMX Music; ESPN Classic; ESPNews; EVINE Live; FOX College Sports Central; FOX College Sports Pacific; Fox Sports 1; Fuse; FYI; Golf Channel; GSN; History International; IFC; Investigation Discovery; NBCSN; Outdoor Channel; OWN: Oprah Winfrey Network; Science Channel; Sundance TV; Trinity Broadcasting Network (TBN); WE tv.
Pay Service 1
Pay Units: N.A.
Programming (via satellite): HBO; Showtime.
Fee: $12.95 monthly (each).
Digital Pay Service 1
Pay Units: N.A.
Programming (via satellite): Cinemax (multiplexed); Flix; HBO (multiplexed); Showtime; Starz (multiplexed); Starz Encore (multiplexed); The Movie Channel (multiplexed).
Fee: $12.95 monthly (Cinemax, HBO, Showtime/TMC or Starz/Encore).
Video-On-Demand: No
Pay-Per-View
iN DEMAND (delivered digitally); Playboy TV (delivered digitally); Club Jenna (delivered digitally); Fresh (delivered digitally); Spice: Xcess (delivered digitally).
Internet Service
Operational: Yes. Began: April 15, 2004.
Broadband Service: Suddenlink High Speed Internet.
Fee: $25.95 monthly.

Cable Systems—Arkansas

Telephone Service
Digital: Operational
Fee: $33.00 monthly
Miles of Plant: 40.0 (coaxial); 3.0 (fiber optic). Homes passed: 2,117.
Senior Vice President, Corporate Finance: Michael Pflantz. Regional Manager: Todd Cruthird. General Manager: Dave Walker. Chief Technician: Carl Miller. Marketing Director: Beverly Gambell.
Ownership: Cequel Communications Holdings I LLC (MSO).

DELIGHT—Formerly served by Almega Cable. No longer in operation. ICA: AR0160.

DES ARC—Alliance Communications, PO Box 9090, Tyler, TX 75711. Phones: 903-561-4411 (Tyler, TX office); 501-679-6619; 800-842-8160. E-mail: marketing@alliancecable.net. Web Site: http://www.alliancecable.net. Also serves Prairie County (portions). ICA: AR0091.
TV Market Ranking: Outside TV Markets (DES ARC, Prairie County (portions)). Franchise award date: N.A. Franchise expiration date: N.A. Began: December 1, 1982.
Channel capacity: 60 (not 2-way capable). Channels available but not in use: N.A.
Basic Service
Subscribers: 49.
Programming (received off-air): KARK-TV (NBC) Little Rock; KASN (CW, The Country Network) Pine Bluff; KATV (ABC, Retro TV) Little Rock; KETS (PBS) Little Rock; KLRT-TV (FOX, This TV) Little Rock; KMYA-DT (MeTV, WeatherNation) Camden; KTHV (Antenna TV, CBS) Little Rock; KVTN-DT (IND) Pine Bluff.
Programming (via satellite): National Geographic Channel.
Fee: $45.00 installation; $22.45 monthly.
Expanded Basic Service 1
Subscribers: N.A.
Programming (via satellite): A&E; AMC; BET; CNN; Discovery Channel; Disney Channel; ESPN; ESPN2; Freeform; Great American Country; HGTV; History; HLN; Lifetime; Nickelodeon; Outdoor Channel; Spike TV; Syfy; TBS; The Weather Channel; TLC; TNT; Trinity Broadcasting Network (TBN); USA Network.
Fee: $27.50 monthly.
Digital Basic Service
Subscribers: N.A.
Programming (via satellite): BBC America; Bloomberg Television; Cloo; Destination America; Discovery Kids Channel; DMX Music; ESPN Classic; ESPN2; ESPNews; EVINE Live; FOX College Sports Central; FOX College Sports Pacific; Fox Sports 1; Fuse; FYI; Golf Channel; GSN; HGTV; History; History International; Investigation Discovery; LMN; NBCSN; Outdoor Channel; Ovation; OWN; Oprah Winfrey Network; Science Channel; Syfy; Trinity Broadcasting Network (TBN); Turner Classic Movies; WE tv.
Pay Service 1
Pay Units: N.A.
Programming (via satellite): HBO; Showtime; The Movie Channel.
Fee: $12.95 monthly (each).
Digital Pay Service 1
Pay Units: N.A.
Programming (via satellite): Cinemax (multiplexed); Flix; HBO (multiplexed); Showtime (multiplexed); Starz (multiplexed); Starz Encore (multiplexed); The Movie Channel (multiplexed).
Video-On-Demand: No

Pay-Per-View
iN DEMAND (delivered digitally); Playboy TV (delivered digitally); Club Jenna (delivered digitally).
Internet Service
Operational: No.
Telephone Service
None
Miles of Plant: 16.0 (coaxial); None (fiber optic). Homes passed: 910.
Chief Financial Officer: David Starrett. Vice President & General Manager: John Brinker. Vice President, Programming: Julie Newman.
Ownership: Buford Media Group LLC (MSO).

DIAMOND CITY—NATCO Communications Inc., 301 East Main St, PO Box 209, Flippin, AR 72634. Phones: 800-775-6682; 870-453-8800. Fax: 870-453-7171. Web Site: http://www.natconet.com. Also serves Lead Hill. ICA: AR0124.
Channel capacity: N.A. Channels available but not in use: N.A.
Basic Service
Subscribers: 114. Commercial subscribers: 5.
Fee: $45.00 monthly.
Internet Service
Operational: Yes.
Fee: $29.95-$79.95 monthly.
Telephone Service
Digital: Operational
Fee: $18.15 monthly
General Manager: Steven G. Sanders Jr. Business Manager: Steve Smith. Plant Manager: Travis Sullivan.
Ownership: Northern Arkansas Telephone Co.

DIERKS—Formerly served by Allegiance Communications. No longer in operation. ICA: AR0108.

DOVER—Suddenlink Communications, 520 Maryville Centre Dr, Ste 300, St. Louis, MO 63141. Phones: 314-315-9400; 888-822-5151. E-mail: Gene.Regan@suddenlink.com. Web Site: http://www.suddenlink.com. Also serves Pope County (unincorporated areas). ICA: AR0113.
TV Market Ranking: Outside TV Markets (DOVER, Pope County (unincorporated areas)). Franchise award date: N.A. Franchise expiration date: N.A. Began: December 7, 1982.
Channel capacity: 60 (not 2-way capable). Channels available but not in use: N.A.
Basic Service
Subscribers: 222.
Programming (received off-air): KAFT (PBS) Fayetteville; KARK-TV (NBC) Little Rock; KATV (ABC, Retro TV) Little Rock; KFSM-TV (CBS, MNT) Fort Smith; KLRT-TV (FOX, This TV) Little Rock; KTHV (Antenna TV, CBS) Little Rock.
Programming (via satellite): Fox News Channel; Trinity Broadcasting Network (TBN).
Fee: $40.00 installation; $36.00 monthly.
Expanded Basic Service 1
Subscribers: N.A.
Programming (via satellite): A&E; AMC; Animal Planet; CNN; Discovery Channel; Disney Channel; ESPN; ESPN2; Food Network; FOX Sports Southwest; Freeform; Great American Country; HGTV; History; HLN; Lifetime; National Geographic Channel; Nickelodeon; Outdoor Channel; QVC; Spike TV; Syfy; TBS; The Weather Channel; TNT; TV Land; USA Network; VH1.
Fee: $22.00 monthly.

CABLE & TV STATION COVERAGE
Atlas 2017

The perfect companion to the Television & Cable Factbook
To order call 800-771-9202 or visit www.warren-news.com

Pay Service 1
Pay Units: N.A.
Programming (via satellite): HBO; Showtime; The Movie Channel.
Fee: $10.95 monthly (Showtime or TMC), $13.00 monthly (HBO).
Video-On-Demand: No
Pay-Per-View
Sports PPV (delivered digitally); ESPN Now (delivered digitally); Playboy TV (delivered digitally); Shorteez (delivered digitally); Fresh (delivered digitally); iN DEMAND (delivered digitally).
Internet Service
Operational: Yes.
Telephone Service
Digital: Operational
Miles of Plant: 36.0 (coaxial); None (fiber optic). Homes passed: 1,073.
Senior Vice President, Corporate Finance: Michael Pflantz. Vice President, Accounting: Sabrina Warr. Regional Manager: Todd Cruthird. Plant Manager: Danny Keith. Marketing Director: Beverly Gambell.
Ownership: Cequel Communications Holdings I LLC (MSO).

DUMAS—BCI Broadband. Now served by McGEHEE, AR [AR0262]. ICA: AR0317.

EARLE—Comcast Cable. Now served by MEMPHIS, TN [TN0001]. ICA: AR0058.

EAST CAMDEN—Formerly served by Cablevision of East Camden. No longer in operation. ICA: AR0127.

EL DORADO—Suddenlink Communications, 1127 North Madison Ave, El Dorado, AR 71730-3805. Phone: 314-315-9400. Fax: 870-852-7080. E-mail: Gene.Regan@suddenlink.com. Web Site: http://www.suddenlink.com. Also serves Union County (portions). ICA: AR0233.
TV Market Ranking: 99 (EL DORADO, Union County (portions)). Franchise award date: N.A. Franchise expiration date: N.A. Began: September 1, 1964.
Channel capacity: 19 (operating 2-way). Channels available but not in use: N.A.
Basic Service
Subscribers: 6,057. Commercial subscribers: 646.
Programming (received off-air): KARD (Bounce TV, FOX) West Monroe; KATV (ABC, Retro TV) Little Rock; KETG (PBS) Arkadelphia; KLMB-CD El Dorado; KMLU (MeTV) Columbia; KNOE-TV (ABC, CBS, CW) Monroe; KTBS-TV (ABC) Shreveport; KTVE (NBC) El Dorado.
Programming (via satellite): CNN; Pop; WGN America.
Fee: $40.00 installation; $32.50 monthly.
Expanded Basic Service 1
Subscribers: N.A.
Programming (via satellite): A&E; AMC; Animal Planet; BET; Cartoon Network; Comedy Central; C-SPAN; Discovery Channel; Disney Channel; ESPN; ESPN2; Food Network; Fox News Channel; FOX Sports Southwest; Freeform; FX; Golf Channel; Great American Country; HGTV;

History; HLN; INSP; ION Television; Lifetime; MSNBC; MTV; Nickelodeon; Oxygen; Spike TV; Syfy; TBS; The Weather Channel; TLC; TNT; Travel Channel; Trinity Broadcasting Network (TBN); Turner Classic Movies; TV Land; USA Network; VH1.
Fee: $22.33 monthly.
Digital Basic Service
Subscribers: N.A.
Programming (via satellite): BBC America; Bloomberg Television; Discovery Digital Networks; Disney XD; DMX Music; ESPNews; Nick Jr.; Outdoor Channel; TeenNick.
Pay Service 1
Pay Units: N.A.
Programming (via satellite): Cinemax; HBO; Showtime.
Fee: $15.00 installation; $9.00 monthly (Cinemax), $10.00 monthly (Showtime), $10.95 monthly (HBO).
Digital Pay Service 1
Pay Units: N.A.
Programming (via satellite): Cinemax (multiplexed); HBO (multiplexed); Showtime (multiplexed); Starz (multiplexed); The Movie Channel (multiplexed).
Fee: $7.95 monthly (Starz), $9.00 monthly (Cinemax), $10.95 monthly (HBO), $11.50 monthly (Showtime/TMC).
Video-On-Demand: No
Pay-Per-View
ESPN Now (delivered digitally); Hot Choice (delivered digitally); iN DEMAND (delivered digitally); NBA TV (delivered digitally); Fresh (delivered digitally); Sports PPV (delivered digitally).
Internet Service
Operational: Yes.
Subscribers: 5,678.
Broadband Service: Suddenlink High Speed Internet.
Fee: $49.95 installation; $26.95 monthly; $39.95 modem lease.
Telephone Service
Digital: Operational
Subscribers: 3,393.
Miles of Plant: 394.0 (coaxial); 154.0 (fiber optic). Homes passed: 15,800.
Senior Vice President, Corporate Finance: Michael Pflantz. Vice President, Accounting: Sabrina Warr. General Manager: Marilyn Warren. Chief Technician: Robbie Lee.
Ownership: Cequel Communications Holdings I LLC (MSO).

EMERSON—Formerly served by Almega Cable. No longer in operation. ICA: AR0186.

EMMET—Formerly served by Almega Cable. No longer in operation. ICA: AR0304.

ENGLAND—Formerly served by Zoom Media. No longer in operation. ICA: AR0082.

EUDORA—Cablevision of Eudora, 1920 Hwy 425 North, Monticello, AR 71655-4463. Phones: 870-367-3166; 870-367-7300. Fax: 870-367-9770. E-mail: cccaccounts@ccc-cable.net. Web Site: http://ccc-cable.com. ICA: AR0088.

Arkansas—Cable Systems

TV Market Ranking: Below 100 (EUDORA). Franchise award date: N.A. Franchise expiration date: N.A. Began: September 1, 1978.
Channel capacity: N.A. Channels available but not in use: N.A.
Basic Service
Subscribers: 345.
Programming (received off-air): KARD (Bounce TV, FOX) West Monroe; KARK-TV (NBC) Little Rock; KARZ-TV (Bounce TV, MNT) Little Rock; KATV (ABC, Retro TV) Little Rock; KKAP (Daystar TV, ETV) Little Rock; KKYK-CD (IND, WeatherNation) Little Rock; KTHV (Antenna TV, CBS) Little Rock; KTVE (NBC) El Dorado; WABG-TV (ABC, FOX) Greenwood; WMAO-TV (PBS) Greenwood; WXVT (CBS) Greenville.
Programming (via satellite): A&E; BET; Bravo; CMT; CNBC; CNN; Discovery Channel; Discovery Life Channel; Disney Channel; E! HD; ESPN; ESPN2; EWTN Global Catholic Network; Fox News Channel; Fox Sports 1; FOX Sports Southwest; Freeform; FX; HGTV; History; Lifetime; MTV; National Geographic Channel; NBCSN; Nickelodeon; Outdoor Channel; Pop; QVC; Spike TV; Syfy; TBS; The Weather Channel; TNT; Trinity Broadcasting Network (TBN); Turner Classic Movies; TV Land; USA Network; WGN America.
Fee: $30.00 installation; $18.95 monthly.
Digital Basic Service
Subscribers: N.A.
Digital Pay Service 1
Pay Units: N.A.
Programming (via satellite): Cinemax; HBO; Showtime; Starz; Starz Encore.
Fee: $12.00 monthly (each).
Internet Service
Operational: Yes.
Fee: $30.00 installation; $29.95 monthly.
Telephone Service
Digital: Operational
Fee: $29.95 monthly
Miles of Plant: 37.0 (coaxial); 6.0 (fiber optic). Homes passed: 1,176.
President: Bill Copeland.
Ownership: Community Communications Co. (MSO).

EUREKA SPRINGS—Cox Communications. Now served by BERRYVILLE, AR [AR0221]. ICA: AR0080.

EVENING SHADE—Indco Cable TV, 2700 North Saint Louis, PO Box 3799, Batesville, AR 72503-3799. Phones: 800-364-0831; 870-793-4175; 800-364-0831. Fax: 870-793-7439. Web Site: http://www.indco.net. ICA: AR0234.
TV Market Ranking: Outside TV Markets (EVENING SHADE).
Channel capacity: N.A. Channels available but not in use: N.A.
Basic Service
Subscribers: 21.
Fee: $40.00 installation; $63.95 monthly.
Miles of Plant: 16.0 (coaxial); None (fiber optic). Homes passed: 140.
President & General Manager: J.D. Pierce.
Ownership: Indco Cable TV (MSO).

EXCELSIOR—Cox Communications. Now served by FORT SMITH, AR [AR0003]. ICA: AR0235.

FAIRFIELD BAY—Vyve Broadband, 707 West Saratoga St, Shawnee, OK 74801. Phones: 800-937-1397; 405-395-1131; 405-275-6923. Web Site: http://vyvebroadband.com. Also serves Cleburne County (portions), Shirley & Van Buren County (portions). ICA: AR0236.
TV Market Ranking: Outside TV Markets (Cleburne County (portions), FAIRFIELD BAY, Shirley, Van Buren County (portions)).
Channel capacity: 33 (operating 2-way). Channels available but not in use: N.A.
Basic Service
Subscribers: 91.
Programming (received off-air): KARK-TV (NBC) Little Rock; KARZ-TV (Bounce TV, MNT) Little Rock; KASN (CW, The Country Network) Pine Bluff; KATV (ABC, Retro TV) Little Rock; KEMV (PBS) Mountain View; KLRT-TV (FOX, This TV) Little Rock; KTHV (Antenna TV, CBS) Little Rock.
Programming (via satellite): C-SPAN; INSP; The Weather Channel.
Fee: $64.95 installation; $25.00 monthly.
Expanded Basic Service 1
Subscribers: N.A.
Programming (via satellite): A&E; AMC; CNBC; CNN; Discovery Channel; Disney Channel; ESPN; Fox News Channel; Freeform; Great American Country; History; HLN; Lifetime; Spike TV; TBS; TLC; TNT; truTV; TV Land; USA Network; WGN America.
Fee: $26.40 monthly.
Digital Basic Service
Subscribers: N.A.
Programming (via satellite): BBC America; Bloomberg Television; Bravo; Chiller; Cloo; CMT; Destination America; Discovery Kids Channel; Discovery Life Channel; Disney XD; DMX Music; ESPN Classic; ESPNews; EVINE Live; Flix; Fox Business Network; FOX College Sports Central; FOX College Sports Pacific; Fox Sports 1; Fuse; FXM; FYI; Golf Channel; GSN; HGTV; History International; IFC; Investigation Discovery; LMN; MTV Classic; MTV Hits; MTV2; National Geographic Channel; NBCSN; Nick Jr.; Nicktoons; Outdoor Channel; OWN: Oprah Winfrey Network; RFD-TV; Science Channel; Starz Encore (multiplexed); Sundance TV; Syfy; TeenNick; Trinity Broadcasting Network (TBN); Turner Classic Movies; VH1 Soul; WE tv.
Pay Service 1
Pay Units: N.A.
Programming (via satellite): HBO.
Fee: $35.00 installation; $11.95 monthly.
Digital Pay Service 1
Pay Units: N.A.
Programming (via satellite): Cinemax (multiplexed); HBO (multiplexed); Showtime (multiplexed); Starz (multiplexed); The Movie Channel (multiplexed).
Video-On-Demand: No
Pay-Per-View
Spice: Xcess (delivered digitally); iN DEMAND (delivered digitally); Playboy TV (delivered digitally); Fresh (delivered digitally); Club Jenna (delivered digitally); Hot Choice (delivered digitally).
Internet Service
Operational: Yes.
Fee: $24.95 installation; $39.95 monthly.
Telephone Service
Digital: Operational
Miles of Plant: 25.0 (coaxial); None (fiber optic).
Chief Executive Officer: Bill Haggarty. Regional Vice President: Andrew Dearth. Senior Vice President, Financial Planning: Daniel White. Vice President, Marketing: Tracy Bass.
Ownership: Vyve Broadband LLC (MSO).

FAYETTEVILLE—Cox Communications. Now served by SPRINGDALE, AR [AR0220]. ICA: AR0007.

FORDYCE—Media3, PO Box 620, Milan, TN 38358. Phone: 866-257-2044. E-mail: customerservice@mymedia3.com. Web Site: http://www.mymedia3.com. ICA: AR0056.
TV Market Ranking: 50 (FORDYCE). Franchise award date: N.A. Franchise expiration date: N.A. Began: January 1, 1977.
Channel capacity: N.A. Channels available but not in use: N.A.
Basic Service
Subscribers: 284.
Programming (received off-air): KARK-TV (NBC) Little Rock; KARZ-TV (Bounce TV, MNT) Little Rock; KASN (CW, The Country Network) Pine Bluff; KATV (ABC, Retro TV) Little Rock; KETS (PBS) Little Rock; KLRT-TV (FOX, This TV) Little Rock; KTHV (Antenna TV, CBS) Little Rock; KTVE (NBC) El Dorado; KVTN-DT (IND) Pine Bluff.
Programming (via satellite): C-SPAN; ESPN; INSP; QVC; The Weather Channel; Trinity Broadcasting Network (TBN); WGN America.
Fee: $24.99 installation; $22.45 monthly.
Expanded Basic Service 1
Subscribers: N.A.
Programming (via satellite): A&E; AMC; Animal Planet; BET; Cartoon Network; CMT; CNBC; CNN; Comedy Central; Discovery Channel; Disney Channel; E! HD; ESPN2; Food Network; Fox News Channel; Freeform; FX; Hallmark Channel; History; HLN; Lifetime; MSNBC; MTV; Nickelodeon; Outdoor Channel; Oxygen; Spike TV; Syfy; TBS; TLC; TNT; Travel Channel; TV Land; USA Network; VH1.
Fee: $42.99 monthly.
Digital Basic Service
Subscribers: N.A.
Programming (via satellite): BBC America; Bloomberg Television; Bravo; Discovery Digital Networks; DMX Music; EVINE Live; Fox Sports 1; FXM; FYI; Golf Channel; GSN; HGTV; History International; IFC; LMN; NBCSN; Nick Jr.; TeenNick; Turner Classic Movies; WE tv.
Pay Service 1
Pay Units: N.A.
Programming (via satellite): HBO; Showtime; The Movie Channel.
Fee: $7.00 monthly (TMC), $9.00 monthly (Showtime), $11.00 monthly (HBO).
Digital Pay Service 1
Pay Units: N.A.
Programming (via satellite): Cinemax (multiplexed); Flix; HBO (multiplexed); Showtime (multiplexed); Starz (multiplexed); Starz Encore (multiplexed); The Movie Channel (multiplexed).
Video-On-Demand: No
Pay-Per-View
Hot Choice (delivered digitally); iN DEMAND (delivered digitally); Playboy TV (delivered digitally); Fresh (delivered digitally); Shorteez (delivered digitally); Urban Xtra (delivered digitally).
Internet Service
Operational: No.
Telephone Service
None
Miles of Plant: 45.0 (coaxial); None (fiber optic). Homes passed: 2,077.
President: Alan Taylor. Chief Financial Officer: Thomas Pate. General Manager: Drew Cannon. Chief Technician: Brian Malley. Marketing Director: Glenda C. Elliott.
Ownership: CableSouth Media3 LLC (MSO).

FORREST CITY—East Arkansas Video Inc, 4804 N Washington St, Forrest City, AR 72335. Phones: 870-633-8934; 870-633-1079 (Headend); 870-633-8932. Fax: 870-633-8898. E-mail: eastarkansasvideocs@cablelynx.com. Web Site: http://www.eastarkansasvideo.com. Also serves Haynes, Lee County (portions), Marianna & Wynne. ICA: AR0026.
TV Market Ranking: Outside TV Markets (FORREST CITY, Haynes, Lee County (portions), Marianna, Wynne). Franchise award date: January 1, 1970. Franchise expiration date: N.A. Began: January 1, 1972.
Channel capacity: 35 (operating 2-way). Channels available but not in use: N.A.
Basic Service
Subscribers: 2,993. Commercial subscribers: 13.
Programming (received off-air): KAIT (ABC, NBC) Jonesboro; KARK-TV (NBC) Little Rock; KATV (ABC, Retro TV) Little Rock; KTEJ (PBS) Jonesboro; KTHV (Antenna TV, CBS) Little Rock; KVTJ-DT (IND) Jonesboro; WATN-TV (ABC) Memphis; WHBQ-TV (Decades, FOX, Movies!) Memphis; WKNO (PBS) Memphis; WLMT (CW, MeTV, MNT) Memphis; WMC-TV (Bounce TV, NBC, This TV) Memphis; WPXX-TV (ION, MNT) Memphis; WREG-TV (Antenna TV, CBS) Memphis; allband FM.
Programming (via satellite): A&E; AMC; Animal Planet; BET; CMT; CNBC; CNN; Comedy Central; C-SPAN; C-SPAN 2; Discovery Channel; Disney Channel; Disney XD; ESPN; ESPN2; EVINE Live; Food Network; Fox News Channel; FOX Sports Southwest; Freeform; FX; HGTV; History; HLN; Lifetime; MTV; Nickelodeon; Pop; Spike TV; Syfy; TBS; The Weather Channel; TLC; TNT; Trinity Broadcasting Network (TBN); Turner Classic Movies; TV Land; Univision Studios; USA Network; VH1; WGN America.
Fee: $79.95 installation; $31.90 monthly; $3.17 converter.
Digital Basic Service
Subscribers: N.A.
Programming (via satellite): BBC America; CMT; Destination America; Discovery Kids Channel; Discovery Life Channel; Disney XD; DMX Music; ESPNews; Fox Sports 1; FSN Digital Atlantic; FSN Digital Central; FSN Digital Pacific; FYI; Golf Channel; Great American Country; GSN; History International; Investigation Discovery; LMN; MTV Classic; MTV Hits; MTV Jams; MTV2; National Geographic Channel; Nick 2; Nick Jr.; Nicktoons; Outdoor Channel; OWN: Oprah Winfrey Network; Science Channel; TeenNick; Tr3s; VH1 Soul; WE tv.
Fee: $4.95 converter.
Digital Expanded Basic Service
Subscribers: N.A.
Programming (via satellite): AXS TV; CNN HD; Discovery Channel HD; ESPN HD; Outdoor Channel 2 HD; TBS HD; TNT HD.
Fee: $5.00 monthly.
Digital Pay Service 1
Pay Units: N.A.
Programming (via satellite): Cinemax (multiplexed); Cinemax HD; HBO (multiplexed); HBO HD; Starz (multiplexed); Starz Encore (multiplexed); Starz HD.
Fee: $12.95 monthly (Cinemax, HBO or Starz/Encore).
Video-On-Demand: No
Pay-Per-View
iN DEMAND (delivered digitally).
Internet Service
Operational: Yes. Began: April 1, 2001.
Broadband Service: Cablelynx.
Fee: $24.95-$44.95 monthly; $10.00 modem lease.
Telephone Service
Analog: Not Operational
Digital: Operational

Cable Systems—Arkansas

Fee: $45.70 monthly
Miles of Plant: 176.0 (coaxial); None (fiber optic). Homes passed: 9,446.
Vice President, Administration: Charlotte A. Dial. General Manager: Laurie Ringler. Chief Technician: Chris Heard. Marketing Director: Lori Haight.
Ownership: WEHCO Video Inc. (MSO).

FORT SMITH—Cox Communications, 6205 Peachtree Dunwoody Rd, 12th Floor, Atlanta, GA 30328. Phones: 479-717-3700; 316-262-4270 (Wichita office). Web Site: http://www.cox.com. Also serves Alma, Arkola, Barling, Bonanza, Cedarville, Central City, Chester, Crawford County, Dyer, Excelsior, Franklin County (western portion), Greenwood, Hackett, Hartford, Huntington, Kibler, Lavaca, Mansfield, Midland, Mountainburg, Mulberry, Rudy, Sugarloaf Lake, Van Buren & Witcherville, AR; Arkoma, Le Flore County (unincorporated areas), Muldrow, Pocola, Roland & Sequoyah County (southern portion), OK. ICA: AR0003.
TV Market Ranking: Below 100 (Alma, Arkola, Arkoma, Barling, Bonanza, Cedarville, Central City, Chester, Crawford County, Dyer, Excelsior, FORT SMITH, Franklin County (western portion), Greenwood, Hackett, Hartford, Kibler, Lavaca, Mansfield, Midland, Mountainburg, Mulberry, Muldrow, Pocola, Roland, Rudy, Sequoyah County (southern portion), Sugarloaf Lake, Van Buren, Witcherville, Huntington, Le Flore County (unincorporated areas)); Outside TV Markets (Le Flore County (unincorporated areas)). Franchise award date: January 1, 1960. Franchise expiration date: N.A. Began: November 11, 1961.
Channel capacity: 65 (operating 2-way). Channels available but not in use: N.A.

Basic Service
Subscribers: 29,061. Commercial subscribers: 1,622.
Programming (received off-air): KAFT (PBS) Fayetteville; KARK-TV (NBC) Little Rock; KFSM-TV (CBS, MNT) Fort Smith; KFTA-TV (FOX, NBC) Fort Smith; KHBS (ABC, CW) Fort Smith; KOET (PBS) Eufaula; KTHV (Antenna TV, CBS) Little Rock; KTUL (ABC, Antenna TV, Retro TV) Tulsa; KWOG (IND) Springdale; KXNW (Antenna TV, MNT) Eureka Springs; 16 FMs.
Programming (via satellite): INSP; Pop; TBS; Trinity Broadcasting Network (TBN); Univision; WGN America.
Fee: $38.00 installation; $21.99 monthly.

Expanded Basic Service 1
Subscribers: N.A.
Programming (via satellite): A&E; AMC; Animal Planet; BET; Bravo; Cartoon Network; CMT; CNBC; CNN; Comedy Central; C-SPAN; C-SPAN 2; Discovery Channel; Disney Channel; E! HD; ESPN; ESPN2; Food Network; Fox News Channel; Fox Sports 1; FOX Sports Southwest; Freeform; FX; Great American Country; HGTV; History; HLN; Lifetime; MSNBC; MTV; NBCSN; Nickelodeon; Oxygen; QVC; Spike TV; The Weather Channel; TLC; TNT; Travel Channel; truTV; TV Land; Univision Studios; USA Network; VH1.
Fee: $43.15 monthly.

Digital Basic Service
Subscribers: N.A.
Programming (via satellite): BBC America; Bloomberg Television; Discovery Digital Networks; Disney XD; ESPN Classic; ESPNews; FYI; Golf Channel; GSN; Hallmark Channel; History; IFC; MC; Syfy; Turner Classic Movies; WE tv.

Digital Pay Service 1
Pay Units: N.A.
Programming (via satellite): Cinemax (multiplexed); HBO (multiplexed); Showtime (multiplexed); Starz (multiplexed); The Movie Channel (multiplexed).
Video-On-Demand: No
Pay-Per-View
NBA TV (delivered digitally); ESPN Now (delivered digitally); iN DEMAND (delivered digitally); Fresh (delivered digitally).
Internet Service
Operational: Yes.
Subscribers: 24,894.
Broadband Service: Cox High Speed Internet.
Fee: $19.99-$59.99 monthly.
Telephone Service
Digital: Operational
Subscribers: 14,174.
Fee: $15.95 monthly
Miles of Plant: 2,667.0 (coaxial); 538.0 (fiber optic). Homes passed: 85,589.
Vice President & General Manager: Kimberly Edmunds. Vice President, Operations: Nelson Mower. Vice President, Marketing: Tony Matthews. Vice President, Tax: Mary Vickers. Marketing Director: Tina Gabbard. Community Relations Manager: Kelly Zaga.
Ownership: Cox Communications Inc. (MSO).

FOUKE—Cable One. Now served by TEXARKANA, TX [TX0031]. ICA: AR0237.

FOUNTAIN HILL—Formerly served by Almega Cable. No longer in operation. ICA: AR0210.

FRIENDSHIP—Formerly served by Community Communications Co. No longer in operation. ICA: AR0123.

FULTON—Formerly served by Allegiance Communications. No longer in operation. ICA: AR0282.

GARLAND CITY—Formerly served by Cebridge Connections. No longer in operation. ICA: AR0305.

GASSVILLE—Yelcot Communications, 225 North Mill St, Yellville, AR 72687. Phone: 800-270-1198. Web Site: http://www.yelcot.com. ICA: AR0327.
Channel capacity: N.A. Channels available but not in use: N.A.
Basic Service
Subscribers: 2.
Fee: $24.95 monthly.
Ownership: Yelcot Communications.

GILLETT—Formerly served by Community Communications Co. No longer in operation. ICA: AR0153.

GLENWOOD—Formerly served by Cablevision of Glenwood. No longer in operation. ICA: AR0238.

GOSNELL—Ritter Communications. Now served by MARKED TREE, AR [AR0072]. ICA: AR0067.

GOULD—Cablevision of Gould, 1920 Hwy 425 North, Monticello, AR 71655-4463. Phones: 870-367-7300; 870-367-3166. Fax: 870-367-9770. E-mail: cccaccounts@ccc-cable.net. Web Site: http://ccc-cable.com. ICA: AR0132.
TV Market Ranking: 50 (GOULD). Franchise award date: N.A. Franchise expiration date: N.A. Began: February 1, 1983.
Channel capacity: N.A. Channels available but not in use: N.A.
Basic Service
Subscribers: 58.
Programming (received off-air): KARK-TV (NBC) Little Rock; KASN (CW, The Country Network) Pine Bluff; KATV (ABC, Retro TV) Little Rock; KETS (PBS) Little Rock; KLRT-TV (FOX, This TV) Little Rock; KTHV (Antenna TV, CBS) Little Rock; KTVE (NBC) El Dorado; WXVT (CBS) Greenville.
Programming (via satellite): AMC; BET; CMT; CNN; Discovery Channel; Discovery Life Channel; Disney Channel; ESPN; ESPN2; FOX Sports Southwest; Freeform; FX; Lifetime; MTV; Nickelodeon; Outdoor Channel; QVC; Spike TV; Syfy; TBS; The Weather Channel; TNT; Trinity Broadcasting Network (TBN); TV Land; USA Network; VH1; WGN America.
Fee: $30.00 installation; $49.90 monthly.
Digital Basic Service
Subscribers: N.A.
Digital Pay Service 1
Pay Units: N.A.
Programming (via satellite): Cinemax; HBO; Showtime; Starz; Starz Encore.
Fee: $12.00 monthly (each).
Video-On-Demand: No
Internet Service
Operational: Yes.
Fee: $30.00 installation; $29.95 monthly.
Telephone Service
Digital: Operational
Fee: $29.95 monthly
Miles of Plant: 7.0 (coaxial); None (fiber optic). Homes passed: 425.
President: Bill Copeland.
Ownership: Community Communications Co. (MSO).

GRADY—Formerly served by Cebridge Connections. No longer in operation. ICA: AR0177.

GREENBRIER—Formerly served by Alliance Communications. Now served by Media3, MAYFLOWER, AR [AR0049]. ICA: AR0077.

GREENE COUNTY (unincorporated areas)—Formerly served by Indco Cable TV. No longer in operation. ICA: AR0319.

GREENWOOD—Formerly served by Eagle Media. No longer in operation. ICA: AR0314.

GREERS FERRY—Formerly served by Alliance Communications Network. No longer in operation. ICA: AR0239.

GUION—Formerly served by Indco Cable TV. No longer in operation. ICA: AR0215.

GUM SPRINGS—Indco Cable TV, 2700 North Saint Louis, PO Box 3799, Batesville, AR 72503-3799. Phones: 800-364-0175; 870-793-4175; 870-793-4174. Fax: 870-793-7439. Web Site: http://www.indco.net. ICA: AR0302.
TV Market Ranking: Below 100 (GUM SPRINGS).
Channel capacity: N.A. Channels available but not in use: N.A.
Basic Service
Subscribers: 135.
Programming (received off-air): KARK-TV (NBC) Little Rock; KASN (CW, The Country Network) Pine Bluff; KATV (ABC, Retro TV) Little Rock; KLRT-TV (FOX, This TV) Little Rock; KMYA-DT (MeTV, WeatherNation) Camden; KTHV (Antenna TV, CBS) Little Rock.
Programming (via satellite): A&E; Cartoon Network; CMT; CNN; C-SPAN; Discovery Channel; Disney Channel; ESPN; ESPN2; Fox News Channel; FOX Sports Southwest; Freeform; FX; Golf Channel; HGTV; History; Lifetime; MSNBC; Nickelodeon; Outdoor Channel; QVC; Spike TV; Syfy; TBS; The Weather Channel; TNT; Trinity Broadcasting Network (TBN); Turner Classic Movies; TV Land; USA Network; WGN America.
Fee: $40.00 installation; $66.95 monthly.
Pay Service 1
Pay Units: 9.
Programming (via satellite): Cinemax.
Fee: $8.00 monthly.
Pay Service 2
Pay Units: 13.
Programming (via satellite): HBO.
Fee: $10.00 monthly.
Pay Service 3
Pay Units: N.A.
Programming (via satellite): The Movie Channel.
Fee: $10.00 monthly.
Video-On-Demand: Planned
Internet Service
Operational: Yes.
Fee: $29.95 monthly.
Telephone Service
None
Miles of Plant: 11.0 (coaxial); None (fiber optic).
President & General Manager: J.D. Pierce. Chief Technician: Tom Barnett. Marketing Director: Connie Barnett.
Ownership: Indco Cable TV (MSO).

GURDON—Suddenlink Communications, 520 Maryville Centre Dr, Ste 300, St. Louis, MO 63141. Phones: 888-592-3861; 314-315-9400. E-mail: Gene.Regan@suddenlink.com. Web Site: http://www.suddenlink.com. ICA: AR0096.
TV Market Ranking: Below 100 (GURDON). Franchise award date: N.A. Franchise expiration date: N.A. Began: September 1, 1976.
Channel capacity: 70 (not 2-way capable). Channels available but not in use: N.A.
Basic Service
Subscribers: 280. Commercial subscribers: 15.
Programming (received off-air): KARK-TV (NBC) Little Rock; KARZ-TV (Bounce TV, MNT) Little Rock; KASN (CW, The Country Network) Pine Bluff; KATV (ABC, Retro TV) Little Rock; KETG (PBS) Arkadelphia;

2017 Edition

Arkansas—Cable Systems

KKAP (Daystar TV, ETV) Little Rock; KLRT-TV (FOX, This TV) Little Rock; KMYA-DT (MeTV, WeatherNation) Camden; KTHV (Antenna TV, CBS) Little Rock; KVTH-DT (IND) Hot Springs.
Programming (via satellite): C-SPAN; FamilyNet; Pop; QVC; TBS; WGN America.
Fee: $40.00 installation; $34.50 monthly.

Expanded Basic Service 1
Subscribers: N.A.
Programming (via satellite): A&E; AMC; Animal Planet; BET; Bravo; Cartoon Network; CMT; CNBC; CNN; Comedy Central; C-SPAN 2; Discovery Channel; Disney Channel; E! HD; ESPN; ESPN2; EWTN Global Catholic Network; Food Network; Fox News Channel; Fox Sports 1; FOX Sports Southwest; Freeform; FX; Great American Country; HGTV; History; HLN; INSP; Jewelry Television; Lifetime; LMN; MSNBC; MTV; NBCSN; Nickelodeon; Outdoor Channel; Spike TV; Syfy; The Weather Channel; TLC; TNT; Travel Channel; Trinity Broadcasting Network (TBN); truTV; Turner Classic Movies; TV Land; USA Network; VH1.

Digital Basic Service
Subscribers: N.A.
Programming (via satellite): A&E HD; AXS TV; BBC America; Bloomberg Television; Boomerang; CBS Sports Network; CMT; Cooking Channel; Cox Sports Television; Destination America; Discovery Kids Channel; Disney XD; DIY Network; ESPN Classic; ESPN HD; ESPNews; FamilyNet; Food Network HD; Fox Sports 2; FSN HD; Fuse; FYI; Golf Network; GSN; Hallmark Channel; HD Theater; HGTV HD; History International; IFC; Investigation Discovery; MC; MTV Classic; MTV Hits; MTV Jams; MTV2; Nat Geo WILD; National Geographic Channel; National Geographic Channel HD; Nick Jr.; Nicktoons; OWN: Oprah Winfrey Network; Oxygen; Science Channel; Starz Encore (multiplexed); Sundance TV; TeenNick; Tennis Channel; TNT HD; TV One; Universal HD; UP; VH1 Soul; WE tv; Weatherscan.

Digital Pay Service 1
Pay Units: N.A.
Programming (via satellite): Cinemax (multiplexed); HBO (multiplexed); HBO HD; Showtime (multiplexed); Showtime HD; Starz (multiplexed); The Movie Channel (multiplexed).

Pay-Per-View
iN DEMAND (delivered digitally); Playboy TV (delivered digitally); Fresh (delivered digitally); Shorteez (delivered digitally); Club Jenna (delivered digitally); Spice: Xcess (delivered digitally).

Internet Service
Operational: Yes.
Broadband Service: Suddenlink High Speed Internet.
Fee: $35.00 monthly.

Telephone Service
Digital: Operational
Fee: $20.00 monthly
Miles of Plant: 249.0 (coaxial); 66.0 (fiber optic). Homes passed: 8,836.
Vice President, Corporate Finance: Sabrina Warr. General Manager: Robbie Lee. Marketing Director: LaDawn Mohr. Chief Technician: Allen Wardlaw.
Ownership: Cequel Communications Holdings I LLC (MSO).

HAMBURG—Formerly served by Zoom Media. No longer in operation. ICA: AR0075.

HAMPTON—SATCO Cable TV, 1st & Main St/Hwy 278, PO Box 778, Hampton, AR 71744-0778. Phones: 870-798-2025; 870-798-2201. Fax: 870-798-2289. E-mail: help@satco.biz. Web Site: http://www.sat-co.net. Also serves Harrell & Hermitage. ICA: AR0321.
TV Market Ranking: 99 (HAMPTON, Harrell, Hermitage).
Channel capacity: N.A. Channels available but not in use: N.A.

Basic Service
Subscribers: N.A.
Programming (received off-air): KARK-TV (NBC) Little Rock; KASN (CW, The Country Network) Pine Bluff; KATV (ABC, Retro TV) Little Rock; KETS (PBS) Little Rock; KKYK-CD (IND, WeatherNation) Little Rock; KLRT-TV (FOX, This TV) Little Rock; KTHV (Antenna TV, CBS) Little Rock; KTVE (NBC) El Dorado.
Programming (via satellite): A&E; AMC; BET; Boomerang; Bravo; Cartoon Network; CMT; CNBC; CNN; Comedy Central; C-SPAN; Discovery Channel; Disney Channel; ESPN; ESPN Classic; ESPN2; ESPNews; Fox Sports 1; Freeform; FXM; Golf Channel; Hallmark Channel; HGTV; History; HLN; Lifetime; MSNBC; MTV; National Geographic Channel; Nickelodeon; Outdoor Channel; Spike TV; Syfy; TBS; The Weather Channel; TLC; TNT; Trinity Broadcasting Network (TBN); Turner Classic Movies; USA Network; WGN America.
Fee: $28.55 monthly.

Digital Basic Service
Subscribers: N.A.
Programming (via satellite): BBC America; Bloomberg Television; Bravo; Cloo; CMT; Destination America; Discovery Kids Channel; Discovery Life Channel; Disney XD; ESPN Classic; ESPN2; ESPNews; FOX College Sports Central; FOX College Sports Pacific; Fox Sports 1; Fuse; FXM; FYI; Golf Channel; Great American Country; GSN; HGTV; History; History International; IFC; Investigation Discovery; LMN; MC; MTV Classic; MTV Hits; MTV2; National Geographic Channel; NBCSN; Nick Jr.; Nicktoons; Outdoor Channel; Ovation; OWN: Oprah Winfrey Network; Science Channel; Starz (multiplexed); Starz Encore (multiplexed); Sundance TV; Syfy; TeenNick; Trinity Broadcasting Network (TBN); Turner Classic Movies; UP; VH1 Soul; WE tv.

Digital Pay Service 1
Pay Units: N.A.
Programming (via satellite): Cinemax (multiplexed); Flix; HBO (multiplexed); Showtime (multiplexed); Sundance TV; The Movie Channel (multiplexed).
Fee: $12.50 monthly (Cinemax, HBO, Showtime/Flix/Sundance or TMC).

Video-On-Demand: No

Pay-Per-View
iN DEMAND (delivered digitally); Playboy TV (delivered digitally); Spice (delivered digitally); Spice 2 (delivered digitally); Club Jenna (delivered digitally).

Internet Service
Operational: No, DSL & dial-up.

Telephone Service
None
General Manager: David Wells. Technology Manager: Mark Lundy.
Ownership: South Arkansas Telephone Co. Inc.

HARDY—Fidelity Communications, 64 North Clark St, Sullivan, MO 63080. Phones: 800-392-8070; 501-859-0384 (Maumelle office); 855-262-7434; 501-315-4405 (Benton office). E-mail: fidelityinfo@fidelitycommunications.com. Web Site: http://www.fidelitycommunications.com. Also serves Cherokee Village & Highland. ICA: AR0040.
TV Market Ranking: Outside TV Markets (Cherokee Village, HARDY, Highland). Franchise award date: June 1, 1965. Franchise expiration date: N.A. Began: June 1, 1996.
Channel capacity: N.A. Channels available but not in use: N.A.

Basic Service
Subscribers: 755. Commercial subscribers: 43.
Programming (received off-air): KAIT (ABC, NBC) Jonesboro; KEMV (PBS) Mountain View; KMYA-LP (MundoMax) Sheridan; KOLR (CBS) Springfield; KVTJ-DT (IND) Jonesboro; KXNW (Antenna TV, MNT) Eureka Springs; WSEE-TV (CBS, CW) Erie.
Programming (via satellite): C-SPAN; EWTN Global Catholic Network; INSP; QVC; Trinity Broadcasting Network (TBN); WGN America; WNBC (COZI TV, NBC) New York.
Fee: $29.99 installation; $28.99 monthly.

Expanded Basic Service 1
Subscribers: N.A.
Programming (via satellite): A&E; AMC; Animal Planet; Bravo; Cartoon Network; CMT; CNBC; CNN; Comedy Central; Discovery Channel; Disney Channel; E! HD; ESPN; ESPN2; Food Network; Fox News Channel; Fox Sports 1; FOX Sports Midwest; Freeform; FX; Golf Channel; HGTV; History; HLN; Lifetime; MSNBC; MTV; National Geographic Channel; Nickelodeon; Outdoor Channel; Oxygen; Spike TV; Syfy; TBS; The Weather Channel; TLC; TNT; Travel Channel; Turner Classic Movies; TV Land; USA Network; VH1.
Fee: $49.99 monthly.

Digital Basic Service
Subscribers: N.A.
Programming (via satellite): BBC America; Bloomberg Television; Discovery Digital Networks; Discovery Life Channel; DIY Network; ESPN Classic; ESPNews; FXM; FYI; GSN; Hallmark Channel; History International; IFC; LMN; MC; Nick 2; Nick Jr.; Nicktoons; Sundance TV; TeenNick; WE tv.

Digital Pay Service 1
Pay Units: N.A.
Programming (via satellite): Cinemax (multiplexed); HBO (multiplexed); Showtime (multiplexed); Starz (multiplexed); Starz Encore; The Movie Channel (multiplexed).
Fee: $10.95 monthly (each).

Video-On-Demand: No

Pay-Per-View
ETC (delivered digitally); The Erotic Network (delivered digitally); Pleasure (delivered digitally); iN DEMAND (delivered digitally).

Internet Service
Operational: Yes.

Telephone Service
None
Miles of Plant: 150.0 (coaxial); None (fiber optic). Homes passed: 3,518.
General Manager, AR/MO/LA/TX: Andy Davis.
Ownership: Fidelity Communications Co. (MSO).

HARMONY GROVE—Formerly served by Almega Cable. No longer in operation. ICA: AR0297.

HARRELL—Formerly served by Suddenlink Communications. No longer in operation. ICA: AR0240.

HARRISBURG—Ritter Communications. Now served by MARKED TREE, AR [AR0072]. ICA: AR0100.

HARRISON—Cox Communications, 6205 Peachtree Dunwoody Rd, 12th Floor, Atlanta, GA 30328. Phones: 316-262-4270 (Wichita office); 404-269-6590. Web Site: http://www.cox.com. Also serves Bellefonte, Bergman, Boone County & Valley Springs. ICA: AR0022.
TV Market Ranking: Below 100 (Bellefonte, Bergman, Boone County, HARRISON, Valley Springs). Franchise award date: N.A. Franchise expiration date: N.A. Began: February 1, 1954.
Channel capacity: 65 (operating 2-way). Channels available but not in use: N.A.

Basic Service
Subscribers: 4,183. Commercial subscribers: 216.
Programming (received off-air): KARK-TV (NBC) Little Rock; KATV (ABC, Retro TV) Little Rock; KEMV (PBS) Mountain View; KOLR (CBS) Springfield; KOZL-TV (IND) Springfield; KSPR (ABC) Springfield; KTHV (Antenna TV, CBS) Little Rock; KWBM (Retro TV) Harrison; KXNW (Antenna TV, MNT) Eureka Springs; KYTV (CW, NBC, WeatherNation) Springfield.
Programming (via satellite): CNN; C-SPAN; TBS; The Weather Channel; Trinity Broadcasting Network (TBN); WGN America.
Fee: $38.00 installation; $21.99 monthly.

Expanded Basic Service 1
Subscribers: N.A.
Programming (via satellite): A&E; AMC; Animal Planet; Bravo; Cartoon Network; CMT; CNBC; Comedy Central; C-SPAN 2; Discovery Channel; Disney Channel; E! HD; ESPN; ESPN2; Food Network; Fox News Channel; Fox Sports 1; FOX Sports Southwest; Freeform; FX; Great American Country; HGTV; History; HLN; Lifetime; MSNBC; MTV; NBCSN; Nickelodeon; Outdoor Channel; OWN: Oprah Winfrey Network; Oxygen; Pop; QVC; Spike TV; Syfy; TLC; TNT; Travel Channel; TV Land; Univision Studios; USA Network; VH1.
Fee: $43.15 monthly.

Digital Basic Service
Subscribers: N.A.
Programming (via satellite): BBC America; Bloomberg Television; Discovery Digital Networks; Disney XD; ESPN Classic; ESPNews; FYI; Golf Channel; GSN; Hallmark Channel; History International; IFC; LMN; MC; Sundance TV; Turner Classic Movies.

Pay Service 1
Pay Units: N.A.
Programming (via satellite): Cinemax; HBO; Showtime; Starz; The Movie Channel.
Fee: $11.95 monthly (each).

Digital Pay Service 1
Pay Units: N.A.
Programming (via satellite): Cinemax (multiplexed); Flix; HBO (multiplexed); Showtime (multiplexed); Starz (multiplexed); The Movie Channel (multiplexed).

Video-On-Demand: No

Pay-Per-View
ESPN Now (delivered digitally); Hot Choice (delivered digitally); iN DEMAND (delivered digitally); NBA TV (delivered digitally); Playboy TV (delivered digitally); Sports PPV (delivered digitally).

Internet Service
Operational: Yes.
Subscribers: 2,497.
Broadband Service: Cox High Speed Internet.
Fee: $19.99-$59.99 monthly.

Cable Systems—Arkansas

Telephone Service
Digital: Operational
Subscribers: 1,764.
Fee: $15.95 monthly
Miles of Plant: 417.0 (coaxial); 98.0 (fiber optic). Homes passed: 10,712.
Vice President & General Manager: Kimberly Edmunds. Vice President, Operations: Nelson Mower. Vice President, Marketing: Tony Matthews. Vice President, Tax: Mary Vickers. Marketing Director: Tina Gabbard. Community Relations Manager: Kelly Zaga.
Ownership: Cox Communications Inc. (MSO).

HATFIELD—Formerly served by Allegiance Communications. No longer in operation. ICA: AR0241.

HAZEN—Suddenlink Communications, 520 Maryville Centre Dr, Ste 300, St. Louis, MO 63141. Phones: 314-315-9400; 888-822-5151. Fax: 314-965-0500. E-mail: Gene.Regan@suddenlink.com.
Web Site: http://www.suddenlink.com. Also serves Carlisle, De Valls Bluff & Prairie County (unincorporated areas). ICA: AR0118.
TV Market Ranking: 50 (Carlisle); Outside TV Markets (De Valls Bluff, HAZEN, Prairie County (unincorporated areas)).
Channel capacity: N.A. Channels available but not in use: N.A.
Basic Service
Subscribers: 231.
Programming (received off-air): KARK-TV (NBC) Little Rock; KARZ-TV (Bounce TV, MNT) Little Rock; KASN (CW, The Country Network) Pine Bluff; KATV (ABC, Retro TV) Little Rock; KETS (PBS) Little Rock; KLRT-TV (FOX, This TV) Little Rock; KTHV (Antenna TV, CBS) Little Rock; KVTN-DT (IND) Pine Bluff.
Fee: $17.95 installation; $28.45 monthly.
Expanded Basic Service 1
Subscribers: N.A.
Programming (via satellite): A&E; AMC; Animal Planet; BET; Bravo; Cartoon Network; CNBC; CNN; Comedy Central; C-SPAN; Discovery Channel; Disney Channel; E! HD; ESPN; ESPN2; Food Network; Fox News Channel; FOX Sports Southwest; Freeform; FX; Golf Channel; Great American Country; Hallmark Channel; HGTV; History; HLN; Lifetime; MSNBC; MTV; National Geographic Channel; Nickelodeon; Outdoor Channel; Spike TV; TBS; The Weather Channel; TLC; TNT; Travel Channel; TV Land; USA Network; VH1.
Fee: $25.00 monthly.
Pay Service 1
Pay Units: N.A.
Programming (via satellite): HBO; Showtime; The Movie Channel.
Fee: $10.95 monthly (each).
Video-On-Demand: No
Pay-Per-View
Sports PPV (delivered digitally); ESPN Now (delivered digitally); Shorteez (delivered digitally); Fresh (delivered digitally); Playboy TV (delivered digitally); iN DEMAND (delivered digitally).
Internet Service
Operational: Yes. Began: October 10, 2003. Broadband Service: Suddenlink High Speed Internet.
Fee: $49.95 installation; $26.95 monthly.
Telephone Service
None
Miles of Plant: 45.0 (coaxial); None (fiber optic). Homes passed: 1,792.
Senior Vice President, Corporate Finance: Michael Pflantz. Regional Manager: Todd Cruthird. Area Manager: Carolyn Wilder. Plant Manager: Randy Oliger. Marketing Director: Beverly Gambell.
Ownership: Cequel Communications Holdings I LLC (MSO).

HEBER SPRINGS—Suddenlink Communications, 903 South 7th St, Heber Springs, AR 72543-4419. Phones: 888-822-5151; 314-315-9400. Fax: 501-362-5070. E-mail: Gene.Regan@suddenlink.com. Web Site: http://www.suddenlink.com. Also serves Cleburne County (portions), Eden Isle & Little Red River. ICA: AR0242.
TV Market Ranking: Outside TV Markets (Cleburne County (portions), Eden Isle, HEBER SPRINGS, Little Red River). Franchise award date: N.A. Franchise expiration date: N.A. Began: January 1, 1960.
Channel capacity: N.A. Channels available but not in use: N.A.
Basic Service
Subscribers: 3,007.
Programming (received off-air): KAIT (ABC, NBC) Jonesboro; KARK-TV (NBC) Little Rock; KARZ-TV (Bounce TV, MNT) Little Rock; KASN (CW, The Country Network) Pine Bluff; KATV (ABC, Retro TV) Little Rock; KEMV (PBS) Mountain View; KKAP (Daystar TV, ETV) Little Rock; KLRT-TV (FOX, This TV) Little Rock; KMYA-DT (MeTV, WeatherNation) Camden; KTHV (Antenna TV, CBS) Little Rock; KVTN-DT (IND) Pine Bluff; allband FM.
Programming (via satellite): C-SPAN; Jewelry Television; QVC; TBS; WGN America.
Fee: $40.00 installation; $35.50 monthly.
Expanded Basic Service 1
Subscribers: N.A.
Programming (via satellite): A&E; AMC; Animal Planet; BET; Bravo; Cartoon Network; CMT; CNBC; CNN; Comedy Central; C-SPAN 2; Discovery Channel; Disney Channel; E! HD; ESPN; ESPN2; Food Network; Fox News Channel; Fox Sports 1; FOX Sports Southwest; Freeform; FX; Great American Country; HGTV; History; HLN; Lifetime; LMN; MSNBC; MTV; NBCSN; Nickelodeon; Outdoor Channel; Oxygen; Spike TV; Syfy; The Weather Channel; TLC; TNT; Travel Channel; truTV; Turner Classic Movies; TV Land; Univision; USA Network; VH1.
Fee: $22.20 monthly.
Digital Basic Service
Subscribers: N.A.
Programming (via satellite): A&E HD; AXS TV; BBC America; Bloomberg Television; Boomerang; CBS Sports Network; CMT; Cooking Channel; Destination America; Discovery Kids Channel; Disney XD; DIY Network; ESPN Classic; ESPN HD; ESPNews; Food Network HD; Fox Sports 2; FSN HD; Fuse; FYI; Golf Channel; GSN; Hallmark Channel; HD Theater; HGTV HD; History International; IFC; Investigation Discovery; MC; MTV Classic; MTV Hits; MTV2; Nat Geo WILD; National Geographic Channel; National Geographic Channel HD; Nick Jr.; Nicktoons; OWN; Oprah Winfrey Network; Science Channel; Starz Encore (multiplexed); Sundance TV; TeenNick; TNT HD; Trinity Broadcasting Network (TBN); Universal HD.
Digital Pay Service 1
Pay Units: N.A.
Programming (via satellite): Cinemax (multiplexed); HBO (multiplexed); HBO HD; Showtime (multiplexed); Showtime HD; Starz (multiplexed); The Movie Channel (multiplexed).
Fee: $11.95 monthly (each).
Video-On-Demand: No

Access the most current data instantly
www.warren-news.com/factbook.htm

Pay-Per-View
iN DEMAND (delivered digitally); Spice: Xcess (delivered digitally); Playboy TV (delivered digitally); Fresh (delivered digitally).
Internet Service
Operational: Yes.
Broadband Service: Suddenlink High Speed Internet.
Fee: $49.95 installation; $26.95 monthly.
Telephone Service
Digital: Operational
Miles of Plant: 160.0 (coaxial); None (fiber optic).
Senior Vice President, Corporate Finance: Michael Pflantz. General Manager: Dewayne Millikin. Chief Technician: Robert Hayes.
Ownership: Cequel Communications Holdings I LLC (MSO).

HECTOR—Formerly served by Suddenlink Communications. No longer in operation. ICA: AR0243.

HELENA—Suddenlink Communications, PO Box 2342, West Helena, AR 72390. Phones: 870-338-8220; 888-822-5151; 314-315-9400. Web Site: http://www.suddenlink.com. Also serves Lexa, Phillips County, Poplar Grove & West Helena. ICA: AR0015.
TV Market Ranking: Outside TV Markets (HELENA, Lexa, Phillips County, Poplar Grove, West Helena). Franchise award date: N.A. Franchise expiration date: N.A. Began: October 20, 1968.
Channel capacity: 60 (operating 2-way). Channels available but not in use: N.A.
Basic Service
Subscribers: 2,410. Commercial subscribers: 424.
Programming (received off-air): KATV (ABC, Retro TV) Little Rock; KETS (PBS) Little Rock; KTHV (Antenna TV, CBS) Little Rock; WATN-TV (ABC) Memphis; WHBQ-TV (Decades, FOX, Movies!) Memphis; WKNO (PBS) Memphis; WLMT (CW, MeTV, MNT) Memphis; WMC-TV (Bounce TV, NBC, This TV) Memphis; WPXX-TV (ION, MNT) Memphis; WREG-TV (Antenna TV, CBS) Memphis; allband FM.
Programming (via satellite): C-SPAN; C-SPAN 2; HLN; Local Cable Weather; TBS; The Weather Channel; Trinity Broadcasting Network (TBN); WGN America.
Fee: $40.00 installation; $21.10 monthly.
Expanded Basic Service 1
Subscribers: N.A.
Programming (via satellite): A&E; AMC; Animal Planet; BET; Bravo; Cartoon Network; CMT; CNBC; CNN; Comedy Central; Discovery Channel; Disney Channel; E! HD; ESPN; ESPN2; Food Network; Fox News Channel; Fox Sports 1; FOX Sports Southwest; Freeform; FX; Great American Country; HGTV; History; Jewelry Television; Lifetime; LMN; MSNBC; MTV; NBCSN; Nickelodeon; Outdoor Channel; Oxygen; Spike TV; Syfy; TLC; TNT; Travel Channel; truTV; TV Land; USA Network; VH1.
Fee: $45.10 monthly.

Digital Basic Service
Subscribers: N.A.
Programming (via satellite): A&E HD; AXS TV; BBC America; Bloomberg Television; Boomerang; CBS Sports Network; CMT; Cooking Channel; Destination America; Discovery Kids Channel; Disney XD; DIY Network; ESPN Classic; ESPN HD; ESPNews; Food Network HD; Fox Sports 2; FSN HD; Fuse; FYI; Golf Channel; GSN; Hallmark Channel; HD Theater; HGTV HD; History International; IFC; Investigation Discovery; MC; MTV Classic; MTV Hits; MTV Jams; MTV2; Nat Geo WILD; National Geographic Channel; National Geographic Channel HD; Nick Jr.; Nicktoons; OWN; Oprah Winfrey Network; Science Channel; Starz Encore (multiplexed); Sundance TV; TeenNick; TNT HD; Turner Classic Movies; Universal HD; VH1 Soul.
Pay Service 1
Pay Units: N.A.
Fee: $35.00 installation; $11.95 monthly (each).
Digital Pay Service 1
Pay Units: N.A.
Programming (via satellite): Cinemax (multiplexed); HBO (multiplexed); HBO HD; Showtime (multiplexed); Showtime HD; Starz (multiplexed); The Movie Channel (multiplexed).
Video-On-Demand: Planned
Pay-Per-View
iN DEMAND (delivered digitally); Fresh (delivered digitally); Spice: Xcess (delivered digitally); Playboy TV (delivered digitally).
Internet Service
Operational: Yes.
Broadband Service: Suddenlink High Speed Internet.
Fee: $29.95 monthly.
Telephone Service
Digital: Operational
Fee: $44.95 monthly
Miles of Plant: 101.0 (coaxial); None (fiber optic). Homes passed: 8,777.
Senior Vice President, Corporate Finance: Michael Pflantz. Vice President, Accounting: Sabrina Warr. General Manager: Russ Hodges. Chief Technician: Wesley Bryan.
Ownership: Cequel Communications Holdings I LLC (MSO).

HERMITAGE—Formerly served by Almega Cable. No longer in operation. ICA: AR0146.

HIGGINSON—White County Cable TV. Now served by SEARCY, AR [AR0017]. ICA: AR0133.

HOLLY GROVE—Formerly served by Cebridge Connections. No longer in operation. ICA: AR0154.

HOOKER/LADD—Formerly served by Community Communications Co. No longer in operation. ICA: AR0157.

HOPE—Hope Community TV, 506 South Walnut St, PO Box 2221, Hope, AR 71801-5355. Phones: 800-903-0508; 870-777-4684. Fax:

Arkansas—Cable Systems

870-777-5159. E-mail: hopecabletvcs@cablelynx.com. Web Site: http://www.hopecabletv.com. Also serves Prescott. ICA: AR0031.
TV Market Ranking: 58 (HOPE); Outside TV Markets (Prescott). Franchise award date: N.A. Franchise expiration date: N.A. Began: December 9, 1967.
Channel capacity: N.A. Channels available but not in use: N.A.

Basic Service
Subscribers: 1,299. Commercial subscribers: 9.
Programming (received off-air): KARK-TV (NBC) Little Rock; KATV (ABC, Retro TV) Little Rock; KETG (PBS) Arkadelphia; KMSS-TV (FOX) Shreveport; KSHV-TV (MNT) Shreveport; KSLA (Bounce TV, CBS, Grit, This TV) Shreveport; KTAL-TV (NBC) Texarkana; KTBS-TV (ABC) Shreveport; KTHV (Antenna TV, CBS) Little Rock; KTSS-LP Hope.
Programming (via satellite): A&E; AMC; Animal Planet; BET; Cartoon Network; CMT; CNBC; CNN; Concert TV; C-SPAN; C-SPAN 2; CW PLUS; Discovery Channel; Disney Channel; ESPN; ESPN2; EVINE Live; FamilyNet; Food Network; Fox News Channel; FOX Sports Southwest; Freeform; FX; HGTV; History; HLN; Lifetime; MTV; Nickelodeon; Pop; Spike TV; Syfy; TBS; Telemundo; The Weather Channel; TLC; TNT; Trinity Broadcasting Network (TBN); Turner Classic Movies; TV Land; Univision; Univision Studios; USA Network; VH1.
Fee: $57.95 installation; $67.90 monthly.

Digital Basic Service
Subscribers: N.A.
Programming (via satellite): BBC America; CMT; Destination America; Discovery Kids Channel; Discovery Life Channel; Disney XD; ESPNews; Fox Sports 1; FSN Digital Atlantic; FSN Digital Central; FSN Digital Pacific; FYI; Golf Channel; Great American Country; GSN; History International; Investigation Discovery; LMN; MC; MTV Classic; MTV Hits; MTV Jams; MTV2; National Geographic Channel; Nick Jr.; Nicktoons; Outdoor Channel; OWN; Oprah Winfrey Network; Science Channel; TeenNick; Tr3s; VH1 Soul; WE tv.

Digital Expanded Basic Service
Subscribers: N.A.
Programming (via satellite): AXS TV; CNN HD; ESPN HD; HD Theater; Outdoor Channel 2 HD; TBS HD; TNT HD.
Fee: $10.00 monthly.

Pay Service 1
Pay Units: N.A.
Programming (via satellite): HBO.
Fee: $12.29 installation; $12.95 monthly.

Digital Pay Service 1
Pay Units: N.A.
Programming (via satellite): Cinemax (multiplexed); Cinemax HD; HBO (multiplexed); HBO HD; Starz (multiplexed); Starz Encore; Starz HD.
Fee: $12.95 monthly (Cinemax/Cinemax HD, HBO/HBO HD or Starz/Encore/Starz HDTV).

Video-On-Demand: No
Pay-Per-View
iN DEMAND (delivered digitally).

Internet Service
Operational: Yes. Began: May 1, 2001.
Broadband Service: Cablelynx.
Fee: $19.95-$74.95 monthly; $10.00 modem lease.

Telephone Service
Analog: Not Operational
Digital: Operational
Fee: $45.70 monthly

Miles of Plant: 160.0 (coaxial); 13.0 (fiber optic).
President & General Manager: David P. Mooney. Vice President, Administration: Charlotta A. Dial. Chief Technical Advisor: Craig Bass. Technical Advisor: Dennis Jenkins. Marketing Director: Robbie Mooney. Finance/Office Manager: Bill Butler. Front Office Manager: Dianna Henderson.
Ownership: WEHCO Video Inc. (MSO).; Gilmer Cable (MSO).

HORSESHOE BEND—Crystal Broadband Networks, PO Box 180336, Chicago, IL 60618. Phones: 877-319-0328; 630-206-0447. E-mail: helpdesk@crystalbn.com. Web Site: http://crystalbn.com. Also serves Franklin & Izard County. ICA: AR0071.
TV Market Ranking: Outside TV Markets (Franklin, HORSESHOE BEND, Izard County). Franchise award date: August 1, 1974. Franchise expiration date: N.A. Began: August 1, 1974.
Channel capacity: 52 (2-way capable). Channels available but not in use: N.A.

Basic Service
Subscribers: 33.
Programming (received off-air): KAIT (ABC, NBC) Jonesboro; KEMV (PBS) Mountain View; KOLR (CBS) Springfield; KOZL-TV (IND) Springfield; KTHV (Antenna TV, CBS) Little Rock; KYTV (CW, NBC, WeatherNation) Springfield; WNBC (COZI TV, NBC) New York; allband FM.
Programming (via satellite): C-SPAN; Trinity Broadcasting Network (TBN); WGN America.
Fee: $29.95 installation; $22.00 monthly.

Expanded Basic Service 1
Subscribers: N.A.
Programming (via satellite): A&E; AMC; Cartoon Network; CNBC; CNN; Discovery Channel; Disney Channel; E! HD; ESPN; ESPN2; Food Network; FOX Sports Southwest; Freeform; Golf Channel; Great American Country; Hallmark Channel; HGTV; History; Lifetime; MTV; Nickelodeon; Spike TV; TBS; The Weather Channel; TLC; TNT; Turner Classic Movies; TV Land; USA Network; VH1.
Fee: $20.00 monthly.

Pay Service 1
Pay Units: N.A.
Programming (via satellite): Cinemax; HBO; Showtime; Starz; Starz Encore; The Movie Channel.
Fee: $5.99 monthly (Encore), $8.99 monthly (Cinemax), $12.99 monthly (HBO), $13.99 monthly (Showtime/TMC).

Video-On-Demand: No
Internet Service
Operational: Yes.
Telephone Service
Digital: Operational
Miles of Plant: 59.0 (coaxial); None (fiber optic). Homes passed: 1,335.
General Manager: Nidhin Johnson. Program Manager: Shawn Smith.
Ownership: Crystal Broadband Networks (MSO).

HOT SPRINGS—Resort TV Cable Co. Inc, 410 Airport Rd, Ste H, Hot Springs, AR 71913-4000. Phones: 501-624-5781; 800-903-0508. Fax: 501-624-0502. E-mail: resort@cablelynx.com. Web Site: http://www.resorttvcable.com. Also serves Garland County (portions) & Mountain Pine. ICA: AR0004.
TV Market Ranking: Below 100 (Garland County (portions), HOT SPRINGS, Mountain Pine). Franchise award date: June 1, 1964. Franchise expiration date: N.A. Began: September 2, 1970.
Channel capacity: N.A. Channels available but not in use: N.A.

Basic Service
Subscribers: 11,486. Commercial subscribers: 49.
Programming (received off-air): KARK-TV (NBC) Little Rock; KARZ-TV (Bounce TV, MNT) Little Rock; KASN (CW, The Country Network) Pine Bluff; KATV (ABC, Retro TV) Little Rock; KETS (PBS) Little Rock; KKAP (Daystar TV, ETV) Little Rock; KLRT-TV (FOX, This TV) Little Rock; KTEJ (PBS) Jonesboro; KTHV (Antenna TV, CBS) Little Rock; KVTJ-DT (IND) Jonesboro.
Programming (via satellite): A&E; AMC; Animal Planet; BET; Cartoon Network; CMT; CNBC; CNN; Comedy Central; C-SPAN; C-SPAN 2; Discovery Channel; Disney Channel; ESPN; ESPN Classic; ESPN2; EVINE Live; Food Network; Fox News Channel; FOX Sports Southwest; Freeform; FX; Hallmark Channel; HGTV; History; HLN; Lifetime; MSNBC; MTV; NASA TV; Nickelodeon; Pop; Spike TV; Syfy; TBS; Telemundo; The Weather Channel; TLC; TNT; Travel Channel; Trinity Broadcasting Network (TBN); truTV; Turner Classic Movies; TV Land; Univision; Univision Studios; USA Network; VH1; WGN America.
Fee: $49.95 installation; $29.95 monthly; $2.19 converter.

Digital Basic Service
Subscribers: N.A.
Programming (via satellite): BBC America; CMT; Destination America; Discovery Kids Channel; Discovery Life Channel; Disney XD; DMX Music; ESPNews; Fox Sports 1; FSN Digital Atlantic; FSN Digital Central; FSN Digital Pacific; FYI; Golf Channel; Great American Country; GSN; History International; Investigation Discovery; LMN; MTV Classic; MTV Hits; MTV Jams; MTV2; National Geographic Channel; Nick 2; Nick Jr.; Nicktoons; OWN; Oprah Winfrey Network; Science Channel; TeenNick; Tr3s; VH1 Soul; WE tv.

Digital Expanded Basic Service
Subscribers: N.A.
Programming (via satellite): AXS TV; CNN HD; Discovery Channel HD; ESPN HD; Outdoor Channel 2 HD; PBS HD; TBS HD; TNT HD.
Fee: $5.00 monthly.

Pay Service 1
Pay Units: N.A.
Programming (via satellite): HBO.

Digital Pay Service 1
Pay Units: N.A.
Programming (via satellite): Cinemax (multiplexed); Cinemax HD; HBO (multiplexed); HBO HD; Starz (multiplexed); Starz Encore (multiplexed); Starz HD.
Fee: $12.95 monthly (Cinemax, HBO or Starz/Encore).

Video-On-Demand: No
Pay-Per-View
iN DEMAND (delivered digitally).

Internet Service
Operational: Yes. Began: April 1, 2001.
Subscribers: 11,347.
Broadband Service: Cablelynx.
Fee: $19.95 monthly; $10.00 modem lease.

Telephone Service
Digital: Operational
Subscribers: 2,399.
Miles of Plant: 1,170.0 (coaxial); 277.0 (fiber optic). Homes passed: 42,405.

President & General Manager: David P. Mooney. Vice President, Administration: Charlotta A. Dial. Chief Technical Advisor: Craig Bass. Technical Advisor: Dennis Jenkins. Marketing Director: Robbie Mooney. Finance/Office Manager: Bill Butler. Front Office Manager: Dianna Henderson.
Ownership: WEHCO Video Inc. (MSO).; Gilmer Cable (MSO).

HOT SPRINGS VILLAGE—Suddenlink Communications, 4656 North Hwy 7, Ste L, PO Box 8067, Hot Springs Village, AR 71909. Phone: 314-315-9400. E-mail: Gene.Regan@suddenlink.com. Web Site: http://www.suddenlink.com. Also serves Garland County (portions) & Saline County (portions). ICA: AR0246.
TV Market Ranking: 50 (Garland County (portions), Saline County (portions)); Below 100 (HOT SPRINGS VILLAGE, Garland County (portions), Saline County (portions)). Franchise award date: July 27, 1972. Franchise expiration date: N.A. Began: January 1, 1973.
Channel capacity: N.A. Channels available but not in use: N.A.

Basic Service
Subscribers: 3,919. Commercial subscribers: 185.
Programming (received off-air): KARK-TV (NBC) Little Rock; KARZ-TV (Bounce TV, MNT) Little Rock; KASN (CW, The Country Network) Pine Bluff; KATV (ABC, Retro TV) Little Rock; KETS (PBS) Little Rock; KLRT-TV (FOX, This TV) Little Rock; KTHV (Antenna TV, CBS) Little Rock; KVTN-DT (IND) Pine Bluff; allband FM.
Programming (via satellite): C-SPAN; Fox News Channel; FOX Sports Southwest; Freeform; Golf Channel; HGTV; TBS; Trinity Broadcasting Network (TBN); TV Land; WGN America.
Fee: $40.00 installation; $35.50 monthly.

Expanded Basic Service 1
Subscribers: N.A.
Programming (via satellite): A&E; AMC; CNBC; CNN; Discovery Channel; Disney Channel; ESPN; ESPN2; Great American Country; History; HLN; Lifetime; Spike TV; Syfy; The Weather Channel; TNT; USA Network.
Fee: $10.00 installation; $13.47 monthly.

Pay Service 1
Pay Units: N.A.
Programming (via satellite): HBO; The Movie Channel.
Fee: $35.00 installation; $8.75 monthly (TMC), $9.75 monthly (HBO).

Video-On-Demand: No
Internet Service
Operational: Yes.
Broadband Service: Suddenlink High Speed Internet.
Fee: $49.95 installation; $26.95 monthly.

Telephone Service
Digital: Operational
Miles of Plant: 54.0 (coaxial); None (fiber optic).
Vice President, Corporate Finance: Sabrina Warr. General Manager: Mark Badgwell. Chief Technician: Chris Raburn.
Ownership: Cequel Communications Holdings I LLC (MSO).

HOXIE—Suddenlink Communications, PO Box 370, Pocahontas, AR 72455. Phones: 888-822-5151; 314-315-9400. Web Site: http://www.suddenlink.com. Also serves College City, Lawrence County & Walnut Ridge. ICA: AR0288.

Cable Systems—Arkansas

TV Market Ranking: Below 100 (College City, HOXIE, Lawrence County, Walnut Ridge). Franchise award date: N.A. Franchise expiration date: N.A. Began: July 1, 1963.
Channel capacity: N.A. Channels available but not in use: N.A.
Basic Service
Subscribers: 1,348. Commercial subscribers: 157.
Programming (received off-air): KAIT (ABC, NBC) Jonesboro; KARK-TV (NBC) Little Rock; KATV (ABC, Retro TV) Little Rock; KTEJ (PBS) Jonesboro; KTHV (Antenna TV, CBS) Little Rock; KVTJ-DT (IND) Jonesboro; WHBQ-TV (Decades, FOX, Movies!) Memphis; WMC-TV (Bounce TV, NBC, This TV) Memphis; WREG-TV (Antenna TV, CBS) Memphis; 3 FMs.
Programming (via satellite): C-SPAN; CW PLUS; ION Television; Lifetime; MTV; Pop; QVC; TBS; WGN America.
Fee: $40.00 installation; $33.50 monthly.
Expanded Basic Service 1
Subscribers: N.A.
Programming (via satellite): A&E; AMC; Animal Planet; Bravo; Cartoon Network; CMT; CNBC; CNN; Comedy Central; Discovery Channel; Disney Channel; E! HD; ESPN; ESPN2; EWTN Global Catholic Network; Food Network; Fox News Channel; Fox Sports 1; FOX Sports Southwest; Freeform; FX; Great American Country; HGTV; History; HLN; INSP; MSNBC; NBCSN; Nickelodeon; Oxygen; Spike TV; Syfy; The Weather Channel; TLC; TNT; Travel Channel; truTV; Turner Classic Movies; TV Land; USA Network; VH1.
Fee: $12.88 monthly.
Digital Basic Service
Subscribers: N.A.
Programming (via satellite): BBC America; Bloomberg Television; Discovery Digital Networks; Disney XD; ESPN Classic; ESPNews; Fuse; FYI; Golf Channel; GSN; Hallmark Channel; History International; IFC; LMN; MC; Outdoor Channel; Starz Encore (multiplexed); Sundance TV.
Digital Pay Service 1
Pay Units: N.A.
Programming (via satellite): Cinemax (multiplexed); HBO (multiplexed); Showtime (multiplexed); Starz (multiplexed); The Movie Channel (multiplexed).
Video-On-Demand: No
Pay-Per-View
Playboy TV (delivered digitally); ESPN Now (delivered digitally); NBA TV (delivered digitally); Fresh (delivered digitally); iN DEMAND (delivered digitally).
Internet Service
Operational: Yes.
Broadband Service: Suddenlink High Speed Internet.
Fee: $35.00 monthly.
Telephone Service
Digital: Operational
Fee: $20.00 monthly
Miles of Plant: 26.0 (coaxial); None (fiber optic).
Senior Vice President, Corporate Finance: Michael Pflantz. Vice President, Corporate Finance: Sabrina Warr. General Manager: Garry Bowman.
Ownership: Cequel Communications Holdings I LLC (MSO).

HUGHES—Suddenlink Communications, 520 Maryville Centre Dr, Ste 300, St. Louis, MO 63141. Phones: 314-315-9400; 888-822-5151. Fax: 314-965-0500. E-mail: Gene.Regan@suddenlink.com. Web Site: http://www.suddenlink.com. Also serves Crittenden County (portions), Horseshoe Lake, Madison & Widener. ICA: AR0112.
TV Market Ranking: 26 (Crittenden County (portions), Horseshoe Lake, HUGHES); Outside TV Markets (Madison, Widener). Franchise award date: N.A. Franchise expiration date: N.A. Began: December 1, 1982.
Channel capacity: N.A. Channels available but not in use: N.A.
Basic Service
Subscribers: 176.
Programming (received off-air): KAIT (ABC, NBC) Jonesboro; KARK-TV (NBC) Little Rock; KATV (ABC, Retro TV) Little Rock; KTHV (Antenna TV, CBS) Little Rock; KVTJ-DT (IND) Jonesboro; WATN-TV (ABC) Memphis; WHBQ-TV (Decades, FOX, Movies!) Memphis; WKNO (PBS) Memphis; WLMT (CW, MeTV, MNT) Memphis; WMC-TV (Bounce TV, NBC, This TV) Memphis; WPXX-TV (ION, MNT) Memphis; WREG-TV (Antenna TV, CBS) Memphis.
Programming (via satellite): National Geographic Channel.
Fee: $17.95 installation; $28.45 monthly.
Expanded Basic Service 1
Subscribers: N.A.
Programming (via satellite): Animal Planet; BET; Cartoon Network; CNBC; CNN; C-SPAN; C-SPAN 2; Discovery Channel; Disney Channel; E! HD; ESPN; ESPN2; Fox News Channel; Freeform; Great American Country; HGTV; HLN; Lifetime; MTV; Nickelodeon; Spike TV; Syfy; TBS; The Weather Channel; TLC; TNT; Travel Channel; Trinity Broadcasting Network (TBN); USA Network.
Fee: $24.00 monthly.
Pay Service 1
Pay Units: N.A.
Programming (via satellite): Cinemax; HBO; Showtime.
Fee: $10.95 monthly (each).
Video-On-Demand: No
Pay-Per-View
Sports PPV (delivered digitally); ESPN Now (delivered digitally); Shorteez (delivered digitally); Fresh (delivered digitally); Playboy TV (delivered digitally); iN DEMAND (delivered digitally).
Internet Service
Operational: Yes. Began: June 3, 2004.
Broadband Service: Suddenlink High Speed Internet.
Fee: $49.95 installation; $26.95 monthly.
Telephone Service
None
Miles of Plant: 72.0 (coaxial); 68.0 (fiber optic). Homes passed: 2,422.
Senior Vice President, Corporate Finance: Michael Pflantz. Regional Manager: Todd Cruthird. Area Manager: Al Harrison. Plant Manager: John Barnett. Marketing Director: Beverly Gambell.
Ownership: Cequel Communications Holdings I LLC (MSO).

HUMNOKE—Formerly served by Cebridge Connections. No longer in operation. ICA: AR0179.

HUMPHREY—Formerly served by Cebridge Connections. No longer in operation. ICA: AR0161.

HUNTSVILLE—Madison County Cable, 113 Court St, PO Box 627, Huntsville, AR 72740. Phones: 888-846-6282; 479-738-6828. Fax: 479-738-2105. Web Site: http://www.madisoncounty.net. ICA: AR0247.
TV Market Ranking: Below 100 (HUNTSVILLE). Franchise award date: N.A. Franchise expiration date: N.A. Began: October 1, 1959.
Channel capacity: N.A. Channels available but not in use: N.A.
Basic Service
Subscribers: 731. Commercial subscribers: 2.
Programming (received off-air): KAFT (PBS) Fayetteville; KFSM-TV (CBS, MNT) Fort Smith; KHOG-TV (ABC, CW) Fayetteville; KNWA-TV (FOX, NBC) Rogers; KOLR (CBS) Springfield; KOZL-TV (IND) Springfield; KSPR (ABC) Springfield; KXNW (Antenna TV, MNT) Eureka Springs; KXUN-LD (UNV) Fort Smith; KYTV (CW, NBC, WeatherNation) Springfield.
Programming (via satellite): A&E; Animal Planet; Bravo; CMT; CNBC; CNN; C-SPAN; C-SPAN 2; CW PLUS; Discovery Channel; Discovery Life Channel; Disney Channel; Disney XD; E! HD; ESPN; ESPN Classic; ESPN2; Food Network; Fox News Channel; FOX Sports Southwest; Freeform; Golf Channel; HGTV; History; HLN; Lifetime; LMN; MSNBC; MTV; MyNetworkTV; Nickelodeon; Outdoor Channel; Pop; QVC; Spike TV; Syfy; TBS; The Weather Channel; TLC; TNT; Travel Channel; Trinity Broadcasting Network (TBN); truTV; Turner Classic Movies; TV Land; USA Network; VH1; WGN America.
Fee: $21.90 installation; $37.00 monthly; $5.00 converter.
Digital Basic Service
Subscribers: N.A.
Programming (via satellite): BBC America; Bloomberg Television; Bravo; Destination America; Discovery Kids Channel; DMX Music; EVINE Live; Fuse; FXM; FYI; Great American Country; GSN; History International; IFC; Investigation Discovery; LMN; MTV Classic; MTV Hits; MTV2; Nick Jr.; Nicktoons; Ovation; OWN: Oprah Winfrey Network; Science Channel; TeenNick; VH1 Country; VH1 Soul; WE tv.
Digital Expanded Basic Service
Subscribers: N.A.
Programming (via satellite): Cinelatino; CNN en Espanol; Fox Deportes; Fox Life; HTV; Tr3s.
Fee: $5.00 monthly.
Digital Expanded Basic Service 2
Subscribers: N.A.
Programming (via satellite): ESPN Classic; ESPNews; Fox Sports 1; FSN Digital Atlantic; FSN Digital Central; FSN Digital Pacific; NBCSN.
Fee: $5.00 monthly.
Pay Service 1
Pay Units: 40.
Programming (via satellite): Cinemax; HBO.
Fee: $16.00 monthly.
Digital Pay Service 1
Pay Units: N.A.
Programming (via satellite): Cinemax (multiplexed); Flix; HBO (multiplexed); Showtime (multiplexed); Starz (multiplexed); Starz Encore (multiplexed); Sundance TV; The Movie Channel.
Fee: $13.00 monthly (Cinemax, Starz/Encore or Showtime/Flix/Sundance/TMC), $15.00 monthly (HBO).
Video-On-Demand: No
Pay-Per-View
iN DEMAND (delivered digitally); Playboy TV (delivered digitally); Spice (delivered digitally); Spice 2 (delivered digitally); ESPN Now (delivered digitally); ESPN (delivered digitally).
Internet Service
Operational: No, DSL.
Telephone Service
Analog: Operational
Miles of Plant: 80.0 (coaxial); None (fiber optic).
President: Joe C. Schrum. Chief Technician: Stewart Markley.
Ownership: Madison Communications Inc. (MSO).

HUTTIG—Bayou Cable TV, 378 Main St, Marion, LA 71260. Phone: 318-292-4774. Fax: 318-292-4775. E-mail: admin@bayoucable.com. Web Site: http://www2.bayoucable.com. ICA: AR0315.
TV Market Ranking: 99 (HUTTIG).
Channel capacity: 57 (not 2-way capable). Channels available but not in use: N.A.
Basic Service
Subscribers: 127.
Programming (received off-air): KARD (Bounce TV, FOX) West Monroe; KATV (ABC, Retro TV) Little Rock; KLTM-TV (PBS) Monroe; KMLU (MeTV) Columbia; KNOE-TV (ABC, CBS, CW) Monroe; KTVE (NBC) El Dorado.
Programming (via satellite): AMC; Hallmark Channel; Trinity Broadcasting Network (TBN); TV Land.
Fee: $25.00 installation; $54.99 monthly.
Expanded Basic Service 1
Subscribers: N.A.
Programming (via satellite): A&E; Animal Planet; BET; CMT; CNN; Discovery Channel; ESPN; ESPN2; Food Network; Fox News Channel; Fox Sports 1; Freeform; FX; History; ION Television; Lifetime; MTV; National Geographic Channel; Nickelodeon; Outdoor Channel; Spike TV; TBS; The Weather Channel; TLC; TNT; USA Network; VH1; WGN America.
Fee: $20.00 monthly.
Pay Service 1
Pay Units: 17.
Programming (via satellite): HBO.
Fee: $10.95 monthly.
Pay Service 2
Pay Units: 7.
Programming (via satellite): Cinemax.
Fee: $8.95 monthly.
Video-On-Demand: No
Internet Service
Operational: Yes.
Subscribers: 96.
Telephone Service
None
Miles of Plant: 13.0 (coaxial); None (fiber optic). Homes passed: 500.
President & General Manager: Allen C. Booker. Chief Technician: Mark Andrews.
Ownership: Bayou Cable TV (MSO).

Arkansas—Cable Systems

JASPER—Ritter Communications. Now served by WESTERN GROVE, AR [AR0183]. ICA: AR0178.

JONES MILL—Formerly served by Cablevision of Jones Mill. No longer in operation. ICA: AR0248.

JONESBORO—Suddenlink Communications, PO Box 19127, Jonesboro, AR 72402. Phones: 314-315-9400; 870-935-3615. Fax: 870-972-8141. E-mail: Gene.Regan@suddenlink.com. Web Site: http://www.suddenlink.com. Also serves Bay & Craighead County (portions). ICA: AR0008.
TV Market Ranking: Below 100 (Bay, Craighead County (portions), JONESBORO). Franchise award date: January 1, 1968. Franchise expiration date: N.A. Began: October 3, 1967.
Channel capacity: 76 (operating 2-way). Channels available but not in use: N.A.
Basic Service
Subscribers: 14,852. Commercial subscribers: 1,565.
Programming (received off-air): KAIT (ABC, NBC) Jonesboro; KARK-TV (NBC) Little Rock; KATV (ABC, Retro TV) Little Rock; KTEJ (PBS) Jonesboro; KTHV (Antenna TV, CBS) Little Rock; KVTJ-DT (IND) Jonesboro; WHBQ-TV (Decades, FOX, Movies!) Memphis; WKNO (PBS) Memphis; WMC-TV (Bounce TV, NBC, This TV) Memphis; WREG-TV (Antenna TV, CBS) Memphis.
Programming (via satellite): CW PLUS; INSP; ION Television; News Plus; Pop; QVC; TBS; WGN America.
Fee: $40.00 installation; $34.50 monthly; $3.83 converter.
Expanded Basic Service 1
Subscribers: N.A.
Programming (via satellite): A&E; AMC; BET; Cartoon Network; CNBC; CNN; Comedy Central; C-SPAN; Discovery Channel; Disney Channel; ESPN; ESPN2; Food Network; Fox News Channel; FOX Sports Southwest; Freeform; FX; Great American Country; History; HLN; Lifetime; MSNBC; MTV; Nickelodeon; Spike TV; The Weather Channel; TLC; TNT; Travel Channel; Trinity Broadcasting Network (TBN); truTV; USA Network; VH1.
Fee: $27.35 monthly.
Digital Basic Service
Subscribers: N.A.
Programming (via satellite): BBC America; Discovery Digital Networks; DMX Music; ESPN Classic; ESPNews; Golf Channel; GSN; HGTV; NBCSN; Syfy; Turner Classic Movies; WE tv.
Pay Service 1
Pay Units: N.A.
Programming (via satellite): Cinemax; HBO; Showtime; Starz.
Fee: $19.95 installation; $11.95 monthly (each).
Digital Pay Service 1
Pay Units: N.A.
Programming (via satellite): Cinemax (multiplexed); HBO (multiplexed); Showtime (multiplexed); Starz (multiplexed); The Movie Channel (multiplexed).
Video-On-Demand: Planned
Pay-Per-View
Hot Choice (delivered digitally); iN DEMAND (delivered digitally); Playboy TV (delivered digitally).
Internet Service
Operational: Yes.
Subscribers: 19,084.
Broadband Service: Suddenlink High Speed Internet.
Fee: $29.95 monthly.
Telephone Service
Digital: Operational
Subscribers: 8,532.
Fee: $44.95 monthly
Miles of Plant: 1,447.0 (coaxial); 392.0 (fiber optic). Homes passed: 46,241.
Senior Vice President, Corporate Finance: Michael Pflantz. Vice President, Accounting: Sabrina Warr. General Manager: Garry Bowman. Chief Technician: Chriss Berry. Program Director: Kevin Shirley. Customer Service Manager: Rhonda McKay.
Ownership: Cequel Communications Holdings I LLC (MSO).

JUNCTION CITY—Alliance Communications, PO Box 9090, Tyler, TX 75711. Phones: 903-561-4411 (Tyler, TX office); 501-679-6619; 800-842-8160. E-mail: marketing@alliancecable.net. Web Site: http://www.alliancecable.net. Also serves Junction City. ICA: AR0249.
TV Market Ranking: 99 (Junction City, JUNCTION CITY).
Channel capacity: 36 (not 2-way capable). Channels available but not in use: N.A.
Basic Service
Subscribers: 42.
Programming (received off-air): KARD (Bounce TV, FOX) West Monroe; KATV (ABC, Retro TV) Little Rock; KLTM-TV (PBS) Monroe; KMLU (MeTV) Columbia; KMYA-DT (MeTV, WeatherNation) Camden; KNOE-TV (ABC, CBS, CW) Monroe; KTVE (NBC) El Dorado.
Programming (via satellite): A&E; Animal Planet; BET; Cartoon Network; CNBC; CNN; Discovery Channel; Disney Channel; ESPN; Freeform; FX; Great American Country; HGTV; History; HLN; Lifetime; MTV; National Geographic Channel; Nickelodeon; Outdoor Channel; Spike TV; Syfy; TBS; The Weather Channel; TLC; TNT; Turner Classic Movies; USA Network.
Fee: $45.00 installation; $22.45 monthly.
Pay Service 1
Pay Units: N.A.
Programming (via satellite): Flix; HBO; Showtime; The Movie Channel.
Video-On-Demand: No
Internet Service
Operational: No.
Telephone Service
None
Miles of Plant: 15.0 (coaxial); None (fiber optic). Homes passed: 551.
Chief Financial Officer: David Starrett. Vice President & General Manager: John Brinker. Vice President, Programming: Julie Newman.
Ownership: Buford Media Group LLC (MSO).

KNOBEL—Formerly served by Cebridge Connections. No longer in operation. ICA: AR0193.

KNOXVILLE—Formerly served by Quality Entertainment Corp. No longer in operation. ICA: AR0310.

LAKE CITY—Ritter Communications. Now served by MARKED TREE, AR [AR0072]. ICA: AR0251.

LAKE ERLING—Formerly served by Cebridge Connections. No longer in operation. ICA: AR0306.

LAKE VIEW—Alliance Communications, PO Box 9090, Tyler, TX 75711. Phones: 903-561-4411 (Tyler, TX office); 800-842-8160; 501-679-6619. E-mail: marketing@alliancecable.net. Also serves Elaine. ICA: AR0181.
TV Market Ranking: Outside TV Markets (Elaine, LAKE VIEW). Franchise award date: N.A. Franchise expiration date: N.A. Began: August 1, 1989.
Channel capacity: N.A. Channels available but not in use: N.A.
Basic Service
Subscribers: 101.
Programming (received off-air): KASN (CW, The Country Network) Pine Bluff; KATV (ABC, Retro TV) Little Rock; WABG-TV (ABC, FOX) Greenwood; WHBQ-TV (Decades, FOX, Movies!) Memphis; WLMT (CW, MeTV, MNT) Memphis; WMAV-TV (PBS) Oxford; WMC-TV (Bounce TV, NBC, This TV) Memphis; WREG-TV (Antenna TV, CBS) Memphis; WXVT (CBS) Greenville.
Programming (via satellite): A&E; Animal Planet; BET; Cartoon Network; CMT; CNN; C-SPAN; Discovery Channel; ESPN; ESPN2; Freeform; FX; History; HLN (multiplexed); Lifetime; MTV; Nickelodeon; Outdoor Channel; Spike TV; Syfy; TBS; The Weather Channel; TLC; TNT; Trinity Broadcasting Network (TBN); truTV; Turner Classic Movies; TV Land; USA Network; VH1; WGN America.
Fee: $45.00 installation; $25.45 monthly.
Digital Basic Service
Subscribers: N.A.
Programming (via satellite): BBC America; Bloomberg Television; Discovery Digital Networks; DMX Music; ESPN Classic; ESPNews; Fox Sports 1; Fuse; FXM; FYI; Golf Channel; GSN; HGTV; History International; IFC; National Geographic Channel; NBCSN; Nick Jr.; Nicktoons; Ovation; Sundance TV; TeenNick; WE tv.
Pay Service 1
Pay Units: N.A.
Programming (via satellite): Cinemax; HBO.
Digital Pay Service 1
Pay Units: N.A.
Programming (via satellite): Cinemax (multiplexed); Flix; HBO; Showtime (multiplexed); Starz (multiplexed); Starz Encore (multiplexed); The Movie Channel (multiplexed).
Fee: $11.95 monthly (each).
Video-On-Demand: No
Pay-Per-View
iN DEMAND (delivered digitally); Playboy TV (delivered digitally); Fresh (delivered digitally); Shorteez (delivered digitally).
Internet Service
Operational: No.
Telephone Service
None
Miles of Plant: 28.0 (coaxial); None (fiber optic). Homes passed: 978.
Vice President & General Manager: John Brinker. Vice President, Programming: Julie Newman.
Ownership: Buford Media Group LLC (MSO).

LAKE VILLAGE—BCI Broadband. Now served by McGEHEE, AR [AR0262]. ICA: AR0253.

LAVACA—Cox Communications. Now served by FORT SMITH, AR [AR0003]. ICA: AR0254.

LEOLA—Formerly served by Cebridge Connections. No longer in operation. ICA: AR0184.

LESLIE—Formerly served by Ritter Communications. No longer in operation. ICA: AR0170.

LEWISVILLE—Formerly served by Alliance Communications. Now served by Media3, PO Box 620, Milan, TN 38358. Phone: 866-257-2044. E-mail: customerservice@mymedia3.com. Web Site: http://www.mymedia3.com. Also serves Buckner & Stamps. ICA: AR0285.
TV Market Ranking: 58 (Buckner, LEWISVILLE, Stamps).
Channel capacity: 54 (not 2-way capable). Channels available but not in use: N.A.
Basic Service
Subscribers: 180.
Programming (received off-air): KATV (ABC, Retro TV) Little Rock; KETG (PBS) Arkadelphia; KMSS-TV (FOX) Shreveport; KSHV-TV (MNT) Shreveport; KSLA (Bounce TV, CBS, Grit, This TV) Shreveport; KTAL-TV (NBC) Texarkana; KTBS-TV (ABC) Shreveport; KTSS-LP Hope.
Programming (via satellite): National Geographic Channel; Trinity Broadcasting Network (TBN).
Fee: $45.00 installation; $22.45 monthly.
Expanded Basic Service 1
Subscribers: N.A.
Programming (via satellite): A&E; AMC; Animal Planet; BET; Cartoon Network; CNBC; CNN; C-SPAN; Discovery Channel; Disney Channel; E! HD; ESPN; ESPN2; Food Network; Fox News Channel; FOX Sports Southwest; Freeform; FX; Great American Country; HGTV; HLN; Lifetime; MTV; Nickelodeon; Outdoor Channel; Spike TV; TBS; The Weather Channel; TNT; Turner Classic Movies; USA Network; VH1.
Fee: $27.50 monthly.
Digital Basic Service
Subscribers: N.A.
Programming (via satellite): BBC America; Bloomberg Television; Cloo; Destination America; Discovery Kids Channel; DMX Music; ESPN Classic; ESPN2; ESPNews; EVINE Live; FOX College Sports Central; FOX College Sports Pacific; Fox Sports 1; Fuse; FYI; Golf Channel; GSN; HGTV; History; History International; Investigation Discovery; LMN; NBCSN; Outdoor Channel; Ovation; OWN: Oprah Winfrey Network; Science Channel; Syfy; Trinity Broadcasting Network (TBN); Turner Classic Movies; WE tv.
Pay Service 1
Pay Units: N.A.
Programming (via satellite): Flix; HBO; Showtime; The Movie Channel.
Fee: $1.95 monthly (Flix), $12.95 monthly (HBO, Showtime or TMC).
Digital Pay Service 1
Pay Units: N.A.
Programming (via satellite): Cinemax (multiplexed); Flix; HBO (multiplexed); Showtime (multiplexed); Starz (multiplexed); Starz Encore (multiplexed); The Movie Channel (multiplexed).
Video-On-Demand: No
Pay-Per-View
iN DEMAND (delivered digitally); Playboy TV (delivered digitally); Club Jenna (delivered digitally).
Internet Service
Operational: No.
Telephone Service
None
Miles of Plant: 56.0 (coaxial); None (fiber optic). Homes passed: 1,983.
Business Manager: Larry Harmon.
Ownership: CableSouth Media3 LLC (MSO).

Cable Systems—Arkansas

LITTLE ROCK—Comcast Cable, 12775 Lyndon St, Detroit, MI 48227. Phone: 800-266-2278. Web Site: http://www.comcast.com. Also serves Alexander, Bryant, Cammack Village, Jacksonville, North Little Rock, Pulaski County (portions) & Sherwood. ICA: AR0001.
TV Market Ranking: 50 (Alexander, Bryant, Cammack Village, Jacksonville, LITTLE ROCK, North Little Rock, Pulaski County (portions), Sherwood).
Channel capacity: 31 (not 2-way capable). Channels available but not in use: N.A.
Basic Service
Subscribers: 48,722.
Fee: $25.20 monthly.
Internet Service
Operational: Yes.
Subscribers: 42,864.
Broadband Service: Comcast High Speed Internet.
Telephone Service
Digital: Operational
Subscribers: 18,588.
Miles of Plant: 3,629.0 (coaxial); 499.0 (fiber optic). Homes passed: 161,970.
Ownership: Comcast Cable Communications Inc. (MSO).

LITTLE ROCK—Formerly served by Charter Communications. No longer in operation. ICA: AR0296.

LOCKESBURG—Formerly served by Lockesburg Cablevision. No longer in operation. ICA: AR0122.

LOCUST BAYOU—Formerly served by Rapid Cable. No longer in operation. ICA: AR0257.

LONDON—Suddenlink Communications, 520 Maryville Centre Dr, Ste 300, St. Louis, MO 63141. Phones: 314-315-9400; 888-822-5151. E-mail: Gene.Regan@suddenlink.com. Web Site: http://www.suddenlink.com. Also serves Pope County (portions). ICA: AR0258.
TV Market Ranking: Outside TV Markets (LONDON, Pope County (portions)). Franchise award date: N.A. Franchise expiration date: N.A. Began: January 1, 1980.
Channel capacity: 36 (not 2-way capable). Channels available but not in use: N.A.
Basic Service
Subscribers: 112.
Programming (received off-air): KAFT (PBS) Fayetteville; KARK-TV (NBC) Little Rock; KATV (ABC, Retro TV) Little Rock; KHBS (ABC, CW) Fort Smith; KLRT-TV (FOX, This TV) Little Rock; KTHV (Antenna TV, CBS) Little Rock.
Programming (via satellite): National Geographic Channel; Trinity Broadcasting Network (TBN).
Fee: $40.00 installation; $31.50 monthly.
Expanded Basic Service 1
Subscribers: N.A.
Programming (via satellite): A&E; Cartoon Network; CNN; Discovery Channel; Disney Channel; ESPN; Freeform; Great American Country; HGTV; History; HLN; Lifetime; Nickelodeon; Spike TV; TBS; The Weather Channel; TLC; TNT; Turner Classic Movies; USA Network.
Fee: $20.74 monthly.
Pay Service 1
Pay Units: N.A.
Programming (via satellite): HBO; Showtime; The Movie Channel.
Fee: $10.95 monthly (Showtime or TMC), $13.00 monthly (HBO).
Video-On-Demand: No

Pay-Per-View
iN DEMAND (delivered digitally); Playboy TV (delivered digitally); Fresh (delivered digitally); Shorteez (delivered digitally).
Internet Service
Operational: No.
Telephone Service
None
Miles of Plant: 18.0 (coaxial); None (fiber optic). Homes passed: 502.
Senior Vice President, Corporate Finance: Michael Pflantz. Vice President, Accounting: Sabrina Warr. Regional Manager: Todd Cruthird. Area Manager: Carl Miller. Plant Manager: Danny Keith. Marketing Director: Beverly Gambell.
Ownership: Cequel Communications Holdings I LLC (MSO).

LONOKE—Media3, PO Box 650, Milan, TN 38358. Phone: 866-257-2044. E-mail: customerservice@mymedia3.com. Web Site: http://www.mymedia3.com. ICA: AR0066.
TV Market Ranking: 50 (LONOKE). Franchise award date: August 10, 1981. Franchise expiration date: N.A. Began: July 1, 1981.
Channel capacity: 36 (2-way capable). Channels available but not in use: N.A.
Basic Service
Subscribers: 81.
Programming (received off-air): KARK-TV (NBC) Little Rock; KARZ-TV (Bounce TV, MNT) Little Rock; KASN (CW, The Country Network) Pine Bluff; KATV (ABC, Retro TV) Little Rock; KETS (PBS) Little Rock; KLRT-TV (FOX, This TV) Little Rock; KMYA-DT (MeTV, WeatherNation) Camden; KTHV (Antenna TV, CBS) Little Rock; KVTN-DT (IND) Pine Bluff; allband FM.
Programming (via satellite): National Geographic Channel; Spike TV; TNT.
Fee: $24.95 installation; $22.45 monthly.
Expanded Basic Service 1
Subscribers: N.A.
Programming (via satellite): BET; Cartoon Network; CNN; C-SPAN; Discovery Channel; Disney Channel; ESPN; ESPN2; Fox News Channel; Freeform; FX; Great American Country; HGTV; History; HLN; Lifetime; Nickelodeon; QVC; TBS; The Weather Channel; TLC; Travel Channel; Turner Classic Movies; TV Land; USA Network; VH1.
Fee: $27.50 monthly.
Pay Service 1
Pay Units: N.A.
Programming (via satellite): HBO; Showtime.
Fee: $12.95 monthly (each).
Video-On-Demand: No
Internet Service
Operational: No.
Telephone Service
None
Miles of Plant: 32.0 (coaxial); None (fiber optic). Homes passed: 964.
Chief Financial Officer: Thomas Pate.
Ownership: CableSouth Media3 LLC (MSO).

LYNN—Formerly served by Ritter Communications. No longer in operation. ICA: AR0188.

MAGAZINE—Formerly served by Almega Cable. No longer in operation. ICA: AR0134.

MAGIC SPRINGS—Formerly served by Cablevision of Magic Springs. No longer in operation. ICA: AR0137.

MAGNOLIA—Suddenlink Communications, 1911 North Jackson St, Magnolia, AR 71753-2053. Phones: 888-592-3861; 314-315-9400. Fax: 870-234-3959. E-mail: Gene.Regan@suddenlink.com. Web Site: http://www.suddenlink.com. Also serves Columbia County & Waldo. ICA: AR0024.
TV Market Ranking: 99 (Columbia County (portions), MAGNOLIA); Below 100 (Waldo, Columbia County (portions)); Outside TV Markets (Columbia County (portions)). Franchise award date: N.A. Franchise expiration date: N.A. Began: June 1, 1964.
Channel capacity: 60 (not 2-way capable). Channels available but not in use: N.A.
Basic Service
Subscribers: 2,391. Commercial subscribers: 385.
Programming (received off-air): KARK-TV (NBC) Little Rock; KATV (ABC, Retro TV) Little Rock; KETG (PBS) Arkadelphia; KMSS-TV (FOX) Shreveport; KPXJ (Antenna TV, CW, MeTV, Movies!) Minden; KSLA (Bounce TV, CBS, Grit, This TV) Shreveport; KTAL-TV (NBC) Texarkana; KTBS-TV (ABC) Shreveport; 5 FMs.
Programming (via satellite): C-SPAN; C-SPAN 2; DMX Music; INSP; Jewelry Television; Local Cable Weather; QVC; TBS; The Weather Channel; Trinity Broadcasting Network (TBN); WGN America.
Fee: $40.00 installation; $32.50 monthly.
Expanded Basic Service 1
Subscribers: N.A.
Programming (via satellite): A&E; AMC; Animal Planet; BET; Bravo; Cartoon Network; CMT; CNBC; CNN; Comedy Central; Discovery Channel; Disney Channel; E! HD; ESPN; ESPN2; Food Network; Fox News Channel; Fox Sports 1; FOX Sports Southwest; Freeform; FX; Great American Country; HGTV; History; HLN; Lifetime; LMN; MSNBC; MTV; NBCSN; Nickelodeon; Spike TV; Syfy; TLC; TNT; Travel Channel; truTV; TV Land; USA Network; VH1.
Fee: $15.60 monthly.
Digital Basic Service
Subscribers: N.A.
Programming (via satellite): A&E HD; AXS TV; BBC America; Bloomberg Television; CBS Sports Network; CMT; Cooking Channel; Destination America; Discovery Kids Channel; Disney XD; DIY Network; ESPN Classic; ESPN HD; ESPNews; Food Network HD; Fox Sports 2; Fuse; FYI; Golf Channel; GSN; Hallmark Channel; HD Theater; HGTV HD; History International; IFC; Investigation Discovery; MC; MTV Classic; MTV Hits; MTV Jams; MTV2; Nat Geo WILD; National Geographic Channel; National Geographic Channel HD; Nick Jr.; Nicktoons; Outdoor Channel; OWN: Oprah Winfrey Network; Science Channel; Starz Encore (multiplexed); Sundance TV; TeenNick; TNT HD; Turner Classic Movies; Universal HD; VH1 Soul.
Digital Pay Service 1
Pay Units: N.A.
Programming (via satellite): Cinemax (multiplexed); HBO (multiplexed); HBO HD; Showtime (multiplexed); Showtime HD; Starz (multiplexed); The Movie Channel (multiplexed).
Fee: $27.95 monthly.
Video-On-Demand: No
Pay-Per-View
iN DEMAND (delivered digitally); Playboy TV (delivered digitally); Fresh (delivered digitally).
Internet Service
Operational: Yes.
Broadband Service: Suddenlink High Speed Internet.
Fee: $29.95 monthly.
Telephone Service
None
Miles of Plant: 50.0 (coaxial); None (fiber optic). Homes passed: 5,700.
Senior Vice President, Corporate Finance: Michael Pflantz. Vice President, Accounting: Sabrina Warr. General Manager: Robert Banks. Marketing Director: Kathy Wyrick. Chief Technician: James Crisp. Customer Service Manager: Jennifer England.
Ownership: Cequel Communications Holdings I LLC (MSO).

MALVERN—Suddenlink Communications, PO Box 2640, Malvern, AR 72104. Phones: 314-315-9400; 888-822-5151; 501-332-6254. Fax: 314-965-0500. E-mail: Gene.Regan@suddenlink.com. Web Site: http://www.suddenlink.com. Also serves Perla & Rockport. ICA: AR0259.
TV Market Ranking: 50 (Perla, Rockport); Below 100 (MALVERN). Franchise award date: N.A. Franchise expiration date: N.A. Began: January 1, 1980.
Channel capacity: N.A. Channels available but not in use: N.A.
Basic Service
Subscribers: 2,002. Commercial subscribers: 236.
Programming (received off-air): KAIT (ABC, NBC) Jonesboro; KARK-TV (NBC) Little Rock; KARZ-TV (Bounce TV, MNT) Little Rock; KASN (CW, The Country Network) Pine Bluff; KATV (ABC, Retro TV) Little Rock; KKAP (Daystar TV, ETV) Little Rock; KLRT-TV (FOX, This TV) Little Rock; KMYA-DT (MeTV, WeatherNation) Camden; KTEJ (PBS) Jonesboro; KTHV (Antenna TV, CBS) Little Rock; KVTJ-DT (IND) Jonesboro; WMC-TV (Bounce TV, NBC, This TV) Memphis.
Programming (via satellite): C-SPAN 2; HLN; Jewelry Television; QVC; TBS; The Weather Channel; WGN America.
Fee: $38.00 installation; $34.50 monthly.
Expanded Basic Service 1
Subscribers: N.A.
Programming (via satellite): A&E; AMC; Animal Planet; BET; Bravo; Cartoon Network; CMT; CNBC; CNN; Comedy Central; C-SPAN; Discovery Channel; Disney Channel; E! HD; ESPN; ESPN2; Food Network; Fox News Channel; Fox Sports 1; FOX Sports Southwest; Freeform; FX; Great American Country; HGTV; History; Lifetime; LMN; MSNBC; MTV; NBCSN; Nickelodeon; Oxygen; Spike TV; Syfy; TLC; TNT; Travel Channel; truTV; Turner Classic Movies; TV Land; USA Network; VH1.
Fee: $16.13 monthly.

Arkansas—Cable Systems

Digital Basic Service
Subscribers: N.A.
Programming (via satellite): BBC America; Bloomberg Television; CBS Sports Network; CMT; Cooking Channel; Destination America; Discovery Kids Channel; Disney XD; DIY Network; ESPN Classic; ESPNews; Fox Sports 2; Fuse; FYI; Golf Channel; GSN; Hallmark Channel; History International; IFC; Investigation Discovery; MC; MTV Classic; MTV Hits; MTV Jams; MTV2; Nat Geo WILD; National Geographic Channel; Nick Jr.; Nicktoons; Outdoor Channel; OWN: Oprah Winfrey Network; Science Channel; Starz Encore (multiplexed); Sundance TV; TeenNick; Trinity Broadcasting Network (TBN); VH1 Soul.

Digital Pay Service 1
Pay Units: N.A.
Programming (via satellite): Cinemax (multiplexed); HBO (multiplexed); Showtime (multiplexed); Starz (multiplexed); The Movie Channel (multiplexed).

Pay-Per-View
iN DEMAND (delivered digitally); Fresh (delivered digitally); Spice: Xcess (delivered digitally).

Internet Service
Operational: Yes.

Telephone Service
Digital: Operational
Miles of Plant: 97.0 (coaxial); None (fiber optic).
Senior Vice President, Corporate Finance: Michael Pflantz. Vice President, Accounting: Sabrina Warr. General Manager: Robbie Lee. Chief Technician: Chuck Davis.
Ownership: Cequel Communications Holdings I LLC (MSO).

MANILA—Ritter Communications. Now served by MARKED TREE, AR [AR0072]. ICA: AR0076.

MARKED TREE—Ritter Communications, 2400 Ritter Dr, Jonesboro, AR 72401. Phones: 870-336-3400; 888-336-4466 (Customer service); 870-336-3434 (Administrative office). Fax: 870-358-4170. E-mail: customerservice@rittermail.com. Web Site: http://rittercommunications.com. Also serves Bassett, Black Oak, Blytheville, Bono, Brookland, Caraway, Cash, Cherry Valley, Craighead County (northwestern portion), Dell, Dyess, Fisher, Gilmore, Gosnell, Grubbs, Harrisburg, Hickory Ridge, Joiner, Jonesboro, Keiser, Lake City, Leachville, Lepanto, Luxora, Manila, Mississippi County (portions), Monette, Osceola, Payneway, Poinsett County (portions), Swifton, Trumann, Turrell, Tyronza, Weiner, Wilson & Wynne, AR; Arbyrd & Cardwell, MO. ICA: AR0072.
TV Market Ranking: 26 (Bassett, Dell, Gilmore, Joiner, Turrell, Tyronza, Wilson) Below 100 (Arbyrd, Black Oak, Bono, Brookland, Caraway, Cardwell, Cash, Cherry Valley, Craighead County (northwestern portion), Dyess, Fisher, Grubbs, Harrisburg, Hickory Ridge, Jonesboro, Keiser, Lake City, Leachville, Lepanto, Manila, MARKED TREE, Monette, Payneway, Poinsett County (portions), Swifton, Trumann, Weiner, Mississippi County (portions)); Outside TV Markets (Blytheville, Gosnell, Luxora, Osceola, Wynne, Mississippi County (portions)). Franchise award date: January 1, 1981. Franchise expiration date: N.A. Began: June 28, 1982.
Channel capacity: N.A. Channels available but not in use: N.A.

Basic Service
Subscribers: 11,984.
Programming (received off-air): KAIT (ABC, NBC) Jonesboro; KTEJ (PBS) Jonesboro; KVTJ-DT (IND) Jonesboro; WATN-TV (ABC) Memphis; WHBQ-TV (Decades, FOX, Movies!) Memphis; WKNO (PBS) Memphis; WLMT (CW, MeTV, MNT) Memphis; WMC-TV (Bounce TV, NBC, This TV) Memphis; WPXX-TV (ION, MNT) Memphis; WREG-TV (Antenna TV, CBS) Memphis; 1 FM.
Programming (via microwave): KARK-TV (NBC) Little Rock; KATV (ABC, Retro TV) Little Rock.
Programming (via satellite): C-SPAN; C-SPAN 2; National Geographic Channel; Pop; QVC; Travel Channel; Trinity Broadcasting Network (TBN).
Fee: $39.95 installation; $35.98 monthly.

Expanded Basic Service 1
Subscribers: N.A.
Programming (via satellite): A&E; AMC; Animal Planet; BET; Bravo; Cartoon Network; CMT; CNBC; CNN; Comedy Central; Discovery Channel; Disney Channel; E! HD; ESPN; ESPN2; Food Network; Fox News Channel; Freeform; FX; Great American Country; Hallmark Channel; HGTV; HLN; Lifetime; LMN; MSNBC; MTV; Nickelodeon; Outdoor Channel; Spike TV; Syfy; TBS; The Weather Channel; TLC; TNT; Turner Classic Movies; TV Land; USA Network; VH1.
Fee: $45.95 monthly.

Digital Basic Service
Subscribers: N.A.
Programming (via satellite): AXS TV; BBC America; CMT; Destination America; Discovery Kids Channel; Discovery Life Channel; Disney XD; DMX Music; ESPN Classic; ESPN HD; ESPNews; FOX College Sports Central; FOX College Sports Pacific; Fox Sports 1; FXM; Golf Channel; GSN; HD Theater; History; IFC; Investigation Discovery; MTV Classic; MTV Hits; MTV2; NBCSN; Nick Jr.; Nicktoons; OWN: Oprah Winfrey Network; Science Channel; Sprout; TeenNick; Universal HD; UP; VH1 Soul; WE tv.

Digital Pay Service 1
Pay Units: N.A.
Programming (via satellite): Cinemax (multiplexed); Flix; HBO (multiplexed); HBO HD; Showtime (multiplexed); Starz (multiplexed); Starz Encore (multiplexed); Starz HD; The Movie Channel (multiplexed).
Fee: $12.95 monthly (Cinemax, HBO, Showtime/TMC/Flix or Starz/Encore).

Video-On-Demand: No

Pay-Per-View
Playboy TV (delivered digitally); iN DEMAND (delivered digitally).

Internet Service
Operational: Yes.
Subscribers: 9,804.
Broadband Service: Cebridge High Speed Cable Internet.
Fee: $39.95 monthly.

Telephone Service
Digital: Operational
Subscribers: 5,800.
Miles of Plant: 1,062.0 (coaxial); 1,258.0 (fiber optic). Homes passed: 28,000.
President: Paul Waits. Vice President: John D. Strode. Vice President, Customer Care: Shanna French. General Manager: Doug Warzecha. Marketing Director: Jane Marie Woodruff.
Ownership: Ritter Communications (MSO).

MARSHALL—Media3, PO Box 650, Milan, TN 38358. Phone: 866-257-2044. E-mail: customerservice@mymedia3.com. Web Site: http://www.mymedia3.com. ICA: AR0098.
TV Market Ranking: Outside TV Markets (MARSHALL). Franchise award date: May 20, 1997. Franchise expiration date: N.A. Began: January 1, 1952.
Channel capacity: N.A. Channels available but not in use: N.A.

Basic Service
Subscribers: 91.
Programming (received off-air): KARK-TV (NBC) Little Rock; KASN (CW, The Country Network) Pine Bluff; KATV (ABC, Retro TV) Little Rock; KETS (PBS) Little Rock; KLRT-TV (FOX, This TV) Little Rock; KTHV (Antenna TV, CBS) Little Rock; KYTV (CW, NBC, WeatherNation) Springfield.
Programming (via satellite): Turner Classic Movies.
Fee: $24.95 installation; $22.45 monthly.

Pay Service 1
Pay Units: N.A.
Programming (via satellite): Cinemax; Flix; HBO; Showtime; Starz; Starz Encore; Sundance TV; The Movie Channel.
Fee: $11.95 monthly (each).

Video-On-Demand: No

Internet Service
Operational: No.

Telephone Service
None
Miles of Plant: 25.0 (coaxial); None (fiber optic). Homes passed: 936.
Chief Financial Officer: Thomas Pate.
Ownership: CableSouth Media3 LLC (MSO).

MARVELL—Suddenlink Communications, PO Box 2342, West Helena, AR 72390. Phones: 888-822-5151; 870-338-8220; 314-315-9400. Fax: 870-338-7642. E-mail: Gene.Regan@suddenlink.com. Web Site: http://www.suddenlink.com. ICA: AR0260.
TV Market Ranking: Outside TV Markets (MARVELL).
Channel capacity: N.A. Channels available but not in use: N.A.

Basic Service
Subscribers: 273. Commercial subscribers: 31.
Programming (received off-air): KATV (ABC, Retro TV) Little Rock; KETS (PBS) Little Rock; KTHV (Antenna TV, CBS) Little Rock; WATN-TV (ABC) Memphis; WHBQ-TV (Decades, FOX, Movies!) Memphis; WKNO (PBS) Memphis; WLMT (CW, MeTV, MNT) Memphis; WMC-TV (Bounce TV, NBC, This TV) Memphis; WREG-TV (Antenna TV, CBS) Memphis.
Programming (via satellite): A&E; AMC; Animal Planet; BET; Bravo; Cartoon Network; CMT; CNBC; CNN; Comedy Central; C-SPAN; Discovery Channel; Disney Channel; E! HD; ESPN; ESPN2; Food Network; Fox News Channel; Fox Sports 1; FOX Sports Southwest; Freeform; FX; Great American Country; HGTV; History; HLN; ION Television; Lifetime; MSNBC; MTV; NBCSN; Nickelodeon; Outdoor Channel; Oxygen; Spike TV; Syfy; TBS; The Weather Channel; TLC; TNT; Travel Channel; Trinity Broadcasting Network (TBN); TV Land; USA Network; VH1; WGN America.
Fee: $40.00 installation; $21.10 monthly.

Digital Basic Service
Subscribers: N.A.
Programming (via satellite): BBC America; Bloomberg Television; Discovery Digital Networks; Disney XD; ESPN Classic; ESPNews; FYI; Golf Channel; GSN; Hallmark Channel; History International; IFC; LMN; MC; Sundance TV; truTV.

Pay Service 1
Pay Units: N.A.
Programming (via satellite): Showtime; The Movie Channel.
Fee: $35.00 installation; $10.00 monthly (each).

Digital Pay Service 1
Pay Units: N.A.
Programming (via satellite): Cinemax (multiplexed); HBO (multiplexed); Showtime; Starz (multiplexed); The Movie Channel (multiplexed).

Video-On-Demand: No

Pay-Per-View
NBA TV (delivered digitally); ESPN Now (delivered digitally); Fresh (delivered digitally); Hot Choice (delivered digitally); iN DEMAND (delivered digitally).

Internet Service
Operational: Yes.
Broadband Service: Suddenlink High Speed Internet.
Fee: $49.95 installation; $26.95 monthly.

Telephone Service
Digital: Operational
Miles of Plant: 210.0 (coaxial); None (fiber optic). Homes passed: 9,200.
Senior Vice President, Corporate Finance: Michael Pflantz. Vice President, Accounting: Sabrina Warr.
Ownership: Cequel Communications Holdings I LLC (MSO).

MAUMELLE—Fidelity Communications, 64 North Clark St, Sullivan, MO 63080. Phones: 800-392-8070; 501-859-0384 (Maumelle office); 855-262-7434; 501-315-4405 (Benton office). E-mail: fidelityinfo@fidelitycommunications.com. Web Site: http://www.fidelitycommunications.com. Also serves Crystal Hill, North Little Rock & Oak Grove. ICA: AR0020.
TV Market Ranking: 50 (Crystal Hill, MAUMELLE, North Little Rock, Oak Grove). Franchise award date: N.A. Franchise expiration date: N.A. Began: August 1, 1983.
Channel capacity: N.A. Channels available but not in use: N.A.

Basic Service
Subscribers: 948. Commercial subscribers: 261.
Programming (received off-air): KARK-TV (NBC) Little Rock; KARZ-TV (Bounce TV, MNT) Little Rock; KASN (CW, The Country Network) Pine Bluff; KATV (ABC, Retro TV) Little Rock; KETS (PBS) Little Rock; KLRT-TV (FOX, This TV) Little Rock; KTHV (Antenna TV, CBS) Little Rock; KVTN-DT (IND) Pine Bluff.
Programming (via satellite): C-SPAN; QVC; WGN America.
Fee: $29.99 installation; $28.99 monthly; $1.18 converter.

Expanded Basic Service 1
Subscribers: N.A.
Programming (via satellite): A&E; CMT; CNN; Comedy Central; E! HD; ESPN; FOX Sports Southwest; Freeform; HLN; Lifetime; MTV; Nickelodeon; VH1.

Digital Basic Service
Subscribers: N.A.
Programming (via satellite): BBC America; Bloomberg Television; Bravo; Discovery Digital Networks; Disney XD; DMX Music; ESPN Classic; ESPNews; EVINE Live; FXM; FYI; GSN; History International; IFC; LMN; NBCSN; Nick Jr.; Outdoor Channel; TeenNick; Trinity Broadcasting Network (TBN); Turner Classic Movies; WE tv.

Cable Systems—Arkansas

Digital Pay Service 1
Pay Units: N.A.
Programming (via satellite): Cinemax (multiplexed); Flix; HBO (multiplexed); Showtime (multiplexed); Starz (multiplexed); Starz Encore (multiplexed); The Movie Channel (multiplexed).
Video-On-Demand: No
Pay-Per-View
ESPN Now (delivered digitally); Hot Choice (delivered digitally); iN DEMAND (delivered digitally); Playboy TV (delivered digitally); Fresh (delivered digitally); Shorteez (delivered digitally); Urban Xtra (delivered digitally).
Internet Service
Operational: Yes.
Fee: $29.99 monthly.
Telephone Service
Digital: Operational
Miles of Plant: 111.0 (coaxial); None (fiber optic). Homes passed: 10,804.
General Manager, AR/MO/LA/TX: Andy Davis.
Ownership: Fidelity Communications Co. (MSO).

MAYFLOWER—Media3, PO Box 650, Milan, TN 38358. Phone: 866-257-2044. E-mail: customerservice@mymedia3.com. Web Site: http://www.mymedia3.com. Also serves Conway, Faulkner County (portions), Greenbrier & Wooster. ICA: AR0049.
TV Market Ranking: 50 (Conway, Faulkner County (portions), Greenbrier, MAYFLOWER, Wooster). Franchise award date: N.A. Franchise expiration date: N.A. Began: August 1, 1984.
Channel capacity: 44 (not 2-way capable). Channels available but not in use: N.A.
Basic Service
Subscribers: 910.
Programming (received off-air): KARK-TV (NBC) Little Rock; KARZ-TV (Bounce TV, MNT) Little Rock; KASN (CW, The Country Network) Pine Bluff; KATV (ABC, Retro TV) Little Rock; KETS (PBS) Little Rock; KKAP (Daystar TV, ETV) Little Rock; KLRT-TV (FOX, This TV) Little Rock; KMYA-DT (MeTV, WeatherNation) Camden; KTHV (Antenna TV, CBS) Little Rock; KVTN-DT (IND) Pine Bluff.
Fee: $24.95 installation; $22.45 monthly.
Expanded Basic Service 1
Subscribers: N.A.
Programming (via satellite): A&E; Animal Planet; BET; Cartoon Network; CNN; C-SPAN; Discovery Channel; Disney Channel; E! HD; ESPN; ESPN2; Fox News Channel; Freeform; FX; Great American Country; HLN; Lifetime; MSNBC; MTV; National Geographic Channel; Nickelodeon; Outdoor Channel; Spike TV; TBS; The Weather Channel; TNT; Turner Classic Movies; USA Network.
Fee: $24.99 monthly.
Digital Basic Service
Subscribers: N.A.
Programming (via satellite): BBC America; Bloomberg Television; Cloo; Destination America; Discovery Kids Channel; DMX Music; ESPN Classic; ESPN2; ESPNews; EVINE Live; FOX College Sports Central; FOX College Sports Pacific; Fox Sports 1; Fuse; FYI; Golf Channel; GSN; HGTV; History; History International; Investigation Discovery; LMN; NBCSN; Outdoor Channel; Ovation; OWN: Oprah Winfrey Network; Science Channel; Syfy; Trinity Broadcasting Network (TBN); Turner Classic Movies; WE tv.

Pay Service 1
Pay Units: N.A.
Programming (via satellite): Cinemax; HBO; Showtime.
Fee: $12.95 monthly (each).
Digital Pay Service 1
Pay Units: N.A.
Programming (via satellite): Cinemax (multiplexed); Flix; HBO (multiplexed); Showtime (multiplexed); Starz (multiplexed); Starz Encore (multiplexed); The Movie Channel (multiplexed).
Video-On-Demand: No
Pay-Per-View
iN DEMAND (delivered digitally); Playboy TV (delivered digitally); Club Jenna (delivered digitally).
Internet Service
Operational: No.
Telephone Service
None
Miles of Plant: 55.0 (coaxial); None (fiber optic). Homes passed: 1,892.
Chief Financial Officer: Thomas Pate.
Ownership: CableSouth Media3 LLC (MSO).

McALMONT—Formerly served by Cobridge Communications. No longer in operation. ICA: AR0034.

McCASKILL—Formerly served by Allegiance Communications. No longer in operation. ICA: AR0261.

McCRORY—Vyve Broadband, 4 International Dr, Ste 330, Rye Brook, NY 10573. Phones: 800-937-1397; 405-275-6923; 405-395-1131. Web Site: http://vyvebroadband.com. Also serves Patterson. ICA: AR0073.
TV Market Ranking: Outside TV Markets (McCRORY, Patterson). Franchise award date: N.A. Franchise expiration date: N.A. Began: April 1, 1974.
Channel capacity: N.A. Channels available but not in use: N.A.
Basic Service
Subscribers: 114. Commercial subscribers: 21.
Programming (received off-air): KAIT (ABC, NBC) Jonesboro; KARK-TV (NBC) Little Rock; KASN (CW, The Country Network) Pine Bluff; KATV (ABC, Retro TV) Little Rock; KLRT-TV (FOX, This TV) Little Rock; KTEJ (PBS) Jonesboro; KTHV (Antenna TV, CBS) Little Rock; KVTJ-DT (IND) Jonesboro; WMC-TV (Bounce TV, NBC, This TV) Memphis.
Programming (via satellite): A&E; AMC; BET; Cartoon Network; CNN; Comedy Central; C-SPAN; Discovery Channel; Disney Channel; ESPN; ESPN Classic; ESPN2; Food Network; FOX Sports Southwest; Freeform; FX; Great American Country; Hallmark Channel; HGTV; History; Lifetime; NFL Network; Nickelodeon; Outdoor Channel; QVC; Spike TV; Syfy; TBS; The Weather Channel; TLC; TNT; Trinity Broadcasting Network (TBN); TV Land; USA Network; VH1; WGN America.
Fee: $64.95 installation; $67.75 monthly.
Digital Basic Service
Subscribers: N.A.
Programming (via satellite): BBC America; Bloomberg Television; Bravo; Cine Mexicano; Cinelatino; Cloo; CMT; CNN en Espanol; Destination America; Discovery Kids Channel; Discovery Life Channel; Disney XD; DMX Music; ESPN Classic; ESPN Deportes; ESPN2; ESPNews; EVINE Live; Flix; FOX College Sports Central; FOX College Sports Pacific; Fox Deportes; Fox Sports 1; Fuse; FXM; FYI; Golf Channel; Great American Country; GSN; HGTV; History; History en Espanol; History International; IFC; Investigation Discovery; LMN; MTV Classic; MTV Hits; MTV2; National Geographic Channel; NBC Universo; NBCSN; Nick Jr.; Nicktoons; Outdoor Channel; OWN: Oprah Winfrey Network; Science Channel; Starz Encore (multiplexed); Sundance TV; Syfy; TeenNick; The Word Network; Tr3s; Trinity Broadcasting Network (TBN); Turner Classic Movies; UP; VH1 Soul; ViendoMovies; WE tv.
Pay Service 1
Pay Units: N.A.
Programming (via satellite): HBO; Showtime.
Fee: $30.00 installation; $11.95 monthly (each).
Digital Pay Service 1
Pay Units: N.A.
Programming (via satellite): Cinemax (multiplexed); HBO (multiplexed); HBO Latino; Showtime (multiplexed); Starz (multiplexed); The Movie Channel (multiplexed).
Video-On-Demand: No
Pay-Per-View
iN DEMAND (delivered digitally); Playboy TV (delivered digitally); Fresh (delivered digitally); Hot Choice (delivered digitally); Spice: Xcess (delivered digitally); Club Jenna (delivered digitally).
Internet Service
Operational: Yes.
Fee: $24.95 installation; $39.95 monthly.
Telephone Service
Digital: Operational
Miles of Plant: 16.0 (coaxial); None (fiber optic). Homes passed: 1,320.
Chief Executive Officer: Bill Haggarty. Regional Vice President: Andrew Dearth. Senior Vice President, Financial Planning: Daniel White. Vice President, Marketing: Tracy Bass.
Ownership: Vyve Broadband LLC (MSO).

McDOUGAL—Formerly served by Almega Cable. No longer in operation. ICA: AR0201.

McGEHEE—Vyve Broadband, 4 International Dr, Ste 330, Rye Brook, NY 10573. Phones: 800-937-1397; 405-275-6923; 405-395-1131. Web Site: http://vyvebroadband.com. Also serves Chicot County (portions), Dermott, Desha County, Dumas, Lake Village & Mitchellville. ICA: AR0262.
TV Market Ranking: Below 100 (Chicot County (portions), Dermott, Desha County (portions), MCGEHEE, Mitchellville, Dumas, Lake Village); Outside TV Markets (Desha County (portions)). Franchise award date: N.A. Franchise expiration date: N.A. Began: March 1, 1964.
Channel capacity: N.A. Channels available but not in use: N.A.
Basic Service
Subscribers: 1,068.
Programming (received off-air): KARK-TV (NBC) Little Rock; KARZ-TV (Bounce TV, MNT) Little Rock; KASN (CW, The Country Network) Pine Bluff; KATV (ABC, Retro TV) Little Rock; KETS (PBS) Little Rock; KLRT-TV (FOX, This TV) Little Rock; KMYA-DT (MeTV, WeatherNation) Camden; KTHV (Antenna TV, CBS) Little Rock; KTVE (NBC) El Dorado; WABG-TV (ABC, FOX) Greenwood; WXVT (CBS) Greenville; allband FM.
Programming (via satellite): CNBC; CNN; C-SPAN; Daystar TV Network; HLN; The Weather Channel; Trinity Broadcasting Network (TBN); WGN America.
Fee: $64.95 installation; $25.00 monthly.
Expanded Basic Service 1
Subscribers: N.A.
Programming (via satellite): A&E; Animal Planet; BET; Cartoon Network; Discovery Channel; Disney Channel; ESPN; ESPN Classic; ESPN2; Fox News Channel; Fox Sports 1; FOX Sports Southwest; Freeform; FX; Great American Country; Hallmark Channel; HGTV; History; Lifetime; Nickelodeon; Outdoor Channel; Oxygen; Spike TV; Syfy; TBS; TLC; TNT; Travel Channel; Turner Classic Movies; TV Land; USA Network; VH1.
Fee: $38.91 monthly.
Digital Basic Service
Subscribers: N.A.
Programming (via satellite): AXS TV; BBC America; Bloomberg Television; Bravo; Cine Mexicano; Cinelatino; Cloo; CMT; CNN en Espanol; Daystar TV Network; Destination America; Discovery Kids Channel; Discovery Life Channel; Disney XD; DMX Music; ESPN Classic; ESPN Deportes; ESPN HD; ESPNews; EVINE Live; Flix; FOX College Sports Central; FOX College Sports Pacific; Fox Deportes; Fox Sports 1; Fuse; FXM; FYI; Golf Channel; Great American Country; GSN; HD Theater; History; History en Espanol; History International; IFC; Investigation Discovery; LMN; MTV Classic; MTV Hits; MTV2; National Geographic Channel; NBCSN; Nick Jr.; Nicktoons; Outdoor Channel; Outdoor Channel 2 HD; OWN: Oprah Winfrey Network; Science Channel; Starz Encore (multiplexed); Sundance TV; Syfy; TeenNick; The Word Network; Tr3s; Trinity Broadcasting Network (TBN); Turner Classic Movies; Universal HD; UP; WE tv.
Digital Pay Service 1
Pay Units: N.A.
Programming (via satellite): Cinemax (multiplexed); HBO (multiplexed); HBO HD; HBO Latino; Showtime (multiplexed); Showtime HD; Starz (multiplexed); The Movie Channel.
Video-On-Demand: No
Pay-Per-View
iN DEMAND (delivered digitally); Hot Choice (delivered digitally); Playboy TV (delivered digitally); Spice (delivered digitally); Spice 2 (delivered digitally).
Internet Service
Operational: Yes.
Subscribers: 642.
Broadband Service: Net Commander.
Fee: $24.95 installation; $39.95 monthly.
Telephone Service
Digital: Operational
Subscribers: 138.
Miles of Plant: 230.0 (coaxial); 99.0 (fiber optic). Homes passed: 8,697.

2017 Edition

D-71

Arkansas—Cable Systems

Chief Executive Officer: Bill Haggarty. Regional Vice President: Andrew Dearth. Senior Vice President, Financial Planning: Daniel White. Vice President, Marketing: Tracy Bass.
Ownership: Vyve Broadband LLC (MSO).

MELBOURNE—Yelcot Communications, 218 East Main St, Mountain View, AR 72560. Phone: 800-270-1198. Web Site: http://www.yelcot.com. ICA: AR0264.
TV Market Ranking: Outside TV Markets (MELBOURNE). Franchise award date: N.A. Franchise expiration date: N.A. Began: August 1, 1966.
Channel capacity: N.A. Channels available but not in use: N.A.
Basic Service
Subscribers: 289.
Programming (received off-air): KAIT (ABC, NBC) Jonesboro; KARK-TV (NBC) Little Rock; KATV (ABC, Retro TV) Little Rock; KEMV (PBS) Mountain View; KOLR (CBS) Springfield; KTHV (Antenna TV, CBS) Little Rock; KYTV (CW, NBC, WeatherNation) Springfield.
Programming (via satellite): CMT; CNN; Discovery Channel; Disney Channel; ESPN; ESPN2; FOX Sports Networks; Freeform; FX; HGTV; HLN; Nickelodeon; Outdoor Channel; QVC; Spike TV; Syfy; TBS; The Weather Channel; TNT; Trinity Broadcasting Network (TBN); Turner Classic Movies; TV Land; USA Network; WGN America; WPIX (Antenna TV, CW, This TV) New York.
Fee: $20.00 installation; $41.00 monthly.
Pay Service 1
Pay Units: 24.
Programming (via satellite): Cinemax.
Fee: $8.00 monthly.
Pay Service 2
Pay Units: 16.
Programming (via satellite): HBO.
Fee: $10.00 monthly.
Video-On-Demand: Planned
Internet Service
Operational: Yes.
Fee: $29.95 monthly.
Telephone Service
None
Miles of Plant: 14.0 (coaxial); None (fiber optic).
Ownership: Yelcot Communications (MSO).

MENA—Vyve Broadband, 4 International Dr, Ste 330, Rye Brook, NY 10573. Phones: 800-937-1397; 405-275-6923; 405-395-1131. Web Site: http://vyvebroadband.com. Also serves Polk County (portions). ICA: AR0265.
TV Market Ranking: Outside TV Markets (MENA, Polk County (portions)). Franchise award date: N.A. Franchise expiration date: N.A. Began: February 1, 1954.
Channel capacity: N.A. Channels available but not in use: N.A.
Basic Service
Subscribers: 555. Commercial subscribers: 167.
Programming (received off-air): KARK-TV (NBC) Little Rock; KARZ-TV (Bounce TV, MNT) Little Rock; KATV (ABC, Retro TV) Little Rock; KETG (PBS) Arkadelphia; KFSM-TV (CBS, MNT) Fort Smith; KHBS (ABC, CW) Fort Smith; KLRT-TV (FOX, This TV) Little Rock; KTHV (Antenna TV, CBS) Little Rock; allband FM.
Programming (via satellite): CNN; C-SPAN; Pop; QVC; The Weather Channel; Trinity Broadcasting Network (TBN); WGN America.
Fee: $64.95 installation; $25.00 monthly.

Expanded Basic Service 1
Subscribers: N.A.
Programming (via satellite): A&E; AMC; Animal Planet; CMT; CNBC; Comedy Central; CW PLUS; Discovery Channel; Disney Channel; ESPN; ESPN Classic; ESPN2; Food Network; Fox News Channel; FOX Sports Southwest; Freeform; FX; Hallmark Channel; HGTV; History; HLN; Lifetime; NFL Network; Nickelodeon; RFD-TV; Spike TV; Syfy; TBS; TLC; TNT; Travel Channel; truTV; Turner Classic Movies; TV Land; USA Network; VH1.
Fee: $31.91 monthly.
Digital Basic Service
Subscribers: N.A.
Programming (via satellite): BBC America; Bloomberg Television; Bravo; Chiller; Cine Mexicano; Cinelatino; Cloo; CMT; CNN en Espanol; Destination America; Discovery Kids Channel; Discovery Life Channel; Disney XD; DMX Music; ESPN Classic; ESPN Deportes; ESPN2; ESPNews; EVINE Live; Flix; FOX College Sports Central; FOX College Sports Pacific; Fox Deportes; Fox Sports 1; Fuse; FXM; FYI; Golf Channel; Great American Country; GSN; HGTV; History; History en Espanol; History International; IFC; Investigation Discovery; LMN; MTV Classic; MTV Hits; MTV2; National Geographic Channel; NBC Universo; NBCSN; Nick Jr.; Nicktoons; Outdoor Channel; Ovation; OWN: Oprah Winfrey Network; Science Channel; Starz Encore (multiplexed); Sundance TV; Syfy; TeenNick; The Word Network; Tr3s; Trinity Broadcasting Network (TBN); Turner Classic Movies; UP; VH1 Soul; ViendoMovies; WE tv.
Pay Service 1
Pay Units: N.A.
Programming (via satellite): HBO; Showtime.
Fee: $35.00 installation; $11.95 monthly (each).
Digital Pay Service 1
Pay Units: N.A.
Programming (via satellite): Cinemax (multiplexed); HBO (multiplexed); HBO Latino; Showtime (multiplexed); Starz (multiplexed); The Movie Channel (multiplexed).
Video-On-Demand: No
Pay-Per-View
iN DEMAND (delivered digitally); Playboy TV (delivered digitally); Hot Choice (delivered digitally); Spice: Xcess (delivered digitally); Club Jenna (delivered digitally); Fresh (delivered digitally).
Internet Service
Operational: Yes.
Fee: $24.95 installation; $39.95 monthly.
Telephone Service
Digital: Operational
Miles of Plant: 41.0 (coaxial); None (fiber optic).
Chief Executive Officer: Bill Haggarty. Regional Vice President: Andrew Dearth. Senior Vice President, Financial Planning: Daniel White. Vice President, Marketing: Tracy Bass.
Ownership: Vyve Broadband LLC (MSO).

MIDLAND—Cox Communications. Now served by FORT SMITH, AR [AR0003]. ICA: AR0266.

MINERAL SPRINGS—Formerly served by Allegiance Communications. No longer in operation. ICA: AR0148.

MONTICELLO—Cablevision of Monticello, 1920 Hwy 425 North, Monticello, AR 71655-4463. Phones: 870-367-7300; 870-367-3166. Fax: 870-367-9770. E-mail: cccaccounts@ccc-cable.net. Web Site: http://ccc-cable.com. Also serves Drew County. ICA: AR0032.
TV Market Ranking: Below 100 (Drew County (portions), MONTICELLO); Outside TV Markets (Drew County (portions)). Franchise award date: N.A. Franchise expiration date: N.A. Began: May 1, 1974.
Channel capacity: N.A. Channels available but not in use: N.A.
Basic Service
Subscribers: 1,845.
Programming (received off-air): KARK-TV (NBC) Little Rock; KARZ-TV (Bounce TV, MNT) Little Rock; KASN (CW, The Country Network) Pine Bluff; KATV (ABC, Retro TV) Little Rock; KETS (PBS) Little Rock; KKAP (Daystar TV, ETV) Little Rock; KLRA-CD (UNV) Little Rock; KLRT-TV (FOX, This TV) Little Rock; KMYA-DT (MeTV, WeatherNation) Camden; KTHV (Antenna TV, CBS) Little Rock; KTVE (NBC) El Dorado; WABG-TV (ABC, FOX) Greenwood; WXVT (CBS) Greenville.
Programming (via satellite): A&E; Animal Planet; BET; Bloomberg Television; Bravo; Cartoon Network; CMT; CNBC; CNN; Comedy Central; Cox Sports Television; C-SPAN; C-SPAN 2; Discovery Channel; Discovery Life Channel; Disney Channel; E! HD; ESPN; ESPN2; EWTN Global Catholic Network; Food Network; Fox News Channel; Fox Sports 1; FOX Sports Southwest; Freeform; FX; Golf Channel; HGTV; History; HLN; Lifetime; MSNBC; MTV; National Geographic Channel; NBCSN; Nickelodeon; Outdoor Channel; Pop; QVC; Spike TV; Syfy; TBS; The Weather Channel; TLC; TNT; Travel Channel; Trinity Broadcasting Network (TBN); Turner Classic Movies; TV Land; USA Network; VH1; WGN America.
Fee: $30.00 installation; $18.95 monthly.
Digital Basic Service
Subscribers: N.A.
Programming (via satellite): BBC America; Cloo; CMT; Cooking Channel; Destination America; Discovery Kids Channel; Disney XD; ESPNews; Fuse; FXM; FYI; GSN; History International; IFC; Investigation Discovery; LMN; MC; MTV Classic; MTV2; Nick Jr.; Nicktoons; OWN: Oprah Winfrey Network; Science Channel; TeenNick; WE tv.
Digital Pay Service 1
Pay Units: N.A.
Programming (via satellite): Cinemax; HBO; Showtime; Starz; Starz Encore.
Fee: $12.00 monthly (each).
Video-On-Demand: No
Pay-Per-View
Club Jenna (delivered digitally); Playboy TV (delivered digitally); Fresh (delivered digitally); special events (delivered digitally).
Internet Service
Operational: Yes.
Fee: $30.00 installation; $29.95 monthly.
Telephone Service
Digital: Operational
Fee: $29.95 monthly
Miles of Plant: 183.0 (coaxial); 20.0 (fiber optic). Homes passed: 3,000.
President: Bill Copeland.
Ownership: Community Communications Co. (MSO).

MONTROSE—Dean Hill Cable, PO Box 128, Parkdale, AR 71661. Phone: 870-473-2802. Fax: 870-737-0020. ICA: AR0322.
TV Market Ranking: Below 100 (MONTROSE).
Channel capacity: N.A. Channels available but not in use: N.A.

Basic Service
Subscribers: N.A.
Programming (received off-air): KATV (ABC, Retro TV) Little Rock; KLTM-TV (PBS) Monroe; KNOE-TV (ABC, CBS, CW) Monroe; KTVE (NBC) El Dorado; WABG-TV (ABC, FOX) Greenwood.
Programming (via satellite): Disney Channel; ESPN; TBS; TNT; WGN America.
Fee: $35.00 installation.
Pay Service 1
Pay Units: N.A.
Programming (via satellite): HBO.
Fee: $10.00 installation; $11.55 monthly.
Internet Service
Operational: No.
Telephone Service
None
General Manager: Dean Hill. Assistant Manager: Kathy Hill.
Ownership: Dean Hill Cable (MSO).

MORO—Formerly served by Indco Cable TV. No longer in operation. ICA: AR0268.

MORRILTON—Suddenlink Communications, PO Box 10010, Russellville, AR 72812. Phones: 888-592-3861; 888-822-5151; 314-315-9400. Fax: 479-969-1343. E-mail: Gene.Regan@suddenlink.com. Web Site: http://www.suddenlink.com. Also serves Conway County (portions). ICA: AR0035.
TV Market Ranking: 50 (MORRILTON (portions)); Outside TV Markets (MORRILTON (portions)). Franchise award date: N.A. Franchise expiration date: N.A. Began: February 1, 1981.
Channel capacity: N.A. Channels available but not in use: N.A.
Basic Service
Subscribers: 1,402.
Programming (received off-air): KAFT (PBS) Fayetteville; KARK-TV (NBC) Little Rock; KARZ-TV (Bounce TV, MNT) Little Rock; KASN (CW, The Country Network) Pine Bluff; KATV (ABC, Retro TV) Little Rock; KFSM-TV (CBS, MNT) Fort Smith; KKAP (Daystar TV, ETV) Little Rock; KLRA-CD (UNV) Little Rock; KLRT-TV (FOX, This TV) Little Rock; KMYA-DT (MeTV, WeatherNation) Camden; KTHV (Antenna TV, CBS) Little Rock.
Programming (via satellite): C-SPAN; QVC; TBS; The Weather Channel; UniMas; WGN America.
Fee: $40.00 installation; $31.50 monthly.
Expanded Basic Service 1
Subscribers: N.A.
Programming (via satellite): A&E; AMC; Animal Planet; BET; Bravo; Cartoon Network; CMT; CNBC; CNN; Comedy Central; C-SPAN 2; Discovery Channel; Disney Channel; E! HD; ESPN; ESPN2; EWTN Global Catholic Network; Food Network; Fox News Channel; Fox Sports 1; FOX Sports Southwest; Freeform; FX; Great American Country; HGTV; History; HLN; INSP; Jewelry Television; Lifetime; LMN; MSNBC; MTV; NBCSN; Nickelodeon; Outdoor Channel; Pop; Spike TV; Syfy; TLC; TNT; Travel Channel; Trinity Broadcasting Network (TBN); truTV; Turner Classic Movies; TV Land; Univision; USA Network; VH1.
Fee: $30.00 installation; $35.75 monthly.
Digital Basic Service
Subscribers: N.A.
Programming (via satellite): A&E HD; AXS TV; Bandamax; BBC America; Bloomberg Television; Boomerang; CBS Sports Network; Cine Mexicano; Cinelatino; CMT; CNN

D-72   TV & Cable Factbook No. 85

Cable Systems—Arkansas

en Espanol; Cooking Channel; Cox Sports Television; De Pelicula; De Pelicula Clasico; Destination America; Discovery Kids Channel; Disney XD; DIY Network; Enlace USA; ESPN Classic; ESPN Deportes; ESPN HD; ESPNews; FamilyNet; Food Network HD; Fox Deportes; Fox Sports 2; FSN HD; Fuse; FYI; Golf Channel; GSN; Hallmark Channel; HD Theater; HGTV HD; History en Espanol; History International; IFC; Investigation Discovery; MC; MTV Classic; MTV Hits; MTV Live; MTV2; mtvU; Nat Geo WILD; National Geographic Channel; National Geographic Channel HD; NBC Universo; Nick Jr.; Nicktoons; NickToons en Espanol; OWN: Oprah Winfrey Network; Oxygen; Ritmoson; Science Channel; Starz Encore (multiplexed); Sundance TV; Sur; TeenNick; Telehit; Telemundo; Tennis Channel; TNT HD; Toon Disney en Espanol; Tr3s; TV One; ULTRA HD-Plex; Universal HD; Univision; UP; Video-Rola; WE tv; Weatherscan.

Digital Pay Service 1
Pay Units: N.A.
Programming (via satellite): Cinemax (multiplexed); HBO (multiplexed); HBO HD; HBO Latino; Showtime (multiplexed); Showtime HD; Starz (multiplexed); The Movie Channel (multiplexed).

Video-On-Demand: Yes

Pay-Per-View
iN DEMAND (delivered digitally); Playboy TV (delivered digitally); Fresh (delivered digitally); Shorteez (delivered digitally); Club Jenna (delivered digitally); Spice: Xcess (delivered digitally); Playboy en Espanol (delivered digitally).

Internet Service
Operational: Yes.
Broadband Service: Suddenlink High Speed Internet.
Fee: $35.00 monthly.

Telephone Service
Digital: Operational
Fee: $20.00 monthly
Miles of Plant: 79.0 (coaxial); None (fiber optic). Homes passed: 3,270.
Senior Vice President, Corporate Finance: Michael Pflantz. Vice President, Accounting: Sabrina Warr. General Manager: Mike Ederington. Marketing Director: Kathy Wyrick. Chief Technician: Clint Petty.
Ownership: Cequel Communications Holdings I LLC (MSO).

MOUNT IDA—Suddenlink Communications, 520 Maryville Centre Dr, Ste 300, St. Louis, MO 63141. Phones: 314-315-9400; 888-822-5151. E-mail: Gene.Regan@suddenlink.com. Web Site: http://www.suddenlink.com. Also serves Montgomery County (unincorporated areas) & Mountain Harbor Resort. ICA: AR0121.
TV Market Ranking: Below 100 (Montgomery County (unincorporated areas), MOUNT IDA, Mountain Harbor Resort). Franchise award date: N.A. Franchise expiration date: N.A. Began: May 1, 1982.
Channel capacity: N.A. Channels available but not in use: N.A.

Basic Service
Subscribers: 465.
Programming (received off-air): KARK-TV (NBC) Little Rock; KARZ-TV (Bounce TV, MNT) Little Rock; KASN (CW, The Country Network) Pine Bluff; KATV (ABC, Retro TV) Little Rock; KETG (PBS) Arkadelphia; KLRT-TV (FOX, This TV) Little Rock; KMYA-DT (MeTV, WeatherNation) Camden; KTHV (Antenna TV, CBS) Little Rock; KVTN-DT (IND) Pine Bluff.

Programming (via satellite): Trinity Broadcasting Network (TBN); WGN America.
Fee: $40.00 installation; $28.45 monthly.

Expanded Basic Service 1
Subscribers: N.A.
Programming (via satellite): A&E; AMC; Animal Planet; BET; Cartoon Network; CNBC; CNN; Comedy Central; Discovery Channel; Disney Channel; E! HD; ESPN; ESPN2; Food Network; Fox News Channel; Fox Sports 1; FOX Sports Southwest; Freeform; FX; Great American Country; Hallmark Channel; HGTV; History; HLN; Lifetime; MSNBC; MTV; National Geographic Channel; Nickelodeon; Outdoor Channel; Spike TV; Syfy; TBS; The Weather Channel; TLC; TNT; Travel Channel; Turner Classic Movies; TV Land; USA Network; VH1.
Fee: $25.00 monthly.

Pay Service 1
Pay Units: N.A.
Programming (via satellite): HBO; Showtime; The Movie Channel.
Fee: $10.95 monthly (Showtime or TMC), $13.00 monthly (HBO).

Video-On-Demand: No

Pay-Per-View
Fresh (delivered digitally); Playboy TV (delivered digitally); iN DEMAND (delivered digitally).

Internet Service
Operational: Yes. Began: May 5, 2003.
Broadband Service: Suddenlink High Speed Internet.
Fee: $49.95 installation; $26.95 monthly.

Telephone Service
None
Miles of Plant: 56.0 (coaxial); None (fiber optic). Homes passed: 1,607.
Vice President, Corporate Finance: Michael Pflantz. Regional Manager: Todd Cruthird. Area Manager: Carolyn Wilder. Plant Manager: Donnie Burton. Marketing Director: Beverly Gambell.
Ownership: Cequel Communications Holdings I LLC (MSO).

MOUNT PLEASANT—Yelcot Communications, 218 East Main St, Mountain View, AR 72560. Phone: 800-270-1198. Web Site: http://www.yelcot.com. ICA: AR0269.
TV Market Ranking: Outside TV Markets (MOUNT PLEASANT). Franchise award date: N.A. Franchise expiration date: N.A. Began: January 1, 1972.
Channel capacity: N.A. Channels available but not in use: N.A.

Basic Service
Subscribers: 511.
Programming (received off-air): KAIT (ABC, NBC) Jonesboro; KARK-TV (NBC) Little Rock; KATV (ABC, Retro TV) Little Rock; KEMV (PBS) Mountain View; KTHV (Antenna TV, CBS) Little Rock.
Programming (via satellite): CNN; Discovery Channel; Disney Channel; ESPN; ESPN2; Freeform; HGTV; Lifetime; Nickelodeon; Outdoor Channel; QVC; Spike TV; TBS; TNT; Turner Classic Movies; WGN America.
Fee: $20.00 installation; $49.95 monthly.

Pay Service 1
Pay Units: 4.
Programming (via satellite): HBO.
Fee: $10.00 monthly.

Video-On-Demand: Planned

Internet Service
Operational: Yes.
Fee: $29.95 monthly.

Access the most current data instantly
FREE TRIAL @ ADVANCED TVFactbook
TELCO/IPTV • CABLE TV • TV STATIONS
www.warren-news.com/factbook.htm

Telephone Service
None
Miles of Plant: 3.0 (coaxial); None (fiber optic).
Ownership: Yelcot Communications (MSO).

MOUNTAIN HOME—Suddenlink Communications, 808 Club Blvd, PO Box 3055, Mountain Home, AR 72654. Phones: 314-315-9400; 870-425-3161. Fax: 870-425-3164. E-mail: Gene.Regan@suddenlink.com. Web Site: http://www.suddenlink.com. Also serves Baxter County (portions), Bull Shoals, Cotter, Flippin, Gassville, Lakeview, Marion County (portions) & Midway. ICA: AR0013.
TV Market Ranking: Below 100 (Bull Shoals, Cotter, Flippin, Gassville, Lakeview, Baxter County (portions), Marion County (portions)); Outside TV Markets (Midway, MOUNTAIN HOME, Baxter County (portions), Marion County (portions)). Franchise award date: N.A. Franchise expiration date: N.A. Began: March 1, 1959.
Channel capacity: 26 (operating 2-way). Channels available but not in use: N.A.

Basic Service
Subscribers: 7,607. Commercial subscribers: 745.
Programming (received off-air): K07XL-D (This TV) Mountain Home; KARK-TV (NBC) Little Rock; KATV (ABC, Retro TV) Little Rock; KEMV (PBS) Mountain View; KOLR (CBS) Springfield; KOZK (PBS) Springfield; KOZL-TV (IND) Springfield; KSPR (ABC) Springfield; KTHV (Antenna TV, CBS) Little Rock; KWBM (Retro TV) Harrison; KYTV (CW, NBC, WeatherNation) Springfield; 9 FMs.
Programming (via satellite): C-SPAN; C-SPAN 2; DMX Music; INSP; LWS Local Weather Station; Pop; QVC; TBS; The Weather Channel; Trinity Broadcasting Network (TBN); WGN America.
Fee: $40.00 installation; $34.50 monthly.

Expanded Basic Service 1
Subscribers: N.A.
Programming (via satellite): A&E; AMC; Animal Planet; Bravo; Cartoon Network; CMT; CNBC; CNN; Comedy Central; Discovery Channel; Disney Channel; E! HD; ESPN; ESPN2; Food Network; Fox News Channel; Fox Sports 1; FOX Sports Southwest; Freeform; FX; Golf Channel; Great American Country; HGTV; History; HLN; Jewelry Television; Lifetime; LMN; MSNBC; MTV; NBCSN; Nickelodeon; Outdoor Channel; Oxygen; Spike TV; Syfy; TLC; TNT; Travel Channel; truTV; Turner Classic Movies; TV Land; USA Network; VH1; WE tv.
Fee: $13.64 monthly.

Digital Basic Service
Subscribers: N.A.
Programming (via satellite): A&E HD; AXS TV; BBC America; Bloomberg Television; CBS Sports Network; CMT; Cooking Channel; Destination America; Discovery Kids Channel; Disney XD; DIY Network; ESPN Classic; ESPN HD; ESPNews; Food Network HD; Fox Sports 2; FSN HD; Fuse; FYI;

GSN; Hallmark Channel; HD Theater; HGTV HD; History International; IFC; Investigation Discovery; MC; MTV Classic; MTV Hits; MTV2; Nat Geo WILD; National Geographic Channel; National Geographic Channel HD; Nick Jr.; Nicktoons; OWN: Oprah Winfrey Network; Science Channel; Starz Encore (multiplexed); Sundance TV; TeenNick; TNT HD; Universal HD.

Digital Pay Service 1
Pay Units: N.A.
Programming (via satellite): Cinemax (multiplexed); HBO (multiplexed); HBO HD; Showtime (multiplexed); Showtime HD; Starz (multiplexed); The Movie Channel (multiplexed).

Video-On-Demand: Planned

Pay-Per-View
iN DEMAND (delivered digitally); Playboy TV (delivered digitally); Fresh (delivered digitally); Club Jenna (delivered digitally); Spice: Xcess (delivered digitally).

Internet Service
Operational: Yes.
Subscribers: 6,895.
Broadband Service: Suddenlink High Speed Internet.
Fee: $29.95 monthly.

Telephone Service
Digital: Operational
Subscribers: 3,888.
Fee: $44.95 monthly
Miles of Plant: 774.0 (coaxial); 763.0 (fiber optic). Homes passed: 17,211.
Senior Vice President, Corporate Finance: Michael Pflantz. Vice President, Accounting: Sabrina Warr. General Manager: Ron Vincent. Chief Technician: Eddie Thorn.
Ownership: Cequel Communications Holdings I LLC (MSO).

MOUNTAIN VIEW—Yelcot Communications, 218 East Main St, Mountain View, AR 72560. Phones: 800-270-1198; 870-269-3232. Web Site: http://www.yelcot.com. ICA: AR0271.
TV Market Ranking: Outside TV Markets (MOUNTAIN VIEW). Franchise award date: N.A. Franchise expiration date: N.A. Began: November 1, 1968.
Channel capacity: N.A. Channels available but not in use: N.A.

Basic Service
Subscribers: 807.
Programming (received off-air): KAIT (ABC, NBC) Jonesboro; KARK-TV (NBC) Little Rock; KASN (CW, The Country Network) Pine Bluff; KATV (ABC, Retro TV) Little Rock; KLRT-TV (FOX, This TV) Little Rock; KTEJ (PBS) Jonesboro; KTHV (Antenna TV, CBS) Little Rock; KYTV (CW, NBC, WeatherNation) Springfield; allband FM.
Programming (via satellite): A&E; CMT; CNN; Discovery Channel; Disney Channel; ESPN; ESPN2; FOX Sports Networks; Freeform; FX; HGTV; History; Lifetime; Nickelodeon; QVC; Spike TV; Syfy; TBS; The Weather Channel; TNT; Trinity Broadcasting Network (TBN); Turner Classic

Arkansas—Cable Systems

Movies; TV Land; USA Network; VH1; WGN America.
Fee: $20.00 installation; $41.00 monthly.
Pay Service 1
Pay Units: 34.
Programming (via satellite): Cinemax.
Fee: $8.00 monthly.
Pay Service 2
Pay Units: 32.
Programming (via satellite): HBO.
Fee: $10.00 monthly.
Pay Service 3
Pay Units: 29.
Programming (via satellite): Cinemax; HBO.
Fee: $16.00 monthly (HBO and Cinemax Combo).
Video-On-Demand: No
Internet Service
Operational: Yes.
Telephone Service
Digital: Operational
Fee: $13.50 monthly
Miles of Plant: 35.0 (coaxial); None (fiber optic).
Ownership: Yelcot Communications (MSO).

MULBERRY—Cox Communications. Now served by FORT SMITH, AR [AR0003]. ICA: AR0052.

MURFREESBORO—Vyve Broadband, 4 International Dr, Ste 330, Rye Brook, NY 10573. Phones: 800-937-1397; 405-395-1131; 405-275-6923. Web Site: http://vyvebroadband.com. ICA: AR0095.
TV Market Ranking: Outside TV Markets (MURFREESBORO). Franchise award date: March 2, 1964. Franchise expiration date: N.A. Began: September 1, 1964.
Channel capacity: N.A. Channels available but not in use: N.A.
Basic Service
Subscribers: 41. Commercial subscribers: 31.
Programming (received off-air): KARK-TV (NBC) Little Rock; KATV (ABC, Retro TV) Little Rock; KETG (PBS) Arkadelphia; KJEP-LP Nashville; KMSS-TV (FOX) Shreveport; KSLA (Bounce TV, CBS, Grit, This TV) Shreveport; KTAL-TV (NBC) Texarkana; KTBS-TV (ABC) Shreveport; KTHV (Antenna TV, CBS) Little Rock; KTSS-LP Hope; KVTH-DT (IND) Hot Springs; allband FM.
Programming (via satellite): CNN; Pop; QVC; The Weather Channel; Trinity Broadcasting Network (TBN); WGN America.
Fee: $64.95 installation; $25.00 monthly.
Expanded Basic Service 1
Subscribers: N.A.
Programming (via satellite): A&E; AMC; Cartoon Network; CMT; CNBC; Comedy Central; Discovery Channel; Disney Channel; ESPN; ESPN2; Fox News Channel; FOX Sports Southwest; Freeform; Hallmark Channel; History; Lifetime; MTV; NFL Network; Nickelodeon; Spike TV; Syfy; TBS; TLC; TNT; TV Land; USA Network; VH1.
Fee: $29.96 monthly.
Digital Basic Service
Subscribers: N.A.
Programming (via satellite): BBC America; Bloomberg Television; Bravo; Cine Mexicano; Cinelatino; CMT; CNN en Espanol; Destination America; Discovery Kids Channel; Discovery Life Channel; Disney XD; DMX Music; ESPN Classic; ESPN Deportes; ESPN2; ESPNews; EVINE Live; Flix; FOX College Sports Central; FOX College Sports Pacific; Fox Deportes; Fox Sports 1; Fuse; FXM; FYI; Golf Channel; Great American Country; GSN; HGTV; History; History en Espanol; History International; IFC; Investigation Discovery; LMN; MTV Classic; MTV Hits; MTV2; National Geographic Channel; NBC Universo; NBCSN; Nick Jr.; Nicktoons; Outdoor Channel; OWN: Oprah Winfrey Network; Science Channel; Starz Encore (multiplexed); Sundance TV; Syfy; TeenNick; The Word Network; Tr3s; Trinity Broadcasting Network (TBN); Turner Classic Movies; UP; VH1 Soul; ViendoMovies; WE tv.
Pay Service 1
Pay Units: N.A.
Programming (via satellite): HBO; Starz; Starz Encore; The Movie Channel.
Fee: $1.75 monthly (Encore), $9.95 monthly (TMC), $10.95 monthly (HBO).
Digital Pay Service 1
Pay Units: N.A.
Programming (via satellite): Cinemax (multiplexed); HBO (multiplexed); HBO Latino; Showtime (multiplexed); Starz (multiplexed); The Movie Channel (multiplexed).
Pay-Per-View
iN DEMAND (delivered digitally); Hot Choice (delivered digitally); Playboy TV (delivered digitally); Fresh (delivered digitally); Spice: Xcess (delivered digitally); Club Jenna (delivered digitally).
Internet Service
Operational: Yes.
Fee: $24.95 installation; $39.95 monthly.
Telephone Service
Digital: Operational
Miles of Plant: 20.0 (coaxial); None (fiber optic). Homes passed: 1,634.
Chief Executive Officer: Bill Haggarty. Regional Vice President: Andrew Dearth. Senior Vice President, Financial Planning: Daniel White. Vice President, Marketing: Tracy Bass.
Ownership: Vyve Broadband LLC (MSO).

NASHVILLE—Suddenlink Communications, 520 Maryville Centre Dr, Ste 300, St. Louis, MO 63141. Phones: 314-315-9400; 888-822-5151. Web Site: http://www.suddenlink.com. Also serves Hempstead County (portions). ICA: AR0272.
TV Market Ranking: Outside TV Markets (Hempstead County (portions), NASHVILLE). Franchise award date: N.A. Franchise expiration date: N.A. Began: September 15, 1967.
Channel capacity: N.A. Channels available but not in use: N.A.
Basic Service
Subscribers: 263.
Programming (received off-air): KARK-TV (NBC) Little Rock; KATV (ABC, Retro TV) Little Rock; KETG (PBS) Arkadelphia; KJEP-LP Nashville; KMSS-TV (FOX) Shreveport; KSLA (Bounce TV, CBS, Grit, This TV) Shreveport; KTAL-TV (NBC) Texarkana; KTBS-TV (ABC) Shreveport; KTHV (Antenna TV, CBS) Little Rock; KTSS-LP Hope; allband FM.
Fee: $28.45 monthly.
Expanded Basic Service 1
Subscribers: N.A.
Programming (via satellite): A&E; AMC; Animal Planet; BET; Cartoon Network; CNBC; CNN; Comedy Central; Discovery Channel; Disney Channel; E! HD; ESPN; ESPN2; Food Network; Fox News Channel; FOX Sports Southwest; Freeform; FX; Great American Country; HGTV; History; HLN; Lifetime; MSNBC; MTV; National Geographic Channel; NBCSN; Nickelodeon; Outdoor Channel; Spike TV; Syfy; TBS; The Weather Channel; TLC; TNT; Travel Channel; Turner Classic Movies; TV Land; USA Network; VH1.
Fee: $24.00 monthly.
Pay Service 1
Pay Units: N.A.
Programming (via satellite): Cinemax; HBO; Showtime.
Fee: $7.00 monthly (Showtime), $9.95 monthly (Cinemax) $10.95 monthly (HBO).
Video-On-Demand: No
Pay-Per-View
iN DEMAND (delivered digitally); Playboy TV (delivered digitally); Fresh (delivered digitally); Shorteez (delivered digitally).
Internet Service
Operational: Yes. Began: July 8, 2003.
Broadband Service: Suddenlink High Speed Internet.
Fee: $49.95 installation; $26.95 monthly.
Telephone Service
None
Miles of Plant: 53.0 (coaxial); None (fiber optic). Homes passed: 2,426.
Vice President, Corporate Finance: Michael Pflantz. Regional Manager: Todd Cruthird. Plant Manager: George Lewis. Marketing Director: Beverly Gambell.
Ownership: Cequel Communications Holdings I LLC (MSO).

NEWARK—Indco Cable TV, 2700 North Saint Louis, PO Box 3799, Batesville, AR 72503-3799. Phones: 800-364-0831; 870-793-4175; 870-793-4174. Fax: 870-793-7439. Web Site: http://www.indco.net. Also serves Magness. ICA: AR0093.
TV Market Ranking: Outside TV Markets (Magness, NEWARK). Franchise award date: N.A. Franchise expiration date: N.A. Began: October 1, 1975.
Channel capacity: 78 (not 2-way capable). Channels available but not in use: N.A.
Basic Service
Subscribers: 171.
Programming (received off-air): KAIT (ABC, NBC) Jonesboro; KARK-TV (NBC) Little Rock; KATV (ABC, Retro TV) Little Rock; KEMV (PBS) Mountain View; KLRT-TV (FOX, This TV) Little Rock; KTHV (Antenna TV, CBS) Little Rock.
Programming (via satellite): A&E; CMT; CNN; Discovery Channel; Disney Channel; ESPN; ESPN2; FOX Sports Southwest; Freeform; FX; HGTV; Lifetime; Nickelodeon; Outdoor Channel; QVC; Spike TV; Syfy; TBS; The Weather Channel; TNT; Turner Classic Movies; USA Network; WGN America.
Fee: $40.00 installation; $66.95 monthly.
Pay Service 1
Pay Units: 9.
Programming (via satellite): Cinemax.
Fee: $8.00 monthly.
Pay Service 2
Pay Units: 3.
Programming (via satellite): HBO.
Fee: $10.00 monthly.
Pay Service 3
Pay Units: 8.
Programming (via satellite): Cinemax; HBO.
Fee: $16.00 monthly.
Internet Service
Operational: Yes.
Subscribers: 169.
Broadband Service: In-house.
Telephone Service
Digital: Operational
Miles of Plant: 32.0 (coaxial); 19.0 (fiber optic). Homes passed: 550.
President & General Manager: J.D. Pierce. Chief Technician: Tommy Barnett. Marketing Director: Connie Barnett.
Ownership: Indco Cable TV (MSO).

NEWPORT—Suddenlink Communications, 300 State St, PO Box 598, Newport, AR 72112. Phone: 314-315-9400. Fax: 870-523-2219. E-mail: Gene.Regan@suddenlink.com. Web Site: http://www.suddenlink.com. Also serves Campbell Station, Diaz, Jackson County, Jacksonport & Tuckerman. ICA: AR0030.
TV Market Ranking: Below 100 (Campbell Station, Diaz, Jackson County (portions), NEWPORT, Tuckerman); Outside TV Markets (Jackson County (portions), Jacksonport). Franchise award date: N.A. Franchise expiration date: N.A. Began: November 2, 1964.
Channel capacity: 61 (operating 2-way). Channels available but not in use: N.A.
Basic Service
Subscribers: 2,039. Commercial subscribers: 246.
Programming (received off-air): KAIT (ABC, NBC) Jonesboro; KARK-TV (NBC) Little Rock; KARZ-TV (Bounce TV, MNT) Little Rock; KASN (CW, The Country Network) Pine Bluff; KATV (ABC, Retro TV) Little Rock; KKAP (Daystar TV, ETV) Little Rock; KLRT-TV (FOX, This TV) Little Rock; KMYA-DT (MeTV, WeatherNation) Camden; KTEJ (PBS) Jonesboro; KTHV (Antenna TV, CBS) Little Rock; KVTJ-DT (IND) Jonesboro; WMC-TV (Bounce TV, NBC, This TV) Memphis; allband FM.
Programming (via satellite): C-SPAN; C-SPAN 2; HLN; Jewelry Television; QVC; TBS; The Weather Channel; WGN America.
Fee: $40.00 installation; $33.50 monthly.
Expanded Basic Service 1
Subscribers: N.A.
Programming (via satellite): A&E; AMC; Animal Planet; BET; Bravo; Cartoon Network; CMT; CNBC; CNN; Comedy Central; Discovery Channel; Disney Channel; E! HD; ESPN; ESPN2; Food Network; Fox News Channel; Fox Sports 1; FOX Sports Southwest; Freeform; FX; Great American Country; HGTV; History; Lifetime; LMN; MSNBC; MTV; NBCSN; Nickelodeon; Oxygen; Spike TV; Syfy; TLC; TNT; Travel Channel; truTV; Turner Classic Movies; TV Land; USA Network; VH1.
Digital Basic Service
Subscribers: N.A.
Programming (via satellite): BBC America; Bloomberg Television; CBS Sports Network; CMT; Cooking Channel; Destination America; Discovery Kids Channel; Disney XD; DIY Network; ESPN Classic; ESPNews; Fox Sports 2; Fuse; FYI; Golf Channel; GSN; Hallmark Channel; History International; IFC; Investigation Discovery; MC; MTV Classic; MTV Hits; MTV Jams; MTV2; Nat Geo WILD; National Geographic Channel; Nick Jr.; Nicktoons; Outdoor Channel; OWN: Oprah Winfrey Network; Science Channel; Starz Encore (multiplexed); Sundance TV; TeenNick; Trinity Broadcasting Network (TBN); VH1 Soul.
Digital Pay Service 1
Pay Units: N.A.
Programming (via satellite): Cinemax (multiplexed); HBO (multiplexed); Showtime (multiplexed); Starz (multiplexed); The Movie Channel (multiplexed).
Pay-Per-View
iN DEMAND (delivered digitally); Fresh (delivered digitally); Spice: Xcess (delivered digitally).
Internet Service
Operational: Yes.
Broadband Service: Suddenlink High Speed Internet.
Fee: $29.95 monthly.

Cable Systems—Arkansas

Telephone Service
Digital: Operational
Fee: $44.95 monthly
Miles of Plant: 80.0 (coaxial); None (fiber optic). Homes passed: 4,905.
Senior Vice President, Corporate Finance: Michael Pflantz. Vice President, Accounting: Sabrina Warr. General Manager: Paul Eddington. Chief Technician: Jerry Raby.
Ownership: Cequel Communications Holdings I LLC (MSO).

NORMAN—Formerly served by Cablevision of Norman. No longer in operation. ICA: AR0167.

OAK GROVE HEIGHTS—Fusion Media, 1910 Mockingbird Ln, Paragould, AR 72450. Phones: 870-215-3456; 870-919-1454. Fax: 870-586-0675. E-mail: support@fusionmedia.tv; goodwintechnologies@gmail.com. Web Site: http://www.fusionmedia.tv. Also serves Bono, Brookland, Craighead County (portions), Greene County (portions), Jonesboro, Lafe, Marmaduke, Paragould & Walcott. ICA: AR0273.
TV Market Ranking: Below 100 (Bono, Brookland, Jonesboro, Lafe, Marmaduke, OAK GROVE HEIGHTS, Paragould, Craighead County (portions), Greene County (portions)). Franchise award date: N.A. Franchise expiration date: N.A. Began: November 1, 1983.
Channel capacity: 57 (not 2-way capable). Channels available but not in use: N.A.

Basic Service
Subscribers: 1,194.
Programming (received off-air): KAIT (ABC, NBC) Jonesboro; KTEJ (PBS) Jonesboro; WATN-TV (ABC) Memphis; WMC-TV (Bounce TV, NBC, This TV) Memphis; WREG-TV (Antenna TV, CBS) Memphis.
Programming (via satellite): Disney Channel; HLN.
Fee: $25.00 installation; $24.95 monthly.

Pay Service 1
Pay Units: 25.
Programming (via satellite): Cinemax.
Fee: $10.00 installation; $9.95 monthly.

Pay Service 2
Pay Units: 25.
Programming (via satellite): HBO.
Fee: $10.95 monthly.

Video-On-Demand: No

Internet Service
Operational: Yes.
Subscribers: 152.
Fee: $29.99-$59.99 monthly.

Telephone Service
Digital: Operational
Miles of Plant: 21.0 (coaxial); 10.0 (fiber optic).
General Manager: Kenneth Goodwin.
Ownership: MM & G Enterprises LLC.

OIL TROUGH—Indco Cable TV, 2700 North Saint Louis, PO Box 3799, Batesville, AR 72503-3799. Phones: 800-364-0831; 870-793-4175; 870-793-4174. Fax: 870-793-7439. Web Site: http://www.indco.net. ICA: AR0274.
TV Market Ranking: Outside TV Markets (OIL TROUGH). Franchise award date: N.A. Franchise expiration date: N.A. Began: January 1, 1984.
Channel capacity: N.A. Channels available but not in use: N.A.

Basic Service
Subscribers: 13.
Programming (received off-air): KAIT (ABC, NBC) Jonesboro; KARK-TV (NBC) Little Rock; KATV (ABC, Retro TV) Little Rock; KEMV (PBS) Mountain View; KTHV (Antenna TV, CBS) Little Rock.
Programming (via satellite): CNN; Discovery Channel; Disney Channel; ESPN; ESPN2; HGTV; Lifetime; Nickelodeon; Spike TV; Syfy; TBS; The Weather Channel; TNT; Turner Classic Movies; USA Network; WGN America.
Fee: $40.00 installation; $63.95 monthly.

Pay Service 1
Pay Units: 1.
Programming (via satellite): HBO.
Fee: $10.00 installation; $10.00 monthly.

Video-On-Demand: Planned

Internet Service
Operational: Yes.
Fee: $29.95 monthly.

Telephone Service
None
Miles of Plant: 2.0 (coaxial); None (fiber optic).
President & General Manager: J.D. Pierce. Chief Technician: Tommy Barnett. Marketing Director: Connie Barnett.
Ownership: Indco Cable TV (MSO).

O'KEAN—Formerly served by Cebridge Connections. No longer in operation. ICA: AR0207.

OSCEOLA—Ritter Communications. Now served by MARKED TREE, AR [AR0072]. ICA: AR0029.

OXFORD—Formerly served by Almega Cable. No longer in operation. ICA: AR0205.

OZARK—Suddenlink Communications, PO Box 10010, Russellville, AR 72812. Phones: 314-315-9400; 800-582-9577. Web Site: http://www.suddenlink.com. Also serves Altus. ICA: AR0275.
TV Market Ranking: Below 100 (OZARK); Outside TV Markets (Altus). Franchise award date: N.A. Franchise expiration date: N.A. Began: July 1, 1965.
Channel capacity: N.A. Channels available but not in use: N.A.

Basic Service
Subscribers: 368. Commercial subscribers: 94.
Programming (received off-air): KAFT (PBS) Fayetteville; KARK-TV (NBC) Little Rock; KFSM-TV (CBS, MNT) Fort Smith; KFTA-TV (FOX, NBC) Fort Smith; KHBS (ABC, CW) Fort Smith; KTHV (Antenna TV, CBS) Little Rock.
Programming (via satellite): A&E; CNN; C-SPAN; C-SPAN 2; Discovery Channel; Disney Channel; ESPN; ESPN2; FOX Sports Southwest; Freeform; Great American Country; HGTV; History; HLN; ION Television; Lifetime; Nickelodeon; Spike TV; TBS; The Weather Channel; TLC; TNT; Trinity Broadcasting Network (TBN); Turner Classic Movies; TV Land; USA Network; VH1; WGN America.
Fee: $40.00 installation; $58.45 monthly.

Digital Basic Service
Subscribers: N.A.
Programming (via satellite): BBC America; Bloomberg Television; Discovery Digital Networks; Disney XD; DMX Music; ESPNews; Fox Sports 1; FYI; Golf Channel; GSN; History International; LMN; NBCSN; Outdoor Channel; Sundance TV.

Communications Daily
Warren Communications News

Get the industry standard FREE —
For a no-obligation trial call 800-771-9202 or visit www.warren-news.com

Pay Service 1
Pay Units: N.A.
Programming (via satellite): Cinemax; HBO; Showtime.
Fee: $30.00 installation; $10.00 monthly (Showtime), $11.95 monthly (Cinemax or HBO).

Digital Pay Service 1
Pay Units: N.A.
Programming (via satellite): Cinemax (multiplexed); HBO (multiplexed); Showtime (multiplexed); Starz (multiplexed); Starz Encore (multiplexed); The Movie Channel.

Video-On-Demand: No

Pay-Per-View
Shorteez (delivered digitally); Fresh (delivered digitally); Playboy TV (delivered digitally); iN DEMAND (delivered digitally); ESPN Now (delivered digitally); Special events, Addressable: No.

Internet Service
Operational: Yes.

Telephone Service
Digital: Operational
Miles of Plant: 38.0 (coaxial); None (fiber optic). Homes passed: 2,721.
Vice President: Mark Williams. General Manager: Jeff Jech. Chief Technician: Clint Petty. Marketing Director: Tina Gabbard. Senior Vice President, Corporate Finance: Michael Pflantz.
Ownership: Cequel Communications Holdings I LLC (MSO).

OZARK ACRES—Formerly served by Cebridge Connections. No longer in operation. ICA: AR0155.

PALESTINE—Formerly served by Almega Cable. No longer in operation. ICA: AR0191.

PANGBURN—Indco Cable TV, 2700 North Saint Louis, PO Box 3799, Batesville, AR 72503-3799. Phones: 800-364-0831; 870-793-4175; 870-793-4174. Fax: 870-793-7439. Web Site: http://www.indco.net. Also serves Cleburne County (portions) & Letona. ICA: AR0276.
TV Market Ranking: Outside TV Markets (Cleburne County (portions), Letona, PANGBURN). Franchise award date: N.A. Franchise expiration date: N.A. Began: January 1, 1984.
Channel capacity: N.A. Channels available but not in use: N.A.

Basic Service
Subscribers: 146.
Programming (received off-air): KARK-TV (NBC) Little Rock; KASN (CW, The Country Network) Pine Bluff; KATV (ABC, Retro TV) Little Rock; KEMV (PBS) Mountain View; KLRT-TV (FOX, This TV) Little Rock; KMYA-DT (MeTV, WeatherNation) Camden; KTHV (Antenna TV, CBS) Little Rock.
Programming (via satellite): A&E; CMT; CNN; Discovery Channel; Disney Channel; ESPN; ESPN2; FOX Sports Southwest; Freeform; FX; HGTV; History; Lifetime; Nickelodeon; Outdoor Channel; QVC; Spike TV; Syfy; TBS; The Weather Channel; TNT; Trinity Broadcasting Network (TBN); Turner Classic Movies; USA Network; WGN America.
Fee: $40.00 installation; $63.95 monthly.

Pay Service 1
Pay Units: 7.
Programming (via satellite): Cinemax.
Fee: $8.00 monthly.

Pay Service 2
Pay Units: 20.
Programming (via satellite): HBO.
Fee: $10.00 monthly.

Video-On-Demand: Planned

Internet Service
Operational: Yes.
Fee: $29.95 monthly.

Telephone Service
None
Miles of Plant: 8.0 (coaxial); None (fiber optic).
President & General Manager: J.D. Pierce. Marketing Director: Connie Barnett. Chief Technician: Tommy Barnett.
Ownership: Indco Cable TV (MSO).

PARAGOULD—Paragould City Light & Water Commission, 1901 Jones Rd, PO Box 9, Paragould, AR 72451-0009. Phone: 870-239-7700. Fax: 870-239-7727. E-mail: support@paragould.net. Web Site: http://www.paragould.com. ICA: AR0016.
TV Market Ranking: Below 100 (PARAGOULD). Franchise award date: December 1, 1989. Franchise expiration date: N.A. Began: January 31, 1991.
Channel capacity: 70 (operating 2-way). Channels available but not in use: N.A.

Basic Service
Subscribers: 9,625.
Programming (received off-air): KAIT (ABC, NBC) Jonesboro; KARK-TV (NBC) Little Rock; KATV (ABC, Retro TV) Little Rock; KTEJ (PBS) Jonesboro; KVTJ-DT (IND) Jonesboro; WATN-TV (ABC) Memphis; WHBQ-TV (Decades, FOX, Movies!) Memphis; WKNO (PBS) Memphis; WLMT (CW, MeTV, MNT) Memphis; WMC-TV (Bounce TV, NBC, This TV) Memphis; WREG-TV (Antenna TV, CBS) Memphis.
Programming (via satellite): C-SPAN; C-SPAN 2; HGTV; Pop; QVC; The Weather Channel; Trinity Broadcasting Network (TBN).
Fee: $19.43 monthly.

Expanded Basic Service 1
Subscribers: 6,745.
Programming (via satellite): A&E; AMC; Animal Planet; Cartoon Network; CMT; CNBC; CNN; Comedy Central; Discovery Channel; Disney Channel; E! HD; ESPN; ESPN Classic; ESPN2; ESPNews; Food Network; Fox News Channel; FOX Sports Southwest; Freeform; FX; Hallmark Channel; History; HLN; Lifetime; MSNBC; MTV; National Geographic Channel; Nickelodeon; Outdoor Channel; Radar Channel; Spike TV; Syfy; TBS; TLC; TNT; Travel Channel; truTV; Turner Classic Movies; TV Land; USA Network; VH1; WGN America.
Fee: $38.79 monthly.

2017 Edition D-75

Arkansas—Cable Systems

Digital Basic Service
Subscribers: 1,154.
Programming (via satellite): Bloomberg Television; CMT; Destination America; Discovery Kids Channel; Disney XD; DIY Network; ESPNU; EWTN Global Catholic Network; FamilyNet; Fox Sports 1; Fox Sports 2; FSN Digital Atlantic; FSN Digital Central; FSN Digital Pacific; FXM; FYI; Golf Channel; History International; Investigation Discovery; MTV Classic; MTV Hits; MTV2; Nat Geo WILD; NBCSN; Nick Jr.; Nicktoons; OWN: Oprah Winfrey Network; Science Channel; Sundance TV; TeenNick; WE tv.
Fee: $23.30 monthly.

Digital Expanded Basic Service
Subscribers: N.A.
Programming (via satellite): A&E HD; AXS TV; Bio HD; Discovery Channel HD; ESPN HD; ESPN2 HD; History HD.
Fee: $7.10 monthly.

Pay Service 1
Pay Units: N.A.
Programming (via satellite): Cinemax; HBO (multiplexed); Showtime; The Movie Channel.
Fee: $9.77 monthly (Cinemax), $11.83 monthly (Showtime/TMC), $14.59 monthly (HBO).

Digital Pay Service 1
Pay Units: N.A.
Programming (via satellite): Cinemax (multiplexed); HBO (multiplexed); Showtime (multiplexed); Starz (multiplexed); Starz Encore (multiplexed); Starz HD; The Movie Channel.
Fee: $9.56 monthly (Starz/Encore), $9.77 monthly (Cinemax), $11.83 monthly (Showtime/TMC), $14.59 monthly (HBO).

Video-On-Demand: No

Pay-Per-View
Hot Choice (delivered digitally); iN DEMAND (delivered digitally).

Internet Service
Operational: Yes, Dial-up. Began: June 1, 1998.
Subscribers: 6,308.
Broadband Service: In-house.
Fee: free installation; $24.95-$62.95 monthly.

Telephone Service
Digital: Operational
Subscribers: 6,308.
Miles of Plant: 225.0 (coaxial); 195.0 (fiber optic). Homes passed: 12,000.
General Manager & Chief Executive Officer: Bill Fisher. Chief Financial Officer: Rhonda Davis. Cable Manager: Farron Toler. Assistant General Manager: Darrell Phillips. Chief Technician: Johnny Estes.
Ownership: Paragould Light Water & Cable.

PARIS—Suddenlink Communications, PO Box 10010, Russellville, AR 72801. Phones: 888-592-3861; 314-315-9400; 800-582-9577. Fax: 479-968-1343. E-mail: Gene.Regan@suddenlink.com. Web Site: http://www.suddenlink.com. ICA: AR0054.
TV Market Ranking: Outside TV Markets (PARIS). Franchise award date: April 7, 1994. Franchise expiration date: N.A. Began: April 1, 1964.
Channel capacity: 62 (operating 2-way). Channels available but not in use: N.A.

Basic Service
Subscribers: 284.
Programming (received off-air): KAFT (PBS) Fayetteville; KFSM-TV (CBS, MNT) Fort Smith; KFTA-TV (FOX, NBC) Fort Smith; KHBS (ABC, CW) Fort Smith; KNWA-TV (FOX, NBC) Rogers; KTHV (Antenna TV, CBS) Little Rock.
Programming (via satellite): C-SPAN; CW PLUS; Pop; QVC; TBS; The Weather Channel; Trinity Broadcasting Network (TBN); WGN America.
Fee: $40.00 installation; $32.50 monthly; $4.15 converter.

Expanded Basic Service 1
Subscribers: N.A.
Programming (via satellite): A&E; AMC; Animal Planet; Cartoon Network; CNBC; CNN; Discovery Channel; Disney Channel; E! HD; ESPN; ESPN2; Food Network; Fox News Channel; Fox Sports 1; FOX Sports Southwest; Freeform; Great American Country; HGTV; History; HLN; Lifetime; NBCSN; Nickelodeon; Outdoor Channel; Spike TV; Syfy; TLC; TNT; TV Land; USA Network; VH1.
Fee: $25.24 monthly.

Digital Basic Service
Subscribers: N.A.
Programming (via satellite): BBC America; Bloomberg Television; Destination America; Discovery Kids Channel; Disney XD; DMX Music; ESPN Classic; ESPNews; Fuse; FYI; Golf Channel; GSN; History International; IFC; Investigation Discovery; LMN; OWN: Oprah Winfrey Network; Science Channel; Sundance TV.

Digital Pay Service 1
Pay Units: N.A.
Programming (via satellite): Cinemax (multiplexed); HBO (multiplexed); Showtime (multiplexed); Starz (multiplexed); Starz Encore (multiplexed); The Movie Channel (multiplexed).

Video-On-Demand: No

Pay-Per-View
iN DEMAND (delivered digitally); Playboy TV (delivered digitally); Fresh (delivered digitally); Spice: Xcess (delivered digitally).

Internet Service
Operational: Yes.
Broadband Service: Suddenlink High Speed Internet.
Fee: $29.95 monthly.

Telephone Service
Digital: Operational
Fee: $44.95 monthly
Miles of Plant: 66.0 (coaxial); 5.0 (fiber optic). Homes passed: 1,849.
Senior Vice President, Corporate Finance: Michael Pflantz. System Manager: Mike Ederington. Field Services Manager: Clint Petty. Field System Manager: Wayne Ollis. Customer Service Manager: Jane Howell.
Ownership: Cequel Communications Holdings I LLC (MSO).

PEARCY—Formerly served by Cablevision of Garland County. No longer in operation. ICA: AR0089.

PERRYVILLE—Formerly served by Alliance Communications Network. No longer in operation. ICA: AR0318.

PFEIFFER—Indco Cable TV, 2700 North Saint Louis, PO Box 3799, Batesville, AR 72503-3799. Phones: 800-364-0831; 870-793-4175; 870-793-4174. Fax: 870-793-7439. Web Site: http://www.indco.net. Also serves Cave City & Independence County (northern portion). ICA: AR0224.
TV Market Ranking: Outside TV Markets (Independence County (northern portion), PFEIFFER, Cave City). Franchise award date: N.A. Franchise expiration date: N.A. Began: August 1, 1963.
Channel capacity: N.A. Channels available but not in use: N.A.

Basic Service
Subscribers: 466.
Programming (received off-air): KAIT (ABC, NBC) Jonesboro; KARK-TV (NBC) Little Rock; KATV (ABC, Retro TV) Little Rock; KEMV (PBS) Mountain View; KLRT-TV (FOX, This TV) Little Rock; KTHV (Antenna TV, CBS) Little Rock; KVTJ-DT (IND) Jonesboro.
Programming (via satellite): CMT; CNN; Discovery Channel; Disney Channel; ESPN; ESPN2; FOX Sports Southwest; Freeform; FX; HGTV; Lifetime; Nickelodeon; Outdoor Channel; QVC; Spike TV; Syfy; TBS; The Weather Channel; TNT; Trinity Broadcasting Network (TBN); Turner Classic Movies; USA Network; VH1; WGN America.
Fee: $40.00 installation; $66.95 monthly.

Pay Service 1
Pay Units: N.A.
Programming (via satellite): Cinemax; HBO; Showtime; The Movie Channel.
Fee: $8.00 monthly (Cinemax), $9.00 monthly (Showtime or TMC), $10.00 monthly (HBO).

Video-On-Demand: Planned

Internet Service
Operational: Yes. Began: December 10, 2004.
Subscribers: 133.
Broadband Service: In-house.
Fee: $29.95 monthly.

Telephone Service
None
Miles of Plant: 57.0 (coaxial); 18.0 (fiber optic). Homes passed: 1,100.
President & General Manager: J.D. Pierce. Chief Technician: Tom Barnett. Marketing Director: Connie Barnett.
Ownership: Indco Cable TV (MSO).

PIKE COUNTY (portions)—Formerly served by Allegiance Communications. No longer in operation. ICA: AR0142.

PINE BLUFF—Pine Bluff Cable TV Co. Inc, 715 South Poplar St, PO Box 9008, Pine Bluff, AR 71601-4842. Phones: 870-879-4734 (Headend); 870-536-0350. Fax: 870-536-0351. E-mail: pinebluffcabletvcs@cablelynx.com. Web Site: http://www.pinebluffcabletv.com. Also serves Jefferson County (portions). ICA: AR0006.
TV Market Ranking: 50 (Jefferson County (portions), PINE BLUFF). Franchise award date: October 1, 1975. Franchise expiration date: N.A. Began: May 31, 1976.
Channel capacity: 116 (operating 2-way). Channels available but not in use: N.A.

Basic Service
Subscribers: 4,104. Commercial subscribers: 8.
Programming (received off-air): KARK-TV (NBC) Little Rock; KASN (CW, The Country Network) Pine Bluff; KATV (ABC, Retro TV) Little Rock; KETS (PBS) Little Rock; KLRT-TV (FOX, This TV) Little Rock; KMYA-DT (MeTV, WeatherNation) Camden; KTHV (Antenna TV, CBS) Little Rock.
Programming (via satellite): A&E; AMC; Animal Planet; BET; Cartoon Network; CMT; CNBC; CNN; Comedy Central; C-SPAN; C-SPAN 2; Discovery Channel; Disney Channel; ESPN; ESPN Classic; ESPN2; EVINE Live; EWTN Global Catholic Network; Food Network; Fox News Channel; FOX Sports Southwest; Freeform; FX; Hallmark Channel; HGTV; History; HLN; Lifetime; MSNBC; MTV; NASA TV; National Geographic Channel; Nickelodeon; Pop; Spike TV; Syfy; TBS; The Weather Channel; TLC; TNT; truTV; Turner Classic Movies; TV Land; USA Network; VH1; WGN America.
Fee: $49.95 installation; $31.90 monthly; $3.19 converter.

Digital Basic Service
Subscribers: N.A.
Programming (via satellite): BBC America; CMT; Destination America; Discovery Kids Channel; Discovery Life Channel; Disney XD; DMX Music; ESPNews; Fox Sports 1; FSN Digital Atlantic; FSN Digital Central; FSN Digital Pacific; FYI; Golf Channel; Great American Country; GSN; History International; Investigation Discovery; LMN; MTV Classic; MTV Hits; MTV Jams; MTV2; National Geographic Channel; Nick 2; Nick Jr.; Nicktoons; Outdoor Channel; OWN: Oprah Winfrey Network; Science Channel; TeenNick; Tr3s; VH1 Soul; WE tv.

Digital Expanded Basic Service
Subscribers: N.A.
Programming (via satellite): AXS TV; CNN HD; Discovery Channel HD; ESPN HD; Outdoor Channel 2 HD; PBS HD; TBS HD; TNT HD.
Fee: $5.00 monthly.

Digital Pay Service 1
Pay Units: N.A.
Programming (via satellite): Cinemax (multiplexed); Cinemax HD; HBO (multiplexed); HBO HD; Starz (multiplexed); Starz Encore (multiplexed); Starz HD.
Fee: $12.95 monthly (Cinemax, HBO or Starz/Encore).

Video-On-Demand: No

Internet Service
Operational: Yes.
Subscribers: 3,511.
Broadband Service: Cablelynx.
Fee: $24.95-$44.95 monthly; $10.00 modem lease.

Telephone Service
Digital: Operational
Subscribers: 672.
Fee: $45.70 monthly
Miles of Plant: 647.0 (coaxial); 108.0 (fiber optic). Homes passed: 26,759.
Vice President, Administration: Charlotte A. Dial. General Manager: Mark Billingsly. Technical Supervisor: Mike Spokes. Customer Service & Office Manager: Jena Jones.
Ownership: WEHCO Video Inc. (MSO).

PINE BLUFF (southern portion)—Formerly served by Almega Cable. No longer in operation. ICA: AR0277.

PINEBERGEN—Formerly served by Zoom Media. No longer in operation. ICA: AR0110.

PLAINVIEW—Formerly served by Rapid Cable. No longer in operation. ICA: AR0085.

PLAINVIEW—Indco Cable TV, 2700 North Saint Louis, PO Box 3799, Batesville, AR 72503-3799. Phones: 800-364-0831; 870-793-4175; 870-793-4174. Fax: 870-793-7439. Web Site: http://www.indco.net. Also serves White County (portions). ICA: AR0303.
TV Market Ranking: Outside TV Markets (PLAINVIEW, White County (portions)).
Channel capacity: N.A. Channels available but not in use: N.A.

Basic Service
Subscribers: 135.
Programming (received off-air): KARK-TV (NBC) Little Rock; KASN (CW, The Country Network) Pine Bluff; KATV (ABC, Retro TV) Little Rock; KLRT-TV (FOX, This TV) Little Rock; KMYA-DT (MeTV, WeatherNa-

tion) Camden; KTHV (Antenna TV, CBS) Little Rock.
Programming (via satellite): A&E; Cartoon Network; CMT; CNN; Discovery Channel; Disney Channel; ESPN; ESPN2; FOX Sports Southwest; Freeform; FX; HGTV; History; Lifetime; Nickelodeon; Outdoor Channel; QVC; Spike TV; Syfy; TBS; The Weather Channel; TNT; Trinity Broadcasting Network (TBN); Turner Classic Movies; TV Land; USA Network; WGN America.
Fee: $40.00 installation; $66.95 monthly.

Pay Service 1
Pay Units: 23.
Programming (via satellite): HBO.
Fee: $10.00 monthly.

Pay Service 2
Pay Units: 13.
Programming (via satellite): The Movie Channel.
Fee: $9.00 monthly.

Video-On-Demand: Planned

Internet Service
Operational: Yes.
Fee: $29.95 monthly.

Telephone Service
None

President & General Manager: J.D. Pierce. Chief Technician: Tommy Barnett. Marketing Director: Connie Barnett.
Ownership: Indco Cable TV (MSO).

PLEASANT PLAINS—Indco Cable TV, 2700 North Saint Louis, PO Box 3799, Batesville, AR 72503-3799. Phones: 800-364-0831; 870-793-4175; 800-364-0831. Fax: 870-793-7439. Web Site: http://www.indco.net. Also serves Independence County (unincorporated areas). ICA: AR0278.
TV Market Ranking: Outside TV Markets (Independence County (unincorporated areas), PLEASANT PLAINS). Franchise award date: N.A. Franchise expiration date: N.A. Began: November 1, 1989.
Channel capacity: N.A. Channels available but not in use: N.A.

Basic Service
Subscribers: 19.
Programming (received off-air): KAIT (ABC, NBC) Jonesboro; KARK-TV (NBC) Little Rock; KASN (CW, The Country Network) Pine Bluff; KATV (ABC, Retro TV) Little Rock; KEMV (PBS) Mountain View; KLRT-TV (FOX, This TV) Little Rock; KTHV (Antenna TV, CBS) Little Rock.
Programming (via satellite): CMT; CNN; Discovery Channel; Disney Channel; ESPN; ESPN2; Freeform; HGTV; Lifetime; Nickelodeon; Outdoor Channel; QVC; Spike TV; Syfy; TBS; The Weather Channel; TNT; Trinity Broadcasting Network (TBN); USA Network; WGN America.
Fee: $40.00 installation; $63.95 monthly.

Pay Service 1
Pay Units: 2.
Programming (via satellite): Cinemax.
Fee: $8.00 monthly.

Pay Service 2
Pay Units: 2.
Programming (via satellite): Cinemax; HBO.
Fee: $16.00 monthly.

Video-On-Demand: Planned

Internet Service
Operational: Yes.
Fee: $29.95 monthly.

Telephone Service
None

Programming Director: J.D. Pierce. Chief Technician: Tommy Barnett. Marketing Director: Connie Barnett.
Ownership: Indco Cable TV (MSO).

PLUMERVILLE—Media3, PO Box 650, Milan, TN 38358. Phone: 866-257-2044. E-mail: customerservice@mymedia3.com. Web Site: http://www.mymedia3.com. Also serves Menifee. ICA: AR0149.
TV Market Ranking: 50 (Menifee, PLUMERVILLE). Franchise award date: N.A. Franchise expiration date: N.A. Began: January 1, 1990.
Channel capacity: N.A. Channels available but not in use: N.A.

Basic Service
Subscribers: 102.
Programming (received off-air): KARK-TV (NBC) Little Rock; KARZ-TV (Bounce TV, MNT) Little Rock; KASN (CW, The Country Network) Pine Bluff; KATV (ABC, Retro TV) Little Rock; KETS (PBS) Little Rock; KKYK-CD (IND, WeatherNation) Little Rock; KLRT-TV (FOX, This TV) Little Rock; KTHV (Antenna TV, CBS) Little Rock.
Programming (via satellite): A&E; AMC; Animal Planet; BET; Cartoon Network; CMT; CNN; C-SPAN; Discovery Channel; Disney Channel; ESPN; ESPN2; Freeform; GSN; Hallmark Channel; HGTV; History; Lifetime; MTV; Nickelodeon; Outdoor Channel; Spike TV; Syfy; TBS; The Weather Channel; TLC; TNT; truTV; Turner Classic Movies; TV Land; USA Network; VH1; WGN America.
Fee: $24.95 installation; $22.45 monthly.

Digital Basic Service
Subscribers: N.A.
Programming (via satellite): BBC America; Bloomberg Television; Discovery Digital Networks; DMX Music; ESPN Classic; ESPNews; Fox Sports 1; Fuse; FXM; FYI; Golf Channel; History International; IFC; National Geographic Channel; NBCSN; Nick Jr.; Nicktoons; Ovation; Sundance TV; TeenNick; WE tv.

Pay Service 1
Pay Units: N.A.
Programming (via satellite): Cinemax; HBO.

Digital Pay Service 1
Pay Units: N.A.
Programming (via satellite): Cinemax (multiplexed); Flix; HBO (multiplexed); Showtime (multiplexed); Starz (multiplexed); Starz Encore; The Movie Channel (multiplexed).
Fee: $11.95 monthly (each).

Video-On-Demand: No

Pay-Per-View
iN DEMAND (delivered digitally); Hot Choice (delivered digitally); Playboy TV (delivered digitally); Fresh (delivered digitally); Shorteez (delivered digitally).

Internet Service
Operational: Yes.

Telephone Service
None

Miles of Plant: 25.0 (coaxial); None (fiber optic). Homes passed: 1,433.
Chief Financial Officer: Thomas Pate.
Ownership: CableSouth Media3 LLC (MSO).

POCAHONTAS—Suddenlink Communications, 2728 Thomasville Rd, PO Box 370, Pocahontas, AR 72455. Phones: 888-822-5151; 314-315-9400. E-mail: Gene.Regan@suddenlink.com. Web Site: http://www.suddenlink.com. Also serves Randolph County (portions). ICA: AR0036.
TV Market Ranking: Below 100 (POCAHONTAS, Randolph County (portions)). Franchise award date: N.A. Franchise expiration date: N.A. Began: January 1, 1961.
Channel capacity: N.A. Channels available but not in use: N.A.

Basic Service
Subscribers: 2,011. Commercial subscribers: 138.
Programming (received off-air): KAIT (ABC, NBC) Jonesboro; KARK-TV (NBC) Little Rock; KATV (ABC, Retro TV) Little Rock; KTEJ (PBS) Jonesboro; KTHV (Antenna TV, CBS) Little Rock; KVTJ-DT (IND) Jonesboro; WHBQ-TV (Decades, FOX, Movies!) Memphis; WMC-TV (Bounce TV, NBC, This TV) Memphis; WREG-TV (Antenna TV, CBS) Memphis; allband FM.
Programming (via satellite): CNN; C-SPAN; CW PLUS; ESPN; ION Television; MTV; Pop; QVC; TBS; The Weather Channel; WGN America.
Fee: $40.00 installation; $33.50 monthly.

Expanded Basic Service 1
Subscribers: N.A.
Programming (via satellite): A&E; AMC; Animal Planet; Bravo; Cartoon Network; CMT; CNBC; Comedy Central; Discovery Channel; Disney Channel; E! HD; ESPN2; EWTN Global Catholic Network; Food Network; Fox News Channel; Fox Sports 1; FOX Sports Southwest; Freeform; FX; Great American Country; HGTV; History; HLN; INSP; Lifetime; MSNBC; NBCSN; Nickelodeon; Oxygen; Spike TV; Syfy; TLC; TNT; Travel Channel; truTV; Turner Classic Movies; TV Land; USA Network; VH1.

Digital Basic Service
Subscribers: N.A.
Programming (via satellite): BBC America; Bloomberg Television; Discovery Digital Networks; Disney XD; ESPN Classic; ESPNews; FYI; Golf Channel; GSN; Hallmark Channel; History International; IFC; LMN; MC; Outdoor Channel; Sundance TV.

Pay Service 1
Pay Units: N.A.
Programming (via satellite): Cinemax; HBO; Showtime.
Fee: $8.00 monthly (Cinemax or Showtime), $9.00 monthly (HBO).

Digital Pay Service 1
Pay Units: N.A.
Programming (via satellite): Cinemax (multiplexed); HBO (multiplexed); Showtime (multiplexed); Starz (multiplexed); The Movie Channel (multiplexed).

Pay-Per-View
Playboy TV (delivered digitally); Fresh (delivered digitally); NBA TV (delivered digitally); ESPN Now (delivered digitally); iN DEMAND (delivered digitally); Special events, Addressable: No.

Internet Service
Operational: Yes.
Broadband Service: Suddenlink High Speed Internet.
Fee: $29.95 monthly.

Telephone Service
Digital: Operational
Miles of Plant: 53.0 (coaxial); None (fiber optic). Homes passed: 3,000.
Senior Vice President, Corporate Finance: Michael Pflantz. General Manager: Gary Bowman.
Ownership: Cequel Communications Holdings I LLC (MSO).

PORTLAND—Dean Hill Cable, PO Box 128, Parkdale, AR 71661. Phone: 870-473-2802. Fax: 870-737-0020. ICA: AR0323.
TV Market Ranking: Below 100 (PORTLAND). Franchise award date: N.A. Franchise expiration date: N.A. Began: September 1, 1981.
Channel capacity: N.A. Channels available but not in use: N.A.

Basic Service
Subscribers: N.A.
Programming (received off-air): KATV (ABC, Retro TV) Little Rock; KLTM-TV (PBS) Monroe; KNOE-TV (ABC, CBS, CW) Monroe; KTVE (NBC) El Dorado; WABG-TV (ABC, FOX) Greenwood.
Programming (via satellite): Disney Channel; ESPN; TBS; TNT; WGN America.
Fee: $35.00 installation.

Pay Service 1
Pay Units: N.A.
Programming (via satellite): HBO; Showtime; The Movie Channel.
Fee: $11.55 monthly (each).

Internet Service
Operational: No.

Telephone Service
None

General Manager: Dean Hill. Assistant Manager: Kathy Hill.
Ownership: Dean Hill Cable (MSO).

PRAIRIE GROVE—Cox Communications. Now served by SPRINGDALE, AR [AR0220]. ICA: AR0279.

RATCLIFF—Formerly served by Eagle Media. No longer in operation. ICA: AR0162.

RAVENDEN SPRINGS—Formerly served by Cebridge Connections. No longer in operation. ICA: AR0211.

RECTOR—NewWave Communications. Now served by DEXTER, MO [MO0039]. ICA: AR0081.

RISON—Cablevision of Rison, 1920 Hwy 425 North, Monticello, AR 71655-4463. Phones: 870-367-7300; 870-367-3166. Fax: 870-367-9770. E-mail: cccaccounts@ccc-cable.net. Web Site: http://ccc-cable.com. ICA: AR0150.
TV Market Ranking: 50 (RISON). Franchise award date: N.A. Franchise expiration date: N.A. Began: July 16, 1982.
Channel capacity: N.A. Channels available but not in use: N.A.

Basic Service
Subscribers: 52.
Programming (received off-air): KARK-TV (NBC) Little Rock; KASN (CW, The Country Network) Pine Bluff; KATV (ABC, Retro TV) Little Rock; KETS (PBS) Little Rock; KLRT-TV (FOX, This TV) Little Rock; KTHV (Antenna TV, CBS) Little Rock; KTVE (NBC) El Dorado; KVTN-DT (IND) Pine Bluff.
Programming (via satellite): A&E; AMC; BET; CMT; CNN; Discovery Channel; Disney Channel; ESPN; ESPN2; Freeform; FX; Lifetime; Nickelodeon; Outdoor Channel;

Arkansas—Cable Systems

QVC; Spike TV; Syfy; TBS; TLC; TNT; Trinity Broadcasting Network (TBN); TV Land; USA Network; VH1; WGN America.
Fee: $30.00 installation; $49.90 monthly.
Digital Basic Service
Subscribers: N.A.
Digital Pay Service 1
Pay Units: N.A.
Programming (via satellite): Cinemax; HBO; Showtime; Starz; Starz Encore.
Fee: $12.00 monthly (each).
Video-On-Demand: No
Internet Service
Operational: Yes.
Fee: $30.00 installation; $29.95 monthly.
Telephone Service
Digital: Operational
Fee: $29.95 monthly
Miles of Plant: 12.0 (coaxial); None (fiber optic). Homes passed: 350.
President: Bill Copeland.
Ownership: Community Communications Co. (MSO).

ROGERS—Cox Communications. Now served by SPRINGDALE, AR [AR0220]. ICA: AR0012.

ROYAL—Formerly served by Cablevision of Royal. No longer in operation. ICA: AR0125.

RUDY—Cox Communications. Now served by FORT SMITH, AR [AR0003]. ICA: AR0281.

RUSSELL—Formerly served by Indco Cable TV. No longer in operation. ICA: AR0212.

RUSSELLVILLE—Suddenlink Communications, PO Box 10010, Russellville, AR 72812. Phones: 888-592-3861; 314-315-9400; 479-968-2223; 800-582-9577. Fax: 479-968-2223. E-mail: Gene.Regan@suddenlink.com. Web Site: http://www.suddenlink.com. Also serves Dardanelle, Pope County (portions) & Pottsville. ICA: AR0014.
TV Market Ranking: Outside TV Markets (Dardanelle, Pope County (portions), Pottsville, RUSSELLVILLE). Franchise award date: N.A. Franchise expiration date: N.A. Began: September 1, 1964.
Channel capacity: 72 (operating 2-way). Channels available but not in use: N.A.
Basic Service
Subscribers: 7,904. Commercial subscribers: 806.
Programming (received off-air): KAFT (PBS) Fayetteville; KARK-TV (NBC) Little Rock; KARZ-TV (Bounce TV, MNT) Little Rock; KASN (CW, The Country Network) Pine Bluff; KATV (ABC, Retro TV) Little Rock; KFSM-TV (CBS, MNT) Fort Smith; KKAP (Daystar TV, ETV) Little Rock; KKYK-CD (IND, WeatherNation) Little Rock; KLRA-CD (UNV) Little Rock; KLRT-TV (FOX, This TV) Little Rock; KTHV (Antenna TV, CBS) Little Rock.
Programming (via satellite): C-SPAN; QVC; TBS; The Weather Channel; UniMas; WGN America.
Fee: $40.00 installation; $31.50 monthly.
Expanded Basic Service 1
Subscribers: N.A.
Programming (via satellite): A&E; AMC; Animal Planet; BET; Bravo; Cartoon Network; CMT; CNBC; CNN; Comedy Central; C-SPAN 2; Discovery Channel; Disney Channel; E! HD; ESPN; ESPN2; EWTN Global Catholic Network; Food Network; Fox News Channel; Fox Sports 1; FOX Sports Southwest; Freeform; FX; Great American Country; HGTV; History; HLN;

INSP; Jewelry Television; Lifetime; LMN; MSNBC; MTV; NBCSN; Nickelodeon; Outdoor Channel; Pop; Spike TV; Syfy; TLC; TNT; Travel Channel; Trinity Broadcasting Network (TBN); truTV; Turner Classic Movies; TV Land; Univision; USA Network; VH1.
Fee: $25.60 monthly.
Digital Basic Service
Subscribers: N.A.
Programming (via satellite): A&E HD; AXS TV; Bandamax; BBC America; Bloomberg Television; Boomerang; CBS Sports Network; Cine Mexicano; Cinelatino; CMT; CNN en Espanol; Cooking Channel; Cox Sports Television; De Pelicula; De Pelicula Clasico; Destination America; Discovery Kids Channel; Disney XD; DIY Network; Enlace USA; ESPN Classic; ESPN Deportes; ESPN HD; ESPNews; FamilyNet; Food Network HD; Fox Deportes; Fox Sports 2; FSN HD; Fuse; FYI; Golf Channel; GSN; Hallmark Channel; HD Theater; HGTV HD; History en Espanol; History International; IFC; Investigation Discovery; MC; MTV Classic; MTV Hits; MTV Live; MTV2; mtvU; Nat Geo WILD; National Geographic Channel; National Geographic Channel HD; NBC Universo; Nick Jr.; Nicktoons; NickToons en Espanol; OWN: Oprah Winfrey Network; Oxygen; Ritmoson; Science Channel; Starz Encore (multiplexed); Sundance TV; Sur; TeenNick; Telehit; Telemundo; Tennis Channel; TNT HD; Toon Disney en Espanol; Tr3s; TV One; ULTRA HD-Plex; Universal HD; Univision; UP; VideoRola; WE tv; Weatherscan.
Digital Pay Service 1
Pay Units: N.A.
Programming (via satellite): Cinemax (multiplexed); HBO (multiplexed); HBO HD; HBO Latino; Showtime (multiplexed); Showtime HD; Starz (multiplexed); The Movie Channel (multiplexed).
Fee: $10.95 monthly (each).
Video-On-Demand: Planned
Pay-Per-View
iN DEMAND (delivered digitally); Playboy TV (delivered digitally); Shorteez (delivered digitally); Fresh (delivered digitally); Club Jenna (delivered digitally); Spice: Xcess (delivered digitally).
Internet Service
Operational: Yes.
Subscribers: 12,447.
Broadband Service: Suddenlink High Speed Internet.
Fee: $29.95 monthly.
Telephone Service
Digital: Operational
Subscribers: 5,339.
Fee: $44.95 monthly
Miles of Plant: 1,291.0 (coaxial); 711.0 (fiber optic). Homes passed: 32,486.
Senior Vice President, Corporate Finance: Michael Pflantz. General Manager: Mike Ederington. Marketing Director: Kathy Wyrick. Chief Engineer: Wayne Ollis. Customer Service Manager: Jane Ollis.
Ownership: Cequel Communications Holdings I LLC (MSO).

SALEM—Salem Cable Vision, 206 South Main St, PO Box 57, Salem, AR 72576. Phones: 870-895-2121; 870-368-7870; 870-895-4993. Fax: 870-895-4905. Also serves Viola. ICA: AR0116.
TV Market Ranking: Outside TV Markets (SALEM, Viola). Franchise award date: N.A. Franchise expiration date: N.A. Began: January 1, 1965.
Channel capacity: N.A. Channels available but not in use: N.A.

Basic Service
Subscribers: 650.
Programming (received off-air): KAIT (ABC, NBC) Jonesboro; KARK-TV (NBC) Little Rock; KEMV (PBS) Mountain View; KOLR (CBS) Springfield; KOZL-TV (IND) Springfield; KTVT (CBS, Decades) Fort Worth; KYTV (CW, NBC, WeatherNation) Springfield.
Programming (via satellite): A&E; CMT; CNN; C-SPAN; Discovery Channel; Disney Channel; ESPN; Freeform; HLN; Lifetime; Nickelodeon; QVC; Spike TV; TBS; The Weather Channel; TLC; TNT; Trinity Broadcasting Network (TBN); USA Network; WGN America.
Fee: $25.00 installation; $32.75 monthly.
Pay Service 1
Pay Units: N.A.
Programming (via satellite): Cinemax; HBO.
Fee: $10.00 installation; $6.00 monthly (Cinemax), $7.50 monthly (HBO).
Video-On-Demand: No
Internet Service
Operational: No.
Telephone Service
None
Miles of Plant: 330.0 (coaxial); None (fiber optic). Homes passed: 700.
General Manager: Monty McCullough. Chief Technician: Mike Innis.
Ownership: Monty McCullough.

SALINE COUNTY (unincorporated areas)—Formerly served by Community Cablevision. No longer in operation. ICA: AR0083.

SCRANTON—Formerly served by Eagle Media. No longer in operation. ICA: AR0173.

SEARCY—White County Cable TV, 1927 West Beebe Capps Expy, PO Box 340, Searcy, AR 72145-0340. Phone: 501-268-4117. Fax: 501-268-1341. E-mail: whitecountycabletvcs@cablelynx.com. Web Site: http://www.whitecountycabletv.com. Also serves Bald Knob, Higginson, Judsonia & Kensett. ICA: AR0017.
TV Market Ranking: Outside TV Markets (Bald Knob, Judsonia, Kensett, SEARCY, Higginson). Franchise award date: N.A. Franchise expiration date: N.A. Began: October 1, 1979.
Channel capacity: N.A. Channels available but not in use: N.A.
Basic Service
Subscribers: 2,945. Commercial subscribers: 6.
Programming (received off-air): KAIT (ABC, NBC) Jonesboro; KARK-TV (NBC) Little Rock; KARZ-TV (Bounce TV, MNT) Little Rock; KASN (CW, The Country Network) Pine Bluff; KATV (ABC, Retro TV) Little Rock; KETS (PBS) Little Rock; KKAP (Daystar TV, ETV) Little Rock; KLRT-TV (FOX, This TV) Little Rock; KMYA-DT (MeTV, WeatherNation) Camden; KTHV (Antenna TV, CBS) Little Rock; KVTN-DT (IND) Pine Bluff; 1 FM.
Programming (via satellite): A&E; AMC; Animal Planet; BET; Cartoon Network; CMT; CNBC; CNN; C-SPAN; C-SPAN 2; Discovery Channel; Disney Channel; ESPN; ESPN2; EVINE Live; Food Network; Fox News Channel; FOX Sports Southwest; Freeform; FX; Hallmark Channel; HGTV; History; HLN; Lifetime; MSNBC; MTV; Nickelodeon; Pop; Spike TV; Syfy; TBS; The Weather Channel; TLC; TNT; Trinity Broadcasting Network (TBN); truTV; Turner Classic Movies;

TV Land; Univision Studios; USA Network; VH1; WGN America.
Fee: $49.95 installation; $67.95 monthly.
Digital Basic Service
Subscribers: N.A.
Programming (via satellite): BBC America; CMT; Destination America; Discovery Kids Channel; Discovery Life Channel; Disney XD; DMX Music; ESPNews; Fox Sports 1; FSN Digital Atlantic; FSN Digital Central; FSN Digital Pacific; FYI; Golf Channel; Great American Country; GSN; History International; Investigation Discovery; LMN; MTV Classic; MTV Hits; MTV Jams; MTV2; National Geographic Channel; Nick 2; Nick Jr.; Nicktoons; Outdoor Channel; OWN: Oprah Winfrey Network; Science Channel; TeenNick; Tr3s; VH1 Soul; WE tv.
Digital Pay Service 1
Pay Units: N.A.
Programming (via satellite): Cinemax (multiplexed); HBO (multiplexed); Starz (multiplexed); Starz Encore (multiplexed).
Fee: $12.95 monthly (Cinemax, HBO or Starz/Encore).
Video-On-Demand: No
Pay-Per-View
iN DEMAND (delivered digitally).
Internet Service
Operational: Yes. Began: April 1, 2001.
Broadband Service: Cablelynx.
Fee: $24.95-$44.95 monthly; $10.00 modem lease.
Telephone Service
Digital: Operational
Fee: $45.70 monthly
Miles of Plant: 452.0 (coaxial); 239.0 (fiber optic). Homes passed: 15,931.
Vice President, Administration: Charlotte A. Dial. Area Manager: Tony Allen. Marketing & Program Director: Lori Haight. Plant Manager: Tyson Sergent. Office Manager: Christian Young.
Ownership: WEHCO Video Inc. (MSO).

SEDGWICK—Formerly served by Cebridge Connections. No longer in operation. ICA: AR0202.

SHERIDAN—Formerly served by Zoom Media. No longer in operation. ICA: AR0051.

SIDNEY—Formerly served by Indco Cable TV. No longer in operation. ICA: AR0320.

SILOAM SPRINGS—Cox Communications. Now served by SPRINGDALE, AR [AR0220]. ICA: AR0283.

SMACKOVER—Formerly served by Zoom Media. No longer in operation. ICA: AR0069.

SONORA—Cox Communications. Now served by SPRINGDALE, AR [AR0220]. ICA: AR0117.

SPRINGDALE—Cox Communications, 6205 Peachtree Dunwoody Rd, 12th Floor, Atlanta, GA 30328. Phones: 800-822-4433; 404-269-6590. Web Site: http://www.cox.com. Also serves Avoca, Beaver Lake, Beaver Shores, Beaverama, Bella Vista, Benton County, Bentonville, Bethel Heights Twp., Cave Springs, Centerton, Crawford County (unincorporated areas), Decatur, Elkins, Elm Springs, Farmington, Fayetteville, Gentry, Goshen, Gravette, Greenland, Johnson, Lincoln, Little Flock, Lowell, Pea Ridge, Prairie Creek, Prairie Grove, Rogers, Siloam Springs, Sonora, Tontitown, Washington County, West Fork & Winslow. ICA: AR0220.

Cable Systems—Arkansas

TV Market Ranking: Below 100 (Avoca, Avoca, Beaver Lake, Beaver Shores, Beaverama, Bella Vista, Benton County, Bentonville, Bethel Heights Twp., Cave Springs, Centerton, Crawford County (unincorporated areas), Decatur, Elkins, Elm Springs, Farmington, Fayetteville, Gentry, Goshen, Gravette, Greenland, Johnson, Lincoln, Little Flock, Lowell, Pea Ridge, Prairie Creek, Prairie Grove, Rogers, Sonora, SPRINGDALE, Tontitown, Washington County, West Fork, Winslow, Siloam Springs). Franchise award date: N.A. Franchise expiration date: N.A. Began: January 1, 1962.
Channel capacity: 65 (operating 2-way). Channels available but not in use: N.A.

Basic Service
Subscribers: 63,670.
Programming (received off-air): KAFT (PBS) Fayetteville; KARK-TV (NBC) Little Rock; KFSM-TV (CBS, MNT) Fort Smith; KHOG-TV (ABC, CW) Fayetteville; KNWA-TV (FOX, NBC) Rogers; KOLR (CBS) Springfield; KSNF (NBC) Joplin; KTUL (ABC, Antenna TV, Retro TV) Tulsa; KWOG (IND) Springdale; allband FM.
Programming (via satellite): C-SPAN; ESPN; ION Television; Pop; TBS; WGN America.
Fee: $35.00 installation; $21.99 monthly.

Digital Basic Service
Subscribers: N.A.
Programming (via satellite): BBC America; Discovery Digital Networks; Disney XD; DMX Music; ESPN Classic; ESPNews; Fox Sports 1; GSN; LMN; NBCSN; WE tv.

Digital Pay Service 1
Pay Units: N.A.
Programming (via satellite): Brazzers TV; Cinemax (multiplexed); HBO (multiplexed); Showtime (multiplexed); The Movie Channel (multiplexed).
Fee: $11.95 monthly (each).

Video-On-Demand: No

Pay-Per-View
iN DEMAND.

Internet Service
Operational: Yes.
Subscribers: 90,629.
Broadband Service: Cox High Speed Internet.
Fee: $24.95 installation; $19.99-$59.99 monthly; $10.00 modem lease.

Telephone Service
Digital: Operational
Subscribers: 42,827.
Miles of Plant: 8,394.0 (coaxial); 1,630.0 (fiber optic). Homes passed: 273,487.
Vice President & General Manager: Kimberly Edmunds. Vice President, Operations: Nelson Mower. Vice President, Marketing: Tony Matthews. Vice President, Tax: Mary Vickers. Marketing Director: Tina Gabbard. Community Relations Manager: Kelly Zaga.
Ownership: Cox Communications Inc.

STAR CITY—Formerly served by Cablevision of Star City. No longer in operation. ICA: AR0086.

STEPHENS—Formerly served by Zoom Media. No longer in operation. ICA: AR0106.

STRONG—Bayou Cable TV, 378 Main St, Marion, LA 71260. Phone: 318-292-4774. Fax: 318-292-4775. E-mail: admin@bayoucable.com. Web Site: http://www2.bayoucable.com. ICA: AR0324.
Channel capacity: N.A. Channels available but not in use: N.A.

Basic Service
Subscribers: 113.
Programming (received off-air): KARD (Bounce TV, FOX) West Monroe; KATV (ABC, Retro TV) Little Rock; KLTM-TV (PBS) Monroe; KMLU (MeTV) Columbia; KNOE-TV (ABC, CBS, CW) Monroe; KTVE (NBC) El Dorado.
Programming (via satellite): AMC; Hallmark Channel; Trinity Broadcasting Network (TBN); TV Land.
Fee: $25.00 installation; $54.99 monthly.

Expanded Basic Service 1
Subscribers: N.A.
Programming (via satellite): A&E; Animal Planet; BET; CMT; CNN; Discovery Channel; ESPN; ESPN2; Food Network; Fox News Channel; Fox Sports 1; Freeform; FX; History; ION Television; Lifetime; MTV; National Geographic Channel; Nickelodeon; Outdoor Channel; Spike TV; TBS; The Weather Channel; TLC; TNT; USA Network; VH1; WGN America.
Fee: $20.00 monthly.

Pay Service 1
Pay Units: 11.
Programming (via satellite): HBO.
Fee: $10.95 monthly.

Pay Service 2
Pay Units: 16.
Programming (via satellite): Cinemax.
Fee: $8.95 monthly.

Internet Service
Operational: No.

Telephone Service
None
Miles of Plant: 8.0 (coaxial); None (fiber optic).
President & General Manager: Allen C. Booker. Chief Technician: Mark Andrews.
Ownership: Bayou Cable TV (MSO).

STUTTGART—Suddenlink Communications, 520 Maryville Centre Dr, Ste 300, St. Louis, MO 63141. Phones: 314-315-9400; 888-822-5151. E-mail: Gene.Regan@suddenlink.com. Web Site: http://www.suddenlink.com. ICA: AR0027.
TV Market Ranking: 50 (STUTTGART). Franchise award date: March 29, 1972. Franchise expiration date: N.A. Began: October 1, 1973.
Channel capacity: 78 (operating 2-way). Channels available but not in use: N.A.

Basic Service
Subscribers: 1,250.
Programming (received off-air): KARK-TV (NBC) Little Rock; KARZ-TV (Bounce TV, MNT) Little Rock; KASN (CW, The Country Network) Pine Bluff; KATV (ABC, Retro TV) Little Rock; KETS (PBS) Little Rock; KKAP (Daystar TV, ETV) Little Rock; KLRT-TV (FOX, This TV) Little Rock; KTHV (Antenna TV, CBS) Little Rock; KVTN-DT (IND) Pine Bluff; allband FM.
Programming (via satellite): WGN America.
Fee: $28.45 monthly.

Expanded Basic Service 1
Subscribers: N.A.
Programming (via satellite): A&E; AMC; Animal Planet; BET; Bravo; Cartoon Network; CNBC; CNN; Comedy Central; C-SPAN; Discovery Channel; Disney Channel; E! HD; ESPN; ESPN2; Food Network; Fox News Channel; Fox Sports 1; FOX Sports Southwest; Freeform; FX; Golf Channel; Great American Country; Hallmark Channel; HGTV; History; HLN; Jewelry Television; Lifetime; MSNBC; MTV; National Geographic Channel; Nickelodeon; Outdoor Channel; Pop; QVC; Spike TV; Syfy; TBS; The Weather Channel; TLC; TNT; Travel Channel; Turner Classic Movies; TV Land; USA Network; VH1.
Fee: $24.00 monthly.

Digital Basic Service
Subscribers: N.A.
Programming (via satellite): BBC America; Bloomberg Television; Cloo; CMT; Destination America; Discovery Kids Channel; Disney XD; DMX Music; ESPN Classic; ESPNews; Fuse; FYI; GSN; History International; IFC; Investigation Discovery; LMN; MTV Classic; MTV Hits; MTV2; NBCSN; Nick Jr.; Nicktoons; OWN: Oprah Winfrey Network; Science Channel; Sundance TV; TeenNick; Trinity Broadcasting Network (TBN); VH1 Soul; WE tv.

Pay Service 1
Pay Units: N.A.
Programming (via satellite): HBO; Showtime; The Movie Channel.
Fee: $5.95 monthly (TMC), $9.95 monthly (Showtime), $10.95 monthly (HBO).

Digital Pay Service 1
Pay Units: N.A.
Programming (via satellite): Cinemax (multiplexed); HBO (multiplexed); Showtime (multiplexed); Starz (multiplexed); Starz Encore (multiplexed); The Movie Channel (multiplexed).

Pay-Per-View
iN DEMAND (delivered digitally); Playboy TV (delivered digitally); Club Jenna (delivered digitally); Fresh (delivered digitally); Spice: Xcess (delivered digitally).

Internet Service
Operational: Yes. Began: June 23, 2002.
Broadband Service: Suddenlink High Speed Internet.
Fee: $29.95 monthly; $9.95 modem lease.

Telephone Service
Digital: Operational
Fee: $44.95 monthly
Miles of Plant: 66.0 (coaxial); None (fiber optic). Homes passed: 3,445.
Senior Vice President, Corporate Finance: Michael Pflantz. Regional Manager: Todd Cruthird. General Manager: Dave Walker. Marketing Director: Beverly Gambell. Chief Technician: Carl Miller.
Ownership: Cequel Communications Holdings I LLC (MSO).

SUBIACO—Formerly served by Eagle Media. No longer in operation. ICA: AR0187.

TAYLOR—Formerly served by Cebridge Connections. No longer in operation. ICA: AR0168.

THORNTON—Formerly served by Almega Cable. No longer in operation. ICA: AR0171.

TILLAR—Cablevision of Tillar Reed, 1920 Hwy 425 North, Monticello, AR 71655-4463. Phones: 870-367-7300; 870-367-3166. Fax: 870-367-9770. E-mail: cccaccounts@ccc-cable.net. Web Site: http://ccc-cable.com. Also serves Reed. ICA: AR0169.
TV Market Ranking: Below 100 (TILLAR, Reed). Franchise award date: N.A. Franchise expiration date: N.A. Began: January 1, 1980.
Channel capacity: N.A. Channels available but not in use: N.A.

Basic Service
Subscribers: 43.
Programming (received off-air): KASN (CW, The Country Network) Pine Bluff; KATV (ABC, Retro TV) Little Rock; KETS (PBS) Little Rock; KLRT-TV (FOX, This TV) Little Rock; KTHV (Antenna TV, CBS) Little Rock; KTVE (NBC) El Dorado; WXVT (CBS) Greenville.
Programming (via satellite): A&E; AMC; BET; CMT; CNN; Discovery Channel; ESPN; ESPN2; Freeform; FX; Lifetime; Nickelodeon; Outdoor Channel; QVC; Spike TV; Syfy; TBS; TLC; TNT; Trinity Broadcasting Network (TBN); TV Land; USA Network; VH1; WGN America.
Fee: $30.00 installation; $49.90 monthly.

Digital Basic Service
Subscribers: N.A.

Digital Pay Service 1
Pay Units: N.A.
Programming (via satellite): Cinemax; HBO; Showtime; Starz; Starz Encore.
Fee: $12.00 monthly (each).

Video-On-Demand: No

Internet Service
Operational: Yes.
Fee: $30.00 installation; $29.95 monthly.

Telephone Service
Digital: Operational
Fee: $29.95 monthly
Miles of Plant: 30.0 (coaxial); None (fiber optic). Homes passed: 250.
President: Bill Copeland.
Ownership: Community Communications Co. (MSO).

TONTITOWN—Cox Communications. Now served by SPRINGDALE, AR [AR0220]. ICA: AR0074.

TRASKWOOD—Formerly served by Cebridge Connections. No longer in operation. ICA: AR0190.

TRUMANN—Ritter Communications. Now served by MARKED TREE, AR [AR0072]. ICA: AR0025.

TUMBLING SHOALS—Indco Cable TV, 2700 North Saint Louis, PO Box 3799, Batesville, AR 72503-3799. Phones: 800-364-0831; 870-793-4175; 870-793-4174. Fax: 870-793-7439. Web Site: http://www.indco.net. ICA: AR0286.
TV Market Ranking: Outside TV Markets (TUMBLING SHOALS). Franchise award date: N.A. Franchise expiration date: N.A. Began: August 1, 1990.
Channel capacity: N.A. Channels available but not in use: N.A.

Basic Service
Subscribers: 70.
Programming (received off-air): KAIT (ABC, NBC) Jonesboro; KARK-TV (NBC) Little Rock; KATV (ABC, Retro TV) Little Rock; KEMV (PBS) Mountain View; KLRT-TV (FOX, This TV) Little Rock; KMYA-DT

Arkansas—Cable Systems

(MeTV, WeatherNation) Camden; KTHV (Antenna TV, CBS) Little Rock.
Programming (via satellite): CNN; Discovery Channel; Disney Channel; ESPN; ESPN2; FOX Sports Southwest; Freeform; FX; HGTV; History; Nickelodeon; Outdoor Channel; QVC; Spike TV; Syfy; TBS; The Weather Channel; TNT; Trinity Broadcasting Network (TBN); Turner Classic Movies; USA Network; WGN America.
Fee: $40.00 installation; $63.95 monthly.
Pay Service 1
Pay Units: 6.
Programming (via satellite): Cinemax.
Fee: $8.00 monthly.
Pay Service 2
Pay Units: 8.
Programming (via satellite): HBO.
Fee: $10.00 monthly.
Video-On-Demand: Planned
Internet Service
Operational: Yes.
Fee: $29.95 monthly.
Telephone Service
None
President & General Manager: J.D. Pierce. Chief Technician: Tommy Barnett. Marketing Director: Connie Barnett.
Ownership: Indco Cable TV (MSO).

TUPELO—Formerly served by Indco Cable TV. No longer in operation. ICA: AR0209.

TURRELL—Ritter Communications. Now served by MARKED TREE, AR [AR0072]. ICA: AR0144.

VAN BUREN—Cox Communications. Now served by FORT SMITH, AR [AR0003]. ICA: AR0287.

VILONIA—Formerly served by Cobridge Communications. No longer in operation. ICA: AR0099.

VIOLA—Salem Cable Vision. Now served by SALEM, AR [AR0116]. ICA: AR0195.

WALDRON—Suddenlink Communications, 520 Maryville Centre Dr, Ste 300, St. Louis, MO 63141. Phones: 314-315-9400; 888-822-5151. E-mail: Gene.Regan@suddenlink.com. Web Site: http://www.suddenlink.com. ICA: AR0078.
TV Market Ranking: Outside TV Markets (WALDRON). Franchise award date: January 1, 1967. Franchise expiration date: N.A. Began: August 1, 1967.
Channel capacity: N.A. Channels available but not in use: N.A.
Basic Service
Subscribers: 266.
Programming (received off-air): KAFT (PBS) Fayetteville; KFSM-TV (CBS, MNT) Fort Smith; KFTA-TV (FOX, NBC) Fort Smith; KHBS (ABC, CW) Fort Smith; KNWA-TV (FOX, NBC) Rogers; KTUL (ABC, Antenna TV, Retro TV) Tulsa; allband FM.
Programming (via satellite): C-SPAN; National Geographic Channel; QVC; Trinity Broadcasting Network (TBN).
Fee: $28.45 monthly.
Expanded Basic Service 1
Subscribers: N.A.
Programming (via satellite): A&E; AMC; Animal Planet; Cartoon Network; CNBC; CNN; Comedy Central; CW PLUS; Discovery Channel; Disney Channel; E! HD; ESPN; ESPN2; Food Network; Fox News Channel; FOX Sports Southwest; Freeform; FX; Great American Country; Hallmark Channel; HGTV; History; HLN; Jewelry Televi-

sion; Lifetime; MSNBC; MTV; Nickelodeon; Outdoor Channel; Spike TV; Syfy; TBS; The Weather Channel; TLC; TNT; Turner Classic Movies; TV Land; Univision Studios; USA Network; VH1.
Fee: $19.95 monthly.
Digital Basic Service
Subscribers: N.A.
Programming (via satellite): BBC America; Bloomberg Television; Cloo; Destination America; Discovery Kids Channel; DMX Music; ESPN Classic; ESPNews; EVINE Live; FOX College Sports Central; FOX College Sports Pacific; Fox Sports 1; Fuse; FYI; Golf Channel; GSN; History International; IFC; Investigation Discovery; NBCSN; OWN; Oprah Winfrey Network; Science Channel; Sundance TV; WE tv.
Pay Service 1
Pay Units: N.A.
Programming (via satellite): HBO; Showtime; The Movie Channel.
Fee: $5.95 monthly (TMC), $9.95 monthly (Showtime), $10.95 monthly (HBO).
Digital Pay Service 1
Pay Units: N.A.
Programming (via satellite): Cinemax (multiplexed); Flix; HBO (multiplexed); Showtime (multiplexed); Starz (multiplexed); Starz Encore (multiplexed); The Movie Channel (multiplexed).
Video-On-Demand: No
Pay-Per-View
iN DEMAND (delivered digitally); Playboy TV (delivered digitally); Fresh (delivered digitally); Club Jenna (delivered digitally); Spice: Xcess (delivered digitally).
Internet Service
Operational: Yes. Began: March 24, 2004. Broadband Service: Suddenlink High Speed Internet.
Fee: $29.95 monthly.
Telephone Service
Digital: Operational
Fee: $44.95 monthly
Miles of Plant: 23.0 (coaxial); None (fiber optic). Homes passed: 1,378.
Vice President, Corporate Finance: Michael Pflantz. Regional Manager: Todd Cruthird. General Manager: Dave Walker. Marketing Director: Beverly Gambell. Chief Technician: Carl Miller.
Ownership: Cequel Communications Holdings I LLC (MSO).

WARREN—Cablevision of Warren, 1920 Hwy 425 North, Monticello, AR 71655-4463. Phones: 870-367-7300; 870-367-3166. Fax: 870-367-9770. E-mail: cccaccounts@ccc-cable.net. Web Site: http://ccc-cable.com. Also serves Bradley County. ICA: AR0041.
TV Market Ranking: 99 (Bradley County (portions)); Outside TV Markets (WARREN, Bradley County (portions)). Franchise award date: N.A. Franchise expiration date: N.A. Began: December 1, 1974.
Channel capacity: N.A. Channels available but not in use: N.A.
Basic Service
Subscribers: 600.
Programming (received off-air): KARK-TV (NBC) Little Rock; KARZ-TV (Bounce TV, MNT) Little Rock; KASN (CW, The Country Network) Pine Bluff; KATV (ABC, Retro TV) Little Rock; KETS (PBS) Little Rock; KLRT-TV (FOX, This TV) Little Rock; KMYA-DT (MeTV, WeatherNation) Camden; KTHV (Antenna TV, CBS) Little Rock; KTVE (NBC) El Dorado.
Programming (via satellite): A&E; Animal Planet; BET; CMT; CNBC; CNN; Comedy Central; C-SPAN; Discovery Channel;

Disney Channel; E! HD; ESPN; ESPN2; ESPNews; Fox News Channel; Fox Sports 1; FOX Sports Southwest; Freeform; FX; History; HLN; Lifetime; MTV; National Geographic Channel; NBCSN; Nickelodeon; Outdoor Channel; Pop; QVC; Spike TV; Syfy; TBS; The Weather Channel; TLC; TNT; Travel Channel; Trinity Broadcasting Network (TBN); Turner Classic Movies; TV Land; Univision; USA Network; VH1; WGN America.
Fee: $30.00 installation; $18.95 monthly.
Digital Basic Service
Subscribers: N.A.
Digital Pay Service 1
Pay Units: N.A.
Programming (via satellite): Cinemax; HBO; Showtime; Starz; Starz Encore.
Fee: $12.00 monthly (each).
Video-On-Demand: No
Internet Service
Operational: Yes.
Fee: $30.00 installation; $29.95 monthly.
Telephone Service
Digital: Operational
Fee: $29.95 monthly
Miles of Plant: 75.0 (coaxial); None (fiber optic). Homes passed: 3,127.
President: Bill Copeland.
Ownership: Community Communications Co. (MSO).

WATSON—Formerly served by Cablevision of Watson. No longer in operation. ICA: AR0198.

WEST FORK—Cox Communications. Now served by SPRINGDALE, AR [AR0220]. ICA: AR0290.

WEST PULASKI (portions)—Fidelity Communications, 64 North Clark St, Sullivan, MO 63080. Phones: 800-392-8070; 501-859-0384 (Maumelle office); 501-315-4405 (Benton office); 855-262-7434. E-mail: fidelityinfo@fidelitycommunications.com. Web Site: http://www.fidelitycommunications.com. ICA: AR0048.
TV Market Ranking: 50 (WEST PULASKI (PORTIONS)).
Channel capacity: N.A. Channels available but not in use: N.A.
Basic Service
Subscribers: 66.
Programming (received off-air): KARK-TV (NBC) Little Rock; KARZ-TV (Bounce TV, MNT) Little Rock; KASN (CW, The Country Network) Pine Bluff; KATV (ABC, Retro TV) Little Rock; KETS (PBS) Little Rock; KLRT-TV (FOX, This TV) Little Rock; KTHV (Antenna TV, CBS) Little Rock; KVTN-DT (IND) Pine Bluff.
Programming (via satellite): A&E; AMC; Bravo; CMT; CNN; Comedy Central; C-SPAN; Discovery Channel; Disney Channel; ESPN; FOX Sports Southwest; Freeform; Lifetime; MTV; Nickelodeon; QVC; Spike TV; Syfy; TBS; TLC; TNT; USA Network; VH1; WGN America.
Fee: $29.99 installation; $30.74 monthly.
Expanded Basic Service 1
Subscribers: N.A.
Programming (via satellite): E! HD; HLN.
Pay Service 1
Pay Units: N.A.
Programming (via satellite): HBO; Showtime; Starz.
Fee: $14.00 monthly (each).
Video-On-Demand: No
Pay-Per-View
ESPN Now (delivered digitally); Hot Choice (delivered digitally); iN DEMAND; iN DE-

MAND (delivered digitally); Playboy TV (delivered digitally); Fresh (delivered digitally); Shorteez (delivered digitally); Urban Xtra (delivered digitally).
Internet Service
Operational: No.
Telephone Service
None
Miles of Plant: 94.0 (coaxial); None (fiber optic). Homes passed: 1,907.
General Manager, AR/MO/LA/TX: Andy Davis.
Ownership: Fidelity Communications Co. (MSO).

WESTERN GROVE—Ritter Communications, 2400 Ritter Dr, Jonesboro, AR 72401. Phones: 888-336-4466; 870-336-3400. E-mail: customerservice@rittermail.com. Web Site: http://rittercommunications.com. Also serves Alpena, Everton & Jasper. ICA: AR0183.
TV Market Ranking: Below 100 (Alpena, Everton, Jasper, WESTERN GROVE). Franchise award date: N.A. Franchise expiration date: N.A. Began: October 1, 1983.
Channel capacity: N.A. Channels available but not in use: N.A.
Basic Service
Subscribers: 355.
Programming (received off-air): KARK-TV (NBC) Little Rock; KATV (ABC, Retro TV) Little Rock; KEMV (PBS) Mountain View; KHOG-TV (ABC, CW) Fayetteville; KOLR (CBS) Springfield; KOZL-TV (IND) Springfield; KSPR (ABC) Springfield; KTHV (Antenna TV, CBS) Little Rock; KTKO-LP Harrison; KWBM (Retro TV) Harrison; KYTV (CW, NBC, WeatherNation) Springfield.
Programming (via satellite): C-SPAN; CW PLUS; Trinity Broadcasting Network (TBN).
Fee: $39.95 installation; $24.48 monthly.
Expanded Basic Service 1
Subscribers: N.A.
Programming (via satellite): A&E; AMC; Animal Planet; CNN; Comedy Central; Discovery Channel; Disney Channel; ESPN; ESPN2; Food Network; Freeform; Great American Country; HGTV; History; HLN; Lifetime; LMN; National Geographic Channel; Nickelodeon; Outdoor Channel; Spike TV; TBS; The Weather Channel; TLC; TNT; Travel Channel; Turner Classic Movies; TV Land; USA Network.
Fee: $23.00 monthly.
Pay Service 1
Pay Units: 12.
Programming (via satellite): HBO.
Fee: $11.95 monthly.
Pay Service 2
Pay Units: 4.
Programming (via satellite): The Movie Channel.
Fee: $11.95 monthly.
Video-On-Demand: No
Internet Service
Operational: Yes, DSL.
Telephone Service
Digital: Operational
Miles of Plant: 97.0 (coaxial); None (fiber optic). Homes passed: 888.
President: Paul Waits. Vice President: John D. Strode. Vice President, Customer Care: Shanna French. General Manager: Bob Mouser. Marketing Director: Jane Marie Woodruff. Chief Technician: Joe Sain.
Ownership: Ritter Communications (MSO).

WHEATLEY—Formerly served by Almega Cable. No longer in operation. ICA: AR0298.

WHITEHALL—Suddenlink Communications, 520 Maryville Centre Dr, Ste 300, St. Louis, MO 63141. Phones: 314-315-9400; 888-

Cable Systems—Arkansas

822-5151. Web Site: http://www.suddenlink.com. Also serves Grant County (portions), Hardin, Jefferson County (portions), Pine Bluff Arsenal & Redfield. ICA: AR0042.
TV Market Ranking: 50 (Grant County (portions), Hardin, Jefferson County (portions), Pine Bluff Arsenal, Redfield, WHITEHALL).
Channel capacity: 36 (operating 2-way). Channels available but not in use: N.A.

Basic Service
Subscribers: 941. Commercial subscribers: 33.
Programming (received off-air): KARK-TV (NBC) Little Rock; KARZ-TV (Bounce TV, MNT) Little Rock; KASN (CW, The Country Network) Pine Bluff; KATV (ABC, Retro TV) Little Rock; KETS (PBS) Little Rock; KLRT-TV (FOX, This TV) Little Rock; KMYA-DT (MeTV, WeatherNation) Camden; KTHV (Antenna TV, CBS) Little Rock; KVTN-DT (IND) Pine Bluff.
Fee: $28.45 monthly.

Expanded Basic Service 1
Subscribers: N.A.
Programming (via satellite): A&E; AMC; Animal Planet; BET; Cartoon Network; CNBC; CNN; Comedy Central; Discovery Channel; Disney Channel; E! HD; ESPN; ESPN2; Food Network; Fox News Channel; FOX Sports Southwest; Freeform; Great American Country; HGTV; History; HLN; Lifetime; MTV; National Geographic Channel; Nickelodeon; Outdoor Channel; Spike TV; Syfy; TBS; The Weather Channel; TLC; TNT; Turner Classic Movies; TV Land; USA Network.
Fee: $24.00 monthly.

Digital Basic Service
Subscribers: N.A.
Programming (via satellite): BBC America; Bloomberg Television; Discovery Digital Networks; Disney XD; ESPN Classic; ESPNews; EVINE Live; FOX College Sports Central; FOX College Sports Pacific; Fox Sports 1; Fuse; FYI; Golf Channel; GSN; History International; IFC; NBCSN; Sundance TV; Trinity Broadcasting Network (TBN); WE tv.

Digital Expanded Basic Service
Subscribers: N.A.
Programming (via satellite): DMX Music.

Pay Service 1
Pay Units: N.A.
Programming (via satellite): Cinemax; HBO; Showtime.
Fee: $9.00 monthly (Cinemax), $10.95 monthly (HBO or Showtime).

Digital Pay Service 1
Pay Units: N.A.
Programming (via satellite): Cinemax (multiplexed); Flix (multiplexed); HBO (multiplexed); Showtime (multiplexed); Starz (multiplexed); Starz Encore (multiplexed); The Movie Channel (multiplexed).

Video-On-Demand: No

Pay-Per-View
Fresh (delivered digitally); Fresh (delivered digitally); Playboy TV (delivered digitally); iN DEMAND (delivered digitally).

Internet Service
Operational: Yes. Began: November 22, 2002.
Broadband Service: Suddenlink High Speed Internet.
Fee: $29.95 monthly.

Telephone Service
Digital: Operational
Fee: $44.95 monthly
Miles of Plant: 127.0 (coaxial); None (fiber optic). Homes passed: 4,375.
Senior Vice President, Corporate Finance: Michael Pflantz. Regional Manager: Todd Cruthird. Area Manager: Carolyn Wilder. Plant Manager: Donnie Burton.
Ownership: Cequel Communications Holdings I LLC (MSO).

WILMAR—Formerly served by Almega Cable. No longer in operation. ICA: AR0164.

WILMOT—Dean Hill Cable, PO Box 128, Parkdale, AR 71661. Phone: 870-473-2802. Fax: 870-737-0020. Also serves Parkdale. ICA: AR0129.
TV Market Ranking: Below 100 (Parkdale); Outside TV Markets (WILMOT). Franchise award date: N.A. Franchise expiration date: N.A. Began: September 1, 1981.
Channel capacity: N.A. Channels available but not in use: N.A.

Basic Service
Subscribers: N.A.
Programming (received off-air): KATV (ABC, Retro TV) Little Rock; KLTM-TV (PBS) Monroe; KNOE-TV (ABC, CBS, CW) Monroe; KTVE (NBC) El Dorado; WABG-TV (ABC, FOX) Greenwood.
Programming (via satellite): Disney Channel; ESPN; TBS; TNT; WGN America.
Fee: $35.00 installation.

Pay Service 1
Pay Units: N.A.
Programming (via satellite): HBO.
Fee: $11.55 monthly.

Video-On-Demand: No

Internet Service
Operational: No.

Telephone Service
None
Miles of Plant: 19.0 (coaxial); None (fiber optic).
General Manager: Dean Hill. Assistant Manager: Kathy Hill.
Ownership: Dean Hill Cable (MSO).

WINSLOW—Cox Communications. Now served by SPRINGDALE, AR [AR0220]. ICA: AR0291.

WITCHERVILLE—Formerly served by Eagle Media. No longer in operation. ICA: AR0311.

YELLVILLE—Yelcot Communications, 225 North Mill St, Yellville, AR 72687. Phones: 800-354-3360; 870-449-4211. Web Site: http://www.yelcot.com. Also serves Marion County & Summit. ICA: AR0292.
TV Market Ranking: Below 100 (Marion County (portions), Summit, YELLVILLE); Outside TV Markets (Marion County (portions)). Franchise award date: September 1, 1991. Franchise expiration date: N.A. Began: August 1, 1961.
Channel capacity: N.A. Channels available but not in use: N.A.

Basic Service
Subscribers: 309.
Programming (received off-air): KARK-TV (NBC) Little Rock; KATV (ABC, Retro TV) Little Rock; KEMV (PBS) Mountain View; KOLR (CBS) Springfield; KOZL-TV (IND) Springfield; KSPR (ABC) Springfield; KTHV (Antenna TV, CBS) Little Rock; KWBM (Retro TV) Harrison; KYTV (CW, NBC, WeatherNation) Springfield.
Programming (via satellite): A&E; CMT; CNBC; CNN; C-SPAN; Discovery Channel; Disney Channel; ESPN; ESPN2; Freeform; FX; HGTV; History; Nickelodeon; Outdoor Channel; QVC; Spike TV; Syfy; TBS; The Weather Channel; TNT; Travel Channel; Trinity Broadcasting Network (TBN); USA Network; WGN America.
Fee: $20.00 installation; $49.95 monthly.

Pay Service 1
Pay Units: 9.
Programming (via satellite): Cinemax.
Fee: $8.00 monthly.

Pay Service 2
Pay Units: 15.
Programming (via satellite): HBO.
Fee: $10.00 monthly.

Video-On-Demand: Planned

Internet Service
Operational: Yes.
Fee: $29.95 monthly.

Telephone Service
Digital: Operational
Fee: $15.60 monthly
Miles of Plant: 26.0 (coaxial); None (fiber optic).
Ownership: Yelcot Communications (MSO).

Access the most current data instantly
FREE TRIAL @ ADVANCED TVFactbook
TELCO/IPTV • CABLE TV • TV STATIONS
www.warren-news.com/factbook.htm

CALIFORNIA

Total Systems: 104	Communities with Applications: 0
Total Communities Served: 922	Number of Basic Subscribers: 4,530,056
Franchises Not Yet Operating: 0	Number of Expanded Basic Subscribers: 0
Applications Pending: 0	Number of Pay Units: 122,239

Top 100 Markets Represented: Sacramento-Stockton-Modesto (25); Los Angeles-San Bernardino-Corona-Riverside-Anaheim (2); San Diego (51); Fresno-Visalia-Hanford-Clovis-Merced-Porterville (72); San Francisco-Oakland-San Jose (7).

For a list of cable communities in this section, see the Cable Community Index located in the back of Cable Volume 2.
For explanation of terms used in cable system listings, see p. D-11.

ADOBE WELLS MOBILE HOME PARK—Formerly served by Comcast Cable. No longer in operation. ICA: CA0305.

AGOURA HILLS—Time Warner Cable. Now served by LOS ANGELES, CA [CA0009]. ICA: CA0024.

ALAMEDA—Comcast Cable. Now served by SAN FRANCISCO, CA [CA0003]. ICA: CA0080.

ALAMEDA—Formerly served by Alameda Power & Telecom. Now served by Comcast Cable, SAN FRANCISCO, CA [CA0003]. ICA: CA0454.

ALTURAS—Charter Communications, 12405 Powerscourt Dr, St. Louis, MO 63131. Phones: 636-207-5100 (Corporate office); 805-544-1962. Fax: 805-541-6042. Web Site: http://www.charter.com. Also serves Modoc County (portions). ICA: CA0230.
TV Market Ranking: Outside TV Markets (ALTURAS, Modoc County (portions)). Franchise award date: N.A. Franchise expiration date: N.A. Began: January 1, 1957. Channel capacity: N.A. Channels available but not in use: N.A.
Digital Basic Service
Subscribers: 261.
Programming (via satellite): BBC America; Bloomberg Television; Bravo; Discovery Digital Networks; Disney XD; DMX Music; ESPN Now; EVINE Live; Fox Sports 1; Fuse; FXM; FYI; Golf Channel; GSN; History International; IFC; LMN; Nick Jr.; Outdoor Channel; TeenNick; Trinity Broadcasting Network (TBN); Turner Classic Movies; WE tv.
Fee: $26.99 monthly.
Digital Expanded Basic Service
Subscribers: N.A.
Programming (via satellite): A&E; AMC; Animal Planet; Cartoon Network; CMT; CNN; Comedy Central; Discovery Life Channel; Disney Channel; E! HD; ESPN; ESPN2; Fox News Channel; Freeform; FX; HGTV; History; HLN; MoviePlex; MTV; NBCSN; Nickelodeon; Spike TV; Syfy; TBS; The Weather Channel; TLC; TNT; truTV; USA Network.
Fee: $14.38 monthly.
Digital Pay Service 1
Pay Units: N.A.
Programming (via satellite): Cinemax (multiplexed); Flix; HBO (multiplexed); Showtime (multiplexed); Starz (multiplexed); Starz Encore (multiplexed); The Movie Channel (multiplexed).
Fee: 11.95-$13.00 monthly.
Video-On-Demand: No
Pay-Per-View
iN DEMAND (delivered digitally); Hot Choice (delivered digitally); Playboy TV (delivered digitally); Fresh (delivered digitally); Shorteez (delivered digitally); ESPN (delivered digitally).
Internet Service
Operational: No.
Telephone Service
None
Miles of Plant: 66.0 (coaxial); 6.0 (fiber optic). Homes passed: 1,691.
Vice President & General Manager: Ed Merrill. Operations Manager: Donna Briggs. Marketing Director: Sarwar Assar. Accounting Director: David Sovanski.
Ownership: Charter Communications Inc. (MSO).

ANAHEIM—Time Warner Cable. Now served by LOS ANGELES, CA [CA0009]. ICA: CA0033.

ARTESIA—Formerly served by Comcast Cable. No longer in operation. ICA: CA0187.

AUBURN—Wave Broadband. Now served by PLACER COUNTY (southwestern portion), CA [CA0131]. ICA: CA0162.

AVALON/CATALINA ISLAND—Catalina Cable TV Co., 222 Metropole Ave, PO Box 2143, Avalon, CA 90704-2143. Phone: 310-510-0255. Fax: 310-510-2565. Web Site: http://www.catalinaisp.com. Also serves Catalina Island. ICA: CA0224.
TV Market Ranking: 2 (CATALINA ISLAND). Franchise award date: December 19, 1986. Franchise expiration date: N.A. Began: October 1, 1986.
Channel capacity: N.A. Channels available but not in use: N.A.
Basic Service
Subscribers: 879.
Programming (received off-air): KABC-TV (ABC, Live Well Network) Los Angeles; KCBS-TV (CBS, Decades) Los Angeles; KCET (ETV) Los Angeles; KCOP-TV (Bounce TV, Buzzr, Heroes & Icons, MNT, Movies!) Los Angeles; KDOC-TV (MeTV) Anaheim; KNBC (COZI TV, NBC) Los Angeles; KOCE-TV (PBS) Huntington Beach; KTLA (Antenna TV, CW, This TV) Los Angeles; KTTV (FOX) Los Angeles.
Programming (via satellite): A&E; AMC; Cartoon Network; CNBC; CNN; Comedy Central; C-SPAN; Discovery Channel; ESPN; ESPN2; Food Network; FOX Sports Networks; Freeform; HLN; Lifetime; MTV; Nick Jr.; Nickelodeon; QVC; Spike TV; TBS; TLC; Travel Channel; Univision; USA Network; VH1; WGN America.
Fee: $29.95 installation; $63.45 monthly.
Digital Basic Service
Subscribers: N.A.
Programming (via satellite): 52MX; A&E HD; Animal Planet HD; BBC America; Bloomberg Television; Bravo; Centric; Cinelatino; Cloo; CMT; CNN en Espanol; Destination America; Discovery Channel HD; Discovery Family; Discovery Life Channel; Disney Channel HD; Disney XD; ESPN Classic; ESPN Deportes; ESPN HD; ESPN2; ESPN2 HD; ESPNews; ESPNU; Food Network HD; Fox Business Network; FOX College Sports Central; FOX College Sports Pacific; Fox Deportes; Fox News HD; Fox Sports 1; Freeform HD; FSN HD; Fuse; FX HD; FXM; FYI; Golf Channel; GSN; HD Theater; HGTV; HGTV HD; History; History en Espanol; History HD; IFC; LMN; MTV Classic; MTV Hits; MTV2; National Geographic Channel; National Geographic Channel HD; NBCSN; Nick Jr.; Outdoor Channel; OWN: Oprah Winfrey Network; Oxygen; RFD-TV; Science Channel; Science HD; Syfy; Syfy HD; Teen-Nick; Trinity Broadcasting Network (TBN); Turner Classic Movies; TVG Network; Univision HD; USA Network HD; VH1 Soul; ViendoMovies; WE tv.
Digital Pay Service 1
Pay Units: N.A.
Programming (via satellite): Flix; HBO (multiplexed); HBO HD; HBO Latino; Showtime (multiplexed); Starz; Starz Encore; Starz HD; Sundance TV; The Movie Channel (multiplexed).
Video-On-Demand: Planned
Pay-Per-View
iN DEMAND (delivered digitally); Hot Choice (delivered digitally); Playboy TV (delivered digitally); Fresh (delivered digitally); Spice: Xcess (delivered digitally); Club Jenna (delivered digitally).
Internet Service
Operational: Yes. Began: August 31, 1999.
Broadband Service: ISP Channel.
Fee: $99.00 installation; $39.95 monthly.
Telephone Service
None
Miles of Plant: 13.0 (coaxial); None (fiber optic). Homes passed: 1,650.
General Manager: Ralph Morrow.
Ownership: Catalina Cable TV Co.

AVENAL—Bright House Networks, 2251 Lucien Way, Ste 200B, Maitland, FL 32751. Phones: 407-667-5200; 661-323-4892; 800-734-4615; 661-634-2200. E-mail: bakersfield.customercare@mybrighthouse.com. Web Site: http://brighthouse.com. ICA: CA0221.
TV Market Ranking: 72 (AVENAL). Franchise award date: April 1, 1968. Franchise expiration date: N.A. Began: April 1, 1968.
Channel capacity: 78 (operating 2-way). Channels available but not in use: N.A.
Basic Service
Subscribers: 318. Commercial subscribers: 1.
Programming (received off-air): KAIL (COZI TV, MNT, WeatherNation) Fresno; KFAZ-CA (Azteca America) Visalia; KFRE-TV (CW, IND) Sanger; KFSN-TV (ABC, Live Well Network) Fresno; KFTV-DT (getTV, UNV) Hanford; KGPE (CBS, The Country Network, Untamed Sports TV) Fresno; KMPH-TV (FOX, This TV) Visalia; KNSO (TMO) Merced; KNXT (ETV) Visalia; KSEE (LATV, NBC) Fresno; KTFF-DT (UniMas) Porterville; KVPT (PBS) Fresno.
Programming (via satellite): California Channel; EVINE Live; Pop; QVC; WGN America.
Fee: $27.00 monthly.
Expanded Basic Service 1
Subscribers: N.A.
Programming (via satellite): A&E; AMC; Animal Planet; Cartoon Network; CNBC; CNN; CNN en Espanol; Comedy Central; C-SPAN; C-SPAN 2; Discovery Channel; Disney Channel; E! HD; ESPN; ESPN Classic; ESPN2; Food Network; Fox Deportes; Fox News Channel; Fox Sports 1; FOX Sports West/Prime Ticket; Freeform; FX; Great American Country; Hallmark Channel; HGTV; History; HLN; Lifetime; LMN; MSNBC; MTV; National Geographic Channel; NBC Universo; NBCSN; Nickelodeon; Spike TV; Syfy; TBS; The Weather Channel; TLC; TNT; Travel Channel; truTV; Turner Classic Movies; TV Land; Univision; USA Network; VH1; WE tv.
Fee: $33.00 monthly.
Digital Basic Service
Subscribers: N.A.
Programming (via satellite): Bloomberg Television; Discovery Digital Networks; Disney XD; DMX Music; ESPNews; FOX College Sports Central; FOX College Sports Pacific; FXM; Golf Channel; GSN; IFC; NBCSN; Nick Jr.; Starz Encore; TeenNick.
Digital Pay Service 1
Pay Units: N.A.
Programming (via satellite): Cinemax (multiplexed); HBO (multiplexed); Showtime (multiplexed); Starz (multiplexed); The Movie Channel (multiplexed).
Fee: $13.95 monthly (each).
Pay-Per-View
iN DEMAND (delivered digitally); Fresh (delivered digitally); Hot Choice (delivered digitally); Playboy TV (delivered digitally); ESPN Now (delivered digitally); Sports PPV (delivered digitally).
Internet Service
Operational: No.
Telephone Service
None
Miles of Plant: 18.0 (coaxial); 2.0 (fiber optic). Homes passed: 2,242.
Chief Financial Officer: William Futera. General Manager: Joe Schoenstein. Marketing Director: Danielle Armstrong. Chief Technician: Chris Gravis. Advertising Manager:

D-82 TV & Cable Factbook No. 85

Cable Systems—California

Don Stone. Customer Service Manager: Becky Mitchell.
Ownership: Bright House Networks LLC (MSO).

AZUSA—Charter Communications. Now served by LOS ANGELES COUNTY (portions), CA [CA0005]. ICA: CA0429.

BAKERSFIELD—Bright House Networks, 3701 North Sillect Ave, Bakersfield, CA 93308-6330. Phones: 661-323-4892 (Customer service); 800-734-4615; 661-634-2200. Fax: 661-634-2245. E-mail: bakersfield.customercare@mybrighthouse.com. Web Site: http://brighthouse.com. Also serves Arvin, Buttonwillow, Delano, Kern County, Lamont, Maricopa, McFarland, Shafter, Taft, Tehachapi & Wasco. ICA: CA0025.
TV Market Ranking: 72 (Delano, Kern County (portions), McFarland); Below 100 (Arvin, BAKERSFIELD, Buttonwillow, Lamont, Maricopa, Shafter, Taft, Wasco, Tehachapi, Kern County (portions)); Outside TV Markets (Kern County (portions)). Franchise award date: September 17, 1966. Franchise expiration date: N.A. Began: September 17, 1966.
Channel capacity: 68 (operating 2-way). Channels available but not in use: N.A.
Basic Service
Subscribers: 65,691. Commercial subscribers: 1,175.
Programming (received off-air): KABC-TV (ABC, Live Well Network) Los Angeles; KABE-CD (UNV) Bakersfield; KBAK-TV (CBS) Bakersfield; KBFX-CD (FOX, This TV) Bakersfield; KCAL-TV (IND) Los Angeles; KCET (ETV) Los Angeles; KCOP-TV (Bounce TV, Buzzr, Heroes & Icons, MNT, Movies!) Los Angeles; KERO-TV (ABC, Azteca America, MeTV) Bakersfield; KGET-TV (CW, NBC) Bakersfield; KTLA (Antenna TV, CW, This TV) Los Angeles; KUVI-DT (getTV, MNT) Bakersfield; KVPT (PBS) Fresno.
Programming (via satellite): California Channel; EVINE Live; Pop; QVC.
Fee: $44.95 installation; $27.00 monthly.
Expanded Basic Service 1
Subscribers: N.A.
Programming (via satellite): A&E; AMC; Animal Planet; Azteca; BET; Bravo; Cartoon Network; CNBC; CNN; Comedy Central; C-SPAN; C-SPAN 2; Discovery Channel; Disney Channel; E! HD; ESPN; ESPN Classic; ESPN2; Food Network; Fox News Channel; FOX Sports West/Prime Ticket; Freeform; Fuse; FX; Golf Channel; Great American Country; Hallmark Channel; HGTV; History; HLN; Lifetime; LMN; MSNBC; MTV; National Geographic Channel; NBCSN; Nickelodeon; Spike TV; Syfy; TBS; Telemundo; The Weather Channel; TLC; TNT; Travel Channel; Trinity Broadcasting Network (TBN); truTV; Turner Classic Movies; TV Land; UniMas; Univision; USA Network; VH1; WE tv.
Fee: $33.00 monthly.
Digital Basic Service
Subscribers: N.A.
Programming (via satellite): A&E HD; AXS TV; BBC America; BBC America On Demand; Beauty & Fashion Channel; Bloomberg Television; Boomerang; CBS Sports Network; Cloo; CMT; CNBC; CNN International; Cooking Channel; C-SPAN 2; C-SPAN 3; Discovery Digital Networks; Disney XD; DIY Network; ESPN HD; ESPNews; EWTN Global Catholic Network; FOX College Sports Central; FOX College Sports Pacific; Fox Sports 1; Fox Sports 2; FXM; FYI; GSN; HD Theater; History International; HITS (Headend In The Sky); IFC; Jewelry Television; MC; MoviePlex; Nat Geo WILD; National Geographic Channel On Demand; NBA TV; Nick Jr.; Nicktoons; Outdoor Channel; Ovation; Starz Encore (multiplexed); TeenNick; Tennis Channel; The Word Network; TNT HD; Universal HD.
Digital Pay Service 1
Pay Units: N.A.
Programming (via satellite): Cinemax (multiplexed); HBO (multiplexed); HBO HD; Showtime (multiplexed); Showtime HD; Starz (multiplexed); The Filipino Channel; The Movie Channel (multiplexed); Zee TV.
Fee: $17.00 monthly (each).
Video-On-Demand: Yes
Pay-Per-View
iN DEMAND; Playboy TV; Fresh; Shorteez.
Internet Service
Operational: Yes. Began: April 15, 2000.
Subscribers: 80,105.
Broadband Service: Road Runner.
Fee: $29.95 monthly.
Telephone Service
Digital: Operational
Subscribers: 33,699.
Fee: $33.95 monthly
Miles of Plant: 3,476.0 (coaxial); 853.0 (fiber optic). Homes passed: 231,675.
Chief Financial Officer: William Futera. Vice President & General Manager: Danielle Wade. Advertising Director: Don Stone. Chief Technician: Chris Gravis. Customer Service Manager: Becky Mitchell.
Ownership: Bright House Networks LLC (MSO).

BAKERSFIELD—Bright House Networks. Now served by BAKERSFIELD, CA [CA0025]. ICA: CA0073.

BANNING—Time Warner Cable, 41725 Cook St, Palm Desert, CA 92211-5100. Phones: 760-340-2225; 858-695-3110 (San Diego administrative office); 760-340-1312. Fax: 760-340-9764. Web Site: http://www.timewarnercable.com. Also serves Beaumont, Cherry Valley (portions), Joshua Tree, Morongo Valley, Riverside County (portions), San Bernardino County (portions), Twentynine Palms, Twentynine Palms Marine Corps Base & Yucca Valley. ICA: CA0176.
TV Market Ranking: 2 (BANNING, Beaumont, Cherry Valley (portions), Riverside County (portions)); Below 100 (Joshua Tree, Morongo Valley, San Bernardino County (portions), Twentynine Palms, Twentynine Palms Marine Corps Base, Yucca Valley). Franchise award date: November 25, 1952. Franchise expiration date: N.A. Began: February 1, 1953.
Channel capacity: N.A. Channels available but not in use: N.A.
Basic Service
Subscribers: 11,119.
Programming (received off-air): KABC-TV (ABC, Live Well Network) Los Angeles; KAZA-TV (Azteca America) Avalon; KCBS-TV (CBS, Decades) Los Angeles; KCET (ETV) Los Angeles; KCOP-TV (Bounce TV, Buzzr, Heroes & Icons, MNT, Movies!) Los Angeles; KESQ-TV (ABC, CW) Palm Springs; KFTR-DT (getTV, UniMas) Ontario; KJLA (LATV) Ventura; KMEX-DT (UNV) Los Angeles; KMIR-TV (IND, Movies!, NBC) Palm Springs; KNBC (COZI TV, NBC) Los Angeles; KPXN-TV (ION) San Bernardino; KRCA (Estrella TV) Riverside; KTLA (Antenna TV, CW, This TV) Los Angeles; KTTV (FOX) Los Angeles; KVCR-DT (PBS) San Bernardino; KXLA (IND) Rancho Palos Verdes; 14 FMs.
Programming (via satellite): C-SPAN; C-SPAN 2; QVC; The Weather Channel; WGN America.
Fee: $33.00 installation; $22.00 monthly.
Expanded Basic Service 1
Subscribers: N.A.
Programming (via satellite): A&E; AMC; Animal Planet; BET; Bravo; Cartoon Network; CNBC; CNN; Comedy Central; Discovery Channel; Disney Channel; E! HD; ESPN; ESPN Classic; ESPN2; EWTN Global Catholic Network; Food Network; Fox News Channel; FOX Sports Networks; Freeform; FX; Hallmark Channel; HGTV; History; HLN; Lifetime; MSNBC; MTV; National Geographic Channel; Nickelodeon; Pop; Spike TV; TBS; The Weather Channel; TLC; TNT; Travel Channel; Trinity Broadcasting Network (TBN); truTV; Turner Classic Movies; TV Land; USA Network; VH1; WE tv.
Fee: $30.00 monthly.
Digital Basic Service
Subscribers: N.A.
Programming (via satellite): A&E; AMC; Animal Planet; BBC America; BET; Bloomberg Television; Bravo; Cartoon Network; CNBC; CNN; CNN International; Comedy Central; Cooking Channel; C-SPAN; C-SPAN 2; C-SPAN 3; Discovery Life Channel; Disney Channel; Disney XD; DIY Network; E! HD; ESPN; ESPN Classic; ESPN2; ESPNews; Flix; Food Network; Fox News Channel; Fox Sports 1; FOX Sports West/Prime Ticket; Freeform; Fuse; FX; FYI; Golf Channel; GSN; Hallmark Channel; HGTV; History; History International; HLN; IFC; INSP; Lifetime; LMN; MoviePlex; MSNBC; MTV; MTV Classic; MTV2; National Geographic Channel; NBCSN; Nick Jr.; Nickelodeon; Ovation; Oxygen; Spike TV; Starz Encore (multiplexed); Sundance TV; Syfy; TBS; The Weather Channel; TLC; TNT; Travel Channel; truTV; Turner Classic Movies; TV Land; USA Network; VH1; WE tv.
Digital Pay Service 1
Pay Units: N.A.
Programming (via satellite): Cinemax (multiplexed); HBO (multiplexed); Showtime (multiplexed); Starz (multiplexed); The Movie Channel (multiplexed).
Fee: $15.00 monthly (Cinemax, HBO, Starz, or Showtime/TMC).
Video-On-Demand: Yes
Pay-Per-View
Playboy TV (delivered digitally); Fresh (delivered digitally); Shorteez (delivered digitally).
Internet Service
Operational: Yes.
Broadband Service: Road Runner.
Fee: $50.00 installation; $44.95 monthly.
Telephone Service
Digital: Operational
Fee: $39.95 monthly
Miles of Plant: 2,442.0 (coaxial); 199.0 (fiber optic).
President: Bob Barlow. Vice President & General Manager: Tad Yo. Technical Operations Director: Dessi Ochoa. Engineering Director: Mike Sagona. Marketing Director: Jimmy Kelly. Government & Community Affairs Director: Kathi Jacobs. Vice President, Customer Service: Armando Rancano.
Ownership: Time Warner Cable (MSO).

BARSTOW—Time Warner Cable, 7800 Crescent Executive Dr, Charlotte, NC 28217. Phones: 858-695-3110; 858-635-8297. Web Site: http://www.timewarnercable.com. Also serves Marine Corps Logistics Base Barstow & San Bernardino County. ICA: CA0151.
TV Market Ranking: Below 100 (BARSTOW, Marine Corps Logistics Base Barstow, San Bernardino County). Franchise award date: January 1, 1952. Franchise expiration date: N.A. Began: November 1, 1952.
Channel capacity: 14 (operating 2-way). Channels available but not in use: N.A.
Basic Service
Subscribers: 4,042.
Programming (received off-air): KILM (IND) Barstow; KJLA (LATV) Ventura; 15 FMs.
Programming (via microwave): KABC-TV (ABC, Live Well Network) Los Angeles; KCAL-TV (IND) Los Angeles; KCBS-TV (CBS, Decades) Los Angeles; KCET (ETV) Los Angeles; KCOP-TV (Bounce TV, Buzzr, Heroes & Icons, MNT, Movies!) Los Angeles; KNBC (COZI TV, NBC) Los Angeles; KTLA (Antenna TV, CW, This TV) Los Angeles; KTTV (FOX) Los Angeles.
Programming (via satellite): A&E; BET; CNBC; CNN; C-SPAN; C-SPAN 2; Discovery Channel; E! HD; ESPN; FOX Sports Networks; Freeform; HLN; ION Television; Lifetime; MTV; Nickelodeon; QVC; Spike TV; TBS; TNT; Trinity Broadcasting Network (TBN); USA Network; VH1.
Fee: $49.99 installation; $16.50 monthly.
Expanded Basic Service 1
Subscribers: N.A.
Programming (via satellite): AMC; Animal Planet; Bravo; California Channel; Cartoon Network; Comedy Central; Disney Channel; ESPN Classic; ESPN2; EVINE Live; Food Network; Fox News Channel; Fox Sports 1; FX; Golf Channel; GSN; HGTV; History; INSP; MSNBC; Outdoor Channel; Pop; Syfy; The Weather Channel; TLC; Travel Channel; Turner Classic Movies; TV Land; Univision; Univision Studios.
Fee: $30.00 monthly.
Digital Basic Service
Subscribers: N.A.
Programming (via satellite): BBC America; Bloomberg Television; CMT; C-SPAN 3; Discovery Life Channel; Disney XD; DIY Network; ESPNews; FXM; Great American Country; HITS (Headend In The Sky); IFC; LMN; MC; MTV2; National Geographic Channel; Nick Jr.; truTV.
Fee: $20.00 installation.
Digital Pay Service 1
Pay Units: N.A.
Programming (via satellite): Cinemax (multiplexed); HBO (multiplexed); Showtime (multiplexed); The Movie Channel (multiplexed).
Fee: $12.00 monthly (each).
Video-On-Demand: Yes
Pay-Per-View
Playboy TV (delivered digitally); iN DEMAND (delivered digitally); Shorteez (delivered digitally); Pleasure (delivered digitally).
Internet Service
Operational: Yes.
Subscribers: 4,545.
Broadband Service: Road Runner.
Fee: $99.95 installation; $44.95 monthly.
Telephone Service
Digital: Operational
Subscribers: 2,074.
Fee: $39.95 monthly
Miles of Plant: 387.0 (coaxial); 78.0 (fiber optic). Homes passed: 18,901.
President: Bob Barlow. Vice President, Engineering: Ron Johnson. Vice President, Technical Services: Bob Jones. Vice President, Public Affairs: Marc Farrar. Vice Pres-

California—Cable Systems

ident, Customer Care: Vinit Ahooja. Senior Accounting Director: Karen Goodfellow. Ownership: Time Warner Cable (MSO).; Advance/Newhouse Partnership (MSO).

BEAR VALLEY—Formerly served by New Day Broadband. No longer in operation. ICA: CA0307.

BELL—Formerly served by Comcast Cable. No longer in operation. ICA: CA0139.

BENICIA—Comcast Cable. Now served by SAN FRANCISCO, CA [CA0003]. ICA: CA0166.

BIG BEAR LAKE—Charter Communications. Now served by HESPERIA, CA [CA0158]. ICA: CA0309.

BISHOP—Suddenlink Communications, 520 Maryville Centre Dr, Ste 300, St. Louis, MO 63141. Phone: 314-315-9400. Web Site: http://www.suddenlink.com. Also serves Big Pine, Independence, Inyo County (portions) & Round Valley. ICA: CA0310.
 TV Market Ranking: Outside TV Markets (Big Pine, BISHOP, Independence, Inyo County (portions), Round Valley). Franchise award date: May 13, 1967. Franchise expiration date: N.A. Began: February 28, 1966.
 Channel capacity: N.A. Channels available but not in use: N.A.
Basic Service
 Subscribers: 2,468. Commercial subscribers: 299.
 Programming (received off-air): KLVX (PBS) Las Vegas; KNBC (COZI TV, NBC) Los Angeles; KOLO-TV (ABC, IND, Movies!) Reno; KTTV (FOX) Los Angeles; 17 FMs.
 Programming (via satellite): Pop; QVC; TBS; The Weather Channel.
 Programming (via translator): KABC-TV (ABC, Live Well Network) Los Angeles; KCBS-TV (CBS, Decades) Los Angeles; KTLA (Antenna TV, CW, This TV) Los Angeles.
 Fee: $40.00 installation; $60.08 monthly.
Expanded Basic Service 1
 Subscribers: N.A.
 Programming (via satellite): A&E; CNBC; CNN; Discovery Channel; Disney Channel; Disney XD; E! HD; ESPN; ESPN2; Fox News Channel; FOX Sports Networks; FX; History; HLN; MSNBC; Nickelodeon; Spike TV; Syfy; TLC; TNT; Trinity Broadcasting Network (TBN); USA Network.
 Fee: $15.54 monthly.
Digital Basic Service
 Subscribers: N.A.
 Programming (via satellite): BBC America; Bravo; Discovery Digital Networks; DMX Music; ESPN Classic; ESPNews; Fox Sports 1; Golf Channel; GSN; HGTV; HITS (Headend In The Sky); IFC; MTV Classic; NBCSN; Starz Encore; Turner Classic Movies; VH1 Country.
Digital Pay Service 1
 Pay Units: N.A.
 Programming (via satellite): Cinemax (multiplexed); HBO (multiplexed); Showtime (multiplexed); The Movie Channel (multiplexed).
 Fee: $10.95 monthly (Cinemax, Showtime or TMC), $13.95 monthly (HBO).
Video-On-Demand: No
Pay-Per-View
 Hot Choice (delivered digitally); iN DEMAND (delivered digitally); Fresh (delivered digitally).

Internet Service
 Operational: Yes. Began: August 7, 2002.
 Broadband Service: Suddenlink High Speed Internet.
 Fee: $99.99 installation; $24.95 monthly.
Telephone Service
 Digital: Operational
 Miles of Plant: 108.0 (coaxial); None (fiber optic).
Senior Vice President, Corporate Finance: Michael Pflantz. Vice President, Accounting: Sabrina Warr. General Manager: Dawn McWithey. Chief Technician: David Gibbs. Marketing Director: Jason Oelkers.
Ownership: Cequel Communications Holdings I LLC (MSO).

BLYTHE—Suddenlink Communications, 520 Maryville Centre Dr, Ste 300, St. Louis, MO 63141. Phones: 314-315-9400; 800-999-6845 (Customer service). Web Site: http://www.suddenlink.com. Also serves Ehrenberg & La Paz County (portions), AZ; East Blythe & Riverside County (eastern portion), CA. ICA: CA0183.
 TV Market Ranking: 2 (East Blythe); Outside TV Markets (BLYTHE, Ehrenberg, La Paz County (portions), Riverside County (eastern portion), East Blythe). Franchise award date: N.A. Franchise expiration date: N.A. Began: July 12, 1957.
 Channel capacity: N.A. Channels available but not in use: N.A.
Basic Service
 Subscribers: 1,149. Commercial subscribers: 258.
 Programming (received off-air): KABC-TV (ABC, Live Well Network) Los Angeles; KASW (CW) Phoenix; KCAL-TV (IND) Los Angeles; KECY-TV (ABC, FOX, MNT, TMO) El Centro; KMOH-TV (MundoMax) Kingman; KSWT (CBS, Estrella TV, Tuff TV) Yuma; KTVW-DT (UNV) Phoenix; KUTP (Buzzr, MNT, Movies!) Phoenix; KYMA-DT (NBC, This TV) Yuma; 10 FMs.
 Programming (via microwave): KAET (PBS) Phoenix; KPHO-TV (CBS, COZI TV) Phoenix; KPNX (NBC) Mesa; KSAZ-TV (Bounce TV, FOX, Heroes & Icons) Phoenix; KTLA (Antenna TV, CW, This TV) Los Angeles; KTTV (FOX) Los Angeles.
 Programming (via satellite): A&E; AMC; Animal Planet; BET; Cartoon Network; CMT; CNBC; CNN; Comedy Central; C-SPAN; Discovery Channel; Disney Channel; E! HD; ESPN; ESPN Classic; ESPN2; EWTN Global Catholic Network; Food Network; Fox News Channel; FOX Sports West/Prime Ticket; Freeform; FX; Great American Country; HGTV; History; HLN; ION Television; Lifetime; MSNBC; MTV; Nickelodeon; OWN: Oprah Winfrey Network; Pop; QVC; Spike TV; Syfy; TBS; Telemundo; The Weather Channel; TLC; TNT; Travel Channel; Trinity Broadcasting Network (TBN); truTV; Turner Classic Movies; TV Land; UniMas; Univision; USA Network; VH1.
 Fee: $40.00 installation; $60.99 monthly; $2.50 converter.
Digital Basic Service
 Subscribers: N.A.
 Programming (via satellite): BBC America; CMT; Cooking Channel; Disney XD; DIY Network; DMX Music; ESPNews; Fox Sports 1; Fox Sports 2; FSN Digital Atlantic; FSN Digital Central; FSN Digital Pacific; FYI; Golf Channel; GSN; Hallmark Channel; HD Theater; History International; HITS (Headend In The Sky); IFC; National Geographic Channel; NBCSN; Nick Jr.; Nicktoons; Outdoor Channel; TeenNick; WE tv.

Digital Pay Service 1
 Pay Units: N.A.
 Programming (via satellite): Cinemax (multiplexed); HBO (multiplexed); Starz (multiplexed); Starz Encore (multiplexed); The Movie Channel (multiplexed).
 Fee: $6.95 monthly (Cinemax), $9.95 monthly (Starz/Encore), $11.95 monthly (Showtime/TMC), $12.00 monthly (HBO).
Video-On-Demand: No
Pay-Per-View
 iN DEMAND (delivered digitally); Fresh (delivered digitally).
Internet Service
 Operational: Yes.
 Broadband Service: Suddenlink High Speed Internet.
 Fee: $59.95 installation; $24.95 monthly; $5.00 modem lease.
Telephone Service
 Analog: Not Operational
 Digital: Operational
 Fee: $39.95 monthly
 Miles of Plant: 189.0 (coaxial); 15.0 (fiber optic). Homes passed: 4,001.
Chief Executive Officer: Jerald L. Kent. Executive Vice President & Chief Operating Officer: Thomas P. McMillin. Senior Vice President, Marketing: Mary R. Meier. Senior Vice President, Corporate Finance: Michael Pflantz. Vice President, Accounting: Sabrina Warr.
Ownership: Cequel Communications Holdings I LLC (MSO).

BOMBAY BEACH—USA Communications, 2455 Stirrup Rd, Borrego Springs, CA 92004. Phones: 800-234-0102; 308-236-1512 (Kearney, NE corporate office); 877-234-0102; 760-767-5607. Fax: 760-767-3609. E-mail: csr@usacommunications.tv. Web Site: http://usacommunications.tv. ICA: CA0275.
 TV Market Ranking: Below 100 (BOMBAY BEACH).
 Channel capacity: N.A. Channels available but not in use: N.A.
Basic Service
 Subscribers: 8.
 Programming (received off-air): KECY-TV (ABC, FOX, MNT, TMO) El Centro; KESQ-TV (ABC, CW) Palm Springs; KSWT (CBS, Estrella TV, Tuff TV) Yuma; KYMA-DT (NBC, This TV) Yuma.
 Programming (via satellite): Cartoon Network; Comedy Central; C-SPAN; C-SPAN 2; E! HD; HLN; KRMA-TV (PBS) Denver; TBS; TLC; Trinity Broadcasting Network (TBN); TV Land; VH1; WGN America.
 Fee: $29.95 installation; $29.95 monthly.
Expanded Basic Service 1
 Subscribers: N.A.
 Programming (via satellite): A&E; AMC; Animal Planet; CNN; Discovery Channel; ESPN; ESPN2; Freeform; History; Lifetime; Nickelodeon; Spike TV; Syfy; TNT; Turner Classic Movies; USA Network.
 Fee: $36.51 monthly.
Pay Service 1
 Pay Units: N.A.
 Programming (via satellite): Cinemax; HBO.
 Fee: $13.00 monthly (Cinemax), $13.50 monthly (HBO).
Internet Service
 Operational: No.
Telephone Service
 None
 Miles of Plant: 10.0 (coaxial); None (fiber optic). Homes passed: 250.

Chief Financial Officer: Amber Reineke. General Manager & Chief Technician: Joe Gustafson.
Ownership: USA Companies LP (MSO).

BORON—Charter Communications. Now served by NORTH EDWARDS, CA [CA0404]. ICA: CA0242.

BORREGO SPRINGS—USA Communications, 2455 Stirrup Rd, Borrego Springs, CA 92004. Phones: 800-234-0102; 308-236-1512 (Kearney, NE corporate office); 877-234-0102; 760-767-5607. Fax: 760-767-3609. E-mail: csr@usacommunications.tv. Web Site: http://usacommunications.tv. ICA: CA0236.
 TV Market Ranking: Outside TV Markets (BORREGO SPRINGS). Franchise award date: June 1, 1963. Franchise expiration date: N.A. Began: June 1, 1963.
 Channel capacity: N.A. Channels available but not in use: N.A.
Basic Service
 Subscribers: 794.
 Programming (received off-air): KSWT (CBS, Estrella TV, Tuff TV) Yuma; KYMA-DT (NBC, This TV) Yuma; various Mexican stations; allband FM.
 Programming (via microwave): KCOP-TV (Bounce TV, Buzzr, Heroes & Icons, MNT, Movies!) Los Angeles; KFMB-TV (CBS, Grit, MeTV) San Diego; KGTV (ABC, Azteca America) San Diego; KNSD (COZI TV, NBC) San Diego; KPBS (PBS) San Diego; KSWB-TV (Antenna TV, FOX, This TV) San Diego; KTLA (Antenna TV, CW, This TV) Los Angeles; KUSI-TV (IND) San Diego.
 Programming (via satellite): EWTN Global Catholic Network; HLN; Pop; QVC; Telemundo; The Weather Channel; Trinity Broadcasting Network (TBN); UniMas; Univision; Univision Studios.
 Fee: $39.95 installation; $33.45 monthly.
Expanded Basic Service 1
 Subscribers: N.A.
 Programming (via satellite): A&E; AMC; Animal Planet; Cartoon Network; CNBC; CNN; Comedy Central; C-SPAN; C-SPAN 2; Discovery Channel; E! HD; ESPN; ESPN Classic; ESPN2; Food Network; Fox News Channel; FOX Sports Networks; Freeform; FX; Golf Channel; Great American Country; Hallmark Channel; HGTV; History; ION Television; Lifetime; MSNBC; MTV; National Geographic Channel; Nickelodeon; Spike TV; Syfy; TBS; TLC; TNT; Travel Channel; truTV; Turner Classic Movies; TV Land; USA Network; VH1; WGN America.
Digital Basic Service
 Subscribers: N.A.
 Programming (via satellite): AZ TV; BBC America; Bloomberg Television; Cloo; CMT; Daystar TV Network; Destination America; Discovery Channel HD; Discovery Kids Channel; Discovery Life Channel; DMX Music; ESPN HD; ESPNews; EVINE Live; FOX College Sports Central; FOX College Sports Pacific; Fox Sports 1; FXM; FYI; GSN; History International; HITS (Headend In The Sky); Investigation Discovery; MTV Classic; MTV Hits; MTV2; NBCSN; Nick Jr.; Outdoor Channel; Ovation; OWN: Oprah Winfrey Network; Science Channel; Starz (multiplexed); Starz Encore (multiplexed); Syfy; TBS HD; TeenNick; TNT HD; VH1 Soul; WE tv.
Digital Pay Service 1
 Pay Units: N.A.
 Programming (via satellite): Cinemax (multiplexed); Flix; HBO (multiplexed);

Cable Systems—California

LMN; Showtime (multiplexed); The Movie Channel (multiplexed).
Video-On-Demand: No
Pay-Per-View
iN DEMAND (delivered digitally); Playboy TV (delivered digitally); Hot Choice (delivered digitally); Fresh (delivered digitally); Spice: Xcess (delivered digitally); Club Jenna (delivered digitally).
Internet Service
Operational: Yes.
Broadband Service: In-house.
Telephone Service
Digital: Operational
Miles of Plant: 100.0 (coaxial); None (fiber optic).
Chief Financial Officer: Amber Reineke. General Manager & Chief Technician: Joe Gustafson.
Ownership: USA Companies LP (MSO).

BOX CANYON—Formerly served by Charter Communications. No longer in operation. ICA: CA0433.

BREA—Formerly served by Adelphia Communications. Now served by Time Warner Cable, LOS ANGELES, CA [CA0009]. ICA: CA0084.

BRENTWOOD—Comcast Cable. Now served by SAN FRANCISCO, CA [CA0003]. ICA: CA0485.

BRIDGEPORT—Formerly served by Satview Broadband. No longer in operation. ICA: CA0292.

BURLINGAME—Comcast Cable. Now served by SAN FRANCISCO, CA [CA0003]. ICA: CA0149.

BURNEY—Zito Media, 102 S Main St, PO Box 665, Coudersport, PA 16915. Phones: 814-260-9055; 800-365-6988. Fax: 913-563-5454. E-mail: info@zitomedia.com. Web Site: http://www.zitomedia.com. Also serves Johnson Park. ICA: CA0217.
TV Market Ranking: Outside TV Markets (BURNEY, Johnson Park). Franchise award date: N.A. Franchise expiration date: N.A. Began: October 1, 1971.
Channel capacity: N.A. Channels available but not in use: N.A.
Basic Service
Subscribers: 280.
Programming (received off-air): KCVU (COZI TV, FOX, This TV) Paradise; KHSL-TV (CBS, CW) Chico; KIXE-TV (PBS) Redding; KNVN (Antenna TV, NBC) Chico; KRCR-TV (ABC, MeTV, Movies!) Redding; KRVU-LD (MNT) Redding.
Programming (via satellite): California Channel; C-SPAN; C-SPAN 2; EVINE Live; Hallmark Channel; KCNC-TV (CBS, Decades) Denver; KUSA (NBC, WeatherNation) Denver; Pop; QVC; TBS; WGN America.
Fee: $49.95 installation; $20.92 monthly.
Expanded Basic Service 1
Subscribers: N.A.
Programming (via satellite): A&E; AMC; Animal Planet; Bravo; Cartoon Network; CMT; CNBC; CNN; Comcast SportsNet Bay Area; Comedy Central; Discovery Channel; Disney Channel; E! HD; ESPN; ESPN2; Food Network; Fox News Channel; Freeform; FX; HGTV; History; HLN; Lifetime; MSNBC; MTV; Nickelodeon; Spike TV; Syfy; The Weather Channel; TLC; TNT; Travel Channel; truTV; Univision Studios; USA Network; VH1.
Fee: $33.93 monthly.

Digital Basic Service
Subscribers: N.A.
Programming (via satellite): BBC America; Bloomberg Television; Discovery Life Channel; Fox Sports 1; Fuse; FXM; Great American Country; GSN; LMN; MTV; MTV Classic; MTV Hits; MTV2; National Geographic Channel; Nick 2; Nick Jr.; Nicktoons; TeenNick; The Word Network; Trinity Broadcasting Network (TBN); Turner Classic Movies; VH1; VH1 Country; VH1 Soul; WE tv.
Digital Expanded Basic Service
Subscribers: N.A.
Programming (via satellite): Disney XD; DIY Network; DMX Music; ESPN Classic; ESPNews; FOX Sports Networks; FYI; Golf Channel; History International; HITS (Headend In The Sky); IFC; NBCSN; Outdoor Channel; Sundance TV.
Digital Pay Service 1
Pay Units: N.A.
Programming (via satellite): ART America; Cinemax (multiplexed); Flix (multiplexed); HBO (multiplexed); RAI Italia; RTN; Showtime (multiplexed); Starz Encore; The Filipino Channel; The Movie Channel (multiplexed); TV Asia; TV5, La Television International; Zee TV.
Fee: $12.00 monthly (Cinemax, HBO, Showtime/TMC or Starz), $15.00 monthly (CCTV, Filipino, ART, TV Asia, TV5, RAI, CTN or RTN).
Video-On-Demand: No
Pay-Per-View
Sports PPV (delivered digitally); Hot Choice (delivered digitally); Playboy TV (delivered digitally); Fresh (delivered digitally).
Internet Service
Operational: Yes.
Broadband Service: In-house.
Fee: $20.99-$49.99 installation; $44.95 monthly.
Telephone Service
Digital: Operational
Fee: $49.95 monthly
Miles of Plant: 42.0 (coaxial); None (fiber optic). Homes passed: 2,000.
President: James Rigas.
Ownership: Zito Media (MSO).

CABAZON—Formerly served by TV Max. No longer in operation. ICA: CA0263.

CALABASAS—Time Warner Cable. Now served by LOS ANGELES, CA [CA0009]. ICA: CA0227.

CALIFORNIA CITY—Charter Communications. Now served by NORTH EDWARDS, CA [CA0404]. ICA: CA0399.

CALIFORNIA HOT SPRINGS—Formerly served by Charter Communications. No longer in operation. ICA: CA0402.

CALIPATRIA—USA Communications, 2455 Stirrup Rd, Borrego Springs, CA 92004. Phones: 800-234-0102; 308-236-1512 (Kearney, NE corporate office); 877-234-0102; 760-767-5607. Fax: 760-767-3609. E-mail: csr@usacommunications.tv. Web Site: http://usacommunications.tv. ICA: CA0256.
TV Market Ranking: Below 100 (CALIPATRIA). Franchise award date: N.A. Franchise expiration date: N.A. Began: January 21, 1982.
Channel capacity: 61 (not 2-way capable). Channels available but not in use: N.A.
Basic Service
Subscribers: 140.
Programming (received off-air): KCET (ETV) Los Angeles; KECY-TV (ABC, FOX, MNT, TMO) El Centro; KESQ-TV (ABC, CW) Palm Springs; KSWT (CBS, Estrella TV, Tuff TV) Yuma; KTLA (Antenna TV, CW, This TV) Los Angeles; KVYE (LATV, UNV) El Centro; KYMA-DT (NBC, This TV) Yuma; various Mexican stations.
Programming (via satellite): CNN en Espanol; Freeform; QVC; Telemundo; UniMas; Univision.
Fee: $39.95 installation; $29.75 monthly.
Expanded Basic Service 1
Subscribers: N.A.
Programming (via satellite): A&E; AMC; Animal Planet; Cartoon Network; CNBC; CNN; Comedy Central; C-SPAN; C-SPAN 2; Discovery Channel; E! HD; ESPN; ESPN2; EWTN Global Catholic Network; Fox News Channel; Great American Country; HGTV; History; HLN; INSP; Lifetime; MSNBC; MTV; Nickelodeon; Spike TV; Syfy; TBS; TLC; TNT; Trinity Broadcasting Network (TBN); truTV; Turner Classic Movies; TV Land; WGN America.
Fee: $36.51 monthly.
Pay Service 1
Pay Units: N.A.
Programming (via satellite): Cinemax; HBO (multiplexed).
Fee: $13.00 monthly (Cinemax), $13.95 monthly (HBO).
Internet Service
Operational: No, DSL.
Telephone Service
Analog: Operational
Miles of Plant: 29.0 (coaxial); 6.0 (fiber optic). Homes passed: 939.
Chief Financial Officer: Amber Reineke. General Manager & Chief Technician: Joe Gustafson.
Ownership: USA Companies LP (MSO).

CAMARILLO—No longer in operation. ICA: CA0311.

CAMARILLO—Time Warner Cable. Now served by LOS ANGELES, CA [CA0009]. ICA: CA0138.

CANYON COUNTRY—Time Warner Cable. Now served by LOS ANGELES, CA [CA0009]. ICA: CA0313.

CAPE COD MOBILE HOME PARK—Formerly served by Comcast Cable. No longer in operation. ICA: CA0314.

CARLSBAD—Time Warner Cable. Now served by SAN DIEGO, CA [CA0007]. ICA: CA0048.

CARSON—Formerly served by Wave Broadband. No longer in operation. ICA: CA0456.

CARSON—Time Warner Cable. Now served by LOS ANGELES, CA [CA0009]. ICA: CA0112.

CASA DE AMIGOS MOBILE HOME PARK—Formerly served by Comcast Cable. No longer in operation. ICA: CA0316.

CEDARVILLE—Formerly served by Almega Cable. No longer in operation. ICA: CA0282.

CENTRAL ORANGE COUNTY—Time Warner Cable. Now served by LOS ANGELES, CA [CA0009]. ICA: CA0042.

CERRITOS—Charter Communications, 12405 Powerscourt Dr, St. Louis, MO 63131. Phones: 636-207-5100 (Corporate office); 626-430-6112; 626-430-3300. Fax: 626-430-3420. Web Site: http://www.charter.com. ICA: CA0137.
TV Market Ranking: 2 (CERRITOS). Franchise award date: February 19, 1987. Franchise expiration date: N.A. Began: September 26, 1988.
Channel capacity: N.A. Channels available but not in use: N.A.
Digital Basic Service
Subscribers: 1,633.
Programming (via satellite): AXS TV; Discovery Digital Networks; Disney XD; DMX Music; E! HD; ESPNews; FOX College Sports Central; FOX College Sports Pacific; Fox Sports 1; GSN; HD Theater; National Geographic Channel; NFL Network; Nick Jr.; Nicktoons; Outdoor Channel; TeenNick; TNT HD; truTV; WE tv.
Fee: $14.99 monthly.
Digital Expanded Basic Service
Subscribers: N.A.
Programming (via satellite): HITS (Headend In The Sky); MBC America; New Tang Dynasty TV; The Filipino Channel; TV Asia; Zee TV.
Fee: $7.00 monthly.
Digital Pay Service 1
Pay Units: N.A.
Programming (via satellite): Cinemax (multiplexed); Flix; HBO (multiplexed); Showtime (multiplexed); Starz (multiplexed); Starz Encore (multiplexed); The Movie Channel (multiplexed).
Fee: $12.00 monthly (Cinemax or Showtime/TMC/Flix or Starz/Encore), $14.00 monthly (HBO).
Video-On-Demand: Yes
Pay-Per-View
Special events (delivered digitally); ESPN (delivered digitally).
Internet Service
Operational: Yes.
Broadband Service: Charter Internet.
Fee: $39.95 monthly.
Telephone Service
Digital: Operational
Miles of Plant: 175.0 (coaxial); None (fiber optic). Homes passed: 15,976.
Vice President & General Manager: Wendy Rasumssen. Technical Operations Manager: Tom Williams. Accounting Director: David Sovanski.
Ownership: Charter Communications Inc. (MSO).

CHALFANT VALLEY—Formerly served by Satview Broadband. No longer in operation. ICA: CA0319.

CHATSWORTH—Time Warner Cable. Now served by LOS ANGELES, CA [CA0009]. ICA: CA0013.

CHICO—Comcast Cable. Now served by SACRAMENTO, CA [CA0002]. ICA: CA0066.

CHINO—Time Warner Cable. Now served by LOS ANGELES, CA [CA0009]. ICA: CA0320.

CHOWCHILLA—Comcast Cable. Now served by FRESNO, CA [CA0011]. ICA: CA0218.

CHULA VISTA—Formerly served by Access Cable. No longer in operation. ICA: CA0113.

CLAREMONT—Time Warner Cable. Now served by LOS ANGELES, CA [CA0009]. ICA: CA0150.

2017 Edition D-85

California—Cable Systems

CLEARLAKE—Mediacom, 13221 East Highway 20, Clearlake Oaks, CA 95423-9329. Phones: 707-998-1187; 800-239-8411 (Customer service). Fax: 707-998-9317. Web Site: http://www.mediacomcable.com. Also serves Clearlake Oaks, Clearlake Park, Cobb, Glenhaven, Kelseyville, Lake County, Lakeport, Loch Lomond, Lower Lake, Lucerne, Middletown, Nice, North Lakeport & Upper Lake. ICA: CA0104.
TV Market Ranking: Below 100 (Lake County (portions), Lower Lake); Outside TV Markets (Clearlake Park, Cobb, Glenhaven, Kelseyville, Lake County (portions), Lakeport, Loch Lomond, Lucerne, Middletown, Nice, North Lakeport, Upper Lake, CLEARLAKE, Clearlake Oaks). Franchise award date: October 1, 1962. Franchise expiration date: N.A. Began: October 1, 1962.
Channel capacity: 80 (operating 2-way). Channels available but not in use: N.A.

Basic Service
Subscribers: 6,536.
Programming (received off-air): KBCW (CW) San Francisco; KCRA-TV (MeTV, NBC) Sacramento; KEMO-TV (Azteca America) Santa Rosa; KGO-TV (ABC, Live Well Network) San Francisco; KICU-TV (Heroes & Icons, IND) San Jose; KNTV (COZI TV, NBC) San Jose; KOVR (CBS, Decades) Stockton; KPIX-TV (CBS, Decades) San Francisco; KQED (PBS) San Francisco; KRON-TV (Antenna TV, MNT) San Francisco; KTNC-TV (Estrella TV, This TV) Concord; KTVU (Buzzr, FOX, LATV, Movies!) Oakland; KTXL (Antenna TV, FOX) Sacramento; 22 FMs.
Programming (via satellite): C-SPAN; Discovery Life Channel; Freeform; Pop; QVC; The Weather Channel.
Fee: $29.50 installation; $39.95 monthly; $2.00 converter.

Expanded Basic Service 1
Subscribers: N.A.
Programming (via satellite): A&E; AMC; Animal Planet; Bravo; Cartoon Network; CMT; CNBC; CNN; Comcast SportsNet Bay Area; Comedy Central; Discovery Channel; Disney Channel; E! HD; ESPN; ESPN2; EVINE Live; Food Network; Fox News Channel; Fox Sports 1; FOX Sports Networks; FX; HGTV; History; HLN; Lifetime; MSNBC; MTV; Nickelodeon; Spike TV; Syfy; TBS; Telemundo; TLC; TNT; Travel Channel; Trinity Broadcasting Network (TBN); truTV; TV Land; Univision Studios; USA Network; VH1; WE tv.
Fee: $25.95 monthly.

Digital Basic Service
Subscribers: N.A.
Programming (via satellite): BBC America; Discovery Digital Networks; ESPN; ESPN2; ESPNews; Golf Channel; GSN; IFC; MC; MTV Classic; National Geographic Channel; NBCSN; Nick Jr.; TNT; Turner Classic Movies.
Fee: $8.00 monthly.

Digital Pay Service 1
Pay Units: N.A.
Programming (via satellite): Cinemax (multiplexed); Flix; HBO (multiplexed); Showtime (multiplexed); Starz (multiplexed); Starz Encore (multiplexed); Sundance TV; The Movie Channel (multiplexed).
Fee: $13.95 monthly (HBO), $9.95 monthly (Showtime or Cinemax), $8.00 monthly (Starz/Encore).

Video-On-Demand: No

Internet Service
Operational: Yes.
Subscribers: 6,564.
Broadband Service: Mediacom High Speed Internet.
Fee: $59.95 installation; $42.95 monthly; $3.00 modem lease; $239.95 modem purchase.

Telephone Service
Digital: Operational
Subscribers: 3,708.
Miles of Plant: 707.0 (coaxial); 159.0 (fiber optic). Homes passed: 39,931.
Vice President, Financial Reporting: Kenneth J. Kohrs. Senior Manager, Operations: Shawn Swatosh. Chief Technician: Mike Caruthers.
Ownership: Mediacom LLC (MSO).

COALINGA—Comcast Cable, 2441 North Grove Industrial Dr, Fresno, CA 93727-1535. Phone: 559-253-4050. Fax: 559-253-4090. Web Site: http://www.comcast.com. ICA: CA0208.
TV Market Ranking: Outside TV Markets (COALINGA). Franchise award date: August 15, 1977. Franchise expiration date: N.A. Began: January 1, 1979.
Channel capacity: 60 (operating 2-way). Channels available but not in use: N.A.

Basic Service
Subscribers: 502.
Programming (received off-air): KAIL (COZI TV, MNT, WeatherNation) Fresno; KFRE-TV (CW, IND) Sanger; KFSN-TV (ABC, Live Well Network) Fresno; KGMC (Antenna TV, Azteca, Daystar, HSN, MeTV, MundoMax) Clovis; KGPE (CBS, The Country Network, Untamed Sports TV) Fresno; KMPH-TV (FOX, This TV) Visalia; KNSO (TMO) Merced; KNXT (ETV) Visalia; KSEE (LATV, NBC) Fresno; KTFF-DT (UniMas) Porterville; KVPT (PBS) Fresno.
Programming (via satellite): A&E; AMC; Animal Planet; CNN; Comcast SportsNet Bay Area; Comedy Central; C-SPAN; Discovery Channel; Disney Channel; E! HD; ESPN; ESPN2; Fox News Channel; Freeform; FX; Great American Country; HGTV; History; HLN; ION Television; Lifetime; MTV; Nickelodeon; Pop; Spike TV; Syfy; TBS; The Weather Channel; TLC; TNT; Trinity Broadcasting Network (TBN); Turner Classic Movies; TV Land; Univision; USA Network; VH1; WGN America.
Fee: $42.00 installation; $19.25 monthly; $1.00 converter.

Digital Basic Service
Subscribers: N.A.
Programming (via satellite): BBC America; Bloomberg Television; Bravo; Discovery Digital Networks; Disney XD; DMX Music; ESPN Classic; ESPN2; ESPNews; EVINE Live; FOX College Sports Central; FOX College Sports Pacific; Fox Sports 1; Fuse; FXM; FYI; Golf Channel; Great American Country; GSN; HGTV; History; History International; HITS (Headend In The Sky); IFC; LMN; National Geographic Channel; NBCSN; Nick Jr.; Nicktoons; Outdoor Channel; Ovation; Sundance TV; Syfy; TeenNick; The Word Network; Trinity Broadcasting Network (TBN); Turner Classic Movies; TV Land; TVG Network; WE tv.

Digital Pay Service 1
Pay Units: N.A.
Programming (via satellite): Cinemax (multiplexed); Flix; HBO (multiplexed); Showtime (multiplexed); Starz (multiplexed); Starz Encore (multiplexed); The Movie Channel (multiplexed).
Fee: $15.99 -19.99 (each).

Video-On-Demand: No

Pay-Per-View
iN DEMAND (delivered digitally); Fresh (delivered digitally); Shorteez (delivered digitally); Playboy TV (delivered digitally); Hot Choice (delivered digitally).

Internet Service
Operational: Yes.

Telephone Service
Digital: Operational
Miles of Plant: 26.0 (coaxial); None (fiber optic). Homes passed: 3,800.
General Manager: Len Falter. Marketing Director: Stewart Butler.
Ownership: Comcast Cable Communications Inc. (MSO).

COARSEGOLD—Northland Cable Television, 40092 Hwy 49, Ste A, Oakhurst, CA 93644. Phones: 800-736-1414; 559-683-7388. Fax: 559-642-2432. E-mail: oakhurst@northlandcabletv.com. Web Site: http://www.yournorthland.com. ICA: CA0259.
TV Market Ranking: 72 (COARSEGOLD). Franchise award date: April 11, 1990. Franchise expiration date: N.A. Began: July 1, 1990.
Channel capacity: N.A. Channels available but not in use: N.A.

Basic Service
Subscribers: N.A.
Programming (received off-air): KAIL (COZI TV, MNT, WeatherNation) Fresno; KFRE-TV (CW, IND) Sanger; KFSN-TV (ABC, Live Well Network) Hanford; KGPE (CBS, The Country Network, Untamed Sports TV) Fresno; KMPH-TV (FOX, This TV) Visalia; KNSO (TMO) Merced; KNXT (ETV) Visalia; KSEE (LATV, NBC) Fresno; KVPT (PBS) Fresno.
Programming (via satellite): A&E; CNN; C-SPAN; Discovery Channel; ESPN; Fox News Channel; Hallmark Channel; HLN; National Geographic Channel; Pop; QVC; TBS; The Weather Channel; TLC; TNT; USA Network; WGN America.
Fee: $55.00 installation.

Expanded Basic Service 1
Subscribers: N.A.
Programming (via satellite): Cartoon Network; CMT; CNBC; Comcast SportsNet Bay Area; E! HD; ESPN2; Food Network; FXM; HGTV; History; Lifetime; Nickelodeon; Spike TV; Turner Classic Movies.
Fee: $39.99 monthly.

Digital Basic Service
Subscribers: 149.
Programming (via satellite): BBC America; Bloomberg Television; Discovery Digital Networks; DMX Music; Fox Sports 1; Golf Channel; Great American Country; GSN; INSP; Outdoor Channel; Syfy; Trinity Broadcasting Network (TBN).
Fee: $75.00 installation; $47.64 monthly.

Digital Expanded Basic Service
Subscribers: N.A.
Programming (via satellite): Bravo; Discovery Life Channel; IFC; WE tv.

Pay Service 1
Pay Units: N.A.
Programming (via satellite): HBO.
Fee: $15.00 installation; $13.50 monthly.

Digital Pay Service 1
Pay Units: N.A.
Programming (via satellite): Cinemax (multiplexed); Flix; HBO (multiplexed); Showtime (multiplexed); Starz (multiplexed); Starz Encore (multiplexed); Sundance TV; The Movie Channel (multiplexed).

Pay-Per-View
Hot Choice (delivered digitally); Playboy TV (delivered digitally); Fresh (delivered digitally).

Internet Service
Operational: Yes.
Broadband Service: Northland Express.
Fee: $42.99 monthly.

Telephone Service
Digital: Operational
Homes passed: 1,032.
Executive Vice President: Richard I. Clark. General Manager: Ken Musgrove. Chief Technician: Roger Conroy. Office Manager: Karen Bradley.
Ownership: Northland Communications Corp. (MSO).

COLEVILLE—Formerly served by Satview Broadband. No longer in operation. ICA: CA0432.

COLTON—Time Warner Cable. Now served by LOS ANGELES, CA [CA0009]. ICA: CA0134.

COMPTON—Time Warner Cable. Now served by LOS ANGELES, CA [CA0009]. ICA: CA0041.

CONCORD—Comcast Cable. Now served by SAN FRANCISCO, CA [CA0003]. ICA: CA0101.

CONCORD—Comcast Cable. Now served by SAN FRANCISCO, CA [CA0003]. ICA: CA0057.

CONCORD—Wave Broadband, 401 Parkplace Center, Ste 500, Kirkland, WA 98033. Phones: 800-427-8686; 925-459-1000. Web Site: http://www.wavebroadband.com. Also serves Contra Costa County (unincorporated areas), Pleasant Hill & Walnut Creek. ICA: CA0457. **Note:** This system is an overbuild.
TV Market Ranking: 7 (CONCORD, Contra Costa County (unincorporated areas), Pleasant Hill, Walnut Creek).
Channel capacity: 70 (operating 2-way). Channels available but not in use: N.A.

Basic Service
Subscribers: 16,519.
Programming (received off-air): KBCW (CW) San Francisco; KCNS (MundoMax, Retro TV) San Francisco; KCRA-TV (MeTV, NBC) Sacramento; KCSM-TV (PBS) San Mateo; KDTV-DT (Bounce TV, getTV, UNV) San Francisco; KFSF-DT (UniMas) Vallejo; KGO-TV (ABC, Live Well Network) San Francisco; KICU-TV (Heroes & Icons, IND) San Jose; KKPX-TV (ION) San Jose; KMTP-TV (ETV) San Francisco; KNTV (COZI TV, NBC) San Jose; KOFY-TV (MeTV) San Francisco; KPIX-TV (CBS, Decades) San Francisco; KQED (PBS) San Francisco; KQEH (PBS) San Jose; KRON-TV (Antenna TV, MNT) San Francisco; KSTS (TMO) San Jose; KTLN-TV (IND) Novato; KTNC-TV (Estrella TV, This TV) Concord; KTSF (IND) San Francisco; KTVU (Buzzr, FOX, LATV, Movies!) Oakland.
Programming (via satellite): California Channel; QVC; TBS; The Weather Channel; Trinity Broadcasting Network (TBN); WGN America.
Fee: $29.95 installation; $25.95 monthly.

Expanded Basic Service 1
Subscribers: N.A.
Programming (via satellite): A&E; AMC; Animal Planet; BET; Bravo; Cartoon Network; CMT; CNBC; CNN; Comcast SportsNet Bay Area; Comedy Central; C-SPAN; C-SPAN 2; Discovery Channel; Disney Channel; Disney XD; E! HD; ESPN; ESPN Classic; ESPN2; ESPNews; Food Network; Fox News Channel; Fox Sports 1;

Cable Systems—California

Freeform; FX; Golf Channel; GSN; Hallmark Channel; HGTV; History; HLN; Lifetime; MSNBC; MTV; NBC Universo; Nickelodeon; OWN: Oprah Winfrey Network; Spike TV; Syfy; TLC; TNT; Travel Channel; truTV; TV Land; Univision; USA Network; VH1.
Fee: $28.00 monthly.

Digital Basic Service
Subscribers: N.A.
Programming (via satellite): A&E HD; AXS TV; BBC America; Bloomberg Television; Boomerang; Classic Arts Showcase; Cloo; Cooking Channel; Discovery Digital Networks; DIY Network; ESPN HD; ESPN2 HD; ESPNU; Food Network HD; FOX College Sports Central; FOX College Sports Pacific; Fox Sports 2; Fuse; FXM; FYI; Great American Country; Hallmark Channel; HD Theater; HGTV HD; History International; IFC; LMN; MC; National Geographic Channel; National Geographic Channel HD; NBCSN; NFL Network; Nick Jr.; Nicktoons; Outdoor Channel; Ovation; Oxygen; Starz Encore Family; TeenNick; TNT HD; Turner Classic Movies; Universal HD; WE tv.

Digital Pay Service 1
Pay Units: N.A.
Programming (via satellite): Cinemax (multiplexed); Cinemax HD; Cinemax On Demand; Flix; HBO (multiplexed); HBO HD; HBO on Demand; here! On Demand; here! TV; HITS (Headend In The Sky); RTN; Showtime (multiplexed); Showtime HD; Showtime On Demand; Starz (multiplexed); Starz Encore (multiplexed); Starz HD; Starz On Demand; The Filipino Channel; The Movie Channel (multiplexed); The Movie Channel HD; The Movie Channel On Demand; Zee TV.
Fee: $8.95 monthly (Starz or Flix, Sundance & TMC), $9.95 monthly (Cinemax, HBO or Showtime), $11.95 monthly (Canales n, CTN or Filipino).

Video-On-Demand: Yes

Pay-Per-View
iN DEMAND (delivered digitally).

Internet Service
Operational: Yes.
Subscribers: 21,131.
Broadband Service: BroadbandNOW!.
Fee: $19.95-$74.95 monthly.

Telephone Service
Digital: Operational
Subscribers: 12,826.
Fee: $24.95-$49.95 monthly
Miles of Plant: 1,205.0 (coaxial); 683.0 (fiber optic). Homes passed: 75,674.
Chief Financial Officer: Wayne Schattenkerk. General Manager: Tim Peters. Marketing Manager: Bob Green.
Ownership: WaveDivision Holdings LLC (MSO).

COPPER COVE COPPEROPOLIS—Formerly served by Mountain View Cable. No longer in operation. ICA: CA0323.

CORONA—Time Warner Cable. Now served by LOS ANGELES, CA [CA0009]. ICA: CA0087.

CORONADO—Time Warner Cable. Now served by SAN DIEGO, CA [CA0007]. ICA: CA0163.

COSTA MESA—Time Warner Cable. Now served by LOS ANGELES, CA [CA0009]. ICA: CA0069.

COVINA—Time Warner Cable. Now served by LOS ANGELES, CA [CA0009]. ICA: CA0110.

CRESCENT CITY—Charter Communications, 12405 Powerscourt Dr, St. Louis, MO 63131. Phones: 636-207-5100 (Corporate office); 360-828-6600 (Vancouver office); 707-464-5722. Fax: 707-464-4849. Web Site: http://www.charter.com. Also serves Del Norte County, Gasquet & Hiouchi, CA; Brookings, Curry County (portions), Gold Beach & North Smith River, OR. ICA: CA0155.
TV Market Ranking: Outside TV Markets (CRESCENT CITY, Curry County (portions), Del Norte County, Gasquet, Hiouchi, North Smith River, Brookings, Gold Beach). Franchise award date: N.A. Franchise expiration date: N.A. Began: January 1, 1958.
Channel capacity: 67 (operating 2-way). Channels available but not in use: N.A.

Digital Basic Service
Subscribers: 7,677.
Programming (via satellite): BBC America; Boomerang; CNN en Espanol; CNN International; Discovery Digital Networks; DMX Music; ESPN Classic; ESPNews; FOX College Sports Central; FOX College Sports Pacific; Fox Deportes; Fox Sports 2; FXM; FYI; History International; IFC; LMN; NFL Network; Nick Jr.; Nicktoons; Sundance TV; TeenNick.
Fee: $26.99 monthly.

Digital Expanded Basic Service
Subscribers: N.A.
Programming (via satellite): A&E; AMC; Animal Planet; Cartoon Network; CMT; CNBC; CNN; Comcast SportsNet Bay Area; Comedy Central; Discovery Channel; Disney Channel; Disney XD; DIY Network; E! HD; ESPN; ESPN2; Food Network; Fox News Channel; Fox Sports 1; Freeform; FX; Golf Channel; Great American Country; GSN; Hallmark Channel; HGTV; History; HLN; Lifetime; MSNBC; MTV; MTV2; National Geographic Channel; NBCSN; Nickelodeon; Northwest Cable News; Oxygen; Spike TV; Syfy; TBS; TLC; TNT; Travel Channel; truTV; Turner Classic Movies; TV Land; USA Network; VH1; WE tv.
Fee: $42.95 monthly.

Digital Pay Service 1
Pay Units: N.A.
Programming (via satellite): Cinemax; Flix; HBO (multiplexed); Showtime (multiplexed); Starz (multiplexed); Starz Encore; The Movie Channel (multiplexed).
Fee: $18.61 monthly (each).

Video-On-Demand: No

Pay-Per-View
iN DEMAND (delivered digitally); Hot Choice (delivered digitally); Playboy TV (delivered digitally); Fresh (delivered digitally); Shorteez (delivered digitally).

Internet Service
Operational: Yes.
Subscribers: 9,742.
Broadband Service: Charter Internet.
Fee: $29.95 monthly.

Telephone Service
Digital: Operational
Subscribers: 1,307.
Miles of Plant: 809.0 (coaxial); 763.0 (fiber optic). Homes passed: 25,087.
Vice President: Frank Antonovich. General Manager: Linda Kimberly. Plant Manager: Earl Desomber. Chief Technician: Dennis Putman. Marketing Director: Diane Long. Accounting Director: David Sovanski. Office Manager: Sandra Milunich.
Ownership: Charter Communications Inc. (MSO).

CRESCENT MILLS—Formerly served by Wave Broadband. No longer in operation. ICA: CA0447.

CROWLEY LAKE—Formerly served by Satview Broadband. No longer in operation. ICA: CA0289.

CUPERTINO—Comcast Cable. Now served by SAN FRANCISCO, CA [CA0003]. ICA: CA0466.

CYPRESS—Time Warner Cable. Now served by LOS ANGELES, CA [CA0009]. ICA: CA0117.

DAVIS—Comcast Cable. Now served by SACRAMENTO, CA [CA0002]. ICA: CA0122.

DESERT CENTER—Formerly served by American Pacific Co. No longer in operation. ICA: CA0327.

DESERT HOT SPRINGS—Time Warner Cable. Now served by PALM SPRINGS, CA [CA0036]. ICA: CA0156.

DIAMOND BAR—Time Warner Cable. Now served by LOS ANGELES, CA [CA0009]. ICA: CA0082.

DORRIS—Formerly served by Almega Cable. No longer in operation. ICA: CA0274.

DOWNEY—Formerly served by Comcast Cable. No longer in operation. ICA: CA0022.

DOWNIEVILLE—Formerly served by Downieville TV Corp. No longer in operation. ICA: CA0287.

EAGLE ROCK—Time Warner Cable. Now served by LOS ANGELES, CA [CA0009]. ICA: CA0472.

EARLIMART—Charter Communications. Now served by PORTERVILLE, CA [CA0152]. ICA: CA0328.

EAST LOS ANGELES—Time Warner Cable. Now served by LOS ANGELES, CA [CA0009]. ICA: CA0063.

EAST SAN FERNANDO VALLEY—Time Warner Cable. Now served by LOS ANGELES, CA [CA0009]. ICA: CA0012.

EL CENTRO—Time Warner Cable, 1289 South 2nd Ave, Yuma, AZ 85364-4715. Phones: 928-782-9853; 928-329-9723. Fax: 928-783-0242. Web Site: http://www.timewarnercable.com. Also serves Brawley, Calexico, El Centro NAF, Holtville, Imperial, Seeley & Westmorland. ICA: CA0088.
TV Market Ranking: Below 100 (Brawley, Calexico, EL CENTRO, El Centro NAF, Holtville, Imperial, Seeley, Westmorland). Franchise award date: March 1, 1960. Franchise expiration date: N.A. Began: March 1, 1960.
Channel capacity: 77 (operating 2-way). Channels available but not in use: N.A.

Basic Service
Subscribers: 12,841.
Programming (received off-air): KECY-TV (ABC, FOX, MNT, TMO) El Centro; KSWT (CBS, Estrella TV, Tuff TV) Yuma; KVYE (LATV, UNV) El Centro; KYMA-DT (NBC, This TV) Yuma; 5 FMs.
Programming (via microwave): KABC-TV (ABC, Live Well Network) Los Angeles; KCOP-TV (Bounce TV, Buzzr, Heroes & Icons, MNT, Movies!) Los Angeles; KPBS (PBS) San Diego.
Programming (via satellite): A&E; AMC; Animal Planet; BET; California Channel; Cartoon Network; CMT; CNBC; CNN; Comedy Central; C-SPAN; C-SPAN 2; Discovery Channel; E! HD; ESPN; ESPN2; EVINE Live; EWTN Global Catholic Network; Food Network; Fox Deportes; Fox News Channel; FOX Sports West/Prime Ticket; Freeform; FX; Hallmark Channel; HGTV; History; HLN; ION Television; Lifetime; MSNBC; MTV; Nickelodeon; Oxygen; QVC; Syfy; TBS; Telemundo; The Weather Channel; TLC; TNT; Travel Channel; truTV; TV Land; Univision; USA Network; VH1.
Fee: $32.99 installation; $23.00 monthly; $2.01 converter.

Expanded Basic Service 1
Subscribers: N.A.
Programming (via satellite): Disney Channel; FOX Sports West/Prime Ticket; Spike TV.
Fee: $7.00 monthly.

Digital Basic Service
Subscribers: N.A.
Programming (via satellite): BBC America; Bloomberg Television; Discovery Digital Networks; Disney XD; DIY Network; ESPN Classic; ESPNews; Fox Sports 1; Fuse; Golf Channel; GSN; HITS (Headend In The Sky); IFC; MC; Hispanic Information and Telecommunications Network; NBCSN; Nick 2; Nick Jr.; Outdoor Channel; Sundance TV; TeenNick; Trinity Broadcasting Network (TBN); Turner Classic Movies; WE tv.
Fee: $6.00 monthly (Variety, Choice, Movies, Sports or Espanol).

Digital Pay Service 1
Pay Units: N.A.
Programming (via satellite): ART America; Cinemax (multiplexed); Flix; HBO (multiplexed); RAI Italia; RTN; Showtime (multiplexed); Starz (multiplexed); Starz Encore (multiplexed); The Filipino Channel; The Movie Channel (multiplexed); TV Asia; TV5, La Television International.
Fee: $12.00 monthly (Cinemax, Encore, HBO, Showtime, TMC or Starz), $15.00 monthly (ART, CCTV, Filipino Channel, RAI, RTN, TV Asia, TV Japan or TV-5).

Video-On-Demand: Planned

Pay-Per-View
Special events; Playboy TV (delivered digitally); Fresh (delivered digitally); Hot Choice (delivered digitally).

Internet Service
Operational: Yes.
Subscribers: 13,265.
Broadband Service: Road Runner.
Fee: $44.95 monthly; $5.00 modem lease.

Telephone Service
Digital: Operational
Subscribers: 5,380.
Fee: $49.95 monthly
Miles of Plant: 721.0 (coaxial); 534.0 (fiber optic). Homes passed: 54,087. Homes passed & miles of plant included in Yuma, AZ.
General Manager: Ricky Rinehart. Operations Manager: Hughie Williams. Marketing Manager: Shayne Abney. Business Manager: Jessica Haggard.
Ownership: Time Warner Cable (MSO).

EL MONTE—Time Warner Cable. Now served by LOS ANGELES, CA [CA0009]. ICA: CA0047.

California—Cable Systems

ESPARTO—Cableview Communications, PO Box 619, Esparto, CA 95627. Phone: 530-787-4656. E-mail: cs@cableview.tv. Web Site: http://cableview.tv. ICA: CA0902.
TV Market Ranking: 25 (ESPARTO).
Channel capacity: N.A. Channels available but not in use: N.A.
Basic Service
Subscribers: 310.
Fee: $52.00 installation; $32.87 monthly.
Secretary: Penny Langhout.
Ownership: Cableview Communications.

ETNA—Formerly served by Siskiyou Cablevision Inc. No longer in operation. ICA: CA0233.

FAIRFIELD—Comcast Cable. Now served by SAN FRANCISCO, CA [CA0003]. ICA: CA0078.

FALL RIVER MILLS—Formerly served by Almega Cable. No longer in operation. ICA: CA0329.

FISH CAMP—Formerly served by Northland Cable Television. No longer in operation. ICA: CA0330.

FORESTHILL—Suddenlink Communications, 520 Maryville Centre Dr, Ste 300, St. Louis, MO 63141. Phones: 314-315-9400; 530-268-3771. Web Site: http://www.suddenlink.com. ICA: CA0238.
TV Market Ranking: Outside TV Markets (FORESTHILL). Franchise award date: April 1, 1987. Franchise expiration date: N.A. Began: September 1, 1989.
Channel capacity: N.A. Channels available but not in use: N.A.
Basic Service
Subscribers: 171.
Programming (received off-air): KCRA-TV (MeTV, NBC) Sacramento; KMAX-TV (CW) Sacramento; KOVR (CBS, Decades) Stockton; KQCA (MNT, Movies!, This TV) Stockton; KTFK-DT (getTV, UniMas) Stockton; KTXL (Antenna TV, FOX) Sacramento; KUVS-DT (Bounce TV, UNV) Modesto; KVIE (PBS) Sacramento; KXTV (ABC) Sacramento.
Programming (via satellite): A&E; Animal Planet; CNBC; CNN; Comedy Central; C-SPAN; C-SPAN 2; Discovery Channel; Disney Channel; E! HD; ESPN; ESPN2; EWTN Global Catholic Network; Food Network; Fox News Channel; Freeform; Great American Country; HGTV; History; HLN; Lifetime; MTV; Nickelodeon; QVC; Spike TV; Syfy; TBS; The Weather Channel; TLC; TNT; Trinity Broadcasting Network (TBN); Turner Classic Movies; TV Land; USA Network; VH1; WGN America.
Fee: $40.00 installation; $35.04 monthly.
Digital Basic Service
Subscribers: N.A.
Programming (via satellite): BBC America; Bravo; Discovery Digital Networks; Disney XD; DMX Music; ESPN Classic; ESPNews; Fox Sports 1; Fuse; FYI; Golf Channel; GSN; History International; IFC; LMN; MTV Classic; MTV2; National Geographic Channel; NBCSN; Nick Jr.; Starz; TeenNick; VH1 Country; WE tv.
Pay Service 1
Pay Units: N.A.
Programming (via satellite): Cinemax; HBO; Showtime; The Movie Channel.
Digital Pay Service 1
Pay Units: N.A.
Programming (via satellite): Cinemax (multiplexed); HBO (multiplexed); Showtime (multiplexed); The Movie Channel (multiplexed).
Video-On-Demand: No
Internet Service
Operational: Yes. Began: January 1, 1998.
Broadband Service: Suddenlink High Speed Internet.
Fee: $99.99 installation; $24.95 monthly.
Telephone Service
Digital: Operational
Miles of Plant: 35.0 (coaxial); None (fiber optic). Homes passed: 1,500.
Senior Vice President, Corporate Finance: Michael Pflantz. Vice President, Accounting: Sabrina Warr. General Manager: Doug Landaker. Marketing Director: Jason Oelkers. Chief Technician: Tim Lenz.
Ownership: Cequel Communications Holdings I LLC (MSO).

FORT BRAGG—Comcast Cable. Now served by SAN FRANCISCO, CA [CA0003]. ICA: CA0481.

FORT IRWIN—Formerly served by Total TV of Fort Irwin Inc. No longer in operation. ICA: CA0405.

FOSTER CITY—Comcast Cable. Now served by SAN FRANCISCO, CA [CA0003]. ICA: CA0136.

FRANCISCAN MOBILE HOME PARK—Formerly served by Comcast Cable. No longer in operation. ICA: CA0331.

FRAZIER PARK—CalNeva Broadband, 322 Ash St, PO Box 1470, Westwood, CA 96137. Phones: 530-256-2028; 866-330-2028. Web Site: http://blog.calneva.org. ICA: CA0225.
TV Market Ranking: Outside TV Markets (FRAZIER PARK). Franchise award date: September 4, 1974. Franchise expiration date: N.A. Began: January 1, 1981.
Channel capacity: N.A. Channels available but not in use: N.A.
Basic Service
Subscribers: 350.
Programming (received off-air): KABC-TV (ABC, Live Well Network) Los Angeles; KBAK-TV (CBS) Bakersfield; KCAL-TV (IND) Los Angeles; KCBS-TV (CBS, Decades) Los Angeles; KCET (ETV) Los Angeles; KCOP-TV (Bounce TV, Buzzr, Heroes & Icons, MNT, Movies!) Los Angeles; KERO-TV (ABC, Azteca America, MeTV) Bakersfield; KGET-TV (CW, NBC) Bakersfield; KMPH-TV (FOX, This TV) Visalia; KNBC (COZI TV, NBC) Los Angeles; KTFF-DT (UniMas) Porterville; KTLA (Antenna TV, CW, This TV) Los Angeles; KTTV (FOX) Los Angeles; KUVI-DT (getTV, MNT) Bakersfield; allband FM.
Programming (via satellite): A&E; Animal Planet; Cartoon Network; CMT; CNN; Comedy Central; C-SPAN; C-SPAN 2; Discovery Channel; E! HD; ESPN; ESPN Classic; ESPN2; Food Network; Fox News Channel; FOX Sports Networks; FX; Hallmark Channel; HGTV; History; Lifetime; MTV; National Geographic Channel; Nickelodeon; Pop; QVC; Spike TV; Syfy; TBS; The Weather Channel; TLC; TNT; Travel Channel; Trinity Broadcasting Network (TBN); truTV; Turner Classic Movies; TV Land; VH1; WGN America.
Fee: $65.00 installation; $31.00 monthly.
Digital Basic Service
Subscribers: N.A.
Programming (via satellite): BBC America; Bloomberg Television; Bravo; CMT; Destination America; Discovery Kids Channel; DMX Music; ESPNews; Fox Sports 1; FXM; FYI; Golf Channel; GSN; History International; IFC; Investigation Discovery; LMN; MTV Classic; MTV Jams; MTV2; Nick Jr.; Nicktoons; Outdoor Channel; Ovation; OWN: Oprah Winfrey Network; Science Channel; Sundance TV; TeenNick; VH1 Soul.
Digital Pay Service 1
Pay Units: N.A.
Programming (via satellite): Cinemax (multiplexed); HBO (multiplexed); Showtime (multiplexed); Starz (multiplexed); Starz Encore (multiplexed); The Movie Channel (multiplexed).
Fee: $12.50 monthly (Cinemax, HBO, Showtime/TMC or Starz/Encore).
Video-On-Demand: No
Pay-Per-View
iN DEMAND (delivered digitally).
Internet Service
Operational: Yes.
Broadband Service: Rapid High Speed Internet.
Fee: $29.25 installation; $24.95 monthly.
Telephone Service
None
Miles of Plant: 90.0 (coaxial); 15.0 (fiber optic). Homes passed: 3,000.
General Manager: Tom Gelardi.
Ownership: CalNeva Broadband LLC (MSO).

FREMONT—Comcast Cable. Now served by SAN FRANCISCO, CA [CA0003]. ICA: CA0046.

FRESNO—Comcast Cable, 2441 North Grove Industrial Dr, Fresno, CA 93727-1535. Phones: 800-266-2278; 559-253-4050. Fax: 559-253-4090. Web Site: http://www.comcast.com. Also serves Armona, Atwater, Buellton, Chowchilla, Clovis, Corcoran, Dinuba, Dos Palos, Firebaugh, Fowler, Fresno County (portions), Hanford, Kerman, Kings County (portions), Kingsburg, Laton, Lemoore, Lemoore Naval Air Station, Lompoc, Los Banos, Los Olivos, Madera, Madera County (portions), Mendota, Merced, Merced County (portions), Mission Hills, Orcutt, Parlier, Reedley, Riverdale, San Joaquin, Sanger, Santa Maria, Santa Ynez, Selma, Solvang, Tulare, Vandenburg Village & Visalia. ICA: CA0011.
TV Market Ranking: 25 (Los Banos, Merced); 25,72 (Atwater, Merced County (portions)); 72 (Armona, Chowchilla, Clovis, Corcoran, Dinuba, Dos Palos, Firebaugh, Fowler, FRESNO, Fresno County (portions), Hanford, Kerman, Kings County (portions), Kingsburg, Laton, Lemoore, Lemoore Naval Air Station, Madera, Madera County (portions), Mendota, Parlier, Reedley, Riverdale, San Joaquin, Sanger, Selma, Tulare, Visalia); Below 100 (Buellton, Los Olivos, Mission Hills, Orcutt, Santa Ynez, Solvang, Vandenburg Village, Lompoc, Santa Maria); Outside TV Markets (Fresno County (portions)). Franchise award date: N.A. Franchise expiration date: N.A. Began: May 9, 1977.
Channel capacity: 70 (operating 2-way). Channels available but not in use: N.A.
Basic Service
Subscribers: 161,999.
Programming (received off-air): KAIL (COZI TV, MNT, WeatherNation) Fresno; KFRE-TV (CW, IND) Sanger; KFSN-TV (ABC, Live Well Network) Fresno; KFTV-DT (getTV, UNV) Hanford; KGMC (Antenna TV, Azteca, Daystar, HSN, MeTV, MundoMax) Clovis; KGPE (CBS, The Country Network, Untamed Sports TV) Fresno; KMPH-TV (FOX, This TV) Visalia; KNSO (TMO) Merced; KNXT (ETV) Visalia; KSEE (LATV, NBC) Fresno; KVPT (PBS) Fresno; 17 FMs.
Programming (via satellite): California Channel; C-SPAN; C-SPAN 2; ION Television; Pop.
Fee: $42.00 installation; $39.12 monthly; $.24 converter.
Expanded Basic Service 1
Subscribers: N.A.
Programming (via satellite): A&E; AMC; Animal Planet; BET; Bravo; Cartoon Network; CNBC; CNN; Comcast SportsNet Bay Area; Comedy Central; Discovery Channel; Disney Channel; E! HD; ESPN; ESPN Classic; ESPN2; Food Network; Fox Deportes; Fox News Channel; Fox Sports 1; Freeform; FX; Golf Channel; Great American Country; HGTV; History; HLN; Lifetime; MSNBC; MTV; NBC Universo; NBCSN; Nickelodeon; Oxygen; Spike TV; Syfy; TBS; The Weather Channel; TLC; TNT; Travel Channel; Trinity Broadcasting Network (TBN); truTV; TV Land; Univision; USA Network; VH1; WE tv; WGN America.
Fee: $37.73 monthly.
Digital Basic Service
Subscribers: N.A.
Programming (via satellite): ABP News; ART America; BBC America; Bloomberg Television; Discovery Digital Networks; Disney XD; DMX Music; ESPNews; EVINE Live; FOX College Sports Central; FOX College Sports Pacific; Fuse; FXM; FYI; History International; HITS (Headend In The Sky); IFC; Life OK; LMN; National Geographic Channel; Nick Jr.; Nicktoons; Outdoor Channel; Ovation; RTN; STAR Plus; Sundance TV; TeenNick; The Filipino Channel; Turner Classic Movies; TV Asia; TV5MONDE USA.
Digital Pay Service 1
Pay Units: N.A.
Programming (via satellite): Cinemax (multiplexed); Flix; HBO (multiplexed); Showtime (multiplexed); Starz (multiplexed); Starz Encore (multiplexed); The Movie Channel (multiplexed).
Fee: $13.00 monthly (each).
Video-On-Demand: Yes
Pay-Per-View
iN DEMAND; ESPN Now (delivered digitally); Hot Choice (delivered digitally); iN DEMAND (delivered digitally); Playboy TV (delivered digitally); Fresh (delivered digitally); Shorteez (delivered digitally).
Internet Service
Operational: Yes.
Subscribers: 166,287.
Broadband Service: Comcast High Speed Internet.
Fee: $42.95 monthly; $3.00 modem lease.
Telephone Service
Analog: Not Operational
Digital: Operational
Subscribers: 79,605.
Miles of Plant: 9,281.0 (coaxial); 2,890.0 (fiber optic). Homes passed: 595,180.
General Manager: Len Falter. Marketing Director: Stewart Butler. Communications Director: Erica Smith.
Ownership: Comcast Cable Communications Inc. (MSO).

FRESNO—Formerly served by Sprint Corp. No longer in operation. ICA: CA0407.

GARBERVILLE—Wave Broadband, 401 Parkplace Center, Ste 500, Kirkland, WA 98033. Phones: 916-652-9479; 866-928-3123. Web Site: http://www.wavebroadband.com. Also serves Benbow & Redway. ICA: CA0244.

Cable Systems—California

TV Market Ranking: Outside TV Markets (Benbow, GARBERVILLE, Redway). Franchise award date: N.A. Franchise expiration date: N.A. Began: June 1, 1975.
Channel capacity: N.A. Channels available but not in use: N.A.
Basic Service
Subscribers: 404.
Programming (received off-air): KEET (PBS) Eureka; KIEM-TV (NBC) Eureka; KRCR-TV (ABC, MeTV, Movies!) Redding; KVIQ (CBS, CW) Eureka; allband FM.
Programming (via microwave): KRON-TV (Antenna TV, MNT) San Francisco; KTVU (Buzzr, FOX, LATV, Movies!) Oakland.
Programming (via satellite): A&E; CNN; Comcast SportsNet Bay Area; Discovery Channel; Disney Channel; ESPN; Freeform; HLN; Lifetime; MTV; Nickelodeon; QVC; Spike TV; TBS; TNT; Turner Classic Movies; USA Network; WGN America.
Fee: $29.95 installation; $49.78 monthly; $2.00 converter.
Pay Service 1
Pay Units: 160.
Programming (via satellite): Cinemax; HBO; Showtime; Starz; Sundance TV; The Movie Channel.
Fee: $10.95 monthly (Starz/Encore), $11.95 monthly (Cinemax, HBO or Showtime/TMC/Sundance).
Video-On-Demand: No
Internet Service
Operational: Yes.
Broadband Service: Wave Broadband.
Fee: $59.95 monthly.
Telephone Service
Digital: Operational
Fee: $49.95 monthly
Miles of Plant: 17.0 (coaxial); None (fiber optic). Homes passed: 1,329.
Chief Financial Officer: Wayne Schattenkerk. General Manager: Tim Peters. Technology Manager: Seth Johannson. Sales Director: Tom Carroll.
Ownership: WaveDivision Holdings LLC (MSO).

GEORGIAN MANOR MOBILE HOME PARK—Formerly served by Comcast Cable. No longer in operation. ICA: CA0333.

GILROY—Charter Communications, 8120 Camino Arrayo Circle, Gilroy, CA 95020. Phones: 636-207-5100 (Corporate office); 805-544-1962 (San Luis Obispo office); 408-847-2020. Fax: 408-847-2993. Web Site: http://www.charter.com. Also serves Capitola, Corralitos, Day Valley, Freedom, Hollister, Morgan Hill, Pajaro Dunes, San Benito County (portions), San Juan Bautista (portions), Santa Clara County (portions), Santa Cruz County (portions) & Watsonville. ICA: CA0425.
TV Market Ranking: 7 (Capitola, Corralitos, Day Valley, Freedom, GILROY, Hollister, Morgan Hill, Pajaro Dunes, San Benito County (portions), Santa Clara County (portions), Santa Cruz County (portions), Watsonville); Below 100 (San Juan Bautista (portions), San Benito County (portions)); Outside TV Markets (San Benito County (portions)).
Channel capacity: 77 (operating 2-way). Channels available but not in use: N.A.
Digital Basic Service
Subscribers: 17,482.
Programming (via satellite): BBC America; Discovery Digital Networks; DIY Network; ESPN Classic; ESPNews; FOX College Sports Pacific; Fox Sports 2; Fuse; FYI; History International; IFC; LMN; MC; NFL Network; Nick 2; Nick Jr.; Outdoor Channel; TeenNick; TVG Network.
Fee: $49.99 installation; $28.63 monthly.
Digital Expanded Basic Service
Subscribers: N.A.
Programming (via satellite): A&E; AMC; Animal Planet; BET; Bravo; Cartoon Network; CMT; CNBC; CNN; Comcast SportsNet Bay Area; Comedy Central; Discovery Channel; Discovery Life Channel; Disney Channel; Disney XD; E! HD; ESPN; ESPN2; Food Network; Fox Deportes; Fox News Channel; Fox Sports 1; FX; Golf Channel; GSN; Hallmark Channel; HGTV; History; HLN; Lifetime; MSNBC; MTV; National Geographic Channel; NBCSN; Nickelodeon; Oxygen; Spike TV; Syfy; TLC; TNT; Travel Channel; truTV; Turner Classic Movies; TV Land; USA Network; VH1; WE tv.
Fee: $38.99 monthly.
Digital Pay Service 1
Pay Units: N.A.
Programming (via satellite): Cinemax (multiplexed); HBO (multiplexed); Starz (multiplexed).
Video-On-Demand: Yes
Pay-Per-View
Hot Choice (delivered digitally); Playboy TV (delivered digitally); Fresh (delivered digitally); Shorteez (delivered digitally).
Internet Service
Operational: Yes.
Subscribers: 5,475.
Broadband Service: Charter Internet.
Fee: $29.99 monthly.
Telephone Service
Digital: Operational
Subscribers: 1,867.
Miles of Plant: 1,106.0 (coaxial); 290.0 (fiber optic). Homes passed: 77,572.
Vice President & General Manager: Ed Merrill. Marketing Director: Sarwar Assar. Accounting Director: Steve Lottmann.
Ownership: Charter Communications Inc. (MSO).

GLENDALE—Charter Communications, 12405 Powerscourt Dr, St. Louis, MO 63131. Phones: 636-207-5100 (Corporate office); 626-430-6112; 626-430-3300. Fax: 626-430-3420. Web Site: http://www.charter.com. Also serves Burbank, La Crescenta & Montrose. ICA: CA0021.
TV Market Ranking: 2 (Burbank, GLENDALE, La Crescenta, Montrose). Franchise award date: January 1, 1962. Franchise expiration date: N.A. Began: January 1, 1962.
Channel capacity: 70 (operating 2-way). Channels available but not in use: N.A.
Digital Basic Service
Subscribers: 39,205.
Programming (via satellite): BBC America; Bloomberg Television; Discovery Digital Networks; FYI; History International; IFC; LMN; MC; Nick Jr.; TeenNick; WE tv.
Fee: $14.99 monthly.
Digital Expanded Basic Service
Subscribers: N.A.
Programming (via satellite): A&E; AMC; Animal Planet; BET; Bravo; Cartoon Network; CNBC; CNN; Comedy Central; C-SPAN; C-SPAN 2; Discovery Channel; Disney Channel; Disney XD; E! HD; ESPN; ESPN Classic; ESPN2; Food Network; Fox News Channel; FOX Sports West/Prime Ticket; Freeform; FX; Golf Channel; GSN; HGTV; History; HLN; Lifetime; MSNBC; MTV; Nickelodeon; Oxygen; Pop; Spike TV; Syfy; The Weather Channel; TLC; TNT; Travel Channel; truTV; Turner Classic Movies; TV Land; Univision; VH1.
Fee: $48.95 monthly.
Digital Pay Service 1
Pay Units: N.A.
Programming (via satellite): Cinemax (multiplexed); Flix; HBO (multiplexed); Showtime (multiplexed); Starz (multiplexed); Starz Encore (multiplexed); Sundance TV; The Movie Channel (multiplexed).
Fee: $10.90 monthly (TMC), $10.95 monthly (Cinemax or Starz/Encore), $12.95 monthly (HBO or Showtime/Flix/Sundance).
Video-On-Demand: Yes
Pay-Per-View
iN DEMAND (delivered digitally); Fresh (delivered digitally); Shorteez (delivered digitally).
Internet Service
Operational: Yes.
Subscribers: 27,453.
Broadband Service: Charter Internet.
Fee: $29.99 monthly; $4.95 modem lease.
Telephone Service
Analog: Not Operational
Digital: Operational
Miles of Plant: 1,155.0 (coaxial); 249.0 (fiber optic). Homes passed: 144,318. Homes passed includes Whittier.
Vice President & General Manager: Wendy Rasmusson. Technical Operations Manager: Tom Williams. Marketing Manager: Lily Ho. Accounting Director: David Sovanski.
Ownership: Charter Communications Inc. (MSO).

GLENDORA—Time Warner Cable. Now served by LOS ANGELES, CA [CA0009]. ICA: CA0035.

GLENWOOD—Comcast Cable. Now served by SAN FRANCISCO, CA [CA0003]. ICA: CA0335.

GRASS VALLEY—Comcast Cable. Now served by SACRAMENTO, CA [CA0002]. ICA: CA0164.

GREENFIELD—Charter Communications, 12405 Powerscourt Dr, St. Louis, MO 63131. Phones: 636-207-5100 (Corporate office); 408-847-2020; 805-544-1962 (San Luis Obispo office). Fax: 408-847-2993. Web Site: http://www.charter.com. Also serves Monterey County (portions). ICA: CA0337.
TV Market Ranking: Below 100 (GREENFIELD, Monterey County (portions)). Franchise award date: N.A. Franchise expiration date: N.A. Began: January 1, 1974.
Channel capacity: N.A. Channels available but not in use: N.A.
Digital Basic Service
Subscribers: 173.
Programming (via satellite): BBC America; Bloomberg Television; Discovery Life Channel; Disney XD; DMX Music; ESPN Classic; ESPN2; ESPNews; EVINE Live; Fox Sports 1; Fuse; FXM; FYI; Golf Channel; GSN; HGTV; History; History International; IFC; INSP; LMN; NBCSN; Nick Jr.; Outdoor Channel; TeenNick; Trinity Broadcasting Network (TBN); Turner Classic Movies; WE tv.
Fee: $26.99 monthly.
Digital Expanded Basic Service
Subscribers: N.A.
Programming (via satellite): CNN; Discovery Channel; Disney Channel; HLN; TBS; TNT; Univision; WGN America.
Fee: $28.99 monthly.
Digital Pay Service 1
Pay Units: N.A.
Programming (via satellite): Cinemax (multiplexed); HBO (multiplexed); Showtime (multiplexed); Starz; Starz Encore (multiplexed); The Movie Channel.
Video-On-Demand: No
Pay-Per-View
iN DEMAND (delivered digitally); ESPN Now (delivered digitally); ESPN Sports PPV (delivered digitally); Hot Choice (delivered digitally); Playboy TV (delivered digitally); Fresh (delivered digitally); Shorteez (delivered digitally).
Internet Service
Operational: Yes.
Broadband Service: Charter Internet.
Telephone Service
Digital: Operational
Miles of Plant: 278.0 (coaxial); 39.0 (fiber optic). Homes passed: 10,356.
Vice President & General Manager: Ed Merrill. Chief Technician: Mark Beech. Marketing Director: Sarwar Assar. Accounting Director: David Sovanski.
Ownership: Charter Communications Inc. (MSO).

GROVELAND—SNC Cable, PO Box 281, Standard, CA 95373. Phones: 209-962-6373; 209-588-9601. E-mail: cust@gosnc.com. Web Site: http://gosnc.com. Also serves Big Oak Flat. ICA: CA0209.
TV Market Ranking: Outside TV Markets (Big Oak Flat, GROVELAND). Franchise award date: N.A. Franchise expiration date: N.A. Began: October 1, 1978.
Channel capacity: N.A. Channels available but not in use: N.A.
Basic Service
Subscribers: N.A.
Programming (received off-air): KCRA-TV (MeTV, NBC) Sacramento; KMAX-TV (CW) Sacramento; KOVR (CBS, Decades) Stockton; KQCA (MNT, Movies!, This TV) Stockton; KTXL (Antenna TV, FOX) Sacramento; KUVS-DT (Bounce TV, UNV) Modesto; KVIE (PBS) Sacramento; KXTV (ABC) Sacramento.
Programming (via satellite): A&E; AMC; Animal Planet; CNN; Comedy Central; C-SPAN; Discovery Channel; Disney Channel; ESPN; Fox News Channel; Freeform; FX; HLN; Lifetime; Nickelodeon; Spike TV; TBS; TNT; USA Network; VH1; WGN America.
Fee: $50.00 installation.
Pay Service 1
Pay Units: N.A.
Programming (via satellite): HBO.
Fee: $13.95 monthly.
Internet Service
Operational: Yes.
Fee: $21.95 monthly.
Telephone Service
Digital: Operational
Miles of Plant: 65.0 (coaxial); None (fiber optic). Homes passed: 4,000.
General Manager: Tim Holden. Product Development & Communications Manager: Bill Manley.
Ownership: Sierra Nevada Communications (MSO).

GUADALUPE—Charter Communications. Now served by SAN LUIS OBISPO, CA [CA0045]. ICA: CA0400.

HACIENDA HEIGHTS—Time Warner Cable. Now served by LOS ANGELES, CA [CA0009]. ICA: CA0027.

2017 Edition — D-89

California—Cable Systems

HACIENDA HEIGHTS—Time Warner Cable. Now served by LOS ANGELES, CA [CA0009]. ICA: CA0338.

HALF MOON BAY—Comcast Cable. Now served by SAN FRANCISCO, CA [CA0003]. ICA: CA0179.

HAPPY CAMP—Formerly served by Almega Cable. No longer in operation. ICA: CA0260.

HAYFORK—Formerly served by New Day Broadband. No longer in operation. ICA: CA0279.

HAYWARD—Comcast Cable. Now served by SAN FRANCISCO, CA [CA0003]. ICA: CA0026.

HEALDSBURG—Comcast Cable. Now served by SAN FRANCISCO, CA [CA0003]. ICA: CA0487.

HEMET—Time Warner Cable. Now served by LOS ANGELES, CA [CA0009]. ICA: CA0044.

HERLONG—Formerly served by Almega Cable. No longer in operation. ICA: CA0340.

HERMOSA BEACH—Time Warner Cable. Now served by LOS ANGELES, CA [CA0009]. ICA: CA0094.

HESPERIA—Charter Communications, 25953 Twenty Muleteam Rd, Boron, CA 93516. Phones: 636-207-5100 (Corporate office); 951-343-5100. Web Site: http://www.charter.com. Also serves Adelanto, Angelus Oaks, Apple Valley, Big Bear, Big Bear City, Big Bear Lake, Forest Falls, Green Valley Lake, Lake Arrowhead, San Bernardino County (portions) & Victorville. ICA: CA0158.
TV Market Ranking: 2 (Adelanto, Angelus Oaks, Apple Valley, Big Bear, Big Bear City, Big Bear Lake, Forest Falls, Green Valley Lake, HESPERIA, Lake Arrowhead, San Bernardino County (portions), Victorville); Below 100 (San Bernardino County (portions)); Outside TV Markets (San Bernardino County (portions)). Franchise award date: May 1, 1981. Franchise expiration date: N.A. Began: N.A.
Channel capacity: 68 (operating 2-way). Channels available but not in use: N.A.
Digital Basic Service
Subscribers: 41,649.
Programming (via satellite): AWE; AXS TV; BBC America; Bloomberg Television; Boomerang; BYUtv; CNN en Espanol; Discovery Digital Networks; Disney XD; DIY Network; ESPN; ESPNews; EWTN Global Catholic Network; FOX College Sports Central; FOX College Sports Pacific; Fox Sports 2; Fuse; FYI; HD Theater; History International; IFC; International Television (ITV); LMN; MC; NFL Network; Nick Jr.; Nicktoons; Sundance TV; TeenNick; TV One; TVG Network.
Fee: $49.99 installation; $14.99 monthly.
Digital Expanded Basic Service
Subscribers: N.A.
Programming (via satellite): A&E; AMC; Animal Planet; BET; Bravo; Cartoon Network; CMT; CNBC; CNN; Comedy Central; Discovery Channel; Disney Channel; E! HD; ESPN; ESPN Classic; ESPN2; EVINE Live; EWTN Global Catholic Network; Food Network; Fox Deportes; Fox News Channel; Fox Sports 1; FOX Sports West/Prime Ticket; Freeform; Golf Channel; Great American Country; GSN; Hallmark Channel; HGTV; History; HLN; ION Television; Lifetime; MSNBC; MTV; MTV2; National Geographic Channel; NBCSN; Nickelodeon; Oxygen; Spike TV; Syfy; The Weather Channel; TLC; TNT; Travel Channel; Trinity Broadcasting Network (TBN); truTV; Turner Classic Movies; TV Land; Univision; Univision Studios; USA Network; VH1; WE tv.
Fee: $29.99 installation; $28.15 monthly.
Digital Pay Service 1
Pay Units: N.A.
Programming (via satellite): Cinemax (multiplexed); HBO; Showtime; Starz (multiplexed); The Filipino Channel.
Fee: $20.00 monthly (each).
Video-On-Demand: Yes
Pay-Per-View
@Max (delivered digitally); Playboy TV (delivered digitally); Fresh (delivered digitally).
Internet Service
Operational: Yes.
Subscribers: 33,031.
Broadband Service: Charter Internet.
Fee: $29.99 monthly; $2.96 modem lease.
Telephone Service
Digital: Operational
Subscribers: 18,469.
Miles of Plant: 2,979.0 (coaxial); 972.0 (fiber optic). Homes passed: 146,358.
Vice President & General Manager: Fred Lutz. Technical Operations Manager: George Noel. Marketing Director: Chris Bailey. Senior Accounting Director: Steve Lottmann.
Ownership: Charter Communications Inc. (MSO).

HUMBOLDT COUNTY (portions)—Suddenlink Communications, 520 Maryville Centre Dr, Ste 300, St. Louis, MO 63141. Phones: 707-443-1661; 877-443-3127; 314-315-9400. Web Site: http://www.suddenlink.com. Also serves Arcata, Blue Lake, Eureka, Ferndale, Fortuna, McKinleyville, Rio Dell & Trinidad. ICA: CA0065.
TV Market Ranking: Below 100 (Arcata, Blue Lake, Eureka, Ferndale, Fortuna, HUMBOLDT COUNTY (PORTIONS), McKinleyville, Rio Dell, Trinidad). Franchise award date: October 1, 1967. Franchise expiration date: N.A. Began: May 1, 1968.
Channel capacity: 72 (operating 2-way). Channels available but not in use: N.A.
Basic Service
Subscribers: 22,023. Commercial subscribers: 1,397.
Programming (received off-air): KAEF-TV (ABC, MeTV, Movies!) Arcata; KBVU (COZI TV, FOX, This TV) Eureka; KEET (PBS) Eureka; KIEM-TV (NBC) Eureka; KVIQ (CBS, CW) Eureka.
Programming (via microwave): KPIX-TV (CBS, Decades) San Francisco; KRON-TV (Antenna TV, MNT) San Francisco.
Programming (via satellite): C-SPAN; TBS.
Fee: $40.00 installation; $28.74 monthly.
Expanded Basic Service 1
Subscribers: N.A.
Programming (via satellite): A&E; AMC; Animal Planet; Bravo; Cartoon Network; CNBC; CNN; Comcast SportsNet Bay Area; Comedy Central; C-SPAN 2; Discovery Channel; Disney Channel; E! HD; ESPN; ESPN2; Food Network; Fox News Channel; Fox Sports 1; Freeform; FX; Golf Channel; HGTV; History; HLN; IFC; ION Television; Lifetime; MSNBC; MTV; NBCSN; Nickelodeon; OWN: Oprah Winfrey Network; Pop; QVC; Spike TV; Syfy; The Weather Channel; TLC; TNT; Travel Channel; Trinity Broadcasting Network (TBN); truTV; Turner Classic Movies; TV Land; USA Network; VH1.
Fee: $30.00 installation; $8.33 monthly.
Digital Basic Service
Subscribers: N.A.
Programming (via satellite): BBC America; Bloomberg Television; Discovery Digital Networks; Disney XD; ESPN Now; ESPNews; Golf Channel; GSN; IFC; LMN; MC; NBA TV; Outdoor Channel; Sundance TV.
Pay Service 1
Pay Units: N.A.
Programming (via satellite): Cinemax (multiplexed); HBO (multiplexed); Showtime (multiplexed); The Movie Channel.
Fee: $10.75 monthly (each).
Digital Pay Service 1
Pay Units: N.A.
Programming (via satellite): Cinemax (multiplexed); HBO (multiplexed); Showtime (multiplexed); Starz (multiplexed); Starz Encore; The Movie Channel.
Video-On-Demand: Yes
Pay-Per-View
Hot Choice (delivered digitally); iN DEMAND; iN DEMAND (delivered digitally); Playboy TV (delivered digitally); Fresh (delivered digitally); Shorteez (delivered digitally).
Internet Service
Operational: Yes.
Subscribers: 23,797.
Broadband Service: Suddenlink High Speed Internet.
Fee: $99.99 installation; $24.95 monthly.
Telephone Service
Digital: Operational
Subscribers: 11,873.
Fee: $39.95 monthly
Miles of Plant: 1,109.0 (coaxial); 260.0 (fiber optic). Homes passed: 55,435.
Senior Vice President, Corporate Finance: Michael Pflantz. Vice President, Accounting: Sabrina Warr. General Manager: Dorothy Lovfald. Marketing Director: Wendy Purnell. Chief Technician: Carl Moon.
Ownership: Cequel Communications Holdings I LLC (MSO).

HURON—Comcast Cable, 2441 North Grove Industrial Dr, Fresno, CA 93727-1535. Phones: 800-266-2278; 559-455-4305. Fax: 559-253-4090. Web Site: http://www.comcast.com. ICA: CA0273.
TV Market Ranking: 72 (HURON). Franchise award date: N.A. Franchise expiration date: N.A. Began: January 1, 1983.
Channel capacity: 36 (2-way capable). Channels available but not in use: N.A.
Basic Service
Subscribers: 83.
Programming (received off-air): KAIL (COZI TV, MNT, WeatherNation) Fresno; KFRE-TV (CW, IND) Sanger; KFSN-TV (ABC, Live Well Network) Fresno; KFTV-DT (getTV, UNV) Hanford; KGPE (CBS, The Country Network, Untamed Sports TV) Fresno; KJEO-LD (America One, IND) Fresno; KMPH-TV (FOX, This TV) Visalia; KSEE (LATV, NBC) Fresno; KVPT (PBS) Fresno.
Programming (via satellite): A&E; AMC; Animal Planet; CNN; Comedy Central; C-SPAN; Discovery Channel; Disney Channel; E! HD; ESPN; ESPN2; FOX Sports Networks; Freeform; FX; HGTV; History; HLN; Lifetime; MTV; Nickelodeon; Pop; Spike TV; Syfy; TBS; Telemundo; The Weather Channel; TLC; TNT; Turner Classic Movies; TV Land; Univision; USA Network; VH1; WGN America.
Fee: $42.00 installation; $19.00 monthly.

Digital Basic Service
Subscribers: N.A.
Programming (via satellite): BBC America; Bloomberg Television; Bravo; Destination America; Discovery Kids Channel; Discovery Life Channel; ESPN Classic; ESPN2; ESPNews; EVINE Live; FOX College Sports Central; FOX College Sports Pacific; Fox Sports 1; Fuse; Golf Channel; Great American Country; GSN; HGTV; History; Investigation Discovery; MTV Classic; MTV Hits; MTV2; National Geographic Channel; NBCSN; Nicktoons; Outdoor Channel; OWN: Oprah Winfrey Network; Science Channel; Syfy; Trinity Broadcasting Network (TBN); TV Land; VH1 Country; VH1 Soul.
Pay Service 1
Pay Units: N.A.
Programming (via satellite): HBO (multiplexed); Starz; Starz Encore.
Fee: $20.00 installation; $11.43 monthly (Starz/Encore), $12.17 monthly (HBO).
Video-On-Demand: Yes
Internet Service
Operational: Yes.
Telephone Service
Digital: Operational
Miles of Plant: 10.0 (coaxial); None (fiber optic). Homes passed: 800.
General Manager: Len Falter. Marketing Director: Stewart Butler.
Ownership: Comcast Cable Communications Inc. (MSO).

IONE—Volcano Vision, 20000 Hwy 88, PO Box 1070, Pine Grove, CA 95665. Phone: 209-296-2288. Fax: 209-296-2230. E-mail: info@volcanotel.com. Web Site: http://www.volcanocommunications.com.
Also serves Amador County, Buena Vista, Kirkwood, Pine Grove, Pioneer & West Point. ICA: CA0265.
TV Market Ranking: 25 (Amador County (portions), Buena Vista, IONE); Outside TV Markets (Kirkwood, Pioneer, West Point, Pine Grove, Amador County (portions)). Franchise award date: December 10, 1976. Franchise expiration date: N.A. Began: May 1, 1977.
Channel capacity: N.A. Channels available but not in use: N.A.
Digital Basic Service
Subscribers: 3,103.
Programming (received off-air): KCRA-TV (MeTV, NBC) Sacramento; KMAX-TV (CW) Sacramento; KOVR (CBS, Decades) Stockton; KQCA (MNT, Movies!, This TV) Stockton; KSPX-TV (ION) Sacramento; KTXL (Antenna TV, FOX) Sacramento; KUVS-DT (Bounce TV, UNV) Modesto; KVIE (PBS) Sacramento; KXTV (ABC) Sacramento.
Programming (via satellite): A&E; A&E HD; AMC; AWE; AXS TV; BBC America; BBC World News; BET; Bloomberg Television; Boomerang; Bravo; Bravo HD; Chiller; CMT; CNBC; CNBC HD+; CNN; Colours; Comcast SportsNet Bay Area; Comcast SportsNet California; Comedy Central; Cooking Channel; Discovery Channel; Discovery Life Channel; Disney XD; DMX Music; E! HD; ESPN; ESPN Classic; ESPN HD; ESPN2; ESPN2 HD; ESPNews; Food Network; Food Network HD; Fox News Channel; Fox Sports 1; Fox Sports 2; FOX Sports West/Prime Ticket; FX; FXM; GSN; HD Theater; HGTV; HGTV HD; History; History HD; HLN; HRTV; iN DEMAND; Lifetime; Lifetime Movie Network HD; LMN; MSNBC; MTV; National Geographic Channel; National Geographic Channel HD; NBCSN; Outdoor Channel; Outdoor Channel 2 HD; Ovation;

Oxygen; Reelz; Smile of a Child TV; Soundtrack Channel; Spike TV; Syfy; Syfy HD; TBS; TBS HD; TNT; TNT HD; Travel Channel; truTV; Turner Classic Movies; TV Land; Universal HD; UP; USA Network; USA Network HD; VH1; WE tv; World Harvest Television.
Fee: $35.00 installation; $29.99 monthly; $2.00 converter.

Digital Expanded Basic Service
Subscribers: N.A.
Programming (via satellite): CBS Sports Network; Cloo; CMT; DIY Network; ESPNU; Fox Business Network; FOX College Sports Central; FOX College Sports Pacific; FYI; Hallmark Movies & Mysteries; History International; MTV Classic; MTV Hits; MTV Jams; MTV2; Nick Jr.; Nicktoons; OWN: Oprah Winfrey Network; RFD-TV; TeenNick; VH1 Soul.
Fee: $13.00 monthly.

Digital Expanded Basic Service 2
Subscribers: N.A.
Programming (via satellite): CMT; Crime & Investigation Network; C-SPAN 3; Fuse; Golf Channel; Great American Country; History; IFC; Tennis Channel.
Fee: $26.00 monthly.

Digital Pay Service 1
Pay Units: N.A.
Programming (via satellite): Cinemax; Flix; HBO (multiplexed); Showtime (multiplexed); Showtime HD; Starz (multiplexed); Starz Encore (multiplexed); Starz HD; Sundance TV; The Movie Channel (multiplexed); The Movie Channel HD.
Fee: $8.95 monthly (Starz or Encore), $12.95 monthly (Cinemax), $14.95 monthly (HBO).

Video-On-Demand: No

Pay-Per-View
iN DEMAND (delivered digitally); Hot Choice (delivered digitally); Playboy TV (delivered digitally); Fresh (delivered digitally); Shorteez (delivered digitally).

Internet Service
Operational: Yes. Began: October 17, 2002.
Broadband Service: Volcano.
Fee: $29.95-$59.95 monthly.

Telephone Service
Digital: Operational
Fee: $39.95 monthly
Miles of Plant: 35.0 (coaxial); None (fiber optic).
General Manager: Ray Crabtree. Chief Technician: Ramel Chand. Marketing Director: Duke Milunovich.
Ownership: Volcano Communications Co. (MSO).

ISLETON—Formerly served by Comcast Cable. No longer in operation. ICA: CA0484.

JACK RANCH/POSEY—Formerly served by Charter Communications. No longer in operation. ICA: CA0403.

JULIAN—USA Communications, 2455 Stirrup Rd, Borrego Springs, CA 92004. Phones: 800-234-0102; 308-236-1512 (Kearney, NE corporate office); 877-234-0102; 760-767-5607. Fax: 760-767-3609. E-mail: csr@usacommunications.tv. Web Site: http://usacommunications.tv. ICA: CA0254.
TV Market Ranking: Outside TV Markets (JULIAN). Franchise award date: N.A. Franchise expiration date: N.A. Began: December 1, 1982.
Channel capacity: N.A. Channels available but not in use: N.A.

Basic Service
Subscribers: 164.
Programming (received off-air): KFMB-TV (CBS, Grit, MeTV) San Diego; KGTV (ABC, Azteca America) San Diego; KNSD (COZI TV, NBC) San Diego; KPBS (PBS) San Diego; KSWB-TV (Antenna TV, FOX, This TV) San Diego; KUSI-TV (IND) San Diego; 15 FMs.
Programming (via microwave): KCAL-TV (IND) Los Angeles; KCOP-TV (Bounce TV, Buzzr, Heroes & Icons, MNT, Movies!) Los Angeles; KTLA (Antenna TV, CW, This TV) Los Angeles.
Programming (via satellite): C-SPAN; EWTN Global Catholic Network; HGTV; HLN; International Television (ITV); QVC; TBS; The Weather Channel; Trinity Broadcasting Network (TBN).
Fee: $39.95 installation; $33.45 monthly.

Expanded Basic Service 1
Subscribers: N.A.
Programming (via satellite): A&E; AMC; CNN; Discovery Channel; ESPN; ESPN2; Freeform; History; Lifetime; MTV; Nickelodeon; Outdoor Channel; Spike TV; TNT; TV Land; USA Network; VH1.
Fee: $39.99 monthly.

Digital Basic Service
Subscribers: N.A.
Programming (via satellite): Bloomberg Television; Discovery Life Channel; DMX Music; ESPN Classic; ESPN2; ESPNews; Flix; Fox Sports 1; Fuse; FXM; FYI; Golf Channel; Great American Country; GSN; HGTV; History; History International; IFC; Lifetime; National Geographic Channel; NBCSN; Outdoor Channel; Starz (multiplexed); Starz Encore (multiplexed); Turner Classic Movies; WE tv.

Digital Pay Service 1
Pay Units: N.A.
Programming (via satellite): Cinemax (multiplexed); Flix; HBO (multiplexed); Showtime (multiplexed); Starz; The Movie Channel (multiplexed).
Fee: $12.00 monthly (Cinemax), $14.00 monthly (Starz or Showtime), $15.00 monthly (HBO).

Video-On-Demand: No

Pay-Per-View
iN DEMAND (delivered digitally); Playboy TV (delivered digitally).

Internet Service
Operational: Yes.
Broadband Service: In-house.
Fee: $35.95 monthly.

Telephone Service
Digital: Operational
Fee: $39.95 monthly
Miles of Plant: 24.0 (coaxial); None (fiber optic). Homes passed: 1,087.
Chief Financial Officer: Amber Reineke. General Manager & Chief Technician: Joe Gustafson.
Ownership: USA Companies LP (MSO).

JUNE LAKE—Suddenlink Communications. Now served by MAMMOTH LAKES, CA [CA0358]. ICA: CA0475.

KERN COUNTY (portions)—Mediacom, 27192 Sun City Blvd, Ste A, Sun City, CA 92586. Phone: 951-679-3977. Fax: 951-679-9087. Web Site: http://www.mediacomcable.com. Also serves Bodfish, Kernville, Lake Isabella, Onyx, Weldon & Wofford Heights. ICA: CA0168.
TV Market Ranking: Below 100 (Bodfish, Lake Isabella, Weldon); Outside TV Markets (KERN COUNTY (PORTIONS), Onyx, Wofford Heights, Kernville).
Channel capacity: N.A. Channels available but not in use: N.A.

Basic Service
Subscribers: 1,036.
Programming (received off-air): KBAK-TV (CBS) Bakersfield; KBFX-CD (FOX, This TV) Bakersfield; KCAL-TV (IND) Los Angeles; KERO-TV (ABC, Azteca America, MeTV) Bakersfield; KGET-TV (CW, NBC) Bakersfield; KTVU (Buzzr, FOX, LATV, Movies!) Oakland; KUVI-DT (getTV, MNT) Bakersfield.
Programming (via satellite): Disney Channel; EWTN Global Catholic Network; FX; Pop; QVC.
Fee: $39.95 monthly.

Expanded Basic Service 1
Subscribers: N.A.
Programming (via satellite): A&E; Animal Planet; Bravo; Cartoon Network; CMT; CNBC; CNN; Comedy Central; C-SPAN; C-SPAN 2; Discovery Channel; E! HD; ESPN; ESPN2; Food Network; Fox News Channel; Fox Sports 1; FOX Sports Networks; Freeform; Golf Channel; HGTV; History; HLN; ION Television; Lifetime; MSNBC; MTV; NBCSN; Nickelodeon; Spike TV; Syfy; TBS; The Weather Channel; TLC; TNT; Travel Channel; Trinity Broadcasting Network (TBN); truTV; Turner Classic Movies; TV Land; USA Network; VH1; WE tv.
Fee: $26.15 monthly.

Digital Basic Service
Subscribers: N.A.
Programming (via satellite): BBC America; Discovery Digital Networks; DMX Music; ESPNews; GSN; IFC; MTV Classic; National Geographic Channel; Nick Jr.
Fee: $13.95 monthly (HBO), $9.95 monthly (Cinemax or Showtime), $8.00 monthly (Starz/Encore).

Digital Pay Service 1
Pay Units: N.A.
Programming (via satellite): Cinemax (multiplexed); HBO (multiplexed); Showtime (multiplexed); Starz (multiplexed); Starz Encore (multiplexed); The Movie Channel (multiplexed).
Fee: $8.00 monthly.

Video-On-Demand: No

Internet Service
Operational: Yes.
Broadband Service: Mediacom High Speed Internet.
Fee: $40.95 monthly.

Telephone Service
None
Miles of Plant: 283.0 (coaxial); 99.0 (fiber optic). Homes passed: 8,826.
General Manager: Allen Boblitz. Engineering Director: Jon Tatilano.
Ownership: Mediacom LLC (MSO).

KING CITY—Charter Communications, 12405 Powerscourt Dr, St. Louis, MO 63131. Phones: 636-207-5100 (Corporate office); 408-847-2020; 805-544-1962 (San Luis Obispo administrative office). Fax: 408-847-2993. Web Site: http://www.charter.com. Also serves Monterey County (portions). ICA: CA0345.
TV Market Ranking: Outside TV Markets (KING CITY, Monterey County (portions)). Franchise award date: N.A. Franchise expiration date: N.A. Began: December 10, 1974.
Channel capacity: N.A. Channels available but not in use: N.A.

Digital Basic Service
Subscribers: 203.
Programming (via satellite): BBC America; Bloomberg Television; Discovery Life Channel; Disney XD; DMX Music; ESPN Classic; ESPN2; ESPNews; EVINE Live; Fox Sports 1; Fuse; FXM; FYI; Golf Channel; GSN; HGTV; History; History International; IFC; INSP; LMN; NBCSN; Nick Jr.; Outdoor Channel; TeenNick; Trinity Broadcasting Network (TBN); Turner Classic Movies; WE tv.
Fee: $26.99 monthly.

Digital Expanded Basic Service
Subscribers: N.A.
Programming (via satellite): A&E; CNN; Disney Channel; HLN; The Weather Channel; TLC; TNT; WGN America.
Fee: $38.99 monthly.

Digital Pay Service 1
Pay Units: N.A.
Programming (via satellite): Cinemax (multiplexed); HBO (multiplexed); Showtime (multiplexed); Starz (multiplexed); Starz Encore (multiplexed); The Movie Channel (multiplexed).
Fee: $10.95 monthly.

Video-On-Demand: No

Pay-Per-View
iN DEMAND (delivered digitally); ESPN Now (delivered digitally); ESPN (delivered digitally); Hot Choice (delivered digitally); Playboy TV (delivered digitally); Fresh (delivered digitally); Shorteez (delivered digitally).

Internet Service
Operational: No.

Telephone Service
None
Miles of Plant: 63.0 (coaxial); None (fiber optic). Homes passed: 3,550.
Vice President & General Manager: Ed Merrill. Chief Technician: Mark Beech. Marketing Director: Sarwar Assar. Accounting Director: David Sovanski.
Ownership: Charter Communications Inc. (MSO).

KLAMATH—Formerly served by Almega Cable. No longer in operation. ICA: CA0228.

KNIGHTSEN—Formerly served by Comcast Cable. No longer in operation. ICA: CA0145.

KYBURZ—Formerly served by Comcast Cable. No longer in operation. ICA: CA0422.

LAGUNA WOODS—Golden Rain Foundation of Laguna Hills Inc., 24351 El Torro Rd, PO Box 2220, Laguna Woods, CA 92654. Phone: 949-441-8804. ICA: CA0904.
TV Market Ranking: 2 (LAGUNA WOODS).
Channel capacity: N.A. Channels available but not in use: N.A.

Basic Service
Subscribers: 12,736.
Fee: $22.99 monthly.
Chief Technician: Mark DeBinion.
Ownership: Golden Rain Foundation of Laguna Hills Inc.

LAKE ALMANOR—CalNeva Broadband, 322 Ash St, PO Box 1470, Westwood, CA 96137. Phones: 530-256-2028; 866-330-2028. Web Site: http://blog.calneva.org. Also serves Chester, Clear Creek, Hamilton Branch & Westwood. ICA: CA0200.
TV Market Ranking: Outside TV Markets (Chester, Clear Creek, Hamilton Branch, LAKE ALMANOR, Westwood). Franchise award date: January 1, 1962. Franchise

California—Cable Systems

expiration date: N.A. Began: January 1, 1962.
Channel capacity: 65 (not 2-way capable). Channels available but not in use: N.A.
Basic Service
Subscribers: 691.
Programming (received off-air): KHSL-TV (CBS, CW) Chico; KIXE-TV (PBS) Redding; KOVR (CBS, Decades) Stockton; KRCR-TV (ABC, MeTV, Movies!) Redding; KRXI-TV (FOX, Retro TV) Reno; allband FM.
Programming (via microwave): KCRA-TV (MeTV, NBC) Sacramento; KMAX-TV (CW) Sacramento.
Programming (via satellite): 3ABN; A&E; AMC; Animal Planet; Cartoon Network; CBS Sports Network; CMT; CNBC; CNN; Comedy Central; C-SPAN; Discovery Channel; E! HD; ESPN; ESPN Classic; ESPN2; Food Network; Fox News Channel; Freeform; FX; Golf Channel; Great American Country; Hallmark Channel; HGTV; History; HLN; Lifetime; MSNBC; MTV; National Geographic Channel; Nickelodeon; Outdoor Channel; Pop; Spike TV; Syfy; TBS; The Weather Channel; TLC; TNT; truTV; Turner Classic Movies; TV Land; USA Network; VH1; WE tv; WGN America.
Fee: $65.00 installation; $31.00 monthly; $1.00 converter.
Digital Basic Service
Subscribers: N.A.
Programming (via satellite): BBC America; Bloomberg Television; Bravo; CMT; Destination America; Discovery Kids Channel; Disney XD; DMX Music; ESPNews; Fox Sports 1; FXM; FYI; GSN; History International; IFC; Investigation Discovery; LMN; MTV Jams; MTV2; Nick Jr.; Nicktoons; Ovation; OWN; Oprah Winfrey Network; Science Channel; Sundance TV; TeenNick; The Movie Channel (multiplexed); VH1 Soul.
Pay Service 1
Pay Units: N.A.
Programming (via satellite): HBO.
Digital Pay Service 1
Pay Units: N.A.
Programming (via satellite): Cinemax (multiplexed); HBO (multiplexed); Showtime (multiplexed); Starz (multiplexed); Starz Encore (multiplexed).
Fee: $8.35 monthly (Starz), $13.00 monthly (HBO or Cinemax).
Pay-Per-View
Fresh (delivered digitally); Playboy TV (delivered digitally).
Internet Service
Operational: Yes.
Fee: $29.95 installation; $24.95 monthly.
Telephone Service
None
Miles of Plant: 97.0 (coaxial); None (fiber optic). Homes passed: 4,070.
General Manager: Tom Gelardi.
Ownership: CalNeva Broadband LLC (MSO).

LAKE ARROWHEAD—Charter Communications. Now served by HESPERIA, CA [CA0158]. ICA: CA0127.

LAKE ELSINORE—Time Warner Cable. Now served by LOS ANGELES, CA [CA0009]. ICA: CA0079.

LAKE HUGHES—Formerly served by Lake Hughes Cable TV Service. No longer in operation. ICA: CA0286.

LAKE OF THE PINES—Suddenlink Communications, 520 Maryville Centre Dr, Ste 300, St. Louis, MO 63141. Phones: 314-315-9400; 530-268-3731. Web Site: http:// www.suddenlink.com. Also serves Alta Sierra, Auburn, Christian Valley & Meadow Vista. ICA: CA0202.
TV Market Ranking: 25 (Auburn, Christian Valley); Outside TV Markets (Alta Sierra, LAKE OF THE PINES, Meadow Vista). Franchise award date: July 1, 1984. Franchise expiration date: N.A. Began: June 2, 1987.
Channel capacity: N.A. Channels available but not in use: N.A.
Basic Service
Subscribers: 3,580. Commercial subscribers: 96.
Programming (received off-air): KCRA-TV (MeTV, NBC) Sacramento; KMAX-TV (CW) Sacramento; KOVR (CBS, Decades) Stockton; KQCA (MNT, Movies!, This TV) Stockton; KSPX-TV (ION) Sacramento; KTFK-DT (getTV, UniMas) Stockton; KTXL (Antenna TV, FOX) Sacramento; KVIE (PBS) Sacramento; KXTV (ABC) Sacramento.
Programming (via satellite): The Weather Channel; WGN-TV (IND) Chicago.
Fee: $40.00 installation; $35.04 monthly.
Expanded Basic Service 1
Subscribers: N.A.
Programming (via satellite): A&E; AMC; Animal Planet; Cartoon Network; CNBC; CNN; Comcast SportsNet Bay Area; Comedy Central; C-SPAN; C-SPAN 2; Discovery Channel; Disney Channel; E! HD; ESPN; ESPN2; EWTN Global Catholic Network; Food Network; Fox News Channel; Freeform; FX; Golf Channel; Great American Country; Hallmark Channel; HGTV; History; HLN; Lifetime; MTV; Nickelodeon; QVC; Spike TV; TBS; TLC; TNT; Travel Channel; Trinity Broadcasting Network (TBN); TV Land; USA Network; VH1.
Fee: $19.04 monthly.
Digital Basic Service
Subscribers: N.A.
Programming (via satellite): BBC America; Bloomberg Television; Discovery Digital Networks; Disney XD; DMX Music; ESPN Classic; ESPNews; Fox Sports 1; Fuse; FXM; FYI; GSN; History; History International; IFC; LMN; National Geographic Channel; NBCSN; Outdoor Channel; Turner Classic Movies; WE tv.
Pay Service 1
Pay Units: N.A.
Programming (via satellite): Cinemax; HBO; Showtime; Starz; Starz Encore; The Movie Channel.
Fee: $1.35 monthly (Encore), $4.99 monthly (Starz), $9.95 monthly (Cinemax, Showtime or TMC), $10.95 monthly (HBO).
Digital Pay Service 1
Pay Units: N.A.
Programming (via satellite): Cinemax; HBO (multiplexed); Showtime (multiplexed); Starz (multiplexed); Starz Encore (multiplexed); The Movie Channel (multiplexed).
Video-On-Demand: No
Pay-Per-View
iN DEMAND (delivered digitally); Playboy TV (delivered digitally); Fresh (delivered digitally).
Internet Service
Operational: Yes.
Broadband Service: Suddenlink High Speed Internet.
Fee: $99.99 installation; $24.95 monthly.
Telephone Service
None
Miles of Plant: 305.0 (coaxial); None (fiber optic). 450/550 MHz
Senior Vice President, Corporate Finance: Michael Pflantz. Vice President, Accounting: Sabrina Warr. General Manager: Doug Landaker. Chief Technician: Tim Lenz. Marketing Director: Jason Oelkers.
Ownership: Cequel Communications Holdings I LLC (MSO).

LAKE WILDWOOD—Comcast Cable. Now served by SACRAMENTO, CA [CA0002]. ICA: CA0207.

LAKEWOOD—Formerly served by Time Warner Cable. No longer in operation. ICA: CA0092.

LE GRAND—Comcast Cable, 2441 North Grove Industrial Dr, Fresno, CA 93727-1535. Phones: 800-266-2278; 559-253-4050. Fax: 559-253-4090. Web Site: http:// www.comcast.com. ICA: CA0349.
TV Market Ranking: 25 (LE GRAND (portions)); Outside TV Markets (LE GRAND (portions)). Franchise award date: N.A. Franchise expiration date: N.A. Began: January 1, 1987.
Channel capacity: 33 (not 2-way capable). Channels available but not in use: N.A.
Basic Service
Subscribers: 34.
Programming (received off-air): KAIL (COZI TV, MNT, WeatherNation) Fresno; KFSN-TV (ABC, Live Well Network) Fresno; KFTV-DT (getTV, UNV) Hanford; KGPE (CBS, The Country Network, Untamed Sports TV) Fresno; KMPH-TV (FOX, This TV) Visalia; KSEE (LATV, NBC) Fresno; KVPT (PBS) Fresno.
Programming (via satellite): A&E; AMC; Cartoon Network; CNN; Concert TV; C-SPAN; Discovery Channel; ESPN; ESPN2; Freeform; FX; HLN; Spike TV; TBS; TLC; TNT; Trinity Broadcasting Network (TBN); Univision; USA Network; WGN America.
Fee: $42.00 installation; $24.50 monthly.
Pay Service 1
Pay Units: N.A.
Programming (via satellite): Cinemax; HBO.
Fee: $10.97 monthly (Cinemax), $12.87 monthly (HBO).
Internet Service
Operational: Yes.
Telephone Service
None
General Manager: Len Falter. Marketing Director: Stewart Butler. Communications Director: Erica Smith.
Ownership: Comcast Cable Communications Inc.

LEE VINING—Formerly served by Satview Broadband. No longer in operation. ICA: CA0350.

LEWISTON—Formerly served by New Day Broadband. No longer in operation. ICA: CA0351.

LODI—Comcast Cable. Now served by SACRAMENTO, CA [CA0002]. ICA: CA0100.

LOMPOC—Comcast Cable. Now served by FRESNO, CA [CA0011]. ICA: CA0477.

LONE PINE—Lone Pine TV Inc, 223 Jackson St, PO Box 867, Lone Pine, CA 93545-0867. Phones: 888-876-5461; 760-876-5461. Fax: 760-876-9101. Web Site: http:// www.lonepinecommunications.com. ICA: CA0353.
TV Market Ranking: Outside TV Markets (LONE PINE). Franchise award date: January 1, 1956. Franchise expiration date: N.A. Began: January 1, 1956.
Channel capacity: N.A. Channels available but not in use: N.A.
Basic Service
Subscribers: 500.
Programming (via satellite): A&E; AMC; Animal Planet; Cartoon Network; CMT; CNBC; CNN; Comedy Central; Discovery Channel; Disney Channel; Disney XD; ESPN; ESPN Classic; ESPN2; EWTN Global Catholic Network; Food Network; Fox News Channel; FOX Sports West/Prime Ticket; Freeform; FX; Great American Country; Hallmark Channel; HGTV; History; HLN; Lifetime; MSNBC; MTV; National Geographic Channel; Nickelodeon; QVC; Spike TV; Syfy; TBS; Telemundo; The Weather Channel; TLC; TNT; Travel Channel; Trinity Broadcasting Network (TBN); truTV; TV Land; UniMas; Univision; Univision Studios; USA Network; VH1.
Programming (via translator): KABC-TV (ABC, Live Well Network) Los Angeles; KCAL-TV (IND) Los Angeles; KCBS-TV (CBS, Decades) Los Angeles; KCET (ETV) Los Angeles; KCOP-TV (Bounce TV, Buzzr, Heroes & Icons, MNT, Movies!) Los Angeles; KNBC (COZI TV, NBC) Los Angeles; KTLA (Antenna TV, CW, This TV) Los Angeles; KTTV (FOX) Los Angeles.
Fee: $25.00 installation; $37.00 monthly.
Digital Basic Service
Subscribers: N.A.
Programming (via satellite): BBC America; Bloomberg Television; Church Channel; Cloo; Cooking Channel; Destination America; Discovery Life Channel; EVINE Live; FYI; History International; Investigation Discovery; JUCE TV; OWN; Oprah Winfrey Network; RFD-TV; Science Channel; The Word Network; UP.
Digital Expanded Basic Service
Subscribers: N.A.
Programming (via satellite): Bravo; FXM; IFC; LMN; Sundance TV; Turner Classic Movies; WE tv.
Fee: $5.00 monthly.
Digital Expanded Basic Service 2
Subscribers: N.A.
Programming (via satellite): Discovery Kids Channel; GSN; Nick Jr.; Nicktoons; Sprout; TeenNick.
Fee: $5.00 monthly.
Digital Expanded Basic Service 3
Subscribers: N.A.
Programming (via satellite): Fuse; MTV Classic; MTV Hits; MTV Jams; MTV2; VH1 Country; VH1 Soul.
Fee: $5.00 monthly.
Digital Expanded Basic Service 4
Subscribers: N.A.
Programming (via satellite): ESPN Classic; ESPN2; ESPNews; FOX College Sports Central; FOX College Sports Pacific; Fox Sports 1; Golf Channel; NBCSN; Outdoor Channel.
Fee: $5.00 monthly.
Digital Expanded Basic Service 5
Subscribers: N.A.
Programming (via satellite): Cine Mexicano; Cinelatino; CNN en Espanol; ESPN Deportes; Fox Deportes; HBO Latino; History en Espanol; NBC Universo; Tr3s; Viendo-Movies.
Fee: $5.00 monthly.
Pay Service 1
Pay Units: 135.
Programming (via satellite): Showtime; The Movie Channel.
Fee: $15.00 installation; $8.00 monthly (each).

Cable Systems—California

Pay Service 2
Pay Units: N.A.
Programming (via satellite): HBO.
Fee: $15.00 installation; $12.00 monthly.
Digital Pay Service 1
Pay Units: N.A.
Programming (via satellite): Cinemax (multiplexed); Flix; HBO (multiplexed); Showtime (multiplexed); Starz (multiplexed); Starz Encore (multiplexed); The Movie Channel (multiplexed).
Fee: $11.99 monthly (Cinemax, HBO, Showtime/Flix/TMC or Starz/Encore).
Internet Service
Operational: Yes.
Broadband Service: In-house.
Fee: $41.99-$61.99 monthly.
Telephone Service
Digital: Operational
Fee: $30.00-$40.00 monthly
Miles of Plant: 8.0 (coaxial); None (fiber optic). Homes passed: 902.
Manager, Marketing & Program Director: Bruce Branson. Chief Technician: Steve Stukas.
Ownership: Lone Pine TV Inc. (MSO).

LONG BARN—SNC Cable, PO Box 281, Standard, CA 95373. Phones: 209-588-9601; 209-588-9601. E-mail: cust@gosnc.com. Web Site: http://gosnc.com. Also serves Cold Springs. ICA: CA0354.
TV Market Ranking: Outside TV Markets (Cold Springs, LONG BARN). Franchise award date: N.A. Franchise expiration date: N.A. Began: January 1, 1984.
Channel capacity: N.A. Channels available but not in use: N.A.
Basic Service
Subscribers: N.A.
Programming (received off-air): KCRA-TV (MeTV, NBC) Sacramento; KMAX-TV (CW) Sacramento; KOVR (CBS, Decades) Stockton; KQCA (MNT, Movies!, This TV) Stockton; KTFK-DT (getTV, UniMas) Stockton; KTNC-TV (Estrella TV, This TV) Concord; KTXL (Antenna TV, FOX) Sacramento; KVIE (PBS) Sacramento; KXTV (ABC) Sacramento; allband FM.
Programming (via satellite): A&E; CNBC; CNN; Discovery Channel; ESPN; Fox News Channel; History; TBS; TNT; Trinity Broadcasting Network (TBN).
Fee: $50.00 installation.
Pay Service 1
Pay Units: N.A.
Programming (via satellite): HBO.
Fee: $13.95 monthly.
Video-On-Demand: No
Internet Service
Operational: Yes.
Fee: $21.95 monthly.
Telephone Service
Digital: Operational
Miles of Plant: 10.0 (coaxial); None (fiber optic). Homes passed: 360.
General Manager: Tim Holden. Product Development & Communications Manager: Bill Manley.
Ownership: Sierra Nevada Communications (MSO).

LONG BEACH—Charter Communications, 12405 Powerscourt Dr, St. Louis, MO 63131. Phones: 636-207-5100 (Corporate office); 626-430-6112; 626-430-3300. Fax: 626-430-3420. Web Site: http://www.charter.com. Also serves Los Angeles County (portions) & Signal Hill. ICA: CA0014.
TV Market Ranking: 2 (LONG BEACH, Los Angeles County (portions), Signal Hill). Franchise award date: N.A. Franchise expiration date: N.A. Began: June 1, 1965.
Channel capacity: 78 (operating 2-way). Channels available but not in use: N.A.
Digital Basic Service
Subscribers: 34,808.
Programming (via satellite): BBC America; Bloomberg Television; Boomerang; CNN en Espanol; Discovery Digital Networks; Disney XD; DIY Network; FOX College Sports Central; FOX College Sports Pacific; Fuse; FYI; Great American Country; History International; HTV; IFC; LMN; MC; National Geographic Channel; NBC Universo; Nick Jr.; Nicktoons; Sundance TV; Syfy; TeenNick; Telemundo.
Fee: $14.99 monthly.
Digital Expanded Basic Service
Subscribers: N.A.
Programming (via satellite): A&E; AMC; Animal Planet; BET; Bravo; Cartoon Network; CMT; CNBC; CNN; Comedy Central; Discovery Channel; Discovery Life Channel; Disney Channel; ESPN; ESPN Classic; ESPN2; EWTN Global Catholic Network; Food Network; Fox Deportes; Fox News Channel; Fox Sports 1; FOX Sports West/Prime Ticket; Freeform; FX; FXM; Golf Channel; GSN; Hallmark Channel; HGTV; History; HLN; Lifetime; MSNBC; MTV; MTV2; NBCSN; Nickelodeon; Oxygen; Pop; QVC; Spike TV; TBS; The Weather Channel; TLC; TNT; Travel Channel; truTV; Turner Classic Movies; TV Land; Univision; USA Network; VH1; WE tv.
Fee: $48.95 monthly.
Digital Pay Service 1
Pay Units: 9,646.
Programming (via satellite): Cinemax (multiplexed); Flix; HBO (multiplexed); HITS (Headend In The Sky); Showtime (multiplexed); Starz (multiplexed); The Movie Channel (multiplexed).
Fee: $10.00 monthly (Cinemax, Showtime or TMC), $11.00 monthly (HBO).
Video-On-Demand: Yes
Pay-Per-View
Playboy TV (delivered digitally); Shorteez (delivered digitally); Sports PPV (delivered digitally); iN DEMAND (delivered digitally); ETC (delivered digitally); Pleasure (delivered digitally).
Internet Service
Operational: Yes.
Subscribers: 42,279.
Broadband Service: Charter Internet.
Fee: $29.99 monthly.
Telephone Service
Digital: Operational
Subscribers: 14,718.
Fee: $29.99 monthly
Miles of Plant: 1,361.0 (coaxial); 265.0 (fiber optic). Homes passed: 192,077.
Vice President & General Manager: Wendy Rasmusson. Technical Operations Manager: Tom Williams. Marketing Manager: Lily Ho. Accounting Director: David Sovanski.
Ownership: Charter Communications Inc. (MSO).

LONG BEACH NAVAL BASE—Formerly served by Americable International. No longer in operation. ICA: CA0355.

LOS ALAMOS—Formerly served by Charter Communications. No longer in operation. ICA: CA0280.

LOS ALTOS HILLS—Comcast Cable. Now served by SAN FRANCISCO, CA [CA0003]. ICA: CA0213.

Communications Daily
Warren Communications News
Get the industry standard FREE —
For a no-obligation trial call 800-771-9202 or visit www.warren-news.com

LOS ANGELES—Time Warner Cable, 550 North Continental Blvd, Ste 250, El Segundo, CA 90245-5050. Phone: 310-647-3000. Fax: 310-647-3036. Web Site: http://www.timewarnercable.com. Also serves Acton, Agoura, Agoura Hills, Anaheim, Arcadia, Artesia, Baldwin Park, Bell, Bell Canyon, Bell Gardens, Bellflower, Beverly Hills, Bloomington, Boyle Heights, Bradbury, Brea, Buena Park, Calabasas, Calimesa, Camarillo, Canoga Park, Canyon Country, Canyon Lake, Carson, Castaic, CBC Naval Base, Central Orange County, Chatsworth, Chino, Chino Hills, Claremont, Colton, Compton, Corona, Corona Del Mar, Costa Mesa, Covina, Cudahy, Culver City, Cypress, Diamond Bar, Downey, Eagle Rock, East Los Angeles, East San Fernando Valley, Eastvale, Edwards AFB, El Monte, El Rio, El Segundo, Elizabeth Lake, Encino, Etiwanda, Fillmore, Fontana, Fountain Valley, Fullerton, Garden Grove, Gardena, Glendora, Granada Hills, Grand Terrace, Green Valley, Hacienda Heights, Harbor City, Hawaiian Gardens, Hawthorne, Hemet, Hermosa Beach, Highland, Hollywood, Homeland, Huntington Beach, Idyllwild, Inglewood, Kagel Canyon, La Habra, La Habra Heights, La Mirada, La Palma, La Puente, La Verne, Lake Elsinore, Lake Los Angeles, Lakewood, Lancaster, Lawndale, Leona Valley, Littlerock, Loma Linda, Lomita, Los Alamitos, Los Angeles County (portions), Lynwood, Manhattan Beach, March AFB, Marina Del Ray, Maywood, Menifee, Mentone, Midway City, Mission Hills, Mission Hills (portions), Monrovia, Montclair, Moorpark, Moreno Valley, Murrieta, Muscoy, Newbury Park, Newhall, Newport Beach, North Hills, Northridge, Nuevo, Oak Park, Ojai, Ontario, Orange City, Orange County (unincorporated areas), Oxnard, Pacific Palisades, Pacoima, Palmdale, Paramount, Pearblossom, Perris, Pico Rivera, Piru, Placentia, Playa Del Ray, Playa Vista, Pomona, Port Hueneme, Quail Valley, Quartz Hill, Rancho Cucamonga, Redlands, Redondo Beach, Reseda, Rialto, Riverside County (portions), Romoland, Rossmoor, Rowland Heights, San Bernardino, San Bernardino County (portions), San Dimas, San Fernando, San Jacinto, San Marino, San Pedro, Santa Ana, Santa Clarita, Santa Fe Springs, Santa Monica, Santa Paula, Saugus, Seal Beach, Seal Beach Naval Station, Sherman Oaks, Sierra Madre, Simi Valley, South El Monte, South Gate, South Pasadena, South Whittier, Stanton, Stevenson Ranch, Studio City, Sun Valley, Sunland, Sunset Beach, Sylmar, Tarzana, Temecula, Thousand Oaks, Torrance, Tujunga, Tustin, Upland, Valencia, Van Nuys, Venice, Ventura, Ventura County (portions), Villa Park, Walnut Park, West Hills, West Hollywood, West Los Angeles, West San Fernando Valley, Westlake Village, Westminster, Wildomar, Wilmington, Winchester, Winnetka, Woodland Hills, Yorba Linda & Yucaipa. ICA: CA0009.
TV Market Ranking: 2 (Agoura, Agoura Hills, Anaheim, Arcadia, Artesia, Baldwin Park, Bell, Bell Canyon, Bell Gardens, Bellflower, Beverly Hills, Bloomington, Boyle Heights, Bradbury, Brea, Buena Park, Calabasas, Calimesa, Canoga Park, Canyon Country, Canyon Lake, Carson, Castaic, Chatsworth, Chino, Chino Hills, Claremont, Compton, Corona, Corona Del Mar, Costa Mesa, Covina, Cudahy, Culver City, Cypress, Diamond Bar, Downey, Eagle Rock, East Los Angeles, East San Fernando Valley, Eastvale, El Monte, El Segundo, Encino, Etiwanda, Fontana, Fullerton, Garden Grove, Gardena, Glendora, Granada Hills, Grand Terrace, Hacienda Heights, Harbor City, Hawaiian Gardens, Hawthorne, Hemet, Hermosa Beach, Hollywood, Homeland, Huntington Beach, Inglewood, Kagel Canyon, La Habra, La Habra Heights, La Mirada, La Palma, La Puente, La Verne, Lake Elsinore, Lake Los Angeles, Lakewood, Lawndale, Loma Linda, Lomita, Los Alamitos, LOS ANGELES, Los Angeles County (portions), Lynwood, Manhattan Beach, March AFB, Marina Del Ray, Maywood, Menifee, Mentone, Midway City, Mission Hills, Mission Hills (portions), Monrovia, Montclair, Moorpark, Moreno Valley, Murrieta, Muscoy, Newbury Park, Newhall, Newport Beach, North Hills, Northridge, Nuevo, Oak Park, Ontario, Orange City, Orange County (unincorporated areas), Pacific Palisades, Pacoima, Paramount, Perris, Pico Rivera, Placentia, Playa Del Ray, Playa Vista, Pomona, Quail Valley, Rancho Cucamonga, Redlands, Redondo Beach, Reseda, Rialto, Riverside County (portions), Romoland, Rossmoor, Rowland Heights, San Bernardino, San Bernardino County (portions), San Dimas, San Fernando, San Jacinto, San Marino, San Pedro, Santa Ana, Santa Clarita, Santa Fe Springs, Santa Monica, Saugus, Seal Beach, Seal Beach Naval Station, Sherman Oaks, Sierra Madre, Simi Valley, South El Monte, South Gate, South Whittier, Stanton, Stevenson Ranch, Studio City, Sun Valley, Sunland, Sunset Beach, Sylmar, Tarzana, Temecula, Thousand Oaks, Torrance, Tujunga, Tustin, Upland, Valencia, Van Nuys, Venice, Ventura County (portions), Villa Park, Walnut Park, West Hills, West Hollywood, West Los Angeles, West San Fernando Valley, Westlake Village, Westminster, Wildomar, Wilmington, Winchester, Winnetka, Woodland Hills, Yorba Linda, Yucaipa); Below 100 (Camarillo, CBC Naval Base, El Rio, Fillmore, Fountain Valley, Idyllwild, Ojai, Oxnard, Piru, Port Hueneme, Santa Paula, Ventura, Ventura County (portions)); Outside TV Markets (Acton, Edwards AFB, Elizabeth Lake, Green Valley, Lancaster, Leona Valley, Littlerock, Palmdale, Pearblossom, Quartz Hill). Franchise award date: N.A. Franchise expiration date: N.A. Began: November 1, 1980.
Channel capacity: 30 (operating 2-way). Channels available but not in use: N.A.
Basic Service
Subscribers: 1,206,754.
Programming (received off-air): KABC-TV (ABC, Live Well Network) Los Angeles; KAZA-TV (Azteca America) Avalon; KBEH (IND) Oxnard; KCAL-TV (IND) Los Angeles; KCBS-TV (CBS, Decades) Los Angeles; KCET (ETV) Los Angeles; KCOP-

2017 Edition D-93

California—Cable Systems

TV (Bounce TV, Buzzr, Heroes & Icons, MNT, Movies!) Los Angeles; KDOC-TV (MeTV) Anaheim; KFTR-DT (getTV, UniMas) Ontario; KILM (IND) Barstow; KJLA (LATV) Ventura; KLCS (PBS) Los Angeles; KMEX-DT (UNV) Los Angeles; KNBC (COZI TV, NBC) Los Angeles; KOCE-TV (PBS) Huntington Beach; KPXN-TV (ION) San Bernardino; KRCA (Estrella TV) Riverside; KSCI (IND) Long Beach; KTBN-TV (TBN) Santa Ana; KTLA (Antenna TV, CW, This TV) Los Angeles; KTTV (FOX) Los Angeles; KVEA (TMO) Corona; KVMD (IND) Twentynine Palms; KWHY-TV (MundoMax) Los Angeles; KXLA (IND) Rancho Palos Verdes.

Programming (via satellite): A&E; AMC; BET; Bravo; Cartoon Network; CNN; Comedy Central; C-SPAN; Discovery Channel; Disney Channel; E! HD; ESPN; ESPN2; EVINE Live; Food Network; Fox News Channel; FOX Sports West/Prime Ticket; Freeform; FX; Golf Channel; HGTV; History; HLN; LATV; Lifetime; MSNBC; MTV; National Geographic Channel; Nickelodeon; Oxygen; QVC; Spike TV; Syfy; TBS; TLC; TNT; truTV; TV Land; Univision; USA Network; VH1; WGN America.

Fee: $32.99 installation; $13.00 monthly.

Digital Basic Service
Subscribers: N.A.
Programming (via satellite): A&E; AMC HD; Animal Planet; Animal Planet HD; Antenna TV; AYM Sports; Bandamax; BBC America; BBC HD; BET; Bio HD; Bloomberg Television; Boomerang; Bravo; Bravo HD; California Channel; Canal 22 Internacional; Canal Sur; Caracol TV; Cartoon Network; Cartoon Network en Espanol; Cartoon Network HD; CB Tu Television Michoacan; CBS Sports Network; CBS Sports Network HD; CCTV-Documentary; Centric; Centroamerica TV; Chiller; Cine Mexicano; Cinelatino; Cloo; CMT; CMT HD; CNBC HD+; CNBC World; CNN; CNN en Espanol; CNN HD; Comedy Central; Comedy Central HD; Cooking Channel; C-SPAN; C-SPAN 2; C-SPAN 3; Daystar TV Network; De Pelicula; De Pelicula Clasico; Destination America; Discovery Channel; Discovery Channel HD; Discovery Familia; Discovery Family; Discovery Life Channel; Disney Channel HD; Disney XD; Disney XD HD; DIY Network; E! HD; Ecuavisa Internacional; ESPN; ESPN Classic; ESPN Deportes; ESPN HD; ESPN2; ESPN2 HD; ESPNews; ESPNews HD; ESPNU; ESPNU HD; EVINE Live; EWTN Global Catholic Network; Flix; Food Network; Food Network HD; Fox Business Network; Fox Business Network HD; FOX College Sports Central; FOX College Sports Pacific; Fox Deportes; Fox Life; Fox News Channel; Fox News HD; Fox Soccer Plus; Fox Sports 1; Fox Sports 2; FOX Sports West/Prime Ticket; Freeform; FSN HD; Fuse; Fuse HD; FX; FX HD; FXM; FYI; GalaVision HD; Golf Channel; Golf Channel HD; GolTV; GSN; Hallmark Channel; Hallmark Channel HD; Hallmark Movie Channel HD; Hallmark Movies & Mysteries; HD Theater; HGTV; HGTV HD; History; History en Espanol; History HD; History International; HLN; HLN HD; HSN; HTV; ID Investigation Discovery HD; IFC; IFC HD; Infinito; INSP; Investigation Discovery; Jewelry Television; Jewish Life TV; La Familia Cosmovision; Latinoamerica Television; Lifetime; Lifetime Movie Network HD; LMN; LOGO; MC; Mexico TV; MGM HD; Mnet; MSNBC; MTV; MTV Classic; MTV Hits; MTV Jams; MTV2; NASA TV; Nat Geo WILD; National Geographic Channel; National Geographic Channel HD; NBA TV; NBA TV HD; NBC Universo; NBCSN; NHL Network; NHL Network HD; Nick HD; Nick Jr.; Nickelodeon; Nicktoons; Outdoor Channel; Ovation; OWN: Oprah Winfrey Network; Oxygen; QVC HD; Reelz; Science Channel; Sky Link TV; Smithsonian Channel HD; Spike TV; Spike TV HD; Sprout; Starz Encore (multiplexed); Sundance TV; Sur; Syfy HD; TBS; TBS HD; TeenNick; TeleFormula; Tennis Channel; The Africa Channel; The Weather Channel; The Weather Channel HD; The Word Network; TLC; TLC HD; TNT; TNT HD; Tr3s; Travel Channel; Travel Channel HD; truTV; Turner Classic Movies; Turner Classic Movies HD; TV Land; TV One; TV One HD; TVG Network; ULTRA HDPlex; Universal HD; Univision; UP; USA Network; USA Network HD; Versus HD; VH1; VH1 HD; VH1 Soul; VideoRola; ViendoMovies; Vme TV; WE tv; WGN America HD.

Fee: $5.00 monthly (each tier).

Digital Pay Service 1
Pay Units: N.A.
Programming (via satellite): ART America; CCTV-Documentary; Cinemax (multiplexed); Cinemax HD; GMA Pinoy TV; HBO (multiplexed); HBO HD; Jade Channel; MBC America; Phoenix Infonews; Phoenix InfoNews; Playboy en Espanol; RAI Italia; RTN; RTVI; Saigon Broadcasting Television Network (SBTN); Showtime (multiplexed); Showtime HD; Sony Entertainment Television Asia; Starz (multiplexed); Starz HD; Tapesh TV; The Movie Channel (multiplexed); The Movie Channel HD; TV Asia; TV5, La Television International; Zee TV.

Fee: $15.00 monthly (each).

Video-On-Demand: Yes

Pay-Per-View
iN DEMAND (delivered digitally); NBA League Pass (delivered digitally); MLS Direct Kick (delivered digitally); MLB Extra Innings (delivered digitally); NHL Center Ice (delivered digitally); Special events (delivered digitally).

Internet Service
Operational: Yes.
Subscribers: 1,553,906.
Broadband Service: Road Runner.
Fee: $49.95 installation; $44.95 monthly.

Telephone Service
Digital: Operational
Subscribers: 581,202.
Fee: $44.95 monthly
Miles of Plant: 45,244.0 (coaxial); 5,479.0 (fiber optic). Homes passed: 4,984,766.
President: Jeffrey Hirsch. Vice President, Technical Operations: Mitchel Christopher. Vice President, Marketing & Sales: Bill Erickson. Vice President, External Affairs: Deane Leavenworth. Vice President, Engineering: Jose Leon. Vice President, Public Relations: Patti Rockenwagner. Corporate Communications Manager: Toni Mathews.
Ownership: Time Warner Cable (MSO).

LOS ANGELES—Time Warner Cable. Now served by LOS ANGELES, CA [CA0009]. ICA: CA0062.

LOS ANGELES (south central portion)—Time Warner Cable. Now served by LOS ANGELES, CA [CA0009]. ICA: CA0008.

LOS ANGELES (western portion)—Time Warner Cable. Now served by LOS ANGELES, CA [CA0009]. ICA: CA0019.

LOS ANGELES COUNTY (portions)—Charter Communications, 4781 Irwindale Dr, Irwindale, CA 91706. Phones: 636-207-5100 (Corporate office); 626-430-6112; 626-430-3300. Web Site: http://www.charter.com. Also serves Alhambra, Altadena, Azusa, Commerce, Duarte, Huntington Park, Irwindale, La Canada Flintridge, Monrovia, Montebello, Monterey Park, Norwalk, Pasadena, Rosemead, San Gabriel, South San Gabriel, Temple City, Walnut & West Covina. ICA: CA0005.

TV Market Ranking: 2 (Alhambra, Altadena, Azusa, Commerce, Duarte, Huntington Park, Irwindale, La Canada Flintridge, LOS ANGELES COUNTY (PORTIONS), Monrovia, Montebello, Monterey Park, Norwalk, Pasadena, Rosemead, San Gabriel, South San Gabriel, Temple City, Walnut, West Covina). Franchise award date: N.A. Franchise expiration date: N.A. Began: August 1, 1981.

Channel capacity: 75 (operating 2-way). Channels available but not in use: N.A.

Digital Basic Service
Subscribers: 65,672.
Programming (via satellite): BBC America; Bloomberg Television; Boomerang; Discovery Digital Networks; Disney XD; DIY Network; FOX College Sports Central; FOX College Sports Pacific; FYI; Great American Country; History International; IFC; LMN; MC; Nick 2; Nick Jr.; Sundance TV; TeenNick; WE tv.

Fee: $49.99 installation; $14.99 monthly.

Digital Expanded Basic Service
Subscribers: N.A.
Programming (via satellite): A&E; AMC; Animal Planet; BET; Bravo; Cartoon Network; CMT; CNBC; CNN; C-SPAN 2; Discovery Channel; Disney Channel; E! HD; ESPN; ESPN Classic; ESPN2; Food Network; Fox Deportes; Fox News Channel; Fox Sports 1; FOX Sports West/Prime Ticket; Freeform; FX; Golf Channel; HGTV; History; HLN; Jade Channel; Lifetime; MSNBC; MTV; Nickelodeon; Oxygen; Spike TV; Syfy; The Movie Channel; TLC; TNT; Travel Channel; truTV; Turner Classic Movies; Univision; USA Network; VH1.

Fee: $48.95 monthly.

Digital Pay Service 1
Pay Units: N.A.
Programming (via satellite): Cinemax (multiplexed); Flix; HBO (multiplexed); Showtime (multiplexed); Starz (multiplexed); Starz Encore (multiplexed); The Movie Channel (multiplexed).

Fee: $10.00 monthly (Cinemax, HBO, Starz/Encore, Showtime/Flix or TMC).

Video-On-Demand: Yes

Pay-Per-View
ETC (delivered digitally); iN DEMAND (delivered digitally); Playboy TV (delivered digitally); Pleasure (delivered digitally); Fresh; Shorteez (delivered digitally); Video On Demand (delivered digitally).

Internet Service
Operational: Yes.
Subscribers: 102,122.
Broadband Service: Charter Internet.
Fee: $29.99 monthly; $4.95 modem lease.

Telephone Service
Digital: Operational
Subscribers: 35,677.
Fee: $29.99 monthly
Miles of Plant: 3,492.0 (coaxial); 583.0 (fiber optic). Homes passed: 351,110.
Vice President & General Manager: Wendy Rasmussen. Accounting Director: David Sovanski. Technical Operations Manager: Tom Williams. Marketing Manager: Lily Ho.
Ownership: Charter Communications Inc. (MSO).

LOS BANOS—Comcast Cable. Now served by FRESNO, CA [CA0011]. ICA: CA0479.

LOS GATOS—Comcast Cable. Now served by SAN FRANCISCO, CA [CA0003]. ICA: CA0144.

LOS GATOS (unincorporated areas)—Comcast Cable. Now served by SAN FRANCISCO, CA [CA0003]. ICA: CA0306.

LOS TRANCOS WOODS—Comcast Cable. Now served by SAN FRANCISCO, CA [CA0003]. ICA: CA0486.

LUSHMEADOWS—Formerly served by Northland Cable Television. No longer in operation. ICA: CA0357.

LYTLE CREEK—Time Warner Cable, 550 North Continental Blvd, Ste 250, El Segundo, CA 90245-5050. Phone: 310-647-3000. Fax: 310-647-3036. Web Site: http://www.timewarnercable.com. ICA: CA0476.

TV Market Ranking: 2 (LYTLE CREEK).
Channel capacity: N.A. Channels available but not in use: N.A.

Basic Service
Subscribers: 90.
Programming (received off-air): KABC-TV (ABC, Live Well Network) Los Angeles; KCAL-TV (IND) Los Angeles; KCBS-TV (CBS, Decades) Los Angeles; KCET (ETV) Los Angeles; KCOP-TV (Bounce TV, Buzzr, Heroes & Icons, MNT, Movies!) Los Angeles; KDOC-TV (MeTV) Anaheim; KFTR-DT (getTV, UniMas) Ontario; KMEX-DT (UNV) Los Angeles; KNBC (COZI TV, NBC) Los Angeles; KPXN-TV (ION) San Bernardino; KRCA (Estrella TV) Riverside; KSCI (IND) Long Beach; KTBN-TV (TBN) Santa Ana; KTLA (Antenna TV, CW, This TV) Los Angeles; KTTV (FOX) Los Angeles; KVCR-DT (PBS) San Bernardino; KVEA (TMO) Corona; KWHY-TV (MundoMax) Los Angeles.

Fee: $19.95 installation; $16.00 monthly.

Expanded Basic Service 1
Subscribers: N.A.
Programming (via satellite): A&E; AMC; Animal Planet; BET; CMT; CNBC; CNN; C-SPAN; Discovery Channel; Disney Channel; E! HD; ESPN; ESPN2; Freeform; FX; HLN; Lifetime; MTV; National Geographic Channel; Nickelodeon; Pop; QVC; Spike TV; Syfy; TBS; TLC; TNT; Travel Channel; Univision; USA Network; VH1; WGN America.

Pay Service 1
Pay Units: N.A.
Programming (via satellite): Cinemax; HBO; Showtime; The Movie Channel.

Internet Service
Operational: Yes.
Broadband Service: Road Runner.

Telephone Service
Digital: Operational
Ownership: Time Warner Cable (MSO).

MALIBU—Charter Communications, 12405 Powerscourt Dr, St. Louis, MO 63131. Phones: 636-207-5100 (Corporate office); 626-430-3300 (Irwindale office); 310-456-9010. Fax: 310-579-7010. Web Site: http://www.charter.com. Also serves Agoura (portions), Agoura Hills, Calabasas, Hidden Hills, Los Angeles (unincorporated areas), Los Angeles County (portions), Topanga & Ventura County (portions). ICA: CA0129.

TV Market Ranking: 2 (Agoura (portions), Agoura Hills, Calabasas, Hidden Hills, Los Angeles (unincorporated areas), Los Ange-

Cable Systems—California

les County (portions), MALIBU, Topanga, Ventura County (portions)). Franchise award date: N.A. Franchise expiration date: N.A. Began: January 1, 1958.
Channel capacity: 75 (operating 2-way). Channels available but not in use: N.A.
Digital Basic Service
Subscribers: 4,365.
Programming (via satellite): BBC America; Bloomberg Television; Boomerang; Discovery Digital Networks; Disney XD; DIY Network; FYI; History International; IFC; LMN; MC; Nick 2; Nick Jr.; Sundance TV; TeenNick; WE tv.
Fee: $14.99 monthly.
Digital Expanded Basic Service
Subscribers: N.A.
Programming (via satellite): AMC; Animal Planet; Bravo; Cartoon Network; CMT; CNN; Comedy Central; Discovery Channel; Disney Channel; ESPN; ESPN2; Food Network; Fox Sports 1; FOX Sports West/Prime Ticket; FX; FXM; Golf Channel; GSN; HGTV; History; HLN; MSNBC; NBCSN; Spike TV; TNT; truTV; Turner Classic Movies; TV Land.
Fee: $48.95 monthly.
Digital Pay Service 1
Pay Units: N.A.
Programming (via satellite): Cinemax (multiplexed); Flix; HBO (multiplexed); Showtime (multiplexed); The Movie Channel (multiplexed).
Fee: $10.00 monthly (each).
Video-On-Demand: Yes
Pay-Per-View
Hot Choice (delivered digitally); iN DEMAND; iN DEMAND (delivered digitally); Playboy TV; Playboy TV (delivered digitally); Fresh (delivered digitally); Shorteez (delivered digitally).
Internet Service
Operational: Yes.
Subscribers: 1,393.
Broadband Service: Charter Internet.
Fee: $29.99 monthly.
Telephone Service
Digital: Operational
Subscribers: 670.
Fee: $29.99 monthly
Miles of Plant: 833.0 (coaxial); 200.0 (fiber optic). Homes passed: 20,177.
Vice President & General Manager: Wendy Rasmusson. Technical Operations Director: Peter Arredondo. Accounting Director: David Sovanski. Marketing Manager: Lily Ho.
Ownership: Charter Communications Inc. (MSO).

MAMMOTH LAKES—Suddenlink Communications, 520 Maryville Centre Dr, Ste 300, St. Louis, MO 63141. Phones: 800-999-6845 (Customer service); 314-315-9400. Web Site: http://www.suddenlink.com. Also serves June Lake. ICA: CA0358.
TV Market Ranking: Outside TV Markets (MAMMOTH LAKES, June Lake). Franchise award date: January 1, 1970. Franchise expiration date: N.A. Began: September 1, 1970.
Channel capacity: N.A. Channels available but not in use: N.A.
Basic Service
Subscribers: 3,312. Commercial subscribers: 1,583.
Programming (received off-air): KAME-TV (MeTV, MNT) Reno; KBEH (IND) Oxnard; KNPB (PBS) Reno; KOLO-TV (ABC, IND, Movies!) Reno; KREN-TV (CW, UNV) Reno; KRNV-DT (NBC, This TV) Reno; KRXI-TV (FOX, Retro TV) Reno; KSRW-LP Mammoth Lakes, etc.; KTVN (Antenna TV, CBS) Reno; allband FM.

Programming (via satellite): A&E; AMC; Animal Planet; Cartoon Network; CMT; CNBC; CNN; Comedy Central; C-SPAN; Discovery Channel; Disney Channel; ESPN; ESPN Classic; ESPN2; Food Network; Fox News Channel; FOX Sports West/Prime Ticket; Freeform; FX; Great American Country; HGTV; History; HLN; INSP; ION Television; KTLA (Antenna TV, CW, This TV) Los Angeles; Lifetime; LMN; MSNBC; MTV; National Geographic Channel; NBCSN; Nickelodeon; OWN: Oprah Winfrey Network; Pop; QVC; Spike TV; Syfy; TBS; The Weather Channel; TLC; TNT; Travel Channel; Turner Classic Movies; TV Land; Univision; Univision Studios; USA Network; VH1.
Fee: $39.95 installation; $60.99 monthly; $2.50 converter.
Digital Basic Service
Subscribers: N.A.
Programming (via satellite): AXS TV; BBC America; Cooking Channel; Discovery Digital Networks; Disney XD; DIY Network; DMX Music; ESPN HD; ESPN2 HD; ESPNews; ESPNU; Food Network HD; Fox Deportes; Fox Sports 1; Fox Sports 2; FSN Digital Atlantic; FSN Digital Central; FSN Digital Pacific; FYI; Golf Channel; GSN; HD Theater; HGTV HD; History International; IFC; Nick Jr.; Nicktoons; TeenNick; TNT HD; Universal HD; WE tv.
Digital Pay Service 1
Pay Units: N.A.
Programming (via satellite): Cinemax (multiplexed); HBO (multiplexed); Showtime (multiplexed); Starz (multiplexed); Starz Encore (multiplexed); The Movie Channel (multiplexed).
Fee: $6.95 monthly (Cinemax), $9.95 monthly (Starz/Encore), $11.95 monthly (Showtime/TMC), $12.00 monthly (HBO).
Video-On-Demand: No
Pay-Per-View
iN DEMAND (delivered digitally); Fresh (delivered digitally).
Internet Service
Operational: Yes.
Broadband Service: Suddenlink High Speed Internet.
Fee: $59.95 installation; $24.95 monthly; $5.00 modem lease.
Telephone Service
Digital: Operational
Miles of Plant: 105.0 (coaxial); 19.0 (fiber optic). Homes passed: 9,000.
Senior Vice President, Corporate Finance: Michael Pflantz. Chief Executive Officer: Jerald L. Kent. Executive Vice President & Chief Operating Officer: Thomas P. McMillin. Senior Vice President, Marketing: Mary R. Meier. Vice President, Accounting: Sabrina Warr.
Ownership: Cequel Communications Holdings I LLC (MSO).

MANTECA—Comcast Cable. Now served by SACRAMENTO, CA [CA0002]. ICA: CA0126.

MARIPOSA—Northland Cable Television, 40092 Hwy 49, Ste A, Oakhurst, CA 93644. Phones: 800-736-1414; 559-683-7388. Fax: 559-642-2432. E-mail: oakhurst@northlandcabletv.com. Web Site: http://www.yournorthland.com. ICA: CA0359.
TV Market Ranking: 72 (MARIPOSA). Franchise award date: January 1, 1981. Franchise expiration date: N.A. Began: N.A.
Channel capacity: N.A. Channels available but not in use: N.A.

Basic Service
Subscribers: 44.
Programming (received off-air): KAIL (COZI TV, MNT, WeatherNation) Fresno; KFRE-TV (CW, IND) Sanger; KFSN-TV (ABC, Live Well Network) Fresno; KFTV-DT (getTV, UNV) Hanford; KGMC (Antenna TV, Azteca, Daystar, HSN, MeTV, MundoMax) Clovis; KGPE (CBS, The Country Network, Untamed Sports TV) Fresno; KMPH-TV (FOX, This TV) Visalia; KNSO (TMO) Merced; KSEE (LATV, NBC) Fresno; KTVU (Buzzr, FOX, LATV, Movies!) Oakland; KVPT (PBS) Fresno; allband FM.
Programming (via satellite): A&E; Animal Planet; Cartoon Network; CNBC; CNN; C-SPAN; Discovery Channel; ESPN; Fox News Channel; History; HLN; Lifetime; QVC; TBS; TLC; TNT; USA Network; WGN America.
Fee: $75.00 installation; $47.64 monthly.
Expanded Basic Service 1
Subscribers: N.A.
Programming (via satellite): AMC; CMT; Comcast SportsNet Bay Area; E! HD; ESPN2; Food Network; Hallmark Channel; HGTV; Nickelodeon; Spike TV; Syfy; Turner Classic Movies.
Fee: $39.99 monthly.
Digital Basic Service
Subscribers: N.A.
Programming (via satellite): BBC America; Bloomberg Television; Discovery Digital Networks; DMX Music; Fox Sports 1; FXM; Golf Channel; Great American Country; GSN; Trinity Broadcasting Network (TBN).
Digital Expanded Basic Service
Subscribers: N.A.
Programming (via satellite): Discovery Life Channel; Outdoor Channel; WE tv.
Pay Service 1
Pay Units: N.A.
Programming (via satellite): HBO.
Fee: $13.50 monthly.
Digital Pay Service 1
Pay Units: N.A.
Programming (via satellite): Cinemax (multiplexed); Flix; HBO (multiplexed); Showtime (multiplexed); Starz Encore; The Movie Channel (multiplexed).
Fee: $10.00 monthly (each).
Pay-Per-View
Fresh (delivered digitally); Playboy TV (delivered digitally); Hot Choice (delivered digitally); Sports PPV (delivered digitally).
Internet Service
Operational: Yes.
Fee: $44.99 monthly.
Telephone Service
None
Miles of Plant: 14.0 (coaxial); None (fiber optic). Homes passed: 956.
Executive Vice President: Richard I. Clark. General Manager: Ken Musgrove. Chief Technician: Roger Conroy. Office Manager: Karen Bradley.
Ownership: Northland Communications Corp. (MSO).

MARSH CREEK MOTOR HOME PARK—Comcast Cable. Now served by SAN FRANCISCO, CA [CA0003]. ICA: CA0291.

CABLE & TV STATION COVERAGE
Atlas 2017
The perfect companion to the Television & Cable Factbook
To order call 800-771-9202 or visit www.warren-news.com

MEADOW VISTA—Formerly served by Cebridge Connections. Now served by Suddenlink Communications, LAKE OF THE PINES, CA [CA0202]. ICA: CA0196.

MECCA—USA Communications, 2455 Stirrup Rd, Borrego Springs, CA 92004. Phones: 800-234-0102; 308-236-1512 (Kearney, NE corporate office); 760-767-5607; 877-234-0102. Fax: 760-767-3609. E-mail: csr@usacommunications.tv. Web Site: http://usacommunications.tv. ICA: CA0281.
TV Market Ranking: Below 100 (MECCA). Franchise award date: N.A. Franchise expiration date: N.A. Began: January 1, 1983.
Channel capacity: N.A. Channels available but not in use: N.A.
Basic Service
Subscribers: 71.
Programming (received off-air): KDFX-CD Indio/Palm Springs; KESQ-TV (ABC, CW) Palm Springs; KFMB-TV (CBS, Grit, MeTV) San Diego; KMIR-TV (IND, Movies!, NBC) Palm Springs; KPBS (PBS) San Diego.
Programming (via satellite): QVC; TBS; The Weather Channel; Trinity Broadcasting Network (TBN); WGN America.
Fee: $39.95 installation; $21.45 monthly.
Expanded Basic Service 1
Subscribers: N.A.
Programming (via satellite): A&E; Animal Planet; Cartoon Network; CMT; CNBC; CNN; CNN en Espanol; C-SPAN; C-SPAN 2; Discovery Channel; E! HD; ESPN; ESPN Classic; ESPN2; EVINE Live; EWTN Global Catholic Network; Food Network; Fox Deportes; Fox News Channel; Freeform; Hallmark Channel; History; HLN; Nickelodeon; Spike TV; Syfy; TLC; TNT; Tr3s; Turner Classic Movies; USA Network; ViendoMovies; WE tv.
Fee: $24.95 installation; $35.45 monthly.
Expanded Basic Service 2
Subscribers: N.A.
Programming (via satellite): 52MX; Cine Mexicano; Cinelatino; History en Espanol; Telemundo; Toon Disney en Espanol; Uni-Mas; Univision; Univision Studios.
Fee: $9.95 monthly.
Pay Service 1
Pay Units: N.A.
Programming (via satellite): Showtime.
Fee: $7.75 monthly.
Internet Service
Operational: No.
Telephone Service
Analog: Operational
Miles of Plant: 5.0 (coaxial); None (fiber optic). Homes passed: 350.
Chief Financial Officer: Amber Reineke. General Manager & Chief Technician: Joe Gustafson.
Ownership: USA Companies LP (MSO).

MENLO PARK—Comcast Cable. Now served by SAN FRANCISCO, CA [CA0003]. ICA: CA0361.

MERCED—Comcast Cable. Now served by FRESNO, CA [CA0011]. ICA: CA0072.

California—Cable Systems

MERCED—Formerly served by Sprint Corp. No longer in operation. ICA: CA0436.

MEYERS—Charter Communications. Now served by RENO, NV [NV0002]. ICA: CA0194.

MIDPINES—Formerly served by Timber TV. No longer in operation. ICA: CA0299.

MILPITAS—Comcast Cable. Now served by SAN FRANCISCO, CA [CA0003]. ICA: CA0142.

MISSION BAY MOBILE HOME PARK—Formerly served by Comcast Cable. No longer in operation. ICA: CA0362.

MODESTO—Comcast Cable. Now served by SACRAMENTO, CA [CA0002]. ICA: CA0040.

MOFFETT FIELD NAVAL AIRSTATION—Formerly served by Americable International-Moffett Inc. No longer in operation. ICA: CA0226.

MOJAVE—Charter Communications, 12405 Powerscourt Dr, St. Louis, MO 63131. Phones: 636-207-5100 (Corporate office); 951-343-5100. Fax: 951-354-5942. Web Site: http://www.charter.com. Also serves Rosamond. ICA: CA0206.
  TV Market Ranking: Outside TV Markets (MOJAVE, Rosamond). Franchise award date: N.A. Franchise expiration date: N.A. Began: May 28, 1984.
  Channel capacity: N.A. Channels available but not in use: N.A.
Digital Basic Service
  Subscribers: 909.
  Programming (via satellite): Bandamax; BBC America; Bloomberg Television; CMT; C-SPAN 3; Discovery Life Channel; Disney XD; DIY Network; ESPN Classic; ESPNews; FOX College Sports Central; FOX College Sports Pacific; Fuse; FYI; GolTV; GSN; Hallmark Channel; History; History International; HITS (Headend In The Sky); IFC; LMN; National Geographic Channel; NBCSN; Nick 2; Nick Jr.; Sundance TV; TeenNick; TV Land; WE tv.
  Fee: $14.99 monthly.
Digital Expanded Basic Service
  Subscribers: N.A.
  Programming (via satellite): A&E; AMC; BET; Bravo; Cartoon Network; CMT; CNBC; CNN; Comedy Central; Discovery Channel; Disney Channel; E! HD; ESPN; ESPN2; Food Network; Fox News Channel; FOX Sports West/Prime Ticket; Freeform; HGTV; History; HLN; Lifetime; MTV; MTV2; Nickelodeon; Outdoor Channel; Oxygen; Spike TV; Syfy; TBS; TLC; TNT; TV One; Univision Studios; USA Network; VH1.
  Fee: $45.45 monthly.
Digital Pay Service 1
  Pay Units: N.A.
  Programming (via satellite): Cinemax (multiplexed); Flix; FXM; HBO (multiplexed); Showtime (multiplexed); Starz (multiplexed); Starz Encore (multiplexed); The Movie Channel (multiplexed).
Video-On-Demand: No
Pay-Per-View
  iN DEMAND (delivered digitally); Playboy TV (delivered digitally); Fresh (delivered digitally); Club Jenna (delivered digitally); Fresh! (delivered digitally).
Internet Service
  Operational: Yes.
  Broadband Service: Charter Internet.
  Fee: $39.99 monthly.

Telephone Service
  None
  Miles of Plant: 85.0 (coaxial); 10.0 (fiber optic). Homes passed: 5,432.
  Vice President & General Manager: Fred Lutz. Technical Operations Manager: George Noel. Marketing Director: Chris Bailey. Accounting Director: David Sovanski.
  Ownership: Charter Communications Inc. (MSO).

MONTEREY—Comcast Cable. Now served by SAN FRANCISCO, CA [CA0003]. ICA: CA0030.

MONTEREY—Formerly served by Sprint Corp. No longer in operation. ICA: CA0437.

MONTEREY—Suddenlink Communications, 520 Maryville Centre Dr, Ste 300, St. Louis, MO 63141. Phones: 314-315-9400; 800-446-6745; 530-587-6100. Web Site: http://www.suddenlink.com. Also serves Del Rey Oaks, Marina, Presidio of Monterey & Seaside. ICA: CA0153.
  TV Market Ranking: Below 100 (Del Rey Oaks, Marina, MONTEREY, Presidio of Monterey, Seaside). Franchise award date: November 19, 1980. Franchise expiration date: N.A. Began: May 5, 1981.
  Channel capacity: N.A. Channels available but not in use: N.A.
Basic Service
  Subscribers: 227. Commercial subscribers: 91.
  Programming (received off-air): KCBA (FOX) Salinas; KION-TV (CBS, CW) Monterey; KSBW (ABC, Estrella TV, NBC) Salinas; KSMS-TV (LATV, UNV) Monterey.
  Programming (via microwave): KICU-TV (Heroes & Icons, IND) San Jose; KNTV (COZI TV, NBC) San Jose; KQED (PBS) San Francisco; KQEH (PBS) San Jose.
  Programming (via satellite): TBS; WGN America.
  Fee: $40.00 installation; $35.04 monthly.
Expanded Basic Service 1
  Subscribers: N.A.
  Programming (via satellite): A&E; BET; CNN; Comcast SportsNet Bay Area; Comedy Central; Discovery Channel; Disney Channel; E! HD; ESPN; Freeform; HLN; Lifetime; MTV; Nickelodeon; Spike TV; TNT; USA Network; VH1.
  Fee: $5.00 monthly.
Pay Service 1
  Pay Units: N.A.
  Programming (via satellite): Flix; HBO; Playboy TV; Showtime; The Movie Channel.
  Fee: $8.95 monthly (Playboy), $9.95 monthly (HBO, Showtime or TMC).
Video-On-Demand: No
Pay-Per-View
  iN DEMAND.
Internet Service
  Operational: No.
Telephone Service
  None
  Miles of Plant: 50.0 (coaxial); None (fiber optic). Homes passed: 5,000.
  Senior Vice President, Corporate Finance: Michael Pflantz. Vice President, Accounting: Sabrina Warr. Marketing Director: Jason Oelkers.
  Ownership: Cequel Communications Holdings I LLC (MSO).

MONTEREY COUNTY (portions)—Charter Communications, 12405 Powerscourt Dr, St. Louis, MO 63131. Phone: 303-323-1423. Web Site: http://www.charter.com. Also serves Carmel Highlands, Castroville, Moss Landing, Oak Hills, Prunedale & Rancho Tierra Grande. ICA: CA0905.
  TV Market Ranking: Below 100 (Carmel Highlands, MONTEREY COUNTY (portions) (portions), Moss Landing, Oak Hills, Prunedale, Rancho Tierra Grande); Outside TV Markets (Castroville, MONTEREY COUNTY (portions) (portions)).
  Channel capacity: N.A. Channels available but not in use: N.A.
Basic Service
  Subscribers: 378.
  Fee: $26.99 monthly.
  Senior Accounting Director: Steve Lottmann.
  Ownership: Charter Communications Inc. (MSO).

MORGAN HILL—Charter Communications. Now served by GILROY, CA [CA0425]. ICA: CA0334.

MOUNT SHASTA—Northland Cable Television, 900 South Mt Shasta Blvd, PO Box 8, Mount Shasta, CA 96067-0008. Phones: 888-667-8452; 530-926-6546; 530-926-6128. Fax: 530-926-6546. E-mail: mtshasta@northlandcabletv.com. Web Site: http://www.yournorthland.com. Also serves Dunsmuir, McCloud, Shasta County (portions), Siskiyou County (portions) & Weed. ICA: CA0171.
  TV Market Ranking: Below 100 (Siskiyou County (portions)); Outside TV Markets (Dunsmuir, McCloud, MOUNT SHASTA, Shasta County (portions), Weed, Siskiyou County (portions)). Franchise award date: N.A. Franchise expiration date: N.A. Began: December 26, 1972.
  Channel capacity: N.A. Channels available but not in use: N.A.
Basic Service
  Subscribers: 1,440.
  Programming (received off-air): KBLN-TV (IND) Grants Pass; KDRV (ABC) Medford; KHSL-TV (CBS, CW) Chico; KIXE-TV (PBS) Redding; KNVN (Antenna TV, NBC) Redding; KOBI (NBC) Medford; KRCR-TV (ABC, MeTV, Movies!) Redding; KRVU-LD (MNT) Redding; KTVL (CBS, CW) Medford.
  Programming (via satellite): A&E; Animal Planet; Cartoon Network; CNBC; CNN; Comcast SportsNet Bay Area; Comedy Central; Cooking Channel; C-SPAN; CW PLUS; Discovery Channel; ESPN; ESPN2; Food Network; Fox News Channel; FX; FXM; Golf Channel; Great American Country; Hallmark Channel; HGTV; History; HLN; Lifetime; MTV; NBCSN; NFL Network; Nickelodeon; Outdoor Channel; QVC; Spike TV; Syfy; TBS; Telemundo; The Weather Channel; TLC; TNT; Turner Classic Movies; TV Land; USA Network; VH1; WGN America.
  Fee: $75.00 installation; $47.64 monthly.
Digital Basic Service
  Subscribers: N.A.
  Programming (via satellite): BBC America; Bloomberg Television; Bravo; Destination America; Discovery Kids Channel; Discovery Life Channel; DMX Music; ESPNews; EWTN Global Catholic Network; Fox Sports 1; IFC; INSP; Investigation Discovery; LMN; National Geographic Channel; OWN: Oprah Winfrey Network; Science Channel; Trinity Broadcasting Network (TBN); WE tv.
Pay Service 1
  Pay Units: N.A.
  Programming (via satellite): HBO.
  Fee: $10.00 installation; $11.45 monthly.
Digital Pay Service 1
  Pay Units: N.A.
  Programming (via satellite): Cinemax (multiplexed); Flix; HBO (multiplexed); Showtime (multiplexed); Starz (multiplexed); Starz Encore (multiplexed); The Movie Channel (multiplexed).
  Fee: $14.75 monthly (Cinemax, HBO, Showtime/TMC/Flix or Starz/Encore).
Video-On-Demand: No
Pay-Per-View
  iN DEMAND (delivered digitally); Playboy TV (delivered digitally); Fresh (delivered digitally); Club Jenna (delivered digitally).
Internet Service
  Operational: Yes.
  Broadband Service: Northland Express.
  Fee: $42.99 monthly.
Telephone Service
  Digital: Operational
  Miles of Plant: 135.0 (coaxial); None (fiber optic). Homes passed: 8,500.
  Executive Vice President: Richard I. Clark. District Manager: Vince Reinig.
  Ownership: Northland Communications Corp. (MSO).

MOUNTAIN MEADOWS—Formerly served by Entertainment Express. No longer in operation. ICA: CA0240.

MOUNTAIN VIEW—Comcast Cable. Now served by SAN FRANCISCO, CA [CA0003]. ICA: CA0090.

NAPA—Comcast Cable. Now served by SAN FRANCISCO, CA [CA0003]. ICA: CA0091.

NAPA—Comcast Cable. Now served by SAN FRANCISCO, CA [CA0003]. ICA: CA0038.

NEEDLES—Golden Valley Cable & Communications, 1058 East Broadway, Needles, CA 92363. Phone: 760-326-4190. E-mail: cs@goldenvalleycable.com. Web Site: http://gvcable.com. Also serves Lower Mohave Valley. ICA: CA0222.
  TV Market Ranking: Below 100 (Lower Mohave Valley, NEEDLES). Franchise award date: N.A. Franchise expiration date: N.A. Began: December 1, 1982.
  Channel capacity: N.A. Channels available but not in use: N.A.
Basic Service
  Subscribers: 370.
  Programming (received off-air): KPHO-TV (CBS, COZI TV) Phoenix.
  Programming (via satellite): A&E; Animal Planet; Cartoon Network; CMT; CNN; C-SPAN; C-SPAN 2; Discovery Channel; Disney Channel; ESPN; ESPN2; Great American Country; History; HLN; KTLA (Antenna TV, CW, This TV) Los Angeles; Lifetime; LMN; MTV; Nickelodeon; Pop; Spike TV; Syfy; TBS; The Weather Channel; TLC; TNT; Trinity Broadcasting Network (TBN); Turner Classic Movies; TV Land; Univision Studios; USA Network; VH1; WGN America.
  Programming (via translator): KAET (PBS) Phoenix; KAZT-TV (MeTV, Retro TV) Phoenix; KHSV (Antenna TV, MNT) Las Vegas; KNXV-TV (ABC) Phoenix; KPNX (NBC) Mesa; KSAZ-TV (Bounce TV, FOX, Heroes & Icons) Phoenix; KTVK (This TV) Phoenix; KUTP (Buzzr, MNT, Movies!) Phoenix; KVVU-TV (Escape, FOX) Henderson.
  Fee: $29.95 installation; $43.00 monthly.
Pay Service 1
  Pay Units: 309.
  Programming (via satellite): Cinemax; HBO; Showtime.
  Fee: $10.45 monthly (each).
Video-On-Demand: No

Cable Systems—California

Internet Service
Operational: Yes.
Broadband Service: Rapid High Speed Internet.
Fee: $29.95 installation; $24.95 monthly.
Telephone Service
None
Miles of Plant: 32.0 (coaxial); None (fiber optic). Homes passed: 1,900.
President: Daniel Huffman.
Ownership: Golden Valley Cable & Communications Inc. (MSO).

NEW CUYAMA—Formerly served by Wave Broadband. No longer in operation. ICA: CA0290.

NEWARK—Comcast Cable. Now served by SAN FRANCISCO, CA [CA0003]. ICA: CA0154.

NEWPORT BEACH—Formerly served by Adelphia Communications. Now served by Time Warner Cable, LOS ANGELES, CA [CA0009]. ICA: CA0115.

NILAND—USA Communications, 2455 Stirrup Rd, Borrego Springs, CA 92004. Phones: 800-234-0102; 308-236-1515 (Kearney, NE corporate office); 760-767-5607; 877-234-0102. Fax: 760-767-3609. E-mail: csr@usacommunications.tv. Web Site: http://usacommunications.tv. ICA: CA0901.
TV Market Ranking: Below 100 (NILAND).
Channel capacity: N.A. Channels available but not in use: N.A.
Basic Service
Subscribers: 33.
Fee: $39.95 installation; $29.75 monthly.
Chief Financial Officer: Amber Reineke.
Ownership: USA Companies LP (MSO).

NORTH EDWARDS—Charter Communications, 12405 Powerscourt Dr, St. Louis, MO 63131. Phones: 636-207-5100 (Corporate office); 951-343-5100. Fax: 951-354-5942. Web Site: http://www.charter.com. Also serves Boron & California City. ICA: CA0404.
TV Market Ranking: Below 100 (Boron); Outside TV Markets (NORTH EDWARDS, California City).
Channel capacity: N.A. Channels available but not in use: N.A.
Digital Basic Service
Subscribers: 1,394.
Programming (via satellite): Bandamax; BBC America; Bloomberg Television; CMT; C-SPAN 3; Discovery Life Channel; Disney XD; DIY Network; ESPN Classic; ESPNews; FOX College Sports Central; FOX College Sports Pacific; Fuse; FYI; GolTV; GSN; Hallmark Channel; History; History International; HITS (Headend In The Sky); IFC; LMN; National Geographic Channel; NBCSN; Nick 2; Nick Jr.; Sundance TV; TeenNick; TV Land; WE tv.
Fee: $14.99 monthly.
Digital Expanded Basic Service
Subscribers: N.A.
Programming (via satellite): A&E; AMC; BET; Bravo; Cartoon Network; CMT; CNBC; CNN; Discovery Channel; Disney Channel; E! HD; ESPN; ESPN2; Food Network; Fox News Channel; FOX Sports West/Prime Ticket; Freeform; HGTV; History; HLN; Lifetime; MTV; MTV2; Nickelodeon; Outdoor Channel; Oxygen; Spike TV; Syfy; TBS; TLC; TNT; TV One; Univision Studios; USA Network; VH1.
Fee: $45.45 monthly.

Digital Pay Service 1
Pay Units: N.A.
Programming (via satellite): Cinemax (multiplexed); Flix; FXM; HBO (multiplexed); Showtime (multiplexed); Starz (multiplexed); Starz Encore (multiplexed); The Movie Channel (multiplexed).
Video-On-Demand: No
Pay-Per-View
iN DEMAND (delivered digitally); Playboy TV (delivered digitally); Fresh (delivered digitally); Club Jenna (delivered digitally); Fresh! (delivered digitally).
Internet Service
Operational: Yes.
Broadband Service: Charter Internet.
Fee: $39.99 monthly.
Telephone Service
None
Miles of Plant: 7.0 (coaxial); None (fiber optic).
Vice President & General Manager: Fred Lutz. Technical Operations Manager: George Noel. Marketing Director: Chris Bailey. Accounting Director: David Sovanski.
Ownership: Charter Communications Inc. (MSO).

NORTH FORK—Ponderosa Cablevision, 47034 Road 201, O'Neals, CA 93645. Phones: 800-682-1878; 559-868-6000. E-mail: customercare@goponderosa.com. Web Site: http://www.goponderosa.com. ICA: CA0469.
TV Market Ranking: 72 (NORTH FORK).
Channel capacity: N.A. Channels available but not in use: N.A.
Basic Service
Subscribers: 180.
Programming (received off-air): KAIL (COZI TV, MNT, WeatherNation) Fresno; KFRE-TV (CW, IND) Sanger; KFSN-TV (ABC, Live Well Network) Fresno; KFTV-DT (getTV, UNV) Hanford; KJEO-LD (America One, IND) Fresno; KMPH-TV (FOX, This TV) Visalia; KSEE (LATV, NBC) Fresno; KTFF-DT (UniMas) Porterville; KVPT (PBS) Fresno.
Programming (via satellite): A&E; AMC; Animal Planet; CMT; CNBC; CNN; Comedy Central; C-SPAN; Discovery Channel; Disney Channel; ESPN; ESPN Classic; ESPN2; Food Network; Fox News Channel; Freeform; Hallmark Channel; HGTV; History; HLN; MSNBC; MTV; Nickelodeon; Outdoor Channel; QVC; Spike TV; Syfy; TBS; TLC; TNT; Travel Channel; Trinity Broadcasting Network (TBN); Turner Classic Movies; TV Land; USA Network; VH1.
Fee: $30.00 installation; $30.95 monthly.
Pay Service 1
Pay Units: 66.
Programming (via satellite): HBO.
Fee: $10.00 installation; $10.95 monthly.
Pay Service 2
Pay Units: 23.
Programming (via satellite): Showtime.
Fee: $10.00 installation; $9.95 monthly.
Pay Service 3
Pay Units: 20.
Programming (via satellite): Cinemax.
Fee: $10.00 installation; $9.95 monthly.
Internet Service
Operational: No, DSL.
Telephone Service
Analog: Operational
Homes passed: 800.
General Manager: Matt Boos. Technical Supervisor: Doug Wickham.
Ownership: Ponderosa Cablevision.

NORTHSTAR—Formerly served by Charter Communications. No longer in operation. ICA: CA0246.

NOVATO—Comcast Cable. Now served by SAN FRANCISCO, CA [CA0003]. ICA: CA0118.

NOVATO—Formerly served by Horizon Cable TV Inc. No longer in operation. ICA: CA0239.

OAKHURST—Northland Cable Television, 40092 Hwy 49, Ste A, Oakhurst, CA 93644. Phones: 800-736-1414; 559-683-7388. Fax: 559-642-2432. E-mail: oakhurst@northlandcabletv.com. Web Site: http://www.yournorthland.com. Also serves Ahwahnee, Bass Lake & Cedar Valley. ICA: CA0364.
TV Market Ranking: 72 (Ahwahnee, Bass Lake, Cedar Valley, OAKHURST). Franchise award date: N.A. Franchise expiration date: N.A. Began: March 1, 1963.
Channel capacity: N.A. Channels available but not in use: N.A.
Basic Service
Subscribers: 923.
Programming (received off-air): KAIL (COZI TV, MNT, WeatherNation) Fresno; KFRE-TV (CW, IND) Sanger; KFSN-TV (ABC, Live Well Network) Fresno; KFTV-DT (getTV, UNV) Hanford; KGPE (CBS, The Country Network, Untamed Sports TV) Fresno; KNSO (TMO) Merced; KSEE (LATV, NBC) Fresno; KVPT (PBS) Fresno; 13 FMs.
Programming (via microwave): KMPH-TV (FOX, This TV) Visalia.
Programming (via satellite): A&E; CNBC; CNN; C-SPAN; Discovery Channel; ESPN; Fox News Channel; Hallmark Channel; HLN; Pop; QVC; TBS; The Weather Channel; TLC; TNT; Travel Channel; Trinity Broadcasting Network (TBN); USA Network.
Fee: $75.00 installation; $47.64 monthly.
Expanded Basic Service 1
Subscribers: N.A.
Programming (via satellite): Animal Planet; Bravo; Cartoon Network; Comcast SportsNet Bay Area; Comedy Central; E! HD; ESPN2; Food Network; FXM; Golf Channel; Great American Country; HGTV; History; Lifetime; NFL Network; Nickelodeon; Spike TV; Syfy; Turner Classic Movies; TV Land.
Fee: $43.29 monthly.
Digital Basic Service
Subscribers: N.A.
Programming (via satellite): BBC America; Bloomberg Television; Destination America; Discovery Kids Channel; Discovery Life Channel; DMX Music; ESPNews; Fox Sports 1; IFC; Investigation Discovery; LMN; OWN; Oprah Winfrey Network; Science Channel; WE tv.
Pay Service 1
Pay Units: N.A.
Programming (via satellite): HBO.
Fee: $15.00 installation; $11.95 monthly.
Digital Pay Service 1
Pay Units: N.A.
Programming (via satellite): Cinemax (multiplexed); Flix; HBO (multiplexed); Showtime (multiplexed); Starz (multiplexed); Starz Encore (multiplexed); Sundance TV; The Movie Channel (multiplexed).
Fee: $14.75 monthly (Cinemax, HBO, Showtime/TMC/Flix or Starz/Encore).
Video-On-Demand: No
Pay-Per-View
iN DEMAND (delivered digitally); Playboy TV (delivered digitally); Fresh (delivered digitally).

Internet Service
Operational: Yes.
Fee: $44.99 monthly.
Telephone Service
None
Miles of Plant: 106.0 (coaxial); None (fiber optic). Homes passed: 4,387.
Executive Vice President: Richard I. Clark. General Manager: Ken Musgrove. Chief Technician: Roger Conroy. Office Manager: Karen Bradley.
Ownership: Northland Communications Corp. (MSO).

OCOTILLO—Formerly served by USA Communications. No longer in operation. ICA: CA0297.

OJAI—Time Warner Cable. Now served by LOS ANGELES, CA [CA0009]. ICA: CA0440.

OLINDA—Formerly served by Almega Cable. No longer in operation. ICA: CA0455.

ONTARIO—Time Warner Cable. Now served by LOS ANGELES, CA [CA0009]. ICA: CA0010.

ORANGE COUNTY (western portion)—Time Warner Cable. Now served by LOS ANGELES, CA [CA0009]. ICA: CA0071.

ORICK—Formerly served by Almega Cable. No longer in operation. ICA: CA0366.

OROVILLE—Comcast Cable. Now served by SACRAMENTO, CA [CA0002]. ICA: CA0077.

OXNARD—Time Warner Cable. Now served by LOS ANGELES, CA [CA0009]. ICA: CA0052.

PACIFICA—Comcast Cable. Now served by SAN FRANCISCO, CA [CA0003]. ICA: CA0116.

PALM SPRINGS—Time Warner Cable, 41725 Cook St, Palm Desert, CA 92211-5100. Phones: 760-340-2225; 858-695-3110 (San Diego office); 760-340-1312. Fax: 760-340-9764. Web Site: http://www.timewarnercable.com. Also serves Cathedral City, Coachella, Desert Hot Springs, Indian Wells, Indio, La Quinta, Palm Desert, Rancho Mirage, Riverside County (portions) & Thousand Palms. ICA: CA0036.
TV Market Ranking: Below 100 (Cathedral City, Coachella, Desert Hot Springs, Indian Wells, Indio, La Quinta, Rancho Mirage, Riverside County (portions), Thousand Palms, Palm Desert, PALM SPRINGS). Franchise award date: N.A. Franchise expiration date: N.A. Began: January 1, 1959.
Channel capacity: 63 (operating 2-way). Channels available but not in use: N.A.
Basic Service
Subscribers: 82,631.
Programming (received off-air): KCWQ-LP Palm Springs; KDFX-CD Indio/Palm Springs; KESQ-TV (ABC, CW) Palm Springs; KEVC-CD (UniMas) Indio; KMIR-TV (IND, Movies!, NBC) Palm Springs; KPSP-CD (CBS) Cathedral City; KUNA-LP (TMO) Indio; KVCR-DT (PBS) San Bernardino; KVER-CA (LATV, UNV) Indio; KYAV-LD (IND) Palm Springs; 11 FMs.
Programming (via microwave): KABC-TV (ABC, Live Well Network) Los Angeles; KCAL-TV (IND) Los Angeles; KCET (ETV) Los Angeles; KNBC (COZI TV, NBC) Los Angeles.

2017 Edition

D-97

California—Cable Systems

Programming (via satellite): C-SPAN; C-SPAN 2; EVINE Live; EWTN Global Catholic Network; ION Television; MyNetworkTV; Pop; QVC; Trinity Broadcasting Network (TBN); WGN America.
Fee: $33.00 installation; $22.00 monthly; $5.00 converter.

Expanded Basic Service 1
Subscribers: N.A.
Programming (via satellite): A&E; AMC; Animal Planet; BET; Bravo; Cartoon Network; CNBC; CNN; Comedy Central; Discovery Channel; Disney Channel; E! HD; ESPN; ESPN2; Food Network; Fox Deportes; Fox News Channel; FOX Sports West/Prime Ticket; Freeform; FX; Golf Channel; Hallmark Channel; HGTV; History; HLN; Lifetime; LMN; MSNBC; MTV; NBCSN; Nickelodeon; Spike TV; Syfy; TBS; The Weather Channel; TLC; TNT; Travel Channel; truTV; Turner Classic Movies; TV Land; USA Network; VH1; WE tv.

Digital Basic Service
Subscribers: N.A.
Programming (via satellite): A&E HD; AXS TV; BBC America; BBC America On Demand; Bloomberg Television; Boomerang; California Channel; Canal Sur; CBS Sports Network; Cinelatino; Cloo; CMT; CNN en Espanol; CNN International; Cooking Channel; C-SPAN 3; Destination America; Discovery Kids Channel; Discovery Life Channel; Disney XD; DIY Network; ESPN Classic; ESPN Deportes; ESPN HD; ESPN2 HD; ESPNews; ESPNU; Flix; Fox Business Network; FOX College Sports Central; FOX College Sports Pacific; Fox Deportes; Fox HD; Fox Sports 2; Fuse; FXM; FYI; GSN; HD Theater; History HD; History International; IFC; INSP; Investigation Discovery; La Familia Cosmovision; LOGO; MC; MTV Classic; MTV2; Nat Geo WILD; National Geographic Channel; National Geographic Channel HD; National Geographic Channel On Demand; NBA TV; NBC Universo; Nick Jr.; Nicktoons; Ovation; OWN; Oprah Winfrey Network; Oxygen; Oxygen On Demand; Science Channel; Starz Encore (multiplexed); Sundance TV; TBS HD; TeenNick; Tennis Channel; TNT HD; Toon Disney en Espanol; Tr3s; TV Guide Network; Universal HD; Versus HD; Video-Rola.

Digital Pay Service 1
Pay Units: N.A.
Programming (via satellite): AXS TV; Cinemax (multiplexed); Cinemax On Demand; HBO (multiplexed); HBO HD; HBO on Demand; Showtime (multiplexed); Showtime HD; Showtime On Demand; Starz (multiplexed); The Movie Channel (multiplexed); The Movie Channel On Demand.
Fee: $15.00 monthly (each).

Video-On-Demand: Yes

Pay-Per-View
iN DEMAND; Playboy TV (delivered digitally); Fresh (delivered digitally); Shorteez (delivered digitally); ESPN (delivered digitally).

Internet Service
Operational: Yes.
Subscribers: 115,441.
Broadband Service: Road Runner, EarthLink, AOL.
Fee: $50.00 installation; $44.95 monthly.

Telephone Service
Digital: Operational
Subscribers: 69,853.
Fee: $39.95 monthly
Miles of Plant: 4,703.0 (coaxial); 574.0 (fiber optic). Homes passed: 274,686. Homes passed included in San Diego. Miles of plant (coax & fiber) included in Banning.

President: Bob Barlow. Vice President & General Manager: Tad Yo. Vice President, Customer Care: Vinit Ahooja. Public Affairs Director: Kathi Jacobs. Marketing Director: Jimmy Kelly. Technical Operations Director: Dessi Ocho. Engineering Director: Mike Sagona.
Ownership: Time Warner Cable (MSO).

PALMDALE—Time Warner Cable. Now served by LOS ANGELES, CA [CA0009]. ICA: CA0031.

PALO ALTO—Comcast Cable. Now served by SAN FRANCISCO, CA [CA0003]. ICA: CA0004.

PALO ALTO—Comcast Cable. Now served by SAN FRANCISCO, CA [CA0003]. ICA: CA0055.

PALO CEDRO—Formerly served by New Day Broadband. No longer in operation. ICA: CA0172.

PALOS VERDES PENINSULA—Cox Communications. Now served by RANCHO PALOS VERDES, CA [CA0903]. ICA: CA0060.

PATTERSON—Comcast Cable, 2441 North Grove Industrial Dr, Fresno, CA 93727-1535. Phones: 559-253-4050; 800-266-2278. Fax: 559-253-4090. Web Site: http://www.comcast.com. Also serves Crow's Landing, Gustine, Newman, Santa Nella & Stanislaus County (portions). ICA: CA0178.
TV Market Ranking: 25 (Crow's Landing, Gustine, Newman, PATTERSON, Stanislaus County (portions)); 72 (Santa Nella).
Channel capacity: N.A. Channels available but not in use: N.A.

Basic Service
Subscribers: 3,252.
Programming (received off-air): KAIL (COZI TV, MNT, WeatherNation) Fresno; KFRE-TV (CW, IND) Sanger; KFSN-TV (ABC, Live Well Network) Fresno; KFTV-DT (getTV, UNV) Hanford; KMAX-TV (CW) Sacramento; KMPH-TV (FOX, This TV) Visalia; KNSO (TMO) Merced; KQED (PBS) San Francisco; KSEE (LATV, NBC) Fresno; KTXL (Antenna TV, FOX) Sacramento.
Programming (via satellite): A&E; CNN; C-SPAN; Discovery Channel; Freeform; HLN; Lifetime; MTV; Nickelodeon; QVC; TBS; TNT.
Fee: $42.00 installation; $30.75 monthly.

Expanded Basic Service 1
Subscribers: N.A.
Programming (via satellite): A&E; AMC; Animal Planet; Bravo; Cartoon Network; CMT; Comcast SportsNet Bay Area; Comedy Central; Disney Channel; E! HD; ESPN; ESPN2; EVINE Live; Food Network; Fox News Channel; FX; Golf Channel; GSN; Hallmark Channel; HGTV; NBCSN; Spike TV; Syfy; TBS; TLC; TNT; TV Land; Univision; USA Network.
Fee: $27.34 -$38.00.

Digital Basic Service
Subscribers: N.A.
Programming (via satellite): BBC America; Bloomberg Television; Bravo; Discovery Digital Networks; Disney XD; DMX Music; ESPN Classic; ESPN Now; ESPN2; ESPNews; EVINE Live; FOX College Sports Central; FOX College Sports Pacific; Fox Sports 1; Fuse; FXM; FYI; Golf Channel; Great American Country; GSN; HGTV; History International; HITS (Headend In The Sky); IFC; LMN; National Geographic Channel; NBCSN; Nick Jr.; Nicktoons; Outdoor Channel; Ovation; Sprout; Sundance TV; Syfy; TeenNick; The Word Network; Trinity Broadcasting Network (TBN); Turner Classic Movies; TV Land; TV One; WE tv.

Digital Pay Service 1
Pay Units: N.A.
Programming (via satellite): Cinemax (multiplexed); Flix; HBO (multiplexed); Showtime (multiplexed); Starz (multiplexed); Starz Encore (multiplexed); The Movie Channel (multiplexed).
Fee: $17.99 monthly (Cinemax, Starz or TMC), $18.99 monthly (HBO or Showtime).

Video-On-Demand: Yes

Pay-Per-View
iN DEMAND (delivered digitally); Urban Xtra (delivered digitally); Fresh (delivered digitally); Shorteez (delivered digitally); Playboy TV (delivered digitally); Hot Choice (delivered digitally); Sports PPV (delivered digitally).

Internet Service
Operational: Yes.
Broadband Service: Comcast High Speed Internet.
Fee: $42.95 monthly; $3.00 modem lease.

Telephone Service
Digital: Operational
Fee: $39.95 monthly
Miles of Plant: 83.0 (coaxial); None (fiber optic). Homes passed: 7,000.
General Manager: Len Falter. Marketing Director: Stewart Butler. Communications Director: Erica Smith.
Ownership: Comcast Cable Communications Inc. (MSO).

PERRIS—Time Warner Cable. Now served by LOS ANGELES, CA [CA0009]. ICA: CA0159.

PESCADERO—Comcast Cable. Now served by SAN FRANCISCO, CA [CA0003]. ICA: CA0483.

PETALUMA—Comcast Cable. Now served by SAN FRANCISCO, CA [CA0003]. ICA: CA0068.

PETALUMA COAST GUARD STATION—Compass Digital Media, 599 Tomales Rd, Petaluma, CA 94952-5000. Phones: 707-765-7341; 707-765-7343 (Office). Fax: 707-765-7329. E-mail: jason.s.vanzant@uscg.mil. ICA: CA0368.
TV Market Ranking: 7 (PETALUMA COAST GUARD STATION). Franchise award date: N.A. Franchise expiration date: N.A. Began: December 22, 1988.
Channel capacity: N.A. Channels available but not in use: N.A.

Basic Service
Subscribers: N.A.
Programming (received off-air): KBCW (CW) San Francisco; KGO-TV (ABC, Live Well Network) San Francisco; KICU-TV (Heroes & Icons, IND) San Jose; KOFY-TV (MeTV) San Francisco; KPIX-TV (CBS, Decades) San Francisco; KQED (PBS) San Francisco; KRON-TV (Antenna TV, MNT) San Francisco; KTVU (Buzzr, FOX, LATV, Movies!) Oakland.
Programming (via satellite): A&E; AMC; Animal Planet; BET; Cartoon Network; CMT; CNN; Comedy Central; Discovery Channel; Disney Channel; Disney XD; E! HD; ESPN; ESPN Classic; ESPN2; ESPNews; Food Network; Fox News Channel; Fox Sports 1; FOX Sports West/Prime Ticket; Freeform; FXM; GSN; HBO (multiplexed); HGTV; History; Lifetime; MTV; Nickelodeon; Spike TV; Syfy; TBS; The Weather Channel; TLC; TNT; Travel Channel; Univision Studios; USA Network; VH1.
Fee: $20.00 installation.

Internet Service
Operational: Yes. Began: October 1, 2004.
Broadband Service: In-house.
Fee: $20.00 installation; $25.00 monthly; $50.00 modem purchase.

Telephone Service
None
Homes passed: 500.
General Manager: Larry Streeter.
Ownership: MWR Cable.

PINE GROVE—Volcano Vision. Now served by IONE, CA [CA0265]. ICA: CA0197.

PINECREST—SNC Cable, PO Box 281, Standard, CA 95373. Phones: 209-588-9601; 209-588-9601. E-mail: cust@gosnc.com. Web Site: http://gosnc.com. Also serves Strawberry. ICA: CA0251.
TV Market Ranking: Outside TV Markets (PINECREST, Strawberry). Franchise award date: N.A. Franchise expiration date: N.A. Began: August 1, 1961.
Channel capacity: N.A. Channels available but not in use: N.A.

Digital Basic Service
Subscribers: N.A.
Programming (received off-air): KCRA-TV (MeTV, NBC) Sacramento; KMAX-TV (CW) Sacramento; KOVR (CBS, Decades) Stockton; KQCA (MNT, Movies!, This TV) Stockton; KTFK-DT (getTV, UniMas) Stockton; KTNC-TV (Estrella TV, This TV) Concord; KTXL (Antenna TV, FOX) Sacramento; KVIE (PBS) Sacramento; KXTV (ABC) Sacramento; allband FM.
Programming (via satellite): A&E; CNBC; CNN; Discovery Channel; ESPN; Fox News Channel; History; TBS; TNT; Trinity Broadcasting Network (TBN).
Fee: $50.00 installation.

Digital Pay Service 1
Pay Units: N.A.
Programming (via satellite): HBO.
Fee: $13.95 monthly.

Video-On-Demand: No

Internet Service
Operational: Yes.
Fee: $21.95 monthly.

Telephone Service
Digital: Operational
Miles of Plant: 18.0 (coaxial); None (fiber optic). Homes passed: 1,000.
General Manager: Tim Holden. Product Development & Communications Manager: Bill Manley.
Ownership: Sierra Nevada Communications (MSO).

PINOLE—Comcast Cable. Now served by SAN FRANCISCO, CA [CA0003]. ICA: CA0032.

PINOLE—Comcast Cable. Now served by SAN FRANCISCO, CA [CA0003]. ICA: CA0018.

PITTSBURG—Comcast Cable. Now served by SAN FRANCISCO, CA [CA0003]. ICA: CA0056.

PLACER COUNTY (southwestern portion)—Wave Broadband, 401 Parkplace Center, Ste 500, Kirkland, WA 98033. Phones: 916-652-9479; 866-928-3123. Web Site: http://www.wavebroadband.com. Also serves Auburn, Colfax, Granite Bay, Lincoln, Loomis, Newcastle, Penryn, Placer

Cable Systems—California

County (western portion) & Rocklin. ICA: CA0131.
TV Market Ranking: 25 (Auburn, Granite Bay, Lincoln, Loomis, Newcastle, Penryn, Placer County (western portion), Rocklin); Below 100 (Placer County (western portion) (portions)); Outside TV Markets (Colfax, Placer County (western portion) (portions)). Franchise award date: May 1, 1980. Franchise expiration date: N.A. Began: January 1, 1981.
Channel capacity: 63 (operating 2-way). Channels available but not in use: N.A.

Basic Service
Subscribers: 16,378.
Programming (received off-air): KCRA-TV (MeTV, NBC) Sacramento; KMAX-TV (CW) Sacramento; KOVR (CBS, Decades) Stockton; KQCA (MNT, Movies!, This TV) Stockton; KSPX-TV (ION) Sacramento; KTFK-DT (getTV, UniMas) Stockton; KTXL (Antenna TV, FOX) Sacramento; KUVS-DT (Bounce TV, UNV) Modesto; KVIE (PBS) Sacramento; KXTV (ABC) Sacramento. Programming (via satellite): California Channel; C-SPAN; C-SPAN 2; Jewelry Television; QVC; WGN America.
Fee: $29.95 installation; $25.95 monthly.

Expanded Basic Service 1
Subscribers: N.A.
Programming (via satellite): A&E; AMC; Animal Planet; Bravo; Cartoon Network; CBS Sports Network; CMT; CNBC; CNN; Comcast SportsNet Bay Area; Comcast SportsNet California; Comedy Central; Discovery Channel; Disney Channel; Disney XD; E! HD; ESPN; ESPN Classic; ESPN2; Food Network; Fox News Channel; Freeform; FX; FXM; Golf Channel; Hallmark Channel; HGTV; History; HLN; INSP; Lifetime; MSNBC; MTV; National Geographic Channel; Nickelodeon; Oxygen; Spike TV; Syfy; TBS; The Weather Channel; TLC; TNT; Travel Channel; truTV; Turner Classic Movies; TV Land; USA Network; VH1.
Fee: $25.55 monthly.

Digital Basic Service
Subscribers: N.A.
Programming (via satellite): BBC America; BYUtv; Cloo; CMT; C-SPAN 2; Destination America; Discovery Kids Channel; Discovery Life Channel; Disney XD; EWTN Global Catholic Network; Fox Business Network; FYI; History International; Investigation Discovery; MC; MTV Classic; MTV Hits; MTV2; Nick Jr.; Nicktoons; OWN: Oprah Winfrey Network; Science Channel; Sprout; TeenNick; Trinity Broadcasting Network (TBN); VH1 Soul.

Digital Expanded Basic Service
Subscribers: N.A.
Programming (via satellite): AWE; Bloomberg Television; Boomerang; Bravo; Cooking Channel; DIY Network; Fuse; FXM; Great American Country; GSN; HGTV; History; IFC; LMN; NBC Universo; Ovation; Syfy; truTV; Turner Classic Movies; UP; WE tv.

Digital Expanded Basic Service 2
Subscribers: N.A.
Programming (via satellite): CBS Sports Network; ESPN Classic; ESPN2; ESPNews; ESPNU; Fox Sports 1; Fox Sports 2; FSN Digital Atlantic; FSN Digital Central; FSN Digital Pacific; Golf Channel; GolTV; NBA TV; NBCSN; NFL Network; Outdoor Channel; Tennis Channel.

Digital Expanded Basic Service 3
Subscribers: N.A.
Programming (via satellite): 52MX; Azteca; Bandamax; Cine Mexicano; Cinelatino; CNN en Espanol; De Pelicula; De Pelicula Clasico; Discovery Familia; ESPN Deportes; GolTV; History en Espanol; Telemundo; Tr3s; ViendoMovies; Vme TV.

Digital Expanded Basic Service 4
Subscribers: N.A.
Programming (via satellite): A&E HD; Animal Planet HD; AXS TV; Discovery Channel HD; Disney Channel HD; ESPN HD; ESPN2 HD; Food Network HD; Hallmark Channel HD; HD Theater; HGTV HD; History HD; MGM HD; National Geographic Channel HD; NFL Network HD; Science HD; TBS HD; TLC HD; TNT HD; Travel Channel HD; Universal HD.

Digital Pay Service 1
Pay Units: N.A.
Programming (via satellite): Cinemax (multiplexed); Flix; HBO (multiplexed); HBO HD; MoviePlex; Showtime (multiplexed); Showtime HD; Starz (multiplexed); Starz Encore (multiplexed); The Filipino Channel; The Movie Channel (multiplexed).
Fee: $12.00 monthly (Showtime/TMC/Flix), $15.00 monthly (Cinemax, HBO or Starz/Encore).

Video-On-Demand: Yes

Pay-Per-View
Playboy TV (delivered digitally); Fresh (delivered digitally); iN DEMAND (delivered digitally); NBA League Pass (delivered digitally).

Internet Service
Operational: Yes.
Subscribers: 19,953.
Broadband Service: Wave Broadband.
Fee: $24.95-$74.95 monthly; $5.00 modem lease.

Telephone Service
Digital: Operational
Subscribers: 8,908.
Fee: $29.95-$49.95 monthly
Miles of Plant: 1,251.0 (coaxial); 417.0 (fiber optic). Homes passed: 62,403.
Chief Financial Officer: Wayne Schattenkerk. Sales Director: Tom Carroll.
Ownership: WaveDivision Holdings LLC (MSO).

PLACERVILLE—Comcast Cable. Now served by SACRAMENTO, CA [CA0002]. ICA: CA0108.

PLANADA—Comcast Cable, 2441 North Grove Industrial Dr, Fresno, CA 93727-1535. Phones: 559-253-4050; 800-266-2278. Fax: 559-253-4090. Web Site: http://www.comcast.com. ICA: CA0268.
TV Market Ranking: 72 (PLANADA). Franchise award date: N.A. Franchise expiration date: N.A. Began: January 1, 1984.
Channel capacity: N.A. Channels available but not in use: N.A.

Basic Service
Subscribers: 46.
Programming (received off-air): KAIL (COZI TV, MNT, WeatherNation) Fresno; KFRE-TV (CW, IND) Sanger; KFSN-TV (ABC, Live Well Network) Fresno; KFTV-DT (getTV, UNV) Hanford; KGPE (CBS, The Country Network, Untamed Sports TV) Fresno; KMPH-TV (FOX, This TV) Visalia; KNSO (TMO) Merced; KSEE (LATV, NBC) Fresno; KVPT (PBS) Fresno.
Programming (via satellite): A&E; AMC; Cartoon Network; CNN; Comcast SportsNet Bay Area; Comedy Central; Discovery Channel; Disney Channel; ESPN; Freeform; Great American Country; HLN; Lifetime; MTV; Nickelodeon; QVC; Spike TV; Syfy; TBS; TLC; TNT; Univision; USA Network; VH1.
Fee: $42.00 installation; $24.50 monthly.

Pay Service 1
Pay Units: N.A.
Programming (via satellite): HBO; Showtime.
Fee: $11.50 monthly (Showtime), $12.87 monthly (HBO).

Internet Service
Operational: Yes.

Telephone Service
Digital: Operational
Miles of Plant: 23.0 (coaxial); None (fiber optic). Homes passed: 180.
General Manager: Len Falter. Marketing Director: Stewart Butler. Communications Director: Erica Smith.
Ownership: Comcast Cable Communications Inc. (MSO).

PLANTATION-BY-THE-SEA—Formerly served by Cox Communications. No longer in operation. ICA: CA0293.

PLEASANT HILL—Comcast Cable. Now served by SAN FRANCISCO, CA [CA0003]. ICA: CA0029.

PLEASANTON—Comcast Cable. Now served by SAN FRANCISCO, CA [CA0003]. ICA: CA0037.

POINT MUGU NAVAL AIR STATION—Communication Services, 4564 Telephone Rd, Ste 805, Ventura, CA 93003-5661. Phones: 805-658-0721; 805-658-1579. Fax: 805-658-0929. E-mail: commserv@cablerocket.com. Web Site: http://cscable.net. ICA: CA0252.
TV Market Ranking: Below 100 (POINT MUGU NAVAL AIR STATION). Franchise award date: N.A. Franchise expiration date: N.A. Began: September 1, 1992.
Channel capacity: 40 (operating 2-way). Channels available but not in use: N.A.

Basic Service
Subscribers: N.A.
Programming (received off-air): KABC-TV (ABC, Live Well Network) Los Angeles; KBEH (IND) Oxnard; KCAL-TV (IND) Los Angeles; KCBS-TV (CBS, Decades) Los Angeles; KCET (ETV) Los Angeles; KCOP-TV (Bounce TV, Buzzr, Heroes & Icons, MNT, Movies!) Los Angeles; KJLA (LATV) Ventura; KMEX-DT (UNV) Los Angeles; KNBC (COZI TV, NBC) Los Angeles; KTLA (Antenna TV, CW, This TV) Los Angeles; KTTV (FOX) Los Angeles.
Programming (via satellite): A&E; Animal Planet; BET; Cartoon Network; CMT; CNBC; CNN; Comedy Central; C-SPAN; Discovery Channel; Disney Channel; E! HD; ESPN; ESPN2; Food Network; Fox News Channel; FOX Sports West/Prime Ticket; Freeform; Great American Country; HGTV; History; HLN; INSP; Lifetime; MTV; National Geographic Channel; Nickelodeon; Pop; QVC; Syfy; TBS; The Weather Channel; TLC; TNT; Travel Channel; Turner Classic Movies; TV Land; USA Network; VH1; WGN America.
Fee: $25.00 installation.

Digital Basic Service
Subscribers: N.A.
Programming (via satellite): BBC America; Bloomberg Television; Discovery Digital Networks; Disney XD; DMX Music; ESPNews; ESPNU; FOX College Sports Central; FOX College Sports Pacific; FXM; Outdoor Channel.

Pay Service 1
Pay Units: N.A.
Programming (via satellite): HBO.
Fee: $10.95 monthly.

Digital Pay Service 1
Pay Units: N.A.
Programming (via satellite): Cinemax (multiplexed); HBO (multiplexed).
Fee: $10.06 monthly (Cinemax), $11.12 monthly (HBO).

Video-On-Demand: Yes

Pay-Per-View
iN DEMAND (delivered digitally); Fresh (delivered digitally); Playboy TV (delivered digitally).

Internet Service
Operational: Yes. Began: July 1, 2000.
Broadband Service: Cable Rocket.
Fee: $99.00 installation; $42.50 monthly; $10.00 modem lease.

Telephone Service
Digital: Operational
Miles of Plant: 13.0 (coaxial); None (fiber optic). Homes passed: 1,000.
General Manager: Phil Shockley. Chief Technician: Wayne Shockley.
Ownership: Coaxial Properties Inc.

POINT REYES STATION—Horizon Cable TV Inc, 520 Mesa Rd, PO Box 1240, Point Reyes Station, CA 94956. Phones: 888-663-9610; 415-663-9610. Fax: 415-663-9608. E-mail: horizon-info@horizoncable.com. Web Site: http://www.horizoncable.com. Also serves Dillon Beach, Inverness, Olema & Stinson Beach. ICA: CA0453.
TV Market Ranking: 7 (Dillon Beach, Inverness, Olema, POINT REYES STATION, Stinson Beach).
Channel capacity: N.A. Channels available but not in use: N.A.

Basic Service
Subscribers: 608.
Programming (received off-air): KBCW (CW) San Francisco; KEMO-TV (Azteca America) Santa Rosa; KGO-TV (ABC, Live Well Network) San Francisco; KNTV (COZI TV, NBC) San Jose; KOFY-TV (MeTV) San Francisco; KPIX-TV (CBS, Decades) San Francisco; KQED (PBS) San Francisco; KRCB (PBS) Cotati; KRON-TV (Antenna TV, MNT) San Francisco; KTLN-TV (IND) Novato; KTSF (IND) San Francisco; KTVU (Buzzr, FOX, LATV, Movies!) Oakland.
Programming (via satellite): A&E; AMC; Animal Planet; Bravo; CNBC; CNN; Comedy Central; C-SPAN; C-SPAN 2; Discovery Channel; Disney Channel; ESPN; ESPN2; FOX Sports Networks; HGTV; History; HLN; Lifetime; MSNBC; MTV; Nickelodeon; QVC; Spike TV; Starz Encore; Syfy; TBS; The Weather Channel; TLC; TNT; Travel Chan-

2017 Edition   D-99

California—Cable Systems

nel; Turner Classic Movies; TV Land; Univision Studios; USA Network; VH1.
Fee: $39.95 installation; $54.95 monthly.
Pay Service 1
Pay Units: N.A.
Programming (via satellite): Cinemax (multiplexed); HBO (multiplexed); Showtime; Sundance TV; The Movie Channel.
Fee: $8.95 monthly (Cinemax), $10.95 monthly (Showtime, TMC or Sundance), $12.95 monthly (HBO).
Video-On-Demand: No
Internet Service
Operational: Yes.
Broadband Service: ISP Alliance.
Fee: $89.95 installation; $19.95-$59.95 monthly; $10.00 modem lease; $199.00 modem purchase.
Telephone Service
Analog: Not Operational
Digital: Planned
Homes passed: 1,994.
General Manager & Program Director: Susan Daniel. Marketing Director & Customer Service Manager: Andrea Clark. Chief Engineer: Kevin Daniel.
Ownership: Horizon Cable TV Inc. (MSO).

POMONA—Time Warner Cable. Now served by LOS ANGELES, CA [CA0009]. ICA: CA0076.

PORTERVILLE—Charter Communications, 1152 West Henderson, Porterville, CA 93257. Phones: 314-543-2236; 636-207-5100 (Corporate office); 805-544-1962. Web Site: http://www.charter.com. Also serves Camp Nelson, Cotton Center, Earlimart, Exeter, Farmersville, Ivanhoe, Lemon Cove, Lindsay, Orange Cove, Orosi, Pixley, Plainview, Poplar, Springville, Strathmore, Terra Bella, Three Rivers, Tipton, Tulare County (northeastern portion), Woodlake & Woodville. ICA: CA0152.
TV Market Ranking: 72 (Camp Nelson, Cotton Center, Earlimart, Exeter, Farmersville, Ivanhoe, Lemon Cove, Lindsay, Orange Cove, Orosi, Pixley, Plainview, Poplar, PORTERVILLE, Springville, Strathmore, Terra Bella, Three Rivers, Tipton, Tulare County (northeastern portion), Woodlake, Woodville). Franchise award date: October 6, 1965. Franchise expiration date: N.A. Began: January 1, 1968.
Channel capacity: 60 (not 2-way capable). Channels available but not in use: N.A.
Digital Basic Service
Subscribers: 4,644.
Programming (via satellite): BBC America; Discovery Digital Networks; Disney XD; ESPNews; Fuse; FYI; Golf Channel; GSN; History International; IFC; LMN; MC; MTV2; NBCSN; Nick Jr.; Syfy; TeenNick; Turner Classic Movies; Vida Vision; WE tv.
Fee: $49.99 installation; $26.99 monthly.
Digital Expanded Basic Service
Subscribers: N.A.
Programming (via satellite): A&E; CMT; CNBC; CNN; Discovery Channel; Disney Channel; ESPN; ESPN2; HLN; Lifetime; Nickelodeon; Spike TV; TNT; USA Network.
Fee: $8.00 installation; $38.99 monthly.
Digital Pay Service 1
Pay Units: N.A.
Programming (via satellite): Cinemax (multiplexed); HBO (multiplexed); Showtime (multiplexed); The Movie Channel (multiplexed).
Video-On-Demand: No
Pay-Per-View
Playboy TV (delivered digitally).

Internet Service
Operational: Yes.
Subscribers: 1,547.
Broadband Service: Charter Internet.
Fee: $29.99 monthly.
Telephone Service
Digital: Operational
Miles of Plant: 1,116.0 (coaxial); 76.0 (fiber optic). Homes passed: 52,590.
Vice President & General Manager: Ed Merrill. Technical Operations Director: Ken Arellano. Marketing Director: Sarwar Assar. Accounting Director: David Sovanski.
Ownership: Charter Communications Inc. (MSO).

PORTOLA—Formerly served by New Day Broadband. No longer in operation. ICA: CA0185.

PORTOLA VALLEY—Comcast Cable. Now served by SAN FRANCISCO, CA [CA0003]. ICA: CA0356.

QUINCY—Formerly served by Quincy Community TV Assn. Inc. No longer in operation. ICA: CA0214.

QUINCY (portions)—Formerly served by New Day Broadband. No longer in operation. ICA: CA0278.

RAINBOW—Formerly served by Venture Communications. No longer in operation. ICA: CA0296.

RANCHO CORDOVA—Comcast Cable. Now served by SACRAMENTO, CA [CA0002]. ICA: CA0215.

RANCHO PALOS VERDES—Cox Communications, 6205 Peachtree Dunwoody Rd, 12th Floor, Atlanta, GA 30328. Phone: 404-269-6590. Web Site: http://www.cox.com. Also serves Los Angeles County (portions), Palos Verdes Estates, Rolling Hills, Rolling Hills Estates & San Pedro. ICA: CA0903.
TV Market Ranking: 2 (Los Angeles County (portions), Palos Verdes Estates, RANCHO PALOS VERDES, Rolling Hills, Rolling Hills Estates, San Pedro); Below 100 (Los Angeles County (portions)); Outside TV Markets (Los Angeles County (portions)).
Channel capacity: 67 (not 2-way capable). Channels available but not in use: N.A.
Basic Service
Subscribers: 19,675. Commercial subscribers: 249.
Fee: $24.99 monthly.
Internet Service
Operational: Yes.
Subscribers: 22,964.
Broadband Service: Cox High Speed Internet.
Telephone Service
Digital: Operational
Subscribers: 12,086.
Miles of Plant: 627.0 (coaxial); 140.0 (fiber optic). Homes passed: 43,753.
Vice President, Tax: Mary Vickers.
Ownership: Cox Communications Inc. (MSO).

RANCHO YOLO MOBILE HOME PARK—Formerly served by Wave Broadband. No longer in operation. ICA: CA0448.

RASNOW—No longer in operation. ICA: CA0439.

RED BLUFF—Charter Communications. Now served by REDDING, CA [CA0058]. ICA: CA0464.

REDDING—Charter Communications, 12405 Powerscourt Dr, St. Louis, MO 63131. Phones: 636-207-5100 (Corporate office); 805-544-1962. Fax: 805-541-6042. Web Site: http://www.charter.com. Also serves Anderson, Red Bluff, Shasta County & Tehama County. ICA: CA0058.
TV Market Ranking: Below 100 (Anderson, REDDING, Shasta County, Tehama County, Red Bluff). Franchise award date: N.A. Franchise expiration date: N.A. Began: May 1, 1967.
Channel capacity: 80 (operating 2-way). Channels available but not in use: N.A.
Digital Basic Service
Subscribers: 18,831.
Programming (via satellite): BBC America; Bloomberg Television; Boomerang; CNN en Espanol; Discovery Digital Networks; DIY Network; ESPNews; FOX College Sports Central; FOX College Sports Pacific; Fox Deportes; Fox Sports 2; Fuse; FYI; Great American Country; History International; IFC; LMN; MC; NFL Network; Nick Jr.; Nicktoons; Outdoor Channel; Sundance TV; TeenNick; Turner Classic Movies; TV Guide Interactive Inc.; TVG Network.
Fee: $26.99 monthly.
Digital Expanded Basic Service
Subscribers: N.A.
Programming (via satellite): A&E; AMC; Animal Planet; BET; Bravo; Cartoon Network; CMT; CNBC; CNN; Comcast SportsNet Bay Area; Comedy Central; Discovery Channel; Disney Channel; Disney XD; E! HD; ESPN; ESPN Classic; ESPN2; Food Network; Fox News Channel; Fox Sports 1; Freeform; FX; Golf Channel; GSN; Hallmark Channel; HGTV; History; HLN; Lifetime; MSNBC; MTV; National Geographic Channel; NBCSN; Nickelodeon; Oxygen; Spike TV; Syfy; TLC; TNT; Travel Channel; truTV; TV Land; USA Network; VH1; WE tv.
Fee: $48.95 monthly.
Digital Pay Service 1
Pay Units: N.A.
Programming (via satellite): Cinemax (multiplexed); Flix; HBO (multiplexed); Showtime (multiplexed); Starz (multiplexed); Starz Encore (multiplexed); The Movie Channel (multiplexed).
Fee: $19.95 installation; $10.95 monthly (each).
Video-On-Demand: Yes
Pay-Per-View
iN DEMAND (delivered digitally); Playboy TV (delivered digitally); Fresh (delivered digitally); Shorteez (delivered digitally).
Internet Service
Operational: Yes.
Subscribers: 17,997.
Broadband Service: Charter Internet.
Fee: $29.99 monthly.
Telephone Service
Digital: Operational
Subscribers: 7,326.
Miles of Plant: 1,332.0 (coaxial); 349.0 (fiber optic). Homes passed: 72,386.
Vice President & General Manager: Ed Merrill. Operations Manager: Donna Briggs. Marketing Director: Sarwar Assar. Accounting Director: David Sovanski.
Ownership: Charter Communications Inc. (MSO).

REDDING—Formerly served by Sprint Corp. No longer in operation. ICA: CA0408.

REDLANDS—Time Warner Cable. Now served by LOS ANGELES, CA [CA0009]. ICA: CA0039.

REDONDO BEACH—Time Warner Cable. Now served by LOS ANGELES, CA [CA0009]. ICA: CA0097.

RIDGECREST—Mediacom, 27192 Sun City Blvd, Ste A, Sun City, CA 92586. Phone: 951-679-3977. Fax: 951-679-9087. Web Site: http://www.mediacomcable.com. Also serves China Lake Naval Weapons Center, Inyokern, Kern County (unincorporated areas) & San Bernardino County (portions). ICA: CA0128.
TV Market Ranking: Below 100 (Kern County (unincorporated areas) (portions)); Outside TV Markets (China Lake Naval Weapons Center, Inyokern, Kern County (unincorporated areas) (portions), RIDGECREST, San Bernardino County (portions)).
Channel capacity: N.A. Channels available but not in use: N.A.
Basic Service
Subscribers: 1,956.
Programming (received off-air): KABC-TV (ABC, Live Well Network) Los Angeles; KCAL-TV (IND) Los Angeles; KCBS-TV (CBS, Decades) Los Angeles; KCET (ETV) Los Angeles; KNBC (COZI TV, NBC) Los Angeles; KTLA (Antenna TV, CW, This TV) Los Angeles; KTTV (FOX) Los Angeles; 16 FMs.
Programming (via satellite): C-SPAN; C-SPAN 2; Food Network; MSNBC; Pop; TBS; WGN America.
Fee: $44.25 installation; $39.95 monthly.
Expanded Basic Service 1
Subscribers: N.A.
Programming (via satellite): A&E; AMC; Animal Planet; BET; Bravo; Cartoon Network; CMT; CNBC; CNN; Comedy Central; Discovery Channel; Disney Channel; E! HD; ESPN; ESPN2; EWTN Global Catholic Network; Fox News Channel; FOX Sports Networks; Freeform; FX; History; HLN; Lifetime; MTV; Nickelodeon; QVC; Spike TV; Syfy; The Weather Channel; TLC; TNT; Trinity Broadcasting Network (TBN); truTV; TV Land; Univision Studios; USA Network; VH1.
Fee: $25.25 monthly.
Digital Basic Service
Subscribers: N.A.
Programming (via satellite): BBC America; Bloomberg Television; Discovery Life Channel; DMX Music; ESPNews; Fox Sports 1; Fuse; FYI; Golf Channel; GSN; HGTV; History International; IFC; LMN; National Geographic Channel; NBCSN; Nick Jr.; Nicktoons; Outdoor Channel; Turner Classic Movies; TV Land.
Digital Pay Service 1
Pay Units: N.A.
Programming (via satellite): Cinemax (multiplexed); HBO (multiplexed); Showtime (multiplexed); Starz (multiplexed); Starz Encore (multiplexed); The Movie Channel (multiplexed).
Fee: $13.95 monthly (HBO), $9.95 monthly (Cinemax or Showtime), $8.00 monthly (Starz/Encore).
Video-On-Demand: No
Internet Service
Operational: Yes.
Subscribers: 3,739.
Broadband Service: Mediacom High Speed Internet.
Fee: $40.95 monthly; $3.00 modem lease; $239.95 modem purchase.
Telephone Service
Digital: Operational
Subscribers: 452.
Miles of Plant: 404.0 (coaxial); 71.0 (fiber optic). Homes passed: 17,545.

Cable Systems—California

General Manager: Allen Bublitz. Engineering Director: Jon Tatilano.
Ownership: Mediacom LLC (MSO).

RIO VISTA—Comcast Cable. Now served by SAN FRANCISCO, CA [CA0003]. ICA: CA0232.

RIO VISTA—Wave Broadband, 401 Parkplace Center, Ste 500, Kirkland, WA 98033. Phones: 866-928-3123; 425-576-8200. Fax: 425-576-8221. Web Site: http://www.wavebroadband.com. ICA: CA0449.
TV Market Ranking: 7,25 (RIO VISTA).
Channel capacity: N.A. Channels available but not in use: N.A.
Basic Service
Subscribers: 57.
Programming (received off-air): KCRA-TV (MeTV, NBC) Sacramento; KMAX-TV (CW) Sacramento; KOVR (CBS, Decades) Stockton; KQCA (MNT, Movies!, This TV) Stockton; KTNC-TV (Estrella TV, This TV) Concord; KTXL (Antenna TV, FOX) Sacramento; KUVS-DT (Bounce TV, UNV) Modesto; KVIE (PBS) Sacramento; KXTV (ABC) Sacramento.
Programming (via satellite): A&E; AMC; BET; California Channel; Cartoon Network; CMT; CNBC; CNN; Comcast SportsNet Bay Area; Comedy Central; C-SPAN; C-SPAN 2; Discovery Channel; Disney Channel; E! HD; ESPN; ESPN2; Food Network; Freeform; Golf Channel; HGTV; History; HLN; Lifetime; MTV; Nickelodeon; Pop; QVC; Spike TV; Syfy; TBS; The Weather Channel; TLC; TNT; Turner Classic Movies; TV Land; USA Network; VH1; WGN America.
Fee: $29.95 installation; $51.95 monthly.
Pay Service 1
Pay Units: N.A.
Programming (via satellite): Cinemax (multiplexed); HBO (multiplexed); Showtime (multiplexed); Starz Encore; The Movie Channel.
Fee: $29.00 monthly.
Video-On-Demand: No
Internet Service
Operational: Yes.
Telephone Service
None
Chief Financial Officer: Wayne Schattenkerk. General Manager: Tim Peters. Marketing Director: Adam Lazara.
Ownership: WaveDivision Holdings LLC (MSO).

RIVERDALE—Comcast Cable. Now served by FRESNO, CA [CA0011]. ICA: CA0270.

RIVERSIDE—Charter Communications, 12405 Powerscourt Dr, St. Louis, MO 63131. Phones: 636-207-5100 (Corporate office); 951-343-5100. Fax: 951-354-5942. Web Site: http://www.charter.com. Also serves Eastvale, Jurupa Valley, Norco, Rancho Cucamonga, Riverside County (portions), San Bernardino & San Bernardino County (portions). ICA: CA0023.
TV Market Ranking: 2 (Eastvale, Jurupa Valley, Norco, Rancho Cucamonga, RIVERSIDE, Riverside County (portions), San Bernardino, San Bernardino County (portions)). Franchise award date: N.A. Franchise expiration date: N.A. Began: September 30, 1980.
Channel capacity: 75 (operating 2-way). Channels available but not in use: N.A.
Digital Basic Service
Subscribers: 51,961.
Programming (via satellite): AWE; BBC America; Bloomberg Television; Boomerang; BYUtv; CNN en Espanol; Discovery Digital Networks; Disney XD; DIY Network; DMX Music; ESPN Classic; ESPN Deportes; ESPNews; EWTN Global Catholic Network; FOX College Sports Central; FOX College Sports Pacific; Fox Deportes; Fox Sports 2; Fuse; FYI; Golf Channel; Great American Country; History International; IFC; International Television (ITV); LMN; NFL Network; Nick Jr.; Nicktoons; Sundance TV; TeenNick; TV One; TVG Network.
Fee: $14.99 monthly.
Digital Expanded Basic Service
Subscribers: N.A.
Programming (via satellite): A&E; AMC; Animal Planet; BET; Bravo; Cartoon Network; CMT; CNBC; CNN; Comedy Central; Discovery Channel; Disney Channel; E! HD; ESPN; ESPN2; Food Network; Fox News Channel; Fox Sports 1; FOX Sports West/Prime Ticket; Freeform; FX; GSN; Hallmark Channel; HGTV; History; HLN; INSP; Lifetime; MSNBC; MTV; National Geographic Channel; NBCSN; Nickelodeon; Oxygen; Spike TV; Syfy; The Weather Channel; TLC; TNT; Travel Channel; truTV; Turner Classic Movies; TV Land; Univision; USA Network; VH1; WE tv.
Fee: $33.20 monthly.
Digital Pay Service 1
Pay Units: N.A.
Programming (via satellite): Cinemax (multiplexed); Flix; HBO (multiplexed); Showtime (multiplexed); Starz (multiplexed); Starz Encore (multiplexed); The Filipino Channel; The Movie Channel (multiplexed).
Video-On-Demand: Yes
Pay-Per-View
iN DEMAND (delivered digitally); Playboy TV (delivered digitally); The Erotic Network (delivered digitally); Spice Hot (delivered digitally); ETC (Erotic TV Clips) (delivered digitally); NHL Center Ice/MLB Extra Innings (delivered digitally).
Internet Service
Operational: Yes.
Subscribers: 26,800.
Broadband Service: Charter Internet.
Fee: $29.99 monthly.
Telephone Service
Digital: Operational
Subscribers: 10,620.
Fee: $29.99 monthly
Miles of Plant: 3,635.0 (coaxial); 813.0 (fiber optic). Homes passed: 222,520.
Vice President & General Manager: Fred Lutz. Technical Operations Manager: George Noel. Marketing Director: Chris Bailey. Accounting Director: David Sovanski.
Ownership: Charter Communications Inc. (MSO).

RIVERSIDE—Formerly served by Cross Country Wireless Cable. No longer in operation. ICA: CA0409.

ROHNERT PARK—Comcast Cable. Now served by SAN FRANCISCO, CA [CA0003]. ICA: CA0050.

ROSEVILLE—Comcast Cable. Now served by SACRAMENTO, CA [CA0002]. ICA: CA0124.

SACRAMENTO—Comcast Cable, 4350 Pell Dr, Sacramento, CA 95838-2531. Phone: 916-927-2225. Fax: 916-927-0805. Web Site: http://www.comcast.com. Also serves Acampo, Amador, Angels Camp, Arbuckle, Auburn Lake Trails, Beale AFB, Biggs, Butte County (portions), Calaveras County (portions), Chico, Citrus Heights, Colusa, Colusa County (portions), Corning, Davis, Durham, El Dorado, El Dorado Hills, Elk Grove, Folsom, Galt, Glenn County (portions), Grass Valley, Gridley, Hamilton City, Jackson, Lake Wildwood, Lathrop, Linda, Live Oak, Lodi, Manteca, Marysville, Maxwell, Modesto, Mokelumne Hill, Nevada City, Nevada County (portions), Oakdale, Olivehurst, Orland, Oroville, Paradise, Penn Valley, Placer County (portions), Placerville, Plymouth, Rancho Cordova, Roseville, Sacramento County (portions), San Andreas, San Joaquin County (portions), Sonora, Stanislaus County (portions), Stockton, Sutter County (portions), Sutter Creek, Tierra Buena, Tower Park, Tracy, Tuolumne County (portions), Wheatland, Williams, Willows & Yuba City. ICA: CA0002.
TV Market Ranking: 25 (Acampo, Calaveras County (portions), Citrus Heights, Davis, El Dorado, El Dorado Hills, Elk Grove, Folsom, Galt, Lathrop, Lodi, Manteca, Modesto, Oakdale, Placer County (portions), Plymouth, Rancho Cordova, Roseville, SACRAMENTO, Sacramento County (portions), San Andreas, San Joaquin County (portions), Stanislaus County (portions), Stockton, Sutter County (portions), Tower Park, Wheatland), 7,25 (Tracy); Below 100 (Biggs, Butte County (portions), Corning, Durham, Glenn County (portions), Gridley, Hamilton City, Lake Wildwood, Live Oak, Orland, Paradise, Penn Valley, Willows, Chico, Colusa County (portions), Oroville); Outside TV Markets (Amador, Angels Camp, Arbuckle, Auburn Lake Trails, Beale AFB, Colusa, Jackson, Linda, Marysville, Maxwell, Mokelumne Hill, Nevada City, Nevada County (portions), Olivehurst, Sutter Creek, Tierra Buena, Tuolumne County (portions), Colusa County (portions), Grass Valley, Placerville, Sonora, Williams, Yuba City, Calaveras County (portions), San Andreas, Sutter County (portions)).
Franchise award date: December 1, 1983. Franchise expiration date: N.A. Began: August 25, 1985.
Channel capacity: 15 (operating 2-way). Channels available but not in use: N.A.
Basic Service
Subscribers: 408,548.
Programming (received off-air): KCRA-TV (MeTV, NBC) Sacramento; KCSO-LD (MeTV, The Country Network, TMO) Sacramento; KMAX-TV (CW) Sacramento; KOVR (CBS, Decades) Stockton; KQCA (MNT, Movies!, This TV) Stockton; KRCA (Estrella TV) Riverside; KSPX-TV (ION) Sacramento; KTFK-DT (getTV, UniMas) Stockton; KTNC-TV (Estrella TV, This TV) Concord; KTXL (Antenna TV, FOX) Sacramento; KUVS-DT (Bounce TV, UNV) Modesto; KVIE (PBS) Sacramento; KXTV (ABC) Sacramento; 28 FMs.
Programming (via satellite): California Channel; C-SPAN; C-SPAN 2; Pop; QVC; Univision.
Fee: $42.00 installation; $29.89 monthly.
Expanded Basic Service 1
Subscribers: N.A.
Programming (via satellite): A&E; AMC; Animal Planet; BET; Bravo; Cartoon Network; CMT; CNBC; CNN; Comcast SportsNet Bay Area; Comedy Central; Discovery Channel; E! HD; ESPN; ESPN2; Food Network; Fox News Channel; Fox Sports 1; Freeform; FX; Golf Channel; GSN; HGTV; History; HLN; Lifetime; MSNBC; MTV; NBCSN; Nickelodeon; Spike TV; Syfy; TBS; The Weather Channel; TLC; TNT; truTV; Turner Classic Movies; TV Land; USA Network; VH1.
Fee: $39.05 monthly.
Digital Basic Service
Subscribers: N.A.
Programming (via satellite): ABP News; BBC America; Bloomberg Television; Discovery Digital Networks; Disney XD; ESPN Classic; ESPNews; EVINE Live; FOX College Sports Central; FOX College Sports Pacific; FXM; Great American Country; History International; IFC; Life OK; LMN; National Geographic Channel; Nick Jr.; Nicktoons; Outdoor Channel; Ovation; STAR Plus; Sundance TV; TeenNick; The Word Network; Trinity Broadcasting Network (TBN); WE tv.
Digital Pay Service 1
Pay Units: N.A.
Programming (via satellite): Cinemax (multiplexed); Flix; HBO (multiplexed); HITS (Headend In The Sky); MC; Showtime (multiplexed); Starz (multiplexed); Starz Encore (multiplexed); The Movie Channel (multiplexed).
Fee: $17.99 monthly (Cinemax, Starz or TMC), $18.99 monthly (HBO or Showtime).
Video-On-Demand: Yes
Pay-Per-View
iN DEMAND (delivered digitally); Hot Choice (delivered digitally); Playboy TV (delivered digitally); Fresh (delivered digitally); Shorteez (delivered digitally); ESPN Now (delivered digitally); Sports PPV (delivered digitally); iN DEMAND.
Internet Service
Operational: Yes.
Subscribers: 425,028.
Broadband Service: Comcast High Speed Internet.
Fee: $42.95 monthly; $7.00 modem lease; $149.00 modem purchase.
Telephone Service
Digital: Operational
Subscribers: 204,203.
Miles of Plant: 19,676.0 (coaxial); 4,487.0 (fiber optic). Homes passed: 1,287,033.
Area Vice President: Dan McCarty. Technical Operations Director: Joe Trassare. Communications Director: Erica Smith. Marketing Manager: Christi Rossi.
Ownership: Comcast Cable Communications Inc. (MSO).

SACRAMENTO—Consolidated Communications. Formerly [CA0459]. This cable system has converted to IPTV, 211 Lincoln St, Roseville, CA 95678. Phones: 916-786-1616; 866-787-3937. Fax: 916-786-4030. Web Site: https://www.consolidated.com. Also serves Antelope, Carmichael, Citrus Heights, Elk Grove, Granite Bay, Lincoln, McClellan Park, Natomas, Orangevale, Rancho Cordova, Rocklin & Roseville. ICA: CA5597.
TV Market Ranking: 25 (Antelope, Carmichael, Citrus Heights, Elk Grove, Lincoln, McClellan Park, Rancho Cordova, Roseville, SACRAMENTO).
Channel capacity: N.A. Channels available but not in use: N.A.
Basic
Subscribers: 27,622. Commercial subscribers: 313.
Fee: $99.95 installation; $26.75 monthly. Includes 29 channels.
Digital Basic
Subscribers: N.A.
Fee: $67.49 monthly. Includes 89 channels & one whole home DVR.
Digital Choice
Subscribers: N.A.
Fee: $74.49 monthly. Includes 154 channels, 50 music channels & one whole home DVR.

2017 Edition · D-101

California—Cable Systems

Digital Encore
Subscribers: N.A.
Fee: $80.49 monthly. Includes 154 channels, 50 music channels, 7 Encore channels & one whole home DVR.
True HD
Subscribers: N.A.
Fee: $11.99 monthly.
International
Subscribers: N.A.
Fee: $2.99-$19.99 monthly.
Sports
Subscribers: N.A.
Fee: $5.99 monthly.
Cinemax
Subscribers: N.A.
Fee: $14.99 monthly. Includes 14 channels.
HBO
Subscribers: N.A.
Fee: $16.99 monthly. Includes 8 channels.
Playboy
Subscribers: N.A.
Fee: $18.99 monthly.
Showtime/TMC
Subscribers: N.A.
Fee: $14.99 monthly. Includes 14 channels.
Starz/Encore
Subscribers: N.A.
Fee: $16.99 monthly. Includes 27 channels.
Video-On-Demand: Yes
Internet Service
Operational: Yes.
Fee: $15.00-$49.95 monthly.
Telephone Service
Digital: Operational
Fee: $12.99 monthly
Homes passed & miles of plant include all SureWest systems.
Ownership: Consolidated Communications Inc.

SACRAMENTO—Formerly served by Wireless Broadcasting Services. No longer in operation. ICA: CA0410.

SACRAMENTO—SureWest Broadband. This cable system has converted to IPTV. See SACRAMENTO, CA [CA5597]. ICA: CA0459.

SALTON CITY—USA Communications, 2455 Stirrup Rd, Borrego Springs, CA 92004. Phones: 800-234-0102; 308-236-1515 (Kearney, NE corporate office); 877-234-0102; 760-767-5607. Fax: 760-767-3609. E-mail: csr@usacommunications.tv. Web Site: http://usacommunications.tv. ICA: CA0473.
TV Market Ranking: Below 100 (SALTON CITY).
Channel capacity: N.A. Channels available but not in use: N.A.
Basic Service
Subscribers: 42.
Programming (received off-air): KDFX-CD Indio/Palm Springs; KESQ-TV (ABC, CW) Palm Springs; KFMB-TV (CBS, Grit, MeTV) San Diego; KMIR-TV (IND, Movies!, NBC) Palm Springs; KPBS (PBS) San Diego.
Programming (via satellite): 52MX; Cine Mexicano; Cinelatino; CNN en Espanol; History en Espanol; QVC; TBS; The Weather Channel; Toon Disney en Espanol; Tr3s; Trinity Broadcasting Network (TBN); ViendoMovies; WGN America.
Fee: $39.95 installation; $21.45 monthly.
Expanded Basic Service 1
Subscribers: N.A.
Programming (via satellite): A&E; Animal Planet; Cartoon Network; CMT; CNBC; CNN; C-SPAN; C-SPAN 2; Discovery Channel; E! HD; ESPN; ESPN Classic; ESPN2; EVINE Live; EWTN Global Catholic Network; Food Network; Fox Deportes; Fox News Channel; Freeform; Hallmark Channel; History; HLN; MTV; Nickelodeon; Spike TV; Syfy; TLC; TNT; Turner Classic Movies; UniMas; Univision; Univision Studios; USA Network; VH1; WE tv.
Digital Basic Service
Subscribers: N.A.
Programming (via satellite): BBC America; Bloomberg Television; CMT; Daystar TV Network; Destination America; Discovery Kids Channel; Discovery Life Channel; DMX Music; ESPN Classic; ESPN2; ESPNews; EVINE Live; FOX College Sports Central; FOX College Sports Pacific; Fox Sports 1; FXM; FYI; Golf Channel; GSN; History International; Investigation Discovery; MTV Classic; MTV Hits; MTV2; National Geographic Channel; NBCSN; Nick Jr.; Outdoor Channel; Ovation; OWN: Oprah Winfrey Network; Science Channel; Syfy; TeenNick; Trinity Broadcasting Network (TBN); UP; VH1 Soul; WE tv.
Digital Expanded Basic Service
Subscribers: N.A.
Programming (via satellite): Cine Mexicano; Cinelatino; CNN en Espanol; Fox Deportes; Fox Life; History en Espanol; Toon Disney en Espanol; Tr3s.
Digital Pay Service 1
Pay Units: N.A.
Programming (via satellite): Cinemax (multiplexed); Flix; FXM; HBO (multiplexed); HBO Latino; LMN; Showtime (multiplexed); Starz (multiplexed); Starz Encore (multiplexed); Sundance TV; The Movie Channel (multiplexed).
Video-On-Demand: No
Pay-Per-View
iN DEMAND (delivered digitally); Hot Choice (delivered digitally); Playboy TV (delivered digitally); Shorteez (delivered digitally); Fresh (delivered digitally); Club Jenna (delivered digitally).
Internet Service
Operational: Yes.
Telephone Service
Analog: Operational
Chief Financial Officer: Amber Reineke. General Manager & Chief Technician: Joe Gustafson.
Ownership: USA Companies LP (MSO).

SALTON SEA BEACH—USA Communications, 2455 Stirrup Rd, Borrego Springs, CA 92004. Phones: 800-234-0102; 308-236-1512 (Kearney, NE corporate office); 877-234-0102; 760-767-5607. Fax: 760-767-3609. E-mail: csr@usacommunications.tv. Web Site: http://usacommunications.tv. ICA: CA0255.
TV Market Ranking: Outside TV Markets (SALTON SEA BEACH). Franchise award date: April 5, 1984. Franchise expiration date: N.A. Began: June 1, 1984.
Channel capacity: N.A. Channels available but not in use: N.A.
Basic Service
Subscribers: 26.
Programming (received off-air): KECY-TV (ABC, FOX, MNT, TMO) El Centro; KESQ-TV (ABC, CW) Palm Springs; KMIR-TV (IND, Movies!, NBC) Palm Springs; KRMA-TV (PBS) Denver; KSWT (CBS, Estrella TV, Tuff TV) Yuma; KTLA (Antenna TV, CW, This TV) Los Angeles.
Programming (via satellite): Cartoon Network; C-SPAN 2; Freeform; Great American Country; HLN; TBS; The Weather Channel; TLC; Trinity Broadcasting Network (TBN); TV Land; WGN America.
Fee: $39.95 installation; $29.75 monthly; $3.00 converter.
Expanded Basic Service 1
Subscribers: N.A.
Programming (via satellite): A&E; AMC; Animal Planet; Comedy Central; Discovery Channel; E! HD; ESPN; ESPN2; History; Lifetime; MTV; Nickelodeon; Spike TV; Syfy; TNT; truTV; Turner Classic Movies; USA Network; VH1.
Pay Service 1
Pay Units: N.A.
Programming (via satellite): HBO; The Movie Channel.
Fee: $13.00 monthly (TMC), $14.50 monthly (HBO).
Internet Service
Operational: No, DSL.
Telephone Service
Analog: Operational
Miles of Plant: 12.0 (coaxial); None (fiber optic). Homes passed: 900.
Chief Financial Officer: Amber Reineke. General Manager & Chief Technician: Joe Gustafson.
Ownership: USA Companies LP (MSO).

SAN ANDREAS—Comcast Cable. Now served by SACRAMENTO, CA [CA0002]. ICA: CA0133.

SAN BERNARDINO—Charter Communications. Now served by RIVERSIDE, CA [CA0023]. ICA: CA0120.

SAN BERNARDINO—Time Warner Cable. Now served by LOS ANGELES, CA [CA0009]. ICA: CA0103.

SAN BRUNO—City of San Bruno Municipal Cable TV, 398 El Camino Real, San Bruno, CA 94066-4946. Phones: 877-646-6407 (Internet technical support); 650-616-3100. Fax: 650-871-5526. E-mail: info@sanbrunocable.com. Web Site: http://www.sanbrunocable.com. ICA: CA0140.
TV Market Ranking: 7 (SAN BRUNO). Franchise award date: January 1, 1971. Franchise expiration date: N.A. Began: October 1, 1971.
Channel capacity: N.A. Channels available but not in use: N.A.
Basic Service
Subscribers: 5,782.
Programming (received off-air): KBCW (CW) San Francisco; KCNS (MundoMax, Retro TV) San Francisco; KCSM-TV (PBS) San Mateo; KDTV-DT (Bounce TV, getTV, UNV) San Francisco; KFSF-DT (UniMas) Vallejo; KGO-TV (ABC, Live Well Network) San Francisco; KICU-TV (Heroes & Icons, IND) San Jose; KKPX-TV (ION) San Jose; KMTP-TV (ETV) San Francisco; KNTV (COZI TV, NBC) San Jose; KOFY-TV (MeTV) San Francisco; KPIX-TV (CBS, Decades) San Francisco; KQED (PBS) San Francisco; KQEH (PBS) San Jose; KRON-TV (Antenna TV, MNT) San Francisco; KSTS (TMO) San Jose; KTLN-TV (IND) Novato; KTNC-TV (Estrella TV, This TV) Concord; KTSF (IND) San Francisco; KTVU (Buzzr, FOX, LATV, Movies!) Oakland.
Programming (via satellite): California Channel; QVC.
Fee: $25.00 installation; $19.39 monthly.
Expanded Basic Service 1
Subscribers: N.A.
Programming (via satellite): A&E; AMC; Animal Planet; BET; Bravo; Cartoon Network; CBS Sports Network; CMT; CNBC; CNN; Comcast SportsNet California; Comedy Central; C-SPAN; Discovery Channel; Disney Channel; Disney XD; E! HD; ESPN; ESPN Classic; ESPN2; ESPNU; Food Network; Fox News Channel; Freeform; FX; Hallmark Channel; HGTV; History; HLN; Lifetime; MSNBC; MTV; MTV2; National Geographic Channel; Nickelodeon; Oxygen; Pop; Spike TV; Sprout; Syfy; TBS; The Weather Channel; TLC; TNT; Travel Channel; truTV; Turner Classic Movies; TV Land; USA Network; VH1.
Fee: $22.32 monthly.
Digital Basic Service
Subscribers: N.A.
Programming (via satellite): BBC America; Bloomberg Television; Boomerang; BYUtv; Cloo; CMT; CNN International; Cooking Channel; C-SPAN 2; Destination America; Discovery Kids Channel; DIY Network; DMX Music; ESPN Deportes; ESPNews; EWTN Global Catholic Network; Fox Business Network; Fox Sports 1; Fuse; FXM; FYI; Golf Channel; GolTV; GSN; Hallmark Movies & Mysteries; History International; HRTV; IFC; Investigation Discovery; LMN; LOGO; MTV Classic; MTV Hits; MTV Jams; NBCSN; Nick Jr.; Nicktoons; Outdoor Channel; Ovation; OWN: Oprah Winfrey Network; Science Channel; Sundance TV; TeenNick; Tennis Channel; Trinity Broadcasting Network (TBN); TVG Network; VH1 Soul; WE tv.
Digital Expanded Basic Service
Subscribers: N.A.
Programming (via satellite): A&E HD; Animal Planet HD; AXS TV; Azteca; Bio HD; CNN HD; Destination America; Discovery Channel HD; ESPN HD; ESPN2 HD; Food Network HD; Fox Business Network HD; Fox News HD; FX HD; Hallmark Movie Channel HD; HD Theater; HGTV HD; History HD; National Geographic Channel HD; Outdoor Channel 2 HD; QVC HD; Science HD; TBS HD; The Weather Channel HD; TLC HD; TNT HD; Universal HD; Versus HD.
Fee: $7.30 monthly (HD Broadcast/Basic or HD Plus).
Digital Expanded Basic Service 2
Subscribers: N.A.
Programming (via satellite): AYM Sports; Bandamax; Canal Sur; Cine Mexicano; Cinelatino; CNN en Espanol; De Pelicula; De Pelicula Clasico; Discovery Familia; Docu TVE; Ecuavisa Internacional; Enlace USA; Fox Deportes; Fox Life; GolTV; History en Espanol; HITN; HTV; Infinito; La Familia Cosmovision; Latinoamerica Television; NBC Universo; Ritmoson; Telefe Internacional; TeleFormula; Telehit; Telemicro Internacional; Tr3s; ULTRA HDPlex; VideoRola; ViendoMovies.
Fee: $15.70 monthly.
Pay Service 1
Pay Units: N.A.
Programming (via satellite): Cinemax; HBO; Showtime; Starz; Starz Encore; The Movie Channel.
Fee: $8.35 monthly (Starz/Encore), $10.95 monthly (Cinemax, HBO, Showtime or TMC).
Digital Pay Service 1
Pay Units: N.A.
Programming (via satellite): ART America; Cinemax (multiplexed); Cinemax HD; GMA Pinoy TV; HBO (multiplexed); HBO HD; Korean Channel; RAI Italia; RTN; Saigon Broadcasting Television Network (SBTN); Showtime (multiplexed); Showtime HD; Smithsonian Channel HD; Starz (multiplexed); Starz Comedy HD; Starz Edge HD; Starz Encore (multiplexed); Starz HD; Starz Kids & Family HD; The Filipino Channel; The Movie Channel (multiplexed); The Movie Channel HD; TV Asia; TV5MONDE USA; Zee TV.

Cable Systems—California

Fee: $3.54 monthly (Encore), $10.45 monthly (Rai or TV5), $12.55 monthly (CCTV/Zhong Tian), $13.60 monthly (ART, Cinemax, HBO, Korean, Showtime, TMC or Starz), $15.70 monthly (Russian, SBTN or TV Asia/Zee TV), $20.95 monthly (Filipino), $26.20 monthly (TV Japan).

Video-On-Demand: Yes

Pay-Per-View
iN DEMAND (delivered digitally); Playboy TV (delivered digitally); Sports PPV (delivered digitally); Fresh (delivered digitally); Hot Choice (delivered digitally); Spice: Xcess (delivered digitally).

Internet Service
Operational: Yes. Began: September 1, 1999.
Subscribers: 5,755.
Broadband Service: sanbrunocable.com.
Fee: $99.00 installation; $37.95 monthly; $75.00 modem purchase.

Telephone Service
Analog: Not Operational
Digital: Operational
Subscribers: 1,001.
Fee: $26.80 monthly

Miles of Plant: 137.0 (coaxial); 42.0 (fiber optic). Homes passed: 15,500.
Director: Tenzin Gyaltsen. Chief Engineer: Al Johnson. Business Manager: Stephen Firpo. Program Manager: Miriam Schalit.
Ownership: San Bruno Municipal Cable TV.

SAN DIEGO—Cox Communications, 6205 Peachtree Dunwoody Rd, 12th Floor, Atlanta, GA 30328. Phones: 404-269-6590; 619-263-9251. Web Site: http://www.cox.com. Also serves Bonita, Bonsall, Camp Pendleton, Chula Vista, Crest, El Cajon, Encinitas, Escondido, Imperial Beach, Jamul, La Mesa, Lemon Grove, Leucadia, National City, Oceanside, Pine Valley, Poway, Ramona, Rancho San Diego, Rancho Santa Fe, San Diego (unincorporated areas), San Diego County, San Marcos, Santee, Solana Beach, Spring Valley & Vista. ICA: CA0001.
TV Market Ranking: 51 (Bonita, Bonsall, Camp Pendleton, Chula Vista, Crest, El Cajon, Encinitas, Escondido, Imperial Beach, Jamul, La Mesa, Lemon Grove, Leucadia, National City, Oceanside, Poway, Ramona, Rancho San Diego, Rancho Santa Fe, SAN DIEGO, San Diego (unincorporated areas), San Marcos, Santee, Solana Beach, Spring Valley, Vista); Outside TV Markets (Pine Valley). Franchise award date: January 1, 1962. Franchise expiration date: N.A. Began: January 1, 1964.
Channel capacity: 67 (operating 2-way). Channels available but not in use: N.A.

Basic Service
Subscribers: 353,499.
Programming (received off-air): KFMB-TV (CBS, Grit, MeTV) San Diego; KGTV (ABC, Azteca America) San Diego; KNSD (COZI TV, NBC) San Diego; KPBS (PBS) San Diego; KSWB-TV (Antenna TV, FOX, This TV) San Diego; KUSI-TV (IND) San Diego; allband FM.
Programming (via microwave): 10 News Channel; KCOP-TV (Bounce TV, Buzzr, Heroes & Icons, MNT, Movies!) Los Angeles; KTLA (Antenna TV, CW, This TV) Los Angeles.
Programming (via satellite): California Channel; C-SPAN; C-SPAN 2; EWTN Global Catholic Network; QVC; TBS; The Weather Channel; WGN America.
Fee: $60.00 installation; $22.99 monthly.

Expanded Basic Service 1
Subscribers: N.A.
Programming (via satellite): A&E; AMC; Animal Planet; BET; Bravo; Cartoon Network; CMT; CNBC; CNN; Comedy Central; Discovery Channel; Disney Channel; E! HD; ESPN; ESPN Classic; ESPN2; EVINE Live; EWTN Global Catholic Network; Food Network; Fox Deportes; Fox News Channel; Fox Sports 1; FOX Sports Networks; Freeform; FX; Golf Channel; HGTV; History; HLN; ION Television; Lifetime; MSNBC; MTV; NBCSN; Nickelodeon; Pop; Spike TV; Syfy; TLC; TNT; Travel Channel; truTV; Turner Classic Movies; TV Land; USA Network; VH1.
Fee: $27.95 monthly.

Digital Basic Service
Subscribers: N.A.
Programming (via satellite): BBC America; Bloomberg Television; Discovery Digital Networks; Disney XD; EWTN Global Catholic Network; Flix; GSN; Hallmark Channel; IFC; LMN; MC; NBA TV; Oxygen; Sundance TV; Trinity Broadcasting Network (TBN); Weatherscan.

Pay Service 1
Pay Units: N.A.
Programming (via satellite): Cinemax; HBO; Showtime.
Fee: $12.50 monthly (each).

Digital Pay Service 1
Pay Units: N.A.
Programming (via satellite): Cinemax (multiplexed); HBO (multiplexed); Saigon Broadcasting Television Network (SBTN); Showtime (multiplexed); Starz (multiplexed); The Filipino Channel; The Movie Channel (multiplexed); TV Japan.
Fee: $9.00 (Cinemax, HBO, Showtime, Starz, TMC); $10.00 monthly (Filipino Channel); $15.00 monthly (Saigon Broadcasting TV Network); $25.00 monthly (TV Japan).

Video-On-Demand: Yes

Pay-Per-View
iN DEMAND; iN DEMAND (delivered digitally).

Internet Service
Operational: Yes. Began: May 1, 1997.
Subscribers: 449,953.
Broadband Service: Cox High Speed Internet.
Fee: $49.95 installation; $29.95 monthly; $10.00 modem lease; $399.00 modem purchase.

Telephone Service
Digital: Operational
Subscribers: 295,482.
Fee: $9.99 monthly

Miles of Plant: 10,423.0 (coaxial); 2,780.0 (fiber optic). Homes passed: 834,712.
Senior Vice President & General Manager: David A. Bialis. Vice President, Marketing: Colette Jelineo. Vice President, Tax: Mary Vickers. Media & Public Relations Manager: Ceanne Guerra.
Ownership: Cox Communications Inc. (MSO).

SAN DIEGO—Time Warner Cable, 10450 Pacific Center Ct, San Diego, CA 92121-2222. Phones: 865-635-8297; 858-695-3110. Fax: 858-566-6248. Web Site: http://www.timewarnercable.com. Also serves Admiral Hartman Navy Housing Project, Carlsbad, Chesterton Navy Housing Project, Coronado, Del Mar, Encinitas (portions), Pomerado Terrace Navy Housing, Poway, San Diego County, San Marcos (portions), Silver Strand Navy Housing, Solana Beach & Vista. ICA: CA0007.
TV Market Ranking: 51 (Admiral Hartman Navy Housing Project, Carlsbad, Chesterton Navy Housing Project, Coronado, Del Mar, Encinitas (portions), Pomerado Terrace Navy Housing, Poway, SAN DIEGO, San Marcos (portions), Silver Strand Navy Housing, Solana Beach, Vista); 51,2 (San Diego County (portions)); Below 100 (San Diego County (portions)); Outside TV Markets (San Diego County (portions)). Franchise award date: January 1, 1964. Franchise expiration date: N.A. Began: January 1, 1964.
Channel capacity: 61 (operating 2-way). Channels available but not in use: N.A.

Basic Service
Subscribers: 135,177.
Programming (received off-air): KBNT-CD (UniMas) San Diego; KFMB-TV (CBS, Grit, MeTV) San Diego; KGTV (ABC, Azteca America) San Diego; KNSD (COZI TV, NBC) San Diego; KPBS (PBS) San Diego; KSWB-TV (Antenna TV, FOX, This TV) San Diego; KUSI-TV (IND) San Diego; allband FM.
Programming (via satellite): Azteca; C-SPAN; C-SPAN 2; Jewelry Television; NASA TV; Pop; TBS; various Mexican stations; WGN America.
Fee: $33.00 installation; $22.00 monthly; $2.19 converter.

Expanded Basic Service 1
Subscribers: N.A.
Programming (via satellite): A&E; AMC; Animal Planet; BET; Bravo; Cartoon Network; CMT; CNBC; CNN; Comedy Central; Discovery Channel; Disney Channel; E! HD; ESPN; ESPN2; Food Network; Fox News Channel; FOX Sports West/Prime Ticket; Freeform; FX; Golf Channel; Hallmark Channel; HGTV; History; HLN; ION Television; Lifetime; LMN; MSNBC; MTV; NBCSN; Nickelodeon; QVC; Spike TV; Syfy; Telemundo; The Weather Channel; TLC; TNT; Travel Channel; truTV; Turner Classic Movies; TV Land; UniMas; USA Network; VH1; WE tv.
Fee: $36.46 monthly.

Digital Basic Service
Subscribers: N.A.
Programming (via microwave): 10 News Channel.
Programming (via satellite): A&E HD; AXS TV; BBC America; BBC America On Demand; Bloomberg Television; Boomerang; Canal Sur; CBS Sports Network; CCTV-Documentary; Cinelatino; Cloo; CNN en Espanol; CNN International; Cooking Channel; C-SPAN 3; Destination America; Discovery Kids Channel; Discovery Life Channel; Disney Channel; Disney XD; DIY Network; ESPN Classic; ESPN Deportes; ESPN HD; ESPN2 HD; ESPNews; ESPNU; EWTN Global Catholic Network; Fox Business Network; FOX College Sports Central; FOX College Sports Pacific; Fox Deportes; Fox Sports 1; Fox Sports 2; FSN HD; Fuse; FXM; FYI; Great American Country; GSN; HD Theater; History International; HRTV; IFC; INSP; Investigation Discovery; La Familia Cosmovision; LOGO; MC; MTV Classic; MTV Live; MTV2; Nat Geo WILD; National Geographic Channel; National Geographic Channel HD; National Geographic Channel On Demand; NBA TV; NBC Universo; Nick Jr.; Nicktoons; Ovation; OWN; Oprah Winfrey Network; Oxygen; Oxygen On Demand; Science Channel; Starz Encore (multiplexed); Sundance TV; TBS HD; TeenNick; Tennis Channel; The Word Network; TNT HD; Toon Disney en Espanol; Tr3s; Trinity Broadcasting Network (TBN); TV Guide Network; Universal HD; UP; Versus HD; VideoRola.

Digital Pay Service 1
Pay Units: 19,400.
Programming (via satellite): Cinemax (multiplexed); Cinemax HD.
Fee: $15.00 monthly.

Digital Pay Service 2
Pay Units: 55,000.
Programming (via satellite): HBO (multiplexed); HBO HD.
Fee: $15.00 monthly.

Digital Pay Service 3
Pay Units: 21,900.
Programming (via satellite): Showtime (multiplexed); Showtime HD.
Fee: $15.00 monthly.

Digital Pay Service 4
Pay Units: 13,000.
Programming (via satellite): Starz; Starz HD.
Fee: $15.00 monthly.

Digital Pay Service 5
Pay Units: 2,500.
Programming (via satellite): Playgirl TV; Saigon Broadcasting Television Network (SBTN); The Filipino Channel.
Fee: $15.00 monthly.

Video-On-Demand: Yes

Pay-Per-View
iN DEMAND (delivered digitally); NHL Center Ice (delivered digitally); Juicy (delivered digitally); MLB Extra Innings (delivered digitally); NBA League Pass (delivered digitally); SexSee (delivered digitally); Playboy TV (delivered digitally); Club Jenna (delivered digitally).

Internet Service
Operational: Yes. Began: January 1, 1997.
Subscribers: 200,134.
Broadband Service: Road Runner.
Fee: $50.00 installation; $44.95 monthly.

Telephone Service
Digital: Operational
Subscribers: 95,945.
Fee: $39.95 monthly
Miles of Plant: 5,262.0 (coaxial); 461.0 (fiber optic). Homes passed: 408,498.
President: Bob Barlow. Vice President, Technical Services: Ron Johnson. Vice President, Engineering: Bob Jones. Vice President, Public Affairs: Marc Farrar. Vice President, Customer Care: Vinit Ahooja.
Ownership: Time Warner Cable (MSO).

SAN DIEGO NAVAL BASE—NWS Communications, 79 Mainline Dr, PO Box 1416, Westfield, MA 01086-1416. Phone: 800-562-7081. Fax: 413-562-5415. E-mail: info@nwscorp.net. Web Site: http://www.nwscorp.net. ICA: CA0372.
TV Market Ranking: 51 (SAN DIEGO NAVAL BASE). Franchise award date: October 1, 1986. Franchise expiration date: N.A. Began: June 1, 1987.
Channel capacity: N.A. Channels available but not in use: N.A.

Basic Service
Subscribers: N.A.
Programming (received off-air): KFMB-TV (CBS, Grit, MeTV) San Diego; KGTV (ABC, Azteca America) San Diego; KNSD (COZI TV, NBC) San Diego; KPBS (PBS) San Diego; KSWB-TV (Antenna TV, FOX, This TV) San Diego; KUSI-TV (IND) San Diego.
Programming (via microwave): KTLA (Antenna TV, CW, This TV) Los Angeles.
Programming (via satellite): A&E; AMC; Animal Planet; BET; Cartoon Network; CMT; CNBC; CNN; Comedy Central; C-SPAN; C-SPAN 2; Discovery Channel; Disney Channel; E! HD; ESPN; ESPN2; EWTN Global Catholic Network; Freeform; FX; FXM; History; HLN; Lifetime; MTV;

2017 Edition
D-103

California—Cable Systems

Nickelodeon; Pop; QVC; Spike TV; Syfy; TBS; The Weather Channel; TLC; TNT; Trinity Broadcasting Network (TBN); Turner Classic Movies; TV Land; USA Network; VH1; WGN America.

Pay Service 1
Pay Units: N.A.
Programming (via satellite): Cinemax; HBO; Showtime; Starz Encore; The Movie Channel.
Fee: $2.95 monthly (Encore), $11.95 monthly (Showtime), $12.95 monthly (Cinemax, HBO or TMC).

Video-On-Demand: No

Internet Service
Operational: No.

Telephone Service
None
Miles of Plant: 50.0 (coaxial); None (fiber optic). Homes passed: 14,811.
General Manager: James Smith.
Ownership: NWS Communications.

SAN FRANCISCO—Comcast Cable, 2055 Folsom St, San Francisco, CA 94110-1330. Phones: 925-973-7000 (San Ramon regional office); 415-863-8500. Fax: 415-863-1659. Web Site: http://www.comcast.com. Also serves Alameda, Alameda Naval Air Station, Albany, American Canyon, Antioch, Atherton, Bay Point, Belmont, Belvedere, Benicia, Berkeley, Brentwood, Brisbane, Broadmoor, Burlingame, Calistoga, Campbell, Carmel Valley (village), Carmel-by-the-Sea, Castro Valley, Clayton, Cloverdale, Clyde, Colma, Concord, Concord Naval Weapons Station, Contra Costa County (portions), Corte Madera, Cotati, Crockett, Cupertino, Daly City, Danville, Del Monte Forest, Del Rey Oaks, Dublin, East Palo Alto, El Cerrito, El Granada, Emeryville, Fairfax, Fairfield, Forest Knolls, Fort Bragg, Foster City, Fremont, Glenwood, Half Moon Bay, Hayward, Healdsburg, Hercules, Hillsborough, La Honda, Lafayette, Larkspur, Livermore, Los Altos, Los Altos Hills, Los Gatos, Los Trancos Woods, Marin County (portions), Marina, Marsh Creek Motor Home Park, Martinez, Mendocino, Mendocino County (portions), Menlo Park, Mill Valley, Millbrae, Milpitas, Montara, Monte Sereno, Monterey, Moraga, Moss Beach, Mountain View, Napa, Napa County (portions), Newark, Novato, Oakland, Oakley, Orinda, Pacific Grove, Pacifica, Palo Alto, Pescadero, Petaluma, Piedmont, Pinole, Pittsburg, Pleasant Hill, Pleasanton, Port Costa, Portola Valley, Redwood City, Richmond, Rio Vista, Rodeo, Rohnert Park, Ross, Salinas, San Anselmo, San Carlos, San Jose, San Leandro, San Lorenzo, San Mateo, San Mateo County (portions), San Pablo, San Rafael, San Ramon, Sand City, Santa Clara, Santa Clara County (portions), Santa Cruz, Santa Cruz County (portions), Santa Rosa, Saratoga, Sausalito, Scotts Valley, Seaside, Sebastopol, Sonoma, Sonoma County (portions), Solano County (western portions), Sonoma, Sonoma County (portions), South San Francisco, St. Helena, Stanford, Suisin City, Sunnyvale, Sunol, Tiburon, Travis AFB, Treasure Island Naval Station, Ukiah, Union City, Vacaville, Vallejo, Walnut Creek, Windsor, Woodside & Yountville. ICA: CA0003.

TV Market Ranking: 25 (Vacaville); 7 (Alameda, Alameda Naval Air Station, Albany, American Canyon, Antioch, Atherton, Bay Point, Belmont, Belvedere, Benicia, Berkeley, Brentwood, Brisbane, Broadmoor, Burlingame, Campbell, Castro Valley, Clayton, Clyde, Colma, Concord, Concord Naval Weapons Station, Contra Costa County (portions), Corte Madera, Crockett, Cupertino, Daly City, Danville, Dublin, East Palo Alto, El Cerrito, El Granada, Emeryville, Fairfax, Fairfield, Forest Knolls, Foster City, Fremont, Half Moon Bay, Hayward, Hercules, Hillsborough, La Honda, Lafayette, Larkspur, Livermore, Los Altos, Los Altos Hills, Los Gatos, Los Trancos Woods, Marin County (portions), Martinez, Menlo Park, Mill Valley, Millbrae, Milpitas, Montara, Monte Sereno, Moraga, Moss Beach, Mountain View, Napa County (portions), Newark, Novato, Oakland, Oakley, Orinda, Pacifica, Palo Alto, Pescadero, Piedmont, Pinole, Pittsburg, Pleasant Hill, Pleasanton, Port Costa, Portola Valley, Redwood City, Richmond, Rio Vista, Rodeo, Ross, San Anselmo, San Carlos, SAN FRANCISCO, San Jose, San Leandro, San Lorenzo, San Mateo, San Mateo County (portions), San Pablo, San Ramon, Santa Clara, Santa Clara County (portions), Santa Cruz, Santa Cruz County (portions), Saratoga, Sausalito, Scotts Valley, Solano County (western portions), South San Francisco, Stanford, Suisin City, Sunnyvale, Sunol, Tiburon, Travis AFB, Treasure Island Naval Station, Union City, Vallejo, Walnut Creek, Woodside); 7,25 (Marsh Creek Motor Home Park (portions), Solano (portions), Solano County (portions)); Below 100 (Calistoga, Carmel Valley (village), Carmel-by-the-Sea, Cloverdale, Cotati, Danville, Del Monte Forest, Del Rey Oaks, Marina, Mendocino, Pacific Grove, Salinas, Sand City, Santa Rosa, Seaside, Sebastopol, Sonoma, St. Helena, Windsor, Fort Bragg, Healdsburg, Mendocino County (portions), Monterey, Napa, Rohnert Park, Yountville, Napa County (portions), Santa Clara County (portions)); Outside TV Markets (Petaluma, Ukiah). Franchise award date: N.A. Franchise expiration date: N.A. Began: January 1, 1953.

Channel capacity: 33 (operating 2-way). Channels available but not in use: N.A.

Basic Service
Subscribers: 1,305,228.
Programming (received off-air): KBCW (CW) San Francisco; KCNS (MundoMax, Retro TV) San Francisco; KCSM-TV (PBS) San Mateo; KDTV-DT (Bounce TV, getTV, UNV) San Francisco; KFSF-DT (UniMas) Vallejo; KGO-TV (ABC, Live Well Network) San Francisco; KICU-TV (Heroes & Icons, IND) San Jose; KKPX-TV (ION) San Jose; KNTV (COZI TV, NBC) San Jose; KOFY-TV (MeTV) San Francisco; KPIX-TV (CBS, Decades) San Francisco; KQED (PBS) San Francisco; KQEH (PBS) San Jose; KRCB (PBS) Cotati; KRON-TV (Antenna TV, MNT) San Francisco; KSTS (TMO) San Jose; KTLN-TV (IND) Novato; KTNC-TV (Estrella TV, This TV) Concord; KTSF (IND) San Francisco; KTVU (Buzzr, FOX, LATV, Movies!) Oakland; 24 FMs.
Programming (via satellite): California Channel; C-SPAN; C-SPAN 2; Discovery Channel; Pop.
Fee: $42.00 installation; $61.81 monthly.

Expanded Basic Service 1
Subscribers: N.A.
Programming (via satellite): A&E; AMC; Animal Planet; BET; Bravo; Cartoon Network; CNBC; CNN; Comcast SportsNet Bay Area; Comedy Central; Disney Channel; E! HD; ESPN; ESPN2; Food Network; Fox News Channel; Freeform; FX; Golf Channel; Hallmark Channel; HGTV; History; HLN; International Television (ITV); Jade Channel; Lifetime; MSNBC; MTV; NBCSN; Nickelodeon; QVC; Spike TV; Syfy; TBS; The Weather Channel; TLC; TNT; Travel Channel; truTV; TV Land; USA Network; VH1.
Fee: $52.50 monthly.

Digital Basic Service
Subscribers: N.A.
Programming (via satellite): ABP News; BBC America; Bloomberg Television; CNN en Espanol; Destination America; Discovery Kids Channel; Discovery Life Channel; Disney XD; ESPN Classic; ESPN Now; ESPNews; EVINE Live; EWTN Global Catholic Network; Fox Deportes; Fox Sports 1; Fuse; FXM; FYI; GolTV; Great American Country; GSN; History International; HITS (Headend In The Sky); IFC; INSP; Investigation Discovery; Life OK; LMN; MC; MTV2; National Geographic Channel; Nick Jr.; Nicktoons; Outdoor Channel; Ovation; OWN; Oprah Winfrey Network; RAI Italia; RTN; Saigon Broadcasting Television Network (SBTN); STAR Plus; Sundance TV; TeenNick; The Filipino Channel; The Word Network; Trinity Broadcasting Network (TBN); Turner Classic Movies; TV Asia; VideoRola; WAM! America's Kidz Network; WE tv; Weatherscan; Zee TV.

Digital Pay Service 1
Pay Units: N.A.
Programming (via satellite): Cinemax (multiplexed); Flix; HBO (multiplexed); Showtime (multiplexed); The Movie Channel (multiplexed).
Fee: $17.00 monthly (each).

Video-On-Demand: Yes

Pay-Per-View
iN DEMAND; Playboy TV (delivered digitally); Fresh (delivered digitally); UrbanXtra (delivered digitally).

Internet Service
Operational: Yes.
Subscribers: 1,325,051.
Broadband Service: Comcast High Speed Internet.
Fee: $42.95 monthly.

Telephone Service
Digital: Operational
Subscribers: 632,254.
Miles of Plant: 34,170.0 (coaxial); 7,536.0 (fiber optic). Homes passed: 3,110,254.
Area Vice President: Doug Schulz. Vice President, Communications: Andrew Johnson. Technical Operations Director: Adam Goyer. Marketing Director: Jeff Farr.
Ownership: Comcast Cable Communications Inc. (MSO).

SAN FRANCISCO—Formerly served by TV Max. No longer in operation. ICA: CA0411.

SAN FRANCISCO (southern portion)—Wave Broadband, 401 Parkplace Center, Ste 500, Kirkland, WA 98033. Phone: 800-427-8686. Web Site: http://www.wavebroadband.com. Also serves Burlingame, Daly City, Redwood City, San Mateo & South San Francisco. ICA: CA0452. **Note:** This system is an overbuild.

TV Market Ranking: 7 (Burlingame, Daly City, Redwood City, San Mateo, South San Francisco). Franchise award date: N.A. Franchise expiration date: N.A. Began: July 28, 1999.

Channel capacity: N.A. Channels available but not in use: N.A.

Basic Service
Subscribers: 11,075.
Programming (received off-air): KBCW (CW) San Francisco; KCNS (MundoMax, Retro TV) San Francisco; KDTV-DT (Bounce TV, getTV, UNV) San Francisco; KGO-TV (ABC, Live Well Network) San Francisco; KICU-TV (Heroes & Icons, IND) San Jose; KKPX-TV (ION) San Jose; KMTP-TV (ETV) San Francisco; KNTV (COZI TV, NBC) San Jose; KOFY-TV (MeTV) San Francisco; KPIX-TV (CBS, Decades) San Francisco; KQED (PBS) San Francisco; KQEH (PBS) San Jose; KRON-TV (Antenna TV, MNT) San Francisco; KSTS (TMO) San Jose; KTLN-TV (IND) Novato; KTNC-TV (Estrella TV, This TV) Concord; KTSF (IND) San Francisco; KTVU (Buzzr, FOX, LATV, Movies!) Oakland.
Programming (via satellite): California Channel; C-SPAN; C-SPAN 2; Pop; UniMas.
Fee: $29.95 installation; $25.95 monthly.

Expanded Basic Service 1
Subscribers: N.A.
Programming (via satellite): A&E; AMC; Animal Planet; BET; Bloomberg Television; Bravo; Cartoon Network; CMT; CNBC; CNN; Comcast SportsNet Bay Area; Comedy Central; Discovery Channel; Disney Channel; Disney XD; E! HD; ESPN; ESPN Classic; ESPN2; ESPNews; EWTN Global Catholic Network; Food Network; Fox News Channel; Fox Sports 1; FOX Sports Networks; Freeform; FX; FXM; Golf Channel; HGTV; History; HLN; IFC; Lifetime; MTV; MTV2; National Geographic Channel; Nickelodeon; Oxygen; QVC; Spike TV; Syfy; TBS; The Weather Channel; TLC; TNT; Travel Channel; truTV; Turner Classic Movies; TV Land; Univision; USA Network; VH1; WE tv.
Fee: $3.45 monthly.

Digital Basic Service
Subscribers: N.A.
Programming (via satellite): AXS TV; BBC America; Boomerang; Comcast SportsNet Bay Area; Discovery Digital Networks; ESPN; Fox Sports 2; FYI; HD Theater; History International; LMN; MC; Nick 2; Nick Jr.; Nicktoons; Sprout; Sundance TV; TeenNick; Tennis Channel.

Digital Pay Service 1
Pay Units: N.A.
Programming (via satellite): ART America; Cinemax; Flix; HBO (multiplexed); RAI Italia; RTN; Showtime (multiplexed); Starz (multiplexed); Starz Encore (multiplexed); Starz HD; The Filipino Channel; The Movie Channel (multiplexed); TV Asia; TV5, La Television International; Zee TV.

Video-On-Demand: Yes

Pay-Per-View
iN DEMAND (delivered digitally); SexSee (delivered digitally); VaVoom (delivered digitally); Juicy (delivered digitally).

Internet Service
Operational: Yes.
Broadband Service: In-house.
Fee: free installation; $19.95-$74.95 monthly.

Telephone Service
Digital: Operational
Fee: $24.95-$49.95 monthly
Homes passed: 92,000.
Chief Financial Officer: Wayne Schattenkerk. General Manager: Tim Peters.
Ownership: WaveDivision Holdings LLC (MSO).

SAN JOSE—Comcast Cable. Now served by SAN FRANCISCO, CA [CA0003]. ICA: CA0467.

SAN JOSE—Formerly served by Pacific Bell Video Services. No longer in operation. ICA: CA0441.

SAN JOSE—Formerly served by TV Max. No longer in operation. ICA: CA0412.

Cable Systems—California

SAN JUAN CAPISTRANO—Cox Communications, 6205 Peachtree Dunwoody Rd, 12th Floor, Atlanta, GA 30328. Phones: 404-269-6590; 949-546-2000 (Administrative office). Web Site: http://www.cox.com. Also serves Aliso Viejo, Coto de Caza, Dana Point, Irvine, Laguna Beach, Laguna Hills, Laguna Niguel, Laguna Woods, Lake Forest, Marine Corps Air Station El Toro, Mission Viejo, Modjeska Canyon, Newport Beach, Orange County, Rancho Santa Margarita, San Clemente, Trabuco Canyon & Tustin. ICA: CA0015.

TV Market Ranking: 2 (Aliso Viejo, Coto de Caza, Dana Point, Irvine, Laguna Beach, Laguna Hills, Laguna Niguel, Laguna Woods, Lake Forest, Marine Corps Air Station El Toro, Mission Viejo, Modjeska Canyon, Newport Beach, Orange County, Rancho Santa Margarita, San Clemente, SAN JUAN CAPISTRANO, Trabuco Canyon).

Channel capacity: 66 (operating 2-way). Channels available but not in use: N.A.

Basic Service
Subscribers: 184,230. Commercial subscribers: 4,594.
Programming (received off-air): KABC-TV (ABC, Live Well Network) Los Angeles; KCBS-TV (CBS, Decades) Los Angeles; KCET (ETV) Los Angeles; KCOP-TV (Bounce TV, Buzzr, Heroes & Icons, MNT, Movies!) Los Angeles; KDOC-TV (MeTV) Anaheim; KFTR-DT (getTV, UniMas) Ontario; KLCS (PBS) Los Angeles; KMEX-DT (UNV) Los Angeles; KNBC (COZI TV, NBC) Los Angeles; KOCE-TV (PBS) Huntington Beach; KPXN-TV (ION) San Bernardino; KRCA (Estrella TV) Riverside; KSCI (IND) Long Beach; KTBN-TV (TBN) Santa Ana; KTLA (Antenna TV, CW, This TV) Los Angeles; KTTV (FOX) Los Angeles; KVEA (TMO) Corona; KWHY-TV (MundoMax) Los Angeles; KXLA (IND) Rancho Palos Verdes.
Programming (via satellite): California Channel; C-SPAN; C-SPAN 2; Pop; QVC; TBS; WGN America.
Fee: $52.50 installation; $24.99 monthly; $7.10 converter.

Expanded Basic Service 1
Subscribers: N.A.
Programming (via satellite): A&E; AMC; Animal Planet; BET; Bravo; Cartoon Network; CNBC; CNN; Comedy Central; Discovery Channel; Disney Channel; E! HD; ESPN; ESPN Classic; ESPN2; Flix; Food Network; Fox News Channel; Fox Sports 1; FOX Sports Networks; FOX Sports West/Prime Ticket; Freeform; FX; Hallmark Channel; HGTV; History; HLN; IFC; Lifetime; MSNBC; MTV; NBCSN; Nickelodeon; Spike TV; Sundance TV; Syfy; The Weather Channel; TLC; TNT; Travel Channel; Turner Classic Movies; TV Land; Univision; USA Network; VH1.
Fee: $44.99 monthly.

Digital Basic Service
Subscribers: N.A.
Programming (via satellite): BBC America; Bloomberg Television; Discovery Digital Networks; Disney XD; DMX Music; Flix; FYI; Golf Channel; GSN; History International; IFC; LMN; Ovation; Sundance TV; Weatherscan.

Pay Service 1
Pay Units: N.A.
Programming (via satellite): Cinemax; HBO; Showtime.
Fee: $20.00 installation; $9.95 monthly (each).

Digital Pay Service 1
Pay Units: N.A.
Programming (via satellite): Cinemax (multiplexed); HBO (multiplexed); Showtime (multiplexed); Starz (multiplexed); Starz Encore (multiplexed); The Movie Channel (multiplexed).
Fee: $9.95 monthly (each).
Video-On-Demand: Yes
Pay-Per-View
Hot Choice; iN DEMAND (delivered digitally); Playboy TV (delivered digitally); Fresh (delivered digitally); Shorteez (delivered digitally).
Internet Service
Operational: Yes.
Subscribers: 240,767.
Broadband Service: Cox High Speed Internet.
Fee: $99.95 installation; $44.95 monthly; $15.00 modem lease; $79.00 modem purchase.
Telephone Service
Digital: Operational
Subscribers: 153,362.
Fee: $10.69 monthly
Miles of Plant: 4,871.0 (coaxial); 1,548.0 (fiber optic). Homes passed: 351,927.
Vice President & General Manager: Duffy Leone. Vice President, Network Operations: Rick Guerrero. Vice President, Tax: Mary Vickers. Marketing Director: Colleen Lagner. Communications Manager: Ayn Craciun.
Ownership: Cox Communications Inc. (MSO).

SAN LUIS OBISPO—Charter Communications, 270 Bridge St, San Luis Obispo, CA 93401. Phones: 314-543-2236; 636-207-5100 (Corporate office); 805-544-1962. Web Site: http://www.charter.com. Also serves Arroyo Grande, Atascadero, Avila Beach, Baywood-Los Osos, Cambria, Cayucos, Country Club Estates, Garden Farms, Grover Beach, Guadalupe, Heritage Ranch, Morro Bay, Nipomo, Oceano, Paso Robles, Pismo/Shell Beach, San Luis Obispo County (portions), San Miguel, Santa Margarita & Templeton. ICA: CA0045.

TV Market Ranking: Below 100 (Arroyo Grande, Atascadero, Avila Beach, Baywood-Los Osos, Cambria, Cayucos, Country Club Estates, Garden Farms, Grover Beach, Guadalupe, Heritage Ranch, Morro Bay, Nipomo, Oceano, Paso Robles, Pismo/Shell Beach, SAN LUIS OBISPO, San Luis Obispo County (portions), San Miguel, Santa Margarita, Templeton). Franchise award date: August 2, 1967. Franchise expiration date: N.A. Began: August 2, 1968.

Channel capacity: 74 (operating 2-way). Channels available but not in use: N.A.

Digital Basic Service
Subscribers: 37,187.
Programming (via satellite): BBC America; Bloomberg Television; Boomerang; Discovery Digital Networks; Disney XD; DIY Network; FOX College Sports Central; FOX College Sports Pacific; FYI; Great American Country; History International; IFC; LMN; MC; Nick Jr.; Nicktoons; Sundance TV; TeenNick; WE tv.
Fee: $26.99 monthly.

Digital Expanded Basic Service
Subscribers: N.A.
Programming (via satellite): A&E; AMC; Animal Planet; Bravo; Cartoon Network; CMT; CNBC; CNN; Comedy Central; Discovery Channel; Disney Channel; E! HD; ESPN; ESPN2; Food Network; Fox News Channel; Fox Sports 1; FOX Sports West/Prime Ticket; Freeform; Golf Channel; Hallmark Channel; HGTV; History; HLN; Lifetime; MSNBC; MTV; National Geographic Channel; NBCSN; Nickelodeon; Oxygen; Spike TV; Syfy; TBS; The Weather Channel; TLC; TNT; Travel Channel; truTV; Turner Classic Movies; TV Land; Univision; USA Network; VH1.
Fee: $38.99 monthly.

Digital Pay Service 1
Pay Units: N.A.
Programming (via satellite): Cinemax (multiplexed); Flix; HBO (multiplexed); Showtime (multiplexed); Starz (multiplexed); Starz Encore (multiplexed); The Movie Channel (multiplexed).
Fee: $10.00 monthly (Cinemax, HBO, TMC, Showtime/Flix or Starz/Encore).
Video-On-Demand: Yes
Pay-Per-View
iN DEMAND; iN DEMAND (delivered digitally); Playboy TV (delivered digitally); Fresh (delivered digitally); Shorteez (delivered digitally).
Internet Service
Operational: Yes. Began: March 1, 2000.
Subscribers: 46,855.
Broadband Service: Charter Internet.
Fee: $29.99 monthly; $4.95 modem lease.
Telephone Service
Digital: Operational
Subscribers: 20,181.
Fee: $29.99 monthly
Miles of Plant: 1,973.0 (coaxial); 373.0 (fiber optic). Homes passed: 116,000.
Vice President & General Manager: Ed Merrill. Chief Technician: Dan Joseph. Marketing Director: Sarwar Assar. Accounting Director: David Sovanski.
Ownership: Charter Communications Inc. (MSO).

SAN LUIS OBISPO—Formerly served by TVCN. No longer in operation. ICA: CA0413.

SAN MATEO—Comcast Cable. Now served by SAN FRANCISCO, CA [CA0003]. ICA: CA0081.

SAN PABLO—Comcast Cable. Now served by SAN FRANCISCO, CA [CA0003]. ICA: CA0123.

SAN RAFAEL—Comcast Cable. Now served by SAN FRANCISCO, CA [CA0003]. ICA: CA0480.

SAN SIMEON ACRES—San Simeon Community Cable Inc, PO Box 544, Cambria, CA 93428. Phones: 805-781-5252; 805-927-5555. Web Site: http://www.slocounty.ca.gov/PW/Franchise_Administration/SanSimeonCable.htm. ICA: CA0295.

TV Market Ranking: Below 100 (SAN SIMEON ACRES). Franchise award date: N.A. Franchise expiration date: N.A. Began: August 1, 1982.

Channel capacity: N.A. Channels available but not in use: N.A.

Basic Service
Subscribers: N.A.
Programming (received off-air): KCOY-TV (CBS) Santa Maria; KSBY (CW, Laff, NBC) San Luis Obispo; KTLA (Antenna TV, CW, This TV) Los Angeles.
Programming (via satellite): A&E; CNBC; CNN; C-SPAN; Discovery Channel; ESPN; History; KRMA-TV (PBS) Denver; KUSA (NBC, WeatherNation) Denver; Lifetime; Nickelodeon; Spike TV; TBS; The Weather Channel; TLC; TNT; Turner Classic Movies; USA Network; WGN America.
Fee: $22.50 monthly.

Pay Service 1
Pay Units: N.A.
Programming (via satellite): Cinemax; HBO.
Fee: $10.00 monthly (each).
Internet Service
Operational: Yes.
Broadband Service: Paralynx.
Fee: $49.00 monthly.
Telephone Service
None
Miles of Plant: 4.0 (coaxial); None (fiber optic). Homes passed: 1,200.
Ownership: San Simeon Community Cable Inc.

SANTA ANA—Formerly served by Adelphia Communications. Now served by Time Warner Cable, LOS ANGELES, CA [CA0009]. ICA: CA0376.

SANTA BARBARA—Cox Communications, 6205 Peachtree Dunwoody Rd, 12th Floor, Atlanta, GA 30328. Phones: 404-269-6590; 805-683-6651 (Customer service). Web Site: http://www.cox.com. Also serves Carpinteria, Goleta & Santa Barbara County (portions). ICA: CA0034.

TV Market Ranking: Below 100 (Carpinteria, Goleta, SANTA BARBARA, Santa Barbara County (portions)). Franchise award date: October 1, 1961. Franchise expiration date: N.A. Began: May 1, 1962.

Channel capacity: 63 (operating 2-way). Channels available but not in use: N.A.

Basic Service
Subscribers: 47,302.
Programming (received off-air): KBEH (IND) Oxnard; KCET (ETV) Los Angeles; KCOP-TV (Bounce TV, Buzzr, Heroes & Icons, MNT, Movies!) Los Angeles; KCOY-TV (CBS) Santa Maria; KEYT-TV (ABC, MNT, Retro TV) Santa Barbara; KNBC (COZI TV, NBC) Los Angeles; KSBY (CW, Laff, NBC) San Luis Obispo; KTAS (TMO) San Luis Obispo; 24 FMs.
Programming (via satellite): CNN; C-SPAN; C-SPAN 2; FX; Lifetime; MSNBC; NBC Universo; Pop; TBS; The Weather Channel; TNT; Trinity Broadcasting Network (TBN); truTV; USA Network; VH1.
Fee: $49.95 installation; $26.99 monthly.

Expanded Basic Service 1
Subscribers: N.A.
Programming (via satellite): A&E; AMC; Animal Planet; Bravo; Cartoon Network; CNBC; Comedy Central; Discovery Channel; Disney Channel; E! HD; ESPN; ESPN2; Food Network; Fox Deportes; Fox News Channel; Fox Sports 1; FOX Sports West/Prime Ticket; Freeform; Golf Channel; Hallmark Channel; HBO; HGTV; History; HITS (Headend In The Sky); HLN; IFC; MTV; NBCSN; Nickelodeon; QVC; Spike TV; Syfy; TLC; Travel Channel; Turner Classic Movies; TV Land; Univision.
Fee: $11.95 monthly.

Digital Basic Service
Subscribers: N.A.
Programming (via satellite): BBC America; Bloomberg Television; Discovery Digital Networks; Disney XD; GSN; IFC; LMN; MC; NBA TV; Oxygen; Sundance TV.

Pay Service 1
Pay Units: N.A.
Programming (via satellite): Cinemax; HBO; Showtime.
Fee: $5.00 installation; $13.95 monthly (each).

Digital Pay Service 1
Pay Units: N.A.
Programming (via satellite): Cinemax (multiplexed); HBO (multiplexed); Showtime

2017 Edition
D-105

California—Cable Systems

The industry bible...
Consumer Electronics Daily
Warren Communications News
Free 30-day trial—call 800-771-9202 or visit www.warren-news.com

(multiplexed); Starz (multiplexed); Starz Encore; The Movie Channel.
Video-On-Demand: No
Pay-Per-View
ESPN Now (delivered digitally); iN DEMAND; Sports PPV (delivered digitally); movies (delivered digitally).
Internet Service
Operational: Yes. Began: December 1, 1999.
Subscribers: 52,165.
Broadband Service: Cox High Speed Internet.
Fee: $149.95 installation; $39.95 monthly; $15.00 modem lease; $199.00 modem purchase.
Telephone Service
Digital: Operational
Subscribers: 18,597.
Fee: $15.25 monthly
Miles of Plant: 1,470.0 (coaxial); 286.0 (fiber optic). Homes passed: 91,198.
Vice President & General Manager: Julie McGovern. Vice President, Tax: Mary Vickers. Chief Technician: Rodney Baker. Marketing Director: Scott James. Government & Public Affairs Director: David Edelman.
Ownership: Cox Communications Inc. (MSO).

SANTA CLARA—Comcast Cable. Now served by SAN FRANCISCO, CA [CA0003]. ICA: CA0075.

SANTA CLARITA—Time Warner Cable. Now served by LOS ANGELES, CA [CA0009]. ICA: CA0083.

SANTA CRUZ—Comcast Cable. Now served by SAN FRANCISCO, CA [CA0003]. ICA: CA0043.

SANTA MARIA—Comcast Cable. Now served by FRESNO, CA [CA0011]. ICA: CA0352.

SANTA MONICA—Time Warner Cable. Now served by LOS ANGELES, CA [CA0009]. ICA: CA0460.

SANTA ROSA—Comcast Cable. Now served by SAN FRANCISCO, CA [CA0003]. ICA: CA0049.

SARATOGA—Comcast Cable. Now served by SAN FRANCISCO, CA [CA0003]. ICA: CA0165.

SEAL BEACH—Formerly served by Adelphia Communications. Time Warner Cable. Now served by LOS ANGELES, CA [CA0009]. ICA: CA0147.

SHAVER LAKE—Suddenlink Communications, 520 Maryville Centre Dr, Ste 300, St. Louis, MO 63141. Phones: 314-315-9400; 760-873-4123. Web Site: http://www.suddenlink.com. ICA: CA0247.
TV Market Ranking: 72 (SHAVER LAKE). Franchise award date: August 23, 1983. Franchise expiration date: N.A. Began: N.A.
Channel capacity: N.A. Channels available but not in use: N.A.
Basic Service
Subscribers: 586. Commercial subscribers: 53.
Programming (received off-air): KFRE-TV (CW, IND) Sanger; KFSN-TV (ABC, Live Well Network) Fresno; KJEO-LD (America One, IND) Fresno; KMPH-TV (FOX, This TV) Visalia; KMSG-LD (Azteca America) Fresno; KNXT (ETV) Visalia; KPXN-TV (ION) San Bernardino; KSEE (LATV, NBC) Fresno; KVPT (PBS) Fresno.
Programming (via satellite): A&E; AMC; Animal Planet; CNBC; CNN; Comcast SportsNet Bay Area; C-SPAN; Discovery Channel; Disney Channel; Disney XD; ESPN; ESPN2; Fox News Channel; Freeform; History; Lifetime; Nickelodeon; Spike TV; TBS; The Weather Channel; TLC; TNT; USA Network; WGN America.
Fee: $40.00 installation; $57.08 monthly.
Pay Service 1
Pay Units: N.A.
Programming (via satellite): HBO; Showtime; Starz Encore; The Movie Channel.
Fee: $10.00 monthly (HBO), $10.95 monthly (Encore, Showtime or TMC).
Video-On-Demand: No
Internet Service
Operational: Yes.
Telephone Service
None
Miles of Plant: 50.0 (coaxial); None (fiber optic). Homes passed: 1,749.
Senior Vice President, Corporate Finance: Michael Pflantz. Marketing Director: Jason Oelkers.
Ownership: Cequel Communications Holdings I LLC (MSO).

SHERMAN OAKS—Time Warner Cable. Now served by LOS ANGELES, CA [CA0009]. ICA: CA0471.

SIERRA DAWN ESTATES—Formerly served by Sierra Dawn Cablevision. No longer in operation. ICA: CA0379.

SIERRA MADRE—Time Warner Cable. Now served by LOS ANGELES, CA [CA0009]. ICA: CA0093.

SIMI VALLEY—Time Warner Cable. Now served by LOS ANGELES, CA [CA0009]. ICA: CA0380.

SOLEDAD—Charter Communications, 12405 Powerscourt Dr, St. Louis, MO 63131. Phones: 636-207-5100 (Corporate office); 408-847-2020; 805-544-1962 (San Luis Obispo administrative office). Fax: 408-847-2993. Web Site: http://www.charter.com. Also serves Gonzales & Monterey County (portions). ICA: CA0382.
TV Market Ranking: Below 100 (Gonzales, Monterey County (portions), SOLEDAD). Franchise award date: N.A. Franchise expiration date: N.A. Began: March 1, 1972.
Channel capacity: N.A. Channels available but not in use: N.A.
Digital Basic Service
Subscribers: 237.
Programming (via satellite): BBC America; Bloomberg Television; Discovery Life Channel; Disney XD; DMX Music; ESPN Classic; ESPN2; ESPNews; EVINE Live; Fox Sports 1; Fuse; FXM; FYI; Golf Channel; GSN; HGTV; History; History International; IFC; INSP; LMN; NBCSN; Nick Jr.; Outdoor Channel; Syfy; TeenNick; Trinity Broadcasting Network (TBN); Turner Classic Movies; WE tv.
Fee: $26.99 monthly.
Digital Expanded Basic Service
Subscribers: N.A.
Programming (via satellite): AMC; Cartoon Network; CMT; CNN; Discovery Channel; Disney Channel; ESPN; Freeform; HLN; Lifetime; Nickelodeon; Spike TV; Univision.
Fee: $8.58 monthly.
Digital Pay Service 1
Pay Units: N.A.
Programming (via satellite): Cinemax (multiplexed); HBO (multiplexed); Showtime (multiplexed); Starz (multiplexed); Starz Encore (multiplexed); The Movie Channel (multiplexed).
Video-On-Demand: No
Pay-Per-View
iN DEMAND (delivered digitally); ESPN Now (delivered digitally); ESPN Sports PPV (delivered digitally); Hot Choice (delivered digitally); Playboy TV (delivered digitally); Fresh (delivered digitally); Shorteez (delivered digitally).
Internet Service
Operational: No.
Telephone Service
None
Miles of Plant: 36.0 (coaxial); None (fiber optic). Homes passed: 4,629.
Vice President & General Manager: Ed Merrill. Chief Technician: Mark Beech. Marketing Director: Sarwar Assar. Accounting Director: David Sovanski.
Ownership: Charter Communications Inc. (MSO).

SONORA—Comcast Cable. Now served by SACRAMENTO, CA [CA0002]. ICA: CA0130.

SONORA—Comcast Cable. Now served by SACRAMENTO, CA [CA0002]. ICA: CA0148.

SOUTH GATE—Time Warner Cable. Now served by LOS ANGELES, CA [CA0009]. ICA: CA0468.

SOUTH LAKE TAHOE—Charter Communications. Now served by RENO, NV [NV0002]. ICA: CA0132.

SOUTH PASADENA—Time Warner Cable. Now served by LOS ANGELES, CA [CA0009]. ICA: CA0161.

SOUTH SAN FRANCISCO—Comcast Cable. Now served by SAN FRANCISCO, CA [CA0003]. ICA: CA0106.

SPANISH RANCH MOBILE HOME PARK—Formerly served by Comcast Cable. No longer in operation. ICA: CA0383.

STEVENSON RANCH—Time Warner Cable. Now served by LOS ANGELES, CA [CA0009]. ICA: CA0465.

STOCKTON—Comcast Cable. Now served by SACRAMENTO, CA [CA0002]. ICA: CA0028.

STRAWBERRY—Formerly served by Comcast Cable. No longer in operation. ICA: CA0421.

STUDIO CITY—Formerly served by Adelphia Communications. Now served by Time Warner Cable, LOS ANGELES, CA [CA0009]. ICA: CA0461.

SUN CITY—Mediacom, 27192 Sun City Blvd, Ste A, Sun City, CA 92586. Phone: 951-679-3977. Fax: 951-679-9087. Web Site: http://www.mediacomcable.com. Also serves Riverside County (western portion). ICA: CA0385.
TV Market Ranking: 2 (Riverside County (western portion), SUN CITY). Franchise award date: April 10, 1964. Franchise expiration date: N.A. Began: April 10, 1964.
Channel capacity: N.A. Channels available but not in use: N.A.
Basic Service
Subscribers: 1,130.
Programming (received off-air): KABC-TV (ABC, Live Well Network) Los Angeles; KCAL-TV (IND) Los Angeles; KCBS-TV (CBS, Decades) Los Angeles; KCET (ETV) Los Angeles; KCOP-TV (Bounce TV, Buzzr, Heroes & Icons, MNT, Movies!) Los Angeles; KDOC-TV (MeTV) Anaheim; KHSC-LP (HSN) Fresno; KJLA (LATV) Ventura; KLCS (PBS) Los Angeles; KMEX-DT (UNV) Los Angeles; KNBC (COZI TV, NBC) Los Angeles; KPXN-TV (ION) San Bernardino; KRCA (Estrella TV) Riverside; KSCI (IND) Long Beach; KTBN-TV (TBN) Santa Ana; KTLA (Antenna TV, CW, This TV) Los Angeles; KTTV (FOX) Los Angeles; KVCR-DT (PBS) San Bernardino; KVEA (TMO) Corona; KWHY-TV (MundoMax) Los Angeles.
Programming (via satellite): California Channel; C-SPAN; C-SPAN 2; FX; Pop; QVC; TBS; truTV; WGN America.
Fee: $29.50 installation; $39.95 monthly; $2.18 converter.
Expanded Basic Service 1
Subscribers: N.A.
Programming (via satellite): A&E; AMC; Animal Planet; BET; CNBC; CNN; Comedy Central; Discovery Channel; Disney Channel; Disney XD; ESPN; ESPN2; Food Network; Fox News Channel; FOX Sports West/Prime Ticket; Freeform; Golf Channel; HGTV; History; HLN; INSP; Lifetime; MSNBC; MTV; Nickelodeon; Spike TV; Syfy; The Weather Channel; TLC; TNT; Travel Channel; Turner Classic Movies; TV Land; USA Network; VH1; WE tv.
Fee: $24.95 monthly.
Digital Basic Service
Subscribers: N.A.
Programming (via satellite): BBC America; Discovery Digital Networks; ESPNews; Fox Sports 1; MC; National Geographic Channel; Nick Jr.
Digital Pay Service 1
Pay Units: N.A.
Programming (via satellite): Cinemax (multiplexed); Flix (multiplexed); HBO (multiplexed); Showtime (multiplexed); Starz (multiplexed); Starz Encore (multiplexed); Sundance TV (multiplexed); The Movie Channel (multiplexed).
Fee: $13.95 monthly (HBO), $9.95 monthly (Showtime or Cinemax), $8.00 monthly (Starz/Encore).
Video-On-Demand: No

Cable Systems—California

Pay-Per-View
iN DEMAND.
Internet Service
Operational: Yes.
Broadband Service: Mediacom High Speed Internet.
Fee: $59.95 installation; $40.95 monthly; $3.00 modem lease; $239.95 modem purchase.
Telephone Service
Analog: Not Operational
Digital: Operational
Miles of Plant: 145.0 (coaxial); None (fiber optic). Homes passed: 10,501.
General Manager: Allen Bublitz. Regional Engineering Director: Jon Tatilano.
Ownership: Mediacom LLC (MSO).

SUNNYVALE—Comcast Cable. Now served by SAN FRANCISCO, CA [CA0003]. ICA: CA0067.

SUSANVILLE—Zito Media, 102 S Main St, PO Box 665, Coudersport, PA 16915. Phones: 814-260-9055; 800-365-6988. E-mail: info@zitomedia.com. Web Site: http://www.zitomedia.com. Also serves Janesville & Lassen County. ICA: CA0191.
TV Market Ranking: Outside TV Markets (Janesville, Lassen County, SUSANVILLE). Franchise award date: January 1, 1955. Franchise expiration date: N.A. Began: January 1, 1965.
Channel capacity: N.A. Channels available but not in use: N.A.
Basic Service
Subscribers: 1,098.
Programming (received off-air): KNPB (PBS) Reno; allband FM.
Programming (via microwave): KAME-TV (MeTV, MNT) Reno; KCRA-TV (MeTV, NBC) Sacramento; KHSL-TV (CBS, CW) Chico; KOLO-TV (ABC, IND, Movies!) Reno; KRNV-DT (NBC, This TV) Reno; KRXI-TV (FOX, Retro TV) Reno; KTVN (Antenna TV, CBS) Reno.
Programming (via satellite): California Channel; C-SPAN; C-SPAN 2; CW PLUS; Daystar TV Network; Pop; QVC; TBS; WGN America.
Fee: $49.95 installation; $28.01 monthly.
Expanded Basic Service 1
Subscribers: N.A.
Programming (via satellite): A&E; AMC; Animal Planet; Bravo; Cartoon Network; CMT; CNBC; CNN; Comcast SportsNet Bay Area; Comedy Central; Discovery Channel; Disney Channel; E! HD; ESPN; ESPN2; Food Network; Fox News Channel; Freeform; FX; Hallmark Channel; HGTV; History; HLN; Lifetime; MSNBC; MTV; Nickelodeon; Spike TV; Syfy; The Weather Channel; TLC; TNT; Travel Channel; truTV; TV Land; USA Network; VH1.
Fee: $33.93 monthly.
Digital Basic Service
Subscribers: N.A.
Programming (via satellite): 52MX; AXS TV; BBC America; Bloomberg Television; Boomerang; CBS Sports Network; Cinelatino; CMT; CNN en Espanol; Cooking Channel; C-SPAN 3; Destination America; Discovery Kids Channel; Discovery Life Channel; Disney XD; DIY Network; ESPN Classic; ESPN HD; ESPN2 HD; ESPNews; ESPNU; EWTN Global Catholic Network; Flix; Fox Business Network; FOX College Sports Central; FOX College Sports Pacific; Fox Deportes; Fox Sports 1; Fox Sports 2; Fuse; FXM; FYI; Golf Channel; Great American Country; GSN; HD Theater; History en Espanol; History International; IFC; Investigation Discovery; LMN; LOGO; MC; MTV Classic; MTV Hits; MTV Jams; MTV2; Nat Geo WILD; National Geographic Channel; NBA TV; NBCSN; Nick 2; Nick Jr.; Nicktoons; Outdoor Channel; OWN; Oprah Winfrey Network; Science Channel; Starz Encore (multiplexed); Sundance TV; TeenNick; The Word Network; TNT HD; Tr3s; Trinity Broadcasting Network (TBN); Turner Classic Movies; Universal HD; UP; VH1 Soul; WE tv.
Digital Pay Service 1
Pay Units: N.A.
Programming (via satellite): ART America; Cinemax (multiplexed); Cinemax HD; HBO (multiplexed); HBO HD; RAI Italia; RTN; Showtime (multiplexed); Showtime HD; Starz (multiplexed); Starz HD; The Filipino Channel; The Movie Channel (multiplexed); TV Asia; TV5; La Television International.
Fee: $12.00 monthly (Cinemax, HBO, Showtime/TMC or Starz), $15.00 monthly (ART, CCTV, Filipino, RAI, Russia, TV Asia, TV Russia, TV5 or Zhong Tian).
Video-On-Demand: No
Pay-Per-View
Playboy TV (delivered digitally); Fresh (delivered digitally); Hot Choice (delivered digitally); Special events (delivered digitally); iN DEMAND (delivered digitally).
Internet Service
Operational: Yes.
Broadband Service: In-house.
Fee: $20.99-$49.99 monthly.
Telephone Service
Digital: Operational
Fee: $49.95 monthly
Miles of Plant: 93.0 (coaxial); None (fiber optic).
President: James Rigas.
Ownership: Zito Media (MSO).

TASSAJARA VALLEY—Formerly served by Comcast Cable. No longer in operation. ICA: CA0387.

TEHACHAPI—Bright House Networks. Now served by BAKERSFIELD, CA [CA0025]. ICA: CA0170.

TEHAMA—Formerly served by New Day Broadband. No longer in operation. ICA: CA0241.

THE SEA RANCH—CalNeva Broadband, 322 Ash St, PO Box 1470, Westwood, CA 96137. Phones: 530-256-2028; 866-330-2028. Web Site: http://blog.calneva.org. Also serves Gualala. ICA: CA0389.
TV Market Ranking: Outside TV Markets (Gualala, THE SEA RANCH). Franchise award date: N.A. Franchise expiration date: N.A. Began: August 13, 1966.
Channel capacity: N.A. Channels available but not in use: N.A.
Basic Service
Subscribers: 636.
Programming (received off-air): KBCW (CW) San Francisco; KGO-TV (ABC, Live Well Network) San Francisco; KICU-TV (Heroes & Icons, IND) San Jose; KNTV (COZI TV, NBC) San Jose; KOFY-TV (MeTV) San Francisco; KPIX-TV (CBS, Decades) San Francisco; KQED (PBS) San Francisco; KRCB (PBS) Cotati; KRON-TV (Antenna TV, MNT) San Francisco; KTVU (Buzzr, FOX, LATV, Movies!) Oakland; 21 FMs.
Programming (via satellite): A&E; AMC; BBC America; Bravo; Cartoon Network; CNBC; CNN; Comedy Central; C-SPAN; C-SPAN 3; Discovery Channel; E! HD; ESPN; ESPN2; ESPNews; Fox News Channel; FOX Sports Networks; FX; FXM; Golf Channel; Great American Country; HGTV; History; HLN; Lifetime; MTV; National Geographic Channel; Nickelodeon; QVC; Syfy; TBS; Telemundo; The Weather Channel; TLC; TNT; Turner Classic Movies; Univision Studios; USA Network; VH1; WGN America.
Fee: $65.00 installation; $31.00 monthly; $1.00 converter.
Pay Service 1
Pay Units: 20.
Programming (via satellite): Cinemax (multiplexed).
Fee: $12.10 monthly.
Pay Service 2
Pay Units: 60.
Programming (via satellite): HBO (multiplexed).
Fee: $13.15 monthly.
Video-On-Demand: No
Internet Service
Operational: Yes.
Broadband Service: Mendocino Community Network (MCN).
Fee: $65.00 installation; $39.99 monthly.
Telephone Service
None
Miles of Plant: 110.0 (coaxial); None (fiber optic).
General Manager: Thomas E. Gelardi.
Ownership: CalNeva Broadband LLC.

THERMAL—Formerly served by USA Communications. No longer in operation. ICA: CA0474.

THOUSAND OAKS—Charter Communications, 12405 Powerscourt Dr, St. Louis, MO 63131. Phones: 636-207-5100 (Corporate office); 626-430-3300 (Irwindale office); 310-456-9010. Fax: 310-579-7010. Web Site: http://www.charter.com. ICA: CA0188.
TV Market Ranking: 2 (THOUSAND OAKS). Franchise award date: September 1, 1967. Franchise expiration date: N.A. Began: September 1, 1967.
Channel capacity: N.A. Channels available but not in use: N.A.
Digital Basic Service
Subscribers: 101.
Programming (received off-air): KABC-TV (ABC, Live Well Network) Los Angeles; KAZA-TV (Azteca America) Avalon; KCAL-TV (IND) Los Angeles; KCBS-TV (CBS, Decades) Los Angeles; KCET (ETV) Los Angeles; KCOP-TV (Bounce TV, Buzzr, Heroes & Icons, MNT, Movies!) Los Angeles; KEYT-TV (ABC, MNT, Retro TV) Santa Barbara; KFTR-DT (getTV, UniMas) Ontario; KJLA (LATV) Ventura; KMEX-DT (UNV) Los Angeles; KNBC (COZI TV, NBC) Los Angeles; KPXN-TV (ION) San Bernardino; KRCA (Estrella TV) Riverside; KSCI (IND) Long Beach; KTBN-TV (TBN) Santa Ana; KTLA (Antenna TV, CW, This TV) Los Angeles; KTTV (FOX) Los Angeles; KVEA (TMO) Corona; KVMD (IND) Twentynine Palms; KWHY-TV (MundoMax) Los Angeles; KXLA (IND) Rancho Palos Verdes.
Programming (via satellite): A&E; AMC; Bravo; CNBC; CNN; Comedy Central; C-SPAN; E! HD; ESPN; Food Network; Freeform; FX; HLN; Lifetime; MTV; Nickelodeon; Oxygen; QVC; Spike TV; USA Network; VH1.
Fee: $65.00 installation; $26.99 monthly; $.98 converter.
Digital Expanded Basic Service
Subscribers: N.A.
Programming (via satellite): Animal Planet; Discovery Channel; Disney Channel; ESPN2; Fox News Channel; FOX Sports West/Prime Ticket; FXM; GSN; History; MSNBC; Syfy; TBS; The Weather Channel; TLC; TNT; Turner Classic Movies; WE tv; WGN America.
Digital Pay Service 1
Pay Units: N.A.
Programming (via satellite): HBO; Showtime.
Fee: $5.00 monthly (each).
Video-On-Demand: No
Pay-Per-View
iN DEMAND (delivered digitally); Playboy TV (delivered digitally); Fresh (delivered digitally); Shorteez (delivered digitally).
Internet Service
Operational: Yes.
Broadband Service: Charter Internet.
Telephone Service
Digital: Operational
Miles of Plant: 65.0 (coaxial); None (fiber optic). Homes passed: 4,709.
Vice President & General Manager: Wendy Rasmussen. Technical Operations Director: Peter Arredondo. Accounting Director: David Sovanski. Marketing Manager: Lily Ho.
Ownership: Charter Communications Inc. (MSO).

THOUSAND OAKS—Time Warner Cable. Now served by LOS ANGELES, CA [CA0009]. ICA: CA0446.

TORRANCE—Time Warner Cable. Now served by LOS ANGELES, CA [CA0009]. ICA: CA0020.

TRACY—Comcast Cable. Now served by SACRAMENTO, CA [CA0002]. ICA: CA0143.

TRAVIS AFB—Comcast Cable. Now served by SAN FRANCISCO, CA [CA0003]. ICA: CA0192.

TRINITY CENTER—Formerly served by Almega Cable. No longer in operation. ICA: CA0391.

TRUCKEE—Suddenlink Communications, 520 Maryville Centre Dr, Ste 300, St. Louis, MO 63141. Phones: 530-550-3900; 314-315-9400; 530-587-6100. Web Site: http://www.suddenlink.com. Also serves Donner Summit, El Dorado County (western portion), Placer County (western portion) & Tahoe City. ICA: CA0181.
TV Market Ranking: 25 (Placer County (western portion) (portions)); Below 100 (Donner Summit, Tahoe City, TRUCKEE, Placer County (western portion) (portions)); Outside TV Markets (El Dorado County (western portion), Placer County (western portion) (portions)). Franchise award date: February 3, 1964. Franchise expiration date: N.A. Began: September 1, 1964.
Channel capacity: 4 (operating 2-way). Channels available but not in use: N.A.
Basic Service
Subscribers: 9,311. Commercial subscribers: 541.
Programming (received off-air): KCRA-TV (MeTV, NBC) Sacramento; KGO-TV (ABC, Live Well Network) San Francisco; KOLO-TV (ABC, IND, Movies!) Reno; KOVR (CBS, Decades) Stockton; KPIX-TV (CBS, Decades) San Francisco; KQED (PBS) San Francisco; KREN-TV (CW, UNV) Reno; KTVU (Buzzr, FOX, LATV, Movies!) Oakland; KTXL (Antenna TV, FOX) Sacramento; allband FM.

California—Cable Systems

Programming (via satellite): A&E; CNBC; CNN; Comcast SportsNet Bay Area; Comedy Central; C-SPAN; Discovery Channel; Disney Channel; Disney XD; ESPN; ESPN2; Fox News Channel; Freeform; Great American Country; HLN; Lifetime; MTV; NBCSN; Nickelodeon; QVC; Spike TV; The Weather Channel; TLC; TNT; USA Network; VH1.
Fee: $49.95 installation; $35.04 monthly.
Digital Basic Service
Subscribers: N.A.
Programming (via satellite): BBC America; Box; Bravo; Discovery Digital Networks; DMX Music; ESPN Classic; ESPNews; Fox Sports 1; Golf Channel; GSN; HGTV; HITS (Headend In The Sky); IFC; Starz Encore; Syfy; Turner Classic Movies.
Pay Service 1
Pay Units: N.A.
Programming (via satellite): HBO; Showtime; Starz; Starz Encore; The Movie Channel; Univision Studios.
Digital Pay Service 1
Pay Units: N.A.
Programming (via satellite): Cinemax (multiplexed); HBO (multiplexed); Showtime (multiplexed); The Movie Channel (multiplexed).
Video-On-Demand: No
Pay-Per-View
Special events (delivered digitally).
Internet Service
Operational: Yes. Began: June 1, 2001.
Subscribers: 7,515.
Broadband Service: Suddenlink High Speed Internet.
Fee: $99.99 installation; $24.95 monthly; $10.00 modem lease; $240.00 modem purchase.
Telephone Service
Digital: Operational
Subscribers: 2,307.
Miles of Plant: 507.0 (coaxial); 193.0 (fiber optic). Homes passed: 20,383.
Senior Vice President, Corporate Finance: Michael Pflantz. General Manager: Dawn McWithey. Marketing Director: Jason Oelkers. Chief Technician: Dave Woods.
Ownership: Cequel Communications Holdings I LLC (MSO).

TUJUNGA—Time Warner Cable. Now served by LOS ANGELES, CA [CA0009]. ICA: CA0470.

TULELAKE—Formerly served by Almega Cable. No longer in operation. ICA: CA0392.

TURLOCK—Charter Communications, 12405 Powerscourt Dr, St. Louis, MO 63131. Phones: 636-207-5100 (Corporate office); 805-544-1962. Fax: 805-541-6042. Web Site: http://www.charter.com. Also serves Ceres, Escalon, Hickman, Hughson, Livingston, Merced County (portions), Ripon, Riverbank, San Joaquin County (portions), Stanislaus County (portions) & Waterford. ICA: CA0095.
TV Market Ranking: 25 (Ceres, Escalon, Ripon, San Joaquin County (portions)); 25,72 (Hickman, Hughson, Livingston, Merced County (portions), Riverbank, Stanislaus County (portions), TURLOCK, Waterford). Franchise award date: N.A. Franchise expiration date: N.A. Began: June 13, 1973.
Channel capacity: 67 (operating 2-way). Channels available but not in use: N.A.
Digital Basic Service
Subscribers: 16,494.
Programming (via satellite): BBC America; Bloomberg Television; Boomerang; Discovery Digital Networks; Disney XD; DIY Network; FYI; History International; LMN; MC; Nick Jr.; Sundance TV; TeenNick; WE tv.
Fee: $26.99 monthly.
Digital Pay Service 1
Pay Units: N.A.
Programming (via satellite): Cinemax (multiplexed); Flix; HBO (multiplexed); Showtime (multiplexed); Starz (multiplexed); Starz Encore (multiplexed); The Movie Channel (multiplexed).
Video-On-Demand: Yes
Pay-Per-View
Hot Choice (delivered digitally); iN DEMAND; Fresh; Fresh (delivered digitally); Shorteez (delivered digitally); Sports PPV (delivered digitally); movies (delivered digitally).
Internet Service
Operational: Yes. Began: December 1, 1999.
Subscribers: 19,903.
Broadband Service: Charter Internet.
Fee: $29.99 monthly; $199.00 modem purchase.
Telephone Service
Digital: Operational
Subscribers: 9,110.
Miles of Plant: 1,417.0 (coaxial); 305.0 (fiber optic). Homes passed: 84,691.
Vice President & General Manager: Ed Merrill. Technical Operations Director: Ken Arellano. Marketing Director: Sarwar Assar. Office Manager: Joanne Yee. Accounting Director: David Sovanski.
Ownership: Charter Communications Inc. (MSO).

TUSTIN—Time Warner Cable. Now served by LOS ANGELES, CA [CA0009]. ICA: CA0121.

UKIAH—Comcast Cable. Now served by SAN FRANCISCO, CA [CA0003]. ICA: CA0111.

UNION CITY—Comcast Cable. Now served by SAN FRANCISCO, CA [CA0003]. ICA: CA0135.

VACAVILLE—Comcast Cable. Now served by SAN FRANCISCO, CA [CA0003]. ICA: CA0098.

VALLEJO—Comcast Cable. Now served by SAN FRANCISCO, CA [CA0003]. ICA: CA0061.

VALLEY CENTER—Mediacom, 27192 Sun City Blvd, Ste A, Sun City, CA 92586. Phone: 951-679-3977. Fax: 951-679-9087. Web Site: http://www.mediacomcable.com. Also serves Pauma Valley & Rincon. ICA: CA0223.
TV Market Ranking: 51 (VALLEY CENTER); Outside TV Markets (Pauma Valley, Rincon). Franchise award date: N.A. Franchise expiration date: N.A. Began: September 1, 1966.
Channel capacity: N.A. Channels available but not in use: N.A.
Basic Service
Subscribers: 229.
Programming (received off-air): KFMB-TV (CBS, Grit, MeTV) San Diego; KGTV (ABC, Azteca America) San Diego; KNSD (COZI TV, NBC) San Diego; KPBS (PBS) San Diego; KSWB-TV (Antenna TV, FOX, This TV) San Diego; KUSI-TV (IND) San Diego; allband FM.
Programming (via satellite): A&E; AMC; Animal Planet; CNBC; CNN; Comedy Central; Concert TV; C-SPAN; C-SPAN 2; Discovery Channel; Disney Channel; Disney XD; E! HD; ESPN; ESPN2; EWTN Global Catholic Network; Food Network; Fox News Channel; FOX Sports West/Prime Ticket; Freeform; Golf Channel; HGTV; History; HLN; KTLA (Antenna TV, CW, This TV) Los Angeles; Lifetime; MSNBC; MTV; Nickelodeon; Outdoor Channel; QVC; Spike TV; Telemundo; The Weather Channel; TLC; TNT; Travel Channel; Trinity Broadcasting Network (TBN); TV Land; Univision Studios; USA Network; VH1; WGN America.
Fee: $41.25 installation; $36.00 monthly.
Digital Basic Service
Subscribers: N.A.
Programming (via satellite): BBC America; Discovery Digital Networks; DMX Music; ESPNews; Fox Sports 1; Fuse; FYI; GSN; History International; IFC; LMN; MTV Classic; National Geographic Channel; NBCSN; Nick Jr.; TeenNick; Turner Classic Movies.
Digital Pay Service 1
Pay Units: N.A.
Programming (via satellite): Cinemax (multiplexed); Flix; HBO (multiplexed); Showtime (multiplexed); Starz (multiplexed); Starz Encore (multiplexed); The Movie Channel (multiplexed).
Fee: $13.95 monthly (HBO), $9.95 monthly (Cinemax or Showtime/TMC), $8.00 monthly (Starz/Encore).
Video-On-Demand: No
Pay-Per-View
iN DEMAND (delivered digitally); Adult PPV (delivered digitally).
Internet Service
Operational: Yes.
Broadband Service: Mediacom High Speed Internet.
Fee: $59.95 installation; $40.95 monthly.
Telephone Service
None
Miles of Plant: 150.0 (coaxial); None (fiber optic). Homes passed: 2,100.
General Manager: Allen Bublitz. Engineering Director: Jon Tatilano.
Ownership: Mediacom LLC.

VAN NUYS—Formerly served by Adelphia Communications. Now served by Time Warner, LOS ANGELES, CA [CA0009]. ICA: CA0462.

VANDENBERG AFB—Vandenberg Broadband, 2312 104th Ave SE, Bellevue, WA 98004. Phones: 425-734-5578 (Local office); 425-451-1470. Fax: 425-451-1471. E-mail: vandenbergcsr@ruralwest.com. Web Site: http://ruralwest.com. ICA: CA0393.
TV Market Ranking: Below 100 (VANDENBERG AFB). Franchise award date: February 1, 1986. Franchise expiration date: N.A. Began: May 10, 1986.
Channel capacity: N.A. Channels available but not in use: N.A.
Basic Service
Subscribers: 35.
Programming (received off-air): KCOY-TV (CBS) Santa Maria; KEYT-TV (ABC, MNT, Retro TV) Santa Barbara; KSBY (CW, Laff, NBC) San Luis Obispo; KTLA (Antenna TV, CW, This TV) Los Angeles; KTVD (MeTV, MNT) Denver.
Programming (via satellite): A&E; AMC; Animal Planet; BET; Boomerang; Cartoon Network; CMT; CNBC; CNN; Comedy Central; C-SPAN; C-SPAN 2; Discovery Channel; Disney Channel; E! HD; ESPN; ESPN Classic; ESPN2; EWTN Global Catholic Network; Food Network; Fox News Channel; Fox Sports 1; FOX Sports Networks; Freeform; FX; Hallmark Channel; HGTV; History; HLN; KRMA-TV (PBS) Denver; Lifetime; MSNBC; MTV; NASA TV; Nickelodeon; Oxygen; QVC; Spike TV; Syfy; TBS; The Weather Channel; TLC; TNT; Travel Channel; Trinity Broadcasting Network (TBN); TV Land; Univision Studios; USA Network; VH1; WE tv; WGN America; WPIX (Antenna TV, CW, This TV) New York.
Fee: $32.95 monthly.
Digital Basic Service
Subscribers: N.A.
Programming (via satellite): BBC America; Bloomberg Television; Bravo; Destination America; Discovery Kids Channel; Discovery Life Channel; Disney XD; DMX Music; ESPN Classic; ESPN2; FOX College Sports Central; FOX College Sports Pacific; Fox Sports 1; Fuse; FXM; FYI; Golf Channel; Great American Country; GSN; HGTV; History; History International; IFC; International Television (ITV); Investigation Discovery; LMN; MTV Classic; MTV Hits; MTV2; National Geographic Channel; Nick Jr.; Nicktoons; Outdoor Channel; Ovation; OWN: Oprah Winfrey Network; Science Channel; Sundance TV; TeenNick; Turner Classic Movies; VH1 Country; VH1 Soul.
Digital Pay Service 1
Pay Units: N.A.
Programming (via satellite): Cinemax (multiplexed); Flix; HBO (multiplexed); Showtime (multiplexed); Starz (multiplexed); Starz Encore (multiplexed); The Movie Channel (multiplexed).
Fee: $10.95 monthly (each).
Video-On-Demand: No
Pay-Per-View
iN DEMAND.
Internet Service
Operational: Yes.
Broadband Service: In-house.
Fee: $34.99 monthly.
Telephone Service
Digital: Operational
Miles of Plant: 25.0 (coaxial); 12.0 (fiber optic). Homes passed: 3,000.
General Manager: Dave Bowland. Chief Technician: Sean Esman.
Ownership: RuralWest - Western Rural Broadband Inc. (MSO).

VENTURA—Charter Communications, PO Box 1458, Ventura, CA 93002. Phones: 314-543-2236; 636-207-5100 (Corporate office); 310-456-9010; 626-430-3300 (Irwindale office). Web Site: http://www.charter.com. Also serves Ventura County (Rincon area). ICA: CA0146.
TV Market Ranking: Below 100 (VENTURA, Ventura County (Rincon area)). Franchise award date: December 31, 1999. Franchise expiration date: N.A. Began: January 1, 1951.
Channel capacity: 80 (operating 2-way). Channels available but not in use: N.A.
Digital Basic Service
Subscribers: 4,961.
Programming (via satellite): A&E HD; AXS TV; BBC America; CMT; Discovery Digital Networks; ESPN HD; ESPN2 HD; Food Network HD; FYI; HD Theater; HGTV HD; History International; INSP; MC; Nat Geo WILD; National Geographic Channel HD; Nick Jr.; Nicktoons; Sprout; TeenNick; TNT HD; Universal HD.
Fee: $49.99 installation; $14.99 monthly.
Digital Expanded Basic Service
Subscribers: N.A.
Programming (via satellite): A&E; AMC; Animal Planet; BET; Bloomberg Television; Boomerang; Bravo; Cartoon Network; Cloo; CMT; CNBC; CNN; Comedy Central; C-

Cable Systems—California

SPAN; C-SPAN 2; Discovery Channel; Discovery Life Channel; Disney Channel; Disney XD; DIY Network; E! HD; ESPN; ESPN Classic; ESPN2; ESPNews; ESPNU; EVINE Live; EWTN Global Catholic Network; Food Network; FOX College Sports Central; FOX College Sports Pacific; Fox Deportes; Fox News Channel; Fox Sports 1; Fox Sports 2; FOX Sports West/Prime Ticket; Freeform; Fuse; FX; FXM; Golf Channel; GolTV; Great American Country; GSN; Hallmark Channel; HGTV; History; HITS (Headend In The Sky); HLN; IFC; ION Television; Lifetime; LMN; MSNBC; MTV; National Geographic Channel; NBCSN; NFL Network; Nickelodeon; Outdoor Channel; OWN: Oprah Winfrey Network; Oxygen; Pop; Spike TV; Syfy; TBS; Tennis Channel; The Weather Channel; TLC; TNT; Travel Channel; truTV; Turner Classic Movies; TV Land; Univision; USA Network; VH1; WE tv.
Fee: $5.00 monthly (variety or sports), $7.00 monthly (Canales).

Digital Pay Service 1
Pay Units: N.A.
Programming (via satellite): Cinemax (multiplexed); Cinemax HD; Flix; HBO (multiplexed); HBO HD; Showtime (multiplexed); Showtime HD; Starz (multiplexed); Starz Encore (multiplexed); Starz HD; The Movie Channel (multiplexed); The Movie Channel HD.
Fee: $10.00 -$20.00.

Video-On-Demand: Planned

Pay-Per-View
Playboy TV (delivered digitally); Fresh (delivered digitally); special events.

Internet Service
Operational: Yes. Began: April 1, 1998.
Subscribers: 1,393.
Broadband Service: Charter Internet.
Fee: $49.95 installation; $39.95 monthly; $3.00 modem lease.

Telephone Service
Digital: Operational
Subscribers: 670.
Miles of Plant: 833.0 (coaxial); 200.0 (fiber optic). Homes passed: 20,177.
Vice President & General Manager: Wendy Rasmussen. Technical Operations Manager: Peter Arrendondo. Accounting Director: David Sovanski. Marketing Manager: Lily Ho.
Ownership: Charter Communications Inc. (MSO).

VENTURA—Time Warner Cable. Now served by LOS ANGELES, CA [CA0009]. ICA: CA0099.

VICTORVILLE—Charter Communications. Now served by HESPERIA, CA [CA0158]. ICA: CA0064.

VISALIA—Charter Communications. Now served by FRESNO, CA [CA0011]. ICA: CA0478.

VISALIA—Formerly served by Sprint Corp. No longer in operation. ICA: CA0420.

WALNUT CREEK—Comcast Cable. Now served by SAN FRANCISCO, CA [CA0003]. ICA: CA0488.

WATSONVILLE—Charter Communications. Now served by GILROY, CA [CA0425]. ICA: CA0107.

WEAVERVILLE—Velocity Telephone Inc, PO Box 246, Weaverville, CA 96093. Phone: 877-623-3550. Fax: 530-625-5279. Web Site: http://www.velotech.net. ICA: CA0249.
TV Market Ranking: Below 100 (WEAVERVILLE). Franchise award date: January 1, 1978. Franchise expiration date: N.A. Began: October 15, 1979.
Channel capacity: N.A. Channels available but not in use: N.A.

Basic Service
Subscribers: N.A.
Programming (received off-air): KCVU (COZI TV, FOX, This TV) Paradise; KHSL-TV (CBS, CW) Chico; KIXE-TV (PBS) Redding; KRCR-TV (ABC, MeTV, Movies!) Redding.
Programming (via satellite): CNN; Disney Channel; ESPN; Freeform; Nickelodeon; TBS; WGN America.
Fee: $15.00 installation; $36.75 monthly.

Pay Service 1
Pay Units: N.A.
Programming (via satellite): HBO; Showtime.
Fee: $11.50 monthly (each).

Internet Service
Operational: No.

Telephone Service
None
Miles of Plant: 23.0 (coaxial); None (fiber optic). Homes passed: 1,680.
Chief Executive Officer: Travis Finch.
Ownership: Velocity Telephone Inc.

WEST HOLLYWOOD—Time Warner Cable. Now served by LOS ANGELES, CA [CA0009]. ICA: CA0463.

WEST LOS ANGELES—Time Warner Cable. Now served by LOS ANGELES, CA [CA0009]. ICA: CA0006.

WEST SACRAMENTO—Wave Broadband, 401 Parkplace Center, Ste 500, Kirkland, WA 98033. Phones: 866-928-3123; 425-576-8200. Fax: 425-576-8221. E-mail: jpenney@wavebroadband.com. Web Site: http://www.wavebroadband.com. Also serves Dixon, Winters & Woodland. ICA: CA0086.
TV Market Ranking: 25 (Dixon, WEST SACRAMENTO, Winters, Woodland). Franchise award date: N.A. Franchise expiration date: N.A. Began: September 14, 1973.
Channel capacity: 81 (operating 2-way). Channels available but not in use: N.A.

Basic Service
Subscribers: 9,761.
Programming (received off-air): KCRA-TV (MeTV, NBC) Sacramento; KCSO-LD (MeTV, The Country Network, TMO) Sacramento; KMAX-TV (CW) Sacramento; KOVR (CBS, Decades) Stockton; KQCA (MNT, Movies!, This TV) Stockton; KQED (PBS) San Francisco; KSPX-TV (ION) Sacramento; KTFK-DT (getTV, UniMas) Stockton; KTNC-TV (Estrella TV, This TV) Concord; KTVU (Buzzr, FOX, LATV, Movies!) Oakland; KTXL (Antenna TV, FOX) Sacramento; KUVS-DT (Bounce TV, UNV) Modesto; KVIE (PBS) Sacramento; KXTV (ABC) Sacramento; 30 FMs.
Programming (via satellite): California Channel; C-SPAN; C-SPAN 2; Jewelry Television; Pop; QVC; Trinity Broadcasting Network (TBN).
Fee: $29.99 installation; $25.95 monthly.

Expanded Basic Service 1
Subscribers: N.A.
Programming (via satellite): A&E; AMC; Animal Planet; BET; Cartoon Network; CMT; CNBC; CNN; Comcast SportsNet California; Comedy Central; Discovery Channel; Disney Channel; Disney XD; E! HD; ESPN; ESPN2; Food Network; Fox Deportes; Fox News Channel; Fox Sports 1; Freeform; FX; Golf Channel; GSN; Hallmark Channel; HGTV; History; HLN; INSP; Lifetime; MSNBC; MTV; National Geographic Channel; NBCSN; Nickelodeon; Oxygen; Spike TV; Syfy; TBS; The Weather Channel; TLC; TNT; Travel Channel; truTV; Turner Classic Movies; TV Land; Univision; USA Network; VH1.
Fee: $38.99 monthly.

Digital Basic Service
Subscribers: N.A.
Programming (via satellite): BBC America; BYUtv; Cloo; CMT; Destination America; Discovery Kids Channel; Discovery Life Channel; EWTN Global Catholic Network; Fox Business Network; FYI; History International; Investigation Discovery; MC; MTV Classic; MTV Hits; MTV Jams; MTV2; mtvU; Nick Jr.; Nicktoons; OWN: Oprah Winfrey Network; Science Channel; Sprout; TeenNick; Tr3s; VH1 Soul.

Digital Expanded Basic Service
Subscribers: N.A.
Programming (via satellite): AWE; Bloomberg Television; Boomerang; Cooking Channel; DIY Network; Fuse; FXM; Great American Country; IFC; LMN; NBC Universo; Ovation; UP; WE tv.

Digital Expanded Basic Service 2
Subscribers: N.A.
Programming (via satellite): 52MX; Azteca; Bandamax; Canal 22 Internacional; Cine Mexicano; Cinelatino; CNN en Espanol; De Pelicula; De Pelicula Clasico; Discovery Familia; ESPN Deportes; Fox Life; GolTV; History en Espanol; HITN; Infinito; La Familia Cosmovision; Tr3s; ULTRA HDPlex; Video-Rola; ViendoMovies.

Digital Expanded Basic Service 3
Subscribers: N.A.
Programming (via satellite): The Filipino Channel.

Digital Expanded Basic Service 4
Subscribers: N.A.
Programming (via satellite): CBS Sports Network; ESPN Classic; ESPNews; ESPNU; Fox Sports 2; FSN Digital Atlantic; FSN Digital Central; FSN Digital Pacific; GolTV; NFL Network; Outdoor Channel; Tennis Channel; TVG Network.

Digital Expanded Basic Service 5
Subscribers: N.A.
Programming (via satellite): A&E HD; Animal Planet HD; AXS TV; Discovery Channel HD; Disney Channel HD; ESPN HD; ESPN2 HD; Food Network HD; Hallmark Movie Channel HD; HD Theater; HGTV HD; History HD; MGM HD; National Geographic Channel HD; NFL Network HD; Science HD; TBS HD; TLC HD; TNT HD; Travel Channel HD; Universal HD.

Digital Pay Service 1
Pay Units: N.A.
Programming (via satellite): Cinemax (multiplexed); Cinemax HD; Flix; HBO (multiplexed); HBO HD; MoviePlex; Showtime (multiplexed); Showtime HD; Starz (multiplexed); Starz Encore (multiplexed); Starz HD; The Movie Channel (multiplexed); The Movie Channel HD.

Video-On-Demand: Yes

Pay-Per-View
iN DEMAND; Playboy TV (delivered digitally); Fresh (delivered digitally); Club Jenna (delivered digitally); Special events (delivered digitally).

Internet Service
Operational: Yes.
Subscribers: 12,094.
Broadband Service: Wave Broadband.
Fee: $24.95-$74.95 monthly.

Telephone Service
Digital: Operational
Subscribers: 4,640.
Fee: $29.95-$49.95 monthly
Miles of Plant: 629.0 (coaxial); 169.0 (fiber optic). Homes passed: 49,131.
Chief Financial Officer: Wayne Schattenkerk. General Manager: Tim Peters. Marketing Director: Adam Lazara.
Ownership: WaveDivision Holdings LLC (MSO).

WHITTIER—Charter Communications, 12405 Powerscourt Dr, St. Louis, MO 63131. Phones: 636-207-5100 (Corporate office); 626-430-6112; 626-430-3300. Fax: 626-430-3420. Web Site: http://www.charter.com. ICA: CA0096.
TV Market Ranking: 2 (WHITTIER). Franchise award date: January 1, 1976. Franchise expiration date: N.A. Began: January 1, 1982.
Channel capacity: 70 (operating 2-way). Channels available but not in use: N.A.

Digital Basic Service
Subscribers: 7,987.
Programming (via satellite): BBC America; Bloomberg Television; Discovery Digital Networks; FYI; History International; LMN; MC; Nick Jr.; TeenNick; WE tv.
Fee: $14.99 monthly.

Digital Expanded Basic Service
Subscribers: N.A.
Programming (via satellite): A&E; AMC; Animal Planet; BET; Bravo; Cartoon Network; CNBC; CNN; Comedy Central; Discovery Channel; Disney Channel; Disney XD; E! HD; ESPN; ESPN Classic; ESPN2; Food Network; Fox News Channel; Fox Sports 1; FOX Sports West/Prime Ticket; Freeform; FX; Golf Channel; GSN; HGTV; History; HLN; Lifetime; MSNBC; MTV; NBCSN; Nickelodeon; Spike TV; Syfy; The Weather Channel; TLC; TNT; Travel Channel; truTV; Turner Classic Movies; TV Land; Univision; USA Network; VH1.
Fee: $48.95 monthly.

Digital Pay Service 1
Pay Units: N.A.
Programming (via satellite): Cinemax (multiplexed); Flix; HBO (multiplexed); Showtime (multiplexed); Starz (multiplexed); Starz Encore (multiplexed); Sundance TV; The Movie Channel (multiplexed).
Fee: $10.90 monthly (TMC), $10.95 monthly (Cinemax or Starz/Encore), $12.95 monthly (Showtime/Flix/Sundance or HBO).

Video-On-Demand: Yes

Pay-Per-View
iN DEMAND; Fresh (delivered digitally); Shorteez (delivered digitally).

Internet Service
Operational: Yes.
Subscribers: 8,013.
Broadband Service: Charter Internet.
Fee: $29.99 monthly; $4.95 modem lease.

Telephone Service
Digital: Operational
Subscribers: 3,333.
Fee: $29.99 monthly
Miles of Plant: 424.0 (coaxial); 49.0 (fiber optic). Homes passed: 31,000. Homes passed included in Glendale.
Vice President & General Manager: Wendy Rasmusson. Technical Operations Manager: Tom Williams. Marketing Manager: Lily Ho. Accounting Director: David Sovanski.
Ownership: Charter Communications Inc. (MSO).

2017 Edition   D-109

California—Cable Systems

WILLIAMS—Comcast Cable. Now served by SACRAMENTO, CA [CA0002]. ICA: CA0229.

WILLITS—Comcast Cable, 1060 North State St, Ukiah, CA 95482. Phone: 800-266-2278. Web Site: http://www.comcast.com. Also serves Mendocino County (portions). ICA: CA0482.
 TV Market Ranking: Below 100 (Mendocino County (portions) (portions), WILLITS); Outside TV Markets (Mendocino County (portions) (portions)).
 Channel capacity: N.A. Channels available but not in use: N.A.
 Basic Service
 Subscribers: 836.
 Fee: $42.00 installation; $61.81 monthly.
 Internet Service
 Operational: Yes.
 Telephone Service
 Digital: Operational
 Ownership: Comcast Cable Communications Inc.

WILLOW CREEK—Formerly served by Almega Cable. No longer in operation. ICA: CA0264.

WILLOW RANCH MOBILE HOME PARK—Formerly served by Comcast Cable. No longer in operation. ICA: CA0394.

WILMINGTON—Time Warner Cable. Now served by LOS ANGELES, CA [CA0009]. ICA: CA0054.

WRIGHTWOOD—Charter Communications, 12405 Powerscourt Dr, St. Louis, MO 63131. Phones: 636-207-5100 (Corporate office); 951-343-5100. Fax: 951-354-5942. Web Site: http://www.charter.com. Also serves Baldy Mesa & Phelan. ICA: CA0398.
 TV Market Ranking: 2 (Baldy Mesa, Phelan, WRIGHTWOOD).
 Channel capacity: N.A. Channels available but not in use: N.A.
 Digital Basic Service
 Subscribers: 154.
 Programming (received off-air): KABC-TV (ABC, Live Well Network) Los Angeles; KCBS-TV (CBS, Decades) Los Angeles; KCET (ETV) Los Angeles; KCOP-TV (Bounce TV, Buzzr, Heroes & Icons, MNT, Movies!) Los Angeles; KILM (IND) Barstow; KNBC (COZI TV, NBC) Los Angeles; KTLA (Antenna TV, CW, This TV) Los Angeles; KTTV (FOX) Los Angeles; KWHY-TV (MundoMax) Los Angeles.
 Programming (via satellite): A&E; AMC; CNN; Comedy Central; ESPN; MTV; Nickelodeon; QVC; Spike TV; TBS; TNT; USA Network; VH1.
 Fee: $35.99 monthly.

Digital Expanded Basic Service
 Subscribers: N.A.
 Programming (via satellite): Discovery Channel; Disney Channel; Food Network; Freeform; HLN; TLC.
 Fee: $7.68 monthly.
Digital Pay Service 1
 Pay Units: N.A.
 Programming (via satellite): Cinemax; FOX Sports Networks; HBO; Showtime; Starz Encore; The Movie Channel.
 Fee: $10.95 monthly (Cinemax, Showtime, or TMC), $11.95 monthly (HBO).
Video-On-Demand: No
Pay-Per-View
 Special events.
Internet Service
 Operational: No.
Telephone Service
 None
 Miles of Plant: 102.0 (coaxial); 17.0 (fiber optic). Homes passed: 3,815.
 Vice President & General Manager: Fred Lutz. Technical Operations Manager: George Noel. Marketing Director: Chris Bailey. Accounting Director: David Sovanski.
 Ownership: Charter Communications Inc. (MSO).

YORBA LINDA—Time Warner Cable. Now served by LOS ANGELES, CA [CA0009]. ICA: CA0397.

YOUNTVILLE—Comcast Cable. Now served by SAN FRANCISCO, CA [CA0003]. ICA: CA0261.

YREKA—Northland Cable Television, 1882 Fort Jones Rd, Ste 2, Yreka, CA 96097. Phones: 888-667-8452; 530-842-4228. Fax: 530-842-2516. E-mail: yreka@northlandcabletv.com. Web Site: http://www.yournorthland.com. Also serves Montague & Siskiyou County (portions). ICA: CA0189.
 TV Market Ranking: Outside TV Markets (Montague, Siskiyou County (portions), YREKA). Franchise award date: N.A. Franchise expiration date: N.A. Began: August 1, 1954.
 Channel capacity: N.A. Channels available but not in use: N.A.
 Basic Service
 Subscribers: 801.
 Programming (received off-air): KBLN-TV (IND) Grants Pass; KDRV (ABC) Medford; KIXE-TV (PBS) Redding; KMVU-DT (FOX, MeTV) Medford; KOBI (NBC) Medford; KRCR-TV (ABC, MeTV, Movies!) Redding; KRVU-LD (MNT) Redding; KTVL (CBS, CW) Medford; allband FM.
 Programming (via satellite): A&E; Animal Planet; Cartoon Network; CNBC; CNN; Comcast SportsNet Bay Area; Comedy Central; C-SPAN; CW PLUS; Discovery Channel; E! HD; ESPN; ESPN2; Food Network; Fox News Channel; FX; FXM; Great American Country; Hallmark Channel; HGTV; History; HLN; Lifetime; National Geographic Channel; NFL Network; Nickelodeon; Outdoor Channel; QVC; Spike TV; Syfy; TBS; The Weather Channel; TLC; TNT; Travel Channel; Trinity Broadcasting Network (TBN); Turner Classic Movies; TV Land; Univision Studios; USA Network; VH1; WGN America.
 Fee: $50.00 installation; $47.64 monthly.
 Digital Basic Service
 Subscribers: N.A.
 Programming (via satellite): BBC America; Bloomberg Television; Bravo; Destination America; Discovery Kids Channel; Discovery Life Channel; DMX Music; ESPNews; Fox Sports 1; Golf Channel; IFC; Investigation Discovery; LMN; NBCSN; OWN; Oprah Winfrey Network; Science Channel; WE tv.
 Pay Service 1
 Pay Units: N.A.
 Programming (via satellite): HBO; Starz Encore.
 Fee: $2.95 monthly (Encore), $13.50 monthly (HBO).
 Digital Pay Service 1
 Pay Units: N.A.
 Programming (via satellite): Cinemax (multiplexed); Flix; HBO (multiplexed); Showtime (multiplexed); Starz (multiplexed); Starz Encore (multiplexed); The Movie Channel (multiplexed).
 Fee: $14.00 monthly (Cinemax, HBO, Showtime/TMC/Flix or Starz/Encore).
 Video-On-Demand: No
 Internet Service
 Operational: Yes.
 Fee: $42.99 monthly.
 Telephone Service
 Digital: Operational
 Miles of Plant: 98.0 (coaxial); 4.0 (fiber optic). Homes passed: 4,381.
 General Manager & Chief Technician: Coralene Arkfeld.
 Ownership: Northland Communications Corp. (MSO).

YUBA CITY—Comcast Cable. Now served by SACRAMENTO, CA [CA0002]. ICA: CA0070.

YUBA CITY—Formerly served by Sprint Corp. No longer in operation. ICA: CA0443.

YUCAIPA—Charter Communications, 7337 Central Ave, Riverside, CA 92504. Phones: 636-207-5100 (Corporate office); 951-343-5100. Web Site: http://www.charter.com. ICA: CA0211.

TV Market Ranking: 2 (YUCAIPA). Franchise award date: N.A. Franchise expiration date: N.A. Began: October 1, 1986.
 Channel capacity: N.A. Channels available but not in use: N.A.
 Digital Basic Service
 Subscribers: 70. Commercial subscribers: 90.
 Programming (received off-air): KABC-TV (ABC, Live Well Network) Los Angeles; KCBS-TV (CBS, Decades) Los Angeles; KCET (ETV) Los Angeles; KCOP-TV (Bounce TV, Buzzr, Heroes & Icons, MNT, Movies!) Los Angeles; KDOC-TV (MeTV) Anaheim; KFTR-DT (getTV, UniMas) Ontario; KILM (IND) Barstow; KMEX-DT (UNV) Los Angeles; KNBC (COZI TV, NBC) Los Angeles; KPXN-TV (ION) San Bernardino; KRCA (Estrella TV) Riverside; KSCI (IND) Long Beach; KTBN-TV (TBN) Santa Ana; KTLA (Antenna TV, CW, This TV) Los Angeles; KTTV (FOX) Los Angeles; KVCR-DT (PBS) San Bernardino; KVEA (TMO) Corona.
 Programming (via satellite): A&E; AMC; BET; Cartoon Network; CMT; CNBC; CNN; Comedy Central; C-SPAN; Discovery Channel; Disney Channel; E! HD; ESPN; ESPN2; EWTN Global Catholic Network; Food Network; Fox News Channel; FOX Sports West/Prime Ticket; Freeform; FX; History; HLN; Lifetime; MSNBC; MTV; Nickelodeon; Oxygen; Pop; QVC; Spike TV; Syfy; TBS; The Weather Channel; TLC; TNT; Turner Classic Movies; USA Network; VH1; WGN America.
 Fee: $29.95 installation; $33.99 monthly.
 Digital Pay Service 1
 Pay Units: N.A.
 Programming (via satellite): Cinemax; HBO (multiplexed); Showtime; The Movie Channel.
 Video-On-Demand: No
 Pay-Per-View
 iN DEMAND.
 Internet Service
 Operational: No.
 Telephone Service
 None
 Miles of Plant: 35.0 (coaxial); None (fiber optic). Homes passed: 850.
 Vice President & General Manager: Fred Lutz. Divisional Controller: David Sovanski. Marketing Director: Chris Bailey. Technical Operations Manager: George Noel.
 Ownership: Charter Communications Inc. (MSO).

YUCCA VALLEY—Time Warner Cable. Now served by BANNING, CA [CA0176]. ICA: CA0119.

COLORADO

Total Systems: 67	Communities with Applications: 0
Total Communities Served: 268	Number of Basic Subscribers: 793,044
Franchises Not Yet Operating: 0	Number of Expanded Basic Subscribers: 3,991
Applications Pending: 0	Number of Pay Units: 5,621

Top 100 Markets Represented: Denver-Castle Rock (32).

For a list of cable communities in this section, see the Cable Community Index located in the back of Cable Volume 2.
For explanation of terms used in cable system listings, see p. D-11.

AKRON (town)—Mediastream. Now served by Vyve Broadband, OTIS (town), CO [CO0128]. ICA: CO0086.

ALAMOSA—Charter Communications, 12405 Powerscourt Dr, St. Louis, MO 63131. Phones: 636-207-5100 (Corporate office); 877-273-7626 (Customer service); 866-213-6572; 516-803-2300 (Corporate office). Web Site: http://www.charter.com. Also serves Alamosa County, Alamosa East, Monte Vista & Rio Grande County (portions). ICA: CO0035.
TV Market Ranking: Outside TV Markets (ALAMOSA, Alamosa County, Alamosa East, Monte Vista, Rio Grande County (portions)). Franchise award date: N.A. Franchise expiration date: N.A. Began: March 1, 1955.
Channel capacity: N.A. Channels available but not in use: N.A.
Digital Basic Service
Subscribers: 2,098.
Programming (via satellite): A&E HD; Animal Planet HD; Bandamax; BBC America; Bloomberg Television; Bravo; CBS Sports Network; Cine Mexicano; Cinelatino; CMT; CNN en Espanol; Cooking Channel; De Pelicula; De Pelicula Clasico; Destination America; Discovery Channel HD; Discovery Kids Channel; Discovery Life Channel; Disney XD; DIY Network; DMX Music; ESPN Classic; ESPN Deportes; ESPN HD; ESPNews; Food Network HD; FOX College Sports Central; FOX College Sports Pacific; Fox Deportes; Fox Sports 1; Fuse; FXM; FYI; Golf Channel; GolTV; GSN; HD Theater; HGTV HD; History en Espanol; History HD; History International; IFC; Investigation Discovery; ION Television; LMN; MTV Classic; MTV Hits; MTV Jams; MTV2; Nat Geo WILD; National Geographic Channel; National Geographic Channel HD; NBC Universo; NBCSN; NFL Network; Nick 2; Nick Jr.; Nicktoons; Outdoor Channel; OWN; Oprah Winfrey Network; RFD-TV; Science Channel; Sprout; Syfy HD; TeenNick; Telehit; Tr3s; Trinity Broadcasting Network (TBN); UniMas; Universal HD; Univision Studios; UP; USA Network HD; VH1 Soul; ViendoMovies.
Fee: $26.99 monthly.
Digital Expanded Basic Service
Subscribers: N.A.
Programming (via satellite): A&E; Altitude Sports & Entertainment; AMC; Animal Planet; Cartoon Network; CMT; CNBC; CNN; Comedy Central; Discovery Channel; Disney Channel; E! HD; ESPN; ESPN2; EWTN Global Catholic Network; Food Network; Fox News Channel; Freeform; Hallmark Channel; HGTV; History; HLN; INSP; MSNBC; MTV; Nickelodeon; Oxygen; Root Sports Rocky Mountain; Spike TV; Syfy; TBS; The Weather Channel; TLC; TNT; Travel Channel; truTV; Turner Classic Movies; TV Land; UniMas; Univision Studios; USA Network; VH1.
Fee: $41.62 monthly.
Digital Pay Service 1
Pay Units: N.A.
Programming (via satellite): Cinemax (multiplexed); Flix; HBO (multiplexed); HBO HD; Showtime (multiplexed); Starz (multiplexed); Starz Encore (multiplexed); Starz HD; The Movie Channel (multiplexed).
Video-On-Demand: No
Pay-Per-View
iN DEMAND (delivered digitally).
Internet Service
Operational: Yes.
Broadband Service: Charter Internet.
Fee: $39.95 monthly.
Telephone Service
Digital: Operational
Fee: $49.99 monthly
Miles of Plant: 80.0 (coaxial); 31.0 (fiber optic). Homes passed: 7,512.
Accounting Director: David Sovanski. President & Chief Executive Officer: Tom Rutledge. General Manager: Jerry Parker. Technical Operations Manager: Doyle Rouna.
Ownership: Charter Communications Inc. (MSO).

ANTONITO—Formerly served by Charter Communications. No longer in operation. ICA: CO0120.

ARRIBA—Rebeltec Communications. Now served by KIT CARSON, CO [CO0152]. ICA: CO0156.

ASPEN—Comcast Cable. Now served by LONGMONT, CO [CO0011]. ICA: CO0017.

AVON—Comcast Cable. Now served by LONGMONT, CO [CO0011]. ICA: CO0020.

BAILEY—Formerly served by US Cable of Coastal Texas LP. No longer in operation. ICA: CO0059.

BAYFIELD—USA Communications, 920 East 56th St, Ste B, Kearney, NE 68847. Phone: 877-234-0102. E-mail: csr@usacommunications.tv. Web Site: http://usacommunications.tv. ICA: CO0105.
TV Market Ranking: Below 100 (BAYFIELD). Franchise award date: July 5, 1983. Franchise expiration date: N.A. Began: March 1, 1984.
Channel capacity: N.A. Channels available but not in use: N.A.
Basic Service
Subscribers: 114.
Programming (received off-air): KREZ-TV (CBS, The Country Network) Durango.
Programming (via microwave): KDVR (Antenna TV, FOX) Denver; KMGH-TV (ABC, Azteca America) Denver; KRMA-TV (PBS) Denver; KUSA (NBC, WeatherNation) Denver; KWGN-TV (CW, This TV) Denver.
Programming (via satellite): Altitude Sports & Entertainment; CNBC; CNN; Discovery Channel; Disney Channel; DIY Network; Food Network; HGTV; History; HLN; Nickelodeon; QVC; TBS; The Weather Channel; TLC; truTV; USA Network.
Fee: $29.95 installation; $19.50 monthly.
Expanded Basic Service 1
Subscribers: N.A.
Programming (via satellite): A&E; Bravo; Cartoon Network; CMT; Comedy Central; ESPN; ESPN2; Fox News Channel; Fox Sports 1; Freeform; FX; Great American Country; GSN; Hallmark Channel; MSNBC; MTV; NBCSN; Outdoor Channel; Root Sports Rocky Mountain; Spike TV; TNT; Turner Classic Movies; TV Land; Univision Studios; WE tv.
Fee: $14.75 monthly.
Pay Service 1
Pay Units: N.A.
Programming (via satellite): HBO (multiplexed).
Fee: $13.49 monthly.
Video-On-Demand: No
Internet Service
Operational: No.
Telephone Service
None
Miles of Plant: 16.0 (coaxial); None (fiber optic). Homes passed: 780.
Chief Financial Officer: Amber Reineke.
Ownership: USA Companies LP (MSO).

BENNETT—Comcast Cable. Now served by DENVER, CO [CO0001]. ICA: CO0157.

BEULAH—Beulah Cable TV, 8611 Central Ave, PO Box 188, Beulah, CO 81023-0188. Phone: 719-485-3400. Fax: 719-485-3500. E-mail: pdtelco@pinedrivetel.com. Web Site: http://www.pinedrivetel.com. ICA: CO0158.
TV Market Ranking: Below 100 (BEULAH). Franchise award date: March 1, 1992. Franchise expiration date: N.A. Began: September 1, 1992.
Channel capacity: 41 (not 2-way capable). Channels available but not in use: N.A.
Basic Service
Subscribers: 196.
Programming (received off-air): KKTV (CBS, MNT) Colorado Springs; KOAA-TV (Grit, NBC) Pueblo; KRDO-TV (ABC, TMO) Colorado Springs; KTSC (PBS) Pueblo; KXRM-TV (FOX, MundoMax) Colorado Springs.
Programming (via microwave): KWGN-TV (CW, This TV) Denver.
Programming (via satellite): The Arts; A&E; Animal Planet; CMT; CNN; Discovery Channel; Disney Channel; ESPN; ESPN2; Food Network; Fox News Channel; Freeform; Hallmark Channel; HGTV; History; HLN; Lifetime; NASA TV; National Geographic Channel; NBCSN; Nickelodeon; Root Sports Rocky Mountain; Spike TV; Syfy; TBS; The Weather Channel; TLC; TNT; Travel Channel; Turner Classic Movies; TV Land; USA Network.
Fee: $125.00 installation; $34.95 monthly.
Pay Service 1
Pay Units: N.A.
Programming (via satellite): HBO; The Movie Channel.
Fee: $10.00 monthly (each).
Video-On-Demand: No
Internet Service
Operational: Yes.
Telephone Service
Analog: Operational
Miles of Plant: 15.0 (coaxial); None (fiber optic). Homes passed: 350.
President & General Manager: Richard J. Sellers.
Ownership: Beulah Land Communications Inc.

BLACK HAWK—USA Communications, 920 East 56th St, Ste B, Kearney, NE 68847. Phone: 877-234-0102. E-mail: csr@usacommunications.tv. Web Site: http://usacommunications.tv. ICA: CO0097.
TV Market Ranking: 32 (BLACK HAWK). Franchise award date: May 8, 1984. Franchise expiration date: N.A. Began: November 20, 1985.
Channel capacity: N.A. Channels available but not in use: N.A.
Basic Service
Subscribers: 177.
Programming (received off-air): KCNC-TV (CBS, Decades) Denver; KDVR (Antenna TV, FOX) Denver; KMGH-TV (ABC, Azteca America) Denver; KRMA-TV (PBS) Denver; KUSA (NBC, WeatherNation) Denver; KWGN-TV (CW, This TV) Denver.
Programming (via satellite): Discovery Channel; Nickelodeon; Nickelodeon; Pop; QVC; TBS; TLC; Travel Channel; TV Land; USA Network; WGN America.
Fee: $29.95 installation; $34.50 monthly.
Expanded Basic Service 1
Subscribers: N.A.
Programming (via satellite): A&E; Animal Planet; Bravo; Cartoon Network; CMT; CNBC; CNN; Comedy Central; Disney Channel; DIY Network; ESPN; ESPN2; Food Network; Fox Sports 1; Freeform; History; HLN; MSNBC; MTV; NBCSN; Outdoor Channel; Root Sports Rocky Mountain; Spike TV; Syfy; The Weather Channel; TNT; Trinity Broadcasting Network (TBN); truTV; Turner Classic Movies; Univision Studios; WE tv.
Fee: $14.75 monthly.
Pay Service 1
Pay Units: 33.
Programming (via satellite): HBO (multiplexed).
Fee: $12.49 monthly.

2017 Edition D-111

Colorado—Cable Systems

Pay Service 2
Pay Units: 67.
Programming (via satellite): Cinemax (multiplexed).
Fee: $13.49 monthly.
Video-On-Demand: No
Pay-Per-View
Spice; Spice2.
Internet Service
Operational: Yes.
Fee: $35.00 installation; $39.95 monthly.
Telephone Service
None
Miles of Plant: 41.0 (coaxial); None (fiber optic). Homes passed: 814.
Chief Financial Officer: Amber Reineke.
Ownership: USA Companies LP (MSO).

BLANCA—Formerly served by Jade Communications. No longer in operation. ICA: CO0198.

BOULDER—Comcast Cable. Now served by DENVER, CO [CO0001]. ICA: CO0007.

BOULDER (portions)—Formerly served by Qwest Choice TV. No longer in operation. ICA: CO5002.

BRECKENRIDGE—Comcast Cable. Now served by LONGMONT, CO [CO0011]. ICA: CO0022.

BRIGHTON—Comcast Cable. Now served by DENVER, CO [CO0001]. ICA: CO0024.

BROOMFIELD—Comcast Cable. Now served by DENVER, CO [CO0001]. ICA: CO0014.

BUENA VISTA—Charter Communications, 12405 Powerscourt Dr, St. Louis, MO 63131. Phones: 636-207-5100 (Corporate office); 719-275-1656; 516-803-2300 (Corporate office); 866-213-6572; 877-273-7626 (Customer service). Web Site: http://www.charter.com. Also serves Chaffee County (central portion). ICA: CO0047.
TV Market Ranking: Outside TV Markets (BUENA VISTA, Chaffee County (central portion)). Franchise award date: N.A. Franchise expiration date: N.A. Began: October 1, 1973.
Channel capacity: N.A. Channels available but not in use: N.A.
Digital Basic Service
Subscribers: 641.
Programming (via satellite): A&E HD; Animal Planet HD; BBC America; Bloomberg Television; Bravo; CBS Sports Network; Cine Mexicano; Cinelatino; CMT; CNN en Espanol; Destination America; Discovery Channel HD; Discovery Life Channel; Disney XD; DMX Music; ESPN Classic; ESPN Deportes; ESPN HD; ESPNews; Food Network HD; FOX College Sports Central; FOX College Sports Pacific; Fox Deportes; Fox Sports 1; FXM; FYI; Golf Channel; GSN; HD Theater; HGTV HD; History en Espanol; History HD; History International; IFC; Investigation Discovery; ION Television; LMN; MTV Classic; MTV Hits; MTV Jams; MTV2; Nat Geo WILD; National Geographic Channel; National Geographic Channel HD; NBC Universo; NBCSN; NFL Network; Nick 2; Nick Jr.; Nicktoons; Outdoor Channel; OWN: Oprah Winfrey Network; RFD-TV; Science Channel; Sprout; Syfy HD; TeenNick; Tr3s; Trinity Broadcasting Network (TBN); Universal HD; UP; USA Network HD; VH1 Soul; ViendoMovies.
Fee: $22.99 monthly.

Digital Expanded Basic Service
Subscribers: N.A.
Programming (via satellite): A&E; Altitude Sports & Entertainment; AMC; Animal Planet; Cartoon Network; CMT; CNBC; CNN; Comedy Central; Discovery Channel; Disney Channel; E! HD; ESPN; ESPN2; EWTN Global Catholic Network; Food Network; Fox News Channel; Freeform; FX; Hallmark Channel; HGTV; History; HLN; IFC; MSNBC; MTV; Nickelodeon; Oxygen; Pop; QVC; Root Sports Rocky Mountain; Spike TV; Syfy; TBS; The Weather Channel; TLC; TNT; Travel Channel; truTV; Turner Classic Movies; TV Land; USA Network; VH1.
Fee: $35.00 monthly.
Digital Pay Service 1
Pay Units: N.A.
Programming (via satellite): Cinemax (multiplexed); Flix; HBO (multiplexed); HBO HD; Showtime (multiplexed); Starz (multiplexed); Starz Encore (multiplexed); Starz HD; The Movie Channel (multiplexed).
Video-On-Demand: No
Internet Service
Operational: Yes.
Broadband Service: Charter Internet.
Fee: $35.00 installation; $55.95 monthly.
Telephone Service
Digital: Operational
Fee: $49.99 monthly
Miles of Plant: 52.0 (coaxial); 9.0 (fiber optic). Homes passed: 2,314.
Accounting Director: David Sovanski. President & Chief Executive Officer: Tom Rutledge. General Manager: Jerry Parker. Technical Operations Manager: Doyle Ruona.
Ownership: Charter Communications Inc. (MSO).

BURLINGTON—Eagle Communications, 2703 Hall St, Ste 15, PO Box 817, Hays, KS 67601. Phones: 877-613-2453; 785-625-4000 (Corporate office). Fax: 785-625-8030. E-mail: support@eaglecom.net. Web Site: http://www.eaglecom.net. ICA: CO0057.
TV Market Ranking: Below 100 (BURLINGTON). Franchise award date: September 1, 1963. Franchise expiration date: N.A. Began: September 1, 1963.
Channel capacity: N.A. Channels available but not in use: N.A.
Basic Service
Subscribers: 327.
Programming (received off-air): KBSL-DT (CBS) Goodland; KLBY (ABC) Colby.
Programming (via microwave): KCNC-TV (CBS, Decades) Denver; KDVR (Antenna TV, FOX) Denver; KMGH-TV (ABC, Azteca America) Denver; KRMA-TV (PBS) Denver; KTVD (MeTV, MNT) Denver; KUSA (NBC, WeatherNation) Denver; KWGN-TV (CW, This TV) Denver.
Programming (via satellite): A&E; AMC; Animal Planet; Bravo; Cartoon Network; CMT; CNBC; CNN; Comedy Central; C-SPAN; Discovery Channel; Disney Channel; E! HD; ESPN; ESPN2; Food Network; Fox News Channel; Fox Sports 1; Freeform; FX; Hallmark Channel; HGTV; History; HLN; Lifetime; MSNBC; MTV; National Geographic Channel; Nickelodeon; QVC; Root Sports Rocky Mountain; Spike TV; Syfy; TBS; The Weather Channel; TLC; TNT; Travel Channel; truTV; Turner Classic Movies; TV Land; Univision Studios; USA Network; VH1; WGN America.
Fee: $24.95 installation; $61.95 monthly.
Digital Basic Service
Subscribers: N.A.
Programming (via satellite): BBC America; Bloomberg Television; CMT; Destination America; Discovery Kids Channel; Discovery Life Channel; Disney XD; ESPNews; Fuse; FXM; FYI; Golf Channel; GSN; History International; IFC; Investigation Discovery; LMN; MC; MTV Classic; MTV2; NBCSN; Nick Jr.; Nicktoons; Outdoor Channel; OWN: Oprah Winfrey Network; Science Channel; TeenNick; Trinity Broadcasting Network (TBN); WE tv.
Digital Pay Service 1
Pay Units: N.A.
Programming (via satellite): Cinemax (multiplexed); HBO (multiplexed); Showtime (multiplexed); Starz; Starz Encore (multiplexed); The Movie Channel (multiplexed).
Fee: $9.95 monthly (each).
Video-On-Demand: No
Pay-Per-View
iN DEMAND (delivered digitally); Club Jenna (delivered digitally); Playboy TV (delivered digitally); Fresh (delivered digitally).
Internet Service
Operational: No.
Telephone Service
None
Miles of Plant: 29.0 (coaxial); None (fiber optic). Homes passed: 1,769.
President & Chief Executive Officer: Gary Shorman. Chief Operating Officer: Kurt K. David. General Manager: Travis Kohlrus. Marketing Manager: Elizabeth Jaeger.
Ownership: Eagle Communications Inc. (MSO).

CALHAN—Formerly served by FairPoint Communications. No longer in operation. ICA: CO0140.

CANON CITY—Charter Communications, 12405 Powerscourt Dr, St. Louis, MO 63131. Phones: 636-207-5100 (Corporate office); 719-275-1656; 516-803-2300 (Corporate office); 866-213-6572; 877-273-7626 (Customer service). Web Site: http://www.charter.com. Also serves Brookside, Coal Creek, Florence, Fremont County, Penrose, Rockvale & Williamsburg. ICA: CO0016.
TV Market Ranking: Below 100 (Brookside, Coal Creek, Florence, Fremont County (portions), Penrose, Rockvale, Williamsburg); Outside TV Markets (CANON CITY, Fremont County (portions)). Franchise award date: July 1, 1978. Franchise expiration date: N.A. Began: October 1, 1978.
Channel capacity: 49 (operating 2-way). Channels available but not in use: N.A.
Digital Basic Service
Subscribers: 6,452.
Programming (via satellite): A&E HD; Animal Planet HD; AXS TV; BBC America; Bloomberg Television; Bravo; Bravo HD; CBS Sports Network; CMT; CNBC HD+; CNN HD; Cooking Channel; Destination America; Discovery Channel HD; Discovery Kids Channel; Discovery Life Channel; Disney Channel HD; Disney XD; DIY Network; DMX Music; ESPN Classic; ESPN HD; ESPN2 HD; ESPNews; Food Network HD; FOX College Sports Central; FOX College Sports Pacific; Fox Sports 1; Freeform HD; FSN HD; Fuse; FXM; FYI; Golf Channel; GSN; HD Theater; HGTV HD; History HD; History International; IFC; Investigation Discovery; ION Television; Jewelry Television; Lifetime Movie Network HD; LMN; MTV Classic; MTV Hits; MTV Jams; MTV Live; MTV2; Nat Geo WILD; National Geographic Channel; National Geographic Channel HD; NBCSN; NFL Network; NFL Network HD; Nick 2; Nick Jr.; Nicktoons; Outdoor Channel; Outdoor Channel 2 HD; OWN: Oprah Winfrey Network; Qubo; RFD-TV; Science Channel; Science HD; Sprout; Syfy HD; TBS HD; TeenNick; The Weather Channel HD; TLC HD; TNT HD; Tr3s; Trinity Broadcasting Network (TBN); Universal HD; UP; USA Network HD; Versus HD; VH1 Soul.
Fee: $26.99 monthly.
Digital Expanded Basic Service
Subscribers: N.A.
Programming (via satellite): A&E; Altitude Sports & Entertainment; AMC; Animal Planet; BYUtv; Cartoon Network; CMT; CNBC; CNN; Comedy Central; Discovery Channel; Disney Channel; E! HD; ESPN; ESPN2; EWTN Global Catholic Network; Food Network; Fox News Channel; Freeform; FX; Hallmark Channel; HGTV; History; HLN; ION Television; Lifetime; MSNBC; MTV; Nickelodeon; Oxygen; Root Sports Rocky Mountain; Spike TV; Syfy; The Weather Channel; TLC; TNT; Travel Channel; truTV; Turner Classic Movies; TV Land; UniMas; Univision Studios; USA Network; VH1.
Fee: $35.00 monthly.
Digital Pay Service 1
Pay Units: 4,000.
Programming (via satellite): Cinemax (multiplexed); Cinemax HD; Flix; HBO (multiplexed); HBO HD; Showtime (multiplexed); Showtime HD; Starz (multiplexed); Starz Encore (multiplexed); Starz HD; The Movie Channel (multiplexed); The Movie Channel HD.
Video-On-Demand: Yes
Pay-Per-View
Hot Choice (delivered digitally), Addressable: No; Fresh (delivered digitally).
Internet Service
Operational: Yes.
Subscribers: 7,515.
Broadband Service: Charter Internet.
Fee: $35.00 installation; $60.95 monthly.
Telephone Service
Digital: Operational
Subscribers: 5,541.
Fee: $49.95 monthly
Miles of Plant: 493.0 (coaxial); 203.0 (fiber optic). Homes passed: 16,906.
President & Chief Executive Officer: Tom Rutledge. General Manager: Jerry Parker. Technical Operations Manager: Doyle Ruona. Accounting Director: David Sovanski.
Ownership: Charter Communications Inc. (MSO).

CANTERBURY PARK—Formerly served by Island Cable. No longer in operation. ICA: CO0160.

CARBONDALE—Comcast Cable, 1605 Grand Ave, Ste 1, Glenwood Springs, CO 81601. Phones: 970-230-9076; 970-928-7784. Fax: 970-945-0270. Web Site: http://www.comcast.com. Also serves Garfield County (portions). ICA: CO0064.
TV Market Ranking: Below 100 (Garfield County (portions), CARBONDALE).
Channel capacity: N.A. Channels available but not in use: N.A.
Basic Service
Subscribers: 1,286.
Fee: $50.00 installation; $30.45 monthly.
Ownership: Comcast Cable Communications Inc. (MSO).

CASTLE ROCK—Comcast Cable. Now served by DENVER, CO [CO0001]. ICA: CO0200.

Cable Systems—Colorado

CENTER—Formerly served by Center Municipal Cable System. No longer in operation. ICA: CO0102.

CENTER—USA Communications, 920 East 56th St, Ste B, Kearney, NE 68847. Phone: 877-234-0102. E-mail: csr@usacommunications.tv. Web Site: http://usacommunications.tv. ICA: CO0216.
TV Market Ranking: Outside TV Markets (CENTER).
Channel capacity: N.A. Channels available but not in use: N.A.
Basic Service
Subscribers: 14.
Fee: $19.50 monthly.
Chief Financial Officer: Amber Reineke.
Ownership: USA Companies LP (MSO).

CENTRAL CITY—USA Communications, 920 E 56th ST, Ste B, Kearney, NE 68847. Phone: 877-234-0102. Web Site: http://www.usacommunications.tv. ICA: CO0215.
TV Market Ranking: 32 (CENTRAL CITY).
Channel capacity: N.A. Channels available but not in use: N.A.
Basic Service
Subscribers: 142.
Fee: $29.95 installation; $34.50 monthly.
Vice President, Operations: Richard Miller.
Ownership: USA Communications (MSO).

CHEYENNE WELLS—Formerly served by NexHorizon Communications. No longer in operation. ICA: CO0104.

COLLBRAN (town)—Formerly served by KiRock Communications. No longer in operation. ICA: CO0147.

COLORADO CITY—Formerly served by Bresnan Communications. No longer in operation. ICA: CO0094.

COLORADO SPRINGS—Comcast Cable, 213 North Union Blvd, Colorado Springs, CO 80909. Phone: 719-457-4501. Fax: 719-457-4503. Web Site: http://www.comcast.com. Also serves Black Forest, Cascade, Chipita Park, El Paso County (portions), Falcon, Fountain, Green Mountain Falls, Manitou Springs, Monument, Palmer Lake, Pueblo, Pueblo County (portions) & Pueblo West. ICA: CO0003.
TV Market Ranking: 32 (Black Forest, Cascade, Chipita Park, El Paso County (portions) (portions), Falcon, Green Mountain Falls, Manitou Springs, Monument, Palmer Lake); Below 100 (COLORADO SPRINGS, Fountain, Pueblo County (portions), Pueblo, El Paso County (portions) (portions)). Franchise award date: N.A. Franchise expiration date: N.A. Began: June 23, 1969.
Channel capacity: 27 (operating 2-way). Channels available but not in use: N.A.
Basic Service
Subscribers: 113,704.
Programming (received off-air): KGHB-CD (UNV) Pueblo, etc.; KKTV (CBS, MNT) Colorado Springs; KOAA-TV (Grit, NBC) Pueblo; KRDO-TV (ABC, TMO) Colorado Springs; KRMZ (PBS) Steamboat Springs; KTSC (PBS) Pueblo; KUSA (NBC, WeatherNation) Denver; KWGN-TV (CW, This TV) Denver; KWHS-LD (COZI TV, IND) Colorado Springs; KXRM-TV (FOX, MundoMax) Colorado Springs; KXTU-LD (CW) Colorado Springs; 24 FMs.
Programming (via microwave): KBDI-TV (PBS) Broomfield; KCNC-TV (CBS, Decades) Denver.
Programming (via satellite): QVC.
Fee: $50.00 installation; $33.60 monthly.
Expanded Basic Service 1
Subscribers: N.A.
Programming (via satellite): A&E; AMC; Animal Planet; BET; Bravo; Cartoon Network; CMT; CNBC; CNN; Comedy Central; C-SPAN; C-SPAN 2; Discovery Channel; Disney Channel; E! HD; ESPN; ESPN2; EVINE Live; EWTN Global Catholic Network; Food Network; Fox Deportes; Fox News Channel; Fox Sports 1; Freeform; FX; Golf Channel; Hallmark Channel; HGTV; History; HLN; INSP; ION Television; Lifetime; MSNBC; MTV; NBCSN; Nickelodeon; Oxygen; Pop; Root Sports Rocky Mountain; Spike TV; Syfy; TBS; The Weather Channel; TLC; TNT; Travel Channel; Turner Classic Movies; TV Land; USA Network; VH1; WE tv; WGN America.
Fee: $27.94 monthly.
Digital Basic Service
Subscribers: N.A.
Programming (via satellite): BBC America; Bloomberg Television; Discovery Life Channel; Disney XD; DIY Network; ESPN Classic; ESPNews; FamilyNet; Fuse; FXM; FYI; Great American Country; GSN; History International; IFC; MC; National Geographic Channel; Nick 2; Nick Jr.; Nicktoons; Outdoor Channel; TeenNick; Trinity Broadcasting Network (TBN).
Digital Expanded Basic Service
Subscribers: N.A.
Programming (via satellite): FOX College Sports Central; FOX College Sports Pacific; HITS (Headend In The Sky); Sundance TV.
Fee: $4.95 monthly.
Digital Pay Service 1
Pay Units: N.A.
Programming (via satellite): ART America; Cinemax (multiplexed); Flix; HBO (multiplexed); HITS (Headend In The Sky); International Television (ITV); RAI Italia; RTN; Showtime (multiplexed); Starz (multiplexed); Starz Encore (multiplexed); The Filipino Channel; The Movie Channel (multiplexed); TV Asia; TV5MONDE USA; Zee TV.
Fee: $18.99 monthly (each).
Video-On-Demand: Planned
Pay-Per-View
Shorteez (delivered digitally); Fresh (delivered digitally); Playboy TV (delivered digitally); Hot Choice (delivered digitally); HITS PPV (delivered digitally).
Internet Service
Operational: Yes.
Subscribers: 122,256.
Broadband Service: Comcast High Speed Internet.
Fee: $42.95 monthly; $6.95 modem lease; $264.99 modem purchase.
Telephone Service
Digital: Operational
Subscribers: 57,444.
Miles of Plant: 6,622.0 (coaxial); 927.0 (fiber optic). Homes passed: 338,237. Homes passed includes Trinidad.
Vice President & General Manager: Jim Commers. Vice President, Marketing: Zach Street. Technical Operations Director: Jim Garcia. Public Relations Manager: Sandra Mann.
Ownership: Comcast Cable Communications Inc. (MSO).

COLORADO SPRINGS—Formerly served by Sprint Corp. No longer in operation. ICA: CO0192.

CONIFER—Formerly served by Baja Broadband. No longer in operation. ICA: CO0163.

COPPER MOUNTAIN—Copper Mountain Consolidated Metropolitan District, 477 Copper Rd, PO Box 3002, Copper Mountain, CO 80443. Phone: 970-968-2537. Fax: 970-968-2932. Web Site: http://www.coppermtnmetro.org. ICA: CO0083.
TV Market Ranking: Outside TV Markets (COPPER MOUNTAIN). Franchise award date: January 1, 1976. Franchise expiration date: N.A. Began: December 31, 1976.
Channel capacity: N.A. Channels available but not in use: N.A.
Basic Service
Subscribers: 1,451.
Programming (via microwave): KCNC-TV (CBS, Decades) Denver; KDVR (Antenna TV, FOX) Denver; KMGH-TV (ABC, Azteca America) Denver; KRMA-TV (PBS) Denver; KTVD (MeTV, MNT) Denver.
Programming (via satellite): A&E; Altitude Sports & Entertainment; AMC; Animal Planet; Bravo; CMT; CNBC; CNN; Comedy Central; C-SPAN; C-SPAN 2; Discovery Channel; Disney Channel; Disney XD; ESPN; ESPN2; Food Network; Fox News Channel; Fox Sports 1; Freeform; Golf Channel; HGTV; History; HLN; IFC; KUSA (NBC, WeatherNation) Denver; KWGN-TV (CW, This TV) Denver; Lifetime; MSNBC; MTV; National Geographic Channel; NBCSN; Nickelodeon; Pop; Spike TV; TBS; The Weather Channel; TLC; TNT; Turner Classic Movies; TV Land; USA Network; VH1; WGN America.
Fee: $30.00 installation; $45.00 monthly.
Digital Basic Service
Subscribers: N.A.
Programming (via satellite): Bravo; DMX Music; ESPN Classic; Flix; Fuse; FYI; HGTV; History; History International; LMN; MTV2; Starz Encore (multiplexed); TeenNick.
Pay Service 1
Pay Units: N.A.
Programming (via satellite): HBO.
Digital Pay Service 1
Pay Units: N.A.
Programming (via satellite): Cinemax (multiplexed); HBO (multiplexed); Showtime (multiplexed); Starz (multiplexed); The Movie Channel (multiplexed).
Fee: $7.00 monthly (Starz), $8.00 monthly (Cinemax), $10.00 monthly (HBO), $12.50 monthly (Showtime/TMC).
Pay-Per-View
Hot Choice; iN DEMAND; movies; special events.
Internet Service
Operational: Yes.
Subscribers: 1,512.
Fee: $25.00 installation; $24.00 monthly.
Telephone Service
None
Miles of Plant: 4,828.0 (coaxial); None (fiber optic). Homes passed: 1,917.
General Manager: David Erickson. Chief Technician: David Arnesen.
Ownership: Copper Mountain Consolidated Metropolitan District.

CORTEZ—Baja Broadband, 525 Junction Rd, Madison, WI 53717. Phones: 877-422-5282; 970-565-4031. E-mail: customersupportco@bajabb.tv. Web Site: http://www.bajabroadband.com. Also serves Towaoc. ICA: CO0044.
TV Market Ranking: Outside TV Markets (CORTEZ, Towaoc). Franchise award date: N.A. Franchise expiration date: N.A. Began: September 1, 1981.
Channel capacity: N.A. Channels available but not in use: N.A.
Basic Service
Subscribers: 486.
Programming (via satellite): C-SPAN; INSP; QVC; WGN America.
Programming (via translator): KASA-TV (COZI TV, FOX) Santa Fe; KGBY (ABC, TMO) Grand Junction; KLUZ-TV (LATV, UNV) Albuquerque; KOAT-TV (ABC, Estrella TV) Albuquerque; KOBF (NBC, This TV) Farmington; KREZ-TV (CBS, The Country Network) Durango; KRMJ (PBS) Grand Junction; KRPV-DT (GLC) Roswell; KTEL-CD (TMO) Albuquerque; KTVD (MeTV, MNT) Denver; KUSA (NBC, WeatherNation) Denver; KWGN-TV (CW, This TV) Denver.
Fee: $29.95-$49.95 installation; $37.20 monthly.
Digital Basic Service
Subscribers: N.A.
Programming (via satellite): A&E; AMC; BBC America; Bloomberg Television; CMT; CNN; Destination America; Discovery Channel; Discovery Kids Channel; Discovery Life Channel; Disney Channel; Disney XD; ESPN; Fox Business Network; Freeform; Fuse; FXM; FYI; History International; HLN; IFC; Investigation Discovery; Lifetime; MC; MTV; MTV Classic; MTV Hits; MTV2; Nat Geo WILD; Nick Jr.; Nickelodeon; OWN: Oprah Winfrey Network; Science Channel; TBS; TeenNick; TNT; Trinity Broadcasting Network (TBN); Turner Classic Movies; USA Network; VH1; VH1 Soul.
Digital Expanded Basic Service
Subscribers: N.A.
Programming (via satellite): A&E HD; ESPN HD; Food Network HD; FSN HD; FX HD; HGTV HD; History HD; National Geographic Channel HD; TBS HD; TNT HD.
Digital Expanded Basic Service 2
Subscribers: N.A.
Programming (via satellite): AXS TV; Universal HD.
Digital Pay Service 1
Pay Units: N.A.
Programming (via satellite): Cinemax (multiplexed); Cinemax HD; Flix; HBO (multiplexed); HBO HD; Showtime (multiplexed); Showtime HD; Starz (multiplexed); Starz Encore (multiplexed); Starz HD; The Movie Channel (multiplexed); The Movie Channel HD.
Fee: $9.00 monthly (each).
Video-On-Demand: No
Pay-Per-View
iN DEMAND (delivered digitally); Juicy (delivered digitally); XTSY (delivered digitally); Sports PPV (delivered digitally); Hot Choice (delivered digitally); VaVoom (delivered digitally); Playboy TV (delivered digitally); Fresh (delivered digitally); Spice: Xcess (delivered digitally); SexSee (delivered digitally).
Internet Service
Operational: Yes. Began: May 1, 2002.
Broadband Service: In-house.
Fee: $49.99 installation; $52.99 monthly; $4.96 modem lease; $69.95 modem purchase.
Telephone Service
Analog: Operational
Miles of Plant: 48.0 (coaxial); None (fiber optic). Homes passed: 2,770.
Area Vice President & General Manager: Tom Jaskiewicz. Vice President, Corporate Finance: Carl Shapiro. Technical Operations Director: Matt Warford.
Ownership: TDS Telecom (MSO).

CRAIG—Charter Communications, 12405 Powerscourt Dr, St. Louis, MO 63131. Phones: 636-207-5100 (Corporate office);

Colorado—Cable Systems

970-824-9221; 877-273-7626; 970-824-3298. Web Site: http://www.charter.com. Also serves Hayden & Moffat County. ICA: CO0039.

TV Market Ranking: Below 100 (Hayden, Moffat County (portions)); Outside TV Markets (CRAIG, Moffat County (portions)). Franchise award date: N.A. Franchise expiration date: N.A. Began: June 1, 1980.

Channel capacity: N.A. Channels available but not in use: N.A.

Digital Basic Service
Subscribers: 1,744.
Programming (via satellite): A&E HD; Animal Planet HD; AXS TV; Bandamax; BBC America; Bloomberg Television; Bravo; CBS Sports Network; Cine Mexicano; Cinelatino; CMT; CNN en Espanol; CNN HD; Cooking Channel; De Pelicula; De Pelicula Clasico; Destination America; Discovery Kids Channel; Discovery Life Channel; Disney XD; DIY Network; DMX Music; ESPN Classic; ESPN Deportes; ESPN HD; ESPN2 HD; ESPNews; Food Network HD; FOX College Sports Central; FOX College Sports Pacific; Fox Deportes; Fox Sports 1; Fuse; FXM; FYI; Golf Channel; GolTV; GSN; HD Theater; HGTV HD; History en Espanol; History HD; History International; IFC; Investigation Discovery; Jewelry Television; Lifetime Movie Network HD; LMN; MTV Classic; MTV Hits; MTV Jams; MTV2; Nat Geo WILD; National Geographic Channel; National Geographic Channel HD; NBC Universo; NBCSN; NFL Network; NFL Network HD; Nick 2; Nick Jr.; Nicktoons; Outdoor Channel; OWN: Oprah Winfrey Network; RFD-TV; Science Channel; Science HD; Sprout; Syfy HD; TBS HD; TeenNick; Telehit; The Weather Channel HD; TLC HD; TNT HD; Tr3s; Trinity Broadcasting Network (TBN); UniMas; Universal HD; Univision; Univision Studios; UP; USA Network HD; Versus HD; VH1 Soul; ViendoMovies.
Fee: $26.99 monthly.

Digital Expanded Basic Service
Subscribers: N.A.
Programming (via satellite): A&E; Altitude Sports & Entertainment; AMC; Animal Planet; Cartoon Network; CMT; CNBC; CNN; Comedy Central; Disney Channel; E! HD; ESPN; ESPN2; EWTN Global Catholic Network; Food Network; Fox News Channel; Freeform; FX; Great American Country; Hallmark Channel; HGTV; History; HLN; MSNBC; MTV; Nickelodeon; Oxygen; Pop; Root Sports Rocky Mountain; Spike TV; Syfy; The Weather Channel; TLC; TNT; Travel Channel; truTV; Turner Classic Movies; TV Land; UniMas; Univision; Univision Studios; USA Network; VH1.
Fee: $35.00 monthly.

Digital Pay Service 1
Pay Units: N.A.
Programming (via satellite): Cinemax (multiplexed); Cinemax HD; Flix; HBO (multiplexed); HBO HD; Showtime (multiplexed); Showtime HD; Starz (multiplexed); Starz Encore (multiplexed); Starz HD; The Movie Channel (multiplexed); The Movie Channel HD.

Video-On-Demand: No

Pay-Per-View
ESPN (delivered digitally); iN DEMAND (delivered digitally).

Internet Service
Operational: Yes.
Broadband Service: Charter Internet.
Fee: $35.00 installation; $55.95 monthly.

Telephone Service
Digital: Operational
Fee: $49.99 monthly
Miles of Plant: 58.0 (coaxial); None (fiber optic). Homes passed: 5,000.

President & Chief Executive Officer: Tom Rutledge. Regional General Manager: Tommy Cotton. Accounting Director: David Sovanski.
Ownership: Charter Communications Inc. (MSO).

CREEDE—Formerly served by Cable USA. No longer in operation. ICA: CO0126.

CRESTED BUTTE—Time Warner Cable, 7800 Crescent Executive Dr, Charlotte, NC 28217. Phone: 970-641-6412. Web Site: http://www.timewarnercable.com. Also serves Gunnison, Gunnison County & Mount Crested Butte. ICA: CO0036.

TV Market Ranking: Outside TV Markets (Gunnison County, Mount Crested Butte, CRESTED BUTTE, Gunnison). Franchise award date: N.A. Franchise expiration date: N.A. Began: March 1, 1984.

Channel capacity: N.A. Channels available but not in use: N.A.

Basic Service
Subscribers: 1,209.
Programming (via microwave): KCNC-TV (CBS, Decades) Denver; KDVR (Antenna TV, FOX) Denver; KMGH-TV (ABC, Azteca America) Denver; KRMA-TV (PBS) Denver; KTVD (MeTV, MNT) Denver; KUSA (NBC, WeatherNation) Denver; KWGN-TV (CW, This TV) Denver.
Programming (via satellite): C-SPAN; C-SPAN 2; ESPNews; EVINE Live; Pop; QVC; TV Land; Univision; WGN America.
Fee: $49.99 installation; $32.00 monthly.

Expanded Basic Service 1
Subscribers: N.A.
Programming (via satellite): A&E; AMC; Animal Planet; Cartoon Network; CMT; CNBC; CNN; Comedy Central; Discovery Channel; Disney Channel; E! HD; ESPN; ESPN2; Food Network; Fox News Channel; Fox Sports 1; Freeform; FX; Hallmark Channel; HGTV; History; HLN; ION Television; Lifetime; MSNBC; MTV; NBCSN; Nickelodeon; Oxygen; Root Sports Rocky Mountain; Spike TV; Syfy; TBS; The Weather Channel; TLC; TNT; Travel Channel; truTV; USA Network; VH1.
Fee: $29.75 monthly.

Digital Basic Service
Subscribers: N.A.
Programming (via satellite): BBC America; Bloomberg Television; Discovery Life Channel; ESPN Classic; ESPNews; FXM; Golf Channel; GSN; INSP; MC; MTV Classic; National Geographic Channel; NBCSN; Nick Jr.; Nicktoons; Outdoor Channel; Trinity Broadcasting Network (TBN); Turner Classic Movies; VH1 Country; WE tv.

Digital Pay Service 1
Pay Units: N.A.
Programming (via satellite): Cinemax (multiplexed); HBO (multiplexed); Showtime (multiplexed); Starz (multiplexed); Starz Encore (multiplexed); The Movie Channel (multiplexed).
Fee: $14.99 monthly (each).

Video-On-Demand: No

Pay-Per-View
Fresh (delivered digitally); Hot Choice (delivered digitally); Playboy TV (delivered digitally); HITS PPV (delivered digitally).

Internet Service
Operational: Yes.
Broadband Service: Road Runner.
Fee: $69.95 installation; $44.95 monthly.

Telephone Service
Digital: Operational
Fee: $44.95 monthly

Miles of Plant: 80.0 (coaxial); None (fiber optic). Homes passed: 4,000.
Senior Accounting Director: Karen Goodfellow. General Manager: Ernie Young.
Ownership: Time Warner Cable (MSO).

CRIPPLE CREEK—Formerly served by Baja Broadband. No longer in operation. ICA: CO0165.

CUCHARA VALLEY—Formerly served by Westcom II LLC. No longer in operation. ICA: CO0130.

DEER TRAIL—Formerly served by Champion Broadband. No longer in operation. ICA: CO0139.

DEL NORTE—Formerly served by Bresnan Communications. No longer in operation. ICA: CO0089.

DELTA—Charter Communications. Now served by MONTROSE, CO [CO0028]. ICA: CO0042.

DENVER—Comcast Cable, 8000 East Iliff Ave, Denver, CO 80231. Phones: 303-532-5886; 303-603-2000. Fax: 303-603-2600. Web Site: http://www.comcast.com. Also serves Adams County (portions), Arapahoe County (portions), Arvada, Aurora, Bennett, Boulder, Boulder County (portions), Bow Mar, Brighton, Broomfield, Byers, Castle Pines, Castle Rock, Centennial, Cherry Hills Village, Clear Creek County (portions), Columbine Valley, Commerce City, Douglas County (portions), Dumont, Edgewater, Elbert County (portions), Elizabeth, Empire, Englewood, Evergreen, Federal Heights, Foxfield, Franktown, Genesee, Georgetown, Glendale, Golden, Greenwood Village, Highlands Ranch, Holly Hills, Idaho Springs, Idledale, Indian Hills, Jefferson County (portions), Kiowa, Kittredge, Lakewood, Larkspur, Littleton, Lochbuie, Lone Tree, Louviers, Morrison, Mountain View, Northglenn, Parker, Perry Park, Roxborough, Roxborough Park, Sedalia, Sheridan, Silver Plume, Strasburg, The Pinery, Thornton, Westminster & Wheat Ridge. ICA: CO0001.

TV Market Ranking: 32 (Adams County (portions), Arapahoe County (portions), Arvada, Aurora, Bennett, Boulder, Boulder County (portions), Bow Mar, Brighton, Broomfield, Byers, Castle Pines, Castle Rock, Centennial, Cherry Hills Village, Clear Creek County (portions) (portions), Columbine Valley, Commerce City, DENVER, Douglas County (portions), Edgewater, Elbert County (portions), Elizabeth, Englewood, Evergreen, Federal Heights, Foxfield, Franktown, Glendale, Golden, Greenwood Village, Highlands Ranch, Highlands Ranch, Holly Hills, Idaho Springs, Idledale, Indian Hills, Jefferson County (portions), Kiowa, Kittredge, Lakewood, Larkspur, Littleton, Littleton, Lochbuie, Lone Tree, Louviers, Morrison, Mountain View, Northglenn, Parker, Perry Park, Roxborough, Roxborough Park, Sedalia, Sheridan, Strasburg, The Pinery, Thornton, Westminster, Wheat Ridge); Below 100 (Dumont, Empire, Georgetown, Silver Plume); Outside TV Markets (Clear Creek County (portions) (portions)).

Channel capacity: 28 (operating 2-way). Channels available but not in use: N.A.

Basic Service
Subscribers: 487,024.
Programming (received off-air): KBDI-TV (PBS) Broomfield; KCEC (Bounce TV, LATV,

UNV) Denver; KCNC-TV (CBS, Decades) Denver; KDEN-TV (TMO) Longmont; KDVR (Antenna TV, FOX) Denver; KETD (Estrella TV) Castle Rock; KMGH-TV (ABC, Azteca America) Denver; KRMA-TV (PBS) Denver; KRMT (Daystar TV, ETV) Denver; KTFD-DT (getTV, UniMas) Boulder; KTVD (MeTV, MNT) Denver; KUSA (NBC, WeatherNation) Denver; KWGN-TV (CW, This TV) Denver.
Programming (via satellite): Azteca; Bravo; C-SPAN; Discovery Channel; Discovery Life Channel; Hallmark Channel; ION Television; QVC; TBS; WGN America.
Fee: $42.00-$50.00 installation; $29.66 monthly.

Expanded Basic Service 1
Subscribers: N.A.
Programming (via satellite): A&E; Altitude Sports & Entertainment; AMC; Animal Planet; BET; Cartoon Network; CNBC; CNN; Comedy Central; Disney Channel; Disney XD; E! HD; ESPN; ESPN2; Food Network; Fox News Channel; Fox Sports 1; Freeform; FX; Golf Channel; HGTV; History; HLN; Lifetime; MSNBC; MTV; NBCSN; Nickelodeon; Oxygen; Root Sports Rocky Mountain; Spike TV; Syfy; The Weather Channel; TLC; TNT; Travel Channel; truTV; Turner Classic Movies; TV Land; Univision; USA Network; VH1.
Fee: $34.50 monthly.

Digital Basic Service
Subscribers: N.A.
Programming (via satellite): BBC America; Bloomberg Television; Bravo; BYUtv; CBS Sports Network; CMT; Cooking Channel; Discovery Digital Networks; DIY Network; ESPN Classic; ESPN HD; ESPN2 HD; ESPNews; EVINE Live; EWTN Global Catholic Network; Flix; FOX College Sports Central; FOX College Sports Pacific; Fuse; FXM; FYI; Great American Country; GSN; HD Theater; History International; HITS (Headend In The Sky); IFC; LMN; LOGO; MoviePlex; MTV Live; Nat Geo WILD; National Geographic Channel; NBA TV; NFL Network; Nick 2; Nick Jr.; Nicktoons; Outdoor Channel; Sprout; Starz Encore (multiplexed); Sundance TV; TeenNick; The Word Network; TNT HD; Trinity Broadcasting Network (TBN); TV One; Universal HD; Versus HD; WE tv; Weatherscan.

Digital Pay Service 1
Pay Units: N.A.
Programming (via satellite): Cinemax (multiplexed); Cinemax HD; Flix; HBO (multiplexed); HBO HD; Showtime (multiplexed); Showtime HD; Starz (multiplexed); Starz HD; The Movie Channel (multiplexed).
Fee: $18.99 monthly (each).

Pay-Per-View
iN DEMAND (delivered digitally); Sports PPV (delivered digitally); NBA League Pass (delivered digitally); NHL Center Ice (delivered digitally); MLB Extra Innings (delivered digitally); Playboy TV (delivered digitally); Hot Choice (delivered digitally).

Internet Service
Operational: Yes.
Subscribers: 536,278.
Broadband Service: Comcast High Speed Internet.
Fee: $42.95 monthly.

Telephone Service
Digital: Operational
Subscribers: 279,888.
Fee: $44.95 monthly

Miles of Plant: 22,296.0 (coaxial); 2,402.0 (fiber optic). Homes passed: 1,232,943.
Senior Vice President: Scott Binder. Vice President, Sales & Marketing: William Mosher. General Manager (northern portion): Rich Jennings. General Manager (southern por-

Cable Systems—Colorado

tion): Dan Buchanan. Technical Operations Director: Dale Kirk. Network Operations Director: David Krook. Marketing Manager: Carolyn O'Hearn. Public Relations Director: Cindy Parsons.
Ownership: Comcast Cable Communications Inc. (MSO).

DENVER—Comcast Cable. Now served by DENVER, CO [CO0001]. ICA: CO0002.

DENVER—Formerly served by Sprint Corp. No longer in operation. ICA: CO0195.

DILLON—Comcast Cable. Now served by LONGMONT, CO [CO0011]. ICA: CO0015.

DOLORES—Charter Communications. Now served by DURANGO, CO [CO0023]. ICA: CO0106.

DOVE CREEK—Formerly served by Bresnan Communications. No longer in operation. ICA: CO0118.

DURANGO—Charter Communications, 12405 Powerscourt Dr, St. Louis, MO 63131. Phones: 636-207-5100 (Corporate office); 516-803-2300; 877-273-7626. Web Site: http://www.charter.com. Also serves Dolores, Hermosa, La Plata County & Mancos. ICA: CO0023.
TV Market Ranking: Below 100 (DURANGO, Hermosa, La Plata County, Mancos); Outside TV Markets (Dolores). Franchise award date: N.A. Franchise expiration date: N.A. Began: December 1, 1954.
Channel capacity: N.A. Channels available but not in use: N.A.
Digital Basic Service
Subscribers: 4,524.
Programming (via satellite): A&E HD; Animal Planet HD; AXS TV; Bandamax; BBC America; Bloomberg Television; Bravo; BYUtv; CBS Sports Network; Cine Mexicano; Cinelatino; CMT; CNN en Espanol; Cooking Channel; De Pelicula; De Pelicula Clasico; Destination America; Discovery Channel HD; Discovery Kids Channel; Discovery Life Channel; Disney XD; DIY Network; DMX Music; ESPN Classic; ESPN Deportes; ESPN HD; ESPN2 HD; ESPNews; Food Network HD; FOX College Sports Central; FOX College Sports Pacific; Fox Deportes; Fox Sports 1; FSN HD; Fuse; FXM; FYI; Golf Channel; GolTV; Great American Country; GSN; HD Theater; HGTV HD; History en Espanol; History HD; History International; IFC; Investigation Discovery; ION Television; Jewelry Television; Lifetime Movie Network HD; LMN; MTV Classic; MTV Hits; MTV Jams; MTV2; Nat Geo WILD; National Geographic Channel; National Geographic Channel HD; NBC Universo; NBCSN; NFL Network; NFL Network HD; NHL Network; Nick 2; Nick Jr.; Nicktoons; Outdoor Channel; OWN: Oprah Winfrey Network; Qubo; RFD-TV; Science Channel; Science HD; Sprout; Syfy HD; TBS HD; TeenNick; Telehit; TLC HD; TNT HD; Tr3s; Trinity Broadcasting Network (TBN); Universal HD; UP; USA Network HD; Versus HD; VH1 Soul; ViendoMovies.
Fee: $26.99 monthly.
Digital Expanded Basic Service
Subscribers: N.A.
Programming (via satellite): A&E; AMC; Animal Planet; Cartoon Network; CMT; CNBC; CNN; Comedy Central; Disney Channel; E! HD; ESPN; ESPN2; Food Network; Fox News Channel; Freeform; FX; Hallmark Channel; HGTV; History; HLN; INSP; ION Television; Lifetime; MSNBC; MTV; Nickelodeon; Oxygen; Pop; Root Sports Rocky Mountain; Spike TV; Syfy; The Weather Channel; TLC; TNT; Travel Channel; truTV; Turner Classic Movies; TV Land; USA Network; VH1.
Fee: $56.99 monthly.
Digital Pay Service 1
Pay Units: N.A.
Programming (via satellite): Cinemax (multiplexed); Cinemax On Demand; Flix; HBO (multiplexed); HBO HD; HBO on Demand; Showtime (multiplexed); Showtime HD; Showtime On Demand; Starz (multiplexed); Starz Encore (multiplexed); Starz HD; Starz On Demand; The Movie Channel (multiplexed); The Movie Channel HD.
Video-On-Demand: Yes
Pay-Per-View
iN DEMAND (delivered digitally); ESPN (delivered digitally); NBA League Pass (delivered digitally); MLS Direct Kick (delivered digitally); MLB Extra Innings (delivered digitally); NHL Center Ice (delivered digitally).
Internet Service
Operational: Yes.
Broadband Service: Charter Internet.
Fee: $39.95 monthly; $3.00 modem lease.
Telephone Service
Digital: Operational
Fee: $49.99 monthly
Miles of Plant: 57.0 (coaxial); None (fiber optic). Homes passed: 11,110.
President & Chief Executive Officer: Tom Rutledge. Regional Vice President: Sean Hogue. Technical Operations Manager: Gary Young. Accounting Director: David Sovanski.
Ownership: Charter Communications Inc. (MSO).

DURANGO WEST—Charter Communications, 12405 Powerscourt Dr, St. Louis, MO 63131. Phones: 636-207-5100 (Corporate office); 516-803-2300 (Corporate office); 877-273-7626. Web Site: http://www.charter.com. ICA: CO0125.
TV Market Ranking: Below 100 (DURANGO WEST). Franchise award date: N.A. Franchise expiration date: N.A. Began: January 1, 1983.
Channel capacity: N.A. Channels available but not in use: N.A.
Digital Basic Service
Subscribers: 33.
Programming (received off-air): KOBF (NBC, This TV) Farmington; KREZ-TV (CBS, The Country Network) Durango.
Programming (via microwave): KASA-TV (COZI TV, FOX) Santa Fe; KCNC-TV (CBS, Decades) Denver; KMGH-TV (ABC, Azteca America) Denver; KRMA-TV (PBS) Denver; KUSA (NBC, WeatherNation) Denver; KWGN-TV (CW, This TV) Denver.
Programming (via satellite): A&E; Altitude Sports & Entertainment; Animal Planet; Cartoon Network; CNN; Comedy Central; C-SPAN; Discovery Channel; Disney Channel; ESPN; Food Network; Fox News Channel; Freeform; FX; HGTV; History; HLN; Lifetime; Nickelodeon; QVC; Root Sports Rocky Mountain; Spike TV; TBS; The Weather Channel; TLC; TNT; USA Network; VH1.
Fee: $34.95 installation; $55.99 monthly.
Pay Service 1
Pay Units: N.A.
Programming (via satellite): Cinemax; HBO; Starz.
Fee: $10.00 installation; $12.00 monthly (each).
Video-On-Demand: No

Internet Service
Operational: Yes.
Broadband Service: Charter Internet.
Fee: $39.95 monthly.
Telephone Service
Digital: Operational
Fee: $49.99 monthly
Miles of Plant: 7.0 (coaxial); None (fiber optic). Homes passed: 586.
President & Chief Executive Officer: Tom Rutledge. Regional Vice President: Sean Hogue. Technical Operations Manager: Gary Young. Accounting Director: David Sovanski.
Ownership: Charter Communications Inc. (MSO).

EADS—Formerly served by NexHorizon Communications. No longer in operation. ICA: CO0114.

EAGLE—CenturyLink. This cable system has converted to IPTV. See EAGLE CITY, CO [CO5010]. ICA: CO0096.

EAGLE CITY—CenturyLink Prism (formerly Qwest), 308 E Pikes Peak Ave, Colorado Springs, CO 80903. Phones: 800-475-7526; 719-636-4576. E-mail: prismtveverywhere@centurylink. net. Web Site: http://www.centurylink.com/prismtv. Also serves Eagle County (portions), Edwards & Gypsum. ICA: CO5010.
TV Market Ranking: Outside TV Markets (Eagle County (portions), Edwards).
Channel capacity: N.A. Channels available but not in use: N.A.
Prism Essential
Subscribers: 763.
Fee: $34.99 monthly. Includes 140+ channels including music channels.
Prism Complete
Subscribers: N.A.
Fee: $39.99 monthly. Includes 190+ channels including music channels.
Prism Preferred
Subscribers: N.A.
Fee: $49.99 monthly. Includes 290+ channels including Showtime/TMC & Starz/Encore.
Prism Premium
Subscribers: N.A.
Fee: $79.99 monthly. Includes 320+ channels including all premium movie channels.
Prism Paquette Latino
Subscribers: N.A.
Fee: $8.49 monthly.
Cinemax
Subscribers: N.A.
Fee: $12.99 monthly.
HBO
Subscribers: N.A.
Fee: $12.99 monthly.
Showtime/TMC
Subscribers: N.A.
Fee: $14.99 monthly.
Starz/Encore
Subscribers: N.A.
Fee: $12.99 monthly.
Video-On-Demand: Yes
Internet Service
Operational: Yes.
Fee: $29.95 monthly.
Telephone Service
Digital: Operational
Vice President, Operations: Penny Larson.
Ownership: CenturyLink.

EATON—Baja Broadband. Now served by FORT COLLINS, CO [CO0073]. ICA: CO0055.

EL PASO COUNTY (eastern portions)—Falcon PTC. Formerly Falcon, CO [CO0213]. This cable system has converted to IPTV, 707 Hathaway Dr, Colorado Springs, CO 80915. Phone: 719-573-5343. Fax: 719-886-7925. E-mail: sales@falconbroadband. net. Web Site: http://falconbroadband.net. ICA: CO5007.
Channel capacity: N.A. Channels available but not in use: N.A.
Internet Service
Operational: Yes.
Ownership: Falcon Broadband.

EMPIRE—Comcast Cable. Now served by DENVER, CO [CO0001]. ICA: CO0080.

ESTES PARK—Baja Broadband, 525 Junction Rd, Madison, WI 53717. Phones: 877-422-5282; 970-577-0199. E-mail: customersupportco@bajabb.tv. Web Site: http://www.bajabroadband.com. Also serves Larimer County (portions). ICA: CO0038.
TV Market Ranking: Below 100 (ESTES PARK, Larimer County (portions)). Franchise award date: N.A. Franchise expiration date: N.A. Began: June 1, 1953.
Channel capacity: 68 (operating 2-way). Channels available but not in use: N.A.
Basic Service
Subscribers: 1,238.
Programming (received off-air): KCNC-TV (CBS, Decades) Denver; KDVR (Antenna TV, FOX) Denver; KMGH-TV (ABC, Azteca America) Denver; KRMA-TV (PBS) Denver; KTVD (MeTV, MNT) Denver; KUSA (NBC, WeatherNation) Denver; KWGN-TV (CW, This TV) Denver; 18 FMs.
Programming (via satellite): C-SPAN; C-SPAN 2; QVC; The Weather Channel; Univision Studios; WGN America.
Fee: $29.95-$49.95 installation; $36.70 monthly.
Expanded Basic Service 1
Subscribers: N.A.
Programming (via satellite): A&E; Altitude Sports & Entertainment; AMC; Animal Planet; Bravo; Cartoon Network; CMT; CNBC; CNN; Comedy Central; Discovery Channel; Discovery Life Channel; Disney Channel; Disney XD; E! HD; ESPN; ESPN2; Food Network; Fox News Channel; Fox Sports 1; Freeform; FX; Golf Channel; GSN; Hallmark Channel; HGTV; History; HLN; Lifetime; MSNBC; MTV; National Geographic Channel; NBCSN; Nickelodeon; Root Sports Rocky Mountain; Spike TV; Syfy; TBS; TLC; TNT; Travel Channel; truTV; Turner Classic Movies; TV Land; USA Network; VH1.
Digital Basic Service
Subscribers: N.A.
Programming (via satellite): BBC America; Bloomberg Television; CMT; Destination America; Discovery Kids Channel; ESPN Classic; Investigation Discovery; MC; MTV Classic; MTV Hits; MTV Jams; MTV2; Nick 2; Nick Jr.; Nicktoons; OWN: Oprah Winfrey Network; Science Channel; TeenNick; Tr3s; VH1 Soul; WE tv.
Digital Expanded Basic Service
Subscribers: N.A.
Programming (via satellite): LOGO.
Digital Expanded Basic Service 2
Subscribers: N.A.
Programming (via satellite): ESPN HD; Golf Channel HD; TNT HD; Versus HD.
Digital Expanded Basic Service 3
Subscribers: N.A.
Programming (via satellite): AXS TV; Universal HD.

2017 Edition
D-115

Colorado—Cable Systems

Digital Pay Service 1
Pay Units: N.A.
Programming (via satellite): Cinemax (multiplexed); Flix; HBO (multiplexed); Showtime (multiplexed); Showtime HD; Starz (multiplexed); Starz Encore (multiplexed); Starz HD; The Movie Channel (multiplexed); The Movie Channel HD.

Video-On-Demand: No

Pay-Per-View
iN DEMAND (delivered digitally); Hot Choice (delivered digitally).

Internet Service
Operational: Yes. Began: September 1, 2000.
Subscribers: 1,497.
Broadband Service: In-house.
Fee: $49.99 installation; $52.99 monthly; $4.95 modem lease; $69.95 modem purchase.

Telephone Service
Digital: Operational
Subscribers: 283.
Miles of Plant: 257.0 (coaxial); 42.0 (fiber optic). Homes passed: 6,557.
Chief Executive Officer: William A. Schuler. Chief Operating Officer: Phillip Klein. Area Vice President & General Manager: Tom Jaskiewicz. Vice President, Corporate Finance: Carl Shapiro. Assistant Treasurer: Noel Hutton. Technical Operations Director: Matt Warford.
Ownership: TDS Telecom (MSO).

FAIRPLAY—Formerly served by Cebridge Connections. No longer in operation. ICA: CO0124.

FLAGLER—Formerly served by NexHorizon Communications. No longer in operation. ICA: CO0133.

FLEMING—PC Telcom. Now served by HOLYOKE, CO [CO0165]. ICA: CO0167.

FORT CARSON—Baja Broadband, 525 Junction Rd, Madison, WI 53717. Phones: 877-422-5282; 719-576-7404. E-mail: customersupportco@bajabb.tv. Web Site: http://www.bajabroadband.com. Also serves Colorado Springs. ICA: CO0026.
TV Market Ranking: Below 100 (Colorado Springs, FORT CARSON). Franchise award date: May 4, 1989. Franchise expiration date: N.A. Began: November 15, 1979.
Channel capacity: N.A. Channels available but not in use: N.A.

Basic Service
Subscribers: 884.
Programming (received off-air): KKTV (CBS, MNT) Colorado Springs; KMAS-LD (TMO) Denver; KOAA-TV (Grit, NBC) Pueblo; KRDO-TV (ABC, TMO) Colorado Springs; KTSC (PBS) Pueblo; KWGN-TV (CW, This TV) Denver; KXRM-TV (FOX, MundoMax) Colorado Springs; KXTU-LD (CW) Colorado Springs.
Programming (via satellite): C-SPAN; INSP; QVC; Trinity Broadcasting Network (TBN); WGN America.
Fee: $29.95-$49.95 installation; $34.60 monthly.

Expanded Basic Service 1
Subscribers: N.A.
Programming (via satellite): A&E; AMC; Animal Planet; BET; Bravo; Cartoon Network; CMT; CNBC; CNN; Comedy Central; Discovery Channel; Disney Channel; E! HD; ESPN; ESPN2; Food Network; Fox News Channel; Fox Sports 1; Freeform; FX; Golf Channel; Great American Country; GSN; Hallmark Channel; HGTV; History; HLN; Lifetime; LMN; MSNBC; MTV; National Geographic Channel; Nickelodeon; Root Sports Rocky Mountain; Spike TV; Syfy; TBS; The Weather Channel; TLC; TNT; Travel Channel; truTV; Turner Classic Movies; TV Land; Univision Studios; USA Network; VH1; WE tv.
Fee: $30.00 monthly.

Digital Basic Service
Subscribers: N.A.
Programming (via satellite): BBC America; Bloomberg Television; CMT; Destination America; Discovery Kids Channel; Discovery Life Channel; Disney XD; DIY Network; ESPN Classic; Fox Business Network; FOX College Sports Central; FOX College Sports Pacific; Fox Sports 2; FXM; FYI; History International; IFC; Investigation Discovery; MC; MTV Classic; MTV Hits; MTV Jams; MTV2; Nat Geo WILD; Nick 2; Nick Jr.; Nicktoons; OWN: Oprah Winfrey Network; Science Channel; Sundance TV; TeenNick; Tr3s; VH1 Soul.

Digital Expanded Basic Service
Subscribers: N.A.
Programming (via satellite): A&E HD; ESPN HD; Food Network HD; FX HD; HGTV HD; History HD; National Geographic Channel HD; TBS HD; TNT HD.

Digital Expanded Basic Service 2
Subscribers: N.A.
Programming (via satellite): AXS TV; Universal HD.

Digital Pay Service 1
Pay Units: N.A.
Programming (via satellite): Cinemax (multiplexed); Cinemax HD; Flix; HBO (multiplexed); HBO HD; Showtime (multiplexed); Showtime HD; Starz (multiplexed); Starz Encore; Starz HD; The Movie Channel (multiplexed); The Movie Channel HD.

Video-On-Demand: No

Pay-Per-View
iN DEMAND (delivered digitally); Hot Choice (delivered digitally); SexSee (delivered digitally).

Internet Service
Operational: Yes. Began: November 1, 2002.
Broadband Service: In-house.
Fee: $9.99 installation; $55.99 monthly; $4.96 modem lease; $69.95 modem purchase.

Telephone Service
Analog: Operational
Miles of Plant: 32.0 (coaxial); None (fiber optic). Homes passed: 5,097.
Area Vice President & General Manager: Tom Jaskiewicz. Vice President, Corporate Finance: Carl Shapiro. Assistant Treasurer: Noel Hutton. Technical Operations Director: Matt Warford.
Ownership: TDS Telecom (MSO).

FORT COLLINS—Baja Broadband, 525 Junction Rd, Madison, WI 53717. Phones: 575-437-3101; 877-422-5282; 970-587-2243; 800-480-7020. E-mail: customersupportco@bajabb.tv. Web Site: http://www.bajabroadband.com. Also serves Ault, Cloverleaf Trailer Park, Collinsaire Trailer Park, Eaton, Johnstown, Larimer County (portions), Milliken, Mt. Range Shadows, Pierce, Poudre Valley, Ptarmigan, Severance, Weld County (portions) & Wellington. ICA: CO0073.
TV Market Ranking: Below 100 (Ault, Eaton, Larimer County (portions), Milliken, Pierce, Poudre Valley, Wellington, FORT COLLINS, Johnstown). Franchise award date: N.A. Franchise expiration date: N.A. Began: July 1, 1982.
Channel capacity: 86 (operating 2-way). Channels available but not in use: N.A.

Basic Service
Subscribers: 2,354.
Programming (received off-air): KBDI-TV (PBS) Broomfield; KCEC (Bounce TV, LATV, UNV) Denver; KCNC-TV (CBS, Decades) Denver; KDEN-TV (TMO) Denver; KDVR (Antenna TV, FOX) Denver; KGWN-TV (CBS, CW) Cheyenne; KMGH-TV (ABC, Azteca America) Denver; KPXC-TV (ION) Denver; KRMA-TV (PBS) Denver; KTFD-DT (getTV, UniMas) Boulder; KTVD (MeTV, MNT) Denver; KUSA (NBC, WeatherNation) Denver; KWGN-TV (CW, This TV) Denver.
Programming (via satellite): A&E; Altitude Sports & Entertainment; AMC; Animal Planet; BYUtv; Cartoon Network; CMT; CNN; Comedy Central; C-SPAN; Discovery Channel; Disney Channel; E! HD; ESPN; ESPN2; EVINE Live; Food Network; Fox News Channel; Fox Sports 1; Freeform; FX; Hallmark Channel; HGTV; History; HLN; Lifetime; MTV; National Geographic Channel; NBC Universo; NBCSN; Nickelodeon; Oxygen; Pop; QVC; Root Sports Rocky Mountain; Spike TV; Syfy; TBS; The Weather Channel; TLC; TNT; Travel Channel; truTV; TV Land; Univision; USA Network; VH1; WGN America.
Fee: $49.95 installation; $32.95 monthly.

Digital Basic Service
Subscribers: N.A.
Programming (via satellite): A&E HD; Animal Planet HD; AXS TV; BBC America; Bloomberg Television; Bravo; Cloo; Daystar TV Network; Discovery Channel HD; Discovery Kids Channel; Disney XD; DMX Music; ESPN Classic; ESPN HD; ESPNews; Food Network HD; Fuse; Golf Channel; Great American Country; GSN; HD Theater; HGTV HD; History HD; IFC; LMN; MTV Classic; MTV2; National Geographic Channel HD; Nick Jr.; OWN: Oprah Winfrey Network; Science Channel; Syfy; Syfy HD; TeenNick; The Word Network; Trinity Broadcasting Network (TBN); Turner Classic Movies; Universal HD; UP; USA Network HD; WE tv.

Digital Expanded Basic Service
Subscribers: N.A.
Programming (via satellite): FOX College Sports Central; FOX College Sports Pacific; NFL Network; Outdoor Channel.
Fee: $2.00 monthly.

Digital Expanded Basic Service 2
Subscribers: N.A.
Programming (via satellite): CMT; Destination America; Discovery Life Channel; FXM; FYI; History International; Investigation Discovery; Ovation; Starz Encore (multiplexed).
Fee: $2.95 monthly.

Digital Pay Service 1
Pay Units: N.A.
Programming (via satellite): Cinemax (multiplexed); Cinemax HD; HBO (multiplexed); HBO HD; Showtime (multiplexed); Showtime HD; The Movie Channel (multiplexed).
Fee: $11.95 monthly (HBO, Cinemax, Showtime or TMC).

Video-On-Demand: No

Pay-Per-View
iN DEMAND (delivered digitally); Playboy TV (delivered digitally); Fresh (delivered digitally); Spice: Xcess (delivered digitally); Club Jenna (delivered digitally).

Internet Service
Operational: Yes.
Broadband Service: Warp Drive Online.
Fee: $27.95 monthly.

Telephone Service
Digital: Operational
Miles of Plant: 13.0 (coaxial); None (fiber optic).
Vice President, Corporate Finance: Carl Shapiro. Assistant Treasurer: Noel Hutton.
Ownership: TDS Telecom (MSO).

FORT COLLINS—Comcast Cable. Now served by LONGMONT, CO [CO0011]. ICA: CO0008.

FORT COLLINS—Formerly served by Sprint Corp. No longer in operation. ICA: CO0197.

FORT LUPTON—Comcast Cable. Now served by LONGMONT, CO [CO0011]. ICA: CO0056.

FORT MORGAN—Charter Communications, 12405 Powerscourt Dr, St. Louis, MO 63131. Phones: 636-207-5100 (Corporate office); 516-803-2300 (Corporate office); 877-273-7626. Web Site: http://www.charter.com. Also serves Brush, Log Lane Village & Morgan County. ICA: CO0029.
TV Market Ranking: Below 100 (Brush, Morgan County (portions)); Outside TV Markets (FORT MORGAN, Log Lane Village, Morgan County (portions)). Franchise award date: N.A. Franchise expiration date: N.A. Began: September 1, 1970.
Channel capacity: N.A. Channels available but not in use: N.A.

Digital Basic Service
Subscribers: 2,408.
Programming (via satellite): A&E HD; Animal Planet HD; AXS TV; Azteca; Bandamax; BBC America; Bloomberg Television; Bravo; CBS Sports Network; Cine Mexicano; Cinelatino; CMT; CNBC HD+; CNN en Espanol; CNN HD; Cooking Channel; De Pelicula; De Pelicula Clasico; Destination America; Discovery Channel HD; Discovery Kids Channel; Discovery Life Channel; Disney Channel HD; Disney XD; DIY Network; DMX Music; ESPN Classic; ESPN Deportes; ESPN HD; ESPN2 HD; ESPNews; Food Network HD; FOX College Sports Central; FOX College Sports Pacific; Fox Deportes; Fox Sports 1; Freeform HD; FSN HD; Fuse; FXM; FYI; Golf Channel; GolTV; GSN; HD Theater; HGTV HD; History en Espanol; History HD; History International; IFC; Investigation Discovery; ION Television; Lifetime Movie Network HD; LMN; MTV Classic; MTV Hits; MTV Jams; MTV2; Nat Geo WILD; National Geographic Channel; National Geographic Channel HD; NBC Universo; NBCSN; NFL Network; NFL Network HD; Nick 2; Nick Jr.; Nicktoons; Outdoor Channel; OWN: Oprah Winfrey Network; RFD-TV; Science Channel; Science HD; Sprout; Syfy HD; TBS HD; TeenNick; Telehit; The Weather Channel HD; TLC HD; TNT HD; Tr3s; Trinity Broadcasting Network (TBN); UniMas; Universal HD; Univision; Univision Studios; UP; USA Network HD; Versus HD; VH1 Soul; ViendoMovies.
Fee: $26.99 monthly.

Digital Expanded Basic Service
Subscribers: N.A.
Programming (via satellite): A&E; Altitude Sports & Entertainment; AMC; Animal Planet; Cartoon Network; CMT; CNBC; CNN; Comedy Central; C-SPAN; Disney Channel; E! HD; ESPN; ESPN2; EWTN Global Catholic Network; Food Network; Fox News Channel; Freeform; FX; Hallmark Channel; HGTV; History; HLN; ION Television; MSNBC; MTV; Nickelodeon;

D-116

TV & Cable Factbook No. 85

Cable Systems—Colorado

Access the most current data instantly
www.warren-news.com/factbook.htm

Pop; Root Sports Rocky Mountain; Spike TV; Syfy; Telemundo; The Weather Channel; TLC; TNT; Travel Channel; truTV; Turner Classic Movies; TV Land; UniMas; Univision; USA Network; VH1.
Fee: $44.90 monthly.
Digital Pay Service 1
Pay Units: N.A.
Programming (via satellite): Cinemax (multiplexed); Cinemax HD; HBO (multiplexed); HBO HD; Showtime (multiplexed); Showtime HD; Starz (multiplexed); Starz Encore (multiplexed); Starz HD; The Movie Channel (multiplexed); The Movie Channel HD.
Video-On-Demand: No
Pay-Per-View
Sports PPV (delivered digitally); ESPN Now (delivered digitally); iN DEMAND (delivered digitally).
Internet Service
Operational: Yes.
Broadband Service: Charter Internet.
Fee: $39.95 monthly.
Telephone Service
Digital: Operational
Fee: $49.99 monthly
Miles of Plant: 100.0 (coaxial); 21.0 (fiber optic). Homes passed: 7,782.
President & Chief Executive Officer: Tom Rutledge. Regional Vice President: Clint Rodeman. General Manager: Wes Frost. Technical Operations Manager: Mitch Winter. Accounting Director: David Sovanski.
Ownership: Charter Communications Inc. (MSO).

FOWLER—Formerly served by Bresnan Communications. Now served by Charter Communications, LA JUNTA, CO [CO0040]. ICA: CO0091.

FREDERICK—Comcast Cable. Now served by LONGMONT, CO [CO0011]. ICA: CO0050.

GENESEE—Comcast Cable. Now served by DENVER, CO [CO0001]. ICA: CO0169.

GILCREST—Formerly served by Baja Broadband. No longer in operation. ICA: CO0170.

GILPIN COUNTY—Formerly served by CAMS Cable. No longer in operation. ICA: CO0060.

GLENWOOD SPRINGS—Comcast Cable, 1605 Grand Ave, Ste 1, Glenwood Springs, CO 81601. Phones: 970-230-9076; 970-928-7784. Fax: 970-945-0270. Web Site: http://www.comcast.com. Also serves Garfield County (portions). ICA: CO0025.
TV Market Ranking: Below 100 (Garfield County (portions)).
Channel capacity: N.A. Channels available but not in use: N.A.
Basic Service
Subscribers: 2,639.
Fee: $50.00 installation; $30.75 monthly.
Ownership: Comcast Cable Communications Inc. (MSO).

GRANADA—Formerly served by NexHorizon Communications. No longer in operation. ICA: CO0144.

GRANBY—Comcast Cable. Now served by LONGMONT, CO [CO0011]. ICA: CO0021.

GRAND JUNCTION—Charter Communications, 12405 Powerscourt Dr, St. Louis, MO 63131. Phones: 636-207-5100 (Corporate office); 877-273-7626; 516-803-2300 (Corporate office). Fax: 970-245-6803. Web Site: http://www.charter.com. Also serves Fruita, Mesa County & Palisade. ICA: CO0006.
TV Market Ranking: Below 100 (Fruita, GRAND JUNCTION, Mesa County, Palisade). Franchise award date: March 1, 1966. Franchise expiration date: N.A. Began: October 1, 1966.
Channel capacity: 49 (operating 2-way). Channels available but not in use: N.A.
Digital Basic Service
Subscribers: 25,658.
Programming (via satellite): A&E HD; Animal Planet HD; AXS TV; Bandamax; BBC America; Bloomberg Television; BlueHighways TV; Bravo HD; CBS Sports Network; Cine Mexicano; Cinelatino; CMT; CNBC HD+; CNN en Espanol; CNN HD; Cooking Channel; C-SPAN 3; De Pelicula; De Pelicula Clasico; Destination America; Discovery Channel HD; Discovery Kids Channel; Discovery Life Channel; Disney Channel HD; Disney XD; DIY Network; DMX Music; ESPN Classic; ESPN Deportes; ESPN HD; ESPN2 HD; ESPNews; Food Network HD; FOX College Sports Central; FOX College Sports Pacific; Fox Deportes; Fox Sports 1; Freeform HD; FSN HD; Fuse; FXM; FYI; Golf Channel; GolTV; Great American Country; GSN; HD Theater; HGTV HD; History en Espanol; History HD; History International; IFC; Investigation Discovery; ION Television; Jewelry Television; Lifetime Movie Network HD; LMN; MTV Classic; MTV Hits; MTV Jams; MTV Live; MTV2; Nat Geo WILD; National Geographic Channel; National Geographic Channel HD; NBC Universo; NBCSN; NFL Network; NFL Network HD; NHL Network; Nick 2; Nick Jr.; Nicktoons; Outdoor Channel; Outdoor Channel 2 HD; OWN: Oprah Winfrey Network; RFD-TV; Science Channel; Science HD; Sprout; Syfy HD; TBS HD; TeenNick; Telehit; The Weather Channel HD; TLC HD; TNT HD; Tr3s; Trinity Broadcasting Network (TBN); UniMas; Universal HD; Univision Studios; UP; USA Network HD; Versus HD; VH1 Soul; ViendoMovies.
Fee: $26.99 monthly.
Digital Expanded Basic Service
Subscribers: N.A.
Programming (via satellite): A&E; Altitude Sports & Entertainment; AMC; Animal Planet; Bravo; BYUtv; Cartoon Network; CMT; CNBC; CNN; Comedy Central; C-SPAN 2; Disney Channel; E! HD; ESPN; ESPN2; EWTN Global Catholic Network; Food Network; Fox News Channel; Freeform; FX; Hallmark Channel; HGTV; History; HLN; INSP; ION Television; MTV; Nickelodeon; Oxygen; Pop; Root Sports Rocky Mountain; Spike TV; Syfy; The Weather Channel; TLC; TNT; Travel Channel; truTV; Turner Classic Movies; TV Land; UniMas; Univision Studios; USA Network; VH1.
Fee: $56.99 monthly.
Digital Pay Service 1
Pay Units: N.A.
Programming (via satellite): Cinemax (multiplexed); Cinemax HD; Cinemax On Demand; Flix; HBO (multiplexed); HBO HD; HBO on Demand; Showtime (multiplexed); Showtime HD; Showtime on Demand; Starz (multiplexed); Starz Encore (multiplexed); Starz HD; Starz On Demand; The Movie Channel (multiplexed); The Movie Channel HD.
Video-On-Demand: Yes
Pay-Per-View
iN DEMAND (delivered digitally); ESPN (delivered digitally); NBA League Pass (delivered digitally); MLS Direct Kick (delivered digitally); MLB Extra Innings (delivered digitally); NHL Center Ice (delivered digitally).
Internet Service
Operational: Yes.
Subscribers: 31,707.
Broadband Service: Charter Internet.
Fee: $39.95 monthly.
Telephone Service
Digital: Operational
Subscribers: 20,560.
Fee: $49.99 monthly
Miles of Plant: 1,609.0 (coaxial); 285.0 (fiber optic). Homes passed: 61,909.
President & Chief Executive Officer: Tom Rutledge. Regional Vice President: Sean Hogue. Technical Operations Manager: Gary Young. Accounting Director: David Sovanski.
Ownership: Charter Communications Inc. (MSO).

GREELEY—Comcast Cable. Now served by LONGMONT, CO [CO0011]. ICA: CO0009.

HAYDEN—Formerly served by Bresnan Communications. Now served by Charter Communications, CRAIG, CO [CO0039]. ICA: CO0098.

HERMOSA—Formerly served by Hermosa Cablevision Inc. Now served by Charter Communications, DURANGO, CO [CO0023]. ICA: CO0087.

HIGHLANDS RANCH—Comcast Cable. Now served by DENVER, CO [CO0001]. ICA: CO0180.

HIGHLANDS RANCH—Formerly served by Qwest Choice TV. IPTV service has been discontinued. ICA: CO0208.

HIGHLANDS RANCH—Formerly served by Qwest Choice TV. IPTV service has been discontinued. ICA: CO5003.

HOLIDAY VILLAGE—Formerly served by Island Cable. No longer in operation. ICA: CO0209.

HOLLY—Formerly served by NexHorizon Communications. No longer in operation. ICA: CO0101.

HOLYOKE—PC Telcom, 240 South Interocean Ave, Ste 2, Holyoke, CO 80734. Phones: 866-854-2111; 970-854-2201. Fax: 970-854-2668. E-mail: customerservice@pctelcom.coop. Web Site: http://my.pctelcom.coop. Also serves Fleming, Haxtun, Julesburg, Ovid & Sedgwick, CO; Chappell, NE. ICA: CO0065.
TV Market Ranking: Below 100 (Haxtun, Fleming); Outside TV Markets (Chappell, HOLYOKE, Ovid, Julesburg, Sedgwick). Franchise award date: N.A. Franchise expiration date: N.A. Began: March 1, 1972.
Channel capacity: N.A. Channels available but not in use: N.A.
Basic Service
Subscribers: 771.
Programming (received off-air): KCDO-TV (IND) Sterling; KPNE-TV (PBS) North Platte; allband FM.
Programming (via microwave): KCNC-TV (CBS, Decades) Denver; KDVR (Antenna TV, FOX) Denver; KMGH-TV (ABC, Azteca America) Denver; KUSA (NBC, WeatherNation) Denver; KWGN-TV (CW, This TV) Denver.
Programming (via satellite): A&E; AMC; Animal Planet; CNBC; CNN; C-SPAN; Discovery Channel; Disney Channel; E! HD; ESPN; ESPN2; Fox News Channel; Freeform; Great American Country; HGTV; History; HLN; Lifetime; MTV; Nickelodeon; Root Sports Rocky Mountain; Spike TV; Syfy; TBS; The Weather Channel; TNT; TV Land; Univision Studios; USA Network; VH1; WGN America.
Fee: $49.95 monthly.
Pay Service 1
Pay Units: N.A.
Programming (via satellite): Cinemax; HBO.
Fee: $11.10 monthly (Cinemax), $13.35 monthly (HBO).
Video-On-Demand: No
Internet Service
Operational: Yes.
Fee: $37.95-$77.95 monthly.
Telephone Service
Digital: Operational
Fee: $38.95 monthly
Miles of Plant: 22.0 (coaxial); None (fiber optic). Homes passed: 1,300.
General Manager: Vincent Kropp. Operations Director: Pete Markle. Chief Technician: J.C. Peckham. Customer Service Manager: Patty Freel.
Ownership: PC Telcorp (MSO).

HOTCHKISS—Formerly served by Rocky Mountain Cable. No longer in operation. ICA: CO0172.

HUDSON—Formerly served by US Cable of Coastal Texas LP. No longer in operation. ICA: CO0173.

HUGO—Formerly served by NexHorizon Communications. No longer in operation. ICA: CO0174.

IDAHO SPRINGS—Comcast Cable. Now served by DENVER, CO [CO0001]. ICA: CO0082.

IGNACIO—USA Communications, 56 Talisman Dr, Ste 200, Pagosa Springs, CO 81147. Phone: 877-234-0102. E-mail: csr@usacommunications.tv. Web Site: http://usacommunications.tv. Also serves Southern Ute Indian Reservation. ICA: CO0076.
TV Market Ranking: Below 100 (IGNACIO, Southern Ute Indian Reservation). Franchise award date: February 1, 1987. Franchise expiration date: N.A. Began: December 1, 1986.
Channel capacity: N.A. Channels available but not in use: N.A.

Colorado—Cable Systems

Basic Service
Subscribers: 157.
Programming (received off-air): KOBF (NBC, This TV) Farmington; KREZ-TV (CBS, The Country Network) Durango.
Programming (via microwave): KLUZ-TV (LATV, UNV) Albuquerque; KOAT-TV (ABC, Estrella TV) Albuquerque; KRMJ (PBS) Grand Junction.
Programming (via satellite): Animal Planet; Cartoon Network; CMT; CNBC; C-SPAN; C-SPAN 2; ESPN2; Food Network; Freeform; FX; HGTV; History; Syfy; TLC; Travel Channel; Trinity Broadcasting Network (TBN); Turner Classic Movies; TV Land; UniMas; WE tv.
Fee: $60.00 installation; $37.00 monthly; $3.00 converter.
Pay Service 1
Pay Units: N.A.
Programming (via satellite): Cinemax; HBO.
Fee: $10.50 monthly (Cinemax), $11.50 monthly (HBO).
Video-On-Demand: No
Internet Service
Operational: Yes. Began: December 31, 1999.
Broadband Service: In-house.
Fee: $150.00 installation; $45.00 monthly.
Telephone Service
None
Miles of Plant: 14.0 (coaxial); None (fiber optic). Homes passed: 1,000.
Ownership: USA Companies LP (MSO).

JULESBURG—PC Telcom. Now served by HOLYOKE, CO [CO0065]. ICA: CO0084.

KERSEY—Formerly served by US Cable. No longer in operation. ICA: CO0116.

KIT CARSON—Rebeltec Communications, PO Box 10, Kit Carson, CO 80825. Phone: 719-767-8902. Fax: 719-767-8906. E-mail: tech@rebeltec.net. Web Site: http://www.rebeltec.net. Also serves Arriba & Seibert. ICA: CO0152.
TV Market Ranking: Outside TV Markets (Arriba, KIT CARSON, Seibert). Franchise award date: January 1, 1991. Franchise expiration date: N.A. Began: June 1, 1991.
Channel capacity: N.A. Channels available but not in use: N.A.
Basic Service
Subscribers: 45.
Programming (received off-air): KOAA-TV (Grit, NBC) Pueblo.
Programming (via microwave): KCNC-TV (CBS, Decades) Denver; KDVR (Antenna TV, FOX) Denver; KKTV (CBS, MNT) Colorado Springs; KMGH-TV (ABC, Azteca America) Denver; KRDO-TV (ABC, TMO) Colorado Springs; KRMA-TV (PBS) Denver; KTVD (MeTV, MNT) Denver; KUSA (NBC, WeatherNation) Denver; KWGN-TV (CW, This TV) Denver.
Programming (via satellite): A&E; Altitude Sports & Entertainment; CMT; CNN; Discovery Channel; Disney Channel; ESPN; ESPN2; Fox News Channel; Freeform; Hallmark Channel; HGTV; History; ION Television; NBCSN; RFD-TV; Root Sports Rocky Mountain; TBS; The Weather Channel; TNT; Trinity Broadcasting Network (TBN); Turner Classic Movies; USA Network; WGN America.
Fee: $30.00 installation; $30.00 monthly; $3.00 converter.
Pay Service 1
Pay Units: N.A.
Programming (via satellite): Cinemax; HBO.
Fee: $15.00 monthly.

Internet Service
Operational: Yes, Dial-up.
Subscribers: 48.
Fee: $75.00 installation; $25.00 monthly.
Telephone Service
Digital: Operational
Subscribers: 3.
Miles of Plant: 4.0 (coaxial); None (fiber optic). Homes passed: 117.
General Manager & Chief Technician: B.J. Mayhan. Marketing Director: Angela Mayhan.
Ownership: Rebeltec Communications LLC (MSO).

KREMMLING—Comcast Cable, 249 Warren Ave, Ste 250, Silverthorne, CO 80498. Phones: 970-262-2605; 970-262-2601. Fax: 970-468-2672. Web Site: http://www.comcast.com. Also serves Grand County (portions). ICA: CO0093.
TV Market Ranking: Below 100 (Grand County (portions) (portions)); Outside TV Markets (Grand County (portions) (portions), KREMMLING). Franchise award date: N.A. Franchise expiration date: N.A. Began: February 1, 1970.
Channel capacity: N.A. Channels available but not in use: N.A.
Basic Service
Subscribers: 27.
Programming (via microwave): KCNC-TV (CBS, Decades) Denver; KDVR (Antenna TV, FOX) Denver; KMGH-TV (ABC, Azteca America) Denver; KRMA-TV (PBS) Denver; KTVD (MeTV, MNT) Denver.
Programming (via satellite): A&E; Animal Planet; CNN; Disney Channel; E! HD; ESPN; Fox News Channel; Freeform; FX; Great American Country; KUSA (NBC, WeatherNation) Denver; KWGN-TV (CW, This TV) Denver; MSNBC; MTV; Nickelodeon; Root Sports Rocky Mountain; Spike TV; TBS; TNT; USA Network.
Fee: $50.00 installation; $58.24 monthly.
Digital Basic Service
Subscribers: N.A.
Programming (via satellite): BBC America; Bravo; Discovery Digital Networks; DMX Music; ESPN Classic; ESPNews; Golf Channel; GSN; HGTV; History; IFC; NBCSN; Nick Jr.; Syfy; Turner Classic Movies; TV Land; WE tv.
Pay Service 1
Pay Units: N.A.
Programming (via satellite): Cinemax; HBO; Starz; Starz Encore.
Fee: $25.00 installation; $9.95 monthly (Cinemax or HBO), $10.45 monthly (Starz & Encore).
Digital Pay Service 1
Pay Units: N.A.
Programming (via satellite): HBO (multiplexed); Showtime; Starz; Starz Encore (multiplexed); The Movie Channel.
Fee: $15.99 monthly (each).
Video-On-Demand: No
Pay-Per-View
iN DEMAND (delivered digitally) Playboy TV (delivered digitally).
Internet Service
Operational: Yes.
Broadband Service: Comcast High Speed Internet.
Fee: $42.95 monthly.
Telephone Service
None
Miles of Plant: 21.0 (coaxial); None (fiber optic). Homes passed: 314.
Vice President: Mike Trueblood. General Manager: Ben Miller. Technical Operations Manager: David Farran. Customer Service Manager: Sherry Higgins.
Ownership: Comcast Cable Communications Inc. (MSO).

LA JUNTA—Charter Communications, 12405 Powerscourt Dr, St. Louis, MO 63131. Phones: 636-207-5100 (Corporate office); 719-383-0424; 516-803-2300 (Corporate office); 877-273-7626. Web Site: http://www.charter.com. Also serves Fowler, Lamar, Manzanola, Otero County (unincorporated areas), Prowers County (unincorporated areas), Rocky Ford & Swink. ICA: CO0040.
TV Market Ranking: Below 100 (Fowler, Otero County (unincorporated areas) (portions)); Outside TV Markets (LA JUNTA, Manzanola, Otero County (unincorporated areas) (portions), Prowers County (unincorporated areas), Rocky Ford, Swink, Lamar). Franchise award date: April 1, 1981. Franchise expiration date: N.A. Began: June 1, 1977.
Channel capacity: N.A. Channels available but not in use: N.A.
Digital Basic Service
Subscribers: 4,089.
Programming (via satellite): A&E HD; Animal Planet HD; Bandamax; BBC America; Bloomberg Television; Bravo; CBS Sports Network; Cine Mexicano; Cinelatino; CMT; CNN en Espanol; Cooking Channel; De Pelicula; De Pelicula Clasico; Destination America; Discovery Channel HD; Discovery Life Channel; Disney Channel HD; Disney XD; DIY Network; DMX Music; ESPN Classic; ESPN Deportes; ESPN HD; ESPNews; Food Network HD; FOX College Sports Central; FOX College Sports Pacific; Fox Deportes; FOX Sports 1; Freeform HD; Fuse; FXM; FYI; Golf Channel; GolTV; GSN; HD Theater; HGTV HD; History en Espanol; History International; IFC; Investigation Discovery; ION Television; LMN; MTV Classic; MTV Hits; MTV Jams; MTV2; Nat Geo WILD; National Geographic Channel; National Geographic Channel HD; NBC Universo; NBCSN; NFL Network; Nick 2; Nick Jr.; Nicktoons; Outdoor Channel; OWN; Oprah Winfrey Network; RFD-TV; Science Channel; Science HD; Sprout; Syfy HD; TeenNick; Telehit; Tr3s; Trinity Broadcasting Network (TBN); UniMas; Universal HD; Univision; Univision Studios; UP; USA Network HD; VH1 Soul; ViendoMovies.
Fee: $26.99 monthly.
Digital Expanded Basic Service
Subscribers: N.A.
Programming (via satellite): A&E; Altitude Sports & Entertainment; AMC; Animal Planet; Cartoon Network; CMT; CNN; Comedy Central; Discovery Channel; Disney Channel; E! HD; ESPN; ESPN2; EWTN Global Catholic Network; Food Network; Fox News Channel; Freeform; FX; Hallmark Channel; HGTV; History; HLN; MSNBC; MTV; Nickelodeon; Oxygen; Root Sports Rocky Mountain; Spike TV; Syfy; TBS; The Weather Channel; TLC; TNT; Travel Channel; truTV; Turner Classic Movies; TV Land; UniMas; Univision; USA Network; VH1.
Fee: $28.56 monthly.
Digital Pay Service 1
Pay Units: 493.
Programming (via satellite): Cinemax (multiplexed); Flix; HBO (multiplexed); HBO HD; Showtime (multiplexed); Starz (multiplexed); Starz Encore (multiplexed); Starz HD; The Movie Channel.
Video-On-Demand: No
Pay-Per-View
iN DEMAND (delivered digitally).

Internet Service
Operational: Yes.
Broadband Service: Charter Internet.
Fee: $39.95 monthly.
Telephone Service
Digital: Operational
Fee: $49.99 monthly
Miles of Plant: 94.0 (coaxial); 20.0 (fiber optic). Homes passed: 5,092.
President & Chief Executive Officer: Tom Rutledge. General Manager: Jerry Parker. Chief Technician: Matt Harris. Accounting Director: David Sovanski.
Ownership: Charter Communications Inc. (MSO).

LA VETA—Formerly served by Westcom II LLC. No longer in operation. ICA: CO0199.

LAKE CITY—USA Communications, 920 East 56th St, Ste B, Kearney, NE 68847. Phone: 877-234-0102. E-mail: csr@usacommunications.tv. Web Site: http://usacommunications.tv. ICA: CO0127.
TV Market Ranking: Outside TV Markets (LAKE CITY). Franchise award date: January 1, 1982. Franchise expiration date: N.A. Began: January 1, 1986.
Channel capacity: N.A. Channels available but not in use: N.A.
Basic Service
Subscribers: 39.
Programming (via microwave): KCNC-TV (CBS, Decades) Denver; KDVR (Antenna TV, FOX) Denver; KMGH-TV (ABC, Azteca America) Denver; KRMA-TV (PBS) Denver; KWGN-TV (CW, This TV) Denver.
Programming (via satellite): A&E; AMC; Animal Planet; Bravo; CMT; CNBC; CNN; Comedy Central; Discovery Channel; Disney Channel; ESPN; ESPN2; Fox News Channel; Freeform; Hallmark Channel; History; KUSA (NBC, WeatherNation) Denver; MSNBC; Nickelodeon; Outdoor Channel; QVC; Spike TV; Syfy; TBS; The Weather Channel; TLC; TNT; Travel Channel; TV Land; USA Network; VH1; WE tv; WGN America.
Fee: $29.95 installation; $42.95 monthly.
Pay Service 1
Pay Units: 11.
Programming (via satellite): HBO.
Fee: $15.00 installation; $13.49 monthly.
Video-On-Demand: No
Internet Service
Operational: No.
Telephone Service
None
Miles of Plant: 11.0 (coaxial); None (fiber optic). Homes passed: 300.
Chief Financial Officer: Amber Reineke.
Ownership: USA Companies LP (MSO).

LAKEWOOD—Comcast Cable. Now served by DENVER, CO [CO0001]. ICA: CO0207.

LAMAR—Charter Communications. Now served by LA JUNTA, CO [CO0040]. ICA: CO0034.

LAPORTE—Formerly served by Baja Broadband. No longer in operation. ICA: CO0177.

LARIMER COUNTY—Formerly served by NexHorizon Communications. No longer in operation. ICA: CO0211.

LAS ANIMAS—Satview Broadband, 3550 Barron Way, Ste 13A, Reno, NV 89511. Phones: 800-225-0605; 775-333-6626 (Elko, NV Office); 775-324-2198. Fax: 775-333-0225. E-mail: satviewreno@yahoo.

Cable Systems—Colorado

FULLY SEARCHABLE • CONTINUOUSLY UPDATED • DISCOUNT RATES FOR PRINT PURCHASERS

For more information call **800-771-9202** or visit **www.warren-news.com**

com. Web Site: http://www.satview.net. ICA: CO0066.
TV Market Ranking: Outside TV Markets (LAS ANIMAS). Franchise award date: N.A. Franchise expiration date: N.A. Began: July 1, 1981.
Channel capacity: 56 (not 2-way capable). Channels available but not in use: N.A.
Basic Service
Subscribers: 142.
Programming (via microwave): KKTV (CBS, MNT) Colorado Springs; KOAA-TV (Grit, NBC) Pueblo; KRDO-TV (ABC, TMO) Colorado Springs; KTSC (PBS) Pueblo; KTVD (MeTV, MNT) Denver; KWGN-TV (CW, This TV) Denver; KXRM-TV (FOX, MundoMax) Colorado Springs.
Programming (via satellite): A&E; AMC; Animal Planet; Bravo; Cartoon Network; CMT; CNBC; CNN; Comedy Central; C-SPAN; Discovery Channel; Disney Channel; E! HD; ESPN; ESPN2; EWTN Global Catholic Network; Food Network; Fox News Channel; Fox Sports 1; Freeform; FX; HGTV; History; HLN; Lifetime; MSNBC; MTV; National Geographic Channel; Nickelodeon; QVC; Root Sports Rocky Mountain; Spike TV; Syfy; TBS; The Weather Channel; TLC; TNT; Travel Channel; Trinity Broadcasting Network (TBN); truTV; Turner Classic Movies; TV Land; Univision Studios; USA Network; VH1; WGN America.
Fee: $49.95 installation; $54.50 monthly.
Digital Basic Service
Subscribers: N.A.
Programming (via satellite): BBC America; Bloomberg Television; CMT; Destination America; Discovery Kids Channel; Discovery Life Channel; Disney XD; ESPNews; Fuse; FXM; FYI; Golf Channel; GSN; History International; IFC; Investigation Discovery; LMN; MC; MTV Classic; MTV2; NBCSN; Nick Jr.; Outdoor Channel; OWN: Oprah Winfrey Network; Science Channel; TeenNick.
Digital Pay Service 1
Pay Units: N.A.
Programming (via satellite): Cinemax (multiplexed); HBO (multiplexed); Showtime (multiplexed); Starz; Starz Encore (multiplexed); The Movie Channel (multiplexed).
Video-On-Demand: No
Pay-Per-View
Club Jenna (delivered digitally); iN DEMAND (delivered digitally); Playboy TV (delivered digitally); Fresh (delivered digitally).
Internet Service
Operational: No.
Telephone Service
None
Homes passed: 1,414.
President: Tariq Ahmad.
Ownership: Satview Broadband Ltd. (MSO).

LEADVILLE—Charter Communications, 12405 Powerscourt Dr, St. Louis, MO 63131. Phones: 719-275-1656; 877-273-7626; 516-803-2300 (Corporate office); 719-275-8356. Web Site: http://www.charter.com. Also serves Lake County & Leadville North. ICA: CO0045.
TV Market Ranking: Outside TV Markets (Lake County, LEADVILLE, Leadville North). Franchise award date: N.A. Franchise expiration date: N.A. Began: March 1, 1954.
Channel capacity: N.A. Channels available but not in use: N.A.
Digital Basic Service
Subscribers: 785.
Programming (via satellite): A&E HD; Animal Planet HD; Bandamax; BBC America; Bloomberg Television; Bravo; CBS Sports Network; Cine Mexicano; Cinelatino; CMT; CNN en Espanol; De Pelicula; De Pelicula Clasico; Discovery Channel HD; Discovery Kids Channel; Discovery Life Channel; Disney XD; DMX Music; ESPN Classic; ESPN Deportes; ESPN HD; ESPNews; Food Network HD; FOX College Sports Central; FOX College Sports Pacific; Fox Deportes; Fox Sports 1; Fuse; FXM; FYI; Golf Channel; GolTV; GSN; HD Theater; HGTV HD; History en Espanol; History HD; History International; IFC; Investigation Discovery; ION Television; LMN; MTV Classic; MTV Hits; MTV Jams; MTV2; Nat Geo WILD; National Geographic Channel; National Geographic Channel HD; NBC Universo; NBCSN; NFL Network; Nick 2; Nick Jr.; Nicktoons; Outdoor Channel; OWN: Oprah Winfrey Network; RFD-TV; Science Channel; Sprout; Syfy HD; TeenNick; Telehit; Tr3s; Trinity Broadcasting Network (TBN); Universal HD; UP; USA Network HD; VH1 Soul; Viendo-Movies.
Fee: $26.99 monthly.
Digital Expanded Basic Service
Subscribers: N.A.
Programming (via satellite): A&E; Altitude Sports & Entertainment; AMC; Animal Planet; Cartoon Network; CMT; CNBC; CNN; Comedy Central; Discovery Channel; Disney Channel; E! HD; ESPN; ESPN2; EWTN Global Catholic Network; Food Network; Fox News Channel; Freeform; FX; Hallmark Channel; HGTV; History; HLN; MSNBC; MTV; Nickelodeon; Oxygen; Pop; Root Sports Rocky Mountain; Spike TV; Syfy; TBS; Telemundo; TLC; TNT; Travel Channel; truTV; Turner Classic Movies; TV Land; USA Network; VH1.
Fee: $12.60 monthly.
Digital Pay Service 1
Pay Units: N.A.
Programming (via satellite): Cinemax (multiplexed); Flix; HBO (multiplexed); HBO HD; Showtime (multiplexed); Starz (multiplexed); Starz Encore (multiplexed); Starz HD; The Movie Channel (multiplexed).
Video-On-Demand: No
Pay-Per-View
iN DEMAND (delivered digitally).
Internet Service
Operational: Yes.
Broadband Service: Charter Internet.
Fee: $39.95 monthly.
Telephone Service
Analog: Not Operational
Digital: Operational
Miles of Plant: 47.0 (coaxial); 19.0 (fiber optic). Homes passed: 3,826.
President & Chief Executive Officer: Tom Rutledge. General Manager: Jerry Parker. Technical Operations Manager: Doyle Ruona. Accounting Director: David Sovanski.
Ownership: Charter Communications Inc. (MSO).

LIMON—Formerly served by CAMS Cable. No longer in operation. ICA: CO0069.

LONGMONT—Comcast Cable, 434 Kimbark St, Longmont, CO 80501-5526. Phone: 303-776-2108. Fax: 303-678-5308. Web Site: http://www.comcast.com. Also serves Aspen, Avon, Basalt, Beaver Creek, Berthoud, Blue River, Boulder County (portions), Breckenridge, Dacono, Dillon, Eagle County (portions), Edwards, Erie, Evans, Evanston, Firestone, Fort Collins, Fort Lupton, Fraser, Frederick, Frisco, Garden City, Garfield County (portions), Granby, Grand County, Grand Lake, Greeley, Hot Sulphur Springs, Keystone, La Salle, Lafayette, Larimer County (portions), Louisville, Loveland, Minturn, Pitkin County (portions), Routt County (portions), Silver Creek, Silverthorne, Snowmass Village, Steamboat Springs, Summit County (portions), Superior, Vail, Weld County (portions), Windsor & Winter Park. ICA: CO0011.
TV Market Ranking: 32 (Boulder County (portions) (portions), Dacono, Erie, Evanston, Firestone, Fort Lupton, Frederick, Lafayette, LONGMONT, Louisville, Superior, Weld County (portions) (portions)); Below 100 (Basalt, Berthoud, Evans, Fraser, Garden City, Garfield County (portions), Grand County (portions), Grand Lake, La Salle, Larimer County (portions), Loveland, Pitkin County (portions) (portions), Routt County (portions), Silver Creek, Snowmass Village, Windsor, Winter Park, Fort Collins, Greeley, Steamboat Springs, Boulder County (portions) (portions), Weld County (portions) (portions)); Outside TV Markets (Beaver Creek, Eagle County (portions), Edwards, Frisco, Grand County (portions), Hot Sulphur Springs, Keystone, Minturn, Pitkin County (portions) (portions), SILVERTHORNE, Vail, Aspen, Avon, Dillon, Granby, Weld County (portions) (portions)). Franchise award date: May 1, 1982. Franchise expiration date: N.A. Began: March 15, 1983.
Channel capacity: 26 (operating 2-way). Channels available but not in use: N.A.
Basic Service
Subscribers: 112,610.
Programming (received off-air): KBDI-TV (PBS) Broomfield; KCEC (Bounce TV, LATV, UNV) Denver; KCNC-TV (CBS, Decades) Denver; KDEN-TV (TMO) Longmont; KDVR (Antenna TV, FOX) Denver; KETD (Estrella TV) Castle Rock; KMGH-TV (ABC, Azteca America) Denver; KPXC-TV (ION) Denver; KRMA-TV (PBS) Denver; KRMT (Daystar TV, ETV) Denver; KTVD (MeTV, MNT) Denver; KUSA (NBC, WeatherNation) Denver; KWGN-TV (CW, This TV) Denver; 1 FM.
Programming (via satellite): C-SPAN; Hallmark Channel; QVC; UniMas; WGN America.
Fee: $50.00 installation; $30.45 monthly.
Expanded Basic Service 1
Subscribers: N.A.
Programming (via satellite): A&E; Altitude Sports & Entertainment; AMC; Animal Planet; Cartoon Network; CMT; CNBC; CNN; Comedy Central; Discovery Channel; Disney Channel; E! HD; ESPN; ESPN2; Food Network; Fox News Channel; Fox Sports 1; Freeform; FX; Golf Channel; HGTV; History; HLN; Lifetime; MSNBC; MTV; NBCSN; Nickelodeon; Root Sports Rocky Mountain; Spike TV; Syfy; TBS; The Weather Channel; TLC; TNT; Travel Channel; truTV; TV Land; USA Network; VH1.
Fee: $35.70 monthly.
Digital Basic Service
Subscribers: N.A.
Programming (via satellite): 52MX; BBC America; Bloomberg Television; Bravo; CBS Sports Network; CMT; Discovery Digital Networks; Disney XD; ESPN Classic; ESPN HD; ESPNews; EVINE Live; Flix; FOX College Sports Central; FOX College Sports Pacific; Fuse; FXM; FYI; Great American Country; GSN; History International; HITS (Headend In The Sky); IFC; LMN; LOGO; MC; MoviePlex; Nat Geo WILD; National Geographic Channel; NFL Network; Nick Jr.; Nicktoons; Outdoor Channel; Pop; Sprout; Starz Encore (multiplexed); Sundance TV; TeenNick; The Word Network; Trinity Broadcasting Network (TBN); Turner Classic Movies; Versus HD; WE tv; Weatherscan.
Fee: $30.45 monthly.
Digital Pay Service 1
Pay Units: 151.
Programming (via satellite): Cinemax (multiplexed); Flix; HBO (multiplexed); Showtime (multiplexed); Starz (multiplexed); The Movie Channel (multiplexed).
Fee: $15.99 monthly (each).
Video-On-Demand: No
Pay-Per-View
iN DEMAND (delivered digitally); ESPN (delivered digitally); Starz (delivered digitally); Playboy TV (delivered digitally).
Internet Service
Operational: Yes.
Subscribers: 79,113.
Broadband Service: Comcast High Speed Internet.
Fee: $42.95 monthly.
Telephone Service
Digital: Operational
Subscribers: 33,186.
Miles of Plant: 4,386.0 (coaxial); 552.0 (fiber optic). Homes passed: 213,661.
Vice President & General Manager: Mike Trueblood. Technical Operations Director: Stan Reifschneider. Marketing Director: Kier Kristenson.
Ownership: Comcast Cable Communications Inc. (MSO).

LOVELAND (Columbine Mobile Home Park)—Formerly served by US Cable of Coastal Texas L.P. No longer in operation. ICA: CO0178.

LYONS (town)—Lyons Communications, PO Box 1403, Lyons, CO 80540. Phone: 303-823-5656. E-mail: lyonstv@gmail.com. Web Site: http://lyonscomm.com. ICA: CO0110.
TV Market Ranking: Below 100 (LYONS (TOWN)). Franchise award date: N.A. Franchise expiration date: N.A. Began: February 1, 1985.
Channel capacity: N.A. Channels available but not in use: N.A.
Basic Service
Subscribers: 154.
Programming (received off-air): KCEC (Bounce TV, LATV, UNV) Denver; KCNC-TV (CBS, Decades) Denver; KDVR (Antenna TV, FOX) Denver; KMGH-TV (ABC, Azteca America) Denver; KRMA-TV (PBS) Denver; KRMT (Daystar TV, ETV) Denver; KTVD (MeTV, MNT) Denver; KUSA (NBC, WeatherNation) Denver; KWGN-TV (CW, This TV) Denver.

Colorado—Cable Systems

Programming (via satellite): Azteca; C-SPAN; QVC; The Weather Channel; WGN America.
Fee: $34.95 installation; $36.00 monthly.

Expanded Basic Service 1
Subscribers: 152.
Programming (via satellite): A&E; AMC; Cartoon Network; CNBC; CNN; Discovery Channel; Disney Channel; ESPN; ESPN2; Fox News Channel; Freeform; FX; Great American Country; Hallmark Channel; HGTV; History; HLN; Lifetime; MSNBC; Root Sports Rocky Mountain; TBS; TLC; TNT; Turner Classic Movies; USA Network.
Fee: $34.95 installation; $39.95 monthly.

Pay Service 1
Pay Units: 20.
Programming (via satellite): Cinemax; HBO; Showtime.
Fee: $10.95 monthly (Cinemax), $11.95 monthly (Showtime) $14.00 monthly (HBO)

Video-On-Demand: No

Internet Service
Operational: Yes.
Subscribers: 60.
Fee: $34.95 installation; $19.95 monthly.

Telephone Service
Analog: Operational
Fee: $34.95 monthly

Miles of Plant: 20.0 (coaxial); None (fiber optic). Homes passed: 850.
General Manager: Robert Jones.
Ownership: Lyons Communications (MSO).

MANASSA—Formerly served by Charter Communications. No longer in operation. ICA: CO0068.

MANCOS—Formerly served by Bresnan Communications. Now served by Charter Communications, DURANGO, CO [CO0023]. ICA: CO0111.

MANZANOLA—Formerly served by Bresnan Communications. Now served by Charter Communications, LA JUNTA, CO [CO0040]. ICA: CO0149.

MEAD—K2 Communications, 339 Main St., PO Box 232, Mead, CO 80542. Phones: 866-525-2253; 303-828-0369; 970-535-6323. Fax: 303-265-9001. E-mail: info@k2cable.com. Web Site: http://www.k2cable.com. ICA: CO0196.
TV Market Ranking: 32 (MEAD). Franchise award date: July 1, 1993. Franchise expiration date: N.A. Began: March 1, 1994.
Channel capacity: N.A. Channels available but not in use: N.A.

Basic Service
Subscribers: N.A.
Programming (received off-air): KBDI-TV (PBS) Broomfield; KCNC-TV (CBS, Decades) Denver; KDVR (Antenna TV, FOX) Denver; KMGH-TV (ABC, Azteca America) Denver; KPXC-TV (ION) Denver; KRMA-TV (PBS) Denver; KTFD-DT (getTV, UniMas) Boulder; KTVD (MeTV, MNT) Denver; KUSA (NBC, WeatherNation) Denver; KWGN-TV (CW, This TV) Denver.
Fee: $35.00 installation.

Expanded Basic Service 1
Subscribers: N.A.
Programming (received off-air): KDEN-TV (TMO) Longmont.
Programming (via satellite): A&E; Altitude Sports & Entertainment; AMC; Animal Planet; Bravo; Cartoon Network; CNBC; CNN; Comedy Central; C-SPAN; Discovery Channel; Disney Channel; DIY Network; ESPN; ESPN Classic; ESPN2; Food Network; Fox Sports 1; FOX Sports Networks; Freeform; FX; Golf Channel; Great American Country; Hallmark Channel; HGTV; History; HLN; IFC; INSP; Lifetime; MoviePlex; MSNBC; National Geographic Channel; NBCSN; Nickelodeon; Oxygen; Spike TV; Starz Encore; Syfy; TBS; The Weather Channel; TLC; TNT; Travel Channel; truTV; Turner Classic Movies; TV Land; USA Network; VH1; WGN America.
Fee: $37.95 monthly.

Pay Service 1
Pay Units: N.A.
Programming (via satellite): Flix; HBO; Showtime; Sundance TV; The Movie Channel.
Fee: $14.95 monthly (HBO or Flix/Sundance/Showtime/TMC).

Video-On-Demand: No

Internet Service
Operational: Yes.
Broadband Service: In-house.
Fee: $49.99 installation; $38.95 monthly.

Telephone Service
Digital: Operational
Fee: $29.99 monthly
Miles of Plant: 14.0 (coaxial); None (fiber optic).
General Manager & Chief Technician: Gary Shields.
Ownership: K2 Communications.

MEEKER—Charter Communications, 12405 Powerscourt Dr, St. Louis, MO 63131. Phones: 636-207-5100 (Corporate office); 970-824-9221; 970-824-3298; 877-273-7626 (Customer service). Web Site: http://www.charter.com. Also serves Rio Blanco County (eastern portion). ICA: CO0078.
TV Market Ranking: Below 100 (Rio Blanco County (eastern portion) (portions)); Outside TV Markets (MEEKER, Rio Blanco County (eastern portion) (portions)). Franchise award date: N.A. Franchise expiration date: N.A. Began: June 1, 1982.
Channel capacity: N.A. Channels available but not in use: N.A.

Digital Basic Service
Subscribers: 29. Commercial subscribers: 15.
Programming (via microwave): KCNC-TV (CBS, Decades) Denver; KDVR (Antenna TV, FOX) Denver; KMGH-TV (ABC, Azteca America) Denver; KRMA-TV (PBS) Denver; KTVD (MeTV, MNT) Denver; KUSA (NBC, WeatherNation) Denver; KWGN-TV (CW, This TV) Denver.
Programming (via satellite): Altitude Sports & Entertainment; AMC; Animal Planet; Cartoon Network; CNBC; CNN; Discovery Channel; Disney Channel; E! HD; ESPN; Fox News Channel; Freeform; FX; Great American Country; HLN; Lifetime; MSNBC; MTV; Nickelodeon; QVC; Root Sports Rocky Mountain; Spike TV; TBS; The Weather Channel; TLC; TNT; truTV; USA Network.
Fee: $34.95 installation; $52.99 monthly; $1.50 converter.

Digital Pay Service 1
Pay Units: N.A.
Programming (via satellite): Cinemax; HBO; Showtime; Starz; Starz Encore.

Video-On-Demand: No

Pay-Per-View
special events.

Internet Service
Operational: Yes.
Broadband Service: Charter Internet.
Fee: $36.95 monthly.

Telephone Service
Digital: Operational
Fee: $46.95 monthly

Miles of Plant: 31.0 (coaxial); 1.0 (fiber optic). Homes passed: 1,090.
President & Chief Executive Officer: Tom Rutledge. General Manager: Tommy Cotton. Accounting Director: David Sovanski.
Ownership: Charter Communications Inc. (MSO).

MERINO—Kentec Communications, 710 West Main St, Sterling, CO 80751. Phone: 970-522-8107. Fax: 970-521-9457. E-mail: support@kci.net. Web Site: http://www.kci.net. ICA: CO0191.
TV Market Ranking: Below 100 (MERINO). Franchise award date: May 4, 1992. Franchise expiration date: N.A. Began: September 1, 1992.
Channel capacity: N.A. Channels available but not in use: N.A.

Basic Service
Subscribers: N.A.
Programming (via satellite): A&E; Altitude Sports & Entertainment; AMC; Animal Planet; CNN; Comedy Central; Discovery Channel; Disney Channel; ESPN; ESPN2; EVINE Live; Fox News Channel; Fox Sports 1; Freeform; HGTV; History; HLN; KUSA (NBC, WeatherNation) Denver; National Geographic Channel; Nickelodeon; OWN: Oprah Winfrey Network; Root Sports Rocky Mountain; Syfy; TBS; The Weather Channel; TLC; TNT; Travel Channel; Trinity Broadcasting Network (TBN); Turner Classic Movies; USA Network; WE tv; WGN America.
Programming (via translator): KCNC-TV (CBS, Decades) Denver; KDVR (Antenna TV, FOX) Denver; KMGH-TV (ABC, Azteca America) Denver; KRMA-TV (PBS) Denver; KTVD (MeTV, MNT) Denver; KWGN-TV (CW, This TV) Denver.
Fee: $30.00 installation.

Pay Service 1
Pay Units: N.A.
Programming (via satellite): HBO.
Fee: $10.00 monthly.

Internet Service
Operational: Yes.

Telephone Service
Digital: Operational
Miles of Plant: 3.0 (coaxial); None (fiber optic). Homes passed: 100.
General Manager & Chief Technician: Kent Sager. Marketing Director: Tiffany Stewart.
Ownership: Kentec Communications Inc. (MSO).

MONTE VISTA—Formerly served by Bresnan Communications. Now served by Charter Communications, ALAMOSA, CO [CO0035]. ICA: CO0048.

MONTROSE—Charter Communications, 12405 Powerscourt Dr, St. Louis, MO 63131. Phones: 636-207-5100 (Corporate office); 516-803-2300 (Corporate office); 877-273-7626. Web Site: http://www.charter.com. Also serves Delta, Delta County (western portion) & Montrose County. ICA: CO0028.
TV Market Ranking: Below 100 (Delta County (western portion), MONTROSE, Montrose County (portions), Delta); Outside TV Markets (Montrose County (portions)). Franchise award date: N.A. Franchise expiration date: N.A. Began: January 1, 1966.
Channel capacity: N.A. Channels available but not in use: N.A.

Digital Basic Service
Subscribers: 5,456.
Programming (via satellite): A&E HD; Altitude Sports & Entertainment; Animal Planet HD; AXS TV; Bandamax; BBC America; Bloomberg Television; Bravo; Bravo HD; BYUtv; CBS Sports Network; Cine Mexicano; Cinelatino; CMT; CNBC HD+; CNN en Espanol; CNN HD; Cooking Channel; De Pelicula; De Pelicula Clasico; Destination America; Discovery Channel HD; Discovery Kids Channel; Discovery Life Channel; Disney Channel HD; Disney XD; DIY Network; DMX Music; ESPN Classic; ESPN Deportes; ESPN HD; ESPN2 HD; ESPNews; Food Network HD; FOX College Sports Central; FOX College Sports Pacific; Fox Deportes; Fox Sports 1; Freeform HD; FSN HD; Fuse; FXM; FYI; Golf Channel; GolTV; GSN; HD Theater; HGTV HD; History en Espanol; History HD; History International; IFC; Investigation Discovery; ION Television; Lifetime Movie Network HD; LMN; MTV Classic; MTV Hits; MTV Jams; MTV Live; MTV2; Nat Geo WILD; National Geographic Channel; National Geographic Channel HD; NBC Universo; NBCSN; NFL Network; NFL Network HD; NHL Network; Nick 2; Nick Jr.; Nicktoons; Outdoor Channel; Outdoor Channel 2 HD; OWN: Oprah Winfrey Network; Qubo; RFD-TV; Science Channel; Science HD; Sprout; Syfy HD; TBS HD; TeenNick; Telehit; The Weather Channel HD; TLC HD; TNT HD; Tr3s; Trinity Broadcasting Network (TBN); UniMas; Universal HD; Univision Studios; UP; USA Network HD; Versus HD; VH1 Soul; ViendoMovies.
Fee: $26.99 monthly.

Digital Expanded Basic Service
Subscribers: 3,500.
Programming (via satellite): A&E; AMC; Animal Planet; Cartoon Network; CMT; CNBC; CNN; Comedy Central; Disney Channel; E! HD; ESPN; ESPN2; EWTN Global Catholic Network; Food Network; Fox News Channel; Freeform; FX; Hallmark Channel; HLN; ION Television; MSNBC; MTV; Nickelodeon; Oxygen; Pop; QVC; Root Sports Rocky Mountain; Syfy; TLC; TNT; Travel Channel; truTV; Turner Classic Movies; TV Land; UniMas; Univision Studios; USA Network; VH1.
Fee: $26.99 monthly.

Digital Pay Service 1
Pay Units: N.A.
Programming (via satellite): Cinemax (multiplexed); Cinemax HD; Cinemax On Demand; Flix; HBO (multiplexed); HBO HD; HBO on Demand; Showtime; Showtime HD; Showtime On Demand; Starz (multiplexed); Starz Encore (multiplexed); Starz HD; Starz On Demand; The Movie Channel (multiplexed); The Movie Channel HD.

Video-On-Demand: Yes

Pay-Per-View
special events (delivered digitally); ESPN (delivered digitally); NBA League Pass (delivered digitally); MLS Direct Kick (delivered digitally); MLB Extra Innings (delivered digitally); NHL Center Ice (delivered digitally).

Internet Service
Operational: Yes.
Broadband Service: Charter Internet.
Fee: $55.95 monthly.

Telephone Service
Digital: Operational
Fee: $39.99 monthly
Miles of Plant: 116.0 (coaxial); None (fiber optic). Homes passed: 9,100.
President & Chief Executive Officer: Tom Rutledge. Regional Vice President: Sean Hogue. Technical Operations Manager: Gary Young. Accounting Director: David Sovanski.
Ownership: Charter Communications Inc. (MSO).

Cable Systems—Colorado

MONTROSE—Spring Creek Cable, 146 West Main St, Ste 104, Montrose, CO 81401. Phone: 970-249-4506. Fax: 970-240-8122. E-mail: springcreek89@yahoo.com. Web Site: http://www.springcreekcable.com. ICA: CO0217.
TV Market Ranking: Below 100 (MONTROSE).
Channel capacity: N.A. Channels available but not in use: N.A.
President & General Manager: Tom Randolph.
Ownership: Spring Creek Cable Inc. (MSO).

MONUMENT—Formerly served by Adelphia Communications. Now served by Comcast Cable, COLORADO SPRINGS, CO [CO0003]. ICA: CO0032.

MOUNTAIN VILLAGE—Mountain Village Cable, 455 Mountain Village Blvd, Ste A, Mountain Village, CO 81435. Phone: 970-728-8000. E-mail: info@mvcable.net. Web Site: https://townofmountainvillage.com/residents/utilities/cable. ICA: CO0219.
TV Market Ranking: Below 100 (MOUNTAIN VILLAGE).
Channel capacity: N.A. Channels available but not in use: N.A.
Chief Technician: Jory Hasler.
Ownership: Town of Mountain Village.

NEDERLAND—USA Communications, 920 East 56th St, Ste B, Kearney, NE 68847. Phone: 877-234-0102. E-mail: csr@usacommunications.tv. Web Site: http://usacommunications.tv. ICA: CO0100.
TV Market Ranking: Below 100 (NEDERLAND). Franchise award date: January 15, 1983. Franchise expiration date: N.A. Began: December 30, 1983.
Channel capacity: N.A. Channels available but not in use: N.A.
Basic Service
  Subscribers: 31.
  Programming (received off-air): KCNC-TV (CBS, Decades) Denver; KDVR (Antenna TV, FOX) Denver; KMGH-TV (ABC, Azteca America) Denver; KRMA-TV (PBS) Denver. Programming (via satellite): Animal Planet; Cartoon Network; Discovery Channel; ESPN; History; KUSA (NBC, WeatherNation) Denver; KWGN-TV (CW, This TV) Denver; MSNBC; Nickelodeon; Outdoor Channel; QVC; TBS; TLC; Travel Channel; TV Land; USA Network; WE tv.
  Fee: $29.95 installation; $46.00 monthly.
Expanded Basic Service 1
  Subscribers: N.A.
  Programming (via satellite): A&E; CMT; CNBC; CNN; Comedy Central; Disney Channel; ESPN2; Freeform; HLN; MTV; NBCSN; Root Sports Rocky Mountain; Spike TV; Syfy; The Weather Channel; TNT; Turner Classic Movies.
  Fee: $14.75 monthly.
Pay Service 1
  Pay Units: 25.
  Programming (via satellite): HBO (multiplexed).
  Fee: $13.49 monthly.
Video-On-Demand: No
Internet Service
  Operational: No.
Telephone Service
  None
Miles of Plant: 14.0 (coaxial); None (fiber optic). Homes passed: 541.
Chief Financial Officer: Amber Reineke.
Ownership: USA Companies LP (MSO).

NEW CASTLE (town)—Comcast Cable. Now served by SILT, CO [CO0108]. ICA: CO0092.

NORWOOD—B & C Cablevision Inc, PO Box 548, Norwood, CO 81423-0548. Phone: 970-327-0122. ICA: CO0137.
TV Market Ranking: Below 100 (NORWOOD). Franchise award date: N.A. Franchise expiration date: N.A. Began: August 1, 1991.
Channel capacity: N.A. Channels available but not in use: N.A.
Basic Service
  Subscribers: 27.
  Programming (received off-air): KGBY (ABC, TMO) Grand Junction.
  Programming (via microwave): KKCO (CW, NBC) Grand Junction; KREY-TV (CBS) Montrose; KRMA-TV (PBS) Denver; KWGN-TV (CW, This TV) Denver.
  Programming (via satellite): A&E; AMC; CNN; Discovery Channel; ESPN; Freeform; Spike TV; TBS; TNT; USA Network.
  Fee: $15.00 installation; $25.00 monthly.
Pay Service 1
  Pay Units: 5.
  Programming (via satellite): Cinemax.
  Fee: $8.00 monthly.
Pay Service 2
  Pay Units: 11.
  Programming (via satellite): HBO.
  Fee: $8.00 monthly.
Pay Service 3
  Pay Units: 7.
  Programming (via satellite): Showtime.
  Fee: $8.00 monthly.
Internet Service
  Operational: No.
Telephone Service
  None
Miles of Plant: 5.0 (coaxial); None (fiber optic). Homes passed: 245.
General Manager & Chief Technician: Craig Greager.
Ownership: B & C Cable.

NUCLA—Formerly served by Charter Communications. No longer in operation. ICA: CO0090.

OAK CREEK—Formerly served by Westcom II LLC. No longer in operation. ICA: CO0119.

OLATHE—Formerly served by Cable USA. No longer in operation. ICA: CO0112.

OLATHE—Spring Creek Cable, 146 West Main St, Ste 104, Montrose, CO 81401. Phone: 970-249-4506. Fax: 970-240-8122. E-mail: springcreek89@yahoo.com. Web Site: http://www.springcreekcable.com. ICA: CO0218.
TV Market Ranking: Below 100 (OLATHE).
Channel capacity: N.A. Channels available but not in use: N.A.
President & General Manager: Tom Randolph.
Ownership: Spring Creek Cable Inc. (MSO).

ORDWAY—Formerly served by NexHorizon Communications. No longer in operation. ICA: CO0099.

OTIS (town)—Vyve Broadband, 4 International Dr, Ste 330, Rye Brook, NY 10573. Phones: 800-937-1397; 307-358-3833; 307-358-3861. Web Site: http://vyvebroadband.com. Also serves Akron & Yuma. ICA: CO0128.
TV Market Ranking: Below 100 (Akron); Outside TV Markets (OTIS (TOWN), Yuma). Franchise award date: January 1, 1969. Franchise expiration date: N.A. Began: December 1, 1969.
Channel capacity: N.A. Channels available but not in use: N.A.
Basic Service
  Subscribers: 149.
  Programming (via microwave): KCNC-TV (CBS, Decades) Denver; KDVR (Antenna TV, FOX) Denver; KMGH-TV (ABC, Azteca America) Denver; KRMA-TV (PBS) Denver; KTVS-LD (IND) Albuquerque; KUSA (NBC, WeatherNation) Denver; KWGN-TV (CW, This TV) Denver.
  Programming (via satellite): QVC; Univision Studios; WGN America.
  Fee: $59.99 installation; $25.00 monthly.
Expanded Basic Service 1
  Subscribers: 39.
  Programming (via satellite): 3ABN; A&E; AMC; Animal Planet; Bravo; Cartoon Network; CMT; CNBC; CNN; Comedy Central; C-SPAN; C-SPAN 2; Discovery Channel; E! HD; ESPN; ESPN Classic; ESPN2; ESPNews; Food Network; Fox News Channel; Freeform; FX; Great American Country; Hallmark Channel; HGTV; History; HLN; MSNBC; MTV; Nick Jr.; Nickelodeon; Outdoor Channel; OWN: Oprah Winfrey Network; Root Sports Rocky Mountain; Spike TV; Syfy; TBS; The Weather Channel; TLC; TNT; Travel Channel; Turner Classic Movies; TV Land; USA Network; VH1; WE tv.
  Fee: $19.04 monthly.
Digital Basic Service
  Subscribers: N.A.
  Programming (via satellite): BBC America; Bloomberg Television; Bravo; Discovery Digital Networks; ESPN Classic; ESPN2; ESPNews; EVINE Live; FOX College Sports Central; FOX College Sports Pacific; Fox Sports 1; Fuse; FXM; FYI; Golf Channel; Great American Country; GSN; HGTV; History; History International; IFC; International Television (ITV); LMN; MBC America; MC; National Geographic Channel; NBCSN; Nick Jr.; Nicktoons; Outdoor Channel; Ovation; Sundance TV; Syfy; TeenNick; The Word Network; Trinity Broadcasting Network (TBN); Turner Classic Movies; TV Land; WE tv.
Digital Pay Service 1
  Pay Units: 5.
  Programming (via satellite): HBO (multiplexed).
  Fee: $15.00 installation; $13.95 monthly.
Digital Pay Service 2
  Pay Units: 5.
  Programming (via satellite): Cinemax (multiplexed).
  Fee: $11.95 monthly.
Digital Pay Service 3
  Pay Units: 4.
  Programming (via satellite): Starz (multiplexed); Starz Encore (multiplexed).
  Fee: $13.95 monthly.
Digital Pay Service 4
  Pay Units: 2.
  Programming (via satellite): Flix; Showtime (multiplexed); The Movie Channel (multiplexed).
  Fee: $13.95 monthly (Showtime/Flix or TMC).
Video-On-Demand: No
Pay-Per-View
  Hot Choice; Playboy TV; Fresh; Shorteez.
Internet Service
  Operational: Yes.
  Broadband Service: Net Commander.
  Fee: $39.95 installation; $21.95 monthly.
Telephone Service
  None
Miles of Plant: 38.0 (coaxial); None (fiber optic). Homes passed: 2,550.
President & Chief Executive Officer: Jeffrey DeMond. Vice President, Residential Services: Vin Zachariah. Vice President, Marketing: Diane Quennoz. Senior Vice President, Financial Planning: Daniel White.
Ownership: Vyve Broadband LLC.

PAGOSA SPRINGS—USA Communications, 920 East 56th St, Ste B, Kearney, NE 68847. Phone: 877-234-0102. E-mail: csr@usacommunications.tv. Web Site: http://usacommunications.tv. Also serves Archuleta County. ICA: CO0053.
TV Market Ranking: Outside TV Markets (Archuleta County, PAGOSA SPRINGS). Franchise award date: February 7, 1984. Franchise expiration date: N.A. Began: August 15, 1984.
Channel capacity: N.A. Channels available but not in use: N.A.
Basic Service
  Subscribers: 835.
  Programming (via microwave): KCNC-TV (CBS, Decades) Denver; KMGH-TV (ABC, Azteca America) Denver; KOAT-TV (ABC, Estrella TV) Albuquerque; KOBF (NBC, This TV) Farmington; KRMA-TV (PBS) Denver; KRPV-DT (GLC) Roswell; KUSA (NBC, WeatherNation) Denver; KWGN-TV (CW, This TV) Denver.
  Programming (via satellite): CNN; Discovery Channel; Fox News Channel; Hallmark Channel; HLN; Lifetime; Pop; QVC; The Weather Channel; TLC; Travel Channel.
  Fee: $29.95 installation; $34.50 monthly.
Expanded Basic Service 1
  Subscribers: N.A.
  Programming (via microwave): KLUZ-TV (LATV, UNV) Albuquerque.
  Programming (via satellite): A&E; AMC; Animal Planet; Bravo; CMT; CNBC; Comedy Central; C-SPAN; Disney Channel; DIY Network; ESPN; ESPN2; Food Network; Fox Sports 1; Freeform; FX; Great American Country; GSN; HGTV; History; MSNBC; MTV; NBCSN; Nickelodeon; Outdoor Channel; Root Sports Rocky Mountain; Spike TV; TBS; TNT; truTV; TV Land; USA Network; VH1; WE tv.
  Fee: $14.75 monthly.
Digital Basic Service
  Subscribers: N.A.
  Programming (via satellite): BBC America; Bloomberg Television; Bravo; Discovery Life Channel; ESPN Classic; ESPN2; ESPNews; Family Friendly Entertainment; Fox Sports 1; Fuse; FXM; FYI; Golf Channel; GSN; HGTV; History; History International; IFC; LMN; NBCSN; Nick Jr.; Nicktoons; Outdoor Channel; TeenNick; Trinity Broadcasting Network (TBN); Turner Classic Movies; TV Land; WE tv.

CABLE & TV STATION COVERAGE
Atlas 2017
The perfect companion to the Television & Cable Factbook
To order call 800-771-9202 or visit www.warren-news.com

Colorado—Cable Systems

Digital Pay Service 1
Pay Units: N.A.
Programming (via satellite): Cinemax (multiplexed); Flix; HBO (multiplexed); Showtime (multiplexed); Starz (multiplexed); Starz Encore (multiplexed); The Movie Channel (multiplexed).
Fee: $12.49 monthly (Cinemax or Starz/Encore), $13.49 monthly (HBO or Showtime).
Video-On-Demand: No
Pay-Per-View
Playboy TV; Spice; Spice2.
Internet Service
Operational: Yes.
Fee: $35.00 installation; $39.95 monthly.
Telephone Service
None
Miles of Plant: 143.0 (coaxial); None (fiber optic).
Chief Financial Officer: Amber Reineke.
Ownership: USA Companies LP (MSO).

PAONIA—Charter Communications, 12405 Powerscourt Dr, St. Louis, MO 63131. Phones: 636-207-5100 (Corporate office); 516-803-2300; 877-273-7626. Web Site: http://www.charter.com. Also serves Delta County (eastern portion). ICA: C00079.
TV Market Ranking: Below 100 (Delta County (eastern portion) (portions), PAONIA); Outside TV Markets (Delta County (eastern portion) (portions)). Franchise award date: N.A. Franchise expiration date: N.A. Began: June 1, 1982.
Channel capacity: N.A. Channels available but not in use: N.A.
Digital Basic Service
Subscribers: 31.
Programming (via satellite): BBC America; Bravo; CBS Sports Network; CMT; Destination America; Discovery Kids Channel; DMX Music; ESPN Classic; ESPN2; ESPNews; Fox Sports 1; Golf Channel; GSN; HGTV; History; IFC; Investigation Discovery; MTV Classic; National Geographic Channel; NBCSN; Nick Jr.; OWN: Oprah Winfrey Network; Science Channel; Syfy; Turner Classic Movies; TV Land.
Fee: $26.99 monthly.
Digital Pay Service 1
Pay Units: N.A.
Programming (via satellite): HBO (multiplexed); Showtime 2; Starz Edge; Starz Encore (multiplexed); The Movie Channel.
Video-On-Demand: No
Internet Service
Operational: Yes.
Broadband Service: Charter Internet.
Fee: $39.95 monthly.
Telephone Service
Digital: Operational
Fee: $49.99 monthly
Miles of Plant: 26.0 (coaxial); None (fiber optic). Homes passed: 990.
President & Chief Executive Officer: Tom Rutledge. Regional Vice President: Sean Hogue. Technical Operations Manager: Gary Young. Accounting Director: David Sovanski.
Ownership: Charter Communications Inc. (MSO).

PARACHUTE—Comcast Cable, 1605 Grand Ave, Ste 1, Glenwood Springs, CO 81601. Phones: 970-230-9076; 970-928-7784. Fax: 970-945-0270. Web Site: http://www.comcast.com. Also serves Battlement Mesa. ICA: C00072.
TV Market Ranking: Outside TV Markets (Battlement Mesa, PARACHUTE). Franchise award date: July 9, 1981. Franchise expiration date: N.A. Began: November 1, 1981.
Channel capacity: 66 (operating 2-way). Channels available but not in use: N.A.
Basic Service
Subscribers: 230.
Programming (received off-air): KGBY (ABC, TMO) Grand Junction.
Programming (via microwave): KCEC (Bounce TV, LATV, UNV) Denver; KCNC-TV (CBS, Decades) Denver; KDVR (Antenna TV, FOX) Denver; KMGH-TV (ABC, Azteca America) Denver; KPXC-TV (ION) Denver; KRMA-TV (PBS) Denver; KTVD (MeTV, MNT) Denver; KUSA (NBC, WeatherNation) Denver; KWGN-TV (CW, This TV) Denver.
Programming (via satellite): Altitude Sports & Entertainment; C-SPAN; ESPN; ESPN2; Freeform; Pop; Root Sports Rocky Mountain.
Fee: $50.00 installation; $230.00 monthly.
Expanded Basic Service 1
Subscribers: N.A.
Programming (via satellite): A&E; AMC; Animal Planet; Bravo; CMT; CNBC; CNN; Comedy Central; Discovery Channel; Disney Channel; Disney XD; EVINE Live; Food Network; Fox News Channel; FYI; Great American Country; HGTV; History; History International; HLN; Lifetime; MSNBC; MTV; National Geographic Channel; Nickelodeon; Outdoor Channel; QVC; Spike TV; Syfy; TBS; The Weather Channel; TLC; TNT; Travel Channel; Trinity Broadcasting Network (TBN); Turner Classic Movies; TV Land; USA Network; VH1; WGN America.
Fee: $35.00 monthly.
Digital Basic Service
Subscribers: N.A.
Programming (via satellite): BBC America; Bloomberg Television; Discovery Kids Channel; Discovery Life Channel; ESPN Classic; ESPNews; FXM; Golf Channel; GSN; IFC; LOGO; MC; MoviePlex; NBCSN; Nick Jr.; Nicktoons; OWN: Oprah Winfrey Network; Sprout; WE tv.
Pay Service 1
Pay Units: N.A.
Programming (via satellite): Cinemax; HBO (multiplexed); Showtime.
Fee: $9.95 monthly (each).
Digital Pay Service 1
Pay Units: N.A.
Programming (via satellite): Showtime; Starz; Starz Encore (multiplexed); The Movie Channel.
Fee: $15.99 monthly (each).
Video-On-Demand: No
Pay-Per-View
Playboy TV; Fresh.
Internet Service
Operational: Yes.
Broadband Service: Comcast High Speed Internet.
Fee: $42.95 monthly.
Telephone Service
None
Miles of Plant: 30.0 (coaxial); None (fiber optic).
Vice President: Mike Trueblood. General Manager: Ben Miller. Technical Operations Manager: James Comiskey. Customer Service Manager: Anita Robinson.
Ownership: Comcast Cable Communications Inc. (MSO).

PENROSE (unincorporated areas)—Formerly served by Bresnan Communications. Now served by Charter Communications, CANON CITY, CO [C00016]. ICA: C00075.

PETERSON AFB—Peterson Broadband, 301 Mitchell Rd, Colorado Springs, CO 80914. Phones: 719-597-0873; 719-597-0164; 425-451-1470 (Corporate office). Fax: 425-451-1471. E-mail: petersoncsr@ruralwest.com. Web Site: http://ruralwest.com. ICA: C00081.
TV Market Ranking: Below 100 (PETERSON AFB). Franchise award date: N.A. Franchise expiration date: N.A. Began: January 1, 1983.
Channel capacity: N.A. Channels available but not in use: N.A.
Basic Service
Subscribers: 20.
Programming (received off-air): KKTV (CBS, MNT) Colorado Springs; KOAA-TV (Grit, NBC) Pueblo; KRDO-TV (ABC, TMO) Colorado Springs; KTSC (PBS) Pueblo; KXRM-TV (FOX, MundoMax) Colorado Springs; KXTU-LD (CW) Colorado Springs.
Programming (via satellite): A&E; AMC; Animal Planet; BBC America; BET; Cartoon Network; CMT; CNBC; CNN; Comedy Central; C-SPAN; C-SPAN 2; Discovery Channel; Discovery Kids Channel; Disney Channel; E! HD; ESPN; ESPN Classic; ESPN2; Food Network; Fox News Channel; Fox Sports 1; Freeform; FX; FXM; FYI; Golf Channel; Hallmark Channel; HGTV; History; History International; HLN; KWGN-TV (CW, This TV) Denver; Lifetime; LMN; MSNBC; MTV; NASA TV; National Geographic Channel; NBCSN; Nickelodeon; Outdoor Channel; Oxygen; QVC; Spike TV; Syfy; TBS; The Weather Channel; TLC; TNT; Travel Channel; Trinity Broadcasting Network (TBN); Turner Classic Movies; TV Land; Univision Studios; USA Network; VH1; WE tv; WGN America.
Fee: $40.00 installation; $37.95 monthly.
Digital Basic Service
Subscribers: N.A.
Programming (via satellite): Bravo; CMT; Destination America; Disney XD; DMX Music; ESPN Classic; Fox Sports 1; Fuse; HGTV; History International; Investigation Discovery; LMN; MTV Classic; MTV2; National Geographic Channel; TeenNick.
Digital Pay Service 1
Pay Units: N.A.
Programming (via satellite): Cinemax (multiplexed); Flix; HBO (multiplexed); Showtime (multiplexed); Starz (multiplexed); Starz Encore (multiplexed); The Movie Channel (multiplexed).
Fee: $10.95 monthly (each).
Video-On-Demand: No
Internet Service
Operational: Yes.
Broadband Service: In-house.
Fee: $26.95 installation; $34.95 monthly.
Telephone Service
Digital: Operational
Miles of Plant: 4.0 (coaxial); 4.0 (fiber optic). Homes passed: 1,549.
General Manager: Kevin Abriam. Office Manager: Kim Abriam.
Ownership: RuralWest - Western Rural Broadband Inc. (MSO).

PEYTON—Falcon Broadband, 555 Hathaway Dr, Colorado Springs, CO 80915. Phone: 719-573-5343. Fax: 719-886-7925. E-mail: sales@falconbroadband.net. Web Site: http://falconbroadband.net. Also serves Colorado Springs (portions), El Paso County (eastern portions) & Falcon. ICA: C00213.
Channel capacity: N.A. Channels available but not in use: N.A.

Basic Service
Subscribers: N.A.
Programming (received off-air): KKTV (CBS, MNT) Colorado Springs; KOAA-TV (Grit, NBC) Pueblo; KRDO-TV (ABC, TMO) Colorado Springs; KXRM-TV (FOX, MundoMax) Colorado Springs; KXTU-LD (CW) Colorado Springs.
Digital Basic Service
Subscribers: N.A.
Internet Service
Operational: Yes.
Fee: $39.95 monthly.
Telephone Service
Digital: Operational
Fee: $28.95 monthly
General Manager: Ben Kley.
Ownership: Falcon Broadband.

PUEBLO—Comcast Cable. Now served by COLORADO SPRINGS, CO [C00003]. ICA: C00005.

PUEBLO WEST—Comcast Cable. Now served by COLORADO SPRINGS, CO [C00003]. ICA: C00077.

RANGELY—Charter Communications, 12405 Powerscourt Dr, St. Louis, MO 63131. Phones: 636-207-5100 (Corporate office); 970-824-9221; 877-273-7626; 970-824-3298. Web Site: http://www.charter.com. Also serves Rio Blanco County (northwestern portion). ICA: C00085.
TV Market Ranking: Outside TV Markets (RANGELY, Rio Blanco County (northwestern portion)). Franchise award date: N.A. Franchise expiration date: N.A. Began: August 1, 1982.
Channel capacity: N.A. Channels available but not in use: N.A.
Digital Basic Service
Subscribers: 12. Commercial subscribers: 18.
Programming (via microwave): KCNC-TV (CBS, Decades) Denver; KDVR (Antenna TV, FOX) Denver; KMGH-TV (ABC, Azteca America) Denver; KRMA-TV (PBS) Denver; KTVD (MeTV, MNT) Denver; KUSA (NBC, WeatherNation) Denver; KWGN-TV (CW, This TV) Denver.
Programming (via satellite): Altitude Sports & Entertainment; AMC; Animal Planet; Cartoon Network; CNBC; CNN; C-SPAN; Discovery Channel; Disney Channel; E! HD; ESPN; Fox News Channel; Freeform; FX; Great American Country; Hallmark Channel; HLN; Lifetime; MoviePlex; MSNBC; MTV; Nickelodeon; QVC; Root Sports Rocky Mountain; Spike TV; TBS; The Weather Channel; TLC; TNT; truTV; USA Network.
Fee: $34.95 installation; $24.99 monthly; $1.50 converter.
Digital Pay Service 1
Pay Units: N.A.
Programming (via satellite): Cinemax; HBO; Showtime; Starz; Starz Encore.
Video-On-Demand: No
Internet Service
Operational: Yes.
Broadband Service: Charter Internet.
Fee: $39.95 monthly.
Telephone Service
Digital: Operational
Fee: $49.99 monthly
Miles of Plant: 34.0 (coaxial); 1.0 (fiber optic). Homes passed: 1,214.
President & Chief Executive Officer: Tom Rutledge. General Manager: Tommy Cotton. Accounting Director: David Sovanski.
Ownership: Charter Communications Inc. (MSO).

Cable Systems—Colorado

Access the most current data instantly
FREE TRIAL @ ADVANCED TVFactbook
TELCO/IPTV • CABLE TV • TV STATIONS
www.warren-news.com/factbook.htm

RIFLE—Comcast Cable, 1605 Grand Ave, Ste 1, Glenwood Springs, CO 81601. Phones: 970-230-9076; 970-928-7784. Fax: 970-945-0270. Web Site: http://www.comcast.com. Also serves Garfield County (portions). ICA: C00043.
TV Market Ranking: Below 100 (Garfield County (portions) (portions), RIFLE); Outside TV Markets (Garfield County (portions) (portions)). Franchise award date: July 1, 1978. Franchise expiration date: N.A. Began: July 31, 1963.
Channel capacity: N.A. Channels available but not in use: N.A.
Basic Service
Subscribers: 1,144.
Programming (received off-air): KGBY (ABC, TMO) Grand Junction; KREG-TV (CBS) Glenwood Springs; 19 FMs.
Programming (via microwave): KCNC-TV (CBS, Decades) Denver; KDVR (Antenna TV, FOX) Denver; KMGH-TV (ABC, Azteca America) Denver; KPXC-TV (ION) Denver; KRMA-TV (PBS) Denver; KTVD (MeTV, MNT) Denver; KUSA (NBC, WeatherNation) Denver; KWGN-TV (CW, This TV) Denver.
Programming (via satellite): A&E; Discovery Channel; QVC; TBS.
Fee: $50.00 installation; $30.45 monthly.
Expanded Basic Service 1
Subscribers: N.A.
Programming (via satellite): Animal Planet; Cartoon Network; CMT; CNBC; CNN; Comedy Central; C-SPAN; Disney Channel; ESPN; ESPN2; Fox News Channel; Freeform; FX; Lifetime; MoviePlex; MSNBC; MTV; Nickelodeon; Oxygen; Root Sports Rocky Mountain; Spike TV; The Weather Channel; TNT; Univision Studios; USA Network.
Fee: $35.00 monthly.
Digital Basic Service
Subscribers: N.A.
Programming (via satellite): BBC America; Bravo; Discovery Digital Networks; DMX Music; ESPN Classic; ESPNews; Golf Channel; GSN; History; IFC; NBCSN; Nick Jr.; Starz Encore; Syfy; Turner Classic Movies; TV Land; WE tv.
Pay Service 1
Pay Units: N.A.
Programming (via satellite): HBO; Starz Encore.
Fee: $10.00 installation; $1.75 monthly (Encore), $10.95 monthly (HBO).
Digital Pay Service 1
Pay Units: N.A.
Programming (via satellite): Cinemax (multiplexed); HBO (multiplexed); Showtime (multiplexed); Starz (multiplexed); The Movie Channel (multiplexed).
Fee: $15.99 monthly (each).
Video-On-Demand: No
Pay-Per-View
iN DEMAND (delivered digitally); Playboy TV (delivered digitally).
Internet Service
Operational: Yes.
Broadband Service: Comcast High Speed Internet.
Fee: $42.95 monthly.
Telephone Service
None
Vice President: Mike Trueblood. General Manager: Amy Lynch. Technical Operations Manager: James Comiskey. Customer Service Supervisor: Anita Robinson.
Ownership: Comcast Cable Communications Inc. (MSO).

ROCKY FORD—Formerly served by Bresnan Communications. Now served by Charter Communications, LA JUNTA, CO [C00040]. ICA: C00051.

SAGUACHE—USA Communications, 920 East 56th St, Ste B, Kearney, NE 68847. Phone: 877-234-0102. E-mail: csr@usacommunications.tv. Web Site: http://usacommunications.tv. ICA: C00138.
TV Market Ranking: Outside TV Markets (SAGUACHE). Franchise award date: N.A. Franchise expiration date: N.A. Began: July 8, 1992.
Channel capacity: N.A. Channels available but not in use: N.A.
Basic Service
Subscribers: 23.
Programming (via microwave): KCNC-TV (CBS, Decades) Denver; KDVR (Antenna TV, FOX) Denver; KKTV (CBS, MNT) Colorado Springs; KMGH-TV (ABC, Azteca America) Denver; KRMA-TV (PBS) Denver; KUSA (NBC, WeatherNation) Denver; KWGN-TV (CW, This TV) Denver.
Programming (via satellite): A&E; Altitude Sports & Entertainment; AMC; Bravo; Cartoon Network; CMT; CNN; Comedy Central; C-SPAN; Discovery Channel; Disney Channel; ESPN; ESPN2; Freeform; History; MSNBC; Nickelodeon; Pop; QVC; Root Sports Rocky Mountain; Spike TV; Syfy; TBS; The Weather Channel; TLC; TNT; Travel Channel; Trinity Broadcasting Network (TBN); Turner Classic Movies; TV Land; Univision Studios; USA Network; VH1; WE tv; WGN America.
Programming (via translator): KOB (NBC, This TV) Albuquerque.
Fee: $29.95 installation; $39.00 monthly.
Pay Service 1
Pay Units: 3.
Programming (via satellite): Cinemax.
Fee: $12.49 monthly.
Pay Service 2
Pay Units: 5.
Programming (via satellite): HBO.
Fee: $13.49 monthly.
Video-On-Demand: No
Internet Service
Operational: No.
Telephone Service
None
Miles of Plant: 5.0 (coaxial); None (fiber optic). Homes passed: 250.
Chief Financial Officer: Amber Reineke.
Ownership: USA Companies LP (MSO).

SALIDA—Charter Communications, 12405 Powerscourt Dr, St. Louis, MO 63131. Phones: 636-207-5100 (Corporate office); 719-275-1656; 516-803-2300; 877-273-7626. Web Site: http://www.charter.com. Also serves Chaffee County (southeastern portion) & Poncha Springs. ICA: C00037.
TV Market Ranking: Outside TV Markets (Chaffee County (southeastern portion), Poncha Springs, SALIDA). Franchise award date: N.A. Franchise expiration date: N.A. Began: August 1, 1954.
Channel capacity: N.A. Channels available but not in use: N.A.
Digital Basic Service
Subscribers: 1,347.
Programming (via satellite): A&E HD; Animal Planet HD; BBC America; Bloomberg Television; Bravo; CBS Sports Network; Cine Mexicano; Cinelatino; CMT; CNN en Espanol; Cooking Channel; Destination America; Discovery Channel HD; Discovery Kids Channel; Discovery Life Channel; Disney XD; DIY Network; DMX Music; ESPN Classic; ESPN Deportes; ESPN HD; ESPNews; Food Network HD; FOX College Sports Central; FOX College Sports Pacific; Fox Deportes; Fox Sports 1; Fuse; FXM; FYI; Golf Channel; GSN; HD Theater; HGTV HD; History en Espanol; History HD; History International; IFC; Investigation Discovery; ION Television; LMN; MTV Classic; MTV Jams; MTV2; Nat Geo WILD; National Geographic Channel; National Geographic Channel HD; NBC Universo; NBCSN; NFL Network; Nick 2; Nick Jr.; Nicktoons; Outdoor Channel; OWN: Oprah Winfrey Network; RFD-TV; Science Channel; Sprout; Syfy HD; TeenNick; Tr3s; Trinity Broadcasting Network (TBN); Universal HD; UP; USA Network HD; VH1 Soul; ViendoMovies.
Fee: $26.99 monthly.
Digital Expanded Basic Service
Subscribers: N.A.
Programming (via satellite): A&E; Altitude Sports & Entertainment; AMC; Animal Planet; Cartoon Network; CMT; CNBC; CNN; Comedy Central; C-SPAN; Disney Channel; E! HD; ESPN; ESPN2; EWTN Global Catholic Network; Food Network; Fox News Channel; Freeform; FX; Hallmark Channel; HGTV; History; HLN; MSNBC; MTV; Nickelodeon; Oxygen; Root Sports Rocky Mountain; Spike TV; Syfy; TBS; The Weather Channel; TLC; TNT; Travel Channel; truTV; Turner Classic Movies; TV Land; USA Network; VH1.
Fee: $12.21 monthly.
Digital Pay Service 1
Pay Units: N.A.
Programming (via satellite): Cinemax (multiplexed); Flix; HBO; HBO HD; Showtime (multiplexed); Starz (multiplexed); Starz Encore (multiplexed); Starz HD; The Movie Channel (multiplexed).
Video-On-Demand: No
Internet Service
Operational: Yes.
Broadband Service: Charter Internet.
Fee: $39.95 monthly.
Telephone Service
Digital: Operational
Fee: $49.99 monthly
Miles of Plant: 50.0 (coaxial); 10.0 (fiber optic). Homes passed: 4,303.
President & Chief Executive Officer: Tom Rutledge. General Manager: Jerry Parker. Technical Operations Manager: Doyle Ruena. Accounting Director: David Sovanski.
Ownership: Charter Communications Inc. (MSO).

SAN LUIS—Formerly served by Charter Communications. No longer in operation. ICA: C00107.

SEDGWICK—PC Telcom. Now served by HOLYOKE, CO [C00065]. ICA: C00214.

SEIBERT—Formerly served by B & C Cablevision Inc. No longer in operation. ICA: C00181.

SILT—Comcast Cable, 1605 Grand Ave, Ste 1, Glenwood Springs, CO 81601. Phones: 970-230-9076; 970-928-7784. Fax: 970-945-0270. Web Site: http://www.comcast.com. Also serves Apple Tree Mobile Home Park, Garfield County (portions) & New Castle. ICA: C00108.
TV Market Ranking: Below 100 (Apple Tree Mobile Home Park, New Castle, SILT).
Channel capacity: N.A. Channels available but not in use: N.A.
Basic Service
Subscribers: 1,177.
Fee: $50.00 installation; $30.45 monthly.
Ownership: Comcast Cable Communications Inc. (MSO).

SILVERTON—Formerly served by Cable USA. No longer in operation. ICA: C00103.

SIMLA—Formerly served by FairPoint Communications. No longer in operation. ICA: C00142.

SOUTH FORK—USA Communications, 920 East 56th St, Ste B, Kearney, NE 68847. Phone: 877-234-0102. E-mail: csr@usacommunications.tv. Web Site: http://usacommunications.tv. ICA: C00131.
TV Market Ranking: Outside TV Markets (SOUTH FORK). Franchise award date: April 19, 1989. Franchise expiration date: N.A. Began: August 26, 1989.
Channel capacity: N.A. Channels available but not in use: N.A.
Basic Service
Subscribers: 63.
Programming (via microwave): KCNC-TV (CBS, Decades) Denver; KDVR (Antenna TV, FOX) Denver; KMGH-TV (ABC, Azteca America) Denver; KRMA-TV (PBS) Denver.
Programming (via satellite): A&E; AMC; Bravo; CMT; CNN; Comedy Central; C-SPAN; Discovery Channel; ESPN; ESPN2; Fox News Channel; Freeform; Hallmark Channel; History; HLN; KUSA (NBC, WeatherNation) Denver; KWGN-TV (CW, This TV) Denver; MSNBC; QVC; Spike TV; Syfy; TBS; The Weather Channel; TLC; Travel Channel; TV Land; USA Network; WE tv; WGN America.
Fee: $29.95 installation; $41.00 monthly.
Pay Service 1
Pay Units: 11.
Programming (via satellite): HBO.
Fee: $13.49 monthly.
Video-On-Demand: No
Internet Service
Operational: No.
Telephone Service
None
Miles of Plant: 26.0 (coaxial); None (fiber optic). Homes passed: 531.
Chief Financial Officer: Amber Reineke.
Ownership: USA Companies LP (MSO).

SPRINGFIELD—Satview Broadband, 3550 Barron Way, Ste 13A, Reno, NV 89511. Phones: 800-225-0605; 775-333-6626 (Elko, NV office); 775-324-2198. Fax: 775-333-0225. E-mail: satviewreno@yahoo.

Colorado—Cable Systems

com. Web Site: http://www.satview.net. ICA: CO0088.
TV Market Ranking: Outside TV Markets (SPRINGFIELD). Franchise award date: N.A. Franchise expiration date: N.A. Began: October 1, 1961.
Channel capacity: N.A. Channels available but not in use: N.A.

Basic Service
Subscribers: 66.
Programming (via microwave): KDVR (Antenna TV, FOX) Denver; KKTV (CBS, MNT) Colorado Springs; KOAA-TV (Grit, NBC) Pueblo; KPXC-TV (ION) Denver; KRDO-TV (ABC, TMO) Colorado Springs; KTSC (PBS) Pueblo; KWGN-TV (CW, This TV) Denver.
Programming (via satellite): A&E; AMC; Animal Planet; Bravo; Cartoon Network; CMT; CNBC; CNN; Comedy Central; C-SPAN; Discovery Channel; Disney Channel; E! HD; ESPN; ESPN2; Food Network; Fox News Channel; Freeform; FX; Hallmark Channel; HGTV; History; HLN; Lifetime; MSNBC; MTV; National Geographic Channel; Nickelodeon; QVC; Root Sports Rocky Mountain; Spike TV; Syfy; TBS; The Weather Channel; TLC; TNT; Travel Channel; truTV; TV Land; Univision Studios; USA Network; VH1; WGN America.
Fee: $54.50 installation; $54.50 monthly.

Digital Basic Service
Subscribers: N.A.
Programming (via satellite): BBC America; Bloomberg Television; CMT; Destination America; Discovery Kids Channel; Discovery Life Channel; Disney XD; ESPNews; Fox Sports 1; Fuse; FXM; FYI; Golf Channel; GSN; History International; IFC; Investigation Discovery; MC; MTV Classic; MTV2; NBCSN; Nick Jr.; Nicktoons; Outdoor Channel; OWN: Oprah Winfrey Network; Science Channel; TeenNick; Trinity Broadcasting Network (TBN); WE tv.

Digital Pay Service 1
Pay Units: N.A.
Programming (via satellite): Cinemax (multiplexed); HBO (multiplexed); Showtime (multiplexed); Starz; Starz Encore (multiplexed); The Movie Channel (multiplexed).
Video-On-Demand: No

Pay-Per-View
iN DEMAND (delivered digitally); Club Jenna (delivered digitally); Playboy TV (delivered digitally); Fresh (delivered digitally).

Internet Service
Operational: No.

Telephone Service
None
Miles of Plant: 28.0 (coaxial); None (fiber optic). Homes passed: 906.
President: Tariq Ahmad.
Ownership: Satview Broadband Ltd. (MSO).

STAGECOACH—Formerly served by Westcom II LLC. No longer in operation. ICA: CO0205.

STEAMBOAT SPRINGS—Comcast Cable. Now served by LONGMONT, CO [CO0011]. ICA: CO0027.

STERLING—Charter Communications, 12405 Powerscourt Dr, St. Louis, MO 63131. Phones: 636-207-5100 (Corporate office); 877-273-7626. Web Site: http://www.charter.com. Also serves Logan County. ICA: CO0019.
TV Market Ranking: Below 100 (Logan County, STERLING). Franchise award date: January 1, 1951. Franchise expiration date: N.A. Began: September 1, 1952.
Channel capacity: N.A. Channels available but not in use: N.A.

Digital Basic Service
Subscribers: 2,596.
Programming (via satellite): A&E HD; Animal Planet HD; AXS TV; Bandamax; BBC America; Bloomberg Television; Bravo; CBS Sports Network; Cinelatino; CMT; CNBC HD+; CNN en Espanol; CNN HD; Cooking Channel; De Pelicula; De Pelicula Clasico; Destination America; Discovery Channel HD; Discovery Kids Channel; Discovery Life Channel; Disney Channel HD; Disney XD; DIY Network; DMX Music; ESPN Classic; ESPN Deportes; ESPN HD; ESPN2 HD; ESPNews; Food Network HD; FOX College Sports Central; FOX College Sports Pacific; Fox Deportes; Fox Sports 1; Freeform HD; FSN HD; Fuse; FXM; FYI; Golf Channel; GolTV; GSN; HD Theater; HGTV HD; History en Espanol; History HD; History International; HRTV; IFC; Investigation Discovery; ION Television; Lifetime Movie Network HD; LMN; MTV Classic; MTV Hits; MTV Jams; MTV2; Nat Geo WILD; National Geographic Channel; National Geographic Channel HD; NBC Universo; NBCSN; NFL Network; NFL Network HD; Nick 2; Nick Jr.; Nicktoons; Outdoor Channel; OWN: Oprah Winfrey Network; RFD-TV; Science Channel; Science HD; Sprout; Syfy HD; TBS HD; TeenNick; Telehit; The Weather Channel HD; TLC HD; TNT HD; Tr3s; Trinity Broadcasting Network (TBN); UniMas; Universal HD; Univision Studios; UP; USA Network HD; Versus HD; VH1 Soul; ViendoMovies.
Fee: $17.99 monthly.

Digital Expanded Basic Service
Subscribers: N.A.
Programming (via satellite): A&E; Altitude Sports & Entertainment; AMC; Animal Planet; Cartoon Network; CMT; CNBC; CNN; Comedy Central; C-SPAN 2; Disney Channel; E! HD; ESPN; ESPN2; EWTN Global Catholic Network; Food Network; Fox News Channel; Freeform; FX; Great American Country; Hallmark Channel; HGTV; History; HLN; INSP; MSNBC; MTV; Nickelodeon; Oxygen; Pop; Root Sports Rocky Mountain; Spike TV; Syfy; The Weather Channel; TLC; TNT; Travel Channel; truTV; Turner Classic Movies; TV Land; UniMas; USA Network; VH1.
Fee: $47.80 monthly.

Pay Service 1
Pay Units: N.A.
Programming (via satellite): HBO; Starz; Starz Encore.
Fee: $20.00 installation; $11.95 monthly (HBO or Showtime).

Digital Pay Service 1
Pay Units: N.A.
Programming (via satellite): Cinemax (multiplexed); Cinemax HD; HBO (multiplexed); HBO HD; Showtime (multiplexed); Showtime HD; Starz (multiplexed); Starz Encore (multiplexed); Starz HD; The Movie Channel (multiplexed); The Movie Channel HD.
Video-On-Demand: No

Pay-Per-View
Sports PPV (delivered digitally); ESPN Now (delivered digitally); iN DEMAND (delivered digitally).

Internet Service
Operational: Yes.
Broadband Service: Charter Internet.
Fee: $39.95 monthly.

Telephone Service
Digital: Operational
Fee: $49.99 monthly

Miles of Plant: 97.0 (coaxial); None (fiber optic). Homes passed: 6,900.
President & Chief Executive Officer: Tom Rutledge. Regional Vice President & General Manager: Clint Rodeman. Technical Operations Manager: Mitch Winter. Accounting Director: David Sovanski.
Ownership: Charter Communications Inc. (MSO).

STRATTON—Formerly served by NexHorizon Communications. No longer in operation. ICA: CO0184.

SUGAR CITY—Formerly served by CableDirect. No longer in operation. ICA: CO0206.

SUNNYSIDE—Rural Route Video, PO Box 640, Ignacio, CO 81137-0640. Phone: 970-563-9593. ICA: CO0154.
TV Market Ranking: Below 100 (SUNNYSIDE). Franchise award date: N.A. Franchise expiration date: N.A. Began: November 1, 1988.
Channel capacity: N.A. Channels available but not in use: N.A.

Basic Service
Subscribers: 3.
Programming (received off-air): KREZ-TV (CBS, The Country Network) Durango.
Programming (via microwave): KRMA-TV (PBS) Denver; KUSA (NBC, WeatherNation) Denver; KWGN-TV (CW, This TV) Denver.
Programming (via satellite): ESPN; Freeform; TBS; USA Network.
Fee: $40.00 installation; $28.00 monthly.

Pay Service 1
Pay Units: N.A.
Programming (via satellite): HBO.
Fee: $10.95 monthly.

Video-On-Demand: No

Internet Service
Operational: No.

Telephone Service
None
Miles of Plant: 2.0 (coaxial); None (fiber optic). Homes passed: 75.
General Manager: Christopher L. May.
Ownership: Rural Route Video (MSO).

SUNSET CREEK—Formerly served by Island Cable. No longer in operation. ICA: CO0210.

TABLE MOUNTAIN—Baja Broadband, 525 Junction Rd, Madison, WI 53717. Phones: 575-437-3101; 303-463-0168; 303-656-2102; 800-480-7020; 877-422-5282. E-mail: customersupport@bajabb.tv. Web Site: http://www.bajabroadband.com. Also serves Arvada & Jefferson County (portions). ICA: CO0185.
TV Market Ranking: 32 (TABLE MOUNTAIN).
Channel capacity: 74 (operating 2-way). Channels available but not in use: N.A.

Basic Service
Subscribers: 777.
Programming (received off-air): KBDI-TV (PBS) Broomfield; KCEC (Bounce TV, LATV, UNV) Denver; KCNC-TV (CBS, Decades) Denver; KDVR (Antenna TV, FOX) Denver; KETD (Estrella TV) Castle Rock; KMGH-TV (ABC, Azteca America) Denver; KPXC-TV (ION) Denver; KRMA-TV (PBS) Denver; KRMT (Daystar TV, ETV) Denver; KTVD (MeTV, MNT) Denver; KUSA (NBC, WeatherNation) Denver; KWGN-TV (CW, This TV) Denver.
Programming (via satellite): A&E; Altitude Sports & Entertainment; AMC; Animal Planet; Bravo; Cartoon Network; CMT; CNBC; CNN; Comedy Central; C-SPAN; C-SPAN 2; Discovery Channel; Disney Channel; E! HD; ESPN; ESPN2; EVINE Live; Food Network; Fox News Channel; Fox Sports 1; Freeform; FX; Hallmark Channel; HGTV; History; HLN; Lifetime; MSNBC; MTV; National Geographic Channel; Nickelodeon; Pop; Root Sports Rocky Mountain; Spike TV; Syfy; TBS; The Weather Channel; TLC; TNT; Travel Channel; truTV; TV Land; USA Network; VH1; WGN America.
Fee: $29.95-$39.96 installation; $32.95 monthly.

Digital Basic Service
Subscribers: N.A.
Programming (via satellite): AZ TV; BBC America; Bloomberg Television; Cloo; Daystar TV Network; Discovery Kids Channel; Disney XD; DMX Music; ESPN Classic; ESPNews; Fuse; Golf Channel; Great American Country; GSN; IFC; LMN; MTV Classic; MTV2; NBCSN; Nick Jr.; Ovation; OWN: Oprah Winfrey Network; Science Channel; TeenNick; The Word Network; Trinity Broadcasting Network (TBN); Turner Classic Movies; WE tv.

Digital Expanded Basic Service
Subscribers: N.A.
Programming (via satellite): FOX College Sports Central; FOX College Sports Pacific; NFL Network; Outdoor Channel.
Fee: $2.00 monthly.

Digital Expanded Basic Service 2
Subscribers: N.A.
Programming (via satellite): Destination America; Discovery Life Channel; FXM; FYI; History International; Investigation Discovery; Starz Encore (multiplexed).
Fee: $2.95 monthly.

Pay Service 1
Pay Units: N.A.
Programming (via satellite): Cinemax; HBO; Showtime.

Digital Pay Service 1
Pay Units: N.A.
Programming (via satellite): Cinemax (multiplexed); HBO (multiplexed); Showtime (multiplexed); Starz; The Movie Channel (multiplexed).
Fee: $6.95 monthly (Starz), $11.95 monthly (Cinemax, HBO, Showtime or TMC).

Video-On-Demand: No

Pay-Per-View
iN DEMAND (delivered digitally); Playboy TV (delivered digitally); Fresh (delivered digitally); Spice: Xcess (delivered digitally); Club Jenna (delivered digitally).

Internet Service
Operational: Yes.
Broadband Service: Warp Drive Online.
Fee: $27.95 monthly.

Telephone Service
Digital: Operational
Vice President, Corporate Finance: Carl Shapiro. Assistant Treasurer: Noel Hutton.
Ownership: TDS Telecom (MSO).

TELLURIDE—Time Warner Cable, 7800 Crescent Executive Dr, Charlotte, NC 28217. Phone: 970-641-6412. Web Site: http://www.timewarnercable.com. Also serves Ophir & San Miguel County. ICA: CO0061.
TV Market Ranking: Outside TV Markets (San Miguel County, TELLURIDE). Franchise award date: January 1, 1980. Franchise expiration date: N.A. Began: January 30, 1981.
Channel capacity: N.A. Channels available but not in use: N.A.

Basic Service
Subscribers: 748.
Programming (via microwave): KCNC-TV (CBS, Decades) Denver; KMGH-TV (ABC,

Cable Systems—Colorado

Azteca America) Denver; KRMA-TV (PBS) Denver; KUSA (NBC, WeatherNation) Denver; KWGN-TV (CW, This TV) Denver.
Programming (via satellite): A&E; CNN; C-SPAN; C-SPAN 2; Disney Channel; Hallmark Channel; MSNBC; OWN: Oprah Winfrey Network; QVC; Spike TV; TBS; The Word Network; WGN America.
Fee: $49.99 installation; $32.00 monthly; $2.00 converter.

Expanded Basic Service 1
Subscribers: N.A.
Programming (via satellite): Altitude Sports & Entertainment; AMC; Animal Planet; Bravo; Cartoon Network; CMT; CNBC; Comedy Central; Discovery Channel; E! HD; ESPN; ESPN2; Food Network; Fox News Channel; Fox Sports 1; Freeform; FX; Great American Country; History; HLN; Lifetime; MTV; NBCSN; Nickelodeon; Oxygen; Root Sports Rocky Mountain; Syfy; The Weather Channel; TLC; TNT; Travel Channel; truTV; Turner Classic Movies; TV Land; Univision; USA Network; VH1.
Fee: $29.75 monthly.

Digital Basic Service
Subscribers: N.A.
Programming (via satellite): BBC America; Bloomberg Television; Destination America; Discovery Kids Channel; Discovery Life Channel; Disney XD; ESPN Classic; ESP-News; EWTN Global Catholic Network; Fox Business Network; FSN Digital Atlantic; FSN Digital Central; FSN Digital Pacific; Fuse; FXM; FYI; Golf Channel; Great American Country; GSN; HGTV; History International; IFC; Investigation Discovery; LMN; MC; MTV Classic; MTV2; National Geographic Channel; NBCSN; Nick Jr.; Nicktoons; Outdoor Channel; OWN: Oprah Winfrey Network; Science Channel; Trinity Broadcasting Network (TBN); UP; VH1 Country; WE tv.

Digital Pay Service 1
Pay Units: N.A.
Programming (via satellite): Cinemax (multiplexed); HBO (multiplexed); Showtime (multiplexed); Starz; Starz Encore (multiplexed); The Movie Channel.
Fee: $14.99 monthly (each package).
Video-On-Demand: Planned
Pay-Per-View
Hot Choice (delivered digitally); Fresh (delivered digitally); Playboy TV (delivered digitally); Sports PPV (delivered digitally).

Internet Service
Operational: Yes.
Subscribers: 874.
Broadband Service: Road Runner.
Fee: $69.95 installation; $44.95 monthly.

Telephone Service
Digital: Operational
Subscribers: 169.
Fee: $44.95 monthly
Miles of Plant: 29.0 (coaxial); 15.0 (fiber optic). Homes passed: 3,044.
General Manager: Mike Miller. Senior Accounting Director: Karen Goodfellow.
Ownership: Time Warner Cable (MSO).

TOWAOC—Ute Mountain Cable TV, 100 Mike Wash Rd, PO Box 68, Towaoc, CO 81334-0068. Phones: 970-564-5490. Fax: 970-564-5489. ICA: CO0121.
TV Market Ranking: Outside TV Markets (TOWAOC). Franchise award date: N.A. Franchise expiration date: N.A. Began: January 1, 1985.
Channel capacity: N.A. Channels available but not in use: N.A.

Basic Service
Subscribers: N.A.
Programming (via satellite): A&E; CNN; C-SPAN; C-SPAN 2; Discovery Channel; Disney Channel; ESPN; FX; FXM; History; HLN; MTV; Nickelodeon; Outdoor Channel; Root Sports Rocky Mountain; Spike TV; Syfy; TBS; TNT; Trinity Broadcasting Network (TBN); Turner Classic Movies; USA Network; WGN America.
Programming (via translator): KCNC-TV (CBS, Decades) Denver; KMGH-TV (ABC, Azteca America) Denver; KOAT-TV (ABC, Estrella TV) Albuquerque; KRMA-TV (PBS) Denver; KUSA (NBC, WeatherNation) Denver; KWGN-TV (CW, This TV) Denver.
Fee: $25.00 installation.

Pay Service 1
Pay Units: N.A.
Programming (via satellite): Cinemax; HBO; Showtime; The Movie Channel.
Fee: $10.00 monthly (each).

Internet Service
Operational: Yes.
Broadband Service: In-house.

Telephone Service
Digital: Planned
Miles of Plant: 25.0 (coaxial); None (fiber optic). Homes passed: 425.
General Manager: Michael Elkriver. Chief Technician: Aldo Hammond. Office Manager: Yvonne House.
Ownership: Ute Mountain Indian Tribe.

TRINIDAD—Comcast Cable, 213 North Union Blvd, Colorado Springs, CO 80909. Phones: 719-457-4501; 800-266-2278. Fax: 719-457-4503. Web Site: http://www.comcast.com. Also serves Las Animas County (portions). ICA: CO0031.
TV Market Ranking: Outside TV Markets (Las Animas County (portions), TRINIDAD). Franchise award date: N.A. Franchise expiration date: N.A. Began: March 1, 1953.
Channel capacity: N.A. Channels available but not in use: N.A.

Basic Service
Subscribers: 1,491.
Programming (received off-air): KTSC (PBS) Pueblo; 15 FMs.
Programming (via microwave): KKTV (CBS, MNT) Colorado Springs; KOAA-TV (Grit, NBC) Pueblo; KRDO-TV (ABC, TMO) Colorado Springs; KWGN-TV (CW, This TV) Denver; KXRM-TV (FOX, MundoMax) Colorado Springs; KXTU-LD (CW) Colorado Springs.
Programming (via satellite): A&E; AMC; Animal Planet; CMT; CNBC; CNN; C-SPAN; Discovery Channel; Disney Channel; ESPN; ESPN2; EWTN Global Catholic Network; Food Network; Fox News Channel; Freeform; FX; Hallmark Channel; HGTV; History; HLN; Lifetime; MTV; Nickelodeon; Oxygen; QVC; Syfy; The Weather Channel; TLC; Trinity Broadcasting Network (TBN); truTV; TV Land; Univision; USA Network; VH1; WGN America.
Fee: $50.00 installation; $53.10 monthly; $1.00 converter.

Expanded Basic Service 1
Subscribers: N.A.
Programming (via satellite): Comedy Central; MSNBC; Root Sports Rocky Mountain; Spike TV; TBS; TNT; Travel Channel.
Fee: $48.20 monthly.

Digital Basic Service
Subscribers: N.A.
Programming (via satellite): BBC America; Bloomberg Television; Bravo; Discovery Life Channel; ESPN Classic; ESPNews; Golf Channel; GSN; INSP; MC; NBCSN; Nick Jr.; Nicktoons; Outdoor Channel; WE tv.

Digital Pay Service 1
Pay Units: N.A.
Programming (via satellite): Cinemax (multiplexed); HBO (multiplexed); Showtime (multiplexed); Starz (multiplexed); Starz Encore (multiplexed); The Movie Channel (multiplexed).
Fee: $14.95 monthly.
Video-On-Demand: Planned
Pay-Per-View
Fresh (delivered digitally); Playboy TV (delivered digitally); HITS PPV (delivered digitally).

Internet Service
Operational: Yes.
Broadband Service: Comcast High Speed Internet.
Fee: $42.95 monthly.

Telephone Service
None
Miles of Plant: 69.0 (coaxial); 69.0 (fiber optic). Homes passed included in Colorado Springs.
Vice President & General Manager: Jim Commers. Senior Vice President, Colorado Region: Scott Binder. Vice President, Marketing: Zach Street. Technical Operations Director: Jim Garcia. Public Relations Manager: Sandra Mann.
Ownership: Comcast Cable Communications Inc. (MSO).

VALDEZ—Formerly served by Wozniak TV. No longer in operation. ICA: CO0135.

VICTOR—Formerly served by Charter Communications. No longer in operation. ICA: CO0123.

WALDEN (village)—Formerly served by Charter Communications. No longer in operation. ICA: CO0115.

WALSENBURG—Charter Communications, 12405 Powerscourt Dr, St. Louis, MO 63131. Phones: 636-207-5100 (Corporate office); 719-275-1656; 516-803-2300 (Corporate office); 970-824-3298; 877-273-7626. Web Site: http://www.charter.com. Also serves Huerfano County (portions). ICA: CO0058.
TV Market Ranking: Outside TV Markets (Huerfano County (portions), WALSENBURG). Franchise award date: July 5, 1977. Franchise expiration date: N.A. Began: October 1, 1969.
Channel capacity: N.A. Channels available but not in use: N.A.

Digital Basic Service
Subscribers: 602.
Programming (via satellite): A&E HD; Animal Planet HD; Bandamax; BBC America; Bloomberg Television; Bravo; CBS Sports Network; Cine Mexicano; Cinelatino; CMT; CNN en Espanol; De Pelicula; De Pelicula Clasico; Destination America; Discovery Channel HD; Discovery Kids Channel; Discovery Life Channel; Disney Channel HD; Disney XD; DMX Music; ESPN Classic; ESPN Deportes; ESPN HD; ESPNews;

FULLY SEARCHABLE • CONTINUOUSLY UPDATED • DISCOUNT RATES FOR PRINT PURCHASERS
For more information call **800-771-9202** or visit **www.warren-news.com**

Food Network HD; FOX College Sports Central; FOX College Sports Pacific; Fox Deportes; Fox Sports 1; Freeform HD; Fuse; FXM; FYI; Golf Channel; GolTV; GSN; HD Theater; HGTV HD; History en Espanol; History HD; History International; IFC; Investigation Discovery; ION Television; LMN; MTV Classic; MTV Hits; MTV Jams; MTV2; Nat Geo WILD; National Geographic Channel; National Geographic Channel HD; NBC Universo; NBCSN; NFL Network; Nick 2; Nick Jr.; Nicktoons; Outdoor Channel; OWN: Oprah Winfrey Network; RFD-TV; Science Channel; Sprout; Syfy HD; Teen-Nick; Telehit; Tr3s; Trinity Broadcasting Network (TBN); TV Land; UniMas; Universal HD; Univision Studios; UP; USA Network HD; VH1 Soul; ViendoMovies.
Fee: $26.99 monthly.

Digital Expanded Basic Service
Subscribers: 300.
Programming (via satellite): A&E; Altitude Sports & Entertainment; AMC; Animal Planet; Cartoon Network; CMT; CNBC; CNN; Comedy Central; C-SPAN 2; Discovery Channel; Disney Channel; E! HD; ESPN; ESPN2; EWTN Global Catholic Network; Food Network; Fox News Channel; Freeform; Hallmark Channel; HGTV; History; HLN; MSNBC; MTV; Nickelodeon; Oxygen; Pop; QVC; Root Sports Rocky Mountain; Spike TV; Syfy; The Weather Channel; TLC; Travel Channel; truTV; Turner Classic Movies; UniMas; Univision Studios; USA Network; VH1.
Fee: $28.99 monthly.

Digital Pay Service 1
Pay Units: N.A.
Programming (via satellite): Cinemax (multiplexed); Flix; HBO (multiplexed); HBO HD; Showtime (multiplexed); Starz (multiplexed); Starz Encore (multiplexed); Starz HD; The Movie Channel (multiplexed).
Video-On-Demand: No

Internet Service
Operational: Yes.
Subscribers: 308.
Broadband Service: Charter Internet.
Fee: $39.95 monthly.

Telephone Service
Digital: Operational
Subscribers: 215.
Fee: $49.99 monthly
Miles of Plant: 38.0 (coaxial); 10.0 (fiber optic). Homes passed: 2,316.
President & Chief Executive Officer: Tom Rutledge. General Manager: Jerry Parker. Chief Technician: Matt Harris. Accounting Director: David Sovanski.
Ownership: Charter Communications Inc. (MSO).

WALSH—Formerly served by NexHorizon Communications. No longer in operation. ICA: CO0113.

WELD COUNTY—Formerly served by Nex-Horizon Communications. No longer in operation. ICA: CO0212.

2017 Edition   D-125

Colorado—Cable Systems

WESTCLIFFE—Formerly served by NexHorizon Communications. No longer in operation. ICA: CO0190.

WIGGINS—Formerly served by Northern Colorado Communications Inc. No longer in operation. ICA: CO0145.

WILEY—Formerly served by NexHorizon Communications. No longer in operation. ICA: CO0150.

WINTER PARK—Comcast Cable. Now served by LONGMONT, CO [CO0011]. ICA: CO0188.

WOODLAND PARK—Baja Broadband, 525 Junction Rd, Madison, WI 53717. Phones: 575-437-3101; 800-480-7020; 877-422-5282. E-mail: customersupportco@bajabb.tv. Web Site: http://www.bajabroadband.com. Also serves Teller County (portions). ICA: CO0189.
TV Market Ranking: 32 (WOODLAND PARK). Franchise award date: January 1, 1981. Franchise expiration date: N.A. Began: June 1, 1982.
Channel capacity: 66 (not 2-way capable). Channels available but not in use: N.A.
Basic Service
Subscribers: 492.
Programming (received off-air): KKTV (CBS, MNT) Colorado Springs; KOAA-TV (Grit, NBC) Pueblo; KRDO-TV (ABC, TMO) Colorado Springs; KTSC (PBS) Pueblo; KUSA (NBC, WeatherNation) Denver; KWGN-TV (CW, This TV) Denver; KXRM-TV (FOX, MundoMax) Colorado Springs.
Programming (via satellite): A&E; Altitude Sports & Entertainment; AMC; Animal Planet; Bravo; Cartoon Network; CMT; CNBC; CNN; Comedy Central; C-SPAN; C-SPAN 2; Discovery Channel; Disney Channel; E! HD; ESPN; ESPN2; EVINE Live; EWTN Global Catholic Network; Food Network; Fox News Channel; Fox Sports 1; Freeform; FX; Hallmark Channel; History; HLN; Lifetime; MTV; National Geographic Channel; Nickelodeon; Pop; QVC; Root Sports Rocky Mountain; Spike TV; Syfy; TBS; The Weather Channel; TLC; TNT; Travel Channel; truTV; Turner Classic Movies; TV Land; USA Network; VH1; WGN America.
Fee: $19.99 installation; $32.95 monthly; $1.15 converter.

Digital Basic Service
Subscribers: N.A.
Programming (via satellite): A&E HD; Animal Planet HD; AXS TV; AZ TV; BBC America; Bloomberg Television; Cloo; Daystar TV Network; Discovery Channel HD; Discovery Kids Channel; Disney XD; DMX Music; ESPN Classic; ESPN HD; ESPNews; Food Network HD; Fuse; Golf Channel; Great American Country; GSN; HD Theater; HGTV; HGTV HD; History HD; IFC; LMN; MBC America; MTV Classic; MTV2; National Geographic Channel HD; NBCSN; Nick Jr.; Ovation; OWN: Oprah Winfrey Network; Science Channel; Syfy HD; TeenNick; The Word Network; Trinity Broadcasting Network (TBN); Universal HD; USA Network HD; WE tv.
Digital Expanded Basic Service
Subscribers: N.A.
Programming (via satellite): FOX College Sports Central; FOX College Sports Pacific; NFL Network; Outdoor Channel.
Fee: $2.95 monthly.
Digital Expanded Basic Service 2
Subscribers: N.A.
Programming (via satellite): Destination America; Discovery Life Channel; FXM; FYI; History International; Investigation Discovery; Starz Encore (multiplexed); VH1 Country.
Fee: $2.00 monthly.
Digital Pay Service 1
Pay Units: N.A.
Programming (via satellite): Cinemax (multiplexed); HBO (multiplexed); Showtime (multiplexed); The Movie Channel (multiplexed).
Fee: $11.95 monthly (each).
Digital Pay Service 2
Pay Units: N.A.
Programming (via satellite): Starz (multiplexed).
Fee: $6.95 monthly.
Video-On-Demand: No
Pay-Per-View
iN DEMAND (delivered digitally); Playboy TV (delivered digitally); Fresh (delivered digitally); Spice: Xcess (delivered digitally); Club Jenna (delivered digitally).
Internet Service
Operational: Yes. Began: September 1, 2003.
Broadband Service: Warp Drive Online.
Fee: $27.95 monthly.

Telephone Service
Digital: Operational
Miles of Plant: 81.0 (coaxial); None (fiber optic).
Vice President, Corporate Finance: Carl Shapiro. Assistant Treasurer: Noel Hutton.
Ownership: TDS Telecom (MSO).

WRAY—Eagle Communications, 2703 Hall St, Ste 15, PO Box 817, Hays, KS 67601. Phones: 785-899-3371; 785-625-5910; 785-625-4000. Fax: 785-625-8030. E-mail: comments@eaglecom.net. Web Site: http://www.eaglecom.net. ICA: CO0071.
TV Market Ranking: Outside TV Markets (WRAY). Franchise award date: July 1, 1980. Franchise expiration date: N.A. Began: December 1, 1980.
Channel capacity: 36 (operating 2-way). Channels available but not in use: N.A.
Basic Service
Subscribers: 73. Commercial subscribers: 4.
Programming (received off-air): KBSL-DT (CBS) Goodland.
Programming (via microwave): KCNC-TV (CBS, Decades) Denver; KDVR (Antenna TV, FOX) Denver; KMGH-TV (ABC, Azteca America) Denver; KRMA-TV (PBS) Denver; KUSA (NBC, WeatherNation) Denver; KWGN-TV (CW, This TV) Denver.
Programming (via satellite): C-SPAN; QVC; The Weather Channel.
Fee: $24.95 installation; $69.95 monthly.
Expanded Basic Service 1
Subscribers: N.A.
Programming (via satellite): A&E; Animal Planet; CMT; CNN; Discovery Channel; Disney Channel; E! HD; ESPN; ESPN2; Fox News Channel; Freeform; Great American Country; History; HLN; Lifetime; MTV; National Geographic Channel; Nickelodeon; Root Sports Rocky Mountain; Spike TV; TBS; TLC; TNT; TV Land; USA Network; VH1.
Fee: $34.00 monthly.
Digital Basic Service
Subscribers: N.A.
Programming (via satellite): BBC America; Bloomberg Television; Cloo; CMT; Cooking Channel; Destination America; Discovery Kids Channel; Discovery Life Channel; Disney XD; DMX Music; ESPN Classic; ESPNews; Fox Sports 1; Fuse; FXM; FYI; Golf Channel; GSN; History International; IFC; Investigation Discovery; LMN; MTV Classic; MTV Hits; MTV2; NBCSN; Nick Jr.; Nicktoons; Outdoor Channel; OWN: Oprah Winfrey Network; RFD-TV; Science Channel; Sprout; Sundance TV; TeenNick; Trinity Broadcasting Network (TBN); Turner Classic Movies; VH1 Soul; WE tv.
Fee: $3.95 monthly (variety, sports or entertainment package), $5.95 monthly (basic); $4.95 converter.
Pay Service 1
Pay Units: N.A.
Programming (via satellite): HBO; Showtime; The Movie Channel.
Fee: $11.95 monthly (each).
Digital Pay Service 1
Pay Units: N.A.
Programming (via satellite): Cinemax (multiplexed); HBO (multiplexed); Showtime (multiplexed); Starz (multiplexed); Starz Encore (multiplexed); The Movie Channel (multiplexed).
Fee: $11.95 monthly (Cinemax, Showtime/TMC/Flix or Starz/Encore), $14.95 monthly (HBO).
Video-On-Demand: No
Pay-Per-View
Spice: Xcess (delivered digitally); Club Jenna (delivered digitally); iN DEMAND (delivered digitally); Playboy TV (delivered digitally); Fresh (delivered digitally).
Internet Service
Operational: Yes.
Fee: $22.95-$42.95 monthly.
Telephone Service
None
Miles of Plant: 12.0 (coaxial); None (fiber optic). Homes passed: 1,104.
Chief Operating Officer: Kurt K. David. General Manager: Travis Kohlrus. Chief Technician: Jim Gall. Ad Sales Manager: Mike Koerner.
Ownership: Eagle Communications Inc. (MSO).

YUMA—Formerly served by Mediastream. Now served by Vyve Broadband, OTIS (town), CO [CO0128]. ICA: CO0063.

CONNECTICUT

Total Systems: 11	Communities with Applications: 0
Total Communities Served: 210	Number of Basic Subscribers: 876,515
Franchises Not Yet Operating: 0	Number of Expanded Basic Subscribers: 0
Applications Pending: 0	Number of Pay Units: 0

Top 100 Markets Represented: Hartford-New Haven-New Britain-Waterbury-New London (19); New York, NY-Linden-Paterson-Newark, NJ (1); Providence, RI-New Bedford, MA (33); Boston-Cambridge-Worcester-Lawrence, MA (6).

For a list of cable communities in this section, see the Cable Community Index located in the back of Cable Volume 2.
For explanation of terms used in cable system listings, see p. D-11.

ANSONIA—Comcast Cable. Now served by NEW BRITAIN, CT [CT0037]. ICA: CT0009.

ASHFORD—Charter Communications, 1320 Main St, Willimantic, CT 06226. Phones: 636-207-5100 (Corporate office); 314-543-2236; 508-853-1515 (Worcester office); 203-304-4001 (Newtown office). Web Site: http://www.charter.com. Also serves Brooklyn, Canterbury, Chaplin, Columbia, Coventry, Eastford, Hampton, Lebanon, Mansfield, Pomfret, Scotland, Storrs (village), Thompson, Willimantic, Willington, Windham & Woodstock. ICA: CT0012.
TV Market Ranking: 19 (Columbia, Coventry, Lebanon, Mansfield, Storrs (village), Willimantic, Windham); 19,33 (Scotland); 33 (Brooklyn, Pomfret); 6,19 (ASHFORD, Canterbury, Chaplin, Eastford, Hampton, Willington); 6,33 (Thompson, Woodstock). Franchise award date: August 3, 1983. Franchise expiration date: N.A. Began: December 1, 1984.
Channel capacity: 72 (operating 2-way). Channels available but not in use: N.A.

Digital Basic Service
Subscribers: 27,032.
Programming (via satellite): BBC America; Bloomberg Television; Discovery Digital Networks; Disney XD; DIY Network; ESPNews; FYI; Great American Country; History International; IFC; LMN; MC; Nick 2; Nick Jr.; Nicktoons; Sundance TV; TeenNick; WE tv.
Fee: $49.99 installation; $26.99 monthly.

Digital Expanded Basic Service
Subscribers: N.A.
Programming (via satellite): A&E; AMC; Animal Planet; BET; Bravo; Cartoon Network; CNBC; CNN; Comcast SportsNet New England; Comedy Central; Discovery Channel; Disney Channel; E! HD; ESPN; ESPN2; Food Network; Fox News Channel; Fox Sports 1; Freeform; Golf Channel; Hallmark Channel; HGTV; History; HLN; INSP; Lifetime; MSNBC; MTV; National Geographic Channel; NBCSN; New England Sports Network; Nickelodeon; Oxygen; Spike TV; Syfy; TBS; The Weather Channel; TLC; TNT; Travel Channel; truTV; Turner Classic Movies; TV Land; Univision; USA Network; VH1.
Fee: $55.00 monthly.

Digital Pay Service 1
Pay Units: N.A.
Programming (via satellite): Cinemax (multiplexed); Flix; HBO (multiplexed); Showtime (multiplexed); Starz (multiplexed); Starz Encore (multiplexed); The Movie Channel (multiplexed).
Fee: $13.95 monthly (Cinemax, HBO, Flix/Showtime/TMC, or Starz/Encore).
Video-On-Demand: Yes

Pay-Per-View
ETC (delivered digitally); Hot Choice (delivered digitally); iN DEMAND; Playboy TV (delivered digitally); Pleasure (delivered digitally); Fresh (delivered digitally).

Internet Service
Operational: Yes.
Subscribers: 25,915.
Broadband Service: Charter Internet.
Fee: $29.99 monthly; $5.00 modem lease; $120.00 modem purchase.

Telephone Service
Digital: Operational
Subscribers: 16,082.
Fee: $29.99 monthly
Miles of Plant: 2,556.0 (coaxial); 829.0 (fiber optic). Homes passed: 52,927.
Vice President & General Manager: Greg Garabedian. Technical Operations Director: George Duffy. Marketing Director: Dennis Jerome. Accounting Director: David Sovanski.
Ownership: Charter Communications Inc. (MSO).

BOLTON—Comcast of Connecticut. Now served by NEW BRITAIN, CT [CT0037]. ICA: CT0036.

BRANFORD—Comcast Cable. Now served by NEW BRITAIN, CT [CT0037]. ICA: CT0006.

BRIDGEPORT—Cablevision, 122 River St, Bridgeport, CT 06604. Phones: 203-750-5703; 516-803-2300; 203-750-5600. Fax: 203-354-0921. Web Site: http://www.cablevision.com. Also serves Fairfield County, Milford, Orange, Stratford & Woodbridge. ICA: CT0003.
TV Market Ranking: 19 (BRIDGEPORT, Fairfield County, Milford, Orange, Stratford, Woodbridge). Franchise award date: N.A. Franchise expiration date: N.A. Began: June 15, 1977.
Channel capacity: N.A. Channels available but not in use: N.A.

Basic Service
Subscribers: 86,991. Commercial subscribers: 4,628.
Programming (received off-air): WABC-TV (ABC, Live Well Network) New York; WCCT-TV (CW, This TV) Waterbury; WEDW (PBS) Bridgeport; WFSB (CBS, Escape, Laff) Hartford; WFUT-DT (getTV, UniMas) Newark; WLIW (PBS) Garden City; WLNY-TV (IND) Riverhead; WNBC (COZI TV, NBC) New York; WNET (PBS) Newark; WNJU (TMO) Linden; WNYW (FOX, Movies!) New York; WPIX (Antenna TV, CW, This TV) New York; WPXN-TV (ION) New York; WRNN-TV (IND) Kingston; WTIC-TV (Antenna TV, FOX) Hartford; WTNH (ABC, Bounce TV) New Haven; WVIT (COZI TV, NBC) New Britain; WWOR-TV (Bounce TV, Buzzr, Heroes & Icons, MNT) Secaucus; WXTV-DT (UNV) Paterson; WZME (Retro TV) Bridgeport; 29 FMs.
Programming (via microwave): News 12 Connecticut; WCBS-TV (CBS, Decades) New York.
Fee: $39.95 installation; $15.70 monthly.

Expanded Basic Service 1
Subscribers: N.A.
Programming (via satellite): A&E; AMC; Animal Planet; BET; Bravo; Cartoon Network; CNBC; CNN; Comedy Central; C-SPAN; C-SPAN 2; CT-N; Discovery Channel; Disney Channel; E! HD; ESPN; ESPN2; EVINE Live; Food Network; Fox News Channel; Fox Sports 1; Freeform; Fuse; FX; GSN; HGTV; History; HLN; Lifetime; MSNBC; MTV; MTV2; News 12 Traffic & Weather; Nickelodeon; QVC; Spike TV; SportsNet New York; Syfy; TBS; The Weather Channel; TLC; TNT; Travel Channel; truTV; Turner Classic Movies; TV Land; Univision; USA Network; VH1; WE tv; YES Network.
Fee: $31.25 monthly.

Digital Basic Service
Subscribers: N.A.
Programming (via satellite): Azteca; BBC World News; Bloomberg Television; Canal Sur; Caracol TV; Cartoon Network en Espanol; CBS Sports Network; Cinelatino; CMT; CNN en Espanol; CNN HD; C-SPAN 3; Destination America; Discovery Kids Channel; Disney XD; Docu TVE; Ecuavisa Internacional; ESPN Classic; ESPN Deportes; ESPN HD; ESPN2 HD; ESPNews; EuroNews; EVINE Live; Food Network HD; FOX College Sports Central; FOX College Sports Pacific; Fox Deportes; Fox Life; Fox Sports 2; FXM; FYI; Golf Channel; GolTV; Great American Country; Hallmark Channel; HD Theater; here! On Demand; HGTV HD; History en Espanol; History International; HTV; Infinito; Investigation Discovery; Jewelry Television; La Familia Cosmovision; LOGO; Mariavision; MC; Momentum; MoviePlex; MSG; MSG Plus; MTV Classic; MTV Hits; National Geographic Channel; National Geographic Channel HD; NBA TV; NBC Universo; NBCSN; New England Cable News; NHL Network; Nick Jr.; Nicktoons; Outdoor Channel; Oxygen; Science Channel; Sundance TV; TBS HD; TeenNick; Telefe Internacional; Telemicro Internacional; TNT HD; Toon Disney en Espanol; Tr3s; TVG Network; ULTRA HD-Plex; Universal HD; Versus HD; VH1 Soul; ViendoMovies; Vme TV; YES HD.

Pay Service 1
Pay Units: N.A.
Programming (via satellite): Cinemax; Flix; HBO (multiplexed); IFC; Showtime (multiplexed); Starz; The Movie Channel.
Fee: $40.00 installation; $9.95 monthly (each).

Digital Pay Service 1
Pay Units: N.A.
Programming (via satellite): Cinemax (multiplexed); Cinemax HD; Cinemax On Demand; GMA Pinoy TV; HBO (multiplexed); HBO HD; HBO on Demand; Korean Channel; MBC America; Portuguese Channel; RTN; Showtime (multiplexed); Showtime HD; Showtime On Demand; Sino TV; Starz (multiplexed); Starz Encore (multiplexed); Starz HD; Starz On Demand; The Filipino Channel; The Jewish Channel; The Movie Channel (multiplexed); The Movie Channel HD; TV Asia; TV Polonia; TV5MONDE USA; Zee TV.
Fee: $9.95 monthly (Cinemax, Showtime/TMC, Starz/Encore or Playboy), $11.95 monthly (HBO).
Video-On-Demand: Yes

Pay-Per-View
Anime Network (delivered digitally); IFC (delivered digitally); Disney Channel (delivered digitally); MSG Plus (delivered digitally); MSG (delivered digitally); MoviePlex (delivered digitally); iN DEMAND (delivered digitally); Playboy TV (delivered digitally).

Internet Service
Operational: Yes.
Subscribers: 81,935.
Broadband Service: Optimum Online.
Fee: $46.95 installation; $34.95 monthly; $299.00 modem purchase.

Telephone Service
Digital: Operational
Subscribers: 67,976.
Fee: $34.95 monthly
Miles of Plant: 1,975.0 (coaxial); 576.0 (fiber optic). Homes passed: 129,611.
Executive Vice President, Programming: Tom Montemagno. Vice President, Field Operations: Mark Fitchett. Area Government Affairs Director: Michael Chowaniec. Government Affairs Director: Jennifer Young.
Ownership: Altice USA (MSO).

CLINTON—Comcast Cable. Now served by NEW BRITAIN, CT [CT0037]. ICA: CT0017.

DANBURY—Comcast Cable. Now served by NEW BRITAIN, CT [CT0037]. ICA: CT0024.

ENFIELD—Cox Communications, 6205 Peachtree Dunwoody Rd, 12th Floor, Atlanta, GA 30328. Phones: 800-955-9515; 404-269-6590. Web Site: http://www.cox.com. Also serves East Granby, East Windsor, Granby, Hartland, Somers, Stafford, Suffield, Union & Windsor Locks, CT; Holland, MA. ICA: CT0011.
TV Market Ranking: 19 (East Granby, East Windsor, ENFIELD, Granby, Hartland, Somers, Suffield, Windsor Locks); 19,6 (Stafford, Union); 6 (Holland). Franchise award date: December 23, 1982. Fran-

Connecticut—Cable Systems

chise expiration date: N.A. Began: April 1, 1984.
Channel capacity: N.A. Channels available but not in use: N.A.

Basic Service
Subscribers: 29,240. Commercial subscribers: 755.
Programming (received off-air): WCCT-TV (CW, This TV) Waterbury; WDMR-LD (TMO) Springfield; WEDH (PBS) Hartford; WFSB (CBS, Escape, Laff) Hartford; WGBY-TV (PBS) Springfield; WGGB-TV (ABC, FOX, MNT) Springfield; WHPX-TV (ION) New London; WTIC-TV (Antenna TV, FOX) Hartford; WTNH (ABC, Bounce TV) New Haven; WUVN (LATV, UNV) Hartford; WVIT (COZI TV, NBC) New Britain; allband FM.
Programming (via satellite): Cox Sports Television; C-SPAN; C-SPAN 2; CT-N; MyNetworkTV; Pop; QVC; TBS.
Fee: $29.99 installation; $24.99 monthly.

Expanded Basic Service 1
Subscribers: N.A.
Programming (via satellite): A&E; AMC; Animal Planet; BET; Bravo; Cartoon Network; CNBC; CNN; Comcast SportsNet Mid-Atlantic; Comedy Central; Discovery Channel; Disney Channel; E! HD; ESPN; ESPN2; EVINE Live; EWTN Global Catholic Network; Food Network; Fox News Channel; Freeform; FX; HGTV; History; HLN; Lifetime; MSNBC; MTV; New England Sports Network; Nickelodeon; OWN: Oprah Winfrey Network; Spike TV; Syfy; The Weather Channel; TLC; TNT; Travel Channel; truTV; TV Land; USA Network; VH1.
Fee: $42.05 installation; $32.59 monthly.

Digital Basic Service
Subscribers: N.A.
Programming (via satellite): A&E HD; AMC HD; Animal Planet HD; Bio HD; Bloomberg Television; Boomerang; Bravo HD; Cartoon Network HD; CBS Sports Network; CMT HD; CNBC HD+; CNN HD; CNN International; Comcast SportsNet Mid-Atlantic; Comedy Central; Destination America; Destination America HD; Discovery Channel HD; Discovery Kids Channel; Discovery Life Channel; E! HD; ESPN Classic; ESPN HD; ESPN2 HD; ESPNews; ESPNU; Food Network HD; Fox Business Network; Fox Business Network HD; Fox News HD; Fox Sports 1; Fox Sports 2; FX HD; FYI; Golf Channel; Golf Channel HD; GolTV; Hallmark Movie Channel HD; HD Theater; HGTV HD; History; History HD; History International; Investigation Discovery; Lifetime HD; Lifetime Movie Network HD; MC; MLB Network; MTV Live; MyNetworkTV; National Geographic Channel; National Geographic Channel HD; NBA TV; NBA TV HD; NBCSN; New England Sports Network; NFL Network; NFL Network HD; NHL Network; NHL Network HD; Nick Jr.; Nick Jr.; Science HD; Spike TV HD; Syfy HD; TBS HD; TLC HD; TNT HD; Travel Channel HD; Trinity Broadcasting Network (TBN); Universal HD; USA Network HD; Versus HD; VH1 HD; Weatherscan.

Digital Expanded Basic Service
Subscribers: N.A.
Programming (via satellite): BBC America; Boomerang; Chiller; CMT; Cooking Channel; Disney XD; Fuse; Great American Country; GSN; Hallmark Channel; IFC; INSP; LMN; LOGO; MTV Classic; MTV Hits; MTV Jams; mtvU; NBC Universo; Nicktoons; Oxygen; Sprout; Sundance TV; TeenNick; Tr3s; Turner Classic Movies; TV One.
Fee: $68.74 monthly.

Digital Expanded Basic Service 2
Subscribers: N.A.
Programming (via satellite): Canal Sur; Cinelatino; CNN en Espanol; De Pelicula; De Pelicula Clasico; ESPN Deportes; Fox Deportes; History en Espanol; NickToons en Espanol; RAI Italia; Ritmoson; TV5MONDE USA; ULTRA HDPlex; Univision.
Fee: $9.95 monthly (RAI Italia), $11.95 monthly (TV5), $44.95 (various Spanish channels).

Digital Pay Service 1
Pay Units: N.A.
Programming (via satellite): Cinemax (multiplexed); Cinemax HD; Flix; HBO (multiplexed); HBO HD; Showtime (multiplexed); Showtime HD; Starz (multiplexed); Starz Encore (multiplexed); Starz HD; The Movie Channel (multiplexed).
Fee: $13.00 monthly (Cinemax, HBO, Starz/Encore or Flix/Showtime/TMC).

Video-On-Demand: Yes

Pay-Per-View
iN DEMAND (delivered digitally); NHL Center Ice (delivered digitally); Playboy TV (delivered digitally); Shorteez (delivered digitally); Club Jenna (delivered digitally); NBA League Pass (delivered digitally); MLS Direct Kick (delivered digitally); MLB Extra Innings (delivered digitally); Spice: Xcess (delivered digitally).

Internet Service
Operational: Yes. Began: May 1, 2000.
Broadband Service: Cox High Speed Internet.
Fee: $79.95 installation; $39.95 monthly; $15.00 modem lease; $299.00 modem purchase.

Telephone Service
Digital: Operational
Fee: $22.00 monthly
Miles of Plant: 956.0 (coaxial); None (fiber optic). Homes passed: 52,988.
Senior Vice President & General Manager: Paul Cronin. Vice President, Network Services: Allan Gardiner. Vice President, Marketing: Doreen Studley. Vice President, Government & Public Affairs: John L Wolfe. Vice President, Tax: Mary Vickers. Residential Product Management Director: Jonathan Leepson. Public Relations Director: Amy Quinn.
Ownership: Cox Communications Inc. (MSO).

GROTON—Comcast Cable. Now served by NEW BRITAIN, CT [CT0037]. ICA: CT0013.

GROTON—Thames Valley Communications, 295 Meridian St, Groton, CT 06340. Phone: 860-446-4009. Fax: 860-446-4752. E-mail: info@tvcconnect.com. Web Site: http://www.tvcconnect.com. ICA: CT0039.
Channel capacity: N.A. Channels available but not in use: N.A.

Basic Service
Subscribers: 6,110.
Fee: $17.95 monthly.

Internet Service
Operational: Yes.
Fee: $29.99-$59.99 monthly.

Telephone Service
Digital: Operational
Chief Executive Officer: William H. Pearson.
Ownership: Thames Valley Communications.

HARTFORD—Comcast Cable. Now served by NEW BRITAIN, CT [CT0037]. ICA: CT0001.

LAKEVILLE—Comcast Cable. Now served by NEW BRITAIN, CT [CT0037]. ICA: CT0023.

LITCHFIELD—Cablevision, 622 Torrington Rd, Litchfield, CT 06757. Phones: 203-750-5703; 516-803-2300 (Corporate office); 203-750-5600. Fax: 203-354-0921. Web Site: http://www.cablevision.com. Also serves Cornwall, Goshen, Morris, Thomaston, Torrington, Warren & Watertown. ICA: CT0015.
TV Market Ranking: 19 (Cornwall, Goshen, LITCHFIELD, Morris, Thomaston, Torrington, Warren, Watertown). Franchise award date: January 1, 1968. Franchise expiration date: N.A. Began: December 1, 1974.
Channel capacity: N.A. Channels available but not in use: N.A.

Basic Service
Subscribers: 24,311. Commercial subscribers: 925.
Programming (received off-air): WCCT-TV (CW, This TV) Waterbury; WCTX (Grit, MNT, TheCoolTV) New Haven; WEDH (PBS) Hartford; WFSB (CBS, Escape, Laff) Hartford; WHPX-TV (ION) New London; WNBC (COZI TV, NBC) New York; WRDM-CD (TMO) Hartford; WTIC-TV (Antenna TV, FOX) Hartford; WTNH (ABC, Bounce TV) New Haven; WVIT (COZI TV, NBC) New Britain; allband FM.
Programming (via satellite): CT-N; EVINE Live; QVC; WGN America.
Fee: $39.95 installation; $12.42 monthly.

Expanded Basic Service 1
Subscribers: N.A.
Programming (received off-air): WUVN (LATV, UNV) Hartford.
Programming (via satellite): A&E; AMC; Animal Planet; BET; Bravo; Cartoon Network; CNBC; CNN; Comedy Central; C-SPAN; C-SPAN 2; Discovery Channel; Disney Channel; E! HD; ESPN; ESPN2; Food Network; Fox News Channel; Fox Sports 1; Freeform; Fuse; FX; GSN; HGTV; History; HLN; Lifetime; MSG; MSNBC; MTV; MTV2; New England Sports Network; Nickelodeon; Spike TV; SportsNet New York; Syfy; TBS; The Weather Channel; TLC; TNT; Travel Channel; truTV; Turner Classic Movies; TV Land; USA Network; VH1; WE tv; Yesterday USA.
Fee: $34.53 monthly.

Digital Basic Service
Subscribers: N.A.
Programming (via satellite): Animal Planet HD; Azteca; BBC World News; Bloomberg Television; Bravo HD; Canal Sur; Caracol TV; Cartoon Network en Espanol; CBS Sports Network; Chiller; Cinelatino; Cloo; CMT; CNBC HD+; CNN en Espanol; CNN HD; C-SPAN 3; Destination America; Discovery Channel HD; Discovery Kids Channel; Disney XD; Docu TVE; Ecuavisa Internacional; ESPN Classic; ESPN Deportes; ESPN HD; ESPN2 HD; ESPNews; EuroNews; Food Network HD; FOX College Sports Central; FOX College Sports Pacific; Fox Deportes; Fox Life; Fox News HD; Fox Sports 2; FX HD; FXM; FYI; GMA Pinoy TV; Golf Channel; GolTV; Great American Country; Hallmark Channel; Hallmark Movie Channel HD; Hallmark Movies & Mysteries; HD Theater; here! On Demand; HGTV HD; History en Espanol; History International; HTV; Infinito; Investigation Discovery; Jewelry Television; Korean Channel; La Familia Cosmovision; LOGO; Mariavision; MBC America; MC; Momentum; MTV Classic; MTV Hits; National Geographic Channel; National Geographic Channel HD; NBA TV; NBC Universo; NBCSN; NHL Network; Nick HD; Nick Jr.; Nicktoons; Outdoor Channel; Oxygen; RTN; Science Channel; Science HD; Spike TV HD; Sundance TV; Syfy HD; TBS HD; TeenNick; Telefe Internacional; Telemicro Internacional; The Filipino Channel; The Weather Channel HD; TLC HD; TNT HD; Toon Disney en Espanol; Tr3s; Travel Channel HD; TV Asia; TV Polonia; TV5MONDE USA; TVG Network; ULTRA HDPlex; Universal HD; USA Network HD; Versus HD; VH1 Soul; ViendoMovies; YES HD; Zee TV.

Pay Service 1
Pay Units: N.A.
Programming (via satellite): Cinemax; Flix; HBO (multiplexed); IFC; Showtime (multiplexed); The Movie Channel.

Digital Pay Service 1
Pay Units: N.A.
Programming (via satellite): Cinemax; Cinemax HD; Cinemax On Demand; HBO (multiplexed); HBO HD; HBO on Demand; Playboy TV HD; Showtime (multiplexed); Showtime HD; Showtime On Demand; Starz (multiplexed); Starz Encore (multiplexed); Starz HD; Starz On Demand; The Movie Channel (multiplexed); The Movie Channel HD.
Fee: $9.95 monthly (Cinemax, Showtime/TMC, Playboy or Starz/Encore), $11.95 monthly (HBO).

Video-On-Demand: Yes

Pay-Per-View
Playboy TV; IFC (delivered digitally); Anime Network (delivered digitally); Disney Channel (delivered digitally); iN DEMAND (delivered digitally); NBA TV (delivered digitally); Playboy TV (delivered digitally).

Internet Service
Operational: Yes.
Subscribers: 22,185.
Broadband Service: Optimum Online.
Fee: $46.95 installation; $34.95 monthly; $299.00 modem purchase.

Telephone Service
Digital: Operational
Subscribers: 17,418.
Fee: $34.95 monthly
Miles of Plant: 1,495.0 (coaxial); 404.0 (fiber optic). Homes passed: 40,217.
Executive Vice President, Programming: Tom Montemagno. Vice President, Field Operations: Mark Fitchett. Government Affairs Area Director: Michael Chowaniec. Government Affairs Director: Jennifer Young.
Ownership: Altice USA (MSO).

MANCHESTER—Cox Communications, 6205 Peachtree Dunwoody Rd, 12th Floor, Atlanta, GA 30328. Phones: 800-955-9515; 404-269-6590. E-mail: newengland.services@cox.com. Web Site: http://www.cox.com. Also serves East Glastonbury, Glastonbury, Newington, Rocky Hill, South Glastonbury, South Windsor & Wethersfield. ICA: CT0005.
TV Market Ranking: 19 (East Glastonbury, Glastonbury, MANCHESTER, Newington, Rocky Hill, South Glastonbury, South Windsor, Wethersfield). Franchise award date: October 13, 1973. Franchise expiration date: N.A. Began: March 1, 1975.
Channel capacity: 57 (operating 2-way). Channels available but not in use: N.A.

Basic Service
Subscribers: 46,761. Commercial subscribers: 1,588.
Programming (received off-air): WCCT-TV (CW, This TV) Waterbury; WEDH (PBS) Hartford; WFSB (CBS, Escape, Laff) Hartford; WGBY-TV (PBS) Springfield; WHPX-TV (ION) New London; WRDM-CD (TMO) Hartford; WTIC-TV (Antenna TV, FOX) Hartford; WTNH (ABC, Bounce TV) New Haven; WUVN (LATV, UNV) Hartford; WVIT (COZI TV, NBC) New Britain; WZME (Retro TV) Bridgeport.

Cable Systems—Connecticut

Programming (via satellite): Cox Sports Television; C-SPAN; C-SPAN 2; CT-N; MyNetworkTV; Pop; QVC; TBS.
Fee: $29.99 installation; $24.99 monthly; $2.84 converter.
Expanded Basic Service 1
Subscribers: N.A.
Programming (via satellite): A&E; AMC; Animal Planet; BET; Bravo; Cartoon Network; CNBC; CNN; Comcast SportsNet Mid-Atlantic; Comedy Central; Discovery Channel; Disney Channel; E! HD; ESPN; ESPN2; EVINE Live; EWTN Global Catholic Network; Food Network; Fox News Channel; Freeform; FX; HGTV; History; HLN; Lifetime; MSNBC; MTV; New England Sports Network; Nickelodeon; OWN; Oprah Winfrey Network; Spike TV; Syfy; The Weather Channel; TLC; TNT; Travel Channel; truTV; TV Land; USA Network; VH1; YES Network.
Fee: $21.35 monthly.
Digital Basic Service
Subscribers: N.A.
Programming (via satellite): A&E HD; AMC HD; Animal Planet HD; Bio HD; Bloomberg Television; Bravo HD; Cartoon Network HD; CBS Sports Network; CMT HD; CNBC HD+; CNN HD; CNN International; Comcast SportsNet Mid-Atlantic; Comedy Central; Destination America; Destination America HD; Discovery Channel HD; Discovery Kids Channel; Discovery Life Channel; E! HD; ESPN Classic; ESPN HD; ESPN2 HD; ESPNews; ESPNU; Food Network HD; Fox Business Network; Fox Business Network HD; Fox News HD; Fox Sports 1; Fox Sports 2; FX HD; FYI; Golf Channel; Golf Channel HD; GolTV; Hallmark Movie Channel HD; HD Theater; HGTV HD; History; History HD; History International; Investigation Discovery; Lifetime HD; Lifetime Movie Network HD; MLB Network; MTV Live; MyNetworkTV; National Geographic Channel; National Geographic Channel HD; NBA TV; NBA TV HD; NBCSN; New England Sports Network; NFL Network; NFL Network HD; NHL Network; NHL Network HD; Nick HD; Nick Jr.; Science Channel; Science HD; Spike TV HD; Syfy HD; TBS HD; TLC HD; TNT HD; Travel Channel HD; Universal HD; USA Network HD; Versus HD; VH1 HD; Weatherscan; YES HD.
Digital Expanded Basic Service
Subscribers: N.A.
Programming (via satellite): BBC America; Boomerang; Chiller; CMT; Cooking Channel; Disney XD; DIY Network; Fuse; Great American Country; GSN; Hallmark Channel; IFC; INSP; LMN; LOGO; MTV Classic; MTV Hits; MTV Jams; MTV2; mtvU; NBC Universo; Nicktoons; Oxygen; Sprout; Sundance TV; TeenNick; Tr3s; Trinity Broadcasting Network (TBN); Turner Classic Movies; TV One; WE tv.
Fee: $68.74 monthly.
Digital Expanded Basic Service 2
Subscribers: N.A.
Programming (via satellite): Canal Sur; Cinelatino; CNN en Espanol; De Pelicula; De Pelicula Clasico; ESPN Deportes; Fox Deportes; History en Espanol; NickToons en Espanol; RAI Italia; Ritmoson; TV5MONDE USA; ULTRA HDPlex; Univision.
Fee: $9.95 monthly (RAI Italia), $11.95 monthly (TV5), $44.39 monthly (various Spanish channels).
Digital Pay Service 1
Pay Units: N.A.
Programming (via satellite): Cinemax (multiplexed); Cinemax HD; Flix; HBO (multiplexed); HBO HD; Showtime (multiplexed);

Showtime HD; Starz (multiplexed); Starz Encore (multiplexed); Starz HD; The Movie Channel (multiplexed).
Fee: $13.00 monthly (Cinemax, HBO, Starz/Encore or Flix/Showtime/TMC).
Video-On-Demand: Yes
Pay-Per-View
iN DEMAND; iN DEMAND (delivered digitally); Club Jenna (delivered digitally); Playboy TV (delivered digitally); Shorteez (delivered digitally); NHL Center Ice (delivered digitally); NBA League Pass (delivered digitally); MLS Direct Kick (delivered digitally); MLB Extra Innings (delivered digitally); Spice: Xcess (delivered digitally).
Internet Service
Operational: Yes. Began: January 1, 1997.
Subscribers: 96,992.
Broadband Service: Cox High Speed Internet.
Fee: $99.95 installation; $39.95 monthly; $15.00 modem lease; $299.00 modem purchase.
Telephone Service
Digital: Operational
Subscribers: 73,296.
Miles of Plant: 4,732.0 (coaxial); 1,611.0 (fiber optic). Homes passed: 204,645.
Senior Vice President & General Manager: Paul Cronin. Vice President, Network Services: Allan Gardiner. Vice President, Government & Public Affairs: John L Wolfe. Vice President, Marketing: Doreen Studley. Vice President, Tax: Mary Vickers. Public Relations Director: Amy Quinn. Residential Product Management Director: Jonathan Leepson.
Ownership: Cox Communications Inc. (MSO).

MERIDEN—Cox Communications, 6205 Peachtree Dunwoody Rd, 12th Floor, Atlanta, GA 30328. Phones: 404-269-6590; 800-955-9515. Web Site: http://www.cox.com. Also serves Cheshire & Southington. ICA: CT0010.
TV Market Ranking: 19 (Cheshire, MERIDEN, Southington). Franchise award date: January 1, 1974. Franchise expiration date: N.A. Began: July 1, 1974.
Channel capacity: 57 (operating 2-way). Channels available but not in use: N.A.
Basic Service
Subscribers: 28,103. Commercial subscribers: 754.
Programming (received off-air): WCCT-TV (CW, This TV) Waterbury; WEDH (PBS) Hartford; WFSB (CBS, Escape, Laff) Hartford; WGBY-TV (PBS) Springfield; WHPX-TV (ION) New London; WRDM-CD (TMO) Hartford; WTIC-TV (Antenna TV, FOX) Hartford; WTNH (ABC, Bounce TV) New Haven; WUVN (LATV, UNV) Hartford; WVIT (COZI TV, NBC) New Britain; WZME (Retro TV) Bridgeport.
Programming (via microwave): WPIX (Antenna TV, CW, This TV) New York.
Programming (via satellite): Cox Sports Television; C-SPAN; C-SPAN 2; CT-N; MyNetworkTV; Pop; TBS.
Fee: $29.99 installation; $24.99 monthly; $1.25 converter.
Expanded Basic Service 1
Subscribers: N.A.
Programming (via satellite): A&E; AMC; Animal Planet; BET; Cartoon Network; CNBC; CNN; Comcast SportsNet Mid-Atlantic; Comedy Central; Discovery Channel; Disney Channel; E! HD; ESPN; ESPN2; EWTN Global Catholic Network; Food Network; Fox News Channel; Freeform; FX; HGTV; History; HLN; Lifetime; MSNBC; MTV; New England Sports Network; Nickelodeon; OWN; Oprah Winfrey Network; QVC; Spike

TV; Syfy; The Weather Channel; TLC; TNT; Travel Channel; truTV; TV Land; USA Network; VH1; YES Network.
Fee: $26.08 installation; $21.35 monthly.
Digital Basic Service
Subscribers: N.A.
Programming (via satellite): A&E HD; AMC HD; Animal Planet HD; Bio HD; Bloomberg Television; Bravo HD; Cartoon Network HD; CBS Sports Network; CMT HD; CNBC HD+; CNN HD; CNN International; Comcast SportsNet Mid-Atlantic; Comedy Central; Destination America; Destination America HD; Discovery Channel HD; Discovery Kids Channel; Discovery Life Channel; E! HD; ESPN Classic; ESPN HD; ESPN2 HD; ESPNews; ESPNU; Food Network HD; Fox Business Network; Fox Business Network HD; Fox News HD; Fox Sports 1; Fox Sports 2; FX HD; FYI; Golf Channel; Golf Channel HD; GolTV; Hallmark Movie Channel HD; HD Theater; HGTV HD; History; History HD; History International; Investigation Discovery; Lifetime HD; Lifetime Movie Network HD; MC; MLB Network; MTV Live; MyNetworkTV; National Geographic Channel; National Geographic Channel HD; NBA TV; NBA TV HD; NBCSN; New England Sports Network; NFL Network; NFL Network HD; NHL Network; NHL Network HD; Nick HD; Nick Jr.; Science Channel; Science HD; Spike TV HD; Syfy HD; TBS HD; TLC HD; TNT HD; Travel Channel HD; Universal HD; USA Network HD; Versus HD; VH1 HD; Weatherscan; YES HD.
Digital Expanded Basic Service
Subscribers: N.A.
Programming (via satellite): BBC America; Boomerang; Chiller; CMT; Cooking Channel; Disney XD; DIY Network; Fuse; Great American Country; GSN; Hallmark Channel; IFC; INSP; LMN; LOGO; MTV Classic; MTV Hits; MTV Jams; MTV2; mtvU; NBC Universo; Nicktoons; Oxygen; Sprout; Sundance TV; TeenNick; Tr3s; Trinity Broadcasting Network (TBN); Turner Classic Movies; TV One; WE tv.
Fee: $68.74 monthly.
Digital Expanded Basic Service 2
Subscribers: N.A.
Programming (via satellite): Canal Sur; Cinelatino; CNN en Espanol; De Pelicula; De Pelicula Clasico; ESPN Deportes; Fox Deportes; History en Espanol; NickToons en Espanol; RAI Italia; Ritmoson; TV5MONDE USA; ULTRA HDPlex; Univision.
Fee: $9.95 monthly (RAI Italia), $11.95 monthly (TV5), $44.39 monthly (various Spanish channels).
Digital Pay Service 1
Pay Units: N.A.
Programming (via satellite): Cinemax (multiplexed); Cinemax HD; Flix; HBO (multiplexed); HBO HD; Showtime (multiplexed); Showtime HD; Starz (multiplexed); Starz Encore (multiplexed); Starz HD; The Movie Channel (multiplexed).
Fee: $13.00 monthly (HBO, Cinemax, Showtime/Flix/TMC or Starz/Encore).
Video-On-Demand: Yes

Pay-Per-View
iN DEMAND (delivered digitally); Fresh (delivered digitally); Playboy TV (delivered digitally); Shorteez (delivered digitally); NHL Center Ice (delivered digitally); NBA League Pass (delivered digitally); MLS Direct Kick (delivered digitally); MLB Extra Innings (delivered digitally); Spice: Xcess (delivered digitally).
Internet Service
Operational: Yes. Began: September 30, 1997.
Broadband Service: Cox High Speed Internet.
Fee: $114.95 installation; $39.95 monthly; $15.00 modem lease; $299.00 modem purchase.
Telephone Service
Digital: Operational
Fee: $11.95 monthly
Miles of Plant: 4,594.0 (coaxial); 1,600.0 (fiber optic). Homes passed: 203,334.
Senior Vice President & General Manager: Paul Cronin. Vice President, Network Services: Allan Gardner. Vice President, Government & Public Affairs: John Wolfe. Vice President, Marketing: Doreen Studley. Vice President, Tax: Mary Vickers. Public Relations Director: Amy Quinn. Residential Product Management Director: Jonathan Leepson.
Ownership: Cox Communications Inc. (MSO).

MIDDLETOWN—Comcast Cable. Now served by NEW BRITAIN, CT [CT0037]. ICA: CT0019.

NEW BRITAIN—Comcast Cable, 676 Island Pond Rd, Manchester, NH 03109. Phones: 800-266-2278; 860-505-6248. Fax: 860-505-3597. Web Site: http://www.comcast.com. Also serves Andover, Ansonia, Avon, Beacon Falls, Berlin, Bethany, Bethel, Bloomfield, Bolton, Bozrah, Branford, Bristol, Burlington, Canaan, Canton, Centerbrook, Chester, Clinton, Colchester, Cromwell, Danbury, Deep River, Derby, Durham, East Haddam, East Hampton, East Hartford, East Haven, Ellington, Essex, Falls Village, Farmington, Franklin, Gales Ferry, Groton, Guilford, Haddam, Hamden, Hartford, Hebron, Higganum, Huntington, Ivoryton, Killingworth, Lakeville, Ledyard, Lisbon, Lyme, Madison, Marlborough, Middlebury, Middlefield, Middletown, Mystic, Naugatuck, New Haven, New London Submarine Base, Norfolk, North Branford, North Canaan, North Haven, North Stonington, Norwich, Old Lyme, Old Mystic, Old Saybrook, Oxford, Pawcatuck, Pequabuck, Plainville (town), Plymouth, Portland, Preston, Prospect, Ridgefield, Rockfall, Salem, Salisbury, Seymour, Sharon, Shelton, Simsbury, Sprague, Stonington, Terryville, Thomaston, Tolland, Vernon, Voluntown, Wallingford, Waterbury, West Hartford, West Haven, Westbrook, Windsor & Wolcott, CT; Beekman (town), Brewster (village), Carmel, Kent (town), Patterson (town), Pawling (town), Pawling (village), Putnam Valley (town), Somers (town) & Southeast (town), NY. ICA: CT0037.

Connecticut—Cable Systems

TV Market Ranking: 19 (Andover, Ansonia, Avon, Beacon Falls, Beekman (town), Berlin, Bethany, Bethel, Bloomfield, Bolton, Bozrah, Branford, Brewster (village), Bristol, Burlington, Canton, Carmel, Centerbrook, Chester, Clinton, Colchester, Cromwell, Danbury, Deep River, Derby, Durham, East Haddam, East Hampton, East Hartford, East Haven, Ellington, Essex, Falls Village, Farmington, Franklin, Gales Ferry, Groton, Guilford, Haddam, Hamden, Hartford, Hebron, Higganum, Huntington, Ivoryton, Killingworth, Ledyard, Lyme, Madison, Marlborough, Middlebury, Middlefield, Middletown, Mystic, Naugatuck, NEW BRITAIN, New Haven, New London Submarine Base, Norfolk, North Branford, North Haven, North Stonington, Norwich, Old Lyme, Old Mystic, Old Saybrook, Oxford, Patterson (town), Pawcatuck, Pawling (town), Pawling (village), Pequabuck, Plainville (town), Plymouth, Portland, Prospect, Putnam Valley (town), Ridgefield, Salem, Seymour, Sharon, Shelton, Simsbury, Somers (town), Southeast (town), Sprague, Stonington, Terryville, Thomaston, Tolland, Vernon, Voluntown, Wallingford, Waterbury, West Hartford, West Haven, Westbrook, Windsor, Wolcott); 33,19 (Lisbon, Preston); Below 100 (Canaan, Kent (town), North Canaan, Salisbury, Lakeville).
Channel capacity: N.A. Channels available but not in use: N.A.

Basic Service
Subscribers: 433,700. Commercial subscribers: 3,303.
Programming (received off-air): WCCT-TV (CW, This TV) Waterbury; WCTX (Grit, MNT, TheCoolTV) New Haven; WFSB (CBS, Escape, Laff) Hartford; WGBY-TV (PBS) Springfield; WHPX-TV (ION) New London; WRDM-CD (TMO) Hartford; WTIC-TV (Antenna TV, FOX) Hartford; WTNH (ABC, Bounce TV) New Haven; WUVN (LATV, UNV) Hartford; WVIT (COZI TV, NBC) New Britain.
Programming (via satellite): Comcast Network Philadelphia; C-SPAN; C-SPAN 2; EWTN Global Catholic Network; National Jewish TV (NJT); New England Cable News; TBS.
Fee: $31.95-$46.00 installation; $31.75 monthly.

Expanded Basic Service 1
Subscribers: N.A.
Programming (via satellite): A&E; AMC; Animal Planet; BET; Cartoon Network; CNBC; CNN; Comcast SportsNet New England; Comedy Central; Discovery Channel; Disney Channel; E! HD; ESPN; ESPN2; EVINE Live; Food Network; Fox News Channel; Freeform; FX; Golf Channel; HGTV; History; HLN; Lifetime; MSNBC; MTV; New England Sports Network; Nickelodeon; Pop; QVC; Spike TV; Syfy; The Weather Channel; TLC; TNT; truTV; TV Land; USA Network; VH1.
Fee: $37.90 monthly.

Expanded Basic Service 2
Subscribers: N.A.
Programming (via satellite): Fuse; NBCSN; Turner Classic Movies.

Digital Basic Service
Subscribers: N.A.
Programming (received off-air): WVIT (COZI TV, NBC) New Britain.
Programming (via satellite): Bloomberg Television; Discovery Life Channel; Disney XD; ESPN; ESPN Classic; ESPNews; Fox Sports 1; FXM; FYI; GSN; History International; HITS (Headend In The Sky); IFC; LMN; National Geographic Channel; NFL Network; Nick 2; Nick Jr.; Nicktoons;

Outdoor Channel; Sundance TV; TeenNick; Trinity Broadcasting Network (TBN); TVG Network; WE tv.

Pay Service 1
Pay Units: N.A.
Programming (via satellite): HBO; The Movie Channel.
Fee: $19.95 monthly.

Digital Pay Service 1
Pay Units: N.A.
Programming (via satellite): Cinemax (multiplexed); HBO (multiplexed); Showtime (multiplexed); Starz (multiplexed); Starz Encore (multiplexed); The Movie Channel (multiplexed).
Fee: $19.95 monthly (each).

Video-On-Demand: Yes

Pay-Per-View
iN DEMAND; iN DEMAND (delivered digitally); Playboy TV (delivered digitally); Fresh (delivered digitally); Shorteez (delivered digitally).

Internet Service
Operational: Yes.
Subscribers: 314,247.
Broadband Service: Comcast High Speed Internet.
Fee: $42.95 monthly; $3.00 modem lease.

Telephone Service
Digital: Operational
Subscribers: 229,576.
Fee: $44.95 monthly
Miles of Plant: 19,399.0 (coaxial); 4,556.0 (fiber optic). Homes passed: 938,739.
Vice President & General Manager: Pamela Mackenzie. Technical Operations Director: Jim Jones. Marketing Director: Carolyne Hannan. Marketing Coordinator: Marcia McElroy. Marketing Manager: Judy Cyr.
Ownership: Comcast Cable Communications Inc. (MSO).

NEW HAVEN—Comcast Cable. Now served by NEW BRITAIN, CT [CT0037]. ICA: CT0004.

NEW LONDON—Atlantic Broadband, 2 Batterymarch Park, Ste 205, Quincy, MA 02169. Phones: 888-536-9600 (Customer service); 617-786-8800. E-mail: info@atlanticbb.com. Web Site: http://atlanticbb.com. Also serves Danielson, Dayville, East Lyme, Griswold, Killingly, Montville, Moosup, Niantic, Oakdale, Oneco, Plainfield, Putnam, Quaker Hill, Rogers, Sterling, Waterford & Wauregan. ICA: CT0008.
TV Market Ranking: 19 (East Lyme, Griswold, Montville, NEW LONDON, Niantic, Oakdale, Plainfield, Quaker Hill, Waterford); 19,33 (Killingly, Moosup, Oneco, Sterling, Wauregan); 19,6 (Danielson); 6,33 (Dayville, Putnam, Rogers). Franchise award date: N.A. Franchise expiration date: N.A. Began: May 1, 1973.
Channel capacity: 78 (operating 2-way). Channels available but not in use: N.A.

Basic Service
Subscribers: 23,043. Commercial subscribers: 1,321.
Programming (received off-air): WCCT-TV (CW, This TV) Waterbury; WCTX (Grit, MNT, TheCoolTV) New Haven; WEDN (PBS) Norwich; WFSB (CBS, Escape, Laff) Hartford; WGBH-TV (PBS) Boston; WHPX-TV (ION) New London; WJAR (MeTV, NBC) Providence; WLNE-TV (ABC) New Bedford; WPRI-TV (CBS, TheCoolTV) Providence; WTIC-TV (Antenna TV, FOX) Hartford; WTNH (ABC, Bounce TV) New Haven; WUVN (LATV, UNV) Hartford; WVIT (COZI TV, NBC) New Britain; 28 FMs.

Programming (via satellite): CMT; C-SPAN; C-SPAN 2; CT-N; Pop; QVC; TBS; WGN America.
Fee: $25.90 installation; $30.95 monthly.

Expanded Basic Service 1
Subscribers: N.A.
Programming (via satellite): A&E; Animal Planet; BET; Bravo; Cartoon Network; CNBC; CNN; Comcast SportsNet New England; Comedy Central; Discovery Channel; Disney Channel; ESPN; ESPN Classic; ESPN2; EWTN Global Catholic Network; Food Network; Fox News Channel; Freeform; FX; HGTV; History; Lifetime; MSNBC; MTV; New England Sports Network; Nickelodeon; Spike TV; Syfy; The Weather Channel; TLC; TNT; Travel Channel; TV Land; USA Network; VH1; YES Network.
Fee: $32.15 monthly.

Digital Basic Service
Subscribers: N.A.
Programming (via satellite): AXS TV; BBC America; Boomerang; CMT; Cooking Channel; Discovery Digital Networks; Disney XD; ESPNews; ESPNU; Hallmark Channel; HD Theater; LMN; LOGO; MC; Nick 2; Nick Jr.; Nicktoons; Sprout; TeenNick; TNT HD; Weatherscan.

Digital Expanded Basic Service
Subscribers: N.A.
Programming (via satellite): Bloomberg Television; FOX College Sports Central; FOX College Sports Pacific; Fox Sports 1; FXM; FYI; Golf Channel; History International; IFC; NBCSN; NFL Network; Turner Classic Movies.
Fee: $8.95 monthly.

Digital Pay Service 1
Pay Units: N.A.
Programming (via satellite): Cinemax (multiplexed); Flix; HBO (multiplexed); Showtime (multiplexed); Sundance TV; The Movie Channel (multiplexed).
Fee: $9.95 monthly (Showtime or Cinemax), $10.95 monthly (HBO).

Video-On-Demand: Planned

Pay-Per-View
iN DEMAND; Fresh; iN DEMAND (delivered digitally); Pleasure (delivered digitally).

Internet Service
Operational: Yes. Began: September 1, 2000.
Subscribers: 17,272.
Broadband Service: In-house.
Fee: $75.00 installation; $39.95 monthly; $2.50 modem lease; $99.00 modem purchase.

Telephone Service
Analog: Not Operational
Digital: Operational
Subscribers: 5,908.
Miles of Plant: 1,867.0 (coaxial); 997.0 (fiber optic). Homes passed: 68,903.
President & Chief Executive Officer: Richard Shea. Vice President & General Manager: Chap Hanley.
Ownership: Atlantic Broadband (MSO).

NEW MILFORD—Charter Communications, 11 Commerce Rd, Newtown, CT 06470. Phones: 636-207-5100 (Corporate office); 203-304-4050; 508-853-1515 (Worcester office); 314-543-2236. Web Site: http://www.charter.com. Also serves Barkhamsted, Bethlehem, Bridgewater, Brookfield, Colebrook, Harwinton, Kent, Monroe, New Fairfield, New Hartford, Newtown (borough), Roxbury, Sherman, Southbury, Trumbull, Warren, Washington, West Hartland, Winchester, Winsted & Woodbury. ICA: CT0014.

TV Market Ranking: 19 (Barkhamsted, Bethlehem, Bridgewater, Brookfield, Colebrook, Harwinton, Kent, Monroe, New Fairfield, New Hartford, NEW MILFORD, Newtown (borough), Roxbury, Sherman, Southbury, Trumbull, Warren, Washington, West Hartland, Winchester, Winsted, Woodbury). Franchise award date: N.A. Franchise expiration date: N.A. Began: July 1, 1978.
Channel capacity: 72 (operating 2-way). Channels available but not in use: N.A.

Digital Basic Service
Subscribers: 52,414.
Programming (via satellite): BBC America; Bloomberg Television; Discovery Digital Networks; Disney XD; DIY Network; ESPNews; FYI; Great American Country; History International; IFC; LMN; MC; Nick 2; Nick Jr.; Nicktoons; Sundance TV; TeenNick; WE tv.
Fee: $49.99 installation; $26.99 monthly.

Digital Expanded Basic Service
Subscribers: N.A.
Programming (via satellite): A&E; AMC; Animal Planet; Bravo; Cartoon Network; CNBC; CNN; Comedy Central; C-SPAN 2; Discovery Channel; Disney Channel; E! HD; ESPN; ESPN Classic; ESPN2; EVINE Live; EWTN Global Catholic Network; Food Network; Fox News Channel; Fox Sports 1; Freeform; Golf Channel; Hallmark Channel; HGTV; History; HLN; INSP; Lifetime; MSG; MSG Plus; MSNBC; MTV; National Geographic Channel; NBCSN; Nickelodeon; Oxygen; Spike TV; Syfy; TBS; The Weather Channel; TLC; TNT; Travel Channel; Trinity Broadcasting Network (TBN); truTV; Turner Classic Movies; TV Land; USA Network; VH1; YES Network.
Fee: $55.00 monthly.

Digital Pay Service 1
Pay Units: N.A.
Programming (via satellite): Cinemax (multiplexed); Flix; HBO (multiplexed); Showtime (multiplexed); Starz (multiplexed); Starz Encore (multiplexed); The Movie Channel (multiplexed).
Fee: $13.95 monthly (Cinemax, HBO, Showtime/TMC/Flix, or Starz/Encore).

Video-On-Demand: Yes

Pay-Per-View
ETC (delivered digitally); iN DEMAND (delivered digitally); Playboy TV (delivered digitally); Pleasure (delivered digitally); Fresh (delivered digitally).

Internet Service
Operational: Yes. Began: May 1, 1998.
Subscribers: 45,662.
Broadband Service: Charter Internet.
Fee: $29.99 monthly; $5.00 modem lease; $79.00 modem purchase.

Telephone Service
Digital: Operational
Subscribers: 31,309.
Fee: $29.99 monthly
Miles of Plant: 5,007.0 (coaxial); 1,845.0 (fiber optic). Homes passed: 98,352.
Vice President & General Manager: Greg Garabedian. Technical Operations Director: George Duffy. Marketing Director: Dennis Jerome. Accounting Director: David Sovanski.
Ownership: Charter Communications Inc. (MSO).

NORWALK—Cablevision, 28 Cross St, Norwalk, CT 06851. Phones: 203-750-5703; 203-750-5600; 516-803-2300 (Corporate office). Fax: 203-354-0921. Web Site: http://www.cablevision.com. Also serves Darien, Easton, Greenwich, New Canaan, Redding, Stamford, Weston, Westport & Wilton. ICA: CT0002.

TV Market Ranking: 1 (Greenwich, Stamford); 19 (Darien, Easton, New Canaan, NORWALK, Redding, Weston, Westport, Wilton). Franchise award date: July 1, 1981. Franchise expiration date: N.A. Began: August 16, 1982.
Channel capacity: N.A. Channels available but not in use: N.A.

Basic Service
Subscribers: 118,810. Commercial subscribers: 6,454.
Programming (received off-air): News 12 Connecticut; WABC-TV (ABC, Live Well Network) New York; WCBS-TV (CBS, Decades) New York; WCCT-TV (CW, This TV) Waterbury; WEDW (PBS) Bridgeport; WFSB (CBS, Escape, Laff) Hartford; WFUT-DT (getTV, UniMas) Newark; WLIW (PBS) Garden City; WLNY-TV (IND) Riverhead; WNBC (COZI TV, NBC) New York; WNET (PBS) Newark; WNJU (TMO) Linden; WNYW (FOX, Movies!) New York; WPIX (Antenna TV, CW, This TV) New York; WPXN-TV (ION) New York; WRNN-TV (IND) Kingston; WTIC-TV (Antenna TV, FOX) Hartford; WTNH (ABC, Bounce TV) New Haven; WVIT (COZI TV, NBC) New Britain; WWOR-TV (Bounce TV, Buzzr, Heroes & Icons, MNT) Secaucus; WXTV-DT (UNV) Paterson; WZME (Retro TV) Bridgeport; 12 FMs.
Fee: $39.95 installation; $16.72 monthly; $3.50 converter.

Expanded Basic Service 1
Subscribers: N.A.
Programming (via satellite): A&E; AMC; Animal Planet; BET; Bravo; Cartoon Network; CNBC; CNN; Comedy Central; C-SPAN; C-SPAN 2; CT-N; Discovery Channel; Disney Channel; E! HD; ESPN; ESPN2; EVINE Live; Food Network; Fox News Channel; Fox Sports 1; Freeform; Fuse; FX; GSN; HGTV; History; HLN; Lifetime; MSG; MSG Plus; MSNBC; MTV; MTV2; News 12 Traffic & Weather; Nickelodeon; QVC; Spike TV; SportsNet New York; Syfy; TBS; The Weather Channel; TLC; TNT; Travel Channel; truTV; Turner Classic Movies; TV Land; USA Network; VH1; WE tv; YES Network.
Fee: $33.23 monthly.

Digital Basic Service
Subscribers: N.A.
Programming (via satellite): Azteca; BBC World News; Bloomberg Television; Canal Sur; Caracol TV; Cartoon Network en Espanol; CBS Sports Network; Cinelatino; CMT; CNN en Espanol; CNN HD; C-SPAN 3; Destination America; Discovery Kids Channel; Disney XD; Docu TVE; Ecuavisa Internacional; ESPN Classic; ESPN Deportes; ESPN HD; ESPN2 HD; ESPNews; EuroNews; EVINE Live; Food Network HD; FOX College Sports Central; FOX College Sports Pacific; Fox Deportes; Fox Life; Fox Sports 2; FXM; FYI; Golf Channel; GolTV; Great American Country; Hallmark Channel; HD Theater; here! On Demand; HGTV HD; History en Espanol; History International; HTV; Infinito; Investigation Discovery; Jewelry Television; La Familia Cosmovision; LOGO; Mariavision; MC; Momentum; MoviePlex; MTV Classic; MTV Hits; National Geographic Channel; National Geographic Channel HD; NBA TV; NBC Universo; NBCSN; New England Cable News; NHL Network; Nick Jr.; Nicktoons; Outdoor Channel; Oxygen; Science Channel; Sundance TV; TBS HD; TeenNick; Telefe Internacional; Telemicro Internacional; The Jewish Channel; TNT HD; Toon Disney en Espanol; Tr3s; TVG Network; ULTRA HDPlex; Universal HD; Versus HD; VH1 Soul; ViendoMovies; YES HD.

Pay Service 1
Pay Units: N.A.
Programming (via satellite): Cinemax; Flix; HBO (multiplexed); IFC; Reality Kings TV (RKTV); Showtime (multiplexed); The Movie Channel (multiplexed).
Fee: $40.00 installation.

Digital Pay Service 1
Pay Units: N.A.
Programming (via satellite): Cinemax (multiplexed); Cinemax HD; Cinemax On Demand; GMA Pinoy TV; HBO (multiplexed); HBO HD; HBO on Demand; Korean Channel; MBC America; Portuguese Channel; RTN; Showtime (multiplexed); Showtime HD; Showtime On Demand; Sino TV; Starz (multiplexed); Starz Encore (multiplexed); Starz HD; Starz On Demand; The Filipino Channel; The Movie Channel (multiplexed); The Movie Channel HD; TV Asia; TV Polonia; TV5MONDE USA; Zee TV.
Fee: $11.95 monthly (Cinemax, Showtime, TMC, Starz/Encore or Playboy), $14.95 monthly (HBO).

Video-On-Demand: Yes

Pay-Per-View
IFC (delivered digitally); Anime Network (delivered digitally); iN DEMAND (delivered digitally); Disney Channel (delivered digitally); Playboy TV (delivered digitally).

Internet Service
Operational: Yes. Began: January 1, 1997.
Subscribers: 119,433.
Broadband Service: Optimum Online.
Fee: $46.95 installation; $34.95 monthly; $299.00 modem purchase.

FULLY SEARCHABLE • CONTINUOUSLY UPDATED • DISCOUNT RATES FOR PRINT PURCHASERS
For more information call **800-771-9202** or visit **www.warren-news.com**

Telephone Service
Digital: Operational
Subscribers: 91,916.
Fee: $34.95 monthly
Miles of Plant: 3,776.0 (coaxial); 941.0 (fiber optic). Homes passed: 142,886.
Executive Vice President, Programming: Tom Montemagno. Vice President, Field Operations: Mark Fitchett. Government Affairs Area Director: Michael Chowaniec. Government Affairs Director: Jennifer Young.
Ownership: Altice USA (MSO).

NORWICH—Comcast Cable. Now served by NEW BRITAIN, CT [CT0037]. ICA: CT0018.

OLD LYME—Comcast Cable. Now served by NEW BRITAIN, CT [CT0037]. ICA: CT0025.

PLAINFIELD—Atlantic Broadband. Now served by NEW LONDON, CT [CT0008]. ICA: CT0038.

VERNON—Comcast Cable. Now served by NEW BRITAIN, CT [CT0037]. ICA: CT0034.

WATERBURY—Comcast Cable. Now served by NEW BRITAIN, CT [CT0037]. ICA: CT0007.

WINSTED—Charter Communications. Now served by NEW MILFORD, CT [CT0014]. ICA: CT0021.

DELAWARE

Total Systems: 1	Communities with Applications: 0
Total Communities Served: 21	Number of Basic Subscribers: 30,049
Franchises Not Yet Operating: 0	Number of Expanded Basic Subscribers: 0
Applications Pending: 0	Number of Pay Units: 0

Top 100 Markets Represented: Baltimore, MD (14); Philadelphia, PA-Burlington, NJ (4).

For a list of cable communities in this section, see the Cable Community Index located in the back of Cable Volume 2.
For explanation of terms used in cable system listings, see p. D-11.

DOVER—Comcast Cable. Now served by TOWSON, MD [MD0003]. ICA: DE0004.

MILFORD—Comcast Cable. Now served by TOWSON, MD [MD0003]. ICA: DE0003.

MILLSBORO—Mediacom, 601 Clayton St, Dagsboro, DE 19939-1738. Phones: 302-732-9332; 302-732-6600 (Customer service). Fax: 302-732-6697. Web Site: http://www.mediacomcable.com. Also serves Bayard, Bethany Beach, Clarksville, Dagsboro, Frankford, Lewes, Middlesex Beach, Millville, Ocean View, Roxana, Selbyville, South Bethany & Sussex County, DE; Bishopville, Ocean Pines, Pittsville, Whaleysville, Wicomico County (eastern portion), Willards & Worcester County (portions), MD. ICA: DE0001.

TV Market Ranking: Below 100 (Bayard, Bethany Beach, Bishopville, Clarksville, Frankford, Lewes, Middlesex Beach, Millville, Ocean Pines, Ocean View, Pittsville, Roxana, Selbyville, South Bethany, Sussex County (portions), Whaleysville, Wicomico County (eastern portion), Willards, Worcester County (portions), Dagsboro, MILLSBORO); Outside TV Markets (Sussex County (portions)). Franchise award date: March 12, 1975. Franchise expiration date: N.A. Began: October 1, 1968.
Channel capacity: 80 (operating 2-way). Channels available but not in use: N.A.

Basic Service
Subscribers: 26,721.
Programming (received off-air): WBOC-TV (CBS, FOX) Salisbury; WCPB (PBS) Salisbury; WDPB (PBS) Seaford; WMDT (ABC, CW, MeTV) Salisbury.
Programming (via microwave): WBAL-TV (NBC) Baltimore; WJZ-TV (CBS, Decades) Baltimore; WTTG (Buzzr, FOX) Washington; WTXF-TV (Buzzr, FOX, Movies!) Philadelphia.
Programming (via satellite): A&E; AMC; Animal Planet; BET; Bravo; Cartoon Network; CMT; CNBC; CNN; Comcast SportsNet Mid-Atlantic; Comedy Central; C-SPAN; C-SPAN 2; Discovery Channel; Disney Channel; E! HD; ESPN; ESPN2; EVINE Live; EWTN Global Catholic Network; Food Network; Fox News Channel; Freeform; FX; Golf Channel; HGTV; History; HLN; Lifetime; MSNBC; MTV; Nickelodeon; Outdoor Channel; Pop; QVC; Spike TV; Syfy; TBS; The Weather Channel; TLC; TNT; Travel Channel; truTV; TV Land; USA Network; VH1; WE tv.
Fee: $29.50 installation; $68.95 monthly; $3.00 converter.

Digital Basic Service
Subscribers: N.A.
Programming (via satellite): AXS TV; BBC America; Bloomberg Television; Bravo; Discovery Digital Networks; DMX Music; ESPN; ESPNews; Fox Sports 1; Fuse; FXM; FYI; GSN; HD Theater; History International; IFC; LMN; Mid-Atlantic Sports Network (MASN); MTV Classic; MTV2; National Geographic Channel; NBCSN; Nick Jr.; Nicktoons; TeenNick; Turner Classic Movies; Weatherscan.

Digital Pay Service 1
Pay Units: N.A.
Programming (via satellite): Cinemax (multiplexed); HBO (multiplexed); HBO HD; Showtime (multiplexed); Showtime HD; Starz (multiplexed); Starz Encore (multiplexed); Starz HD; The Movie Channel (multiplexed).
Fee: $8.00 monthly (Starz), $9.95 monthly (Showtime or Cinemax), $13.95 monthly (HBO).

Video-On-Demand: Planned

Pay-Per-View
ESPN (delivered digitally); Mediacom PPV (delivered digitally).

Internet Service
Operational: Yes.
Subscribers: 22,286.
Broadband Service: Mediacom High Speed Internet.
Fee: $59.95 installation; $42.95 monthly; $3.00 modem lease; $239.00 modem purchase.

Telephone Service
Digital: Operational
Subscribers: 9,926.
Miles of Plant: 1,828.0 (coaxial); 167.0 (fiber optic). Homes passed: 60,859. Miles of plant (coax) includes miles (fiber)
Regional Vice President: David Kane. Area Technical Operations Manager: Gary McEachern. Chief Technician: Tim Baker. Customer Service Manager: Dulce Olexo. Marketing Director: Martin Wills.
Ownership: Mediacom LLC (MSO).

WILMINGTON—Comcast Cable. Now served by PHILADELPHIA, PA [PA0005]. ICA: DE0006.

DISTRICT OF COLUMBIA

Total Systems: 1	Communities with Applications: 0
Total Communities Served: 24	Number of Basic Subscribers: 33,231
Franchises Not Yet Operating: 0	Number of Expanded Basic Subscribers: 0
Applications Pending: 0	Number of Pay Units: 0

Top 100 Markets Represented: Washington, DC (9).

For a list of cable communities in this section, see the Cable Community Index located in the back of Cable Volume 2.
For explanation of terms used in cable system listings, see p. D-11.

BOLLING AFB—Comcast Cable. Now served by FREDERICK COUNTY (portions), MD [MD0009]. ICA: DC0007.

BOLLING AFB—Formerly served by Mid-Atlantic Communications. Now served by Comcast Cable, FREDERICK COUNTY, MD [MD0009]. ICA: DC0002.

U.S. SOLDIERS' & AIRMEN'S HOME—Comcast Cable. Now served by FREDERICK COUNTY (portions), MD [MD0009]. ICA: DC0009.

U.S. SOLDIERS' & AIRMEN'S HOME—Formerly served by Chesapeake Cable Partners. Now served by Comcast Cable, FREDERICK COUNTY, MD [MD0009]. ICA: DC0003.

WALTER REED ARMY MEDICAL CENTER—Comcast Cable. Now served by FREDERICK COUNTY (portions), MD [MD0009]. ICA: DC0008.

WASHINGTON (northwestern portion)—RCN. This cable system has converted to IPTV. See WASHINGTON, DC (portions) [DC5001]. ICA: DC0005.

WASHINGTON (portions)—Comcast Cable. Served by FREDERICK COUNTY (portions), MD [MD0009]. ICA: DC0001.

WASHINGTON (portions)—RCN. Formerly [DC0006]. This cable system has converted to IPTV. 196 Van Buren St, Ste 300, Herndon, VA 20170. Phones: 800-746-4726; 609-681-2281. Web Site: http://www.rcn.com. Also serves Adams Morgan, American University Park, Anacostia, Benning Road, Berkley, Brightwood, Brookland, Capitol Hill, Chevy Chase, Chinatown, Cleveland Park, Colonial Village, Columbia Heights, Congress Heights, Dupont Circle, Edgewood, Foggy Bottom, Fort Dupont, Fort Totten, Foxhall, Friendship Heights, Glover Park, Hillcrest, Ivy City, Judiciary Square, Kenilworth, Kent, Lamond Riggs, Manor Park, McLean Gardens, Michigan Park, Mount Pleasant, Mount Vernon Square, Palisades, Petworth, Pleasant Hill, River Terrace, Shaw, Shepherd Park, Sixteenth Street Heights, Tenleytown, Van Ness, Wesley Heights, West End, Woodley Park & Woodridge, DC; Bethesda, Chevy Chase, College Park, Gaithersburg, Lanham, Montgomery County (portions), Montgomery Village, Silver Spring & Takoma Park, MD; Arlington & Falls Church, VA. ICA: DC5001.
TV Market Ranking: 9 (Anacostia, Benning Road, Bethesda, Brookland, Capitol Hill, Chevy Chase, Chinatown, Cleveland Park, Columbia Heights, Congress Heights, Dupont Circle, Fort Totten, Friendship Heights, Gaithersburg, Glover Park, Mount Pleasant, Mount Vernon Square, Petworth, Shaw, Silver Spring, Takoma Park, Tenleytown, Van Ness, WASHINGTON (PORTIONS)).
Channel capacity: 4 (not 2-way capable). Channels available but not in use: N.A.

Limited Basic
Subscribers: 33,231. Commercial subscribers: 1,544.
Programming (received off-air): WDCA (Heroes & Icons, MNT, Movies!, MundoMax) Washington; WDCW (Antenna TV, CW, This TV) Washington; WETA-TV (PBS) Washington; WFDC-DT (getTV, UNV) Arlington; WHUT-TV (PBS) Washington; WJLA-TV (ABC, MeTV, Retro TV) Washington; WMDO-CD (LATV, UniMas) Washington; WMPT (PBS) Annapolis; WPXW-TV (ION) Manassas; WRC-TV (COZI TV, NBC) Washington; WTTG (Buzzr, FOX) Washington; WUSA (Bounce TV, CBS, WeatherNation) Washington.
Programming (via satellite): Antenna TV; Home Shopping Network HD; HSN; HSN2; NewsChannel 8; QVC; QVC HD; Telemundo; This TV; WETA UK; WGN America.
Fee: $38.02 monthly. Includes 43 channels - 40 in SD & 3 in HD. Additional $9.95 HD equipment fee for HD channels.

Signature Digital Cable
Subscribers: N.A.
Fee: $59.99 monthly. Includes 218 channels - 161 in SD & 57 in HD. Additional $9.95 HD equipment fee for HD channels.

HD Expanded Pack
Subscribers: N.A.
Fee: $8.99 monthly. Includes 6 additional HD channels. Additional $9.95 HD equipment fee for HD channels.

Premiere Family & Children
Subscribers: N.A.
Fee: $5.99 monthly. Includes 19 channels - 17 in SD & 2 in HD. Additional $9.95 HD equipment fee for HD channels.

Premiere Movies & Entertainment
Subscribers: N.A.
Fee: $10.99 monthly. Includes 31 channels - 27 in SD & 4 in HD. Additional $9.95 HD equipment fee for HD channels.

Premiere News & Information
Subscribers: N.A.
Fee: $5.99 monthly. Includes 21 channels - 16 in SD & 5 in HD. Additional $9.95 HD equipment fee for HD channels.

Premiere Sports
Subscribers: N.A.
Fee: $9.99 monthly. Includes 28 channels - 20 in SD & 8 in HD. Additional $9.95 HD equipment fee for HD channels.

Premiere Total Pack
Subscribers: N.A.
Fee: $20.95 monthly. Includes 105 channels - 87 in SD & 18 in HD. Additional $9.95 HD equipment fee for HD channels.

MiVision Lite
Subscribers: N.A.
Fee: $12.00 monthly. Includes 40 channels in Spanish.

MiVision Plus
Subscribers: N.A.
Fee: $22.95 monthly. Includes 44 channels in Spanish.

Cinemax
Subscribers: N.A.
Fee: $9.99 monthly. Includes 16 channels - 8 in SD & 8 in HD plus Cinemax on Demand & MAXGo. Additional $9.95 HD equipment fee for HD channels.

HBO
Subscribers: N.A.
Fee: $15.95 monthly. Includes 14 channels - 7 in SD & 7 in HD plus HBO on Demand & HBO Go. Additional $9.95 HD equipment fee for HD channels.

Cinemax/HBO
Subscribers: N.A.
Fee: $19.95 monthly. Includes 16 channels of Cinemax - 8 in SD & 8 in HD & 14 channels of HBO - 7 in SD & 7 in HD plus Cinemax on Demand, HBO on Demand, MAXGo & HBO Go. Additional $9.95 HD equipment fee for HD channels.

Showtime/TMC
Subscribers: N.A.
Fee: $4.95 monthly. Includes 20 channels - 9 in SD & 11 in HD plus Showtime on Demand & The Movie Channel on Demand. Additional $9.95 HD equipment fee for HD channels.

Starz
Subscribers: N.A.
Fee: $5.00 monthly. Includes 13 channels - 9 in SD & 4 in HD plus Starz on Demand. Additional $9.95 HD equipment fee for HD channels.

Video-On-Demand: Yes
Internet Service
Operational: Yes.
Fee: $34.99-$74.99 monthly.
Telephone Service
Digital: Operational
Fee: $29.99 monthly
Miles of Plant: 1,733.0 (coaxial); 1,693.0 (fiber optic). Homes passed: 192,270.
Vice President & General Manager: Jamie Hill.
Ownership: RCN Corp. (MSO).

WASHINGTON (portions)—RCN. This cable system has converted to IPTV. See WASHINGTON, DC (portions) [DC5001]. ICA: DC0006.

FLORIDA

Total Systems: 56	Communities with Applications: 0
Total Communities Served: 673	Number of Basic Subscribers: 3,626,593
Franchises Not Yet Operating: 0	Number of Expanded Basic Subscribers: 34,945
Applications Pending: 0	Number of Pay Units: 4,035

Top 100 Markets Represented: Miami (21); Tampa-St. Petersburg-Clearwater (28); Orlando-Daytona Beach-Melbourne-Cocoa-Clermont (55); Mobile, AL-Pensacola, FL (59); Jacksonville (68).

For a list of cable communities in this section, see the Cable Community Index located in the back of Cable Volume 2.
For explanation of terms used in cable system listings, see p. D-11.

ADVENT CHRISTIAN VILLAGE—Formerly served by Advent Christian Village Cable TV. No longer in operation. ICA: FL0315.

ALACHUA—Formerly served by Altitude Communications. No longer in operation. ICA: FL0209.

ALLIGATOR POINT—Mediacom. Now served by EASTPOINT, FL [FL0180]. ICA: FL0191.

ALVA—Comcast Cable. Now served by SARASOTA, FL [FL0017]. ICA: FL0324.

APALACHICOLA—Mediacom. Now served by EASTPOINT, FL [FL0180]. ICA: FL0103.

ARCADIA—Comcast Cable. Now served by SARASOTA, FL [FL0017]. ICA: FL0101.

ARCHER—Comcast Cable, 8130 CR 44, Leg A, Leesburg, FL 34788. Phones: 352-787-9601 (Leesburg office); 352-489-0939. Fax: 352-365-6279. Web Site: http://www.comcast.com. Also serves Beverly Hills, Brandon, Celebration, Citrus County (northern portion), DeBary, Dunnellon, Eustis, Fruitland Park, Hillsborough County (portions), Howey-in-the-Hills, Inglis, Inverness, Lady Lake, Lake County (unincorporated areas), Leesburg (village), Levy County (portions), Marion County (southwestern portion), Mont Verde, Mount Dora, Mount Plymouth, Orange County (unincorporated areas), Osceola County (portions), Polk County (portions), Sorrento, Sumter County (unincorporated areas), Tampa (portions), Tavares, The Villages, Trenton, Umatilla, Volusia County (unincorporated areas), Williston & Yankeetown. ICA: FL0189.
TV Market Ranking: 28 (Hillsborough County (portions), Tampa (portions)); 28,55 (Orange County (unincorporated areas), Osceola County (portions), Polk County (portions)); 55 (Celebration, DeBary, Eustis, Howey-in-the-Hills, Lady Lake, Lake County (unincorporated areas), Leesburg (village), Mont Verde, Mount Dora, Mount Plymouth, Sorrento, Sumter County (unincorporated areas), Tavares, The Villages, Umatilla, Volusia County (unincorporated areas)); Below 100 (ARCHER, Beverly Hills, Citrus County (northern portion), Dunnellon, Inglis, Marion County (southwestern portion), Fruitland Park, Inverness, Levy County (portions), Trenton, Williston); Outside TV Markets (Levy County (portions)). Franchise award date: N.A. Franchise expiration date: N.A. Began: January 1, 1984.
Channel capacity: N.A. Channels available but not in use: N.A.

Basic Service
Subscribers: 90,072. Commercial subscribers: 9,706.
Programming (received off-air): WCJB-TV (ABC, CW) Gainesville; WOGX (Buzzr, FOX) Ocala; WUFT (PBS) Gainesville.
Programming (via microwave): WESH (MeTV, NBC) Daytona Beach; WJXT (LATV, This TV) Jacksonville.
Programming (via satellite): CNN; Discovery Channel; ESPN; Freeform; HLN; TBS; TNT; USA Network; WGN America.
Fee: $45.95-$67.95 installation; $50.20 monthly.

Pay Service 1
Pay Units: N.A.
Programming (via satellite): Cinemax; HBO.
Fee: $10.00 installation; $11.60 monthly (each).

Video-On-Demand: No

Internet Service
Operational: Yes.
Subscribers: 46,440.
Broadband Service: Comcast High Speed Internet.

Telephone Service
Digital: Operational
Subscribers: 23,382.
Miles of Plant: 5,220.0 (coaxial); 1,047.0 (fiber optic). Homes passed: 144,699.
General Manager: Mike Davenport. Marketing Manager: Melanie Melvin.
Ownership: Comcast Cable Communications Inc. (MSO).

ASTOR—Florida Fiber Networks, 23505 State Rd 40, PO Box 498, Astor, FL 32102-0498. Phones: 888-860-4088; 352-702-4990. E-mail: info@flfibernet.com. Web Site: http://www.flfibernet.com. Also serves Altoona, Astatula, Eustis, Lake County (unincorporated areas), Pierson, Sorrento, Volusia & Volusia County (unincorporated areas). ICA: FL0171.
TV Market Ranking: 55 (Altoona, Astatula, ASTOR, Eustis, Lake County (unincorporated areas), Pierson, Sorrento, Volusia, Volusia County (unincorporated areas)). Franchise award date: N.A. Franchise expiration date: N.A. Began: September 15, 1984.
Channel capacity: N.A. Channels available but not in use: N.A.

Basic Service
Subscribers: N.A.
Programming (received off-air): WDSC-TV (ETV) New Smyrna Beach; WESH (MeTV, NBC) Daytona Beach; WFTV (ABC, Escape) Orlando; WKCF (CW, Estrella TV, This TV) Clermont; WKMG-TV (CBS, Retro TV) Orlando; WOFL (Bounce TV, FOX) Orlando; WRBW (Buzzr, Heroes & Icons, MNT, Movies!) Orlando; WRDQ (Antenna TV) Orlando; WUCF-TV (ETV) Orlando.
Programming (via satellite): A&E; AMC; Animal Planet; Cartoon Network; CMT; CNBC; CNN; C-SPAN; Discovery Channel; E! HD; ESPN; ESPN2; Food Network; Fox News Channel; Fox Sports 1; FOX Sports Florida/Sun Sports; Freeform; FX; HGTV; History; HLN; Lifetime; MTV; Nickelodeon; Pop; Spike TV; Syfy; TBS; The Weather Channel; TLC; TNT; Travel Channel; Turner Classic Movies; TV Land; Univision; Univision Studios; USA Network; VH1; WGN America.
Fee: $25.00 installation; $11.95 monthly.

Digital Basic Service
Subscribers: N.A.
Programming (via satellite): BBC America; Bloomberg Television; Bravo; Discovery Life Channel; DMX Music; ESPN Classic; ESPNews; EVINE Live; Fuse; FXM; FYI; Golf Channel; Great American Country; GSN; History International; HITS (Headend In The Sky); IFC; LMN; National Geographic Channel; NBCSN; Nick Jr.; Outdoor Channel; Ovation; Sundance TV; TeenNick; The Word Network; Trinity Broadcasting Network (TBN); WE tv.

Digital Pay Service 1
Pay Units: N.A.
Programming (via satellite): Cinemax (multiplexed); HBO (multiplexed); Showtime (multiplexed); Starz (multiplexed); Starz Encore (multiplexed); The Movie Channel (multiplexed).
Fee: $9.95 installation; $10.50 monthly (each).

Video-On-Demand: No

Pay-Per-View
iN DEMAND (delivered digitally); Hot Choice (delivered digitally); Playboy TV (delivered digitally); Fresh (delivered digitally); Shorteez (delivered digitally).

Internet Service
Operational: Yes. Began: January 1, 2000.
Broadband Service: USA2net.net.
Fee: $49.95 installation; $24.95 monthly.

Telephone Service
None
Miles of Plant: 22.0 (coaxial); None (fiber optic).
Chief Executive Officer: David Suarez. Chief Marketing Officer: David Orshan.
Ownership: Florida Fiber Networks.

AUBURNDALE—Bright House Networks. Now served by HILLSBOROUGH COUNTY (portions), FL [FL0003]. ICA: FL0036.

BAKER—Mediacom. Now served by GULF BREEZE, FL [FL0070]. ICA: FL0182.

BARTOW—Comcast Cable. Now served by SARASOTA, FL [FL0017]. ICA: FL0050.

BAY INDIES MOBILE HOME PARK—Formerly served by Mobile Home Properties Inc. No longer in operation. ICA: FL0213.

BELLE GLADE—Comcast Cable. Now served by WEST PALM BEACH, FL [FL0008]. ICA: FL0073.

BEVERLY BEACH—Formerly served by TV Max. No longer in operation. ICA: FL0186.

BIG CYPRESS SEMINOLE INDIAN RESERVATION—Formerly served by Comcast Cable. No longer in operation. ICA: FL0376.

BLOUNTSTOWN—Bright House Networks, 2251 Lucien Way, Ste 200B, Maitland, FL 32751. Phones: 407-667-5200; 850-892-4972; 800-288-1664; 727-791-7730. Web Site: http://brighthouse.com. Also serves Bristol, Calhoun County (portions) & Liberty County. ICA: FL0133.
TV Market Ranking: Below 100 (BLOUNTSTOWN, Bristol, Calhoun County (portions), Liberty County). Franchise award date: N.A. Franchise expiration date: N.A. Began: January 1, 1971.
Channel capacity: N.A. Channels available but not in use: N.A.

Basic Service
Subscribers: 564. Commercial subscribers: 524.
Programming (received off-air): WCTV (CBS, MNT, This TV) Thomasville; WFSU-TV (PBS) Tallahassee; WJHG-TV (CW, MNT, NBC) Panama City; WMBB (ABC, This TV) Panama City; WPGX (FOX) Panama City; WTVY (CBS, CW, MeTV, MNT, This TV) Dothan.
Programming (via satellite): A&E; AMC; Animal Planet; BET; Bravo; Cartoon Network; CMT; CNBC; CNN; C-SPAN; Discovery Channel; Disney Channel; E! HD; ESPN; ESPN2; EVINE Live; Food Network; Fox News Channel; FOX Sports Florida/Sun Sports; Freeform; FX; HGTV; History; HLN; Lifetime; LMN; MSNBC; MTV; National Geographic Channel; Nickelodeon; Oxygen; QVC; Spike TV; Syfy; TBS; The Weather Channel; TLC; TNT; Travel Channel; Trinity Broadcasting Network (TBN); USA Network; VH1; WE tv.
Fee: $38.35 installation; $27.00 monthly.

Digital Basic Service
Subscribers: N.A.
Programming (via satellite): BBC America; Bloomberg Television; Discovery Digital Networks; Disney XD; DMX Music; ESPN Classic; ESPN Now; ESPNews; Fox Sports 1; Golf Channel; GSN; MTV Classic; MTV2; NBCSN; Nick Jr.; Outdoor Channel; Ovation; TeenNick; Turner Classic Movies.

Digital Pay Service 1
Pay Units: N.A.
Programming (via satellite): Cinemax (multiplexed); HBO (multiplexed); IFC; Showtime (multiplexed); Starz Encore (multiplexed); Sundance TV; The Movie Channel

D-134 TV & Cable Factbook No. 85

Cable Systems—Florida

(multiplexed); WAM! America's Kidz Network.
Fee: $10.50 monthly (each).
Video-On-Demand: No
Pay-Per-View
Fresh (delivered digitally); Shorteez (delivered digitally); Hot Choice (delivered digitally); iN DEMAND (delivered digitally); Sports PPV (delivered digitally).
Internet Service
Operational: Yes.
Broadband Service: Road Runner.
Fee: $49.95 installation; $29.95 monthly.
Telephone Service
Digital: Operational
Fee: $39.95 monthly
Miles of Plant: 72.0 (coaxial); None (fiber optic). Homes passed: 2,330.
Chief Financial Officer: William Futera. Vice President, Finance: John Ogden. Chief Technician: Edward Harrison. Marketing Director: Nicole Hardy. Technical Operations Manager: Lynn Miller. Business Manager: Elaine West.
Ownership: Bright House Networks LLC (MSO).

BOCA RATON—Comcast Cable. Now served by WEST PALM BEACH, FL [FL0008]. ICA: FL0035.

BOCA RATON—Comcast Cable. Now served by WEST PALM BEACH, FL [FL0008]. ICA: FL0051.

BONIFAY—Mediacom. Now served by WALTON COUNTY (portions), FL [FL0159]. ICA: FL0152.

BOWLING GREEN—Bright House Networks, 2251 Lucien Way, Ste 200B, Maitland, FL 32751. Phones: 407-667-5200; 727-329-5020 (Customer service); 727-329-2000. Web Site: http://brighthouse.com. ICA: FL0167.
TV Market Ranking: 28 (BOWLING GREEN).
Channel capacity: N.A. Channels available but not in use: N.A.
Basic Service
Subscribers: 15. Commercial subscribers: 2.
Fee: $39.95 installation; $27.00 monthly.
Chief Financial Officer: William Futera.
Ownership: Bright House Networks LLC (MSO).

BRADENTON—Bright House Networks. Now served by HILLSBOROUGH COUNTY (portions), FL [FL0003]. ICA: FL0019.

BRADENTON—Formerly served by Florida Cable. No longer in operation. ICA: FL0348.

BRADENTON—Formerly served by Sprint Corp. No longer in operation. ICA: FL0301.

BRADENTON (unincorporated areas)—Formerly served by Universal Cablevision Inc. No longer in operation. ICA: FL0215.

BRANDON—Comcast Cable. Now served by ARCHER, FL [FL0189]. ICA: FL0085.

BRANFORD—Formerly served by Altitude Communications. No longer in operation. ICA: FL0197.

BRATT—Formerly served by CableSouth Inc. No longer in operation. ICA: FL0184.

BRIGHTON SEMINOLE RESERVE—Formerly served by Comcast Cable. No longer in operation. ICA: FL0314.

BRONSON (town)—Florida Fiber Networks, 301 South Collins St, Ste 105, Plant City, FL 33563. Phones: 888-860-4088; 352-702-4990. E-mail: info@flfibernet.com. Web Site: http://www.flfibernet.com. Also serves Levy County. ICA: FL0169.
TV Market Ranking: Below 100 (BRONSON (TOWN), Levy County). Franchise award date: June 9, 1985. Franchise expiration date: N.A. Began: July 1, 1988.
Channel capacity: N.A. Channels available but not in use: N.A.
Basic Service
Subscribers: N.A.
Programming (received off-air): WCJB-TV (ABC, CW) Gainesville; WGFL (CBS, MNT) High Springs; WOGX (Buzzr, FOX) Ocala; WUFT (PBS) Gainesville.
Programming (via satellite): A&E; Cartoon Network; CNN; Comedy Central; Discovery Channel; Disney Channel; Disney XD; E! HD; ESPN; ESPN2; Food Network; Fox News Channel; Fox Sports 1; Freeform; Fuse; FX; Great American Country; HLN; Lifetime; Syfy; TBS; The Weather Channel; TLC; TNT; Turner Classic Movies; USA Network; WGN America; WNBC (COZI TV, NBC) New York.
Programming (via translator): WACX (IND) Leesburg.
Fee: $39.45 monthly.
Pay Service 1
Pay Units: N.A.
Programming (via satellite): Cinemax; HBO; Showtime; The Movie Channel.
Fee: $10.95 monthly (each).
Internet Service
Operational: No.
Telephone Service
None
Miles of Plant: 49.0 (coaxial); None (fiber optic). Homes passed: 977.
Chief Executive Officer: David Suarez. Chief Marketing Officer: David Orshan.
Ownership: Florida Fiber Networks (MSO).

BROOKER—New River Cablevision Inc, 11401 Southwest State Rd 231, PO Box 128, Brooker, FL 32622. Phone: 352-485-1362. Fax: 352-485-1352. Also serves Worthington Springs. ICA: FL0196.
TV Market Ranking: Below 100 (BROOKER, Worthington Springs). Franchise award date: January 1, 1989. Franchise expiration date: N.A. Began: N.A.
Channel capacity: 54 (2-way capable). Channels available but not in use: N.A.
Basic Service
Subscribers: N.A.
Programming (received off-air): WCJB-TV (ABC, CW) Gainesville; WGFL (CBS, MNT) High Springs; WJAX-TV (CBS, Decades, getTV) Jacksonville; WJXT (LATV, This TV) Jacksonville; WOGX (Buzzr, FOX) Ocala; WTLV (Antenna TV, NBC, The Country Network) Jacksonville; WUFT (PBS) Gainesville.
Programming (via satellite): A&E; AMC; CMT; CNN; Discovery Channel; Disney Channel; ESPN; ESPN2; Freeform; History; HLN; INSP; Lifetime; Nickelodeon; Spike TV; Syfy; TBS; The Weather Channel; TLC; TNT; Trinity Broadcasting Network (TBN); TV Land; USA Network; VH1.
Fee: $24.95 installation.
Pay Service 1
Pay Units: N.A.
Programming (via satellite): HBO; Showtime.
Fee: $9.95 monthly (each).
Video-On-Demand: No
Internet Service
Operational: No.
Telephone Service
None
Miles of Plant: 25.0 (coaxial); None (fiber optic). Homes passed: 574.
General Manager & Chief Technician: Mike McCoy.
Ownership: New River Cablevision Inc.

BROWARD COUNTY (portions)—Comcast Cable. Now served by WEST PALM BEACH, FL [FL0008]. ICA: FL0016.

CALLAHAN (town)—Comcast Cable. Now served by JACKSONVILLE, FL [FL0002]. ICA: FL0128.

CAMPBELLTON—Formerly served by Campbellton Cable. No longer in operation. ICA: FL0323.

CANTONMENT—Bright House Networks, 2251 Lucien Way, Ste 200B, Maitland, FL 32751. Phones: 407-667-5200; 850-968-6959; 800-866-2061; 205-591-6880. Web Site: http://brighthouse.com. Also serves Baldwin County (portions) & Flomaton, AL; Century, Escambia County, Jay & Santa Rosa, FL. ICA: FL0090.
TV Market Ranking: 59 (Baldwin County (portions), CANTONMENT, Escambia County (portions), Santa Rosa (portions)); Outside TV Markets (Flomaton, Jay, Century, Escambia County (portions), Santa Rosa (portions)). Franchise award date: February 1, 1987. Franchise expiration date: N.A. Began: May 1, 1987.
Channel capacity: N.A. Channels available but not in use: N.A.
Basic Service
Subscribers: 4,729. Commercial subscribers: 43.
Programming (received off-air): WALA-TV (FOX) Mobile; WEAR-TV (ABC, The Country Network) Pensacola; WHBR (Christian TV Network) Pensacola; WJTC (IND) Pensacola; WKRG-TV (CBS, MeTV) Mobile; WMPV-TV (TBN) Mobile; WPAN (Soul of the South) Fort Walton Beach [LICENSED & SILENT]; WPMI-TV (NBC) Mobile; WSRE (PBS) Pensacola.
Programming (via satellite): A&E; AMC; Animal Planet; BET; Cartoon Network; CMT; CNBC; CNN; Comedy Central; C-SPAN; C-SPAN 2; Discovery Channel; Disney Channel; E! HD; ESPN; ESPN2; EWTN Global Catholic Network; Food Network; Fox News Channel; FOX Sports Florida/Sun Sports; Freeform; FX; Hallmark Channel; HGTV; History; HLN; Lifetime; MSNBC; MTV; National Geographic Channel; Nickelodeon; Oxygen; QVC; Spike TV; Syfy; TBS; The Weather Channel; TLC; TNT; Travel Channel; truTV; USA Network; VH1; WE tv.
Fee: $38.35 installation; $27.00 monthly.
Digital Basic Service
Subscribers: N.A.
Programming (via satellite): BBC America; Bloomberg Television; Discovery Digital Networks; Disney XD; DMX Music; ESPN Classic; ESPN Now; ESPNews; Fox Sports 1; Golf Channel; GSN; MTV Classic; MTV2; NBCSN; Nick Jr.; Outdoor Channel; Ovation; TeenNick; Turner Classic Movies.
Digital Pay Service 1
Pay Units: N.A.
Programming (via satellite): Cinemax (multiplexed); FXM; HBO (multiplexed); IFC; Showtime (multiplexed); Starz (multiplexed); Starz Encore (multiplexed); Sundance TV; The Movie Channel (multiplexed).
Fee: $10.50 monthly (each).
Video-On-Demand: Yes
Pay-Per-View
Hot Choice (delivered digitally); iN DEMAND (delivered digitally); Fresh (delivered digitally); Shorteez (delivered digitally); Sports PPV (delivered digitally).
Internet Service
Operational: Yes.
Subscribers: 4,745.
Broadband Service: Road Runner.
Fee: $29.95 monthly.
Telephone Service
Digital: Operational
Subscribers: 3,054.
Fee: $39.95 monthly
Miles of Plant: 620.0 (coaxial); 209.0 (fiber optic). Homes passed: 13,809.
Chief Financial Officer: William Futera. Marketing Director: Nicole Hardy. Chief Technician: Ed Harrison.
Ownership: Bright House Networks LLC (MSO).

CAPE CORAL—Comcast Cable. Now served by SARASOTA, FL [FL0017]. ICA: FL0039.

CAPE SAN BLAS—Mediacom. Now served by WALTON COUNTY (portions), FL [FL0159]. ICA: FL0206.

CEDAR KEY—Bright House Networks, 2251 Lucien Way, Ste 200B, Maitland, FL 32751. Phones: 407-667-5200; 863-965-7766; 727-791-7730. Web Site: http://brighthouse.com. ICA: FL0190.
TV Market Ranking: Outside TV Markets (CEDAR KEY). Franchise award date: September 1, 1977. Franchise expiration date: N.A. Began: September 1, 1977.
Channel capacity: N.A. Channels available but not in use: N.A.
Basic Service
Subscribers: 302. Commercial subscribers: 10.
Programming (received off-air): WCLF (Christian TV Network) Clearwater; WEDU (PBS) Tampa; WFLA-TV (MeTV, NBC) Tampa; WFTS-TV (ABC, Grit, Laff) Tampa; WFTT-DT (getTV, UniMas) Tampa; WMOR-TV (Estrella TV, This TV) Lakeland; WTOG (CW, Decades) St. Petersburg; WTSP (CBS) St. Petersburg; WTTA (COZI TV, MNT) St. Petersburg; WTVT (Buzzr, FOX, Heroes & Icons, Movies!) Tampa; WUSF-TV (PBS) Tampa; WVEA-TV (Bounce TV, LATV, UNV) Venice; WXPX-TV (ION) Bradenton.
Programming (via satellite): Bay News 9; EVINE Live; National Geographic Channel; Pop; QVC; WGN America.
Fee: $39.95 installation; $51.00 monthly.
Expanded Basic Service 1
Subscribers: N.A.
Programming (via satellite): A&E; AMC; Animal Planet; BET; Bravo; Bright House Sports Network; Cartoon Network; CMT; CNBC; CNN; Comedy Central; C-SPAN; C-SPAN 2; Discovery Channel; Disney Channel; ESPN; ESPN Classic; ESPN2; EWTN Global Catholic Network; Food Network; Fox News Channel; FOX Sports Florida/Sun Sports; FOX Sports Networks; Freeform; FX; Golf Channel; Hallmark Channel; HGTV; History; HLN; Lifetime; LMN; MoviePlex; MSNBC; MTV; National Geographic Channel; NBCSN; Nickelodeon; OWN: Oprah Winfrey Network; Oxygen; ReacTV; Spike TV; Syfy; TBS; The Weather

Florida—Cable Systems

Channel; TLC; TNT; Travel Channel; truTV; Turner Classic Movies; TV Land; Univision; USA Network; VH1; WE tv.

Digital Basic Service
Subscribers: N.A.
Programming (via satellite): A&E HD; AXS TV; Bay News 9; BBC America; Bloomberg Television; Cloo; Cooking Channel; C-SPAN 3; Discovery Digital Networks; Disney Channel; Disney XD; DIY Network; ESPN HD; ESPNews; EWTN Global Catholic Network; Flix; FOX College Sports Central; FOX College Sports Pacific; Fox Sports 1; Fox Sports 2; Fuse; FXM; FYI; Great American Country; GSN; HD Theater; History International; HITS (Headend In The Sky); IFC; Jewelry Television; LOGO; MC; MTV Live; Nat Geo WILD; NBA TV; Nick Jr.; Nicktoons; Outdoor Channel; Ovation; Starz Encore; Sundance TV; TeenNick; Tennis Channel; TNT HD; Trinity Broadcasting Network (TBN); TV Guide Network; TV One; Universal HD.

Digital Pay Service 1
Pay Units: N.A.
Programming (via satellite): Cinemax (multiplexed); Cinemax On Demand; HBO (multiplexed); HBO HD; HBO on Demand; Showtime (multiplexed); Showtime HD; Showtime On Demand; Starz (multiplexed); The Movie Channel (multiplexed); The Movie Channel On Demand.
Fee: $16.00 monthly (each).

Pay-Per-View
iN DEMAND (delivered digitally); Pleasure (delivered digitally); Playboy TV (delivered digitally); NBA League Pass (delivered digitally); NHL Center Ice (delivered digitally); MLS Direct Kick (delivered digitally).

Internet Service
Operational: Yes.

Telephone Service
Digital: Operational
Miles of Plant: 21.0 (coaxial); 1.0 (fiber optic). Homes passed: 963.
Division President: Kevin Hyman. Chief Financial Officer: William Futera. Vice President, Engineering: Gene White. Chief Technician: Roger Carroll.
Ownership: Bright House Networks LLC (MSO).

CELEBRATION—Comcast Cable. Now served by ARCHER, FL [FL0189]. ICA: FL0334.

CENTURY—Bright House Networks. Now served by CANTONMENT [FL0090]. ICA: FL0217.

CHASEWOOD—Formerly served by Comcast Cable. No longer in operation. ICA: FL0219.

CHATTAHOOCHEE—Bright House Networks, 2251 Lucien Way, Ste 200B, Maitland, FL 32751. Phones: 407-667-5200; 850-892-4972; 800-288-1664; 727-791-7730. Web Site: http://brighthouse.com. Also serves Gadsden County (portions). ICA: FL0151.
TV Market Ranking: Below 100 (CHATTAHOOCHEE, Gadsden County (portions)). Franchise award date: N.A. Franchise expiration date: N.A. Began: February 1, 1971.
Channel capacity: N.A. Channels available but not in use: N.A.

Basic Service
Subscribers: 274. Commercial subscribers: 8.
Programming (received off-air): WCTV (CBS, MNT, This TV) Thomasville; WFSU-TV (PBS) Tallahassee; WJHG-TV (CW, MNT, NBC) Panama City; WMBB (ABC, This TV) Panama City; WTLH (CW, FOX, MeTV) Bainbridge; WTVY (CBS, CW, MeTV, MNT, This TV) Dothan; WTWC-TV (NBC, The Country Network) Tallahassee; WTXL-TV (ABC, Bounce TV) Tallahassee.
Programming (via satellite): A&E; AMC; Animal Planet; BET; Bravo; Cartoon Network; CMT; CNBC; CNN; C-SPAN; Discovery Channel; Disney Channel; E! HD; ESPN; ESPN2; EVINE Live; Food Network; Fox News Channel; FOX Sports Florida/Sun Sports; Freeform; FX; Hallmark Channel; HGTV; History; HLN; Lifetime; LMN; MSNBC; MTV; National Geographic Channel; Nickelodeon; Oxygen; QVC; Spike TV; Syfy; TBS; The Weather Channel; TLC; TNT; Travel Channel; Trinity Broadcasting Network (TBN); USA Network; VH1; WE tv; WGN America.
Fee: $38.35 installation; $27.00 monthly.

Digital Basic Service
Subscribers: N.A.
Programming (via satellite): BBC America; Bloomberg Television; Discovery Life Channel; Disney XD; DMX Music; ESPN Classic; ESPN Now; ESPNews; Fox Sports 1; Golf Channel; GSN; MTV Classic; MTV2; NBCSN; Nick Jr.; Outdoor Channel; Ovation; TeenNick; Turner Classic Movies.

Digital Pay Service 1
Pay Units: N.A.
Programming (via satellite): Cinemax (multiplexed); FXM; HBO (multiplexed); IFC; Showtime (multiplexed); Starz Encore (multiplexed); Sundance TV; The Movie Channel (multiplexed).
Fee: $15.00 monthly (each).

Video-On-Demand: No

Pay-Per-View
Hot Choice (delivered digitally); Fresh (delivered digitally); iN DEMAND (delivered digitally); Shorteez (delivered digitally).

Internet Service
Operational: Yes.
Broadband Service: Road Runner.
Fee: $49.95 installation; $29.95 monthly.

Telephone Service
Digital: Operational
Fee: $39.95 monthly
Miles of Plant: 26.0 (coaxial); None (fiber optic). Homes passed: 1,432.
Chief Financial Officer: William Futera. Chief Technician: Edward Harrison. Marketing Director: Nicole Hardy. Technical Operations Manager: Lynn Miller. Business Manager: Elaine West.
Ownership: Bright House Networks LLC (MSO).

CHIEFLAND—Formerly served by Altitude Communications. No longer in operation. ICA: FL0140.

CHIPLEY—Bright House Networks, 2251 Lucien Way, Ste 200B, Maitland, FL 32751. Phones: 407-667-5200; 850-892-4972; 800-288-1664; 205-290-1300. Web Site: http://brighthouse.com. Also serves Eunola, Geneva, Geneva County, Hartford, Samson & Slocomb, AL; Graceville, Jackson County & Washington County, FL. ICA: FL0126.
TV Market Ranking: Below 100 (CHIPLEY, Geneva County (portions), Graceville, Jackson County, Slocomb, Washington County, Geneva, Samson); Outside TV Markets (Geneva County (portions)). Franchise award date: N.A. Franchise expiration date: N.A. Began: August 1, 1970.
Channel capacity: N.A. Channels available but not in use: N.A.

Basic Service
Subscribers: 3,096. Commercial subscribers: 129.
Programming (received off-air): WCTV (CBS, MNT, This TV) Thomasville; WFSU-TV (PBS) Tallahassee; WJHG-TV (CW, MNT, NBC) Panama City; WMBB (ABC, This TV) Panama City; WPGX (FOX) Panama City; WTVY (CBS, CW, MeTV, MNT, This TV) Dothan.
Programming (via satellite): A&E; AMC; Animal Planet; BET; Bravo; Cartoon Network; CMT; CNBC; CNN; C-SPAN; Discovery Channel; Disney Channel; E! HD; ESPN; ESPN2; EVINE Live; Food Network; FOX Sports Florida/Sun Sports; Freeform; FX; Hallmark Channel; HGTV; History; HLN; Lifetime; LMN; MSNBC; MTV; National Geographic Channel; Nickelodeon; Oxygen; QVC; Spike TV; Syfy; TBS; The Weather Channel; TLC; TNT; Travel Channel; Trinity Broadcasting Network (TBN); USA Network; VH1; WE tv.
Fee: $38.35 installation; $27.00 monthly.

Digital Basic Service
Subscribers: N.A.
Programming (via satellite): BBC America; Bloomberg Television; Discovery Digital Networks; Disney XD; ESPN Now; ESPNews; Fox Sports 1; Golf Channel; GSN; MTV Classic; MTV2; NBCSN; Nick Jr.; Outdoor Channel; Ovation; TeenNick; Turner Classic Movies.

Digital Pay Service 1
Pay Units: N.A.
Programming (via satellite): HBO (multiplexed); Showtime (multiplexed); Starz Encore (multiplexed); The Movie Channel (multiplexed).
Fee: $15.00 monthly (each).

Video-On-Demand: No

Pay-Per-View
Special events.

Internet Service
Operational: Yes.
Fee: $49.95 installation; $29.95 monthly.

Telephone Service
Digital: Operational
Fee: $39.95 monthly
Miles of Plant: 91.0 (coaxial); None (fiber optic).
Chief Financial Officer: William Futera. Technical Operations Manager: Lynn Miller. Marketing Director: Nicole Hardy. Chief Technician: Edward Harrison.
Ownership: Bright House Networks LLC (MSO).

CHRISTMAS—Formerly served by Florida Cable. No longer in operation. ICA: FL0342.

CITRA—Florida Fiber Networks, 301 South Collins St, Ste 105, Plant City, FL 33563. Phones: 888-860-4088; 352-702-4990. E-mail: info@flfibernet.com. Web Site: http://www.flfibernet.com. Also serves Anthony, Hideaway Mobile Home Park, Marion County (northern portion) & Sparr. ICA: FL0153.
TV Market Ranking: Below 100 (Anthony, CITRA, Hideaway Mobile Home Park, Marion County (northern portion), Sparr). Franchise award date: N.A. Franchise expiration date: N.A. Began: July 1, 1988.
Channel capacity: N.A. Channels available but not in use: N.A.

Basic Service
Subscribers: N.A.
Programming (received off-air): WACX (IND) Leesburg; WCJB-TV (ABC, CW) Gainesville; WESH (MeTV, NBC) Daytona Beach; WFTV (ABC, Escape) Orlando; WGFL (CBS, MNT) High Springs; WKMG-TV (CBS, Retro TV) Orlando; WOGX (Buzzr, FOX) Ocala; WUFT (PBS) Gainesville.
Programming (via satellite): A&E; Animal Planet; CNN; Comedy Central; Discovery Channel; Disney Channel; ESPN; Food Network; Fox News Channel; Fox Sports 1; Freeform; Fuse; FX; Great American Country; History; HLN; Lifetime; QVC; Syfy; TBS; The Weather Channel; TNT; Travel Channel; Turner Classic Movies; USA Network; WGN America.
Fee: $39.45 monthly.

Pay Service 1
Pay Units: N.A.
Programming (via satellite): Cinemax; HBO; Showtime.

Video-On-Demand: No

Internet Service
Operational: No.

Telephone Service
None
Miles of Plant: 99.0 (coaxial); None (fiber optic). Homes passed: 2,100.
Chief Executive Officer: David Suarez. Chief Marketing Officer: David Orshan.
Ownership: Florida Fiber Networks (MSO).

CLAY COUNTY (portions)—Florida Fiber Networks, 301 South Collins St, Ste 105, Plant City, FL 33563. Phones: 888-860-4088; 352-702-4990. E-mail: info@flfibernet.com. Web Site: http://www.flfibernet.com. Also serves Clay Hill & Middleburg. ICA: FL0125.
TV Market Ranking: 68 (CLAY COUNTY (PORTIONS), Clay Hill, Middleburg); Below 100 (CLAY COUNTY (PORTIONS)). Franchise award date: May 26, 1987. Franchise expiration date: N.A. Began: July 26, 1988.
Channel capacity: N.A. Channels available but not in use: N.A.

Basic Service
Subscribers: N.A.
Programming (received off-air): WCWJ (Bounce TV, CW) Jacksonville; WFOX-TV (FOX, MeTV, MNT) Jacksonville; WJAX-TV (CBS, Decades, getTV) Jacksonville; WJCT (PBS) Jacksonville; WJEB-TV (TBN) Jacksonville; WJXT (LATV, This TV) Jacksonville; WJXX (ABC) Orange Park; WTLV (Antenna TV, NBC, The Country Network) Jacksonville; WUFT (PBS) Gainesville.
Programming (via satellite): A&E; AMC; Cartoon Network; CNBC; CNN; Comedy Central; Discovery Channel; Disney Channel; ESPN; Food Network; Fox News Channel; Fox Sports 1; FOX Sports Florida/Sun Sports; Freeform; Fuse; FX; Great American Country; History; HLN; Lifetime; QVC; TBS; The Weather Channel; TNT; Travel Channel; USA Network; WGN America.
Fee: $30.00 installation; $36.45 monthly.

Pay Service 1
Pay Units: N.A.
Programming (via satellite): Cinemax; HBO; Showtime; The Movie Channel.
Fee: $9.95 monthly (each).

Video-On-Demand: No

Internet Service
Operational: Yes.
Fee: $24.95-$49.95 monthly.

Telephone Service
Digital: Planned
Miles of Plant: 86.0 (coaxial); None (fiber optic). Homes passed: 1,909.
Plant Manager: Larry English. Chief Executive Officer: David Suarez. Chief Marketing Officer: David Orshan.
Ownership: Florida Fiber Networks (MSO).

CLEWISTON—Comcast Cable. Now served by WEST PALM BEACH, FL [FL0008]. ICA: FL0105.

Cable Systems—Florida

CORAL SPRINGS—Advanced Cable Communications, 12409 NW 35th St, Coral Springs, FL 33065. Phone: 954-753-0100. Fax: 954-345-0783. E-mail: info@advancedcable.net. Web Site: http://www.advancedcable.net. Also serves Broward County (portions). ICA: FL0045.
TV Market Ranking: 21 (Broward County (portions), CORAL SPRINGS). Franchise award date: June 12, 1980. Franchise expiration date: N.A. Began: September 1, 1975.
Channel capacity: N.A. Channels available but not in use: N.A.
Basic Service
Subscribers: 12,327.
Programming (received off-air): WAMI-DT (Bounce TV, getTV, UniMas) Hollywood; WBFS-TV (MNT) Miami; WFOR-TV (CBS, Decades) Miami; WGEN-TV (IND, MundoMax) Key West; WHFT-TV (TBN) Miami; WLRN-TV (PBS) Miami; WLTV-DT (Bounce TV, Laff, UNV) Miami; WPBT (PBS) Miami; WPLG (ABC, MeTV, Movies) Miami; WPXM-TV (ION) Miami; WSBS-TV (IND) Key West; WSCV (TMO) Fort Lauderdale; WSFL-TV (Antenna TV, Azteca America, CW, This TV) Miami; WSVN (Estrella TV, FOX) Miami; WTVJ (COZI TV, NBC) Miami; WXEL-TV (PBS) West Palm Beach.
Programming (via satellite): C-SPAN; Pop; QVC; The Weather Channel; WGN America.
Fee: $28.64-$68.04 installation; $27.00 monthly; $2.32 converter.
Expanded Basic Service 1
Subscribers: N.A.
Programming (via satellite): A&E; AMC; Animal Planet; BET; Bravo; Cartoon Network; CMT; CNBC; CNN; Comedy Central; Discovery Channel; Disney Channel; E! HD; ESPN; ESPN2; ESPNU; EWTN Global Catholic Network; Food Network; Fox News Channel; Fox Sports 1; FOX Sports Florida/Sun Sports; Freeform; FX; Golf Channel; Hallmark Channel; HGTV; History; HLN; Lifetime; MSNBC; MTV; MTV2; National Geographic Channel; NBCSN; Nickelodeon; OWN: Oprah Winfrey Network; Spike TV; Syfy; TBS; TLC; TNT; Travel Channel; truTV; Turner Classic Movies; TV Land; USA Network; VH1; WE tv.
Fee: $30.75 monthly.
Digital Basic Service
Subscribers: N.A.
Programming (via satellite): A&E HD; AXS TV; BBC America; Bloomberg Television; CBS Sports Network; Cloo; CMT; Cooking Channel; C-SPAN 3; Destination America; Discovery Kids Channel; Disney XD; DMX Music; ESPN HD; ESPN2 HD; ESPNews; EVINE Live; FOX College Sports Central; FOX College Sports Pacific; Fox Deportes; Fox Sports 2; FSN HD; Fuse; FXM; FYI; GolTV; GSN; HD Theater; History HD; History International; Investigation Discovery; LATV; LMN; MTV Classic; MTV Hits; Nat Geo WILD; National Geographic Channel HD; NBC Universo; NFL Network; NFL Network HD; Nick Jr.; Nicktoons; Science Channel; Sprout; TBS HD; TeenNick; TNT HD; Universal HD; VH1 Soul.
Fee: $2.32 converter.
Digital Expanded Basic Service
Subscribers: N.A.
Programming (via satellite): 52MX; Canal Sur; Cine Mexicano; Cinelatino; CNN en Espanol; Docu TVE; ESPN Deportes; Fox Deportes; GolTV; History en Espanol; NBC Universo; Telefe Internacional; Toon Disney en Espanol; Tr3s; ULTRA HDPlex; Viendo-Movies.
Fee: $10.95 monthly.

Digital Pay Service 1
Pay Units: N.A.
Programming (via satellite): Cinemax (multiplexed); Cinemax HD; Flix; HBO (multiplexed); HBO HD; Showtime (multiplexed); Showtime HD; Starz (multiplexed); Starz Encore (multiplexed); Starz HD; Sundance TV; The Movie Channel (multiplexed).
Fee: $10.00 monthly (Cinemax), $16.95 monthly (Starz/Encore or Showtime/TMC/Flix/Sundance), $18.95 monthly (HBO).
Video-On-Demand: Planned
Pay-Per-View
iN DEMAND; iN DEMAND (delivered digitally); Playboy TV (delivered digitally); Fresh (delivered digitally); special events; special events (delivered digitally).
Internet Service
Operational: Yes. Began: August 1, 1998.
Subscribers: 18,399.
Broadband Service: In-house.
Fee: $99.00 installation; $42.95 monthly; $10.00 modem lease.
Telephone Service
Analog: Not Operational
Digital: Operational
Subscribers: 3,570.
Fee: $33.00-$39.00 monthly
Miles of Plant: 1,412.0 (coaxial); 233.0 (fiber optic). Homes passed: 66,738.
President & General Manager: James Pagano. Vice President, Engineering: Rick Scheller. Program Director & Production Manager: Mike Milo. Customer Service Manager: Michelle Martinie. Secretary: Michelle Fitzpatrick.
Ownership: Advocate Communications Inc. (MSO).

CRAWFORDVILLE—Comcast Cable. Now served by TALLAHASSEE, FL [FL0283]. ICA: FL0116.

CRESCENT CITY—Comcast Cable. Now served by JACKSONVILLE, FL [FL0002]. ICA: FL0131.

CRESTVIEW—Cox Communications. Now served by PENSACOLA, FL [FL0018]. ICA: FL0074.

CROSS CITY—Formerly served by Altitude Communications. No longer in operation. ICA: FL0158.

DAVIE—Comcast Cable. Now served by WEST PALM BEACH, FL [FL0008]. ICA: FL0022.

DE FUNIAK SPRINGS—Bright House Networks, 2251 Lucien Way, Ste 200B, Maitland, FL 32751. Phones: 407-667-5200; 850-892-4972; 850-892-3155; 205-290-1300. Web Site: http://brighthouse.com. Also serves Florala & Lockhart, AL; Paxton & Walton County (portions), FL. ICA: FL0111.
TV Market Ranking: Below 100 (Walton County (portions)); Outside TV Markets (DE FUNIAK SPRINGS, Lockhart, Paxton, Florala, Walton County (portions)). Franchise award date: N.A. Franchise expiration date: N.A. Began: November 1, 1969.
Channel capacity: N.A. Channels available but not in use: N.A.
Basic Service
Subscribers: 3,542. Commercial subscribers: 120.
Programming (received off-air): WFSU-TV (PBS) Tallahassee; WJHG-TV (CW, MNT, NBC) Panama City; WMBB (ABC, This TV) Panama City; WPGX (FOX) Panama City;

WTVY (CBS, CW, MeTV, MNT, This TV) Dothan; WWEO-LD De Funiak Springs.
Programming (via satellite): A&E; AMC; Animal Planet; BET; Bravo; Cartoon Network; CMT; CNBC; CNN; C-SPAN; Discovery Channel; Disney Channel; E! HD; ESPN; ESPN2; EVINE Live; Food Network; Fox News Channel; FOX Sports Florida/Sun Sports; Freeform; FX; Hallmark Channel; HGTV; History; HLN; Lifetime; LMN; MSNBC; MTV; National Geographic Channel; Nickelodeon; Oxygen; QVC; Spike TV; Syfy; TBS; The Weather Channel; TLC; TNT; Travel Channel; Trinity Broadcasting Network (TBN); USA Network; VH1; WE tv.
Fee: $38.35 installation; $27.00 monthly; $.65 converter.
Digital Basic Service
Subscribers: N.A.
Programming (via satellite): Discovery Digital Networks; Disney XD; GSN; MTV Classic; MTV2; Nick Jr.; Ovation; TeenNick; Turner Classic Movies.
Digital Pay Service 1
Pay Units: N.A.
Programming (via satellite): Cinemax (multiplexed); FXM; HBO (multiplexed); Showtime (multiplexed); Starz Encore; Sundance TV; The Movie Channel (multiplexed).
Fee: $10.50 monthly (each).
Video-On-Demand: No
Internet Service
Operational: Yes.
Broadband Service: Road Runner.
Fee: $49.95 monthly.
Telephone Service
Digital: Operational
Fee: $39.95 monthly
Miles of Plant: 167.0 (coaxial); None (fiber optic).
Chief Financial Officer: William Futera. Chief Technician: Edward Harrison. Marketing Director: Nicole Hardy. Technical Operations Manager: Lynn Miller. Business Manager: Elaine West.
Ownership: Bright House Networks LLC (MSO).

DE LAND—Formerly served by Bright House Networks. No longer in operation. ICA: FL0033.

DEBARY—Comcast Cable. Now served by ARCHER, FL [FL0189]. ICA: FL0124.

DELRAY BEACH—Comcast Cable. Now served by WEST PALM BEACH, FL [FL0008]. ICA: FL0091.

DOWLING PARK—Formerly served by KLiP Interactive. No longer in operation. ICA: FL0347.

DUNNELLON—Comcast Cable. Now served by ARCHER, FL [FL0189]. ICA: FL0227.

EAST MILTON—Mediacom. Now served by GULF BREEZE, FL [FL0070]. ICA: FL0170.

EASTPOINT—Mediacom, 1613 Nantahala Beach Rd, Gulf Breeze, FL 32563-8944. Phones: 845-695-2762; 850-934-7700. Fax: 850-934-2506. Web Site: http://www.mediacomcable.com. Also serves Alligator Point, Apalachicola, Carrabelle, Franklin County (portions), Lanark Village, Port St. Joe & St. George Island. ICA: FL0180.
TV Market Ranking: Below 100 (Port St. Joe); Outside TV Markets (Alligator Point, Apalachicola, Carrabelle, Franklin County

(portions), Lanark Village, St. George Island, EASTPOINT).
Channel capacity: N.A. Channels available but not in use: N.A.
Basic Service
Subscribers: 3,165.
Fee: $41.00 monthly.
Vice President, Financial Reporting: Kenneth J. Kohrs.
Ownership: Mediacom LLC (MSO).

ENGLEWOOD—Comcast Cable. Now served by SARASOTA, FL [FL0017]. ICA: FL0229.

EVERGLADES CITY—Comcast Cable. Now served by SARASOTA, FL [FL0017]. ICA: FL0150.

FANNING SPRINGS—Florida Fiber Networks, 301 South Collins St, Ste 105, Plant City, FL 33563. Phones: 888-860-4088; 352-702-4990. Web Site: http://www.flfibernet.com. Also serves Old Town. ICA: FL0378.
TV Market Ranking: Below 100 (FANNING SPRINGS, Old Town).
Channel capacity: N.A. Channels available but not in use: N.A.
Basic Service
Subscribers: N.A.
Programming (received off-air): WCJB-TV (ABC, CW) Gainesville; WESH (MeTV, NBC) Daytona Beach; WGFL (CBS, MNT) High Springs; WOGX (Buzzr, FOX) Ocala; WUFT (PBS) Gainesville.
Programming (via satellite): A&E; Cartoon Network; CMT; CNN; C-SPAN; C-SPAN 2; Discovery Channel; ESPN; ESPN2; Freeform; HGTV; History; HLN; Lifetime; MTV; Nickelodeon; QVC; Spike TV; Syfy; TBS; The Weather Channel; TLC; TNT; Trinity Broadcasting Network (TBN); Turner Classic Movies; USA Network; VH1; WGN America.
Pay Service 1
Pay Units: N.A.
Programming (via satellite): HBO (multiplexed).
Internet Service
Operational: No.
Telephone Service
None
Plant Manager: Larry English. Chief Executive Officer: David Suarez. Chief Marketing Officer: David Orshan.
Ownership: Florida Fiber Networks (MSO).

FERNANDINA BEACH—Comcast Cable. Now served by JACKSONVILLE, FL [FL0002]. ICA: FL0088.

FLORAHOME—Florida Fiber Networks, 23505 State Rd 40, PO Box 498, Astor, FL 32102-0498. Phones: 888-860-4088; 352-702-4990. E-mail: info@flfibernet.com. Web Site: http://www.flfibernet.com. Also serves Grandin & Keystone Heights. ICA: FL0221.
TV Market Ranking: Below 100 (FLORAHOME, Grandin, Keystone Heights). Franchise award date: August 29, 1990. Franchise expiration date: N.A. Began: December 1, 1990.
Channel capacity: N.A. Channels available but not in use: N.A.
Basic Service
Subscribers: N.A.
Programming (received off-air): WCJB-TV (ABC, CW) Gainesville; WCWJ (Bounce TV, CW) Jacksonville; WFOX-TV (FOX, MeTV, MNT) Jacksonville; WJAX-TV (CBS, Decades, getTV) Jacksonville; WJCT (PBS) Jacksonville; WJXT (LATV, This TV) Jack-

Florida—Cable Systems

sonville; WJXX (ABC) Orange Park; WOGX (Buzzr, FOX) Ocala; WTLV (Antenna TV, NBC, The Country Network) Jacksonville; WUFT (PBS) Gainesville.
Programming (via satellite): A&E; AMC; Animal Planet; Cartoon Network; CMT; CNBC; CNN; Comedy Central; Cooking Channel; C-SPAN; Discovery Channel; Disney Channel; DIY Network; ESPN; ESPN2; ESPNews; Food Network; Fox News Channel; Fox Sports 1; Freeform; FX; GSN; Hallmark Channel; HGTV; History; HLN; Lifetime; MoviePlex; MTV; Nickelodeon; Outdoor Channel; OWN; Oprah Winfrey Network; QVC; Spike TV; Syfy; TBS; The Weather Channel; TLC; TNT; Travel Channel; Trinity Broadcasting Network (TBN); truTV; Turner Classic Movies; TV Land; USA Network; VH1; WE tv; WGN America.
Fee: $45.00 installation; $33.42 monthly.
Pay Service 1
Pay Units: N.A.
Programming (via satellite): Cinemax; HBO; The Movie Channel.
Fee: $8.95 monthly (TMC), $10.95 monthly (Cinemax or HBO).
Video-On-Demand: No
Internet Service
Operational: No.
Telephone Service
None
Chief Executive Officer: David Suarez. Chief Marketing Officer: David Orshan.
Ownership: Florida Fiber Networks (MSO).

FLORIDA HIGHLANDS—Formerly served by KLiP Interactive. No longer in operation. ICA: FL0231.

FOREST GLEN—Formerly served by Comcast Cable. No longer in operation. ICA: FL0232.

FORT LAUDERDALE—Comcast Cable. Now served by WEST PALM BEACH, FL [FL0008]. ICA: FL0014.

FORT MYERS—Comcast Cable. Now served by SARASOTA, FL [FL0017]. ICA: FL0025.

FORT PIERCE—Comcast Cable. Now served by WEST PALM BEACH, FL [FL0008]. ICA: FL0043.

FORT PIERCE—Formerly served by Wireless Broadcasting of Fort Pierce. No longer in operation. ICA: FL0303.

FORT WALTON BEACH—Cox Communications. Now served by PENSACOLA, FL [FL0018]. ICA: FL0023.

FREEPORT—Cox Communications. Now served by PENSACOLA, FL [FL0018]. ICA: FL0357.

FRUITLAND PARK—Comcast Cable. Now served by ARCHER, FL [FL0189]. ICA: FL0350.

GADSDEN COUNTY (portions)—Mediacom. Now served by HAVANA (town), FL [FL0144]. ICA: FL0360.

GAINESVILLE—Cox Communications, 6205 Peachtree Dunwoody Rd, 12th Floor, Atlanta, GA 30328. Phone: 404-269-6590. Web Site: http://www.cox.com. Also serves Alachua, Alachua County (portions), Marion County (portions), Newberry & Ocala. ICA: FL0027.

TV Market Ranking: Below 100 (Alachua, Alachua County (portions), GAINESVILLE, Marion County (portions), Newberry, Ocala). Franchise award date: January 1, 1963. Franchise expiration date: N.A. Began: May 1, 1965.
Channel capacity: N.A. Channels available but not in use: N.A.
Basic Service
Subscribers: 73,610. Commercial subscribers: 1,228.
Programming (received off-air): WCJB-TV (ABC, CW) Gainesville; WESH (MeTV, NBC) Daytona Beach; WGFL (CBS, MNT) High Springs; WKCF (CW, Estrella TV, This TV) Clermont; WNBW-DT (MeTV, NBC) Gainesville; WOGX (Buzzr, FOX) Ocala; WOPX-TV (ION, Movies!) Melbourne; WRUF-LD Gainesville; WUFT (PBS) Gainesville.
Programming (via microwave): WJXT (LATV, This TV) Jacksonville.
Programming (via satellite): C-SPAN; C-SPAN 2; EVINE Live; MyNetworkTV; Pop; QVC; TBS; WGN America.
Fee: $21.36 installation; $23.99 monthly; $.81 converter.
Expanded Basic Service 1
Subscribers: N.A.
Programming (via satellite): A&E; AMC; Animal Planet; BET; Bravo; Cartoon Network; CMT; CNBC; CNN; Comedy Central; Discovery Channel; Disney Channel; E! HD; ESPN; ESPN2; Food Network; Fox News Channel; Fox Sports 1; FOX Sports Florida/Sun Sports; Freeform; FX; Golf Channel; HGTV; History; HLN; Lifetime; MSNBC; MTV; MTV2; NBCSN; Nickelodeon; OWN; Oprah Winfrey Network; Spike TV; Syfy; The Weather Channel; TLC; TNT; Travel Channel; Turner Classic Movies; TV Land; Univision Studios; USA Network; VH1.
Fee: $34.89 monthly.
Digital Basic Service
Subscribers: N.A.
Programming (via satellite): Destination America; Discovery Kids Channel; History International; Investigation Discovery; MC; MLB Network; National Geographic Channel; Nick Jr.; Science Channel; Weatherscan.
Digital Expanded Basic Service
Subscribers: N.A.
Programming (via satellite): IFC; LMN; LOGO; Starz Encore (multiplexed); Sundance TV.
Fee: $5.00 monthly.
Digital Expanded Basic Service 2
Subscribers: N.A.
Programming (via satellite): BBC America; Boomerang; BYUtv; Chiller; CMT; Cooking Channel; Disney XD; EWTN Global Catholic Network; Fuse; GSN; Hallmark Channel; MTV Classic; MTV Hits; MTV Jams; mtvU; Nat Geo WILD; Nicktoons; Oxygen; Sprout; Starz Encore Family; TeenNick; Tr3s; truTV; TV One; VH1 Soul; WE tv.
Fee: $5.00 monthly.
Digital Expanded Basic Service 3
Subscribers: N.A.
Programming (via satellite): Bloomberg Television; Cox Sports Television; Discovery Life Channel; DIY Network; ESPN Classic; ESPNews; ESPNU; Fox Business Network; Fox Sports 2; FYI; History International; HRTV; NBA TV; NFL Network; NHL Network; Tennis Channel; TVG Network.
Fee: $5.00 monthly.
Digital Expanded Basic Service 4
Subscribers: N.A.
Programming (via satellite): Canal Sur; CNN en Espanol; De Pelicula; Discovery Familia; ESPN Deportes; Fox Deportes; History en Espanol; Ritmoson; Telehit; Telemundo; Tr3s; Univision; Univision Studios.
Fee: $5.00 monthly.
Digital Expanded Basic Service 5
Subscribers: N.A.
Programming (via satellite): A&E HD; AMC HD; Animal Planet HD; Bravo HD; CNBC HD+; CNN HD; Destination America HD; Discovery Channel HD; ESPN HD; ESPN2 HD; Food Network HD; Golf Channel HD; Hallmark Movie Channel HD; HD Theater; History HD; Lifetime HD; Lifetime Movie Network HD; MTV Live; National Geographic Channel HD; NFL Network HD; Science HD; Syfy HD; TBS HD; TLC HD; TNT HD; Universal HD; USA Network HD; Versus HD.
Digital Pay Service 1
Pay Units: N.A.
Programming (via satellite): Cinemax (multiplexed); Cinemax HD; HBO (multiplexed); HBO HD; Showtime (multiplexed); Showtime HD; Starz (multiplexed); Starz Encore; Starz HD; The Movie Channel (multiplexed).
Fee: $11.99 monthly (Cinemax, HBO, Showtime/TMC or Starz/Encore).
Video-On-Demand: Yes
Pay-Per-View
Hot Choice (delivered digitally); Spice: Xcess (delivered digitally); Club Jenna (delivered digitally); iN DEMAND; iN DEMAND (delivered digitally); Playboy TV (delivered digitally); Fresh; Shorteez (delivered digitally).
Internet Service
Operational: Yes.
Subscribers: 90,987.
Broadband Service: Cox High Speed Internet.
Fee: $29.95 installation; $19.99-$44.99 monthly; $10.00 modem lease; $299.95 modem purchase.
Telephone Service
Digital: Operational
Subscribers: 24,330.
Fee: $9.97-$39.95 monthly
Miles of Plant: 3,899.0 (coaxial); 708.0 (fiber optic). Homes passed: 177,618. Miles of plant (coax) includes miles of plant (fiber).
Vice President & General Manager: Mike Giampietro. Vice President, Human Resources: Kia Painter. Vice President, Tax: Mary Vickers. Network Operations Director: Brad Spatz. Sales & Marketing Director: David Saldarriago. Business Operations Director: Steve Chapman. Public Affairs Specialist: Devon Chestnut.
Ownership: Cox Communications Inc. (MSO).

GAINESVILLE—Formerly served by Brytlink. No longer in service. ICA: FL5224.

GOLDEN GATE—Comcast Cable. Now served by SARASOTA, FL [FL0017]. ICA: FL0062.

GOLF VILLAGE—Formerly served by Comcast Cable. No longer in operation. ICA: FL0193.

GREENACRES CITY—Comcast Cable. Now served by WEST PALM BEACH, FL [FL0008]. ICA: FL0053.

GREENSBORO—Mediacom. Now served by HAVANA (town), FL [FL0144]. ICA: FL0204.

GREENVILLE—Formerly served by KLiP Interactive. No longer in operation. ICA: FL0235.

GRETNA—Mediacom. Now served by HAVANA (town), FL [FL0144]. ICA: FL0202.

GULF BREEZE—Mediacom, 4435 Gulf Breeze Pkwy, Gulf Breeze, FL 32561. Phones: 850-934-2520 (Southern division office); 850-934-7700. Web Site: http://www.mediacomcable.com. Also serves Atmore, Brewton & East Brewton, AL; Baker, East Milton, Escambia County (portions), Holt, Milton, Navarre Beach, Pace, Pensacola Beach, Santa Rosa County (portions) & Whiting Field Naval Air Station, FL. ICA: FL0070.
TV Market Ranking: 59 (East Milton, Escambia County (portions), GULF BREEZE, Milton, Navarre Beach, Pace, Pensacola Beach, Santa Rosa County (portions), Whiting Field Naval Air Station); Below 100 (Baker, Holt); Outside TV Markets (Atmore, Brewton, East Brewton). Franchise award date: March 21, 1977. Franchise expiration date: N.A. Began: December 29, 1978.
Channel capacity: N.A. Channels available but not in use: N.A.
Basic Service
Subscribers: 16,801.
Programming (received off-air): WALA-TV (FOX) Mobile; WEAR-TV (ABC, The Country Network) Pensacola; WFGX (MNT, This TV) Fort Walton Beach; WFNA (Bounce TV, CW) Gulf Shores; WHBR (Christian TV Network) Pensacola; WJTC (IND) Pensacola; WKRG-TV (CBS, MeTV) Mobile; WMPV-TV (TBN) Mobile; WPAN (Soul of the South) Fort Walton Beach [LICENSED & SILENT]; WPMI-TV (NBC) Mobile; WSRE (PBS) Pensacola.
Programming (via satellite): A&E; AMC; Animal Planet; BET; Bravo; Cartoon Network; CMT; CNBC; CNN; Comedy Central; C-SPAN; C-SPAN 2; Discovery Channel; Discovery Family; Disney Channel; E! HD; ESPN; ESPN2; EWTN Global Catholic Network; Food Network; Fox News Channel; Fox Sports 1; FOX Sports Florida/Sun Sports; Freeform; FX; Golf Channel; Hallmark Channel; HGTV; History; HLN; ION Television; Lifetime; MSNBC; MTV; Nickelodeon; Outdoor Channel; Oxygen; Pop; QVC; Spike TV; Syfy; TBS; The Weather Channel; TLC; TNT; Travel Channel; truTV; TV Land; USA Network; VH1; WE tv; WGN America.
Fee: $47.13 monthly; $2.95 converter.
Digital Basic Service
Subscribers: N.A.
Programming (via satellite): BBC America; Discovery Digital Networks; Fuse; FXM; FYI; GSN; History International; IFC; LMN; MC; Turner Classic Movies.
Digital Pay Service 1
Pay Units: 4,035.
Programming (via satellite): Cinemax (multiplexed); Flix; HBO (multiplexed); Showtime (multiplexed); Starz (multiplexed); Starz Encore (multiplexed); Sundance TV; The Movie Channel (multiplexed).
Video-On-Demand: Yes
Pay-Per-View
ESPN Now (delivered digitally); ETC (delivered digitally); Pleasure (delivered digitally); Vubiquity Inc. (delivered digitally).
Internet Service
Operational: Yes.
Subscribers: 20,166.
Broadband Service: Mediacom High Speed Internet.
Fee: $42.95 monthly.
Telephone Service
Digital: Operational
Subscribers: 9,125.

Cable Systems—Florida

Miles of Plant: 1,863.0 (coaxial); 215.0 (fiber optic). Homes passed: 68,824.
Vice President: David Servies. Vice President, Financial Reporting: Kenneth J. Kohrs. Regional Technical Operations Director: Eddie Arnold. Engineering Director: Powell Bedgood. Government Relations Director: Barbara Bonowicz. Sales & Marketing Manager: Joey Nagem. Technical Operations Manager: Shayne Routhe.
Ownership: Mediacom LLC (MSO).

HAMPTON—Florida Fiber Networks, 301 South Collins St, Ste 105, Plant City, FL 33563. Phones: 888-860-4088; 352-702-4990. E-mail: info@flfibernet.com. Web Site: http://www.flfibernet.com. Also serves Starke. ICA: FL0237.
TV Market Ranking: Below 100 (HAMPTON, Starke). Franchise award date: August 8, 1989. Franchise expiration date: N.A. Began: N.A.
Channel capacity: N.A. Channels available but not in use: N.A.
Basic Service
Subscribers: N.A.
Programming (received off-air): WCWJ (Bounce TV, CW) Jacksonville; WFOX-TV (FOX, MeTV, MNT) Jacksonville; WJAX-TV (CBS, Decades, getTV) Jacksonville; WJCT (PBS) Jacksonville; WJEB-TV (TBN) Jacksonville; WJXT (LATV, This TV) Jacksonville; WJXX (ABC) Orange Park; WTLV (Antenna TV, NBC, The Country Network) Jacksonville; WUFT (PBS) Gainesville.
Programming (via satellite): A&E; Animal Planet; Cartoon Network; CNN; Comedy Central; Discovery Channel; Disney Channel; Disney XD; E! HD; ESPN; Food Network; Fox News Channel; Fox Sports 1; Freeform; Fuse; FX; Great American Country; HLN; Lifetime; Syfy; TBS; The Weather Channel; TNT; USA Network; WGN America.
Fee: $30.00 installation; $39.45 monthly.
Pay Service 1
Pay Units: N.A.
Programming (via satellite): Cinemax; HBO; Showtime; The Movie Channel.
Fee: $9.95 monthly (each).
Internet Service
Operational: No.
Telephone Service
None
Miles of Plant: 19.0 (coaxial); None (fiber optic). Homes passed: 1,492.
Chief Executive Officer: David Suarez. Chief Marketing Officer: David Orshan.
Ownership: Florida Fiber Networks (MSO).

HASTINGS—Comcast Cable. Now served by JACKSONVILLE, FL [FL0002]. ICA: FL0187.

HAVANA (town)—Mediacom, 275 Norman Dr, Valdosta, GA 31601. Phones: 229-244-4182; 229-244-3852. Fax: 229-244-0724. Web Site: http://www.mediacomcable.com. Also serves Gadsden County (portions), Greensboro & Gretna. ICA: FL0144.
TV Market Ranking: Below 100 (Gadsden County (portions), Greensboro, Gretna, HAVANA (TOWN)). Franchise award date: October 3, 1977. Franchise expiration date: N.A. Began: December 1, 1977.
Channel capacity: N.A. Channels available but not in use: N.A.
Basic Service
Subscribers: 1,173.
Programming (received off-air): WCTV (CBS, MNT, This TV) Thomasville; WFSU-TV (PBS) Tallahassee; WJHG-TV (CW, MNT, NBC) Panama City; WMBB (ABC, This TV) Panama City; WTLH (CW, FOX, MeTV) Bainbridge; WTWC-TV (NBC, The Country Network) Tallahassee; WTXL-TV (ABC, Bounce TV) Tallahassee.
Programming (via satellite): A&E; AMC; Animal Planet; BET; Bravo; Cartoon Network; CMT; CNBC; CNN; Comedy Central; C-SPAN; C-SPAN 2; Discovery Channel; Disney Channel; Disney XD; E! HD; ESPN; ESPN2; EVINE Live; EWTN Global Catholic Network; Food Network; Fox News Channel; Fox Sports 1; FOX Sports Florida/Sun Sports; Freeform; FX; Golf Channel; Hallmark Channel; HGTV; History; HLN; INSP; ION Television; Jewelry Television; Lifetime; MSNBC; MTV; MTV2; Nickelodeon; Outdoor Channel; Pop; QVC; Spike TV; Syfy; TBS; The Weather Channel; TLC; TNT; Travel Channel; Trinity Broadcasting Network (TBN); truTV; TV Land; Univision Studios; USA Network; VH1; WE tv; WGN America.
Fee: $29.50 installation; $69.95 monthly; $3.35 converter.
Digital Basic Service
Subscribers: N.A.
Programming (via satellite): AXS TV; BBC America; Bloomberg Television; CCTV-Documentary; Cloo; CMT; Destination America; Discovery Kids Channel; DMX Music; ESPN HD; ESPN2 HD; ESPNews; Fuse; FXM; FYI; Golf Channel; Great American Country; GSN; History International; IFC; Investigation Discovery; ION Television; LMN; MTV Classic; MTV Hits; National Geographic Channel; NBCSN; Nick Jr.; Nicktoons; Ovation; OWN: Oprah Winfrey Network; Qubo; Reelz; RFD-TV; TeenNick; The Word Network; Turner Classic Movies; Universal HD; VH1 Soul.
Fee: $5.00 converter.
Digital Pay Service 1
Pay Units: N.A.
Programming (via satellite): Cinemax (multiplexed); HBO (multiplexed); HBO HD; Showtime (multiplexed); Showtime HD; Starz (multiplexed); Starz Encore (multiplexed); Starz HD; The Movie Channel (multiplexed); The Movie Channel HD.
Fee: $9.95 monthly (Cinemax, Showtime or Starz), $11.95 monthly (HBO).
Video-On-Demand: Yes
Pay-Per-View
iN DEMAND (delivered digitally); Sports PPV (delivered digitally).
Internet Service
Operational: Yes.
Broadband Service: Mediacom High Speed Internet.
Fee: $49.95 installation; $45.95 monthly.
Telephone Service
Analog: Not Operational
Digital: Operational
Homes passed: 4,537. Miles of plant (coax & fiber) included in Thomasville, GA.
Vice President, Financial Reporting: Kenneth J. Kohrs. Regional Vice President: Sue Misiunas. Regional Technical Operations Manager: Gary McDougall. Regional Marketing Director: Melanie Hannasch. Marketing Manager: Daryl Channey.
Ownership: Mediacom LLC (MSO).

HAWTHORNE—Formerly served by Altitude Communications. No longer in operation. ICA: FL0183.

HERNANDO COUNTY—Bright House Networks. Now served by HILLSBOROUGH COUNTY (portions), FL [FL0003]. ICA: FL0238.

HERNANDO COUNTY—Florida Fiber Networks, 301 South Collins St, Ste 105, Plant City, FL 33563. Phones: 888-860-4088; 352-702-4990. E-mail: info@flfibernet.com. Web Site: http://www.flfibernet.com. Also serves Brooksville, Nobleton, Sumter County & Webster. ICA: FL0148.
TV Market Ranking: 55 (Brooksville, HERNANDO COUNTY, Nobleton, Sumter County, Webster). Franchise award date: May 18, 1989. Franchise expiration date: N.A. Began: N.A.
Channel capacity: N.A. Channels available but not in use: N.A.
Basic Service
Subscribers: N.A.
Programming (received off-air): WACX (IND) Leesburg; WEDU (PBS) Tampa; WFLA-TV (MeTV, NBC) Tampa; WFTS-TV (ABC, Grit, Laff) Tampa; WFTT-DT (getTV, UniMas) Tampa; WKCF (CW, Estrella TV, This TV) Clermont; WMOR-TV (Estrella TV, This TV) Lakeland; WTOG (CW, Decades) St. Petersburg; WTSP (CBS) St. Petersburg; WTVT (Buzzr, FOX, Heroes & Icons, Movies!) Tampa.
Programming (via satellite): A&E; Animal Planet; Cartoon Network; CNN; Comedy Central; Discovery Channel; Disney Channel; ESPN; Food Network; Fox News Channel; Fox Sports 1; FOX Sports Florida/Sun Sports; Freeform; Fuse; FX; Great American Country; HLN; Lifetime; QVC; Showtime; TBS; The Weather Channel; TNT; USA Network; WGN America.
Fee: $30.00 installation; $39.45 monthly.
Pay Service 1
Pay Units: N.A.
Programming (via satellite): Cinemax; HBO; Showtime.
Fee: $9.95 monthly (each).
Video-On-Demand: No
Internet Service
Operational: No.
Telephone Service
None
Miles of Plant: 63.0 (coaxial); None (fiber optic). Homes passed: 1,414.
Plant Manager: Larry English. Chief Executive Officer: David Suarez. Chief Marketing Officer: David Orshan.
Ownership: Florida Fiber Networks (MSO).

HIALEAH—Comcast Cable. Now served by WEST PALM BEACH, FL [FL0008]. ICA: FL0010.

HIDDEN ACRES—Formerly served by Comcast Cable. No longer in operation. ICA: FL0240.

HIGH SPRINGS—Formerly served by Altitude Communications. No longer in operation. ICA: FL0160.

HIGHLAND BEACH—Comcast Cable. Now served by WEST PALM BEACH, FL [FL0008]. ICA: FL0117.

HILLIARD—Comcast Cable. Now served by JACKSONVILLE, FL [FL0002]. ICA: FL0157.

HILLSBOROUGH COUNTY (portions)—Bright House Networks, 2251 Lucien Way, Ste 200B, Maitland, FL 32751. Phones: 407-667-5200; 813-436-2128 (Customer service); 813-684-6400. Web Site: http://brighthouse.com. Also serves Anna Maria, Apollo Beach, Auburndale, Bayonet, Belleair, Belleair Beach, Belleair Bluffs, Bradenton, Bradenton Beach, Brooksville (portions), Citrus County, Clearwater, Crystal River, Dade City, Davenport, Dundee, Dunedin, Eagle Lake, Elfers, Gibsonton, Gulfport, Haines City, Hernando County, Holiday, Holmes Beach, Hudson, Indian Rocks Beach, Inverness, Kenneth City, Lake Alfred, Lake Hamilton, Lake Wales, Lakeland, Land O' Lakes, Largo, MacDill AFB, Madeira Beach, Manatee County, Mulberry, New Port Richey, North Redington Beach, Oldsmar, Palmetto, Pasco County (portions), Pinellas County (portions), Pinellas Park, Plant City, Polk City, Polk County (portions), Port Richey, Redington Shores, Riverview, Ruskin, Safety Harbor, San Antonio, Seminole, South Pasadena, St. Leo, St. Petersburg, St. Petersburg Beach, Sun City Center, Tampa, Tarpon Springs, Temple Terrace, Treasure Island, Wesley Chapel, Wimauma, Winter Haven & Zephyrhills. ICA: FL0003.
TV Market Ranking: 28 (Anna Maria, Apollo Beach, Auburndale, Bayonet, Belleair, Belleair Bluffs, Bradenton, Bradenton Beach, Clearwater, Dade City, Dundee, Dunedin, Eagle Lake, Elfers, Gibsonton, Gulfport, Hernando County (portions), HILLSBOROUGH COUNTY (PORTIONS), Holiday, Holmes Beach, Hudson, Indian Rocks Beach, Kenneth City, Lake Alfred, Lake Hamilton, Lake Wales, Lakeland, Land O' Lakes, Largo, MacDill AFB, Madeira Beach, Manatee County (portions), Mulberry, New Port Richey, North Redington Beach, Oldsmar, Palmetto, Pinellas County (portions), Pinellas Park, Plant City, Polk City, Port Richey, Redington Shores, Riverview, Ruskin, Safety Harbor, San Antonio, Seminole, South Pasadena, St. Leo, St. Petersburg, St. Petersburg Beach, Sun City Center, Tampa, Tarpon Springs, Temple Terrace, Treasure Island, Wesley Chapel, Wimauma, Winter Haven, Zephyrhills); 28,55 (Pasco County (portions), Polk County (portions)); 55 (Davenport, Haines City); Below 100 (Citrus County (portions), Crystal River, Inverness, Hernando County (portions), Manatee County (portions)); Outside TV Markets (Brooksville (portions), Citrus County (portions), Hernando County (portions), Polk County (portions)). Franchise award date: April 1, 1970. Franchise expiration date: N.A. Began: February 10, 1971.
Channel capacity: 68 (operating 2-way). Channels available but not in use: N.A.
Basic Service
Subscribers: 897,463. Commercial subscribers: 13,159.
Programming (received off-air): WCLF (Christian TV Network) Clearwater; WEDU (PBS) Tampa; WFLA-TV (MeTV, NBC) Tampa; WFTS-TV (ABC, Grit, Laff) Tampa; WFTT-DT (getTV, UniMas) Tampa; WMOR-TV (Estrella TV, This TV) Lakeland; WRMD-CD (TMO) Tampa; WTOG (CW, Decades) St. Petersburg; WTSP (CBS) St. Petersburg; WTTA (COZI TV, MNT) St. Petersburg; WTVT (Buzzr, FOX, Heroes & Icons, Movies!) Tampa; WUSF-TV (PBS) Tampa; WXPX-TV (ION) Bradenton; 3 FMs.
Programming (via satellite): Bay News 9; BET; C-SPAN; EVINE Live; Pop; TBS; WGN America.
Fee: $69.95 installation; $27.00 monthly.
Expanded Basic Service 1
Subscribers: N.A.
Programming (via satellite): A&E; AMC; Animal Planet; Bravo; Cartoon Network; CMT; CNBC; CNN; Comedy Central; C-SPAN 2; Discovery Channel; Disney Channel; E! HD; ESPN; ESPN Classic; ESPN2; EWTN Global Catholic Network; Food Network; Fox News Channel; FOX Sports Florida/Sun Sports; FOX Sports Networks; Freeform;

2017 Edition D-139

Florida—Cable Systems

FX; Golf Channel; Hallmark Channel; HGTV; History; HLN; Lifetime; LMN; MoviePlex; MSNBC; MTV; National Geographic Channel; NBCSN; Nickelodeon; Oxygen; QVC; Spike TV; Syfy; The Weather Channel; TLC; TNT; Travel Channel; truTV; Turner Classic Movies; TV Land; USA Network; VH1; WE tv.
Fee: $31.95 monthly.

Digital Basic Service
Subscribers: N.A.
Programming (via satellite): AXS TV; Bay News 9; BBC America; Bloomberg Television; Bright House Sports Network; Cooking Channel; C-SPAN 3; Discovery Digital Networks; Disney Channel; Disney XD; DIY Network; ESPN; ESPNews; EWTN Global Catholic Network; Flix; Food Network; Fox Sports 1; Fuse; FYI; Great American Country; GSN; HD Theater; HGTV; History International; HITS (Headend In The Sky); IFC; InfoMas; MC; MTV Classic; MTV2; Nick Jr.; Nicktoons; Ovation; Sundance TV; Tampa Bay; TeenNick; TNT HD; Trinity Broadcasting Network (TBN); TV One; Universal HD.

Digital Expanded Basic Service
Subscribers: N.A.
Programming (via satellite): FOX College Sports Central; FOX College Sports Pacific; Fox Sports 2; FXM; NBA TV; Outdoor Channel; Starz Encore; Tennis Channel.

Digital Pay Service 1
Pay Units: N.A.
Programming (via satellite): Cinemax (multiplexed); HBO (multiplexed); HBO HD; HBO on Demand; Showtime (multiplexed); Showtime HD; Showtime On Demand; Starz (multiplexed); The Movie Channel (multiplexed); The Movie Channel On Demand.
Fee: $10.50 installation; $9.95 monthly (each).

Video-On-Demand: Yes

Pay-Per-View
Hot Choice (delivered digitally); iN DEMAND (delivered digitally); Playboy TV (delivered digitally); Pleasure (delivered digitally); Fresh (delivered digitally); Shorteez (delivered digitally).

Internet Service
Operational: Yes.
Subscribers: 798,203.
Broadband Service: AOL for Broadband, EarthLink, Internet Junction, Road Runner.
Fee: $44.95 monthly.

Telephone Service
Digital: Operational
Subscribers: 514,528.
Fee: $49.95 monthly
Miles of Plant: 34,317.0 (coaxial); 7,939.0 (fiber optic). Homes passed: 1,807,961.
Division President: Kevin Hyman. Vice President, Engineering: Gene White. General Manager: Harry F. Sheraw. Chief Financial Officer: William Futera. Marketing Director: Robb Bennett. Engineering Director: Mike Vanderkodde.
Ownership: Bright House Networks LLC (MSO).

HOLLYWOOD—Formerly served by Advanced Cable Communications. No longer in operation. ICA: FL0109.

HOLOPAW—Formerly served by Florida Cable. No longer in operation. ICA: FL0242.

HOMOSASSA—Formerly served by Bright House Networks. No longer in operation. ICA: FL0046.

HOSFORD—Formerly served by Southeast Cable TV Inc. No longer in operation. ICA: FL0312.

IMMOKALEE—Comcast Cable. Now served by SARASOTA, FL [FL0017]. ICA: FL0099.

IMMOKALEE SEMINOLE INDIAN RESERVATION—Formerly served by Comcast Cable. No longer in operation. ICA: FL0375.

INDIAN SPRINGS—Formerly served by Formerly served by Comcast Cable. No longer in operation. ICA: FL0243.

INDIANTOWN—Comcast Cable. Now served by WEST PALM BEACH, FL [FL0008]. ICA: FL0244.

INVERNESS—Comcast Cable. Now served by ARCHER, FL [FL0189]. ICA: FL0319.

JACKSONVILLE—AT&T U-verse. This cable system has converted to IPTV. See JACKSONVILLE BEACH, FL [FL5236]. ICA: FL0358.

JACKSONVILLE—Comcast Cable, 4600 Touchton Rd East, Bldg 200, Jacksonville, FL 32246. Phones: 904-733-8489; 904-374-8000. E-mail: doug_mcmillan2@cable.comcast.com. Web Site: http://www.comcast.com. Also serves Alachua County (portions), Atlantic Beach, Baker County (portions), Baldwin, Bradford County (portions), Callahan, Clay County (portions), Columbia, Crescent Beach, Crescent City, Duval County (portions), Fernandina Beach, Fruitland, Georgetown, Glen St. Mary, Green Cove Springs, Hastings, Hilliard, Interlachen, Jacksonville Beach, Jacksonville Naval Air Station, Jennings, Keystone Heights, Lake Butler, Lake City, Live Oak, MacClenny, Mayo, Mayport Naval Air Station, Nassau County (portions), Neptune Beach, Orange Park, Palatka, Pomona Park, Putnam County (portions), St. Augustine, St. Augustine Beach, St. Johns County (portions), Starke, Suwannee County (portions), Union County (portions), Waldo, Welaka (town) & Yulee, FL; Brunswick, Camden County (portions), Charlton County (portions), Folkston, Glynn County (portions), Homeland, Jekyll Island, Nahunta, St. Mary's, Waynesville & Woodbine, GA. ICA: FL0002.
TV Market Ranking: 55 (Crescent City, Putnam County (portions)); 68 (Atlantic Beach, Baker County (portions), Baldwin, Bradford County (portions), Callahan, Camden County (portions), Clay County (portions), Duval County (portions), Fernandina Beach, Glen St. Mary, Green Cove Springs, Hilliard, JACKSONVILLE, Jacksonville Beach, Jacksonville Naval Air Station, MacClenny, Mayport Naval Air Station, Nassau County (portions), Neptune Beach, Orange Park, St. Johns County (portions), St. Mary's, Union County (portions), Yulee); Below 100 (Alachua County (portions), Columbia, Georgetown, Glynn County (portions), Interlachen, Keystone Heights, Live Oak, Starke, Suwannee County (portions), Charlton County (portions), Jekyll Island, Jennings, Lake Butler, Nahunta, Waldo, Waynesville & Welaka (town), Woodbine, Putnam County (portions), Baker County (portions), Bradford County (portions), Camden County (portions), Clay County (portions), Union County (portions), Outside TV Markets (Crescent Beach, Fruitland, Homeland, Pomona Park, St. Augustine Beach, Charlton County (portions), Folkston, Hastings, Lake City, Mayo, Palatka, St. Augustine, Putnam County (portions), Baker County (portions)). Franchise award date: N.A. Franchise expiration date: N.A. Began: June 15, 1979.
Channel capacity: 29 (operating 2-way). Channels available but not in use: N.A.

Basic Service
Subscribers: 295,770. Commercial subscribers: 25,234.
Programming (received off-air): WCWJ (Bounce TV, CW) Jacksonville; WFOX-TV (FOX, MeTV, MNT) Jacksonville; WJAX-TV (CBS, Decades, getTV) Jacksonville; WJCT (PBS) Jacksonville; WJEB-TV (TBN) Jacksonville; WJXT (LATV, This TV) Jacksonville; WJXX (ABC) Orange Park; WPXC-TV (ION) Brunswick; WTLV (Antenna TV, NBC, The Country Network) Jacksonville; WUFT (PBS) Gainesville.
Programming (via satellite): C-SPAN; EVINE Live; EWTN Global Catholic Network; HSN; QVC; WGN America.
Fee: $29.55-$99.00 installation; $28.00 monthly; $3.00 converter.

Expanded Basic Service 1
Subscribers: N.A.
Programming (via satellite): A&E; AMC; Animal Planet; BET; Bravo; CNBC; CNN; Comedy Central; Discovery Channel; Disney Channel; E! HD; ESPN; ESPN2; Food Network; Fox News Channel; Fox Sports 1; FOX Sports Florida/Sun Sports; Freeform; Fuse; FX; Golf Channel; HGTV; HLN; Lifetime; MTV; MTV2; NBCSN; Nickelodeon; Pop; Root Sports Southwest; Spike TV; Syfy; TBS; The Weather Channel; TLC; TNT; TV Land; Univision; USA Network; VH1; Weatherscan.
Fee: $49.99 monthly.

Digital Basic Service
Subscribers: N.A.
Programming (via satellite): A&E HD; AMC HD; Animal Planet HD; BBC America; Bio HD; Bloomberg Television; Bravo HD; BTN; Cartoon Network; Cartoon Network HD; CBS Sports Network HD; Centric; Cine Mexicano; Cinelatino; CMT; CMT HD; CNBC HD+; CNN en Espanol; CNN HD; Comcast SportsNet New England; Comedy Central HD; Cooking Channel; Crime & Investigation Network; C-SPAN 2; C-SPAN 3; Daystar TV Network; Destination America; Destination America HD; Discovery Channel HD; Discovery Family; Discovery Life Channel; Disney Channel HD; Disney XD; Disney XD HD; DIY Network; E! HD; ESPN Classic; ESPN Deportes; ESPN HD; ESPN2 HD; ESPNews; ESPNews HD; ESPNU; ESPNU HD; EVINE Live; FamilyNet; Flix; Food Network HD; Fox Business Network; Fox Business Network HD; FOX College Sports Central; FOX College Sports Pacific; Fox Deportes; Fox News HD; FOX Sports Florida/Sun Sports; Freeform HD; FSN HD; Fuse; Fuse HD; FX HD; FYI; gmcHD; Golf Channel HD; GolTV; Gran Cine; Great American Country; GSN; Hallmark Channel; Hallmark Channel HD; Hallmark Movie Channel HD; Hallmark Movies & Mysteries; HD Theater; HGTV HD; History; History en Espanol; History HD; History International; HLN HD; Home Shopping Network HD; ID Investigation Discovery HD; IFC; IFC HD; Investigation Discovery; Jewelry Television; JUCE TV; Lifetime HD; Lifetime Movie Network HD; LMN; LOGO; MC; MGM HD; MLB Network; MLB Network HD; MoviePlex; MSNBC; MTV Classic; MTV Hits; MTV Jams; MTV Live; Nat Geo WILD; National Geographic Channel; National Geographic Channel HD; NBA TV; NBA TV HD; NBC Universo; NFL Network; NFL Network HD; NFL RedZone; NHL Network; NHL Network HD; Nick 2; Nick HD; Nick Jr.; Nicktoons; Outdoor Channel; Outdoor Channel HD; Ovation; OWN: Oprah Winfrey Network; Oxygen; QVC HD; Reelz; Retirement Living TV; RFD-TV; Science Channel; Science HD; Spike TV HD; SportsNet New York; Sprout; Starz Encore (multiplexed); Starz Encore HD; Sundance TV; Syfy HD; TBS HD; TeenNick; Tennis Channel; Tennis Channel HD; The Sportsman Channel; The Weather Channel HD; The Word Network; TLC HD; TNT HD; Tr3s; Travel Channel; Travel Channel HD; Trinity Broadcasting Network (TBN); truTV; truTV HD; Turner Classic Movies; Turner Classic Movies HD; TV One; TV One HD; TVG Network; Universal HD; Univision; UP; USA Network HD; Versus HD; VH1 HD; VH1 Soul; Viendo-Movies; WAM! America's Kidz Network; WE tv; WGN America HD; World Fishing Network.

Pay Service 1
Pay Units: N.A.
Programming (via satellite): HBO (multiplexed).
Fee: $15.95 monthly.

Digital Pay Service 1
Pay Units: N.A.
Programming (via satellite): Cinemax (multiplexed); Cinemax HD (multiplexed); Flix; HBO (multiplexed); HBO HD (multiplexed); Showtime (multiplexed); Showtime HD (multiplexed); Starz (multiplexed); Starz HD (multiplexed); The Movie Channel (multiplexed); The Movie Channel HD (multiplexed).
Fee: $15.95 monthly (each).

Video-On-Demand: Yes

Pay-Per-View
NBA TV (delivered digitally); iN DEMAND (delivered digitally); Fresh (delivered digitally); Shorteez (delivered digitally); Playboy TV (delivered digitally); Sports PPV (delivered digitally).

Internet Service
Operational: Yes.
Subscribers: 266,318.
Broadband Service: Comcast High Speed Internet.
Fee: $39.95 installation; $42.95 monthly; $10.00 modem lease.

Telephone Service
Digital: Operational
Subscribers: 140,954.
Fee: $44.95 monthly
Miles of Plant: 18,298.0 (coaxial); 8,284.0 (fiber optic). Homes passed: 804,006.
Vice President & General Manager: Doug McMillan. Vice President, Marketing: Vic Scarborough. Government Affairs Director: Bill Ferry. Engineering Director: Mke Humprey.
Ownership: Comcast Cable Communications Inc. (MSO).

JACKSONVILLE BEACH—AT&T U-verse. Formerly [FL0358]. This cable system has converted to IPTV. This is the regional video hub for the JACKSONVILLE BEACH area, 208 South Akard St, Dallas, TX 75202. Phone: 800-288-2020. Web Site: http://www.att.com. Also serves Arlington, Atlantic Beach, Baldwin, Callahan, Clay County (unincorporated areas), Columbia County (unincorporated areas), Duval County (unincorporated areas), East Palatka, Fernandina Beach, Fleming Island, Fort George Island, Green Cove Springs, Hawthorne, Keystone Heights, Lake City, Maxville, Middleburg, Nassau County (unincorporated areas), Neptune Beach,

Cable Systems—Florida

Northside, Oceanway, Orange Park, Palatka, Palm Valley, Penney Farms, Pomona Park, Ponte Vedra Beach, Putnam County (unincorporated areas), San Jose, San Marco, San Pablo, Sawgrass, St. Augustine, St. Augustine Beach, St. Johns County (unincorporated areas), Watertown, Welaka, Wesconnett & Yulee, FL; Blackshear, Brantley County (unincorporated areas), Brunswick, Camden County (unincorporated areas), Deenwood, Dock Junction, Glynn County (unincorporated areas), Jekyll Island, St. Simons Island, Ware County (unincorporated areas) & Waycross, GA. ICA: FL5236.

TV Market Ranking: Franchise award date: July 2, 2007. Franchise expiration date: N.A. Began: November 13, 2008.

Channel capacity: N.A. Channels available but not in use: N.A.

U-basic
Subscribers: 83,687 Subscriber counts include all areas in the JACKSONVILLE BEACH regional video hub. Commercial subscribers: 54.
Fee: $199.00 installation; $19.00 monthly. Includes only local channels.

U-family
Subscribers: N.A.
Fee: $67.00 monthly. Up to 130 channels, including 38 music channels & 1 DVR.

U200
Subscribers: N.A.
Fee: $83.00 monthly. Up to 290 channels, including 46 music channels & 1 DVR.

U200 Latino
Subscribers: N.A.
Fee: $93.00 monthly. Up to 350 channels, including 46 music channels & 1 DVR.

U300
Subscribers: N.A.
Fee: $99.00 monthly. Up to 390 channels, including 46 music channels, The Movie Package & 1 DVR.

U300 Latino
Subscribers: N.A.
Fee: $109.00 monthly. Up to 440 channels, including 46 music channels, 60 Spanish language channels, The Movie Package & 1 DVR.

U450
Subscribers: N.A.
Fee: $131.00 monthly. Up to 460 channels, including 46 music channels, The Movie Package, HBO/Cinemax, The Sports Package, HD Tech Fee & 1 DVR.

U450 Latino
Subscribers: N.A.
Fee: $141.00 monthly. Up to 510 channels, including 46 music channels, 60 Spanish language channels, The Movie Package, HBO/Cinemax, The Sports Package, HD Tech Fee & 1 DVR.

HD
Subscribers: N.A.
Fee: $10.00 monthly. Includes up to 205 channels in HD.

HD Premium
Subscribers: N.A.
Fee: $7.00 monthly. Includes 31 additional channels in HD.

Cinemax
Subscribers: N.A.
Fee: $14.00 monthly. Includes 24 channels.

HBO
Subscribers: N.A.
Fee: $16.00 monthly. Includes 28 channels.

Cinemax/HBO
Subscribers: N.A.
Fee: $26.00 monthly. Includes 52 channels.

Encore
Subscribers: N.A.
Fee: $14.00 monthly. Includes 10 channels.

Showtime Unlimited
Subscribers: N.A.
Fee: $14.00 monthly. Includes 29 channels of Showtime, TMC & Flix.

Starz
Subscribers: N.A.
Fee: $14.00 monthly. Includes 14 channels.

Movie Package
Subscribers: N.A.
Fee: $20.00 monthly. Includes 55 channels of Showtime, TMC, Starz, Encore & Flix.

Sports Package
Subscribers: N.A.
Fee: $10.00 monthly. Includes 28 channels.

International Channels
Subscribers: N.A.
Fee: $5.00 -$35.00.

Video-On-Demand: Yes

Internet Service
Operational: Yes.
Fee: $29.95-$64.95 monthly.

Telephone Service
Digital: Operational
Fee: $30.00 monthly
Ownership: AT&T Inc.

JASPER—Comcast Cable, 3760 Hartsfiled Rd, Tallahassee, FL 32303-1121. Phones: 850-574-4016 (Tallahassee office); 386-792-1820 (Jasper office). Fax: 386-792-2415. Web Site: http://www.comcast.com. Also serves Hamilton County (portions). ICA: FL0168.

TV Market Ranking: Below 100 (JASPER, Hamilton County (portions)); Outside TV Markets (Hamilton County (portions)). Franchise award date: N.A. Franchise expiration date: N.A. Began: January 1, 1969.

Channel capacity: N.A. Channels available but not in use: N.A.

Basic Service
Subscribers: 237.
Programming (received off-air): WALB (ABC, NBC, This TV) Albany; WCJB-TV (ABC, CW) Gainesville; WCTV (CBS, MNT, This TV) Thomasville; WJCT (PBS) Jacksonville; WJXT (LATV, This TV) Jacksonville; WTLH (CW, FOX, MeTV) Bainbridge.
Programming (via satellite): QVC; TBS; The Weather Channel; WGN America.
Fee: $52.95 installation; $17.20 monthly.

Expanded Basic Service 1
Subscribers: N.A.
Programming (via satellite): A&E; AMC; BET; Cartoon Network; CMT; CNBC; CNN; Comcast/Charter Sports Southeast (CSS); Comedy Central; C-SPAN; Discovery Channel; Disney Channel; E! HD; ESPN; ESPN2; Food Network; Fox News Channel; Fox Sports 1; FOX Sports Florida/Sun Sports; Freeform; FX; Golf Channel; Great American Country; GSN; Hallmark Channel; HGTV; History; HLN; Lifetime; MTV; NBCSN; Nickelodeon; OWN; Oprah Winfrey Network; Spike TV; TLC; TNT; Travel Channel; Trinity Broadcasting Network (TBN); truTV; TV Land; TV One; USA Network; VH1.
Fee: $36.55 monthly.

Pay Service 1
Pay Units: N.A.
Programming (via satellite): Cinemax; HBO.
Fee: $11.95 monthly (Cinemax), $13.94 monthly (HBO).

Video-On-Demand: No

Internet Service
Operational: Yes.

Telephone Service
Digital: Operational
Miles of plant (coax) & homes passed included in Tallahassee.

General Manager: K. C. McWilliams. Technical Operations Director: Terry Pullen. Area Technical Manager: Andy Musgrove. Chief Technician: Dwayne Hicks. Marketing Director: Claire Evans.
Ownership: Comcast Cable Communications Inc. (MSO).

JENNINGS—Comcast Cable. Now served by JACKSONVILLE, FL [FL0002]. ICA: FL0203.

KEATON BEACH—Formerly served by Southeast Cable TV Inc. No longer in operation. ICA: FL0225.

KENANSVILLE—Formerly served by Florida Cable. No longer in operation. ICA: FL0246.

KENDALL—Comcast Cable. Now served by WEST PALM BEACH, FL [FL0008]. ICA: FL0021.

KEY COLONY BEACH—Comcast Cable. Now served by WEST PALM BEACH, FL [FL0008]. ICA: FL0081.

KEY LARGO—Comcast Cable. Now served by WEST PALM BEACH, FL [FL0008]. ICA: FL0068.

KEY WEST—Comcast Cable. Now served by WEST PALM BEACH, FL [FL0008]. ICA: FL0055.

LA BELLE—Comcast Cable. Now served by SARASOTA, FL [FL0017]. ICA: FL0106.

LAKE BUTLER—Comcast Cable. Now served by JACKSONVILLE, FL [FL0002]. ICA: FL0155.

LAKE CITY—Comcast Cable. Now served by JACKSONVILLE, FL [FL0002]. ICA: FL0079.

LAKE MARY JANE—Formerly served by Florida Cable. No longer in operation. ICA: FL0344.

LAKE PLACID—Comcast Cablevision of West Florida Inc. Now served by SARASOTA, FL [FL0017]. ICA: FL0250.

LAKE WALES—Comcast Cable. Now served by SARASOTA, FL [FL0017]. ICA: FL0251.

LAWTEY—Florida Fiber Networks, 301 South Collins St, Ste 105, Plant City, FL 33563. Phones: 888-860-4088; 352-702-4990. E-mail: info@flfibernet.com. Web Site: http://www.flfibernet.com. Also serves Bradford County, Clay County, Kingsley Lake, Raiford & Union County. ICA: FL0137.

TV Market Ranking: 68 (Bradford County (portions), Clay County (portions), Kingsley Lake, LAWTEY, Union County (portions)); Below 100 (Raiford, Bradford County (portions), Clay County (portions), Union County (portions)). Franchise award date: December 7, 2002. Franchise expiration date: N.A. Began: N.A.

Channel capacity: N.A. Channels available but not in use: N.A.

Basic Service
Subscribers: N.A.
Programming (received off-air): WCWJ (Bounce TV, CW) Jacksonville; WFOX-TV (FOX, MeTV, MNT) Jacksonville; WJAX-TV (CBS, Decades, getTV) Jacksonville; WJCT (PBS) Jacksonville; WJEB (TBN) Jacksonville; WJXT (LATV, This TV) Jacksonville; WJXX (ABC) Orange Park; WTLV (Antenna TV, NBC, The Country Network) Jacksonville; WUFT (PBS) Gainesville.
Programming (via satellite): A&E; AMC; BET; Cartoon Network; CNBC; CNN; Comedy Central; Discovery Channel; Disney Channel; ESPN; Food Network; Fox News Channel; Fox Sports 1; FOX Sports Florida/Sun Sports; Freeform; Fuse; FX; Great American Country; HLN; Lifetime; QVC; TBS; The Weather Channel; TNT; USA Network; WGN America.
Fee: $30.00 installation; $39.45 monthly.

Pay Service 1
Pay Units: N.A.
Programming (via satellite): Cinemax; HBO; Showtime; The Movie Channel.
Fee: $9.95 monthly (each).

Video-On-Demand: No

Internet Service
Operational: No.

Telephone Service
None

Miles of Plant: 108.0 (coaxial); None (fiber optic). Homes passed: 1,954.
Chief Executive Officer: David Suarez. Chief Marketing Officer: David Orshan.
Ownership: Florida Fiber Networks (MSO).

LEE—Formerly served by KLiP Interactive. No longer in operation. ICA: FL0349.

LEESBURG (village)—Comcast Cable. Now served by ARCHER, FL [FL0189]. ICA: FL0034.

LEESBURG LAKESHORE MOBILE HOME PARK—Formerly served by Leesburg Lakeshore Mobile Home Park Inc. No longer in operation. ICA: FL0205.

LEHIGH ACRES—Comcast Cable. Now served by SARASOTA, FL [FL0017]. ICA: FL0095.

LITTLE TORCH KEY—Comcast Cable. Now served by WEST PALM BEACH, FL [FL0008]. ICA: FL0089.

LIVE OAK—Comcast Cable. Now served by JACKSONVILLE, FL [FL0002]. ICA: FL0100.

LIVE OAK—Formerly served by Florida Cable. No longer in operation. ICA: FL0361.

LIVE OAK—Formerly served by KLiP Interactive. No longer in operation. ICA: FL0352.

MACCLENNY—Comcast Cable. Now served by JACKSONVILLE, FL [FL0002]. ICA: FL0107.

MADISON—Comcast Cable. Now served by TALLAHASSEE, FL [FL0283]. ICA: FL0138.

MARCO ISLAND—Marco Island Cable Inc, 914 Park Ave, Marco Island, FL 34145. Phones: 242-300-2200; 239-394-4895; 239-642-4545 (Customer service). Fax: 239-394-4895. E-mail: marcocable@marcocable.com. Web Site: http://www.cablebahamas.com. Also serves Naples. ICA: FL0359.

TV Market Ranking: Below 100 (MARCO ISLAND, Naples).
Channel capacity: 263 (operating 2-way). Channels available but not in use: N.A.

Basic Service
Subscribers: 15,783.
Programming (received off-air): WBBH-TV (NBC) Fort Myers; WFTX-TV (Escape, FOX, LATV) Cape Coral; WGCU (PBS) Fort Myers; WINK-TV (CBS) Fort Myers; WRXY-

2017 Edition

Florida—Cable Systems

TV (Christian TV Network) Tice; WXCW (CW, MundoMax) Naples; WZVN-TV (ABC, MeTV) Naples; 15 FMs.
Programming (via satellite): A&E; AMC; Animal Planet; Bravo; CMT; CNBC; CNN; Comedy Central; C-SPAN; C-SPAN 2; Discovery Channel; Disney Channel; Disney XD; E! HD; ESPN; ESPN2; EWTN Global Catholic Network; Food Network; Fox News Channel; Freeform; Golf Channel; HGTV; History; HLN; Lifetime; MSNBC; MTV; Nickelodeon; Pop; QVC; Spike TV; Syfy; TBS; The Weather Channel; TLC; TNT; Travel Channel; truTV; Turner Classic Movies; TV Land; USA Network; VH1; WGN America.
Fee: $12.00 monthly.

Digital Basic Service
Subscribers: N.A.
Programming (via satellite): BBC America; Cinemax; Cooking Channel; Discovery Digital Networks; ESPN; MC; NFL Network; Nick 2; Nick Jr.; Nicktoons; TeenNick; Tennis Channel.
Fee: $25.00 installation.

Digital Pay Service 1
Pay Units: N.A.
Programming (via satellite): Cinemax (multiplexed); Deutsche Welle TV; Flix; HBO (multiplexed); Playboy TV; Showtime (multiplexed); Starz (multiplexed); The Movie Channel (multiplexed).
Fee: $9.95 monthly (Deutsche Welle), $10.00 monthly (Showtime/TMC/Flix or Starz), $10.95 monthly (Cinemax), $15.95 monthly (HBO), $29.95 monthly (Playboy).

Video-On-Demand: No

Pay-Per-View
Playboy TV (delivered digitally); iN DEMAND (delivered digitally); MLB Extra Innings (delivered digitally); Hot Choice (delivered digitally); Pleasure (delivered digitally); Fresh (delivered digitally); Shorteez (delivered digitally); ESPN Now (delivered digitally); NHL Center Ice (delivered digitally).

Internet Service
Operational: Yes.
Broadband Service: Marco Island Cable.
Fee: $50.00 installation; $29.95 monthly; $5.00 modem lease; $99.00 modem purchase.

Telephone Service
Digital: Operational
President: William Gaston.
Ownership: Cable Bahamas Ltd.

MARGATE—Comcast Cable. Now served by WEST PALM BEACH, FL [FL0008]. ICA: FL0041.

MARIANNA—Comcast Cable. Now served by TALLAHASSEE, FL [FL0283]. ICA: FL0134.

MARION COUNTY (southern portion)—Florida Fiber Networks, 301 South Collins St, Ste 105, Plant City, FL 33563. Phones: 888-860-4088; 352-702-4990. E-mail: info@flfibernet.com. Web Site: http://www.flfibernet.com. Also serves Eustis, Lake Yale Estates, Palm Shores Mobile Home Park, Sandpiper Mobile Home Park & Umatilla. ICA: FL0364.
TV Market Ranking: 55 (Eustis, Lake Yale Estates, MARION COUNTY (SOUTHERN PORTION), Palm Shores Mobile Home Park, Sandpiper Mobile Home Park, Umatilla).
Channel capacity: N.A. Channels available but not in use: N.A.

Basic Service
Subscribers: N.A.
Programming (received off-air): WACX (IND) Leesburg; WESH (MeTV, NBC) Daytona Beach; WFTV (ABC, Escape) Orlando; WKCF (CW, Estrella TV, This TV) Clermont; WKMG-TV (CBS, Retro TV) Orlando; WOFL (Bounce TV, FOX) Orlando; WOGX (Buzzr, FOX) Ocala; WRBW (Buzzr, Heroes & Icons, MNT, Movies!) Orlando; WUCF-TV (ETV) Orlando.
Programming (via satellite): A&E; Animal Planet; Cartoon Network; CNBC; CNN; Comedy Central; C-SPAN; Discovery Channel; Disney Channel; ESPN; Food Network; Fox Sports 1; Freeform; Fuse; Great American Country; HLN; Lifetime; QVC; Syfy; TBS; The Weather Channel; TNT; USA Network; WGN America.
Fee: $26.45 monthly.

Pay Service 1
Pay Units: N.A.
Programming (via satellite): Cinemax; HBO; Showtime.

Internet Service
Operational: No.

Telephone Service
None
Miles of Plant: 41.0 (coaxial); None (fiber optic). Homes passed: 1,180.
Chief Executive Officer: David Suarez. Chief Marketing Officer: David Orshan.
Ownership: Florida Fiber Networks (MSO).

MARION COUNTY (unincorporated areas)—Cablevision of Marion County, 8296 Southwest 103rd Rd, Ste 3, Ocala, FL 34481. Phone: 352-854-0408. Fax: 352-854-1829. E-mail: comc@lightningspeed.net. Web Site: http://www.lightningspeed.net. Also serves Fairfield, Marion County (southwestern portion), Palm Cay, Pedro, Spruce Creek & Summerfield. ICA: FL0368.
TV Market Ranking: Below 100 (Fairfield, Marion County (southwestern portion), MARION COUNTY (UNINCORPORATED AREAS), Palm Cay, Pedro, Summerfield).
Channel capacity: N.A. Channels available but not in use: N.A.

Basic Service
Subscribers: 2,708.
Programming (received off-air): WACX (IND) Leesburg; WCJB-TV (ABC, CW) Gainesville; WESH (MeTV, NBC) Daytona Beach; WFTV (ABC, Escape) Orlando; WKCF (CW, Estrella TV, This TV) Clermont; WKMG-TV (CBS, Retro TV) Orlando; WOFL (Bounce TV, FOX) Orlando; WOGX (Buzzr, FOX) Ocala; WRBW (Buzzr, Heroes & Icons, MNT, Movies!) Orlando; WUFT (PBS) Gainesville.
Programming (via satellite): A&E; AMC; Animal Planet; Bravo; Cartoon Network; CNBC; CNN; C-SPAN; C-SPAN 2; Discovery Channel; ESPN; ESPN2; Food Network; Fox News Channel; Fox Sports 1; FOX Sports Florida/Sun Sports; Freeform; FX; FXM; Golf Channel; Great American Country; HGTV; History; HLN; Lifetime; MSNBC; Pop; QVC; Syfy; TBS; The Weather Channel; TLC; TNT; Travel Channel; truTV; Turner Classic Movies; TV Land; Univision Studios; USA Network; WGN America.
Fee: $25.00 installation; $12.72 monthly.

Digital Basic Service
Subscribers: N.A.
Programming (via satellite): BBC America; Bloomberg Television; Cloo; Discovery Life Channel; Disney XD; DMX Music; ESPN Classic; ESPNews; Fox Sports 1; FOX Sports Networks; Fuse; FXM; FYI; GSN; History International; INSP; LMN; National Geographic Channel; Outdoor Channel; WE tv.

Pay Service 1
Pay Units: N.A.
Programming (via satellite): Cinemax; HBO (multiplexed); Showtime; The Movie Channel.
Fee: $10.25 monthly (Showtime or TMC), $10.95 monthly (Cinemax), $14.95 monthly (HBO).

Digital Pay Service 1
Pay Units: N.A.
Programming (via satellite): Cinemax (multiplexed); Flix; HBO (multiplexed); Showtime (multiplexed); Starz (multiplexed); Starz Encore (multiplexed); The Movie Channel (multiplexed).
Fee: $14.95 monthly (Starz/Encore), $23.95 monthly (HBO or Movieplex).

Video-On-Demand: No

Pay-Per-View
iN DEMAND (delivered digitally); Playboy TV (delivered digitally); Fresh (delivered digitally); Shorteez (delivered digitally); Hot Choice (delivered digitally).

Internet Service
Operational: Yes.
Subscribers: 2,136.
Fee: $50.00 installation; $34.95 monthly.

Telephone Service
Digital: Operational
Subscribers: 804.
Fee: $49.99 monthly
Miles of Plant: 581.0 (coaxial); 77.0 (fiber optic). Homes passed: 15,000.
President: Kerri King. Vice President, Plant Services: Ben Ardiles. Office Manager: Louise Brush.
Ownership: Cablevision of Marion County LLC (MSO).

MAYO—Comcast Cable. Now served by JACKSONVILLE, FL [FL0002]. ICA: FL0192.

MELBOURNE—Bright House Networks. Now served by ORLANDO, FL [FL0001]. ICA: FL0015.

MELBOURNE—Formerly served by Wireless Broadcasting of Melbourne. No longer in operation. ICA: FL0305.

MEXICO BEACH—Mediacom. Now served by WALTON COUNTY (portions), FL [FL0159]. ICA: FL0141.

MIAMI—AT&T U-verse. This is the regional video hub for the MIAMI area, 208 South Akard St, Dallas, TX 75202. Phone: 800-288-2020. Web Site: http://www.att.com. Also serves Allapattah, Arch Creek, Aventura, Bal Harbour, Bay Harbor Islands, Big Coppitt, Big Pine Key, Biscayne Park, Boca Chica Key, Broadview Park, Broward County (unincorporated areas), Brownsville, Carol City, Coconut Creek, Cooper City, Coral Gables, Coral Springs, Cutler Bay, Dania Beach, Davie, Deerfield Beach, Doral, Duck Key, El Portal, Florida City, Fort Lauderdale, Golden Beach, Golden Glades, Goulds, Hallandale Beach, Hialeah, Hialeah Gardens, Hillcrest, Hillsboro Beach, Hollywood, Homestead, Indian Creek (village), Islamorada, Kendall, Key Biscayne, Key Largo, Key West, Lake Forest, Lauderdale Lakes, Lauderdale-By-The-Sea, Lauderhill, Lazy Lake, Leisure City, Lighthouse Point, Marathon, Margate, Medley, Miami Beach, Miami Gardens (Broward County), Miami Gardens (Miami-Dade County), Miami Lakes, Miami Shores, Miami Springs, Miami-Dade County (unincorporated areas), Miramar, Monroe County (unincorporated areas), Naranja, Norland, Normandy, North Bay Village, North Key Largo, North Lauderdale, North Miami, North Miami Beach, Oakland Park, Ojus, Olympia Heights, Opa Locka, Palm Springs North, Palmetto Bay, Parkland, Pembroke Park, Pembroke Pines, Perrine, Pinecrest (Miami-Dade County), Plantation, Pompano Beach, Princeton, Richmond Heights, Sea Ranch Lakes, Snapper Creek, South Miami, South Miami Heights, Southwest Ranches, Stock Island, Sugarloaf Key, Sunny Isles Beach, Sunrise, Surfside, Sweetwater, Tamarac, Tavernier, Vaca Key, West Hollywood, West Miami, West Park, Weston, Westwood Lakes & Wilton Manors. ICA: FL5430.
Channel capacity: N.A. Channels available but not in use: N.A.

U-basic
Subscribers: 252,393 Subscriber counts include all areas in the MIAMI regional video hub. Commercial subscribers: 258.
Fee: $199.00 installation; $19.00 monthly. Includes only local channels.

U-family
Subscribers: N.A.
Fee: $67.00 monthly. Up to 130 channels, including 38 music channels & 1 DVR.

U200
Subscribers: N.A.
Fee: $83.00 monthly. Up to 290 channels, including 46 music channels & 1 DVR.

U200 Latino
Subscribers: N.A.
Fee: $93.00 monthly. Up to 350 channels, including 46 music channels & 1 DVR.

U300
Subscribers: N.A.
Fee: $99.00 monthly. Up to 390 channels, including 46 music channels, The Movie Package & 1 DVR.

U300 Latino
Subscribers: N.A.
Fee: $109.00 monthly. Up to 440 channels, including 46 music channels, 60 Spanish language channels, The Movie Package & 1 DVR.

U450
Subscribers: N.A.
Fee: $131.00 monthly. Up to 460 channels, including 46 music channels, The Movie Package, HBO/Cinemax, The Sports Package, HD Tech Fee & 1 DVR.

U450 Latino
Subscribers: N.A.
Fee: $141.00 monthly. Up to 510 channels, including 46 music channels, 60 Spanish language channels, The Movie Package, HBO/Cinemax, The Sports Package, HD Tech Fee & 1 DVR.

HD
Subscribers: N.A.
Fee: $10.00 monthly. Includes up to 205 channels in HD.

HD Premium
Subscribers: N.A.
Fee: $7.00 monthly. Includes 31 additional channels in HD.

Cinemax
Subscribers: N.A.
Fee: $14.00 monthly. Includes 24 channels.

HBO
Subscribers: N.A.
Fee: $16.00 monthly. Includes 28 channels.

Cinemax/HBO
Subscribers: N.A.
Fee: $26.00 monthly. Includes 52 channel.

Encore
Subscribers: N.A.
Fee: $14.00 monthly. Includes 10 channels.

Showtime Unlimited
Subscribers: N.A.
Fee: $14.00 monthly. Includes 29 channels of Showtime, TMC & Flix.

Cable Systems—Florida

Access the most current data instantly
FREE TRIAL @ ADVANCED TVFactbook
TELCO/IPTV • CABLE TV • TV STATIONS
www.warren-news.com/factbook.htm

Starz
Subscribers: N.A.
Fee: $14.00 monthly. Includes 14 channels.
Movie Package
Subscribers: N.A.
Fee: $20.00 monthly. Includes 55 channels of Showtime, TMC, Starz, Encore & Flix.
Sports Package
Subscribers: N.A.
Fee: $10.00 monthly. Includes 28 channels.
International Channels
Subscribers: N.A.
Fee: $5.00 -$35.00.
Video-On-Demand: Yes
Internet Service
Operational: Yes.
Fee: $29.95-$64.95 monthly.
Telephone Service
Digital: Operational
Fee: $30.00 monthly
Ownership: AT&T Inc.

MIAMI—Comcast Cable. Now served by WEST PALM BEACH, FL [FL0008]. ICA: FL0011.

MIAMI—Comcast Cable. Now served by WEST PALM BEACH, FL [FL0008]. ICA: FL0006.

MIAMI (portions)—Formerly served by Bright House Networks. No longer in operation. ICA: FL0355.

MIAMI BEACH—Atlantic Broadband, 1681 Kennedy Cswy, Miami, FL 33141. Phones: 305-868-5086; 888-752-4222; 305-861-1564; 305-861-8069. Fax: 305-861-9047. E-mail: info@atlanticbb.com. Web Site: http://atlanticbb.com. Also serves Aventura, Bal Harbour, Bay Harbor Islands, Dade County (portions), Golden Beach, North Bay Village, Pinecrest (portions), South Miami, Sunny Isles & Surfside. ICA: FL0020.
TV Market Ranking: 21 (Aventura, Bal Harbour, Bay Harbor Islands, Dade County (portions), Golden Beach, MIAMI BEACH, North Bay Village, Pinecrest (portions), South Miami, Sunny Isles, Surfside). Franchise award date: July 1, 1978. Franchise expiration date: N.A. Began: March 1, 1980.
Channel capacity: N.A. Channels available but not in use: N.A.
Basic Service
Subscribers: 33,455.
Programming (received off-air): WAMI-DT (Bounce TV, getTV, UniMas) Hollywood; WBFS-TV (MNT) Miami; WFOR-TV (CBS, Decades) Miami; WGEN-TV (IND, Mundo-Max) Key West; WHFT-TV (TBN) Miami; WJAN-CD Miami; WLRN-TV (PBS) Miami; WLTV-DT (Bounce TV, Laff, UNV) Miami; WPBT (PBS) Miami; WPLG (ABC, MeTV, Movies) Miami; WPXM-TV (ION) Miami; WSBS-TV (IND) Key West; WSCV (TMO) Fort Lauderdale; WSFL-TV (Antenna TV, Azteca America, CW, This TV) Miami; WSVN (Estrella TV, FOX) Miami; WTVJ (COZI TV, NBC) Miami.
Programming (via satellite): America CV Network LLC; BeachTV; C-SPAN; C-SPAN 2; QVC; Telemiami; The Weather Channel; TV Guide.
Fee: $40.00 installation; $31.99 monthly; $3.05 converter.
Expanded Basic Service 1
Subscribers: 32,853.
Programming (via satellite): A&E; AMC; Animal Planet; BET; Bravo; Cartoon Network; CMT; CNBC; CNN; Comedy Central; Discovery Channel; Disney Channel; E! HD; ESPN; ESPN2; Food Network; Fox News Channel; Fox Sports 1; FOX Sports Florida/Sun Sports; Freeform; FX; Golf Channel; GSN; Hallmark Channel; HGTV; History; HLN; Lifetime; MSNBC; MTV; MTV2; National Geographic Channel; NBCSN; Nickelodeon; Oxygen; Spike TV; Syfy; TBS; TLC; TNT; Travel Channel; truTV; TV Land; Univision; USA Network; VH1.
Fee: $40.81 monthly.
Digital Basic Service
Subscribers: 31,871.
Programming (via satellite): A&E HD; Animal Planet HD; AXS TV; BBC America; Bloomberg Television; Chiller; Cooking Channel; Destination America; Discovery Channel HD; Discovery Kids Channel; Disney Channel HD; Disney XD; DIY Network; ESPN Classic; ESPN HD; ESPN2 HD; ESPNews; ESPNU; EWTN Global Catholic Network; Fox Sports 2; FOX Sports Florida/Sun Sports; Fuse; FYI; GolTV; Great American Country; HD Theater; History International; IFC; INSP; Investigation Discovery; Jewelry Television; LATV; LMN; LOGO; MC; MTV Classic; MTV Hits; MTV Jams; NBC Universo; NFL Network; NFL Network HD; Nick 2; Nick Jr.; Nicktoons; OWN: Oprah Winfrey Network; Science Channel; Soundtrack Channel; Starz; Starz Encore; Syfy HD; TBS HD; TeenNick; Tennis Channel; TNT HD; Turner Classic Movies; USA Network HD; VH1 Country; VH1 Soul; WE tv; Weatherscan.
Fee: $9.95 monthly.
Digital Pay Service 1
Pay Units: N.A.
Programming (via satellite): Canal Sur; Caracol TV; Cinelatino; Cinemax (multiplexed); Cinemax HD; CNN en Espanol; De Pelicula; De Pelicula Clasico; Discovery Familia; Docu TVE; Enlace USA; ESPN Deportes; Flix; Fox Deportes; Fox Life; HBO (multiplexed); HBO HD; History en Espanol; HTV; Infinito; Ole TV; Portuguese Channel; Ritmoson; RTN; Showtime (multiplexed); Showtime HD; Starz HD; Sundance TV; Telefe Internacional; Telehit; The Movie Channel (multiplexed); Tr3s; ULTRA HDPlex.
Fee: $2.99 monthly (Sundance), $8.95 monthly (HERE!), $17.95 monthly (Cinemax, HBO, Mundo Latino, Portuguese, Russian or Showtime/TMC/Flix).
Video-On-Demand: Yes
Pay-Per-View
iN DEMAND (delivered digitally); Playboy TV (delivered digitally); Hot Choice (delivered digitally).
Internet Service
Operational: Yes. Began: January 1, 1998.
Subscribers: 77,133.
Broadband Service: Atlantic Broadband High-Speed Internet.
Fee: $24.95 monthly; $5.00 modem lease.
Telephone Service
Digital: Operational
Subscribers: 11,452.
Fee: $49.95 monthly
Miles of Plant: 391.0 (coaxial); 154.0 (fiber optic). Homes passed: 152,706.
Senior Vice President & General Counsel: Bartlett Leber. Vice President & General Manager: Jim Waldo. Chief Technician: David Conkle. Marketing Administrator: Ira Levy.
Ownership: Atlantic Broadband (MSO).

MIAMI/DADE COUNTY—AT&T U-verse. This cable system has converted to IPTV. See MIAMI, FL [FL5430]. ICA: FL0353.

MICANOPY (town)—Formerly served by CommuniComm Services. No longer in operation. ICA: FL0201.

MIDWAY—Comcast Cablevision of Tallahassee Inc. Now served by TALLAHASSEE, FL [FL0283]. ICA: FL0194.

MILTON—Mediacom. Now served by GULF BREEZE, FL [FL0070]. ICA: FL0380.

MIMS—Comcast Cable. Now served by WEST PALM BEACH, FL [FL0008]. ICA: FL0130.

MONTICELLO—Comcast Cable, 3760 Hartsfield Rd, Tallahassee, FL 32303-1121. Phones: 850-574-4000; 850-574-4016. Fax: 850-574-4030. E-mail: claire_evans@cable.comcast.com. Web Site: http://www.comcast.com. Also serves Jefferson County (portions). ICA: FL0165.
TV Market Ranking: Below 100 (Jefferson County (portions), MONTICELLO). Franchise award date: April 1, 1980. Franchise expiration date: N.A. Began: April 1, 1980.
Channel capacity: N.A. Channels available but not in use: N.A.
Basic Service
Subscribers: 158.
Programming (received off-air): WABW-TV (PBS) Pelham; WCTV (CBS, MNT, This TV) Thomasville; WFSU-TV (PBS) Tallahassee; WTLH (CW, FOX, MeTV) Bainbridge; WTWC-TV (NBC, The Country Network) Tallahassee; WTXL-TV (ABC, Bounce TV) Tallahassee.
Programming (via satellite): C-SPAN; CW PLUS; Pop; QVC; WGN America.
Fee: $52.95 installation; $19.20 monthly.
Expanded Basic Service 1
Subscribers: N.A.
Programming (via satellite): A&E; AMC; Animal Planet; BET; Cartoon Network; CMT; CNN; Comcast/Charter Sports Southeast (CSS); Comedy Central; Discovery Channel; Disney Channel; E! HD; ESPN; ESPN2; Food Network; Fox News Channel; Fox Sports 1; FOX Sports Florida/Sun Sports; Freeform; Golf Channel; Great American Country; GSN; Hallmark Channel; HGTV; History; HLN; ION Television; Lifetime; MSNBC; MTV; NBCSN; Nickelodeon; OWN: Oprah Winfrey Network; Spike TV; TBS; The Weather Channel; TLC; TNT; Travel Channel; Trinity Broadcasting Network (TBN); truTV; TV Land; TV One; USA Network.
Fee: $13.49 monthly.
Pay Service 1
Pay Units: N.A.
Programming (via satellite): HBO; Showtime; The Movie Channel.
Fee: $10.00 monthly (each).
Internet Service
Operational: Yes.
Telephone Service
None
Miles of Plant: 47.0 (coaxial); 10.0 (fiber optic). Homes passed: 841. Miles of plant (coax) & homes passed included in Tallahassee.
General Manager: K. C. McWilliams. Technical Operations Director: Terry Pullen. Marketing Director: Claire Evans. Technical Operations Manager: Dave Morawski.
Ownership: Comcast Cable Communications Inc. (MSO).

MOORE HAVEN—Comcast Cable. Now served by WEST PALM BEACH, FL [FL0008]. ICA: FL0146.

NAPLES (town)—Comcast Cable. Now served by SARASOTA, FL [FL0017]. ICA: FL0028.

NAPLES (town)—Comcast Cable. Now served by SARASOTA, FL [FL0017]. ICA: FL0029.

NEWBERRY—Cox Communications. Now served by GAINESVILLE, FL [FL0027]. ICA: FL0257.

NORTH DADE COUNTY—Formerly served by Comcast Cable. No longer in operation. ICA: FL0007.

NORTH OLD TOWN—Florida Fiber Networks, 301 South Collins St, Ste 105, Plant City, FL 33563. Phones: 888-860-4088; 352-702-4990. E-mail: info@flfibernet.com. Web Site: http://www.flfibernet.com. Also serves Gilchrist County (portions). ICA: FL0379.
TV Market Ranking: Below 100 (Gilchrist County (portions), NORTH OLD TOWN).
Channel capacity: N.A. Channels available but not in use: N.A.
Basic Service
Subscribers: N.A.
Programming (received off-air): WCJB-TV (ABC, CW) Gainesville; WESH (MeTV, NBC) Daytona Beach; WGFL (CBS, MNT) High Springs; WOGX (Buzzr, FOX) Ocala; WUFT (PBS) Gainesville.
Programming (via satellite): A&E; Cartoon Network; CMT; CNN; C-SPAN; Discovery Channel; ESPN; ESPN2; Freeform; HGTV; History; HLN; Lifetime; Outdoor Channel; Spike TV; Syfy; TBS; The Weather Channel; TNT; Trinity Broadcasting Network (TBN); USA Network; WGN America.
Pay Service 1
Pay Units: N.A.
Programming (via satellite): HBO.
Internet Service
Operational: No.
Telephone Service
None
General Manager: Jim Pierce. Plant Manager: Larry English. Office Manager: Alita Dawson.
Ownership: Florida Fiber Networks (MSO).

OCALA—Cox Cable Greater Ocala. Now served by GAINESVILLE, FL [FL0027]. ICA: FL0038.

OCALA/OAK RUN—Oak Run Associates LTD, 10983 SW 89th Ave, Ocala, FL 34481. Phone: 352-854-3223. Also serves Pine Run. ICA: FL0382.

2017 Edition

D-143

Florida—Cable Systems

TV Market Ranking: Below 100 (OCALA/OAK RUN).
Channel capacity: N.A. Channels available but not in use: N.A.
Basic Service
Subscribers: 3,476.
Fee: $45.00 installation; $44.75 monthly.
Expanded Basic Service 1
Subscribers: 2,092.
Fee: $44.75 monthly.
Digital Basic Service
Subscribers: 331.
Fee: $16.50 monthly.
Internet Service
Operational: Yes.
Fee: $29.99-$69.99 monthly.
Telephone Service
Digital: Operational
Fee: $39.99 monthly
Vice President, Administration: Carol Olson.
Ownership: Oak Run Associates Ltd.

OKEECHOBEE—Comcast Cable. Now served by WEST PALM BEACH, FL [FL0008]. ICA: FL0064.

ORANGE COUNTY (unincorporated areas)—Comcast Cable. Now served by ARCHER, FL [FL0189]. ICA: FL0037.

ORANGE LAKE—Formerly served by Altitude Communications. No longer in operation. ICA: FL0260.

ORANGE PARK—Comcast Cable. Now served by JACKSONVILLE, FL [FL0002]. ICA: FL0047.

ORANGE SPRINGS—Florida Fiber Networks, 23505 State Rd 40, PO Box 498, Astor, FL 32102-0498. Phones: 888-860-4088; 352-702-4990. E-mail: info@flfibernet.com. Web Site: http://www.flfibernet.com. Also serves Johnson & Marion County (portions). ICA: FL0261.
TV Market Ranking: Below 100 (Johnson, Marion County (portions), ORANGE SPRINGS). Franchise award date: N.A. Franchise expiration date: N.A. Began: May 1, 1990.
Channel capacity: N.A. Channels available but not in use: N.A.
Basic Service
Subscribers: N.A.
Programming (received off-air): WCJB-TV (ABC, CW) Gainesville; WESH (MeTV, NBC) Daytona Beach; WFOX-TV (FOX, MeTV, MNT) Jacksonville; WFTV (ABC, Escape) Orlando; WGFL (CBS, MNT) High Springs; WJXT (LATV, This TV) Jacksonville; WKCF (CW, Estrella TV, This TV) Clermont; WKMG-TV (CBS, Retro TV) Orlando; WOFL (Bounce TV, FOX) Orlando; WOGX (Buzzr, FOX) Ocala; WUFT (PBS) Gainesville.
Programming (via satellite): A&E; AMC; Animal Planet; Cartoon Network; CMT; CNBC; CNN; Comedy Central; Cooking Channel; C-SPAN; Discovery Channel; Disney Channel; DIY Network; ESPN; ESPN2; ESPNews; Food Network; Fox News Channel; Fox Sports 1; Freeform; FX; GSN; Hallmark Channel; HGTV; History; HLN; Lifetime; MoviePlex; MTV; Nickelodeon; Outdoor Channel; OWN: Oprah Winfrey Network; QVC; Spike TV; Syfy; TBS; The Weather Channel; TLC; TNT; Travel Channel; Trinity Broadcasting Network (TBN); truTV; Turner Classic Movies; TV Land; USA Network; WE tv; WGN America.
Fee: $40.00 installation.
Pay Service 1
Pay Units: N.A.
Programming (via satellite): Cinemax; HBO; The Movie Channel.
Fee: $10.95 monthly (each).
Internet Service
Operational: Yes.
Fee: $49.95 installation; $24.95 monthly.
Telephone Service
None
Chief Executive Officer: David Suarez. Chief Marketing Officer: David Orshan.
Ownership: Florida Fiber Networks (MSO).

ORLANDO—Bright House Networks, 2251 Lucien Way, Ste 200B, Maitland, FL 32751. Phone: 407-667-5200. Web Site: http://brighthouse.com. Also serves Altamonte Springs, Apopka, Barefoot Bay, Belle Isle, Belleview, Beverly Beach, Brevard County, Bunnell, Bushnell, Cape Canaveral, Casselberry, Center Hill, Clermont, Cocoa, Cocoa Beach, Coleman, Daytona Beach, Daytona Beach Shores, De Bary, DeLand, Deltona, Eatonville, Edgewater, Edgewood, Flagler Beach, Flagler County, Grand Island, Groveland, Holly Hill, Indian Harbour Beach, Indiatlantic, Kissimmee, Lake County (portions), Lake Helen, Lake Mary, Longwood, Maitland, Malabar, Marion County (portions), Marion Oaks, Mascotte, Melbourne, Melbourne Beach, Melbourne Village, Minneola, Mount Dora, New Smyrna, Oak Hill, Oakland, Ocoee, Orange City, Orange County, Ormond Beach, Osceola County, Oviedo, Palm Bay, Palm Coast, Palm Shores, Patrick AFB, Pennbrooke, Ponce Inlet, Port Orange, Rockledge, Sanford, Satellite Beach, Seminole County, Snug Harbor Village, South Daytona, St. Cloud, Sumter County (portions), Titusville, Volusia County, Webster, West Melbourne, Wildwood, Windermere, Winter Garden, Winter Park, Winter Springs; 85 (Beverly Beach); Below 100 (Belleview, Marion County (portions), Marion Oaks, Southgate); Outside TV Markets (Osceola County). Franchise award date: N.A. Franchise expiration date: N.A. Began: January 7, 1985.
Channel capacity: N.A. Channels available but not in use: N.A.
Basic Service
Subscribers: 744,445. Commercial subscribers: 11,096.
Programming (received off-air): WACX (IND) Leesburg; WDSC-TV (ETV) New Smyrna Beach; WEFS (PBS) Cocoa; WESH (MeTV, NBC) Daytona Beach; WFTV (ABC, Escape) Orlando; WHLV-TV (TBN) Cocoa; WKCF (CW, Estrella TV, This TV) Clermont; WKMG-TV (CBS, Retro TV) Orlando; WOFL (Bounce TV, FOX) Orlando; WOPX-TV (ION, Movies!) Melbourne; WOTF-DT (getTV, TEL) Melbourne; WRBW (Buzzr, Heroes & Icons, MNT, Movies!) Orlando; WRDQ (Antenna TV) Orlando; WTGL (ETV) Leesburg; WUCF-TV (ETV) Orlando.
Programming (via satellite): A&E; AMC; Animal Planet; BET; Bravo; Cartoon Network; Central Florida News 13; CMT; CNBC; CNN; Comedy Central; C-SPAN; C-SPAN 2; Discovery Channel; Disney Channel; E! HD; ESPN; ESPN2; EVINE Live; Food Network; Fox News Channel; Fox Sports 1; FOX Sports Florida/Sun Sports; FX; Golf Channel; Hallmark Channel; HGTV; History; HLN; Lifetime; LMN; MSNBC; MTV; Nickelodeon; Oxygen; QVC; Spike TV; Syfy; TBS; Telemundo; The Weather Channel; TLC; TNT; Travel Channel; truTV; Turner Classic Movies; TV Land; Univision; USA Network; VH1; WE tv; WGN America.
Fee: $69.95 installation; $27.00 monthly.
Digital Basic Service
Subscribers: N.A.
Programming (via satellite): BBC America; Bloomberg Television; C-SPAN 2; C-SPAN 3; Discovery Digital Networks; Disney XD; DIY Network; DMX Music; ESPN Classic; ESPN Now; ESPNews; EWTN Global Catholic Network; Freeform; Fuse; NASA TV; National Geographic Channel; NBCSN; Nick Jr.; Outdoor Channel; Ovation; TeenNick; Weatherscan.
Digital Expanded Basic Service
Subscribers: N.A.
Programming (via satellite): HITS (Headend In The Sky).
Digital Pay Service 1
Pay Units: N.A.
Programming (via satellite): Cinemax (multiplexed); Flix; HBO (multiplexed); IFC; MoviePlex; Showtime (multiplexed); Starz (multiplexed); Starz Encore; Sundance TV; The Movie Channel (multiplexed).
Fee: $24.99 monthly (each).
Video-On-Demand: Yes
Pay-Per-View
Sports PPV (delivered digitally); ESPN Now (delivered digitally); Fresh (delivered digitally); Shorteez (delivered digitally); Playboy TV (delivered digitally); iN DEMAND (delivered digitally); Pleasure (delivered digitally); Fresh; Playboy TV; Pleasure; Hot Choice (delivered digitally); iN DEMAND.
Internet Service
Operational: Yes.
Subscribers: 896,120.
Broadband Service: Road Runner.
Fee: $29.95 monthly.
Telephone Service
Digital: Operational
Subscribers: 477,759.
Fee: $32.95 monthly.
Miles of Plant: 36,231.0 (coaxial); 9,287.0 (fiber optic). Homes passed: 1,748,217.
Division President: J. Christian Fenger. Vice President & General Manager: Michel Champagne. Senior Operations Director: Mark Clark. Engineering Director: Fred Celi. Senior Customer Service Director: Susan Bonsor. Marketing Director: Sue Ruwe. Program Director: Jeff Pashley. Chief Financial Officer: William Futera.
Ownership: Bright House Networks LLC (MSO).

ORLANDO—Bright House Networks. Now served by ORLANDO, FL [FL0001]. ICA: FL0113.

ORTONA—Formerly served by Comcast Cable. No longer in operation. ICA: FL0262.

OSCEOLA COUNTY (portions)—Comcast Cable. Now served by ARCHER, FL [FL0189]. ICA: FL0094.

OSCEOLA COUNTY (western portion)—Comcast Cable. Now served by ARCHER, FL [FL0189]. ICA: FL0139.

OZELLO—Formerly served by KLiP Interactive. No longer in operation. ICA: FL0263.

PAISLEY—Florida Fiber Networks, 301 South Collins St, Ste 105, Plant City, FL 33563. Phones: 888-860-4088; 352-702-4990. E-mail: info@flfibernet.com. Web Site: http://www.flfibernet.com. Also serves Lake County (eastern portion). ICA: FL0248.
TV Market Ranking: 55 (Lake County (eastern portion), PAISLEY). Franchise award date: May 3, 1988. Franchise expiration date: N.A. Began: N.A.
Channel capacity: N.A. Channels available but not in use: N.A.
Basic Service
Subscribers: N.A.
Programming (received off-air): WACX (IND) Leesburg; WESH (MeTV, NBC) Daytona Beach; WFTV (ABC, Escape) Orlando; WKCF (CW, Estrella TV, This TV) Clermont; WKMG-TV (CBS, Retro TV) Orlando; WOFL (Bounce TV, FOX) Orlando; WRBW (Buzzr, Heroes & Icons, MNT, Movies!) Orlando; WUCF-TV (ETV) Orlando.
Programming (via satellite): A&E; AMC; Animal Planet; Cartoon Network; CMT; CNBC; CNN; Comedy Central; C-SPAN; Discovery Channel; E! HD; ESPN; ESPN2; EWTN Global Catholic Network; Food Network; Fox News Channel; Fox Sports 1; FOX Sports Florida/Sun Sports; Freeform; FX; HGTV; History; HLN; Lifetime; MSNBC; MTV; Nickelodeon; Spike TV; Syfy; TBS; The Weather Channel; TLC; TNT; Travel Channel; Trinity Broadcasting Network (TBN); Turner Classic Movies; TV Land; USA Network; VH1; WGN America.
Fee: $30.00 installation; $38.45 monthly.
Pay Service 1
Pay Units: N.A.
Programming (via satellite): HBO; Showtime; The Movie Channel.
Fee: $10.95 monthly (each).
Video-On-Demand: No

Cable Systems—Florida

Internet Service
Operational: No.
Telephone Service
None
Miles of Plant: 67.0 (coaxial); None (fiber optic). Homes passed: 1,629.
Chief Executive Officer: David Suarez. Chief Marketing Officer: David Orshan.
Ownership: Florida Fiber Networks (MSO).

PALATKA—Comcast Cable. Now served by JACKSONVILLE, FL [FL0002]. ICA: FL0076.

PALM BAY—Comcast Cable. Now served by WEST PALM BEACH, FL [FL0008]. ICA: FL0377.

PALM BEACH COUNTY (portions)—Comcast Cable. Now served by WEST PALM BEACH, FL [FL0008]. ICA: FL0057.

PALM BEACH COUNTY (southeastern portion)—Comcast Cable. Now served by WEST PALM BEACH, FL [FL0008]. ICA: FL0264.

PALM BEACH GARDENS—Comcast Cable. Now served by WEST PALM BEACH, FL [FL0008]. ICA: FL0030.

PALM CAY—Cablevision of Marion County. Now served by MARION COUNTY (unincorporated areas), FL [FL0368]. ICA: FL0311.

PALM CHASE—Formerly served by Comcast Cable. No longer in operation. ICA: FL0265.

PALM COAST—Bright House Networks. Now served by ORLANDO, FL [FL0001]. ICA: FL0097.

PALM SPRINGS—Comcast Cable. Now served by WEST PALM BEACH, FL [FL0008]. ICA: FL0266.

PANAMA CITY—Comcast Cable. Now served by TALLAHASSEE, FL [FL0283]. ICA: FL0267.

PANAMA CITY BEACH—Comcast Cable. Now served by TALLAHASSEE, FL [FL0283]. ICA: FL0075.

PANAMA CITY BEACH—WOW! Internet, Cable & Phone, 7887 East Belleview Ave, Ste 1000, Englewood, CO 80111. Phones: 720-479-3500; 850-215-6100; 706-645-8553 (Corporate office); 850-215-1000. Fax: 720-479-3585. E-mail: wow_general@wideopenwest.com. Web Site: http://www.wowway.com. Also serves Callaway, Cedar Grove, Lynn Haven, Panama City, Parker & Springfield. ICA: FL0336. **Note:** This system is an overbuild.
TV Market Ranking: Below 100 (Callaway, Cedar Grove, Lynn Haven, Panama City, PANAMA CITY BEACH, Parker, Springfield).
Channel capacity: 80 (operating 2-way). Channels available but not in use: N.A.
Basic Service
Subscribers: 15,318.
Programming (received off-air): WBIF (IND) Marianna; WFSG (PBS) Panama City; WJHG-TV (CW, MNT, NBC) Panama City; WMBB (ABC, This TV) Panama City; WPCT (IND) Panama City Beach; WPGX (FOX) Panama City; WTVY (CBS, CW, MeTV, MNT, This TV) Dothan.
Programming (via satellite): A&E; AMC; Animal Planet; BET; Bravo; Cartoon Network; CMT; CNBC; CNN; Comedy Central;

C-SPAN; C-SPAN 2; CW PLUS; Discovery Channel; Disney Channel; Disney XD; E! HD; ESPN; ESPN2; EVINE Live; EWTN Global Catholic Network; Food Network; Fox News Channel; Fox Sports 1; FOX Sports Florida/Sun Sports; Freeform; FX; Golf Channel; Hallmark Channel; HGTV; History; HLN; INSP; Lifetime; LMN; MoviePlex; MSNBC; MTV; MyNetworkTV; NASA TV; NBCSN; Nick At Nite; Nickelodeon; Outdoor Channel; Oxygen; Pop; QVC; Spike TV; Syfy; TBS; The Weather Channel; TLC; TNT; Travel Channel; Trinity Broadcasting Network (TBN); truTV; Turner Classic Movies; TV Land; Univision Studios; USA Network; VH1; WE tv; Weatherscan; WGN America.
Fee: $50.00 installation; $33.00 monthly.
Digital Basic Service
Subscribers: N.A.
Programming (via satellite): AXS TV; BBC America; Bloomberg Television; Boomerang; CBS Sports Network; Church Channel; CMT; C-SPAN 3; Destination America; Discovery Kids Channel; Discovery Life Channel; ESPN HD; ESPN2 HD; ESPNews; ESPNU; FamilyNet; Florida Channel; FOX College Sports Central; FOX College Sports Pacific; Fox Sports 2; GSN; HD Theater; IFC; Investigation Discovery; Jewelry Television; JUCE TV; MC; MTV Classic; MTV Hits; MTV Jams; MTV2; mtvU; National Geographic Channel; NFL Network; Nick 2; Nick Jr.; Nicktoons; Ovation; OWN: Oprah Winfrey Network; Science Channel; Starz HD; TeenNick; Tennis Channel; TNT HD; Tr3s; Universal HD; VH1 Soul.
Pay Service 1
Pay Units: N.A.
Programming (via satellite): HBO (multiplexed); Showtime (multiplexed).
Fee: $7.95 monthly (Showtime), $9.95 monthly (HBO).
Digital Pay Service 1
Pay Units: N.A.
Programming (via satellite): Cinemax (multiplexed); Flix; HBO (multiplexed); HBO HD; Showtime (multiplexed); Starz (multiplexed); Starz Encore (multiplexed); Sundance TV; The Movie Channel (multiplexed).
Fee: $3.00 monthly (Encore), $4.50 monthly (Starz), $7.95 monthly (Showtime or Sundance/TMC), $8.95 monthly (Cinemax), $9.95 monthly (HBO).
Video-On-Demand: Yes
Pay-Per-View
Urban Xtra (delivered digitally); ESPN Now (delivered digitally); Spice: Xcess (delivered digitally); Club Jenna (delivered digitally); iN DEMAND (delivered digitally); Playboy TV (delivered digitally); Fresh (delivered digitally); Shorteez (delivered digitally).
Internet Service
Operational: Yes.
Subscribers: 20,148.
Fee: $29.95 installation; $59.95 monthly.
Telephone Service
Analog: Not Operational
Digital: Operational
Subscribers: 21,052.
Fee: $18.60 monthly
Miles of Plant: 1,454.0 (coaxial); 318.0 (fiber optic). Homes passed: 71,106.
Chief Executive Officer: Colleen Abdoulah.
Chief Financial Officer: Rich Fish. President: Steven Cochran.
Ownership: WideOpenWest LLC (MSO).

PASCO COUNTY (central & eastern portions)—Bright House Networks. Now served by HILLSBOROUGH COUNTY (portions), FL [FL0003]. ICA: FL0042.

PASCO COUNTY (western portion)—Bright House Networks. Now served by HILLSBOROUGH COUNTY (portions), FL [FL0003]. ICA: FL0009.

PEDRO—Cablevision of Marion County. Now served by MARION COUNTY (unincorporated areas), FL [FL0368]. ICA: FL0362.

PEMBROKE PINES—Comcast Cable. Now served by WEST PALM BEACH, FL [FL0008]. ICA: FL0372.

PENNEY FARMS—Florida Fiber Networks, 301 South Collins St, Ste 105, Plant City, FL 33563. Phones: 888-860-4088; 352-702-4990. E-mail: info@flfibernet.com. Web Site: http://www.flfibernet.com. ICA: FL0363.
TV Market Ranking: 68 (PENNEY FARMS).
Channel capacity: N.A. Channels available but not in use: N.A.
Basic Service
Subscribers: N.A.
Programming (received off-air): WCWJ (Bounce TV, CW) Jacksonville; WFOX-TV (FOX, MeTV, MNT) Jacksonville; WJAX-TV (CBS, Decades, getTV) Jacksonville; WJCT (PBS) Jacksonville; WJEB-TV (TBN) Jacksonville; WJXT (LATV, This TV) Jacksonville; WJXX (ABC) Orange Park; WTLV (Antenna TV, NBC, The Country Network) Jacksonville; WUFT (PBS) Gainesville.
Programming (via satellite): A&E; AMC; Cartoon Network; CNBC; CNN; Comedy Central; Discovery Channel; Disney Channel; ESPN; Food Network; Fox News Channel; Fox Sports 1; Freeform; Fuse; FX; Great American Country; HLN; Lifetime; QVC; Syfy; TBS; The Weather Channel; TNT; Travel Channel; Turner Classic Movies; USA Network; WGN America.
Fee: $32.45 monthly.
Pay Service 1
Pay Units: N.A.
Programming (via satellite): Cinemax; HBO; Showtime; The Movie Channel.
Internet Service
Operational: No.
Telephone Service
None
Miles of Plant: 40.0 (coaxial); None (fiber optic). Homes passed: 1,359.
Chief Executive Officer: David Suarez. Chief Marketing Officer: David Orshan.
Ownership: Florida Fiber Networks (MSO).

PENSACOLA—Cox Communications, 6205 Peachtree Dunwoody Rd, 12th Floor, Atlanta, GA 30328. Phone: 404-269-6590. Web Site: http://www.cox.com. Also serves Cinco Bayou, Crestview, Destin, Eglin AFB, Escambia County, Fort Walton Beach, Freeport, Hurlburt Field, Mary Esther, Niceville, Okaloosa County (portions), Okaloosa Island, Shalimar, University of West Florida & Walton County (portions). ICA: FL0018.

TV Market Ranking: 59 (Cinco Bayou, Escambia County (portions), Fort Walton Beach, Hurlburt Field, Mary Esther, Okaloosa Island, PENSACOLA, University of West Florida); Below 100 (Crestview, Destin, Eglin AFB, Niceville, Shalimar); Outside TV Markets (Escambia County (portions)). Franchise award date: January 26, 1967. Franchise expiration date: N.A. Began: January 1, 1969.
Channel capacity: N.A. Channels available but not in use: N.A.
Basic Service
Subscribers: 119,204 Includes Fort Walton Beach.
Programming (received off-air): WALA-TV (FOX) Mobile; WEAR-TV (ABC, The Country Network) Pensacola; WFGX (MNT, This TV) Fort Walton Beach; WFNA (Bounce TV, CW) Gulf Shores; WHBR (Christian TV Network) Pensacola; WJTC (IND) Pensacola; WKRG-TV (CBS, MeTV) Mobile; WMPV-TV (TBN) Mobile; WPAN (Soul of the South) Fort Walton Beach [LICENSED & SILENT]; WPMI-TV (NBC) Mobile; WSRE (PBS) Pensacola.
Programming (via satellite): C-SPAN; C-SPAN 2; Pop; QVC; TBS; WGN America.
Fee: $56.50 installation; $23.99 monthly; $1.25 converter.
Expanded Basic Service 1
Subscribers: N.A.
Programming (via satellite): A&E; AMC; Animal Planet; BET; Bravo; Cartoon Network; CMT; CNBC; CNN; Comedy Central; Discovery Channel; Disney Channel; E! HD; ESPN; ESPN2; EVINE Live; Food Network; Fox News Channel; Fox Sports 1; FOX Sports Florida/Sun Sports; Freeform; FX; Golf Channel; HGTV; History; HLN; Lifetime; MSNBC; MTV; NBCSN; Nickelodeon; Oxygen; Spike TV; Syfy; The Weather Channel; TLC; TNT; Travel Channel; Turner Classic Movies; TV Land; USA Network; VH1.
Fee: $31.69 monthly.
Digital Basic Service
Subscribers: N.A.
Programming (via satellite): BBC America; Bloomberg Television; Discovery Digital Networks; Disney XD; ESPN; ESPNews; EWTN Global Catholic Network; Golf Channel; Great American Country; GSN; HD Theater; IFC; LMN; MC; NBA TV; Sundance TV; TNT; Universal HD; Univision.
Pay Service 1
Pay Units: N.A.
Programming (via satellite): Cinemax (multiplexed); HBO (multiplexed); Showtime (multiplexed); The Movie Channel.
Fee: $11.00 monthly (each).
Digital Pay Service 1
Pay Units: N.A.
Programming (via satellite): Cinemax (multiplexed); HBO (multiplexed); HBO HD; Showtime (multiplexed); Showtime HD; Starz (multiplexed); Starz Encore.
Fee: $11.00 monthly (each).
Video-On-Demand: Planned
Pay-Per-View
Hot Choice; iN DEMAND; iN DEMAND (delivered digitally); Fresh; Shorteez.

Florida—Cable Systems

Internet Service
Operational: Yes.
Subscribers: 197,899.
Broadband Service: Cox High Speed Internet.
Fee: $149.00 installation; $19.95-$59.95 monthly; $15.00 modem lease; $175.00 modem purchase.

Telephone Service
Digital: Operational
Subscribers: 47,628.
Fee: $10.99-$44.79 monthly
Miles of Plant: 4,994.0 (coaxial); 1,335.0 (fiber optic). Homes passed: 253,087. Miles of plant & homes passed include Fort Walton Beach.
Vice President & General Manager: Keith Gregory. Vice President, Network Operations: Mark O'Ceallaigh. Vice President, Marketing: Dale Tapley. Vice President, Tax: Mary Vickers. Government & Public Affairs Director: Sheila Nichols. Marketing Manager: Bob Hartnett.
Ownership: Cox Communications Inc. (MSO).

PERRY—Comcast Cable. Now served by TALLAHASSEE, FL [FL0283]. ICA: FL0269.

PINELLAS COUNTY (portions)—Bright House Networks. Now served by HILLSBOROUGH COUNTY (portions), FL [FL0003]. ICA: FL0005.

PINELLAS COUNTY (portions)—WOW! Internet, Cable & Phone, 7887 East Belleview Ave, Ste 1000, Englewood, CO 80111. Phones: 720-479-3500; 727-239-0211; 727-239-1000 (Customer service); 706-645-8553 (Corporate office). Fax: 720-479-3585. E-mail: wow_general@wideopenwest.com. Web Site: http://www.wowway.com. Also serves Clearwater, Dunedin, Largo, Oldsmar, Safety Harbor, Seminole, St. Petersburg & Tarpon Springs. ICA: FL0339. **Note:** This system is an overbuild.
TV Market Ranking: 28 (Clearwater, Dunedin, Largo, Oldsmar, PINELLAS COUNTY (PORTIONS), Safety Harbor, Seminole, St. Petersburg, Tarpon Springs).
Channel capacity: N.A. Channels available but not in use: N.A.

Basic Service
Subscribers: 13,144.
Programming (received off-air): WCLF (Christian TV Network) Clearwater; WEDU (PBS) Tampa; WFLA-TV (MeTV, NBC) Tampa; WFTS-TV (ABC, Grit, Laff) Tampa; WFTT-DT (getTV, UniMas) Tampa; WMOR-TV (Estrella TV, This TV) Lakeland; WTOG (CW, Decades) St. Petersburg; WTSP (CBS) St. Petersburg; WTTA (COZI TV, MNT) St. Petersburg; WTVT (Buzzr, FOX, Heroes & Icons, Movies!) Tampa; WUSF-TV (PBS) Tampa; WVEA-TV (Bounce TV, LATV, UNV) Venice.
Programming (via satellite): A&E; AMC; Animal Planet; BET; Bravo; Cartoon Network; CMT; CNBC; CNN; Comedy Central; C-SPAN; Discovery Channel; Discovery Life Channel; Disney Channel; E! HD; ESPN; ESPN Classic; ESPN2; EVINE Live; Food Network; Fox News Channel; Fox Sports 1; FOX Sports Florida/Sun Sports; Freeform; FX; FYI; Golf Channel; GSN; Hallmark Channel; HGTV; History; HLN; ION Television; Lifetime; LMN; Local Cable Weather; MTV; National Geographic Channel; NBCSN; Nickelodeon; Outdoor Channel; OWN: Oprah Winfrey Network; Oxygen; QVC; Spike TV; Syfy; TBS; The Weather Channel; TLC; TNT; Travel Channel; truTV; Turner Classic Movies; TV Land; Univision; USA Network; VH1; WGN America.
Fee: $50.00 installation; $33.00 monthly.

Digital Basic Service
Subscribers: N.A.
Programming (via satellite): Animal Planet HD; AXS TV; BBC America; Boomerang; CBS Sports Network; CMT; C-SPAN 2; C-SPAN 3; Destination America; Discovery Channel HD; Discovery Kids Channel; DIY Network; ESPN HD; ESPN2 HD; ESPNews; ESPNU; EWTN Global Catholic Network; Florida Channel; FOX College Sports Central; FOX College Sports Pacific; Fox Sports 2; FSN HD; Fuse; Hallmark Movies & Mysteries; HD Theater; History International; IFC; INSP; Investigation Discovery; Jewelry Television; MC; MSNBC; MTV Classic; MTV Hits; MTV Jams; MTV2; mtvU; National Geographic Channel HD; NFL Network; NFL Network HD; Nick 2; Nick Jr.; Nicktoons; QVC HD; Science Channel; TBS HD; TeenNick; Telemundo; Tennis Channel; TLC HD; TNT HD; Tr3s; Trinity Broadcasting Network (TBN); Universal HD; Versus HD; VH1 Soul; Vme TV; WE tv; Weatherscan; World.

Digital Pay Service 1
Pay Units: N.A.
Programming (via satellite): Cinemax (multiplexed); Cinemax HD; Flix; HBO (multiplexed); HBO HD; Playboy TV; Showtime (multiplexed); Showtime HD; Starz (multiplexed); Starz Encore (multiplexed); Starz HD; The Movie Channel (multiplexed).

Video-On-Demand: No

Pay-Per-View
iN DEMAND (delivered digitally); ESPN (delivered digitally); Hot Choice (delivered digitally); Spice: Xcess (delivered digitally); Playboy TV (delivered digitally); Club Jenna (delivered digitally); SexSee (delivered digitally).

Internet Service
Operational: Yes.
Subscribers: 16,000.
Fee: $29.95 installation; $54.95 monthly.

Telephone Service
Digital: Operational
Subscribers: 10,719.
Fee: $18.91 monthly
Miles of Plant: 5,417.0 (coaxial); 853.0 (fiber optic). Homes passed: 277,914. Miles of plant (coax) includes miles of plant (fiber).
Chief Executive Officer: Colleen Abdoulah. President: Steven Cochran. Chief Financial Officer: Rich Fish.
Ownership: WideOpenWest LLC (MSO).

POLK COUNTY (portions)—Formerly served by People's Wireless Cable. No longer in operation. ICA: FL0307.

PORT CHARLOTTE—Comcast Cable. Now served by SARASOTA, FL [FL0017]. ICA: FL0044.

PORT ST. JOE—Mediacom. Now served by EASTPOINT, FL [FL0180]. ICA: FL0142.

PUTNAM COUNTY—Formerly served by Florida Cable. No longer in operation. ICA: FL0272.

PUTNAM COUNTY (eastern portion)—Florida Fiber Networks, 301 South Collins St, Ste 105, Plant City, FL 33563. Phones: 888-860-4088; 352-702-4990. E-mail: info@flfibernet.com. Web Site: http://www.flfibernet.com. Also serves Bostwick & Palatka. ICA: FL0271.
TV Market Ranking: Below 100 (Bostwick, PUTNAM COUNTY (EASTERN PORTION) (portions)); Outside TV Markets (Palatka, PUTNAM COUNTY (EASTERN PORTION) (portions)).
Channel capacity: N.A. Channels available but not in use: N.A.

Basic Service
Subscribers: N.A.
Programming (received off-air): WCWJ (Bounce TV, CW) Jacksonville; WFOX-TV (FOX, MeTV, MNT) Jacksonville; WJAX-TV (CBS, Decades, getTV) Jacksonville; WJCT (PBS) Jacksonville; WJGV-CD (IND) Palatka; WJXT (LATV, This TV) Jacksonville; WJXX (ABC) Orange Park; WTLV (Antenna TV, NBC, The Country Network) Jacksonville; WUFT (PBS) Gainesville.
Programming (via satellite): A&E; Animal Planet; Cartoon Network; CNN; Comedy Central; C-SPAN; Discovery Channel; Disney Channel; ESPN; Food Network; Fox News Channel; Fox Sports 1; Freeform; Fuse; FX; Great American Country; HLN; Lifetime; Syfy; TBS; The Weather Channel; TNT; Travel Channel; USA Network; WGN America.
Fee: $39.45 monthly.

Pay Service 1
Pay Units: N.A.
Programming (via satellite): Cinemax; HBO; Showtime; The Movie Channel.
Fee: $9.95 monthly (each).

Internet Service
Operational: No.

Telephone Service
None
Miles of Plant: 45.0 (coaxial); None (fiber optic). Homes passed: 916.
Chief Executive Officer: David Suarez. Chief Marketing Officer: David Orshan.
Ownership: Florida Fiber Networks (MSO).

PUTNAM COUNTY (western portion)—Florida Fiber Networks, 301 South Collins St, Ste 105, Plant City, FL 33563. Phones: 888-860-4088; 352-702-4990. E-mail: info@flfibernet.com. Web Site: http://www.flfibernet.com. Also serves Hawthorne. ICA: FL0371.
TV Market Ranking: Below 100 (Hawthorne, PUTNAM COUNTY (WESTERN PORTION)).
Channel capacity: N.A. Channels available but not in use: N.A.

Basic Service
Subscribers: N.A.
Programming (received off-air): WCJB-TV (ABC, CW) Gainesville; WCWJ (Bounce TV, CW) Jacksonville; WESH (MeTV, NBC) Daytona Beach; WFOX-TV (FOX, MeTV, MNT) Jacksonville; WJAX-TV (CBS, Decades, getTV) Jacksonville; WJXT (LATV, This TV) Jacksonville; WJXX (ABC) Orange Park; WKMG-TV (CBS, Retro TV) Orlando; WOGX (Buzzr, FOX) Ocala; WTLV (Antenna TV, NBC, The Country Network) Jacksonville; WUFT (PBS) Gainesville.
Programming (via satellite): A&E; Animal Planet; BET; Cartoon Network; CNN; Comedy Central; Discovery Channel; Disney Channel; ESPN; Fox News Channel; Fox Sports 1; Freeform; Fuse; FX; Great American Country; HLN; Lifetime; QVC; Syfy; TBS; The Weather Channel; TNT; Turner Classic Movies; USA Network; WGN America.

Pay Service 1
Pay Units: N.A.
Programming (via satellite): Cinemax; HBO; Showtime.

Internet Service
Operational: No.

Telephone Service
None
Miles of Plant: 7.0 (coaxial); None (fiber optic). Homes passed: 1,083.
Chief Executive Officer: David Suarez. Chief Marketing Officer: David Orshan.
Ownership: Florida Fiber Networks (MSO).

QUINCY—Comcast Cable. Now served by TALLAHASSEE, FL [FL0283]. ICA: FL0273.

RIVER RANCH—SAT STAR Communications, 11449 Challenger Ave, Odessa, FL 33556. Phone: 800-445-1139. Web Site: http://www.satstartech.com. ICA: FL0161.
TV Market Ranking: 28 (RIVER RANCH). Franchise award date: December 1, 1989. Franchise expiration date: N.A. Began: June 1, 1990.
Channel capacity: N.A. Channels available but not in use: N.A.

Basic Service
Subscribers: N.A.
Programming (received off-air): WEDU (PBS) Tampa; WFLA-TV (MeTV, NBC) Tampa; WFTS-TV (ABC, Grit, Laff) Tampa; WFTV (ABC, Escape) Orlando; WKMG-TV (CBS, Retro TV) Orlando; WMOR-TV (Estrella TV, This TV) Lakeland; WOPX-TV (ION, Movies!) Melbourne; WTOG (CW, Decades) St. Petersburg; WTVT (Buzzr, FOX, Heroes & Icons, Movies!) Tampa.
Programming (via satellite): A&E; AMC; CMT; CNBC; CNN; C-SPAN; Discovery Channel; Disney Channel; ESPN; Freeform; HLN; Lifetime; QVC; Spike TV; Syfy; TBS; The Weather Channel; TNT; Travel Channel; USA Network; WGN America.
Fee: $40.00 installation.

Pay Service 1
Pay Units: N.A.
Programming (via satellite): HBO; Showtime; Starz Encore; The Movie Channel.
Fee: $6.95 monthly (Encore), $10.95 monthly (Showtime or TMC), $12.95 monthly (HBO).

Internet Service
Operational: No.

Telephone Service
None
Miles of Plant: 1.0 (coaxial); None (fiber optic).
Vice President, Operations: George Gioe.
Ownership: SAT STAR Communications LLC.

SAMSULA—Formerly served by Consolidated Cablevision. No longer in operation. ICA: FL0287.

SANDESTIN BEACH RESORT—Mediacom. Now served by WALTON COUNTY (portions), FL [FL0159]. ICA: FL0276.

SAND-N-SEA—Formerly served by Formerly served by Comcast Cable. No longer in operation. ICA: FL0275.

SARALAKE ESTATES MOBILE HOME PARK—Formerly served by Nalman Electronics. No longer in operation. ICA: FL0277.

SARASOTA—Comcast Cable, 5205 Fruitville Rd, Sarasota, FL 34232. Phone: 941-371-6700 (Customer service). Fax: 941-371-5097. Web Site: http://www.comcast.com. Also serves Alva, Arcadia, Avon Park, Bartow, Boca Grande, Boca Grande Island, Bonita Beach, Bonita Springs, Burnt Store Marina, Cape Coral, Cape Haze, Captiva Island, Charlotte County (portions), Charlotte Harbor, Cleveland, Collier County (portions), DeSoto County (portions), El Jobean, Englewood, Es-

Cable Systems—Florida

tero, Everglades City, Fort Meade, Fort Myers, Fort Myers Beach, Fort Ogden, Frostproof, Glades County (portions), Golden Gate, Hendry County (portions), Highlands County (portions), Hillcrest Heights, Immokalee, La Belle, Lake Placid, Lake Wales, Lehigh Acres, Longboat Key, Manatee County (portions), Marco Island, Murdock, Naples, North Fort Myers, North Port, Pine Island, Plantation (Sarasota County), Port Charlotte, Punta Gorda, Sanibel Island, Sarasota County (portions), Sebring (village), Venice, Waterford & West Arcadia. ICA: FL0017.

TV Market Ranking: 28 (Bartow, Fort Meade, Frostproof, Hillcrest Heights, Lake Wales, Longboat Key, Manatee County (portions), SARASOTA, Sarasota County (portions), Waterford); Below 100 (Alva, Boca Grande, Boca Grande Island, Bonita Beach, Bonita Springs, Burnt Store Marina, Cape Coral, Cape Haze, Captiva Island, Charlotte County (portions), Charlotte Harbor, Cleveland, El Jobean, Estero, Everglades City, Fort Myers, Fort Myers Beach, Fort Ogden, Golden Gate, Immokalee, La Belle, Lehigh Acres, Marco Island, Murdock, North Fort Myers, North Port, Pine Island, Plantation (Sarasota County), Punta Gorda, Sanibel Island, West Arcadia, Collier County (portions), DeSoto County (portions), Englewood, Glades County (portions), Hendry County (portions), Naples, Port Charlotte, Venice, Manatee County (portions), Sarasota County (portions)); Outside TV Markets (Avon Park, Highlands County (portions), Lake Placid, Arcadia, DeSoto County (portions), Glades County (portions), Hendry County (portions), Sebring (village)). Franchise award date: August 1, 1962. Franchise expiration date: N.A. Began: January 1, 1962.

Channel capacity: 22 (operating 2-way). Channels available but not in use: N.A.

Basic Service
Subscribers: 301,594. Commercial subscribers: 151,044.
Programming (received off-air): WCLF (Christian TV Network) Clearwater; WEDU (PBS) Tampa; WFLA-TV (MeTV, NBC) Tampa; WFTS-TV (ABC, Grit, Laff) Tampa; WMOR-TV (Estrella TV, This TV) Lakeland; WTOG (CW, Decades) St. Petersburg; WTSP (CBS) St. Petersburg; WTTA (COZI TV, MNT) St. Petersburg; WTVT (Buzzr, FOX, Heroes & Icons, Movies!) Tampa; WUSF-TV (PBS) Tampa; WVEA-TV (Bounce TV, LATV, UNV) Venice; WWSB (ABC) Sarasota; WXPX-TV (ION) Bradenton; 16 FMs.
Programming (via satellite): C-SPAN; FOX Sports Networks; FX; Jewelry Television; Pop; QVC; WGN America.
Fee: $43.75-$64.95 installation; $27.20 monthly.

Expanded Basic Service 1
Subscribers: N.A.
Programming (via satellite): A&E; AMC; Animal Planet; BET; Bravo; Cartoon Network; CMT; CNBC; CNN; Comcast/Charter Sports Southeast (CSS); Comedy Central; C-SPAN 2; Discovery Channel; E! HD; ESPN; ESPN2; Food Network; Fox News Channel; Fox Sports 1; FOX Sports Florida/Sun Sports; Freeform; Golf Channel; GSN; HGTV; History; HLN; Lifetime; MSNBC; MTV; NBCSN; Nickelodeon; OWN: Oprah Winfrey Network; Spike TV; Syfy; TBS; The Weather Channel; TLC; TNT; truTV; Turner Classic Movies; TV Land; USA Network; VH1; WE tv.
Fee: $34.95 monthly.

Digital Basic Service
Subscribers: N.A.
Programming (via satellite): A&E HD; Animal Planet HD; AXS TV; BBC America; BTN; Cartoon Network; CMT; CNN HD; Cooking Channel; C-SPAN 2; C-SPAN 3; Destination America; Discovery Channel HD; Discovery Kids Channel; Disney Channel; Disney Channel HD; Disney XD; DIY Network; ESPN HD; ESPN2 HD; ESPNews; EVINE Live; EWTN Global Catholic Network; Flix; Food Network HD; Fox Business Network; FOX College Sports Central; FOX College Sports Florida/Sun Sports; Freeform HD; Fuse; FX HD; FYI; Golf Channel HD; GolTV; Great American Country; GSN; Hallmark Movies & Mysteries; HGTV HD; History; History HD; History International; IFC; Investigation Discovery; Jewelry Television; LMN; LOGO; MC; MLB Network; MoviePlex; MTV Classic; MTV Hits; MTV2; Nat Geo WILD; National Geographic Channel; National Geographic Channel HD; NBA TV; NFL Network; NHL Network; Nick 2; Nick Jr.; Nicktoons; Outdoor Channel; Oxygen; RTV; Science Channel; Science HD; Sprout; Starz Encore (multiplexed); Sundance TV; Syfy HD; TBS HD; TeenNick; Tennis Channel; TLC HD; TNT HD; Tr3s; TV One; TVG Network; Universal HD; USA Network HD; Versus HD; VH1 Soul; WE tv.

Digital Pay Service 1
Pay Units: N.A.
Programming (via satellite): Cinemax (multiplexed); Cinemax HD; HBO (multiplexed); HBO HD; Showtime (multiplexed); Showtime HD; Starz (multiplexed); Starz HD; The Movie Channel (multiplexed).
Fee: $13.50 monthly (each).

Video-On-Demand: Yes

Pay-Per-View
iN DEMAND (delivered digitally); Playboy TV (delivered digitally); Fresh (delivered digitally); Shorteez (delivered digitally); Pleasure (delivered digitally).

Internet Service
Operational: Yes.
Subscribers: 303,881.
Broadband Service: Comcast High Speed Internet.
Fee: $42.95 monthly; $7.00 modem lease; $199.00 modem purchase.

Telephone Service
Digital: Operational
Subscribers: 141,524.
Fee: $44.95 monthly

Miles of Plant: 6,723.0 (coaxial); 2,250.0 (fiber optic). Homes passed: 873,337.
Regional Vice President: Rod Dagenais. Vice President & General Manager: Steve Dvoskin. Technical Operations Director: Danny Maxwell. Marketing Director: Vince Maffeo. Technical Operations Manager: Andrew Behn.
Ownership: Comcast Cable Communications Inc. (MSO).

SEBASTIAN—Comcast Cable. Now served by WEST PALM BEACH, FL [FL0008]. ICA: FL0077.

SEBRING (village)—Comcast Cable. Now served by SARASOTA, FL [FL0017]. ICA: FL0063.

SHARPES FERRY—Florida Fiber Networks, 301 South Collins St, Ste 105, Plant City, FL 33563. Phones: 888-860-4088; 352-702-4990. E-mail: info@flfibernet.com. Web Site: http://www.flfibernet.com. ICA: FL0365.

TV Market Ranking: Below 100 (SHARPES FERRY).
Channel capacity: N.A. Channels available but not in use: N.A.

Basic Service
Subscribers: N.A.
Programming (received off-air): WACX (IND) Leesburg; WCJB-TV (ABC, CW) Gainesville; WESH (MeTV, NBC) Daytona Beach; WFTV (ABC, Escape) Orlando; WKCF (CW, Estrella TV, This TV) Clermont; WKMG-TV (CBS, Retro TV) Orlando; WOFL (Bounce TV, FOX) Orlando; WOGX (Buzzr, FOX) Ocala; WRBW (Buzzr, Heroes & Icons, MNT, Movies!) Orlando; WUFT (PBS) Gainesville.
Programming (via satellite): A&E; Cartoon Network; CNN; Comedy Central; Discovery Channel; Disney Channel; ESPN; Food Network; Fox News Channel; Fox Sports 1; Freeform; FX; Great American Country; HLN; Lifetime; Spike TV; Syfy; TBS; The Weather Channel; Turner Classic Movies; USA Network; WGN America.
Fee: $39.45 monthly.

Pay Service 1
Pay Units: N.A.
Programming (via satellite): Cinemax; HBO; Showtime.

Internet Service
Operational: No.

Telephone Service
None
Miles of Plant: 20.0 (coaxial); None (fiber optic). Homes passed: 550.
Chief Executive Officer: David Suarez. Chief Marketing Officer: David Orshan.
Ownership: Florida Fiber Networks (MSO).

SILVER SPRINGS SHORES—Formerly served by Comcast Cable. No longer in operation. ICA: FL0112.

SMITH LAKE SHORES MOBILE HOME PARK—Formerly served by Florida Cable. No longer in operation. ICA: FL0366.

SOUTH BROWARD COUNTY—Formerly served by Comcast Cable. No longer in operation. ICA: FL0374.

SOUTHPORT—Mediacom. Now served by WALTON COUNTY (portions), FL [FL0159]. ICA: FL0119.

SPRING LAKE—Comcast Cable. Now served by WAUCHULA, FL [FL0288]. ICA: FL0280.

SPRINGFIELD—Formerly served by FiberCast Cable. No longer in operation. ICA: FL0122.

SPRUCE CREEK NORTH—Formerly served by Galaxy Cablevision. No longer in operation. ICA: FL0367.

ST. AUGUSTINE—Comcast Cable. Now served by JACKSONVILLE, FL [FL0002]. ICA: FL0059.

ST. GEORGE ISLAND—St. George Cable Inc, PO Box 1090, St. George Island, FL 32328. Phone: 850-927-3200. Fax: 850-927-2060. E-mail: charles@stgeorgecable.com. Web Site: http://www.stgeorgecable.com. ICA: FL0384.
TV Market Ranking: Outside TV Markets (ST. GEORGE ISLAND).
Channel capacity: N.A. Channels available but not in use: N.A.
Miles of Plant: 64.0 (coaxial); None (fiber optic). Homes passed: 2,200.
Ownership: St. George Cable Inc.

STEINHATCHEE—Formerly served by Altitude Communications. No longer in operation. ICA: FL0179.

STUART—Circle Bay Yacht Club Condo Assoc Inc, 1950 SW Palm City Rd, Stuart, FL 34994. Phones: 772-287-1002; 772-287-0990. Fax: 772-287-1002. E-mail: office@circlebay.net. Web Site: http://circlebay.net. ICA: FL0383.
TV Market Ranking: Below 100 (STUART).
Channel capacity: N.A. Channels available but not in use: N.A.
Basic Service
Subscribers: 295.
Fee: $1.20 monthly.
Treasurer: E. Hudgins. Secretary: Glenn H. Meyer.
Ownership: Circle Bay Yacht Club Condominium Association Inc.

STUART—Comcast Cable. Now served by WEST PALM BEACH, FL [FL0008]. ICA: FL0024.

SUMTER COUNTY—Formerly served by Florida Cable. Now served by Florida Fiber Networks, HERNANDO COUNTY, FL [FL0148]. ICA: FL0369.

SUNNY HILLS—Formerly served by Community Cable. No longer in operation. ICA: FL0200.

SUWANNEE CAMPGROUND—Formerly served by KLiP Interactive. No longer in operation. ICA: FL0351.

SWEETWATER GOLF & TENNIS CLUB EAST—Formerly served by Sweetwater Golf & Tennis Club East Inc. No longer in operation. ICA: FL0318.

SWEETWATER OAKS—Formerly served by Galaxy Cablevision. No longer in operation. ICA: FL0370.

TALLAHASSEE—Comcast Cable, 3760 Hartsfield Rd, Tallahassee, FL 32303-1121. Phones: 850-574-4000; 850-574-4016. Fax: 850-574-4030. Web Site: http://www.comcast.com. Also serves Abbeville, Ashford, Avon, Cottonwood, Cowarts, Dothan, Headland, Henry County (portions), Houston County (portions), Kinsey, Madrid & Newville, AL; Alford, Bascom, Bay County (portions), Calhoun County (portions), Call-

Florida—Cable Systems

away, Cedar Grove, Cottondale, Crawfordville, Gadsden County (portions), Grand Ridge, Greenwood, Jackson County (portions), Killearn Lakes, Leon County (portions), Lynn Haven, Madison, Madison County (portions), Malone, Marianna, Midway, Noma, Panama City, Panama City Beach, Parker, Perry, Quincy, Sneads, Sopchoppy, Springfield, St. Mark's, Taylor County (portions) & Wakulla, FL; Brooks County (portions) & Quitman, GA. ICA: FL0283.

TV Market Ranking: Below 100 (Alford, Ashford, Avon, Bascom, Bay County (portions), Brooks County (portions), Calhoun County (portions), Callaway, Cedar Grove, Cottondale, Cottonwood, Cowarts, Crawfordville, Dothan, Gadsden County (portions), Grand Ridge, Greenwood, Headland, Henry County (portions), Houston County (portions), Jackson County (portions), Killearn Lakes, Kinsey, Leon County (portions), Lynn Haven, Madrid, Malone, Midway, Newville, Noma, Panama City Beach, Parker, Quincy, Sneads, Sopchoppy, Springfield, St. Mark's, TALLAHASSEE, Wakulla, Abbeville, Madison, Madison County (portions), Marianna, Panama City, Quitman, Taylor County (portions)); Outside TV Markets (Madison County (portions), Perry, Taylor County (portions)). Franchise award date: N.A. Franchise expiration date: N.A. Began: January 1, 1962.

Channel capacity: N.A. Channels available but not in use: N.A.

Basic Service
Subscribers: 108,700. Commercial subscribers: 10,051.
Programming (received off-air): WABW-TV (PBS) Pelham; WBXT-LD (IND) Tallahassee; WCTV (CBS, MNT, This TV) Thomasville; WFSU-TV (PBS) Tallahassee; WTLF (CW) Tallahassee; WTLH (CW, FOX, MeTV) Bainbridge; WTWC-TV (NBC, The Country Network) Tallahassee; WTXL-TV (ABC, Bounce TV) Tallahassee; 12 FMs.
Programming (via satellite): A&E; AMC; Animal Planet; BET; Bravo; Cartoon Network; CMT; CNBC; CNN; Comcast/Charter Sports Southeast (CSS); Comedy Central; Concert TV; C-SPAN; C-SPAN 3; Discovery Channel; E! HD; ESPN; ESPN Classic; ESPN2; Food Network; Fox News Channel; Fox Sports 1; FOX Sports Florida/Sun Sports; Freeform; FX; Golf Channel; Great American Country; GSN; HGTV; History; HLN; HSN2; ION Television; Lifetime; MSNBC; MTV; NBCSN; Nickelodeon; OWN: Oprah Winfrey Network; Pop; QVC; Spike TV; Syfy; TBS; The Weather Channel; TLC; TNT; truTV; Turner Classic Movies; TV Land; Univision Studios; USA Network; VH1; Weatherscan; WGN America.
Fee: $29.50-$50.00 installation; $69.20 monthly.

Digital Basic Service
Subscribers: N.A.
Programming (via satellite): BBC America; C-SPAN 3; Discovery Digital Networks; Disney Channel; Disney XD; ESPNews; EWTN Global Catholic Network; Flix; INSP; MC; National Geographic Channel; Nick 2; Nick Jr.; Sundance TV; TeenNick; The Word Network; Trinity Broadcasting Network (TBN).

Pay Service 1
Pay Units: N.A.
Programming (via satellite): HBO; Showtime.
Fee: $9.95 monthly (Showtime), $13.95 monthly (HBO).

Digital Pay Service 1
Pay Units: N.A.
Programming (via satellite): Cinemax (multiplexed); HBO (multiplexed); Showtime (multiplexed); Starz (multiplexed); The Movie Channel (multiplexed).
Video-On-Demand: Yes
Pay-Per-View
iN DEMAND; iN DEMAND (delivered digitally); Playboy TV (delivered digitally); Fresh (delivered digitally); Shorteez (delivered digitally); Pleasure (delivered digitally).
Internet Service
Operational: Yes.
Subscribers: 95,266.
Broadband Service: Comcast High Speed Internet.
Fee: $149.00 installation; $42.95 monthly; $7.00 modem lease; $199.00 modem purchase.
Telephone Service
Digital: Operational
Subscribers: 42,094.
Miles of Plant: 7,930.0 (coaxial); 1,192.0 (fiber optic). Homes passed: 278,763. Miles of plant (coax) & homes passed include Jasper & Monticello.
Regional Vice President: Rod Dagenais. General Manager: K. C. McWilliams. Marketing Director: Claire Evans. Engineering Manager: Mike Gainey.
Ownership: Comcast Cable Communications Inc. (MSO).

TAMPA—Formerly served by V TV Video Television. No longer in operation. ICA: FL0309.

TEQUESTA—Comcast Cable. Now served by WEST PALM BEACH, FL [FL0008]. ICA: FL0284.

TRENTON—Comcast Cable. Now served by ARCHER, FL [FL0189]. ICA: FL0188.

TYNDALL AFB—Mediacom. Now served by WALTON COUNTY (portions), FL [FL0159]. ICA: FL0143.

VALPARAISO—Valparaiso Communications System, 465 Valparaiso Pkwy, Valparaiso, FL 32580-1274. Phones: 850-729-5404; 850-389-3026. Fax: 850-678-4553. E-mail: support@valp.net. Web Site: http://www.valp.net. ICA: FL0145.
TV Market Ranking: Below 100 (VALPARAISO). Franchise award date: N.A. Franchise expiration date: N.A. Began: June 12, 1976.
Channel capacity: N.A. Channels available but not in use: N.A.

Basic Service
Subscribers: N.A.
Programming (received off-air): WALA-TV (FOX) Mobile; WEAR-TV (ABC, The Country Network) Pensacola; WFBD (America One) Destin; WFGX (MNT, This TV) Fort Walton Beach; WFNA (Bounce TV, CW) Gulf Shores; WJHG-TV (CW, MNT, NBC) Panama City; WJTC (IND) Pensacola; WKRG-TV (CBS, MeTV) Mobile; WPAN (Soul of the South) Fort Walton Beach [LICENSED & SILENT]; WPMI-TV (NBC) Mobile; WSRE (PBS) Pensacola; WTVY (CBS, CW, MeTV, MNT, This TV) Dothan; allband FM.
Programming (via satellite): A&E; AMC; Animal Planet; BET; Bravo; Cartoon Network; CMT; CNBC; CNN; Comedy Central; C-SPAN; C-SPAN 2; Discovery Channel; Disney Channel; Disney XD; DIY Network; ESPN; ESPN2; EWTN Global Catholic Network; Food Network; Fox News Channel; Freeform; FX; HGTV; History; HLN; INSP; Lifetime; MSNBC; MTV; National Geographic Channel; Nickelodeon; Pop; QVC; Spike TV; Syfy; TBS; The Weather Channel; TLC; TNT; Travel Channel; Trinity Broadcasting Network (TBN); Turner Classic Movies; TV Land; USA Network; VH1; WGN America.
Fee: Free installation.

Digital Basic Service
Subscribers: N.A.
Programming (via satellite): BBC America; Bloomberg Television; Chiller; Church Channel; Cloo; CMT; Cooking Channel; Destination America; Discovery Kids Channel; Discovery Life Channel; DMX Music; ESPNews; Fox Business Network; Fox Sports 1; Fuse; FXM; FYI; Golf Channel; GSN; History International; IFC; Investigation Discovery; JUCE TV; LMN; LOGO; MTV Classic; MTV Hits; MTV Jams; MTV2; Nat Geo WILD; NBCSN; Nick Jr.; Nicktoons; Outdoor Channel; Ovation; OWN: Oprah Winfrey Network; RFD-TV; Science Channel; Sprout; Starz Encore (multiplexed); TeenNick; TV One; TVG Network; VH1 Soul; WE tv.

Digital Pay Service 1
Pay Units: N.A.
Programming (via satellite): Cinemax (multiplexed); Flix; HBO (multiplexed); Showtime (multiplexed); Starz (multiplexed); Sundance TV; The Movie Channel (multiplexed).
Fee: $7.50 monthly (Cinemax), $10.50 monthly (Starz), $12.50 motnthly (HBO or Showtime/TMC/Sundance).
Video-On-Demand: No
Pay-Per-View
Playboy TV (delivered digitally); Fresh (delivered digitally); iN DEMAND (delivered digitally); Hot Choice (delivered digitally); Club Jenna (delivered digitally); Spice: Xcess (delivered digitally).
Internet Service
Operational: Yes. Began: July 1, 2000.
Broadband Service: Valparaiso Communication Systems.
Fee: $29.95-$44.95 installation; $10.00 modem lease; $99.95 modem purchase.
Telephone Service
Digital: Operational
Fee: $29.95-$49.95 monthly
Miles of Plant: 28.0 (coaxial); None (fiber optic). Homes passed: 1,850.
General Manager: Burt B. Bennett. Chief Technician: Jerry Richter.
Ownership: Valparaiso Communication Systems.

VENICE—Comcast Cable. Now served by SARASOTA, FL [FL0017]. ICA: FL0032.

VERO BEACH—Comcast Cable. Now served by WEST PALM BEACH, FL [FL0008]. ICA: FL0040.

WALDO—Comcast Cable. Now served by JACKSONVILLE, FL [FL0002]. ICA: FL0185.

WALTON COUNTY (portions)—Mediacom, 1613 Nantahala Beach Rd, Gulf Breeze, FL 32563-8944. Phone: 850-934-7700. Fax: 850-934-2506. Web Site: http://www.mediacomcable.com. Also serves Bay County (portions), Bonifay, Cape San Blas, Gulf County (portions), Holmes County (portions), Mexico Beach, Panama City (portions), Sandestin Beach Resort, Southport, Tyndall AFB, Vernon & Wewahitchka. ICA: FL0159.
TV Market Ranking: Below 100 (Bay County (portions), Bonifay, Cape San Blas, Holmes County (portions), Mexico Beach, Panama City (portions), Sandestin Beach Resort, Southport, Tyndall AFB, Vernon, Gulf County (portions), WALTON COUNTY (PORTIONS), Wewahitchka); Outside TV Markets (Gulf County (portions)). Franchise award date: August 24, 1982. Franchise expiration date: N.A. Began: June 1, 1983.
Channel capacity: N.A. Channels available but not in use: N.A.

Basic Service
Subscribers: 11,069.
Programming (received off-air): WFSU-TV (PBS) Tallahassee; WJHG-TV (CW, MNT, NBC) Panama City; WMBB (ABC, This TV) Panama City; WPGX (FOX) Panama City; WTVY (CBS, CW, MeTV, MNT, This TV) Dothan.
Programming (via satellite): A&E; AMC; Animal Planet; BET; Bravo; Cartoon Network; CMT; CNBC; CNN; Comedy Central; C-SPAN; C-SPAN 2; Discovery Channel; Discovery Life Channel; Disney Channel; Disney XD; E! HD; ESPN; ESPN2; EWTN Global Catholic Network; Food Network; Fox News Channel; Fox Sports 1; FOX Sports Florida/Sun Sports; Freeform; FX; Golf Channel; Hallmark Channel; HGTV; History; HLN; INSP; ION Television; Lifetime; MSNBC; MTV; Nickelodeon; Outdoor Channel; Oxygen; Pop; QVC; Spike TV; Syfy; TBS; The Weather Channel; TLC; TNT; Travel Channel; Trinity Broadcasting Network (TBN); truTV; TV Land; Univision; Univision Studios; USA Network; VH1; WE tv; WGN America.
Fee: $29.50 installation; $42.00 monthly; $3.35 converter.

Digital Basic Service
Subscribers: N.A.
Programming (via satellite): BBC America; Bloomberg Television; Discovery Digital Networks; DMX Music; FYI; GSN; History International; IFC; LMN; Turner Classic Movies.

Digital Pay Service 1
Pay Units: N.A.
Programming (via satellite): Cinemax (multiplexed); HBO (multiplexed); Showtime (multiplexed); Starz (multiplexed); Starz Encore (multiplexed).
Fee: $9.95 monthly (Cinemax, Showtime or Starz/Encore), $11.95 monthly (HBO).
Video-On-Demand: No
Internet Service
Operational: Yes.
Broadband Service: Mediacom High Speed Internet.
Fee: $49.95 installation; $40.95 monthly.
Telephone Service
Digital: Operational
Vice President: David Servies. Vice President, Financial Reporting: Kenneth J. Kohrs. Engineering Director: Powell Bedgood. Regional Technical Operations Director: Eddie Arnold. Government Relations Director: Barbara Bonowicz. Sales & Marketing Manager: Joey Nagem. Technical Operations Manager: Shayne Routhe.
Ownership: Mediacom LLC (MSO).

WAUCHULA—Comcast Cable, 3010 Herring Ave, Sebring, FL 33870. Phones: 941-371-6700 (Customer service); 941-371-4444. Fax: 941-371-5097. Web Site: http://www.comcast.com. Also serves Hardee County (portions), Spring Lake & Zolfo Springs. ICA: FL0288.

Cable Systems—Florida

TV Market Ranking: Outside TV Markets (WAUCHULA, Zolfo Springs, Spring Lake). Franchise award date: N.A. Franchise expiration date: N.A. Began: June 1, 1970. Channel capacity: N.A. Channels available but not in use: N.A.

Basic Service
Subscribers: 921. Commercial subscribers: 151.
Programming (received off-air): WCLF (Christian TV Network) Clearwater; WEDU (PBS) Tampa; WFLA-TV (MeTV, NBC) Tampa; WFTS-TV (ABC, Grit, Laff) Tampa; WFTT-DT (getTV, UniMas) Tampa; WFTV (ABC, Escape) Orlando; WKMG-TV (CBS, Retro TV) Orlando; WMOR-TV (Estrella TV, This TV) Lakeland; WTOG (CW, Decades) St. Petersburg; WTSP (CBS) St. Petersburg; WTTA (COZI TV, MNT) St. Petersburg; WTVT (Buzzr, FOX, Heroes & Icons, Movies!) Tampa; WUSF-TV (PBS) Tampa; WVEA-TV (Bounce TV, LATV, UNV) Venice; WXPX-TV (ION) Bradenton.
Programming (via satellite): A&E; AMC; Animal Planet; BET; Cartoon Network; CMT; CNBC; CNN; Comcast/Charter Sports Southeast (CSS); Comedy Central; C-SPAN; C-SPAN 2; Discovery Channel; E! HD; ESPN; ESPN2; Food Network; Fox News Channel; Fox Sports 1; FOX Sports Florida/Sun Sports; Freeform; FX; Golf Channel; GSN; Hallmark Channel; HGTV; History; HLN; Lifetime; MTV; NBCSN; Nickelodeon; OWN: Oprah Winfrey Network; Pop; QVC; Spike TV; Syfy; TBS; The Weather Channel; TLC; TNT; TV Land; USA Network; VH1; WGN America.
Fee: $50.00 installation; $25.20 monthly.

Digital Basic Service
Subscribers: N.A.
Programming (via satellite): BBC America; Discovery Digital Networks; Disney Channel; Disney XD; ESPNews; Flix; MC; Nick 2; Nick Jr.; Sundance TV; TeenNick; WAM! America's Kidz Network; WE tv.

Pay Service 1
Pay Units: N.A.
Programming (via satellite): Cinemax; HBO; Showtime.
Fee: $24.95 installation; $9.50 monthly (each).

Digital Pay Service 1
Pay Units: N.A.
Programming (via satellite): Cinemax (multiplexed); HBO (multiplexed); Showtime (multiplexed); Starz (multiplexed); Starz Encore (multiplexed); The Movie Channel (multiplexed).

Video-On-Demand: No
Pay-Per-View
iN DEMAND; Hot Choice (delivered digitally); Playboy TV (delivered digitally); Pleasure (delivered digitally); Fresh (delivered digitally); Shorteez (delivered digitally).

Internet Service
Operational: Yes.

Telephone Service
Analog: Not Operational
Digital: Operational
Miles of Plant: 87.0 (coaxial); None (fiber optic).
Regional Vice President: Rod Dagenais. Vice President & General Manager: Steve Dvoskin. Technical Operations Director: Danny Maxwell. Marketing Director: Vince Maffeo. Technical Operations Manager: Andrew Behn.
Ownership: Comcast Cable Communications Inc. (MSO).

WELAKA (town)—Comcast Cable. Now served by JACKSONVILLE, FL [FL0002]. ICA: FL0326.

WELLINGTON—Formerly served by Bright House Networks. No longer in operation. ICA: FL0356.

WEST PALM BEACH—Comcast Cable, 1401 Northpoint Pkwy, West Palm Beach, FL 33407-1965. Phones: 561-478-5866; 561-227-4240. Fax: 561-640-3996. Web Site: http://www.comcast.com. Also serves Atlantis, Aventura, Belle Glade, Biscayne Park, Boca Raton, Boynton Beach, Broward County (portions), Buckhead Ridge, Clewiston, Cloud Lake, Coconut Creek, Cooper City, Coral Gables, Cutler Bay, Dade County (portions), Dania, Davie, Deerfield Beach, Delray Beach, Delray Shores, Doral, El Portal, Fellsmere, Florida City, Fort Lauderdale, Fort Pierce, Gifford, Glen Ridge, Greenacres, Hallandale, Haverhill, Hialeah, Hialeah Gardens, Highland Beach, Hillsboro Beach, Hollywood, Homestead, Hypoluxo, Indian River, Indian River County (portions), Indian River Shores, Indiantown, Islamorada (portions), Jensen Beach, Juno Beach, Jupiter, Jupiter Inlet Colony, Jupiter Island, Kendall, Key Biscayne, Key Colony Beach, Key Largo, Key West, Lake Clarke Shores, Lake Park, Lake Worth, Lakeport, Lantana, Lauderdale Lakes, Lauderdale-by-the-Sea, Lauderhill, Layton, Lazy Lake, Lighthouse Point, Little Torch Key, Manalapan, Mangonia Park, Marathon, Marathon Shores, Margate, Martin County (portions), Medley, Miami, Miami Shores, Miami Springs, Micco, Mims, Miramar, Moore Haven, North Lauderdale, North Miami, North Miami Beach, North Palm Beach, Oakland Park, Ocean Breeze Park, Ocean Reef Club, Ocean Ridge, Okeechobee, Okeechobee County (portions), Opa-Locka, Orchid, Pahokee, Palm Bay, Palm Beach (town), Palm Beach City, Palm Beach County (portions), Palm Beach Gardens, Palm Beach Shores, Palm City, Palm Springs, Palmetto Bay, Parkland, Pembroke, Pembroke Park, Pembroke Pines, Pinecrest, Plantation (Broward County), Pompano Beach, Port St. Lucie, Riviera Beach, Roseland, Royal Palm Beach, Sea Ranch Lakes, Sebastian, Sewall's Point, South Bay, South Palm Beach, Southwest Ranches, St. Lucie County (portions), St. Lucie Village, St. Lucie West, Stuart, Summerland Key, Sunrise, Sweetwater, Tamarac, Tequesta, Vero Beach, Virginia Gardens, Wellington, West Miami, Weston, Wilton Manors & Wynmoor Village. ICA: FL0008.
TV Market Ranking: 21 (Aventura, Biscayne Park, Broward County (portions), Coconut Creek, Cooper City, Coral Gables, Cutler Bay, Dade County (portions), Dania, Davie, Doral, El Portal, Florida City, Fort Lauderdale, Hallandale, Hialeah, Hialeah Gardens, Hollywood, Homestead, Kendall, Key Biscayne, Lauderdale Lakes, Lauderdale-by-the-Sea, Lauderhill, Lazy Lake, Margate, Medley, Miami, Miami Shores, Miami Springs, Miramar, North Lauderdale, North Miami, North Miami Beach, Oakland Park, Opa-Locka, Parkland, Pembroke Park, Pembroke Pines, Pinecrest, Plantation (Broward County), Pompano Beach, Sea Ranch Lakes, Southwest Ranches, Sunrise, Sweetwater, Tamarac, Virginia Gardens, West Miami, Weston, Wilton Manors, Wynmoor Village); 28 (Pembroke); 55 (Fellsmere, Gifford, Indian River, Indian River County (portions), Indian River Shores, Micco, Mims, Orchid, Palm Bay, Roseland, Sebastian); Below 100 (Atlantis, Boca Raton, Boynton Beach, Cloud Lake, Deerfield Beach, Delray Shores, Fort Lauderdale, Glen Ridge, Greenacres, Haverhill, Highland Beach, Hillsboro Beach, Hypoluxo, Indiantown, Jensen Beach, Juno Beach, Jupiter, Jupiter Inlet Colony, Jupiter Island, Lake Clarke Shores, Lake Park, Lake Worth, Lantana, Lighthouse Point, Little Torch Key, Manalapan, Mangonia Park, Martin County (portions), North Palm Beach, Ocean Breeze Park, Ocean Ridge, Pahokee, Palm Beach (town), Palm Beach City, Palm Beach Shores, Palm City, Palm Springs, Port St. Lucie, Riviera Beach, Royal Palm Beach, Sewall's Point, South Palm Beach, St. Lucie County (portions), St. Lucie Village, St. Lucie West, Summerland Key, Tequesta, Wellington, WEST PALM BEACH, Belle Glade, Delray Beach, Key West, Okeechobee, Okeechobee County (portions), Palm Beach Gardens, Stuart, Vero Beach, Broward County (portions)); Outside TV Markets (Buckhead Ridge, Clewiston, Islamorada (portions), Key Colony Beach, Key Largo, Lakeport, Layton, Marathon, Marathon Shores, Ocean Reef Club, South Bay, Moore Haven, Okeechobee County (portions), Broward County (portions), Dade County (portions)). Franchise award date: N.A. Franchise expiration date: N.A. Began: December 15, 1968.
Channel capacity: 27 (operating 2-way). Channels available but not in use: N.A.

Basic Service
Subscribers: 813,001. Commercial subscribers: 167,735.
Programming (received off-air): WFGC (Christian TV Network) Palm Beach; WFLX (Bounce TV, FOX, Grit) West Palm Beach; WLPH-CD (WeatherNation) Miami; WLTV-DT (Bounce TV, Laff, UNV) Miami; WPBF (ABC, Estrella TV) Tequesta; WPBT (PBS) Miami; WPEC (CBS, WeatherNation) West Palm Beach; WPLG (ABC, MeTV, Movies) Miami; WPTV-TV (IND, MeTV, NBC) West Palm Beach; WPXP-TV (ION) Lake Worth; WSCV (TMO) Fort Lauderdale; WTCE-TV (TBN) Fort Pierce; WTVX (CW, LATV) Fort Pierce; WXEL-TV (PBS) West Palm Beach; 12 FMs.
Programming (via satellite): AMC; Discovery Channel; History; TBS; TNT; WGN America.
Fee: $52.95-$67.95 installation; $28.40 monthly.

Expanded Basic Service 1
Subscribers: N.A.
Programming (via satellite): A&E; Animal Planet; BET; Bravo; Cartoon Network; CNBC; CNN; Comedy Central; C-SPAN; C-SPAN 2; Disney Channel; E! HD; ESPN; ESPN2; EWTN Global Catholic Network; Food Network; Fox News Channel; FOX Sports Florida/Sun Sports; Freeform; FX; Golf Channel; Hallmark Channel; HGTV; HLN; Lifetime; MSNBC; MTV; Nickelodeon; Pop; QVC; Spike TV; Syfy; The Weather Channel; TLC; Travel Channel; truTV; TV Land; USA Network; VH1.
Fee: $18.30 monthly.

Digital Basic Service
Subscribers: N.A.
Programming (via satellite): A&E HD; Animal Planet HD; AXS TV; BBC America; Bloomberg Television; CBS Sports Network; Cine Mexicano; Cinelatino; CMT; CNN en Espanol; Cooking Channel; C-SPAN 2; C-SPAN 3; Destination America; Discovery Channel HD; Discovery Kids Channel; Discovery Life Channel; Disney XD; DIY Network; ESPN Classic; ESPN Deportes; ESPN HD; ESPN2 HD; ESPNews; FamilyNet; Flix; Food Network HD; Fox Business Network; FOX College Sports Central; FOX College Sports Pacific; Fox Deportes; Fox Sports 1; Fox Sports 2; FSN HD; Fuse; FXM; Golf Channel HD; GolTV; Great American Country; GSN; HGTV HD; History HD; History International; IFC; Investigation Discovery; Jewelry Television; La Familia Cosmovision; LMN; LOGO; MC; MLB Network; MoviePlex; MTV Classic; MTV Hits; MTV2; Nat Geo WILD; National Geographic Channel; National Geographic Channel HD; NBA TV; NBC Universo; NBCSN; NFL Network; NHL Network; Nick 2; Nick Jr.; Outdoor Channel; OWN: Oprah Winfrey Network; Oxygen; RLTV; RTV; Science Channel; Sprout; Starz Encore (multiplexed); Sundance TV; Syfy HD; TeenNick; Tennis Channel; TNT HD; Toon Disney en Espanol; Tr3s; Trinity Broadcasting Network (TBN); Turner Classic Movies; TV One; TVG Network; Universal HD; UP; USA Network HD; Versus HD; VH1 Soul; ViendoMovies; Vubiquity Inc.; WE tv.

Digital Pay Service 1
Pay Units: N.A.
Programming (via satellite): Cinemax (multiplexed); HBO (multiplexed); HBO HD; Showtime (multiplexed); Showtime HD; Starz (multiplexed); Starz HD; The Movie Channel (multiplexed).

Video-On-Demand: Yes

Pay-Per-View
iN DEMAND; Club Jenna (delivered digitally); Playboy TV (delivered digitally); Fresh; Shorteez (delivered digitally).

Internet Service
Operational: Yes.
Subscribers: 927,064.
Broadband Service: Comcast High Speed Internet.
Fee: $42.95 monthly.

Telephone Service
Digital: Operational
Subscribers: 435,057.
Miles of Plant: 28,250.0 (coaxial); 4,559.0 (fiber optic). Homes passed: 2,595,901.
Area Vice President: Gary Waterfield. General Manager: Beth Fulcher. Technical Operations Director: Barry Rhodes. Community & Government Affairs Director: Marta Casas Celayas. Marketing Director: Christopher Derario. Chief Technician: Skip Buck. Marketing Manager: Dianne Bissoon. Technical Operations Manager: Van Gordon. Marketing Coordinator: Janet Epstien.; Gary Goldman.
Ownership: Comcast Cable Communications Inc. (MSO).

WESTON—Advocate Communications, 12409 NW 35th St, Coral Springs, FL 33065. Phones: 954-384-3090; 954-753-0100. ICA: FL0321.

Florida—Cable Systems

Communications Daily
Warren Communications News

Get the industry standard FREE —
For a no-obligation trial call 800-771-9202 or visit www.warren-news.com

TV Market Ranking: 21 (WESTON). Franchise award date: September 1, 1983. Franchise expiration date: N.A. Began: April 1, 1986. Channel capacity: N.A. Channels available but not in use: N.A.

Basic Service
Subscribers: 7,980.
Programming (received off-air): WAMI-DT (Bounce TV, getTV, UniMas) Hollywood; WBFS-TV (MNT) Miami; WFOR-TV (CBS, Decades) Miami; WHFT-TV (TBN) Miami; WLRN-TV (PBS) Miami; WLTV-DT (Bounce TV, Laff, UNV) Miami; WPBT (PBS) Miami; WPLG (ABC, MeTV, Movies) Miami; WPXM-TV (ION) Miami; WSBS-TV (IND) Key West; WSCV (TMO) Fort Lauderdale; WSFL-TV (Antenna TV, Azteca America, CW, This TV) Miami; WSVN (Estrella TV, FOX) Miami; WTVJ (COZI TV, NBC) Miami; WXEL-TV (PBS) West Palm Beach.
Programming (via satellite): A&E; AMC; Animal Planet; BET; Bravo; Cartoon Network; CMT; CNBC; CNN; Comedy Central; C-SPAN; Discovery Channel; Disney Channel; E! HD; ESPN; ESPN2; EWTN Global Catholic Network; Food Network; Fox News Channel; Fox Sports 1; FOX Sports Florida/Sun Sports; Freeform; FX; FXM; Golf Channel; Hallmark Channel; HGTV; History; HLN; Lifetime; MSNBC; MTV; MTV2; National Geographic Channel; NBCSN; Nickelodeon; OWN: Oprah Winfrey Network; Pop; QVC; Spike TV; Syfy; TBS; The Weather Channel; TLC; TNT; Travel Channel; truTV; Turner Classic Movies; TV Land; USA Network; VH1; WE tv; WGN America.
Fee: $68.74 installation; $67.25 monthly; $2.32 converter.

Digital Basic Service
Subscribers: N.A.
Programming (via satellite): A&E HD; AXS TV; BBC America; Bloomberg Television; CBS Sports Network; Cloo; CMT; Cooking Channel; C-SPAN 3; Destination America; Discovery Kids Channel; Disney XD; DMX Music; ESPN Classic; ESPN HD; ESPN2 HD; ESPNews; ESPNU; EVINE Live; FOX College Sports Central; FOX College Sports Pacific; Fox Deportes; Fox Sports 2; FSN HD; Fuse; FYI; GolTV; GSN; HD Theater; History HD; History International; Investigation Discovery; LATV; LMN; MTV Classic; MTV Hits; Nat Geo WILD; National Geographic Channel HD; NBC Universo; NFL Network; NFL Network HD; Nick Jr.; Nicktoons; Science Channel; Sprout; TBS HD; TeenNick; TNT HD; Universal HD; VH1 Soul.

Digital Expanded Basic Service
Subscribers: N.A.
Programming (via satellite): 52MX; Canal Sur; Cine Mexicano; Cinelatino; CNN en Espanol; Docu TVE; ESPN Deportes; Fox Deportes; GolTV; History en Espanol; NBC Universo; Telefe Internacional; Toon Disney en Espanol; Tr3s; ULTRA HDPlex; Viendo-Movies.
Fee: $10.95 monthly.

Digital Pay Service 1
Pay Units: N.A.
Programming (via satellite): Cinemax (multiplexed); Cinemax HD; Flix; HBO (multiplexed); HBO HD; Showtime (multiplexed); Showtime HD; Starz (multiplexed); Starz Encore (multiplexed); Starz HD; Sundance TV; The Movie Channel (multiplexed).
Fee: $13.00 -$18.95 monthly (each).
Video-On-Demand: Yes
Pay-Per-View
iN DEMAND; Playboy TV (delivered digitally); Fresh (delivered digitally); special events (delivered digitally).
Internet Service
Operational: Yes.
Broadband Service: In-house.
Fee: $47.95 monthly; $10.00 modem lease.
Telephone Service
Analog: Not Operational
Digital: Operational
Fee: $33.00-$39.00 monthly
Miles of Plant: 100.0 (coaxial); 1.0 (fiber optic). Homes passed: 17,000.
President & General Manager: James Pagano. Vice President, Engineering: Rick Scheller. Secretary: Michelle Fitzpatrick.
Ownership: Advocate Communications Inc. (MSO).

WESTVILLE—Formerly served by Community Cable. No longer in operation. ICA: FL0289.

WHITE SPRINGS—Formerly served by Southeast Cable TV Inc. No longer in operation. ICA: FL0290.

WILDWOOD—Bright House Networks. Now served by ORLANDO, FL [FL0001]. ICA: FL0291.

WILLISTON—Comcast Cable. Now served by ARCHER, FL [FL0189]. ICA: FL0166.

WOODFIELD—Formerly served by Formerly served by Comcast Cable. No longer in operation. ICA: FL0295.

WYNMOOR VILLAGE—Comcast Cable. Now served by WEST PALM BEACH, FL [FL0008]. ICA: FL0373.

YANKEETOWN—Comcast Cable. Now served by ARCHER, FL [FL0189]. ICA: FL0177.

YULEE—Comcast Cable. Now served by JACKSONVILLE, FL [FL0002]. ICA: FL0129.

ZELLWOOD—Florida Fiber Networks, 301 South Collins St, Ste 105, Plant City, FL 33563. Phones: 888-860-4088; 352-702-4990. E-mail: info@flfibernet.com. Web Site: http://www.flfibernet.com. ICA: FL0346.
TV Market Ranking: 55 (ZELLWOOD).
Channel capacity: 52 (not 2-way capable). Channels available but not in use: N.A.

Basic Service
Subscribers: N.A.
Programming (received off-air): WESH (MeTV, NBC) Daytona Beach; WFTV (ABC, Escape) Orlando; WHLV-TV (TBN) Cocoa; WKCF (CW, Estrella TV, This TV) Clermont; WKMG-TV (CBS, Retro TV) Orlando; WOFL (Bounce TV, FOX) Orlando; WRBW (Buzzr, Heroes & Icons, MNT, Movies!) Orlando; WRDQ (Antenna TV) Orlando; WTGL (ETV) Leesburg; WUCF-TV (ETV) Orlando.
Programming (via satellite): A&E; AMC; Animal Planet; CMT; CNBC; CNN; C-SPAN; Discovery Channel; ESPN; ESPN2; Fox News Channel; FOX Sports Florida/Sun Sports; Freeform; FX; History; Lifetime; MTV; Nickelodeon; Spike TV; TBS; The Weather Channel; TLC; TNT; Travel Channel; Trinity Broadcasting Network (TBN); USA Network; VH1; WGN America.

Pay Service 1
Pay Units: N.A.
Programming (via satellite): Cinemax; HBO.
Internet Service
Operational: No.
Telephone Service
None
Miles of Plant: 14.0 (coaxial); None (fiber optic).
Chief Executive Officer: David Suarez. Chief Marketing Officer: David Orshan.
Ownership: Florida Fiber Networks (MSO).

GEORGIA

Total Systems: 95	Communities with Applications: 0
Total Communities Served: 698	Number of Basic Subscribers: 1,437,945
Franchises Not Yet Operating: 0	Number of Expanded Basic Subscribers: 8,162
Applications Pending: 0	Number of Pay Units: 3,065

Top 100 Markets Represented: Atlanta-Rome (18); Greenville-Spartanburg-Anderson, SC-Asheville, NC (46); Jacksonville, FL (68); Chattanooga, TN (78); Columbus (94).

For a list of cable communities in this section, see the Cable Community Index located in the back of Cable Volume 2. For explanation of terms used in cable system listings, see p. D-11.

ABBEVILLE—Bulldog Cable, PO Box 1288, Watkinsville, GA 30677. Phones: 706-997-9003; 800-388-6577. Web Site: http://www.bulldogcable.com. ICA: GA0146.
TV Market Ranking: Below 100 (ABBEVILLE). Franchise award date: N.A. Franchise expiration date: N.A. Began: March 1, 1983.
Channel capacity: N.A. Channels available but not in use: N.A.
Basic Service
Subscribers: 28.
Programming (received off-air): WALB (ABC, NBC, This TV) Albany; WFXL (Bounce TV, FOX) Albany; WGXA (ABC, FOX) Macon; WMAZ-TV (CBS) Macon; WMGT-TV (Escape, MNT, NBC) Macon; WMUM-TV (PBS) Cochran; WPGA-TV (Bounce TV, IND, MeTV) Perry; WSST-TV (IND) Cordele.
Programming (via satellite): A&E; BET; CMT; CNN; Discovery Channel; Disney Channel; ESPN; ESPN2; Fox News Channel; Freeform; History; Lifetime; MTV; Nickelodeon; QVC; Spike TV; TBS; The Weather Channel; TLC; TNT; Trinity Broadcasting Network (TBN); TV Land; USA Network; VH1; WGN America.
Fee: $44.95 installation; $49.00 monthly.
Pay Service 1
Pay Units: 20.
Programming (via satellite): HBO.
Fee: $12.00 monthly.
Pay Service 2
Pay Units: 10.
Programming (via satellite): Cinemax.
Fee: $12.00 monthly.
Internet Service
Operational: No.
Telephone Service
None
Miles of Plant: 10.0 (coaxial); None (fiber optic). Homes passed: 360.
President: Mark Wilson. General Manager East: Mark Miller. General Manager West: Vance Johnson. Controller: Ashley Hull.
Ownership: Bulldog Cable (MSO).

ACWORTH—Formerly served by KLiP Interactive. No longer in operation. ICA: GA0292.

ADEL—Mediacom, 100 Crystal Run Rd, Middletown, NY 10941. Phones: 845-695-2762; 229-244-3852 (Regional office). Web Site: http://www.mediacomcable.com. Also serves Alapaha, Berrien County (portions), Cook County (portions), Enigma, Lakeland, Lenox, Nashville, Pearson, Ray City, Sparks, Tift County (portions) & Willacoochee. ICA: GA0063.
TV Market Ranking: Below 100 (Cook County (portions), Enigma, Lakeland, Lenox, Nashville, Ray City, Sparks, Tift County (portions)), ADEL, Berrien County (portions)); Outside TV Markets (Alapaha, Willacoochee, Berrien County (portions), Pearson). Franchise award date: N.A. Franchise expiration date: N.A. Began: April 1, 1968.
Channel capacity: N.A. Channels available but not in use: N.A.
Basic Service
Subscribers: 5,339.
Programming (received off-air): WALB (ABC, NBC, This TV) Albany; WCTV (CBS, MNT, This TV) Thomasville; WFXL (Bounce TV, FOX) Albany; WSB-TV (ABC, MeTV) Atlanta; WSWG (CBS, CW, MeTV, MNT) Valdosta; WTXL-TV (ABC, Bounce TV) Tallahassee; WXGA-TV (PBS) Waycross; 9 FMs.
Programming (via satellite): C-SPAN; C-SPAN 2; EWTN Global Catholic Network; Hallmark Channel; ION Television; QVC; Trinity Broadcasting Network (TBN); WSBK-TV (MNT) Boston.
Fee: $27.67 installation; $69.95 monthly; $2.72 converter.
Expanded Basic Service 1
Subscribers: N.A.
Programming (via satellite): A&E; AMC; Animal Planet; BET; Cartoon Network; CMT; CNBC; CNN; Comedy Central; Discovery Channel; Discovery Life Channel; Disney Channel; ESPN; ESPN2; Food Network; Fox News Channel; Freeform; FX; Golf Channel; HGTV; History; HLN; Lifetime; MSNBC; MTV; Nickelodeon; Oxygen; Pop; Spike TV; Syfy; TBS; The Weather Channel; TLC; TNT; Travel Channel; truTV; TV Land; Univision; Univision Studios; USA Network; VH1; WE tv.
Fee: $28.84 monthly.
Digital Basic Service
Subscribers: N.A.
Programming (via satellite): BBC America; Bloomberg Television; Discovery Digital Networks; Disney XD; DMX Music; Fox Sports 1; Fuse; FXM; FYI; Golf Channel; GSN; History International; HITS (Headend In The Sky); IFC; LMN; National Geographic Channel; NBCSN; Nick Jr.; Outdoor Channel; Ovation; TeenNick; Turner Classic Movies.
Digital Pay Service 1
Pay Units: N.A.
Programming (via satellite): Cinemax (multiplexed); Flix; HBO (multiplexed); Showtime (multiplexed); Starz (multiplexed); Starz Encore (multiplexed); Sundance TV; The Movie Channel (multiplexed).
Fee: $10.30 monthly (Cinemax, HBO, Showtime/Sundance/TMC or Starz/Encore).
Video-On-Demand: Yes
Pay-Per-View
ESPN Now (delivered digitally); ETC (delivered digitally); Vubiquity Inc. (delivered digitally).
Internet Service
Operational: Yes.
Subscribers: 3,490.
Broadband Service: Mediacom High Speed Internet.
Fee: $70.00 installation; $40.95 monthly.
Telephone Service
Digital: Operational
Subscribers: 2,325.
Miles of Plant: 797.0 (coaxial); 202.0 (fiber optic). Homes passed: 19,973. Miles of plant included in Fitzgerald.
Regional Vice President: Sue Misiunas. Vice President, Financial Reporting: Kenneth J. Kohrs. General Manager: Gary Crosby. Regional Technical Operations Manager: Gary McDougall. Regional Marketing Director: Melanie Hannasch. Marketing Manager: Daryl Channey.
Ownership: Mediacom LLC (MSO).

ADRIAN—Comcast Cable. Now served by SAVANNAH, GA [GA0005]. ICA: GA0136.

ALBANY—Mediacom, 509 Flint Ave, Albany, GA 31701. Phones: 229-244-3852 (Valdosta regional office); 229-888-0242. Fax: 229-436-4819. Web Site: http://www.mediacomcable.com. Also serves Camilla, Dawson, Dougherty County (portions), Lee County (portions), Leesburg, Meigs, Mitchell County (portions), Pelham, Pine Glen, Poulan, Putney, Sylvester, Terrell County (southern portion), Thomas County (portions), U.S. Marine Logistics Base (Government Reserve) & Worth County (eastern portion). ICA: GA0011.
TV Market Ranking: Below 100 (ALBANY, Dawson, Dougherty County (portions), Lee County (portions), Leesburg, Meigs, Mitchell County (portions), Pelham, Pine Glen, Poulan, Putney, Sylvester, Terrell County (southern portion), Thomas County (portions), U.S. Marine Logistics Base (Government Reserve), Worth County (eastern portion), Camilla). Franchise award date: May 1, 1966. Franchise expiration date: N.A. Began: October 1, 1965.
Channel capacity: N.A. Channels available but not in use: N.A.
Basic Service
Subscribers: 21,970.
Programming (received off-air): WABW-TV (PBS) Pelham; WALB (ABC, NBC, This TV) Albany; WCTV (CBS, MNT, This TV) Thomasville; WFXL (Bounce TV, FOX) Albany; WRBL (CBS, MeTV) Columbus; WSST-TV (IND) Cordele; WSWG (CBS, CW, MeTV, MNT) Valdosta; WTVM (ABC, Bounce TV) Columbus.
Programming (via microwave): WSB-TV (ABC, MeTV) Atlanta.
Programming (via satellite): CNBC; C-SPAN; C-SPAN 2; CW PLUS; EWTN Global Catholic Network; Hallmark Channel; QVC; Trinity Broadcasting Network (TBN).
Fee: $19.95 installation; $69.95 monthly; $1.90 converter.
Expanded Basic Service 1
Subscribers: N.A.
Programming (via satellite): A&E; AMC; Animal Planet; BET; Bravo; Cartoon Network; CMT; CNN; Comedy Central; Discovery Channel; Disney Channel; ESPN; ESPN2; Food Network; Fox News Channel; Freeform; FX; HGTV; History; HLN; INSP; ION Television; Lifetime; MSNBC; MTV; Nickelodeon; Pop; Spike TV; Syfy; TBS; The Weather Channel; TLC; TNT; truTV; TV Land; USA Network; VH1; WE tv.
Fee: $21.66 monthly.
Digital Basic Service
Subscribers: N.A.
Programming (via satellite): BBC America; Discovery Digital Networks; Disney XD; DMX Music; Fox Sports 1; Fuse; FYI; Golf Channel; GSN; History International; IFC; LMN; National Geographic Channel; NBCSN; Nick Jr.; Ovation; TeenNick; Turner Classic Movies.
Digital Pay Service 1
Pay Units: N.A.
Programming (via satellite): Cinemax (multiplexed); HBO (multiplexed); Showtime (multiplexed); Starz (multiplexed); Starz Encore (multiplexed); Sundance TV; The Movie Channel (multiplexed).
Fee: $10.30 monthly (Cinemax, HBO, Showtime, Sundance/TMC or Starz/Encore).
Video-On-Demand: Yes
Pay-Per-View
ESPN Now (delivered digitally); ETC (delivered digitally); Vubiquity Inc. (delivered digitally).
Internet Service
Operational: Yes.
Subscribers: 14,423.
Broadband Service: Mediacom High Speed Internet.
Fee: $70.00 installation; $42.95 monthly; $3.00 modem lease.
Telephone Service
Analog: Not Operational
Digital: Operational
Subscribers: 7,680.
Miles of Plant: 1,895.0 (coaxial); 405.0 (fiber optic). Homes passed: 67,065.
Regional Vice President: Sue Misiunas. Vice President, Financial Reporting: Kenneth J. Kohrs. General Manager: Gary Crosby. Regional Technical Operations Manager: Gary McDougall. Regional Marketing Director: Melanie Hannasch. Marketing Manager: Daryl Channey. Technical Operations Manager: David Jones.
Ownership: Mediacom LLC (MSO).

Georgia—Cable Systems

ALLENTOWN—Formerly served by KLiP Interactive. No longer in operation. ICA: GA0186.

ALMA—Dixie Cable TV, 407 West 11th St, PO Box 2027, Alma, GA 31510-2027. Phone: 912-632-8603. Fax: 912-634-4519. E-mail: info@atcbroadband.com. Web Site: http://www.atcbroadband.com. ICA: GA0098.
TV Market Ranking: Below 100 (ALMA). Franchise award date: January 1, 1979. Franchise expiration date: N.A. Began: December 31, 1965.
Channel capacity: N.A. Channels available but not in use: N.A.

Basic Service
Subscribers: 1,332.
Programming (received off-air): WCWJ (Bounce TV, CW) Jacksonville; WFOX-TV (FOX, MeTV, MNT) Jacksonville; WGSA (CW) Baxley; WJAX-TV (CBS, Decades, getTV) Jacksonville; WJCL (ABC) Savannah; WJXT (LATV, This TV) Jacksonville; WJXX (ABC) Orange Park; WPXC-TV (ION) Brunswick; WSAV-TV (MeTV, MNT, NBC) Savannah; WTGS (Antenna TV, FOX) Hardeeville; WTLV (Antenna TV, NBC, The Country Network) Jacksonville; WTOC-TV (Bounce TV, CBS, This TV) Savannah; WXGA-TV (PBS) Waycross; allband FM.
Programming (via satellite): A&E; AMC; Animal Planet; BET; Cartoon Network; CMT; CNBC; CNN; Comcast/Charter Sports Southeast (CSS); Comedy Central; C-SPAN; C-SPAN 2; Discovery Channel; Discovery Life Channel; Disney Channel; E! HD; ESPN; ESPN Classic; ESPN2; Food Network; Fox News Channel; Fox Sports 1; FOX Sports South/SportSouth; Freeform; FX; Golf Channel; Hallmark Channel; HGTV; History; HLN; INSP; Lifetime; Local Cable Weather; MTV; National Geographic Channel; Nickelodeon; Outdoor Channel; Pop; QVC; Spike TV; Syfy; TBS; The Weather Channel; TLC; TNT; Travel Channel; Trinity Broadcasting Network (TBN); truTV; TV Land; USA Network; VH1.
Fee: $35.00 installation; $15.95 monthly; $3.00 converter.

Digital Basic Service
Subscribers: N.A.
Programming (via satellite): BBC America; Bloomberg Television; Boomerang; Cloo; Discovery Life Channel; Disney XD; DMX Music; ESPN Classic; ESPN2; ESPNews; ESPNU; Flix; Fox Sports 1; FSN Digital Atlantic; FSN Digital Central; FSN Digital Pacific; Fuse; FXM; FYI; Golf Channel; Great American Country; GSN; Hallmark Movies & Mysteries; HGTV; History; History International; Investigation Discovery; LMN; MTV Classic; MTV Hits; MTV2; National Geographic Channel; NBCSN; Nick Jr.; Nicktoons; Outdoor Channel; RFD-TV; Science Channel; Sundance TV; TeenNick; Trinity Broadcasting Network (TBN); Turner Classic Movies; UP; WE tv.

Digital Expanded Basic Service
Subscribers: N.A.
Programming (via satellite): A&E HD; Animal Planet HD; Bravo HD; CNBC HD+; CNN HD; Discovery Channel HD; ESPN HD; ESPN2 HD; Golf Channel HD; History HD; National Geographic Channel HD; Outdoor Channel 2 HD; Science HD; Syfy HD; TBS HD; The Weather Channel HD; TLC HD; TNT HD; USA Network HD; Versus HD.

Digital Expanded Basic Service 2
Subscribers: N.A.
Programming (via satellite): AXS TV; HD Theater; Universal HD.

Digital Pay Service 1
Pay Units: 141.
Programming (via satellite): HBO (multiplexed); HBO HD.
Fee: $12.95 monthly.

Digital Pay Service 2
Pay Units: 71.
Programming (via satellite): Showtime (multiplexed); Showtime HD; The Movie Channel (multiplexed).
Fee: $12.95 monthly.

Digital Pay Service 3
Pay Units: 34.
Programming (via satellite): Cinemax (multiplexed); Cinemax HD.
Fee: $8.00 monthly.

Digital Pay Service 4
Pay Units: 85.
Programming (via satellite): Starz (multiplexed); Starz Encore (multiplexed); Starz HD.
Fee: $12.95 monthly.

Video-On-Demand: No

Pay-Per-View
iN DEMAND (delivered digitally); Playboy TV (delivered digitally); Fresh (delivered digitally); Spice: Xcess (delivered digitally); Club Jenna (delivered digitally).

Internet Service
Operational: Yes.

Telephone Service
Analog: Operational
Miles of Plant: 80.0 (coaxial); 10.0 (fiber optic). Homes passed: 2,600.
General Manager: Kevin Brooks. Chief Technician: Tony McKinnon.
Ownership: ATC (Alma, GA).

AMERICUS—Mediacom, 100 Crystal Run Rd, Middletown, NY 10941. Phones: 229-244-3852 (Valdosta regional office); 845-695-2762. Web Site: http://www.mediacomcable.com. Also serves Ellaville, Schley County (portions) & Sumter County (portions). ICA: GA0039.
TV Market Ranking: Below 100 (AMERICUS, Schley County (portions), Sumter County (portions)); Outside TV Markets (Ellaville, Schley County (portions), Sumter County (portions)). Franchise award date: N.A. Franchise expiration date: N.A. Began: January 1, 1969.
Channel capacity: N.A. Channels available but not in use: N.A.

Basic Service
Subscribers: 4,200.
Programming (received off-air): WACS-TV (PBS) Dawson; WALB (ABC, NBC, This TV) Albany; WLTZ (CW, NBC) Columbus; WMAZ-TV (CBS) Macon; WRBL (CBS, MeTV) Columbus; WSB-TV (ABC, MeTV) Atlanta; WSST-TV (IND) Cordele; WTVM (ABC, Bounce TV) Columbus; WXTX (FOX, Movies!, This TV) Columbus; allband FM.
Programming (via satellite): Hallmark Channel; Lifetime; The Weather Channel.
Fee: $27.67 installation; $43.95 monthly; $1.77 converter.

Expanded Basic Service 1
Subscribers: N.A.
Programming (via satellite): A&E; AMC; Animal Planet; BET; Cartoon Network; CMT; CNBC; CNN; C-SPAN; Discovery Channel; Disney Channel; ESPN; ESPN2; Fox News Channel; FOX Sports South/SportSouth; Freeform; FX; HGTV; HLN; ION Television; MoviePlex; MSNBC; MTV; Nickelodeon; Pop; QVC; Spike TV; Syfy; TBS; TLC; TNT; Travel Channel; Trinity Broadcasting Network (TBN); truTV; USA Network; VH1.
Fee: $17.45 monthly.

Digital Basic Service
Subscribers: N.A.
Programming (via satellite): BBC America; Bravo; Discovery Digital Networks; DMX Music; ESPN Classic; ESPNews; Fox Sports 1; Golf Channel; GSN; History; IFC; MTV Classic; National Geographic Channel; NBCSN; Nick Jr.; Turner Classic Movies; TV Land; VH1 Country; WE tv.

Digital Pay Service 1
Pay Units: N.A.
Programming (via satellite): Cinemax (multiplexed); HBO (multiplexed); Showtime (multiplexed); Starz (multiplexed); Starz Encore (multiplexed); The Movie Channel (multiplexed).

Video-On-Demand: Yes

Pay-Per-View
Playboy TV (delivered digitally).

Internet Service
Operational: Yes.
Subscribers: 2,389.
Broadband Service: Mediacom High Speed Internet.
Fee: $42.95 monthly; $3.00 modem lease.

Telephone Service
Analog: Not Operational
Digital: Operational
Subscribers: 1,364.
Miles of Plant: 342.0 (coaxial); 125.0 (fiber optic). Homes passed: 12,617.
Regional Vice President: Sue Misiunas. Vice President, Financial Reporting: Kenneth J. Kohrs. General Manager: Gary Crosby. Regional Marketing Director: Melanie Hannasch. Regional Technical Operations Manager: Gary McDougall. Technical Operations Manager: David Jones. Marketing Manager: Daryl Channey.
Ownership: Mediacom LLC (MSO).

ANDERSONVILLE—Formerly served by Andersonville Cable. No longer in operation. ICA: GA0326.

ARABI—Formerly served by Citizens Cable TV. No longer in operation. ICA: GA0168.

ARNOLDSVILLE—Formerly served by Allegiance Communications. No longer in operation. ICA: GA0125.

ATHENS—Charter Communications, 12405 Powerscourt Dr, St. Louis, MO 63131. Phones: 636-207-5100 (Corporate office); 770-806-7060. Fax: 706-806-7099. Web Site: http://www.charter.com. Also serves Arnoldsville, Bogart, Clarke County (portions), Colbert, Comer, Danielsville, Hull, Lexington, Madison County, Oconee County, Oglethorpe County (portions), Watkinsville & Winterville. ICA: GA0014.
TV Market Ranking: Below 100 (ATHENS, Bogart, Clarke County (portions), Colbert, Comer, Danielsville, Hull, Madison County, Oconee County, Watkinsville, Winterville). Franchise award date: N.A. Franchise expiration date: N.A. Began: January 1, 1964.
Channel capacity: 69 (operating 2-way). Channels available but not in use: N.A.

Digital Basic Service
Subscribers: 24,461.
Programming (via satellite): BBC America; Bloomberg Television; Boomerang; Discovery Digital Networks; DIY Network; ESPN Classic; ESPNews; FOX College Sports Central; FOX College Sports Pacific; Fuse; FYI; Great American Country; History International; HITS (Headend In The Sky); IFC; LMN; MC; Nick 2; Nick Jr.; Nicktoons; Sundance TV; TeenNick; TV Guide Interactive Inc.
Fee: $26.99 monthly.

Digital Expanded Basic Service
Subscribers: N.A.
Programming (via satellite): A&E; AMC; Animal Planet; Bravo; Cartoon Network; CMT; CNBC; CNN; Comedy Central; Discovery Channel; Disney Channel; Disney XD; E! HD; ESPN; ESPN2; EVINE Live; Food Network; Fox News Channel; Fox Sports 1; FOX Sports South/SportSouth; Freeform; FX; Golf Channel; GSN; Hallmark Channel; HGTV; History; HLN; Lifetime; MSNBC; MTV; National Geographic Channel; NBCSN; Nickelodeon; Outdoor Channel; Oxygen; Spike TV; Syfy; Telemundo; The Weather Channel; TLC; TNT; Travel Channel; truTV; Turner Classic Movies; TV Land; Univision; USA Network; VH1; WE tv.
Fee: $48.99 monthly.

Digital Pay Service 1
Pay Units: N.A.
Programming (via satellite): Cinemax (multiplexed); Flix; HBO (multiplexed); Showtime (multiplexed); Starz (multiplexed); Starz Encore (multiplexed); The Movie Channel (multiplexed).

Video-On-Demand: Yes

Pay-Per-View
iN DEMAND (delivered digitally); Playboy TV (delivered digitally); Fresh (delivered digitally); Shorteez (delivered digitally).

Internet Service
Operational: Yes.
Subscribers: 25,136.
Broadband Service: Charter Internet.
Fee: $29.99 monthly.

Telephone Service
Digital: Operational
Subscribers: 9,558.
Fee: $29.99 monthly.
Miles of Plant: 2,067.0 (coaxial); 423.0 (fiber optic). Homes passed: 72,422.
Vice President & General Manager: Matt Favre. Operations Director: Jeff Osbourne. Sales & Marketing Director: Antoinette Carpenter. Accounting Director: David Sovanski.
Ownership: Charter Communications Inc. (MSO).

ATLANTA—Comcast Cable, 2925 Courtyards Dr, Norcross, GA 30071. Phones: 770-559-2424 (Regional office); 770-559-6807. Fax: 770-559-2479. E-mail: kenny_faust@cable.comcast.com. Web Site: http://www.comcast.com. Also serves Acworth, Adairsville, Alpharetta, Arcade, Auburn, Austell, Avondale Estates, Banks County (portions), Barrow County (portions), Bartow County (portions), Berkeley Lake, Bethlehem, Between, Braselton, Braswell, Bremen, Brooks, Calhoun, Canton, Carl (town), Carroll County (portions), Carrollton, Cartersville, Chamblee, Chattahoochee Hills, Cherokee County (portions), Clarke County (portions), Clarkston, Clayton, Clermont, Cobb County (portions), College Park, Conley, Conyers, Coweta County (portions), Cumming, Dallas, Decatur, DeKalb County (portions), Dobbins Air Force Base, Doraville, Douglas County (portions), Douglasville, Duluth, Dunwoody, East Point, Ellenwood, Emerson, Euharlee, Fairburn, Fairmount, Fayette County (portions), Fayetteville, Floyd County (portions), Forest Park, Forsyth County (portions), Fort Gillem, Fort McPherson, Fulton County (portions), Gillsville, Gordon County (portions), Grantville, Grayson, Griffin, Gwinnett County (portions), Hall County (portions), Hapeville, Haralson County (portions), Henry County (portions), Hiram, Hogansville, Holly Springs,

Cable Systems—Georgia

Hoschton, Jackson County (portions), Jersey, Jonesboro, Kennesaw, Kingston, Lake City, Lawrenceville, Lilburn, Lithonia, Loganville, Lovejoy, Lula, Mansfield, Marietta, Maysville, Monticello, Morrow, Mount Zion, Newborn, Newton County (portions), Norcross, Oconee County, Orchard Hill, Palmetto, Paulding County (portions), Peachtree City, Pendergrass, Pine Lake, Plainville, Polk County (portions), Powder Springs, Resaca, Riverdale, Rockdale County (portions), Rome, Roswell, Senoia, Smyrna, Snellville, Social Circle, Spalding County (portions), Statham, Stockbridge, Stone Mountain, Sunny Side, Tallapoosa, Talmo, Taylorsville, Troup County (portions), Tyrone, Union City, Villa Rica, Waco, Waleska, Walnut Grove, Walton County (portions), White, Whitesburg, Winder, Woodstock & Woolsey. ICA: GA0017.

TV Market Ranking: 18 (Acworth, Adairsville, Alpharetta, ATLANTA, Austell, Avondale Estates, Bartow County (portions), Berkeley Lake, Braswell, Brooks, Calhoun, Canton, Carroll County (portions), Cartersville, Chamblee, Chattahoochee Hills, Cherokee County (portions), Clarkston, Clayton, Cobb County (portions), College Park, Conley, Conyers, Coweta County (portions), Cumming, Dallas, Decatur, DeKalb County (portions), Dobbins Air Force Base, Doraville, Douglas County (portions), Douglasville, Duluth, Dunwoody, East Point, Ellenwood, Emerson, Euharlee, Fairburn, Fairmount, Fayette County (portions), Fayetteville, Floyd County (portions), Forest Park, Forsyth County (portions), Fort Gillem, Fort McPherson, Fulton County (portions), Gordon County (portions), Grayson, Gwinnett County (portions), Hapeville, Haralson County (portions), Henry County (portions), Hiram, Hogansville, Holly Springs, Jonesboro, Kennesaw, Kingston, Lake City, Lawrenceville, Lilburn, Lithonia, Loganville, Lovejoy, Mansfield, Marietta, Morrow, Newborn, Newton County (portions), Norcross, Palmetto, Paulding County (portions), Peachtree City, Pine Lake, Plainville, Polk County (portions), Powder Springs, Resaca, Riverdale, Rockdale County (portions), Rome, Roswell, Senoia, Smyrna, Snellville, Spalding County (portions), Stockbridge, Stone Mountain, Sunny Side, Taylorsville, Tyrone, Union City, Villa Rica, Walnut Grove, Walton County (portions), White, Whitesburg, Woodstock, Woolsey); 94 (Troup County (portions)); Below 100 (Arcade, Auburn, Banks County (portions), Barrow County (portions), Bethlehem, Between, Braselton, Carl (town), Clarke County (portions), Clermont, Gillsville, Hoschton, Jersey, Lula, Maysville, Monticello, Mount Zion, Oconee County, Pendergrass, Social Circle, Statham, Talmo, Winder, Tallapoosa, Cherokee County (portions), Gwinnett County (portions), Haralson County (portions)); Outside TV Markets (Bremen, Carrollton, Griffin, Orchard Hill, Waco, Waleska, Cherokee County (portions), Haralson County (portions), Spalding County (portions), Troup County (portions)).

Franchise award date: August 21, 1978. Franchise expiration date: N.A. Began: October 28, 1967.

Channel capacity: 20 (operating 2-way). Channels available but not in use: N.A.

Basic Service
Subscribers: 741,462.
Programming (received off-air): WAGA-TV (Buzzr, FOX, Movies!) Atlanta; WATC-DT (ETV) Atlanta; WATL (Antenna TV, Bounce TV, MNT) Atlanta; WGCL-TV (CBS, COZI TV, Grit) Atlanta; WGTV (PBS) Athens; WHSG-TV (TBN) Monroe; WPBA (PBS) Atlanta; WPCH-TV (IND) Atlanta; WPXA-TV (ION) Rome; WRCB (Antenna TV, NBC) Chattanooga; WSB-TV (ABC, MeTV) Atlanta; WUPA (CW, Decades) Atlanta; WUVG-DT (getTV, UNV) Athens; WXIA-TV (NBC) Atlanta; allband FM.
Programming (via microwave): Atlanta Interfaith Broadcasters.
Programming (via satellite): Pop; QVC.
Fee: $25.00 installation; $35.20 monthly.

Expanded Basic Service 1
Subscribers: N.A.
Programming (via satellite): A&E; AMC; Animal Planet; BET; Bravo; Cartoon Network; CMT; CNBC; CNN; Comcast/Charter Sports Southeast (CSS); Comedy Central; C-SPAN; C-SPAN 2; Discovery Channel; Disney Channel; E! HD; ESPN; ESPN2; Food Network; Fox News Channel; Fox Sports 1; FOX Sports South/SportSouth; Freeform; FX; Golf Channel; HGTV; History; HLN; Lifetime; MTV; Nickelodeon; Oxygen; Spike TV; Syfy; Telemundo; The Weather Channel; TLC; TNT; Travel Channel; truTV; Turner Classic Movies; TV Land; USA Network; VH1; WE tv.
Fee: $35.00 installation; $33.04 monthly.

Digital Basic Service
Subscribers: N.A.
Programming (via satellite): C-SPAN 3; Discovery Digital Networks; Disney XD; ESPN Classic; ESPNews; EVINE Live; GSN; MC; NASA TV; Nick Jr.; TeenNick; Weatherscan.

Digital Expanded Basic Service
Subscribers: N.A.
Programming (via satellite): BBC America; Bloomberg Television; Concert TV; Daystar TV Network; EWTN Global Catholic Network; FamilyNet; FOX College Sports Central; FOX College Sports Pacific; FXM; FYI; Great American Country; History International; IFC; LMN; MSNBC; National Geographic Channel; NBCSN; Nicktoons; Outdoor Channel; Ovation; Sundance TV.
Fee: $4.00 monthly.

Digital Pay Service 1
Pay Units: N.A.
Programming (via satellite): Cinemax (multiplexed); Flix; HBO (multiplexed); HITS (Headend In The Sky); Korean Channel; Showtime (multiplexed); Starz (multiplexed); The Movie Channel (multiplexed).
Fee: $5.99 monthly (Canales n), $14.99 monthly (Cinemax, HBO, Showtime, Starz, or TMC/Flix), $14.99 monthly (Korean), $29.95 monthly (TV Japan).

Video-On-Demand: Yes

Pay-Per-View
ESPN Now (delivered digitally); Hot Choice (delivered digitally); iN DEMAND (delivered digitally); Playboy TV (delivered digitally); Fresh (delivered digitally); Shorteez (delivered digitally).

Internet Service
Operational: Yes. Began: April 1, 2001.
Subscribers: 633,275.
Broadband Service: Comcast High Speed Internet.
Fee: $49.95 installation; $42.95 monthly; $3.00 modem lease; $139.00 modem purchase.

Telephone Service
Digital: Operational
Subscribers: 290,862.
Fee: $44.95 monthly
Miles of Plant: 42,364.0 (coaxial); 7,163.0 (fiber optic). Homes passed: 1,767,367.
Regional Vice President: Gene Shatlock. Regional Vice President Operations: Michael Hewitt. General Manager: Kenny Faust. Marketing Manager: Maleka Burnett. Technical Operations Manager: Deborah Collins. Communications Manager: Cindy Kicklighter.
Ownership: Comcast Cable Communications Inc. (MSO).

ATLANTA (metro area 2)—Formerly served by BellSouth Entertainment. No longer in operation. ICA: GA0271.

ATLANTA (metro area)—Comcast Cable. Now served by ATLANTA, GA [GA0017]. ICA: GA0001.

ATLANTA (northern portion)—Comcast Cable. Now served by ATLANTA, GA [GA0017]. ICA: GA0007.

ATLANTA (perimeter north)—Comcast Cable. Now served by ATLANTA, GA [GA0017]. ICA: GA0033.

ATTAPULGUS—Formerly served by KLiP Interactive. No longer in operation. ICA: GA0173.

AUGUSTA—Comcast Cable, 105 River Shoals Pkwy, Augusta, GA 30909. Phones: 706-733-7712; 706-738-0091. Fax: 706-739-1871. Web Site: http://www.comcast.com. Also serves Bartow, Blythe, Burke County (portions), Camak, Columbia County (portions), Dearing, Hephzibah, Hiltonia, Jefferson County (portions), Jenkins County (portions), Louisville, McDuffie County (portions), Millen, Screven County (portions), Sylvania, Thomson, Wadley, Warren County (portions), Warrenton & Waynesboro, GA; Aiken County (portions), Beech Island, Burnettown, Edgefield, North Augusta & Trenton, SC. ICA: GA0004.

TV Market Ranking: Below 100 (Aiken County (portions), AUGUSTA, Beech Island, Blythe, Burke County (portions), Burnettown, Columbia County (portions), Dearing, Edgefield, Hephzibah, North Augusta, Thomson, Trenton, Waynesboro, Jefferson County (portions), McDuffie County (portions), Warren County (portions)); Outside TV Markets (Bartow, Camak, Hiltonia, Jenkins County (portions), Screven County (portions), Wadley, Jefferson County (portions), Louisville, McDuffie County (portions), Millen, Sylvania, Warren County (portions), Warrenton).
Franchise award date: March 1, 1970. Franchise expiration date: N.A. Began: March 1, 1970.
Channel capacity: N.A. Channels available but not in use: N.A.

Basic Service
Subscribers: 75,753. Commercial subscribers: 3,931.
Programming (received off-air): WAGT (CW, NBC) Augusta; WBPI-CD (My Family TV) Augusta; WCES-TV (PBS) Wrens; WEBA-TV (PBS) Allendale; WFXG (Bounce TV, FOX, This TV) Augusta; WIS (Bounce TV, NBC, This TV) Columbia; WJBF (ABC, MeTV) Augusta; WRDW-TV (CBS, MNT, The Country Network) Augusta; 24 FMs.
Programming (via satellite): Comcast/Charter Sports Southeast (CSS); EWTN Global Catholic Network; ION Television; MyNetworkTV; QVC; TBS; USA Network; WGN America.
Fee: $42.50-$64.95 installation; $27.20 monthly.

Expanded Basic Service 1
Subscribers: N.A.
Programming (via satellite): A&E; AMC; Animal Planet; BET; Cartoon Network; CNBC; CNN; Comedy Central; C-SPAN; C-SPAN 2; Discovery Channel; Disney Channel; E! HD; ESPN; ESPN2; Food Network; Fox News Channel; Fox Sports 1; Freeform; FX; Golf Channel; Great American Country; Hallmark Channel; HGTV; History; HLN; Lifetime; MTV; NBCSN; Nickelodeon; OWN: Oprah Winfrey Network; Spike TV; SportSouth; Syfy; The Weather Channel; TLC; TNT; Travel Channel; truTV; Turner Classic Movies; TV Land; Univision Studios; VH1.
Fee: $30.04 monthly.

Digital Basic Service
Subscribers: N.A.
Programming (via satellite): BBC America; CBS Sports Network; CMT; Cooking Channel; C-SPAN 3; Discovery Digital Networks; Disney XD; DIY Network; DMX Music; ESPN HD; ESPN2 HD; ESPNews; Family Friendly Entertainment; Flix; FOX College Sports Central; FOX College Sports Pacific; FYI; GolTV; GSN; HD Theater; History International; LMN; MoviePlex; MSNBC; MTV Live; Nat Geo WILD; National Geographic Channel; NBA TV; NFL Network; Nick 2; Nick Jr.; Outdoor Channel; Oxygen; Sprout; Starz Encore (multiplexed); Sundance TV; TeenNick; Tennis Channel; The Word Network; TNT HD; Trinity Broadcasting Network (TBN); TV Asia; TV One; WE tv; Weatherscan; Zee TV.

Pay Service 1
Pay Units: N.A.
Programming (via satellite): HBO.
Fee: $9.50 monthly.

Digital Pay Service 1
Pay Units: N.A.
Programming (via satellite): Cinemax (multiplexed); Cinemax HD; HBO (multiplexed); HBO HD; Showtime (multiplexed); Showtime HD; Starz (multiplexed); Starz HD; The Movie Channel (multiplexed).
Fee: $12.05 monthly (each).

Video-On-Demand: Yes

Pay-Per-View
iN DEMAND (delivered digitally); Hot Choice (delivered digitally); Playboy TV (delivered digitally); Sports PPV (delivered digitally).

Internet Service
Operational: Yes.
Subscribers: 67,998.
Broadband Service: Comcast High Speed Internet.
Fee: $42.95 monthly.

Telephone Service
Digital: Operational
Subscribers: 38,195.
Miles of Plant: 5,216.0 (coaxial); 1,788.0 (fiber optic). Homes passed: 208,817.
Engineering Director: Harry Hess. Technical Operations Director: Butch Jernigan. Marketing Director: Joey Fortier.
Ownership: Comcast Cable Communications Inc. (MSO).

AUGUSTA—WOW! Internet, Cable & Phone, 7887 East Belleview Ave, Ste 1000, Englewood, CO 80111. Phones: 720-479-3500; 706-364-2100; 706-645-8553 (Corporate office); 706-364-1000 (Customer service). Fax: 720-479-3585. E-mail: wow_general@wideopenwest.com. Web Site: http://www.wowway.com. Also serves Columbia County (portions), Fort Gordon, Grovetown, Harlem & Richmond County (portions). ICA: GA0288. **Note:** This system is an overbuild.
TV Market Ranking: Below 100 (AUGUSTA, Columbia County (portions), Fort Gordon, Grovetown, Harlem, Richmond County (portions)).
Channel capacity: 80 (operating 2-way). Channels available but not in use: N.A.

Georgia—Cable Systems

Basic Service
Subscribers: 13,983.
Programming (received off-air): WAGT (CW, NBC) Augusta; WAGT-CD (America One) Augusta; WBPI-CD (My Family TV) Augusta; WCES-TV (PBS) Wrens; WEBA-TV (PBS) Allendale; WFXG (Bounce TV, FOX, This TV) Augusta; WJBF (ABC, MeTV) Augusta; WRDW-TV (CBS, MNT, The Country Network) Augusta.
Programming (via satellite): A&E; AMC; Animal Planet; BET; Bravo; Cartoon Network; CMT; CNBC; CNN; Comedy Central; C-SPAN; C-SPAN 2; CW PLUS; Discovery Channel; Disney Channel; Disney XD; E! HD; ESPN; ESPN Classic; ESPN2; EVINE Live; Food Network; Fox News Channel; Fox Sports 1; FOX Sports South/SportSouth; Freeform; FX; Golf Channel; Great American Country; Hallmark Channel; HGTV; History; HLN; Lifetime; LMN; MSNBC; MTV; MTV2; MyNetworkTV; Nick At Nite; Nickelodeon; Outdoor Channel; OWN: Oprah Winfrey Network; Oxygen; Pop; QVC; Spike TV; Syfy; TBS; The Weather Channel; TLC; TNT; Travel Channel; Trinity Broadcasting Network (TBN); truTV; Turner Classic Movies; TV Land; Univision Studios; USA Network; VH1; WGN America.
Fee: $50.00 installation; $33.00 monthly.

Digital Basic Service
Subscribers: N.A. Included in Valley Twp., AL
Programming (via satellite): Animal Planet HD; AXS TV; BBC America; Bloomberg Television; Boomerang; CBS Sports Network; Church Channel; CMT; Cooking Channel; C-SPAN 3; Destination America; Discovery Channel HD; Discovery Kids Channel; Discovery Life Channel; DIY Network; ESPN HD; ESPN2 HD; ESPNews; ESPNU; EWTN Global Catholic Network; FOX College Sports Central; FOX College Sports Pacific; Fox Sports 2; GSN; Hallmark Movies & Mysteries; HD Theater; IFC; INSP; Investigation Discovery; Jewelry Television; JUCE TV; MC; MTV Classic; MTV Hits; MTV Jams; mtvU; National Geographic Channel HD; NBCSN; NFL Network; Nick 2; Nick Jr.; Nicktoons; Outdoor Channel On Demand; QVC HD; Science Channel; Science HD; Starz HD; TBS HD; TeenNick; Tennis Channel; The Word Network; TLC HD; TNT HD; Tr3s; Universal HD; UP; Versus HD; VH1 Soul; WE tv.

Pay Service 1
Pay Units: N.A.
Programming (via satellite): HBO; Showtime.
Fee: $8.95 monthly (Showtime), $9.95 monthly (HBO).

Digital Pay Service 1
Pay Units: N.A.
Programming (via satellite): Cinemax (multiplexed); Cinemax HD; Cinemax On Demand; Flix; Flix On Demand; HBO (multiplexed); HBO HD; HBO on Demand; Showtime (multiplexed); Showtime HD; Showtime On Demand; Starz (multiplexed); Starz Encore (multiplexed); Sundance TV; The Movie Channel (multiplexed); The Movie Channel On Demand.
Video-On-Demand: Yes

Pay-Per-View
iN DEMAND (delivered digitally); Hot Choice (delivered digitally); Playboy TV (delivered digitally); Fresh (delivered digitally); Shorteez (delivered digitally); Spice: Xcess (delivered digitally); Club Jenna (delivered digitally); ESPN Now (delivered digitally).

Internet Service
Operational: Yes.
Subscribers: 16,786.
Broadband Service: Knology.Net.
Fee: $29.95 installation; $61.95 monthly; $7.00 modem lease; $199.00 modem purchase.

Telephone Service
Analog: Not Operational
Digital: Operational
Subscribers: 17,344.
Fee: $23.80 monthly
Miles of Plant: 1,711.0 (coaxial); 512.0 (fiber optic). Homes passed: 72,872.
Chief Executive Officer: Colleen Abdoulah. President: Steven Cochran. Chief Financial Officer: Rich Fish.
Ownership: WideOpenWest LLC (MSO).

AVALON—Formerly served by Galaxy Cablevision. Now served by Hart Communications, HART COUNTY, GA [GA0293]. ICA: GA0126.

AVERA—Formerly served by National Cable Inc. No longer in operation. ICA: GA0174.

BACONTON—CNS, 30 East Broad St, PO Box 328, Camilla, GA 31730. Phone: 229-336-2220. E-mail: answers@cns-internet.com. Web Site: http://www.cns-internet.com. ICA: GA0294.
TV Market Ranking: Below 100 (BACONTON).
Channel capacity: N.A. Channels available but not in use: N.A.

Basic Service
Subscribers: N.A.
Programming (received off-air): WABW-TV (PBS) Pelham; WALB (ABC, NBC, This TV) Albany; WFSU-TV (PBS) Tallahassee; WFXL (Bounce TV, FOX) Albany; WSB-TV (ABC, MeTV) Atlanta; WSWG (CBS, CW, MeTV, MNT) Valdosta; WTXL-TV (ABC, Bounce TV) Tallahassee.
Programming (via satellite): C-SPAN; C-SPAN 2; CW Television Network; HSN; QVC; The Weather Channel; Trinity Broadcasting Network (TBN).
Fee: $25.00 installation.

Expanded Basic Service 1
Subscribers: N.A.
Programming (via satellite): A&E; AMC; Animal Planet; BET; Bloomberg Television; Bravo; Cartoon Network; CMT; CNBC; CNN; Comcast/Charter Sports Southeast (CSS); Comedy Central; Discovery Channel; Discovery Life Channel; Disney Channel; Disney XD; E! HD; ESPN; ESPN Classic; ESPN2; FamilyNet; Food Network; Fox News Channel; Fox Sports 1; FOX Sports South/SportSouth; Freeform; FX; Golf Channel; Great American Country; GSN; Hallmark Channel; HGTV; History; ION Television; Lifetime; MSNBC; MTV; National Geographic Channel; Nickelodeon; Outdoor Channel; Oxygen; Spike TV; Syfy; TBS; Telemundo; TLC; TNT; Travel Channel; truTV; Turner Classic Movies; TV Land; Univision; USA Network; VH1; WE tv; WGN America.

Digital Basic Service
Subscribers: N.A.
Programming (via satellite): American Heroes Channel; BBC America; Boomerang; Chiller; Church Channel; cloo; CMT; CNN en Espanol; CNN International; Cooking Channel; Destination America; Discovery Kids Channel; DIY Network; Enlace USA; ESPNews; ESPNU; EWTN Global Catholic Network; FamilyNet; Fox Business Network; FOX Sports Florida/Sun Sports; Fuse; FXM; FYI; Hallmark Movies & Mysteries; History International; IFC; Investigation Discovery; JUCE TV; LMN; MC; MTV Classic; MTV Hits; MTV Jams; MTV2; NASA TV; NBC Universo; NBCSN; Nick 2; Nick Jr.; Nicktoons; OWN: Oprah Winfrey Network; RFD-TV; Science Channel; Sprout; TeenNick; Tennis Channel; The Sportsman Channel; VH1 Soul.

Digital Expanded Basic Service
Subscribers: N.A.
Programming (via satellite): A&E HD; Animal Planet HD; AXS TV; Bio HD; Bravo HD; CNBC HD+; E! HD; ESPN HD; ESPN2 HD; ESPNews HD; ESPNU HD; Food Network HD; Fox Business Network HD; FSN HD; FX HD; Golf Channel HD; HD Theater; HGTV HD; History HD; Lifetime HD; MSNBC HD; National Geographic Channel HD; Syfy HD; TBS HD; TLC HD; TNT HD; Universal HD; USA Network HD; Versus HD.

Digital Pay Service 1
Pay Units: N.A.
Programming (via satellite): Cinemax (multiplexed); Flix; HBO (multiplexed); Showtime (multiplexed); Starz (multiplexed); Starz Encore (multiplexed); The Movie Channel (multiplexed).
Video-On-Demand: No

Internet Service
Operational: Yes.

Telephone Service
Digital: Operational
Broadband Engineer: Chris White. Marketing Coordinator: Sherri Nix. Marketing Representative: Angela Boat.
Ownership: Community Network Services (MSO).

BAINBRIDGE—Mediacom, 275 Norman Dr, Valdosta, GA 31601. Phone: 866-755-2225. Web Site: http://www.mediacomcable.com. Also serves Decatur County (portions), Donalsonville & Seminole County (portions). ICA: GA0060.
TV Market Ranking: Below 100 (BAINBRIDGE, Decatur County (portions), Donalsonville, Seminole County (portions)). Franchise award date: N.A. Franchise expiration date: N.A. Began: July 20, 1968.
Channel capacity: N.A. Channels available but not in use: N.A.

Basic Service
Subscribers: 2,993.
Programming (received off-air): WABW-TV (PBS) Pelham; WALB (ABC, NBC, This TV) Albany; WBXT-LD (IND) Tallahassee; WCTV (CBS, MNT, This TV) Thomasville; WFSU-TV (PBS) Tallahassee; WMBB (ABC, This TV) Panama City; WSWG (CBS, CW, MeTV, MNT) Valdosta; WTLH (CW, FOX, MeTV) Bainbridge; WTVY (CBS, CW, MeTV, MNT, This TV) Dothan; WTWC-TV (NBC, The Country Network) Tallahassee; WTXL-TV (ABC, Bounce TV) Tallahassee; allband FM.
Programming (via microwave): WSB-TV (ABC, MeTV) Atlanta.
Programming (via satellite): A&E; BET; CNBC; CNN; Comedy Central; C-SPAN; Discovery Channel; Freeform; HLN; Lifetime; Nickelodeon; TBS; The Weather Channel; TNT; VH1.
Fee: $43.95 monthly.

Expanded Basic Service 1
Subscribers: N.A.
Programming (via satellite): AMC; Animal Planet; Bravo; Cartoon Network; CMT; C-SPAN 2; Discovery Life Channel; Disney Channel; E! HD; ESPN; ESPN2; EWTN Global Catholic Network; Food Network; Fox News Channel; Fox Sports 1; FOX Sports South/SportSouth; FX; Golf Channel; Hallmark Channel; HGTV; History; INSP; ION Television; MSNBC; MTV; Outdoor Channel; Pop; QVC; Spike TV; Syfy; TLC; Travel Channel; Trinity Broadcasting Network (TBN); truTV; TV Land; USA Network; WE tv.
Fee: $11.13 monthly.

Digital Basic Service
Subscribers: N.A.
Programming (via satellite): BBC America; Discovery Digital Networks; GSN; IFC; International Television (ITV); MC; National Geographic Channel; NBCSN; Nick Jr.; Ovation; Turner Classic Movies.

Digital Pay Service 1
Pay Units: N.A.
Programming (via satellite): Cinemax (multiplexed); HBO (multiplexed); Showtime (multiplexed); Starz (multiplexed); Starz Encore (multiplexed); Sundance TV; The Movie Channel (multiplexed).
Fee: $10.00 installation; $1.75 monthly (Encore), $4.75 monthly (Starz), $10.75 monthly (Cinemax/Sundance), $11.75 monthly (Showtime/TMC), $13.15 monthly (HBO).
Video-On-Demand: Yes

Pay-Per-View
ETC (delivered digitally); ESPN Now (delivered digitally); Sports PPV (delivered digitally).

Internet Service
Operational: Yes.
Broadband Service: Mediacom High Speed Internet.
Fee: $59.95 installation; $42.95 monthly; $3.00 modem lease.

Telephone Service
Analog: Not Operational
Digital: Operational
Homes passed: 8,111. Miles of plant (coax & fiber) included in Thomasville.
Regional Vice President: Sue Misiunas. Vice President, Financial Reporting: Kenneth J. Kohrs. Regional Technical Operations Manager: Gary McDougall. Regional Marketing Director: Melanie Hannasch. Marketing Manager: Daryl Channey.
Ownership: Mediacom LLC (MSO).

BALDWIN COUNTY (eastern portion)—Formerly served by KLiP Interactive. No longer in operation. ICA: GA0175.

BAXLEY—ATC Broadband, 371 West Parker St, Baxley, GA 31513. Phones: 877-217-2842 (Sales); 912-705-5000. Fax: 912-705-2959. E-mail: cabletv.signals@gmail.com. Web Site: http://www.atcbroadband.com. ICA: GA0082.
TV Market Ranking: Below 100 (BAXLEY). Franchise award date: N.A. Franchise expiration date: N.A. Began: April 1, 1966.
Channel capacity: N.A. Channels available but not in use: N.A.

Basic Service
Subscribers: 1,111.
Programming (received off-air): WCWJ (Bounce TV, CW) Jacksonville; WFOX-TV (FOX, MeTV, MNT) Jacksonville; WGSA (CW) Baxley; WJAX-TV (CBS, Decades, getTV) Jacksonville; WJCL (ABC) Savannah; WJCT (PBS) Jacksonville; WJXT (LATV, This TV) Jacksonville; WJXX (ABC) Orange Park; WPXC-TV (ION) Brunswick; WSAV-TV (MeTV, MNT, NBC) Savannah; WTGS (Antenna TV, FOX) Hardeeville; WTLV (Antenna TV, NBC, The Country Network) Jacksonville; WTOC-TV (Bounce TV, CBS, This TV) Savannah; WXGA-TV (PBS) Waycross; allband FM.
Programming (via satellite): A&E; AMC; Animal Planet; BET; Cartoon Network;

Cable Systems—Georgia

CMT; CNBC; CNN; Comcast/Charter Sports Southeast (CSS); Comedy Central; C-SPAN; C-SPAN 2; Discovery Channel; Discovery Life Channel; Disney Channel; E! HD; ESPN; ESPN Classic; ESPN2; Food Network; Fox News Channel; Fox Sports 1; FOX Sports South/SportSouth; Freeform; FX; Golf Channel; Hallmark Channel; HGTV; History; HLN; INSP; Lifetime; Local Cable Weather; MTV; National Geographic Channel; Nickelodeon; Outdoor Channel; Pop; QVC; Spike TV; Syfy; TBS; The Weather Channel; TLC; TNT; Travel Channel; Trinity Broadcasting Network (TBN); truTV; TV Land; USA Network; VH1.
Fee: $35.00 installation; $15.95 monthly.
Digital Basic Service
Subscribers: 396.
Programming (via satellite): BBC America; Bloomberg Television; Boomerang; Cloo; Discovery Life Channel; Disney XD; DMX Music; ESPN Classic; ESPN2; ESPNews; ESPNU; Flix; Fox Sports 1; FSN Digital Atlantic; FSN Digital Central; FSN Digital Pacific; Fuse; FXM; FYI; Golf Channel; Great American Country; GSN; Hallmark Movies & Mysteries; HGTV; History; History International; Investigation Discovery; LMN; MTV Classic; MTV Hits; MTV2; National Geographic Channel; NBCSN; Nick Jr.; Nicktoons; Outdoor Channel; RFD-TV; Science Channel; Sundance TV; TeenNick; Trinity Broadcasting Network (TBN); Turner Classic Movies; UP; WE tv.
Fee: $1.95 monthly.
Digital Expanded Basic Service
Subscribers: N.A.
Programming (via satellite): A&E HD; Animal Planet HD; Bravo HD; CNBC HD+; CNN HD; Discovery Channel HD; ESPN HD; ESPN2 HD; Golf Channel HD; History HD; National Geographic Channel HD; Outdoor Channel 2 HD; Science HD; Syfy HD; TBS HD; The Weather Channel HD; TLC HD; TNT HD; USA Network HD; Versus HD.
Digital Expanded Basic Service 2
Subscribers: N.A.
Programming (via satellite): AXS TV; HD Theater; Universal HD.
Digital Pay Service 1
Pay Units: N.A.
Programming (via satellite): Cinemax (multiplexed); Cinemax HD; HBO (multiplexed); HBO HD; Showtime (multiplexed); Showtime HD; Starz (multiplexed); Starz Encore (multiplexed); Starz HD; The Movie Channel (multiplexed).
Fee: $8.00 monthly (Cinemax), $12.95 monthly (HBO, Showtime/TMC or Starz/Encore).
Video-On-Demand: No
Pay-Per-View
iN DEMAND (delivered digitally); Playboy TV (delivered digitally); Fresh (delivered digitally); Spice: Xcess (delivered digitally); Club Jenna (delivered digitally).
Internet Service
Operational: Yes, DSL.
Broadband Service: atcnet.
Fee: $49.95-$64.95 monthly.
Telephone Service
Analog: Operational
Miles of Plant: 48.0 (coaxial); None (fiber optic). Homes passed: 2,300.
General Manager: Kevin Brooks. Chief Technician: Tony McKinnon. Customer Service: Jennifer Barnette.
Ownership: ATC (Alma, GA) (MSO).

BENT TREE—Ellijay Telephone Cooperative. Now served by ELLIJAY, GA [GA0044]. ICA: GA0138.

BERLIN—Formerly served by Mega Cable LLC. No longer in operation. ICA: GA0122.

BIBB COUNTY (portions)—Suburban Cable, 4931 Mercer University Dr, Macon, GA 31210. Phone: 478-477-6881. ICA: GA0334.
TV Market Ranking: Below 100 (BIBB COUNTY (portions)).
Channel capacity: N.A. Channels available but not in use: N.A.
Vice President: Robbie Watson.
Ownership: Suburban Cable Ltd.

BIG CANOE—Teleview. Now served by DAHLONEGA, GA [GA0099]. ICA: GA0095.

BISHOP—Formerly served by KLiP Interactive. No longer in operation. ICA: GA0144.

BLACKSHEAR—ATC Broadband, 3349 Hwy 84 West, Ste 104, Blackshear, GA 31516. Phones: 912-449-5443; 877-552-5946. Fax: 912-449-2602. E-mail: cabletv.signals@gmail.com. Web Site: http://www.atcbroadband.com. ICA: GA0100.
TV Market Ranking: Below 100 (BLACKSHEAR). Franchise award date: N.A. Franchise expiration date: N.A. Began: December 1, 1968.
Channel capacity: N.A. Channels available but not in use: N.A.
Basic Service
Subscribers: 1,550.
Programming (received off-air): WCWJ (Bounce TV, CW) Jacksonville; WFOX-TV (FOX, MeTV, MNT) Jacksonville; WGSA (CW) Baxley; WJAX-TV (CBS, Decades, getTV) Jacksonville; WJCL (ABC) Savannah; WJCT (PBS) Jacksonville; WJXT (LATV, This TV) Jacksonville; WJXX (ABC) Orange Park; WPXC-TV (ION) Brunswick; WSAV-TV (MeTV, MNT, NBC) Savannah; WTGS (Antenna TV, FOX) Hardeeville; WTLV (Antenna TV, NBC, The Country Network) Jacksonville; WTOC-TV (Bounce TV, CBS, This TV) Savannah; WXGA-TV (PBS) Waycross; allband FM.
Programming (via satellite): A&E; AMC; Animal Planet; BET; Cartoon Network; CMT; CNBC; CNN; Comcast/Charter Sports Southeast (CSS); Comedy Central; C-SPAN; C-SPAN 2; Discovery Channel; Discovery Life Channel; Disney Channel; E! HD; ESPN; ESPN Classic; ESPN2; Food Network; Fox News Channel; Fox Sports 1; FOX Sports South/SportSouth; Freeform; FX; Golf Channel; Hallmark Channel; HGTV; History; HLN; INSP; Lifetime; Local Cable Weather; MTV; National Geographic Channel; Nickelodeon; Outdoor Channel; Pop; QVC; Spike TV; Syfy; TBS; The Weather Channel; TLC; TNT; Travel Channel; Trinity Broadcasting Network (TBN); truTV; TV Land; USA Network; VH1.
Fee: $35.00 installation; $15.95 monthly.
Digital Basic Service
Subscribers: 729.
Programming (via satellite): BBC America; Bloomberg Television; Boomerang; Cloo; Discovery Life Channel; Disney XD; DMX Music; ESPN Classic; ESPN2; ESPNews; ESPNU; Flix; Fox Sports 1; FSN Digital Atlantic; FSN Digital Central; FSN Digital Pacific; Fuse; FXM; FYI; Golf Channel; Great American Country; GSN; Hallmark Movies & Mysteries; HGTV; History; History International; Investigation Discovery; LMN; Local Cable Weather; MTV Classic; MTV Hits; MTV2; NBCSN; Nick Jr.; Nicktoons; Outdoor Channel; RFD-TV; Science Channel; Sundance TV; TeenNick; Trinity Broadcasting Network (TBN); Turner Classic Movies; UP; WE tv.
Fee: $15.95 monthly.
Digital Expanded Basic Service
Subscribers: N.A.
Programming (via satellite): A&E HD; Animal Planet HD; Bravo HD; CNBC HD+; CNN HD; Discovery Channel HD; ESPN HD; ESPN2 HD; Golf Channel HD; History HD; National Geographic Channel HD; Outdoor Channel 2 HD; Science HD; Syfy HD; TBS HD; The Weather Channel HD; TLC HD; TNT HD; USA Network HD; Versus HD.
Digital Expanded Basic Service 2
Subscribers: N.A.
Programming (via satellite): AXS TV; HD Theater; Universal HD.
Digital Pay Service 1
Pay Units: 78.
Programming (via satellite): Showtime (multiplexed); Showtime HD.
Fee: $12.95 monthly.
Digital Pay Service 2
Pay Units: 72.
Programming (via satellite): HBO (multiplexed); HBO HD.
Fee: $12.95 monthly.
Digital Pay Service 3
Pay Units: 12.
Programming (via satellite): Starz (multiplexed); Starz HD.
Fee: $12.95 monthly.
Digital Pay Service 4
Pay Units: N.A.
Programming (via satellite): Cinemax (multiplexed); Cinemax HD; Starz Encore (multiplexed); The Movie Channel (multiplexed).
Fee: $8.00 monthly.
Video-On-Demand: No
Pay-Per-View
iN DEMAND (delivered digitally); Playboy TV (delivered digitally); Fresh (delivered digitally); Spice: Xcess (delivered digitally); Club Jenna (delivered digitally).
Internet Service
Operational: Yes, DSL & dial-up.
Broadband Service: atcnet.
Fee: $49.95-$64.95 monthly.
Telephone Service
Analog: Operational
Miles of Plant: 35.0 (coaxial); None (fiber optic). Homes passed: 2,500.
General Manager: Kevin Brooks. Chief Technician: Tony McKinnon. Customer Service: Jennifer Barnette.
Ownership: ATC (Alma, GA) (MSO).

BLAIRSVILLE—Teleview. Now served by DAHLONEGA, GA [GA0099]. ICA: GA0113.

BLAKELY—Blakely Cable TV Inc, 113 West Liberty St, Blakely, GA 31723. Phone: 229-723-3555. Fax: 229-723-2000. Also serves Columbia. ICA: GA0085.
TV Market Ranking: Below 100 (BLAKELY, Columbia). Franchise award date: N.A. Franchise expiration date: N.A. Began: December 1, 1979.
Channel capacity: N.A. Channels available but not in use: N.A.
Basic Service
Subscribers: N.A.
Programming (received off-air): WACS-TV (PBS) Dawson; WALB (ABC, NBC, This TV) Albany; WCTV (CBS, MNT, This TV) Thomasville; WDHN (ABC) Dothan; WTVM (ABC, Bounce TV) Columbus; WTVY (CBS, CW, MeTV, MNT, This TV) Dothan; WXTX (FOX, Movies!, This TV) Columbus.
Programming (via satellite): A&E; Animal Planet; BET; Cartoon Network; CMT; CNBC; CNN; Comedy Central; C-SPAN; C-SPAN 2; Discovery Channel; Disney Channel; E! HD; ESPN; ESPN2; Food Network; Fox News Channel; Fox Sports 1; FOX Sports South/SportSouth; Freeform; FX; Golf Channel; Hallmark Channel; HGTV; History; HLN; Lifetime; MTV; National Geographic Channel; NBCSN; Nickelodeon; Spike TV; SportSouth; Syfy; TBS; The Weather Channel; TLC; TNT; Travel Channel; Trinity Broadcasting Network (TBN); truTV; Turner Classic Movies; TV Land; USA Network; VH1; WGN America.
Fee: $25.00 installation.
Pay Service 1
Pay Units: N.A.
Programming (via satellite): Cinemax; HBO.
Fee: $8.95 - $10.00 monthly (each).
Video-On-Demand: No
Internet Service
Operational: No.
Telephone Service
None
Miles of Plant: 35.0 (coaxial); None (fiber optic). Homes passed: 2,200.
General Manager: William C. De Loach Jr. Office Manager: Anne Harroll.
Ownership: Blakely Cable TV Inc. (MSO).

BLUE RIDGE—Community Cable Television Co. Now served by ELLIJAY, GA [GA0044]. ICA: GA0075.

BOLINGBROKE—Reynolds Cable TV Inc, 528 South Main St, PO Box 782, Swainsboro, GA 30401. Phones: 800-822-8650; 478-289-9949; 478-237-2853. Fax: 47-237-8730. E-mail: reynoldscable@reynoldscable.net. Web Site: http://www.reynoldscable.net. ICA: GA0123.
TV Market Ranking: Below 100 (BOLINGBROKE). Franchise award date: N.A. Franchise expiration date: N.A. Began: August 1, 1989.
Channel capacity: N.A. Channels available but not in use: N.A.
Basic Service
Subscribers: N.A.
Programming (received off-air): WGNM (Christian TV Network) Macon; WGXA (ABC, FOX) Macon; WMAZ-TV (CBS) Macon; WMGT-TV (Escape, MNT, NBC) Macon; WMUM-TV (PBS) Cochran; WPGA-TV (Bounce TV, IND, MeTV) Perry; WSB-TV (ABC, MeTV) Atlanta.
Programming (via satellite): A&E; AMC; Animal Planet; Cartoon Network; CMT; CNBC; CNN; Comcast/Charter Sports Southeast (CSS); Comedy Central; C-SPAN; CW PLUS; Discovery Channel; Disney Channel; E! HD; ESPN; ESPN2; Food Network; Fox News Channel; FOX Sports South/SportSouth; Freeform; FX; Golf Channel; Hallmark Channel; HGTV; History; HLN; Lifetime; MTV; NFL Network; Nickelodeon; Outdoor Channel; QVC; Radar Channel; Spike TV; Syfy; TBS; The Weather Channel; TLC; TNT; Travel Channel; Trinity Broadcasting Network (TBN); truTV; TV Land; USA Network; VH1.
Fee: $23.99 monthly.
Digital Basic Service
Subscribers: N.A.
Programming (via satellite): BBC America; Bloomberg Television; Bravo; Chiller; Church Channel; Cloo; CMT; Cooking Channel; Daystar TV Network; Destination America; Discovery Kids Channel; Discovery Life Channel; Disney XD; DMX Music; ESPN Classic; ESPN2; ESPNews; EVINE Live; FOX College Sports Central; FOX College Sports Pacific; Fox Sports 1; Fuse; FXM; FYI; Golf Channel; Great American Country; GSN; HGTV; History; History Interna-

2017 Edition D-155

Georgia—Cable Systems

tional; IFC; Investigation Discovery; JUCE TV; LMN; MTV Classic; MTV Hits; MTV2; Nat Geo WILD; NBCSN; Nick Jr.; Nicktoons; Outdoor Channel; Ovation; OWN: Oprah Winfrey Network; RFD-TV; Science Channel; Sprout; Syfy; TeenNick; The Word Network; Trinity Broadcasting Network (TBN); Turner Classic Movies; TV Land; TVG Network; UP; VH1 Soul; WE tv.

Digital Expanded Basic Service
Subscribers: N.A.
Programming (via satellite): A&E HD; AXS TV; Discovery Channel HD; ESPN HD; ESPN2 HD; HGTV HD; NFL Network HD; Outdoor Channel 2 HD.
Fee: $9.99 monthly.

Digital Pay Service 1
Pay Units: N.A.
Programming (via satellite): Cinemax (multiplexed); HBO (multiplexed); Playboy TV; Showtime (multiplexed); Starz (multiplexed); Starz Encore (multiplexed); The Movie Channel (multiplexed).
Fee: $4.00 monthly (Encore), $10.95 monthly (Starz/Encore), $15.95 monthly (Cinemax), $15.99 monthly (Showtime/TMC) or $18.99 monthly (HBO).

Video-On-Demand: No

Internet Service
Operational: Yes.
Fee: $29.99 monthly.

Telephone Service
Digital: Operational
Fee: $39.99 monthly
Miles of Plant: 55.0 (coaxial); None (fiber optic). Homes passed: 1,350.
General Manager: Terry Reynolds.
Ownership: Reynolds Cable TV Inc. (MSO).

BOSTON—Formerly served by Southeast Cable TV Inc. No longer in operation. ICA: GA0176.

BOWMAN—Comcast Cablevision of the South. Now served by ELBERTON, GA [GA0192]. ICA: GA0147.

BRONWOOD—Formerly served by Citizens Cable TV. No longer in operation. ICA: GA0158.

BROOKLET—Bulloch Telephone, 2903 Northside Dr. West, Statesboro, GA 30458. Phone: 912-865-1100. Fax: 912-865-2500. E-mail: bullnet@bulloch.net. Web Site: http://www.bulloch.net. Also serves Portal. ICA: GA0330.
TV Market Ranking: Outside TV Markets (BROOKLET).
Channel capacity: N.A. Channels available but not in use: N.A.

Basic Service
Subscribers: 2,416.
Fee: $16.95 monthly.
General Manager: John D. Scott, Jr.
Ownership: Bulloch Telephone Cooperative (MSO).

BROWNS CROSSING—Formerly served by National Cable Inc. No longer in operation. ICA: GA0276.

BRUNSWICK—Comcast Cable. Now served by JACKSONVILLE, FL [FL0002]. ICA: GA0019.

BUENA VISTA—Flint Cable TV. Now served by REYNOLDS, GA [GA0236]. ICA: GA0130.

BUTLER—Flint Cable TV. Now served by REYNOLDS, GA [GA0236]. ICA: GA0128.

CAIRO—CNS, 100 2nd St SW, Cairo, GA 39828. Phone: 229-307-0332. E-mail: answers@cns-internet.com. Web Site: http://www.cns-internet.com. ICA: GA0306. **Note:** This system is an overbuild.
TV Market Ranking: Below 100 (CAIRO). Franchise award date: N.A. Franchise expiration date: N.A. Began: June 27, 2001.
Channel capacity: N.A. Channels available but not in use: N.A.

Basic Service
Subscribers: N.A.
Programming (received off-air): WABW-TV (PBS) Pelham; WALB (ABC, NBC, This TV) Albany; WCTV (CBS, MNT, This TV) Thomasville; WFSU-TV (PBS) Tallahassee; WSB-TV (ABC, MeTV) Atlanta; WTLF (CW) Tallahassee; WTLH (CW, FOX, MeTV) Bainbridge; WTWC-TV (NBC, The Country Network) Tallahassee; WTXL-TV (ABC, Bounce TV) Tallahassee.
Programming (via satellite): C-SPAN; C-SPAN 2; HSN; QVC; The Weather Channel; Trinity Broadcasting Network (TBN).

Expanded Basic Service 1
Subscribers: N.A.
Programming (via satellite): A&E; AMC; Animal Planet; BET; Bloomberg Television; Bravo; Cartoon Network; CNBC; CNN; Comcast/Charter Sports Southeast (CSS); Comedy Central; Discovery Channel; Discovery Life Channel; Disney Channel; Disney XD; E! HD; ESPN; ESPN Classic; ESPN2; FamilyNet; Food Network; Fox News Channel; Fox Sports 1; FOX Sports South/SportSouth; Freeform; FX; Golf Channel; Great American Country; GSN; Hallmark Channel; HGTV; History; ION Television; Lifetime; MSNBC; MTV; National Geographic Channel; Nickelodeon; Outdoor Channel; Oxygen; Spike TV; Syfy; TBS; Telemundo; TLC; TNT; Travel Channel; truTV; Turner Classic Movies; TV Land; Univision Studios; USA Network; VH1; WE tv; WGN America.
Fee: $29.95 monthly.

Digital Basic Service
Subscribers: N.A.
Programming (via satellite): BBC America; Boomerang; CMT; CNN en Espanol; CNN International; Discovery Digital Networks; DIY Network; Family Friendly Entertainment; Fuse; FXM; FYI; History International; IFC; LMN; MC; NASA TV; Nick 2; Nick Jr.; TeenNick.

Digital Pay Service 1
Pay Units: N.A.
Programming (via satellite): Cinemax (multiplexed); Flix; HBO (multiplexed); Showtime (multiplexed); Starz (multiplexed); Starz Encore (multiplexed); The Movie Channel (multiplexed).
Fee: $10.00 monthly (each).

Pay-Per-View
iN DEMAND.

Internet Service
Operational: Yes.
Broadband Service: SyrupCity.net.
Fee: $28.95 monthly.

Telephone Service
Digital: Operational
Miles of Plant: 100.0 (coaxial); None (fiber optic).
Broadband Engineer: Chris White. Marketing Coordinator: Sherri Nix. Marketing Representative: Angela Boat.
Ownership: Community Network Services (MSO).

CAMILLA—CNS, 30 East Broad St, PO Box 328, Camilla, GA 31730. Phones: 229-336-2220; 229-336-7856. E-mail: answers@cns-internet.com. Web Site: http://www.cns-internet.com. ICA: GA0307. **Note:** This system is an overbuild.
TV Market Ranking: Below 100 (CAMILLA).
Channel capacity: 88 (operating 2-way). Channels available but not in use: N.A.

Basic Service
Subscribers: 19,483.
Programming (received off-air): WABW-TV (PBS) Pelham; WALB (ABC, NBC, This TV) Albany; WCTV (CBS, MNT, This TV) Thomasville; WFSU-TV (PBS) Tallahassee; WFXL (Bounce TV, FOX) Albany; WSB-TV (ABC, MeTV) Atlanta; WSWG (CBS, CW, MeTV, MNT) Valdosta; WTXL-TV (ABC, Bounce TV) Tallahassee.
Programming (via satellite): Bloomberg Television; C-SPAN; C-SPAN 2; CW PLUS; Discovery Channel; Discovery Life Channel; Disney Channel; Disney XD; Family Friendly Entertainment; FamilyNet; Fox News Channel; FOX Sports South/SportSouth; Hallmark Channel; HLN; ION Television; QVC; TBS; The Weather Channel; Travel Channel; Trinity Broadcasting Network (TBN).

Expanded Basic Service 1
Subscribers: N.A.
Programming (via satellite): A&E; AMC; Animal Planet; BET; Bravo; Cartoon Network; CNBC; CNN; Comedy Central; E! HD; ESPN; ESPN2; Food Network; Fox Sports 1; Freeform; FX; Golf Channel; Great American Country; GSN; HGTV; History; Lifetime; MSNBC; MTV; Nickelodeon; Outdoor Channel; Spike TV; Syfy; TLC; TNT; truTV; Turner Classic Movies; TV Land; Univision Studios; USA Network; VH1; WE tv; WGN America.
Fee: $32.95 monthly.

Digital Basic Service
Subscribers: N.A.
Programming (via satellite): BBC America; Boomerang; CNN en Espanol; CNN International; Discovery Digital Networks; DIY Network; Fox Deportes; Fuse; FXM; FYI; History International; IFC; LMN; MC; National Geographic Channel; Nick 2; Nick Jr.; TeenNick.

Pay Service 1
Pay Units: N.A.
Programming (via satellite): Cinemax; HBO; Showtime; Starz; Starz Encore.
Fee: $8.95 monthly (HBO).

Digital Pay Service 1
Pay Units: N.A.
Programming (via satellite): Cinemax (multiplexed); Flix; HBO (multiplexed); Showtime (multiplexed); Starz (multiplexed); Starz Encore (multiplexed); Sundance TV; The Movie Channel (multiplexed).
Fee: $10.00 monthly (each).

Video-On-Demand: Yes

Pay-Per-View
iN DEMAND.

Internet Service
Operational: Yes.
Subscribers: 13,219.
Broadband Service: SyrupCity.net.
Fee: $28.95 monthly.

Telephone Service
Digital: Operational
Subscribers: 6,675.
Miles of Plant: 1,246.0 (coaxial); 624.0 (fiber optic). Homes passed: 34,800.
Broadband Engineer: Chris White. Marketing Coordinator: Sherri Nix. Marketing Representative: Angela Boat.
Ownership: Community Network Services (MSO).

CAMILLA—Mediacom. Now served by ALBANY, GA [GA0011]. ICA: GA0065.

CARNESVILLE—TruVista Communications, 112 York St, PO Box 160, Chester, SC 29706. Phones: 800-768-1212; 706-356-1714. Web Site: http://truvista.net. Also serves Franklin County (portions), Lavonia & Martin. ICA: GA0290.
TV Market Ranking: 46 (CARNESVILLE, Franklin County (portions), Lavonia, Martin).
Channel capacity: N.A. Channels available but not in use: N.A.

Basic Service
Subscribers: 800.
Programming (received off-air): WAGA-TV (Buzzr, FOX, Movies!) Atlanta; WGGS-TV (IND) Greenville; WGTA (Decades, Heroes & Icons, Movies!) Toccoa; WGTV (PBS) Athens; WHNS (COZI TV, Escape, FOX) Greenville; WLOS (ABC, Antenna TV) Asheville; WNTV (PBS) Greenville; WSB-TV (ABC, MeTV) Atlanta; WXIA-TV (NBC) Atlanta; WYCW (CW) Asheville; WYFF (NBC, Movies!) Greenville.
Programming (via satellite): A&E; Cartoon Network; CMT; CNBC; CNN; Comedy Central; C-SPAN; C-SPAN 2; Discovery Channel; Disney Channel; E! HD; ESPN; ESPN2; Fox News Channel; FOX Sports South/SportSouth; Freeform; HGTV; HLN; Lifetime; MTV; Nickelodeon; Outdoor Channel; QVC; Spike TV; Syfy; TBS; The Weather Channel; TLC; TNT; Trinity Broadcasting Network (TBN); Turner Classic Movies; TV Land; USA Network; WGN America.
Fee: $30.00 installation; $20.99 monthly.

Digital Basic Service
Subscribers: N.A.
Programming (via satellite): BBC America; Bloomberg Television; Bravo; Discovery Life Channel; DMX Music; ESPN Classic; ESPNews; Fox Sports 1; Golf Channel; GSN; History; IFC; MTV Classic; NBCSN; Nick Jr.; Nicktoons; Outdoor Channel; VH1 Country; WE tv.

Pay Service 1
Pay Units: N.A.
Programming (via satellite): Cinemax; HBO; Showtime.
Fee: $10.95 monthly (Cinemax), $12.95 monthly (HBO), $11.95 monthly (Showtime).

Digital Pay Service 1
Pay Units: N.A.
Programming (via satellite): Cinemax (multiplexed); HBO (multiplexed); Showtime (multiplexed); Starz (multiplexed); Starz Encore (multiplexed); The Movie Channel (multiplexed).
Fee: $10.05 monthly (each).

Pay-Per-View
iN DEMAND (delivered digitally); Playboy TV (delivered digitally); Hot Choice (delivered digitally); Fresh (delivered digitally).

Internet Service
Operational: Yes.
Broadband Service: Depot Street Comm.
Fee: $39.95-$69.95 monthly.

Telephone Service
Digital: Operational
Miles of Plant: 15.0 (coaxial); None (fiber optic).
Chief Executive Officer: Brian Singleton. Senior Vice President, Sales & Marketing: Allison A. Jakubecy.
Ownership: TruVista Communications (MSO).

CARROLLTON—Charter Communications. Now served by NEWNAN, GA [GA0042]. ICA: GA0054.

Cable Systems—Georgia

CARTERSVILLE—Comcast Cable. Now served by ATLANTA, GA [GA0017]. ICA: GA0026.

CEDARTOWN—Charter Communications. Now served by NEWNAN, GA [GA0042]. ICA: GA0178.

CHATSWORTH—Charter Communications, 12405 Powerscourt Dr, St. Louis, MO 63131. Phones: 636-207-5100 (Corporate office); 706-272-0647; 865-984-1400 (Maryville, TN office). Fax: 706-260-2520. Web Site: http://www.charter.com. Also serves Eton & Murray County (central portion). ICA: GA0051.
TV Market Ranking: 78 (CHATSWORTH, Eton). Franchise award date: September 12, 1977. Franchise expiration date: N.A. Began: N.A.
Channel capacity: N.A. Channels available but not in use: N.A.
Digital Basic Service
Subscribers: 5,079.
Programming (via satellite): AXS TV; BBC America; Bloomberg Television; CBS Sports Network; CMT; CNN International; Cooking Channel; Discovery Digital Networks; DIY Network; ESPN Classic; ESPN HD; ESPN2 HD; ESPNews; ESPNU; FOX College Sports Central; FOX College Sports Pacific; Fox Sports 2; Fuse; FXM; FYI; Great American Country; HD Theater; History International; HITS (Headend In The Sky); IFC; INSP; Jewelry Television; LMN; MC; MTV Live; Nick 2; Nick Jr.; Nicktoons; Sundance TV; TeenNick; Tennis Channel; TNT HD; TV Guide Interactive Inc.; Universal HD; UP.
Fee: $26.99 monthly.
Digital Expanded Basic Service
Subscribers: N.A.
Programming (via satellite): A&E; AMC; Animal Planet; BET; Bravo; Cartoon Network; CMT; CNBC; CNN; Comcast/Charter Sports Southeast (CSS); Comedy Central; Disney Channel; Disney XD; E! HD; ESPN; ESPN2; Food Network; Fox News Channel; Fox Sports 1; FOX Sports South/SportSouth; Freeform; FX; Golf Channel; GSN; Hallmark Channel; HGTV; History; HLN; Lifetime; MSNBC; MTV; National Geographic Channel; NBCSN; Nickelodeon; Oxygen; Spike TV; Syfy; TBS; Telemundo; The Weather Channel; TLC; TNT; Travel Channel; truTV; Turner Classic Movies; TV Land; Univision; Univision Studios; USA Network; VH1; WE tv.
Fee: $50.99 monthly.
Digital Pay Service 1
Pay Units: N.A.
Programming (via satellite): Cinemax (multiplexed); Flix; HBO (multiplexed); HBO HD; Showtime (multiplexed); Showtime HD; Starz (multiplexed); Starz Encore (multiplexed); Starz HD; The Movie Channel (multiplexed).
Video-On-Demand: Yes
Pay-Per-View
Hot Choice (delivered digitally); iN DEMAND (delivered digitally).
Internet Service
Operational: Yes. Began: December 1, 2002.
Subscribers: 15,632.
Broadband Service: Charter Internet.
Fee: $29.99 monthly.
Telephone Service
Digital: Operational
Subscribers: 3,112.
Miles of Plant: 3,487.0 (coaxial); 629.0 (fiber optic). Homes passed: 76,461.

Operations Manager: Mike Burns. Technical Operations Director: Grant Evans. Marketing Director: Pat Hollenbeck. Accounting Director: David Sovanski.
Ownership: Charter Communications Inc. (MSO).

CHAUNCEY—Formerly served by KLiP Interactive. No longer in operation. ICA: GA0179.

CHESTER—Bulldog Cable, 455 Gees Mill Business Ct, Conyers, GA 30013. Phones: 706-997-9003; 800-388-6577. Web Site: http://www.bulldogcable.com. Also serves Dexter. ICA: GA0209.
TV Market Ranking: Below 100 (CHESTER); Outside TV Markets (Dexter). Franchise award date: N.A. Franchise expiration date: N.A. Began: January 1, 1988.
Channel capacity: N.A. Channels available but not in use: N.A.
Basic Service
Subscribers: 40.
Programming (received off-air): WGXA (ABC, FOX) Macon; WMAZ-TV (CBS) Macon; WMGT-TV (Escape, MNT, NBC) Macon; WMUM-TV (PBS) Cochran; WPCH-TV (IND) Atlanta; WPGA-TV (Bounce TV, IND, MeTV) Perry.
Programming (via satellite): A&E; BET; CMT; CNBC; CNN; C-SPAN; Discovery Channel; Disney Channel; E! HD; ESPN; ESPN2; FOX Sports South/SportSouth; Freeform; FX; History; HLN; Lifetime; MTV; Nickelodeon; QVC; Spike TV; Syfy; The Weather Channel; TNT; Trinity Broadcasting Network (TBN); truTV; USA Network; WGN America.
Fee: $44.95 installation; $49.00 monthly.
Digital Basic Service
Subscribers: N.A.
Programming (via satellite): BBC America; Bloomberg Television; Bravo; Cloo; Discovery Life Channel; DMX Music; ESPN Classic; ESPNews; Fox Sports 1; Fuse; FXM; FYI; Golf Channel; GSN; HGTV; History; History International; IFC; INSP; LMN; NBCSN; Outdoor Channel; Ovation; Sundance TV; Turner Classic Movies; WE tv.
Pay Service 1
Pay Units: 39.
Programming (via satellite): HBO.
Fee: $10.95 monthly.
Pay Service 2
Pay Units: 32.
Programming (via satellite): Showtime.
Fee: $10.95 monthly.
Pay Service 3
Pay Units: 9.
Programming (via satellite): The Movie Channel.
Fee: $10.95 monthly.
Digital Pay Service 1
Pay Units: N.A.
Programming (via satellite): Cinemax (multiplexed); Flix; HBO (multiplexed); Showtime (multiplexed); Starz (multiplexed); Starz Encore (multiplexed); The Movie Channel (multiplexed).
Fee: $12.00 monthly (HBO, Showtime or TMC).
Pay-Per-View
iN DEMAND (delivered digitally); Playboy TV (delivered digitally); Fresh (delivered digitally); Shorteez (delivered digitally); Sports PPV (delivered digitally); Hot Choice (delivered digitally).
Internet Service
Operational: No.
Telephone Service
None
Miles of Plant: 48.0 (coaxial); None (fiber optic). Homes passed: 1,527.

President: Mark Wlson. General Manager East: Mark Miller. General Manager West: Vance Johnson. Controller: Ashley Hull.
Ownership: Bulldog Cable (MSO).

CLAXTON—Comcast Cable. Now served by SAVANNAH, GA [GA0005]. ICA: GA0180.

CLAYTON—TruVista Communications, 112 York St, PO Box 160, Chester, SC 29706. Phones: 803-581-9190; 800-768-1212. Web Site: http://truvista.net. Also serves Dillard, Lake Rabun, Mountain City, Rabun County (portions) & Tiger. ICA: GA0096.
TV Market Ranking: Below 100 (CLAYTON, Dillard, Lake Rabun, Mountain City, Rabun County (portions), Tiger). Franchise award date: N.A. Franchise expiration date: N.A. Began: March 1, 1969.
Channel capacity: N.A. Channels available but not in use: N.A.
Basic Service
Subscribers: 1,047.
Programming (received off-air): WAGA-TV (Buzzr, FOX, Movies!) Atlanta; WATL (Antenna TV, Bounce TV, MNT) Atlanta; WGCL-TV (CBS, COZI TV, Grit) Atlanta; WGTA (Decades, Heroes & Icons, Movies!) Toccoa; WGTV (PBS) Athens; WHNS (COZI TV, Escape, FOX) Greenville; WSB-TV (ABC, MeTV) Atlanta; WUVG-DT (getTV, UNV) Athens; WYFF (NBC, Movies!) Greenville; allband FM.
Programming (via satellite): A&E; Animal Planet; Cartoon Network; CNBC; CNN; Comedy Central; C-SPAN; Discovery Channel; E! HD; ESPN; ESPN2; Food Network; Fox News Channel; Fox Sports 1; FXM; Great American Country; Hallmark Channel; HGTV; History; HLN; Lifetime; National Geographic Channel; Nickelodeon; QVC; RFD-TV; Spike TV; SportSouth; Syfy; TBS; The Weather Channel; TLC; TNT; Trinity Broadcasting Network (TBN); Turner Classic Movies; TV Land; USA Network.
Fee: $55.00 installation; $31.99 monthly.
Digital Basic Service
Subscribers: N.A.
Programming (via satellite): Destination America; Discovery Kids Channel; DMX Music; ESPNews; Golf Channel; Investigation Discovery; NBCSN; Outdoor Channel; OWN: Oprah Winfrey Network; Science Channel; WE tv.
Pay Service 1
Pay Units: N.A.
Programming (via satellite): Cinemax; HBO; Starz; Starz Encore.
Fee: $11.50 monthly (Cinemax), $13.50 monthly (HBO).
Digital Pay Service 1
Pay Units: N.A.
Programming (via satellite): Cinemax (multiplexed); Flix; HBO (multiplexed); Showtime (multiplexed); Starz (multiplexed); Starz Encore (multiplexed); The Movie Channel (multiplexed).
Fee: $14.75 monthly (each).
Pay-Per-View
iN DEMAND (delivered digitally), Addressable: No.

Access the most current data instantly
FREE TRIAL @ ADVANCED TVFactbook
TELCO/IPTV • CABLE TV • TV STATIONS
www.warren-news.com/factbook.htm

Internet Service
Operational: Yes.
Fee: $42.99 monthly.
Telephone Service
None
Miles of Plant: 120.0 (coaxial); None (fiber optic). Homes passed: 4,020.
Senior Vice President, Sales & Marketing: Allison Jacubecy. Senior Director, Field Operations: Tracy D. Starnes. Video Manager: Tony Helms.
Ownership: TruVista Communications (MSO).

CLERMONT—Comcast Cable. Now served by ATLANTA, GA [GA0017]. ICA: GA0101.

CLEVELAND—Teleview. Now served by DAHLONEGA, GA [GA0099]. ICA: GA0181.

CLIMAX—Formerly served by KLiP Interactive. No longer in operation. ICA: GA0159.

COBB—Citizens Cable TV, PO Box 465, Leslie, GA 31764. Phones: 866-341-3050; 229-268-2288; 229-874-4145; 229-853-1600. Fax: 229-874-2211. Web Site: http://www.citizenscatv.com. Also serves Crisp County (southern portion), De Soto, Dooly County (portions), Drayton, Leslie, Lilly, Plains, Smithville, Sumter County (portions), Vienna, Warwick, Wiley Acres & Worth County (portions). ICA: GA0150.
TV Market Ranking: Below 100 (COBB, Crisp County (southern portion), De Soto, Dooly County (portions), Drayton, Leslie, Lilly, Plains, Sumter County (portions), Worth County (portions), Smithville, Warwick, Wiley Acres). Franchise award date: N.A. Franchise expiration date: N.A. Began: January 1, 1990.
Channel capacity: N.A. Channels available but not in use: N.A.
Basic Service
Subscribers: 1,570.
Programming (received off-air): WACS-TV (PBS) Dawson; WALB (ABC, NBC, This TV) Albany; WFXL (Bounce TV, FOX) Albany; WLGA (WeatherNation) Opelika; WLTZ (CW, NBC) Columbus; WMAZ-TV (CBS) Macon; WRBL (CBS, MeTV) Columbus; WSST-TV (IND) Cordele; WTVM (ABC, Bounce TV) Columbus; WXTX (FOX, Movies!, This TV) Columbus.
Programming (via microwave): WSB-TV (ABC, MeTV) Atlanta.
Programming (via satellite): A&E; Animal Planet; BET; Bloomberg Television; Cartoon Network; CMT; CNN; Comedy Central; Discovery Channel; ESPN; ESPN2; Food Network; Fox News Channel; Fox Sports 1; Freeform; Hallmark Channel; History; ION Television; Lifetime; Nickelodeon; Spike TV; SportSouth; TBS; The Weather Channel; TLC; TNT; Travel Channel; Trinity Broadcasting Network (TBN); Turner Classic Movies; TV Land; USA Network; VH1; WPIX (Antenna TV, CW, This TV) New York.
Fee: $19.95 installation; $19.95 monthly.

2017 Edition — D-157

Georgia—Cable Systems

Digital Basic Service
Subscribers: N.A.
Programming (via satellite): BBC America; Bloomberg Television; Bravo; Cloo; Discovery Digital Networks; Disney XD; DMX Music; ESPN Classic; ESPN2; ESPNews; FOX College Sports Central; FOX College Sports Pacific; Fox Sports 1; Fuse; FXM; FYI; Golf Channel; Great American Country; GSN; HGTV; History; History International; IFC; LMN; National Geographic Channel; NBCSN; Nick Jr.; Nicktoons; Outdoor Channel; Ovation; Sprout; TeenNick; Trinity Broadcasting Network (TBN); WE tv.

Pay Service 1
Pay Units: 61.
Programming (via satellite): HBO.
Fee: $10.95 monthly.

Pay Service 2
Pay Units: 33.
Programming (via satellite): Cinemax.
Fee: $10.95 monthly.

Pay Service 3
Pay Units: 47.
Programming (via satellite): Starz; Starz Encore.
Fee: $9.00 monthly.

Digital Pay Service 1
Pay Units: N.A.
Programming (via satellite): Cinemax (multiplexed); HBO (multiplexed); Showtime (multiplexed); Starz (multiplexed); Starz Encore (multiplexed); The Movie Channel.

Internet Service
Operational: Yes.
Fee: $35.00 installation; $39.95 monthly.

Telephone Service
None
Miles of Plant: 36.0 (coaxial); None (fiber optic).
Chief Executive Officer: Joseph A. Sheehan. General Manager West: Vance Johnson. General Manager East: Mark Miller. Chief Technician: Bill Gregory. Administrative Assistant: Gloria Taylor.
Ownership: Citizens Cable TV (MSO).

COLLINS—Formerly served by Worth Cable. No longer in operation. ICA: GA0156.

COLONELS ISLAND—Comcast Cable. Now served by SAVANNAH, GA [GA0005]. ICA: GA0165.

COLQUITT—Bulldog Cable, PO Box 1288, Watkinsville, GA 30677. Phone: 800-388-6577. Web Site: http://www.bulldogcable.com. Also serves Miller County (portions). ICA: GA0114.
TV Market Ranking: Below 100 (COLQUITT, Miller County (portions)).
Channel capacity: N.A. Channels available but not in use: N.A.

Basic Service
Subscribers: 189.
Programming (received off-air): WABW-TV (PBS) Pelham; WALB (ABC, NBC, This TV) Albany; WCTV (CBS, MNT, This TV) Thomasville; WDHN (ABC) Dothan; WPCH-TV (IND) Atlanta; WTLH (CW, FOX, MeTV) Bainbridge; WTWC-TV (NBC, The Country Network) Tallahassee; WTXL-TV (ABC, Bounce TV) Tallahassee.
Programming (via satellite): A&E; Animal Planet; BET; CMT; CNBC; CNN; Comedy Central; C-SPAN; Discovery Channel; Disney Channel; E! HD; ESPN; ESPN2; Fox Sports 1; Freeform; FX; HLN; Lifetime; MTV; National Geographic Channel; Nickelodeon; QVC; Spike TV; The Weather Channel; TLC; TNT; Trinity Broadcasting Network (TBN); TV Land; USA Network; WGN America.
Fee: $44.95 installation; $49.00 monthly.

Pay Service 1
Pay Units: 21.
Programming (via satellite): Cinemax.
Fee: $25.00 installation; $12.00 monthly.

Pay Service 2
Pay Units: 44.
Programming (via satellite): HBO.
Fee: $12.00 monthly.

Internet Service
Operational: No.

Telephone Service
None
Miles of Plant: 42.0 (coaxial); None (fiber optic). Homes passed: 911.
President: Mark Wilson. General Manager East: Mark Miller. General Manager West: Vance Johnson. Controller: Ashley Hull.
Ownership: Bulldog Cable (MSO).

COLUMBUS—Charter Communications. Now served by NEWNAN, GA [GA0042]. ICA: GA0018.

COLUMBUS—Mediacom, 6700 Macon Rd, Columbus, GA 31907-5735. Phones: 229-244-3852 (Valdosta regional office); 229-888-0242 (Albany administrative office). Fax: 706-568-8270. Web Site: http://www.mediacomcable.com. Also serves Cataula, Ellerslie & Harris County (southern portion). ICA: GA0012.
TV Market Ranking: 94 (Cataula, COLUMBUS, Ellerslie, Harris County (southern portion)). Franchise award date: N.A. Franchise expiration date: N.A. Began: December 1, 1970.
Channel capacity: N.A. Channels available but not in use: N.A.

Basic Service
Subscribers: 13,740.
Programming (received off-air): WJSP-TV (PBS) Columbus; WLGA (WeatherNation) Opelika; WLTZ (CW, NBC) Columbus; WRBL (CBS, MeTV) Columbus; WTVM (ABC, Bounce TV) Columbus; WXTX (FOX, Movies!, This TV) Columbus; WYBU-CD (Christian TV Network) Columbus; 1 FM.
Programming (via satellite): BET; Bravo; CMT; CNBC; Comedy Central; C-SPAN; C-SPAN 2; E! HD; Freeform; Hallmark Channel; Pop; QVC; TBS; The Weather Channel; TLC; Travel Channel; Trinity Broadcasting Network (TBN); truTV; VH1; WGN America.
Fee: $44.25 installation; $69.95 monthly.

Expanded Basic Service 1
Subscribers: N.A.
Programming (via satellite): A&E; AMC; Animal Planet; Cartoon Network; CNN; Discovery Channel; Disney Channel; ESPN; ESPN2; Food Network; Fox News Channel; FOX Sports South/SportSouth; FX; HGTV; History; HLN; ION Television; Lifetime; MSNBC; MTV; Nickelodeon; Spike TV; Syfy; TNT; TV Land; Univision; USA Network; WE tv.
Fee: $15.00 installation; $7.53 monthly.

Digital Basic Service
Subscribers: N.A.
Programming (via satellite): BBC America; Bloomberg Television; Discovery Digital Networks; Disney XD; ESPN Classic; ESPNews; Fox Sports 1; Fuse; FXM; FYI; Golf Channel; GSN; History International; HITS (Headend In The Sky); IFC; LMN; MC; National Geographic Channel; NBCSN; Nick Jr.; Outdoor Channel; Ovation; TeenNick; Turner Classic Movies.

Digital Pay Service 1
Pay Units: N.A.
Programming (via satellite): Cinemax (multiplexed); HBO (multiplexed); Showtime (multiplexed); Starz (multiplexed); Starz Encore (multiplexed); Sundance TV; The Movie Channel (multiplexed).
Fee: $10.00 monthly (Cinemax, HBO, Showtime, Starz/Encore or Sundance/TMC).

Video-On-Demand: Yes

Pay-Per-View
Sports PPV (delivered digitally); ETC (delivered digitally); Pleasure (delivered digitally).

Internet Service
Operational: Yes.
Subscribers: 11,092.
Broadband Service: Mediacom High Speed Internet.
Fee: $49.00 installation; $40.95 monthly; $10.00 modem lease; $249.00 modem purchase.

Telephone Service
Analog: Not Operational
Digital: Operational
Subscribers: 6,488.
Miles of Plant: 1,518.0 (coaxial); 257.0 (fiber optic). Homes passed: 60,490. Miles of plant (coax) includes miles of plant (fiber).
Regional Vice President: Sue Misiunas. Vice President, Financial Reporting: Kenneth J. Kohrs. General Manager: Gary Crosby. Regional Marketing Director: Melanie Hannasch. Regional Technical Operations Manager: Gary McDougall. Chief Technician: Darrin Best. Marketing Manager: Daryl Channey.
Ownership: Mediacom LLC (MSO).

COLUMBUS—WOW! Internet, Cable & Phone, 7887 East Belleview Ave, Ste 1000, Englewood, CO 80111. Phones: 720-479-3500; 706-221-2100; 706-645-8553 (Corporate office); 706-221-1000 (Customer service). Fax: 720-479-3585. E-mail: wow_general@wideopenwest.com. Web Site: http://www.wowway.com. Also serves Auburn, AL; Harris County (portions), GA. ICA: GA0029. **Note:** This system is an overbuild.
TV Market Ranking: 94 (Auburn, COLUMBUS, Harris County (portions)). Franchise award date: June 1, 1988. Franchise expiration date: N.A. Began: October 7, 1988.
Channel capacity: N.A. Channels available but not in use: N.A.

Basic Service
Subscribers: 20,872.
Programming (received off-air): WJSP-TV (PBS) Columbus; WLGA (WeatherNation) Opelika; WLTZ (CW, NBC) Columbus; WRBL (CBS, MeTV) Columbus; WTVM (ABC, Bounce TV) Columbus; WXTX (FOX, Movies!, This TV) Columbus; WYBU-CD (Christian TV Network) Columbus.
Programming (via satellite): A&E; AMC; Animal Planet; BET; Bravo; Cartoon Network; CMT; CNBC; CNN; Comedy Central; C-SPAN; C-SPAN 2; Discovery Channel; Disney Channel; Disney XD; E! HD; ESPN; ESPN Classic; ESPN2; EVINE Live; Food Network; Fox News Channel; Fox Sports 1; FOX Sports South/SportSouth; Freeform; FX; Great American Country; Hallmark Channel; HGTV; History; HLN; Lifetime; LMN; MSNBC; MTV; National Geographic Channel; Nickelodeon; Outdoor Channel; OWN: Oprah Winfrey Network; Oxygen; Pop; QVC; Spike TV; Syfy; TBS; The Weather Channel; TLC; TNT; Travel Channel; Trinity Broadcasting Network (TBN); truTV; Turner Classic Movies; TV Land; Univision Studios; USA Network; VH1; WGN America.
Fee: $50.00 installation; $33.00 monthly.

Digital Basic Service
Subscribers: N.A.
Programming (via satellite): AXS TV; BBC America; Bloomberg Television; Boomerang; CBS Sports Network; Church Channel; CMT; C-SPAN 3; Destination America; Discovery Channel HD; Discovery Kids Channel; DIY Network; ESPN HD; ESPN2 HD; ESPNews; ESPNU; EWTN Global Catholic Network; FOX College Sports Central; FOX College Sports Pacific; Fox Sports 2; FSN HD; Golf Channel; GSN; Hallmark Movies & Mysteries; HD Theater; IFC; INSP; Investigation Discovery; Jewelry Television; JUCE TV; MC; MTV Classic; MTV Hits; MTV Jams; MTV2; mtvU; National Geographic Channel HD; NBCSN; NFL Network; Nick 2; Nick Jr.; Nicktoons; QVC HD; Science Channel; TBS HD; TeenNick; Tennis Channel; TLC HD; TNT HD; Tr3s; Universal HD; UP; Versus HD; VH1 Soul; WE tv.

Pay Service 1
Pay Units: N.A.
Programming (via satellite): HBO; Showtime.
Fee: $13.95 monthly (HBO).

Digital Pay Service 1
Pay Units: N.A.
Programming (via satellite): Cinemax (multiplexed); Cinemax HD; Cinemax On Demand; Flix; Flix On Demand; HBO (multiplexed); HBO HD; HBO on Demand; Showtime (multiplexed); Showtime HD; Showtime On Demand; Starz (multiplexed); Starz Encore (multiplexed); Starz HD; Sundance TV; The Movie Channel (multiplexed); The Movie Channel On Demand.
Fee: $32.35 monthly.

Video-On-Demand: Yes

Pay-Per-View
ESPN (delivered digitally); iN DEMAND (delivered digitally); Playboy TV (delivered digitally); Fresh (delivered digitally); Shorteez (delivered digitally); Spice: Xcess (delivered digitally); Hot Choice (delivered digitally); Club Jenna (delivered digitally).

Internet Service
Operational: Yes.
Subscribers: 23,268.
Fee: $29.95 installation; $61.95 monthly.

Telephone Service
Analog: Not Operational
Digital: Operational
Subscribers: 21,139.
Fee: $23.25 monthly
Miles of Plant: 1,579.0 (coaxial); 352.0 (fiber optic). Homes passed: 80,014.
Chief Executive Officer: Colleen Abdoulah. President: Steven Cochran. Chief Financial Officer: Rich Fish.
Ownership: WideOpenWest LLC (MSO).

COMER—Charter Communications. Now served by ATHENS, GA [GA0014]. ICA: GA0086.

CONCORD—Formerly served by Georgia Broadband. No longer in operation. ICA: GA0319.

COOLIDGE—Formerly served by Southeast Cable TV Inc. No longer in operation. ICA: GA0182.

CORDELE—Mediacom. Now served by FITZGERALD, GA [GA0052]. ICA: GA0047.

CORNELIA—Windstream Teleview. Now served by DAHLONEGA, GA [GA0099]. ICA: GA0183.

Cable Systems—Georgia

COVINGTON—Charter Communications. Now served by STOCKBRIDGE, GA [GA0083]. ICA: GA0040.

CRAWFORD—Formerly served by Allegiance Communications. No longer in operation. ICA: GA0273.

CRAWFORD COUNTY (Eastern portion)—Formerly served by Piedmont Cable Corp. No longer in operation. ICA: GA0120.

CRAWFORDVILLE—Formerly served by CommuniComm Services. No longer in operation. ICA: GA0148.

CUMMING—Comcast Cable. Now served by ATLANTA, GA [GA0017]. ICA: GA0027.

CUSSETA—Formerly served by Almega Cable. No longer in operation. ICA: GA0127.

CUTHBERT—Mediacom, 509 Flint Ave, Albany, GA 31701. Phones: 229-244-3852 (Valdosta office); 229-888-0242. Fax: 229-436-4819. Web Site: http://www.mediacomcable.com. Also serves Arlington, Edison, Fort Gaines, Lumpkin, Randolph County (portions), Richland & Shellman. ICA: GA0184.
TV Market Ranking: 94 (Lumpkin, Richland); Below 100 (Arlington, Edison, Fort Gaines, Randolph County (portions) (portions), Shellman); Outside TV Markets (CUTHBERT, Randolph County (portions) (portions)). Franchise award date: September 4, 1979. Franchise expiration date: N.A. Began: October 1, 1980.
Channel capacity: N.A. Channels available but not in use: N.A.
Basic Service
Subscribers: 799.
Programming (received off-air): WACS-TV (PBS) Dawson; WALB (ABC, NBC, This TV) Albany; WLTZ (CW, NBC) Columbus; WRBL (CBS, MeTV) Columbus; WSB-TV (ABC, MeTV) Atlanta; WSST-TV (IND) Cordele; WTVM (ABC, Bounce TV) Columbus; WXTX (FOX, Movies!, This TV) Columbus.
Programming (via satellite): INSP; Pop; QVC; The Weather Channel.
Fee: $47.78 installation; $43.95 monthly; $2.50 converter.
Expanded Basic Service 1
Subscribers: N.A.
Programming (via satellite): A&E; Animal Planet; BET; Cartoon Network; CMT; CNBC; CNN; Comedy Central; C-SPAN; C-SPAN 2; CW PLUS; Discovery Channel; Disney Channel; ESPN; ESPN2; EWTN Global Catholic Network; Fox News Channel; FOX Sports South/SportSouth; Freeform; History; HLN; ION Television; Lifetime; MSNBC; MTV; Nickelodeon; Spike TV; TBS; TLC; TNT; TV Land; USA Network; VH1; Weatherscan; WGN America.
Fee: $30.00 installation; $3.95 monthly.
Digital Basic Service
Subscribers: N.A.
Programming (via satellite): 3ABN; BBC America; Bloomberg Television; Cloo; CMT; Discovery Digital Networks; Disney XD; ESPNews; Fox Sports 1; FXM; FYI; Golf Channel; GSN; History International; IFC; Investigation Discovery; ION Television; LMN; MTV Hits; MTV2; National Geographic Channel; NBCSN; Nick Jr.; Nicktoons; Outdoor Channel; Ovation; Qubo; Reelz; Science Channel; TeenNick; Turner Classic Movies; TV One; VH1 Soul.
Digital Pay Service 1
Pay Units: N.A.
Programming (via satellite): Cinemax (multiplexed); HBO (multiplexed); Showtime (multiplexed); Starz (multiplexed); Starz Encore (multiplexed); The Movie Channel (multiplexed).
Video-On-Demand: No
Internet Service
Operational: Yes.
Broadband Service: Mediacom High Speed Internet.
Fee: $42.95 monthly; $3.00 modem lease.
Telephone Service
Analog: Not Operational
Digital: Operational
Homes passed: 4,453.
Regional Vice President: Sue Misiunas. Vice President, Financial Reporting: Kenneth J. Kohrs. General Manager: Gary Crosby. Regional Marketing Director: Melanie Hannasch. Regional Technical Operations Manager: Gary McDougall. Marketing Manager: Daryl Channey. Technical Operations Manager: David Jones.
Ownership: Mediacom LLC (MSO).

DAHLONEGA—Windstream Teleview, 4001 Rodney Parham Rd, Little Rock, AR 72212. Phones: 877-759-9020; 501-748-7000; 877-807-9463. Fax: 501-748-6392. E-mail: support@windstream.net. Web Site: http://www.windstream.com. Also serves Alto, Arcade, Baldwin, Banks County (portions), Big Canoe, Blairsville, Clarkesville, Cleveland, Commerce, Cornelia, Dawson County (portions), Dawsonville, Demorest, Habersham County (portions), Helen, Hiawassee, Homer, Jackson County (portions), Jefferson, Lumpkin County (portions), Mount Airy, Nicholson, Towns County (portions), Union County (portions), White County (portions) & Young Harris, GA; Clay County (western portions) & Hayesville, NC. ICA: GA0099.
TV Market Ranking: Below 100 (Alto, Arcade, Baldwin, Banks County (portions), Clarkesville, Cornelia, DAHLONEGA, Demorest, Habersham County (portions), Homer, Jackson County (portions), Mount Airy, Nicholson, White County (portions), Cleveland, Helen, Jefferson, Towns County (portions), Union County (portions)); Outside TV Markets (Clay County (western portions), Dawson County (portions), Hayesville, Young Harris, Big Canoe, Blairsville, Dawsonville, Hiawassee, Towns County (portions), Union County (portions)). Franchise award date: December 18, 1982. Franchise expiration date: N.A. Began: September 1, 1981.
Channel capacity: N.A. Channels available but not in use: N.A.
Basic Service
Subscribers: 15,201.
Programming (received off-air): WAGA-TV (Buzzr, FOX, Movies!) Atlanta; WATL (Antenna TV, Bounce TV, MNT) Atlanta; WGCL-TV (CBS, COZI TV, Grit) Atlanta; WGTA (Decades, Heroes & Icons, Movies!) Toccoa; WGTV (PBS) Athens; WHSG-TV (TBN) Monroe; WPBA (PBS) Atlanta; WPCH-TV (IND) Atlanta; WPXA-TV (ION) Rome; WSB-TV (ABC, MeTV) Atlanta; WUPA (CW, Decades) Atlanta; WUVG-DT (getTV, UNV) Athens; WXIA-TV (NBC) Atlanta; WYFF (NBC, Movies!) Greenville.
Programming (via satellite): C-SPAN; Pop.
Fee: $25.00 monthly; $1.00 converter.
Expanded Basic Service 1
Subscribers: N.A.
Programming (via satellite): A&E; AMC; BET; Boomerang; Bravo; Cartoon Network; CMT; CNBC; CNN; Comedy Central; Discovery Channel; ESPN; ESPN Classic; ESPN2; Food Network; Fox News Channel; Fox Sports 1; FOX Sports South/SportSouth; Freeform; Fuse; FX; Golf Channel; HGTV; History; HLN; Lifetime; MSNBC; MTV; National Geographic Channel; Nickelodeon; QVC; Spike TV; The Weather Channel; TLC; TNT; Turner Classic Movies; TV Land; USA Network; VH1; WGN America.
Fee: $28.70 monthly.
Digital Basic Service
Subscribers: N.A.
Programming (via satellite): BBC America; CBS Sports Network; Cloo; Cooking Channel; Discovery Digital Networks; DMX Music; ESPNews; EWTN Global Catholic Network; Family Friendly Entertainment; FamilyNet; FOX College Sports Central; FOX College Sports Pacific; Fox Sports 2; FXM; FYI; GSN; Hallmark Channel; History International; HITS (Headend In The Sky); IFC; LMN; MTV Classic; MTV2; NBCSN; Nick Jr.; Nicktoons; Outdoor Channel; Praise Television; TeenNick; VH1 Country; WE tv.
Digital Pay Service 1
Pay Units: N.A.
Programming (via satellite): Cinemax (multiplexed); HBO (multiplexed); Showtime (multiplexed); Starz (multiplexed); Starz Encore (multiplexed); The Movie Channel (multiplexed).
Fee: $10.95 monthly (Starz/Encore), $12.99 monthly (Showtime/TMC), $24.95 monthly (HBO/Cinemax).
Video-On-Demand: No
Pay-Per-View
iN DEMAND (delivered digitally).
Internet Service
Operational: Yes.
Telephone Service
Digital: Operational
Miles of Plant: 2,632.0 (coaxial); 878.0 (fiber optic). Homes passed: 57,996.
President & Chief Executive Officer: Tony Thomas. Chief Financial Officer & Treasurer: Bob Gunderman. Executive Vice President, Operations: Mark Farris. Executive Vice President, Engineering & Chief Technology Officer: Randy Nicklas.
Ownership: Windstream Communications Inc. (MSO).

DAHLONEGA—Windstream Teleview. Now served by DAHLONEGA, GA [GA0099]. ICA: GA0185.

DALTON—Charter Communications, 1103 S Hamilton St, Dalton, GA 30720. Phones: 636-207-5100 (Corporate office); 314-543-2236; 706-428-2290; 865-984-1400 (Maryville office). Web Site: http://www.charter.com. Also serves Cohutta, Tunnel Hill, Varnell & Whitfield County. ICA: GA0025.
TV Market Ranking: 18,78 (Whitfield County (portions)); 78 (Cohutta, DALTON, Tunnel Hill, Varnell). Franchise award date: N.A. Franchise expiration date: N.A. Began: September 24, 1965.
Channel capacity: N.A. Channels available but not in use: N.A.
Digital Basic Service
Subscribers: 9,114.
Programming (via satellite): BBC America; Discovery Digital Networks; DIY Network; FOX College Sports Central; FOX College Sports Pacific; FYI; Great American Country; History International; HITS (Headend In The Sky); IFC; MC; Nick Jr.; Sundance TV; TV Guide Interactive Inc.
Fee: $49.99 installation; $26.99 monthly.
Digital Expanded Basic Service
Subscribers: N.A.
Programming (via satellite): A&E; AMC; Animal Planet; BET; Bravo; Cartoon Network; CMT; CNBC; CNN; Comcast/Charter Sports Southeast (CSS); Comedy Central; C-SPAN 2; Discovery Channel; Disney Channel; E! HD; ESPN; ESPN2; EWTN Global Catholic Network; Fox News Channel; Fox Sports 1; FOX Sports South/SportSouth; Freeform; FX; Golf Channel; GSN; Hallmark Channel; HGTV; History; HLN; INSP; Lifetime; MSNBC; MTV; National Geographic Channel; NBCSN; Nickelodeon; Oxygen; Pop; Syfy; Telemundo; The Weather Channel; TLC; Travel Channel; TV Land; Univision; USA Network; VH1.
Digital Pay Service 1
Pay Units: N.A.
Programming (via satellite): Cinemax (multiplexed); Flix (multiplexed); HBO (multiplexed); Showtime (multiplexed); Starz (multiplexed); Starz Encore (multiplexed); The Movie Channel (multiplexed).
Video-On-Demand: Yes
Pay-Per-View
Hot Choice (delivered digitally); iN DEMAND (delivered digitally); Playboy TV (delivered digitally); Playboy TV en Espanol (delivered digitally); Fresh (delivered digitally); Shorteez (delivered digitally).
Internet Service
Operational: Yes. Began: November 1, 2001.
Broadband Service: Charter Internet.
Fee: $29.99 monthly.
Telephone Service
None
Miles of Plant: 631.0 (coaxial); None (fiber optic). Homes passed: 26,173.
Operations Manager: Mike Burns. Technical Operations Director: Grant Evans. Marketing Director: Pat Hollenbeck. Accounting Director: David Sovanski.
Ownership: Charter Communications Inc. (MSO).

DARIEN—Comcast Cable, One Comcast Center, Philadelphia, PA 19103. Phones: 912-354-7531; 912-356-3113. Web Site: http://www.comcast.com. Also serves Crescent, Eulonia, McIntosh County (portions), Shellman Bluff & Townsend. ICA: GA0117.
TV Market Ranking: Below 100 (Crescent, DARIEN, McIntosh County (portions), Shellman Bluff, Townsend, Eulonia). Franchise award date: N.A. Franchise expiration date: N.A. Began: November 1, 1982.
Channel capacity: N.A. Channels available but not in use: N.A.

Georgia—Cable Systems

Basic Service
Subscribers: 811. Commercial subscribers: 21.
Programming (received off-air): WJCL (ABC) Savannah; WPXC-TV (ION) Brunswick; WSAV-TV (MeTV, MNT, NBC) Savannah; WTGS (Antenna TV, FOX) Hardeeville; WTLV (Antenna TV, NBC, The Country Network) Jacksonville; WTOC-TV (Bounce TV, CBS, This TV) Savannah; WVAN-TV (PBS) Savannah.
Programming (via satellite): BET; C-SPAN; Freeform; Lifetime; Trinity Broadcasting Network (TBN).
Fee: $20.00 installation; $25.05 monthly.

Expanded Basic Service 1
Subscribers: N.A.
Programming (via satellite): A&E; AMC; Animal Planet; Cartoon Network; CMT; CNBC; CNN; Comcast/Charter Sports Southeast (CSS); Comedy Central; C-SPAN 2; Discovery Channel; Disney Channel; E! HD; ESPN; ESPNews; EVINE Live; Food Network; Fox News Channel; Fox Sports 1; FOX Sports Networks; FOX Sports South/SportSouth; FX; Golf Channel; Great American Country; Hallmark Channel; HGTV; History; HLN; MTV; NBCSN; Nickelodeon; Outdoor Channel; OWN: Oprah Winfrey Network; Pop; Spike TV; Syfy; TBS; The Weather Channel; TLC; TNT; Travel Channel; truTV; Turner Classic Movies; TV Land; TV One; USA Network; VH1; WGN America.
Fee: $33.49 monthly.

Digital Basic Service
Subscribers: N.A.
Programming (via satellite): BBC America; Bloomberg Television; Cooking Channel; Discovery Digital Networks; Disney XD; DIY Network; DMX Music; ESPN Classic; ESPNews; Flix (multiplexed); FYI; GSN; History International; National Geographic Channel; NFL Network; Nick 2; Nick Jr.; Nicktoons; Starz Encore (multiplexed); Sundance TV; TeenNick; The Word Network; WE tv.

Pay Service 1
Pay Units: N.A.
Programming (via satellite): HBO.
Fee: $18.88 installation; $13.95 monthly.

Digital Pay Service 1
Pay Units: N.A.
Programming (via satellite): Cinemax (multiplexed); HBO (multiplexed); Showtime (multiplexed); The Movie Channel (multiplexed).

Video-On-Demand: No

Pay-Per-View
iN DEMAND (delivered digitally); Hot Choice (delivered digitally); Playboy TV (delivered digitally); Fresh (delivered digitally); Pleasure (delivered digitally).

Internet Service
Operational: Yes.
Subscribers: 221.
Fee: $42.95 monthly.

Telephone Service
Digital: Operational
Subscribers: 102.
Miles of Plant: 218.0 (coaxial); 55.0 (fiber optic). Homes passed: 1,200. Homes passed & miles of plant (coax & fiber) included in Savannah.
Vice President, Accounting: Joan Ritchie. General Manager: Michael Daves. Technical Operations Director: Joel Godsen. Marketing Director: Jerry Avery. Marketing Manager: Ken Torres.
Ownership: Comcast Cable Communications Inc.

DARIEN—Darien Communications, 1011 North Way, PO Box 575, Darien, GA 31305. Phone: 912-437-4111. Fax: 912-437-7006. E-mail: dtcadmin@darientel.net. Web Site: http://www.darientelephone.com. Also serves McIntosh County & Townsend. ICA: GA0270.
TV Market Ranking: Below 100 (DARIEN, McIntosh County, Townsend). Franchise award date: N.A. Franchise expiration date: N.A. Began: January 3, 1992.
Channel capacity: N.A. Channels available but not in use: N.A.

Basic Service
Subscribers: 2,427.
Programming (received off-air): WJCL (ABC) Savannah; WPXC-TV (ION) Brunswick; WSAV-TV (MeTV, MNT, NBC) Savannah; WTGS (Antenna TV, FOX) Hardeeville; WTLV (Antenna TV, NBC, The Country Network) Jacksonville; WTOC-TV (Bounce TV, CBS, This TV) Savannah; WVAN-TV (PBS) Savannah.
Programming (via satellite): C-SPAN; C-SPAN 2; EWTN Global Catholic Network; Pop; QVC; TBS; Trinity Broadcasting Network (TBN); WGN America.
Fee: $70.00 installation; $15.00 monthly.

Expanded Basic Service 1
Subscribers: 2,322.
Programming (via satellite): A&E; Animal Planet; BET; Bravo; Cartoon Network; CMT; CNBC; CNN; Comedy Central; Discovery Channel; Disney Channel; E! HD; ESPN; ESPN Classic; ESPN2; ESPNews; FamilyNet; Food Network; Fox News Channel; Fox Sports 1; FOX Sports South/SportSouth; Freeform; FX; FYI; Golf Channel; GSN; Hallmark Channel; HGTV; History; History International; HLN; Lifetime; MSNBC; MTV; National Geographic Channel; Nickelodeon; Outdoor Channel; Oxygen; Spike TV; Syfy; The Weather Channel; TLC; TNT; Travel Channel; truTV; TV Land; Univision Studios; USA Network; VH1.
Fee: $40.00 monthly.

Digital Basic Service
Subscribers: 724.
Programming (via satellite): BBC America; Bloomberg Television; Discovery Digital Networks; FXM; Great American Country; IFC; LMN; MC; Nick Jr.; Nicktoons; Starz Encore; Sundance TV; TeenNick; Turner Classic Movies.
Fee: $18.95 monthly.

Digital Pay Service 1
Pay Units: N.A.
Programming (via satellite): Cinemax (multiplexed); HBO (multiplexed); Showtime (multiplexed); Starz (multiplexed); The Movie Channel (multiplexed).
Fee: $10.95 monthly (Cinemax, HBO, Showtime/TMC or Starz).

Video-On-Demand: No

Pay-Per-View
iN DEMAND (delivered digitally); Playboy TV (delivered digitally); Fresh (delivered digitally).

Internet Service
Operational: Yes.
Fee: $100.00 installation; $42.95-$62.95 monthly; $3.95 modem lease.

Telephone Service
Analog: Operational
Miles of Plant: 35.0 (coaxial); None (fiber optic). Homes passed: 7,000.
President: Mary Lou Jackson Forsyth. Chief Operating Officer: Johnny Zoucks. Central Office Manager: Chuck Durant. Technical Operations Manager: Neil Elder. Chief Engineer: Robert Brigman. Marketing Manager: Julia Dodd. Customer Service Manager: Bess Wolfes.
Ownership: Darien Communications.

DAVISBORO—Formerly served by Walker Cablevision. No longer in operation. ICA: GA0166.

DAWSONVILLE—Windstream Teleview. Now served by DAHLONEGA, GA [GA0099]. ICA: GA0187.

DOERUN—Doerun Cable TV, 223 West Broad Ave, PO Box 37, Doerun, GA 31744. Phone: 229-782-5444. Fax: 229-782-5224. ICA: GA0286.
TV Market Ranking: Below 100 (DOERUN).
Channel capacity: 48 (not 2-way capable). Channels available but not in use: N.A.

Basic Service
Subscribers: 193.
Programming (received off-air): WALB (ABC, NBC, This TV) Albany; WCTV (CBS, MNT, This TV) Thomasville; WFXL (Bounce TV, FOX) Albany; WSWG (CBS, CW, MeTV, MNT) Valdosta; WTXL-TV (ABC, Bounce TV) Tallahassee.
Programming (via satellite): A&E; AMC; Animal Planet; BET; Cartoon Network; CMT; CNN; C-SPAN; C-SPAN 2; Discovery Channel; Disney Channel; DIY Network; ESPN; ESPN2; Food Network; Fox News Channel; Freeform; Hallmark Channel; HGTV; History; HLN; Lifetime; National Geographic Channel; Nickelodeon; Outdoor Channel; QVC; Spike TV; TBS; The Weather Channel; TLC; TNT; Trinity Broadcasting Network (TBN); TV Land; USA Network; WE tv; WGN America.
Fee: $25.00 installation; $35.63 monthly.

Pay Service 1
Pay Units: 54.
Programming (via satellite): HBO.
Fee: $16.00 monthly.

Pay Service 2
Pay Units: 79.
Programming (via satellite): Starz Encore.
Fee: $3.50 monthly.

Pay Service 3
Pay Units: 45.
Programming (via satellite): The Movie Channel.
Fee: $9.00 monthly.

Internet Service
Operational: No.

Telephone Service
None

Miles of Plant: 10.0 (coaxial); None (fiber optic). Homes passed: 370.
General Manager & Chief Technician: Herchel Finch. Office Manager: Patrice Bryant.
Ownership: City of Doerun.

DONALSONVILLE—Mediacom. Now served by BAINBRIDGE, GA [GA0060]. ICA: GA0110.

DOUGLAS—Vyve Broadband, 4 International Dr, Ste 330, Rye Brook, NY 10573. Phones: 800-937-1397; 706-342-7271; 706-485-2288; 800-392-2662. Web Site: http://vyvebroadband.com. Also serves Ambrose, Broxton, Coffee County (unincorporated areas) & Nicholls. ICA: GA0037.
TV Market Ranking: Below 100 (Broxton, Coffee County (unincorporated areas) (portions), DOUGLAS, Nicholls); Outside TV Markets (Ambrose, Coffee County (unincorporated areas) (portions)). Franchise award date: N.A. Franchise expiration date: N.A. Began: December 1, 1963.
Channel capacity: N.A. Channels available but not in use: N.A.

Basic Service
Subscribers: 2,851.
Programming (received off-air): WALB (ABC, NBC, This TV) Albany; WFXL (Bounce TV, FOX) Albany; WTOC-TV (Bounce TV, CBS, This TV) Savannah; WXGA-TV (PBS) Waycross; 6 FMs.
Programming (via microwave): WAGA-TV (Buzzr, FOX, Movies!) Atlanta; WSB-TV (ABC, MeTV) Atlanta; WXIA-TV (NBC) Atlanta.
Programming (via satellite): INSP; QVC; WGN America.
Fee: $64.95 installation; $25.00 monthly.

Expanded Basic Service 1
Subscribers: N.A.
Programming (via satellite): A&E; AMC; Animal Planet; BET; Bravo; Cartoon Network; CMT; CNBC; CNN; Comcast/Charter Sports Southeast (CSS); Comedy Central; C-SPAN; C-SPAN 2; CW PLUS; Discovery Channel; Disney Channel; Disney XD; E! HD; ESPN; ESPN2; EVINE Live; EWTN Global Catholic Network; Food Network; Fox News Channel; Fox Sports 1; FOX Sports South/SportSouth; Freeform; FX; Golf Channel; GSN; Hallmark Channel; HGTV; History; HLN; ION Television; Lifetime; MSNBC; MTV; National Geographic Channel; NBCSN; Nickelodeon; Oxygen; Pop; Spike TV; Syfy; TBS; Telemundo; The Weather Channel; TLC; TNT; Travel Channel; Trinity Broadcasting Network (TBN); truTV; Turner Classic Movies; TV Land; Univision; USA Network; VH1; WE tv.
Fee: $48.99 monthly.

Digital Basic Service
Subscribers: N.A.
Programming (via satellite): BBC America; Bloomberg Television; Boomerang; Discovery Digital Networks; DIY Network; ESPN Classic; ESPNews; FYI; History International; HITS (Headend In The Sky); IFC; LMN; MC; Nick 2; Nick Jr.; Nicktoons; Sundance TV; TeenNick; TV Guide Interactive Inc.

Digital Pay Service 1
Pay Units: N.A.
Programming (via satellite): Cinemax (multiplexed); Flix; HBO (multiplexed); Showtime (multiplexed); Starz (multiplexed); Starz Encore (multiplexed); The Movie Channel (multiplexed).
Fee: $10.95 monthly (each).

Video-On-Demand: Yes

Pay-Per-View
iN DEMAND (delivered digitally); Playboy TV (delivered digitally); Fresh (delivered digitally); Shorteez (delivered digitally).

Internet Service
Operational: Yes.
Subscribers: 2,574.
Broadband Service: Net Commander.

Telephone Service
Digital: Operational
Subscribers: 1,539.
Miles of Plant: 608.0 (coaxial); 787.0 (fiber optic). Homes passed: 14,838.
President & Chief Executive Officer: Jeffrey DeMond. Senior Vice President, Financial Planning: Daniel White. Vice President, Residential Services: Vin Zachariah. Vice President, Marketing: Diane Quennoz.
Ownership: Vyve Broadband LLC (MSO).

DRY BRANCH—Formerly served by KLiP Interactive. No longer in operation. ICA: GA0189.

DUBLIN—Charter Communications, 12405 Powerscourt Dr, St. Louis, MO 63131. Phones: 636-207-5100 (Corporate office); 478-272-1162. Web Site: http://www.charter.com. Also serves East Dublin & Laurens County. ICA: GA0043.

Cable Systems—Georgia

Access the most current data instantly
www.warren-news.com/factbook.htm

TV Market Ranking: Below 100 (Laurens County (portions)); Outside TV Markets (DUBLIN, East Dublin, Laurens County (portions)). Franchise award date: July 8, 1965. Franchise expiration date: N.A. Began: July 8, 1965.
Channel capacity: N.A. Channels available but not in use: N.A.

Digital Basic Service
Subscribers: 5,369.
Programming (via satellite): BBC America; Boomerang; Discovery Digital Networks; DIY Network; FYI; History International; HITS (Headend In The Sky); IFC; LMN; MC; Nick 2; Nick Jr.; Nicktoons; Sundance TV; TeenNick; TV Guide Interactive Inc.
Fee: $26.99 monthly.

Digital Expanded Basic Service
Subscribers: N.A.
Programming (via satellite): A&E; AMC; Animal Planet; BET; Bravo; Cartoon Network; CMT; CNBC; CNN; Comedy Central; Discovery Channel; Disney Channel; E! HD; ESPN; ESPN Classic; ESPN2; ESPNews; Food Network; Fox News Channel; Fox Sports 1; FOX Sports South/SportSouth; Freeform; FX; Golf Channel; Hallmark Channel; HGTV; History; HLN; Lifetime; MTV; National Geographic Channel; NBCSN; Nickelodeon; Oxygen; Spike TV; Syfy; TBS; Telemundo; The Weather Channel; TLC; TNT; Travel Channel; truTV; Turner Classic Movies; TV Land; USA Network; VH1; WE tv.
Fee: $48.99 monthly.

Digital Pay Service 1
Pay Units: N.A.
Programming (via satellite): Cinemax (multiplexed); Flix; HBO (multiplexed); Showtime (multiplexed); Starz (multiplexed); Starz Encore (multiplexed); The Movie Channel (multiplexed).
Fee: $40.00 installation; $12.20 monthly (Showtime), $12.70 monthly (Cinemax or HBO).

Video-On-Demand: Yes

Pay-Per-View
iN DEMAND (delivered digitally); Playboy TV (delivered digitally); Fresh (delivered digitally); Shorteez (delivered digitally).

Internet Service
Operational: Yes.
Subscribers: 2,826.
Broadband Service: Charter Internet.
Fee: $29.99 monthly.

Telephone Service
Digital: Operational
Subscribers: 2,276.
Fee: $29.99 monthly.
Miles of Plant: 507.0 (coaxial); 78.0 (fiber optic). Homes passed: 13,842.
Vice President & General Manager: Matt Favre. Operations Manager: David Spriggs. Technical Operations Manager: Tim Hardeman. Sales & Marketing Director: Antoinette Carpenter. Accounting Director: David Sovanski.
Ownership: Charter Communications Inc. (MSO).

DUDLEY—Bulldog Cable, 455 Gees Mill Business Ct, Conyers, GA 30013. Phones: 706-997-9003; 800-388-6577. Web Site: http://www.bulldogcable.com. Also serves Laurens County (portions). ICA: GA0298.
TV Market Ranking: Outside TV Markets (DUDLEY, Laurens County (portions)).
Channel capacity: N.A. Channels available but not in use: N.A.

Basic Service
Subscribers: 33.
Programming (received off-air): WGNM (Christian TV Network) Macon; WGXA (ABC, FOX) Macon; WMAZ-TV (CBS) Macon; WMGT-TV (Escape, MNT, NBC) Macon; WMUM-TV (PBS) Cochran; WPCH-TV (IND) Atlanta; WPGA-TV (Bounce TV, IND, MeTV) Perry.
Programming (via satellite): A&E; BET; Bravo; CMT; CNBC; CNN; C-SPAN; Discovery Channel; Disney Channel; ESPN; ESPN2; Fox News Channel; FOX Sports South/SportSouth; Freeform; FX; History; HLN; Lifetime; MTV; Nickelodeon; QVC; Spike TV; Syfy; The Weather Channel; TNT; Trinity Broadcasting Network (TBN); USA Network; WGN America.
Fee: $44.95 installation; $49.00 monthly.

Digital Basic Service
Subscribers: N.A.
Programming (via satellite): BBC America; Bloomberg Television; Cloo; Discovery Life Channel; DMX Music; ESPN Classic; ESPNews; Fox Sports 1; Fuse; FXM; FYI; Golf Channel; GSN; HGTV; History; History International; IFC; INSP; LMN; NBCSN; Outdoor Channel; Ovation; Sundance TV; Turner Classic Movies; WE tv.

Pay Service 1
Pay Units: 28.
Programming (via satellite): HBO.
Fee: $10.95 monthly.

Pay Service 2
Pay Units: 9.
Programming (via satellite): Showtime.
Fee: $10.95 monthly.

Pay Service 3
Pay Units: 2.
Programming (via satellite): The Movie Channel.
Fee: $10.95 monthly.

Digital Pay Service 1
Pay Units: N.A.
Programming (via satellite): Cinemax (multiplexed); Flix; HBO (multiplexed); Showtime (multiplexed); Starz (multiplexed); Starz Encore (multiplexed); The Movie Channel (multiplexed).
Fee: $12.00 monthly (HBO, Showtime or TMC).

Pay-Per-View
iN DEMAND (delivered digitally); Hot Choice (delivered digitally); Playboy TV (delivered digitally); Fresh (delivered digitally); Shorteez (delivered digitally).

Internet Service
Operational: No.

Telephone Service
None

Miles of Plant: 41.0 (coaxial); None (fiber optic). Homes passed: 532.
President: Mark Wilson. General Manager East: Mark Miller. General Manager West: Vance Johnson. Controller: Ashley Hull.
Ownership: Bulldog Cable (MSO).

EAST DUBLIN—Charter Communications. Now served by DUBLIN, GA [GA0043]. ICA: GA0299.

EAST DUBLIN—Formerly served by Bulldog Cable. No longer in operation. ICA: GA0327.

EASTMAN—Mediacom, 509 Flint Ave, Albany, GA 31701. Phones: 229-888-0242; 229-244-3852 (Valdosta regional office). Fax: 229-436-4819. Web Site: http://www.mediacomcable.com. Also serves Dodge County (portions), Helena, McRae, Scotland & Telfair County (portions). ICA: GA0076.
TV Market Ranking: Below 100 (Dodge County (portions), Helena, McRae, Scotland, Telfair County (portions)); Outside TV Markets (Dodge County (portions), EASTMAN, Telfair County (portions)). Franchise award date: June 1, 1966. Franchise expiration date: N.A. Began: May 1, 1966.
Channel capacity: N.A. Channels available but not in use: N.A.

Basic Service
Subscribers: 1,574.
Programming (received off-air): WALB (ABC, NBC, This TV) Albany; WGXA (ABC, FOX) Macon; WMAZ-TV (CBS) Macon; WPGA-TV (Bounce TV, IND, MeTV) Perry; WSST-TV (IND) Cordele; 1 FM.
Programming (via microwave): WSB-TV (ABC, MeTV) Atlanta.
Programming (via satellite): A&E; BET; CNBC; CNN; Comedy Central; C-SPAN; Discovery Channel; Freeform; Hallmark Channel; HLN; MTV; Nickelodeon; QVC; TBS; The Weather Channel; TNT; VH1.
Fee: $35.00 installation; $43.95 monthly.

Expanded Basic Service 1
Subscribers: N.A.
Programming (via satellite): AMC; Animal Planet; Bravo; Cartoon Network; CMT; C-SPAN 2; CW PLUS; Discovery Life Channel; Disney Channel; E! HD; ESPN; EWTN Global Catholic Network; Food Network; Fox News Channel; FOX Sports South/SportSouth; FX; HGTV; History; ION Television; Lifetime; MSNBC; Oxygen; Pop; Spike TV; TLC; Travel Channel; Trinity Broadcasting Network (TBN); truTV; TV Land; Univision; Univision Studios; USA Network; WE tv.
Fee: $22.43 monthly.

Digital Basic Service
Subscribers: N.A.
Programming (via satellite): BBC America; Bloomberg Television; Discovery Digital Networks; Disney XD; Fox Sports 1; Fuse; FXM; FYI; Golf Channel; GSN; History International; HITS (Headend In The Sky); IFC; LMN; MC; National Geographic Channel; NBCSN; Nick Jr.; Outdoor Channel; Ovation; TeenNick; Turner Classic Movies.

Digital Pay Service 1
Pay Units: N.A.
Programming (via satellite): Cinemax (multiplexed); Flix; HBO (multiplexed); Showtime (multiplexed); Starz (multiplexed); Starz Encore (multiplexed); Sundance TV; The Movie Channel (multiplexed).
Fee: $25.00 installation; $11.95 monthly (each).

Video-On-Demand: Yes

Pay-Per-View
Vubiquity Inc. (delivered digitally); Pleasure (delivered digitally); ETC (delivered digitally); ESPN Now (delivered digitally); Sports PPV (delivered digitally).

Internet Service
Operational: Yes. Began: April 1, 2003.
Broadband Service: Mediacom High Speed Internet.
Fee: $42.95 monthly; $3.00 modem lease.

Telephone Service
Digital: Operational
Homes passed: 5,592. Miles of plant included in Fitzgerald.
Regional Vice President: Sue Misiunas. General Manager: Gary Crosby. Regional Marketing Director: Melanie Hannasch. Regional Technical Operations Manager: Gary McDougall. Marketing Manager: Daryl Channey. Vice President, Financial Reporting: Kenneth J. Kohrs.
Ownership: Mediacom LLC (MSO).

EATONTON—Charter Communications. Now served by MILLEDGEVILLE, GA [GA0046]. ICA: GA0191.

ELBERTON—Comcast Cable, 254 Heard St, Elberton, GA 30635. Phones: 706-738-0091 (Administrative office); 706-733-7712 (Customer service). Fax: 706-739-1871. Web Site: http://www.comcast.com. Also serves Bowman, Elbert County (portions), Hart County (portions) & Hartwell, GA; Abbeville County (portions) & Calhoun Falls, SC. ICA: GA0192.
TV Market Ranking: 46 (Abbeville County (portions), Bowman, Calhoun Falls, Elbert County (portions), ELBERTON, Hart County (portions), Hartwell); Below 100 (Elbert County (portions)). Franchise award date: N.A. Franchise expiration date: N.A. Began: September 1, 1966.
Channel capacity: N.A. Channels available but not in use: N.A.

Basic Service
Subscribers: 2,935. Commercial subscribers: 29.
Programming (received off-air): WAGA-TV (Buzzr, FOX, Movies!) Atlanta; WGGS-TV (IND) Greenville; WGTA (Decades, Heroes & Icons, Movies!) Toccoa; WGTV (PBS) Athens; WHNS (COZI TV, Escape, FOX) Greenville; WLOS (ABC, Antenna TV) Asheville; WMYA-TV (MNT, The Country Network) Anderson; WNTV (PBS) Greenville; WOLO-TV (ABC, MeTV) Columbia; WSB-TV (ABC, MeTV) Atlanta; WSPA-TV (CBS, MeTV) Spartanburg; WXIA-TV (NBC) Atlanta; WYCW (CW) Asheville; WYFF (NBC, Movies!) Greenville.
Programming (via satellite): ION Television; QVC; WGN America.
Fee: $29.50-$64.00 installation; $22.89 monthly.

Expanded Basic Service 1
Subscribers: 2,325.
Programming (via satellite): A&E; AMC; Animal Planet; BET; Cartoon Network; CMT; CNBC; CNN; Comcast/Charter Sports Southeast (CSS); Comedy Central; C-SPAN; C-SPAN 2; Discovery Channel; Disney Channel; E! HD; ESPN; ESPN2; Food Network; Fox News Channel; Fox Sports 1; FOX Sports South/SportSouth; Freeform; FX; Golf Channel; GSN; HGTV; History; HLN; MSNBC; MTV; NBCSN; Nickelodeon; Pop; Spike TV; Syfy; TBS; The Weather Channel; TLC; TNT; Travel Channel; Trinity Broadcasting Network (TBN); truTV; Turner Classic Movies; TV Land; USA Network; VH1.
Fee: $42.95 monthly.

Digital Basic Service
Subscribers: N.A.
Programming (via satellite): BBC America; CMT; Destination America; Discovery Kids Channel; DMX Music; ESPN HD; Flix; Investigation Discovery; MTV Classic; MTV2;

2017 Edition   D-161

Georgia—Cable Systems

Nick Jr.; Nicktoons; Science Channel; Starz Encore (multiplexed); Sundance TV; TeenNick; Tr3s; VH1 Soul.

Pay Service 1
Pay Units: N.A.
Programming (via satellite): HBO.
Fee: $9.95 monthly.

Digital Pay Service 1
Pay Units: N.A.
Programming (via satellite): Cinemax (multiplexed); HBO (multiplexed); Showtime (multiplexed); The Movie Channel (multiplexed).
Fee: $7.05 monthly (each).

Video-On-Demand: Planned

Pay-Per-View
iN DEMAND (delivered digitally); Hot Choice (delivered digitally); Playboy TV (delivered digitally); Fresh (delivered digitally); Shorteez (delivered digitally); Pleasure (delivered digitally).

Internet Service
Operational: Yes.
Broadband Service: Comcast High Speed Internet.
Fee: $42.95 monthly.

Telephone Service
Digital: Operational
Miles of Plant: 324.0 (coaxial); None (fiber optic).
Technical Operations Director: Butch Jernigan. Engineering Director: Harry Hess. Marketing Director: Joey Fortier. Chief Technician: Jeff Bartlett.
Ownership: Comcast Cable Communications Inc. (MSO).

ELBERTON—ElbertonNET. Formerly [GA0304]. This cable system has converted to IPTV, 234 North McIntosh St, PO Box 70, Elberton, GA 30635. Phones: 706-283-1400; 706-213-3278. Fax: 706-213-3279. E-mail: customerservice@cityofelberton.net. Web Site: http://www.elberton.net. ICA: GA5280.
TV Market Ranking: 46 (ELBERTON).
Channel capacity: N.A. Channels available but not in use: N.A.

Basic
Subscribers: 2,696.
Programming (received off-air): WAGA-TV (Buzzr, FOX, Movies!) Atlanta; WGGS-TV (IND) Greenville; WGTA (Decades, Heroes & Icons, Movies!) Toccoa; WGTV (PBS) Athens; WHNS (COZI TV, Escape, FOX) Greenville; WLOS (ABC, Antenna TV) Asheville; WMYA-TV (MNT, The Country Network) Anderson; WRDW-TV (CBS, MNT, The Country Network) Augusta; WSPA-TV (CBS, MeTV) Spartanburg; WXIA-TV (NBC) Atlanta; WYCW (CW) Asheville; WYFF (NBC, Movies!) Greenville. Programming (via satellite): C-SPAN; C-SPAN 2; Pop; QVC; TBS; The Weather Channel; Trinity Broadcasting Network (TBN); Univision Studios; Weatherscan; WGN America.
Fee: $25.00 installation; $22.95 monthly.

Expanded
Subscribers: 1,814.
Programming (via satellite): A&E; AMC; Animal Planet; BET; Boomerang; Bravo; Cartoon Network; CMT; CNBC; CNN; Comedy Central; Discovery Channel; Disney Channel; Disney XD; E! HD; ESPN; ESPN Classic; ESPN2; ESPNews; Food Network; Fox News Channel; Fox Sports 1; FOX Sports South/SportSouth; Freeform; FX; Golf Channel; GSN; Hallmark Channel; HGTV; History; HLN; Lifetime; LMN; MSNBC; MTV; National Geographic Channel; Nickelodeon; Outdoor Channel; Ovation; Oxygen; Spike TV; Syfy; Telemundo; TLC; TNT; Travel Channel; truTV; Turner Classic Movies; TV Land; UniMas; USA Network; VH1; WE tv.
Fee: $62.95 monthly.

Digital/HD
Subscribers: N.A.
Programming (via satellite): A&E HD; BBC America; Bloomberg Television; Cloo; CMT; Destination America; Discovery Kids Channel; Discovery Life Channel; DMX Music; Food Network HD; FOX College Sports Central; FOX College Sports Pacific; Fuse; FXM; FYI; Great American Country; Hallmark Movies & Mysteries; HGTV HD; History International; IFC; Investigation Discovery; LOGO; MTV Classic; MTV Hits; MTV2; Nat Geo WILD; National Geographic Channel HD; NBCSN; Nick Jr.; Nicktoons; OWN: Oprah Winfrey Network; RFD-TV; Science Channel; Science HD; Sprout; TeenNick; Universal HD; UP; VH1 Soul.
Fee: $74.95 monthly.

Cinemax
Subscribers: N.A.
Programming (via satellite): Cinemax.
Fee: $11.00 monthly.

HBO
Subscribers: N.A.
Programming (via satellite): HBO (multiplexed).
Fee: $14.00 monthly.

Showtime/TMC/Flix
Subscribers: N.A.
Programming (via satellite): Flix; Showtime (multiplexed); The Movie Channel (multiplexed).
Fee: $13.00 monthly.

Starz/Encore
Subscribers: N.A.
Programming (via satellite): Starz (multiplexed); Starz Encore; Starz HD.
Fee: $11.00 monthly.

Pay-Per-View
iN DEMAND (delivered digitally).

Internet Service
Operational: Yes.
Broadband Service: In-house.
Fee: $39.95-$59.95 monthly; $10.00 modem lease.

Telephone Service
Digital: Operational
Fee: $44.95 monthly
City Manager: Lanier Dunn.
Ownership: Elberton Utilities.

ELBERTON—ElbertonNET. This cable system has converted to IPTV. See ELBERTON, GA [GA5280]. ICA: GA0304.

ELLIJAY—Community Cable Television Co, 224 Dalton St, PO Box 0, Ellijay, GA 30540-3119. Phones: 706-276-2281; 800-660-6826; 706-276-2271. Fax: 706-276-9888. E-mail: info@ellijay.com. Web Site: http://www.etcnow.com. Also serves Ball Ground, Bent Tree, Blue Ridge, Cherokee County (portions), East Ellijay, Fannin County (portions), Gilmer County, Jasper, McCaysville, Mineral Bluff, Morganton, Nelson, Pickens County (portions), Talking Rock & Tate, GA; Copperhill & Ducktown, TN. ICA: GA0044.
TV Market Ranking: Below 100 (Copperhill, Ducktown, East Ellijay, ELLIJAY, Gilmer County (portions)); Outside TV Markets (Ball Ground, Bent Tree, Blue Ridge, Cherokee County (portions), Fannin County (portions), Gilmer County (portions), Jasper, McCaysville, Mineral Bluff, Morganton, Nelson, Pickens County (portions), Talking Rock, Tate). Franchise award date: N.A. Franchise expiration date: N.A. Began: May 1, 1968.
Channel capacity: N.A. Channels available but not in use: N.A.

Basic Service
Subscribers: 14,824.
Programming (received off-air): WAGA-TV (Buzzr, FOX, Movies!) Atlanta; WATC-DT (ETV) Atlanta; WATL (Antenna TV, Bounce TV, MNT) Atlanta; WDEF-TV (Bounce TV, CBS, Escape) Chattanooga; WDSI-TV (FOX, MNT) Chattanooga; WGCL-TV (CBS, COZI TV, Grit) Atlanta; WGTV (PBS) Athens; WPCH-TV (IND) Atlanta; WPXA-TV (ION) Rome; WRCB (Antenna TV, NBC) Chattanooga; WSB-TV (ABC, MeTV) Atlanta; WTVC (ABC, This TV, WeatherNation) Chattanooga; WUPA (CW, Decades) Atlanta; WUVG-DT (getTV, UNV) Athens; WXIA-TV (NBC) Atlanta.
Programming (via satellite): A&E; Animal Planet; Cartoon Network; CMT; CNBC; CNN; Comedy Central; C-SPAN; C-SPAN 2; Discovery Channel; Disney Channel; Disney XD; ESPN; ESPN2; FamilyNet; Food Network; Fox News Channel; FOX Sports South/SportSouth; Freeform; FX; Hallmark Channel; HGTV; History; HLN; Lifetime; MTV; Nickelodeon; Outdoor Channel; Pop; QVC; Spike TV; Syfy; TBS; The Weather Channel; TLC; TNT; Travel Channel; Trinity Broadcasting Network (TBN); Turner Classic Movies; TV Land; UP; USA Network; VH1.
Fee: $46.99 monthly.

Digital Basic Service
Subscribers: N.A.
Programming (via satellite): AXS TV; BBC America; Bloomberg Television; Discovery Digital Networks; DMX Music; ESPN Classic; ESPNews; Fox Sports 1; Fox Sports 2; FXM; FYI; Golf Channel; GSN; Hallmark Movies & Mysteries; HD Theater; History International; IFC; LMN; NBCSN; Nick Jr.; Nicktoons; Starz Encore; TeenNick; TNT HD; WE tv.

Digital Pay Service 1
Pay Units: N.A.
Programming (via satellite): Cinemax; Flix; HBO (multiplexed); Showtime (multiplexed); Starz; The Movie Channel (multiplexed).
Fee: $4.95 monthly (Encore), $6.95 monthly (Cinemax), $11.95 monthly (Starz/Encore), $12.95 monthly (HBO or Showtime/TMC/Flix).

Video-On-Demand: No

Internet Service
Operational: Yes.
Fee: $49.95 monthly.

Telephone Service
None
Miles of Plant: 1,100.0 (coaxial); None (fiber optic). Homes passed: 20,000.
President: Dwight Roeland. Assistant Vice President: Daryl Harper. Engineering Director: Frank Rigdon.
Ownership: Ellijay Telephone Co. (MSO).

ENIGMA—Mediacom. Now served by ADEL, GA [GA0063]. ICA: GA0119.

EULONIA—Comcast Cable. Now served by DARIEN, GA [GA0117]. ICA: GA0091.

FAIRBURN—Comcast Cable. Now served by ATLANTA, GA [GA0017]. ICA: GA0305.

FITZGERALD—Mediacom, 100 Crystal Run Rd, Middletown, NY 10941. Phones: 229-244-3852 (Valdosta regional office); 845-695-2762. Web Site: http://www.mediacomcable.com. Also serves Ben Hill County (portions), Cordele, Crisp County (portions), Dooly County (portions), Irwin County (portions), Ocilla & Vienna. ICA: GA0052.
TV Market Ranking: Below 100 (Ben Hill County (portions), Cordele, Crisp County (portions), Dooly County (portions), Irwin County (portions), Vienna); Outside TV Markets (Ben Hill County (portions), FITZGERALD, Irwin County (portions), Ocilla). Franchise award date: N.A. Franchise expiration date: N.A. Began: November 1, 1962.
Channel capacity: N.A. Channels available but not in use: N.A.

Basic Service
Subscribers: 5,186.
Programming (received off-air): WALB (ABC, NBC, This TV) Albany; WFXL (Bounce TV, FOX) Albany; WMAZ-TV (CBS) Macon; WPGA-TV (Bounce TV, IND, MeTV) Perry; WSST-TV (IND) Cordele; WXGA-TV (PBS) Waycross; 1 FM.
Programming (via microwave): WSB-TV (ABC, MeTV) Atlanta.
Programming (via satellite): A&E; BET; CNBC; CNN; C-SPAN; Discovery Channel; Freeform; Hallmark Channel; HLN; Lifetime; MTV; Nickelodeon; QVC; TBS; The Weather Channel; TNT.
Fee: $35.00 installation; $43.95 monthly; $.11 converter.

Expanded Basic Service 1
Subscribers: N.A.
Programming (via satellite): AMC; Animal Planet; Bravo; Cartoon Network; CMT; Comedy Central; C-SPAN 2; CW PLUS; Discovery Life Channel; Disney Channel; E! HD; ESPN; ESPN2; EWTN Global Catholic Network; Food Network; Fox News Channel; FOX Sports South/SportSouth; FX; Golf Channel; HGTV; History; ION Television; MSNBC; Oxygen; Pop; Spike TV; Syfy; TLC; Travel Channel; Trinity Broadcasting Network (TBN); truTV; TV Land; Univision; Univision Studios; USA Network; VH1; WE tv.
Fee: $2.15 monthly.

Digital Basic Service
Subscribers: N.A.
Programming (via satellite): BBC America; Bloomberg Television; Discovery Digital Networks; Disney XD; Fox Sports 1; Fuse; FXM; FYI; GSN; History International; HITS (Headend In The Sky); IFC; LMN; MC; National Geographic Channel; NBCSN; Nick Jr.; Outdoor Channel; Ovation; TeenNick; Turner Classic Movies.

Digital Pay Service 1
Pay Units: N.A.
Programming (via satellite): Cinemax (multiplexed); Flix; HBO (multiplexed); Showtime (multiplexed); Starz (multiplexed); Starz Encore (multiplexed); Sundance TV; The Movie Channel (multiplexed).

Video-On-Demand: Yes

Pay-Per-View
Vubiquity Inc. (delivered digitally); Pleasure (delivered digitally); ETC (delivered digitally); ESPN Now (delivered digitally); Sports PPV (delivered digitally).

Internet Service
Operational: Yes. Began: November 1, 2001.
Subscribers: 2,833.
Broadband Service: Mediacom High Speed Internet.
Fee: $50.00 installation; $42.95 monthly; $3.00 modem lease.

Cable Systems—Georgia

Telephone Service
Analog: Not Operational
Digital: Operational
Subscribers: 1,971.
Miles of Plant: 605.0 (coaxial); 163.0 (fiber optic). Homes passed: 18,463. Miles of plant (coax & fiber) includes Adel, Eastman, & Hazlehurst.
Regional Vice President: Sue Misiunas. Vice President, Financial Reporting: Kenneth J. Kohrs. General Manager: Gary Crosby. Regional Marketing Director: Melanie Hannasch. Regional Technical Operations Manager: Gary McDougall. Marketing Manager: Daryl Chaney.
Ownership: Mediacom LLC (MSO).

FLINT RIVER—Formerly served by KLiP Interactive. No longer in operation. ICA: GA0280.

FOLKSTON—Comcast Cable. Now served by JACKSONVILLE, FL [FL0002]. ICA: GA0093.

FORSYTH—Forsyth CableNet, PO Box 669, Reynolds, GA 31076. Phones: 478-994-7623; 478-885-4111. Web Site: http://www.forsythcable.com. Also serves Monroe County (portions). ICA: GA0080.
TV Market Ranking: Below 100 (FORSYTH, Monroe County (portions)). Franchise award date: N.A. Franchise expiration date: N.A. Began: February 20, 1979.
Channel capacity: N.A. Channels available but not in use: N.A.
Basic Service
Subscribers: 1,061.
Programming (received off-air): WAGA-TV (Buzzr, FOX, Movies!) Atlanta; WATL (Antenna TV, Bounce TV, MNT) Atlanta; WGCL-TV (CBS, COZI TV, Grit) Atlanta; WGNM (Christian TV Network) Macon; WGTV (PBS) Athens; WGXA (ABC, FOX) Macon; WMGT-TV (Escape, MNT, NBC) Macon; WPGA-TV (Bounce TV, IND, MeTV) Perry; WSB-TV (ABC, MeTV) Atlanta; WXIA-TV (NBC) Atlanta; 1 FM.
Programming (via satellite): Disney Channel; HLN; ION Television; Pop; truTV; WGN America.
Fee: $54.95 installation; $29.95 monthly.
Expanded Basic Service 1
Subscribers: 848.
Programming (via satellite): A&E; AMC; Animal Planet; BET; Bloomberg Television; Cartoon Network; CMT; CNBC; CNN; Comedy Central; C-SPAN; C-SPAN 2; Discovery Channel; Discovery Life Channel; Disney XD; ESPN; ESPN2; ESPNews; Food Network; Fox News Channel; FOX Sports South/SportSouth; Freeform; FX; Golf Channel; HGTV; History; INSP; Lifetime; MSNBC; MTV; Nickelodeon; Outdoor Channel; QVC; Spike TV; Syfy; TBS; The Weather Channel; TLC; TNT; Travel Channel; Trinity Broadcasting Network (TBN); Turner Classic Movies; TV Land; USA Network; VH1; WE tv.
Fee: $37.00 monthly.
Pay Service 1
Pay Units: N.A.
Programming (via satellite): Cinemax (multiplexed); HBO (multiplexed); Showtime (multiplexed); Starz; Starz Encore (multiplexed).
Fee: $10.84 monthly (Starz/Encore), $10.94 monthly (Showtime), $12.04 monthly (Cinemax), $14.25 monthly (HBO).
Video-On-Demand: No
Pay-Per-View
iN DEMAND.

Internet Service
Operational: Yes. Began: January 1, 2000.
Broadband Service: Metropolitan Electrical Association of Georgia.
Fee: $99.00 installation; $24.95-$49.95 monthly.
Telephone Service
None
Miles of Plant: 40.0 (coaxial); 80.0 (fiber optic). Homes passed: 2,600.
President: James L. Bond. General Manager: Dennis Rolling. Chief Technician: Mark Beaubien.
Ownership: Forsyth Cable.

FORT BENNING—Charter Communications. Now served by NEWNAN, GA [GA0042]. ICA: GA0071.

FORT GORDON—WOW! Internet, Cable & Phone. Now served by AUGUSTA, GA [GA0288]. ICA: GA0198.

FORT VALLEY—ComSouth. Now served by PERRY, GA [GA0229]. ICA: GA0077.

FORT VALLEY—Flint Cable TV. Now served by REYNOLDS, GA [GA0236]. ICA: GA0324.

FRANKLIN COUNTY—TruVista Communications, 112 York St, PO Box 160, Chester, SC 29706. Phones: 803-581-9190; 800-768-1212. Web Site: http://truvista.net. Also serves Bowersville, Canon, Franklin Springs & Hart County (portions). ICA: GA0078.
TV Market Ranking: 46 (Bowersville, Canon, FRANKLIN COUNTY (portions), Franklin Springs, Hart County (portions)); Below 100 (FRANKLIN COUNTY (portions)).
Franchise award date: N.A. Franchise expiration date: N.A. Began: October 30, 1981.
Channel capacity: N.A. Channels available but not in use: N.A.
Basic Service
Subscribers: 88.
Programming (received off-air): WAGA-TV (Buzzr, FOX, Movies!) Atlanta; WGGS-TV (IND) Greenville; WGTA (Decades, Heroes & Icons, Movies!) Toccoa; WGTV (PBS) Athens; WHNS (COZI TV, Escape, FOX) Greenville; WLOS (ABC, Antenna TV) Asheville; WMYA-TV (MNT, The Country Network) Anderson; WSB-TV (ABC, MeTV) Atlanta; WXIA-TV (NBC) Atlanta; WYCW (CW) Asheville; WYFF (NBC, Movies!) Greenville.
Programming (via satellite): A&E; BET; Cartoon Network; CNN; C-SPAN; Discovery Channel; ESPN; ESPN2; FOX Sports South/SportSouth; Freeform; FX; Great American Country; Hallmark Channel; HGTV; HLN; INSP; Lifetime; Nickelodeon; Pop; QVC; TBS; The Weather Channel; TLC; TNT; Turner Classic Movies; USA Network.
Fee: $40.00 installation; $28.99 monthly.
Pay Service 1
Pay Units: N.A.
Programming (via satellite): Cinemax; HBO; Showtime.
Video-On-Demand: No
Internet Service
Operational: Yes.
Fee: $39.99 monthly.
Telephone Service
Analog: Not Operational
Digital: Operational
Fee: $23.99 monthly
Miles of Plant: 90.0 (coaxial); None (fiber optic). Homes passed: 2,800.
Ownership: TruVista Communications (MSO).

Communications Daily
Warren Communications News
Get the industry standard FREE —
For a no-obligation trial call 800-771-9202 or visit www.warren-news.com

FUNSTON—Formerly served by Wainwright Cable Inc. No longer in operation. ICA: GA0269.

GAINESVILLE—Charter Communications. Now served by LAWRENCEVILLE, GA [GA0009]. ICA: GA0016.

GIBSON—Formerly served by KLiP Interactive. No longer in operation. ICA: GA0195.

GLENNVILLE—Comcast Cable, 209 Council St, PO Box 548, Waynesboro, GA 30830. Phones: 912-354-7531; 912-356-3113. Web Site: http://www.comcast.com. Also serves Tattnall County (portions). ICA: GA0115.
TV Market Ranking: Below 100 (GLENNVILLE, Tattnall County (portions)); Outside TV Markets (Tattnall County (portions)). Franchise award date: October 21, 1970. Franchise expiration date: N.A. Began: December 1, 1971.
Channel capacity: N.A. Channels available but not in use: N.A.
Basic Service
Subscribers: 336. Commercial subscribers: 67.
Programming (received off-air): WGSA (CW) Baxley; WJCL (ABC) Savannah; WSAV-TV (MeTV, MNT, NBC) Savannah; WTGS (Antenna TV, FOX) Hardeeville; WTOC-TV (Bounce TV, CBS, This TV) Savannah; WVAN-TV (PBS) Savannah.
Programming (via satellite): Comcast/Charter Sports Southeast (CSS); ION Television; QVC; TBS; WGN America.
Fee: $39.95-$50.00 installation; $17.45 monthly.
Expanded Basic Service 1
Subscribers: N.A.
Programming (via satellite): A&E; AMC; Animal Planet; BET; Cartoon Network; CMT; CNBC; CNN; C-SPAN; Discovery Channel; Disney Channel; E! HD; ESPN; ESPN2; Food Network; Fox News Channel; Fox Sports 1; FOX Sports Networks; FOX Sports South/SportSouth; Freeform; FX; Golf Channel; GSN; Hallmark Channel; HGTV; HLN; Lifetime; MTV; NBCSN; Nickelodeon; OWN: Oprah Winfrey Network; Spike TV; Syfy; The Weather Channel; TLC; TNT; Trinity Broadcasting Network (TBN); truTV; Turner Classic Movies; TV Land; USA Network; VH1.
Fee: $30.99 monthly.
Digital Basic Service
Subscribers: N.A.
Programming (via satellite): BBC America; CMT; Destination America; DMX Music; Investigation Discovery; MTV Classic; MTV2; Nick 2; Nick Jr.; Science Channel; Starz Encore (multiplexed); TeenNick; Tr3s; VH1 Soul.
Pay Service 1
Pay Units: N.A.
Programming (via satellite): HBO; Showtime.
Digital Pay Service 1
Pay Units: N.A.
Programming (via satellite): Cinemax (multiplexed); HBO (multiplexed); Showtime (multiplexed); Starz (multiplexed); The Movie Channel (multiplexed).
Fee: $3.50 monthly (TMC), $7.95 monthly (Starz), $11.95 monthly (Cinemax, HBO or Showtime).
Video-On-Demand: No
Pay-Per-View
iN DEMAND (delivered digitally); Hot Choice (delivered digitally).
Internet Service
Operational: Yes.
Telephone Service
Digital: Operational
Homes passed & miles of plant (coax & fiber) included in Savannah.
General Manager: Michael Daves. Technical Operations Director: Joel Godsen. Marketing Director: Jerry Avery. Marketing Manager: Ken Torres.
Ownership: Comcast Cable Communications Inc. (MSO).

GORDON—Bulldog Cable, 455 Gees Mill Business Ct, Conyers, GA 30013. Phones: 706-997-9003; 800-388-6577. Web Site: http://www.bulldogcable.com. ICA: GA0090.
TV Market Ranking: Below 100 (GORDON). Franchise award date: N.A. Franchise expiration date: N.A. Began: December 1, 1982.
Channel capacity: N.A. Channels available but not in use: N.A.
Basic Service
Subscribers: 23.
Programming (received off-air): WGNM (Christian TV Network) Macon; WGXA (ABC, FOX) Macon; WMAZ-TV (CBS) Macon; WMGT-TV (Escape, MNT, NBC) Macon; WMUM-TV (PBS) Cochran; WPCH-TV (IND) Atlanta; WPGA-TV (Bounce TV, IND, MeTV) Perry.
Programming (via satellite): A&E; AMC; Animal Planet; BET; Cartoon Network; CMT; CNN; Comedy Central; CW PLUS; Discovery Channel; Disney Channel; ESPN; ESPN2; Fox News Channel; FOX Sports South/SportSouth; Freeform; FX; GSN; Hallmark Channel; Lifetime; MTV; National Geographic Channel; NBCSN; Nickelodeon; Spike TV; The Weather Channel; TLC; TNT; Trinity Broadcasting Network (TBN); truTV; TV Land; USA Network; WE tv.
Fee: $44.95 installation; $46.00 monthly; $.45 converter.
Pay Service 1
Pay Units: N.A.
Programming (via satellite): HBO; Showtime.
Fee: $12.00 monthly.
Internet Service
Operational: No.
Telephone Service
None
Miles of Plant: 55.0 (coaxial); None (fiber optic). Homes passed: 1,704.
President: Mark Wilson. General Manager East: Mark Miller. General Manager West: Vance Johnson. Controller: Ashley Hull.
Ownership: Bulldog Cable (MSO).

GRAY—Formerly served by Allegiance Communications. No longer in operation. ICA: GA0196.

2017 Edition   D-163

Georgia—Cable Systems

GREENE COUNTY (unincorporated areas)—Plantation Cablevision Inc, 865 Harmony Rd, PO Box 4494, Eatonton, GA 31024-4494. Phones: 877-830-5454; 706-485-7740. Fax: 706-485-2590. Web Site: http://www.plantationcable.net. Also serves Lake Oconee & Putnam County (unincorporated areas). ICA: GA0197.
  TV Market Ranking: Below 100 (GREENE COUNTY (UNINCORPORATED AREAS) (portions), Lake Oconee, Putnam County (unincorporated areas) (portions)); Outside TV Markets (GREENE COUNTY (UNINCORPORATED AREAS) (portions), Putnam County (unincorporated areas) (portions)).
  Channel capacity: N.A. Channels available but not in use: N.A.
Basic Service
  Subscribers: 4,135.
  Programming (received off-air): WAGA-TV (Buzzr, FOX, Movies!) Atlanta; WATL (Antenna TV, Bounce TV, MNT) Atlanta; WGCL-TV (CBS, COZI TV, Grit) Atlanta; WGTV (PBS) Athens; WGXA (ABC, FOX) Macon; WHSG-TV (TBN) Monroe; WMAZ-TV (CBS) Macon; WMGT-TV (Escape, MNT, NBC) Macon; WPBA (PBS) Atlanta; WPCH-TV (IND) Atlanta; WPGA-TV (Bounce TV, IND, MeTV) Perry; WSB-TV (ABC, MeTV) Atlanta; WUPA (CW, Decades) Atlanta; WUVG-DT (getTV, UNV) Athens; WXIA-TV (NBC) Atlanta.
  Programming (via satellite): A&E; AMC; Animal Planet; CMT; CNBC; CNN; Comedy Central; C-SPAN; C-SPAN 2; Discovery Channel; Disney Channel; DIY Network; E! HD; ESPN; ESPN2; Food Network; Fox News Channel; FOX Sports Networks; FOX Sports South/SportSouth; FX; Golf Channel; HGTV; History; HLN; ION Television; Lifetime; MSNBC; MTV; National Geographic Channel; Nickelodeon; Outdoor Channel; Pop; QVC; Spike TV; The Weather Channel; TLC; TNT; Travel Channel; truTV; TV Land; USA Network; VH1.
  Fee: $50.00 installation; $60.55 monthly.
Digital Basic Service
  Subscribers: N.A.
  Programming (via satellite): BBC America; Destination America; Discovery Kids Channel; Disney XD; ESPN Now; Investigation Discovery; National Geographic Channel; Nick Jr.; Nicktoons; Outdoor Channel; OWN: Oprah Winfrey Network; Science Channel; Syfy; Turner Classic Movies.
Pay Service 1
  Pay Units: N.A.
  Programming (via satellite): HBO.
  Fee: $12.95 monthly.
Digital Pay Service 1
  Pay Units: N.A.
  Programming (via satellite): Cinemax; HBO; Showtime; Starz; Starz Encore; The Movie Channel.
  Fee: $5.95 monthly (Encore), $10.95 monthly (Cinemax, Showtime/TMC or Starz/Encore), $12.95 monthly (HBO).
Video-On-Demand: No
Pay-Per-View
  special events.
Internet Service
  Operational: Yes. Began: December 31, 1998.
  Broadband Service: Plantation Cable.net.
  Fee: $39.95 monthly; $9.95 modem lease.
Telephone Service
  Analog: Not Operational
  Digital: Operational
  Fee: $39.95 monthly
  Miles of Plant: 150.0 (coaxial); None (fiber optic). Homes passed: 5,000.
  General Manager: Joel Hall. Chief Engineer: John H. Hall.
  Ownership: Hargray Communications Group Inc.

GREENSBORO—Formerly served by Allegiance Communications. Now served by Charter Communications, MILLEDGEVILLE, GA [GA0046]. ICA: GA0323.

GREENVILLE—Formerly served by Almega Cable. No longer in operation. ICA: GA0317.

GREENVILLE—Formerly served by Charter Communications. No longer in operation. ICA: GA0132.

GREENVILLE—Formerly served by Georgia Broadband. No longer in operation. ICA: GA0321.

GRIFFIN—Comcast Cable. Now served by ATLANTA, GA [GA0017]. ICA: GA0028.

GUYTON—Comcast Cable. Now served by SAVANNAH, GA [GA0005]. ICA: GA0199.

HADDOCK—Formerly served by KLiP Interactive. No longer in operation. ICA: GA0160.

HARRISON—Formerly served by Walker Cablevision. No longer in operation. ICA: GA0169.

HART COUNTY—Hart Communications, 196 North Forest Ave, PO Box 750, Hartwell, GA 30643. Phones: 706-856-2288; 800-276-3925; 706-376-4701. Fax: 706-376-2009. Web Site: http://www.htconline.net. Also serves Avalon, Franklin County (northern portion), Hartwell & Martin. ICA: GA0293.
  TV Market Ranking: 46 (Avalon, HART COUNTY, Hartwell, Martin); Below 100 (Franklin County (northern portion)).
  Channel capacity: N.A. Channels available but not in use: N.A.
Basic Service
  Subscribers: 2,471.
  Programming (received off-air): WAGA-TV (Buzzr, FOX, Movies!) Atlanta; WGGS-TV (IND) Greenville; WGTA (Decades, Heroes & Icons, Movies!) Toccoa; WGTV (PBS) Athens; WHNS (COZI TV, Escape, FOX) Greenville; WLOS (ABC, Antenna TV) Asheville; WMYA-TV (MNT, The Country Network) Anderson; WNTV (PBS) Greenville; WSB-TV (ABC, MeTV) Atlanta; WSPA-TV (CBS, MeTV) Spartanburg; WXIA-TV (NBC) Atlanta; WYCW (CW) Asheville; WYFF (NBC, Movies!) Greenville.
  Programming (via satellite): A&E; AMC; Animal Planet; BET; Cartoon Network; CMT; CNBC; CNN; C-SPAN; C-SPAN 2; Discovery Channel; Disney Channel; E! HD; ESPN; ESPN2; Food Network; Fox News Channel; Fox Sports 1; Freeform; FX; Golf Channel; GSN; HGTV; History; Lifetime; MTV; Nickelodeon; Outdoor Channel; QVC; Spike TV; SportSouth; Syfy; TBS; The Weather Channel; TLC; TNT; Travel Channel; Turner Classic Movies; TV Land; USA Network; VH1; WGN America.
  Fee: $45.00 installation; $19.50 monthly; $2.50 converter.
Digital Basic Service
  Subscribers: 656.
  Programming (via satellite): BBC America; Bloomberg Television; Bravo; Cloo; Discovery Digital Networks; Disney XD; ESPN Classic; ESPNews; FXM; FYI; History International; IFC; LMN; NBCSN; Nick Jr.; Nicktoons; Starz (multiplexed); Starz Encore (multiplexed); TeenNick; Trinity Broadcasting Network (TBN).
  Fee: $26.00 monthly.
Pay Service 1
  Pay Units: N.A.
  Programming (via satellite): HBO; Showtime.
  Fee: $12.95 monthly (each).
Digital Pay Service 1
  Pay Units: N.A.
  Programming (via satellite): Cinemax (multiplexed); Flix; HBO (multiplexed); Showtime (multiplexed); The Movie Channel (multiplexed).
  Fee: $13.00 monthly (Showtime/TMC/Flix), $15.00 monthly (Cinemax/HBO).
Internet Service
  Operational: Yes, DSL.
  Fee: $49.95 monthly.
Telephone Service
  Analog: Operational
  President: Randy Daniel. Vice President, Network Operations: J.R. Anderson. Customer Service Manager: Debbie Anderson.
  Ownership: Hart Cable.

HARTWELL—Comcast Cablevision of the South. Now served by ELBERTON, GA [GA0192]. ICA: GA0200.

HAWKINSVILLE—ComSouth Telesys Inc. Now served by PERRY, GA [GA0229]. ICA: GA0062.

HAYNEVILLE—ComSouth Telesys Inc. Now served by PERRY, GA [GA0229]. ICA: GA0281.

HAZLEHURST—Mediacom, 509 Flint Ave, Albany, GA 31701. Phones: 229-244-3852 (Valdosta Regional office); 229-888-0242. Fax: 229-436-4819. Web Site: http://www.mediacomcable.com. Also serves Jeff Davis County (portions) & Lumber City. ICA: GA0073.
  TV Market Ranking: Below 100 (HAZLEHURST, Jeff Davis County (portions), Lumber City). Franchise award date: N.A. Franchise expiration date: N.A. Began: January 1, 1965.
  Channel capacity: N.A. Channels available but not in use: N.A.
Basic Service
  Subscribers: 1,100.
  Programming (received off-air): WALB (ABC, NBC, This TV) Albany; WGSA (CW) Baxley; WJCL (ABC) Savannah; WSAV-TV (MeTV, MNT, NBC) Savannah; WTGS (Antenna TV, FOX) Hardeeville; WTOC-TV (Bounce TV, CBS, This TV) Savannah; WXGA-TV (PBS) Waycross.
  Programming (via microwave): WSB-TV (ABC, MeTV) Atlanta; WXIA-TV (NBC) Atlanta.
  Programming (via satellite): A&E; BET; CNBC; CNN; C-SPAN; Discovery Channel; Disney Channel; Freeform; HLN; MTV; Nickelodeon; QVC; TBS; The Weather Channel; TNT.
  Fee: $35.00 installation; $43.95 monthly; $.11 converter.
Digital Basic Service
  Subscribers: N.A.
  Programming (via satellite): BBC America; Bloomberg Television; Discovery Digital Networks; Disney XD; Food Network; Fox Sports 1; Fuse; FXM; FYI; Golf Channel; GSN; HGTV; History International; HITS (Headend In The Sky); IFC; LMN; MC; National Geographic Channel; NBCSN; Nick Jr.; Outdoor Channel; Ovation; TeenNick; Travel Channel; Turner Classic Movies.
Digital Pay Service 1
  Pay Units: N.A.
  Programming (via satellite): Cinemax (multiplexed); Flix; HBO (multiplexed); Showtime (multiplexed); Starz (multiplexed); Starz Encore (multiplexed); Sundance TV; The Movie Channel (multiplexed).
  Fee: $20.00 installation; $11.95 monthly (Cinemax or HBO), $12.50 monthly (Showtime).
Video-On-Demand: Yes
Pay-Per-View
  Vubiquity Inc. (delivered digitally); ETC (delivered digitally); Pleasure; ESPN Now (delivered digitally); Sports PPV (delivered digitally).
Internet Service
  Operational: Yes. Began: March 14, 2003.
  Broadband Service: Mediacom High Speed Internet.
  Fee: $42.95 monthly; $3.00 modem lease.
Telephone Service
  Digital: Operational
  Miles of Plant: 88.0 (coaxial); None (fiber optic). Homes passed: 3,584. Miles of plant (coax & fiber) included in Fitzgerald.
  Regional Vice President: Sue Misiunas. General Manager: Gary Crosby. Regional Technical Operations Manager: Gary McDougall. Regional Marketing Director: Melanie Hannasch. Marketing Manager: Daryl Channey. Vice President, Financial Reporting: Kenneth J. Kohrs.
  Ownership: Mediacom LLC (MSO).

HELEN—Teleview. Now served by DAHLONEGA, GA [GA0099]. ICA: GA0201.

HIAWASSEE—Windstream Teleview. Now served by DAHLONEGA, GA [GA0099]. ICA: GA0202.

HINESVILLE—Comcast Cable. Now served by SAVANNAH, GA [GA0005]. ICA: GA0024.

HOBOKEN—Worth Cable, 3 Commissioner Dr, PO Box 2056, Darien, GA 31305-2056. Phones: 912-437-3422; 866-206-0656. Fax: 912-437-2065. Also serves Brantley County (unincorporated areas). ICA: GA0203.
  TV Market Ranking: Below 100 (Brantley County (unincorporated areas) (portions)); Outside TV Markets (Brantley County (unincorporated areas) (portions), HOBOKEN).
  Channel capacity: 45 (not 2-way capable). Channels available but not in use: N.A.
Basic Service
  Subscribers: 107.
  Programming (received off-air): WCWJ (Bounce TV, CW) Jacksonville; WFOX-TV (FOX, MeTV, MNT) Jacksonville; WJCL (ABC) Savannah; WJXT (LATV, This TV) Jacksonville; WPXC-TV (ION) Brunswick; WTLV (Antenna TV, NBC, The Country Network) Jacksonville; WTOC-TV (Bounce TV, CBS, This TV) Savannah; WXGA-TV (PBS) Waycross.
  Programming (via satellite): A&E; AMC; Animal Planet; BET; CMT; CNN; Disney Channel; ESPN; Fox News Channel; Freeform; Nickelodeon; Spike TV; TBS; The Weather Channel; TLC; TNT; Travel Channel; Trinity Broadcasting Network (TBN); TV Land; USA Network; WGN America.
  Fee: $29.95 installation; $30.45 monthly.

Pay Service 1
Pay Units: 48.
Programming (via satellite): HBO.
Fee: $10.95 monthly.
Video-On-Demand: No
Internet Service
Operational: No.
Telephone Service
None
Miles of Plant: 12.0 (coaxial); None (fiber optic). Homes passed: 300.
General Manager: Dennis Wortham.
Ownership: Worth Cable Services (MSO).

HOMERVILLE—Comcast Cable, 3760 Hartsfiled Rd, Tallahassee, FL 32303-1121. Phones: 850-574-4016 (Tallahassee office); 912-487-2224. Fax: 850-574-4030. E-mail: claire_evans@cable.comcast.com. Web Site: http://www.comcast.com. Also serves Argyle & Clinch County (portions). ICA: GA0204.
TV Market Ranking: Below 100 (HOMERVILLE, Clinch County (portions)); Outside TV Markets (Argyle, Clinch County (portions)). Franchise award date: August 1, 1968. Franchise expiration date: N.A. Began: November 1, 1968.
Channel capacity: N.A. Channels available but not in use: N.A.
Basic Service
Subscribers: 511.
Programming (received off-air): WALB (ABC, NBC, This TV) Albany; WBXT-LD (IND) Tallahassee; WCTV (CBS, MNT, This TV) Thomasville; WFXL (Bounce TV, FOX) Albany; WJXT (LATV, This TV) Jacksonville; WTLV (Antenna TV, NBC, The Country Network) Jacksonville; WTXL-TV (ABC, Bounce TV) Tallahassee; WXGA-TV (PBS) Waycross.
Programming (via satellite): Disney Channel; ESPN; Great American Country; QVC; WGN America.
Fee: $31.00 installation; $14.00 monthly.
Expanded Basic Service 1
Subscribers: N.A.
Programming (via satellite): A&E; AMC; Animal Planet; BET; Cartoon Network; CMT; CNBC; CNN; Comcast/Charter Sports Southeast (CSS); Comedy Central; C-SPAN; C-SPAN 2; Discovery Channel; E! HD; ESPN2; Food Network; Fox News Channel; Fox Sports 1; FOX Sports South/SportSouth; Freeform; FX; Golf Channel; GSN; Hallmark Channel; HGTV; History; HLN; INSP; ION Television; Lifetime; MTV; NBCSN; Nickelodeon; OWN: Oprah Winfrey Network; Pop; Spike TV; Syfy; TBS; The Weather Channel; TLC; TNT; Travel Channel; Trinity Broadcasting Network (TBN); truTV; Turner Classic Movies; TV Land; TV One; USA Network; VH1.
Fee: $37.60 monthly.
Digital Basic Service
Subscribers: N.A.
Programming (via satellite): CMT; Destination America; Discovery Kids Channel; Flix; Investigation Discovery; LMN; MC; MoviePlex; MTV Classic; MTV2; Nick 2; Nick Jr.; RTV; Science Channel; Sprout; Starz Encore (multiplexed); TeenNick; Tr3s; UP; VH1 Soul.
Pay Service 1
Pay Units: N.A.
Programming (via satellite): HBO; Showtime.
Fee: $15.00 installation; $9.95 monthly (Showtime), $11.95 monthly (HBO).
Digital Pay Service 1
Pay Units: N.A.
Programming (via satellite): Cinemax (multiplexed); HBO (multiplexed); Showtime (multiplexed); Starz (multiplexed); The Movie Channel (multiplexed).
Fee: $9.95 monthly (each).
Video-On-Demand: No
Pay-Per-View
iN DEMAND (delivered digitally); Hot Choice (delivered digitally); Playboy TV (delivered digitally); Fresh (delivered digitally); Shorteez (delivered digitally).
Internet Service
Operational: Yes.
Telephone Service
Digital: Operational
General Manager: K. C. McWilliams. Technical Operations Director: Terry Pullen. Area Technical Manager: Andy Musgrove. Marketing Director: Claire Evans. System Coordinator: Carla Musgrove.
Ownership: Comcast Cable Communications Inc. (MSO).

IRON CITY—Formerly served by KLiP Interactive. No longer in operation. ICA: GA0137.

IRWINTON—Windstream Teleview, 4001 Rodney Parham Rd, Little Rock, AR 72212. Phones: 877-759-9020; 866-971-9463; 501-748-7000. Fax: 501-748-6392. E-mail: support@windstream.net. Web Site: http://www.windstream.com. Also serves Gordon, Ivey, McIntyre, Toomsboro & Wilkinson County (portions). ICA: GA0300.
TV Market Ranking: Below 100 (Gordon, IRWINTON, Ivey, McIntyre, Wilkinson County (portions), Toomsboro).
Channel capacity: N.A. Channels available but not in use: N.A.
Basic Service
Subscribers: 586.
Programming (received off-air): WGNM (Christian TV Network) Macon; WGXA (ABC, FOX) Macon; WMAZ-TV (CBS) Macon; WMGT-TV (Escape, MNT, NBC) Macon; WMUM-TV (PBS) Cochran; WPCH-TV (IND) Atlanta; WPGA-TV (Bounce TV, IND, MeTV) Perry.
Programming (via satellite): AMC; Animal Planet; BET; Bravo; CMT; CNN; Comedy Central; CW PLUS; Discovery Channel; Disney Channel; ESPN; ESPN2; Fox News Channel; Freeform; FX; GSN; MTV; Nickelodeon; Spike TV; The Weather Channel; TLC; TNT; Trinity Broadcasting Network (TBN); TV Land; USA Network.
Fee: $50.00 installation; $25.00 monthly.
Pay Service 1
Pay Units: N.A.
Programming (via satellite): HBO.
Fee: $10.95 monthly.
Pay Service 2
Pay Units: N.A.
Programming (via satellite): Showtime.
Fee: $10.95 monthly.
Internet Service
Operational: Yes.
Telephone Service
Digital: Operational
Miles of Plant: 45.0 (coaxial); None (fiber optic). Homes passed: 600.
President & Chief Executive Officer: Tony Thomas. Chief Financial Officer & Treasurer: Bob Gunderman. Executive Vice President, Operations: Mark Farris. Executive Vice President, Engineering & Chief Technology Officer: Randy Nicklas.
Ownership: Windstream Communications Inc. (MSO).

JACKSON COUNTY (portions)—Comcast Cable. Now served by ATLANTA, GA [GA0017]. ICA: GA0112.

JEFFERSON—Windstream Teleview. Now served by DAHLONEGA, GA [GA0099]. ICA: GA0206.

JEFFERSONVILLE—Formerly served by Windstream Teleview. No longer in operation. ICA: GA0207.

JEKYLL ISLAND—Comcast Cable. Now served by JACKSONVILLE, FL [FL0002]. ICA: GA0121.

JESUP—Comcast Cable. Now served by AUGUSTA, GA [GA0004]. ICA: GA0036.

KINGSLAND—Kings Bay Communications Inc, 220 East King Ave, PO Box 1267, Kingsland, GA 31548. Phone: 912-729-3153. Also serves Camden County (portions). ICA: GA0329.
TV Market Ranking: 68 (Camden County (portions), KINGSLAND).
Channel capacity: N.A. Channels available but not in use: N.A.
Basic Service
Subscribers: 1,712.
Fee: $13.36 monthly.
President: Don Trednick. Director: Joel Trednick.
Ownership: Kings Bay Communications Inc.

KITE—Formerly served by Walker Cablevision. No longer in operation. ICA: GA0170.

LAFAYETTE—Comcast Cable. Now served by KNOXVILLE, TN [TN0004]. ICA: GA0074.

LAGRANGE—Charter Communications, 127 Mattox Ct, LaGrange, GA 30241. Phones: 314-543-2236; 636-207-5100 (Corporate office); 770-253-2668 (Newnan office); 770-806-7060 (Duluth office). Web Site: http://www.charter.com. Also serves Centralhatchee, Chalybeate Springs, Corinth, Franklin, Harris County (portions), Heard County (portions), Manchester, Meriwether County (portions), Shiloh, Talbot County, Talbotton, Troup County (portions), Warm Springs & Woodland. ICA: GA0208.
TV Market Ranking: 94 (Chalybeate Springs, Harris County (portions), Manchester, Meriwether County (portions), Shiloh, Talbot County, Talbotton, Troup County (portions), Warm Springs, Woodland); Outside TV Markets (Centralhatchee, Corinth, Franklin, Heard County (portions), LAGRANGE, Meriwether County (portions), Troup County (portions)). Franchise award date: January 1, 1965. Franchise expiration date: N.A. Began: September 1, 1966.
Channel capacity: 71 (operating 2-way). Channels available but not in use: N.A.
Digital Basic Service
Subscribers: 11,947.
Programming (via satellite): BBC America; Bloomberg Television; Boomerang; CNN International; Discovery Digital Networks; Disney XD; DIY Network; ESPN Classic; ESPNews; FYI; Great American Country; History International; HITS (Headend In The Sky); IFC; LMN; MC; Nick Jr.; Nicktoons; Sundance TV.
Fee: $49.99 installation; $26.99 monthly.
Digital Expanded Basic Service
Subscribers: N.A.
Programming (via satellite): A&E; AMC; Animal Planet; BET; Bravo; Cartoon Network; CMT; CNBC; CNN; Comedy Central; Discovery Channel; Disney Channel; E! HD; ESPN; ESPN2; EWTN Global Catholic Network; Food Network; Fox News Channel; Fox Sports 1; FOX Sports South/SportSouth; Freeform; FX; Golf Channel; GSN; Hallmark Channel; HGTV; History; HLN; INSP; Lifetime; MSNBC; MTV; National Geographic Channel; NBCSN; Nickelodeon; Oxygen; Pop; QVC; Spike TV; Syfy; Telemundo; The Weather Channel; TLC; TNT; Travel Channel; truTV; Turner Classic Movies; TV Land; Univision; USA Network; VH1; WE tv.
Fee: $48.99 monthly.
Digital Pay Service 1
Pay Units: N.A.
Programming (via satellite): Cinemax (multiplexed); Flix; HBO (multiplexed); Showtime (multiplexed); Starz (multiplexed); Starz Encore (multiplexed); The Movie Channel (multiplexed).
Fee: $24.99 monthly (each).
Video-On-Demand: Yes
Pay-Per-View
iN DEMAND (delivered digitally); Playboy TV (delivered digitally); Fresh (delivered digitally); Shorteez (delivered digitally); Sports PPV (delivered digitally).
Internet Service
Operational: Yes.
Subscribers: 8,180.
Broadband Service: Charter Internet.
Fee: $29.99 monthly; $5.00 modem lease.
Telephone Service
Digital: Operational
Subscribers: 6,047.
Fee: $29.99 monthly
Miles of Plant: 5,363.0 (coaxial); 1,184.0 (fiber optic). Homes passed: 144,317.
Vice President & General Manager: Matt Favre. Accounting Director: David Sovanski. Sales & Marketing Manager: Antoinette Carpenter. Technical Operations Manager: Brenda Ivey. Operations Manager: David Spriggs.
Ownership: Charter Communications Inc. (MSO).

LAKE PARK—Formerly served by Altitude Communications. No longer in operation. ICA: GA0214.

LAKELAND—Mediacom. Now served by ADEL, GA [GA0063]. ICA: GA0108.

LAWRENCEVILLE—Charter Communications, 12405 Powerscourt Dr, St. Louis, MO 63131. Phones: 636-207-5100 (Corporate office); 770-806-7060. Fax: 770-806-7099. Web Site: http://www.charter.com. Also serves Buford, Cobb County, Dacula, Duluth, Flowery Branch, Gainesville, Gwinnett County, Gwinnett County (portions), Hall County, Johns Creek, Mountain Park, Oakwood, Rest Haven, Roswell, Smyrna, Sugar Hill & Suwanee. ICA: GA0009.

Georgia—Cable Systems

TV Market Ranking: 18 (Buford, Cobb County, Dacula, Duluth, Gwinnett County (portions), LAWRENCEVILLE, Mountain Park, Roswell, Smyrna, Sugar Hill, Suwanee); Below 100 (Flowery Branch, Hall County (portions), Oakwood, Rest Haven, Gainesville); Outside TV Markets (Hall County (portions)). Franchise award date: October 15, 1979. Franchise expiration date: N.A. Began: October 15, 1979.
Channel capacity: 65 (operating 2-way). Channels available but not in use: N.A.

Digital Basic Service
Subscribers: 71,914.
Programming (via satellite): BBC America; Bloomberg Television; Boomerang; Discovery Digital Networks; DIY Network; ESP-News; FOX College Sports Central; FOX College Sports Pacific; Fuse; FYI; Great American Country; History International; HITS (Headend In The Sky); IFC; LMN; Nick 2; Nick Jr.; Nicktoons; Sundance TV; Teen-Nick; TV Guide Interactive Inc.; Weatherscan.
Fee: $14.99 monthly.

Digital Expanded Basic Service
Subscribers: N.A.
Programming (via satellite): A&E; AMC; Animal Planet; BET; Bravo; Cartoon Network; CMT; CNBC; CNN; Comcast/Charter Sports Southeast (CSS); Comedy Central; C-SPAN; C-SPAN 2; Discovery Channel; Discovery Life Channel; Disney Channel; Disney XD; E! HD; ESPN; ESPN Classic; ESPN2; EWTN Global Catholic Network; Food Network; Fox News Channel; Fox Sports 1; FOX Sports South/SportSouth; Freeform; FX; Golf Channel; GSN; Hallmark Channel; HGTV; History; HLN; Lifetime; MSNBC; MTV; National Geographic Channel; NBCSN; Nickelodeon; Oxygen; Spike TV; Telemundo; The Weather Channel; TLC; TNT; Travel Channel; truTV; Turner Classic Movies; TV Land; Univision; USA Network; VH1; WE tv.
Fee: $48.99 monthly.

Digital Pay Service 1
Pay Units: N.A.
Programming (via satellite): Cinemax (multiplexed); Flix; HBO (multiplexed); Showtime (multiplexed); Starz (multiplexed); Starz Encore (multiplexed); The Movie Channel (multiplexed).
Fee: $14.00 monthly (each).
Video-On-Demand: Yes
Pay-Per-View
iN DEMAND (delivered digitally); NBA League Pass/WNBA (delivered digitally); NHL Center Ice/MLB Extra Innings (delivered digitally); Playboy TV (delivered digitally); Fresh (delivered digitally); Shorteez (delivered digitally).
Internet Service
Operational: Yes.
Subscribers: 82,576.
Broadband Service: Charter Internet.
Fee: $29.99 monthly; $5.00 modem lease; $99.00 modem purchase.
Telephone Service
Digital: Operational
Subscribers: 37,501.
Fee: $29.99 monthly
Miles of Plant: 5,826.0 (coaxial); 911.0 (fiber optic). Homes passed: 232,631.
Vice President & General Manager: Matt Favre. Marketing Director: Antoinette Carpenter. Operations Director: Jeff Osborne. Accounting Director: David Sovanski. Marketing Manager: Christopher Bolton.
Ownership: Charter Communications Inc. (MSO).

LEARY—Formerly served by Blakely Cable TV Inc. No longer in operation. ICA: GA0295.

LESLIE—Citizens Cable TV. Now served by COBB, GA [GA0150]. ICA: GA0210.

LINCOLNTON—Comcast Cable. Now served by WASHINGTON, GA [GA0260]. ICA: GA0311.

LINCOLNTON—Formerly served by KLiP Interactive. No longer in operation. ICA: GA0211.

LIZELLA—Flint Cable TV. Now served by REYNOLDS, GA [GA0236]. ICA: GA0325.

LOUISVILLE—Comcast Cable. Now served by AUGUSTA, GA [GA0004]. ICA: GA0213.

LULA—Comcast Cable. Now served by ATLANTA, GA [GA0017]. ICA: GA0141.

LUTHERSVILLE—Luthersville Cablevision, 6301 Broad Branch Rd, Chevy Chase, MD 20815-3343. Phone: 855-821-0524. E-mail: LuthersvilleCable@mail.com. Also serves Meriwether County. ICA: GA0131.
TV Market Ranking: Outside TV Markets (LUTHERSVILLE, Meriwether County).
Channel capacity: N.A. Channels available but not in use: N.A.

Basic Service
Subscribers: 825.
Programming (received off-air): WAGA-TV (Buzzr, FOX, Movies!) Atlanta; WGCL-TV (CBS, COZI TV, Grit) Atlanta; WJSP-TV (PBS) Columbus; WLTZ (CW, NBC) Columbus; WPCH-TV (IND) Atlanta; WRBL (CBS, MeTV) Columbus; WSB-TV (ABC, MeTV) Atlanta; WTVM (ABC, Bounce TV) Columbus; WUPA (CW, Decades) Atlanta; WXIA-TV (NBC) Atlanta.
Programming (via satellite): A&E; AMC; Cartoon Network; CMT; CNN; C-SPAN; Discovery Channel; Disney Channel; E! HD; ESPN; Freeform; Hallmark Channel; HLN; Lifetime; MTV; Nickelodeon; QVC; Spike TV; Starz Encore; The Weather Channel; TLC; TNT; USA Network; VH1.
Fee: $39.95 installation; $23.95 monthly.

Pay Service 1
Pay Units: 213.
Programming (via satellite): Cinemax; HBO; Showtime.
Fee: $25.00 installation; $10.95 monthly (Cinemax or Showtime), $11.95 monthly (HBO).

Internet Service
Operational: No.
Miles of Plant: 41.0 (coaxial); None (fiber optic). Homes passed: 845.
General Manager: Sarah Chet. Chief Technician: Morgan Madigan.
Ownership: South Shore Cable TV Inc. (MSO).

MACON—Cox Communications, 6205 Peachtree Dunwoody Rd, 12th Floor, Atlanta, GA 30328. Phone: 404-269-6590. Web Site: http://www.cox.com. Also serves Bibb County, Byron, Centerville, Houston County, Jones County (portions), Monroe County (portions), Payne City, Peach County (portions), Perry, Robins AFB & Warner Robins. ICA: GA0003.
TV Market Ranking: Below 100 (Bibb County, Byron, Centerville, Houston County, Jones County (portions), MACON, Monroe County (portions), Payne City, Peach County (portions), Perry, Robins AFB, Warner Robins. Franchise award date:

December 14, 1964. Franchise expiration date: N.A. Began: December 31, 1964.
Channel capacity: N.A. Channels available but not in use: N.A.

Basic Service
Subscribers: 58,065.
Programming (received off-air): WGNM (Christian TV Network) Macon; WGXA (ABC, FOX) Macon; WMAZ-TV (CBS) Macon; WMGT-TV (Escape, MNT, NBC) Macon; WMUM-TV (PBS) Cochran; WPGA-TV (Bounce TV, IND, MeTV) Perry; WSB-TV (ABC, MeTV) Atlanta.
Programming (via satellite): C-SPAN; CW PLUS; INSP; TBS; WGN America.
Fee: $56.50 installation; $23.99 monthly; $1.00 converter.

Expanded Basic Service 1
Subscribers: N.A.
Programming (via satellite): A&E; AMC; Animal Planet; BET; Bravo; Cartoon Network; CMT; CNBC; CNN; Comedy Central; C-SPAN 2; Discovery Channel; Disney Channel; E! HD; ESPN; ESPN2; EWTN Global Catholic Network; Food Network; Fox News Channel; Fox Sports 1; FOX Sports South/SportSouth; Freeform; FX; Golf Channel; Hallmark Channel; HGTV; History; HLN; ION Television; Lifetime; MSNBC; MTV; NBCSN; Nickelodeon; OWN; Oprah Winfrey Network; Pop; QVC; Spike TV; Syfy; The Weather Channel; TLC; TNT; Travel Channel; Trinity Broadcasting Network (TBN); truTV; TV Land; Univision Studios; USA Network; VH1.
Fee: $35.99 monthly.

Digital Basic Service
Subscribers: N.A.
Programming (via satellite): BYUtv; Daystar TV Network; Destination America; Discovery Kids Channel; EVINE Live; EWTN Global Catholic Network; FamilyNet; GSN; Investigation Discovery; Jewelry Television; MC; National Geographic Channel; Nick Jr.; Science Channel; Trinity Broadcasting Network (TBN); UP; Weatherscan.

Digital Expanded Basic Service
Subscribers: N.A.
Programming (via satellite): Flix; Hallmark Movies & Mysteries; IFC; LMN; MoviePlex; Starz Encore (multiplexed); Sundance TV; Turner Classic Movies.
Fee: $10.51 monthly.

Digital Expanded Basic Service 2
Subscribers: N.A.
Programming (via satellite): Bloomberg Television; CNN International; Cooking Channel; Cox Sports Television; Discovery Life Channel; DIY Network; ESPN Classic; ESPNews; ESPNU; Fox Sports 2; FYI; History International; NBA TV; NFL Network; NHL Network; Outdoor Channel; Tennis Channel.
Fee: $10.51 monthly.

Digital Expanded Basic Service 3
Subscribers: N.A.
Programming (via satellite): BBC America; Boomerang; CMT; Disney XD; Fuse; Great American Country; GSN; MTV Classic; MTV Hits; MTV Jams; MTV2; Nicktoons; Oxygen; Sprout; Starz Encore Family; TeenNick; The Africa Channel; Tr3s; TV One; VH1 Soul; WE tv.
Fee: $10.51 monthly.

Digital Expanded Basic Service 4
Subscribers: N.A.
Programming (via satellite): CNN en Espanol; Discovery Familia; ESPN Deportes; Fox Deportes; GolTV; Telemundo; Tr3s; Uni-Mas; Univision; ViendoMovies.
Fee: $30.71 monthly.

Digital Pay Service 1
Pay Units: N.A.
Programming (via satellite): Cinemax (multiplexed); Cinemax HD; HBO (multiplexed); HBO HD; Showtime (multiplexed); Showtime HD; Starz (multiplexed); Starz Encore; Starz HD; The Movie Channel (multiplexed).
Fee: $11.00 monthly (HBO, Cinemax, Showtime/TMC or Starz/Encore).
Video-On-Demand: Yes
Pay-Per-View
Spice: Xcess (delivered digitally); MLB Extra Innings (delivered digitally); NHL Center Ice (delivered digitally); Club Jenna (delivered digitally); NBA League Pass (delivered digitally); iN DEMAND; iN DEMAND (delivered digitally); MLS Direct Kick (delivered digitally); Playboy TV (delivered digitally); Juicy (delivered digitally); SexSee (delivered digitally).
Internet Service
Operational: Yes.
Subscribers: 82,005.
Broadband Service: Cox High Speed Internet.
Fee: $79.99 installation; $29.99-$56.99 monthly; $15.00 modem lease.
Telephone Service
Digital: Operational
Subscribers: 25,587.
Fee: $15.70-$54.95 monthly
Miles of Plant: 3,444.0 (coaxial); 761.0 (fiber optic). Homes passed: 150,247.
Vice President & General Manager: J. Michael Dyer. Vice President, Operations: Karen Whitaker. Vice President, Tax: Mary Vickers. Marketing Director: Mark Watkins. Community & Government Relations Director: Lynn Murphey.
Ownership: Cox Communications Inc. (MSO).

MANCHESTER—Charter Communications. Now served by LaGRANGE, GA [GA0208]. ICA: GA0097.

McRAE—Mediacom. Now served by EASTMAN, GA [GA0076]. ICA: GA0084.

METTER—Comcast Cable. Now served by SAVANNAH, GA [GA0005]. ICA: GA0218.

METTER—Pineland Telephone Coop. Inc. This cable system has converted to IPTV. Now served by METTER, GA [GA5005]. ICA: GA5256.

METTER—Pineland Telephone Coop. This cable system has converted to IPTV, 30 South Roundtree St, PO Box 678, Metter, GA 30439. Phones: 800-247-1266; 912-685-2121. Fax: 912-685-7439. E-mail: pineland@pineland.net. Web Site: http://www.pineland.net. Also serves Adrian, Bartow, Cobbtown, Davisboro, Garfield, Kite, Lexsy, Midville, Nunez, Oak Park, Pulaski, Stillmore, Swainsboro & Twin City. ICA: GA5005.
TV Market Ranking: Franchise award date: January 14, 2011. Franchise expiration date: N.A. Began: N.A.
Channel capacity: N.A. Channels available but not in use: N.A.

Local Channels
Subscribers: 3,840. Commercial subscribers: 2.
Fee: $19.50 monthly.
20+ channels
Subscribers: 3,836.
Fee: $29.99 monthly.
80+ channels
Subscribers: 3,735.
Fee: $61.99 monthly.

Cable Systems—Georgia

Access the most current data instantly

www.warren-news.com/factbook.htm

100+ channels
Subscribers: 3,014.
Fee: $71.99 monthly.
Programacion En Espanol
Subscribers: N.A.
Fee: $5.99 monthly.
Movie Channels
Subscribers: N.A.
Fee: $13.50 monthly/one movie package, $23.50 monthly/two movie packages, $33.50/three movie packages, $43.50/ four movie packages. Packages include Cinemax (7 channels), HBO (6 channels), Showtime/TMC/Flix (8 channels) & Starz/Encore (13 channels).
Internet Service
Operational: Yes.
Fee: $45.00 installation; $34.95-$49.95 monthly.
Telephone Service
Digital: Operational
Fee: $19.54 monthly
General Manager: Dustin Durden. Operations Director: Jinks Durden. Plant Operations Director: Eddy Jones. Plant Manager: Wayne Foskey. Engineering & Construction Manager: Mike Purvis.
Ownership: Pineland Telephone Cooperative Inc.

MIDVILLE—Pineland Telephone Coop. Inc. This cable system has converted to IPTV. Now served by METTER, GA [GA5005]. ICA: GA0152.

MILAN—Formerly served by Bulldog Cable. No longer in operation. ICA: GA0219.

MILLEDGEVILLE—Charter Communications, 12405 Powerscourt Dr, St. Louis, MO 63131. Phones: 636-207-5100 (Corporate office); 478-451-3056; 770-806-7060 (Duluth). Fax: 478-452-1942. Web Site: http://www.charter.com. Also serves Baldwin County, Eatonton, Gray, Greene County (portions), Greensboro, Jones County (portions), Madison, Morgan County (portions), Putnam County (portions), Rutledge, Union Point & Woodville. ICA: GA0046.
TV Market Ranking: Below 100 (Baldwin County, Gray, Jones County (portions), Madison, MILLEDGEVILLE, Morgan County (portions), Rutledge, Union Point, Woodville, Greene County (portions), Greensboro, Putnam County (portions)); Outside TV Markets (Eatonton, Greene County (portions), Putnam County (portions)). Franchise award date: January 1, 1964. Franchise expiration date: N.A. Began: September 20, 1965.
Channel capacity: 69 (operating 2-way). Channels available but not in use: N.A.
Digital Basic Service
Subscribers: 8,976.
Programming (via satellite): BBC America; Bloomberg Television; Boomerang; Discovery Digital Networks; DIY Network; ESPN Classic; ESPNews; FYI; History International; IFC; LMN; MC; Nick 2; Nick Jr.; Nicktoons; Sundance TV; TeenNick; TV Guide Interactive Inc.; WE tv.
Fee: $14.99 monthly.
Digital Expanded Basic Service
Subscribers: N.A.
Programming (via satellite): A&E; AMC; Animal Planet; Bravo; Cartoon Network; CMT; CNBC; CNN; Comcast/Charter Sports Southeast (CSS); Comedy Central; Discovery Channel; Disney Channel; Disney XD; E! HD; ESPN; ESPN2; Fox News Channel; Fox Sports 1; FOX Sports South/ SportSouth; Freeform; FX; Golf Channel; Hallmark Channel; HGTV; History; HLN; Lifetime; MSNBC; MTV; National Geographic Channel; NBCSN; Nickelodeon; Oxygen; Spike TV; Syfy; TBS; The Weather Channel; TLC; TNT; Travel Channel; Turner Classic Movies; TV Land; USA Network; VH1.
Fee: $48.99 monthly.
Digital Pay Service 1
Pay Units: N.A.
Programming (via satellite): Cinemax (multiplexed); HBO (multiplexed); Showtime (multiplexed); Starz (multiplexed); Starz Encore (multiplexed); The Movie Channel (multiplexed).
Fee: $25.00 installation; $24.99 monthly (each).
Video-On-Demand: Yes
Pay-Per-View
iN DEMAND (delivered digitally); Playboy TV (delivered digitally); Fresh (delivered digitally); Shorteez (delivered digitally).
Internet Service
Operational: Yes. Began: December 1, 2001.
Broadband Service: Charter Internet.
Fee: $29.99 monthly.
Telephone Service
Digital: Operational
Fee: $29.99 monthly
Miles of Plant: 1,317.0 (coaxial); 475.0 (fiber optic). Homes passed: 33,455.
Vice President & General Manager: Matt Favre. Sales & Marketing Director: Antoinette Carpenter. Operations Director: Jeff Osborne. Accounting Director: David Sovanski. Technical Supervisor: Marcus Webb.
Ownership: Charter Communications Inc. (MSO).

MILLEN—Comcast Cable. Now served by AUGUSTA, GA [GA0004]. ICA: GA0220.

MONROE—Monroe Utilities Network, 215 North Broad St, PO Box 725, Monroe, GA 30655-0725. Phones: 770-266-5312; 770-267-3429. Fax: 770-267-3698. Web Site: http://www.monroega.com/departments/ utility-department. Also serves Between, Bostwick, Good Hope & Social Circle. ICA: GA0068.
TV Market Ranking: Below 100 (Between, Bostwick, Good Hope, MONROE, Social Circle). Franchise award date: N.A. Franchise expiration date: N.A. Began: February 15, 1972.
Channel capacity: N.A. Channels available but not in use: N.A.
Basic Service
Subscribers: 4,308.
Programming (received off-air): WAGA-TV (Buzzr, FOX, Movies!) Atlanta; WATL (Antenna TV, Bounce TV, MNT) Atlanta; WGCL-TV (CBS, COZI TV, Grit) Atlanta; WGTV (PBS) Athens; WHSG-TV (TBN) Monroe; WPCH-TV (IND) Atlanta; WSB-TV (ABC, MeTV) Atlanta; WUPA (CW, Decades) Atlanta; WUVG-DT (getTV, UNV) Athens; WXIA-TV (NBC) Atlanta; allband FM.
Programming (via satellite): A&E; AMC; Animal Planet; BET; Cartoon Network; CMT; CNBC; CNN; Comedy Central; C-SPAN; Discovery Channel; Disney Channel; E! HD; ESPN; ESPN2; Food Network; Fox News Channel; Fox Sports 1; FOX Sports South/ SportSouth; Freeform; Golf Channel; HGTV; History; HLN; INSP; Lifetime; MTV; Nickelodeon; Outdoor Channel; Pop; QVC; Spike TV; Syfy; Telemundo; The Weather Channel; TLC; TNT; Travel Channel; truTV; Turner Classic Movies; TV Land; USA Network; VH1; WE tv; WGN America.
Fee: $35.00-$55.00 installation; $16.28 monthly.
Pay Service 1
Pay Units: N.A.
Programming (via satellite): Cinemax; HBO; Playboy TV; Showtime.
Fee: $10.00 installation; $9.95 monthly (Cinemax, HBO or Showtime), $10.95 monthly (Playboy).
Video-On-Demand: No
Pay-Per-View
iN DEMAND, Addressable: No.
Internet Service
Operational: Yes.
Broadband Service: In-house.
Fee: $25.00 installation; $39.95 monthly.
Telephone Service
None
Miles of Plant: 267.0 (coaxial); 277.0 (fiber optic). Homes passed: 7,800.
Cable TV Division Chief: Brian Thompson. City Administrator: Julian L. Jackson.
Ownership: City of Monroe, Water, Light & Gas Commission.

MONTEZUMA—Comcast Cable, 209 Council St, PO Box 548, Waynesboro, GA 30830. Phones: 912-354-7531; 912-356-3113. Web Site: http://www.comcast.com. Also serves Macon County (portions) & Oglethorpe. ICA: GA0081.
TV Market Ranking: Below 100 (Macon County (portions), MONTEZUMA, Oglethorpe). Franchise award date: June 14, 1976. Franchise expiration date: N.A. Began: October 1, 1977.
Channel capacity: N.A. Channels available but not in use: N.A.
Basic Service
Subscribers: 620. Commercial subscribers: 29.
Programming (received off-air): WACS-TV (PBS) Dawson; WALB (ABC, NBC, This TV) Albany; WGNM (Christian TV Network) Macon; WLTZ (CW, NBC) Columbus; WMAZ-TV (CBS) Macon; WPGA-TV (Bounce TV, IND, MeTV) Perry; WTVM (ABC, Bounce TV) Columbus; WXTX (FOX, Movies!, This TV) Columbus; 7 FMs.
Programming (via satellite): Pop; QVC; WGN America.
Fee: $32.00-$43.00 installation; $17.45 monthly.
Expanded Basic Service 1
Subscribers: N.A.
Programming (via satellite): A&E; AMC; Animal Planet; BET; Cartoon Network; CMT; CNBC; CNN; Comcast/Charter Sports Southeast (CSS); Comedy Central; CW PLUS; Discovery Channel; Disney Channel; E! HD; ESPN; ESPN2; Food Network; Fox News Channel; Fox Sports 1; FOX Sports Networks; FOX Sports South/ SportSouth; Freeform; Golf Channel; GSN; HGTV; HLN; INSP; ION Television; Lifetime; MTV; NBCSN; Nickelodeon; OWN: Oprah Winfrey Network; Spike TV; Syfy; TBS; The Weather Channel; TLC; TNT; truTV; TV Land; USA Network.
Fee: $26.99 monthly.

Digital Basic Service
Subscribers: N.A.
Programming (via satellite): BBC America; CMT; Discovery Digital Networks; Flix; MC; Nick 2; Nick Jr.; TeenNick.
Pay Service 1
Pay Units: N.A.
Programming (via satellite): Cinemax; HBO; Showtime.
Fee: $20.00 installation; $7.95 monthly (Showtime), $10.95 monthly (HBO).
Digital Pay Service 1
Pay Units: N.A.
Programming (via satellite): Cinemax (multiplexed); HBO (multiplexed); Showtime (multiplexed); The Movie Channel (multiplexed).
Fee: $10.05 monthly (each).
Video-On-Demand: No
Internet Service
Operational: Yes.
Telephone Service
Digital: Operational
Homes passed & miles of plant (coax & fiber) included in Savannah.
General Manager: Michael Daves. Technical Operations Director: Joel Godsen. Marketing Director: Jerry Avery. Marketing Manager: Ken Torres.
Ownership: Comcast Cable Communications Inc. (MSO).

MORGAN—Formerly served by Blakely Cable TV Inc. No longer in operation. ICA: GA0314.

MOULTRIE—CNS, 21st Avenue NE, PO Box 3368, Moultrie, GA 31776. Phone: 229-985-5400. E-mail: answers@cns-internet.com. Web Site: http://www.cns-internet.com. ICA: GA0308. **Note:** This system is an overbuild.
TV Market Ranking: Below 100 (MOULTRIE). Franchise award date: N.A. Franchise expiration date: N.A. Began: December 12, 2001.
Channel capacity: N.A. Channels available but not in use: N.A.
Basic Service
Subscribers: N.A.
Programming (received off-air): WABW-TV (PBS) Pelham; WALB (ABC, NBC, This TV) Albany; WCTV (CBS, MNT, This TV) Thomasville; WFSU-TV (PBS) Tallahassee; WFXL (Bounce TV, FOX) Albany; WSB-TV (ABC, MeTV) Atlanta; WSWG (CBS, CW, MeTV, MNT) Valdosta; WTXL-TV (ABC, Bounce TV) Tallahassee.
Programming (via satellite): Bloomberg Television; C-SPAN; C-SPAN 2; CW PLUS; Discovery Channel; Discovery Life Channel; Disney Channel; Disney XD; Family Friendly Entertainment; FamilyNet; Fox News Channel; FOX Sports South/SportSouth; Hallmark Channel; HLN; ION Television; QVC; TBS; The Weather Channel; Travel Channel; Trinity Broadcasting Network (TBN).
Expanded Basic Service 1
Subscribers: N.A.
Programming (via satellite): A&E; AMC; Animal Planet; BET; Bravo; Cartoon Network; CNBC; CNN; Comedy Central; E! HD; ESPN; ESPN2; Food Network; Fox Sports

2017 Edition D-167

Georgia—Cable Systems

1; Freeform; FX; Golf Channel; Great American Country; GSN; HGTV; History; Lifetime; MSNBC; MTV; Nickelodeon; Outdoor Channel; Spike TV; Syfy; TLC; TNT; truTV; Turner Classic Movies; TV Land; Univision Studios; USA Network; VH1; WE tv; WGN America.
Fee: $34.95 monthly.

Digital Basic Service
Subscribers: N.A.
Programming (via satellite): BBC America; Boomerang; CNN en Espanol; CNN International; Discovery Digital Networks; DIY Network; Fox Deportes; Fuse; FXM; FYI; History International; IFC; LMN; MC; National Geographic Channel; Nick 2; Nick Jr.; TeenNick.

Pay Service 1
Pay Units: N.A.
Programming (via satellite): Cinemax; HBO; Showtime; Starz; Starz Encore.
Fee: $8.95 monthly.

Digital Pay Service 1
Pay Units: N.A.
Programming (via satellite): Cinemax (multiplexed); Flix; HBO (multiplexed); Showtime (multiplexed); Starz (multiplexed); Starz Encore (multiplexed); Sundance TV; The Movie Channel (multiplexed).
Fee: $10.00 monthly (each).

Pay-Per-View
iN DEMAND.

Internet Service
Operational: Yes.
Subscribers: 13,219.
Broadband Service: SyrupCity.net.
Fee: $28.95 monthly.

Telephone Service
Digital: Operational
Subscribers: 6,675.
Miles of Plant: 220.0 (coaxial); None (fiber optic).
Broadband Engineer: Chris White. Marketing Coordinator: Sherri Nix. Marketing Representative: Angela Boat.
Ownership: Community Network Services (MSO).

MOULTRIE—Mediacom. Now served by TIFTON, GA [GA0032]. ICA: GA0041.

MOUNT VERNON—Comcast Cable, 315 East Second Ave, PO Box 615, Glenwood, GA 30428. Phones: 912-354-7531; 912-356-3113. Web Site: http://www.comcast.com. Also serves Ailey, Alamo, Glenwood, Montgomery County (portions) & Wheeler County (portions). ICA: GA0106.
TV Market Ranking: Below 100 (Ailey, Glenwood, MOUNT VERNON, Montgomery County (portions), Wheeler County (portions)); Outside TV Markets (Alamo, Montgomery County (portions), Wheeler County (portions)). Franchise award date: March 6, 1978. Franchise expiration date: N.A. Began: March 7, 1978.
Channel capacity: N.A. Channels available but not in use: N.A.

Basic Service
Subscribers: 517. Commercial subscribers: 158.
Programming (received off-air): WJCL (ABC) Savannah; WSAV-TV (MeTV, MNT, NBC) Savannah; WTGS (Antenna TV, FOX) Hardeeville; WTOC-TV (Bounce TV, CBS, This TV) Savannah; WVAN-TV (PBS) Savannah.
Programming (via satellite): Comcast/Charter Sports Southeast (CSS); ION Television; QVC; TBS; WGN America.
Fee: $11.50 installation; $18.00 monthly.

Expanded Basic Service 1
Subscribers: N.A.
Programming (via satellite): A&E; AMC; Animal Planet; BET; Cartoon Network; CMT; CNBC; CNN; C-SPAN; Discovery Channel; Disney Channel; E! HD; ESPN; ESPN2; Food Network; Fox News Channel; Fox Sports 1; FOX Sports Networks; FOX Sports South/SportSouth; Freeform; FX; Golf Channel; GSN; Hallmark Channel; HGTV; HLN; Lifetime; MTV; NBCSN; Nickelodeon; OWN; Oprah Winfrey Network; Spike TV; Syfy; The Weather Channel; TLC; TNT; Trinity Broadcasting Network (TBN); truTV; Turner Classic Movies; TV Land; USA Network; VH1.
Fee: $32.49 monthly.

Digital Basic Service
Subscribers: N.A.
Programming (via satellite): BBC America; CMT; Discovery Digital Networks; MC; Nick 2; Nick Jr.; Starz Encore; TeenNick.

Pay Service 1
Pay Units: N.A.
Programming (via satellite): HBO; Showtime.
Fee: $20.00 installation; $10.00 monthly (each).

Digital Pay Service 1
Pay Units: N.A.
Programming (via satellite): Cinemax (multiplexed); HBO (multiplexed); Showtime (multiplexed); Starz (multiplexed); The Movie Channel (multiplexed).

Video-On-Demand: No

Internet Service
Operational: Yes.

Telephone Service
Digital: Operational
Homes passed & miles of plant (coax & fiber) included in Savannah.
General Manager: Michael Daves. Technical Operations Director: Joel Godson. Marketing Director: Jerry Avery. Marketing Manager: Ken Torres.
Ownership: Comcast Cable Communications Inc. (MSO).

NAHUNTA—Comcast Cable. Now served by JACKSONVILLE, FL [FL0002]. ICA: GA0134.

NEWINGTON—Formerly served by Planters Telephone Cooperative. No longer in operation. ICA: GA5258.

NEWNAN—Charter Communications, 127 Mattox Ct, LaGrange, GA 30241. Phones: 314-543-2236; 636-207-5100 (Corporate office); 770-806-7060 (Duluth office); 877-581-3485. Web Site: http://www.charter.com. Also serves Beulah, Chambers County (portions), Fairfax, Huguley, Lafayette, Lanett & Valley, AL; Aragon, Bibb City, Bowdon, Bremen, Buchanan, Carroll County, Carrollton, Cave Spring, Cedartown, Columbus, Coweta County, Floyd County, Fort Benning, Hamilton, Haralson County, Harris County (portions), Heard County (portions), Lone Oak, Luthersville, Meriwether County (portions), Moreland, Pine Mountain, Pine Mountain Valley, Polk County, Rockmart, Sharpsburg, Temple, Troup County (portions), Turin, Villa Rica, Waverly Hall & West Point, GA. ICA: GA0042.
TV Market Ranking: 18 (Aragon, Buchanan, Cave Spring, Cedartown, Coweta County (portions), Floyd County, NEWNAN, Polk County, Rockmart, Sharpsburg, Turin, Villa Rica); 94 (Beulah, Bibb City, Chambers County (portions), Columbus, Fairfax, Fort Benning, Hamilton, Harris County (portions), Huguley, Lanett, Meriwether County (portions), Pine Mountain, Pine Mountain Valley, Troup County (portions), Valley, Waverly Hall, West Point); Below 100 (Bowdon, Haralson County, Chambers County (portions)); Outside TV Markets (Bremen, Carroll County, Heard County (portions), Lafayette, Lone Oak, Luthersville, Moreland, Temple, Carrollton, Coweta County (portions), Meriwether County (portions), Troup County (portions)). Franchise award date: January 1, 1971. Franchise expiration date: N.A. Began: March 25, 1972.
Channel capacity: 80 (operating 2-way). Channels available but not in use: N.A.

Digital Basic Service
Subscribers: 44,119.
Programming (via satellite): BBC America; Bloomberg Television; Boomerang; Discovery Digital Networks; DIY Network; ESPNews; FOX College Sports Central; FOX College Sports Pacific; Fuse; FYI; Great American Country; History International; HITS (Headend In The Sky); IFC; LMN; MC; Nick 2; Nick Jr.; Nicktoons; Sundance TV; TeenNick.
Fee: $49.99 installation; $26.99 monthly.

Digital Expanded Basic Service
Subscribers: N.A.
Programming (via satellite): A&E; AMC; Animal Planet; BET; Bravo; Cartoon Network; CMT; CNBC; CNN; Comcast/Charter Sports Southeast (CSS); Comedy Central; Discovery Channel; Discovery Life Channel; Disney Channel; Disney XD; E! HD; ESPN; ESPN Classic; ESPN2; EVINE Live; EWTN Global Catholic Network; Food Network; Fox News Channel; Fox Sports 1; FOX Sports South/SportSouth; Freeform; FX; Golf Channel; GSN; Hallmark Channel; HGTV; History; HLN; Lifetime; MSNBC; MTV; National Geographic Channel; NBCSN; Nickelodeon; Outdoor Channel; Spike TV; Syfy; Telemundo; The Weather Channel; TLC; Travel Channel; truTV; Turner Classic Movies; TV Land; Univision; USA Network; VH1; WE tv.
Fee: $48.99 monthly.

Digital Pay Service 1
Pay Units: N.A.
Programming (via satellite): Cinemax (multiplexed); Flix; HBO (multiplexed); Showtime (multiplexed); Starz (multiplexed); Starz Encore (multiplexed); The Movie Channel (multiplexed).
Fee: $17.99 monthly (each).

Video-On-Demand: Yes

Pay-Per-View
iN DEMAND (delivered digitally); NBA League Pass/WNBA (delivered digitally); NHL Center Ice/MLB Extra Innings (delivered digitally); Playboy TV (delivered digitally); Fresh (delivered digitally); Shorteez (delivered digitally).

Internet Service
Operational: Yes.
Subscribers: 27,983.
Broadband Service: Charter Internet.
Fee: $29.99 monthly; $199.00 modem purchase.

Telephone Service
Digital: Operational
Subscribers: 13,943.
Fee: $29.99 monthly
Miles of Plant: 6,624.0 (coaxial); 1,653.0 (fiber optic). Homes passed: 204,548.
Vice President & General Manager: Matt Favre. Sales & Marketing Director: Antoinette Carpenter. Accounting Director: David Sovanski. Technical Operations Manager: Brenda Ivey. Operations Manager: David Spriggs.
Ownership: Charter Communications Inc. (MSO).

NEWNAN—NuLink Digital, 2 A Jackson St., Newnan, GA 30263. Phones: 770-683-6988; 770-683-6988. E-mail: info@nulinkdigital.com. Web Site: http://nulinkdigital.com. Also serves Coweta County (portions), Palmetto, Peachtree City, Sharpsburg & Tyrone. ICA: GA0310. **Note:** This system is an overbuild.
TV Market Ranking: 18 (Coweta County (portions), NEWNAN, Palmetto, Peachtree City, Sharpsburg, Tyrone).
Channel capacity: N.A. Channels available but not in use: N.A.

Basic Service
Subscribers: 10,346.
Programming (received off-air): WAGA-TV (Buzzr, FOX, Movies!) Atlanta; WATL (Antenna TV, Bounce TV, MNT) Atlanta; WGCL-TV (CBS, COZI TV, Grit) Atlanta; WGTV (PBS) Athens; WPBA (PBS) Atlanta; WPCH-TV (IND) Atlanta; WSB-TV (ABC, MeTV) Atlanta; WUPA (CW, Decades) Atlanta; WUVG-DT (getTV, UNV) Athens; WXIA-TV (NBC) Atlanta.
Programming (via satellite): Disney Channel; ION Television; Pop; The Weather Channel; Trinity Broadcasting Network (TBN).
Fee: $21.95 monthly.

Expanded Basic Service 1
Subscribers: N.A.
Programming (via satellite): A&E; AMC; Animal Planet; BET; Bravo; Cartoon Network; CMT; CNBC; CNN; Comedy Central; C-SPAN; Daystar TV Network; Discovery Channel; Disney XD; E! HD; ESPN; ESPN2; EWTN Global Catholic Network; Family Friendly Entertainment; Food Network; Fox News Channel; Fox Sports 1; FOX Sports South/SportSouth; Freeform; FX; FXM; Golf Channel; Great American Country; Hallmark Channel; HGTV; History; HLN; Lifetime; MSNBC; MTV; Nickelodeon; Outdoor Channel; OWN; Oprah Winfrey Network; Spike TV; Syfy; The Weather Channel; TLC; TNT; Travel Channel; truTV; Turner Classic Movies; TV Land; USA Network; VH1; WGN America.
Fee: $34.60 monthly.

Digital Basic Service
Subscribers: N.A.
Programming (via satellite): BBC America; Bloomberg Television; Boomerang; CNN en Espanol; C-SPAN 2; Discovery Digital Networks; DIY Network; ESPNews; Fox Deportes; Fuse; FYI; GSN; History International; IFC; MC; National Geographic Channel; NBCSN; Nick Jr.; Nicktoons; Oxygen; QVC; TeenNick; WAM! America's Kidz Network.

Pay Service 1
Pay Units: N.A.
Programming (via satellite): Cinemax; HBO; Showtime; Starz Encore.
Fee: $12.85 monthly (each).

Digital Pay Service 1
Pay Units: N.A.
Programming (via satellite): Cinemax (multiplexed); Flix; HBO (multiplexed); Showtime (multiplexed); Starz (multiplexed); Starz Encore (multiplexed); Sundance TV; The Movie Channel (multiplexed).
Fee: $13.60 monthly (each).

Video-On-Demand: Yes

Pay-Per-View
iN DEMAND; iN DEMAND (delivered digitally); Playboy TV (delivered digitally); Pleasure (delivered digitally); Fresh (delivered digitally).

Internet Service
Operational: Yes.
Subscribers: 11,904.
Broadband Service: In-house.
Fee: $44.20 monthly.

Cable Systems—Georgia

Telephone Service
Digital: Operational
Subscribers: 4,626.
Miles of Plant: 1,260.0 (coaxial); 385.0 (fiber optic). Homes passed: 38,717.
Chief Executive Officer: Daniel Shoemaker. Vice President, Technical Operations: Scott Madison. Marketing Director: Scott Werner. Commercial Sales: Lana Mobley.
Ownership: H C Cable Holdings LLC.

NEWTON—Formerly served by Blakely Cable TV Inc. No longer in operation. ICA: GA0313.

NEWTON COUNTY—Bulldog Cable, PO Box 1288, Watkinsville, GA 30677. Phones: 706-997-9003; 800-388-6577. Web Site: http://www.bulldogcable.com. Also serves Butts County & Jasper County. ICA: GA0328. Note: This system is an overbuild.
TV Market Ranking: 18 (NEWTON COUNTY (portions)); Below 100 (NEWTON COUNTY (portions)); Outside TV Markets (Jasper County).
Channel capacity: N.A. Channels available but not in use: N.A.
Basic Service
Subscribers: 67.
Fee: $44.95 installation; $49.00 monthly.
Internet Service
Operational: No.
President: Mark Wilson. Controller: Ashley Hull.
Ownership: Bulldog Cable (MSO).

NEWTON COUNTY (southern portion)—Formerly served by KLiP Interactive. No longer in operation. ICA: GA0301.

NORMAN PARK—Formerly served by Wainwright Cable Inc. No longer in operation. ICA: GA0140.

OAK PARK—Pineland Telephone Coop. Inc. This cable system has converted to IPTV. Now served by METTER, GA [GA5005]. ICA: GA0224.

OCHLOCKNEE—Formerly served by Southeast Cable TV Inc. No longer in operation. ICA: GA0225.

OCONEE—Formerly served by National Cable Inc. No longer in operation. ICA: GA0226.

OMEGA—Formerly served by Plant Telenet. No longer in operation.. ICA: GA5262.

PATTERSON—ATC Broadband, 5660 Railroad Rd West, Patterson, GA 31557. Phones: 877-552-5946 (Sales); 912-449-5443. Fax: 912-449-2602. E-mail: info@atc.cc. Web Site: http://www.atcbroadband.com. Also serves Offerman. ICA: GA0272.
TV Market Ranking: Below 100 (Offerman, PATTERSON).
Channel capacity: N.A. Channels available but not in use: N.A.
Basic Service
Subscribers: 235.
Programming (received off-air): WCWJ (Bounce TV, CW) Jacksonville; WFOX-TV (FOX, MeTV, MNT) Jacksonville; WGSA (CW) Baxley; WJAX-TV (CBS, Decades, getTV) Jacksonville; WJCL (ABC) Savannah; WJCT (PBS) Jacksonville; WJXT (LATV, This TV) Jacksonville; WJXX (ABC) Orange Park; WPXC-TV (ION) Brunswick; WSAV-TV (MeTV, MNT, NBC) Savannah; WTGS (Antenna TV, FOX) Hardeeville; WTLV (Antenna TV, NBC, The Country Network) Jacksonville; WTOC-TV (Bounce TV, CBS, This TV) Savannah; WXGA-TV (PBS) Waycross.
Programming (via satellite): A&E; AMC; Animal Planet; BET; Cartoon Network; CMT; CNBC; CNN; Comcast/Charter Sports Southeast (CSS); Comedy Central; C-SPAN; C-SPAN 2; Discovery Channel; Discovery Life Channel; Disney Channel; E! HD; ESPN; ESPN Classic; ESPN2; Food Network; Fox News Channel; Fox Sports 1; FOX Sports South/SportSouth; Freeform; FX; Golf Channel; Hallmark Channel; HGTV; History; HLN; INSP; Lifetime; Local Cable Weather; MTV; National Geographic Channel; Nickelodeon; Outdoor Channel; Pop; QVC; Spike TV; Syfy; TBS; The Weather Channel; TLC; TNT; Travel Channel; Trinity Broadcasting Network (TBN); truTV; TV Land; USA Network; VH1.
Fee: $15.95 monthly.
Digital Basic Service
Subscribers: N.A.
Programming (via satellite): BBC America; Bloomberg Television; Boomerang; Cloo; Discovery Life Channel; Disney XD; DMX Music; ESPN Classic; ESPN2; ESPNews; ESPNU; Flix; Fox Sports 1; FSN Digital Atlantic; FSN Digital Central; FSN Digital Pacific; Fuse; FXM; FYI; Golf Channel; Great American Country; GSN; Hallmark Movies & Mysteries; HGTV; History; History International; Investigation Discovery; LMN; MTV Classic; MTV Hits; MTV2; National Geographic Channel; NBCSN; Nick Jr.; Nicktoons; Outdoor Channel; RFD-TV; Science Channel; Sundance TV; TeenNick; Trinity Broadcasting Network (TBN); Turner Classic Movies; UP; WE tv.
Digital Expanded Basic Service
Subscribers: N.A.
Programming (via satellite): A&E HD; Animal Planet HD; Bravo HD; CNBC HD+; CNN HD; Discovery Channel HD; ESPN HD; ESPN2 HD; Golf Channel HD; History HD; National Geographic Channel HD; Outdoor Channel 2 HD; Science HD; Syfy HD; TBS HD; The Weather Channel HD; TLC HD; TNT HD; USA Network HD; Versus HD.
Digital Expanded Basic Service 2
Subscribers: N.A.
Programming (via satellite): AXS TV; HD Theater; Universal HD.
Digital Pay Service 1
Pay Units: N.A.
Programming (via satellite): Cinemax (multiplexed); Cinemax HD; HBO (multiplexed); HBO HD; Showtime (multiplexed); Showtime HD; Starz (multiplexed); Starz Encore (multiplexed); Starz HD; The Movie Channel (multiplexed).
Fee: $12.95 monthly (each).
Pay-Per-View
iN DEMAND (delivered digitally); Playboy TV (delivered digitally); Fresh (delivered digitally); Spice: Xcess (delivered digitally); Club Jenna (delivered digitally).
Internet Service
Operational: Yes, DSL.
Broadband Service: atcnet.
Telephone Service
Analog: Operational
Miles of Plant: 20.0 (coaxial); None (fiber optic). Homes passed: 600.
General Manager: Kevin Brooks. Chief Technician: Tony McKinnon. Customer Service: Jennifer Barnette.
Ownership: ATC (Alma, GA) (MSO).

PAVO—Formerly served by Southeast Cable TV Inc. No longer in operation. ICA: GA0227.

PEMBROKE—Comcast Cable. Now served by SAVANNAH, GA [GA0005]. ICA: GA0228.

PERRY—ComSouth Telesys Inc, 1357-D Sam Nunn Blvd, PO Box 910, Perry, GA 31069. Phones: 478-224-4001; 478-987-0172. Fax: 478-987-9932. Web Site: http://comsouth.net. Also serves Bleckley County (portions), Bonaire, Cochran, Dooly County (portions), Fort Valley, Hawkinsville, Hayneville, Houston County (portions), Kathleen, Marshallville, Peach County, Pinehurst, Pulaski County (portions), Unadilla & Warner Robins. ICA: GA0229.
TV Market Ranking: Below 100 (Bleckley County (portions), Bonaire, Cochran, Dooly County (portions), Hawkinsville, Hayneville, Houston County (portions), Kathleen, Marshallville, Peach County, PERRY, Pinehurst, Pulaski County (portions), Unadilla, Warner Robins, Fort Valley). Franchise award date: N.A. Franchise expiration date: N.A. Began: January 1, 1968.
Channel capacity: N.A. Channels available but not in use: N.A.
Basic Service
Subscribers: 4,326.
Programming (received off-air): WGNM (Christian TV Network) Macon; WGXA (ABC, FOX) Macon; WMAZ-TV (CBS) Macon; WMGT-TV (Escape, MNT, NBC) Macon; WMUM-TV (PBS) Cochran; WPGA-TV (Bounce TV, IND, MeTV) Perry; WSB-TV (ABC, MeTV) Atlanta.
Programming (via satellite): Pop; TBS; WGN America.
Fee: $50.00 installation; $44.00 monthly; $3.25 converter.
Expanded Basic Service 1
Subscribers: N.A.
Programming (via satellite): A&E; AMC; Animal Planet; BET; Cartoon Network; CMT; CNBC; CNN; Comedy Central; C-SPAN; Discovery Channel; Disney Channel; E! HD; ESPN; ESPN Classic; ESPN2; Fox News Channel; Fox Sports 1; Freeform; FX; Golf Channel; Hallmark Channel; HGTV; History; HLN; Lifetime; MTV; National Geographic Channel; NBCSN; Nickelodeon; QVC; Spike TV; Syfy; The Weather Channel; TLC; TNT; Travel Channel; truTV; Turner Classic Movies; TV Land; USA Network; VH1.
Fee: $27.00 monthly.
Digital Basic Service
Subscribers: 2,644.
Programming (via satellite): A&E; BBC America; Bloomberg Television; Bravo; Discovery Digital Networks; FOX Sports South/SportSouth; FXM; GSN; History International; IFC; LMN; Outdoor Channel; Ovation; WE tv.
Fee: $8.95 installation; $19.00 monthly.
Digital Pay Service 1
Pay Units: N.A.
Programming (via satellite): Cinemax; HBO (multiplexed); Showtime (multiplexed); Starz; Starz Encore; Sundance TV; The Movie Channel.
Fee: $11.00 monthly (Cinemax, HBO, Showtime/TMC/Flix or Starz/Encore).
Video-On-Demand: No
Pay-Per-View
iN DEMAND (delivered digitally); Playboy TV (delivered digitally); Fresh (delivered digitally); Shorteez (delivered digitally).
Internet Service
Operational: Yes.
Subscribers: 4,941.
Fee: $19.95 installation; $29.95 monthly.
Telephone Service
Analog: Operational
Fee: $19.95 monthly
Digital: Operational
Subscribers: 3,990.
Miles of Plant: 773.0 (coaxial); 564.0 (fiber optic). Homes passed: 20,000.
General Manager: Jeff Leonard. Chief Technician: Larry Smiddle. Customer Service Manager: Debra Wells. Assistant Controller: Neysa Atkinson.
Ownership: ComSouth Corp. (MSO).

PINE MOUNTAIN—Charter Communications. Now served by NEWNAN, GA [GA0042]. ICA: GA0230.

PINEHURST—ComSouth Telesys Inc. Now served by PERRY, GA [GA0229]. ICA: GA0231.

PINEVIEW—Formerly served by KLiP Interactive. No longer in operation. ICA: GA0154.

PITTS—Formerly served by KLiP Interactive. No longer in operation. ICA: GA0151.

PLAINS—Citizens Cable TV. Now served by COBB, GA [GA0150]. ICA: GA0232.

POOLER—Hargray. Now served by BLUFFTON (village), SC [SC0020]. ICA: GA0315.

PORT WENTWORTH (portions)—Comcast Cable. Now served by SAVANNAH, GA [GA0005]. ICA: GA0233.

PORTAL—Formerly served by KLiP Interactive. No longer in operation. ICA: GA0153.

PRESTON—Formerly served by Citizens Cable TV. No longer in operation. ICA: GA0162.

PUTNAM COUNTY—Bulldog Cable, PO Box 1288, Watkinsville, GA 30677. Phones: 706-997-9003; 800-388-6577. Web Site: http://www.bulldogcable.com. Also serves Baldwin County (northern portion). ICA: GA0129.
TV Market Ranking: Below 100 (Baldwin County (northern portion), PUTNAM COUNTY).
Channel capacity: N.A. Channels available but not in use: N.A.
Basic Service
Subscribers: 24.
Programming (received off-air): WGXA (ABC, FOX) Macon; WMAZ-TV (CBS) Macon; WMGT-TV (Escape, MNT, NBC) Macon; WMUM-TV (PBS) Cochran; WPCH-

Georgia—Cable Systems

TV (IND) Atlanta; WPGA-TV (Bounce TV, IND, MeTV) Perry.
Programming (via satellite): A&E; AMC; Animal Planet; BET; Cartoon Network; CMT; CNBC; CNN; CW PLUS; Discovery Channel; Disney Channel; ESPN; ESPN2; Fox News Channel; Fox Sports 1; FOX Sports South/SportSouth; Freeform; FX; GSN; Lifetime; National Geographic Channel; Nickelodeon; Outdoor Channel; QVC; Spike TV; The Weather Channel; TLC; TNT; Trinity Broadcasting Network (TBN); truTV; TV Land; USA Network; WGN America.
Fee: $44.95 installation; $49.00 monthly.
Pay Service 1
  Pay Units: N.A.
  Programming (via satellite): Cinemax.
  Fee: $12.00 monthly.
Pay Service 2
  Pay Units: N.A.
  Programming (via satellite): HBO.
  Fee: $12.00 monthly.
Internet Service
  Operational: No.
Telephone Service
  None
Miles of Plant: 40.0 (coaxial); None (fiber optic). Homes passed: 1,500.
President: Mark Wilson. General Manager East: Mark Miller. General Manager West: Vance Johnson. Controller: Ashley Hull.
Ownership: Bulldog Cable (MSO).

QUITMAN—Camellia City Cable, 100 West Screven St, PO Box 208, Quitman, GA 31643. Phone: 229-263-4166. Web Site: http://www.cityofquitmanga.com/CableTelevision.aspx. ICA: GA0332.
  TV Market Ranking: Below 100 (QUITMAN).
  Channel capacity: N.A. Channels available but not in use: N.A.
  Chief Technician: Greg Swann.
  Ownership: City of Quitman.

QUITMAN—Comcast Cable. Now served by TALLAHASSEE, FL [FL0283]. ICA: GA0234.

RANGER—Formerly served by 3D Cable Inc. No longer in operation. ICA: GA0171.

RAYLE—Formerly served by KLiP Interactive. No longer in operation. ICA: GA0303.

RAYSVILLE—Formerly served by KLiP Interactive. No longer in operation. ICA: GA0302.

REBECCA—Formerly served by KLiP Interactive. No longer in operation. ICA: GA0235.

RECOVERY—Formerly served by KLiP Interactive. No longer in operation. ICA: GA0296.

REIDSVILLE—Hargray. Now served by BLUFFTON (village), SC [SC0020]. ICA: GA0103.

RENTZ—Progressive Rural Telephone. This cable system has converted to IPTV., 890 Simpson Ave, PO Box 89, Rentz, GA 31075. Phones: 877-599-3939; 478-984-4201. Fax: 478-984-4205. E-mail: prtc@progressivetel.com. Web Site: http://progressivetel.com. Also serves Cadwell, Chester, Dexter, Dudley & Laurens County (portions). ICA: GA5268.
  TV Market Ranking: Below 100 (Chester, Laurens County (portions)); Outside TV Markets (Cadwell, Dudley, RENTZ, Laurens County (portions)).
  Channel capacity: N.A. Channels available but not in use: N.A.

Basic
  Subscribers: 1,610.
  Fee: $50.00 installation; $24.95 monthly.
Expanded
  Subscribers: N.A.
  Fee: $71.95 monthly.
Full
  Subscribers: N.A.
  Fee: $127.95 monthly.
HD
  Subscribers: N.A.
  Fee: $7.50 monthly.
Cinemax
  Subscribers: N.A.
  Fee: $15.50 monthly.
Encore
  Subscribers: N.A.
  Fee: $12.00 monthly.
HBO
  Subscribers: N.A.
  Fee: $17.00 monthly.
Showtime/TMC
  Subscribers: N.A.
  Fee: $15.50 monthly.
Starz
  Subscribers: N.A.
  Fee: $13.00 monthly.
Internet Service
  Operational: Yes.
  Fee: $49.95-$99.95 monthly.
Telephone Service
  Digital: Operational
  Fee: $9.25 monthly
General Manager: Wayne Dixon. Office Manager: Ron Chambers. Central Office Supervisor: Larry Stevenson. Outside Plant Supervisor: Donnie Alligood.
Ownership: Progressive Rural Telephone Co-Op Inc.

RENTZ—Progressive Rural Telephone. This cable system has converted to IPTV. See RENTZ, GA [GA5268]. ICA: GA0331.

REYNOLDS—Flint Cable TV, PO Box 669, Reynolds, GA 31076. Phones: 855-593-3278; 478-847-3101; 478-847-4111. Fax: 478-847-2010. Web Site: http://www.flintrvr.com. Also serves Box Springs, Buena Vista, Butler, Crawford County (portions), Culloden, Fort Valley, Lizella, Mauk, Monroe County (portions), Roberta, Upson County (portions) & Yatesville. ICA: GA0236.
  TV Market Ranking: 94 (Buena Vista); Below 100 (Box Springs, Culloden, Mauk, Monroe County (portions), REYNOLDS, Upson County (portions), Butler, Crawford County (portions), Fort Valley, Lizella, Roberta, Yatesville). Franchise award date: October 21, 1981. Franchise expiration date: N.A. Began: N.A.
  Channel capacity: 40 (not 2-way capable). Channels available but not in use: N.A.
Basic Service
  Subscribers: 1,362.
  Programming (received off-air): WGNM (Christian TV Network) Macon; WGXA (ABC, FOX) Macon; WLGA (WeatherNation) Opelika; WLTZ (CW, NBC) Columbus; WMAZ-TV (CBS) Macon; WMGT-TV (Escape, MNT, NBC) Macon; WMUM-TV (PBS) Cochran; WPGA-TV (Bounce TV, IND, MeTV) Perry; WRBL (CBS, MeTV) Columbus; WTVM (ABC, Bounce TV) Columbus; WXTX (FOX, Movies!, This TV) Columbus.
  Programming (via satellite): INSP; QVC; TBS; The Weather Channel.
  Fee: $59.95 installation; $29.95 monthly.
Expanded Basic Service 1
  Subscribers: 853.
  Programming (via satellite): A&E; Animal Planet; BET; Bloomberg Television; Boomerang; Bravo; Cartoon Network; CMT; CNBC; CNN; Comedy Central; C-SPAN; C-SPAN 2; C-SPAN 3; Discovery Channel; Disney Channel; E! HD; ESPN; ESPN Classic; ESPN2; Food Network; Fox News Channel; Fox Sports 1; FOX Sports South/SportSouth; Freeform; FX; GSN; Hallmark Channel; HGTV; History; HLN; Lifetime; MSNBC; MTV; National Geographic Channel; Nickelodeon; RFD-TV; Spike TV; Syfy; TLC; TNT; Travel Channel; Trinity Broadcasting Network (TBN); truTV; Turner Classic Movies; TV Land; UP; USA Network; VH1; WE tv; WGN America; WPIX (Antenna TV, CW, This TV) New York.
  Fee: $37.00 monthly.
Digital Basic Service
  Subscribers: 234.
  Programming (via satellite): BBC America; Chiller; Destination America; Discovery Kids Channel; DMX Music; IFC; International Television (ITV); Investigation Discovery; Nick Jr.; OWN: Oprah Winfrey Network; Science Channel.
  Fee: $5.00 monthly.
Digital Expanded Basic Service
  Subscribers: N.A.
  Programming (via satellite): 52MX; Cine Mexicano; Cinelatino; Cloo; CMT; CNN en Espanol; Disney XD; ESPN Deportes; ESPNews; Flix; FOX College Sports Central; FOX College Sports Pacific; Fox Deportes; Fuse; FXM; FYI; Golf Channel; Great American Country; History en Espanol; History International; MTV Classic; MTV Hits; MTV2; NBCSN; Nicktoons; Outdoor Channel; Ovation; Starz Encore (multiplexed); Sundance TV; TeenNick; Tr3s; UP; VH1 Soul.
Pay Service 1
  Pay Units: N.A.
  Programming (via satellite): Cinemax; HBO; Starz Encore.
  Fee: $2.99 monthly (Encore), $11.99 monthly (Cinemax or HBO).
Digital Pay Service 1
  Pay Units: N.A.
  Programming (via satellite): Cinemax (multiplexed); HBO (multiplexed); Showtime (multiplexed); Starz (multiplexed); The Movie Channel (multiplexed).
  Fee: $11.99 monthly (HBO, Cinemax, Showtime/TMC or Starz).
Video-On-Demand: No
Internet Service
  Operational: No.
Telephone Service
  None
President & General Manager: James L. Bond. Marketing Manager: Laurie Long.
Ownership: Flint Cable Television Inc. (MSO).

RHINE—Formerly served by KLiP Interactive. No longer in operation. ICA: GA0164.

RINGGOLD—Charter Communications, 1103 S Hamilton St, Dalton, GA 30720. Phones: 314-543-2236; 636-207-5100 (Corporate office); 706-272-0647; 865-984-1400 (Maryville, TN office). Web Site: http://www.charter.com. Also serves Catoosa County. ICA: GA0238.
  TV Market Ranking: 78 (Catoosa County, RINGGOLD). Franchise award date: January 16, 1984. Franchise expiration date: N.A. Began: N.A.
  Channel capacity: N.A. Channels available but not in use: N.A.
Digital Basic Service
  Subscribers: 5,426.
  Programming (via satellite): BBC America; Discovery Digital Networks; DIY Network; FOX College Sports Central; FOX College Sports Pacific; Fox Deportes; FYI; Great American Country; History International; IFC; MC; Nick Jr.; Sundance TV; TV Guide Interactive Inc.
  Fee: $49.99 installation; $26.99 monthly.
Digital Expanded Basic Service
  Subscribers: N.A.
  Programming (via satellite): A&E; AMC; Animal Planet; BET; Bravo; Cartoon Network; CMT; CNBC; CNN; Comcast/Charter Sports Southeast (CSS); Comedy Central; Discovery Channel; Disney Channel; E! HD; ESPN; ESPN2; EWTN Global Catholic Network; Food Network; Fox News Channel; Fox Sports 1; FOX Sports South/SportSouth; Freeform; FX; Golf Channel; GSN; Hallmark Channel; HGTV; History; HLN; Lifetime; MTV; National Geographic Channel; NBCSN; Nickelodeon; Syfy; TLC; TNT; Travel Channel; Turner Classic Movies; TV Land; Univision; Univision Studios; USA Network; VH1; WE tv.
  Fee: $50.99 monthly.
Digital Pay Service 1
  Pay Units: N.A.
  Programming (via satellite): Cinemax (multiplexed); Flix; HBO (multiplexed); Showtime (multiplexed); Starz (multiplexed); Starz Encore (multiplexed); The Movie Channel (multiplexed).
  Fee: $20.00 monthly (each).
Video-On-Demand: No
Pay-Per-View
  Hot Choice (delivered digitally); iN DEMAND (delivered digitally); Playboy TV (delivered digitally); Fresh (delivered digitally); Shorteez (delivered digitally).
Internet Service
  Operational: Yes. Began: September 1, 2001.
  Broadband Service: Charter Internet.
  Fee: $29.99 monthly.
Telephone Service
  Digital: Operational
Miles of Plant: 170.0 (coaxial); None (fiber optic). Homes passed: 7,207.
Technical Operations Director: Grant Evans. Marketing Director: Pat Hollenbeck. Accounting Director: David Sovanski. Operations Manager: Mike Burns.
Ownership: Charter Communications Inc. (MSO).

RINGGOLD—Formerly served by Ringgold Telephone. No longer in operation. ICA: GA5001.

ROBERTA—Flint Cable TV. Now served by REYNOLDS, GA [GA0236]. ICA: GA0240.

ROBINS AFB—Watson Cable, 1127 Leverett Rd, Warner Robins, GA 31088. Phone: 478-922-9440. E-mail: watsoncable@wastononline.net. Web Site: http://www.watsononline.net. ICA: GA0333.
  TV Market Ranking: Below 100 (ROBINS AFB).
  Channel capacity: N.A. Channels available but not in use: N.A.
Basic Service
  Subscribers: 395.
  Fee: $12.95 monthly.
Vice President: Robbie Watson.
Ownership: RGW Communications Inc.

ROCHELLE—Bulldog Cable, PO Box 1288, Watkinsville, GA 30677. Phones: 706-997-9003; 800-388-6577. Web Site: http://www.bulldogcable.com. ICA: GA0241.

Cable Systems—Georgia

TV Market Ranking: Below 100 (ROCHELLE). Franchise award date: N.A. Franchise expiration date: N.A. Began: August 1, 1982.
Channel capacity: N.A. Channels available but not in use: N.A.
Basic Service
Subscribers: 81.
Programming (received off-air): WALB (ABC, NBC, This TV) Albany; WFXL (Bounce TV, FOX) Albany; WGXA (ABC, FOX) Macon; WMAZ-TV (CBS) Macon; WMGT-TV (Escape, MNT, NBC) Macon; WMUM-TV (PBS) Cochran; WPCH-TV (IND) Atlanta; WPGA-TV (Bounce TV, IND, MeTV) Perry; WSST-TV (IND) Cordele.
Programming (via satellite): A&E; Animal Planet; BET; CMT; CNN; Discovery Channel; Disney Channel; ESPN; ESPN2; Fox News Channel; Freeform; Hallmark Channel; Lifetime; MTV; Nickelodeon; Spike TV; The Weather Channel; TLC; TNT; TV Land; USA Network; VH1; WGN America.
Fee: $44.95 installation; $47.49 monthly.
Pay Service 1
Pay Units: 21.
Programming (via satellite): Cinemax.
Fee: $10.95 monthly.
Pay Service 2
Pay Units: 36.
Programming (via satellite): HBO.
Fee: $10.95 monthly.
Internet Service
Operational: No.
Telephone Service
None
Miles of Plant: 15.0 (coaxial); None (fiber optic). Homes passed: 500.
President: Mark Wilson. General Manager East: Mark Miller. General Manager West: Vance Johnson. Controller: Ashley Hull.
Ownership: Bulldog Cable (MSO).

ROCKMART—Charter Communications. Now served by NEWNAN, GA [GA0042]. ICA: GA0242.

ROSSVILLE—Comcast Cable. Now served by KNOXVILLE, TN [TN0004]. ICA: GA0022.

ROSWELL—Charter Communications. Now served by LAWRENCEVILLE, GA [GA0009]. ICA: GA0274.

SANDERSVILLE—Charter Communications, 1827 Joiner Rd, Sandersville, GA 31089. Phone: 314-543-2236. Web Site: http://www.charter.com. Also serves Tennille & Washington County (portions). ICA: GA0069.
TV Market Ranking: Outside TV Markets (SANDERSVILLE, Tennille, Washington County (portions)). Franchise award date: N.A. Franchise expiration date: N.A. Began: September 1, 1966.
Channel capacity: N.A. Channels available but not in use: N.A.
Basic Service
Subscribers: 1,516.
Programming (received off-air): WAGA-TV (Buzzr, FOX, Movies!) Atlanta; WCES-TV (PBS) Wrens; WGNM (Christian TV Network) Macon; WGXA (ABC, FOX) Macon; WJBF (ABC, MeTV) Augusta; WMAZ-TV (CBS) Macon; WMGT-TV (Escape, MNT, NBC) Macon.
Programming (via satellite): CW PLUS; Hallmark Channel; The Weather Channel; Trinity Broadcasting Network (TBN).
Fee: $49.99 installation; $26.99 monthly.
Expanded Basic Service 1
Subscribers: N.A.
Programming (via satellite): A&E; Animal Planet; BET; Cartoon Network; CNBC; CNN; C-SPAN; Discovery Channel; ESPN; ESPN2; Food Network; Fox News Channel; Freeform; FX; FXM; Golf Channel; Great American Country; HGTV; History; HLN; Lifetime; MTV; Nickelodeon; Outdoor Channel; QVC; Spike TV; SportSouth; Syfy; TBS; TLC; TNT; Travel Channel; truTV; Turner Classic Movies; TV Land; USA Network.
Fee: $49.99 monthly.
Digital Basic Service
Subscribers: N.A.
Programming (via satellite): BBC America; Bloomberg Television; Bravo; Destination America; Discovery Kids Channel; Discovery Life Channel; DMX Music; ESPNews; Fox Sports 1; IFC; Investigation Discovery; LMN; National Geographic Channel; OWN: Oprah Winfrey Network; Science Channel; WE tv.
Pay Service 1
Pay Units: N.A.
Programming (via satellite): HBO; Showtime.
Fee: $10.00 installation; $13.95 monthly (Showtime), $14.60 monthly (HBO).
Digital Pay Service 1
Pay Units: N.A.
Programming (via satellite): Cinemax (multiplexed); Flix; HBO (multiplexed); Showtime (multiplexed); Starz (multiplexed); Starz Encore (multiplexed); The Movie Channel (multiplexed).
Fee: $14.75 monthly (Cinemax, HBO, Showtime/TMC/Flix or Starz/Encore).
Video-On-Demand: No
Internet Service
Operational: Yes.
Fee: $42.99 monthly.
Telephone Service
Digital: Operational
Miles of Plant: 1,317.0 (coaxial); 475.0 (fiber optic). Homes passed: 33,455.
Accounting Director: David Sovanski.
Ownership: Charter Communications Inc. (MSO).

SANFORD—Formerly served by KLiP Interactive. No longer in operation. ICA: GA0105.

SARDIS—Formerly served by KLiP Interactive. No longer in operation. ICA: GA0243.

SASSER—Formerly served by Citizens Cable TV. No longer in operation. ICA: GA0167.

SAVANNAH—Comcast Cable, 5515 Abercorn St, Savannah, GA 31405. Phones: 912-354-7531 (Customer service); 912-356-3113. Fax: 912-353-6063. Web Site: http://www.comcast.com. Also serves Adrian, Allenhurst, Bellville, Blitchton County (portions), Bloomingdale, Bryan County (portions), Candler County (portions), Chatham County (portions), Claxton, Colonels Island, Daisy, Dutch Island, Effingham County (portions), Ellabelle, Emanuel County (portions), Evans, Evans County (portions), Fleming, Flemington, Fort Stewart, Garden City, Gumbranch, Guyton, Hagan, Highland Woods Motor Home Park, Hinesville, Hunter Army Airfield, Jesup, Lake George, Liberty County (portions), Long County (portions), Ludowici, Metter, Midway, Odum, Pembroke, Pooler, Port Wentworth, Regency Motor Home Park, Riceboro, Richmond Hill, Rincon, Screven, Silverwood Plantation, Skidaway Island, Springfield, Thunderbolt, Twin City, Tybee Island, Vernonburg, Walthourville, Wayne County (portions) & Woodland Lakes Resort. ICA: GA0005.
TV Market Ranking: Below 100 (Allenhurst, Bellville, Blitchton County (portions), Bloomingdale, Bryan County (portions), Chatham County (portions), Dutch Island, Effingham County (portions), Ellabelle, Evans, Fleming, Flemington, Fort Stewart, Garden City, Gumbranch, Highland Woods Motor Home Park, Hunter Army Airfield, Jesup, Lake George, Liberty County (portions), Midway, Odum, Pooler, Port Wentworth, Regency Motor Home Park, Riceboro, Richmond Hill, Rincon, SAVANNAH, Screven, Skidaway Island, Springfield, Thunderbolt, Vernonburg, Walthourville, Wayne County (portions), Woodland Lakes Resort, Colonels Island, Evans County (portions), Guyton, Hinesville, Long County (portions), Pembroke, Tybee Island); Outside TV Markets (Candler County (portions), Daisy, Hagan, Ludowici, Adrian, Claxton, Emanuel County (portions), Evans County (portions), Long County (portions), Metter, Twin City). Franchise award date: N.A. Franchise expiration date: N.A. Began: January 1, 1965.
Channel capacity: N.A. Channels available but not in use: N.A.
Basic Service
Subscribers: 93,010. Commercial subscribers: 6,105.
Programming (received off-air): WGSA (CW) Baxley; WJCL (ABC) Savannah; WSAV-TV (MeTV, MNT, NBC) Savannah; WTGS (Antenna TV, FOX) Hardeeville; WTOC-TV (Bounce TV, CBS, This TV) Savannah; WVAN-TV (PBS) Savannah; 15 FMs.
Programming (via satellite): INSP; ION Television; Pop; QVC; WGN America.
Fee: $42.91-$54.95 installation; $25.05 monthly; $3.25 converter.
Expanded Basic Service 1
Subscribers: N.A.
Programming (via satellite): A&E; AMC; Animal Planet; BET; Bravo; Cartoon Network; CMT; CNBC; CNN; Comcast/Charter Sports Southeast (CSS); Comedy Central; C-SPAN; C-SPAN 2; Discovery Channel; Disney Channel; E! HD; ESPN; ESPN2; EWTN Global Catholic Network; Food Network; Fox News Channel; Fox Sports 1; FOX Sports South/SportSouth; Freeform; FX; Golf Channel; Great American Country; GSN; Hallmark Channel; HGTV; History; HLN; Lifetime; MSNBC; MTV; NBCSN; Nickelodeon; OWN: Oprah Winfrey Network; Spike TV; Syfy; TBS; The Weather Channel; TLC; TNT; Travel Channel; Trinity Broadcasting Network (TBN); TV Land; TV One; Univision Studios; USA Network; VH1; WE tv.
Fee: $51.99 monthly.
Digital Basic Service
Subscribers: N.A.
Programming (via satellite): BBC America; CMT; Cooking Channel; C-SPAN 3; Discovery Digital Networks; Disney XD; DIY Network; ESPN HD; ESPN2 HD; ESPNews; Flix; FOX College Sports Central; FOX College Sports Pacific; FYI; GolTV; HD Theater; History International; HITS (Head-end In The Sky); Jewelry Television; LMN; LOGO; MC; MoviePlex; MTV Live; Nat Geo WILD; National Geographic Channel; NBA TV; NFL Network; Nick 2; Nick Jr.; Nicktoons; Outdoor Channel; Sprout; Starz Encore (multiplexed); Sundance TV; TeenNick; Tennis Channel; The Word Network; TNT HD; truTV; Turner Classic Movies; UP; Versus HD; Weatherscan.
Digital Pay Service 1
Pay Units: N.A.
Programming (via satellite): Cinemax (multiplexed); Cinemax HD; HBO (multiplexed); HBO HD; Showtime (multiplexed); Showtime HD; Starz (multiplexed); Starz HD; The Movie Channel (multiplexed).
Fee: $51.98 monthly.
Video-On-Demand: Yes
Pay-Per-View
Hot Choice (delivered digitally); iN DEMAND (delivered digitally); Playboy TV (delivered digitally); NBA League Pass (delivered digitally); MLB Extra Innings (delivered digitally).
Internet Service
Operational: Yes. Began: July 28, 2000.
Subscribers: 72,630.
Broadband Service: Comcast High Speed Internet.
Fee: $42.95 monthly; $7.00 modem lease.
Telephone Service
Digital: Operational
Subscribers: 31,205.
Miles of Plant: 5,686.0 (coaxial); 1,389.0 (fiber optic). Homes passed: 231,195. Homes passed & miles of plant (coax & fiber) include Darien, Glennville, Montezuma, Mount Vernon, Soperton, & Wrightsville
General Manager: Michael Daves. Technical Operations Director: Joel Godsen. Marketing Director: Jerry Avery. Marketing Manager: Ken Torres.
Ownership: Comcast Cable Communications Inc. (MSO).

SEMINOLE COUNTY—Formerly served by Bulldog Cable. No longer in operation. ICA: GA0244.

SKIDAWAY ISLAND—Formerly served by US Cable of Coastal Texas L.P. Now served by Comcast Cable, SAVANNAH, GA [GA0005]. ICA: GA0107.

SMITHVILLE—Citizens Cable TV. Now served by COBB, GA [GA0150]. ICA: GA0246.

SMYRNA—Charter Communications. Now served by LAWRENCEVILLE, GA [GA0009]. ICA: GA0013.

SOPERTON—Comcast Cable, 141 Park of Commerce Dr, Savannah, GA 31405. Phones: 912-354-7531; 912-354-2813. Fax: 912-353-6063. Web Site: http://www.comcast.com. Also serves Treutlen County (portions). ICA: GA0247.
TV Market Ranking: Outside TV Markets (SOPERTON, Treutlen County (portions)). Fran-

Georgia—Cable Systems

chise award date: April 15, 1975. Franchise expiration date: N.A. Began: April 1, 1975. Channel capacity: N.A. Channels available but not in use: N.A.

Basic Service
Subscribers: 554.
Programming (received off-air): WJBF (ABC, MeTV) Augusta; WMAZ-TV (CBS) Macon; WMGT-TV (Escape, MNT, NBC) Macon; WMUM-TV (PBS) Cochran; WTOC-TV (Bounce TV, CBS, This TV) Savannah.
Programming (via satellite): MTV; QVC; TBS; The Weather Channel; WGN America.
Fee: $47.99 installation; $11.00 monthly.

Expanded Basic Service 1
Subscribers: N.A.
Programming (via satellite): BET; CNN; Disney Channel; ESPN; Freeform; HLN; Nickelodeon; Spike TV; TNT; USA Network; VH1.
Fee: $25.00 installation; $19.95 monthly; $20.00 additional installation.

Pay Service 1
Pay Units: N.A.
Programming (via satellite): Cinemax; HBO.
Fee: $15.00 installation; $10.00 monthly (Cinemax), $10.95 monthly (HBO).

Video-On-Demand: No

Internet Service
Operational: Yes.

Telephone Service
Digital: Operational
Homes passed & miles of plant (coax & fiber) included in Savannah.
General Manager: Michael Daves. Technical Operations Director: Joel Godsen. Marketing Director: Jerry Avery. Marketing Manager: Ken Torres.
Ownership: Comcast Cable Communications Inc. (MSO).

SOUTHBRIDGE—Formerly served by Comcast Cable. No longer in operation. ICA: GA0248.

SPARTA—Bulldog Cable, PO Box 1288, Watkinsville, GA 30677. Phones: 706-997-9003; 800-388-6577. Web Site: http://www.bulldogcable.com. Also serves Hancock County. ICA: GA0116.
TV Market Ranking: Outside TV Markets (Hancock County, SPARTA).
Channel capacity: N.A. Channels available but not in use: N.A.

Basic Service
Subscribers: 150.
Programming (received off-air): WGTV (PBS) Athens; WGXA (ABC, FOX) Macon; WMAZ-TV (CBS) Macon; WMGT-TV (Escape, MNT, NBC) Macon; WPCH-TV (IND) Atlanta; WPGA-TV (Bounce TV, IND, MeTV) Perry; WXIA-TV (NBC) Atlanta.
Programming (via satellite): A&E; Animal Planet; BET; CNN; Comedy Central; Discovery Channel; Disney Channel; E! HD; ESPN; ESPN2; Fox News Channel; Fox Sports 1; Freeform; FX; GSN; Lifetime; National Geographic Channel; Nickelodeon; Spike TV; The Weather Channel; TLC; TNT; Trinity Broadcasting Network (TBN); truTV; TV Land; USA Network.
Fee: $44.95 installation; $49.00 monthly.

Digital Basic Service
Subscribers: N.A.
Programming (via satellite): BBC America; Bloomberg Television; Bravo; Cloo; Discovery Life Channel; DMX Music; ESPN Classic; ESPNews; Fuse; FXM; FYI; Golf Channel; HGTV; History; History International; IFC; INSP; LMN; NBCSN; Outdoor Channel; Ovation; Sundance TV; Turner Classic Movies; WE tv.

Pay Service 1
Pay Units: 51.
Programming (via satellite): HBO.
Fee: $10.95 monthly.

Pay Service 2
Pay Units: 72.
Programming (via satellite): Showtime.
Fee: $10.95 monthly.

Digital Pay Service 1
Pay Units: N.A.
Programming (via satellite): Cinemax (multiplexed); Flix; HBO (multiplexed); Showtime (multiplexed); Starz (multiplexed); Starz Encore (multiplexed); The Movie Channel (multiplexed).
Fee: $12.00 monthly (HBO or Showtime).

Pay-Per-View
iN DEMAND (delivered digitally); Hot Choice (delivered digitally); Playboy TV (delivered digitally); Fresh (delivered digitally); Shorteez (delivered digitally).

Internet Service
Operational: No.

Telephone Service
None
Miles of Plant: 25.0 (coaxial); None (fiber optic). Homes passed: 1,180.
President: Mark Wilson. General Manager East: Mark Miller. General Manager West: Vance Johnson. Controller: Ashley Hull.
Ownership: Bulldog Cable (MSO).

ST. MARY'S—Comcast Cable. Now served by JACKSONVILLE, FL [FL0002]. ICA: GA0055.

STAPLETON—Formerly served by KLiP Interactive. No longer in operation. ICA: GA0249.

STATESBORO—Northland Cable Television, 32 East Vine St, PO Box 407, Statesboro, GA 30458-4843. Phones: 888-667-8452; 912-489-8715. Fax: 912-489-5479. Web Site: http://www.yournorthland.com. Also serves Brooklet & Bulloch County (portions). ICA: GA0038.
TV Market Ranking: Below 100 (Bulloch County (portions)); Outside TV Markets (Brooklet, STATESBORO, Bulloch County (portions)). Franchise award date: January 1, 1970. Franchise expiration date: N.A. Began: December 1, 1970.
Channel capacity: N.A. Channels available but not in use: N.A.

Basic Service
Subscribers: 4,106.
Programming (received off-air): WGSA (CW) Baxley; WJCL (ABC) Savannah; WSAV-TV (MeTV, MNT, NBC) Savannah; WTGS (Antenna TV, FOX) Hardeeville; WTOC-TV (Bounce TV, CBS, This TV) Savannah; WVAN-TV (PBS) Savannah.
Programming (via satellite): A&E; Animal Planet; BET; Bravo; Cartoon Network; CNBC; CNN; Comcast/Charter Sports Southeast (CSS); Comedy Central; C-SPAN; Discovery Channel; E! HD; ESPN; ESPN2; Food Network; Fox News Channel; FX; FXM; Golf Channel; Great American Country; Hallmark Channel; HGTV; History; HLN; Lifetime; MTV; National Geographic Channel; NFL Network; Nickelodeon; QVC; Spike TV; SportSouth; Syfy; TBS; The Weather Channel; TLC; TNT; Travel Channel; Trinity Broadcasting Network (TBN); Turner Classic Movies; USA Network.
Fee: $75.00 installation; $47.64 monthly.

Digital Basic Service
Subscribers: N.A.
Programming (via satellite): AXS TV; BBC America; Bloomberg Television; Destination America; Discovery Kids Channel; Discovery Life Channel; DMX Music; ESPN HD; ESPN2 HD; ESPNews; Food Network HD; Fox Sports 1; HD Theater; IFC; Investigation Discovery; NBCSN; Outdoor Channel; TNT HD; Universal HD; Versus HD; WE tv.

Pay Service 1
Pay Units: N.A.
Programming (via satellite): Cinemax; HBO.
Fee: $11.50 monthly (Cinemax), $13.50 monthly (HBO).

Digital Pay Service 1
Pay Units: N.A.
Programming (via satellite): Cinemax (multiplexed); Flix; HBO (multiplexed); Showtime (multiplexed); Starz (multiplexed); Starz Encore; The Movie Channel.
Fee: $14.75 monthly (Cinemax, HBO, Showtime/TMC/Flix or Starz/Encore).

Video-On-Demand: Planned

Pay-Per-View
iN DEMAND (delivered digitally); Playboy TV (delivered digitally); Fresh (delivered digitally); Hot Choice (delivered digitally).

Internet Service
Operational: Yes.
Subscribers: 5,679.
Fee: $42.99 monthly.

Telephone Service
Digital: Operational
Subscribers: 1,110.
Fee: $29.99 monthly
Miles of Plant: 668.0 (coaxial); 77.0 (fiber optic). Homes passed: 21,657.
Executive Vice President: Richard I. Clark. Regional Manager: Richard W. Hutchison. Marketing Director: Steve Hudgins. Chief Technician: Daniel Cullimore. Customer Service Manager: Danielle Nixon.
Ownership: Northland Communications Corp. (MSO).

STATHAM—Comcast Cable. Now served by ATLANTA, GA [GA0017]. ICA: GA0250.

STILLMORE—Pineland Telephone Coop. Inc. This cable system has converted to IPTV. Now served by METTER, GA [GA5005]. ICA: GA0161.

STOCKBRIDGE—Charter Communications, 1920 Brannan Rd, McDonough, GA 30253. Phones: 314-543-2236; 636-207-5100 (Corporate office); 877-581-3485. Web Site: http://www.charter.com. Also serves Aldora, Barnesville, Butts County (portions), Clayton County (portions), Covington, Flovilla, Hampton, Henry County, Jackson, Jenkinsburg, Lamar County, Locust Grove, McDonough, Milner, Newton County, Oxford, Porterdale & Rockdale County (unincorporated areas). ICA: GA0083.
TV Market Ranking: 18 (Clayton County (portions), Covington, Hampton, Henry County, Locust Grove, McDonough, Newton County (portions), Oxford, Porterdale, Rockdale County (unincorporated areas), STOCKBRIDGE; Below 100 (Aldora, Barnesville, Flovilla, Lamar County (portions), Newton County (portions)); Outside TV Markets (Jackson, Jenkinsburg, Lamar County (portions), Milner). Franchise award date: September 5, 1989. Franchise expiration date: N.A. Began: April 26, 1990.
Channel capacity: N.A. Channels available but not in use: N.A.

Digital Basic Service
Subscribers: 34,190.
Programming (via satellite): BBC America; Bloomberg Television; Boomerang; Discovery Digital Networks; FOX College Sports Central; FOX College Sports Pacific; FYI; Great American Country; History International; HITS (Headend In The Sky); IFC; MC; Nick 2; Nick Jr.; Nicktoons; Sundance TV; TeenNick; Turner Classic Movies; TV Guide Interactive Inc.
Fee: $49.99 installation; $26.99 monthly.

Digital Expanded Basic Service
Subscribers: N.A.
Programming (via satellite): A&E; AMC; Animal Planet; BET; Bravo; Cartoon Network; CMT; CNBC; CNN; Comcast/Charter Sports Southeast (CSS); Comedy Central; C-SPAN; C-SPAN 2; Discovery Channel; Disney Channel; Disney XD; E! HD; ESPN; ESPN2; Food Network; Fox News Channel; Fox Sports 1; FOX Sports South/SportSouth; Freeform; FX; Golf Channel; GSN; Hallmark Channel; HGTV; History; HLN; INSP; Lifetime; MSNBC; MTV; National Geographic Channel; Nickelodeon; Oxygen; Pop; Spike TV; Syfy; Telemundo; The Weather Channel; TLC; TNT; Travel Channel; truTV; TV Land; Univision; USA Network; VH1; WE tv.
Fee: $48.99 monthly.

Digital Pay Service 1
Pay Units: N.A.
Programming (via satellite): Cinemax (multiplexed); Flix; HBO (multiplexed); Showtime (multiplexed); Starz (multiplexed); Starz Encore (multiplexed); The Movie Channel (multiplexed).
Fee: $7.95 monthly (Cinemax), $9.95 monthly (HBO or Showtime).

Video-On-Demand: Yes

Pay-Per-View
iN DEMAND (delivered digitally); Playboy TV (delivered digitally); NBA League Pass/WNBA (delivered digitally); NHL Center Ice/MLB Extra Innings (delivered digitally); Fresh (delivered digitally); Shorteez (delivered digitally).

Internet Service
Operational: Yes.
Subscribers: 30,345.
Broadband Service: Charter Internet.
Fee: $29.99 monthly.

Telephone Service
Digital: Operational
Subscribers: 19,086.
Miles of Plant: 3,494.0 (coaxial), 734.0 (fiber optic). Homes passed: 99,879.
Vice President & General Manager: Matt Favre. Sales & Marketing Director: Antoinette Carpenter. Accounting Director: David Sovanski. Technical Operations Manager: Bob Ballew. Operations Manager: David Spriggs.
Ownership: Charter Communications Inc. (MSO).

SUMMERVILLE—Charter Communications, 12405 Powerscourt Dr, St. Louis, MO 63131. Phones: 636-207-5100 (Corporate office); 706-272-0647; 865-984-1400 (Maryville, TN office). Fax: 706-260-2520. Web Site: http://www.charter.com. Also serves Chattooga County, Lyerly, Menlo & Trion. ICA: GA0251.
TV Market Ranking: 18 (Chattooga County, Lyerly, Menlo, SUMMERVILLE); 18,78 (Trion). Franchise award date: N.A. Franchise expiration date: N.A. Began: January 1, 1972.
Channel capacity: N.A. Channels available but not in use: N.A.

Digital Basic Service
Subscribers: 3,293.
Programming (via satellite): BBC America; Bloomberg Television; Bravo; Discovery Digital Networks; DMX Music; EVINE Live; FXM; FYI; Golf Channel; GSN; History

Cable Systems—Georgia

International; IFC; LMN; Nick Jr.; Outdoor Channel; TeenNick; Turner Classic Movies. Fee: $14.99 monthly.

Digital Expanded Basic Service
Subscribers: N.A.
Programming (via satellite): A&E; AMC; Animal Planet; BET; Cartoon Network; CMT; CNBC; CNN; Comedy Central; Discovery Channel; Discovery Life Channel; Disney Channel; Disney XD; E! HD; ESPN; ESPN2; Fox News Channel; Fox Sports 1; FOX Sports South/SportSouth; Freeform; FX; Golf Channel; HGTV; History; HLN; Lifetime; MSNBC; MTV; NBCSN; Nickelodeon; Oxygen; Spike TV; Syfy; The Weather Channel; TLC; TNT; Travel Channel; TV Land; USA Network; VH1; WE tv.
Fee: $50.99 monthly.

Digital Pay Service 1
Pay Units: N.A.
Programming (via satellite): Cinemax (multiplexed); HBO (multiplexed); Showtime (multiplexed); Starz (multiplexed); Starz Encore (multiplexed); The Movie Channel (multiplexed).

Video-On-Demand: No

Pay-Per-View
ESPN Now (delivered digitally); Hot Choice (delivered digitally); iN DEMAND (delivered digitally); Playboy TV (delivered digitally); Fresh (delivered digitally); Shorteez (delivered digitally).

Internet Service
Operational: Yes.
Broadband Service: Charter Internet.
Fee: $29.99 monthly.

Telephone Service
Digital: Operational
Miles of Plant: 60.0 (coaxial); None (fiber optic).
Technical Operations Director: Grant Evans. Marketing Director: Pat Hollenbeck. Accounting Director: David Sovanski. Operations Manager: Mike Burns.
Ownership: Charter Communications Inc. (MSO).

SURRENCY—Worth Cable, 3 Commissioner Dr, PO Box 2056, Darien, GA 31305-2056. Phones: 866-206-0656; 912-437-3422. Fax: 912-437-2065. Also serves Appling County (unincorporated areas). ICA: GA0252.
TV Market Ranking: Below 100 (Appling County (unincorporated areas), SURRENCY).
Channel capacity: 45 (not 2-way capable). Channels available but not in use: N.A.

Basic Service
Subscribers: 50.
Programming (received off-air): WGSA (CW) Baxley; WJCL (ABC) Savannah; WPXC-TV (ION) Brunswick; WSAV-TV (MeTV, MNT, NBC) Savannah; WTGS (Antenna TV, FOX) Hardeeville; WTOC-TV (Bounce TV, CBS, This TV) Savannah; WXGA-TV (PBS) Waycross.
Programming (via satellite): A&E; Animal Planet; BET; CNN; Discovery Channel; Disney Channel; ESPN; Freeform; History; Lifetime; Nickelodeon; Spike TV; TBS; The Weather Channel; TLC; TNT; Travel Channel; TV Land; USA Network; WGN America.
Fee: $29.95 installation; $29.45 monthly.

Pay Service 1
Pay Units: 5.
Programming (via satellite): HBO.
Fee: $10.95 monthly.

Video-On-Demand: No

Internet Service
Operational: No.

Telephone Service
None
Miles of Plant: 4.0 (coaxial); None (fiber optic). Homes passed: 67.
General Manager: Dennis Wortham.
Ownership: Worth Cable Services (MSO).

SWAINSBORO—Northland Cable Television, 123 Roger Shaw St, PO Box 417, Swainsboro, GA 30401-0417. Phones: 888-667-8452; 478-237-8182; 478-237-6434. Fax: 478-237-9569. Web Site: http://www.yournorthland.com. Also serves Emanuel County (portions). ICA: GA0072.
TV Market Ranking: Outside TV Markets (Emanuel County (portions), SWAINSBORO). Franchise award date: N.A. Franchise expiration date: N.A. Began: April 15, 1965.
Channel capacity: N.A. Channels available but not in use: N.A.

Basic Service
Subscribers: 1,127.
Programming (received off-air): WAGT (CW, NBC) Augusta; WFXG (Bounce TV, FOX, This TV) Augusta; WJBF (ABC, MeTV) Augusta; WJCL (ABC) Savannah; WRDW-TV (CBS, MNT, The Country Network) Augusta; WSAV-TV (MeTV, MNT, NBC) Savannah; WTOC-TV (Bounce TV, CBS, This TV) Savannah; WVAN-TV (PBS) Savannah; allband FM.
Programming (via satellite): C-SPAN; QVC.
Fee: $60.00 installation; $43.65 monthly; $2.00 converter.

Expanded Basic Service 1
Subscribers: N.A.
Programming (via satellite): A&E; BET; Cartoon Network; CMT; CNBC; CNN; Discovery Channel; E! HD; ESPN; ESPN2; Food Network; Fox News Channel; FX; FXM; Golf Channel; Great American Country; Hallmark Channel; HGTV; History; HLN; Lifetime; MTV; Nickelodeon; Outdoor Channel; Spike TV; SportSouth; Syfy; TBS; The Weather Channel; TLC; TNT; Travel Channel; Trinity Broadcasting Network (TBN); Turner Classic Movies; TV Land; USA Network.

Digital Basic Service
Subscribers: N.A.
Programming (via satellite): BBC America; Bravo; Discovery Kids Channel; DMX Music; ESPNews; Fox Sports 1; IFC; Investigation Discovery; National Geographic Channel; OWN: Oprah Winfrey Network; Science Channel; WE tv.

Pay Service 1
Pay Units: N.A.
Programming (via satellite): HBO.
Fee: $11.95 monthly (HBO).

Digital Pay Service 1
Pay Units: N.A.
Programming (via satellite): Cinemax (multiplexed); Flix; HBO (multiplexed); Showtime (multiplexed); Starz (multiplexed); Starz Encore (multiplexed); The Movie Channel (multiplexed).
Fee: $14.75 monthly (Cinemax, HBO, Showtime/TMC/Flix or Starz/Encore).

Video-On-Demand: No

Pay-Per-View
iN DEMAND (delivered digitally); Hot Choice (delivered digitally); Playboy TV (delivered digitally); Fresh (delivered digitally).

Internet Service
Operational: Yes.
Fee: $42.99 monthly.

Telephone Service
None
Miles of Plant: 99.0 (coaxial); None (fiber optic). Homes passed: 3,620.

Communications Daily
Warren Communications News
Get the industry standard FREE —
For a no-obligation trial call 800-771-9202 or visit www.warren-news.com

Executive Vice President: Richard I. Clark. Regional Manager: Richard Hutchinson. Chief Technician: Arthur Jones. Office Manager: Becky Williams.
Ownership: Northland Communications Corp. (MSO).

SYLVANIA—Comcast Cable. Now served by AUGUSTA, GA [GA0004]. ICA: GA0253.

TALLAPOOSA—Comcast Cable. Now served by ATLANTA, GA [GA0017]. ICA: GA0104.

THOMASTON—Charter Communications, 127 Mattox Ct, LaGrange, GA 30241. Phones: 314-543-2236; 636-207-5100 (Corporate office); 770-806-7060 (Administrative office); 706-647-1575. Web Site: http://www.charter.com. Also serves Upson County (unincorporated areas). ICA: GA0061.
TV Market Ranking: Outside TV Markets (THOMASTON, Upson County (unincorporated areas)). Franchise award date: January 1, 1969. Franchise expiration date: N.A. Began: August 1, 1972.
Channel capacity: N.A. Channels available but not in use: N.A.

Digital Basic Service
Subscribers: 4,829.
Programming (via satellite): BBC America; Bloomberg Television; Boomerang; Discovery Digital Networks; DIY Network; FOX College Sports Central; FOX College Sports Pacific; Fuse; FYI; History International; HITS (Headend In The Sky); IFC; LMN; MC; Nick 2; Nick Jr.; Nicktoons; Sundance TV; TeenNick.
Fee: $49.99 installation; $26.99 monthly.

Digital Expanded Basic Service
Subscribers: N.A.
Programming (via satellite): A&E; AMC; Animal Planet; BET; Cartoon Network; CMT; CNBC; CNN; Comcast/Charter Sports Southeast (CSS); Comedy Central; C-SPAN; C-SPAN 2; Discovery Channel; Disney Channel; Disney XD; E! HD; ESPN; ESPN Classic; ESPN2; Food Network; Fox News Channel; Fox Sports 1; FOX Sports South/SportSouth; Freeform; FX; Golf Channel; Hallmark Channel; HGTV; History; HLN; INSP; ION Television; Lifetime; MSNBC; MTV; National Geographic Channel; NBCSN; Nickelodeon; Oxygen; Pop; QVC; Spike TV; Syfy; Telemundo; The Weather Channel; TLC; TNT; Travel Channel; Trinity Broadcasting Network (TBN); truTV; Turner Classic Movies; TV Land; Univision; Univision Studios; USA Network; VH1; WE tv.
Fee: $48.99 monthly.

Digital Pay Service 1
Pay Units: N.A.
Programming (via satellite): Cinemax (multiplexed); Flix; HBO (multiplexed); Showtime (multiplexed); Starz (multiplexed); Starz Encore; The Movie Channel (multiplexed).
Fee: $9.95 monthly (each).

Video-On-Demand: Yes

Pay-Per-View
iN DEMAND (delivered digitally); NBA League Pass/WNBA (delivered digitally); NHL Center Ice/MLB Extra Innings (delivered digitally); Playboy TV (delivered digitally); Fresh (delivered digitally); Shorteez (delivered digitally).

Internet Service
Operational: Yes.
Broadband Service: Charter Internet.
Fee: $29.99 monthly; $200.00 modem purchase.

Telephone Service
Digital: Operational
Fee: $29.99 monthly
Miles of Plant: 434.0 (coaxial); 125.0 (fiber optic). Homes passed: 12,283.
Vice President & General Manager: Matt Favre. Sales & Marketing Director: Antoinette Carpenter. Accounting Director: David Sovanski. Technical Operations Manager: Tim Hardeman. Operations Manager: David Spriggs.
Ownership: Charter Communications Inc. (MSO).

THOMASVILLE—CNS, 111 Victoria Pl, PO Box 1540, Thomasville, GA 31799. Phone: 229-227-7001. E-mail: answers@cns-internet.com. Web Site: http://www.cns-internet.com. ICA: GA0309. **Note:** This system is an overbuild.
TV Market Ranking: Below 100 (THOMASVILLE). Franchise award date: N.A. Franchise expiration date: N.A. Began: May 14, 2001.
Channel capacity: N.A. Channels available but not in use: N.A.

Basic Service
Subscribers: N.A.
Programming (received off-air): WABW-TV (PBS) Pelham; WALB (ABC, NBC, This TV) Albany; WBXT-LD (IND) Tallahassee; WCTV (CBS, MNT, This TV) Thomasville; WFSU-TV (PBS) Tallahassee; WSB-TV (ABC, MeTV) Atlanta; WTLF (CW) Tallahassee; WTLH (CW, FOX, MeTV) Bainbridge; WTWC-TV (NBC, The Country Network) Tallahassee; WTXL-TV (ABC, Bounce TV) Tallahassee; WXIA-TV (NBC) Atlanta.
Programming (via satellite): Bloomberg Television; C-SPAN; C-SPAN 2; Discovery Channel; Discovery Life Channel; Disney Channel; Disney XD; Family Friendly Entertainment; FamilyNet; Fox News Channel; FOX Sports South/SportSouth; Hallmark Channel; HLN; ION Television; QVC; TBS; The Weather Channel; Travel Channel; Trinity Broadcasting Network (TBN).

Expanded Basic Service 1
Subscribers: N.A.
Programming (via satellite): A&E; AMC; Animal Planet; BET; Bravo; Cartoon Network; CNBC; CNN; Comedy Central; E! HD; ESPN; ESPN Classic; ESPN2; Food Network; Fox Sports 1; Freeform; FX; Golf Channel; Great American Country; GSN; HGTV; History; Lifetime; MSNBC; MTV; Nickelodeon; Outdoor Channel; Spike TV; Syfy; TLC; TNT; truTV; Turner Classic Movies; TV Land; USA Network; VH1; WE tv; WGN America.
Fee: $34.95 monthly.

2017 Edition
D-173

Georgia—Cable Systems

Digital Basic Service
Subscribers: N.A.
Programming (via satellite): BBC America; Boomerang; CNN en Espanol; CNN International; Discovery Digital Networks; DIY Network; Fox Deportes; Fuse; FXM; FYI; History International; IFC; LMN; MC; National Geographic Channel; Nick 2; Nick Jr.; TeenNick.

Pay Service 1
Pay Units: N.A.
Programming (via satellite): Cinemax (multiplexed); Flix; HBO (multiplexed); Showtime; Starz (multiplexed); Starz Encore (multiplexed); Sundance TV; The Movie Channel.
Fee: $8.95 monthly (HBO).

Digital Pay Service 1
Pay Units: N.A.
Programming (via satellite): Cinemax (multiplexed); Flix; HBO (multiplexed); Showtime (multiplexed); Starz (multiplexed); Starz Encore (multiplexed); Sundance TV; The Movie Channel (multiplexed).
Fee: $10.00 monthly (Cinemax, Encore, Flix, HBO, Showtime, Starz, Sundance, or TMC).

Pay-Per-View
iN DEMAND.

Internet Service
Operational: Yes.
Subscribers: 13,219.
Broadband Service: SyrupCity.net.
Fee: $28.95 monthly.

Telephone Service
Digital: Operational
Subscribers: 6,675.
Miles of Plant: 280.0 (coaxial); None (fiber optic).
Broadband Engineer: Chris White. Marketing Coordinator: Sherri Nix. Marketing Representative: Angela Boat.
Ownership: Community Network Services (MSO).

THOMASVILLE—Mediacom, 275 Norman Dr, Valdosta, GA 31601. Phones: 229-244-4182; 229-244-3852. Fax: 229-244-0724. Web Site: http://www.mediacomcable.com. Also serves Cairo, Grady County & Thomas County. ICA: GA0035.
TV Market Ranking: Below 100 (Cairo, Grady County, Thomas County, THOMASVILLE). Franchise award date: N.A. Franchise expiration date: N.A. Began: March 1, 1969.
Channel capacity: N.A. Channels available but not in use: N.A.

Basic Service
Subscribers: 2,223.
Programming (received off-air): WABW-TV (PBS) Pelham; WALB (ABC, NBC, This TV) Albany; WBXT-LD (IND) Tallahassee; WCTV (CBS, MNT, This TV) Thomasville; WFSU-TV (PBS) Tallahassee; WSWG (CBS, CW, MeTV, MNT) Valdosta; WTLH (CW, FOX, MeTV) Bainbridge; WTWC-TV (NBC, The Country Network) Tallahassee; WTXL-TV (ABC, Bounce TV) Tallahassee; 15 FMs.
Programming (via microwave): WSB-TV (ABC, MeTV) Atlanta.
Fee: $69.95 monthly; $2.00 converter.

Expanded Basic Service 1
Subscribers: N.A.
Programming (via satellite): A&E; AMC; Animal Planet; BET; Bravo; Cartoon Network; CMT; CNBC; CNN; Comedy Central; C-SPAN; C-SPAN 2; Discovery Channel; Disney Channel; E! HD; ESPN; EWTN Global Catholic Network; Food Network; Fox News Channel; Fox Sports 1; FOX Sports South/SportSouth; Freeform; FX; Hallmark Channel; HGTV; History; HLN; INSP; ION Television; Lifetime; MSNBC; MTV; Nickelodeon; Outdoor Channel; Pop; QVC; Spike TV; Syfy; TBS; The Weather Channel; TLC; TNT; Travel Channel; Trinity Broadcasting Network (TBN); truTV; TV Land; Univision Studios; USA Network; VH1; WE tv.
Fee: $60.00 installation; $9.43 monthly.

Digital Basic Service
Subscribers: N.A.
Programming (via satellite): BBC America; Discovery Digital Networks; DMX Music; Golf Channel; GSN; IFC; National Geographic Channel; NBCSN; Nick Jr.; Ovation; Turner Classic Movies.

Digital Pay Service 1
Pay Units: N.A.
Programming (via satellite): Cinemax (multiplexed); HBO (multiplexed); Showtime (multiplexed); Starz (multiplexed); Starz Encore (multiplexed); Sundance TV; The Movie Channel.

Video-On-Demand: Yes

Pay-Per-View
Vubiquity Inc. (delivered digitally); ETC (delivered digitally); ESPN Now (delivered digitally); Sports PPV (delivered digitally).

Internet Service
Operational: Yes.
Broadband Service: Mediacom High Speed Internet.
Fee: $40.95 monthly.

Telephone Service
Digital: Operational
Miles of Plant: 886.0 (coaxial); 329.0 (fiber optic). Homes passed: 26,040. Miles of plant (coax & fiber) includes Bainbridge & Havana FL.
Regional Vice President: Sue Misiunas. Vice President, Financial Reporting: Kenneth J. Kohrs. Regional Marketing Director: Melanie Hannasch. Regional Technical Operations Manager: Gary McDougall. Marketing Manager: Daryl Channey.
Ownership: Mediacom LLC (MSO).

TIFTON—Mediacom, 275 Norman Dr, Valdosta, GA 31601. Phones: 229-244-4182; 229-244-3852. Fax: 229-244-0724. Web Site: http://www.mediacomcable.com. Also serves Ashburn, Colquitt County (portions), Moultrie, Omega, Sycamore, Turner County (southern portion) & Ty Ty. ICA: GA0032.
TV Market Ranking: Below 100 (Ashburn, Colquitt County (portions), Sycamore, Turner County (southern portion), Ty Ty, Moultrie); Outside TV Markets (Omega, TIFTON). Franchise award date: N.A. Franchise expiration date: N.A. Began: February 1, 1969.
Channel capacity: N.A. Channels available but not in use: N.A.

Basic Service
Subscribers: 4,337.
Programming (received off-air): WALB (ABC, NBC, This TV) Albany; WCTV (CBS, MNT, This TV) Thomasville; WFXL (Bounce TV, FOX) Albany; WSST-TV (IND) Cordele; WSWG (CBS, CW, MeTV, MNT) Valdosta; WTWC-TV (NBC, The Country Network) Tallahassee; WTXL-TV (ABC, Bounce TV) Tallahassee; allband FM.
Programming (via microwave): WGCL-TV (CBS, COZI TV, Grit) Atlanta; WSB-TV (ABC, MeTV) Atlanta.
Programming (via satellite): C-SPAN; C-SPAN 2; QVC.
Fee: $43.95 monthly.

Expanded Basic Service 1
Subscribers: N.A.
Programming (via satellite): A&E; AMC; Animal Planet; BET; Bravo; Cartoon Network; CMT; CNBC; CNN; Comedy Central; Discovery Channel; Discovery Life Channel; Disney Channel; Disney XD; DIY Network; E! HD; ESPN; ESPN Classic; ESPN2; Food Network; Fox News Channel; Fox Sports 1; FOX Sports South/SportSouth; Freeform; FX; FYI; Golf Channel; Great American Country; Hallmark Channel; HGTV; History; HLN; Lifetime; LMN; MSNBC; MTV; National Geographic Channel; NBCSN; Nickelodeon; Outdoor Channel; OWN: Oprah Winfrey Network; Oxygen; Pop; Spike TV; Syfy; TBS; The Weather Channel; TLC; TNT; Travel Channel; Trinity Broadcasting Network (TBN); truTV; TV Land; Univision; Univision Studios; USA Network; VH1; WE tv; WGN America; WPIX (Antenna TV, CW, This TV) New York.
Fee: $27.73 monthly.

Digital Basic Service
Subscribers: N.A.
Programming (via satellite): 3ABN; AXS TV; BBC America; Bloomberg Television; Boomerang; BYUtv; Church Channel; CNN International; Daystar TV Network; Discovery Digital Networks; ESPNews; EWTN Global Catholic Network; Family Friendly Entertainment; FOX College Sports Central; FOX College Sports Pacific; Fuse; FXM; GEB America; GSN; HD Theater; History International; IFC; INSP; JUCE TV; Nick Jr.; Nicktoons; Outdoor Channel 2 HD; Ovation; TeenNick; Tennis Channel; Turner Classic Movies; Universal HD.

Pay Service 1
Pay Units: N.A.
Programming (via satellite): Cinemax; HBO (multiplexed); Showtime; Starz; Starz Encore (multiplexed).
Fee: $10.00 installation; $1.75 monthly (Encore), $4.75 monthly (Starz), $11.75 monthly (Cinemax or Showtime), $13.15 monthly (HBO).

Digital Pay Service 1
Pay Units: N.A.
Programming (via satellite): Cinemax (multiplexed); Flix; HBO (multiplexed); HBO HD; Showtime (multiplexed); Starz (multiplexed); Starz Encore (multiplexed); Starz HD; Sundance TV; The Movie Channel (multiplexed).
Fee: $10.30 monthly (Cinemax, HBO, Showtime, Starz/Encore or Sundance/TMC).

Video-On-Demand: Yes

Pay-Per-View
ESPN Now (delivered digitally); ETC (delivered digitally); Vubiquity Inc. (delivered digitally).

Internet Service
Operational: Yes.
Subscribers: 2,886.
Broadband Service: Mediacom High Speed Internet.
Fee: $70.00 installation; $40.95 monthly.

Telephone Service
Digital: Operational
Subscribers: 2,090.
Fee: $39.99 monthly
Miles of Plant: 752.0 (coaxial); 405.0 (fiber optic). Homes passed: 22,051.
Vice President: Don Zagorski. General Manager: Sally A. Bloom. Technical Operations Manager: Donald Swanson. Chief Technician: Wendell Pitts. Vice President, Financial Reporting: Kenneth J. Kohrs.
Ownership: Mediacom LLC (MSO).

TIGNALL—Formerly served by Almega Cable. No longer in operation. ICA: GA0254.

TOCCOA—TruVista Communications, 112 York St, PO Box 160, Chester, SC 29706. Phones: 803-385-2191; 800-768-1212; 864-545-2291; 800-768-1212. Fax: 803-581-2226. Web Site: http://truvista.net. Also serves Royston, Stephens County & Toccoa Falls. ICA: GA0050.
TV Market Ranking: 46 (Royston); Below 100 (Stephens County, TOCCOA, Toccoa Falls). Franchise award date: N.A. Franchise expiration date: N.A. Began: January 1, 1965.
Channel capacity: N.A. Channels available but not in use: N.A.

Basic Service
Subscribers: 2,943.
Programming (received off-air): WAGA-TV (Buzzr, FOX, Movies!) Atlanta; WGGS-TV (IND) Greenville; WGTA (Decades, Heroes & Icons, Movies!) Toccoa; WGTV (PBS) Athens; WHNS (COZI TV, Escape, FOX) Greenville; WLOS (ABC, Antenna TV) Asheville; WMYA-TV (MNT, The Country Network) Anderson; WSB-TV (ABC, MeTV) Atlanta; WXIA-TV (NBC) Atlanta; WYCW (CW) Asheville; WYFF (NBC, Movies!) Greenville; 3 FMs.
Programming (via satellite): A&E; BET; Cartoon Network; C-SPAN; Discovery Channel; ESPN; ESPN2; Fox News Channel; FXM; HGTV; History; Nickelodeon; Pop; QVC; The Weather Channel; TLC; Trinity Broadcasting Network (TBN).
Fee: $35.00 installation; $31.99 monthly.

Expanded Basic Service 1
Subscribers: N.A.
Programming (via satellite): AMC; Animal Planet; CMT; CNBC; CNN; Comedy Central; E! HD; Food Network; Fox Sports 1; FOX Sports South/SportSouth; Freeform; FX; Great American Country; Hallmark Channel; HLN; Lifetime; MTV; Spike TV; Syfy; TBS; TNT; Turner Classic Movies; TV Land; USA Network.
Fee: $40.00 installation.

Digital Basic Service
Subscribers: N.A.
Programming (via satellite): BBC America; Discovery Digital Networks; DMX Music; Golf Channel; GSN; INSP; Outdoor Channel.

Pay Service 1
Pay Units: N.A.
Programming (via satellite): HBO; Showtime; The Movie Channel.
Fee: $12.20 monthly (HBO, Showtime, or TMC).

Digital Pay Service 1
Pay Units: N.A.
Programming (via satellite): Cinemax (multiplexed); Flix; HBO (multiplexed); Showtime (multiplexed); Starz (multiplexed); Starz Encore; The Movie Channel (multiplexed).
Fee: $14.75 monthly (HBO, Cinemax, Showtime/TMC/Flix or Starz/Encore).

Video-On-Demand: No

Pay-Per-View
Playboy TV (delivered digitally); Fresh (delivered digitally).

Internet Service
Operational: Yes.
Fee: $42.99 monthly.

Telephone Service
Analog: Not Operational
Digital: Operational
Fee: $29.99 monthly
Miles of Plant: 196.0 (coaxial); None (fiber optic). Homes passed: 7,403.
Senior Vice President, Sales & Marketing: Allison Jakubecy. Senior Director, Field Oper-

Cable Systems—Georgia

ations: Tracy D. Starnes. Video Manager: Tony Helms.
Ownership: TruVista Communications (MSO).

TOOMSBORO—Formerly served by KLiP Interactive. Now served by Windstream Teleview, IRWINTON, GA [GA0300]. ICA: GA0157.

TRENTON—Charter Communications. Now served by JASPER, TN [TN0070]. ICA: GA0255.

TWIN CITY—Comcast Cable. Now served by SAVANNAH, GA [GA0005]. ICA: GA0256.

TYBEE ISLAND—Comcast Cable. Now served by SAVANNAH, GA [GA0005]. ICA: GA0087.

UNADILLA—Formerly served by CommuniComm Services. Now served by ComSouth Telesys Inc., PERRY, GA [GA0229]. ICA: GA0275.

UVALDA—Worth Cable, 3 Commissioner Dr, PO Box 2056, Darien, GA 31305-2056. Phones: 912-437-3422; 866-206-0656. Fax: 912-437-2065. Also serves Montgomery County (portions) & Toombs County (portions). ICA: GA0135.
TV Market Ranking: Below 100 (Montgomery County (portions), Toombs County (portions), UVALDA).
Channel capacity: 45 (not 2-way capable). Channels available but not in use: N.A.
Basic Service
Subscribers: 195.
Programming (received off-air): WFXL (Bounce TV, FOX) Albany; WGSA (CW) Baxley; WJCL (ABC) Savannah; WSAV-TV (MeTV, MNT, NBC) Savannah; WTOC-TV (Bounce TV, CBS, This TV) Savannah; WVAN-TV (PBS) Savannah.
Programming (via satellite): A&E; Animal Planet; BET; CNN; Discovery Channel; Disney Channel; ESPN; Fox News Channel; Freeform; History; Lifetime; Nickelodeon; Spike TV; TBS; The Weather Channel; TLC; TNT; Travel Channel; TV Land; USA Network; WGN America.
Fee: $29.95 installation; $32.50 monthly.
Pay Service 1
Pay Units: 50.
Programming (via satellite): HBO.
Fee: $10.95 monthly.
Video-On-Demand: No
Internet Service
Operational: No.
Telephone Service
None
Miles of Plant: 15.0 (coaxial); None (fiber optic). Homes passed: 370.
General Manager: Dennis Wortham.
Ownership: Worth Cable Services (MSO).

VALDOSTA—Mediacom, 100 Crystal Run Rd, Middletown, NY 10941. Phones: 845-695-2762; 229-244-3852. Web Site: http://www.mediacomcable.com. Also serves Brooks County (eastern portion), Cecil, Hahira, Lowndes County & Remerton. ICA: GA0020.
TV Market Ranking: Below 100 (Brooks County (eastern portion), Cecil, Hahira, Lowndes County, Remerton, VALDOSTA). Franchise award date: N.A. Franchise expiration date: N.A. Began: July 1, 1965.
Channel capacity: N.A. Channels available but not in use: N.A.

Basic Service
Subscribers: 11,558.
Programming (received off-air): WALB (ABC, NBC, This TV) Albany; WBXT-LD (IND) Tallahassee; WCTV (CBS, MNT, This TV) Thomasville; WFXU (IND, Soul of the South) Live Oak; WSWG (CBS, CW, MeTV, MNT) Valdosta; WTLH (CW, FOX, MeTV) Bainbridge; WTWC-TV (NBC, The Country Network) Tallahassee; WTXL-TV (ABC, Bounce TV) Tallahassee; WXGA-TV (PBS) Waycross; 19 FMs.
Programming (via microwave): WPCH-TV (IND) Atlanta; WSB-TV (ABC, MeTV) Atlanta.
Programming (via satellite): A&E; BET; CNBC; CNN; Comedy Central; C-SPAN; Discovery Channel; Freeform; Hallmark Channel; HLN; Lifetime; MTV; Nickelodeon; QVC; The Weather Channel; TNT; VH1.
Fee: $43.95 monthly.
Expanded Basic Service 1
Subscribers: N.A.
Programming (via satellite): AMC; Animal Planet; Bravo; Cartoon Network; CMT; C-SPAN 2; Discovery Life Channel; E! HD; ESPN; ESPN2; EWTN Global Catholic Network; Food Network; Fox News Channel; FOX Sports South/SportSouth; FX; Golf Channel; HGTV; History; ION Television; MSNBC; Oxygen; Pop; Spike TV; Syfy; TLC; Travel Channel; Trinity Broadcasting Network (TBN); truTV; TV Land; Univision; USA Network; WE tv.
Digital Basic Service
Subscribers: N.A.
Programming (via satellite): BBC America; Bloomberg Television; Discovery Digital Networks; Disney XD; Fox Sports 1; Fuse; FXM; FYI; GSN; History International; HITS (Headend In The Sky); IFC; LMN; MC; National Geographic Channel; NBCSN; Nick Jr.; Outdoor Channel; Ovation; TeenNick; Turner Classic Movies.
Digital Pay Service 1
Pay Units: N.A.
Programming (via satellite): Cinemax (multiplexed); Flix; HBO (multiplexed); Showtime (multiplexed); Starz (multiplexed); Starz Encore (multiplexed); Sundance TV; The Movie Channel (multiplexed).
Video-On-Demand: Yes
Pay-Per-View
Vubiquity Inc. (delivered digitally); Pleasure (delivered digitally); ETC (delivered digitally); ESPN Now (delivered digitally); Sports PPV (delivered digitally).
Internet Service
Operational: Yes.
Subscribers: 8,972.
Broadband Service: Mediacom High Speed Internet.
Fee: $59.95 installation; $42.95 monthly; $3.00 modem lease.
Telephone Service
Analog: Not Operational
Digital: Operational
Subscribers: 3,490.
Miles of Plant: 1,127.0 (coaxial); 178.0 (fiber optic). Homes passed: 39,960.
Regional Vice President: Sue Misiunas. Vice President, Financial Reporting: Kenneth J. Kohrs. Regional Marketing Director: Melanie Hannasch. Regional Technical Operations Manager: Gary McDougall. Government Affairs Director: Sally Bloom. Marketing Manager: Daryl Channey.
Ownership: Mediacom LLC (MSO).

VIDALIA—Northland Cable Television, 320 Commerce Way, PO Box 547, Vidalia, GA 30474. Phones: 888-667-8452; 912-

537-3200. Fax: 912-537-7395. Web Site: http://www.yournorthland.com. Also serves Higgston, Lyons, Montgomery County (portions), Santa Claus & Toombs County (portions). ICA: GA0049.
TV Market Ranking: Below 100 (Higgston, Lyons, Santa Claus, VIDALIA, Montgomery County (portions), Toombs County (portions)); Outside TV Markets (Montgomery County (portions), Toombs County (portions)). Franchise award date: N.A. Franchise expiration date: N.A. Began: June 1, 1963.
Channel capacity: N.A. Channels available but not in use: N.A.
Basic Service
Subscribers: 2,166.
Programming (received off-air): WGSA (CW) Baxley; WJCL (ABC) Savannah; WMAZ-TV (CBS) Macon; WSAV-TV (MeTV, MNT, NBC) Savannah; WTGS (Antenna TV, FOX) Hardeeville; WTOC-TV (Bounce TV, CBS, This TV) Savannah; WVAN-TV (PBS) Savannah; 6 FMs.
Programming (via microwave): WXIA-TV (NBC) Atlanta.
Programming (via satellite): Animal Planet; BET; CNBC; CNN; C-SPAN; Discovery Channel; ESPN; FOX Sports South/SportSouth; FX; Great American Country; Hallmark Channel; INSP; Nickelodeon; Pop; QVC; TBS; The Weather Channel; TLC; Travel Channel; TV Land; Univision Studios.
Fee: $75.00 installation; $47.64 monthly; $3.00 converter.
Expanded Basic Service 1
Subscribers: N.A.
Programming (via satellite): A&E; AMC; Cartoon Network; E! HD; ESPN2; Food Network; Fox Sports 1; FX; Golf Channel; HGTV; History; HLN; Lifetime; MTV; Spike TV; Syfy; TNT; Turner Classic Movies; USA Network.
Fee: $42.29 monthly.
Digital Basic Service
Subscribers: N.A.
Programming (via satellite): BBC America; Bloomberg Television; Discovery Digital Networks; DMX Music; GSN; INSP; Outdoor Channel; Trinity Broadcasting Network (TBN).
Digital Expanded Basic Service
Subscribers: N.A.
Programming (via satellite): Bravo; Discovery Life Channel; IFC; NBCSN; WE tv.
Pay Service 1
Pay Units: N.A.
Programming (via satellite): HBO; Showtime.
Fee: $11.95 monthly (each).
Digital Pay Service 1
Pay Units: N.A.
Programming (via satellite): Cinemax (multiplexed); Flix; HBO (multiplexed); Showtime (multiplexed); Starz Encore; The Movie Channel (multiplexed).
Video-On-Demand: No
Pay-Per-View
Playboy TV (delivered digitally); Fresh (delivered digitally).

Internet Service
Operational: Yes.
Fee: $42.99 monthly.
Telephone Service
Analog: Not Operational
Digital: Operational
Fee: $29.99 monthly
Miles of Plant: 168.0 (coaxial); None (fiber optic). Homes passed: 7,192.
Executive Vice President: Richard I. Clark. General Manager: Diana Joyner. Chief Technician: Mike Dawkins.
Ownership: Northland Communications Corp. (MSO).

VILLA RICA—Charter Communications. Now served by NEWNAN, GA [GA0042]. ICA: GA0258.

WARRENTON—Comcast Cable. Now served by AUGUSTA, GA [GA0004]. ICA: GA0124.

WARWICK—Citizens Cable TV. Now served by COBB, GA [GA0150]. ICA: GA0259.

WASHINGTON—Comcast Cable, 5 West Robert Toombs Ave, Washington, GA 30673. Phones: 706-738-0091 (Administrative office); 706-733-7712. Fax: 706-739-1871. Web Site: http://www.comcast.com. Also serves Lincoln County (portions), Lincolnton & Wilkes County (portions). ICA: GA0260.
TV Market Ranking: Below 100 (Lincoln County (portions), Wilkes County (portions)); Outside TV Markets (WASHINGTON, Lincoln County (portions), Lincolnton, Wilkes County (portions)). Franchise award date: N.A. Franchise expiration date: N.A. Began: December 1, 1978.
Channel capacity: N.A. Channels available but not in use: N.A.
Basic Service
Subscribers: 699. Commercial subscribers: 49.
Programming (received off-air): WAGA-TV (Buzzr, FOX, Movies!) Atlanta; WAGT (CW, NBC) Augusta; WCES-TV (PBS) Wrens; WFXG (Bounce TV, FOX, This TV) Augusta; WGGS-TV (IND) Greenville; WGTV (PBS) Athens; WJBF (ABC, MeTV) Augusta; WPCH-TV (IND) Atlanta; WRDW-TV (CBS, MNT, The Country Network) Augusta; WSB-TV (ABC, MeTV) Atlanta; WXIA-TV (NBC) Atlanta; 1 FM.
Programming (via satellite): C-SPAN; C-SPAN 2; ION Television; Nickelodeon; QVC; Trinity Broadcasting Network (TBN); WGN America.
Fee: $49.95-$64.00 installation; $21.67 monthly.
Expanded Basic Service 1
Subscribers: N.A.
Programming (via satellite): A&E; Animal Planet; BET; Cartoon Network; CMT; CNBC; CNN; Comcast/Charter Sports Southeast (CSS); Comedy Central; Discovery Channel; Disney Channel; E! HD; ESPN; ESPN2; Food Network; Fox News Channel; Fox Sports 1; Freeform; FX; Golf Channel; GSN; HGTV; History; HLN; Lifetime; MSNBC;

Georgia—Cable Systems

MTV; NBCSN; Spike TV; SportSouth; Syfy; The Weather Channel; TLC; TNT; Travel Channel; Turner Classic Movies; TV Land; USA Network.
Fee: $42.50 monthly.
Digital Basic Service
Subscribers: N.A.
Programming (via satellite): MC.
Digital Pay Service 1
Pay Units: N.A.
Programming (via satellite): Cinemax (multiplexed); Flix; HBO (multiplexed); Showtime (multiplexed); The Movie Channel (multiplexed).
Video-On-Demand: No
Pay-Per-View
Hot Choice (delivered digitally); iN DEMAND (delivered digitally); Playboy TV (delivered digitally); Pleasure (delivered digitally); Fresh (delivered digitally); Shorteez (delivered digitally).
Internet Service
Operational: Yes.
Broadband Service: DSL service only.
Telephone Service
None
Miles of Plant: 50.0 (coaxial); None (fiber optic).
Engineering Director: Harry Hess. Technical Operations Director: Butch Jernigan. Area Marketing Director: Joey Fortier.
Ownership: Comcast Cable Communications Inc. (MSO).

WAVERLY HALL—Charter Communications. Now served by NEWNAN, GA [GA0042]. ICA: GA0261.

WAYCROSS—Vyve Broadband, 4 International Dr, Ste 330, Rye Brook, NY 10573. Phones: 800-937-1397; 912-548-0528; 912-283-2332. Web Site: http://vyvebroadband.com. Also serves Ware County (eastern portion). ICA: GA0031.
TV Market Ranking: Below 100 (Ware County (eastern portion) (portions)); Outside TV Markets (Ware County (eastern portion) (portions), WAYCROSS). Franchise award date: January 1, 1962. Franchise expiration date: N.A. Began: May 1, 1964.
Channel capacity: 73 (operating 2-way). Channels available but not in use: N.A.
Basic Service
Subscribers: 4,215.
Programming (received off-air): WALB (ABC, NBC, This TV) Albany; WCWJ (Bounce TV, CW) Jacksonville; WFOX-TV (FOX, MeTV, MNT) Jacksonville; WJAX-TV (CBS, Decades, getTV) Jacksonville; WJCL (ABC) Savannah; WJXT (LATV, This TV) Jacksonville; WJXX (ABC) Orange Park; WPXC-TV (ION) Brunswick; WTGS (Antenna TV, FOX) Hardeeville; WTLV (Antenna TV, NBC, The Country Network) Jacksonville; WTOC-TV (Bounce TV, CBS, This TV) Savannah; WXGA-TV (PBS) Waycross; allband FM.
Programming (via satellite): A&E; AMC; Animal Planet; BET; Boomerang; Bravo; Cartoon Network; CMT; CNBC; CNN; Comedy Central; Cooking Channel; C-SPAN; Discovery Channel; Discovery Life Channel; Disney Channel; DIY Network; E! HD; ESPN; ESPN Classic; ESPN2; EWTN Global Catholic Network; Family Friendly Entertainment; FamilyNet; Food Network; Fox News Channel; Fox Sports 1; Freeform; FX; Golf Channel; Hallmark Channel; HGTV; History; HLN; INSP; Lifetime; LWS Local Weather Station; MSNBC; MTV; National Geographic Channel; NBCSN;

Nickelodeon; Pop; QVC; Spike TV; SportSouth; Syfy; TBS; The Weather Channel; TLC; TNT; Travel Channel; Trinity Broadcasting Network (TBN); truTV; Turner Classic Movies; TV Land; USA Network; VH1; WGN America.
Fee: $21.45 monthly; $4.95 converter.
Digital Basic Service
Subscribers: N.A.
Programming (via satellite): BBC America; Bloomberg Television; Cloo; CMT; Destination America; Discovery Kids Channel; Disney XD; ESPNews; ESPNU; FOX College Sports Central; FOX College Sports Pacific; Great American Country; GSN; Hallmark Movies & Mysteries; Investigation Discovery; LMN; MC; MTV Classic; MTV Hits; MTV2; NFL Network; Nick Jr.; Outdoor Channel; Ovation; OWN: Oprah Winfrey Network; Science Channel; TeenNick; TVG Network; VH1 Soul; WE tv.
Digital Expanded Basic Service
Subscribers: N.A.
Programming (via satellite): ESPN HD; ESPN2 HD; Outdoor Channel 2 HD; Universal HD.
Fee: $13.95 monthly.
Digital Pay Service 1
Pay Units: 662.
Programming (via satellite): Cinemax (multiplexed); Cinemax HD; HBO (multiplexed); HBO HD.
Fee: $8.95 monthly (Cinemax), $13.95 monthly (HBO).
Digital Pay Service 2
Pay Units: 291.
Programming (via satellite): Flix; Showtime (multiplexed); Showtime HD; Sundance TV; The Movie Channel (multiplexed); The Movie Channel HD.
Fee: $11.95 monthly.
Digital Pay Service 3
Pay Units: 486.
Programming (via satellite): Starz (multiplexed); Starz Encore (multiplexed); Starz HD.
Fee: $11.95 monthly.
Video-On-Demand: No
Pay-Per-View
iN DEMAND (delivered digitally); Playboy TV (delivered digitally).
Internet Service
Operational: Yes.
Subscribers: 5,294.
Broadband Service: In-house.
Fee: $19.95-$49.95 monthly.
Telephone Service
Digital: Operational
Subscribers: 2,167.
Fee: $39.95 monthly
Miles of Plant: 579.0 (coaxial); 700.0 (fiber optic). Homes passed: 15,141.
President & Chief Executive Officer: Jeffrey DeMond. Senior Vice President, Financial Planning: Daniel White. Vice President, Marketing: Diane Quennoz. Vice President, Residential Services: Vin Zachariah.
Ownership: Vyve Broadband LLC (MSO).

WAYNESBORO—Comcast Cablevision of the South. Now served by AUGUSTA, GA [GA0004]. ICA: GA0262.

WAYNESVILLE—Comcast Cable. Now served by JACKSONVILLE, FL [FL0002]. ICA: GA0143.

WEST POINT—Charter Communications. Now served by NEWNAN, GA [GA0042]. ICA: GA0034.

WHIGHAM—Formerly served by KLiP Interactive. No longer in operation. ICA: GA0263.

WILEY ACRES—Citizens Cable TV. Now served by COBB, GA [GA0150]. ICA: GA0297.

WILKINSON COUNTY (portions)—Windstream Teleview. Now served by IRWINTON, GA [GA0300]. ICA: GA0312.

WILLIAMSON—Formerly served by Georgia Broadband. No longer in operation. ICA: GA0320.

WINDER—Comcast Cable. Now served by ATLANTA, GA [GA0017]. ICA: GA0066.

WOODBINE—Comcast Cable. Now served by JACKSONVILLE, FL [FL0002]. ICA: GA0111.

WOODBURY—Formerly served by Almega Cable. No longer in operation. ICA: GA0318.

WOODBURY—Formerly served by Georgia Broadband. No longer in operation. ICA: GA0322.

WRENS—Bulldog Cable, PO Box 1288, Watkinsville, GA 30677. Phones: 706-997-9003; 800-388-6577. Web Site: http://www.bulldogcable.com. ICA: GA0118.
TV Market Ranking: Below 100 (WRENS). Channel capacity: N.A. Channels available but not in use: N.A.
Basic Service
Subscribers: 165.
Programming (received off-air): WAGT (CW, NBC) Augusta; WCES-TV (PBS) Wrens; WFXG (Bounce TV, FOX, This TV) Augusta; WJBF (ABC, MeTV) Augusta; WPCH-TV (IND) Atlanta; WRDW-TV (CBS, MNT, The Country Network) Augusta.
Programming (via satellite): A&E; AMC; Animal Planet; BET; Boomerang; Cartoon Network; CMT; CNN; C-SPAN; CW PLUS; Discovery Channel; Disney Channel; E! HD; ESPN; ESPN2; EVINE Live; Food Network; Fox News Channel; Fox Sports 1; FOX Sports South/SportSouth; Freeform; FX; Hallmark Channel; HGTV; History; HLN; INSP; Lifetime; LMN; MTV; Nickelodeon; Pop; Spike TV; Syfy; The Weather Channel; TLC; TNT; Travel Channel; Turner Classic Movies; TV Land; USA Network; VH1; WGN America.
Fee: $44.95 installation; $49.00 monthly.
Pay Service 1
Pay Units: 32.
Programming (via satellite): Cinemax.
Fee: $12.00 monthly.
Pay Service 2
Pay Units: 72.
Programming (via satellite): HBO.
Fee: $12.00 monthly.
Internet Service
Operational: Yes.
Fee: $34.95 monthly.
Telephone Service
None
Miles of Plant: 20.0 (coaxial); None (fiber optic). Homes passed: 1,575.
President: Mark Wilson. General Manager East: Mark Miller. General Manager West: Vance Johnson. Controller: Ashley Hull.
Ownership: Bulldog Cable (MSO).

WRIGHTSVILLE—Comcast Cable, 141 Park of Commerce Dr, Savannah, GA 31405. Phones: 912-354-7531; 912-356-3113. Web Site: http://www.comcast.com. Also serves Johnson County (portions). ICA: GA0265.
TV Market Ranking: Outside TV Markets (Johnson County (portions), WRIGHTSVILLE). Franchise award date: August 17, 1979. Franchise expiration date: N.A. Began: January 16, 1981.
Channel capacity: N.A. Channels available but not in use: N.A.
Basic Service
Subscribers: 512.
Programming (received off-air): WGXA (ABC, FOX) Macon; WJBF (ABC, MeTV) Augusta; WMAZ-TV (CBS) Macon; WMGT-TV (Escape, MNT, NBC) Macon; WMUM-TV (PBS) Cochran; WPGA-TV (Bounce TV, IND, MeTV) Perry.
Programming (via satellite): TBS; Trinity Broadcasting Network (TBN); WGN America.
Fee: $47.99 installation; $11.50 monthly.
Expanded Basic Service 1
Subscribers: N.A.
Programming (via satellite): A&E; Animal Planet; BET; Cartoon Network; CMT; CNBC; CNN; Comcast/Charter Sports Southeast (CSS); C-SPAN; CW PLUS; Discovery Channel; Disney Channel; E! HD; ESPN; ESPN2; Food Network; Fox News Channel; Fox Sports 1; FOX Sports Networks; FOX Sports South/SportSouth; Freeform; FX; Golf Channel; Great American Country; Hallmark Channel; HGTV; History; HLN; Lifetime; NBCSN; Nickelodeon; OWN: Oprah Winfrey Network; QVC; Spike TV; Syfy; The Weather Channel; TLC; TNT; truTV; Turner Classic Movies; TV Land; USA Network.
Fee: $34.32 monthly.
Digital Basic Service
Subscribers: N.A.
Programming (via satellite): BBC America; Discovery Digital Networks; DMX Music; Flix; Nick 2; Nick Jr.; Starz Encore (multiplexed); TeenNick; WAM! America's Kidz Network.
Digital Pay Service 1
Pay Units: N.A.
Programming (via satellite): Cinemax (multiplexed); HBO (multiplexed); Showtime (multiplexed); Starz (multiplexed); The Movie Channel (multiplexed).
Fee: $7.95 monthly (each).
Video-On-Demand: No
Pay-Per-View
iN DEMAND (delivered digitally); Hot Choice (delivered digitally).
Internet Service
Operational: Yes.
Telephone Service
Digital: Operational
Homes passed & miles of plant (coax & fiber) included in Savannah.
General Manager: Michael Daves. Technical Operations Director: Joel Godsen. Marketing Director: Jerry Avery. Marketing Manager: Ken Torres.
Ownership: Comcast Cable Communications Inc. (MSO).

YATESVILLE—Flint Cable TV. Now served by REYNOLDS, GA [GA0236]. ICA: GA0289.

ZEBULON—Formerly served by Georgia Broadband. No longer in operation. ICA: GA0316.

HAWAII

Total Systems: 4	Communities with Applications: 0
Total Communities Served: 86	Number of Basic Subscribers: 307,097
Franchises Not Yet Operating: 0	Number of Expanded Basic Subscribers: 0
Applications Pending: 0	Number of Pay Units: 0

Top 100 Markets Represented: N.A.

For a list of cable communities in this section, see the Cable Community Index located in the back of Cable Volume 2.
For explanation of terms used in cable system listings, see p. D-11.

BELLOWS AFB—Oceanic Time Warner Cable. Now served by OAHU ISLAND, HI [HI0001]. ICA: HI0008.

HAWAII KAI—Oceanic Time Warner Cable. Now served by OAHU ISLAND, HI [HI0001]. ICA: HI0009.

HAWI—Oceanic Time Warner Cable. Now served by KEALAKEKUA (formerly KONA), HI [HI0011]. ICA: HI0010.

HICKAM AFB—Formerly served by Cable TV Services. No longer in operation. ICA: HI0006.

HILO—Oceanic Time Warner Cable. Now served by KEALAKEKUA (formerly KONA), HI [HI0011]. ICA: HI0002.

HONOLULU—Formerly served by Craig Wireless Honolulu Inc. No longer in operation. ICA: HI0017.

KAUAI ISLAND—Oceanic Time Warner Cable, 3022 Peleke St, Lihue, HI 96766-2100. Phones: 808-245-1947; 808-625-2100 (Administrative office). Fax: 808-625-5888. Web Site: http://www.oceanic.com. Also serves Barking Sands Naval Base. ICA: HI0004.
TV Market Ranking: Outside TV Markets (Barking Sands Naval Base, KAUAI ISLAND). Franchise award date: August 4, 1981. Franchise expiration date: N.A. Began: August 4, 1981.
Channel capacity: N.A. Channels available but not in use: N.A.
Basic Service
Subscribers: 19,669. Commercial subscribers: 1,363.
Programming (received off-air): KIKU (IND) Honolulu; 12 FMs.
Programming (via microwave): KFVE (MNT) Honolulu; KGMB (CBS, This TV) Honolulu; KHET (PBS) Honolulu; KHNL (Antenna TV, NBC) Honolulu; KHON-TV (CW, FOX) Honolulu; KITV (ABC, MeTV) Honolulu.
Programming (via satellite): C-SPAN; C-SPAN 2; GSN; Trinity Broadcasting Network (TBN).
Fee: $75.00 installation; $14.38 monthly.
Expanded Basic Service 1
Subscribers: N.A.
Programming (via satellite): A&E; AMC; Animal Planet; Bravo; Cartoon Network; CNBC; CNN; Comedy Central; Discovery Channel; Discovery Life Channel; Disney Channel; E! HD; ESPN; ESPN2; EVINE Live; Food Network; Fox News Channel; FOX Sports West/Prime Ticket; Freeform; FX; Golf Channel; GSN; Hallmark Channel; HGTV; History; HLN; Lifetime; LMN; MSNBC; MTV; National Geographic Channel; NBCSN; Nickelodeon; Oxygen; QVC; Spike TV; Syfy; TBS; TLC; TNT; Travel Channel; truTV; Turner Classic Movies; TV Land; USA Network; VH1; WE tv.
Fee: $43.60 monthly.
Digital Basic Service
Subscribers: N.A.
Programming (via satellite): BBC America; CMT; Cooking Channel; Discovery Digital Networks; Disney XD; DIY Network; ESPN Classic; ESPNews; Fox Sports 1; Fuse; FYI; Great American Country; History International; HITS (Headend In The Sky); INSP; MC; Nick Jr.; Outdoor Channel; Ovation.
Digital Pay Service 1
Pay Units: N.A.
Programming (taped): Nippon Golden Network.
Programming (via satellite): Cinemax (multiplexed); HBO (multiplexed); Showtime (multiplexed); Starz Encore (multiplexed); Sundance TV; The Filipino Channel; The Movie Channel (multiplexed).
Fee: $13.95 monthly (each).
Video-On-Demand: Yes
Pay-Per-View
iN DEMAND (delivered digitally); Hot Choice (delivered digitally); Playboy TV (delivered digitally).
Internet Service
Operational: Yes.
Subscribers: 15,750.
Broadband Service: EarthLink, Road Runner, AOL.
Fee: $69.95 installation; $44.95 monthly.
Telephone Service
Digital: Operational
Subscribers: 5,069.
Fee: $44.95 monthly
Miles of Plant: 937.0 (coaxial); 582.0 (fiber optic). Homes passed: 36,139. Homes passed & miles of plant (coax & fiber) included in Oahu Island.
President: Bob Barlow. Vice President, Engineering: Mike Goodish. Vice President, Operations: Norman Santos. Marketing Director: Allan Pollack. Controller: Ann Butack.
Ownership: Time Warner Cable (MSO).

KEALAKEKUA—Oceanic Time Warner Cable, 74-5605 Luhia St, Ste B1, Kona, HI 96740-1678. Phones: 808-329-2418; 202-625-2100 (Administrative office). Fax: 808-625-5888. Web Site: http://www.oceanic.com. Also serves Captain Cook, Hau, Hawaii, Hawi, Hilo, Holualoa, Honaunau, Honokaa, Honomu, Kailua (portions), Kalaoa, Kamuela, Kau, Kawaiabe, Kawaihae, Keauhou, Keeau, Kona, Kurtistown, Laupahoehoe, Mauna Kea, Mauna Lani, Mountain View, North Kohala District, Paauilo, Paia, Papaaloa, Papaikou, Pepeekeo, Puako, Puna, Volcano Village, Waikoloa Resort & Waikoloa Village. ICA: HI0011.
TV Market Ranking: Below 100 (Captain Cook, HILO, Holualoa, Honaunau, Kamuela, Kawaihae, Keauhou, Kona, Mauna Kea, Mauna Lani, Pahoa, Puna, Volcano Village, Waikoloa Resort, Waikoloa Village, Kailua (portions), KEALAKEKUA); Outside TV Markets (Hawi, Honokaa, North Kohala District). Franchise award date: January 1, 1973. Franchise expiration date: N.A. Began: October 1, 1974.
Channel capacity: N.A. Channels available but not in use: N.A.
Basic Service
Subscribers: 40,813. Commercial subscribers: 1,538.
Programming (via microwave): KFVE (MNT) Honolulu; KGMB (CBS, This TV) Honolulu; KHET (PBS) Honolulu; KHNL (Antenna TV, NBC) Honolulu; KHON-TV (CW, FOX) Honolulu; KITV (ABC, MeTV) Honolulu; KWHE (COZI TV, IND) Honolulu.
Programming (via satellite): A&E; AMC; Bravo; Cartoon Network; CNBC; CNN; Comedy Central; C-SPAN; C-SPAN 2; Discovery Channel; Discovery Life Channel; Disney Channel; E! HD; ESPN; ESPN2; EVINE Live; Food Network; Fox News Channel; FOX Sports West/Prime Ticket; Freeform; FX; Golf Channel; GSN; Hallmark Channel; HGTV; HLN; Lifetime; LMN; MSNBC; MTV; National Geographic Channel; NBCSN; Nickelodeon; Oxygen; QVC; Spike TV; Syfy; TBS; TLC; TNT; Travel Channel; truTV; Turner Classic Movies; TV Land; USA Network; VH1; WE tv.
Fee: $50.00 installation; $14.38 monthly.
Digital Basic Service
Subscribers: N.A.
Programming (via satellite): BBC America; CMT; Cooking Channel; Discovery Digital Networks; Disney XD; DIY Network; ESPN Classic; ESPNews; Fox Sports 1; Fox Sports 2; FOX Sports Networks (multiplexed); Fuse; FYI; Great American Country; MC; MTV Classic; MTV2; Nick Jr.; Outdoor Channel; Ovation; Tennis Channel.
Fee: $33.00 installation.
Digital Pay Service 1
Pay Units: N.A.
Programming (via satellite): Cinemax (multiplexed); HBO (multiplexed); HITS (Headend In The Sky); Showtime (multiplexed); Starz Encore; Sundance TV; The Filipino Channel; The Movie Channel (multiplexed).
Fee: $75.00 installation; $15.95 monthly (each).
Video-On-Demand: Yes
Pay-Per-View
Hot Choice (delivered digitally); Playboy TV (delivered digitally); iN DEMAND (delivered digitally).
Internet Service
Operational: Yes. Began: December 31, 2001.
Subscribers: 35,845.
Broadband Service: EarthLink, Road Runner, AOL.
Fee: $69.95 installation; $44.95 monthly.
Telephone Service
Digital: Operational
Subscribers: 12,605.
Fee: $44.95 monthly
Miles of Plant: 2,899.0 (coaxial); 1,220.0 (fiber optic). Homes passed: 79,820. Homes passed & miles of plant (coax & fiber) included in Oahu Island.
President: Bob Barlow. Vice President, Engineering: Mike Goodish. Vice President, Operations: Norman Santos. Marketing Director: Allan Pollack. Chief Technician: Met LeBar. Controller: Ann Butak.
Ownership: Time Warner Cable (MSO).

MAUI—Formerly served by Hawaiian Cablevision. Now served by Oceanic Time Warner Cable, MAUI ISLAND, HI [HI0013]. ICA: HI0003.

MAUI—Formerly served by Maui Cablevision Corp. No longer in operation. ICA: HI0016.

MAUI ISLAND—Oceanic Time Warner Cable, 350 Hoohana St, Kahului, HI 96732-2931. Phones: 808-877-4425; 808-625-2100 (Administrative office). Fax: 808-625-5888. Web Site: http://www.oceanic.com. Also serves Hana, Kahului, Kalaupapa, Kaunakakai, Kihei, Kula, Lahaina, Lanai City, Maalaea, Makawao, Paia, Pukalani, Wailea & Wailuku. ICA: HI0013.
TV Market Ranking: Below 100 (Hana, Kahului, Kaunakakai, Kihei, Kula, Lahaina, Lanai City, Maalaea, Makawao, MAUI ISLAND, Paia, Pukalani, Wailea, Wailuku); Outside TV Markets (Kalaupapa). Franchise award date: N.A. Franchise expiration date: N.A. Began: May 3, 1978.
Channel capacity: N.A. Channels available but not in use: N.A.
Basic Service
Subscribers: 40,683. Commercial subscribers: 2,130.
Programming (received off-air): KWHM (IND) Wailuku; allband FM.
Programming (via microwave): KAAH-TV (TBN) Honolulu; KFVE (MNT) Honolulu; KGMB (CBS, This TV) Honolulu; KHET (PBS) Honolulu; KHNL (Antenna TV, NBC) Honolulu; KHON-TV (CW, FOX) Honolulu; KIKU (IND) Honolulu; KITV (ABC, MeTV) Honolulu.
Programming (via satellite): Cartoon Network; CNBC; CNN; C-SPAN; C-SPAN 2; Disney Channel; ESPN; Freeform; HLN; Lifetime; MTV; Nickelodeon; QVC; TBS; TLC; TNT; Travel Channel; USA Network; VH1.
Fee: $61.00 installation; $15.25 monthly; $3.00 converter.
Digital Basic Service
Subscribers: N.A.
Programming (via satellite): A&E; AMC; Animal Planet; BBC America; Bravo; CMT; CNBC; Comedy Central; Cooking Channel; Discovery Digital Networks; Disney XD; DIY

2017 Edition D-177

Hawaii—Cable Systems

Network; DMX Music; E! HD; ESPN Classic; ESPN2; ESPNews; EVINE Live; Flix; Food Network; FOX College Sports Pacific; Fox News Channel; Fox Sports 1; Fox Sports 2; FOX Sports West/Prime Ticket; Fuse; FX; FXM; FYI; Golf Channel; Great American Country; GSN; Hallmark Channel; HGTV; History; History International; IFC; INSP; LMN; MSNBC; MTV Classic; National Geographic Channel; NBA TV; NBCSN; Nick Jr.; Outdoor Channel; Ovation; Oxygen; Spike TV; Syfy; Tennis Channel; truTV; Turner Classic Movies; TV Land; WE tv.
Fee: $33.00 installation.

Digital Pay Service 1
Pay Units: N.A.
Programming (taped): Nippon Golden Network.
Programming (via satellite): Cinemax (multiplexed); HBO (multiplexed); HITS (Head-end In The Sky); Showtime; Starz Encore (multiplexed); Sundance TV; The Filipino Channel; The Movie Channel (multiplexed).
Fee: $15.95 monthly (each).

Video-On-Demand: Yes

Pay-Per-View
iN DEMAND (delivered digitally); UH Football PPV (delivered digitally); PPV Highlights (delivered digitally); Hot Choice (delivered digitally); Playboy TV (delivered digitally).

Internet Service
Operational: Yes.
Subscribers: 41,316.
Broadband Service: Road Runner, EarthLink, Internet.
Fee: $69.95 installation; $44.95 monthly.

Telephone Service
Analog: Not Operational
Digital: Operational
Subscribers: 10,246.
Fee: $44.95 monthly
Miles of Plant: 1,815.0 (coaxial); 791.0 (fiber optic). Homes passed: 83,140. Homes passed & miles of plant (coax & fiber) included in Oahu Island.
President: Bob Barlow. Vice President, Operations: Norman Santos. Vice President, Engineering: Mike Goodish. Marketing Director: Allan Pollack. Chief Technician: Met LeBar. Controller: Ann Butack.
Ownership: Time Warner Cable (MSO).

OAHU ISLAND—Oceanic Time Warner Cable, 200 Akamainui St, Mililani, HI 96789-3999. Phones: 808-625-8510; 808-625-2100 (Administrative office). Fax: 808-625-5888. Web Site: http://www.oceanic.com. Also serves Ahuimanu, Aliamanu Government Reserve, Bellows AFB, East Honolulu, Enchanted Hills, Ewa, Ewa Beach, Haleiwa, Hauula, Hawaii Kai, Hickam AFB, Honolulu, Iwelei, Kaaawa, Kahaluu, Kailua (portions), Kaimuki, Kalihi, Kaneohe, Kaneohe Bay Marine Corps Base, Kapahulu, Laie, Makaha, Maunawili, Miliani, Moanalua, North Shore, Palolo, Pearl Harbor Government Reserve, Salt Lake, Wahiawa, Waialua, Waianae, Waimanalo & Waipio. ICA: HI0001.
TV Market Ranking: Below 100 (Ahuimanu, Aliamanu Government Reserve, Bellows AFB, East Honolulu, Enchanted Hills, Ewa, Ewa Beach, Haleiwa, Hauula, Hawaii Kai, Hickam AFB, Honolulu, Iwelei, Kaaawa, Kahaluu, Kailua (portions), Kaimuki, Kalihi, Kaneohe, Kaneohe Bay Marine Corps Base, Kapahulu, Laie, Makaha, Maunawili, Miliani, Moanalua, North Shore, OAHU ISLAND, Palolo, Pearl Harbor Government Reserve, Salt Lake, Wahiawa, Waialua, Waianae, Waimanalo, Waipio). Franchise award date: January 1, 1970. Franchise expiration date: N.A. Began: September 1, 1968.
Channel capacity: N.A. Channels available but not in use: N.A.

Basic Service
Subscribers: 205,932. Commercial subscribers: 4,810.
Programming (received off-air): KAAH-TV (TBN) Honolulu; KALO (ETV) Honolulu; KBFD-DT (IND) Honolulu; KFVE (MNT) Honolulu; KGMB (CBS, This TV) Honolulu; KHET (PBS) Honolulu; KHNL (Antenna TV, NBC) Honolulu; KHON-TV (CW, FOX) Honolulu; KIKU (IND) Honolulu; KITV (ABC, MeTV) Honolulu; KWHE (COZI TV, IND) Honolulu; 13 FMs.
Programming (via satellite): CNBC; CNN; C-SPAN; EVINE Live; Fox News Channel; HLN; Lifetime; QVC; TBS.
Fee: $61.00 installation; $16.04 monthly.

Expanded Basic Service 1
Subscribers: N.A.
Programming (via satellite): A&E; AMC; Animal Planet; BBC America; Bravo; Cartoon Network; CMT; Comedy Central; Cooking Channel; C-SPAN 2; Discovery Channel; Discovery Kids Channel; Discovery Life Channel; Disney Channel; DIY Network; E! HD; ESPN; ESPN Classic; ESPN2; ESPNews; Flix; Food Network; Fox Sports 1; Fox Sports 2; FOX Sports West/Prime Ticket; Freeform; Golf Channel; Hallmark Channel; HGTV; History; History International; MSNBC; MTV; National Geographic Channel; NBA TV; NBCSN; Nickelodeon; Outdoor Channel; OWN: Oprah Winfrey Network; Spike TV; Tennis Channel; TLC; TNT; Travel Channel; truTV; Turner Classic Movies; USA Network; VH1.
Fee: $43.60 monthly.

Digital Basic Service
Subscribers: N.A.
Programming (via satellite): Disney XD; DMX Music; FOX College Sports Pacific; FOX Sports Networks (multiplexed); Fuse; FX; FXM; FYI; Great American Country; GSN; IFC; INSP; LMN; MTV Classic; MTV2; Nick Jr.; Ovation; Oxygen; Sundance TV; Syfy; TV Land; WAM! America's Kidz Network; WE tv.

Digital Pay Service 1
Pay Units: N.A.
Programming (taped): Nippon Golden Network.
Programming (via satellite): Cinemax (multiplexed); HBO (multiplexed); HITS (Head-end In The Sky); Playboy TV; Showtime (multiplexed); The Filipino Channel; The Movie Channel (multiplexed).
Fee: $15.95 monthly (each).

Video-On-Demand: Yes

Pay-Per-View
iN DEMAND; special events; Hot Choice (delivered digitally); Playboy TV (delivered digitally); UH Football PPV (delivered digitally); NBA (delivered digitally).

Internet Service
Operational: Yes.
Subscribers: 203,603.
Broadband Service: AOL for Broadband; EarthLink; Road Runner.
Fee: $69.95 installation; $44.95 monthly.

Telephone Service
Digital: Operational
Subscribers: 57,153.
Fee: $44.95 monthly
Miles of Plant: 4,739.0 (coaxial); 2,302.0 (fiber optic). Homes passed: 412,459. Homes passed & miles of plant (coax & fiber) includes Kauai Island, Kealakekua, & Maui Island.
President: Bob Barlow. Vice President, Operations: Norman Santos. Vice President, Engineering: Mike Goodish. Marketing Director: Allan Pollack. Chief Technician: Met LeBar. Controller: Ann Butack.
Ownership: Time Warner Cable (MSO).

PAHALA—Formerly served by Time Warner Cable. No longer in operation. ICA: HI0015.

IDAHO

Total Systems: 26	Communities with Applications: 0
Total Communities Served: 156	Number of Basic Subscribers: 99,741
Franchises Not Yet Operating: 0	Number of Expanded Basic Subscribers: 1,327
Applications Pending: 0	Number of Pay Units: 374

Top 100 Markets Represented: Spokane, WA (76).

For a list of cable communities in this section, see the Cable Community Index located in the back of Cable Volume 2.
For explanation of terms used in cable system listings, see p. D-11.

ABERDEEN TWP.—Direct Communications, 150 South Main, PO Box 858, Rockland, ID 83271. Phones: 800-245-4329; 208-548-2345. Web Site: http://directcom.com. ICA: ID0099.
TV Market Ranking: Below 100 (ABERDEEN TWP.). Franchise award date: N.A. Franchise expiration date: N.A. Began: January 1, 2006.
Channel capacity: N.A. Channels available but not in use: N.A.
Basic Service
Subscribers: 53.
Programming (received off-air): KIDK (CBS, FOX, MNT) Idaho Falls; KIFI-TV (ABC, CW, UniMas) Idaho Falls; KISU-TV (PBS) Pocatello; KPVI-DT (Antenna TV, NBC, This TV) Pocatello; KUWB-LD Bloomington; KVUI (MeTV) Pocatello.
Programming (via satellite): A&E; Animal Planet; CMT; CNN; Discovery Channel; Disney Channel; ESPN; Fox News Channel; Freeform; FX; HGTV; History; HLN; ION Television; Lifetime; MTV; Nickelodeon; Root Sports Rocky Mountain; Spike TV; Syfy; TBS; Telemundo; The Weather Channel; TLC; TNT; Turner Classic Movies; TV Land; Univision Studios; USA Network; VH1; WGN America.
Fee: $39.95 monthly.
Pay Service 1
Pay Units: N.A.
Programming (via satellite): Cinemax; HBO; Starz; Starz Encore.
Fee: $7.99 monthly (Starz & Encore), $14.95 monthly (HBO or Showtime).
Internet Service
Operational: Yes.
Telephone Service
None
Miles of Plant: 16.0 (coaxial); None (fiber optic). Homes passed: 300.
General Manager: Jeremy Smith. Marketing Director: Brigham Griffin.
Ownership: Direct Communications (MSO).

ADA COUNTY (unincorporated areas)—Formerly served by Ada Cable Vision Inc. No longer in operation. ICA: ID0056.

ALBION (town)—Formerly served by Telsat Systems Inc. No longer in operation. ICA: ID0068.

AMERICAN FALLS—Cable One. Now served by POCATELLO, ID [ID0004]. ICA: ID0014.

ARCO—ATC Communications, 205 Era West Ave, Arco, ID 83213. Phone: 208-673-5335. Web Site: http://www.atcnet.net. Also serves Mackay. ICA: ID0030.
TV Market Ranking: Outside TV Markets (ARCO, Mackay). Franchise award date: N.A. Franchise expiration date: N.A. Began: July 1, 1982.
Channel capacity: 54 (not 2-way capable). Channels available but not in use: N.A.
Basic Service
Subscribers: 162.
Programming (received off-air): KBYU-TV (PBS) Provo; KIDK (CBS, FOX, MNT) Idaho Falls; KIFI-TV (ABC, CW, UniMas) Idaho Falls; KISU-TV (PBS) Pocatello; KPVI-DT (Antenna TV, NBC, This TV) Pocatello.
Programming (via satellite): A&E; Animal Planet; Boomerang; Bravo; Cartoon Network; CNBC; CNN; C-SPAN; Discovery Channel; Disney Channel; ESPN; ESPN2; Fox News Channel; Fox Sports 1; FOX Sports West/Prime Ticket; Freeform; FX; Golf Channel; Great American Country; Hallmark Channel; HGTV; History; HLN; INSP; Lifetime; MSNBC; Nickelodeon; Outdoor Channel; QVC; Spike TV; Syfy; TBS; The Weather Channel; TLC; TNT; Travel Channel; Turner Classic Movies; TV Land; USA Network; VH1; WGN America.
Programming (via translator): KJZZ-TV (IND) Salt Lake City; KSL-TV (NBC) Salt Lake City.
Fee: $43.95 monthly.
Pay Service 1
Pay Units: 48.
Programming (via satellite): Cinemax.
Fee: $9.00 monthly.
Pay Service 2
Pay Units: 30.
Programming (via satellite): HBO.
Fee: $9.00 monthly.
Video-On-Demand: No
Internet Service
Operational: Yes.
Telephone Service
Digital: Operational
Miles of Plant: 17.0 (coaxial); None (fiber optic). Homes passed: 523.
President & Chief Executive Officer: ODeen Redman. Vice President: Rich Redman. Executive Secretary: Darla Redman.
Ownership: ATC Communications (MSO).

ASHTON—Formerly served by Silver Star Broadband. No longer in operation. ICA: ID0040.

AVERY—Formerly served by Rapid Cable. No longer in operation. ICA: ID0093.

BOISE—Cable One, 8400 Westpark St, Boise, ID 83704-8365. Phones: 877-692-2253 (Technical support); 208-375-8288. Fax: 208-472-8330. E-mail: celynda.roach@cableone.net. Web Site: http://www.cableone.net. Also serves Ada County (portions), Caldwell, Canyon County (portions), Cascade, Donnelly, Eagle, Emmett, Fruitland, Garden City, Gem County (portions), Greenleaf, Homedale, Horseshoe Bend, Kuna, Marsing, McCall, Meridian, Middleton, Nampa, New Meadows, New Plymouth, Notus, Owyhee County (northwestern portion), Parma, Payette, Purple Sage, Star, Weiser & Wilder, ID; Malheur County (portions), Nyssa, Ontario & Vale, OR. ICA: ID0001.
TV Market Ranking: Below 100 (Ada County (portions), BOISE, Canyon County (portions), Eagle, Emmett, Fruitland, Garden City, Gem County (portions), Greenleaf, Homedale, Horseshoe Bend, Horseshoe Bend, Kuna, Malheur County (portions), Marsing, Meridian, Middleton, Nampa, New Plymouth, Notus, Nyssa, Ontario, Owyhee County (northwestern portion), Parma, Payette, Purple Sage, Star, Wilder, Caldwell); Outside TV Markets (Cascade, Donnelly, McCall, New Meadows, Vale, Weiser). Franchise award date: N.A. Franchise expiration date: N.A. Began: September 9, 1979.
Channel capacity: 72 (operating 2-way). Channels available but not in use: N.A.
Basic Service
Subscribers: 35,356.
Programming (received off-air): KAID (PBS) Boise; KBOI-TV (CBS, CW) Boise; KIVI-TV (ABC, Escape, FOX) Nampa; KKJB (MundoMax) Boise; KNIN-TV (FOX) Caldwell; KTRV-TV (MeTV, MNT, Movies!, This TV) Nampa; KTVB (NBC) Boise; 11 FMs.
Programming (via satellite): C-SPAN; C-SPAN 2; ION Television; Pop; QVC; Telemundo; UniMas; Univision Studios.
Fee: $60.00 installation; $35.00 monthly.
Expanded Basic Service 1
Subscribers: N.A.
Programming (via satellite): 24/7 News Channel; A&E; AMC; Animal Planet; Bravo; Cartoon Network; Celebrity Shopping Network; CMT; CNBC; CNN; Comedy Central; Discovery Channel; Disney Channel; ESPN; ESPN Classic; ESPN2; EVINE Live; Food Network; Fox News Channel; Freeform; FX; HGTV; History; HLN; Lifetime; MSNBC; MTV; Nickelodeon; Spike TV; Syfy; TBS; The Weather Channel; TLC; TNT; Travel Channel; truTV; Turner Classic Movies; TV Land; USA Network; VH1.
Digital Basic Service
Subscribers: N.A.
Programming (via satellite): 3ABN; A&E HD; Boomerang; BYUtv; Cine Mexicano; CNN en Espanol; Discovery Channel HD; Discovery Kids Channel; Disney XD; ESPN Classic; ESPN Deportes; ESPN HD; ESPN2 HD; ESPNews; ESPNU; FamilyNet; Food Network HD; FOX College Sports Central; FOX College Sports Pacific; Fox Deportes; Fox Sports 1; Fox Sports 2; Freeform HD; FXM; FYI; Golf Channel; Great American Country; GSN; Hallmark Channel; HD Theater; HGTV HD; History HD; History International; INSP; La Familia Cosmovision; MC; National Geographic Channel; National Geographic Channel HD; Outdoor Channel; OWN: Oprah Winfrey Network; Science Channel; TBS HD; Telemundo; TLC HD; TNT HD; Toon Disney en Espanol; Trinity Broadcasting Network (TBN); TVG Network; Universal HD; WE tv.
Digital Pay Service 1
Pay Units: N.A.
Programming (via satellite): Cinemax (multiplexed); Flix; HBO (multiplexed); HBO HD; HBO Latino; Showtime (multiplexed); Showtime HD; Starz (multiplexed); Starz Encore (multiplexed); Sundance TV; The Movie Channel (multiplexed); The Movie Channel HD.
Fee: $7.00 monthly (each).
Video-On-Demand: No
Pay-Per-View
iN DEMAND (delivered digitally); ESPN (delivered digitally); SexSee (delivered digitally); Juicy (delivered digitally).
Internet Service
Operational: Yes.
Subscribers: 65,609.
Broadband Service: CableONE.net.
Fee: $75.00 installation; $43.00 monthly; $5.00 modem lease.
Telephone Service
Digital: Operational
Subscribers: 24,195.
Fee: $39.95 monthly
Miles of Plant: 3,151.0 (coaxial); 386.0 (fiber optic). Homes passed: 231,281.
Vice President: Patrick A. Dolohanty. General Manager: Celynda Roach. Chief Technician: Dave Rehder. Marketing Manager: Jane Shanley. Ad Sales Manager: Rick Street.
Ownership: Cable ONE Inc. (MSO).

BOISE—Formerly served by Wireless Broadcasting Systems. No longer in operation. ICA: ID0086.

BONNERS FERRY—Country Cable, 7520 North Market St, Ste 14, Spokane, WA 99217. Phone: 509-633-2283. Also serves Boundary County. ICA: ID0027.
TV Market Ranking: Outside TV Markets (BONNERS FERRY, Boundary County). Franchise award date: January 1, 1981. Franchise expiration date: N.A. Began: November 1, 1981.
Channel capacity: N.A. Channels available but not in use: N.A.
Basic Service
Subscribers: 109.
Programming (via satellite): CNN; C-SPAN; E! HD; Freeform; Nickelodeon; Northwest Cable News; QVC; TBS; WGN America.
Programming (via translator): KAYU-TV (FOX, This TV) Spokane; KHQ-TV (NBC) Spokane; KREM (CBS, TheCoolTV) Spokane; KSPS-TV (PBS) Spokane; KUID-TV (PBS) Moscow; KXLY-TV (ABC, MeTV) Spokane.
Fee: $39.95 installation; $27.82 monthly.

2017 Edition   D-179

Idaho—Cable Systems

Expanded Basic Service 1
Subscribers: 84.
Programming (via satellite): A&E; AMC; Animal Planet; Discovery Channel; Disney Channel; ESPN; Fox News Channel; HLN; MTV; Spike TV; The Weather Channel; TLC; TNT; truTV; USA Network; VH1.
Fee: $28.86 monthly.
Digital Basic Service
Subscribers: N.A.
Programming (via satellite): BBC America; Bloomberg Television; Bravo; Discovery Life Channel; ESPN Classic; ESPNews; Golf Channel; GSN; HGTV; History; INSP; NBCSN; Outdoor Channel; Trinity Broadcasting Network (TBN); WE tv.
Digital Expanded Basic Service
Subscribers: N.A.
Programming (via satellite): DMX Music; FXM; IFC; Nick Jr.; Turner Classic Movies.
Fee: $11.49 monthly.
Digital Pay Service 1
Pay Units: N.A.
Programming (via satellite): Cinemax (multiplexed); HBO (multiplexed); Showtime (multiplexed); Starz (multiplexed); Starz Encore (multiplexed).
Fee: $15.95 monthly (each).
Video-On-Demand: No
Pay-Per-View
Shorteez (delivered digitally); Fresh (delivered digitally); Urban Extra (delivered digitally); Hot Choice (delivered digitally); Playboy TV (delivered digitally); HITS PPV (delivered digitally).
Internet Service
Operational: Yes.
Broadband Service: Road Runner.
Fee: $19.95 monthly.
Telephone Service
Digital: Operational
Fee: $49.95 monthly
Vice President: Carl Sherwood. General Manager & Chief Technician: Jon Cooke.
Ownership: Country Cable LLC (MSO).

BOVILL—Formerly served by Adelphia Communications. No longer in operation. ICA: ID0065.

BOVILL—Formerly served by Elk River TV Cable Co. No longer in operation. ICA: ID0095.

BUHL—Formerly served by Millennium Digital Media. Now served by Cable One, TWIN FALLS, ID [ID0088]. ICA: ID0019.

CALDWELL—Cable One. Now served by BOISE, ID [ID0001]. ICA: ID0008.

CAMBRIDGE—Cambridge Cable TV, 85 North Superior St, Cambridge, ID 83610. Phone: 208-229-1000. Fax: 208-257-3310. E-mail: support@ctcweb.net. Web Site: http://ctcweb.net. Also serves Council. ICA: ID0075.
TV Market Ranking: Outside TV Markets (CAMBRIDGE, Council). Franchise award date: N.A. Franchise expiration date: N.A. Began: January 1, 1984.
Channel capacity: N.A. Channels available but not in use: N.A.
Basic Service
Subscribers: 200 Includes Council.
Programming (received off-air): KAID (PBS) Boise; KBOI-TV (CBS, CW) Boise; KIVI-TV (ABC, Escape, FOX) Nampa; KTRV-TV (MeTV, MNT, Movies!, This TV) Nampa; KTVB (NBC) Boise.
Programming (via satellite): A&E; AMC; Cartoon Network; CMT; CNBC; CNN; C-SPAN; Discovery Channel; Disney Channel; ESPN; ESPN2; Freeform; Hallmark Channel; History; Lifetime; MSNBC; Nickelodeon; Northwest Cable News; Outdoor Channel; QVC; Spike TV; Syfy; TBS; TNT; Trinity Broadcasting Network (TBN); Turner Classic Movies; TV Land; USA Network; VH1; WGN America.
Fee: $22.50 installation; $41.95 monthly.
Pay Service 1
Pay Units: 54.
Programming (via satellite): Starz (multiplexed).
Fee: $6.00 monthly.
Pay Service 2
Pay Units: 58.
Programming (via satellite): Starz; Starz Encore.
Fee: $2.50 monthly (Encore), $7.50 monthly (Encore & Starz).
Video-On-Demand: No
Internet Service
Operational: Yes, DSL & dial-up.
Fee: $19.95 monthly.
Telephone Service
Digital: Operational
Fee: $25.76 monthly
President & General Manager: Richard Wiggins. Facilities Manager: Dan Morris. Controller: J. Kowalski. Chief Technician: Gordon Huff. Marketing Director: Jerry Piper.
Ownership: CTC Telecom.

CASCADE—Cable One. Now served by BOISE, ID [ID0001]. ICA: ID0035.

CASTLEFORD—Formerly served by WDB Communications. No longer in operation. ICA: ID0070.

CATALDO—Suddenlink Communications. Now served by OSBURN, ID [ID0015]. ICA: ID0076.

CHALLIS—Custer Telephone Broadband Services, 400 Shoup St, Salmon, ID 83467. Phone: 208-756-4111. Web Site: http://www.custertel.net. ICA: ID0077.
TV Market Ranking: Outside TV Markets (CHALLIS).
Channel capacity: 45 (not 2-way capable). Channels available but not in use: N.A.
Basic Service
Subscribers: 116.
Programming (received off-air): KIDK (CBS, FOX, MNT) Idaho Falls; KIFI-TV (ABC, CW, UniMas) Idaho Falls; KISU-TV (PBS) Pocatello; KPVI-DT (Antenna TV, NBC, This TV) Pocatello.
Programming (via satellite): A&E; Cartoon Network; CMT; CNN; Discovery Channel; Disney Channel; ESPN; Fox News Channel; FOX Sports West/Prime Ticket; Freeform; INSP; KUSA (NBC, WeatherNation) Denver; QVC; Spike TV; TBS; TNT; Turner Classic Movies; USA Network; WGN America.
Fee: $29.95 installation; $29.45 monthly.
Pay Service 1
Pay Units: 28.
Programming (via satellite): HBO.
Fee: $14.50 monthly.
Video-On-Demand: No
Internet Service
Operational: Yes.
Telephone Service
Digital: Operational
Miles of Plant: 16.0 (coaxial); None (fiber optic). Homes passed: 520.
President & Chief Executive Officer: ODeen Redman. Vice President: Rich Redman. Executive Secretary: Darla Redman.
Ownership: Custer Telephone Cooperative Inc. (MSO).

COEUR D'ALENE—Time Warner Cable, 2305 West Kathleen Ave, Coeur D'Alene, ID 83815-9402. Phones: 208-769-8300; 888-892-2253. Fax: 208-666-0488. Web Site: http://www.timewarnercable.com. Also serves Athol, Bayview, Dalton Gardens, Fernan Lake, Hauser Lake, Hayden, Hayden Lake, Huetter, Kootenai County (portions), Post Falls & Rathdrum. ICA: ID0003.
TV Market Ranking: 76 (COEUR D'ALENE, Dalton Gardens, Fernan Lake, Hauser Lake, Hayden, Hayden Lake, Huetter, Kootenai County (portions), Post Falls, Rathdrum). Outside TV Markets (Athol, Bayview). Franchise award date: January 26, 1979. Franchise expiration date: N.A. Began: September 15, 1970.
Channel capacity: N.A. Channels available but not in use: N.A.
Basic Service
Subscribers: 16,909.
Programming (received off-air): KAYU-TV (FOX, This TV) Spokane; KHQ-TV (NBC) Spokane; KREM (CBS, TheCoolTV) Spokane; KSKN (CW) Spokane; KSPS-TV (PBS) Spokane; KUID-TV (PBS) Moscow; KXLY-TV (ABC, MeTV) Spokane.
Programming (via satellite): C-SPAN; C-SPAN 2; E! HD; ION Television; MSNBC; Northwest Cable News; Pop; QVC; The Weather Channel.
Fee: $32.99 installation; $30.00 monthly.
Expanded Basic Service 1
Subscribers: N.A.
Programming (via satellite): A&E; AMC; Animal Planet; Bravo; Cartoon Network; CMT; CNBC; CNN; Comedy Central; Discovery Channel; Disney Channel; Disney XD; ESPN; ESPN Classic; ESPN2; EVINE Live; EWTN Global Catholic Network; Food Network; Fox News Channel; Freeform; FX; Golf Channel; Great American Country; Hallmark Channel; HGTV; History; HLN; Lifetime; MTV; NBCSN; Nickelodeon; Oxygen; Spike TV; Syfy; TBS; TLC; TNT; Travel Channel; truTV; TV Land; USA Network; VH1; WE tv; WGN America.
Fee: $28.29 monthly.
Digital Basic Service
Subscribers: N.A.
Programming (via satellite): BBC America; Bloomberg Television; Discovery Digital Networks; DIY Network; ESPNews; FOX College Sports Central; FOX College Sports Pacific; Fox Sports 1; Fuse; FXM; FYI; GSN; History International; HITS (Headend In The Sky); IFC; LMN; MC; National Geographic Channel; Nick Jr.; Nicktoons; Outdoor Channel; Starz Encore (multiplexed); Sundance TV; TeenNick; Trinity Broadcasting Network (TBN); Turner Classic Movies.
Fee: $1.97 monthly access, $6.00 monthly (each tier).
Digital Pay Service 1
Pay Units: N.A.
Programming (via satellite): ART America; Cinemax (multiplexed); HBO (multiplexed); RAI Italia; RTN; Showtime (multiplexed); Starz (multiplexed); The Filipino Channel; The Movie Channel (multiplexed); TV Asia; TV5, La Television International; Zee TV.
Fee: $14.00 monthly (each).
Video-On-Demand: Planned
Pay-Per-View
iN DEMAND (delivered digitally).
Internet Service
Operational: Yes.
Subscribers: 27,461.
Broadband Service: Road Runner.
Fee: $39.95 installation; $45.95 monthly.
Telephone Service
Digital: Operational
Subscribers: 8,041.
Fee: $49.95 monthly
Miles of Plant: 1,273.6 (coaxial); 288.0 (fiber optic). Homes passed: 59,555.
Mountain West-Area Manager: Correen Stauffer. Technical Operations Manager: Ted Chesley. Marketing Manager: Jody Veeder. Business Manager: Kirk Hobson.
Ownership: Time Warner Cable (MSO).

COUNCIL—Cambridge Cable TV, 130 North Superior St, PO Box 88, Cambridge, ID 83610. Phone: 208-257-3314. Fax: 208-257-3310. E-mail: support@ctcweb.net. Web Site: http://ctcweb.net. ICA: ID0032.
TV Market Ranking: Outside TV Markets (COUNCIL). Franchise award date: February 5, 1985. Franchise expiration date: N.A. Began: January 1, 1984.
Channel capacity: N.A. Channels available but not in use: N.A.
Basic Service
Subscribers: N.A. Included in Cambridge
Programming (received off-air): KAID (PBS) Boise; KBOI-TV (CBS, CW) Boise; KIVI-TV (ABC, Escape, FOX) Nampa; KTRV-TV (MeTV, MNT, Movies!, This TV) Nampa; KTVB (NBC) Boise.
Programming (via satellite): CMT; CNN; ESPN; Freeform; HLN; Lifetime; Nickelodeon; QVC; TBS; TLC; TNT; Trinity Broadcasting Network (TBN); WGN America.
Fee: $41.45 monthly.
Expanded Basic Service 1
Subscribers: N.A.
Programming (via satellite): A&E; AMC; Discovery Channel; Disney Channel; Northwest Cable News; Spike TV; Syfy; USA Network.
Fee: $3.07 monthly.
Digital Basic Service
Subscribers: N.A.
Programming (via satellite): BBC America; Bloomberg Television; Bravo; Discovery Life Channel; Disney XD; DMX Music; ESPN Classic; ESPN2; EVINE Live; Fox Sports 1; Fuse; FXM; FYI; Golf Channel; GSN; HGTV; History; History International; IFC; LMN; NBCSN; Nick Jr.; Outdoor Channel; TeenNick; Turner Classic Movies; WE tv.
Pay Service 1
Pay Units: N.A.
Programming (via satellite): HBO; Showtime.
Fee: $10.95 monthly (Showtime), $11.95 monthly (HBO).
Digital Pay Service 1
Pay Units: N.A.
Programming (via satellite): Cinemax (multiplexed); Flix; HBO (multiplexed); Showtime (multiplexed); Starz (multiplexed); Starz Encore (multiplexed); The Movie Channel (multiplexed).
Video-On-Demand: No
Pay-Per-View
iN DEMAND (delivered digitally); Hot Choice (delivered digitally); Playboy TV (delivered digitally); Fresh (delivered digitally); Shorteez (delivered digitally).
Internet Service
Operational: Yes.
Broadband Service: CableONE.net.
Fee: $75.00 installation; $43.00 monthly.
Telephone Service
Digital: Operational
Fee: $39.95 monthly
Miles of Plant: 12.0 (coaxial); None (fiber optic). Homes passed: 330.
President & General Manager: Richard Wiggins.
Ownership: CTC Telecom (MSO).

Cable Systems—Idaho

CULDESAC—Formerly served by Rapid Cable. No longer in operation. ICA: ID0066.

DEARY—Formerly served by Elk River TV Cable Co. No longer in operation. ICA: ID0058.

DONNELLY—Cable One. Now served by BOISE, ID [ID0001]. ICA: ID0053.

DOWNEY—Formerly served by Independent Cable. Now served by Silver Star Communications, SODA SPRINGS, ID [ID0022]. ICA: ID0055.

DRIGGS—Formerly served by Independent Cable. Now served by Silver Star Broadband, VICTOR, ID [ID0062]. ICA: ID0038.

ELK RIVER—Formerly served by Elk River TV Cable Co. No longer in operation. ICA: ID0069.

EMMETT—Cable One. Now served by BOISE, ID [ID0001]. ICA: ID0017.

FILER—Formerly served by Filer Mutual Telephone. No longer in operation. ICA: ID5000.

FISH HAVEN—Formerly served by Independent Cable. Now served by Silver Star Communications, SODA SPRINGS, ID [ID0022]. ICA: ID0073.

GLENNS FERRY—RTI-Rural Telecom, 892 West Madison Ave, Glenns Ferry, ID 83623-2374. Phones: 888-366-7821; 208-366-2614. Fax: 208-366-2615. E-mail: mark@rtci.net. Web Site: http://www.rtci.net. ICA: ID0029.
TV Market Ranking: Outside TV Markets (GLENNS FERRY). Franchise award date: July 16, 1981. Franchise expiration date: N.A. Began: May 1, 1981.
Channel capacity: N.A. Channels available but not in use: N.A.
Basic Service
 Subscribers: N.A.
 Programming (received off-air): KAID (PBS) Boise; KBOI-TV (CBS, CW) Boise; KIVI-TV (ABC, Escape, FOX) Nampa; KMVT (CBS, CW) Twin Falls; KNIN-TV (FOX) Caldwell; KTRV-TV (MeTV, MNT, Movies!, This TV) Nampa; KTVB (NBC) Boise.
 Programming (via satellite): A&E; AMC; Animal Planet; Cartoon Network; CMT; CNN; Comedy Central; C-SPAN; Discovery Channel; Disney Channel; DIY Network; ESPN; ESPN2; Food Network; Fox News Channel; Freeform; FX; GSN; HGTV; History; HLN; MoviePlex; MSNBC; MTV; Nickelodeon; Outdoor Channel; Pop; Root Sports Rocky Mountain; Spike TV; Syfy; TBS; The Weather Channel; TLC; TNT; Travel Channel; Turner Classic Movies; TV Land; Univision; Univision Studios; USA Network; VH1; WGN America.
 Fee: $45.00 installation; $35.99 monthly; $8.00 converter.
Digital Basic Service
 Subscribers: N.A.
 Programming (via satellite): BBC America; Bloomberg Television; Bravo; Cine Mexicano; Cinelatino; CNN en Espanol; Daystar TV Network; Destination America; Discovery Kids Channel; Discovery Life Channel; Disney XD; DMX Music; ESPN Classic; ESPNews; EVINE Live; Fox Deportes; Fox Sports 1; FSN Digital Atlantic; FSN Digital Central; FSN Digital Pacific; Fuse; FXM; FYI; Golf Channel; Great American Country; History International; IFC; INSP; Investigation Discovery; MTV Classic; MTV Hits; MTV2; NBCSN; Nick Jr.; Nicktoons; Outdoor Channel; Ovation; Science Channel; Sundance TV; Syfy; TeenNick; The Word Network; Trinity Broadcasting Network (TBN); TVG Network; VH1 Country; VH1 Soul; WE tv.
Digital Pay Service 1
 Pay Units: N.A.
 Programming (via satellite): Cinemax (multiplexed); Flix; HBO (multiplexed); HBO Latino; Showtime (multiplexed); Starz (multiplexed); Starz Encore (multiplexed); The Movie Channel (multiplexed).
 Fee: $12.99 monthly (each).
Internet Service
 Operational: No, DSL.
 Subscribers: 77.
Telephone Service
 Analog: Operational
Miles of Plant: 16.0 (coaxial); 5.0 (fiber optic). Homes passed: 640.
General Manager: Mark R. Martell. Assistant Manager: Susan Case.
Ownership: Rural Telephone Co.

HARRISON—Formerly served by Rapid Cable. No longer in operation. ICA: ID0096.

HAZELTON—Formerly served by WDB Communications. No longer in operation. ICA: ID0061.

IDAHO CITY—Formerly served by Idaho City Cable TV. No longer in operation. ICA: ID0067.

IDAHO FALLS—Cable One, 1525 Sherry Ave, Idaho Falls, ID 83401. Phone: 208-523-4567. Web Site: http://www.cableone.net. Also serves Ammon, Basalt, Bingham County, Blackfoot, Bonneville County, Firth, Fremont County (southern portion), Iona, Jefferson County, Madison County (northern portion), Rexburg, Rigby, Ririe, Rockford, Shelley, St. Anthony, Sugar City, Teton & Ucon. ICA: ID0002.
TV Market Ranking: Below 100 (Ammon, Basalt, Bingham County, Blackfoot, Bonneville County, Firth, IDAHO FALLS, Iona, Jefferson County, Madison County (northern portion), Rexburg, Rigby, Ririe, Rockford, Shelley, Sugar City, Ucon); Outside TV Markets (St. Anthony, Teton). Franchise award date: N.A. Franchise expiration date: N.A. Began: December 15, 1970.
Channel capacity: 72 (operating 2-way). Channels available but not in use: N.A.
Basic Service
 Subscribers: 10,009.
 Programming (received off-air): KIDK (CBS, FOX, MNT) Idaho Falls; KIFI-TV (ABC, CW, UniMas) Idaho Falls; KISU-TV (PBS) Pocatello; KPVI-DT (Antenna TV, NBC, This TV) Pocatello; KVUI (MeTV) Pocatello.
 Programming (via microwave): KBYU-TV (PBS) Provo; KSL-TV (NBC) Salt Lake City.
 Programming (via satellite): C-SPAN; C-SPAN 2; ION Television; Pop; QVC; Telemundo; Univision Studios.
 Fee: $90.00 installation; $35.00 monthly.
Expanded Basic Service 1
 Subscribers: N.A.
 Programming (via satellite): A&E; AMC; Animal Planet; Bravo; Cartoon Network; CMT; CNBC; CNN; Comedy Central; Discovery Channel; Disney Channel; ESPN; ESPN2; EVINE Live; Food Network; Fox News Channel; Freeform; FX; HGTV; History; HLN; Jewelry Television; Lifetime; MSNBC; MTV; Nickelodeon; Root Sports Rocky Mountain; Spike TV; Syfy; TBS; The Weather Channel; TLC; TNT; Travel Channel; Turner Classic Movies; TV Land; USA Network; VH1.
 Fee: $1.80 monthly.
Digital Basic Service
 Subscribers: N.A.
 Programming (via satellite): 3ABN; Boomerang; BYUtv; Cinelatino; CNN en Espanol; Disney XD; ESPN Classic; ESPN Deportes; ESPN HD; ESPNews; FamilyNet; FOX College Sports Central; FOX College Sports Pacific; Fox Deportes; Fox Sports 1; Fox Sports 2; FXM; FYI; Golf Channel; Great American Country; GSN; Hallmark Channel; History International; INSP; La Familia Cosmovision; MC; National Geographic Channel; Outdoor Channel; OWN; Oprah Winfrey Network; Science Channel; Toon Disney en Espanol; Trinity Broadcasting Network (TBN); TVG Network; Universal HD; WE tv.
Digital Pay Service 1
 Pay Units: N.A.
 Programming (via satellite): Cinemax (multiplexed); Flix; HBO (multiplexed); HBO HD; HBO Latino; Showtime (multiplexed); Showtime HD; Starz (multiplexed); Starz Encore (multiplexed); Sundance TV; The Movie Channel (multiplexed); The Movie Channel HD.
 Fee: $20.00 installation; $10.00 monthly (each).
Video-On-Demand: No
Pay-Per-View
 iN DEMAND (delivered digitally); SexSee (delivered digitally); Juicy (delivered digitally); VaVoom (delivered digitally).
Internet Service
 Operational: Yes. Began: March 1, 2001.
 Subscribers: 30,209.
 Broadband Service: CableONE.net.
 Fee: $75.00 installation; $43.00 monthly; $5.00 modem lease.
Telephone Service
 Digital: Operational
 Subscribers: 11,571.
 Fee: $39.95 monthly
Miles of Plant: 2,240.0 (coaxial); 628.0 (fiber optic). Homes passed: 97,373.
Vice President: Patrick A. Dolohanty. General Manager: Dean Jones. Chief Technician: Brett Young. Marketing Director: Penny Schultz.
Ownership: Cable ONE Inc. (MSO).

KOOSKIA—Formerly served by Rapid Cable. No longer in operation. ICA: ID0060.

KOOTENAI COUNTY (portions)—Formerly served by Rapid Cable. No longer in operation. ICA: ID0100.

LAVA HOT SPRINGS—Formerly served by Independent Cable. Now served by Silver Star Communications, SODA SPRINGS, ID [ID0022]. ICA: ID0043.

LEWISTON—Cable One, 2360 Nez Perce Dr, PO Box 876, Lewiston, ID 83501. Phone: 208-746-3325. Fax: 208-746-0290. Web Site: http://www.cableone.net. Also serves Nez Perce County (portions), ID; Asotin, Asotin County & Clarkston, WA. ICA: ID0007.

Access the most current data instantly
FREE TRIAL @ ADVANCED TVFactbook
TELCO/IPTV • CABLE TV • TV STATIONS
www.warren-news.com/factbook.htm

TV Market Ranking: Below 100 (Asotin, Asotin County, Clarkston, LEWISTON, Nez Perce County (portions)). Franchise award date: N.A. Franchise expiration date: N.A. Began: July 1, 1953.
Channel capacity: N.A. Channels available but not in use: N.A.
Basic Service
 Subscribers: 8,378.
 Programming (received off-air): KLEW-TV (CBS) Lewiston; 9 FMs.
 Programming (via microwave): KHQ-TV (NBC) Spokane; KREM (CBS, TheCoolTV) Spokane; KSPS-TV (PBS) Spokane; KWSU-TV (PBS) Pullman; KXLY-TV (ABC, MeTV) Spokane.
 Programming (via satellite): A&E; AMC; Animal Planet; Bravo; Cartoon Network; CMT; CNBC; CNN; Comedy Central; C-SPAN; C-SPAN 2; Discovery Channel; Discovery Channel; ESPN; ESPN Classic; ESPN2; EVINE Live; EWTN Global Catholic Network; Food Network; Fox News Channel; FX; HGTV; History; HLN; Lifetime; MSNBC; MTV; Nickelodeon; Pop; QVC; Syfy; TBS; The Weather Channel; TLC; TNT; Travel Channel; Turner Classic Movies; TV Land; USA Network; VH1.
 Programming (via translator): KAYU-TV (FOX, This TV) Spokane.
 Fee: $90.00 installation; $35.00 monthly; $1.44 converter.
Digital Basic Service
 Subscribers: N.A.
 Programming (via satellite): Boomerang; Discovery Digital Networks; Disney XD; ESPN Classic; ESPNews; FOX College Sports Central; FOX College Sports Pacific; Fox Sports 1; Fox Sports 2; Freeform; FXM; FYI; Golf Channel; Great American Country; GSN; Hallmark Channel; History; History International; HITS (Headend In The Sky) (multiplexed); INSP; LMN; MC; National Geographic Channel; Outdoor Channel; Trinity Broadcasting Network (TBN); truTV.
Digital Pay Service 1
 Pay Units: N.A.
 Programming (via satellite): Cinemax (multiplexed); HBO (multiplexed); Showtime (multiplexed); Starz (multiplexed); Starz Encore (multiplexed); The Movie Channel (multiplexed).
 Fee: $15.00 monthly for first premium channel, $7.00 for each additional.
Video-On-Demand: No
Pay-Per-View
 TEN (delivered digitally); iN DEMAND (delivered digitally); ESPN (delivered digitally); Sports PPV (delivered digitally); Pleasure (delivered digitally); ETC (delivered digitally); Playboy TV (delivered digitally); Fresh (delivered digitally); Shorteez (delivered digitally).
Internet Service
 Operational: Yes. Began: October 1, 1999.
 Subscribers: 2,793.
 Broadband Service: CableONE.net.
 Fee: $75.00 installation; $43.00 monthly; $10.00 modem lease.
Telephone Service
 Digital: Operational
 Subscribers: 3,994.

2017 Edition D-181

Idaho—Cable Systems

Fee: $39.95 monthly
Miles of Plant: 441.0 (coaxial); 135.0 (fiber optic). Homes passed: 24,778.
Vice President: Patrick A. Dolohanty. General Manager: Jerry Giedt. Chief Technician: Les Shriver.
Ownership: Cable ONE Inc. (MSO).

MACKAY—Formerly served by Independent Cable. Now served by ATC Communications, ARCO, ID [ID0030]. ICA: ID0047.

MALAD CITY—ATC Communications, 89 North Main St, Malad, ID 83252. Phone: 208-673-5335. Web Site: http://www.atcnet.net. ICA: ID0028.
TV Market Ranking: Outside TV Markets (MALAD CITY). Franchise award date: N.A. Franchise expiration date: N.A. Began: January 1, 1983.
Channel capacity: 45 (not 2-way capable). Channels available but not in use: N.A.
Basic Service
Subscribers: 116.
Programming (received off-air): KUCW (CW, Movies!, The Country Network) Ogden.
Programming (via satellite): A&E; CMT; CNBC; CNN; Comedy Central; C-SPAN; Discovery Channel; Disney Channel; ESPN; ESPN2; Fox News Channel; FOX Sports West/Prime Ticket; Freeform; HGTV; Lifetime; NBCSN; QVC; Spike TV; TBS; TNT; Turner Classic Movies; TV Land; USA Network; WGN America.
Programming (via translator): KBYU-TV (PBS) Provo; KIDK (CBS, FOX, MNT) Idaho Falls; KIFI-TV (ABC, CW, UniMas) Idaho Falls; KJZZ-TV (IND) Salt Lake City; KSL-TV (NBC) Salt Lake City; KSTU (Antenna TV, FOX) Salt Lake City; KTVX (ABC, MeTV) Salt Lake City; KUTV (CBS, This TV) Salt Lake City.
Fee: $43.95 monthly.
Pay Service 1
Pay Units: 16.
Programming (via satellite): Cinemax.
Fee: $9.00 monthly.
Pay Service 2
Pay Units: 39.
Programming (via satellite): HBO.
Fee: $9.00 monthly.
Video-On-Demand: No
Internet Service
Operational: Yes.
Telephone Service
Digital: Operational
Miles of Plant: 17.0 (coaxial); None (fiber optic). Homes passed: 720.
President & Chief Executive Officer: ODeen Redman. Vice President: Rich Redman. Executive Secretary: Darla Redman.
Ownership: ATC Communications (MSO).

McCALL—Cable One. Now served by BOISE, ID [ID0001]. ICA: ID0023.

McCAMMON—Formerly served by Independent Cable. Now served by Silver Star Communications, SODA SPRINGS, ID [ID0022]. ICA: ID0052.

MIDVALE—Midvale Telephone Exchange Inc., 2205 Keithley Creek Rd, PO Box 7, Midvale, ID 83645-5019. Phones: 800-462-4523; 208-355-2211. Fax: 208-355-2222. E-mail: info@mtecom.net. Web Site: http://www.mtecom.net. ICA: ID0080.
TV Market Ranking: Outside TV Markets (MIDVALE).
Channel capacity: N.A. Channels available but not in use: N.A.
Basic Service
Subscribers: 36.
Programming (received off-air): KAID (PBS) Boise; KBOI-TV (CBS, CW) Boise; KIVI-TV (ABC, Escape, FOX) Nampa; KTRV-TV (MeTV, MNT, Movies!, This TV) Nampa; KTVB (NBC) Boise.
Programming (via satellite): Cartoon Network; CMT; CNN; C-SPAN; Discovery Channel; Disney Channel; ESPN; Freeform; History; HLN; NBCSN; Nickelodeon; Northwest Cable News; QVC; Spike TV; TBS; TLC; TNT; Trinity Broadcasting Network (TBN); Turner Classic Movies; USA Network; WGN America.
Fee: $35.00 installation; $35.00 monthly.
Pay Service 1
Pay Units: 5.
Programming (via satellite): Cinemax.
Fee: $9.00 monthly.
Pay Service 2
Pay Units: N.A.
Programming (via satellite): HBO.
Fee: $9.00 monthly.
Internet Service
Operational: Yes.
Telephone Service
Analog: Operational
Miles of Plant: 4.0 (coaxial); None (fiber optic).
Chief Executive Officer & General Manager: John Stuart. Marketing & Tech Manager: John Stall.
Ownership: Midvale Telephone Exchange Inc. (MSO).

MOUNTAIN HOME—Zito Media, 102 S Main St, PO Box 665, Coudersport, PA 16915. Phones: 814-260-9055; 800-365-6988. E-mail: info@zitomedia.com. Web Site: http://www.zitomedia.com. Also serves Elmore County & Mountain Home AFB. ICA: ID0010.
TV Market Ranking: Below 100 (Elmore County (portions)); Outside TV Markets (Elmore County (portions), MOUNTAIN HOME, Mountain Home AFB). Franchise award date: January 1, 1964. Franchise expiration date: N.A. Began: April 1, 1968.
Channel capacity: N.A. Channels available but not in use: N.A.
Basic Service
Subscribers: 1,392.
Programming (received off-air): KAID (PBS) Boise; KBOI-TV (CBS, CW) Boise; KIVI-TV (ABC, Escape, FOX) Nampa; KNIN-TV (FOX) Caldwell; KTRV-TV (MeTV, MNT, Movies!, This TV) Nampa; KTVB (NBC) Boise.
Programming (via satellite): A&E; AMC; Animal Planet; BET; Cartoon Network; CNN; Comedy Central; C-SPAN; Discovery Channel; Disney Channel; ESPN; ESPN2; FX; History; HLN; Lifetime; MSNBC; MTV; Nickelodeon; Northwest Cable News; QVC; Spike TV; Syfy; The Weather Channel; TLC; TNT; Travel Channel; truTV; TV Land; USA Network; VH1; WGN America.
Fee: $29.95 installation; $24.94 monthly.
Expanded Basic Service 1
Subscribers: N.A.
Programming (via satellite): CMT; Freeform; HGTV; Root Sports Rocky Mountain; TBS.
Fee: $7.44 monthly.
Digital Basic Service
Subscribers: N.A.
Programming (via satellite): BBC America; Bloomberg Television; Discovery Digital Networks; Disney XD; DIY Network; DMX Music; ESPN Classic; ESPNews; Fox Sports 1; Fuse; FXM; FYI; Golf Channel; GSN; History International; HITS (Headend In The Sky); INSP; National Geographic Channel; NBCSN; Nick Jr.; Nicktoons; Outdoor Channel; Trinity Broadcasting Network (TBN); WE tv.
Digital Pay Service 1
Pay Units: N.A.
Programming (via satellite): ART America; Cinemax (multiplexed); Flix; HBO (multiplexed); RAI Italia; Showtime (multiplexed); Starz (multiplexed); Starz Encore (multiplexed); The Filipino Channel; The Movie Channel (multiplexed); TV Asia; TV5, La Television International; Zee TV.
Fee: $12.00 monthly (Cinemax, HBO, Showtime/TMC or Starz), $15.00 monthly (TV Japan, Zhong Tian, CCTV, TV Asia, TV5, Filipino, RAI or ART).
Video-On-Demand: No
Pay-Per-View
Shorteez (delivered digitally); Fresh (delivered digitally); Urban Extra (delivered digitally); Hot Choice (delivered digitally); Playboy TV (delivered digitally); HITS PPV 1-30 (delivered digitally).
Internet Service
Operational: Yes.
Telephone Service
Digital: Operational
Fee: $49.95 monthly
President: James Rigas.
Ownership: Zito Media (MSO).

MULLAN—Mullan Cable TV Inc, 202 North 2nd St, PO Box 615, Mullan, ID 83846-0615. Phone: 208-744-1223. Fax: 208-556-5609. E-mail: cs@mctvusa.tv. Web Site: http://www.mctvusa.tv. ICA: ID0033.
TV Market Ranking: Outside TV Markets (MULLAN). Franchise award date: May 16, 2005. Franchise expiration date: N.A. Began: August 25, 1954.
Channel capacity: N.A. Channels available but not in use: N.A.
Basic Service
Subscribers: 129.
Programming (received off-air): KAYU-TV (FOX, This TV) Spokane; KHQ-TV (NBC) Spokane; KREM (CBS, TheCoolTV) Spokane; KSPS-TV (PBS) Spokane; KXLY-TV (ABC, MeTV) Spokane; allband FM.
Programming (via satellite): A&E; Animal Planet; Bravo; Cartoon Network; Church Channel; CMT; CNN; Comedy Central; C-SPAN; Discovery Channel; Disney Channel; Disney XD; ESPN; ESPN2; Food Network; Freeform; HGTV; History; HLN; JUCE TV; Lifetime; LMN; MTV; Nickelodeon; Outdoor Channel; QVC; Spike TV; Syfy; TBS; The Weather Channel; TLC; TNT; Travel Channel; Trinity Broadcasting Network (TBN); Turner Classic Movies; TV Land; USA Network; VH1; WGN America.
Fee: $15.00 installation; $57.50 monthly.
Pay Service 1
Pay Units: 96.
Programming (via satellite): Cinemax; HBO; The Movie Channel.
Video-On-Demand: No
Internet Service
Operational: Yes. Began: September 14, 2005.
Fee: $25.00 installation; $44.95 monthly; $30.00 modem purchase.
Telephone Service
Digital: Operational
Miles of Plant: 9.0 (coaxial); None (fiber optic). Homes passed: 420.
President & General Manager: James R. Dahl.
Ownership: Mullan Cable TV Inc.

MURRAY—Formerly served by Rapid Cable. No longer in operation. ICA: ID0097.

NEW MEADOWS—Cable One. Now served by BOISE, ID [ID0001]. ICA: ID0082.

OROFINO—Suddenlink Communications, 520 Maryville Centre Dr, Ste 300, St. Louis, MO 63141. Phones: 314-315-9400; 800-326-8206; 208-476-5111. Web Site: http://www.suddenlink.com. Also serves Cottonwood, Grangeville & Kamiah. ICA: ID0016.
TV Market Ranking: Below 100 (OROFINO); Outside TV Markets (Cottonwood, Grangeville, Kamiah). Franchise award date: October 25, 1988. Franchise expiration date: N.A. Began: January 1, 1954.
Channel capacity: 150 (operating 2-way). Channels available but not in use: N.A.
Basic Service
Subscribers: 607.
Programming (received off-air): KAYU-TV (FOX, This TV) Spokane; KHQ-TV (NBC) Spokane; KLEW-TV (CBS) Lewiston; KREM (CBS, TheCoolTV) Spokane; KUID-TV (PBS) Moscow; KXLY-TV (ABC, MeTV) Spokane; allband FM.
Programming (via satellite): C-SPAN; Fox News Channel; Freeform; HLN; Northwest Cable News; WGN America.
Fee: $24.95 monthly.
Expanded Basic Service 1
Subscribers: N.A.
Programming (via satellite): A&E; AMC; Animal Planet; Cartoon Network; CNBC; CNN; Comedy Central; Discovery Channel; Disney Channel; Disney XD; ESPN; ESPN2; EWTN Global Catholic Network; Great American Country; History; Lifetime; MTV; Nickelodeon; Outdoor Channel; QVC; Spike TV; TBS; The Weather Channel; TLC; TNT; USA Network; VH1.
Fee: $39.95 installation; $15.04 monthly.
Digital Basic Service
Subscribers: N.A.
Programming (via satellite): BBC America; Bravo; Discovery Digital Networks; DMX Music; ESPN Classic; ESPNews; Fox Sports 1; Golf Channel; GSN; HGTV; IFC; MTV Classic; NBCSN; Nick Jr.; Starz (multiplexed); Starz Encore; Syfy; Turner Classic Movies; VH1 Country; WE tv.
Pay Service 1
Pay Units: N.A.
Programming (via satellite): Cinemax; HBO (multiplexed); Showtime; Starz; Starz Encore; The Movie Channel.
Fee: $15.00 installation; $5.95 monthly (Starz/Encore), $9.95 monthly (Showtime or TMC), $10.00 monthly (Cinemax), $11.00 monthly (HBO).
Digital Pay Service 1
Pay Units: N.A.
Programming (via satellite): Cinemax (multiplexed); Flix; HBO (multiplexed); Showtime (multiplexed); The Movie Channel.
Video-On-Demand: No
Internet Service
Operational: Yes.
Broadband Service: Suddenlink High Speed Internet.
Fee: $99.99 installation; $24.95 monthly.
Telephone Service
None
Miles of Plant: 23.0 (coaxial); None (fiber optic).
Vice President, Corporate Finance: Michael Pflantz. General Manager: Sam Richardson. Chief Technician: Josh Kellburg. Marketing Director: Theresa Richardson.
Ownership: Cequel Communications Holdings I LLC (MSO).

Cable Systems—Idaho

OSBURN—Suddenlink Communications, 520 Maryville Centre Dr, Ste 300, St. Louis, MO 63141. Phones: 314-315-9400; 800-326-8206; 208-752-1151. Web Site: http://www.suddenlink.com. Also serves Cataldo, Elizabeth Park, Enaville, Kellogg, Kingston, Pinehurst, Silverton, Smelterville, Wallace & Wardner. ICA: ID0015.

TV Market Ranking: Outside TV Markets (Cataldo, Elizabeth Park, Enaville, Kellogg, Kingston, OSBURN, Pinehurst, Silverton, Smelterville, Wallace, Wardner). Franchise award date: December 1, 1953. Franchise expiration date: N.A. Began: December 1, 1953.

Channel capacity: N.A. Channels available but not in use: N.A.

Basic Service
Subscribers: 1,670.
Programming (received off-air): KAYU-TV (FOX, This TV) Spokane; KHQ-TV (NBC) Spokane; KREM (CBS, TheCoolTV) Spokane; KSPS-TV (PBS) Spokane; KUID-TV (PBS) Moscow; KXLY-TV (ABC, MeTV) Spokane; allband FM.
Programming (via satellite): A&E; AMC; Animal Planet; Cartoon Network; CNBC; CNN; Comedy Central; C-SPAN; Discovery Channel; Disney Channel; Disney XD; E! HD; ESPN; ESPN2; EWTN Global Catholic Network; Fox News Channel; Freeform; FX; Great American Country; HGTV; History; HLN; Lifetime; MTV; Nickelodeon; Northwest Cable News; Outdoor Channel; QVC; Spike TV; Syfy; TBS; The Weather Channel; TLC; TNT; Trinity Broadcasting Network (TBN); TV Land; USA Network; VH1; WGN America.
Fee: $24.95 monthly.

Digital Basic Service
Subscribers: N.A.
Programming (via satellite): BBC America; Bravo; Discovery Kids Channel; DMX Music; ESPN Classic; ESPNews; Fox Sports 1; Golf Channel; GSN; MTV Classic; NBCSN; Nick Jr.; VH1 Country; WE tv.

Pay Service 1
Pay Units: N.A.
Programming (via satellite): Cinemax; HBO; Showtime; Starz; Starz Encore; The Movie Channel.
Fee: $5.95 monthly (Starz/Encore), $9.95 monthly (Showtime or TMC), $10.00 monthly (Cinemax), $11.00 monthly (HBO).

Digital Pay Service 1
Pay Units: N.A.
Programming (via satellite): Cinemax (multiplexed); Flix; HBO (multiplexed); IFC; Showtime (multiplexed); Starz Encore (multiplexed); The Movie Channel (multiplexed); Turner Classic Movies.

Video-On-Demand: No

Pay-Per-View
Special events (delivered digitally).

Internet Service
Operational: Yes. Began: January 1, 2002.
Subscribers: 319.
Broadband Service: Suddenlink High Speed Internet.
Fee: $99.99 installation; $24.95 monthly; $10.00 modem lease.

Telephone Service
None
Miles of Plant: 150.0 (coaxial); None (fiber optic). Homes passed: 6,970.
Senior Vice President, Corporate Finance: Michael Pflantz. General Manager: Sam Richardson. Chief Technician: Josh Kellberg. Marketing Director: Teresa Richardson.
Ownership: Cequel Communications Holdings I LLC (MSO).

POCATELLO—Cable One, 204 West Alameda Rd, Pocatello, ID 83201-4463. Phone: 208-232-1784. Web Site: http://www.cableone.net. Also serves American Falls, Bannock County, Chubbock & Inkom. ICA: ID0004.

TV Market Ranking: Below 100 (American Falls, Bannock County, Chubbock, Inkom, POCATELLO). Franchise award date: January 1, 1954. Franchise expiration date: N.A. Began: January 1, 1954.

Channel capacity: N.A. Channels available but not in use: N.A.

Basic Service
Subscribers: 4,938.
Programming (received off-air): KIDK (CBS, FOX, MNT) Idaho Falls; KIFI-TV (ABC, CW, UniMas) Idaho Falls; KISU-TV (PBS) Pocatello; KPVI-DT (Antenna TV, NBC, This TV) Pocatello; KVUI (MeTV) Pocatello; 14 FMs.
Programming (via microwave): KBYU-TV (PBS) Provo; KSL-TV (NBC) Salt Lake City.
Programming (via satellite): Cartoon Network; Disney Channel; ION Television; Pop; QVC.
Fee: $90.00 installation; $35.00 monthly.

Expanded Basic Service 1
Subscribers: N.A.
Programming (via satellite): A&E; AMC; Animal Planet; Bravo; CMT; CNBC; CNN; Comedy Central; C-SPAN; C-SPAN 2; Discovery Channel; E! HD; ESPN; ESPN2; EVINE Live; Fox News Channel; Freeform; FX; HGTV; History; HLN; Jewelry Television; Lifetime; MSNBC; MTV; Nickelodeon; Root Sports Rocky Mountain; Spike TV; Syfy; TBS; Telemundo; The Weather Channel; TLC; TNT; Travel Channel; Turner Classic Movies; TV Land; Univision Studios; USA Network; VH1.

Digital Basic Service
Subscribers: N.A.
Programming (via satellite): 3ABN; Boomerang; BYUtv; Discovery Digital Networks; Disney XD; ESPN Classic; ESPNews; FamilyNet; FOX College Sports Central; FOX College Sports Pacific; Fox Sports 1; Fox Sports 2; FXM; FYI; Golf Channel; GSN; Hallmark Channel; History International; HITS (Headend In The Sky); INSP; National Geographic Channel; Outdoor Channel; TNT HD; Trinity Broadcasting Network (TBN); truTV; Universal HD.

Digital Pay Service 1
Pay Units: N.A.
Programming (via satellite): Cinemax (multiplexed); Flix; HBO (multiplexed); Showtime (multiplexed); Showtime HD; Starz; Starz Encore (multiplexed); Sundance TV; The Movie Channel (multiplexed); The Movie Channel HD.
Fee: $15.15 monthly (Showtime/Showtime HD), $16.95 monthly (HBO).

Video-On-Demand: No

Pay-Per-View
iN Demand; Pleasure (delivered digitally); SexSee (delivered digitally); Juicy (delivered digitally); VaVoom (delivered digitally); ESPN Now (delivered digitally); ESPN (delivered digitally).

Internet Service
Operational: Yes. Began: December 31, 2001.
Broadband Service: CableONE.net.
Fee: $75.00 installation; $43.00 monthly; $5.00 modem lease.

Telephone Service
Digital: Operational
Fee: $39.95 monthly
Miles of Plant: 277.0 (coaxial); None (fiber optic). Homes passed: 29,817.

Communications Daily
Warren Communications News

Get the industry standard FREE —
For a no-obligation trial call 800-771-9202 or visit www.warren-news.com

---

Vice President: Patrick A. Dolohanty. General Manager: Judy Drennen. Chief Technician: Neil Ransbottom. Marketing Director: Nadine Singleton.
Ownership: Cable ONE Inc. (MSO).

PRESTON—Formerly served by Direct Communications. Now served by Silver Star Communications, SODA SPRINGS, ID [ID0022]. ICA: ID0094.

PRICHARD—Formerly served by Rapid Cable. No longer in operation. ICA: ID0083.

RICHFIELD—Formerly served by WDB Communications. No longer in operation. ICA: ID0084.

RIGGINS—Formerly served by Elk River TV Cable Co. No longer in operation. ICA: ID0037.

SALMON—Custer Telephone Broadband Services, 400 Shoup St, Salmon, ID 83467. Phone: 208-756-4111. Web Site: http://www.custertel.net. ICA: ID0098.

TV Market Ranking: Outside TV Markets (SALMON). Franchise award date: N.A. Franchise expiration date: N.A. Began: December 1, 2005.

Channel capacity: N.A. Channels available but not in use: N.A.

Basic Service
Subscribers: 326.
Programming (received off-air): KECI-TV (MeTV, Movies!, NBC, This TV) Missoula; KIDK (CBS, FOX, MNT) Idaho Falls; KIFI-TV (ABC, CW, UniMas) Idaho Falls; KISU-TV (PBS) Pocatello.
Programming (via satellite): A&E; AMC; Animal Planet; Bravo; BYUtv; Cartoon Network; CMT; CNBC; CNN; Comedy Central; C-SPAN; C-SPAN 2; CW PLUS; Discovery Channel; Disney Channel; ESPN; ESPN2; Food Network; Fox News Channel; Freeform; FX; Hallmark Channel; HGTV; History; HLN; ION Television; Lifetime; MSNBC; MTV; Nickelodeon; Pop; QVC; Root Sports Rocky Mountain; Spike TV; Syfy; TBS; The Weather Channel; TLC; TNT; Travel Channel; Turner Classic Movies; TV Land; USA Network; VH1.
Programming (via translator): KSL-TV (NBC) Salt Lake City.
Fee: $39.95 monthly.

Digital Basic Service
Subscribers: N.A.
Programming (via satellite): Discovery Digital Networks; Disney XD; DMX Music; ESPN Classic; ESPNews; Fox Sports 1; FXM; FYI; Golf Channel; History International; National Geographic Channel; Outdoor Channel.

Digital Pay Service 1
Pay Units: N.A.
Programming (via satellite): Cinemax (multiplexed); HBO (multiplexed); Starz (multiplexed); Starz Encore (multiplexed).
Fee: $9.95 monthly (Starz or Encore), $11.95 monthly (Cinemax), $14.95 monthly (HBO).

Pay-Per-View
iN DEMAND (delivered digitally).

Internet Service
Operational: Yes.
Fee: $24.95-$59.95 monthly; $5.00 modem lease.

Telephone Service
Digital: Operational
General Manager: Dennis L. Thornock.
Ownership: Custer Telephone Cooperative Inc. (MSO).

SANDPOINT—Northland Cable Television, 509 North 5th Ave, Ste B, Sandpoint, ID 83864. Phones: 888-667-8452; 208-263-4070. Fax: 208-263-1713. E-mail: sandpoint@northlandcabletv.com. Web Site: http://www.yournorthland.com. Also serves Bonner County (portions), Dover, Kootenai, Ponderay & Sandpoint (unincorporated areas). ICA: ID0012.

TV Market Ranking: Outside TV Markets (Bonner County (portions), Dover, Kootenai, Ponderay, SANDPOINT, Sandpoint (unincorporated areas)). Franchise award date: April 1, 1974. Franchise expiration date: N.A. Began: May 1, 1975.

Channel capacity: N.A. Channels available but not in use: N.A.

Basic Service
Subscribers: 1,003.
Programming (received off-air): KAYU-TV (FOX, This TV) Spokane; KCDT (PBS) Coeur d'Alene; KHQ-TV (NBC) Spokane; KQUP (IND) Pullman; KREM (CBS, TheCoolTV) Spokane; KSPS-TV (PBS) Spokane; KXLY-TV (ABC, MeTV) Spokane.
Programming (via satellite): A&E; Animal Planet; Cartoon Network; CNBC; CNN; Comedy Central; C-SPAN; CW PLUS; Discovery Channel; ESPN; ESPN2; Food Network; Fox News Channel; FXM; Great American Country; Hallmark Channel; HGTV; History; HLN; Lifetime; National Geographic Channel; Nickelodeon; Northwest Cable News; Outdoor Channel; QVC; Syfy; TBS; The Weather Channel; TLC; TNT; Travel Channel; Trinity Broadcasting Network (TBN); Turner Classic Movies; TV Land; USA Network; VH1; WGN America.
Fee: $60.00 installation; $47.64 monthly.

Digital Basic Service
Subscribers: N.A.
Programming (via satellite): BBC America; Bloomberg Television; Bravo; Destination America; Discovery Kids Channel; Discovery Life Channel; DMX Music; ESPNews; Fox Sports 1; Golf Channel; IFC; Investigation Discovery; OWN: Oprah Winfrey Network; WE tv.

Pay Service 1
Pay Units: N.A.
Programming (via satellite): Cinemax; HBO.
Fee: $20.00 installation; $14.00 monthly (HBO).

Digital Pay Service 1
Pay Units: N.A.
Programming (via satellite): Cinemax (multiplexed); Flix; HBO (multiplexed); Showtime (multiplexed); Starz (multiplexed); Starz Encore (multiplexed); The Movie Channel (multiplexed).

2017 Edition
D-183

Idaho—Cable Systems

Fee: $14.75 monthly (Cinemax, HBO, Starz/Encore or Showtime/TMC/Flix).
Video-On-Demand: Yes
Pay-Per-View
iN DEMAND (delivered digitally); Fresh (delivered digitally); Playboy TV (delivered digitally); Hot Choice (delivered digitally).
Internet Service
Operational: Yes.
Fee: $42.99 monthly.
Telephone Service
Digital: Operational
Miles of Plant: 76.0 (coaxial); None (fiber optic). Homes passed: 4,000.
Executive Vice President: Richard I. Clark. General Manager: Mary Strickley. Chief Technician: Justin Custis.
Ownership: Northland Communications Corp. (MSO).

SHOSHONE—Formerly served by Millennium Digital Media. Now served by Cable One, TWIN FALLS, ID [ID0088]. ICA: ID0031.

SODA SPRINGS—Silver Star Communications, 132 South Main St, PO Box 226, Freedom, WY 83276. Phone: 208-909-5000. Fax: 208-909-5001. E-mail: silverstar@silverstar.com. Web Site: http://www.silverstar.com. Also serves Bancroft, Downey, Fish Haven, Georgetown, Grace, Lava Hot Springs, McCammon, Montpelier, Paris, Preston & St. Charles, ID; Garden City, UT. ICA: ID0022.
TV Market Ranking: 48 (Preston); Below 100 (Bancroft, Garden City, Lava Hot Springs, McCammon, St. Charles, Fish Haven, Preston); Outside TV Markets (Downey, Georgetown, Grace, Montpelier, Paris, SODA SPRINGS). Franchise award date: N.A. Franchise expiration date: N.A. Began: January 1, 1955.
Channel capacity: 65 (not 2-way capable). Channels available but not in use: N.A.
Basic Service
Subscribers: 1,401.
Programming (via satellite): BYUtv; CNN; Discovery Channel; Fox News Channel; Lifetime; Pop; QVC; The Weather Channel; TLC; Travel Channel; WGN America.
Programming (via translator): KBYU-TV (PBS) Provo; KIDK (CBS, FOX, MNT) Idaho Falls; KIFI-TV (ABC, CW, UniMas) Idaho Falls; KISU-TV (PBS) Pocatello; KJZZ-TV (IND) Salt Lake City; KPNZ (Estrella TV) Ogden; KPVI-DT (Antenna TV, NBC, This TV) Pocatello; KSL-TV (NBC) Salt Lake City; KTVX (ABC, MeTV) Salt Lake City; KUCW (CW, Movies!, The Country Network) Ogden; KUTV (CBS, This TV) Salt Lake City; KVUI (MeTV) Pocatello.
Fee: $28.50 monthly.
Expanded Basic Service 1
Subscribers: 1,243.
Programming (via satellite): A&E; AMC; Animal Planet; BBC America; Boomerang; Bravo; Cartoon Network; CMT; CNBC; Comedy Central; C-SPAN; Disney Channel; DIY Network; E! HD; ESPN; ESPN Classic; ESPN2; Food Network; Fox Sports 1; Freeform; FX; FXM; Great American Country; GSN; Hallmark Channel; HGTV; History; HLN; MoviePlex; MSNBC; MTV; National Geographic Channel; NBCSN; NFL Network; Nickelodeon; Outdoor Channel; OWN: Oprah Winfrey Network; RFD-TV; Root Sports Rocky Mountain; Spike TV; Syfy; TBS; TNT; truTV; Turner Classic Movies; TV Land; UP; USA Network; VH1; WE tv.
Fee: $18.95 monthly.
Video-On-Demand: No

Internet Service
Operational: Yes.
Fee: $23.95 monthly.
Telephone Service
Digital: Operational
Fee: $29.95 monthly
Miles of Plant: 92.0 (coaxial); None (fiber optic).
General Manager: Jeremy Smith. Marketing Director: Brigham Griffin.
Ownership: Silver Star Communications (MSO).

SPIRIT LAKE—Formerly served by Cebridge Connections. Now served by Suddenlink Communications, SPIRIT LAKE, ID [ID0092]. ICA: ID0050.

SPIRIT LAKE—Suddenlink Communications, 520 Maryville Centre Dr, Ste 300, St. Louis, MO 63141. Phones: 800-326-8206; 314-315-9400; 208-752-1151. Web Site: http://www.suddenlink.com. Also serves Twin Lakes. ICA: ID0092.
TV Market Ranking: 76 (SPIRIT LAKE); Below 100 (Twin Lakes).
Channel capacity: N.A. Channels available but not in use: N.A.
Basic Service
Subscribers: 297.
Programming (received off-air): KAYU-TV (FOX, This TV) Spokane; KHQ-TV (NBC) Spokane; KREM (CBS, TheCoolTV) Spokane; KSKN (CW) Spokane; KSPS-TV (PBS) Spokane; KUID-TV (PBS) Moscow; KXLY-TV (ABC, MeTV) Spokane.
Programming (via satellite): A&E; Animal Planet; Cartoon Network; CNBC; CNN; Comedy Central; C-SPAN; Discovery Channel; Disney Channel; E! HD; ESPN; ESPN2; Food Network; Fox News Channel; Freeform; FX; Golf Channel; Great American Country; HGTV; History; HLN; INSP; Lifetime; MTV; Nickelodeon; Northwest Cable News; Outdoor Channel; QVC; Spike TV; Syfy; TBS; The Weather Channel; TLC; TNT; Travel Channel; Turner Classic Movies; TV Land; USA Network; VH1; WGN America.
Fee: $24.95 monthly.
Digital Basic Service
Subscribers: N.A.
Programming (via satellite): BBC America; Bravo; Cloo; Discovery Digital Networks; Disney XD; DMX Music; ESPN Classic; ESPNews; Fox Sports 1; Fuse; FYI; GSN; History International; IFC; LMN; NBCSN; Nick Jr.; TeenNick; WE tv.
Pay Service 1
Pay Units: N.A.
Programming (via satellite): HBO; Showtime; The Movie Channel.
Fee: $10.00 monthly (Showtime or TMC), $11.00 monthly (HBO).
Digital Pay Service 1
Pay Units: N.A.
Programming (via satellite): Cinemax (multiplexed); Flix; HBO (multiplexed); Showtime (multiplexed); Starz (multiplexed); Starz Encore (multiplexed); The Movie Channel (multiplexed).
Video-On-Demand: No
Pay-Per-View
iN DEMAND (delivered digitally); Playboy TV (delivered digitally).
Internet Service
Operational: Yes.
Broadband Service: Suddenlink High Speed Internet.
Telephone Service
Digital: Operational
Miles of Plant: 131.0 (coaxial); None (fiber optic). Homes passed: 1,484.

Vice President, Corporate Finance: Michael Pflantz. General Manager: Sam Richardson. Marketing Director: Teresa Richardson. Chief Technician: Josh Kellberg.
Ownership: Cequel Communications Holdings I LLC (MSO).

ST. MARIES—Suddenlink Communications, 520 Maryville Centre Dr, Ste 300, St. Louis, MO 63141. Phones: 314-315-9400; 800-326-8206; 208-752-1151. Web Site: http://www.suddenlink.com. ICA: ID0085.
TV Market Ranking: Outside TV Markets (ST. MARIES). Franchise award date: N.A. Franchise expiration date: N.A. Began: March 1, 1959.
Channel capacity: N.A. Channels available but not in use: N.A.
Basic Service
Subscribers: 143. Commercial subscribers: 46.
Programming (received off-air): KAYU-TV (FOX, This TV) Spokane; KHQ-TV (NBC) Spokane; KREM (CBS, TheCoolTV) Spokane; KSKN (CW) Spokane; KSPS-TV (PBS) Spokane; KXLY-TV (ABC, MeTV) Spokane; allband FM.
Programming (via satellite): C-SPAN; C-SPAN 2; Northwest Cable News; WGN America.
Fee: $24.95 monthly.
Expanded Basic Service 1
Subscribers: N.A.
Programming (via satellite): A&E; AMC; Cartoon Network; CNBC; CNN; Comedy Central; Discovery Channel; Disney Channel; Disney XD; E! HD; ESPN; ESPN2; Fox News Channel; Freeform; Great American Country; History; HLN; Lifetime; MSNBC; MTV; Nickelodeon; Outdoor Channel; QVC; Spike TV; Syfy; TBS; The Weather Channel; TLC; TNT; USA Network; VH1.
Fee: $39.95 installation; $16.04 monthly.
Digital Basic Service
Subscribers: N.A.
Programming (via satellite): BBC America; Bravo; Cloo; Discovery Digital Networks; DMX Music; ESPN Classic; ESPNews; Fox Sports 1; Fuse; FYI; Golf Channel; GSN; HGTV; History International; IFC; LMN; NBCSN; Nick Jr.; TeenNick; Turner Classic Movies; WE tv.
Pay Service 1
Pay Units: N.A.
Programming (via satellite): Cinemax; HBO; Showtime; Starz; Starz Encore; The Movie Channel.
Fee: $15.00 installation; $5.95 monthly (Starz/Encore), $9.95 monthly (Showtime or TMC), $10.00 monthly (Cinemax), $11.00 monthly (HBO).
Digital Pay Service 1
Pay Units: N.A.
Programming (via satellite): Cinemax (multiplexed); Flix; HBO (multiplexed); Showtime (multiplexed); Starz (multiplexed); Starz Encore (multiplexed); The Movie Channel (multiplexed).
Video-On-Demand: No
Pay-Per-View
iN DEMAND (delivered digitally); Playboy TV (delivered digitally).
Internet Service
Operational: Yes.
Broadband Service: Suddenlink High Speed Internet.
Fee: $99.99 installation; $24.95 monthly.
Telephone Service
None
Miles of Plant: 50.0 (coaxial); None (fiber optic). Homes passed: 1,729.
Vice President, Corporate Finance: Michael Pflantz. General Manager: Sam Richardson.

Chief Technician: Josh Kellberg. Marketing Director: Teresa Richardson.
Ownership: Cequel Communications Holdings I LLC (MSO).

SUN VALLEY—Cox Communications, 6205 Peachtree Dunwoody Rd, 12th Floor, Atlanta, GA 30328. Phone: 404-269-6590. Web Site: http://www.cox.com. Also serves Bellevue, Blaine County, Hailey & Ketchum. ICA: ID0079.
TV Market Ranking: Below 100 (Bellevue, Blaine County (portions), Hailey, Ketchum, SUN VALLEY); Outside TV Markets (Blaine County (portions)). Franchise award date: N.A. Franchise expiration date: N.A. Began: January 1, 1954.
Channel capacity: N.A. Channels available but not in use: N.A.
Basic Service
Subscribers: 8,421. Commercial subscribers: 278.
Programming (received off-air): KIPT (PBS) Twin Falls; KMVT (CBS, CW) Twin Falls; KSAW-LD (ABC, Escape) Twin Falls; KXTF (This TV) Twin Falls; allband FM.
Programming (via satellite): C-SPAN; C-SPAN 2; CW PLUS; HLN; Pop; QVC; TBS; The Weather Channel; TLC; Travel Channel; WGN America.
Fee: $38.00 installation; $21.99 monthly.
Expanded Basic Service 1
Subscribers: N.A.
Programming (via satellite): A&E; AMC; Animal Planet; Bravo; Cartoon Network; CMT; CNBC; CNN; Comedy Central; C-SPAN 2; Discovery Channel; Disney Channel; E! HD; ESPN; ESPN2; Food Network; Fox News Channel; Fox Sports 1; Freeform; FX; HGTV; History; Lifetime; MSNBC; MTV; NBCSN; Nickelodeon; Root Sports Rocky Mountain; Spike TV; Syfy; TNT; truTV; Turner Classic Movies; TV Land; Univision; Univision Studios; USA Network; VH1.
Fee: $26.29 monthly.
Digital Basic Service
Subscribers: N.A.
Programming (via satellite): A&E HD; Animal Planet HD; Bandamax; BBC America; Bloomberg Television; Bravo HD; Canal Sur; Cine Mexicano; Cinelatino; CMT; CNBC HD+; CNN en Espanol; CNN HD; Cooking Channel; De Pelicula; De Pelicula Clasico; Destination America; Discovery Channel HD; Discovery Kids Channel; Discovery Life Channel; Disney XD; DIY Network; Enlace USA; ESPN Classic; ESPN Deportes; ESPN HD; ESPN2 HD; ESPNews; ESPNU; Food Network HD; Fox Deportes; Fox Sports 2; FSN HD; Fuse; FYI; Golf Channel; GolTV; GSN; Hallmark Channel; HD Theater; HGTV HD; History en Espanol; History HD; History International; IFC; Investigation Discovery; Lifetime HD; LMN; MC; MTV Classic; MTV Hits; MTV Jams; MTV Live; Nat Geo WILD; National Geographic Channel; National Geographic Channel HD; NBA TV; NBC Universo; NFL Network; NFL Network HD; NHL Network; Nick Jr.; Nicktoons; NickToons en Espanol; OWN: Oprah Winfrey Network; Oxygen; Ritmoson; Science Channel; Science HD; Starz Encore (multiplexed); Sundance TV; Syfy HD; TBS HD; TeenNick; Telehit; Telemundo; Tennis Channel; TLC HD; TNT HD; Tr3s; Travel Channel HD; Trinity Broadcasting Network (TBN); UniMas; Universal HD; Univision; Univision Studios; USA Network HD; Versus HD; VideoRola.
Digital Pay Service 1
Pay Units: N.A.
Programming (via satellite): Cinemax (multiplexed); Cinemax HD; Flix; HBO (multiplexed); HBO HD; HBO Latino; Showtime

Cable Systems—Idaho

(multiplexed); Showtime HD; Starz; Starz HD; The Movie Channel (multiplexed).
Fee: $12.99 monthly (Cinemax, HBO, Starz or Showtime/TMC/Flix.

Video-On-Demand: No

Pay-Per-View
NHL Center Ice (delivered digitally); MLB Extra Innings (delivered digitally); MLS Direct Kick (delivered digitally); NBA League Pass (delivered digitally); Club Jenna (delivered digitally); iN DEMAND (delivered digitally); Playboy TV (delivered digitally); Hot Choice (delivered digitally); Fresh (delivered digitally); ESPN Now (delivered digitally).

Internet Service
Operational: Yes. Began: December 31, 2000.
Subscribers: 7,474.
Broadband Service: Cox High Speed Internet.
Fee: $29.99-$56.99 monthly.

Telephone Service
Digital: Operational
Subscribers: 3,186.
Fee: $10.35-$49.95 monthly

Miles of Plant: 457.0 (coaxial); 131.0 (fiber optic). Homes passed: 16,637.
Vice President: Percy Kick. Vice President, Public & Government Affairs: Kristin Peck. Vice President, Tax: Mary Vickers. Operations Director: Dan Wherry. General Manager: Guy Cherp.
Ownership: Cox Communications Inc. (MSO).

TROY—Formerly served by Elk River TV Cable Co. No longer in operation. ICA: ID0044.

TWIN FALLS—Cable One, 261 Eastland Dr, Twin Falls, ID 83301. Phone: 208-733-6230. Fax: 208-733-6296. E-mail: russ.young@cableone.net. Web Site: http://www.cableone.net. Also serves Buhl, Burley, Cassia County (northern portion), Filer, Gooding, Gooding County (portions), Hagerman, Hansen, Heyburn, Jerome, Kimberly, Minidoka County (southern portion), Paul, Rupert, Shoshone, Twin Falls County (portions) & Wendell. ICA: ID0088.
TV Market Ranking: Below 100 (Buhl, Burley, Filer, Gooding, Gooding County (portions), Hagerman, Hansen, Jerome, Kimberly, Paul, Shoshone, TWIN FALLS, Twin Falls County (portions), Wendell); Outside TV Markets (Gooding County (portions), Heyburn, Rupert). Franchise award date: January 1, 1954. Franchise expiration date: N.A. Began: N.A.
Channel capacity: N.A. Channels available but not in use: N.A.

Basic Service
Subscribers: 7,900.
Programming (received off-air): KIPT (PBS) Twin Falls; KIVI-TV (ABC, Escape, FOX) Nampa; KMVT (CBS, CW) Twin Falls; KTRV-TV (MeTV, MNT, Movies!, This TV) Nampa; KXTF (This TV) Twin Falls.
Programming (via satellite): A&E; AMC; Animal Planet; Bravo; Cartoon Network; CMT; CNBC; CNN; Comedy Central; C-SPAN; C-SPAN 2; Discovery Channel; Disney Channel; E! HD; ESPN; ESPN Classic; ESPN2; EVINE Live; Food Network; Fox News Channel; Freeform; FX; HGTV; History; HLN; INSP; Lifetime; MSNBC; MTV; Nickelodeon; Pop; QVC; Root Sports Rocky Mountain; Spike TV; Syfy; TBS; Telemundo; The Weather Channel; TLC; TNT; Travel Channel; Turner Classic Movies; TV Land; UniMas; Univision; Univision Studios; USA Network; VH1.
Programming (via translator): KSL-TV (NBC) Salt Lake City.
Fee: $90.00 installation; $20.00 monthly.

Digital Basic Service
Subscribers: N.A.
Programming (via satellite): Boomerang; Discovery Digital Networks; Disney XD; ESPN Classic; ESPNews; FOX College Sports Central; FOX College Sports Pacific; Fox Sports 1; Fox Sports 2; FXM; FYI; Golf Channel; Great American Country; GSN; Hallmark Channel; History; History International; INSP; MC (multiplexed); National Geographic Channel; Outdoor Channel; Trinity Broadcasting Network (TBN); truTV.

Digital Expanded Basic Service
Subscribers: N.A.
Programming (via satellite): HITS (Headend In The Sky).
Fee: $4.00 installation; $4.00 monthly.

Digital Pay Service 1
Pay Units: N.A.
Programming (via satellite): Cinemax (multiplexed); HBO (multiplexed); Showtime (multiplexed); Starz (multiplexed); Starz Encore (multiplexed); The Movie Channel (multiplexed).

Video-On-Demand: No

Pay-Per-View
ETC (delivered digitally); iN DEMAND; Playboy TV (delivered digitally); Fresh (delivered digitally); Shorteez (delivered digitally).

Internet Service
Operational: Yes. Began: April 1, 2002.
Subscribers: 12,259.
Broadband Service: CableONE.net.
Fee: $75.00 installation; $43.00 monthly; $5.00 modem lease.

Telephone Service
Analog: Not Operational
Digital: Operational
Subscribers: 5,419.
Fee: $39.95 monthly

Miles of Plant: 1,314.0 (coaxial); 382.0 (fiber optic). Homes passed: 40,350.
Vice President: Patrick A. Dolohanty. General Manager: Russ Young. Marketing Director: Mark Wolfe. Customer Service Manager: Eddy Cordova.
Ownership: Cable ONE Inc. (MSO).

VICTOR—Silver Star Broadband, 132 South Main St, Soda Springs, ID 83276. Phone: 208-909-5000. Fax: 208-909-5001. Web Site: http://www.silverstar.com. Also serves Driggs. ICA: ID0062.
TV Market Ranking: Below 100 (Driggs, VICTOR).
Channel capacity: 53 (not 2-way capable). Channels available but not in use: N.A.

Basic Service
Subscribers: 70.
Programming (via satellite): A&E; Cartoon Network; CNBC; CNN; Discovery Channel; Disney Channel; ESPN; Freeform; FX; HGTV; Spike TV; TBS; TNT; Turner Classic Movies; USA Network; WGN America.
Programming (via translator): KIDK (CBS, FOX, MNT) Idaho Falls; KIFI-TV (ABC, CW, UniMas) Idaho Falls; KISU-TV (PBS) Pocatello; KPVI-DT (Antenna TV, NBC, This TV) Pocatello.
Fee: $29.95 installation; $32.45 monthly.

Pay Service 1
Pay Units: N.A.
Programming (via satellite): HBO.
Fee: $10.00 installation; $9.00 monthly.

Video-On-Demand: No

Internet Service
Operational: Yes.

Telephone Service
Digital: Operational

Miles of Plant: 5.0 (coaxial); None (fiber optic). Homes passed: 440.
General Manager: Jeremy Smith. Marketing Director: Brigham Griffin.
Ownership: Silver Star Communications (MSO).; Direct Communications (MSO).

WEISER—Cable One. Now served by BOISE, ID [ID0001]. ICA: ID0018.

WORLEY—Formerly served by Elk River TV Cable Co. No longer in operation. ICA: ID0046.

ILLINOIS

Total Systems: 151
Total Communities Served: 1,338
Franchises Not Yet Operating: 0
Applications Pending: 0
Communities with Applications: 0
Number of Basic Subscribers: 2,143,203
Number of Expanded Basic Subscribers: 12,026
Number of Pay Units: 11,284

Top 100 Markets Represented: St. Louis, MO (11); Chicago (3); Davenport, IA-Rock Island-Moline, IL (60); Springfield-Decatur-Champaign (64); Cape Girardeau, MO-Paducah, KY-Harrisburg, IL (69); Peoria (83); Evansville, IN (86); Rockford-Freeport (97).

For a list of cable communities in this section, see the Cable Community Index located in the back of Cable Volume 2.
For explanation of terms used in cable system listings, see p. D-11.

ABINGDON—Mediacom. Now served by ELMWOOD, IL [IL0205]. ICA: IL0186.

ADAIR (unincorporated areas)—Formerly served by CableDirect. No longer in operation. ICA: IL0439.

ADDIEVILLE—Charter Communications. Now served by ST. LOUIS, MO [MO0009]. ICA: IL0633.

ALBION—NewWave Communications. Now served by McLEANSBORO, IL [IL0177]. ICA: IL0457.

ALEXANDER COUNTY (portions)—Zito Media, 102 S Main St, PO Box 665, Coudersport, PA 16915. Phones: 814-260-9055; 800-365-6988. E-mail: info@zitomedia.com. Web Site: http://www.zitomedia.com. Also serves East Cape Girardeau, McClure, Pulaski, Pulaski County, Thebes & Ullin. ICA: IL0458.
TV Market Ranking: 69 (ALEXANDER COUNTY (PORTIONS), East Cape Girardeau, McClure, Pulaski, Pulaski County, Thebes, Ullin).
Channel capacity: N.A. Channels available but not in use: N.A.
Basic Service
Subscribers: 66.
Programming (received off-air): KBSI (FOX) Cape Girardeau; KFVS-TV (CBS, CW, MeTV) Cape Girardeau; WDKA (MNT, The Country Network) Paducah; WKPD (PBS) Paducah; WPSD-TV (Antenna TV, NBC) Paducah; WSIL-TV (ABC) Harrisburg; WTCT (IND) Marion.
Programming (via satellite): A&E; AMC; Animal Planet; BET; Cartoon Network; CNN; Comedy Central; C-SPAN; Discovery Channel; Disney Channel; Disney XD; E! HD; ESPN; ESPN2; Fox News Channel; Freeform; Fuse; FX; Great American Country; HGTV; History; HLN; Lifetime; Outdoor Channel; QVC; TBS; The Weather Channel; TLC; TNT; Turner Classic Movies; USA Network; WGN America.
Fee: $49.95 installation; $47.00 monthly.
Digital Basic Service
Subscribers: N.A.
Pay Service 1
Pay Units: N.A.
Programming (via satellite): HBO; Showtime; Starz Encore; The Movie Channel.
Internet Service
Operational: No.
Telephone Service
None
Miles of Plant: 5.0 (coaxial); None (fiber optic). Homes passed: 400.
President: James Rigas.
Ownership: Zito Media (MSO).

ALEXIS—Mediacom. Now served by GENESEO, IL [IL0170]. ICA: IL0302.

ALHAMBRA—Madison Communications. Now served by STAUNTON, IL [IL0171]. ICA: IL0367.

ALLERTON (village)—Clearvision Cable Systems Inc, 1785 US Rte 40, Greenup, IL 62428-3501. Phone: 217-923-5594. Fax: 217-923-5681. ICA: IL0699.
TV Market Ranking: Below 100 (ALLERTON (VILLAGE)).
Channel capacity: N.A. Channels available but not in use: N.A.
Basic Service
Subscribers: 15.
Fee: $47.95 monthly.
President: Michael Bauguss. Secretary: Gwyndolyn S. Bauguss.
Ownership: Clearvision Cable Systems Inc. (MSO).

ALPHA—Diverse Communications Inc., 246 N Division St, PO Box 117, Woodhull, IL 61490. Phone: 309-334-2150. Fax: 309-334-2989. E-mail: woodhulltel@yahoo.com. Web Site: http://www.woodhulltel.com. Also serves Ophiem & Woodhull. ICA: IL0459.
TV Market Ranking: 60 (ALPHA, Ophiem, Woodhull). Franchise award date: N.A. Franchise expiration date: N.A. Began: July 1, 1984.
Channel capacity: N.A. Channels available but not in use: N.A.
Basic Service
Subscribers: N.A.
Programming (received off-air): KIIN (PBS) Iowa City; KLJB (CW, FOX, MeTV) Davenport; KWQC-TV (NBC) Davenport; WHBF-TV (CBS) Rock Island; WQAD-TV (ABC, Antenna TV) Moline; WQPT-TV (PBS) Moline.
Programming (via satellite): QVC; WGN America.
Fee: $24.95 monthly.
Expanded Basic Service 1
Subscribers: N.A.
Programming (via satellite): A&E; AMC; Animal Planet; CMT; CNBC; CNN; Comcast SportsNet Chicago; Comedy Central; Discovery Channel; Disney Channel; ESPN; ESPN Classic; ESPN2; ESPNews; Fox News Channel; FOX Sports Midwest; Freeform; FX; HGTV; History; HLN; Lifetime; MSNBC; MTV; National Geographic Channel; Nickelodeon; Spike TV; Syfy; TBS; The Weather Channel; TLC; TNT; Travel Channel; TV Land; USA Network; VH1.
Fee: $28.05 monthly.
Pay Service 1
Pay Units: N.A.
Programming (via satellite): Cinemax; HBO.
Fee: $40.00 installation; $13.00 monthly (Cinemax), $17.00 monthly (HBO).

Internet Service
Operational: No, DSL & dial-up.
Telephone Service
Analog: Operational
Miles of Plant: 22.0 (coaxial); None (fiber optic).
General Manager: George Wirt. Chief Technician: Jeremy Hand.
Ownership: Diverse Communications Inc.

ALSEY TWP.—Formerly served by Longview Communications. No longer in operation. ICA: IL0454.

ALTAMONT—Mediacom, 4290 Blue Stem Rd, PO Box 288, Charleston, IL 61920. Phone: 217-348-5533. Fax: 217-345-7074. Web Site: http://www.mediacomcable.com. Also serves Effingham County (portions), Fayette County (portions) & St. Elmo. ICA: IL0160.
TV Market Ranking: Outside TV Markets (ALTAMONT, Effingham County (portions), Fayette County (portions), St. Elmo). Franchise award date: N.A. Franchise expiration date: N.A. Began: January 1, 1968.
Channel capacity: N.A. Channels available but not in use: N.A.
Basic Service
Subscribers: 643.
Programming (received off-air): KMOV (CBS) St. Louis; KPLR-TV (CW, This TV) St. Louis; KSDK (Bounce TV, NBC) St. Louis; WAND (NBC) Decatur; WBUI (CW, This TV) Decatur; WCCU (FOX, MNT) Urbana; WCIA (CBS, MNT) Champaign; WCIX (CBS, MNT) Springfield; WEIU-TV (PBS) Charleston; WICS (ABC, The Country Network) Springfield; WILL-TV (PBS) Urbana; WPXS (IND) Mount Vernon; WSIU-TV (PBS) Carbondale; WTHI-TV (CBS, FOX) Terre Haute; WTWO (NBC) Terre Haute; allband FM.
Programming (via satellite): C-SPAN; QVC; WGN America.
Fee: $45.00 installation; $43.00 monthly.
Expanded Basic Service 1
Subscribers: N.A.
Programming (via satellite): A&E; AMC; Animal Planet; Cartoon Network; CMT; CNBC; CNN; Comedy Central; C-SPAN 2; Discovery Channel; Disney Channel; E! HD; ESPN; ESPN Classic; ESPN2; EVINE Live; EWTN Global Catholic Network; Food Network; Fox News Channel; Fox Sports 1; FOX Sports Midwest; Freeform; Fuse; FX; Hallmark Channel; HGTV; History; HLN; INSP; ION Television; Jewelry Television; Lifetime; LMN; MSNBC; MTV; Nickelodeon; Outdoor Channel; Pop; Spike TV; Syfy; TBS; The Weather Channel; TLC; TNT; Travel Channel; Trinity Broadcasting Network (TBN);

truTV; TV Land; USA Network; VH1; WE tv.
Fee: $34.00 monthly.
Digital Basic Service
Subscribers: N.A.
Programming (via satellite): AXS TV; BBC America; Bloomberg Television; Bravo; Cloo; CMT; Discovery Life Channel; ESPN HD; ESPN2 HD; ESPNews; FXM; FYI; Golf Channel; GSN; HD Theater; History; History International; IFC; ION Television; MC; MTV Classic; MTV Hits; MTV2; Nat Geo WILD; National Geographic Channel; NBCSN; Nick Jr.; Nicktoons; Qubo; Reelz; Science Channel; TeenNick; Turner Classic Movies; Universal HD.
Digital Expanded Basic Service
Subscribers: N.A.
Programming (via satellite): CBS Sports Network; ESPNU; FOX College Sports Central; FOX College Sports Pacific; Fox Sports 2; GolTV; Tennis Channel; TVG Network.
Fee: $3.95 monthly.
Digital Pay Service 1
Pay Units: N.A.
Programming (via satellite): Cinemax (multiplexed); HBO (multiplexed); HBO HD; Showtime (multiplexed); Showtime HD; Starz (multiplexed); Starz Encore (multiplexed); Starz HD; The Movie Channel (multiplexed); The Movie Channel HD.
Fee: $11.95 monthly (each).
Video-On-Demand: Yes
Pay-Per-View
iN DEMAND (delivered digitally); Playboy TV (delivered digitally); SexSee (delivered digitally); Juicy (delivered digitally); ESPN (delivered digitally); AXS TV (delivered digitally).
Internet Service
Operational: Yes.
Broadband Service: Mediacom High Speed Internet.
Fee: $59.95 installation; $40.95 monthly.
Telephone Service
Digital: Operational
Fee: $39.95 monthly
Miles of Plant: 38.0 (coaxial); None (fiber optic). Homes passed: 1,832.
General Manager: Todd Acker. Technical Operations Manager: Jerry Ferguson. Marketing Director: James Friske.
Ownership: Mediacom LLC (MSO).

ALTONA (village)—Mediacom. Now served by GENESEO, IL [IL0170]. ICA: IL0369.

AMBOY—Comcast Cable. Now served by MOUNT PROSPECT, IL [IL0036]. ICA: IL0689.

ANNA—NewWave Communications, One Montgomery Plaza, 4th Floor, Sikeston, MO 63801. Phone: 888-863-9928 (Customer service). Fax: 573-481-9809. E-mail: info@

D-186 TV & Cable Factbook No. 85

Cable Systems—Illinois

newwavecom.com. Web Site: http://www.newwavecom.com. Also serves Jonesboro & Union County (portions). ICA: IL0127.
TV Market Ranking: 69 (ANNA, Jonesboro, Union County (portions)). Franchise award date: N.A. Franchise expiration date: N.A. Began: December 15, 1977.
Channel capacity: N.A. Channels available but not in use: N.A.

Basic Service
Subscribers: 568. Commercial subscribers: 22.
Programming (received off-air): KBSI (FOX) Cape Girardeau; KFVS-TV (CBS, CW, MeTV) Cape Girardeau; WDKA (MNT, The Country Network) Paducah; WPSD-TV (Antenna TV, NBC) Paducah; WSIL-TV (ABC) Harrisburg; WSIU-TV (PBS) Carbondale; WTCT (IND) Marion.
Programming (via satellite): C-SPAN; QVC; WGN America.
Fee: $40.00 installation; $34.78 monthly; $.98 converter.

Expanded Basic Service 1
Subscribers: N.A.
Programming (via satellite): A&E; AMC; Animal Planet; Cartoon Network; CMT; CNBC; CNN; Comedy Central; Discovery Channel; Disney Channel; E! HD; ESPN; ESPN2; Food Network; Fox News Channel; Fox Sports 1; FOX Sports Midwest; Freeform; FX; HGTV; History; HLN; Lifetime; MSNBC; MTV; National Geographic Channel; Nickelodeon; Oxygen; Spike TV; Syfy; TBS; The Weather Channel; TLC; TNT; Travel Channel; truTV; TV Land; USA Network; VH1.
Fee: $24.80 monthly.

Digital Basic Service
Subscribers: N.A.
Programming (via satellite): BBC America; Bloomberg Television; Discovery Digital Networks; Disney XD; DIY Network; FYI; GSN; History International; IFC; MC; Nick 2; Nick Jr.; Nicktoons; Sundance TV; TeenNick; TV Guide Interactive Inc.; WE tv.

Digital Pay Service 1
Pay Units: N.A.
Programming (via satellite): Cinemax (multiplexed); Flix; HBO (multiplexed); LOGO; Showtime (multiplexed); Starz (multiplexed); Starz Encore (multiplexed); The Movie Channel (multiplexed).
Fee: $9.50 monthly (each).

Video-On-Demand: No

Pay-Per-View
iN DEMAND (delivered digitally); Pleasure (delivered digitally); ETC (delivered digitally).

Internet Service
Operational: Yes.
Subscribers: 342.
Fee: $40.00 installation; $31.99 monthly.

Telephone Service
Digital: Operational
Subscribers: 223.
Fee: $34.99 monthly
Miles of Plant: 66.0 (coaxial); None (fiber optic). Homes passed: 3,134.
Chief Financial Officer: Rod Siemers. General Manager: John Helmers.
Ownership: NewWave Communications LLC (MSO).

APOLLO ACRES—Mediacom. Now served by ROANOKE, IL [IL0068]. ICA: IL0340.

ARENZVILLE—Mediacom, 4290 Blue Stem Rd, PO Box 288, Charleston, IL 61920. Phone: 217-348-5533. Fax: 217-345-7074. Web Site: http://www.mediacomcable.com. ICA: IL0391.

TV Market Ranking: Outside TV Markets (ARENZVILLE). Franchise award date: N.A. Franchise expiration date: N.A. Began: March 1, 1984.
Channel capacity: N.A. Channels available but not in use: N.A.

Basic Service
Subscribers: 12.
Programming (received off-air): KHQA-TV (ABC, CBS) Hannibal; WAND (NBC) Decatur; WGEM-TV (CW, FOX, NBC) Quincy; WHOI (Comet) Peoria; WICS (ABC, The Country Network) Springfield; WRSP-TV (Antenna TV, FOX, MeTV) Springfield; WSEC (PBS) Jacksonville; WTVP (PBS) Peoria.
Programming (via satellite): A&E; CMT; CNN; C-SPAN; Discovery Channel; ESPN; ESPN2; Food Network; Fox Sports 1; Freeform; HGTV; History; Lifetime; Nickelodeon; Spike TV; Syfy; TBS; The Weather Channel; TNT; Travel Channel; truTV; Turner Classic Movies; USA Network; WGN America.
Fee: $45.00 installation; $69.95 monthly.

Pay Service 1
Pay Units: N.A.
Programming (via satellite): Cinemax.
Fee: $13.50 monthly.

Video-On-Demand: No

Internet Service
Operational: No.

Telephone Service
None
Miles of Plant: 4.0 (coaxial); 1.0 (fiber optic). Homes passed: 193.
General Manager: Todd Acker. Technical Operations Manager: Jerry Ferguson. Marketing Director: Jim Friske.
Ownership: Mediacom LLC (MSO).

ARGENTA—NewWave Communications, One Montgomery Plaza, 4th Floor, Sikeston, MO 63801. Phone: 888-863-9928. Fax: 573-481-9809. E-mail: info@newwavecom.com. Web Site: http://www.newwavecom.com. Also serves Macon County (portions) & Oreana. ICA: IL0228.
TV Market Ranking: 64 (ARGENTA, Macon County (portions), Oreana). Franchise award date: January 8, 1980. Franchise expiration date: N.A. Began: March 1, 1982.
Channel capacity: N.A. Channels available but not in use: N.A.

Basic Service
Subscribers: 213.
Programming (received off-air): WAND (NBC) Decatur; WBUI (CW, This TV) Decatur; WCIA (CBS, MNT) Champaign; WCIX (CBS, MNT) Springfield; WICS (ABC, The Country Network) Springfield; WILL-TV (PBS) Urbana; WRSP-TV (Antenna TV, FOX, MeTV) Springfield.
Programming (via satellite): C-SPAN; WGN America.
Fee: $40.00 installation; $34.78 monthly.

Expanded Basic Service 1
Subscribers: N.A.
Programming (via satellite): A&E; AMC; Animal Planet; BET; Comcast SportsNet Chicago; C-SPAN 2; Discovery Channel; Disney Channel; Disney XD; ESPN; ESPN2; Fox News Channel; Fox Sports 1; FOX Sports Midwest; Freeform; FX; Great American Country; Hallmark Channel; HGTV; History; Lifetime; MTV; Nickelodeon; Radar Channel; Spike TV; Syfy; TBS; The Weather Channel; TLC; TNT; Trinity Broadcasting Network (TBN); TV Land; USA Network; VH1.
Fee: $25.00 monthly.

Digital Basic Service
Subscribers: N.A.
Programming (via satellite): BBC America; Bloomberg Television; Discovery Digital Networks; ESPN Classic; ESPNews; EVINE Live; FOX College Sports Central; FOX College Sports Pacific; Fuse; FXM; FYI; Golf Channel; GSN; History; History International; IFC; LMN; National Geographic Channel; NBCSN; Outdoor Channel; Turner Classic Movies; WE tv.

Pay Service 1
Pay Units: N.A.
Programming (via satellite): Cinemax; HBO; Starz Encore.
Fee: $25.00 installation; $3.99 monthly (Encore), $7.95 monthly (Cinemax), $11.99 monthly (HBO or TMC).

Digital Pay Service 1
Pay Units: N.A.
Programming (via satellite): Cinemax (multiplexed); Flix; HBO (multiplexed); Showtime (multiplexed); Starz (multiplexed); Starz Encore (multiplexed); The Movie Channel (multiplexed).

Video-On-Demand: No

Pay-Per-View
iN DEMAND (delivered digitally); Playboy TV (delivered digitally); Fresh (delivered digitally).

Internet Service
Operational: Yes. Began: November 1, 2004.
Broadband Service: Suddenlink High Speed Internet.
Fee: $99.99 installation; $24.95 monthly.

Telephone Service
None
Miles of Plant: 31.0 (coaxial); None (fiber optic). Homes passed: 892.
Chief Financial Officer: Rod Siemers.
Ownership: NewWave Communications LLC (MSO).

ARMINGTON—Formerly served by Heartland Cable Inc. No longer in operation. ICA: IL0419.

ARMSTRONG—Park TV & Electronics Inc, 205 East Railroad Ave, PO Box 9, Cissna Park, IL 60924. Phones: 800-825-3882; 815-457-2659. Fax: 815-457-2735. Web Site: http://www.parktvcable.com. ICA: IL0678.
TV Market Ranking: 64 (ARMSTRONG).
Channel capacity: N.A. Channels available but not in use: N.A.

Basic Service
Subscribers: 28.
Programming (received off-air): WAND (NBC) Decatur; WBUI (CW, This TV) Decatur; WCCU (FOX, MeTV) Urbana; WCIA (CBS, MNT) Champaign; WICD (ABC) Champaign; WILL-TV (PBS) Urbana.
Programming (via satellite): A&E; Animal Planet; CMT; CNN; Discovery Channel; E! HD; ESPN; ESPN2; Freeform; History; Lifetime; Nickelodeon; QVC; Spike TV; TBS; TNT; Travel Channel; Trinity Broadcasting Network (TBN); USA Network; WGN America.
Fee: $35.00 installation; $47.00 monthly.

Pay Service 1
Pay Units: N.A.
Programming (via satellite): HBO.
Fee: $10.50 monthly.

Video-On-Demand: No

Internet Service
Operational: Yes.
Broadband Service: West Michigan Internet Service.
Fee: $99.00 installation; $39.95 monthly.

Telephone Service
None
Homes passed & miles of plant included in Cissna Park
President & General Manager: Joe Young.
Ownership: Park TV & Electronics Inc. (MSO).

ASTORIA—Formerly served by Mediacom. Now served by Nova Cablevision, IPAVA, IL [IL0357]. ICA: IL0258.

ATLANTA—Mediacom, 609 South 4th St, PO Box 334, Chillicothe, IL 61523. Phones: 309-469-2027; 309-274-4500. Fax: 309-274-3188. Web Site: http://www.mediacomcable.com. Also serves Heyworth, McLean, Wapella & Waynesville. ICA: IL0197.
TV Market Ranking: 64 (Heyworth, McLean, Wapella, Waynesville); 64,83 (ATLANTA). Franchise award date: N.A. Franchise expiration date: N.A. Began: September 1, 1982.
Channel capacity: N.A. Channels available but not in use: N.A.

Basic Service
Subscribers: 710.
Programming (received off-air): WAND (NBC) Decatur; WAOE (Antenna TV, MNT) Peoria; WCCU (FOX, MeTV) Urbana; WCIA (CBS, MNT) Champaign; WEEK-TV (ABC, CW, NBC) Peoria; WHOI (Comet) Peoria; WICS (ABC, The Country Network) Springfield; WILL-TV (PBS) Urbana; WMBD-TV (Bounce TV, CBS) Peoria; WPXU-TV (ION) Jacksonville; WYZZ-TV (FOX, The Country Network) Bloomington.
Programming (via satellite): WGN America.
Fee: $45.00 installation; $43.00 monthly.

Expanded Basic Service 1
Subscribers: N.A.
Programming (via satellite): A&E; AMC; Animal Planet; BET; Bravo; Cartoon Network; CMT; CNBC; CNN; Comcast SportsNet Chicago; Comedy Central; C-SPAN; C-SPAN 2; Discovery Channel; Disney Channel; E! HD; ESPN; ESPN2; EVINE Live; EWTN Global Catholic Network; Food Network; Fox News Channel; Fox Sports 1; Freeform; Fuse; FX; Hallmark Channel; HGTV; History; HLN; ION Television; Lifetime; MSNBC; MTV; Nickelodeon; Pop; QVC; Spike TV; Syfy; TBS; The Weather Channel; TLC; TNT; Travel Channel; Trinity Broadcasting Network (TBN); truTV; TV Land; Univision Studios; USA Network; VH1; WE tv; Weatherscan.
Fee: $34.00 monthly.

Digital Basic Service
Subscribers: N.A.
Programming (via satellite): BBC America; Bloomberg Television; Cloo; Discovery Digital Networks; ESPNews; FXM; FYI; Golf Channel; GSN; History International; IFC; LMN; MC; National Geographic Channel; NBCSN; Nick Jr.; Nicktoons; Outdoor Channel; Sundance TV (multiplexed); TeenNick; Turner Classic Movies.

Digital Expanded Basic Service
Subscribers: N.A.
Programming (via satellite): AXS TV; ESPN HD; ESPN2 HD; HD Theater; Universal HD.
Fee: $6.95 monthly.

Digital Pay Service 1
Pay Units: N.A.
Programming (via satellite): Cinemax (multiplexed); Flix (multiplexed); HBO (multiplexed); HBO HD; Showtime (multiplexed); Showtime HD; Starz (multiplexed); Starz Encore (multiplexed); Starz HD; The Movie Channel (multiplexed); The Movie Channel HD.

Video-On-Demand: Yes

2017 Edition D-187

Illinois—Cable Systems

Pay-Per-View
iN DEMAND (delivered digitally); Playboy TV (delivered digitally); ESPN (delivered digitally); FOX Sports Networks (delivered digitally).

Internet Service
Operational: Yes, DSL.
Broadband Service: Mediacom High Speed Internet.
Fee: $59.95 installation; $45.95 monthly.

Telephone Service
Analog: Not Operational
Digital: Operational
Fee: $39.95 monthly

Miles of Plant: 37.0 (coaxial); None (fiber optic). Homes passed: 1,316.
Vice President: Don Hagwell. Operations Director: Gary Wightman. Technical Operations Manager: Lary Brackman. Marketing Director: Stephanie Law.
Ownership: Mediacom LLC (MSO).

AUGUSTA—Adams Telcom. Now served by BOWDEN, IL [IL0702]. ICA: IL0356.

AURORA—Comcast Cable. Now served by PEORIA, IL [IL0012]. ICA: IL0017.

AVA—Formerly served by Longview Communications. No longer in operation. ICA: IL0461.

AVON—Mediacom. Now served by ELMWOOD, IL [IL0205]. ICA: IL0300.

BARDOLPH—Formerly served by CableDirect. No longer in operation. ICA: IL0462.

BARRINGTON HILLS—Comcast Cable. Now served by MOUNT PROSPECT, IL [IL0036]. ICA: IL0110.

BARRY—Formerly served by Crystal Broadband Networks. No longer in operation. ICA: IL0262.

BARTELSO—Formerly served by CableDirect. No longer in operation. ICA: IL0463.

BATAVIA—Comcast Cable. Now served by PEORIA, IL [IL0012]. ICA: IL0080.

BAYLIS (village)—Formerly served by Cass Cable TV Inc. No longer in operation. ICA: IL0464.

BEARDSTOWN—Cass Cable TV Inc, 100 Redbud Rd, PO Box 200, Virginia, IL 62691. Phones: 217-452-7934; 800-252-1799; 217-452-7725. Fax: 217-452-7030. E-mail: casscatv@casscomm.com; solutions@casscomm.com. Web Site: http://www.casscomm.com. Also serves Ashland, Bath, Bluff Springs, Buzzville, Chandlerville, Easton, Forest City, Goofy Ridge, Havana, Kilbourne, Manito, Mason City, Mount Sterling, Oakford (village), Pleasant Plains, Quiver Twp., Rushville, Talbott, Tallula, Versailles & Virginia. ICA: IL0598.
TV Market Ranking: 64 (Ashland, Chandlerville, Mason City, Oakford (village), Pleasant Plains, Quiver Twp., Tallula, Virginia); 83 (Easton, Forest City, Goofy Ridge, Kilbourne, Manito, Talbott); Below 100 (Buzzville, Havana, Mount Sterling); Outside TV Markets (Bath, Bluff Springs, Rushville, Versailles, BEARDSTOWN). Franchise award date: N.A. Franchise expiration date: N.A. Began: June 1, 1976.
Channel capacity: N.A. Channels available but not in use: N.A.

Basic Service
Subscribers: 6,365.
Programming (received off-air): KHQA-TV (ABC, CBS) Hannibal; WAND (NBC) Decatur; WCIA (CBS, MNT) Champaign; WGEM-TV (CW, FOX, NBC) Quincy; WHOI (Comet) Peoria; WICS (ABC, The Country Network) Springfield; WMBD-TV (Bounce TV, CBS) Peoria; WRSP-TV (Antenna TV, FOX, MeTV) Springfield; WSEC (PBS) Jacksonville; WTVP (PBS) Peoria.
Programming (via satellite): WGN America.
Fee: $45.00 installation; $17.95 monthly; $4.00 converter.

Expanded Basic Service 1
Subscribers: N.A.
Programming (via satellite): A&E; AMC; Animal Planet; Cartoon Network; CMT; CNBC; CNN; Comcast SportsNet Chicago; Comedy Central; C-SPAN; Discovery Channel; Disney Channel; Disney XD; E! HD; ESPN; ESPN Classic; ESPN2; Food Network; Fox News Channel; Fox Sports 1; FOX Sports Midwest; Freeform; FX; Golf Channel; GSN; Hallmark Channel; HGTV; History; HLN; ION Television; Lifetime; MSNBC; MTV; NBCSN; Nickelodeon; QVC; Spike TV; Syfy; TBS; Telemundo; The Weather Channel; TLC; TNT; Travel Channel; Trinity Broadcasting Network (TBN); truTV; TV Land; Univision Studios; USA Network; VH1.
Fee: $32.00 monthly.

Digital Basic Service
Subscribers: N.A.
Programming (via satellite): BBC America; Bloomberg Television; Bravo; Discovery Life Channel; DMX Music; ESPNews; FXM; FYI; History International; IFC; INSP; LMN; National Geographic Channel; Nick Jr.; Outdoor Channel; Ovation; Syfy; Teen-Nick; Trinity Broadcasting Network (TBN); Turner Classic Movies; WE tv; Weatherscan.

Pay Service 1
Pay Units: 536.
Programming (via satellite): Cinemax.
Fee: $20.00 installation; $11.35 monthly.

Pay Service 2
Pay Units: 429.
Programming (via satellite): Showtime; The Movie Channel.
Fee: $20.00 installation; $12.95 monthly.

Pay Service 3
Pay Units: 728.
Programming (via satellite): Starz; Starz Encore.
Fee: $20.00 installation; $8.95 monthly.

Pay Service 4
Pay Units: 881.
Programming (via satellite): HBO.
Fee: $20.00 installation; $13.55 monthly.

Digital Pay Service 1
Pay Units: N.A.
Programming (via satellite): Cinemax (multiplexed); DMX Music; HBO (multiplexed); Showtime (multiplexed); Starz Encore; The Movie Channel (multiplexed).

Video-On-Demand: No

Pay-Per-View
ESPN Extra; ESPN Now; iN DEMAND; Playboy TV; Spice.

Internet Service
Operational: Yes. Began: January 1, 1999.
Broadband Service: casscomm.com.
Fee: $39.95 monthly.

Telephone Service
Digital: Operational
Fee: $34.95 monthly

Miles of Plant: 240.0 (coaxial); 14.0 (fiber optic). Homes passed: 12,155.
CATV Manager: Chad Winters. Plant Manager: Lance Allen. Chief Technician: Gary Lowe. Marketing & Public Relations Manager: Erynn Snedeker. Advertising Director: Laymon Carter. Office Manager: Cindy Kilby.
Ownership: Cass Cable TV Inc. (MSO).

BEAVERVILLE TWP.—Formerly served by CableDirect. No longer in operation. ICA: IL0449.

BEECHER CITY—Clearvision Cable Systems Inc, 1785 US Rte 40, Greenup, IL 62428-3501. Phone: 217-923-5594. Fax: 217-923-5681. ICA: IL0279.
TV Market Ranking: Outside TV Markets (BEECHER CITY). Franchise award date: N.A. Franchise expiration date: N.A. Began: August 25, 1989.
Channel capacity: N.A. Channels available but not in use: N.A.

Basic Service
Subscribers: 9.
Programming (received off-air): WAND (NBC) Decatur; WBUI (CW, This TV) Decatur; WCIA (CBS, MNT) Champaign; WEIU-TV (PBS) Charleston; WICS (ABC, The Country Network) Springfield; WPXS (IND) Mount Vernon; WRSP-TV (Antenna TV, FOX, MeTV) Springfield; WUSI-TV (PBS) Olney.
Programming (via satellite): A&E; AMC; Bravo; Cartoon Network; CMT; CNBC; CNN; Comedy Central; C-SPAN; Discovery Channel; Disney Channel; ESPN; Fox News Channel; Freeform; History; HLN; Lifetime; MSNBC; MTV; Nickelodeon; QVC; Spike TV; Syfy; TBS; The Weather Channel; TLC; TNT; Trinity Broadcasting Network (TBN); USA Network; VH1; WGN America.
Fee: $47.95 monthly.

Pay Service 1
Pay Units: N.A.
Programming (via satellite): Cinemax; HBO.
Fee: $14.00 monthly (both), or $6.50 monthly (Cinemax), $9.50 monthly (HBO).

Video-On-Demand: No

Internet Service
Operational: No.

Telephone Service
None

Miles of Plant: 6.0 (coaxial); None (fiber optic). Homes passed: 192.
President & General Manager: Michael Bauguss. Secretary: Gwyndolyn S. Bauguss.
Ownership: Clearvision Cable Systems Inc. (MSO).

BELLE RIVE—Formerly served by Longview Communications. No longer in operation. ICA: IL0668.

BELLEVILLE—Charter Communications. Now served by ST. LOUIS, MO [MO0009]. ICA: IL0020.

BELLMONT—Formerly served by CableDirect. No longer in operation. ICA: IL0400.

BELVIDERE—Formerly served by Insight Communications. Now served by Comcast Cable, MOUNT PROSPECT, IL [IL0036]. ICA: IL0097.

BELVIDERE TWP.—Mediacom, 3900 26th Ave, Moline, IL 61265. Phone: 309-797-2580. Fax: 309-797-2414. Web Site: http://www.mediacomcable.com. Also serves Argyle, Caledonia, Candlewick Lake, Capron, Chemung, Garden Prairie, Hebron (village), McHenry County (portions), Poplar Grove, Richmond, Ringwood, Rockford (unincorporated areas) & Spring Grove (village). ICA: IL0282.
TV Market Ranking: 97 (Argyle, BELVIDERE TWP., Caledonia, Candlewick Lake, Capron, Chemung, Garden Prairie, McHenry County (portions) (portions), Poplar Grove); Below 100 (Richmond, Ringwood, Hebron (village), Spring Grove (village), McHenry County (portions) (portions)). Franchise award date: May 28, 1985. Franchise expiration date: N.A. Began: August 1, 1985.
Channel capacity: N.A. Channels available but not in use: N.A.

Basic Service
Subscribers: 1,574.
Programming (received off-air): WFLD (FOX) Chicago; WIFR (Antenna TV, CBS) Freeport; WPWR-TV (Buzzr, CW, MNT, Movies!) Gary; WQRF-TV (Bounce TV, FOX) Rockford; WREX (CW, MeTV, NBC) Rockford; WTTW (PBS) Chicago; WTVO (ABC, MNT) Rockford.
Programming (via satellite): CW PLUS; QVC; WGN America.
Fee: $45.00 installation; $43.00 monthly.

Expanded Basic Service 1
Subscribers: N.A.
Programming (via satellite): A&E; AMC; Animal Planet; Bravo; Cartoon Network; CMT; CNBC; CNN; Comcast SportsNet Chicago; Comedy Central; C-SPAN; Discovery Channel; Discovery Life Channel; Disney Channel; E! HD; ESPN; ESPN2; Food Network; Fox Sports 1; Freeform; HGTV; History; HLN; Lifetime; MSNBC; MTV; Nickelodeon; Spike TV; Syfy; TBS; The Weather Channel; TLC; TNT; Travel Channel; Trinity Broadcasting Network (TBN); truTV; TV Land; USA Network; VH1.
Fee: $34.00 monthly.

Digital Basic Service
Subscribers: N.A.
Programming (via satellite): BBC America; Bloomberg Television; Cloo; Destination America; Discovery Kids Channel; ESPNews; Fuse; FXM; FYI; Golf Channel; History International; IFC; Investigation Discovery; LMN; MC; MTV Classic; MTV Hits; MTV2; National Geographic Channel; Nick Jr.; Nicktoons; Outdoor Channel; OWN: Oprah Winfrey Network; Science Channel; TeenNick; Turner Classic Movies; TVG Network.

Digital Pay Service 1
Pay Units: N.A.
Programming (via satellite): Cinemax (multiplexed); HBO (multiplexed); Showtime (multiplexed); Starz (multiplexed); Starz Encore (multiplexed); The Movie Channel (multiplexed).
Fee: $11.95 monthly (HBO, Cinemax, Starz/Encore or Showtime/TMC).

Video-On-Demand: No

Internet Service
Operational: Yes.
Broadband Service: Mediacom High Speed Internet.
Fee: $59.95 installation; $40.95 monthly.

Telephone Service
Digital: Operational
Fee: $39.95 monthly

Homes passed: 1,937. Miles of plant included in Moline
Regional Vice President: Cari Fenzel. Engineering Director: Mitch Carlson. Technical Operations Manager: Chris Toalson. Marketing Director: Greg Evans.
Ownership: Mediacom LLC (MSO).

BELVIDERE TWP.—Mediacom. Now served by BELVIDERE TWP. (formerly POPLAR GROVE), IL [IL0282]. ICA: IL0663.

D-188   TV & Cable Factbook No. 85

Cable Systems—Illinois

BENTON—NewWave Communications, One Montgomery Plaza, 4th Floor, Sikeston, MO 63801. Phone: 888-863-9928. Fax: 573-481-9809. E-mail: info@newwavecom.com. Web Site: http://www.newwavecom.com. Also serves Buckner, Christopher, Du Quoin, Ewing, Franklin County (portions), Mulkeytown, North City, Perry County (portions), Pinckneyville, St. Johns (village), Tamaroa & West City (village). ICA: IL0117.
TV Market Ranking: 69 (BENTON, Buckner, Christopher, Ewing, Franklin County (portions) (portions), Mulkeytown, North City, West City (village)); Below 100 (Mulkeytown, Perry County (portions), Pinckneyville, St. Johns (village), Tamaroa, Du Quoin, Franklin County (portions) (portions)). Franchise award date: January 1, 1975. Franchise expiration date: N.A. Began: October 1, 1976.
Channel capacity: N.A. Channels available but not in use: N.A.
Basic Service
Subscribers: 3,526. Commercial subscribers: 25.
Programming (received off-air): KBSI (FOX) Cape Girardeau; KFVS-TV (CBS, CW, MeTV) Cape Girardeau; KSDK (Bounce TV, NBC) St. Louis; WDKA (MNT, The Country Network) Paducah; WPSD-TV (Antenna TV, NBC) Paducah; WPXS (IND) Mount Vernon; WQWQ-LP (CW, MeTV) Paducah; WSIL-TV (ABC) Harrisburg; WSIU-TV (PBS) Carbondale; WTCT (IND) Marion.
Programming (via satellite): A&E; AMC; Animal Planet; BET; Cartoon Network; CMT; CNBC; CNN; Comedy Central; C-SPAN; Discovery Channel; Disney Channel; Disney XD; E! HD; ESPN; ESPN Classic; ESPN2; ESPNews; EVINE Live; EWTN Global Catholic Network; Food Network; Fox News Channel; FOX Sports Midwest; Freeform; FX; GSN; Hallmark Channel; HGTV; History; HLN; Lifetime; MSNBC; MTV; Nickelodeon; OWN: Oprah Winfrey Network; Pop; QVC; Spike TV; Syfy; TBS; The Weather Channel; TLC; TNT; Travel Channel; truTV; TV Land; USA Network; VH1; WGN America.
Fee: $50.00 installation; $34.78 monthly.
Digital Basic Service
Subscribers: N.A.
Programming (via satellite): BBC America; Discovery Digital Networks; Fox Sports 1; LMN; MC; NFL Network; Nick 2; Nick Jr.; Nicktoons; TeenNick.
Pay Service 1
Pay Units: N.A.
Programming (via satellite): Cinemax; HBO; Showtime.
Digital Pay Service 1
Pay Units: N.A.
Programming (via satellite): Cinemax (multiplexed); HBO (multiplexed); Showtime (multiplexed); Starz (multiplexed); Starz Encore (multiplexed); The Movie Channel (multiplexed); WAM! America's Kidz Network.
Fee: $11.95 monthly (each).
Video-On-Demand: No
Pay-Per-View
Fresh (delivered digitally).
Internet Service
Operational: Yes.
Broadband Service: Comcast High Speed Internet.
Fee: $42.95 monthly.
Telephone Service
Digital: Operational
Miles of Plant: 302.0 (coaxial); None (fiber optic). Homes passed: 13,281.

General Manager: John Helmers.
Ownership: NewWave Communications LLC (MSO).

BETHANY—Formerly served by Suddenlink Communications. Now served by NewWave Communications, MOWEAQUA, IL [IL0185]. ICA: IL0245.

BIGGSVILLE—Formerly served by CableDirect. No longer in operation. ICA: IL0466.

BIRDS—Formerly served by Park TV & Electronics Inc. No longer in operation. ICA: IL0499.

BISMARCK—Park TV & Electronics Inc, 205 East Railroad Ave, PO Box 9, Cissna Park, IL 60924. Phones: 815-457-2659; 800-825-3882. Web Site: http://www.parktvcable.com. ICA: IL0669.
TV Market Ranking: Below 100 (BISMARCK).
Channel capacity: N.A. Channels available but not in use: N.A.
Basic Service
Subscribers: 34.
Programming (received off-air): WAND (NBC) Decatur; WBUI (CW, This TV) Decatur; WCCU (FOX, MeTV) Urbana; WCIA (CBS, MNT) Champaign; WICD (ABC) Champaign; WILL-TV (PBS) Urbana; WLFI-TV (CBS, TheCoolTV) Lafayette.
Programming (via satellite): A&E; CNN; Comedy Central; Discovery Channel; Disney Channel; ESPN; Freeform; HLN; Lifetime; MTV; Nickelodeon; QVC; Spike TV; TBS; The Weather Channel; TLC; TNT; Travel Channel; USA Network; VH1; WGN America.
Fee: $46.95 monthly.
Pay Service 1
Pay Units: N.A.
Programming (via satellite): Showtime; The Movie Channel.
Fee: $9.95 monthly (each).
Video-On-Demand: No
Internet Service
Operational: No.
Telephone Service
None
Miles of Plant: 27.0 (coaxial); None (fiber optic). Homes passed: 601.
President & General Manager: Joe Young.
Ownership: Park TV & Electronics Inc. (MSO).

BLOOMINGTON—Comcast Cable. Now served by PEORIA, IL [IL0012]. ICA: IL0026.

BLUE MOUND—Formerly served by Suddenlink Communications. Now served by NewWave Communications, MOWEAQUA, IL [IL0185]. ICA: IL0229.

BLUFFS—Formerly served by Crystal Broadband Networks. No longer in operation. ICA: IL0227.

BLUFORD—Formerly served by Longview Communications. No longer in operation. ICA: IL0360.

BONE GAP—Formerly served by CableDirect. No longer in operation. ICA: IL0418.

BONFIELD (village)—Formerly served by CableDirect. No longer in operation. ICA: IL0467.

BONNIE—Formerly served by Longview Communications. No longer in operation. ICA: IL0395.

BOODY—Formerly served by CableDirect. No longer in operation. ICA: IL0468.

BOWEN—Adams Telcom, 405 Emminga Rd, PO Box 217, Golden, IL 62339. Phones: 877-696-4611; 217-696-4611. E-mail: service@adams.net; marketing@adams.net. Web Site: http://www.adams.net. Also serves Augusta, Coatsburg, Fowler, Golden, Lima, Loraine, Marcelline, Mendon, Paloma, Plymouth, Quincy & Ursa. ICA: IL0702.
Channel capacity: N.A. Channels available but not in use: N.A.
Digital Basic Service
Subscribers: 292.
Programming (received off-air): KHQA-TV (ABC, CBS) Hannibal; KTVO (ABC) Kirksville; WGEM-TV (CW, FOX, NBC) Quincy; WQEC (PBS) Quincy; WTJR (Christian TV Network) Quincy.
Programming (via satellite): A&E; Animal Planet; Cartoon Network; CNN; CW Television Network; Discovery Channel; Disney Channel; Disney XD; ESPN; ESPN2; Fox Business Network; Fox News Channel; FOX Sports Midwest; Freeform; Hallmark Channel; History; Lifetime; TBS; The Weather Channel; TLC; TNT; USA Network; WGN America.
Fee: $99.95 installation; $54.95 monthly.
Digital Expanded Basic Service
Subscribers: 194.
Programming (via satellite): American Heroes Channel; BBC America; Cloo; Cooking Channel; Discovery Family; Discovery Life Channel; Disney Junior; ESPN Classic; ESPNews; Esquire Network; FXM; FYI; Golf Channel; GSN; Halogen TV; HGTV; Syfy; Trinity Broadcasting Network (TBN); Turner Classic Movies.
Fee: $53.95 monthly.
Digital Pay Service 1
Pay Units: N.A.
Fee: $11.95 monthly (Cinemax, Showtime/TMC or Starz/Encore), $15.95 monthly (HBO).
Internet Service
Operational: Yes.
Fee: $44.95-$64.95 monthly.
Telephone Service
Digital: Operational
Fee: $28.89 monthly
Miles of Plant: 9.0 (coaxial); 2.0 (fiber optic). Homes passed: 265.
Chief Executive Officer & General Manager: James W. Broemmer Jr.
Ownership: Adams Telephone Co-Operative.

BRADFORD—Mediacom. Now served by WYOMING, IL [IL0196]. ICA: IL0323.

BREESE—Charter Communications. Now served by ST. LOUIS, MO [MO0009]. ICA: IL0149.

BRIGHTON—Formerly served by Greene County Partners. Now served by NewWave Communications, JERSEYVILLE, IL [IL0130]. ICA: IL0210.

BRIMFIELD—Mediacom. Now served by CHILLICOTHE, IL [IL0118]. ICA: IL0330.

BRIMFIELD—Mediacom. Now served by CHILLICOTHE, IL [IL0118]. ICA: IL0201.

BROCTON—Clearvision Cable Systems Inc, 1785 US Rte 40, Greenup, IL 62428-3501. Phone: 217-923-5594. Fax: 217-923-5681. ICA: IL0666.
TV Market Ranking: 64 (BROCTON).
Channel capacity: N.A. Channels available but not in use: N.A.
Basic Service
Subscribers: 13.
Programming (received off-air): WAND (NBC) Decatur; WBUI (CW, This TV) Decatur; WCIA (CBS, MNT) Champaign; WCIX (CBS, MNT) Springfield; WEIU-TV (PBS) Charleston; WICD (ABC) Champaign; WILL-TV (PBS) Urbana.
Programming (via satellite): A&E; AMC; Bravo; Cartoon Network; CNBC; CNN; Comedy Central; C-SPAN; Discovery Channel; Disney Channel; ESPN; ESPN2; Fox News Channel; Freeform; Great American Country; History; HLN; Lifetime; MSNBC; MTV; Nickelodeon; QVC; Spike TV; Syfy; TBS; The Weather Channel; TLC; TNT; Trinity Broadcasting Network (TBN); USA Network; VH1; WGN America.
Fee: $47.95 monthly.
Pay Service 1
Pay Units: N.A.
Programming (via satellite): Showtime; The Movie Channel.
Fee: $9.45 monthly (each).
Video-On-Demand: No
Internet Service
Operational: No.
Telephone Service
None
Miles of Plant: 4.0 (coaxial); None (fiber optic). Homes passed: 188.
President & General Manager: Michael Bauguss. Secretary: Gwyndolyn S. Bauguss.
Ownership: Clearvision Cable Systems Inc. (MSO).

BRYANT (village)—Formerly served by CableDirect. No longer in operation. ICA: IL0472.

BUCKLEY (village)—Park TV & Electronics Inc, 205 East Railroad Ave, PO Box 9, Cissna Park, IL 60924. Phones: 800-825-3882; 815-457-2659. Web Site: http://www.parktvcable.com. ICA: IL0473.
TV Market Ranking: Below 100 (BUCKLEY (VILLAGE)). Franchise award date: N.A. Franchise expiration date: N.A. Began: December 1, 1983.
Channel capacity: N.A. Channels available but not in use: N.A.
Basic Service
Subscribers: 102.
Programming (received off-air): WAND (NBC) Decatur; WBUI (CW, This TV) Decatur; WCCU (FOX, MeTV) Urbana; WCIA (CBS, MNT) Champaign; WICD (ABC) Champaign; WILL-TV (PBS) Urbana.
Programming (via satellite): A&E; AMC; Animal Planet; BTN; Cartoon Network; CMT; CNBC; CNN; Comedy Central; Discovery Channel; Disney Channel; E! HD; ESPN; ESPN2; Food Network; Fox News Channel; Fox Sports 1; Freeform; FX; GSN; Hallmark Channel; HGTV; History; Lifetime; MTV; Nickelodeon; Outdoor Channel; Oxygen; QVC; Spike TV; Syfy; TBS; The Weather Channel; TLC; TNT; Travel Channel; Trinity Broadcasting Network (TBN); Turner Classic Movies; TV Land; USA Network; VH1; WGN America.
Fee: $47.00 monthly.
Pay Service 1
Pay Units: N.A.
Programming (via satellite): Cinemax; HBO; Showtime; The Movie Channel.
Video-On-Demand: No
Internet Service
Operational: Yes.
Fee: $29.95-$54.95 monthly.

2017 Edition

Illinois—Cable Systems

Telephone Service
None
Homes passed & miles of plant included in Cissna Park
President & General Manager: Joe Young.
Ownership: Park TV & Electronics Inc. (MSO).

BUFFALO—Mediacom. Now served by KINCAID, IL [IL0176]. ICA: IL0259.

BUNCOMBE—Zito Media, 102 S Main St, PO Box 665, Coudersport, PA 16915. Phones: 814-260-9055; 800-365-6988. E-mail: info@zitomedia.com. Web Site: http://www.zitomedia.com. Also serves Johnson County (portions) & Vienna. ICA: IL0266.
TV Market Ranking: 69 (BUNCOMBE, Vienna). Franchise award date: N.A. Franchise expiration date: N.A. Began: September 1, 1982.
Channel capacity: N.A. Channels available but not in use: N.A.
Basic Service
Subscribers: 91.
Programming (received off-air): KBSI (FOX) Cape Girardeau; KFVS-TV (CBS, CW, MeTV) Cape Girardeau; WDKA (MNT, The Country Network) Paducah; WPSD-TV (Antenna TV, NBC) Paducah; WSIL-TV (ABC) Harrisburg; WSIU-TV (PBS) Carbondale; WTCT (IND) Marion.
Programming (via satellite): A&E; AMC; Cartoon Network; CNN; Comedy Central; Discovery Channel; Disney Channel; E! HD; ESPN; ESPN2; Fox News Channel; Freeform; Fuse; FX; Great American Country; HGTV; History; HLN; Lifetime; Outdoor Channel; TBS; The Weather Channel; TLC; TNT; Turner Classic Movies; USA Network; WGN America.
Fee: $49.95 installation; $47.41 monthly.
Pay Service 1
Pay Units: N.A.
Programming (via satellite): HBO; Showtime; Starz Encore.
Fee: $12.00 monthly.
Internet Service
Operational: No.
Telephone Service
None
Miles of Plant: 13.0 (coaxial); None (fiber optic). Homes passed: 897.
President: James Rigas.
Ownership: Zito Media (MSO).

BUREAU—Mediacom. Now served by MOUNT PROSPECT, IL [IL0036]. ICA: IL0388.

BURLINGTON (village)—Formerly served by Mediacom. No longer in operation. ICA: IL0474.

BUSHNELL—Formerly served by Insight Communications. Now served by Comcast Cable, PEORIA, IL [IL0012]. ICA: IL0190.

CAHOKIA—Charter Communications. Now served by ST. LOUIS, MO [MO0009]. ICA: IL0088.

CAIRO—NewWave Communications, One Montgomery Plaza, 4th Floor, Sikeston, MO 63801. Phone: 888-863-9928 (Customer service). Fax: 573-481-9809. E-mail: info@newwavecom.com. Web Site: http://www.newwavecom.com. ICA: IL0136.
TV Market Ranking: 69 (CAIRO). Franchise award date: N.A. Franchise expiration date: N.A. Began: August 1, 1981.
Channel capacity: N.A. Channels available but not in use: N.A.

Basic Service
Subscribers: 169. Commercial subscribers: 9.
Programming (received off-air): KBSI (FOX) Cape Girardeau; KFVS-TV (CBS, CW, MeTV) Cape Girardeau; WDKA (MNT, The Country Network) Paducah; WPSD-TV (Antenna TV, NBC) Paducah; WSIL-TV (ABC) Harrisburg; WSIU-TV (PBS) Carbondale; WTCT (IND) Marion.
Programming (via satellite): C-SPAN; C-SPAN 2; Hallmark Channel; QVC; TBS; The Weather Channel; TLC; WGN America.
Fee: $40.00 installation; $34.78 monthly.
Expanded Basic Service 1
Subscribers: N.A.
Programming (via satellite): A&E; AMC; BET; Bravo; Cartoon Network; CMT; CNN; Comedy Central; Discovery Channel; Disney Channel; Disney XD; E! HD; ESPN; ESPN Classic; ESPN2; EWTN Global Catholic Network; Fox News Channel; Fox Sports 1; FOX Sports Midwest; Freeform; HGTV; HLN; Lifetime; MTV; NBCSN; Nickelodeon; Spike TV; Syfy; TNT; Travel Channel; truTV; TV Land; USA Network; VH1.
Fee: $12.95 monthly.
Pay Service 1
Pay Units: N.A.
Programming (via satellite): Cinemax; HBO (multiplexed); Showtime; The Movie Channel.
Fee: $7.95 monthly (TMC), $8.95 monthly (Cinemax), $9.95 monthly (HBO or Showtime).
Video-On-Demand: No
Internet Service
Operational: Yes.
Telephone Service
Digital: Operational
Miles of Plant: 23.0 (coaxial); None (fiber optic). Homes passed: 2,373.
Chief Financial Officer: Rod Siemers. General Manager: John Helmers.
Ownership: NewWave Communications LLC (MSO).

CALEDONIA—Mediacom. Now served by BELVIDERE TWP, IL [IL0282]. ICA: IL0465.

CALHOUN COUNTY (portions)—Formerly served by CableDirect. No longer in operation. ICA: IL0438.

CAMERON—Nova1Net, 677 West Main St, PO Box 1412, Galesburg, IL 61401. Phones: 800-397-6682; 309-342-9681. Fax: 309-342-4408. Web Site: http://www.novacablevision.com. ICA: IL0444.
TV Market Ranking: Below 100 (CAMERON). Franchise award date: N.A. Franchise expiration date: N.A. Began: September 16, 1989.
Channel capacity: 60 (not 2-way capable). Channels available but not in use: N.A.
Basic Service
Subscribers: N.A.
Programming (received off-air): KGCW (CW, MeTV, This TV) Burlington; KIIN (PBS) Iowa City; KLJB (CW, FOX, MeTV) Davenport; KWQC-TV (NBC) Davenport; WEEK-TV (ABC, CW, NBC) Peoria; WHBF-TV (CBS) Rock Island; WHOI (Comet) Peoria; WMBD-TV (Bounce TV, CBS) Peoria; WQAD-TV (ABC, Antenna TV) Moline; WQPT-TV (PBS) Moline; WTVP (PBS) Peoria.
Programming (via satellite): A&E; AMC; Animal Planet; Cartoon Network; CMT; CNBC; CNN; Comedy Central; Discovery Channel; Disney Channel; ESPN; ESPN2; Food Network; Freeform; HGTV; History; Lifetime; MTV; Nickelodeon; QVC; Spike TV; Syfy; TBS; The Weather Channel; TLC; TNT; TV Land; USA Network; WGN America.
Fee: $60.00 installation.
Digital Basic Service
Subscribers: N.A.
Programming (via satellite): Bloomberg Television; CMT; Destination America; Discovery Kids Channel; Disney XD; DMX Music; ESPN Classic; ESPN2; ESPNews; EVINE Live; Fox Sports 1; FSN Digital Atlantic; FSN Digital Central; FSN Digital Pacific; FXM; FYI; Golf Channel; Great American Country; GSN; HGTV; History; History International; IFC; Investigation Discovery; LMN; MTV Classic; MTV Hits; MTV2; NBCSN; Nicktoons; Noggin; Outdoor Channel; OWN: Oprah Winfrey Network; Science Channel; Syfy; TeenNick; Trinity Broadcasting Network (TBN); Turner Classic Movies; VH1 Soul; WE tv.
Pay Service 1
Pay Units: N.A.
Programming (via satellite): Cinemax; HBO.
Fee: $12.85 monthly (each).
Digital Pay Service 1
Pay Units: N.A.
Programming (via satellite): Cinemax (multiplexed); Flix; HBO (multiplexed); Showtime (multiplexed); Starz (multiplexed); Starz Encore (multiplexed); Sundance TV; The Movie Channel (multiplexed).
Fee: $12.85 monthly (HBO, Showtime/TMC/Flix/Sundance, Cinemax, or Starz/Encore).
Pay-Per-View
Hot Choice (delivered digitally); Playboy TV (delivered digitally); Fresh (delivered digitally); Spice; Xcess (delivered digitally); Club Jenna (delivered digitally).
Internet Service
Operational: Yes. Began: January 1, 2005.
Fee: $30.00 installation; $39.95 monthly; $3.95 modem lease.
Telephone Service
None
Miles of Plant: 2.0 (coaxial); None (fiber optic). Homes passed: 97.
General Manager: Robert G. Fischer Jr. Office Manager: Hazel Harden.
Ownership: Nova Cablevision Inc. (MSO).

CAMP POINT—Adams Telcom. Formerly [IL0206]. This cable system has converted to IPTV, 405 Emminga Rd, PO Box 217, Golden, IL 62339. Phones: 217-696-4611; 877-696-4611. E-mail: service@adams.net; marketing@adams.net. Web Site: http://www.adams.net. Also serves Clayton. ICA: IL5313.
Channel capacity: N.A. Channels available but not in use: N.A.
Family Video
Subscribers: 597.
Fee: $99.95 installation; $54.95 monthly. Includes 60 channels.
Entertainment Video
Subscribers: 112.
Fee: $60.95 monthly. Includes 93 channels plus music channels.
Cinemax
Subscribers: N.A.
Fee: $11.95 monthly. Includes 4 channels.
HBO
Subscribers: N.A.
Fee: $15.95 monthly. Includes 6 channels.
Showtime/TMC
Subscribers: N.A.
Fee: $11.95 monthly. Includes 10 channels.
Starz/Encore
Subscribers: N.A.
Fee: $11.95 monthly. Includes 12 channels.
Internet Service
Operational: Yes.
Telephone Service
Digital: Operational
Fee: $44.95-$64.95 monthly
Chief Executive Officer & General Manager: James W. Broemmer Jr.
Ownership: Adams Telephone Co-Operative.

CAMP POINT—Adams Telephone. This cable system has converted to IPTV. See CAMP POINT, IL [IL5313]. ICA: IL0206.

CAMPTON TWP.—Formerly served by Comcast Cable. No longer in operation. ICA: IL0108.

CANTON—Comcast Cable. Now served by PEORIA, IL [IL0012]. ICA: IL0087.

CANTRALL—Mediacom. Now served by DELEVAN, IL [IL0172]. ICA: IL0308.

CARLINVILLE—NewWave Communications. Now served by TAYLORVILLE, IL [IL0098]. ICA: IL0081.

CARLOCK—Formerly served by CableDirect. No longer in operation. ICA: IL0670.

CARLYLE—Charter Communications. Now served by ST. LOUIS, MO [MO0009]. ICA: IL0184.

CARMI—Formerly served by Charter Communications. No longer in operation. ICA: IL0126.

CARPENTERSVILLE—Comcast Cable. Now served by MOUNT PROSPECT, IL [IL0036]. ICA: IL0023.

CARRIER MILLS—Zito Media, 102 S Main St, PO Box 665, Coudersport, PA 16915. Phones: 814-260-9055; 800-365-6988. E-mail: info@zitomedia.com. Web Site: http://www.zitomedia.com. Also serves Saline County (portions). ICA: IL0195.
TV Market Ranking: 69 (CARRIER MILLS, Saline County (portions)). Franchise award date: N.A. Franchise expiration date: N.A. Began: August 1, 1982.
Channel capacity: N.A. Channels available but not in use: N.A.
Basic Service
Subscribers: 353.
Programming (received off-air): KBSI (FOX) Cape Girardeau; KFVS-TV (CBS, CW, MeTV) Cape Girardeau; WDKA (MNT, The Country Network) Paducah; WPXS (IND) Mount Vernon; WQWQ-LP (CW, MeTV) Paducah; WSIL-TV (ABC) Harrisburg; WSIU-TV (PBS) Carbondale; WTCT (IND) Marion.
Programming (via satellite): A&E; AMC; Animal Planet; BET; Cartoon Network; CNBC; CNN; Comedy Central; C-SPAN; Discovery Channel; Disney Channel; Disney XD; E! HD; ESPN; ESPN Classic; ESPN2; Food Network; Fox News Channel; FOX Sports Networks; Freeform; Fuse; FX; Great American Country; HGTV; History; HLN; INSP; Lifetime; National Geographic Channel; Outdoor Channel; QVC; Syfy; TBS; The Weather Channel; TLC;

Cable Systems—Illinois

TNT; Travel Channel; truTV; Turner Classic Movies; USA Network; WGN America.
Fee: $49.95 installation; $17.35 monthly; $3.00 converter.
Digital Basic Service
Subscribers: N.A.
Programming (via satellite): BBC America; Bloomberg Television; Cloo; Destination America; Discovery Kids Channel; Discovery Life Channel; Disney XD; ESPN Classic; ESPNews; FOX College Sports Central; FOX College Sports Pacific; Fox Sports 1; Fuse; FXM; FYI; Golf Channel; GSN; History International; Investigation Discovery; LMN; National Geographic Channel; Outdoor Channel; OWN: Oprah Winfrey Network; Science Channel; Turner Classic Movies; UP; WE tv.
Pay Service 1
Pay Units: N.A.
Programming (via satellite): HBO; Showtime; Starz Encore; The Movie Channel.
Fee: $12.00 monthly (each).
Digital Pay Service 1
Pay Units: N.A.
Programming (via satellite): Cinemax (multiplexed); Flix; HBO (multiplexed); Showtime (multiplexed); Starz (multiplexed); Starz Encore (multiplexed); The Movie Channel (multiplexed).
Pay-Per-View
iN DEMAND (delivered digitally); Hot Choice (delivered digitally); Playboy TV (delivered digitally); Spice: Xcess (delivered digitally).
Internet Service
Operational: Yes.
Broadband Service: Galaxy Cable Internet.
Fee: $49.95 installation; $35.00 monthly.
Telephone Service
Digital: Operational
Miles of Plant: 41.0 (coaxial); 12.0 (fiber optic). Homes passed: 1,419.
President: James Rigas.
Ownership: Zito Media (MSO).

CARROLLTON—NewWave Communications. Now served by JERSEYVILLE, IL [IL0130]. ICA: IL0221.

CARTHAGE—Mediacom, 609 South 4th St, PO Box 334, Chillicothe, IL 61523. Phones: 309-469-2027; 309-274-4500. Fax: 309-274-3188. Web Site: http://www.mediacomcable.com. ICA: IL0183.
TV Market Ranking: Below 100 (CARTHAGE). Franchise award date: May 8, 1969. Franchise expiration date: N.A. Began: April 1, 1970.
Channel capacity: N.A. Channels available but not in use: N.A.
Basic Service
Subscribers: 388.
Programming (received off-air): KHQA-TV (ABC, CBS) Hannibal; KIIN (PBS) Iowa City; KTVO (ABC) Kirksville; KWQC-TV (NBC) Davenport; KYOU-TV (FOX) Ottumwa; WGEM-TV (CW, FOX, NBC) Quincy; WHBF-TV (CBS) Rock Island; WMEC (PBS) Macomb; WQAD-TV (ABC, Antenna TV) Moline; WTJR (Christian TV Network) Quincy.
Programming (via microwave): KPLR-TV (CW, This TV) St. Louis.
Programming (via satellite): WGN America.
Fee: $45.00 installation; $43.00 monthly.
Expanded Basic Service 1
Subscribers: N.A.
Programming (via satellite): A&E; AMC; Animal Planet; Cartoon Network; CNN; C-SPAN; C-SPAN 2; Discovery Channel; Disney Channel; E! HD; ESPN; ESPN2; EVINE Live; Food Network; Fox News Channel; Fox Sports 1; Freeform; FX; HGTV; History; HLN; Lifetime; MSNBC; MTV; NBCSN; Nickelodeon; Pop; QVC; Spike TV; TBS; The Weather Channel; TLC; TNT; USA Network.
Fee: $34.00 monthly.
Digital Basic Service
Subscribers: N.A.
Programming (via satellite): BBC America; Bloomberg Television; Cloo; Discovery Digital Networks; ESPNews; Fuse; FXM; FYI; Golf Channel; History International; IFC; LMN; MC; National Geographic Channel; NBCSN; Nick Jr.; Nicktoons; Outdoor Channel; Sundance TV; TeenNick; Turner Classic Movies; TVG Network.
Digital Expanded Basic Service
Subscribers: N.A.
Programming (via satellite): AXS TV; ESPN HD; ESPN2 HD; HD Theater.
Fee: $6.95 monthly.
Digital Pay Service 1
Pay Units: N.A.
Programming (via satellite): Cinemax (multiplexed); Flix; HBO (multiplexed); HBO HD; Showtime (multiplexed); Showtime HD; Starz (multiplexed); Starz Encore (multiplexed); Starz HD; The Movie Channel (multiplexed); The Movie Channel HD.
Fee: $11.95 monthly (HBO, Cinemax, Showtime/TMC or Starz/Encore).
Video-On-Demand: Yes
Pay-Per-View
iN DEMAND (delivered digitally); Playboy TV (delivered digitally); TEN Clip, TEN, & TEN BLOX (delivered digitally).
Internet Service
Operational: Yes.
Subscribers: 414.
Broadband Service: Mediacom High Speed Internet.
Fee: $59.95 installation; $45.95 monthly.
Telephone Service
Digital: Operational
Subscribers: 149.
Fee: $39.95 monthly
Miles of Plant: 37.0 (coaxial); 65.0 (fiber optic). Homes passed: 1,493.
Vice President: Don Hagwell. Operations Director: Gary Wightman. Technical Operations Manager: Larry Brackman. Marketing Director: Stephanie Law.
Ownership: Mediacom LLC (MSO).

CASEY—Mediacom. Now served by MARTINSVILLE, IL [IL0217]. ICA: IL0477.

CAVE-IN-ROCK—Formerly served by Vital Communications. No longer in operation. ICA: IL0662.

CEDAR POINT—Formerly served by McNabb Cable & Satellite Inc. No longer in operation. ICA: IL0434.

CERRO GORDO—Mediacom. Now served by SULLIVAN, IL [IL0154]. ICA: IL0478.

CHAMPAIGN—Comcast Cable, 303 Fairlawn Dr, Urbana, IL 61801-5141. Phone: 217-384-2530. Fax: 217-384-2021. Web Site: http://www.comcast.com. Also serves Alsip, Aroma, Aroma Park, Ashkum, Beecher, Blue Island, Bondville, Bourbonais, Bradley, Burnham, Calumet City, Calumet Park, Champaign County (portions), Chebanse, Chicago Heights, Chicago Ridge, Chrisman, Clifton, Cook County (portions), Country Club Hills, Crestwood, Crete, Danville, Dixmoor, Dolton, East Hazel Crest, Eugene, Evergreen Park, Fairmount, Fithian, Flossmoor, Ford Heights, Glenwood, Harvey, Hazel Crest, Herscher, Hickory Hills, Homer, Hometown, Homewood, Indianola, Iroquois County (portions), Kankakee, Lansing, Limestone, Lynwood, Manteno, Markham, Matteson, Merrionette Park, Midlothian, Monee, Muncie, Oak Forest, Oak Lawn, Oakwood, Ogden, Olivet, Olympia Fields, Orland Hills, Orland Park, Otto, Palos Heights, Palos Hills, Palos Park, Park Forest (Cook County), Park Forest (Will County), Peotone, Philo, Phoenix, Posen, Richton Park, Ridge Farm, Riverdale, Robbins (village), Sauk Village, Savoy, Sidney, South Chicago Heights, South Holland, St. Anne, St. Joseph, Steger, Sun River Terrace, Thornton, Thornton Twp., Tinley Park, University Park, Urbana, Vermilion County (portions), Will, Will County (northwestern portion), Will County (portions) & Worth, IL; Akron, Beverly Shores, Bristol, Burket, Burns Harbor, Cayuga, Cedar Lake, Chesterton, Crown Point, Demotte, Dune Acres, Duneland Beach, Dyer, East Chicago, Elkhart, Elkhart County (portions), Etna Green, Fulton County (portions), Gary, Goshen, Griffith, Hammond, Hebron, Highland, Hobart, Jasper County (portions), Jefferson Twp., Kingsbury, Kingsford Heights, Kosciusko County (portions), La Porte, La Porte County (portions), Lake County (portions), Lake Station, Lakes of the Four Seasons, Lodi, Long Beach, Lowell, Marshall County (portions), Mentone, Merrillville, Michiana Shores, Michigan City, Middlebury, Mishawaka, Munster, New Carlisle (town), New Chicago, Notre Dame, Ogden Dunes, Osceola, Pines Twp., Plymouth, Portage, Porter, Porter County (portions), Pottawattomie Park, Rochester, Roseland, Schererville, Silver Lake, Silverwood, South Bend, St. John, St. Joseph County (portions), St. Joseph County (unincorporated areas), Trail Creek, Valparaiso, Wakarusa, Warsaw, Whiting, Winfield & Winona Lake, IN; Bainbridge Twp., Baroda (village), Baroda Twp., Benton Harbor, Benton Twp. (Berrien County), Berrien Springs (village), Berrien Twp., Bertrand Twp., Bridgman, Buchanan, Buchanan Twp., Calvin Twp., Cassopolis, Chikaming Twp., Coloma, Coloma Twp., Dowagiac, Edwardsburg, Grand Beach, Hagar Twp., Hartford Twp., Howard Twp., Jefferson Twp. (Cass County), LaGrange Twp., Lake Twp., Lincoln Twp. (Berrien County), Mason Twp., Mason Twp. (Cass County), Michiana, Milton Twp. (Cass County), New Buffalo, New Buffalo Twp., Niles, Niles Twp., Ontwa Twp., Oronoko Twp., Park Twp., Penn Twp. (portions), Pipestone Twp., Pokagon Twp., Porter Twp., Royalton Twp., Shoreham (village), Silver Creek Twp., Sodus Twp., St. Joseph, St. Joseph Twp., Stevensville (village), Three Oaks, Three Oaks Twp., Washington Twp., Washington Twp. (Macomb County), Watervliet, Watervliet Twp., Wayne Twp. & Weesaw, MI. ICA: IL0019.
TV Market Ranking: 3 (Alsip, Beecher, Blue Island, Burnham, Burns Harbor, Calumet City, Calumet Park, Chicago Heights, Chicago Ridge, Cook County (portions), Country Club Hills, Crestwood, Crete, Crown Point, Demotte, Dixmoor, Dolton, Dune Acres, Dyer, East Chicago, East Hazel Crest, Evergreen Park, Flossmoor, Ford Heights, Gary, Glenwood, Griffith, Hammond, Harvey, Hazel Crest, Hickory Hills, Highland, Hobart, Hometown, Homewood, Lake County (portions), Lake Station, Lakes of the Four Seasons, Lansing, Lynwood, Manteno, Markham, Matteson, Merrillville, Merrionette Park, Midlothian, Monee, Munster, New Chicago, Oak Forest, Oak Lawn, Ogden Dunes, Olympia Fields, Orland Hills, Orland Park, Palos Heights, Palos Hills, Palos Park, Park Forest (Cook County), Park Forest (Will County), Peotone, Phoenix, Portage, Porter, Porter County (portions) (portions), Posen, Richton Park, Riverdale, Robbins (village), Sauk Village, Schererville, South Chicago Heights, South Holland, St. John, Steger, Thornton, Thornton Twp., Tinley Park, University Park, Whiting, Will, Will County (northwestern portion), Winfield, Worth); 37 (Bainbridge Twp., Calvin Twp., Dowagiac, Edwardsburg, Park Twp., Penn Twp. (portions), Pokagon Twp., Porter Twp., Silver Creek Twp., Wayne Twp.); 37,80 (Berrien Springs (village), Berrien Twp., Cassopolis, Hartford Twp., Jefferson Twp. (Cass County), LaGrange Twp., St. Joseph Twp., Stevensville (village), Watervliet); 5 (Washington Twp., Washington Twp. (Macomb County)); 64 (Bondville, CHAMPAIGN, Champaign County (portions), Danville, Fairmount, Fithian, Homer, Indianola, Iroquois County (portions), Muncie, Oakwood, Ogden, Philo, Savoy, Sidney, St. Joseph, Urbana, Vermilion County (portions) (portions)); 80 (Baroda (village), Baroda Twp., Benton Harbor, Benton Twp. (Berrien County), Bertrand Twp., Bridgman, Bristol, Buchanan, Buchanan Twp., Burket, Chikaming Twp., Duneland Beach, Elkhart, Elkhart County (portions), Etna Green, Goshen, Grand Beach, Hagar Twp., Howard Twp., Jefferson Twp., Kingsbury, Kingsford Heights, Kosciusko County (portions), La Porte, La Porte County (portions) (portions), Lake Twp., Lincoln Twp. (Berrien County), Long Beach, Marshall County (portions), Mason Twp. (Cass County), Michiana, Michiana Shores, Michigan City, Middlebury, Milton Twp. (Cass County), Mishawaka, New Buffalo, New Buffalo Twp., New Carlisle (town), Niles, Niles Twp., Notre Dame, Ontwa Twp., Oronoko Twp., Osceola, Pipestone Twp., Plymouth, Pottawattomie Park, Roseland, Royalton Twp., Shoreham (village), Sodus Twp., South Bend, St. Joseph, St. Joseph County (portions), Three Oaks, Three Oaks Twp., Trail Creek, Wakarusa, Weesaw); 82 (Akron, Silver Lake, Warsaw); Below 100 (Aroma, Aroma Park, Beverly Shores, Bourbonais, Bradley, Cedar Lake, Chesterton, Chrisman, Eugene, Hebron, Herscher, Limestone, Lodi, Lowell, Otto, Pines Twp., Ridge Farm, Silverwood, Sun River Terrace, Valparaiso, Will County (portions), Fulton County (portions), Jasper County (portions), Kankakee, Lake County (portions), Porter County (portions) (portions), Iroquois County (portions) (portions), Vermilion County (portions) (portions), La Porte County (portions) (portions)); Outside TV Markets (Ashkum, Chebanse,

Illinois—Cable Systems

Clifton, Coloma, Coloma Twp., Rochester, St. Anne, Fulton County (portions), Jasper County (portions), Mason Twp., Iroquois County (portions) (portions), Vermilion County (portions) (portions), Kosciusko County (portions)). Franchise award date: April 1, 1979. Franchise expiration date: N.A. Began: April 1, 1979.
Channel capacity: N.A. Channels available but not in use: N.A.

Basic Service
Subscribers: 409,278. Commercial subscribers: 3,585.
Programming (received off-air): WAND (NBC) Decatur; WBUI (CW, This TV) Decatur; WCCU (FOX, MeTV) Urbana; WCIA (CBS, MNT) Champaign; WCIX (CBS, MNT) Springfield; WEIU-TV (PBS) Charleston; WICD (ABC) Champaign; WILL-TV (PBS) Urbana.
Programming (via satellite): Comcast SportsNet Chicago; C-SPAN; C-SPAN 2; Pop; QVC; TBS; Weatherscan; WGN America.
Fee: $29.00-$42.00 installation; $29.49 monthly.

Expanded Basic Service 1
Subscribers: N.A.
Programming (via satellite): A&E; AMC; Animal Planet; BET; Bravo; Cartoon Network; CMT; CNBC; CNN; Comcast SportsNet Chicago; Comedy Central; Discovery Channel; Disney Channel; E! HD; ESPN; ESPN2; EWTN Global Catholic Network; Food Network; Fox News Channel; Fox Sports 1; FOX Sports Midwest; Freeform; FX; Hallmark Channel; HGTV; History; HLN; Lifetime; MSNBC; MTV; MTV2; National Geographic Channel; Nickelodeon; Oxygen; Spike TV; The Weather Channel; TLC; TNT; Travel Channel; Trinity Broadcasting Network (TBN); truTV; Turner Classic Movies; TV Land; USA Network; VH1.
Fee: $40.00 monthly.

Digital Basic Service
Subscribers: N.A.
Programming (via satellite): AXS TV; BBC America; Bloomberg Television; CBS Sports Network; CMT; Cooking Channel; C-SPAN 3; Discovery Digital Networks; Disney XD; DIY Network; DMX Music; ESPN Classic; ESPN HD; ESPN2 HD; ESPNews; ESPNU; Fuse; FXM; FYI; Golf Channel; Great American Country; GSN; HD Theater; History International; HRTV; IFC; LMN; LOGO; MTV Live; Nat Geo WILD; NBCSN; NFL Network; Nick 2; Nick Jr.; Nicktoons; Outdoor Channel; Sprout; Starz Encore (multiplexed); Sundance TV; Syfy; TeenNick; Tennis Channel; TNT HD; TVG Network; Universal HD; WE tv.

Digital Expanded Basic Service
Subscribers: N.A.
Programming (via satellite): HITS (Headend In The Sky).
Fee: $10.00 monthly.

Digital Pay Service 1
Pay Units: N.A.
Programming (via satellite): Cinemax (multiplexed); Flix; HBO (multiplexed); Showtime (multiplexed); Showtime HD; Starz (multiplexed); The Movie Channel (multiplexed).
Fee: $10.00 monthly (Cinemax or Starz), $13.00 monthly (HBO or Showtime/TMC).
Video-On-Demand: Yes
Pay-Per-View
ESPN (delivered digitally); iN DEMAND (delivered digitally); Playboy TV (delivered digitally); Special events (delivered digitally).

Internet Service
Operational: Yes.
Subscribers: 403,870.
Broadband Service: Comcast High Speed Internet.
Fee: $99.95 installation; $44.95 monthly; $10.00 modem lease; $149.95 modem purchase.

Telephone Service
Digital: Operational
Subscribers: 232,654.
Miles of Plant: 26,015.0 (coaxial); 6,668.0 (fiber optic). Homes passed: 1,288,432.
District Director: Melody Brucker. Chief Technician: Jim Lee.
Ownership: Comcast Cable Communications Inc. (MSO).

CHANNAHON—Comcast Cable. Now served by PEORIA, IL [IL0012]. ICA: IL0693.

CHAPIN—Mediacom. Now served by JACKSONVILLE, IL [IL0065]. ICA: IL0366.

CHARLESTON—Mediacom, 4290 Blue Stem Rd, PO Box 288, Charleston, IL 61920. Phones: 217-345-7071; 217-348-5533; 309-274-4500 (Chillicothe regional office). Fax: 217-345-7074. Web Site: http://www.mediacomcable.com. Also serves Ashmore, Kansas & Westfield. ICA: IL0064.
TV Market Ranking: Below 100 (Ashmore, Kansas, Westfield); Outside TV Markets (CHARLESTON). Franchise award date: N.A. Franchise expiration date: N.A. Began: July 1, 1967.
Channel capacity: N.A. Channels available but not in use: N.A.

Basic Service
Subscribers: 2,148. Commercial subscribers: 6.
Programming (received off-air): WAND (NBC) Decatur; WBUI (CW, This TV) Decatur; WCCU (FOX, MeTV) Urbana; WCIA (CBS, MNT) Champaign; WCIX (CBS, MNT) Springfield; WEIU-TV (PBS) Charleston; WICD (ABC) Champaign; WILL-TV (PBS) Urbana; WSIU-TV (PBS) Carbondale; WTHI-TV (CBS, FOX) Terre Haute; WTWO (NBC) Terre Haute; 5 FMs.
Programming (via satellite): C-SPAN; Disney Channel; INSP; Pop; QVC.
Fee: $45.00 installation; $43.00 monthly.

Expanded Basic Service 1
Subscribers: N.A.
Programming (via satellite): A&E; AMC; Animal Planet; BET; Cartoon Network; CMT; CNBC; CNN; Comcast SportsNet Chicago; Comedy Central; C-SPAN 2; Discovery Channel; Discovery Life Channel; E! HD; ESPN; ESPN Classic; ESPN2; EVINE Live; EWTN Global Catholic Network; Food Network; Fox News Channel; Fox Sports 1; FOX Sports Midwest; Freeform; FX; Hallmark Channel; HGTV; History; HLN; ION Television; Jewelry Television; Lifetime; LMN; MSNBC; MTV; Nickelodeon; Outdoor Channel; Oxygen; Spike TV; Syfy; TBS; The Weather Channel; TLC; TNT; Travel Channel; Trinity Broadcasting Network (TBN); truTV; USA Network; VH1; WE tv; WGN America.
Fee: $34.00 monthly.

Digital Basic Service
Subscribers: N.A.
Programming (via satellite): AXS TV; BBC America; Bloomberg Television; Bravo; CBS Sports Network; CCTV-Documentary; Cloo; CMT; Destination America; Discovery Kids Channel; Discovery Life Channel; Disney XD; ESPN HD; ESPN2 HD; ESPNews; ESPNU; FOX College Sports Central; FOX College Sports Pacific; Fox Sports 2; Fuse; FXM; FYI; Golf Channel; GolTV; GSN; HD Theater; History International; IFC; Investigation Discovery; ION Television; MC; MTV Classic; MTV Hits; MTV2; Nat Geo WILD; National Geographic Channel; NBCSN; Nick Jr.; Nicktoons; OWN: Oprah Winfrey Network; Qubo; Reelz; Science Channel; TeenNick; Tennis Channel; Turner Classic Movies; TV Land; TVG Network; Universal HD.

Digital Pay Service 1
Pay Units: N.A.
Programming (via satellite): Cinemax (multiplexed); Cinemax On Demand; HBO (multiplexed); HBO HD; HBO on Demand; Showtime (multiplexed); Showtime HD; Showtime On Demand; Starz (multiplexed); Starz Encore (multiplexed); Starz HD; Starz On Demand; The Movie Channel (multiplexed); The Movie Channel HD; The Movie Channel On Demand.
Fee: $11.95 monthly (HBO, Cinemax, Showtime/TMC or Starz/Encore).
Video-On-Demand: Yes
Pay-Per-View
iN DEMAND (delivered digitally); Playboy TV (delivered digitally); SexSee (delivered digitally); Juicy (delivered digitally); ESPN (delivered digitally).

Internet Service
Operational: Yes. Began: December 1, 2002.
Subscribers: 3,529.
Broadband Service: Mediacom High Speed Internet.
Fee: $59.95 installation; $40.95 monthly.

Telephone Service
Analog: Not Operational
Digital: Operational
Subscribers: 903.
Fee: $39.95 monthly
Miles of Plant: 206.0 (coaxial); 60.0 (fiber optic). Homes passed: 9,659.
Vice President: Don Hagwell. Area Operations Director: Todd Acker. Technical Operations Manager: Jerry Ferguson. Sales & Marketing Director: Stephanie Law. Customer Service Manager: Angie McHenry.
Ownership: Mediacom LLC (MSO).

CHATHAM—Formerly served by Insight Communications. Now served by Comcast Cable, SPRINGFIELD, IL [IL0016]. ICA: IL0114.

CHEMUNG—Mediacom. Now served by BELVIDERE TWP, IL [IL0282]. ICA: IL0479.

CHESTER—Formerly served by Charter Communications. Now served by NewWave Communications, SPARTA, IL [IL0147]. ICA: IL0144.

CHESTERFIELD (village)—Formerly served by CableDirect. No longer in operation. ICA: IL0480.

CHICAGO—Comcast Cable, 1255 West North Ave, Chicago, IL 60622. Phones: 847-281-5510; 630-600-6347; 773-394-8796; 847-585-6300 (Regional office). Fax: 773-486-2847. Web Site: http://www.comcast.com. ICA: IL0001.
TV Market Ranking: 3 (CHICAGO). Franchise award date: March 16, 1984. Franchise expiration date: N.A. Began: March 1, 1984.
Channel capacity: N.A. Channels available but not in use: N.A.

Basic Service
Subscribers: 305,109. Commercial subscribers: 23,667.
Programming (received off-air): WBBM-TV (CBS, Decades) Chicago; WCIU-TV (MeTV) Chicago; WCPX-TV (ION) Chicago; WFLD (FOX) Chicago; WGBO-DT (getTV, UNV) Joliet; WGN-TV (IND) Chicago; WJYS (IND) Hammond; WLS-TV (ABC, Live Well Network) Chicago; WMAQ-TV (COZI TV, NBC) Chicago; WPWR-TV (Buzzr, CW, MNT, Movies!) Gary; WSNS-TV (TMO) Chicago; WTTW (PBS) Chicago; WXFT-DT (UniMas) Aurora; WYCC (PBS) Chicago; WYIN (PBS) Gary; 28 FMs.
Programming (via satellite): BET; C-SPAN; C-SPAN 2; Pop; TBS.
Fee: $29.00-$42.00 installation; $33.24 monthly.

Expanded Basic Service 1
Subscribers: N.A.
Programming (via satellite): A&E; AMC; Animal Planet; Bravo; Cartoon Network; CLTV; CNBC; CNN; Comcast SportsNet Chicago; Comedy Central; Discovery Channel; Disney Channel; Disney XD; E! HD; ESPN; ESPN2; EWTN Global Catholic Network; Food Network; Fox News Channel; Freeform; FX; Golf Channel; HGTV; History; HLN; Lifetime; MoviePlex; MSNBC; MTV; MTV2; NBCSN; Nickelodeon; Oxygen; QVC; Spike TV; The Weather Channel; TLC; TNT; Total Living Network; Travel Channel; truTV; TV Land; Univision; USA Network; VH1.
Fee: $34.00 monthly.

Digital Basic Service
Subscribers: N.A.
Programming (via satellite): BBC America; Bloomberg Television; CMT; Cooking Channel; Discovery Digital Networks; Disney XD; DIY Network; ESPN Classic; ESPN HD; ESPN2 HD; ESPNews; EVINE Live; Flix; FOX College Sports Central; FOX College Sports Pacific; Fox Sports 1; Fuse; FXM; FYI; GolTV; Great American Country; GSN; Hallmark Channel; HD Theater; History International; HITS (Headend In The Sky); IFC; LMN; LOGO; MC; MTV Live; Nat Geo WILD; National Geographic Channel; NFL Network; Nick 2; Nick Jr.; Nicktoons; Outdoor Channel; Ovation; Sprout; Starz Encore (multiplexed); Sundance TV; Syfy; TeenNick; The Word Network; TNT HD; Trinity Broadcasting Network (TBN); Turner Classic Movies; TVG Network; Universal HD; UP; Versus HD; WE tv; Weatherscan.

Digital Pay Service 1
Pay Units: N.A.
Programming (via satellite): Cinemax (multiplexed); Cinemax HD; Flix; HBO (multiplexed); HBO HD; Showtime (multiplexed); Showtime HD; Starz (multiplexed); Starz HD; The Movie Channel (multiplexed); TV Polonia.
Fee: $16.00 monthly (each).
Video-On-Demand: Yes
Pay-Per-View
Playboy TV (delivered digitally); Fresh (delivered digitally); iN DEMAND; ESPN (delivered digitally); Sports PPV (delivered digitally); NBA TV (delivered digitally); Shorteez (delivered digitally); iN DEMAND (delivered digitally).

Internet Service
Operational: Yes.
Subscribers: 437,434.
Broadband Service: Comcast High Speed Internet.
Fee: $99.00 installation; $42.95 monthly.

Telephone Service
Digital: Operational
Subscribers: 206,120.
Fee: $44.95 monthly
Miles of Plant: 14,792.0 (coaxial); 5,443.0 (fiber optic). Homes passed: 1,251,760.

Cable Systems—Illinois

Regional Senior Vice President: Steve Reimer. Area Vice President: Mark Allen. Vice President, Technical Operations: Bob Curtis. Vice President, Marketing & Sales: Eric Schaefer. Vice President, Communications: Rich Ruggiero.
Ownership: Comcast Cable Communications Inc. (MSO).

CHICAGO—Formerly served by Preferred Entertainment of Chicago. No longer in operation. ICA: IL0615.

CHICAGO—RCN Corp. Formerly [IL0661]. This cable system has converted to IPTV. 196 Van Buren St, Ste 300, Herndon, VA 20170. Phones: 800-746-4726; 609-681-2281. Web Site: http://www.rcn.com. Also serves Andersonville, Avondale, Belmont Harbor, Bridgeport, Bronzeville, Buena Park, Clybourn Corridor, Edgewater, Evanston, Gold Coast, Hollywood Park, Hyde Park, Irving Park, Lakeview, Lincoln Park, Morton Grove, Old Town, Ravenswood, River North, Rogers Park (portions), Roscoe Village, Skokie, Southport Corridor, Streeterville, The Loop, Uptown & Wrigleyville. ICA: IL5236.
TV Market Ranking: 3 (ANDERSONVILLE, CHICAGO, EDGEWATER, GOLD COAST, HYDE PARK, LAKEVIEW, LINCOLN PARK, ROGERS PARK (PORTIONS), SKOKIE).
Channel capacity: N.A. Channels available but not in use: N.A.
Limited Basic
Subscribers: 75,476. Commercial subscribers: 3,828.
Fee: $28.74 monthly. 57 channels - 40 in SD & 17 in HD. $9.95 HD equipment fee for HD channels.
Signature Digital Cable
Subscribers: N.A.
Fee: $59.99 monthly. 304 channels - 237 in SD & 67 in HD. $9.95 HD equipment fee for HD channels.
HD Expanded Pack
Subscribers: N.A.
Fee: $8.99 monthly. 6 additional HD channels.
Premiere Movies & Entertainment
Subscribers: N.A.
Fee: $10.99 monthly. 33 channels - 29 in SD & 4 in HD. $9.95 HD equipment fee for HD channels.
Premiere Family & Children
Subscribers: N.A.
Fee: $5.99 monthly. 19 channels - 17 in SD & 2 in HD. $9.95 HD equipment fee for HD channels.
Premiere News & Information
Subscribers: N.A.
Fee: $5.99 monthly. 21 channels - 16 in SD & 5 in HD. $9.95 HD equipment fee for HD channels.
Premiere Sports
Subscribers: N.A.
Fee: $9.99 monthly. 36 channels - 28 in SD & 8 in HD. $9.95 HD equipment fee for HD channels.
Premiere Total Pack
Subscribers: N.A.
Fee: $20.95 monthly. 121 channels - 96 in SD & 25 in HD. $9.95 HD equipment fee for HD channels.
MiVision Lite
Subscribers: N.A.
Fee: $12.00 monthly. 40 channels in Spanish.
MiVision Plus
Subscribers: N.A.
Fee: $22.95 monthly. 44 channels in Spanish.
Cinemax
Subscribers: N.A.
Fee: $9.99 monthly. 16 channels - 8 in SD & 8 in HD including Cinemax on Demand & MAXGo. $9.95 HD equipment fee for HD channels.
HBO
Subscribers: N.A.
Fee: $15.95 monthly. 14 channels - 7 in SD & 7 in HD including HBO on Demand & HBO Go. $9.95 HD equipment fee for HD channels.
Cinemax/HBO
Subscribers: N.A.
Fee: $19.95 monthly. 16 channels of Cinemax- 8 in SD & 8 in HD & 14 channels of HBO - 7 in SD & 7 in SD plus Cinemax on Demand, HBO in Demand, MAXGo & HBO Go. $9.95 HD equipment fee for HD channels.
Showtime/TMC
Subscribers: N.A.
Fee: $4.95 monthly. 20 channels - 9 in SD & 11 in HD plus Showtime on Demand & The Movie Channel on Demand. $9.95 HD equipment fee for HD channels.
Starz
Subscribers: N.A.
Fee: $5.00 monthly. 13 channels - 9 in SD & 4 in HD plus Starz on Demand. $9.95 HD equipment fee for HD channels.
Video-On-Demand: Yes
Internet Service
Operational: Yes.
Fee: $39.99-$59.99 monthly.
Telephone Service
Digital: Operational
Fee: $29.99 monthly
Vice President & General Manager: Jamie Hill.
Ownership: RCN Corp. (MSO).

CHICAGO (Area 4)—Comcast Cable. Now served by CHICAGO, IL [IL0001]. ICA: IL0003.

CHICAGO (Area 5)—Comcast Cable. Now served by CHICAGO, IL [IL0001]. ICA: IL0005.

CHICAGO (Areas 1, 4 & 5)—Comcast Cable. Now served by CHICAGO, IL [IL0001]. ICA: IL0002.

CHICAGO (portions)—RCN Corp. This cable system has converted to IPTV. See CHICAGO, IL [IL5236]. ICA: IL0661.

CHICAGO (southern portion)—WOW! Internet, Cable & Phone. Now served by NAPERVILLE, IL [IL0655]. ICA: IL0680.

CHILLICOTHE—Mediacom, 3900 26th Ave, Moline, IL 61265. Phones: 309-797-2580 (Moline regional office); 309-274-4500 (Chillicothe office). Fax: 309-797-2414. Web Site: http://www.mediacomcable.com. Also serves Brimfield, Bureau, Dunlap, Granville, Hennepin, Henry, Hopewell, Mark, Oak Park Estates, Peoria County, Princeville, Putnam County (northeastern portion), Rome, Sparland & Standard. ICA: IL0118.
TV Market Ranking: 83 (Brimfield, CHILLICOTHE, Dunlap, Henry, Hopewell, Peoria County, Princeville, Rome, Sparland); Below 100 (Bureau, Granville, Hennepin, Mark, Oak Park Estates, Putnam County (northeastern portion), Standard). Franchise award date: January 15, 1980. Franchise expiration date: N.A. Began: February 1, 1980.
Channel capacity: N.A. Channels available but not in use: N.A.
Basic Service
Subscribers: 3,000.
Programming (received off-air): WAOE (Antenna TV, MNT) Peoria; WEEK-TV (ABC, CW, NBC) Peoria; WHOI (Comet) Peoria; WMBD-TV (Bounce TV, CBS) Peoria; WTVP (PBS) Peoria; WYZZ-TV (FOX, The Country Network) Bloomington.
Programming (via satellite): EWTN Global Catholic Network; TBS; Trinity Broadcasting Network (TBN); WGN America.
Fee: $45.00 installation; $43.00 monthly.
Expanded Basic Service 1
Subscribers: N.A.
Programming (via satellite): A&E; AMC; Animal Planet; Bloomberg Television; Cartoon Network; CMT; CNBC; CNN; Comcast SportsNet Chicago; Comedy Central; C-SPAN; Discovery Channel; Disney Channel; E! HD; ESPN; ESPN2; Food Network; Fox News Channel; Fox Sports 1; FOX Sports Networks; Freeform; FX; FXM; FYI; HGTV; History; History International; HLN; Lifetime; LMN; MSNBC; MTV; Nickelodeon; Pop; QVC; Spike TV; Syfy; The Weather Channel; TLC; TNT; TV Land; USA Network; VH1.
Fee: $34.00 monthly.
Digital Basic Service
Subscribers: N.A.
Programming (via satellite): BBC America; Discovery Digital Networks; DMX Music; Golf Channel; GSN; IFC; NBCSN; Turner Classic Movies.
Digital Pay Service 1
Pay Units: N.A.
Programming (via satellite): Cinemax (multiplexed); HBO (multiplexed); Showtime (multiplexed); Starz (multiplexed); The Movie Channel (multiplexed).
Fee: $11.95 monthly (HBO, Cinemax, Showtime/TMC or Starz/Encore).
Video-On-Demand: No
Pay-Per-View
Hot Choice; Hot Choice (delivered digitally); iN DEMAND; iN DEMAND (delivered digitally); Playboy TV; Playboy TV (delivered digitally); Pleasure (delivered digitally); Fresh; Fresh (delivered digitally); Shorteez (delivered digitally).
Internet Service
Operational: Yes.
Broadband Service: Mediacom High Speed Internet.
Fee: $59.95 installation; $40.95 monthly.
Telephone Service
Analog: Not Operational
Digital: Operational
Fee: $39.95 monthly
Homes passed: 5,348. Miles of plant (coax & fiber) included in Moline
Regional Vice President: Cari Fenzel. Area Manager: Don DeMay. Engineering Director: Mitch Carlson. Marketing Director: Greg Evans. Technical Operations Manager: Chris Toalson.
Ownership: Mediacom LLC (MSO).

CISCO (village)—Formerly served by Longview Communications. No longer in operation. ICA: IL0481.

CISNE—Wabash Independent Networks. Now served by FLORA, IL [IL0140]. ICA: IL0320.

CISSNA PARK (village)—Park TV & Electronics Inc, 205 East Railroad Ave, PO Box 9, Cissna Park, IL 60924. Phones: 800-825-3882; 815-457-2659. Web Site: http://www.parktvcable.com. ICA: IL0482.
TV Market Ranking: Outside TV Markets (CISSNA PARK (VILLAGE)). Franchise award date: N.A. Franchise expiration date: N.A. Began: April 1, 1984.
Channel capacity: N.A. Channels available but not in use: N.A.
Basic Service
Subscribers: 198.
Programming (received off-air): WAND (NBC) Decatur; WBUI (CW, This TV) Decatur; WCCU (FOX, MeTV) Urbana; WCIA (CBS, MNT) Champaign; WICD (ABC) Champaign; WILL-TV (PBS) Urbana.
Programming (via satellite): A&E; AMC; Animal Planet; BTN; Cartoon Network; CMT; CNBC; CNN; Comedy Central; Discovery Channel; Disney Channel; E! HD; ESPN; ESPN2; Food Network; Fox News Channel; Fox Sports 1; Freeform; FX; GSN; Hallmark Channel; HGTV; History; Lifetime; MTV; Nickelodeon; Outdoor Channel; Oxygen; QVC; Spike TV; Syfy; TBS; The Weather Channel; TLC; TNT; Travel Channel; Trinity Broadcasting Network (TBN); Turner Classic Movies; TV Land; USA Network; VH1; WGN America.
Fee: $47.00 monthly.
Pay Service 1
Pay Units: N.A.
Programming (via satellite): Cinemax; HBO.
Video-On-Demand: No
Internet Service
Operational: Yes.
Fee: $29.95-$54.95 monthly.
Telephone Service
None
Miles of Plant: 15.0 (coaxial); None (fiber optic). Homes passed: 900. Miles of plant & homes passed includes Armstrong, Buckley (village), Potomac (village) & Rankin (village)
President & General Manager: Joe Young.
Ownership: Park TV & Electronics Inc. (MSO).

CLAREMONT—Formerly served by CableDirect. No longer in operation. ICA: IL0437.

CLAY CITY—Mediacom, 4290 Blue Stem Rd, PO Box 288, Charleston, IL 61920. Phone: 217-348-5533. Fax: 217-348-5533. Web Site: http://www.mediacomcable.com. ICA: IL0686.
TV Market Ranking: Outside TV Markets (CLAY CITY).
Channel capacity: N.A. Channels available but not in use: N.A.
Internet Service
Operational: Yes.
Telephone Service
None
Operations Director: Todd Acker. Technical Operations Manager: Jerry Ferguson.
Ownership: Mediacom LLC (MSO).

CLINTON—Mediacom. Now served by RANTOUL, IL [IL0089]. ICA: IL0113.

COBDEN—Mediacom. Now served by ZEIGLER, IL [IL0123]. ICA: IL0260.

COFFEEN—Mediacom, 4290 Blue Stem Rd, PO Box 288, Charleston, IL 61920. Phone: 217-348-5533. Fax: 217-345-7074. Web Site: http://www.mediacomcable.com. ICA: IL0344.
TV Market Ranking: Outside TV Markets (COFFEEN). Franchise award date: N.A. Franchise expiration date: N.A. Began: December 15, 1983.
Channel capacity: N.A. Channels available but not in use: N.A.
Basic Service
Subscribers: 16.
Programming (received off-air): KDNL-TV (ABC, The Country Network) St. Louis;

2017 Edition   D-193

Illinois—Cable Systems

KETC (PBS) St. Louis; KMOV (CBS) St. Louis; KPLR-TV (CW, This TV) St. Louis; WAND (NBC) Decatur; WICS (ABC, The Country Network) Springfield; WRSP-TV (Antenna TV, FOX, MeTV) Springfield. Programming (via satellite): A&E; AMC; Animal Planet; Bravo; Cartoon Network; CMT; CNN; Comedy Central; Discovery Channel; ESPN; ESPN2; Freeform; HGTV; History; Lifetime; MTV; Nickelodeon; Spike TV; Syfy; TBS; The Weather Channel; TLC; TNT; TV Land; USA Network; WGN America.
Fee: $45.00 installation; $69.95 monthly.

Pay Service 1
Pay Units: N.A.
Programming (via satellite): Cinemax; HBO.
Fee: $25.00 installation; $7.95 monthly (Cinemax), $13.50 monthly (HBO).

Video-On-Demand: No
Internet Service
Operational: No.
Telephone Service
None
Miles of Plant: 9.0 (coaxial); None (fiber optic). Homes passed: 315.
Area Operations Director: Todd Acker. Technical Operations Manager: Jerry Ferguson.
Ownership: Mediacom LLC (MSO).

COLFAX—Mediacom. Now served by LE ROY, IL [IL0539]. ICA: IL0319.

COMPTON—Formerly served by Compton Cable TV Co. No longer in operation. ICA: IL0483.

COMPTON—Formerly served by Heartland Cable Broadband. No longer in operation. ICA: IL0685.

CONGERVILLE—Tel-Star Cablevision Inc. Now served by METAMORA, IL [IL0326]. ICA: IL0484.

CORNELL—Mediacom. Now served by PONTIAC, IL [IL0109]. ICA: IL0374.

CORTLAND (village)—Mediacom, 3900 26th Ave, Moline, IL 61265. Phone: 309-797-2580. Fax: 309-797-2414. Web Site: http://www.mediacomcable.com. Also serves Davis Junction, DeKalb County (portions), Gilberts, Hampshire, Kirkland, Malta, Maple Park (village), Monroe Center & Rolling Meadows Mobile Home Park. ICA: IL0485.
TV Market Ranking: 97 (CORTLAND (VILLAGE), Davis Junction, Hampshire, Kirkland, Malta, Maple Park (village), Monroe Center, Rolling Meadows Mobile Home Park); Below 100 (Gilberts). Franchise award date: November 25, 1985. Franchise expiration date: N.A. Began: N.A.
Channel capacity: N.A. Channels available but not in use: N.A.

Basic Service
Subscribers: 1,633.
Programming (received off-air): WBBM-TV (CBS, Decades) Chicago; WCIU-TV (MeTV) Chicago; WCPX-TV (ION) Chicago; WFLD (FOX) Chicago; WGBO-DT (getTV, UNV) Joliet; WGN-TV (IND) Chicago; WIFR (Antenna TV, CBS) Freeport; WLS-TV (ABC, Live Well Network) Chicago; WMAQ-TV (COZI TV, NBC) Chicago; WPWR-TV (Buzzr, CW, MNT, Movies!) Gary; WQRF-TV (Bounce TV, FOX) Rockford; WREX (CW, MeTV, NBC) Rockford; WSNS-TV (TMO) Chicago; WTTW (PBS) Chicago; WWTO-TV (TBN) La Salle; WYCC (PBS) Chicago.
Programming (via satellite): TBS.
Fee: $45.00 installation; $43.00 monthly.

Expanded Basic Service 1
Subscribers: N.A.
Programming (via satellite): A&E; AMC; Animal Planet; Bravo; Cartoon Network; CNBC; CNN; Comcast SportsNet Chicago; Comedy Central; C-SPAN; C-SPAN 2; Discovery Channel; Disney Channel; E! HD; ESPN; ESPN2; EVINE Live; EWTN Global Catholic Network; Food Network; Fox News Channel; Fox Sports 1; Freeform; FX; Hallmark Channel; HGTV; History; HLN; Lifetime; LMN; MSNBC; MTV; Nickelodeon; Pop; QVC; Spike TV; Syfy; The Weather Channel; TLC; TNT; Travel Channel; Trinity Broadcasting Network (TBN); truTV; Turner Classic Movies; TV Land; USA Network; VH1.
Fee: $34.00 monthly.

Digital Basic Service
Subscribers: N.A.
Programming (via satellite): BBC America; Bloomberg Television; CCTV-Documentary; Cloo; Destination America; Discovery Kids Channel; Discovery Life Channel; ESPN HD; ESPN2 HD; ESPNews; ESPNU; Fox Sports 2; Fuse; FXM; FYI; Golf Channel; GSN; History International; IFC; Investigation Discovery; ION Television; MC; MTV Classic; MTV Hits; MTV2; Nat Geo WILD; National Geographic Channel; Nick Jr.; Nicktoons; Outdoor Channel; OWN: Oprah Winfrey Network; Qubo; Reelz; Science Channel; Sundance TV; TeenNick; TVG Network; WE tv.

Digital Expanded Basic Service
Subscribers: N.A.
Programming (via satellite): CBS Sports Network; FOX College Sports Central; FOX College Sports Pacific; GolTV; Tennis Channel.
Fee: $3.95 monthly.

Digital Expanded Basic Service 2
Subscribers: N.A.
Programming (via satellite): AXS TV; HD Theater; Universal HD.
Fee: $6.95 monthly.

Digital Pay Service 1
Pay Units: N.A.
Programming (via satellite): Cinemax (multiplexed); Flix; HBO (multiplexed); HBO HD; Showtime (multiplexed); Showtime HD; Starz (multiplexed); Starz Encore (multiplexed); Starz HD; Sundance TV; The Movie Channel (multiplexed); The Movie Channel HD.
Fee: $11.95 monthly (HBO, Cinemax, Showtime/TMC or Starz/Encore).

Video-On-Demand: Yes
Pay-Per-View
iN DEMAND (delivered digitally); Playboy TV (delivered digitally); SexSee (delivered digitally); ESPN (delivered digitally).

Internet Service
Operational: Yes, DSL.
Broadband Service: Mediacom High Speed Internet.
Fee: $59.95 installation; $45.95 monthly.

Telephone Service
Digital: Operational
Fee: $39.95 monthly
Homes passed: 2,420. Miles of plant included in Moline.
Regional Vice President: Cari Fenzel. Engineering Director: Mitch Carlson. Technical Operations Manager: Chris Toalson. Marketing Director: Greg Evans.
Ownership: Mediacom LLC (MSO).

COULTERVILLE—Mediacom, 90 Main St, Benton, KY 42025-1132. Phones: 417-875-5560 (Springfield regional office); 270-527-2909. Fax: 270-527-0813. Web Site: http://www.mediacomcable.com. Also serves Hecker, Monroe County (portions), Red Bud, Smithton & Tilden. ICA: IL0152.
TV Market Ranking: 11 (Hecker, Monroe County (portions), Red Bud, Smithton); Outside TV Markets (COULTERVILLE, Tilden). Franchise award date: October 1, 1982. Franchise expiration date: N.A. Began: December 1, 1983.
Channel capacity: N.A. Channels available but not in use: N.A.

Basic Service
Subscribers: 568.
Programming (received off-air): KDNL-TV (ABC, The Country Network) St. Louis; KETC (PBS) St. Louis; KFVS-TV (CBS, CW, MeTV) Cape Girardeau; KMOV (CBS) St. Louis; KNLC (IND, My Family TV) St. Louis; KPLR-TV (CW, This TV) St. Louis; KSDK (Bounce TV, NBC) St. Louis; KTVI (Antenna TV, Escape, FOX) St. Louis; WRBU (ION) East St. Louis; WSIU-TV (PBS) Carbondale.
Programming (via satellite): C-SPAN; Pop; QVC; WGN America.
Fee: $36.95 installation; $42.00 monthly.

Expanded Basic Service 1
Subscribers: N.A.
Programming (via satellite): A&E; AMC; Animal Planet; BET; Bravo; Cartoon Network; CMT; CNBC; CNN; Comedy Central; C-SPAN 2; Discovery Channel; Discovery Life Channel; Disney Channel; E! HD; ESPN; ESPN2; EVINE Live; Food Network; Fox News Channel; Fox Sports 1; FOX Sports Midwest; Freeform; FX; Great American Country; Hallmark Channel; HGTV; History; HLN; INSP; Lifetime; MSNBC; MTV; Nickelodeon; Outdoor Channel; Spike TV; Syfy; TBS; The Weather Channel; TLC; TNT; Travel Channel; Trinity Broadcasting Network (TBN); truTV; TV Land; USA Network; VH1; WE tv.

Digital Basic Service
Subscribers: N.A.
Programming (via satellite): BBC America; Destination America; Discovery Kids Channel; Fuse; FXM; FYI; Golf Channel; History International; IFC; Investigation Discovery; LMN; MC; National Geographic Channel; NBCSN; Nick Jr.; Nicktoons; OWN: Oprah Winfrey Network; TeenNick; Turner Classic Movies.

Digital Pay Service 1
Pay Units: N.A.
Programming (via satellite): Cinemax (multiplexed); Flix; HBO (multiplexed); Showtime (multiplexed); Starz (multiplexed); Starz Encore; Sundance TV; The Movie Channel (multiplexed).

Video-On-Demand: Yes
Internet Service
Operational: Yes.
Broadband Service: Mediacom High Speed Internet.

Telephone Service
Digital: Operational
Miles of Plant: 77.0 (coaxial); None (fiber optic). Homes passed: 2,763.
Regional Vice President: Bill Copeland. General Manager: Dale Haney. Regional Technical Operations Director: Alan Freedman. Marketing Director: Will Kuebler. Technical Operations Manager: Jeff Brown. Marketing Manager: Melanie Westerman.
Ownership: Mediacom LLC (MSO).

COULTERVILLE—Mediacom. Now served by COULTERVILLE (formerly RED BUD), IL [IL0152]. ICA: IL0234.

COWDEN—Clearvision Cable Systems Inc, 1785 US Rte 40, Greenup, IL 62428-3501. Phone: 217-923-5594. Fax: 217-923-5681. ICA: IL0337.
TV Market Ranking: Outside TV Markets (COWDEN). Franchise award date: N.A. Franchise expiration date: N.A. Began: April 1, 1985.
Channel capacity: N.A. Channels available but not in use: N.A.

Basic Service
Subscribers: 25.
Programming (received off-air): WAND (NBC) Decatur; WICS (ABC, The Country Network) Springfield; WPXS (IND) Mount Vernon; WRSP-TV (Antenna TV, FOX, MeTV) Springfield; WTOL (CBS, MeTV) Toledo; WUSI-TV (PBS) Olney.
Programming (via satellite): CMT; CNN; Discovery Channel; Disney Channel; ESPN; Freeform; HGTV; MTV; Nickelodeon; Spike TV; TBS; TNT; Turner Classic Movies; USA Network; VH1; WGN America.
Fee: $47.95 monthly.

Pay Service 1
Pay Units: N.A.
Programming (via satellite): Cinemax; HBO.

Video-On-Demand: No
Internet Service
Operational: No.
Telephone Service
None
Miles of Plant: 7.0 (coaxial); None (fiber optic). Homes passed: 277.
President & General Manager: Michael Bauguss. Secretary: Gwyndolyn S. Bauguss.
Ownership: Clearvision Cable Systems Inc. (MSO).

CULLOM—Mediacom. Now served by PONTIAC, IL [IL0109]. ICA: IL0289.

CUSTER PARK—Comcast Cable. Now served by PEORIA, IL [IL0012]. ICA: IL0487.

DAHLGREN—Hamilton County Communications. Formerly [IL0381]. This cable system has converted to IPTV, Rte 142E, PO Box 40, Dahlgren, IL 62828. Phones: 618-736-2242; 800-447-8725; 618-736-2211. Fax: 617-736-2616. Web Site: http://www.hcc.coop. Also serves Belle Rive, Broughton, Ewing, Galatia, Macedonia, McLeansboro, Opdyke, Springerton, Thompsonville & Wayne City. ICA: IL5024.
Channel capacity: N.A. Channels available but not in use: N.A.

Essential
Subscribers: 115.
Fee: $50.00 installation; $62.59 monthly. Includes 60+ channels.

Extended
Subscribers: 58.
Fee: $74.95 monthly. Includes 111+ channels plus 50 music channels.

Entire
Subscribers: 5.
Fee: $124.95 monthly. Includes 170+ channels plus 50 music channels & all premium channels.

Cinemax
Subscribers: N.A.
Fee: $12.95 monthly. Includes 11 channels.

Epix
Subscribers: N.A.
Fee: $6.95 monthly. Includes 4 channels.

HBO
Subscribers: N.A.
Fee: $15.95 monthly. Includes 7 channels.

Showtime/TMC
Subscribers: N.A.
Fee: $12.95 monthly. Includes 11 channels.

Cable Systems—Illinois

Starz/Encore
Subscribers: N.A.
Fee: $12.95 monthly. Includes 16 channels.
Internet Service
Operational: Yes.
Fee: $35.99-$49.99 monthly.
Telephone Service
Digital: Operational
Fee: $7.95 monthly
Executive Vice President & General Manager: Kevin Pyle.
Ownership: Hamilton County Communications Inc.

DAHLGREN—Hamilton County Communications. This cable system has converted to IPTV. See DAHLGREN, IL [IL5024]. ICA: IL0381.

DALLAS CITY—Mediacom, 609 South 4th St, PO Box 334, Chillicothe, IL 61523. Phones: 309-469-2027; 309-274-4500. Fax: 309-274-3188. Web Site: http://www.mediacomcable.com. Also serves Lomax, Nauvoo, Oquawka, Pontoosuc, Roseville & Stronghurst. ICA: IL0274.
TV Market Ranking: Below 100 (DALLAS CITY, Lomax, Oquawka, Pontoosuc, Stronghurst, Nauvoo, Roseville). Franchise award date: N.A. Franchise expiration date: N.A. Began: N.A.
Channel capacity: N.A. Channels available but not in use: N.A.
Basic Service
Subscribers: 799.
Programming (received off-air): KIIN (PBS) Iowa City; KLJB (CW, FOX, MeTV) Davenport; KWQC-TV (NBC) Davenport; WHBF-TV (CBS) Rock Island; WHOI (Comet) Peoria; WQAD-TV (ABC, Antenna TV) Moline.
Programming (via satellite): Freeform; INSP; Radar Channel; WGN America.
Fee: $45.00 installation; $72.95 monthly.
Digital Basic Service
Subscribers: N.A.
Programming (via satellite): BBC America; Bloomberg Television; CBS Sports Network; CCTV-Documentary; Cloo; Destination America; Discovery Kids Channel; ESPNews; FOX College Sports Central; FOX College Sports Pacific; Fuse; FXM; FYI; Golf Channel; GolTV; History International; IFC; Investigation Discovery; ION Television; LMN; MTV Classic; MTV Hits; MTV2; Nat Geo WILD; National Geographic Channel; NBCSN; Nick Jr.; Nicktoons; Outdoor Channel; OWN; Oprah Winfrey Network; Qubo; Reelz; Science Channel; Sundance TV; TeenNick; Tennis Channel; Turner Classic Movies; TVG Network.
Digital Expanded Basic Service
Subscribers: N.A.
Programming (via satellite): AXS TV; ESPN HD; ESPN2 HD; HD Theater; Universal HD.
Fee: $6.95 monthly.
Digital Pay Service 1
Pay Units: N.A.
Programming (via satellite): Cinemax (multiplexed); Flix (multiplexed); HBO (multiplexed); HBO HD; Showtime (multiplexed); Showtime HD; Starz (multiplexed); Starz Encore (multiplexed); Starz HD; The Movie Channel (multiplexed); The Movie Channel HD.
Fee: $11.95 monthly (HBO, Cinemax, Starz/Encore or Showtime/TMC).
Video-On-Demand: No
Pay-Per-View
iN DEMAND (delivered digitally); Playboy TV (delivered digitally).

Internet Service
Operational: Yes.
Broadband Service: Mediacom High Speed Internet.
Fee: $59.95 installation; $45.95 monthly.
Telephone Service
Digital: Operational
Fee: $39.95 monthly
Miles of Plant: 51.0 (coaxial); None (fiber optic). Homes passed: 2,697.
Vice President: Don Hagwell. Operations Director: Gary Wightman. Technical Operations Manager: Larry Brackman. Marketing Director: Stephanie Law.
Ownership: Mediacom LLC (MSO).

DALLAS CITY—Mediacom. Now served by DALLAS CITY (formerly Roseville), IL [IL0274]. ICA: IL0230.

DANVERS—Mediacom. Now served by ROANOKE, IL [IL0068]. ICA: IL0303.

DANVILLE—Formerly served by Insight Communications. Now served by Comcast Cable, CHAMPAIGN, IL [IL0019]. ICA: IL0041.

DECATUR—Formerly served by Insight Communications. Now served by Comcast Cable, SPRINGFIELD, IL [IL0016]. ICA: IL0024.

DEER CREEK—Mediacom. Now served by ROANOKE, IL [IL0068]. ICA: IL0306.

DEKALB—Comcast Cable. Now served by MOUNT PROSPECT, IL [IL0036]. ICA: IL0046.

DELAVAN—Mediacom, 4290 Blue Stem Rd, PO Box 288, Charleston, IL 61920. Phone: 217-348-5533. Fax: 217-345-7074. Web Site: http://www.mediacomcable.com. Also serves Cantrall, Elkhart, Emden, Green Valley, Greenview, Hartsburg, Middletown, New Holland, San Jose & Sangamon County (portions). ICA: IL0172.
TV Market Ranking: 64 (Cantrall, Elkhart, Hartsburg, Middletown, New Holland, Sangamon County (portions)); 64,83 (Emden, Green Valley, San Jose); 83 (Greenview); 83,83 (DELAVAN). Franchise award date: N.A. Franchise expiration date: N.A. Began: September 1, 1982.
Channel capacity: N.A. Channels available but not in use: N.A.
Basic Service
Subscribers: 726.
Programming (received off-air): WAND (NBC) Decatur; WAOE (Antenna TV, MNT) Peoria; WBUI (CW, This TV) Decatur; WCIA (CBS, MNT) Champaign; WCIX (CBS, MNT) Springfield; WEEK-TV (ABC, CW, NBC) Peoria; WHOI (Comet) Peoria; WICS (ABC, The Country Network) Springfield; WILL-TV (PBS) Urbana; WMBD-TV (Bounce TV, CBS) Peoria; WRSP-TV (Antenna TV, FOX, MeTV) Springfield; WSEC (PBS) Jacksonville; WTVP (PBS) Peoria; WYZZ-TV (FOX, The Country Network) Bloomington.
Programming (via satellite): A&E; AMC; Animal Planet; BET; Bravo; Cartoon Network; CMT; CNBC; CNN; Comcast SportsNet Chicago; Comedy Central; C-SPAN; C-SPAN 2; Discovery Channel; Discovery Life Channel; Disney Channel; E! HD; ESPN; ESPN2; EVINE Live; EWTN Global Catholic Network; Food Network; Fox News Channel; Fox Sports 1; Freeform; FX; Hallmark Channel; HGTV; History; HLN; INSP; ION Television; Lifetime; MoviePlex; MSNBC; MTV; Nickelodeon; Pop; QVC; RFD-TV; Spike TV;

Syfy; TBS; The Weather Channel; TLC; TNT; Travel Channel; Trinity Broadcasting Network (TBN); truTV; TV Land; USA Network; VH1; WE tv; WGN America.
Fee: $45.00 installation; $72.95 monthly.
Digital Basic Service
Subscribers: N.A.
Programming (via satellite): AXS TV; BBC America; Bloomberg Television; CCTV-Documentary; Cloo; Destination America; Discovery Kids Channel; ESPN HD; ESPNews; Fuse; FXM; FYI; Golf Channel; GSN; HD Theater; History International; IFC; Investigation Discovery; ION Television; LMN; MC; MTV Classic; MTV Hits; MTV2; Nat Geo WILD; National Geographic Channel; NBCSN; Nick Jr.; Nicktoons; Outdoor Channel; OWN; Oprah Winfrey Network; Qubo; Reelz; Science Channel; TeenNick; Turner Classic Movies; TVG Network; Universal HD.
Digital Expanded Basic Service
Subscribers: N.A.
Programming (via satellite): CBS Sports Network; ESPNU; FOX College Sports Central; FOX College Sports Pacific; Fox Sports 2; GolTV; Tennis Channel.
Fee: $3.95 monthly.
Digital Pay Service 1
Pay Units: N.A.
Programming (via satellite): Cinemax (multiplexed); Cinemax On Demand; HBO (multiplexed); HBO HD; HBO on Demand; Showtime (multiplexed); Showtime HD; Showtime On Demand; Starz (multiplexed); Starz Encore (multiplexed); Starz HD; Starz On Demand; The Movie Channel (multiplexed); The Movie Channel HD; The Movie Channel On Demand.
Fee: $11.95 monthly (each).
Video-On-Demand: Yes
Pay-Per-View
iN DEMAND (delivered digitally); Juicy (delivered digitally); Playboy TV (delivered digitally); SexSee (delivered digitally).
Internet Service
Operational: Yes.
Broadband Service: Mediacom High Speed Internet.
Fee: $59.95 installation; $40.95 monthly.
Telephone Service
Digital: Operational
Fee: $39.95 monthly
Miles of Plant: 46.0 (coaxial); 19.0 (fiber optic). Homes passed: 2,179.
General Manager: Todd Acker. Technical Operations Manager: Jerry Ferguson. Marketing Director: James Friske.
Ownership: Mediacom LLC (MSO).

DIETERICH—Clearvision Cable Systems Inc, 1785 US Rte 40, Greenup, IL 62428-3501. Phone: 217-923-5594. Fax: 217-923-5681. Also serves Montrose. ICA: IL0659.
TV Market Ranking: Outside TV Markets (DIETERICH, Montrose).
Channel capacity: N.A. Channels available but not in use: N.A.
Basic Service
Subscribers: 76.
Programming (received off-air): WAND (NBC) Decatur; WAWV-TV (ABC) Terre Haute; WBUI (CW, This TV) Decatur; WPXS (IND) Mount Vernon; WTHI-TV (CBS, FOX) Terre Haute; WTWO (NBC) Terre Haute; WUSI-TV (PBS) Olney.
Programming (via satellite): A&E; AMC; Animal Planet; CMT; CNN; C-SPAN; Discovery Channel; Disney Channel; ESPN; Freeform; History; Lifetime; Spike TV; Syfy; TBS; TLC; TNT; Travel Channel; Trinity Broadcasting Network (TBN); USA Network; WGN America.
Fee: $47.95 monthly.
Pay Service 1
Pay Units: N.A.
Programming (via satellite): Cinemax; HBO; Showtime; The Movie Channel.
Fee: $6.50 monthly (Cinemax), $11.50 monthly (HBO).
Video-On-Demand: No
Internet Service
Operational: No.
Telephone Service
None
Miles of Plant: 100.0 (coaxial); None (fiber optic).
President & General Manager: Michael Bauguss. Secretary: Gwyndolyn S. Bauguss.
Ownership: Clearvision Cable Systems Inc. (MSO).

DIX—Formerly served by Beck's Cable Systems. No longer in operation. ICA: IL0490.

DIXON—Comcast Cable. Now served by MOUNT PROSPECT, IL [IL0036]. ICA: IL0082.

DOLTON—Comcast Cable. Now served by CHAMPAIGN, IL [IL0019]. ICA: IL0030.

DONGOLA—Formerly served by Longview Communications. No longer in operation. ICA: IL0328.

DONOVAN TWP.—Formerly served by CableDirect. No longer in operation. ICA: IL0405.

DUNLAP—Mediacom. Now served by CHILLICOTHE, IL [IL0118]. ICA: IL0313.

DUPAGE COUNTY (portions)—Comcast Cable. Now served by PEORIA, IL [IL0012]. ICA: IL0694.

DURAND (village)—Mediacom. Now served by LENA, IL [IL0223]. ICA: IL0179.

DWIGHT—Mediacom. Now served by PONTIAC, IL [IL0109]. ICA: IL0163.

EAST DUBUQUE—Mediacom. Now served by DUBUQUE, IA [IA0007]. ICA: IL0188.

EAST ST. LOUIS—Charter Communications. Now served by ST. LOUIS, MO [M00009]. ICA: IL0062.

EDGEWOOD—Clearvision Cable Systems Inc, 1785 US Rte 40, Greenup, IL 62428-3501. Phone: 217-923-5594. Fax:

Illinois—Cable Systems

217-923-5681. Also serves Mason. ICA: IL0495.
TV Market Ranking: Outside TV Markets (EDGEWOOD, Mason).
Channel capacity: N.A. Channels available but not in use: N.A.

Basic Service
Subscribers: 36.
Programming (received off-air): WAND (NBC) Decatur; WBUI (CW, This TV) Decatur; WCIA (CBS, MNT) Champaign; WCIX (CBS, MNT) Springfield; WICS (ABC, The Country Network) Springfield; WPXS (IND) Mount Vernon; WRSP-TV (Antenna TV, FOX, MeTV) Springfield; WTHI-TV (CBS, FOX) Terre Haute; WUSI-TV (PBS) Olney.
Programming (via satellite): A&E; Bravo; Cartoon Network; CMT; CNBC; CNN; Comedy Central; C-SPAN; Discovery Channel; Disney Channel; FOX Sports Networks; Freeform; FX; Hallmark Channel; History; HLN; Lifetime; MTV; National Geographic Channel; Nickelodeon; Oxygen; QVC; Spike TV; Syfy; TBS; The Weather Channel; TLC; TNT; Trinity Broadcasting Network (TBN); TV Land; USA Network; VH1; WGN America.
Fee: $47.95 monthly.

Pay Service 1
Pay Units: N.A.
Programming (via satellite): Cinemax; HBO.
Fee: $11.00 monthly (each).
Video-On-Demand: No

Internet Service
Operational: No.

Telephone Service
None
Miles of Plant: 6.0 (coaxial); None (fiber optic). Homes passed: 390.
President & General Manager: Michael Bauguss. Secretary: Gwyndolyn S. Bauguss.
Ownership: Clearvision Cable Systems Inc. (MSO).

EFFINGHAM—Mediacom, 4290 Blue Stem Rd, PO Box 288, Charleston, IL 61920. Phones: 217-348-5533 (Local office); 217-347-7454 (Effingham). Fax: 217-345-7074. Web Site: http://www.mediacomcable.com. Also serves Effingham County (unincorporated areas), Lake Sara, Sigel & Teutopolis. ICA: IL0094.
TV Market Ranking: Outside TV Markets (EFFINGHAM, Effingham County (unincorporated areas), Lake Sara, Sigel, Teutopolis). Franchise award date: N.A. Franchise expiration date: N.A. Began: August 19, 1962.
Channel capacity: N.A. Channels available but not in use: N.A.

Basic Service
Subscribers: 2,618. Commercial subscribers: 8.
Programming (received off-air): KPLR-TV (CW, This TV) St. Louis; KSDK (Bounce TV, NBC) St. Louis; WAND (NBC) Decatur; WBUI (CW, This TV) Decatur; WCCU (FOX, MeTV) Urbana; WCIA (CBS, MNT) Champaign; WCIX (CBS, MNT) Charleston; WEIU-TV (PBS) Charleston; WICS (ABC, The Country Network) Springfield; WILL-TV (PBS) Urbana; WPXS (IND) Mount Vernon; WTHI-TV (CBS, FOX) Terre Haute; WTWO (NBC) Terre Haute; WUSI-TV (PBS) Olney. 5 FMs.
Programming (via satellite): C-SPAN 2; Discovery Digital Networks; Nick Jr.; QVC; WGN America.
Fee: $45.00 installation; $43.00 monthly; $1.18 converter.

Expanded Basic Service 1
Subscribers: N.A.
Programming (via satellite): A&E; AMC; Animal Planet; Cartoon Network; CMT; CNBC; CNN; Comedy Central; C-SPAN 2; Discovery Channel; Disney Channel; E! HD; ESPN; ESPN Classic; ESPN2; EVINE Live; EWTN Global Catholic Network; Food Network; Fox News Channel; Fox Sports 1; FOX Sports Midwest; Freeform; Fuse; FX; Hallmark Channel; HGTV; History; HLN; INSP; ION Television; Jewelry Television; Lifetime; LMN; MSNBC; MTV; Nickelodeon; Outdoor Channel; Pop; Spike TV; Syfy; TBS; The Weather Channel; TLC; TNT; Travel Channel; Trinity Broadcasting Network (TBN); truTV; TV Land; USA Network; VH1; WE tv.
Fee: $34.00 monthly.

Digital Basic Service
Subscribers: N.A.
Programming (via satellite): AXS TV; BBC America; Bloomberg Television; Bravo; Cloo; CMT; Discovery Life Channel; Disney XD; ESPN HD; ESPN2 HD; ESPNews; Fuse; FXM; FYI; Golf Channel; GSN; HD Theater; History; History International; IFC; ION Television; MC; MTV Classic; MTV Hits; MTV2; Nat Geo WILD; National Geographic Channel; NBCSN; Nicktoons; Qubo; Reelz; Science Channel; TeenNick; Turner Classic Movies; Universal HD.

Digital Expanded Basic Service
Subscribers: N.A.
Programming (via satellite): CBS Sports Network; ESPNU; FOX College Sports Central; FOX College Sports Pacific; Fox Sports 2; GolTV; Tennis Channel; TVG Network.
Fee: $3.95 monthly.

Digital Pay Service 1
Pay Units: N.A.
Programming (via satellite): Cinemax (multiplexed); HBO (multiplexed); HBO HD; Showtime (multiplexed); Showtime HD; Starz (multiplexed); Starz Encore (multiplexed); Starz HD; The Movie Channel (multiplexed); The Movie Channel HD.
Fee: $11.95 monthly (each).
Video-On-Demand: Yes

Pay-Per-View
iN DEMAND (delivered digitally); Playboy TV (delivered digitally); SexSee (delivered digitally); Juicy (delivered digitally); ESPN (delivered digitally); AXS TV (delivered digitally).

Internet Service
Operational: Yes.
Broadband Service: Mediacom High Speed Internet.
Fee: $59.95 installation; $40.95 monthly.

Telephone Service
Analog: Not Operational
Digital: Operational
Fee: $39.95 monthly
Miles of Plant: 111.0 (coaxial); None (fiber optic).
General Manager: Todd Acker. Technical Operations Manager: Jerry Ferguson. Marketing Director: James Friske.
Ownership: Mediacom LLC (MSO).

ELDRED—Formerly served by Longview Communications. No longer in operation. ICA: IL0626.

ELGIN—Comcast Cable. Now served by PEORIA, IL [IL0012]. ICA: IL0032.

ELIZABETH—Mediacom. Now served by LENA, IL [IL0223]. ICA: IL0305.

ELKHART TWP.—Formerly served by Mediacom. No longer in operation. ICA: IL0398.

ELLISVILLE—Mid Century Communications, 285 Mid Century Ln, PO Box 380, Fairview, IL 61432-0380. Phones: 309-879-2900; 877-643-2368; 309-778-8611. Fax: 309-783-3297. E-mail: info@midcentury.com. Web Site: http://www.midcentury.com. Also serves Altona, Bishop Hill, Fairview, Fulton County (unincorporated areas), Gilson, Henry County (unincorporated areas), Knox County (unincorporated areas), LaFayette, Maquon, Marietta, McDonough County (unincorporated areas), Peoria County (unincorporated areas), Smithfield, Stark County (unincorporated areas), Summum, Table Grove, Victoria, Williamsfield & Yates City. ICA: IL5238.
Channel capacity: N.A. Channels available but not in use: N.A.

Lifeline
Subscribers: N.A.
Fee: $33.95 monthly. Includes 13+ channels.

Expanded Basic Lifeline
Subscribers: N.A.
Fee: $79.95 monthly. Includes 153+ channels.

Cinemax
Subscribers: N.A.
Fee: $10.00 monthly. Includes 4+ channels.

HBO
Subscribers: N.A.
Fee: $17.00 monthly. Includes 6+ channels.

Starz/Encore
Subscribers: N.A.
Fee: $10.00 monthly. Includes 13+ channels.

Video-On-Demand: Yes

Internet Service
Operational: Yes.
Fee: $79.95-$94.95 monthly.

Telephone Service
Digital: Operational
Chief Executive Officer: James Sherburne. President: Sidney Smith. Vice President: John Wherley.
Ownership: Mid Century Telephone Cooperative.

ELMHURST—Comcast Cable. Now served by PEORIA, IL [IL0012]. ICA: IL0006.

ELMWOOD—Mediacom, 609 South 4th St, PO Box 334, Chillicothe, IL 61523. Phones: 309-469-2027; 309-274-4500. Fax: 309-274-3188. Web Site: http://www.mediacomcable.com. Also serves Abingdon, Avon, Dunfermline, Fairview, Farmington, Glasford, Hanna City, London Mills, Maquon, Smithville, St. Augustine, St. David & Yates City, IL; Clear Lake, IN. ICA: IL0205.
TV Market Ranking: 83 (Dunfermline, ELMWOOD, Fairview, Farmington, Glasford, Hanna City, London Mills, Maquon, Smithville, St. Augustine, St. David, Yates City); Below 100 (Clear Lake); Outside TV Markets (Avon, Abingdon).
Channel capacity: N.A. Channels available but not in use: N.A.

Basic Service
Subscribers: 1,959.
Programming (received off-air): WAOE (Antenna TV, MNT) Peoria; WEEK-TV (ABC, CW, NBC) Peoria; WHOI (Comet) Peoria; WMBD-TV (Bounce TV, CBS) Peoria; WTVP (PBS) Peoria; WYZZ-TV (FOX, The Country Network) Bloomington.
Programming (via satellite): WGN America.
Fee: $45.00 installation; $69.95 monthly.

Expanded Basic Service 1
Subscribers: N.A.
Programming (via satellite): A&E; AMC; Animal Planet; Cartoon Network; CMT; CNBC; CNN; Comcast SportsNet Chicago; Comedy Central; C-SPAN; CW PLUS; Discovery Channel; Discovery Life Channel; Disney Channel; E! HD; ESPN; ESPN Classic; ESPN2; EVINE Live; Food Network; Fox News Channel; Fox Sports 1; Freeform; FX; Great American Country; Hallmark Channel; HGTV; History; HLN; INSP; ION Television; Lifetime; LMN; MSNBC; MTV; Nickelodeon; QVC; Spike TV; Syfy; TBS; The Weather Channel; TLC; TNT; Travel Channel; Trinity Broadcasting Network (TBN); truTV; TV Land; TVG Network; USA Network; VH1; WE tv.
Fee: $34.00 monthly.

Digital Basic Service
Subscribers: N.A.
Programming (via satellite): BBC America; Bloomberg Television; CBS Sports Network; CCTV-Documentary; Cloo; Destination America; Discovery Kids Channel; ESPN HD; ESPN2 HD; ESPNews; ESPNU; FOX College Sports Central; FOX College Sports Pacific; Fuse; FXM; FYI; Golf Channel; GolTV; History International; IFC; Investigation Discovery; ION Television; MTV Classic; MTV Hits; MTV2; National Geographic Channel; NBCSN; Nick Jr.; Nicktoons; Outdoor Channel; OWN: Oprah Winfrey Network; Qubo; Science Channel; TeenNick; Tennis Channel; Turner Classic Movies; TVG Network.

Digital Expanded Basic Service
Subscribers: N.A.
Programming (via satellite): AXS TV; CNN HD; HD Theater; TBS HD; TNT HD.
Fee: $6.95 monthly.

Digital Pay Service 1
Pay Units: N.A.
Programming (via satellite): Cinemax (multiplexed); Flix; HBO (multiplexed); HBO HD; Showtime (multiplexed); Showtime HD; Starz (multiplexed); Starz Encore (multiplexed); Starz HD; Sundance TV; The Movie Channel (multiplexed); The Movie Channel HD.
Fee: $11.95 monthly (HBO, Cinemax, Showtime/TMC or Starz/Encore).
Video-On-Demand: Yes

Pay-Per-View
iN DEMAND (delivered digitally); Playboy TV (delivered digitally); SexSee (delivered digitally); Juicy (delivered digitally).

Internet Service
Operational: Yes.
Broadband Service: Mediacom High Speed Internet.
Fee: $59.95 installation; $45.95 monthly.

Telephone Service
Digital: Operational
Fee: $39.95 monthly
Miles of Plant: 58.0 (coaxial); 8.0 (fiber optic). Homes passed: 4,396.
Vice President: Don Hagwell. Operations Director: Gary Wightman. Technical Operations Manager: Larry Brackman. Marketing Director: Stephanie Law.
Ownership: Mediacom LLC (MSO).

ENFIELD—NewWave Communications. Now served by McLEANSBORO, IL [IL0177]. ICA: IL0321.

EVANSVILLE—NewWave Communications, One Montgomery Plaza, 4th Floor, Sikeston, MO 63801. Phone: 888-863-9928. Fax: 573-481-9809. E-mail: info@newwavecom.com. Web Site: http://www.newwavecom.com. Also serves Prairie du Rocher & Ruma. ICA: IL0237.
TV Market Ranking: Outside TV Markets (EVANSVILLE, Prairie du Rocher, Ruma). Franchise award date: October 1, 1987.

Cable Systems—Illinois

Franchise expiration date: N.A. Began: June 13, 1988.
Channel capacity: N.A. Channels available but not in use: N.A.
Basic Service
Subscribers: 46. Commercial subscribers: 31.
Programming (received off-air): KDNL-TV (ABC, The Country Network) St. Louis; KETC (PBS) St. Louis; KFVS-TV (CBS, CW, MeTV) Cape Girardeau; KMOV (CBS) St. Louis; KPLR-TV (CW, This TV) St. Louis; KSDK (Bounce TV, NBC) St. Louis; KTVI (Antenna TV, Escape, FOX) St. Louis; WRBU (ION) East St. Louis; WSIL-TV (ABC) Harrisburg; WSIU-TV (PBS) Carbondale.
Programming (via satellite): AMC; C-SPAN; TBS; The Weather Channel; TLC; Trinity Broadcasting Network (TBN); WGN America.
Fee: $40.00 installation; $26.34 monthly.
Expanded Basic Service 1
Subscribers: N.A.
Programming (via satellite): CMT; CNN; Comedy Central; Discovery Channel; Disney Channel; ESPN; ESPN2; Fox News Channel; FOX Sports Midwest; Freeform; HLN; Lifetime; MTV; Nickelodeon; Spike TV; Syfy; TNT; TV Land; USA Network; VH1.
Fee: $12.95 monthly.
Digital Basic Service
Subscribers: N.A.
Programming (via satellite): BBC America; Bloomberg Television; Bravo; Discovery Digital Networks; Disney XD; DMX Music; EVINE Live; Fox Sports 1; FXM; FYI; Golf Channel; GSN; HGTV; History; History International; IFC; LMN; NBCSN; Nick Jr.; Outdoor Channel; TeenNick; Turner Classic Movies; WE tv.
Pay Service 1
Pay Units: N.A.
Programming (via satellite): Cinemax; HBO (multiplexed); Showtime.
Fee: $8.95 monthly.
Digital Pay Service 1
Pay Units: N.A.
Programming (via satellite): Cinemax (multiplexed); Flix; HBO (multiplexed); Showtime (multiplexed); Starz (multiplexed); Starz Encore (multiplexed); The Movie Channel (multiplexed).
Video-On-Demand: No
Pay-Per-View
iN DEMAND (delivered digitally); Hot Choice (delivered digitally); ESPN Now (delivered digitally); Playboy TV (delivered digitally); Fresh (delivered digitally); Shorteez (delivered digitally).
Internet Service
Operational: No.
Telephone Service
None
Miles of Plant: 25.0 (coaxial); None (fiber optic). Homes passed: 779.
General Manager: John Helmers.
Ownership: NewWave Communications LLC (MSO).

FAIRBURY—Mediacom. Now served by ROANOKE, IL [IL0068]. ICA: IL0116.

FAIRBURY—Mediacom. Now served by ROANOKE, IL [IL0068]. ICA: IL0346.

FAIRFIELD—NewWave Communications. Now served by McLEANSBORO, IL [IL0177]. ICA: IL0148.

FAIRVIEW—Mediacom. Now served by ELMWOOD, IL [IL0205]. ICA: IL0385.

FARMER CITY—Mediacom. Now served by RANTOUL, IL [IL0089]. ICA: IL0231.

FARMERSVILLE—NewWave Communications. Now served by TAYLORVILLE, IL [IL0098]. ICA: IL0370.

FAYETTEVILLE—Formerly served by CableDirect. No longer in operation. ICA: IL0422.

FIELDON—Formerly served by CableDirect. No longer in operation. ICA: IL0451.

FILLMORE—Formerly served by CableDirect. No longer in operation. ICA: IL0498.

FINDLAY—Formerly served by Almega Cable. No longer in operation. ICA: IL0364.

FLANAGAN—Heartland Cable Inc, 167 West 5th St, PO Box 7, Minonk, IL 61760. Phones: 800-448-4320; 309-432-2075. Fax: 309-432-2500. Web Site: http://www.hcable.net. Also serves Rutland. ICA: IL0304.
TV Market Ranking: Below 100 (FLANAGAN, Rutland). Franchise award date: January 1, 1971. Franchise expiration date: N.A. Began: March 1, 1972.
Channel capacity: N.A. Channels available but not in use: N.A.
Basic Service
Subscribers: N.A.
Programming (received off-air): WEEK-TV (ABC, CW, NBC) Peoria; WHOI (Comet) Peoria; WMBD-TV (Bounce TV, CBS) Peoria; WTVP (PBS) Peoria; WYZZ-TV (FOX, The Country Network) Bloomington.
Programming (via satellite): A&E; CNN; Discovery Channel; Disney Channel; ESPN; Freeform; Lifetime; Nickelodeon; Spike TV; TBS; The Weather Channel; TNT; VH1; WGN America.
Fee: $39.00 installation.
Pay Service 1
Pay Units: N.A.
Programming (via satellite): HBO; Showtime.
Fee: $8.95 - $10.95 monthly (each).
Video-On-Demand: Yes
Pay-Per-View
Movies; special events.
Internet Service
Operational: Yes.
Fee: $39.00 installation; $29.99 monthly.
Telephone Service
None
Miles of Plant: 10.0 (coaxial); None (fiber optic). Homes passed: 450.
Chief Executive Officer: Jim Frances. President & General Manager: Steve Allen.
Ownership: Heartland Cable Inc. (MSO).

FLORA—Wabash Independent Networks, 113 Hagen Dr, PO Box 719, Flora, IL 62839. Phones: 618-662-3636; 877-878-2120; 618-665-3311. Fax: 618-665-3400. E-mail: winita@wabash.net. Web Site: http://www.wabash.net. Also serves Bible Grove, Bone Gap, Browns, Cisne, Clay County (portions), Geff, Louisville, Noble & Xenia. ICA: IL0140.
TV Market Ranking: Below 100 (FLORA, Xenia, Cisne, Clay County (portions)); Outside TV Markets (Noble, Clay County (portions), Geff, Louisville). Franchise award date: N.A. Franchise expiration date: N.A. Began: December 1, 1963.
Channel capacity: N.A. Channels available but not in use: N.A.

ADVANCED TVFactbook
FULLY SEARCHABLE • CONTINUOUSLY UPDATED • DISCOUNT RATES FOR PRINT PURCHASERS
For more information call **800-771-9202** or visit **www.warren-news.com**

Basic Service
Subscribers: 2,559.
Programming (received off-air): KFVS-TV (CBS, CW, MeTV) Cape Girardeau; KMOV (CBS) St. Louis; KPLR-TV (CW, This TV) St. Louis; KSDK (Bounce TV, NBC) St. Louis; WEHT (ABC) Evansville; WFIE (NBC, This TV) Evansville; WSIL-TV (ABC) Harrisburg; WTHI-TV (CBS, FOX) Terre Haute; WTVW (CW, MeTV) Evansville; WTWO (NBC) Terre Haute; WUSI-TV (PBS) Olney.
Programming (via satellite): C-SPAN; C-SPAN 2; EVINE Live; EWTN Global Catholic Network; ION Television; MSNBC; QVC; TBS; The Weather Channel; Trinity Broadcasting Network (TBN); WGN America.
Fee: $25.00 installation; $30.98 monthly.
Expanded Basic Service 1
Subscribers: N.A.
Programming (via satellite): A&E; AMC; Animal Planet; Boomerang; BTN; Cartoon Network; CMT; CNN; Comedy Central; Discovery Channel; Disney Channel; DIY Network; E! HD; ESPN; ESPN Classic; ESPN2; FamilyNet; Food Network; Fox News Channel; FOX Sports Networks; Freeform; FX; Hallmark Channel; History; HLN; Lifetime; MTV; National Geographic Channel; Nickelodeon; Outdoor Channel; Oxygen; Spike TV; TLC; TNT; Travel Channel; truTV; Turner Classic Movies; TV Land; UP; USA Network; VH1.
Fee: $35.00 monthly.
Digital Basic Service
Subscribers: N.A.
Programming (via satellite): AZ TV; BBC America; Bloomberg Television; Bravo; Cloo; CMT; Destination America; Discovery Kids Channel; Discovery Life Channel; Disney XD; DMX Music; ESPNews; Fox Sports 1; FSN Digital Atlantic; FSN Digital Central; FSN Digital Pacific; Fuse; FXM; FYI; Golf Channel; Great American Country; GSN; HGTV; History International; IFC; Investigation Discovery; LMN; MTV Classic; MTV Hits; MTV2; National Geographic Channel; NBCSN; Nick Jr.; Outdoor Channel; Ovation; OWN: Oprah Winfrey Network; RFD-TV; Science Channel; Syfy; TeenNick; The Word Network; VH1 Soul; WE tv.
Fee: $86.98 monthly.
Pay Service 1
Pay Units: N.A.
Programming (via satellite): HBO; Showtime; The Movie Channel.
Fee: $15.00 installation; $11.95 monthly (TMC), $12.95 monthly (Showtime), $13.95 monthly (HBO).
Digital Pay Service 1
Pay Units: N.A.
Programming (via satellite): Cinemax (multiplexed); Flix; HBO (multiplexed); Showtime (multiplexed); Starz (multiplexed); Starz Encore (multiplexed); The Movie Channel (multiplexed).
Fee: $13.95 monthly (Cinemax, Showtime/TMC/Flix or Starz/Encore), $17.95 monthly (HBO).
Video-On-Demand: Yes

Pay-Per-View
iN DEMAND (delivered digitally); Playboy TV (delivered digitally); Fresh (delivered digitally); Club Jenna (delivered digitally); Spice: Xcess (delivered digitally).
Internet Service
Operational: Yes.
Fee: $25.00 installation; $35.00-$85.00 monthly.
Telephone Service
Digital: Operational
Miles of Plant: 57.0 (coaxial); None (fiber optic). Homes passed: 3,823.
President: Dave Grahn. Executive Vice President & General Manager: Jeffrey Williams. Controller: Tanya Wells.
Ownership: Wabash Independent Networks (MSO).

FRANKLIN GROVE—Comcast Cable. Now served by MOUNT PROSPECT, IL [IL0036]. ICA: IL0690.

FREEMAN SPUR—Zito Media, 102 S Main St, PO Box 665, Coudersport, PA 16915. Phones: 814-260-9055; 800-365-6988. E-mail: info@zitomedia.com. Web Site: http://www.zitomedia.com. Also serves Cedar Grove, Franklin County & Orient. ICA: IL0232.
TV Market Ranking: 69 (Cedar Grove, Franklin County, FREEMAN SPUR, Orient). Franchise award date: N.A. Franchise expiration date: N.A. Began: September 26, 1989.
Channel capacity: N.A. Channels available but not in use: N.A.
Basic Service
Subscribers: 69.
Programming (received off-air): KBSI (FOX) Cape Girardeau; KFVS-TV (CBS, CW, MeTV) Cape Girardeau; WDKA (MNT, The Country Network) Paducah; WPSD-TV (Antenna TV, NBC) Paducah; WSIL-TV (ABC) Harrisburg; WSIU-TV (PBS) Carbondale; WTCT (IND) Marion.
Programming (via satellite): A&E; AMC; Cartoon Network; CNN; Comedy Central; C-SPAN; Discovery Channel; Disney Channel; E! HD; ESPN; ESPN2; Fox News Channel; Freeform; Fuse; FX; Great American Country; HGTV; History; HLN; Lifetime; Outdoor Channel; TBS; The Weather Channel; TLC; TNT; USA Network; WGN America.
Fee: $49.95 installation; $50.15 monthly.
Digital Basic Service
Subscribers: N.A.
Pay Service 1
Pay Units: N.A.
Programming (via satellite): HBO; Showtime; Starz Encore.
Fee: $12.00 monthly (each).
Internet Service
Operational: No.
Telephone Service
None
Miles of Plant: 20.0 (coaxial); None (fiber optic). Homes passed: 755.
President: James Rigas.
Ownership: Zito Media (MSO).

2017 Edition
D-197

Illinois—Cable Systems

FREEPORT—Comcast Cable. Now served by MOUNT PROSPECT, IL [IL0036]. ICA: IL0049.

GALENA—Mediacom. Now served by DUBUQUE, IA [IA0007]. ICA: IL0657.

GALESBURG—Comcast Cable. Now served by PEORIA, IL [IL0012]. ICA: IL0038.

GARDEN PRAIRIE—Mediacom. Now served by BELVIDERE TWP, IL [IL0282]. ICA: IL0428.

GARDNER—Gardner Cable TV Co., 305 State St, PO Box 11, Manhattan, IL 60442. Phones: 815-478-4000; 815-478-4444. Fax: 815-478-3386. Web Site: http://www.krausonline.com. ICA: IL0269.
TV Market Ranking: Below 100 (GARDNER). Franchise award date: August 27, 1984. Franchise expiration date: N.A. Began: October 1, 1985.
Channel capacity: N.A. Channels available but not in use: N.A.
Basic Service
Subscribers: 207.
Programming (received off-air): WBBM-TV (CBS, Decades) Chicago; WCIU-TV (MeTV) Chicago; WCPX-TV (ION) Chicago; WFLD (FOX) Chicago; WGBO-DT (getTV, UNV) Joliet; WGN-TV (IND) Chicago; WJYS (IND) Hammond; WLS-TV (ABC, Live Well Network) Chicago; WMAQ-TV (COZI TV, NBC) Chicago; WPWR-TV (Buzzr, CW, MNT, Movies!) Gary; WSNS-TV (TMO) Chicago; WTTW (PBS) Chicago; WWTO-TV (TBN) La Salle; WYCC (PBS) Chicago; WYIN (PBS) Gary.
Programming (via satellite): HLN; QVC.
Fee: $35.00 installation; $23.00 monthly.
Expanded Basic Service 1
Subscribers: N.A.
Programming (via satellite): A&E; AMC; Animal Planet; Cartoon Network; CMT; CNBC; CNN; Comcast SportsNet Chicago; Comedy Central; C-SPAN; C-SPAN 2; Discovery Channel; Disney Channel; ESPN; ESPN Classic; ESPN2; EWTN Global Catholic Network; Food Network; Fox News Channel; Freeform; FX; GSN; Hallmark Channel; HGTV; History; Lifetime; MTV; National Geographic Channel; Nickelodeon; Spike TV; Syfy; TBS; The Weather Channel; TLC; TNT; truTV; TV Land; USA Network; VH1.
Digital Basic Service
Subscribers: N.A.
Programming (via satellite): BBC America; Bloomberg Television; Bravo; Discovery Digital Networks; Disney XD; DMX Music; ESPNews; FOX College Sports Central; FOX College Sports Pacific; Fox Sports 1; Fuse; FXM; FYI; Golf Channel; Great American Country; GSN; History; History International; IFC; LMN; Nick Jr.; Nicktoons; Outdoor Channel; TeenNick; Turner Classic Movies; WE tv.
Pay Service 1
Pay Units: N.A.
Programming (via satellite): Cinemax; HBO.
Digital Pay Service 1
Pay Units: N.A.
Programming (via satellite): Cinemax (multiplexed); HBO (multiplexed); Showtime (multiplexed); Starz (multiplexed); Starz Encore (multiplexed); The Movie Channel (multiplexed).
Video-On-Demand: No
Pay-Per-View
Playboy TV (delivered digitally); Fresh (delivered digitally); Shorteez (delivered digitally).
Internet Service
Operational: Yes.
Broadband Service: In-house.
Fee: $9.95 monthly.
Telephone Service
Digital: Operational
Fee: $26.95-$34.95 monthly
Miles of Plant: 8.0 (coaxial); None (fiber optic). Homes passed: 525.
Vice President: Arthur Kraus. General Manager: Mike Bordeaux. Chief Technician: Skip Kraus.
Ownership: Arthur J. Kraus (MSO).

GAYS (village)—Formerly served by CableDirect. No longer in operation. ICA: IL0502.

GEFF—Wabash Independent Networks. Now served by FLORA, IL [IL0140]. ICA: IL0683.

GEM SUBURBAN MOBILE HOME PARK—Packerland Broadband, 105 Kent St., PO Box 885, Iron Mountain, MI 49801. Phones: 906-774-1291; 800-236-8434; 906-774-6621. Fax: 906-776-2811. E-mail: service@plbb.net. Web Site: http://www.packerlandbroadband.com. ICA: IL0503.
TV Market Ranking: 97 (GEM SUBURBAN MOBILE HOME PARK). Franchise award date: N.A. Franchise expiration date: N.A. Began: April 1, 1988.
Channel capacity: N.A. Channels available but not in use: N.A.
Basic Service
Subscribers: N.A.
Programming (received off-air): WHA-TV (PBS) Madison; WIFR (Antenna TV, CBS) Freeport; WQRF-TV (Bounce TV, FOX) Rockford; WREX (CW, MeTV, NBC) Rockford; WTVO (ABC, MNT) Rockford.
Programming (via satellite): A&E; AMC; CNN; Comedy Central; Discovery Channel; Disney Channel; ESPN; ESPN2; Freeform; Lifetime; MTV; Nickelodeon; QVC; Spike TV; Syfy; TBS; The Weather Channel; TLC; TNT; TV Land; USA Network; VH1; WGN America.
Fee: $24.95 installation; $2.00 converter.
Pay Service 1
Pay Units: N.A.
Programming (via satellite): HBO.
Fee: $14.95 installation; $10.95 monthly.
Internet Service
Operational: No.
Telephone Service
None
Miles of Plant: 3.0 (coaxial); None (fiber optic). Homes passed: 37.
General Manager: Dan Plante. Technical Supervisor: Chad Kay.
Ownership: Packerland Broadband (MSO).

GENESEO—Mediacom, 3900 26th Ave, Moline, IL 61265. Phone: 309-797-2580. Fax: 309-797-2414. Web Site: http://www.mediacomcable.com. Also serves Aledo, Alexis, Altona, Andover, Annawan, Atkinson, Boden, Buda, Cambridge, Cordova, Frye Lake, Galva, Henderson, Henry County (unincorporated areas), Hillsdale, Manlius (village), Matherville, Mineral, Mobet, Neponset, Osco Twp., Port Bryon, Preemption, Rapids City, Reynolds, Sheffield, Sherrard, Viola, Walnut & Wataga. ICA: IL0170.
TV Market Ranking: 60 (Aledo, Alexis, Altona, Andover, Annawan, Atkinson, Boden, Cambridge, Cordova, Frye Lake, Galva, GENESEO, Henderson, Henry County (unincorporated areas), Hillsdale, Matherville, Mineral, Mobet, Osco Twp., Preemption, Rapids City, Reynolds, Sherrard, Viola, Wataga); Below 100 (Buda, Manlius (village), Sheffield, Walnut); Outside TV Markets (Neponset). Franchise award date: December 1, 1982. Franchise expiration date: N.A. Began: February 1, 1983.
Channel capacity: N.A. Channels available but not in use: N.A.
Basic Service
Subscribers: 5,631.
Programming (received off-air): KGCW (CW, MeTV, This TV) Burlington; KIIN (PBS) Iowa City; KLJB (CW, FOX, MeTV) Davenport; KWQC-TV (NBC) Davenport; WHBF-TV (CBS) Rock Island; WQAD-TV (ABC, Antenna TV) Moline; WQPT-TV (PBS) Moline.
Programming (via satellite): TBS; Trinity Broadcasting Network (TBN); WGN America.
Fee: $45.00 installation; $43.00 monthly.
Expanded Basic Service 1
Subscribers: N.A.
Programming (via satellite): A&E; AMC; Animal Planet; Bravo; Cartoon Network; CMT; CNBC; CNN; Comcast SportsNet Chicago; Comedy Central; C-SPAN; C-SPAN 2; Discovery Channel; Disney Channel; E! HD; ESPN; ESPN2; EWTN Global Catholic Network; Food Network; Fox News Channel; Fox Sports 1; FOX Sports Midwest; Freeform; FX; Hallmark Channel; HGTV; History; HLN; INSP; Lifetime; MSNBC; MTV; Nickelodeon; Pop; QVC; Spike TV; Syfy; The Weather Channel; TLC; TNT; Travel Channel; truTV; TV Land; USA Network; VH1; WE tv.
Fee: $24.00 monthly.
Digital Basic Service
Subscribers: N.A.
Programming (via satellite): BBC America; Bloomberg Television; Discovery Digital Networks; DMX Music; FXM; FYI; Golf Channel; GSN; History International; IFC; LMN; NBCSN; Outdoor Channel; Turner Classic Movies.
Pay Service 1
Pay Units: N.A.
Programming (via satellite): Cinemax; HBO; Starz; Starz Encore.
Fee: $3.99 monthly (Encore), $5.99 monthly (Starz/Encore); $7.95 monthly (Cinemax); $11.99 monthly (HBO).
Digital Pay Service 1
Pay Units: N.A.
Programming (via satellite): Cinemax (multiplexed); Flix; HBO (multiplexed); Showtime (multiplexed); Starz (multiplexed); Starz Encore (multiplexed); Sundance TV; The Movie Channel (multiplexed).
Video-On-Demand: No
Pay-Per-View
Hot Choice (delivered digitally); Vubiquity Inc.; Playboy TV (delivered digitally); Fresh (delivered digitally); Shorteez (delivered digitally).
Internet Service
Operational: Yes.
Broadband Service: Mediacom High Speed Internet.
Telephone Service
Digital: Operational
Miles of Plant: 496.0 (coaxial); 144.0 (fiber optic). Homes passed: 21,487.
Vice President: Scott Westerman. Technical Operations Manager: Mitch Carlson. Marketing Manager: Greg Evans. Business Operations Manager: Cari Venzell.
Ownership: Mediacom LLC (MSO).

GENOA—Charter Communications. Now served by MADISON, WI [WI0002]. ICA: IL0200.

GERMAN VALLEY—Mediacom, 3900 26th Ave, Moline, IL 61265. Phones: 309-797-2580 (Moline regional office); 563-557-8025. Fax: 309-797-2414. Web Site: http://www.mediacomcable.com. Also serves Ridott Twp. ICA: IL0505.
TV Market Ranking: 97 (GERMAN VALLEY, Ridott Twp.). Franchise award date: N.A. Franchise expiration date: N.A. Began: November 1, 1988.
Channel capacity: N.A. Channels available but not in use: N.A.
Basic Service
Subscribers: 15.
Programming (received off-air): WHA-TV (PBS) Madison; WIFR (Antenna TV, CBS) Freeport; WQRF-TV (Bounce TV, FOX) Rockford; WREX (CW, MeTV, NBC) Rockford; WTVO (ABC, MNT) Rockford.
Programming (via satellite): A&E; AMC; Animal Planet; CMT; CNN; Comedy Central; C-SPAN; Discovery Channel; ESPN; ESPN2; FOX Sports Networks; Freeform; History; Lifetime; Nickelodeon; QVC; Spike TV; TBS; The Weather Channel; TLC; TNT; Travel Channel; USA Network; VH1; WGN America.
Fee: $45.00 installation; $69.95 monthly.
Pay Service 1
Pay Units: N.A.
Programming (via satellite): Starz; Starz Encore.
Fee: $9.95 monthly.
Internet Service
Operational: No.
Telephone Service
None
Miles of Plant: 12.0 (coaxial); None (fiber optic). Homes passed: 310. Miles of plant (coax & fiber) included in Moline
Regional Vice President: Cari Fenzel. Area Manager: Kathleen McMullen. Engineering Director: Mitch Carlson. Technical Operations Manager: Darren Dean. Marketing Director: Greg Evans.
Ownership: Mediacom LLC (MSO).

GIBSON CITY—Mediacom, 609 South 4th St, PO Box 334, Chillicothe, IL 61523. Phones: 309-469-2027; 309-274-4500. Fax: 309-274-3188. Web Site: http://www.mediacomcable.com. ICA: IL0164.
TV Market Ranking: 64 (GIBSON CITY). Franchise award date: N.A. Franchise expiration date: N.A. Began: March 15, 1972.
Channel capacity: N.A. Channels available but not in use: N.A.
Basic Service
Subscribers: 525.
Programming (received off-air): WAND (NBC) Decatur; WBUI (CW, This TV) Decatur; WCCU (FOX, MeTV) Urbana; WCIA (CBS, MNT) Champaign; WICD (ABC) Champaign; WILL-TV (PBS) Urbana; WRSP-TV (Antenna TV, FOX, MeTV) Springfield; 12 FMs.
Programming (via satellite): Freeform; INSP; Radar Channel; WGN America.
Fee: $45.00 installation; $43.00 monthly.
Expanded Basic Service 1
Subscribers: N.A.
Programming (received off-air): WCIX (CBS, MNT) Springfield.
Programming (via satellite): A&E; AMC; Animal Planet; BET; Bravo; Cartoon Network; CMT; CNBC; CNN; Comcast SportsNet Chicago; Comedy Central; C-SPAN; C-SPAN 2; Discovery Channel; Discovery Life Channel; Disney Channel;

Cable Systems—Illinois

E! HD; ESPN; ESPN2; EVINE Live; EWTN Global Catholic Network; Food Network; Fox News Channel; Fox Sports 1; FX; Hallmark Channel; HGTV; History; HLN; ION Television; Jewelry Television; Lifetime; LMN; MSNBC; MTV; Nickelodeon; Pop; QVC; Spike TV; Syfy; TBS; The Weather Channel; TLC; TNT; Travel Channel; Trinity Broadcasting Network (TBN); truTV; TV Land; Univision Studios; USA Network; VH1; WE tv.
Fee: $34.00 monthly.
Digital Basic Service
Subscribers: N.A.
Programming (via satellite): AXS TV; BBC America; Bloomberg Television; Cloo; Destination America; Discovery Kids Channel; ESPN HD; ESPN2 HD; ESPNU; Fox Sports 2; Fuse; FXM; FYI; Golf Channel; GSN; HD Theater; History International; IFC; Investigation Discovery; ION Television; MC; MTV Classic; MTV Hits; MTV2; Nat Geo WILD; National Geographic Channel; NBCSN; Nick Jr.; Nicktoons; Outdoor Channel; OWN: Oprah Winfrey Network; Qubo; Reelz; Science Channel; Sundance TV; TeenNick; Turner Classic Movies; TVG Network; Universal HD.
Digital Expanded Basic Service
Subscribers: N.A.
Programming (via satellite): CBS Sports Network; ESPNU; FOX College Sports Central; FOX College Sports Pacific; Fox Sports 2; GolTV; Tennis Channel; TVG Network.
Fee: $3.95 monthly.
Digital Pay Service 1
Pay Units: N.A.
Programming (via satellite): Cinemax (multiplexed); Cinemax On Demand; Flix; HBO (multiplexed); HBO HD; HBO on Demand; Showtime (multiplexed); Showtime HD; Showtime On Demand; Starz (multiplexed); Starz Encore (multiplexed); Starz HD; Starz On Demand; Sundance TV; The Movie Channel (multiplexed); The Movie Channel HD; The Movie Channel On Demand.
Fee: $11.95 monthly (HBO, Cinemax, Showtime/TMC/Sundance/Flix or Starz/Encore).
Video-On-Demand: Yes
Pay-Per-View
Juicy (delivered digitally); iN DEMAND (delivered digitally); Playboy TV (delivered digitally); SexSee (delivered digitally); ESPN (delivered digitally); FOX Sports Networks (delivered digitally).
Internet Service
Operational: Yes.
Broadband Service: Mediacom High Speed Internet.
Fee: $59.95 installation; $45.95 monthly.
Telephone Service
Digital: Operational
Fee: $39.95 monthly
Miles of Plant: 83.0 (coaxial); 21.0 (fiber optic). Homes passed: 4,626.
Vice President: Don Hagwell. Operations Director: Gary Wightman. Technical Operations Manager: Larry Brackman. Marketing Director: Stephanie Law.
Ownership: Mediacom LLC (MSO).

GILBERTS—Mediacom. Now served by CORTLAND (village), IL [IL0485]. ICA: IL0507.

GILLESPIE—NewWave Communications. Now served by TAYLORVILLE, IL [IL0098]. ICA: IL0610.

GINGER RIDGE—Formerly served by Universal Cable Inc. No longer in operation. ICA: IL0508.

GLADSTONE—Nova1Net, 677 West Main St, PO Box 1412, Galesburg, IL 61401. Phones: 800-397-6682; 309-342-9681. Fax: 309-342-4408. Web Site: http://www.novacablevision.com. ICA: IL0415.
TV Market Ranking: Below 100 (GLADSTONE). Franchise award date: N.A. Franchise expiration date: N.A. Began: April 1, 1989.
Channel capacity: N.A. Channels available but not in use: N.A.
Basic Service
Subscribers: N.A.
Programming (received off-air): KGCW (CW, MeTV, This TV) Burlington; KIIN (PBS) Iowa City; KLJB (CW, FOX, MeTV) Davenport; KWQC-TV (NBC) Davenport; WEEK-TV (ABC, CW, NBC) Peoria; WHBF-TV (CBS) Rock Island; WHOI (Comet) Peoria; WMBD-TV (Bounce TV, CBS) Peoria; WQAD-TV (ABC, Antenna TV) Moline; WQPT-TV (PBS) Moline; WTVP (PBS) Peoria.
Programming (via satellite): A&E; AMC; Animal Planet; BTN; Cartoon Network; CMT; CNBC; CNN; Comcast SportsNet Chicago; Comedy Central; C-SPAN; C-SPAN 2; Discovery Channel; Disney Channel; DIY Network; E! HD; ESPN; ESPN2; ESPNU; EWTN Global Catholic Network; Food Network; Fox News Channel; Fox Sports 1; FOX Sports Midwest; Freeform; FX; Golf Channel; Great American Country; Hallmark Channel; HGTV; History; HLN; HRTV; INSP; Lifetime; MSNBC; MTV; National Geographic Channel; Nickelodeon; QVC; RFD-TV; Spike TV; Syfy; TBS; The Weather Channel; TLC; TNT; Travel Channel; truTV; TV Land; USA Network; VH1; WGN America.
Fee: $60.00 installation.
Digital Basic Service
Subscribers: N.A.
Programming (via satellite): Bloomberg Television; CMT; Destination America; Discovery Kids Channel; Disney XD; DMX Music; ESPN Classic; ESPN2; ESPNews; EVINE Live; Fox Sports 1; FSN Digital Atlantic; FSN Digital Central; FSN Digital Pacific; Fuse; FXM; FYI; Golf Channel; Great American Country; GSN; HGTV; History; History International; IFC; Investigation Discovery; LMN; MTV Classic; MTV Hits; MTV2; NBCSN; Nicktoons; Noggin; Outdoor Channel; OWN: Oprah Winfrey Network; Science Channel; Syfy; TeenNick; Trinity Broadcasting Network (TBN); Turner Classic Movies; VH1 Soul; WE tv.
Pay Service 1
Pay Units: N.A.
Programming (via satellite): Cinemax; HBO.
Fee: $12.85 monthly (each).
Digital Pay Service 1
Pay Units: N.A.
Programming (via satellite): Cinemax (multiplexed); Flix; HBO (multiplexed); Showtime (multiplexed); Starz (multiplexed); Starz Encore (multiplexed); Sundance TV; The Movie Channel (multiplexed).
Fee: $12.85 monthly (HBO, Cinemax, Showtime/TMC/Flix/Sundance or Starz/Encore).
Video-On-Demand: No
Pay-Per-View
Hot Choice (delivered digitally); Playboy TV (delivered digitally); Fresh (delivered digitally); Spice: Xcess (delivered digitally); Club Jenna (delivered digitally).
Internet Service
Operational: Yes. Began: January 1, 2005.
Fee: $30.00 installation; $39.95 monthly; $3.95 modem lease.
Telephone Service
None
Miles of Plant: 11.0 (coaxial); None (fiber optic). Homes passed: 285.
General Manager: Robert G. Fischer Jr. Office Manager: Hazel Harden.
Ownership: Nova Cablevision Inc. (MSO).

GLASFORD—Mediacom. Now served by ELMWOOD, IL [IL0205]. ICA: IL0214.

GLENDALE HEIGHTS—Comcast Cable. Now served by PEORIA, IL [IL0012]. ICA: IL0022.

GLENVIEW—Comcast Cable. Now served by MOUNT PROSPECT, IL [IL0036]. ICA: IL0236.

GOLCONDA—Zito Media, 102 S Main St, PO Box 665, Coudersport, PA 16915. Phones: 814-260-9055; 800-365-6988. E-mail: info@zitomedia.com. Web Site: http://www.zitomedia.com. ICA: IL0297.
TV Market Ranking: 69 (GOLCONDA). Franchise award date: N.A. Franchise expiration date: N.A. Began: July 1, 1985.
Channel capacity: N.A. Channels available but not in use: N.A.
Basic Service
Subscribers: 30.
Programming (received off-air): KBSI (FOX) Cape Girardeau; KFVS-TV (CBS, CW, MeTV) Cape Girardeau; WDKA (MNT, The Country Network) Paducah; WKPD (PBS) Paducah; WPSD-TV (Antenna TV, NBC) Paducah; WSIL-TV (ABC) Harrisburg; WTCT (IND) Marion.
Programming (via satellite): A&E; AMC; Animal Planet; Cartoon Network; CNN; Comedy Central; Discovery Channel; Disney Channel; E! HD; ESPN; ESPN2; Food Network; Fox News Channel; Freeform; Fuse; Great American Country; HGTV; Lifetime; Outdoor Channel; TBS; The Weather Channel; TLC; TNT; USA Network; WGN America.
Fee: $49.95 installation; $49.85 monthly.
Pay Service 1
Pay Units: N.A.
Programming (via satellite): HBO; Showtime; The Movie Channel.
Fee: $12.00 monthly.
Internet Service
Operational: No.
Telephone Service
None
Miles of Plant: 7.0 (coaxial); None (fiber optic). Homes passed: 345.
President: James Rigas.
Ownership: Zito Media (MSO).

GOLDEN—Adams Telcom. Now served by BOWDEN, IL [IL0702]. ICA: IL0257.

GOOD HOPE—Mediacom, 609 South 4th St, PO Box 334, Chillicothe, IL 61523. Phones: 309-469-2027; 309-274-4500. Fax: 309-274-3188. Web Site: http://www.mediacomcable.com. Also serves Prairie City. ICA: IL0396.
TV Market Ranking: Below 100 (GOOD HOPE, Prairie City). Franchise award date: N.A. Franchise expiration date: N.A. Began: January 1, 1985.
Channel capacity: 42 (operating 2-way). Channels available but not in use: N.A.
Basic Service
Subscribers: 88.
Programming (received off-air): KHQA-TV (ABC, CBS) Hannibal; WEEK-TV (ABC, CW, NBC) Peoria; WGEM-TV (CW, FOX, NBC) Quincy; WMBD-TV (Bounce TV, CBS) Peoria; WMEC (PBS) Macomb; WQAD-TV (ABC, Antenna TV) Moline; WRSP-TV (Antenna TV, FOX, MeTV) Springfield; WTVP (PBS) Peoria.
Programming (via satellite): A&E; AMC; Animal Planet; Cartoon Network; CNN; Comcast SportsNet Chicago; Discovery Channel; Disney Channel; ESPN; ESPN2; Food Network; FOX Sports Networks; Freeform; HGTV; History; HLN; Lifetime; Nickelodeon; Spike TV; Syfy; TBS; The Weather Channel; TLC; TNT; USA Network; WGN America.
Fee: $45.00 installation; $43.00 monthly.
Digital Basic Service
Subscribers: N.A.
Programming (via satellite): BBC America; Bloomberg Television; Cloo; Discovery Digital Networks; ESPNews; Fuse; FXM; FYI; Golf Channel; History International; IFC; LMN; National Geographic Channel; NBCSN; Nick Jr.; Nicktoons; Outdoor Channel; TeenNick; Turner Classic Movies; TVG Network.
Digital Expanded Basic Service
Subscribers: N.A.
Programming (via satellite): AXS TV; ESPN; ESPN2; HD Theater; Universal HD.
Digital Pay Service 1
Pay Units: N.A.
Programming (via satellite): Cinemax (multiplexed); Flix (multiplexed); HBO (multiplexed); Showtime (multiplexed); Starz (multiplexed); Starz Encore (multiplexed); Starz HD; Sundance TV (multiplexed); The Movie Channel (multiplexed).
Video-On-Demand: No
Pay-Per-View
iN DEMAND (delivered digitally); Playboy TV (delivered digitally).
Internet Service
Operational: Yes.
Broadband Service: Mediacom High Speed Internet.
Telephone Service
Digital: Operational
Miles of Plant: 3.0 (coaxial); None (fiber optic). Homes passed: 229.
Vice President: Jim Waldo. Operations Director: Gary Wightman. Technical Operations Manager: Larry Brackman.
Ownership: Mediacom LLC (MSO).

GORHAM TWP.—Formerly served by CableDirect. No longer in operation. ICA: IL0511.

GRAFTON—Formerly served by Almega Cable. No longer in operation. ICA: IL0315.

Illinois—Cable Systems

GRAND RIDGE—Heartland Cable Inc, 167 West 5th St, PO Box 7, Minonk, IL 61760. Phones: 800-448-4320; 309-432-2075. Web Site: http://www.hcable.net. Also serves Ransom. ICA: IL0325.
TV Market Ranking: Below 100 (GRAND RIDGE, Ransom). Franchise award date: January 1, 1960. Franchise expiration date: N.A. Began: November 1, 1960.
Channel capacity: N.A. Channels available but not in use: N.A.
Basic Service
Subscribers: N.A.
Programming (received off-air): WCIU-TV (MeTV) Chicago; WEEK-TV (ABC, CW, NBC) Peoria; WFLD (FOX) Chicago; WGN-TV (IND) Chicago; WHOI (Comet) Peoria; WLS-TV (ABC, Live Well Network) Chicago; WMBD-TV (Bounce TV, CBS) Peoria; WPWR-TV (Buzzr, CW, MNT, Movies!) Gary; WTTW (PBS) Chicago; WWTO-TV (TBN) La Salle; WYZZ-TV (FOX, The Country Network) Bloomington.
Programming (via satellite): A&E; AMC; CNN; C-SPAN; Discovery Channel; Disney Channel; ESPN; ESPN2; Fox Sports 1; Freeform; HGTV; History; HLN; ION Television; QVC; Spike TV; Syfy; TBS; The Weather Channel; TLC; TNT; TV Land; USA Network; WGN America.
Fee: $30.00 installation.
Pay Service 1
Pay Units: N.A.
Programming (via satellite): HBO.
Fee: $10.00 monthly.
Internet Service
Operational: No.
Telephone Service
None
Miles of Plant: 5.0 (coaxial); None (fiber optic). Homes passed: 350.
Ownership: Heartland Cable Inc.

GRAND TOWER (village)—Formerly served by CableDirect. No longer in operation. ICA: IL0514.

GRANT PARK (village)—Mediacom. Now served by NEWTON COUNTY (portions), IN [IN0316]. ICA: IL0516.

GRANTFORK (village)—Clearvision Cable Systems Inc, 1785 US Rte 40, Greenup, IL 62428-3501. Phones: 866-923-5594; 217-923-5594. Fax: 217-923-5681. ICA: IL0517.
TV Market Ranking: 11 (GRANTFORK (VILLAGE)).
Channel capacity: N.A. Channels available but not in use: N.A.
Basic Service
Subscribers: 8.
Programming (received off-air): KDNL-TV (ABC, The Country Network) St. Louis; KETC (PBS) St. Louis; KMOV (CBS) St. Louis; KPLR-TV (CW, This TV) St. Louis; KSDK (Bounce TV, NBC) St. Louis; KTVI (Antenna TV, Escape, FOX) St. Louis.
Programming (via satellite): A&E; AMC; Animal Planet; CMT; CNN; C-SPAN; Discovery Channel; Disney Channel; ESPN; ESPN2; Freeform; History; HLN; Lifetime; Spike TV; Syfy; TBS; TLC; TNT; Travel Channel; USA Network; WGN America.
Fee: $42.50 installation; $47.95 monthly.
Pay Service 1
Pay Units: N.A.
Programming (via satellite): Showtime; The Movie Channel.
Video-On-Demand: No
Internet Service
Operational: No.
Telephone Service
None
Miles of Plant: 4.0 (coaxial); None (fiber optic). Homes passed: 118.
President & General Manager: Michael Bauguss. Secretary: Gwyndolyn S. Bauguss.
Ownership: Clearvision Cable Systems Inc. (MSO).

GRAYVILLE—NewWave Communications. Now served by McLEANSBORO, IL [IL0177]. ICA: IL0211.

GREAT LAKES NAVAL TRAINING CENTER—Comcast Cable. Now served by MOUNT PROSPECT, IL [IL0036]. ICA: IL0518.

GREENFIELD—Formerly served by BrightGreen Cable. No longer in operation. ICA: IL0284.

GREENUP—Mediacom, 4290 Blue Stem Rd, PO Box 288, Charleston, IL 61920. Phone: 217-348-5533. Fax: 217-345-7074. Web Site: http://www.mediacomcable.com. Also serves Toledo. ICA: IL0192.
TV Market Ranking: Outside TV Markets (GREENUP, Toledo). Franchise award date: January 1, 1981. Franchise expiration date: N.A. Began: February 25, 1981.
Channel capacity: N.A. Channels available but not in use: N.A.
Basic Service
Subscribers: 472.
Programming (received off-air): WAND (NBC) Decatur; WBUI (CW, This TV) Decatur; WCCU (FOX, MeTV) Urbana; WCIA (CBS, MNT) Champaign; WCIX (CBS, MNT) Springfield; WEIU-TV (PBS) Charleston; WICD (ABC) Champaign; WILL-TV (PBS) Urbana; WSIU-TV (PBS) Carbondale; WTHI-TV (CBS, FOX) Terre Haute; WTWO (NBC) Terre Haute; 7 FMs.
Programming (via satellite): C-SPAN; INSP; Pop; QVC; WGN America.
Fee: $45.00 installation; $43.00 monthly.
Expanded Basic Service 1
Subscribers: N.A.
Programming (via satellite): A&E; AMC; Animal Planet; BET; Cartoon Network; CMT; CNBC; CNN; Comedy Central; C-SPAN 2; Discovery Channel; Discovery Life Channel; Disney Channel; E! HD; ESPN; ESPN Classic; ESPN2; EVINE Live; EWTN Eternal Global Catholic Network; Food Network; Fox News Channel; Fox Sports 1; FOX Sports Midwest; Freeform; FX; Hallmark Channel; HGTV; History; HLN; ION Television; Jewelry Television; Lifetime; LMN; MSNBC; MTV; Nickelodeon; Outdoor Channel; Oxygen; Spike TV; Syfy; TBS; The Weather Channel; TLC; TNT; Travel Channel; Trinity Broadcasting Network (TBN); truTV; TV Land; USA Network; VH1; WE tv.
Fee: $34.00 monthly.
Digital Basic Service
Subscribers: N.A.
Programming (via satellite): AXS TV; BBC America; Bloomberg Television; Bravo; CBS Sports Network; CCTV-Documentary; Cloo; CMT; Destination America; Discovery Kids Channel; Discovery Life Channel; Disney XD; ESPN HD; ESPN2 HD; ESPNews; ESPNU; FOX College Sports Central; FOX College Sports Pacific; Fox Sports 2; Fuse; FXM; FYI; Golf Channel; GolTV; GSN; HD Theater; History; IFC; Investigation Discovery; ION Television; MC; MTV Classic; MTV Hits; MTV2; Nat Geo WILD; NBCSN; Nick Jr.; Nicktoons; OWN: Oprah Winfrey Network; Qubo; Reelz; Science Channel; TeenNick; Tennis Channel; Turner Classic Movies; TVG Network; Universal HD.
Digital Pay Service 1
Pay Units: N.A.
Programming (via satellite): Cinemax (multiplexed); Cinemax On Demand; HBO (multiplexed); HBO HD; HBO on Demand; Showtime (multiplexed); Showtime HD; Showtime On Demand; Starz (multiplexed); Starz Encore (multiplexed); Starz HD; Starz On Demand; The Movie Channel (multiplexed); The Movie Channel HD; The Movie Channel On Demand.
Fee: $11.95 monthly (HBO, Cinemax, Showtime/TMC or Starz/Encore).
Video-On-Demand: Yes
Internet Service
Operational: Yes.
Broadband Service: Mediacom High Speed Internet.
Fee: $59.95 installation; $40.95 monthly.
Telephone Service
Digital: Operational
Fee: $39.95 monthly
Miles of Plant: 27.0 (coaxial); None (fiber optic). Homes passed: 1,281.
General Manager: Todd Acker. Technical Operations Manager: Jerry Ferguson. Marketing Director: James Friske.
Ownership: Mediacom LLC (MSO).

GREENVIEW—Mediacom. Now served by DELAVAN, IL [IL0172]. ICA: IL0331.

GREENVILLE—NewWave Communications. Now served by TAYLORVILLE, IL [IL0098]. ICA: IL0137.

GRIDLEY—Gridley Cable, 108 East Third St, PO Box 247, Gridley, IL 61744. Phones: 309-747-2221; 309-747-2324. Fax: 309-747-2888. E-mail: info@gridcom.net. Web Site: http://www.gridtel.com. ICA: IL0280.
TV Market Ranking: Below 100 (GRIDLEY). Franchise award date: N.A. Franchise expiration date: N.A. Began: September 1, 1982.
Channel capacity: N.A. Channels available but not in use: N.A.
Basic Service
Subscribers: 349.
Programming (received off-air): WAOE (Antenna TV, MNT) Peoria; WEEK-TV (ABC, CW, NBC) Peoria; WHOI (Comet) Peoria; WMBD-TV (Bounce TV, CBS) Peoria; WTVP (PBS) Peoria; WYZZ-TV (FOX, The Country Network) Bloomington.
Programming (via satellite): A&E; AMC; Animal Planet; Bravo; BTN; Cartoon Network; CMT; CNBC; CNN; Comcast SportsNet Chicago; Comedy Central; C-SPAN; Discovery Channel; Disney Channel; Disney XD; ESPN; ESPN Classic; ESPN2; Food Network; Fox News Channel; FOX Sports Midwest; Freeform; FX; Great American Country; Hallmark Channel; HGTV; History; Lifetime; MTV; National Geographic Channel; NFL Network; Nickelodeon; Spike TV; Syfy; TBS; The Weather Channel; TLC; TNT; Travel Channel; Turner Classic Movies; TV Land; USA Network; VH1; WGN America.
Fee: $50.00 installation; $55.95 monthly.
Digital Basic Service
Subscribers: 186.
Programming (via satellite): BBC America; Bloomberg Television; Bravo; CMT; Destination America; Discovery Kids Channel; Discovery Life Channel; DMX Music; ESPN Classic; ESPN2; ESPNews; ESPNU; Fox Sports 1; Fuse; FXM; FYI; Golf Channel; Great American Country; GSN; HGTV; History; History International; IFC; Investigation Discovery; LMN; MTV Classic; MTV Hits; MTV2; National Geographic Channel; Nick Jr.; Nicktoons; Outdoor Channel; Ovation; OWN: Oprah Winfrey Network; Science Channel; Syfy; TeenNick; Trinity Broadcasting Network (TBN); Turner Classic Movies; VH1 Soul; WE tv.
Fee: $56.95 monthly.
Pay Service 1
Pay Units: N.A.
Programming (via satellite): Starz Encore.
Fee: $1.95 monthly.
Digital Pay Service 1
Pay Units: N.A.
Programming (via satellite): Cinemax (multiplexed); Flix; HBO (multiplexed); Showtime (multiplexed); Starz (multiplexed); Starz Encore (multiplexed); The Movie Channel (multiplexed).
Fee: $8.95 monthly (Cinemax), $10.95 monthly (Showtime/TMC/Flix), $12.95 monthly (Starz/Encore), $16.00 monthly (HBO).
Video-On-Demand: No
Pay-Per-View
iN DEMAND (delivered digitally).
Internet Service
Operational: Yes.
Fee: $39.95-$59.95 installation.
Telephone Service
Digital: Operational
Fee: $9.00 monthly
Miles of Plant: 9.0 (coaxial); None (fiber optic).
Vice President & General Manager: Herbert Flesher.
Ownership: Gridley Telephone (MSO).

GRIGGSVILLE—Cass Cable TV Inc. Now served by PITTSFIELD, IL [IL0158]. ICA: IL0246.

HAMEL—Madison Communications. Now served by STAUNTON, IL [IL0171]. ICA: IL0393.

HAMPSHIRE—Mediacom. Now served by CORTLAND (village), IL [IL0485]. ICA: IL0253.

HANOVER—Mediacom. Now served by LENA, IL [IL0223]. ICA: IL0285.

HARDIN—Formerly served by BrightGreen Cable. No longer in operation. ICA: IL0333.

HARRISBURG—Mediacom. Now served by MARION, IL [IL0083]. ICA: IL0086.

HARTSBURG—Mediacom. Now served by DELAVAN, IL [IL0172]. ICA: IL0413.

HARVARD—Charter Communications. Now served by MADISON, WI [WI0002]. ICA: IL0073.

HARVEL—Mediacom. Now served by KINCAID, IL [IL0176]. ICA: IL0433.

HARVEY—Comcast Cable. Now served by CHAMPAIGN, IL [IL0019]. ICA: IL0055.

HEBRON (village)—Mediacom. Now served by BELVIDERE TWP., IL [IL0282]. ICA: IL0519.

HENNING—Formerly served by CableDirect. No longer in operation. ICA: IL0453.

HERITAGE LAKE—Tel-Star Cablevision Inc. Now served by METAMORA, IL [IL0326]. ICA: IL0520.

Cable Systems—Illinois

HERRICK—Mediacom, 4290 Blue Stem Rd, PO Box 288, Charleston, IL 61920. Phones: 217-348-5533; 309-274-4500. Fax: 217-345-7074. Web Site: http://www.mediacomcable.com. ICA: IL0368.
TV Market Ranking: Outside TV Markets (HERRICK). Franchise award date: N.A. Franchise expiration date: N.A. Began: N.A.
Channel capacity: N.A. Channels available but not in use: N.A.
Basic Service
Subscribers: 6.
Programming (received off-air): WAND (NBC) Decatur; WCIA (CBS, MNT) Champaign; WICS (ABC, The Country Network) Springfield; WILL-TV (PBS) Urbana; WPXS (IND) Mount Vernon; WRSP-TV (Antenna TV, FOX, MeTV) Springfield.
Programming (via satellite): A&E; AMC; Animal Planet; CNN; Comedy Central; Discovery Channel; ESPN; ESPN2; Fox Sports 1; Freeform; HGTV; History; HLN; Lifetime; MTV; Nickelodeon; Spike TV; Syfy; TBS; The Weather Channel; TLC; TNT; Travel Channel; USA Network; WGN America.
Fee: $45.00 installation; $69.95 monthly.
Pay Service 1
Pay Units: N.A.
Programming (via satellite): Cinemax; HBO.
Fee: $7.95 monthly (Cinemax), $13.50 monthly (HBO).
Video-On-Demand: No
Internet Service
Operational: No.
Telephone Service
None
Miles of Plant: 5.0 (coaxial); None (fiber optic). Homes passed: 244.
General Manager: Todd Acker. Technical Operations Manager: Jerry Ferguson. Marketing Director: James Friske.
Ownership: Mediacom LLC (MSO).

HERRIN—Mediacom. Now served by MARION, IL [IL0083]. ICA: IL0063.

HERSCHER—Comcast Cable. Now served by CHAMPAIGN, IL [IL0019]. ICA: IL0298.

HETTICK (village)—Formerly served by CableDirect. No longer in operation. ICA: IL0521.

HEYWORTH—Mediacom. Now served by ATLANTA, IL [IL0197]. ICA: IL0226.

HICKORY HILLS—Comcast Cable. Now served by CHAMPAIGN, IL [IL0019]. ICA: IL0695.

HIGHLAND PARK—Comcast Cable. Now served by MOUNT PROSPECT, IL [IL0036]. ICA: IL0031.

HILLSBORO—NewWave Communications. Now served by TAYLORVILLE, IL [IL0098]. ICA: IL0143.

HOFFMAN—Formerly served by CableDirect. No longer in operation. ICA: IL0622.

HOMEWOOD—Comcast Cable. Now served by CHAMPAIGN, IL [IL0019]. ICA: IL0052.

HOOPESTON—Formerly served by Avenue Broadband Communications. Now served by NewWave Communications, WESTVILLE, IL [IL0079]. ICA: IL0112.

HOOPPOLE—Formerly served by CableDirect. No longer in operation. ICA: IL0429.

HOYLETON—Formerly served by CableDirect. No longer in operation. ICA: IL0430.

HUDSON—Mediacom. Now served by ROANOKE, IL [IL0068]. ICA: IL0342.

HUME (village)—Clearvision Cable Systems Inc, 1785 US Rte 40, Greenup, IL 62428-3501. Phone: 217-923-5594. Fax: 217-923-5681. Also serves Metcalf (village). ICA: IL0526.
TV Market Ranking: 64 (HUME (VILLAGE), Metcalf (village)). Franchise award date: N.A. Franchise expiration date: N.A. Began: May 1, 1983.
Channel capacity: 36 (not 2-way capable). Channels available but not in use: N.A.
Basic Service
Subscribers: 23.
Programming (received off-air): WAND (NBC) Decatur; WBUI (CW, This TV) Decatur; WCCU (FOX, MeTV) Urbana; WCIA (CBS, MNT) Champaign; WCIX (CBS, MNT) Springfield; WEIU-TV (PBS) Charleston; WICD (ABC) Champaign; WILL-TV (PBS) Urbana.
Programming (via satellite): A&E; AMC; Bravo; Cartoon Network; CMT; CNBC; CNN; Comedy Central; C-SPAN; C-SPAN 2; Discovery Channel; Disney Channel; ESPN; ESPN2; Fox News Channel; History; HLN; Lifetime; MSNBC; MTV; Nickelodeon; QVC; Spike TV; Syfy; TBS; The Weather Channel; TLC; TNT; Trinity Broadcasting Network (TBN); Turner Classic Movies; TV Land; USA Network; VH1; WGN America.
Fee: $47.95 monthly.
Pay Service 1
Pay Units: N.A.
Programming (via satellite): Showtime; The Movie Channel.
Fee: $11.95 monthly (each).
Video-On-Demand: No
Internet Service
Operational: No.
Telephone Service
None
Miles of Plant: 9.0 (coaxial); None (fiber optic). Homes passed: 314.
President & General Manager: Michael Bauguss. Secretary: Gwyndolyn S. Bauguss.
Ownership: Clearvision Cable Systems Inc. (MSO).

INA—Formerly served by Longview Communications. No longer in operation. ICA: IL0392.

INDUSTRY—Mediacom, 609 South 4th St, PO Box 334, Chillicothe, IL 61523. Phones: 309-469-2027; 309-274-4500. Fax: 309-274-3188. Web Site: http://www.mediacomcable.com. ICA: IL0365.
TV Market Ranking: Outside TV Markets (INDUSTRY). Franchise award date: N.A. Franchise expiration date: N.A. Began: December 1, 1983.
Channel capacity: N.A. Channels available but not in use: N.A.
Basic Service
Subscribers: 2.
Programming (received off-air): KHQA-TV (ABC, CBS) Hannibal; WGEM-TV (CW, FOX, NBC) Quincy; WHOI (Comet) Peoria; WRSP-TV (Antenna TV, FOX, MeTV) Springfield; WTVP (PBS) Peoria.
Programming (via satellite): A&E; AMC; Cartoon Network; CNN; Comedy Central; Discovery Channel; ESPN; Freeform; HGTV; History; Lifetime; Nickelodeon; Spike TV; TBS; The Weather Channel; TLC; TNT; Trin-

ity Broadcasting Network (TBN); TV Land; USA Network; WGN America.
Fee: $45.00 installation; $69.95 monthly.
Pay Service 1
Pay Units: N.A.
Programming (via satellite): Cinemax; HBO.
Fee: $7.95 monthly (Cinemax), $13.50 monthly (HBO).
Video-On-Demand: No
Internet Service
Operational: No.
Telephone Service
None
Miles of Plant: 5.0 (coaxial); None (fiber optic). Homes passed: 260.
Vice President: Don Hagwell. Operations Director: Gary Wightman. Technical Operations Manager: Larry Brackman. Marketing Director: Stephanie Law.
Ownership: Mediacom LLC (MSO).

IPAVA—Nova1Net, 677 West Main St, PO Box 1412, Galesburg, IL 61402. Phones: 800-397-6682; 309-469-2027. Fax: 309-342-4408. Web Site: http://www.novacablevision.com. Also serves Astoria. ICA: IL0357.
TV Market Ranking: Outside TV Markets (IPAVA, Astoria). Franchise award date: N.A. Franchise expiration date: N.A. Began: March 1, 1984.
Channel capacity: N.A. Channels available but not in use: N.A.
Basic Service
Subscribers: N.A.
Programming (received off-air): WEEK-TV (ABC, CW, NBC) Peoria; WHOI (Comet) Peoria; WMBD-TV (Bounce TV, CBS) Peoria; WRSP-TV (Antenna TV, FOX, MeTV) Springfield; WTVP (PBS) Peoria.
Programming (via satellite): A&E; AMC; Animal Planet; Cartoon Network; CMT; CNN; Comedy Central; Discovery Channel; ESPN; ESPN2; Freeform; HGTV; Lifetime; Nickelodeon; Spike TV; Syfy; TBS; TNT; USA Network; VH1; WGN America.
Fee: $45.00 installation; $47.95 monthly.
Pay Service 1
Pay Units: N.A.
Programming (via satellite): HBO.
Fee: $12.00 monthly.
Video-On-Demand: No
Internet Service
Operational: No.
Telephone Service
None
Miles of Plant: 6.0 (coaxial); None (fiber optic). Homes passed: 181.
Ownership: Nova Cablevision Inc. (MSO).

IROQUOIS (village)—Formerly served by CableDirect. No longer in operation. ICA: IL0527.

IRVING—Mediacom, 4290 Blue Stem Rd, PO Box 288, Charleston, IL 61920. Phone: 217-348-5533. Fax: 217-345-7074. Web Site: http://www.mediacomcable.com. ICA: IL0687.

TV Market Ranking: Outside TV Markets (IRVING).
Channel capacity: N.A. Channels available but not in use: N.A.
Internet Service
Operational: No.
Telephone Service
None
Area Operations Director: Todd Acker. Technical Operations Manager: Jerry Ferguson.
Ownership: Mediacom LLC (MSO).

IRVING—Mediacom. Now served by IRVING, IL [IL0687]. ICA: IL0390.

IUKA—Formerly served by Advanced Technologies & Technical Resources Inc. No longer in operation. ICA: IL0528.

JACKSON COUNTY (portions)—Zito Media, 102 S Main St, PO Box 665, Coudersport, PA 16915. Phones: 814-260-9055; 800-365-6988. E-mail: info@zitomedia.com. Web Site: http://www.zitomedia.com. ICA: IL0634.
TV Market Ranking: 69 (JACKSON COUNTY (PORTIONS) (portions)); Below 100 (JACKSON COUNTY (PORTIONS) (portions)); Outside TV Markets (JACKSON COUNTY (PORTIONS) (portions)).
Channel capacity: N.A. Channels available but not in use: N.A.
Basic Service
Subscribers: 269.
Programming (received off-air): KBSI (FOX) Cape Girardeau; KFVS-TV (CBS, CW, MeTV) Cape Girardeau; WDKA (MNT, The Country Network) Paducah; WPSD-TV (Antenna TV, NBC) Paducah; WSIL-TV (ABC) Harrisburg; WSIU-TV (PBS) Carbondale; WTCT (IND) Marion.
Programming (via satellite): A&E; AMC; Animal Planet; Cartoon Network en Espanol; CNBC; CNN; Comedy Central; C-SPAN; Discovery Channel; Disney Channel; E! HD; ESPN; ESPN2; Food Network; Fox News Channel; Freeform; Fuse; FX; Great American Country; HGTV; History; HLN; Lifetime; Outdoor Channel; TBS; The Weather Channel; TLC; TNT; Turner Classic Movies; USA Network; WGN America.
Fee: $49.95 installation; $17.20 monthly.
Digital Basic Service
Subscribers: N.A.
Programming (via satellite): BBC America; Bloomberg Television; Discovery Life Channel; Disney XD; DMX Music; ESPN Classic; ESPNews; FYI; Golf Channel; GSN; History International; National Geographic Channel; Syfy; WE tv.
Digital Expanded Basic Service
Subscribers: N.A.
Programming (via satellite): DMX Music; FXM; LMN; Starz Encore.
Fee: $13.95 monthly.
Pay Service 1
Pay Units: N.A.
Programming (via satellite): HBO; Showtime; Starz Encore.

Illinois—Cable Systems

Digital Pay Service 1
Pay Units: N.A.
Programming (via satellite): Cinemax (multiplexed); Flix; HBO (multiplexed); Showtime (multiplexed); The Movie Channel (multiplexed).
Fee: $14.30 monthly.

Pay-Per-View
ESPN Now (delivered digitally); Hot Choice (delivered digitally); Playboy TV (delivered digitally); Fresh (delivered digitally); Shorteez (delivered digitally); Urban Xtra (delivered digitally).

Internet Service
Operational: Yes.
Fee: $49.95 installation; $35.00 monthly.

Telephone Service
Digital: Operational
Miles of Plant: 53.0 (coaxial); None (fiber optic). Homes passed: 1,295.
President: James Rigas.
Ownership: Zito Media (MSO).

JACKSONVILLE—Mediacom, 4290 Blue Stem Rd, PO Box 288, Charleston, IL 61920. Phone: 217-348-5533. Fax: 217-345-7074. Web Site: http://www.mediacomcable.com. Also serves Chapin, Morgan County (portions) & South Jacksonville. ICA: IL0065.
TV Market Ranking: 64 (JACKSONVILLE, Morgan County (portions) (portions), South Jacksonville); Outside TV Markets (Chapin, Morgan County (portions) (portions)). Franchise award date: October 19, 1964. Franchise expiration date: N.A. Began: October 14, 1964.
Channel capacity: N.A. Channels available but not in use: N.A.

Basic Service
Subscribers: 3,534. Commercial subscribers: 7.
Programming (received off-air): KETC (PBS) St. Louis; KHQA-TV (ABC, CBS) Hannibal; KPLR-TV (CW, This TV) St. Louis; KTVI (Antenna TV, Escape, FOX) St. Louis; WAND (NBC) Decatur; WBUI (CW, This TV) Decatur; WCIA (CBS, MNT) Champaign; WCIX (CBS, MNT) Springfield; WICS (ABC, The Country Network) Springfield; WILL-TV (PBS) Urbana; WRSP-TV (Antenna TV, FOX, MeTV) Springfield; WSEC (PBS) Jacksonville; allband FM.
Programming (via satellite): Freeform; QVC; TBS; WGN America.
Fee: $45.00 installation; $43.00 monthly.

Expanded Basic Service 1
Subscribers: N.A.
Programming (via satellite): A&E; AMC; Animal Planet; BET; Bravo; Cartoon Network; CMT; CNBC; CNN; Comedy Central; C-SPAN; C-SPAN 2; Discovery Channel; Disney Channel; Disney XD; E! HD; ESPN; ESPN2; ESPNews; EWTN Global Catholic Network; Food Network; Fox News Channel; Fox Sports 1; FOX Sports Midwest; FX; Golf Channel; Hallmark Channel; HGTV; History; HLN; INSP; Lifetime; MoviePlex; MSNBC; MTV; Nickelodeon; Pop; Spike TV; Syfy; The Weather Channel; TLC; TNT; Travel Channel; Trinity Broadcasting Network (TBN); truTV; Turner Classic Movies; TV Land; USA Network; VH1; WE tv.
Fee: $34.00 monthly.

Digital Basic Service
Subscribers: N.A.
Programming (via satellite): BBC America; Bloomberg Television; Cloo; Destination America; Discovery Kids Channel; DMX Music; ESPNews; Fuse; FXM; FYI; Golf Channel; GSN; History International; IFC; Investigation Discovery; LMN; MTV2; National Geographic Channel; NBCSN; Nick Jr.; Nicktoons; Outdoor Channel; OWN; Oprah Winfrey Network; Science Channel; Turner Classic Movies; TVG Network.

Digital Pay Service 1
Pay Units: N.A.
Programming (via satellite): Cinemax (multiplexed); HBO (multiplexed); Showtime (multiplexed); Starz (multiplexed); Starz Encore (multiplexed); The Movie Channel (multiplexed).
Fee: $11.95 monthly (HBO, Cinemax, Showtime/TMC or Starz/Encore).

Video-On-Demand: Yes

Pay-Per-View
iN DEMAND (delivered digitally); Playboy TV (delivered digitally); Pleasure (delivered digitally); Fresh (delivered digitally); Shorteez (delivered digitally).

Internet Service
Operational: Yes.
Subscribers: 3,535.
Broadband Service: Mediacom High Speed Internet.
Fee: $59.95 installation; $40.95 monthly.

Telephone Service
Digital: Operational
Subscribers: 1,119.
Fee: $39.95 monthly
Miles of Plant: 266.0 (coaxial); 85.0 (fiber optic). Homes passed: 11,690.
Area Operations Director: Todd Acker. Technical Operations Manager: Jerry Ferguson.
Ownership: Mediacom LLC (MSO).

JERSEYVILLE—NewWave Communications, One Montgomery Plaza, 4th Floor, Sikeston, MO 63801. Phone: 888-863-9928. Fax: 573-481-9809. E-mail: info@newwavecom.com. Web Site: http://www.newwavecom.com. Also serves Brighton, Carrollton, Jersey County (portions), Manchester, Roodhouse & White Hall. ICA: IL0130.
TV Market Ranking: 11 (Brighton, Jersey County (portions), JERSEYVILLE, Manchester); Outside TV Markets (Roodhouse, White Hall, Carrollton). Franchise award date: May 1, 1979. Franchise expiration date: N.A. Began: May 29, 1980.
Channel capacity: N.A. Channels available but not in use: N.A.

Basic Service
Subscribers: 1,911.
Programming (received off-air): KDNL-TV (ABC, The Country Network) St. Louis; KETC (PBS) St. Louis; KMOV (CBS) St. Louis; KPLR-TV (CW, This TV) St. Louis; KSDK (Bounce TV, NBC) St. Louis; KTVI (CW, MeTV, NBC) Sioux City; KTVI (Antenna TV, Escape, FOX) St. Louis;

Programming (via satellite): C-SPAN; QVC; WGN America.
Fee: $40.00 installation; $17.95 monthly.

Expanded Basic Service 1
Subscribers: N.A.
Programming (via satellite): A&E; AMC; Animal Planet; Bravo; Cartoon Network; CMT; CNBC; CNN; Comedy Central; Discovery Channel; Disney Channel; E! HD; ESPN; ESPN2; Food Network; Fox News Channel; FOX Sports Midwest; Freeform; FX; Hallmark Channel; HGTV; History; HLN; Lifetime; MSNBC; MTV; National Geographic Channel; Nickelodeon; Outdoor Channel; Pop; Spike TV; Syfy; TBS; The Weather Channel; TLC; TNT; Travel Channel; TV Land; USA Network; VH1.
Fee: $30.40 monthly.

Digital Basic Service
Subscribers: N.A.
Programming (via satellite): AXS TV; BET; Bloomberg Television; CMT; CW PLUS; Destination America; Discovery Channel HD; Discovery Kids Channel; Discovery Life Channel; Disney XD; ESPN Classic; ESPN HD; ESPNews; EVINE Live; Food Network HD; Fox Sports 1; Fuse; FXM; FYI; Golf Channel; HGTV HD; History; IFC; Investigation Discovery; LMN; MTV Classic; MTV Hits; MTV2; NBCSN; Nick 2; Nick Jr.; Nicktoons; Outdoor Channel 2 HD; OWN; Oprah Winfrey Network; Science Channel; Trinity Broadcasting Network (TBN); Turner Classic Movies; Universal HD; VH1 Soul; WE tv.

Digital Pay Service 1
Pay Units: 204.
Programming (via satellite): Cinemax (multiplexed); Cinemax HD; Flix; HBO (multiplexed); HBO HD; Showtime (multiplexed); Showtime HD; Starz (multiplexed); Starz Encore (multiplexed); The Movie Channel (multiplexed); The Movie Channel HD.

Video-On-Demand: No

Pay-Per-View
iN DEMAND (delivered digitally); Shorteez (delivered digitally); Hot Choice (delivered digitally); ESPN Now (delivered digitally); Playboy TV (delivered digitally); Fresh (delivered digitally).

Internet Service
Operational: Yes.
Subscribers: 295.
Fee: $30.00 or $99.95 installation; $29.95-$99.95 monthly.

Telephone Service
Digital: Operational
Subscribers: 60.
Fee: $34.95 monthly
Miles of Plant: 48.0 (coaxial); None (fiber optic). Homes passed: 4,123.
Chief Financial Officer: Rod Siemers.
Ownership: NewWave Communications LLC (MSO).

JEWETT—Clearvision Cable Systems Inc, 1785 US Rte 40, Greenup, IL 62428-3501. Phone: 217-923-5594. Fax: 217-923-5681. ICA: IL0700.
TV Market Ranking: Outside TV Markets (JEWETT).
Channel capacity: N.A. Channels available but not in use: N.A.

Basic Service
Subscribers: 4.
Fee: $47.95 monthly.
President & General Manager: Michael Bauguss. Secretary: Gwyndolyn S. Bauguss.
Ownership: Clearvision Cable Systems Inc. (MSO).

KAMPSVILLE (village)—Formerly served by Cass Cable TV Inc. No longer in operation. ICA: IL0397.

KANKAKEE—Comcast Cable. Now served by CHAMPAIGN, IL [IL0019]. ICA: IL0035.

KARNAK—Formerly served by Longview Communications. No longer in operation. ICA: IL0358.

KEITHSBURG—Nova1Net, 677 West Main St, PO Box 1412, Galesburg, IL 61401. Phones: 800-397-6682; 309-342-9681. Fax: 309-342-4408. Web Site: http://www.novacablevision.com. ICA: IL0318.
TV Market Ranking: 60 (KEITHSBURG). Franchise award date: N.A. Franchise expiration date: N.A. Began: September 7, 1984.
Channel capacity: N.A. Channels available but not in use: N.A.

Basic Service
Subscribers: N.A.
Programming (received off-air): KGCW (CW, MeTV, This TV) Burlington; KIIN (PBS) Iowa City; KWQC-TV (NBC) Davenport; WEEK-TV (ABC, CW, NBC) Peoria; WHBF-TV (CBS) Rock Island; WHOI (Comet) Peoria; WMBD-TV (Bounce TV, CBS) Peoria; WQAD-TV (ABC, Antenna TV) Moline; WQPT-TV (PBS) Moline; WTVP (PBS) Peoria.
Programming (via satellite): A&E; AMC; Animal Planet; BTN; Cartoon Network; CMT; CNBC; CNN; Comcast SportsNet Chicago; Comedy Central; C-SPAN; C-SPAN 2; Discovery Channel; Disney Channel; DIY Network; E! HD; ESPN; ESPN2; ESPNU; EWTN Global Catholic Network; Food Network; Fox News Channel; Fox Sports 1; FOX Sports Midwest; Freeform; FX; Golf Channel; Hallmark Channel; HGTV; History; HLN; HRTV; INSP; Lifetime; MSNBC; MTV; National Geographic Channel; Nickelodeon; QVC; RFD-TV; Spike TV; Syfy; TBS; The Weather Channel; TLC; TNT; Travel Channel; truTV; TV Land; USA Network; VH1; WGN America.
Fee: $60.00 installation.

Digital Basic Service
Subscribers: N.A.
Programming (via satellite): Bloomberg Television; CMT; Destination America; Discovery Kids Channel; Disney XD; DMX Music; ESPN Classic; ESPN2; ESPNews; EVINE Live; Fox Sports 1; FSN Digital Atlantic; FSN Digital Central; FSN Digital Pacific; Fuse; FXM; FYI; Golf Channel; Great American Country; GSN; HGTV; History; History International; IFC; Investigation Discovery; LMN; MTV Classic; MTV Hits; MTV2; NBCSN; Nicktoons; Noggin; Outdoor Channel; OWN: Oprah Winfrey Network; Science Channel; Syfy; TeenNick; Trinity Broadcasting Network (TBN); Turner Classic Movies; VH1 Soul; WE tv.

Pay Service 1
Pay Units: N.A.
Programming (via satellite): Cinemax; HBO.
Fee: $11.95 monthly (each).

Digital Pay Service 1
Pay Units: N.A.
Programming (via satellite): Cinemax (multiplexed); Flix; HBO (multiplexed); Showtime (multiplexed); Starz (multiplexed); Starz Encore (multiplexed); Sundance TV; The Movie Channel (multiplexed).
Fee: $12.85 monthly (HBO, Cinemax, Starz/Encore or Showtime/TMC/Flix/Sundance).

Video-On-Demand: No

D-202   TV & Cable Factbook No. 85

Cable Systems—Illinois

Internet Service
Operational: Yes.
Fee: $30.00 installation; $39.95 monthly; $3.95 modem lease.
Telephone Service
None
Miles of Plant: 10.0 (coaxial); None (fiber optic). Homes passed: 323.
General Manager: Robert G. Fischer Jr. Office Manager: Hazel Harden.
Ownership: Nova Cablevision Inc. (MSO).

KENNEY—Heartland Cable Inc, 167 West 5th St, PO Box 7, Minonk, IL 61760. Phones: 800-448-4320; 309-432-2075. Web Site: http://www.hcable.net. ICA: IL0531.
TV Market Ranking: 64 (KENNEY). Franchise award date: August 1, 1987. Franchise expiration date: N.A. Began: January 1, 1988.
Channel capacity: N.A. Channels available but not in use: N.A.
Basic Service
Subscribers: N.A.
Programming (received off-air): WAND (NBC) Decatur; WCCU (FOX, MeTV) Urbana; WCIA (CBS, MNT) Champaign; WICD (ABC) Champaign; WILL-TV (PBS) Urbana.
Programming (via satellite): A&E; CNN; Discovery Channel; Disney Channel; ESPN; Freeform; Spike TV; TBS; TNT; USA Network; WGN America.
Fee: $39.00 installation.
Pay Service 1
Pay Units: N.A.
Programming (via satellite): HBO; Showtime.
Fee: $8.95 - $10.95 monthly (each).
Video-On-Demand: Yes
Internet Service
Operational: Yes.
Fee: $39.00 installation; $29.99 monthly.
Telephone Service
None
Miles of Plant: 3.0 (coaxial); None (fiber optic).
Chief Executive Officer: Jim Frances. President & General Manager: Steve Allen.
Ownership: Heartland Cable Inc. (MSO).

KEWANEE—Comcast Cable. Now served by MOUNT PROSPECT, IL [IL0036]. ICA: IL0085.

KEYESPORT—Formerly served by CableDirect. No longer in operation. ICA: IL0348.

KINCAID—Mediacom, 4290 Blue Stem Rd, PO Box 288, Charleston, IL 61920. Phone: 217-348-5533. Fax: 217-345-7074. Web Site: http://www.mediacomcable.com. Also serves Buffalo, Bulpitt, Clear Lake (village), Dawson, Edinburg, Harvel, Jeisyville, Loami, Mechanicsburg, Morrisonville, Mount Auburn, New Berlin, Palmer, River Oaks (village) & Tovey. ICA: IL0176.
TV Market Ranking: 64 (Buffalo, Bulpitt, Clear Lake (village), Dawson, Edinburg, Harvel, Jeisyville, KINCAID, Loami, Mechanicsburg, Morrisonville, Mount Auburn, New Berlin, Palmer, River Oaks (village), Tovey). Franchise award date: N.A. Franchise expiration date: N.A. Began: March 1, 1983.
Channel capacity: N.A. Channels available but not in use: N.A.
Basic Service
Subscribers: 1,242.
Programming (received off-air): WAND (NBC) Decatur; WBUI (CW, This TV) Decatur; WCIA (CBS, MNT) Champaign; WCIX (CBS, MNT) Springfield; WICD (ABC) Champaign; WICS (ABC, The Country Network) Springfield; WILL-TV (PBS) Urbana; WRSP-TV (Antenna TV, FOX, MeTV) Springfield; WSEC (PBS) Jacksonville.
Programming (via satellite): Freeform; QVC; TBS; Weatherscan; WGN America.
Fee: $45.00 installation; $43.00 monthly.
Expanded Basic Service 1
Subscribers: N.A.
Programming (via satellite): A&E; AMC; Animal Planet; BET; Bravo; Cartoon Network; CMT; CNBC; CNN; Comcast SportsNet Chicago; Comedy Central; C-SPAN; C-SPAN 2; Discovery Channel; Discovery Life Channel; Disney Channel; E! HD; ESPN; ESPN2; EVINE Live; EWTN Global Catholic Network; Food Network; Fox News Channel; Fox Sports 1; FX; Hallmark Channel; HGTV; History; HLN; INSP; ION Television; Lifetime; MoviePlex; MSNBC; MTV; Nickelodeon; Pop; RFD-TV; Spike TV; Syfy; The Weather Channel; TLC; TNT; Travel Channel; Trinity Broadcasting Network (TBN); truTV; TV Land; USA Network; VH1; WE tv.
Fee: $34.00 monthly.
Digital Basic Service
Subscribers: N.A.
Programming (via satellite): AXS TV; BBC America; Bloomberg Television; CCTV-Documentary; Cloo; Destination America; Discovery Kids Channel; ESPN HD; ESPN2 HD; ESPNews; Fuse; FXM; FYI; Golf Channel; GSN; HD Theater; History International; IFC; Investigation Discovery; ION Television; LMN; MC; MTV Classic; MTV Hits; MTV2; Nat Geo WILD; National Geographic Channel; NBCSN; Nick Jr.; Nicktoons; Outdoor Channel; OWN; Oprah Winfrey Network; Qubo; Reelz; Science Channel; TeenNick; Turner Classic Movies; TVG Network; Universal HD.
Digital Expanded Basic Service
Subscribers: N.A.
Programming (via satellite): CBS Sports Network; ESPNU; FOX College Sports Central; FOX College Sports Pacific; Fox Sports 2; GolTV; Tennis Channel.
Fee: $3.95 monthly.
Digital Pay Service 1
Pay Units: N.A.
Programming (via satellite): Cinemax (multiplexed); Cinemax On Demand; HBO (multiplexed); HBO HD; HBO on Demand; Showtime (multiplexed); Showtime HD; Showtime On Demand; Starz (multiplexed); Starz Encore (multiplexed); Starz HD; Starz On Demand; The Movie Channel (multiplexed); The Movie Channel HD; The Movie Channel On Demand.
Fee: $11.95 monthly (each).
Video-On-Demand: Yes
Pay-Per-View
iN DEMAND (delivered digitally); Playboy TV (delivered digitally); SexSee (delivered digitally); Juicy (delivered digitally).
Internet Service
Operational: Yes.
Broadband Service: Mediacom High Speed Internet.
Fee: $59.95 installation; $40.95 monthly.
Telephone Service
Digital: Operational
Fee: $39.95 monthly
Miles of Plant: 127.0 (coaxial); 26.0 (fiber optic). Homes passed: 5,747.
Area Operations Director: Todd Acker. Technical Operations Manager: Jerry Ferguson. Customer Service Manager: Angie McHenry.
Ownership: Mediacom LLC (MSO).

KINDERHOOK—Formerly served by Almega Cable. No longer in operation. ICA: IL0276.

KINGSTON—Formerly served by Kingston Cable TV Co. No longer in operation. ICA: IL0532.

KINGSTON MINES—KMHC Inc, 207 3rd St, PO Box 107, Kingston Mines, IL 61539-0107. Phone: 309-389-5782. ICA: IL0440.
TV Market Ranking: 83 (KINGSTON MINES). Franchise award date: October 1, 1983. Franchise expiration date: N.A. Began: October 1, 1983.
Channel capacity: N.A. Channels available but not in use: N.A.
Basic Service
Subscribers: N.A.
Programming (received off-air): WEEK-TV (ABC, CW, NBC) Peoria; WHOI (Comet) Peoria; WMBD-TV (Bounce TV, CBS) Peoria; WTVP (PBS) Peoria; WYZZ-TV (FOX, The Country Network) Bloomington.
Programming (via satellite): CMT; Comedy Central; Discovery Channel; Disney Channel; ESPN; ESPN2; Freeform; Spike TV; Syfy; TBS; TNT; USA Network; WGN America.
Fee: $10.00 installation.
Pay Service 1
Pay Units: N.A.
Programming (via satellite): HBO; Showtime.
Fee: $6.50 monthly (each).
Internet Service
Operational: No.
Telephone Service
None
Miles of Plant: 2.0 (coaxial); None (fiber optic). Homes passed: 100.
General Manager: Tom Hedge.
Ownership: KMHC Inc. (MSO).

KINMUNDY—Clearvision Cable Systems Inc, 1785 US Rte 40, Greenup, IL 62428-3501. Phone: 217-923-5594. Fax: 217-923-5681. Also serves Alma. ICA: IL0338.
TV Market Ranking: Below 100 (Alma, KINMUNDY). Franchise award date: N.A. Franchise expiration date: N.A. Began: January 1, 1984.
Channel capacity: N.A. Channels available but not in use: N.A.
Basic Service
Subscribers: 95.
Programming (received off-air): KDNL-TV (ABC, The Country Network) St. Louis; KMOV (CBS) St. Louis; KPLR-TV (CW, This TV) St. Louis; KSDK (Bounce TV, NBC) St. Louis; WPXS (IND) Mount Vernon; WRAL-TV (NBC, This TV) Raleigh; WSIU-TV (PBS) Carbondale.
Programming (via satellite): A&E; AMC; CMT; CNN; Discovery Channel; Disney Channel; ESPN; Fox News Channel; FOX Sports Networks; Freeform; History; Lifetime; Nickelodeon; Spike TV; TBS; The Weather Channel; TLC; TNT; Trinity Broadcasting Network (TBN); TV Land; USA Network; WABC-TV (ABC, Live Well Network) New York; WGN America; WNBC (COZI TV, NBC) New York.
Fee: $47.95 monthly.
Pay Service 1
Pay Units: N.A.
Programming (via satellite): HBO.
Fee: $10.75 monthly.
Video-On-Demand: No
Internet Service
Operational: No.
Telephone Service
None
Miles of Plant: 6.0 (coaxial); None (fiber optic). Homes passed: 719.
President & General Manager: Michael Bauguss. Secretary: Gwyndolyn S. Bauguss.
Ownership: Clearvision Cable Systems Inc. (MSO).

KIRKLAND—Mediacom. Now served by CORTLAND (village), IL [IL0485]. ICA: IL0277.

KIRKWOOD—Nova1Net, 677 West Main St, PO Box 1412, Galesburg, IL 61401. Phones: 800-397-6682; 309-342-9681. Fax: 309-342-4408. Web Site: http://www.novacablevision.com. ICA: IL0327.
TV Market Ranking: Below 100 (KIRKWOOD). Franchise award date: N.A. Franchise expiration date: N.A. Began: June 1, 1984.
Channel capacity: N.A. Channels available but not in use: N.A.
Basic Service
Subscribers: N.A.
Programming (received off-air): KGCW (CW, MeTV, This TV) Burlington; KIIN (PBS) Iowa City; KLJB (CW, FOX, MeTV) Davenport; KWQC-TV (NBC) Davenport; WEEK-TV (ABC, CW, NBC) Peoria; WHBF-TV (CBS) Rock Island; WHOI (Comet) Peoria; WMBD-TV (Bounce TV, CBS) Peoria; WQAD-TV (ABC, Antenna TV) Moline; WQPT-TV (PBS) Moline; WTVP (PBS) Peoria.
Programming (via satellite): A&E HD; AMC; Animal Planet; BTN HD; Cartoon Network; CMT; CNBC; CNN; Comcast SportsNet Chicago; Comedy Central; C-SPAN; C-SPAN 2; Discovery Channel; Disney Channel; DIY Network; E! HD; ESPN HD; ESPN2; ESPNU; EWTN Global Catholic Network; Food Network; Fox News Channel; Fox Sports 1; FOX Sports Midwest; Freeform; FX; Golf Channel; Great American Country; Hallmark Channel; HGTV; History; HLN; HRTV; INSP; Lifetime; MSNBC; MTV; National Geographic Channel; Nickelodeon; QVC; RFD-TV; Spike TV; Syfy; TBS; The Weather Channel; TLC; TNT; Travel Channel; truTV; TV Land; USA Network; VH1; WGN America.
Fee: $30.00 installation.
Digital Basic Service
Subscribers: N.A.
Programming (via satellite): Bloomberg Television; CMT; Destination America; Discovery Kids Channel; Disney XD; DMX Music; ESPN Classic; ESPN2; ESPNews; EVINE Live; Fox Sports 1; FSN Digital Atlantic; FSN Digital Central; FSN Digital Pacific; Fuse; FXM; FYI; Golf Channel; Great American Country; GSN; HGTV; History; History International; IFC; Investigation Discovery; LMN; MTV Classic; MTV Hits; MTV2; NBCSN; Nicktoons; Noggin; Outdoor Channel; OWN; Oprah Winfrey Network; Science Channel; Syfy; TeenNick; Trinity Broadcasting Network (TBN); Turner Classic Movies; VH1 Soul; WE tv.
Pay Service 1
Pay Units: N.A.
Programming (via satellite): Cinemax; HBO.
Fee: $12.85 monthly (each).
Digital Pay Service 1
Pay Units: N.A.
Programming (via satellite): Cinemax (multiplexed); Flix; HBO (multiplexed); Showtime (multiplexed); Starz (multiplexed); Starz Encore (multiplexed); Sundance TV; The Movie Channel (multiplexed).

Illinois—Cable Systems

Fee: $12.95 monthly (HBO, Showtime/TMC/Flix/Sundance, Cinemax, or Starz/Encore).
Video-On-Demand: No
Pay-Per-View
Hot Choice (delivered digitally); Playboy TV (delivered digitally); Fresh (delivered digitally); Spice: Xcess (delivered digitally); Club Jenna (delivered digitally).
Internet Service
Operational: Yes.
Fee: $30.00 installation; $39.95 monthly; $3.95 modem lease.
Telephone Service
None
Miles of Plant: 7.0 (coaxial); None (fiber optic). Homes passed: 346.
General Manager: Robert G. Fischer Jr. Office Manager: Hazel Harden.
Ownership: Nova Cablevision Inc. (MSO).

LA GRANGE—Comcast Cable. Now served by PEORIA, IL [IL0012]. ICA: IL0696.

LA HARPE—Formerly served by Insight Communications. Now served by Comcast Cable, PEORIA, IL [IL0012]. ICA: IL0222.

LA MOILLE (village)—Formerly served by CableDirect. No longer in operation. ICA: IL0533.

LA PLACE—Formerly served by Longview Communications. No longer in operation. ICA: IL0534.

LA ROSE—Formerly served by Tel-Star Cablevision Inc. No longer in operation. ICA: IL0535.

LACON—Mediacom. Now served by ROANOKE, IL [IL0068]. ICA: IL0394.

LACON—Mediacom. Now served by ROANOKE, IL [IL0068]. ICA: IL0225.

LADD—Comcast Cable. Now served by MOUNT PROSPECT, IL [IL0036]. ICA: IL0161.

LAKE BRACKEN—Nova1Net, 677 West Main St, PO Box 1412, Galesburg, IL 61401. Phones: 800-397-6682; 309-342-9681. Fax: 309-342-4408. E-mail: novariocable@hotmail.com. Web Site: http://www.novacablevision.com. ICA: IL0611.
TV Market Ranking: Outside TV Markets (LAKE BRACKEN). Franchise award date: N.A. Franchise expiration date: N.A. Began: January 1, 1990.
Channel capacity: 40 (operating 2-way). Channels available but not in use: N.A.
Basic Service
Subscribers: N.A.
Programming (received off-air): KGCW (CW, MeTV, This TV) Burlington; KIIN (PBS) Iowa City; KLJB (CW, FOX, MeTV) Davenport; KWQC-TV (NBC) Davenport; WEEK-TV (ABC, CW, NBC) Peoria; WHBF-TV (CBS) Rock Island; WHOI (Comet) Peoria; WMBD-TV (Bounce TV, CBS) Peoria; WQAD-TV (ABC, Antenna TV) Moline; WQPT-TV (PBS) Moline; WTVP (PBS) Peoria.
Programming (via satellite): A&E; AMC; Animal Planet; BTN; CMT; CNBC; CNN; Comcast SportsNet Chicago; Comedy Central; C-SPAN; C-SPAN 2; Discovery Channel; Disney Channel; E! HD; ESPN; ESPN2; EWTN Global Catholic Network; Food Network; Fox News Channel; Fox Sports 1; FOX Sports Midwest; Freeform; Golf Channel; Great American Country; Hallmark Channel; HGTV; History; HLN; HRTV; INSP; Lifetime; MSNBC; MTV; National Geographic Channel; Nickelodeon; QVC; RFD-TV; Spike TV; Syfy; TBS; The Weather Channel; TLC; TNT; Travel Channel; truTV; TV Land; USA Network; VH1; WGN America.
Fee: $60.00 installation.
Digital Basic Service
Subscribers: N.A.
Programming (via satellite): Bloomberg Television; CMT; Destination America; Discovery Kids Channel; Disney XD; DMX Music; ESPN Classic; ESPN2; ESPNews; EVINE Live; Fox Sports 1; FSN Digital Atlantic; FSN Digital Central; FSN Digital Pacific; Fuse; FXM; FYI; Golf Channel; Great American Country; GSN; History; History International; IFC; Investigation Discovery; LMN; MTV Classic; MTV Hits; MTV2; NBCSN; Nick Jr.; Nicktoons; Outdoor Channel; OWN: Oprah Winfrey Network; Science Channel; Syfy; TeenNick; Trinity Broadcasting Network (TBN); Turner Classic Movies; VH1 Soul; WE tv.
Pay Service 1
Pay Units: N.A.
Programming (via satellite): Cinemax; HBO.
Fee: $11.95 monthly (each).
Digital Pay Service 1
Pay Units: N.A.
Programming (via satellite): Cinemax (multiplexed); Flix; HBO (multiplexed); Showtime (multiplexed); Starz (multiplexed); Starz Encore (multiplexed); Sundance TV; The Movie Channel (multiplexed).
Fee: $12.95 monthly (HBO, Cinemax, Showtime/TMC/Sundance/Flix or Starz/Encore).
Video-On-Demand: No
Pay-Per-View
Club Jenna (delivered digitally); Hot Choice (delivered digitally); iN DEMAND (delivered digitally); Playboy TV (delivered digitally); Fresh (delivered digitally); Spice: Xcess (delivered digitally).
Internet Service
Operational: Yes. Began: January 1, 2005.
Fee: $25.00 installation; $34.95 monthly.
Telephone Service
None
Miles of Plant: 8.0 (coaxial); None (fiber optic). Homes passed: 271.
General Manager & Chief Technician: Robert G. Fischer Jr.
Ownership: Nova Cablevision Inc. (MSO).

LAKE CAMELOT—Tel-Star Cablevision Inc. Now served by METAMORA, IL [IL0326]. ICA: IL0536.

LAKE HOLIDAY—Comcast Cable. Now served by PEORIA, IL [IL0012]. ICA: IL0486.

LAKE OF EGYPT—Zito Media, 102 S Main St, PO Box 665, Coudersport, PA 16915. Phones: 814-260-9055; 800-365-6988. E-mail: info@zitomedia.com. Web Site: http://www.zitomedia.com. Also serves Creal Springs, Goreville, Johnson County (northern portion) & Williamson County (southern portion). ICA: IL0510.
TV Market Ranking: 69 (Creal Springs, Goreville, LAKE OF EGYPT). Franchise award date: N.A. Franchise expiration date: N.A. Began: June 1, 1986.
Channel capacity: N.A. Channels available but not in use: N.A.
Basic Service
Subscribers: 143.
Programming (received off-air): KBSI (FOX) Cape Girardeau; KFVS-TV (CBS, CW, MeTV) Cape Girardeau; WDKA (MNT, The Country Network) Paducah; WPSD-TV (Antenna TV, NBC) Paducah; WSIL-TV (ABC) Harrisburg; WSIU-TV (PBS) Carbondale; WTCT (IND) Marion.
Programming (via satellite): A&E; AMC; Animal Planet; Cartoon Network; CNBC; CNN; Comedy Central; Discovery Channel; Disney Channel; Disney XD; E! HD; ESPN; ESPN2; Fox News Channel; Freeform; Fuse; FX; Great American Country; HGTV; History; HLN; Lifetime; Outdoor Channel; TBS; The Weather Channel; TLC; TNT; Turner Classic Movies; USA Network; WGN America.
Fee: $49.95 installation; $50.65 monthly.
Digital Basic Service
Subscribers: N.A.
Pay Service 1
Pay Units: N.A.
Programming (via satellite): Cinemax; HBO; Showtime; The Movie Channel.
Video-On-Demand: No
Internet Service
Operational: No.
Telephone Service
None
Miles of Plant: 10.0 (coaxial); None (fiber optic). Homes passed: 400.
President: James Rigas.
Ownership: Zito Media (MSO).

LAKE ZURICH—Comcast Cable. Now served by MOUNT PROSPECT, IL [IL0036]. ICA: IL0047.

LANSING—Comcast Cable. Now served by CHAMPAIGN, IL [IL0019]. ICA: IL0060.

LAWRENCEVILLE—NewWave Communications. Now served by VINCENNES, IN [IN0035]. ICA: IL0119.

LE ROY—Mediacom, 609 South 4th St, PO Box 334, Chillicothe, IL 61523. Phones: 309-469-2027; 309-274-4500. Fax: 309-274-3188. Web Site: http://www.mediacomcable.com. Also serves Bellflower, Colfax, Downs, McLean County (portions) & Saybrook. ICA: IL0539.
TV Market Ranking: 64 (Bellflower, LE ROY, McLean County (portions), Saybrook); Below 100 (Colfax, Downs). Franchise award date: N.A. Franchise expiration date: N.A. Began: December 4, 1981.
Channel capacity: N.A. Channels available but not in use: N.A.
Basic Service
Subscribers: 1,100.
Programming (received off-air): WAND (NBC) Decatur; WAOE (Antenna TV, MNT) Peoria; WCIA (CBS, MNT) Champaign; WEEK-TV (ABC, CW, NBC) Peoria; WHOI (Comet) Peoria; WILL-TV (PBS) Urbana; WMBD-TV (Bounce TV, CBS) Peoria; WTVP (PBS) Peoria; WYZZ-TV (FOX, The Country Network) Bloomington.
Programming (via satellite): Freeform; WGN America.
Fee: $45.00 installation; $43.00 monthly.
Expanded Basic Service 1
Subscribers: N.A.
Programming (via satellite): A&E; AMC; Animal Planet; BET; Bravo; Cartoon Network; CMT; CNBC; CNN; Comcast SportsNet Chicago; Comedy Central; C-SPAN; C-SPAN 2; CW PLUS; Discovery Channel; Discovery Life Channel; Disney Channel; E! HD; ESPN; ESPN2; EVINE Live; EWTN Global Catholic Network; Food Network; Fox News Channel; Fox Sports 1; FX; Hallmark Channel; HGTV; History; HLN; INSP; ION Television; Jewelry Television; Lifetime; LMN; MSNBC; MTV; Nickelodeon; Pop; QVC; Radar Channel; Spike TV; Syfy; TBS; The Weather Channel; TLC; TNT; Travel Channel; Trinity Broadcasting Network (TBN); truTV; TV Land; Univision Studios; USA Network; VH1; WE tv.
Fee: $34.00 monthly.
Digital Basic Service
Subscribers: N.A.
Programming (via satellite): BBC America; Bloomberg Television; CBS Sports Network; CCTV-Documentary; Cloo; Destination America; Discovery Kids Channel; ESPN HD; ESPN2 HD; ESPNews; ESPNU; FOX College Sports Central; FOX College Sports Pacific; Fox Sports 2; Fuse; FXM; FYI; Golf Channel; GolTV; GSN; History International; IFC; Investigation Discovery; ION Television; MC; MTV Classic; MTV Hits; MTV2; Nat Geo WILD; National Geographic Channel; NBCSN; Nick Jr.; Nicktoons; Outdoor Channel; OWN: Oprah Winfrey Network; Qubo; Reelz; Science Channel; Sundance TV; TeenNick; Tennis Channel; Turner Classic Movies; TVG Network.
Digital Expanded Basic Service
Subscribers: N.A.
Programming (via satellite): AXS TV; HD Theater; Universal HD.
Fee: $6.95 monthly.
Digital Pay Service 1
Pay Units: N.A.
Programming (via satellite): Cinemax (multiplexed); Cinemax On Demand; Flix; HBO (multiplexed); HBO GO; HBO HD; Showtime (multiplexed); Showtime On Demand; Starz (multiplexed); Starz Encore (multiplexed); Starz HD; Starz On Demand; Sundance TV; The Movie Channel (multiplexed); The Movie Channel HD; The Movie Channel On Demand.
Fee: $11.95 monthly (HBO, Cinemax, Starz/Encore or Showtime/TMC).
Video-On-Demand: Yes
Pay-Per-View
iN DEMAND (delivered digitally); Playboy TV (delivered digitally); Sports PPV (delivered digitally); SexSee (delivered digitally); Juicy (delivered digitally).
Internet Service
Operational: Yes.
Broadband Service: Mediacom High Speed Internet.
Fee: $59.95 installation; $45.95 monthly.
Telephone Service
Digital: Operational
Miles of Plant: 63.0 (coaxial); 11.0 (fiber optic). Homes passed: 3,652.
Vice President: Don Hagwell. Operations Director: Gary Wightman. Technical Operations Manager: Larry Brackman. Marketing Director: Stephanie Law.
Ownership: Mediacom LLC (MSO).

LEAF RIVER—Formerly served by Grand River Cablevision. No longer in operation. ICA: IL0540.

LEONORE—Formerly served by HI Cablevision. No longer in operation. ICA: IL0691.

LERNA—Formerly served by CableDirect. No longer in operation. ICA: IL0450.

LEWISTOWN—Formerly served by Insight Communications. Now served by Comcast Cable, PEORIA, IL [IL0012]. ICA: IL0156.

Cable Systems—Illinois

LEXINGTON—Mediacom. Now served by ROANOKE, IL [IL0068]. ICA: IL0240.

LIBERTY—Adams Telcom. Now served by BOWDEN, IL [IL0702]. ICA: IL0379.

LIBERTYVILLE—Comcast Cable. Now served by MOUNT PROSPECT, IL [IL0036]. ICA: IL0044.

LINCOLN—Formerly served by Insight Communications. Now served by Comcast Cable, SPRINGFIELD, IL [IL0016]. ICA: IL0078.

LISLE—Comcast Cable. Now served by PEORIA, IL [IL0012]. ICA: IL0054.

LITCHFIELD—NewWave Communications. Now served by TAYLORVILLE, IL [IL0098]. ICA: IL0101.

LITTLE YORK—Nova1Net, 677 West Main St, PO Box 1412, Galesburg, IL 61401. Phones: 800-397-6682; 309-342-9681. Fax: 309-342-4408. Web Site: http://www.novacablevision.com. ICA: IL0414.
TV Market Ranking: 60 (LITTLE YORK). Franchise award date: N.A. Franchise expiration date: N.A. Began: July 29, 1988.
Channel capacity: N.A. Channels available but not in use: N.A.
Basic Service
Subscribers: N.A.
Programming (received off-air): KGCW (CW, MeTV, This TV) Burlington; KIIN (PBS) Iowa City; KLJB (CW, FOX, MeTV) Davenport; KWQC-TV (NBC) Davenport; WEEK-TV (ABC, CW, NBC) Peoria; WHBF-TV (CBS) Rock Island; WHOI (Comet) Peoria; WMBD-TV (Bounce TV, CBS) Peoria; WQAD-TV (ABC, Antenna TV) Moline; WQPT-TV (PBS) Moline; WTVP (PBS) Peoria.
Programming (via satellite): A&E; AMC; Animal Planet; BTN; Cartoon Network; CMT; CNBC; CNN; Comcast SportsNet Chicago; Comedy Central; C-SPAN; C-SPAN 2; Discovery Channel; Disney Channel; DIY Network; E! HD; ESPN; ESPN2; ESPNU; EWTN Global Catholic Network; Food Network; Fox News Channel; Fox Sports 1; FOX Sports Midwest; Freeform; FX; Golf Channel; Great American Country; Hallmark Channel; HGTV; History; HLN; HRTV; Lifetime; MSNBC; MTV; National Geographic Channel; Nickelodeon; QVC; RFD-TV; Spike TV; Syfy; TBS; The Weather Channel; TLC; TNT; Travel Channel; truTV; TV Land; USA Network; VH1; WGN America.
Fee: $60.00 installation.
Digital Basic Service
Subscribers: N.A.
Programming (via satellite): Bloomberg Television; CMT; Destination America; Discovery Kids Channel; Disney XD; DMX Music; ESPN Classic; ESPN2; ESPNews; EVINE Live; Fox Sports 1; FSN Digital Atlantic; FSN Digital Central; FSN Digital Pacific; Fuse; FXM; FYI; Golf Channel; Great American Country; GSN; HGTV; History; History International; IFC; Investigation Discovery; LMN; MTV Classic; MTV Hits; MTV2; NBCSN; Nicktoons; Noggin; Outdoor Channel; OWN: Oprah Winfrey Network; Science Channel; Syfy; Teen-Nick; Trinity Broadcasting Network (TBN); Turner Classic Movies; VH1 Soul; WE tv.
Pay Service 1
Pay Units: N.A.
Programming (via satellite): Cinemax; HBO.
Fee: $12.85 monthly (each).

Digital Pay Service 1
Pay Units: N.A.
Programming (via satellite): Cinemax (multiplexed); Flix; HBO (multiplexed); Showtime (multiplexed); Starz (multiplexed); Starz Encore (multiplexed); Sundance TV; The Movie Channel (multiplexed).
Fee: $12.85 monthly (HBO, Showtime/TMC/Flix/Sundance), Cinemax, or Starz/Encore).
Video-On-Demand: No
Pay-Per-View
Hot Choice (delivered digitally); Playboy TV (delivered digitally); Fresh (delivered digitally); Spice: Xcess (delivered digitally); Club Jenna (delivered digitally).
Internet Service
Operational: Yes. Began: January 1, 2005. Fee: $30.00 installation; $39.95 monthly; $3.95 modem lease.
Telephone Service
None
Miles of Plant: 3.0 (coaxial); None (fiber optic). Homes passed: 142.
General Manager: Robert G. Fischer Jr. Office Manager: Hazel Harden.
Ownership: Nova Cablevision Inc. (MSO).

LOAMI—Mediacom. Now served by KINCAID, IL [IL0176]. ICA: IL0362.

LONDON MILLS—Mediacom. Now served by ELMWOOD, IL [IL0205]. ICA: IL0387.

LONG POINT (village)—Formerly served by Longview Communications. No longer in operation. ICA: IL0543.

LOSTANT—HI Cablevision, 102 South Main St, Lostant, IL 61334. Phone: 815-368-3744. Fax: 815-368-3590. Web Site: http://www.hihart.com. ICA: IL0692.
TV Market Ranking: Below 100 (LOSTANT). Channel capacity: N.A. Channels available but not in use: N.A.
Basic Service
Subscribers: N.A.
Programming (received off-air): KWQC-TV (NBC) Davenport; WCIU-TV (MeTV) Chicago; WHOI (Comet) Peoria; WMAQ-TV (COZI TV, NBC) Chicago; WMBD-TV (Bounce TV, CBS) Peoria; WTVP (PBS) Peoria; WWTO-TV (TBN) La Salle; WYZZ-TV (FOX, The Country Network) Bloomington.
Programming (via satellite): A&E; AMC; Animal Planet; BTN; Cartoon Network; Church Channel; Cinemax; CMT; CNBC; CNN; Comcast SportsNet Chicago; Comedy Central; CW PLUS; Discovery Channel; Disney Channel; Enlace USA; ESPN; ESPN2; EWTN Global Catholic Network; Food Network; Fox News Channel; Fox Sports 1; Freeform; FX; HGTV; History; HLN; JUCE TV; Nickelodeon; QVC; Radar Channel; Spike TV; Syfy; TBS; The Movie Channel; The Weather Channel; TLC; TNT; TV Land; USA Network; VH1; WGN America.
Fee: $24.00 monthly.
Pay Service 1
Pay Units: N.A.
Programming (via satellite): HBO; Showtime.
Fee: $9.00 monthly (each).
Internet Service
Operational: Yes.
Telephone Service
None
General Manager: Fred Hartenbower.
Ownership: Hart Electric Inc. (MSO).

LOUISVILLE—Mediacom, 4290 Blue Stem Rd, PO Box 288, Charleston, IL 61920. Phone: 217-348-5533. Fax: 217-345-7074. Web Site: http://www.mediacomcable.com. Also serves Farina. ICA: IL0157.
TV Market Ranking: Outside TV Markets (Farina, LOUISVILLE). Franchise award date: January 1, 1976. Franchise expiration date: N.A. Began: June 15, 1977.
Channel capacity: N.A. Channels available but not in use: N.A.
Basic Service
Subscribers: 141.
Programming (received off-air): WBAK (FOX) Terre Haute; KDNL-TV (ABC, The Country Network) St. Louis; KMOV (CBS) St. Louis; KPLR-TV (CW, This TV) St. Louis; KSDK (Bounce TV, NBC) St. Louis; WAND (NBC) Decatur; WCCU (FOX, MeTV, Urbana; WCIA (CBS, MNT) Champaign; WICD (ABC) Champaign; WILL-TV (PBS) Urbana; WPXS (IND) Mount Vernon; WTHI-TV (CBS, FOX) Terre Haute; WTWO (NBC) Terre Haute; WUSI-TV (PBS) Olney.
Programming (via satellite): C-SPAN; QVC; WGN America.
Fee: $45.00 installation; $43.00 monthly.
Expanded Basic Service 1
Subscribers: N.A.
Programming (via satellite): A&E; AMC; Animal Planet; BET; Bravo; Cartoon Network; CMT; CNBC; CNN; Comedy Central; C-SPAN 2; Discovery Channel; Disney Channel; E! HD; ESPN; ESPN Classic; ESPN2; EVINE Live; Food Network; Fox News Channel; Fox Sports 1; FOX Sports Midwest; Freeform; FX; Hallmark Channel; HGTV; History; HLN; ION Television; Jewelry Television; Lifetime; LMN; MSNBC; MTV; Nickelodeon; Oxygen; Spike TV; Syfy; TBS; The Weather Channel; TLC; TNT; Travel Channel; Trinity Broadcasting Network (TBN); truTV; TV Land; USA Network; VH1; WE tv.
Fee: $34.00 monthly.
Digital Basic Service
Subscribers: N.A.
Programming (via satellite): BBC America; Bloomberg Television; Cloo; CMT; Discovery Life Channel; Disney XD; ESPN HD; ESPN2 HD; ESPNews; Fuse; FXM; FYI; Golf Channel; GSN; History; History International; IFC; ION Television; MC; MTV Classic; MTV Hits; MTV2; Nat Geo WILD; National Geographic Channel; NBCSN; Nick Jr.; Nicktoons; Outdoor Channel; Qubo; Reelz; Science Channel; TeenNick; Turner Classic Movies.
Digital Expanded Basic Service
Subscribers: N.A.
Programming (via satellite): CBS Sports Network; ESPNU; FOX College Sports Central; FOX College Sports Pacific; Fox Sports 2; GolTV; Tennis Channel; TVG Network.
Fee: $3.95 monthly.
Digital Expanded Basic Service 2
Subscribers: N.A.
Programming (via satellite): AXS TV; HD Theater; Universal HD.
Fee: $6.95 monthly.
Digital Pay Service 1
Pay Units: N.A.
Programming (via satellite): Cinemax (multiplexed); HBO (multiplexed); HBO HD; Showtime (multiplexed); Showtime HD; Starz (multiplexed); Starz Encore (multiplexed); Starz HD; The Movie Channel (multiplexed); The Movie Channel HD.
Fee: $11.95 monthly (each).
Video-On-Demand: Yes
Pay-Per-View
iN DEMAND (delivered digitally); Playboy TV (delivered digitally); SexSee (delivered digitally); Juicy (delivered digitally); ESPN (delivered digitally); AXS TV (delivered digitally).
Internet Service
Operational: Yes.
Broadband Service: Mediacom High Speed Internet.
Fee: $59.95 installation; $40.95 monthly.
Telephone Service
Digital: Operational
Fee: $39.95 monthly
Miles of Plant: 46.0 (coaxial); None (fiber optic). Homes passed: 1,885.
General Manager: Todd Acker. Technical Operations Manager: Jerry Ferguson. Marketing Director: James Friske.
Ownership: Mediacom LLC (MSO).

LOUISVILLE—Wabash Independent Networks. Now served by FLORA, IL [IL0140]. ICA: IL0684.

LOVINGTON—Moultrie Telecommunications, 111 State St & Broadway, PO Box 350, Lovington, IL 61937. Phone: 217-873-5215. Fax: 217-873-4990. E-mail: dbowers@moultrie.com. Web Site: http://www.moultriemulticorp.com. ICA: IL0544.
TV Market Ranking: 64 (LOVINGTON). Franchise award date: October 13, 1980. Franchise expiration date: N.A. Began: June 26, 1982.
Channel capacity: N.A. Channels available but not in use: N.A.
Basic Service
Subscribers: 243.
Programming (received off-air): WAND (NBC) Decatur; WBUI (CW, This TV) Decatur; WCIA (CBS, MNT) Champaign; WEIU-TV (PBS) Charleston; WICD (ABC) Champaign; WICS (ABC, The Country Network) Springfield; WILL-TV (PBS) Urbana; WRSP-TV (Antenna TV, FOX, MeTV) Springfield; allband FM.
Programming (via satellite): AMC; CMT; Disney Channel; ESPN; ESPN2; Freeform; History; Syfy; TBS; The Weather Channel; TLC; TNT; Turner Classic Movies; WGN America.
Fee: $50.00 installation; $68.48 monthly; $2.00 converter.
Expanded Basic Service 1
Subscribers: N.A.
Programming (via satellite): A&E; CNN; Comcast SportsNet Chicago; C-SPAN; Discovery Channel; Nickelodeon; Spike TV; USA Network; VH1.
Fee: $9.44 monthly.
Pay Service 1
Pay Units: N.A.
Programming (via satellite): HBO.
Fee: $13.05 monthly.
Video-On-Demand: No
Internet Service
Operational: Yes, DSL.
Telephone Service
Analog: Operational
Miles of Plant: 16.0 (coaxial); None (fiber optic). Homes passed: 626.
President & General Manager: David A. Bowers. Customer Service Manager: Marcia Franklin.
Ownership: Moultrie Telecommunications Inc.

LOWPOINT—Formerly served by Tel-Star Cablevision Inc. No longer in operation. ICA: IL0545.

MACOMB—Comcast Cable. Now served by PEORIA, IL [IL0012]. ICA: IL0076.

2017 Edition
D-205

Illinois—Cable Systems

MAHOMET—Mediacom. Now served by RANTOUL, IL [IL0089]. ICA: IL0115.

MALDEN—HI Cablevision, 102 South Main St, Lostant, IL 61334. Phone: 815-368-3744. Fax: 815-368-3590. Web Site: http://www.hihart.com. ICA: IL0421.
   TV Market Ranking: Below 100 (MALDEN). Franchise award date: August 1, 1985. Franchise expiration date: N.A. Began: February 1, 1986.
   Channel capacity: 62 (not 2-way capable). Channels available but not in use: N.A.
   Basic Service
   Subscribers: N.A.
   Programming (received off-air): WEEK-TV (ABC, CW, NBC) Peoria; WMBD-TV (Bounce TV, CBS) Peoria; WQAD-TV (ABC, Antenna TV) Moline; WTVP (PBS) Peoria; WYZZ-TV (FOX, The Country Network) Bloomington.
   Programming (via satellite): CMT; CNN; Discovery Channel; Disney Channel; ESPN; FOX Sports Midwest; Freeform; Nickelodeon; QVC; Spike TV; TBS; TNT; USA Network; WGN America.
   Pay Service 1
   Pay Units: N.A.
   Programming (via satellite): HBO; Showtime.
   Fee: $8.45 installation; $10.45 monthly (Showtime or HBO).
   Video-On-Demand: No
   Internet Service
   Operational: Yes.
   Fee: $20.00 monthly.
   Telephone Service
   None
   Homes passed: 134.
   General Manager: Fred Hartenbower.
   Ownership: Hart Electric Inc. (MSO).

MALTA—Mediacom. Now served by KIRKLAND, IL [IL0277]. ICA: IL0296.

MANCHESTER (village)—Formerly served by Longview Communications. No longer in operation. ICA: IL0548.

MANHATTAN—Kraus Electronics Systems Inc, 305 State St, PO Box 11, Manhattan, IL 60442. Phones: 815-478-4444; 815-478-4000. Fax: 815-478-3386. Web Site: http://www.krausonline.com. Also serves Elwood. ICA: IL0252.
   TV Market Ranking: 3 (MANHATTAN); Below 100 (Elwood). Franchise award date: N.A. Franchise expiration date: N.A. Began: September 1, 1981.
   Channel capacity: 50 (operating 2-way). Channels available but not in use: N.A.
   Basic Service
   Subscribers: 833.
   Programming (received off-air): WBBM-TV (CBS, Decades) Chicago; WCIU-TV (MeTV) Chicago; WCPX-TV (ION) Chicago; WFLD (FOX) Chicago; WGBO-DT (getTV, UNV) Joliet; WGN-TV (IND) Chicago; WJYS (IND) Hammond; WLS-TV (ABC, Live Well Network) Chicago; WPWR-TV (Buzzr, CW, MNT, Movies!) Gary; WSNS-TV (TMO) Chicago; WTTW (PBS) Chicago; WWTO-TV (TBN) La Salle; WXFT-DT (UniMas) Aurora; WYCC (PBS) Chicago; WYIN (PBS) Gary; allband FM.
   Programming (via satellite): HLN; QVC.
   Fee: $23.00 monthly.
   Expanded Basic Service 1
   Subscribers: N.A.
   Programming (via satellite): A&E; AMC; Animal Planet; Cartoon Network; CMT; CNBC; CNN; Comcast SportsNet Chicago; Comedy Central; C-SPAN; C-SPAN 2; Discovery Channel; Disney Channel; ESPN; ESPN Classic; ESPN2; EWTN Global Catholic Network; FamilyNet; Food Network; Fox News Channel; FX; GSN; Hallmark Channel; HGTV; History; Lifetime; MTV; National Geographic Channel; Nickelodeon; Spike TV; Syfy; TBS; The Weather Channel; TLC; TNT; truTV; TV Land; USA Network; VH1.
   Digital Basic Service
   Subscribers: N.A.
   Programming (via satellite): BBC America; Bloomberg Television; Bravo; Destination America; Discovery Kids Channel; Discovery Life Channel; Disney XD; DMX Music; ESPNews; FSN Digital Atlantic; FSN Digital Central; FSN Digital Pacific; Fuse; FXM; FYI; Golf Channel; Great American Country; History; History International; IFC; Investigation Discovery; LMN; MTV Classic; MTV Hits; MTV2; Nick Jr.; Nicktoons; Outdoor Channel; TeenNick; Turner Classic Movies; VH1 Country; WE tv.
   Digital Pay Service 1
   Pay Units: N.A.
   Programming (via satellite): Cinemax (multiplexed); HBO (multiplexed); Showtime (multiplexed); Starz (multiplexed); Starz Encore (multiplexed); The Movie Channel (multiplexed).
   Video-On-Demand: No
   Pay-Per-View
   Playboy TV (delivered digitally); Fresh (delivered digitally); Shorteez (delivered digitally).
   Internet Service
   Operational: Yes.
   Broadband Service: In-house.
   Fee: $39.95 monthly.
   Telephone Service
   Digital: Operational
   Fee: $26.95-$34.95 monthly
   Miles of Plant: 10.0 (coaxial); None (fiber optic).
   Vice President: Arthur Kraus. General Manager: Mike Bordeaux. Chief Technician: Skip Kraus.
   Ownership: Arthur J. Kraus (MSO).

MANITO—Cass Cable TV Inc. Now served by BEARDSTOWN, IL [IL0598]. ICA: IL0220.

MANLIUS (village)—Mediacom. Now served by GENESEO, IL [IL0170]. ICA: IL0549.

MANSFIELD—Mediacom. Now served by RANTOUL, IL [IL0089]. ICA: IL0322.

MAQUON—Mediacom. Now served by ELMWOOD, IL [IL0205]. ICA: IL0406.

MARION—Mediacom. Now served by MURPHYSBORO, IL [IL0059]. ICA: IL0083.

MAROA—Formerly served by Crystal Broadband Networks. No longer in operation. ICA: IL0263.

MARTINSVILLE—Mediacom, 4290 Blue Stem Rd, PO Box 288, Charleston, IL 61920. Phone: 217-348-5533. Fax: 217-345-7074. Web Site: http://www.mediacomcable.com. Also serves Casey, Clark County & Marshall. ICA: IL0217.
   TV Market Ranking: Below 100 (Casey, Clark County (portions), Marshall, MARTINSVILLE); Outside TV Markets (Clark County (portions)). Franchise award date: January 1, 1982. Franchise expiration date: N.A. Began: January 11, 1982.
   Channel capacity: N.A. Channels available but not in use: N.A.
   Basic Service
   Subscribers: 1,102.
   Programming (received off-air): WAND (NBC) Decatur; WAWV-TV (ABC) Terre Haute; WBUI (CW, This TV) Decatur; WCCU (FOX, MeTV) Urbana; WCIA (CBS, MNT) Champaign; WCIX (CBS, MNT) Springfield; WEIU-TV (PBS) Charleston; WICD (ABC) Champaign; WILL-TV (PBS) Urbana; WSIU-TV (PBS) Carbondale; WTHI-TV (CBS, FOX) Terre Haute; WTWO (NBC) Terre Haute; 6 FMs.
   Programming (via satellite): C-SPAN; INSP; Pop; QVC; WGN America.
   Fee: $45.00 installation; $43.00 monthly.
   Expanded Basic Service 1
   Subscribers: N.A.
   Programming (via satellite): A&E; AMC; Animal Planet; BET; Bravo; Cartoon Network; CMT; CNBC; CNN; Comedy Central; C-SPAN 2; Discovery Channel; Discovery Life Channel; Disney Channel; E! HD; ESPN; ESPN Classic; ESPN2; EVINE Live; EWTN Global Catholic Network; Food Network; Fox News Channel; Fox Sports 1; FOX Sports Midwest; Freeform; FX; Hallmark Channel; HGTV; History; HLN; ION Television; Jewelry Television; Lifetime; LMN; MSNBC; MTV; Nickelodeon; Outdoor Channel; Oxygen; Spike TV; Syfy; TBS; The Weather Channel; TLC; TNT; Travel Channel; Trinity Broadcasting Network (TBN); truTV; TV Land; USA Network; VH1; WE tv.
   Fee: $34.00 monthly.
   Digital Basic Service
   Subscribers: N.A.
   Programming (via satellite): BBC America; Bloomberg Television; CCTV-Documentary; Cloo; CMT; Destination America; Discovery Kids Channel; Discovery Life Channel; ESPNews; ESPNU; Fox Sports 2; Fuse; FXM; FYI; Golf Channel; GSN; History International; IFC; Investigation Discovery; ION Television; MC; MTV Classic; MTV Hits; MTV2; Nat Geo WILD; National Geographic Channel; NBCSN; Nick Jr.; Nicktoons; OWN: Oprah Winfrey Network; Qubo; Reelz; Science Channel; TeenNick; Turner Classic Movies; TVG Network.
   Digital Expanded Basic Service
   Subscribers: N.A.
   Programming (via satellite): CBS Sports Network; ESPNU; FOX College Sports Central; FOX College Sports Pacific; Fox Sports 2; GolTV; Tennis Channel; TVG Network.
   Fee: $3.95 monthly.
   Digital Expanded Basic Service 2
   Subscribers: N.A.
   Programming (via satellite): AXS TV; ESPN HD; ESPN2 HD; HD Theater; Universal HD.
   Fee: $6.95 monthly.
   Digital Pay Service 1
   Pay Units: N.A.
   Programming (via satellite): Cinemax (multiplexed); Cinemax On Demand; HBO (multiplexed); HBO HD; HBO on Demand; Showtime (multiplexed); Showtime HD; Showtime On Demand; Starz (multiplexed); Starz Encore (multiplexed); Starz HD; Starz On Demand; The Movie Channel (multiplexed); The Movie Channel HD; The Movie Channel On Demand.
   Fee: $11.95 monthly (each).
   Video-On-Demand: Yes
   Internet Service
   Operational: Yes. Began: November 1, 2002.
   Broadband Service: Mediacom High Speed Internet.
   Fee: $59.95 installation; $40.95 monthly.
   Telephone Service
   Digital: Operational
   Fee: $39.95 monthly.
   Miles of Plant: 42.0 (coaxial); None (fiber optic).
   Area Operations Director: Todd Acker. Technical Operations Manager: Jerry Ferguson.
   Ownership: Mediacom LLC (MSO).

MARTINTON (village)—Formerly served by CableDirect. No longer in operation. ICA: IL0552.

MARYVILLE—Charter Communications. Now served by ST. LOUIS, MO [MO0009]. ICA: IL0018.

MASON CITY—Formerly served by Greene County Cable. Now served by Cass Cable TV Inc., BEARDSTOWN, IL [IL0598]. ICA: IL0209.

MATTESON—Comcast Cable. Now served by CHAMPAIGN, IL [IL0019]. ICA: IL0028.

MATTOON—Mediacom, 4290 Blue Stem Rd, PO Box 288, Charleston, IL 61920. Phone: 217-348-5533. Fax: 217-345-7074. Web Site: http://www.mediacomcable.com. Also serves Coles County. ICA: IL0072.
   TV Market Ranking: 64 (Coles County (portions)); Below 100 (Coles County (portions)); Outside TV Markets (MATTOON, Coles County (portions)). Franchise award date: N.A. Franchise expiration date: N.A. Began: May 1, 1967.
   Channel capacity: N.A. Channels available but not in use: N.A.
   Basic Service
   Subscribers: 1,764. Commercial subscribers: 246.
   Programming (received off-air): WAND (NBC) Decatur; WBUI (CW, This TV) Decatur; WCCU (FOX, MeTV) Urbana; WCIA (CBS, MNT) Champaign; WCIX (CBS, MNT) Springfield; WEIU-TV (PBS) Charleston; WICD (ABC) Champaign; WILL-TV (PBS) Urbana; WSIU-TV (PBS) Carbondale; WTHI-TV (CBS, FOX) Terre Haute; WTWO (NBC) Terre Haute; 11 FMs.
   Programming (via satellite): C-SPAN; INSP; Pop; QVC; WGN America.
   Fee: $45.00 installation; $43.00 monthly; $.91 converter.
   Expanded Basic Service 1
   Subscribers: N.A.
   Programming (via satellite): A&E; AMC; Animal Planet; BET; Cartoon Network; CMT; CNBC; CNN; Comcast SportsNet Chicago; C-SPAN 2; Discovery Channel; Discovery Life Channel; Disney Channel; E! HD; ESPN; ESPN Classic; ESPN2; EVINE Live; EWTN Global Catholic Network; Food Network; Fox News Channel; Fox Sports 1; FOX Sports Midwest; Freeform; FX; Hallmark Channel; HGTV; History; HLN; ION Television; Jewelry Television; Lifetime; LMN; MSNBC; MTV; Nickelodeon; Outdoor Channel; Oxygen; Spike TV; Syfy; TBS; The Weather Channel; TLC; TNT; Travel Channel; Trinity Broadcasting Network (TBN); truTV; TV Land; USA Network; VH1; WE tv.
   Fee: $34.00 monthly.
   Digital Basic Service
   Subscribers: N.A.
   Programming (via satellite): AXS TV; BBC America; Bloomberg Television; Bravo;

Cable Systems—Illinois

FULLY SEARCHABLE • CONTINUOUSLY UPDATED • DISCOUNT RATES FOR PRINT PURCHASERS

For more information call 800-771-9202 or visit www.warren-news.com

CBS Sports Network; CCTV-Documentary; Cloo; CMT; Destination America; Discovery Kids Channel; Disney XD; ESPN HD; ESPN2 HD; ESPNews; ESPNU; FOX College Sports Central; FOX College Sports Pacific; Fox Sports 2; Fuse; FXM; FYI; Golf Channel; GolTV; GSN; HD Theater; History International; IFC; Investigation Discovery; ION Television; MC; MTV Classic; MTV Hits; MTV2; Nat Geo WILD; National Geographic Channel; NBCSN; Nick Jr.; Nicktoons; OWN: Oprah Winfrey Network; Qubo; Reelz; Science Channel; TeenNick; Tennis Channel; Turner Classic Movies; TVG Network; Universal HD.

Digital Pay Service 1
Pay Units: N.A.
Programming (via satellite): Cinemax (multiplexed); Cinemax On Demand; HBO (multiplexed); HBO HD; HBO on Demand; Showtime (multiplexed); Showtime HD; Showtime On Demand; Starz (multiplexed); Starz Encore (multiplexed); Starz HD; Starz On Demand; The Movie Channel (multiplexed); The Movie Channel HD; The Movie Channel On Demand.
Fee: $11.95 monthly (HBO, Cinemax, Showtime/TMC or Starz/Encore).

Video-On-Demand: Yes

Pay-Per-View
iN DEMAND (delivered digitally); Playboy TV (delivered digitally); SexSee (delivered digitally); Juicy (delivered digitally); ESPN (delivered digitally).

Internet Service
Operational: Yes. Began: December 1, 2002.
Broadband Service: Mediacom High Speed Internet.
Fee: $59.95 installation; $40.95 monthly.

Telephone Service
Digital: Operational
Fee: $39.95 monthly
Miles of Plant: 332.0 (coaxial); 18.0 (fiber optic). Homes passed: 8,385.
General Manager: Todd Acker. Technical Operations Manager: Jerry Ferguson. Marketing Director: James Friske.
Ownership: Mediacom LLC (MSO).

MAYWOOD—Comcast Cable. Now served by PEORIA, IL [IL0012]. ICA: IL0071.

MAZON (village)—Formerly served by CableDirect. No longer in operation. ICA: IL0553.

MCHENRY—Comcast Cable. Now served by MOUNT PROSPECT, IL [IL0036]. ICA: IL0034.

McLEANSBORO—NewWave Communications, One Montgomery Plaza, 4th Floor, Sikeston, MO 63801. Phone: 888-863-9928. Fax: 573-481-9809. E-mail: info@newwavecom.com. Web Site: http://www.newwavecom.com. Also serves Albion (town), Carmi, Crossville, Enfield, Fairfield, Grayville, Mount Carmel, Norris City, Sesser, Valier, Wabash County (portions), Wayne City, Wayne County (portions) & White County, IL; New Harmony, Posey County (portions) & Vanderburgh County (western portion), IN. ICA: IL0177.
TV Market Ranking: 69 (Carmi, Crossville, Enfield, MCLEANSBORO, Norris City, Valier, White County (portions)); 86 (Grayville, New Harmony, Posey County (portions), Vanderburgh County (western portion)); Below 100 (Fairfield, Sesser, Wayne City, White County (portions)); Outside TV Markets (Albion (town), White County

(portions)). Franchise award date: N.A. Franchise expiration date: N.A. Began: October 1, 1980.
Channel capacity: N.A. Channels available but not in use: N.A.

Basic Service
Subscribers: 4,015.
Programming (received off-air): KBSI (FOX) Cape Girardeau; KFVS-TV (CBS, CW, MeTV) Cape Girardeau; WDKA (MNT, The Country Network) Paducah; WEVV-TV (CBS, FOX) Evansville; WPSD-TV (Antenna TV, NBC) Paducah; WPXS (IND) Mount Vernon; WSIL-TV (ABC) Harrisburg; WSIU-TV (PBS) Carbondale; WTCT (IND) Marion; WTVW (CW, MeTV) Evansville; 1 FM.
Programming (via satellite): C-SPAN; INSP; QVC; Trinity Broadcasting Network (TBN); WGN America.
Fee: $45.00 installation; $34.78 monthly.

Expanded Basic Service 1
Subscribers: 519.
Programming (via satellite): A&E; AMC; Animal Planet; Bravo; BTN; Cartoon Network; CMT; CNBC; CNN; Comedy Central; Discovery Channel; Disney Channel; Disney XD; E! HD; ESPN; ESPN Classic; ESPN2; EVINE Live; EWTN Global Catholic Network; Food Network; Fox News Channel; Fox Sports 1; FOX Sports Midwest; Freeform; FX; Golf Channel; GSN; Hallmark Channel; HGTV; History; HLN; Lifetime; MSNBC; MTV; National Geographic Channel; NBCSN; Nickelodeon; Outdoor Channel; Oxygen; Spike TV; Syfy; TBS; The Weather Channel; TLC; TNT; Travel Channel; truTV; Turner Classic Movies; TV Land; USA Network; VH1.
Fee: $12.95 monthly.

Digital Basic Service
Subscribers: 107.
Programming (via satellite): AXS TV; BBC America; Bloomberg Television; Cloo; CMT; Cooking Channel; Destination America; Discovery Kids Channel; Discovery Life Channel; DIY Network; ESPN HD; ESPN2 HD; ESPNews; FOX College Sports Central; FOX College Sports Pacific; FSN HD; FXM; FYI; Great American Country; HD Theater; History International; IFC; Investigation Discovery; LMN; MC; MTV Classic; MTV Hits; MTV Jams; MTV2; Nick 2; Nick Jr.; Nicktoons; OWN: Oprah Winfrey Network; RFD-TV; Science Channel; TeenNick; TNT HD; Universal HD; USA Network HD; VH1 Soul; WE tv.
Fee: $19.55 monthly.

Digital Pay Service 1
Pay Units: 246.
Programming (via satellite): Cinemax (multiplexed); Cinemax HD; Flix; HBO (multiplexed); HBO HD; Showtime (multiplexed); Starz (multiplexed); Starz Encore (multiplexed); Starz HD; The Movie Channel (multiplexed).

Video-On-Demand: No

Pay-Per-View
iN DEMAND (delivered digitally); Spice: Xcess (delivered digitally); Club Jenna (delivered digitally); Shorteez (delivered digitally); Playboy TV (delivered digitally); Fresh (delivered digitally).

Internet Service
Operational: Yes.
Subscribers: 277.

Telephone Service
Digital: Operational
Subscribers: 153.
General Manager: John Helmers.
Ownership: NewWave Communications LLC (MSO).

MCNABB—McNabb TV Cable, 308 West Main St, PO Box 218, McNabb, IL 61335-0218. Phones: 815-882-2206; 815-882-2201. Fax: 815-882-2141. E-mail: jsmith@nabbnet.com. Web Site: http://www.nabbnet.com. ICA: IL0431.
TV Market Ranking: Below 100 (MCNABB). Franchise award date: September 19, 1984. Franchise expiration date: N.A. Began: January 1, 1985.
Channel capacity: 36 (not 2-way capable). Channels available but not in use: N.A.

Basic Service
Subscribers: 46.
Programming (received off-air): WAOE (Antenna TV, MNT) Peoria; WEEK-TV (ABC, CW, NBC) Peoria; WHOI (Comet) Peoria; WMBD-TV (Bounce TV, CBS) Peoria; WTVP (PBS) Peoria; WYZZ-TV (FOX, The Country Network) Bloomington.
Programming (via satellite): A&E; AMC; Bravo; CMT; CNN; Comcast SportsNet Chicago; Comedy Central; Discovery Channel; Disney Channel; ESPN; ESPN2; Fox News Channel; Freeform; History; Lifetime; MSNBC; MTV; Nickelodeon; QVC; Spike TV; Syfy; TBS; The Weather Channel; TLC; TNT; Travel Channel; TV Land; USA Network; VH1; WGN America.
Fee: $35.00 installation; $37.44 monthly.

Pay Service 1
Pay Units: N.A.
Programming (via satellite): Cinemax; HBO.
Fee: $9.00 installation; $9.00 monthly (each).

Video-On-Demand: No

Internet Service
Operational: No, DSL & dial-up.

Telephone Service
None
Miles of Plant: 5.0 (coaxial); None (fiber optic). Homes passed: 114.
President: Robin Pletsch. General Manager: Jackie Smith. Chief Technician: David Haworth. Marketing Director: Bertie Soeder.
Ownership: McNabb Cable & Satellite Inc. (MSO).

MEDORA—Formerly served by CableDirect. No longer in operation. ICA: IL0441.

MELVIN—Mediacom. Now served by RANTOUL, IL [IL0089]. ICA: IL0377.

MENDOTA—Comcast Cable. Now served by MOUNT PROSPECT, IL [IL0036]. ICA: IL0053.

METAMORA—Tel-Star Cablevision Inc, 1295 Lourdes Rd, Metamora, IL 61548-7710. Phones: 888-842-0258; 309-383-2677. Fax: 309-383-2657. E-mail: cdecker@telstar-online.net. Web Site: http://www.telstar-online.net. Also serves Brimfield, Congerville, Edwards, Eureka, Fox Creek, Glasford, Goodfield, Heritage Lake, Kickapoo, Lake Camelot, Lake Windermere, Mackinaw, Mapleton, Morton, Peoria County (portions), Tremont & Washington. ICA: IL0326.
TV Market Ranking: 83 (Brimfield, Congerville, Edwards, Eureka, Fox Creek, Glasford, Goodfield, Heritage Lake, Kickapoo, Lake Camelot, Lake Windermere, Mackinaw, Mapleton, METAMORA, Morton, Peoria County (portions), Tremont, Washington). Franchise award date: July 1, 1989. Franchise expiration date: N.A. Began: July 1, 1989.
Channel capacity: N.A. Channels available but not in use: N.A.

Basic Service
Subscribers: 949.
Programming (received off-air): WAOE (Antenna TV, MNT) Peoria; WEEK-TV (ABC, CW, NBC) Peoria; WHOI (Comet) Peoria; WMBD-TV (Bounce TV, CBS) Peoria; WTVP (PBS) Peoria; WYZZ-TV (FOX, The Country Network) Bloomington.
Programming (via satellite): A&E; AMC; Animal Planet; Cartoon Network; CMT; CNN; Comedy Central; C-SPAN; Discovery Channel; Disney Channel; ESPN; ESPN2; Fox News Channel; Fox Sports 1; Freeform; FX; Hallmark Channel; HGTV; History; HLN; INSP; Lifetime; MTV; National Geographic Channel; Nickelodeon; QVC; Spike TV; Syfy; TBS; The Weather Channel; TLC; TNT; Travel Channel; TV Land; USA Network; VH1; WGN America.
Fee: $19.95 installation; $72.45 monthly; $2.95 converter.

Digital Basic Service
Subscribers: N.A.
Programming (via satellite): BBC America; Bloomberg Television; Discovery Life Channel; Disney XD; DMX Music; ESPN Classic; ESPN Now; ESPNews; FXM; FYI; Golf Channel; GSN; History International; LMN; NBCSN; Nick Jr.; Nicktoons; Outdoor Channel; TeenNick; Trinity Broadcasting Network (TBN); Turner Classic Movies; WE tv.

Digital Pay Service 1
Pay Units: N.A.
Programming (via satellite): Cinemax (multiplexed); HBO (multiplexed); Showtime; Starz (multiplexed); Starz Encore; The Movie Channel.
Fee: $11.00 monthly (each).

Pay-Per-View
iN DEMAND (delivered digitally); Playboy TV (delivered digitally); Fresh (delivered digitally); Sports PPV (delivered digitally).

Internet Service
Operational: Yes.
Broadband Service: Tel-Star High Speed Internet.
Fee: $24.95-$49.95 monthly; $5.00 modem lease.

Telephone Service
Digital: Operational
Subscribers: 753.
Fee: $29.95-$59.95 monthly
Homes passed: 5,657.
President: James Perry. General Manager: John Gregory. Network Operations Manager: Chris Decker. Customer Service Manager: Patti Sanders.
Ownership: Tel-Star Cablevision Inc. (MSO).

MIDDLETOWN—Mediacom. Now served by DELAVAN, IL [IL0172]. ICA: IL0383.

2017 Edition
D-207

Illinois—Cable Systems

MILL SHOALS—Formerly served by CableDirect. No longer in operation. ICA: IL0410.

MILLINGTON—Comcast Cable. Now served by PEORIA, IL [IL0012]. ICA: IL0556.

MILTON—Formerly served by Cass Cable TV Inc. No longer in operation. ICA: IL0417.

MINIER—Mediacom. Now served by ROANOKE, IL [IL0068]. ICA: IL0173.

MINOOKA—Comcast Cable. Now served by PEORIA, IL [IL0012]. ICA: IL0150.

MOLINE—Mediacom, 3900 26th Ave, Moline, IL 61265. Phones: 800-332-0245; 800-824-6047. Fax: 309-797-2414. Web Site: http://www.mediacomcable.com. Also serves Andalusia, Andalusia Twp., Barstow, Campbells Island, Carbon Cliff, Cleveland, Coal Valley, Colona, East Moline, Green Rock, Hampton, Henry County (northwestern portion), Milan, Oak Grove, Orion, Rock Island, Rock Island Arsenal, Rock Island County, Silvis & Taylor Ridge, IL; Bettendorf, Blue Grass, Buffalo, Davenport, Durant, Eldridge, Le Claire, Long Grove, Mount Joy, Panorama Park, Park View, Pleasant Valley, Princeton, Riverdale, Scott County (portions), Walcott & Wilton, IA. ICA: IL0011.
TV Market Ranking: 60 (Andalusia, Andalusia Twp., Barstow, Bettendorf, Blue Grass, Buffalo, Campbells Island, Carbon Cliff, Cleveland, Coal Valley, Colona, Davenport, Durant, East Moline, Eldridge, Green Rock, Hampton, Henry County (northwestern portion), Le Claire, Long Grove, Milan, MOLINE, Mount Joy, Oak Grove, Orion, Panorama Park, Park View, Pleasant Valley, Princeton, Riverdale, Rock Island, Rock Island Arsenal, Rock Island County, Scott County (portions), Silvis, Taylor Ridge, Walcott, Wilton). Franchise award date: November 18, 1969. Franchise expiration date: N.A. Began: December 1, 1972.
Channel capacity: N.A. Channels available but not in use: N.A.
Basic Service
Subscribers: 37,016. Commercial subscribers: 104.
Programming (received off-air): KDIN-TV (PBS) Des Moines; KGCW (CW, MeTV, This TV) Burlington; KLJB (CW, FOX, MeTV) Davenport; KWQC-TV (NBC) Davenport; WHBF-TV (CBS) Rock Island; WQAD-TV (ABC, Antenna TV) Moline; WQPT-TV (PBS) Moline; allband FM.
Programming (via satellite): C-SPAN; Discovery Channel; Local Cable Weather; Pop; QVC; TBS; Univision Studios; WGN America.
Fee: $45.00 installation; $43.00 monthly.
Expanded Basic Service 1
Subscribers: N.A.
Programming (via satellite): A&E; AMC; Animal Planet; BET; Bravo; Cartoon Network; CMT; CNBC; CNN; Comcast SportsNet Chicago; Comedy Central; C-SPAN 2; Discovery Life Channel; Disney Channel; E! HD; ESPN; ESPN2; EVINE Live; EWTN Global Catholic Network; Food Network; Fox News Channel; Fox Sports 1; Freeform; FX; Hallmark Channel; HGTV; History; HLN; INSP; ION Television; Lifetime; LMN; MSNBC; MTV; National Geographic Channel; NBCSN; Nickelodeon; Spike TV; Syfy; The Weather Channel; TLC; TNT; Travel Channel; Trinity Broadcasting Network (TBN); truTV; Turner Classic Movies; TV Land; UniMas; Univision; USA Network; VH1; WE tv.
Fee: $34.00 monthly.
Digital Basic Service
Subscribers: N.A.
Programming (via satellite): 52MX; BBC America; Bloomberg Television; CCTV-Documentary; Cine Mexicano; Cinelatino; Cloo; CMT; CNN en Espanol; Destination America; Discovery Kids Channel; Disney XD; ESPN Deportes; ESPN HD; ESPN2 HD; ESPNews; ESPNU; Fox Sports 2; Fuse; FXM; FYI; Golf Channel; GSN; History en Espanol; History International; IFC; Investigation Discovery; ION Television; MC; MTV Classic; MTV Hits; MTV2; Nat Geo WILD; Nick Jr.; Nicktoons; Outdoor Channel; Ovation; OWN; Oprah Winfrey Network; Qubo; Reelz; RFD-TV; Science Channel; Sundance TV; TeenNick; Tr3s; TVG Network; VH1 Soul; ViendoMovies.
Digital Expanded Basic Service
Subscribers: N.A.
Programming (via satellite): CBS Sports Network; FOX College Sports Central; FOX College Sports Pacific; GolTV; Tennis Channel.
Fee: $3.95 monthly.
Digital Expanded Basic Service 2
Subscribers: N.A.
Programming (via satellite): AXS TV; HD Theater; Universal HD.
Fee: $6.95 monthly.
Digital Pay Service 1
Pay Units: N.A.
Programming (via satellite): Cinemax (multiplexed); Flix; HBO (multiplexed); HBO HD; Showtime (multiplexed); Showtime HD; Starz (multiplexed); Starz Encore (multiplexed); Starz HD; Sundance TV; The Movie Channel (multiplexed); The Movie Channel HD.
Fee: $11.95 monthly (HBO, Cinemax, Showtime/TMC/Sundance/Flix or Starz/Encore).
Video-On-Demand: Yes
Pay-Per-View
iN DEMAND (delivered digitally); SexSee (delivered digitally); Playboy TV (delivered digitally).
Internet Service
Operational: Yes.
Subscribers: 41,038.
Broadband Service: Mediacom High Speed Internet.
Fee: $59.95 installation; $40.95 monthly.
Telephone Service
Digital: Operational
Subscribers: 19,466.
Fee: $39.95 monthly
Miles of Plant: 1,920.0 (coaxial); 348.0 (fiber optic). Homes passed: 111,749. Miles of plant (coax & fiber combined) includes all Northern IL, Albany WI, Argyle WI, Blanchardville WI, Cuba City WI, Monticello WI, Orfordville WI, & Sugar Creek WI)
Regional Vice President: Cari Fenzel. Business Operations Manager: Leonard Lipe. Technical Operations Manager: Chris Toalson. Engineering Director: Mitch Carlson. Marketing Director: Greg Evans. Government Affairs Manager: LeeAnn Herrera. Customer Service Manager: Jody Jones. Human Relations Manager: Hazel Butter.
Ownership: Mediacom LLC (MSO).

MOMENCE—Mediacom. Now served by NEWTON COUNTY (portions), IN [IN0316]. ICA: IL0182.

MONMOUTH—Comcast Cable, 533 North Henderson, PO Box 151, Galesburg, IL 61401. Phones: 309-682-3767; 309-686-2600. Fax: 309-686-9828. Web Site: http://www.comcast.com. Also serves Warren County (portions). ICA: IL0557.
TV Market Ranking: 60 (Warren County (portions) (portions)); Below 100 (MONMOUTH, Warren County (portions) (portions)).
Channel capacity: N.A. Channels available but not in use: N.A.
Basic Service
Subscribers: 690. Commercial subscribers: 93.
Programming (received off-air): KIIN (PBS) Iowa City; KLJB (CW, FOX, MeTV) Davenport; KWQC-TV (NBC) Davenport; WEEK-TV (ABC, CW, NBC) Peoria; WHBF-TV (CBS) Rock Island; WMBD-TV (Bounce TV, CBS) Peoria; WMEC (PBS) Macomb; WQAD-TV (ABC, Antenna TV) Moline; WQPT-TV (PBS) Moline.
Programming (via satellite): A&E; AMC; Animal Planet; BET; Cartoon Network; CNBC; CNN; Comedy Central; C-SPAN; C-SPAN 2; Discovery Channel; Discovery Life Channel; Disney Channel; E! HD; ESPN; Food Network; Fox News Channel; FOX Sports Midwest; Freeform; FX; Great American Country; Hallmark Channel; HGTV; HLN; Lifetime; MoviePlex; MSNBC; MTV; Nickelodeon; Oxygen; QVC; Spike TV; Syfy; TBS; The Weather Channel; TLC; TNT; truTV; USA Network; WGN America.
Fee: $29.00-$42.00 installation; $20.24 monthly.
Digital Basic Service
Subscribers: N.A.
Programming (via satellite): BBC America; Bravo; Discovery Digital Networks; DMX Music; ESPN Classic; ESPN2; ESPNews; Fox Sports 1; Golf Channel; GSN; History International; IFC; NBCSN; Nick Jr.; Starz Encore (multiplexed); Turner Classic Movies; TV Land; WE tv.
Digital Pay Service 1
Pay Units: N.A.
Programming (via satellite): Cinemax (multiplexed); HBO (multiplexed); Showtime (multiplexed); Starz (multiplexed); The Movie Channel.
Fee: $10.00 monthly (Cinemax or Starz), $13.00 monthly (HBO or Showtime/TMC).
Video-On-Demand: No
Pay-Per-View
Hot Choice (delivered digitally); Playboy TV (delivered digitally); iN DEMAND (delivered digitally); ESPN Now (delivered digitally); Sports PPV (delivered digitally).
Internet Service
Operational: Yes.
Broadband Service: Comcast High Speed Internet.
Fee: $99.95 installation; $44.95 monthly; $10.00 modem lease; $99.95 modem purchase.
Telephone Service
Digital: Operational
General Manager: John Nieber. Chief Technician: Mike Vandergraft.
Ownership: Comcast Cable Communications Inc. (MSO).

MONROE CENTER—Mediacom. Now served by KIRKLAND, IL [IL0277]. ICA: IL0664.

MONTICELLO—Mediacom, 5290 Blue Stem Rd, PO Box 288, Charleston, IL 61920. Phone: 855-633-4226. Fax: 217-345-7074. Web Site: https://mediacomcable.com. Also serves Bement, Pesotum & Tolono. ICA: IL0133.
TV Market Ranking: 64 (Bement, MONTICELLO, Pesotum, Tolono).
Channel capacity: N.A. Channels available but not in use: N.A.
Basic Service
Subscribers: 1,533.
Fee: $53.00 monthly.
Ownership: Mediacom LLC (MSO).

MORRIS (town)—Comcast Cable. Now served by PEORIA, IL [IL0012]. ICA: IL0084.

MORRIS (town)—Mediacom, 3900 26th Ave, Moline, IL 61265. Phone: 309-797-2580. Fax: 309-797-2414. Web Site: http://www.mediacomcable.com. Also serves Minooka & Shady Oaks Trailer Park. ICA: IL0402.
TV Market Ranking: Below 100 (Minooka, MORRIS (TOWN), Shady Oaks Trailer Park). Franchise award date: N.A. Franchise expiration date: N.A. Began: December 1, 1989.
Channel capacity: N.A. Channels available but not in use: N.A.
Basic Service
Subscribers: 2.
Programming (received off-air): WBBM-TV (CBS, Decades) Chicago; WCIU-TV (MeTV) Chicago; WFLD (FOX) Chicago; WGN-TV (IND) Chicago; WLS-TV (ABC, Live Well Network) Chicago; WMAQ-TV (COZI TV, NBC) Chicago; WPWR-TV (Buzzr, CW, MNT, Movies!) Gary; WTTW (PBS) Chicago; WYCC (PBS) Chicago.
Programming (via satellite): A&E; AMC; Animal Planet; CNN; Comedy Central; Discovery Channel; Disney Channel; ESPN; ESPN2; EWTN Global Catholic Network; Freeform; History; HLN; Lifetime; MTV; Nickelodeon; Spike TV; TBS; The Weather Channel; TLC; TNT; Trinity Broadcasting Network (TBN); USA Network.
Fee: $45.00 installation; $69.95 monthly.
Pay Service 1
Pay Units: N.A.
Programming (via satellite): Showtime.
Fee: $10.95 monthly.
Video-On-Demand: No
Internet Service
Operational: No.
Telephone Service
None
Miles of plant included in Moline
Technical Operations Manager: Mitch Carlson. Marketing Director: Greg Evans.
Ownership: Mediacom LLC (MSO).

MORRISONVILLE—Mediacom. Now served by KINCAID, IL [IL0176]. ICA: IL0286.

MORTON GROVE—Comcast Cable. Now served by MOUNT PROSPECT, IL [IL0036]. ICA: IL0027.

MOUNDS—Mediacom. Now served by ZEIGLER, IL [IL0123]. ICA: IL0207.

MOUNT AUBURN—Mediacom. Now served by KINCAID, IL [IL0176]. ICA: IL0371.

MOUNT CARMEL—NewWave Communications. Now served by McLEANSBORO, IL [IL0177]. ICA: IL0124.

MOUNT CARROLL—Mediacom, 3033 Asbury Rd, Dubuque, IA 52001. Phone: 563-557-8024. Fax: 563-557-7413. Web Site: http://www.mediacomcable.com. Also serves Apple River, Carroll County (western portion), Chadwick, Dakota, Davis, Durand, Elizabeth, Hanover, Lake Summerset,

Cable Systems—Illinois

Lanark, Lena, McConnell, Milledgeville, Orangeville, Pearl City (village), Pecatonica, Rock City, Scales Mound, Shannon, Stephenson County, Stockton, Warren, Winnebago County (portions) & Winslow, IL; Albany, Albany Twp., Argyle, Blanchardville, Browntown, Martintown & South Wayne, WI. ICA: IL0223.

TV Market Ranking: 93 (Albany, Albany Twp., Blanchardville); 97 (Apple River, Browntown, Carroll County (western portion), Chadwick, Dakota, Davis, Durand, Elizabeth, Hanover, Lake Summerset, Lanark, Lena, Martintown, McConnell, Milledgeville, MOUNT CARROLL, Orangeville, Pearl City (village), Pecatonica, Rock City, Shannon, South Wayne, Stephenson County, Stockton, Warren, Winnebago County (portions), Winslow); Outside TV Markets (Argyle). Franchise award date: January 1, 1982. Franchise expiration date: N.A. Began: January 28, 1983.

Channel capacity: N.A. Channels available but not in use: N.A.

Basic Service
Subscribers: 2,444.
Programming (received off-air): WHA-TV (PBS) Madison; WIFR (Antenna TV, CBS) Freeport; WISC-TV (CBS, MNT) Madison; WMSN-TV (FOX, The Country Network) Madison; WQRF-TV (Bounce TV, FOX) Rockford; WREX (CW, MeTV, NBC) Rockford; WTVO (ABC, MNT) Rockford.
Programming (via satellite): TBS; Trinity Broadcasting Network (TBN); WGN America.
Fee: $45.00 installation; $43.00 monthly.

Expanded Basic Service 1
Subscribers: N.A.
Programming (via satellite): A&E; AMC; Animal Planet; Cartoon Network; CMT; CNBC; CNN; Comcast SportsNet Chicago; Comedy Central; C-SPAN; Discovery Channel; Disney Channel; E! HD; ESPN; ESPN2; EWTN Global Catholic Network; Fox News Channel; Fox Sports 1; FOX Sports Networks; Freeform; FX; Hallmark Channel; HGTV; History; HLN; Lifetime; MTV; Nickelodeon; QVC; Spike TV; Syfy; The Weather Channel; TLC; TNT; Travel Channel; TV Land; USA Network; VH1.
Fee: $24.00 monthly.

Pay Service 1
Pay Units: N.A.
Programming (via satellite): Cinemax; HBO; Showtime; Starz; Starz Encore.
Fee: $3.99 monthly (Encore), $5.99 monthly (Starz/Encore), $7.95 monthly (Cinemax), $11.99 monthly (HBO or Showtime).

Video-On-Demand: Yes

Internet Service
Operational: Yes.
Broadband Service: Mediacom High Speed Internet.

Telephone Service
Digital: Operational
Miles of Plant: 6.0 (coaxial); None (fiber optic). Homes passed: 3,684.
Vice President: Scott Westerman. Area Manager: Kathleen McMullen. Chief Technician: Darren Dean.
Ownership: Mediacom LLC (MSO).

MOUNT CARROLL—Mediacom. Now served by LENA, IL [IL0223]. ICA: IL0141.

MOUNT PROSPECT—Comcast Cable, 1500 McConnor Pkwy, Schaumburg, IL 60173. Phones: 847-281-5510; 630-600-6347; 847-585-6300. Fax: 847-585-6733. Web Site: http://www.comcast.com. Also serves Algonquin, Amboy, Antioch, Arlington Heights, Ashton, Bannockburn, Barrington, Barrington Hills, Bartlett, Beach Park, Belvidere, Boone County (portions), Buffalo Grove, Bureau County (portions), Byron, Carpentersville, Cary, Cedarville, Cherry, Cherry Valley, Coloma Twp., Cook County (portions), Creston, Crystal Lake, Dalzell, Deer Park, Deerfield, DeKalb, Del Mar Woods, Depue, Des Plaines, Dixon, DuPage County (portions), East Dundee, Elk Grove, Evanston, Forreston, Fort Sheridan, Fox Lake, Fox River Grove, Franklin Grove, Freeport, Glencoe, Glenview, Glenview Naval Air Station, Golf, Grayslake, Great Lakes Naval Training Center, Green Oaks, Gurnee, Hainesville, Hanover Park, Hawthorne Woods, Henry County (portions), Highland Park, Highwood, Hillcrest, Hoffman Estates, Holiday Hills, Hopkins Twp., Huntley, Indian Creek, Inverness, Island Lake, Johnsburg, Kane County (portions), Kenilworth, Kewanee, Kewanee Twp., Kildeer, La Salle, Ladd, Lake Barrington, Lake Bluff, Lake County (portions), Lake Forest, Lake in the Hills, Lake Villa, Lake Zurich, Lakemoor, Lakewood, Libertyville, Lincolnshire, Lindenhurst, Long Grove, Loves Park, Machesney Park, Maine Twp., McCollum Lake, McHenry, McHenry County (portions), Mendota, Mettawa, Montmorency Twp., Morton Grove, Mount Morris, Mundelein, New Milford, New Trier Twp., Niles, North Barrington (village), North Chicago, North Utica, Northbrook, Northfield, Oakwood Hills, Ogle County (portions), Oglesby, Oregon, Palatine, Park City, Park Ridge, Peru, Pingree Grove, Polo, Poplar Grove, Port Barrington, Prairie Grove, Princeton, Prospect Heights, Riverwoods, Rochelle, Rock Falls, Rockford, Rolling Meadows, Round Lake, Round Lake Beach, Round Lake Heights, Round Lake Park, Schaumburg, Skokie, Sleepy Hollow, South Barrington, Spring Valley, Stephenson County, Sterling, Sterling Twp., Stillman Valley, Streamwood, Sycamore, Third Lake, Tiskilwa, Tower Lakes, Vernon Hills, Volo, Wadsworth, Wauconda, Waukegan, West Dundee, Wheeling, Wilmette, Winnebago County (portions), Winnetka, Winthrop Harbor, Wonder Lake, Woodstock, Wyanet & Zion. ICA: IL0036.

TV Market Ranking: 3 (Arlington Heights, Arlington Heights, Bannockburn, Barrington, Barrington Hills, Barrington Hills, Bartlett, Bartlett, Beach Park, Buffalo Grove, Deer Park, Deerfield, Del Mar Woods (portions), Del Mar Woods, Des Plaines, East Dundee, Elk Grove, Evanston, Fort Sheridan, Glencoe, Glenview, Glenview Naval Air Station, Golf, Great Lakes Naval Training Center, Green Oaks, Hanover Park, Hawthorne Woods, Highland Park, Highwood, Hoffman Estates, Indian Creek, Inverness, Kane County (portions), Kenilworth, Kildeer, Lake Barrington, Lake Bluff, Lake County (portions) (portions), Lake Forest, Lake Zurich, Libertyville, Lincolnshire, Long Grove, Maine Twp., Mettawa, Morton Grove, MOUNT PROSPECT, Mundelein, New Trier Twp., Niles, North Barrington (village), North Chicago, Northbrook, Northfield, Palatine, Park Ridge, Park Ridge, Prospect Heights, Riverwoods, Rolling Meadows, Schaumburg, Skokie, South Barrington, Streamwood, Tower Lakes, Vernon Hills, Wheeling, Wilmette, Winnetka); 60 (Henry County (portions) (portions), Kewanee, Kewanee Twp.); 97 (Ashton, Belvidere, Boone County (portions), Byron, Cedarville, Cherry Valley, Creston, DeKalb, Dixon, Forreston, Franklin Grove, Freeport, Hillcrest, Hopkins Twp., Huntley, Lakewood, Loves Park, Machesney Park, McHenry County (portions) (portions), Mount Morris, New Milford, Ogle County (portions), Oregon, Polo, Poplar Grove, Rochelle, Rockford, Stephenson County, Sterling, Sterling Twp., Stillman Valley, Sycamore, Winnebago County (portions), Wonder Lake); Below 100 (Algonquin, Antioch, Bureau County (portions) (portions), Cary, Cherry, Crystal Lake, Dalzell, Depue, Fox Lake, Fox River Grove, Grayslake, Gurnee, Hainesville, Holiday Hills, Island Lake, Island Lake, Johnsburg, Lake in the Hills, Lake Villa, Lakemoor, Lindenhurst, McCollum Lake, North Utica, Oakwood Hills, Oglesby, Park City, Pingree Grove, Port Barrington, Prairie Grove, Round Lake, Round Lake Beach, Round Lake Heights, Round Lake Park, Sleepy Hollow, Spring Valley, Third Lake, Tiskilwa, Volo, Wadsworth, Wauconda, West Dundee, Winthrop Harbor, Woodstock, Wyanet, Zion, Amboy, Carpentersville, Ladd, McHenry, Mendota, Peru, Princeton, Del Mar Woods (portions), Kane County (portions), Lake County (portions) (portions), McHenry County (portions) (portions)); Outside TV Markets (Coloma Twp., Montmorency Twp., Rock Falls, Henry County (portions) (portions)). Franchise award date: N.A. Franchise expiration date: N.A. Began: August 1, 1982.

Channel capacity: N.A. Channels available but not in use: N.A.

Basic Service
Subscribers: 504,711. Commercial subscribers: 3,728.
Programming (received off-air): WBBM-TV (CBS, Decades) Chicago; WCIU-TV (MeTV) Chicago; WCPX-TV (ION) Chicago; WFLD (FOX) Chicago; WGBO-DT (getTV, UNV) Joliet; WGN-TV (IND) Chicago; WJYS (IND) Hammond; WLS-TV (ABC, Live Well Network) Chicago; WMAQ-TV (COZI TV, NBC) Chicago; WPWR-TV (Buzzr, CW, MNT, Movies!) Gary; WSNS-TV (TMO) Chicago; WTTW (PBS) Chicago; WXFT-DT (UniMas) Aurora; WYCC (PBS) Chicago.
Programming (via satellite): C-SPAN; C-SPAN 2; Discovery Channel; Pop; QVC; TBS; TLC; Turner Classic Movies.
Fee: $29.00-$42.00 installation; $30.24 monthly.

Expanded Basic Service 1
Subscribers: N.A.
Programming (via satellite): A&E; AMC; Animal Planet; BET; Cartoon Network; CLTV; CNBC; CNN; Comcast SportsNet Chicago; Comedy Central; Disney Channel; E! HD; ESPN; ESPN Classic; ESPN2; EWTN Global Catholic Network; Food Network; Fox News Channel; Freeform; FX; Golf Channel; Hallmark Channel; HGTV; History; HLN; HSN2; Lifetime; MSNBC; MTV; Nickelodeon; Oxygen; Spike TV; Syfy; The Weather Channel; TNT; Total Living Network; Travel Channel; truTV; TV Land; USA Network; VH1.
Fee: $29.60 monthly.

Digital Basic Service
Subscribers: N.A.
Programming (via satellite): BBC America; Bloomberg Television; Bravo; Discovery Life Channel; Disney XD; ESPNews; EVINE Live; FOX College Sports Central; FOX College Sports Pacific; Fox Sports 1; Fuse; FXM; FYI; Great American Country; GSN; History International; HITS (Headend In The Sky); IFC; LMN; MC; National Geographic Channel; NBCSN; Nick Jr.; Nicktoons; Outdoor Channel; Ovation; Sundance TV; TeenNick; The Word Network; Trinity Broadcasting Network (TBN); WE tv; Weatherscan.

Pay Service 1
Pay Units: N.A.
Programming (via satellite): Cinemax; HBO; Showtime; Starz Encore.

Digital Pay Service 1
Pay Units: N.A.
Programming (via satellite): Cinemax (multiplexed); Flix; HBO (multiplexed); Showtime (multiplexed); Starz (multiplexed); Starz Encore (multiplexed); The Movie Channel (multiplexed).
Fee: $10.00 monthly (each).

Video-On-Demand: Yes

Pay-Per-View
iN DEMAND; ESPN Now (delivered digitally); Sports PPV (delivered digitally); iN DEMAND (delivered digitally); Fresh (delivered digitally); Shorteez (delivered digitally); Playboy TV (delivered digitally); Hot Choice (delivered digitally).

Internet Service
Operational: Yes.
Subscribers: 480,254.
Broadband Service: Comcast High Speed Internet.
Fee: $99.99 installation; $45.95 monthly.

Telephone Service
Digital: Operational
Subscribers: 251,379.
Fee: $44.95 monthly
Miles of Plant: 21,869.0 (coaxial); 5,380.0 (fiber optic). Homes passed: 1,408,575.
Regional Senior Vice President: Steve Reimer. Area Vice President: Brian Sullivan. Vice President, Technical Operations: Bob Curtis. Vice President, Sales & Marketing: Eric Schaefer. Vice President, Communications: Rich Ruggiero. Operations Director: Robert Rogola. Technical Operations Director: Bob Cole. Sales & Marketing Director: Lori Tybon.
Ownership: Comcast Cable Communications Inc. (MSO).

MOUNT PULASKI—Formerly served by Insight Communications. Now served by Comcast Cable, SPRINGFIELD, IL [IL0016]. ICA: IL0090.

MOUNT STERLING—Cass Cable TV Inc. Now served by BEARDSTOWN, IL [IL0598]. ICA: IL0208.

MOWEAQUA—NewWave Communications, One Montgomery Plaza, 4th Floor, Sikeston, MO 63801. Phone: 888-863-9928 (Customer service). Fax: 573-481-9809. E-mail: info@newwavecom.com. Web Site: http://www.newwavecom.com. Also serves Assumption, Bethany, Blue Mound, Dalton City, Macon & Stonington. ICA: IL0185.

Illinois—Cable Systems

TV Market Ranking: 64 (Assumption, Bethany, Blue Mound, Dalton City, Macon, MOWEAQUA, Stonington). Franchise award date: N.A. Franchise expiration date: N.A. Began: October 1, 1982.
Channel capacity: N.A. Channels available but not in use: N.A.
Basic Service
Subscribers: 798.
Programming (received off-air): WAND (NBC) Decatur; WBUI (CW, This TV) Decatur; WCIA (CBS, MNT) Champaign; WCIX (CBS, MNT) Springfield; WEIU-TV (PBS) Charleston; WICS (ABC, The Country Network) Springfield; WILL-TV (PBS) Urbana; WRSP-TV (Antenna TV, FOX, MeTV) Springfield.
Programming (via satellite): WGN America.
Fee: $59.95 installation; $24.25 monthly.
Expanded Basic Service 1
Subscribers: N.A.
Programming (via satellite): A&E; AMC; Animal Planet; Cartoon Network; CMT; CNN; Comcast SportsNet Chicago; C-SPAN; C-SPAN 2; Discovery Channel; Disney Channel; E! HD; ESPN; ESPN Classic; ESPN2; Fox News Channel; Fox Sports 1; FOX Sports Midwest; Freeform; FX; Great American Country; HGTV; History; HLN; INSP; Lifetime; MSNBC; MTV; National Geographic Channel; Nickelodeon; Radar Channel; Spike TV; Syfy; TBS; The Weather Channel; TLC; TNT; Trinity Broadcasting Network (TBN); Turner Classic Movies; TV Land; USA Network; VH1; WE tv.
Digital Basic Service
Subscribers: N.A.
Programming (via satellite): BBC America; Bloomberg Television; CMT; Destination America; Discovery Kids Channel; Disney XD; DMX Music; ESPNews; EVINE Live; FOX College Sports Central; FOX College Sports Pacific; Fuse; FXM; FYI; Golf Channel; GSN; History International; IFC; Investigation Discovery; LMN; MTV Classic; MTV2; NBCSN; Nick Jr.; Nicktoons; Outdoor Channel; OWN: Oprah Winfrey Network; Science Channel; TeenNick.
Pay Service 1
Pay Units: N.A.
Programming (via satellite): Cinemax; HBO; Showtime; Starz Encore; The Movie Channel.
Fee: $25.00 installation; $3.99 monthly (Encore), $7.95 monthly (Cinemax), $11.99 monthly (HBO, Showtime or TMC).
Digital Pay Service 1
Pay Units: N.A.
Programming (via satellite): Cinemax (multiplexed); HBO (multiplexed); Showtime (multiplexed); Starz (multiplexed); Starz Encore (multiplexed); The Movie Channel.
Video-On-Demand: No
Pay-Per-View
iN DEMAND (delivered digitally); Playboy TV (delivered digitally); Fresh (delivered digitally); Club Jenna (delivered digitally).
Internet Service
Operational: Yes.
Telephone Service
None
Miles of Plant: 35.0 (coaxial); None (fiber optic). Homes passed: 1,911.
Chief Financial Officer: Rod Siemers.
Ownership: NewWave Communications LLC (MSO).

MULBERRY GROVE—Clearvision Cable Systems Inc, 1785 US Rte 40, Greenup, IL 62428-3501. Phone: 217-923-5594. Fax: 217-923-5681. ICA: IL0355.

TV Market Ranking: Outside TV Markets (MULBERRY GROVE). Franchise award date: N.A. Franchise expiration date: N.A. Began: April 1, 1986.
Channel capacity: N.A. Channels available but not in use: N.A.
Basic Service
Subscribers: 6.
Programming (received off-air): KDNL-TV (ABC, The Country Network) St. Louis; KETC (PBS) St. Louis; KMOV (CBS) St. Louis; KPLR-TV (CW, This TV) St. Louis; KSDK (Bounce TV, NBC) St. Louis; KTVI (Antenna TV, Escape, FOX) St. Louis; WPXS (IND) Mount Vernon; WRBU (ION) East St. Louis.
Programming (via satellite): A&E; AMC; Bravo; Cartoon Network; CMT; CNBC; CNN; Comedy Central; C-SPAN; Discovery Channel; Disney Channel; ESPN; Fox News Channel; Freeform; History; HLN; Lifetime; MSNBC; MTV; Nickelodeon; QVC; Spike TV; Syfy; TBS; The Weather Channel; TLC; TNT; Trinity Broadcasting Network (TBN); USA Network; VH1; WGN America.
Fee: $47.95 monthly.
Pay Service 1
Pay Units: N.A.
Programming (via satellite): Showtime; The Movie Channel.
Video-On-Demand: No
Internet Service
Operational: No.
Telephone Service
None
Miles of Plant: 7.0 (coaxial); None (fiber optic). Homes passed: 292.
President & General Manager: Michael Bauguss. Secretary: Gwyndolyn S. Bauguss.
Ownership: Clearvision Cable Systems Inc. (MSO).

MURPHYSBORO—Mediacom, 90 Main St, Benton, KY 42025-1132. Phones: 417-875-5560 (Springfield regional office); 270-527-9939. Fax: 270-527-0813. Web Site: http://www.mediacomcable.com. Also serves Carbondale, Carbondale Twp., Carterville, Colp (village), Crainville, De Soto, Eldorado, Energy, Harrisburg, Herrin, Jackson County (portions), Johnston City, Marion, West Frankfort, Whiteash & Williamson County (portions). ICA: IL0059.
TV Market Ranking: 60 (Eldorado); 69 (Carbondale, Carbondale Twp., Carterville, Colp (village), Crainville, Energy, Harrisburg, Herrin, Jackson County (portions), Johnston City, Marion, MURPHYSBORO, West Frankfort, Whiteash, Williamson County (portions)); Below 100 (De Soto, Jackson County (portions) (portions)). Franchise award date: N.A. Franchise expiration date: N.A. Began: July 1, 1971.
Channel capacity: N.A. Channels available but not in use: N.A.
Basic Service
Subscribers: 12,144.
Programming (received off-air): KBSI (FOX) Cape Girardeau; KETC (PBS) St. Louis; KFVS-TV (CBS, CW, MeTV) Cape Girardeau; WPSD-TV (Antenna TV, NBC) Paducah; WPXS (IND) Mount Vernon; WQWQ-LP (CW, MeTV) Paducah; WSIL-TV (ABC) Harrisburg; WSIU-TV (PBS) Carbondale; WTCT (IND) Marion; allband FM.
Programming (via satellite): A&E; AMC; Animal Planet; BET; Bravo; Cartoon Network; CMT; CNN; Comedy Central; C-SPAN; C-SPAN 2; Discovery Channel; Disney Channel; E! HD; ESPN; ESPN2; Food Channel; Fox News Channel; Fox Sports 1; FOX Sports Midwest; Freeform; FX; Hallmark Channel; HGTV; History; HLN; INSP; Lifetime; MSNBC; MTV; Nickelodeon; Outdoor Channel; Pop; QVC; Spike TV; Syfy; TBS; The Weather Channel; TLC; TNT; Travel Channel; truTV; TV Land; USA Network; VH1; WGN America.
Fee: $43.64 installation; $56.96 monthly; $2.59 converter.
Digital Basic Service
Subscribers: N.A.
Programming (via satellite): BBC America; Bloomberg Television; Discovery Digital Networks; FXM; Golf Channel; History International; IFC; LMN; National Geographic Channel; NBCSN; Nick Jr.; Nicktoons; TeenNick; Turner Classic Movies.
Digital Pay Service 1
Pay Units: N.A.
Programming (via satellite): Cinemax (multiplexed); DMX Music; HBO (multiplexed); Showtime; Starz; Starz Encore (multiplexed).
Fee: $1.70 monthly (Encore), $4.75 monthly (Starz), $9.95 monthly (DMX), $13.60 monthly (Cinemax), $14.10 monthly (Showtime), $14.30 monthly (HBO).
Video-On-Demand: Yes
Pay-Per-View
Playboy Entertainment Group Inc. (delivered digitally); Pleasure (delivered digitally).
Internet Service
Operational: Yes.
Subscribers: 10,479.
Broadband Service: Mediacom High Speed Internet.
Telephone Service
Digital: Operational
Subscribers: 4,189.
Miles of Plant: 1,103.0 (coaxial); 297.0 (fiber optic). Homes passed: 60,249.
Regional Vice President: Bill Copeland. General Manager: Dale Haney. Regional Technical Operations Director: Alan Freedman. Marketing Director: Will Kuebler. Marketing Manager: Melanie Westerman. Technical Operations Manager: Jeff Brown.
Ownership: Mediacom LLC (MSO).

MURRAYVILLE—Formerly served by Almega Cable. No longer in operation. ICA: IL0294.

NAPERVILLE—Comcast Cable. Now served by PEORIA, IL [IL0012]. ICA: IL0029.

NAPERVILLE—WOW! Internet, Cable & Phone, 7887 East Belleview Ave, Ste 1000, Englewood, CO 80111. Phones: 866-496-9669; 720-479-3500; 630-536-3100 (Customer service). Fax: 720-479-3585. E-mail: wow_general@wideopenwest.com. Web Site: http://www.wowway.com. Also serves Arlington Heights, Calumet City, Chicago (southern portion), Chicago Heights, Crestwood, Des Plaines, DuPage County (portions), Elgin, Glen Ellyn, Glendale Heights, Glenview, Mount Prospect, Oak Forest, Palos Park, Posen, Prospect Heights, Robbins, Schaumburg, South Holland & Streamwood, IL; Hammond, IN. ICA: IL0655. **Note:** This system is an overbuild.
TV Market Ranking: 3 (Arlington Heights, Calumet City, Chicago Heights, Crestwood, Des Plaines, DuPage County (portions), Elgin, Glen Ellyn, Glendale Heights, Glenview, Hammond, Mount Prospect, NAPERVILLE, Oak Forest, Palos Park, Posen, Prospect Heights, Robbins, Schaumburg, South Holland, Streamwood). Franchise award date: February 1, 1996. Franchise expiration date: N.A. Began: N.A.
Channel capacity: N.A. Channels available but not in use: N.A.
Basic Service
Subscribers: 56,875.
Programming (received off-air): WBBM-TV (CBS, Decades) Chicago; WCIU-TV (MeTV) Chicago; WCPX-TV (ION) Chicago; WFLD (FOX) Chicago; WGBO-DT (getTV, UNV) Joliet; WGN-TV (IND) Chicago; WJYS (IND) Hammond; WLS-TV (ABC, Live Well Network) Chicago; WMAQ-TV (COZI TV, NBC) Chicago; WPWR-TV (Buzzr, CW, MNT, Movies!) Gary; WSNS-TV (TMO) Chicago; WTTW (PBS) Chicago; WXFT-DT (UniMas) Aurora; WYCC (PBS) Chicago.
Programming (via satellite): INSP; TBS; Vme TV.
Fee: $50.00 installation; $32.00 monthly.
Expanded Basic Service 1
Subscribers: N.A.
Programming (via satellite): A&E; AMC; Animal Planet; BET; Bravo; BTN; Cartoon Network; CMT; CNBC; CNN; Comcast SportsNet Chicago; Comedy Central; C-SPAN; Discovery Channel; Disney Channel; Disney XD; E! HD; ESPN; ESPN Classic; ESPN2; EVINE Live; Food Network; Fox News Channel; Fox Sports 1; Freeform; FX; Golf Channel; GSN; Hallmark Channel; HGTV; History; HLN; Lifetime; MSNBC; MTV; MTV2; Nickelodeon; Nicktoons; OWN: Oprah Winfrey Network; Oxygen; QVC; Spike TV; Syfy; The Weather Channel; TLC; TNT; Travel Channel; truTV; Turner Classic Movies; TV Land; USA Network; VH1.
Fee: $34.76 monthly.
Digital Basic Service
Subscribers: N.A.
Programming (via satellite): BBC America; Bloomberg Television; Bridges TV; BTN; CMT; Cooking Channel; Destination America; Discovery Kids Channel; DIY Network; DMX Music; ESPNews; ESPNU; EWTN Global Catholic Network; Fox Business Network; FOX College Sports Central; FOX College Sports Pacific; FXM; FYI; History International; Investigation Discovery; LMN; MTV Classic; MTV Hits; Nat Geo WILD; National Geographic Channel; NFL Network; Nick 2; Nick Jr.; Outdoor Channel; Science Channel; Sprout; Starz (multiplexed); Starz Encore (multiplexed); Sundance TV; TeenNick; Tennis Channel; The Word Network.
Digital Expanded Basic Service
Subscribers: N.A.
Programming (via satellite): A&E HD; Animal Planet HD; AXS TV; Discovery Channel HD; Disney Channel HD; ESPN HD; ESPN2 HD; Food Network HD; Fox News HD; Freeform HD; FX HD; HD Theater; HGTV HD; History HD; National Geographic Channel HD; NFL Network HD; Starz HD; TLC HD; TNT HD.
Fee: $13.00 monthly.
Digital Pay Service 1
Pay Units: N.A.
Programming (via satellite): Cinemax (multiplexed); Cinemax HD; Cinemax On Demand; HBO (multiplexed); HBO HD; HBO on Demand; Showtime (multiplexed); Showtime HD; Showtime On Demand; The Movie Channel (multiplexed); The Movie Channel On Demand.
Fee: $15.00 monthly (HBO, Cinemax, Starz or Showtime/TMC/Flix).
Video-On-Demand: Yes

Cable Systems—Illinois

Pay-Per-View
ETC; iN DEMAND (delivered digitally); Pleasure (delivered digitally); Playboy TV (delivered digitally); Sports PPV (delivered digitally).
Internet Service
Operational: Yes.
Subscribers: 78,852.
Broadband Service: WOW! Internet.
Fee: $40.99 monthly; $2.50 modem lease.
Telephone Service
Digital: Operational.
Subscribers: 46,868.
Miles of Plant: 5,081.0 (coaxial); 1,314.0 (fiber optic). Homes passed: 461,260.
Chief Financial Officer: Rich Fish. Vice President & General Manager: Kelvin Fee. Vice President, Sales & Marketing: Cathy Kuo. Chief Technician: Cash Hagan.
Ownership: WideOpenWest LLC (MSO).

NAUVOO—Medicom. Now served by DALLAS CITY, IL [IL0274]. ICA: IL0299.

NEOGA—Mediacom, 4290 Blue Stem Rd, PO Box 288, Charleston, IL 61920. Phone: 217-348-5533. Fax: 217-345-7074. Web Site: http://www.mediacomcable.com. Also serves Stewardson, Strasburg & Windsor. ICA: IL0249.
TV Market Ranking: 64 (Windsor); Outside TV Markets (NEOGA, Stewardson, Strasburg). Franchise award date: January 1, 1981. Franchise expiration date: N.A. Began: May 26, 1981.
Channel capacity: N.A. Channels available but not in use: N.A.
Basic Service
Subscribers: 407.
Programming (received off-air): WAND (NBC) Decatur; WBUI (CW, This TV) Decatur; WCCU (FOX, MeTV) Urbana; WCIA (CBS, MNT) Champaign; WCIX (CBS, MNT) Springfield; WEIU-TV (PBS) Charleston; WICD (ABC) Champaign; WILL-TV (PBS) Urbana; WSIU-TV (PBS) Carbondale; WTHI-TV (CBS, FOX) Terre Haute; WTWO (NBC) Terre Haute; 6 FMs.
Programming (via satellite): C-SPAN; INSP; Pop; QVC; WGN America.
Fee: $45.00 installation; $43.00 monthly.
Expanded Basic Service 1
Subscribers: N.A.
Programming (via satellite): A&E; AMC; Animal Planet; BET; Cartoon Network; CMT; CNBC; CNN; Comedy Central; C-SPAN 2; Discovery Channel; Discovery Life Channel; Disney Channel; E! HD; ESPN; ESPN Classic; ESPN2; EVINE Live; EWTN Global Catholic Network; Food Network; Fox News Channel; Fox Sports 1; FOX Sports Midwest; Freeform; FX; Hallmark Channel; HGTV; History; HLN; ION Television; Jewelry Television; Lifetime; LMN; MSNBC; MTV; Nickelodeon; Outdoor Channel; Oxygen; Spike TV; Syfy; TBS; The Weather Channel; TLC; TNT; Travel Channel; Trinity Broadcasting Network (TBN); truTV; TV Land; USA Network; VH1; WE tv.
Fee: $34.00 monthly.
Digital Basic Service
Subscribers: N.A.
Programming (via satellite): BBC America; Bloomberg Television; CCTV-Documentary; Cloo; Destination America; Discovery Kids Channel; Discovery Life Channel; Disney XD; ESPN HD; ESPN2 HD; ESPNews; ESPNU; Fox Sports 1; Fox Sports 2; Fuse; FXM; FYI; Golf Channel; GSN; History International; ION Television; MC; MTV Classic; MTV Hits; MTV2;

Nat Geo WILD; National Geographic Channel; NBCSN; Nick Jr.; Nicktoons; OWN: Oprah Winfrey Network; Qubo; Reelz; Science Channel; TeenNick; Turner Classic Movies; TVG Network.
Digital Expanded Basic Service
Subscribers: N.A.
Programming (via satellite): CBS Sports Network; FOX College Sports Central; FOX College Sports Pacific; GolTV; Tennis Channel.
Fee: $3.95 monthly.
Digital Expanded Basic Service 2
Subscribers: N.A.
Programming (via satellite): AXS TV; HD Theater; Universal HD.
Fee: $6.95 monthly.
Digital Pay Service 1
Pay Units: N.A.
Programming (via satellite): Cinemax (multiplexed); Cinemax On Demand; HBO (multiplexed); HBO GO; HBO HD; Showtime (multiplexed); Showtime HD; Showtime On Demand; Starz (multiplexed); Starz Encore; Starz HD; Starz On Demand; The Movie Channel (multiplexed); The Movie Channel HD; The Movie Channel On Demand.
Fee: $11.95 monthly (HBO, Cinemax, Showtime/TMC or Starz/Encore).
Video-On-Demand: Planned
Pay-Per-View
iN DEMAND (delivered digitally); Playboy TV (delivered digitally); SexSee (delivered digitally); Juicy (delivered digitally); ESPN (delivered digitally).
Internet Service
Operational: Yes.
Broadband Service: Mediacom High Speed Internet.
Fee: $59.95 installation; $40.95 monthly; $15.00 modem lease.
Telephone Service
Digital: Operational
Fee: $39.95 monthly
Miles of Plant: 51.0 (coaxial); 66.0 (fiber optic). Homes passed: 1,912.
General Manager: Todd Acker. Technical Operations Manager: Jerry Ferguson. Marketing Director: James Friske.
Ownership: Mediacom LLC (MSO).

NEW BERLIN—Mediacom. Now served by KINCAID, IL [IL0176]. ICA: IL0334.

NEW BOSTON—Nova1Net, 677 West Main St, PO Box 1412, Galesburg, IL 61401. Phones: 800-397-6682; 309-342-9681. Fax: 309-342-4408. Web Site: http://www.novacablevision.com. ICA: IL0558.
TV Market Ranking: 60 (NEW BOSTON). Franchise award date: N.A. Franchise expiration date: N.A. Began: October 1, 1984.
Channel capacity: N.A. Channels available but not in use: N.A.
Basic Service
Subscribers: N.A.
Programming (received off-air): KGCW (CW, MeTV, This TV) Burlington; KIIN (PBS) Iowa City; KLJB (CW, FOX, MeTV) Davenport; KWQC-TV (NBC) Davenport; WEEK-TV (ABC, CW, NBC) Peoria; WHBF-TV (CBS) Rock Island; WHOI (Comet) Peoria; WMBD-TV (Bounce TV, CBS) Peoria; WQAD-TV (ABC, Antenna TV) Moline; WQPT-TV (PBS) Moline; WTVP (PBS) Peoria.
Programming (via satellite): A&E; AMC; Animal Planet; BTN; Cartoon Network; CMT; CNBC; CNN; Comcast SportsNet Chicago; Comedy Central; C-SPAN; C-SPAN 2; Discovery Channel; Disney Channel; DIY Net-

work; E! HD; ESPN; ESPN2; ESPNU; EWTN Global Catholic Network; Food Network; Fox News Channel; FOX Sports Midwest; Freeform; FX; Golf Channel; Great American Country; Hallmark Channel; HGTV; History; HLN; HRTV; Lifetime; MSNBC; MTV; National Geographic Channel; Nickelodeon; QVC; RFD-TV; Spike TV; Syfy; TBS; The Weather Channel; TLC; TNT; Travel Channel; truTV; TV Land; USA Network; VH1; WGN America.
Fee: $60.00 installation.
Digital Basic Service
Subscribers: N.A.
Programming (via satellite): Bloomberg Television; CMT; Destination America; Discovery Kids Channel; Disney XD; DMX Music; ESPN Classic; ESPN2; ESPNews; EVINE Live; Fox Sports 1; FSN Digital Atlantic; FSN Digital Central; FSN Digital Pacific; Fuse; FXM; FYI; Golf Channel; Great American Country; GSN; HGTV; History; History International; IFC; Investigation Discovery; LMN; MTV Classic; MTV Hits; MTV2; NBCSN; Nicktoons; Noggin; Outdoor Channel; OWN: Oprah Winfrey Network; Science Channel; Syfy; TeenNick; Trinity Broadcasting Network (TBN); Turner Classic Movies; VH1 Soul; WE tv.
Pay Service 1
Pay Units: N.A.
Programming (via satellite): Cinemax; HBO.
Fee: $12.85 monthly (each).
Digital Pay Service 1
Pay Units: N.A.
Programming (via satellite): Cinemax (multiplexed); Flix; HBO (multiplexed); Showtime (multiplexed); Starz (multiplexed); Starz Encore (multiplexed); Sundance TV; The Movie Channel (multiplexed).
Fee: $12.85 monthly (HBO, Showtime/TMC/Flix/Sundance, Cinemax, or Starz/Encore).
Video-On-Demand: No
Pay-Per-View
Hot Choice (delivered digitally); Playboy TV (delivered digitally); Fresh (delivered digitally); Spice: Xcess (delivered digitally); Club Jenna (delivered digitally).
Internet Service
Operational: Yes.
Fee: $39.95 monthly; $3.95 modem lease.
Telephone Service
None
Miles of Plant: 8.0 (coaxial); None (fiber optic). Homes passed: 422.
General Manager: Robert G. Fischer Jr. Office Manager: Hazel Harden.
Ownership: Nova Cablevision Inc. (MSO).

NEW DOUGLAS—Madison Communications. Now served by STAUNTON, IL [IL0171]. ICA: IL0354.

NEW DOUGLAS—Madison Communications. Now served by STAUNTON, IL [IL0171]. ICA: IL0404.

NEW HAVEN (village)—Formerly served by CableDirect. No longer in operation. ICA: IL0442.

NEW HOLLAND—Mediacom. Now served by DELAVAN, IL [IL0172]. ICA: IL0416.

NEWMAN—Comcast Cable, 303 Fairlawn Dr, Urbana, IL 61801-5141. Phone: 217-384-2530. Fax: 217-384-2021. Web Site: http://www.comcast.com. Also serves Broadlands & Douglas County (portions). ICA: IL0255.
TV Market Ranking: 64 (Broadlands, Douglas County (portions), NEWMAN). Franchise award date: N.A. Franchise expiration date: N.A. Began: September 28, 1981.
Channel capacity: 36 (not 2-way capable). Channels available but not in use: N.A.
Basic Service
Subscribers: 22. Commercial subscribers: 8.
Programming (received off-air): WAND (NBC) Decatur; WBUI (CW, This TV) Decatur; WCCU (FOX, MeTV) Urbana; WCIA (CBS, MNT) Champaign; WEIU-TV (PBS) Charleston; WICD (ABC) Champaign; WILL-TV (PBS) Urbana; 6 FMs.
Programming (via satellite): A&E; Animal Planet; Cartoon Network; CNN; C-SPAN; C-SPAN 2; Discovery Channel; Disney Channel; ESPN; Fox News Channel; Freeform; FX; HGTV; HLN; Lifetime; MTV; Nickelodeon; QVC; Spike TV; TBS; The Weather Channel; TLC; TNT; USA Network; WGN America.
Fee: $29.00-$42.00 installation; $19.24 monthly.
Pay Service 1
Pay Units: N.A.
Programming (via satellite): Cinemax; HBO; Starz; Starz Encore.
Fee: $8.50 installation; $10.00 monthly (Cinemax, HBO or Starz/Encore).
Internet Service
Operational: Yes.
Telephone Service
Digital: Operational
Miles of Plant: 22.0 (coaxial); None (fiber optic). Homes passed: 620.
District Director: Melody Brucker. Chief Technician: Jim Lee.
Ownership: Comcast Cable Communications Inc. (MSO).

NEWTON—NewWave Communications, One Montgomery Plaza, 4th Floor, Sikeston, MO 63801. Phone: 888-863-9928. Fax: 573-481-9809. E-mail: info@newwavecom.com. Web Site: http://www.newwavecom.com. Also serves Jasper County (southern portion), Olney & Richland County (portions), IL; Daviess County (portions), Elnora, Knox County (portions), Newberry, Odon, Plainville & Sandborn, IN. ICA: IL0559.
TV Market Ranking: 16 (Newberry, Odon); Outside TV Markets (Elnora, Jasper County (southern portion), Knox County (portions), NEWTON, Plainville, Richland County (portions), Sandborn, Olney). Franchise award date: N.A. Franchise expiration date: N.A. Began: October 1, 1964.
Channel capacity: N.A. Channels available but not in use: N.A.

Illinois—Cable Systems

Basic Service
Subscribers: 2,723. Commercial subscribers: 32.
Programming (received off-air): WAWV-TV (ABC) Terre Haute; WEHT (ABC) Evansville; WPXS (IND) Mount Vernon; WTHI-TV (CBS, FOX) Terre Haute; WTWO (NBC) Terre Haute; WUSI-TV (PBS) Olney; allband FM.
Programming (via satellite): C-SPAN; QVC; Spike TV; Trinity Broadcasting Network (TBN); WGN America.
Fee: $40.00 installation; $34.78 monthly; $2.00 converter.
Expanded Basic Service 1
Subscribers: 613.
Programming (via satellite): A&E; AMC; Animal Planet; Bravo; Cartoon Network; CMT; CNBC; CNN; Comedy Central; Discovery Channel; Disney Channel; E! HD; ESPN; ESPN2; Food Network; Fox News Channel; Fox Sports 1; FOX Sports Midwest; Freeform; FX; GSN; Hallmark Channel; HGTV; History; HLN; Lifetime; MTV; MTV2; National Geographic Channel; Nickelodeon; Outdoor Channel; Syfy; TBS; The Weather Channel; TLC; TNT; Travel Channel; truTV; Turner Classic Movies; TV Land; USA Network; VH1.
Digital Basic Service
Subscribers: N.A.
Programming (via satellite): BBC America; Bloomberg Television; CMT; Destination America; Discovery Kids Channel; Discovery Life Channel; Disney XD; DMX Music; ESPNews; EVINE Live; FXM; FYI; Golf Channel; History International; IFC; Investigation Discovery; LMN; MTV Classic; MTV Hits; NBCSN; Nick Jr.; OWN: Oprah Winfrey Network; Science Channel; TeenNick; VH1 Soul; WE tv.
Pay Service 1
Pay Units: 226.
Programming (via satellite): HBO; Showtime; Starz Encore; The Movie Channel.
Fee: $20.00 installation; $10.75 monthly (each).
Digital Pay Service 1
Pay Units: N.A.
Programming (via satellite): Cinemax (multiplexed); Flix; HBO (multiplexed); Showtime (multiplexed); Starz (multiplexed); Starz Encore (multiplexed); The Movie Channel (multiplexed).
Video-On-Demand: No
Pay-Per-View
Hot Choice (delivered digitally); iN DEMAND (delivered digitally); Playboy TV (delivered digitally); Fresh (delivered digitally); Shorteez (delivered digitally).
Internet Service
Operational: No.
Telephone Service
None
Chief Financial Officer: Rod Siemers. General Manager: John Helmers.
Ownership: NewWave Communications LLC (MSO).

NOBLE—Wabash Independent Networks. Now served by FLORA, IL [IL0140]. ICA: IL0339.

NOKOMIS—NewWave Communications. Now served by TAYLORVILLE, IL [IL0098]. ICA: IL0199.

NORRIS—Formerly served by Insight Communications. Now served by Comcast Cable, PEORIA, IL [IL0012]. ICA: IL0353.

NORRIS CITY—NewWave Communications. Now served by McLEANSBORO, IL [IL0177]. ICA: IL0235.

NORTH HENDERSON—Nova1Net, 677 West Main St, PO Box 1412, Galesburg, IL 61402. Phones: 309-342-9681; 800-397-6682. Fax: 309-342-4408. E-mail: cableme@nova1net.com. Web Site: http://nova1net.com. ICA: IL0705.
TV Market Ranking: 60 (NORTH HENDERSON).
Channel capacity: N.A. Channels available but not in use: N.A.
President: Robert Fischer.
Ownership: Nova Cablevision Inc. (MSO).

OAK FOREST—Comcast Cable. Now served by CHAMPAIGN, IL [IL0019]. ICA: IL0050.

OAK LAWN—Comcast Cable. Now served by CHAMPAIGN, IL [IL0019]. ICA: IL0021.

OCONEE—Formerly served by Mediacom. No longer in operation. ICA: IL0447.

ODELL—Mediacom. Now served by PONTIAC, IL [IL0109]. ICA: IL0310.

OKAWVILLE—Charter Communications. Now served by ST. LOUIS, MO [MO0009]. ICA: IL0075.

OLNEY—NewWave Communications. Now served by NEWTON, IL [IL0559]. ICA: IL0103.

OMAHA—Formerly served by CableDirect. No longer in operation. ICA: IL0624.

ONARGA—Comcast Cable. Now served by SPRINGFIELD, IL [IL0016]. ICA: IL0168.

ONEIDA—Oneida Cablevision Inc. Formerly [IL0361]. This cable system has converted to IPTV, 129 West Hwy 34, PO Box 445, Oneida, IL 61467-0445. Phone: 309-483-3111. Fax: 309-483-7777. E-mail: info@oneidatel.net. Web Site: http://oneidatel.com. Also serves Aldo (unincorporated areas), Alpha, Altona, Bishop Hill, Cameron, Canton, Cuba, Ellisville, Fairview, Fiatt, Gilson, Gladstone, Joy, Keithsburg, Kirkwood, Lafayette, Lake Bracken, Lake Warren, Little York, Maquon, Marietta, Milan (unincorporated areas), New Boston, New Windsor, North Henderson, Reynolds, Rio, Smithfield, Summum, Table Grove, Taylor Ridge (unincorporated areas), Victoria, Viola, Williamsfield, Woodhull & Yates City. ICA: IL5332.
TV Market Ranking: 60 (North Henderson, ONEIDA, Rio).
Channel capacity: N.A. Channels available but not in use: N.A.
Internet Service
Operational: Yes.
General Manager: David Olson.
Ownership: Oneida Cablevision.

ONEIDA—Oneida Cablevision Inc. This cable system has converted to IPTV. See ONEIDA, IL [IL5332]. ICA: IL0361.

OQUAWKA—Mediacom. Now served by DALLAS CITY, IL [IL0274]. ICA: IL0250.

OREGON—Formerly served by Insight Communications. No longer in operation. ICA: IL0074.

ORLAND PARK—Comcast Cable. Now served by CHAMPAIGN, IL [IL0019]. ICA: IL0048.

ORLAND PARK—Comcast Cable. Now served by CHAMPAIGN, IL [IL0019]. ICA: IL0008.

OSWEGO—Comcast Cable. Now served by PEORIA, IL [IL0012]. ICA: IL0697.

OTTAWA—Mediacom. Now served by STREATOR, IL [IL0069]. ICA: IL0058.

PALMER—Mediacom. Now served by KINCAID, IL [IL0176]. ICA: IL0435.

PALMYRA—Formerly served by Almega Cable. No longer in operation. ICA: IL0290.

PALOS PARK—Formerly served by TV Max. No longer in operation. ICA: IL0167.

PANA—NewWave Communications. Now served by TAYLORVILLE, IL [IL0098]. ICA: IL0562.

PANAMA—Formerly served by Beck's Cable Systems. No longer in operation. ICA: IL0350.

PARIS—Formerly served by Avenue Broadband Communications. Now served by NewWave Communications, WESTVILLE, IL [IL0079]. ICA: IL0122.

PARK FOREST—Comcast Cable. Now served by CHAMPAIGN, IL [IL0019]. ICA: IL0066.

PARKERSBURG—Formerly served by CableDirect. No longer in operation. ICA: IL0424.

PATOKA—Clearvision Cable Systems Inc, 1785 US Rte 40, Greenup, IL 62428-3501. Phone: 217-923-5594. Fax: 217-923-5681. Also serves Vernon. ICA: IL0159.
TV Market Ranking: Below 100 (PATOKA, Vernon). Franchise award date: N.A. Franchise expiration date: N.A. Began: September 1, 1984.
Channel capacity: N.A. Channels available but not in use: N.A.
Basic Service
Subscribers: 37.
Programming (received off-air): KDNL-TV (ABC, The Country Network) St. Louis; KMOV (CBS) St. Louis; KPLR-TV (CW, This TV) St. Louis; KSDK (Bounce TV, NBC) St. Louis; KTVI (Antenna TV, Escape, FOX) St. Louis; WPXS (IND) Mount Vernon; WSIU-TV (PBS) Carbondale.
Programming (via satellite): TBS; Trinity Broadcasting Network (TBN); WGN America.
Fee: $47.95 monthly; $2.00 converter.
Expanded Basic Service 1
Subscribers: N.A.
Programming (via satellite): A&E; AMC; CMT; CNBC; CNN; Discovery Channel; Disney Channel; ESPN; FOX Sports Midwest; Freeform; History; HLN; Lifetime; Nickelodeon; Spike TV; Syfy; The Weather Channel; TNT; USA Network.
Fee: $20.00 installation; $6.00 monthly.
Digital Basic Service
Subscribers: N.A.
Programming (via satellite): BBC America; Bloomberg Television; Bravo; Discovery Life Channel; Disney XD; DMX Music; EVINE Live; Fox Sports 1; Fuse; FXM; FYI; Golf Channel; GSN; HGTV; History International; IFC; LMN; NBCSN; Nick Jr.; Outdoor Channel; TeenNick; Turner Classic Movies; WE tv.
Pay Service 1
Pay Units: N.A.
Programming (via satellite): HBO.
Fee: $20.00 installation; $11.00 monthly.
Digital Pay Service 1
Pay Units: N.A.
Programming (via satellite): Cinemax (multiplexed); Flix; HBO (multiplexed); Showtime (multiplexed); Starz (multiplexed); Starz Encore (multiplexed); The Movie Channel (multiplexed).
Video-On-Demand: No
Pay-Per-View
ESPN Now (delivered digitally); Hot Choice (delivered digitally); iN DEMAND (delivered digitally); Playboy TV (delivered digitally); Fresh (delivered digitally); Shorteez (delivered digitally).
Internet Service
Operational: No.
Telephone Service
None
Miles of Plant: 12.0 (coaxial); None (fiber optic). Homes passed: 437.
President & General Manager: Michael Bauguss. Secretary: Gwyndolyn S. Bauguss.
Ownership: Clearvision Cable Systems Inc. (MSO).

PAYSON—Formerly served by Adams Telcom. No longer in operation. ICA: IL0288.

PEARL CITY (village)—Mediacom. Now served by LENA, IL [IL0223]. ICA: IL0565.

PECATONICA—Mediacom. Now served by LENA, IL [IL0223]. ICA: IL0233.

PEKIN—Comcast Cable. Now served by PEORIA, IL [IL0012]. ICA: IL0045.

PENFIELD—Formerly served by CableDirect. No longer in operation. ICA: IL0456.

PEORIA—Comcast Cable, 3517 North Dries Ln, Peoria, IL 61604. Phones: 309-682-3767; 309-686-2600. Fax: 309-688-9828. Web Site: http://www.comcast.com. Also serves Adams County (portions), Addison, Aurora, Bartonville, Batavia, Bedford Park, Bellevue, Bellwood, Bensenville, Berkeley, Berwyn, Blandinsville (village), Bloomingdale, Bloomington, Bolingbrook, Boulder Hill, Braidwood, Bridgeview, Bristol, Broadview, Brookfield, Burbank, Burr Ridge, Bushnell, Campton Hills, Canton, Carbon Hill, Carol

Cable Systems—Illinois

Stream, Channahon, Cicero, Clarendon Hills, Coal City, Colchester, Cook County (portions), Countryside, Crest Hill, Creve Coeur, Cuba, Custer Park, Darien, Diamond, Downers Grove, Du Page County (unincorporated areas), DuPage County (portions), DuPage County (southwestern portion), East Galesburg, East Peoria, Elgin, Elgin Twp., Elmhurst, Elmwood Park, Forest Park, Forest View, Frankfort (village), Frankfort Twp., Franklin Park, Fulton County (portions), Galesburg, Geneva, Glen Ellyn, Glendale Heights, Goose Lake, Groveland, Grundy County (portions), Harwood Heights, Hillside, Hinsdale, Hodgkins, Homer Twp., Indian Head Park, Itasca, Joliet, Justice, Kane County (portions), Kendall County (portions), Knoxville, La Grange, La Grange Park, La Harpe, Lake Holiday, Lemont, Lewistown, Lily Lake (village), Lisle, Lockport, Lockport Twp., Lombard, Lyons, Macomb, Marquette Heights, Maywood, Mazon (village), McCook, McDonough County (portions), McLean County (portions), Melrose Park, Millington, Minooka, Mokena, Montgomery, Morris, Morton, Naperville, New Lenox, New Lenox Twp., Newark, Normal, Norridge, Norris, North Aurora, North Pekin, North Riverside, Northlake, Norwood, Oak Brook, Oak Park, Oakbrook Terrace, Oswego, Pekin, Peoria County (portions), Peoria Heights, Plainfield, Plainfield Twp., Plano, Proviso Twp., Quincy, River Forest, River Grove, Riverside, Rockdale, Romeoville, Roselle, Rosemont, Sandwich, Schiller Park, Shorewood, South Elgin, South Pekin, St. Charles, Stickney, Stone Park, Summit, Tazewell County (portions), Tremont, Troy Twp., Villa Park, Warrenville, Washington, West Chicago, West Peoria, Westchester, Western Springs, Westmont, Wheaton, Will County (portions), Willow Springs, Willowbrook, Wilmington, Winfield, Wood Dale, Woodridge & Yorkville. ICA: IL0012.

TV Market Ranking: 3 (Addison, Aurora, Batavia, Bedford Park, Bensenville, Berkeley, Berwyn, Bloomingdale, Bolingbrook, Bridgeview, Broadview, Brookfield, Burbank, Burr Ridge, Campton Hills, Carol Stream, Cicero, Clarendon Hills, Cook County (portions), Cook County (portions), Countryside, Crest Hill, Darien, Downers Grove, Du Page County (unincorporated areas), DuPage County (portions), DuPage County (southwestern portion), Elgin, Elgin Twp., Elmhurst, Elmwood Park, Forest Park, Forest View, Frankfort (village), Frankfort Twp., Franklin Park, Geneva, Glen Ellyn, Glendale Heights, Hillside, Hinsdale, Hodgkins, Homer Twp., Indian Head Park, Itasca, Joliet, Justice, Kane County (portions) (portions), Kendall County (portions) (portions), La Grange, La Grange Park, Lemont, Lisle, Lockport, Lockport Twp., Lombard, Lyons, Maywood, McCook, Melrose Park, Mokena, Montgomery, Naperville, Naperville, New Lenox, New Lenox Twp., Norridge, North Aurora, North Riverside, Northlake, Oak Brook, Oak Park, Oakbrook Terrace, Oswego, PEORIA, Plainfield, Plainfield Twp., Proviso Twp., River Forest, River Grove, Riverside, Romeoville, Roselle, Roselle, Rosemont, Schiller Park, South Elgin, St. Charles, Stickney, Stone Park, Summit, Troy Twp., Villa Park, Warrenville, West Chicago, Westchester, Western Springs, Westmont, Wheaton, Will County (portions) (portions), Willow Springs, Willowbrook, Winfield, Wood Dale, Woodridge); 3,97 (Elgin); 83 (Bartonville, Bellevue, Canton, Creve Coeur, East Peoria, Fulton County (portions), Groveland, Mar-

quette Heights, Morton, Norris, North Pekin, Norwood, Pekin, PEORIA, Peoria County (portions), Peoria Heights, South Pekin, Tazewell County (portions), Tremont, Washington, West Peoria); 83,64 (McLean County (portions) (portions)); Below 100 (Adams County (portions), Blandinsville (village), Boulder Hill, Braidwood, Bristol, Carbon Hill, Coal City, Colchester, Cuba, Custer Park, Diamond, Goose Lake, Grundy County (portions), La Harpe, Lewistown, Lily Lake (village), Mazon (village), McDonough County (portions) (portions), Millington, Minooka, Morris, Newark, Normal, Plano, Rockdale, Sandwich, Shorewood, Wilmington, Yorkville, Bloomington, Channahon, Macomb, Quincy, Kane County (portions) (portions), Kendall County (portions) (portions), Will County (portions) (portions), Elgin (portions), McLean County (portions) (portions)); Outside TV Markets (Bushnell, East Galesburg, Knoxville, McDonough County (portions) (portions), Galesburg, Kane County (portions) (portions), Fulton County (portions) (portions)). Franchise award date: N.A. Franchise expiration date: N.A. Began: April 16, 1973.

Channel capacity: N.A. Channels available but not in use: N.A.

Basic Service
Subscribers: 557,197. Commercial subscribers: 2,357.
Programming (received off-air): WAOE (Antenna TV, MNT) Peoria; WEEK-TV (ABC, CW, NBC) Peoria; WHOI (Comet) Peoria; WMBD-TV (Bounce TV, CBS) Peoria; WTVP (PBS) Peoria; WYZZ-TV (FOX, The Country Network) Bloomington; 18 FMs.
Programming (via satellite): C-SPAN 2; Discovery Channel; EWTN Global Catholic Network; ION Television; Pop; QVC; The Weather Channel; Trinity Broadcasting Network (TBN); WGN America.
Fee: $29.00-$42.00 installation; $30.99 monthly; $1.06 converter.

Expanded Basic Service 1
Subscribers: N.A.
Programming (via satellite): A&E; AMC; Animal Planet; BET; Bravo; Cartoon Network; CMT; CNBC; CNN; Comcast SportsNet Chicago; Comedy Central; Disney Channel; Disney XD; E! HD; ESPN; ESPN2; EVINE Live; Food Network; Fox News Channel; Fox Sports 1; FOX Sports Midwest; Freeform; FX; Golf Channel; Great American Country; Hallmark Channel; HGTV; History; HLN; Lifetime; MSNBC; MTV; National Geographic Channel; Nickelodeon; Oxygen; Spike TV; Syfy; TBS; TLC; TNT; Travel Channel; truTV; USA Network; VH1.
Fee: $37.15 monthly.

Digital Basic Service
Subscribers: N.A.
Programming (via satellite): AXS TV; BBC America; Bloomberg Television; CBS Sports Network; Cloo; CMT; Cooking Channel; C-SPAN 3; Discovery Digital Networks; Disney XD; DIY Network; ESPN Classic; ESPN HD; ESPN2 HD; ESPNews; ESPNU; FOX College Sports Central; FOX College Sports Pacific; Fuse; FXM; FYI; GSN; HD Theater; History International; HRTV; IFC; LMN; MTV Live; Nat Geo WILD; NBCSN; NFL Network; Nick 2; Nick Jr.; Nicktoons; Outdoor Channel; Ovation; Sprout; Starz Encore (multiplexed); Sundance TV; TeenNick; Tennis Channel; TNT HD; Turner Classic Movies; TV Land; TVG Network; Universal HD; WE tv.

Digital Pay Service 1
Pay Units: N.A.
Programming (via satellite): Cinemax (multiplexed); Flix; HBO (multiplexed); HBO HD; Showtime (multiplexed); Starz (multiplexed); The Movie Channel (multiplexed).
Fee: $10.00 monthly (Cinemax or Starz), $13.00 monthly (HBO or Showtime/TMC).
Video-On-Demand: Yes
Pay-Per-View
ESPN Now (delivered digitally); iN DEMAND (delivered digitally); Playboy TV (delivered digitally); Special events (delivered digitally).
Internet Service
Operational: Yes.
Subscribers: 554,426.
Broadband Service: Comcast High Speed Internet.
Fee: $99.95 installation; $44.95 monthly; $10.00 modem lease; $99.95 modem purchase.
Telephone Service
Digital: Operational
Subscribers: 280,989.
Miles of Plant: 25,196.0 (coaxial); 7,679.0 (fiber optic). Homes passed: 1,694,163.
General Manager: John Nieber. Chief Technician: Mike Vandergraft.
Ownership: Comcast Cable Communications Inc. (MSO).

PEOTONE—Comcast Cable. Now served by CHAMPAIGN, IL [IL0019]. ICA: IL0107.

PIERRON—Clearvision Cable Systems Inc, 1785 US Rte 40, Greenup, IL 62428-3501. Phone: 217-923-5594. Fax: 217-923-5681. ICA: IL0620.
TV Market Ranking: 11 (PIERRON).
Channel capacity: N.A. Channels available but not in use: N.A.
Basic Service
Subscribers: 8.
Programming (received off-air): KDNL-TV (ABC, The Country Network) St. Louis; KETC (PBS) St. Louis; KMOV (CBS) St. Louis; KPLR-TV (CW, This TV) St. Louis; KSDK (Bounce TV, NBC) St. Louis; KTVI (Antenna TV, Escape, FOX) St. Louis; WPXS (IND) Mount Vernon.
Programming (via satellite): A&E; AMC; Bravo; Cartoon Network; CMT; CNBC; CNN; Comedy Central; C-SPAN; Discovery Channel; Disney Channel; ESPN; Freeform; History; HLN; Lifetime; MSNBC; MTV; Nickelodeon; QVC; Spike TV; Syfy; TBS; The Weather Channel; TLC; TNT; Trinity Broadcasting Network (TBN); USA Network; VH1; WGN America.
Fee: $42.45 monthly.
Pay Service 1
Pay Units: N.A.
Programming (via satellite): Showtime; The Movie Channel.
Video-On-Demand: No
Internet Service
Operational: No.
Telephone Service
None
Homes passed: 253.
General Manager: Michael Baugus. Secretary: Gwyndolyn S. Baugus.
Ownership: Clearvision Cable Systems Inc. (MSO).

PIPER CITY—Comcast Cable, 7720 West 98th St, Hickory Hills, IL 60457. Phones: 708-576-8168; 847-585-6310 (Kankakee office); 708-237-3260. Fax: 708-237-3292.

Web Site: http://www.comcast.com. ICA: IL0309.
TV Market Ranking: Outside TV Markets (PIPER CITY). Franchise award date: N.A. Franchise expiration date: N.A. Began: January 1, 1975.
Channel capacity: N.A. Channels available but not in use: N.A.
Basic Service
Subscribers: 20.
Programming (received off-air): WAND (NBC) Decatur; WCCU (FOX, MeTV) Urbana; WCIA (CBS, MNT) Champaign; WFLD (FOX) Chicago; WGN-TV (IND) Chicago; WICD (ABC) Champaign; WILL-TV (PBS) Urbana; WLS-TV (ABC, Live Well Network) Chicago; allband FM.
Programming (via satellite): Discovery Channel; TBS.
Fee: $29.00-$42.00 installation; $20.24 monthly; $3.00 converter.
Expanded Basic Service 1
Subscribers: N.A.
Programming (via satellite): AMC; Animal Planet; Cartoon Network; CNN; Comcast SportsNet Chicago; Disney Channel; ESPN; Fox News Channel; Freeform; HGTV; Lifetime; Nickelodeon; QVC; TLC; TNT; USA Network.
Fee: $23.73 monthly.
Pay Service 1
Pay Units: N.A.
Programming (via satellite): Showtime; Starz; Starz Encore.
Fee: $1.75 monthly (Encore), $6.75 monthly (Starz), $13.10 monthly (Showtime).
Internet Service
Operational: Yes.
Telephone Service
Digital: Operational
Miles of Plant: 6.0 (coaxial); None (fiber optic). Homes passed: 393.
Area Vice President: Sandy Weicher. Vice President, Technical Operations: Bob Curtis. Vice President, Sales & Marketing: Eric Schaefer. Vice President, Communications: Rich Ruggiero.
Ownership: Comcast Cable Communications Inc. (MSO).

PITTSFIELD—Cass Cable TV Inc, 100 Redbud Rd, PO Box 200, Virginia, IL 62691. Phones: 217-452-7934; 800-252-1799; 217-452-7725. Fax: 217-452-7030. E-mail: casscatv@casscomm.com; solutions@casscomm.com. Web Site: http://www.casscomm.com. Also serves Griggsville. ICA: IL0158.
TV Market Ranking: Below 100 (PITTSFIELD, Griggsville). Franchise award date: N.A. Franchise expiration date: N.A. Began: February 1, 1980.
Channel capacity: N.A. Channels available but not in use: N.A.
Basic Service
Subscribers: 1,087.
Programming (received off-air): KDNL-TV (ABC, The Country Network) St. Louis; KETC (PBS) St. Louis; KHQA-TV (ABC, CBS) Hannibal; KPLR-TV (CW, This TV) St. Louis; KSDK (Bounce TV, NBC) St. Louis; KTVI (Antenna TV, Escape, FOX) St. Louis; WGEM-TV (CW, FOX, NBC) Quincy; WKRN-TV (ABC) Nashville; WRSP-TV (Antenna TV, FOX, MeTV) Springfield; WSEC (PBS) Jacksonville; WTJR (Christian TV Network) Quincy.
Programming (via satellite): Animal Planet; Disney XD.
Fee: $45.00 installation; $17.95 monthly; $4.00 converter.

2017 Edition
D-213

Illinois—Cable Systems

Expanded Basic Service 1
Subscribers: N.A.
Programming (via satellite): A&E; AMC; Cartoon Network; CMT; CNBC; CNN; Comcast SportsNet Chicago; Comedy Central; C-SPAN; Discovery Channel; Disney Channel; E! HD; ESPN; ESPN Classic; ESPN2; Food Network; Fox News Channel; Fox Sports 1; FOX Sports Midwest; Freeform; FX; Golf Channel; GSN; HGTV; History; HLN; Lifetime; MSNBC; MTV; NBCSN; Nickelodeon; QVC; Spike TV; Syfy; TBS; The Weather Channel; TLC; TNT; Travel Channel; Trinity Broadcasting Network (TBN); truTV; TV Land; USA Network; VH1; WGN America.
Fee: $32.00 monthly.

Digital Basic Service
Subscribers: N.A.
Programming (via satellite): A&E; BBC America; Bloomberg Television; Bravo; Discovery Life Channel; DMX Music; ESPNews; Fuse; History International; MTV2; National Geographic Channel; Nick Jr.; Outdoor Channel; Ovation; TeenNick; Trinity Broadcasting Network (TBN); WE tv.

Pay Service 1
Pay Units: 77.
Programming (via satellite): Cinemax.
Fee: $20.00 installation; $11.35 monthly.

Pay Service 2
Pay Units: 44.
Programming (via satellite): Showtime; The Movie Channel.
Fee: $20.00 installation; $12.95 monthly.

Pay Service 3
Pay Units: 81.
Programming (via satellite): Starz; Starz Encore.
Fee: $20.00 installation; $8.95 monthly.

Pay Service 4
Pay Units: 125.
Programming (via satellite): HBO.
Fee: $20.00 installation; $13.55 monthly.

Digital Pay Service 1
Pay Units: N.A.
Programming (via satellite): Cinemax (multiplexed); HBO (multiplexed); Showtime (multiplexed); Starz (multiplexed); Starz Encore (multiplexed); The Movie Channel (multiplexed).
Fee: $8.95 monthly (Starz/Encore), $11.35 monthly (Cinemax), $12.95 monthly (Showtime/TMC), $13.55 monthly (HBO).

Video-On-Demand: No
Pay-Per-View
iN DEMAND (delivered digitally); ESPN Now (delivered digitally); Playboy TV (delivered digitally); Fresh (delivered digitally); ESPN (delivered digitally); Sports PPV (delivered digitally).

Internet Service
Operational: Yes. Began: January 1, 2002.
Broadband Service: casscomm.com.
Fee: $39.95 monthly.

Telephone Service
Analog: Operational
Fee: $34.95 monthly
Digital: Operational
Fee: $34.95 monthly
Miles of Plant: 29.0 (coaxial); None (fiber optic). Homes passed: 1,941.
Vice President & CATV Manager: Chad Winters. Plant Manager: Lance Allen. Chief Technician: Gary Lowe. Marketing & Public Relations Manager: Erynn Snedeker. Advertising Director: Laymon Carter. Office Manager: Cindy Kilby.
Ownership: Cass Cable TV Inc. (MSO).

PLAINFIELD—Comcast Cable. Now served by PEORIA, IL [IL0012]. ICA: IL0351.

PLANO—Comcast Cable. Now served by PEORIA, IL [IL0012]. ICA: IL0100.

PLEASANT HILL—Formerly served by Crystal Broadband Networks. No longer in operation. ICA: IL0248.

POCAHONTAS—Clearvision Cable Systems Inc, 1785 US Rte 40, Greenup, IL 62428-3501. Phone: 217-923-5594. Fax: 217-923-5681. ICA: IL0332.
TV Market Ranking: Outside TV Markets (POCAHONTAS). Franchise award date: N.A. Franchise expiration date: N.A. Began: August 1, 1985.
Channel capacity: 40 (not 2-way capable). Channels available but not in use: N.A.

Basic Service
Subscribers: 11.
Programming (received off-air): KDNL-TV (ABC, The Country Network) St. Louis; KETC (PBS) St. Louis; KMOV (CBS) St. Louis; KPLR-TV (CW, This TV) St. Louis; KSDK (Bounce TV, NBC) St. Louis; KTVI (Antenna TV, Escape, FOX) St. Louis; WPXS (IND) Mount Vernon.
Programming (via satellite): A&E; AMC; Bravo; Cartoon Network; CMT; CNBC; CNN; Comedy Central; C-SPAN; Discovery Channel; Disney Channel; Freeform; History; HLN; Lifetime; MSNBC; MTV; Nickelodeon; QVC; Spike TV; Syfy; TBS; The Weather Channel; TLC; TNT; Trinity Broadcasting Network (TBN); USA Network; VH1; WGN America.
Fee: $47.95 monthly.

Pay Service 1
Pay Units: N.A.
Programming (via satellite): Showtime; The Movie Channel.
Fee: $11.00 monthly (each).

Video-On-Demand: No
Internet Service
Operational: No.
Telephone Service
None
Miles of Plant: 6.0 (coaxial); None (fiber optic). Homes passed: 322.
President & General Manager: Michael Bauguss. Secretary: Gwyndolyn S. Bauguss.
Ownership: Clearvision Cable Systems Inc. (MSO).

PONTIAC—Mediacom, 903 East Howard St, Pontiac, IL 61764. Phones: 815-844-4800; 309-274-4500 (Chillicothe office); 815-844-3142. Fax: 815-844-6755. Web Site: http://www.mediacomcable.com. Also serves Cornell, Cullom, Dwight, Livingston County (portions), Odell, Saunemin & South Wilmington (village). ICA: IL0109.
TV Market Ranking: Below 100 (Cornell, Dwight, PONTIAC, South Wilmington (village)); Outside TV Markets (Cullom, Odell, Saunemin). Franchise award date: October 1, 1964. Franchise expiration date: N.A. Began: April 1, 1964.
Channel capacity: N.A. Channels available but not in use: N.A.

Basic Service
Subscribers: 3,178. Commercial subscribers: 7.
Programming (received off-air): WCIA (CBS, MNT) Champaign; WCIX (CBS, MNT) Springfield; WEEK-TV (ABC, CW, NBC) Peoria; WFLD (FOX) Chicago; WGN-TV (IND) Chicago; WHOI (Comet) Peoria; WILL-TV (PBS) Urbana; WLS-TV (ABC, Live Well Network) Chicago; WMAQ-TV (COZI TV, NBC) Chicago; WMBD-TV (Bounce TV, CBS) Peoria; WTTW (PBS) Chicago; WYZZ-TV (FOX, The Country Network) Bloomington; 22 FMs.
Fee: $45.00 installation; $72.95 monthly.

Expanded Basic Service 1
Subscribers: N.A.
Programming (via satellite): A&E; AMC; Animal Planet; BET; Bravo; Cartoon Network; CMT; CNBC; CNN; Comcast SportsNet Chicago; Comedy Central; C-SPAN; C-SPAN 2; Discovery Channel; Disney Channel; E! HD; ESPN; ESPN2; EVINE Live; EWTN Global Catholic Network; Food Network; Fox News Channel; Fox Sports 1; Freeform; Fuse; FX; Hallmark Channel; HGTV; History; HLN; INSP; Lifetime; MSNBC; MTV; Nickelodeon; Pop; QVC; Spike TV; Syfy; TBS; The Weather Channel; TLC; TNT; Travel Channel; Trinity Broadcasting Network (TBN); truTV; TV Land; Univision Studios; USA Network; VH1; WE tv.
Fee: $34.00 monthly.

Digital Basic Service
Subscribers: N.A.
Programming (via satellite): AXS TV; BBC America; Bloomberg Television; Discovery Digital Networks; DMX Music; ESPN; FXM; FYI; Golf Channel; GSN; HD Theater; History International; IFC; LMN; National Geographic Channel; NBCSN; Nick Jr.; Nicktoons; Outdoor Channel; TeenNick; Turner Classic Movies; Universal HD.

Digital Pay Service 1
Pay Units: N.A.
Programming (via satellite): Cinemax (multiplexed); Flix (multiplexed); HBO (multiplexed); Showtime (multiplexed); Starz (multiplexed); Starz Encore (multiplexed); Starz HD (multiplexed); Sundance TV (multiplexed); The Movie Channel (multiplexed).
Fee: $11.95 monthly (HBO, Cinemax, Starz/Encore or Showtime/TMC).

Video-On-Demand: Yes
Pay-Per-View
Hot Choice; Playboy TV; Fresh; Shorteez.
Internet Service
Operational: Yes.
Broadband Service: Mediacom High Speed Internet.
Fee: $59.95 installation; $45.95 monthly.

Telephone Service
Digital: Operational
Fee: $39.95 monthly
Miles of Plant: 104.0 (coaxial); 7.0 (fiber optic). Homes passed: 9,108.
Vice President: Don Hagwell. Operations Director: Gary Wightman. Technical Operations Manager: Larry Brackman. Marketing Director: Stephanie Law.
Ownership: Mediacom LLC (MSO).

POTOMAC (village)—Park TV & Electronics Inc, 205 East Railroad Ave, PO Box 9, Cissna Park, IL 60924. Phones: 800-825-3882; 815-457-2659. Web Site: http://www.parktvcable.com. ICA: IL0568.
TV Market Ranking: 64 (POTOMAC (VILLAGE)). Franchise award date: N.A. Franchise expiration date: N.A. Began: September 1, 1984.
Channel capacity: N.A. Channels available but not in use: N.A.

Basic Service
Subscribers: 85.
Programming (received off-air): WAND (NBC) Decatur; WBUI (CW, This TV) Decatur; WCCU (FOX, MeTV) Urbana; WCIA (CBS, MNT) Champaign; WICD (ABC) Champaign; WILL-TV (PBS) Urbana.
Programming (via satellite): A&E; AMC; Animal Planet; BTN; Cartoon Network; CMT; CNBC; CNN; Comedy Central; Discovery Channel; Disney Channel; E! HD; ESPN; ESPN2; Food Network; Fox News Channel; Fox Sports 1; Freeform; FX; GSN; Hallmark Channel; HGTV; History; Lifetime; MTV; Nickelodeon; Outdoor Channel; Oxygen; QVC; Spike TV; Syfy; TBS; The Weather Channel; TLC; TNT; Travel Channel; Trinity Broadcasting Network (TBN); Turner Classic Movies; TV Land; USA Network; VH1; WGN America.
Fee: $47.00 monthly.

Pay Service 1
Pay Units: N.A.
Programming (via satellite): Cinemax; HBO; Showtime; The Movie Channel.
Video-On-Demand: No
Internet Service
Operational: Yes.
Fee: $29.95-$54.95 monthly.
Telephone Service
None
Miles of Plant: 9.0 (coaxial); None (fiber optic). Homes passed: 355. Homes passed & miles of plant included in Cissna Park (village)
President & General Manager: Joe Young.
Ownership: Park TV & Electronics Inc. (MSO).

PRAIRIE CITY—Formerly served by CableDirect. No longer in operation. ICA: IL0569.

PRINCETON—Comcast Cable. Now served by MOUNT PROSPECT, IL [IL0036]. ICA: IL0105.

PRINCEVILLE—Mediacom. Now served by CHILLICOTHE, IL [IL0118]. ICA: IL0254.

QUINCY—Comcast Cable. Now served by PEORIA, IL [IL0012]. ICA: IL0039.

RAMSEY—NewWave Communications. Now served by TAYLORVILLE, IL [IL0098]. ICA: IL0316.

RANKIN (village)—Park TV & Electronics Inc, 205 East Railroad Ave, PO Box 9, Cissna Park, IL 60924. Phones: 800-825-3882; 815-457-2659. Web Site: http://www.parktvcable.com. ICA: IL0571.
TV Market Ranking: 64 (RANKIN (VILLAGE)). Franchise award date: N.A. Franchise expiration date: N.A. Began: November 1, 1984.
Channel capacity: N.A. Channels available but not in use: N.A.

Basic Service
Subscribers: 70.
Programming (received off-air): WAND (NBC) Decatur; WBUI (CW, This TV) Decatur; WCCU (FOX, MeTV) Urbana; WCIA (CBS, MNT) Champaign; WICD (ABC) Champaign; WILL-TV (PBS) Urbana.
Programming (via satellite): A&E; AMC; Animal Planet; BTN; Cartoon Network; CMT; CNBC; CNN; Comcast SportsNet Chicago; Comedy Central; Discovery Channel; Disney Channel; E! HD; ESPN; ESPN2; Food Network; Fox News Channel; Fox Sports 1; Freeform; FX; GSN; Hallmark Channel; HGTV; History; Lifetime; MTV; Nickelodeon; Outdoor Channel; Oxygen; QVC; Spike TV; Syfy; TBS; The Weather Channel; TLC; TNT; Travel Channel; Trinity Broadcasting Network (TBN); Turner Classic Movies; TV Land; USA Network; VH1; WGN America.
Fee: $47.00 monthly.

Pay Service 1
Pay Units: N.A.
Programming (via satellite): Cinemax; HBO; Showtime; The Movie Channel.
Video-On-Demand: No

Cable Systems—Illinois

Internet Service
Operational: Yes.
Fee: $29.95-$54.95 monthly.
Telephone Service
None
Miles of plant & homes passed included in Cissna Park (village)
President & General Manager: Joe Young.
Ownership: Park TV & Electronics Inc. (MSO).

RANTOUL—Mediacom, 609 South 4th St, PO Box 334, Chillicothe, IL 61523. Phones: 309-469-2027; 309-274-4500. Fax: 309-274-3188. Web Site: http://www.mediacomcable.com. Also serves Bayles Lake, Champaign County (portions), Clinton, De Land, Farmer City, Fisher, Gifford (village), Lake of the Woods, Loda, Ludlow (village), Mahomet, Mansfield, Melvin, Paxton, Thomasboro, Triangle Mobile Home Park & Weldon. ICA: IL0089.
TV Market Ranking: 64 (Bayles Lake, Champaign County (portions), Clinton, De Land, Farmer City, Fisher, Gifford (village), Lake of the Woods, Loda, Ludlow (village), Mahomet, Mansfield, Melvin, Paxton, RANTOUL, Thomasboro, Triangle Mobile Home Park, Weldon). Franchise award date: N.A. Franchise expiration date: N.A. Began: December 7, 1974.
Channel capacity: N.A. Channels available but not in use: N.A.
Basic Service
Subscribers: 7,468. Commercial subscribers: 19.
Programming (received off-air): WAND (NBC) Decatur; WBUI (CW, This TV) Decatur; WCCU (FOX, MeTV) Urbana; WCIA (CBS, MNT) Champaign; WCIX (CBS, MNT) Springfield; WICD (ABC) Champaign; WILL-TV (PBS) Urbana; 14 FMs.
Programming (via satellite): Freeform; INSP; Radar Channel; WGN America.
Fee: $45.00 installation; $55.00 monthly.
Expanded Basic Service 1
Subscribers: N.A.
Programming (via satellite): A&E; AMC; Animal Planet; BET; Bravo; Cartoon Network; CMT; CNBC; CNN; Comcast SportsNet Chicago; Comedy Central; C-SPAN; C-SPAN 2; Discovery Channel; Discovery Life Channel; Disney Channel; Disney XD; E! HD; ESPN; ESPN2; EVINE Live; EWTN Global Catholic Network; Food Network; Fox News Channel; Fox Sports 1; FX; Hallmark Channel; HGTV; History; HLN; ION Television; Jewelry Television; Lifetime; LMN; MSNBC; MTV; Nickelodeon; QVC; Spike TV; Syfy; TBS; The Weather Channel; TLC; TNT; Travel Channel; Trinity Broadcasting Network (TBN); truTV; TV Land; Univision Studios; USA Network; VH1; WE tv.
Fee: $34.00 monthly.
Digital Basic Service
Subscribers: N.A.
Programming (via satellite): BBC America; Bloomberg Television; Cloo; Discovery Digital Networks; ESPN HD; ESPN2 HD; ESPNews; Fuse; FXM; FYI; Golf Channel; GSN; History; History International; IFC; ION Television; MC; MTV Classic; MTV Hits; MTV2; Nat Geo WILD; National Geographic Channel; NBCSN; Nick Jr.; Nicktoons; Outdoor Channel; Qubo; Reelz; Science Channel; Sundance TV; TeenNick; Turner Classic Movies.
Digital Expanded Basic Service
Subscribers: N.A.
Programming (via satellite): CBS Sports Network; ESPNU; FOX College Sports Central; FOX College Sports Pacific; Fox Sports 2; GolTV; Tennis Channel; TVG Network.
Fee: $3.95 monthly.
Digital Expanded Basic Service 2
Subscribers: N.A.
Programming (via satellite): AXS TV; HD Theater; Universal HD.
Fee: $6.95 monthly.
Digital Pay Service 1
Pay Units: N.A.
Programming (via satellite): Cinemax (multiplexed); Flix; HBO (multiplexed); HBO HD; Showtime (multiplexed); Showtime HD; Starz (multiplexed); Starz Encore (multiplexed); Starz HD; The Movie Channel (multiplexed); The Movie Channel HD.
Fee: $11.95 monthly (HBO, Cinemax, Showtime/TMC or Starz/Encore).
Video-On-Demand: Yes
Pay-Per-View
SexSee (delivered digitally); Juicy (delivered digitally); iN DEMAND (delivered digitally); Playboy TV (delivered digitally); ESPN (delivered digitally); FOX Sports Networks (delivered digitally).
Internet Service
Operational: Yes.
Subscribers: 8,488.
Broadband Service: Mediacom High Speed Internet.
Fee: $59.95 installation; $45.95 monthly.
Telephone Service
Digital: Operational
Subscribers: 4,067.
Fee: $39.95 monthly
Miles of Plant: 493.0 (coaxial); 249.0 (fiber optic). Homes passed: 22,854.
Vice President: Don Hagwell. Operations Director: Gary Wightman. Technical Operations Manager: Larry Brackman. Marketing Director: Stephanie Law.
Ownership: Mediacom LLC (MSO).

RAYMOND—NewWave Communications. Now served by TAYLORVILLE, IL [IL0098]. ICA: IL0291.

REDMON—Formerly served by CableDirect. No longer in operation. ICA: IL0627.

RICHVIEW—Formerly served by CableDirect. No longer in operation. ICA: IL0425.

RIDGE FARM—Formerly served by Insight Communications. Now served by Comcast Cable, CHAMPAIGN, IL [IL0019]. ICA: IL0215.

RIO—Formerly served by Nova Cablevision Inc. No longer in operation. ICA: IL0612.

RIVER OAKS (village)—Mediacom. Now served by KINCAID, IL [IL0176]. ICA: IL0251.

ROANOKE—Mediacom, 609 South 4th St, PO Box 334, Chillicothe, IL 61523. Phones: 309-469-2027; 309-274-4500; 309-923-6061. Fax: 309-274-3188. Web Site: http://www.mediacomcable.com. Also serves Apollo Acres, Bayview Gardens, Benson, Chatsworth, Chenoa, Danvers, Deer Creek, El Paso, Eureka, Fairbury, Far Hills, Forrest, Germantown Hills, Goodfield, Hopedale, Hudson, Lacon, Lamplighter, Lexington, Mackinaw, Mackinaw Trailer Park, Metamora, Minier, Minonk, Secor, Spring Bay, Stanford, Timber Ridge, Toluca, Towanda, Varna, Washburn, Wenona & Woodford County. ICA: IL0068.
TV Market Ranking: 83 (Bayview Gardens, Benson, Chatsworth, Chenoa, Danvers, Deer Creek, El Paso, Eureka, Far Hills, Germantown Hills, Goodfield, Hopedale, Hudson, Lacon, Mackinaw, Mackinaw Trailer Park, Metamora, Minier, Minonk, ROANOKE, Secor, Spring Bay, Stanford, Toluca, Varna, Washburn, Woodford County); Below 100 (Chenoa, Lamplighter, Lexington, Timber Ridge, Towanda, Wenona, Apollo Acres, Fairbury); Outside TV Markets (Chatsworth, Forrest).
Channel capacity: N.A. Channels available but not in use: N.A.
Basic Service
Subscribers: 6,507.
Programming (received off-air): WAOE (Antenna TV, MNT) Peoria; WCIA (CBS, MNT) Champaign; WEEK-TV (ABC, CW, NBC) Peoria; WHOI (Comet) Peoria; WILL-TV (PBS) Urbana; WMBD-TV (Bounce TV, CBS) Peoria; WTVP (PBS) Peoria; WYZZ-TV (FOX, The Country Network) Bloomington.
Programming (via satellite): Freeform; WGN America.
Fee: $45.00 installation; $72.95 monthly.
Expanded Basic Service 1
Subscribers: 6,318.
Programming (via satellite): A&E; AMC; Animal Planet; BET; Bravo; Cartoon Network; CMT; CNBC; CNN; Comcast SportsNet Chicago; Comedy Central; C-SPAN; C-SPAN 2; CW PLUS; Discovery Channel; Discovery Life Channel; Disney Channel; E! HD; ESPN; ESPN2; EVINE Live; EWTN Global Catholic Network; Food Network; Fox News Channel; Fox Sports 1; FX; Hallmark Channel; HGTV; History; HLN; INSP; ION Television; Jewelry Television; Lifetime; LMN; MSNBC; MTV; Nickelodeon; Pop; QVC; Radar Channel; Spike TV; Syfy; TBS; The Weather Channel; TLC; TNT; Travel Channel; truTV; TV Land; Univision Studios; USA Network; VH1; WE tv.
Fee: $34.00 monthly.
Digital Basic Service
Subscribers: N.A.
Programming (via satellite): BBC America; Bloomberg Television; Cloo; Destination America; Discovery Kids Channel; ESPN HD; ESPN2 HD; ESPNews; ESPNU; Fox Sports 2; Fuse; FXM; FYI; Golf Channel; GSN; History International; IFC; Investigation Discovery; ION Television; MTV Classic; MTV Hits; MTV2; Nat Geo WILD; National Geographic Channel; NBCSN; Nick Jr.; Nicktoons; Outdoor Channel; OWN: Oprah Winfrey Network; Qubo; Reelz; Science Channel; Sundance TV; TeenNick; Turner Classic Movies.
Digital Expanded Basic Service
Subscribers: N.A.
Programming (via satellite): AXS TV; CBS Sports Network; ESPNU; FOX College Sports Central; FOX College Sports Pacific; Fox Sports 2; GolTV; HD Theater; Tennis Channel; TVG Network; Universal HD.
Fee: $3.95 monthly (Sports Pak), $6.95 monthly (HD Pac).
Digital Pay Service 1
Pay Units: 2,502.
Programming (via satellite): Cinemax (multiplexed); Cinemax On Demand; Flix; HBO (multiplexed); HBO HD; HBO on Demand; Showtime (multiplexed); Showtime HD; Starz (multiplexed); Starz Encore (multiplexed); Starz HD; Starz On Demand; Sundance TV; The Movie Channel (multiplexed); The Movie Channel HD; The Movie Channel On Demand.
Fee: $11.95 monthly (HBO, Cinemax, Showtime/TMC/Sundance/Flix or Starz/Encore).
Video-On-Demand: Yes
Pay-Per-View
ESPN Now (delivered digitally); Hot Choice (delivered digitally); iN DEMAND; iN DE-MAND (delivered digitally); Playboy TV (delivered digitally); Pleasure (delivered digitally); Fresh (delivered digitally); Shorteez (delivered digitally).
Internet Service
Operational: Yes.
Subscribers: 7,374.
Broadband Service: Mediacom High Speed Internet.
Fee: $59.95 installation; $45.95 monthly.
Telephone Service
Analog: Not Operational
Digital: Operational
Subscribers: 3,705.
Fee: $39.95 monthly
Miles of Plant: 663.0 (coaxial); 494.0 (fiber optic). Homes passed: 23,570.
Vice President: Don Hagwell. Operations Director: Gary Wightman. Technical Operations Manager: Larry Brackman. Chief Technician: Scott Rocke. Marketing Director: Stephanie Law.
Ownership: Mediacom LLC (MSO).

ROBBINS—Comcast Cable. Now served by CHAMPAIGN, IL [IL0019]. ICA: IL0146.

ROBERTS—Park TV & Electronics Inc, 205 East Railroad Ave, PO Box 9, Cissna Park, IL 60924. Phones: 800-825-3882; 815-457-2659. Web Site: http://www.parktvcable.com. ICA: IL0698.
TV Market Ranking: 64 (ROBERTS).
Channel capacity: N.A. Channels available but not in use: N.A.
Basic Service
Subscribers: 54.
Fee: $47.00 monthly.
President & General Manager: Joe Young.
Ownership: Park TV & Electronics Inc. (MSO).

ROBINSON—Mediacom, 4290 Blue Stem Rd, PO Box 288, Charleston, IL 61920. Phone: 217-348-5533. Fax: 217-345-7074. Web Site: http://www.mediacomcable.com. Also serves Crawford County, Hutsonville, Oblong & Palestine. ICA: IL0106.
TV Market Ranking: Below 100 (Crawford County (portions), Hutsonville, Palestine); Outside TV Markets (Crawford County (portions), Oblong, ROBINSON).
Channel capacity: N.A. Channels available but not in use: N.A.
Basic Service
Subscribers: 1,464.
Programming (received off-air): WAND (NBC) Decatur; WBUI (CW, This TV) Decatur; WCCU (FOX, MeTV) Urbana; WCIA (CBS, MNT) Champaign; WCIX (CBS, MNT) Springfield; WEIU-TV (PBS) Charleston; WICD (ABC) Champaign; WILL-TV (PBS) Urbana; WSIU-TV (PBS) Carbondale; WTHI-TV (CBS, FOX) Terre Haute; WTWO (NBC) Terre Haute; 1 FM.
Programming (via satellite): C-SPAN; INSP; Pop; QVC; WGN America.
Fee: $45.00 installation; $43.00 monthly.
Expanded Basic Service 1
Subscribers: N.A.
Programming (via satellite): A&E; AMC; Animal Planet; BET; Cartoon Network; CMT; CNBC; CNN; Comcast SportsNet Chicago; Comedy Central; C-SPAN 2; Discovery Channel; Discovery Life Channel; Disney Channel; E! HD; ESPN; ESPN Classic; ESPN2; EVINE Live; EWTN Global Catholic Network; Food Network; Fox News Channel; Fox Sports 1; FOX Sports Midwest; Freeform; FX; Hallmark Channel; HGTV; History; HLN; ION Television; Jewelry Television; Lifetime; LMN; MSNBC; MTV; Nickelodeon; Outdoor Channel; Oxy-

2017 Edition   D-215

Illinois—Cable Systems

gen; Spike TV; Syfy; TBS; The Weather Channel; TLC; TNT; Travel Channel; Trinity Broadcasting Network (TBN); truTV; TV Land; USA Network; VH1; WE tv.
Fee: $34.00 monthly.
Digital Basic Service
Subscribers: N.A.
Programming (via satellite): AXS TV; BBC America; Bloomberg Television; Bravo; CBS Sports Network; CCTV-Documentary; Cloo; CMT; Destination America; Discovery Kids Channel; Disney XD; ESPNews; ESPNU; FOX College Sports Central; FOX College Sports Pacific; Fox Sports 2; Fuse; FXM; FYI; Golf Channel; GolTV; GSN; HD Theater; History International; IFC; Investigation Discovery; ION Television; MC; MTV Classic; MTV Hits; MTV2; Nat Geo WILD; National Geographic Channel; NBCSN; Nick Jr.; Nicktoons; OWN: Oprah Winfrey Network; Qubo; Reelz; Science Channel; TeenNick; Tennis Channel; Turner Classic Movies; TVG Network; Universal HD.
Digital Pay Service 1
Pay Units: N.A.
Programming (via satellite): Cinemax (multiplexed); Cinemax On Demand; HBO (multiplexed); HBO HD; HBO on Demand; Showtime (multiplexed); Showtime HD; Showtime On Demand; Starz (multiplexed); Starz Encore (multiplexed); Starz HD; Starz On Demand; The Movie Channel (multiplexed); The Movie Channel HD; The Movie Channel On Demand.
Fee: $11.95 monthly (HBO, Cinemax, Showtime/TMC or Starz/Encore).
Video-On-Demand: Yes
Pay-Per-View
iN DEMAND (delivered digitally); Playboy TV; SexSee (delivered digitally); Juicy (delivered digitally); ESPN (delivered digitally).
Internet Service
Operational: Yes.
Broadband Service: Mediacom High Speed Internet.
Fee: $59.95 installation; $40.95 monthly.
Telephone Service
Digital: Operational
Fee: $39.95 monthly
Miles of Plant: 88.0 (coaxial); 9.0 (fiber optic). Homes passed: 5,691.
General Manager: Todd Acker. Technical Operations Manager: Jerry Ferguson. Marketing Director: James Friske.
Ownership: Mediacom LLC (MSO).

ROCK ISLAND—Mediacom. Now served by MOLINE, IL [IL0011]. ICA: IL0042.

ROCKFORD—Comcast Cable. Now served by MOUNT PROSPECT, IL [IL0036]. ICA: IL0010.

ROCKFORD—Formerly served by Wireless Cable Systems Inc. No longer in operation. ICA: IL0617.

ROLLING MEADOWS—Comcast Cable. Now served by MOUNT PROSPECT, IL [IL0036]. ICA: IL0013.

ROMEOVILLE—Comcast Cable. Now served by PEORIA, IL [IL0012]. ICA: IL0009.

ROSAMOND—Formerly served by Beck's Cable Systems. No longer in operation. ICA: IL0681.

ROSICLARE—Zito Media, 102 S Main St, PO Box 665, Coudersport, PA 16915. Phones: 814-260-9055; 800-365-6988. E-mail: info@zitomedia.com. Web Site: http://www.zitomedia.com. Also serves Elizabethtown & Hardin County. ICA: IL0216.
TV Market Ranking: 69 (Elizabethtown, Hardin County, ROSICLARE). Franchise award date: N.A. Franchise expiration date: N.A. Began: October 1, 1982.
Channel capacity: N.A. Channels available but not in use: N.A.
Basic Service
Subscribers: 97.
Programming (received off-air): KBSI (FOX) Cape Girardeau; KFVS-TV (CBS, CW, MeTV) Cape Girardeau; WDKA (MNT, The Country Network) Paducah; WKPD (PBS) Paducah; WPSD-TV (Antenna TV, NBC) Paducah; WSIL-TV (ABC) Harrisburg; WTCT (IND) Marion.
Programming (via satellite): A&E; AMC; Animal Planet; Cartoon Network; CNBC; CNN; Comedy Central; C-SPAN; Discovery Channel; Disney Channel; E! HD; ESPN; ESPN2; Fox News Channel; Freeform; Fuse; FX; Great American Country; HGTV; History; HLN; Lifetime; Outdoor Channel; TBS; The Weather Channel; TLC; TNT; Travel Channel; Trinity Broadcasting Network (TBN); USA Network; WGN America.
Fee: $49.95 installation; $48.40 monthly; $3.00 converter.
Pay Service 1
Pay Units: N.A.
Programming (via satellite): Cinemax; HBO; Showtime.
Fee: $12.00 monthly (each).
Internet Service
Operational: No.
Telephone Service
None
Miles of Plant: 16.0 (coaxial); None (fiber optic). Homes passed: 834.
President: James Rigas.
Ownership: Zito Media (MSO).

ROXANA—Charter Communications. Now served by ST. LOUIS, MO [MO0009]. ICA: IL0025.

ROYAL—Formerly served by CableDirect. No longer in operation. ICA: IL0640.

RUSHVILLE—Cass Cable TV Inc. Now served by BEARDSTOWN, IL [IL0598]. ICA: IL0191.

SADORUS—Formerly served by Longview Communications. No longer in operation. ICA: IL0575.

SALEM—Charter Communications. Now served by ST. LOUIS, MO [MO0009]. ICA: IL0121.

SALINE COUNTY (portions)—Zito Media, 102 S Main St, PO Box 665, Coudersport, PA 16915. Phones: 814-260-9055; 800-365-6988. E-mail: info@zitomedia.com. Web Site: http://www.zitomedia.com. Also serves Galatia & Raleigh. ICA: IL0501.
TV Market Ranking: 69 (Raleigh, SALINE COUNTY (PORTIONS). Franchise award date: N.A. Franchise expiration date: N.A. Began: November 1, 1986.
Channel capacity: N.A. Channels available but not in use: N.A.
Basic Service
Subscribers: N.A.
Programming (received off-air): KBSI (FOX) Cape Girardeau; KFVS-TV (CBS, CW, MeTV) Cape Girardeau; WDKA (MNT, The Country Network) Paducah; WPSD-TV (Antenna TV, NBC) Paducah; WSIL-TV (ABC) Harrisburg; WSIU-TV (PBS) Carbondale; WTCT (IND) Marion.
Programming (via satellite): A&E; Animal Planet; Cartoon Network; CNN; Comedy Central; Discovery Channel; Disney Channel; E! HD; ESPN; ESPN2; Fox News Channel; Freeform; Fuse; FX; Great American Country; HGTV; History; HLN; Lifetime; Outdoor Channel; TBS; The Weather Channel; TLC; TNT; Turner Classic Movies; USA Network; WGN America.
Fee: $49.95 installation; $49.85 monthly.
Pay Service 1
Pay Units: N.A.
Programming (via satellite): Cinemax; HBO.
Internet Service
Operational: Yes.
Telephone Service
Digital: Operational
Miles of Plant: 22.0 (coaxial); None (fiber optic). Homes passed: 934.
President: James Rigas.
Ownership: Zito Media (MSO).

SAYBROOK—Mediacom. Now served by LE ROY, IL [IL0539]. ICA: IL0283.

SCALES MOUND—Mediacom. Now served by MOUNT CARROLL, IL [IL0223]. ICA: IL0688.

SCOTT AFB—Charter Communications. Now served by ST. LOUIS, MO [MO0009]. ICA: IL0057.

SEATONVILLE (village)—Formerly served by CableDirect. No longer in operation. ICA: IL0576.

SENECA—Kraus Electronics Systems Inc, 305 State St, PO Box 11, Manhattan, IL 60442. Phones: 815-478-4000; 815-478-4444. Fax: 815-478-3386. Web Site: http://www.krausonline.com. ICA: IL0238.
TV Market Ranking: Below 100 (SENECA). Franchise award date: N.A. Franchise expiration date: N.A. Began: March 1, 1972.
Channel capacity: N.A. Channels available but not in use: N.A.
Basic Service
Subscribers: 428.
Programming (received off-air): WBBM-TV (CBS, Decades) Chicago; WCIU-TV (MeTV) Chicago; WCPX-TV (ION) Chicago; WFLD (FOX) Chicago; WGBO-DT (getTV, UNV) Joliet; WGN-TV (IND) Chicago; WJYS (IND) Hammond; WLS-TV (ABC, Live Well Network) Chicago; WMAQ-TV (COZI TV, NBC) Chicago; WPWR-TV (Buzzr, CW, MNT, Movies!) Gary; WSNS-TV (TMO) Chicago; WTTW (PBS) Chicago; WWTO-TV (TBN) La Salle; WXFT-DT (UniMas) Aurora; WYCC (PBS) Chicago; WYIN (PBS) Gary; allband FM.
Programming (via satellite): HLN; QVC.
Fee: $35.00 installation; $23.00 monthly.
Expanded Basic Service 1
Subscribers: N.A.
Programming (via satellite): A&E; AMC; Animal Planet; Cartoon Network; CMT; CNBC; CNN; Comcast SportsNet Chicago; Comedy Central; C-SPAN; C-SPAN 2; Discovery Channel; Disney Channel; ESPN; ESPN Classic; ESPN2; EWTN Global Catholic Network; Food Network; Fox News Channel; Freeform; FX; GSN; Hallmark Channel; HGTV; History; Lifetime; MTV; National Geographic Channel; Nickelodeon; Spike TV; Syfy; TBS; The Weather Channel; TLC; TNT; truTV; TV Land; USA Network; VH1.
Digital Basic Service
Subscribers: N.A.
Programming (via satellite): BBC America; Bloomberg Television; Bravo; Destination America; Discovery Kids Channel; Discovery Life Channel; Disney XD; DMX Music; ESPNews; Fox Sports 1; FSN Digital Atlantic; FSN Digital Central; FSN Digital Pacific; Fuse; FXM; FYI; Golf Channel; Great American Country; History; History International; IFC; Investigation Discovery; LMN; MTV Classic; MTV Hits; MTV2; Nick Jr.; Nicktoons; Outdoor Channel; TeenNick; Turner Classic Movies; VH1 Country; WE tv.
Pay Service 1
Pay Units: N.A.
Programming (via satellite): Cinemax; HBO.
Fee: $10.00 monthly (Cinemax), $13.95 monthly (HBO).
Digital Pay Service 1
Pay Units: N.A.
Programming (via satellite): Cinemax (multiplexed); HBO (multiplexed); Showtime (multiplexed); Starz (multiplexed); Starz Encore (multiplexed); The Movie Channel (multiplexed).
Video-On-Demand: No
Pay-Per-View
Playboy TV (delivered digitally); Fresh (delivered digitally); Shorteez (delivered digitally).
Internet Service
Operational: Yes.
Broadband Service: In-house.
Fee: $9.95 monthly.
Telephone Service
Digital: Operational
Fee: $26.95-$34.95 monthly
Miles of Plant: 12.0 (coaxial); None (fiber optic).
Vice President: Arthur Kraus. General Manager: Mike Bordeaux. Chief Technician: Skip Kraus.
Ownership: Arthur J. Kraus (MSO).

SESSER—NewWave Communications. Now served by McLEANSBORO, IL [IL0177]. ICA: IL0189.

SHAWNEETOWN—Time Warner Cable. Now served by OWENSBORO, KY [KY0004]. ICA: IL0198.

SHELBYVILLE—NewWave Communications. Now served by TAYLORVILLE, IL [IL0098]. ICA: IL0162.

SHERIDAN (village)—Mediacom. Now served by STREATOR, IL [IL0069]. ICA: IL0577.

SHIPMAN—Formerly served by Mediacom. Now served by Madison Communications, STAUNTON, IL [IL0171]. ICA: IL0384.

SHUMWAY—Clearvision Cable Systems Inc, 1785 US Rte 40, Greenup, IL 62428-3501. Phone: 217-923-5594. Fax: 217-923-5681. ICA: IL0701.
TV Market Ranking: Outside TV Markets (SHUMWAY).
Channel capacity: N.A. Channels available but not in use: N.A.
Basic Service
Subscribers: 11.
Fee: $47.95 monthly.
Secretary: Gwyndolyn S. Bauguss.
Ownership: Clearvision Cable Systems Inc. (MSO).

Cable Systems—Illinois

SIBLEY (village)—Heartland Cable Inc, 167 West 5th St, PO Box 7, Minonk, IL 61760. Phones: 800-448-4320; 309-432-2075. Web Site: http://www.hcable.net. Also serves Elliott & Ellsworth. ICA: IL0409.
TV Market Ranking: 64 (Elliott, Ellsworth, SIBLEY (VILLAGE)). Franchise award date: June 1, 1987. Franchise expiration date: N.A. Began: January 1, 1988.
Channel capacity: N.A. Channels available but not in use: N.A.
Basic Service
Subscribers: N.A.
Programming (received off-air): WAND (NBC) Decatur; WCIA (CBS, MNT) Champaign; WICD (ABC) Champaign; WILL-TV (PBS) Urbana; WYZZ-TV (FOX, The Country Network) Bloomington.
Programming (via satellite): CNN; Discovery Channel; Disney Channel; ESPN; Freeform; Spike TV; TBS; TNT; USA Network; WGN America.
Fee: $39.00 installation.
Pay Service 1
Pay Units: N.A.
Programming (via satellite): HBO; Showtime.
Fee: $8.95 - $10.95 monthly (each).
Video-On-Demand: Yes
Pay-Per-View
Movies; special events.
Internet Service
Operational: Yes.
Fee: $39.00 installation; $29.99 monthly.
Telephone Service
None
Miles of Plant: 3.0 (coaxial); None (fiber optic).
Chief Executive Officer: Jim Frances. President & General Manager: Steve Allen.
Ownership: Heartland Cable Inc. (MSO).

SIDELL (village)—Clearvision Cable Systems Inc, 1785 US Rte 40, Greenup, IL 62428-3501. Phone: 217-923-5594. Fax: 217-923-5681. ICA: IL0578.
TV Market Ranking: 64 (SIDELL (VILLAGE)). Franchise award date: N.A. Franchise expiration date: N.A. Began: October 1, 1984.
Channel capacity: 36 (not 2-way capable). Channels available but not in use: N.A.
Basic Service
Subscribers: 22.
Programming (received off-air): WAND (NBC) Decatur; WBUI (CW, This TV) Decatur; WCCU (FOX, MeTV) Urbana; WCIA (CBS, MNT) Champaign; WCIX (CBS, MNT) Springfield; WEIU-TV (PBS) Charleston; WICD (ABC) Champaign; WILL-TV (PBS) Urbana.
Programming (via satellite): A&E; AMC; Bravo; Cartoon Network; CNBC; CNN; Comedy Central; C-SPAN; Discovery Channel; Disney Channel; ESPN; ESPN2; Fox News Channel; Freeform; Great American Country; Hallmark Channel; HGTV; History; HLN; Lifetime; MSNBC; MTV; Nickelodeon; QVC; Spike TV; Syfy; TBS; The Weather Channel; TLC; TNT; Trinity Broadcasting Network (TBN); Turner Classic Movies; TV Land; USA Network; VH1; WGN America.
Fee: $47.95 monthly.
Pay Service 1
Pay Units: N.A.
Programming (via satellite): Showtime; The Movie Channel.
Fee: $12.95 monthly (each).
Video-On-Demand: No
Internet Service
Operational: No.

Telephone Service
None
Miles of Plant: 4.0 (coaxial); None (fiber optic). Homes passed: 267.
President & General Manager: Michael Bauguss. Secretary: Gwyndolyn S. Bauguss.
Ownership: Clearvision Cable Systems Inc. (MSO).

SIMS—Formerly served by CableDirect. No longer in operation. ICA: IL0420.

SKOKIE—Comcast Cable. Now served by MOUNT PROSPECT, IL [IL0036]. ICA: IL0040.

SKOKIE—Formerly served by RCN Corp. No longer in operation. ICA: IL0665.

SMITHFIELD—Formerly served by CableDirect. No longer in operation. ICA: IL0427.

SOUTH HOLLAND—Comcast Cable. Now served by CHAMPAIGN, IL [IL0019]. ICA: IL0077.

SOUTH WILMINGTON (village)—Mediacom. Now served by PONTIAC, IL [IL0109]. ICA: IL0579.

SPARTA—NewWave Communications, One Montgomery Plaza, 4th Floor, Sikeston, MO 63801. Phone: 888-863-9928. Fax: 573-481-9809. E-mail: info@newwavecom.com. Web Site: http://www.newwavecom.com. Also serves Chester, Lenzburg, Marissa, New Athens, Percy, Randolph County (portions), St. Clair County (portions) & Steeleville. ICA: IL0147.
TV Market Ranking: 11 (Lenzburg, New Athens, St. Clair County (portions) (portions)); Outside TV Markets (Chester, Marissa, Percy, Randolph County (portions), SPARTA, Steeleville, St. Clair County (portions) (portions)). Franchise award date: N.A. Franchise expiration date: N.A. Began: October 1, 1981.
Channel capacity: N.A. Channels available but not in use: N.A.
Basic Service
Subscribers: 2,040. Commercial subscribers: 376.
Programming (received off-air): KBSI (FOX) Cape Girardeau; KDNL-TV (ABC, The Country Network) St. Louis; KETC (PBS) St. Louis; KFVS-TV (CBS, CW, MeTV) Cape Girardeau; KMOV (CBS) St. Louis; KNLC (IND, My Family TV) St. Louis; KPLR-TV (CW, This TV) St. Louis; KSDK (Bounce TV, NBC) St. Louis; KTVI (Antenna TV, Escape, FOX) St. Louis; WPXS (IND) Mount Vernon; WRBU (ION) East St. Louis.
Programming (via satellite): C-SPAN; C-SPAN 2; EWTN Global Catholic Network; Hallmark Channel; Jewelry Television; QVC; TBS; The Weather Channel; Trinity Broadcasting Network (TBN); WGN America.
Fee: $40.00 installation; $34.78 monthly.
Expanded Basic Service 1
Subscribers: N.A.
Programming (via satellite): A&E; AMC; Animal Planet; BET; Bravo; BTN; Cartoon Network; CMT; CNBC; CNN; Comedy Central; Discovery Channel; Disney Channel; Disney XD; E! HD; ESPN; ESPN2; Food Network; Fox News Channel; Fox Sports 1; FOX Sports Midwest; Freeform; FX; Golf Channel; Great American Country; GSN; HGTV; History; HLN; Lifetime; MSNBC; MTV; MTV2; National Geographic Channel;

NBCSN; Nickelodeon; Outdoor Channel; Spike TV; Syfy; TLC; TNT; Travel Channel; truTV; TV Land; USA Network; VH1; WE tv.
Digital Basic Service
Subscribers: 606.
Programming (via satellite): AXS TV; BBC America; CMT; Destination America; Discovery Kids Channel; Discovery Life Channel; DIY Network; ESPN HD; ESPN2 HD; FOX College Sports Central; FOX College Sports Pacific; FSN HD; FXM; FYI; HD Theater; History International; Investigation Discovery; LMN; MC; MTV Classic; MTV Hits; MTV Jams; Nick 2; Nick Jr.; Nicktoons; OWN: Oprah Winfrey Network; Science Channel; TeenNick; TNT HD; Tr3s; Universal HD; VH1 Soul.
Fee: $10.00 monthly.
Digital Pay Service 1
Pay Units: 1,731.
Programming (via satellite): Cinemax (multiplexed); Cinemax HD; HBO (multiplexed); HBO HD; Showtime (multiplexed); Starz (multiplexed); Starz Encore (multiplexed); Starz HD; The Movie Channel (multiplexed).
Fee: $10.95 monthly (Cinemax, Showtime or TMC), $11.95 monthly (HBO).
Video-On-Demand: No
Pay-Per-View
iN DEMAND (delivered digitally); Playboy TV (delivered digitally); Fresh (delivered digitally); Shorteez (delivered digitally); Spice: Xcess (delivered digitally); Club Jenna (delivered digitally).
Internet Service
Operational: Yes.
Subscribers: 1,417.
Fee: $40.00 installation; $31.99 monthly.
Telephone Service
Digital: Operational
Subscribers: 778.
Fee: $34.99 monthly
Miles of Plant: 150.0 (coaxial); None (fiber optic). Homes passed: 9,019.
Chief Financial Officer: Rod Siemers. General Manager: John Helmers.
Ownership: NewWave Communications LLC (MSO).

SPRING GROVE (village)—Mediacom. Now served by BELVIDERE TWP, IL [IL0282]. ICA: IL0574.

SPRINGFIELD—Comcast Cable, 701 South Dirksen Pkwy, PO Box 3066, Springfield, IL 62703. Phones: 217-788-5659; 217-788-5898. Fax: 217-788-8093. Web Site: http://www.comcast.com. Also serves Ball Twp., Bissel, Chatham, Curran, Danforth, Decatur, Divernon, Forsyth (village), Gardner Twp., Gilman, Glenarm, Grandview, Harristown (village), Illiopolis (village), Jerome, Leland Grove, Lincoln, Logan County (portions), Long Creek (village), Macon County (portions), Mount Pulaski, Mount Zion (village), Niantic (village), Onarga, Pawnee, Rochester, Rochester Twp., Sangamon County (portions), Southern View, Spaulding, Springfield Twp. & Woodside Twp. ICA: IL0016.
TV Market Ranking: 64 (Ball Twp., Bissel, Chatham, Curran, Decatur, Divernon, Forsyth (village), Gardner Twp., Glenarm,

Grandview, Harristown (village), Illiopolis (village), Jerome, Leland Grove, Lincoln, Logan County (portions), Long Creek (village), Macon County (portions), Mount Pulaski, Mount Zion (village), Niantic (village), Pawnee, Rochester, Rochester Twp., Sangamon County (portions), Southern View, Spaulding, SPRINGFIELD, Springfield Twp., Woodside Twp.); Outside TV Markets (Danforth, Gilman, Onarga). Franchise award date: October 20, 2003. Franchise expiration date: N.A. Began: February 1, 1967.
Channel capacity: N.A. Channels available but not in use: N.A.
Basic Service
Subscribers: 61,979. Commercial subscribers: 3,783.
Programming (received off-air): WAND (NBC) Decatur; WBUI (CW, This TV) Decatur; WCIA (CBS, MNT) Champaign; WCIX (CBS, MNT) Springfield; WICS (ABC, The Country Network) Springfield; WILL-TV (PBS) Urbana; WRSP-TV (Antenna TV, FOX, MeTV) Springfield; WSEC (PBS) Jacksonville; 22 FMs.
Programming (via satellite): C-SPAN; C-SPAN 2; EVINE Live; EWTN Global Catholic Network; ION Television; Pop; QVC; WGN America.
Fee: $29.00-$42.00 installation; $28.24 monthly; $1.75 converter.
Expanded Basic Service 1
Subscribers: N.A.
Programming (via satellite): A&E; AMC; Animal Planet; BET; Bravo; Cartoon Network; CMT; CNBC; CNN; Comcast SportsNet Chicago; Comedy Central; Discovery Channel; Disney Channel; Disney XD; E! HD; ESPN; ESPN2; Food Network; Fox News Channel; Fox Sports 1; FOX Sports Midwest; Freeform; FX; Golf Channel; Hallmark Channel; HGTV; History; HLN; Lifetime; MSNBC; MTV; MTV2; National Geographic Channel; Nickelodeon; Oxygen; Spike TV; Syfy; TBS; The Weather Channel; TLC; TNT; Travel Channel; truTV; TV Land; USA Network; VH1.
Fee: $37.87 monthly.
Digital Basic Service
Subscribers: N.A.
Programming (via satellite): AXS TV; BBC America; Bloomberg Television; CBS Sports Network; Cloo; CMT; Cooking Channel; C-SPAN 3; Discovery Digital Networks; Disney XD; DIY Network; DMX Music; ESPN Classic; ESPN HD; ESPN2 HD; ESPNews; ESPNU; FOX College Sports Central; FOX College Sports Pacific; Fuse; FXM; FYI; Great American Country; GSN; HD Theater; History International; HRTV; IFC; LMN; MTV Live; NBCSN; NFL Network; Nick 2; Nick Jr.; Nicktoons; Outdoor Channel; Ovation; Sprout; Starz Encore (multiplexed); Sundance TV; TeenNick; Tennis Channel; TNT HD; Trinity Broadcasting Network (TBN); Turner Classic Movies; TVG Network; Universal HD; WE tv.
Digital Pay Service 1
Pay Units: N.A.
Programming (via satellite): Cinemax (multiplexed); Flix; HBO (multiplexed); Show-

Illinois—Cable Systems

time (multiplexed); Starz (multiplexed); The Movie Channel (multiplexed).
Fee: $10.00 monthly (Cinemax or Starz), $13.00 monthly (HBO or Showtime/TMC).
Video-On-Demand: Yes
Pay-Per-View
ESPN (delivered digitally); iN DEMAND (delivered digitally); Playboy TV (delivered digitally); Special events (delivered digitally).
Internet Service
Operational: Yes.
Subscribers: 59,944.
Broadband Service: Comcast High Speed Internet.
Fee: $99.95 installation; $44.95 monthly; $10.00 modem lease; $39.99 modem purchase.
Telephone Service
Digital: Operational
Subscribers: 25,023.
Miles of Plant: 2,633.0 (coaxial); 845.0 (fiber optic). Homes passed: 199,287.
Chief Technician: Terry Blackwell. Community & Government Affairs Director: Libbie Stehn. Customer Service Manager: Holt Lisa.
Ownership: Comcast Cable Communications Inc. (MSO).

ST. DAVID—Mediacom. Now served by ELMWOOD, IL [IL0205]. ICA: IL0301.

ST. FRANCISVILLE—NewWave Communications. Now served by VINCENNES, IN [IN0035]. ICA: IL0317.

ST. JACOB—HomeTel Cable TV, 501 North Douglas St, PO Box 215, St. Jacob, IL 62281. Phone: 618-644-2111. E-mail: admin@hometel.com. Web Site: http://www.hometel.com. ICA: IL0703.
TV Market Ranking: 11 (ST. JACOB, ST. JACOB).
Channel capacity: N.A. Channels available but not in use: N.A.
Basic Service
Subscribers: 139.
Fee: $15.95 monthly.
Expanded Basic Service 1
Subscribers: N.A.
Fee: $38.00 monthly.
Digital Basic Service
Subscribers: N.A.
Secretary: Rachel Stopka.
Ownership: HomeTel Entertainment Inc.

ST. LIBORY—Formerly served by CableDirect. No longer in operation. ICA: IL0641.

ST. PETER—Clearvision Cable Systems Inc, 1785 US Rte 40, Greenup, IL 62428-3501. Phone: 217-923-5594. Fax: 217-923-5681. ICA: IL0667.
TV Market Ranking: Outside TV Markets (ST. PETER).
Channel capacity: 42 (not 2-way capable). Channels available but not in use: N.A.
Basic Service
Subscribers: 23.
Programming (received off-air): KMOV (CBS) St. Louis; WAND (NBC) Decatur; WICS (ABC, The Country Network) Springfield; WPXS (IND) Mount Vernon; WRSP-TV (Antenna TV, FOX, MeTV) Springfield; WUSI-TV (PBS) Olney.
Programming (via satellite): A&E; AMC; CMT; CNBC; CNN; Discovery Channel; Disney Channel; ESPN; Freeform; History; HLN; Nickelodeon; QVC; Spike TV; TBS;

The Weather Channel; TNT; USA Network; WGN America.
Fee: $47.95 monthly.
Pay Service 1
Pay Units: N.A.
Programming (via satellite): Showtime; The Movie Channel.
Fee: $9.45 monthly.
Video-On-Demand: No
Internet Service
Operational: No.
Telephone Service
None
Miles of Plant: 3.0 (coaxial); None (fiber optic). Homes passed: 152.
President & General Manager: Michael Bauguss. Secretary: Gwyndolyn S. Bauguss.
Ownership: Clearvision Cable Systems Inc. (MSO).

STAUNTON—Madison Communications, 21668 Double Arch Rd, PO Box 29, Staunton, IL 62088. Phones: 800-422-4848; 618-633-2267 (Business office); 618-635-5456. Fax: 618-633-2713. E-mail: infomtc@madisontelco.com. Web Site: http://www.gomadison.com. Also serves Alhambra, Benld, Bunker Hill, Hamel, Holiday Shores, Livingston, Mount Clare, Mount Olive, New Douglas, Sawyerville, Shipman, Williamson, Wilsonville & Worden. ICA: IL0171.
TV Market Ranking: 11 (Alhambra, Bunker Hill, Hamel, Holiday Shores, Livingston, Worden); Outside TV Markets (Benld, Mount Clare, Mount Olive, Sawyerville, STAUNTON, Williamson, New Douglas, Shipman, Wilsonville). Franchise award date: N.A. Franchise expiration date: N.A. Began: June 1, 1981.
Channel capacity: N.A. Channels available but not in use: N.A.
Basic Service
Subscribers: 733. Commercial subscribers: 22.
Programming (received off-air): KDNL-TV (ABC, The Country Network) St. Louis; KETC (PBS) St. Louis; KMOV (CBS) St. Louis; KNLC (IND, My Family TV) St. Louis; KPLR-TV (CW, This TV) St. Louis; KSDK (Bounce TV, NBC) St. Louis; KTVI (Antenna TV, Escape, FOX) St. Louis; WPXS (IND) Mount Vernon; WRBU (ION) East St. Louis.
Programming (via satellite): Classic Arts Showcase; C-SPAN; C-SPAN 2; C-SPAN 3; ESPN Classic; EVINE Live; EWTN Global Catholic Network; INSP; Jewelry Television; QVC; Trinity Broadcasting Network (TBN); WGN America.
Fee: $49.99 installation; $35.47 monthly.
Expanded Basic Service 1
Subscribers: N.A.
Programming (via satellite): A&E; AMC; Animal Planet; Boomerang; Bravo; Cartoon Network; CMT; CNBC; CNN; Comedy Central; Cooking Channel; Discovery Channel; Disney Channel; DIY Network; E! HD; ESPN; ESPN2; FamilyNet; Food Network; Fox News Channel; Fox Sports 1; FOX Sports Midwest; Freeform; FX; Great American Country; Hallmark Channel; HGTV; History; HLN; Lifetime; MSNBC; MTV; National Geographic Channel; Nickelodeon; Oxygen; Spike TV; Syfy; TBS; The Weather Channel; TLC; TNT; Travel Channel; truTV; TV Land; USA Network; VH1.
Fee: $26.45 monthly.
Digital Basic Service
Subscribers: N.A.
Programming (via satellite): AXS TV; BBC America; Bloomberg Television; Bravo; Discovery Digital Networks; DMX Music; ESPN; ESPN Classic; ESPNews; FOX Col-

lege Sports Central; FOX College Sports Pacific; Fox Sports 1; Fuse; FXM; FYI; Golf Channel; GSN; HD Theater; History International; IFC; International Television (ITV); LMN; National Geographic Channel; NBCSN; Nick Jr.; Nicktoons; Outdoor Channel; Ovation; TeenNick; Trinity Broadcasting Network (TBN); Turner Classic Movies; WE tv.
Digital Pay Service 1
Pay Units: N.A.
Programming (via satellite): Cinemax (multiplexed); Cinemax HD; Flix; HBO (multiplexed); HBO HD; Showtime (multiplexed); Showtime HD; Starz (multiplexed); Starz Encore (multiplexed); Starz HD; Sundance TV; The Movie Channel (multiplexed).
Fee: $12.95 monthly (HBO), $10.95 monthly (Cinemax, Showtime, Encore, or TMC).
Video-On-Demand: No
Internet Service
Operational: Yes, DSL & dial-up. Began: June 1, 2002.
Broadband Service: In-house.
Fee: $75.00 installation; $39.95 monthly.
Telephone Service
Digital: Operational
Miles of Plant: 100.0 (coaxial); None (fiber optic).
President: Robert Schwartz. General Manager: Mary Schwartz. Chief Technician: Dave Black. Marketing Manager: Linda Prante.
Ownership: Madison Communications Co. (MSO).

STE. MARIE TWP.—Formerly served by Advanced Technologies & Technical Resources Inc. No longer in operation. ICA: IL0583.

STERLING—Comcast Cable. Now served by MOUNT PROSPECT, IL [IL0036]. ICA: IL0051.

STOCKTON—Mediacom. Now served by LENA, IL [IL0223]. ICA: IL0247.

STRASBURG—Mediacom. Now served by NEOGA, IL [IL0249]. ICA: IL0585.

STREAMWOOD—Comcast Cable. Now served by MOUNT PROSPECT, IL [IL0036]. ICA: IL0061.

STREATOR—Mediacom, 3900 26th Ave, Moline, IL 61265. Phones: 309-797-2580; 815-672-5071 (Streator office). Fax: 309-797-2414. Web Site: http://www.mediacomcable.com. Also serves Bruce Twp., Dayton Twp., Eagle Twp., Kangley, La Salle Twp., Marseilles, Naplate, Ottawa, Otter Creek Twp., Reading Twp., Sheridan & South Ottawa Twp. ICA: IL0069.
TV Market Ranking: Below 100 (Bruce Twp., Dayton Twp., Eagle Twp., Kangley, La Salle Twp., Marseilles, Naplate, Ottawa, Otter Creek Twp., Reading Twp., Sheridan, South Ottawa Twp., STREATOR). Franchise award date: February 1, 1963. Franchise expiration date: N.A. Began: February 1, 1963.
Channel capacity: N.A. Channels available but not in use: N.A.
Basic Service
Subscribers: 3,240. Commercial subscribers: 7.
Programming (received off-air): WBBM-TV (CBS, Decades) Chicago; WCIU-TV (MeTV) Chicago; WCPX-TV (ION) Chicago; WEEK-TV (ABC, CW, NBC) Peoria; WFLD (FOX) Chicago; WGN (IND) Chicago;

WHOI (Comet) Peoria; WLS-TV (ABC, Live Well Network) Chicago; WMAQ-TV (COZI TV, NBC) Chicago; WMBD-TV (Bounce TV, CBS) Peoria; WTTW (PBS) Chicago; WWTO-TV (TBN) La Salle; WYZZ-TV (FOX, The Country Network) Bloomington; 21 FMs.
Programming (via satellite): C-SPAN; Freeform; Pop; QVC; TBS.
Fee: $45.00 installation; $43.00 monthly.
Expanded Basic Service 1
Subscribers: N.A.
Programming (via satellite): A&E; AMC; Animal Planet; Bravo; Cartoon Network; CMT; CNBC; CNN; Comcast SportsNet Chicago; Comedy Central; C-SPAN 2; Discovery Channel; Disney Channel; E! HD; ESPN; ESPN2; EVINE Live; EWTN Global Catholic Network; Food Network; Fox News Channel; Fox Sports 1; FX; HGTV; History; HLN; Lifetime; MSNBC; MTV; Nickelodeon; Spike TV; Syfy; The Weather Channel; TLC; TNT; Travel Channel; Trinity Broadcasting Network (TBN); truTV; TV Land; USA Network; VH1.
Fee: $34.00 monthly.
Digital Basic Service
Subscribers: N.A.
Programming (via satellite): BBC America; Discovery Digital Networks; DMX Music; Golf Channel; GSN; IFC; Turner Classic Movies.
Digital Pay Service 1
Pay Units: N.A.
Programming (via satellite): Cinemax (multiplexed); HBO (multiplexed); Showtime (multiplexed); Starz (multiplexed); Starz Encore (multiplexed); The Movie Channel (multiplexed).
Fee: $11.95 monthly (HBO, Cinemax, Starz/Encore or Showtime/TMC).
Video-On-Demand: Yes
Pay-Per-View
ESPN Now (delivered digitally); Hot Choice (delivered digitally); iN DEMAND; iN DEMAND (delivered digitally); Playboy TV (delivered digitally); Pleasure (delivered digitally); Fresh (delivered digitally); Shorteez (delivered digitally).
Internet Service
Operational: Yes.
Subscribers: 4,575.
Broadband Service: Mediacom High Speed Internet.
Fee: $59.95 installation; $45.95 monthly.
Telephone Service
Analog: Not Operational
Digital: Operational
Subscribers: 1,425.
Fee: $39.95 monthly
Miles of Plant: 299.0 (coaxial); 123.0 (fiber optic). Homes passed: 14,292. Miles of plant included in Moline
Vice President: Cari Fenzel. Engineering Director: Mitch Carlson. Technical Operations Manager: Chris Toalson. Lead Technician: Bobby Brown. Marketing Director: Greg Evans.
Ownership: Mediacom LLC (MSO).

STRONGHURST—Mediacom. Now served by DALLAS CITY, IL [IL0274]. ICA: IL0314.

SUBLETTE (village)—Heartland Cable Broadband, 156 West 5th South, PO Box 7, Minonk, IL 61760. Phones: 309-432-2075; 866-428-0490. Web Site: http://www.hcable.net. ICA: IL0408.
TV Market Ranking: Below 100 (SUBLETTE VILLAGE). Franchise award date: May 1,

Cable Systems—Illinois

1989. Franchise expiration date: N.A. Began: January 1, 1990.
Channel capacity: N.A. Channels available but not in use: N.A.

Basic Service
Subscribers: N.A.
Programming (received off-air): WIFR (Antenna TV, CBS) Freeport; WQRF-TV (Bounce TV, FOX) Rockford; WREX (CW, MeTV, NBC) Rockford; WTTW (PBS) Chicago; WTVO (ABC, MNT) Rockford.
Programming (via satellite): A&E; Animal Planet; Cartoon Network; CNN; Comcast/Charter Sports Southeast (CSS); Comedy Central; Discovery Channel; Disney Channel; ESPN; ESPN2; Food Network; Fox News Channel; Fox Sports 1; Freeform; FX; FXM; Great American Country; GSN; HGTV; History; HLN; Lifetime; MSNBC; MTV; Nickelodeon; Outdoor Channel; QVC; Spike TV; Syfy; TBS; The Weather Channel; TLC; TNT; Travel Channel; truTV; TV Land; USA Network; VH1; WE tv; WGN America.
Fee: $39.00 installation.

Pay Service 1
Pay Units: N.A.
Programming (via satellite): HBO.
Fee: $10.90 monthly.

Video-On-Demand: Yes

Internet Service
Operational: Yes.
Fee: $39.00 installation; $45.00 monthly.

Telephone Service
None
Miles of Plant: 3.0 (coaxial); None (fiber optic). Homes passed: 160.
Chief Executive Officer: Jim Frances. President & General Manager: Steve Allen.
Ownership: Heartland Cable Inc. (MSO).

SUGAR GROVE—Mediacom, 3900 26th Ave, Moline, IL 61265. Phones: 630-365-0045 (Local office); 309-797-2580. Fax: 309-797-2414. Web Site: http://www.mediacomcable.com. Also serves Big Rock, DeKalb County (portions), Earlville, Elburn, Hinckley, Kane County, Kaneville, Leland, Shabbona, Somonauk & Waterman. ICA: IL0131.
TV Market Ranking: 3,97 (Kane County (portions)); Below 100 (Big Rock, DeKalb County (portions), Earlville, Elburn, Hinckley, Kaneville, Leland, Shabbona, Somonauk, SUGAR GROVE, Waterman, Kane County (portions)). Franchise award date: N.A. Franchise expiration date: Began: December 12, 1984.
Channel capacity: N.A. Channels available but not in use: N.A.

Basic Service
Subscribers: 4,053.
Programming (received off-air): WBBM-TV (CBS, Decades) Chicago; WCIU-TV (MeTV) Chicago; WCPX-TV (ION) Chicago; WFLD (FOX) Chicago; WGBO-DT (getTV, UNV) Joliet; WGN-TV (IND) Chicago; WJYS (IND) Hammond; WLS-TV (ABC, Live Well Network) Chicago; WMAQ-TV (COZI TV, NBC) Chicago; WPWR-TV (Buzzr, CW, MNT, Movies!) Gary; WQRF-TV (Bounce TV, FOX) Rockford; WREX (CW, MeTV, NBC) Rockford; WSNS-TV (TMO) Chicago; WTTW (PBS) Chicago; WYCC (PBS) Chicago.
Programming (via satellite): Pop; TBS.
Fee: $45.00 installation; $43.00 monthly.

Expanded Basic Service 1
Subscribers: N.A.
Programming (via satellite): A&E; AMC; Animal Planet; Bravo; Comcast SportsNet Chicago; CNBC; CNN; Comcast SportsNet Chicago; Comedy Central; C-SPAN; Dis-

covery Channel; Disney Channel; E! HD; ESPN; ESPN2; Food Network; Fox News Channel; Fox Sports 1; FOX Sports Networks; Freeform; HGTV; History; INSP; Lifetime; MSNBC; MTV; Nickelodeon; Spike TV; Syfy; The Weather Channel; TLC; TNT; Travel Channel; Trinity Broadcasting Network (TBN); TV Land; USA Network; VH1.
Fee: $34.00 monthly.

Digital Basic Service
Subscribers: N.A.
Programming (via satellite): BBC America; Discovery Digital Networks; DMX Music; Golf Channel; GSN; IFC; NBCSN; Turner Classic Movies.

Digital Pay Service 1
Pay Units: N.A.
Programming (via satellite): Cinemax (multiplexed); HBO (multiplexed); Showtime (multiplexed); Starz (multiplexed); Starz Encore (multiplexed); The Movie Channel (multiplexed).
Fee: $11.95 monthly (each).

Video-On-Demand: Yes

Pay-Per-View
iN DEMAND; iN DEMAND (delivered digitally); Playboy TV (delivered digitally); Fresh (delivered digitally); Shorteez (delivered digitally).

Internet Service
Operational: Yes.
Broadband Service: Mediacom High Speed Internet.
Fee: $59.95 installation; $45.95 monthly.

Telephone Service
Analog: Not Operational
Digital: Operational
Homes passed: 9,212. Miles of plant included in Moline
Vice President: Cari Fenzel. Area Manager: Don DeMay. Engineering Director: Mitch Carlson. Marketing Director: Greg Evans. Business Operations Manager: Leonard Lipe. Technical Operations Manager: Chris Toalson.
Ownership: Mediacom LLC (MSO).

SULLIVAN—Mediacom, 4290 Blue Stem Rd, PO Box 288, Charleston, IL 61920. Phones: 217-348-5533; 309-274-4500. Fax: 217-345-7074. Web Site: http://www.mediacomcable.com. Also serves Cerro Gordo. ICA: IL0154.
TV Market Ranking: 64 (Cerro Gordo, SULLIVAN). Franchise award date: N.A. Franchise expiration date: N.A. Began: January 1, 1980.
Channel capacity: N.A. Channels available but not in use: N.A.

Basic Service
Subscribers: 822.
Programming (received off-air): WAND (NBC) Decatur; WBUI (CW, This TV) Decatur; WCCU (FOX, MeTV) Urbana; WCIA (CBS, MNT) Champaign; WCIX (CBS, MNT) Springfield; WEIU-TV (PBS) Charleston; WICD (ABC) Champaign; WILL-TV (PBS) Urbana; WSIU-TV (PBS) Carbondale; WTHI-TV (CBS, FOX) Terre Haute; WTWO (NBC) Terre Haute; 1 FM.
Programming (via satellite): C-SPAN; INSP; Pop; QVC; WGN America.
Fee: $45.00 installation; $43.00 monthly.

Expanded Basic Service 1
Subscribers: N.A.
Programming (via satellite): A&E; AMC; Animal Planet; BET; Cartoon Network; CMT; CNBC; CNN; Comcast SportsNet Chicago; Comedy Central; C-SPAN 2; Discovery Channel; Discovery Life Channel; Disney Channel; E! HD; ESPN; ESPN Clas-

sic; ESPN2; EVINE Live; EWTN Global Catholic Network; Food Network; Fox News Channel; Fox Sports 1; FOX Sports Midwest; Freeform; FX; Hallmark Channel; HGTV; History; HLN; ION Television; Jewelry Television; Lifetime; LMN; MSNBC; MTV; NBCSN; Nickelodeon; Outdoor Channel; Oxygen; Spike TV; Syfy; TBS; The Weather Channel; TLC; TNT; Travel Channel; Trinity Broadcasting Network (TBN); truTV; TV Land; USA Network; VH1; WE tv.
Fee: $34.00 monthly.

Digital Basic Service
Subscribers: N.A.
Programming (via satellite): AXS TV; BBC America; Bloomberg Television; Bravo; CBS Sports Network; CCTV-Documentary; Cloo; CMT; Destination America; Discovery Kids Channel; Discovery Life Channel; Disney XD; ESPN HD; ESPN2 HD; ESPNews; ESPNU; FOX College Sports Central; FOX College Sports Pacific; Fox Sports 2; Fuse; FXM; FYI; Golf Channel; GolTV; GSN; HD Theater; History International; IFC; Investigation Discovery; ION Television; MC; MTV Classic; MTV Hits; MTV2; Nat Geo WILD; National Geographic Channel; NBCSN; Nick Jr.; Nicktoons; OWN: Oprah Winfrey Network; Qubo; Reelz; Science Channel; TeenNick; Tennis Channel; Turner Classic Movies; TVG Network; Universal HD.

Digital Pay Service 1
Pay Units: N.A.
Programming (via satellite): Cinemax (multiplexed); Cinemax On Demand; HBO (multiplexed); HBO HD; HBO on Demand; Showtime (multiplexed); Showtime HD; Showtime On Demand; Starz (multiplexed); Starz Encore (multiplexed); Starz HD; Starz On Demand; The Movie Channel (multiplexed); The Movie Channel HD; The Movie Channel On Demand.
Fee: $11.95 monthly (HBO, Cinemax, Showtime/TMC or Starz/Encore).

Video-On-Demand: Yes

Pay-Per-View
iN DEMAND (delivered digitally); Playboy TV (delivered digitally); SexSee (delivered digitally); Juicy (delivered digitally); ESPN (delivered digitally).

Internet Service
Operational: Yes.
Subscribers: 1,200.
Broadband Service: Mediacom High Speed Internet.
Fee: $59.95 installation; $40.95 monthly.

Telephone Service
Digital: Operational
Subscribers: 419.
Fee: $39.95 monthly
Miles of Plant: 63.0 (coaxial); 70.0 (fiber optic). Homes passed: 3,086.
General Manager: Todd Acker. Technical Operations Manager: Jerry Ferguson. Marketing Director: James Friske.
Ownership: Mediacom LLC (MSO).

SUMNER—NewWave Communications. Now served by VINCENNES, IN [IN0035]. ICA: IL0268.

TABLE GROVE—Mid Century Telephone Cooperative. Formerly [IL0587]. This cable system has converted to IPTV. Now served by ELLISVILLE, IL [IL5238]. ICA: IL5244.

TABLE GROVE—Mid Century Telephone Cooperative. This cable system has converted to IPTV. Now served by ELLISVILLE, IL [IL5238]. ICA: IL0587.

TAMMS—NewWave Communications, One Montgomery Plaza, 4th Floor, Sikeston, MO 63801. Phones: 888-863-9928; 844-546-3278; 618-283-4567. Fax: 573-481-9809. E-mail: info@newwavecom.com. Web Site: http://www.newwavecom.com. ICA: IL0329.
TV Market Ranking: 69 (TAMMS). Franchise award date: N.A. Franchise expiration date: N.A. Began: January 27, 1988.
Channel capacity: N.A. Channels available but not in use: N.A.

Basic Service
Subscribers: 25.
Programming (received off-air): KBSI (FOX) Cape Girardeau; KFVS-TV (CBS, CW, MeTV) Cape Girardeau; WDKA (MNT, The Country Network) Paducah; WPSD-TV (Antenna TV, NBC) Paducah; WSIL-TV (ABC) Harrisburg; WSIU-TV (PBS) Carbondale; WTCT (IND) Marion.
Programming (via satellite): A&E; AMC; BET; Cartoon Network; CMT; CNN; Comedy Central; C-SPAN; Discovery Channel; Disney Channel; ESPN; ESPN2; Fox News Channel; Freeform; HLN; Lifetime; MTV; Nickelodeon; Spike TV; Syfy; TBS; The Weather Channel; TLC; TNT; TV Land; USA Network; VH1; WGN America.
Fee: $40.00 installation; $25.62 monthly.

Pay Service 1
Pay Units: N.A.
Programming (via satellite): Cinemax; HBO (multiplexed); Showtime.

Video-On-Demand: No

Pay-Per-View
iN DEMAND (delivered digitally); Hot Choice (delivered digitally); ESPN Now (delivered digitally); Playboy TV (delivered digitally); Fresh (delivered digitally); Shorteez (delivered digitally).

Internet Service
Operational: No.

Telephone Service
None
Miles of Plant: 8.0 (coaxial); None (fiber optic). Homes passed: 332.
General Manager: John Helmers.
Ownership: NewWave Communications LLC (MSO).

TAMPICO—Mediacom, 3900 26th Ave, Moline, IL 61265. Phone: 309-797-2580. Fax: 309-797-2414. Web Site: http://www.mediacomcable.com. ICA: IL0347.
TV Market Ranking: Outside TV Markets (TAMPICO). Franchise award date: November 1, 1982. Franchise expiration date: N.A. Began: November 1, 1984.
Channel capacity: N.A. Channels available but not in use: N.A.

The industry bible...
Consumer Electronics Daily
Warren Communications News
Free 30-day trial—call 800-771-9202 or visit www.warren-news.com

2017 Edition

D-219

Illinois—Cable Systems

Basic Service
Subscribers: 23.
Programming (received off-air): KIIN (PBS) Iowa City; KLJB (CW, FOX, MeTV) Davenport; KWQC-TV (NBC) Davenport; WHBF-TV (CBS) Rock Island; WQAD-TV (ABC, Antenna TV) Moline.
Programming (via satellite): TBS; Trinity Broadcasting Network (TBN); WGN America.
Fee: $45.00 installation; $40.00 monthly.
Expanded Basic Service 1
Subscribers: N.A.
Programming (via satellite): A&E; AMC; Animal Planet; Bravo; CMT; CNN; Comcast SportsNet Chicago; Discovery Channel; Disney Channel; ESPN; ESPN2; Fox Sports 1; FOX Sports Networks; Freeform; History; Lifetime; MTV; Nickelodeon; QVC; Spike TV; Syfy; The Weather Channel; TLC; TNT; Travel Channel; TV Land; USA Network.
Fee: $34.00 monthly.
Pay Service 1
Pay Units: N.A.
Programming (via satellite): HBO; Showtime.
Fee: $11.99 monthly (each).
Video-On-Demand: No
Internet Service
Operational: No.
Telephone Service
None
Miles of Plant: 6.0 (coaxial); None (fiber optic). Homes passed: 364.
Regional Vice President: Cari Fenzel. Area Manager: Don DeMay. Engineering Director: Mitch Carlson. Technical Operations Manager: Chris Toalson. Marketing Director: Greg Evans.
Ownership: Mediacom LLC (MSO).

TAYLORVILLE—NewWave Communications, One Montgomery Plaza, 4th Floor, Sikeston, MO 63801. Phone: 888-863-9928. Fax: 573-481-9809. E-mail: info@newwavecom.com. Web Site: http://www.newwavecom.com. Also serves Auburn, Bluff City, Bond County (portions), Brownstown, Carlinville, Christian County (portions), Coalton, East Gillespie, Farmersville, Gillespie, Girard, Greenville, Hewittville, Hillsboro, Litchfield, Macoupin County (portions), Montgomery County (portions), Nilwood, Nokomis, Owaneco, Pana, Ramsey, Raymond, Schram City, Shelby County (portions), Shelbyville, Sunset Lake, Taylor Springs, Thayer, Vandalia, Vera, Virden & Witt. ICA: IL0098.
TV Market Ranking: 64 (Auburn, Christian County (portions), Farmersville, Girard, Hewittville, Nilwood, Owaneco, Pana, Raymond, Shelby County (portions), Shelbyville, Sunset Lake, TAYLORVILLE, Thayer, Virden); Outside TV Markets (Bluff City, Bond County (portions), Brownstown, Coalton, East Gillespie, Macoupin County (portions), Montgomery County (portions), Schram City, Taylor Springs, Vera, Witt, Carlinville, Gillespie, Greenville, Hillsboro, Litchfield, Ramsey, Vandalia). Franchise award date: November 1, 1977. Franchise expiration date: N.A. Began: November 1, 1951.
Channel capacity: N.A. Channels available but not in use: N.A.
Basic Service
Subscribers: 10,815.
Programming (received off-air): KPLR-TV (CW, This TV) St. Louis; KSDK (Bounce TV, NBC) St. Louis; WAND (NBC) Decatur; WBUI (CW, This TV) Decatur; WCIA (CBS, MNT) Champaign; WICS (ABC, The Country Network) Springfield; WILL-TV (PBS) Urbana; WRSP-TV (Antenna TV, FOX, MeTV) Springfield.
Programming (via satellite): C-SPAN; C-SPAN 2; QVC; WGN America.
Fee: $40.00 installation; $34.78 monthly.
Expanded Basic Service 1
Subscribers: 4,382.
Programming (via satellite): A&E; AMC; Animal Planet; Bravo; Cartoon Network; CMT; CNBC; CNN; Comedy Central; Discovery Channel; Disney Channel; Disney XD; E! HD; ESPN; ESPN2; Food Network; Fox News Channel; FOX Sports Midwest; Freeform; FX; Golf Channel; GSN; Hallmark Channel; HGTV; History; HLN; Lifetime; MSNBC; MTV; National Geographic Channel; Nickelodeon; Oxygen; Pop; Spike TV; Syfy; TBS; The Weather Channel; TLC; TNT; Travel Channel; Trinity Broadcasting Network (TBN); truTV; TV Land; USA Network; VH1.
Fee: $1.48 monthly.
Digital Basic Service
Subscribers: N.A.
Programming (via satellite): BBC America; Discovery Digital Networks; DIY Network; FYI; History International; IFC; LMN; Nick 2; Nick Jr.; Nicktoons; Sundance TV; TeenNick.
Digital Pay Service 1
Pay Units: 285.
Programming (via satellite): Cinemax (multiplexed).
Fee: $15.00 installation; $10.45 monthly.
Digital Pay Service 2
Pay Units: 476.
Programming (via satellite): HBO (multiplexed).
Fee: $15.00 installation; $11.00 monthly.
Digital Pay Service 3
Pay Units: 127.
Programming (via satellite): Showtime (multiplexed).
Fee: $10.45 monthly.
Digital Pay Service 4
Pay Units: 187.
Programming (via satellite): The Movie Channel (multiplexed).
Fee: $15.00 installation; $10.45 monthly.
Digital Pay Service 5
Pay Units: N.A.
Programming (via satellite): Flix; Starz (multiplexed); Starz Encore (multiplexed).
Video-On-Demand: No
Pay-Per-View
iN DEMAND (delivered digitally); Hot Choice (delivered digitally); Fresh (delivered digitally); Shorteez (delivered digitally); Playboy TV (delivered digitally).
Internet Service
Operational: Yes. Began: July 1, 2004. Broadband Service: Charter Internet.
Fee: $39.99 monthly.
Telephone Service
None
Miles of Plant: 84.0 (coaxial); None (fiber optic). Homes passed: 13,315.
General Manager: John Helmers.
Ownership: NewWave Communications LLC (MSO).

THAWVILLE—Formerly served by CableDirect. No longer in operation. ICA: IL0590.

TOLONO—Mediacom. Now served by TUSCOLA, IL [IL0135]. ICA: IL0592.

TONICA—Heartland Cable Inc, 167 West 5th St, PO Box 7, Minonk, IL 61760. Phones: 800-448-4320; 309-432-2075. Web Site: http://www.hcable.net. ICA: IL0677.
TV Market Ranking: Below 100 (TONICA). Channel capacity: N.A. Channels available but not in use: N.A.
Basic Service
Subscribers: N.A.
Programming (received off-air): WEEK-TV (ABC, CW, NBC) Peoria; WGN-TV (IND) Chicago; WHOI (Comet) Peoria; WMBD-TV (Bounce TV, CBS) Peoria; WTVP (PBS) Peoria; WYZZ-TV (FOX, The Country Network) Bloomington.
Programming (via satellite): A&E; CMT; CNN; C-SPAN; Discovery Channel; Disney Channel; ESPN; ESPN2; FOX Sports Networks; Freeform; HGTV; History; HLN; Lifetime; Nickelodeon; QVC; Spike TV; TBS; The Weather Channel; TNT; TV Land; USA Network.
Fee: $39.00 installation.
Pay Service 1
Pay Units: N.A.
Programming (via satellite): HBO; Showtime.
Fee: $8.95 - $10.95 monthly (each).
Video-On-Demand: Yes
Pay-Per-View
Movies; special events.
Internet Service
Operational: Yes.
Fee: $39.00 installation; $29.99 monthly.
Telephone Service
None
Miles of Plant: 3.0 (coaxial); None (fiber optic). Homes passed: 350.
Chief Executive Officer: Jim Frances. President & General Manager: Steve Allen.
Ownership: Heartland Cable Inc. (MSO).

TOWER HILL—Mediacom, 4290 Blue Stem Rd, PO Box 288, Charleston, IL 61920. Phone: 217-348-5533. Fax: 217-345-7074. Web Site: http://www.mediacomcable.com. ICA: IL0363.
TV Market Ranking: 64 (TOWER HILL). Franchise award date: N.A. Franchise expiration date: N.A. Began: April 7, 1986.
Channel capacity: N.A. Channels available but not in use: N.A.
Basic Service
Subscribers: 3.
Programming (received off-air): WAND (NBC) Decatur; WCIX (CBS, MNT) Springfield; WICS (ABC, The Country Network) Springfield; WILL-TV (PBS) Urbana; WPXS (IND) Mount Vernon; WRSP-TV (Antenna TV, FOX, MeTV) Springfield.
Programming (via satellite): A&E; AMC; Animal Planet; CNN; Discovery Channel; ESPN; Freeform; History; HLN; Lifetime; MTV; Nickelodeon; TBS; The Weather Channel; TLC; TNT; TV Land; USA Network; WGN America.
Fee: $45.00 installation; $67.95 monthly.
Pay Service 1
Pay Units: N.A.
Programming (via satellite): Cinemax.
Fee: $7.95 monthly.
Video-On-Demand: No
Internet Service
Operational: No.
Telephone Service
None
Miles of Plant: 6.0 (coaxial); None (fiber optic). Homes passed: 277.
General Manager: Todd Acker. Technical Operations Manager: Jerry Ferguson. Marketing Director: James Friske.
Ownership: Mediacom LLC (MSO).

TRIVOLI—Nova1Net, 677 West Main St, PO Box 1412, Galesburg, IL 61401. Phones: 800-397-6682; 309-342-9681. Fax: 309-342-4408. Web Site: http://www.novacablevision.com. ICA: IL0411.
TV Market Ranking: 83 (TRIVOLI). Franchise award date: N.A. Franchise expiration date: N.A. Began: June 18, 1989.
Channel capacity: N.A. Channels available but not in use: N.A.
Basic Service
Subscribers: 38.
Programming (received off-air): WEEK-TV (ABC, CW, NBC) Peoria; WHOI (Comet) Peoria; WICS (ABC, The Country Network) Springfield; WMBD-TV (Bounce TV, CBS) Peoria; WRSP-TV (Antenna TV, FOX, MeTV) Springfield; WTVP (PBS) Peoria; WYZZ-TV (FOX, The Country Network) Bloomington.
Programming (via satellite): A&E; CNN; Discovery Channel; Disney Channel; ESPN; Freeform; Spike TV; Syfy; TBS; TNT; USA Network; WGN America.
Fee: $50.00 installation; $54.95 monthly.
Pay Service 1
Pay Units: 1.
Programming (via satellite): Cinemax.
Fee: $10.00 monthly.
Pay Service 2
Pay Units: 3.
Programming (via satellite): HBO.
Fee: $10.00 monthly.
Video-On-Demand: No
Internet Service
Operational: Yes. Began: January 1, 2005.
Fee: $30.00 installation; $39.95 monthly.
Telephone Service
None
Miles of Plant: 3.0 (coaxial); None (fiber optic). Homes passed: 150.
General Manager: Robert G. Fischer Jr. Office Manager: Hazel Harden.
Ownership: Nova Cablevision Inc. (MSO).

TROY GROVE (village)—Formerly served by CableDirect. No longer in operation. ICA: IL0594.

TUSCOLA—Mediacom, 4290 Blue Stem Rd, PO Box 288, Charleston, IL 61920. Phones: 217-348-5533; 217-253-9028 (Tuscola office). Fax: 217-345-7074. Web Site: http://www.mediacomcable.com. Also serves Arcola, Arthur, Atwood, Camargo, Douglas County (portions), Garrett, Hammond, Hindsboro, Humboldt, Ivesdale, Oakland, Pierson & Villa Grove. ICA: IL0135.
TV Market Ranking: 64 (Arcola, Arthur, Atwood, Camargo, Douglas County (portions), Garrett, Hammond, Hindsboro, Ivesdale, Oakland, Pierson, TUSCOLA, Villa Grove); Outside TV Markets (Humboldt). Franchise award date: February 12, 1979. Franchise expiration date: N.A. Began: May 1, 1980.
Channel capacity: N.A. Channels available but not in use: N.A.
Basic Service
Subscribers: 1,772.
Programming (received off-air): WAND (NBC) Decatur; WBUI (CW, This TV) Decatur; WCCU (FOX, MeTV) Urbana; WCIA (CBS, MNT) Champaign; WCIX (CBS, MNT) Springfield; WEIU-TV (PBS) Charleston; WICD (ABC) Champaign; WICS (ABC, The Country Network) Springfield; WILL-TV (PBS) Urbana.
Programming (via satellite): C-SPAN; Pop; QVC; Radar Channel; WGN America.
Fee: $45.00 installation; $43.00 monthly.
Expanded Basic Service 1
Subscribers: N.A.
Programming (via satellite): A&E; AMC; Animal Planet; BET; Bravo; Cartoon Network; CMT; CNBC; CNN; Comedy Central;

Cable Systems—Illinois

C-SPAN 2; Discovery Channel; Discovery Life Channel; Disney Channel; Disney XD; E! HD; ESPN; ESPN Classic; ESPN2; EVINE Live; EWTN Global Catholic Network; Food Network; Fox News Channel; Fox Sports 1; FOX Sports Networks; Freeform; FX; Hallmark Channel; HGTV; History; HLN; ION Television; Lifetime; LMN; MSNBC; MTV; Nickelodeon; Outdoor Channel; Spike TV; Syfy; TBS; The Weather Channel; TLC; TNT; Travel Channel; Trinity Broadcasting Network (TBN); truTV; TV Land; USA Network; VH1; WE tv.
Fee: $34.00 monthly.

Digital Basic Service
Subscribers: N.A.
Programming (via satellite): AXS TV; BBC America; Bloomberg Television; CBS Sports Network; CCTV-Documentary; Cloo; CNN HD; Destination America; Discovery Kids Channel; Discovery Life Channel; ESPN HD; ESPN2 HD; ESPNews; ESPNU; FOX College Sports Central; FOX College Sports Pacific; Fuse; FXM; FYI; Golf Channel; GolTV; GSN; HD Theater; History International; IFC; Investigation Discovery; ION Television; LMN; MTV Classic; MTV Hits; MTV2; National Geographic Channel; NBCSN; Nick Jr.; Nicktoons; OWN: Oprah Winfrey Network; Qubo; Reelz; Science Channel; TBS HD; TeenNick; Tennis Channel; TNT HD; Turner Classic Movies; TVG Network; Universal HD.

Digital Pay Service 1
Pay Units: N.A.
Programming (via satellite): Cinemax (multiplexed); HBO (multiplexed); HBO HD; Showtime (multiplexed); Showtime HD; Starz (multiplexed); Starz Encore (multiplexed); The Movie Channel (multiplexed); The Movie Channel HD.
Fee: $11.95 monthly (HBO, Cinemax, Starz/Encore or Showtime/TMC).

Video-On-Demand: Yes

Pay-Per-View
iN DEMAND (delivered digitally); Playboy TV (delivered digitally); SexSee (delivered digitally); Juicy (delivered digitally).

Internet Service
Operational: Yes.
Broadband Service: Mediacom High Speed Internet.
Fee: $59.95 installation; $40.95 monthly.

Telephone Service
Analog: Not Operational
Digital: Operational
Fee: $39.95 monthly
Miles of Plant: 210.0 (coaxial); 106.0 (fiber optic). Homes passed: 7,743.
General Manager: Todd Acker. Technical Operations Manager: Jerry Ferguson. Marketing Director: James Friske. Office Manager: Karl McClelland.
Ownership: Mediacom LLC (MSO).

UNION—Packerland Broadband, 105 Kent St., PO Box 885, Iron Mountain, MI 49801. Phones: 906-774-1291; 800-236-8434; 906-774-6621. Fax: 906-776-2811. E-mail: service@plbb.net. Web Site: http://www.packerlandbroadband.com. ICA: IL0380.
TV Market Ranking: 97 (UNION). Franchise award date: N.A. Franchise expiration date: N.A. Began: December 1, 1986.
Channel capacity: N.A. Channels available but not in use: N.A.

Basic Service
Subscribers: N.A.
Programming (received off-air): WBBM-TV (CBS, Decades) Chicago; WCIU-TV (MeTV) Chicago; WFLD (FOX) Chicago; WGBO-DT (getTV, UNV) Joliet; WGN-TV (IND) Chicago; WIFR (Antenna TV, CBS) Freeport; WLS-TV (ABC, Live Well Network) Chicago; WMAQ-TV (COZI TV, NBC) Chicago; WPWR-TV (Buzzr, CW, MNT, Movies!) Gary; WQRF-TV (Bounce TV, FOX) Rockford; WREX (CW, MeTV, NBC) Rockford; WSNS-TV (TMO) Chicago; WTTW (PBS) Chicago; WTVO (ABC, MNT) Rockford; WYCC (PBS) Chicago.
Programming (via satellite): A&E; AMC; Animal Planet; Bravo; Cartoon Network; CMT; CNBC; CNN; Comcast SportsNet Chicago; Comedy Central; C-SPAN; C-SPAN 2; Discovery Channel; E! HD; ESPN; ESPN2; Food Network; Freeform; Hallmark Channel; HGTV; History; HLN; Lifetime; MTV; Nickelodeon; Spike TV; Syfy; TBS; The Weather Channel; TLC; TNT; Travel Channel; truTV; UniMas; USA Network; VH1.
Fee: $25.00 installation.

Pay Service 1
Pay Units: N.A.
Programming (via satellite): Cinemax; HBO; Showtime; The Movie Channel.
Fee: $14.72 monthly.

Internet Service
Operational: No.

Telephone Service
None
Miles of Plant: 3.0 (coaxial); None (fiber optic). Homes passed: 160.
General Manager: Dan Plante. Technical Supervisor: Chad Kay.
Ownership: Packerland Broadband (MSO).

VANDALIA—NewWave Communications. Now served by TAYLORVILLE, IL [IL0098]. ICA: IL0596.

VERGENNES—Formerly served by CableDirect. No longer in operation. ICA: IL0625.

VERMILLION (village)—Formerly served by CableDirect. No longer in operation. ICA: IL0597.

VERMONT—Nova1Net, 677 West Main St, PO Box 1412, Galesburg, IL 61402. Phones: 309-342-9681; 800-397-6682. Fax: 309-342-4408. Web Site: http://www.novacablevision.com. ICA: IL0311.
TV Market Ranking: Outside TV Markets (VERMONT). Franchise award date: N.A. Franchise expiration date: N.A. Began: December 1, 1982.
Channel capacity: N.A. Channels available but not in use: N.A.

Basic Service
Subscribers: N.A.
Programming (received off-air): WEEK-TV (ABC, CW, NBC) Peoria; WHOI (Comet) Peoria; WMBD-TV (Bounce TV, CBS) Peoria; WRSP-TV (Antenna TV, FOX, MeTV) Springfield; WTVP (PBS) Peoria.
Programming (via satellite): A&E; AMC; CMT; CNN; Comedy Central; Discovery Channel; ESPN; ESPN2; Fox Sports 1; Freeform; History; HLN; Lifetime; Nickelodeon; Spike TV; TBS; The Weather Channel; TLC; TNT; Travel Channel; USA Network; WGN America.
Fee: $45.00 installation; $47.95 monthly.

Pay Service 1
Pay Units: N.A.
Programming (via satellite): HBO.
Fee: $12.00 monthly.

Video-On-Demand: No

Internet Service
Operational: No.

Telephone Service
None
Miles of Plant: 8.0 (coaxial); None (fiber optic). Homes passed: 389.
Ownership: Nova Cablevision Inc. (MSO).

VERSAILLES—Cass Cable TV Inc. Now served by BEARDSTOWN, IL [IL0598]. ICA: IL0382.

VICTORIA—Mediacom, 3900 26th Ave, Moline, IL 61265. Phone: 309-797-2580. Fax: 309-797-2414. Web Site: http://www.mediacomcable.com. ICA: IL0436.
TV Market Ranking: 83 (VICTORIA).
Channel capacity: N.A. Channels available but not in use: N.A.

Basic Service
Subscribers: 3.
Fee: $45.00 installation; $69.95 monthly.

Pay Service 1
Pay Units: N.A.
Programming (via satellite): Cinemax; HBO.

Internet Service
Operational: No.

Telephone Service
None
Miles of Plant: 4.0 (coaxial); None (fiber optic). Homes passed: 134. Miles of plant included in Moline
Area Manager: Don DeMay. Engineering Director: Mitch Carlson. Technical Operations Manager: Chris Toalson. Marketing Director: Greg Evans.
Ownership: Mediacom LLC (MSO).

VILLA PARK—Comcast Cable. Now served by PEORIA, IL [IL0012]. ICA: IL0070.

VIRDEN—NewWave Communications. Now served by TAYLORVILLE, IL [IL0098]. ICA: IL0609.

WALNUT—Mediacom. Now served by GENESEO, IL [IL0170]. ICA: IL0600.

WALTONVILLE—Formerly served by Longview Communications. No longer in operation. ICA: IL0623.

WARREN—Mediacom. Now served by LENA, IL [IL0223]. ICA: IL0243.

WARRENSBURG—Formerly served by Crystal Broadband Networks. No longer in operation. ICA: IL0264.

WASHINGTON PARK—Mediacom, 4290 Blue Stem Rd, PO Box 288, Charleston, IL 61920. Phone: 217-348-5533. Fax: 217-345-7074. Web Site: http://www.mediacomcable.com. Also serves Fairmont City, Madison County, St. Clair County (unincorporated portions) & St. Clair Twp. ICA: IL0093.
TV Market Ranking: 11 (Fairmont City, Madison County (portions), St. Clair County (unincorporated portions), St. Clair Twp., WASHINGTON PARK); Below 100 (Madison County (portions)). Franchise award date: N.A. Franchise expiration date: N.A. Began: June 23, 1983.
Channel capacity: N.A. Channels available but not in use: N.A.

Basic Service
Subscribers: 175.
Programming (received off-air): KDNL-TV (ABC, The Country Network) St. Louis; KETC (PBS) St. Louis; KMOV (CBS) St. Louis; KNLC (IND, My Family TV) St. Louis; KPLR-TV (CW, This TV) St. Louis; KSDK (Bounce TV, NBC) St. Louis; KTVI (Antenna TV, Escape, FOX) St. Louis; WSIU-TV (PBS) Carbondale.
Programming (via satellite): TBS; Trinity Broadcasting Network (TBN).
Fee: $45.00 installation; $46.37 monthly.

Expanded Basic Service 1
Subscribers: N.A.
Programming (via satellite): A&E; AMC; Animal Planet; BET; Cartoon Network; CMT; CNN; Comedy Central; Discovery Channel; Disney Channel; E! HD; ESPN; ESPN2; FOX Sports Networks; Freeform; History; Lifetime; MTV; Nickelodeon; Spike TV; Syfy; The Weather Channel; TNT; TV Land; USA Network; VH1; WGN America.
Fee: $27.00 monthly.

Pay Service 1
Pay Units: N.A.
Programming (via satellite): Cinemax; HBO; Showtime; The Movie Channel.
Fee: $7.95 monthly (Cinemax), $11.99 monthly (Showtime or TMC), $13.50 monthly (HBO).

Video-On-Demand: No

Internet Service
Operational: No.

Telephone Service
None
Miles of Plant: 60.0 (coaxial); 8.0 (fiber optic). Homes passed: 6,018.
General Manager: Todd Acker. Technical Operations Manager: Jerry Ferguson. Marketing Director: James Friske.
Ownership: Mediacom LLC (MSO).

WATAGA—Mediacom. Now served by GENESEO, IL [IL0170]. ICA: IL0261.

WATERLOO—Charter Communications. Now served by ST. LOUIS, MO [MO0009]. ICA: IL0175.

WATSEKA—Mediacom, 109 East 5th St, Ste A, Auburn, IN 46706. Phone: 260-927-3015. Fax: 260-347-4433. Web Site: http://www.mediacomcable.com. Also serves Crescent City, Iroquois County (portions), Sheldon & Woodland (village), IL; Brook, Goodland & Kentland, IN. ICA: IL0092.
TV Market Ranking: Below 100 (Goodland); Outside TV Markets (Brook, Crescent City, Iroquois County (portions), Sheldon, WATSEKA, Woodland (village), Kentland). Franchise award date: January 1, 1966. Franchise expiration date: N.A. Began: June 1, 1966.
Channel capacity: N.A. Channels available but not in use: N.A.

Illinois—Cable Systems

CABLE & TV STATION COVERAGE
Atlas2017
The perfect companion to the Television & Cable Factbook
To order call 800-771-9202 or visit www.warren-news.com

Basic Service
Subscribers: 1,728. Commercial subscribers: 3.
Programming (received off-air): WAND (NBC) Decatur; WBBM-TV (CBS, Decades) Chicago; WCCU (FOX, MeTV) Urbana; WCIA (CBS, MNT) Champaign; WCIX (CBS, MNT) Springfield; WFLD (FOX) Chicago; WGN-TV (IND) Chicago; WICD (ABC) Champaign; WILL-TV (PBS) Urbana; WLS-TV (ABC, Live Well Network) Chicago; WMAQ-TV (COZI TV, NBC) Chicago; WPWR-TV (Buzzr, CW, MNT, Movies!) Gary; WPXU-TV (ION) Jacksonville; WTTW (PBS) Chicago; allband FM.
Fee: $45.00 installation; $72.95 monthly.

Expanded Basic Service 1
Subscribers: N.A.
Programming (via satellite): A&E; AMC; Animal Planet; Cartoon Network; CMT; CNBC; CNN; Comcast SportsNet Chicago; Comedy Central; C-SPAN; C-SPAN 2; Discovery Channel; Discovery Life Channel; Disney Channel; E! HD; ESPN; ESPN2; EVINE Live; Food Network; Fox News Channel; Fox Sports 1; Freeform; FX; Great American Country; Hallmark Channel; HGTV; History; HLN; ION Television; Lifetime; MSNBC; MTV; Nickelodeon; Outdoor Channel; Pop; QVC; RFD-TV; Spike TV; Syfy; TBS; The Weather Channel; TLC; TNT; Travel Channel; Trinity Broadcasting Network (TBN); truTV; TV Land; USA Network; VH1; WE tv.
Fee: $33.00 monthly.

Digital Basic Service
Subscribers: N.A.
Programming (via satellite): BBC America; Bloomberg Television; Discovery Kids Channel; ESPNews; Fuse; FXM; FYI; Golf Channel; GSN; History International; IFC; LMN; MC; National Geographic Channel; NBCSN; Nick Jr.; Nicktoons; Outdoor Channel; TeenNick; Turner Classic Movies; TVG Network.

Digital Expanded Basic Service
Subscribers: N.A.
Programming (via satellite): AXS TV; ESPN; ESPN2; HD Theater; iN DEMAND.

Digital Pay Service 1
Pay Units: N.A.
Programming (via satellite): Cinemax (multiplexed); Flix (multiplexed); HBO (multiplexed); Showtime (multiplexed); Starz (multiplexed); Starz Encore (multiplexed); Sundance TV (multiplexed); The Movie Channel (multiplexed).
Fee: $11.95 monthly (each).

Video-On-Demand: Yes

Pay-Per-View
iN DEMAND (delivered digitally); Playboy TV (delivered digitally); TENClips, TEN by the Movie, TEN Blox (delivered digitally).

Internet Service
Operational: Yes.
Subscribers: 395.
Broadband Service: Mediacom High Speed Internet.
Fee: $59.95 installation; $40.95 monthly.

Telephone Service
Digital: Operational
Subscribers: 281.
Fee: $39.95 monthly
Miles of Plant: 55.0 (coaxial); 91.0 (fiber optic). Homes passed: 1,834.
Operations Director: Joe Poffenberger. Technical Operations Manager: Craig Grey.
Ownership: Mediacom LLC (MSO).

WATSON—Clearvision Cable Systems Inc, 1785 US Rte 40, Greenup, IL 62428-3501. Phone: 217-923-5594. Fax: 217-923-5681. Also serves Effingham County & Heartville. ICA: IL0349.
TV Market Ranking: Outside TV Markets (Heartville, Effingham County, WATSON).
Channel capacity: N.A. Channels available but not in use: N.A.

Basic Service
Subscribers: 57.
Programming (received off-air): WAND (NBC) Decatur; WBUI (CW, This TV) Decatur; WICS (ABC, The Country Network) Springfield; WPXS (IND) Mount Vernon; WRSP-TV (Antenna TV, FOX, MeTV) Springfield; WTHI-TV (CBS, FOX) Terre Haute; WTWO (NBC) Terre Haute; WUSI-TV (PBS) Olney.
Programming (via satellite): ESPN; QVC; TBS; WGN America.
Fee: $47.95 monthly.

Expanded Basic Service 1
Subscribers: N.A.
Programming (via satellite): A&E; CNN; C-SPAN; Discovery Channel; Disney Channel; ESPN2; EWTN Global Catholic Network; Fox News Channel; FOX Sports Midwest; Freeform; History; Lifetime; MTV; Nickelodeon; Spike TV; The Weather Channel; TNT; Trinity Broadcasting Network (TBN); USA Network.
Fee: $13.09 monthly.

Digital Basic Service
Subscribers: N.A.
Programming (via satellite): BBC America; Bloomberg Television; Discovery Channel; Disney XD; DMX Music; EVINE Live; Fox Sports 1; FXM; FYI; Golf Channel; GSN; HGTV; History International; IFC; LMN; NBCSN; Nick Jr.; Outdoor Channel; Syfy; TeenNick; Trinity Broadcasting Network (TBN); Turner Classic Movies; WE tv.

Pay Service 1
Pay Units: N.A.
Programming (via satellite): HBO; Showtime; The Movie Channel.
Fee: $9.50 monthly (Showtime).

Digital Pay Service 1
Pay Units: N.A.
Programming (via satellite): Cinemax (multiplexed); Flix; HBO (multiplexed); Showtime (multiplexed); Starz (multiplexed); Starz Encore (multiplexed); The Movie Channel (multiplexed).

Video-On-Demand: No

Pay-Per-View
Shorteez (delivered digitally); Fresh (delivered digitally); Playboy TV (delivered digitally); iN DEMAND (delivered digitally); Hot Choice (delivered digitally); ESPN Now (delivered digitally).

Internet Service
Operational: No.

Telephone Service
None
Homes passed: 613.
President & General Manager: Michael Bauguss. Secretary: Gwyndolyn S. Bauguss.
Ownership: Clearvision Cable Systems Inc. (MSO).

WAUKEGAN—Comcast Cable. Now served by MOUNT PROSPECT, IL [IL0036]. ICA: IL0014.

WAYNE CITY—NewWave Communications. Now served by McLEANSBORO, IL [IL0177]. ICA: IL0270.

WEE-MA-TUK HILLS—Nova1Net, 677 West Main St, PO Box 1412, Galesburg, IL 61401. Phones: 800-397-6682; 309-342-9681. Fax: 309-342-4408. Web Site: http://www.novacablevision.com. Also serves Fiatt. ICA: IL0603.
TV Market Ranking: 83 (Fiatt, WEE-MA-TUK HILLS). Franchise award date: N.A. Franchise expiration date: N.A. Began: October 1, 1990.
Channel capacity: 40 (operating 2-way). Channels available but not in use: N.A.

Basic Service
Subscribers: 120.
Programming (received off-air): KGCW (CW, MeTV, This TV) Burlington; KIIN (PBS) Iowa City; KLJB (CW, FOX, MeTV) Davenport; KWQC-TV (NBC) Davenport; WAOE (Antenna TV, MNT) Peoria; WEEK-TV (ABC, CW, NBC) Peoria; WHBF-TV (CBS) Rock Island; WHOI (Comet) Peoria; WMBD-TV (Bounce TV, CBS) Peoria; WQAD-TV (ABC, Antenna TV) Moline; WQPT-TV (PBS) Moline; WTVP (PBS) Peoria.
Programming (via satellite): A&E; AMC; Animal Planet; BTN; Cartoon Network; CMT; CNBC; CNN; Comcast SportsNet Chicago; Comedy Central; C-SPAN; C-SPAN 2; Discovery Channel; Disney Channel; E! HD; ESPN; ESPN2; EWTN Global Catholic Network; Food Network; Fox News Channel; Fox Sports 1; FOX Sports Midwest; Freeform; FX; Golf Channel; Great American Country; Hallmark Channel; HGTV; History; HLN; HRTV; INSP; Lifetime; MSNBC; MTV; National Geographic Channel; Nickelodeon; QVC; RFD-TV; Spike TV; Syfy; TBS; The Weather Channel; TLC; TNT; Travel Channel; truTV; TV Land; USA Network; VH1; WGN America.
Fee: $60.00 installation; $58.95 monthly.

Digital Basic Service
Subscribers: N.A.
Programming (via satellite): Bloomberg Television; CMT; Destination America; Discovery Kids Channel; Disney XD; ESPN Classic; ESPN2; ESPNews; EVINE Live; Fox Sports 1; FSN Digital Atlantic; FSN Digital Central; FSN Digital Pacific; Fuse; FXM; FYI; Golf Channel; Great American Country; GSN; HGTV; History; History International; IFC; Investigation Discovery; LMN; MC; MTV Classic; MTV Hits; MTV2; NBCSN; Nick Jr.; Nicktoons; Outdoor Channel; OWN: Oprah Winfrey Network; Science Channel; Syfy; TeenNick; Trinity Broadcasting Network (TBN); Turner Classic Movies; VH1 Soul; WE tv.

Pay Service 1
Pay Units: 1.
Programming (via satellite): Cinemax.
Fee: $11.95 monthly.

Pay Service 2
Pay Units: 14.
Programming (via satellite): HBO.
Fee: $11.95 monthly.

Digital Pay Service 1
Pay Units: N.A.
Programming (via satellite): Cinemax (multiplexed); Flix; HBO (multiplexed); Showtime (multiplexed); Starz (multiplexed); Starz Encore (multiplexed); Sundance TV; The Movie Channel (multiplexed).
Fee: $12.95 monthly (HBO, Cinemax, Showtime/TMC/Flix/Sundance or Starz/Encore).

Video-On-Demand: No

Pay-Per-View
Hot Choice (delivered digitally); Fresh (delivered digitally); Spice: Xcess (delivered digitally); Club Jenna (delivered digitally).

Internet Service
Operational: Yes. Began: January 1, 2005.
Fee: $25.00 installation; $35.95-$39.95 monthly.

Telephone Service
None
Miles of Plant: 12.0 (coaxial); None (fiber optic). Homes passed: 285.
General Manager & Chief Technician: Robert G. Fischer Jr.
Ownership: Nova Cablevision Inc. (MSO).

WELDON—Mediacom. Now served by RANTOUL, IL [IL0089]. ICA: IL0295.

WEST CHICAGO—Comcast Cable. Now served by PEORIA, IL [IL0012]. ICA: IL0015.

WEST SALEM—Formerly served by Park TV & Electronics Inc. No longer in operation. ICA: IL0275.

WEST UNION—Formerly served by Longview Communications. No longer in operation. ICA: IL0619.

WESTERN SPRINGS—Comcast Cable. Now served by PEORIA, IL [IL0012]. ICA: IL0043.

WESTVILLE—NewWave Communications, One Montgomery Plaza, 4th Floor, Sikeston, MO 63801. Phone: 888-863-9928. Fax: 573-481-9809. E-mail: info@newwavecom.com. Web Site: http://www.newwavecom.com. Also serves Belgium, Catlin, Danville, Edgar County (portions), Georgetown, Hegeler, Hoopeston, Milford, Paris, Rossville, Tilton, Vermilion County (portions) & Wellington. ICA: IL0079.
TV Market Ranking: 64 (Belgium, Catlin, Danville, Georgetown, Hegeler, Tilton, Vermilion County (portions), WESTVILLE); Below 100 (Edgar County (portions), Rossville, Paris); Outside TV Markets (Milford, Wellington, Hoopeston). Franchise award date: N.A. Franchise expiration date: N.A. Began: December 27, 1965.
Channel capacity: N.A. Channels available but not in use: N.A.

Basic Service
Subscribers: 5,807.
Programming (received off-air): WAND (NBC) Decatur; WBUI (CW, This TV) Decatur; WCCU (FOX, MeTV) Urbana; WCIA (CBS, MNT) Champaign; WICD (ABC) Champaign; WILL-TV (PBS) Urbana; WRTV (ABC, Grit) Indianapolis; WTHI-TV (CBS, FOX) Terre Haute; WTTV (CBS, This TV) Bloomington; WTWO (NBC) Terre Haute; allband FM.

Cable Systems—Illinois

Programming (via satellite): Pop; WGN America.
Fee: $29.99 installation; $34.78 monthly.

Expanded Basic Service 1
Subscribers: N.A.
Programming (via satellite): A&E; AMC; Animal Planet; Bravo; Cartoon Network; CMT; CNBC; CNN; Comedy Central; C-SPAN; C-SPAN 2; Discovery Channel; Discovery Life Channel; Disney Channel; Disney XD; E! HD; ESPN; ESPN2; EWTN Global Catholic Network; Food Network; Fox News Channel; Fox Sports 1; Freeform; FX; Golf Channel; Hallmark Channel; HGTV; History; HLN; ION Television; Lifetime; MSNBC; MTV; National Geographic Channel; NBCSN; Nickelodeon; Outdoor Channel; Oxygen; QVC; Spike TV; Syfy; TBS; The Weather Channel; TLC; TNT; Travel Channel; Trinity Broadcasting Network (TBN); truTV; Turner Classic Movies; TV Land; USA Network; VH1; WE tv.
Fee: $49.99 monthly.

Digital Basic Service
Subscribers: N.A.
Programming (via satellite): BBC America; Discovery Digital Networks; DIY Network; FYI; History International; IFC; LMN; MC; Nick 2; Nick Jr.; Nicktoons; Sundance TV; TeenNick; TV Guide Interactive Inc.

Digital Pay Service 1
Pay Units: 557.
Programming (via satellite): Cinemax (multiplexed); Flix; HBO (multiplexed); Showtime (multiplexed); Starz (multiplexed); Starz Encore (multiplexed); The Movie Channel (multiplexed).
Fee: $2.95 monthly (Encore), $8.95 monthly (Cinemax or Showtime), $10.95 monthly (HBO).

Video-On-Demand: Yes

Pay-Per-View
iN DEMAND (delivered digitally); NHL Center Ice/MLB Extra Innings (delivered digitally); Hot Choice (delivered digitally); Playboy TV (delivered digitally); Fresh (delivered digitally); Shorteez (delivered digitally).

Internet Service
Operational: Yes. Began: July 1, 2001.
Subscribers: 2,421.
Broadband Service: In-house.
Fee: $50.00 installation; $29.99 monthly.

Telephone Service
Digital: Operational
Subscribers: 685.
Miles of Plant: 226.0 (coaxial); 103.0 (fiber optic). Homes passed: 8,411.
Chief Financial Officer: Rod Siemers. General Manager: John Helmers.
Ownership: NewWave Communications LLC (MSO).

WHITE HEATH—Formerly served by Park TV & Electronics Inc. No longer in operation. ICA: IL0642.

WILLIAMSFIELD—Mediacom. Now served by WYOMING, IL [IL0196]. ICA: IL0389.

WILLIAMSON COUNTY (portions)—Zito Media, 102 S Main St, PO Box 665, Coudersport, PA 16915. Phones: 814-260-9055; 800-365-6988. E-mail: info@zitomedia.com. Web Site: http://www.zitomedia.com. Also serves Pittsburg. ICA: IL0372.
TV Market Ranking: 69 (Pittsburg, WILLIAMSON COUNTY (PORTIONS)). Franchise award date: N.A. Franchise expiration date: N.A. Began: June 1, 1986.
Channel capacity: N.A. Channels available but not in use: N.A.

Basic Service
Subscribers: 26.
Programming (received off-air): KBSI (FOX) Cape Girardeau; KFVS-TV (CBS, CW, MeTV) Cape Girardeau; WDKA (MNT, The Country Network) Paducah; WPSD-TV (Antenna TV, NBC) Paducah; WSIL-TV (ABC) Harrisburg; WSIU-TV (PBS) Carbondale; WTCT (IND) Marion.
Programming (via satellite): AMC; Cartoon Network; CNN; Comedy Central; Discovery Channel; Disney Channel; E! HD; ESPN; ESPN2; Fox News Channel; Freeform; Fuse; FX; Great American Country; HGTV; History; HLN; Lifetime; Outdoor Channel; Starz Encore; TBS; The Weather Channel; TLC; TNT; Turner Classic Movies; USA Network; WGN America.
Fee: $49.95 installation; $48.89 monthly.

Pay Service 1
Pay Units: N.A.
Programming (via satellite): HBO; Starz.

Internet Service
Operational: No.

Telephone Service
None
Miles of Plant: 17.0 (coaxial); None (fiber optic). Homes passed: 200.
President: James Rigas.
Ownership: Zito Media (MSO).

WILLIAMSVILLE—Greene County Partners Inc, PO Box 230, Virginia, IL 62691. Phones: 800-252-1799; 800-274-5789; 217-452-7725. Fax: 217-452-7797. E-mail: chadwinters@casscomm.com. Web Site: http://www.casscomm.com. Also serves Athens, Menard County (portions), Petersburg, Riverton & Sherman. ICA: IL0244.
TV Market Ranking: 64 (Athens, Menard County (portions), Petersburg, Riverton, Sherman, WILLIAMSVILLE). Franchise award date: N.A. Franchise expiration date: N.A. Began: April 1, 1980.
Channel capacity: N.A. Channels available but not in use: N.A.

Basic Service
Subscribers: 2,808.
Programming (received off-air): WAND (NBC) Decatur; WBUI (CW, This TV) Decatur; WCIA (CBS, MNT) Champaign; WCIX (CBS, MNT) Springfield; WICS (ABC, The Country Network) Springfield; WILL-TV (PBS) Urbana; WRSP-TV (Antenna TV, FOX, MeTV) Springfield; WSEC (PBS) Jacksonville.
Programming (via satellite): A&E; AMC; Animal Planet; Bravo; Cartoon Network; CMT; CNBC; CNN; Comedy Central; C-SPAN; C-SPAN 2; Discovery Channel; Disney Channel; E! HD; ESPN; ESPN Classic; ESPN2; ESPNews; EVINE Live; EWTN Global Catholic Network; Food Network; Fox News Channel; FOX Sports Midwest; Freeform; FX; FXM; Golf Channel; Great American Country; HGTV; History; HLN; Lifetime; MSNBC; MTV; National Geographic Channel; Nickelodeon; Outdoor Channel; Pop; QVC; Spike TV; Syfy; TBS; The Weather Channel; TLC; TNT; Travel Channel; Trinity Broadcasting Network (TBN); truTV; Turner Classic Movies; TV Land; USA Network; VH1; WE tv; WGN America.
Fee: $45.00 installation; $17.95 monthly; $2.00 converter.

Digital Basic Service
Subscribers: 543.
Programming (via satellite): BBC America; Discovery Digital Networks; DMX Music; FOX College Sports Central; FOX College Sports Pacific; Fox Sports 1; GSN; IFC; MTV Classic; National Geographic Channel; NBCSN; Nick Jr.; Nicktoons; VH1 Country.

Pay Service 1
Pay Units: N.A. Included in Digital Pay Service 1
Programming (via satellite): Cinemax; HBO; Starz Encore.
Fee: $40.00 installation; $4.95 monthly (Encore), $10.95 monthly (Cinemax), $11.95 monthly (HBO).

Digital Pay Service 1
Pay Units: 1,761 Includes Pay Service 1.
Programming (via satellite): Cinemax; HBO (multiplexed); Showtime (multiplexed); Starz (multiplexed); Starz Encore (multiplexed); The Movie Channel (multiplexed).

Video-On-Demand: No

Pay-Per-View
iN DEMAND (delivered digitally); Fresh (delivered digitally); Playboy TV (delivered digitally); Hot Choice (delivered digitally).

Internet Service
Operational: Yes. Began: June 1, 1999.
Broadband Service: Netlink.
Fee: $30.00 or $99.00 installation; $29.95-$99.95 monthly.

Telephone Service
Digital: Operational
Subscribers: 349.
Miles of Plant: 147.0 (coaxial); 37.0 (fiber optic). Homes passed: 4,657.
General Manager: Chad Winters. Chief Technician: Lance Allen. Marketing Director: Erynn Snedeker. Plant Manager: G.R. Mansfield. Office Manager: Cindy Kilby.
Ownership: Greene County Partners Inc. (MSO).

WILLOW HILL TWP.—Formerly served by Advanced Technologies & Technical Resources Inc. No longer in operation. ICA: IL0605.

WILMINGTON—Comcast Cable. Now served by PEORIA, IL [IL0012]. ICA: IL0099.

WILSONVILLE—Formerly served by Mediacom. Now served by Madison Communications, STAUNTON, IL [IL0171]. ICA: IL0359.

WINCHESTER—Formerly served by Crystal Broadband Networks. No longer in operation. ICA: IL0241.

WINDSOR—Mediacom. Now served by NEOGA, IL [IL0249]. ICA: IL0271.

WINSLOW—Mediacom. Now served by LENA, IL [IL0223]. ICA: IL0606.

WOLF LAKE—Formerly served by CableDirect. No longer in operation. ICA: IL0607.

WOODLAND HEIGHTS—Tel-Star Cablevision Inc, 1295 Lourdes Rd, Metamora, IL 61548-7710. Phones: 888-842-0258; 309-383-2677. Fax: 309-383-2657. E-mail: cdecker@telstar-online.net. Web Site: http://www.telstar-online.net. ICA: IL0448.
TV Market Ranking: 83 (WOODLAND HEIGHTS). Franchise award date: July 1, 1989. Franchise expiration date: N.A. Began: July 11, 1989.
Channel capacity: N.A. Channels available but not in use: N.A.

Basic Service
Subscribers: 13.
Programming (received off-air): WAOE (Antenna TV, MNT) Peoria; WEEK-TV (ABC, CW, NBC) Peoria; WHOI (Comet) Peoria; WMBD-TV (Bounce TV, CBS) Peoria; WTVP (PBS) Peoria; WYZZ-TV (FOX, The Country Network) Bloomington.
Programming (via satellite): A&E; AMC; Animal Planet; CMT; CNN; Discovery Channel; Disney Channel; ESPN; ESPN2; Food Network; Fox Sports 1; Freeform; Hallmark Channel; HGTV; History; Lifetime; MSNBC; National Geographic Channel; Nickelodeon; QVC; Spike TV; Syfy; TBS; The Weather Channel; TLC; TNT; Travel Channel; USA Network; WGN America.
Fee: $49.95 installation; $47.20 monthly; $2.95 converter.

Pay Service 1
Pay Units: 4.
Programming (via satellite): HBO.
Fee: $10.95 monthly.

Video-On-Demand: No

Internet Service
Operational: Yes.
Broadband Service: Tel-Star High Speed Internet.
Fee: $44.95 monthly; $5.00 modem lease.

Telephone Service
Digital: Operational
Fee: $24.95-$54.95 monthly
Miles of Plant: 7.0 (coaxial); None (fiber optic). Homes passed: 98.
General Manager: John Gregory. Network Operations Manager: Chris Decker. Customer Service Manager: Patti Sanders.
Ownership: Tel-Star Cablevision Inc. (MSO).

WOODLAWN—Charter Communications. Now served by ST. LOUIS, MO [MO0009]. ICA: IL0067.

WOODLAWN—Charter Communications. Now served by ST. LOUIS, MO [MO0009]. ICA: IL0256.

WOODSTOCK—Comcast Cable. Now served by MOUNT PROSPECT, IL [IL0036]. ICA: IL0608.

WORDEN—Madison Communications. Now served by STAUNTON, IL [IL0171]. ICA: IL0312.

WYOMING—Mediacom, 3900 26th Ave, Moline, IL 61265. Phone: 309-797-2580. Fax: 309-797-2414. Web Site: http://www.mediacomcable.com. Also serves Bradford, Toulon & Williamsfield. ICA: IL0196.
TV Market Ranking: 60 (Williamsfield); 83 (Bradford, Toulon, WYOMING). Franchise award date: N.A. Franchise expiration date: N.A. Began: October 1, 1982.
Channel capacity: N.A. Channels available but not in use: N.A.

Basic Service
Subscribers: 643.
Programming (received off-air): KLJB (CW, FOX, MeTV) Davenport; KWQC-TV (NBC) Davenport; WAOE (Antenna TV, MNT) Peoria; WEEK-TV (ABC, CW, NBC) Peoria; WHBF-TV (CBS) Rock Island; WHOI (Comet) Peoria; WMBD-TV (Bounce TV, CBS) Peoria; WQAD-TV (ABC, Antenna TV) Moline; WTVP (PBS) Peoria; WYZZ-TV (FOX, The Country Network) Bloomington.
Programming (via satellite): WGN America.
Fee: $45.00 installation; $43.00 monthly.

Digital Basic Service
Subscribers: N.A.
Programming (via satellite): BBC America; Bloomberg Television; CCTV-Documentary; Cloo; Destination America; Discovery Kids Channel; Discovery Life Channel; ESPN HD; ESPN2 HD; ESPNews;

Illinois—Cable Systems

ESPNU; Fox Sports 2; Fuse; FXM; FYI; Golf Channel; GSN; History International; IFC; Investigation Discovery; ION Television; LMN; MC; MTV Classic; MTV Hits; MTV2; Nat Geo WILD; National Geographic Channel; Nick Jr.; Nicktoons; Outdoor Channel; OWN: Oprah Winfrey Network; Qubo; Reelz; RFD-TV; Science Channel; Sundance TV; TeenNick; Turner Classic Movies; TVG Network.

Digital Expanded Basic Service
Subscribers: N.A.
Programming (via satellite): CBS Sports Network; FOX College Sports Central; FOX College Sports Pacific; GolTV; Tennis Channel.
Fee: $6.95 monthly.

Digital Expanded Basic Service 2
Subscribers: N.A.
Programming (via satellite): AXS TV; HD Theater; Universal HD.
Fee: $3.95 monthly.

Digital Pay Service 1
Pay Units: N.A.
Programming (via satellite): Cinemax (multiplexed); Flix; HBO (multiplexed); HBO HD; Showtime (multiplexed); Showtime HD; Starz (multiplexed); Starz Encore (multiplexed); Starz HD; Sundance TV; The Movie Channel (multiplexed); The Movie Channel HD.
Fee: $11.95 monthly (HBO, Cinemax, Starz/Encore or Showtime/TMC).
Video-On-Demand: No

Pay-Per-View
ESPN (delivered digitally); Playboy TV (delivered digitally); SexSee (delivered digitally).

Internet Service
Operational: Yes.
Broadband Service: Mediacom High Speed Internet.
Fee: $59.95 installation; $45.95 monthly.

Telephone Service
Digital: Operational
Fee: $39.95 monthly
Homes passed: 2,304. Miles of plant (coax & fiber) included in Moline
Regional Vice President: Cari Fenzel. Area Manager: Don DeMay. Engineering Director: Mitch Carlson. Technical Operations Manager: Chris Toalson. Marketing Director: Greg Evans.
Ownership: Mediacom LLC (MSO).

XENIA—Wabash Independent Networks. Now served by FLORA, IL [IL0140]. ICA: IL0373.

ZEIGLER—Mediacom, 90 Main St, Benton, KY 42025-1132. Phones: 417-875-5560 (Springfield regional office); 270-527-9939. Fax: 270-527-0813. Web Site: http://www.mediacomcable.com. Also serves Alto Pass, Blairsville, Bush, Cambria, Cobden, Dowell, Elkville, Franklin County, Hurst, Jackson County (portions), Mound City, Mounds, Perry County, Pulaski County (portions), Royalton, Union County (portions) & Williamson County (portions). ICA: IL0123.
TV Market Ranking: 69 (Alto Pass, Blairsville, Bush, Cambria, Cobden, Franklin County, Hurst, Mound City, Mounds, Pulaski County (portions), Royalton, Union County (portions), Williamson County (portions), ZEIGLER); Below 100 (Dowell, Elkville, Perry County (portions)); Outside TV Markets (Perry County (portions)). Franchise award date: N.A. Franchise expiration date: N.A. Began: January 1, 1982.
Channel capacity: N.A. Channels available but not in use: N.A.

Basic Service
Subscribers: 1,304.
Programming (received off-air): KBSI (FOX) Cape Girardeau; KFVS-TV (CBS, CW, MeTV) Cape Girardeau; WDKA (MNT, The Country Network) Paducah; WPSD-TV (Antenna TV, NBC) Paducah; WPXS (IND) Mount Vernon; WQWQ-LP (CW, MeTV) Paducah; WSIL-TV (ABC) Harrisburg; WSIU-TV (PBS) Carbondale; WTCT (IND) Marion.
Programming (via satellite): C-SPAN; Freeform; Pop; WGN America.
Fee: $36.95 installation; $42.00 monthly.

Expanded Basic Service 1
Subscribers: N.A.
Programming (via satellite): A&E; AMC; Animal Planet; BET; Bravo; Cartoon Network; CMT; CNBC; CNN; Comedy Central; C-SPAN 2; Discovery Channel; Discovery Life Channel; Disney Channel; E! HD; ESPN; ESPN2; EVINE Live; Food Network; Fox News Channel; Fox Sports 1; FOX Sports Midwest; FX; Great American Country; Hallmark Channel; HGTV; History; HLN; INSP; Lifetime; MSNBC; MTV; Nickelodeon; Outdoor Channel; QVC; Spike TV; Syfy; TBS; The Weather Channel; TLC; TNT; Travel Channel; Trinity Broadcasting Network (TBN); TV Land; USA Network; VH1; WE tv.

Digital Basic Service
Subscribers: N.A.
Programming (via satellite): BBC America; Destination America; Discovery Kids Channel; DMX Music; Fuse; FXM; FYI; Golf Channel; History International; IFC; Investigation Discovery; LMN; National Geographic Channel; NBCSN; Nick Jr.; Nicktoons; OWN: Oprah Winfrey Network; TeenNick; Turner Classic Movies.

Digital Pay Service 1
Pay Units: N.A.
Programming (via satellite): Cinemax (multiplexed); Flix; HBO; Showtime (multiplexed); Starz (multiplexed); Starz Encore (multiplexed); Sundance TV; The Movie Channel (multiplexed).
Video-On-Demand: Yes

Internet Service
Operational: Yes.
Broadband Service: Mediacom High Speed Internet.

Telephone Service
Digital: Operational
Miles of Plant: 116.0 (coaxial); None (fiber optic). Homes passed: 5,142.
Regional Vice President: Bill Copeland. General Manager: Dale Haney. Regional Technical Operations Director: Alan Freedman. Technical Operations Manager: Jeff Brown. Marketing Director: Will Kuebler. Marketing Manager: Melanie Westerman.
Ownership: Mediacom LLC (MSO).

INDIANA

Total Systems: 53	Communities with Applications: 0
Total Communities Served: 557	Number of Basic Subscribers: 641,319
Franchises Not Yet Operating: 0	Number of Expanded Basic Subscribers: 324
Applications Pending: 0	Number of Pay Units: 1,492

Top 100 Markets Represented: Indianapolis-Bloomington (16); Cincinnati, OH-Newport, KY (17); Louisville, KY (38); Chicago (3); Dayton-Kettering, OH (41); Cape Girardeau, MO-Paducah, KY-Harrisburg, IL (69); South Bend-Elkhart (80); Fort Wayne-Roanoke (82); Evansville (86).

For a list of cable communities in this section, see the Cable Community Index located in the back of Cable Volume 2.
For explanation of terms used in cable system listings, see p. D-11.

AKRON (town)—Comcast Cable. Now served by CHAMPAIGN, IL [IL0019]. ICA: IN0170.

ALLEN COUNTY—Mediacom. Now served by AUBURN, IN [IN0066]. ICA: IN0087.

AMBOY—Formerly served by CableDirect. No longer in operation. ICA: IN0222.

ANDERSON—Comcast Cable. Now served by HENDRICKS COUNTY (portions), IN [IN0001]. ICA: IN0012.

ANDERSON—Formerly served by Broadcast Cable Inc. No longer in operation. ICA: IN0344.

ANDREWS—Formerly served by Longview Communications. No longer in operation. ICA: IN0223.

ANGOLA—Mediacom, PO Box 334, Chillicothe, IN 61523. Phones: 260-927-3015; 845-695-2762. Web Site: http://www.mediacomcable.com. Also serves Butler, Fremont, Hamilton & Steuben County (portions). ICA: IN0034.
TV Market Ranking: 82 (Butler, Hamilton, Steuben County (portions)); Below 100 (ANGOLA, Fremont, Steuben County (portions)). Franchise award date: N.A. Franchise expiration date: N.A. Began: September 1, 1966.
Channel capacity: N.A. Channels available but not in use: N.A.
Basic Service
Subscribers: 2,958.
Programming (received off-air): WANE-TV (Antenna TV, CBS) Fort Wayne; WFFT-TV (FOX, MeTV) Fort Wayne; WFWA (PBS) Fort Wayne; WHME-TV (COZI TV, IND) South Bend; WINM (IND) Angola; WISE-TV (CW) Fort Wayne; WNIT (PBS) South Bend; WPTA (ABC, MNT, NBC) Fort Wayne; 20 FMs.
Programming (via satellite): A&E; AMC; Animal Planet; Cartoon Network; CMT; CNBC; CNN; Comedy Central; C-SPAN; Discovery Channel; Disney Channel; E! HD; ESPN; ESPN2; Food Network; Fox News Channel; Fox Sports 1; FOX Sports Midwest; Freeform; FX; Hallmark Channel; HGTV; History; HLN; Lifetime; MSNBC; MTV; Nickelodeon; Pop; QVC; Spike TV; Syfy; TBS; The Weather Channel; TLC; TNT; Travel Channel; Trinity Broadcasting Network (TBN); TV Land; Univision Studios; USA Network; VH1; WE tv; WGN America.
Fee: $45.00 installation; $43.00 monthly.
Digital Basic Service
Subscribers: N.A.
Programming (via satellite): BBC America; Bloomberg Television; Discovery Digital Networks; DMX Music; FYI; Golf Channel; GSN; History International; HITS (Head-end In The Sky); IFC; LMN; NBCSN; Turner Classic Movies.
Digital Pay Service 1
Pay Units: N.A.
Programming (via satellite): Cinemax (multiplexed); HBO (multiplexed); Showtime (multiplexed); Starz Encore (multiplexed); The Movie Channel (multiplexed).
Fee: $11.95 monthly (each).
Video-On-Demand: Yes
Pay-Per-View
Playboy TV (delivered digitally).
Internet Service
Operational: Yes.
Broadband Service: Mediacom High Speed Internet.
Fee: $59.95 installation; $40.95 monthly.
Telephone Service
Analog: Not Operational
Digital: Operational
Fee: $39.95 monthly
Homes passed: 11,515.
Vice President, Financial Reporting: Kenneth J. Kohrs. Operations Director: Joe Poffenberger. Technical Operations Manager: Craig Grey. Chief Technician: Mike Parr.
Ownership: Mediacom LLC (MSO).

ARGOS—Mediacom. Now served by NORTH WEBSTER, IN [IN0038]. ICA: IN0154.

ASHLEY—Formerly served by Longview Communications. No longer in operation. ICA: IN0225.

AUBURN—Mediacom, 1102 North 4th St, PO Box 334, Chillicothe, IN 61523. Phones: 845-695-2762; 309-274-4500 (Chillicothe regional office); 260-927-3015. Web Site: http://www.mediacomcable.com. Also serves Adams Lake, Albion, Allen County, Cedarville, Churubusco, Columbia City, Cromwell, DeKalb County, Garrett, Grabill, Harlan, Kendallville, Laketon, Laotto, Leo, Ligonier, Noble County (portions), North Manchester, Rome City, Skinner Lake, South Whitley, Spencerville, St. Joe, Tri-Lakes, Wabash, Waterloo & Wolcottville. ICA: IN0066.
TV Market Ranking: 80 (Cromwell); 80,82 (Adams Lake, Albion, Rome City, Skinner Lake, Wolcottville); 82 (Allen County, AUBURN, Cedarville, Churubusco, Columbia City, DeKalb County, Garrett, Grabill, Harlan, Kendallville, Laketon, Laotto, Leo, Ligonier, Noble County (portions), North Manchester, South Whitley, Spencerville, St. Joe, Tri-Lakes, Wabash, Waterloo). Franchise award date: N.A. Franchise expiration date: N.A. Began: May 1, 1975.
Channel capacity: N.A. Channels available but not in use: N.A.
Basic Service
Subscribers: 7,592.
Programming (received off-air): WANE-TV (Antenna TV, CBS) Fort Wayne; WFFT-TV (FOX, MeTV) Fort Wayne; WFWA (PBS) Fort Wayne; WHME-TV (COZI TV, IND) South Bend; WINM (IND) Angola; WISE-TV (CW) Fort Wayne; WNIT (PBS) South Bend; WPTA (ABC, MNT, NBC) Fort Wayne; WTTK (CW, This TV) Kokomo; 1 FM.
Programming (via satellite): WGN America.
Fee: $45.00 installation; $53.91 monthly.
Expanded Basic Service 1
Subscribers: N.A.
Programming (via satellite): A&E; AMC; Animal Planet; Bravo; Cartoon Network; CMT; CNBC; CNN; Comedy Central; C-SPAN; CW PLUS; Discovery Channel; Disney Channel; E! HD; ESPN; ESPN2; Food Network; Fox News Channel; Fox Sports 1; FOX Sports Networks; Freeform; FX; Hallmark Channel; HGTV; History; HLN; Lifetime; MSNBC; MTV; Nickelodeon; Pop; QVC; Radar Channel; Spike TV; Syfy; TBS; The Weather Channel; TLC; TNT; Travel Channel; Trinity Broadcasting Network (TBN); TV Land; Univision Studios; USA Network; VH1; WE tv.
Fee: $34.00 monthly.
Digital Basic Service
Subscribers: N.A.
Programming (via satellite): BBC America; Bloomberg Television; Cinelatino; CNN en Espanol; Destination America; Discovery Kids Channel; Discovery Life Channel; Fox Deportes; Fox Life; FXM; FYI; Golf Channel; GSN; History International; IFC; Investigation Discovery; LMN; MTV Hits; National Geographic Channel; NBCSN; Outdoor Channel; OWN: Oprah Winfrey Network; Science Channel; Toon Disney en Espanol; Tr3s; Turner Classic Movies.
Pay Service 1
Pay Units: N.A.
Programming (via satellite): Cinemax; HBO; Showtime; Starz; Starz Encore.
Digital Pay Service 1
Pay Units: N.A.
Programming (via satellite): Cinemax (multiplexed); HBO (multiplexed); Showtime (multiplexed); Starz (multiplexed); Starz Encore (multiplexed); The Movie Channel (multiplexed).
Fee: $11.95 monthly (Cinemax, HBO, Showtime/TMC or Starz/Encore).
Video-On-Demand: Yes
Internet Service
Operational: Yes.
Subscribers: 2,377.
Broadband Service: Mediacom High Speed Internet.
Fee: $59.95 installation; $40.95 monthly.
Telephone Service
Analog: Not Operational
Digital: Operational
Subscribers: 993.
Fee: $39.95 monthly
Miles of Plant: 213.0 (coaxial); 54.0 (fiber optic). Homes passed: 8,251.
Vice President: Don Hagwell. Vice President, Financial Reporting: Kenneth J. Kohrs. Sales & Marketing Director: Stephanie Law. Technical Operations Manager: Craig Grey. Operations Manager: Joe Poffenberger.
Ownership: Mediacom LLC (MSO).

AVILLA—NewWave Communications, One Montgomery Plaza, 4th Floor, Sikeston, MO 63801. Phones: 888-863-9928; 888-863-9928. Fax: 573-481-9809. E-mail: info@newwavecom.com. Web Site: http://www.newwavecom.com. Also serves Noble County (portions). ICA: IN0357.
TV Market Ranking: 82 (AVILLA); Below 100 (Noble County (portions)). Franchise award date: June 1, 1981. Franchise expiration date: N.A. Began: N.A.
Channel capacity: N.A. Channels available but not in use: N.A.
Basic Service
Subscribers: 97. Commercial subscribers: 1.
Programming (received off-air): WANE-TV (Antenna TV, CBS) Fort Wayne; WFFT-TV (FOX, MeTV) Fort Wayne; WFWA (PBS) Fort Wayne; WINM (IND) Angola; WISE-TV (CW) Fort Wayne; WPTA (ABC, MNT, NBC) Fort Wayne.
Programming (via satellite): Freeform.
Fee: $50.00 installation; $20.15 monthly.
Expanded Basic Service 1
Subscribers: N.A.
Programming (via satellite): A&E; AMC; CMT; CNBC; CNN; C-SPAN; Discovery Channel; Disney Channel; E! HD; ESPN; ESPN2; EWTN Global Catholic Network; HLN; Lifetime; MTV; Nickelodeon; QVC; Spike TV; Syfy; TBS; TNT; USA Network; VH1; WGN America.
Fee: $39.98 monthly.
Pay Service 1
Pay Units: N.A.
Programming (via satellite): Cinemax; HBO; Showtime.
Fee: $15.95 monthly (each).
Internet Service
Operational: Yes.
Telephone Service
Digital: Operational
General Manager: John Helmers.
Ownership: NewWave Communications LLC (MSO).

BAINBRIDGE—Formerly served by Global Com Inc. No longer in operation. ICA: IN0205.

Indiana—Cable Systems

BATESVILLE—Formerly served by Comcast Cable. Now served by Enhanced Telecommunications Corp., BROOKVILLE, IN [IN0108]. ICA: IN0078.

BEDFORD—Comcast Cable. Now served by HENDRICKS COUNTY (portions), IN [IN0001]. ICA: IN0033.

BICKNELL—Formerly served by Charter Communications. Now served by NewWave Communications, VINCENNES, IN [IN0035]. ICA: IN0092.

BIRDSEYE—Formerly served by CableDirect. No longer in operation. ICA: IN0319.

BLOOMFIELD—Formerly served by Insight Communications. Now served by Comcast Cable, HENDRICKS COUNTY (portions), IN [IN0001]. ICA: IN0228.

BLOOMINGTON—Comcast Cable. Now served by HENDRICKS COUNTY (portions), IN [IN0001]. ICA: IN0016.

BOONVILLE—Time Warner Cable. Now served by EVANSVILLE, IN [IN0006]. ICA: IN0086.

BOSWELL—Benton County Cable Co, 205 East Railroad Ave, PO Box 9, Cissna Park, IL 60924. Phones: 800-825-3882; 800-474-9488. Web Site: http://www.parktvcable.com. ICA: IN0229.
TV Market Ranking: Below 100 (BOSWELL).
Channel capacity: N.A. Channels available but not in use: N.A.
Basic Service
  Subscribers: 19.
  Programming (received off-air): WAND (NBC) Decatur; WCCU (FOX, MeTV) Urbana; WCIA (CBS, MNT) Champaign; WHMB-TV (IND) Indianapolis; WILL-TV (PBS) Urbana; WLFI-TV (CBS, TheCoolTV) Lafayette; WRTV (ABC, Grit) Indianapolis; WTHR (COZI TV, MeTV, NBC) Indianapolis; WTTV (CBS, This TV) Bloomington; WXIN (Antenna TV, FOX) Indianapolis.
  Programming (via satellite): QVC; The Weather Channel; Trinity Broadcasting Network (TBN).
  Fee: $32.50 installation; $21.98 monthly.
Video-On-Demand: No
Internet Service
  Operational: No.
Telephone Service
  None
Miles of Plant: 5.0 (coaxial); None (fiber optic). Homes passed: 356.
President: Joe Young.
Ownership: Park TV & Electronics Inc. (MSO).

BOURBON—Mediacom. Now served by NORTH WEBSTER, IN [IN0038]. ICA: IN0128.

BRAZIL—NewWave Communications. Now served by VINCENNES, IN [IN0035]. ICA: IN0027.

BREMEN—Mediacom. Now served by NORTH WEBSTER, IN [IN0038]. ICA: IN0067.

BRISTOL—Comcast Cable. Now served by CHAMPAIGN, IL [IL0019]. ICA: IN0231.

BROOKLYN—Formerly served by CableDirect. No longer in operation. ICA: IN0232.

BROOKVILLE—Enhanced Telecommunications Corp, 123 Nieman St, Sunman, IN 47041. Phones: 866-382-4968; 812-623-2122. Fax: 812-623-4159. Web Site: http://www.etczone.com. Also serves Batesville, Flat Rock & Liberty. ICA: IN0108.
TV Market Ranking: 16 (Flat Rock); 17 (BROOKVILLE); Below 100 (Liberty); Outside TV Markets (Batesville). Franchise award date: N.A. Franchise expiration date: N.A. Began: January 1, 1982.
Channel capacity: 90 (not 2-way capable). Channels available but not in use: N.A.
Basic Service
  Subscribers: 3,851.
  Programming (received off-air): WCET (PBS) Cincinnati; WCPO-TV (ABC, Escape) Cincinnati; WKRC-TV (CBS, CW) Cincinnati; WLWT (MeTV, NBC) Cincinnati; WPTD (PBS) Dayton; WPTO (PBS) Oxford; WSTR-TV (Antenna TV, MNT) Cincinnati; WTTV (CBS, This TV) Bloomington; WXIX-TV (Bounce TV, FOX) Newport.
  Programming (via satellite): C-SPAN; Trinity Broadcasting Network (TBN); WGN America.
  Fee: $15.00 installation; $14.95 monthly.
Digital Basic Service
  Subscribers: N.A.
  Programming (via satellite): A&E; AMC; Animal Planet; CMT; CNBC; CNN; C-SPAN 2; Discovery Channel; Disney Channel; Disney XD; E! HD; ESPN; ESPN2; ESPNews; Esquire Network; EWTN Global Catholic Network; Fox Business Network; Fox News Channel; Freeform; Fuse; FX; GSN; Hallmark Channel; HGTV; History; HLN; Lifetime; MSNBC; MTV; NBCSN; Nickelodeon; Spike TV; Syfy; TBS; The Weather Channel; TLC; TNT; Travel Channel; TV Land; USA Network; VH1.
Digital Pay Service 1
  Pay Units: N.A.
  Programming (via satellite): Cinemax; HBO; Showtime; Starz; Starz Encore; The Movie Channel.
  Fee: $12.95 monthly (each).
Video-On-Demand: Yes
Internet Service
  Operational: Yes.
  Fee: $75.00 installation; $26.95-$99.95 monthly.
Telephone Service
  Digital: Operational
  Fee: $27.57 monthly
Miles of Plant: 21.0 (coaxial); None (fiber optic).
President & Chief Executive Officer: Chad Miles. Chief Financial Officer: Mike Alig. Chief Technical Officer: Kevin McGuire. Vice President, Operations: Mike Fledderman. Network Operations Manager: Matt Anderson. Customer Service/Sales Manager: Becky Brashear. Business Development Manager: Lori Feldbauer. Marketing Manager: Anita Fledderman. Video Operations Manager: Ryan Ibold. Facilities/Safety Manager: Dave Smith.
Ownership: Enhanced Telecommunications Corp. (MSO).

BROWNSTOWN—Comcast Cable. Now served by HENDRICKS COUNTY (portions), IN [IN0001]. ICA: IN0127.

BUTLER—Mediacom. Now served by ANGOLA, IN [IN0034]. ICA: IN0359.

CAMPBELLSBURG—Formerly served by Insight Communications. Now served by Time Warner Cable, LOUISVILLE, KY [KY0001]. ICA: IN0233.

CARBON—NewWave Communications. Now served by VINCENNES, IN [IN0035]. ICA: IN0374.

CARLISLE—Formerly served by Almega Cable. No longer in operation. ICA: IN0199.

CARMEL—FirstMile Technologies, 750 Liberty Drive, PO Box 788, Westfield, IN 46074. Phone: 317-569-2800. E-mail: info@firstmileusa.com. Also serves Fishers, Westfield & Zionsville. ICA: IN0380.
TV Market Ranking: 16 (CARMEL, Fishers, Westfield, Zionsville).
Channel capacity: N.A. Channels available but not in use: N.A.
Basic Service
  Subscribers: 685.
  Fee: $49.95 installation; $42.95 monthly.
President: Craig Kunkle.
Ownership: E.com Technologies LLC.

CATARACT LAKE—Formerly served by Longview Communications. No longer in operation. ICA: IN0235.

CENTER POINT—Formerly served by CableDirect. No longer in operation. ICA: IN0236.

CENTERTON—NewWave Communications. Now served by MORGAN COUNTY (portions), IN [IN0098]. ICA: IN0367.

CHRISNEY—Formerly served by CableDirect. No longer in operation. ICA: IN0237.

CLAY CITY—Formerly served by Global Com Inc. No longer in operation. ICA: IN0174.

CLEAR LAKE—Mediacom. Now served by ELMWOOD, IL [IL0205]. ICA: IN0239.

CLINTON—NewWave Communications. Now served by VINCENNES, IN [IN0035]. ICA: IN0049.

CLOVERDALE—Formerly served by Indiana Communications. No longer in operation. ICA: IN0240.

COAL CITY—Formerly served by CableDirect. No longer in operation. ICA: IN0241.

COATESVILLE—NewWave Communications. Now served by VINCENNES, IN [IN0035]. ICA: IN0261.

COLUMBUS—Comcast Cable. Now served by HENDRICKS COUNTY (portions), IN [IN0001]. ICA: IN0022.

CONNERSVILLE—Comcast Cable. Now served by HENDRICKS COUNTY (portions), IN [IN0001]. ICA: IN0040.

CORUNNA—Formerly served by CableDirect. No longer in operation. ICA: IN0242.

COVINGTON—NewWave Communications, One Montgomery Plaza, 4th Floor, Sikeston, MO 63801. Phones: 888-863-9928; 888-863-9928. Fax: 573-481-9809. E-mail: info@newwavecom.com. Web Site: http://www.newwavecom.com. Also serves Fountain County (portions) & Veedersburg. ICA: IN0124.
TV Market Ranking: Below 100 (COVINGTON, Fountain County (portions) (portions), Veedersburg). Outside TV Markets (Fountain County (portions) (portions)). Franchise award date: N.A. Franchise expiration date: N.A. Began: September 1, 1965.
Channel capacity: 52 (operating 2-way). Channels available but not in use: N.A.
Basic Service
  Subscribers: 517.
  Programming (received off-air): WCIA (CBS, MNT) Champaign; WHMB-TV (IND) Indianapolis; WILL-TV (PBS) Urbana; WISH-TV (CW) Indianapolis; WLFI-TV (CBS, TheCoolTV) Lafayette; WRTV (ABC, Grit) Indianapolis; WTHR (COZI TV, MeTV, NBC) Indianapolis; WTTV (CBS, This TV) Bloomington; WTWO (NBC) Terre Haute; WXIN (Antenna TV, FOX) Indianapolis.
  Programming (via satellite): C-SPAN; C-SPAN 2; WGN America.
  Fee: $40.00 installation; $32.93 monthly.
Expanded Basic Service 1
  Subscribers: N.A.
  Programming (via satellite): A&E; AMC; Animal Planet; CMT; CNBC; CNN; Comedy Central; Discovery Channel; Disney Channel; E! HD; ESPN; ESPN2; ESPNews; Food Network; Freeform; FX; Golf Channel; HGTV; History; Lifetime; MSNBC; MTV; NBCSN; Nickelodeon; Spike TV; TBS; The Weather Channel; TLC; TNT; USA Network; VH1.
Digital Basic Service
  Subscribers: N.A.
  Programming (via satellite): BBC America; CMT; Discovery Digital Networks; Disney XD; Flix; Fuse; FYI; GSN; History International; LMN; MC; National Geographic Channel; Nick Jr.; Nicktoons; Outdoor Channel; Sprout; Starz Encore; Sundance TV; Syfy; TeenNick; Trinity Broadcasting Network (TBN); Turner Classic Movies; TV Land; WE tv.
Digital Pay Service 1
  Pay Units: N.A.
  Programming (via satellite): Cinemax (multiplexed); HBO (multiplexed); Showtime (multiplexed); Starz (multiplexed); The Movie Channel (multiplexed).
Video-On-Demand: No
Pay-Per-View
  iN DEMAND (delivered digitally); Playboy TV (delivered digitally).
Internet Service
  Operational: Yes.
Telephone Service
  Digital: Operational
Miles of Plant: 27.0 (coaxial); None (fiber optic). Homes passed: 1,371.
Chief Financial Officer: Rod Siemers. General Manager: John Helmers.
Ownership: NewWave Communications LLC (MSO).

CRAWFORD COUNTY (portions)—Formerly served by NewWave Communications. No longer in operation. ICA: IN0134.

CRAWFORDSVILLE—Comcast Cable. Now served by HENDRICKS COUNTY (portions), IN [IN0001]. ICA: IN0043.

CRAWFORDSVILLE—Formerly served by Acceplus. Now served by Metronet, GREENCASTLE, IN [IN5142]. ICA: IN5130.

CYNTHIANA—Time Warner Cable. Now served by EVANSVILLE, IN [IN0006]. ICA: IN0201.

DARLINGTON—Formerly served by Indiana Communications. No longer in operation. ICA: IN0195.

Cable Systems—Indiana

DECATUR—Mediacom, 109 East 5th St, Ste A, Auburn, IN 46706. Phones: 845-695-2762; 260-927-3015. Fax: 260-347-4433. Web Site: http://www.mediacomcable.com. Also serves Bluffton (village), Craigville, Kingsland, Liberty Center, Magley, Monmouth, Monroe, Murray, Pleasant Mills, Poneto, Preble, Tocsin, Uniondale, Vera Cruz & Wells County. ICA: IN0059.

TV Market Ranking: 82 (Bluffton (village), Craigville, DECATUR, Kingsland, Liberty Center, Magley, Monmouth, Monroe, Murray, Pleasant Mills, Poneto, Preble, Tocsin, Uniondale, Vera Cruz, Wells County). Franchise award date: January 1, 1975. Franchise expiration date: N.A. Began: February 1, 1976.

Channel capacity: N.A. Channels available but not in use: N.A.

Basic Service
Subscribers: 2,124.
Programming (received off-air): WANE-TV (Antenna TV, CBS) Fort Wayne; WFFT-TV (FOX, MeTV) Fort Wayne; WFWA (PBS) Fort Wayne; WHME-TV (COZI TV, IND) South Bend; WINM (IND) Angola; WIPB (PBS) Muncie; WISE-TV (CW) Fort Wayne; WPTA (ABC, MNT, NBC) Fort Wayne; WTTK (CW, This TV) Kokomo; allband FM.
Programming (via satellite): Bravo; CW PLUS; WGN America.
Fee: $45.00 installation; $43.00 monthly; $2.75 converter.

Expanded Basic Service 1
Subscribers: N.A.
Programming (via satellite): A&E; AMC; Animal Planet; Cartoon Network; CMT; CNBC; CNN; Comedy Central; C-SPAN; Discovery Channel; Disney Channel; E! HD; ESPN; ESPN2; Food Network; Fox News Channel; Fox Sports 1; FOX Sports Networks; Freeform; FX; Hallmark Channel; HGTV; History; HLN; Lifetime; MSNBC; MTV; MyNetworkTV; Nickelodeon; QVC; Radar Channel; Spike TV; Syfy; TBS; The Weather Channel; TLC; TNT; Travel Channel; Trinity Broadcasting Network (TBN); TV Land; Univision Studios; USA Network; VH1; WE tv.
Fee: $34.00 monthly.

Digital Basic Service
Subscribers: N.A.
Programming (via satellite): AXS TV; BBC America; Bloomberg Television; CBS Sports Network; CCTV-Documentary; Cinelatino; Cloo; CNN en Espanol; CNN HD; Destination America; Discovery Kids Channel; Discovery Life Channel; ESPN HD; ESPN2 HD; ESPNews; ESPNU; FOX College Sports Central; FOX College Sports Pacific; Fox Deportes; Fox Life; FSN HD; FXM; FYI; Golf Channel; GolTV; GSN; HD Theater; History International; IFC; Investigation Discovery; ION Television; LMN; MTV Classic; MTV Hits; MTV2; National Geographic Channel; NBCSN; Nick Jr.; Nicktoons; Outdoor Channel; OWN: Oprah Winfrey Network; Reelz; Science Channel; TBS HD; TeenNick; Tennis Channel; TNT HD; Toon Disney en Espanol; Tr3s; Turner Classic Movies; TVG Network; Universal HD.

Digital Pay Service 1
Pay Units: N.A.
Programming (via satellite): Cinemax (multiplexed); Flix; HBO (multiplexed); HBO HD; Showtime (multiplexed); Showtime HD; Starz (multiplexed); Starz Encore (multiplexed); Sundance TV; The Movie Channel (multiplexed); The Movie Channel HD.
Fee: $11.95 monthly (Cinemax, HBO, Showtime/TMC or Starz/Encore).
Video-On-Demand: Yes

Pay-Per-View
special events; iN DEMAND.
Internet Service
Operational: Yes.
Broadband Service: Mediacom High Speed Internet.
Fee: $40.95 monthly.
Telephone Service
Analog: Not Operational
Digital: Operational
Fee: $39.95 monthly
Miles of Plant: 262.0 (coaxial); 44.0 (fiber optic). Homes passed: 12,482.
Vice President, Financial Reporting: Kenneth J. Kohrs. Operations Director: Joe Poffenberger. Technical Operations Manager: Craig Grey.
Ownership: Mediacom LLC (MSO).

DECKER—Formerly served by CableDirect. No longer in operation. ICA: IN0244.

DESOTO—Comcast Cable. Now served by HENDRICKS COUNTY (portions), IN [IN0001]. ICA: IN0187.

DISTRICT OF SWEETWATER—Formerly served by NewWave Communications. No longer in operation. ICA: IN0373.

DUBOIS COUNTY—Formerly served by CableDirect. No longer in operation. ICA: IN0247.

DUPONT—Formerly served by CableDirect. No longer in operation. ICA: IN0248.

ECONOMY—Formerly served by CableDirect. No longer in operation. ICA: IN0219.

EDINBURGH—Formerly served by Avenue Broadband Communications. Now served by NewWave Communications, VINCENNES, IN [IN0035]. ICA: IN0105.

ELBERFELD—NewWave Communications, One Montgomery Plaza, 4th Floor, Sikeston, MO 63801. Phone: 888-863-9928. Fax: 573-481-9809. E-mail: info@newwavecom.com. Web Site: http://www.newwavecom.com. Also serves Warrick County (portions). ICA: IN0190.
TV Market Ranking: 86 (ELBERFELD, Warrick County (portions)). Franchise award date: September 10, 1981. Franchise expiration date: N.A. Began: January 1, 1982.
Channel capacity: N.A. Channels available but not in use: N.A.

Basic Service
Subscribers: 43.
Programming (received off-air): WEHT (ABC) Evansville; WEVV-TV (CBS, FOX) Evansville; WFIE (NBC, This TV) Evansville; WNIN (PBS) Evansville; WTVW (CW, MeTV) Evansville.
Programming (via satellite): QVC; TBS; WGN America.
Fee: $45.25 installation; $23.66 monthly; $1.81 converter.

Expanded Basic Service 1
Subscribers: N.A.
Programming (via satellite): A&E; Animal Planet; CNN; Comedy Central; Discovery Channel; Disney Channel; ESPN; ESPN2; Fox News Channel; Freeform; HGTV; HLN; Lifetime; MTV; Nickelodeon; Spike TV; Syfy; The Weather Channel; TNT; Turner Classic Movies; TV Land; USA Network; VH1.
Fee: $9.31 monthly.

Pay Service 1
Pay Units: N.A.
Programming (via satellite): Cinemax; HBO.
Fee: $20.00 installation; $9.50 monthly (each).
Video-On-Demand: No
Internet Service
Operational: No.
Telephone Service
None
Miles of Plant: 12.0 (coaxial); None (fiber optic). Homes passed: 521.
General Manager: John Helmers.
Ownership: NewWave Communications LLC (MSO).

ELIZABETH (town)—Formerly served by Windjammer Cable. No longer in operation. ICA: IN0249.

ELKHART—Comcast Cable. Now served by CHAMPAIGN, IL [IL0019]. ICA: IN0010.

ENGLISH—Formerly served by NewWave Communications. No longer in operation. ICA: IN0379.

EVANSVILLE—Time Warner Cable, 60 Columbus Circle, 17th Fl, New York, NY 10023. Phones: 212-364-8200; 212-364-8200; 800-824-4003; 812-838-2044; 812-422-1167. Fax: 212-364-8252. Web Site: http://www.timewarnercable.com. Also serves Boonville, Cynthiana, Darmstadt, Dubois County (portions), Fort Branch, Gibson County (portions), Haubstadt, Huntingburg, Jasper, Mount Vernon, Owensville, Patoka, Posey County (portions), Poseyville, Princeton, Vanderburgh County (portions) & Warrick County (portions), IN; Henderson & Henderson County (portions), KY. ICA: IN0006.
TV Market Ranking: 86 (Boonville, Cynthiana, Darmstadt, Dubois County (portions), EVANSVILLE, Fort Branch, Gibson County (portions), Haubstadt, Henderson, Henderson County (portions), Mount Vernon, Owensville, Patoka, Posey County (portions), Poseyville, Princeton, Princeton, Vanderburgh County (portions), Warrick County (portions)); Outside TV Markets (Huntingburg, Jasper, Dubois County (portions)). Franchise award date: March 14, 1976. Franchise expiration date: N.A. Began: March 1, 1979.
Channel capacity: N.A. Channels available but not in use: N.A.

Basic Service
Subscribers: 45,161. Commercial subscribers: 395.
Programming (received off-air): WEHT (ABC) Evansville; WEVV-TV (CBS, FOX) Evansville; WFIE (NBC, This TV) Evansville; WNIN (PBS) Evansville; WTVW (CW, MeTV) Evansville.
Programming (via satellite): C-SPAN; C-SPAN 2; Discovery Channel; EWTN Global Catholic Network; QVC; TBS; Trinity Broadcasting Network (TBN); WGN America.
Fee: $35.00 monthly; $19.95 monthly; $1.01 converter.

Expanded Basic Service 1
Subscribers: N.A.
Programming (via satellite): A&E; AMC; Animal Planet; BET; Bravo; Cartoon Network; CMT; CNBC; CNN; Comedy Central; Disney Channel; Disney XD; E! HD; ESPN; ESPN2; Food Network; Fox News Channel; Fox Sports 1; FOX Sports Midwest; FOX Sports Ohio/Sports Time Ohio; Freeform; FX; Golf Channel; Hallmark Channel; History; HLN; Lifetime; MSNBC; MTV; National Geographic Channel; Nickelodeon; Oxygen; Pop; Spike TV; Syfy; The Weather Channel; TLC; TNT; Travel Channel; truTV; TV Land; USA Network; VH1.
Fee: $40.00 monthly.

Digital Basic Service
Subscribers: N.A.
Programming (via satellite): AXS TV; BBC America; Bloomberg Television; BTN; CBS Sports Network; Cloo; Cooking Channel; Discovery Digital Networks; DIY Network; ESPN; ESPN Classic; ESPNews; ESPNU; Fuse; FXM; FYI; GSN; HD Theater; History International; IFC; LMN; MC; NBCSN; NFL Network; Nick 2; Nick Jr.; Nicktoons; Outdoor Channel; Sprout; Starz Encore (multiplexed); Sundance TV; TeenNick; Turner Classic Movies; Universal HD; WE tv.

Digital Pay Service 1
Pay Units: N.A.
Programming (via satellite): Cinemax (multiplexed); Flix; HBO (multiplexed); HBO HD; Showtime (multiplexed); Showtime HD; Starz (multiplexed); The Movie Channel (multiplexed).
Fee: $10.00 monthly (Cinemax or Starz), $13.00 monthly (HBO or Showtime/TMC).
Video-On-Demand: Yes
Pay-Per-View
iN DEMAND (delivered digitally); ESPN (delivered digitally).
Internet Service
Operational: Yes.
Subscribers: 51,924.
Broadband Service: InsightBB.com.
Fee: $99.95 installation; $40.00 monthly; $10.00 modem lease; $99.00 modem purchase.
Telephone Service
Digital: Operational
Subscribers: 31,669.
Fee: $25.00 monthly
Miles of Plant: 2,616.0 (coaxial); 5,227.0 (fiber optic). Homes passed: 142,137.
Chief Executive Officer: Glenn A. Britt. President & Chief Operations Officer: Robert D. Marcus.
Ownership: Time Warner Cable (MSO).

EVANSVILLE—WOW! Internet, Cable & Phone, 7887 East Belleview Ave, Ste 1000, Englewood, CO 80111. Phones: 866-496-9669; 812-437-0345. E-mail: wow_general@wideopenwest.com. Web Site: http://www.wowway.com. Also serves Boonville, Chandler, Mount Vernon, Newburgh, Vanderburgh County (portions) & Warrick County (portions). ICA: IN0365.
Note: This system is an overbuild.
TV Market Ranking: 86 (Boonville, Chandler, EVANSVILLE, Mount Vernon, Newburgh, Vanderburgh County (portions), Warrick County (portions)). Franchise award date: N.A. Franchise expiration date: N.A. Began: April 1, 1999.
Channel capacity: 14 (operating 2-way). Channels available but not in use: N.A.

Basic Service
Subscribers: 23,995.
Programming (received off-air): WEHT (ABC) Evansville; WEVV-TV (CBS, FOX) Evansville; WFIE (NBC, This TV) Evansville; WNIN (PBS) Evansville; WTVW (CW, MeTV) Evansville.
Programming (via satellite): A&E; AMC; Animal Planet; BET; Bloomberg Television; Bravo; BTN; Cartoon Network; CMT; CNBC; CNN; Comedy Central; C-SPAN; C-SPAN 2; Discovery Channel; Disney Channel; Disney XD; E! HD; ESPN; ESPN Classic; ESPN2; ESPNews; EVINE Live; EWTN Global Catholic Network; Food Network; Fox News Channel; Fox Sports

Indiana—Cable Systems

1; FOX Sports Midwest; Freeform; FX; FYI; Golf Channel; Great American Country; Hallmark Channel; HGTV; History; HLN; Lifetime; MSNBC; MTV; National Geographic Channel; Nickelodeon; OWN: Oprah Winfrey Network; Oxygen; QVC; Spike TV; Syfy; TBS; The Weather Channel; TLC; TNT; Travel Channel; truTV; TV Land; USA Network; VH1; WGN America.
Fee: $50.00 installation; $32.00 monthly.

Digital Basic Service
Subscribers: N.A.
Programming (via satellite): A&E HD; Animal Planet HD; AXS TV; BBC America; Boomerang; BTN; BTN HD; BYUtv; CBS Sports Network; Church Channel; CMT; CNBC World; Cooking Channel; Daystar TV Network; Destination America; Discovery Channel; Discovery Channel HD; Discovery Kids Channel; Discovery Life Channel; DIY Network; ESPN HD; ESPN2 HD; ESPNU; Food Network HD; Fox Business Network; FOX College Sports Central; FOX College Sports Pacific; Fox HD; Fox News HD; FX HD; FXM; HD Theater; here! On Demand; HGTV HD; History HD; History International; HRTV; IFC; Investigation Discovery; LMN; MTV Classic; MTV Hits; MTV Jams; MTV2; National Geographic Channel HD; NBC Universo; NFL Network; NFL Network HD; Nick 2; Nick Jr.; Nicktoons; Outdoor Channel; PBS HD; Science Channel; Sprout; Starz (multiplexed); Starz Encore (multiplexed); Starz On Demand; Sundance TV; TeenNick; Tennis Channel; TLC HD; TNT HD; Tr3s; Trinity Broadcasting Network (TBN); Turner Classic Movies; TVG Network; Universal HD; VH1 Soul; WAM! America's Kidz Network.

Digital Pay Service 1
Pay Units: N.A.
Programming (via satellite): Cinemax (multiplexed); Cinemax On Demand; Flix; HBO (multiplexed); HBO HD; HBO on Demand; Showtime (multiplexed); Showtime HD; Showtime On Demand; Starz HD; The Movie Channel (multiplexed); The Movie Channel On Demand.
Fee: $15.00 monthly (Cinemax, HBO, Showtime/TMC/Flix or Starz).

Video-On-Demand: Yes

Pay-Per-View
Playboy TV (delivered digitally); Fresh (delivered digitally); Shorteez (delivered digitally); Hustler TV (delivered digitally); Hot Choice (delivered digitally); ESPN (delivered digitally); iN DEMAND (delivered digitally).

Internet Service
Operational: Yes.
Subscribers: 24,641.
Broadband Service: In-house.
Fee: $40.99-$72.99 monthly.

Telephone Service
Digital: Operational
Subscribers: 16,175.
Miles of Plant: 1,961.0 (coaxial); 798.0 (fiber optic). Homes passed: 88,056.
Chief Financial Officer: Rich Fish. Vice President & General Manager: Kelvin Fee. Vice President, Sales & Marketing: Cathy Kuo. Chief Technician: Cash Hagen.
Ownership: WideOpenWest LLC (MSO).

FERDINAND—NewWave Communications. Now served by SPENCER COUNTY (portions), IN [IN0089]. ICA: IN0378.

FILLMORE—Formerly served by Global Com Inc. No longer in operation. ICA: IN0210.

FISH LAKE—Formerly served by CableDirect. No longer in operation. ICA: IN0317.

FLAT ROCK—Formerly served by Comcast Cable. No longer in operation. ICA: IN0252.

FLORA—NewWave Communications, One Montgomery Plaza, 4th Floor, Sikeston, MO 63801. Phones: 888-863-9928; 888-863-9928. Fax: 573-481-9809. E-mail: info@newwavecom.com. Web Site: http://www.newwavecom.com. Also serves Bringhurst, Burlington, Camden, Carroll County (portions), Delphi, Pittsburg, Rockfield & Tippecanoe County (portions). ICA: IN0371.
TV Market Ranking: Below 100 (Bringhurst, Burlington, Camden, Carroll County (portions), Delphi, FLORA, Pittsburg, Rockfield, Tippecanoe County (portions)).
Channel capacity: N.A. Channels available but not in use: N.A.

Basic Service
Subscribers: 928. Commercial subscribers: 6.
Programming (received off-air): WFYI (PBS) Indianapolis; WHMB-TV (IND) Indianapolis; WISH-TV (CW) Indianapolis; WLFI-TV (CBS, TheCoolTV) Lafayette; WNDY-TV (Bounce TV, Grit, MNT, TheCoolTV) Marion; WRTV (ABC, Grit) Indianapolis; WTHR (COZI TV, MeTV, NBC) Indianapolis; WTTK (CW, This TV) Kokomo; WXIN (Antenna TV, FOX) Indianapolis.
Programming (via satellite): C-SPAN; C-SPAN 2; Pop; QVC; WGN America.
Fee: $40.00 installation; $33.97 monthly.

Expanded Basic Service 1
Subscribers: N.A.
Programming (via satellite): A&E; AMC; Animal Planet; Bravo; Cartoon Network; CMT; CNBC; CNN; Comedy Central; Discovery Channel; Disney Channel; Disney XD; E! HD; ESPN; ESPN2; ESPNews; Food Network; Fox News Channel; Fox Sports 1; FOX Sports Midwest; Freeform; FX; Golf Channel; HGTV; History; HLN; Lifetime; MSNBC; MTV; NBCSN; Nickelodeon; Spike TV; Syfy; TBS; The Weather Channel; TLC; TNT; Travel Channel; Trinity Broadcasting Network (TBN); truTV; Turner Classic Movies; TV Land; Univision; Univision Studios; USA Network; VH1.

Digital Basic Service
Subscribers: N.A.
Programming (via satellite): BBC America; CMT; Destination America; Discovery Kids Channel; Disney XD; Flix; Fuse; FYI; History International; Investigation Discovery; LMN; MTV Classic; MTV Hits; MTV2; National Geographic Channel; Nick Jr.; Nicktoons; Outdoor Channel; OWN: Oprah Winfrey Network; Science Channel; Sprout; Starz Encore; Sundance TV; Syfy; TeenNick; Trinity Broadcasting Network (TBN); Turner Classic Movies; TV Land; TVG Network; VH1 Soul; WAM! America"s Kidz Network.

Digital Pay Service 1
Pay Units: N.A.
Programming (via satellite): Cinemax (multiplexed); HBO (multiplexed); Showtime (multiplexed); Starz (multiplexed); The Movie Channel (multiplexed).

Pay-Per-View
iN DEMAND (delivered digitally); Playboy TV (delivered digitally); Fresh (delivered digitally); Spice: Xcess (delivered digitally).

Internet Service
Operational: Yes.

Telephone Service
Digital: Operational
Miles of Plant: 83.0 (coaxial); 44.0 (fiber optic). Homes passed: 5,196.
Chief Financial Officer: Rod Siemers. General Manager: John Helmers.
Ownership: NewWave Communications LLC (MSO).

FORT BRANCH—Time Warner Cable. Now served by EVANSVILLE, IN [IN0006]. ICA: IN0088.

FORT WAYNE—Comcast Cable. Now served by HENDRICKS COUNTY (portions), IN [IN0001]. ICA: IN0003.

FOWLER—Benton County Cable Inc., 205 East Railroad Ave, PO Box 9, Cissna Park, IL 60924. Phones: 800-825-3882; 815-457-2659. Web Site: http://www.parktvcable.com. ICA: IN0091.
TV Market Ranking: Below 100 (FOWLER).
Franchise award date: January 1, 1962.
Franchise expiration date: N.A. Began: May 1, 1963.
Channel capacity: N.A. Channels available but not in use: N.A.

Basic Service
Subscribers: 116.
Programming (received off-air): WFYI (PBS) Indianapolis; WHMB-TV (IND) Indianapolis; WILL-TV (PBS) Urbana; WLFI-TV (CBS, TheCoolTV) Lafayette; WNDY-TV (Bounce TV, Grit, MNT, TheCoolTV) Marion; WRTV (ABC, Grit) Indianapolis; WTHR (COZI TV, MeTV, NBC) Indianapolis; WTTV (CBS, This TV) Bloomington; WXIN (Antenna TV, FOX) Indianapolis; 1 FM.
Programming (via satellite): C-SPAN; C-SPAN 2; Hallmark Channel; Iowa Communications Network; QVC; Weatherscan; WGN America.
Fee: $50.00 installation; $53.75 monthly; $2.00 converter.

Expanded Basic Service 1
Subscribers: N.A.
Programming (via satellite): A&E; AMC; Animal Planet; BET; Bravo; Cartoon Network; CMT; CNBC; CNN; Comedy Central; Discovery Channel; Disney Channel; E! HD; ESPN; ESPN2; EWTN Global Catholic Network; Food Network; Fox News Channel; Freeform; FX; HGTV; History; HLN; Lifetime; MSNBC; MTV; Nickelodeon; Pop; Spike TV; Syfy; TBS; The Weather Channel; TLC; TNT; Travel Channel; TV Land; USA Network; VH1.
Fee: $30.00 monthly.

Digital Basic Service
Subscribers: N.A.
Programming (via satellite): BBC America; Bloomberg Television; C-SPAN 3; Discovery Digital Networks; Disney XD; DIY Network; DMX Music; ESPN Classic; ESPNews; Fox Sports 1; FYI; Golf Channel; GSN; History International; HITS (Headend In The Sky); IFC; LMN; MTV2; National Geographic Channel; NBCSN; Nick 2; Nick Jr.; Ovation; Starz Encore (multiplexed); Sundance TV; TeenNick; truTV; Turner Classic Movies; WE tv.

Digital Pay Service 1
Pay Units: N.A.
Programming (via satellite): Cinemax (multiplexed); Flix; HBO (multiplexed); Showtime (multiplexed); Starz (multiplexed); The Movie Channel (multiplexed).
Fee: $10.00 monthly (Cinemax or Starz), $13.00 monthly (HBO or Showtime/TMC/Flix).

Video-On-Demand: Yes

Pay-Per-View
iN DEMAND; Adult (delivered digitally); iN DEMAND (delivered digitally).

Internet Service
Operational: Yes. Began: September 1, 2002.
Broadband Service: Comcast High Speed Internet.
Fee: $99.95 installation; $44.95 monthly; $15.00 modem lease; $129.95 modem purchase.

Telephone Service
Analog: Not Operational
Digital: Operational
Fee: $39.95 monthly
Miles of Plant: 35.0 (coaxial); None (fiber optic). Homes passed: 1,275.
President: Joe Young.
Ownership: Park TV & Electronics Inc.

FRANCESVILLE—Mediacom. Now served by KNOX, IN [IN0060]. ICA: IN0253.

FRANCISCO—Formerly served by Almega Cable. No longer in operation. ICA: IN0152.

FRANKFORT—Comcast Cable. Now served by HENDRICKS COUNTY (portions), IN [IN0001]. ICA: IN0048.

FRANKLIN—Formerly served by Insight Communications. Now served by Comcast Cable, HENDRICKS COUNTY (portions), IN [IN0001]. ICA: IN0062.

FRANKTON—Swayzee Communications, 214 South Washington St, PO Box 97, Swayzee, IN 46986. Phones: 800-435-8353; 765-922-7916. Fax: 765-922-4545. E-mail: swayzee@swayzee.com. Web Site: http://swayzee.com. ICA: IN0143.
TV Market Ranking: 16 (FRANKTON).
Channel capacity: N.A. Channels available but not in use: N.A.

Basic Service
Subscribers: 66.
Fee: $20.00 installation; $20.98 monthly.
Office Manager: Audra Hicks.
Ownership: Swayzee Communications Corp. (MSO).

FREETOWN—Formerly served by CableDirect. No longer in operation. ICA: IN0254.

FRENCH LICK—Formerly served by Avenue Broadband Communications. Now served by NewWave Communications, VINCENNES, IN [IN0035]. ICA: IN0117.

GARY—Comcast Cable. Now served by CHAMPAIGN, IL [IL0019]. ICA: IN0013.

GASTON—Formerly served by Longview Communications. No longer in operation. ICA: IN0191.

GLENWOOD—Formerly served by CableDirect. No longer in operation. ICA: IN0256.

GOLDEN LAKE—Formerly served by CableDirect. No longer in operation. ICA: IN0362.

GOSPORT—Formerly served by Insight Communications. Now served by Comcast Cable, HENDRICKS COUNTY (portions), IN [IN0001]. ICA: IN0189.

GREENCASTLE—Comcast Cable. Now served by HENDRICKS COUNTY (portions), IN [IN0001]. ICA: IN0079.

GREENS FORK—Formerly served by CableDirect. No longer in operation. ICA: IN0258.

Cable Systems—Indiana

GREENSBURG—Comcast Cable. Now served by HENDRICKS COUNTY (portions), IN [IN0001]. ICA: IN0072.

GREENWOOD—Comcast Cable. Now served by HENDRICKS COUNTY (portions), IN [IN0001]. ICA: IN0023.

GRIFFIN (town)—Formerly served by CableDirect. No longer in operation. ICA: IN0259.

HAMLET—Formerly served by CableDirect. No longer in operation. ICA: IN0202.

HAMMOND—Comcast Cable. Now served by CHAMPAIGN, IL [IL0019]. ICA: IN0008.

HAMMOND—WOW! Internet, Cable & Phone. Now served by NAPERVILLE, IL [IL0655]. ICA: IN0366.

HARDINSBURG—Formerly served by CableDirect. No longer in operation. ICA: IN0260.

HARMONY—NewWave Communications. Now served by VINCENNES, IN [IN0035]. ICA: IN0377.

HARTFORD CITY—Comcast Cable. Now served by HENDRICKS COUNTY (portions), IN [IN0001]. ICA: IN0047.

HATFIELD—Time Warner Cable. Now served by OWENSBORO, KY [KY0004]. ICA: IN0179.

HAYDEN—Formerly served by CableDirect. No longer in operation. ICA: IN0351.

HEBRON—Comcast Cable. Now served by CHAMPAIGN, IL [IL0019]. ICA: IN0070.

HENDRICKS COUNTY (portions)—Comcast Cable, 5330 East 65th St, Indianapolis, IN 46220-0911. Phone: 317-275-6370. Fax: 317-275-6340. Web Site: http://www.comcast.com. Also serves Albany, Alexandria, Allen County (portions), Anderson, Andrews, Arcadia, Atlanta, Attica (village), Aurora, Bargersville, Bartholomew County (portions), Battle Ground, Bedford, Beech Grove, Benton County (portions), Berne, Blackford County (portions), Bloomfield, Bloomington, Blountsville, Boone County (portions), Brookston, Brown County (northwest portion), Brownsburg, Brownstown, Bryant, Buffalo, Bunker Hill, Burnettsville, Cadiz, Cambridge City, Carroll County (portions), Carthage, Cass County (portions), Centerville, Chalmers, Charlottesville, Chesterfield, Cicero, Clarks Hill, Clermont, Clifford, Clinton County (portions), Columbus, Connersville, Cowan, Crawfordsville, Cumberland (town), Daleville, Danville, Dayton, Dearborn County (portions), Decatur County (portions), Delaware County (portions), Denver, Desoto, Dublin, Dunkirk, Dunreith, Eaton, Edgewood, Elizabethtown, Ellettsville, Elwood, Fairmount, Farmland, Fayette County (portions), Fishers, Fort Wayne, Fountain City, Fountain County (portions), Fowlerton, Frankfort, Franklin, Galveston, Geneva, Gosport, Grant County (portions), Greencastle, Greendale, Greene County (portions), Greenfield, Greensboro, Greensburg, Greentown, Greenwood, Grissom AFB, Guilford, Hagerstown, Hamilton County (portions), Hancock County (portions), Hartford City, Hartsville, Henry County (portions), Hidden Valley Lake, Homecroft, Hope, Howard County (portions), Huntertown, Huntington, Huntington County (portions), Idaville, Indianapolis, Jackson County (portions), Jay County (portions), Jennings County (portions), Johnson County (portions), Jonesville, Kennard, Knightstown, Kokomo, Lafayette, Lake Cicott, Lawrence, Lawrence County (portions), Lawrenceburg, Lebanon, Lewisville, Linton, Logansport, Losantville, Lynn, Lyons, Madison County (portions), Markleville, Martinsville, McCordsville, Medora, Meridian Hills, Mexico, Miami County (portions), Middletown, Milan, Milton, Modoc, Monon, Monroe County (portions), Montgomery County (portions), Monticello, Mooreland, Moores Hill, Mooresville, Morgan County (portions), Mount Auburn, Mount Summit, Mulberry, Muncie, New Castle, New Haven, New Palestine, New Waverly, New Whiteland, Noblesville, North Vernon, Oakville, Ohio County (portions), Oolitic, Orestes, Osgood, Ossian, Otterbein, Owen County (portions), Parker City, Pendleton, Pennville, Pershing, Peru, Plainfield, Portland, Putnam County (portions), Randolph County (portions), Redkey, Remington, Reynolds, Richmond, Ridgeville, Ripley County (portions), Rising Sun, Roanoke, Rush County (portions), Rushville, Russiaville, Saratoga, Selma, Seymour, Shadeland, Shamrock, Sharpsville, Shelby County (portions), Shelbyville, Shirley, Southport, Speedway, Spencer, Spiceland, Spring Grove, Spring Lake, Springport, Stinesville, Straughn, Sullivan, Sullivan County (portions), Sulphur Springs, Switzerland County (portions), Thorntown, Tippecanoe County (portions), Tipton, Tipton County (portions), Ulen, Upland, Vernon, Versailles, Wabash, Wabash County (portions), Warren County (portions), Warren Park, Wayne County (portions), Wells County (portions), West Lafayette, Westfield, Westport, White County (portions), Whiteland, Whitley County (portions), Wilkinson, Williams Creek, Williamsport, Winchester, Windfall, Wolcott, Woodburn, Wynnedale & Yorktown, IN; Fort Recovery, OH. ICA: IN0001.

TV Market Ranking: 16 (Anderson, Arcadia, Atlanta, Atlanta, Bargersville, Bartholomew County (portions), Bedford, Beech Grove, Bloomfield, Bloomington, Brown County (northwest portion), Brownsburg, Brownstown, Carthage, Charlottesville, Cicero, Clermont, Clinton County (portions), Columbus, Cumberland (town), Danville, Edgewood, Ellettsville, Fishers, Franklin, Gosport, Greene County (portions), Greenfield, Greenwood, Hamilton County (portions), Hancock County (portions), HENDRICKS COUNTY (PORTIONS), Henry County (portions), Homecroft, Indianapolis, Jackson County (portions), Johnson County (portions), Jonesville, Kennard, Knightstown, Lawrence, Lawrence County (portions), Lebanon, Lyons, Markleville, Martinsville, McCordsville, Medora, Meridian Hills, Monroe County (portions), Mooresville, Morgan County (portions), New Palestine, New Whiteland, Noblesville, Oolitic, Owen County (portions), Pendleton, Plainfield, Rush County (portions), Shelby County (portions), Shelbyville, Southport, Speedway, Spencer, Spring Lake, Stinesville, Thorntown, Tipton County (portions), Ulen, Warren Park, Westfield, Whiteland, Wilkinson, Williams Creek, Wynnedale); 17 (Aurora, Dearborn County (portions), Dillsboro, Greendale, Guilford, Hidden Valley Lake, Lawrenceburg, Milan, Moores Hill, Ohio County (portions), Ripley County (portions), Rising Sun, Switzerland County (portions)); 19 (Boone County (portions)); 82 (Allen County (portions), Andrews, Berne, Blackford County (portions), Fort Wayne, Geneva, Grant County (portions), Hartford City, Huntertown, Huntington, Huntington County (portions), Jay County (portions), Miami County (portions), New Haven, Ossian, Pennville, Roanoke, Upland, Wabash, Wabash County (portions), Wells County (portions), Whitley County (portions), Woodburn); Below 100 (Albany, Alexandria, Battle Ground, Blountsville, Brookston, Buffalo, Bunker Hill, Burnettsville, Cadiz, Cambridge City, Carroll County (portions), Cass County (portions), Centerville, Chalmers, Chesterfield, Clarks Hill, Cowan, Daleville, Dayton, Delaware County (portions), Denver, Desoto, Dublin, Dunkirk, Dunreith, Eaton, Elwood, Fairmount, Farmland, Fayette County (portions), Fountain City, Fowlerton, Galveston, Greensboro, Greentown, Grissom AFB, Hagerstown, Howard County (portions), Idaville, Kokomo, Lake Cicott, Lewisville, Losantville, Lynn, Mexico, Middletown, Milton, Modoc, Monon, Montgomery County (portions), Mooreland, Mount Auburn, Mount Summit, Mulberry, New Castle, New Waverly, Oakville, Orestes, Otterbein, Parker City, Pershing, Peru, Randolph County (portions), Redkey, Remington, Reynolds, Ridgeville, Russiaville, Saratoga, Selma, Shadeland, Shamrock, Sharpsville, Shirley, Spiceland, Spring Grove, Springport, Straughn, Sullivan, Sulphur Springs, Tippecanoe County (portions), Tipton, Wayne County (portions), West Lafayette, White County (portions), Williamsport, Windfall, Wolcott, Yorktown, Attica (village), Benton County (portions), Connersville, Crawfordsville, Fountain County (portions), Frankfort, Greencastle, Lafayette, Linton, Logansport, Monticello, Muncie, Richmond, Rushville, Seymour, Sullivan County (portions), Warren County (portions), Winchester, Clinton County (portions), Henry County (portions), Jackson County (portions), Rush County (portions), Tipton County (portions), Blackford County (portions), Grant County (portions), Jay County (portions), Miami County (portions)); Outside TV Markets (Bryant, Clifford, Decatur County (portions), Elizabethtown, Hartsville, Hope, Jennings County (portions), North Vernon, Osgood, Sullivan, Vernon, Versailles, Westport, Benton County (portions), Fort Recovery, Fountain County (portions), Greensburg, Portland, Sullivan County (portions), Warren County (portions), Bartholomew County (portions), Ripley County (portions), Switzerland County (portions), Jay County (portions)). Franchise award date: May 19, 1967. Franchise expiration date: N.A. Began: August 1, 1979.

Channel capacity: N.A. Channels available but not in use: N.A.

Basic Service
Subscribers: 414,550. Commercial subscribers: 2,847.
Programming (received off-air): WFYI (PBS) Indianapolis; WHMB-TV (IND) Indianapolis; WIPB (PBS) Muncie; WIPX-TV (ION) Bloomington; WISH-TV (CW) Indianapolis; WNDY-TV (Bounce TV, Grit, MNT, TheCoolTV) Marion; WRTV (ABC, Grit) Indianapolis; WTHR (COZI TV, MeTV, NBC) Indianapolis; WTTV (CBS, This TV) Bloomington; WXIN (Antenna TV, FOX) Indianapolis.
Programming (via satellite): A&E; AMC; Animal Planet; BET; Cartoon Network; CMT; CNBC; CNN; Comedy Central; C-SPAN; C-SPAN 2; Discovery Channel; Disney Channel; E! HD; ESPN; ESPN2; Food Network; Fox News Channel; Fox Sports 1; FOX Sports Midwest; Freeform; FX; Golf Channel; GSN; HGTV; History; HLN; Lifetime; MSNBC; MTV; NBCSN; Nickelodeon; Pop; QVC; Spike TV; Syfy; TBS; The Weather Channel; TLC; TNT; Travel Channel; truTV; Turner Classic Movies; TV Land; USA Network; VH1; WGN America.
Fee: $50.00 installation; $25.20 monthly.

Digital Basic Service
Subscribers: N.A.
Programming (via satellite): BBC America; Discovery Digital Networks; Flix; Nick 2; Nick Jr.; Sundance TV; TeenNick.

Digital Pay Service 1
Pay Units: N.A.
Programming (via satellite): Cinemax (multiplexed); DMX Music; Flix; HBO (multiplexed); Showtime (multiplexed); Starz (multiplexed); The Movie Channel (multiplexed).

Video-On-Demand: Yes

Pay-Per-View
iN DEMAND (delivered digitally); Playboy TV (delivered digitally); Fresh (delivered digitally); Fresh; iN DEMAND (delivered digitally); Shorteez (delivered digitally); Pleasure (delivered digitally).

Internet Service
Operational: Yes.
Subscribers: 368,727.
Broadband Service: Comcast High Speed Internet.
Fee: $42.95 monthly; $7.00 modem lease.

Telephone Service
Digital: Operational
Subscribers: 170,734.
Fee: $39.95 monthly
Miles of Plant: 26,673.0 (coaxial); 6,015.0 (fiber optic). Homes passed: 1,114,882.
Regional Vice President: Scott Tenney. Regional Vice President, Communications: Mark Apple. Regional Vice President, Technical Operations: Max Woolsey. Vice President, Marketing: Aaron Geisel. Marketing Manager: Marci Hefley.
Ownership: Comcast Cable Communications Inc. (MSO).

HERITAGE LAKE—Formerly served by Global Com Inc. No longer in operation. ICA: IN0188.

HILLSBORO—Formerly served by Longview Communications. No longer in operation. ICA: IN0265.

HILLSDALE TWP.—Formerly served by CableDirect. No longer in operation. ICA: IN0266.

HOAGLAND—Formerly served by CableDirect. No longer in operation. ICA: IN0267.

HOLLAND—Formerly served by CableDirect. No longer in operation. ICA: IN0268.

HOLTON—Formerly served by CableDirect. No longer in operation. ICA: IN0269.

HUNTINGTON—Comcast Cable. Now served by HENDRICKS COUNTY (portions), IN [IN0001]. ICA: IN0051.

INDIANAPOLIS—Formerly served by Sprint Corp. No longer in operation. ICA: IN0348.

Indiana—Cable Systems

INDIANAPOLIS (portions)—Bright House Networks, 2251 Lucien Way, Ste 200B, Maitland, FL 32751. Phones: 407-667-5200; 317-713-1720; 317-972-9700 (Customer service); 317-632-9077 (Administrative office). E-mail: customersupport.indiana@ mybrighthouse.com. Web Site: http:// brighthouse.com. Also serves Boone County, Carmel, Fishers, Fortville, Hamilton County (portions), Hancock County (portions), Hendricks County (portions), Ingalls, Lizton, Madison County (portions), McCordsville, Pittsboro, Plainfield, Whitestown & Zionsville. ICA: IN0002.
TV Market Ranking: 16 (Boone County, Carmel, Fishers, Fortville, Hamilton County (portions), Hancock County (portions), Hendricks County (portions), INDIANAPOLIS (PORTIONS), Ingalls, Lizton, Madison County (portions), McCordsville, Pittsboro, Plainfield, Whitestown, Zionsville). Franchise award date: February 7, 1981. Franchise expiration date: N.A. Began: December 7, 1981.
Channel capacity: N.A. Channels available but not in use: N.A.
Basic Service
Subscribers: 68,772. Commercial subscribers: 1,144.
Programming (received off-air): WCLJ-TV (TBN) Bloomington; WDNI-CD (TMO) Indianapolis; WFYI (PBS) Indianapolis; WHMB-TV (IND) Indianapolis; WIPX-TV (ION) Bloomington; WISH-TV (CW) Indianapolis; WNDY-TV (Bounce TV, Grit, MNT, TheCoolTV) Marion; WRTV (ABC, Grit) Indianapolis; WTHR (COZI TV, MeTV, NBC) Indianapolis; WTTV (CBS, This TV) Bloomington; WXIN (Antenna TV, FOX) Indianapolis; 7 FMs.
Programming (via satellite): C-SPAN 2; QVC; The Weather Channel; WGN America.
Fee: $38.35 installation; $27.00 monthly.
Expanded Basic Service 1
Subscribers: N.A.
Programming (via satellite): A&E; AMC; Animal Planet; BET; Bravo; Cartoon Network; CMT; CNBC; CNN; Comedy Central; C-SPAN; Discovery Channel; E! HD; ESPN; ESPN Classic; ESPN2; EVINE Live; Food Network; Fox News Channel; Fox Sports 1; FOX Sports Midwest; Freeform; FX; Golf Channel; GSN; Hallmark Channel; HGTV; History; HLN; IFC; Lifetime; MSNBC; MTV; NBCSN; Nickelodeon; Oxygen; QVC; Spike TV; Syfy; TBS; TLC; TNT; Travel Channel; truTV; Turner Classic Movies; TV Land; Univision Studios; USA Network; VH1; WE tv.
Fee: $34.95 monthly.
Digital Basic Service
Subscribers: N.A.
Programming (via satellite): BBC America; C-SPAN 3; Discovery Digital Networks; Disney Channel; Disney XD; DIY Network; DMX Music; ESPNews; LMN; MTV Classic; MTV2; National Geographic Channel; Nick Jr.; Outdoor Channel.
Digital Pay Service 1
Pay Units: N.A.
Programming (via satellite): Cinemax (multiplexed); FXM; HBO (multiplexed); IFC; Showtime (multiplexed); Starz (multiplexed); Starz Encore (multiplexed); Sundance TV; The Movie Channel (multiplexed).
Fee: $17.00 monthly (each).
Video-On-Demand: No
Pay-Per-View
Shorteez (delivered digitally); Fresh (delivered digitally); Pleasure (delivered digitally); Playboy TV (delivered digitally); NHL Center Ice (delivered digitally); NBA League Pass (delivered digitally); MLB Extra Innings (delivered digitally); Pay-Per-View movies, sports, events (delivered digitally).
Internet Service
Operational: Yes.
Subscribers: 72,042.
Broadband Service: Road Runner.
Fee: $24.95 installation; $44.95 monthly.
Telephone Service
Digital: Operational
Subscribers: 31,839.
Fee: $49.95 monthly
Miles of Plant: 4,896.0 (coaxial); 938.0 (fiber optic). Homes passed: 246,640.
Division President: Buz Nesbit. Chief Financial Officer: William Futera. Vice President, Engineering: Kerry Fouts. Vice President, Marketing & Customer Service: Wayde Klein. Vice President, Finance: Rick Langhals. Vice President, Sales & Area Operations: Ray Pawulich. General Manager: Cal Blumharst. Public Affairs Director: Al Aldridge. Customer Service Director: Anita Hendricks. Digital Services Director: Doug Murray.
Ownership: Bright House Networks LLC (MSO).

JAMESTOWN—Formerly served by Indiana Communications. No longer in operation. ICA: IN0132.

JASONVILLE—NewWave Communications, One Montgomery Plaza, 4th Floor, Sikeston, MO 63801. Phone: 888-863-9928. Fax: 573-481-9809. E-mail: info@newwavecom.com. Web Site: http://www.newwavecom.com. Also serves Bloomingdale, Coalmont, Dugger, Farmersburg, Greene County (western portion), Hymera, Marshall, Mecca, Midland, Montezuma, Parke County, Rockville, Shelburn, Vigo, Wilfred & Worthington. ICA: IN0106.
TV Market Ranking: 16 (Worthington); Below 100 (Bloomingdale, Coalmont, Dugger, Farmersburg, Greene County (western portion), Hymera, JASONVILLE, Marshall, Mecca, Midland, Parke County, Shelburn, Vigo, Wilfred, Montezuma, Rockville). Franchise award date: March 16, 1981. Franchise expiration date: N.A. Began: November 1, 1981.
Channel capacity: 39 (operating 2-way). Channels available but not in use: N.A.
Basic Service
Subscribers: 1,339.
Programming (received off-air): WAWV-TV (ABC) Terre Haute; WRTV (ABC, Grit) Indianapolis; WTHI-TV (CBS, FOX) Terre Haute; WTTV (CBS, This TV) Bloomington; WTWO (NBC) Terre Haute; WVUT (PBS) Vincennes.
Programming (via satellite): INSP; The Weather Channel; Trinity Broadcasting Network (TBN); WGN America.
Fee: $40.00 installation; $32.93 monthly.
Expanded Basic Service 1
Subscribers: N.A.
Programming (via satellite): A&E; AMC; Animal Planet; Cartoon Network; CNN; Comedy Central; Discovery Channel; Disney Channel; E! HD; ESPN; ESPN2; Food Network; Fox News Channel; Fox Sports 1; FOX Sports Midwest; Freeform; FX; Great American Country; Hallmark Channel; HGTV; History; HLN; Lifetime; MSNBC; MTV; National Geographic Channel; Nickelodeon; Spike TV; Syfy; TBS; TLC; TNT; Travel Channel; TV Land; USA Network; VH1.
Fee: $25.00 monthly.

Digital Basic Service
Subscribers: N.A.
Programming (via satellite): BBC America; Bloomberg Television; Discovery Digital Networks; Disney XD; DMX Music; ESPN Classic; ESPNews; EVINE Live; FOX College Sports Central; FOX College Sports Pacific; Fuse; FXM; FYI; Golf Channel; GSN; History International; LMN; NBCSN; Outdoor Channel; Turner Classic Movies; WE tv.
Pay Service 1
Pay Units: N.A.
Programming (via satellite): Cinemax; HBO; Showtime; Starz Encore; The Movie Channel.
Fee: $10.00 installation; $3.99 monthly (Encore), $8.99 monthly (Cinemax), $12.99 monthly (HBO), $13.99 monthly (Showtime/TMC).
Digital Pay Service 1
Pay Units: N.A.
Programming (via satellite): Cinemax (multiplexed); HBO (multiplexed); Showtime (multiplexed); Starz (multiplexed); Starz Encore (multiplexed); The Movie Channel (multiplexed).
Pay-Per-View
iN DEMAND (delivered digitally); Playboy TV (delivered digitally); Fresh (delivered digitally).
Internet Service
Operational: Yes. Began: April 15, 2004.
Broadband Service: Suddenlink High Speed Internet.
Fee: $49.95 installation; $20.95 monthly.
Telephone Service
None
Miles of Plant: 127.0 (coaxial); None (fiber optic). Homes passed: 4,144.
Chief Financial Officer: Rod Siemers.
Ownership: NewWave Communications LLC (MSO).

JASPER—Formerly served by NewWave Communications. No longer in operation. ICA: IN0368.

JASPER—Time Warner Cable. Now served by EVANSVILLE, IN [IN0006]. ICA: IN0044.

JEFFERSON TWP.—Comcast Cable. Now served by CHAMPAIGN, IL [IL0019]. ICA: IN0159.

JEFFERSONVILLE—Time Warner Cable. Now served by LOUISVILLE, KY [KY0001]. ICA: IN0015.

KEMPTON—Formerly served by Country Cablevision Ltd. No longer in operation. ICA: IN0273.

KENTLAND—Mediacom. Now served by WATSEKA, IL [IL0092]. ICA: IN0097.

KEWANNA—Formerly served by CableDirect. No longer in operation. ICA: IN0274.

KIMMEL—Formerly served by CableDirect. No longer in operation. ICA: IN0275.

KINGMAN—Formerly served by CableDirect. No longer in operation. ICA: IN0276.

KNIGHTSTOWN—Formerly served by Insight Communications. Now served by Comcast Cable, HENDRICKS COUNTY (portions), IN [IN0001]. ICA: IN0077.

KNIGHTSVILLE—NewWave Communications. Now served by VINCENNES, IN [IN0035]. ICA: IN0376.

KNOX—Mediacom, 109 East 5th St, Ste A, Auburn, IN 46706. Phone: 260-927-3015. Fax: 260-347-4433. Web Site: http://www.mediacomcable.com. Also serves Culver, Francesville, Grovertown, Koontz Lake, La Paz, Lakeville, LaPorte County (portions), Marshall County, Medaryville, North Judson, North Liberty, San Pierre, St. Joseph County, Starke County & Walkerton. ICA: IN0060.
TV Market Ranking: 80 (Culver, Grovertown, KNOX, Koontz Lake, La Paz, Lakeville, LaPorte County (portions), Marshall County, North Liberty, St. Joseph County, Starke County (portions), Walkerton); Outside TV Markets (Francesville, Medaryville, North Judson, San Pierre, Starke County (portions)). Franchise award date: N.A. Franchise expiration date: N.A. Began: August 1, 1983.
Channel capacity: N.A. Channels available but not in use: N.A.
Basic Service
Subscribers: 2,498.
Programming (received off-air): WCWW-LD (CW, Movies!, This TV) South Bend; WFLD (FOX) Chicago; WHME-TV (COZI TV, IND) South Bend; WNDU-TV (NBC) South Bend; WNIT (PBS) South Bend; WSBT-TV (CBS, FOX) South Bend; WSJV (Heroes & Icons) Elkhart; WYIN (PBS) Gary.
Programming (via satellite): WGN America.
Fee: $45.00 installation; $72.95 monthly.
Expanded Basic Service 1
Subscribers: N.A.
Programming (via satellite): A&E; AMC; Animal Planet; Cartoon Network; CMT; CNBC; CNN; Comcast SportsNet Chicago; Comedy Central; C-SPAN; C-SPAN 2; Discovery Channel; Disney Channel; E! HD; ESPN; ESPN2; Food Network; Fox News Channel; Fox Sports 1; Freeform; FX; Great American Country; Hallmark Channel; HGTV; History; HLN; Lifetime; MSNBC; MTV; Nickelodeon; Pop; QVC; RFD-TV; Spike TV; Syfy; TBS; The Weather Channel; TLC; TNT; Travel Channel; Trinity Broadcasting Network (TBN); truTV; TV Land; USA Network; VH1; WE tv.
Fee: $34.00 monthly.
Digital Basic Service
Subscribers: N.A.
Programming (via satellite): AXS TV; BBC America; Bloomberg Television; Cloo; Discovery Digital Networks; ESPN HD; ESPN2 HD; ESPNews; Fuse; FXM; FYI; Golf Channel; GSN; HD Theater; History International; IFC; LMN; MC; National Geographic Channel; NBCSN; Nick Jr.; Nicktoons; Outdoor Channel; TeenNick; Turner Classic Movies; TVG Network; Universal HD.
Digital Pay Service 1
Pay Units: N.A.
Programming (via satellite): Cinemax (multiplexed); Flix (multiplexed); HBO (multiplexed); HBO HD; Showtime (multiplexed); Showtime HD; Starz (multiplexed); Starz Encore; Starz HD; Sundance TV (multiplexed); The Movie Channel (multiplexed); The Movie Channel HD.
Fee: $11.95 monthly (Cinemax, HBO, Showtime/TMC/Flix/Sundance or Starz/Encore.
Video-On-Demand: Yes
Pay-Per-View
iN DEMAND (delivered digitally); Playboy TV (delivered digitally).
Internet Service
Operational: Yes.
Broadband Service: Mediacom High Speed Internet.
Fee: $59.95 installation; $40.95 monthly.

Cable Systems—Indiana

Telephone Service
Digital: Operational
Fee: $39.95 monthly
Miles of Plant: 270.0 (coaxial); 43.0 (fiber optic). Homes passed: 4,843.
Vice President, Financial Reporting: Kenneth J. Kohrs. Operations Director: Joe Poffenberger. Technical Operations Manager: Craig Grey.
Ownership: Mediacom LLC (MSO).

KOKOMO—Comcast Cable. Now served by HENDRICKS COUNTY (portions), IN [IN0001]. ICA: IN0017.

KOUTS—Mediacom. Now served by NEWTON COUNTY (portions), IN [IN0316]. ICA: IN0277.

LA FONTAINE—Swayzee Communications, 214 South Washington St, PO Box 97, Swayzee, IN 46986. Phones: 800-435-8353; 765-922-7916. Fax: 765-922-4545. E-mail: swayzee@swayzee.com. Web Site: http://swayzee.com. ICA: IN0196.
TV Market Ranking: 82 (LA FONTAINE).
Channel capacity: N.A. Channels available but not in use: N.A.
Basic Service
Subscribers: 16.
Fee: $20.00 installation; $21.98 monthly.
Office Manager: Audra Hicks.
Ownership: Swayzee Communications Corp. (MSO).

LA PORTE—Comcast Cable. Now served by CHAMPAIGN, IL [IL0019]. ICA: IN0009.

LA PORTE MOBILE HOME PARK—Formerly served by North American Cablevision. Now served by Comcast Cable, CHAMPAIGN, IL [IL0019]. ICA: IN0278.

LAFAYETTE—Comcast Cable. Now served by HENDRICKS COUNTY (portions), IN [IN0001]. ICA: IN0007.

LAGRANGE—Mediacom, 109 East 5th St, Ste A, Auburn, IN 46706. Phone: 260-927-3015. Fax: 260-347-4433. Web Site: http://www.mediacomcable.com. Also serves Howe & Lagrange County (portions). ICA: IN0123.
TV Market Ranking: 80 (Howe, LAGRANGE, Lagrange County (portions)). Franchise award date: N.A. Franchise expiration date: N.A. Began: June 1, 1981.
Channel capacity: N.A. Channels available but not in use: N.A.
Basic Service
Subscribers: 414.
Programming (received off-air): WANE-TV (Antenna TV, CBS) Fort Wayne; WCWW-LD (CW, Movies!, This TV) South Bend; WFWA (PBS) Fort Wayne; WHME-TV (COZI TV, IND) South Bend; WISE-TV (CW) Fort Wayne; WNDU-TV (NBC) South Bend; WNIT (PBS) South Bend; WSBT-TV (CBS, FOX) South Bend; WSJV (Heroes & Icons) Elkhart.
Programming (via satellite): C-SPAN; Trinity Broadcasting Network (TBN).
Fee: $45.00 installation; $43.00 monthly.
Expanded Basic Service 1
Subscribers: N.A.
Programming (via satellite): A&E; AMC; Animal Planet; Bloomberg Television; Cartoon Network; CMT; CNBC; CNN; Comedy Central; Discovery Channel; Disney Channel; E! HD; ESPN; ESPN2; Fox News Channel; Fox Sports 1; Freeform; FX; FXM; FYI; Hallmark Channel; HGTV; History; History International; HLN; Lifetime; LMN; MSNBC; MTV;

NBCSN; Nickelodeon; Pop; QVC; Spike TV; Syfy; TBS; The Weather Channel; TLC; TNT; Travel Channel; TV Land; USA Network; VH1; WGN America.
Fee: $34.00 monthly.
Digital Basic Service
Subscribers: N.A.
Programming (via satellite): BBC America; Discovery Digital Networks; DMX Music; ESPN Classic; Golf Channel; GSN; IFC; Turner Classic Movies.
Digital Pay Service 1
Pay Units: N.A.
Programming (via satellite): Cinemax (multiplexed); HBO (multiplexed); Showtime (multiplexed); Starz (multiplexed); Starz Encore (multiplexed); The Movie Channel (multiplexed).
Fee: $11.95 monthly (Cinemax, HBO, Showtime/TMC or Starz/Encore).
Video-On-Demand: Yes
Pay-Per-View
iN DEMAND; iN DEMAND (delivered digitally); Playboy TV (delivered digitally); Pleasure (delivered digitally); Fresh (delivered digitally); Shorteez (delivered digitally).
Internet Service
Operational: Yes.
Broadband Service: Mediacom High Speed Internet.
Fee: $59.95 installation; $40.95 monthly.
Telephone Service
Digital: Operational
Fee: $39.95 monthly
Miles of Plant: 29.0 (coaxial); 8.0 (fiber optic). Homes passed: 2,041.
Vice President, Financial Reporting: Kenneth J. Kohrs. Operations Director: Joe Poffenberger. Technical Operations Manager: Craig Grey.
Ownership: Mediacom LLC (MSO).

LAGRO—Formerly served by CableDirect. No longer in operation. ICA: IN0279.

LAKE CICOTT—Formerly served by Insight Communications. Now served by Comcast Cable, HENDRICKS COUNTY (portions), IN [IN0001]. ICA: IN0171.

LAKE SANTEE—Formerly served by CableDirect. No longer in operation. ICA: IN0281.

LAKES OF THE FOUR SEASONS—Comcast Cable. Now served by CHAMPAIGN, IL [IL0019]. ICA: IN0280.

LAKEVILLE—Mediacom. Now served by KNOX, IN [IN0060]. ICA: IN0115.

LAPEL—Swayzee Communications, 214 South Washington St, PO Box 97, Swayzee, IN 46986. Phones: 765-922-7916; 800-435-8353. Fax: 765-922-4545. E-mail: swayzee@swayzee.com. Web Site: http://swayzee.com. ICA: IN0144.
TV Market Ranking: 16 (LAPEL).
Channel capacity: N.A. Channels available but not in use: N.A.
Basic Service
Subscribers: 83.
Fee: $20.00 installation; $22.98 monthly.
Office Manager: Audra Hicks.
Ownership: Swayzee Communications Corp. (MSO).

LARWILL—Formerly served by CableDirect. No longer in operation. ICA: IN0282.

LAUREL TWP.—Formerly served by CableDirect. No longer in operation. ICA: IN0213.

LAWRENCEBURG—Comcast Cable. Now served by HENDRICKS COUNTY (portions), IN [IN0001]. ICA: IN0050.

LEAVENWORTH—Formerly served by CableDirect. No longer in operation. ICA: IN0283.

LEBANON—Comcast Cable. Now served by HENDRICKS COUNTY (portions), IN [IN0001]. ICA: IN0056.

LEITERS FORD—Formerly served by CableDirect. No longer in operation. ICA: IN0245.

LIBERTY—Formerly served by Comcast Cable. Now served by Enhanced Telecommunications Corp., BROOKVILLE, IN [IN0108]. ICA: IN0137.

LIBERTY MILLS—Formerly served by CableDirect. No longer in operation. ICA: IN0284.

LIGONIER—LigTel Communications. This cable system has converted to IPTV, 414 South Cavin St, Ligonier, IN 46767. Phones: 866-544-8350; 260-894-7161. Fax: 260-894-7711. E-mail: billing@ligtel.com. Web Site: http://www.ligoniertelephone.com. ICA: IN5133.
TV Market Ranking: 80 (LIGONIER).
Channel capacity: N.A. Channels available but not in use: N.A.
Digital Basic
Subscribers: 378.
Programming (received off-air): WANE-TV (Antenna TV, CBS) Fort Wayne; WFWA (PBS) Fort Wayne; WHME-TV (COZI TV, IND) South Bend; WINM (IND) Angola; WISE-TV (CW) Fort Wayne; WNDU-TV (NBC) South Bend; WNIT (PBS) South Bend; WPTA (ABC, MNT, NBC) Fort Wayne; WSJV (Heroes & Icons) Elkhart; WTTV (CBS, This TV) Bloomington.
Programming (via satellite): A&E; AMC; Animal Planet; BBC America; Boomerang; Bravo; Cartoon Network; CMT; CNBC; CNN; Comedy Central; C-SPAN; C-SPAN 2; Discovery Channel; Discovery Kids Channel; Disney Channel; Disney XD; E! HD; ESPN; ESPN Classic; ESPN2; ESPNews; EVINE Live; EWTN Global Catholic Network; Food Network; Fox News Channel; Fox Sports 1; FOX Sports Midwest; Freeform; FX; Hallmark Channel; HGTV; History; HLN; Lifetime; LMN; MC; MTV; MTV Classic; MTV Hits; MTV2; National Geographic Channel; Nick Jr.; Nickelodeon; Nicktoons; Outdoor Channel; OWN: Oprah Winfrey Network; Oxygen; QVC; Radar Channel; Spike TV; Syfy; TBS; TeenNick; The Weather Channel; The Word Network; TLC; TNT; Travel Channel; TV Land; Univision Studios; USA Network; VH1; WE tv; WGN America.
Fee: $35.00 installation; $54.95 monthly. Includes 130 channels.
Digital Choice
Subscribers: N.A.
Programming (via satellite): Bloomberg Television; Daystar TV Network; Destination America; Discovery Life Channel; DIY Network; FSN Digital Atlantic; FSN Digital Central; FSN Digital Pacific; FXM; FYI; Golf Channel; Great American Country; GSN; History International; Investigation Discovery; MSNBC; NBCSN; Science Channel; Starz Encore (multiplexed); Turner Classic Movies.
Fee: $64.95 monthly. Includes 172 channels.

Digital Complete
Subscribers: N.A.
Programming (via satellite): Cinelatino; Fox Deportes; HITN; NBC Universo; Tr3s; Uni-Mas; Univision.
Fee: $110.95 monthly. Includes 229 channels.
HD
Subscribers: N.A.
Fee: $10.99 monthly.
Spanish
Subscribers: N.A.
Fee: $3.95 monthly.
Cinemax
Subscribers: N.A.
Programming (via satellite): Cinemax (multiplexed).
Fee: $12.00 monthly.
HBO
Subscribers: N.A.
Programming (via satellite): HBO (multiplexed).
Fee: $18.00 monthly.
Showtime/TMC/Flix
Subscribers: N.A.
Programming (via satellite): Flix; Showtime; The Movie Channel (multiplexed).
Fee: $12.00 monthly.
Starz/Encore
Subscribers: N.A.
Programming (via satellite): Starz (multiplexed); Starz Encore.
Fee: $12.00 monthly.
Video-On-Demand: Yes
Pay-Per-View
Playboy TV (delivered digitally); Spice 2 (delivered digitally); Spice (delivered digitally).
Internet Service
Operational: Yes.
Fee: $44.95-$99.95 monthly.
Telephone Service
Digital: Operational
Fee: $14.72 monthly
Executive Vice President & General Manager: Don Johnson.
Ownership: Ligonier Telephone Co. (MSO).

LIGONIER—LigTel Communications. This cable system has converted to IPTV. See LIGONIER, IN [IN5133]. ICA: IN0372.

LIGONIER—Mediacom. Now served by AUBURN, IN [IN0066]. ICA: IN0156.

LINDEN—Tri-County Communications, 117 East Washington St, PO Box 186, New Richmond, IN 47967. Phones: 866-734-0704; 765-538-3333; 765-538-3424; 765-339-4651. Fax: 765-339-7999. Web Site: http://www.tdstelecom.com. Also serves Colfax, New Richmond, Romney, Tippecanoe County (southern portion) & Wingate. ICA: IN0103.
TV Market Ranking: Below 100 (Colfax, LINDEN, New Richmond, Romney, Tippecanoe County (southern portion), Wingate). Franchise award date: N.A. Franchise expiration date: N.A. Began: February 1, 1982.
Channel capacity: N.A. Channels available but not in use: N.A.
Basic Service
Subscribers: 426.
Programming (received off-air): WFYI (PBS) Indianapolis; WHMB-TV (IND) Indianapolis; WISH-TV (CW) Indianapolis; WLFI-TV (CBS, TheCoolTV) Lafayette; WNDY-TV (Bounce TV, Grit, MNT, TheCoolTV) Marion; WRTV (ABC, Grit) Indianapolis; WTHR (COZI TV, MeTV, NBC) Indianapolis; WTTK (CW, This TV) Kokomo; WXIN (Antenna TV, FOX) Indianapolis.

2017 Edition D-231

Indiana—Cable Systems

Programming (via satellite): Pop; QVC; WGN America.
Fee: $49.95 monthly.

Expanded Basic Service 1
Subscribers: N.A.
Programming (via satellite): A&E; AMC; Animal Planet; BTN; CMT; CNBC; CNN; Comedy Central; C-SPAN; Discovery Channel; Discovery Life Channel; Disney Channel; Disney XD; DIY Network; ESPN; ESPN2; EWTN Global Catholic Network; Food Network; Fox News Channel; Fox Sports 1; FOX Sports Midwest; Freeform; FX; Great American Country; GSN; Hallmark Channel; HGTV; History; HLN; Lifetime; MTV; National Geographic Channel; NBCSN; Nickelodeon; Spike TV; Syfy; TBS; The Weather Channel; TLC; TNT; Travel Channel; truTV; Turner Classic Movies; TV Land; USA Network; VH1.
Fee: $43.00 installation; $47.95 monthly; $1.38 converter.

Pay Service 1
Pay Units: 300.
Programming (via satellite): Cinemax; HBO; Showtime.
Fee: $10.00 installation; $13.00 monthly (Cinemax or Showtime), $16.00 monthly (HBO).

Video-On-Demand: No
Pay-Per-View
iN DEMAND, Addressable: No.

Internet Service
Operational: Yes.

Telephone Service
Analog: Operational
Miles of Plant: 30.0 (coaxial); 29.0 (fiber optic). Homes passed: 1,945.
Chief Technician: Mark Grote. Customer Service Manager: Myra Goings.
Ownership: TDS Telecom (MSO).

LINTON—Comcast Cable. Now served by BLOOMINGTON, IN [IN0016]. ICA: IN0052.

LOGANSPORT—Comcast Cable. Now served by HENDRICKS COUNTY (portions), IN [IN0001]. ICA: IN0037.

LOOGOOTEE—Formerly served by Avenue Broadband Communications. Now served by NewWave Communications, VINCENNES, IN [IN0035]. ICA: IN0102.

LOON LAKE—Formerly served by CableDirect. No longer in operation. ICA: IN0286.

LYNNVILLE—Formerly served by Avenue Broadband Communications. No longer in operation. ICA: IN0209.

LYONS—Formerly served by Insight Communications. Now served by Comcast Cable, HENDRICKS COUNTY (portions), IN [IN0001]. ICA: IN0186.

MACY—Formerly served by Longview Communications. No longer in operation. ICA: IN0349.

MADISON—Time Warner Cable, 7800 Crescent Executive Dr, Charlotte, NC 28217. Phones: 859-625-6600; 859-626-4800; 859-624-9666; 812-265-5499 (Local office). Web Site: http://www.timewarnercable.com. Also serves Hanover (town), Jefferson Twp. & Vevay (town). ICA: IN0046.
TV Market Ranking: Below 100 (Hanover (town)); Outside TV Markets (MADISON, Vevay (town)). Franchise award date:

N.A. Franchise expiration date: N.A. Began: June 3, 1951.
Channel capacity: N.A. Channels available but not in use: N.A.

Basic Service
Subscribers: 2,432.
Programming (received off-air): WAVE (Bounce TV, NBC, This TV) Louisville; WBKI-TV (CW, IND, Movies!) Campbellsville; WBNA (ION, Retro TV) Louisville; WCPO-TV (ABC, Escape) Cincinnati; WDRB (Antenna TV, FOX) Louisville; WHAS-TV (ABC) Louisville; WKPC-TV (PBS) Louisville; WLKY (CBS, MeTV) Louisville; WLWT (MeTV, NBC) Cincinnati; WMYO (MNT, My Family TV) Salem; WTTV (CBS, This TV) Bloomington; WXIX-TV (Bounce TV, FOX) Newport; allband FM.
Programming (via satellite): C-SPAN; C-SPAN 2; Disney Channel; Freeform; Pop; QVC; TBS; TNT; WGN America.
Fee: $49.99 installation; $21.25 monthly.

Expanded Basic Service 1
Subscribers: N.A.
Programming (via satellite): A&E; AMC; Animal Planet; BET; Bravo; Cartoon Network; CMT; CNBC; CNN; Comedy Central; Discovery Channel; E! HD; ESPN; ESPN2; EWTN Global Catholic Network; Food Network; Fox News Channel; FOX Sports Ohio/Sports Time Ohio; FX; Great American Country; Hallmark Channel; HGTV; History; HLN; INSP; MSNBC; MTV; Oxygen; Spike TV; Syfy; The Weather Channel; TLC; Travel Channel; Trinity Broadcasting Network (TBN); truTV; Turner Classic Movies; TV Land; USA Network; VH1.
Fee: $38.20 monthly.

Digital Basic Service
Subscribers: N.A.
Programming (via satellite): BBC America; Bloomberg Television; CNBC; Discovery Life Channel; Disney XD; DIY Network; ESPN Classic; ESPNews; FOX College Sports Central; FOX College Sports Pacific; Fox Sports 1; FYI; Golf Channel; GSN; HITS (Headend In The Sky); IFC; INSP; NBCSN; Outdoor Channel; WE tv.

Digital Expanded Basic Service
Subscribers: 324.
Programming (via satellite): FX; History International; Lifetime; National Geographic Channel; Nick 2; Nick Jr.; Nickelodeon; Nicktoons; Sundance TV; TeenNick.
Fee: $6.00 monthly.

Digital Pay Service 1
Pay Units: N.A.
Programming (via satellite): ART America; Cinemax (multiplexed); DMX Music; Flix; HBO (multiplexed); RAI Italia; RTN; Showtime (multiplexed); Starz (multiplexed); Starz Encore (multiplexed); The Filipino Channel; The Movie Channel (multiplexed); TV Asia; TV5, La Television International; Zee TV.
Fee: $14.00 monthly (each).

Video-On-Demand: No
Pay-Per-View
Urban Extra (delivered digitally); Hot Choice (delivered digitally); Fresh (delivered digitally); Playboy TV (delivered digitally); HITS PPV 1-30 (delivered digitally).

Internet Service
Operational: Yes.
Subscribers: 2,256.
Broadband Service: Road Runner.
Fee: $44.95 monthly.

Telephone Service
Digital: Operational
Subscribers: 968.
Fee: $44.95 monthly
Miles of Plant: 256.0 (coaxial); 120.0 (fiber optic). Homes passed: 12,490.

General Manager: Robert Trott. Senior Accounting Director: Karen Goodfellow. Technical Operations Manager: Dennis Lester. Marketing Director: Betrina Morse. Chief Technician: Mardy Osterman. Government & Public Affairs Manager: Carla Deaton.
Ownership: Time Warner Cable (MSO).

MANILLA—Formerly served by CableDirect. No longer in operation. ICA: IN0270.

MARENGO—Formerly served by NewWave Communications. No longer in operation. ICA: IN0370.

MARION—Bright House Networks, 2251 Lucien Way, Ste 200B, Maitland, FL 32751. Phones: 407-667-5200; 317-713-1720; 765-662-0071 (Customer service); 765-668-5456 (Administrative office). E-mail: customersupport.indiana@mybrighthouse.com. Web Site: http://brighthouse.com. Also serves Gas City, Grant County & Jonesboro. ICA: IN0021.
TV Market Ranking: 82 (Grant County (portions), MARION); Below 100 (Gas City, Jonesboro, Grant County (portions)). Franchise award date: January 4, 1966. Franchise expiration date: N.A. Began: May 1, 1966.
Channel capacity: N.A. Channels available but not in use: N.A.

Basic Service
Subscribers: 9,408. Commercial subscribers: 280.
Programming (received off-air): WANE-TV (Antenna TV, CBS) Fort Wayne; WFFT-TV (FOX, MeTV) Fort Wayne; WFWA (PBS) Fort Wayne; WHMB-TV (IND) Indianapolis; WIPB (PBS) Muncie; WISE-TV (CW) Fort Wayne; WISH-TV (CW) Indianapolis; WIWU-CD (IND) Marion; WNDY-TV (Bounce TV, Grit, MNT, TheCoolTV) Marion; WPTA (ABC, MNT, NBC) Fort Wayne; WRTV (ABC, Grit) Indianapolis; WSOT-LD (My Family TV) Marion; WTHR (COZI TV, MeTV, NBC) Indianapolis; WTTK (CW, This TV) Kokomo; WXIN (Antenna TV, FOX) Indianapolis.
Programming (via satellite): C-SPAN; C-SPAN 2; EVINE Live; Hallmark Channel; ION Television; Pop; QVC; TBS; Travel Channel; Trinity Broadcasting Network (TBN); WGN America.
Fee: $38.35 installation; $27.00 monthly; $6.95 converter.

Expanded Basic Service 1
Subscribers: N.A.
Programming (via satellite): A&E; AMC; Animal Planet; BET; Cartoon Network; CMT; CNBC; CNN; Discovery Channel; Disney Channel; E! HD; ESPN; ESPN2; Food Network; Fox News Channel; FOX Sports Midwest; Freeform; FX; Golf Channel; HGTV; History; HLN; Lifetime; MSNBC; MTV; NBCSN; Nickelodeon; Oxygen; Spike TV; The Weather Channel; TLC; TNT; USA Network; VH1; WE tv.
Fee: $31.30 monthly.

Digital Basic Service
Subscribers: N.A.
Programming (via satellite): BBC America; Comedy Central; C-SPAN 3; Discovery Digital Networks; Disney Channel; Disney XD; DIY Network; DMX Music; ESPN Classic; ESPNews; Flix; Fox Sports 1; GSN; LMN; MTV Classic; MTV2; National Geographic Channel; Nick Jr.; Outdoor Channel; Syfy; truTV; TV Land.

Digital Pay Service 1
Pay Units: N.A.
Programming (via satellite): Cinemax (multiplexed); HBO (multiplexed); Showtime

(multiplexed); Starz (multiplexed); Starz Encore (multiplexed); The Movie Channel (multiplexed).
Fee: $15.00 monthly (each).

Video-On-Demand: Yes
Pay-Per-View
iN DEMAND (delivered digitally); MLB Extra Innings (delivered digitally); NBA League Pass (delivered digitally); NHL Center Ice (delivered digitally); Playboy TV (delivered digitally); Pleasure (delivered digitally); Fresh (delivered digitally); Shorteez (delivered digitally).

Internet Service
Operational: Yes. Began: April 1, 2001.
Broadband Service: Road Runner.
Fee: $19.95 installation; $44.95 monthly.

Telephone Service
Digital: Operational
Fee: $44.95 monthly
Miles of Plant: 322.0 (coaxial); 25.0 (fiber optic). Homes passed: 25,572.
Division President: Buz Nesbit. General Manager: Cal Blumhorst. Chief Financial Officer: William Futera. Public Affairs Director: Al Aldridge. Community Program Director: Inge Harte-North. Technical Operations Manager: Michael Buckles.
Ownership: Bright House Networks LLC (MSO).

MARKLE—Swayzee Communications, 214 South Washington St, PO Box 97, Swayzee, IN 46986. Phones: 765-922-7916; 800-435-8353. Fax: 765-922-4545. E-mail: swayzee@swayzee.com. Web Site: http://swayzee.com. ICA: IN0192.
TV Market Ranking: 82 (MARKLE).
Channel capacity: N.A. Channels available but not in use: N.A.

Basic Service
Subscribers: 26.
Fee: $20.00 installation; $22.98 monthly.
Office Manager: Audra Hicks.
Ownership: Swayzee Communications Corp. (MSO).

MARSHALL COUNTY—Formerly served by Windjammer Cable. No longer in operation. ICA: IN0341.

MARTINSVILLE—Comcast Cable. Now served by HENDRICKS COUNTY (portions), IN [IN0001]. ICA: IN0054.

MEDORA—Formerly served by Insight Communications. Now served by Comcast Cable, HENDRICKS COUNTY (portions), IN [IN0001]. ICA: IN0291.

MENTONE—Formerly served by Longview Communications. No longer in operation. ICA: IN0193.

MEROM—Formerly served by CableDirect. No longer in operation. ICA: IN0217.

MERRILLVILLE—Comcast Cable. Now served by CHAMPAIGN, IL [IL0019]. ICA: IN0004.

METAMORA—Formerly served by CableDirect. No longer in operation. ICA: IN0293.

MIAMI—Formerly served by CableDirect. No longer in operation. ICA: IN0214.

MICHIANA—Formerly served by Sprint Corp. No longer in operation. ICA: IN0342.

MICHIGAN CITY—Comcast Cable. Now served by CHAMPAIGN, IL [IL0019]. ICA: IN0024.

Cable Systems—Indiana

MICHIGANTOWN—Formerly served by Country Cablevision Ltd. No longer in operation. ICA: IN0294.

MIDDLEBURY—Comcast Cable. Now served by CHAMPAIGN, IL [IL0019]. ICA: IN0114.

MIDDLETOWN (town)—Formerly served by Insight Communications. Now served by Comcast Cable, HENDRICKS COUNTY (portions), IN [IN0001]. ICA: IN0121.

MILROY—Formerly served by CableDirect. No longer in operation. ICA: IN0295.

MITCHELL—NewWave Communications. Now served by VINCENNES, IN [IN0035]. ICA: IN0061.

MONROE CITY—Formerly served by Cebridge Connections. Now served by NewWave Communications, VINCENNES, IN [IN0035]. ICA: IN0177.

MONROEVILLE—NewWave Communications, One Montgomery Plaza, 4th Floor, Sikeston, MO 63801. Phones: 888-863-9928; 888-863-9928. Fax: 573-481-9809. E-mail: info@newwavecom.com. Web Site: http://www.newwavecom.com. Also serves Convoy & Payne. ICA: IN0358.
TV Market Ranking: 82 (Convoy, Payne); Below 100 (MONROEVILLE). Franchise award date: May 20, 1981. Franchise expiration date: N.A. Began: N.A.
Channel capacity: N.A. Channels available but not in use: N.A.
Basic Service
Subscribers: 195. Commercial subscribers: 1.
Programming (received off-air): WANE-TV (Antenna TV, CBS) Fort Wayne; WFFT-TV (FOX, MeTV) Fort Wayne; WFWA (PBS) Fort Wayne; WINM (IND) Angola; WISE-TV (CW) Fort Wayne; WPTA (ABC, MNT, NBC) Fort Wayne.
Programming (via satellite): Freeform.
Fee: $50.00 installation; $20.15 monthly.
Expanded Basic Service 1
Subscribers: N.A.
Programming (via satellite): A&E; AMC; BTN; Cartoon Network; CNBC; CNN; C-SPAN; Discovery Channel; Disney Channel; E! HD; ESPN; ESPN2; EWTN Global Catholic Network; Fox Sports 1; Great American Country; HGTV; History; HLN; ION Television; Lifetime; MSNBC; MTV; Nickelodeon; QVC; Spike TV; Syfy; TBS; TNT; TV Land; USA Network; VH1; WGN America.
Fee: $37.98 monthly.
Pay Service 1
Pay Units: N.A.
Programming (via satellite): Cinemax; HBO; Showtime.
Fee: $15.95 monthly (each).
Internet Service
Operational: Yes.
Telephone Service
Digital: Operational
General Manager: John Helmers.
Ownership: NewWave Communications LLC (MSO).

MONTEREY—Formerly served by CableDirect. No longer in operation. ICA: IN0298.

MONTEZUMA—Formerly served by Indiana Communications. Now served by JASONVILLE, IN [IN0106]. ICA: IN0136.

MONTGOMERY TWP. (Indiana County)—Formerly served by CableDirect. No longer in operation. ICA: IN0204.

MONTICELLO—Comcast Cable. Now served by HENDRICKS COUNTY (portions), IN [IN0001]. ICA: IN0025.

MONTPELIER—Formerly served by Comcast Cable. No longer in operation. ICA: IN0029.

MORGAN COUNTY (portions)—NewWave Communications, One Montgomery Plaza, 4th Floor, Sikeston, MO 63801. Phones: 888-863-9928; 888-863-9928. Fax: 573-481-9809. E-mail: info@newwavecom.com. Web Site: http://www.newwavecom.com. Also serves Camby, Centerton, Hendricks County (portions), Monrovia, Mooresville & Paragon. ICA: IN0098.
TV Market Ranking: 16 (Camby, Centerton, Hendricks County (portions), Monrovia, Mooresville, MORGAN COUNTY (PORTIONS), Paragon).
Channel capacity: 50 (operating 2-way). Channels available but not in use: N.A.
Basic Service
Subscribers: 241. Commercial subscribers: 1.
Programming (received off-air): WFYI (PBS) Indianapolis; WHMB-TV (IND) Indianapolis; WISH-TV (CW) Indianapolis; WNDY-TV (Bounce TV, Grit, MNT, TheCoolTV) Marion; WRTV (ABC, Grit) Indianapolis; WTHR (COZI TV, MeTV, NBC) Indianapolis; WTTV (CBS, This TV) Bloomington; WXIN (Antenna TV, FOX) Indianapolis.
Programming (via satellite): A&E; AMC; Cartoon Network; CNBC; CNN; Comedy Central; C-SPAN; C-SPAN 2; Discovery Channel; E! HD; ESPN; ESPN Classic; ESPN2; Food Network; Fox Sports 1; FOX Sports Midwest; Freeform; Golf Channel; Great American Country; GSN; HGTV; History; HLN; Lifetime; MSNBC; MTV; Nickelodeon; QVC; Spike TV; Syfy; TBS; The Weather Channel; TLC; TNT; Trinity Broadcasting Network (TBN); TV Land; USA Network; VH1; WPIX (Antenna TV, CW, This TV) New York.
Fee: $40.00 installation; $32.93 monthly.
Digital Basic Service
Subscribers: N.A.
Programming (via satellite): BBC America; C-SPAN 3; Discovery Digital Networks; Disney Channel; Disney XD; ESPNews; HITS (Headend In The Sky); Nick 2; Nick Jr.; TeenNick; Weatherscan.
Digital Pay Service 1
Pay Units: N.A.
Programming (via satellite): Cinemax (multiplexed); Flix; HBO (multiplexed); Showtime (multiplexed); Starz (multiplexed); Starz Encore (multiplexed); Sundance TV; The Movie Channel (multiplexed).
Fee: $9.95 monthly (each).
Pay-Per-View
iN DEMAND (delivered digitally); Playboy TV (delivered digitally); Fresh (delivered digitally); Shorteez (delivered digitally); Pleasure (delivered digitally); ESPN Now (delivered digitally); NBA TV (delivered digitally).
Internet Service
Operational: Yes.
Telephone Service
Digital: Operational
Miles of Plant: 17.0 (coaxial); None (fiber optic). Homes passed: 2,000.

Chief Financial Officer: Rod Siemers. General Manager: John Helmers.
Ownership: NewWave Communications LLC (MSO).

MORGANTOWN—NewWave Communications, One Montgomery Plaza, 4th Floor, Sikeston, MO 63801. Phone: 888-863-9928. Fax: 573-481-9809. E-mail: info@newwavecom.com. Web Site: http://www.newwavecom.com. ICA: IN0369.
TV Market Ranking: 16 (MORGANTOWN).
Channel capacity: N.A. Channels available but not in use: N.A.
Basic Service
Subscribers: 34. Commercial subscribers: 3.
Programming (received off-air): WCLJ-TV (TBN) Bloomington; WFYI (PBS) Indianapolis; WHMB-TV (IND) Indianapolis; WIPX-TV (ION) Bloomington; WISH-TV (CW) Indianapolis; WNDY-TV (Bounce TV, Grit, MNT, TheCoolTV) Marion; WRTV (ABC, Grit) Indianapolis; WTHR (COZI TV, MeTV, NBC) Indianapolis; WTTV (CBS, This TV) Bloomington; WXIN (Antenna TV, FOX) Indianapolis.
Programming (via satellite): TBS; WGN America.
Fee: $40.00 installation; $30.78 monthly.
Expanded Basic Service 1
Subscribers: N.A.
Programming (via satellite): A&E; AMC; CMT; CNN; C-SPAN; Discovery Channel; Disney Channel; ESPN; ESPN2; FOX Sports Midwest; Freeform; History; HLN; Lifetime; MTV; Nickelodeon; Spike TV; The Weather Channel; TLC; TNT; USA Network; VH1.
Pay Service 1
Pay Units: N.A.
Programming (via satellite): Cinemax; HBO; Showtime.
Video-On-Demand: No
Internet Service
Operational: No.
Telephone Service
None
Miles of Plant: None (coaxial); 10.0 (fiber optic). Homes passed: 485.
Chief Financial Officer: Rod Siemers. General Manager: John Helmers.
Ownership: NewWave Communications LLC (MSO).

MOROCCO—TV Cable of Rensselaer Inc, 215 West Kellner Blvd, Ste 19, PO Box 319, Rensselaer, IN 47978-0319. Phones: 219-866-7101; 800-621-2344. Fax: 219-866-5785. E-mail: tvcable@rensselaer.tv. Web Site: http://www.rensselaer.tv. ICA: IN0162.
TV Market Ranking: Outside TV Markets (MOROCCO). Franchise award date: N.A. Franchise expiration date: N.A. Began: May 1, 1984.
Channel capacity: N.A. Channels available but not in use: N.A.
Basic Service
Subscribers: 157.
Programming (received off-air): WCIU-TV (MeTV) Chicago; WCPX-TV (ION) Chicago; WFLD (FOX) Chicago; WGBO-DT (getTV, UNV) Joliet; WGN-TV (IND) Chicago; WJYS (IND) Hammond; WLFI-TV (CBS, TheCoolTV) Lafayette; WLS-TV (ABC, Live Well Network) Chicago; WMAQ-TV (COZI TV, NBC) Chicago; WNDU-TV (NBC) South Bend; WPWR-TV (Buzzr, CW, MNT, Movies!) Gary; WSBT-TV (CBS, FOX) South Bend; WSNS-TV (TMO) Chicago; WTTK (CW, This TV) Kokomo; WTTW (PBS) Chicago; WXFT-DT (UniMas) Aurora; WYIN (PBS) Gary.
Programming (via satellite): A&E; AMC; Animal Planet; Cartoon Network; CMT; CNBC; CNN; Comcast SportsNet Mid-Atlantic; Comedy Central; C-SPAN; Discovery Channel; Disney Channel; Disney XD; E! HD; ESPN; ESPN Classic; ESPN2; EVINE Live; Food Network; Fox News Channel; Fox Sports 1; Freeform; FX; FXM; Golf Channel; Hallmark Channel; HGTV; History; HLN; Lifetime; MSNBC; MTV; National Geographic Channel; Nickelodeon; Outdoor Channel; OWN: Oprah Winfrey Network; Pop; QVC; Spike TV; Syfy; TBS; The Weather Channel; TLC; TNT; Travel Channel; truTV; Turner Classic Movies; TV Land; USA Network; VH1; WE tv.
Fee: $50.00 installation; $67.50 monthly; $2.30 converter.
Pay Service 1
Pay Units: 21.
Programming (via satellite): HBO.
Fee: $5.00 installation; $12.65 monthly.
Pay Service 2
Pay Units: 19.
Programming (via satellite): Cinemax.
Fee: $5.00 installation; $8.20 monthly.
Pay Service 3
Pay Units: 6.
Programming (via satellite): Starz; Starz Encore.
Fee: $5.00 installation; $9.95 monthly.
Video-On-Demand: No
Pay-Per-View
iN DEMAND.
Internet Service
Operational: No, DSL.
Telephone Service
Analog: Operational
Miles of Plant: 160.0 (coaxial); 40.0 (fiber optic). Homes passed: 3,150.
Vice President & General Manager: Eric Galbreath. Chief Technician: Eric Sampson. Marketing Director: Karen Maki. Office Manager: Sue Shuey. Customer Service Representative: Lisa Cawby.
Ownership: TV Cable of Rensselaer Inc. (MSO).

MORRISTOWN—Formerly served by Longview Communications. No longer in operation. ICA: IN0299.

MOUNT SUMMIT—Comcast Cable. Now served by HENDRICKS COUNTY (portions), IN [IN0001]. ICA: IN0111.

MOUNT VERNON—Time Warner Cable. Now served by EVANSVILLE, IN [IN0006]. ICA: IN0074.

2017 Edition　　　D-233

Indiana—Cable Systems

MUNCIE—Comcast Cable. Now served by HENDRICKS COUNTY (portions), IN [IN0001]. ICA: IN0014.

NASHVILLE—NewWave Communications. Now served by VINCENNES, IN [IN0035]. ICA: IN0099.

NEW ALBANY—Formerly served by Insight Communications. Now served by Time Warner Cable, LOUISVILLE, KY [KY0001]. ICA: IN0019.

NEW CASTLE—Formerly served by Insight Communications. Now served by Comcast Cable, HENDRICKS COUNTY (portions), IN [IN0001]. ICA: IN0031.

NEW MARKET—Formerly served by Indiana Communications. No longer in operation. ICA: IN0185.

NEW PARIS—Quality Cablevision, 19066 East Market St, New Paris, IN 46553. Phones: 260-768-9152; 574-831-2225. Fax: 574-831-7125. E-mail: qualcabl@bnin.net. Web Site: http://qualitycablevision.com. Also serves Benton Twp., Goshen & Millersburg. ICA: IN0100. **Note:** This system is an overbuild.
TV Market Ranking: 80 (Benton Twp., Goshen, Millersburg, NEW PARIS). Franchise award date: May 1, 1986. Franchise expiration date: N.A. Began: October 24, 1986.
Channel capacity: N.A. Channels available but not in use: N.A.
Basic Service
Subscribers: 1,740.
Programming (received off-air): WCWW-LD (CW, Movies!, This TV) South Bend; WHME-TV (COZI TV, IND) South Bend; WNDU-TV (NBC) South Bend; WNIT (PBS) South Bend; WSBT-TV (CBS, FOX) South Bend; WSJV (Heroes & Icons) Elkhart.
Programming (via satellite): AMC; CMT; CNBC; CNN; Comedy Central; Discovery Channel; Disney Channel; ESPN; ESPN Classic; ESPN2; Fox News Channel; Fox Sports 1; FOX Sports Networks; Freeform; HGTV; History; HLN; Lifetime; LMN; Nickelodeon; QVC; Spike TV; Syfy; TBS; The Weather Channel; TNT; Trinity Broadcasting Network (TBN); TV Land; USA Network; VH1; WGN America.
Fee: $19.95 installation; $42.20 monthly; $3.35 converter.
Expanded Basic Service 1
Subscribers: N.A.
Programming (via satellite): A&E; Animal Planet; Cartoon Network; C-SPAN; C-SPAN 2; Disney XD; E! HD; Flix; Food Network; FX; FXM; GSN; Hallmark Channel; ION Television; MSNBC; MTV; Outdoor Channel; Telemundo; TLC; Travel Channel; truTV; Turner Classic Movies; WE tv.
Fee: $13.00 monthly.
Pay Service 1
Pay Units: 29.
Programming (via satellite): HBO.
Fee: $9.25 monthly.
Pay Service 2
Pay Units: 16.
Programming (via satellite): Cinemax.
Fee: $7.75 monthly.
Pay Service 3
Pay Units: 6.
Programming (via satellite): Showtime.
Fee: $8.75 monthly.
Pay Service 4
Pay Units: N.A.
Programming (via satellite): The Movie Channel.
Fee: $7.75 monthly.
Video-On-Demand: No
Internet Service
Operational: Yes.
Broadband Service: Brightnet.
Fee: $29.95 installation; $19.95-$74.95 monthly; $10.00 modem lease; $69.95 modem purchase.
Telephone Service
Digital: Operational
Fee: $19.95-$34.95 monthly
Miles of Plant: 63.0 (coaxial); None (fiber optic). Homes passed: 5,315.
General Manager: Mark Grady. Chief Technician: Jim Farst. Plant Manager: Robin Loucks.
Ownership: New Paris Telephone Co.

NEWBURGH—Time Warner Cable, 7800 Crescent Executive Dr, Charlotte, NC 28217. Phone: 270-852-2000. Web Site: http://www.timewarnercable.com. Also serves Ohio Twp. (eastern portion) & Warrick County. ICA: IN0032.
TV Market Ranking: 86 (NEWBURGH, Ohio Twp. (eastern portion), Warrick County). Franchise award date: June 14, 1979. Franchise expiration date: N.A. Began: April 8, 1980.
Channel capacity: N.A. Channels available but not in use: N.A.
Basic Service
Subscribers: 1,846.
Programming (received off-air): WEHT (ABC) Evansville; WEVV-TV (CBS, FOX) Evansville; WFIE (NBC, This TV) Evansville; WNIN (PBS) Evansville; WTVW (CW, MeTV) Evansville.
Programming (via satellite): A&E; AMC; Animal Planet; BET; Bravo; Cartoon Network; CMT; CNBC; CNN; Comedy Central; C-SPAN; C-SPAN 2; Discovery Channel; Disney Channel; E! HD; ESPN; ESPN Classic; ESPN2; EVINE Live; EWTN Global Catholic Network; Food Network; Fox News Channel; FOX Sports Midwest; Freeform; FX; Golf Channel; Hallmark Channel; HGTV; History; HLN; Lifetime; MSNBC; MTV; Nickelodeon; Oxygen; QVC; Spike TV; Syfy; TBS; The Weather Channel; TLC; TNT; Travel Channel; Trinity Broadcasting Network (TBN); truTV; Turner Classic Movies; TV Land; USA Network; VH1; WE tv; WGN America.
Fee: $49.99 installation; $19.95 monthly; $1.00 converter.
Digital Basic Service
Subscribers: N.A.
Programming (via satellite): BBC America; Bloomberg Television; Discovery Life Channel; DIY Network; ESPNews; Fox Sports 1; FYI; Great American Country; GSN; History International; INSP; NBCSN; Outdoor Channel; The Word Network.
Digital Expanded Basic Service
Subscribers: N.A.
Programming (via satellite): FOX College Sports Central; FOX College Sports Pacific; FXM; IFC; National Geographic Channel; Nick 2; Nick Jr.; Nicktoons; Sundance TV; TeenNick.
Fee: $6.00 monthly (per tier).
Digital Pay Service 1
Pay Units: N.A.
Programming (via satellite): ART America; Cinemax (multiplexed); DMX Music; Flix; HBO (multiplexed); HITS (Headend In The Sky); RAI Italia; RTN; Showtime (multiplexed); Starz (multiplexed); Starz Encore (multiplexed); The Filipino Channel; The Movie Channel (multiplexed); TV Asia; TV5; La Television International; Zee TV.
Fee: $14.00 monthly (each).
Video-On-Demand: Planned

Pay-Per-View
Urban Extra (delivered digitally); Hot Choice (delivered digitally); Shorteez (delivered digitally); Fresh (delivered digitally); Playboy TV (delivered digitally); HITS PPV 1-30 (delivered digitally).
Internet Service
Operational: Yes.
Broadband Service: Road Runner.
Fee: $44.95 monthly.
Telephone Service
Digital: Operational
Fee: $49.95 monthly
Miles of Plant: 1,349.0 (coaxial); None (fiber optic).
General Manager: Chris Poynter. Senior Accounting Director: Karen Goodfellow. Technical Operations Director: Don Collins. Marketing Manager: Doug Rodgers.
Ownership: Time Warner Cable (MSO).

NEWPORT—NewWave Communications, One Montgomery Plaza, 4th Floor, Sikeston, MO 63801. Phone: 888-863-9928. Fax: 573-481-9809. E-mail: info@newwavecom.com. Web Site: http://www.newwavecom.com. Also serves Perrysville. ICA: IN0304.
TV Market Ranking: Below 100 (NEWPORT); Outside TV Markets (Perrysville). Franchise award date: N.A. Franchise expiration date: N.A. Began: October 1, 1984.
Channel capacity: N.A. Channels available but not in use: N.A.
Basic Service
Subscribers: 141.
Programming (received off-air): WAWV-TV (ABC) Terre Haute; WRTV (ABC, Grit) Indianapolis; WTHI-TV (CBS, FOX) Terre Haute; WTTV (CBS, This TV) Bloomington; WTWO (NBC) Terre Haute.
Programming (via satellite): C-SPAN; C-SPAN 2; INSP; QVC; Trinity Broadcasting Network (TBN); WGN America.
Fee: $40.00 installation; $32.93 monthly.
Expanded Basic Service 1
Subscribers: N.A.
Programming (via satellite): A&E; AMC; Animal Planet; CNN; Discovery Channel; Disney Channel; E! HD; ESPN; ESPN2; Fox News Channel; Fox Sports 1; Freeform; Great American Country; History; HLN; Lifetime; MSNBC; TBS; The Weather Channel; TLC; TNT; USA Network.
Fee: $17.97 monthly.
Pay Service 1
Pay Units: N.A.
Programming (via satellite): Cinemax; HBO; Showtime; The Movie Channel.
Fee: $8.95 monthly (TMC), $10.95 monthly (Cinemax or Showtime), $12.95 monthly (HBO).
Video-On-Demand: No
Internet Service
Operational: No.
Telephone Service
None
Miles of Plant: 4.0 (coaxial); None (fiber optic). Homes passed: 270.
Chief Financial Officer: Rod Siemers.
Ownership: NewWave Communications LLC (MSO).

NEWTON COUNTY (portions)—Mediacom, 109 East 5th St, Ste A, Auburn, IN 46706. Phone: 260-927-3015. Fax: 260-347-4433. Web Site: http://www.mediacomcable.com. Also serves Grant Park (village), Kankakee County & Momence, IL; Jasper County (western portion), Kouts, La Crosse, Lake County (southern portion), Lake Village, Malden, New Durham Twp., Roselawn, Rosewood Manor, Schneider, Sumava Resorts, Thayer, Wanatah, Westville & Wheatfield, IN. ICA: IN0316.
TV Market Ranking: 80 (New Durham Twp., Westville); Below 100 (Grant Park (village), Jasper County (western portion), Kankakee County (portions), Kouts, La Crosse, Lake County (southern portion), Lake Village, Malden, Momence, Rosewood Manor, Schneider, Sumava Resorts, Thayer, Wanatah, Wheatfield, NEWTON COUNTY (PORTIONS), Roselawn); Outside TV Markets (Kankakee County (portions)).
Franchise award date: N.A. Franchise expiration date: N.A. Began: May 1, 1989.
Channel capacity: N.A. Channels available but not in use: N.A.
Basic Service
Subscribers: 1,678.
Programming (received off-air): WBBM-TV (CBS, Decades) Chicago; WCIU-TV (MeTV) Chicago; WCPX-TV (ION) Chicago; WFLD (FOX) Chicago; WGBO-DT (getTV, UNV) Joliet; WGN-TV (IND) Chicago; WJYS (IND) Hammond; WLS-TV (ABC, Live Well Network) Chicago; WMAQ-TV (COZI TV, NBC) Chicago; WPWR-TV (Buzzr, CW, MNT, Movies!) Gary; WSNS-TV (TMO) Chicago; WTTW (PBS) Chicago; WWTO-TV (TBN) La Salle; WYCC (PBS) Chicago; WYIN (PBS) Gary.
Fee: $45.00 installation; $72.95 monthly; $4.00 converter.
Expanded Basic Service 1
Subscribers: N.A.
Programming (via satellite): A&E; AMC; Animal Planet; Cartoon Network; CMT; CNBC; CNN; Comcast SportsNet Chicago; Comedy Central; C-SPAN; C-SPAN 2; Discovery Channel; Discovery Life Channel; Disney Channel; E! HD; ESPN; ESPN2; EVINE Live; Food Network; Fox News Channel; Fox Sports 1; Freeform; FX; Great American Country; Hallmark Channel; HGTV; History; HLN; Lifetime; MSNBC; MTV; Nickelodeon; Pop; QVC; RFD-TV; Spike TV; Syfy; TBS; The Weather Channel; TLC; TNT; Travel Channel; Trinity Broadcasting Network (TBN); truTV; TV Land; USA Network; VH1; WE tv.
Fee: $34.00 monthly.
Digital Basic Service
Subscribers: N.A.
Programming (via satellite): AXS TV; BBC America; Bloomberg Television; Cloo; Discovery Digital Networks; ESPN HD; ESPN2 HD; ESPNews; Fuse; FXM; FYI; Golf Channel; GSN; HD Theater; History International; IFC; LMN; National Geographic Channel; NBCSN; Nick Jr.; Nicktoons; Outdoor Channel; TeenNick; Turner Classic Movies; TVG Network; Universal HD.
Digital Pay Service 1
Pay Units: N.A.
Programming (via satellite): Cinemax (multiplexed); Flix (multiplexed); HBO (multiplexed); HBO HD; Showtime (multiplexed); Showtime HD; Starz (multiplexed); Starz Encore; Starz HD; Sundance TV (multiplexed); The Movie Channel (multiplexed); The Movie Channel HD.
Fee: $11.95 monthly (Cinemax, HBO, Showtime/TMC/Flix/Sundance or Starz/Encore).
Video-On-Demand: Yes
Pay-Per-View
iN DEMAND (delivered digitally); Playboy TV (delivered digitally).
Internet Service
Operational: Yes.
Broadband Service: Mediacom High Speed Internet.
Fee: $59.95 installation; $40.95 monthly.

Cable Systems—Indiana

FULLY SEARCHABLE • CONTINUOUSLY UPDATED • DISCOUNT RATES FOR PRINT PURCHASERS
For more information call **800-771-9202** or visit **www.warren-news.com**

Telephone Service
Digital: Operational
Fee: $39.95 monthly
Homes passed: 3,005.
Vice President, Financial Reporting: Kenneth J. Kohrs. Operations Director: Joe Poffenberger. Technical Operations Manager: Craig Grey.
Ownership: Mediacom LLC (MSO).

NOBLESVILLE—Comcast Cable. Now served by HENDRICKS COUNTY (portions), IN [IN0001]. ICA: IN0020.

NORTH MANCHESTER—Mediacom. Now served by AUBURN, IN [IN0066]. ICA: IN0093.

NORTH VERNON—Comcast Cable. Now served by HENDRICKS COUNTY (portions), IN [IN0001]. ICA: IN0069.

NORTH WEBSTER—Mediacom, 1102 North 4th St, PO Box 334, Chillicothe, IN 61523. Phone: 845-695-2762. Web Site: http://www.mediacomcable.com. Also serves Argos, Bourbon, Bremen, Elkhart County (portions), Kosciusko County, Leesburg, Milford, Nappanee, Pierceton, Syracuse & Tippecanoe. ICA: IN0038.
TV Market Ranking: 80 (Argos, Bourbon, Bremen, Elkhart County (portions), Milford, Nappanee, Syracuse, Tippecanoe); 80,82 (Kosciusko County (portions), Leesburg, NORTH WEBSTER); 82 (Pierceton); Outside TV Markets (Kosciusko County (portions)). Franchise award date: N.A. Franchise expiration date: N.A. Began: January 1, 1984.
Channel capacity: N.A. Channels available but not in use: N.A.
Basic Service
Subscribers: 4,968.
Programming (received off-air): WCWW-LD (CW, Movies!, This TV) South Bend; WFFT-TV (FOX, MeTV) Fort Wayne; WHME-TV (COZI TV, IND) South Bend; WISE-TV (CW) Fort Wayne; WNDU-TV (NBC) South Bend; WNIT (PBS) South Bend; WPTA (ABC, MNT, NBC) Fort Wayne; WSBT-TV (CBS, FOX) South Bend; WSJV (Heroes & Icons) Elkhart; WTTW (PBS) Chicago.
Programming (via satellite): TBS; WGN America.
Fee: $45.00 installation; $53.11 monthly.
Expanded Basic Service 1
Subscribers: N.A.
Programming (via satellite): A&E; AMC; Animal Planet; Cartoon Network; CMT; CNBC; CNN; Comedy Central; C-SPAN; Discovery Channel; Disney Channel; E! HD; ESPN; ESPN2; Fox News Channel; Fox Sports 1; Freeform; FX; HGTV; History; HLN; Lifetime; MTV; Nickelodeon; Pop; QVC; Spike TV; Syfy; The Weather Channel; TLC; TNT; Travel Channel; Trinity Broadcasting Network (TBN); TV Land; USA Network; VH1.
Fee: $34.00 monthly.
Digital Basic Service
Subscribers: N.A.
Programming (via satellite): BBC America; Discovery Digital Networks; DMX Music; Golf Channel; GSN; IFC; NBCSN; Turner Classic Movies.
Digital Pay Service 1
Pay Units: N.A.
Programming (via satellite): Cinemax (multiplexed); HBO (multiplexed); Showtime (multiplexed); Starz (multiplexed); Starz Encore (multiplexed); The Movie Channel (multiplexed).

Fee: $11.95 monthly (Cinemax, HBO, Showtime/TMC or Starz/Encore).
Video-On-Demand: Yes
Pay-Per-View
iN DEMAND; iN DEMAND (delivered digitally); Playboy TV (delivered digitally); Pleasure (delivered digitally); Fresh (delivered digitally); Shorteez (delivered digitally).
Internet Service
Operational: Yes.
Broadband Service: Mediacom High Speed Internet.
Fee: $59.95 installation; $40.95 monthly.
Telephone Service
Digital: Operational
Fee: $39.95 monthly
Vice President, Financial Reporting: Kenneth J. Kohrs. Operations Director: Joe Poffenberger. Technical Operations Manager: Craig Grey.
Ownership: Mediacom LLC (MSO).

OAKLAND CITY—Formerly served by Charter Communications. Now served by NewWave Communications, VINCENNES, IN [IN0035]. ICA: IN0122.

OAKTOWN—Formerly served by Almega Cable. No longer in operation. ICA: IN0203.

ODON—Formerly served by Suddenlink Communications. Now served by NewWave Communications, NEWTON, IL [IL0559]. ICA: IN0107.

OLIVER LAKE—Formerly served by CableDirect. No longer in operation. ICA: IN0306.

OTTER LAKE—Formerly served by CableDirect. No longer in operation. ICA: IN0363.

OTWELL—Formerly served by CableDirect. No longer in operation. ICA: IN0309.

OWENSBURG—Formerly served by CableDirect. No longer in operation. ICA: IN0310.

OWENSVILLE (village)—Formerly served by Sigecom. Now served by Time Warner Cable, EVANSVILLE, IN [IN0006]. ICA: IN0178.

OXFORD—Formerly served by Indiana Communications. No longer in operation. ICA: IN0176.

PAINT MILL LAKE—Formerly served by CableDirect. No longer in operation. ICA: IN0311.

PATOKA—Formerly served by Almega Cable. No longer in operation. ICA: IN0173.

PATRICKSBURG—Formerly served by CableDirect. No longer in operation. ICA: IN0312.

PEKIN—Time Warner Cable. Now served by LOUISVILLE, KY [KY0001]. ICA: IN0164.

PENN TWP.—Crystal Broadband Networks, 5860 Main St, Clay City, KY 40312. Phone: 877-319-0328. E-mail: helpdesk@crystalbn.com. Web site: http://crystalbn.com. Also serves Greene Twp. & St. Joseph County (portions). ICA: IN0381.
TV Market Ranking: 80 (Greene Twp., PENN TWP., St. Joseph County (portions)).
Channel capacity: N.A. Channels available but not in use: N.A.

General Manager: Mitch Johnson.
Ownership: Crystal Broadband Networks (MSO).

PERRYSVILLE—Formerly served by Indiana Communications. Now served by NewWave Communications, NEWPORT, IN [IN0304]. ICA: IN0314.

PINE VILLAGE—Formerly served by CableDirect. No longer in operation. ICA: IN0218.

PLYMOUTH—Crystal Broadband Network, 5860 Main St, Clay City, KY 40312. Phone: 877-319-0328. E-mail: helpdesk@crystalbn.com. Web Site: http://crystalbn.com. Also serves Marshall County (portions). ICA: IN0382.
TV Market Ranking: 80 (PLYMOUTH).
Channel capacity: N.A. Channels available but not in use: N.A.
General Manager: Mitch Johnson.
Ownership: Crystal Broadband Networks (MSO).

PORTAGE—Comcast Cable. Now served by CHAMPAIGN, IL [IL0019]. ICA: IN0028.

PORTLAND—Comcast Cable. Now served by HENDRICKS COUNTY (portions), IN [IN0001]. ICA: IN0083.

POSEYVILLE—Time Warner Cable. Now served by EVANSVILLE, IN [IN0006]. ICA: IN0180.

PRETTY LAKE—Formerly served by Longview Communications. No longer in operation. ICA: IN0227.

PRINCES LAKES—Formerly served by Avenue Broadband Communications. Now served by NewWave Communications, VINCENNES, IN [IN0035]. ICA: IN0147.

PRINCETON—Time Warner Cable. Now served by EVANSVILLE, IN [IN0006]. ICA: IN0071.

RENSSELAER (town)—TV Cable of Rensselaer Inc, 215 West Kellner Blvd, Ste 19, PO Box 319, Rensselaer, IN 47978-0319. Phones: 800-621-2344; 219-866-7101. Fax: 219-866-5785. E-mail: tvcable@rensselaer.tv. Web Site: http://www.rensselaer.tv. Also serves Jasper County (portions). ICA: IN0082.
TV Market Ranking: Outside TV Markets (Jasper County (portions), RENSSELAER (TOWN)). Franchise award date: N.A. Franchise expiration date: N.A. Began: January 1, 1966.
Channel capacity: N.A. Channels available but not in use: N.A.
Basic Service
Subscribers: 1,289. Commercial subscribers: 74.
Programming (received off-air): WCIU-TV (MeTV) Chicago; WCPX-TV (ION) Chicago; WFLD (FOX) Chicago; WGBO-DT (getTV,

UNV) Joliet; WGN-TV (IND) Chicago; WJYS (IND) Hammond; WLFI-TV (CBS, TheCoolTV) Lafayette; WLS-TV (ABC, Live Well Network) Chicago; WMAQ-TV (COZI TV, NBC) Chicago; WNDU-TV (NBC) South Bend; WPWR-TV (Buzzr, CW, MNT, Movies!) Gary; WSBT-TV (CBS, FOX) South Bend; WSNS-TV (TMO) Chicago; WTTK (CW, This TV) Kokomo; WTTW (PBS) Chicago; WXFT-DT (UniMas) Aurora; WYIN (PBS) Gary.
Programming (via satellite): A&E; AMC; Animal Planet; Cartoon Network; CMT; CNBC; CNN; Comcast SportsNet Chicago; Comedy Central; C-SPAN; Discovery Channel; Disney Channel; Disney XD; E! HD; ESPN; ESPN Classic; ESPN2; EVINE Live; Food Network; Fox News Channel; Fox Sports 1; Freeform; FX; FXM; Golf Channel; Hallmark Channel; HGTV; History; HLN; Lifetime; MSNBC; MTV; National Geographic Channel; Nickelodeon; Outdoor Channel; OWN: Oprah Winfrey Network; Pop; QVC; Spike TV; Syfy; TBS; The Weather Channel; TLC; TNT; Travel Channel; truTV; Turner Classic Movies; TV Land; USA Network; VH1; WE tv.
Fee: $50.00 installation; $67.50 monthly (city); $41.13 monthly (rural areas); $2.30 converter.
Pay Service 1
Pay Units: 234.
Programming (via satellite): HBO.
Fee: $5.00 installation; $12.65 monthly.
Pay Service 2
Pay Units: 121.
Programming (via satellite): Cinemax.
Fee: $5.00 installation; $8.20 monthly.
Pay Service 3
Pay Units: N.A.
Programming (via satellite): Starz; Starz Encore.
Video-On-Demand: No
Pay-Per-View
special events; iN DEMAND.
Internet Service
Operational: Yes. Began: December 31, 2002.
Broadband Service: Northwest Internet Services.
Fee: $30.00 installation; $39.95 monthly; $4.95 modem lease; $69.95 modem purchase.
Telephone Service
Digital: Operational
Miles of Plant: 21.0 (coaxial); 5.0 (fiber optic). Homes passed: 2,800.
Vice President & General Manager: Eric Galbreath. Chief Technician: Eric Sampson. Marketing Director: Karen Maki. Office Manager: Sue Shuey.
Ownership: TV Cable of Rensselaer Inc. (MSO).

RICHLAND—Formerly served by Time Warner Cable. No longer in operation. ICA: IN0315.

RICHMOND—Comcast Cable. Now served by HENDRICKS COUNTY (portions), IN [IN0001]. ICA: IN0018.

2017 Edition D-235

Indiana—Cable Systems

ROACHDALE—Formerly served by Indiana Communications. No longer in operation. ICA: IN0163.

ROANN—Formerly served by CableDirect. No longer in operation. ICA: IN0350.

ROCKPORT—Time Warner Cable. Now served by OWENSBORO, KY [KY0004]. ICA: IN0120.

ROCKVILLE—Formerly served by Cequel Communications. Now served by JASONVILLE, IN [IN0106]. ICA: IN0101.

ROME CITY—Mediacom. Now served by AUBURN, IN [IN0066]. ICA: IN0095.

ROSEDALE—Formerly served by Rapid Cable. Now served by NewWave Communications, VINCENNES, IN [IN0035]. ICA: IN0200.

ROYAL CENTER—Park TV & Electronics Inc, 205 East Railroad Ave, PO Box 9, Cissna Park, IL 60924. Phones: 815-457-2659; 800-825-3882. Web site: http://www.parktvcable.com. ICA: IN0194.
TV Market Ranking: Below 100 (ROYAL CENTER).
Channel capacity: N.A. Channels available but not in use: N.A.
Basic Service
Subscribers: 15.
Fee: $17.98 monthly.
President & General Manager: Joe Young.
Ownership: Park TV & Electronics Inc. (MSO).

RUSHVILLE—Comcast Cable. Now served by HENDRICKS COUNTY (portions), IN [IN0001]. ICA: IN0076.

RUSSELLVILLE—Formerly served by CableDirect. No longer in operation. ICA: IN0364.

SALEM—Formerly served by Insight Communications. No longer in operation. ICA: IN0084.

SAN PIERRE—Mediacom. Now served by KNOX, IN [IN0060]. ICA: IN0221.

SCOTTSBURG—Formerly served by Insight Communications. Now served by Time Warner Cable, LOUISVILLE, KY [KY0001]. ICA: IN0053.

SEYMOUR—Comcast Cable. Now served by HENDRICKS COUNTY (portions), IN [IN0001]. ICA: IN0039.

SHELBYVILLE—Comcast Cable. Now served by HENDRICKS COUNTY (portions), IN [IN0001]. ICA: IN0042.

SHERIDAN—Swayzee Communications, 214 South Washington St, PO Box 97, Swayzee, IN 46986. Phones: 765-922-7916; 800-435-8353. Fax: 765-922-4545. E-mail: swayzee@swayzee.com. Web Site: http://swayzee.com. ICA: IN0116.
TV Market Ranking: 16 (SHERIDAN).
Channel capacity: N.A. Channels available but not in use: N.A.
Basic Service
Subscribers: 141.
Fee: $20.00 installation; $22.98 monthly.
President: Tim Miles.
Ownership: Swayzee Communications Corp. (MSO).

SHIPSHEWANA—Formerly served by Longview Communications. No longer in operation. ICA: IN0320.

SHOALS—Formerly served by Almega Cable. No longer in operation. ICA: IN0168.

SILVER LAKE—Comcast Cable. Now served by CHAMPAIGN, IL [IL0019]. ICA: IN0165.

SOMERSET (village)—Formerly served by CableDirect. No longer in operation. ICA: IN0321.

SOUTH BEND—Comcast Cable. Now served by CHAMPAIGN, IL [IL0019]. ICA: IN0005.

SOUTH BEND—Formerly served by Sprint Corp. No longer in operation. ICA: IN0355.

SOUTH WHITLEY—Mediacom. Now served by AUBURN, IN [IN0066]. ICA: IN0146.

SPENCER—Formerly served by Insight Communications. Now served by Comcast Cable, HENDRICKS COUNTY (portions), IN [IN0001]. ICA: IN0104.

SPENCER COUNTY (portions)—NewWave Communications, One Montgomery Plaza, 4th Floor, Sikeston, MO 63801. Phone: 888-863-9928. Fax: 573-481-9809. E-mail: info@newwavecom.com. Web Site: http://www.newwavecom.com. Also serves Dale, Ferdinand, Mariah Hill & Santa Claus. ICA: IN0089.
TV Market Ranking: 86 (Dale, Santa Claus, SPENCER COUNTY (PORTIONS)); Outside TV Markets (Mariah Hill, Ferdinand, SPENCER COUNTY (PORTIONS)). Franchise award date: September 10, 1981. Franchise expiration date: N.A. Began: April 19, 1982.
Channel capacity: N.A. Channels available but not in use: N.A.
Basic Service
Subscribers: 93.
Programming (received off-air): WAVE (Bounce TV, NBC, This TV) Louisville; WDRB (Antenna TV, FOX) Louisville; WEHT (ABC) Evansville; WEVV-TV (CBS, FOX) Evansville; WFIE (NBC, This TV) Evansville; WHAS-TV (ABC) Louisville; WJTS-CD (America One, IND) Jasper; WNIN (PBS) Evansville; WTWW (CW, MeTV) Evansville.
Programming (via satellite): EWTN Global Catholic Network; QVC; WGN America.
Fee: $36.50 installation; $21.81 monthly; $1.46 converter.
Expanded Basic Service 1
Subscribers: N.A.
Programming (via satellite): A&E; Animal Planet; CNN; Comedy Central; Discovery Channel; Disney Channel; E! HD; ESPN; ESPN2; Freeform; HLN; MTV; Nickelodeon; Spike TV; Syfy; TBS; The Weather Channel; TLC; TNT; Turner Classic Movies; USA Network; VH1.
Fee: $11.71 monthly.
Pay Service 1
Pay Units: N.A.
Programming (via satellite): HBO; Showtime; The Movie Channel.
Fee: $9.50 monthly (each).
Video-On-Demand: No
Internet Service
Operational: No.
Telephone Service
None
Miles of Plant: 84.0 (coaxial); None (fiber optic). Homes passed: 2,144.

General Manager: John Helmers.
Ownership: NewWave Communications LLC (MSO).

SPURGEON—Formerly served by CableDirect. No longer in operation. ICA: IN0353.

ST. PAUL—Formerly served by Longview Communications. No longer in operation. ICA: IN0157.

SULLIVAN—Formerly served by Insight Communications. Now served by Comcast Cable, HENDRICKS COUNTY (portions), IN [IN0001]. ICA: IN0090.

SUMMITVILLE—Swayzee Communications, 214 South Washington St, PO Box 97, Swayzee, IN 46986. Phones: 765-922-7916; 800-435-8353. Fax: 765-922-4545. E-mail: swayzee@swayzee.com. Web Site: http://swayzee.com. ICA: IN0175.
TV Market Ranking: 16 (SUMMITVILLE).
Channel capacity: N.A. Channels available but not in use: N.A.
Basic Service
Subscribers: 42.
Fee: $20.00 installation; $21.98 monthly.
Office Manager: Audra Hicks.
Ownership: Swayzee Communications Corp. (MSO).

SUNMAN—Enhanced Telecommunications Corp, 123 Nieman St, Sunman, IN 47041. Phones: 866-382-4968; 812-623-2122. Fax: 812-623-4159. Web Site: http://www.etczone.com. Also serves Napoleon & St. Leon. ICA: IN0183.
TV Market Ranking: 17 (Napoleon, St. Leon, SUNMAN). Franchise award date: May 24, 1984. Franchise expiration date: N.A. Began: May 1, 1984.
Channel capacity: N.A. Channels available but not in use: N.A.
Basic Service
Subscribers: 3,160.
Programming (received off-air): WCET (PBS) Cincinnati; WCPO-TV (ABC, Escape) Cincinnati; WISH-TV (CW) Indianapolis; WKOI-TV (TBN) Richmond; WKRC-TV (CBS, CW) Cincinnati; WLWT (MeTV, NBC) Cincinnati; WNDY-TV (Bounce TV, Grit, MNT, TheCoolTV) Marion; WPTO (PBS) Oxford; WRTV (ABC, Grit) Indianapolis; WSTR-TV (Antenna TV, MNT) Cincinnati; WTHR (COZI TV, MeTV, NBC) Indianapolis; WTTV (CBS, This TV) Bloomington; WXIN (Antenna TV, FOX) Indianapolis; WXIX-TV (Bounce TV, FOX) Newport.
Programming (via satellite): EWTN Global Catholic Network; QVC; The Weather Channel; WGN America.
Fee: $15.00 installation; $14.95 monthly.
Digital Basic Service
Subscribers: N.A.
Programming (via satellite): A&E; BBC America; Bloomberg Television; Bravo; Cartoon Network; CMT; CNN; Comedy Central; Discovery Channel; Discovery Life Channel; Disney Channel; DMX Music; E! HD; ESPN; ESPN Classic; ESPN2; ESPNews; Food Network; Fox News Channel; Fox Sports 1; FOX Sports Networks; Freeform; FYI; Golf Channel; GSN; HGTV; History; HLN; IFC; Lifetime; LMN; MSNBC; MTV; National Geographic Channel; NBCSN; Nick Jr.; Nickelodeon; Outdoor Channel; Ovation; Spike TV; Sundance TV; Syfy; TBS; TeenNick; TLC; TNT; Turner Classic Movies; USA Network; VH1.

Digital Pay Service 1
Pay Units: N.A.
Programming (via satellite): Cinemax (multiplexed); HBO (multiplexed); Showtime (multiplexed); Starz; Starz Encore; The Movie Channel (multiplexed).
Fee: $49.95 installation; $11.00 monthly.
Video-On-Demand: Yes
Internet Service
Operational: Yes.
Fee: $75.00 installation; $26.95-$99.95 monthly.
Telephone Service
Digital: Operational
Fee: $23.95-$27.57 monthly
Miles of Plant: 100.0 (coaxial); 26.0 (fiber optic).
President & Chief Executive Officer: Chad Miles. Chief Financial Officer: Mike Alig. Chief Technical Officer: Kevin McGuire. Vice President, Operations: Mike Fledderman. Network Operations Manager: Matt Anderson. Outside Plant Manager, Sunman: Bruce Bauman. Customer Service/Sales Manager: Becky Brashear. Business Development Manager: Lori Feldbauer. Marketing Manager: Anita Fledderman. Video Operations Manager: Ryan Ibold. Outside Plant Manager, Batesville/Greensburg: Gabe Nobbe. Facilities/Safety Manager: Dave Smith.
Ownership: Enhanced Telecommunications Corp. (MSO).

SWAYZEE—The Swayzee Telephone Co, 214 South Washington St, PO Box 97, Swayzee, IN 46986. Phones: 765-922-7929; 800-435-8353; 765-922-7916. Fax: 765-922-4545. E-mail: swayzee@swayzee.com. Web Site: http://swayzee.com. ICA: IN0323.
TV Market Ranking: Below 100 (SWAYZEE). Franchise award date: N.A. Franchise expiration date: N.A. Began: January 1, 1983.
Channel capacity: 53 (not 2-way capable). Channels available but not in use: N.A.
Basic Service
Subscribers: 248.
Programming (received off-air): WHMB-TV (IND) Indianapolis; WIPB (PBS) Muncie; WISH-TV (CW) Indianapolis; WNDY-TV (Bounce TV, Grit, MNT, TheCoolTV) Marion; WRTV (ABC, Grit) Indianapolis; WSOT-LD (My Family TV) Marion; WTHR (COZI TV, MeTV, NBC) Indianapolis; WTTV (CBS, This TV) Bloomington; WXIN (Antenna TV, FOX) Indianapolis.
Programming (via satellite): A&E; AMC; Animal Planet; Boomerang; BTN; Cartoon Network; CMT; CNN; Comedy Central; Discovery Channel; Disney Channel; DIY Network; ESPN; ESPN2; Food Network; Fox News Channel; Fox Sports 1; Freeform; FX; Great American Country; Hallmark Channel; HGTV; History; HLN; Lifetime; MSNBC; MTV; National Geographic Channel; Nickelodeon; Oxygen; QVC; Spike TV; Syfy; TBS; The Weather Channel; TLC; TNT; Travel Channel; Turner Classic Movies; TV Land; USA Network; VH1; WGN America.
Fee: $20.00 installation; $39.95 monthly; $4.00 converter.
Pay Service 1
Pay Units: 18.
Programming (via satellite): Cinemax.
Fee: $13.00 monthly.
Pay Service 2
Pay Units: 22.
Programming (via satellite): HBO.
Fee: $13.00 monthly.
Video-On-Demand: No
Internet Service
Operational: No, DSL & dial-up.

Cable Systems—Indiana

Telephone Service
Analog: Operational
Miles of Plant: 15.0 (coaxial); None (fiber optic). Homes passed: 650.
General Manager: Tim Miles. Plant Manager & Chief Technician: Jeff Duncan. Office Manager: Audra Hicks. Customer Service Manager: Sue Whitlow.
Ownership: Swayzee Communications Corp.

SWEETSER—Oak Hill Cablevision Inc, 210 North Main St, Sweetser, IN 46987. Phone: 765-384-7873. Fax: 765-384-7002. E-mail: sweetser@comteck.com. Web Site: http://www.comteck.com. Also serves Converse & Jalapa. ICA: IN0129.
TV Market Ranking: 82 (Jalapa, SWEETSER); Below 100 (Converse). Franchise award date: March 24, 1983. Franchise expiration date: N.A. Began: July 1, 1983.
Channel capacity: N.A. Channels available but not in use: N.A.
Basic Service
Subscribers: 510.
Programming (received off-air): WFFT-TV (FOX, MeTV) Fort Wayne; WFTC (MNT, Movies!) Minneapolis; WHMB-TV (IND) Indianapolis; WIPB (PBS) Muncie; WISE-TV (CW) Fort Wayne; WISH-TV (CW) Indianapolis; WLFI-TV (CBS, TheCoolTV) Lafayette; WNDY-TV (Bounce TV, Grit, MNT, TheCoolTV) Marion; WPTA (ABC, MNT, NBC) Fort Wayne; WRTV (ABC, Grit) Indianapolis; WSOT-LD (My Family TV) Marion; WTHR (COZI TV, MeTV, NBC) Indianapolis; WXIN (Antenna TV, FOX) Indianapolis.
Programming (via satellite): A&E; Cartoon Network; CMT; CNN; C-SPAN; Discovery Channel; Disney Channel; ESPN; ESPN2; Freeform; HGTV; History; Nickelodeon; QVC; Spike TV; TBS; The Weather Channel; TLC; TNT; Turner Classic Movies; USA Network; VH1; WGN America.
Fee: $20.00 installation; $31.50 monthly; $1.00 converter.
Pay Service 1
Pay Units: 213.
Programming (via satellite): Cinemax.
Fee: $11.95 monthly.
Pay Service 2
Pay Units: 109.
Programming (via satellite): HBO.
Fee: $11.95 monthly.
Video-On-Demand: No
Internet Service
Operational: No.
Telephone Service
None
Miles of Plant: 51.0 (coaxial); None (fiber optic). Homes passed: 1,275.
General Manager: Rocky Bradshaw.
Ownership: Scott Winger.

SYRACUSE—Mediacom. Now served by NORTH WEBSTER, IN [IN0038]. ICA: IN0340.

TALMA—Formerly served by CableDirect. No longer in operation. ICA: IN0324.

TELL CITY—Comcast Cable, 2919 Ring Rd, Elizabethtown, KY 42701. Phones: 270-605-7719; 270-737-2731. Fax: 270-737-3379. E-mail: tim_hagen@cable.comcast.com. Web Site: http://www.comcast.com. Also serves Cannelton & Perry County (portions). ICA: IN0063.
TV Market Ranking: Outside TV Markets (Cannelton, Perry County (portions), TELL CITY). Franchise award date: July 1, 1965. Franchise expiration date: N.A. Began: September 1, 1965.
Channel capacity: N.A. Channels available but not in use: N.A.
Basic Service
Subscribers: 1,036. Commercial subscribers: 211.
Programming (received off-air): WAVE (Bounce TV, NBC, This TV) Louisville; WDRB (Antenna TV, FOX) Louisville; WEHT (ABC) Evansville; WEVV-TV (CBS, FOX) Evansville; WFIE (NBC, This TV) Evansville; WHAS-TV (ABC) Louisville; WKOH (PBS) Owensboro; WLKY (CBS, MeTV) Louisville; WNIN (PBS) Evansville; WTVW (CW, MeTV) Evansville.
Programming (via satellite): CMT; CNN; Discovery Channel; Disney Channel; ESPN; Food Network; FOX Sports Ohio/Sports Time Ohio; Freeform; HGTV; HLN; Lifetime; MSNBC; MTV; Nickelodeon; Spike TV; Syfy; TBS; TNT; USA Network; VH1; WGN America.
Fee: $52.95-$67.00 installation; $22.75 monthly.
Digital Basic Service
Subscribers: N.A.
Programming (via satellite): BBC America; CMT; C-SPAN 3; Discovery Digital Networks; Disney XD; ESPNews; Flix; LMN; MC; MoviePlex; National Geographic Channel; NFL Network; Nick 2; Nick Jr.; Nicktoons; Sprout; Starz Encore (multiplexed); Sundance TV; TeenNick.
Digital Pay Service 1
Pay Units: N.A.
Programming (via satellite): Cinemax (multiplexed); HBO (multiplexed); Showtime (multiplexed); Starz (multiplexed); The Movie Channel (multiplexed).
Fee: $13.05 monthly (each).
Video-On-Demand: No
Pay-Per-View
iN DEMAND (delivered digitally); Hot Choice (delivered digitally); Playboy TV (delivered digitally).
Internet Service
Operational: Yes.
Broadband Service: Comcast High Speed Internet.
Fee: $42.95 monthly.
Telephone Service
None
Miles of Plant: 65.0 (coaxial); None (fiber optic). Homes passed: 4,000.
General Manager: Tim Hagan. Marketing Director: Laurie Nicholson. Technical Operations Director: Bob Tharp.
Ownership: Comcast Cable Communications Inc. (MSO).

TERRE HAUTE—Time Warner Cable, 1605 Wabash Ave, Terre Haute, IN 47807. Phone: 812-232-5808. Fax: 812-232-7453. Web Site: http://www.timewarnercable.com. Also serves Riley, Vigo County (portions) & West Terre Haute. ICA: IN0011.
TV Market Ranking: Below 100 (Riley, TERRE HAUTE, Vigo County (portions), West Terre Haute). Franchise award date: N.A. Franchise expiration date: N.A. Began: October 18, 1966.
Channel capacity: N.A. Channels available but not in use: N.A.
Basic Service
Subscribers: 13,986.
Programming (received off-air): WAWV-TV (ABC) Terre Haute; WFYI (PBS) Indianapolis; WRTV (ABC, Grit) Indianapolis; WTHI-TV (CBS, FOX) Terre Haute; WTIU (PBS) Bloomington; WTTV (CBS, This TV) Bloomington; WTWO (NBC) Terre Haute; WXIN (Antenna TV, FOX) Indianapolis; 22 FMs.

The industry bible…
Consumer Electronics Daily
Warren Communications News
Free 30-day trial–call 800-771-9202 or visit www.warren-news.com

Programming (via satellite): Boomerang; C-SPAN; C-SPAN 2; Discovery Life Channel; EVINE Live; Food Network; Fox News Channel; FX; INSP; LMN; OWN: Oprah Winfrey Network; Oxygen; TBS; WE tv; WGN America.
Fee: $24.95-$61.55 installation; $18.50 monthly.
Expanded Basic Service 1
Subscribers: N.A.
Programming (via satellite): A&E; AMC; Animal Planet; BET; Bravo; Cartoon Network; CMT; CNBC; CNN; Comedy Central; Discovery Channel; Disney Channel; E! HD; ESPN; ESPN2; EWTN Global Catholic Network; FOX Sports Midwest; FOX Sports Ohio/Sports Time Ohio; Freeform; HGTV; History; HLN; ION Television; Lifetime; MSNBC; MTV; Nickelodeon; Pop; QVC; Spike TV; The Weather Channel; TLC; TNT; Travel Channel; Trinity Broadcasting Network (TBN); Turner Classic Movies; TV Land; USA Network; VH1.
Fee: $39.96 monthly.
Digital Basic Service
Subscribers: N.A.
Programming (via satellite): BBC America; Bloomberg Television; Cooking Channel; Discovery Digital Networks; Disney XD; DIY Network; ESPN Now; ESPNews; FOX College Sports Central; FOX College Sports Pacific; Fox Sports 1; Fuse; FXM; FYI; Golf Channel; Great American Country; GSN; History International; IFC; MC; MTV Classic; MTV Hits; MTV2; National Geographic Channel; NBA TV; NBCSN; Nick Jr.; Nicktoons; Outdoor Channel; Ovation; Sundance TV; TeenNick.
Fee: $6.00 monthly (per tier).
Digital Pay Service 1
Pay Units: N.A.
Programming (via satellite): Cinemax (multiplexed); Flix (multiplexed); HBO (multiplexed); Showtime (multiplexed); Starz Encore (multiplexed); The Movie Channel (multiplexed).
Fee: $14.00 monthly (each).
Video-On-Demand: Yes
Pay-Per-View
MLB Extra Innings (delivered digitally); Fresh (delivered digitally); Shorteez (delivered digitally); Playboy TV (delivered digitally); Hot Choice (delivered digitally).
Internet Service
Operational: Yes.
Subscribers: 15,358.
Broadband Service: Road Runner.
Fee: $99.00 installation; $44.95 monthly.
Telephone Service
Digital: Operational
Subscribers: 6,379.
Fee: $44.95 monthly
Miles of Plant: 868.0 (coaxial); 167.0 (fiber optic). Homes passed: 49,304.
General Manager: Irene Christopher. Business Manager: Terry Goodman. Technical Operations Manager: Patrick Rafferty.
Ownership: Time Warner Cable (MSO).

THORNTOWN—Comcast Cable. Now served by HENDRICKS COUNTY (portions), IN [IN0001]. ICA: IN0325.

TIPTON (portions)—Formerly served by Country Cablevision Ltd. No longer in operation. ICA: IN0326.

TOPEKA—Formerly served by Lig TV. No longer in operation. ICA: IN0198.

TRAFALGAR—Formerly served by CableDirect. No longer in operation. ICA: IN0327.

TROY—Formerly served by Avenue Broadband Communications. No longer in operation. ICA: IN0207.

TWELVE MILE—Formerly served by CableDirect. No longer in operation. ICA: IN0328.

TWIN LAKES—Formerly served by CableDirect. No longer in operation. ICA: IN0329.

UNION CITY—Time Warner Cable. Now served by AMBERLEY (village), OH [OH0001]. ICA: IN0080.

URBANA—Formerly served by CableDirect. No longer in operation. ICA: IN0330.

VAN BUREN—Swayzee Communications, 214 South Washington St, PO Box 97, Swayzee, IN 46986. Phones: 765-922-7916; 800-435-8353. Fax: 765-922-4545. E-mail: swayzee@swayzee.com. Web Site: http://swayzee.com. ICA: IN0331.
TV Market Ranking: 82 (VAN BUREN).
Channel capacity: N.A. Channels available but not in use: N.A.
Basic Service
Subscribers: 19.
Fee: $20.00 installation; $21.98 monthly.
Office Manager: Audra Hicks.
Ownership: Swayzee Communications Corp. (MSO).

VEEDERSBURG—NewWave Communications. Now served by COVINGTON, IN [IN0124]. ICA: IN0145.

VEVAY—Formerly served by Adelphia Communications. Now served by Time Warner Cable, MADISON, IN [IN0046]. ICA: IN0153.

VINCENNES—NewWave Communications, One Montgomery Plaza, 4th Floor, Sikeston, MO 63801. Phone: 888-863-9928 (Corporate office). Fax: 573-481-9809. E-mail: info@newwavecom.com. Web Site: http://www.newwavecom.com. Also serves Bridgeport, Lawrence County (portions), Lawrenceville, St. Francisville & Sumner, IL; Arno, Bartholomew County (portions), Bedford, Bicknell, Brazil, Brown County, Bruceville, Carbon, Clay County (north central portion), Clayton, Clinton, Coatesville, Cordry Lake, Daviess County, Edinburgh, Edwardsport, Fairview Park, Freelandville, French Lick, Gibson County (portions), Harmony, Hendricks County (southern portion), Knightsville, Knox County, Lawrence County (unincorporated areas), Loogootee, Martin County (portions), Mitchell, Monroe City,

2017 Edition — D-237

Indiana—Cable Systems

CABLE & TV STATION COVERAGE
Atlas 2017
The perfect companion to the Television & Cable Factbook
To order call 800-771-9202 or visit www.warren-news.com

Nashville, Nineveh, Oakland City, Orange County (unincorporated areas), Orleans, Paoli, Parke County (portions), Petersburg, Pike County (portions), Princes Lakes, Rosedale, Seelyville, Shoals, Staunton, Stilesville, Terre Haute City, Universal, Vermillion County (portions), Vigo County (portions), Washington, West Baden Springs, Wheatland & Winslow, IN. ICA: IN0035.

TV Market Ranking: 16 (Amo, Bartholomew County (portions), Bedford, Brown County, Clayton, Coatesville, Cordry Lake, Edinburgh, Hendricks County (southern portion), Lawrence County (unincorporated areas), Mitchell, Nashville, Nineveh, Orange County (unincorporated areas) (portions), Orleans, Princes Lakes, Stilesville); 86 (Gibson County (portions), Oakland City, Winslow); Below 100 (Clay County (north central portion), Fairview Park, Paoli, Parke County (portions), Rosedale, Seelyville, Staunton, Terre Haute City, Universal, Vermillion County (portions), Vigo County (portions), West Baden Springs, Brazil, Carbon, Clinton, French Lick, Knightsville, Orange County (unincorporated areas) (portions)); Outside TV Markets (Bicknell, Bridgeport, Bruceville, Daviess County, Edwardsport, Freelandville, Knox County, Lawrence County (portions), Lawrenceville, Martin County (portions), Monroe City, Petersburg, Pike County (portions), Shoals, VINCENNES, Washington, Wheatland, Loogootee, St. Francisville, Sumner, Bartholomew County (portions)).

Channel capacity: N.A. Channels available but not in use: N.A.

Basic Service
Subscribers: 19,874.
Programming (received off-air): WAWV-TV (ABC) Terre Haute; WEHT (ABC) Evansville; WEVV-TV (CBS, FOX) Evansville; WFIE (NBC, This TV) Evansville; WNIN (PBS) Evansville; WTHI-TV (CBS, FOX) Terre Haute; WTTV (CBS, This TV) Bloomington; WTWO (NBC) Terre Haute; WVUT (PBS) Vincennes; allband FM.
Programming (via satellite): C-SPAN; C-SPAN 2; EVINE Live; EWTN Global Catholic Network; INSP; Jewelry Television; QVC; Trinity Broadcasting Network (TBN); WGN America.
Fee: $40.00 installation; $34.78 monthly.

Expanded Basic Service 1
Subscribers: N.A.
Programming (via satellite): A&E; AMC; Animal Planet; BET; Bravo; Cartoon Network; CMT; CNBC; CNN; Comedy Central; Discovery Channel; Discovery Life Channel; Disney Channel; Disney XD; E! HD; ESPN; ESPN2; Food Network; Fox Sports 1; FOX Sports Midwest; Freeform; FX; Golf Channel; GSN; Hallmark Channel; HGTV; History; HLN; ION Television; Lifetime; MSNBC; MTV; National Geographic Channel; NBCSN; Nickelodeon; Oxygen; Spike TV; Syfy; TBS; The Weather Channel; TLC; TNT; Travel Channel; truTV; Turner Classic Movies; TV Land; Univision Studios; USA Network; VH1.
Fee: $33.00 monthly.

Digital Basic Service
Subscribers: N.A.
Programming (via satellite): BBC America; Discovery Digital Networks; DIY Network; ESPN Classic; ESPNews; Fuse; FYI; History International; IFC; LMN; MC; Nick 2; Nick Jr.; Nicktoons; Sundance TV; TeenNick; TV Guide Interactive Inc.; WE tv.

Digital Pay Service 1
Pay Units: N.A.
Programming (via satellite): Cinemax (multiplexed); Flix; HBO (multiplexed); Showtime (multiplexed); Starz (multiplexed); Starz Encore (multiplexed); The Movie Channel (multiplexed).
Fee: $6.95 monthly (Cinemax or HBO).

Video-On-Demand: No

Pay-Per-View
iN DEMAND (delivered digitally); NHL Center Ice (delivered digitally); MLB Extra Innings (delivered digitally); Hot Choice (delivered digitally); Playboy TV (delivered digitally); Fresh (delivered digitally); Shorteez (delivered digitally).

Internet Service
Operational: Yes.
Broadband Service: In-house.
Fee: $46.95 installation; $33.99 monthly.

Telephone Service
Digital: Operational
Fee: $25.99 monthly
Miles of Plant: 520.0 (coaxial); None (fiber optic). Homes passed: 29,228.
Chief Financial Officer: Rod Siemers. General Manager: John Helmers.
Ownership: NewWave Communications LLC (MSO).

WABASH—Comcast Cable. Now served by HENDRICKS COUNTY (portions), IN [IN0001]. ICA: IN0045.

WADESVILLE—Formerly served by NewWave Communications. No longer in operation. ICA: IN0301.

WAKARUSA—Comcast Cable. Now served by CHAMPAIGN, IL [IL0019]. ICA: IN0149.

WALKERTON—Mediacom. Now served by KNOX, IN [IN0060]. ICA: IN0081.

WALTON—Park TV & Electronics Inc, 205 East Railroad Ave, PO Box 9, Cissna Park, IL 60924. Phones: 800-825-3882; 815-457-2659. Web Site: http://www.parktvcable.com. ICA: IN0181.
TV Market Ranking: Below 100 (WALTON).
Channel capacity: N.A. Channels available but not in use: N.A.

Basic Service
Subscribers: 3.
Fee: $17.98 monthly.
President & General Manager: Joe Young.
Ownership: Park TV & Electronics Inc. (MSO).

WANATAH—Mediacom. Now served by NEWTON COUNTY (portions), IN [IN0316]. ICA: IN0333.

WARREN—Warren Cable, 426 North Wayne St, PO Box 330, Warren, IN 46792. Phones: 260-375-2111; 260-375-2115. Fax: 260-375-2244. E-mail: info@citznet.com. Web Site: http://www.citznet.com. Also serves Huntington. ICA: IN0172.
TV Market Ranking: 82 (Huntington, WARREN). Franchise award date: November 22, 1983. Franchise expiration date: N.A. Began: July 1, 1985.
Channel capacity: N.A. Channels available but not in use: N.A.

Basic Service
Subscribers: 493. Commercial subscribers: 336.
Programming (received off-air): WANE-TV (Antenna TV, CBS) Fort Wayne; WFFT-TV (FOX, MeTV) Fort Wayne; WFWA (PBS) Fort Wayne; WIPB (PBS) Muncie; WISH-TV (CW) Indianapolis; WNDY-TV (Bounce TV, Grit, MNT, TheCoolTV) Marion; WPTA (ABC, MNT, NBC) Fort Wayne; WTHR (COZI TV, MeTV, NBC) Indianapolis; WTTK (CW, This TV) Kokomo.
Programming (via satellite): A&E; AMC; CMT; CNN; Concert TV; C-SPAN; Discovery Channel; Disney Channel; ESPN; ESPN2; Fox News Channel; Freeform; HGTV; History; Lifetime; Nickelodeon; Spike TV; TBS; The Weather Channel; TLC; TNT; Travel Channel; USA Network; WGN America.
Fee: $15.00 installation; $40.00 monthly; $1.00 converter.

Pay Service 1
Pay Units: 189.
Programming (via satellite): HBO; Showtime.
Fee: $5.00 installation; $10.00 monthly (HBO or Showtime), $15.00 monthly (HBO/Showtime).

Internet Service
Operational: Yes.

Telephone Service
Analog: Operational
Miles of Plant: 28.0 (coaxial); 705.0 (fiber optic). Homes passed: 893.
President & General Manager: Neil Laymon. Marketing Director: Ellen Laymon. Chief Technician: Jack Roberts.
Ownership: Citizens Telephone Corp.

WARSAW—Comcast Cable. Now served by CHAMPAIGN, IL [IL0019]. ICA: IN0030.

WASHINGTON—Formerly served by Charter Communications. Now served by NewWave Communications, VINCENNES, IN [IN0035]. ICA: IN0055.

WAVELAND—Formerly served by CableDirect. No longer in operation. ICA: IN0332.

WAYNETOWN—Formerly served by Indiana Communications. No longer in operation. ICA: IN0184.

WEST LEBANON—Park TV & Electronics Inc, 205 East Railroad Ave, PO Box 9, Cissna Park, IL 60924. Phones: 815-457-2659; 800-825-3882. Web Site: http://www.parktvcable.com. ICA: IN0197.
TV Market Ranking: Below 100 (WEST LEBANON). Franchise award date: N.A. Franchise expiration date: N.A. Began: November 1, 1988.
Channel capacity: N.A. Channels available but not in use: N.A.

Basic Service
Subscribers: 38.
Programming (received off-air): WCCU (FOX, MeTV) Urbana; WCIA (CBS, MNT) Champaign; WICD (ABC) Champaign; WILL-TV (PBS) Urbana; WLFI-TV (CBS, TheCoolTV) Lafayette; WRTV (ABC, Grit) Indianapolis; WTHR (COZI TV, MeTV, NBC) Indianapolis; WTTV (CBS, This TV) Bloomington.
Fee: $39.90 installation; $43.95 monthly.

Expanded Basic Service 1
Subscribers: N.A.
Programming (via satellite): CNN; Discovery Channel; Disney Channel; ESPN; Freeform; HLN; MTV; Nickelodeon; TBS; TNT; VH1; WGN America.
Fee: $17.97 monthly.

Pay Service 1
Pay Units: N.A.
Programming (via satellite): Cinemax; HBO; Showtime; The Movie Channel.
Fee: $8.95 monthly (TMC), $10.95 monthly (Cinemax or Showtime), $12.95 monthly (HBO).

Video-On-Demand: No

Internet Service
Operational: No.

Telephone Service
None
Miles of Plant: 4.0 (coaxial); None (fiber optic). Homes passed: 340.
President & General Manager: Joe Young.
Ownership: Park TV & Electronics Inc. (MSO).

WESTPORT—Comcast Cable. Now served by HENDRICKS COUNTY (portions), IN [IN0001]. ICA: IN0166.

WHEATFIELD—Mediacom. Now served by NEWTON COUNTY (portions), IN [IN0316]. ICA: IN0334.

WHITESTOWN—Formerly served by Longview Communications. No longer in operation. ICA: IN0160.

WILKINSON—Formerly served by Insight Communications. Now served by Comcast Cable, HENDRICKS COUNTY (portions), IN [IN0001]. ICA: IN0148.

WILLIAMSBURG—Formerly served by CableDirect. No longer in operation. ICA: IN0335.

WILLIAMSBURG—Formerly served by Vital Communications. No longer in operation. ICA: IN0360.

WINAMAC—LightStream, 306 South State Rd 39, PO Box 408, Buffalo, IN 47925. Phones: 574-946-1377; 800-760-0848; 574-278-7121. Fax: 574-278-8448. E-mail: customerservice@pwrtc.net. Web Site: http://www.lightstreamin.com. Also serves Bruce Lake, Fulton County (western portion), Pulaski County (southern portion) & Star City. ICA: IN0130.
TV Market Ranking: Below 100 (Fulton County (western portion) (portions), Pulaski County (southern portion) (portions)); Outside TV Markets (Bruce Lake, Fulton County (western portion) (portions), Pulaski County (southern portion) (portions), Star City, WINAMAC). Franchise award date: March 1, 1970. Franchise expiration date: N.A. Began: March 1, 1971.
Channel capacity: N.A. Channels available but not in use: N.A.

Basic Service
Subscribers: 878. Commercial subscribers: 73.
Programming (received off-air): WCIU-TV (MeTV) Chicago; WCWW-LD (CW, Movies!, This TV) South Bend; WGN-TV (IND) Chicago; WHME-TV (COZI TV, IND)

Cable Systems—Indiana

South Bend; WLFI-TV (CBS, TheCoolTV) Lafayette; WLS-TV (ABC, Live Well Network) Chicago; WNDU-TV (NBC) South Bend; WNIT (PBS) South Bend; WSBT-TV (CBS, FOX) South Bend; WSJV (Heroes & Icons) Elkhart; WTHR (COZI TV, MeTV, NBC) Indianapolis; WTTK (CW, This TV) Kokomo; WTTW (PBS) Chicago.
Programming (via satellite): A&E; AMC; Animal Planet; Cartoon Network; CMT; CNBC; CNN; Comcast SportsNet Chicago; Comedy Central; C-SPAN; Discovery Channel; Disney Channel; Disney XD; E! HD; ESPN; ESPN Classic; ESPN2; EVINE Live; Food Network; Fox News Channel; Fox Sports 1; Freeform; FX; FXM; Hallmark Channel; HGTV; History; HLN; Lifetime; MSNBC; MTV; National Geographic Channel; Nickelodeon; OWN: Oprah Winfrey Network; QVC; Spike TV; Syfy; TBS; The Weather Channel; TLC; TNT; truTV; Turner Classic Movies; TV Land; USA Network; VH1; WE tv.
Fee: $99.00 installation; $58.52 monthly; $2.30 converter.

Pay Service 1
Pay Units: 91.
Programming (via satellite): HBO.
Fee: $5.00 installation; $12.65 monthly.

Pay Service 2
Pay Units: 47.
Programming (via satellite): Cinemax.
Fee: $5.00 installation; $8.20 monthly.

Pay Service 3
Pay Units: 51.
Programming (via satellite): Starz; Starz Encore.
Fee: $5.00 installation; $9.95 monthly.

Video-On-Demand: No

Pay-Per-View
iN DEMAND; special events.

Internet Service
Operational: Yes. Began: January 1, 2004.
Broadband Service: Nortwest Indiana Internet Services (NWIIS).
Fee: $30.00 installation; $19.95-$39.95 monthly; $4.95 modem lease; $69.95 modem purchase.

Telephone Service
Digital: Operational
Miles of Plant: 30.0 (coaxial); None (fiber optic). Homes passed: 1,650.
President & Chief Executive Officer: Mark Dickerson.
Ownership: Pulaski White Rural Telephone Cooperative (MSO).

WINCHESTER—Comcast Cable. Now served by HENDRICKS COUNTY (portions), IN [IN0001]. ICA: IN0068.

WINSLOW—NewWave Communications. Now served by VINCENNES, IN [IN0035]. ICA: IN0118.

WORTHINGTON—Formerly served by Indiana Communications. Now served by JASONVILLE, IN [IN0106]. ICA: IN0138.

YANKEETOWN—Formerly served by Time Warner Cable. No longer in operation. ICA: IN0336.

YOUNG AMERICA—Formerly served by CableDirect. No longer in operation. ICA: IN0338.

ZANESVILLE—Formerly served by CableDirect. No longer in operation. ICA: IN0339.

IOWA

Total Systems: 193	Communities with Applications: 0
Total Communities Served: 704	Number of Basic Subscribers: 351,724
Franchises Not Yet Operating: 0	Number of Expanded Basic Subscribers: 2,592
Applications Pending: 0	Number of Pay Units: 3,506

Top 100 Markets Represented: Omaha, NE (53); Davenport, IA-Rock Island-Moline, IL (60); Cedar Rapids-Waterloo (65); Des Moines-Ames (66); Sioux Falls-Mitchell, SD (85); Rockford-Freeport, IL (97).

For a list of cable communities in this section, see the Cable Community Index located in the back of Cable Volume 2.
For explanation of terms used in cable system listings, see p. D-11.

ADAIR—Formerly served by B & L Technologies LLC. No longer in operation. ICA: IA0216.

ADEL—Mediacom. Now served by DEXTER, IA [IA0015]. ICA: IA0030.

AFTON—Formerly served by B & L Technologies LLC. No longer in operation. ICA: IA0222.

AINSWORTH—Formerly served by Starwest Inc. No longer in operation. ICA: IA0614.

AKRON—Premier Communications. Now served by SIOUX CENTER, IA [IA0076]. ICA: IA0150.

ALBIA—Mediacom, 6300 Council St NE, Ste A, Cedar Rapids, IA 52402. Phones: 319-393-1914; 319-395-9699; 641-682-1695 (Ottumwa office). Fax: 319-393-7017. Web Site: http://www.mediacomcable.com. Also serves Appanoose County, Bloomfield, Centerville, Eddyville, Eldon & Monroe County (portions). ICA: IA0039.
 TV Market Ranking: Below 100 (ALBIA, Appanoose County (portions), Bloomfield, Centerville, Eddyville, Eldon, Monroe County (portions); Outside TV Markets (Appanoose County (portions)). Franchise award date: N.A. Franchise expiration date: N.A. Began: April 1, 1970.
 Channel capacity: N.A. Channels available but not in use: N.A.
Basic Service
 Subscribers: 2,237. Commercial subscribers: 141.
 Programming (received off-air): KCCI (CBS, MeTV) Des Moines; KCWI-TV (CW) Ames; KDSM-TV (FOX, The Country Network) Des Moines; KFPX-TV (ION) Newton; KIIN (PBS) Iowa City; KTVO (ABC) Kirksville; KYOU-TV (FOX) Ottumwa; WHO-DT (Antenna TV, NBC) Des Moines; WOI-DT (ABC) Ames; allband FM.
 Programming (via satellite): C-SPAN; C-SPAN 2; QVC; The Weather Channel; WGN America.
 Fee: $43.00 monthly; $1.01 converter.
Expanded Basic Service 1
 Subscribers: N.A.
 Programming (via satellite): A&E; AMC; Animal Planet; BET; Bravo; Cartoon Network; CMT; CNBC; CNN; Comedy Central; Discovery Channel; Discovery Life Channel; Disney Channel; E! HD; ESPN; ESPN2; EWTN Global Catholic Network; Food Network; Fox News Channel; Fox Sports 1; FOX Sports Midwest; Freeform; FX; Hallmark Channel; HGTV; History; HLN; INSP; Lifetime; LMN; MSNBC; MTV; National Geographic Channel; NBCSN; Nickelodeon; Oxygen; RFD-TV; Spike TV; Syfy; TBS; Telemundo; The Weather Channel; TLC; TNT; Travel Channel; Trinity Broadcasting Network (TBN); truTV; TV Land; Univision Studios; USA Network; VH1; WE tv.
 Fee: $17.57 monthly.
Digital Basic Service
 Subscribers: N.A.
 Programming (via satellite): AXS TV; BBC America; Bloomberg Television; CBS Sports Network; Cloo; CMT; Destination America; Discovery Kids Channel; Disney XD; DMX Music; ESPN HD; ESPN2 HD; ESPNews; ESPNU; FOX College Sports Central; FOX College Sports Pacific; Fox Sports 2; Fuse; FXM; FYI; Golf Channel; GolTV; GSN; HD Theater; History International; IFC; Investigation Discovery; MTV Classic; MTV Hits; MTV2; Nat Geo WILD; Nick Jr.; Nicktoons; Outdoor Channel; Ovation; OWN: Oprah Winfrey Network; Science Channel; TeenNick; Tennis Channel; Turner Classic Movies; TVG Network; Universal HD; VH1 Soul.
Digital Pay Service 1
 Pay Units: N.A.
 Programming (via satellite): Cinemax (multiplexed); Flix; HBO (multiplexed); HBO HD; Showtime (multiplexed); Showtime HD; Starz (multiplexed); Starz Encore (multiplexed); Starz HD; Sundance TV; The Movie Channel (multiplexed); The Movie Channel HD.
 Fee: $10.00 installation; $9.50 monthly (Cinemax, HBO, Showtime/Flix/Sundance/TMC or Starz/Encore).
Video-On-Demand: Yes
Pay-Per-View
 ESPN Now (delivered digitally); ETC (delivered digitally); Playboy TV (delivered digitally); Pleasure (delivered digitally); Fresh (delivered digitally); Shorteez (delivered digitally); Vubiquity Inc. (delivered digitally).
Internet Service
 Operational: Yes.
 Subscribers: 1,477.
 Broadband Service: Mediacom High Speed Internet.
Telephone Service
 Digital: Operational
 Subscribers: 884.
 Miles of Plant: 183.0 (coaxial); 165.0 (fiber optic). Homes passed: 8,850.
 Regional Vice President: Doug Frank. Technical Operations Director: Greg Nank. Technical Operations Manager: Steve Angren. Marketing Director: Steve Schuh.
 Ownership: Mediacom LLC (MSO).

ALBION—Heart of Iowa Telecommunications. This cable system has converted to IPTV. See UNION, IA [IA5001]. ICA: IA0623.

ALDEN—Formerly served by Latimer/Coulter Cablevision. No longer in operation. ICA: IA0389.

ALEXANDER—Formerly served by CableDirect. No longer in operation. ICA: IA0390.

ALGONA—Algona Municipal Utilities, 104 West Call St, PO Box 10, Algona, IA 50511. Phone: 515-295-3584. Fax: 515-295-3364. E-mail: info@netamu.com. Web Site: http://www.netamu.com. ICA: IA0598. **Note:** This system is an overbuild.
 TV Market Ranking: Outside TV Markets (ALGONA).
 Channel capacity: N.A. Channels available but not in use: N.A.
Basic Service
 Subscribers: 213.
 Programming (received off-air): KAAL (ABC, This TV) Austin; KCCI (CBS, MeTV) Des Moines; KCWI-TV (CW) Ames; KDIN-TV (PBS) Des Moines; KDMI (MNT, This TV) Des Moines; KDSM-TV (FOX, The Country Network) Des Moines; KEYC-TV (CBS, FOX) Mankato; KIMT (CBS, MNT) Mason City; KTIN (PBS) Fort Dodge; WHO-DT (Antenna TV, NBC) Des Moines; WOI-DT (ABC) Ames.
 Programming (via satellite): C-SPAN; C-SPAN 2; EWTN Global Catholic Network; QVC; TBS; The Weather Channel; Trinity Broadcasting Network (TBN); WGN America.
 Fee: $17.95 monthly.
Expanded Basic Service 1
 Subscribers: N.A.
 Programming (via satellite): A&E; AMC; Animal Planet; Bravo; BTN; Cartoon Network; CMT; CNBC; CNN; Comedy Central; Discovery Channel; Disney Channel; Disney XD; DIY Network; E! HD; ESPN; ESPN Classic; ESPN2; Food Network; Fox News Channel; Fox Sports 1; FOX Sports North; Freeform; FX; FXM; Golf Channel; Hallmark Channel; HGTV; History; HLN; Lifetime; LMN; MoviePlex; MSNBC; MTV; NFL Network; Nickelodeon; OWN: Oprah Winfrey Network; Spike TV; Syfy; TLC; TNT; Travel Channel; truTV; Turner Classic Movies; TV Land; USA Network; VH1.
 Fee: $55.95 monthly.
Digital Basic Service
 Subscribers: N.A.
 Programming (via satellite): BBC America; CMT; Destination America; Discovery Kids Channel; DMX Music; ESPNews; ESPNU; FOX College Sports Central; FOX College Sports Pacific; GSN; Investigation Discovery; MTV Classic; MTV2; National Geographic Channel; NBCSN; Nick Jr.; Nicktoons; Outdoor Channel; RFD-TV; RTN; Science Channel; TeenNick; VH1 Soul; WE tv; World.
Digital Expanded Basic Service
 Subscribers: N.A.
 Programming (via satellite): BTN HD.
Digital Expanded Basic Service 2
 Subscribers: N.A.
 Programming (via satellite): AXS TV; Discovery Channel HD; ESPN HD; ESPN2 HD; NFL Network HD.
Digital Pay Service 1
 Pay Units: 150.
 Programming (via satellite): HBO (multiplexed); HBO HD.
 Fee: $14.95 monthly.
Digital Pay Service 2
 Pay Units: 98.
 Programming (via satellite): Cinemax (multiplexed); Cinemax HD.
 Fee: $14.95 monthly.
Digital Pay Service 3
 Pay Units: 91.
 Programming (via satellite): Flix; IFC; Showtime (multiplexed); Showtime HD; Sundance TV; The Movie Channel (multiplexed); The Movie Channel HD.
 Fee: $16.95 monthly.
Digital Pay Service 4
 Pay Units: 142.
 Programming (via satellite): Starz (multiplexed); Starz Encore (multiplexed); Starz HD.
 Fee: $12.95 monthly.
Pay-Per-View
 iN DEMAND (delivered digitally).
Internet Service
 Operational: Yes.
 Broadband Service: In-house.
 Fee: $22.95 monthly.
Telephone Service
 Analog: Operational
 Miles of Plant: 63.0 (coaxial); None (fiber optic). Homes passed: 3,100.
 General Manager: John Bilsten. Marketing Director: Robert M. Jennings. Communications Supervisor: Lowell Roethler.
 Ownership: Algona Municipal Utilities.

ALGONA—Mediacom. Now served by FORT DODGE, IA [IA0011]. ICA: IA0045.

ALLEMAN—Formerly served by Huxley Communications Corp. No longer in operation. ICA: IA0391.

ALLERTON—Formerly served by Longview Communications. No longer in operation. ICA: IA0297.

ALTA—ALTA-TEC, 223 Main St, Alta, IA 51002-1345. Phone: 712-200-1122. Fax: 712-200-9600. E-mail: altatec@alta-tec.net. Web Site: http://www.alta-tec.net. ICA: IA0599. **Note:** This system is an overbuild.
 TV Market Ranking: Outside TV Markets (ALTA).
 Channel capacity: N.A. Channels available but not in use: N.A.

Cable Systems—Iowa

Basic Service
Subscribers: 408.
Programming (received off-air): KCAU-TV (ABC) Sioux City; KCCI (CBS, MeTV) Des Moines; KCSD-TV (PBS) Sioux Falls; KDSM-TV (FOX, The Country Network) Des Moines; KMEG (Azteca America, CBS, Decades) Sioux City; KPTH (FOX, MNT, This TV) Sioux City; KSIN-TV (PBS) Sioux City; KTIV (CW, MeTV, NBC) Sioux City; WOI-DT (ABC) Ames.
Fee: $58.75 monthly.
Expanded Basic Service 1
Subscribers: N.A.
Programming (via satellite): A&E; AMC; Animal Planet; Cartoon Network; CMT; CNBC; CNN; Comedy Central; C-SPAN; C-SPAN 2; CW PLUS; Discovery Channel; Disney Channel; DIY Network; ESPN; ESPN Classic; ESPN Deportes; ESPN2; ESPNews; Food Network; Fox News Channel; Fox Sports 1; FOX Sports North; Freeform; FX; Hallmark Channel; HGTV; History; HLN; Lifetime; MoviePlex; MSNBC; MTV; Nickelodeon; Outdoor Channel; QVC; RFD-TV; Spike TV; Starz Encore; Syfy; TBS; The Weather Channel; TLC; TNT; Travel Channel; Trinity Broadcasting Network (TBN); truTV; Turner Classic Movies; TV Land; Univision Studios; USA Network; VH1; WGN America.
Fee: $28.00 monthly.
Digital Basic Service
Subscribers: N.A.
Programming (via satellite): BBC America; Cooking Channel; Destination America; Discovery Kids Channel; Discovery Life Channel; Disney XD; DIY Network; ESPNews; ESPNU; FOX College Sports Central; FOX College Sports Pacific; FXM; FYI; Great American Country; GSN; History International; IFC; Investigation Discovery; NBCSN; OWN; Oprah Winfrey Network; Pivot; RFD-TV; Science Channel; WE tv.
Digital Expanded Basic Service
Subscribers: N.A.
Programming (via satellite): AXS TV; BTN HD; Discovery Channel HD; ESPN HD; ESPN2 HD; Fox HD; Fuse HD.
Fee: $9.95 monthly.
Digital Expanded Basic Service 2
Subscribers: N.A.
Programming (via satellite): Bandamax; De Pelicula; De Pelicula Clasico; ESPN Deportes; Fox Deportes; Ritmoson; Telehit.
Fee: $2.99 monthly.
Pay Service 1
Pay Units: N.A.
Programming (via satellite): Cinemax (multiplexed); Flix; HBO (multiplexed); Showtime; Starz; The Movie Channel.
Fee: $12.00 monthly (Showtime/TMC/Flix), $14.00 monthly (Cinemax or HBO).
Digital Pay Service 1
Pay Units: N.A.
Programming (via satellite): Cinemax (multiplexed); HBO (multiplexed); Starz (multiplexed); Starz Encore (multiplexed).
Fee: $7.10 monthly (Starz/Encore), $14.00 monthly (HBO or Cinemax).
Internet Service
Operational: Yes.
Broadband Service: In-house.
Fee: $39.95-$59.95 monthly; $150.00 modem purchase.
Telephone Service
Analog: Operational.
Miles of Plant: 11.0 (coaxial); None (fiber optic). Homes passed: 750.
Utility Manager: Randy Tilk. Utilities Superintendent: Ron Chapman. Telecommunications Clerk: April Meyer.
Ownership: Alta Municipal Utilities.

ALTA VISTA (town)—Formerly served by Alta Vista Municipal Cable. No longer in operation. ICA: IA0392.

AMANA—Mediacom, 6300 Council St NE, Ste A, Cedar Rapids, IA 52402. Phones: 319-393-1914; 319-395-9699; 800-332-0245. Fax: 319-393-7017. Web Site: http://www.mediacomcable.com. ICA: IA0631.
TV Market Ranking: 65 (AMANA).
Channel capacity: N.A. Channels available but not in use: N.A.
Basic Service
Subscribers: 175.
Fee: $43.00 monthly.
Ownership: Mediacom LLC (MSO).

AMES—Mediacom, 2205 Ingersoll Ave, Des Moines, IA 50312. Phone: 515-246-1890. Fax: 515-246-2211. Web Site: http://www.mediacomcable.com. Also serves Boone, Boone County (eastern portion), Boone County (southern portion), Dysart, Greene County, Huxley, Jefferson, Madrid, Nevada, Polk City, Polk County (northwestern portion), Randall, Sheldahl, Slater, Story City, Story County, Toledo, Traer & Woodward. ICA: IA0008.
TV Market Ranking: 65 (Dysart, Traer); 66 (AMES, Boone, Boone County (eastern portion), Boone County (southern portion), Greene County (portions), Huxley, Madrid, Nevada, Polk City, Polk County (northwestern portion), Randall, Sheldahl, Slater, Story City, Story County, Woodward); Below 100 (Toledo); Outside TV Markets (Jefferson, Greene County (portions)). Franchise award date: January 1, 1983. Franchise expiration date: N.A. Began: January 1, 1980.
Channel capacity: N.A. Channels available but not in use: N.A.
Basic Service
Subscribers: 5,757. Commercial subscribers: 2,139.
Programming (received off-air): KCCI (CBS, MeTV) Des Moines; KCWI-TV (CW) Ames; KDIN-TV (PBS) Des Moines; KDSM-TV (FOX, The Country Network) Des Moines; KFPX-TV (ION) Newton; WHO-DT (Antenna TV, NBC) Des Moines; WOI-DT (ABC) Ames.
Programming (via satellite): CNN; C-SPAN; Discovery Channel; QVC; TBS; WGN America.
Fee: $60.00 installation; $43.00 monthly.
Expanded Basic Service 1
Subscribers: N.A.
Programming (via satellite): A&E; AMC; Animal Planet; BET; Bravo; Cartoon Network; CMT; CNBC; Comedy Central; C-SPAN 2; Disney Channel; E! HD; ESPN; ESPN2; EVINE Live; EWTN Global Catholic Network; Food Network; Fox News Channel; Fox Sports 1; Freeform; FX; Hallmark Channel; HGTV; History; HLN; INSP; Lifetime; LMN; MoviePlex; MSNBC; MTV; Nickelodeon; Pop; RFD-TV; Spike TV; Syfy; Telemundo; The Weather Channel; TLC; TNT; Travel Channel; Trinity Broadcasting Network (TBN); truTV; Turner Classic Movies; TV Land; Univision Studios; USA Network; VH1; WE tv.
Fee: $31.46 monthly.
Digital Basic Service
Subscribers: N.A.
Programming (via satellite): BBC America; Bloomberg Television; Discovery Digital Networks; Disney XD; DMX Music; Fuse; FXM; FYI; Golf Channel; GSN; History International; IFC; National Geographic Channel; NBCSN; Nick Jr.; Outdoor Channel; Ovation; TeenNick.

Digital Pay Service 1
Pay Units: N.A.
Programming (via satellite): Cinemax (multiplexed); Flix; HBO (multiplexed); Showtime (multiplexed); Starz (multiplexed); Starz Encore (multiplexed); Sundance TV; The Movie Channel (multiplexed).
Fee: $9.95 monthly (Cinemax, HBO, Showtime, Flix/Sundance/TMC or Starz/Encore).
Video-On-Demand: Yes
Pay-Per-View
ESPN Now (delivered digitally); ETC (delivered digitally); Playboy TV (delivered digitally); Pleasure (delivered digitally); Fresh (delivered digitally); Shorteez (delivered digitally); Vubiquity Inc. (delivered digitally).
Internet Service
Operational: Yes.
Subscribers: 8,012.
Broadband Service: Mediacom High Speed Internet.
Fee: $49.95 installation; $29.95 monthly; $10.00 modem lease.
Telephone Service
Analog: Not Operational
Digital: Operational
Subscribers: 2,516.
Miles of Plant: 445.0 (coaxial); 118.0 (fiber optic). Homes passed: 31,607.
Vice President: Steve Purcell. Marketing Director: LeAnn Treloar. Government & Media Relations Manager: Bill Peard. Technical Operations Manager: Cliff Waggener.
Ownership: Mediacom LLC (MSO).

ANAMOSA—Mediacom, 6300 Council St NE, Ste A, Cedar Rapids, IA 52402. Phones: 800-332-0245; 319-393-1914; 319-395-9699. Fax: 319-393-7017. Web Site: http://www.mediacomcable.com. Also serves Jones County (portions). ICA: IA0630.
TV Market Ranking: 65 (ANAMOSA).
Channel capacity: N.A. Channels available but not in use: N.A.
Basic Service
Subscribers: 1,158.
Fee: $43.00 monthly.
Ownership: Mediacom LLC (MSO).

ANDREW—Andrew Telephone Co. Inc, 105 North West St, PO Box 229, Truro, IA 50257-0229. Phones: 641-765-4201 (Truro office); 712-824-7231 (Emerson office); 563-672-3277. Fax: 641-765-4204. E-mail: customerservice@interstatecom.com. Web Site: http://www.interstatecom.com. ICA: IA0351.
TV Market Ranking: Below 100 (ANDREW). Franchise award date: July 1, 1985. Franchise expiration date: N.A. Began: October 1, 1985.
Channel capacity: N.A. Channels available but not in use: N.A.
Basic Service
Subscribers: 45.
Programming (received off-air): KCRG-TV (ABC, MNT) Cedar Rapids; KIIN (PBS) Iowa City; KLJB (CW, FOX, MeTV) Davenport; KWQC-TV (NBC) Davenport; KWWL (CW, MeTV, NBC) Waterloo; WHBF-TV (CBS) Rock Island; WQAD-TV (ABC, Antenna TV) Moline.
Programming (via satellite): A&E; CNN; Disney Channel; ESPN; Freeform; Spike TV; TBS; TNT; Turner Classic Movies; WGN America.
Fee: $59.95 monthly.
Video-On-Demand: No
Internet Service
Operational: No.
Telephone Service
None
Miles of Plant: 3.0 (coaxial); None (fiber optic). Homes passed: 155.
General Manager: Mike Weis. Customer Service: Carla Ehlers.
Ownership: Interstate Communications.

ANITA—WesTel Systems, 012 East 3rd St, PO Box 330, Remsen, IA 51050. Phones: 800-352-0006; 402-654-3344; 712-786-1181. Fax: 712-786-2400. E-mail: acctinfo@westelsystems.com. Web Site: http://www.westelsystems.com. ICA: IA0188.
TV Market Ranking: Outside TV Markets (ANITA). Franchise award date: N.A. Franchise expiration date: N.A. Began: March 1, 1983.
Channel capacity: 30 (not 2-way capable). Channels available but not in use: N.A.
Basic Service
Subscribers: 253.
Programming (received off-air): KCCI (CBS, MeTV) Des Moines; KDIN-TV (PBS) Des Moines; KDSM-TV (FOX, The Country Network) Des Moines; KETV (ABC, MeTV) Omaha; KMTV-TV (Antenna TV, CBS, Escape) Omaha; WHO-DT (Antenna TV, NBC) Des Moines; WOI-DT (ABC) Ames; WOWT (IND, NBC) Omaha.
Programming (via satellite): A&E; Animal Planet; BTN; CMT; CNBC; CNN; Comedy Central; CW PLUS; Discovery Channel; Disney Channel; DIY Network; ESPN; ESPN2; Food Network; Fox News Channel; Fox Sports 1; Freeform; FX; HGTV; History; HLN; Lifetime; MTV; NBCSN; Nickelodeon; Spike TV; Syfy; TBS; The Weather Channel; TLC; TNT; Travel Channel; Turner Classic Movies; TV Land; USA Network; VH1; WE tv; WGN America.
Fee: $20.00 installation; $39.95 monthly.
Digital Basic Service
Subscribers: N.A.
Programming (via satellite): BBC America; Bloomberg Television; CMT; Destination America; Discovery Kids Channel; Discovery Life Channel; Disney XD; DMX Music; ESPN Classic; ESPNews; EVINE Live; Fuse; FXM; FYI; Golf Channel; Great American Country; GSN; History International; Investigation Discovery; LMN; MTV Classic; MTV Hits; MTV2; Nick Jr.; Nicktoons; Outdoor Channel; OWN; Oprah Winfrey Network; RFD-TV; Science Channel; TeenNick; The Word Network; Trinity Broadcasting Network (TBN); VH1 Soul.
Pay Service 1
Pay Units: N.A.
Programming (via satellite): Cinemax; HBO.
Fee: $11.00 monthly (Cinemax), $12.95 monthly (HBO).
Digital Pay Service 1
Pay Units: N.A.
Programming (via satellite): Cinemax (multiplexed); Flix; HBO (multiplexed); Showtime (multiplexed); Starz (multiplexed); Starz Encore (multiplexed); The Movie Channel (multiplexed).
Pay-Per-View
iN DEMAND (delivered digitally).
Internet Service
Operational: Yes.
Telephone Service
Analog: Operational
Miles of Plant: 10.0 (coaxial); None (fiber optic). Homes passed: 477.
Chief Executive Officer: Robert Gannon. General Manager: William Daubendiek II.
Ownership: WesTel Systems.

Iowa—Cable Systems

ANTHON—Long Lines. Now served by SALIX, IA [IA0510]. ICA: IA0243.

ARLINGTON—Formerly served by Alpine Communications LC. No longer in operation. ICA: IA0393.

ARTHUR—Sac County Mutual Telco, 108 South Maple St, PO Box 488, Odebolt, IA 51458. Phone: 712-668-2200. Fax: 712-668-2100. E-mail: scmtco@netins.net. Web Site: http://www.scmtco.com. ICA: IA0361.
TV Market Ranking: Outside TV Markets (ARTHUR). Franchise award date: August 1, 1988. Franchise expiration date: N.A. Began: January 1, 1989.
Channel capacity: N.A. Channels available but not in use: N.A.
Basic Service
  Subscribers: 216.
  Programming (received off-air): KCAU-TV (ABC) Sioux City; KMEG (Azteca America, CBS, Decades) Sioux City; KPTH (FOX, MNT, This TV) Sioux City; KTIV (CW, MeTV, NBC) Sioux City.
  Programming (via satellite): A&E; Cartoon Network; CMT; CNN; C-SPAN; C-SPAN 2; Discovery Channel; Disney Channel; ESPN; ESPN2; Food Network; Fox News Channel; Fox Sports 1; Freeform; FX; Hallmark Channel; HGTV; History; ION Television; NBCSN; Nickelodeon; Spike TV; TBS; The Weather Channel; TLC; TNT; truTV; Turner Classic Movies; TV Land; USA Network; WE tv; WGN America.
  Fee: $30.00 installation; $47.65 monthly; $2.00 converter.
Pay Service 1
  Pay Units: 4.
  Programming (via satellite): Cinemax; HBO.
  Fee: $15.00 installation; $11.00 monthly (Cinemax), $12.95 monthly (HBO).
Internet Service
  Operational: No, DSL.
Telephone Service
  Analog: Operational
  Miles of Plant: 2.0 (coaxial); None (fiber optic).
  General Manager: Ronald Sorensen.
  Ownership: Sac County Mutual Telephone Co. (MSO).

ASHTON—Formerly served by Premier Communications. Now served by HTC Communications, HOSPERS, IA [IA0060]. ICA: IA0300.

ATKINS—Atkins Telephone, 85 Main Ave, PO Box 157, Atkins, IA 52206-9750. Phone: 319-446-7331. Fax: 319-446-9100. E-mail: jtraut@atkinstelephone.com. Web Site: http://www.atkinstelephone.com. ICA: IA0269.
TV Market Ranking: 65 (ATKINS). Franchise award date: N.A. Franchise expiration date: N.A. Began: November 1, 1981.
Channel capacity: N.A. Channels available but not in use: N.A.
Basic Service
  Subscribers: 334.
  Programming (received off-air): KCRG-TV (ABC, MNT) Cedar Rapids; KFXA (FOX, The Country Network) Cedar Rapids; KGAN (CBS) Cedar Rapids; KIIN (PBS) Iowa City; KPXR-TV (ION) Cedar Rapids; KWKB (The Works, This TV) Iowa City; KWWL (CW, MeTV, NBC) Waterloo.
  Programming (via satellite): A&E; AMC; Animal Planet; Cartoon Network; CMT; CNBC; CNN; Comedy Central; C-SPAN; Discovery Channel; Disney Channel; E!; HD; ESPN; ESPN2; EWTN Global Catholic Network; Food Network; Fox News Channel; Fox Sports 1; Freeform; FX; HGTV; History; HLN; Lifetime; MTV; Nickelodeon; QVC; Spike TV; TBS; The Weather Channel; TLC; TNT; Travel Channel; Trinity Broadcasting Network (TBN); truTV; Turner Classic Movies; TV Land; USA Network; VH1; WGN America.
  Fee: $10.00 installation; $39.00 monthly.
Pay Service 1
  Pay Units: 59.
  Programming (via satellite): HBO.
  Fee: $10.00 monthly.
Pay Service 2
  Pay Units: 6.
  Programming (via satellite): Showtime.
  Fee: $10.00 monthly.
Pay Service 3
  Pay Units: 2.
  Programming (via satellite): Cinemax.
  Fee: $10.00 monthly.
Video-On-Demand: No
Internet Service
  Operational: No, DSL & dial-up.
Telephone Service
  Analog: Operational
  Miles of Plant: 6.0 (coaxial); None (fiber optic).
  General Manager: Jerry Spaight. Chief Technician: Chad Carlson. Cable Administrator: Jody Traut.
  Ownership: Atkins Telephone Co.

ATLANTIC—Mediacom, 2205 Ingersoll Ave, Des Moines, IA 50312. Phone: 515-246-1890. Fax: 515-246-2211. Web Site: http://www.mediacomcable.com. ICA: IA0032.
TV Market Ranking: Outside TV Markets (ATLANTIC). Franchise award date: April 27, 1972. Franchise expiration date: N.A. Began: October 15, 1973.
Channel capacity: N.A. Channels available but not in use: N.A.
Basic Service
  Subscribers: 1,351.
  Programming (received off-air): KCCI (CBS, MeTV) Des Moines; KDIN-TV (PBS) Des Moines; KDSM-TV (FOX, The Country Network) Des Moines; KETV (ABC, MeTV) Omaha; KMTV-TV (Antenna TV, CBS, Escape) Omaha; KPTM (Estrella TV, FOX, MNT, This TV) Omaha; KXVO (Azteca America, CW) Omaha; WHO-DT (Antenna TV, NBC) Des Moines; WOI-DT (ABC) Ames; WOWT (IND, NBC) Omaha.
  Programming (via satellite): C-SPAN; C-SPAN 2; ION Television; Pop; QVC; The Weather Channel; WGN America.
  Fee: $43.00 monthly; $2.31 converter.
Expanded Basic Service 1
  Subscribers: N.A.
  Programming (via satellite): A&E; AMC; Animal Planet; Cartoon Network; CMT; CNBC; CNN; Discovery Channel; Disney Channel; ESPN; ESPN2; Fox News Channel; Fox Sports 1; FOX Sports Midwest; Freeform; FX; Hallmark Channel; HGTV; History; HLN; Lifetime; MSNBC; MTV; Nickelodeon; RFD-TV; Spike TV; Syfy; TBS; Telemundo; The Weather Channel; TLC; TNT; truTV; Univision Studios; USA Network; WE tv.
  Fee: $19.78 monthly.
Digital Basic Service
  Subscribers: N.A.
  Programming (via satellite): BBC America; Bloomberg Television; Bravo; Discovery Digital Networks; DMX Music; Fuse; FXM; FYI; Golf Channel; GSN; History International; IFC; LMN; National Geographic Channel; NBCSN; Nick Jr.; Outdoor Channel; Ovation; TeenNick; TV Land.
Digital Pay Service 1
  Pay Units: N.A.
  Programming (via satellite): Cinemax (multiplexed); Flix; HBO (multiplexed); Showtime (multiplexed); Starz (multiplexed); Starz Encore (multiplexed); Sundance TV; The Movie Channel (multiplexed).
  Fee: $20.00 installation; $9.50 monthly (Cinemax, HBO, Showtime, Flix/Sundance/TMC or Starz/Encore).
Video-On-Demand: Yes
Pay-Per-View
  ESPN Now (delivered digitally); ETC (delivered digitally); Playboy TV (delivered digitally); Pleasure (delivered digitally); Vubiquity Inc. (delivered digitally).
Internet Service
  Operational: Yes. Began: September 1, 2002.
  Broadband Service: Mediacom High Speed Internet.
  Fee: $45.95 monthly.
Telephone Service
  Digital: Operational
  Miles of Plant: 324.0 (coaxial); None (fiber optic). Homes passed: 9,228.
  Vice President: Steve Purcell. Marketing Director: LeAnn Treloar. Government & Media Relations Manager: Bill Peard. Technical Operations Manager: Cliff Waggoner.
  Ownership: Mediacom LLC (MSO).

AURELIA—NU-Telecom. Formerly [IA0212]. This cable system has converted to IPTV, 221 Main St, Aurelia, IA 51005. Phones: 844-354-4111; 888-873-6853; 712-434-5989. Fax: 712-434-5555. E-mail: onlinecustservice@nu-telcom.net. Web Site: http://www.nutelecom.net. ICA: IA5021.
TV Market Ranking: Outside TV Markets (AURELIA).
Channel capacity: N.A. Channels available but not in use: N.A.
NU-Basic
  Subscribers: 260.
  Fee: $50.00 installation; $20.95 monthly. Includes 17 channels.
Nu Entertainment
  Subscribers: N.A.
  Fee: $52.95 monthly. Includes 55 channels.
NU-Variety
  Subscribers: N.A.
  Fee: $7.95 monthly. Includes 27 channels.
HD
  Subscribers: N.A.
  Fee: $10.95 monthly. Includes 34 channels.
Premium Channels
  Subscribers: N.A.
  Fee: $44.95 monthly (all premium channels), $15.95 (Cinemax, HBO, Showtime/TMC or Starz/Encore), $26.95 monthly (HBO/Starz/Encore), $34.95 monthly (Cinemax/HBO/Starz/Encore).
Internet Service
  Operational: Yes.
  Fee: $54.95-$79.95 monthly.
Telephone Service
  Digital: Operational
  Fee: $14.00 monthly
President & Chief Executive Officer: Bill Otis.
Ownership: New Ulm Telecom (MSO).

AURELIA—NU-Telecom. This cable system has converted to IPTV. See AURELIA, IA [IA5021]. ICA: IA0212.

AURORA—Formerly served by Alpine Communications LC. No longer in operation. ICA: IA0395.

AYRSHIRE—ATC Cablevision. Now served by GILLETT GROVE, IA [IA0386]. ICA: IA0368.

BADGER—Formerly served by Goldfield Communication Services Corp. No longer in operation. ICA: IA0396.

BAGLEY—Panora Communications Cooperative. Now served by PANORA, IA [IA0108]. ICA: IA0356.

BALDWIN—Baldwin Nashville Telephone Co, PO Box 50, Baldwin, IA 52207. Phone: 563-673-2001. Also serves Monmouth. ICA: IA0625.
TV Market Ranking: Below 100 (BALDWIN).
Channel capacity: N.A. Channels available but not in use: N.A.
Basic Service
  Subscribers: 187.
  Fee: $25.00 installation; $48.95 monthly.
Chief Executive Officer: Brian Rickels. Secretary: Robert W. Rohwedder.
Ownership: Baldwin Nashville Telephone Co.

BATAVIA—Formerly served by Westcom. No longer in operation. ICA: IA0398.

BATTLE CREEK—Sac County Mutual Telco, 108 South Maple St, PO Box 488, Odebolt, IA 51458. Phone: 712-668-2200. Fax: 712-668-2100. E-mail: scmtco@netins.net. Web Site: http://www.scmtco.com. ICA: IA0238.
TV Market Ranking: Outside TV Markets (BATTLE CREEK). Franchise award date: N.A. Franchise expiration date: N.A. Began: October 1, 1984.
Channel capacity: N.A. Channels available but not in use: N.A.
Basic Service
  Subscribers: 733.
  Programming (received off-air): KCAU-TV (ABC) Sioux City; KMEG (Azteca America, CBS, Decades) Sioux City; KSIN-TV (PBS) Sioux City; KTIV (CW, MeTV, NBC) Sioux City.
  Programming (via satellite): A&E; Cartoon Network; CMT; CNN; Discovery Channel; Disney Channel; ESPN; ESPN2; Food Network; Fox News Channel; Fox Sports 1; Freeform; FX; Hallmark Channel; HGTV; History; NBCSN; Nickelodeon; Spike TV; Starz Encore; Starz Encore Westerns; TBS; The Weather Channel; TNT; truTV; Turner Classic Movies; TV Land; USA Network; WE tv; WGN America.
  Fee: $30.00 installation; $47.65 monthly.
Pay Service 1
  Pay Units: 9.
  Programming (via satellite): Cinemax; HBO.
  Fee: $15.00 installation; $11.00 monthly (Cinemax), $12.95 monthly (HBO).
Pay Service 2
  Pay Units: 22.
  Programming (via satellite): Flix; Showtime; The Movie Channel.
  Fee: $12.75 monthly.
Internet Service
  Operational: No, DSL.
Telephone Service
  Analog: Operational
  Miles of Plant: 8.0 (coaxial); None (fiber optic).
  General Manager: Ronald Sorenson.
  Ownership: Sac County Mutual Telephone Co. (MSO).

BAYARD—Formerly served by Tele-Services Ltd. No longer in operation. ICA: IA0260.

Cable Systems—Iowa

BELLE PLAINE—Mediacom, 6300 Council St NE, Ste A, Cedar Rapids, IA 52402. Phones: 319-395-9699; 319-393-1914; 800-332-0245. Fax: 319-393-7017. Web Site: http://www.mediacomcable.com. Also serves Marengo. ICA: IA0633.
TV Market Ranking: 65 (Marengo); Outside TV Markets (BELLE PLAINE).
Channel capacity: N.A. Channels available but not in use: N.A.
Basic Service
Subscribers: 578.
Fee: $43.00 monthly.
Internet Service
Operational: Yes.
Subscribers: 369.
Broadband Service: Mediacom High Speed Internet.
Telephone Service
Digital: Operational
Subscribers: 190.
Miles of Plant: 67.0 (coaxial); 60.0 (fiber optic). Homes passed: 2,954.
Ownership: Mediacom LLC (MSO).

BELLEVUE—IVUE Network. Formerly [IA0553]. This cable system has converted to IPTV, 106 North 3rd St, Bellevue, IA 52031. Phone: 563-872-4456. E-mail: bellevue@ivuenet.com. Web Site: http://www.bellevueia.gov. ICA: IA5033.
Channel capacity: N.A. Channels available but not in use: N.A.
Lifeline
Subscribers: N.A.
Fee: $32.99 monthly. Includes 32 channels.
Basic
Subscribers: 735.
Fee: $54.99 monthly. Includes 93 channels.
Enhanced Basic
Subscribers: N.A.
Fee: $13.49 monthly. Includes 24 additional channels.
Cinemax
Subscribers: N.A.
Fee: $8.99 monthly. Includes 8 channels.
HBO
Subscribers: N.A.
Fee: $14.99 monthly. Includes 6 channels.
Showtime
Subscribers: N.A.
Fee: $12.99 monthly. Includes 8 channels.
Internet Service
Operational: Yes.
Fee: $39.99 monthly.
Ownership: City of Bellevue.

BELLEVUE—IVUE Network. This cable system has converted to IPTV. See BELLEVUE, IA [IA5033]. ICA: IA0553.

BENNETT—F&B Communications. This cable system has converted to IPTV. Now served by WHEATLAND, IA [IA5105]. ICA: IA0400.

BIRMINGHAM—Starwest Inc. Now served by KEOSAUQUA, IA [IA0186]. ICA: IA0401.

BLAIRSBURG—Milford Cable TV, 806 Okoboji Ave, PO Box 163, Milford, IA 51351. Phones: 855-722-3450; 712-338-4967. Fax: 712-338-4719. E-mail: mplagman@milfordcable.net. Web Site: http://milfordcomm.net. ICA: IA0545.
TV Market Ranking: 66 (BLAIRSBURG). Franchise award date: N.A. Franchise expiration date: N.A. Began: January 1, 1990.
Channel capacity: N.A. Channels available but not in use: N.A.

Basic Service
Subscribers: 17.
Programming (received off-air): KCCI (CBS, MeTV) Des Moines; KCWI-TV (CW) Ames; KDIN-TV (PBS) Des Moines; KDSM-TV (FOX, The Country Network) Des Moines; KPXD-TV (ION) Arlington; WHO-DT (Antenna TV, NBC) Des Moines; WOI-DT (ABC) Ames.
Programming (via satellite): A&E; Bravo; CMT; CNBC; CNN; Discovery Channel; Disney Channel; ESPN; Freeform; HGTV; History; Lifetime; MSNBC; MTV; Nickelodeon; Spike TV; TBS; TNT; USA Network; VH1; WGN America.
Fee: $35.00 installation; $32.86 monthly.
Digital Basic Service
Subscribers: N.A.
Programming (via satellite): BBC America; Bloomberg Television; Discovery Life Channel; Disney XD; DMX Music; ESPN Classic; ESPN2; ESPNews; Fox Sports 1; FOX Sports Networks; FXM; FYI; Golf Channel; GSN; HGTV; History; History International; LMN; National Geographic Channel; Nick Jr.; Nicktoons; Outdoor Channel; Sundance TV; TeenNick; Trinity Broadcasting Network (TBN); Turner Classic Movies; WE tv.
Pay Service 1
Pay Units: N.A.
Programming (via satellite): HBO (multiplexed).
Fee: $10.00 monthly.
Digital Pay Service 1
Pay Units: N.A.
Programming (via satellite): Cinemax (multiplexed); Flix; HBO (multiplexed); Showtime; Starz (multiplexed); Starz Encore (multiplexed); The Movie Channel (multiplexed).
Internet Service
Operational: Yes.
Telephone Service
None
Miles of Plant: 1.0 (coaxial); None (fiber optic). Homes passed: 90.
Ownership: Milford Communications (MSO).

BLAIRSTOWN—Coon Creek Telephone & Cablevision, 312 Locust St, PO Box 150, Blairstown, IA 52209-0150. Phones: 888-823-6234; 319-454-6234. Fax: 319-454-6480. E-mail: cooncrek@netins.net; csr@cooncreektelephone.com. Web Site: http://www.cooncreektelephone.com. Also serves Belle Plaine & Marengo. ICA: IA0402.
TV Market Ranking: 65 (BLAIRSTOWN, Marengo). Franchise award date: N.A. Franchise expiration date: N.A. Began: January 1, 1984.
Channel capacity: N.A. Channels available but not in use: N.A.
Basic Service
Subscribers: 405.
Fee: $20.95 monthly.
Digital Basic Service
Subscribers: 374.
Programming (received off-air): KCRG-TV (ABC, MNT) Cedar Rapids; KGAN (CBS) Cedar Rapids; KIIN (PBS) Iowa City; KWWL (CW, MeTV, NBC) Waterloo.
Programming (via satellite): A&E; CNN; Discovery Channel; Disney Channel; ESPN; ESPN2; Freeform; Lifetime; Nickelodeon; Syfy; TBS; TLC; TNT; Trinity Broadcasting Network (TBN); truTV; USA Network; WGN America.
Fee: $48.00 monthly.

Digital Pay Service 1
Pay Units: N.A.
Programming (via satellite): Cinemax; HBO; Showtime; Starz.
Fee: $9.50 monthly (Cinemax/Starz or HBO/Showtime).
Internet Service
Operational: Yes.
Telephone Service
None
Chief Executive Officer & General Manager: Debra Lucht. Office Manager: Kami Thenhaus. Plant Superintendent: Craig Von Scoyoc.
Ownership: Coon Creek Telephone & Cablevision.

BLAKESBURG—Formerly served by Telnet South LC. No longer in operation. ICA: IA0303.

BLENCOE—Formerly served by Sky Scan Cable Co. No longer in operation. ICA: IA0352.

BLENCOE—Long Lines. Now served by SALIX, IA [IA0510]. ICA: IA0604.

BLOCKTON—Formerly served by B & L Technologies LLC. No longer in operation. ICA: IA0357.

BLOOMFIELD—Citizens Mutual Telephone, 114 West Jefferson St, PO Box 130, Bloomfield, IA 52537. Phones: 800-746-4268; 641-664-2074. E-mail: jsnyder@cmtel.com. Web Site: http://www.cmtel.com. Also serves Drakesville, Floris & Pulaski. ICA: IA0626.
TV Market Ranking: Below 100 (BLOOMFIELD, Drakesville, Floris, Pulaski).
Channel capacity: N.A. Channels available but not in use: N.A.
Basic Service
Subscribers: 820.
Fee: $99.00 installation; $69.95 monthly.
General Manager: Joe Snyder. Plant Manager: Trent Gregory. Office Manager: Sherri Guiter.
Ownership: Citizens Mutual Telephone Cooperative (MSO).

BLUE GRASS—Mediacom. Now served by MOLINE, IL [IL0011]. ICA: IA0071.

BODE—Video Services Ltd, PO Box 23, Livermore, IA 50558. Phone: 515-379-1471. Fax: 515-379-1472. ICA: IA0329.
TV Market Ranking: Outside TV Markets (BODE). Franchise award date: N.A. Franchise expiration date: N.A. Began: October 1, 1969.
Channel capacity: 30 (not 2-way capable). Channels available but not in use: N.A.
Basic Service
Subscribers: N.A.
Programming (received off-air): KCCI (CBS, MeTV) Des Moines; KDIN-TV (PBS) Des Moines; KDSM-TV (FOX, The Country Network) Des Moines; KEYC-TV (CBS, FOX) Mankato; KTIN (PBS) Fort Dodge; KTTC (CW, NBC) Rochester; WHO-DT (Antenna TV, NBC) Des Moines; WOI-DT (ABC) Ames.
Programming (via satellite): Discovery Channel; Disney Channel; Freeform; TBS.
Fee: $30.00 installation; $8.00 monthly.
Expanded Basic Service 1
Subscribers: N.A.
Programming (via satellite): A&E; CNN; ESPN; Lifetime; Nickelodeon; QVC; Spike TV; TNT; Travel Channel; USA Network; WGN America.
Fee: $21.00 monthly.

Pay Service 1
Pay Units: N.A.
Programming (via satellite): HBO; Showtime.
Fee: $9.00 monthly (Showtime), $10.00 monthly (HBO).
Internet Service
Operational: No.
Telephone Service
None
Miles of Plant: 3.0 (coaxial); None (fiber optic).
General Manager: Mark Steil.
Ownership: Video Services Ltd.

BONAPARTE—Formerly served by Mediacom. Now served by Starwest Inc., KEOSAUQUA, IA [IA0186]. ICA: IA0278.

BOYDEN—Premier Communications. Now served by SIOUX CENTER, IA [IA0076]. ICA: IA0307.

BRADDYVILLE—Formerly served by CableDirect. No longer in operation. ICA: IA0582.

BRANDON—Formerly served by New Path Communications LC. No longer in operation. ICA: IA0579.

BREDA—Western Iowa Networks, 112 East Main St, PO Box 190, Breda, IA 51436-0190. Phones: 888-508-2946; 712-673-2311. Fax: 712-673-2800. Web Site: http://www.westIANet.com. Also serves Arcadia, Auburn, Carroll, Lidderdale & Westside. ICA: IA0318.
TV Market Ranking: Outside TV Markets (Arcadia, Auburn, BREDA, Carroll, Lidderdale, Westside). Franchise award date: N.A. Franchise expiration date: N.A. Began: January 1, 1983.
Channel capacity: N.A. Channels available but not in use: N.A.
Basic Service
Subscribers: 435.
Programming (received off-air): KCCI (CBS, MeTV) Des Moines; KDIN-TV (PBS) Des Moines; KDSM-TV (FOX, The Country Network) Des Moines; KPTH (FOX, MNT, This TV) Sioux City; KTIV (CW, MeTV, NBC) Sioux City; WHO-DT (Antenna TV, NBC) Des Moines; WOI-DT (ABC) Ames.
Programming (via satellite): AMC; CMT; CNN; Discovery Channel; Disney Channel; ESPN; HGTV; Lifetime; Nickelodeon; Spike TV; TBS; TNT; TV Land; USA Network; WGN America.
Fee: $30.00 installation; $44.99 monthly.
Pay Service 1
Pay Units: N.A.
Programming (via satellite): HBO.
Fee: $10.95 monthly.
Video-On-Demand: No
Internet Service
Operational: No, DSL.
Telephone Service
Analog: Operational
Miles of Plant: 4.0 (coaxial); None (fiber optic).
Chief Executive Officer: Chuck Deisbeck. Chief Technician: Mike Ludwig. Marketing & Sales Manager: Megan Badding.
Ownership: BTC Inc. (MSO).

BRIGHTON—Starwest Inc, 15235 235th St, Milton, IA 52570-8016. Phones: 319-397-2283; 319-293-6336. ICA: IA0403.
TV Market Ranking: Below 100 (BRIGHTON).
Channel capacity: N.A. Channels available but not in use: N.A.

Iowa—Cable Systems

Basic Service
Subscribers: N.A.
Programming (received off-air): KCRG-TV (ABC, MNT) Cedar Rapids; KGAN (CBS) Cedar Rapids; KWWL (CW, MeTV, NBC) Waterloo.
Programming (via satellite): CNN; Discovery Channel; ESPN; Freeform; HLN; MTV; Nickelodeon; TBS; USA Network; VH1; WGN America.
Fee: $30.00 installation; $14.50 monthly.
Pay Service 1
Pay Units: N.A.
Programming (via satellite): Showtime.
Fee: $10.00 monthly.
Internet Service
Operational: No.
General Manager & Chief Technician: John Stooksberry.
Ownership: Starwest Inc. (MSO).

BRISTOW—Formerly served by Dumont Cablevision. No longer in operation. ICA: IA0371.

BRONSON—Formerly served by TelePartners. Now served by Wiatel, LAWTON (village), IA [IA0330]. ICA: IA0372.

BROOKLYN—Inter-County Cable Co, PO Box 578, Brooklyn, IA 52211. Phones: 641-522-9211; 641-522-7000. Fax: 641-522-5001. E-mail: brookmt@netins.net. ICA: IA0158.
TV Market Ranking: Below 100 (BROOKLYN). Franchise award date: July 29, 1982. Franchise expiration date: N.A. Began: July 29, 1982.
Channel capacity: N.A. Channels available but not in use: N.A.
Basic Service
Subscribers: 397.
Programming (received off-air): KCCI (CBS, MeTV) Des Moines; KCRG-TV (ABC, MNT) Cedar Rapids; KDIN-TV (PBS) Des Moines; KDSM-TV (FOX, The Country Network) Des Moines; KGAN (CBS) Cedar Rapids; KWWL (CW, MeTV, NBC) Waterloo; WHO-DT (Antenna TV, NBC) Des Moines; WOI-DT (ABC) Ames.
Programming (via satellite): A&E; AMC; Animal Planet; Cartoon Network; CMT; CNN; Comedy Central; C-SPAN; Discovery Channel; Disney Channel; E! HD; ESPN; ESPN2; ESPNews; Food Network; Fox News Channel; FOX Sports Midwest; Freeform; FX; Golf Channel; Great American Country; GSN; Hallmark Channel; HGTV; History; INSP; Lifetime; MTV; Nickelodeon; Outdoor Channel; QVC; Spike TV; Syfy; TBS; The Weather Channel; TLC; TNT; Travel Channel; Trinity Broadcasting Network (TBN); truTV; Turner Classic Movies; TV Land; USA Network; VH1; WE tv; WGN America.
Fee: $25.00 installation; $49.00 monthly.
Digital Basic Service
Subscribers: N.A.
Programming (via satellite): Bloomberg Television; Bravo; DMX Music; ESPN Classic; EVINE Live; FOX College Sports Central; FOX College Sports Pacific; FYI; History International; LMN; National Geographic Channel; NBCSN; Nick Jr.; TeenNick.
Pay Service 1
Pay Units: 204.
Programming (via satellite): Cinemax; HBO.
Fee: $9.95 monthly (each).
Digital Pay Service 1
Pay Units: N.A.
Programming (via satellite): Cinemax (multiplexed); HBO (multiplexed); Showtime (multiplexed); Starz (multiplexed); Starz Encore (multiplexed); The Movie Channel (multiplexed).
Pay-Per-View
Action Max (delivered digitally); Sports PPV (delivered digitally); Hot Choice (delivered digitally); Playboy TV (delivered digitally); Fresh (delivered digitally); Shorteez (delivered digitally); ESPN Now (delivered digitally).
Internet Service
Operational: No, DSL.
Telephone Service
Analog: Operational
Miles of Plant: 26.0 (coaxial); 8.0 (fiber optic).
General Manager: Tim Atkinson. Plant Manager: Don Gepner. Office Manager: Martina Korns.
Ownership: Inter-County Cable Co.

BUFFALO CENTER—Mediacom. Now served by SWEA CITY, IA [IA0226]. ICA: IA0179.

BUFFALO CENTER—Winnebago Cooperative Telephone Assn. Now served by LAKE MILLS, IA [IA0590]. ICA: IA0588.

BURLINGTON—Mediacom, 6300 Council St NE, Ste A, Cedar Rapids, IA 52402. Phones: 319-393-1914; 319-395-9699 (Cedar Rapids office); 319-753-6576 (Local office). Fax: 319-393-7017. Web Site: http://www.mediacomcable.com. Also serves Columbus City, Columbus Junction, Danville, Des Moines County (portions), Fredonia, Iowa Army Munitions Plant, Louisa County, Middletown, Morning Sun, Wappello & West Burlington. ICA: IA0405.
TV Market Ranking: Below 100 (BURLINGTON, Columbus City, Columbus Junction, Danville, Des Moines County (portions), Fredonia, Iowa Army Munitions Plant, Louisa County, Middletown, Morning Sun, Wappello, West Burlington). Franchise award date: N.A. Franchise expiration date: N.A. Began: December 31, 1979.
Channel capacity: N.A. Channels available but not in use: N.A.
Basic Service
Subscribers: 7,026. Commercial subscribers: 14.
Programming (received off-air): KGCW (CW, MeTV, This TV) Burlington; KIIN (PBS) Iowa City; KLJB (CW, FOX, MeTV) Davenport; KWQC-TV (NBC) Davenport; KYOU-TV (FOX) Ottumwa; WGEM-TV (CW, FOX, NBC) Quincy; WHBF-TV (CBS) Rock Island; WQAD-TV (ABC, Antenna TV) Moline; 18 FMs.
Programming (via satellite): C-SPAN; C-SPAN 2; ION Television; Local Cable Weather; Pop; QVC; WGN America.
Fee: $52.40 monthly.
Expanded Basic Service 1
Subscribers: N.A.
Programming (via satellite): A&E; AMC; Animal Planet; BET; Bravo; Cartoon Network; CMT; CNBC; CNN; Comedy Central; Discovery Channel; Discovery Life Channel; Disney Channel; E! HD; ESPN; ESPN2; EWTN Global Catholic Network; Food Network; Fox News Channel; Fox Sports 1; FOX Sports Midwest; Freeform; FX; Hallmark Channel; HGTV; History; HLN; INSP; Lifetime; LMN; MSNBC; MTV; National Geographic Channel; NBCSN; Nickelodeon; Spike TV; Syfy; TBS; Telemundo; The Weather Channel; TLC; TNT; Travel Channel; Trinity Broadcasting Network (TBN); truTV; TV Land; Univision Studios; USA Network; VH1; WE tv.
Fee: $21.31 monthly.
Digital Basic Service
Subscribers: N.A.
Programming (via satellite): AXS TV; BBC America; Bloomberg Television; Cloo; Discovery Digital Networks; Disney XD; ESPN HD; ESPN2 HD; ESPNews; Fuse; FXM; FYI; Golf Channel; GSN; HD Theater; History International; IFC; MC; Nick Jr.; Nicktoons; Outdoor Channel; Ovation; TeenNick; Turner Classic Movies; TVG Network; Universal HD.
Digital Pay Service 1
Pay Units: N.A.
Programming (via satellite): Cinemax (multiplexed); Flix (multiplexed); HBO (multiplexed); HBO HD; Showtime (multiplexed); Showtime HD; Starz (multiplexed); Starz Encore (multiplexed); Starz HD; Sundance TV (multiplexed); The Movie Channel (multiplexed); The Movie Channel HD.
Fee: $10.00 installation; $8.95 monthly (Cinemax, HBO, Showtime, Flix/Sundance/TMC or Starz/Encore).
Video-On-Demand: No
Pay-Per-View
ESPN Now (delivered digitally); ETC (delivered digitally); Playboy TV (delivered digitally); Pleasure (delivered digitally); Vubiquity Inc. (delivered digitally).
Internet Service
Operational: Yes.
Subscribers: 5,298.
Broadband Service: Mediacom High Speed Internet.
Fee: $49.95 installation; $45.95 monthly; $10.00 modem lease.
Telephone Service
Digital: Operational
Subscribers: 3,247.
Fee: $39.95 monthly
Miles of Plant: 381.0 (coaxial); 242.0 (fiber optic). Homes passed: 20,438. Miles of plant (coax) includes miles of plant (fiber).
Technical Operations Manager: Joel Hanger. Sales & Marketing Director: Michelle Harper.
Ownership: Mediacom LLC (MSO).

CALAMUS—F&B Communications. This cable system has converted to IPTV. Now served by WHEATLAND, IA [IA5105]. ICA: IA0556.

CALHOUN COUNTY (portions)—Formerly served by Gowrie Cablevision. No longer in operation. ICA: IA0609.

CALMAR—Mediacom, 4010 Alexandra Dr, Waterloo, IA 50702. Phone: 319-235-2197. Fax: 319-232-7841. Web Site: http://www.mediacomcable.com. Also serves Elgin, Fayette, Fort Atkinson, Fredericksburg, New Hampton, Ossian, Spillville, Sumner & West Union. ICA: IA0074.
TV Market Ranking: 65 (Fredericksburg, Sumner); Outside TV Markets (CALMAR, Elgin, Fayette, Fort Atkinson, New Hampton, Ossian, Spillville, West Union). Franchise award date: N.A. Franchise expiration date: N.A. Began: January 1, 1982.
Channel capacity: N.A. Channels available but not in use: N.A.
Basic Service
Subscribers: 2,052.
Programming (received off-air): KAAL (ABC, This TV) Austin; KCRG-TV (ABC, MNT) Cedar Rapids; KFXA (FOX, The Country Network) Cedar Rapids; KGAN (CBS) Cedar Rapids; KIMT (CBS, MNT) Mason City; KRIN (PBS) Waterloo; KTTC (CW, NBC) Rochester; KWKB (The Works, This TV) Iowa City; KWWL (CW, MeTV, NBC) Waterloo; KXLT-TV (FOX, MeTV) Rochester.
Programming (via satellite): C-SPAN; INSP; Nickelodeon; Pop; QVC.
Fee: $20.00 installation; $43.00 monthly.
Expanded Basic Service 1
Subscribers: N.A.
Programming (via satellite): A&E; AMC; Animal Planet; Bravo; Cartoon Network; CMT; CNBC; CNN; Comcast SportsNet Chicago; Comedy Central; C-SPAN 2; Discovery Channel; Disney Channel; E! HD; ESPN; ESPN2; EWTN Global Catholic Network; Food Network; Fox News Channel; Fox Sports 1; Freeform; FX; Hallmark Channel; HGTV; History; HLN; Lifetime; MSNBC; MTV; RFD-TV; Spike TV; Syfy; TBS; Telemundo; The Weather Channel; TLC; TNT; Travel Channel; Trinity Broadcasting Network (TBN); truTV; Turner Classic Movies; TV Land; USA Network; VH1; WE tv; WGN America.
Fee: $10.00 installation; $29.95 monthly.
Digital Basic Service
Subscribers: N.A.
Programming (via satellite): BBC America; Bloomberg Television; Discovery Digital Networks; Disney XD; DMX Music; Fuse; FXM; FYI; Golf Channel; GSN; History International; IFC; LMN; National Geographic Channel; NBCSN; Nick Jr.; Outdoor Channel; Ovation; TeenNick.
Digital Pay Service 1
Pay Units: N.A.
Programming (via satellite): Cinemax (multiplexed); Flix; HBO (multiplexed); Showtime (multiplexed); Starz (multiplexed); Starz Encore (multiplexed); Sundance TV; The Movie Channel (multiplexed).
Fee: $10.00 installation; $9.95 monthly (Cinemax, HBO, Showtime, Flix/Sundance/TMC or Starz/Encore).
Video-On-Demand: Yes
Pay-Per-View
ESPN Now (delivered digitally); ETC (delivered digitally); Playboy TV (delivered digitally); Pleasure (delivered digitally); Fresh (delivered digitally); Shorteez (delivered digitally); Vubiquity Inc. (delivered digitally).
Internet Service
Operational: Yes.
Broadband Service: Mediacom High Speed Internet.
Fee: $99.00 installation; $40.00 monthly.
Telephone Service
Digital: Operational
Miles of Plant: 105.0 (coaxial); None (fiber optic). Homes passed: 5,650.
Regional Vice President: Doug Frank. General Manager: Doug Nix. Technical Operations Director: Greg Nank. Marketing Coordinator: Joni Lindauer. Marketing Director: Steve Schuh.
Ownership: Mediacom LLC (MSO).

CAMBRIDGE—Huxley Communications Corp. Now served by HUXLEY, IA [IA0595]. ICA: IA0406.

CARROLL—Mediacom, 510 North Clark St, Carroll, IA 51401. Phone: 800-332-0245. Web Site: http://www.mediacomcable.com. Also serves Audubon & Glidden. ICA: IA0025.
TV Market Ranking: Outside TV Markets (Audubon, Glidden).
Channel capacity: N.A. Channels available but not in use: N.A.

Cable Systems—Iowa

Basic Service
Subscribers: 2,273. Commercial subscribers: 165.
Fee: $43.00 monthly.
Internet Service
Operational: Yes.
Broadband Service: Mediacom High Speed Internet.
Telephone Service
Digital: Operational
Ownership: Mediacom LLC (MSO).

CARROLL—Western Iowa Networks. Now served by BREDA, IA [IA0318]. ICA: IA0618.

CARSON—Formerly served by Interstate Communications. No longer in operation. ICA: IA0198.

CASCADE—Cascade Communications, 106 Taylor St. SE, PO Box 250, Cascade, IA 52033. Phone: 563-852-3710. Fax: 563-852-9935. E-mail: info@cascadecomm.com. Web Site: http://www.cascadecomm.com. ICA: IA0608.
TV Market Ranking: Below 100 (CASCADE).
Channel capacity: N.A. Channels available but not in use: N.A.
Basic Service
Subscribers: 417 Includes IPTV subscribers.
Programming (received off-air): KCRG-TV (ABC, MNT) Cedar Rapids; KFXA (FOX, The Country Network) Cedar Rapids; KFXB-TV (Christian TV Network) Dubuque; KGAN (CBS) Cedar Rapids; KPXR-TV (ION) Cedar Rapids; KRIN (PBS) Waterloo; KWKB (The Works, This TV) Iowa City; KWWL (CW, MeTV, NBC) Waterloo.
Programming (via satellite): C-SPAN; EVINE Live; Pop; QVC.
Fee: $94.95 monthly.
Expanded Basic Service 1
Subscribers: N.A.
Programming (via satellite): A&E; AMC; Animal Planet; BET; Bravo; Cartoon Network; CMT; CNBC; CNN; Comcast SportsNet Chicago; Comedy Central; Discovery Channel; Disney Channel; E! HD; ESPN; ESPN Classic; ESPN2; EWTN Global Catholic Network; Food Network; Fox News Channel; Fox Sports 1; Freeform; FX; Great American Country; Hallmark Channel; HGTV; History; HLN; INSP; Lifetime; MSNBC; MTV; National Geographic Channel; Nickelodeon; Spike TV; Syfy; TBS; The Weather Channel; TLC; TNT; Travel Channel; Trinity Broadcasting Network (TBN); truTV; Turner Classic Movies; TV Land; USA Network; VH1; WE tv; WGN America.
Fee: $49.95 monthly.
Pay Service 1
Pay Units: N.A.
Programming (via satellite): Cinemax; HBO; Showtime.
Internet Service
Operational: Yes.
Fee: $34.95-$79.00 monthly.
Telephone Service
Digital: Operational
Fee: $16.00 monthly
Homes passed: 1,000.
General Manager: Dave Gibson.
Ownership: Cascade Communications Co.

CASEY—Casey Cable Co, 108 East Logan St, Casey, IA 50048-1012. Phone: 641-746-2222. Fax: 641-746-2221. ICA: IA0286.
TV Market Ranking: Outside TV Markets (CASEY). Franchise award date: February 1, 1984. Franchise expiration date: N.A. Began: February 1, 1984.
Channel capacity: 45 (not 2-way capable). Channels available but not in use: N.A.
Basic Service
Subscribers: 142.
Programming (received off-air): KCCI (CBS, MeTV) Des Moines; KDSM-TV (FOX, The Country Network) Des Moines; WHO-DT (Antenna TV, NBC) Des Moines; WOI-DT (ABC) Ames.
Programming (via satellite): A&E; AMC; CMT; CNN; Discovery Channel; Disney Channel; ESPN; ESPN2; Freeform; HLN; Nickelodeon; Spike TV; Syfy; TBS; TLC; TNT; USA Network; WGN America.
Fee: $20.00 monthly.
Pay Service 1
Pay Units: 42.
Programming (via satellite): HBO.
Fee: $10.00 monthly.
Pay Service 2
Pay Units: 28.
Programming (via satellite): Flix; Showtime; The Movie Channel.
Fee: $10.95 monthly.
Internet Service
Operational: No, DSL.
Telephone Service
None
Miles of Plant: 6.0 (coaxial); None (fiber optic). Homes passed: 228.
General Manager & Chief Technician: John Breining. Customer Service Manager: Traci Clarke.
Ownership: Casey Mutual Telephone Co.

CEDAR FALLS—Cedar Falls Municipal Communications Utility, 1 Utility Pkwy, PO Box 769, Cedar Falls, IA 50613. Phone: 319-266-1761. Fax: 319-266-8158. E-mail: cfu@cfunet.net. Web Site: http://www.cfu.net. ICA: IA0564.
TV Market Ranking: 65 (CEDAR FALLS). Franchise award date: N.A. Franchise expiration date: N.A. Began: March 1, 1996.
Channel capacity: 78 (operating 2-way). Channels available but not in use: N.A.
Basic Service
Subscribers: 11,915. Commercial subscribers: 318.
Programming (received off-air): KCRG-TV (ABC, MNT) Cedar Rapids; KFXA (FOX, The Country Network) Cedar Rapids; KGAN (CBS) Cedar Rapids; KPXR-TV (ION) Cedar Rapids; KRIN (PBS) Waterloo; KWKB (The Works, This TV) Iowa City; KWWF (Untamed Sports TV) Waterloo; KWWL (CW, MeTV, NBC) Waterloo.
Programming (via satellite): Church Channel; C-SPAN; C-SPAN 2; Disney XD; QVC; TBS; The Weather Channel; WGN America.
Fee: $25.00 installation; $23.00 monthly; $2.00 converter.
Expanded Basic Service 1
Subscribers: N.A.
Programming (via satellite): A&E; AMC; Animal Planet; BET; Bravo; Cartoon Network; CMT; CNBC; CNN; Comcast SportsNet Chicago; Comedy Central; Discovery Channel; Disney Channel; E! HD; ESPN; ESPN Classic; ESPN2; ESPNews; ESPNU; Food Network; Fox News Channel; Fox Sports 1; Freeform; FX; Golf Channel; Hallmark Channel; HGTV; History; HLN; Lifetime; MoviePlex; MSNBC; MTV; National Geographic Channel; NBCSN; Nickelodeon; Oxygen; Spike TV; Syfy; TLC; TNT; Travel Channel; truTV; Turner Classic Movies; TV Land; USA Network; VH1; WE tv.
Fee: $35.00 monthly.
Digital Basic Service
Subscribers: N.A.
Programming (via satellite): AXS TV; BBC America; Bloomberg Television; CBS Sports Network; Discovery Digital Networks; DMX Music; ESPN2 HD; ESPNU; Fox HD; Fuse; FXM; FYI; Golf Channel; GSN; Hallmark Movies & Mysteries; HD Theater; History International; IFC; NFL Network; Nick Jr.; Outdoor Channel; Ovation; RFD-TV; Starz Encore (multiplexed); TeenNick; Trinity Broadcasting Network (TBN).
Fee: $7.00 converter.
Pay Service 1
Pay Units: N.A.
Programming (via satellite): HBO; Starz; Starz Encore.
Fee: $6.00 monthly (Starz), $12.00 monthly (HBO).
Digital Pay Service 1
Pay Units: N.A.
Programming (via satellite): Cinemax (multiplexed); HBO (multiplexed); Showtime (multiplexed); Starz (multiplexed); Sundance TV; The Movie Channel (multiplexed).
Fee: $6.00 monthly (Starz/Encore), $10.00 monthly (Cinemax or Showtime/TMC), $12.00 monthly (HBO).
Video-On-Demand: No
Pay-Per-View
iN DEMAND (delivered digitally); Urban Xtra PPV (delivered digitally); Hot Choice (delivered digitally); Playboy TV (delivered digitally); Fresh (delivered digitally); Shorteez (delivered digitally); ESPN Now (delivered digitally); Sports PPV (delivered digitally).
Internet Service
Operational: Yes. Began: January 9, 1997.
Subscribers: 5,028.
Broadband Service: In-house.
Fee: $25.00 installation; $29.95-$43.50 monthly.
Telephone Service
None
Miles of Plant: 344.0 (coaxial); 1,517.0 (fiber optic). Homes passed: 15,950.
General Manager: Jim Krieg. Chief Engineer: Dave Schilling. Marketing Manager: Betty Zeman. Customer Service Manager: Julie Brunscheon.
Ownership: Cedar Falls Municipal Communications Utility (MSO).

CEDAR RAPIDS—ImOn Communications, 625 First St SE, Ste 100, Cedar Rapids, IA 52401. Phones: 319-298-6484; 319-298-3484. E-mail: support@ImOn.net. Web Site: http://www.imon.net. Also serves Hiawatha, Linn County (portions) & Marion. ICA: IA0638.
TV Market Ranking: 65 (CEDAR RAPIDS, Hiawatha, Linn County (portions), Marion).
Channel capacity: N.A. Channels available but not in use: N.A.
Basic Service
Subscribers: 11,411. Commercial subscribers: 248.
Fee: $29.98 installation; $27.98 monthly.
Internet Service
Operational: Yes.
Subscribers: 12,738.
Telephone Service
Digital: Operational
Subscribers: 9,061.
Miles of Plant: 395.0 (coaxial); 479.0 (fiber optic). Homes passed: 40,083.
President & Chief Executive Officer: Patrice Carroll.
Ownership: ImOn Communications.

CEDAR RAPIDS—Mediacom, 6300 Council St NE, Ste A, Cedar Rapids, IA 52402. Phones: 319-393-1914; 800-332-0245; 319-395-9699. Fax: 319-393-7017. Web Site: http://www.mediacomcable.com. Also serves Bertram, Fairfax, Hiawatha, Linn County (unincorporated areas), Marion & Monticello. ICA: IA0002.
TV Market Ranking: 65 (Bertram, CEDAR RAPIDS, Fairfax, Hiawatha, Linn County (unincorporated areas), Marion, Monticello). Franchise award date: June 21, 1978. Franchise expiration date: N.A. Began: April 30, 1979.
Channel capacity: N.A. Channels available but not in use: N.A.
Basic Service
Subscribers: 25,214. Commercial subscribers: 62.
Programming (received off-air): KCRG-TV (ABC, MNT) Cedar Rapids; KFXA (FOX, The Country Network) Cedar Rapids; KGAN (CBS) Cedar Rapids; KIIN (PBS) Iowa City; KPXR-TV (ION) Cedar Rapids; KWKB (The Works, This TV) Iowa City; KWWF (Untamed Sports TV) Waterloo; KWWL (CW, MeTV, NBC) Waterloo.
Programming (via satellite): C-SPAN; C-SPAN 2; EVINE Live; Pop; QVC; TBS; WGN America.
Fee: $41.99 installation; $43.00 monthly; $3.50 converter.
Expanded Basic Service 1
Subscribers: N.A.
Programming (via satellite): A&E; AMC; Animal Planet; BET; Bravo; Cartoon Network; CMT; CNBC; CNN; Comedy Central; Discovery Channel; Discovery Life Channel; Disney Channel; E! HD; ESPN; ESPN2; EWTN Global Catholic Network; Food Network; Fox News Channel; Fox Sports 1; Freeform; FX; Great American Country; Hallmark Channel; HGTV; History; HLN; INSP; Lifetime; MSNBC; MTV; National Geographic Channel; NBCSN; Nickelodeon; Spike TV; Syfy; The Weather Channel; TLC; TNT; Travel Channel; Trinity Broadcasting Network (TBN); truTV; TV Land; Univision Studios; USA Network; VH1; WE tv.
Fee: $45.95 monthly.
Digital Basic Service
Subscribers: N.A.
Programming (via satellite): AXS TV; BBC America; Bloomberg Television; Cloo; Discovery Digital Networks; Disney XD; DMX Music; ESPN; Fuse; FXM; FYI; Golf Channel; GSN; HD Theater; History International; IFC; LMN; Nick Jr.; Outdoor Channel; Ovation; TeenNick; Turner Classic Movies; Universal HD.
Digital Pay Service 1
Pay Units: N.A.
Programming (via satellite): Cinemax (multiplexed); Flix; HBO (multiplexed); Showtime (multiplexed); Starz (multiplexed); Starz Encore (multiplexed); Sundance TV; The Movie Channel (multiplexed).
Fee: $10.00 installation; $2.10 monthly (Encore), $7.10 monthly (Starz), $9.50 monthly (TMC/Sundance/Flix), $10.50 monthly (Cinemax or Showtime).
Video-On-Demand: Yes
Pay-Per-View
ESPN Now (delivered digitally); Playboy TV (delivered digitally); Pleasure (delivered digitally); Fresh (delivered digitally); Shorteez (delivered digitally); SexSee (delivered digitally).
Internet Service
Operational: Yes. Began: November 24, 1998.
Subscribers: 27,739.

2017 Edition D-245

Iowa—Cable Systems

Broadband Service: Mediacom High Speed Internet.
Fee: $150.00 installation; $39.95 monthly; $10.00 modem lease.
Telephone Service
Digital: Operational
Subscribers: 10,573.
Miles of Plant: 1,486.0 (coaxial); 295.0 (fiber optic). Homes passed: 93,415.
Regional Vice President: Doug Frank. Marketing & Sales Director: Steve Schuh. Technical Operations Director: Greg Nank.
Ownership: Mediacom LLC (MSO).

CENTER JUNCTION—Center Junction Telephone Co, 513 Main St, PO Box 67, Center Junction, IA 52212-0067. Phone: 563-487-2631. Fax: 563-487-3701. E-mail: cntrjct@netins.net. ICA: IA0407.
TV Market Ranking: 65 (CENTER JUNCTION). Franchise award date: May 2, 1990. Franchise expiration date: N.A. Began: November 1, 1990.
Channel capacity: N.A. Channels available but not in use: N.A.
Basic Service
Subscribers: 23.
Programming (received off-air): KCRG-TV (ABC, MNT) Cedar Rapids; KFXA (FOX, The Country Network) Cedar Rapids; KGAN (CBS) Cedar Rapids; KIIN (PBS) Iowa City; KLJB (CW, FOX, MeTV) Davenport; KWKB (The Works, This TV) Iowa City; KWQC-TV (NBC) Davenport; KWWL (CW, MeTV, NBC) Waterloo; WHBF-TV (CBS) Rock Island; WQAD-TV (ABC, Antenna TV) Moline. Programming (via satellite): A&E; AMC; Animal Planet; Cartoon Network; CMT; CNBC; CNN; Comedy Central; C-SPAN; Discovery Channel; Disney Channel; E! HD; ESPN; ESPN2; Food Network; Fox News Channel; Fox Sports 1; Freeform; FX; Great American Country; GSN; HGTV; History; INSP; Lifetime; MTV; Nickelodeon; Outdoor Channel; QVC; Spike TV; Syfy; TBS; The Weather Channel; TLC; TNT; Travel Channel; Trinity Broadcasting Network (TBN); Turner Classic Movies; TV Land; USA Network; VH1; WGN America.
Fee: $12.50 installation; $48.50 monthly.
Pay Service 1
Pay Units: N.A.
Programming (via satellite): Cinemax; HBO; Showtime.
Fee: $9.95 monthly (each).
Internet Service
Operational: No.
Telephone Service
None
Homes passed: 72.
Chief Operating Officer: Russ Benke. General Manager: John Heiken. Chief Technician: Jim Petersen.
Ownership: Center Junction Telephone Co.

CENTRAL CITY—USA Communications. Now served by SHELLSBURG, IA [IA0255]. ICA: IA0200.

CHARITON—Mediacom, 2205 Ingersoll Ave, Des Moines, IA 50312. Phone: 800-790-8187. Fax: 515-246-2211. Web Site: http://www.mediacomcable.com. Also serves Clive, Corydon, Creston, Decatur, Greenfield, Kellerton, Lamoni, Leon, Lucas, Mount Ayr, Osceola, Wayne County (portions), Winterset & Woodburn. ICA: IA0017.
TV Market Ranking: 66 (Clive); Outside TV Markets (Corydon, Creston, Decatur, Greenfield, Kellerton, Lamoni, Leon, Lu-

cas, Mount Ayr, Osceola, Wayne County (portions), Winterset, Woodburn).
Channel capacity: N.A. Channels available but not in use: N.A.
Basic Service
Subscribers: 4,796. Commercial subscribers: 4.
Fee: $41.99 installation; $43.00 monthly.
Ownership: Mediacom LLC (MSO).

CHARLES CITY—Mediacom, 4010 Alexandra Dr, Waterloo, IA 50702. Phone: 319-235-2197. Fax: 319-232-7841. Web Site: http://www.mediacomcable.com. Also serves Floyd County (portions). ICA: IA0037.
TV Market Ranking: Below 100 (CHARLES CITY, Floyd County (portions)). Franchise award date: August 3, 1979. Franchise expiration date: N.A. Began: August 3, 1981.
Channel capacity: N.A. Channels available but not in use: N.A.
Basic Service
Subscribers: 1,461.
Programming (received off-air): KAAL (ABC, This TV) Austin; KCRG-TV (ABC, MNT) Cedar Rapids; KGAN (CBS) Cedar Rapids; KIMT (CBS, MNT) Mason City; KTTC (CW, NBC) Rochester; KWWL (CW, MeTV, NBC) Waterloo; KXLT-TV (FOX, MeTV) Rochester; KYIN (PBS) Mason City.
Programming (via satellite): C-SPAN; C-SPAN 2; QVC; WGN America.
Fee: $40.95 installation; $43.00 monthly.
Expanded Basic Service 1
Subscribers: N.A.
Programming (via satellite): A&E; AMC; Animal Planet; Bravo; Cartoon Network; CMT; CNBC; CNN; Comcast SportsNet Chicago; Comedy Central; Discovery Channel; Disney Channel; E! HD; ESPN; ESPN2; EWTN Global Catholic Network; Fox News Channel; Fox Sports 1; Freeform; FX; HGTV; History; INSP; ION Television; Lifetime; MSNBC; MTV; Nickelodeon; Oxygen; Pop; Spike TV; Syfy; TBS; The Weather Channel; TLC; TNT; Travel Channel; Trinity Broadcasting Network (TBN); truTV; TV Land; USA Network; VH1; WE tv.
Fee: $21.91 monthly.
Digital Basic Service
Subscribers: N.A.
Programming (via satellite): BBC America; Bloomberg Television; Discovery Digital Networks; Disney XD; DMX Music; Fuse; FXM; FYI; Golf Channel; GSN; History International; IFC; LMN; National Geographic Channel; NBCSN; Nick Jr.; Outdoor Channel; Ovation; TeenNick; Turner Classic Movies.
Digital Pay Service 1
Pay Units: N.A.
Programming (via satellite): Cinemax (multiplexed); HBO (multiplexed); Showtime (multiplexed); Starz (multiplexed); Starz Encore (multiplexed); Sundance TV; The Movie Channel (multiplexed).
Fee: $2.10 monthly (Encore), $7.10 monthly (Starz), $12.95 monthly (Cinemax or Showtime), $13.95 monthly (HBO).
Video-On-Demand: Yes
Pay-Per-View
ESPN Now (delivered digitally); ETC (delivered digitally); Playboy TV (delivered digitally); Pleasure (delivered digitally); Vubuity Inc. (delivered digitally).
Internet Service
Operational: Yes.
Broadband Service: Mediacom High Speed Internet.
Telephone Service
Analog: Not Operational
Digital: Operational

Miles of Plant: 64.0 (coaxial); 2.0 (fiber optic). Homes passed: 4,163.
Regional Vice President: Doug Frank. General Manager: Doug Nix. Technical Operations Director: Greg Nank. Marketing Director: Steve Schuh. Marketing Coordinator: Joni Lindauer.
Ownership: Mediacom LLC (MSO).

CHARTER OAK—Formerly served by Tip Top Communication. No longer in operation. ICA: IA0237.

CHESTER—Formerly served by CableDirect. No longer in operation. ICA: IA0410.

CHURDAN—Formerly served by Western Iowa Networks. No longer in operation. ICA: IA0616.

CINCINNATI—Formerly served by B & L Technologies LLC. No longer in operation. ICA: IA0301.

CLARENCE—Clarence Cablevision, 608 Lombard St, PO Box 246, Clarence, IA 52216-0246. Phones: 800-695-3896; 563-452-3852. Fax: 563-452-3883. E-mail: clarence@netins.net. Web Site: http://www.clarencetelinc.com. Also serves Stanwood. ICA: IA0213.
TV Market Ranking: 65 (CLARENCE, Stanwood). Franchise award date: July 15, 1983. Franchise expiration date: N.A. Began: January 1, 1984.
Channel capacity: N.A. Channels available but not in use: N.A.
Basic Service
Subscribers: 176.
Programming (received off-air): KCRG-TV (ABC, MNT) Cedar Rapids; KFXA (FOX, The Country Network) Cedar Rapids; KGAN (CBS) Cedar Rapids; KIIN (PBS) Iowa City; KLJB (CW, FOX, MeTV) Davenport; KWKB (The Works, This TV) Iowa City; KWQC-TV (NBC) Davenport; KWWL (CW, MeTV, NBC) Waterloo; WHBF-TV (CBS) Rock Island; WQAD-TV (ABC, Antenna TV) Moline.
Programming (via satellite): A&E; AMC; Animal Planet; Cartoon Network; CMT; CNBC; CNN; Comcast/Charter Sports Southeast (CSS); Comedy Central; C-SPAN; Discovery Channel; Disney Channel; E! HD; ESPN; ESPN2; Food Network; Fox News Channel; Fox Sports 1; Freeform; FX; Great American Country; GSN; HGTV; History; INSP; Lifetime; MTV; Nickelodeon; Outdoor Channel; QVC; Spike TV; Syfy; TBS; The Weather Channel; TLC; TNT; Travel Channel; Trinity Broadcasting Network (TBN); Turner Classic Movies; TV Land; USA Network; VH1; WGN America.
Fee: $20.00 installation; $48.95 monthly.
Pay Service 1
Pay Units: 56.
Programming (via satellite): Cinemax.
Fee: $9.00 monthly.
Pay Service 2
Pay Units: 76.
Programming (via satellite): HBO.
Fee: $9.00 monthly.
Pay Service 3
Pay Units: N.A.
Programming (via satellite): Showtime.
Fee: $8.50 monthly.
Video-On-Demand: No
Internet Service
Operational: Yes.
Telephone Service
Analog: Operational
Miles of Plant: 8.0 (coaxial); None (fiber optic). Homes passed: 400.

General Manager & Chief Technician: Curtis Eldred.
Ownership: Clarence Telephone Co. Inc.

CLEARFIELD—Formerly served by B & L Technologies LLC. No longer in operation. ICA: IA0341.

CLEGHORN—Wetherell Cable TV System, 407 West Grace St, PO Box 188, Cleghorn, IA 51014-0188. Phone: 712-436-2266. Fax: 712-436-2672. E-mail: info@wetherellmfg.com. Also serves Early, Galva, Marathon, Meriden, Pierson, Rembrandt & Washta. ICA: IA0132.
TV Market Ranking: Below 100 (Pierson, Washta); Outside TV Markets (CLEGHORN, Early, Galva, Marathon, Meriden, Rembrandt). Franchise award date: June 1, 1983. Franchise expiration date: N.A. Began: December 1, 1983.
Channel capacity: N.A. Channels available but not in use: N.A.
Basic Service
Subscribers: 335.
Programming (received off-air): KCAU-TV (ABC) Sioux City; KELO-TV (CBS, MNT) Sioux Falls; KMEG (Azteca America, CBS, Decades) Sioux City; KPTH (FOX, MNT, This TV) Sioux City; KSFY-TV (ABC, CW) Sioux Falls; KSIN-TV (PBS) Sioux City; KTIV (CW, MeTV, NBC) Sioux City.
Programming (via satellite): A&E; Cartoon Network; CNN; Discovery Channel; ESPN; ESPN2; Food Network; Fox Business Network; Fox News Channel; Fox Sports 1; Freeform; FX; Great American Country; HGTV; History; Lifetime; MoviePlex; MTV; Nickelodeon; Spike TV; TBS; The Weather Channel; TLC; TNT; truTV; Turner Classic Movies; USA Network; WGN America.
Fee: $25.00 installation; $64.95 monthly.
Pay Service 1
Pay Units: 75.
Programming (via satellite): The Movie Channel.
Fee: $7.00 monthly.
Internet Service
Operational: No.
Telephone Service
None
Miles of Plant: 4.0 (coaxial); None (fiber optic).
General Manager: Ronald Wetherell. Chief Technician: Boyd White.
Ownership: Wetherell Cable TV System.

CLERMONT—Formerly served by Alpine Communications LC. No longer in operation. ICA: IA0412.

CLINTON—Mediacom, 3900 26th Ave, Moline, IL 61265. Phone: 309-797-2580. Fax: 309-797-2414. Web Site: http://www.mediacomcable.com. Also serves Albany, Carroll County (portions), Erie, Fulton, Lyndon, Morrison, Prophetstown, Savanna, Thomson & Whiteside County (portions), IL; Camanche, Clinton County, DeWitt, Low Moor, McCausland & Sabula, IA. ICA: IA0006.
TV Market Ranking: 60 (Albany, Camanche, CLINTON, Clinton County, DeWitt, Erie, Fulton, Low Moor, Lyndon, McCausland, Prophetstown, Whiteside County (portions)); 97 (Carroll County (portions), Sabula, Savanna, Thomson); Outside TV Markets (Morrison). Franchise award date: June 1, 1963. Franchise expiration date: N.A. Began: October 16, 1974.
Channel capacity: N.A. Channels available but not in use: N.A.

Cable Systems—Iowa

Basic Service
Subscribers: 9,968.
Programming (received off-air): KGCW (CW, MeTV, This TV) Burlington; KIIN (PBS) Iowa City; KLJB (CW, FOX, MeTV) Davenport; KWQC-TV (NBC) Davenport; WHBF-TV (CBS) Rock Island; WQAD-TV (ABC, Antenna TV) Moline; WQPT-TV (PBS) Moline.
Programming (via satellite): C-SPAN; Discovery Channel; Pop; QVC; TBS; Trinity Broadcasting Network (TBN); Univision Studios; WGN America.
Fee: $45.00 installation; $55.75 monthly.

Expanded Basic Service 1
Subscribers: N.A.
Programming (via satellite): A&E; AMC; Animal Planet; BET; Bravo; Cartoon Network; CMT; CNBC; CNN; Comcast SportsNet Chicago; Comedy Central; C-SPAN 2; Disney Channel; E! HD; ESPN; ESPN2; EWTN Global Catholic Network; Food Network; Fox News Channel; Fox Sports 1; Freeform; Fuse; FX; Hallmark Channel; HGTV; History; HLN; INSP; ION Television; Lifetime; MSNBC; MTV; Nickelodeon; Spike TV; Syfy; The Weather Channel; TLC; TNT; Travel Channel; truTV; TV Land; USA Network; VH1; WE tv.
Fee: $34.00 monthly.

Digital Basic Service
Subscribers: N.A.
Programming (via satellite): BBC America; Discovery Digital Networks; Disney XD; DMX Music; ESPN Classic; ESPNews; FYI; Golf Channel; GSN; History International; HITS (Headend In The Sky); IFC; LMN; National Geographic Channel; NBCSN; Nick Jr.; Outdoor Channel; Ovation; Sundance TV; TeenNick; Turner Classic Movies.

Digital Pay Service 1
Pay Units: N.A.
Programming (via satellite): Cinemax (multiplexed); HBO (multiplexed); Showtime (multiplexed); Starz (multiplexed); Starz Encore (multiplexed); The Movie Channel (multiplexed).
Fee: $11.95 monthly (Cinemax, HBO, Showtime/TMC or Starz/Encore).

Video-On-Demand: Yes

Pay-Per-View
ESPN Now (delivered digitally); ETC (delivered digitally); Playboy TV (delivered digitally); Pleasure (delivered digitally); Vubiquity Inc. (delivered digitally).

Internet Service
Operational: Yes.
Subscribers: 9,294.
Broadband Service: Mediacom High Speed Internet.
Fee: $59.95 installation; $40.95 monthly.

Telephone Service
Analog: Not Operational
Digital: Operational
Subscribers: 4,386.
Fee: $39.95 monthly.
Miles of Plant: 627.0 (coaxial); 212.0 (fiber optic). Homes passed: 28,631.
Regional Vice President: Cari Fenzel. Engineering Director: Mitch Carlson. Technical Operations Manager: Chris Toalson. Marketing Director: Greg Evans.
Ownership: Mediacom LLC (MSO).

CLUTIER—FCTC. Formerly [IA0413]. This cable system has converted to IPTV, 332 Main St, PO Box 280, Dysart, IA 52224. Phone: 319-476-7800. Fax: 319-476-7911. E-mail: fctcdysart@fctc.coop. Web Site: http://www.fctc.coop. Also serves Dysart. ICA: IA5077.
Channel capacity: N.A. Channels available but not in use: N.A.

Basic
Subscribers: N.A.
Fee: $29.50 monthly. Includes 30 channels.

Standard Plus HD
Subscribers: N.A.
Fee: $58.80 monthly. Includes 120 channels.

Cinemax
Subscribers: N.A.
Fee: $11.99 monthly. Includes 8 channels.

HBO
Subscribers: N.A.
Fee: $14.99 monthly. Includes 6 channels.

Showtime
Subscribers: N.A.
Fee: $12.99 monthly. Includes 11 channels.

Starz/Encore
Subscribers: N.A.
Fee: $12.99 monthly. Includes 9 channels.

Internet Service
Operational: Yes.
Fee: $39.95-$69.95 monthly.

Telephone Service
Digital: Operational
General Manager: Mark Harvey.
Ownership: Farmers Cooperative Telephone Co.

CLUTIER—FCTC. This cable system has converted to IPTV. See CLUTIER, IA [IA5077]. ICA: IA0413.

COGGON—USA Communications. Now served by SHELLSBURG, IA [IA0255]. ICA: IA0287.

COLESBURG—Formerly served by Alpine Communications LC. No longer in operation. ICA: IA0414.

COLLINS—Formerly served by Huxley Communications Corp. No longer in operation. ICA: IA0415.

COLO—Colo Telephone Co. Formerly [IA0416]. This cable system has converted to IPTV, 303 Main St, PO Box 315, Colo, IA 50056. Phones: 641-377-2202; 641-377-2202. Fax: 641-377-2209. E-mail: colo@netins.net. Web Site: http://www.colotel.org. ICA: IA5003.
TV Market Ranking: 66 (COLO).
Channel capacity: N.A. Channels available but not in use: N.A.

Basic
Subscribers: 288. Commercial subscribers: 1.
Fee: 50/hour installation; $54.95 monthly.

Cinemax
Subscribers: N.A.
Fee: $10.95 monthly.

HBO
Subscribers: N.A.
Fee: $12.95 monthly.

Showtime
Subscribers: N.A.
Fee: $11.95 monthly.

Starz/Encore
Subscribers: N.A.
Fee: $11.95 monthly.

Internet Service
Operational: Yes.

Telephone Service
Digital: Operational
Fee: $14.00 monthly
President: Fred Cerka. Vice President: Pete Heintz. Secretary: Edythe Lounsbury-Meller. Chief Executive Officer & General Manager: Larry Springer. Office Manager: Luke DeAnne. Customer Service Representative: Julie Willis.
Ownership: Colo Telephone Co.

COLO—Colo Telephone Co. This cable system has converted to IPTV. See COLO, IA [IA5003]. ICA: IA0416.

COLUMBUS JUNCTION—Mediacom. Now served by BURLINGTON, IA [IA0405]. ICA: IA0111.

COON RAPIDS—Coon Rapids Municipal Cable System, 123 3rd Ave South, PO Box 207, Coon Rapids, IA 50058. Phone: 712-999-2225. Fax: 712-999-5148. E-mail: crmuinfo@gmail.com. Web Site: http://www.crmu.net. ICA: IA0172.
TV Market Ranking: Outside TV Markets (COON RAPIDS). Franchise award date: N.A. Franchise expiration date: N.A. Began: October 1, 1982.
Channel capacity: N.A. Channels available but not in use: N.A.

Basic Service
Subscribers: 51.
Programming (received off-air): KCCI (CBS, MeTV) Des Moines; KDIN-TV (PBS) Des Moines; KDSM-TV (FOX, The Country Network) Des Moines; WHO-DT (Antenna TV, NBC) Des Moines; WOI-DT (ABC) Ames; allband FM.
Programming (via satellite): CNN; Freeform; Hallmark Channel; HLN; LWS Local Weather Station; The Weather Channel; WGN America.
Fee: $15.00 installation; $59.95 monthly; $3.00 converter.

Digital Basic Service
Subscribers: N.A.
Programming (via satellite): AXS TV; ESPN; ESPN2; HD Theater; Outdoor Channel 2 HD.

Pay Service 1
Pay Units: N.A.
Programming (via satellite): Cinemax; HBO.
Fee: $5.00 installation; $12.95 monthly (each).

Internet Service
Operational: Yes.
Broadband Service: In-house.
Fee: $15.00 installation; $49.95 monthly.

Telephone Service
Digital: Operational
Fee: $13.95 monthly
Miles of Plant: 11.0 (coaxial); None (fiber optic). Homes passed: 555.
General Manager: Bradley A. Hunold.
Ownership: Coon Rapids Municipal Cable System.

CORWITH—Comm1. Now served by KANAWHA, IA [IA5095]. ICA: IA0417.

COULTER—Formerly served by Latimer/Coulter Cablevision. No longer in operation. ICA: IA0418.

CRESCO—Mediacom. Now served by OSAGE, IA [IA0085]. ICA: IA0081.

CRESTON—Mediacom. Now served by CHARITON, IA [IA0017]. ICA: IA0028.

CYLINDER—Formerly served by ATC Cablevision. No longer in operation. ICA: IA0384.

DANBURY—Long Lines. Now served by SALIX, IA [IA0510]. ICA: IA0316.

DAVIS CITY—Formerly served by Telnet South LC. No longer in operation. ICA: IA0373.

DAYTON—Lehigh Services Inc. Now served by LEHIGH, IA [IA5319]. ICA: IA0232.

DECATUR—Formerly served by Telnet South LC. Now served by Mediacom, CHARITON, IA [IA0017]. ICA: IA0383.

DECORAH—Mediacom, 4010 Alexandra Dr, Waterloo, IA 50702. Phones: 319-235-2197; 319-232-7841; 563-387-0825 (Decorah office). Fax: 319-232-7841. Web Site: http://www.mediacomcable.com. ICA: IA0034.
TV Market Ranking: Outside TV Markets (DECORAH). Franchise award date: January 1, 1957. Franchise expiration date: N.A. Began: January 1, 1957.
Channel capacity: N.A. Channels available but not in use: N.A.

Basic Service
Subscribers: 1,753.
Programming (received off-air): KAAL (ABC, This TV) Austin; KCRG-TV (ABC, MNT) Cedar Rapids; KFXA (FOX, The Country Network) Cedar Rapids; KGAN (CBS) Cedar Rapids; KIMT (CBS, MNT) Mason City; KRIN (PBS) Waterloo; KTTC (CW, NBC) Rochester; KWKB (The Works, This TV) Iowa City; KWWF (Untamed Sports TV) Waterloo; KWWL (CW, MeTV, NBC) Waterloo; KXLT-TV (FOX, MeTV) Rochester; WHLA-TV (PBS) La Crosse; WLAX (FOX, MeTV) La Crosse; allband FM.
Programming (via satellite): C-SPAN; ION Television; Pop; QVC; WGN America.
Fee: $15.00 installation; $43.00 monthly.

Expanded Basic Service 1
Subscribers: N.A.
Programming (via satellite): A&E; AMC; Animal Planet; BET; Bravo; Cartoon Network; CMT; CNBC; CNN; Comedy Central; C-SPAN 2; Discovery Channel; Discovery Life Channel; Disney Channel; E! HD; ESPN; ESPN Classic; ESPN2; EWTN Global Catholic Network; Food Network; Fox News Channel; Fox Sports 1; Freeform; FX; Hallmark Channel; HGTV; History; HLN; INSP; Lifetime; LMN; MSNBC; MTV; NBCSN; Nickelodeon; Outdoor Channel; RFD-TV; Spike TV; Syfy; TBS; Telemundo; The Weather Channel; TLC; TNT; Travel Channel; Trinity Broadcasting Network (TBN); truTV; Turner Classic Movies; TV Land; USA Network; VH1; WE tv.
Fee: $10.00 installation; $4.45 monthly.

Digital Basic Service
Subscribers: N.A.
Programming (via satellite): AXS TV; BBC America; Bloomberg Television; Cloo; CMT; Destination America; Discovery Channel HD; Discovery Kids Channel; ESPN HD; ESPN2 HD; ESPNews; ESPNU; Fox Sports 2; Fuse; FXM; FYI; Golf Channel; GSN; History International; IFC; Investigation Discovery; ION Television; MTV Classic; MTV Hits; MTV2; Nat Geo WILD; National Geographic Channel; Nick Jr.; Nicktoons; Ovation; Oprah Winfrey Network; Qubo; Reelz; Science Channel; TeenNick; TNT HD; TVG Network; Universal HD; VH1 Soul.

Digital Expanded Basic Service
Subscribers: N.A.
Programming (via satellite): CBS Sports Network; ESPNU; FOX College Sports Central; FOX College Sports Pacific; Fox Sports 2; GolTV; Tennis Channel; TVG Network.

Digital Pay Service 1
Pay Units: N.A.
Programming (via satellite): Cinemax (multiplexed); Flix; HBO (multiplexed); HBO HD; Showtime (multiplexed); Showtime HD; Starz (multiplexed); Starz Encore (multiplexed); Starz HD; Sundance TV; The

Iowa—Cable Systems

Movie Channel (multiplexed); The Movie Channel HD.
Video-On-Demand: Yes
Pay-Per-View
iN DEMAND (delivered digitally); ESPN (delivered digitally); Fresh (delivered digitally); Spice: Xcess (delivered digitally); Playboy TV (delivered digitally); SexSee (delivered digitally).
Internet Service
Operational: Yes.
Subscribers: 1,785.
Broadband Service: Mediacom High Speed Internet.
Telephone Service
Digital: Operational
Subscribers: 838.
Miles of Plant: 88.0 (coaxial); 38.0 (fiber optic). Homes passed: 5,582.
Regional Vice President: Doug Frank. General Manager: Doug Nix. Technical Operations Director: Greg Nank. Marketing Director: Steve Schuh. Technical Operations Manager: Chip Piper. Marketing Coordinator: Joni Lindauer.
Ownership: Mediacom LLC (MSO).

DEDHAM—Templeton Telephone Co., 115 North Main St, PO Box 77, Templeton, IA 51463. Phones: 712-669-3311; 888-669-3311. Fax: 712-669-3312. E-mail: temptel@netins.net. Web Site: http://www.templetoniowa.com. ICA: IA0362.
TV Market Ranking: Outside TV Markets (DEDHAM).
Channel capacity: N.A. Channels available but not in use: N.A.
Basic Service
Subscribers: 62.
Fee: $52.95 monthly.
General Manager: Patricia Snyder.
Ownership: Templeton Telephone Co. (MSO).

DEEP RIVER—Montezuma Mutual Telephone & Cable Co., 107 North 4th St, PO Box 10, Montezuma, IA 50171. Phone: 641-623-5654. Fax: 641-623-2199. Also serves Barnes City & Montezuma. ICA: IA0419.
TV Market Ranking: Below 100 (Barnes City, Montezuma); Outside TV Markets (DEEP RIVER). Franchise award date: N.A. Franchise expiration date: N.A. Began: September 1, 1989.
Channel capacity: N.A. Channels available but not in use: N.A.
Basic Service
Subscribers: 778.
Programming (received off-air): KCCI (CBS, MeTV) Des Moines; KCRG-TV (ABC, MNT) Cedar Rapids; KCWI-TV (CW) Ames; KDIN-TV (PBS) Des Moines; KDSM-TV (FOX, The Country Network) Des Moines; KFXA (FOX, The Country Network) Cedar Rapids; KGAN (CBS) Cedar Rapids; KWWL (CW, MeTV, NBC) Waterloo; KYOU-TV (FOX) Ottumwa; WHO-DT (Antenna TV, NBC) Des Moines; WOI-DT (ABC) Ames.
Programming (via satellite): A&E; AMC; Animal Planet; Cartoon Network; CMT; CNBC; CNN; Comedy Central; C-SPAN; C-SPAN 2; Discovery Channel; Disney Channel; DIY Network; ESPN; ESPN Classic; ESPN2; Food Network; Fox News Channel; FOX Sports Networks; Freeform; FX; Hallmark Channel; HGTV; History; ION Television; Lifetime; MTV; Nickelodeon; Spike TV; Syfy; TBS; The Weather Channel; TLC; TNT; Travel Channel; Trinity Broadcasting Network (TBN); truTV; TV Land; USA Network; VH1; WGN America.
Fee: $10.00 installation; $25.00 monthly.
Digital Basic Service
Subscribers: N.A.
Programming (via satellite): Bravo; CMT; Destination America; Discovery Kids Channel; Disney XD; ESPN Classic; Fox Sports 1; FYI; Golf Channel; History International; Investigation Discovery; LMN; MTV Classic; MTV2; National Geographic Channel; NBCSN; Nick Jr.; Outdoor Channel; OWN: Oprah Winfrey Network; Science Channel; TeenNick; Turner Classic Movies.
Fee: $20.00 installation.
Pay Service 1
Pay Units: N.A.
Programming (via satellite): Cinemax; HBO; Showtime; Starz; Starz Encore; The Movie Channel.
Digital Pay Service 1
Pay Units: N.A.
Programming (via satellite): Cinemax (multiplexed); Flix (multiplexed); HBO (multiplexed); Showtime (multiplexed); Starz (multiplexed); Starz Encore (multiplexed); The Movie Channel (multiplexed).
Internet Service
Operational: Yes.
Broadband Service: Netins.
Fee: free installation; $34.95 monthly.
Telephone Service
None
Miles of Plant: 35.0 (coaxial); 14.0 (fiber optic).
General Manager: Dave Stevenson.
Ownership: Montezuma Mutual Telephone Co.

DEFIANCE—Formerly served by Farmers Mutual Telephone Co. Now served by Mutual Communications Services, IRWIN, IA [IA0302]. ICA: IA0280.

DELHI (town)—New Century Communications, 3588 Kennebec Dr, Eagan, MN 55122-1001. Phones: 800-247-1566; 651-688-2623. Fax: 651-688-2624. ICA: IA0420.
TV Market Ranking: Below 100 (DELHI (TOWN)). Franchise award date: October 13, 1987. Franchise expiration date: N.A. Began: July 1, 1988.
Channel capacity: N.A. Channels available but not in use: N.A.
Basic Service
Subscribers: 84.
Programming (received off-air): KCRG-TV (ABC, MNT) Cedar Rapids; KFXA (FOX, The Country Network) Cedar Rapids; KGAN (CBS) Cedar Rapids; KIIN (PBS) Iowa City; KPXR-TV (ION) Cedar Rapids; KWKB (The Works, This TV) Iowa City; KWWL (CW, MeTV, NBC) Waterloo.
Programming (via satellite): A&E; AMC; CNN; Discovery Channel; Disney Channel; DIY Network; ESPN; ESPN2; Freeform; History; HLN; Lifetime; MTV; Nickelodeon; QVC; Spike TV; TBS; The Weather Channel; TLC; TNT; Turner Classic Movies; USA Network; VH1; WGN America.
Fee: $30.00 installation; $32.95 monthly.
Pay Service 1
Pay Units: 22.
Programming (via satellite): Cinemax.
Fee: $10.00 monthly.
Pay Service 2
Pay Units: 31.
Programming (via satellite): HBO.
Fee: $10.00 monthly.
Pay Service 3
Pay Units: 8.
Programming (via satellite): Showtime.
Fee: $10.00 monthly.
Video-On-Demand: No
Internet Service
Operational: No.
Telephone Service
None
Miles of Plant: 4.0 (coaxial); None (fiber optic). Homes passed: 213.
Executive Vice President: Marty Walch. General Manager & Chief Technician: Todd Anderson.
Ownership: New Century Communications (MSO).

DELMAR—F&B Communications. This cable system has converted to IPTV. Now served by WHEATLAND, IA [IA5105]. ICA: IA0421.

DELOIT—Formerly served by Tip Top Communications. No longer in operation. ICA: IA0422.

DELTA—Formerly served by Longview Communications. No longer in operation. ICA: IA0540.

DENISON—Mediacom, 2205 Ingersoll Ave, Des Moines, IA 50312. Phone: 515-246-1890. Fax: 515-246-2211. Web Site: http://www.mediacomcable.com. Also serves Avoca, Crawford County (southern portion) & Harlan. ICA: IA0005.
TV Market Ranking: Outside TV Markets (Avoca, Crawford County (southern portion), Harlan).
Channel capacity: N.A. Channels available but not in use: N.A.
Basic Service
Subscribers: 1,202. Commercial subscribers: 118.
Fee: $41.99 installation; $43.00 monthly.
Internet Service
Operational: Yes.
Broadband Service: Mediacom High Speed Internet.
Telephone Service
Digital: Operational
Miles of Plant: 118.0 (coaxial); 120.0 (fiber optic). Homes passed: 7,133.
Ownership: Mediacom LLC (MSO).

DENMARK—Formerly served by Longview Communications. No longer in operation. ICA: IA0424.

DES MOINES—Mediacom, 2205 Ingersoll Ave, Des Moines, IA 50312. Phone: 515-246-1890. Fax: 515-246-2211. Web Site: http://www.mediacomcable.com. Also serves Altoona, Ankeny, Bondurant, Carlisle, Dallas, Grimes, Hartford, Indianola, Johnston, Norwalk, Pleasant Hill, Polk, Urbandale, Warren County (portions), Waukee, West Des Moines & Windsor Heights. ICA: IA0001.
TV Market Ranking: 66 (Altoona, Ankeny, Bondurant, Carlisle, Dallas, DES MOINES, Grimes, Hartford, Indianola, Johnston, Marion County (portions), Norwalk, Pleasant Hill, Polk, Urbandale, Warren County (portions), Waukee, West Des Moines, Windsor Heights; Below 100 (Marion County (portions)); Outside TV Markets (Marion County (portions)). Franchise award date: January 1, 1972. Franchise expiration date: N.A. Began: June 1, 1974.
Channel capacity: N.A. Channels available but not in use: N.A.
Basic Service
Subscribers: 58,194. Commercial subscribers: 143.
Programming (received off-air): KCCI (CBS, MeTV) Des Moines; KCWI-TV (CW) Ames; KDIN-TV (PBS) Des Moines; KDSM-TV (FOX, The Country Network) Des Moines; KFPX-TV (ION) Newton; WHO-DT (Antenna TV, NBC) Des Moines; WOI-DT (ABC) Ames; 14 FMs.
Programming (via satellite): CNN; C-SPAN; Discovery Channel; Nickelodeon; QVC; TBS; WGN America.
Fee: $41.99 installation; $49.45 monthly.
Expanded Basic Service 1
Subscribers: N.A.
Programming (via satellite): A&E; AMC; Animal Planet; BET; Bravo; Cartoon Network; CMT; CNBC; Comedy Central; C-SPAN 2; Disney Channel; E! HD; ESPN; ESPN2; EWTN Global Catholic Network; Food Network; Fox News Channel; Fox Sports 1; Freeform; FX; Hallmark Channel; HGTV; History; HLN; Lifetime; MSNBC; MTV; Pop; RFD-TV; Spike TV; Syfy; Telemundo; The Weather Channel; TLC; TNT; Trinity Broadcasting Network (TBN); truTV; TV Land; Univision Studios; USA Network; VH1; WE tv.
Fee: $31.23 monthly.
Digital Basic Service
Subscribers: N.A.
Programming (via satellite): BBC America; Bloomberg Television; Discovery Digital Networks; Disney XD; DMX Music; Fuse; FXM; FYI; Golf Channel; GSN; History International; IFC; LMN; National Geographic Channel; NBCSN; Nick Jr.; Outdoor Channel; Ovation; TeenNick; Turner Classic Movies.
Digital Pay Service 1
Pay Units: N.A.
Programming (via satellite): Cinemax (multiplexed); Flix; HBO (multiplexed); Showtime (multiplexed); Starz (multiplexed); Sundance TV; The Movie Channel (multiplexed).
Fee: $15.00 installation; $9.95 monthly (Cinemax, HBO, Showtime, Flix/Sundance/TMC or Starz/Encore).
Video-On-Demand: Yes
Pay-Per-View
ESPN Now (delivered digitally); ETC (delivered digitally); Playboy TV (delivered digitally); Pleasure (delivered digitally); Fresh (delivered digitally); Shorteez (delivered digitally); Vubiquity Inc. (delivered digitally).
Internet Service
Operational: Yes.
Subscribers: 57,710.
Broadband Service: Mediacom High Speed Internet.
Fee: $55.95 installation; $29.95 monthly; $10.00 modem lease.
Telephone Service
Digital: Operational
Subscribers: 24,597.
Miles of Plant: 4,000.0 (coaxial); 551.0 (fiber optic). Homes passed: 237,627.
Regional Vice President: Steve Purcell. Division Vice President: Ed Pardini. Technical

Cable Systems—Iowa

Operations Manager: Cliff Waggoner. Marketing Director: LeAnn Treloar. Government & Media Relations Manager: Bill Peard.
Ownership: Mediacom LLC (MSO).

DEXTER—Mediacom, 2205 Ingersoll Ave, Des Moines, IA 50312. Phone: 515-246-1890. Fax: 515-246-2211. Web Site: http://www.mediacomcable.com. Also serves Adel, Booneville, Dallas Center, Dallas County, Desoto, Earlham, Granger, Perry, Redfield, Stuart & Van Meter. ICA: IA0015.
TV Market Ranking: 66 (Adel, Booneville, Dallas Center, Dallas County, Desoto, DEXTER, Earlham, Granger, Perry, Redfield, Van Meter); Outside TV Markets (Stuart).
Channel capacity: N.A. Channels available but not in use: N.A.
Basic Service
Subscribers: 2,663. Commercial subscribers: 200.
Fee: $41.99 installation; $43.00 monthly.
Ownership: Mediacom LLC (MSO).

DIAGONAL—Formerly served by B & L Technologies LLC. No longer in operation. ICA: IA0353.

DICKENS—Premier Communications. Now served by SIOUX CENTER, IA [IA0076]. ICA: IA0379.

DIXON—Central Scott Telephone, 125 North Second St, PO Box 260, Eldridge, IA 52748. Phone: 563-285-9611. Fax: 563-285-9648. Web Site: http://centralscott.com. Also serves Donahue, Maysville & New Liberty. ICA: IA0639.
Channel capacity: N.A. Channels available but not in use: N.A.
Basic Service
Subscribers: N.A.
Fee: $55.95 monthly.
Digital Basic Service
Subscribers: N.A.
Fee: $22.95 monthly.
Digital Expanded Basic Service
Subscribers: N.A.
Fee: $20.00 monthly.
Digital Pay Service 1
Pay Units: N.A.
Fee: $12.95 monthly (Starz), $13.62 monthly (Cinemax), $15.49 monthly (Showtime), $20.58 monthly (HBO).
Internet Service
Operational: Yes.
Fee: $22.99-$99.00 monthly.
Telephone Service
Digital: Operational
Fee: $15.00 monthly
President & Chief Operating Officer: Charles Rebman.
Ownership: Central Scott Telephone.

DIXON—Dixon Telephone Co, 608 Davenport St, PO Box 10, Dixon, IA 52745-0010. Phone: 563-843-2901. Fax: 563-843-2481. E-mail: dixontel@netins.net. Also serves Calamus, Donahue, Maysville & New Liberty. ICA: IA0358.
TV Market Ranking: 60 (DIXON, Donahue, Maysville, New Liberty). Franchise award date: N.A. Franchise expiration date: N.A. Began: September 1, 1990.
Channel capacity: N.A. Channels available but not in use: N.A.
Basic Service
Subscribers: 456.
Programming (received off-air): KIIN (PBS) Iowa City; KLJB (CW, FOX, MeTV) Davenport; KWQC-TV (NBC) Davenport; WHBF-TV (CBS) Rock Island; WQAD-TV (ABC, Antenna TV) Moline.
Programming (via satellite): A&E; AMC; Animal Planet; BTN; Cartoon Network; CMT; CNN; Discovery Channel; Disney Channel; E! HD; ESPN; ESPN Classic; ESPN2; Fox News Channel; Fox Sports 1; FOX Sports Networks; Freeform; FX; HGTV; History; HLN; Lifetime; MTV; Nickelodeon; Outdoor Channel; Pop; RFD-TV; Spike TV; Syfy; TBS; The Weather Channel; TNT; Turner Classic Movies; USA Network; VH1; WGN America.
Fee: $10.00 installation; $55.95 monthly.
Pay Service 1
Pay Units: N.A.
Programming (via satellite): Cinemax; HBO; Showtime.
Fee: $9.95 monthly (each).
Video-On-Demand: No
Internet Service
Operational: Yes. Began: April 1, 2002.
Broadband Service: Netins.
Fee: $39.45 monthly.
Telephone Service
None
Miles of Plant: 65.0 (coaxial); 30.0 (fiber optic). Homes passed: 750.
General Manager: Howard Hunt.
Ownership: Dixon Telephone Co.

DONAHUE—Dixon Telephone Co. Now served by DIXON, IA [IA0358]. ICA: IA0425.

DONNELLSON—Formerly served by Longview Communications. No longer in operation. ICA: IA0426.

DOW CITY—Formerly served by Tip Top Communications. No longer in operation. ICA: IA0272.

DOWS—Formerly served by Dows Cablevision. No longer in operation. ICA: IA0427.

DUBUQUE—Mediacom, 3033 Asbury Rd, Dubuque, IA 52001. Phone: 563-557-8025 (Local office). Fax: 563-557-7413. Web Site: http://www.mediacomcable.com. Also serves East Dubuque, Galena & Jo Daviess County, IL; Asbury, Dubuque County, Dyersville, Epworth, Farley, Peosta & Sageville, IA. ICA: IA0007.
TV Market Ranking: 97 (Jo Daviess County (portions)); Below 100 (Asbury, DUBUQUE, Dubuque County, Dyersville, East Dubuque, Epworth, Farley, Galena, Peosta, Sageville, Jo Daviess County (portions)). Franchise award date: January 1, 1954. Franchise expiration date: N.A. Began: April 1, 1954.
Channel capacity: 80 (operating 2-way). Channels available but not in use: N.A.
Basic Service
Subscribers: 15,723. Commercial subscribers: 1,319.
Programming (received off-air): KCRG-TV (ABC, MNT) Cedar Rapids; KFXB-TV (Christian TV Network) Dubuque; KGAN (CBS) Cedar Rapids; KIIN (PBS) Iowa City; KPXR-TV (ION) Cedar Rapids; KWKB (The Works, This TV) Iowa City; KWQC-TV (NBC) Davenport; KWWL (CW, MeTV, NBC) Waterloo; WHA-TV (PBS) Madison; WISC-TV (CBS, MNT) Madison; WQAD-TV (ABC, Antenna TV) Moline; 25 FMs.
Programming (via satellite): A&E; AMC; Animal Planet; BET; Bravo; Cartoon Network; CMT; CNBC; CNN; Comedy Central; C-SPAN; C-SPAN 2; Discovery Channel; Disney Channel; E! HD; ESPN; ESPN2; EWTN Global Catholic Network; Food Network; Fox News Channel; Fox Sports 1; Freeform; FX; Hallmark Channel; HGTV; History; HLN; Lifetime; MoviePlex; MSNBC; MTV; NBCSN; Nickelodeon; Pop; QVC; Spike TV; Syfy; TBS; The Weather Channel; TLC; TNT; Travel Channel; Trinity Broadcasting Network (TBN); truTV; Turner Classic Movies; TV Land; USA Network; VH1; WE tv; WGN America.
Fee: $45.00 installation; $46.05 monthly; $2.00 converter.
Digital Basic Service
Subscribers: N.A.
Programming (via satellite): BBC America; Discovery Digital Networks; Disney XD; DMX Music; Fox Sports 1; Fuse; FYI; Golf Channel; GSN; History International; IFC; LMN; National Geographic Channel; Nick Jr.; Outdoor Channel; TeenNick.
Digital Pay Service 1
Pay Units: N.A.
Programming (via satellite): Cinemax (multiplexed); Flix; HBO (multiplexed); Showtime (multiplexed); Starz (multiplexed); Starz Encore (multiplexed); Sundance TV; The Movie Channel (multiplexed).
Fee: $11.95 monthly (each).
Video-On-Demand: Yes
Pay-Per-View
Playboy TV (delivered digitally); Pleasure (delivered digitally).
Internet Service
Operational: Yes. Began: December 31, 2001.
Subscribers: 15,165.
Broadband Service: Mediacom High Speed Internet.
Fee: $59.95 installation; $45.95 monthly.
Telephone Service
Digital: Operational
Subscribers: 7,379.
Fee: $39.95 monthly
Miles of Plant: 1,020.0 (coaxial); 342.0 (fiber optic). Homes passed: 44,572.
Regional Vice President: Cari Fenzel. Area Manager: Kathleen McMullen. Technical Operations Manager: Darren Dean. Engineering Director: Mitch Carlson. Marketing Director: Greg Evans.
Ownership: Mediacom LLC (MSO).

DUMONT—Dumont Cablevision, 506 Pine St, PO Box 349, Dumont, IA 50625-0349. Phones: 319-267-2300; 641-857-3211; 800-328-6543; 641-857-3213. Fax: 641-857-3300. E-mail: dumontel@netins.net. Web Site: http://www.dumonttelephone.com. Also serves Allison. ICA: IA0250.
TV Market Ranking: 65 (Allison); Below 100 (DUMONT). Franchise award date: N.A. Franchise expiration date: N.A. Began: August 5, 1983.
Channel capacity: N.A. Channels available but not in use: N.A.
Digital Basic Service
Subscribers: 307.
Programming (received off-air): KCRG-TV (ABC, MNT) Cedar Rapids; KFXA (FOX, The Country Network) Cedar Rapids; KGAN (CBS) Cedar Rapids; KIMT (CBS, MNT) Mason City; KWKB (The Works, This TV) Iowa City; KWWF (Untamed Sports TV) Waterloo; KWWL (CW, MeTV, NBC) Waterloo; KYIN (PBS) Mason City.
Programming (via satellite): A&E; AMC; Animal Planet; Bloomberg Television; BTN; Cartoon Network; CMT; CNN; CNN International; Comedy Central; C-SPAN; C-SPAN 2; CW PLUS; Discovery Channel; Disney Channel; Disney XD; E! HD; ESPN; ESPN Classic; ESPN2; ESPNews; ESPNU; Food Network; Fox News Channel; Fox Sports 1; FOX Sports Midwest; FOX Sports North; Freeform; FX; Golf Channel; GSN; Hallmark Channel; HGTV; History; HLN; ION Television; Lifetime; LMN; MC; MTV; MTV Classic; MTV Hits; MTV2; Nick Jr.; Nickelodeon; Nicktoons; Outdoor Channel; QVC; RFD-TV; Spike TV; Syfy; TBS; TeenNick; The Weather Channel; TLC; TNT; Travel Channel; Trinity Broadcasting Network (TBN); Turner Classic Movies; TV Land; USA Network; VH1; WGN America.
Fee: $35.00 installation; $94.34 monthly.
Digital Pay Service 1
Pay Units: 20.
Programming (via satellite): Cinemax (multiplexed); HBO (multiplexed).
Fee: $10.00 installation; $14.95 monthly.
Digital Pay Service 2
Pay Units: 30.
Fee: $10.00 installation; $14.95 monthly.
Pay-Per-View
Special events (delivered digitally); Playboy TV (delivered digitally); Fresh (delivered digitally); Club Jenna (delivered digitally).
Internet Service
Operational: No, DSL.
Telephone Service
Analog: Operational
Miles of Plant: 6.0 (coaxial); None (fiber optic). Homes passed: 399.
General Manager: Roger Kregel. Office Manager: Brooke Gulick. Operations Manager: Terry Arenholz.
Ownership: Dumont Telephone Co. (MSO).

DUNKERTON (portions)—Dunkerton Telephone Coop, 701 South Canfield St, PO Box 188, Dunkerton, IA 50626. Phone: 319-822-4512. Fax: 319-822-2206. Web Site: http://www.dunkerton.net. ICA: IA0428.
Channel capacity: N.A. Channels available but not in use: N.A.
Basic Service
Subscribers: 125.
Programming (received off-air): KFXA (FOX, The Country Network) Cedar Rapids; KPXR-TV (ION) Cedar Rapids; KRIN (PBS) Waterloo; KWWF (Untamed Sports TV) Waterloo.
Programming (via satellite): A&E; AMC; Animal Planet; BTN; Cartoon Network; CMT; CNBC; CNN; Comcast SportsNet Chicago; Comedy Central; C-SPAN; C-SPAN 2; Discovery Channel; Disney Channel; DIY Network; E! HD; ESPN; ESPN Classic; ESPN2; ESPNU; EWTN Global Catholic Network; Food Network; Fox News Channel; Fox Sports 1; FX; Golf Channel; GSN; Hallmark Channel; HGTV; History; HLN; Lifetime; MTV; National Geographic Channel; Nickelodeon; Outdoor Channel; OWN: Oprah Winfrey Network; Pop; QVC;

Iowa—Cable Systems

RFD-TV; Spike TV; Syfy; TBS; The Weather Channel; TLC; TNT; Travel Channel; Trinity Broadcasting Network (TBN); truTV; Turner Classic Movies; TV Land; USA Network; VH1.
Fee: $54.99 monthly.
Pay Service 1
Pay Units: N.A.
Programming (via satellite): HBO; HBO 2; HBO Signature.
Fee: $13.95 monthly.
Internet Service
Operational: Yes.
Fee: $29.95-$99.00 monthly.
Telephone Service
Digital: Operational
Fee: $13.50 monthly
General Manager: Sue Bruns. Plant Superintendent: Brett Delagardelle.
Ownership: Dunkerton Telephone Cooperative.

DUNLAP—Formerly served by Tip Top Communications. No longer in operation. ICA: IA0184.

EAGLE GROVE—Mediacom, 2205 Ingersoll Ave, Des Moines, IA 50312. Phone: 515-246-1890. Fax: 515-246-1890. Web Site: http://www.mediacomcable.com. ICA: IA0077.
Channel capacity: N.A. Channels available but not in use: N.A.
Basic Service
Subscribers: 412. Commercial subscribers: 32.
Fee: $41.99 installation; $43.00 monthly.
Ownership: Mediacom LLC.

EARLVILLE—Formerly served by Alpine Communications LC. No longer in operation. ICA: IA0429.

EDDYVILLE—Mediacom. Now served by ALBIA, IA [IA0039]. ICA: IA0203.

ELDON—Mediacom. Now served by ALBIA, IA [IA0039]. ICA: IA0183.

ELK HORN—Marne & Elk Horn Telephone Co, 4242 Main St, PO Box 120, Elk Horn, IA 51531-0120. Phones: 712-764-6161; 888-764-6141. Fax: 712-764-2773. E-mail: metc@metc.net. Web Site: http://www.metc.net. Also serves Brayton, Exira, Kimballton & Marne. ICA: IA0123.
TV Market Ranking: Outside TV Markets (Brayton, ELK HORN, Exira, Kimballton, Marne). Franchise award date: N.A. Franchise expiration date: N.A. Began: January 1, 1984.
Channel capacity: N.A. Channels available but not in use: N.A.
Basic Service
Subscribers: 769.
Programming (received off-air): KCCI (CBS, MeTV) Des Moines; KDIN-TV (PBS) Des Moines; KDSM-TV (FOX, The Country Network) Des Moines; KETV (ABC, MeTV) Omaha; KMTV-TV (Antenna TV, CBS, Escape) Omaha; KPTM (Estrella TV, FOX, MNT, This TV) Omaha; KXVO (Azteca America, CW) Omaha; WHO-DT (Antenna TV, NBC) Des Moines; WOI-DT (ABC) Ames; WOWT (IND, NBC) Omaha.
Programming (via satellite): A&E; Animal Planet; Bloomberg Television; BTN; CMT; CNN; C-SPAN; C-SPAN 2; Discovery Channel; Disney Channel; ESPN; ESPN Classic; ESPN2; EWTN Global Catholic Network; Food Network; Fox News Channel; Fox Sports 1; FOX Sports Midwest; Freeform; FX; Golf Channel; Hallmark Channel; Hallmark Movies & Mysteries; HGTV; History;

HLN; Lifetime; LMN; MTV; NASA TV; Nickelodeon; Outdoor Channel; Radar Channel; RFD-TV; Spike TV; Syfy; TBS; The Weather Channel; TLC; TNT; Travel Channel; Turner Classic Movies; TV Land; USA Network; VH1; WGN America.
Fee: $20.00 installation; $58.95 monthly; $2.00 converter.
Pay Service 1
Pay Units: 59.
Programming (via satellite): Cinemax.
Fee: $12.00 monthly.
Pay Service 2
Pay Units: 26.
Programming (via satellite): Showtime.
Fee: $12.00 monthly.
Pay Service 3
Pay Units: 119.
Programming (via satellite): HBO (multiplexed).
Fee: $12.00 monthly.
Internet Service
Operational: No, DSL & dial-up.
Telephone Service
Analog: Operational
Miles of Plant: 41.0 (coaxial); None (fiber optic). Homes passed: 957.
Chief Executive Officer & General Manager: Janell Hansen. Marketing Director: Doug Pals. Plant Manager: Bruce Poldberg. Chief Technician: Kennard Mertz. Office Manager: Jill Madsen.
Ownership: Marne & Elk Horn Telephone Co.

ELKHART—Huxley Communications Corp. Now served by HUXLEY, IA [IA0595]. ICA: IA0594.

ELY—South Slope Coop. Communications Co. Formerly served by NORTH LIBERTY, IA [IA0432]. This cable system has converted to IPTV, 980 North Front St, PO Box 19, North Liberty, IA 52317. Phones: 800-272-6449; 319-626-2211. Fax: 319-665-7000. E-mail: info@southslope.com. Web Site: http://www.southslope.com. Also serves Amana, Cedar Rapids (portions), Coralville (portions), Fairfax, Newhall, North Liberty, Norway, Oxford, Shueyville, Solon, Swisher, Tiffin, Walford & Watkins. ICA: IA5004.
TV Market Ranking: 65 (ELY, North Liberty, Oxford, Shueyville, Solon, Tiffin, Walford). Franchise award date: January 12, 2004. Franchise expiration date: N.A. Began: N.A.
Channel capacity: N.A. Channels available but not in use: N.A.
Saver
Subscribers: N.A.
Fee: $29.95 monthly.
Standard
Subscribers: 153.
Fee: $25.00 installation; $59.95 monthly.
Superior
Subscribers: N.A.
Fee: $84.95 monthly.
Supreme
Subscribers: N.A.
Fee: $129.95 monthly.
Cinemax
Subscribers: N.A.
Fee: $13.95 monthly.
HBO
Subscribers: N.A.
Fee: $17.95 monthly.
Showtime/TMC/Flix
Subscribers: N.A.
Fee: $14.95 monthly.
Starz/Encore
Subscribers: N.A.
Fee: $12.95 monthly.

Internet Service
Operational: Yes.
Fee: $39.95 monthly; $10.00 modem lease; $130.00 modem purchase.
Telephone Service
Digital: Operational
Fee: $14.50 monthly
Ownership: South Slope Cooperative Communications Co.

EMERSON—Interstate Communications, 105 North West St, PO Box 229, Truro, IA 50257-0229. Phones: 800-765-3738; 641-765-4201; 712-824-7231; 712-824-7227. Fax: 641-765-4204. Web Site: http://www.interstatecom.com. ICA: IA0288.
TV Market Ranking: Outside TV Markets (EMERSON). Franchise award date: January 1, 1982. Franchise expiration date: N.A. Began: January 1, 1983.
Channel capacity: N.A. Channels available but not in use: N.A.
Digital Basic Service
Subscribers: 118.
Programming (received off-air): KETV (ABC, MeTV) Omaha; KFPX-TV (ION) Newton; KMTV-TV (Antenna TV, CBS, Escape) Omaha; KPTM (Estrella TV, FOX, MNT, This TV) Omaha; KXVO (Azteca America, CW) Omaha; WOWT (IND, NBC) Omaha.
Programming (via satellite): A&E; AMC; Animal Planet; BBC America; Bloomberg Television; Boomerang; Bravo; BTN; Cartoon Network; CMT; CNBC; CNN; CNN International; Comcast SportsNet California; Comedy Central; C-SPAN; C-SPAN 2; Destination America; Discovery Channel; Discovery Kids Channel; Disney Channel; DIY Network; E! HD; ESPN; ESPN Classic; ESPN2; ESPNews; ESPNU; EWTN Global Catholic Network; Food Network; Fox News Channel; Fox Sports 1; FOX Sports Midwest; Freeform; FX; FYI; Golf Channel; GSN; Hallmark Channel; HGTV; History; History International; HLN; Investigation Discovery; Lifetime; LMN; MC; MSNBC; MTV; MTV Classic; MTV Hits; MTV2; National Geographic Channel; NBCSN; Nick Jr.; Nickelodeon; Nicktoons; Outdoor Channel; OWN: Oprah Winfrey Network; Oxygen; QVC; RFD-TV; Science Channel; Spike TV; Syfy; TBS; TeenNick; The Weather Channel; TLC; TNT; Travel Channel; Trinity Broadcasting Network (TBN); truTV; Turner Classic Movies; TV Land; Univision; Univision Studios; USA Network; VH1; WE tv; WGN America.
Fee: $35.00 installation; $79.95 monthly.
Digital Pay Service 1
Pay Units: 14.
Programming (via satellite): Cinemax (multiplexed); HBO (multiplexed); Starz (multiplexed); Starz Encore (multiplexed).
Fee: $9.00 monthly (each).
Video-On-Demand: No
Internet Service
Operational: Yes.
Telephone Service
Analog: Operational
Miles of Plant: 3.0 (coaxial); None (fiber optic). Homes passed: 225.
General Manager: Mike Weis. Chief Technician: Rick Lunn.
Ownership: Interstate Communications (MSO).

ESTHERVILLE—Mediacom, 1504 2nd St SE, PO Box 110, Waseca, MN 56093. Phone: 507-835-2356. Fax: 507-835-4567. Web Site: http://www.mediacomcable.com. Also serves Emmet County (portions), Emmetsburg, Graettinger, Spencer & Wallingford. ICA: IA0022.

TV Market Ranking: Outside TV Markets (Emmet County (portions), Emmetsburg, Graettinger, Spencer, Wallingford). Franchise award date: July 8, 1958. Franchise expiration date: N.A. Began: December 24, 1968.
Channel capacity: N.A. Channels available but not in use: N.A.
Basic Service
Subscribers: 2,758.
Programming (received off-air): KCAU-TV (ABC) Sioux City; KELO-TV (CBS, MNT) Sioux Falls; KEYC-TV (CBS, FOX) Mankato; KMEG (Azteca America, CBS, Decades) Sioux City; KPTH (FOX, MNT, This TV) Sioux City; KSFY-TV (ABC, CW) Sioux Falls; KSIN-TV (PBS) Sioux City; KTIN (PBS) Fort Dodge; KTIV (CW, MeTV, NBC) Sioux City; WHO-DT (Antenna TV, NBC) Des Moines; 11 FMs.
Programming (via satellite): A&E; AMC; Animal Planet; Bravo; BTN; Cartoon Network; CMT; CNBC; CNN; Comedy Central; C-SPAN; C-SPAN 2; CW PLUS; Discovery Channel; Disney Channel; DIY Network; E! HD; ESPN; ESPN Classic; ESPN2; ESPNU; EWTN Global Catholic Network; Food Network; Fox News Channel; Fox Sports 1; FOX Sports North; Freeform; FX; FXM; Golf Channel; Hallmark Channel; HGTV; History; HLN; INSP; ION Television; Lifetime; MSNBC; MTV; NFL Network; Nickelodeon; OWN: Oprah Winfrey Network; Pop; Radar Channel; Spike TV; Syfy; TBS; The Weather Channel; TLC; TNT; Travel Channel; Trinity Broadcasting Network (TBN); truTV; Turner Classic Movies; TV Land; USA Network; VH1; WGN America.
Fee: $20.00 installation; $43.00 monthly; $2.38 converter.
Digital Basic Service
Subscribers: N.A.
Programming (via satellite): AXS TV; BBC America; Destination America; Discovery Kids Channel; Discovery Life Channel; Disney XD; DMX Music; ESPN Deportes; ESPN HD; ESPN2 HD; ESPNews; Fox Business Network; Fox Sports 1; FYI; Golf Channel; GSN; History International; IFC; Investigation Discovery; LMN; MTV Hits; MyNetworkTV; NBC Universo; Nick Jr.; Outdoor Channel; RFD-TV; Science Channel; Telemundo; Universal HD; VH1 Soul.
Digital Pay Service 1
Pay Units: N.A.
Programming (via satellite): Cinemax (multiplexed); Flix; HBO (multiplexed); Showtime (multiplexed); Starz (multiplexed); Starz Encore (multiplexed); Sundance TV; The Movie Channel (multiplexed).
Fee: $9.95 monthly (Cinemax, HBO, Showtime, Flix/Sundance/TMC or Starz/Encore).
Video-On-Demand: Yes
Pay-Per-View
ESPN Now (delivered digitally); Hot Choice (delivered digitally); Playboy TV (delivered digitally); Fresh (delivered digitally); Shorteez (delivered digitally); Vubiquity Inc. (delivered digitally).
Internet Service
Operational: Yes.
Broadband Service: Mediacom High Speed Internet.
Fee: $99.00 installation; $40.00 monthly.
Telephone Service
Digital: Operational
Miles of Plant: 926.0 (coaxial); 123.0 (fiber optic). Homes passed: 10,775.

Cable Systems—Iowa

Vice President: Bill Jensen. Engineering Manager: Kraig Kaiser. Marketing & Sales Manager: Lori Huberty.
Ownership: Mediacom LLC (MSO).

EXIRA—Marne & Elk Horn Telephone Co. Now served by ELK HORN, IA [IA0123]. ICA: IA0433.

FAIRBANK—Mediacom. Now served by WAVERLY, IA [IA0021]. ICA: IA0217.

FAIRFAX—Formerly served by Starwest Inc. No longer in operation. ICA: IA0284.

FARMINGTON—Starwest Inc, 15235 235th St, Milton, IA 52570-8016. Phones: 319-397-2283; 319-293-6336. ICA: IA0228.
TV Market Ranking: Below 100 (FARMINGTON). Franchise award date: N.A. Franchise expiration date: N.A. Began: December 1, 1982.
Channel capacity: N.A. Channels available but not in use: N.A.
Basic Service
Subscribers: N.A.
Programming (via satellite): ESPN; TBS; WGN America.
Fee: $30.00 installation; $10.50 monthly.
Pay Service 1
Pay Units: N.A.
Programming (via satellite): Showtime.
Fee: $6.95 monthly.
Internet Service
Operational: No.
Miles of Plant: 6.0 (coaxial); None (fiber optic). Homes passed: 350.
General Manager & Chief Technician: John Stooksberry.
Ownership: Starwest Inc. (MSO).

FARRAGUT—Formerly served by Western Iowa Networks. No longer in operation. ICA: IA0434.

FENTON—Fenton Cablevision, 300 2nd St, PO Box 77, Fenton, IA 50539-0077. Phone: 515-889-2785. Fax: 515-889-2255. E-mail: fntn@netins.net. ICA: IA0327.
TV Market Ranking: Outside TV Markets (FENTON). Franchise award date: N.A. Franchise expiration date: N.A. Began: August 1, 1967.
Channel capacity: N.A. Channels available but not in use: N.A.
Basic Service
Subscribers: 65.
Programming (received off-air): KAAL (ABC, This TV) Austin; KCAU-TV (ABC) Sioux City; KCCI (CBS, MeTV) Des Moines; KEYC-TV (CBS, FOX) Mankato; KIMT (CBS, MNT) Mason City; KTIN (PBS) Fort Dodge; KTTC (CW, NBC) Rochester; WHO-DT (Antenna TV, NBC) Des Moines; WOI-DT (ABC) Ames; allband FM.
Programming (via satellite): CNN; Discovery Channel; ESPN; Freeform; HLN; Spike TV; TBS; TNT; USA Network; WGN America.
Fee: $10.00 installation; $55.95 monthly.
Pay Service 1
Pay Units: N.A.
Programming (via satellite): Cinemax; HBO.
Fee: $9.00 monthly (each).
Internet Service
Operational: No.
Broadband Service: DSL service only.
Telephone Service
None
Miles of Plant: 3.0 (coaxial); None (fiber optic). Homes passed: 175.

General Manager: Steven Longhenry.
Ownership: Fenton Cooperative Telephone Co.

FERTILE—Formerly served by Westcom. No longer in operation. ICA: IA0580.

FONDA—Formerly served by TelePartners. No longer in operation. ICA: IA0219.

FONTANELLE—Formerly served by B & L Technologies LLC. No longer in operation. ICA: IA0246.

FOREST CITY—Winnebago Cooperative Telephone Assn. Now served by LAKE MILLS, IA [IA0590]. ICA: IA0589.

FORT DODGE—Mediacom, 2205 Ingersoll Ave, Des Moines, IA 50312. Phone: 515-246-1890. Fax: 515-246-2211. Web Site: http://www.mediacomcable.com. Also serves Algona, Barnum, Belmond, Calhoun County (portions), Clare, Clarion, Coalville, Cornelia, Dakota City, Hamilton County, Humboldt, Lake City, Lakota, Laurens, Manson, Moorland, Pocahontas, Rockwell City, Sac City, Webster City, Webster County & Wright County (central portion). ICA: IA0011.
TV Market Ranking: 66 (Hamilton County, Webster City, Webster County (portions)); Below 100 (Belmond); Outside TV Markets (Algona, Barnum, Calhoun County (portions), Clare, Clarion, Coalville, Cornelia, Dakota City, FORT DODGE, Humboldt, Lake City, Lakota, Laurens, Manson, Moorland, Pocahontas, Rockwell City, Sac City, Wright County (central portion), Webster County (portions)). Franchise award date: June 11, 1977. Franchise expiration date: N.A. Began: November 1, 1978.
Channel capacity: N.A. Channels available but not in use: N.A.
Basic Service
Subscribers: 8,704. Commercial subscribers: 16.
Programming (received off-air): KCCI (CBS, MeTV) Des Moines; KCWI-TV (CW) Ames; KDIN-TV (PBS) Des Moines; KDSM-TV (FOX, The Country Network) Des Moines; WHO-DT (Antenna TV, NBC) Des Moines; WOI-DT (ABC) Ames; allband FM.
Programming (via satellite): C-SPAN; C-SPAN 2; MyNetworkTV; Pop; QVC; The Weather Channel; WGN America.
Fee: $41.99 installation; $49.45 monthly; $1.60 converter.
Expanded Basic Service 1
Subscribers: N.A.
Programming (via satellite): A&E; AMC; Animal Planet; Bravo; Cartoon Network; CMT; CNBC; CNN; Comedy Central; Discovery Channel; Disney Channel; E! HD; ESPN; ESPN Classic; ESPN2; EWTN Global Catholic Network; Food Network; Fox News Channel; Fox Sports 1; FOX Sports North; Freeform; FX; FXM; Hallmark Channel; HGTV; History; HLN; INSP; Lifetime; MoviePlex; MSNBC; MTV; National Geographic Channel; NBCSN; Nickelodeon; Oxygen; RFD-TV; Spike TV; Syfy; TBS; Telemundo; TLC; TNT; Travel Channel; Trinity Broadcasting Network (TBN); truTV; Turner Classic Movies; TV Land; Univision Studios; USA Network; VH1; WE tv.
Fee: $13.95 installation; $29.96 monthly.
Digital Basic Service
Subscribers: N.A.
Programming (via satellite): 52MX; AXS TV; BBC America; Bloomberg Television; CBS Sports Network; Cinelatino; Cloo; CMT; CNN en Espanol; Destination America; Discovery Kids Channel; Discovery Life Channel; Disney XD; DMX Music; ESPN HD; ESPN2 HD; ESPNews; ESPNU; FOX College Sports Central; FOX College Sports Pacific; Fox Deportes; Fox Sports 2; Fuse; FYI; Golf Channel; GolTV; GSN; HD Theater; History en Espanol; History International; IFC; Investigation Discovery; LMN; MTV Classic; MTV Hits; MTV2; Nick Jr.; Nicktoons; Outdoor Channel; Ovation; OWN; Oprah Winfrey Network; Science Channel; TeenNick; Tennis Channel; Tr3s; TVG Network; Universal HD; VH1 Soul; ViendoMovies.
Digital Pay Service 1
Pay Units: N.A.
Programming (via satellite): Cinemax (multiplexed); Flix; HBO (multiplexed); HBO HD; Showtime (multiplexed); Showtime HD; Starz (multiplexed); Starz Encore (multiplexed); Starz HD; Sundance TV; The Movie Channel (multiplexed); The Movie Channel HD.
Fee: $13.95 installation; $2.52 monthly (Encore), $8.52 monthly (Starz/Starz HDTV), $9.54 monthly (TMC/TMC HD/Flix/Sundance), $14.00 monthly (Cinemax, HBO/HBO HD or Showtime/Showtime HD).
Video-On-Demand: Yes
Pay-Per-View
ESPN Now (delivered digitally); ETC (delivered digitally); Playboy TV (delivered digitally); Pleasure (delivered digitally); Fresh (delivered digitally); Shorteez (delivered digitally); Vubiquity Inc. (delivered digitally).
Internet Service
Operational: Yes.
Subscribers: 5,937.
Broadband Service: Mediacom High Speed Internet.
Fee: $55.95 monthly.
Telephone Service
Digital: Operational
Subscribers: 3,488.
Miles of Plant: 657.0 (coaxial); 575.0 (fiber optic). Homes passed: 33,138.
Vice President: Steve Purcell. Technical Operations Manager: Cliff Waggoner. Marketing Director: LeAnn Treloar. Government & Media Relations Manager: Bill Peard.
Ownership: Mediacom LLC (MSO).

FORT MADISON—Mediacom, 6300 Council St NE, Ste A, Cedar Rapids, IA 52402. Phones: 319-393-1914; 319-395-9699; 319-753-6576 (Burlington office). Fax: 319-393-9017. Web Site: http://www.mediacomcable.com. Also serves Henry County, Lee County (portions), Mount Pleasant, New London, West Point & Westwood. ICA: IA0611.
TV Market Ranking: Below 100 (FORT MADISON, Henry County, Lee County (portions), Mount Pleasant, New London, West Point, Westwood).
Channel capacity: N.A. Channels available but not in use: N.A.
Basic Service
Subscribers: 3,838. Commercial subscribers: 9.
Programming (received off-air): KCRG-TV (ABC, MNT) Cedar Rapids; KIIN (PBS) Iowa City; KLJB (CW, FOX, MeTV) Davenport; KTVO (ABC) Kirksville; KWQC-TV (NBC) Davenport; KYOU-TV (FOX) Ottumwa; WHBF-TV (CBS) Rock Island; WQAD-TV (ABC, Antenna TV) Moline.
Programming (via satellite): C-SPAN; C-SPAN 2; ION Television; Pop; QVC; The Weather Channel; WGN America.
Fee: $41.99 installation; $43.00 monthly.
Expanded Basic Service 1
Subscribers: N.A.
Programming (via satellite): A&E; AMC; Animal Planet; BET; Cartoon Network; CMT; CNBC; CNN; Comedy Central; Discovery Channel; Disney Channel; E! HD; ESPN; ESPN2; EWTN Global Catholic Network; Food Network; Fox News Channel; Fox Sports 1; FOX Sports Midwest; Freeform; FX; Hallmark Channel; HGTV; History; HLN; INSP; Lifetime; MSNBC; MTV; National Geographic Channel; Nickelodeon; Spike TV; Syfy; TBS; Telemundo; TLC; TNT; truTV; TV Land; Univision Studios; USA Network; VH1; WE tv.
Digital Basic Service
Subscribers: N.A.
Programming (via satellite): BBC America; Bloomberg Television; Bravo; Discovery Digital Networks; DMX Music; Fuse; FXM; FYI; Golf Channel; GSN; History International; IFC; LMN; NBCSN; Nick Jr.; Outdoor Channel; Ovation; TeenNick; Trinity Broadcasting Network (TBN); Turner Classic Movies.
Digital Pay Service 1
Pay Units: N.A.
Programming (via satellite): Cinemax (multiplexed); Flix; HBO (multiplexed); Showtime (multiplexed); Starz (multiplexed); Starz Encore (multiplexed); Sundance TV; The Movie Channel (multiplexed).
Video-On-Demand: Yes
Pay-Per-View
ETC (delivered digitally); Playboy TV (delivered digitally); Pleasure (delivered digitally); Vubiquity Inc. (delivered digitally); Sports PPV (delivered digitally).
Internet Service
Operational: Yes.
Broadband Service: Mediacom High Speed Internet.
Fee: $45.95 monthly.
Telephone Service
Digital: Operational
Fee: $39.95 monthly
Miles of Plant: 210.0 (coaxial); None (fiber optic). Miles of plant (fiber) included in miles of plant (coax).
Regional Vice President: Doug Frank. Technical Operations Director: Greg Nank. Marketing Director: Steve Schuh. Technical Operations Manager: Joel Hanger.
Ownership: Mediacom LLC (MSO).

2017 Edition

D-251

Iowa—Cable Systems

FREMONT—Starwest Inc, 15235 235th St, Milton, IA 52570-8016. Phones: 319-397-2283; 319-293-6336. ICA: IA0291.
TV Market Ranking: Below 100 (FREMONT). Franchise award date: N.A. Franchise expiration date: N.A. Began: August 1, 1984.
Channel capacity: N.A. Channels available but not in use: N.A.
Basic Service
Subscribers: N.A.
Programming (received off-air): KCCI (CBS, MeTV) Des Moines; KDIN-TV (PBS) Des Moines; KTVO (ABC) Kirksville; WHO-DT (Antenna TV, NBC) Des Moines; WOI-DT (ABC) Ames.
Programming (via satellite): ESPN; TBS; WGN America.
Pay Service 1
Pay Units: N.A.
Programming (via satellite): Showtime.
Fee: $8.95 monthly.
Internet Service
Operational: No.
Miles of Plant: 4.0 (coaxial); None (fiber optic). Homes passed: 220.
General Manager & Chief Technician: John Stooksberry.
Ownership: Starwest Inc. (MSO).

GARBER—Formerly served by Alpine Communications LC. No longer in operation. ICA: IA0435.

GARNAVILLO—Mediacom. Now served by BOSCOBEL, WI [WI0341]. ICA: IA0547.

GENEVA—Formerly served by Dumont Cablevision. No longer in operation. ICA: IA0382.

GEORGE—Formerly served by Siebring Cable TV. Now served by Premier Communications, SIOUX CENTER, IA [IA0076]. ICA: IA0199.

GILLETT GROVE—ATC Cablevision, 1405 Silver Lake Ave, PO Box 248, Ayrshire, IA 50515-0248. Phones: 712-426-2800; 800-642-2884; 712-426-2815. Fax: 712-426-2008. E-mail: ayrshire@ayrshireia.com. Web Site: http://www.ayrshireia.com. Also serves Ayrshire & Whittemore. ICA: IA0386.
TV Market Ranking: Outside TV Markets (Ayrshire, GILLETT GROVE, Whittemore). Franchise award date: N.A. Franchise expiration date: N.A. Began: April 1, 1987.
Channel capacity: 36 (not 2-way capable). Channels available but not in use: N.A.
Basic Service
Subscribers: 202.
Programming (received off-air): KCAU-TV (ABC) Sioux City; KELO-TV (CBS, MNT) Sioux Falls; KEYC-TV (CBS, FOX) Mankato; KMEG (Azteca America, CBS, Decades) Sioux City; KPTH (FOX, MNT, This TV) Sioux City; KSFY-TV (ABC, CW) Sioux Falls; KTIN (PBS) Fort Dodge; KTIV (CW, MeTV, NBC) Sioux City; WOI-DT (ABC) Ames.
Programming (via satellite): A&E; Animal Planet; Cartoon Network; CMT; CNBC; CNN; Comedy Central; C-SPAN; C-SPAN 2; Discovery Channel; Disney Channel; E! HD; ESPN; ESPN Classic; ESPN2; Food Network; Fox News Channel; Freeform; FX; Hallmark Channel; HGTV; History; HLN; ION Television; Lifetime; MTV; Nickelodeon; Outdoor Channel; Pop; QVC; Spike TV; Syfy; TBS; The Weather Channel; TLC; TNT; Travel Channel; Turner Classic Movies; TV Land; USA Network; VH1; WGN America.
Fee: $30.00 installation; $69.70 monthly.

Digital Basic Service
Subscribers: N.A.
Programming (via satellite): BBC America; Discovery Life Channel; Disney XD; DMX Music; ESPNews; Fox Sports 1; FXM; FYI; Golf Channel; GSN; History; IFC; MTV Classic; MTV2; National Geographic Channel; Nick Jr.; Nicktoons; Outdoor Channel; TeenNick; VH1 Country.
Digital Pay Service 1
Pay Units: 3.
Programming (via satellite): Cinemax (multiplexed); Flix; HBO (multiplexed); Showtime (multiplexed); Starz (multiplexed); Starz Encore (multiplexed); Sundance TV; The Movie Channel (multiplexed).
Fee: $9.50 monthly (Cinemax), $11.00 monthly (Showtime/TMC or Starz/Encore), $12.00 monthly (HBO).
Digital Pay Service 2
Pay Units: 2.
Programming (via satellite): Showtime HD; The Movie Channel HD.
Video-On-Demand: No
Pay-Per-View
Sports PPV (delivered digitally); Special events (delivered digitally).
Internet Service
Operational: No, DSL.
Telephone Service
Analog: Operational
General Manager: Donald D. Miller. Plant Manager: Chase Cox. Chief Technician: Derek Franker. Office Manager: Sheila Akridge.
Ownership: Ayrshire Communications (MSO).

GILMAN—Partner Communications, 101 East Church St, PO Box 8, Gilman, IA 50106. Phones: 877-433-7701; 800-647-2355; 641-498-7701. Fax: 641-498-7308. E-mail: custsvc@partnercom.net; customercare@pcctel.net. Web Site: http://www.pcctel.net. Also serves Baxter, Harvester Community, Kellogg, Laurel, Melbourne, Montour, Oakland Acres, Rhodes, Rock Creek Lake & State Center. ICA: IA0128.
TV Market Ranking: 66 (Baxter, Melbourne, Rhodes, State Center); Below 100 (GILMAN, Harvester Community, Kellogg, Laurel, Montour, Oakland Acres, Rock Creek Lake). Franchise award date: N.A. Franchise expiration date: N.A. Began: January 1, 1984.
Channel capacity: N.A. Channels available but not in use: N.A.
Basic Service
Subscribers: 379.
Programming (received off-air): KCCI (CBS, MeTV) Des Moines; KDIN-TV (PBS) Des Moines; KDSM-TV (FOX, The Country Network) Des Moines; KFPX-TV (ION) Newton; WHO-DT (Antenna TV, NBC) Des Moines; WOI-DT (ABC) Ames.
Programming (via satellite): A&E; Animal Planet; Cartoon Network; CMT; CNN; Comcast SportsNet Chicago; Comedy Central; C-SPAN; C-SPAN 2; Discovery Channel; Disney Channel; DIY Network; ESPN; ESPN Classic; ESPN2; ESPNU; Fox News Channel; Fox Sports 1; FOX Sports Midwest; Freeform; FX; Hallmark Channel; HGTV; History; HLN; INSP; Lifetime; MTV; National Geographic Channel; NFL Network; Nickelodeon; Spike TV; Syfy; TBS; The Weather Channel; TLC; TNT; Travel Channel; Trinity Broadcasting Network (TBN); truTV; Turner Classic Movies; TV Land; USA Network; VH1; WGN America.
Fee: $9.95 installation; $60.95 monthly.

Digital Basic Service
Subscribers: 338.
Programming (via satellite): BBC America; Bloomberg Television; Discovery Digital Networks; Disney XD; DMX Music; ESPN Classic; ESPN2; ESPNews; Fox Sports 1; FSN Digital Atlantic; FSN Digital Central; FSN Digital Pacific; FXM; FYI; Golf Channel; GSN; HGTV; History; History International; LMN; National Geographic Channel; NBCSN; Nick Jr.; Nicktoons; Outdoor Channel; Syfy; TeenNick; Trinity Broadcasting Network (TBN); Turner Classic Movies.
Fee: $12.00 monthly.
Pay Service 1
Pay Units: N.A.
Programming (via satellite): HBO (multiplexed); Showtime (multiplexed); Starz (multiplexed); Starz Encore (multiplexed).
Fee: $12.95 monthly (each).
Digital Pay Service 1
Pay Units: 146.
Programming (via satellite): HBO.
Digital Pay Service 2
Pay Units: 29.
Programming (via satellite): Showtime (multiplexed); The Movie Channel (multiplexed).
Fee: $10.00 monthly.
Digital Pay Service 3
Pay Units: 57.
Programming (via satellite): Starz (multiplexed); Starz Encore (multiplexed).
Fee: $10.00 monthly.
Video-On-Demand: Planned
Pay-Per-View
Hot Choice (delivered digitally); iN DEMAND (delivered digitally); ESPN Classic (delivered digitally); Hot Choice (delivered digitally); iN DEMAND (delivered digitally).
Internet Service
Operational: Yes, DSL.
Fee: $39.95-$129.95 monthly.
Telephone Service
Digital: Operational
Miles of Plant: 52.0 (coaxial); None (fiber optic). Homes passed: 2,390.
Executive Vice President: Donald S. Jennings. Secretary: Daniel Carnahan. Chief Technician: Dave Grewell. Customer Service Manager: Dot Burgess. Marketing Coordinator: Deb Heater.
Ownership: Partner Communications Cooperative.

GILMORE CITY—Mediacom, 2205 Ingersoll Ave, Des Moines, IA 50312. Phone: 515-246-1890. Fax: 515-246-2211. Web Site: http://www.mediacomcable.com. ICA: IA0251.
TV Market Ranking: Outside TV Markets (GILMORE CITY). Franchise award date: N.A. Franchise expiration date: N.A. Began: January 1, 1983.
Channel capacity: N.A. Channels available but not in use: N.A.
Basic Service
Subscribers: 54.
Programming (received off-air): KCCI (CBS, MeTV) Des Moines; KDSM-TV (FOX, The Country Network) Des Moines; KTIN (PBS) Fort Dodge; WHO-DT (Antenna TV, NBC) Des Moines; WOI-DT (ABC) Ames.
Programming (via satellite): A&E; Animal Planet; CMT; CNBC; CNN; Discovery Channel; ESPN; ESPN2; Fox News Channel; Freeform; HGTV; Lifetime; Nickelodeon; QVC; Spike TV; Syfy; TBS; The Weather Channel; TNT; Turner Classic Movies; TV Land; USA Network; VH1; WGN America.
Fee: $19.95 installation; $43.00 monthly.
Pay Service 1
Pay Units: N.A.
Programming (via satellite): Cinemax; HBO.

Fee: $10.00 installation; $9.95 monthly (each).
Video-On-Demand: No
Internet Service
Operational: No.
Telephone Service
None
Miles of Plant: 5.0 (coaxial); None (fiber optic). Homes passed: 300.
Division Vice President: Ed Pardini. Regional Vice President: Steve Purcell. Technical Operations Director: Cliff Waggoner. Marketing Director: LeAnn Treloar. Government Relations Manager: Bill Peard.
Ownership: Mediacom LLC (MSO).

GLADBROOK—Mediacom, 2205 Ingersoll Ave, Des Moines, IA 50312. Phone: 515-246-1890. Fax: 515-246-2211. Web Site: http://www.mediacomcable.com. Also serves Beaman, Conrad, Eldora, Garwin, Grundy Center, Hardin County, Tama & Tama County (portions). ICA: IA0087.
TV Market Ranking: 65 (Beaman, Conrad, Eldora, Garwin, GLADBROOK, Grundy Center, Tama County (portions) (portions)); 65,66 (Hardin County (portions)); Below 100 (Tama, Tama County (portions) (portions)); Outside TV Markets (Hardin County (portions)). Franchise award date: N.A. Franchise expiration date: N.A. Began: October 1, 1984.
Channel capacity: N.A. Channels available but not in use: N.A.
Basic Service
Subscribers: 1,584.
Programming (received off-air): KCCI (CBS, MeTV) Des Moines; KCRG-TV (ABC, MNT) Cedar Rapids; KCWI-TV (CW) Ames; KDIN-TV (PBS) Des Moines; KDSM-TV (FOX, The Country Network) Des Moines; KFPX-TV (ION) Newton; KFXA (FOX, The Country Network) Cedar Rapids; KGAN (CBS) Cedar Rapids; KPXR-TV (ION) Cedar Rapids; KWKB (The Works, This TV) Iowa City; KWWL (CW, MeTV, NBC) Waterloo; WHO-DT (Antenna TV, NBC) Des Moines; WOI-DT (ABC) Ames.
Programming (via satellite): A&E; AMC; Animal Planet; Bravo; Cartoon Network; CMT; CNBC; CNN; Comedy Central; C-SPAN; C-SPAN 2; Discovery Channel; Disney Channel; E! HD; ESPN; ESPN2; EWTN Global Catholic Network; Food Network; Fox News Channel; Fox Sports 1; FOX Sports Networks; Freeform; FX; Hallmark Channel; HGTV; History; HLN; Lifetime; MSNBC; MTV; Nickelodeon; Pop; Spike TV; Syfy; TBS; The Weather Channel; TLC; TNT; Travel Channel; Trinity Broadcasting Network (TBN); truTV; Turner Classic Movies; TV Land; USA Network; VH1; WGN America.
Fee: $43.00 monthly.
Digital Basic Service
Subscribers: N.A.
Programming (via satellite): BBC America; Bloomberg Television; Discovery Digital Networks; Disney XD; Fuse; FXM; FYI; Golf Channel; GSN; History International; IFC; LMN; MC; MTV2; National Geographic Channel; NBCSN; Nick Jr.; Outdoor Channel; Ovation; TeenNick.
Digital Pay Service 1
Pay Units: N.A.
Programming (via satellite): Cinemax (multiplexed); HBO (multiplexed); Showtime (multiplexed); Starz; Starz Encore; The Movie Channel.
Fee: $9.95 monthly (each).
Video-On-Demand: Yes
Pay-Per-View
Sports PPV (delivered digitally).

D-252   TV & CABLE Factbook No. 85

Cable Systems—Iowa

Internet Service
Operational: Yes.
Broadband Service: Mediacom High Speed Internet.
Fee: $99.00 installation; $55.95 monthly.
Telephone Service
Digital: Operational
Miles of Plant: 40.0 (coaxial); None (fiber optic).
Regional Vice President: Steve Purcell. Technical Operations Director: Cliff Waggoner. Marketing Director: LeAnn Treloar. Government & Media Relations Manager: Bill Peard.
Ownership: Mediacom LLC (MSO).

GOLDFIELD—Goldfield Communication Services Corp, 536 North Main St, PO Box 67, Goldfield, IA 50542. Phones: 800-825-9753; 515-825-3996; 515-825-3888. Fax: 515-825-3801. E-mail: gold@goldfieldaccess.net. Web Site: http://www.goldfieldaccess.net. Also serves Clarion, Humboldt, Renwick & Woolstock. ICA: IA0252.
TV Market Ranking: Outside TV Markets (GOLDFIELD, Humboldt, Woolstock). Franchise award date: March 31, 1980. Franchise expiration date: N.A. Began: December 30, 1982.
Channel capacity: N.A. Channels available but not in use: N.A.
Basic Service
Subscribers: 19.
Programming (received off-air): KCCI (CBS, MeTV) Des Moines; KIMT (CBS, MNT) Mason City; WHO-DT (Antenna TV, NBC) Des Moines; WOI-DT (ABC) Ames; allband FM.
Programming (via satellite): CNN; Freeform; TBS; USA Network; WGN America.
Fee: $20.00 installation; $22.95 monthly; $.50 converter.
Expanded Basic Service 1
Subscribers: N.A.
Programming (via satellite): A&E; AMC; Bravo; Discovery Channel; Disney Channel; ESPN; ESPN2; Fox News Channel; HLN; Lifetime; MTV; Nickelodeon; Spike TV; The Weather Channel; TNT; VH1.
Fee: $10.00 installation; $36.95 monthly.
Pay Service 1
Pay Units: N.A.
Programming (via satellite): Cinemax; Flix; HBO; Showtime; Sundance TV; The Movie Channel.
Fee: $7.00 - $9.85 monthly (each).
Video-On-Demand: No
Internet Service
Operational: Yes.
Telephone Service
Analog: Operational
Miles of Plant: 50.0 (coaxial); None (fiber optic). Homes passed: 450.
General Manager: Darrell L. Seaba. Operations Director: Ron Massingill. Chief Technician: Dean Schipull.
Ownership: Goldfield Communication Services Corp. (MSO).

GOODELL (village)—Formerly served by New Path Communications LC. No longer in operation. ICA: IA0438.

GOWRIE—Gowrie Cablevision, PO Box 415, Gowrie, IA 50543. Phones: 800-292-8989; 515-352-5227. Fax: 515-352-5226. E-mail: gowrie@wccta.net. Web Site: http://www.gowrie.org/utilities/gowrie_catv.htm. Also serves Paton. ICA: IA0439.

TV Market Ranking: 66 (Paton); Outside TV Markets (GOWRIE). Franchise award date: N.A. Franchise expiration date: N.A. Began: December 1, 1983.
Channel capacity: N.A. Channels available but not in use: N.A.
Basic Service
Subscribers: 68.
Programming (received off-air): KCCI (CBS, MeTV) Des Moines; KDIN-TV (PBS) Des Moines; KDSM-TV (FOX, The Country Network) Des Moines; WHO-DT (Antenna TV, NBC) Des Moines; WOI-DT (ABC) Ames.
Programming (via satellite): CNN; ESPN; HLN; Nickelodeon; Spike TV; TBS; WGN America.
Fee: $25.00 installation; $26.95 monthly.
Pay Service 1
Pay Units: N.A.
Programming (via satellite): HBO; Showtime.
Fee: $10.00 monthly (each).
Video-On-Demand: No
Internet Service
Operational: No, DSL & dial-up.
Telephone Service
None
Miles of Plant: 8.0 (coaxial); None (fiber optic). Homes passed: 425.
General Manager: Paul Johnson.
Ownership: Gowrie Cablevision Inc. (MSO).

GRAETTINGER—River Valley Telecommunications Coop, 106 East Robins Ave, PO Box 250, Graettinger, IA 51342. Phone: 712-859-3300. Fax: 712-859-3290. E-mail: questions@rvtc.net. Web Site: http://www.rvtc.net. Also serves Wallingford. ICA: IA0637.
Channel capacity: N.A. Channels available but not in use: N.A.
Basic Service
Subscribers: 813.
Fee: $25.00 installation; $60.00 monthly.
Digital Basic Service
Subscribers: N.A.
Fee: $6.00 monthly.
Internet Service
Operational: Yes.
Fee: $34.95-$149.95 monthly.
Telephone Service
Digital: Operational
Fee: $25.00 monthly
President: Robert Louwagie.
Ownership: River Valley Telecommunications Coop.

GRAFTON—Formerly served by Westcom. No longer in operation. ICA: IA0568.

GRAND JUNCTION—Jefferson Telecom, 105 West Harrison St, Jefferson, IA 50129. Phone: 515-386-4141. Fax: 515-386-2600. E-mail: jtcobob@netins.net. Web Site: http://www.jeffersontelephone.com. ICA: IA0440.
TV Market Ranking: 66 (GRAND JUNCTION). Franchise award date: N.A. Franchise expiration date: N.A. Began: January 1, 1985.
Channel capacity: N.A. Channels available but not in use: N.A.
Basic Service
Subscribers: 1,096.
Programming (received off-air): KCCI (CBS, MeTV) Des Moines; KCWI-TV (CW) Ames; KDIN-TV (PBS) Des Moines; KDSM-TV (FOX, The Country Network) Des Moines; WHO-DT (Antenna TV, NBC) Des Moines; WOI-DT (ABC) Ames.
Programming (via satellite): C-SPAN; C-SPAN 2; EWTN Global Catholic Network; HSN; ION Television; Pop; QVC; Trinity Broadcasting Network (TBN); WGN America.
Fee: $20.00 installation; $52.95 monthly.
Expanded Basic Service 1
Subscribers: N.A.
Programming (via satellite): A&E; AMC; Animal Planet; Bravo; BTN; Cartoon Network; CMT; CNBC; CNN; Comedy Central; Discovery Channel; Disney Channel; DIY Network; E! HD; ESPN; ESPN Classic; ESPN2; Food Network; Fox News Channel; Freeform; FX; Hallmark Channel; HGTV; History; HLN; Lifetime; LMN; MTV; National Geographic Channel; Nickelodeon; RFD-TV; Spike TV; Syfy; TBS; The Weather Channel; TLC; TNT; Travel Channel; truTV; TV Land; USA Network; VH1; WE tv.
Fee: $21.00 monthly.
Digital Basic Service
Subscribers: N.A.
Programming (via satellite): A&E HD; American Heroes Channel; Animal Planet HD; Antenna TV; BBC America; Bravo HD; BTN; Chiller; Cloo; CNBC HD+; Destination America; Destination America HD; Discovery Channel HD; Discovery Family; Discovery Life Channel; Disney Channel HD; ESPN HD; ESPN2 HD; ESPNews; ESPNU; Food Network HD; Fox News HD; Freeform HD; FX HD; FXM; FYI; Golf Channel; GSN; HGTV HD; History HD; Investigation Discovery; Lifetime HD; Lifetime Movie Network HD; MC; MTV Classic; MTV Hits; MTV2; National Geographic Channel HD; NFL Network; NFL Network HD; Nick Jr.; Nicktoons; Outdoor Channel; Outdoor Channel HD; OWN: Oprah Winfrey Network; Science Channel; Science HD; Syfy HD; TBS HD; TeenNick; TheCoolTV; TLC HD; Travel Channel HD; USA Network HD; Velocity.
Digital Expanded Basic Service
Subscribers: N.A.
Programming (via satellite): Bloomberg Television; Centric; CMT; Disney XD; Fox Sports 1; Fuse; IFC; NBCSN; Turner Classic Movies; VH1 Soul.
Fee: $5.95 monthly.
Pay Service 1
Pay Units: N.A.
Programming (via satellite): Cinemax; HBO; Starz; Starz Encore.
Fee: $9.20 monthly (Starz/Encore), $14.00 monthly (Cinemax/HBO).
Digital Pay Service 1
Pay Units: N.A.
Programming (via satellite): Cinemax (multiplexed); Flix; HBO (multiplexed); Showtime (multiplexed); Starz (multiplexed); Starz Encore; The Movie Channel (multiplexed).
Video-On-Demand: No
Internet Service
Operational: Yes.
Telephone Service
Analog: Operational
General Manager: Jim Daubendiek.
Ownership: Jefferson Telephone & Cablevision (MSO).

GRAND MOUND—Grand Mound Communications Corp., 705 Clinton St, PO Box 316, Grand Mound, IA 52751-0316. Phones: 888-732-1378; 563-847-3000. Fax: 563-847-3001. E-mail: grmd@gmcta.coop. Web Site: http://www.gmtel.net. Also serves De Witt. ICA: IA0557. **Note:** This system is an overbuild.
TV Market Ranking: 60 (De Witt, GRAND MOUND). Franchise award date: N.A. Franchise expiration date: N.A. Began: January 17, 1994.
Channel capacity: N.A. Channels available but not in use: N.A.
Basic Service
Subscribers: 228.
Programming (received off-air): KCRG-TV (ABC, MNT) Cedar Rapids; KGAN (CBS) Cedar Rapids; KIIN (PBS) Iowa City; KLJB (CW, FOX, MeTV) Davenport; KWQC-TV (NBC) Davenport; KWWL (CW, MeTV, NBC) Waterloo; WHBF-TV (CBS) Rock Island; WQAD-TV (ABC, Antenna TV) Moline.
Programming (via satellite): A&E; AMC; Cartoon Network; CMT; CNN; C-SPAN; Discovery Channel; ESPN; Freeform; MTV; Nickelodeon; Spike TV; Syfy; TBS; TNT; USA Network; VH1; WGN America.
Fee: $20.00 installation; $75.95 monthly.
Pay Service 1
Pay Units: N.A.
Programming (via satellite): Cinemax; HBO; Showtime.
Fee: $9.95 monthly (each).
Video-On-Demand: No; No
Internet Service
Operational: Yes.
Fee: $37.95-$62.95 monthly.
Telephone Service
Digital: Operational
Fee: $15.50 monthly
Miles of Plant: 9.0 (coaxial); None (fiber optic). Homes passed: 242.
President: Kurt Crosthwaite. General Manager: Marcus Behnken. Office Manager: Terri Bumann.
Ownership: Grand Mound Cooperative Telephone Assn.

GRAND RIVER—Formerly served by B & L Technologies LLC. No longer in operation. ICA: IA0364.

GRANVILLE—Premier Communications. Now served by SIOUX CENTER, IA [IA0076]. ICA: IA0597.

GRAVITY—Formerly served by CableDirect. No longer in operation. ICA: IA0558.

GREELEY—Formerly served by Alpine Communications LC. No longer in operation. ICA: IA0441.

GREENE (town)—Formerly served by Mediacom. No longer in operation. ICA: IA0162.

GRISWOLD—Griswold Cable TV, 607 Main St, PO Box 640, Griswold, IA 51535-0640. Phone: 712-778-2121. Fax: 712-778-2500. E-mail: gctc@netins.net. Web Site: http://www.griswoldtelco.com. Also serves Elliot, Grant, Lewis & Lyman. ICA: IA0442.
TV Market Ranking: Outside TV Markets (Grant, GRISWOLD, Lewis, Lyman). Franchise award date: N.A. Franchise expiration date: N.A. Began: January 1, 1985.
Channel capacity: N.A. Channels available but not in use: N.A.
Digital Basic Service
Subscribers: 617.
Programming (received off-air): KCCI (CBS, MeTV) Des Moines; KDSM-TV (FOX, The Country Network) Des Moines; KETV (ABC, MeTV) Omaha; KHIN (PBS) Red Oak; KMTV-TV (Antenna TV, CBS, Escape) Omaha; KPTM (Estrella TV, FOX, MNT, This TV) Omaha; KXVO (Azteca America, CW) Omaha; WHO-DT (Antenna TV, NBC) Des Moines; WOI-DT (ABC) Ames; WOWT (IND, NBC) Omaha.

2017 Edition   D-253

Iowa—Cable Systems

Programming (via satellite): A&E; AMC; Animal Planet; BBC America; Boomerang; BTN; Cartoon Network; CMT; CNN; CNN International; C-SPAN; C-SPAN 2; Destination America; Discovery Channel; Discovery Kids Channel; Disney Channel; Disney XD; ESPN; ESPN Classic; ESPN2; ESPNews; Food Network; Fox News Channel; Fox Sports 1; FOX Sports Midwest; Freeform; FX; Hallmark Channel; HGTV; History; HLN; Investigation Discovery; Lifetime; LMN; MTV; MTV Classic; MTV Jams; MTV2; National Geographic Channel; NBCSN; Nick Jr.; Nickelodeon; Nicktoons; Outdoor Channel; OWN: Oprah Winfrey Network; Oxygen; QVC; RFD-TV; Science Channel; Spike TV; Syfy; TBS; The Weather Channel; TLC; TNT; Travel Channel; Turner Classic Movies; TV Land; USA Network; VH1; WGN America.
Fee: $30.00 installation; $59.95 monthly.
Digital Pay Service 1
Pay Units: N.A.
Programming (via satellite): Cinemax; HBO; Playboy TV; Starz; Starz Encore.
Fee: $20.00 installation; $11.00 monthly (Cinemax, HBO, Playboy or Starz/Encore).
Video-On-Demand: No
Internet Service
Operational: Yes.
Telephone Service
Digital: Operational
Homes passed: 800.
Executive Vice President & General Manager: Robert A. Drogo. Chief Technician: Mark Gronewold. Marketing Director: Amy Carlisle.
Ownership: Griswold Co-op Telephone Co. (MSO).

GRUNDY CENTER—Grundy Center Municipal Utilities, 706 6th St, PO Box 307, Grundy Center, IA 50638-1536. Phone: 319-825-5207. Web Site: http://www.gcmuni.net. ICA: IA0600. **Note:** This system is an overbuild.
TV Market Ranking: 65 (GRUNDY CENTER).
Channel capacity: N.A. Channels available but not in use: N.A.
Basic Service
Subscribers: 935.
Programming (received off-air): KCCI (CBS, MeTV) Des Moines; KCRG-TV (ABC, MNT) Cedar Rapids; KFXA (FOX, The Country Network) Cedar Rapids; KGAN (CBS) Cedar Rapids; KPXR-TV (ION) Cedar Rapids; KRIN (PBS) Waterloo; KWWL (CW, MeTV, NBC) Waterloo; WHO-DT (Antenna TV, NBC) Des Moines; WOI-DT (ABC) Ames.
Programming (via satellite): A&E; AMC; Animal Planet; Cartoon Network; CMT; CNN; Comedy Central; Discovery Channel; Disney Channel; E! HD; ESPN; ESPN2; Fox News Channel; FOX Sports Midwest; Freeform; Golf Channel; HGTV; History; Lifetime; MSNBC; MTV; Nickelodeon; QVC; Syfy; TBS; The Weather Channel; TLC; TNT; Travel Channel; truTV; Turner Classic Movies; TV Land; USA Network; VH1; WGN America.
Fee: $26.95 monthly.
Pay Service 1
Pay Units: N.A.
Programming (via satellite): HBO; Showtime; Starz; Starz Encore; The Movie Channel.
Fee: $10.00 monthly (each).
Internet Service
Operational: Yes, Dial-up.
Broadband Service: In-house.
Fee: $39.95 monthly; $15.00 modem lease.

Telephone Service
Digital: Operational
Miles of Plant: 16.0 (coaxial); None (fiber optic).
General Manager: Jeff Carson. Chief Technician: Darrel Shuey.
Ownership: Grundy Center Municipal Light & Power.

HAMBURG—Rock Port Cablevision, 107 West Opp St, PO Box 147, Rock Port, MO 64482. Phones: 660-744-5311; 660-744-2020; 877-202-1764. E-mail: rptel@rpt.coop. Web Site: http://www.rptel.net. ICA: IA0443.
TV Market Ranking: Outside TV Markets (HAMBURG). Franchise award date: N.A. Franchise expiration date: N.A. Began: July 1, 1981.
Channel capacity: N.A. Channels available but not in use: N.A.
Basic Service
Subscribers: 108.
Programming (received off-air): KETV (ABC, MeTV) Omaha; KHIN (PBS) Red Oak; KMTV-TV (Antenna TV, CBS, Escape) Omaha; KPTM (Estrella TV, FOX, MNT, This TV) Omaha; KUON-TV (PBS) Lincoln; KXVO (Azteca America, CW) Omaha; WOWT (IND, NBC) Omaha.
Programming (via satellite): A&E; AMC; CNN; Comedy Central; Discovery Channel; Disney Channel; ESPN; ESPN2; Freeform; History; HLN; Lifetime; Nickelodeon; Spike TV; Syfy; TBS; The Weather Channel; TNT; TV Land; USA Network; WGN America.
Fee: $20.00 installation; $48.00 monthly.
Pay Service 1
Pay Units: N.A.
Programming (via satellite): HBO; The Movie Channel.
Fee: $10.95 monthly (each).
Video-On-Demand: No
Internet Service
Operational: No, DSL.
Telephone Service
None
General Manager: Raymond Henagan. Chief Technician: Gary McGuire.
Ownership: Rock Port Telephone Co. (MSO).

HAMILTON—Mediacom, 2205 Ingersoll Ave, Des Moines, IA 50312. Phone: 800-479-2070. Fax: 515-246-2211. Web Site: http://www.mediacomcable.com. Also serves Bussey, Knoxville, Lovilia, Marion County, Melcher & Pleasantville. ICA: IA0018.
TV Market Ranking: 66 (Knoxville, Melcher, Pleasantville); Below 100 (Bussey, HAMILTON, Lovilia).
Channel capacity: N.A. Channels available but not in use: N.A.
Basic Service
Subscribers: 1,489. Commercial subscribers: 69.
Fee: $41.99 installation; $43.00 monthly.
Ownership: Mediacom LLC (MSO).

HAMPTON—Mediacom, 4010 Alexandra Dr, Waterloo, IA 50702. Phone: 319-235-2197. Fax: 319-232-7841. Web Site: http://www.mediacomcable.com. Also serves Rockwell & Sheffield. ICA: IA0070.
TV Market Ranking: Below 100 (HAMPTON, Rockwell, Sheffield). Franchise award date: N.A. Franchise expiration date: N.A. Began: December 1, 1981.
Channel capacity: N.A. Channels available but not in use: N.A.
Basic Service
Subscribers: 797.
Programming (received off-air): KAAL (ABC, This TV) Austin; KCCI (CBS, MeTV)

Des Moines; KCRG-TV (ABC, MNT) Cedar Rapids; KCWI-TV (CW) Ames; KFPX-TV (ION) Newton; KFXA (FOX, The Country Network) Cedar Rapids; KIMT (CBS, MNT) Mason City; KTTC (CW, NBC) Rochester; KWWL (CW, MeTV, NBC) Waterloo; KYIN (PBS) Mason City; WHO-DT (Antenna TV, NBC) Des Moines; WOI-DT (ABC) Ames.
Programming (via satellite): CMT; CNBC; CNN; C-SPAN; Discovery Channel; HLN; Lifetime; MTV; Nickelodeon; TBS; The Weather Channel; TNT; WGN America.
Fee: $60.00 installation; $43.00 monthly; $.69 converter.
Expanded Basic Service 1
Subscribers: N.A.
Programming (via satellite): A&E; AMC; Animal Planet; Bravo; Cartoon Network; Comedy Central; Disney Channel; E! HD; ESPN; ESPN2; EWTN Global Catholic Network; Fox News Channel; Fox Sports 1; FOX Sports Midwest; Freeform; FX; HGTV; History; INSP; Pop; Spike TV; Syfy; Telemundo; TLC; Trinity Broadcasting Network (TBN); TV Land; USA Network; VH1; WE tv.
Fee: $11.45 monthly.
Digital Basic Service
Subscribers: N.A.
Programming (via satellite): BBC America; Bloomberg Television; Discovery Digital Networks; Disney XD; DMX Music; Fuse; FXM; FYI; Golf Channel; GSN; History International; IFC; LMN; National Geographic Channel; NBCSN; Nick Jr.; Outdoor Channel; Ovation; TeenNick; Turner Classic Movies.
Digital Pay Service 1
Pay Units: N.A.
Programming (via satellite): Cinemax (multiplexed); HBO (multiplexed); Showtime (multiplexed); Starz (multiplexed); Starz Encore (multiplexed); Sundance TV; The Movie Channel (multiplexed).
Fee: $9.95 monthly (Cinemax, HBO, Showtime, Starz/Encore or Sundance/TMC).
Video-On-Demand: Yes
Pay-Per-View
ESPN Now (delivered digitally); ETC (delivered digitally); Hot Choice (delivered digitally); Playboy TV (delivered digitally); Pleasure (delivered digitally); Fresh (delivered digitally); Vubiquity Inc. (delivered digitally).
Internet Service
Operational: Yes.
Broadband Service: Mediacom High Speed Internet.
Fee: $49.95 installation; $55.95 monthly.
Telephone Service
Digital: Operational
Miles of Plant: 48.0 (coaxial); None (fiber optic). Homes passed: 2,458.
Regional Vice President: Doug Frank. General Manager: Doug Nix. Technical Operations Director: Greg Nank. Marketing Director: Steve Schuh. Marketing Coordinator: Joni Lindauer.
Ownership: Mediacom LLC (MSO).

HARLAN—Harlan Municipal Utilities, 2412 Southwest Ave, PO Box 71, Harlan, IA 51537. Phones: 712-755-2074; 712-755-5182. Fax: 712-755-2320. E-mail: hmu@harlannet.com. Web Site: http://www.harlannet.com. ICA: IA0586. **Note:** This system is an overbuild.
TV Market Ranking: Outside TV Markets (HARLAN).
Channel capacity: N.A. Channels available but not in use: N.A.

Basic Service
Subscribers: 1,303.
Programming (received off-air): KCCI (CBS, MeTV) Des Moines; KETV (ABC, MeTV) Omaha; KHIN (PBS) Red Oak; KMTV-TV (Antenna TV, CBS, Escape) Omaha; KPTM (Estrella TV, FOX, MNT, This TV) Omaha; KXVO (Azteca America, CW) Omaha; WHO-DT (Antenna TV, NBC) Des Moines; WOI-DT (ABC) Ames; WOWT (IND, NBC) Omaha.
Programming (via satellite): C-SPAN.
Fee: $23.99 monthly; $15.00 converter.
Expanded Basic Service 1
Subscribers: N.A.
Programming (via satellite): A&E; AMC; Animal Planet; BTN; Cartoon Network; CMT; CNBC; CNN; Comedy Central; C-SPAN 2; Discovery Channel; Disney Channel; Disney XD; E! HD; ESPN; ESPN Classic; ESPN2; ESPNews; Food Network; Fox News Channel; Fox Sports 1; FOX Sports Midwest; Freeform; FX; GSN; Hallmark Movies & Mysteries; HGTV; History; HLN; Lifetime; LMN; MSNBC; MTV; MyNetworkTV; National Geographic Channel; Nickelodeon; Outdoor Channel; QVC; RFD-TV; Spike TV; Syfy; TBS; The Weather Channel; TLC; TNT; Travel Channel; Turner Classic Movies; TV Land; USA Network; VH1; WGN America.
Fee: $44.95 monthly.
Digital Basic Service
Subscribers: 341.
Programming (via satellite): A&E HD; Animal Planet HD; BBC America; Bloomberg Television; BTN HD; Chiller; Cloo; CMT; CNN HD; Destination America; Discovery Channel HD; Discovery Kids Channel; Discovery Life Channel; ESPN2 HD; ESPNU; EVINE Live; Fox Business Network; FOX College Sports Central; FOX College Sports Pacific; Fox News HD; FOX Sports Midwest; FX HD; FYI; Golf Channel; History HD; History International; Investigation Discovery; Lifetime Movie Network HD; MTV Classic; MTV Hits; MTV2; National Geographic Channel HD; NBCSN; Nick Jr.; Nicktoons; OWN: Oprah Winfrey Network; Oxygen; Science Channel; Syfy HD; TBS HD; TeenNick; TLC HD; TNT HD; USA Network HD; VH1 Soul.
Fee: $11.99 monthly.
Digital Pay Service 1
Pay Units: N.A.
Programming (via satellite): Cinemax (multiplexed); Cinemax HD (multiplexed); HBO HD; Showtime (multiplexed); Showtime HD; Starz (multiplexed); Starz Encore (multiplexed); Starz HD.
Fee: $10.00 monthly (Cinemax, Showtime or Starz/Encore), $14.00 monthly (HBO).
Video-On-Demand: No
Pay-Per-View
iN DEMAND (delivered digitally); Club Jenna (delivered digitally); Fresh (delivered digitally); Playboy TV (delivered digitally); Spice: Xcess (delivered digitally).
Internet Service
Operational: Yes.
Broadband Service: In-house.
Fee: $42.95-$52.95 monthly.
Telephone Service
Digital: Operational
Miles of Plant: 44.0 (coaxial); 9.0 (fiber optic).
Chief Executive Officer: Darrel Wenzel. Marketing Director: Doug Hammer. Telecommunications Director: Jim Gedwillo. Operations Manager: Tim Hodapp. Chief Technician: Dan Murray. Customer Service Director: John Doonan.
Ownership: Harlan Municipal Utilities.

Cable Systems—Iowa

HARTFORD—Formerly served by Telnet South LC. Now served by Mediacom, DES MOINES, IA [IA0001]. ICA: IA0445.

HAVELOCK—Northwest Telephone Co-operative Association, 844 Wood St, PO Box 186, Havelock, IA 50546. Phones: 800-247-2776; 712-776-2222. Fax: 712-776-4444. E-mail: nis@ncn.net. Web Site: http://northwest.coop. Also serves Mallard, Plover, Rolfe & West Bend. ICA: IA0365.
TV Market Ranking: Outside TV Markets (HAVELOCK, Mallard, Plover, Rolfe, West Bend). Franchise award date: N.A. Franchise expiration date: N.A. Began: January 1, 1987.
Channel capacity: N.A. Channels available but not in use: N.A.
Digital Basic Service
Subscribers: 360.
Programming (received off-air): KCAU-TV (ABC) Sioux City; KCCI (CBS, MeTV) Des Moines; KCWI-TV (CW) Ames; KDSM-TV (FOX, The Country Network) Des Moines; KEYC-TV (CBS, FOX) Mankato; KMEG (Azteca America, CBS, Decades) Sioux City; KPTH (FOX, MNT, This TV) Sioux City; KTIN (PBS) Fort Dodge; KTIV (CW, MeTV, NBC) Sioux City; WHO-DT (Antenna TV, NBC) Des Moines; WOI-DT (ABC) Ames; 10 FMs.
Programming (via satellite): A&E; AMC; Animal Planet; Bravo; Cartoon Network; CMT; CNN; Comedy Central; C-SPAN; C-SPAN 2; Discovery Channel; Disney Channel; DIY Network; E! HD; ESPN; ESPN Classic; ESPN2; ESPNU; EWTN Global Catholic Network; Food Network; Fox News Channel; Fox Sports 1; Freeform; FX; FXM; Golf Channel; Hallmark Channel; HGTV; History; HLN; INSP; ION Television; Lifetime; MSNBC; MTV; Nickelodeon; Outdoor Channel; OWN: Oprah Winfrey Network; Pop; QVC; Radar Channel; Spike TV; Syfy; TBS; The Weather Channel; TLC; TNT; Travel Channel; Trinity Broadcasting Network (TBN); truTV; Turner Classic Movies; TV Land; USA Network; VH1; WGN America.
Fee: $30.00 installation; $79.85 monthly.
Digital Expanded Basic Service
Subscribers: N.A.
Programming (via satellite): AXS TV; BBC America; CMT; Destination America; Discovery Kids Channel; Discovery Life Channel; ESPN HD; ESPN2 HD; ESPNews; FYI; GSN; HD Theater; History; IFC; Investigation Discovery; LMN; MTV Classic; MTV2; National Geographic Channel; Nick Jr.; Nicktoons; Science Channel; TeenNick; Universal HD.
Fee: $50.00 monthly.
Digital Pay Service 1
Pay Units: N.A.
Programming (via satellite): Cinemax (multiplexed); Cinemax HD; HBO (multiplexed); HBO HD; Starz (multiplexed); Starz Encore (multiplexed); Starz HD.
Fee: $9.50 monthly (Cinemax), $11.00 monthly (Starz/Encore) or $15.00 monthly (HBO).
Video-On-Demand: No
Internet Service
Operational: No.
Telephone Service
Digital: Operational
Fee: $23.75 monthly
Miles of Plant: 50.0 (coaxial); 36.0 (fiber optic). Homes passed: 1,000.
Chief Executive Officer: Don Miller. Chief Technical Officer: Chase Cox. Marketing & Customer Service Manager: Sheila Akridge. Plant Manager: Andy Wilta.
Ownership: Northwest Telephone Cooperative Association.

HAWARDEN—Formerly served by Premier Communications. No longer in operation. ICA: IA0092.

HAWARDEN—HiTec Cable, 1150 Central Ave, Hawarden, IA 51023-0231. Phone: 712-551-2565. Fax: 712-551-1117. E-mail: city@cityofhawarden.com. Web Site: http://www.cityofhawarden.com. ICA: IA0566.
TV Market Ranking: Below 100 (HAWARDEN). Franchise award date: N.A. Franchise expiration date: N.A. Began: November 1, 1997.
Channel capacity: N.A. Channels available but not in use: N.A.
Basic Service
Subscribers: 663.
Programming (received off-air): KCAU-TV (ABC) Sioux City; KDLT-TV (Antenna TV, NBC) Sioux Falls; KELO-TV (CBS, MNT) Sioux Falls; KMEG (Azteca America, CBS, Decades) Sioux City; KPTH (FOX, MNT, This TV) Sioux City; KSFY-TV (ABC, CW) Sioux Falls; KSIN-TV (PBS) Sioux City; KTIV (CW, MeTV, NBC) Sioux City; KTTW (FOX, This TV) Sioux Falls; KUSD-TV (PBS) Vermillion.
Programming (via satellite): C-SPAN; National Geographic Channel.
Fee: $47.00 monthly; $2.00 converter.
Expanded Basic Service 1
Subscribers: N.A.
Programming (via satellite): A&E; AMC; Animal Planet; Cartoon Network; CMT; CNN; Comedy Central; CW PLUS; Discovery Channel; Disney Channel; ESPN; ESPN Classic; ESPN2; ESPNU; Food Network; Fox News Channel; Freeform; FX; Hallmark Channel; HGTV; History; HLN; Lifetime; MTV; NASA TV; Nickelodeon; Outdoor Channel; QVC; Spike TV; Syfy; TBS; The Weather Channel; TLC; TNT; Turner Classic Movies; TV Land; USA Network; VH1; WGN America.
Fee: $27.50 monthly.
Digital Basic Service
Subscribers: 59.
Programming (via satellite): BBC America; Bloomberg Television; Bravo; Discovery Life Channel; Disney XD; DMX Music; ESPN Classic; ESPNews; FOX College Sports Central; FOX College Sports Pacific; Fox Sports 1; FXM; FYI; Golf Channel; Great American Country; GSN; History International; HITS (Headend In The Sky); IFC; International Television (ITV); NBCSN; Nick Jr.; Nicktoons; Ovation; Sundance TV; TeenNick; WE tv.
Fee: $26.00 monthly.
Pay Service 1
Pay Units: N.A.
Programming (via satellite): Cinemax; Flix; HBO; Showtime; Sundance TV; The Movie Channel.
Fee: $7.50 monthly (Cinemax), $9.95 monthly (HBO), $10.95 monthly (Flix, Showtime, Sundance or TMC).
Digital Pay Service 1
Pay Units: N.A.
Programming (via satellite): Cinemax (multiplexed); Flix; HBO (multiplexed); Showtime (multiplexed); Starz (multiplexed); Starz Encore (multiplexed); The Movie Channel (multiplexed).
Fee: $10.00 monthly (Cinemax), $12.50 monthly (HBO, Starz/Encore or Showtime/TMC).
Video-On-Demand: No

Pay-Per-View
iN DEMAND (delivered digitally); Hot Choice (delivered digitally); Playboy TV (delivered digitally); Spice (delivered digitally); Spice 2 (delivered digitally); ESPN Now (delivered digitally).
Internet Service
Operational: Yes.
Fee: $100.00 installation; $14.95 monthly.
Telephone Service
Digital: Operational
Fee: $36.10 monthly
Miles of Plant: 35.0 (coaxial); 4.0 (fiber optic). Homes passed: 1,214.
City Administrator: Gary Tucker. Chief Engineer: Ron Prothero. Telecommunications Assistant: Kristi Hansman.
Ownership: City of Hawarden.

HAWKEYE—Hawkeye Telephone Co. This cable system has converted to IPTV, 115 West Main St, PO Box 250, Hawkeye, IA 52147-0250. Phones: 800-369-9131; 563-427-3222. Fax: 563-427-7553. E-mail: hawkeyetelinfo@netins.net. Web Site: http://www.hawkeyetelephone.com. ICA: IA5322.
TV Market Ranking: Outside TV Markets (HAWKEYE). Franchise award date: N.A. Franchise expiration date: N.A. Began: January 1, 1985.
Channel capacity: N.A. Channels available but not in use: N.A.
Basic
Subscribers: N.A.
Programming (received off-air): KCRG-TV (ABC, MNT) Cedar Rapids; KGAN (CBS) Cedar Rapids; KIIN (PBS) Iowa City; KWWL (CW, MeTV, NBC) Waterloo.
Programming (via satellite): A&E; AMC; CNN; Discovery Channel; Disney Channel; ESPN; ESPN2; Freeform; HGTV; History; Nickelodeon; Outdoor Channel; Spike TV; TBS; TNT; USA Network; WGN America.
Fee: $10.00 installation; $34.00 monthly; $2.00 converter.
Video-On-Demand: No
Internet Service
Operational: Yes.
Telephone Service
Digital: Operational
Ownership: Hawkeye Telephone Co.

HAWKEYE—Hawkeye Telephone Co. This cable system has converted to IPTV. See HAWKEYE, IA [IA5322]. ICA: IA0298.

HEDRICK—Starwest Inc, 15235 235th St, Milton, IA 52570-8016. Phones: 319-293-6336; 319-397-2283. ICA: IA0270.
TV Market Ranking: Below 100 (HEDRICK). Franchise award date: N.A. Franchise expiration date: N.A. Began: January 1, 1984.
Channel capacity: N.A. Channels available but not in use: N.A.
Basic Service
Subscribers: N.A.
Programming (received off-air): KCCI (CBS, MeTV) Des Moines; KDIN-TV (PBS) Des Moines; WHO-DT (Antenna TV, NBC) Des Moines; WOI-DT (ABC) Ames.
Programming (via satellite): TBS; WGN America.
Internet Service
Operational: No.
Miles of Plant: 4.0 (coaxial); None (fiber optic). Homes passed: 260.
General Manager & Chief Technician: John Stooksberry.
Ownership: Starwest Inc. (MSO).

HINTON—Premier Communications. Now served by SIOUX CENTER, IA [IA0076]. ICA: IA0309.

HOLLAND—Formerly served by CableDirect. No longer in operation. ICA: IA0446.

HOPKINTON—Formerly served by New Century Communications. No longer in operation. ICA: IA0447.

HORNICK—Formerly served by Telepartners. Now served by Wiatel, LAWTON (village), IA [IA0330]. ICA: IA0363.

HOSPERS—HTC Communications, 107 2nd Ave South, PO Box 142, Hospers, IA 51238. Phones: 712-752-8100; 712-752-8500. Fax: 712-752-8280. E-mail: htc@hosperstel.com. Web Site: http://www.hosperstel.com. Also serves Ashton, Ocheyedan, Sheldon & Sibley. ICA: IA0060.
TV Market Ranking: Outside TV Markets (Ashton, HOSPERS, Sibley, Ocheyedan, Sheldon). Franchise award date: N.A. Franchise expiration date: N.A. Began: August 1, 1979.
Channel capacity: N.A. Channels available but not in use: N.A.
Basic Service
Subscribers: 106.
Programming (received off-air): KCAU-TV (ABC) Sioux City; KDLT-TV (Antenna TV, NBC) Sioux Falls; KELO-TV (CBS, MNT) Sioux Falls; KMEG (Azteca America, CBS, Decades) Sioux City; KPTH (FOX, MNT, This TV) Sioux City; KSFY-TV (ABC, CW) Sioux Falls; KSIN-TV (PBS) Sioux City; KTIV (CW, MeTV, NBC) Sioux City; KUSD-TV (PBS) Vermillion.
Programming (via satellite): C-SPAN; CW PLUS; Pop; QVC.
Fee: $25.00 installation; $17.00 monthly.
Expanded Basic Service 1
Subscribers: N.A.
Programming (via satellite): A&E; Animal Planet; Bloomberg Television; BTN; Cartoon Network; CMT; CNN; Comedy Central; Discovery Channel; Disney Channel; ESPN; ESPN Classic; ESPN2; Family Friendly Entertainment; Food Network; Fox News Channel; Fox Sports 1; FOX Sports North; Freeform; FX; Great American Country; Hallmark Channel; HGTV; History; ION Television; Lifetime; MTV; Nickelodeon; Outdoor Channel; OWN: Oprah Winfrey Network; Spike TV; Syfy; TBS; The Weather Channel; TLC; TNT; Travel Channel; Trinity Broadcasting Network (TBN); Turner Classic Movies; TV Land; USA Network; VH1; WGN America.
Fee: $26.95 monthly.
Digital Basic Service
Subscribers: N.A.
Programming (via satellite): DMX Music; Fuse.
Digital Expanded Basic Service
Subscribers: N.A.
Programming (via satellite): UPN; BBC America; Bravo; CBS Sports Network; Cloo; CMT; Discovery Digital Networks; DIY Network; ESPNews; ESPNU; EVINE Live; FOX College Sports Central; FOX College Sports Pacific; FXM; FYI; Golf Channel; GSN; History International; IFC; LMN; National Geographic Channel; NBCSN; Nick Jr.; Nicktoons; RFD-TV; Science Channel; TeenNick.
Fee: $14.95 monthly.
Digital Expanded Basic Service 2
Subscribers: N.A.
Programming (via satellite): A&E HD; AXS TV; BTN HD; ESPN HD; ESPN2 HD; Food

Iowa—Cable Systems

Network HD; FOX Sports North; HD Theater; HGTV HD; HITS (Headend In The Sky); National Geographic Channel HD; Outdoor Channel 2 HD; Universal HD.
Fee: $7.95 monthly (Spanish), $17.95 monthly (HD).
Pay Service 1
Pay Units: N.A.
Programming (via satellite): HBO.
Fee: $10.95 monthly.
Digital Pay Service 1
Pay Units: N.A.
Programming (via satellite): Flix; HBO (multiplexed); Showtime (multiplexed); Starz (multiplexed); Starz Encore (multiplexed); The Movie Channel (multiplexed).
Fee: $7.95 monthly (Encore), $12.95 monthly (HBO, Starz/Encore or Showtime/TMC/Flix).
Video-On-Demand: No
Pay-Per-View
World Wrestling Entertainment Inc.
Internet Service
Operational: Yes, DSL & dial-up.
Broadband Service: In-house.
Fee: $39.95 installation; $32.95-$199.95 monthly.
Telephone Service
Analog: Operational
Miles of Plant: 16.0 (coaxial); None (fiber optic). Homes passed: 3,724.
President & General Manager: David Raak. Chief Technician: Gregg Andringa.
Ownership: HTC Cablecom.

HOSPERS—HTC Communications. Now served by HOSPERS, IA [IA0060]. ICA: IA0275.

HUBBARD—Hubbard Co-op Cable, 306 East Maple St, PO Box 428, Hubbard, IA 50122. Phone: 641-864-2216. Fax: 641-864-2666. E-mail: hubbard@netins.net. ICA: IA0448.
TV Market Ranking: 66 (HUBBARD). Franchise award date: N.A. Franchise expiration date: N.A. Began: January 1, 1985.
Channel capacity: 36 (not 2-way capable). Channels available but not in use: N.A.
Basic Service
Subscribers: 103.
Programming (received off-air): KCCI (CBS, MeTV) Des Moines; KDIN-TV (PBS) Des Moines; KDSM-TV (FOX, The Country Network) Des Moines; WHO-DT (Antenna TV, NBC) Des Moines; WOI-DT (ABC) Ames.
Programming (via satellite): A&E; AMC; CMT; CNN; Discovery Channel; Disney Channel; ESPN; ESPN2; Freeform; History; ION Television; Nickelodeon; Spike TV; TBS; The Weather Channel; TLC; TNT; Travel Channel; USA Network; WGN America.
Fee: $10.00 installation; $40.22 monthly.
Pay Service 1
Pay Units: N.A.
Programming (via satellite): HBO.
Fee: $8.95 monthly.
Video-On-Demand: No
Internet Service
Operational: No, DSL & dial-up.
Telephone Service
Analog: Operational
Miles of Plant: 6.0 (coaxial); None (fiber optic).
Chief Executive Officer & General Manager: David Lowe. Chief Technician: Ken Kissinger.
Ownership: Hubbard Co-op Cable.

HUDSON—Mediacom, 4010 Alexandra Dr, Waterloo, IA 50702. Phones: 800-332-0245; 319-235-2197. Fax: 319-232-7841. Web Site: http://www.mediacomcable.com. ICA: IA0130.
TV Market Ranking: 65 (HUDSON). Channel capacity: N.A. Channels available but not in use: N.A.
Basic Service
Subscribers: 454.
Fee: $51.45 monthly.
Ownership: Mediacom LLC (MSO).

HUMESTON—Formerly served by B & L Technologies LLC. No longer in operation. ICA: IA0268.

HUXLEY—Huxley Communications Corp, 102 North Main Ave, PO Box 70, Huxley, IA 50124-0070. Phones: 515-597-2212; 800-231-4922; 515-597-2281. Fax: 515-597-2899. E-mail: huxtel@huxcomm.net. Web Site: http://www.huxcomm.net. Also serves Cambridge, Elkhart & Kelley. ICA: IA0595. **Note:** This system is an overbuild.
TV Market Ranking: 66 (Cambridge, Elkhart, HUXLEY, Kelley).
Channel capacity: N.A. Channels available but not in use: N.A.
Basic Service
Subscribers: 111.
Programming (received off-air): KCCI (CBS, MeTV) Des Moines; KDSM-TV (FOX, The Country Network) Des Moines; WHO-DT (Antenna TV, NBC) Des Moines; WOI-DT (ABC) Ames.
Programming (via satellite): A&E; AMC; Animal Planet; Cartoon Network; CMT; CNBC; CNN; Comedy Central; Cooking Channel; Discovery Channel; Disney Channel; Disney XD; DIY Network; E! HD; ESPN; ESPN Classic; ESPN2; ESPNews; Food Network; Fox News Channel; Fox Sports 1; FOX Sports Midwest; Freeform; FX; FXM; Golf Channel; Hallmark Channel; HGTV; History; HLN; ION Television; Lifetime; MSNBC; MTV; Nickelodeon; Outdoor Channel; RFD-TV; Spike TV; TBS; The Weather Channel; TLC; TNT; Travel Channel; Trinity Broadcasting Network (TBN); truTV; Turner Classic Movies; TV Land; USA Network; VH1; WGN America.
Fee: $30.00 installation; $70.00 monthly.
Digital Basic Service
Subscribers: N.A.
Programming (via satellite): BBC America; Bloomberg Television; Bravo; Discovery Digital Networks; Disney XD; DMX Music; ESPN Classic; ESPN2; ESPNews; EVINE Live; FOX College Sports Central; FOX College Sports Pacific; Fox Sports 1; Fuse; FXM; FYI; Golf Channel; Great American Country; GSN; HGTV; History; History International; IFC; INSP; International Television (ITV); LMN; National Geographic Channel; NBCSN; Nick Jr.; Nicktoons; Outdoor Channel; Ovation; Sundance TV; TeenNick; The Word Network; Trinity Broadcasting Network (TBN); Turner Classic Movies; WE tv.
Pay Service 1
Pay Units: N.A.
Programming (via satellite): Cinemax (multiplexed); HBO (multiplexed); Showtime (multiplexed); Starz (multiplexed); Starz Encore (multiplexed).
Fee: $10.00 monthly (Cinemax, Showtime or Starz/Encore), $15.00 monthly (HBO).
Digital Pay Service 1
Pay Units: N.A.
Programming (via satellite): Cinemax (multiplexed); HBO (multiplexed); Showtime (multiplexed); Starz (multiplexed); Starz Encore (multiplexed); The Movie Channel.
Fee: $10.00 monthly (Cinemax, Showtime or Starz/Encore), $15.00 monthly (HBO).
Video-On-Demand: Planned
Pay-Per-View
Playboy TV (delivered digitally); Fresh (delivered digitally); Shorteez (delivered digitally); ESPN Now (delivered digitally); Sports PPV (delivered digitally); iN DEMAND (delivered digitally).
Internet Service
Operational: No, DSL.
Telephone Service
Analog: Operational
Homes passed: 977.
General Manager: Gary Clark. Operations Director: Terry Ferguson. Plant Manager: Brant Strumpfer.
Ownership: Huxley Communications Corp. (MSO).

INDEPENDENCE—Independence Light & Power Telecommunications, 700 7th Ave Northeast, PO Box 754, Independence, IA 50644-0754. Phones: 319-332-3880; 319-332-0100. Fax: 319-332-0101. E-mail: darrel@indytel.com. Web Site: http://www.indytel.com. ICA: IA0591. **Note:** This system is an overbuild.
TV Market Ranking: 65 (INDEPENDENCE). Franchise award date: N.A. Franchise expiration date: N.A. Began: May 1, 2000.
Channel capacity: N.A. Channels available but not in use: N.A.
Basic Service
Subscribers: 1,807.
Programming (received off-air): KCRG-TV (ABC, MNT) Cedar Rapids; KFXA (FOX, The Country Network) Cedar Rapids; KGAN (CBS) Cedar Rapids; KPXR-TV (ION) Cedar Rapids; KRIN (PBS) Waterloo; KWKB (The Works, This TV) Iowa City; KWWF (Untamed Sports TV) Waterloo; KWWL (CW, MeTV, NBC) Waterloo.
Programming (via satellite): C-SPAN; C-SPAN 2; EWTN Global Catholic Network; Nicktoons; Pop; QVC; The Weather Channel; Trinity Broadcasting Network (TBN); WGN America.
Fee: $20.00 installation; $20.95 monthly.
Expanded Basic Service 1
Subscribers: N.A.
Programming (via satellite): A&E; AMC; Animal Planet; BTN; Cartoon Network; CMT; CNBC; CNN; Comcast SportsNet Chicago; Comedy Central; Discovery Channel; Disney Channel; DIY Network; E! HD; ESPN Classic; ESPN2; Food Network; Fox News Channel; Fox Sports 1; Freeform; FX; Golf Channel; GSN; Hallmark Channel; HGTV; History; HLN; Lifetime; MoviePlex; MTV; National Geographic Channel; NFL Network; Outdoor Channel; RFD-TV; Spike TV; Syfy; TBS; TLC; TNT; Travel Channel; truTV; Turner Classic Movies; TV Land; USA Network; VH1; WE tv.
Fee: $27.95 monthly.
Digital Basic Service
Subscribers: 444.
Programming (via satellite): AXS TV; BBC America; Bloomberg Television; BTN HD; Destination America; Discovery Kids Channel; Discovery Life Channel; Disney XD; DMX Music; ESPN HD; ESPN2 HD; ESPNews; ESPNU; FXM; FYI; HD Theater; History; International Television (ITV); Investigation Discovery; LMN; MTV Classic; MTV Hits; MTV2; NBCSN; Nick Jr.; OWN: Oprah Winfrey Network; Science Channel; TeenNick; VH1 Country; VH1 Soul.
Fee: $16.00 monthly.
Pay Service 1
Pay Units: N.A.
Programming (via satellite): Cinemax (multiplexed); HBO (multiplexed); Starz; Starz Encore.
Fee: $1.75 monthly (Encore), $6.95 monthly (Starz), $12.95 monthly (HBO).
Digital Pay Service 1
Pay Units: N.A.
Programming (via satellite): Cinemax (multiplexed); Cinemax HD; HBO (multiplexed); HBO HD; Showtime (multiplexed); Starz (multiplexed); Starz Encore (multiplexed); Sundance TV; The Movie Channel (multiplexed).
Fee: $7.95 monthly (Starz/Encore), $12.95 monthly (Cinemax, HBO or Showtime/TMC/Sundance).
Video-On-Demand: No
Pay-Per-View
iN DEMAND (delivered digitally); Fresh (delivered digitally); Shorteez (delivered digitally); Playboy TV (delivered digitally).
Internet Service
Operational: Yes. Began: May 1, 2001.
Broadband Service: In-house.
Fee: $50.00 installation; $31.95 monthly.
Telephone Service
Analog: Not Operational
Digital: Operational
General Manager: Darrel L. Wenzel. Chief Technician: Ron Curry. Office Manager: Linda Kress. Chairperson: Jerry Stelter.
Ownership: Independence Light & Power Telecommunications.

INDEPENDENCE—Mediacom, 4010 Alexandra Dr, Waterloo, IA 50702. Phones: 800-332-0245; 319-235-2197. Fax: 319-232-7841. Web Site: http://www.mediacomcable.com. ICA: IA0059.
TV Market Ranking: 65 (INDEPENDENCE). Franchise award date: April 23, 1979. Franchise expiration date: N.A. Began: May 1, 1986.
Channel capacity: N.A. Channels available but not in use: N.A.
Basic Service
Subscribers: 164.
Programming (received off-air): KCRG-TV (ABC, MNT) Cedar Rapids; KFXA (FOX, The Country Network) Cedar Rapids; KGAN (CBS) Cedar Rapids; KPXR-TV (ION) Cedar Rapids; KRIN (PBS) Waterloo; KWKB (The Works, This TV) Iowa City; KWWL (CW, MeTV, NBC) Waterloo.
Programming (via satellite): TBS.
Fee: $40.95 installation; $43.00 monthly.
Expanded Basic Service 1
Subscribers: N.A.
Programming (via satellite): A&E; AMC; Animal Planet; BET; Bravo; Cartoon Network; CMT; CNBC; CNN; Comedy Cen-

Cable Systems—Iowa

tral; C-SPAN; C-SPAN 2; Discovery Channel; Disney Channel; E! HD; ESPN; ESPN2; EWTN Global Catholic Network; Food Network; Fox News Channel; Fox Sports 1; FOX Sports Midwest; Freeform; FX; Golf Channel; Hallmark Channel; HGTV; History; HLN; Lifetime; MoviePlex; MSNBC; MTV; NBC Universo; Nickelodeon; Pop; QVC; Spike TV; Syfy; The Weather Channel; TLC; TNT; Travel Channel; Trinity Broadcasting Network (TBN); truTV; Turner Classic Movies; TV Land; USA Network; VH1; WE tv; WGN America.
Fee: $60.00 installation; $7.04 monthly.
Digital Basic Service
Subscribers: N.A.
Programming (via satellite): BBC America; Bloomberg Television; Discovery Digital Networks; Disney XD; DMX Music; Fuse; FXM; FYI; GSN; History International; IFC; LMN; National Geographic Channel; NBCSN; Nick Jr.; Outdoor Channel; Ovation; Sundance TV; TeenNick.
Digital Pay Service 1
Pay Units: N.A.
Programming (via satellite): Cinemax (multiplexed); HBO (multiplexed); Showtime (multiplexed); Starz (multiplexed); Starz Encore (multiplexed); The Movie Channel (multiplexed).
Fee: $8.95 monthly (each).
Video-On-Demand: Yes
Pay-Per-View
Vubiquity Inc. (delivered digitally); Shorteez (delivered digitally); Fresh (delivered digitally); Playboy TV (delivered digitally); Pleasure (delivered digitally); ETC (delivered digitally); ESPN Now (delivered digitally); Sports PPV (delivered digitally).
Internet Service
Operational: Yes.
Subscribers: 185.
Broadband Service: Mediacom High Speed Internet.
Telephone Service
Digital: Operational
Subscribers: 88.
Miles of Plant: 64.0 (coaxial); 76.0 (fiber optic). Homes passed: 3,118.
Regional Vice President: Doug Frank. General Manager: Doug Nix. Technical Operations Director: Greg Nank. Marketing Coordinator: Joni Lindauer.
Ownership: Mediacom LLC (MSO).

INWOOD—Alliance Communications. Now served by GARRETSON, SD [SD0016]. ICA: IA0449.

IONIA—Formerly served by Mid-American Cable Systems. No longer in operation. ICA: IA0450.

IOWA CITY—Mediacom, 6300 Council St NE, Ste A, Cedar Rapids, IA 52402. Phones: 800-332-0245; 319-393-1914; 319-395-9699. Fax: 319-393-7017. Web Site: http://www.mediacomcable.com. Also serves Coralville, Hills & University Heights. ICA: IA0628.
TV Market Ranking: 65 (Coralville, Hills, IOWA CITY, University Heights).
Channel capacity: N.A. Channels available but not in use: N.A.
Basic Service
Subscribers: 13,729. Commercial subscribers: 36.
Fee: $41.99 installation; $58.00 monthly.
Internet Service
Operational: Yes.
Subscribers: 15,898.
Broadband Service: Mediacom High Speed Internet.
Telephone Service
Digital: Operational
Subscribers: 4,552.
Miles of Plant: 697.0 (coaxial); 75.0 (fiber optic). Homes passed: 43,534.
Ownership: Mediacom LLC (MSO).

IOWA FALLS—Mediacom, 4010 Alexandra Dr, Waterloo, IA 50702. Phone: 319-235-2197. Fax: 319-232-7841. Web Site: http://www.mediacomcable.com. Also serves Ackley. ICA: IA0053.
TV Market Ranking: Outside TV Markets (Ackley, IOWA FALLS). Franchise award date: October 12, 1979. Franchise expiration date: N.A. Began: N.A.
Channel capacity: N.A. Channels available but not in use: N.A.
Basic Service
Subscribers: 1,182.
Programming (received off-air): KCCI (CBS, MeTV) Des Moines; KCRG-TV (ABC, MNT) Cedar Rapids; KCWI-TV (CW) Ames; KDIN-TV (PBS) Des Moines; KDSM-TV (FOX, The Country Network) Des Moines; KFPX-TV (ION) Newton; KFXA (FOX, The Country Network) Cedar Rapids; KGAN (CBS) Cedar Rapids; KPXR-TV (ION) Cedar Rapids; KWKB (The Works, This TV) Iowa City; KWWL (CW, MeTV, NBC) Waterloo; WHO-DT (Antenna TV, NBC) Des Moines; WOI-DT (ABC) Ames.
Programming (via satellite): C-SPAN; Pop; QVC; WGN America.
Fee: $40.95 installation; $43.00 monthly.
Expanded Basic Service 1
Subscribers: N.A.
Programming (via satellite): A&E; AMC; Animal Planet; Bravo; Cartoon Network; CMT; CNBC; CNN; Comcast SportsNet Chicago; Comedy Central; C-SPAN 2; Discovery Channel; Disney Channel; E! HD; ESPN; ESPN2; EWTN Global Catholic Network; Food Network; Fox News Channel; Fox Sports 1; Freeform; FX; Hallmark Channel; HGTV; History; HLN; Lifetime; MSNBC; Nickelodeon; Spike TV; Syfy; TBS; The Weather Channel; TLC; TNT; Travel Channel; Trinity Broadcasting Network (TBN); truTV; Turner Classic Movies; TV Land; USA Network; VH1; WE tv.
Fee: $29.76 monthly.
Digital Basic Service
Subscribers: N.A.
Programming (via satellite): BBC America; Bloomberg Television; Discovery Digital Networks; Disney XD; DMX Music; ESPN Classic; ESPNews; Fuse; FXM; FYI; Golf Channel; GSN; History International; IFC; LMN; NBCSN; Nick Jr.; Outdoor Channel; Ovation; TeenNick.
Digital Pay Service 1
Pay Units: N.A.
Programming (via satellite): Cinemax (multiplexed); HBO (multiplexed); Showtime (multiplexed); Starz (multiplexed); Starz Encore (multiplexed); Sundance TV; The Movie Channel (multiplexed).
Fee: $2.10 monthly (Encore), $7.10 monthly (Starz), $12.95 monthly (Cinemax or Showtime), $13.95 monthly (HBO).
Video-On-Demand: Yes
Pay-Per-View
ESPN Now (delivered digitally); ETC (delivered digitally); Playboy TV (delivered digitally); Pleasure (delivered digitally); Fresh (delivered digitally); Shorteez (delivered digitally); Vubiquity Inc. (delivered digitally).

Access the most current data instantly
www.warren-news.com/factbook.htm

Internet Service
Operational: Yes.
Broadband Service: Mediacom High Speed Internet.
Fee: $55.95 monthly.
Telephone Service
Analog: Not Operational
Digital: Not Operational
Digital: Operational
Miles of Plant: 81.0 (coaxial); 56.0 (fiber optic). Homes passed: 3,663.
Regional Vice President: Doug Frank. General Manager: Doug Nix. Technical Operations Director: Greg Nank. Marketing Director: Steve Schuh. Marketing Coordinator: Joni Lindauer.
Ownership: Mediacom LLC (MSO).

IRETON—Premier Communications. Now served by SIOUX CENTER, IA [IA0076]. ICA: IA0451.

IRWIN—Mutual Communications Services, 801 19th St, PO Box 311, Harlan, IA 51537. Phone: 712-744-3131. Fax: 712-744-3100. E-mail: fmctc@fmctc.com. Web Site: http://www.farmersmutualcoop.com. Also serves Corley, Defiance, Earling, Hancock, Jacksonville, Kirkman, Manilla, Panama, Tennant & Westphalia. ICA: IA0302.
TV Market Ranking: 53 (Hancock); Outside TV Markets (Corley, Defiance, IRWIN, Jacksonville, Kirkman, Manilla, Panama, Tennant, Westphalia, Earling). Franchise award date: May 24, 1988. Franchise expiration date: N.A. Began: January 1, 1989.
Channel capacity: 62 (not 2-way capable). Channels available but not in use: N.A.
Basic Service
Subscribers: 802.
Programming (received off-air): KCAU-TV (ABC) Sioux City; KCCI (CBS, MeTV) Des Moines; KETV (ABC, MeTV) Omaha; KHIN (PBS) Red Oak; KMEG (Azteca America, CBS, Decades) Sioux City; KMTV-TV (Antenna TV, CBS, Escape) Omaha; KPTM (Estrella TV, FOX, MNT, This TV) Omaha; KTIV (CW, MeTV, NBC) Sioux City; KXVO (Azteca America, CW) Omaha; KYNE-TV (PBS) Omaha; WHO-DT (Antenna TV, NBC) Des Moines; WOI-DT (ABC) Ames; WOWT (IND, NBC) Omaha.
Programming (via satellite): A&E; AMC; Cartoon Network; CMT; CNN; Comedy Central; C-SPAN; C-SPAN 2; Discovery Channel; Disney Channel; ESPN; ESPN Classic; ESPN2; EWTN Global Catholic Network; Fox News Channel; Freeform; HGTV; History; HLN; Lifetime; LMN; MTV; NASA TV; Nickelodeon; Outdoor Channel; RFD-TV; Spike TV; TBS; The Weather Channel; TLC; TNT; Turner Classic Movies; TV Land; USA Network; VH1; WGN America.
Fee: $20.00 installation; $59.95 monthly.
Pay Service 1
Pay Units: 56.
Programming (via satellite): Cinemax.
Fee: $9.00 monthly.
Pay Service 2
Pay Units: 154.
Programming (via satellite): HBO.
Fee: $10.00 monthly.
Pay Service 3
Pay Units: 25.
Programming (via satellite): Showtime.
Fee: $9.00 monthly.
Internet Service
Operational: Yes.
Subscribers: 43.
Telephone Service
Digital: Operational
Miles of Plant: 40.0 (coaxial); None (fiber optic). Homes passed: 1,381.
Chief Executive Officer: Thomas Conry. General Manager: Kevin Cabbage. Assistant Manager: Dennis Crawford. Central Office Manager: Scott Boatman. Outside Plant Manager: Brad Sunderman. Customer Service Manager: Kathie Bell.
Ownership: Farmers Mutual Cooperative Telephone Co. (Moulton, IA).

JAMAICA—Panora Cooperative Cablevision Assn. Inc. Now served by PANORA, IA [IA0108]. ICA: IA0380.

JEFFERSON—Mediacom. Now served by AMES, IA [IA0008]. ICA: IA0054.

JESUP—Jesup Cablevision, 541 Young St, PO Box 249, Jesup, IA 50648-0249. Phone: 319-827-1151. Fax: 319-827-1110. Web Site: http://www.jtt.net. Also serves Littleton. ICA: IA0116.
TV Market Ranking: 65 (JESUP, Littleton). Franchise award date: January 1, 1982. Franchise expiration date: N.A. Began: December 1, 1982.
Channel capacity: N.A. Channels available but not in use: N.A.
Basic Service
Subscribers: 507.
Programming (received off-air): KCRG-TV (ABC, MNT) Cedar Rapids; KFXA (FOX, The Country Network) Cedar Rapids; KGAN (CBS) Cedar Rapids; KPXR-TV (ION) Cedar Rapids; KRIN (PBS) Waterloo; KWKB (The Works, This TV) Iowa City; KWWF (Untamed Sports TV) Waterloo; KWWL (CW, MeTV, NBC) Waterloo.
Programming (via satellite): A&E; AMC; Animal Planet; Bloomberg Television; BTN; Cartoon Network; CMT; CNBC; CNN; Comedy Central; C-SPAN; C-SPAN 2; Discovery Channel; Disney Channel; DIY Network; E! HD; ESPN; ESPN Classic; ESPN2; ESPNU; EWTN Global Catholic Network; Food Network; Fox News Channel; Fox Sports 1; Freeform; FX; Golf Channel; GSN; Hallmark Channel; HGTV; History; HLN; Lifetime; MoviePlex; MTV; National Geographic Channel; Nickelodeon; Outdoor Channel; Pop; QVC; RFD-TV; Spike TV; Syfy; TBS; The Weather Channel; TLC; TNT; Travel Channel; Trinity Broadcasting Network (TBN); truTV; Turner Classic Movies; TV Land; USA Network; VH1; WE tv; WGN America.
Fee: $18.00 installation; $54.99 monthly; $.75 converter.

2017 Edition   D-257

Iowa—Cable Systems

Digital Basic Service
Subscribers: N.A.
Programming (via satellite): AMC; Bloomberg Television; Boomerang; Bravo; Cartoon Network; Chiller; CMT; CNBC World; CNN; CNN International; Comcast SportsNet Chicago; Comedy Central; Cooking Channel; C-SPAN; C-SPAN 2; Discovery Channel; Disney Channel; Disney XD; DIY Network; E! HD; ESPN; ESPN Classic; ESPN2; ESPNews; ESPNU; EWTN Global Catholic Network; Food Network; Fox News Channel; Fox Sports 1; FOX Sports Midwest; FOX Sports North; FX; FXM; FYI; Golf Channel; Great American Country; GSN; Hallmark Channel; HGTV; History; History International; HLN; HSN; IFC; Lifetime; LMN; MC; MSNBC; MTV; MTV Classic; MTV Hits; MTV Jams; MTV2; National Geographic Channel; NBCSN; Nick 2; Nickelodeon; Nicktoons; Noggin; Outdoor Channel; Oxygen; QVC; RFD-TV; Spike TV; Syfy; TBS; TeenNick; The Weather Channel; TLC; TNT; Travel Channel; Trinity Broadcasting Network (TBN); truTV; Turner Classic Movies; TV Land; USA Network; VH1; WE tv; WGN America.

Digital Expanded Basic Service
Subscribers: N.A.
Programming (via satellite): A&E HD; AXS TV; BTN HD; CNBC HD+; ESPN HD; ESPN2 HD; Food Network HD; FSN HD; FX HD; HGTV HD; History HD; Lifetime HD; National Geographic Channel HD; Outdoor Channel HD; USA Network HD.
Fee: $10.00 monthly.

Pay Service 1
Pay Units: 128.
Programming (via satellite): HBO (multiplexed); Starz; Starz Encore.
Fee: $16.00 installation; $8.50 monthly (Starz/Encore), $10.00 monthly (HBO).

Digital Pay Service 1
Pay Units: N.A.
Programming (via satellite): Cinemax (multiplexed); Flix; HBO (multiplexed); Showtime (multiplexed); Showtime HD; Starz (multiplexed); Starz Encore (multiplexed); Starz HD; The Movie Channel (multiplexed); The Movie Channel HD.
Fee: $10.50 monthly (Starz/Encore), $12.50 monthly (Showtime/TMC/Flix), $15.50 monthly (Cinemax/HBO).

Internet Service
Operational: No, DSL.

Telephone Service
Analog: Operational
Miles of Plant: 20.0 (coaxial); None (fiber optic). Homes passed: 1,800.
President: Robert Bloes. General Manager: Robert Venem. Chief Technician: Ben Wehrspann.
Ownership: Jesup Farmer's Mutual Telephone Co.

JOICE (village)—Formerly served by Westcom. No longer in operation. ICA: IA0452.

KANAWHA—Comm1. Formerly [IA0229]. This cable system has converted to IPTV, 105 South Main, PO Box 20, Kanawha, IA 50447. Phones: 800-469-3772; 641-762-3772. Fax: 641-762-8201. E-mail: comm1net@comm1net.net. Web Site: http://home.comm1net.net. Also serves Corwith & Klemme. ICA: IA5095.
Channel capacity: N.A. Channels available but not in use: N.A.

Digital Basic Service
Subscribers: 584.
Fee: $47.00 installation; $54.95 monthly. Includes 100+ channels plus 45 music channels.

Cinemax
Subscribers: N.A.
Fee: $12.95 monthly. Includes 8 channels.

HBO
Subscribers: N.A.
Fee: $12.95 monthly. Includes 6 channels.

Showtime/TMC
Subscribers: N.A.
Fee: $12.95 monthly. Includes 10+ channels.

Starz/Encore
Subscribers: N.A.
Fee: $12.95 monthly. Includes 9+ channels.

Showtime/TMC
Subscribers: N.A.
Fee: $12.95 monthly. Includes 10+ channels.

Video-On-Demand: No

Internet Service
Operational: Yes.
Fee: $39.95-$59.95 monthly.

Telephone Service
Digital: Operational
Chief Executive Officer & Director: Randolph Yeakel.
Ownership: Communications 1 Network Inc.

KANAWHA—Comm1. This cable system has converted to IPTV. See KANAWHA, IA [IA5095]. ICA: IA0229.

KELLERTON—Formerly served by Telnet South LC. Now served by Mediacom, CHARITON, IA [IA0017]. ICA: IA0349.

KELLEY—Huxley Communications Corp. Now served by HUXLEY, IA [IA0595]. ICA: IA0560.

KEOKUK—Mediacom, 6300 Council St NE, Ste A, Cedar Rapids, IA 52402. Phones: 319-393-1914; 319-753-6576 (Burlington office); 319-395-9699. Fax: 319-393-7017. Web Site: http://www.mediacomcable.com. Also serves Hamilton County (portions) & Warsaw, IL; Hamilton County (portions), Lee County (portions) & Montrose, IA. ICA: IA0612.
TV Market Ranking: Below 100 (Hamilton, Hamilton County (portions), Hancock County (portions), KEOKUK, Lee County (portions), Montrose, Warsaw).
Channel capacity: N.A. Channels available but not in use: N.A.

Basic Service
Subscribers: 2,930. Commercial subscribers: 4.
Programming (received off-air): KHQA-TV (ABC, CBS) Hannibal; KIIN (PBS) Iowa City; KTVO (ABC) Kirksville; KWQC-TV (NBC) Davenport; KYOU-TV (FOX) Ottumwa; WGEM-TV (CW, FOX, NBC) Quincy; WQAD-TV (ABC, Antenna TV) Moline; WTJR (Christian TV Network) Quincy.
Programming (via satellite): C-SPAN; C-SPAN 2; ION Television; Pop; QVC; The Weather Channel; WGN America.
Fee: $41.99 installation; $43.00 monthly.

Expanded Basic Service 1
Subscribers: N.A.
Programming (via satellite): A&E; AMC; Animal Planet; BET; Cartoon Network; CMT; CNBC; CNN; Comedy Central; Disney Channel; Disney Channel; E! HD; ESPN; ESPN2; EWTN Global Catholic Network; Food Network; Fox News Channel; Fox Sports 1; FOX Sports Midwest; Freeform; FX; Hallmark Channel; HGTV; History; HLN; INSP; Lifetime; MSNBC; MTV; National Geographic Channel; Nickelodeon; Spike TV;

Syfy; TBS; Telemundo; TLC; TNT; truTV; TV Land; Univision Studios; USA Network; VH1; WE tv.

Digital Basic Service
Subscribers: N.A.
Programming (via satellite): BBC America; Bloomberg Television; Bravo; Discovery Digital Networks; DMX Music; Fuse; FXM; FYI; Golf Channel; GSN; History International; IFC; LMN; NBCSN; Nick Jr.; Outdoor Channel; Ovation; TeenNick; Trinity Broadcasting Network (TBN); Turner Classic Movies.

Digital Pay Service 1
Pay Units: N.A.
Programming (via satellite): Cinemax (multiplexed); Flix; HBO (multiplexed); Showtime (multiplexed); Starz (multiplexed); Starz Encore (multiplexed); Sundance TV; The Movie Channel (multiplexed).

Video-On-Demand: Yes

Pay-Per-View
ETC (delivered digitally); Playboy TV (delivered digitally); Pleasure (delivered digitally); Vubiquity Inc. (delivered digitally); Sports PPV (delivered digitally).

Internet Service
Operational: Yes.
Broadband Service: Mediacom High Speed Internet.
Fee: $45.95 monthly.

Telephone Service
Digital: Operational
Fee: $39.95 monthly
Miles of Plant: 210.0 (coaxial); None (fiber optic). Miles of plant (fiber) included in miles of plant (coax)
Regional Vice President: Doug Frank. Technical Operations Director: Greg Nank. Technical Operations Manager: Joel Hanger. Marketing Director: Steve Schuh.
Ownership: Mediacom LLC (MSO).

KEOSAUQUA—Starwest Inc, 15235 235th St, Milton, IA 52570-8016. Phones: 319-397-2283; 319-293-6336. Also serves Birmingham, Bonaparte, Cantril, Milton & Stockport. ICA: IA0186.
TV Market Ranking: Below 100 (Birmingham, Bonaparte, Cantril, KEOSAUQUA, Stockport).
Channel capacity: N.A. Channels available but not in use: N.A.

Basic Service
Subscribers: N.A.
Fee: $30.00 installation; $14.50 monthly.

Pay Service 1
Pay Units: N.A.
Programming (via satellite): Showtime.
Fee: $14.95 monthly.

Internet Service
Operational: No.
Miles of Plant: 5.0 (coaxial); None (fiber optic). Homes passed: 490.
General Manager & Chief Technician: John Stooksberry.
Ownership: Starwest Inc. (MSO).

KEOTA—Mediacom, 6300 Council St NE, Ste A, Cedar Rapids, IA 52402. Phones: 319-393-1914; 319-395-9699; 800-332-0245. Fax: 319-393-7017. Web Site: http://www.mediacomcable.com. Also serves Sigourney & What Cheer. ICA: IA0632.
TV Market Ranking: Below 100 (KEOTA, Sigourney, What Cheer).
Channel capacity: N.A. Channels available but not in use: N.A.

Basic Service
Subscribers: 472.
Fee: $43.00 monthly.
Ownership: Mediacom LLC (MSO).

KESWICK—Formerly served by Longview Communications. No longer in operation. ICA: IA0359.

KEYSTONE—Keystone Communications, 86 Main St, PO Box 277, Keystone, IA 52249. Phones: 800-568-9584; 319-442-3241. Fax: 319-442-3210. E-mail: keystone@netins.net. Web Site: http://www.keystonecommunications.com. ICA: IA0187.
TV Market Ranking: 65 (KEYSTONE). Franchise award date: N.A. Franchise expiration date: N.A. Began: January 1, 1985.
Channel capacity: N.A. Channels available but not in use: N.A.

Basic Service
Subscribers: 1,845.
Programming (received off-air): KCRG-TV (ABC, MNT) Cedar Rapids; KFXA (FOX, The Country Network) Cedar Rapids; KGAN (CBS) Cedar Rapids; KPXR-TV (ION) Cedar Rapids; KWWL (CW, MeTV, NBC) Waterloo; WOI-DT (ABC) Ames.
Programming (via satellite): Cartoon Network; CMT; CNBC; CNN; Discovery Channel; Disney Channel; ESPN; ESPN2; Freeform; History; HLN; Lifetime; MTV; Nickelodeon; Outdoor Channel; Spike TV; Syfy; TBS; The Weather Channel; TLC; TNT; Turner Classic Movies; USA Network; VH1; WGN America.
Fee: $35.00 installation; $64.95 monthly.

Pay Service 1
Pay Units: N.A.
Programming (via satellite): HBO; Showtime.
Fee: $10.00 monthly (each).

Video-On-Demand: No

Internet Service
Operational: No, DSL.

Telephone Service
Analog: Operational
Miles of Plant: 7.0 (coaxial); 8.0 (fiber optic).
General Manager: Byran Kimm.
Ownership: Keystone Farmers Cooperative Telephone Co.

KINGSLEY—Wiatel, 202 Cedar St, PO Box 38, Lawton, IA 51030-0038. Phones: 800-469-0811; 712-944-5711. Fax: 712-944-5722. E-mail: wiatel@wiatel.com. Web Site: http://www.wiatel.com. ICA: IA0197.
TV Market Ranking: Below 100 (KINGSLEY). Franchise award date: N.A. Franchise expiration date: N.A. Began: February 1, 1984.
Channel capacity: 35 (not 2-way capable). Channels available but not in use: N.A.

Basic Service
Subscribers: 201.
Programming (received off-air): KCAU-TV (ABC) Sioux City; KMEG (Azteca America, CBS, Decades) Sioux City; KSIN-TV (PBS) Sioux City; KTIV (CW, MeTV, NBC) Sioux City.
Programming (via satellite): A&E; Animal Planet; CMT; CNN; C-SPAN; Discovery Channel; Disney Channel; ESPN; ESPN2; Freeform; History; HLN; Lifetime; Nickelodeon; Spike TV; Syfy; TBS; The Weather Channel; TLC; TNT; Turner Classic Movies; USA Network; VH1; WGN America.
Fee: $45.00 installation; $34.99 monthly.

Pay Service 1
Pay Units: N.A.
Programming (via satellite): Cinemax; HBO; Showtime; The Movie Channel.
Fee: $11.00 monthly (Cinemax or HBO), $15.95 monthly (Showtime/TMC).

Video-On-Demand: No

Cable Systems—Iowa

Internet Service
Operational: Yes.
Fee: $60.00 installation; $24.95 monthly.
Telephone Service
None
Miles of Plant: 6.0 (coaxial); None (fiber optic). Homes passed: 440.
Ownership: Western Iowa Telephone (MSO).

KLEMME—Comm1. Now served by KANAWHA, IA [IA5095]. ICA: IA0454.

KNOXVILLE—Mediacom. Now served by HAMILTON, IA [IA0018]. ICA: IA0029.

KNOXVILLE (unincorporated areas)—Formerly served by Telnet South LC. Now served by Mediacom, HAMILTON, IA [IA0018]. ICA: IA0578.

LACONA—Formerly served by Telnet South LC. No longer in operation. ICA: IA0456.

LAKE MILLS—Winnebago Cooperative Telecom Assn, 704 East Main St, Lake Mills, IA 50450-1420. Phones: 641-592-6105; 800-592-6105. Fax: 641-592-6102. E-mail: wcta@wctatel.net. Web Site: http://www.wctatel.net. Also serves Buffalo Center, Forest City & Thompson. ICA: IA0590.
TV Market Ranking: Below 100 (LAKE MILLS, Thompson, Forest City); Outside TV Markets (Buffalo Center).
Channel capacity: N.A. Channels available but not in use: N.A.
Basic Service
Subscribers: 17.
Programming (received off-air): KAAL (ABC, This TV) Austin; KFPX-TV (ION) Newton; KIMT (CBS, MNT) Mason City; KTTC (CW, NBC) Rochester; KXLT-TV (FOX, MeTV) Rochester; KYIN (PBS) Mason City.
Fee: $20.00 installation; $24.95 monthly.
Expanded Basic Service 1
Subscribers: N.A.
Programming (via satellite): A&E; AMC; CMT; CNN; C-SPAN; CW PLUS; Discovery Channel; ESPN; ESPN Classic; ESPN2; Food Network; FOX Sports North; Freeform; HGTV; History; HLN; Lifetime; MTV; Nickelodeon; Spike TV; TBS; The Weather Channel; TLC; TNT; TV Land; USA Network; VH1; WGN America.
Fee: $18.05 monthly.
Video-On-Demand: No
Internet Service
Operational: Yes.
Fee: $39.90 monthly.
Telephone Service
Analog: Operational
Miles of Plant: 41.0 (coaxial); 110.0 (fiber optic). Homes passed: 4,417.
General Manager: Mark Thoma. Senior Network Administrator: Steve Savoy. Plant Administrator: Bob Klebsch.
Ownership: Winnebago Cooperative Telecom Assn. (MSO).

LAKE PARK—Mediacom. Now served by SPIRIT LAKE, IA [IA0036]. ICA: IA0457.

LAKE VIEW—Corn Belt Telephone Co. Now served by WALL LAKE, IA [IA0256]. ICA: IA0159.

LAKOTA—Formerly served by Heck's TV & Cable. No longer in operation. ICA: IA0458.

LAMONI—Formerly served by Telnet South LC. Now served by Mediacom, CHARITON, IA [IA0017]. ICA: IA0143.

LAMONT—Formerly served by Alpine Communications LC. No longer in operation. ICA: IA0459.

LAMOTTE—LaMotte Telephone Co, 400 Pine St, PO Box 8, La Motte, IA 52054. Phone: 563-773-2213. Also serves Bellevue (village), St. Donatus & Zwingle. ICA: IA0624.
TV Market Ranking: Below 100 (Bellevue (village), LAMOTTE, St. Donatus).
Channel capacity: N.A. Channels available but not in use: N.A.
Basic Service
Subscribers: 94.
Fee: $79.95 monthly.
Miles of Plant: None (coaxial); 8.0 (fiber optic). Homes passed: 200.
General Manager: JoAnne Gregorich.
Ownership: LaMotte Telephone Co. Inc.

LANSING—Mediacom. Now served by BOSCOBEL, WI [WI0341]. ICA: IA0177.

LARCHWOOD—Alliance Communications. Now served by GARRETSON, SD [SD0016]. ICA: IA0271.

LATIMER—Formerly served by Latimer/Coulter Cablevision. No longer in operation. ICA: IA0460.

LAURENS—Laurens Municipal Power & Communications, 272 North 3rd St, Laurens, IA 50554-0148. Phones: 712-841-4610; 712-841-4526. Fax: 712-841-4611. E-mail: chadc@laurens-ia.com. Web Site: http://laurens-ia.com. ICA: IA0601. **Note:** This system is an overbuild.
TV Market Ranking: Outside TV Markets (LAURENS).
Channel capacity: N.A. Channels available but not in use: N.A.
Basic Service
Subscribers: 379. Commercial subscribers: 54.
Programming (received off-air): KCAU-TV (ABC) Sioux City; KCCI (CBS, MeTV) Des Moines; KCWI-TV (CW) Ames; KDSM-TV (FOX, The Country Network) Des Moines; KEYC-TV (CBS, FOX) Mankato; KMEG (Azteca America, CBS, Decades) Sioux City; KPTH (FOX, MNT, This TV) Sioux City; KTIN (PBS) Fort Dodge; KTIV (CW, MeTV, NBC) Sioux City; WHO-DT (Antenna TV, NBC) Des Moines; WOI-DT (ABC) Ames.
Programming (via satellite): Pop; QVC; The Weather Channel.
Fee: $30.00 monthly.
Expanded Basic Service 1
Subscribers: N.A.
Programming (via satellite): A&E; AMC; Animal Planet; Cartoon Network; CMT; CNBC; CNN; Comedy Central; C-SPAN; C-SPAN 2; Discovery Channel; Disney Channel; DIY Network; E! HD; ESPN; ESPN Classic; ESPN2; EWTN Global Catholic Network; Food Network; Fox News Channel; Fox Sports 1; FOX Sports North; Freeform; FX; Hallmark Channel; Hallmark Movies & Mysteries; HGTV; History; HLN; INSP; Lifetime; LWS Local Weather Station; MSNBC; MTV; National Geographic Channel; NBCSN; NFL Network; Nickelodeon; Outdoor Channel; Oxygen; Spike TV; Syfy; TBS; TLC; TNT; Travel Channel; truTV; Turner Classic Movies; TV Land; USA Network; VH1; WE tv; WGN America.
Fee: $40.00 monthly.
Digital Basic Service
Subscribers: N.A.
Programming (via satellite): BBC America; Destination America; Discovery Kids Channel; Discovery Life Channel; DMX Music; ESPNews; FXM; FYI; Golf Channel; GSN; History International; IFC; Investigation Discovery; LMN; MTV Classic; MTV2; Nick Jr.; Nicktoons; OWN: Oprah Winfrey Network; Science Channel; TeenNick; VH1 Country.
Digital Pay Service 1
Pay Units: 46.
Programming (via satellite): Cinemax (multiplexed).
Digital Pay Service 2
Pay Units: 54.
Programming (via satellite): HBO (multiplexed).
Digital Pay Service 3
Pay Units: 64.
Programming (via satellite): Starz (multiplexed); Starz Encore (multiplexed).
Internet Service
Operational: Yes.
Broadband Service: Future Net.
Fee: $35.00-$90.00 monthly.
Telephone Service
Digital: Operational
Homes passed: 750.
General Manager: Chad Cleveland. Operations Manager: Tom Schmidt.
Ownership: Laurens Municipal Power & Communications.

LAWLER—Formerly served by Alpine Communications LC. No longer in operation. ICA: IA0462.

LAWTON (village)—Wiatel, 202 Cedar St, PO Box 38, Lawton, IA 51030-0038. Phones: 800-469-0811; 712-944-5711. Fax: 712-944-5722. E-mail: wiatel@wiatel.com. Web Site: http://www.wiatel.com. Also serves Bronson, Hornick, Moville, Oto, Rodney & Smithland. ICA: IA0330.
TV Market Ranking: Below 100 (Bronson, Hornick, LAWTON (VILLAGE), Moville, Oto, Rodney, Smithland). Franchise award date: N.A. Franchise expiration date: N.A. Began: February 1, 1984.
Channel capacity: N.A. Channels available but not in use: N.A.
Basic Service
Subscribers: 970.
Programming (received off-air): KCAU-TV (ABC) Sioux City; KELO-TV (CBS, MNT) Sioux Falls; KETV (ABC, MeTV) Omaha; KMEG (Azteca America, CBS, Decades) Sioux City; KPTH (FOX, MNT, This TV) Sioux City; KSFY-TV (ABC, CW) Sioux Falls; KSIN-TV (PBS) Sioux City; KTIV (CW, MeTV, NBC) Sioux City; KUSD-TV (PBS) Vermillion.
Programming (via satellite): A&E; AMC; Animal Planet; BTN; Cartoon Network; CMT; CNBC; CNN; Comedy Central; C-SPAN; C-SPAN 2; CW PLUS; Discovery Channel; Disney Channel; E! HD; ESPN; ESPN Classic; ESPN2; EWTN Global Catholic Network; Food Network; Fox News Channel; Fox Sports 1; FOX Sports North; Freeform; FX; Golf Channel; Hallmark Channel; HGTV; History; HLN; Lifetime; LMN; MSNBC; MTV; Nickelodeon; Pop; QVC; Spike TV; Syfy; TBS; The Weather Channel; TLC; TNT; Travel Channel; Trinity Broadcasting Network (TBN); truTV; Turner Classic Movies; TV Land; USA Network; VH1; WGN America.
Fee: $25.00 installation; $37.95 monthly.
Digital Basic Service
Subscribers: N.A.
Programming (via satellite): AXS TV; BBC America; BTN HD; Cooking Channel; Destination America; Discovery Channel HD; Discovery Kids Channel; Discovery Life Channel; Disney XD; DIY Network; ESPN HD; ESPN2 HD; ESPNews; ESPNU; FSN Digital Atlantic; FSN Digital Central; FSN Digital Pacific; FXM; FYI; Great American Country; GSN; History International; IFC; Investigation Discovery; MC; MTV Classic; MTV Hits; MTV Jams; MTV2; NBCSN; Nick Jr.; Nicktoons; Outdoor Channel; Outdoor Channel 2 HD; OWN: Oprah Winfrey Network; RFD-TV; Science Channel; TeenNick; VH1 Country; VH1 Soul; WE tv.
Digital Expanded Basic Service
Subscribers: N.A.
Programming (via satellite): Bandamax; De Pelicula; De Pelicula Clasico; ESPN Deportes; Fox Deportes; Ritmoson; Telehit.
Fee: $2.99 monthly.
Digital Pay Service 1
Pay Units: N.A.
Programming (via satellite): Cinemax (multiplexed); Cinemax HD; Flix; HBO (multiplexed); HBO HD; Showtime (multiplexed); Starz (multiplexed); Starz Encore (multiplexed); Starz HD; The Movie Channel (multiplexed).
Fee: $11.95 monthly (Cinemax), 13.95 monthly (Starz/Encore), $14.95 monthly (HBO or Showtime/Flix/TMC).
Video-On-Demand: Yes
Internet Service
Operational: No, DSL & dial-up.
Telephone Service
Analog: Operational
Homes passed: 1,360.
General Manager: Heath Mallory. Marketing & Sales Manager: Pam Clark. Office Manager: Susan Kolker. Operations Manager: Phil Robinson. Chief Technician: Mark Livermore.
Ownership: Western Iowa Telephone (MSO).

LE MARS—Premier Communications. Now served by SIOUX CENTER, IA [IA0076]. ICA: IA0027.

LEDYARD (village)—Formerly served by New Path Communications LC. No longer in operation. ICA: IA0463.

LEHIGH—Lehigh Valley Cooperative Telephone Assn. Formerly LEHIGH, IA [IA0464]. This cable system has converted to IPTV, 9090 Taylor Rd, PO Box 137, Lehigh, IA 50557. Phone: 515-359-2211. Fax: 515-359-2424. E-mail: lvcta@lvcta.com. Web Site: http://www.lvcta.net. Also serves Callender, Dayton, Harcourt & Otho. ICA: IA5319.
TV Market Ranking: 66 (Harcourt, LEHIGH); Outside TV Markets (Callender, Otho). Franchise award date: N.A. Franchise ex-

Iowa—Cable Systems

piration date: N.A. Began: September 1, 1984.
Channel capacity: N.A. Channels available but not in use: N.A.
Economy
Subscribers: 584.
Programming (received off-air): KCCI (CBS, MeTV) Des Moines; KCWI-TV (CW) Ames; KDIN-TV (PBS) Des Moines; KDSM-TV (FOX, The Country Network) Des Moines; KFPX-TV (ION) Newton; WHO-DT (Antenna TV, NBC) Des Moines; WOI-DT (ABC) Ames.
Programming (via satellite): A&E; AMC; Animal Planet; Cartoon Network; CMT; CNN; CNN International; Discovery Channel; Disney Channel; E! HD; ESPN; ESPN Classic; ESPN2; Food Network; Fox News Channel; FOX Sports Networks; Freeform; FX; Great American Country; Hallmark Channel; HGTV; History; HLN; Lifetime; LMN; MTV; National Geographic Channel; Nickelodeon; OWN: Oprah Winfrey Network; Spike TV; Syfy; TBS; The Weather Channel; TLC; TNT; Travel Channel; Trinity Broadcasting Network (TBN); Turner Classic Movies; TV Land; USA Network; VH1; WGN America.
Fee: $50.00 installation; $30.00 monthly. Includes 22 channels.
Basic
Subscribers: N.A.
Programming (via satellite): BBC America; Destination America; Discovery Kids Channel; DMX Music; ESPN Classic; ESPNews; Fox Sports 1; FSN Digital Atlantic; FSN Digital Central; FSN Digital Pacific; FXM; Golf Channel; GSN; IFC; Investigation Discovery; MTV Hits; MTV2; NBCSN; Nick Jr.; Nicktoons; Outdoor Channel; OWN: Oprah Winfrey Network; Science Channel; TeenNick; TV Land; VH1 Soul; WE tv.
Fee: $52.00 monthly. Includes 84 channels.
Extended Basic
Subscribers: N.A.
Programming (via satellite): Cinemax (multiplexed); Flix; HBO (multiplexed); Showtime (multiplexed); Starz (multiplexed); Starz Encore (multiplexed); The Movie Channel (multiplexed).
Fee: $61.00 monthly. Includes 143 channels.
Cinemax
Subscribers: N.A.
Fee: $14.95 monthly.
HBO
Subscribers: N.A.
Fee: $15.95 monthly.
Showtime/TMC/Flix
Subscribers: N.A.
Fee: $14.95 monthly.
Starz/Encore
Subscribers: N.A.
Fee: $14.95 monthly.
Internet Service
Operational: Yes.
Fee: $25.95-$55.95 monthly.
Telephone Service
Digital: Operational
Fee: $17.00 monthly.
Chief Executive Officer & General Manager: James Suchan.
Ownership: Lehigh Valley Cooperative Telephone Association.

LEHIGH—Lehigh Valley Cooperative Telephone Assn. This cable system has converted to IPTV. See LEHIGH, IA [IA5318]. ICA: IA0464.

LENOX—Lenox Municipal Cablevision, 205 South Main St, Lenox, IA 50851-0096. Phone: 641-333-2550. Fax: 641-333-2582.
Web Site: http://lenoxia.com/cityoflenox.htm. ICA: IA0180.
TV Market Ranking: Outside TV Markets (LENOX). Franchise award date: N.A. Franchise expiration date: N.A. Began: September 1, 1976.
Channel capacity: N.A. Channels available but not in use: N.A.
Basic Service
Subscribers: 286.
Programming (received off-air): KCCI (CBS, MeTV) Des Moines; KDIN-TV (PBS) Des Moines; KDMI (MNT, This TV) Des Moines; KDSM-TV (FOX, The Country Network) Des Moines; KETV (ABC, MeTV) Omaha; KMTV-TV (Antenna TV, CBS, Escape) Omaha; KPTM (Estrella TV, FOX, MNT, This TV) Omaha; WHO-DT (Antenna TV, NBC) Des Moines; WOI-DT (ABC) Ames; WOWT (IND, NBC) Omaha; allband FM.
Programming (via satellite): A&E; AMC; CMT; CNN; Comedy Central; Discovery Channel; Disney Channel; ESPN; ESPN2; Freeform; History; Lifetime; LMN; MTV; Nickelodeon; Spike TV; TBS; The Weather Channel; TNT; TV Land; USA Network; VH1; WGN America.
Fee: $30.00 installation; $30.00 monthly.
Expanded Basic Service 1
Subscribers: N.A.
Fee: $20.00 monthly.
Digital Basic Service
Subscribers: 29.
Fee: $5.00 monthly.
Digital Expanded Basic Service
Subscribers: N.A.
Fee: $37.00 monthly.
Pay Service 1
Pay Units: N.A.
Programming (via satellite): Cinemax; HBO.
Fee: $10.00 monthly (each).
Internet Service
Operational: No.
Telephone Service
Digital: Operational
Subscribers: 200.
Miles of Plant: None (coaxial); 100.0 (fiber optic). Homes passed: 707.
General Manager: Keith Bennett. Cable Manager: David Ferris. Chief Technician: John Borland.
Ownership: Lenox Municipal Cablevision.

LIBERTYVILLE—Formerly served by Westcom. No longer in operation. ICA: IA0570.

LISCOMB—Formerly served by New Path Communications LC. No longer in operation. ICA: IA0571.

LITTLE ROCK—Premier Communications, 339 1st Ave Northeast, PO Box 200, Sioux Center, IA 51250. Phones: 800-741-8351; 712-722-3451. Fax: 712-722-1113. Web Site: http://www.mypremieronline.com. ICA: IA0292.
TV Market Ranking: Outside TV Markets (LITTLE ROCK). Franchise award date: N.A. Franchise expiration date: N.A. Began: January 1, 1984.
Channel capacity: N.A. Channels available but not in use: N.A.
Basic Service
Subscribers: N.A.
Programming (received off-air): KCAU-TV (ABC) Sioux City; KDLT-TV (Antenna TV, NBC) Sioux Falls; KELO-TV (CBS, MNT) Sioux Falls; KPTH (FOX, MNT, This TV) Sioux City; KSFY-TV (ABC, CW) Sioux Falls; KSIN-TV (PBS) Sioux City; KTIV (CW, MeTV, NBC) Sioux City.
Programming (via satellite): A&E; CNN; C-SPAN; Discovery Channel; Disney Channel; ESPN; ESPN2; Fox News Channel; Fox Sports 1; Freeform; Great American Country; Hallmark Channel; HGTV; History; HLN; Lifetime; Nickelodeon; Spike TV; TBS; The Weather Channel; TLC; TNT; Trinity Broadcasting Network (TBN); TV Land; USA Network; WGN America.
Fee: $16.00 installation; $29.00 monthly.
Pay Service 1
Pay Units: N.A.
Programming (via satellite): HBO; Showtime.
Fee: $16.00 installation; $8.95 monthly (each).
Video-On-Demand: No
Internet Service
Operational: Yes, DSL & dial-up.
Broadband Service: Premier Internet.
Fee: $50.00 installation; $47.50 monthly.
Telephone Service
None
Miles of Plant: 4.0 (coaxial); None (fiber optic). Homes passed: 253.
Chief Executive Officer: Douglas A. Boone. Chief Technician: Leslie Sybesma. Marketing Director: Scott Te Stroete. Technology & Product Development Manager: Frank Bulk.
Ownership: Premier Communications Inc. (MSO).

LITTLE SIOUX—Formerly served by TelePartners. No longer in operation. ICA: IA0333.

LITTLETON—Formerly served by Farmers Mutual Cooperative Telephone Co. Now served by Jesup Cablevision, JESUP, IA [IA0116]. ICA: IA0467.

LIVERMORE—Livermore Cable, 806 Okoboji Ave, PO Box 163, Milford, IA 51351. Phones: 855-722-3450; 712-338-4967. Fax: 712-338-4719. E-mail: support@milfordcable.net. Web Site: http://milfordcomm.net. ICA: IA0320.
TV Market Ranking: Outside TV Markets (LIVERMORE). Franchise award date: November 2, 1980. Franchise expiration date: N.A. Began: February 1, 1981.
Channel capacity: N.A. Channels available but not in use: N.A.
Digital Basic Service
Subscribers: 91.
Programming (received off-air): KCCI (CBS, MeTV) Des Moines; KCWI-TV (CW) Ames; KDMI (MNT, This TV) Des Moines; KDSM-TV (FOX, The Country Network) Des Moines; KEYC-TV (CBS, FOX) Mankato; KTIN (PBS) Fort Dodge; WHO-DT (Antenna TV, NBC) Des Moines; WOI-DT (ABC) Ames.
Programming (via satellite): C-SPAN; C-SPAN 2; EWTN Global Catholic Network; HSN; QVC; The Weather Channel; Trinity Broadcasting Network (TBN).
Fee: $35.00 installation; $49.92 monthly.
Digital Expanded Basic Service
Subscribers: N.A.
Programming (via satellite): A&E; Animal Planet; Bravo; BTN; Cartoon Network; CMT; CNBC; CNN; Comedy Central; Discovery Channel; DIY Network; ESPN; ESPN2; Food Network; Fox News Channel; Fox Sports 1; FOX Sports North; Freeform; FX; FXM; Great American Country; Hallmark Channel; HGTV; History; ION Television; Lifetime; MSNBC; MTV; National Geographic Channel; Nickelodeon; OWN: Oprah Winfrey Network; Radar Channel; RFD-TV; Spike TV; Syfy; TBS; TLC; TNT; Travel Channel; Turner Classic Movies; TV Land; USA Network; VH1; WGN America.
Fee: $18.50 monthly.
Digital Pay Service 1
Pay Units: N.A.
Programming (via satellite): Cinemax; HBO; Showtime; Starz; Starz Encore.
Fee: $2.14 monthly (Encore), $9.63 monthly (Cinemax or Starz/Encore), $10.17 monthly (Showtime), $10.70 monthly (HBO).
Video-On-Demand: No
Internet Service
Operational: Yes.
Broadband Service: Milford Cable.
Fee: $25.95-$45.00 monthly.
Telephone Service
None
Miles of Plant: 5.0 (coaxial); None (fiber optic). Homes passed: 186.
General Manager: Kirk Hundertmark.
Ownership: Milford Communications.

LOCKRIDGE—Formerly served by Westcom. No longer in operation. ICA: IA0572.

LOGAN—Long Lines. Now served by SALIX, IA [IA0510]. ICA: IA0155.

LOHRVILLE—Formerly served by Tele-Services Ltd. No longer in operation. ICA: IA0468.

LOST NATION—LN Satellite. Formerly [IA0279]. This cable system has converted to IPTV, 304 Long Ave, PO Box 97, Lost Nation, IA 52254. Phone: 563-678-2470. Fax: 563-678-2300. E-mail: lnation@netins.net. Web Site: http://www.lnetelco.com. Also serves Elwood & Oxford Junction. ICA: IA5107.
TV Market Ranking: 60 (Elwood, LOST NATION, Oxford Junction).
Channel capacity: N.A. Channels available but not in use: N.A.
Digital Light
Subscribers: 133.
Fee: $24.95 monthly.
Digital Basic
Subscribers: 126.
Fee: $49.95 monthly.
Digital Extended
Subscribers: 59.
Fee: $56.95 monthly.
HD
Subscribers: N.A.
Fee: $10.00 monthly.
Cinemax
Subscribers: N.A.
Fee: $12.00 monthly.
HBO
Subscribers: N.A.
Fee: $15.00 monthly.
Playboy
Subscribers: N.A.
Fee: $15.00 monthly.
Showtime
Subscribers: N.A.
Fee: $15.00 monthly.
Starz/Encore
Subscribers: N.A.
Fee: $12.00 monthly.
Video-On-Demand: No
Internet Service
Operational: Yes.
Fee: $34.95-$99.95 monthly.
Telephone Service
Digital: Operational
Fee: $14.00 monthly
General Manager: Glenn Short.
Ownership: Lost Nation-Elwood Telephone Co.

Cable Systems—Iowa

LOST NATION—Lost Nation-Elwood Telephone Co. This cable system has converted to IPTV. See LOST NATION, IA [IA5107]. ICA: IA0279.

LU VERNE—Signal Inc, PO Box 435, West Bend, IA 50597. Phone: 515-887-4591. E-mail: msignal@ncn.net. ICA: IA0342.
TV Market Ranking: Outside TV Markets (LU VERNE). Franchise award date: N.A. Franchise expiration date: N.A. Began: September 1, 1968.
Channel capacity: N.A. Channels available but not in use: N.A.
Basic Service
Subscribers: 35.
Programming (received off-air): KAAL (ABC, This TV) Austin; KCCI (CBS, MeTV) Des Moines; KCWI-TV (CW) Ames; KDIN-TV (PBS) Des Moines; KDSM-TV (FOX, The Country Network) Des Moines; KEYC-TV (CBS, FOX) Mankato; KIMT (CBS, MNT) Mason City; KTTC (CW, NBC) Rochester; WHO-DT (Antenna TV, NBC) Des Moines; WOI-DT (ABC) Ames; allband FM.
Fee: $50.00 installation; $64.49 monthly.
Pay Service 1
Pay Units: 1.
Programming (via satellite): HBO.
Miles of Plant: 3.0 (coaxial); None (fiber optic). Homes passed: 110.
General Manager: Michael Steil.
Ownership: Signal Inc.

LUCAS—Formerly served by Telnet South LC. Now served by Mediacom, CHARITON, IA [IA0017]. ICA: IA0573.

LUXEMBURG—New Century Communications, 3588 Kennebec Dr, Eagan, MN 55122-1001. Phone: 651-688-2623. Fax: 651-688-2624. Also serves Holy Cross & New Vienna. ICA: IA0554.
TV Market Ranking: Below 100 (Holy Cross, LUXEMBURG, New Vienna). Franchise award date: February 6, 1989. Franchise expiration date: N.A. Began: November 14, 1989.
Channel capacity: N.A. Channels available but not in use: N.A.
Basic Service
Subscribers: 134.
Programming (received off-air): KCRG-TV (ABC, MNT) Cedar Rapids; KFXA (FOX, The Country Network) Cedar Rapids; KGAN (CBS) Cedar Rapids; KIIN (PBS) Iowa City; KPXR-TV (ION) Cedar Rapids; KWKB (The Works, This TV) Iowa City; KWWL (CW, MeTV, NBC) Waterloo.
Programming (via satellite): A&E; AMC; CNN; Discovery Channel; Disney Channel; DIY Network; ESPN; ESPN2; EWTN Global Catholic Network; Freeform; History; HLN; Lifetime; MTV; Nickelodeon; QVC; Spike TV; TBS; The Weather Channel; TLC; TNT; Turner Classic Movies; USA Network; VH1; WGN America.
Fee: $30.00 installation; $32.95 monthly.
Pay Service 1
Pay Units: 17.
Programming (via satellite): Cinemax.
Fee: $10.00 monthly.
Pay Service 2
Pay Units: 15.
Programming (via satellite): HBO.
Fee: $10.00 monthly.
Pay Service 3
Pay Units: 8.
Programming (via satellite): Showtime.
Fee: $10.00 monthly.
Video-On-Demand: No

Internet Service
Operational: No.
Telephone Service
None
Miles of Plant: 19.0 (coaxial); None (fiber optic). Homes passed: 378.
Executive Vice President: Marty Walch. General Manager & Chief Technician: Todd Anderson.
Ownership: New Century Communications (MSO).

LYTTON—Formerly served by TelePartners. No longer in operation. ICA: IA0328.

MALCOM—Inter-County Cable Co, PO Box 578, Brooklyn, IA 52211. Phones: 641-522-7000; 641-522-9211. Fax: 641-522-5001. ICA: IA0635.
TV Market Ranking: Below 100 (MALCOM).
Channel capacity: N.A. Channels available but not in use: N.A.
Basic Service
Subscribers: 76.
Fee: $25.00 installation; $49.00 monthly.
General Manager: Tim Atkinson.
Ownership: Inter-County Cable Co. (MSO).

MALVERN BOROUGH—Rock Port Cablevision, 107 West Opp St, PO Box 147, Rock Port, MO 64482. Phones: 660-744-5311; 877-202-1764; 660-744-2020. E-mail: rptel@rpt.coop. Web Site: http://www.rptel.net. ICA: IA0471.
TV Market Ranking: 53 (MALVERN BOROUGH). Franchise award date: N.A. Franchise expiration date: N.A. Began: January 1, 1985.
Channel capacity: N.A. Channels available but not in use: N.A.
Basic Service
Subscribers: 39.
Programming (received off-air): KETV (ABC, MeTV) Omaha; KHIN (PBS) Red Oak; KMTV-TV (Antenna TV, CBS, Escape) Omaha; KPTM (Estrella TV, FOX, MNT, This TV) Omaha; KXVO (Azteca America, CW) Omaha; KYNE-TV (PBS) Omaha; WOWT (IND, NBC) Omaha.
Programming (via satellite): A&E; CMT; CNN; Discovery Channel; Disney Channel; ESPN; ESPN2; Freeform; HGTV; HLN; Lifetime; Spike TV; Syfy; TBS; TLC; TNT; Trinity Broadcasting Network (TBN); TV Land; USA Network; WGN America.
Fee: $20.00 installation; $31.95 monthly.
Pay Service 1
Pay Units: N.A.
Programming (via satellite): HBO; Showtime.
Fee: $10.95 monthly (each).
Video-On-Demand: No
Internet Service
Operational: No, DSL.
Telephone Service
None
General Manager: Raymond Henagan. Chief Technician: Gary McGuire.
Ownership: Rock Port Telephone Co. (MSO).

MANILLA—Formerly served by Manilla Municipal Cable. Now served by Mutual Communications Services, IRWIN, IA [IA0302]. ICA: IA0202.

MANNING—Manning Municipal Cable TV, 719 3rd St, PO Box 386, Manning, IA 51455. Phone: 712-655-2660. Fax: 712-655-3304. E-mail: info@mmctsu.com. Web Site: http://www.mmctsu.com. ICA: IA0145.
TV Market Ranking: Outside TV Markets (MANNING). Franchise award date: N.A. Franchise expiration date: N.A. Began: October 1, 1982.
Channel capacity: N.A. Channels available but not in use: N.A.
Basic Service
Subscribers: 417.
Programming (received off-air): KCCI (CBS, MeTV) Des Moines; KDIN-TV (PBS) Des Moines; KDSM-TV (FOX, The Country Network) Des Moines; KETV (ABC, MeTV) Omaha; KMTV-TV (Antenna TV, CBS, Escape) Omaha; KPTM (Estrella TV, FOX, MNT, This TV) Omaha; KTVO (ABC) Kirksville; WHO-DT (Antenna TV, NBC) Des Moines; WOI-DT (ABC) Ames; WOWT (IND, NBC) Omaha; allband FM.
Programming (via satellite): A&E; AMC; Animal Planet; CMT; CNN; Comedy Central; Discovery Channel; Disney Channel; Disney XD; ESPN; ESPN Classic; ESPN2; EWTN Global Catholic Network; Food Network; Fox News Channel; Fox Sports 1; FOX Sports Networks; Freeform; FX; Golf Channel; Hallmark Channel; HGTV; History; HLN; Lifetime; MSNBC; MTV; NBCSN; Nickelodeon; Outdoor Channel; Pop; QVC; RFD-TV; Spike TV; Starz Encore Westerns; Syfy; TBS; The Weather Channel; TLC; TNT; Travel Channel; Trinity Broadcasting Network (TBN); Turner Classic Movies; TV Land; USA Network; VH1; WGN America.
Fee: $15.00 installation; $56.95 monthly.
Pay Service 1
Pay Units: N.A.
Programming (via satellite): Cinemax; HBO (multiplexed); Showtime; Starz; The Movie Channel.
Fee: $9.50 monthly (Cinemax or HBO).
Video-On-Demand: No
Internet Service
Operational: Yes.
Fee: $34.95-$79.95 monthly.
Telephone Service
Analog: Operational
Miles of Plant: 18.0 (coaxial); 3.0 (fiber optic). Homes passed: 670.
General Manager: Wendel Kahl.
Ownership: Manning Municipal Communication & TV System Utility.

MAPLETON—Long Lines. Now served by SALIX, IA [IA0510]. ICA: IA0153.

MAQUOKETA—Mediacom, 3900 26th Ave, Moline, IL 61265. Phone: 855-633-4226. Fax: 309-797-2414. Web Site: http://www.mediacomcable.com. ICA: IA0619.
TV Market Ranking: Below 100 (MAQUOKETA).
Channel capacity: N.A. Channels available but not in use: N.A.
Basic Service
Subscribers: 904.
Fee: $43.00 monthly.
Miles of Plant: 57.0 (coaxial); 46.0 (fiber optic). Homes passed: 3,679.
Ownership: Mediacom LLC (MSO).

MARBLE ROCK—Omnitel Communications. Now served by RUDD, IA [IA0503]. ICA: IA0473.

MARCUS—WesTel Systems, 012 East 3rd St, PO Box 330, Remsen, IA 51050. Phones: 800-352-0006; 402-654-3344; 712-786-1181. Fax: 712-786-2400. E-mail: acctinfo@westelsystems.com. Web Site: http://www.westelsystems.com. Also serves Alton, Calumet, Oyens, Peterson, Quimby, Remsen, Sioux Rapids & Sutherland. ICA: IA0171.

TV Market Ranking: Below 100 (Remsen); Outside TV Markets (Alton, Calumet, MARCUS, Oyens, Peterson, Peterson, Quimby, Sioux Rapids, Sutherland). Franchise award date: N.A. Franchise expiration date: N.A. Began: October 1, 1982.
Channel capacity: N.A. Channels available but not in use: N.A.
Basic Service
Subscribers: 232.
Programming (received off-air): KCAU-TV (ABC) Sioux City; KELO-TV (CBS, MNT) Sioux Falls; KMEG (Azteca America, CBS, Decades) Sioux City; KPTH (FOX, MNT, This TV) Sioux City; KSFY-TV (ABC, CW) Sioux Falls; KSIN-TV (PBS) Sioux City; KTIV (CW, MeTV, NBC) Sioux City.
Programming (via satellite): A&E; AMC; Animal Planet; BTN; CMT; CNN; Comedy Central; CW PLUS; Discovery Channel; Disney Channel; DIY Network; ESPN; ESPN Classic; ESPN2; Food Network; Fox News Channel; Fox Sports 1; Freeform; FX; Great American Country; GSN; HGTV; History; Lifetime; MTV; NBCSN; Nickelodeon; Pop; QVC; Spike TV; Syfy; TBS; The Weather Channel; TLC; TNT; Travel Channel; TV Land; USA Network; VH1; WE tv; WGN America.
Fee: $20.00 installation; $39.95 monthly.
Digital Basic Service
Subscribers: N.A.
Programming (via satellite): BBC America; Bloomberg Television; Cloo; CMT; Destination America; Discovery Kids Channel; Discovery Life Channel; Disney XD; DMX Music; ESPN Classic; ESPNews; EVINE Live; Fuse; FXM; FYI; Golf Channel; History International; Investigation Discovery; LMN; MTV Classic; MTV Hits; MTV2; Nick Jr.; Nicktoons; Outdoor Channel; OWN: Oprah Winfrey Network; PBS HD; RFD-TV; Science Channel; TeenNick; The Word Network; Trinity Broadcasting Network (TBN); Turner Classic Movies; VH1 Soul.
Pay Service 1
Pay Units: N.A.
Programming (via satellite): HBO.
Fee: $10.00 installation; $9.95 monthly.
Digital Pay Service 1
Pay Units: N.A.
Programming (via satellite): Cinemax (multiplexed); Flix; HBO (multiplexed); Showtime (multiplexed); Starz (multiplexed); Starz Encore (multiplexed); The Movie Channel (multiplexed).
Video-On-Demand: No
Pay-Per-View
iN DEMAND (delivered digitally).
Internet Service
Operational: Yes.
Telephone Service
Analog: Operational
Miles of Plant: 8.0 (coaxial); None (fiber optic).
Chief Executive Officer: Robert Gannon. General Manager: William Daubendiek II.
Ownership: WesTel Systems (MSO).

MARSHALLTOWN—Mediacom, 2205 Ingersoll Ave, Des Moines, IA 50312. Phone: 515-246-2277. Web Site: http://www.mediacomcable.com. Also serves Green Mountain, Le Grand & Marshall County. ICA: IA0012.
TV Market Ranking: 65 (Marshall County (portions)); Below 100 (Green Mountain, Le Grand, Marshall County (portions)).
Channel capacity: N.A. Channels available but not in use: N.A.
Basic Service
Subscribers: 4,320.
Fee: $50.98 monthly.

2017 Edition

Iowa—Cable Systems

Internet Service
Operational: Yes.
Subscribers: 3,489.
Broadband Service: Mediacom High Speed Internet.
Telephone Service
Digital: Operational
Subscribers: 2,216.
Miles of Plant: 271.0 (coaxial); 94.0 (fiber optic). Homes passed: 14,431.
Vice President, Engineering & Network Development: Chad Ernst.
Ownership: Mediacom LLC (MSO).

MARTELLE—Martelle Communications Co-op, 204 South St, PO Box 128, Martelle, IA 52305-0128. Phones: 319-462-2812; 319-482-2381. Fax: 319-482-3018. E-mail: martelle@martellecom.com. Web Site: http://www.martellecom.com. Also serves Fairview, Morley & Stone City. ICA: IA0262.
TV Market Ranking: 65 (Fairview, MARTELLE, Morley, Stone City). Franchise award date: February 1, 1990. Franchise expiration date: N.A. Began: February 1, 1990.
Channel capacity: N.A. Channels available but not in use: N.A.
Basic Service
Subscribers: N.A.
Programming (received off-air): KCRG-TV (ABC, MNT) Cedar Rapids; KFXA (FOX, The Country Network) Cedar Rapids; KGAN (CBS) Cedar Rapids; KIIN (PBS) Iowa City; KPXR-TV (ION) Cedar Rapids; KWKB (The Works, This TV) Iowa City; KWWL (CW, MeTV, NBC) Waterloo.
Programming (via satellite): A&E; AMC; CMT; CNN; Comedy Central; Discovery Channel; Disney Channel; ESPN; ESPN2; FOX Sports Midwest; Freeform; HGTV; History; National Geographic Channel; Nickelodeon; Spike TV; Syfy; TBS; TLC; TNT; Turner Classic Movies; TV Land; USA Network; WGN America.
Fee: $30.00 installation.
Digital Basic Service
Subscribers: N.A.
Programming (via satellite): A&E; AMC; Animal Planet; Bloomberg Television; Bravo; Cartoon Network; CMT; CNBC; CNN; Comcast SportsNet Chicago; Comedy Central; Discovery Channel; Discovery Kids Channel; Disney Channel; DIY Network; E! HD; ESPN; ESPN2; ESPNews; ESPNU; Food Network; Fox News Channel; Fox Sports 1; Freeform; FX; Golf Channel; Hallmark Channel; HGTV; History; HLN; HSN; Investigation Discovery; Lifetime; MSNBC; MTV; National Geographic Channel; NBCSN; Nickelodeon; Outdoor Channel; OWN: Oprah Winfrey Network; Oxygen; QVC; RFD-TV; Science Channel; Spike TV; Syfy; TBS; TLC; TNT; Travel Channel; Trinity Broadcasting Network (TBN); truTV; Turner Classic Movies; TV Land; USA Network; VH1; WGN America.
Fee: $10.00 converter.
Digital Expanded Basic Service
Subscribers: N.A.
Programming (via satellite): A&E HD; Animal Planet HD; BBC America; Bio HD; Boomerang; Bravo HD; BTN HD; Cartoon Network HD; CMT; CMT HD; CNBC HD+; CNN HD; Comedy Central HD; Destination America; Discovery Channel HD; Disney Channel HD; Disney XD; E! HD; ESPN Classic; ESPNews; EVINE Live; Food Network HD; Fox Business Network; Fox Business Network HD; FOX College Sports Central; FOX College Sports Pacific; Fox News HD; Freeform HD; Fuse; FX HD; FYI; Golf Channel HD; Great American Country; GSN; Hallmark Movie Channel HD; HD Theater; HGTV HD; History HD; History International; HLN HD; Lifetime HD; Lifetime Movie Network HD; MC; MLB Network HD; MTV Classic; MTV Hits; MTV Live; MTV2; National Geographic Channel HD; NFL Network; NFL Network HD; Nick HD; Nick Jr.; Nicktoons; Outdoor Channel HD; Science HD; Spike TV HD; Syfy HD; TBS HD; TLC HD; TNT HD; Travel Channel HD; Universal HD; USA Network HD; Versus HD; VH1 Soul; WGN America HD.
Fee: $22.00 monthly.
Digital Pay Service 1
Pay Units: N.A.
Programming (via satellite): HBO (multiplexed); HBO HD; Showtime (multiplexed); Showtime HD (multiplexed).
Fee: $26.00 - $26.00 monthly (each).
Internet Service
Operational: Yes, DSL.
Telephone Service
Analog: Operational
Miles of Plant: 65.0 (coaxial); None (fiber optic). Homes passed: 1,500.
General Manager: Sandra M. Davis. Plant Manager: Greg Conrad. Chief Technician & Program Director: Allen H. Heefner.
Ownership: Martelle Cooperative Telephone Association.

MARTENSDALE—Interstate Communications. Now served by TRURO, IA [IA0344]. ICA: IA0474.

MASON CITY—Mediacom, 4010 Alexandra Dr, Waterloo, IA 50702. Phone: 319-235-2197. Fax: 319-232-7841. Web Site: http://www.mediacomcable.com. Also serves Britt, Cerro Gordo, Clear Lake, Duncan, Forest City, Garner, Kensett, Leland, Manly, Northwood & Ventura. ICA: IA0010.
TV Market Ranking: Below 100 (Britt, Cerro Gordo, Clear Lake, Duncan, Forest City, Garner, Kensett, Leland, Manly, MASON CITY, Northwood, Ventura). Franchise award date: N.A. Franchise expiration date: N.A. Began: November 1, 1980.
Channel capacity: N.A. Channels available but not in use: N.A.
Basic Service
Subscribers: 7,727. Commercial subscribers: 463.
Programming (received off-air): KAAL (ABC, This TV) Austin; KIMT (CBS, MNT) Mason City; KSMQ-TV (PBS) Austin; KTTC (CW, NBC) Rochester; KXLT-TV (FOX, MeTV) Rochester; KYIN (PBS) Mason City.
Programming (via satellite): CMT; CNBC; C-SPAN; Discovery Channel; HLN; MTV; TBS; The Weather Channel; WGN America.
Fee: $60.00 installation; $57.00 monthly; $.70 converter.
Expanded Basic Service 1
Subscribers: N.A.
Programming (via satellite): A&E; AMC; Animal Planet; Bravo; Cartoon Network; CNN; Comedy Central; C-SPAN 2; Discovery Life Channel; Disney Channel; E! HD; ESPN; EWTN Global Catholic Network; Fox News Channel; Fox Sports 1; FOX Sports North; Freeform; FX; Golf Channel; Hallmark Channel; HGTV; History; INSP; ION Television; Lifetime; MoviePlex; MSNBC; Nickelodeon; Oxygen; Pop; Spike TV; Syfy; Telemundo; TLC; TNT; Travel Channel; Trinity Broadcasting Network (TBN); truTV; Turner Classic Movies; TV Land; USA Network; VH1; WE tv.
Fee: $28.27 monthly.
Digital Basic Service
Subscribers: N.A.
Programming (via satellite): BBC America; Bloomberg Television; Discovery Digital Networks; Disney XD; DMX Music; Fuse; FXM; FYI; GSN; History International; IFC; LMN; National Geographic Channel; NBCSN; Nick Jr.; Outdoor Channel; Ovation; TeenNick; Turner Classic Movies.
Digital Pay Service 1
Pay Units: N.A.
Programming (via satellite): Cinemax (multiplexed); HBO (multiplexed); Showtime (multiplexed); Starz (multiplexed); Starz Encore (multiplexed); The Movie Channel (multiplexed).
Fee: $9.95 monthly (Cinemax, HBO, Showtime, TMC or Starz/Encore).
Video-On-Demand: Yes
Pay-Per-View
ESPN Now (delivered digitally); ETC (delivered digitally); Playboy TV (delivered digitally); Pleasure (delivered digitally); Fresh (delivered digitally); Shorteez (delivered digitally); Vubiquity Inc. (delivered digitally).
Internet Service
Operational: Yes.
Subscribers: 6,161.
Broadband Service: Mediacom High Speed Internet.
Fee: $49.95 installation; $29.95 monthly; $10.00 modem lease.
Telephone Service
Analog: Not Operational
Digital: Operational
Subscribers: 3,798.
Miles of Plant: 504.0 (coaxial); 239.0 (fiber optic). Homes passed: 28,684.
Regional Vice President: Doug Frank. General Manager: Doug Nix. Technical Operations Director: Greg Nank. Marketing Director: Steve Schuh. Marketing Coordinator: Joni Lindauer.
Ownership: Mediacom LLC (MSO).

MASSENA—Formerly served by B & L Technologies LLC. No longer in operation. ICA: IA0306.

MAURICE—Premier Communications. Now served by SIOUX CENTER, IA [IA0076]. ICA: IA0475.

MAXWELL—Formerly served by Huxley Communications Corp. No longer in operation. ICA: IA0476.

MAYNARD—Mediacom. Now served by WAVERLY, IA [IA0021]. ICA: IA0293.

MAYSVILLE—Dixon Telephone Co. Now served by DIXON, IA [IA0358]. ICA: IA0477.

MECHANICSVILLE—Mechanicsville Telephone, 107 North John St, PO Box 159, Mechanicsville, IA 52306. Phone: 563-432-7221. Fax: 563-432-7721. E-mail: mtco@netins.net. Web Site: http://www.mechanicsvilletel.net. ICA: IA0194.
TV Market Ranking: 65 (MECHANICSVILLE). Franchise award date: N.A. Franchise expiration date: N.A. Began: October 1, 1983.
Channel capacity: N.A. Channels available but not in use: N.A.
Basic Service
Subscribers: 279.
Programming (received off-air): KCRG-TV (ABC, MNT) Cedar Rapids; KFXA (FOX, The Country Network) Cedar Rapids; KGAN (CBS) Cedar Rapids; KIIN (PBS) Iowa City; KLJB (CW, FOX, MeTV) Davenport; KWQC-TV (NBC) Davenport; KWWL (CW, MeTV, NBC) Waterloo; WHBF-TV (CBS) Rock Island; WQAD-TV (ABC, Antenna TV) Moline.
Programming (via satellite): A&E; AMC; BTN; Cartoon Network; CMT; CNBC; CNN; Comcast SportsNet Chicago; Comedy Central; C-SPAN; Discovery Channel; Disney Channel; ESPN; ESPN Classic; ESPN2; Food Network; Fox News Channel; Fox Sports 1; Freeform; FX; Great American Country; GSN; Hallmark Channel; HGTV; History; INSP; ION Television; Lifetime; Nickelodeon; Outdoor Channel; QVC; Spike TV; Syfy; TBS; The Weather Channel; TLC; TNT; Travel Channel; Trinity Broadcasting Network (TBN); Turner Classic Movies; TV Land; USA Network; VH1; WGN America.
Fee: $15.00 installation; $62.00 monthly.
Pay Service 1
Pay Units: 174.
Programming (via satellite): Cinemax; HBO.
Fee: $9.50 monthly.
Pay Service 2
Pay Units: N.A.
Programming (via satellite): Showtime.
Internet Service
Operational: Yes, DSL.
Fee: $34.95-$74.95 monthly.
Telephone Service
Analog: Operational
Fee: $24.00 monthly
Miles of Plant: 8.0 (coaxial); None (fiber optic). Homes passed: 450.
General Manager: Hans Arwine. Secretary-Treasurer: Robert G. Horner. Office Coordinator: Angie Entwisle.
Ownership: Mechanicsville Telephone Co.

MEDIAPOLIS—MTC Technologies, 652 Main St, PO Box 398, Mediapolis, IA 52637-0398. Phones: 800-762-1527; 319-394-3456. Fax: 319-394-9155. E-mail: office@mepotelco.net. Web Site: http://www.mtctech.net. ICA: IA0142.
TV Market Ranking: Below 100 (MEDIAPOLIS). Franchise award date: N.A. Franchise expiration date: N.A. Began: June 15, 1984.
Channel capacity: N.A. Channels available but not in use: N.A.
Basic Service
Subscribers: N.A.
Programming (received off-air): KGCW (CW, This TV) Burlington; KIIN (PBS) Iowa City; KLJB (CW, FOX, MeTV) Davenport; KWQC-TV (NBC) Davenport; KYOU-TV (FOX) Ottumwa; WHBF-TV (CBS) Rock Island; WQAD-TV (ABC, Antenna TV) Moline; WQPT-TV (PBS) Moline.
Programming (via satellite): The Weather Channel; WGN America.
Fee: $15.00 installation; $15.95 monthly; $1.00 converter.
Expanded Basic Service 1
Subscribers: N.A.
Programming (via satellite): A&E; AMC; Animal Planet; BET; Bravo; BTN; Cartoon Network; CMT; CNBC; CNN; Comcast SportsNet Chicago; Comedy Central; C-SPAN; C-SPAN 2; Discovery Channel; Discovery Life Channel; Disney Channel; Disney XD; E! HD; ESPN; ESPN Classic; ESPN2; EWTN Global Catholic Network; Food Network; Fox Deportes; Fox News Channel; Fox Sports 1; FOX Sports Midwest; Freeform; FX; FXM; Golf Channel; Hallmark Channel; HGTV; History; HLN; INSP; Lifetime; MSNBC; MTV; National Geographic Channel; Nickelodeon; Outdoor Channel; OWN: Oprah Winfrey Network; Pop; QVC; Spike TV; Syfy; TBS; TLC;

TNT; Travel Channel; truTV; Turner Classic Movies; TV Land; Univision; Univision Studios; USA Network; VH1.
Fee: $38.00 monthly.
Digital Basic Service
Subscribers: N.A.
Programming (via satellite): AXS TV; BBC America; Discovery Digital Networks; ESPN HD; ESPN2 HD; ESPNews; ESPNU; Fox Sports 1; GSN; HD Theater; IFC; MC; NBCSN; Nick 2; Nick Jr.; Nicktoons; TeenNick; WE tv.
Pay Service 1
Pay Units: N.A.
Programming (via satellite): Cinemax; HBO; Showtime.
Digital Pay Service 1
Pay Units: N.A.
Programming (via satellite): Cinemax (multiplexed); Flix; HBO (multiplexed); HBO HD; Starz (multiplexed); Starz Encore (multiplexed); Starz HD; The Movie Channel (multiplexed).
Fee: $10.00 monthly (each).
Video-On-Demand: Yes
Internet Service
Operational: No, DSL.
Telephone Service
Analog: Operational
Miles of Plant: 20.0 (coaxial); None (fiber optic). Homes passed: 800.
General Manager: Bill Malcom. Office Manager: Angie Rupe. Plant Supervisor: Paul Kuntz.
Ownership: Mediapolis Cablevision Co.

MELVIN—Premier Communications, 339 1st Ave Northeast, PO Box 200, Sioux Center, IA 51250. Phones: 800-741-8351; 712-722-3451. Fax: 712-722-1113. Web Site: http://www.mypremieronline.com. ICA: IA0354.
TV Market Ranking: Outside TV Markets (MELVIN). Franchise award date: N.A. Franchise expiration date: N.A. Began: June 1, 1985.
Channel capacity: N.A. Channels available but not in use: N.A.
Basic Service
Subscribers: 58.
Programming (received off-air): KCAU-TV (ABC) Sioux City; KDLT-TV (Antenna TV, NBC) Sioux Falls; KELO-TV (CBS, MNT) Sioux Falls; KPTH (FOX, MNT, This TV) Sioux City; KSFY-TV (ABC, CW) Sioux Falls; KSIN-TV (PBS) Sioux City; KTIV (CW, MeTV, NBC) Sioux City.
Programming (via satellite): A&E; CNN; C-SPAN; Discovery Channel; Disney Channel; ESPN; ESPN2; Fox News Channel; Fox Sports 1; Freeform; Great American Country; Hallmark Channel; HGTV; History; HLN; Lifetime; Nickelodeon; Spike TV; TBS; The Weather Channel; TLC; TNT; TV Land; USA Network; WGN America.
Fee: $16.00 installation; $24.95 monthly.
Pay Service 1
Pay Units: N.A.
Programming (via satellite): HBO; Showtime.
Fee: $8.95 monthly (each).
Internet Service
Operational: No.
Telephone Service
None
Miles of Plant: 3.0 (coaxial); None (fiber optic). Homes passed: 139.
Chief Executive Officer: Douglas A. Boone. Chief Technician: Leslie Sybesma. Marketing Director: Scott Te Stroete.
Ownership: Premier Communications Inc. (MSO).

MENLO—Coon Valley Cooperative Telephone, 516 Sherman St, PO Box 108, Menlo, IA 50164. Phones: 641-345-2626; 641-524-2111. Fax: 641-524-2112. Web Site: http://www.coonvalleytelco.com. ICA: IA0340.
TV Market Ranking: Outside TV Markets (MENLO). Franchise award date: May 1, 1988. Franchise expiration date: N.A. Began: July 15, 1988.
Channel capacity: N.A. Channels available but not in use: N.A.
Basic Service
Subscribers: N.A.
Programming (received off-air): KCCI (CBS, MeTV) Des Moines; KCWI-TV (CW) Ames; KDIN-TV (PBS) Des Moines; KDSM-TV (FOX, The Country Network) Des Moines; WHO-DT (Antenna TV, NBC) Des Moines; WOI-DT (ABC) Ames.
Programming (via satellite): A&E; AMC; CMT; CNN; Comedy Central; Discovery Channel; Disney Channel; ESPN; ESPN2; Freeform; History; HLN; Lifetime; Nickelodeon; Outdoor Channel; Syfy; TBS; The Weather Channel; TLC; TNT; USA Network; WGN America.
Fee: $30.00 installation; $1.50 converter.
Pay Service 1
Pay Units: N.A.
Programming (via satellite): Flix; HBO; Showtime (multiplexed); The Movie Channel.
Fee: $10.00 installation; $10.95 monthly (each).
Internet Service
Operational: No, DSL.
Telephone Service
None
Miles of Plant: 3.0 (coaxial); None (fiber optic). Homes passed: 152.
General Manager: Jim Nelson. Chief Technician: Michael Clarke.
Ownership: Coon Valley Cablevision.

MERRILL—Premier Communications. Now served by SIOUX CENTER, IA [IA0076]. ICA: IA0311.

MESERVEY—Rockwell Communications Systems Inc, 111 North 4th St, PO Box 416, Rockwell, IA 50469-0416. Phone: 641-822-3211. Fax: 641-822-3550. E-mail: rockwell@netins.net. Web Site: http://www.rockwellcoop.com. ICA: IA0478.
TV Market Ranking: Below 100 (MESERVEY). Franchise award date: N.A. Franchise expiration date: N.A. Began: January 1, 1990.
Channel capacity: N.A. Channels available but not in use: N.A.
Basic Service
Subscribers: 12.
Fee: $26.45 monthly.
Video-On-Demand: No
Pay-Per-View
ESPN (delivered digitally).
Internet Service
Operational: No, DSL & dial-up.
Telephone Service
Analog: Operational
Homes passed: 140.
General Manager: David Severin. Chief Technician: Jason Dick.
Ownership: Rockwell Cooperative Telephone Association (MSO).

MILFORD—Milford Cable TV, 806 Okoboji Ave, PO Box 163, Milford, IA 51351. Phones: 855-722-3450; 712-338-4967. E-mail: infoweb@milfordcomm.com. Web Site: http://milfordcomm.com. Also serves Fostoria. ICA: IA0109.
TV Market Ranking: Outside TV Markets (Fostoria, MILFORD). Franchise award date: N.A. Franchise expiration date: N.A. Began: January 1, 1982.
Channel capacity: N.A. Channels available but not in use: N.A.
Basic Service
Subscribers: 731.
Programming (received off-air): KCAU-TV (ABC) Sioux City; KDLT-TV (Antenna TV, NBC) Sioux Falls; KELO-TV (CBS, MNT) Sioux Falls; KEYC-TV (CBS, FOX) Mankato; KMEG (Azteca America, CBS, Decades) Sioux City; KPTH (FOX, MNT, This TV) Sioux City; KSFY-TV (ABC, CW) Sioux Falls; KTIN (PBS) Fort Dodge; KTIV (CW, MeTV, NBC) Sioux City; KTTW (FOX, This TV) Sioux Falls.
Programming (via satellite): A&E; Animal Planet; Bravo; CMT; CNBC; CNN; Comedy Central; Cooking Channel; C-SPAN; C-SPAN 2; Discovery Channel; Disney Channel; Disney XD; DIY Network; ESPN; ESPN Classic; ESPN2; EWTN Global Catholic Network; Food Network; Fox News Channel; FOX Sports Networks; Freeform; FX; FXM; Great American Country; Hallmark Channel; HGTV; History; HLN; ION Television; Lifetime; MSNBC; MTV; National Geographic Channel; Nickelodeon; Outdoor Channel; OWN: Oprah Winfrey Network; QVC; RFD-TV; Spike TV; Syfy; TBS; The Weather Channel; TLC; TNT; Travel Channel; Trinity Broadcasting Network (TBN); truTV; Turner Classic Movies; TV Land; USA Network; VH1; WGN America.
Fee: $30.00 installation; $28.05 monthly.
Digital Basic Service
Subscribers: N.A.
Programming (via satellite): BBC America; Bloomberg Television; Discovery Digital Networks; Disney XD; DMX Music; ESPN Classic; ESPN2; ESPNews; FOX College Sports Central; FOX College Sports Pacific; Fox Sports 1; FXM; FYI; Golf Channel; GSN; HGTV; History; History International; LMN; National Geographic Channel; Nick Jr.; Nicktoons; Outdoor Channel; Sundance TV; TeenNick; Trinity Broadcasting Network (TBN); Turner Classic Movies; WE tv.
Pay Service 1
Pay Units: N.A.
Programming (via satellite): Cinemax; HBO; Starz; Starz Encore.
Fee: $9.65 monthly (Starz/Encore), $10.70 monthly (Cinemax or HBO).
Digital Pay Service 1
Pay Units: N.A.
Programming (via satellite): Cinemax (multiplexed); Flix; HBO (multiplexed); Showtime (multiplexed); Starz (multiplexed); Starz Encore (multiplexed); The Movie Channel (multiplexed).
Fee: $10.70 monthly (each).
Video-On-Demand: No
Internet Service
Operational: Yes, DSL. Began: January 1, 2001.
Broadband Service: Milford Cable.
Fee: $25.95-$45.00 monthly; $6.42 modem lease; $80.00 modem purchase.
Telephone Service
None
Miles of Plant: 17.0 (coaxial); 7.0 (fiber optic). Homes passed: 1,300.
Vice President: Douglas A. Boone.
Ownership: Milford Communications.

MILO—Formerly served by Telnet South LC. No longer in operation. ICA: IA0479.

MILTON—Starwest Inc. Now served by KEOSAUQUA, IA [IA0186]. ICA: IA0480.

MINBURN—Minburn Cablevision Inc., 416 Chestnut St, PO Box 206, Minburn, IA 50167. Phones: 877-386-2933; 515-438-2200; 515-677-2264; 515-677-2100. Fax: 515-677-2007. E-mail: minburn@minburncomm.com. Web Site: http://www.minburncomm.com. Also serves Perry & Woodward. ICA: IA0339.
TV Market Ranking: 66 (MINBURN, Perry, Woodward). Franchise award date: May 1, 1989. Franchise expiration date: N.A. Began: December 20, 1989.
Channel capacity: N.A. Channels available but not in use: N.A.
Basic Service
Subscribers: 93.
Programming (received off-air): KCCI (CBS, MeTV) Des Moines; KDIN-TV (PBS) Des Moines; KDSM-TV (FOX, The Country Network) Des Moines; WHO-DT (Antenna TV, NBC) Des Moines; WOI-DT (ABC) Ames.
Programming (via satellite): AMC; CMT; CNN; Discovery Channel; Disney Channel; ESPN; ESPN2; Freeform; History; ION Television; Lifetime; Spike TV; Syfy; TBS; The Weather Channel; TLC; TNT; USA Network; WGN America.
Fee: $15.00 installation; $36.95 monthly.
Expanded Basic Service 1
Subscribers: 84.
Fee: $81.63 monthly.
Pay Service 1
Pay Units: 57.
Programming (via satellite): HBO; Showtime.
Fee: $15.00 installation; $9.50 monthly (each).
Internet Service
Operational: No, DSL & dial-up.
Telephone Service
Analog: Operational
Miles of Plant: 3.0 (coaxial); None (fiber optic). Homes passed: 161.
General Manager & Assistant Secretary: Debra Lucht.
Ownership: Minburn Cablevision Inc.

MINDEN—Walnut Communications. Now served by WALNUT, IA [IA0241]. ICA: IA0304.

MINGO—Formerly served by Huxley Communications Corp. No longer in operation. ICA: IA0593.

MISSOURI VALLEY—Long Lines. Now served by SALIX, IA [IA0510]. ICA: IA0096.

MODALE—Formerly served by TelePartners. No longer in operation. ICA: IA0574.

MONDAMIN—Formerly served by TelePartners. No longer in operation. ICA: IA0315.

MONONA—Northeast Iowa Telephone Co, 800 South Main St, Monona, IA 52159. Phones: 877-638-2122; 563-539-2122. Fax: 563-539-2003. E-mail: neitel@neitel.com. Web Site: http://neitel.com. Also serves Farmersburg, Luana & St. Olaf. ICA: IA0122.
TV Market Ranking: Outside TV Markets (Farmersburg, Luana, MONONA, St. Olaf). Franchise award date: January 1, 1983. Franchise expiration date: N.A. Began: March 1, 1983.
Channel capacity: N.A. Channels available but not in use: N.A.
Basic Service
Subscribers: 197.
Programming (received off-air): KCRG-TV (ABC, MNT) Cedar Rapids; KFXA (FOX,

Iowa—Cable Systems

CABLE & TV STATION COVERAGE
Atlas 2017
The perfect companion to the Television & Cable Factbook
To order call 800-771-9202 or visit www.warren-news.com

The Country Network) Cedar Rapids; KFXB-TV (Christian TV Network) Dubuque; KGAN (CBS) Cedar Rapids; KPXR-TV (ION) Cedar Rapids; KRIN (PBS) Waterloo; KWKB (The Works, This TV) Iowa City; KWWL (CW, MeTV, NBC) Waterloo.
  Programming (via satellite): A&E; AMC; BTN; CMT; CNBC; CNN; Discovery Channel; ESPN; Fox News Channel; FOX Sports Midwest; Freeform; FX; Hallmark Channel; HGTV; History; MTV; Nickelodeon; Outdoor Channel; Spike TV; Syfy; TBS; The Weather Channel; TLC; TNT; TV Land; USA Network; VH1; WGN America.
  Fee: $10.00 installation; $41.95 monthly.
Digital Basic Service
  Subscribers: N.A.
  Programming (via satellite): BBC America; Destination America; Discovery Kids Channel; Discovery Life Channel; DMX Music; ESPN Classic; ESPNews; FOX College Sports Central; FOX College Sports Pacific; Fox Sports 1; Fuse; FYI; Great American Country; GSN; History International; Investigation Discovery; MTV Classic; MTV2; Nick Jr.; Nicktoons; OWN: Oprah Winfrey Network; Science Channel; TeenNick; Trinity Broadcasting Network (TBN); VH1 Country.
Pay Service 1
  Pay Units: N.A.
  Programming (via satellite): Cinemax; HBO.
  Fee: $10.00 installation; $11.00 monthly (Cinemax), $12.00 monthly (HBO).
Digital Pay Service 1
  Pay Units: N.A.
  Programming (via satellite): Cinemax (multiplexed); Flix; HBO (multiplexed); Showtime (multiplexed); Starz (multiplexed); Starz Encore (multiplexed); The Movie Channel (multiplexed).
  Fee: $11.00 monthly (Cinemax), $12.00 monthly (HBO), $13.50 monthly (Showtime/TMC/Flix), $14.50 monthly (Starz/Encore).
Internet Service
  Operational: Yes.
Telephone Service
  Digital: Operational
  Miles of Plant: 17.0 (coaxial); None (fiber optic).
  General Manager: David Byers. Marketing Manager: Steve Hanson. Plant Manager: Dennis Landt.
  Ownership: Northeast Iowa Telephone Co.

MONROE—Formerly served by Telnet South LC. Now served by Mediacom, NEWTON, IA [IA0016]. ICA: IA0139.

MONTROSE—Mediacom. Now served by KEOKUK, IA [IA0612]. ICA: IA0192.

MOORHEAD—Formerly served by Soldier Valley Telephone. Now served by Long Lines, SALIX, IA [IA0510]. ICA: IA0347.

MOORHEAD—Long Lines. Now served by SALIX, IA [IA0510]. ICA: IA0602.

MORAVIA—Formerly served by B & L Communications LLC. No longer in operation. ICA: IA0273.

MOULTON—Formerly served by B & L Technologies LLC. No longer in operation. ICA: IA0535.

MOVILLE—Wiatel, 202 Cedar St, PO Box 38, Lawton, IA 51030-0038. Phones: 800-469-0811; 712-944-5711. Fax: 712-944-5722. E-mail: wiatel@wiatel.com. Web Site: http://www.wiatel.com. ICA: IA0189.
  TV Market Ranking: Below 100 (MOVILLE). Franchise award date: N.A. Franchise expiration date: N.A. Began: February 1, 1984.
  Channel capacity: 35 (not 2-way capable). Channels available but not in use: N.A.
Basic Service
  Subscribers: N.A.
  Programming (received off-air): KCAU-TV (ABC) Sioux City; KMEG (Azteca America, CBS, Decades) Sioux City; KSIN-TV (PBS) Sioux City; KTIV (CW, MeTV, NBC) Sioux City.
  Programming (via satellite): A&E; AMC; Animal Planet; CMT; CNN; C-SPAN; Discovery Channel; Disney Channel; ESPN; ESPN2; Freeform; History; HLN; Lifetime; Nickelodeon; Spike TV; Syfy; TBS; The Weather Channel; TLC; TNT; USA Network; VH1; WGN America.
  Fee: $45.00 installation.
Pay Service 1
  Pay Units: N.A.
  Programming (via satellite): Cinemax; HBO; Showtime; The Movie Channel.
  Fee: $11.00 monthly (Cinemax or HBO), $12.95 monthly (Showtime/TMC).
Video-On-Demand: No
Internet Service
  Operational: No.
Telephone Service
  None
  Miles of Plant: 10.0 (coaxial); 1.0 (fiber optic). Homes passed: 290.
  Ownership: Western Iowa Telephone (MSO).

MURRAY—Formerly served by Interstate Communications. This cable system has converted to IPTV. Now served by GRM Networks, MURRAY, IA [IA5135]. ICA: IA0257.

MURRAY—GRM Networks, 1001 Kentucky St, Princeton, MO 64673. Phones: 800-451-2301; 660-748-4235. Fax: 660-748-4747. E-mail: help@grm.net. Web Site: http://www2.grm.net. Also serves Allerton, Grand River, Leon, Lineville, Lorimor, Millerton, Princeton & Sun Valley Lake, IA; Bethany, New Hampton & Powersville (village), MO. ICA: IA5135.
  Channel capacity: N.A. Channels available but not in use: N.A.
Essential
  Subscribers: 213.
  Fee: $22.95 monthly.
Preferred
  Subscribers: N.A.
  Fee: $59.95 monthly.

Premier
  Subscribers: N.A.
  Fee: $74.95 monthly.
Internet Service
  Operational: Yes.
  Fee: $42.95 monthly.
Telephone Service
  Digital: Operational
  General Manager: Ron Hinds. Assistant General Manager: Tom Anderson. Marketing Director: Shannon Erb. Plant Operations Director: Dirk Schwartzkopf. Network Supervisor: Doug Hulsabeck. Outside Plant Supervisor: Mike Noe.
  Ownership: Grand River Mutual Telephone.

MUSCATINE—MPW Cable, 3205 Cedar St, PO Box 899, Muscatine, IA 52761. Phone: 563-263-2631. Fax: 563-262-3373. E-mail: onlinecs@mpw.org. Web Site: http://www.mpw.org. Also serves Fruitland, Louisa County, Mediapolis, Muscatine County & Wilton. ICA: IA0587.
  TV Market Ranking: 60 (Fruitland, Louisa County (portions), MUSCATINE, Muscatine County, Wilton); Below 100 (Mediapolis, Louisa County (portions)); Outside TV Markets (Louisa County (portions)).
  Channel capacity: N.A. Channels available but not in use: N.A.
Digital Basic Service
  Subscribers: 7,696.
  Programming (received off-air): KGCW (CW, MeTV, This TV) Burlington; KIIN (PBS) Iowa City; KLJB (CW, FOX, MeTV) Davenport; KWQC-TV (NBC) Davenport; WHBF-TV (CBS) Rock Island; WQAD-TV (ABC, Antenna TV) Moline; WQPT-TV (PBS) Moline.
  Programming (via satellite): A&E; A&E HD; AMC; AMC HD; Animal Planet; Animal Planet HD; AXS TV; BBC America; BET; Bravo; Bravo HD; BTN; BTN HD; Cartoon Network; Cartoon Network HD; Chiller; Cine Mexicano; Cloo; CMT; CMT HD; CNBC; CNBC HD+; CNN; CNN en Espanol; CNN HD; Comcast SportsNet Chicago; Comedy Central; Comedy Central HD; Cooking Channel; Crime & Investigation Network; C-SPAN; C-SPAN 2; Destination America; Destination America HD; Discovery Channel; Discovery Channel HD; Discovery Familia; Discovery Family; Discovery Life Channel; Disney Channel; Disney Channel HD; Disney XD; Disney XD HD; DIY Network; E! HD; ESPN; ESPN Classic; ESPN Deportes; ESPN HD; ESPN2; ESPN2 HD; ESPNews; ESPNews HD; ESPNU; ESPNU HD; EWTN Global Catholic Network; Food Network; Food Network HD; Fox Business Network; Fox Business Network HD; Fox Deportes; Fox News Channel; Fox News HD; Fox Sports 1; FOX Sports Midwest; Freeform; Freeform HD; FSN HD; FX; FX HD; FXM; FYI; Golf Channel; Golf Channel HD; Great American Country; GSN; Hallmark Channel; Hallmark Channel HD; Hallmark Movie Channel HD; Hallmark Movies & Mysteries; HD Theater; HGTV; HGTV HD; History; History en Espanol; History HD; History International; HLN; HLN HD; Home Shopping Network HD; HSN; IFC; INSP; Investigation Discovery; Lifetime; Lifetime HD; Lifetime Movie Network HD; LMN; MC; MSNBC; MTV; MTV Classic; MTV Hits; MTV Jams; MTV2; Nat Geo WILD; Nat Geo WILD HD; National Geographic Channel; National Geographic Channel HD; NBCSN; NFL Network; NFL RedZone; Nick 2; Nick HD; Nick Jr.; Nickelodeon; Nicktoons; Outdoor Channel; Outdoor Channel HD; OWN: Oprah Winfrey Network; Oxygen; Pop; QVC; QVC HD; RFD-TV; RTV; Science Channel; Science HD; Smithsonian Channel; Spike TV; Spike TV HD; Syfy; Syfy HD; TBS; TBS HD; The Weather Channel; The Weather Channel HD; TLC; TLC HD; TNT; TNT HD; Tr3s; Travel Channel; Travel Channel HD; truTV; truTV HD; Turner Classic Movies; TV Land; Universal HD; Univision; USA Network; USA Network HD; Versus HD; VH1; VH1 HD; VH1 Soul; WE tv; WE tv HD; WGN America; WGN America HD.
  Fee: $40.00 installation; $26.99 monthly.
Digital Pay Service 1
  Pay Units: N.A.
  Programming (via satellite): Cinemax (multiplexed); Cinemax HD; HBO (multiplexed); HBO HD; Showtime (multiplexed); Showtime HD; Starz (multiplexed); Starz Encore (multiplexed); Starz Encore HD; Starz HD; The Movie Channel (multiplexed); The Movie Channel HD.
Video-On-Demand: Yes
Pay-Per-View
  Movies.
Internet Service
  Operational: Yes.
  Subscribers: 7,148.
  Broadband Service: In-house.
  Fee: $40.00 installation; $21.95-$64.95 monthly.
Telephone Service
  None
  Miles of Plant: 355.0 (coaxial); 157.0 (fiber optic). Homes passed: 13,293.
  General Manager: Salvatore L. LoBianco. Marketing Manager: Tina Campbell. Sales Manager: Terry Curry. Director of Utility Service Delivery: Tim Reed. Telecommunications Manager: David Fyffe.
  Ownership: Muscatine Power & Water.

MUSCATINE—MPW Cable. Now served by MUSCATINE, IA [IA0587]. ICA: IA0014.

MYSTIC—Formerly served by B & L Technologies LLC. No longer in operation. ICA: IA0263.

NEOLA—Walnut Communications. Now served by WALNUT, IA [IA0241]. ICA: IA0481.

NEW ALBIN—Mediacom, 4010 Alexandra Dr, Waterloo, IA 50702. Phone: 319-235-2197. Fax: 319-232-7841. Web Site: http://www.mediacomcable.com. ICA: IA0482.
  TV Market Ranking: Below 100 (NEW ALBIN). Franchise award date: N.A. Franchise expiration date: N.A. Began: January 1, 1967.
  Channel capacity: N.A. Channels available but not in use: N.A.
Basic Service
  Subscribers: 29.
  Programming (received off-air): KAAL (ABC, This TV) Austin; KGAN (CBS) Cedar Rapids; KIMT (CBS, MNT) Mason City; KPXM-TV (ION) St. Cloud; KTTC (CW, NBC) Rochester; KXLT-TV (FOX, MeTV) Rochester; WEAU (NBC) Eau Claire; WHLA-TV (PBS) La Crosse; WKBT-DT (CBS, MNT) La Crosse; WLAX (FOX, MeTV) La Crosse; WXOW (ABC, CW, This TV) La Crosse.
  Fee: $41.99 installation; $43.00 monthly.
Expanded Basic Service 1
  Subscribers: N.A.
  Programming (via satellite): A&E; AMC; Animal Planet; Bravo; Cartoon Network; CMT; CNBC; CNN; Comedy Central; C-SPAN; Discovery Channel; Disney Channel; E! HD; ESPN; ESPN2; Fox News Channel; Fox Sports 1; FOX Sports Midwest;

Cable Systems—Iowa

Freeform; FX; HGTV; History; HLN; Lifetime; MTV; Nickelodeon; QVC; Spike TV; Syfy; TBS; The Weather Channel; TLC; TNT; truTV; TV Land; USA Network; VH1; WGN America.
Digital Basic Service
Subscribers: N.A.
Programming (via satellite): BBC America; Bloomberg Television; Discovery Digital Networks; Fuse; FXM; FYI; Golf Channel; GSN; History International; IFC; LMN; MC; Outdoor Channel.
Digital Pay Service 1
Pay Units: N.A.
Programming (via satellite): Cinemax (multiplexed); Flix; HBO (multiplexed); Showtime (multiplexed); Starz (multiplexed); Starz Encore (multiplexed); Sundance TV; The Movie Channel (multiplexed).
Fee: $20.00 installation; $10.00 monthly (each).
Video-On-Demand: Yes
Pay-Per-View
Vubiquity Inc. (delivered digitally); ESPN Now (delivered digitally); Sports PPV (delivered digitally); Fresh (delivered digitally); Shorteez (delivered digitally); Playboy TV (delivered digitally); Pleasure (delivered digitally); ETC (delivered digitally).
Internet Service
Operational: Yes.
Broadband Service: Mediacom High Speed Internet.
Telephone Service
Digital: Operational
Miles of Plant: 4.0 (coaxial); None (fiber optic). Homes passed: 480.
Regional Vice President: Doug Frank. General Manager: Doug Nix. Technical Operations Director: Greg Nank. Marketing Director: Steve Schuh. Marketing Coordinator: Joni Lindauer.
Ownership: Mediacom LLC (MSO).

NEW LIBERTY—Dixon Telephone Co. Now served by DIXON, IA [IA0358]. ICA: IA0483.

NEW MARKET—Farmers Mutual Telephone Co. Now served by STANTON, IA [IA0264]. ICA: IA0294.

NEW VIRGINIA—Interstate Communications. Now served by TRURO, IA [IA0344]. ICA: IA0343.

NEWELL—Formerly served by TelePartners. No longer in operation. ICA: IA0205.

NEWTON—Mediacom, 2205 Ingersoll Ave, Des Moines, IA 50312. Phone: 515-246-1890. Fax: 515-246-2211. Web Site: http://www.mediacomcable.com. Also serves Colfax, Grinnell, Jasper County (central portion), Lambs Grove, Lynnville, Mitchellville, Monroe, Pella, Poweshiek County (portions), Prairie City & Sully. ICA: IA0016.
TV Market Ranking: 66 (Colfax, Jasper County (central portion), Lambs Grove, Mitchellville, Monroe, NEWTON, Prairie City); Below 100 (Grinnell, Lynnville, Pella, Poweshiek County (portions), Sully).
Channel capacity: N.A. Channels available but not in use: N.A.
Basic Service
Subscribers: 4,932. Commercial subscribers: 12.
Fee: $41.99 installation; $43.00 monthly.
Internet Service
Operational: Yes.
Subscribers: 3,648.
Broadband Service: Mediacom High Speed Internet.
Telephone Service
Digital: Operational
Subscribers: 2,133.
Miles of Plant: 457.0 (coaxial); 302.0 (fiber optic). Homes passed: 23,066.
Ownership: Mediacom LLC (MSO).

NICHOLS—Formerly served by PEC Cablevision. No longer in operation. ICA: IA0485.

NORTH LIBERTY—Mediacom, 6300 Council St NE, Ste A, Cedar Rapids, IA 52402. Phones: 319-393-1914; 800-332-0245; 319-395-9699. Fax: 319-393-7017. Web Site: http://www.mediacomcable.com. Also serves Solon Mills, IL; Atalissa, Johnson County (portions), Lisbon, Mount Vernon, Oxford, Shueyville, Swisher, Tiffin, West Branch & West Liberty, IA. ICA: IA0627.
TV Market Ranking: 60 (Atalissa, West Liberty); 65 (Johnson County (portions), Lisbon, Mount Vernon, NORTH LIBERTY, Oxford, Swisher, Tiffin, West Branch).
Channel capacity: N.A. Channels available but not in use: N.A.
Basic Service
Subscribers: 4,396. Commercial subscribers: 11.
Fee: $41.99 installation; $43.00 monthly.
Internet Service
Operational: Yes.
Subscribers: 5,252.
Broadband Service: Mediacom High Speed Internet.
Telephone Service
Digital: Operational
Subscribers: 1,597.
Miles of Plant: 284.0 (coaxial); 195.0 (fiber optic). Homes passed: 17,964.
Ownership: Mediacom LLC (MSO).

NORTH LIBERTY—South Slope Communications Co. This cable system has converted to IPTV. Now served by ELY, IA [IA5004]. ICA: IA0432.

NORTHWOOD—Mediacom. Now served by MASON CITY, IA [IA0010]. ICA: IA0131.

NORWAY—Mediacom, 6300 Council St NE, Ste A, Cedar Rapids, IA 52402. Phones: 319-395-9699; 319-393-1914; 800-332-0245. Fax: 319-393-7017. Web Site: http://www.mediacomcable.com. ICA: IA0634.
TV Market Ranking: Outside TV Markets (NORWAY).
Channel capacity: N.A. Channels available but not in use: N.A.
Basic Service
Subscribers: 48.
Fee: $43.00 monthly.
Ownership: Mediacom LLC (MSO).

OAKLAND—Formerly served by Our Cable. No longer in operation. ICA: IA0486.

OAKVILLE—Formerly served by Longview Communications. No longer in operation. ICA: IA0323.

OCHEYEDAN—HTC Communications. Now served by HOSPERS, IA [IA0060]. ICA: IA0276.

ODEBOLT—Sac County Mutual Telco, 108 South Maple St, PO Box 488, Odebolt, IA 51458. Phone: 712-668-2200. Fax: 712-668-2100. E-mail: scmtco@netins.net. Web Site: http://www.scmtco.com. ICA: IA0636.

TV Market Ranking: Outside TV Markets (ODEBOLT).
Channel capacity: N.A. Channels available but not in use: N.A.
Basic Service
Subscribers: 1,240.
Fee: $30.00 installation; $59.95 monthly.
General Manager: Robert Sorensen.
Ownership: Sac County Mutual Telephone Co. (MSO).

OELWEIN—Mediacom. Now served by WAVERLY, IA [IA0021]. ICA: IA0044.

OGDEN—Ogden Telephone Co. Cablevision, 202 West Walnut St, PO Box 457, Ogden, IA 50212. Phone: 515-275-2050. Fax: 515-275-2599. E-mail: ogdentel@netins.net. Web Site: http://www.ogdentelephone.com. ICA: IA0126.
TV Market Ranking: 66 (OGDEN). Franchise award date: N.A. Franchise expiration date: N.A. Began: July 1, 1983.
Channel capacity: N.A. Channels available but not in use: N.A.
Basic Service
Subscribers: 20.
Programming (received off-air): KCCI (CBS, MeTV) Des Moines; KCWI-TV (CW) Ames; KDIN-TV (PBS) Des Moines; KDSM-TV (FOX, The Country Network) Des Moines; KFPX-TV (ION) Newton; WHO-DT (Antenna TV, NBC) Des Moines; WOI-DT (ABC) Ames.
Programming (via satellite): Trinity Broadcasting Network (TBN); WGN America.
Fee: $20.50 installation; $14.95 monthly.
Expanded Basic Service 1
Subscribers: N.A.
Programming (via satellite): A&E; AMC; Animal Planet; Cartoon Network; CNN; C-SPAN; C-SPAN 2; Discovery Channel; Disney Channel; ESPN; EWTN Global Catholic Network; FOX Sports Midwest; Freeform; FX; Great American Country; Hallmark Channel; HGTV; History; HLN; Lifetime; MTV; National Geographic Channel; NBCSN; Nickelodeon; Spike TV; Starz Encore; Syfy; The Weather Channel; TLC; TNT; Travel Channel; TV Land; USA Network.
Fee: $35.95 monthly.
Digital Basic Service
Subscribers: N.A.
Pay Service 1
Pay Units: 21.
Programming (via satellite): Cinemax; HBO; Showtime; Starz.
Fee: $6.95 monthly (Starz), $10.95 monthly (Cinemax), $11.95 monthly (Showtime), $15.95 monthly (HBO).
Video-On-Demand: No
Internet Service
Operational: No, DSL.
Broadband Service: Offers dial-up and DSL only; no cable modem service.
Telephone Service
Analog: Operational
Miles of Plant: 13.0 (coaxial); None (fiber optic). Homes passed: 800.
General Manager: John P. Ellis.
Ownership: Ogden Telephone Co.

OLDS—Farmers & Merchants Mutual Telephone. Formerly served by Wayland, IA [IA0525]. This cable system has converted to IPTV, 210 West Main St, PO Box 247, Wayland, IA 52654. Phone: 319-256-2736. Fax: 319-256-7210. E-mail: manager@farmtel.com. Web Site: http://www.farmtelcommunications.com. ICA: IA5075.
Channel capacity: N.A. Channels available but not in use: N.A.
Internet Service
Operational: Yes.
Telephone Service
Digital: Operational
General Manager: Rex McGuire.
Ownership: Farmers & Merchants Mutual Telephone Co.

OLIN—Olin Telephone & Cablevision Co, 318 Jackson St, Olin, IA 52320. Phone: 319-484-2200. Fax: 319-484-2800. E-mail: olintel@netins.net. Web Site: http://www.olintelephone.com. ICA: IA0615.
TV Market Ranking: 65 (OLIN). Franchise award date: N.A. Franchise expiration date: N.A. Began: December 31, 1996.
Channel capacity: N.A. Channels available but not in use: N.A.
Basic Service
Subscribers: 181. Commercial subscribers: 10.
Programming (received off-air): KCRG-TV (ABC, MNT) Cedar Rapids; KFXA (FOX, The Country Network) Cedar Rapids; KGAN (CBS) Cedar Rapids; KIIN (PBS) Iowa City; KLJB (CW, FOX, MeTV) Davenport; KWKB (The Works, This TV) Iowa City; KWQC-TV (NBC) Davenport; KWWL (CW, MeTV, NBC) Waterloo; WHBF-TV (CBS) Rock Island; WQAD-TV (ABC, Antenna TV) Moline.
Programming (via satellite): A&E; AMC; Animal Planet; BTN; Cartoon Network; CMT; CNBC; CNN; Comcast SportsNet Chicago; Comedy Central; C-SPAN; Discovery Channel; Disney Channel; E! HD; ESPN; ESPN Classic; ESPN2; Food Network; Fox News Channel; Fox Sports 1; Freeform; FX; Great American Country; GSN; Hallmark Channel; HGTV; History; INSP; ION Television; Lifetime; MTV; Nickelodeon; Outdoor Channel; QVC; Spike TV; Syfy; TBS; The Weather Channel; TLC; TNT; Travel Channel; Trinity Broadcasting Network (TBN); Turner Classic Movies; TV Land; USA Network; VH1; WGN America.
Fee: $55.95 monthly.
Pay Service 1
Pay Units: N.A.
Programming (via satellite): Cinemax; HBO; Showtime.
Fee: $11.50 monthly (Cinemax & Showtime), $14.50 monthly (HBO).
Video-On-Demand: No
Internet Service
Operational: No, DSL & dial-up.
Telephone Service
Analog: Operational
Miles of Plant: 5.0 (coaxial); None (fiber optic). Homes passed: 250.

Access the most current data instantly
FREE TRIAL @ ADVANCED TVFactbook
TELCO/IPTV • CABLE TV • TV STATIONS
www.warren-news.com/factbook.htm

Iowa—Cable Systems

General Manager: Rodney Cozart. Chief Technician: Frank Wood. Office Manager: Sheila Rouse.
Ownership: Olin Telephone & Cablevision Co.

ONAWA—Long Lines. Now served by SALIX, IA [IA0510]. ICA: IA0090.

ONSLOW—Onslow Cooperative Telephone Assn, 102 Anamosa Ave, PO Box 6, Onslow, IA 52321. Phone: 563-485-2833. Fax: 563-485-3891. ICA: IA0487.
TV Market Ranking: 65 (ONSLOW). Franchise award date: N.A. Franchise expiration date: N.A. Began: October 1, 1990.
Channel capacity: N.A. Channels available but not in use: N.A.
Basic Service
  Subscribers: 38.
  Programming (received off-air): KCRG-TV (ABC, MNT) Cedar Rapids; KFXA (FOX, The Country Network) Cedar Rapids; KGAN (CBS) Cedar Rapids; KIIN (PBS) Iowa City; KLJB (CW, FOX, MeTV) Davenport; KWQC-TV (NBC) Davenport; KWWL (CW, MeTV, NBC) Waterloo; WHBF-TV (CBS) Rock Island; WQAD-TV (ABC, Antenna TV) Moline.
  Programming (via satellite): A&E; AMC; Animal Planet; Cartoon Network; CMT; CNBC; CNN; Comedy Central; C-SPAN; Discovery Channel; Disney Channel; E! HD; ESPN; ESPN2; Food Network; Fox Sports 1; Freeform; FX; Great American Country; GSN; HGTV; History; INSP; Lifetime; MTV; Nickelodeon; Outdoor Channel; QVC; Spike TV; Syfy; TBS; The Weather Channel; TLC; TNT; Travel Channel; Trinity Broadcasting Network (TBN); Turner Classic Movies; TV Land; USA Network; VH1; WGN America.
  Fee: $46.95 monthly.
Pay Service 1
  Pay Units: N.A.
  Programming (via satellite): Cinemax; HBO.
  Fee: $9.95 monthly (Cinemax), $11.50 monthly (HBO).
Video-On-Demand: No
Internet Service
  Operational: No, DSL & dial-up.
Telephone Service
  Analog: Operational
General Manager: Russ Benke.
Ownership: Onslow Cooperative Telephone Association.

ORANGE CITY—Formerly served by Orange City Communications. Now served by Long Lines, SALIX, IA [IA0510]. ICA: IA0605.

ORANGE CITY—Premier Communications. Now served by SIOUX CENTER, IA [IA0076]. ICA: IA0488.

OSAGE—Mediacom, 4010 Alexandra Dr, Waterloo, IA 50702. Phone: 319-235-2197. Fax: 319-232-7841. Web Site: http://www.mediacomcable.com. Also serves Cresco, Elma & Lime Springs. ICA: IA0085.
TV Market Ranking: Below 100 (OSAGE); Outside TV Markets (Cresco, Elma, Lime Springs). Franchise award date: N.A. Franchise expiration date: N.A. Began: January 1, 1981.
Channel capacity: N.A. Channels available but not in use: N.A.
Basic Service
  Subscribers: 970.
  Programming (received off-air): KAAL (ABC, This TV) Austin; KCRG-TV (ABC, MNT) Cedar Rapids; KGAN (CBS) Cedar Rapids; KIMT (CBS, MNT) Mason City; KTTC (CW, NBC) Rochester; KWWL (CW, MeTV, NBC) Waterloo; KXLT-TV (FOX, MeTV) Rochester; KYIN (PBS) Mason City.
  Programming (via satellite): CNN; C-SPAN; Discovery Channel; Freeform; HLN; Lifetime; MTV; Nickelodeon; TBS; The Weather Channel; TNT; WGN America.
  Fee: $60.00 installation; $43.00 monthly; $.69 converter.
Expanded Basic Service 1
  Subscribers: N.A.
  Programming (via satellite): A&E; AMC; Animal Planet; Bravo; Cartoon Network; CMT; CNBC; Comedy Central; C-SPAN 2; Disney Channel; E! HD; ESPN; ESPN2; EWTN Global Catholic Network; Food Network; Fox News Channel; Fox Sports 1; FOX Sports Midwest; FX; Golf Channel; Hallmark Channel; HGTV; History; INSP; ION Television; MoviePlex; MSNBC; Outdoor Channel; Oxygen; Pop; QVC; Spike TV; Syfy; TLC; Travel Channel; Trinity Broadcasting Network (TBN); truTV; Turner Classic Movies; TV Land; USA Network; VH1; WE tv.
  Fee: $10.45 monthly.
Digital Basic Service
  Subscribers: N.A.
  Programming (via satellite): BBC America; Bloomberg Television; Discovery Digital Networks; ESPN Classic; ESPNews; Fuse; FYI; GSN; History International; IFC; LMN; MC; National Geographic Channel; NBCSN; Nick Jr.
Digital Pay Service 1
  Pay Units: N.A.
  Programming (via satellite): Cinemax (multiplexed); HBO (multiplexed); Showtime (multiplexed); Starz (multiplexed); Starz Encore (multiplexed); The Movie Channel (multiplexed).
  Fee: $9.95 monthly (each).
Video-On-Demand: Yes
Pay-Per-View
  Vubiquity Inc. (delivered digitally); iN DEMAND (delivered digitally); Fresh (delivered digitally); Shorteez (delivered digitally); Playboy TV (delivered digitally); Hot Choice (delivered digitally); ESPN Now (delivered digitally); Sports PPV (delivered digitally).
Internet Service
  Operational: Yes.
  Broadband Service: Mediacom High Speed Internet.
  Fee: $49.95 installation; $55.95 monthly.
Telephone Service
  Analog: Not Operational
  Digital: Operational
Miles of Plant: 64.0 (coaxial); None (fiber optic). Homes passed: 3,191.
Regional Vice President: Doug Frank. General Manager: Doug Nix. Technical Operations Director: Greg Nank. Marketing Director: Steve Schuh. Marketing Coordinator: Joni Lindauer.
Ownership: Mediacom LLC (MSO).

OSAGE—Osage Municipal Utilities, 720 Chestnut St, Osage, IA 50461. Phone: 641-832-3731. E-mail: support@osage.net. Web Site: http://osage.net. ICA: IA0640.
TV Market Ranking: Below 100 (OSAGE).
Channel capacity: N.A. Channels available but not in use: N.A.
Chief Technician: Dave Milton.
Ownership: Osage Municipal Utilities.

OSKALOOSA—Mediacom, 6300 Council St NE, Ste A, Cedar Rapids, IA 52402. Phones: 319-393-1914; 641-682-1695 (Ottumwa office); 319-395-9699. Fax: 319-393-7017. Web Site: http://www.mediacomcable.com. Also serves Beacon, New Sharon & University Park. ICA: IA0026.
TV Market Ranking: Below 100 (Beacon, New Sharon, OSKALOOSA, University Park). Franchise award date: N.A. Franchise expiration date: N.A. Began: January 1, 1980.
Channel capacity: N.A. Channels available but not in use: N.A.
Basic Service
  Subscribers: 870.
  Programming (received off-air): KCCI (CBS, MeTV) Des Moines; KCRG-TV (ABC, MNT) Cedar Rapids; KDSM-TV (FOX, The Country Network) Des Moines; KIIN (PBS) Iowa City; KYOU-TV (FOX) Ottumwa; WHO-DT (Antenna TV, NBC) Des Moines; WOI-DT (ABC) Ames.
  Programming (via satellite): C-SPAN; C-SPAN 2; QVC; WGN America.
  Fee: $33.59 installation; $43.00 monthly; $2.00 converter.
Expanded Basic Service 1
  Subscribers: N.A.
  Programming (via satellite): A&E; AMC; Animal Planet; BET; Bravo; Cartoon Network; CMT; CNBC; CNN; Comcast SportsNet Chicago; Comedy Central; Discovery Channel; Disney Channel; E! HD; ESPN; ESPN2; EWTN Global Catholic Network; Food Network; Fox News Channel; Fox Sports 1; Freeform; FX; Hallmark Channel; HGTV; History; HLN; INSP; Lifetime; LMN; MSNBC; MTV; National Geographic Channel; NBCSN; Nickelodeon; RFD-TV; Spike TV; Syfy; TBS; Telemundo; The Weather Channel; TLC; TNT; Travel Channel; Trinity Broadcasting Network (TBN); truTV; TV Land; Univision Studios; USA Network; VH1; WE tv.
  Fee: $31.97 monthly.
Digital Basic Service
  Subscribers: N.A.
  Programming (via satellite): AXS TV; BBC America; Bloomberg Television; CBS Sports Network; Cloo; CMT; Destination America; Discovery Kids Channel; Disney XD; DMX Music; ESPN HD; ESPN2 HD; ESPNews; ESPNU; FOX College Sports Central; FOX College Sports Pacific; Fox Sports 2; Fuse; FXM; FYI; Golf Channel; GolTV; GSN; HD Theater; History International; IFC; Investigation Discovery; MTV Classic; MTV Hits; MTV2; Nat Geo WILD; Nick Jr.; Nicktoons; Outdoor Channel; Ovation; OWN: Oprah Winfrey Network; Science Channel; TeenNick; Tennis Channel; Turner Classic Movies; TVG Network; Universal HD; VH1 Soul.
Digital Pay Service 1
  Pay Units: N.A.
  Programming (via satellite): Cinemax (multiplexed); Flix; HBO (multiplexed); HBO HD; Showtime (multiplexed); Showtime HD; Starz (multiplexed); Starz Encore (multiplexed); Starz HD; Sundance TV; The Movie Channel (multiplexed); The Movie Channel HD.
  Fee: $9.95 monthly (Cinemax, HBO, Showtime, Flix/Sundance/TMC or Starz/Encore).
Video-On-Demand: Yes
Pay-Per-View
  ESPN Now (delivered digitally); ETC (delivered digitally); Playboy TV (delivered digitally); Pleasure (delivered digitally); Fresh (delivered digitally); Shorteez (delivered digitally); Vubiquity Inc. (delivered digitally).
Internet Service
  Operational: Yes.
  Broadband Service: Mediacom High Speed Internet.
  Fee: $55.95 monthly.
Telephone Service
  Digital: Operational
Miles of Plant: 112.0 (coaxial); None (fiber optic). Homes passed: 6,036.
Regional Vice President: Doug Frank. Technical Operations Director: Greg Nank. Technical Operations Manager: Steve Angren. Marketing Director: Steve Schuh.
Ownership: Mediacom LLC (MSO).

OTTUMWA—Mediacom, 6300 Council St NE, Ste A, Cedar Rapids, IA 52402. Phones: 319-393-1914; 319-395-9699. Fax: 319-393-7017. Web Site: http://www.mediacomcable.com. Also serves Agency, Fairfield, Jefferson County & Wapello County. ICA: IA0013.
TV Market Ranking: Below 100 (Agency, Fairfield, Jefferson County, OTTUMWA, Wapello County). Franchise award date: N.A. Franchise expiration date: N.A. Began: July 27, 1971.
Channel capacity: N.A. Channels available but not in use: N.A.
Basic Service
  Subscribers: 5,403.
  Programming (received off-air): KCCI (CBS, MeTV) Des Moines; KDSM-TV (FOX, The Country Network) Des Moines; KFPX-TV (ION) Newton; KIIN (PBS) Iowa City; KTVO (ABC) Kirksville; KYOU-TV (FOX) Ottumwa; WHO-DT (Antenna TV, NBC) Des Moines; WOI-DT (ABC) Ames; allband FM.
  Programming (via satellite): A&E; Cartoon Network; CNBC; CNN; Comedy Central; C-SPAN; Discovery Channel; Freeform; Hallmark Channel; HLN; ION Television; Lifetime; Nickelodeon; QVC; TBS; The Weather Channel; TNT; VH1; WGN America.
  Fee: $60.00 installation; $43.00 monthly; $2.00 converter.
Expanded Basic Service 1
  Subscribers: N.A.
  Programming (via satellite): AMC; Animal Planet; BET; Bravo; CMT; Comcast SportsNet Chicago; Discovery Life Channel; Disney Channel; E! HD; ESPN; ESPN2; EWTN Global Catholic Network; Food Network; Fox News Channel; Fox Sports 1; FX; HGTV; History; INSP; MSNBC; MTV; National Geographic Channel; Spike TV; Syfy; Telemundo; TLC; Travel Channel; Trinity Broadcasting Network (TBN); truTV; TV Land; USA Network; WE tv.
  Fee: $21.16 monthly.
Digital Basic Service
  Subscribers: N.A.
  Programming (via satellite): BBC America; Bloomberg Television; Discovery Digital Networks; Disney XD; DMX Music; Fuse; FXM; FYI; Golf Channel; GSN; History International; IFC; LMN; NBCSN; Nick Jr.; Outdoor Channel; Ovation; TeenNick.
Digital Pay Service 1
  Pay Units: N.A.
  Programming (via satellite): Cinemax (multiplexed); Flix; HBO (multiplexed); Showtime (multiplexed); Starz (multiplexed); Starz Encore (multiplexed); Sundance TV; The Movie Channel (multiplexed).
  Fee: $9.95 monthly (Cinemax, HBO, Showtime, Flix/Sundance/TMC or Starz/Encore).
Video-On-Demand: Yes
Pay-Per-View
  ESPN Now (delivered digitally); ETC (delivered digitally); Playboy TV (delivered digitally); Pleasure (delivered digitally); Fresh (delivered digitally); Shorteez (delivered digitally); Vubiquity Inc. (delivered digitally).

Cable Systems—Iowa

Internet Service
 Operational: Yes. Began: January 1, 2003.
 Subscribers: 3,655.
 Broadband Service: Mediacom High Speed Internet.
 Fee: $50.95 monthly.
Telephone Service
 Analog: Not Operational
 Digital: Operational
 Subscribers: 1,887.
Miles of Plant: 320.0 (coaxial); 116.0 (fiber optic). Homes passed: 14,425.
Regional Vice President: Doug Frank. Technical Operations Director: Greg Nank. Technical Operations Manager: Steve Angren. Marketing Director: Steve Schuh.
Ownership: Mediacom LLC (MSO).

OXFORD JUNCTION—Mediacom, 6300 Council St NE, Ste A, Cedar Rapids, IA 52402. Phones: 319-395-9699; 319-393-1914; 800-332-0245. Fax: 319-393-7017. Web Site: http://www.mediacomcable.com. Also serves Tipton & Wyoming. ICA: IA0163.
TV Market Ranking: 60,65 (Tipton); 65 (OXFORD JUNCTION, Wyoming).
Channel capacity: N.A. Channels available but not in use: N.A.
Basic Service
 Subscribers: 489.
 Fee: $43.00 monthly.
Ownership: Mediacom LLC (MSO).

PALMER—Palmer Mutual Telephone Co, 306 Main St, PO Box 155, Palmer, IA 50571-0155. Phones: 800-685-7417; 712-359-2411. Fax: 712-359-2200. E-mail: palmerone@palmerone.com. Web Site: http://www.palmerone.com. ICA: IA0490.
TV Market Ranking: Outside TV Markets (PALMER). Franchise award date: February 13, 1990. Franchise expiration date: N.A. Began: September 15, 1990.
Channel capacity: N.A. Channels available but not in use: N.A.
Basic Service
 Subscribers: 51.
 Programming (received off-air): KCAU-TV (ABC) Sioux City; KCCI (CBS, MeTV) Des Moines; KDSM-TV (FOX, The Country Network) Des Moines; KEYC-TV (CBS, FOX) Mankato; KMEG (Azteca America, CBS, Decades) Sioux City; KPTH (FOX, MNT, This TV) Sioux City; KTIN (PBS) Fort Dodge; KTIV (CW, MeTV, NBC) Sioux City; WHO-DT (Antenna TV, NBC) Des Moines; WOI-DT (ABC) Ames; 2 FMs.
 Programming (via satellite): A&E; AMC; Animal Planet; Bravo; Cartoon Network; CMT; CNBC; CNN; Comedy Central; C-SPAN; C-SPAN 2; Discovery Channel; Disney Channel; DIY Network; E! HD; ESPN; ESPN Classic; ESPN2; ESPNU; EWTN Global Catholic Network; Food Network; Fox News Channel; Fox Sports 1; Freeform; FX; FXM; Golf Channel; Hallmark Channel; HGTV; History; HLN; INSP; ION Television; Lifetime; LMN; MSNBC; MTV; NFL Network; Nickelodeon; Outdoor Channel; OWN: Oprah Winfrey Network; Pop; QVC; Radar Network; Spike TV; Syfy; TBS; The Weather Channel; TLC; TNT; Travel Channel; Trinity Broadcasting Network (TBN); truTV; Turner Classic Movies; TV Land; USA Network; VH1; WGN America.
 Fee: $30.00 installation; $70.00 monthly.
Digital Basic Service
 Subscribers: N.A.
 Programming (via satellite): AXS TV; BBC America; Destination America; Discovery Kids Channel; Discovery Life Channel; Disney XD; ESPN HD; ESPN2 HD; ESPNews; FYI; GSN; HD Theater; History; IFC; Investigation Discovery; LMN; MC; MTV Classic; MTV2; National Geographic Channel; NBCSN; Nick Jr.; Nicktoons; Outdoor Channel; RFD-TV; Science Channel; TeenNick; Universal HD; VH1 Country.
Digital Pay Service 1
 Pay Units: N.A.
 Programming (via satellite): Cinemax (multiplexed); Cinemax HD; HBO (multiplexed); HBO HD; Starz (multiplexed); Starz Encore; Starz HD.
 Fee: $10.00 monthly (Cinemax), $11.00 monthly (Starz/Encore), $14.00 monthly (HBO).
Internet Service
 Operational: No, DSL.
Telephone Service
 Analog: Operational
Miles of Plant: 3.0 (coaxial); 3.0 (fiber optic). Homes passed: 100.
General Manager: Steve Trimble.
Ownership: Palmer Mutual Telephone Co.

PALO—Palo Cooperative Telephone Association, 807 Second St, PO Box 169, Palo, IA 52324. Phone: 319-851-3431. Fax: 319-851-6970. E-mail: pctafo@netins.net. Web Site: http://www.gopcta.com. ICA: IA0319.
Channel capacity: N.A. Channels available but not in use: N.A.
Basic Service
 Subscribers: 630.
 Fee: $34.95 monthly.
Internet Service
 Operational: Yes.
 Fee: $44.95-$94.95 monthly.
Telephone Service
 Digital: Operational
 Fee: $18.00 monthly
General Manager: Kirby Underberg.
Ownership: Palo Cooperative Telephone Assn.

PANORA—Panora Communications Cooperative, 114 East Main St, PO Box 189, Panora, IA 50216. Phone: 641-755-2424. Fax: 641-755-2425. E-mail: panora@netins.net. Web Site: http://panoratelco.com. Also serves Bagley, Guthrie Center, Jamaica, Lake Panorama, Linden & Yale. ICA: IA0108.
TV Market Ranking: 66 (Linden); Outside TV Markets (Bagley, Lake Panorama, PANORA, Yale, Jamaica). Franchise award date: January 1, 1981. Franchise expiration date: N.A. Began: January 1, 1981.
Channel capacity: N.A. Channels available but not in use: N.A.
Basic Service
 Subscribers: 1,387.
 Programming (received off-air): KCCI (CBS, MeTV) Des Moines; KCWI-TV (CW) Ames; KDIN-TV (PBS) Des Moines; KDSM-TV (FOX, The Country Network) Des Moines; WHO-DT (Antenna TV, NBC) Des Moines; WOI-DT (ABC) Ames.
 Programming (via satellite): A&E; AMC; Animal Planet; BTN; CMT; CNBC; CNN; Comcast SportsNet Chicago; C-SPAN; Discovery Channel; Disney Channel; Disney XD; ESPN; ESPN2; Fox News Channel; Freeform; FX; HGTV; History; HLN; INSP; ION Television; Lifetime; Nickelodeon; Outdoor Channel; Pop; Spike TV; TBS; The Weather Channel; TLC; TNT; Travel Channel; USA Network; WGN America.
 Fee: $20.00 installation; $51.95 monthly; $1.50 converter.
Pay Service 1
 Pay Units: N.A.
 Programming (via satellite): HBO; Starz; Starz Encore.
 Fee: $13.00 monthly (Starz/Encore), $15.00 monthly (HBO).
Video-On-Demand: No
Pay-Per-View
 Special events (delivered digitally).
Internet Service
 Operational: Yes.
 Subscribers: 74.
 Fee: $39.95-$59.95 monthly.
Telephone Service
 Analog: Operational
Miles of Plant: 49.0 (coaxial); 56.0 (fiber optic).
General Manager: Andy Randol. Plant Manager/Co Manager: Bill Dorsett.
Ownership: Panora Communications Cooperative (MSO).

PATON—Gowrie Cablevision. Now served by GOWRIE, IA [IA0439]. ICA: IA0492.

PAULINA—Formerly served by WesTel Systems. Now served by Community Cable TV Agency of O'Brien County, SANBORN, IA [IA0104]. ICA: IA0164.

PERSIA—Formerly served by TelePartners. Now served by Walnut Communications, WALNUT, IA [IA0241]. ICA: IA0575.

PETERSON—WesTel Systems. Now served by MARCUS, IA [IA0171]. ICA: IA0312.

PISGAH—Formerly served by TelePartners. No longer in operation. ICA: IA0494.

PLYMOUTH—OmniTel Communications. This system has converted to IPTV. See PLYMOUTH, IA [IA5127]. ICA: IA0495.

POMEROY—Formerly served by TelePartners. No longer in operation. ICA: IA0220.

POSTVILLE—CenturyLink, PO Box 4065, Monroe, LA 71211. Phones: 913-353-7298; 888-835-2485. Web Site: http://www.centurylink.com. Also serves Allamakee County (portions) & Clayton County (portions). ICA: IA0161.
Channel capacity: N.A. Channels available but not in use: N.A.
Basic Service
 Subscribers: 160.
 Programming (received off-air): KCRG-TV (ABC, MNT) Cedar Rapids; KFXA (FOX, The Country Network) Cedar Rapids; KFXB-TV (Christian TV Network) Dubuque; KGAN (CBS) Cedar Rapids; KPXR-TV (ION) Cedar Rapids; KRIN (PBS) Waterloo; KWWL (CW, MeTV, NBC) Waterloo; WGN-TV (IND) Chicago.
 Fee: $20.95 monthly.
Digital Basic Service
 Subscribers: N.A.
Digital Pay Service 1
 Pay Units: N.A.
 Programming (via satellite): Cinemax (multiplexed); HBO (multiplexed); Showtime (multiplexed); Starz (multiplexed); Starz Encore (multiplexed).
 Fee: $10.95 monthly (Cinemax), $11.95 monthly (Starz/Encore), $13.50 monthly (HBO), $20.95 (Cinemax/HBO).
Internet Service
 Operational: Yes.
Telephone Service
 Digital: Operational
Vice President, Operations: Tim White. Assistant Secretary: Joan Randazzo.
Ownership: CenturyLink.

PRAIRIEBURG—Prairieburg Telephone Co, 120 West Main St, Ste 2, Prairieburg, IA 52219. Phone: 319-437-3611. ICA: IA0641.
TV Market Ranking: 65 (PRAIRIEBURG).
Channel capacity: N.A. Channels available but not in use: N.A.
Basic Service
 Subscribers: 38.
 Fee: $33.00 monthly.
Plant Manager: Don Reichenauer.
Ownership: Prairieburg Telephone Co Inc.

PRESTON—Mediacom, 3900 26th Ave, Moline, IL 61265. Phone: 309-797-2580. Fax: 309-797-2414. Web Site: http://www.mediacomcable.com. Also serves Charlotte, Goose Lake, Jackson County & Miles. ICA: IA0148.
TV Market Ranking: 60 (Charlotte, Goose Lake); Below 100 (Jackson County, Miles, PRESTON).
Channel capacity: N.A. Channels available but not in use: N.A.
Basic Service
 Subscribers: 330.
 Fee: $43.00 monthly.
Ownership: Mediacom LLC (MSO).

PROTIVIN—Protivin Cablevision, 117 North Main St, PO Box 53, Protivin, IA 52163. Phone: 563-569-8401. Fax: 563-569-8401. ICA: IA0561.
TV Market Ranking: Outside TV Markets (PROTIVIN).
Channel capacity: N.A. Channels available but not in use: N.A.
Basic Service
 Subscribers: N.A.
 Programming (received off-air): KCRG-TV (ABC, MNT) Cedar Rapids; KIMT (CBS, MNT) Mason City; KTTC (CW, NBC) Rochester; KWWL (CW, MeTV, NBC) Waterloo; KYIN (PBS) Mason City; WLAX (FOX, MeTV) La Crosse.
 Programming (via satellite): CNN; Discovery Channel; ESPN; EWTN Global Catholic Network; Freeform; Nickelodeon; Spike TV; TBS; TNT; Turner Classic Movies; USA Network; WGN America.
 Fee: $17.36 monthly.
Pay Service 1
 Pay Units: N.A.
 Programming (via satellite): Cinemax; HBO.
 Fee: $7.50 monthly (each).
Internet Service
 Operational: No.

Iowa—Cable Systems

Telephone Service
None
Miles of Plant: 2.0 (coaxial); None (fiber optic). Homes passed: 150.
General Manager: Michael Pecinovsky.
Ownership: City of Protivin.

RADCLIFFE—Radcliffe Cablevision. Formerly [IA0265]. This cable system has converted to IPTV, 202 Isabella St, PO Box 140, Radcliffe, IA 50230-7714. Phone: 515-899-2341. Fax: 515-899-2499. E-mail: info@radcliffetelephone.com. Web Site: http://radcliffetelephone.com. ICA: IA5020.
TV Market Ranking: 66 (RADCLIFFE).
Channel capacity: N.A. Channels available but not in use: N.A.
Digital Vision
Subscribers: 106.
Fee: $42.20 monthly.
Expanded Vision
Subscribers: 65.
Fee: $53.15 monthly.
HD
Subscribers: N.A.
Fee: $10.95 monthly.
Cinemax
Subscribers: N.A.
Fee: $12.95 monthly.
HBO
Subscribers: N.A.
Fee: $15.95 monthly.
Showtime
Subscribers: N.A.
Fee: $15.95 monthly.
Starz/Encore
Subscribers: N.A.
Fee: $12.95 monthly.
Video-On-Demand: Planned
Internet Service
Operational: Yes.
Telephone Service
Digital: Operational
General Manager & Chief Technician: Ed Drake.
Ownership: Radcliffe Cablevision Inc.

RADCLIFFE—Radcliffe Cablevision. This cable system has converted to IPTV. See RADCLIFFE, IA [IA5020]. ICA: IA0265.

RANDOLPH—Formerly served by Westcom. No longer in operation. ICA: IA0366.

READLYN—RTC Communications (formerly Readlyn Telephone Co.) This cable system has converted to IPTV. See READLYN, IA [IA5325]. ICA: IA0245.

READLYN—RTC Communications. This cable system has converted to IPTV, 121 Main St, PO Box 159, Readlyn, IA 50668. Phones: 800-590-7747; 319-279-3375. Fax: 319-279-7575. E-mail: readlyn@netins.net. Web Site: http://www.readlyntelco.com. ICA: IA5325.
TV Market Ranking: 65 (READLYN). Franchise award date: December 1, 1983. Franchise expiration date: N.A. Began: January 1, 1984.
Channel capacity: N.A. Channels available but not in use: N.A.
Essential
Subscribers: N.A.
Programming (received off-air): KCRG-TV (ABC, MNT) Cedar Rapids; KFXA (FOX, The Country Network) Cedar Rapids; KGAN (CBS) Cedar Rapids; KIMT (CBS, MNT) Mason City; KPXR-TV (ION) Cedar Rapids; KRIN (PBS) Waterloo; KWWL (CW, MeTV, NBC) Waterloo.
Programming (via satellite): A&E; AMC; Animal Planet; BTN; Cartoon Network; CMT; CNN; Comedy Central; Discovery Channel; Disney Channel; Disney XD; DIY Network; E! HD; ESPN; ESPN Classic; ESPN2; Food Network; Fox News Channel; Fox Sports 1; Freeform; FX; Golf Channel; GSN; Hallmark Channel; Hallmark Movies & Mysteries; HGTV; History; HLN; Lifetime; MSNBC; MTV; National Geographic Channel; Nickelodeon; Outdoor Channel; OWN: Oprah Winfrey Network; Pop; QVC; RFD-TV; Spike TV; Syfy; TBS; The Weather Channel; TLC; TNT; Travel Channel; truTV; Turner Classic Movies; TV Land; USA Network; VH1; WE tv; WGN America.
Fee: $17.95 monthly. Includes 35 channels.
Elite
Subscribers: N.A.
Fee: $62.95 monthly. Includes 100 channels plus music channels.
Extreme
Subscribers: N.A.
Fee: $72.95 monthly. Includes 190 channels plus music channels.
Cinemax
Subscribers: N.A.
Fee: $10.95 monthly. Includes 8 channels.
HBO
Subscribers: N.A.
Fee: $16.95 monthly. Includes 6 channels.
Starz/Encore
Subscribers: N.A.
Fee: $10.95 monthly. Includes 11 channels.
Video-On-Demand: No
Internet Service
Operational: Yes.
Fee: $39.95 monthly.
Telephone Service
Digital: Operational
General Manager: Sharon K. Huck.
Ownership: Readlyn Telephone Co.

RED OAK—Mediacom, 310 Commerce Dr, Red Oak Dr, IA 51566. Phone: 800-332-0245. Web Site: http://www.mediacomcable.com. Also serves Bedford, Clarinda, Corning, Essex, Glenwood, Mills County (eastern portion), Shenandoah & Villisca. ICA: IA0040.
TV Market Ranking: 53 (Glenwood, Mills County (eastern portion)); Outside TV Markets (Bedford, Clarinda, Corning, Essex, Shenandoah, Villisca).
Channel capacity: N.A. Channels available but not in use: N.A.
Basic Service
Subscribers: 4,237. Commercial subscribers: 6.
Fee: $41.99 installation; $43.00 monthly.
Internet Service
Operational: Yes.
Subscribers: 4,491.
Broadband Service: Mediacom High Speed Internet.
Telephone Service
Digital: Operational
Subscribers: 2,349.
Miles of Plant: 315.0 (coaxial); 409.0 (fiber optic). Homes passed: 15,739.
Ownership: Mediacom LLC (MSO).

RENWICK—Formerly served by Heck's TV & Cable. Now served by Goldfield Communication Services, GOLDFIELD, IA [IA0252]. ICA: IA0497.

RICHLAND—Starwest Inc, 15235 235th St, Milton, IA 52570-8016. Phones: 319-397-2283; 319-293-6336. ICA: IA0498.
TV Market Ranking: Below 100 (RICHLAND).
Channel capacity: N.A. Channels available but not in use: N.A.
Basic Service
Subscribers: N.A.
Programming (received off-air): KCRG-TV (ABC, MNT) Cedar Rapids; KGAN (CBS) Cedar Rapids; KWWL (CW, MeTV, NBC) Waterloo.
Programming (via satellite): ESPN; Freeform; TBS; USA Network; WGN America.
Fee: $30.00 installation; $10.50 monthly.
Pay Service 1
Pay Units: N.A.
Programming (via satellite): Showtime.
Fee: $9.95 monthly.
Internet Service
Operational: No.
General Manager & Chief Technician: John Stooksberry.
Ownership: Starwest Inc. (MSO).

RINGSTED—Ringsted Cablevision, 19 West Maple St, PO Box 187, Ringsted, IA 50578-0187. Phones: 712-866-8000; 712-866-1456. Fax: 712-866-0002. E-mail: tjohnson@ringtelco.com. Web Site: http://www.ringstedtelephone.com. ICA: IA0285.
TV Market Ranking: Outside TV Markets (RINGSTED). Franchise award date: N.A. Franchise expiration date: N.A. Began: September 1, 1973.
Channel capacity: N.A. Channels available but not in use: N.A.
Basic Service
Subscribers: 46.
Programming (received off-air): KAAL (ABC, This TV) Austin; KCAU-TV (ABC) Sioux City; KELO-TV (CBS, MNT) Sioux Falls; KEYC-TV (CBS, FOX) Mankato; KIMT (CBS, MNT) Mason City; KMEG (Azteca America, CBS, Decades) Sioux City; KPTH (FOX, MNT, This TV) Sioux City; KSFY-TV (ABC, CW) Sioux Falls; KTIN (PBS) Fort Dodge; KTIV (CW, MeTV, NBC) Sioux City; WHO-DT (Antenna TV, NBC) Des Moines; allband FM.
Programming (via satellite): A&E; AMC; Animal Planet; Cartoon Network; CMT; CNBC; CNN; Comedy Central; C-SPAN; C-SPAN 2; Disney Channel; E! HD; ESPN; ESPN Classic; ESPN2; ESPNU; Food Network; Fox News Channel; FOX Sports Networks; Freeform; FX; Hallmark Channel; HGTV; History; HLN; ION Television; Lifetime; MTV; National Geographic Channel; Nickelodeon; Outdoor Channel; QVC; Spike TV; Syfy; TBS; The Weather Channel; TLC; TNT; Travel Channel; Turner Classic Movies; TV Land; USA Network; VH1; WGN America.
Fee: $50.00 monthly.
Digital Basic Service
Subscribers: N.A.
Programming (via satellite): BBC America; CMT; Destination America; Discovery Kids Channel; Discovery Life Channel; Disney XD; ESPNews; Fox Sports 1; FXM; FYI; Golf Channel; GSN; History International; IFC; Investigation Discovery; MTV Classic; MTV2; National Geographic Channel; Nick Jr.; Nicktoons; Outdoor Channel; OWN: Oprah Winfrey Network; Science Channel; TeenNick.
Digital Pay Service 1
Pay Units: 14.
Programming (via satellite): HBO (multiplexed).
Fee: $11.00 monthly.
Digital Pay Service 2
Pay Units: 4.
Programming (via satellite): Cinemax (multiplexed).
Fee: $11.00 monthly.
Digital Pay Service 3
Pay Units: 7.
Programming (via satellite): Starz (multiplexed); Starz Encore (multiplexed).
Fee: $11.00 monthly.
Video-On-Demand: No
Internet Service
Operational: No, DSL.
Telephone Service
Analog: Operational
Miles of Plant: 4.0 (coaxial); None (fiber optic). Homes passed: 230.
General Manager: Tim Johnson. Customer Service Manager: Suzanne Bonnicksen.
Ownership: Ringsted Telephone Co.

ROCK RAPIDS—Premier Communications. Now served by SIOUX CENTER, IA [IA0076]. ICA: IA0100.

ROWLEY (village)—Formerly served by New Path Communications LC. No longer in operation. ICA: IA0502.

ROYAL—Royal Telephone Co, 307 Main St, PO Box 80, Royal, IA 51357. Phone: 712-933-2615. Fax: 712-933-0015. E-mail: info@royaltelco.com. Web Site: http://www.royaltelco.com. ICA: IA0299.
TV Market Ranking: Outside TV Markets (ROYAL). Franchise award date: N.A. Franchise expiration date: N.A. Began: March 1, 1983.
Channel capacity: N.A. Channels available but not in use: N.A.
Basic Service
Subscribers: 231.
Programming (received off-air): KCAU-TV (ABC) Sioux City; KELO-TV (CBS, MNT) Sioux Falls; KEYC-TV (CBS, FOX) Mankato; KMEG (Azteca America, CBS, Decades) Sioux City; KPTH (FOX, MNT, This TV) Sioux City; KSFY-TV (ABC, CW) Sioux Falls; KTIN (PBS) Fort Dodge; KTIV (CW, MeTV, NBC) Sioux City; WOI-DT (ABC) Ames.
Programming (via satellite): CW PLUS; ION Television; Radar Channel; The Weather Channel; WGN America.
Fee: $46.00 monthly.
Expanded Basic Service 1
Subscribers: N.A.
Programming (via satellite): A&E; AMC; Animal Planet; Bravo; Cartoon Network; CMT; CNBC; CNN; Comedy Central; C-SPAN; C-SPAN 2; Discovery Channel; Disney Channel; DIY Network; E! HD; ESPN; ESPN Classic; ESPN2; EWTN Global Catholic Network; Food Network; Fox News Channel; Fox Sports 1; FOX Sports North; Freeform; FX; FXM; Golf Channel; Hallmark Channel; HGTV; History; HLN; INSP; Lifetime; MSNBC; MTV; Nickelodeon; Outdoor Channel; OWN: Oprah Winfrey Network; Pop; Spike TV; Syfy; TBS; TLC; TNT; Travel Channel; Trinity Broadcasting Network (TBN); truTV; Turner Classic Movies; TV Land; USA Network; VH1.
Fee: $26.75 monthly.
Digital Basic Service
Subscribers: N.A.
Programming (via satellite): BBC America; Destination America; Discovery Kids Channel; Discovery Life Channel; ESPNews; FYI; GSN; History International; IFC; Investigation Discovery; MC; MTV Classic; MTV2; mtvU; National Geographic Channel; Nick Jr.; Nicktoons; Science Channel; TeenNick; VH1 Country.
Digital Expanded Basic Service
Subscribers: N.A.
Programming (via satellite): AXS TV; Bravo; Discovery Channel HD; ESPN HD.
Fee: $8.50 monthly.

Cable Systems—Iowa

Digital Pay Service 1
Pay Units: N.A.
Programming (via satellite): Cinemax (multiplexed); Cinemax HD; Flix; HBO (multiplexed); HBO HD; Showtime (multiplexed); Showtime HD; Starz (multiplexed); Starz Encore (multiplexed); Starz HD; Sundance TV; The Movie Channel (multiplexed); The Movie Channel HD.
Fee: $9.00 monthly (each).
Pay-Per-View
Sports PPV (delivered digitally).
Internet Service
Operational: No, DSL.
Telephone Service
Analog: Operational
Miles of Plant: 3.0 (coaxial); None (fiber optic).
General Manager: Doug Nelson. Chief Technician: Rob Wassom. Marketing Director: Sherry Toft.
Ownership: Royal Telephone Co.

RUDD—Omnitel Communications, 608 East Congress St, Nora Springs, IA 50458-8634. Phones: 877-666-4835; 641-749-2531. Fax: 641-749-9510. E-mail: question@omnitelcom.com. Web Site: http://www.omnitel.biz. Also serves Floyd, Greene, Lime Springs, Marble Rock, Nora Springs, Osage, Rockford & Staceyville. ICA: IA0503.
TV Market Ranking: Below 100 (Greene, Marble Rock, Nora Springs, Osage, Rockford, RUDD, Staceyville); Outside TV Markets (Lime Springs). Franchise award date: N.A. Franchise expiration date: N.A. Began: October 1, 1989.
Channel capacity: 75 (operating 2-way).
Channels available but not in use: N.A.
Digital Basic Service
Subscribers: 3,244 Includes IPTV. Commercial subscribers: 794.
Programming (received off-air): KAAL (ABC, This TV) Austin; KCRG-TV (ABC, MNT) Cedar Rapids; KGAN (CBS) Cedar Rapids; KIMT (CBS, MNT) Mason City; KSMQ-TV (PBS) Austin; KTTC (CW, NBC) Rochester; KWWL (CW, MeTV, NBC) Waterloo; KXLT-TV (FOX, MeTV) Rochester; KYIN (PBS) Mason City.
Programming (via satellite): A&E; AMC; Animal Planet; BTN; Cartoon Network; CMT; CNBC; CNN; Comedy Central; C-SPAN; Discovery Channel; Disney Channel; DIY Network; E! HD; ESPN; ESPN Classic; ESPN2; ESPNU; EWTN Global Catholic Network; Food Network; Fox News Channel; Fox Sports 1; FOX Sports Networks; Freeform; FX; Golf Channel; Hallmark Channel; HGTV; History; HLN; Lifetime; MoviePlex; MSNBC; MTV; National Geographic Channel; Nickelodeon; Outdoor Channel; Pop; QVC; Radar Channel; RFD-TV; Spike TV; Syfy; TBS; The Weather Channel; TLC; TNT; Travel Channel; truTV; Turner Classic Movies; TV Land; USA Network; VH1; WGN America.
Fee: $25.00 installation; $46.45 monthly.
Digital Expanded Basic Service
Subscribers: 1,669 Includes IPTV.
Programming (via satellite): AXS TV; BBC America; Bloomberg Television; Bravo; Discovery Digital Networks; DMX Music; ESPN Classic; ESPNews; FXM; GSN; IFC; National Geographic Channel; Nick Jr.; Nicktoons; Ovation; Trinity Broadcasting Network (TBN); WE tv.
Fee: $55.95 monthly.
Digital Expanded Basic Service 2
Subscribers: 705.
Programming (via satellite): ESPN HD.
Fee: $11.95 monthly.

Digital Pay Service 1
Pay Units: N.A.
Programming (via satellite): Cinemax (multiplexed); HBO (multiplexed); HBO HD; Showtime (multiplexed); Starz (multiplexed); Starz Encore (multiplexed); Sundance TV; The Movie Channel (multiplexed).
Fee: $12.00 monthly (Starz/Encore), $14.00 monthly (Showtime or Cinemax), $18.00 monthly (HBO).
Pay-Per-View
iN DEMAND (delivered digitally); Playboy TV (delivered digitally); Fresh (delivered digitally); Shorteez (delivered digitally).
Internet Service
Operational: Yes, DSL.
Subscribers: 723.
Telephone Service
Digital: Operational
Miles of Plant: 133.0 (coaxial); 170.0 (fiber optic). Homes passed: 4,000.
President & Chief Executive Officer: Ronald Laudner. Accounting Manager: Melanie Johanns.
Ownership: Farmers Mutual Telephone Co. (Nora Springs) (MSO).

RUDD—Omnitel Communications. This system has converted to IPTV, 608 East Congress St, Nora Springs, IA 50458-8634. Phones: 877-666-4835; 641-749-2531. Fax: 641-749-9510. E-mail: question@omnitel.biz. Web Site: http://www.omnitel.biz. Also serves Elma, Floyd, Lime Springs, Little Cedar, Marble Rock, McIntire, New Haven, Nora Springs, Plymouth, Riceville, Rock Falls, St. Ansgar & Stacyville. ICA: IA5127.
TV Market Ranking: Below 100 (Marble Rock, Nora Springs, Plymouth, Riceville, RUDD, St. Ansgar, Stacyville); Outside TV Markets (Elma, Lime Springs). Franchise award date: N.A. Franchise expiration date: N.A. Began: July 1, 1989.
Channel capacity: N.A. Channels available but not in use: N.A.
OmniTelevision
Subscribers: N.A. Included in Rudd (cable) Commercial subscribers: 794.
Programming (received off-air): KAAL (ABC, This TV) Austin; KCRG-TV (ABC, MNT) Cedar Rapids; KGAN (CBS) Cedar Rapids; KIMT (CBS, MNT) Mason City; KSMQ-TV (PBS) Austin; KTTC (CW, NBC) Rochester; KWWL (CW, MeTV, NBC) Waterloo; KXLT-TV (FOX, MeTV) Rochester; KYIN (PBS) Mason City.
Programming (via satellite): A&E; AMC; Animal Planet; Bravo; BTN; Cartoon Network; CMT; CNBC; CNN; Comedy Central; C-SPAN; Discovery Channel; Disney Channel; DIY Network; DMX Music; E! HD; ESPN; ESPN Classic; ESPN2; ESPNU; EWTN Global Catholic Network; Food Network; Fox News Channel; Fox Sports 1; FOX Sports Networks; Freeform; FX; Golf Channel; Hallmark Channel; HGTV; History; HLN; Lifetime; MoviePlex; MSNBC; MTV; National Geographic Channel; NBCSN; Nickelodeon; Outdoor Channel; Pop; QVC; Radar Channel; RFD-TV; Spike TV; Syfy; TBS; The Weather Channel; TLC; TNT; Travel Channel; Trinity Broadcasting Network (TBN); truTV; Turner Classic Movies; TV Land; USA Network; VH1; WGN America.
Fee: $25.00 installation; $46.45 Includes 65+ channels.
OmniTelevision Plus
Subscribers: N.A. Included in Rudd (cable)
Programming (via satellite): BBC America; Bloomberg Television; Discovery Digital Networks; ESPN HD; ESPNews; FXM; GSN; IFC; Nick Jr.; Nicktoons; WE tv.
Fee: $55.95 Includes 95+ channels.
HD
Subscribers: N.A. Included in Rudd (cable)
Fee: $11.95 monthly.
Cinemax
Subscribers: N.A.
Programming (via satellite): Cinemax.
Fee: $14.00 monthly.
HBO
Subscribers: N.A.
Programming (via satellite): HBO.
Fee: $18.00 monthly.
Showtime
Subscribers: N.A.
Programming (via satellite): Showtime.
Fee: $14.00 monthly.
Starz/Encore
Subscribers: N.A.
Programming (via satellite): Starz; Starz Encore.
Fee: $12.00 monthly.
Pay-Per-View
iN DEMAND (delivered digitally); Fresh (delivered digitally); Playboy TV (delivered digitally); Shorteez (delivered digitally).
Internet Service
Operational: Yes. Began: June 1, 2002.
Telephone Service
Digital: Operational
President & Chief Executive Officer: Ronald Laudner. Accounting Manager: Melanie Johanns.
Ownership: Farmers Mutual Telephone Co. (Nora Springs) (MSO).

RUNNELLS—Formerly served by Telnet South LC. No longer in operation. ICA: IA0504.

RUSSELL—Formerly served by Longview Communications. No longer in operation. ICA: IA0283.

RUTHVEN—Formerly served by Terril Cable Systems. No longer in operation. ICA: IA0551.

RYAN—USA Communications. Now served by SHELLSBURG, IA [IA0255]. ICA: IA0346.

SALEM—Formerly served by Longview Communications. No longer in operation. ICA: IA0505.

SALIX—Long Lines, 501 4th St, PO Box 67, Sergeant Bluff, IA 51054-8509. Phones: 866-901-5664; 712-884-2203; 712-271-4400; 712-271-4000. Fax: 712-271-2727. E-mail: info@longlines.biz. Web Site: http://www.longlines.com. Also serves Anthon, Blencoe, Correctionville, Danbury, Holstein, Ida Grove, Logan, Magnolia, Mapleton, Missouri Valley, Moorhead, Onawa, Orange City, Sergeant Bluff, Sloan, Soldier, Ute, Whiting & Woodbine, IA; South Sioux City, NE; Dakota Dunes & Jefferson, SD. ICA: IA0510.
TV Market Ranking: 53 (Logan, Magnolia, Missouri Valley); Below 100 (Correctionville, Jefferson, SALIX, Sergeant Bluff, Sloan, South Sioux City, Anthon, Dakota Dunes, Whiting); Outside TV Markets (Holstein, Ida Grove, Mapleton, Woodbine, Blencoe, Danbury, Moorhead, Onawa, Orange City, Soldier, Ute).
Channel capacity: N.A. Channels available but not in use: N.A.
Basic Service
Subscribers: 7,405.
Programming (received off-air): KCAU-TV (ABC) Sioux City; KMEG (Azteca America, CBS, Decades) Sioux City; KPTH (FOX, MNT, This TV) Sioux City; KSIN-TV (PBS) Sioux City; KTIV (CW, MeTV, NBC) Sioux City.
Programming (via satellite): A&E; AMC; Animal Planet; BTN; Cartoon Network; CMT; CNBC; CNN; Comedy Central; C-SPAN; C-SPAN 2; CW PLUS; Discovery Channel; Disney Channel; E! HD; ESPN; ESPN Classic; ESPN2; EWTN Global Catholic Network; Food Network; Fox News Channel; Fox Sports 1; FOX Sports North; Freeform; FX; Golf Channel; Hallmark Channel; HGTV; History; HLN; INSP; Lifetime; LMN; MSNBC; MTV; Nickelodeon; QVC; Spike TV; Syfy; TBS; The Weather Channel; TLC; TNT; Travel Channel; Trinity Broadcasting Network (TBN); truTV; Turner Classic Movies; TV Guide; TV Land; USA Network; VH1; WGN America.
Fee: $15.00 installation; $59.95 monthly.
Digital Basic Service
Subscribers: N.A.
Programming (via satellite): BBC America; Cooking Channel; Destination America; Discovery Kids Channel; Discovery Life Channel; Disney XD; DIY Network; DMX Music; ESPNews; ESPNU; FOX College Sports Central; FOX College Sports Pacific; FXM; FYI; Great American Country; GSN; History International; IFC; Investigation Discovery; MTV Classic; MTV Hits; MTV Jams; MTV2; NBCSN; Nick Jr.; Nicktoons; Outdoor Channel; OWN; Oprah Winfrey Network; RFD-TV; Science Channel; TeenNick; VH1 Country; VH1 Soul; WE tv.
Digital Expanded Basic Service
Subscribers: N.A.
Programming (via satellite): AXS TV; BTN HD; Discovery Channel HD; ESPN HD; ESPN2 HD; Outdoor Channel 2 HD.
Fee: $9.95 monthly.
Digital Expanded Basic Service 2
Subscribers: N.A.
Programming (via satellite): Bandamax; De Pelicula; De Pelicula Clasico; ESPN Deportes; Fox Deportes; Ritmoson; Telehit.
Fee: $2.95 monthly.
Pay Service 1
Pay Units: 92.
Programming (via satellite): HBO (multiplexed).
Fee: $14.95 monthly.
Pay Service 2
Pay Units: 40.
Programming (via satellite): Flix; Showtime (multiplexed); The Movie Channel.
Fee: $14.45 monthly.
Digital Pay Service 1
Pay Units: N.A.
Programming (via satellite): Cinemax (multiplexed); Cinemax HD; Flix; HBO (multiplexed); HBO HD; Showtime (multiplexed); Starz (multiplexed); Starz Encore (multiplexed); Starz HD; Starz On Demand; The Movie Channel (multiplexed).
Fee: $11.95 monthly (Cinemax), $13.95 monthly (Starz/Encore), $14.45 monthly (Showtime/TMC/Flix), $14.95 monthly (HBO).
Video-On-Demand: Yes
Internet Service
Operational: Yes.
Fee: $24.95-$64.95 monthly.
Telephone Service
Digital: Operational
Fee: $12.00 monthly
Miles of Plant: 8.0 (coaxial); None (fiber optic).
Chief Executive Officer: Jon Winkel. President & Chief Financial Officer: Brent Olson. General Manager & Chief Operations Officer: Paul Bergmann. Chief Technician:

Iowa—Cable Systems

Tony Seubert. Marketing Director: Denise Moberg.
Ownership: Long Lines (MSO).

SANBORN—Community Cable TV Agency of O'Brien County, 102 South Eastern St, PO Box 489, Sanborn, IA 51248. Phone: 712-930-5593. Fax: 712-930-5595. E-mail: tca@tcaexpress.net. Web Site: http://www.tcaexpress.net. Also serves Hartley, Paulina & Primghar. ICA: IA0104.
TV Market Ranking: Outside TV Markets (Hartley, Paulina, Primghar, SANBORN). Franchise award date: N.A. Franchise expiration date: N.A. Began: April 1, 1982.
Channel capacity: 78 (operating 2-way). Channels available but not in use: N.A.
Basic Service
Subscribers: 1,544.
Programming (received off-air): KCAU-TV (ABC) Sioux City; KDLT-TV (Antenna TV, NBC) Sioux Falls; KELO-TV (CBS, MNT) Sioux Falls; KMEG (Azteca America, CBS, Decades) Sioux City; KPTH (FOX, MNT, This TV) Sioux City; KSFY-TV (ABC, CW) Sioux Falls; KSIN-TV (PBS) Sioux City; KTIV (CW, MeTV, NBC) Sioux City.
Programming (via satellite): C-SPAN; Pop; QVC; TBS; The Weather Channel; Trinity Broadcasting Network (TBN); WGN America.
Fee: $30.00 installation; $55.35 monthly.
Expanded Basic Service 1
Subscribers: N.A.
Programming (via satellite): A&E; AMC; Animal Planet; Bravo; BTN; Cartoon Network; CMT; CNBC; CNN; Comedy Central; Discovery Channel; Discovery Life Channel; Disney Channel; DIY Network; ESPN; ESPN Classic; ESPN2; Food Network; Fox News Channel; Fox Sports 1; FOX Sports North; Freeform; FX; Great American Country; Hallmark Channel; HGTV; History; Lifetime; MSNBC; MTV; National Geographic Channel; NFL Network; Nickelodeon; Outdoor Channel; Oxygen; RFD-TV; Spike TV; Syfy; TLC; TNT; Travel Channel; Turner Classic Movies; TV Land; USA Network; VH1.
Fee: $21.95 monthly.
Digital Basic Service
Subscribers: N.A.
Programming (via satellite): AZN Television; BBC America; Bloomberg Television; Bravo; Centric; Church Channel; Cloo; CMT; Destination America; Discovery Kids Channel; Discovery Life Channel; Disney XD; DMX Music; ESPN Classic; ESPN2; ESPNews; ESPNU; EVINE Live; Fox Business Network; FOX College Sports Central; FOX College Sports Pacific; Fox Sports 1; Fuse; FXM; FYI; Golf Channel; Great American Country; GSN; HGTV; History; History International; IFC; Investigation Discovery; JUCE TV; LMN; MTV Classic; MTV Hits; MTV Jams; MTV2; National Geographic Channel; NBCSN; Nick Jr.; Nicktoons; Outdoor Channel; Ovation; OWN: Oprah Winfrey Network; Pivot; Science Channel; Syfy; TeenNick; Trinity Broadcasting Network (TBN); Turner Classic Movies; VH1 Soul; WE tv.
Fee: $10.00 installation; $4.00 converter.
Digital Expanded Basic Service
Subscribers: N.A.
Programming (via satellite): A&E HD; AXS TV; BTN HD; Discovery Channel HD; ESPN HD; ESPN2 HD; Food Network HD; HGTV HD; Lifetime HD; National Geographic Channel HD; NFL Network HD; Outdoor Channel 2 HD; TNT HD; Travel Channel HD; Universal HD.
Fee: $5.95 monthly; $8.00 converter.

Pay Service 1
Pay Units: N.A.
Programming (via satellite): Cinemax; HBO (multiplexed); Showtime; The Movie Channel.
Fee: $9.95 - $12.95 monthly (each).
Digital Pay Service 1
Pay Units: N.A.
Programming (via satellite): Cinemax (multiplexed); Flix; HBO (multiplexed); Showtime (multiplexed); Showtime HD; Starz (multiplexed); Starz Encore (multiplexed); Starz HD; The Movie Channel (multiplexed).
Fee: $9.95 monthly (Cinemax), $10.00 monthly (Starz/Encore), $11.95 monthly (Showtime/TMC), $12.95 monthly (HBO).
Video-On-Demand: No
Pay-Per-View
iN DEMAND; Fresh.
Internet Service
Operational: Yes.
Broadband Service: In-house.
Fee: $40.00 installation; $18.95-$62.95 monthly; $10.00 modem lease; $180.00 modem purchase.
Telephone Service
None
Miles of Plant: 50.0 (coaxial); 50.0 (fiber optic). Homes passed: 2,600.
General Manager: Denny Weber.
Ownership: Community Cable TV Corp.

SCHALLER—Comserv Ltd, 111 West 2nd St, PO Box 9, Schaller, IA 51053. Phones: 712-275-4215; 800-469-9099; 712-275-4211. Fax: 712-275-4121. E-mail: sbrink@schallertel.net. Web Site: http://www.schallertel.net. Also serves Cushing, Galva & Kiron. ICA: IA0253.
TV Market Ranking: Outside TV Markets (Cushing, Galva, Kiron, SCHALLER). Franchise award date: N.A. Franchise expiration date: N.A. Began: December 1, 1983.
Channel capacity: N.A. Channels available but not in use: N.A.
Basic Service
Subscribers: 313.
Programming (received off-air): KCAU-TV (ABC) Sioux City; KMEG (Azteca America, CBS, Decades) Sioux City; KSIN-TV (PBS) Sioux City; KTIV (CW, MeTV, NBC) Sioux City.
Programming (via satellite): A&E; AMC; Animal Planet; CMT; CNN; Comedy Central; C-SPAN; C-SPAN 2; Discovery Channel; Disney Channel; Disney XD; ESPN; ESPN Classic; ESPN2; ESPNews; Fox News Channel; Freeform; FX; Golf Channel; GSN; HGTV; History; HLN; Lifetime; MTV; Nickelodeon; Outdoor Channel; Spike TV; Syfy; TBS; The Weather Channel; TLC; TNT; Travel Channel; truTV; Turner Classic Movies; TV Land; USA Network; VH1; WE tv; WGN America.
Fee: $45.00 installation; $49.99 monthly.
Pay Service 1
Pay Units: N.A.
Programming (via satellite): Showtime.
Fee: $11.00 monthly.
Pay Service 2
Pay Units: 39.
Programming (via satellite): The Movie Channel.
Fee: $11.00 monthly.
Pay Service 3
Pay Units: 31.
Programming (via satellite): HBO.
Fee: $12.00 monthly.
Pay Service 4
Pay Units: 15.
Programming (via satellite): Cinemax.
Fee: $12.00 monthly.

Pay Service 5
Pay Units: 15.
Programming (via satellite): Starz; Starz Encore.
Fee: $11.00 monthly.
Video-On-Demand: No
Internet Service
Operational: No, DSL.
Broadband Service: DSL service only.
Telephone Service
Analog: Operational
Miles of Plant: 46.0 (coaxial); None (fiber optic).
General Manager: Missy Kestel. Chief Technician: Doug Thomas. Marketing Director: Diana Myrtue.
Ownership: Schaller Telephone Co.

SCHLESWIG—Formerly served by Tip Top Communications. No longer in operation. ICA: IA0231.

SCRANTON—Scranton Community Antenna Television, PO Box 8, Scranton, IA 51462. Phone: 712-652-3355. Fax: 712-652-3777. E-mail: jingles@netins.net. Web Site: http://www.scrantontelephone.com. ICA: IA0254.
TV Market Ranking: Outside TV Markets (SCRANTON). Franchise award date: January 4, 1983. Franchise expiration date: N.A. Began: November 1, 1983.
Channel capacity: N.A. Channels available but not in use: N.A.
Basic Service
Subscribers: 210.
Programming (received off-air): KCCI (CBS, MeTV) Des Moines; KDIN-TV (PBS) Des Moines; KDSM-TV (FOX, The Country Network) Des Moines; WHO-DT (Antenna TV, NBC) Des Moines; WOI-DT (ABC) Ames.
Programming (via satellite): A&E; CMT; CNN; Comedy Central; Discovery Channel; Disney Channel; ESPN; ESPN2; FOX Sports Networks; Freeform; HGTV; History; Lifetime; Nickelodeon; Spike TV; Starz Encore; Syfy; TBS; The Weather Channel; TNT; TV Land; USA Network; WGN America.
Fee: $55.35 monthly.
Pay Service 1
Pay Units: 20.
Programming (via satellite): Cinemax.
Fee: $7.50 monthly.
Pay Service 2
Pay Units: N.A.
Programming (via satellite): Starz.
Fee: $7.50 monthly.
Pay Service 3
Pay Units: 18.
Programming (via satellite): HBO.
Fee: $7.50 monthly.
Internet Service
Operational: No, DSL.
Telephone Service
None
Miles of Plant: 7.0 (coaxial); None (fiber optic). Homes passed: 270.
General Manager: Sam Fengel.
Ownership: Scranton Telephone Co.

SEYMOUR—Formerly served by Longview Communications. No longer in operation. ICA: IA0207.

SHELBY—Walnut Communications. Now served by WALNUT, IA [IA0241]. ICA: IA0537.

SHELLSBURG—USA Communications, 124 Main St, PO Box 389, Shellsburg, IA 52332. Phones: 800-248-8007; 319-436-2224. Fax: 319-436-2228. E-mail: webmaster@fmtcs.com. Web Site: http://www.usacomm.coop. Also serves Alburnett, Center Point, Central City, Coggon, Robins, Ryan & Urbana. ICA: IA0255.
TV Market Ranking: 65 (Alburnett, Center Point, Central City, Robins, SHELLSBURG, Urbana). Franchise award date: N.A. Franchise expiration date: N.A. Began: November 1, 1984.
Channel capacity: 35 (operating 2-way). Channels available but not in use: N.A.
Basic Service
Subscribers: 1,029.
Programming (received off-air): KCRG-TV (ABC, MNT) Cedar Rapids; KFXA (FOX, The Country Network) Cedar Rapids; KGAN (CBS) Cedar Rapids; KPXR-TV (ION) Cedar Rapids; KRIN (PBS) Waterloo; KWKB (The Works, This TV) Iowa City; KWWF (Untamed Sports TV) Waterloo; KWWL (CW, MeTV, NBC) Waterloo.
Programming (via satellite): A&E; AMC; Animal Planet; BTN; Cartoon Network; CMT; CNBC; CNN; Comcast SportsNet Chicago; Comedy Central; C-SPAN; Discovery Channel; Disney Channel; DIY Network; E! HD; ESPN; ESPN Classic; ESPN2; ESPNU; EWTN Global Catholic Network; Food Network; Fox News Channel; Fox Sports 1; Freeform; FX; Great American Country; Hallmark Channel; Hallmark Movies & Mysteries; HGTV; History; HLN; Lifetime; MTV; National Geographic Channel; Nickelodeon; QVC; RFD-TV; Spike TV; Syfy; TBS; The Weather Channel; TLC; TNT; Travel Channel; Trinity Broadcasting Network (TBN); truTV; Turner Classic Movies; TV Land; UP; USA Network; VH1; WGN America.
Fee: $40.00 installation; $53.50 monthly.
Expanded Basic Service 1
Subscribers: 69.
Fee: $15.00 monthly.
Digital Basic Service
Subscribers: 229.
Programming (via satellite): Bloomberg Television; Bravo; Cloo; Cooking Channel; Destination America; Discovery Kids Channel; Discovery Life Channel; Disney XD; DMX Music; ESPN Classic; ESPNews; FXM; FYI; Golf Channel; GSN; History International; Investigation Discovery; LMN; MTV2; NBCSN; Nick Jr.; Nicktoons; Outdoor Channel; OWN: Oprah Winfrey Network; Science Channel; TeenNick; WE tv.
Fee: $40.00 installation; $56.45 monthly.
Digital Expanded Basic Service
Subscribers: N.A.
Programming (via satellite): A&E HD; AXS TV; Discovery Channel HD; ESPN HD; ESPN2 HD; TNT HD; Universal HD.
Fee: $20.95 monthly.
Pay Service 1
Pay Units: N.A.
Programming (via satellite): Cinemax; HBO; Showtime.
Fee: $10.00 monthly (Cinemax), $12.00 monthly (Showtime), $16.00 monthly (HBO).
Digital Pay Service 1
Pay Units: N.A.
Programming (via satellite): Cinemax (multiplexed); HBO (multiplexed); Showtime (multiplexed); Starz (multiplexed); Starz Encore (multiplexed).
Fee: $10.00 monthly (Cinemax or Starz/Encore), $12 monthly (Showtime), $16 monthly (HBO).
Internet Service
Operational: No, DSL.

Cable Systems—Iowa

Telephone Service
Analog: Operational
Fee: $14.00-$16.00 monthly
Miles of Plant: 12.0 (coaxial); None (fiber optic).
General Manager: Mark Harrison. Plant Manager: Mitch Kuhn. Office Manager: Nancy Seely.
Ownership: Shellsburg Cablevision Inc. (MSO).

SHERRILL—Formerly served by Alpine Communications LC. No longer in operation. ICA: IA0507.

SIBLEY—HTC Communications. Now served by HOSPERS, IA [IA0060]. ICA: IA0097.

SIDNEY (town)—Rock Port Cablevision, 107 West Opp St, PO Box 147, Rock Port, MO 64482. Phones: 660-744-5311; 660-744-2020; 877-202-1764. E-mail: rptel@rpt.coop. Web Site: http://www.rptel.net. ICA: IA0508.
TV Market Ranking: Outside TV Markets (SIDNEY (TOWN)). Franchise award date: N.A. Franchise expiration date: N.A. Began: November 2, 1981.
Channel capacity: N.A. Channels available but not in use: N.A.
Basic Service
Subscribers: 79.
Programming (received off-air): KETV (ABC, MeTV) Omaha; KHIN (PBS) Red Oak; KMTV-TV (Antenna TV, CBS, Escape) Omaha; KPTM (Estrella TV, FOX, MNT, This TV) Omaha; KUON-TV (PBS) Lincoln; KXVO (Azteca America, CW) Omaha; WOWT (IND, NBC) Omaha.
Programming (via satellite): A&E; AMC; CNN; Discovery Channel; Disney Channel; ESPN; ESPN2; Freeform; History; HLN; Lifetime; Nickelodeon; Spike TV; Syfy; TBS; The Weather Channel; TNT; TV Land; USA Network; VH1; WGN America.
Fee: $20.00 installation; $48.00 monthly.
Pay Service 1
Pay Units: N.A.
Programming (via satellite): HBO; The Movie Channel.
Fee: $10.95 monthly (each).
Video-On-Demand: No
Internet Service
Operational: No, DSL.
Telephone Service
None
General Manager: Raymond Henagan. Chief Technician: Gary McGuire.
Ownership: Rock Port Telephone Co. (MSO).

SIGOURNEY—Mediacom. Now served by KEOTA, IA [IA0632]. ICA: IA0107.

SILVER CITY—Formerly served by Interstate Communications. No longer in operation. ICA: IA0509.

SIOUX CENTER—Premier Communications, 339 1st Ave Northeast, PO Box 200, Sioux Center, IA 51250. Phones: 800-741-8351; 712-722-3451. Fax: 712-722-1113. Web Site: http://www.mypremieronline.com. Also serves Akron, Boyden, Dickens, Doon, George, Granville, Hinton, Hull, Ireton, Le Mars, Maurice, Merrill, Orange City, Plymouth County, Rock Rapids, Rock Valley, Sanborn & Webb. ICA: IA0076.
TV Market Ranking: 85 (Doon, Rock Rapids, Rock Valley); Below 100 (Akron, Hinton, Ireton, Maurice, Merrill, Plymouth County (portions), Le Mars); Outside TV Markets (Boyden, George, Granville, Hull, Orange City, Plymouth County (portions), Sanborn, SIOUX CENTER, Webb, Dickens). Franchise award date: March 1, 1982. Franchise expiration date: N.A. Began: N.A.
Channel capacity: N.A. Channels available but not in use: N.A.
Basic Service
Subscribers: 8,852.
Programming (received off-air): KCAU-TV (ABC) Sioux City; KELO-TV (CBS, MNT) Sioux Falls; KMEG (Azteca America, CBS, Decades) Sioux City; KPTH (FOX, MNT, This TV) Sioux City; KSFY-TV (ABC, CW) Sioux Falls; KSIN-TV (PBS) Sioux City; KTIV (CW, MeTV, NBC) Sioux City; KUSD-TV (PBS) Vermillion; 11 FMs.
Programming (via satellite): Disney Channel; Freeform; Pop; TBS; The Weather Channel.
Fee: $29.95 installation; $29.00 monthly; $2.95 converter.
Expanded Basic Service 1
Subscribers: N.A.
Programming (via satellite): A&E; Animal Planet; Bloomberg Television; CMT; CNN; Comedy Central; C-SPAN; CW PLUS; Discovery Channel; Disney XD; ESPN; ESPN Classic; ESPN2; Food Network; Fox News Channel; Fox Sports 1; FOX Sports Midwest; FX; Great American Country; Hallmark Channel; HGTV; History; HLN; Lifetime; MSNBC; MTV; Nickelodeon; Outdoor Channel; QVC; Spike TV; TLC; TNT; Travel Channel; Trinity Broadcasting Network (TBN); truTV; Turner Classic Movies; TV Land; Univision Studios; USA Network; VH1; WGN America.
Fee: $28.95 monthly.
Digital Basic Service
Subscribers: N.A.
Programming (via satellite): AXS TV; BBC America; Bravo; CBS Sports Network; Discovery Digital Networks; DIY Network; DMX Music; ESPNews; ESPNU; EVINE Live; FOX College Sports Central; FOX College Sports Pacific; FXM; FYI; Golf Channel; GSN; History International; HITS (Headend In The Sky); LMN; National Geographic Channel; NBCSN; Nick Jr.; Nicktoons; RFD-TV; TeenNick.
Pay Service 1
Pay Units: N.A.
Programming (via satellite): HBO.
Fee: $20.00 installation; $8.00 monthly.
Digital Pay Service 1
Pay Units: N.A.
Programming (via satellite): Cinemax; HBO (multiplexed); Starz (multiplexed); Starz Encore (multiplexed); The Movie Channel.
Fee: $7.95 monthly (Encore), $8.95 monthly (Cinemax or TMC), $12.95 monthly (HBO or Starz/Encore).
Video-On-Demand: Yes
Internet Service
Operational: Yes, DSL & dial-up.
Fee: $21.95 monthly.
Telephone Service
Analog: Operational
Miles of Plant: 115.0 (coaxial); 8,181.0 (fiber optic).
Chief Executive Officer: Douglas A. Boone. Marketing Director: Scott Te Stroete. Chief Technician: Les Sybesma. Technology & Product Development Manager: Frank Bulk.
Ownership: Premier Communications Inc.

SIOUX CITY—Cable One, 900 Steuben St, Sioux City, IA 51101. Phone: 712-233-2000. Web Site: http://www.cableone.net. Also serves Sergeant Bluff & Woodbury County, IA; Dakota City, Dakota County (portions) & South Sioux City, NE; Dakota Dunes, North Sioux City & Union County (portions), SD. ICA: IA0004.
TV Market Ranking: Below 100 (Dakota City, Dakota County (portions), North Sioux City, Sergeant Bluff, SIOUX CITY, South Sioux City, Union County (portions), Woodbury County (portions)); Outside TV Markets (Dakota Dunes, Woodbury County (portions)). Franchise award date: December 16, 1978. Franchise expiration date: N.A. Began: July 1, 1979.
Channel capacity: N.A. Channels available but not in use: N.A.
Basic Service
Subscribers: 10,893.
Programming (received off-air): KCAU-TV (ABC) Sioux City; KMEG (Azteca America, CBS, Decades) Sioux City; KPTH (FOX, MNT, This TV) Sioux City; KSIN-TV (PBS) Sioux City; KTIV (CW, MeTV, NBC) Sioux City.
Programming (via satellite): A&E; AMC; Animal Planet; Azteca; Cartoon Network; CMT; CNBC; CNN; Comedy Central; C-SPAN; C-SPAN 2; CW PLUS; Discovery Channel; Disney Channel; ESPN; ESPN2; EVINE Live; Food Network; Fox News Channel; FOX Sports North; Freeform; FX; HGTV; History; HLN; INSP; Lifetime; MSNBC; MTV; Nickelodeon; Pop; QVC; Spike TV; Syfy; The Weather Channel; TLC; TNT; Travel Channel; Turner Classic Movies; TV Land; USA Network; VH1; WGN America.
Fee: $90.00 installation; $35.00 monthly.
Digital Basic Service
Subscribers: N.A.
Programming (via satellite): 3ABN; Boomerang; BYUtv; Discovery Digital Networks; Disney XD; DMX Music; ESPN Classic; ESPNews; FamilyNet; FOX College Sports Central; FOX College Sports Pacific; Fox Sports 1; Fox Sports 2; FXM; FYI; Golf Channel; Great American Country; Hallmark Channel; History International; HITS (Headend In The Sky); INSP; National Geographic Channel; Outdoor Channel; TNT HD; Trinity Broadcasting Network (TBN); truTV; TVG Network; Universal HD.
Digital Pay Service 1
Pay Units: N.A.
Programming (via satellite): Cinemax (multiplexed); Flix; HBO (multiplexed); Showtime (multiplexed); Showtime HD; Starz (multiplexed); Starz Encore (multiplexed); Sundance TV; The Movie Channel (multiplexed); The Movie Channel HD.
Fee: $15.00 monthly.
Video-On-Demand: No
Pay-Per-View
Juicy (delivered digitally); VaVoom (delivered digitally); Pleasure (delivered digitally); SexSee (delivered digitally).
Internet Service
Operational: Yes. Began: October 1, 2000.
Subscribers: 16,027.
Broadband Service: CableONE.net.
Fee: $75.00 installation; $43.00 monthly.
Telephone Service
Digital: Operational
Subscribers: 7,402.
Fee: $39.95 monthly
Miles of Plant: 424.0 (coaxial); 105.0 (fiber optic). Homes passed: 49,925.
Vice President: Patrick A. Dolohanty. General Manager: Cheryl Goettsche. Chief Technician: Robert Wignes. Marketing Director: Paula Todd.
Ownership: Cable ONE Inc. (MSO).

SIOUX RAPIDS—WesTel Systems. Now served by MARCUS, IA [IA0171]. ICA: IA0209.

SMITHLAND—Formerly served by TelePartners. Now served by Wiatel, LAWTON (village), IA [IA0330]. ICA: IA0350.

SOLDIER—Formerly served by Soldier Valley Telephone. Now served by Long Lines, SALIX, IA [IA0510]. ICA: IA0360.

SOLDIER—Long Lines. Now served by SALIX, IA [IA0510]. ICA: IA0603.

SPENCER—SMU Cable TV, 520 2nd Ave East, Ste 1, Spencer, IA 51301. Phone: 712-580-5800. Fax: 712-580-5888. E-mail: customerservice@smunet.com. Web Site: http://www.smunet.net. Also serves Fostoria. ICA: IA0592. **Note:** This system is an overbuild.
TV Market Ranking: Outside TV Markets (Fostoria, SPENCER). Franchise award date: May 1, 1999. Franchise expiration date: N.A. Began: December 1, 2000.
Channel capacity: N.A. Channels available but not in use: N.A.
Basic Service
Subscribers: 2,741.
Programming (received off-air): KCAU-TV (ABC) Sioux City; KELO-TV (CBS, MNT) Sioux Falls; KMEG (Azteca America, CBS, Decades) Sioux City; KPTH (FOX, MNT, This TV) Sioux City; KSFY-TV (ABC, CW) Sioux Falls; KTIN (PBS) Fort Dodge; KTIV (CW, MeTV, NBC) Sioux City.
Programming (via satellite): EWTN Global Catholic Network; ION Television; Pop; TBS; The Weather Channel; WGN America.
Fee: $64.75 monthly.
Expanded Basic Service 1
Subscribers: N.A.
Programming (via satellite): A&E; AMC; Animal Planet; Bravo; Cartoon Network; CMT; CNBC; CNN; Comedy Central; C-SPAN; C-SPAN 2; Discovery Channel; Disney Channel; E! HD; ESPN; ESPN2; EWTN Global Catholic Network; Food Network; Fox News Channel; FOX Sports North; Freeform; FX; FXM; HGTV; History; HLN; INSP; Lifetime; MTV; Nickelodeon; Outdoor Channel; OWN: Oprah Winfrey Network; Spike TV; Syfy; TLC; TNT; Travel Channel; Trinity Broadcasting Network (TBN); Turner Classic Movies; TV Land; USA Network; VH1.
Fee: $18.00 monthly.
Digital Basic Service
Subscribers: 1,000.
Programming (via satellite): BBC America; Discovery Life Channel; DMX Music; ESPNews; Fox Sports 1; FYI; Golf Channel; GSN; History International; IFC; MTV Classic; Nick Jr.; VH1 Country.
Fee: $4.00 monthly; $3.00 converter.
Digital Pay Service 1
Pay Units: N.A.
Programming (via satellite): Cinemax (multiplexed); HBO (multiplexed); Showtime (multiplexed); Starz (multiplexed); Starz Encore (multiplexed); The Movie Channel (multiplexed).
Fee: $7.00 monthly (Cinemax), $7.50 monthly (Starz/Encore), $10.50 monthly (Showtime/TMC), $14.00 monthly (HBO).
Video-On-Demand: No
Pay-Per-View
Playboy TV (delivered digitally); Fresh (delivered digitally).
Internet Service
Operational: Yes.
Subscribers: 2,000.
Fee: $29.99 monthly.

2017 Edition   D-271

Iowa—Cable Systems

Telephone Service
Analog: Operational
Miles of Plant: 330.0 (coaxial); 21.0 (fiber optic). Homes passed: 5,100.
General Manager: Steve Pick. Telecom Manager: Jeff Rezabek. Marketing Director: Amanda Gloyd. Customer Service Manager: Keetah Dodson.
Ownership: Spencer Municipal Utilities.

SPIRIT LAKE—Mediacom, 1504 2nd St SE, PO Box 110, Waseca, MN 56093. Phone: 507-835-2356. Fax: 507-835-4567. Web Site: http://www.mediacomcable.com. Also serves Arnolds Park, Dickinson County (portions), Harris, Lake Park, Okoboji, Orleans, Wahpeton & West Okoboji. ICA: IA0036.
TV Market Ranking: Outside TV Markets (Arnolds Park, Dickinson County (portions), Harris, Lake Park, Okoboji, Orleans, SPIRIT LAKE, Wahpeton, West Okoboji). Franchise award date: N.A. Franchise expiration date: N.A. Began: October 1, 1976.
Channel capacity: N.A. Channels available but not in use: N.A.
Basic Service
Subscribers: 3,702. Commercial subscribers: 4.
Programming (received off-air): KCAU-TV (ABC) Sioux City; KDIN-TV (PBS) Des Moines; KELO-TV (CBS, MNT) Sioux Falls; KMEG (Azteca America, CBS, Decades) Sioux City; KPTH (FOX, MNT, This TV) Sioux City; KSFY-TV (ABC, CW) Sioux Falls; KTIN (PBS) Fort Dodge; KTIV (CW, MeTV, NBC) Sioux City; WOI-DT (ABC) Ames.
Programming (via satellite): A&E; AMC; Animal Planet; Bravo; Cartoon Network; CMT; CNBC; CNN; Comedy Central; C-SPAN; C-SPAN 2; Discovery Channel; Disney Channel; Disney XD; E! HD; ESPN; ESPN Classic; ESPN2; EWTN Global Catholic Network; Fox News Channel; Fox Sports 1; FOX Sports Midwest; Freeform; FX; FXM; Hallmark Channel; HGTV; History; HLN; Lifetime; MoviePlex; MSNBC; MTV; Nickelodeon; Oxygen; Pop; Radar Channel; Spike TV; Syfy; TBS; Telemundo; The Weather Channel; TLC; TNT; Travel Channel; Trinity Broadcasting Network (TBN); truTV; Turner Classic Movies; TV Land; Univision Studios; USA Network; VH1; WGN America.
Fee: $20.00 installation; $43.00 monthly.
Digital Basic Service
Subscribers: N.A.
Programming (via satellite): 52MX; AXS TV; BBC America; Bloomberg Television; CBS Sports Network; CCTV-Documentary; Cinelatino; Cloo; CMT; CNN en Espanol; CNN HD; Destination America; Discovery Kids Channel; Discovery Life Channel; ESPN Deportes; ESPN HD; ESPN2 HD; ESPNews; ESPNU; FOX College Sports Central; FOX College Sports Pacific; Fox Deportes; Fox Sports 2; Fuse; FYI; Golf Channel; GolTV; GSN; HD Theater; History en Espanol; History International; IFC; Investigation Discovery; ION Television; LMN; MC; MTV Classic; MTV Hits; MTV2; Nat Geo WILD; National Geographic Channel; Nick Jr.; Nicktoons; Outdoor Channel; Ovation; OWN: Oprah Winfrey Network; Qubo; Reelz; Science Channel; TBS HD; TeenNick; Tennis Channel; TNT HD; Tr3s; TVG Network; Universal HD; VH1 Soul; ViendoMovies.
Digital Pay Service 1
Pay Units: N.A.
Programming (via satellite): Cinemax (multiplexed); Flix; HBO (multiplexed); HBO HD; Showtime (multiplexed); Showtime HD; Starz (multiplexed); Starz Encore (multiplexed); Starz HD; Sundance TV; The Movie Channel (multiplexed); The Movie Channel HD.
Fee: $10.00 monthly (each).
Video-On-Demand: Yes
Pay-Per-View
iN DEMAND (delivered digitally); SexSee (delivered digitally); Playboy TV (delivered digitally); Spice: Xcess (delivered digitally).
Internet Service
Operational: Yes.
Subscribers: 3,046.
Broadband Service: Mediacom High Speed Internet.
Telephone Service
Digital: Operational
Subscribers: 1,447.
Miles of Plant: 257.0 (coaxial); 108.0 (fiber optic). Homes passed: 12,123.
Vice President: Bill Jensen. Engineering Manager: Kraig Kaiser. Marketing & Sales Manager: Lori Huberty.
Ownership: Mediacom LLC (MSO).

SPRINGVILLE—Springville Cooperative Telephone Assn Inc, 207 Broadway, PO Box 9, Springville, IA 52336-0009. Phones: 319-854-6107; 319-854-6500. Fax: 319-854-9010. E-mail: springvl@netins.net. Web Site: http://www.springvilletelephone.com. Also serves Paralta, Viola & Whittier. ICA: IA0144.
TV Market Ranking: 65 (Paralta, SPRINGVILLE, Viola, Whittier). Franchise award date: January 1, 1983. Franchise expiration date: N.A. Began: January 1, 1983.
Channel capacity: N.A. Channels available but not in use: N.A.
Basic Service
Subscribers: 154.
Programming (received off-air): KCRG-TV (ABC, MNT) Cedar Rapids; KFXA (FOX, The Country Network) Cedar Rapids; KGAN (CBS) Cedar Rapids; KIIN (PBS) Iowa City; KPXR-TV (ION) Cedar Rapids; KWKB (The Works, This TV) Iowa City; KWWL (CW, MeTV, NBC) Waterloo.
Programming (via satellite): A&E; AMC; Animal Planet; BTN; Cartoon Network; CMT; CNN; Comedy Central; Discovery Channel; Discovery Life Channel; Disney Channel; ESPN; ESPN2; Food Network; Fox News Channel; Fox Sports 1; Freeform; FX; Great American Country; Hallmark Channel; HGTV; History; Lifetime; MTV; NBCSN; Nickelodeon; Spike TV; Syfy; TBS; The Weather Channel; TLC; TNT; Turner Classic Movies; TV Land; USA Network; VH1; WGN America.
Fee: $40.00 installation; $50.00 monthly; $5.00 converter.
Digital Basic Service
Subscribers: N.A.
Programming (via satellite): C-SPAN; C-SPAN 2; HSN; The Weather Channel; Trinity Broadcasting Network (TBN).
Fee: $20.00 monthly.
Digital Expanded Basic Service
Subscribers: N.A.
Programming (via satellite): A&E; A&E HD; AMC; Animal Planet; Boomerang; Bravo; Bravo HD; BTN; Cartoon Network; Chiller; CMT; CNBC; CNBC World; CNN; CNN International; Comedy Central; Discovery Channel; Discovery Life Channel; Disney Channel; E! HD; ESPN; ESPN Classic; ESPN HD; ESPN2; ESPN2 HD; ESPNews; ESPNU; Food Network; Food Network HD; Fox News Channel; Fox Sports 1; Freeform; FX; FX HD; FYI; Golf Channel; Great American Country; GSN; Hallmark Channel; HGTV; HGTV HD; History; History HD; History International; HLN; Lifetime; Lifetime HD; Lifetime Movie Network HD; MC; MSNBC; MTV; MTV Classic; MTV Hits; MTV Jams; MTV2; National Geographic Channel; National Geographic Channel HD; NBCSN; Nickelodeon; Outdoor Channel; Outdoor Channel HD; OWN: Oprah Winfrey Network; RFD-TV; Spike TV; Syfy; Syfy HD; TBS; TLC; TNT; Travel Channel; truTV; Turner Classic Movies; TV Land; USA Network; USA Network HD; VH1; WGN America.
Fee: $40.00 monthly.
Pay Service 1
Pay Units: 55.
Programming (via satellite): HBO.
Fee: $30.00 installation; $15.00 monthly.
Pay Service 2
Pay Units: 42.
Programming (via satellite): Cinemax.
Fee: $11.00 monthly.
Digital Pay Service 1
Pay Units: N.A.
Programming (via satellite): Cinemax (multiplexed); HBO (multiplexed); Showtime (multiplexed); Starz (multiplexed); Starz Encore (multiplexed); The Movie Channel (multiplexed).
Fee: $15.00 monthly (Cinemax, HBO, Showtime/TMC or Starz/Encore.
Internet Service
Operational: No, DSL & dial-up.
Telephone Service
Analog: Operational
Miles of Plant: 33.0 (coaxial); None (fiber optic). Homes passed: 813.
General Office Manager & Treasurer: Jean Johnston. Executive Office Manager: Jean Schilling. Chief Technician: Todd McWherter.
Ownership: Springville Cooperative Telephone Assn. Inc.

ST. CHARLES—Interstate Communications. Now served by TRURO, IA [IA0344]. ICA: IA0295.

ST. LUCAS—Formerly served by Alpine Communications LC. No longer in operation. ICA: IA0559.

STANTON—Farmers Mutual Telephone Co, 410 Broad Ave, PO Box 220, Stanton, IA 51573-0220. Phones: 800-469-2111; 712-829-2111. Fax: 712-829-2509. E-mail: customerservice@myfmtc.com. Web Site: http://www.farmersmutualcoop.com. Also serves New Market. ICA: IA0264.
TV Market Ranking: Outside TV Markets (New Market, STANTON). Franchise award date: N.A. Franchise expiration date: N.A. Began: August 1, 1983.
Channel capacity: N.A. Channels available but not in use: N.A.
Basic Service
Subscribers: 56.
Programming (received off-air): KETV (ABC, MeTV) Omaha; KHIN (PBS) Red Oak; KMTV-TV (Antenna TV, CBS, Escape) Omaha; KPTM (Estrella TV, FOX, MNT, This TV) Omaha; KXVO (Azteca America, CW) Omaha; WHO-DT (Antenna TV, NBC) Des Moines; WOWT (IND, NBC) Omaha.
Programming (via satellite): A&E; AMC; Animal Planet; CNN; Comedy Central; Discovery Channel; Disney Channel; ESPN; ESPN2; Fox News Channel; Fox Sports 1; FOX Sports Midwest; Freeform; Great American Country; Hallmark Channel; HGTV; History; HLN; Lifetime; Nickelodeon; Spike TV; TBS; TLC; TNT; Travel Channel; TV Land; USA Network; WGN America.
Fee: $20.00 installation; $40.00 monthly; $1.00 converter.
Pay Service 1
Pay Units: 46.
Programming (via satellite): HBO.
Fee: $20.00 installation; $12.00 monthly.
Pay Service 2
Pay Units: 20.
Programming (via satellite): Cinemax.
Fee: $20.00 installation; $12.00 monthly.
Internet Service
Operational: Yes.
Telephone Service
Digital: Operational
General Manager: Kevin Cabbage. Assistant Manager: Dennis Crawford. Outside Plant Manager: Brad Sunderman. Central Office Manager: Scott Boatman. Customer Service Manager: Kathie Bell.
Ownership: Farmers Mutual Cooperative Telephone Co. (Moulton, IA) (MSO).

STANWOOD—Clarence Cablevision. Now served by CLARENCE, IA [IA0213]. ICA: IA0174.

STATE CENTER—Partner Communications. Now served by GILMAN, IA [IA0128]. ICA: IA0513.

STEAMBOAT ROCK—Formerly served by Steamboat Rock Cablevision. No longer in operation. ICA: IA0514.

STORM LAKE—Clarity Telecom. Now served by VIBORG, SD [SD0071]. ICA: IA0596.

STORM LAKE—Mediacom, 2205 Ingersoll Ave, Des Moines, IA 50312. Phone: 800-790-8187. Fax: 515-246-2211. Web Site: http://www.mediacomcable.com. Also serves Alta, Buena Vista County, Cherokee & Lakeside. ICA: IA0020.
TV Market Ranking: Outside TV Markets (Alta, Buena Vista County, Cherokee, Lakeside).
Channel capacity: N.A. Channels available but not in use: N.A.
Basic Service
Subscribers: 1,463. Commercial subscribers: 164.
Fee: $41.99 installation; $43.00 monthly.
Internet Service
Operational: Yes.
Subscribers: 1,114.
Broadband Service: Mediacom High Speed Internet.

Cable Systems—Iowa

Access the most current data instantly
FREE TRIAL @ **ADVANCED TVFactbook** TELCO/IPTV • CABLE TV • TV STATIONS
www.warren-news.com/factbook.htm

Telephone Service
Digital: Operational
Subscribers: 832.
Miles of Plant: 166.0 (coaxial); 163.0 (fiber optic). Homes passed: 9,148.
Ownership: Mediacom LLC.

STRATFORD—Stratford Mutual Telephone, 1001 Tennyson Ave, PO Box 438, Stratford, IA 50249. Phones: 800-426-1649; 515-838-2390. Fax: 515-838-9998. Web Site: http://www.globalccs.net. Also serves Gilbert, Jewell & Roland. ICA: IA5024.
TV Market Ranking: 66 (Jewell, Roland, STRATFORD). Franchise award date: July 11, 1983. Franchise expiration date: N.A. Began: January 1, 1983.
Channel capacity: N.A. Channels available but not in use: N.A.
Basic
Subscribers: N.A.
Programming (received off-air): KCCI (CBS, MeTV) Des Moines; KCWI-TV (CW) Ames; KDIN-TV (PBS) Des Moines; KDSM-TV (FOX, The Country Network) Des Moines; KFPX-TV (ION) Newton; WHO-DT (Antenna TV, NBC) Des Moines; WOI-DT (ABC) Ames.
Programming (via satellite): A&E; AMC; Animal Planet; CMT; CNN; Comedy Central; Discovery Channel; Disney Channel; E! HD; ESPN; ESPN2; Food Network; Fox News Channel; FOX Sports Networks; Freeform; FX; Great American Country; Hallmark Channel; HGTV; History; HLN; Lifetime; MTV; Nickelodeon; RFD-TV; Spike TV; Syfy; TBS; The Weather Channel; TLC; TNT; Travel Channel; Trinity Broadcasting Network (TBN); TV Land; USA Network; VH1; WGN America.
Fee: $51.95 monthly. Includes 141+ channels - 92+ in SD & 49+ in HD plus 1 STB.
Expanded Basic
Subscribers: N.A.
Fee: $74.90 monthly. Includes 209+ channels - 135+ in SD & 74+ in HD plus 1 STB.
Cinemax
Subscribers: N.A.
Fee: $12.95 monthly.
HBO
Subscribers: N.A.
Fee: $16.95 monthly.
Showtime/TMC/Flix
Subscribers: N.A.
Fee: $15.95 monthly.
Starz/Encore
Subscribers: N.A.
Fee: $12.95 monthly.
Video-On-Demand: No
Internet Service
Operational: Yes.
Fee: $44.95-$84.95 monthly.
Telephone Service
Digital: Operational
Fee: $25.00 monthly
General Manager: Randy Baker. Programming & Marketing Director: Darcy Runestad. Telephone Plant Manager: Vance Cook. Accounting & Office Manager: Jen Frank. Cable Plant Manager: Scott Henderson. Outside Plant Technician: Doran Erickson.
Ownership: Stratford Mutual Telephone (MSO).

STRATFORD—Stratford Mutual Telephone. This cable system has converted to IPTV. See STRATFORD, IA [IA5024]. ICA: IA0248.

STRAWBERRY POINT—Mediacom. Now served by WAVERLY, IA [IA0021]. ICA: IA0168.

SUN VALLEY LAKE—Formerly served by Interstate Communications. This cable system has converted to IPTV. Now served by GRM Networks, MURRAY, IA [IA5135]. ICA: IA0515.

SUTHERLAND—WesTel Systems. Now served by MARCUS, IA [IA0171]. ICA: IA0208.

SWALEDALE (village)—Formerly served by New Path Communications LC. No longer in operation. ICA: IA0516.

SWEA CITY—Mediacom, 1504 2nd St SE, PO Box 110, Waseca, MN 56093. Phone: 507-835-2356. Fax: 507-835-4567. Web Site: http://www.mediacomcable.com. Also serves Bancroft, Buffalo Center & Burt. ICA: IA0226.
TV Market Ranking: Outside TV Markets (Bancroft, Buffalo Center, Burt, SWEA CITY). Franchise award date: N.A. Franchise expiration date: N.A. Began: October 1, 1974.
Channel capacity: N.A. Channels available but not in use: N.A.
Basic Service
Subscribers: 355.
Programming (received off-air): KAAL (ABC, This TV) Austin; KELO-TV (CBS, MNT) Sioux Falls; KEYC-TV (CBS, FOX) Mankato; KIMT (CBS, MNT) Mason City; KPTH (FOX, MNT, This TV) Sioux City; KTIN (PBS) Fort Dodge; KTTC (CW, NBC) Rochester; WFTC (MNT, Movies!) Minneapolis; WHO-DT (Antenna TV, NBC) Des Moines; allband FM.
Programming (via satellite): A&E; AMC; Animal Planet; Bravo; Cartoon Network; CMT; CNBC; CNN; Comedy Central; C-SPAN 2; CW PLUS; Discovery Channel; Disney Channel; Disney XD; E! HD; ESPN; ESPN Classic; ESPN2; EWTN Global Catholic Network; Food Network; Fox News Channel; Fox Sports 1; FOX Sports Midwest; Freeform; FX; FXM; Hallmark Channel; HGTV; History; HLN; INSP; Lifetime; MoviePlex; MSNBC; MTV; NBCSN; Nickelodeon; Oxygen; Pop; QVC; Radar Channel; Spike TV; Syfy; TBS; Telemundo; The Weather Channel; TLC; TNT; Travel Channel; Trinity Broadcasting Network (TBN); truTV; Turner Classic Movies; TV Land; Univision Studios; USA Network; VH1; WE tv; WGN America.
Fee: $9.95 installation; $43.00 monthly.
Digital Basic Service
Subscribers: N.A.
Programming (via satellite): 52MX; AXS TV; BBC America; Bloomberg Television; CBS Sports Network; CCTV-Documentary; Cinelatino; Cloo; CMT; CNN en Espanol; Destination America; Discovery Kids Channel; Discovery Life Channel; ESPN HD; ESPN2 HD; ESPNews; ESPNU; FOX College Sports Central; FOX College Sports Pacific; Fox Deportes; Fox Sports 2; Fuse; FYI; Golf Channel; GolTV; GSN; History en Espanol; History International; IFC; Investigation Discovery; LMN; MC; MTV Classic; MTV Hits; MTV2; Nat Geo WILD; National Geographic Channel; Nick Jr.; Nicktoons; Outdoor Channel; Ovation; OWN; Oprah Winfrey Network; Science Channel; TeenNick; Tennis Channel; Toon Disney en Espanol; Tr3s; TVG Network; Universal HD; VH1 Soul; ViendoMovies.
Digital Pay Service 1
Pay Units: N.A.
Programming (via satellite): Cinemax (multiplexed); Flix; HBO (multiplexed); HBO HD; Showtime (multiplexed); Showtime HD; Starz (multiplexed); Starz Encore (multiplexed); Starz HD; Sundance TV; The Movie Channel (multiplexed); The Movie Channel HD.
Video-On-Demand: Yes
Pay-Per-View
Vubiquity Inc. (delivered digitally); Playboy TV (delivered digitally); Fresh (delivered digitally); Shorteez (delivered digitally); Hot Choice (delivered digitally); ESPN Now (delivered digitally); Sports PPV (delivered digitally).
Internet Service
Operational: Yes.
Subscribers: 561.
Broadband Service: Mediacom High Speed Internet.
Fee: $99.00 installation; $40.00 monthly.
Telephone Service
Digital: Operational
Subscribers: 431.
Miles of Plant: 107.0 (coaxial); 111.0 (fiber optic). Homes passed: 4,820.
Vice President: Bill Jensen. Engineering Manager: Kraig Kaiser. Marketing & Sales Manager: Lori Huberty.
Ownership: Mediacom LLC (MSO).

TABOR—Rock Port Cablevision, 107 West Opp St, PO Box 147, Rock Port, MO 64482. Phones: 660-744-5311; 877-202-1764; 660-744-2020. E-mail: rptel@rpt.coop. Web Site: http://www.rptel.net. ICA: IA0517.
TV Market Ranking: 53 (TABOR). Franchise award date: N.A. Franchise expiration date: N.A. Began: January 1, 1985.
Channel capacity: N.A. Channels available but not in use: N.A.
Basic Service
Subscribers: 52.
Programming (received off-air): KBIN-TV (PBS) Council Bluffs; KETV (ABC, MeTV) Omaha; KMTV-TV (Antenna TV, CBS, Escape) Omaha; KPTM (Estrella TV, FOX, MNT, This TV) Omaha; KUON-TV (PBS) Lincoln; KXVO (Azteca America, CW) Omaha; WOWT (IND, NBC) Omaha.
Programming (via satellite): A&E; CMT; CNN; Discovery Channel; Disney Channel; ESPN; ESPN2; Freeform; History; HLN; Lifetime; Spike TV; TBS; TLC; TNT; Trinity Broadcasting Network (TBN); truTV; TV Land; USA Network; WGN America.
Fee: $20.00 installation; $31.95 monthly.
Pay Service 1
Pay Units: N.A.
Programming (via satellite): Showtime.
Fee: $10.95 monthly.
Video-On-Demand: No
Internet Service
Operational: No, DSL.
Telephone Service
None
General Manager: Raymond Henagan. Chief Technician: Gary McGuire.
Ownership: Rock Port Telephone Co. (MSO).

TEMPLETON—Templeton Telephone Co, 115 North Main St, PO Box 77, Templeton, IA 51463. Phones: 888-669-3311; 712-669-3311. Fax: 712-669-3312. E-mail: temptel@netins.net. Web Site: http://www.templetoniowa.com. ICA: IA0338.
TV Market Ranking: Outside TV Markets (TEMPLETON). Franchise award date: July 1, 1988. Franchise expiration date: N.A. Began: January 1, 1989.
Channel capacity: N.A. Channels available but not in use: N.A.
Basic Service
Subscribers: 112.
Programming (received off-air): KCAU-TV (ABC) Sioux City; KCCI (CBS, MeTV) Des Moines; KDSM-TV (FOX, The Country Network) Des Moines; KETV (ABC, MeTV) Omaha; KHIN (PBS) Red Oak; KMTV-TV (Antenna TV, CBS, Escape) Omaha; KPTM (Estrella TV, FOX, MNT, This TV) Omaha; KTIV (CW, MeTV, NBC) Sioux City; KTVO (ABC) Kirksville; WHO-DT (Antenna TV, NBC) Des Moines; WOI-DT (ABC) Ames; WOWT (IND, NBC) Omaha.
Programming (via satellite): A&E; AMC; Animal Planet; CMT; CNN; Comedy Central; Discovery Channel; Disney Channel; Disney XD; ESPN; ESPN Classic; ESPN2; EWTN Global Catholic Network; Food Network; Fox News Channel; Fox Sports 1; FOX Sports Networks; Freeform; FX; Golf Channel; Hallmark Channel; HGTV; History; HLN; Lifetime; MSNBC; MTV; NBCSN; Nickelodeon; Outdoor Channel; Pop; QVC; RFD-TV; Spike TV; Starz Encore Westerns; Syfy; TBS; The Movie Channel; The Weather Channel; TLC; TNT; Travel Channel; Trinity Broadcasting Network (TBN); Turner Classic Movies; TV Land; USA Network; VH1; WGN America.
Fee: $10.00 installation; $52.95 monthly.
Pay Service 1
Pay Units: 40.
Programming (via satellite): Cinemax; HBO (multiplexed); Showtime; Starz; Starz Encore.
Fee: $9.50 monthly (each).
Internet Service
Operational: No, DSL & dial-up.
Telephone Service
Analog: Operational
Miles of Plant: 5.0 (coaxial); None (fiber optic). Homes passed: 294.
General Manager: Patricia Snyder.
Ownership: Templeton Telephone Co.

TERRIL—Terril Telephone Cooperative, 107 S State St, Terril, IA 51364. Phone: 712-853-6121. Fax: 712-853-6185. Web Site: http://www.terril.com. ICA: IA5327.
TV Market Ranking: Outside TV Markets (TERRIL). Franchise award date: N.A. Franchise expiration date: N.A. Began: March 1, 1983.
Channel capacity: N.A. Channels available but not in use: N.A.
Basic
Subscribers: 92.
Programming (received off-air): KCAU-TV (ABC) Sioux City; KDIN-TV (PBS) Des Moines; KELO-TV (CBS, MNT) Sioux Falls; KEYC-TV (CBS, FOX) Mankato; KMEG (Azteca America, CBS, Decades) Sioux City; KPTH (FOX, MNT, This TV) Sioux City; KSFY-TV (ABC, CW) Sioux Falls; KTIV (CW,

Iowa—Cable Systems

MeTV, NBC) Sioux City; WOI-DT (ABC) Ames.
Programming (via satellite): A&E; AMC; Animal Planet; BBC America; Cartoon Network; CMT; CNBC; CNN; Comedy Central; C-SPAN; C-SPAN 2; CW PLUS; Destination America; Discovery Channel; Discovery Kids Channel; Discovery Life Channel; Disney Channel; Disney XD; E! HD; ESPN; ESPN Classic; ESPN HD; ESPN2; ESPNews; Food Network; Fox News Channel; Fox Sports 1; Freeform; FX; FXM; FYI; Golf Channel; GSN; Hallmark Channel; HGTV; History; History International; HLN; IFC; Investigation Discovery; ION Television; Lifetime; MC; MTV; MTV Classic; MTV2; National Geographic Channel; Nick Jr.; Nickelodeon; Nicktoons; Outdoor Channel; OWN: Oprah Winfrey Network; Pop; QVC; Science Channel; Spike TV; Syfy; TBS; TeenNick; The Weather Channel; TLC; TNT; Travel Channel; Turner Classic Movies; TV Land; Univision Studios; USA Network; VH1; VH1 Country; WGN America.
Fee: $30.00 installation; $52.14 monthly.
Video-On-Demand: No
Pay-Per-View
iN DEMAND (delivered digitally); Spice (delivered digitally); Playboy TV (delivered digitally); Spice (delivered digitally).
Internet Service
Operational: Yes.
Fee: $25.00-$82.95 monthly.
Telephone Service
Digital: Operational
Chief Executive Officer & General Manager: Douglas R. Nelson.
Ownership: Ter Tel Enterprises (MSO).

TERRIL—Terril Telephone Cooperative. This cable system has converted to IPTV. See TERRIL, IA [IA5327]. ICA: IA0317.

THOMPSON—Winnebago Cooperative Telecom Assn. Now served by LAKE MILLS, IA [IA0590]. ICA: IA0086.

THOR—Milford Cable TV, 806 Okoboji Ave, PO Box 163, Milford, IA 51351. Phones: 855-722-3450; 712-338-4967. Fax: 712-338-4719. E-mail: mplagman@milfordcable.net. Web Site: http://milfordcomm.net. Also serves Vincent. ICA: IA0541.
TV Market Ranking: Outside TV Markets (THOR, Vincent). Franchise award date: N.A. Franchise expiration date: N.A. Began: January 1, 1990.
Channel capacity: N.A. Channels available but not in use: N.A.
Basic Service
Subscribers: 24.
Programming (received off-air): KCCI (CBS, MeTV) Des Moines; KCWI-TV (CW) Ames; KDIN-TV (PBS) Des Moines; KDSM-TV (FOX, The Country Network) Des Moines; WHO-DT (Antenna TV, NBC) Des Moines; WOI-DT (ABC) Ames.
Programming (via satellite): A&E; Bravo; CMT; CNBC; CNN; Discovery Channel; Disney Channel; ESPN; Freeform; HGTV; History; Lifetime; MSNBC; MTV; Nickelodeon; Spike TV; TBS; TNT; USA Network; VH1; WGN America.
Fee: $35.00 installation; $35.39 monthly.
Digital Basic Service
Subscribers: N.A.
Programming (via satellite): BBC America; Bloomberg Television; Discovery Life Channel; Disney XD; DMX Music; ESPN Classic; ESPN2; ESPNews; Fox Sports 1; FXM; FYI; Golf Channel; GSN; HGTV; History; History International; LMN; National Geographic Channel; Nick Jr.; Nicktoons; Outdoor Channel; Sundance TV; TeenNick; Trinity Broadcasting Network (TBN); Turner Classic Movies; WE tv.
Pay Service 1
Pay Units: N.A.
Programming (via satellite): HBO (multiplexed).
Fee: $10.70 monthly.
Digital Pay Service 1
Pay Units: N.A.
Programming (via satellite): Cinemax (multiplexed); Flix; HBO (multiplexed); Showtime (multiplexed); Starz (multiplexed); Starz Encore (multiplexed); The Movie Channel (multiplexed).
Fee: $10.70 monthly (each).
Internet Service
Operational: Yes.
Telephone Service
None
Miles of Plant: 1.0 (coaxial); None (fiber optic). Homes passed: 160.
Ownership: Milford Communications (MSO).

THORNTON—Rockwell Communications Systems Inc, 111 North 4th St, PO Box 416, Rockwell, IA 50469. Phone: 641-822-3211. Fax: 641-822-3550. E-mail: rockwell@netins.net. Web Site: http://www.rockwellcoop.com. ICA: IA0518.
TV Market Ranking: Below 100 (THORNTON). Franchise award date: N.A. Franchise expiration date: N.A. Began: July 1, 1985.
Channel capacity: N.A. Channels available but not in use: N.A.
Basic Service
Subscribers: 39.
Fee: $26.45 monthly.
Video-On-Demand: No
Pay-Per-View
ESPN (delivered digitally).
Internet Service
Operational: No, DSL & dial-up.
Telephone Service
Analog: Operational
Homes passed: 206.
General Manager: David Severin. Chief Technician: Jason Dick.
Ownership: Rockwell Cooperative Telephone Association (MSO).

THURMAN—Formerly served by Tele-Services Ltd. No longer in operation. ICA: IA0519.

TITONKA—Titonka-Burt Communications, 247 Main St North, PO Box 321, Titonka, IA 50480-0321. Phones: 515-928-2110; 800-753-2016. Fax: 515-928-2111. E-mail: titonka@tbctel.com. Web Site: http://www.tbctel.com. ICA: IA0249.
TV Market Ranking: Outside TV Markets (TITONKA). Franchise award date: January 1, 1982. Franchise expiration date: N.A. Began: January 1, 1983.
Channel capacity: N.A. Channels available but not in use: N.A.
Basic Service
Subscribers: 189.
Programming (received off-air): KAAL (ABC, This TV) Austin; KEYC-TV (CBS, FOX) Mankato; KIMT (CBS, MNT) Mason City; KTIN (PBS) Fort Dodge; KTTC (CW, NBC) Rochester; KXLT-TV (FOX, MeTV) Rochester; WHO-DT (Antenna TV, NBC) Des Moines; allband FM.
Programming (via satellite): A&E; CMT; CNN; Discovery Channel; Disney Channel; ESPN; ESPN2; Food Network; FOX Sports North; Freeform; HGTV; History; HLN; ION Television; Lifetime; MTV; Nickelodeon; Spike TV; TBS; The Weather Channel; TLC; TNT; Turner Classic Movies; TV Land; USA Network; VH1; WGN America.
Fee: $25.00 installation; $25.00 monthly.
Pay Service 1
Pay Units: 20.
Programming (via satellite): HBO.
Fee: $10.00 installation; $11.00 monthly.
Video-On-Demand: No
Internet Service
Operational: No, DSL & dial-up.
Telephone Service
Analog: Operational
Miles of Plant: 5.0 (coaxial); None (fiber optic). Homes passed: 301.
General Manager: Jim Mayland. Secretary: Denise Heyer. Secretary-Treasurer: Vicky Nelson.
Ownership: Titonka Telephone Co.

TOLEDO—Mediacom. Now served by AMES, IA [IA0008]. ICA: IA0052.

TORONTO—Formerly served by F&B Communications. No longer in operation. ICA: IA0617.

TRAER—Mediacom. Now served by AMES, IA [IA0008]. ICA: IA0083.

TREYNOR—Formerly served by Our Cable. No longer in operation. ICA: IA0520.

TRIPOLI—Butler-Bremer Communications, 715 Main St, PO Box 99, Plainfield, IA 50666. Phones: 800-830-1146; 319-276-4458. Fax: 319-276-7530. E-mail: comments@butler-bremer.com. Web Site: http://butler-bremer.com. Also serves Clarksville, Frederika, Nashua & Plainfield. ICA: IA0127.
TV Market Ranking: 65 (Clarksville, Frederika, Nashua, Plainfield, TRIPOLI). Franchise award date: September 1, 1983. Franchise expiration date: N.A. Began: September 1, 1983.
Channel capacity: N.A. Channels available but not in use: N.A.
Basic Service
Subscribers: 774.
Programming (received off-air): KCRG-TV (ABC, MNT) Cedar Rapids; KFXA (FOX, The Country Network) Cedar Rapids; KIMT (CBS, MNT) Mason City; KPXR-TV (ION) Cedar Rapids; KRIN (PBS) Waterloo; KWKB (The Works, This TV) Iowa City; KWWL (CW, MeTV, NBC) Waterloo.
Programming (via satellite): A&E; AMC; Animal Planet; Cartoon Network; CMT; CNN; Comedy Central; Discovery Channel; Disney Channel; Disney XD; DIY Network; E! HD; ESPN; ESPN Classic; ESPN2; Food Network; Fox News Channel; Fox Sports 1; Freeform; FX; Golf Channel; GSN; Hallmark Channel; HGTV; History; HLN; Lifetime; MSNBC; MTV; Nickelodeon; Outdoor Channel; OWN: Oprah Winfrey Network; Pop; QVC; RFD-TV; Spike TV; Syfy; TBS; The Weather Channel; TLC; TNT; Travel Channel; truTV; Turner Classic Movies; TV Land; USA Network; VH1; WE tv; WGN America.
Fee: $45.00 installation; $56.00 monthly.
Pay Service 1
Pay Units: 85.
Programming (via satellite): Cinemax.
Fee: $10.00 monthly.
Pay Service 2
Pay Units: 72.
Programming (via satellite): HBO.
Fee: $15.00 monthly.
Pay Service 3
Pay Units: 52.
Programming (via satellite): Starz; Starz Encore.
Fee: $10.00 monthly.
Internet Service
Operational: Yes.
Fee: $25.00 installation; $25.00-$44.95 monthly.
Telephone Service
Digital: Operational
Fee: $14.00 monthly
Miles of Plant: 14.0 (coaxial); 32.0 (fiber optic).
Chief Executive Officer: Richard McBurney. Chief Technician: James Chesnut.
Ownership: Butler-Bremer Communications.

TRURO—Interstate Communications, 105 North West St, PO Box 229, Truro, IA 50257-0229. Phones: 712-824-7227; 641-765-4201. Fax: 641-765-4204. Web Site: http://www.interstatecom.com. Also serves Martensdale, New Virginia, St. Charles & St. Marys. ICA: IA0344.
TV Market Ranking: 66 (Martensdale, New Virginia, St. Charles, St. Marys, TRURO).
Channel capacity: N.A. Channels available but not in use: N.A.
Basic Service
Subscribers: 266.
Programming (received off-air): KCCI (CBS, MeTV) Des Moines; KDIN-TV (PBS) Des Moines; KDSM-TV (FOX, The Country Network) Des Moines; KOFY-TV (MeTV) San Francisco; WHO-DT (Antenna TV, NBC) Des Moines; WOI-DT (ABC) Ames.
Programming (via satellite): A&E; AMC; Animal Planet; Cartoon Network; CMT; CNN; C-SPAN; Discovery Channel; Disney Channel; ESPN; ESPN2; FOX Sports Networks; Freeform; FX; HGTV; History; ION Television; Iowa Communications Network; Lifetime; Nickelodeon; Spike TV; Syfy; TBS; The Weather Channel; TLC; TNT; TV Land; USA Network; WGN America.
Fee: $35.00 installation; $79.95 monthly.
Pay Service 1
Pay Units: N.A.
Programming (via satellite): Cinemax; HBO.
Fee: $9.00 monthly (each).
Video-On-Demand: No
Internet Service
Operational: Yes.
Telephone Service
Analog: Operational
Subscribers: 190.
Miles of Plant: None (coaxial); 57.0 (fiber optic).
General Manager: Mike Weis. Chief Technician: Rick Lunn.
Ownership: Interstate Communications (MSO).

UNDERWOOD—Formerly served by TelePartners. Now served by Walnut Communications, WALNUT, IA [IA0241]. ICA: IA0296.

UNION—Heart of Iowa Communications. Formerly [IA0521]. This cable system has converted to IPTV. 502 Main St, PO Box 130, Union, IA 50258-0130. Phones: 800-806-4482; 641-486-2211. Fax: 641-486-2205. Web Site: http://www.heartofiowa.coop. Also serves Albion, Beaman, Conrad, Eldora, Ferguson, Garwin, Grundy County (unincorporated areas), Hardin County (unincorporated areas), Haverhill, Laurel, Liscomb, Marshall County (unincorporated areas), Marshalltown, New Providence, Steamboat Rock & Whitten. ICA: IA5001.

Cable Systems—Iowa

TV Market Ranking: 66 (UNION); Below 100 (Albion).
Channel capacity: N.A. Channels available but not in use: N.A.
XTreme TV
Subscribers: 927.
Fee: $67.00 monthly. Includes 211 channels plus music.
HD
Subscribers: N.A.
Fee: $11.95 monthly.
Cinemax
Subscribers: N.A.
Fee: $13.95 monthly. Includes 8 channels.
HBO
Subscribers: N.A.
Fee: $14.95 monthly. Includes 6 channels.
Cinemax/HBO
Subscribers: N.A.
Fee: $22.95 monthly. Includes 14 channels.
Playboy
Subscribers: N.A.
Fee: $14.95 monthly.
Showtime/TMC/Flix
Subscribers: N.A.
Fee: $13.95 monthly. Includes 12 channels.
Starz/Encore
Subscribers: N.A.
Fee: $13.95 monthly. Includes 9 channels.
Video-On-Demand: Yes
Internet Service
Operational: Yes.
Fee: $39.95-$99.95 monthly.
Telephone Service
Digital: Operational
Fee: $16.00-$30.35 monthly
General Manager: Bryan Amundson. Marketing & Sales Director: Janell King-Squires. Plant Manager: Jay Duncan. Customer Service Manager: Heidi Mitchell. IT Manager: Rich Twinkle.
Ownership: Heart of Iowa Communications Cooperative.

UNION GROVE VILLAGE—Heart of Iowa Telecommunications. This cable system has converted to IPTV. See UNION, IA [IA5001]. ICA: IA0521.

UTE—Long Lines. Now served by SALIX, IA [IA0510]. ICA: IA0289.

VAIL—Formerly served by Tip Top Communications. No longer in operation. ICA: IA0322.

VAN HORNE—Van Horne Telephone Co, 204 Main St, Van Horne, IA 52346-9712. Phone: 319-228-8791. Fax: 319-228-8784. ICA: IA0261.
TV Market Ranking: 65 (VAN HORNE). Franchise award date: February 8, 1983. Franchise expiration date: N.A. Began: N.A.
Channel capacity: N.A. Channels available but not in use: N.A.
Basic Service
Subscribers: 252.
Programming (received off-air): KCRG-TV (ABC, MNT) Cedar Rapids; KFXA (FOX, The Country Network) Cedar Rapids; KGAN (CBS) Cedar Rapids; KPXR-TV (ION) Cedar Rapids; KRIN (PBS) Waterloo; KWKB (The Works, This TV) Iowa City; KWWF (Untamed Sports TV) Waterloo; KWWL (CW, MeTV, NBC) Waterloo.
Programming (via satellite): A&E; AMC; Animal Planet; BTN; Cartoon Network; CMT; CNBC; CNN; Comcast SportsNet Chicago; Comedy Central; C-SPAN; Discovery Channel; Disney Channel; DIY Network; E! HD; ESPN; ESPN Classic; ESPN2; ESPNU; EWTN Global Catholic Network; Food Network; Fox News Channel; Fox Sports 1; Freeform; FX; Great American Country; Hallmark Channel; Hallmark Movies & Mysteries; HGTV; History; HLN; Lifetime; MTV; National Geographic Channel; Nickelodeon; QVC; RFD-TV; Spike TV; Syfy; TBS; The Weather Channel; TLC; TNT; Travel Channel; Trinity Broadcasting Network (TBN); truTV; Turner Classic Movies; TV Land; UP; USA Network; VH1; WGN America.
Fee: $20.00 installation; $50.00 monthly.
Pay Service 1
Pay Units: 17.
Programming (via satellite): HBO.
Fee: $10.00 installation; $10.95 monthly.
Pay Service 2
Pay Units: 9.
Programming (via satellite): Showtime.
Fee: $10.00 installation; $9.95 monthly.
Pay Service 3
Pay Units: 7.
Programming (via satellite): Cinemax.
Fee: $10.00 installation; $9.95 monthly.
Video-On-Demand: No
Pay-Per-View
special events (delivered digitally).
Internet Service
Operational: No.
Telephone Service
None
Miles of Plant: 5.0 (coaxial); None (fiber optic). Homes passed: 275.
General Manager: Donald Whipple. Chief Technician: Ronald Schnor.
Ownership: Van Horne Telephone Co.

VAN WERT—Formerly served by B & L Technologies LLC. No longer in operation. ICA: IA0555.

VINTON—Mediacom, 6300 Council St NE, Ste A, Cedar Rapids, IA 52402. Phones: 800-332-0245; 319-393-1914; 319-395-9699. Fax: 319-393-7017. Web Site: http://www.mediacomcable.com. Also serves Newhall. ICA: IA0629.
TV Market Ranking: 65 (Newhall, VINTON).
Channel capacity: N.A. Channels available but not in use: N.A.
Basic Service
Subscribers: 1,406.
Fee: $43.00 monthly.
Ownership: Mediacom LLC (MSO).

VOLGA—Formerly served by Alpine Communications LC. No longer in operation. ICA: IA0522.

WADENA (village)—Formerly served by Alpine Communications LC. No longer in operation. ICA: IA0523.

WALKER—Formerly served by Mid American Cable Systems. No longer in operation. ICA: IA0581.

WALL LAKE—Corn Belt Telephone Co, 108 Main St, PO Box 445, Wall Lake, IA 51466. Phone: 712-664-2221. Fax: 712-664-2083. E-mail: cbtelco@netins.net. Web Site: http://www.cornbelttelephone.com. Also serves Lake View. ICA: IA0256.
TV Market Ranking: Outside TV Markets (WALL LAKE, Lake View). Franchise award date: N.A. Franchise expiration date: N.A. Began: February 1, 1984.
Channel capacity: N.A. Channels available but not in use: N.A.
Basic Service
Subscribers: 3,517. Commercial subscribers: 192.
Programming (received off-air): KCAU-TV (ABC) Sioux City; KCCI (CBS, MeTV) Des Moines; KDIN-TV (PBS) Des Moines; KDSM-TV (FOX, The Country Network) Des Moines; KMEG (Azteca America, CBS, Decades) Sioux City; KPTH (FOX, MNT, This TV) Sioux City; KTIV (CW, MeTV, NBC) Sioux City; WHO-DT (Antenna TV, NBC) Des Moines; WOI-DT (ABC) Ames.
Programming (via satellite): A&E; AMC; CNN; Discovery Channel; Disney Channel; ESPN; ESPN2; FOX Sports Midwest; HGTV; History; Nickelodeon; Spike TV; Syfy; TBS; The Weather Channel; TLC; TNT; TV Land; USA Network; VH1; WGN America.
Fee: $79.95 monthly.
Pay Service 1
Pay Units: N.A.
Programming (via satellite): Cinemax; HBO.
Fee: $12.00 monthly (each).
Internet Service
Operational: Yes.
Telephone Service
Analog: Operational
Miles of Plant: 5.0 (coaxial); None (fiber optic).
Vice President: Bill Brotherton. General Manager: Larry Neppl. Chief Technician: Bill Cates. Office Manager: Heather Boger.
Ownership: Corn Belt Telephone Co. (MSO).

WALNUT—Walnut Communications, 510 Highland St, PO Box 346, Walnut, IA 51577-0346. Phones: 888-784-2211; 712-784-2211. Fax: 712-784-2010. E-mail: info@walnutel.net. Web Site: http://www.walnutcommunications.com.
Also serves Avoca, McClelland, Minden, Neola, Persia, Shelby & Underwood. ICA: IA0241. **Note:** This system is an overbuild.
TV Market Ranking: 53 (Minden, Neola, Persia, Shelby, Underwood); Outside TV Markets (Avoca, WALNUT). Franchise award date: N.A. Franchise expiration date: N.A. Began: October 1, 1983.
Channel capacity: N.A. Channels available but not in use: N.A.
Basic Service
Subscribers: 1,208.
Programming (received off-air): KCCI (CBS, MeTV) Des Moines; KETV (ABC, MeTV) Omaha; KHIN (PBS) Red Oak; KMTV-TV (Antenna TV, CBS, Escape) Omaha; KPTM (Estrella TV, FOX, MNT, This TV) Omaha; KXVO (Azteca America, CW) Omaha; WHO-DT (Antenna TV, NBC) Des Moines; WOI-DT (ABC) Ames; WOWT (IND, NBC) Omaha; allband FM.
Programming (via satellite): A&E; AMC; Animal Planet; Bravo; BTN; Cartoon Network; CMT; CNBC; CNN; Comedy Central; C-SPAN; C-SPAN 2; Discovery Channel; Disney Channel; Disney XD; E! HD; ESPN; ESPN Classic; ESPN2; ESPNews; EWTN Global Catholic Network; Food Network; Fox News Channel; Fox Sports 1; FOX Sports Midwest; Freeform; FX; GSN; Hallmark Channel; Hallmark Movies & Mysteries; HGTV; History; HLN; Lifetime; LMN; MSNBC; MTV; MyNetworkTV; National Geographic Channel; Nickelodeon; Outdoor Channel; QVC; RFD-TV; Spike TV; Syfy; TBS; The Weather Channel; TLC; TNT; Travel Channel; Turner Classic Movies; TV Land; USA Network; VH1; WGN America.
Fee: $25.00 installation; $59.00 monthly.
Pay Service 1
Pay Units: N.A.
Programming (via satellite): Cinemax (multiplexed); HBO (multiplexed); Showtime (multiplexed); Starz (multiplexed); Starz Encore (multiplexed).
Fee: $10.00 monthly (Cinemax, Showtime or Starz/Encore), $14.00 monthly (HBO).
Video-On-Demand: No
Pay-Per-View
iN DEMAND (delivered digitally); ESPN (delivered digitally).
Internet Service
Operational: Yes.
Subscribers: 125.
Fee: $32.00-$70.00 monthly.
Telephone Service
Digital: Operational
Subscribers: 63.
Miles of Plant: 34.0 (coaxial); None (fiber optic). Homes passed: 2,227.
General Manager: Bruce Heyne. Plant Manager: Denny Book. Marketing Manager: LeAnne Blotzer. Office Manager: Rachel Becorra.
Ownership: Walnut Communications (MSO).

WASHINGTON—Mediacom, 6300 Council St NE, Ste A, Cedar Rapids, IA 52402. Phone: 319-235-2197. Fax: 319-393-7017. Web Site: http://www.mediacomcable.com. Also serves Kalona, Lone Tree, Riverside & Wellman. ICA: IA0009.
TV Market Ranking: 65 (Kalona, Riverside); Below 100 (Lone Tree, Wellman).
Channel capacity: N.A. Channels available but not in use: N.A.
Basic Service
Subscribers: 1,567.
Fee: $41.99 installation; $43.00 monthly.
Ownership: Mediacom LLC (MSO).

WATERLOO—Formerly served by Wireless Cable TV of Waterloo. No longer in operation. ICA: IA0562.

WATERLOO—Mediacom, 4010 Alexandra Dr, Waterloo, IA 50702. Phones: 319-395-9699 (Cedar Rapids regional office); 319-235-2197. Fax: 319-232-7841. Web Site: http://www.mediacomcable.com. Also serves Black Hawk County (portions), Cedar Falls, Dewar, Elk Run Heights, Evansdale, Gilbertville, Raymond & Washburn. ICA: IA0003.
TV Market Ranking: 65 (Black Hawk County (portions), Cedar Falls, Dewar, Elk Run Heights, Evansdale, Gilbertville, Raymond, Washburn, WATERLOO). Franchise award date: March 20, 1978. Franchise expiration date: N.A. Began: June 7, 1979.
Channel capacity: N.A. Channels available but not in use: N.A.
Basic Service
Subscribers: 15,593. Commercial subscribers: 1,106.
Programming (received off-air): KCRG-TV (ABC, MNT) Cedar Rapids; KFXA (FOX, The Country Network) Cedar Rapids; KGAN

Iowa—Cable Systems

(CBS) Cedar Rapids; KPXR-TV (ION) Cedar Rapids; KRIN (PBS) Waterloo; KWKB (The Works, This TV) Iowa City; KWWF (Untamed Sports TV) Waterloo; KWWL (CW, MeTV, NBC) Waterloo.
Programming (via satellite): A&E; AMC; Animal Planet; BET; Bravo; Cartoon Network; CMT; CNBC; CNN; Comcast SportsNet Chicago; Comedy Central; C-SPAN; C-SPAN 2; Discovery Channel; Disney Channel; E! HD; ESPN; ESPN Classic; ESPN2; EWTN Global Catholic Network; Food Network; Fox News Channel; Fox Sports 1; FOX Sports Midwest; Freeform; FX; Golf Channel; Hallmark Channel; HGTV; History; HLN; INSP; Lifetime; MoviePlex; MSNBC; MTV; NBC Universo; NBCSN; Nickelodeon; Outdoor Channel; Pop; QVC; RFD-TV; Spike TV; Syfy; TBS; The Weather Channel; TLC; TNT; Travel Channel; Trinity Broadcasting Network (TBN); truTV; Turner Classic Movies; TV Land; USA Network; VH1; WGN America.
Fee: $40.95 installation; $60.85 monthly.
Digital Basic Service
Subscribers: N.A.
Programming (via satellite): AXS TV; BBC America; Bloomberg Television; Cloo; Discovery Digital Networks; Disney XD; ESPN; ESPN2; ESPNews; Fuse; FXM; FYI; GSN; HD Theater; History International; IFC; LMN; MC; National Geographic Channel; Nick Jr.; Nicktoons; Ovation; TeenNick; TVG Network; Universal HD.
Digital Pay Service 1
Pay Units: N.A.
Programming (via satellite): Cinemax (multiplexed); Flix (multiplexed); HBO (multiplexed); HBO HD; Showtime (multiplexed); Showtime HD; Starz (multiplexed); Starz Encore (multiplexed); Sundance TV (multiplexed); The Movie Channel (multiplexed); The Movie Channel HD.
Video-On-Demand: Yes
Pay-Per-View
SexSee (delivered digitally); ESPN (delivered digitally); Playboy TV (delivered digitally); Fresh (delivered digitally); Shorteez (delivered digitally); Pleasure (delivered digitally).
Internet Service
Operational: Yes.
Subscribers: 13,796.
Broadband Service: Mediacom High Speed Internet.
Fee: $49.95 installation; $39.95 monthly; $10.00 modem lease.
Telephone Service
Digital: Operational
Subscribers: 6,000.
Fee: $49.95 monthly
Miles of Plant: 998.0 (coaxial); 252.0 (fiber optic). Homes passed: 57,943.
Regional Vice President: Doug Frank. General Manager: Doug Nix. Technical Operations Director: Greg Nank. Marketing Director: Steve Schuh. Marketing Coordinator: Joni Lindauer.
Ownership: Mediacom LLC (MSO).

WAVERLY—Mediacom, 4010 Alexandra Dr, Waterloo, IA 50702. Phone: 319-235-2197. Fax: 319-232-7841. Web Site: http://www.mediacomcable.com. Also serves Aplington, Delaware County (portions), Denver, Dike, Edgewood, Fairbank, Fayette County (portions), Hazleton, Janesville, La Porte, Manchester, Maynard, New Hartford, Oelwein, Parkersburg, Reinbeck, Shell Rock & Strawberry Point. ICA: IA0021.
TV Market Ranking: 65 (Aplington, Denver, Dike, Fairbank, Hazleton, Janesville, La Porte, Maynard, New Hartford, Oelwein, Parkersburg, Reinbeck, Shell Rock, WAVERLY); Outside TV Markets (Edgewood, Manchester, Strawberry Point). Franchise award date: N.A. Franchise expiration date: N.A. Began: September 1, 1982.
Channel capacity: N.A. Channels available but not in use: N.A.
Basic Service
Subscribers: 2,291.
Programming (received off-air): KCRG-TV (ABC, MNT) Cedar Rapids; KFXA (FOX, The Country Network) Cedar Rapids; KGAN (CBS) Cedar Rapids; KPXR-TV (ION) Cedar Rapids; KRIN (PBS) Waterloo; KWKB (The Works, This TV) Iowa City; KWWL (CW, MeTV, NBC) Waterloo.
Programming (via satellite): C-SPAN; C-SPAN 2; INSP; Nickelodeon; Pop; QVC; WGN America.
Fee: $60.00 installation; $54.82 monthly; $.70 converter.
Expanded Basic Service 1
Subscribers: N.A.
Programming (via satellite): A&E; Animal Planet; Bravo; Cartoon Network; CMT; CNBC; CNN; Comcast SportsNet Chicago; Comedy Central; Discovery Channel; Disney Channel; E! HD; ESPN; ESPN2; EWTN Global Catholic Network; Food Network; Fox News Channel; Fox Sports 1; Freeform; FX; Hallmark Channel; HGTV; History; HLN; Lifetime; MSNBC; MTV; RFD-TV; Spike TV; Syfy; TBS; Telemundo; The Weather Channel; TLC; TNT; Travel Channel; Trinity Broadcasting Network (TBN); truTV; Turner Classic Movies; TV Land; USA Network; VH1; WE tv.
Fee: $22.08 monthly.
Digital Basic Service
Subscribers: N.A.
Programming (via satellite): BBC America; Bloomberg Television; Discovery Digital Networks; Disney XD; DMX Music; Fuse; FXM; FYI; Golf Channel; GSN; History International; IFC; LMN; National Geographic Channel; NBCSN; Nick Jr.; Outdoor Channel; Ovation; TeenNick; Turner Classic Movies.
Digital Pay Service 1
Pay Units: N.A.
Programming (via satellite): Cinemax (multiplexed); HBO (multiplexed); Showtime (multiplexed); Starz (multiplexed); Starz Encore (multiplexed); Sundance TV; The Movie Channel (multiplexed).
Fee: $9.95 monthly (Cinemax, HBO, Showtime, Starz/Encore, or Sundance/TMC).
Video-On-Demand: Yes
Pay-Per-View
ESPN Now (delivered digitally); ETC (delivered digitally); Playboy TV (delivered digitally); Pleasure (delivered digitally); Fresh (delivered digitally); Shorteez (delivered digitally); Vubiquity Inc. (delivered digitally).
Internet Service
Operational: Yes.
Subscribers: 1,863.
Broadband Service: Mediacom High Speed Internet.
Telephone Service
Digital: Operational
Subscribers: 1,267.
Fee: $39.95 monthly
Miles of Plant: 187.0 (coaxial); 255.0 (fiber optic). Homes passed: 8,952.
Regional Vice President: Doug Frank. General Manager: Doug Nix. Technical Operations Director: Greg Nank. Marketing Director: Steve Schuh. Marketing Coordinator: Joni Lindauer.
Ownership: Mediacom LLC (MSO).

WAYLAND—Farmers & Merchants Mutual Telephone. Formerly served by Wayland, IA [IA0525]. This cable system has converted to IPTV, 210 West Main St, PO Box 247, Wayland, IA 52654. Phones: 800-822-2736; 319-256-2736. Fax: 319-256-7210. E-mail: manager@farmtel.com. Web Site: http://www.farmtelcommunications.com. ICA: IA5076.
Channel capacity: N.A. Channels available but not in use: N.A.
Internet Service
Operational: Yes.
Ownership: Farmers & Merchants Mutual Telephone Co.

WAYLAND—Farmers & Merchants Mutual Telephone. This cable system has converted to IPTV. See WAYLAND, IA [IA5076]. ICA: IA0525.

WELLSBURG—Formerly served by Union Cablevision. No longer in operation. ICA: IA0526.

WESLEY—Formerly served by Comm1. No longer in operation. ICA: IA0527.

WESLEY—Formerly served by Comm1. No longer in operation. ICA: IA5126.

WESTGATE (village)—Formerly served by Alpine Communications LC. No longer in operation. ICA: IA0528.

WESTSIDE—Western Iowa Networks. Now served by BREDA, IA [IA0318]. ICA: IA0242.

WHEATLAND—F&B Communications. Formerly [IA0529]. This cable system has converted to IPTV., 103 North Main St, PO Box 309, Wheatland, IA 52777-0309. Phones: 800-866-6545; 563-374-1236. Fax: 563-374-1930. E-mail: info@fbc-tele.com. Web Site: http://www.fbc-tele.com. Also serves Bennett, Calamus, Delmar & Lowden. ICA: IA5105.
Channel capacity: N.A. Channels available but not in use: N.A.
Digital Video Lite
Subscribers: 52.
Fee: $37.99 monthly. Includes 35+ channels plus music channels.
Digital Video Basic
Subscribers: 872.
Fee: $81.99 monthly. Includes 120+ channels in SD & 75+ channels in HD plus music channels.
HD
Subscribers: N.A.
Fee: $5.00 monthly. Includes 3 channels.
Premium Channels
Subscribers: N.A.
Fee: $18.00 monthly/one movie package, $31.00/two movie packages, $42.00/three movie packages, $50.00/four movie packages. Packages include Cinemax (8 channels), HBO (6 channels), Showtime/TMC/Flix (12 channels), Starz/Encore (12 channels).
Internet Service
Operational: Yes.
Fee: $125.00 installation; $44.99-$104.99 monthly.
Telephone Service
Digital: Operational
Fee: $15.00 monthly
General Manager: Ken Laursen. Assistant General Manager: Aaron Hoffman. Office Manager: Julie Steines. Plant Supervisor: Jeff Cerda.
Ownership: F & B Communications.

WHEATLAND—F&B Communications. This cable system has converted to IPTV. Now served by WHEATLAND, IA [IA5105]. ICA: IA0529.

WHITING—Long Lines. Now served by SALIX, IA [IA0510]. ICA: IA0267.

WHITTEMORE—ATC Cablevision. Now served by GILLETT GROVE, IA [IA0386]. ICA: IA0266.

WILLIAMS—Formerly served by Williams Cablevision. No longer in operation. ICA: IA0530.

WILLIAMSBURG—Mediacom, 6300 Council St NE, Ste A, Cedar Rapids, IA 52402. Phones: 319-395-9699; 319-393-1914; 800-332-0245. Fax: 319-393-7017. Web Site: http://www.mediacomcable.com. Also serves North English. ICA: IA0124.
TV Market Ranking: 65 (WILLIAMSBURG); Below 100 (North English).
Channel capacity: N.A. Channels available but not in use: N.A.
Basic Service
Subscribers: 574.
Fee: $43.00 monthly.
Ownership: Mediacom LLC (MSO).

WINFIELD—Formerly served by Longview Communications. No longer in operation. ICA: IA0201.

WINTHROP—East Buchanan Telephone Cooperative, 214 3rd St North, PO Box 100, Winthrop, IA 50682-0100. Phones: 866-327-2748; 319-935-3011. Fax: 319-935-3010. E-mail: ebtccw@netins.net. Web Site: http://www.eastbuchanan.com. Also serves Quasqueton. ICA: IA0531.
TV Market Ranking: 65 (Quasqueton, WINTHROP). Franchise award date: January 1, 1981. Franchise expiration date: N.A. Began: January 1, 1983.
Channel capacity: N.A. Channels available but not in use: N.A.
Basic Service
Subscribers: 230.
Programming (received off-air): KCRG-TV (ABC, MNT) Cedar Rapids; KFXA (FOX, The Country Network) Cedar Rapids; KGAN (CBS) Cedar Rapids; KRIN (PBS) Waterloo; KWKB (The Works, This TV) Iowa City; KWWL (CW, MeTV, NBC) Waterloo.
Programming (via satellite): A&E; AMC; Animal Planet; Cartoon Network; CMT; CNBC; CNN; Comedy Central; C-SPAN; C-SPAN 2; Discovery Channel; Disney Channel; DIY Network; E! HD; ESPN; ESPN Classic; ESPN2; EWTN Global Catholic Network; Food Network; Fox News Channel; Fox Sports 1; Freeform; FX; Golf Channel; GSN; Hallmark Channel; HGTV; History; HLN; ION Television; Lifetime; MoviePlex; MTV; National Geographic Channel; NFL Network; Nickelodeon; Outdoor Channel; Pop; QVC; RFD-TV; Spike TV; Syfy; TBS; The Weather Channel; TLC; TNT; Travel Channel; Trinity Broadcasting Network (TBN); truTV; Turner Classic Movies; TV Land; USA Network; VH1; WE tv; WGN America.
Fee: $25.00 installation; $66.85 monthly.
Pay Service 1
Pay Units: 78.
Programming (via satellite): HBO (multiplexed).
Fee: $15.00 installation; $13.49 monthly (each).

Cable Systems—Iowa

Internet Service
Operational: Yes, DSL.
Fee: $49.00 installation; $29.95-$54.95 monthly; $10.00 modem lease; $69.95 modem purchase.
Telephone Service
Analog: Operational
Fee: $16.00 monthly
Miles of Plant: 5.0 (coaxial); None (fiber optic). Homes passed: 500.
General Manager: Butch Rorabaugh. Plant Manager: Roger Olsen. Office Manager: Christy Wolfe.
Ownership: East Buchanan Telephone Cooperative (MSO).

WODEN—Formerly served by Heck's TV & Cable. No longer in operation. ICA: IA0355.

WOODBURN—Formerly served by Telnet South LC. Now served by Mediacom, CHARITON, IA [IA0017]. ICA: IA0577.

WOOLSTOCK—Goldfield Communication Services Corp. Now served by GOLDFIELD, IA [IA0252]. ICA: IA0552.

WORTHINGTON—New Century Communications, 3588 Kennebec Dr, Eagan, MN 55122-1001. Phone: 651-688-2623. Fax: 651-688-2624. ICA: IA0613.
TV Market Ranking: Below 100 (WORTHINGTON). Franchise award date: February 6, 1989. Franchise expiration date: N.A. Began: February 6, 1989.
Channel capacity: N.A. Channels available but not in use: N.A.

Basic Service
Subscribers: 60.
Programming (received off-air): KCRG-TV (ABC, MNT) Cedar Rapids; KFXA (FOX, The Country Network) Cedar Rapids; KGAN (CBS) Cedar Rapids; KIIN (PBS) Iowa City; KPXR-TV (ION) Cedar Rapids; KWKB (The Works, This TV) Iowa City; KWWL (CW, MeTV, NBC) Waterloo.
Programming (via satellite): A&E; AMC; CNN; Discovery Channel; Disney Channel; DIY Network; ESPN; ESPN2; EWTN Global Catholic Network; Freeform; History; HLN; Lifetime; MTV; Nickelodeon; QVC; Spike TV; TBS; The Weather Channel; TLC; TNT; Turner Classic Movies; USA Network; VH1; WGN America.
Fee: $32.95 monthly.
Pay Service 1
Pay Units: N.A.
Programming (via satellite): Cinemax; HBO; Showtime.
Fee: $10.00 monthly (each).
Video-On-Demand: No
Internet Service
Operational: No.
Telephone Service
None
Homes passed: 175.
Executive Vice President: Marty Walch. General Manager & Chief Technician: Todd Anderson.
Ownership: New Century Communications (MSO).

WORTHINGTON—New Century Communications. Now served by WORTHINGTON, IA [IA0613]. ICA: IA0532.

ZEARING—Minerva Valley Cablevision, 104 North Pine St, PO Box 176, Zearing, IA 50278. Phone: 641-487-7399. Fax: 641-487-7599. E-mail: minerva@netins.net. Web Site: http://www.minervavalley.com. Also serves Clemons, McCallsburg & St. Anthony. ICA: IA0533.
TV Market Ranking: 66 (Clemons, McCallsburg, St. Anthony, ZEARING). Franchise award date: N.A. Franchise expiration date: N.A. Began: April 1, 1985.
Channel capacity: 37 (operating 2-way). Channels available but not in use: N.A.
Basic Service
Subscribers: N.A.
Programming (received off-air): KCCI (CBS, MeTV) Des Moines; KCWI-TV (CW) Ames; KDIN-TV (PBS) Des Moines; KDSM-TV (FOX, The Country Network) Des Moines; KFPX-TV (ION) Newton; WHO-DT (Antenna TV, NBC) Des Moines; WOI-DT (ABC) Ames.
Programming (via satellite): A&E; AMC; Animal Planet; Bravo; BTN; CMT; CNBC; CNN; Comedy Central; Discovery Channel; Disney Channel; ESPN; ESPN2; Flix; Food Network; Fox News Channel; Freeform; FX; Hallmark Channel; HLN; Lifetime; LMN; MSNBC; MTV; Nickelodeon; Spike TV; Syfy; TBS; The Weather Channel; TLC; TNT; Trinity Broadcasting Network (TBN); TV Land; USA Network; VH1; WGN America.
Fee: $20.00 installation.
Digital Basic Service
Subscribers: N.A.
Programming (via satellite): BBC America; Bloomberg Television; Bravo; Destination America; Discovery Kids Channel; Discovery Life Channel; Disney XD; DMX Music; ESPN Classic; ESPN2; ESPNews; Fox Sports 1; Fuse; FXM; FYI; Golf Channel; Great American Country; GSN; HGTV; History; History International; IFC; Investigation Discovery; LMN; MBC America; MTV Classic; MTV Hits; MTV2; NBCSN; Nick Jr.; Nicktoons; Outdoor Channel; Ovation; OWN; Oprah Winfrey Network; RFD-TV; Science Channel; Sundance TV; Syfy; TeenNick; Trinity Broadcasting Network (TBN); Turner Classic Movies; VH1 Country; VH1 Soul; WE tv.
Pay Service 1
Pay Units: N.A.
Programming (via satellite): HBO.
Fee: $10.25 monthly.
Digital Pay Service 1
Pay Units: N.A.
Programming (via satellite): Cinemax (multiplexed); Flix; HBO (multiplexed); Showtime (multiplexed); Starz (multiplexed); Starz Encore (multiplexed); The Movie Channel (multiplexed).
Fee: $10.00 monthly (Cinemax), $12.95 monthly (Starz/Encore), $14.00 monthly (HBO or Showtime).
Internet Service
Operational: No, DSL.
Telephone Service
Analog: Operational
Miles of Plant: 8.0 (coaxial); None (fiber optic).
General Manager: Levi Bappe. Office Manager: Mary Phillips.
Ownership: Minerva Valley Cablevision Inc.

KANSAS

Total Systems: 110	Communities with Applications: 0
Total Communities Served: 373	Number of Basic Subscribers: 332,549
Franchises Not Yet Operating: 0	Number of Expanded Basic Subscribers: 13,849
Applications Pending: 0	Number of Pay Units: 22,080

Top 100 Markets Represented: Kansas City, MO (22); Wichita-Hutchinson (67).

For a list of cable communities in this section, see the Cable Community Index located in the back of Cable Volume 2.
For explanation of terms used in cable system listings, see p. D-11.

ABBYVILLE—Formerly served by Cox Communications. No longer in operation. ICA: KS0359.

ABILENE—Eagle Communications, 2703 Hall St, Ste 15, PO Box 817, Hays, KS 67601. Phones: 785-899-3371; 785-625-5910; 785-625-4000 (Corporate office); 785-263-2529. Fax: 785-625-8030. E-mail: gary.shorman@eaglecom.net. Web Site: http://www.eaglecom.net. Also serves Chapman, Clay Center, Clay County (portions), Dickinson County, Enterprise, Solomon & Wakefield. ICA: KS0034.
TV Market Ranking: Below 100 (ABILENE, Clay County (portions) (portions), Dickinson County (portions), Enterprise, Chapman, Solomon); Outside TV Markets (Clay County (portions) (portions), Dickinson County (portions), Clay Center, Wakefield). Franchise award date: September 2, 1962. Franchise expiration date: N.A. Began: September 1, 1962.
Channel capacity: 51 (operating 2-way). Channels available but not in use: N.A.
Basic Service
 Subscribers: 2,485. Commercial subscribers: 69.
 Programming (received off-air): KAAS-TV (FOX) Salina; KSNT (FOX, NBC) Topeka; KTWU (PBS) Topeka; KWCH-DT (CBS) Hutchinson; WIBW-TV (CBS, MeTV, MNT) Topeka.
 Programming (via microwave): KAKE (ABC, MeTV) Wichita; KCTV (CBS) Kansas City; KSCW-DT (CW, Decades) Wichita; KSNW (NBC) Wichita; WDAF-TV (Antenna TV, FOX) Kansas City.
 Fee: $29.95 installation; $69.95 monthly.
Expanded Basic Service 1
 Subscribers: N.A.
 Programming (via satellite): A&E; AMC; Cartoon Network; CNBC; CNN; Comedy Central; C-SPAN; Discovery Channel; Disney Channel; E! HD; ESPN; ESPN2; EWTN Global Catholic Network; Food Network; Fox News Channel; FOX Sports Midwest; Freeform; FX; Great American Country; HGTV; History; HLN; INSP; Lifetime; MSNBC; MTV; National Geographic Channel; NFL Network; Nickelodeon; Outdoor Channel; Spike TV; Syfy; TBS; The Weather Channel; TLC; TNT; Travel Channel; TV Land; USA Network; VH1.
 Fee: $25.50 monthly.
Digital Basic Service
 Subscribers: N.A.
 Programming (via satellite): BBC America; Bloomberg Television; Cloo; Destination America; Discovery Kids Channel; Disney XD; ESPN Classic; ESPNews; Fox Sports 1; Fuse; FYI; Golf Channel; GSN; History International; LMN; NBCSN; OWN: Oprah Winfrey Network; Science Channel; Trinity Broadcasting Network (TBN); Turner Classic Movies; WE tv.
 Fee: $4.95 monthly (Discovery, Entertainment or Sports Package).
Digital Pay Service 1
 Pay Units: N.A.
 Programming (via satellite): Cinemax (multiplexed); HBO (multiplexed); Showtime (multiplexed); Starz; Starz Encore (multiplexed); The Movie Channel (multiplexed).
 Fee: $11.95 monthly (Cinemax, HBO, Starz/Encore or Showtime/TMC).
Video-On-Demand: No
Pay-Per-View
 iN DEMAND; Playboy TV (delivered digitally); Club Jenna (delivered digitally); Fresh (delivered digitally).
Internet Service
 Operational: Yes. Began: January 2, 2004. Broadband Service: Eagle Internet.
 Fee: $22.95 monthly.
Telephone Service
 Analog: Not Operational
 Digital: Operational
 Fee: $18.00 monthly
Miles of Plant: 50.0 (coaxial); None (fiber optic). Homes passed: 4,945.
Chief Operating Officer: Kurt K. David. General Manager: Travis Kohlrus. Chief Technician: Jim Gall. Ad Sales Manager: Mike Koerner.
Ownership: Eagle Communications Inc. (MSO).

AGRA—Nex-Tech. Formerly served by LENORA, KS [KS0450]. This cable system has converted to IPTV, 2418 Vine St, Hays, KS 67601. Phones: 877-567-7872; 785-625-7070. Fax: 785-625-4479. E-mail: webmaster@nex-tech.com. Web Site: http://www.nex-tech.com. ICA: KS5059.
TV Market Ranking: Franchise award date: April 27, 2007. Franchise expiration date: N.A. Began: N.A.
Channel capacity: N.A. Channels available but not in use: N.A.
Essentials
 Subscribers: 85.
 Fee: $30.00 installation; $24.95 monthly. Includes 51 channels.
Premiere
 Subscribers: 83.
 Fee: $61.95 monthly. Includes 119 channels plus music channels.
HD
 Subscribers: N.A.
 Fee: $11.95 monthly. Includes 75+ channels.
Sports & Entertainment
 Subscribers: N.A.
 Fee: $12.95 monthly. Includes 34 channels.
Cinemax
 Subscribers: N.A.
 Fee: $8.95 monthly. Includes 8 channels.
HBO
 Subscribers: N.A.
 Fee: $14.95 monthly. Includes 12 channels.
Showtime/TMC
 Subscribers: N.A.
 Fee: $13.95 monthly. Includes 16 channels.
Starz/Encore
 Subscribers: N.A.
 Fee: $10.95 monthly. Includes 18 channels.
Video-On-Demand: Yes
Internet Service
 Operational: Yes.
 Fee: $22.95-$42.95 monthly.
Telephone Service
 Digital: Operational
 Fee: $16.75 monthly
Chief Executive Officer & General Manager: Larry Sevier. Video Solutions Manager: Scott Roe.
Ownership: Nex-Tech.

ALMA—Formerly served by Zito Media. No longer in operation. ICA: KS0181.

ALMENA—Nex-Tech. Formerly [KS0360]. This cable system has converted to IPTV, 2418 Vine St, Hays, KS 67601. Phones: 877-567-7872; 785-625-7070. Fax: 785-625-4479. E-mail: webmaster@nex-tech.com. Web Site: http://www.nex-tech.com. Also serves Norton. ICA: KS5146.
TV Market Ranking: Franchise award date: N.A. Franchise expiration date: N.A. Began: December 7, 2010.
Channel capacity: N.A. Channels available but not in use: N.A.
Essentials
 Subscribers: 1,217.
 Fee: $30.00 installation; $24.95 monthly. Includes 53 channels.
Premiere
 Subscribers: 1,123.
 Fee: $61.95 monthly. Includes 121 channels plus music channels.
HD
 Subscribers: N.A.
 Fee: $11.95 monthly. Includes 76+ channels.
Sports & Entertainment
 Subscribers: N.A.
 Fee: $12.95 monthly. Includes 34 channels.
Cinemax
 Subscribers: N.A.
 Fee: $8.95 monthly. Includes 8 channels.
HBO
 Subscribers: N.A.
 Fee: $14.95 monthly. Includes 12 channels.
Showtime/TMC
 Subscribers: N.A.
 Fee: $13.95 monthly. Includes 16 channels.
Starz/Encore
 Subscribers: N.A.
 Fee: $10.95 monthly. Includes 18 channels.
Video-On-Demand: Yes
Internet Service
 Operational: Yes.
 Fee: $22.95-$207.95 monthly.
Telephone Service
 Digital: Operational
 Fee: $16.75 monthly
Chief Executive Officer & General Manager: Larry Sevier. Video Solutions Manager: Scott Roe.
Ownership: Nex-Tech.

ALMENA—Nex-Tech. This cable system has converted to IPTV. See ALMENA, KS [KS5146]. ICA: KS0360.

ALTA VISTA—Formerly served by Galaxy Cablevision. No longer in operation. ICA: KS0219.

ALTAMONT—Wave Wireless, 2130 Corning Ave, PO Box 921, Parsons, KS 67357. Phone: 620-423-9283. Fax: 620-784-5882. E-mail: support@wavewls.com. Web Site: http://www.wavewls.com. ICA: KS0170.
TV Market Ranking: Outside TV Markets (ALTAMONT). Franchise award date: N.A. Franchise expiration date: N.A. Began: October 21, 1983.
Channel capacity: N.A. Channels available but not in use: N.A.
Basic Service
 Subscribers: N.A.
 Programming (received off-air): KOAM-TV (CBS) Pittsburg; KODE-TV (ABC) Joplin; KOED-TV (PBS) Tulsa; KOKI-TV (FOX, MeTV) Tulsa; KSNF (NBC) Joplin.
 Programming (via satellite): A&E; Cartoon Network; CMT; CNN; Comedy Central; C-SPAN; Discovery Channel; Disney Channel; ESPN; ESPN2; FOX Sports Midwest; Freeform; Hallmark Channel; Hallmark Movies & Mysteries; History; Lifetime; MTV; Nickelodeon; QVC; Spike TV; TBS; The Weather Channel; TLC; TNT; Travel Channel; Trinity Broadcasting Network (TBN); Turner Classic Movies; TV Land; USA Network; VH1; WGN America.
 Fee: $20.00 installation; $25.50 monthly.
Pay Service 1
 Pay Units: N.A.
 Programming (via satellite): Cinemax; HBO.
 Fee: $10.95 monthly (each).
Video-On-Demand: No
Internet Service
 Operational: No, Wireless.
Telephone Service
 None
Miles of Plant: 20.0 (coaxial); None (fiber optic). Homes passed: 440.
Ownership: Wave Wireless LLC.

ALTOONA—Mediacom, 901 North College Ave, Columbia, MO 65201. Phones: 417-875-5560 (Springfield regional office); 573-443-1536. Fax: 417-883-0265. Web

D-278 TV & Cable Factbook No. 85

Cable Systems—Kansas

Site: http://www.mediacomcable.com. ICA: KS0266.
TV Market Ranking: Outside TV Markets (ALTOONA). Franchise award date: February 21, 1984. Franchise expiration date: N.A. Began: January 1, 1985.
Channel capacity: N.A. Channels available but not in use: N.A.
Basic Service
Subscribers: 15.
Programming (received off-air): KOAM-TV (CBS) Pittsburg; KODE-TV (ABC) Joplin; KSNF (NBC) Joplin; KTWU (PBS) Topeka.
Programming (via satellite): A&E; CMT; CNBC; CNN; Discovery Channel; ESPN; ESPN2; Freeform; HLN; Nickelodeon; QVC; Spike TV; TBS; The Weather Channel; TNT; USA Network; WGN America.
Fee: $35.00 installation; $41.05 monthly.
Pay Service 1
Pay Units: N.A.
Programming (via satellite): Flix; HBO; The Movie Channel.
Fee: $10.50 monthly (each).
Video-On-Demand: No
Internet Service
Operational: No.
Telephone Service
None
Miles of Plant: 12.0 (coaxial); None (fiber optic). Homes passed: 232.
Vice President, Financial Reporting: Kenneth J. Kohrs. Regional Vice President: Bill Copeland. Regional Technical Operations Director: Alan Freedman. Operations Director: Bryan Gann. Marketing Director: Will Kuebler. Technical Operations Manager: Roger Shearer.
Ownership: Mediacom LLC (MSO).

AMERICUS—Zito Media, 102 S Main St, PO Box 665, Coudersport, PA 16915. Phones: 814-260-9055; 800-365-6988. E-mail: info@zitomedia.com. Web Site: http://www.zitomedia.com. ICA: KS0183.
TV Market Ranking: Outside TV Markets (AMERICUS). Franchise award date: N.A. Franchise expiration date: N.A. Began: November 1, 1976.
Channel capacity: N.A. Channels available but not in use: N.A.
Basic Service
Subscribers: 19.
Programming (received off-air): KSNT (FOX, NBC) Topeka; KTKA-TV (ABC, CW) Topeka; KTWU (PBS) Topeka; WIBW-TV (CBS, MeTV, MNT) Topeka.
Programming (via satellite): A&E; AMC; Cartoon Network; CNN; Comedy Central; Discovery Channel; Disney Channel; ESPN; ESPN2; Fox News Channel; Freeform; Fuse; FX; Great American Country; HGTV; History; HLN; Lifetime; MSNBC; Outdoor Channel; QVC; TBS; The Weather Channel; TLC; TNT; USA Network; WGN America.
Fee: $25.00 installation; $42.75 monthly.
Pay Service 1
Pay Units: N.A.
Programming (via satellite): Cinemax; HBO; Showtime; Starz; The Movie Channel.
Fee: $25.00 installation; $11.00 monthly.
Internet Service
Operational: No.
Telephone Service
None
Miles of Plant: 6.0 (coaxial); None (fiber optic). Homes passed: 344.
President: James Rigas.
Ownership: Zito Media (MSO).

ANDALE—Formerly served by Almega Cable. No longer in operation. ICA: KS0264.

ANTHONY—Suddenlink Communications, 520 Maryville Centre Dr, Ste 300, St. Louis, MO 63141. Phones: 314-315-9400; 800-999-6845 (Customer service). Web Site: http://www.suddenlink.com. ICA: KS0362.
TV Market Ranking: Outside TV Markets (ANTHONY). Franchise award date: N.A. Franchise expiration date: N.A. Began: June 1, 1977.
Channel capacity: N.A. Channels available but not in use: N.A.
Basic Service
Subscribers: 154.
Programming (received off-air): KAKE (ABC, MeTV) Wichita; KETA-TV (PBS) Oklahoma City; KPTS (PBS) Hutchinson; KSAS-TV (Antenna TV, FOX) Wichita; KSCW-DT (CW, Decades) Wichita; KSNW (NBC) Wichita; KWCH-DT (CBS) Hutchinson.
Programming (via satellite): EWTN Global Catholic Network; National Geographic Channel; QVC; TV Land.
Fee: $28.45 monthly.
Expanded Basic Service 1
Subscribers: N.A.
Programming (via satellite): A&E; Animal Planet; CNN; C-SPAN; Discovery Channel; Disney Channel; E! HD; ESPN; Fox News Channel; FOX Sports Midwest; Freeform; FX; Great American Country; HGTV; History; HLN; Nickelodeon; Spike TV; TBS; The Weather Channel; TLC; TNT; Turner Classic Movies; USA Network; VH1.
Fee: $24.00 monthly.
Pay Service 1
Pay Units: N.A.
Programming (via satellite): HBO; Showtime; The Movie Channel.
Fee: $35.00 installation; $5.95 monthly (TMC), $9.95 monthly (Showtime), $10.95 monthly (HBO).
Video-On-Demand: No
Pay-Per-View
Fresh (delivered digitally); Playboy TV (delivered digitally); iN DEMAND (delivered digitally).
Internet Service
Operational: Yes. Began: May 26, 2003.
Broadband Service: Suddenlink High Speed Internet.
Fee: $49.95 installation; $26.95 monthly.
Telephone Service
None
Miles of Plant: 42.0 (coaxial); None (fiber optic). Homes passed: 798.
Senior Vice President, Corporate Finance: Michael Pflantz. Regional Manager: Todd Cruthird. Chief Technician: Norm Schwatken. Marketing Director: Beverly Gambell.
Ownership: Cequel Communications Holdings I LLC (MSO).

ARCADIA—Formerly served by National Cable Inc. No longer in operation. ICA: KS0257.

ARGONIA—Formerly served by Almega Cable. No longer in operation. ICA: KS0260.

ARLINGTON—Formerly served by Almega Cable. No longer in operation. ICA: KS0231.

ASHLAND—Formerly served by Cebridge Connections. Now served by United Communications Assn. Inc., CIMARRON, KS [KS0126]. ICA: KS0148.

ASSARIA—Home Communications Inc. Formerly [KS0363]. This cable system has converted to IPTV. Now served by GALVA, KS [KS5068]. ICA: KS5061.

ASSARIA—Home Communications Inc. This cable system has converted to IPTV. Now served by GALVA, KS [KS5068]. ICA: KS0363.

ATCHISON—Vyve Broadband, 4 International Dr, Ste 330, Rye Brook, NY 10573. Phones: 800-937-1397; 405-395-1131; 405-275-6923. Web Site: http://vyvebroadband.com. Also serves Atchison County (portions) & Lancaster, KS; Buchanan County, Lewis & Clark Village, Platte County (western portion) & Rushville, MO. ICA: KS0026.
TV Market Ranking: 22 (Buchanan County, Platte County (western portion)); Below 100 (ATCHISON, Atchison County (portions), Lancaster, Lewis & Clark Village, Rushville). Franchise award date: N.A. Franchise expiration date: N.A. Began: April 5, 1968.
Channel capacity: 78 (operating 2-way). Channels available but not in use: N.A.
Basic Service
Subscribers: 804. Commercial subscribers: 75.
Programming (received off-air): KCPT (PBS) Kansas City; KCTV (CBS) Kansas City; KCWE (CW, Movies!, This TV) Kansas City; KMBC-TV (ABC, MeTV) Kansas City; KMCI-TV (Bounce TV, Escape, IND) Lawrence; KPXE-TV (ION) Kansas City; KQTV (ABC) St. Joseph; KSHB-TV (COZI TV, Grit, NBC) Kansas City; KSMO-TV (Bounce TV, MNT) Kansas City; KTWU (PBS) Topeka; WDAF-TV (Antenna TV, FOX) Kansas City; WIBW-TV (CBS, MeTV, MNT) Topeka; allband FM.
Programming (via satellite): C-SPAN; EWTN Global Catholic Network; Pop; Trinity Broadcasting Network (TBN); WGN America.
Fee: $64.95 installation; $25.00 monthly.
Expanded Basic Service 1
Subscribers: N.A.
Programming (via satellite): A&E; AMC; Animal Planet; BET; Bravo; Cartoon Network; CMT; CNBC; CNN; Comedy Central; C-SPAN 2; Discovery Channel; Discovery Life Channel; Disney Channel; E! HD; ESPN; ESPN2; Food Network; Fox News Channel; Fox Sports 1; FOX Sports Midwest; Freeform; FX; Golf Channel; Hallmark Channel; HGTV; History; HLN; Lifetime; MSNBC; MTV; National Geographic Channel; NBCSN; Nickelodeon; Oxygen; RFD-TV; Spike TV; Syfy; TBS; The Weather Channel; TLC; TNT; Travel Channel; truTV; Turner Classic Movies; TV Land; USA Network; VH1.
Fee: $44.16 monthly.
Digital Basic Service
Subscribers: N.A.
Programming (via satellite): A&E HD; AXS TV; BBC America; Bloomberg Television; Chiller; Cloo; CMT; Destination America; Discovery Kids Channel; Disney XD; ESPN Classic; ESPN HD; ESPN2 HD; ESPNews; ESPNU; EVINE Live; Flix; Food Network HD; FOX College Sports Central; FOX College Sports Pacific; Fuse; FXM; FYI; Great American Country; GSN; HD Theater; HGTV HD; History International; IFC; Investigation Discovery; LMN; MC; MTV Classic; MTV Hits; MTV2; National Geographic Channel HD; Nick Jr.; Nicktoons; Outdoor Channel; Outdoor Channel 2 HD; OWN: Oprah Winfrey Network; Science Channel; Starz Encore (multiplexed); Sundance TV; TeenNick; The Word Network; Universal HD; UP; VH1 Soul; WE tv.

Digital Pay Service 1
Pay Units: N.A.
Programming (via satellite): Cinemax (multiplexed); Flix; HBO (multiplexed); HBO HD; Showtime (multiplexed); Showtime HD; Starz (multiplexed); Starz Encore (multiplexed); Starz HD; The Movie Channel (multiplexed).
Video-On-Demand: No
Pay-Per-View
Fresh (delivered digitally); iN DEMAND (delivered digitally); Club Jenna (delivered digitally); Spice: Xcess (delivered digitally); Playboy TV (delivered digitally).
Internet Service
Operational: Yes.
Broadband Service: Charter Internet.
Fee: $24.95 installation; $39.99 monthly.
Telephone Service
Digital: Operational
Miles of Plant: 63.0 (coaxial); 53.0 (fiber optic).
Chief Executive Officer: Bill Haggarty. Regional Vice President: Andrew Dearth. Senior Vice President, Financial Planning: Daniel White. Vice President, Marketing: Tracy Bass.
Ownership: Vyve Broadband LLC (MSO).

ATTICA (village)—Formerly served by Almega Cable. No longer in operation. ICA: KS0205.

ATWOOD—Atwood Cable Systems Inc, 423 State St, Atwood, KS 67730-1928. Phone: 785-626-3261. Fax: 785-626-9005. E-mail: acsi@atwoodtv.net; cableinfo@atwoodtv.net. Web Site: http://www.atwoodcable.com. ICA: KS0135.
TV Market Ranking: Below 100 (ATWOOD). Franchise award date: May 1, 1982. Franchise expiration date: N.A. Began: May 1, 1982.
Channel capacity: N.A. Channels available but not in use: N.A.
Basic Service
Subscribers: 275.
Programming (received off-air): KBSL-DT (CBS) Goodland; KLBY (ABC) Colby; KOOD (PBS) Hays; KPNE-TV (PBS) North Platte; KSNK (NBC) McCook; KWNB-TV (ABC) Hayes Center; 5 FMs.
Programming (via satellite): A&E; CNN; Comedy Central; Discovery Channel; Disney Channel; ESPN; ESPN2; EWTN Global Catholic Network; Freeform; Great American Country; HGTV; History; HLN; ION Television; MTV; Nickelodeon; Outdoor Channel; QVC; Spike TV; Syfy; TBS; The Weather Channel; TLC; TNT; Turner Classic Movies; TV Land; USA Network; VH1; WGN America.
Fee: $20.00 installation; $35.00 monthly.
Digital Basic Service
Subscribers: N.A.
Programming (via satellite): BBC America; Bloomberg Television; Bravo; Discovery Life Channel; DMX Music; ESPN Classic; ESPN2; ESPNews; Fox Sports 1; FXM; FYI; Golf Channel; GSN; History International; IFC; National Geographic Channel; NBCSN; Nick Jr.; Ovation; TeenNick; Trinity Broadcasting Network (TBN); WE tv.
Pay Service 1
Pay Units: N.A.
Programming (via satellite): HBO; The Movie Channel.
Fee: $12.95 monthly (each).
Digital Pay Service 1
Pay Units: N.A.
Programming (via satellite): Cinemax (multiplexed); HBO (multiplexed); Show-

Kansas—Cable Systems

time (multiplexed); The Movie Channel (multiplexed).
Fee: $10.00 installation; $9.00 monthly (Cinemax), $10.95 monthly (HBO), $12.95 monthly (Showtime/TMC).
Video-On-Demand: No
Pay-Per-View
Sports PPV (delivered digitally); Shorteez (delivered digitally); Fresh (delivered digitally); Playboy TV (delivered digitally); iN DEMAND (delivered digitally); Hot Choice (delivered digitally); ESPN Now (delivered digitally).
Internet Service
Operational: Yes.
Subscribers: 205.
Fee: $39.99 monthly.
Telephone Service
Analog: Not Operational
Digital: Operational
Miles of Plant: 12.0 (coaxial); None (fiber optic). Homes passed: 625.
President & General Manager: Robert J. Dunker. Chief Technician: Kerry Dunker.
Ownership: Atwood Cable Systems Inc.

AXTELL—Blue Valley Tele-Communications, 1559 Pony Express Hwy, Home, KS 66438. Phones: 877-876-1228; 785-799-3311. E-mail: info@bluevalley.net. Web Site: http://www.bluevalley.net. Also serves Centralia, Frankfort, Hanover, Marysville, Onaga, Washington, Waterville, Westmoreland & Wheaton. ICA: KS0424.
TV Market Ranking: Outside TV Markets (Centralia). Franchise award date: N.A. Franchise expiration date: N.A. Began: December 1, 1981.
Channel capacity: N.A. Channels available but not in use: N.A.
Digital Basic Service
Subscribers: 3,773 Includes IPTV subscribers. Commercial subscribers: 473.
Programming (received off-air): KOLN (CBS, MNT, NBC) Lincoln; KPTM (Estrella TV, FOX, MNT, This TV) Omaha; KSNT (FOX, NBC) Topeka; KTKA-TV (ABC, CW) Topeka; KTMJ-CD (Escape, FOX) Topeka; KTWU (PBS) Topeka; WIBW-TV (CBS, MeTV, MNT) Topeka.
Programming (via satellite): A&E; AMC; Animal Planet; Bravo; Cartoon Network; Church Channel; CMT; CNBC; CNN; C-SPAN; C-SPAN 2; CW PLUS; Discovery Channel; Disney Channel; DIY Network; DMX Music; E! HD; ESPN; ESPN Classic; ESPN2; EWTN Global Catholic Network; FamilyNet; Food Network; Fox Business Network; Fox News Channel; FOX Sports Midwest; Freeform; FX; Hallmark Channel; Hallmark Movies & Mysteries; HGTV; History; HLN; HSN; JUCE TV; Lifetime; LMN; MSNBC; MTV; National Geographic Channel; NFL Network; Nickelodeon; Oxygen; QVC; RFD-TV; Smile of a Child TV; Spike TV; Syfy; TBS; The Sportsman Channel; The Weather Channel; TLC; TNT; Travel Channel; Trinity Broadcasting Network (TBN); truTV; TV Land; USA Network; VH1; WGN America.
Fee: $29.95 installation; $29.00 monthly.
Digital Expanded Basic Service
Subscribers: N.A.
Programming (via satellite): A&E HD; Animal Planet HD; AXS TV; BBC America; Bloomberg Television; Boomerang; Cine Mexicano; Cloo; CMT; Comedy Central; Daystar TV Network; Destination America; Destination America HD; Discovery Channel HD; Discovery Family; Discovery Life Channel; Disney Channel HD; Disney XD; Enlace USA; ESPN HD; ESPN2 HD; ESPNews; ESPNews HD; ESPNU; ESPNU HD;

FOX College Sports Central; FOX College Sports Pacific; Fox Sports 1; Fuse; FXM; FYI; God TV; Golf Channel; Great American Country; GSN; HD Theater; History HD; History International; IFC; Investigation Discovery; La Familia Cosmovision; Lifetime HD; MTV Classic; MTV Live; MTV2; NBCSN; NFL Network HD; Nick Jr.; Nicktoons; Outdoor Channel; Outdoor Channel HD; OWN; Oprah Winfrey Network; Science Channel; Science HD; TeenNick; The Weather Channel HD; The Word Network; TLC HD; Turner Classic Movies; ULTRA HDPlex; Universal HD; Versus HD; WE tv; World Harvest Television.
Fee: $11.00 monthly.
Digital Expanded Basic Service 2
Subscribers: N.A.
Fee: $10.00 monthly.
Digital Pay Service 1
Pay Units: N.A.
Programming (via satellite): Cinemax (multiplexed); Flix; HBO (multiplexed); Playboy TV; Showtime (multiplexed); Showtime HD; Starz (multiplexed); Starz Encore (multiplexed); Starz HD; The Movie Channel (multiplexed); The Movie Channel HD.
Fee: $12.95 monthly (Cinemax, Showtime/TMC or Starz/Encore), $15.95 monthly (HBO).
Video-On-Demand: No
Internet Service
Operational: Yes.
Fee: $39.95-$59.95 monthly.
Telephone Service
Digital: Operational
Fee: $16.75 monthly
Miles of Plant: 105.0 (coaxial); 150.0 (fiber optic).
Chief Executive Officer & General Manager: Brian Thomason. Chief Financial Officer: Candice Wright. Public Relations & Community Development Director: Jada Ackerman. Marketing Manager: Angie Armstrong. Network Operations Center Supervisor: Kent Kucklelman. Customer Service Supervisor: Deb Runnebaum.
Ownership: Blue Valley Telecommunications (MSO).

AXTELL—Blue Valley Tele-Communications. Now served by AXTELL (formerly Frankfort & Home), KS [KS0424]. ICA: KS0242.

BAILEYVILLE—Formerly served by Rainbow Communications. No longer in operation. ICA: KS0451.

BALDWIN CITY—Mediacom. Now served by BURLINGTON, KS [KS0064]. ICA: KS0055.

BARNES—Formerly served by Eagle Communications. No longer in operation. ICA: KS0365.

BASEHOR—Formerly served by Knology (formerly Sunflower Broadband). Now served by WOW! Internet, Cable & Phone, LAWRENCE, KS [KS0004]. ICA: KS0164.

BAXTER SPRINGS—City of Baxter Springs, 1445 Military Ave, PO Box 577, Baxter Springs, KS 66713. Phone: 620-856-2114. Fax: 620-856-2460. Web Site: http://baxtersprings.us. ICA: KS0042.
TV Market Ranking: Below 100 (BAXTER SPRINGS). Franchise award date: N.A. Franchise expiration date: N.A. Began: February 1, 1980.
Channel capacity: N.A. Channels available but not in use: N.A.

Basic Service
Subscribers: 822.
Programming (received off-air): KOAM-TV (CBS) Pittsburg; KODE-TV (ABC) Joplin; KOED-TV (PBS) Tulsa; KOKI-TV (FOX, MeTV) Tulsa; KOZJ (PBS) Joplin; KSNF (NBC) Joplin.
Programming (via satellite): CNN; Discovery Channel; ESPN; Freeform; QVC; TBS; TNT; Travel Channel; Trinity Broadcasting Network (TBN); USA Network; WGN America.
Fee: $10.00 installation; $24.99 monthly.
Expanded Basic Service 1
Subscribers: N.A.
Programming (via satellite): A&E; AMC; Cartoon Network; CMT; C-SPAN; Disney Channel; ESPN2; HGTV; History; HLN; Lifetime; MTV; Nickelodeon; Outdoor Channel; Spike TV; Syfy; The Weather Channel; TLC; Turner Classic Movies; VH1.
Fee: $20.00 monthly.
Pay Service 1
Pay Units: N.A.
Programming (via satellite): Cinemax; HBO.
Fee: $4.00 monthly (Cinemax), $8.00 monthly (HBO).
Video-On-Demand: No
Internet Service
Operational: Yes. Began: November 30, 2008.
Fee: $34.95 monthly.
Telephone Service
None
Miles of Plant: 34.0 (coaxial); None (fiber optic). Homes passed: 1,451.
General Manager: Jim Thiele. Marketing Director: Donna Wickson.
Ownership: City of Baxter Springs.

BAZINE—Formerly served by Cebridge Connections. Now served by GBT Communications Inc., RUSH CENTER, KS [KS5143]. ICA: KS0288.

BEATTIE—Formerly served by Allegiance Communications. No longer in operation. ICA: KS0278.

BELLE PLAINE—SKT Entertainment. Now served by CLEARWATER, KS [KS0136]. ICA: KS0128.

BELLEVILLE—Cunningham Cable TV. Now served by GLEN ELDER, KS [KS0228]. ICA: KS0073.

BELOIT—Cunningham Cable TV. Now served by GLEN ELDER, KS [KS0228]. ICA: KS0046.

BELVUE—Formerly served by Giant Communications. No longer in operation. ICA: KS0443.

BENNINGTON—Twin Valley Communications. This system has converted to IPTV. Now served by MILTONVALE, KS [KS5032]. ICA: KS0214.

BENTLEY—IdeaTek Communications LLC, 111 Old Mill St, Buhler, KS 67522. Phones: 855-433-2835; 620-543-5000. Web Site: http://www.ideatek.com. ICA: KS0282.
TV Market Ranking: 67 (BENTLEY). Franchise award date: December 1, 1988. Franchise expiration date: N.A. Began: July 15, 1989.
Channel capacity: N.A. Channels available but not in use: N.A.
Basic Service
Subscribers: 45.
Programming (received off-air): KAKE (ABC, MeTV) Wichita; KMTW (MNT, The

Country Network) Hutchinson; KPTS (PBS) Hutchinson; KSAS-TV (Antenna TV, FOX) Wichita; KSNW (NBC) Wichita; KWCH-DT (CBS) Hutchinson.
Programming (via satellite): A&E; AMC; CMT; CNBC; CNN; C-SPAN; C-SPAN 2; Discovery Channel; Disney Channel; ESPN; ESPN2; Freeform; Great American Country; HGTV; History; Lifetime; Nickelodeon; Outdoor Channel; QVC; Spike TV; Syfy; TBS; The Weather Channel; TLC; TNT; Trinity Broadcasting Network (TBN); TV Land; USA Network; WGN America.
Fee: $25.00 installation; $16.00 monthly.
Pay Service 1
Pay Units: N.A.
Programming (via satellite): Cinemax (multiplexed); HBO (multiplexed); MoviePlex; Showtime; Starz; The Movie Channel.
Fee: $15.00 monthly (each).
Internet Service
Operational: Yes.
Broadband Service: In-house.
Fee: $55.00 installation; $34.95 monthly.
Telephone Service
None
Miles of Plant: 4.0 (coaxial); None (fiber optic). Homes passed: 153.
Ownership: IdeaTek Communications LLC (MSO).

BERN—Formerly served by Rainbow Communications. No longer in operation. ICA: KS0366.

BLUE MOUND—Formerly served by National Cable Inc. No longer in operation. ICA: KS0292.

BLUE RAPIDS—Zito Media, 102 S Main St, PO Box 665, Coudersport, PA 16915. Phones: 814-260-9055; 800-365-6988. E-mail: info@zitomedia.com. Web Site: http://www.zitomedia.com. ICA: KS0096.
TV Market Ranking: Outside TV Markets (BLUE RAPIDS). Franchise award date: N.A. Franchise expiration date: N.A. Began: May 1, 1978.
Channel capacity: N.A. Channels available but not in use: N.A.
Basic Service
Subscribers: 52.
Programming (received off-air): KOLN (CBS, MNT, NBC) Lincoln; KSAS-TV (Antenna TV, FOX) Wichita; KSNT (FOX, NBC) Topeka; KTKA-TV (ABC, CW) Topeka; KTWU (PBS) Topeka; WIBW-TV (CBS, MeTV, MNT) Topeka.
Programming (via satellite): A&E; AMC; Cartoon Network; CNN; Discovery Channel; Disney Channel; E! HD; ESPN; ESPN2; Fox News Channel; FOX Sports Midwest; Freeform; FX; Great American Country; History; HLN; Lifetime; MSNBC; Outdoor Channel; TBS; The Weather Channel; TNT; Trinity Broadcasting Network (TBN); USA Network; WGN America.
Fee: $49.95 installation; $44.40 monthly; $1.00 converter.
Digital Basic Service
Subscribers: N.A.
Programming (via satellite): BBC America; Bloomberg Television; Discovery Life Channel; Disney XD; DMX Music; ESPN Classic; ESPNews; Fuse; FYI; Golf Channel; GSN; HGTV; History International; INSP; National Geographic Channel; WE tv.
Digital Expanded Basic Service
Subscribers: N.A.
Programming (via satellite): DMX Music; FXM; LMN; Starz Encore; Turner Classic Movies.
Fee: $13.95 monthly.

Cable Systems—Kansas

Pay Service 1
Pay Units: N.A.
Programming (via satellite): Cinemax; HBO; Showtime; The Movie Channel.
Fee: $25.00 installation; $13.00 monthly (each).

Digital Pay Service 1
Pay Units: N.A.
Programming (via satellite): Cinemax (multiplexed); Flix; HBO (multiplexed); Showtime (multiplexed); The Movie Channel (multiplexed).
Fee: $16.55 monthly.

Pay-Per-View
Playboy TV (delivered digitally); Fresh (delivered digitally).

Internet Service
Operational: No.

Telephone Service
None
Miles of Plant: 11.0 (coaxial); None (fiber optic). Homes passed: 550.
President: James Rigas.
Ownership: Zito Media (MSO).

BREWSTER—S&T Cable, 320 Kansas Ave, PO Box 99, Brewster, KS 67732-0099. Phones: 800-432-8294; 785-694-2000; 785-694-2256. Fax: 785-694-2750. Web Site: http://www.sttelcom.com. Also serves Colby, Goodland, Grinnell, Kanorado, Oakley & Winona. ICA: KS0315.
TV Market Ranking: Below 100 (BREWSTER, Grinnell, Kanorado, Winona, Colby, Goodland, Oakley). Franchise award date: N.A. Franchise expiration date: N.A. Began: January 1, 1984.
Channel capacity: N.A. Channels available but not in use: N.A.

Basic Service
Subscribers: 3,323.
Programming (received off-air): KAKE (ABC, MeTV) Wichita; KBSL-DT (CBS) Goodland; KLBY (ABC) Colby; KMTW (MNT, The Country Network) Hutchinson; KOOD (PBS) Hays; KSAS-TV (Antenna TV, FOX) Wichita; KSCW-DT (CW, Decades) Wichita; KSNK (NBC) McCook; KWCH-DT (CBS) Hutchinson.
Programming (via satellite): KUSA (NBC, WeatherNation) Denver; KWGN-TV (CW, This TV) Denver; LWS Local Weather Station; QVC.
Fee: $9.95 installation; $21.55 monthly.

Expanded Basic Service 1
Subscribers: N.A.
Programming (via satellite): A&E; AMC; Animal Planet; Bravo; Cartoon Network; CMT; CNBC; CNN; Comedy Central; C-SPAN; C-SPAN 2; Daystar TV Network; Discovery Channel; Discovery Kids Channel; Disney Channel; DIY Network; E! HD; ESPN; ESPN Classic; ESPN2; EWTN Global Catholic Network; Food Network; Fox News Channel; Fox Sports 1; FOX Sports Networks; Freeform; FX; Golf Channel; Hallmark Channel; HGTV; History; HLN; Lifetime; MSNBC; MTV; National Geographic Channel; NBCSN; NFL Network; Nickelodeon; Oxygen; Pop; RFD-TV; Spike TV; Syfy; TBS; The Weather Channel; TLC; TNT; Travel Channel; Trinity Broadcasting Network (TBN); truTV; Turner Classic Movies; TV Land; Univision Studios; USA Network; VH1; WE tv; WGN America.
Fee: $21.95 monthly.

Digital Basic Service
Subscribers: 890.
Programming (via satellite): BBC America; Bloomberg Television; CMT; Destination America; Discovery Kids Channel; Discovery Life Channel; Disney XD; ESPNews; ESPNU; FSN Digital Atlantic; FSN Digital Central; FSN Digital Pacific; Fuse; FYI; Great American Country; GSN; History International; IFC; Investigation Discovery; LMN; MC; MTV Classic; MTV Hits; MTV Jams; MTV2; Nick 2; Nick Jr.; Nicktoons; Outdoor Channel; OWN: Oprah Winfrey Network; Science Channel; Starz Encore (multiplexed); TeenNick; The Word Network; Tr3s; UP; VH1 Soul.
Fee: $50.15 monthly.

Digital Expanded Basic Service
Subscribers: N.A.
Programming (via satellite): Cinelatino; CNN en Espanol; ESPN Deportes; Fox Deportes; History en Espanol.
Fee: $15.95 monthly.

Digital Expanded Basic Service 2
Subscribers: N.A.
Programming (via satellite): A&E HD; AXS TV; Discovery Channel HD; ESPN HD; ESPN2 HD; NFL Network HD; Universal HD.
Fee: $14.95 monthly.

Digital Pay Service 1
Pay Units: N.A.
Programming (via satellite): Cinemax (multiplexed); Cinemax HD; Flix; FXM; HBO (multiplexed); HBO HD; Showtime (multiplexed); Showtime HD; Starz (multiplexed); Starz HD; Sundance TV (multiplexed); The Movie Channel.
Fee: $11.75 monthly (each).

Video-On-Demand: No

Pay-Per-View
special events (delivered digitally).

Internet Service
Operational: No, DSL & dial-up.

Telephone Service
Analog: Operational
Miles of Plant: 11.0 (coaxial); 100.0 (fiber optic).
Chief Financial Officer: Carolyn R. Somers. General Manager: Clint Felzien. Chief Technician: Craig Grantz. Marketing Manager: Shawna Kersenbrock.
Ownership: S & T Communications Inc. (MSO).

BROOKVILLE—Wilson Communications, 2504 Ave D, PO Box 509, Wilson, KS 67490. Phones: 800-432-7607; 785-658-2111. Fax: 785-658-3344. E-mail: customerservice@wilsoncom.us. Web Site: http://www.wilsoncom.us. Also serves Lucas, Sylvan Grove, Tipton & Wilson. ICA: KS0162.
TV Market Ranking: Below 100 (BROOKVILLE, Wilson); Outside TV Markets (Lucas, Sylvan Grove, Tipton). Franchise award date: N.A. Franchise expiration date: N.A. Began: January 28, 1999.
Channel capacity: N.A. Channels available but not in use: N.A.

Basic Service
Subscribers: 584.
Programming (received off-air): KAKE (ABC, MeTV) Wichita; KMTW (MNT, The Country Network) Hutchinson; KOOD (PBS) Hays; KPTS (PBS) Hutchinson; KSAS-TV (Antenna TV, FOX) Wichita; KSCW-DT (CW, Decades) Wichita; KSNC (NBC) Great Bend; KSNW (NBC) Wichita; KWCH-DT (CBS) Hutchinson; 15 FMs.
Programming (via satellite): A&E; AMC; CMT; CNN; C-SPAN; C-SPAN 2; Discovery Channel; Disney Channel; ESPN Classic; ESPN2; ESPNews; EWTN Global Catholic Network; Food Network; Fox News Channel; Freeform; FX; Hallmark Channel; HGTV; HLN; ION Television; Lifetime; MTV; National Geographic Channel; Nickelodeon; Root Sports Rocky Mountain; Spike TV; Syfy; TBS; The Weather Channel; TLC; TNT; TV Land; USA Network; VH1; WGN America.
Fee: $25.00 installation; $56.95 monthly.

Digital Basic Service
Subscribers: N.A.
Programming (via satellite): A&E HD; BBC America; Bravo; Cloo; CMT; Destination America; Discovery Kids Channel; DMX Music; ESPN; ESPN HD; ESPN2 HD; ESPNU; ESPNU HD; Food Network HD; Fox Sports 1; Fuse; FYI; Golf Channel; GSN; HD Theater; HGTV HD; History; History HD; History International; IFC; Investigation Discovery; LMN; MTV Classic; MTV2; NBCSN; Nick Jr.; OWN: Oprah Winfrey Network; RFD-TV; Science Channel; TeenNick; Turner Classic Movies; Universal HD; WE tv.
Fee: $49.95 installation.

Digital Pay Service 1
Pay Units: N.A.
Programming (via satellite): Cinemax (multiplexed); HBO (multiplexed); Showtime (multiplexed); Starz (multiplexed); Starz Encore (multiplexed); Starz HD; The Movie Channel (multiplexed).
Fee: $13.95 monthly (Showtime/TMC or Starz/Encore), $18.95 monthly (Cinemax or HBO).

Video-On-Demand: No

Internet Service
Operational: No, DSL & dial-up.

Telephone Service
Analog: Operational
Miles of Plant: 9.0 (coaxial); None (fiber optic). Homes passed: 1,466.
President: Scott Grauer. Chief Executive Officer & General Manager: Brian Boisvert. Operations Director: Mary Zorn. Network Engineer: Mike Halle. Marketing Manager: Tim Henry. Controller: Devin Weis.
Ownership: Wilson Communications (MSO).

BROOKVILLE—Wilson Communications. Now served by BROOKVILLE, KS [KS0162]. ICA: KS0368.

BUCKLIN—United Communications Assn. Inc. Now served by CIMARRON, KS [KS0126]. ICA: KS0369.

BUFFALO—Formerly served by National Cable Inc. No longer in operation. ICA: KS0283.

BUHLER—Formerly served by Vyve Broadband. No longer in operation. ICA: KS0160.

BURDEN—SKT Entertainment. Now served by CLEARWATER, KS [KS0136]. ICA: KS0370.

BURLINGTON—Mediacom, 901 North College Ave, Columbia, MO 65201. Phones: 417-875-5560 (Springfield regional office); 573-443-1536. Fax: 417-883-0265. Web Site: http://www.mediacomcable.com. Also serves Baldwin City, Burlingame, Carbondale, Edgerton, Gridley, Lebo, LeRoy, Lyndon, New Strawn, Osage City, Scranton & Wellsville. ICA: KS0064.
TV Market Ranking: Below 100 (Burlingame, Carbondale, Edgerton, Lyndon, Osage City, Scranton, Wellsville, Baldwin City); Outside TV Markets (BURLINGTON, Gridley, Lebo, LeRoy, New Strawn). Franchise award date: N.A. Franchise expiration date: N.A. Began: January 1, 1966.
Channel capacity: N.A. Channels available but not in use: N.A.

Basic Service
Subscribers: 2,175.
Programming (received off-air): KAKE (ABC, CW) Wichita; KCTV (CBS) Kansas City; KMBC-TV (ABC, MeTV) Kansas City; KSHB-TV (COZI TV, Grit, NBC) Kansas City; KSNT (FOX, NBC) Topeka; KTKA-TV (ABC, CW) Topeka; KTMJ-CD (Escape, FOX) Topeka; KTWU (PBS) Topeka; WDAF-TV (Antenna TV, FOX) Kansas City; WIBW-TV (CBS, MeTV, MNT) Topeka; allband FM.
Programming (via satellite): C-SPAN; Pop; WGN America.
Fee: $35.00 installation; $44.45 monthly.

Expanded Basic Service 1
Subscribers: N.A.
Programming (via satellite): A&E; AMC; Animal Planet; BET; Bravo; Cartoon Network; CMT; CNBC; CNN; Comedy Central; Discovery Channel; Disney Channel; E! HD; ESPN; ESPN2; EVINE Live; Food Network; Fox News Channel; Fox Sports 1; FOX Sports Networks; Freeform; FX; Hallmark Channel; HGTV; History; HLN; Lifetime; MSNBC; MTV; Nickelodeon; Outdoor Channel; QVC; Spike TV; Syfy; TBS; The Weather Channel; TLC; TNT; Travel Channel; Trinity Broadcasting Network (TBN); truTV; TV Land; USA Network; VH1; WE tv.
Fee: $3.95 monthly.

Digital Basic Service
Subscribers: N.A.
Programming (via satellite): BBC America; Bloomberg Television; Cloo; Destination America; Discovery Kids Channel; ESPNews; Fuse; FXM; FYI; Golf Channel; GSN; History International; IFC; Investigation Discovery; LMN; MC; MTV Classic; MTV Hits; MTV2; National Geographic Channel; NBCSN; Nick Jr.; Nicktoons; OWN: Oprah Winfrey Network; RFD-TV; Science Channel; TeenNick; Turner Classic Movies; TVG Network.

Digital Pay Service 1
Pay Units: N.A.
Programming (via satellite): Cinemax (multiplexed); Flix; HBO (multiplexed); Showtime (multiplexed); Starz (multiplexed); Starz Encore (multiplexed); Sundance TV; The Movie Channel (multiplexed).

Video-On-Demand: No

Pay-Per-View
iN DEMAND (delivered digitally); Playboy TV (delivered digitally); SexSee (delivered digitally); Juicy (delivered digitally).

Internet Service
Operational: Yes.
Broadband Service: Mediacom High Speed Internet.

Telephone Service
None
Miles of Plant: 49.0 (coaxial); None (fiber optic). Homes passed: 6,013.
Regional Vice President: Bill Copeland. Operations Director: Bryan Gann. Regional Technical Operations Director: Alan Freedman. Technical Operations Manager: Roger Shearer. Marketing Director: Will Kuebler. Vice President, Financial Reporting: Kenneth J. Kohrs.
Ownership: Mediacom LLC (MSO).

BURNS—Formerly served by Blue Sky Cable LLC. No longer in operation. ICA: KS0311.

BURR OAK—Nex-Tech. Formerly [KS0265]. This cable system has converted to IPTV, 2418 Vine St, Hays, KS 67601. Phones: 877-567-7872; 785-625-7070. Fax: 785-625-4479. E-mail: webmaster@nex-tech.

Kansas—Cable Systems

com. Web Site: http://www.nex-tech.com. ICA: KS5042.
Channel capacity: N.A. Channels available but not in use: N.A.

Essentials
Subscribers: 122.
Fee: $30.00 installation; $24.95 monthly. Includes 51 channels.

Premiere
Subscribers: 115.
Fee: $61.95 monthly. Includes 119 channels plus music channels.

HD
Subscribers: N.A.
Fee: $11.95 monthly. Includes 74+ channels.

Sports & Entertainment
Subscribers: N.A.
Fee: $12.95 monthly. Includes 34 channels.

Cinemax
Subscribers: N.A.
Fee: $8.95 monthly. Includes 8 channels.

HBO
Subscribers: N.A.
Fee: $14.95 monthly. Includes 12 channels.

Showtime/TMC
Subscribers: N.A.
Fee: $13.95 monthly. Includes 16 channels.

Starz/Encore
Subscribers: N.A.
Fee: $10.95 monthly. Includes 18 channels.

Video-On-Demand: Yes

Internet Service
Operational: Yes.
Fee: $22.95-$202.95 monthly.

Telephone Service
Digital: Operational
Fee: $17.80 monthly

Chief Executive Officer & General Manager: Larry Sevier. Video Solutions Manager: Scott Roe.
Ownership: Nex-Tech.

BURR OAK—Nex-Tech. This cable system has converted to IPTV. See BURR OAK, KS [KS5042]. ICA: KS0265.

BURRTON—Formerly served by Cebridge Connections. No longer in operation. ICA: KS0195.

CALDWELL—Formerly served by Almega Cable. No longer in operation. ICA: KS0151.

CANTON—Formerly served by Cox Communications. No longer in operation. ICA: KS0371.

CANTON—Formerly served by Home Communications Inc. No longer in operation. ICA: KS0472.

CAWKER CITY—Formerly served by City of Cawker City. Now served by Blue Valley Tele-Communications, GLEN ELDER, KS [KS0228]. ICA: KS0202.

CENTRALIA—Blue Valley Tele-Communications. Now served by AXTELL (formerly Frankfort & Home), KS [KS0424]. ICA: KS0230.

CHANUTE—Cable One, 2229 Broadway St, Ste 200, Parsons, KS 67357. Phone: 620-431-2440. Web Site: http://www.cableone.net. Also serves Neosho County (portions). ICA: KS0027.
TV Market Ranking: Outside TV Markets (CHANUTE, Neosho County (portions)). Franchise award date: N.A. Franchise expiration date: N.A. Began: April 1, 1964.
Channel capacity: N.A. Channels available but not in use: N.A.

Basic Service
Subscribers: 1,470.
Programming (received off-air): KFJX (FOX) Pittsburg; KOAM-TV (CBS) Pittsburg; KODE-TV (ABC) Joplin; KSNF (NBC) Joplin.
Programming (via microwave): KJRH-TV (NBC) Tulsa; KMBC-TV (ABC, MeTV) Kansas City; KTWU (PBS) Topeka; WIBW-TV (CBS, MeTV, MNT) Topeka.
Programming (via satellite): A&E; Animal Planet; Bravo; Cartoon Network; CNBC; CNN; Comedy Central; C-SPAN; C-SPAN 2; Discovery Channel; Disney Channel; ESPN; ESPN Classic; ESPN2; EVINE Live; Food Network; Fox News Channel; FOX Sports Midwest; Freeform; FX; Great American Country; Hallmark Channel; HGTV; History; HLN; Lifetime; MoviePlex; MSNBC; MTV; Nickelodeon; Outdoor Channel; Oxygen; Pop; QVC; Spike TV; Syfy; TBS; The Weather Channel; TLC; TNT; Travel Channel; Trinity Broadcasting Network (TBN); Turner Classic Movies; TV Land; USA Network; WE tv.
Fee: $90.00 installation; $35.00 monthly.

Digital Basic Service
Subscribers: N.A.
Programming (via satellite): Boomerang; BYUtv; Discovery Digital Networks; Disney XD; DMX Music; ESPN Classic; ESPNews; FamilyNet; FOX College Sports Central; FOX College Sports Pacific; Fox Sports 1; Fox Sports 2; FXM; FYI; Golf Channel; Hallmark Channel; History; History International; HITS (Headend In The Sky) (multiplexed); INSP; National Geographic Channel; Outdoor Channel; Trinity Broadcasting Network (TBN); truTV.

Digital Pay Service 1
Pay Units: N.A.
Programming (via satellite): Cinemax (multiplexed); HBO (multiplexed); Showtime (multiplexed); Starz Encore; Sundance TV; The Movie Channel (multiplexed).
Fee: $15.00 monthly (each).

Video-On-Demand: No

Pay-Per-View
Shorteez (delivered digitally); Fresh (delivered digitally); Hot Choice (delivered digitally).

Internet Service
Operational: Yes.
Broadband Service: CableONE.net.
Fee: $75.00 installation; $43.00 monthly.

Telephone Service
Digital: Operational
Fee: $39.95 monthly
Miles of Plant: 63.0 (coaxial); None (fiber optic). Homes passed: 4,800.
Vice President: Patrick A. Dolohanty. General Manager: Clarence Matlock. Chief Technician: B. A. Swalley.
Ownership: Cable ONE Inc. (MSO).

CHAPMAN—Eagle Communications. Now served by ABILENE, KS [KS0034]. ICA: KS0074.

CHASE—H&B Communications, 108 North Main St, Holyrood, KS 67450. Phones: 785-252-3598; 800-432-8296; 785-252-4000. Fax: 785-252-3229. E-mail: hbsupport@hbcomm.net; commentsquestions@hbcomm.net. Web Site: http://www.hbcomm.net. Also serves Dorrance & Lorraine. ICA: KS0476.
TV Market Ranking: 67 (CHASE); Below 100 (Dorrance, Lorraine, CHASE). Franchise award date: January 1, 1982. Franchise expiration date: October 1, 1982.
Channel capacity: N.A. Channels available but not in use: N.A.

Basic Service
Subscribers: 1,091.
Programming (received off-air): KAKE (ABC, MeTV) Wichita; KMTW (MNT, The Country Network) Hutchinson; KOOD (PBS) Hays; KPTS (PBS) Hutchinson; KSAS-TV (Antenna TV, FOX) Wichita; KSCW-DT (CW, Decades) Wichita; KSNC (NBC) Great Bend; KWCH-DT (CBS) Hutchinson.
Programming (via satellite): A&E; AMC; CMT; CNN; C-SPAN; C-SPAN 2; Discovery Channel; Disney Channel; ESPN; EWTN Global Catholic Network; Food Network; Freeform; Hallmark Channel; HGTV; HLN; ION Television; Lifetime; Nickelodeon; Root Sports Rocky Mountain; Spike TV; TBS; The Weather Channel; TLC; TNT; TV Land; USA Network; VH1; WGN America.
Fee: $25.00 installation; $65.50 monthly.

Digital Basic Service
Subscribers: N.A.
Programming (via satellite): BBC America; Bravo; Discovery Digital Networks; ESPN Classic; ESPN2; ESPNews; Fox Sports 1; Fuse; FYI; Golf Channel; GSN; History; History International; IFC; LMN; MC; National Geographic Channel; NBCSN; Nick Jr.; Syfy; TeenNick; Turner Classic Movies; WE tv.

Digital Expanded Basic Service
Subscribers: N.A.
Fee: $67.26 monthly.

Digital Pay Service 1
Pay Units: N.A.
Programming (via satellite): Cinemax (multiplexed); HBO (multiplexed); Showtime (multiplexed); Starz (multiplexed); Starz Encore (multiplexed); The Movie Channel (multiplexed).
Fee: $7.95 monthly (Encore), $14.23 (Showtime/TMC) $16.95 (Cinemax/Starz or HBO).

Video-On-Demand: No

Internet Service
Operational: No, DSL.

Telephone Service
Digital: Operational
Miles of Plant: 38.0 (coaxial); 48.0 (fiber optic). Homes passed: 1,125.
President & General Manager: Robert Koch. Chief Technician: Tim Herber. Marketing Director: D.J. Nash.
Ownership: H & B Cable Service Inc.

CHETOPA—Formerly served by Allegiance Communications. No longer in operation. ICA: KS0131.

CIMARRON—United Communications Assn. Inc, 1107 McArtor Rd, PO Box 117, Dodge City, KS 67801. Phones: 620-635-9898; 800-794-9999; 620-227-8641. Fax: 620-855-4009. Web Site: http://www.unitedtelcom.net. Also serves Ashland, Bucklin, Coldwater, Copeland, Ensign, Ford, Hanston, Ingalls, Jetmore, Montezuma, Protection & Spearville. ICA: KS0126.
TV Market Ranking: Below 100 (Bucklin, CIMARRON, Copeland, Ensign, Ford, Ingalls, Jetmore, Montezuma, Spearville); Outside TV Markets (Ashland, Hanston). Franchise award date: March 2, 1983. Franchise expiration date: N.A. Began: November 1, 1981.
Channel capacity: N.A. Channels available but not in use: N.A.

Basic Service
Subscribers: 210.
Programming (received off-air): KBSD-DT (CBS) Ensign; KMTW (MNT, The Country Network) Hutchinson; KOOD (PBS) Hays; KSAS-TV (Antenna TV, FOX) Wichita; KSCW-DT (CW, Decades) Wichita; KSNG (NBC) Garden City; KUPK (ABC) Garden City.
Programming (via satellite): Gracenote; ION Television; TBS; The Weather Channel.
Fee: $36.00 installation; $25.40 monthly.

Expanded Basic Service 1
Subscribers: N.A.
Programming (via satellite): A&E; AMC; Animal Planet; Bloomberg Television; Cartoon Network; CMT; CNBC; CNN; Comedy Central; C-SPAN; C-SPAN 2; Discovery Channel; Disney Channel; Disney XD; DIY Network; E! HD; ESPN; ESPN Classic; ESPN2; EWTN Global Catholic Network; Food Network; Fox News Channel; Fox Sports 1; FOX Sports Midwest; Freeform; FX; FXM; Golf Channel; Great American Country; GSN; Hallmark Channel; HGTV; History; HLN; INSP; Lifetime; MSNBC; MTV; NBCSN; NFL Network; Nickelodeon; Outdoor Channel; Oxygen; QVC; RFD-TV; Science Channel; Spike TV; Starz Encore; Syfy; TLC; TNT; Travel Channel; Trinity Broadcasting Network (TBN); truTV; Turner Classic Movies; TV Land; Univision; Univision Studios; USA Network; VH1; WGN America.
Fee: $48.98 monthly.

Digital Basic Service
Subscribers: N.A.
Programming (via satellite): A&E HD; Animal Planet HD; BBC America; Bravo; Chiller; Cloo; CMT; Cooking Channel; Destination America; Destination America HD; Discovery Channel HD; Discovery Kids Channel; Discovery Life Channel; Disney Channel HD; Disney XD; DMX Music; ESPN Classic; ESPN HD; ESPN2; ESPN2 HD; ESPNews; ESPNU; Food Network HD; Fox Business Network; FOX College Sports Central; FOX College Sports Pacific; Fox News HD; Fox Sports 1; Freeform HD; FX HD; FXM; FYI; Golf Channel; Great American Country; GSN; HD Theater; HGTV HD; History; History HD; History International; IFC; Investigation Discovery; Lifetime Movie Network HD; LMN; MTV Classic; MTV Hits; MTV2; National Geographic Channel; National Geographic Channel HD; NBCSN; Nick Jr.; Nicktoons; Outdoor Channel; Outdoor Channel 2 HD; OWN: Oprah Winfrey Network; RFD-TV; Science Channel; Science HD; Sprout; Starz Encore (multiplexed); Syfy; Syfy HD; The Weather Channel HD; TLC HD; Travel Channel HD; Turner Classic Movies; Universal HD; USA Network HD; VH1 Soul; WE tv.

Digital Expanded Basic Service
Subscribers: N.A.
Programming (via satellite): Cine Mexicano; Cinelatino; CNN en Espanol; ESPN Deportes; Fox Deportes; History en Espanol; Tr3s; ViendoMovies.
Fee: $5.00 monthly.

Digital Pay Service 1
Pay Units: N.A.
Programming (via satellite): Cinemax (multiplexed); HBO (multiplexed); Showtime (multiplexed); Starz (multiplexed); Starz HD.
Fee: $11.95 monthly (Cinemax, HBO, Showtime or Starz).

Video-On-Demand: No

Internet Service
Operational: Yes.
Fee: $57.48-$87.98 monthly.

Telephone Service
Analog: Operational
Miles of Plant: 62.0 (coaxial); 141.0 (fiber optic). Homes passed: 2,215.

Cable Systems—Kansas

General Manager: Craig Mock. Chief Technician: Keith Brack. Customer Service Manager: Jennifer Pachner.
Ownership: United Communications Assn. Inc. (MSO).

CLAY CENTER—Eagle Communications. Now served by ABILENE, KS [KS0034]. ICA: KS0043.

CLEARWATER—SKT Entertainment, 112 South Lee, PO Box 800, Clearwater, KS 67026. Phones: 888-758-8976; 620-584-2077; 888-568-3509; 620-584-2255. Fax: 620-584-2260. E-mail: customerservice@sktc.net. Web Site: http://www.sktmainstreet.com. Also serves Atlanta, Belle Plaine, Burden, Cedar Vale, Dexter, Elk County, Grenola, Howard, Leon, Longton, Moline, Sedgwick County (portions), Severy, Sumner County (portions) & Viola. ICA: KS0136.
TV Market Ranking: 67 (Belle Plaine, CLEARWATER, Leon, Sedgwick County (portions), Sumner County (portions), Viola); Outside TV Markets (Atlanta, Burden, Cedar Vale, Dexter, Elk County, Grenola, Howard, Longton, Moline, Severy). Franchise award date: N.A. Franchise expiration date: N.A. Began: February 1, 1981.
Channel capacity: N.A. Channels available but not in use: N.A.
Basic Service
Subscribers: 2,184.
Programming (received off-air): KAKE (ABC, MeTV) Wichita; KMTW (MNT, The Country Network) Hutchinson; KPTS (PBS) Hutchinson; KSAS-TV (Antenna TV, FOX) Wichita; KSCW-DT (CW, Decades) Wichita; KSNW (NBC) Wichita; KWCH-DT (CBS) Hutchinson.
Programming (via satellite): A&E; AMC; Animal Planet; Cartoon Network; CMT; CNBC; CNN; Comedy Central; C-SPAN; C-SPAN 2; Discovery Channel; Discovery Life Channel; Disney Channel; ESPN; ESPN Classic; ESPN2; EWTN Global Catholic Network; Food Network; Fox News Channel; Fox Sports 1; FOX Sports Networks; Freeform; FX; Hallmark Channel; HGTV; History; HLN; INSP; Lifetime; MTV; National Geographic Channel; NFL Network; Nickelodeon; Outdoor Channel; Pop; QVC; Spike TV; Syfy; TBS; The Weather Channel; TLC; TNT; Travel Channel; truTV; Turner Classic Movies; TV Land; USA Network; VH1; WGN America.
Fee: $22.00 monthly.
Digital Basic Service
Subscribers: N.A.
Programming (via satellite): A&E HD; Animal Planet HD; BBC America; Bravo; Cloo; CMT; CNN HD; Destination America; Discovery Channel HD; Discovery Kids Channel; Discovery Life Channel; Disney XD; DMX Music; ESPN HD; Food Network HD; Fox Sports 1; FYI; HD Theater; HGTV HD; History International; IFC; Investigation Discovery; LMN; MTV Classic; MTV Hits; MTV2; National Geographic Channel; National Geographic Channel HD; NBCSN; Nick Jr.; Nicktoons; Outdoor Channel 2 HD; OWN: Oprah Winfrey Network; RFD-TV; Science Channel; Science HD; TBS HD; TeenNick; TLC HD; TNT HD; VH1 Soul; WE tv.
Digital Expanded Basic Service
Subscribers: N.A.
Programming (via satellite): Bloomberg Television; Cloo; ESPN Classic; ESPNews; FOX College Sports Central; FOX College Sports Pacific; Fuse; FXM; Golf Channel; Great American Country; GSN; Outdoor

Channel; Trinity Broadcasting Network (TBN).
Fee: $9.95 monthly.
Pay Service 1
Pay Units: N.A.
Programming (via satellite): Cinemax; HBO; Showtime; The Movie Channel.
Fee: $11.00 monthly (Cinemax), $12.95 monthly (HBO or Showtime/TMC).
Digital Pay Service 1
Pay Units: N.A.
Programming (via satellite): Cinemax (multiplexed); Cinemax HD; Flix; HBO (multiplexed); HBO HD; Showtime (multiplexed); Showtime HD; Starz (multiplexed); Starz Encore (multiplexed); Starz HD; Sundance TV; The Movie Channel (multiplexed); The Movie Channel HD.
Fee: $11.00 monthly (Cinemax), $12.95 monthly (HBO, Showtime/TMC or Starz/Encore).
Video-On-Demand: No
Internet Service
Operational: Yes, DSL.
Broadband Service: TurboLink.
Fee: $44.95 monthly.
Telephone Service
Analog: Operational
Miles of Plant: 72.0 (coaxial); None (fiber optic).
Chief Financial Officer: William R. McVey. President: Kendall Mikesell. Cable TV Services Manager: Philip Brown. Chief Technical Officer: Jason Gibs. Marketing & Program Director: Donna Van Allen.
Ownership: Southern Kansas Telephone Co.

CLIFTON—Formerly served by Zito Media. No longer in operation. ICA: KS0120.

COFFEYVILLE—Cox Communications. Now served by PITTSBURG, KS [KS0011]. ICA: KS0016.

COLBY—S&T Cable. Now served by BREWSTER, KS [KS0315]. ICA: KS0039.

COLDWATER—United Communications Assn. Inc. Now served by CIMARRON, KS [KS0126]. ICA: KS0169.

COLUMBUS—Columbus Telephone Co. Formerly [KS0056]. This cable system has converted to IPTV, 224 South Kansas Ave, Columbus, KS 66725. Phone: 620-429-3132. Fax: 620-429-1159. E-mail: coltelco@columbus-ks.com. Web Site: http://columbus-telephone.com. ICA: KS0041.
TV Market Ranking: Below 100 (COLUMBUS).
Channel capacity: N.A. Channels available but not in use: N.A.
Basic
Subscribers: 208.
Fee: $7.00 monthly.
Internet Service
Operational: Yes, DSL & dial-up.
Telephone Service
Digital: Operational
Fee: $23.00 monthly
Ownership: Columbus Telephone Co.

COLUMBUS—Columbus Telephone Co. This cable system has converted to IPTV. See COLUMBUS, KS [KS5041]. ICA: KS0056.

COLWICH—Formerly served by Almega Cable. No longer in operation. ICA: KS0211.

CONCORDIA—Cunningham Cable TV. Now served by GLEN ELDER, KS [KS0228]. ICA: KS0035.

CONWAY SPRINGS—Formerly served by Allegiance Communications. No longer in operation. ICA: KS0161.

COPELAND—United Communications Assn. Inc. Now served by CIMARRON, KS [KS0126]. ICA: KS0318.

COUNCIL GROVE—TCT. This cable system has converted to IPTV, 1568 South 1000 Rd, PO Box 299, Council Grove, KS 66872. Phones: 800-362-2576; 785-366-7000; 620-767-5153. Fax: 620-767-6006; 785-366-7007. Web Site: http://www.tctelco.net. Also serves Morris County (portions). ICA: KS5218.
TV Market Ranking: Outside TV Markets (COUNCIL GROVE, Morris County (portions)). Franchise award date: June 1, 2002. Franchise expiration date: N.A. Began: October 1, 1964.
Channel capacity: N.A. Channels available but not in use: N.A.
Local Basics
Subscribers: N.A.
Fee: $24.95 monthly. Includes 28 channels.
Nu-Vision
Subscribers: N.A.
Fee: $69.95 monthly. Includes 135+ channels.
Hispanic
Subscribers: N.A.
Fee: $12.95 monthly. Includes 10 channels.
Lifestyle & Sports Pass
Subscribers: N.A.
Fee: $8.95 monthly. Includes 31+ channels.
Cinemax
Subscribers: N.A.
Fee: $14.95 monthly. Includes 8+ channels.
HBO
Subscribers: N.A.
Fee: $16.95 monthly. Includes 7+ channels.
Showtime/TMC
Subscribers: N.A.
Fee: $14.95 monthly. Includes 20+ channels.
Starz/Encore
Subscribers: N.A.
Fee: $7.00 monthly. Includes 21+ channels.
Internet Service
Operational: Yes.
Fee: $34.95-$69.95 monthly.
Telephone Service
None
General Manager: Dale Jones.
Ownership: Council Grove Telecommunications (MSO).

COUNCIL GROVE—Tri-County Telecom (TCT). This cable system has converted to IPTV. See COUNCIL GROVE, KS [KS5218]. ICA: KS0079.

COURTLAND—Nex-Tech. Formerly [KS0271]. This cable system has converted to IPTV, 2418 Vine St, Hays, KS 67601. Phone: 785-625-4479. Fax: 785-625-4479. E-mail: webmaster@nex-tech.com. Web Site: http://www.nex-tech.com. ICA: KS5043.
Channel capacity: N.A. Channels available but not in use: N.A.
Essentials
Subscribers: 189.
Fee: $30.00 installation; $24.95 monthly. Includes 52 channels.
Premiere
Subscribers: 183.
Fee: $61.95 monthly. Includes 120 channels plus music channels.
HD
Subscribers: N.A.
Fee: $11.95 monthly. Includes 75+ channels.
Sports & Entertainment
Subscribers: N.A.
Fee: $12.95 monthly. Includes 34 channels.
Cinemax
Subscribers: N.A.
Fee: $8.95 monthly. Includes 8 channels.
HBO
Subscribers: N.A.
Fee: $14.95 monthly. Includes 12 channels.
Showtime/TMC
Subscribers: N.A.
Fee: $13.95 monthly. Includes 16 channels.
Starz/Encore
Subscribers: N.A.
Fee: $10.95 monthly. Includes 18 channels.
Video-On-Demand: Yes
Internet Service
Operational: Yes.
Fee: $22.95-$207.95 monthly.
Telephone Service
Digital: Operational
Fee: $17.80 monthly
Chief Executive Officer & General Manager: Larry Sevier. Video Solutions Manager: Scott Roe.
Ownership: Nex-Tech.

COURTLAND—Nex-Tech. This cable system has converted to IPTV. See COURTLAND, KS [KS5043]. ICA: KS0271.

CUBA—Formerly served by Eagle Communications. No longer in operation. ICA: KS0372.

CUNNINGHAM—Cox Communications. Now served by WICHITA, KS [KS0001]. ICA: KS0223.

DEARING—Formerly served by SKT Entertainment. Now served by Cox Communications, PITTSBURG, KS [KS0011]. ICA: KS0255.

DELPHOS—Formerly served by Cunningham Cable TV. No longer in operation. ICA: KS0374.

DENISON—Formerly served by Rainbow Communications. No longer in operation. ICA: KS0324.

Kansas—Cable Systems

FULLY SEARCHABLE • CONTINUOUSLY UPDATED • DISCOUNT RATES FOR PRINT PURCHASERS
For more information call **800-771-9202** or visit **www.warren-news.com**

DIGHTON—S&T Cable, 320 Kansas Ave, PO Box 99, Brewster, KS 67732-0099. Phones: 620-397-2111 (Dighton office); 785-694-2256. Fax: 785-694-2750. Web Site: http://www.sttelcom.com. Also serves Healy. ICA: KS0144.
TV Market Ranking: Outside TV Markets (DIGHTON, Healy).
Channel capacity: N.A. Channels available but not in use: N.A.
Basic Service
Subscribers: 409. Commercial subscribers: 1.
Programming (received off-air): KSNG (NBC) Garden City; KUPK (ABC) Garden City; KWCH-DT (CBS) Hutchinson.
Programming (via microwave): KAKE (ABC, MeTV) Wichita; KMTW (MNT, The Country Network) Hutchinson; KOOD (PBS) Hays; KSAS-TV (Antenna TV, FOX) Wichita; KSCW-DT (CW, Decades) Wichita; KSWK (PBS) Lakin.
Programming (via satellite): KUSA (NBC, WeatherNation) Denver; KWGN-TV (CW, This TV) Denver; QVC.
Fee: $9.95 installation; $21.55 monthly.
Expanded Basic Service 1
Subscribers: N.A.
Programming (via satellite): A&E; AMC; Animal Planet; Bravo; Cartoon Network; CMT; CNBC; CNN; Comedy Central; C-SPAN; C-SPAN 2; Daystar TV Network; Discovery Channel; Discovery Kids Channel; Disney Channel; DIY Network; E! HD; ESPN; ESPN Classic; ESPN2; EWTN Global Catholic Network; Food Network; Fox News Channel; Fox Sports 1; Freeform; FX; Golf Channel; Hallmark Channel; HGTV; History; HLN; Lifetime; MSNBC; MTV; National Geographic Channel; NBCSN; NFL Network; Nickelodeon; Oxygen; Pop; RFD-TV; Root Sports Rocky Mountain; Spike TV; Syfy; TBS; The Weather Channel; TLC; TNT; Travel Channel; Trinity Broadcasting Network (TBN); truTV; Turner Classic Movies; TV Land; Univision Studios; USA Network; VH1; WE tv; WGN America.
Fee: $21.95 monthly.
Digital Basic Service
Subscribers: 72.
Programming (via satellite): BBC America; Bloomberg Television; CMT; Destination America; Discovery Kids Channel; Discovery Life Channel; Disney XD; ESPNews; ESPNU; FSN Digital Atlantic; FSN Digital Central; FSN Digital Pacific; Fuse; FYI; Great American Country; GSN; History International; IFC; Investigation Discovery; LMN; MC; MTV Classic; MTV Hits; MTV Jams; MTV2; Nick 2; Nick Jr.; Nicktoons; Outdoor Channel; OWN: Oprah Winfrey Network; Science Channel; Starz Encore (multiplexed); TeenNick; The Word Network; Tr3s; UP; VH1 Soul.
Fee: $50.15 monthly.
Digital Expanded Basic Service
Subscribers: N.A.
Programming (via satellite): Cinelatino; CNN en Espanol; ESPN Deportes; Fox Deportes; History en Espanol.
Fee: $15.95 monthly.

Digital Pay Service 1
Pay Units: N.A.
Programming (via satellite): Cinemax (multiplexed); Flix; FXM; HBO (multiplexed); Showtime (multiplexed); Starz (multiplexed); Sundance TV; The Movie Channel (multiplexed).
Fee: $11.75 monthly (each).
Video-On-Demand: No
Pay-Per-View
special events (delivered digitally).
Internet Service
Operational: No, DSL & dial-up.
Telephone Service
Analog: Operational
Miles of Plant: 21.0 (coaxial); 36.0 (fiber optic). Homes passed: 1,120.
Chief Financial Officer: Carolyn R. Somers. General Manager: Clint Felzien. System Manager: Fritz Doke. Marketing Manager: Shawna Kersenbrock.
Ownership: S & T Communications Inc. (MSO).

DODGE CITY—Cox Communications, 6205 Peachtree Dunwoody Rd, 12th Floor, Atlanta, GA 30328. Phones: 316-260-7000 (Wichita office); 404-269-6590. Web Site: http://www.cox.com. Also serves Ford County & Kinsley. ICA: KS0015.
TV Market Ranking: Below 100 (DODGE CITY, Ford County); Outside TV Markets (Kinsley). Franchise award date: N.A. Franchise expiration date: N.A. Began: June 1, 1970.
Channel capacity: N.A. Channels available but not in use: N.A.
Basic Service
Subscribers: 5,081. Commercial subscribers: 219.
Programming (received off-air): KBSD-DT (CBS) Ensign; KDCK (PBS) Dodge City; KMTW (MNT, The Country Network) Hutchinson; KSAS-TV (Antenna TV, FOX) Wichita; KSCW-DT (CW, Decades) Wichita; KSMI-LD (My Family TV, PBJ, Retro TV, Tuff TV) Wichita; KSNG (NBC) Garden City; KUPK (ABC) Garden City.
Programming (via satellite): C-SPAN; C-SPAN 2; EVINE Live; Pop; The Weather Channel; Univision Studios; Vubiquity Inc.; WGN America.
Fee: $29.95 installation; $21.99 monthly.
Expanded Basic Service 1
Subscribers: N.A.
Programming (via satellite): A&E; AMC; Animal Planet; BET; Bravo; Cartoon Network; CMT; CNBC; CNN; Comedy Central; Discovery Channel; Disney Channel; E! HD; ESPN; ESPN2; EWTN Global Catholic Network; Food Network; Fox News Channel; Fox Sports 1; FOX Sports Midwest; Freeform; FX; Hallmark Channel; HGTV; History; HLN; INSP; Jewelry Television; Lifetime; MSNBC; MTV; MTV2; Nickelodeon; OWN: Oprah Winfrey Network; QVC; Spike TV; Syfy; TBS; Telemundo; TLC; TNT; Travel Channel; truTV; Turner Classic Movies; TV Land; Univision; USA Network; VH1.
Fee: $43.15 monthly.

Digital Basic Service
Subscribers: N.A.
Programming (via satellite): BBC America; Bloomberg Television; Boomerang; CBS Sports Network; Cooking Channel; Daystar TV Network; Discovery Life Channel; Disney XD; DIY Network; ESPN Classic; ESPN HD; ESPNews; Family Friendly Entertainment; FamilyNet; Fox Sports 2; Fuse; FYI; Golf Channel; GoScout Homes; Great American Country; GSN; Hallmark Movies & Mysteries; HBO HD; HD Theater; History; History International; HITS (Headend In The Sky); IFC; LMN; MC; MTV Live; NASA TV; Nat Geo WILD; National Geographic Channel; NBA TV; NBCSN; NFL Network; Nick 2; Nick Jr.; Nicktoons; Outdoor Channel; Oxygen; Showtime HD; Sprout; Starz HD; Sundance TV; TeenNick; Tennis Channel; Trinity Broadcasting Network (TBN); TV One; Universal HD; WE tv.
Digital Pay Service 1
Pay Units: N.A.
Programming (via satellite): Cinemax (multiplexed); Flix; HBO (multiplexed); Showtime (multiplexed); Starz (multiplexed); Starz Encore (multiplexed); The Movie Channel (multiplexed).
Fee: $11.50 monthly (each).
Video-On-Demand: Planned
Pay-Per-View
iN DEMAND; iN DEMAND (delivered digitally); ESPN (delivered digitally); NBA/WNBA League Pass (delivered digitally); NHL Center Ice/MLB Extra Innings (delivered digitally); NBA TV (delivered digitally); Adult Swim (delivered digitally).
Internet Service
Operational: Yes.
Subscribers: 824.
Broadband Service: Cox High Speed Internet.
Fee: $19.99-$59.99 monthly.
Telephone Service
Digital: Operational
Fee: $15.95-$48.95 monthly
Miles of Plant: 126.0 (coaxial); 27.0 (fiber optic). Homes passed included in Wichita.
Vice President & General Manager: Kimberly Edmonds. Vice President, Engineering: Nick DiPonzio. Vice President, Marketing: Tony Matthews. Vice President, Tax: Mary Vickers. Field Operations Regional Manager: Jim Fronk. Marketing Director: Tina Gabbard. Public Affairs Director: Sarah Kauffman. Office Manager: Edgar Cardenas.
Ownership: Cox Communications Inc. (MSO).

DOUGLASS—Formerly served by Allegiance Communications. No longer in operation. ICA: KS0129.

DOWNS—Cunningham Cable TV. Now served by GLEN ELDER, KS [KS0228]. ICA: KS0463.

DOWNS—Formerly served by Cebridge Connections. No longer in operation. ICA: KS0154.

DURHAM—Formerly served by Eagle Communications. No longer in operation. ICA: KS0431.

DWIGHT—Formerly served by Eagle Communications. No longer in operation. ICA: KS0289.

EASTON—Formerly served by Giant Communications. No longer in operation. ICA: KS0276.

EDMOND—Nex-Tech. Formerly served by LENORA, KS [KS0450]. This cable system has converted to IPTV, 2418 Vine St, Hays, KS 67601. Phones: 877-567-7872; 785-625-7070. Fax: 785-625-4479. E-mail: webmaster@nex-tech.com. Web Site: http://www.nex-tech.com. Also serves Densmore, Jennings, Lenora, Logan, Rexford & Selden. ICA: KS5045.
Channel capacity: N.A. Channels available but not in use: N.A.
Essentials
Subscribers: 661.
Fee: $30.00 installation; $24.95 monthly. Includes 52 channels.
Premiere
Subscribers: 625.
Fee: $61.95 monthly. Includes 120 channels plus music channels.
HD
Subscribers: N.A.
Fee: $11.95 monthly. Includes 76+ channels.
Sports & Entertainment
Subscribers: N.A.
Fee: $12.95 monthly. Includes 34 channels.
Cinemax
Subscribers: N.A.
Fee: $8.95 monthly. Includes 8 channels.
HBO
Subscribers: N.A.
Fee: $14.95 monthly. Includes 12 channels.
Showtime/TMC
Subscribers: N.A.
Fee: $13.95 monthly. Includes 16 channels.
Starz/Encore
Subscribers: N.A.
Fee: $10.95 monthly. Includes 18 channels.
Video-On-Demand: Yes
Internet Service
Operational: Yes.
Fee: $22.95-$202.95 monthly.
Telephone Service
Digital: Operational
Fee: $16.75 monthly
Chief Executive Officer & General Manager: Larry Sevier. Video Solutions Manager: Scott Roe.
Ownership: Nex-Tech.

EDNA—Craw-Kan. Now served by GIRARD, KS [KS0446]. ICA: KS0244.

EDNA—Formerly served by GIRARD, KS [KS0446]. Craw-Kan Telephone Co-op. This cable system has converted to IPTV, 200 North Ozark St, PO Box 100, Girard, KS 66743-0100. Phones: 620-724-8838; 800-362-0316; 620-724-8235. Fax: 620-724-4099. E-mail: webmaster@ckt.net. Web Site: http://web.ckt.net. ICA: KS5102.
TV Market Ranking: Outside TV Markets (EDNA).
Channel capacity: N.A. Channels available but not in use: N.A.
Internet Service
Operational: Yes.
Telephone Service
Digital: Operational
Ownership: Craw-Kan Telephone Cooperative.

EFFINGHAM—Rainbow Communications. No longer in operation. ICA: KS0209.

ELK CITY—Formerly served by SKT Entertainment. No longer in operation. ICA: KS0258.

ELKHART—Epic Touch Co, 610 South Cosmos, PO Box 1260, Elkhart, KS 67950-1260. Phones: 800-554-4250; 620-697-2111. Fax: 620-697-4262. Web Site: http://www.

Cable Systems—Kansas

epictouch.com. Also serves Keyes. ICA: KS0068.
TV Market Ranking: Outside TV Markets (ELKHART, Keyes). Franchise award date: N.A. Franchise expiration date: N.A. Began: July 1, 1960.
Channel capacity: N.A. Channels available but not in use: N.A.

Basic Service
Subscribers: N.A.
Programming (received off-air): KMTW (MNT, The Country Network) Hutchinson; KSAS-TV (Antenna TV, FOX) Wichita; KSCW-DT (CW, Decades) Wichita; KSNG (NBC) Garden City; KSWK (PBS) Lakin; KUPK (ABC) Garden City; KWCH-DT (CBS) Hutchinson.
Programming (via satellite): A&E; AMC; Animal Planet; Bravo; Cartoon Network; CMT; CNBC; CNN; Comedy Central; C-SPAN; C-SPAN 2; Discovery Channel; Disney Channel; E! HD; ESPN; ESPN Classic; ESPN2; ESPNews; EWTN Global Catholic Network; Food Network; Fox News Channel; FOX Sports Midwest; Freeform; FX; Golf Channel; Hallmark Channel; HGTV; History; HLN; HSN; Lifetime; LMN; MSNBC; MTV; NFL Network; Nickelodeon; Ovation; Pop; QVC; Spike TV; Syfy; TBS; Telemundo; The Weather Channel; TLC; TNT; Travel Channel; Trinity Broadcasting Network (TBN); truTV; Turner Classic Movies; TV Land; UniMas; Univision Studios; USA Network; VH1; WGN America; Youtoo America.
Fee: $29.00 installation.

Digital Basic Service
Subscribers: N.A.
Programming (via satellite): American Heroes Channel; BBC America; Boomerang; BYUtv; Chiller; CMT; Destination America; Discovery Family; Discovery Life Channel; DIY Network; ESPNU; FamilyNet; FOX College Sports Central; FOX College Sports Pacific; Fox Sports 1; FXM; FYI; Great American Country; History International; Investigation Discovery; MC; MTV Classic; MTV Hits; MTV Jams; MTV2; NBCSN; Nick 2; Nick Jr.; Nicktoons; Outdoor Channel; OWN: Oprah Winfrey Network; RFD-TV; Science Channel; Starz Encore (multiplexed); TeenNick; VH1 Soul; World Harvest Television.

Digital Expanded Basic Service
Subscribers: N.A.
Programming (via satellite): Cine Mexicano; Cinelatino; CNN en Espanol; Enlace USA; ESPN Deportes; History en Espanol; NBC Universo; Tr3s; VeneMovies.
Fee: $10.95 monthly.

Digital Expanded Basic Service 2
Subscribers: N.A.
Programming (via satellite): Bravo HD; CNBC HD+; Disney Channel HD; ESPN HD; ESPN2 HD; Fox News HD; FSN HD; Syfy HD; TBS HD; TNT HD; Travel Channel HD; USA Network HD.
Fee: $6.95 monthly.

Digital Expanded Basic Service 3
Subscribers: N.A.
Programming (via satellite): A&E HD; AXS TV; Food Network HD; Hallmark Channel HD; HD Theater; HGTV HD; History HD; NFL Network HD; Outdoor Channel HD.
Fee: $5.00 monthly.

Digital Pay Service 1
Pay Units: N.A.
Programming (via satellite): Cinemax (multiplexed); Flix; HBO (multiplexed); Showtime (multiplexed); Starz (multiplexed); The Movie Channel (multiplexed).

Fee: $11.95 monthly (Cinemax or Starz), $14.95 monthly HBO or Showtime/TMC/Flix).
Video-On-Demand: Planned
Internet Service
Operational: Yes.
Telephone Service
Digital: Operational
Miles of Plant: 38.0 (coaxial); None (fiber optic). Homes passed: 1,378.
President: Bob Boaldin. Vice President, Operations: Trent Boaldin. Marketing & Advertising Director: Linda Ward. Assistant Manager: Mike Shannon.
Ownership: Bob & Dian Boaldin.

ELLINWOOD—Vyve Broadband, 4 International Dr, Ste 330, Rye Brook, NY 10573. Phones: 800-937-1397; 405-275-6923; 405-395-1131. Web Site: http://vyvebroadband.com. ICA: KS0080.
TV Market Ranking: Below 100 (ELLINWOOD). Franchise award date: N.A. Franchise expiration date: N.A. Began: September 1, 1976.
Channel capacity: N.A. Channels available but not in use: N.A.

Basic Service
Subscribers: 90. Commercial subscribers: 14.
Programming (received off-air): KAKE (ABC, MeTV) Wichita; KMTW (MNT, The Country Network) Hutchinson; KOOD (PBS) Hays; KPTS (PBS) Hutchinson; KSAS-TV (Antenna TV, FOX) Wichita; KSCW-DT (CW, Decades) Wichita; KSNC (NBC) Great Bend; KWCH-DT (CBS) Hutchinson; alband FM.
Programming (via satellite): Comedy Central; C-SPAN; Food Network; Hallmark Channel; QVC; truTV; WGN America.
Fee: $64.95 installation; $25.00 monthly.

Expanded Basic Service 1
Subscribers: N.A.
Programming (via satellite): A&E; AMC; Animal Planet; Cartoon Network; CMT; CNBC; CNN; Comedy Central; Discovery Channel; Disney Channel; E! HD; ESPN; ESPN2; EWTN Global Catholic Network; Fox News Channel; Fox Sports 1; FOX Sports Midwest; Freeform; FX; HGTV; History; HLN; Lifetime; MSNBC; MTV; National Geographic Channel; Nickelodeon; Oxygen; Spike TV; Syfy; TBS; The Weather Channel; TLC; TNT; Travel Channel; Turner Classic Movies; TV Land; USA Network; VH1.
Fee: $38.91 monthly.

Digital Basic Service
Subscribers: N.A.
Programming (via satellite): BBC America; Bloomberg Television; Bravo; Chiller; Cloo; CMT; Destination America; Discovery Kids Channel; Discovery Life Channel; Disney XD; DMX Music; ESPN Classic; ESPNews; EVINE Live; Flix; FOX College Sports Central; FOX College Sports Pacific; Fuse; FXM; FYI; Golf Channel; Great American Country; GSN; History International; IFC; Investigation Discovery; LMN; MTV Classic; MTV Hits; MTV2; NBCSN; Nick Jr.; Nicktoons; Outdoor Channel; OWN: Oprah Winfrey Network; RFD-TV; Science Channel; Starz Encore (multiplexed); Sundance TV; TeenNick; Trinity Broadcasting Network (TBN); VH1 Soul; WE tv.

Digital Pay Service 1
Pay Units: N.A.
Programming (via satellite): Cinemax (multiplexed); HBO (multiplexed); Showtime (multiplexed); Starz (multiplexed); The Movie Channel (multiplexed).
Video-On-Demand: No

Pay-Per-View
iN DEMAND (delivered digitally); Club Jenna (delivered digitally); Spice: Xcess (delivered digitally); Playboy TV (delivered digitally); Fresh (delivered digitally).
Internet Service
Operational: Yes.
Fee: $24.95 installation; $39.99 monthly.
Telephone Service
Digital: Operational
Miles of Plant: 14.0 (coaxial); None (fiber optic).
Chief Executive Officer: Bill Haggarty. Regional Vice President: Andrew Dearth. Vice President, Marketing: Tracy Bass. Senior Vice President, Financial Planning: Daniel White.
Ownership: Vyve Broadband LLC (MSO).

ELLSWORTH—Eagle Communications, 2703 Hall St, Ste 15, PO Box 817, Hays, KS 67601. Phones: 785-899-3371; 785-625-5910; 785-263-2529; 785-625-4000 (Corporate office). Fax: 785-625-8030. Web Site: http://www.eaglecom.net. Also serves Kanopolis. ICA: KS0069.
TV Market Ranking: Below 100 (ELLSWORTH, Kanopolis). Franchise award date: November 1, 1976. Franchise expiration date: N.A. Began: November 1, 1976.
Channel capacity: N.A. Channels available but not in use: N.A.

Basic Service
Subscribers: 415. Commercial subscribers: 10.
Programming (received off-air): KAKE (ABC, MeTV) Wichita; KMTW (MNT, The Country Network) Hutchinson; KOOD (PBS) Hays; KPTS (PBS) Hutchinson; KSAS-TV (Antenna TV, FOX) Wichita; KSCW-DT (CW, Decades) Wichita; KSNC (NBC) Great Bend; KWCH-DT (CBS) Hutchinson; alband FM.
Programming (via satellite): C-SPAN; QVC; The Weather Channel; Trinity Broadcasting Network (TBN); WGN America.
Fee: $24.95 installation; $69.95 monthly.

Expanded Basic Service 1
Subscribers: N.A.
Programming (via satellite): A&E; AMC; Animal Planet; Bravo; Cartoon Network; CMT; CNBC; CNN; Comedy Central; Discovery Channel; Disney Channel; E! HD; ESPN; ESPN Classic; ESPN2; Food Network; Fox News Channel; FOX Sports Midwest; Freeform; FX; Great American Country; Hallmark Channel; HGTV; History; HLN; Lifetime; MSNBC; MTV; National Geographic Channel; NFL Network; Nickelodeon; Outdoor Channel; Spike TV; Syfy; TBS; TLC; TNT; Travel Channel; Turner Classic Movies; TV Land; USA Network; VH1.
Fee: $25.50 monthly.

Digital Basic Service
Subscribers: N.A.
Programming (via satellite): BBC America; Bloomberg Television; Cloo; CMT; Cooking Channel; Discovery Life Channel; Disney XD; DMX Music; Fox News Channel; Fox Sports 1; Fuse; FXM; FYI; Golf Channel; GSN; IFC; Investigation Discovery; LMN; MTV Classic; MTV Hits; MTV2; Nick Jr.; Nicktoons; OWN: Oprah Winfrey Network; RFD-TV; Sprout; Sundance TV; TeenNick; VH1 Soul.
Fee: $3.95 monthly (entertainment or variety tier), $5.95 monthly (basic).

Pay Service 1
Pay Units: N.A.
Programming (via satellite): HBO; Showtime; The Movie Channel.
Fee: $11.95 monthly (each).

Digital Pay Service 1
Pay Units: N.A.
Programming (via satellite): Cinemax (multiplexed); Flix; HBO (multiplexed); Showtime (multiplexed); Starz (multiplexed); Starz Encore (multiplexed); The Movie Channel.
Fee: $11.95 monthly (Cinemax, HBO, Starz/Encore or Showtime/TMC/Flix).
Video-On-Demand: No
Pay-Per-View
iN DEMAND (delivered digitally); Playboy TV (delivered digitally); Fresh (delivered digitally).
Internet Service
Operational: Yes. Began: May 15, 2003.
Broadband Service: Eagle Internet.
Fee: $22.95 monthly.
Telephone Service
Analog: Not Operational
Digital: Operational
Fee: $18.00 monthly
Miles of Plant: 29.0 (coaxial); None (fiber optic). Homes passed: 1,355.
Chief Operating Officer: Kurt K. David. General Manager: Travis Kohlrus. Chief Technician: Jim Gall. Ad Sales Manager: Mike Koerner.
Ownership: Eagle Communications Inc. (MSO).

EMMETT—Formerly served by Rainbow Communications. No longer in operation. ICA: KS0346.

EMPORIA—Cable One, 714 Commercial St, PO Box 867, Emporia, KS 66801. Phones: 620-341-9783; 620-342-3535. Fax: 620-342-3620. Web Site: http://www.cableone.net. Also serves Lyon County. ICA: KS0009.
TV Market Ranking: Below 100 (Lyon County); Outside TV Markets (EMPORIA). Franchise award date: N.A. Franchise expiration date: N.A. Began: February 1, 1961.
Channel capacity: N.A. Channels available but not in use: N.A.

Basic Service
Subscribers: 3,328.
Programming (received off-air): KSNT (FOX, NBC) Topeka; KTKA-TV (ABC, CW) Topeka; KTMJ-CD (Escape, FOX) Topeka; KTWU (PBS) Topeka; WIBW-TV (CBS, MeTV, MNT) Topeka; 14 FMs.
Programming (via microwave): KAKE (ABC, MeTV) Wichita; KMBC-TV (ABC, MeTV) Kansas City; KSHB-TV (COZI TV, Grit, NBC) Kansas City; KSNW (NBC) Wichita; KWCH-DT (CBS) Hutchinson; WDAF-TV (Antenna TV, FOX) Kansas City.
Programming (via satellite): A&E; AMC; Animal Planet; BET; Bravo; Cartoon Network; CNBC; CNN; Comedy Central; C-SPAN; C-SPAN 2; CW PLUS; Discovery Channel; Disney Channel; ESPN; ESPN2; Food Network; Fox News Channel; FOX Sports Midwest; Freeform; FX; Great American Country; HGTV; History; HLN; Lifetime; MSNBC; MTV; Nickelodeon; QVC; Spike TV; Syfy; TBS; The Weather Channel; TLC; TNT; Travel Channel; Trinity Broadcasting Network (TBN); Turner Classic Movies; TV Land; Univision Studios; USA Network; WGN America.
Fee: $90.00 installation; $35.00 monthly.

Digital Basic Service
Subscribers: N.A.
Programming (via satellite): 3ABN; Boomerang; BYUtv; Discovery Digital Networks; Disney XD; ESPN Classic; ESPNews; FamilyNet; FOX College Sports Central; FOX College Sports Pacific; Fox Sports 1; Fox Sports 2; FXM; FYI; Golf

2017 Edition   D-285

Kansas—Cable Systems

Channel; Hallmark Channel; History International; HITS (Headend In The Sky); INSP; National Geographic Channel; Outdoor Channel; TNT HD; Trinity Broadcasting Network (TBN); truTV; Universal HD.

Digital Pay Service 1
Pay Units: N.A.
Programming (via satellite): Cinemax (multiplexed); Flix; HBO (multiplexed); Showtime (multiplexed); Showtime HD; Starz (multiplexed); Starz Encore (multiplexed); Sundance TV; The Movie Channel HD.
Fee: $14.95 monthly (each).
Video-On-Demand: No

Pay-Per-View
Pleasure (delivered digitally); SexSee (delivered digitally); Juicy (delivered digitally); VaVoom (delivered digitally).

Internet Service
Operational: Yes.
Subscribers: 3,956.
Broadband Service: CableONE.net.
Fee: $75.00 installation; $43.00 monthly.

Telephone Service
Digital: Operational
Subscribers: 1,187.
Fee: $39.95 monthly
Miles of Plant: 217.0 (coaxial); 61.0 (fiber optic). Homes passed: 13,917.
Vice President: Patrick A. Dolohanty. General Manager: Joe Michaels. Technical Operations Manager: Ron Davis. Marketing Director: Chris Harris.
Ownership: Cable ONE Inc. (MSO).

ENSIGN—United Communications Assn. Inc. Now served by CIMARRON, KS [KS0126]. ICA: KS0312.

ESKRIDGE—Formerly served by Zito Media. No longer in operation. ICA: KS0206.

EUREKA—Mediacom, 901 North College Ave, Columbia, MO 65201. Phones: 417-875-5560 (Customer service); 573-443-1536. Fax: 417-883-0265. Web Site: http://www.mediacomcable.com. ICA: KS0058.
TV Market Ranking: Outside TV Markets (EUREKA). Franchise award date: N.A. Franchise expiration date: N.A. Began: May 1, 1981.
Channel capacity: N.A. Channels available but not in use: N.A.

Basic Service
Subscribers: 259.
Programming (received off-air): KAKE (ABC, MeTV) Wichita; KSAS-TV (Antenna TV, FOX) Wichita; KSCW-DT (CW, Decades) Wichita; KSNT (FOX, NBC) Topeka; KSNW (NBC) Wichita; KTKA-TV (ABC, CW) Topeka; KTWU (PBS) Topeka; KWCH-DT (CBS) Hutchinson; WIBW-TV (CBS, MeTV, MNT) Topeka.
Programming (via satellite): C-SPAN; Pop; WGN America.
Fee: $35.00 installation; $42.00 monthly.

Expanded Basic Service 1
Subscribers: N.A.
Programming (via satellite): A&E; AMC; Animal Planet; BET; Bravo; Cartoon Network; CMT; CNBC; CNN; Comedy Central; Discovery Channel; Discovery Life Channel; E! HD; ESPN; ESPN2; EVINE Live; Food Network; Fox News Channel; Fox Sports 1; FOX Sports Networks; Freeform; FX; Hallmark Channel; HGTV; History; HLN; INSP; Lifetime; MSNBC; MTV; Nickelodeon; Outdoor Channel; QVC; Spike TV; Syfy; TBS; The Weather Channel; TLC; TNT; Travel Channel; Trinity Broadcasting Network (TBN); truTV; TV Land; USA Network; VH1; WE tv.
Fee: $3.95 monthly.

Digital Basic Service
Subscribers: N.A.
Programming (via satellite): BBC America; Bloomberg Television; Cloo; Destination America; Discovery Kids Channel; DMX Music; ESPNews; EWTN Global Catholic Network; Fuse; FXM; FYI; Golf Channel; GSN; History International; IFC; Investigation Discovery; LMN; MTV Hits; MTV2; National Geographic Channel; NBCSN; Nick Jr.; Nicktoons; OWN: Oprah Winfrey Network; RFD-TV; Science Channel; TeenNick; Turner Classic Movies; TVG Network.

Digital Pay Service 1
Pay Units: N.A.
Programming (via satellite): Cinemax (multiplexed); Flix; HBO (multiplexed); Showtime; Starz (multiplexed); Starz Encore (multiplexed); Sundance TV; The Movie Channel.
Fee: $2.95 monthly (Flix/Sundance), $10.50 monthly (Cinemax, HBO, Showtime or TMC).
Video-On-Demand: No

Pay-Per-View
Events (delivered digitally); Playboy TV (delivered digitally); TEN Clips; Pleasure (delivered digitally).

Internet Service
Operational: Yes.
Broadband Service: Mediacom High Speed Internet.

Telephone Service
None
Miles of Plant: 40.0 (coaxial); None (fiber optic). Homes passed: 2,573.
Regional Vice President: Bill Copeland. Operations Director: Bryan Gann. Regional Technical Operations Director: Alan Freedman. Technical Operations Director: Roger Shearer. Marketing Director: Will Kuebler. Vice President, Financial Reporting: Kenneth J. Kohrs.
Ownership: Mediacom LLC (MSO).

FAIRVIEW—Formerly served by Carson Communications. Now served by Rainbow Communications, HIAWATHA, KS [KS0059]. ICA: KS0293.

FORD—United Communications Assn. Inc. Now served by CIMARRON, KS [KS0126]. ICA: KS0307.

FORMOSO—Cunningham Cable TV. Now served by GLEN ELDER, KS [KS0228]. ICA: KS0344.

FORT RILEY—Vyve Broadband, 4 International Dr, Ste 330, Rye Brook, NY 10573. Phones: 800-937-1397; 405-275-6923; 405-395-1131. Web Site: http://vyvebroadband.com. ICA: KS0023.
TV Market Ranking: Outside TV Markets (FORT RILEY). Franchise award date: N.A. Franchise expiration date: N.A. Began: January 1, 1980.
Channel capacity: N.A. Channels available but not in use: N.A.

Basic Service
Subscribers: 536. Commercial subscribers: 91.
Programming (received off-air): KSNT (FOX, NBC) Topeka; KTKA-TV (ABC, CW) Topeka; KTMJ-CD (Escape, FOX) Topeka; KTWU (PBS) Topeka; WIBW-TV (CBS, MeTV, MNT) Topeka.
Programming (via satellite): C-SPAN; CW PLUS; ION Television; QVC; TBS; The Weather Channel; WGN America.
Fee: $64.95 installation; $25.00 monthly.

Expanded Basic Service 1
Subscribers: N.A.
Programming (via satellite): A&E; AMC; Animal Planet; BET; Bravo; Cartoon Network; Cloo; CMT; CNBC; CNN; Comedy Central; Discovery Channel; Disney Channel; Disney XD; E! HD; ESPN; ESPN2; ESPNU; Food Network; Fox News Channel; FOX Sports Midwest; Freeform; FX; Golf Channel; GSN; Hallmark Channel; HGTV; History; HLN; Lifetime; MSNBC; MTV; National Geographic Channel; Nickelodeon; Oxygen; Pop; Spike TV; Syfy; TLC; TNT; Travel Channel; truTV; Turner Classic Movies; TV Land; Univision Studios; USA Network; VH1.
Fee: $43.11 monthly.

Digital Basic Service
Subscribers: N.A.
Programming (via satellite): A&E HD; AXS TV; BBC America; Bloomberg Television; Chiller; Cine Mexicano; Cinelatino; CMT; CNN en Espanol; Destination America; Discovery Kids Channel; Discovery Life Channel; ESPN Classic; ESPN Deportes; ESPN HD; ESPN2 HD; ESPNews; EVINE Live; Flix; Food Network HD; FOX College Sports Central; FOX College Sports Pacific; Fox Deportes; Fox Sports 1; Fuse; FXM; FYI; Great American Country; HD Theater; HGTV HD; History en Espanol; History International; IFC; Investigation Discovery; LMN; MC; MTV Classic; MTV Hits; MTV2; National Geographic Channel; National Geographic Channel HD; NBC Universo; NBCSN; Nick Jr.; Nicktoons; Outdoor Channel; Outdoor Channel 2 HD; OWN: Oprah Winfrey Network; Science Channel; Starz Encore (multiplexed); Sundance TV; TeenNick; The Word Network; Tr3s; Trinity Broadcasting Network (TBN); Universal HD; UP; VH1 Soul; ViendoMovies; WE tv.

Digital Pay Service 1
Pay Units: N.A.
Programming (via satellite): Cinemax (multiplexed); HBO (multiplexed); HBO HD; HBO Latino; Showtime (multiplexed); Showtime HD; Starz (multiplexed); Starz Encore (multiplexed); Starz HD; The Movie Channel (multiplexed).
Video-On-Demand: No

Pay-Per-View
iN DEMAND (delivered digitally); Spice: Xcess (delivered digitally); Fresh (delivered digitally); Playboy TV (delivered digitally); Club Jenna (delivered digitally).

Internet Service
Operational: Yes. Began: January 1, 2003.
Broadband Service: Charter Internet.
Fee: $24.95 installation; $39.99 monthly.

Telephone Service
Digital: Operational
Miles of Plant: 55.0 (coaxial); None (fiber optic). Homes passed: 6,600.
Chief Executive Officer: Bill Haggarty. Regional Vice President: Andrew Dearth. Vice President, Marketing: Tracy Bass. Senior Vice President, Financial Planning: Daniel White.
Ownership: Vyve Broadband LLC (MSO).

FORT SCOTT—Suddenlink Communications, 520 Maryville Centre Dr, Ste 300, St. Louis, MO 63141. Phones: 620-223-1804; 314-315-9400. Web Site: http://www.suddenlink.com. Also serves Bourbon County (unincorporated areas). ICA: KS0028.
TV Market Ranking: Below 100 (Bourbon County (unincorporated areas) (portions), FORT SCOTT); Outside TV Markets (Bourbon County (unincorporated areas) (portions)). Franchise award date: N.A. Franchise expiration date: N.A. Began: October 1, 1966.
Channel capacity: 61 (operating 2-way). Channels available but not in use: N.A.

Basic Service
Subscribers: 1,113.
Programming (received off-air): K30AL-D (PBS) Iola; KCPT (PBS) Kansas City; KCTV (CBS) Kansas City; KCWE (CW, Movies!, This TV) Kansas City; KMBC-TV (ABC, MeTV) Kansas City; KOAM-TV (CBS) Pittsburg; KODE-TV (ABC) Joplin; KSHB-TV (COZI TV, Grit, NBC) Kansas City; KSMO-TV (Bounce TV, MNT) Kansas City; KSNF (NBC) Joplin; WDAF-TV (Antenna TV, FOX) Kansas City; allband FM.
Programming (via satellite): A&E; BET; CNBC; CNN; C-SPAN; C-SPAN 2; Discovery Channel; Disney Channel; ESPN; Food Network; FOX Sports Midwest; Freeform; Great American Country; HGTV; History; HLN; Lifetime; National Geographic Channel; Nickelodeon; QVC; Spike TV; TBS; The Weather Channel; TLC; TNT; Travel Channel; Trinity Broadcasting Network (TBN); Turner Classic Movies; TV Land; USA Network.
Fee: $28.45 monthly.

Expanded Basic Service 1
Subscribers: N.A.
Programming (via satellite): EWTN Global Catholic Network; Fox News Channel; ION Television; VH1.
Fee: $25.00 monthly.

Digital Basic Service
Subscribers: N.A.
Programming (via satellite): BBC America; Bloomberg Television; Discovery Digital Networks; DMX Music; ESPN Classic; ESPN2; ESPNews; EVINE Live; Fox Sports 1; Fuse; FYI; Golf Channel; GSN; HGTV; History; History International; IFC; LMN; NBCSN; Outdoor Channel; Ovation; Syfy; Trinity Broadcasting Network (TBN); Turner Classic Movies; WE tv.

Pay Service 1
Pay Units: N.A.
Programming (via satellite): HBO; Showtime; The Movie Channel.
Fee: $9.00 installation; $7.95 monthly (TMC), $9.95 monthly (Showtime), $10.95 monthly (HBO).

Digital Pay Service 1
Pay Units: N.A.
Programming (via satellite): Cinemax (multiplexed); HBO (multiplexed); Showtime (multiplexed); Starz; The Movie Channel.
Video-On-Demand: No

Pay-Per-View
Sports PPV (delivered digitally); ESPN Now (delivered digitally); Shorteez (delivered digitally); Fresh (delivered digitally); Playboy TV (delivered digitally); iN DEMAND (delivered digitally).

Internet Service
Operational: Yes. Began: June 23, 2002.
Broadband Service: Suddenlink High Speed Internet.
Fee: $49.95 installation; $26.95 monthly.

Telephone Service
None
Miles of Plant: 93.0 (coaxial); None (fiber optic). Homes passed: 4,400.
Senior Vice President, Corporate Finance: Michael Pflantz. Regional Manager: Todd Cruthird. Plant Manager: Lee Mott. Regional Marketing Manager: Beverly Gambell.
Ownership: Cequel Communications Holdings I LLC (MSO).

Cable Systems—Kansas

FRANKFORT—Blue Valley Tele-Communications. Now served by AXTELL, KS [KS0424]. ICA: KS0167.

FREDONIA—Vyve Broadband, 4 International Dr, Ste 330, Rye Brook, NY 10573. Phones: 800-937-1397; 405-395-1131; 405-275-6923. Web Site: http://www.vyvebroadband.com. Also serves Wilson County. ICA: KS0052.
TV Market Ranking: Outside TV Markets (FREDONIA, Wilson County).
Channel capacity: 60 (not 2-way capable). Channels available but not in use: N.A.
Basic Service
  Subscribers: 119. Commercial subscribers: 15.
  Programming (received off-air): KAKE (ABC, MeTV) Wichita; KFJX (FOX) Pittsburg; KOAM-TV (CBS) Pittsburg; KODE-TV (ABC) Joplin; KOED-TV (PBS) Tulsa; KSNF (NBC) Joplin; WIBW-TV (CBS, MeTV, MNT) Topeka.
  Programming (via satellite): CNN; C-SPAN; C-SPAN 2; CW PLUS; EVINE Live; Pop; QVC; The Weather Channel; WGN America.
  Fee: $64.95 installation; $25.00 monthly; $2.00 converter.
Expanded Basic Service 1
  Subscribers: N.A.
  Programming (via satellite): A&E; AMC; Animal Planet; Bravo; Cartoon Network; CMT; CNBC; Comedy Central; Discovery Channel; Disney Channel; ESPN; ESPN2; Food Network; Fox News Channel; FOX Sports Midwest; Freeform; FX; Great American Country; Hallmark Channel; HGTV; History; HLN; Lifetime; MSNBC; MTV; NFL Network; Nickelodeon; Outdoor Channel; Spike TV; Syfy; TBS; TLC; TNT; Travel Channel; truTV; TV Land; USA Network; VH1.
  Fee: $33.66 monthly.
Digital Basic Service
  Subscribers: N.A.
  Programming (via satellite): BBC America; Bloomberg Television; Bravo; Cine Mexicano; Cinelatino; Cloo; CMT; CNN en Espanol; Destination America; Discovery Kids Channel; Discovery Life Channel; Disney XD; DMX Music; ESPN Classic; ESPN Deportes; ESPN2; ESPNews; EVINE Live; Flix; FOX College Sports Central; FOX College Sports Pacific; Fox Deportes; Fox Sports 1; Fuse; FXM; FYI; Golf Channel; Great American Country; GSN; HGTV; History; History en Espanol; History International; IFC; Investigation Discovery; LMN; MTV Classic; MTV Hits; MTV2; National Geographic Channel; NBC Universo; NBCSN; Nick Jr.; Nicktoons; Outdoor Channel; Ovation; OWN; Oprah Winfrey Network; Science Channel; Starz Encore (multiplexed); Sundance TV; Syfy; TeenNick; The Word Network; Tr3s; Trinity Broadcasting Network (TBN); Turner Classic Movies; UP; VH1 Soul; ViendoMovies; WE tv.
Pay Service 1
  Pay Units: N.A.
  Programming (via satellite): Cinemax; HBO; Showtime; Starz; Starz Encore.
  Fee: $10.00 installation; $11.95 monthly (Cinemax or HBO).
Digital Pay Service 1
  Pay Units: N.A.
  Programming (via satellite): Cinemax (multiplexed); HBO (multiplexed); HBO Latino; Showtime (multiplexed); Starz (multiplexed); The Movie Channel (multiplexed).
Video-On-Demand: No
Pay-Per-View
  iN DEMAND (delivered digitally); Hot Choice (delivered digitally); Playboy TV (delivered digitally); Fresh (delivered digitally); Club Jenna (delivered digitally); Spice: Xcess (delivered digitally).
Internet Service
  Operational: Yes.
  Subscribers: 75.
Telephone Service
  Digital: Operational
  Subscribers: 28.
  Miles of Plant: 43.0 (coaxial); 12.0 (fiber optic). Homes passed: 1,784.
Chief Executive Officer: Bill Haggarty. Regional Vice President: Andrew Dearth. Vice President, Marketing: Tracy Bass. Senior Vice President, Financial Planning: Daniel White.
Ownership: Vyve Broadband LLC (MSO).

FRONTENAC—Formerly served by Almena Cable. No longer in operation. ICA: KS0037.

GALENA—Mediacom. Now served by CARL JUNCTION, MO [MO0094]. ICA: KS0075.

GALVA—Formerly served by Home Communications Inc. No longer in operation. ICA: KS0378.

GALVA—Home Communications Inc, 211 South Main, PO Box 8, Galva, KS 67443. Phones: 620-654-3673; 620-654-4663; 800-362-9336; 620-654-3381. Fax: 620-654-3122. E-mail: hciservice@homecomminc.com. Web Site: http://www.homecomminc.com. Also serves Assaria, Bridgeport, Canton, Falun, Geneseo, Gypsum, Mentor, Salemsborg, Salina (southwest rural portions) & Smolan. ICA: KS5068.
TV Market Ranking: 67 (Canton); Below 100 (Assaria, Gypsum).
Channel capacity: N.A. Channels available but not in use: N.A.
Skitter TV
  Subscribers: 620.
Internet Service
  Operational: Yes.
  Fee: $2.00 modem lease.
Telephone Service
  Digital: Operational
  Fee: $17.42 monthly
Chief Executive Officer: Richard Baldwin. Billing Account Manager: Tina Anderson. Sales & Marketing Manager: Jill Beltz. Service Operations Manager: Brian Williams. Central Office & Headend Supervisor: Chris Flaherty.
Ownership: Home Communications Inc.

GARDEN CITY—Cox Communications, 6205 Peachtree Dunwoody Rd, 12th Floor, Atlanta, GA 30328. Phones: 404-269-6590; 316-260-7000 (Wichita office). Web Site: http://www.cox.com. Also serves Finney County (portions). ICA: KS0010.
TV Market Ranking: Below 100 (Finney County (portions), GARDEN CITY). Franchise award date: December 1, 1969. Franchise expiration date: N.A. Began: September 1, 1971.
Channel capacity: N.A. Channels available but not in use: N.A.
Basic Service
  Subscribers: 5,062. Commercial subscribers: 218.
  Programming (received off-air): KBSD-DT (CBS) Ensign; KDCK (PBS) Dodge City; KMTW (MNT, The Country Network) Hutchinson; KSAS-TV (Antenna TV, FOX) Wichita; KSCW-DT (CW, Decades) Wichita; KSNG (NBC) Garden City; KUPK (ABC) Garden City; KWCH-DT (CBS) Hutchinson; 4 FMs.
  Programming (via satellite): C-SPAN; C-SPAN 2; EVINE Live; Pop; The Weather Channel; Univision Studios; Vubiquity Inc.; WGN America.
  Fee: $29.95 installation; $21.99 monthly; $2.00 converter.
Expanded Basic Service 1
  Subscribers: N.A.
  Programming (via satellite): A&E; AMC; Animal Planet; BET; Bravo; Cartoon Network; CMT; CNBC; CNN; Comedy Central; Discovery Channel; Disney Channel; E! HD; ESPN; ESPN2; EWTN Global Catholic Network; Food Network; Fox News Channel; Fox Sports 1; FOX Sports Midwest; Freeform; FX; Hallmark Channel; HGTV; History; HLN; INSP; Lifetime; MSNBC; MTV; MTV2; Nickelodeon; OWN: Oprah Winfrey Network; QVC; Spike TV; Syfy; TBS; Telemundo; TLC; TNT; Travel Channel; truTV; Turner Classic Movies; TV Land; Univision; USA Network; VH1.
  Fee: $43.15 monthly.
Digital Basic Service
  Subscribers: N.A.
  Programming (via satellite): Azteca; BBC America; Bloomberg Television; Boomerang; CBS Sports Network; CMT; Cooking Channel; Daystar TV Network; Discovery Digital Networks; Disney XD; DIY Network; ESPN Classic; ESPN HD; ESPNews; ESPNU; FamilyNet; Fox HD; Fox Sports 2; Fuse; FYI; Golf Channel; Great American Country; GSN; HD Theater; History International; HITS (Headend In The Sky); IFC; LMN; MC; MTV Live; NASA TV; Nat Geo WILD; National Geographic Channel; NBA League Pass; NBA TV; NBCSN; NFL Network; Nick 2; Nick Jr.; Nicktoons; Outdoor Channel; Oxygen; PBS HD; Sprout; Sundance TV; TeenNick; Tennis Channel; Trinity Broadcasting Network (TBN); TV One; Universal HD; UP; WE tv.
Digital Pay Service 1
  Pay Units: N.A.
  Programming (via satellite): Cinemax (multiplexed); Flix; HBO (multiplexed); HBO HD; Showtime (multiplexed); Showtime HD; Starz (multiplexed); Starz Encore (multiplexed); Starz HD; The Movie Channel (multiplexed).
  Fee: $11.50 monthly (each).
Video-On-Demand: Planned
Pay-Per-View
  Fresh (delivered digitally); iN DEMAND (delivered digitally); MLB Extra Innings (delivered digitally); ESPN (delivered digitally); Playboy TV (delivered digitally); SexSee (delivered digitally); Juicy (delivered digitally); NBA League Pass (delivered digitally); MLS Direct Kick (delivered digitally); NHL Center Ice (delivered digitally).
Internet Service
  Operational: Yes.
  Broadband Service: Cox High Speed Internet.
  Fee: $19.99-$59.99 monthly; $15.00 modem lease; $199.95 modem purchase.
Telephone Service
  Digital: Operational
  Fee: $15.95-$48.95 monthly
  Miles of Plant: 124.0 (coaxial); None (fiber optic). Homes passed included in Wichita.
Vice President & General Manager: Kimberly Edmonds. Vice President, Engineering: Nick DiPonzio. Vice President, Marketing: Tony Matthews. Vice President, Tax: Mary Vickers. Field Operations Regional Manager: Jim Fronk. Marketing Director: Tina Gabbard. Public Affairs Director: Sarah Kauffman. Office Manager: Edgar Cardenas.
Ownership: Cox Communications Inc. (MSO).

GARDEN PLAIN—Formerly served by Cebridge Connections. No longer in operation. ICA: KS0218.

GARNETT—Vyve Broadband, 4 International Dr, Ste 330, Rye Brook, NY 10573. Phone: 800-937-1397. Web Site: http://vyvebroadband.com. ICA: KS0474.
TV Market Ranking: Outside TV Markets (GARNETT).
Channel capacity: N.A. Channels available but not in use: N.A.
Basic Service
  Subscribers: 181. Commercial subscribers: 19.
  Fee: $64.95 installation; $25.00 monthly.
Expanded Basic Service 1
  Subscribers: N.A.
  Fee: $41.06 monthly.
Chief Executive Officer: Bill Haggarty. Senior Vice President, Financial Planning: Daniel White.
Ownership: Vyve Broadband LLC (MSO).

GENESEO—Formerly served by Eagle Communications. No longer in operation. ICA: KS0251.

GIRARD—Craw-Kan, 200 North Ozark St, PO Box 100, Girard, KS 66743-0100. Phones: 800-362-0316; 620-724-8235. Fax: 620-724-4099. Web Site: http://web.ckt.net. Also serves Arma, Bartlett, Brazilton, Bronson, Cherokee, Columbus, Edna, Farlington, Galesburg, Hepler, Hiattville, McCune, Pleasanton, Prescott, Savonburg, Uniontown, Walnut, Weir & West Mineral, KS; Asbury & Purcell, MO. ICA: KS5099.
TV Market Ranking: Below 100 (GIRARD, Mc-Cune, Uniontown, Walnut); Outside TV Markets (Prescott).
Channel capacity: N.A. Channels available but not in use: N.A.
CKtv Economy
  Subscribers: N.A.
  Programming (received off-air): KCTV (CBS) Kansas City; KCWE (CW, Movies!, This TV) Kansas City; KFJX (FOX) Pittsburg; KMBC-TV (ABC, MeTV) Kansas City; KMCI-TV (Bounce TV, Escape, IND) Lawrence; KOAM-TV (CBS) Pittsburg; KODE-TV (ABC) Joplin; KOZJ (PBS) Joplin; KSHB-TV (COZI TV, Grit, NBC) Kansas City; KSNF (NBC) Joplin; KTWU (PBS) Topeka; WDAF-TV (Antenna TV, FOX) Kansas City.

2017 Edition

D-287

Kansas—Cable Systems

FULLY SEARCHABLE • CONTINUOUSLY UPDATED • DISCOUNT RATES FOR PRINT PURCHASERS
For more information call 800-771-9202 or visit www.warren-news.com

Programming (via satellite): 3ABN; AWE; BYUtv; Chiller; Church Channel; Cloo; CMT; C-SPAN; C-SPAN 2; C-SPAN 3; EVINE Live; EWTN Global Catholic Network; God TV; Great American Country; HSN; Jewelry Television; JUCE TV; Lifetime; LMN; MavTV; MTV; MTV Classic; MTV Hits; MTV Jams; MTV2; mtvU; NASA TV; Oxygen; QVC; RFD-TV; Spike TV; Syfy; TBS; TCT; The Weather Channel; TNT; Tr3s; Travel Channel; Trinity Broadcasting Network (TBN); truTV; Turner Classic Movies; TV Land; VH1; VH1 Soul; WE tv; WGN America; World Harvest Television.
Fee: $25.00 installation; $29.99 monthly. 30 channels.

CKtv Basic
Subscribers: 728.
Programming (via satellite): A&E; AMC; American Heroes Channel; Animal Planet; BBC America; BET; Bloomberg Television; Boomerang; Bravo; Cartoon Network; Centric; CNBC; CNBC World; CNN; Comedy Central; Cooking Channel; Crime & Investigation Network; Daystar TV Network; Discovery Channel; Discovery Family; Disney Channel; Disney Junior; Disney XD; DIY Network; E! HD; ESPN; ESPN Classic; ESPN2; ESPNews; ESPNU; Food Network; Fox Business Network; Fox News Channel; Fox Sports 1; FOX Sports Midwest; Freeform; FSN Digital Atlantic; FSN Digital Central; FSN Digital Pacific; FX; FXM; FYI; Golf Channel; GSN; Hallmark Channel; Hallmark Movies & Mysteries; History; HLN; INSP; Investigation Discovery; MSNBC; National Geographic Channel; NBCSN; NFL Network; Nick 2; Nick Jr.; Nickelodeon; Nicktoons; Outdoor Channel; OWN: Oprah Winfrey Network; Planet Green; Rural TV; Science Channel; Smile of a Child TV; SonLife Broadcasting Network; Sprout; TeenNick; Tennis Channel; The Sportsman Channel; TLC; USA Network.
Fee: $58.99 monthly. 100+ channels & 45 music channels.

HD
Subscribers: N.A.
Fee: $11.99 monthly. 70 channels.

Premium Packages
Subscribers: N.A.
Fee: $12.99 monthly/1 movie package, $24.99/2 movie packages, $34.99/3 movie packages or $42.99/all movie packages. Packages include Cinemax (3 channels), HBO (5 channels), Showtime/TMC (9 channels) or Starz/Encore (12 channels).

Internet Service
Operational: Yes.
Fee: $29.99-$59.99 monthly.

Telephone Service
Digital: Operational
General Manager: Craig Wilbert.
Ownership: Craw-Kan Telephone Cooperative.

GIRARD—Craw-Kan, 200 North Ozark St, PO Box 100, Girard, KS 66743-0100. Phones: 800-362-0316; 620-724-8235. Fax: 620-724-4099. Web Site: http://web.ckt.net. Also serves Arcadia & Mulberry, KS; Amoret, Amsterdam & Hume, MO. ICA: KS0446.
Channel capacity: N.A. Channels available but not in use: N.A.

Basic Service
Subscribers: N.A.
Programming (received off-air): KFJX (FOX) Pittsburg; KOAM-TV (CBS) Pittsburg; KODE-TV (ABC) Joplin; KOZJ (PBS) Joplin; KSNF (NBC) Joplin.

Digital Basic Service
Subscribers: 1,479.
Programming (received off-air): KCTV (CBS) Kansas City; KFJX (FOX) Pittsburg; KMCI-TV (Bounce TV, Escape, IND) Lawrence; KOAM-TV (CBS) Pittsburg; KODE-TV (ABC) Joplin; KOZJ (PBS) Joplin; KSHB-TV (COZI TV, Grit, NBC) Kansas City; KSNF (NBC) Joplin; KTWU (PBS) Topeka; WDAF-TV (Antenna TV, FOX) Kansas City.
Programming (via satellite): A&E; AMC; American Heroes Channel; Animal Planet; BBC America; BET; Bloomberg Television; Boomerang; Bravo; Cartoon Network; CMT; CNBC; CNN; Comedy Central; C-SPAN; C-SPAN 2; Discovery Channel; Discovery Family; Disney Channel; Disney XD; DIY Network; E! HD; ESPN; ESPN Classic; ESPN2; ESPNews; EWTN Global Catholic Network; Food Network; Fox News Channel; FOX Soccer PLUS; Fox Sports 1; FOX Sports Midwest; Freeform; FSN Digital Atlantic; FSN Digital Central; FSN Digital Pacific; FX; Golf Channel; Great American Country; GSN; Hallmark Channel; HGTV; History; HLN; HSN; INSP; Investigation Discovery; Lifetime; LMN; MSNBC; MTV; National Geographic Channel; NBCSN; Nickelodeon; Outdoor Channel; OWN: Oprah Winfrey Network; Oxygen; Planet Green; QVC; RFD-TV; Science Channel; Spike TV; Syfy; TBS; The Weather Channel; TLC; TNT; Travel Channel; Trinity Broadcasting Network (TBN); truTV; Turner Classic Movies; TV Land; USA Network; VH1; WE tv; WGN America.
Fee: $73.99 monthly.

Digital Pay Service 1
Pay Units: N.A.
Programming (via satellite): Cinemax (multiplexed); Flix; HBO (multiplexed); Showtime (multiplexed); Starz (multiplexed); The Movie Channel.
Fee: $12.99 -$42.99.

Internet Service
Operational: Yes.
Fee: $29.95-$59.99 monthly.

Telephone Service
Digital: Operational
General Manager: Craig Wilbert.
Ownership: Craw-Kan Telephone Cooperative.

GIRARD—Formerly served by Craw-Kan Telephone Co-op. No longer in operation. ICA: KS0470.

GLASCO—Formerly served by Cunningham Cable TV. No longer in operation. ICA: KS0186.

GLEN ELDER—Cunningham Cable, 220 West Main St, Glen Elder, KS 67446-9795. Phones: 800-287-8495; 785-545-3215. E-mail: brent@ctctelephony.tv. Web Site: http://cunninghamtelephoneandcable.com. Also serves Belleville, Beloit, Cawker City, Concordia, Downs, Formoso, Jamestown, Jewell, Mankato, Mitchell County (portions), Randall & Scandia. ICA: KS0228.
TV Market Ranking: Below 100 (Belleville, Formoso, Jamestown, Jewell, Mankato, Randall, Scandia); Outside TV Markets (Beloit, Cawker City, Concordia, Downs, GLEN ELDER, Mitchell County (portions)). Franchise award date: N.A. Franchise expiration date: N.A. Began: July 1, 1977.
Channel capacity: N.A. Channels available but not in use: N.A.

Basic Service
Subscribers: 1,508.
Programming (received off-air): KAKE (ABC, MeTV) Wichita; KBSH-DT (CBS) Hays; KGIN (CBS, MNT, NBC) Grand Island; KHGI-TV (ABC) Kearney; KNHL (IND) Hastings; KOOD (PBS) Hays; KSHB-TV (COZI TV, Grit, NBC) Kansas City; KSNB-TV (MeTV, MNT, NBC) Superior; KSNC (NBC) Great Bend; WIBW-TV (CBS, MeTV, MNT) Topeka.
Programming (via satellite): The Weather Channel.
Fee: $31.95 monthly.

Expanded Basic Service 1
Subscribers: N.A.
Programming (received off-air): KSAS-TV (Antenna TV, FOX) Wichita.
Programming (via satellite): A&E; AMC; Animal Planet; Cartoon Network; CMT; CNBC; CNN; Comedy Central; C-SPAN; Discovery Channel; Disney Channel; E! HD; ESPN; ESPN Classic; ESPN2; EWTN Global Catholic Network; Food Network; Fox News Channel; Fox Sports 1; FOX Sports Midwest; Freeform; FX; Great American Country; Hallmark Channel; Hallmark Movies & Mysteries; HGTV; History; HLN; ION Television; Lifetime; MTV; MyNetworkTV; National Geographic Channel; Nickelodeon; Outdoor Channel; QVC; RFD-TV; Spike TV; Syfy; TBS; TLC; TNT; Travel Channel; Trinity Broadcasting Network (TBN); Turner Classic Movies; TV Land; USA Network; VH1; WGN America.
Fee: $60.95 monthly.

Digital Basic Service
Subscribers: 144.
Programming (via satellite): BBC America; Bloomberg Television; Bravo; Cloo; Discovery Digital Networks; Disney XD; DMX Music; ESPN Classic; ESPN2; ESPNews; EVINE Live; Fox Sports 1; FSN Digital Atlantic; FSN Digital Central; FSN Digital Pacific; Fuse; FXM; FYI; Golf Channel; Great American Country; GSN; HGTV; History; History International; IFC; LMN; National Geographic Channel; NBCSN; Nick Jr.; Nicktoons; Outdoor Channel; Syfy; TeenNick; Trinity Broadcasting Network (TBN); Turner Classic Movies; WE tv.
Fee: $31.95 monthly.

Digital Pay Service 1
Pay Units: N.A.
Programming (via satellite): Cinemax (multiplexed); Flix; HBO (multiplexed); Showtime (multiplexed); Starz (multiplexed); Starz Encore (multiplexed); The Movie Channel (multiplexed).
Fee: $10.95 monthly (Cinemax), $12.95 monthly (Starz/Encore), $13.95 monthly (Showtime/TMC/Flix), $16.95 monthly (HBO), $22.95 monthly (Showtime/Starz), $23.95 monthly (Cinemax/HBO).

Pay-Per-View
ESPN Now (delivered digitally); Sports PPV (delivered digitally); iN DEMAND (delivered digitally).

Internet Service
Operational: Yes.
Fee: $29.95-$79.95 monthly.

Telephone Service
Analog: Operational
Fee: $16.75-$16.95 monthly
Miles of Plant: 107.0 (coaxial); None (fiber optic).
Owner & President: John Cunningham. Vice President & General Manager: Brent Cunningham. Vice President & Outside Plant Supervisor: Terry Cunningham. Advertising/Marketing Director: Megan Duskie. Billing Director: Denise Jackson. Cable Plant Supervisor: Jeremy Easter.
Ownership: Cunningham Communications (MSO).

GOESSEL—Mid-Kansas Cable Services Inc. Now served by MOUNDRIDGE, KS [KS0133]. ICA: KS0379.

GOFF—Formerly served by Rainbow Communications. No longer in operation. ICA: KS0340.

GOODLAND—Eagle Communications, 2703 Hall St, Ste 15, PO Box 817, Hays, KS 67601. Phones: 785-263-2529; 785-625-5910; 785-625-4000 (Corporate office); 785-899-3371. Fax: 785-625-8030. Web Site: http://www.eaglecom.net. ICA: KS0045.
TV Market Ranking: Below 100 (GOODLAND). Franchise award date: October 5, 1965. Franchise expiration date: N.A. Began: November 1, 1966.
Channel capacity: N.A. Channels available but not in use: N.A.

Basic Service
Subscribers: 121.
Programming (received off-air): KBSL-DT (CBS) Goodland; KLBY (ABC) Colby; KOOD (PBS) Hays; KSAS-TV (Antenna TV, FOX) Wichita; KSCW-DT (CW, Decades) Wichita; KSNK (NBC) McCook; 10 FMs.
Programming (via satellite): C-SPAN; QVC; The Weather Channel; WGN America.
Programming (via translator): KUSA (NBC, WeatherNation) Denver; KWGN-TV (CW, This TV) Denver.
Fee: $24.95 installation; $69.95 monthly.

Expanded Basic Service 1
Subscribers: N.A.
Programming (via satellite): A&E; Animal Planet; Bravo; CMT; CNBC; CNN; Comedy Central; Discovery Channel; Discovery Life Channel; Disney Channel; Disney XD; E! HD; ESPN; ESPN2; ESPNews; EWTN Global Catholic Network; Food Network; Fox News Channel; Freeform; FX; FXM; Hallmark Channel; HGTV; History; HLN; Lifetime; MSNBC; MTV; NFL Network; Nickelodeon; Root Sports Rocky Mountain; Spike TV; Syfy; TBS; TLC; TNT; Travel Channel; TV Land; Univision Studios; USA Network; VH1.
Fee: $20.50 monthly.

Digital Basic Service
Subscribers: N.A.
Programming (via satellite): BBC America; Bloomberg Television; Bravo; Cloo; CMT; Destination America; Discovery Kids Channel; DMX Music; ESPN Classic; ESPNews; Fox Sports 1; Fuse; FYI; Golf Channel; GSN; HGTV; History International; IFC; Investigation Discovery; LMN; MTV Classic; MTV2; National Geographic Channel; NBCSN; Nick Jr.; Nicktoons; Outdoor Chan-

Cable Systems—Kansas

nel; OWN: Oprah Winfrey Network; Science Channel; TeenNick; Trinity Broadcasting Network (TBN); Turner Classic Movies; WE tv.
Pay Service 1
Pay Units: N.A.
Programming (via satellite): HBO.
Fee: $11.95 monthly.
Digital Pay Service 1
Pay Units: N.A.
Programming (via satellite): Cinemax (multiplexed); HBO (multiplexed); Showtime; Starz (multiplexed); Starz Encore (multiplexed); The Movie Channel (multiplexed).
Fee: $11.95 monthly (Cinemax, Showtime, TMC, HBO or Starz/Encore).
Video-On-Demand: No
Pay-Per-View
iN DEMAND (delivered digitally); Spice Xcess (delivered digitally); Fresh (delivered digitally); Playboy TV (delivered digitally); Club Jenna (delivered digitally).
Internet Service
Operational: Yes.
Broadband Service: Eagle Internet.
Fee: $13.00 monthly.
Telephone Service
Analog: Not Operational
Digital: Operational
Fee: $23.00 monthly
Miles of Plant: 35.0 (coaxial); None (fiber optic). Homes passed: 1,700.
Chief Operating Officer: Kurt K. David. General Manager: Travis Kohlrus. Chief Technician: Jim Gall. Ad Sales Manager: Mike Koerner.
Ownership: Eagle Communications Inc. (MSO).

GOODLAND—S&T Cable. Now served by BREWSTER, KS [KS0315]. ICA: KS0471.

GORHAM—Gorham Tele-Com (formerly Nex-Tech). This cable system has converted to IPTV. See GORHAM, KS [KS5164]. ICA: KS0380.

GORHAM—Gorham Tele-Com. Formerly [KS0380]. This cable system has converted to IPTV, 100 Market St, PO Box 235, Gorham, KS 67640-0235. Phone: 785-637-5300. Fax: 785-637-5590. E-mail: gtc@gorhamtel.com. Web Site: http://gorhamtel.com. Also serves Luray, Paradise & Waldo. ICA: KS5164.
TV Market Ranking: Outside TV Markets (Luray).
Channel capacity: N.A. Channels available but not in use: N.A.
Basic
Subscribers: 140.
Fee: $30.00 installation; $57.95 monthly. Includes 83 SD channels, 32 HD channels & 2 set top boxes.
Expanded Basic
Subscribers: 28.
Fee: $69.95 monthly. Includes 109 SD channels, 33 HD channels, 50 music channels & 2 set top boxes.
Spanish
Subscribers: N.A.
Fee: $9.95 monthly. Includes 7 channels.
Cinemax
Subscribers: N.A.
Fee: $9.95 monthly. Includes 8 SD channels & 8 HD channels.
HBO
Subscribers: N.A.
Fee: $16.95 monthly. Includes 6 SD channels & 6 HD channels.
Showtime/TMC/Flix
Subscribers: N.A.
Fee: $15.95 monthly. Includes 13 SD channels & 5 HD channels.

Starz/Encore
Subscribers: N.A.
Fee: $15.95 monthly. Includes 13 SD & 5 HD channels.
Internet Service
Operational: Yes.
Fee: $30.00 installation; $39.95-$89.95 monthly.
Telephone Service
Digital: Operational
Fee: $16.75-$17.80 monthly
President: Michael Murphy. Secretary-Treasurer: Tonya Murphy.
Ownership: Gorham Telephone Co.

GRAINFIELD—Nex-Tech. Formerly [KS0381]. This cable system has converted to IPTV, 2418 Vine St, Hays, KS 67601. Phones: 877-625-7872; 785-625-7070. Fax: 785-625-4479. E-mail: webmaster@nex-tech.com. Web Site: http://www.nex-tech.com. Also serves Collyer, Gove, Park & Quinter. ICA: KS5071.
TV Market Ranking: Franchise award date: April 27, 2007. Franchise expiration date: N.A. Began: N.A.
Channel capacity: N.A. Channels available but not in use: N.A.
Essentials
Subscribers: 547.
Fee: $30.00 installation; $24.95 monthly. Includes 50 channels.
Premiere
Subscribers: 518.
Fee: $61.95 monthly. Includes 118 channels plus music channels.
HD
Subscribers: N.A.
Fee: $11.95 monthly. Includes 72+ channels.
Sports & Entertainment
Subscribers: N.A.
Fee: $12.95 monthly. Includes 34 channels.
Cinemax
Subscribers: N.A.
Fee: $8.95 monthly. Includes 8 channels.
HBO
Subscribers: N.A.
Fee: $14.95 monthly. Includes 12 channels.
Showtime/TMC
Subscribers: N.A.
Fee: $13.95 monthly. Includes 16 channels.
Starz/Encore
Subscribers: N.A.
Fee: $10.95 monthly. Includes 18 channels.
Video-On-Demand: Yes
Internet Service
Operational: Yes.
Fee: $22.95-$42.95 monthly.
Telephone Service
Digital: Operational
Fee: $16.75 monthly
Chief Executive Officer & General Manager: Larry Sevier. Video Solutions Manager: Scott Roe.
Ownership: Nex-Tech.

GRAINFIELD—Nex-Tech. This cable system has converted to IPTV. See GRAINFIELD, KS [KS5071]. ICA: KS0381.

GRANTVILLE—Formerly served by Cox Communications. No longer in operation. ICA: KS0224.

GREAT BEND—Cox Communications, 6205 Peachtree Dunwoody Rd, 12th Floor, Atlanta, GA 30328. Phone: 404-269-6590. Web Site: http://www.cox.com. Also serves Barton County, Hoisington, Larned, Lyons, Rice County & Sterling. ICA: KS0012. **Note:** This system is an overbuild.

TV Market Ranking: 67 (Lyons, Rice County, Sterling); Below 100 (Barton County, GREAT BEND, Hoisington, Larned). Franchise award date: January 18, 1968. Franchise expiration date: N.A. Began: January 18, 1968.
Channel capacity: N.A. Channels available but not in use: N.A.
Basic Service
Subscribers: 6,083.
Programming (received off-air): KAKE (ABC, MeTV) Wichita; KBSH-DT (CBS) Hays; KOOD (PBS) Hays; KPTS (PBS) Hutchinson; KSAS-TV (Antenna TV, FOX) Wichita; KSCW-DT (CW, Decades) Wichita; KSNC (NBC) Great Bend; KWCH-DT (CBS) Hutchinson; 12 FMs.
Programming (via satellite): C-SPAN; C-SPAN 2; Pop; The Weather Channel; WGN America.
Fee: $29.95 installation; $21.99 monthly.
Expanded Basic Service 1
Subscribers: N.A.
Programming (via satellite): A&E; AMC; Animal Planet; BET; Cartoon Network; CMT; CNBC; CNN; Comedy Central; Discovery Channel; Discovery Life Channel; Disney Channel; E! HD; ESPN; ESPN2; EVINE Live; EWTN Global Catholic Network; Food Network; Fox News Channel; Fox Sports 1; FOX Sports Midwest; Freeform; FX; Hallmark Channel; HGTV; History; HLN; INSP; ION Television; Lifetime; MSNBC; MTV; Nickelodeon; QVC; Spike TV; Syfy; TBS; TLC; TNT; Travel Channel; truTV; Turner Classic Movies; TV Land; Univision Studios; USA Network; VH1.
Fee: $33.68 monthly.
Digital Basic Service
Subscribers: N.A.
Programming (via satellite): BBC America; Bloomberg Television; Discovery Digital Networks; Disney XD; DMX Music; ESPN Classic; ESPNews; FYI; Golf Channel; Great American Country; GSN; History International; HITS (Headend In The Sky); IFC; LMN; NBA TV; NBCSN; Nick 2; Nick Jr.; Outdoor Channel; Oxygen; Sundance TV; TeenNick.
Digital Pay Service 1
Pay Units: N.A.
Programming (via satellite): Cinemax (multiplexed); DMX Music; HBO (multiplexed); Showtime (multiplexed); Starz (multiplexed); Starz Encore (multiplexed).
Fee: $12.95 monthly (each).
Video-On-Demand: No
Pay-Per-View
iN DEMAND (delivered digitally).
Internet Service
Operational: Yes.
Subscribers: 4,462.
Broadband Service: Cox High Speed Internet.
Fee: $19.99-$59.99 monthly; $15.00 modem lease; $259.00 modem purchase.
Telephone Service
Digital: Operational
Subscribers: 2,990.
Fee: $15.95-$48.95 monthly

Miles of Plant: 355.0 (coaxial); 272.0 (fiber optic). Homes passed: 17,135. Homes passed included in Wichita.
Vice President & General Manager: Kimberly Edmonds. Vice President, Engineering: Nick DiPonzio. Vice President, Tax: Mary Vickers. Vice President, Marketing: Tony Matthews. Marketing Director: Tina Gabbard. Public Affairs Director: Sarah Kauffman.
Ownership: Cox Communications Inc. (MSO).

GREEN—Formerly served by Eagle Communications. No longer in operation. ICA: KS0464.

GREENLEAF—Formerly served by Allegiance Communications. No longer in operation. ICA: KS0246.

GREENSBURG—Formerly served by Allegiance Communications. No longer in operation. ICA: KS0110.

GYPSUM—Home Communications Inc. This cable system has converted to IPTV. Now served by GALVA, KS [KS5068]. ICA: KS0383.

HADDAM—Formerly served by Westcom. No longer in operation. ICA: KS0303.

HAMILTON—Mediacom, 901 North College Ave, Columbia, MO 65201. Phones: 845-695-2762; 573-443-1536. Fax: 417-883-0265. Web Site: http://www.mediacomcable.com. ICA: KS0273.
TV Market Ranking: Outside TV Markets (HAMILTON).
Channel capacity: N.A. Channels available but not in use: N.A.
Basic Service
Subscribers: 35.
Fee: $42.00 monthly.
Vice President, Financial Reporting: Kenneth J. Kohrs.
Ownership: Mediacom LLC (MSO).

HANOVER—Blue Valley Tele-Communications. Now served by AXTELL (formerly Frankfort & Home), KS [KS0424]. ICA: KS0179.

HANSTON—United Communications Assn. Inc. Now served by CIMARRON, KS [KS0126]. ICA: KS0291.

HARPER—Formerly served by Allegiance Communications. No longer in operation. ICA: KS0121.

HARTFORD—Formerly served by Zito Media. No longer in operation. ICA: KS0245.

HARVEYVILLE—Formerly served by Galaxy Cablevision. No longer in operation. ICA: KS0297.

HAVEN—Formerly served by Allegiance Communications. No longer in operation. ICA: KS0163.

Kansas—Cable Systems

HAVENSVILLE—Formerly served by Blue Valley Tele-Communications. No longer in operation. ICA: KS5058.

HAVENSVILLE—Formerly served by Rainbow Communications. No longer in operation. ICA: KS0465.

HAVILAND—Haviland Cable-Vision, 104 North Main St, PO Box 308, Haviland, KS 67059-0308. Phones: 800-339-8052; 620-862-5211. Fax: 620-862-5204. Web Site: http://www.havilandtelco.com. ICA: KS0235.
TV Market Ranking: Outside TV Markets (HAVILAND). Franchise award date: N.A. Franchise expiration date: N.A. Began: April 1, 1975.
Channel capacity: N.A. Channels available but not in use: N.A.
Basic Service
Subscribers: 43.
Programming (received off-air): KAKE (ABC, MeTV) Wichita; KPTS (PBS) Hutchinson; KSAS-TV (Antenna TV, FOX) Wichita; KSNC (NBC) Great Bend; KWCH-DT (CBS) Hutchinson; allband FM.
Programming (via satellite): CNN; Discovery Channel; Disney Channel; ESPN; Freeform; Hallmark Channel; Local Cable Weather; Nickelodeon; Spike TV; Syfy; TBS; TLC; TNT; Travel Channel; TV Land; USA Network.
Fee: $10.00 installation; $25.00 monthly.
Video-On-Demand: No
Internet Service
Operational: No, DSL.
Telephone Service
Analog: Operational
Miles of Plant: 6.0 (coaxial); None (fiber optic). Homes passed: 224.
President: Gene Morris. Vice President, Operations: Mark Wade. Chief Technician: Dan King.
Ownership: Haviland Telephone Co.

HAYS—Eagle Communications, 2703 Hall St, Ste 15, PO Box 817, Hays, KS 67601. Phones: 785-263-2529; 785-632-3118; 785-625-4000 (Corporate office); 785-625-5910. Fax: 785-625-3465. E-mail: gary.shorman@eaglecom.net. Web Site: http://www.eaglecom.net. Also serves Ellis, Munjor, Russell, Victoria & Wakeeney. ICA: KS0384.
TV Market Ranking: Below 100 (Ellis, HAYS, Munjor, Victoria, Russell, Wakeeney). Franchise award date: February 1, 1967. Franchise expiration date: N.A. Began: February 1, 1967.
Channel capacity: N.A. Channels available but not in use: N.A.
Basic Service
Subscribers: 3,366. Commercial subscribers: 150.
Programming (received off-air): KAKE (ABC, MeTV) Wichita; KBSH-DT (CBS) Hays; KMTW (MNT, The Country Network) Hutchinson; KOOD (PBS) Hays; KSAS-TV (Antenna TV, FOX) Wichita; KSCW-DT (CW, Decades) Wichita; KSNC (NBC) Great Bend; 11 FMs.
Programming (via satellite): C-SPAN; Pop; QVC; The Weather Channel; WGN America.
Fee: $29.95 installation; $69.95 monthly.
Expanded Basic Service 1
Subscribers: N.A.
Programming (via satellite): A&E; AMC; Animal Planet; Boomerang; Bravo; Cartoon Network; CMT; CNBC; CNN; Comedy Central; Discovery Channel; Discovery Life Channel; Disney Channel; Disney XD; DIY Network; E! HD; ESPN; ESPN Classic; ESPN2; ESPNews; EWTN Global Catholic Network; Food Network; Fox News Channel; FOX Sports Midwest; Freeform; FX; FXM; Hallmark Channel; HGTV; History; HLN; Lifetime; MSNBC; MTV; National Geographic Channel; NFL Network; Nickelodeon; Spike TV; Syfy; TBS; TLC; TNT; Travel Channel; truTV; TV Land; USA Network; VH1.
Fee: $30.00 monthly.
Digital Basic Service
Subscribers: N.A.
Programming (via satellite): BBC America; Bloomberg Television; Bravo; Church Channel; Cloo; CMT; Cooking Channel; Destination America; Discovery Kids Channel; Disney XD; DMX Music; ESPN Classic; ESPN2; ESPNews; ESPNU; Fox Business Network; FOX College Sports Central; FOX College Sports Pacific; Fox Sports 1; Fuse; FXM; FYI; Golf Channel; Great American Country; GSN; HGTV; History; History International; IFC; Investigation Discovery; JUCE TV; LMN; MTV; MTV Classic; MTV Hits; MTV Jams; MTV2; National Geographic Channel; NBCSN; Nick Jr.; Nicktoons; Outdoor Channel; OWN: Oprah Winfrey Network; RFD-TV; Science Channel; Sprout; Syfy; TeenNick; The Word Network; Trinity Broadcasting Network (TBN); Turner Classic Movies; UP; VH1 Soul; WE tv.
Digital Expanded Basic Service
Subscribers: N.A.
Programming (via satellite): A&E HD; Animal Planet HD; Discovery Channel HD; ESPN HD; Food Network HD; HD Theater; HGTV HD; History HD; National Geographic Channel HD; NFL Network HD; Science HD; TBS HD; TLC HD; TNT HD; Universal HD.
Fee: $9.95 monthly.
Pay Service 1
Pay Units: N.A.
Programming (via satellite): Cinemax; HBO.
Fee: $11.95 monthly (each).
Digital Pay Service 1
Pay Units: N.A.
Programming (via satellite): Cinemax; Cinemax HD; HBO (multiplexed); HBO HD; Showtime (multiplexed); Showtime HD; Starz (multiplexed); Starz Encore (multiplexed); Starz HD; The Movie Channel (multiplexed); The Movie Channel HD.
Fee: $11.95 monthly (Cinemax, HBO, Starz/Encore or Showtime/TMC/Flix).
Video-On-Demand: No
Pay-Per-View
iN DEMAND (delivered digitally); Playboy TV (delivered digitally); Fresh (delivered digitally); Hot Choice (delivered digitally); Club Jenna (delivered digitally); Spice; Xcess (delivered digitally).
Internet Service
Operational: Yes.
Broadband Service: Eagle Internet.
Fee: $19.95 monthly.
Telephone Service
Analog: Not Operational
Digital: Operational
Fee: $18.00 monthly
Miles of Plant: 129.0 (coaxial); 9.0 (fiber optic). Homes passed: 11,297.
Chief Operating Officer: Kurt K. David. General Manager: Travis Kohlrus. Chief Technician: Jim Gall. Ad Sales Manager: Mike Koerner.
Ownership: Eagle Communications Inc. (MSO).

HEALY—S&T Cable. Now served by DIGHTON, KS [KS0144]. ICA: KS0385.

HERINGTON—Vyve Broadband, 4 International Dr, Ste 330, Rye Brook, NY 10573. Phones: 800-937-1397; 405-395-1131; 405-275-6923. Web Site: http://vyvebroadband.com. Also serves Dickinson County (portions). ICA: KS0054.
TV Market Ranking: Below 100 (Dickinson County (portions) (portions)); Outside TV Markets (Dickinson County (portions) (portions), HERINGTON). Franchise award date: May 14, 1968. Franchise expiration date: N.A. Began: April 1, 1969.
Channel capacity: N.A. Channels available but not in use: N.A.
Basic Service
Subscribers: 104. Commercial subscribers: 14.
Programming (received off-air): KAKE (ABC, MeTV) Wichita; KPTS (PBS) Hutchinson; KSAS-TV (Antenna TV, FOX) Wichita; KSNW (NBC) Wichita; KTKA-TV (ABC, CW) Topeka; KWCH-DT (CBS) Hutchinson; WIBW-TV (CBS, MeTV, MNT) Topeka; 7 FMs.
Programming (via satellite): A&E; AMC; Animal Planet; Cartoon Network; CMT; CNN; Comedy Central; C-SPAN; CW PLUS; Discovery Channel; Disney Channel; ESPN; ESPN Classic; ESPN2; Food Network; Fox News Channel; FOX Sports Midwest; Freeform; Hallmark Channel; HGTV; History; HLN; Lifetime; LMN; MTV; NFL Network; Nickelodeon; Spike TV; Syfy; TBS; The Weather Channel; TLC; TNT; Travel Channel; TV Land; USA Network; WGN America.
Fee: $64.95 installation; $67.75 monthly.
Digital Basic Service
Subscribers: N.A.
Programming (via satellite): 52MX; BBC America; Bloomberg Television; Bravo; Cine Mexicano; Cinelatino; Cloo; CMT; CNN en Espanol; Destination America; Discovery Kids Channel; Discovery Life Channel; Disney XD; DMX Music; ESPN Classic; ESPN2; ESPNews; EVINE Live; Flix; FOX College Sports Central; FOX College Sports Pacific; Fox Deportes; Fox Sports 1; Fuse; FXM; FYI; Golf Channel; Great American Country; GSN; HGTV; History; History en Espanol; History International; IFC; Investigation Discovery; LMN; MTV Classic; MTV Hits; MTV2; National Geographic Channel; NBCSN; Nick Jr.; Nicktoons; Outdoor Channel; Ovation; OWN: Oprah Winfrey Network; Science Channel; Starz Encore (multiplexed); Sundance TV; Syfy; TeenNick; The Word Network; Toon Disney en Espanol; Tr3s; Trinity Broadcasting Network (TBN); Turner Classic Movies; VH1 Soul; WE tv.

Pay Service 1
Pay Units: N.A.
Programming (via satellite): Cinemax; HBO.
Fee: $14.95 installation; $8.95 monthly (each).
Digital Pay Service 1
Pay Units: N.A.
Programming (via satellite): Cinemax (multiplexed); HBO (multiplexed); Showtime (multiplexed); Starz (multiplexed); The Movie Channel (multiplexed).
Video-On-Demand: No
Pay-Per-View
iN DEMAND (delivered digitally); Hot Choice (delivered digitally); Playboy TV (delivered digitally); Fresh (delivered digitally); Shorteez (delivered digitally).
Internet Service
Operational: Yes.
Broadband Service: Cox High Speed Internet.
Fee: $24.95 installation; $39.95 monthly.
Telephone Service
Digital: Operational
Miles of Plant: 21.0 (coaxial); None (fiber optic). Homes passed: 1,633.
Chief Executive Officer: Bill Haggarty. Regional Vice President: Andrew Dearth. Vice President, Marketing: Tracy Bass. Senior Vice President, Financial Planning: Daniel White.
Ownership: Vyve Broadband LLC (MSO).

HERNDON—Formerly served by Pinpoint Cable TV. No longer in operation. ICA: KS0304.

HIAWATHA—Rainbow Communications, 608 Main St, PO Box 147, Everest, KS 66424. Phones: 800-892-0163; 785-548-7511. Fax: 785-548-7517. Web Site: http://www.rainbowtel.net. Also serves Elwood, Everest, Fairview, Highland, Horton, Robinson, Sabetha, Seneca, Troy & Wathena. ICA: KS0059.
TV Market Ranking: Below 100 (Elwood, Everest, Highland, Robinson, Troy, Wathena); Outside TV Markets (Fairview, HIAWATHA, Horton, Sabetha, Seneca). Franchise award date: January 1, 1965. Franchise expiration date: N.A. Began: November 1, 1966.
Channel capacity: N.A. Channels available but not in use: N.A.
Digital Basic Service
Subscribers: 4,168 Includes IPTV subscriber counts.
Programming (received off-air): KCPT (PBS) Kansas City; KCTV (CBS) Kansas City; KMBC-TV (ABC, MeTV) Kansas City; KPXE-TV (ION) Kansas City; KQTV (ABC) St. Joseph; KSHB-TV (COZI TV, Grit, NBC) Kansas City; KSNT (FOX, NBC) Topeka; KTKA-TV (ABC, CW) Topeka; KTWU (PBS) Topeka; WDAF-TV (Antenna TV, FOX) Kansas City; WIBW-TV (CBS, MeTV, MNT) Topeka; allband FM.
Programming (via satellite): QVC; The Weather Channel.
Fee: $29.95 installation; $37.00 monthly.
Digital Expanded Basic Service
Subscribers: N.A.
Programming (via satellite): A&E; AMC; Animal Planet; CNN; Comedy Central; C-SPAN; Discovery Channel; Disney Channel; ESPN; ESPN2; Food Network; FOX Sports Networks; Freeform; Great American Country; HGTV; History; HLN; Lifetime; MTV; Nickelodeon; Spike TV; Syfy; TBS; TLC; TNT; Trinity Broadcasting Network (TBN); USA Network; VH1; WGN America.
Fee: $59.50 monthly.

Cable Systems—Kansas

Digital Expanded Basic Service 2
Subscribers: N.A.
Programming (via satellite): BBC America; Bloomberg Television; Discovery Digital Networks; DMX Music; ESPN Classic; ESPNews; Fox Sports 1; FXM; FYI; Golf Channel; GSN; History; LMN; National Geographic Channel; Nick Jr.; Outdoor Channel; TeenNick; WE tv.
Fee: $74.50 monthly.

Digital Pay Service 1
Pay Units: N.A.
Programming (via satellite): Cinemax (multiplexed); HBO (multiplexed); Showtime (multiplexed); Starz (multiplexed); Starz Encore (multiplexed); The Movie Channel (multiplexed).
Fee: $14.00 monthly (Cinemax, Showtime/TMC or Starz/Encore), $16.00 monthly (HBO).

Video-On-Demand: No

Pay-Per-View
ESPN Now (delivered digitally); Hot Choice (delivered digitally); iN DEMAND (delivered digitally); Playboy TV (delivered digitally); Fresh (delivered digitally).

Internet Service
Operational: Yes.
Fee: $44.95-$64.95 monthly.

Telephone Service
Digital: Operational
Miles of Plant: 74.0 (coaxial); 2.0 (fiber optic). Homes passed: 4,891.
General Manager: James Lednicky. Assistant General Manager: Jason Smith. Accounting & Billing Manager: Beverly Armstrong. Network Operations Manager: Chris McMullen. Marketing Manager: Jackie Petersen. Customer Service Manager: Vicky Ptomey. Plant Manager: Pat Streeter. Purchasing & Programming Coordinator: Kelly Beach.
Ownership: Rainbow Communications (MSO).

HILL CITY—Nex-Tech, 2418 Vine St, Hays, KS 67601. Phones: 877-625-7872; 785-625-7070. Fax: 785-625-4479. E-mail: webmaster@nex-tech.com. Web Site: http://www.nex-tech.com. ICA: KS0447.
Channel capacity: N.A. Channels available but not in use: N.A.

Basic Service
Subscribers: 996.
Programming (received off-air): KAKE (ABC, MeTV) Wichita; KBSH-DT (CBS) Hays; KMTW (MNT, The Country Network) Hutchinson; KOOD (PBS) Hays; KSAS-TV (Antenna TV, FOX) Wichita; KSCW-DT (CW, Decades) Wichita; KSNC (NBC) Great Bend; KSNK (NBC) McCook.
Programming (via satellite): C-SPAN; EWTN Global Catholic Network; QVC; WGN America.
Fee: $24.95 monthly.

Expanded Basic Service 1
Subscribers: N.A.
Programming (via satellite): Animal Planet; CNBC; CNN; E! HD; ESPN; ESPN Classic; ESPN2; FOX Sports Midwest; FX; HGTV; HLN; Lifetime; NBCSN; Outdoor Channel; Spike TV; Travel Channel.
Fee: $61.95 monthly.

Internet Service
Operational: Yes.
Fee: $22.95-$32.95 monthly.

Telephone Service
Analog: Operational
Fee: $16.75 monthly

Chief Executive Officer & General Manager: Larry Sevier. Video Solutions Manager: Scott Roe.
Ownership: Nex-Tech.

HOLTON—Giant Communications, 418 West 5th St, Ste C, Holton, KS 66436. Phones: 620-672-9991; 785-362-2532; 800-346-9084; 785-362-9331. Fax: 785-362-2144. E-mail: billbarton@giantcomm.net. Web Site: http://www.giantcomm.net. Also serves Circleville, Hoyt, Mayetta, McLouth, Netawaka, Nortonville, Oskaloosa, Ozawkie, Valley Falls, Wetmore & Winchester. ICA: KS0066.
TV Market Ranking: Below 100 (Circleville, HOLTON, Netawaka, Oskaloosa, Hoyt, Mayetta, McLouth, Nortonville, Ozawkie, Valley Falls, Winchester; Outside TV Markets (Wetmore). Franchise award date: N.A. Franchise expiration date: N.A. Began: May 15, 1979.
Channel capacity: N.A. Channels available but not in use: N.A.

Basic Service
Subscribers: 1,028.
Programming (received off-air): KCWE (CW, Movies!, This TV) Kansas City; KSNT (FOX, NBC) Topeka; KTKA-TV (ABC, CW) Topeka; KTMJ-CD (Escape, FOX) Topeka; KTWU (PBS) Topeka; WDAF-TV (Antenna TV, FOX) Kansas City; WIBW-TV (CBS, MeTV, MNT) Topeka.
Programming (via satellite): A&E; AMC; Animal Planet; CMT; CNN; Comedy Central; Discovery Channel; Disney Channel; Disney XD; DIY Network; ESPN Classic; ESPN2; EWTN Global Catholic Network; Food Network; Fox News Channel; Fox Sports 1; FOX Sports Midwest; Freeform; Great American Country; Hallmark Channel; HGTV; History; HLN; Lifetime; MSNBC; MTV; National Geographic Channel; Nickelodeon; Spike TV; Syfy; TBS; The Weather Channel; TLC; TNT; Travel Channel; Trinity Broadcasting Network (TBN); truTV; Turner Classic Movies; TV Land; USA Network; VH1; WGN America.
Fee: $49.95 installation; $57.95 monthly; $4.00 converter.

Digital Basic Service
Subscribers: N.A.
Programming (via satellite): BBC America; Bloomberg Television; Discovery Life Channel; DMX Music; ESPN Classic; ESPNews; Fuse; FXM; FYI; Golf Channel; GSN; History International; IFC; National Geographic Channel; NBCSN; Nick Jr.; Nicktoons; Syfy; TeenNick; Turner Classic Movies; WE tv.

Pay Service 1
Pay Units: N.A.
Programming (via satellite): Cinemax; HBO; Showtime; The Movie Channel.
Fee: $8.95 monthly (Cinemax), $11.95 monthly (HBO, Showtime or TMC).

Digital Pay Service 1
Pay Units: N.A.
Programming (via satellite): Cinemax (multiplexed); HBO (multiplexed); Showtime (multiplexed); Starz (multiplexed); Starz Encore (multiplexed); The Movie Channel (multiplexed).

Video-On-Demand: No

Pay-Per-View
special events (delivered digitally).

Internet Service
Operational: Yes, Dial-up.
Subscribers: 1,033.
Broadband Service: WildBlue Satellite Internet.
Fee: $34.95-$64.95 monthly.

Telephone Service
Digital: Operational
Subscribers: 140.

Miles of Plant: 100.0 (coaxial); 135.0 (fiber optic). Homes passed: 4,816.
President: Mark Wade. Chief Tech Engineer: Bill Barton. Headend Technician: Jay Stewart.; Julian Rodriguez.
Ownership: Giant Communications (MSO).

HOLYROOD—H&B Communications. This cable system has converted to IPTV. See HOLYROOD, KS [KS5105]. ICA: KS0097.

HOLYROOD—H&B Communications. This system has converted to IPTV, 108 North Main St, Holyrood, KS 67450. Phones: 785-252-3598; 800-432-8296; 785-252-4000. Fax: 785-252-3229. E-mail: hbsupport@hbcomm.net; commentsquestions@hbcomm.net. Web Site: http://www.hbcomm.net. Also serves Bushton, Bushton (rural), Claflin, Dorrance (rural), Dubuque, Ellinwood, Hitschman & Odin. ICA: KS5105.
Channel capacity: N.A. Channels available but not in use: N.A.

Limited Basic
Subscribers: N.A.
Fee: $30.36-$31.71 monthly. Includes 65 channels.

Limited Plus
Subscribers: N.A.
Fee: $57.01-$62.93 monthly. Includes 144 channels.

Digital Basic
Subscribers: N.A.
Fee: $62.76-$69.99 monthly. Includes 178 channels.

Digital Value
Subscribers: N.A.
Fee: $69.26-$77.80 monthly. Includes 185 channels.

Digital Value & Sports
Subscribers: N.A.
Fee: $69.26-$77.80 monthly. Includes 192 channels.

Digital Value & Family
Subscribers: N.A.
Fee: $70.76-$77.95 monthly. Includes 191 channels.

Cinemax
Subscribers: N.A.
Fee: $11.95 monthly. Includes 4 channels.

Cinemax/HBO
Subscribers: N.A.
Fee: $16.95 monthly. Includes 10 channels.

Encore
Subscribers: N.A.
Fee: $7.95 monthly. Includes 7 channels.

HBO
Subscribers: N.A.
Fee: $16.95 monthly. Includes 6 channels.

Showtime/TMC
Subscribers: N.A.
Fee: $14.25 monthly. Includes 10 channels.

Starz
Subscribers: N.A.
Fee: $8.95 monthly. Includes 6 channels.

Internet Service
Operational: Yes.
Fee: $29.95-$69.95 monthly.

Telephone Service
Digital: Operational
President & General Manager: Robert Koch.
Ownership: H & B Cable Service Inc.

HOPE—Formerly served by Eagle Communications. No longer in operation. ICA: KS0386.

HOXIE—Eagle Communications, 2703 Hall St, Ste 15, PO Box 817, Hays, KS 67601. Phones: 785-263-2529; 785-625-5910; 785-675-2310 (Hoxie office); 785-625-4000 (Corporate office). Fax: 785-625-8030. Web Site: http://www.eaglecom.net. ICA: KS0137.
TV Market Ranking: Below 100 (HOXIE). Franchise award date: N.A. Franchise expiration date: N.A. Began: October 10, 1988.
Channel capacity: N.A. Channels available but not in use: N.A.

Basic Service
Subscribers: 21. Commercial subscribers: 4.
Programming (received off-air): KBSL-DT (CBS) Goodland; KLBY (ABC) Colby; KMTW (MNT, The Country Network) Hutchinson; KOOD (PBS) Hays; KSAS-TV (Antenna TV, FOX) Wichita; KSCW-DT (CW, Decades) Wichita; KSNK (NBC) McCook.
Programming (via satellite): C-SPAN; The Weather Channel; WGN America.
Fee: $24.95 installation; $69.95 monthly.

Expanded Basic Service 1
Subscribers: N.A.
Programming (via satellite): A&E; AMC; Animal Planet; CMT; CNBC; CNN; Comedy Central; Discovery Channel; Disney Channel; Disney XD; DIY Network; ESPN; ESPN2; ESPNews; EWTN Global Catholic Network; Food Network; Fox News Channel; FOX Sports Midwest; Freeform; FX; FXM; Great American Country; Hallmark Channel; HGTV; History; HLN; Lifetime; MTV; NFL Network; Nickelodeon; Outdoor Channel; Spike TV; Syfy; TBS; TLC; TNT; Travel Channel; Trinity Broadcasting Network (TBN); TV Land; USA Network; VH1.
Fee: $27.20 monthly.

Digital Basic Service
Subscribers: N.A.
Programming (via satellite): BBC America; Bloomberg Television; Cloo; CMT; Discovery Digital Networks; Disney XD; DMX Music; ESPN Classic; ESPN2; ESPNews; Fox Sports 1; Fuse; FXM; FYI; Golf Channel; HGTV; History; History International; IFC; LMN; National Geographic Channel; NBCSN; Nick Jr.; Nicktoons; Outdoor Channel; TeenNick; Trinity Broadcasting Network (TBN); Turner Classic Movies; WE tv.
Fee: $4.95 converter.

Digital Pay Service 1
Pay Units: N.A.
Programming (via satellite): Cinemax (multiplexed); HBO (multiplexed); Showtime (multiplexed); Starz (multiplexed); Starz Encore (multiplexed); The Movie Channel (multiplexed).
Fee: $14.95 monthly (Cinemax, HBO, Showtime/TMC, or Starz/Encore).

Video-On-Demand: No

Pay-Per-View
iN DEMAND (delivered digitally); Playboy TV (delivered digitally); Fresh (delivered digitally); Spice: Xcess (delivered digitally).

Kansas—Cable Systems

FULLY SEARCHABLE • CONTINUOUSLY UPDATED • DISCOUNT RATES FOR PRINT PURCHASERS

For more information call **800-771-9202** or visit **www.warren-news.com**

Internet Service
Operational: Yes. Began: December 31, 2004.
Broadband Service: Eagle Internet.
Fee: $19.95 monthly.
Telephone Service
Analog: Not Operational
Digital: Operational
Fee: $18.00 monthly
Miles of Plant: 11.0 (coaxial); None (fiber optic). Homes passed: 640.
Chief Operating Officer: Kurt K. David. General Manager: Travis Kohlrus. Chief Technician: Jim Gall. Ad Sales Manager: Mike Koerner.
Ownership: Eagle Communications Inc. (MSO).

HOYT—Giant Communications. Now served by HOLTON, KS [KS0066]. ICA: KS0281.

HUTCHINSON—Cox Communications. Now served by WICHITA, KS [KS0001]. ICA: KS0388.

INDEPENDENCE—Cable One, 2229 Broadway St, Ste 200, Parsons, KS 67357. Phones: 620-331-3699 (Ad sales); 800-794-9128; 620-331-3630. E-mail: mike.flood@cableone.net. Web Site: http://www.cableone.net. Also serves Montgomery County (portions) & Neodesha. ICA: KS0022.
TV Market Ranking: Outside TV Markets (INDEPENDENCE, Neodesha). Franchise award date: N.A. Franchise expiration date: N.A. Began: October 1, 1961.
Channel capacity: N.A. Channels available but not in use: N.A.
Basic Service
Subscribers: 2,335.
Programming (received off-air): KDOR-TV (TBN) Bartlesville; KFJX (FOX) Pittsburg; KMBC-TV (ABC, MeTV) Kansas City; KOAM-TV (CBS) Pittsburg.
Programming (via microwave): KJRH-TV (NBC) Tulsa; KOED-TV (PBS) Tulsa; KOKI-TV (FOX, MeTV) Tulsa; KOTV-DT (CBS, IND) Tulsa; KSNT (FOX, NBC) Topeka; KTUL (ABC, Antenna TV, Retro TV) Tulsa; KTWU (PBS) Topeka; WIBW-TV (CBS, MeTV, MNT) Topeka.
Programming (via satellite): BET; C-SPAN; C-SPAN 2; Pop; QVC.
Fee: $90.00 installation; $35.00 monthly.
Expanded Basic Service 1
Subscribers: N.A.
Programming (via satellite): A&E; AMC; Animal Planet; Bravo; Cartoon Network; CMT; CNBC; CNN; Comedy Central; Discovery Channel; Disney Channel; ESPN; ESPN2; EVINE Live; EWTN Global Catholic Network; Food Network; Fox News Channel; FOX Sports Midwest; Freeform; FX; HGTV; History; HLN; Lifetime; MSNBC; MTV; Nickelodeon; Oxygen; Spike TV; Syfy; TBS; The Weather Channel; TLC; TNT; Travel Channel; Turner Classic Movies; TV Land; USA Network; WE tv.
Digital Basic Service
Subscribers: N.A.
Programming (via satellite): 3ABN; Boomerang; BYUtv; Discovery Digital Networks; Disney XD; ESPN Classic; ESPNews; FamilyNet; FOX College Sports Central; FOX College Sports Pacific; Fox HD; Fox Sports 1; Fox Sports 2; FXM; FYI; Golf Channel; Hallmark Channel; History International; HITS (Headend In The Sky); INSP; MC; National Geographic Channel; Outdoor Channel; TNT HD; Trinity Broadcasting Network (TBN); truTV; Universal HD.
Digital Pay Service 1
Pay Units: N.A.
Programming (via satellite): Cinemax (multiplexed); Flix; HBO (multiplexed); Showtime (multiplexed); Showtime HD; Starz (multiplexed); Starz Encore; Sundance TV; The Movie Channel (multiplexed); The Movie Channel HD.
Fee: $15.00 monthly (each).
Video-On-Demand: No
Pay-Per-View
Shorteez (delivered digitally); Fresh (delivered digitally); Hot Choice (delivered digitally).
Internet Service
Operational: Yes.
Broadband Service: CableONE.net.
Fee: $75.00 installation; $43.00 monthly.
Telephone Service
Digital: Operational
Fee: $39.95 monthly
Miles of Plant: 93.0 (coaxial); None (fiber optic).
Vice President: Patrick A. Dolohanty. General Manager: Mike Flood. Technical Operations Manager: Jerry Millis.
Ownership: Cable ONE Inc. (MSO).

INGALLS—United Communications Assn. Inc. Now served by CIMARRON, KS [KS0126]. ICA: KS0313.

INMAN—Vyve Broadband, 4 International Dr, Ste 330, Rye Brook, NY 10573. Phone: 800-937-1397. Web Site: http://vyvebroadband.com. ICA: KS0475.
TV Market Ranking: 67 (INMAN).
Channel capacity: N.A. Channels available but not in use: N.A.
Basic Service
Subscribers: 5. Commercial subscribers: 1.
Fee: $64.95 installation; $50.75 monthly.
Chief Executive Officer: Bill Haggarty. Senior Vice President, Financial Planning: Daniel White.
Ownership: Vyve Broadband LLC (MSO).

IOLA—Cox Communications. Now served by PITTSBURG, KS [KS0011]. ICA: KS0030.

IUKA—Formerly served by Cox Communications. No longer in operation. ICA: KS0389.

JAMESTOWN—Cunningham Cable TV. Now served by GLEN ELDER, KS [KS0228]. ICA: KS0256.

JETMORE—United Communications Assn. Inc. Now served by CIMARRON, KS [KS0126]. ICA: KS0185.

JEWELL—Cunningham Cable TV. Now served by GLEN ELDER, KS [KS0228]. ICA: KS0220.

JOHNSON COUNTY (portions)—Comcast Cable. Now served by INDEPENDENCE, MO [MO0004]. ICA: KS0005.

KANSAS CITY (unincorporated areas)—Formerly served by Charter Communications. Now served by WOW! Internet, Cable & Phone, LAWRENCE, KS [KS0004]. ICA: KS0390.

KENSINGTON—Formerly served by Cunningham Cable TV. No longer in operation. ICA: KS0392.

KENSINGTON—Nex-Tech. Formerly served by LENORA, KS [KS0450]. This cable system has converted to IPTV, 2418 Vine St, Hays, KS 67601. Phones: 877-625-7872; 785-625-7070. Fax: 785-625-4479. E-mail: webmaster@nex-tech.com. Web Site: http://www.nex-tech.com. ICA: KS5074.
TV Market Ranking: Franchise award date: April 27, 2007. Franchise expiration date: N.A. Began: N.A.
Channel capacity: N.A. Channels available but not in use: N.A.
Essentials
Subscribers: 188.
Fee: $30.00 installation; $24.95 monthly. Includes 51 channels.
Premiere
Subscribers: 177.
Fee: $61.95 monthly. Includes 119 channels plus music channels.
HD
Subscribers: N.A.
Fee: $11.95 monthly. Includes 75+ channels.
Sports & Entertainment
Subscribers: N.A.
Fee: $12.95 monthly. Includes 34 channels.
Cinemax
Subscribers: N.A.
Fee: $8.95 monthly. Includes 8 channels.
HBO
Subscribers: N.A.
Fee: $14.95 monthly. Includes 12 channels.
Showtime/TMC
Subscribers: N.A.
Fee: $13.95 monthly. Includes 16 channels.
Starz/Encore
Subscribers: N.A.
Fee: $10.95 monthly. Includes 18 channels.
Video-On-Demand: Yes
Internet Service
Operational: Yes.
Fee: $22.95–$207.95 monthly.
Telephone Service
Digital: Operational
Fee: $16.75 monthly
Chief Executive Officer & General Manager: Larry Sevier. Video Solutions Manager: Scott Roe.
Ownership: Nex-Tech.

KINSLEY—Cox Communications. Now served by DODGE CITY, KS [KS0015]. ICA: KS0093.

KIOWA—Formerly served by Almega Cable. No longer in operation. ICA: KS0115.

KIRWIN—Nex-Tech, 2418 Vine St, Hays, KS 67601. Phones: 877-625-7872; 785-625-7070. Fax: 785-625-4479. E-mail: webmaster@nex-tech.com. Web Site: http://www.nex-tech.com. ICA: KS0287.
Channel capacity: N.A. Channels available but not in use: N.A.
Basic Service
Subscribers: 21.
Programming (received off-air): CNN; KBSH-DT (CBS) Hays; KGIN (CBS, MNT, NBC) Grand Island; KHGI-TV (ABC) Kearney; KLNE-TV (PBS) Lexington.
Programming (via satellite): A&E; Discovery Channel; ESPN; Freeform; Hallmark Channel; History; KNHL (IND) Hastings; Outdoor Channel; TBS; The Weather Channel; TLC; TNT; TV Land; USA Network; WGN America.
Fee: $30.00 installation; $39.95 monthly.
Pay Service 1
Pay Units: N.A.
Programming (via satellite): Showtime.
Fee: $13.45 monthly.
Internet Service
Operational: Yes.
Fee: $22.95-$42.95 monthly.
Telephone Service
Analog: Operational
Fee: $16.75 monthly
Chief Executive Officer & General Manager: Larry Sevier. Video Solutions Manager: Scott Roe.
Ownership: Nex-Tech.

LA CROSSE—Formerly served by Cox Communications. Now served by GBT Communications Inc., RUSH CENTER, KS [KS0418]. ICA: KS0132.

LA CYGNE—Formerly served by Almega Cable. No longer in operation. ICA: KS0153.

LA HARPE—Formerly served by CableDirect. No longer in operation. ICA: KS0393.

LAKE DABINAWA—Formerly served by Rainbow Communications. No longer in operation. ICA: KS0308.

LAKE OF THE FOREST—Time Warner Cable. Now served by KANSAS CITY, MO [MO0001]. ICA: KS0394.

LAKE WABAUNSEE—Formerly served by Galaxy Cablevision. No longer in operation. ICA: KS0241.

LANE—Formerly served by National Cable Inc. No longer in operation. ICA: KS0338.

LAWRENCE—WOW! Internet, Cable & Phone, 7887 East Belleview Ave, Ste 1000, Englewood, CO 80111. Phones: 720-479-3500; 706-645-8553; 706-645-3000. Fax: 720-479-3585. E-mail: wow_general@wideopenwest.com. Web Site: http://www.wowway.com. Also serves Basehor, Douglas County (unincorporated areas), Eudora, Kansas City (unincorporated areas), Lansing, Leavenworth County (unincorporated areas), Linwood, Tonganoxie & Wyandotte County (portions). ICA: KS0004.
TV Market Ranking: 22 (Basehor, Douglas County (unincorporated areas) (portions), Eudora, Kansas City (unincorporated areas), Lansing, Leavenworth County (unincorporated areas), Linwood, Tonganoxie, Wyandotte County (portions)); Below 100 (LAWRENCE, Douglas County (unincorporated areas) (portions)). Franchise award date: January 1, 1971. Franchise expiration date: N.A. Began: January 1, 1972.
Channel capacity: 38 (operating 2-way). Channels available but not in use: N.A.

Cable Systems—Kansas

Basic Service
Subscribers: 14,813.
Programming (received off-air): KCPT (PBS) Kansas City; KCTV (CBS) Kansas City; KCWE (CW, Movies!, This TV) Kansas City; KMBC-TV (ABC, MeTV) Kansas City; KMCI-TV (Bounce TV, Escape, IND) Lawrence; KPXE-TV (ION) Kansas City; KSHB-TV (COZI TV, Grit, NBC) Kansas City; KSMO-TV (Bounce TV, MNT) Kansas City; KSNT (FOX, NBC) Topeka; KTKA-TV (ABC, CW) Topeka; KTWU (PBS) Topeka; WDAF-TV (Antenna TV, FOX) Kansas City; WIBW-TV (CBS, MeTV, MNT) Topeka.
Programming (via satellite): C-SPAN; C-SPAN 2; C-SPAN 3; EVINE Live; Jewelry Television; Pop; QVC; WGN America.
Fee: $50.00 installation; $31.95 monthly.

Expanded Basic Service 1
Subscribers: N.A.
Programming (via satellite): A&E; AMC; Animal Planet; BET; BlueHighways TV; Bravo; Cartoon Network; CMT; CNBC; CNN; Comedy Central; Discovery Channel; Disney Channel; Disney XD; E! HD; ESPN; ESPN Classic; ESPN2; EWTN Global Catholic Network; FamilyNet; Food Network; Fox News Channel; FOX Sports Midwest; Freeform; FX; Great American Country; Hallmark Channel; HGTV; History; HLN; INSP; Lifetime; LMN; MSNBC; MTV; MTV2; National Geographic Channel; NBCSN; Nick Jr.; Nickelodeon; Nicktoons; Oxygen; RLTV; Spike TV; Sprout; Syfy; TBS; TeenNick; The Weather Channel; Time Warner Cable SportsChannel (Kansas City); TLC; TNT; Travel Channel; Trinity Broadcasting Network (TBN); truTV; TV Land; USA Network; VH1.
Fee: $28.00 monthly.

Digital Basic Service
Subscribers: N.A.
Programming (via satellite): A&E HD; Animal Planet HD; AWE; BBC America; Bio HD; Bloomberg Television; Boomerang; Bravo HD; BTN; BTN HD; Cartoon Network HD; CBS Sports Network; CBS Sports Network HD; Chiller; Cloo; CMT; CMT HD; CNBC HD+; CNN HD; Cooking Channel; Crime & Investigation Network; Destination America; Discovery Channel HD; Discovery Kids Channel; Discovery Life Channel; Disney Channel HD; DIY Network; ESPN HD; ESPN2 HD; ESPNews; ESPNews HD; ESPNU; Flix; Food Network HD; FOX College Sports Central; FOX College Sports Pacific; Fox News HD; Fox Sports 1; Freeform HD; FSN HD; FX HD; FXM; FYI; Golf Channel; GSN; Hallmark Movie Channel HD; Hallmark Movies & Mysteries; HGTV HD; History; History HD; History International; IFC; Investigation Discovery; Lifetime HD; Lifetime Movie Network HD; MC; MTV Classic; MTV Hits; MTV Jams; NFL Network; Nick HD; Outdoor Channel; Outdoor Channel 2 HD; OWN; Oprah Winfrey Network; QVC HD; Science Channel; Science HD; Spike TV HD; Sundance TV; Syfy HD; TBS HD; Tennis Channel; Tennis Channel HD; The Weather Channel HD; TLC HD; TNT HD; Toon Disney HD; Travel Channel HD; Turner Classic Movies; USA Network HD; Versus HD; VH1 HD; VH1 Soul; WE tv.
Fee: $5.00 converter.

Digital Expanded Basic Service
Subscribers: 13,800.
Programming (via satellite): AXS TV; HD Theater; National Geographic Channel HD; NFL Network HD; Smithsonian Channel HD; Universal HD.
Fee: $39.00 installation; $9.95 monthly; $5.00 converter.

Digital Pay Service 1
Pay Units: 4,900.
Programming (via satellite): HBO (multiplexed); HBO HD.
Fee: $15.95 monthly; $5.00 converter.

Digital Pay Service 2
Pay Units: 2,600.
Programming (via satellite): Cinemax (multiplexed); Cinemax HD.
Fee: $9.95 monthly; $5.00 converter.

Digital Pay Service 3
Pay Units: 2,200.
Programming (via satellite): Showtime (multiplexed); Showtime HD; The Movie Channel (multiplexed).
Fee: $13.95 monthly; $5.00 converter.

Digital Pay Service 4
Pay Units: 2,200.
Programming (via satellite): Starz (multiplexed); Starz Encore (multiplexed); Starz HD.
Fee: $13.95 monthly; $5.00 converter.

Video-On-Demand: Yes

Pay-Per-View
Hot Choice (delivered digitally); iN DEMAND (delivered digitally); Playboy TV (delivered digitally); Shorteez (delivered digitally); Fresh (delivered digitally); Sports PPV (delivered digitally).

Internet Service
Operational: Yes. Began: September 1, 1996.
Subscribers: 25,021.
Broadband Service: Sprint/UUNET.
Fee: $39.00 installation; $17.95-$59.95 monthly; $5.00 modem lease; $79.95 modem purchase.

Telephone Service
Digital: Operational
Subscribers: 12,955.
Fee: $18.95 monthly
Miles of Plant: 1,465.0 (coaxial); 519.0 (fiber optic). Homes passed: 64,464.
Chief Executive Officer: Colleen Abdoulah.
President: Steven Cochran. Chief Financial Officer: Rich Fish.
Ownership: WideOpenWest LLC (MSO).

LEBANON—Nex-Tech. Formerly [KS0397]. This cable system has converted to IPTV, 2418 Vine St, Hays, KS 67601. Phones: 877-625-7872; 785-625-7070. Fax: 785-625-4479. E-mail: webmaster@nex-tech.com. Web Site: http://www.nex-tech.com. Also serves Esbon. ICA: KS0049.
Channel capacity: N.A. Channels available but not in use: N.A.

Essentials
Subscribers: 188.
Fee: $30.00 installation; $24.95 monthly. Includes 51 channels.

Premiere
Subscribers: N.A.
Fee: $61.95 monthly. Includes 119 channels plus music channels.

HD
Subscribers: N.A.
Fee: $11.95 monthly. Includes 75+ channels.

Sports & Entertainment
Subscribers: N.A.
Fee: $12.95 monthly. Includes 34 channels.

Cinemax
Subscribers: N.A.
Fee: $8.95 monthly. Includes 8 channels.

HBO
Subscribers: N.A.
Fee: $14.95 monthly. Includes 12 channels.

Showtime/TMC
Subscribers: N.A.
Fee: $13.95 monthly. Includes 16 channels.

Starz/Encore
Subscribers: N.A.
Fee: $10.95 monthly. Includes 18 channels.

Video-On-Demand: Yes

Internet Service
Operational: Yes.
Fee: $31.95 monthly.

Telephone Service
Digital: Operational
Fee: $17.81 monthly
Chief Executive Officer & General Manager: Larry Sevier. Video Solutions Manager: Scott Roe.
Ownership: Nex-Tech.

LEBANON—Nex-Tech. This cable system has converted to IPTV. See LEBANON, KS [KS0049]. ICA: KS0397.

LEHIGH—Formerly served by Eagle Communications. No longer in operation. ICA: KS0466.

LENEXA—SureWest Broadband. This cable system has converted to IPTV. See LENEXA, KS [KS5122]. ICA: KS0462.

LENEXA—SureWest Communications. Formerly [KS0462]. This cable system has converted to IPTV, 14859 West 95th St, Lenexa, KS 66215. Phones: 918-825-3000; 913-825-2882. E-mail: inquiries@surewest.com. Web Site: http://mycci.net. Also serves Fairway, Kansas City, Merriam, Mission, Mission Woods, Olathe, Overland Park, Prairie Village, Roeland Park, Shawnee, Westwood & Westwood Hills, KS; Kansas City, MO. ICA: KS5122.
TV Market Ranking: 22 (LENEXA, Overland Park, Shawnee).
Channel capacity: 77 (not 2-way capable). Channels available but not in use: N.A.

Basic
Subscribers: 38,388. Commercial subscribers: 249.
Fee: $45.00 installation; $53.99 monthly. Includes 131 channels & one STB.

Digital
Subscribers: N.A.
Fee: $10.00 monthly. Includes 31 channels plus 41 music channels.

HD
Subscribers: N.A.
Fee: $8.00 monthly. Includes 21 channels.

Cinemax
Subscribers: N.A.
Fee: $13.99 monthly. Includes 12 channels.

HBO
Subscribers: N.A.
Fee: $16.99 monthly. Includes 14 channels.

Showtime/TMC
Subscribers: N.A.
Fee: $13.99 monthly. Includes 11 channels.

Starz/Encore
Subscribers: N.A.
Fee: $13.99 monthly. Includes 21 channels.

Video-On-Demand: Yes

Internet Service
Operational: Yes.
Fee: $24.00-$149.99 monthly.

Telephone Service
Digital: Operational
Fee: $12.75 monthly
Ownership: Consolidated Communications Inc.

LENORA—Nex-Tech. This cable system has converted to IPTV. Now served by EDMOND, KS [KS5045]. ICA: KS0450.

LEONARDVILLE—Formerly served by Giant Communications. No longer in operation. ICA: KS0263.

LEOTI—Formerly served by Cebridge Connections. Now served by Pioneer Communications, ULYSSES, KS [KS0044]. ICA: KS0122.

LIBERAL—Zito Media, 102 S Main St, PO Box 665, Coudersport, PA 16915. Phones: 814-260-9055; 800-365-6988. E-mail: info@zitomedia.com. Web Site: http://www.zitomedia.com. ICA: KS0017.
TV Market Ranking: Outside TV Markets (LIBERAL). Franchise award date: February 24, 1956. Franchise expiration date: N.A. Began: February 24, 1956.
Channel capacity: N.A. Channels available but not in use: N.A.

Basic Service
Subscribers: 1,472.
Programming (received off-air): KAMR-TV (IND, NBC) Amarillo; KBSD-DT (CBS) Ensign; KCIT (FOX, This TV) Amarillo; KFDA-TV (CBS, TMO) Amarillo; KSNG (NBC) Garden City; KSWK (PBS) Lakin; KUPK (ABC) Garden City; KWET (PBS) Cheyenne; WCVB-TV (ABC, MeTV) Boston.
Programming (via satellite): A&E; AMC; Animal Planet; BET; Bravo; Cartoon Network; CMT; CNBC; CNN; Comedy Central; C-SPAN; C-SPAN 2; Discovery Channel; E! HD; ESPN; ESPN2; EVINE Live; EWTN Global Catholic Network; Food Network; Fox Deportes; Fox News Channel; FOX Sports Midwest; Freeform; FX; Hallmark Channel; HGTV; History; HLN; INSP; Lifetime; MSNBC; MTV; Nickelodeon; Oxygen; Pop; QVC; Root Sports Rocky Mountain; Spike TV; Syfy; The Weather Channel; TLC; Travel Channel; Trinity Broadcasting Network (TBN); truTV; Turner Classic Movies; TV Land; Univision; USA Network; VH1; WGN America.
Fee: $49.95 installation; $18.59 monthly.

Expanded Basic Service 1
Subscribers: N.A.
Programming (via satellite): Disney Channel; TBS; TNT.
Fee: $7.91 monthly.

Digital Basic Service
Subscribers: N.A.
Programming (via satellite): BBC America; Bloomberg Television; Discovery Digital Networks; Disney XD; DIY Network; ESPN Classic; ESPNews; FOX College Sports Central; FOX College Sports Pacific; Fox Sports 1; Fuse; FXM; FYI; Golf Channel; Great American Country; GSN; History International; HITS (Headend In The Sky);

Kansas—Cable Systems

CABLE & TV STATION COVERAGE
Atlas 2017
The perfect companion to the Television & Cable Factbook
To order call 800-771-9202 or visit www.warren-news.com

IFC; MC; National Geographic Channel; NBCSN; Nick 2; Nick Jr.; Outdoor Channel; Sundance TV; TeenNick; WE tv.
Digital Pay Service 1
Pay Units: N.A.
Programming (via satellite): ART America; Cinemax (multiplexed); Flix; HBO (multiplexed); RAI Italia; RTN; Showtime (multiplexed); Starz (multiplexed); Starz Encore (multiplexed); The Filipino Channel; The Movie Channel (multiplexed); TV Asia; TV5, La Television International; Zee TV.
Fee: $12.00 monthly (Cinemax, HBO, Showtime Unlimited or Starz), $15.00 monthly (CCTV, TV Asia, TV5, Filipino, RAI, ART or TV Russia).
Video-On-Demand: No
Pay-Per-View
Playboy TV (delivered digitally); Shorteez (delivered digitally); Fresh (delivered digitally); Hot Choice (delivered digitally); Playboy TV (delivered digitally); HITS PPV (delivered digitally).
Internet Service
Operational: Yes.
Broadband Service: In-house.
Fee: $19.95-$49.99 installation; $44.95 monthly.
Telephone Service
Digital: Operational
Fee: $49.95 monthly
Miles of Plant: 95.0 (coaxial); 14.0 (fiber optic). Homes passed: 7,785.
President: James Rigas.
Ownership: Zito Media (MSO).

LINCOLN—Eagle Communications, 2703 Hall St, Ste 15, PO Box 817, Hays, KS 67601. Phones: 785-625-5910; 785-263-2529; 785-625-4000 (Corporate office). Fax: 785-625-8030. Web Site: http://www.eaglecom.net. ICA: KS0134.
TV Market Ranking: Below 100 (LINCOLN). Franchise award date: N.A. Franchise expiration date: N.A. Began: October 1, 1975.
Channel capacity: N.A. Channels available but not in use: N.A.
Basic Service
Subscribers: 51. Commercial subscribers: 3.
Programming (received off-air): KAAS-TV (FOX) Salina; KAKE (ABC, MeTV) Wichita; KBSH-DT (CBS) Hays; KOOD (PBS) Hays; KSNC (NBC) Great Bend; KWCH-DT (CBS) Hutchinson; 1 FM.
Programming (via satellite): EWTN Global Catholic Network; KMGH-TV (ABC, Azteca America) Denver; QVC; The Weather Channel.
Fee: $24.95 installation; $59.95 monthly.
Expanded Basic Service 1
Subscribers: N.A.
Programming (via satellite): A&E; Animal Planet; CNN; C-SPAN; Discovery Channel; Disney Channel; ESPN; ESPN2; Fox News Channel; FOX Sports Midwest; Freeform; Great American Country; History; HLN; Lifetime; National Geographic Channel; Nickelodeon; Spike TV; TBS; TLC; TNT; TV Land; USA Network; VH1.
Fee: $21.50 monthly.

Pay Service 1
Pay Units: N.A.
Programming (via satellite): HBO; Showtime; The Movie Channel.
Fee: $11.95 monthly (each).
Video-On-Demand: No
Pay-Per-View
iN DEMAND (delivered digitally); Playboy TV (delivered digitally); Fresh (delivered digitally); Shorteez (delivered digitally).
Internet Service
Operational: Yes.
Fee: $34.95-$54.95 monthly.
Telephone Service
None
Miles of Plant: 18.0 (coaxial); None (fiber optic). Homes passed: 611.
Chief Operating Officer: Kurt K. David. General Manager: Travis Kohlrus. Chief Technician: Jim Gall. Ad Sales Manager: Mike Koerner.
Ownership: Eagle Communications Inc. (MSO).

LINN—Formerly served by Allegiance Communications. No longer in operation. ICA: KS0253.

LINSBORG—Cox Communications. Now served by WICHITA, KS [KS0001]. ICA: KS0070.

LOUISBURG—Formerly served by Almega Cable. No longer in operation. ICA: KS0123.

LOUISVILLE—WTC Communications. Now served by WAMEGO, KS [KS5017]. ICA: KS5040.

LOWELL—Formerly served by Riverton-Lowell Cablevision. No longer in operation. ICA: KS0399.

LUCAS—Wilson Communications. Now served by BROOKVILLE, KS [KS0162]. ICA: KS0216.

LURAY—Gorham Tele-Com (formerly NexTech). This cable system has converted to IPTV. See GORHAM, KS [KS5164]. ICA: KS0298.

LYON COUNTY—Formerly served by Galaxy Cablevision. No longer in operation. ICA: KS0467.

LYONS—Cox Communications. Now served by GREAT BEND, KS [KS0012]. ICA: KS0047.

MACKSVILLE—Formerly served by Almega Cable. No longer in operation. ICA: KS0225.

MADISON—Mediacom, 901 North College Ave, Columbia, MO 65201. Phones: 845-695-2762; 573-443-1536. Fax: 417-883-0265. Web Site: http://www.mediacomcable.com. ICA: KS0155.
TV Market Ranking: Outside TV Markets (MADISON).
Channel capacity: N.A. Channels available but not in use: N.A.

Basic Service
Subscribers: 88.
Fee: $42.00 monthly.
Vice President, Financial Reporting: Kenneth J. Kohrs.
Ownership: Mediacom LLC (MSO).

MAHASKA—Formerly served by Westcom. No longer in operation. ICA: KS0348.

MANHATTAN—Cox Communications, 6205 Peachtree Dunwoody Rd, 12th Floor, Atlanta, GA 30328. Phones: 404-269-6590; 316-260-7000 (Wichita office); 785-215-6700. Fax: 785-215-6127. Web Site: http://www.cox.com. Also serves Grandview Plaza, Junction City, Kansas State University, Milford (portions), Ogden, Pottawatomie County (southeastern portion), Riley County (southern portion) & St. George. ICA: KS0006.
TV Market Ranking: Outside TV Markets (Grandview Plaza, Kansas State University, MANHATTAN, Manhattan, Milford (portions), Ogden, Pottawatomie County (southeastern portion), Riley County (southern portion), St. George, Junction City). Franchise award date: June 1, 1987. Franchise expiration date: N.A. Began: December 1, 1961.
Channel capacity: N.A. Channels available but not in use: N.A.
Basic Service
Subscribers: 15,435. Commercial subscribers: 604.
Programming (received off-air): KCTV (CBS) Kansas City; KMBC-TV (ABC, MeTV) Kansas City; KSNT (FOX, NBC) Topeka; KTKA-TV (ABC, CW) Topeka; KTMJ-CD (Escape, FOX) Topeka; KTWU (PBS) Topeka; WIBW-TV (CBS, MeTV, MNT) Topeka.
Programming (via satellite): C-SPAN; C-SPAN 2; Pop; The Weather Channel; WGN America.
Fee: $29.95 installation; $21.99 monthly.
Expanded Basic Service 1
Subscribers: N.A.
Programming (via satellite): A&E; AMC; Animal Planet; BET; CMT; CNBC; CNN; Comedy Central; Discovery Channel; Disney Channel; E! HD; ESPN; ESPN2; EWTN Global Catholic Network; Food Network; Fox News Channel; Fox Sports 1; FOX Sports Midwest; Freeform; FX; Hallmark Channel; HGTV; History; HLN; INSP; Lifetime; MSNBC; MTV; Nickelodeon; QVC; Spike TV; Syfy; TBS; TLC; TNT; Travel Channel; truTV; Turner Classic Movies; TV Land; USA Network; VH1.
Fee: $43.15 monthly.
Digital Basic Service
Subscribers: N.A.
Programming (via satellite): BBC America; Bloomberg Television; Discovery Digital Networks; Disney XD; DMX Music; ESPN Classic; ESPNews; FYI; Golf Channel; Great American Country; GSN; History International; HITS (Headend In The Sky); IFC; International Television (ITV); LMN; NBA TV; NBCSN; Nick 2; Nick Jr.; Outdoor Channel; Oxygen; Sundance TV; TeenNick.
Digital Pay Service 1
Pay Units: N.A.
Programming (via satellite): Cinemax (multiplexed); HBO (multiplexed); Showtime (multiplexed); Starz (multiplexed); Starz Encore (multiplexed).
Fee: $11.50 monthly (each).
Video-On-Demand: No
Pay-Per-View
iN DEMAND (delivered digitally); ESPN Now (delivered digitally); NBA/WNBA League Pass (delivered digitally); NHL Center Ice/MLB Extra Innings (delivered digitally).
Internet Service
Operational: Yes.
Subscribers: 16,011.
Broadband Service: Cox High Speed Internet.
Fee: $19.99-$59.99 monthly; $15.00 modem lease; $199.95 modem purchase.
Telephone Service
Digital: Operational
Subscribers: 7,297.
Fee: $15.95-$48.95 monthly
Miles of Plant: 741.0 (coaxial); 239.0 (fiber optic). Homes passed: 43,022. Homes passed included in Wichita.
Vice President & General Manager: Kimberly Edmunds. Vice President, Engineering: Nick DiPonzio. Vice President, Marketing: Tony Matthews. Vice President, Tax: Mary Vickers. Field Operations Regional Manager: Scott Terry. Marketing Director: Tina Gabbard. Public Affairs Director: Sarah Kauffman.
Ownership: Cox Communications Inc. (MSO).

MANKATO—Cunningham Cable TV. Now served by GLEN ELDER, KS [KS0228]. ICA: KS0156.

MAPLE HILL—Formerly served by Zito Media. No longer in operation. ICA: KS0275.

MARION—Eagle Communications, 2703 Hall St, Ste 15, PO Box 817, Hays, KS 67601. Phone: 877-613-2453. Fax: 785-625-8030. Web site: http://www.eaglecom.net. Also serves Florence, Hillsboro, Lincolnville & Marion County (portions). ICA: KS0089.
TV Market Ranking: Outside TV Markets (Florence, Hillsboro, Lincolnville, MARION, Marion County (portions)).
Channel capacity: N.A. Channels available but not in use: N.A.
Basic Service
Subscribers: 734. Commercial subscribers: 19.
Fee: $24.95 installation; $69.95 monthly.
Chief Operating Officer: Kurt K. David.
Ownership: Eagle Communications Inc. (MSO).

MARQUETTE—MTC, 365 Main St, Little River, KS 67457. Phones: 877-216-9951; 620-897-6200. E-mail: service@lrmutual.com. Web Site: http://mtc4me.com. ICA: KS0212.
TV Market Ranking: 67 (MARQUETTE). Franchise award date: January 1, 1982. Franchise expiration date: N.A. Began: June 1, 1983.
Channel capacity: N.A. Channels available but not in use: N.A.
Basic Service
Subscribers: 85.
Programming (received off-air): KAKE (ABC, MeTV) Wichita; KMTW (MNT, The Country Network) Hutchinson; KPTS (PBS) Hutchinson; KSAS-TV (Antenna TV, FOX) Wichita; KSNW (NBC) Wichita; KWCH-DT (CBS) Hutchinson.
Programming (via satellite): A&E; AMC; CMT; CNBC; CNN; C-SPAN; C-SPAN 2; Discovery Channel; Disney Channel; ESPN; ESPN2; Freeform; Great American Country; HGTV; History; Lifetime; Nickelodeon; Outdoor Channel; QVC; Spike TV; Syfy; TBS; The Weather Channel; TLC; TNT; Trinity Broadcasting Network (TBN); TV Land; USA Network; WGN America.
Fee: $32.00 monthly.

Cable Systems—Kansas

Pay Service 1
Pay Units: 5.
Programming (via satellite): Cinemax (multiplexed); HBO (multiplexed); MoviePlex; Showtime; Starz; The Movie Channel.
Fee: $15.00 monthly.
Internet Service
Operational: Yes.
Broadband Service: In-house.
Fee: $25.00 installation; $34.95 monthly.
Telephone Service
None
Miles of Plant: 5.0 (coaxial); None (fiber optic). Homes passed: 262.
General Manager: John Tietjens. Operations Manager: Heath Eberle. Sales & Marketing Manager: Shayla Grasser.
Ownership: Mutual Telephone Co. (MSO).

MARYSVILLE—Blue Valley Tele-Communications. Now served by AXTELL (formerly Frankfort & Home), KS [KS0424]. ICA: KS0048.

MAYETTA—Giant Communications. Now served by HOLTON, KS [KS0066]. ICA: KS0321.

McCUNE—Formerly served by Craw-Kan Telephone Co-op. No longer in operation. ICA: KS0213.

McDONALD—Eagle Communications, 2703 Hall St, Ste 15, PO Box 817, Hays, KS 67601. Phones: 785-263-2529; 785-625-5910; 785-899-3371; 785-625-4000 (Corporate office). Fax: 785-625-8030. Web Site: http://www.eaglecom.net. Also serves Bird City. ICA: KS0084.
TV Market Ranking: Below 100 (Bird City, MCDONALD). Franchise award date: N.A. Franchise expiration date: N.A. Began: December 1, 1976.
Channel capacity: N.A. Channels available but not in use: N.A.
Basic Service
Subscribers: 43.
Programming (received off-air): KBSL-DT (CBS) Goodland; KLBY (ABC) Colby; KSAS-TV (Antenna TV, FOX) Wichita; KSNK (NBC) McCook; 1 FM.
Programming (via microwave): KOOD (PBS) Hays.
Programming (via satellite): Great American Country; KCNC-TV (CBS, Decades) Denver; KMGH-TV (ABC, Azteca America) Denver; KUSA (NBC, WeatherNation) Denver; KWGN-TV (CW, This TV) Denver; National Geographic Channel; QVC; The Weather Channel; TV Land.
Fee: $24.95 installation; $69.95 monthly.
Expanded Basic Service 1
Subscribers: N.A.
Programming (via satellite): A&E; Animal Planet; CNN; Discovery Channel; Disney Channel; ESPN; FOX Sports Midwest; Freeform; HGTV; History; HLN; Nickelodeon; Spike TV; TBS; TLC; TNT; USA Network.
Fee: $21.50 monthly.
Pay Service 1
Pay Units: N.A.
Programming (via satellite): HBO; Showtime; The Movie Channel.
Fee: $11.95 monthly (each).
Video-On-Demand: No
Internet Service
Operational: Yes.
Fee: $34.95-$54.95 monthly.
Telephone Service
None
Miles of Plant: 22.0 (coaxial); None (fiber optic). Homes passed: 278.

Chief Operating Officer: Kurt K. David. General Manager: Travis Kohlrus. Chief Technician: Jim Gall. Ad Sales Manager: Mike Koerner.
Ownership: Eagle Communications Inc. (MSO).

McFARLAND—Formerly served by Galaxy Cablevision. No longer in operation. ICA: KS0327.

McLOUTH—Giant Communications. Now served by HOLTON, KS [KS0066]. ICA: KS0191.

McPHERSON—Cox Communications. Now served by WICHITA, KS [KS0001]. ICA: KS0019.

MEADE—Vyve Broadband, 4 International Dr, Ste 330, Rye Brook, NY 10573. Phones: 800-937-1397; 405-395-1131; 405-275-6923. Web Site: http://vyvebroadband.com. Also serves Fowler, Kismet, Minneola, Plains & Seward County (portions). ICA: KS0124.
TV Market Ranking: Below 100 (Fowler, MEADE, Minneola, Plains); Outside TV Markets (Kismet, Seward County (portions)). Franchise award date: N.A. Franchise expiration date: N.A. Began: February 1, 1976.
Channel capacity: N.A. Channels available but not in use: N.A.
Basic Service
Subscribers: 151. Commercial subscribers: 66.
Programming (received off-air): KBSD-DT (CBS) Ensign; KSAS-TV (Antenna TV, FOX) Wichita; KSNG (NBC) Garden City; KSWK (PBS) Lakin; KUPK (ABC) Garden City; 7 FMs.
Programming (via satellite): C-SPAN; EVINE Live; EWTN Global Catholic Network; QVC; Trinity Broadcasting Network (TBN); WGN America.
Fee: $64.95 installation; $25.00 monthly.
Expanded Basic Service 1
Subscribers: N.A.
Programming (via satellite): A&E; AMC; Animal Planet; Bravo; Cartoon Network; CMT; CNBC; CNN; Comedy Central; Discovery Channel; Disney Channel; E! HD; ESPN; ESPN2; Food Network; Fox News Channel; Fox Sports 1; FOX Sports Midwest; Freeform; FX; Golf Channel; Hallmark Channel; HGTV; History; HLN; Lifetime; MSNBC; MTV; National Geographic Channel; Nickelodeon; Outdoor Channel; Oxygen; Spike TV; Syfy; TBS; Telemundo; The Weather Channel; TLC; TNT; Travel Channel; truTV; Turner Classic Movies; TV Land; Univision Studios; USA Network; VH1.
Fee: $39.96 monthly.
Digital Basic Service
Subscribers: N.A.
Programming (via satellite): BBC America; Bloomberg Television; Cloo; CMT; Destination America; Discovery Kids Channel; Discovery Life Channel; Disney XD; DMX Music; ESPN Classic; ESPNews; EVINE Live; Flix; FOX College Sports Central; FOX College Sports Pacific; Fuse; FXM; FYI; Great American Country; GSN; History International; IFC; Investigation Discovery; LMN; MTV Classic; MTV Hits; MTV2; NBCSN; Nick Jr.; Nickelodeon; Nicktoons; Ovation; OWN; Oprah Winfrey Network; Science Channel; Starz Encore (multiplexed); Sundance TV; TeenNick; The Word Network; VH1 Soul; WE tv.
Digital Pay Service 1
Pay Units: N.A.
Programming (via satellite): Cinemax (multiplexed); Flix; HBO (multiplexed);

Showtime (multiplexed); Starz (multiplexed); Starz Encore (multiplexed); The Movie Channel (multiplexed).
Video-On-Demand: No
Pay-Per-View
Shorteez (delivered digitally); iN DEMAND (delivered digitally); Playboy TV (delivered digitally); Fresh (delivered digitally).
Internet Service
Operational: Yes.
Telephone Service
Digital: Operational
Miles of Plant: 37.0 (coaxial); 56.0 (fiber optic). Homes passed: 2,439.
Chief Executive Officer: Bil Haggarty. Regional Vice President: Andrew Dearth. Vice President, Marketing: Tracy Bass. Senior Vice President, Financial Planning: Daniel White.
Ownership: Vyve Broadband LLC (MSO).

MEDICINE LODGE—Vyve Broadband, 4 International Dr, Ste 330, Rye Brook, NY 10573. Phones: 800-937-1397; 405-395-1131; 405-275-6923. Web Site: http://vyvebroadband.com. Also serves Barber County (portions). ICA: KS0067.
TV Market Ranking: Outside TV Markets (Barber County (portions), MEDICINE LODGE). Franchise award date: N.A. Franchise expiration date: N.A. Began: December 1, 1968.
Channel capacity: N.A. Channels available but not in use: N.A.
Basic Service
Subscribers: 112. Commercial subscribers: 34.
Programming (received off-air): KAKE (ABC, MeTV) Wichita; KPTS (PBS) Hutchinson; KSAS-TV (Antenna TV, FOX) Wichita; KSNW (NBC) Wichita; KWCH-DT (CBS) Hutchinson; 9 FMs.
Programming (via satellite): A&E; Animal Planet; Cartoon Network; CMT; CNN; Comedy Central; C-SPAN; CW PLUS; Discovery Channel; Disney Channel; ESPN; ESPN Classic; ESPN2; Food Network; Fox News Channel; Fox Sports 1; FOX Sports Midwest; Freeform; FX; Hallmark Channel; HGTV; History; HLN; Lifetime; MSNBC; MTV; NFL Network; Nickelodeon; Pop; Spike TV; Syfy; TBS; The Weather Channel; TLC; TNT; Travel Channel; TV Land; USA Network; WGN America.
Fee: $64.95 installation; $67.75 monthly.
Digital Basic Service
Subscribers: N.A.
Programming (via satellite): BBC America; Bloomberg Television; Bravo; Cloo; CMT; Discovery Digital Networks; Disney XD; DMX Music; ESPN Classic; ESPN2; ESPNews; EVINE Live; Flix; FOX College Sports Central; FOX College Sports Pacific; Fox Sports 1; Fuse; FXM; FYI; Golf Channel; Great American Country; GSN; HGTV; History; History International; HITS (Headend In The Sky); IFC; LMN; National Geographic Channel; NBCSN; Nick Jr.; Nicktoons; Outdoor Channel; Ovation; Starz Encore (multiplexed); Sundance TV; Syfy; TeenNick; The Word Network; Trinity Broadcasting Network (TBN); Turner Classic Movies; WE tv.

Pay Service 1
Pay Units: N.A.
Programming (via satellite): Cinemax; HBO.
Fee: $14.95 installation; $8.95 monthly (each).
Digital Pay Service 1
Pay Units: N.A.
Programming (via satellite): Cinemax (multiplexed); HBO (multiplexed); Showtime (multiplexed); Starz (multiplexed); The Movie Channel (multiplexed).
Pay-Per-View
iN DEMAND (delivered digitally); Hot Choice (delivered digitally); Playboy TV (delivered digitally); Fresh (delivered digitally); Shorteez (delivered digitally).
Internet Service
Operational: Yes.
Fee: $24.95 installation; $39.95 monthly.
Telephone Service
Digital: Operational
Miles of Plant: 22.0 (coaxial); None (fiber optic). Homes passed: 1,437.
Chief Executive Officer: Bill Haggarty. Regional Vice President: Andrew Dearth. Vice President, Marketing: Tracy Bass. Senior Vice President, Financial Planning: Daniel White.
Ownership: Vyve Broadband LLC (MSO).

MELVERN—Formerly served by Zito Media. No longer in operation. ICA: KS0400.

MERIDEN—Formerly served by SCI Cable. Now served by Cox Communications, TOPEKA, KS [KS0002]. ICA: KS0221.

MILFORD—Eagle Communications, 2703 Hall St, Ste 15, PO Box 817, Hays, KS 67601. Phones: 785-632-3118; 785-625-5910; 785-625-4000 (Corporate office); 785-263-2529. Fax: 785-625-8030. Web Site: http://www.eaglecom.net. ICA: KS0239.
TV Market Ranking: Outside TV Markets (MILFORD). Franchise award date: N.A. Franchise expiration date: N.A. Began: June 1, 1976.
Channel capacity: N.A. Channels available but not in use: N.A.
Basic Service
Subscribers: 16.
Programming (received off-air): KAAS-TV (FOX) Salina; WIBW-TV (CBS, MeTV, MNT) Topeka.
Programming (via microwave): KSNT (FOX, NBC) Topeka; KTKA-TV (ABC, CW) Topeka; KTWU (PBS) Topeka; KWCH-DT (CBS) Hutchinson.
Programming (via satellite): A&E; AMC; Cartoon Network; CNN; Comedy Central; Discovery Channel; Disney Channel; E! HD; ESPN; ESPN2; FOX Sports Midwest; Freeform; Fuse; Great American Country; History; HLN; KUSA (NBC, WeatherNation) Denver; Lifetime; Outdoor Channel; QVC; Syfy; TBS; The Weather Channel; TLC; TNT; USA Network; WGN America.
Fee: $24.95 installation; $69.95 monthly.

2017 Edition

D-295

Kansas—Cable Systems

FULLY SEARCHABLE • CONTINUOUSLY UPDATED • DISCOUNT RATES FOR PRINT PURCHASERS
For more information call 800-771-9202 or visit www.warren-news.com

Pay Service 1
Pay Units: N.A.
Programming (via satellite): HBO; Showtime; The Movie Channel.
Fee: $11.95 monthly (Showtime or TMC), $14.95 monthly (HBO).
Internet Service
Operational: Yes.
Fee: $25.95-$49.95 monthly.
Telephone Service
Digital: Operational
Miles of Plant: 7.0 (coaxial); None (fiber optic). Homes passed: 245.
Chief Operating Officer: Kurt K. David. General Manager: Travis Kohlrus. Chief Technician: Jim Gall. Ad Sales Manager: Mike Koerner.
Ownership: Eagle Communications Inc. (MSO).

MILTONVALE—Twin Valley Communications. Formerly served by BENNINGTON, KS [KS0214]. This cable system has converted to IPTV, 618 6th St, Clay Center, KS 67432. Phones: 800-515-3311; 785-427-2288. E-mail: tvtinc@twinvalley.net. Web Site: http://www.twinvalley.net. Also serves Aurora, Barnard, Bennington, Beverly, Clay Center, Clifton, Clyde, Delphos, Glasco, Green, Greenleaf, Leonardville, Longford, Milford, Morganville, Olsburg, Riley, Tescott & Wakefield. ICA: KS5032.
TV Market Ranking: Below 100 (Bennington). Channel capacity: N.A. Channels available but not in use: N.A.
Local
Subscribers: 3,369.
Fee: $12.99 monthly. Includes 25 channels.
Internet Service
Operational: Yes.
Telephone Service
Digital: Operational
Fee: $16.75 monthly
Chief Financial Officer: Gary Abbott. Sales & Marketing Manager: Joe Green.
Ownership: Twin Valley Communications Inc.

MINNEAPOLIS—Eagle Communications, 2703 Hall St, Ste 15, PO Box 817, Hays, KS 67601. Phones: 785-743-5616; 785-899-3371; 785-625-4000 (Corporate office); 785-625-5910. Fax: 785-625-8030. Web Site: http://www.eaglecom.net. Also serves Bennington. ICA: KS0117.
TV Market Ranking: Below 100 (Bennington, MINNEAPOLIS). Franchise award date: May 1, 1974. Franchise expiration date: N.A. Began: September 1, 1975.
Channel capacity: N.A. Channels available but not in use: N.A.
Basic Service
Subscribers: 232. Commercial subscribers: 6.
Programming (received off-air): KAAS-TV (FOX) Salina; KOOD (PBS) Hays; KSCW-DT (CW, Decades) Wichita; allband FM.
Programming (via microwave): KAKE (ABC, MeTV) Wichita; KMTW (MNT, The Country Network) Hutchinson; KSNC (NBC) Great Bend; WIBW-TV (CBS, MeTV, MNT) Topeka.

Programming (via satellite): C-SPAN; KMGH-TV (ABC, Azteca America) Denver; KUSA (NBC, WeatherNation) Denver; QVC; The Weather Channel.
Fee: $24.95 installation; $69.95 monthly.
Expanded Basic Service 1
Subscribers: N.A.
Programming (via satellite): A&E; AMC; Animal Planet; Bravo; CNBC; CNN; C-SPAN 2; Discovery Channel; Discovery Life Channel; Disney Channel; Disney XD; E! HD; ESPN; ESPN Classic; ESPN2; ESPNews; Food Network; Fox News Channel; FOX Sports Midwest; Freeform; Fuse; FX; FXM; Great American Country; Hallmark Channel; HGTV; History; Jewelry Television; Lifetime; MSNBC; National Geographic Channel; NFL Network; Nickelodeon; Outdoor Channel; RFD-TV; Syfy; TBS; TLC; TNT; Travel Channel; Trinity Broadcasting Network (TBN); truTV; TV Land; USA Network; WGN America.
Fee: $24.00 monthly.
Digital Basic Service
Subscribers: N.A.
Programming (via satellite): BBC America; Bloomberg Television; Church Channel; Cloo; Cooking Channel; Destination America; Discovery Kids Channel; DIY Network; DMX Music; EWTN Global Catholic Network; FOX College Sports Central; FOX College Sports Pacific; Fox Sports 1; FYI; Golf Channel; GSN; Hallmark Movies & Mysteries; History International; IFC; INSP; Investigation Discovery; JUCE TV; LMN; NBCSN; OWN; Oprah Winfrey Network; Science Channel; Sundance TV; The Word Network; Turner Classic Movies; UP; WE tv.
Fee: $4.95 monthly (sports, variety or entertainment tier), $5.95 monthly (basic).
Digital Pay Service 1
Pay Units: N.A.
Programming (via satellite): Cinemax (multiplexed); Flix; HBO (multiplexed); Showtime (multiplexed); Starz (multiplexed); Starz Encore (multiplexed); The Movie Channel (multiplexed).
Fee: $11.95 monthly (Showtime or TMC), $14.95 monthly (HBO).
Pay-Per-View
iN DEMAND (delivered digitally); Playboy TV (delivered digitally); Fresh (delivered digitally); Spice 2 (delivered digitally); Club Jenna (delivered digitally).
Internet Service
Operational: Yes.
Fee: $24.95-$49.95 monthly.
Telephone Service
Digital: Operational
Fee: $18.00 monthly
Miles of Plant: 15.0 (coaxial); None (fiber optic). Homes passed: 460.
Chief Operating Officer: Kurt K. David. General Manager: Travis Kohlrus. Chief Technician: Jim Gall. Ad Sales Manager: Mike Koerner.
Ownership: Eagle Communications Inc. (MSO).

MONTEZUMA—United Communications Assn. Inc. Now served by CIMARRON, KS [KS0126]. ICA: KS0259.

MORGANVILLE—Formerly served by Eagle Communications. No longer in operation. ICA: KS0401.

MORRILL—Formerly served by Rainbow Communications. No longer in operation. ICA: KS0402.

MORROWVILLE—Formerly served by Diode Cable Co. No longer in operation. ICA: KS0350.

MOUND VALLEY—Formerly served by National Cable Inc. No longer in operation. ICA: KS0274.

MOUNDRIDGE—Mid-Kansas Cable Services Inc., 109 North Christian Ave, PO Box 960, Moundridge, KS 67107-0960. Phone: 620-345-2831. Fax: 620-345-6106. Also serves Goessel. ICA: KS0133.
TV Market Ranking: 67 (Goessel, MOUNDRIDGE). Franchise award date: April 15, 1980. Franchise expiration date: N.A. Began: April 1, 1981.
Channel capacity: 36 (2-way capable). Channels available but not in use: N.A.
Basic Service
Subscribers: 145. Commercial subscribers: 4.
Programming (received off-air): KAKE (ABC, MeTV) Wichita; KMTW (MNT, The Country Network) Hutchinson; KPTS (PBS) Hutchinson; KSAS-TV (Antenna TV, FOX) Wichita; KSCW-DT (CW, Decades) Wichita; KSNW (NBC) Wichita; KWCH-DT (CBS) Hutchinson.
Programming (via satellite): A&E; AMC; CMT; C-SPAN; Discovery Channel; Disney Channel; ESPN; ESPN2; Fox News Channel; FOX Sports Networks; Freeform; HGTV; History; Lifetime; Nickelodeon; Spike TV; TBS; The Weather Channel; TNT; Turner Classic Movies; TV Land; USA Network; WGN America.
Fee: $20.00 installation; $40.15 monthly; $3.00 converter.
Pay Service 1
Pay Units: N.A.
Programming (via satellite): HBO.
Fee: $20.00 installation; $10.50 monthly.
Video-On-Demand: No
Internet Service
Operational: No, DSL.
Telephone Service
None
Miles of Plant: 15.0 (coaxial); None (fiber optic). Homes passed: 646.
Vice President & General Manager: H.M. Weelborg. Chief Technician: Tom Stucky. Marketing Director: Kay Koehn.
Ownership: Mid-Kansas Cable Services Inc. (MSO).

MOUNT HOPE—Formerly served by Almega Cable. No longer in operation. ICA: KS0208.

MULLINVILLE—Formerly served by Mullinville Cable TV. No longer in operation. ICA: KS0309.

MULVANE—Cox Communications. Now served by WICHITA, KS [KS0001]. ICA: KS0095.

MULVANE (unincorporated areas)—Formerly served by CableDirect. No longer in operation. ICA: KS0403.

MUNDEN—Formerly served by Westcom. No longer in operation. ICA: KS0354.

MUNJOR—Nex-Tech. Formerly [KS0473]. This cable system has converted to IPTV, 2418 Vine St, Hays, KS 67601. Phones: 877-625-7872; 785-625-7070. Fax: 785-625-4479. E-mail: webmaster@nex-tech.com. Web Site: http://www.nex-tech.com. ICA: KS5193.
TV Market Ranking: Below 100 (MUNJOR). Channel capacity: N.A. Channels available but not in use: N.A.
Essentials
Subscribers: 59.
Programming (received off-air): KAKE (ABC, MeTV) Wichita; KBSH-DT (CBS) Hays; KGIN (CBS, MNT, NBC) Grand Island; KHGI-TV (ABC) Kearney; KLNE-TV (PBS) Lexington; KMTW (MNT, The Country Network) Hutchinson; KOOD (PBS) Hays; KSAS-TV (Antenna TV, FOX) Wichita; KSCW-DT (CW, Decades) Wichita; KSNC (NBC) Great Bend; KSNK (NBC) McCook.
Programming (via satellite): C-SPAN; EWTN Global Catholic Network; Pop; QVC; The Weather Channel; WGN America.
Fee: $30.00 installation; $24.95 monthly. Includes 50 channels.
Premiere
Subscribers: 58.
Programming (via satellite): Bloomberg Television; Discovery Kids Channel; Disney XD; DMX Music; ESPN Classic; ESPNews; EVINE Live; FXM; Golf Channel; Investigation Discovery; LMN; NBCSN.
Fee: $61.95 monthly. Includes 118 channels plus music channels.
HD
Subscribers: N.A.
Fee: $11.95 monthly. Includes 72 channels.
Sports & Entertainment
Subscribers: N.A.
Programming (via satellite): BBC America; CMT; Destination America; FOX College Sports Central; FOX College Sports Pacific; IFC; MTV Classic; MTV Hits; MTV2; National Geographic Channel; Nick Jr.; OWN; Oprah Winfrey Network; Science Channel; TeenNick; VH1 Soul; WE tv.
Fee: $12.95 monthly. Includes 34 channels.
Cinemax
Subscribers: N.A.
Programming (via satellite): Cinemax (multiplexed); Flix; HBO (multiplexed); Showtime (multiplexed); Starz (multiplexed); Starz Encore (multiplexed); Sundance TV; The Movie Channel (multiplexed).
Fee: $8.95 monthly. Includes 8 channels.
HBO
Subscribers: N.A.
Fee: $14.95 monthly. Includes 12 channels.
Showtime/TMC
Subscribers: N.A.
Fee: $13.95 monthly. Includes 16 channels.
Starz/Encore
Subscribers: N.A.
Fee: $10.95 monthly. Includes 18 channels.
Video-On-Demand: Yes
Pay-Per-View
Hot Choice (delivered digitally); Playboy TV (delivered digitally); Fresh (delivered digitally); Club Jenna (delivered digitally).
Internet Service
Operational: Yes.
Fee: $22.95-$202.95 monthly.
Telephone Service
Digital: Operational
Fee: $16.75 monthly
Chief Operating Officer & General Manager: Larry Sevier. Video Solutions Manager: Scott Roe.
Ownership: Nex-Tech (MSO).

Cable Systems—Kansas

MUNJOR—Nex-Tech. This cable system has converted to IPTV. See MUNJOR, KS [KS5193]. ICA: KS0473.

MUSCOTAH—Rainbow Communications. This cable system has converted to IPTV. Now served by WILLIS, SD [KS5177]. ICA: KS0345.

NARKA—Formerly served by Westcom. No longer in operation. ICA: KS0460.

NATOMA—Formerly served by Eagle Communications. No longer in operation. ICA: KS0222.

NATOMA—Nex-Tech. Formerly served by LENORA, KS [KS0450]. This cable system has converted to IPTV, 2418 Vine St, Hays, KS 67601. Phones: 877-625-7872; 785-625-7070. Fax: 785-625-4479. E-mail: webmaster@nex-tech.com. Web Site: http://www.nex-tech.com. ICA: KS5078.
TV Market Ranking: Franchise award date: April 27, 2007. Franchise expiration date: N.A. Began: N.A.
Channel capacity: N.A. Channels available but not in use: N.A.
Essentials
  Subscribers: 110.
  Fee: $30.00 installation; $24.95 monthly. Includes 45 channels.
Premiere
  Subscribers: 98.
  Fee: $61.95 monthly. Includes 113 channels plus music channels.
HD
  Subscribers: N.A.
  Fee: $11.95 monthly. Includes 72+ channels.
Sports & Entertainment
  Subscribers: N.A.
  Fee: $12.95 monthly. Includes 34 channels.
Cinemax
  Subscribers: N.A.
  Fee: $8.95 monthly. Includes 8 channels.
HBO
  Subscribers: N.A.
  Fee: $14.95 monthly. Includes 12 channels.
Showtime/TMC
  Subscribers: N.A.
  Fee: $13.95 monthly. Includes 16 channels.
Starz/Encore
  Subscribers: N.A.
  Fee: $10.95 monthly. Includes 18 channels.
Video-On-Demand: Yes
Internet Service
  Operational: Yes.
  Fee: $22.95-$42.95 monthly.
Telephone Service
  Digital: Operational
  Fee: $16.75 monthly
Chief Executive Officer & General Manager: Larry Sevier. Video Solutions Manager: Scott Roe.
Ownership: Nex-Tech.

NEODESHA—Cable One. Now served by INDEPENDENCE, KS [KS0022]. ICA: KS0063.

NEOSHO RAPIDS—Formerly served by Zito Media. No longer in operation. ICA: KS0433.

NESS CITY—Formerly served by Cebridge Connections. Now served by GBT Communications Inc., RUSH CENTER, KS [KS0418]. ICA: KS0109.

NEWTON—Cox Communications. Now served by WICHITA, KS [KS0001]. ICA: KS0018.

NORCATUR—Nex-Tech (formerly Pinpoint Cable TV) This cable system has converted to IPTV. ICA: KS0314.

NORCATUR—Nex-Tech. Formerly [KS0314]. This cable system has converted to IPTV, 2418 Vine St, Hays, KS 67601. Phones: 877-625-7872; 785-625-7070. Fax: 785-625-4479. E-mail: webmaster@nex-tech.com. Web Site: http://www.nex-tech.com. ICA: KS5194.
Channel capacity: N.A. Channels available but not in use: N.A.
Essentials
  Subscribers: 59.
  Fee: $30.00 installation; $24.95 monthly. Includes 50 channels.
Premiere
  Subscribers: 58.
  Fee: $61.95 monthly. Includes 118 channels including music channels.
HD
  Subscribers: N.A.
  Fee: $11.95 monthly. Includes 72+ channels.
Sports & Entertainment
  Subscribers: N.A.
  Fee: $12.95 monthly. Includes 34 channels.
Cinemax
  Subscribers: N.A.
  Fee: $8.95 monthly. Includes 8 channels.
HBO
  Subscribers: N.A.
  Fee: $14.95 monthly. Includes 12 channels.
Showtime/TMC
  Subscribers: N.A.
  Fee: $13.95 monthly. Includes 16 channels.
Starz/Encore
  Subscribers: N.A.
  Fee: $10.95 monthly. Includes 18 channels.
Internet Service
  Operational: Yes.
  Fee: $22.95-$202.95 monthly.
Telephone Service
  Digital: Operational
  Fee: $16.75 monthly
Chief Executive Officer & General Manager: Larry Sevier. Video Solutions Manager: Scott Roe.
Ownership: Nex-Tech.

NORTON—Nex-Tech, 2418 Vine St, Hays, KS 67601. Phones: 877-625-7872; 785-625-7070. Fax: 785-625-4479. E-mail: webmaster@nex-tech.com. Web Site: http://www.nex-tech.com. ICA: KS0050.
Channel capacity: N.A. Channels available but not in use: N.A.
Basic Service
  Subscribers: 1,069.
  Programming (received off-air): KAKE (ABC, MeTV) Wichita; KBSH-DT (CBS) Hays; KGIN (CBS, MNT, NBC) Grand Island; KHGI-TV (ABC) Kearney; KLNE-TV (PBS) Lexington; KMTW (MNT, The Country Network) Hutchinson; KOOD (PBS) Hays; KSAS-TV (Antenna TV, FOX) Wichita; KSCW-DT (CW, Decades) Wichita; KSNC (NBC) Great Bend; KSNK (NBC) McCook.
  Programming (via satellite): C-SPAN; QVC; The Weather Channel; WGN America.
  Fee: $24.95 monthly.
Expanded Basic Service 1
  Subscribers: N.A.
  Programming (via satellite): ESPN; ESPN Classic; ESPN2; EWTN Global Catholic Network; Outdoor Channel; Travel Channel.
  Fee: $61.95 monthly.

Pay Service 1
  Pay Units: N.A.
  Programming (via satellite): HBO.
  Fee: $14.95 monthly.
Internet Service
  Operational: Yes.
  Fee: $22.95-$72.95 monthly.
Telephone Service
  Analog: Operational
  Fee: $16.75 monthly
Chief Executive Officer & General Manager: Larry Sevier. Video Solutions Manager: Scott Roe.
Ownership: Nex-Tech.

NORTONVILLE—Giant Communications. Now served by HOLTON, KS [KS0066]. ICA: KS0196.

NORWICH—Formerly served by Almega Cable. No longer in operation. ICA: KS0247.

OAKLEY—S&T Cable. Now served by BREWSTER, KS [KS0315]. ICA: KS0099.

OBERLIN—Eagle Communications, 2703 Hall St, Ste 15, PO Box 817, Hays, KS 67601. Phones: 785-899-3371; 785-625-5910; 785-743-5616; 785-625-4000 (Corporate office). Fax: 785-625-8030. Web Site: http://www.eaglecom.net. ICA: KS0090.
TV Market Ranking: Below 100 (OBERLIN). Franchise award date: N.A. Franchise expiration date: N.A. Began: April 1, 1970.
Channel capacity: N.A. Channels available but not in use: N.A.
Basic Service
  Subscribers: 221. Commercial subscribers: 3.
  Programming (received off-air): KBSL-DT (CBS) Goodland; KLBY (ABC) Colby; KMTW (MNT, The Country Network) Hutchinson; KOOD (PBS) Hays; KSAS-TV (Antenna TV, FOX) Wichita; KSNK (NBC) McCook; KWNB-TV (ABC) Hayes Center; 4 FMs.
  Programming (via satellite): EWTN Global Catholic Network; KWGN-TV (CW, This TV) Denver; QVC; The Weather Channel; Trinity Broadcasting Network (TBN).
  Fee: $24.95 installation; $69.95 monthly.
Expanded Basic Service 1
  Subscribers: N.A.
  Programming (received off-air): KSCW-DT (CW, Decades) Wichita.
  Programming (via satellite): A&E; AMC; Animal Planet; Cartoon Network; CMT; CNBC; CNN; Comedy Central; Discovery Channel; Disney Channel; E! HD; ESPN; ESPN2; Food Network; Fox News Channel; Fox Sports 1; FOX Sports Midwest; Freeform; FX; Great American Country; Hallmark Channel; HGTV; History; HLN; Lifetime; MSNBC; MTV; National Geographic Channel; NFL Network; Nickelodeon; Outdoor Channel; Spike TV; Syfy; TBS; TLC; TNT; Travel Channel; Turner Classic Movies; TV Land; USA Network; VH1.
  Fee: $25.00 monthly.

Pay Service 1
  Pay Units: N.A.
  Programming (via satellite): HBO; Showtime; The Movie Channel.
  Fee: $11.95 monthly (Showtime or TMC), $14.95 monthly (HBO).
Video-On-Demand: No
Internet Service
  Operational: Yes. Began: June 23, 2002. Broadband Service: Eagle Internet.
  Fee: $25.95-$49.95 monthly.
Telephone Service
  Analog: Not Operational
  Digital: Operational
  Fee: $18.00 monthly
Miles of Plant: 14.0 (coaxial); None (fiber optic). Homes passed: 954.
Chief Operating Officer: Kurt K. David. General Manager: Travis Kohlrus. Chief Technician: Jim Gall. Ad Sales Manager: Mike Koerner.
Ownership: Eagle Communications Inc. (MSO).

OFFERLE—GBT Communications Inc, 103 Lincoln St, PO Box 229, Rush Center, KS 67575. Phones: 800-946-4282; 800-432-7965; 785-372-4236. Fax: 785-372-4210. E-mail: custservice@gbtlive.com. Web Site: http://www.gbta.net. ICA: KS0405.
TV Market Ranking: Outside TV Markets (OFFERLE). Franchise award date: N.A. Franchise expiration date: N.A. Began: January 1, 1977.
Channel capacity: N.A. Channels available but not in use: N.A.
Basic Service
  Subscribers: 11.
  Programming (received off-air): KBSD-DT (CBS) Ensign; KOOD (PBS) Hays; KSAS-TV (Antenna TV, FOX) Wichita; KSNC (NBC) Great Bend; KUPK (ABC) Garden City; all-band FM.
  Programming (via satellite): C-SPAN; C-SPAN 2; EWTN Global Catholic Network; LWS Local Weather Station; TBS; WGN America.
  Fee: $18.95 monthly.
Expanded Basic Service 1
  Subscribers: N.A.
  Programming (via satellite): A&E; AMC; Animal Planet; Cartoon Network; CMT; CNN; Comedy Central; Discovery Channel; Disney Channel; E! HD; ESPN; ESPN Classic; ESPN2; ESPNews; Food Network; Fox News Channel; Fox Sports 1; Freeform; FX; Hallmark Channel; HGTV; History; HLN; INSP; Lifetime; MSNBC; MTV; NFL Network; Nickelodeon; Outdoor Channel; QVC; Spike TV; Syfy; The Weather Channel; TLC; TNT; Travel Channel; Trinity Broadcasting Network (TBN); truTV; Turner Classic Movies; TV Land; USA Network; VH1.
  Fee: $39.95 monthly.
Pay Service 1
  Pay Units: N.A.
  Programming (via satellite): Cinemax; Flix; HBO; Showtime; The Movie Channel.
  Fee: $7.00 monthly (Cinemax), $10.95 monthly (Showtime/TMC/Flix), $14.95 monthly (HBO).
Internet Service
  Operational: No.

Communications Daily
Warren Communications News

Get the industry standard FREE —
For a no-obligation trial call 800-771-9202 or visit www.warren-news.com

Kansas—Cable Systems

Telephone Service
None
Miles of Plant: 2.0 (coaxial); None (fiber optic).
General Manager: Beau Rebel. Plant Manager: Kirby Hagans. Office Manager: Debra Tuzicka.
Ownership: Golden Belt Telephone Association Inc. (MSO).

OLPE—Formerly served by Zito Media. No longer in operation. ICA: KS0233.

OLSBURG—Formerly served by Giant Communications. No longer in operation. ICA: KS0436.

ONAGA—Blue Valley Tele-Communications. Now served by AXTELL (formerly Frankfort & Home), KS [KS0424]. ICA: KS0407.

OSAGE CITY—Mediacom. Now served by BURLINGTON, KS [KS0064]. ICA: KS0072.

OSAGE COUNTY—Formerly served by Galaxy Cablevision. No longer in operation. ICA: KS0269.

OSKALOOSA—Giant Communications. Now served by HOLTON, KS [KS0066]. ICA: KS0175.

OSWEGO—Mediacom, 1533 South Enterprise Ave, Springfield, MO 65804. Phones: 417-875-5500; 417-875-5560. Fax: 417-883-0265. Web Site: http://www.mediacomcable.com. ICA: KS0103.
TV Market Ranking: Below 100 (OSWEGO). Franchise award date: N.A. Franchise expiration date: N.A. Began: October 27, 1980.
Channel capacity: N.A. Channels available but not in use: N.A.
Basic Service
Subscribers: 76.
Programming (received off-air): KOAM-TV (CBS) Pittsburg; KODE-TV (ABC) Joplin; KOED-TV (PBS) Tulsa; KOKI-TV (FOX, MeTV) Tulsa; KSNF (NBC) Joplin.
Programming (via satellite): A&E; AMC; Animal Planet; CMT; CNN; C-SPAN; Discovery Channel; Disney Channel; ESPN; ESPN2; Freeform; HLN; Lifetime; MTV; Nickelodeon; QVC; Spike TV; Syfy; TBS; The Weather Channel; TLC; TNT; TV Land; USA Network; WGN America.
Fee: $35.00 installation; $47.00 monthly.
Pay Service 1
Pay Units: N.A.
Programming (via satellite): Cinemax; HBO; Showtime; The Movie Channel.
Fee: $10.50 monthly (each).
Video-On-Demand: No
Internet Service
Operational: No.
Telephone Service
None
Miles of Plant: 17.0 (coaxial); None (fiber optic). Homes passed: 1,001.
Vice President: Bill Copeland. Technical Operations Director: Alan Freedman. Technical Operations Manager: Glen Parrish. Sales & Marketing Manager: Will Kuebler. Vice President, Financial Reporting: Kenneth J. Kohrs.
Ownership: Mediacom LLC (MSO).

OTTAWA—Vyve Broadband, 4 International Dr, Ste 330, Rye Brook, NY 10573. Phones: 800-937-1397; 405-275-6923; 405-395-1131. Web Site: http://vyvebroadband.com. ICA: KS0025.
TV Market Ranking: Below 100 (OTTAWA). Franchise award date: N.A. Franchise expiration date: N.A. Began: January 1, 1972.
Channel capacity: N.A. Channels available but not in use: N.A.
Basic Service
Subscribers: 851. Commercial subscribers: 207.
Programming (received off-air): KCPT (PBS) Kansas City; KCTV (CBS) Kansas City; KCWE (CW, Movies!, This TV) Kansas City; KMBC-TV (ABC, MeTV) Kansas City; KMCI-TV (Bounce TV, Escape, IND) Lawrence; KSHB-TV (COZI TV, Grit, NBC) Kansas City; KSMO-TV (Bounce TV, MNT) Kansas City; KSNT (FOX, NBC) Topeka; KTKA-TV (ABC, CW) Topeka; KTWU (PBS) Topeka; WDAF-TV (Antenna TV, FOX) Kansas City; WIBW-TV (CBS, MeTV, MNT) Topeka; allband FM.
Programming (via satellite): C-SPAN; ION Television; Pop; The Weather Channel.
Fee: $64.95 installation; $25.00 monthly; $2.00 converter.
Expanded Basic Service 1
Subscribers: N.A.
Programming (via satellite): A&E; AMC; Animal Planet; Cartoon Network; CMT; CNBC; CNN; Comedy Central; C-SPAN 2; Discovery Channel; Disney Channel; E! HD; ESPN; ESPN2; EWTN Global Catholic Network; Food Network; Fox News Channel; Fox Sports 1; FOX Sports Midwest; Freeform; FX; Hallmark Channel; HGTV; History; HLN; Lifetime; MSNBC; MTV; NBCSN; Nickelodeon; OWN: Oprah Winfrey Network; QVC; Spike TV; Starz Encore (multiplexed); Syfy; TBS; TLC; TNT; Travel Channel; truTV; Turner Classic Movies; TV Land; USA Network; VH1; WGN America.
Fee: $39.96 monthly.
Digital Basic Service
Subscribers: N.A.
Programming (via satellite): BBC America; Discovery Digital Networks; Disney XD; DMX Music; ESPN Classic; ESPNews; Fuse; Golf Channel; GSN; HITS (Headend In The Sky); IFC; LMN; Sundance TV.
Digital Pay Service 1
Pay Units: N.A.
Programming (via satellite): Cinemax (multiplexed); HBO (multiplexed); Starz (multiplexed); The Movie Channel (multiplexed).
Video-On-Demand: No
Pay-Per-View
iN DEMAND (delivered digitally); ESPN (delivered digitally).
Internet Service
Operational: Yes.
Fee: $24.95 installation; $39.95 monthly.

Telephone Service
Digital: Operational
Miles of Plant: 88.0 (coaxial); None (fiber optic). Homes passed: 6,558.
Chief Executive Officer: Bill Haggarty. Regional Vice President: Andrew Dearth. Vice President, Marketing: Tracy Bass. Senior Vice President, Financial Planning: Daniel White.
Ownership: Vyve Broadband LLC (MSO).

OVERBROOK—Formerly served by Zito Media. No longer in operation. ICA: KS0408.

OVERLAND PARK—Formerly served by Time Warner Cable of Johnson County. No longer in operation. ICA: KS0003.

OXFORD—Formerly served by Allegiance Communications. No longer in operation. ICA: KS0158.

OZAWKIE—Giant Communications. Now served by HOLTON, KS [KS0066]. ICA: KS0409.

PALMER—Formerly served by Eagle Communications. No longer in operation. ICA: KS0468.

PAOLA—Suddenlink Communications, 520 Maryville Centre Dr, Ste 300, St. Louis, MO 63141. Phones: 800-999-6845 (Customer service); 314-315-9400. Web Site: http://www.suddenlink.com. Also serves Johnson County (southern portion), Miami County (unincorporated areas), Osawatomie & Spring Hill. ICA: KS0029.
TV Market Ranking: 22 (Johnson County (southern portion), Miami County (unincorporated areas) (portions), Spring Hill; Below 100 (PAOLA, Miami County (unincorporated areas) (portions)); Outside TV Markets (Osawatomie, Miami County (unincorporated areas) (portions)). Franchise award date: N.A. Franchise expiration date: N.A. Began: August 1, 1974.
Channel capacity: 78 (operating 2-way). Channels available but not in use: N.A.
Basic Service
Subscribers: 2,200.
Programming (received off-air): KCPT (PBS) Kansas City; KCTV (CBS) Kansas City; KCWE (CW, Movies!, This TV) Kansas City; KMBC-TV (ABC, MeTV) Kansas City; KMCI-TV (Bounce TV, Escape, IND) Lawrence; KPXE-TV (ION) Kansas City; KSHB-TV (COZI TV, Grit, NBC) Kansas City; KSMO-TV (Bounce TV, MNT) Kansas City; KSNT (FOX, NBC) Topeka; KTWU (PBS) Topeka; WDAF-TV (Antenna TV, FOX) Kansas City; WIBW-TV (CBS, MeTV, MNT) Topeka; 14 FMs.
Programming (via satellite): A&E; Cartoon Network; CNN; C-SPAN; Discovery Channel; Disney Channel; ESPN; EWTN Global Catholic Network; Freeform; History; HLN; Lifetime; Nickelodeon; QVC; Spike TV; TBS; The Weather Channel; TLC; TNT; Turner Classic Movies; TV Land; USA Network; WGN America.
Fee: $28.45 monthly.
Expanded Basic Service 1
Subscribers: N.A.
Programming (via satellite): Fox News Channel; FX; Great American Country; HGTV; MSNBC; Root Sports Rocky Mountain; VH1.
Fee: $25.00 monthly.

Digital Basic Service
Subscribers: N.A.
Programming (via satellite): BBC America; Discovery Digital Networks; DMX Music; ESPN Classic; ESPN2; Fox Sports 1; Golf Channel; NBCSN; Outdoor Channel.
Pay Service 1
Pay Units: N.A.
Programming (via satellite): Cinemax; HBO; Showtime; The Movie Channel.
Fee: $7.95 monthly (TMC), $9.95 monthly (Showtime), $10.95 monthly (HBO).
Digital Pay Service 1
Pay Units: N.A.
Programming (via satellite): Cinemax (multiplexed); HBO (multiplexed); Showtime (multiplexed); The Movie Channel (multiplexed).
Video-On-Demand: No
Pay-Per-View
iN DEMAND (delivered digitally); Fresh (delivered digitally).
Internet Service
Operational: Yes. Began: June 23, 2002.
Broadband Service: Suddenlink High Speed Internet.
Fee: $49.95 installation; $26.95 monthly.
Telephone Service
None
Miles of Plant: 97.0 (coaxial); None (fiber optic).
Senior Vice President, Corporate Finance: Michael Pflantz. Regional Manager: Todd Cruthird. Plant Manager: Lee Mott. Regional Marketing Manager: Beverly Gambell.
Ownership: Cequel Communications Holdings I LLC (MSO).

PARKER—Formerly served by National Cable Inc. No longer in operation. ICA: KS0316.

PARSONS—Cable One, 2229 Broadway St, Ste 200, Parsons, KS 67357. Phone: 620-421-2510. Fax: 620-421-2719. Web Site: http://www.cableone.net. ICA: KS0024.
TV Market Ranking: Below 100 (PARSONS). Franchise award date: N.A. Franchise expiration date: N.A. Began: January 1, 1966.
Channel capacity: N.A. Channels available but not in use: N.A.
Basic Service
Subscribers: 1,432.
Programming (received off-air): KFJX (FOX) Pittsburg; KOAM-TV (CBS) Pittsburg; KODE-TV (ABC) Joplin; KSNF (NBC) Joplin; 12 FMs.
Programming (via microwave): KJRH-TV (NBC) Tulsa; KMBC-TV (ABC, MeTV) Kansas City; KOED-TV (PBS) Tulsa; WIBW-TV (CBS, MeTV, MNT) Topeka.
Programming (via satellite): A&E; Animal Planet; BET; Bravo; Cartoon Network; CMT; CNBC; CNN; Comedy Central; C-SPAN; C-SPAN 2; CW PLUS; Discovery Channel; Disney Channel; ESPN; ESPN Classic; ESPN2; EVINE Live; EWTN Global Catholic Network; Food Network; Fox News Channel; FOX Sports Midwest; Freeform; FX; Hallmark Channel; HGTV; History; HLN; Lifetime; MSNBC; MTV; Nickelodeon; Outdoor Channel; Oxygen; Pop; QVC; Spike TV; Starz Encore; Syfy; TBS; The Weather Channel; TLC; TNT; Travel Channel; Trinity Broadcasting Network (TBN); Turner Classic Movies; TV Land; USA Network; WE tv; WGN America.
Fee: $90.00 installation; $35.00 monthly; $.23 converter.
Digital Basic Service
Subscribers: N.A.
Programming (via satellite): 3ABN; Boomerang; BYUtv; Discovery Digital

Cable Systems—Kansas

Networks; Disney XD; ESPN Classic; ESPNews; FamilyNet; FOX College Sports Central; FOX College Sports Pacific; Fox Sports 1; Fox Sports 2; FXM; FYI; Golf Channel; Hallmark Channel; History International; HITS (Headend In The Sky); INSP; MC; National Geographic Channel; Outdoor Channel; TNT HD; Trinity Broadcasting Network (TBN); truTV; Universal HD.

Digital Pay Service 1
Pay Units: N.A.
Programming (via satellite): Cinemax (multiplexed); Flix; HBO (multiplexed); Showtime (multiplexed); Showtime HD; Starz (multiplexed); Starz Encore (multiplexed); Sundance TV; The Movie Channel (multiplexed); The Movie Channel HD.
Fee: $7.50 installation; $15.00 monthly (each package).

Video-On-Demand: No

Pay-Per-View
iN DEMAND (delivered digitally); Sports PPV (delivered digitally); Fresh (delivered digitally); Shorteez (delivered digitally); Hot Choice (delivered digitally).

Internet Service
Operational: Yes.
Broadband Service: CableONE.net.
Fee: $75.00 installation; $43.00 monthly.

Telephone Service
Analog: Not Operational
Digital: Operational
Fee: $39.95 monthly
Miles of Plant: 72.0 (coaxial); None (fiber optic). Homes passed: 5,071.
Vice President: Patrick A. Dolohanty. General Manager: Clarence Matlock. Chief Technician: Roger Lee. Marketing Director: Chris Harris.
Ownership: Cable ONE Inc. (MSO).

PARTRIDGE—Formerly served by CableDirect. No longer in operation. ICA: KS0410.

PAWNEE ROCK—GBT Communications Inc. Now served by RUSH CENTER, KS [KS0418]. ICA: KS0412.

PAXICO—Formerly served by Zito Media. No longer in operation. ICA: KS0347.

PEABODY—Vyve Broadband, 4 International Dr, Ste 330, Rye Brook, NY 10573. Phones: 800-937-1397; 405-395-1131; 405-275-6923. Web Site: http://vyvebroadband.com. ICA: KS0141.
TV Market Ranking: Outside TV Markets (PEABODY).
Channel capacity: N.A. Channels available but not in use: N.A.

Basic Service
Subscribers: 67.
Programming (received off-air): KAKE (ABC, MeTV); KAKE; KPTS (PBS) Hutchinson; KSAS-TV (Antenna TV, FOX) Wichita; KSNW (NBC) Wichita; KWCH-DT (CBS) Hutchinson.
Programming (via satellite): A&E; AMC; Animal Planet; Cartoon Network; CMT; CNN; C-SPAN; CW PLUS; Discovery Channel; Disney Channel; ESPN; ESPN2; Food Network; Fox News Channel; FOX Sports Midwest; Freeform; FX; Great American Country; Hallmark Channel; HGTV; History; HLN; Lifetime; MSNBC; MTV; NFL Network; Nickelodeon; Outdoor Channel; QVC; Spike TV; Syfy; TBS; The Weather Channel; TLC; TNT; truTV; TV Land; USA Network; VH1; WGN America.
Fee: $64.95 installation; $65.55 monthly.

Digital Basic Service
Subscribers: N.A.
Programming (via satellite): BBC America; Bloomberg Television; Bravo; Cine Mexicano; Cinelatino; Cloo; CMT; CNN en Espanol; Destination America; Discovery Kids Channel; Disney XD; DMX Music; ESPN Classic; ESPN Deportes; ESPN2; ESPNews; EVINE Live; Flix; FOX College Sports Central; FOX College Sports Pacific; Fox Deportes; Fox Sports 1; Fuse; FXM; FYI; Golf Channel; Great American Country; GSN; HGTV; History; History en Espanol; History International; IFC; Investigation Discovery; LMN; National Geographic Channel; NBC Universo; NBCSN; Nick Jr.; Nicktoons; Outdoor Channel; Ovation; OWN; Oprah Winfrey Network; Science Channel; Starz Encore (multiplexed); Sundance TV; Syfy; TeenNick; The Word Network; Tr3s; Trinity Broadcasting Network (TBN); Turner Classic Movies; UP; ViendoMovies; WE tv.

Pay Service 1
Pay Units: N.A.
Programming (via satellite): Cinemax; HBO.
Fee: $11.95 monthly (each).

Digital Pay Service 1
Pay Units: N.A.
Programming (via satellite): Cinemax (multiplexed); HBO (multiplexed); Showtime (multiplexed); Starz (multiplexed); The Movie Channel (multiplexed).

Pay-Per-View
iN DEMAND (delivered digitally); Hot Choice (delivered digitally); Playboy TV (delivered digitally); Fresh (delivered digitally); Spice: Xcess (delivered digitally); Spice: Xcess (delivered digitally).

Internet Service
Operational: Yes.

Telephone Service
Digital: Operational
Miles of Plant: 11.0 (coaxial); None (fiber optic). Homes passed: 723.
Chief Executive Officer: Bill Haggarty. Regional Vice President: Andrew Dearth. Vice President, Marketing: Tracy Bass. Senior Vice President, Financial Planning: Daniel White.
Ownership: Vyve Broadband LLC (MSO).

PERRY—Cox Communications. Now served by TOPEKA, KS [KS0002]. ICA: KS0147.

PHILLIPSBURG—Nex-Tech. Formerly [KS0060]. This cable system has converted to IPTV, 2418 Vine St, Hays, KS 67601. Phones: 877-625-7872; 785-625-7070. Fax: 785-625-4479. E-mail: webmaster@nex-tech.com. Web Site: http://www.nex-tech.com. ICA: KS5201.
TV Market Ranking: Outside TV Markets (PHILLIPSBURG). Franchise award date: N.A. Franchise expiration date: N.A. Began: August 1, 1966.
Channel capacity: N.A. Channels available but not in use: N.A.

Essentials
Subscribers: 870.
Programming (received off-air): KBSH-DT (CBS) Hays; KGIN (CBS, MNT, NBC) Grand Island; KHGI-TV (ABC) Kearney; KLNE-TV (PBS) Lexington; KNHL (IND) Hastings; KOOD (PBS) Hays; KSNK (NBC) McCook.
Programming (via satellite): National Geographic Channel.
Fee: $30.00 installation; $24.95 monthly. Includes 51 channels.

Premiere
Subscribers: 835.
Programming (via satellite): A&E; Animal Planet; Cartoon Network; CNN; C-SPAN; Discovery Channel; Disney Channel; DMX Music; ESPN; ESPN Classic; ESPN2; ESPNews; FOX Sports Midwest; Freeform; FX; Golf Channel; Great American Country; GSN; HGTV; History; INSP; ION Television; Nickelodeon; Outdoor Channel; QVC; Spike TV; TBS; The Weather Channel; TLC; TNT; Turner Classic Movies; TV Land; USA Network; VH1.
Fee: $61.95 monthly. Includes 119 channels plus music channels.

HD
Subscribers: N.A.
Fee: $11.95 monthly. Includes 75 channels.

Sports & Entertainment
Subscribers: N.A.
Programming (via satellite): BBC America; Bloomberg Television; Discovery Digital Networks; EVINE Live; Fox Sports 1; FYI; History International; LMN; NBCSN; Ovation; Syfy; Trinity Broadcasting Network (TBN).
Fee: $12.95 monthly. Includes 34 channels.

Cinemax
Subscribers: N.A.
Programming (via satellite): Cinemax; HBO; Showtime; The Movie Channel.
Fee: $8.95 monthly. Includes 8 channels.

HBO
Subscribers: N.A.
Fee: $14.95 monthly. Includes 12 channels.

Showtime/TMC
Subscribers: N.A.
Fee: $13.95 monthly. Includes 16 channels.

Starz/Encore
Subscribers: N.A.
Fee: $10.95 monthly. Includes 18 channels.

Video-On-Demand: Yes

Pay-Per-View
iN DEMAND (delivered digitally); Sports PPV (delivered digitally); Fresh (delivered digitally); Shorteez (delivered digitally).

Internet Service
Operational: Yes.

Telephone Service
Digital: Operational
Fee: $16.75 monthly
Chief Executive Officer & General Manager: Larry Sevier. Video Solutions Manager: Scott Roe.
Ownership: Nex-Tech (MSO).

PHILLIPSBURG—Nex-Tech. This cable system has converted to IPTV. See PHLLIPSBURG, KA [KS5201]. ICA: KS0060.

PITTSBURG—Cox Communications, 6205 Peachtree Dunwoody Rd, 12th Floor, Atlanta, GA 30328. Phones: 316-260-7000 (Wichita office); 404-269-6590. Web Site: http://www.cox.com. Also serves Allen County (portions), Arma, Caney, Cherokee County (northern portion), Cherryvale, Chicopee, Coffeyville, Crawford County (eastern portion), Dearing, Erie, Franklin, Frontenac, Gas, Humboldt, Iola, Montgomery County (portions), Neosho County (portions), Tyro & Yates Center, KS; South Coffeyville, OK. ICA: KS0011. **Note:** This system is an overbuild.
TV Market Ranking: Below 100 (Arma, Caney, Cherokee County (northern portion), Chicopee, Crawford County (eastern portion), Dearing, Erie, Franklin, Frontenac, Neosho County (portions), PITTSBURG, South Coffeyville, Tyro, Coffeyville); Outside TV Markets (Allen County (portions), Cherryvale, Gas, Humboldt, Yates Center, Iola). Franchise award date: May 10, 1966. Franchise expiration date: N.A. Began: September 1, 1967.
Channel capacity: N.A. Channels available but not in use: N.A.

Basic Service
Subscribers: 12,231. Commercial subscribers: 528.
Programming (received off-air): K30AL-D (PBS) Iola; KFJX (FOX) Pittsburg; KMBC-TV (ABC, MeTV) Kansas City; KOAM-TV (CBS) Pittsburg; KODE-TV (ABC) Joplin; KOZJ (PBS) Joplin; KQCW-DT (CW, This TV) Muskogee; KSNF (NBC) Joplin; WDAF-TV (Antenna TV, FOX) Kansas City.
Programming (via satellite): C-SPAN; C-SPAN 2; Pop; The Weather Channel; WGN America.
Fee: $29.95 installation; $21.99 monthly.

Expanded Basic Service 1
Subscribers: N.A.
Programming (via satellite): A&E; AMC; Animal Planet; BET; Bravo; Cartoon Network; CMT; CNBC; CNN; Comedy Central; Cox Sports Television; Discovery Channel; Disney Channel; E! HD; ESPN; ESPN2; EWTN Global Catholic Network; Food Network; Fox News Channel; Fox Sports 1; FOX Sports Midwest; Freeform; FX; Hallmark Channel; HGTV; History; HLN; INSP; Lifetime; MSNBC; MTV; MTV2; Nickelodeon; OWN; Oprah Winfrey Network; QVC; Spike TV; Syfy; TBS; TLC; TNT; Travel Channel; Trinity Broadcasting Network (TBN); truTV; Turner Classic Movies; TV Land; Univision Studios; USA Network; VH1.
Fee: $29.95 installation; $18.02 monthly.

Digital Basic Service
Subscribers: N.A.
Programming (via satellite): BBC America; Bloomberg Television; Boomerang; CBS Sports Network; Cooking Channel; Daystar TV Network; Discovery Life Channel; Disney XD; DIY Network; DMX Music; ESPN Classic; ESPNews; FamilyNet; Fox Sports 2; Fuse; FYI; Golf Channel; Great American Country; GSN; Hallmark Movies & Mysteries; History International; HITS (Headend In The Sky); IFC; LMN; NASA TV; Nat Geo WILD; National Geographic Channel; NBA League Pass; NBCSN; NFL Network; Nick 2; Nick Jr.; Nicktoons; Outdoor Channel; Oxygen; Sundance TV; TeenNick; Tennis Channel; Trinity Broadcasting Network (TBN); TV One; UP; WE tv.

Digital Expanded Basic Service
Subscribers: N.A.
Programming (via satellite): HD Theater.

Digital Pay Service 1
Pay Units: N.A.
Programming (via satellite): Cinemax (multiplexed); Flix; HBO (multiplexed); Showtime (multiplexed); Starz (multiplexed); Starz Encore (multiplexed); Starz HD.
Fee: $11.50 monthly (each).

Video-On-Demand: Planned

2017 Edition   D-299

Kansas—Cable Systems

Pay-Per-View
iN DEMAND (delivered digitally); ESPN (delivered digitally); NBA/WNBA League Pass (delivered digitally); NHL Center Ice/MLB Extra Innings (delivered digitally).
Internet Service
Operational: Yes.
Subscribers: 383.
Broadband Service: Cox High Speed Internet.
Fee: $41.95 monthly; $15.00 modem lease; $199.95 modem purchase.
Telephone Service
Digital: Operational
Miles of Plant: 723.0 (coaxial); 246.0 (fiber optic). Homes passed: 32,854. Homes passed included in Wichita.
Vice President & General Manager: Kimberly Edmonds. Vice President, Marketing: Tony Matthews. Vice President, Engineering: Nick DiPonzio. Vice President, Tax: Mary Vickers. Field Operations Regional Manager: Joe Michael. Technical Operations Manager: Rick Fox. Marketing Director: Tina Gabbard. Public Affairs Director: Sarah Kauffman.
Ownership: Cox Communications Inc. (MSO).

PLAINVILLE—Nex-Tech. Formerly [KS0445]. This cable system has converted to IPTV, 2418 Vine St, Hays, KS 67601. Phones: 877-625-7872; 785-625-7070. Fax: 785-625-4479. E-mail: webmaster@nex-tech.com. Web Site: http://www.nex-tech.com. ICA: KS5202.
TV Market Ranking: Below 100 (PLAINVILLE). Channel capacity: N.A. Channels available but not in use: N.A.
Essentials
Subscribers: 594.
Programming (received off-air): KBSH-DT (CBS) Hays; KOOD (PBS) Hays; KSNK (NBC) McCook.
Programming (via microwave): KSAS-TV (Antenna TV, FOX) Wichita.
Programming (via satellite): KMGH-TV (ABC, Azteca America) Denver; KUSA (NBC, WeatherNation) Denver; QVC; The Weather Channel.
Fee: $30.00 installation; $24.95 monthly. Includes 47 channels.
Premiere
Subscribers: 562.
Programming (via satellite): A&E; Animal Planet; BBC America; Bloomberg Television; CNN; Discovery Channel; Discovery Kids Channel; Disney Channel; DMX Music; E! HD; ESPN; ESPN Classic; ESPN2; ESPNews; EVINE Live; EWTN Global Catholic Network; Fox Sports 1; Freeform; FX; FYI; Golf Channel; Great American Country; GSN; HGTV; History; History International; HLN; Lifetime; MSNBC; NBCSN; Nickelodeon; Outdoor Channel; Ovation; Spike TV; Syfy; TBS; TNT; Trinity Broadcasting Network (TBN); Turner Classic Movies; TV Land; USA Network; VH1.
Fee: $61.95 monthly. Includes 115 channels plus music channels.
HD
Subscribers: N.A.
Fee: $11.95 monthly. Includes 72+ channels.
Sports & Entertainment
Subscribers: N.A.
Fee: $12.95 monthly. Includes 34 channels.
Cinemax
Subscribers: N.A.
Programming (via satellite): Cinemax; HBO; Showtime; Starz; Starz Encore; The Movie Channel.
Fee: $8.95 monthly. Includes 8 channels.

HBO
Subscribers: N.A.
Fee: $14.95 monthly. Includes 12 channels.
Showtime/TMC
Subscribers: N.A.
Fee: $13.95 monthly. Includes 16 channels.
Starz/Encore
Subscribers: N.A.
Fee: $10.95 monthly. Includes 18 channels.
Video-On-Demand: Yes
Pay-Per-View
iN DEMAND (delivered digitally); Playboy TV (delivered digitally); Fresh (delivered digitally); Shorteez (delivered digitally); Sports PPV (delivered digitally).
Internet Service
Operational: Yes.
Fee: $22.95-$202.95 monthly.
Telephone Service
Digital: Operational
Fee: $16.75 monthly
Chief Executive Officer & General Manager: Larry Sevier. Video Solutions Manager: Scott Roe.
Ownership: Nex-Tech (MSO).

PLAINVILLE—Nex-Tech. This cable system has converted to IPTV. See PLAINVILLE, KS [KS5202]. ICA: KS0445.

PLEASANTON—Formerly served by Almega Cable. No longer in operation. ICA: KS0083.

POMONA—Formerly served by Zito Media. No longer in operation. ICA: KS0414.

POTTAWATOMIE COUNTY (portions)—WTC Communications. Now served by WAMEGO, KS [KS5017]. ICA: KS5037.

PRATT—Cox Communications. Now served by WICHITA, KS [KS0001]. ICA: KS0031.

PRESCOTT—Craw-Kan Telephone Co-op. This cable system has converted to IPTV. Now served by GIRARD, KS [KS5099]. ICA: KS0341.

PRETTY PRAIRIE—Formerly served by Almega Cable. No longer in operation. ICA: KS0194.

PRINCETON—Formerly served by CableDirect. No longer in operation. ICA: KS0325.

PROTECTION—United Communications Assn. Inc. Now served by CIMARRON, KS [KS0126]. ICA: KS0207.

QUENEMO—Formerly served by Galaxy Cablevision. No longer in operation. ICA: KS0290.

QUINTER—Formerly served by Quinter Cable Co. No longer in operation. ICA: KS0415.

RANDALL—Cunningham Cable TV. Now served by GLEN ELDER, KS [KS0228]. ICA: KS0351.

RANDOLPH—Formerly served by Rainbow Communications. No longer in operation. ICA: KS0352.

READING—Formerly served by Galaxy Cablevision. No longer in operation. ICA: KS0301.

REPUBLIC—Formerly served by Diode Cable Co. No longer in operation. ICA: KS0349.

RESERVE TWP.—Formerly served by Rainbow Communications. No longer in operation. ICA: KS0356.

RICHMOND—Formerly served by Zito Media. No longer in operation. ICA: KS0262.

RILEY—Eagle Communications, 2703 Hall St, Ste 15, PO Box 817, Hays, KS 67601. Phones: 785-263-2529; 785-625-5910; 785-625-4000 (Corporate office); 785-632-3118. Fax: 785-625-8030. Web Site: http://www.eaglecom.net. ICA: KS0190.
TV Market Ranking: Outside TV Markets (RILEY). Franchise award date: March 1, 1977. Franchise expiration date: N.A. Began: June 1, 1978.
Channel capacity: N.A. Channels available but not in use: N.A.
Basic Service
Subscribers: 53.
Programming (received off-air): KAAS-TV (FOX) Salina; KSNT (FOX, NBC) Topeka; KTKA-TV (ABC, CW) Topeka; KTMJ-CD (Escape, FOX) Topeka; KTWU (PBS) Topeka; WIBW-TV (CBS, MeTV, MNT) Topeka; allband FM.
Programming (via satellite): A&E; AMC; Animal Planet; Cartoon Network; CNN; Comedy Central; Discovery Channel; Disney Channel; Disney XD; E! HD; ESPN; ESPN2; Fox News Channel; Fox Sports 1; FOX Sports Midwest; Freeform; FX; Great American Country; HGTV; History; HLN; INSP; Lifetime; MTV; Outdoor Channel; QVC; Syfy; TBS; The Weather Channel; TLC; TNT; Trinity Broadcasting Network (TBN); Turner Classic Movies; TV Land; USA Network; VH1; WGN America.
Fee: $24.95 installation; $69.95 monthly.
Digital Basic Service
Subscribers: N.A.
Programming (via satellite): BBC America; Bloomberg Television; Cloo; Destination America; Discovery Kids Channel; Discovery Life Channel; Disney XD; ESPN Classic; ESPNews; Fox Sports 1; Fuse; FXM; FYI; Golf Channel; GSN; History International; IFC; Investigation Discovery; LMN; NBCSN; Outdoor Channel; OWN; Oprah Winfrey Network; Science Channel; Turner Classic Movies; WE tv.
Fee: $4.95 converter.
Pay Service 1
Pay Units: N.A.
Programming (via satellite): HBO; Showtime; The Movie Channel.
Fee: $11.95 monthly (each).
Digital Pay Service 1
Pay Units: N.A.
Programming (via satellite): Cinemax (multiplexed); Flix; HBO (multiplexed); Showtime (multiplexed); Starz (multiplexed); Starz Encore (multiplexed); The Movie Channel (multiplexed).
Fee: $11.95 monthly (Cinemax, Showtime, TMC or Starz/Encore), $14.95 monthly (HBO).
Pay-Per-View
iN DEMAND (delivered digitally); Playboy TV (delivered digitally); Fresh (delivered digitally); Spice: Xcess (delivered digitally); Club Jenna (delivered digitally).
Internet Service
Operational: Yes.
Broadband Service: Eagle Internet.
Fee: $25.95-$49.95 monthly.
Telephone Service
Digital: Operational
Fee: $18.00 monthly
Miles of Plant: 6.0 (coaxial); None (fiber optic). Homes passed: 406.

Chief Operating Officer: Kurt K. David. General Manager: Travis Kohlrus. Chief Technician: Jim Gall. Ad Sales Manager: Mike Koerner.
Ownership: Eagle Communications Inc. (MSO).

ROSALIA—Formerly served by CableDirect. No longer in operation. ICA: KS0353.

ROSSVILLE—Zito Media, 102 S Main St, PO Box 665, Coudersport, PA 16915. Phones: 814-260-9055; 800-365-6988. E-mail: info@zitomedia.com. Web Site: http://www.zitomedia.com. Also serves Silver Lake. ICA: KS0417.
TV Market Ranking: Below 100 (ROSSVILLE, Silver Lake). Franchise award date: N.A. Franchise expiration date: N.A. Began: November 1, 1982.
Channel capacity: N.A. Channels available but not in use: N.A.
Basic Service
Subscribers: 58.
Programming (received off-air): KCTV (CBS) Kansas City; KCWE (CW, Movies!, This TV) Kansas City; KSHB-TV (COZI TV, Grit, NBC) Kansas City; KSNT (FOX, NBC) Topeka; KTKA-TV (ABC, CW) Topeka; KTWU (PBS) Topeka; WDAF-TV (Antenna TV, FOX) Kansas City; WIBW-TV (CBS, MeTV, MNT) Topeka.
Programming (via satellite): A&E; AMC; Animal Planet; Cartoon Network; CNN; C-SPAN; Discovery Channel; Disney Channel; E!; ESPN; ESPN2; Fox News Channel; Freeform; Fuse; Great American Country; HGTV; HLN; Lifetime; Outdoor Channel; TBS; The Weather Channel; TLC; TNT; USA Network; WGN America.
Fee: $49.95 installation; $48.50 monthly.
Digital Basic Service
Subscribers: N.A.
Programming (via satellite): BBC America; Bloomberg Television; Discovery Life Channel; Disney XD; DMX Music; ESPN Classic; ESPNews; FYI; Golf Channel; GSN; History International; National Geographic Channel; WE tv; Weatherscan.
Digital Expanded Basic Service
Subscribers: N.A.
Programming (via satellite): DMX Music; FXM; LMN; Starz Encore; Turner Classic Movies.
Fee: $15.00 monthly.
Pay Service 1
Pay Units: N.A.
Programming (via satellite): HBO; Showtime; The Movie Channel.
Fee: $12.00 installation; $11.00 monthly (HBO).
Digital Pay Service 1
Pay Units: N.A.
Programming (via satellite): Cinemax (multiplexed); Flix; HBO (multiplexed); Showtime (multiplexed); The Movie Channel (multiplexed).
Fee: $15.50 monthly.
Pay-Per-View
ESPN Now (delivered digitally); Urban Xtra (delivered digitally).
Internet Service
Operational: Yes.
Broadband Service: Galaxy Cable Internet.
Fee: $49.95 installation; $44.95 monthly.
Telephone Service
None
Miles of Plant: 16.0 (coaxial); None (fiber optic). Homes passed: 879.
President: James Rigas.
Ownership: Zito Media (MSO).

Cable Systems—Kansas

RUSH CENTER—GBT Communications Inc, 103 Lincoln St, PO Box 229, Rush Center, KS 67575. Phones: 800-946-4282; 785-372-4236; 800-432-7965. Fax: 785-372-4210. E-mail: custservice@gbtlive.com. Web Site: http://www.gbta.net. Also serves Albert, Albert (rural portions), Alexander, Alexander (rural portions), Bazine, Bazine (rural portions), Beeler, Beeler (rural portions), Bison, Bison (rural portions), Brownell, Brownell (rural portions), Burdett, Burdett (rural portions), Ellis (rural portions), Garfield, Garfield (rural portions), Lewis, Lewis (rural portions), McCracken, McCracken (rural portions), Ness City (rural portions), Otis (rural portions), Ransom (rural portions), Rozel (rural portions), Timken (rural portions) & Utica. ICA: KS5143.
Channel capacity: N.A. Channels available but not in use: N.A.
Basic
Subscribers: 2,627 Includes cable subscribers.
Fee: $13.95 monthly; $27.96-$37.79 monthly (rural areas). Includes 15 channels.
Upper Tier
Subscribers: N.A.
Fee: $39.55 monthly; $31.55 monthly (rural areas). Includes 66 channels.
Digital Basic
Subscribers: N.A.
Fee: $10.95 monthly. Includes 102 channels.
Digital Movie Madness
Subscribers: N.A.
Fee: $12.95 monthly. Includes 16 channels.
Cinemax
Subscribers: N.A.
Fee: $7.00 monthly. Includes 4 channels.
HBO
Subscribers: N.A.
Fee: $14.45 monthly. Includes 6 channels.
Showtime/TMC/Flix
Subscribers: N.A.
Fee: $10.95 monthly. Includes 10 channels.
Internet Service
Operational: Yes.
Fee: $37.95-$149.95 monthly.
Telephone Service
Digital: Operational
Fee: $18.25 monthly
General Manager: Beau Rebel. Plant Manager: Kirby Hagans. Office Manager: Debra Tuzicka.
Ownership: Golden Belt Telephone Association Inc.

RUSH CENTER—GBT Communications Inc, 103 Lincoln St, PO Box 229, Rush Center, KS 67575. Phones: 800-432-7965; 800-946-4282; 785-372-4236. Fax: 785-372-4210. E-mail: custservice@gbtlive.com. Web Site: http://www.gbta.net. Also serves Ellis, La Crosse, Liebenthal, Macksville, Ness City, Pawnee Rock, Ransom, Rozel, Schoenchen, St. John & Timken. ICA: KS0418. **Note:** This system is an overbuild.
TV Market Ranking: Below 100 (Ellis, La Crosse, Liebenthal, Pawnee Rock, Rozel, RUSH CENTER, Schoenchen, St. John, Timken); Outside TV Markets (Ness City, Ransom). Franchise award date: N.A. Franchise expiration date: N.A. Began: March 1, 1982.
Channel capacity: N.A. Channels available but not in use: N.A.
Basic Service
Subscribers: 2,298 Includes IPTV subscribers.
Programming (received off-air): KAKE (ABC, MeTV) Wichita; KBSH-DT (CBS) Hays; KOOD (PBS) Hays; KSAS-TV (Antenna TV, FOX) Wichita; KSNC (NBC) Great Bend; KSNW (NBC) Wichita.
Programming (via satellite): C-SPAN; Disney Channel; TBS; WGN America.
Fee: $18.95 monthly; $3.00 converter.
Expanded Basic Service 1
Subscribers: N.A.
Programming (received off-air): KSCW-DT (CW, Decades) Wichita.
Programming (via satellite): A&E; AMC; Animal Planet; Cartoon Network; CMT; CNN; Comedy Central; C-SPAN 2; Discovery Channel; E! HD; ESPN; ESPN Classic; ESPN2; EWTN Global Catholic Network; Food Network; Fox News Channel; Fox Sports 1; FOX Sports Midwest; Freeform; FX; GSN; Hallmark Channel; HGTV; History; HLN; INSP; Lifetime; MSNBC; MTV; National Geographic Channel; NFL Network; Nickelodeon; Outdoor Channel; QVC; RFD-TV; Spike TV; Syfy; The Weather Channel; TLC; TNT; Travel Channel; Trinity Broadcasting Network (TBN); truTV; Turner Classic Movies; TV Land; Univision Studios; USA Network; VH1.
Fee: $39.55 monthly.
Digital Basic Service
Subscribers: N.A.
Programming (via satellite): 52MX; BBC America; Bloomberg Television; Cinelatino; CNN en Espanol; Destination America; Discovery Channel HD; Discovery Kids Channel; Discovery Life Channel; Disney XD; DMX Music; ESPN Deportes; ESPN HD; ESPNews; Fox Deportes; FXM; Golf Channel; History en Espanol; History International; IFC; Investigation Discovery; LMN; MTV Classic; MTV Hits; MTV2; MyNetworkTV; National Geographic Channel; NBCSN; NFL Network HD; Nick Jr.; OWN: Oprah Winfrey Network; Science Channel; Starz (multiplexed); Starz Encore (multiplexed); TBS HD; TeenNick; TNT HD; Tr3s; Trinity Broadcasting Network (TBN); VH1 Country; ViendoMovies; WE tv.
Digital Pay Service 1
Pay Units: N.A.
Programming (via satellite): Cinemax (multiplexed); Cinemax HD; Flix; FXM; HBO (multiplexed); HBO HD; HBO Latino; IFC; Showtime (multiplexed); Showtime HD; The Movie Channel (multiplexed); The Movie Channel HD; WE tv.
Fee: $7.00 monthly (Cinemax), $10.95 monthly (Showtime/TMC/Flix), $14.95 monthly (Starz/Encore/FXM/IFC/WE).
Pay-Per-View
ESPN Now (delivered digitally); Hot Choice (delivered digitally); Playboy TV (delivered digitally); Fresh (delivered digitally); movies (delivered digitally).
Internet Service
Operational: Yes, DSL.
Fee: $29.95-$79.95 monthly.
Telephone Service
Digital: Operational
Fee: $14.70-$18.25 monthly
Miles of Plant: 50.0 (coaxial); 79.0 (fiber optic).
General Manager: Beau Rebel. Plant Manager: Kirby Hagans. Office Manager: Debra Tuzicka.
Ownership: Golden Belt Telephone Association Inc. (MSO).

RUSSELL—Eagle Communications. Now served by HAYS, KS [KS0384]. ICA: KS0038.

SALINA—Cox Communications, 6205 Peachtree Dunwoody Rd, 12th Floor, Atlanta, GA 30328. Phone: 404-269-6590. Web Site: http://www.cox.com. Also serves Saline County (portions). ICA: KS0007.
TV Market Ranking: Below 100 (SALINA, Saline County (portions)). Franchise award date: N.A. Franchise expiration date: N.A. Began: November 1, 1962.
Channel capacity: N.A. Channels available but not in use: N.A.
Basic Service
Subscribers: 10,411. Commercial subscribers: 380.
Programming (received off-air): KAAS-TV (FOX) Salina; KAKE (ABC, MeTV) Wichita; KMBC-TV (ABC, MeTV) Kansas City; KMTW (MNT, The Country Network) Hutchinson; KOOD (PBS) Hays; KPTS (PBS) Hutchinson; KSCW-DT (CW, Decades) Wichita; KSNW (NBC) Wichita; KWCH-DT (CBS) Hutchinson; WCWF (CW) Suring.
Programming (via satellite): C-SPAN; C-SPAN 2; Pop; QVC; The Weather Channel; WGN America.
Fee: $29.95 installation; $21.99 monthly.
Expanded Basic Service 1
Subscribers: N.A.
Programming (via satellite): A&E; AMC; Animal Planet; BET; Cartoon Network; CMT; CNBC; CNN; Comedy Central; Discovery Channel; Disney Channel; E! HD; ESPN; ESPN2; Food Network; Fox News Channel; Fox Sports 1; FOX Sports Midwest; Freeform; FX; Hallmark Channel; HGTV; HLN; Lifetime; MSNBC; MTV; Nickelodeon; Spike TV; Syfy; TBS; TLC; TNT; truTV; TV Land; USA Network; VH1.
Fee: $43.15 monthly.
Digital Basic Service
Subscribers: N.A.
Programming (via satellite): BBC America; Bloomberg Television; Discovery Digital Networks; Disney XD; DMX Music; ESPN Classic; ESPNews; FYI; Golf Channel; GSN; History; History International; HITS (Head-end In The Sky); IFC; LMN; NBCSN; Sundance TV; Turner Classic Movies.
Digital Pay Service 1
Pay Units: N.A.
Programming (via satellite): Cinemax (multiplexed); HBO (multiplexed); Showtime (multiplexed); Starz (multiplexed); Starz Encore (multiplexed); The Movie Channel (multiplexed).
Fee: $29.95 installation; $11.50 monthly (each).
Video-On-Demand: Yes
Pay-Per-View
iN DEMAND (delivered digitally).
Internet Service
Operational: Yes.
Subscribers: 8,457.
Broadband Service: Cox High Speed Internet.
Fee: $19.99-$59.99 monthly; $15.00 modem lease; $199.95 modem purchase.
Telephone Service
Digital: Operational
Subscribers: 5,688.
Fee: $15.95 monthly
Miles of Plant: 405.0 (coaxial); 153.0 (fiber optic). Homes passed: 24,627. Homes passed included in Wichita.
Vice President & General Manager: Kimberly Edmonds. Vice President, Engineering: Nick DiPonzio. Vice President, Marketing: Tony Matthews. Vice President, Tax: Mary Vickers. Marketing Director: Tina Gabbard. Public Affairs Director: Sarah Kauffman.
Ownership: Cox Communications Inc. (MSO).

SALINA—Formerly served by TVCN. No longer in operation. ICA: KS0426.

SCANDIA—Cunningham Cable TV. Now served by GLEN ELDER, KS [KS0228]. ICA: KS0227.

SCOTT CITY—Pioneer Communications. Now served by ULYSSES, KS [KS0044]. ICA: KS0053.

SEDAN—Formerly served by Allegiance Communications. No longer in operation. ICA: KS0125.

SEDGWICK COUNTY (portions)—Formerly served by Westcom. No longer in operation. ICA: KS0420.

SENECA—Formerly served by Carson Communications. Now served by Rainbow Communications, HIAWATHA, KS [KS0059]. ICA: KS0087.

SHARON—Formerly served by Allegiance Communications. No longer in operation. ICA: KS0254.

SHARON SPRINGS—Formerly served by Cebridge Connections. Now served by Pioneer Communications, ULYSSES, KS [KS0044]. ICA: KS0178.

SMITH CENTER—Nex-Tech. Formerly [KS0102]. This cable system has converted to IPTV, 2418 Vine St, Hays, KS 67601. Phones: 877-625-7872; 785-625-7070. Fax: 785-625-4479. E-mail: webmaster@nex-tech.com. Web Site: http://www.nex-tech.com. ICA: KS5204.
TV Market Ranking: Outside TV Markets (SMITH CENTER). Franchise award date: N.A. Franchise expiration date: N.A. Began: January 1, 1977.
Channel capacity: N.A. Channels available but not in use: N.A.
Essentials
Subscribers: 651.
Programming (received off-air): KBSH-DT (CBS) Hays; KGIN (CBS, MNT, NBC) Grand Island; KHGI-TV (ABC) Kearney; KLNE-TV (PBS) Lexington; KNHL (IND) Hastings; KOOD (PBS) Hays; KSNB-TV (MeTV, MNT, NBC) Superior; KSNC (NBC) Great Bend.
Programming (via satellite): EVINE Live; Trinity Broadcasting Network (TBN).
Fee: $30.00 installation; $24.95 monthly. Includes 51 channels.
Premiere
Subscribers: 613.
Programming (via satellite): A&E; Animal Planet; Cartoon Network; CNN; Discovery Channel; Disney Channel; E! HD; ESPN;

2017 Edition

D-301

Kansas—Cable Systems

ESPN Classic; ESPN2; ESPNews; Fox News Channel; FOX Sports Midwest; Freeform; FX; Golf Channel; Great American Country; GSN; HGTV; History; HLN; Lifetime; LMN; Nickelodeon; Outdoor Channel; QVC; Spike TV; Syfy; TBS; The Weather Channel; TNT; Turner Classic Movies; TV Land; USA Network; VH1.
Fee: $61.95 monthly. Includes 119 channels plus music channels.
HD
Subscribers: N.A.
Fee: $11.95 monthly. Includes 75+ channels.
Sports & Entertainment
Subscribers: N.A.
Programming (via satellite): BBC America; DMX Music; FYI; History International; WE tv.
Fee: $12.95 monthly. Includes 34 channels.
Cinemax
Subscribers: N.A.
Programming (via satellite): HBO.
Fee: $8.95 monthly. Includes 8 channels.
HBO
Subscribers: N.A.
Fee: $14.95 monthly. Includes 12 channels.
Showtime/TMC
Subscribers: N.A.
Fee: $13.95 monthly. Includes 16 channels.
Starz/Encore
Subscribers: N.A.
Fee: $10.95 monthly. Includes 18 channels.
Video-On-Demand: Yes
Pay-Per-View
Sports PPV (delivered digitally); ESPN Now (delivered digitally); Shorteez (delivered digitally); Fresh (delivered digitally); Playboy TV (delivered digitally); iN DEMAND (delivered digitally).
Internet Service
Operational: Yes.
Fee: $22.95-$202.95 monthly.
Telephone Service
Digital: Operational
Fee: $16.75 monthly
Chief Executive Officer & General Manager: Larry Sevier. Video Solutions Manager: Scott Roe.
Ownership: Nex-Tech (MSO).

SMITH CENTER—Nex-Tech. This cable system has converted to IPTV. See SMITH CENTER, KS [KS5204]. ICA: KS0102.

SMOLAN—Formerly served by Home Communications Inc. No longer in operation. ICA: KS0355.

SOLOMON—Eagle Communications. Now served by ABILENE, KS [KS0034]. ICA: KS0177.

SOUTH HAVEN—Formerly served by Almega Cable. No longer in operation. ICA: KS0270.

SPEARVILLE—United Communications Assn. Inc. Now served by CIMARRON, KS [KS0126]. ICA: KS0188.

SPRING HILL—Formerly served by Cebridge Connections. Now served by Suddenlink Communications, PAOLA, KS [KS0029]. ICA: KS0119.

ST. FRANCIS—Eagle Communications, 2703 Hall St, Ste 15, PO Box 817, Hays, KS 67601. Phones: 785-263-2529; 785-625-5910; 785-899-3371; 785-625-4000 (Corporate office). Fax: 785-625-8030. Web Site: http://www.eaglecom.net. ICA: KS0444.
TV Market Ranking: Below 100 (ST. FRANCIS).
Channel capacity: N.A. Channels available but not in use: N.A.
Basic Service
Subscribers: 108.
Programming (received off-air): KLBY (ABC) Colby; KOOD (PBS) Hays; KSAS-TV (Antenna TV, FOX) Wichita; KSNK (NBC) McCook.
Programming (via satellite): CNBC; Comedy Central; FX; KCNC-TV (CBS, Decades) Denver; KMGH-TV (ABC, Azteca America) Denver; KUSA (NBC, WeatherNation) Denver; MSNBC; QVC.
Fee: $24.95 installation; $69.95 monthly.
Expanded Basic Service 1
Subscribers: N.A.
Programming (via satellite): Animal Planet; CNN; Discovery Channel; Disney Channel; ESPN; ESPN2; Fox News Channel; FOX Sports Midwest; Freeform; Great American Country; HGTV; HLN; KWGN-TV (CW, This TV) Denver; National Geographic Channel; Nickelodeon; Spike TV; TBS; The Weather Channel; TLC; TNT; Travel Channel; TV Land; USA Network; VH1.
Fee: $24.00 monthly.
Pay Service 1
Pay Units: N.A.
Programming (via satellite): HBO; Showtime; The Movie Channel.
Fee: $11.95 monthly (Showtime or TMC); $14.95 monthly (HBO).
Video-On-Demand: No
Internet Service
Operational: Yes.
Fee: $34.95-$54.95 monthly.
Telephone Service
None
Miles of Plant: 19.0 (coaxial); None (fiber optic). Homes passed: 793.
Chief Operating Officer: Kurt K. David. General Manager: Travis Kohlrus. Chief Technician: Jim Gall. Ad Sales Manager: Mike Koerner.
Ownership: Eagle Communications Inc. (MSO).

ST. GEORGE—Formerly served by Kansas Cable. Now served by Cox Communications, MANHATTAN, KS [KS0006]. ICA: KS0114.

ST. MARY'S—WTC Communications. Now served by WAMEGO, KS [KS5017]. ICA: KS5014.

ST. PAUL—Formerly served by Cable TV of St. Paul. No longer in operation. ICA: KS0240.

STAFFORD—Vyve Broadband, 4 International Dr, Ste 330, Rye Brook, NY 10573. Phones: 800-937-1397; 405-395-1131; 405-275-6923. Web Site: http://vyvebroadband.com. ICA: KS0469.
TV Market Ranking: Below 100 (STAFFORD).
Channel capacity: N.A. Channels available but not in use: N.A.
Basic Service
Subscribers: 55.
Programming (received off-air): KAKE (ABC, MeTV) Wichita; KMTW (MNT, The Country Network) Hutchinson; KOOD (PBS) Hays; KPTS (PBS) Hutchinson; KSAS-TV (Antenna TV, FOX) Wichita; KSCW-DT (CW, Decades) Wichita; KSNC (NBC) Great Bend; KWCH-DT (CBS) Hutchinson.
Programming (via satellite): E! HD; QVC; WGN America.
Fee: $64.95 installation; $27.59 monthly.
Expanded Basic Service 1
Subscribers: 49.
Programming (via satellite): A&E; AMC; Animal Planet; Cartoon Network; CMT; CNBC; CNN; Comedy Central; Discovery Channel; Disney Channel; ESPN; ESPN2; Food Network; Fox News Channel; Fox Sports 1; FOX Sports Midwest; Freeform; FX; Hallmark Channel; HGTV; History; HLN; Lifetime; MSNBC; MTV; National Geographic Channel; Nickelodeon; Oxygen; Spike TV; Syfy; TBS; The Weather Channel; TLC; TNT; Travel Channel; TV Land; USA Network; VH1.
Fee: $38.91 monthly.
Digital Basic Service
Subscribers: N.A.
Programming (via satellite): BBC America; Bloomberg Television; Bravo; Chiller; Cloo; CMT; Destination America; Discovery Kids Channel; Discovery Life Channel; Disney XD; DMX Music; ESPN Classic; ESPNews; Flix; Fuse; FXM; FYI; Golf Channel; GSN; History International; IFC; Investigation Discovery; LMN; MTV Classic; MTV Hits; MTV2; NBCSN; Nick Jr.; Nicktoons; Outdoor Channel; OWN: Oprah Winfrey Network; RFD-TV; Science Channel; Starz Encore (multiplexed); Sundance TV; TeenNick; Trinity Broadcasting Network (TBN); Turner Classic Movies; VH1 Soul; WE tv.
Pay Service 1
Pay Units: N.A.
Programming (via satellite): Cinemax; HBO; Showtime; The Movie Channel.
Digital Pay Service 1
Pay Units: N.A.
Programming (via satellite): Cinemax (multiplexed); HBO (multiplexed); Showtime (multiplexed); Starz (multiplexed); The Movie Channel (multiplexed).
Video-On-Demand: No
Pay-Per-View
iN DEMAND (delivered digitally); Spice Xcess (delivered digitally); Fresh (delivered digitally); Playboy TV (delivered digitally); Club Jenna (delivered digitally).
Internet Service
Operational: No.
Telephone Service
None
Miles of Plant: 12.0 (coaxial); None (fiber optic).
Chief Executive Officer: Bill Haggerty. Regional Vice President: Andrew Dearth. Vice President, Marketing: Tracy Bass. Senior Vice President, Financial Planning: Daniel White.
Ownership: Vyve Broadband LLC (MSO).

STERLING—Formerly served by Eagle Communications. Now served by Cox Communications, GREAT BEND, KS [KS0012]. ICA: KS0091.

STOCKTON—Nex-Tech. Formerly [KS0051]. This cable system has converted to IPTV, 2418 Vine St, Hays, KS 67601. Phones: 877-625-7872; 785-625-7070. Fax: 785-625-4479. E-mail: webmaster@nex-tech.com. Web Site: http://www.nex-tech.com. ICA: KS5055.
Channel capacity: N.A. Channels available but not in use: N.A.
Essentials
Subscribers: 364.
Fee: $30.00 installation; $24.95 monthly. Includes 46 channels.
Premiere
Subscribers: 341.
Fee: $61.95 monthly. Includes 114 channels plus music channels.
HD
Subscribers: N.A.
Fee: $11.95 monthly. Includes 72+ channels.
Sports & Entertainment
Subscribers: N.A.
Fee: $12.95 monthly. Includes 34 channels.
Cinemax
Subscribers: N.A.
Fee: $8.95 monthly. Includes 8 channels.
HBO
Subscribers: N.A.
Fee: $14.95 monthly. Includes 12 channels.
Showtime/TMC
Subscribers: N.A.
Fee: $13.95 monthly. Includes 16 channels.
Starz/Encore
Subscribers: N.A.
Fee: $10.95 monthly. Includes 18 channels.
Video-On-Demand: Yes
Internet Service
Operational: Yes.
Fee: $22.95-$202.95 monthly.
Telephone Service
Digital: Operational
Fee: $16.75 monthly
Chief Executive Officer & General Manager: Larry Sevier. Video Solutions Manager: Scott Roe.
Ownership: Nex-Tech.

STOCKTON—Nex-Tech. This cable system has converted to IPTV. See STOCKTON, KS [KS5055]. ICA: KS0051.

STRONG CITY—Zito Media, 102 S Main St, PO Box 665, Coudersport, PA 16915. Phones: 814-260-9055; 800-365-6988. E-mail: info@zitomedia.com. Web Site: http://www.zitomedia.com. Also serves Cottonwood Falls. ICA: KS0421.
TV Market Ranking: Outside TV Markets (Cottonwood Falls, STRONG CITY). Franchise award date: N.A. Franchise expiration date: N.A. Began: May 1, 1976.
Channel capacity: N.A. Channels available but not in use: N.A.
Basic Service
Subscribers: 39.
Programming (received off-air): KAKE (ABC, MeTV) Wichita; KMTW (MNT, The Country Network) Hutchinson; KSAS-TV (Antenna TV, FOX) Wichita; KSCW-DT (CW, Decades) Wichita; KSNT (FOX, NBC) Topeka; KTKA-TV (ABC, CW) Topeka; KTWU (PBS) Topeka; KWCH-DT (CBS) Hutchinson; WIBW-TV (CBS, MeTV, MNT) Topeka.
Programming (via satellite): A&E; Cartoon Network; CNN; Discovery Channel; Disney

Cable Systems—Kansas

Channel; ESPN; ESPN2; Fox News Channel; Freeform; Fuse; FX; Great American Country; HGTV; History; Lifetime; Outdoor Channel; Starz; TBS; The Weather Channel; TLC; TNT; Trinity Broadcasting Network (TBN); USA Network.
Fee: $49.95 installation; $44.40 monthly.
Pay Service 1
Pay Units: N.A.
Programming (via satellite): Cinemax; HBO; Showtime; The Movie Channel.
Internet Service
Operational: No.
Telephone Service
None
Miles of Plant: 16.0 (coaxial); None (fiber optic). Homes passed: 719.
President: James Rigas.
Ownership: Zito Media (MSO).

SUMMERFIELD—Blue Valley Tele-Communications. Now served by AXTELL (formerly Frankfort & Home), KS [KS0424]. ICA: KS0452.

SYLVAN GROVE—Wilson Communications. Now served by BROOKVILLE, KS [KS0162]. ICA: KS0279.

SYLVIA—Formerly served by Cox Communications. No longer in operation. ICA: KS0280.

TAMPA—Formerly served by Eagle Communications. No longer in operation. ICA: KS0434.

THAYER—Mediacom, 901 North College Ave, Columbia, MO 65201. Phones: 417-875-5560 (Springfield regional office); 573-443-1536. Fax: 417-883-0255. Web Site: http://www.mediacomcable.com. ICA: KS0237.
TV Market Ranking: Outside TV Markets (THAYER). Franchise award date: N.A. Franchise expiration date: N.A. Began: December 1, 1985.
Channel capacity: N.A. Channels available but not in use: N.A.
Basic Service
Subscribers: 9.
Programming (received off-air): KOAM-TV (CBS) Pittsburg; KODE-TV (ABC) Joplin; KSNF (NBC) Joplin; KTWU (PBS) Topeka.
Programming (via satellite): A&E; CMT; CNN; Discovery Channel; ESPN; Freeform; HLN; Lifetime; Nickelodeon; QVC; Spike TV; TBS; The Weather Channel; TNT; USA Network; WGN America.
Fee: $35.00 installation; $46.05 monthly.
Pay Service 1
Pay Units: N.A.
Programming (via satellite): Showtime; The Movie Channel.
Fee: $10.50 monthly (each).
Video-On-Demand: No
Internet Service
Operational: No.
Telephone Service
None
Miles of Plant: 12.0 (coaxial); None (fiber optic). Homes passed: 240.
Regional Vice President: Bill Copeland. Operations Director: Bryan Gann. Regional Technical Operations Manager: Alan Freedman. Technical Operations Manager: Roger Shearer. Marketing Director: Will Kuebler. Vice President, Financial Reporting: Kenneth J. Kohrs.
Ownership: Mediacom LLC (MSO).

TIPTON—Wilson Communications. Now served by BROOKVILLE, KS [KS0162]. ICA: KS0326.

TOPEKA—Cox Communications, 6205 Peachtree Dunwoody Rd, 12th Floor, Atlanta, GA 30328. Phones: 404-269-6590; 316-260-7000 (Wichita office). Web Site: http://www.cox.com. Also serves Auburn, Berryton, Jefferson County (portions), Lecompton, Meriden, Pauline, Perry, Shawnee County & Silver Lake. ICA: KS0002.
TV Market Ranking: Below 100 (Auburn, Berryton, Jefferson County (portions), Lecompton, Pauline, Shawnee County, Silver Lake, TOPEKA, Meriden, Perry). Franchise award date: N.A. Franchise expiration date: N.A. Began: December 12, 1977.
Channel capacity: N.A. Channels available but not in use: N.A.
Basic Service
Subscribers: 31,660. Commercial subscribers: 1,132.
Programming (received off-air): KCTV (CBS) Kansas City; KMBC-TV (ABC, MeTV) Kansas City; KSHB-TV (COZI TV, Grit, NBC) Kansas City; KSNT (FOX, NBC) Topeka; KTKA-TV (ABC, CW) Topeka; KTWU (PBS) Topeka; WDAF-TV (Antenna TV, FOX) Kansas City; WIBW-TV (CBS, MeTV, MNT) Topeka; 15 FMs.
Programming (via satellite): C-SPAN; Pop; The Weather Channel; WGN America.
Fee: $29.95 installation; $21.99 monthly.
Expanded Basic Service 1
Subscribers: N.A.
Programming (via satellite): A&E; AMC; Animal Planet; BET; Cartoon Network; CMT; CNBC; CNN; Comedy Central; Concert TV; C-SPAN 2; Discovery Channel; Disney Channel; E! HD; ESPN; ESPN2; EVINE Live; EWTN Global Catholic Network; Food Network; Fox News Channel; Fox Sports 1; FOX Sports Midwest; Freeform; FX; Hallmark Channel; HGTV; History; HLN; INSP; Lifetime; MSNBC; MTV; Nickelodeon; QVC; Spike TV; Syfy; TBS; TLC; TNT; Travel Channel; truTV; Turner Classic Movies; TV Land; USA Network; VH1.
Fee: $43.15 monthly.
Digital Basic Service
Subscribers: N.A.
Programming (via satellite): BBC America; Bloomberg Television; Discovery Digital Networks; Disney XD; DMX Music; ESPN Classic; ESPNews; FYI; Golf Channel; Great American Country; GSN; History International; HITS (Headend In The Sky); IFC; LMN; NBA TV; NBCSN; Nick 2; Nick Jr.; Outdoor Channel; Oxygen; Sundance TV; TeenNick.
Digital Pay Service 1
Pay Units: N.A.
Programming (via satellite): Cinemax (multiplexed); HBO (multiplexed); Showtime (multiplexed); Starz (multiplexed); Starz Encore (multiplexed); The Movie Channel (multiplexed).
Fee: $11.50 monthly (each).
Video-On-Demand: Yes
Pay-Per-View
iN DEMAND; ESPN (delivered digitally); NBA/WNBA League Pass (delivered digitally); NHL Center Ice/MLB Extra Innings (delivered digitally).
Internet Service
Operational: Yes.
Subscribers: 25,201.
Broadband Service: Cox High Speed Internet.
Fee: $19.99-$59.99 monthly; $15.00 modem lease; $199.95 modem purchase.
Telephone Service
Digital: Operational
Subscribers: 16,299.
Fee: $15.95 monthly

Miles of Plant: 1,736.0 (coaxial); 429.0 (fiber optic). Homes passed: 85,400. Homes passed included in Wichita.
Vice President & General Manager: Kimberly Edmonds. Vice President, Marketing: Tony Matthews. Vice President, Engineering: Nick DiPonzio. Vice President, Tax: Mary Vickers. Field Operations Regional Manager: Scott Terry. Marketing Director: Tina Gabbard. Public Affairs Director: Sarah Kauffman.
Ownership: Cox Communications Inc. (MSO).

TORONTO—Mediacom, 901 North College Ave, Columbia, MO 65201. Phones: 845-695-2762; 417-875-5560 (Springfield regional office); 573-443-1536. Fax: 417-883-0265. Web Site: http://www.mediacomcable.com. ICA: KS0250.
TV Market Ranking: Outside TV Markets (TORONTO). Franchise award date: N.A. Franchise expiration date: N.A. Began: September 1, 1984.
Channel capacity: N.A. Channels available but not in use: N.A.
Basic Service
Subscribers: 17.
Programming (received off-air): KAKE (ABC, MeTV) Wichita; KOAM-TV (CBS) Pittsburg; KSNF (NBC) Joplin; KSNW (NBC) Wichita; KTWU (PBS) Topeka; WIBW-TV (CBS, MeTV, MNT) Topeka.
Programming (via satellite): A&E; CMT; CNN; Discovery Channel; ESPN; Freeform; HLN; Nickelodeon; QVC; Spike TV; TBS; The Weather Channel; TNT; USA Network; WGN America.
Fee: $35.00 installation; $43.05 monthly.
Pay Service 1
Pay Units: N.A.
Programming (via satellite): HBO; Showtime.
Fee: $10.50 monthly (each).
Video-On-Demand: No
Internet Service
Operational: No.
Telephone Service
None
Miles of Plant: 6.0 (coaxial); None (fiber optic). Homes passed: 251.
Regional Vice President: Bill Copeland. Operations Director: Bryan Gann. Regional Technical Operations Director: Alan Freedman. Technical Operations Manager: Roger Shearer. Marketing Director: Will Kuebler. Vice President, Financial Reporting: Kenneth J. Kohrs.
Ownership: Mediacom LLC (MSO).

TRIBUNE—Formerly served by Cebridge Connections. Now served by Pioneer Communications, ULYSSES, KS [KS0044]. ICA: KS0168.

TURON—Formerly served by Cox Communications. No longer in operation. ICA: KS0217.

UDALL—Wheat State Telecable Inc., 106 West First St, PO Box 320, Udall, KS 67146. Phones: 800-442-6835; 620-782-3341. Fax: 620-782-3302. E-mail: support@wheatstate.com. Web Site: http://www.wheatstate.com. Also serves Butler County (portions), Cassoday, Chase County (portions), Greenwood County (portions), Lyon County (portions), Matfield Green, Olpe & Potwin. ICA: KS0197.
TV Market Ranking: 67 (Butler County (portions), Cassoday, Potwin, UDALL); Outside TV Markets (Chase County (portions), Greenwood County (portions), Lyon County (portions), Matfield Green, Olpe). Franchise award date: July 1, 1983. Franchise expiration date: N.A. Began: September 1, 1983.
Channel capacity: N.A. Channels available but not in use: N.A.
Basic Service
Subscribers: 8.
Programming (received off-air): KAKE (ABC, MeTV) Wichita; KMTW (MNT, The Country Network) Hutchinson; KPTS (PBS) Hutchinson; KSAS-TV (Antenna TV, FOX) Wichita; KSCW-DT (CW, Decades) Wichita; KSNW (NBC) Wichita; KWCH-DT (CBS) Hutchinson.
Programming (via satellite): A&E; CNBC; C-SPAN; C-SPAN 2; Discovery Channel; Disney Channel; ESPN; ESPN2; EWTN Global Catholic Network; Fox News Channel; HGTV; HLN; INSP; Lifetime; MSNBC; MTV; Nickelodeon; Outdoor Channel; QVC; The Weather Channel; TLC; Trinity Broadcasting Network (TBN); TV Land; USA Network; VH1.
Fee: $25.00 installation; $18.95 monthly.
Expanded Basic Service 1
Subscribers: N.A.
Programming (via satellite): CNN; Hallmark Channel; Spike TV; Syfy; TBS; TNT; WGN America.
Fee: $7.50 monthly.
Expanded Basic Service 2
Subscribers: N.A.
Programming (via satellite): AMC; Animal Planet; Cartoon Network; CMT; Comedy Central; Fox Sports 1; Freeform; History.
Fee: $7.00 monthly.
Pay Service 1
Pay Units: N.A.
Programming (via satellite): Cinemax; HBO; Showtime.
Fee: $11.00 monthly (each).
Video-On-Demand: No
Internet Service
Operational: No, DSL.
Telephone Service
Analog: Operational
Miles of Plant: 5.0 (coaxial); None (fiber optic). Homes passed: 275.
General Manager: Arturo Macias. Chief Technician: Bruce Cardwell.
Ownership: Wheat State Telecable Inc.

ULYSSES—Pioneer Communications, 120 West Kansas Ave, PO Box 707, Ulysses, KS 67880. Phones: 800-308-7536; 620-356-3211. Fax: 620-356-3242. E-mail: marketing@pioncomm.net; info@pioncomm.net. Web Site: http://www.pioncomm.net. Also serves Big Bow, Coolidge, Deerfield, Greeley County (portions), Hickok, Holcomb, Horace, Hugoton, Johnson City, Kendall, Lakin, Leoti, Manter,

2017 Edition

D-303

Kansas—Cable Systems

Marienthal, Moscow, Richfield, Rolla, Satanta, Scott City, Sharon Springs, Sublette, Syracuse & Tribune. ICA: KS0044.
TV Market Ranking: Below 100 (Deerfield, Holcomb, Lakin, Scott City, Sharon Springs, Sublette); Outside TV Markets (Big Bow, Coolidge, Greeley County (portions), Hickok, Hickok, Horace, Hugoton, Johnson City, Kendall, Leoti, Manter, Marienthal, Moscow, Richfield, Rolla, Satanta, Syracuse, Tribune, ULYSSES). Franchise award date: N.A. Franchise expiration date: N.A. Began: February 1, 1975.
Channel capacity: N.A. Channels available but not in use: N.A.

Basic Service
Subscribers: 6,914.
Programming (received off-air): KBSD-DT (CBS) Ensign; KMTW (MNT, The Country Network) Hutchinson; KSAS-TV (Antenna TV, FOX) Wichita; KSCW-DT (CW, Decades) Wichita; KSNG (NBC) Garden City; KSWK (PBS) Lakin; KUPK (ABC) Garden City.
Programming (via satellite): A&E; AMC; Animal Planet; Bravo; Cartoon Network; CMT; CNBC; CNN; Comedy Central; C-SPAN; C-SPAN 2; Discovery Channel; Disney Channel; E! HD; ESPN; ESPN Classic; ESPN2; ESPNews; EVINE Live; EWTN Global Catholic Network; Food Network; Fox News Channel; FOX Sports Midwest; Freeform; FX; Golf Channel; Hallmark Channel; HGTV; History; HLN; ION Television; Lifetime; LMN; MSNBC; MTV; Nickelodeon; Ovation; Pop; QVC; Spike TV; Syfy; TBS; Telemundo; The Weather Channel; TLC; TNT; Travel Channel; Trinity Broadcasting Network (TBN); truTV; Turner Classic Movies; TV Land; Univision Studios; USA Network; VH1; WGN America.
Fee: $35.00 installation; $59.99 monthly.

Digital Basic Service
Subscribers: N.A.
Programming (via satellite): BBC America; Bloomberg Television; Discovery Life Channel; DMX Music; FOX College Sports Central; FOX College Sports Pacific; Fox Sports 1; FXM; Great American Country; NBCSN; Nick 2; Nick Jr.; Nicktoons; Outdoor Channel; TeenNick.

Digital Pay Service 1
Pay Units: 1,913.
Programming (via satellite): HBO (multiplexed).
Fee: $12.95 monthly.

Digital Pay Service 2
Pay Units: 845.
Programming (via satellite): Showtime (multiplexed); The Movie Channel.
Fee: $12.95 monthly.

Digital Pay Service 3
Pay Units: 644.
Programming (via satellite): Cinemax (multiplexed).
Fee: $10.95 monthly.

Digital Pay Service 4
Pay Units: 716.
Programming (via satellite): Starz (multiplexed); Starz Encore (multiplexed).
Fee: $10.95 monthly.

Digital Pay Service 5
Pay Units: N.A.
Programming (via satellite): AXS TV; HD Theater; HITS (Headend In The Sky); TNT HD.

Video-On-Demand: Planned

Pay-Per-View
special events (delivered digitally).

Internet Service
Operational: Yes, DSL.
Broadband Service: Pioneer.
Fee: $45.00 installation; $39.95 monthly; $6.00 modem lease; $50.00 modem purchase.

Telephone Service
None
Miles of Plant: 153.0 (coaxial); 11.0 (fiber optic). Homes passed: 13,000.
CEO & General Manager: Catherine Moyer. Chief Engineer: Matt Schonlau. Program Director & Ad Sales Manager: Taylor R. Summers. Telephony & Network Sales Manager: Tim Nemechek.
Ownership: Pioneer Communications.

UNIONTOWN—Craw-Kan Telephone Co-op. This cable system has converted to IPTV. Now served by GIRARD, KS [KS5099]. ICA: KS0310.

VALLEY FALLS—Giant Communications. Now served by HOLTON, KS [KS0066]. ICA: KS0145.

VERMILLION—Blue Valley Tele-Communications. Now served by AXTELL (formerly Frankfort & Home), KS [KS0424]. ICA: KS0339.

VICTORIA—Nex-Tech, 2418 Vine St, Hays, KS 67601. Phones: 877-625-7872; 785-625-7070. Fax: 785-625-4479. E-mail: webmaster@nex-tech.com. Web Site: http://www.nex-tech.com. ICA: KS0157.
Channel capacity: N.A. Channels available but not in use: N.A.

Basic Service
Subscribers: 418.
Programming (received off-air): KAKE (ABC, MeTV) Wichita; KBSH-DT (CBS) Hays; KMTW (MNT, The Country Network) Hutchinson; KOOD (PBS) Hays; KSAS-TV (Antenna TV, FOX) Wichita; KSCW-DT (CW, Decades) Wichita; KSNC (NBC) Great Bend; KSNK (NBC) McCook.
Programming (via satellite): C-SPAN; EWTN Global Catholic Network; QVC; WGN America.
Fee: $30.00 installation; $24.95 monthly.

Expanded Basic Service 1
Subscribers: N.A.
Programming (via satellite): Animal Planet; CNBC; CNN; ESPN; ESPN Classic; ESPN2; FOX Sports Midwest; HGTV; Lifetime; NBCSN; Outdoor Channel; Spike TV; Travel Channel.
Fee: $61.95 monthly.

Pay Service 1
Pay Units: N.A.
Programming (via satellite): HBO.
Fee: $14.95 monthly.

Internet Service
Operational: Yes.
Fee: $22.95-$202.95 monthly.

Telephone Service
Analog: Operational
Fee: $16.75 monthly
Chief Executive Officer & General Manager: Larry Sevier. Video Solutions Manager: Scott Roe.
Ownership: Nex-Tech.

WAKEENEY—Eagle Communications. Now served by HAYS, KS [KS0384]. ICA: KS0100.

WAKEFIELD—Eagle Communications. Now served by ABILENE, KS [KS0034]. ICA: KS0200.

WALNUT—Craw-Kan Telephone Co-op. This cable system has converted to IPTV. Now served by GIRARD, KS [KS5099]. ICA: KS0343.

WALTON—Formerly served by Galaxy Cablevision. No longer in operation. ICA: KS0435.

WAMEGO—WTC Communications, 1009 Lincoln Ave, Wamego, KS 66547. Phones: 877-982-1912; 785-456-1000. Fax: 785-456-9903. E-mail: info@wtcks.com. Web Site: http://www.wtcks.com. Also serves Belvue, Louisville, Paxico, Pottawatomie County (unincorporated areas), St. George, St. Marys & Wabaunsee County (unincorporated areas). ICA: KS0057.
Channel capacity: N.A. Channels available but not in use: N.A.

Basic Service
Subscribers: 2,694.
Fee: $24.95 monthly.

Internet Service
Operational: Yes.
Fee: $31.95-$99.95 monthly.

Telephone Service
Digital: Operational
Fee: $17.00 monthly
General Manager: Jeff Wick.
Ownership: WTC Communications Inc.

WAMEGO—WTC Communications, 1009 Lincoln St, Wamego, KS 66547. Phones: 877-492-6835; 785-456-1000. Fax: 785-456-9903. E-mail: info@wtcks.com. Web Site: http://www.wtcks.com. Also serves Belvue, Louisville, Paxico, Pottawatomie County (unincorporated areas), St. George, St. Mary's & Wabaunsee County (unincorporated areas). ICA: KS5017.
TV Market Ranking: Outside TV Markets (Louisville, WAMEGO, Pottawatomie County (unincorporated areas), St. Mary's).
Channel capacity: N.A. Channels available but not in use: N.A.

Essentials
Subscribers: 2,567.
Fee: $24.95 monthly. Includes 32 channels.

Premiere
Subscribers: N.A.
Fee: $37.95 monthly. Includes 107 channels.

Sports & Variety Pak
Subscribers: N.A.
Fee: $11.95 monthly. Includes 40 channels.

Sports & Outdoor
Subscribers: N.A.
Fee: $4.95 monthly. Includes 9 channels.

Cinemax
Subscribers: N.A.
Fee: $13.95 monthly. Includes 4 channels.

HBO
Subscribers: N.A.
Fee: $17.95 monthly. Includes 7 channels.

Showtime/TMC/Flix
Subscribers: N.A.
Fee: $13.95 monthly. Includes 10 channels.

Starz Super Pak
Subscribers: N.A.
Fee: $13.95 monthly. Includes 11 channels.

Internet Service
Operational: Yes.
Fee: $31.95-$99.95 monthly.

Telephone Service
Digital: Operational
Fee: $17.00 monthly
General Manager: Jeff Wick.
Ownership: WTC Communications Inc.

WASHINGTON—Formerly served by Cunningham Cable TV. Now served by Blue Valley Tele-Communications, AXTELL, KS [KS0424]. ICA: KS0139.

WATERVILLE—Blue Valley Tele-Communications. Now served by AXTELL (formerly Frankfort & Home), KS [KS0424]. ICA: KS0193.

WAVERLY—Formerly served by Zito Media. No longer in operation. ICA: KS0210.

WEIR—Formerly served by WSC Cablevision. No longer in operation. ICA: KS0422.

WELLINGTON—Sumner Cable TV Inc., 117 West Harvey Ave, Wellington, KS 67152-3840. Phone: 620-326-8989. Fax: 620-326-5332. E-mail: sumnertv@sutv.com. Web Site: http://www.sutv.com. ICA: KS0032.
TV Market Ranking: 67 (WELLINGTON). Franchise award date: September 1, 2005. Franchise expiration date: N.A. Began: April 5, 1977.
Channel capacity: N.A. Channels available but not in use: N.A.

Basic Service
Subscribers: 1,733.
Programming (received off-air): KAKE (ABC, MeTV) Wichita; KMTW (MNT, The Country Network) Hutchinson; KPTS (PBS) Hutchinson; KSAS-TV (Antenna TV, FOX) Wichita; KSCW-DT (CW, Decades) Wichita; KSNW (NBC) Wichita; KWCH-DT (CBS) Hutchinson.
Programming (via satellite): Bravo; C-SPAN; Freeform; QVC; The Weather Channel.
Fee: $40.00 installation; $61.00 monthly; $3.00 converter.

Expanded Basic Service 1
Subscribers: N.A.
Programming (via satellite): AMC; Animal Planet; Cartoon Network; CMT; Discovery Channel; Disney Channel; DIY Network; E! HD; ESPN; ESPN Classic; ESPN2; EWTN Global Catholic Network; Food Network; FOX Sports Networks; FX; Great American Country; Hallmark Channel; Hallmark Movies & Mysteries; HGTV; History; HLN; Lifetime; MSNBC; MTV; NFL Network; Nickelodeon; Spike TV; Syfy; TBS; TNT; Travel Channel; truTV; TV Land; USA Network; VH1; WE tv; WGN America.
Fee: $31.95 installation; $22.20 monthly.

Digital Basic Service
Subscribers: N.A.
Programming (via satellite): BBC America; Bloomberg Television; Bravo; Cloo; CMT; Comedy Central; C-SPAN 2; Destination America; Discovery Kids Channel; Discovery Life Channel; Disney XD; DMX Music; ESPN Classic; ESPNews; Fox Sports 1; FSN Digital Atlantic; FSN Digital Central; FSN Digital Pacific; Fuse; FXM; FYI; Golf Channel; Great American Country; GSN; HGTV; History International; IFC; INSP; Investigation Discovery; ION Television; LMN; MTV Hits; MTV2; National Geographic Channel; NBCSN; Nick Jr.; Nicktoons; Outdoor Channel; Ovation; OWN; Oprah Winfrey Network; Pop; RFD-TV; Science Channel; Sundance TV; Syfy; TeenNick; Telemundo; Trinity Broadcasting Network (TBN); Turner Classic Movies; UP; VH1 Soul; WE tv.

Digital Pay Service 1
Pay Units: N.A.
Programming (via satellite): Cinemax (multiplexed); Flix; HBO (multiplexed); Showtime (multiplexed); Starz (multi-

Cable Systems—Kansas

plexed); Starz Encore (multiplexed); The Movie Channel (multiplexed).
Fee: $13.25 monthly (Cinemax or HBO), $13.75 monthly (Showtime/TMC/Flix), $14.35 monthly (Starz/Encore).

Video-On-Demand: No

Pay-Per-View
Playboy TV (delivered digitally); Fresh (delivered digitally); Club Jenna (delivered digitally); Shorteez (delivered digitally).

Internet Service
Operational: Yes. Began: October 1, 1997.
Broadband Service: In-house.
Fee: $25.00 installation; $27.45 monthly; $135.00 modem purchase.

Telephone Service
Digital: Operational
Fee: $30.95 monthly
Miles of Plant: 60.0 (coaxial); None (fiber optic). Homes passed: 3,300.
General Manager & Chief Technician: David Steinbach. Marketing Director: Alda Boyd. Office Manager: Jill Bales.
Ownership: Sumner Communications.

WESTMORELAND—Formerly served by Giant Communications. No longer in operation. ICA: KS0198.

WETMORE—Rainbow Communications. No longer in operation. ICA: KS0285.

WHITE CITY—Formerly served by Eagle Communications. No longer in operation. ICA: KS0248.

WHITE CLOUD—Formerly served by Rainbow Communications. No longer in operation. ICA: KS0302.

WHITING—Formerly served by Rainbow Communications. No longer in operation. ICA: KS0358.

WICHITA—Cox Communications, 6205 Peachtree Dunwoody Rd, 12th Floor, Atlanta, GA 30328. Phones: 404-269-6590; 316-260-7000; 316-262-4270. Web Site: http://www.cox.com. Also serves Andover, Arkansas City, Augusta, Bel Aire, Burrton, Butler County (portions), Cheney, Cunningham, Derby, Eastborough, El Dorado, Garden Plain (portions), Goddard, Halstead, Harvey County (unincorporated areas), Haysville, Hesston, Hutchinson, Kechi, Kingman, Kingman County, Linsborg, Maize, Marion County (southern portion), McConnell AFB, McPherson, McPherson County (portions), Mulvane, Newton, Nickerson, North Newton, Park City, Pratt, Pratt County, Reno County (portions), Rose Hill, Sedgwick, Sedgwick County (portions), South Hutchinson, Towanda, Valley Center, Willowbrook & Winfield. ICA: KS0001.
TV Market Ranking: 67 (Andover, Augusta, Bel Aire, Burrton, Butler County (portions), Cheney, Derby, Eastborough, El Dorado, Garden Plain (portions), Goddard, Halstead, Harvey County (unincorporated areas), Haysville, Hesston, Hutchinson, Kechi, Maize, Marion County (southern portion), McConnell AFB, McPherson, McPherson County (portions) (portions), Mulvane, Newton, Nickerson, North Newton, Park City, Reno County (portions), Rose Hill, Sedgwick, Sedgwick County (portions), South Hutchinson, Towanda, Valley Center, WICHITA, Willowbrook); Below 100 (Linsborg, McPherson County (portions) (portions)); Outside TV Markets (Arkansas City, Cunningham, Kingman, Kingman County, Pratt, Pratt County, Winfield). Franchise award date: December 1, 1978. Franchise expiration date: N.A. Began: January 1, 1979.
Channel capacity: N.A. Channels available but not in use: N.A.

Basic Service
Subscribers: 123,955. Commercial subscribers: 4,567.
Programming (received off-air): KAKE (ABC, MeTV) Wichita; KMTW (MNT, The Country Network) Hutchinson; KPTS (PBS) Hutchinson; KSAS-TV (Antenna TV, FOX) Wichita; KSCW-DT (CW, Decades) Wichita; KSNW (NBC) Wichita; KWCH-DT (CBS) Hutchinson.
Programming (via satellite): C-SPAN; C-SPAN 2; Pop; The Weather Channel; WGN America.
Fee: $29.95 installation; $21.99 monthly; $3.00 converter.

Expanded Basic Service 1
Subscribers: N.A.
Programming (via satellite): A&E; AMC; Animal Planet; BET; Cartoon Network; CMT; CNBC; CNN; Comedy Central; Discovery Channel; Discovery Life Channel; Disney Channel; E! HD; ESPN; ESPN2; EVINE Live; EWTN Global Catholic Network; Food Network; Fox News Channel; Fox Sports 1; FOX Sports Midwest; Freeform; FX; Hallmark Channel; HGTV; History; HLN; INSP; ION Television; Lifetime; MSNBC; MTV; Nickelodeon; QVC; Spike TV; Syfy; TBS; TLC; TNT; Travel Channel; truTV; Turner Classic Movies; TV Land; Univision Studios; USA Network; VH1.
Fee: $29.95 installation; $43.15 monthly.

Digital Basic Service
Subscribers: N.A.
Programming (via satellite): BBC America; Bloomberg Television; Discovery Digital Networks; Disney XD; DMX Music; ESPN Classic; ESPNews; FYI; Golf Channel; Great American Country; GSN; History International; HITS (Headend In The Sky); IFC; LMN; NBA TV; NBCSN; Nick 2; Nick Jr.; Outdoor Channel; Oxygen; Sundance TV; TeenNick.

Digital Pay Service 1
Pay Units: N.A.
Programming (via satellite): Cinemax (multiplexed); HBO (multiplexed); Showtime (multiplexed); Starz (multiplexed); Starz Encore (multiplexed).
Fee: $29.95 installation; $10.50 monthly (each).

Video-On-Demand: Yes

Pay-Per-View
iN DEMAND; ESPN Now (delivered digitally); NBA/WNBA League Pass (delivered digitally); NHL Center Ice/MLB Extra Innings (delivered digitally).

Internet Service
Operational: Yes.
Subscribers: 107,680.
Broadband Service: Cox High Speed Internet.
Fee: $41.95 monthly; $15.00 modem lease; $19.95 modem purchase.

Telephone Service
Digital: Operational
Subscribers: 73,273.
Fee: $15.95 monthly
Miles of Plant: 6,222.0 (coaxial); 1,878.0 (fiber optic). Homes passed: 323,722. Homes passed includes all Cox Kansas systems.
Vice President & General Manager: Kimberly Edmunds. Vice President, Engineering: Nick Difonzio. Vice President, Marketing: Tony Matthews. Vice President, Tax: Mary Vickers. Marketing Director: Tina Gabbard. Public Affairs Director: Sarah Kauffman.
Ownership: Cox Communications Inc. (MSO).

WICHITA—Formerly served by Sprint Corp. No longer in operation. ICA: KS0428.

WILLIAMSBURG—Formerly served by Zito Media. No longer in operation. ICA: KS0300.

WILSEY—Formerly served by CableDirect. No longer in operation. ICA: KS0335.

WINCHESTER—Giant Communications. Now served by HOLTON, KS [KS0066]. ICA: KS0249.

WOODBINE—Formerly served by Eagle Communications. No longer in operation. ICA: KS0423.

WOODSTON—Nex-Tech. Formerly [KS0306]. This cable system has converted to IPTV, 2418 Vine St, Hays, KS 67601. Phones: 877-625-7872; 785-625-7070. Fax: 785-625-4479. E-mail: webmaster@nex-tech.com. Web Site: http://www.nex-tech.com. Also serves Alton, Gaylord & Osborne. ICA: KS5088.
TV Market Ranking: Franchise award date: April 27, 2007. Franchise expiration date: N.A. Began: N.A.
Channel capacity: N.A. Channels available but not in use: N.A.

Essentials
Subscribers: 730.
Fee: $30.00 installation; $24.95 monthly. Includes 46 channels.

Premiere
Subscribers: 668.
Fee: $61.95 monthly. Includes 114 channels plus music channels.

HD
Subscribers: N.A.
Fee: $11.95 monthly. Includes 72+ channels.

Sports & Entertainment
Subscribers: N.A.
Fee: $12.95 monthly. Includes 34 channels.

Cinemax
Subscribers: N.A.
Fee: $8.95 monthly. Includes 8 channels.

HBO
Subscribers: N.A.
Fee: $14.95 monthly. Includes 12 channels.

Showtime/TMC
Subscribers: N.A.
Fee: $13.95 monthly. Includes 16 channels.

Starz/Encore
Subscribers: N.A.
Fee: $10.95 monthly. Includes 18 channels.

Video-On-Demand: Yes

Internet Service
Operational: Yes.
Fee: $22.95-$202.95 monthly.

Telephone Service
Digital: Operational
Fee: $16.75 monthly
Chief Executive Officer & General Manager: Larry Sevier. Video Solutions Manager: Scott Roe.
Ownership: Nex-Tech.

WOODSTON—Nex-Tech. This cable system has converted to IPTV. See WOODSTON, KS [KS5088]. ICA: KS0306.

KENTUCKY

Total Systems: 110
Total Communities Served: 908
Franchises Not Yet Operating: 0
Applications Pending: 0
Communities with Applications: 0
Number of Basic Subscribers: 751,675
Number of Expanded Basic Subscribers: 14,671
Number of Pay Units: 2,658

Top 100 Markets Represented: Cincinnati, OH-Newport, KY (17); Nashville, TN (30); Charleston-Huntington, WV (36); Louisville (38); Cape Girardeau, MO-Paducah, KY-Harrisburg, IL (69); Evansville, IN (86).

For a list of cable communities in this section, see the Cable Community Index located in the back of Cable Volume 2.
For explanation of terms used in cable system listings, see p. D-11.

ADAIRVILLE—Suddenlink Communications, 520 Maryville Centre Dr, Ste 300, St. Louis, MO 63141. Phones: 800-999-6845 (Customer service); 314-315-9400. Web Site: http://www.suddenlink.com. ICA: KY0197.
TV Market Ranking: 30 (ADAIRVILLE). Franchise award date: October 14, 1986. Franchise expiration date: N.A. Began: January 1, 1980.
Channel capacity: N.A. Channels available but not in use: N.A.
Basic Service
Subscribers: 22.
Programming (received off-air): WBKO (ABC, CW, FOX) Bowling Green; WKLE (PBS) Lexington; WKYU-TV (PBS) Bowling Green; WNAB (CW, The Country Network) Nashville; WNKY (CBS, NBC) Bowling Green; WNPT (PBS) Nashville; WNPX-TV (ION) Cookeville; WPGD-TV (TBN) Hendersonville; WSMV-TV (COZI TV, NBC, TNN) Nashville; WTVF (CBS, Laff, This TV) Nashville; WUXP-TV (MNT) Nashville; WZTV (Antenna TV, FOX, WeatherNation) Nashville.
Programming (via satellite): Pop; WGN America.
Fee: $22.99 monthly.
Expanded Basic Service 1
Subscribers: N.A.
Programming (via satellite): A&E; AMC; Animal Planet; BET; Cartoon Network; CMT; CNBC; CNN; C-SPAN; Discovery Channel; Disney Channel; ESPN; ESPN Classic; ESPN2; Fox News Channel; Freeform; FX; HGTV; History; HLN; Lifetime; MTV; Nickelodeon; QVC; Spike TV; Syfy; TBS; The Weather Channel; TLC; TNT; Turner Classic Movies; TV Land; USA Network; VH1.
Fee: $22.00 monthly.
Video-On-Demand: No
Pay-Per-View
iN DEMAND (delivered digitally); Playboy TV (delivered digitally); Fresh (delivered digitally).
Internet Service
Operational: Yes.
Broadband Service: Suddenlink High Speed Internet.
Telephone Service
None
Miles of Plant: 8.0 (coaxial); None (fiber optic). Homes passed: 411.
Vice President: Robert Herrald. Senior Vice President, Corporate Finance: Michael Pflantz. General Manager: Wayne Harrison. Chief Technician: Jim Adkins.
Ownership: Cequel Communications Holdings I LLC (MSO).

ALBANY—Mediacom. Now served by SUMMER SHADE, KY [KY0092]. ICA: KY0108.

ALTRO—Formerly served by Altro TV Inc. No longer in operation. ICA: KY0115.

ASHLAND—Formerly served by Adelphia Communications. No longer in operation. ICA: KY0009.

ASHLAND—Time Warner Cable, 225 Russell Rd, Ashland, KY 41101. Phones: 606-326-6800; 606-329-2201. Fax: 606-329-9579. Web Site: http://www.timewarnercable.com. Also serves Bellefonte, Boyd County (portions), Flatwoods, Greenup County (portions), Raceland, Russell, Westwood & Worthington, KY; Coal Grove (village), Fayette Twp., Franklin Furnace, Green Twp. (Scioto County), Hamilton Twp. (Lawrence County), Hanging Rock, Hanging Rock (village), Ironton, Lawrence Twp., Perry Twp. (Lawrence County), Union Twp. (Lawrence County) & Upper Twp., OH. ICA: KY0326.
TV Market Ranking: 36 (ASHLAND, Bellefonte, Boyd County (portions), Coal Grove (village), Fayette Twp., Flatwoods, Franklin Furnace, Green Twp. (Scioto County), Greenup County (portions), Hamilton Twp. (Lawrence County), Hanging Rock, Hanging Rock (village), Ironton, Lawrence Twp., Perry Twp. (Lawrence County), Raceland, Russell, Union Twp. (Lawrence County), Upper Twp., Westwood, Worthington).
Channel capacity: 65 (not 2-way capable). Channels available but not in use: N.A.
Basic Service
Subscribers: 14,968.
Programming (received off-air): WCHS-TV (ABC, Antenna TV) Charleston; WKAS (PBS) Ashland; WKYT-TV (CBS, CW) Lexington; WLPX-TV (ION) Charleston; WOWK-TV (CBS) Huntington; WQCW (CW) Portsmouth; WSAZ-TV (MNT, NBC, This TV) Huntington; WTSF (Daystar TV) Ashland; WVAH-TV (FOX, The Country Network) Charleston; WVPB-TV (PBS) Huntington.
Programming (via satellite): C-SPAN; EWTN Global Catholic Network; Freeform; INSP; MyNetworkTV; Pop; QVC; TBS; The Weather Channel; WGN America.
Fee: $24.95-$61.55 installation; $24.50 monthly.
Expanded Basic Service 1
Subscribers: N.A.
Programming (via satellite): A&E; AMC; Animal Planet; BET; Bravo; Cartoon Network; CMT; CNBC; CNN; Comedy Central; C-SPAN 2; Discovery Channel; Disney Channel; Disney XD; E! HD; ESPN; ESPN2; EVINE Live; Food Network; Fox News Channel; Fox Sports 1; FOX Sports Ohio/Sports Time Ohio; FX; FYI; Golf Channel; Great American Country; Hallmark Channel; HGTV; History; HLN; Lifetime; MSNBC; MTV; MTV2; National Geographic Channel; Nickelodeon; Outdoor Channel; Oxygen; Spike TV; Syfy; TLC; TNT; Travel Channel; truTV; TV Land; USA Network; VH1.
Fee: $37.12 monthly.

Digital Basic Service
Subscribers: N.A.
Programming (via satellite): 52MX; AXS TV; BBC America; Bloomberg Television; Boomerang; CBS Sports Network; Cinelatino; Cloo; CNN en Espanol; Cooking Channel; C-SPAN 3; Daystar TV Network; Destination America; Discovery Kids Channel; Discovery Life Channel; DIY Network; ESPN Classic; ESPN Deportes; ESPN HD; ESPN2 HD; ESPNews; ESPNU; EWTN Global Catholic Network; FamilyNet; Flix; Fox Business Network; FOX College Sports Central; FOX College Sports Pacific; Fox Deportes; Fox Sports 2; Fuse; FXM; GSN; HD Theater; History en Espanol; History International; IFC; Investigation Discovery; LMN; LOGO; MC; MTV Classic; MTV Hits; MTV Jams; MTV2; Nat Geo WILD; NBA TV; NBCSN; Nick 2; Nick Jr.; Nicktoons; Outdoor Channel; Ovation; OWN; Oprah Winfrey Network; Reelz; Science Channel; Starz Encore (multiplexed); Sundance TV; TeenNick; Tennis Channel; The Word Network; TNT HD; Toon Disney en Espanol; Tr3s; Trinity Broadcasting Network (TBN); Turner Classic Movies; TVG Network; Universal HD; VH1 Country; VH1 Soul; WE tv.
Fee: $6.00 monthly (each tier).
Digital Pay Service 1
Pay Units: N.A.
Programming (via satellite): ART America; Cinemax (multiplexed); Cinemax HD; HBO (multiplexed); HBO HD; RAI Italia; RTN; Showtime (multiplexed); Showtime HD; Starz (multiplexed); Starz HD; The Filipino Channel; The Movie Channel (multiplexed); TV Asia; TV5, La Television International.
Fee: $14.00 monthly (each).
Video-On-Demand: Yes
Pay-Per-View
iN DEMAND (delivered digitally); NHL Center Ice (delivered digitally); MLB Extra Innings (delivered digitally); ESPN (delivered digitally); Fresh (delivered digitally); Hot Choice (delivered digitally); Playboy TV (delivered digitally).
Internet Service
Operational: Yes.
Subscribers: 12,720.
Broadband Service: Road Runner.
Fee: $99.95 installation; $44.95 monthly.
Telephone Service
Digital: Operational
Subscribers: 5,793.
Fee: $49.95 monthly
Miles of Plant: 645.0 (coaxial); 294.0 (fiber optic). Homes passed: 41,270.
General Manager: Russ Pomfrey. Technical Operations Manager: Mike Jones. Marketing Manager: Mark Cole. Business Manager: Tracy Tackett. Technical Supervisor: Rod Frost.
Ownership: Time Warner Cable (MSO).

AUBURN—Suddenlink Communications. Now served by RUSSELLVILLE, KY [KY0032]. ICA: KY0198.

AUGUSTA—Formerly served by Bracken County Cablevision Inc. Now served by Limestone Bracken Cablevision, AUGUSTA, KY [KY0316]. ICA: KY0100.

AUGUSTA—Limestone Bracken Cablevision, 626 Forest Ave, PO Box 100, Maysville, KY 41056. Phone: 606-564-9220. Fax: 606-564-4291. E-mail: jcracraft@maysvilleky.net. Web Site: http://www.limestonecable.com. Also serves Bracken County (portions), Brooksville, Germantown & Mount Olivet. ICA: KY0316.
TV Market Ranking: 17 (AUGUSTA, Bracken County (portions)); Outside TV Markets (Brooksville, Germantown, Mount Olivet, Bracken County (portions)).
Channel capacity: N.A. Channels available but not in use: N.A.
Basic Service
Subscribers: 893.
Programming (received off-air): WCPO-TV (ABC, Escape) Cincinnati; WKRC-TV (CBS, CW) Cincinnati; WKYT-TV (CBS, CW) Lexington; WLEX-TV (MeTV, NBC) Lexington; WLWT (MeTV, NBC) Cincinnati; WSTR-TV (Antenna TV, MNT) Cincinnati; WTVQ-DT (ABC, Antenna TV, Laff, MNT) Lexington; WXIX-TV (Bounce TV, FOX) Newport.
Programming (via satellite): TBS; WGN America.
Fee: $40.00 installation; $27.00 monthly.
Expanded Basic Service 1
Subscribers: 102.
Programming (via satellite): A&E; AMC; CMT; CNN; C-SPAN; Discovery Channel; ESPN; FOX Sports Ohio/Sports Time Ohio; Freeform; MTV; Nickelodeon; QVC; The Weather Channel; TNT; Trinity Broadcasting Network (TBN); USA Network; VH1.
Fee: $35.00 installation; $37.30 monthly.
Pay Service 1
Pay Units: 6.
Programming (via satellite): HBO.
Fee: $12.95 monthly.
Pay Service 2
Pay Units: 1.
Programming (via satellite): Showtime.
Fee: $12.95 monthly.
Internet Service
Operational: Yes.
Fee: $21.95-$64.95 monthly.
Telephone Service
None
Miles of Plant: 20.0 (coaxial); None (fiber optic).
Vice President: Jeff Cracraft. General Manager: Ron Beurkley. Chief Technician: Jeff

Cable Systems—Kentucky

Mason. Customer Service Manager: Jean Black.
Ownership: Standard Tobacco Co. Inc. (MSO).

BARBOURVILLE—Barbourville Utility Commission, 202 Daniel Boone Dr, PO Box 1600, Barbourville, KY 40906. Phones: 606-545-9205; 606-546-3187. Fax: 606-546-4848. Web Site: http://www.barbourville.com. Also serves Artemus, Heidrick & Knox County. ICA: KY0057.
TV Market Ranking: Below 100 (Artemus, BARBOURVILLE, Heidrick, Knox County (portions)). Franchise award date: September 8, 1952. Franchise expiration date: N.A. Began: October 1, 1952.
Channel capacity: N.A. Channels available but not in use: N.A.

Basic Service
Subscribers: 2,521.
Programming (received off-air): WAGV (IND) Harlan; WATE-TV (ABC, Laff) Knoxville; WBIR-TV (MeTV, NBC) Knoxville; WBXX-TV (CW, Escape) Crossville; WDKY-TV (FOX) Danville; WKSO-TV (PBS) Somerset; WKYT-TV (CBS, CW) Lexington; WLEX-TV (MeTV, NBC) Lexington; WLFG (IND, PBJ, Retro TV) Grundy; WLJC-TV (TBN) Beattyville; WTVQ-DT (ABC, Antenna TV, Laff, MNT) Lexington; WVLT-TV (CBS, MNT) Knoxville; WYMT-TV (CBS, CW) Hazard.
Programming (via satellite): A&E; AMC; Animal Planet; Bravo; Cartoon Network; CMT; CNBC; CNN; Comedy Central; Cooking Channel; C-SPAN; CW PLUS; Discovery Channel; Disney Channel; DIY Network; E! HD; ESPN; ESPN Classic; ESPN2; Food Network; Fox News Channel; Fox Sports 1; Freeform; FX; Golf Channel; HGTV; History; HLN; Lifetime; MSNBC; MTV; Nickelodeon; Outdoor Channel; Oxygen; Pop; QVC; Spike TV; Syfy; TBS; The Weather Channel; TLC; TNT; Travel Channel; Turner Classic Movies; TV Land; USA Network; VH1; WGN America.
Fee: $20.00 installation; $16.00 monthly.

Digital Basic Service
Subscribers: N.A.
Programming (via satellite): BBC America; Bloomberg Television; CMT; Destination America; Discovery Kids Channel; Discovery Life Channel; Disney XD; DMX Music; E! HD; ESPNews; ESPNU; FX; FYI; GSN; History International; Investigation Discovery; LMN; MTV Classic; MTV Hits; MTV2; Nick Jr.; Nicktoons; Ovation; OWN: Oprah Winfrey Network; Science Channel; Sprout; TeenNick; Trinity Broadcasting Network (TBN); TVG Network; VH1 Soul; WE tv.

Digital Expanded Basic Service
Subscribers: N.A.
Programming (via satellite): AXS TV; ESPN HD; ESPN2 HD; Outdoor Channel 2 HD; TNT HD.
Fee: $12.00 monthly.

Digital Pay Service 1
Pay Units: N.A.
Programming (via satellite): Cinemax (multiplexed); Flix; HBO (multiplexed); Showtime (multiplexed); Showtime HD; Starz (multiplexed); Starz Encore (multiplexed); Starz HD; The Movie Channel (multiplexed); The Movie Channel HD.
Fee: $9.00 monthly (Starz/Encore), $12.95 monthly (Showtime/TMC/Cinemax), $18.00 monthly (HBO/Cinemax).

Video-On-Demand: No

Pay-Per-View
iN DEMAND (delivered digitally).

Internet Service
Operational: Yes.
Broadband Service: In-house.
Fee: $103.00 installation; $19.95-$54.95 monthly; $29.95 modem lease.

Telephone Service
None
Miles of Plant: 75.0 (coaxial); 30.0 (fiber optic). Homes passed: 3,000.
General Manager: Josh Callihan. Chief Technician: Ron Bowling. Controller: Barry Hubbard.
Ownership: Barbourville Utility Commission.

BARDSTOWN—Bardstown Cable TV, 220 North 5th St, Ste 2, Bardstown, KY 40004-1458. Phones: 502-348-1701; 502-348-5947. Fax: 502-348-2433. E-mail: support@bardstowncable.net. Web Site: http://www.bardstowncable.net. Also serves Fredericktown & Nelson County (portions). ICA: KY0026.
TV Market Ranking: 38 (BARDSTOWN, Fredericktown, Nelson County (portions) (portions)); Below 100 (Nelson County (portions) (portions)). Franchise award date: October 1, 1964. Franchise expiration date: N.A. Began: May 5, 1965.
Channel capacity: N.A. Channels available but not in use: N.A.

Basic Service
Subscribers: 3,745.
Programming (received off-air): WAVE (Bounce TV, NBC, This TV) Louisville; WBKI-TV (CW, IND, Movies!) Campbellsville; WBNA (ION, Retro TV) Louisville; WDRB (Antenna TV, FOX) Louisville; WHAS-TV (ABC) Louisville; WKMJ-TV (PBS) Louisville; WKPC-TV (PBS) Louisville; WKZT-TV (PBS) Elizabethtown; WLKY (CBS, MeTV) Louisville; WMYO (MNT, My Family TV) Salem.
Programming (via satellite): A&E; AMC; Animal Planet; BET; Cartoon Network; CMT; CNBC; CNN; Comedy Central; C-SPAN; Discovery Channel; Disney Channel; Disney XD; E! HD; ESPN; ESPN2; EWTN Global Catholic Network; Food Network; Fox News Channel; Freeform; FX; GSN; Hallmark Channel; HGTV; History; HLN; Lifetime; MTV; National Geographic Channel; Nickelodeon; Outdoor Channel; Pop; QVC; Spike TV; Syfy; TBS; The Weather Channel; TLC; TNT; Travel Channel; Turner Classic Movies; TV Land; USA Network; VH1; WGN America.
Fee: $18.86 monthly; $3.00 converter.

Digital Basic Service
Subscribers: N.A.
Programming (via satellite): Cloo; Discovery Digital Networks; DMX Music; ESPN Classic; IFC; LMN; MTV Classic; MTV2; Nick Jr.; TeenNick.

Digital Expanded Basic Service
Subscribers: N.A.
Programming (via satellite): BBC America; Bloomberg Television; Discovery Health Channel; ESPNews; Fox Sports 1; Fuse; FXM; FYI; Golf Channel; History International; NBCSN; Ovation.
Fee: $3.95 monthly.

Pay Service 1
Pay Units: N.A.
Programming (via satellite): Cinemax; Flix; HBO (multiplexed); Showtime; Sundance TV; The Movie Channel.
Fee: $8.95 - $12.95 monthly (each).

Digital Pay Service 1
Pay Units: N.A.
Programming (via satellite): Cinemax (multiplexed); Flix; HBO (multiplexed); Showtime (multiplexed); Starz (multiplexed); Starz Encore (multiplexed); The Movie Channel (multiplexed); WE tv.
Fee: $9.00 monthly.

Video-On-Demand: No

Pay-Per-View
iN DEMAND (delivered digitally).

Internet Service
Operational: Yes. Began: December 1, 1999.
Subscribers: 7,796.
Broadband Service: Bardstown Cable Internet Service.
Fee: $39.95 installation; $19.95-$45.95 monthly; $5.00 modem lease; $99.00 modem purchase.

Telephone Service
None
Miles of Plant: 1,000.0 (coaxial); 370.0 (fiber optic). Homes passed: 15,000.
General Manager: Larry Hamilton. Chief Financial Officer: Mike Abell. Electrical Engineer: Jeffrey Mills.
Ownership: City of Bardstown.

BEATTYVILLE—Crystal Broadband Networks, PO Box 180336, Chicago, IL 60618. Phones: 877-319-0328; 630-206-0447. E-mail: helpdesk@crystalbn.com. Web Site: http://crystalbn.com. Also serves Booneville & Owsley County (northern portion). ICA: KY0141.
TV Market Ranking: Below 100 (BEATTYVILLE, Booneville). Franchise award date: N.A. Franchise expiration date: N.A. Began: January 1, 1958.
Channel capacity: N.A. Channels available but not in use: N.A.

Basic Service
Subscribers: 231.
Programming (received off-air): WDKY-TV (FOX) Danville; WKHA (PBS) Hazard; WKYT-TV (CBS, CW) Lexington; WLEX-TV (MeTV, NBC) Lexington; WLJC-TV (TBN) Beattyville; WTVQ-DT (ABC, Antenna TV, Laff, MNT) Lexington; WUPX-TV (ION) Morehead; WYMT-TV (CBS, CW) Hazard.
Programming (via satellite): QVC; TBS; WGN America.
Fee: $39.95 installation; $52.75 monthly.

Expanded Basic Service 1
Subscribers: N.A.
Programming (via satellite): A&E; AMC; CMT; CNN; Discovery Channel; Disney Channel; ESPN; ESPN2; Fox News Channel; Freeform; FX; Hallmark Channel; HLN; Lifetime; Nickelodeon; Spike TV; The Weather Channel; TLC; TNT; USA Network; VH1.
Fee: $31.95 monthly.

Digital Basic Service
Subscribers: N.A.
Programming (via satellite): BBC America; Bloomberg Television; Bravo; Discovery Digital Networks; ESPN Classic; ESPNews; EVINE Live; Fox Sports 1; FSN Digital Atlantic; FSN Digital Central; FSN Digital Pacific; FYI; Golf Channel; Great American Country; GSN; HGTV; History; History International; HITS (Headend In The Sky); IFC; National Geographic Channel; NBCSN; Nick 2; Nicktoons; Outdoor Channel; Syfy; TeenNick; Trinity Broadcasting Network (TBN); Turner Classic Movies; WE tv.

Digital Pay Service 1
Pay Units: N.A.
Programming (via satellite): Cinemax (multiplexed); Flix; HBO (multiplexed); Showtime (multiplexed); Starz Encore; The Movie Channel (multiplexed).
Fee: $15.95 monthly (each).

Video-On-Demand: No

Pay-Per-View
HITS PPV (delivered digitally).

Internet Service
Operational: No.
Telephone Service
None
Miles of Plant: 139.0 (coaxial); None (fiber optic). Homes passed: 2,419.
Ownership: Crystal Broadband Networks (MSO).

BEAVER DAM—Time Warner Cable. Now served by MADISONVILLE, KY [KY0013]. ICA: KY0054.

BENHAM—Access Cable Television Inc. Now served by CUMBERLAND, KY [KY0075]. ICA: KY0176.

BENTON—Formerly served by Charter Communications. Now served by Time Warner Cable, MAYFIELD, KY [KY0037]. ICA: KY0085.

BIG CLIFTY—Mediacom. Now served by CANEYVILLE, KY [KY0291]. ICA: KY0200.

BLACK MOUNTAIN—Zito Media, 102 S Main St, PO Box 665, Coudersport, PA 16915. Phones: 814-260-9055; 800-365-6988. E-mail: info@zitomedia.com. Web Site: http://www.zitomedia.com. Also serves Baxter, Brookside, Cawood, Chevrolet, Coalgood, Cranks, Crummies, Dizney, Holmes Mill, Lejunior, Louellen, Putney, Rosspoint & Totz. ICA: KY0042.
TV Market Ranking: Below 100 (Baxter, BLACK MOUNTAIN, Brookside, Cawood, Chevrolet, Coalgood, Cranks, Crummies, Dizney, Holmes Mill, Lejunior, Louellen, Putney, Rosspoint, Totz).
Channel capacity: N.A. Channels available but not in use: N.A.

Basic Service
Subscribers: 144.
Programming (received off-air): WAGV (IND) Harlan; WATE-TV (ABC, Laff) Knoxville; WBIR-TV (MeTV, NBC) Knoxville; WBXX-TV (CW, Escape) Crossville; WEMT (FOX, Movies!, This TV) Greeneville; WETP-TV (PBS) Sneedville; WKHA (PBS) Hazard; WKYT-TV (CBS, CW) Lexington; WVLT-TV (CBS, MNT) Knoxville; WYMT-TV (CBS, CW) Hazard.
Programming (via satellite): WGN America.
Fee: $49.95 installation; $18.70 monthly; $.73 converter.

Expanded Basic Service 1
Subscribers: N.A.
Programming (via satellite): A&E; AMC; CMT; CNN; C-SPAN; Discovery Channel; Disney Channel; E! HD; ESPN; Freeform; Lifetime; MTV; Nickelodeon; Outdoor Channel; Spike TV; Syfy; TBS; The Weather Channel; TNT; Trinity Broadcasting Network (TBN); USA Network.
Fee: $16.89 monthly.

Digital Basic Service
Subscribers: N.A.
Programming (via satellite): BBC America; Bloomberg Television; Discovery Life Channel; Disney XD; DMX Music; ESPN Classic; ESPN2; Fox Sports 1; Fuse; FXM; FYI; Golf Channel; GSN; HGTV; History; History International; IFC; INSP; LMN; NBCSN; Nick Jr.; Outdoor Channel; Syfy; TeenNick; Turner Classic Movies; WE tv.

Pay Service 1
Pay Units: N.A.
Programming (via satellite): Cinemax; HBO; Showtime; Starz Encore; The Movie Channel.
Fee: $3.99 monthly (Encore), $7.99 monthly (Cinemax), $11.99 monthly (HBO, Showtime or TMC).

2017 Edition   D-307

Kentucky—Cable Systems

Digital Pay Service 1
Pay Units: N.A.
Programming (via satellite): Cinemax (multiplexed); Flix; HBO (multiplexed); Showtime (multiplexed); Starz (multiplexed); Starz Encore (multiplexed); The Movie Channel (multiplexed); WAM! America's Kidz Network.
Video-On-Demand: No
Pay-Per-View
iN DEMAND (delivered digitally); Hot Choice (delivered digitally); Playboy TV (delivered digitally); Fresh (delivered digitally); Shorteez (delivered digitally).
Internet Service
Operational: No.
Telephone Service
None
Miles of Plant: 116.0 (coaxial); None (fiber optic). Homes passed: 4,270.
President: James Rigas.
Ownership: Zito Media (MSO).

BLAINE—Formerly served by Lycom Communications. No longer in operation. ICA: KY0302.

BLOOMFIELD—Formerly served by Insight Communications. No longer in operation. ICA: KY0160.

BONNYMAN—TVS Cable, PO Box 1410, Hindman, KY 41822-1410. Phones: 606-946-2600; 606-633-0778; 606-785-3450. Fax: 606-785-3110. E-mail: tvs@tvscable.com. Web Site: http://www.tvscable.com. Also serves Browns Fork, Chavies, Grapevine & Typo. ICA: KY0201.
TV Market Ranking: Below 100 (BONNYMAN, Browns Fork, Chavies, Grapevine, Typo).
Channel capacity: N.A. Channels available but not in use: N.A.
Basic Service
Subscribers: 578. Commercial subscribers: 42.
Fee: $50.00 installation; $23.50 monthly.
Vice President & General Manager: William K. Grigsby.
Ownership: TV Service Inc. (MSO).

BOONEVILLE—Peoples Telecom, 1080 Main St South, McKee, KY 40447. Phones: 606-593-5000; 606-287-7101. E-mail: prtccs@prtcnet.org. Web Site: http://www.prtcnet.org. Also serves Owsley County (portions). ICA: KY0328.
TV Market Ranking: Below 100 (BOONEVILLE).
Channel capacity: N.A. Channels available but not in use: N.A.
Basic Service
Subscribers: N.A.
Programming (received off-air): WBKI-TV (CW, IND, Movies!) Campbellsville; WDKY-TV (FOX) Danville; WKLE (PBS) Lexington; WKYT-TV (CBS, CW) Lexington; WLEX-TV (MeTV, NBC) Lexington; WLJC-TV (TBN) Beattyville; WTVQ-DT (ABC, Antenna TV, Laff, MNT) Lexington; WUPX-TV (ION) Morehead; WYMT-TV (CBS, CW) Hazard.
Programming (via satellite): WGN-TV (IND) Chicago.
Expanded Basic Service 1
Subscribers: N.A.
Programming (via satellite): A&E; Animal Planet; Cartoon Network; CMT; CNN; Discovery Channel; Disney Channel; ESPN; ESPN2; Fox News Channel; FOX Sports Ohio/Sports Time Ohio; Freeform; FX; HGTV; History; Lifetime; Nickelodeon; QVC; Spike TV; TBS; The Weather Channel; TLC; TNT; TV Land; USA Network; VH1.

Digital Basic Service
Subscribers: N.A.
Programming (via satellite): BBC America; Bloomberg Television; Bravo; CMT; Destination America; Discovery Kids Channel; Discovery Life Channel; Disney XD; DMX Music; ESPN Classic; ESPN2; ESPNews; Fox Sports 1; Fuse; FXM; FYI; Golf Channel; HGTV; History; History International; Investigation Discovery; LMN; MTV Classic; MTV Hits; MTV2; Nick Jr.; Nicktoons; Outdoor Channel; Ovation; OWN: Oprah Winfrey Network; RFD-TV; Science Channel; Sprout; TeenNick; Trinity Broadcasting Network (TBN); Turner Classic Movies; VH1 Soul.
Digital Pay Service 1
Pay Units: N.A.
Programming (via satellite): Cinemax (multiplexed); Flix; HBO (multiplexed); Showtime (multiplexed); Starz (multiplexed); Starz Encore (multiplexed); The Movie Channel (multiplexed).
Fee: $9.95 monthly (Cinemax or Starz/Encore), $11.95 monthly (HBO or Showtime/TMC/Flix).
Video-On-Demand: No
Internet Service
Operational: No, DSL.
Telephone Service
Analog: Operational
Homes passed: 1,000.
General Manager: Keith Grabbard. Chief Technician: Jeff Bingham.
Ownership: Peoples Rural Telephone Cooperative (MSO).

BOWLING GREEN—Time Warner Cable, 60 Columbus Circle, 17th Fl, New York, NY 10023. Phones: 212-364-8200; 859-431-0300; 212-364-8200; 270-782-0903. Fax: 212-364-8252. Web Site: http://www.timewarnercable.com. Also serves Oakland, Plum Springs, Smiths Grove, Warren County (portions) & Woodburn. ICA: KY0007.
TV Market Ranking: Below 100 (BOWLING GREEN, Oakland, Plum Springs, Smiths Grove, Warren County (portions), Woodburn). Franchise award date: September 1, 1980. Franchise expiration date: N.A. Began: July 21, 1981.
Channel capacity: N.A. Channels available but not in use: N.A.
Basic Service
Subscribers: 23,763. Commercial subscribers: 459.
Programming (received off-air): WBKO (ABC, CW, FOX) Bowling Green; WKGB-TV (PBS) Bowling Green; WKYU-TV (PBS) Bowling Green; WLKY (CBS, MeTV) Louisville; WNKY (CBS, NBC) Bowling Green; WPSD-TV (Antenna TV, NBC) Paducah; WTVF (CBS, Laff, This TV) Nashville; 30 FMs.
Programming (via satellite): C-SPAN; C-SPAN 2; INSP; Pop; QVC; Trinity Broadcasting Network (TBN); WGN America.
Fee: $30.00 installation; $12.95 monthly.
Expanded Basic Service 1
Subscribers: N.A.
Programming (via satellite): A&E; AMC; Animal Planet; BET; Cartoon Network; CMT; CNBC; CNN; Comedy Central; Discovery Channel; Disney Channel; E! HD; ESPN; EWTN Global Catholic Network; Food Network; Fox News Channel; FOX Sports Ohio/Sports Time Ohio; Freeform; FX; Golf Channel; Hallmark Channel; HGTV; History; HLN; ION Television; Lifetime; MSNBC; MTV; National Geographic Channel; Nickelodeon; Oxygen; Spike TV; TBS; The Weather Channel; TLC; TNT; Travel Channel; truTV; Univision Studios; USA Network; VH1.
Fee: $40.00 monthly.
Digital Basic Service
Subscribers: N.A.
Programming (via satellite): AXS TV; BBC America; Bloomberg Television; Bravo; BTN; CBS Sports Network; Cloo; CMT; Cooking Channel; C-SPAN 3; Discovery Digital Networks; Disney XD; DIY Network; ESPN Classic; ESPN HD; ESPN2 HD; ESPNews; ESPNU; FOX College Sports Central; FOX College Sports Pacific; Fox Sports 1; Fuse; FXM; FYI; Great American Country; GSN; HD Theater; History International; HRTV; IFC; LMN; MC; MTV Live; NBCSN; NFL Network; Nick 2; Nick Jr.; Nicktoons; Outdoor Channel; Ovation; Sprout; Starz Encore (multiplexed); Sundance TV; Syfy; TeenNick; Tennis Channel; TNT HD; Turner Classic Movies; TV Land; TVG Network; Universal HD; WE tv.
Digital Pay Service 1
Pay Units: N.A.
Programming (via satellite): Cinemax (multiplexed); Flix; HBO (multiplexed); HBO HD; Showtime; Showtime HD; Starz (multiplexed); The Movie Channel (multiplexed).
Fee: $10.00 monthly (Cinemax or Starz), $13.00 monthly (HBO or Showtime/TMC).
Video-On-Demand: Yes
Pay-Per-View
iN DEMAND (delivered digitally); ESPN (delivered digitally); Playboy TV (delivered digitally); Fresh (delivered digitally).
Internet Service
Operational: Yes.
Subscribers: 24,378.
Fee: $99.95 installation; $44.95 monthly; $15.00 modem lease.
Telephone Service
Digital: Operational
Subscribers: 10,882.
Miles of Plant: 1,271.0 (coaxial); 473.0 (fiber optic). Homes passed: 46,535. Miles of plant (coax) includes miles of plant (fiber).
Chief Executive Officer: Glenn A. Britt. President & Chief Operations Officer: Robert D. Marcus.
Ownership: Time Warner Cable (MSO).

BRADFORDSVILLE—Formerly served by Charter Communications. No longer in operation. ICA: KY0298.

BREMEN—Inside Connect Cable, 4890 Knob Creek Rd, Brooks, KY 40109. Phones: 502-955-4882; 855-552-2253. Fax: 502-543-7553. E-mail: sales@insideconnect.net. Also serves Central City & Sacramento. ICA: KY0130.
TV Market Ranking: Below 100 (BREMEN, Sacramento).
Channel capacity: N.A. Channels available but not in use: N.A.
Basic Service
Subscribers: 153.
Programming (received off-air): WBKO (ABC, CW, FOX) Bowling Green; WEHT (ABC) Evansville; WEVV-TV (CBS, FOX) Evansville; WFIE (NBC, This TV) Evansville; WKMA-TV (PBS) Madisonville; WNIN (PBS) Evansville; WTVW (CW, MeTV) Evansville.
Programming (via satellite): Nickelodeon; QVC; TBS; WGN America.
Fee: $39.95 installation; $24.95 monthly.
Expanded Basic Service 1
Subscribers: N.A.
Programming (via satellite): A&E; AMC; Animal Planet; Bravo; Cartoon Network; CMT; CNBC; CNN; Comedy Central; C-SPAN; Discovery Channel; Discovery Life Channel; E! HD; ESPN; ESPN2; Food Network; Freeform; HGTV; History; HLN; Lifetime; MTV; Outdoor Channel; Spike TV; Syfy; The Weather Channel; TLC; TNT; Travel Channel; truTV; TV Land; USA Network.
Fee: $27.69 monthly.
Pay Service 1
Pay Units: N.A.
Programming (via satellite): Cinemax; HBO (multiplexed); Showtime; The Movie Channel.
Fee: $15.95 monthly (each).
Video-On-Demand: No
Internet Service
Operational: Yes, DSL.
Telephone Service
Digital: Operational
Miles of Plant: 32.0 (coaxial); None (fiber optic).
Ownership: Inside Connect Cable LLC (MSO).

BRODHEAD—Wilcop Cable TV, 101 Pine Ave, PO Box 558, Brodhead, KY 40409-0558. Phone: 606-758-8320. Fax: 606-758-8320. Also serves Crab Orchard. ICA: KY0173.
TV Market Ranking: Below 100 (BRODHEAD, Crab Orchard). Franchise award date: N.A. Franchise expiration date: N.A. Began: January 1, 1952.
Channel capacity: N.A. Channels available but not in use: N.A.
Basic Service
Subscribers: 169.
Programming (received off-air): WDRB (Antenna TV, FOX) Louisville; WKLE (PBS) Lexington; WKYT-TV (CBS, CW) Lexington; WLEX-TV (MeTV, NBC) Lexington; WLKY (CBS, MeTV) Louisville; WTVQ-DT (ABC, Antenna TV, Laff, MNT) Lexington.
Programming (via satellite): ESPN; TBS; WGN America.
Fee: $25.00 installation; $49.00 monthly.
Pay Service 1
Pay Units: 18.
Programming (via satellite): HBO (multiplexed).
Fee: $10.00 monthly.
Video-On-Demand: No
Internet Service
Operational: No.
Telephone Service
None
Miles of Plant: 20.0 (coaxial); None (fiber optic). Homes passed: 850.
General Manager: Johnny Wilcop.
Ownership: Wilcop Cable TV (MSO).

BROOKS—Inside Connect Cable, 4890 Knob Creek Rd, Brooks, KY 40109. Phones: 855-552-2253; 502-955-4882. Fax: 502-543-7553. E-mail: sales@insideconnect.net. Also serves Shepherdsville & West Point. ICA: KY0199.
TV Market Ranking: 38 (BROOKS, Shepherdsville, West Point).
Channel capacity: N.A. Channels available but not in use: N.A.
Basic Service
Subscribers: 336.
Programming (received off-air): WAVE (Bounce TV, NBC, This TV) Louisville; WDRB (Antenna TV, FOX) Louisville; WHAS-TV (ABC) Louisville; WKPC-TV (PBS) Louisville; WLKY (CBS, MeTV) Louisville; WMYO (MNT, My Family TV) Salem; WUPX-TV (ION) Morehead.
Programming (via satellite): A&E; AMC; CMT; CNN; Discovery Channel; Disney Channel; ESPN; Freeform; MTV; Nickelodeon; Spike TV; TBS; TLC; TNT;

Cable Systems—Kentucky

Trinity Broadcasting Network (TBN); USA Network; VH1; WGN America.
Fee: $29.95 installation; $16.37 monthly.
Pay Service 1
Pay Units: N.A.
Programming (via satellite): Flix; Showtime.
Digital Pay Service 1
Pay Units: N.A.
Programming (via satellite): Cinemax (multiplexed); HBO (multiplexed); Showtime (multiplexed); Starz (multiplexed); Starz Encore (multiplexed); The Movie Channel (multiplexed).
Fee: $15.95 monthly (each).
Video-On-Demand: No
Pay-Per-View
iN DEMAND (delivered digitally); Fresh (delivered digitally); Playboy TV (delivered digitally).
Internet Service
Operational: Yes, DSL.
Telephone Service
Digital: Operational
Miles of Plant: 305.0 (coaxial); None (fiber optic). Homes passed: 445.
Ownership: Inside Connect Cable LLC (MSO).

BROOKSVILLE—Formerly served by Bracken County Cablevision Inc. Now served by Limestone Bracken Cablevision, AUGUSTA, KY [KY0316]. ICA: KY0204.

BROWNSVILLE—Mediacom. Now served by MORGANTOWN, KY [KY0096]. ICA: KY0088.

BRYANTSVILLE—Formerly served by Charter Communications. No longer in operation. ICA: KY0205.

BULAN—Time Warner Cable, 7800 Crescent Executive Dr, Charlotte, NC 28217. Phones: 859-626-4800; 606-678-9215. Web Site: http://www.timewarnercable.com. Also serves Breathitt County (portions), Darfork, Fisty, Hardburly, Hardshell, Knott County (portions), Perry County (portions), Rowdy & Tribbey. ICA: KY0062.
TV Market Ranking: Below 100 (BULAN, Darfork, Fisty, Hardburly, Hardshell, Rowdy, Tribbey). Franchise award date: N.A. Franchise expiration date: N.A. Began: January 1, 1952.
Channel capacity: N.A. Channels available but not in use: N.A.
Basic Service
Subscribers: 971. Commercial subscribers: 16.
Programming (received off-air): WAGV (IND) Harlan; WDKY-TV (FOX) Danville; WKPI-TV (PBS) Pikeville; WKYT-TV (CBS, CW) Lexington; WLEX-TV (MeTV, NBC) Lexington; WLJC-TV (TBN) Beattyville; WTVQ-DT (ABC, Antenna TV, Laff, MNT) Lexington; WUPX-TV (ION) Morehead; WYMT-TV (CBS, CW) Hazard.
Programming (via satellite): C-SPAN; ESPN Classic; QVC; The Weather Channel; WGN America.
Fee: $49.99 installation; $23.99 monthly.
Expanded Basic Service 1
Subscribers: N.A.
Programming (via satellite): A&E; AMC; Animal Planet; Bravo; Cartoon Network; CMT; CNBC; CNN; Comcast/Charter Sports Southeast (CSS); Comedy Central; Discovery Channel; Disney Channel; Disney XD; E! HD; ESPN; ESPN2; EVINE Live; Food Network; Fox News Channel; Fox Sports 1; FOX Sports Ohio/Sports Time Ohio; Freeform; FX; Golf Channel; Hallmark Channel; HGTV; History; HLN; INSP; Jewelry Television; Lifetime; MSNBC; MTV; National Geographic Channel; NBCSN; Nickelodeon; Oxygen; Spike TV; Syfy; TBS; TLC; TNT; Travel Channel; Trinity Broadcasting Network (TBN); truTV; Turner Classic Movies; TV Land; USA Network; VH1; WE tv.
Digital Basic Service
Subscribers: N.A.
Programming (via satellite): BBC America; Bloomberg Television; CMT; Destination America; Discovery Kids Channel; Discovery Life Channel; DIY Network; ESPN Classic; ESPNews; FOX College Sports Central; FOX College Sports Pacific; FXM; FYI; Great American Country; History International; IFC; Investigation Discovery; LMN; MC; MTV Classic; MTV Hits; MTV Jams; MTV2; Nick 2; Nick Jr.; Nicktoons; OWN: Oprah Winfrey Network; Science Channel; TeenNick; Tr3s; VH1 Soul.
Digital Pay Service 1
Pay Units: N.A.
Programming (via satellite): Cinemax (multiplexed); Flix; HBO (multiplexed); Showtime (multiplexed); Starz (multiplexed); Starz Encore (multiplexed); The Movie Channel (multiplexed).
Video-On-Demand: No
Pay-Per-View
iN DEMAND (delivered digitally); Special events (delivered digitally); SexSee (delivered digitally); VaVoom (delivered digitally); Juicy (delivered digitally).
Internet Service
Operational: No.
Telephone Service
None
Miles of Plant: 154.0 (coaxial); None (fiber optic). Homes passed: 3,698.
General Manager: Tim Jones. Senior Accounting Director: Karen Goodfellow. Marketing Manager: Brandon Cummins. Technical Operations Manager: James Thompson.
Ownership: Time Warner Cable (MSO).

BULLSKIN CREEK—Formerly served by Bullskin Cable TV. No longer in operation. ICA: KY0206.

BURKESVILLE—Mediacom, 90 Main St, Benton, KY 42025-1132. Phones: 845-695-2762; 417-875-5560 (Springfield regional office); 270-527-9939. Fax: 270-527-0813. Web Site: http://www.mediacomcable.com. Also serves Cumberland County (portions) & Marrowbone. ICA: KY0116.
TV Market Ranking: Below 100 (Marrowbone); Outside TV Markets (BURKESVILLE). Franchise award date: N.A. Franchise expiration date: N.A. Began: September 1, 1961.
Channel capacity: N.A. Channels available but not in use: N.A.
Basic Service
Subscribers: 457.
Programming (received off-air): WAVE (Bounce TV, NBC, This TV) Louisville; WBKO (ABC, CW, FOX) Bowling Green; WDRB (Antenna TV, FOX) Louisville; WKSO-TV (PBS) Somerset; WKYU-TV (PBS) Bowling Green; WLKY (CBS, MeTV) Louisville; WNKY (CBS, NBC) Bowling Green; WSMV-TV (COZI TV, NBC, TNN) Nashville; WTVF (CBS, Laff, This TV) Nashville; allband FM.
Programming (via satellite): Pop; WGN America.
Fee: $36.95 installation; $49.46 monthly.
Digital Basic Service
Subscribers: N.A.
Programming (via satellite): BBC America; Bloomberg Television; Discovery Digital Networks; DMX Music; Fuse; FXM; FYI; Golf Channel; GSN; History International; IFC; LMN; NBCSN; Nick Jr.; Nicktoons; TeenNick; Turner Classic Movies.
Digital Pay Service 1
Pay Units: N.A.
Programming (via satellite): Cinemax (multiplexed); Flix (multiplexed); HBO (multiplexed); Showtime (multiplexed); Starz (multiplexed); Sundance TV (multiplexed); The Movie Channel (multiplexed).
Video-On-Demand: No
Pay-Per-View
Barker (delivered digitally); Mediacom PPV (delivered digitally); Playboy TV (delivered digitally); TEN Clips (delivered digitally); TEN (delivered digitally); TEN Blox (delivered digitally); Pleasure (delivered digitally).
Internet Service
Operational: Yes, DSL.
Broadband Service: Mediacom High Speed Internet.
Telephone Service
Digital: Operational
Miles of Plant: 174.0 (coaxial); 4.0 (fiber optic). Homes passed: 2,507.
Regional Vice President: Bill Copeland. Vice President, Financial Reporting: Kenneth J. Kohrs. Regional Technical Operations Director: Alan Freedman. General Manager: Dale Haney. Marketing Director: Will Kuebler. Technical Operations Manager: Jeff Brown. Chief Technician: Richard Hanning. Marketing Manager: Melanie Westerman.
Ownership: Mediacom LLC (MSO).

BURNING SPRINGS—C & W Cable, 7920 Hwy 30 West, PO Box 490, Annville, KY 40402. Phone: 606-364-5357. Fax: 606-364-2138. ICA: KY0341.
TV Market Ranking: Below 100 (BURNING SPRINGS).
Channel capacity: N.A. Channels available but not in use: N.A.
Basic Service
Subscribers: 641.
Fee: $18.00 monthly.
Vice President: Veola R. Williams.
Ownership: C & W Cable Inc. (MSO).

BURNSIDE—Formerly served by Charter Communications. Now served by Time Warner Cable, CORBIN, KY [KY0030]. ICA: KY0039.

BUSY—TVS Cable, PO Box 1410, Hindman, KY 41822-1410. Phones: 606-785-3450; 606-946-2600; 606-633-0778. Fax: 606-785-3110. E-mail: tvs@tvscable.com. Web Site: http://www.tvscable.com. Also serves Butterfly, Krypton & Yerkes. ICA: KY0334.
TV Market Ranking: Below 100 (BUSY, Butterfly, Krypton, Yerkes).
Channel capacity: N.A. Channels available but not in use: N.A.
Basic Service
Subscribers: 250. Commercial subscribers: 2.
Fee: $50.00 installation; $23.50 monthly.

Vice President & General Manager: William K. Grigsby.
Ownership: TV Service Inc. (MSO).

CADIZ—Mediacom, 90 Main St, Benton, KY 42025-1132. Phones: 845-695-2762; 417-875-5560 (Springfield regional office); 270-527-9939. Fax: 270-527-0813. Web Site: http://www.mediacomcable.com. Also serves Trigg County. ICA: KY0079.
TV Market Ranking: 69 (Trigg County (portions)); Below 100 (Trigg County (portions)); Outside TV Markets (CADIZ, Trigg County (portions). Franchise award date: August 1, 1977. Franchise expiration date: N.A. Began: January 1, 1980.
Channel capacity: N.A. Channels available but not in use: N.A.
Basic Service
Subscribers: 1,093.
Programming (received off-air): WEHT (ABC) Evansville; WKMA-TV (PBS) Madisonville; WKRN-TV (ABC) Nashville; WNAB (CW, The Country Network) Nashville; WNPT (PBS) Nashville; WPSD-TV (Antenna TV, NBC) Paducah; WSMV-TV (COZI TV, NBC, TNN) Nashville; WTVF (CBS, Laff, This TV) Nashville; WUXP-TV (MNT) Nashville; WZTV (Antenna TV, FOX, WeatherNation) Nashville.
Programming (via satellite): Pop; WGN America.
Fee: $36.95 installation; $43.45 monthly.
Expanded Basic Service 1
Subscribers: N.A.
Programming (via satellite): A&E; AMC; Animal Planet; BET; Bravo; Cartoon Network; CMT; CNBC; CNN; Comedy Central; C-SPAN; Discovery Channel; Discovery Life Channel; Disney Channel; E! HD; ESPN; ESPN2; Food Network; Fox News Channel; Fox Sports 1; Freeform; FX; Hallmark Channel; HGTV; History; HLN; INSP; Lifetime; MSNBC; MTV; Nickelodeon; Outdoor Channel; QVC; Spike TV; Syfy; TBS; The Weather Channel; TLC; TNT; Travel Channel; Trinity Broadcasting Network (TBN); TV Land; Univision Studios; USA Network; VH1; WE tv.
Digital Basic Service
Subscribers: N.A.
Programming (via satellite): BBC America; Bloomberg Television; Discovery Digital Networks; Fuse; FXM; FYI; Golf Channel; GSN; History International; IFC; LMN; MC; National Geographic Channel; NBCSN; Nick Jr.; Nicktoons; TeenNick; Turner Classic Movies.
Digital Pay Service 1
Pay Units: N.A.
Programming (via satellite): Cinemax (multiplexed); Flix (multiplexed); HBO (multiplexed); Showtime (multiplexed); Starz (multiplexed); Starz Encore (multiplexed); Sundance TV (multiplexed); The Movie Channel (multiplexed).
Video-On-Demand: No
Pay-Per-View
Mediacom PPV (delivered digitally); Playboy TV (delivered digitally); TEN Clips (delivered digitally); TEN Blox (delivered digitally).

Kentucky—Cable Systems

Internet Service
Operational: Yes.
Broadband Service: Mediacom High Speed Internet.
Telephone Service
Digital: Operational
Miles of Plant: 85.0 (coaxial); None (fiber optic). Homes passed: 2,200.
Regional Vice President: Bill Copeland. Vice President, Financial Reporting: Kenneth J. Kohrs. General Manager: Dale Haney. Regional Technical Operations Director: Alan Freedman. Marketing Director: Will Kuebler. Technical Operations Manager: Jeff Brown. Marketing Manager: Melanie Westerman.
Ownership: Mediacom LLC (MSO).

CALLOWAY COUNTY—Mediacom. Now served by MARSHALL COUNTY, KY [KY0035]. ICA: KY0323.

CALVERT CITY—Formerly served by Charter Communications. Now served by Time Warner Cable, MAYFIELD, KY [KY0037]. ICA: KY0117.

CAMPBELLSVILLE—Comcast Cablevision of the South. Now served by ELIZABETHTOWN, KY [KY0012]. ICA: KY0029.

CAMPTON—MTTV. This cable system has converted to IPTV. Now served by WEST LIBERTY, KY [KY5013]. ICA: KY0249.

CANEYVILLE—Mediacom, 90 Main St, Benton, KY 42025-1132. Phones: 845-695-2762; 417-875-5560 (Springfield regional office); 270-527-9939. Fax: 270-527-0813. Web Site: http://www.mediacomcable.com. Also serves Big Clifty, Breckinridge County (portions), Grayson County (portions), Millwood & St. Paul. ICA: KY0291.
TV Market Ranking: Below 100 (Breckinridge County (portions), CANEYVILLE, Grayson County (portions), Millwood); Outside TV Markets (Big Clifty, St. Paul). Franchise award date: September 20, 1988. Franchise expiration date: N.A. Began: January 1, 1988.
Channel capacity: N.A. Channels available but not in use: N.A.
Basic Service
Subscribers: 316.
Programming (received off-air): WAVE (Bounce TV, NBC, This TV) Louisville; WBKO (ABC, CW, FOX) Bowling Green; WDRB (Antenna TV, FOX) Louisville; WDYL-LD (Daystar TV) Louisville; WHAS-TV (ABC) Louisville; WKYU-TV (PBS) Bowling Green; WKZT-TV (PBS) Elizabethtown; WMYO (MNT, My Family TV) Salem.
Fee: $29.95 installation; $39.95 monthly; $3.95 converter.
Expanded Basic Service 1
Subscribers: N.A.
Programming (via satellite): A&E; AMC; Animal Planet; Bravo; Cartoon Network; CMT; CNBC; CNN; Comedy Central; C-SPAN; Discovery Channel; Disney Channel; E! HD; ESPN; ESPN2; EVINE Live; Food Network; Fox News Channel; Fox Sports 1; Freeform; FX; Great American Country; Hallmark Channel; HGTV; History; HLN; INSP; Lifetime; MSNBC; MTV; National Geographic Channel; Nickelodeon; Outdoor Channel; QVC; Spike TV; Syfy; TBS; The Weather Channel; TLC; TNT; Travel Channel; Trinity Broadcasting Network (TBN); truTV; Turner Classic Movies; TV Land; USA Network; VH1; WE tv; WGN America.

Digital Basic Service
Subscribers: N.A.
Programming (via satellite): BBC America; Destination America; Discovery Kids Channel; Discovery Life Channel; DMX Music; ESPN Classic; ESPNews; Fuse; FXM; FYI; Golf Channel; GSN; History International; IFC; Investigation Discovery; LMN; National Geographic Channel; NBCSN; Nick Jr.; Nicktoons; Outdoor Channel; OWN: Oprah Winfrey Network; TeenNick; Turner Classic Movies.
Digital Pay Service 1
Pay Units: N.A.
Programming (via satellite): Cinemax (multiplexed); HBO (multiplexed); Showtime (multiplexed); Starz (multiplexed); Starz Encore (multiplexed); The Movie Channel (multiplexed).
Video-On-Demand: No
Internet Service
Operational: Yes.
Broadband Service: Mediacom High Speed Internet.
Telephone Service
None
Miles of Plant: 89.0 (coaxial); None (fiber optic). Homes passed: 2,054.
Regional Vice President: Bill Copeland. Vice President, Financial Reporting: Kenneth J. Kohrs. General Manager: Dale Haney. Regional Technical Operations Director: Alan Freedman. Marketing Director: Will Kuebler. Technical Operations Manager: Jeff Brown. Marketing Manager: Melanie Westerman.
Ownership: Mediacom LLC (MSO).

CARLISLE—Time Warner Cable. Now served by RICHMOND, KY [KY0008]. ICA: KY0208.

CASEY COUNTY (portions)—Mediacom. Now served by RUSSELL COUNTY, KY [KY0114]. ICA: KY0144.

CHARLEY—Lycom Communications, 305 East Pike St, PO Box 1114, Louisa, KY 41230. Phones: 606-638-4278; 800-489-0640; 606-638-3600. Fax: 606-638-4278. E-mail: info@lycomonline.com. Web Site: http://lycomonline.com. ICA: KY0329.
TV Market Ranking: 36 (CHARLEY).
Channel capacity: N.A. Channels available but not in use: N.A.
Basic Service
Subscribers: 124.
Fee: $69.95 installation; $40.06 monthly.
Expanded Basic Service 1
Subscribers: 109.
Fee: $42.95 monthly.
President: Steven J. Lycans. Chief Technician: Aaron Lycans.
Ownership: Lycom Communications Inc. (MSO).

CLAY (town)—Time Warner Cable, 7800 Crescent Executive Dr, Charlotte, NC 28217. Phone: 270-852-2000. Web Site: http://www.timewarnercable.com. Also serves Dixon, Webster County (portions) & Wheatcroft. ICA: KY0218.
TV Market Ranking: 86 (Dixon); Below 100 (Webster County (portions), Wheatcroft, CLAY (TOWN)). Franchise award date: October 12, 1987. Franchise expiration date: N.A. Began: N.A.
Channel capacity: N.A. Channels available but not in use: N.A.
Basic Service
Subscribers: 159.
Programming (received off-air): WEHT (ABC) Evansville; WEVV-TV (CBS, FOX) Evansville; WFIE (NBC, This TV) Evansville; WKMA-TV (PBS) Madisonville; WNIN (PBS) Evansville; WPSD-TV (Antenna TV, NBC) Paducah; WTVW (CW, MeTV) Evansville.
Programming (via satellite): A&E; AMC; Animal Planet; CMT; C-SPAN; Discovery Channel; E! HD; ESPN; ESPN2; EVINE Live; Food Network; Freeform; FX; HLN; Lifetime; MSNBC; MTV; Nickelodeon; QVC; Spike TV; Syfy; The Weather Channel; TLC; TNT; Travel Channel; Trinity Broadcasting Network (TBN); truTV; TV Land; USA Network; VH1; WGN America.
Fee: $49.99 installation; $54.99 monthly.
Expanded Basic Service 1
Subscribers: N.A.
Programming (via satellite): CNN; Disney Channel; Fox News Channel; HGTV; History; TBS.
Fee: $9.15 monthly.
Digital Basic Service
Subscribers: N.A.
Programming (via satellite): BBC America; Bloomberg Television; Discovery Digital Networks; DMX Music; ESPN Classic; ESPNews; FXM; Golf Channel; GSN; MC; NBCSN; Nick Jr.; Nicktoons; Outdoor Channel; WE tv.
Digital Pay Service 1
Pay Units: N.A.
Programming (via satellite): Cinemax (multiplexed); HBO (multiplexed); Showtime (multiplexed); Starz (multiplexed); Starz Encore (multiplexed); The Movie Channel (multiplexed).
Fee: $14.00 monthly (each).
Video-On-Demand: No
Pay-Per-View
iN DEMAND (delivered digitally); Playboy TV (delivered digitally); Fresh (delivered digitally).
Internet Service
Operational: Yes.
Broadband Service: Road Runner.
Fee: $44.95 monthly.
Telephone Service
None
Miles of Plant: 19.0 (coaxial); None (fiber optic).
Senior Accounting Director: Karen Goodfellow. General Manager: Chris Poynter. Technical Operations Director: Don Collins. Marketing Manager: Doug Rodgers.
Ownership: Time Warner Cable (MSO).

CLAY (town)—Time Warner Cable. Now served by CLAY (town) (formerly Dixon), KY [KY0218]. ICA: KY0133.

CLINTON COUNTY—Mediacom. Now served by SUMMER SHADE, KY [KY0092]. ICA: KY0212.

CLOVER BOTTOM—Formerly served by McKee TV Enterprises Inc. No longer in operation. ICA: KY0179.

CLOVERPORT—Formerly served by Inside Connect Cable (formerly Crystal Broadband). No longer in operation. ICA: KY0121.

COLUMBIA—Duo County Telephone. Now served by RUSSELL SPRINGS, KY [KY0243]. ICA: KY0213.

CORBIN—Time Warner Cable, 60 Columbus Circle, 17th Fl, New York, NY 10023. Phones: 859-431-0300; 212-364-8200. Fax: 203-328-0604. Web Site: http://www.timewarnercable.com. Also serves Arjay, Baughman, Bell County (portions), Big Creek, Bimble, Bronston, Burnside, Calvin, Casey County (portions), Clear Creek, Conway, Cubage, Dewitt, East Pineville, Eubank, Faber, Ferguson, Flat Lick, Fogertown, Fourmile, Garrard, Girdler, Goose Rock, Harlan, Hima, Hinkle, Kettle Island, Knox County (portions), Laurel County (portions), Leslie County (portions), Liberty, Lily, Log Mountain, McKinney, Middleburg, Middlesboro, Miracle, Mount Vernon, Nancy, Oneida, Pineville, Pulaski County (portions), Renfro Valley, Rockcastle County (portions), Rockholds, Salt Gum, Scalf, Science Hill, Sibert, Sloans Valley, Somerset, Stoney Fork, Straight Creek, Tateville, Walker, Waynesburg, Whitley County (portions), Williamsburg, Woodbine & Yosemite, KY; Claiborne County (portions), TN. ICA: KY0030.
TV Market Ranking: Below 100 (Arjay, Baughman, Bell County (portions), Big Creek, Bimble, Calvin, Casey County (portions), Claiborne County (portions), Clear Creek, Conway, Cubage, Dewitt, East Pineville, Eubank, Fogertown, Fourmile, Goose Rock, Harlan, Hima, Kettle Island, Knox County (portions), Laurel County (portions), Leslie County (portions), Lily, Log Mountain, Middleburg, Middlesboro, Miracle, Mount Vernon, Oneida, Renfro Valley, Rockcastle County (portions), Salt Gum, Scalf, Science Hill, Sloans Valley, Walker, Waynesburg, Whitley County (portions), Woodbine, Yosemite, CORBIN, Flat Lick, Garrard, Liberty, McKinney, Pineville, Pulaski County (portions), Williamsburg); Outside TV Markets (Bronston, Burnside, Ferguson, Nancy, Tateville, Pulaski County (portions), Somerset). Franchise award date: August 3, 1988. Franchise expiration date: N.A. Began: March 1, 1956.
Channel capacity: N.A. Channels available but not in use: N.A.
Basic Service
Subscribers: 34,110. Commercial subscribers: 1,246.
Programming (received off-air): WAGV (IND) Harlan; WATE-TV (ABC, Laff) Knoxville; WBIR-TV (MeTV, NBC) Knoxville; WBXX-TV (CW, Escape) Crossville; WDKY-TV (FOX) Danville; WKSO-TV (PBS) Somerset; WKYT-TV (CBS, CW) Lexington; WLEX-TV (MeTV, NBC) Lexington; WLJC-TV (TBN) Beattyville; WTVQ-DT (ABC, Antenna TV, Laff, MNT) Lexington; WUPX-TV (ION) Morehead; WVTN-LP Corbin; WYMT-TV (CBS, CW) Hazard; 1 FM.
Programming (via satellite): EVINE Live; Pop; QVC; WGN America.
Fee: $40.00 installation; $20.99 monthly.
Expanded Basic Service 1
Subscribers: 7,050.
Programming (via satellite): A&E; AMC; Animal Planet; Bravo; Cartoon Network; CMT; CNBC; CNN; Comcast/Charter Sports Southeast (CSS); Comedy Central; C-SPAN; C-SPAN 2; Discovery Channel; Discovery Life Channel; Disney Channel; Disney XD; E! HD; ESPN; ESPN2; Food Network; Fox News Channel; Fox Sports 1; FOX Sports Ohio/Sports Time Ohio; Freeform; FX; Golf Channel; Hallmark Channel; HGTV; History; HLN; INSP; Lifetime; MSNBC; MTV; National Geographic Channel; NBCSN; Nickelodeon; Oxygen; Spike TV; Syfy; TBS; The Weather Channel; TLC; TNT; Travel Channel; Trinity Broadcasting Network (TBN); truTV; Turner Classic Movies; TV Land; USA Network; VH1; WE tv.
Digital Basic Service
Subscribers: N.A.
Programming (via satellite): BBC America; Bloomberg Television; Discovery Digital Networks; DIY Network; ESPN Classic;

Cable Systems—Kentucky

ESPNews; FOX College Sports Central; FOX College Sports Pacific; Fox Sports 2; Fuse; FXM; FYI; Great American Country; History International; IFC; Jewelry Television; LMN; MC; NFL Network; Nick 2; Nick Jr.; Nicktoons; Sundance TV; TeenNick; TV Guide Interactive Inc.

Digital Pay Service 1
Pay Units: N.A.
Programming (via satellite): Cinemax (multiplexed); Flix; HBO (multiplexed); Showtime (multiplexed); Starz (multiplexed); Starz Encore (multiplexed); The Movie Channel (multiplexed).

Video-On-Demand: No

Pay-Per-View
iN DEMAND (delivered digitally); NHL Center Ice (delivered digitally); MLB Extra Innings (delivered digitally); Playboy TV (delivered digitally); Fresh (delivered digitally); Shorteez (delivered digitally).

Internet Service
Operational: Yes.
Subscribers: 15,328.
Fee: $40.00 installation; $23.95 monthly.

Telephone Service
Digital: Operational
Subscribers: 5,783.
Miles of Plant: 2,741.0 (coaxial); 988.0 (fiber optic). Homes passed: 66,644.
Chairman & Chief Executive Officer: Glenn A. Britt. President & Chief Operations Officer: Robert D. Marcus.
Ownership: Time Warner Cable (MSO).

CORINTH—Formerly served by City of Williamstown. No longer in operation. ICA: KY0307.

CORYDON—Time Warner Cable. Now served by OWENSBORO, KY [KY0004]. ICA: KY0214.

COVINGTON—Time Warner Cable, 60 Columbus Circle, 17th Fl, New York, NY 10023. Phones: 212-364-8200; 212-364-8200; 888-735-0300; 859-431-0300. Fax: 212-364-8252. Web Site: http://www.timewarnercable.com. Also serves Alexandria, Bellevue, Boone County (portions), Bromley, Butler, California, Campbell County (portions), Cold Spring, Crescent Park, Crescent Springs, Crestview, Crestview Hills, Crittenden, Dayton, Dry Ridge, Edgewood, Elsmere, Erlanger, Fairview, Falmouth, Florence, Fort Mitchell, Fort Thomas, Fort Wright, Gallatin County (portions), Grant County (portions), Highland Heights, Independence, Kenton County (portions), Kenton Vale, Lakeside Park, Latonia Lakes, Ludlow, Melbourne, Mentor, Morning View, Newport, Park Hills, Pendleton County (portions), Ryland Heights, Silver Grove, Southgate, Taylor Mill, Union, Villa Hills, Walton, Warsaw, Wilder & Woodlawn. ICA: KY0002.
TV Market Ranking: 17 (Alexandria, Bellevue, Boone County (portions), Bromley, Butler, Campbell County (portions), Cold Spring, COVINGTON, Crescent Park, Crescent Springs, Crestview Hills, Crittenden, Dry Ridge, Edgewood, Elsmere, Erlanger, Falmouth, Florence, Fort Mitchell, Fort Thomas, Fort Wright, Grant County (portions), Highland Heights, Independence, Kenton County (portions), Kenton Vale, Lakeside Park, Latonia Lakes, Ludlow, Melbourne, Mentor, Morning View, Newport, Park Hills, Ryland Heights, Silver Grove, Southgate, Taylor Mill, Union, Villa Hills, Walton, Warsaw, Wilder, Woodlawn)); Below 100 (Grant County (portions)).
Franchise award date: December 1, 1980. Franchise expiration date: N.A. Began: January 1, 1981.
Channel capacity: N.A. Channels available but not in use: N.A.

Basic Service
Subscribers: 90,778. Commercial subscribers: 471.
Programming (received off-air): WCET (PBS) Cincinnati; WCPO-TV (ABC, Escape) Cincinnati; WCVN-TV (PBS) Covington; WKRC-TV (CBS, CW) Cincinnati; WLWT (MeTV, NBC) Cincinnati; WPTO (PBS) Oxford; WSTR-TV (Antenna TV, MNT) Cincinnati; WXIX-TV (Bounce TV, FOX) Newport.
Programming (via satellite): C-SPAN; C-SPAN 2; Pop; QVC; WGN America.
Fee: $30.00 installation; $13.25 monthly.

Expanded Basic Service 1
Subscribers: N.A.
Programming (via satellite): A&E; AMC; Animal Planet; BET; BTN; Cartoon Network; CMT; CNBC; CNN; Comedy Central; Discovery Channel; Disney Channel; E! HD; ESPN; ESPN2; EWTN Global Catholic Network; Food Network; Fox News Channel; FOX Sports Ohio/Sports Time Ohio; Freeform; FX; Golf Channel; Hallmark Channel; HGTV; History; HLN; ION Television; Lifetime; MSNBC; MTV; Nickelodeon; Spike TV; Syfy; TBS; The Weather Channel; TLC; TNT; Travel Channel; truTV; TV Land; Univision Studios; USA Network; VH1; Weatherscan.
Fee: $40.00 monthly.

Digital Basic Service
Subscribers: N.A.
Programming (via satellite): BBC America; Bloomberg Television; Bravo; Discovery Digital Networks; Disney XD; DMX Music; ESPN Classic; ESPNews; Fox Sports 1; Fuse; FXM; FYI; GSN; History International; IFC; LMN; National Geographic Channel; NBCSN; Nick 2; Nick Jr.; Outdoor Channel; Ovation; Starz Encore (multiplexed); Sundance TV; TeenNick; Trinity Broadcasting Network (TBN); Turner Classic Movies; WE tv.

Digital Pay Service 1
Pay Units: N.A.
Programming (via satellite): Cinemax (multiplexed); Flix; HBO (multiplexed); Showtime (multiplexed); Starz (multiplexed); The Movie Channel (multiplexed).
Fee: $10.00 monthly (Cinemax or Starz), $13.00 monthly (HBO or Showtime/TMC/Flix).

Video-On-Demand: Yes

Pay-Per-View
Hot Choice (delivered digitally); iN DEMAND (delivered digitally); BET Action Pay-Per-View (delivered digitally); Shorteez (delivered digitally); Fresh (delivered digitally); Sports PPV (delivered digitally).

Internet Service
Operational: Yes.
Subscribers: 71,543.
Fee: $99.95 installation; $40.00 monthly; $10.00 modem lease; $140.00 modem purchase.

Telephone Service
Digital: Operational
Subscribers: 33,348.
Miles of Plant: 3,429.0 (coaxial); 1,227.0 (fiber optic). Homes passed: 172,075.
Chief Executive Officer: Glenn A. Britt. President & Chief Operations Officer: Robert D. Marcus.
Ownership: Time Warner Cable (MSO).

COWAN CREEK—TVS Cable, PO Box 1410, Hindman, KY 41822-1410. Phones: 606-633-0778; 606-946-2600; 606-785-3450. Fax: 606-785-3110. E-mail: tvs@tvscable.com. Web Site: http://www.tvscable.com. Also serves Gordon, Linefork & Whitco. ICA: KY0332.
TV Market Ranking: Below 100 (COWAN CREEK, Gordon, Linefork, Whitco).
Channel capacity: N.A. Channels available but not in use: N.A.

Basic Service
Subscribers: 646. Commercial subscribers: 12.
Fee: $50.00 installation; $23.50 monthly.
Vice President & General Manager: William K. Grigsby.
Ownership: TV Service Inc. (MSO).

CRAB ORCHARD—Wilcop Cable TV. Now served by BRODHEAD, KY [KY0173]. ICA: KY0175.

CRITTENDEN—Formerly served by Insight Communications. Now served by Time Warner Cable, COVINGTON, KY [KY0002]. ICA: KY0068.

CROMWELL—Formerly served by Vital Communications. No longer in operation. ICA: KY0215.

CUMBERLAND—Access Cable Television Inc, 302 Enterprise Dr, Somerset, KY 42501. Phone: 606-677-2444. Fax: 606-677-2443. E-mail: cable@accesshsd.net. Web Site: http://www.accesshsd.com. Also serves Benham, Blair, Harlan County (portions), Hiram & Lynch. ICA: KY0075.
TV Market Ranking: Below 100 (Benham, Blair, CUMBERLAND, Hiram, Lynch, Harlan County (portions)); Outside TV Markets (Harlan County (portions)).
Channel capacity: N.A. Channels available but not in use: N.A.

Basic Service
Subscribers: 1,167.
Programming (received off-air): WAGV (IND) Harlan; WATE-TV (ABC, Laff) Knoxville; WCYB-TV (CW, Decades, NBC) Bristol; WKHA (PBS) Hazard; WKPT-TV (COZI TV, Escape, MeTV, MNT) Kingsport; WKYT-TV (CBS, CW) Lexington; WLEX-TV (MeTV, NBC) Lexington; WTNZ (FOX, This TV) Knoxville; WTVQ-DT (ABC, Antenna TV, Laff, MNT) Lexington; WVLT-TV (CBS, MNT) Knoxville; WYMT-TV (CBS, CW) Hazard; allband FM.
Programming (via satellite): A&E; AMC; CMT; CW PLUS; Discovery Channel; ESPN; ESPN2; History; Lifetime; MTV; Nickelodeon; QVC; Syfy; TBS; TNT; Trinity Broadcasting Network (TBN); VH1; WGN America.
Fee: $25.00 installation; $28.50 monthly; $3.00 converter.

Expanded Basic Service 1
Subscribers: 901.
Programming (via satellite): Animal Planet; BET; Cartoon Network; CNN; Disney Channel; Food Network; Fox News Channel; Fox Sports 1; Freeform; FX; Hallmark Channel; HGTV; HLN; Outdoor Channel; Spike TV; The Weather Channel; TLC; truTV; Turner Classic Movies; TV Land; USA Network.
Fee: $9.50 monthly.

Pay Service 1
Pay Units: 58.
Programming (via satellite): Cinemax.
Fee: $15.00 installation; $11.95 monthly.

Pay Service 2
Pay Units: 58.
Programming (via satellite): HBO.
Fee: $15.00 installation; $11.95 monthly.

Video-On-Demand: No

Internet Service
Operational: Yes.

Telephone Service
Digital: Operational
Fee: $24.95 monthly
Miles of Plant: 48.0 (coaxial); None (fiber optic). Homes passed: 2,200.
President & Manager: Roy Baker. Technical Manager: Allen Slavin.
Ownership: Access Cable Television Inc. (MSO).

CUTSHIN—Formerly served by Craft Cable Service. Now served by TVS Cable, VICCO, KY [KY0339]. ICA: KY0217.

CYNTHIANA—Time Warner Cable. Now served by RICHMOND, KY [KY0008]. ICA: KY0051.

DANVILLE—Time Warner Cable. Now served by RICHMOND, KY [KY0008]. ICA: KY0024.

DAWSON SPRINGS—Time Warner Cable, 116 South Main St, Dawson Springs, KY 42408. Phones: 212-364-8200; 859-431-0300; 212-364-8200; 270-797-5061. Web Site: http://www.timewarnercable.com. Also serves Caldwell County (portions), Hopkins County (portions) & St. Charles. ICA: KY0069.
TV Market Ranking: 69 (Caldwell County (portions)); 86 (Hopkins County (portions)); Below 100 (DAWSON SPRINGS, St. Charles, Caldwell County (portions), Hopkins County (portions)). Franchise award date: N.A. Franchise expiration date: N.A. Began: April 1, 1969.
Channel capacity: N.A. Channels available but not in use: N.A.

Basic Service
Subscribers: 1,092. Commercial subscribers: 4.
Programming (received off-air): WEHT (ABC) Evansville; WEVV-TV (CBS, FOX) Evansville; WFIE (NBC, This TV) Evansville; WKMA-TV (PBS) Madisonville; WNIN (PBS) Evansville; WPSD-TV (Antenna TV, NBC) Paducah; WTVF (CBS, Laff, This TV) Nashville; WTVW (CW, MeTV) Evansville; allband FM.
Programming (via satellite): WGN America.
Fee: $24.95 installation; $19.95 monthly; $2.00 converter.

Expanded Basic Service 1
Subscribers: N.A.
Programming (via satellite): AMC; Cartoon Network; CNBC; CNN; C-SPAN; Discovery Channel; Disney Channel; ESPN; ESPN2; Fox News Channel; Freeform; FX; HLN; Life-

2017 Edition
D-311

Kentucky—Cable Systems

time; MoviePlex; MTV; Nickelodeon; QVC; Spike TV; TBS; The Weather Channel; TLC; TNT; USA Network.
Fee: $19.63 monthly.
Pay Service 1
Pay Units: N.A.
Programming (via satellite): Cinemax; HBO; Showtime; Starz; Starz Encore.
Fee: $10.00 monthly (Cinemax, HBO, Showtime or Starz/Encore).
Video-On-Demand: No
Internet Service
Operational: No.
Telephone Service
None
Miles of Plant: 99.0 (coaxial); None (fiber optic). Homes passed: 2,444.
Chief Executive Officer: Glenn A. Britt. President & Chief Operations Officer: Robert D. Marcus.
Ownership: Time Warner Cable (MSO).

DUNMOR—Formerly served by Windjammer Cable. No longer in operation. ICA: KY0248.

ELIZABETHTOWN—Comcast Cable, One Comcast Center, Philadelphia, PA 19103. Phones: 270-605-7719; 270-765-2731. Web Site: http://www.comcast.com. Also serves Brookport, Massac County (portions) & Metropolis, IL; Campbellsville, Clarkson, Grayson County (portions), Hardin County (portions), Hodgenville, Kevil, Larue County (portions), Ledbetter, Leitchfield, Lone Oak (Grayson County), McCracken County (portions), Paducah, Radcliff, Taylor County (portions) & Vine Grove, KY. ICA: KY0012.
TV Market Ranking: 38 (Hardin County (portions), Radcliff, Vine Grove); 69 (Brookport, Kevil, Ledbetter, Massac County (portions), McCracken County (portions), Metropolis, Paducah); Below 100 (Campbellsville, Grayson County (portions), Hodgenville, Larue County (portions), Taylor County (portions)); Outside TV Markets (Clarkson, ELIZABETHTOWN, Lone Oak (Grayson County), Leitchfield). Franchise award date: October 18, 1965. Franchise expiration date: N.A. Began: February 10, 1965.
Channel capacity: N.A. Channels available but not in use: N.A.
Basic Service
Subscribers: 33,927. Commercial subscribers: 3,204.
Programming (received off-air): WAVE (Bounce TV, NBC, This TV) Louisville; WBKI-TV (CW, IND, Movies!) Campbellsville; WBKO (ABC, CW, FOX) Bowling Green; WBNA (ION, Retro TV) Louisville; WHAS-TV (ABC) Louisville; WKMJ-TV (PBS) Louisville; WKYT-TV (CBS, CW) Lexington; WKZT-TV (PBS) Elizabethtown; WLKY (CBS, MeTV) Louisville; WMYO (MNT, My Family TV) Salem; allband FM.
Programming (via satellite): Freeform; QVC; TBS; WGN America.
Fee: $59.95 installation; $25.20 monthly.
Expanded Basic Service 1
Subscribers: N.A.
Programming (via satellite): A&E; AMC; Animal Planet; BET; Cartoon Network; CMT; CNBC; CNN; Comcast/Charter Sports Southeast (CSS); Comedy Central; C-SPAN; C-SPAN 2; Discovery Channel; Disney Channel; E! HD; ESPN; ESPN2; EWTN Global Catholic Network; Food Network; Fox News Channel; FOX Sports Ohio/Sports Time Ohio; FX; Golf Channel; Great American Country; Hallmark Channel; HGTV; History; HLN;

INSP; Lifetime; MTV; NBCSN; Nickelodeon; Outdoor Channel; Pop; Spike TV; Syfy; The Weather Channel; TLC; TNT; Travel Channel; Trinity Broadcasting Network (TBN); truTV; TV Land; USA Network; VH1.
Fee: $29.64 monthly.
Digital Basic Service
Subscribers: 20,772.
Programming (received off-air): WDRB (Antenna TV, FOX) Louisville.
Programming (via satellite): A&E HD; BBC America; CBS Sports Network; CMT; C-SPAN 3; Discovery Digital Networks; Disney XD; ESPN HD; ESPN2 HD; ESPNews; Flix; FOX College Sports Central; FOX College Sports Pacific; FYI; GolTV; GSN; HD Theater; History International; LMN; MC; MoviePlex; MSNBC; MTV Live; Nat Geo WILD; National Geographic Channel; National Geographic Channel HD; NBA TV; NFL Network; Nick 2; Nick Jr.; Nicktoons; Sprout; Starz Encore (multiplexed); Sundance TV; TeenNick; Tennis Channel; TNT HD; TV One; TVG Network; Universal HD; Versus HD.
Pay Service 1
Pay Units: N.A.
Programming (via satellite): HBO.
Fee: $8.69 monthly.
Digital Pay Service 1
Pay Units: N.A.
Programming (via satellite): Cinemax (multiplexed); Cinemax HD; HBO (multiplexed); HBO HD; Showtime (multiplexed); Showtime HD; Starz (multiplexed); Starz HD; The Movie Channel (multiplexed).
Fee: $13.05 monthly (each).
Video-On-Demand: Yes
Pay-Per-View
iN DEMAND; iN DEMAND (delivered digitally); Hot Choice (delivered digitally); Playboy TV (delivered digitally).
Internet Service
Operational: Yes.
Subscribers: 24,026.
Broadband Service: Comcast High Speed Internet.
Fee: $42.95 monthly.
Telephone Service
Digital: Operational
Subscribers: 8,165.
Miles of Plant: 2,549.0 (coaxial); 445.0 (fiber optic). Homes passed: 90,514.
Vice President, Accounting: Donald S. Tyrie. General Manager: Tim Hagan. Marketing Director: Laurie Nicholson. Technical Operations Director: Bob Tharp.
Ownership: Comcast Cable Communications Inc. (MSO).

ELKHORN CITY—Formerly served by Cebridge Connections. Now served by Suddenlink Communications, PIKEVILLE, KY [KY0045]. ICA: KY0059.

ELKTON—Mediacom. Now served by TRENTON, KY [KY0101]. ICA: KY0132.

EOLIA—Formerly served by Charter Communications. Now served by Inter Mountain Cable Inc., JENKINS, KY [KY0041]. ICA: KY0127.

EVARTS—Evarts TV Inc, 113 Yocum St, PO Box 8, Evarts, KY 40828. Phone: 606-837-2505. Fax: 606-837-3738. Also serves Harlan County (unincorporated areas). ICA: KY0135.
TV Market Ranking: Below 100 (EVARTS, Harlan County (unincorporated areas)). Franchise award date: N.A. Franchise expiration date: N.A. Began: June 1, 1987.
Channel capacity: 42 (not 2-way capable). Channels available but not in use: N.A.

Basic Service
Subscribers: N.A.
Programming (received off-air): WATE-TV (ABC, Laff) Knoxville; WBIR-TV (MeTV, NBC) Knoxville; WBXX-TV (CW, Escape) Crossville; WEMT (FOX, Movies!, This TV) Greeneville; WKYT-TV (CBS, CW) Lexington; WLEX-TV (MeTV, NBC) Lexington; WLJC-TV (TBN) Beattyville; WTNZ (FOX, This TV) Knoxville; WTVQ-DT (ABC, Antenna TV, Laff, MNT) Lexington; WVLT-TV (CBS, MNT) Knoxville; WYMT-TV (CBS, CW) Hazard.
Programming (via satellite): AMC; Cartoon Network; CMT; CNN; Discovery Channel; ESPN; ESPN2; Fox News Channel; Freeform; Hallmark Channel; HGTV; History; Lifetime; LMN; Nickelodeon; Outdoor Channel; Spike TV; Syfy; TBS; The Weather Channel; TNT; TV Land; USA Network; WGN America.
Fee: $40.00 installation.
Pay Service 1
Pay Units: N.A.
Programming (via satellite): Cinemax; HBO.
Fee: $7.00 monthly (Cinemax), $12.00 monthly (HBO).
Internet Service
Operational: No.
Telephone Service
None
Miles of Plant: 25.0 (coaxial); None (fiber optic).
General Manager: Bob Cornett. Chief Technician: John Lutrell.
Ownership: Evarts TV Inc.

FALLSBURG—Formerly served by Lycom Communications. No longer in operation. ICA: KY0166.

FALMOUTH—Formerly served by Insight Communications. Now served by Time Warner Cable, COVINGTON, KY [KY0002]. ICA: KY0087.

FEDSCREEK—Formerly served by Fuller's TV. Now served by Inter Mountain Cable Inc., HAROLD, KY [KY0006]. ICA: KY0188.

FIVE STAR—Formerly served by Insight Communications. No longer in operation. ICA: KY0162.

FLAT LICK—Time Warner Cable. Now served by CORBIN, KY [KY0030]. ICA: KY0078.

FLEMINGSBURG—Formerly served by Adelphia Communications. Now served by Time Warner Cable, RICHMOND, KY [KY0008]. ICA: KY0077.

FORT CAMPBELL—Comcast Cable. Now served by NASHVILLE, TN [TN0002]. ICA: KY0019.

FRAKES—Formerly served by Suddenlink Communications. No longer in operation. ICA: KY0225.

FRANKFORT—Frankfort Plant Board Cable Service, 317 West 2nd St, PO Box 308, Frankfort, KY 40601-2645. Phones: 502-352-4505; 888-312-4372; 502-352-4372. Fax: 502-223-4449. Web Site: http://fpb.cc. ICA: KY0010.
TV Market Ranking: Below 100 (FRANKFORT). Franchise award date: N.A. Franchise expiration date: N.A. Began: October 1, 1952.
Channel capacity: N.A. Channels available but not in use: N.A.

Basic Service
Subscribers: 13,145.
Programming (received off-air): KETS (PBS) Little Rock; WAVE (Bounce TV, NBC, This TV) Louisville; WBKI-TV (CW, IND, Movies!) Campbellsville; WDKY-TV (FOX) Danville; WDRB (Antenna TV, FOX) Louisville; WHAS-TV (ABC) Louisville; WKYT-TV (CBS, CW) Lexington; WLEX-TV (MeTV, NBC) Lexington; WLKY (CBS, MeTV) Louisville; WTVQ-DT (ABC, Antenna TV, Laff, MNT) Lexington; WUPX-TV (ION) Morehead; 9 FMs.
Programming (via satellite): CW PLUS; QVC; Weatherscan.
Fee: $30.00 installation; $64.43 monthly.
Expanded Basic Service 1
Subscribers: N.A.
Programming (via satellite): A&E; AMC; Animal Planet; BET; Cartoon Network; CMT; CNBC; CNN; Comedy Central; C-SPAN; C-SPAN 2; C-SPAN 3; Discovery Channel; Discovery Life Channel; E! HD; ESPN; ESPN Classic; ESPN2; EWTN Global Catholic Network; Food Network; Fox News Channel; Freeform; Hallmark Channel; HGTV; History; HLN; HRTV; Lifetime; MTV; NASA TV; National Geographic Channel; Nickelodeon; Outdoor Channel; Pop; Spike TV; Syfy; TBS; The Weather Channel; TLC; TNT; Travel Channel; Trinity Broadcasting Network (TBN); truTV; Turner Classic Movies; TV Land; USA Network; VH1.
Fee: $20.00 monthly.
Digital Basic Service
Subscribers: N.A.
Programming (via satellite): A&E HD; AXS TV; BBC America; Bloomberg Television; CMT; Destination America; Discovery Kids Channel; Disney XD; DMX Music; ESPN HD; ESPN2 HD; ESPNews; ESPNU; Fox Sports 1; FXM; FYI; Golf Channel; Great American Country; GSN; HD Theater; History International; International Television (ITV); Investigation Discovery; LMN; MTV Classic; MTV Hits; MTV2; Nick Jr.; Nicktoons; Outdoor Channel 2 HD; Ovation; OWN: Oprah Winfrey Network; Science Channel; Sprout; TeenNick; TNT HD; Universal HD; VH1 Soul; WE tv.
Pay Service 1
Pay Units: N.A.
Programming (via satellite): HBO.
Fee: $8.00 installation; $10.45 monthly.
Digital Pay Service 1
Pay Units: N.A.
Programming (via satellite): Cinemax (multiplexed); Cinemax HD; HBO (multiplexed); HBO HD; Showtime (multiplexed); Showtime HD; Starz (multiplexed); Starz Encore (multiplexed); Starz HD; The Movie Channel (multiplexed); The Movie Channel HD.
Fee: $10.45 monthly (Cinemax, HBO, Showtime/TMC or Starz/Encore).
Video-On-Demand: Planned
Pay-Per-View
iN DEMAND (delivered digitally).
Internet Service
Operational: Yes. Began: February 1, 2001.
Subscribers: 12,425.
Broadband Service: FPB ISP.
Fee: $100.00 installation; $26.00-$54.00 monthly; $7.00 modem lease; $250.00 modem purchase.
Telephone Service
Digital: Operational
Subscribers: 9,506.
Miles of Plant: 890.0 (coaxial); 453.0 (fiber optic). Homes passed: 22,500.
General Manager: Jim Smith. Cable Superintendent: John Higginbotham. Chief Technician: Adam Hellard. Marketing & Program

Cable Systems—Kentucky

Director: Will Bell. Finance Director: David Denton.
Ownership: Frankfort Plant Board.

FRANKFORT/STONEWALL—Formerly served by Vital Communications. No longer in operation. ICA: KY0284.

FRANKLIN—Comcast Cable. Now served by NASHVILLE, TN [TN0002]. ICA: KY0050.

FRENCHBURG—MTTV. This cable system has converted to IPTV. Now served by WEST LIBERTY, KY [KY5013]. ICA: KY0292.

FULTON—Time Warner Cable. Now served by MAYFIELD, KY [KY0037]. ICA: KY0226.

GARRARD—Time Warner Cable. Now served by CORBIN, KY [KY0030]. ICA: KY0058.

GARRISON—Formerly served by Adelphia Communications. Now served by Time Warner Cable, VANCEBURG, KY [KY0286]. ICA: KY0125.

GEORGETOWN—Time Warner Cable. Now served by RICHMOND, KY [KY0008]. ICA: KY0044.

GLASGOW—Glasgow Electric Power Board-CATV Division. This cable system has converted to IPTV. See GLASGOW, KY [KY5022]. ICA: KY0038.

GLASGOW—Glasgow EPB. Formerly [KY0038]. This cable system has converted to IPTV, PO Box 1809, Glasgow, KY 42142-1809. Phones: 800-648-6056; 270-651-8341. Fax: 270-651-7572. E-mail: epb@glasgow-ky.com. Web Site: http://www.glasgowepb.net. ICA: KY5022.
Channel capacity: N.A. Channels available but not in use: N.A.
Basic
Subscribers: 6,916.
Fee: $34.50 monthly. Includes 70 channels.
Video-On-Demand: Yes
Internet Service
Operational: Yes.
Telephone Service
Digital: Operational
President: Ray Williams. General Manager: Eddie Russell. Marketing Director: Sheila Hogue. Engineering Manager: Todd Barbour.
Ownership: Glasgow Electric Plant Board-CATV Division.

GRAVES COUNTY—Zito Media, 102 S Main St, PO Box 665, Coudersport, PA 16915. Phones: 814-260-9055; 800-365-6988. E-mail: info@zitomedia.com. Web Site: http://www.zitomedia.com. Also serves Ballard County (portions), Carlisle County (portions), Cunningham, Fancy Farm, Hickory, Lovelaceville, Mayfield, Pryorsburg, Sedalia, Symsonia & Wingo. ICA: KY0065.
TV Market Ranking: 69 (Ballard County (portions), Carlisle County (portions), Cunningham, Fancy Farm, GRAVES COUNTY (portions), Hickory, Lovelaceville, Mayfield, Pryorsburg, Sedalia, Symsonia, Wingo); Outside TV Markets (GRAVES COUNTY (portions)). Franchise award date: N.A. Franchise expiration date: N.A. Began: May 1, 1984.
Channel capacity: N.A. Channels available but not in use: N.A.

Basic Service
Subscribers: 441.
Programming (received off-air): KBSI (FOX) Cape Girardeau; KFVS-TV (CBS, CW, MeTV) Cape Girardeau; WDKA (MNT, The Country Network) Paducah; WKMU (PBS) Murray; WPSD-TV (Antenna TV, NBC) Paducah; WQTV-LP (CW) Murray; WSIL-TV (ABC) Harrisburg; WTCT (IND) Marion.
Programming (via satellite): A&E; AMC; Animal Planet; Cartoon Network; CNBC; CNN; Comedy Central; C-SPAN; Discovery Channel; Disney Channel; E! HD; ESPN; ESPN2; EWTN Global Catholic Network; Fox News Channel; Freeform; Fuse; FX; Great American Country; HGTV; History; HLN; Lifetime; Outdoor Channel; QVC; Syfy; TBS; The Weather Channel; TLC; TNT; USA Network; WGN America.
Fee: $49.95 installation; $20.05 monthly.
Digital Basic Service
Subscribers: N.A.
Programming (via satellite): BBC America; Bloomberg Television; Discovery Life Channel; Disney XD; DMX Music; ESPN Classic; ESPNews; Fox Sports 1; FYI; Golf Channel; GSN; History International; INSP; National Geographic Channel; WE tv.
Digital Expanded Basic Service
Subscribers: N.A.
Programming (via satellite): DMX Music; FXM; LMN; Starz Encore; Turner Classic Movies.
Fee: $12.95 monthly.
Pay Service 1
Pay Units: N.A.
Programming (via satellite): HBO; Showtime; Starz Encore.
Fee: $10.00 monthly (Showtime), $11.00 monthly (HBO).
Digital Pay Service 1
Pay Units: N.A.
Programming (via satellite): Cinemax (multiplexed); Flix; HBO (multiplexed); Showtime (multiplexed); The Movie Channel (multiplexed).
Fee: $17.15 monthly.
Video-On-Demand: No
Pay-Per-View
ESPN Now (delivered digitally).
Internet Service
Operational: Yes.
Telephone Service
None
Miles of Plant: 190.0 (coaxial); 28.0 (fiber optic). Homes passed: 4,261.
President: James Rigas.
Ownership: Zito Media (MSO).

GRAY—Eastern Cable Corp, PO Box 126, Corbin, KY 40702-0126. Phone: 606-528-6400. Fax: 606-523-0427. E-mail: cablecsr@2geton.net. Web Site: http://www.easterncable.net. Also serves Barbourville, Cannon & Girdler. ICA: KY0066.
TV Market Ranking: Below 100 (Barbourville, Cannon, Girdler, GRAY). Franchise award date: April 4, 1972. Franchise expiration date: N.A. Began: April 1, 1981.
Channel capacity: N.A. Channels available but not in use: N.A.
Basic Service
Subscribers: 89.
Programming (received off-air): WBIR-TV (MeTV, NBC) Knoxville; WDKY-TV (FOX) Danville; WKYT-TV (CBS, CW) Lexington; WTVQ-DT (ABC, Antenna TV, Laff, MNT) Lexington; WYMT-TV (CBS, CW) Hazard.
Programming (via satellite): A&E; CMT; CNN; Discovery Channel; Disney Channel; ESPN; Freeform; INSP; Lifetime; Nickelodeon; Spike TV; TBS; The Weather Channel; TNT; USA Network; WGN America.
Programming (via translator): WKSO-TV (PBS) Somerset.
Fee: $48.33 installation; $45.00 monthly.
Expanded Basic Service 1
Subscribers: N.A.
Fee: $51.25 monthly.
Video-On-Demand: No
Internet Service
Operational: Yes.
Fee: $20.00 installation; $29.95 monthly.
Telephone Service
None
Miles of Plant: 140.0 (coaxial); None (fiber optic). Homes passed: 2,516.
President & General Manager: Dallas R. Eubanks.
Ownership: Eastern Cable.

GRAYSON—Suddenlink Communications, 520 Maryville Centre Dr, Ste 300, St. Louis, MO 63141. Phones: 800-999-6845 (Customer service); 314-315-9400; 314-415-9346. Fax: 903-561-5485. Web Site: http://www.suddenlink.com. Also serves Boyd County (portions) & Carter County (portions). ICA: KY0061.
TV Market Ranking: 36 (Boyd County (portions), GRAYSON); Below 100 (Carter County (portions), Boyd County (portions)). Franchise award date: N.A. Franchise expiration date: N.A. Began: July 1, 1977.
Channel capacity: N.A. Channels available but not in use: N.A.
Basic Service
Subscribers: 1,074. Commercial subscribers: 158.
Programming (received off-air): WCHS-TV (ABC, Antenna TV) Charleston; WKMR (PBS) Morehead; WKYT-TV (CBS, CW) Lexington; WLPX-TV (ION) Charleston; WOWK-TV (CBS) Huntington; WQCW (CW) Portsmouth; WSAZ-TV (MNT, NBC, This TV) Huntington; WTSF (Daystar TV) Ashland; WTVQ-DT (ABC, Antenna TV, Laff, MNT) Lexington; WVAH-TV (FOX, The Country Network) Charleston; WVPB-TV (PBS) Huntington; allband FM.
Programming (via satellite): A&E; AMC; Animal Planet; Cartoon Network; CMT; CNBC; CNN; Comedy Central; C-SPAN; Discovery Channel; Disney Channel; E! HD; ESPN; ESPN2; Food Network; Fox News Channel; Fox Sports 1; FOX Sports Ohio/Sports Time Ohio; Freeform; FX; Hallmark Channel; HGTV; History; HLN; Lifetime; MTV; National Geographic Channel; Nickelodeon; Outdoor Channel; QVC; Spike TV; Syfy; TBS; The Weather Channel; TLC; TNT; Trinity Broadcasting Network (TBN); TV Land; USA Network; VH1; WGN-TV (IND) Chicago.
Fee: $59.95 installation; $64.31 monthly.
Digital Basic Service
Subscribers: N.A.
Programming (via satellite): BBC America; Bloomberg Television; C-SPAN 3; Discovery Digital Networks; Disney XD; DIY Network; ESPN Classic; ESPNews; FOX College Sports Central; FOX College Sports Pacific; Fuse; FXM; FYI; GSN; History; History International; IFC; LMN; MC; Sundance TV; WE tv.
Pay Service 1
Pay Units: N.A.
Programming (via satellite): Cinemax; HBO.
Fee: $9.95 monthly (each).
Digital Pay Service 1
Pay Units: N.A.
Programming (via satellite): Cinemax (multiplexed); Flix; HBO (multiplexed); Showtime (multiplexed); Starz (multiplexed); Starz Encore; The Movie Channel.
Video-On-Demand: No
Pay-Per-View
iN DEMAND (delivered digitally); Playboy TV (delivered digitally).
Internet Service
Operational: Yes. Began: December 31, 2005.
Broadband Service: Suddenlink High Speed Internet.
Fee: $59.95 monthly.
Telephone Service
Digital: Operational
Miles of Plant: 108.0 (coaxial); None (fiber optic). Homes passed: 3,896.
Senior Vice President, Corporate Finance: Michael Pflantz. District Manager: Robert Herrald. General Manager: Dale Thaxton. Office Manager: Anthony Cochran. Local Manager: Bill Glore.
Ownership: Cequel Communications Holdings I LLC (MSO).

GREASY CREEK—Formerly served by Suddenlink Communications. No longer in operation. ICA: KY0239.

GREENSBURG—Access Cable Television Inc, 302 Enterprise Dr, Somerset, KY 42501. Phone: 606-677-2444. Fax: 606-677-2443. E-mail: cable@accesshsd.net. Web Site: http://www.accesshsd.com. Also serves Green County (portions) & Summersville. ICA: KY0110.
TV Market Ranking: Below 100 (Green County (portions), GREENSBURG, Summersville). Franchise award date: September 6, 1982. Franchise expiration date: N.A. Began: March 1, 1955.
Channel capacity: N.A. Channels available but not in use: N.A.
Basic Service
Subscribers: 657.
Programming (received off-air): WAVE (Bounce TV, NBC, This TV) Louisville; WBKI-TV (CW, IND, Movies!) Campbellsville; WBKO (ABC, CW, FOX) Bowling Green; WDKY-TV (FOX) Danville; WDRB (Antenna TV, FOX) Louisville; WHAS-TV (ABC) Louisville; WKYT-TV (CBS, CW) Lexington; WKZT-TV (PBS) Elizabethtown; WLEX-TV (MeTV, NBC) Lexington; WLKY (CBS, MeTV) Louisville; WNKY (CBS, NBC) Bowling Green; allband FM.
Programming (via satellite): A&E; AMC; CMT; CNN; C-SPAN; C-SPAN 2; Discovery Channel; E! HD; ESPN; ESPN2; HGTV; HLN; INSP; ION Television; Nickelodeon; QVC;

Kentucky—Cable Systems

Spike TV; TLC; TNT; Trinity Broadcasting Network (TBN); VH1; WGN America.
Fee: $25.50 monthly.

Expanded Basic Service 1
Subscribers: 472.
Programming (via satellite): Animal Planet; BET; Cartoon Network; CNBC; Disney Channel; ESPN Classic; Fox News Channel; Fox Sports 1; Freeform; FX; Hallmark Channel; History; Lifetime; MSNBC; MTV; Outdoor Channel; Syfy; TBS; The Weather Channel; Travel Channel; TV Land; UP; USA Network.
Fee: $11.55 monthly.

Pay Service 1
Pay Units: N.A.
Programming (via satellite): Cinemax; Showtime; The Movie Channel.
Fee: $15.00 installation; $11.95 monthly (Showtime/TMC), $12.95 monthly (Cinemax).

Video-On-Demand: No

Internet Service
Operational: Yes.

Telephone Service
Digital: Operational
Fee: $24.95 monthly

Miles of Plant: 92.0 (coaxial); None (fiber optic). Homes passed: 2,098.
President & Manager: Roy Baker. Technical Manager: Allen Slavin.
Ownership: Access Cable Television Inc. (MSO).

GREENUP—Formerly served by Charter Communications. Now served by Armstrong Cable Services, ZELIENOPLE, PA [PA0053]. ICA: KY0195.

GREENVILLE—Comcast Cable, 2919 Ring Rd, Elizabethtown, KY 42701. Phones: 270-605-7719; 270-765-2731. Fax: 270-737-3379. Web Site: http://www.comcast.com. Also serves Central City, Drakesboro, Muhlenberg County, Powderly & South Carrollton. ICA: KY0023.
TV Market Ranking: Below 100 (Central City, Drakesboro, GREENVILLE, Muhlenberg County (portions), Powderly, South Carrollton); Outside TV Markets (Muhlenberg County (portions)). Franchise award date: April 4, 1964. Franchise expiration date: N.A. Began: March 1, 1965.
Channel capacity: N.A. Channels available but not in use: N.A.

Basic Service
Subscribers: 2,947. Commercial subscribers: 234.
Programming (received off-air): WBKO (ABC, CW, FOX) Bowling Green; WEHT (ABC) Evansville; WEVV-TV (CBS, FOX) Evansville; WFIE (NBC, This TV) Evansville; WKMA-TV (PBS) Madisonville; WKYU-TV (PBS) Bowling Green; WTVF (CBS, Laff, This TV) Nashville; WTVW (CW, MeTV) Evansville; allband FM.
Programming (via satellite): QVC; WGN America.
Fee: $52.95-$67.00 installation; $25.20 monthly.

Expanded Basic Service 1
Subscribers: N.A.
Programming (via satellite): A&E; AMC; Animal Planet; BET; Cartoon Network; CNBC; CNN; Comcast/Charter Sports Southeast (CSS); Comedy Central; C-SPAN; Discovery Channel; Disney Channel; E! HD; ESPN; ESPN2; Food Network; Fox News Channel; Fox Sports 1; Freeform; FX; Golf Channel; Great American Country; GSN; Hallmark Channel; HGTV; History; HLN; Lifetime; MSNBC; MTV; National Geographic Channel; NBCSN; Nickelodeon; Outdoor Channel; OWN: Oprah Winfrey Network; Spike TV; Syfy; TBS; The Weather Channel; TLC; TNT; Travel Channel; Trinity Broadcasting Network (TBN); truTV; TV Land; USA Network; VH1.
Fee: $33.91 monthly.

Digital Basic Service
Subscribers: N.A.
Programming (via satellite): BBC America; CMT; C-SPAN 3; Discovery Digital Networks; Disney XD; ESPNews; Flix; LMN; MoviePlex; NFL Network; Nick 2; Nick Jr.; Nicktoons; Sprout; Starz Encore; Sundance TV; TeenNick; WAM! America's Kidz Network.

Digital Pay Service 1
Pay Units: N.A.
Programming (via satellite): Cinemax (multiplexed); HBO (multiplexed); Showtime (multiplexed); Starz (multiplexed); The Movie Channel (multiplexed).
Fee: $13.05 monthly (each).

Video-On-Demand: No

Pay-Per-View
Playboy TV (delivered digitally); Fresh (delivered digitally); Shorteez (delivered digitally); Pleasure (delivered digitally); Hot Choice (delivered digitally).

Internet Service
Operational: Yes.
Broadband Service: Comcast High Speed Internet.
Fee: $42.95 monthly.

Telephone Service
Digital: Operational
Miles of Plant: 230.0 (coaxial); None (fiber optic). Homes passed: 8,634.
General Manager: Tim Hagan. Technical Operations Director: Bob Tharp. Marketing Director: Laurie Nicholson.
Ownership: Comcast Cable Communications Inc. (MSO).

HARDINSBURG—Crystal Broadband Networks, PO Box 180336, Chicago, IL 60618. Phones: 817-685-9588; 630-206-0447. E-mail: sales@crystalbn.com. Web Site: http://crystalbn.com. Also serves Breckinridge County. ICA: KY0098.
TV Market Ranking: Outside TV Markets (Breckinridge County, HARDINSBURG). Franchise award date: March 10, 1987. Franchise expiration date: N.A. Began: June 1, 1982.
Channel capacity: N.A. Channels available but not in use: N.A.

Basic Service
Subscribers: 8.
Programming (received off-air): WAVE (Bounce TV, NBC, This TV) Louisville; WDRB (Antenna TV, FOX) Louisville; WHAS-TV (ABC) Louisville; WKZT-TV (PBS) Elizabethtown; WLKY (CBS, MeTV) Louisville; WNIN (PBS) Evansville; WTVW (CW, MeTV) Evansville.
Programming (via satellite): MTV; QVC; TBS; WGN America.
Fee: $39.95 installation; $45.87 monthly; $1.50 converter.

Expanded Basic Service 1
Subscribers: N.A.
Programming (via satellite): AMC; CMT; CNN; Discovery Channel; ESPN; Freeform; Lifetime; Nickelodeon; Spike TV; TNT; USA Network.
Fee: $15.95 monthly.

Pay Service 1
Pay Units: N.A.
Programming (via satellite): Cinemax; HBO.
Fee: $15.95 monthly (each).

Video-On-Demand: No

Internet Service
Operational: No.

Telephone Service
None

Miles of Plant: 27.0 (coaxial); None (fiber optic).
General Manager: Ron Page. Program Manager: Shawn Smith.
Ownership: Crystal Broadband Networks (MSO).

HARLAN—Harlan Community TV Inc, 124 South First St, PO Box 592, Harlan, KY 40831. Phone: 606-573-2945. Fax: 606-573-6959. E-mail: hctv@harlanonline.net. Web Site: http://www.harlanonline.net. Also serves Baxter, Coldiron, Dayhoit, Grays Knob, Harlan County, Loyall, Mary Alice & Wallins. ICA: KY0230.
TV Market Ranking: Below 100 (Baxter, Grays Knob, HARLAN, Harlan County, Loyall, Mary Alice). Franchise award date: N.A. Franchise expiration date: N.A. Began: January 1, 1953.
Channel capacity: N.A. Channels available but not in use: N.A.

Basic Service
Subscribers: 3,378. Commercial subscribers: 202.
Programming (received off-air): WAGV (IND) Harlan; WATE-TV (ABC, Laff) Knoxville; WBIR-TV (MeTV, NBC) Knoxville; WBXX-TV (CW, Escape) Crossville; WDKY-TV (FOX) Danville; WEMT (FOX, Movies!, This TV) Greeneville; WJHL-TV (ABC, CBS, MeTV) Johnson City; WKHA (PBS) Hazard; WKPT-TV (COZI TV, Escape, MeTV, MNT) Kingsport; WKYT-TV (CBS, CW) Lexington; WLEX-TV (MeTV, NBC) Lexington; WTNZ (FOX, This TV) Knoxville; WTVQ-DT (ABC, Antenna TV, Laff, MNT) Lexington; WVLT-TV (CBS, MNT) Knoxville; WYMT-TV (CBS, CW) Hazard; allband FM.
Programming (via satellite): A&E; AMC; Animal Planet; Cartoon Network; CMT; CNBC; CNN; C-SPAN; C-SPAN 2; Discovery Channel; ESPN; ESPN Classic; ESPN2; Food Network; Fox News Channel; Fox Sports 1; FX; Golf Channel; Hallmark Channel; Hallmark Movies & Mysteries; HGTV; History; HLN; ION Television; Lifetime; MTV; Nickelodeon; Outdoor Channel; Spike TV; Syfy; TBS; The Weather Channel; TLC; TNT; Trinity Broadcasting Network (TBN); Turner Classic Movies; TV Land; USA Network; VH1; WGN America; WPIX (Antenna TV, CW, This TV) New York.
Fee: $50.00 installation; $18.00 monthly.

Pay Service 1
Pay Units: N.A.
Programming (via satellite): Cinemax; HBO; Showtime.
Fee: $7.00 monthly (Cinemax), $10.00 monthly (HBO or Showtime).

Video-On-Demand: No

Internet Service
Operational: Yes. Began: April 18, 2000.
Broadband Service: In-house.
Fee: $29.95-$49.90 monthly; $9.95 modem lease; $100.00 modem purchase.

Telephone Service
Analog: Not Operational
Digital: Operational
Fee: $43.98 monthly

Miles of Plant: 100.0 (coaxial); None (fiber optic).
President & General Manager: Jack B. Hale. Vice President: Mark Lawrence. Office Manager: Joy Taylor. Secretary-Treasurer: David Smith.
Ownership: Harlan Community TV Inc.

HAROLD—Inter Mountain Cable Inc, 20 Laynesville Rd, PO Box 159, Harold, KY 41635. Phones: 800-635-7052; 606-452-2345; 606-478-9406. Fax: 606-478-1680. E-mail: imcable@gearheart.com. Web Site: http://www.imctv.com. Also serves Allen, Argo, Banner, Belfry, Betsy Layne, Bevinsville, Blackberry Creek, Blair Town, Blue River, Boldman, Broad Bottom, Canada, Coal Run, David, Dorton, Dwale, Eastern, Emma, Fedscreek, Floyd County, Freeburn, Galveston, Garrett, Grethel, Hardy, Hi Hat, Hippo, Hite, Hueysville, Hunter, Island Creek, Ivel, Johnny Young Branch, Johnson County, Kimper, Knott County (portions), Little Mud Creek, Little Robinson, Magoffin, Majestic, Manton, Martin, Maytown, McCarr, McVeigh, Melvin, Meta, Myra, Peter Fork, Phelps, Phyllis, Pike County, Pikeville, Pinsonfork, Prater Creek, Prater Fork, Prestonsburg, Printer, Pyramid, Ransom, Risner, Robinette Knob, Robinson Creek, Rockhouse, Shelby Gap, Stanville, Stone Coal, Stopover, Teaberry, Toler Creek, Tram, Upper Johns Creek, Varney, Watergap, Weeksbury, Wells Addition, West Prestonsburg, Wheelwright & Zebulon, KY; Buchanan County & Hurley, VA; Blackberry City, Hatfield Bottom, Lynn, Matewan, Mingo County, Newtown, North Matewan, Red Jacket & Thacker, WV. ICA: KY0006.
TV Market Ranking: 36 (Mingo County (portions)); Below 100 (Argo, Belfry, Betsy Layne, Bevinsville, Blackberry City, Blackberry Creek, Blair Town, Blue River, Boldman, Broad Bottom, Buchanan County (portions), Canada, Coal Run, David, Dorton, Eastern, Fedscreek, Floyd County (portions), Freeburn, Galveston, Garrett, Grethel, Hardy, HAROLD, Hatfield Bottom, Hi Hat, Hippo, Hite, Hueysville, Hunter, Hurley, Island Creek, Johnson County (portions), Kimper, Little Mud Creek, Little Robinson, Lynn, Magoffin, Majestic, Manton, Martin, Matewan, Maytown, McCarr, McVeigh, Melvin, Meta, Myra, Newtown, North Matewan, Peter Fork, Phelps, Phyllis, Pike County (portions), Pikeville, Pinsonfork, Prater Fork, Printer, Pyramid, Ransom, Red Jacket, Risner, Robinson Creek, Rockhouse, Shelby Gap, Stanville, Stopover, Teaberry, Thacker, Weeksbury, Wells Addition, Wheelwright, Zebulon); Outside TV Markets (Allen, Banner, Buchanan County (portions), Dwale, Emma, Floyd County (portions), Ivel, Johnny Young Branch, Johnson County (portions), Pike County (portions), Prater Creek, Prestonsburg, Robinette Knob, Stone Coal, Toler Creek, Tram, Upper Johns Creek, Watergap, West

Cable Systems—Kentucky

Prestonsburg, Mingo County (portions)). Franchise award date: N.A. Franchise expiration date: N.A. Began: April 1, 1948. Channel capacity: 70 (operating 2-way). Channels available but not in use: N.A.

Basic Service
Subscribers: 16,752.
Programming (received off-air): WCHS-TV (ABC, Antenna TV) Charleston; WKPI-TV (PBS) Pikeville; WLJC-TV (TBN) Beattyville; WOWK-TV (CBS) Huntington; WQCW (CW) Portsmouth; WSAZ-TV (MNT, NBC, This TV) Huntington; WUPX-TV (ION) Morehead; WVAH-TV (FOX, The Country Network) Charleston; WYMT-TV (CBS, CW) Hazard; allband FM.
Programming (via satellite): EVINE Live; Pop; QVC; Syfy; The Weather Channel; WGN America.
Fee: $40.00 installation; $22.69 monthly.

Expanded Basic Service 1
Subscribers: N.A.
Programming (via satellite): A&E; AMC; Animal Planet; Boomerang; Bravo; Cartoon Network; CMT; CNBC; CNN; Comedy Central; C-SPAN; Discovery Channel; Disney Channel; E! HD; ESPN; ESPN Classic; ESPN2; Food Network; Fox News Channel; FOX Sports Networks; Freeform; FX; Great American Country; GSN; Hallmark Channel; History; JUCE TV; Lifetime; MSNBC; MTV; National Geographic Channel; NFL Network; Nickelodeon; Outdoor Channel; Spike TV; TBS; TLC; TNT; Travel Channel; truTV; TV Land; TVG Network; USA Network; VH1.
Fee: $40.10 monthly.

Digital Basic Service
Subscribers: 5,867.
Programming (via satellite): Anime Network; AXS TV; BBC America; Bloomberg Television; Bravo; CBS Sports Network; Discovery Digital Networks; DMX Music; ESPN Classic; ESPN2; ESPNews; EVINE Live; FOX College Sports Central; FOX College Sports Pacific; Fox Sports 1; FOX Sports Networks; Fuse; FXM; Golf Channel; Great American Country; GSN; HD Theater; HGTV; HITS (Headend In The Sky); IFC; LMN; NBCSN; Nick Jr.; Outdoor Channel; Ovation; Syfy; Trinity Broadcasting Network (TBN); Turner Classic Movies; TV One; TVG Network; Universal HD; WE tv.
Fee: $14.95 monthly; $3.99 converter.

Digital Pay Service 1
Pay Units: 416.
Programming (via satellite): Cinemax (multiplexed).
Fee: $7.95 monthly; $3.99 converter.

Digital Pay Service 2
Pay Units: 453.
Programming (via satellite): HBO (multiplexed).
Fee: $12.95 monthly; $3.99 converter.

Digital Pay Service 3
Pay Units: 144.
Programming (via satellite): Flix; Showtime (multiplexed); Sundance TV; The Movie Channel.
Fee: $11.95 monthly; $3.99 converter.

Digital Pay Service 4
Pay Units: 407.
Programming (via satellite): Starz; Starz Encore (multiplexed).
Fee: $13.95 monthly; $3.99 converter.

Video-On-Demand: Yes

Pay-Per-View
iN DEMAND (delivered digitally); Hot Choice (delivered digitally); movies (delivered digitally); Fresh (delivered digitally); Shorteez (delivered digitally).

Internet Service
Operational: Yes.
Subscribers: 7,528.
Fee: $24.95 monthly.

Telephone Service
Digital: Operational
Subscribers: 4,634.
Fee: $19.99-$32.99 monthly
Miles of Plant: 2,398.0 (coaxial); 1,319.0 (fiber optic). Homes passed: 37,055.
Vice President & General Manager: Paul Douglas Gearheart. Chief Financial Officer: James O. Campbell. Operations Director: John C. Schmoldt. Marketing Director: Heath Wiley. Chief Engineer: Jefferson Thacker. Ad Sales Manager: Adam Gearheart. Billing & Services Manager: Rebecca A Walters. Field Engineer: Roy A Harlow.
Ownership: Inter-Mountain Cable Inc. (MSO).

HARRODSBURG—Time Warner Cable. Now served by RICHMOND, KY [KY0008]. ICA: KY0231.

HAWESVILLE—Inside Connect Cable, 4890 Knob Creek Rd, Brooks, KY 40109. Phones: 502-955-4882; 855-552-2253. Fax: 502-543-7553. E-mail: sales@insideconnect.net. Also serves Hancock County (portions) & Lewisport. ICA: KY0232.
TV Market Ranking: Outside TV Markets (Hancock County (portions), HAWESVILLE, Lewisport). Franchise award date: January 1, 1979. Franchise expiration date: N.A. Began: November 8, 1979.
Channel capacity: N.A. Channels available but not in use: N.A.

Basic Service
Subscribers: 122.
Programming (received off-air): WAVE (Bounce TV, NBC, This TV) Louisville; WDRB (Antenna TV, FOX) Louisville; WEHT (ABC) Evansville; WEVV-TV (CBS, FOX) Evansville; WFIE (NBC, This TV) Evansville; WHAS-TV (ABC) Louisville; WKOH (PBS) Owensboro; WLKY (CBS, MeTV) Louisville; WNIN (PBS) Evansville; WTVW (CW, MeTV) Evansville; 2 FMs.
Programming (via satellite): TBS; USA Network; WGN America.
Fee: $39.95 installation; $20.54 monthly; $1.98 converter.

Expanded Basic Service 1
Subscribers: N.A.
Programming (via satellite): A&E; AMC; Cartoon Network; CMT; CNN; Discovery Channel; Disney Channel; ESPN; ESPN2; Freeform; HGTV; History; HLN; Lifetime; MTV; Nickelodeon; QVC; Spike TV; The Weather Channel; TLC; TNT; Turner Classic Movies.
Fee: $17.00 monthly.

Pay Service 1
Pay Units: N.A.
Programming (via satellite): HBO.
Fee: $15.95 monthly.

Video-On-Demand: No

Internet Service
Operational: Yes, DSL.

Telephone Service
Digital: Operational
Miles of Plant: 32.0 (coaxial); None (fiber optic).
Ownership: Inside Connect Cable LLC (MSO).

HAYMOND—TVS Cable, PO Box 1410, Hindman, KY 41822-1410. Phones: 606-946-2600; 606-785-3450; 606-633-0778. Fax: 606-785-3110. E-mail: tvs@tvscable.com. Web Site: http://www.tvscable.com. Also serves Cromona, Millstone, Seco & Whitesburg. ICA: KY0340.
TV Market Ranking: Below 100 (Cromona, Millstone, Seco, Whitesburg, HAYMOND).
Channel capacity: N.A. Channels available but not in use: N.A.

Basic Service
Subscribers: 822. Commercial subscribers: 28.
Fee: $50.00 installation; $23.50 monthly.
Vice President & General Manager: William K. Grigsby.
Ownership: TV Service Inc. (MSO).

HAZARD—Formerly served by Hazard TV Cable Co. Inc. No longer in operation. ICA: KY0119.

HAZEL—Zito Media, 102 S Main St, PO Box 665, Coudersport, PA 16915. Phones: 814-260-9055; 800-365-6988. E-mail: info@zitomedia.com. Web Site: http://www.zitomedia.com. Also serves Puryear. ICA: KY0233.
TV Market Ranking: Outside TV Markets (HAZEL, Puryear). Franchise award date: N.A. Franchise expiration date: N.A. Began: February 1, 1984.
Channel capacity: N.A. Channels available but not in use: N.A.

Basic Service
Subscribers: 63.
Programming (received off-air): KBSI (FOX) Cape Girardeau; KFVS-TV (CBS, CW, MeTV) Cape Girardeau; WBBJ-TV (ABC, CBS, MeTV) Jackson; WDKA (MNT, The Country Network) Paducah; WKMU (PBS) Murray; WPSD-TV (Antenna TV, NBC) Paducah; WQTV-LP (CW) Murray.
Programming (via satellite): A&E; AMC; Animal Planet; Cartoon Network; CNBC; CNN; Comedy Central; C-SPAN; Discovery Channel; Disney Channel; E! HD; ESPN; ESPN2; Food Network; Fox News Channel; Freeform; Fuse; FX; Great American Country; HGTV; History; HLN; Lifetime; Outdoor Channel; QVC; Syfy; TBS; The Weather Channel; TLC; TNT; Turner Classic Movies; USA Network; WGN America.
Fee: $49.95 installation; $49.83 monthly; $3.00 converter.

Digital Basic Service
Subscribers: N.A.
Programming (via satellite): BBC America; Bloomberg Television; Cloo; Destination America; Discovery Kids Channel; Discovery Life Channel; ESPN Classic; ESPNews; Fox Sports 1; Fuse; FXM; FYI; Golf Channel; GSN; History International; IFC; Investigation Discovery; LMN; National Geographic Channel; OWN: Oprah Winfrey Network; RFD-TV; Science Channel; Sprout; WE tv.

Pay Service 1
Pay Units: N.A.
Programming (via satellite): Cinemax (multiplexed); Flix; HBO (multiplexed); Showtime (multiplexed); Starz (multiplexed); Starz Encore (multiplexed); The Movie Channel (multiplexed).

Pay-Per-View
iN DEMAND (delivered digitally); Playboy TV (delivered digitally); Fresh (delivered digitally); Shorteez (delivered digitally); Club Jenna (delivered digitally).

Internet Service
Operational: Yes.
Fee: $49.95 installation; $44.95 monthly.

Telephone Service
None
Miles of Plant: 15.0 (coaxial); None (fiber optic). Homes passed: 604.
President: James Rigas.
Ownership: Zito Media (MSO).

HENDERSON (portions)—Time Warner Cable. Now served by EVANSVILLE, IN [IN0006]. ICA: KY0016.

HENDERSON (town)—Time Warner Cable. Now served by OWENSBORO, KY [KY0004]. ICA: KY0306.

HENDERSON COUNTY (portions)—Mediacom, 90 Main St, Benton, KY 42025-1132. Phones: 845-695-2762; 417-875-5560 (Springfield regional office); 270-527-9939. Fax: 270-527-0813. Web Site: http://www.mediacomcable.com. Also serves Henderson. ICA: KY0112.
TV Market Ranking: 86 (HENDERSON COUNTY (PORTIONS)). Franchise award date: April 11, 1989. Franchise expiration date: N.A. Began: January 1, 1989.
Channel capacity: N.A. Channels available but not in use: N.A.

Basic Service
Subscribers: 53.
Programming (received off-air): WEHT (ABC) Evansville; WEVV-TV (CBS, FOX) Evansville; WFIE (NBC, This TV) Evansville; WKMA-TV (PBS) Madisonville; WNIN (PBS) Evansville; WTVW (CW, MeTV) Evansville.
Programming (via satellite): A&E; AMC; Animal Planet; Cartoon Network; CMT; CNN; Comedy Central; Discovery Channel; Disney Channel; E! HD; ESPN; ESPN2; Food Network; Fox News Channel; Fox Sports 1; Freeform; FX; Great American Country; HGTV; History; HLN; Lifetime; MSNBC; MTV; National Geographic Channel; Nickelodeon; Outdoor Channel; QVC; Spike TV; Syfy; TBS; The Weather Channel; TLC; TNT; Travel Channel; Trinity Broadcasting Network (TBN); truTV; Turner Classic Movies; TV Land; USA Network; WGN America.
Fee: $29.95 installation; $64.95 monthly; $3.95 converter.

Pay Service 1
Pay Units: N.A.
Programming (via satellite): Cinemax; HBO; Starz; Starz Encore.
Fee: $10.00 installation; $7.00 monthly (Starz/Encore), $9.00 monthly (Cinemax), $10.00 monthly (HBO).

Video-On-Demand: No
Internet Service
Operational: No.

Kentucky—Cable Systems

CABLE & TV STATION COVERAGE Atlas 2017
The perfect companion to the Television & Cable Factbook
To order call 800-771-9202 or visit www.warren-news.com

Telephone Service
None
Miles of Plant: 35.0 (coaxial); None (fiber optic). Homes passed: 1,036.
Regional Vice President: Bill Copeland. Vice President, Financial Reporting: Kenneth J. Kohrs. Regional Technical Operations Director: Alan Freedman. General Manager: Dale Haney. Marketing Director: Will Kuebler. Technical Operations Manager: Jeff Brown. Marketing Manager: Melanie Westerman.
Ownership: Mediacom LLC (MSO).

HICKMAN—Zito Media, 102 S Main St, PO Box 665, Coudersport, PA 16915. Phones: 814-260-9055; 800-365-6988. E-mail: info@zitomedia.com. Web Site: http://www.zitomedia.com. ICA: KY0234.
TV Market Ranking: Outside TV Markets (HICKMAN). Franchise award date: N.A. Franchise expiration date: N.A. Began: December 1, 1980.
Channel capacity: N.A. Channels available but not in use: N.A.

Basic Service
Subscribers: 202.
Programming (received off-air): KBSI (FOX) Cape Girardeau; KFVS-TV (CBS, CW, MeTV) Cape Girardeau; WBBJ-TV (ABC, CBS, MeTV) Jackson; WKMU (PBS) Murray; WPSD-TV (Antenna TV, NBC) Paducah; WSIL-TV (ABC) Harrisburg.
Programming (via satellite): A&E; AMC; Animal Planet; BET; Cartoon Network; CNBC; CNN; Comedy Central; Discovery Channel; Disney Channel; Disney XD; E! HD; ESPN; ESPN2; Food Network; Fox News Channel; Fox Sports 1; Freeform; Fuse; FX; Great American Country; HGTV; History; HLN; INSP; Lifetime; Outdoor Channel; Syfy; TBS; The Weather Channel; TLC; TNT; Turner Classic Movies; USA Network; WGN America.
Fee: $49.95 installation; $15.26 monthly; $3.00 converter.

Digital Basic Service
Subscribers: N.A.
Programming (via satellite): BBC America; Bloomberg Television; Discovery Life Channel; Disney XD; DMX Music; ESPN Classic; ESPNews; FYI; Golf Channel; GSN; History International; National Geographic Channel; WE tv.

Digital Expanded Basic Service
Subscribers: N.A.
Programming (via satellite): FXM; LMN; Starz Encore (multiplexed).
Fee: $13.95 monthly.

Pay Service 1
Pay Units: N.A.
Programming (via satellite): Cinemax; HBO; Showtime; The Movie Channel.

Digital Pay Service 1
Pay Units: N.A.
Programming (via satellite): Cinemax (multiplexed); Flix; HBO (multiplexed); Showtime (multiplexed); The Movie Channel (multiplexed).
Fee: $14.05 monthly.

Pay-Per-View
ESPN Now; Hot Choice (delivered digitally); Playboy TV (delivered digitally); Fresh (delivered digitally); Shorteez (delivered digitally).

Internet Service
Operational: Yes.
Subscribers: 101.
Fee: $49.95 installation; $44.95 monthly.

Telephone Service
None
Miles of Plant: 54.0 (coaxial); 16.0 (fiber optic). Homes passed: 1,000.
President: James Rigas.
Ownership: Zito Media (MSO).

HINDMAN—TVS Cable, PO Box 1410, Hindman, KY 41822-1410. Phones: 606-946-2600; 606-633-0778; 606-785-3450. Fax: 606-785-3110. E-mail: tvs@tvscable.com. Web Site: http://www.tvscable.com. Also serves Brinkley, Carrie, Estill County (portions), Knott County, Leburn, Littcarr, Mallie, Perry County (portions), Pine Top, Pippa Passes & Vest. ICA: KY0027.
TV Market Ranking: Below 100 (Brinkley, Carrie, HINDMAN, Knott County, Leburn, Littcarr, Mallie, Pippa Passes, Vest). Franchise award date: N.A. Franchise expiration date: N.A. Began: April 1, 1966.
Channel capacity: N.A. Channels available but not in use: N.A.

Basic Service
Subscribers: 8,389. Commercial subscribers: 45.
Programming (received off-air): WCYB-TV (CW, Decades, NBC) Bristol; WDKY-TV (FOX) Danville; WKHA (PBS) Hazard; WKYT-TV (CBS, CW) Lexington; WLEX-TV (MeTV, NBC) Lexington; WLFG (IND, PBJ, Retro TV) Grundy; WLJC-TV (TBN) Beattyville; WTVQ-DT (ABC, Antenna TV, Laff, MNT) Lexington; WYMT-TV (CBS, CW) Hazard.
Programming (via satellite): CW PLUS; ION Television; WGN America.
Fee: $50.00 installation; $25.00 monthly.

Expanded Basic Service 1
Subscribers: N.A.
Programming (via satellite): A&E; Animal Planet; Bloomberg Television; Boomerang; Cartoon Network; CMT; CNN; Comedy Central; C-SPAN; Discovery Channel; Disney Channel; E! HD; ESPN; ESPN Classic; ESPN2; ESPNU; Family Friendly Entertainment; Food Network; Fox News Channel; FOX Sports Ohio/Sports Time Ohio; Freeform; FX; Great American Country; Hallmark Channel; HGTV; History; HLN; HRTV; Lifetime; MTV; National Geographic Channel; Nickelodeon; Outdoor Channel; QVC; Spike TV; Syfy; TBS; The Weather Channel; TLC; TNT; Travel Channel; truTV; Turner Classic Movies; TV Land; USA Network; VH1.
Fee: $34.05 monthly.

Digital Basic Service
Subscribers: N.A.
Programming (via satellite): BBC America; Church Channel; Cloo; CMT; Daystar TV Network; Destination America; Discovery Kids Channel; Discovery Life Channel; Disney XD; DMX Music; ESPNews; EVINE Live; FOX College Sports Central; FOX College Sports Pacific; Fox Sports 1; Fuse; FYI; Golf Channel; GSN; History International; IFC; Investigation Discovery; JUCE TV; LMN; MTV Classic; MTV Hits; MTV Jams; MTV2; NBCSN; Nick Jr.; Nicktoons; OWN: Oprah Winfrey Network; RFD-TV; Science Channel; TeenNick; The Word Network; Trinity Broadcasting Network (TBN); VH1 Soul; WE tv.
Fee: $3.50 converter.

Digital Pay Service 1
Pay Units: N.A.
Programming (via satellite): Cinemax (multiplexed); Flix; HBO (multiplexed); Showtime (multiplexed); Starz (multiplexed); Starz Encore (multiplexed); Sundance TV; The Movie Channel (multiplexed).
Fee: $8.50 monthly (Cinemax or TMC), $10.95 monthly (Starz/Encore), $11.50 monthly (HBO or Showtime); $3.50 converter.

Video-On-Demand: No

Pay-Per-View
iN DEMAND (delivered digitally); Playboy TV (delivered digitally); Fresh (delivered digitally); Spice: Xcess (delivered digitally); Club Jenna (delivered digitally).

Internet Service
Operational: Yes. Began: December 1, 2001.
Broadband Service: In-house.
Fee: $89.95 installation; $24.95-$79.95 monthly; $9.95 modem lease.

Telephone Service
Digital: Operational
Fee: $39.99-$59.99 monthly
Miles of Plant: 975.0 (coaxial); 425.0 (fiber optic). Homes passed: 17,615.
Vice President & General Manager: William K. Grigsby. Assistant Manager: Kenny Salmons. Program Director: Betty Thomas. Chief Technician: Tony Everage.
Ownership: TV Service Inc. (MSO).

HODGENVILLE—Comcast Cablevision of the South. Now served by ELIZABETHTOWN, KY [KY0012]. ICA: KY0080.

HOPKINSVILLE—Time Warner Cable. Now served by MADISONVILLE, KY [KY0013]. ICA: KY0014.

HORSE CAVE—Comcast Cable, 2919 Ring Rd, Elizabethtown, KY 42701. Phones: 270-605-7719; 270-765-2731. Fax: 270-737-3379. Web Site: http://www.comcast.com. Also serves Cave City & Hiseville. ICA: KY0236.
TV Market Ranking: Below 100 (Cave City, Hiseville, HORSE CAVE). Franchise award date: February 3, 1964. Franchise expiration date: N.A. Began: July 1, 1964.
Channel capacity: N.A. Channels available but not in use: N.A.

Basic Service
Subscribers: 615. Commercial subscribers: 194.
Programming (received off-air): WAVE (Bounce TV, NBC, This TV) Louisville; WBKO (ABC, CW, FOX) Bowling Green; WDRB (Antenna TV, FOX) Louisville; WHAS-TV (ABC) Louisville; WKGB-TV (PBS) Bowling Green; WKYU-TV (PBS) Bowling Green; WLKY (CBS, MeTV) Louisville; WSMV-TV (COZI TV, NBC, TNN) Nashville; WTVF (CBS, Laff, This TV) Nashville; WUXP-TV (MNT) Nashville; allband FM.
Programming (via satellite): A&E; AMC; Animal Planet; BET; Cartoon Network; Cinemax; CMT; CNBC; CNN; Comedy Central; C-SPAN; Discovery Channel; Disney Channel; E! HD; ESPN; ESPN2; Food Network; Fox News Channel; Freeform; FX; HBO (multiplexed); HGTV; History; HLN; HSN2; ION Television; Lifetime; MTV; NBCSN; Nickelodeon; QVC; Showtime; Spike TV; Syfy; TBS; The Weather Channel; TLC; TNT; Travel Channel; Trinity Broadcasting Network (TBN); Turner Classic Movies; TV Land; USA Network; VH1; WGN America.
Fee: $49.99-$71.00 installation; $14.00 monthly.

Digital Basic Service
Subscribers: N.A.
Programming (via satellite): BBC America; C-SPAN 3; Discovery Digital Networks; Disney XD; ESPNews; MTV Classic; Nick 2; Nick Jr.; TeenNick; VH1 Country; VH1 Soul; WAM! America's Kidz Network.

Digital Pay Service 1
Pay Units: N.A.
Programming (via satellite): Cinemax (multiplexed); Flix; HBO (multiplexed); Showtime (multiplexed); Starz Encore (multiplexed); Sundance TV; The Movie Channel (multiplexed).

Video-On-Demand: No

Pay-Per-View
Hot Choice (delivered digitally).

Internet Service
Operational: Yes.
Broadband Service: Comcast High Speed Internet.
Fee: $42.95 monthly.

Telephone Service
Digital: Operational
Miles of Plant: 97.0 (coaxial); None (fiber optic).
General Manager: Tim Hagan. Marketing Director: Laurie Nicholson. Technical Operations Director: Bob Tharp.
Ownership: Comcast Cable Communications Inc. (MSO).

HUSTONVILLE—Access Cable Television Inc, 302 Enterprise Dr, Somerset, KY 42501. Phone: 606-676-2444. Fax: 606-677-2443. E-mail: cable@accesshsd.net. Web Site: http://www.accesshsd.com. Also serves Lincoln County (portions) & Moreland. ICA: KY0296.
TV Market Ranking: Below 100 (HUSTONVILLE, Lincoln County (portions), Moreland).
Channel capacity: N.A. Channels available but not in use: N.A.

Basic Service
Subscribers: 18.
Programming (received off-air): WDKY-TV (FOX) Danville; WDRB (Antenna TV, FOX) Louisville; WHAS-TV (ABC) Louisville; WKSO-TV (PBS) Somerset; WKYT-TV (CBS, CW) Lexington; WLEX-TV (MeTV, NBC) Lexington; WTVQ-DT (ABC, Antenna TV, Laff, MNT) Lexington; WUPX-TV (ION) Morehead.
Programming (via satellite): A&E; AMC; CMT; CNN; C-SPAN; Discovery Channel; E! HD; ESPN; HLN; Lifetime; MTV; Nickelodeon; QVC; Syfy; TLC; TNT; USA Network; VH1.
Fee: $20.95 monthly.

Expanded Basic Service 1
Subscribers: N.A.
Programming (via satellite): Disney Channel; Freeform; MSNBC; Spike TV; TBS; WGN America.
Fee: $9.95 monthly.

Cable Systems—Kentucky

Pay Service 1
Pay Units: N.A.
Programming (via satellite): HBO.
Fee: $11.95 monthly.
Video-On-Demand: No
Internet Service
Operational: Yes.
Telephone Service
Digital: Operational
Miles of Plant: 44.0 (coaxial); None (fiber optic). Homes passed: 529.
President & Manager: Roy Baker. Chief Technician: Allen Slavin.
Ownership: Access Cable Television Inc. (MSO).

HYDEN—Bowling Cable TV, 652 Owls Nest Rd, PO Box 522, Hyden, KY 41749-0522. Phone: 606-672-3479. Fax: 606-672-7575. Also serves Leslie County (portions). ICA: KY0238.
TV Market Ranking: Below 100 (HYDEN, Leslie County (portions)). Franchise award date: N.A. Franchise expiration date: N.A. Began: July 1, 1954.
Channel capacity: N.A. Channels available but not in use: N.A.
Basic Service
Subscribers: 196.
Programming (received off-air): WATE-TV (ABC, Laff) Knoxville; WCYB-TV (CW, Decades, NBC) Bristol; WJHL-TV (ABC, CBS, MeTV) Johnson City; WKHA (PBS) Hazard; WKPT-TV (COZI TV, Escape, MeTV, MNT) Kingsport; WKYT-TV (CBS, CW) Lexington; WLOS (ABC, Antenna TV) Asheville; WSBN-TV (PBS) Norton; WYMT-TV (CBS, CW) Hazard; allband FM.
Programming (via satellite): CMT; CNN; ESPN; Freeform; TBS; TNT; WGN America; WPIX (Antenna TV, CW, This TV) New York.
Fee: $49.95 installation; $59.95 monthly.
Pay Service 1
Pay Units: 46.
Programming (via satellite): HBO.
Fee: $14.95 monthly.
Video-On-Demand: No
Internet Service
Operational: No.
Telephone Service
None
Miles of Plant: 30.0 (coaxial); None (fiber optic). Homes passed: 1,100.
President & General Manager: Daniel Bowling.
Ownership: Dan Bowling.

INEZ—Formerly served by Charter Communications. Now served by Suddenlink Communications, KERMIT, WV [WV0038]. ICA: KY0072.

IRVINE—Irvine Community TV Inc, 251 Broadway St, PO Box 186, Irvine, KY 40336. Phones: 606-723-3668; 606-723-4240. Fax: 606-723-4723. E-mail: irvtv@irvineonline.net. Web Site: http://www.irvine-cable.net. Also serves Estill County & Ravenna. ICA: KY0052.
TV Market Ranking: Below 100 (Estill County, IRVINE, Ravenna). Franchise award date: N.A. Franchise expiration date: N.A. Began: January 1, 1951.
Channel capacity: N.A. Channels available but not in use: N.A.
Basic Service
Subscribers: 2,490.
Programming (received off-air): WDKY-TV (FOX) Danville; WKYT-TV (CBS, CW) Lexington; WLEX-TV (MeTV, NBC) Lexington; WLJC-TV (TBN) Beattyville; WTVQ-DT (ABC, Antenna TV, Laff, MNT) Lexington; allband FM.
Programming (via satellite): A&E; AMC; Animal Planet; Cartoon Network; CMT; CNN; C-SPAN; Discovery Channel; ESPN; ESPN2; Family Friendly Entertainment; Fox News Channel; Freeform; FX; Hallmark Channel; HGTV; History; HLN; ION Television; Kentucky Educational Television (KET); Lifetime; MTV; Nickelodeon; Pop; QVC; Spike TV; Syfy; TBS; The Weather Channel; TLC; TNT; Travel Channel; truTV; Turner Classic Movies; TV Land; USA Network; VH1; WGN America.
Fee: $23.98 installation; $29.12 monthly.
Digital Basic Service
Subscribers: N.A.
Programming (via satellite): BBC America; Bloomberg Television; Discovery Life Channel; DMX Music; ESPN Classic; ESPNews; Golf Channel; GSN; INSP; Outdoor Channel; Trinity Broadcasting Network (TBN).
Pay Service 1
Pay Units: N.A.
Programming (via satellite): HBO; Showtime.
Fee: $10.50 monthly (each).
Digital Pay Service 1
Pay Units: N.A.
Programming (via satellite): Cinemax (multiplexed); HBO (multiplexed); Showtime (multiplexed); Starz (multiplexed); Starz Encore (multiplexed); The Movie Channel (multiplexed).
Fee: $5.60 monthly (Encore), $8.49 monthly (Cinemax or TMC), $10.00 monthly (Showtime), $10.50 monthly (HBO), $12.95 monthly (Starz/Encore).
Video-On-Demand: No
Pay-Per-View
iN DEMAND (delivered digitally); ESPN (delivered digitally); Sports PPV (delivered digitally); Hot Choice (delivered digitally); Fresh (delivered digitally).
Internet Service
Operational: Yes.
Broadband Service: In-house.
Fee: $22.90 monthly.
Telephone Service
Digital: Operational
Miles of Plant: 277.0 (coaxial); 57.0 (fiber optic). Homes passed: 5,500.
President & General Manager: Jim Hays.
Ownership: Jim Hays.

IRVINGTON—Crystal Broadband Networks, PO Box 180336, Chicago, IL 60618. Phones: 817-685-9588; 630-206-0447. E-mail: sales@crystalbn.com. Web Site: http://crystalbn.com. Also serves Irvington (village). ICA: KY0126.
TV Market Ranking: Below 100 (Irvington (village)); Outside TV Markets (IRVINGTON, Irvington (village)). Franchise award date: March 14, 1986. Franchise expiration date: N.A. Began: December 15, 1987.
Channel capacity: N.A. Channels available but not in use: N.A.
Basic Service
Subscribers: 7.
Programming (received off-air): WAVE (Bounce TV, NBC, This TV) Louisville; WDRB (Antenna TV, FOX) Louisville; WHAS-TV (ABC) Louisville; WKPC-TV (PBS) Louisville; WLKY (CBS, MeTV) Louisville; WMYO (MNT, My Family TV) Salem.
Programming (via satellite): Animal Planet; QVC; TBS; WGN America.
Fee: $39.95 installation; $42.33 monthly; $1.50 converter.

Communications Daily

Warren Communications News

Get the industry standard FREE —
For a no-obligation trial call 800-771-9202 or visit www.warren-news.com

Expanded Basic Service 1
Subscribers: N.A.
Programming (via satellite): AMC; CMT; CNN; Discovery Channel; Disney Channel; ESPN; Freeform; HLN; Lifetime; Nickelodeon; Spike TV; TNT; USA Network.
Fee: $16.61 monthly.
Pay Service 1
Pay Units: N.A.
Programming (via satellite): HBO.
Fee: $15.95 monthly.
Video-On-Demand: No
Internet Service
Operational: No.
Telephone Service
None
Miles of Plant: 15.0 (coaxial); None (fiber optic).
General Manager: Ron Page. Program Manager: Shawn Smith.
Ownership: Crystal Broadband Networks (MSO).

ISLAND—Formerly served by Crystal Broadband Networks. No longer in operation. ICA: KY0308.

ISLAND CITY—Formerly served by City TV Cable. No longer in operation. ICA: KY0177.

JACKSON—Crystal Broadband Networks, PO Box 180336, Chicago, IL 60618. Phones: 817-685-9588; 630-206-0447. E-mail: sales@crystalbn.com. Web Site: http://crystalbn.com. ICA: KY0242.
TV Market Ranking: Below 100 (JACKSON).
Channel capacity: N.A. Channels available but not in use: N.A.
Basic Service
Subscribers: N.A.
Programming (received off-air): WDKY-TV (FOX) Danville; WKHA (PBS) Hazard; WKYT-TV (CBS, CW) Lexington; WLEX-TV (MeTV, NBC) Lexington; WLJC-TV (TBN) Beattyville; WTVQ-DT (ABC, Antenna TV, Laff, MNT) Lexington; WUPX-TV (ION) Morehead; WYMT-TV (CBS, CW) Hazard.
Programming (via satellite): QVC; TBS; WGN America.
Fee: $39.95 installation; $50.71 monthly; $.73 converter.
Expanded Basic Service 1
Subscribers: N.A.
Programming (via satellite): A&E; AMC; CMT; CNN; Discovery Channel; Disney Channel; ESPN; ESPN2; Fox News Channel; Freeform; FX; Hallmark Channel; HLN; Lifetime; Nickelodeon; Spike TV; The Weather Channel; TLC; TNT; USA Network; VH1.
Fee: $28.17 monthly.
Digital Basic Service
Subscribers: N.A.
Programming (via satellite): BBC America; Bloomberg Television; Bravo; Discovery Life Channel; Disney XD; ESPN Classic; ESPNews; FOX College Sports Central; FOX College Sports Pacific; Fox Sports 1; Fuse; FXM; FYI; Golf Channel; Great American Country; GSN; HGTV; History; History International; IFC; INSP; LMN; MTV Classic; MTV2; National Geographic Channel; NBCSN; Nick Jr.; Nicktoons; Outdoor Channel; Syfy; TeenNick; The Word Network; Trinity Broadcasting Network (TBN); Turner Classic Movies; VH1 Country; WE tv.
Digital Pay Service 1
Pay Units: N.A.
Programming (via satellite): Cinemax (multiplexed); HBO (multiplexed); Showtime (multiplexed); Starz (multiplexed); Starz Encore (multiplexed); The Movie Channel (multiplexed).
Fee: $15.95 monthly (each).
Video-On-Demand: No
Pay-Per-View
Playboy (delivered digitally); Fresh (delivered digitally).
Internet Service
Operational: No.
Telephone Service
None
Miles of Plant: 83.0 (coaxial); None (fiber optic). Homes passed: 2,243.
General Manager: Ron Page. Program Manager: Shawn Smith.
Ownership: Crystal Broadband Networks (MSO).

JENKINS—Inter Mountain Cable Inc, 20 Laynesville Rd, PO Box 159, Harold, KY 41635. Phones: 800-635-7052; 606-452-2345; 866-917-4688; 606-478-9406. Fax: 606-478-1680. E-mail: imcable@gearheart.com. Web Site: http://www.imctv.com. Also serves Bottom, Burdine, Collier Creek, Deane, Eolia, Eversole, Fleming, Gibbo, Jackhorn, Lewis Creek, McRoberts, Neon, Oven Fork, Partridge, Payne Gap, Rado Hollow & Roberts Branch, KY; Pound & Wise County (northern portion), VA. ICA: KY0041.
TV Market Ranking: Below 100 (Bottom, Burdine, Collier Creek, Deane, Eolia, Eversole, Fleming, Gibbo, Jackhorn, JENKINS, Lewis Creek, McRoberts, Neon, Oven Fork, Partridge, Payne Gap, Pound, Rado Hollow, Roberts Branch, Wise County (northern portion)). Franchise award date: N.A. Franchise expiration date: N.A. Began: January 1, 1961.
Channel capacity: N.A. Channels available but not in use: N.A.
Basic Service
Subscribers: 2,112.
Programming (received off-air): WCHS-TV (ABC, Antenna TV) Charleston; WCYB-TV (CW, Decades, NBC) Bristol; WJHL-TV (ABC, CBS, MeTV) Johnson City; WKPI-TV (PBS) Pikeville; WKPT-TV (COZI TV, Escape, MeTV, MNT) Kingsport; WLFG (IND, PBJ, Retro TV) Grundy; WSAZ-TV (MNT, NBC, This TV) Huntington; WSBN-TV (PBS) Norton; WUPX-TV (ION) Morehead; WVAH-TV (FOX, The Country Network) Charleston; WYMT-TV (CBS, CW) Hazard; allband FM.
Programming (via satellite): C-SPAN; CW PLUS; Pop; QVC; The Weather Channel; WGN America.
Fee: $47.50 installation; $25.78 monthly; $.73 converter.

2017 Edition   D-317

Kentucky—Cable Systems

Expanded Basic Service 1
Subscribers: N.A.
Programming (via satellite): A&E; AMC; Animal Planet; Boomerang; Cartoon Network; CMT; CNBC; CNN; Comedy Central; Discovery Channel; Disney Channel; E! HD; ESPN; ESPN2; EVINE Live; Food Network; Fox News Channel; Freeform; FX; Hallmark Channel; HGTV; History; Lifetime; MSNBC; MTV; MyNetworkTV; National Geographic Channel; NFL Network; Nickelodeon; Spike TV; Syfy; TBS; TLC; TNT; Travel Channel; truTV; TV Land; USA Network; VH1.
Fee: $49.54 monthly.

Digital Basic Service
Subscribers: 480.
Programming (via satellite): Anime Network; AXS TV; AZ TV; BBC America; Bloomberg Television; Bravo; Church Channel; Cloo; CMT; Daystar TV Network; Discovery Life Channel; Disney XD; DMX Music; ESPN Classic; ESPN HD; ESPNews; FOX College Sports Central; FOX College Sports Pacific; Fox Sports 1; Fuse; FXM; FYI; Golf Channel; Great American Country; GSN; HD Theater; History; History International; IFC; JUCE TV; LMN; NBCSN; Nick Jr.; Nicktoons; Outdoor Channel; Ovation; Sundance TV; TeenNick; The Word Network; Trinity Broadcasting Network (TBN); Turner Classic Movies; TV One; TVG Network; Universal HD; UP; WE tv.
Fee: $14.30 monthly.

Pay Service 1
Pay Units: N.A.
Programming (via satellite): Flix; Showtime (multiplexed); The Movie Channel (multiplexed).
Fee: $7.95 monthly (Cinemax), $11.95 monthly (Showtime/TMC), $12.95 monthly (HBO), $13.95 monthly (Starz/Encore).

Digital Pay Service 1
Pay Units: N.A.
Programming (via satellite): Cinemax; Flix; HBO (multiplexed); Showtime (multiplexed); Starz (multiplexed); Starz Encore (multiplexed); The Movie Channel (multiplexed).
Fee: $3.95 monthly (Canales), $7.95 monthly (Cinemax), $11.95 monthly (Showtime/TMC), $12.95 monthly (HBO), $13.95 monthly (Starz/Encore).

Video-On-Demand: No

Pay-Per-View
Playboy TV (delivered digitally); Club Jenna (delivered digitally); Hot Choice (delivered digitally); Fresh (delivered digitally); iN DEMAND (delivered digitally).

Internet Service
Operational: Yes.
Subscribers: 737.
Fee: $34.95 monthly.

Telephone Service
Digital: Operational
Subscribers: 329.
Fee: $19.99-$32.99 monthly
Miles of Plant: 115.0 (coaxial); 55.0 (fiber optic). Homes passed: 4,350.
Vice President & General Manager: Paul Douglas Gearheart. Chief Financial Officer: James Campbell. Operations Director: John Schmoldt. Marketing Director: Heath Wiley. Chief Engineer: Jefferson Thacker. Ad Sales Manager: Adam Gearheart. Customer Service Manager: Rebecca Walters. Field Engineer: Roy A. Harlow.
Ownership: Inter-Mountain Cable Inc. (MSO).

JEREMIAH—TVS Cable, PO Box 1410, Hindman, KY 41822-1410. Phones: 606-946-2600; 606-785-3450; 606-633-0778. Fax: 606-785-3110. E-mail: tvs@tvscable.com. Web Site: http://www.tvscable.com. Also serves Blackey, Carcassonne, Colson, Isom, Letcher County (portions), Premium & Redfox. ICA: KY0333.
TV Market Ranking: Below 100 (Blackey, Carcassonne, Colson, Isom, JEREMIAH, Premium, Redfox, Letcher County (portions)); Outside TV Markets (Letcher County (portions)).
Channel capacity: N.A. Channels available but not in use: N.A.

Basic Service
Subscribers: 1,355. Commercial subscribers: 17.
Fee: $50.00 installation; $23.50 monthly.

Internet Service
Operational: Yes.
Fee: $24.95-$79.95 monthly.
Vice President & General Manager: William K. Grigsby.
Ownership: TV Service Inc. (MSO).

KUTTAWA—Zito Media, 102 S Main St, PO Box 665, Coudersport, PA 16915. Phones: 814-260-9055; 800-365-6988. E-mail: info@zitomedia.com. Web Site: http://www.zitomedia.com. Also serves Eddyville, Grand Rivers, Livingston County (portions), Lyon County & Smithland. ICA: KY0255.
TV Market Ranking: 69 (Eddyville, Grand Rivers, KUTTAWA, Lyon County, Smithland).
Channel capacity: N.A. Channels available but not in use: N.A.

Basic Service
Subscribers: 626.
Programming (received off-air): KBSI (FOX) Cape Girardeau; KFVS-TV (CBS, CW, MeTV) Cape Girardeau; WDKA (MNT, The Country Network) Paducah; WKMA-TV (PBS) Madisonville; WPSD-TV (Antenna TV, NBC) Paducah; WQWQ-LP (CW, MeTV) Paducah; WSIL-TV (ABC) Harrisburg; WTCT (IND) Marion.
Programming (via satellite): A&E; Animal Planet; Cartoon Network; CNBC; CNN; C-SPAN; Discovery Channel; Disney Channel; ESPN; ESPN2; Fox News Channel; Freeform; Fuse; FX; Great American Country; HGTV; History; HLN; Lifetime; Outdoor Channel; TBS; The Weather Channel; TLC; TNT; Travel Channel; Turner Classic Movies; USA Network; WGN America.
Fee: $49.95 installation; $49.28 monthly.

Digital Basic Service
Subscribers: N.A.
Programming (via satellite): BBC America; Bloomberg Television; Discovery Life Channel; Disney XD; DMX Music; ESPN Classic; ESPNews; Fox Sports 1; FYI; Golf Channel; GSN; History International; National Geographic Channel; WE tv.

Digital Expanded Basic Service
Subscribers: N.A.
Programming (via satellite): DMX Music; FXM; LMN; Starz Encore.
Fee: $13.95 monthly.

Pay Service 1
Pay Units: N.A.
Programming (via satellite): Cinemax; HBO; Showtime; The Movie Channel.

Digital Pay Service 1
Pay Units: N.A.
Programming (via satellite): Cinemax (multiplexed); Flix; HBO (multiplexed); Showtime (multiplexed); The Movie Channel (multiplexed).
Fee: $19.55 monthly.

Video-On-Demand: No

Pay-Per-View
Playboy TV (delivered digitally); Fresh (delivered digitally).

Internet Service
Operational: No.

Telephone Service
None
Miles of Plant: 121.0 (coaxial); None (fiber optic). Homes passed: 2,000.
President: James Rigas.
Ownership: Zito Media (MSO).

LAFAYETTE—Formerly served by Adelphia Communications. No longer in operation. ICA: KY0246.

LAWRENCE COUNTY (southern portion)—Lycom Communications, 305 East Pike St, PO Box 1114, Louisa, KY 41230. Phones: 800-489-0640; 606-638-4278; 606-638-3600. Fax: 606-638-4278. E-mail: info@lycomonline.com. Web Site: http://lycomonline.com. ICA: KY0251.
TV Market Ranking: Franchise award date: N.A. Franchise expiration date: N.A. Began: January 1, 1983.
Channel capacity: N.A. Channels available but not in use: N.A.

Basic Service
Subscribers: 533.
Programming (received off-air): WCHS-TV (ABC, Antenna TV) Charleston; WKAS (PBS) Ashland; WKYT-TV (CBS, CW) Lexington; WLPX-TV (ION) Charleston; WOWK-TV (CBS) Huntington; WSAZ-TV (MNT, NBC, This TV) Huntington; WTSF (Daystar TV) Ashland; WVAH-TV (FOX, The Country Network) Charleston; WVPB-TV (PBS) Huntington; WYMT-TV (CBS, CW) Hazard.
Programming (via satellite): A&E; AMC; Animal Planet; Cartoon Network; CMT; CNBC; CNN; Comedy Central; C-SPAN; C-SPAN 2; CW PLUS; Discovery Channel; Disney Channel; E! HD; ESPN; ESPN Classic; ESPN2; Food Network; Fox News Channel; Fox Sports 1; FOX Sports Ohio/Sports Time Ohio; Freeform; FX; Great American Country; Hallmark Channel; HGTV; History; HLN; Lifetime; MTV; National Geographic Channel; Nickelodeon; Pop; QVC; RFD-TV; Spike TV; Syfy; TBS; The Weather Channel; TLC; TNT; Travel Channel; Trinity Broadcasting Network (TBN); truTV; Turner Classic Movies; TV Land; UP; USA Network; VH1; WGN America.
Fee: $129.95 installation; $23.25 monthly; $3.00 converter.

Expanded Basic Service 1
Subscribers: 491.
Fee: $26.70 monthly.

Digital Basic Service
Subscribers: 111.
Programming (via satellite): BBC America; Bloomberg Television; Boomerang; CMT; Destination America; Discovery Kids Channel; Discovery Life Channel; DIY Network; DMX Music; ESPN Classic; ESPN2; ESPNews; ESPNU; Fox Sports 1; FXM; Golf Channel; GSN; IFC; Investigation Discovery; MTV Classic; NBCSN; Nick Jr.; Nicktoons; OWN: Oprah Winfrey Network; Science Channel.
Fee: $13.75 monthly.

Digital Pay Service 1
Pay Units: N.A.
Programming (via satellite): Cinemax (multiplexed); Flix; HBO (multiplexed); Showtime (multiplexed); Starz (multiplexed); Starz Encore (multiplexed); The Movie Channel (multiplexed).
Fee: $11.95 monthly (Cinemax, HBO, Showtime/TMC/Flix or Starz/Encore).

Video-On-Demand: No

Internet Service
Operational: Yes.
Broadband Service: Lycom Online.
Fee: $31.95 monthly.

Telephone Service
Digital: Operational
Miles of Plant: 30.0 (coaxial); None (fiber optic).
President: Steven J. Lycans. Chief Technician: Aaron Lycans.
Ownership: Lycom Communications Inc.

LAWRENCEBURG—Time Warner Cable. Now served by RICHMOND, KY [KY0008]. ICA: KY0252.

LEBANON—Time Warner Cable, 1615 Foxhaven Dr, Richmond, KY 40475. Phones: 859-625-6600; 859-626-4800; 859-624-9666. Fax: 859-624-0060. Web Site: http://www.timewarnercable.com. Also serves Loretto, Marion County (portions), Nelson County (portions), New Haven & Springfield. ICA: KY0049.
TV Market Ranking: Below 100 (LEBANON, Loretto, Marion County (portions), Nelson County (portions), New Haven, Springfield). Franchise award date: N.A. Franchise expiration date: N.A. Began: March 9, 1970.
Channel capacity: N.A. Channels available but not in use: N.A.

Basic Service
Subscribers: 2,574.
Programming (received off-air): WAVE (Bounce TV, NBC, This TV) Louisville; WBKI-TV (CW, IND, Movies!) Campbellsville; WBNA (ION, Retro TV) Louisville; WDRB (Antenna TV, FOX) Louisville; WHAS-TV (ABC) Louisville; WKLE (PBS) Lexington; WKYT-TV (CBS, CW) Lexington; WLEX-TV (MeTV, NBC) Lexington; WLJC-TV (TBN) Beattyville; WLKY (CBS, MeTV) Louisville; WMYO (MNT, My Family TV) Salem; WOAY-TV (ABC) Oak Hill; allband FM.
Programming (via satellite): QVC.
Fee: $24.95-$61.55 installation; $24.50 monthly.

Expanded Basic Service 1
Subscribers: N.A.
Programming (via satellite): A&E; AMC; Animal Planet; BET; Bravo; Cartoon Network; CMT; CNBC; CNN; Comedy Central; C-SPAN; C-SPAN 2; Discovery Channel; Disney Channel; E! HD; ESPN; ESPN2; EVINE Live; EWTN Global Catholic Network; Food Network; Fox News Channel; FOX Sports Ohio/Sports Time Ohio; Freeform; FX; Hall-

mark Channel; HGTV; History; HLN; Lifetime; MSNBC; MTV; Nickelodeon; OWN: Oprah Winfrey Network; Oxygen; Pop; Spike TV; Syfy; TBS; The Weather Channel; TLC; TNT; Travel Channel; Trinity Broadcasting Network (TBN); truTV; TV Land; USA Network; VH1; WGN America.
Fee: $32.98 monthly.
Digital Basic Service
Subscribers: N.A.
Programming (via satellite): AXS TV; BBC America; Bloomberg Television; Boomerang; CBS Sports Network; Cloo; CMT; Cooking Channel; C-SPAN 3; Daystar TV Network; Discovery Digital Networks; Disney XD; DIY Network; ESPN Classic; ESPN HD; ESPN2 HD; ESPNews; ESPNU; FamilyNet; Flix; FOX College Sports Central; FOX College Sports Pacific; Fox Sports 1; Fox Sports 2; Fuse; FYI; Golf Channel; Great American Country; GSN; HD Theater; History International; HITS (Headend In The Sky); IFC; LMN; LOGO; MC; Nat Geo WILD; National Geographic Channel; NBA TV; NBCSN; Nick 2; Nick Jr.; Nicktoons; Outdoor Channel; Ovation; Reelz; Starz Encore (multiplexed); Sundance TV; TeenNick; Tennis Channel; The Word Network; TNT HD; Turner Classic Movies; TVG Network; Universal HD; UP; WE tv.
Fee: $6.00 monthly (each tier).
Digital Pay Service 1
Pay Units: N.A.
Programming (via satellite): Cinemax (multiplexed); Cinemax HD; HBO (multiplexed); HBO HD; RAI Italia; RTN; Showtime (multiplexed); Showtime HD; Starz (multiplexed); Starz HD; TAC TV; The Filipino Channel; The Movie Channel (multiplexed); TV Asia; TV5, La Television International.
Fee: $14.00 monthly (each).
Video-On-Demand: No
Pay-Per-View
iN DEMAND (delivered digitally); Fresh (delivered digitally); Hot Choice (delivered digitally); Sports PPV (delivered digitally); Playboy TV (delivered digitally).
Internet Service
Operational: Yes.
Broadband Service: Road Runner.
Fee: $44.95 monthly.
Telephone Service
Digital: Operational
Fee: $44.95 monthly
Miles of Plant: 305.0 (coaxial); None (fiber optic). Homes passed: 5,045.
General Manager: Robert Trott. Marketing Director: Betrina Morse. Technical Operations Manager: Dennis Lester. Government & Public Affairs Manager: Carla Deaton. Office Manager: Laverne Farris.
Ownership: Time Warner Cable (MSO).

LEITCHFIELD—Comcast Cable. Now served by ELIZABETHTOWN, KY [KY0012]. ICA: KY0067.

LEROSE—Formerly served by Phil's Cablevision. No longer in operation. ICA: KY0161.

LESLIE COUNTY (northern portion)—Crystal Broadband Networks, PO Box 180336, Chicago, IL 60618. Phones: 817-685-9588; 630-206-0447. E-mail: sales@crystalbn.com. Web Site: http://crystalbn.com. Also serves Greasy Creek, Perry County (portions), Stinnett & Wooton. ICA: KY0289.
TV Market Ranking: Below 100 (LESLIE COUNTY (NORTHERN PORTION), Perry County (portions), Stinnett). Outside TV Markets (Greasy Creek). Franchise award date: N.A. Franchise expiration date: N.A. Began: March 1, 1971.
Channel capacity: N.A. Channels available but not in use: N.A.
Basic Service
Subscribers: N.A.
Programming (received off-air): WAGV (IND) Harlan; WCYB-TV (CW, Decades, NBC) Bristol; WEMT (FOX, Movies!, This TV) Greeneville; WJHL-TV (ABC, CBS, MeTV) Johnson City; WKHA (PBS) Hazard; WKPT-TV (COZI TV, Escape, MeTV, MNT) Kingsport; WYMT-TV (CBS, CW) Hazard.
Programming (via satellite): Freeform; QVC; Trinity Broadcasting Network (TBN); WGN America.
Fee: $39.95 installation; $49.36 monthly.
Expanded Basic Service 1
Subscribers: N.A.
Programming (via satellite): A&E; AMC; CMT; CNN; C-SPAN; Discovery Channel; Disney Channel; E! HD; ESPN; ESPN2; Fox News Channel; FX; HLN; INSP; Nickelodeon; Spike TV; TBS; The Weather Channel; TLC; TNT; USA Network; VH1.
Fee: $24.52 monthly.
Digital Basic Service
Subscribers: N.A.
Programming (via satellite): BBC America; Bloomberg Television; Bravo; Discovery Life Channel; Disney XD; ESPN Classic; ESPNews; Fox Sports 1; FOX Sports Networks; Fuse; FXM; FYI; Golf Channel; Great American Country; GSN; HGTV; History; History International; IFC; LMN; MTV Classic; MTV2; National Geographic Channel; NBCSN; Nick Jr.; Nicktoons; Outdoor Channel; Syfy; TeenNick; The Word Network; Turner Classic Movies; VH1 Country; WE tv.
Digital Pay Service 1
Pay Units: N.A.
Programming (via satellite): Cinemax (multiplexed); HBO; Showtime (multiplexed); Starz Encore; The Movie Channel (multiplexed).
Fee: $12.00 monthly (each).
Video-On-Demand: No
Pay-Per-View
Fresh (delivered digitally); Playboy TV (delivered digitally).
Internet Service
Operational: No.
Telephone Service
None
Miles of Plant: 102.0 (coaxial); None (fiber optic). Homes passed: 2,297.
General Manager: Ron Page. Program Manager: Shawn Smith.
Ownership: Crystal Broadband Networks (MSO).

LEWISPORT—Formerly served by Crystal Broadband Networks. Now served by Inside Connect Cable, HAWESVILLE, KY [KY0232]. ICA: KY0136.

LEXINGTON—Formerly served by Wireless Associates LP. No longer in operation. ICA: KY0303.

LEXINGTON—Time Warner Cable, 60 Columbus Circle, 17th Fl, New York, NY 10023. Phones: 212-364-8200; 212-364-8200; 859-514-1400; 859-514-1439. Fax: 212-364-8252. Web Site: http://www.timewarnercable.com. Also serves Fayette County (portions) & Jessamine County (northern portion). ICA: KY0003.
TV Market Ranking: Below 100 (Fayette County (portions), Jessamine County (northern portion), LEXINGTON). Franchise award date: N.A. Franchise expiration date: N.A. Began: October 1, 1980.
Channel capacity: N.A. Channels available but not in use: N.A.
Basic Service
Subscribers: 68,618. Commercial subscribers: 1,015.
Programming (received off-air): KETS (PBS) Little Rock; WBKI-TV (CW, IND, Movies!) Campbellsville; WDKY-TV (FOX) Danville; WKLE (PBS) Lexington; WKYT-TV (CBS, CW) Lexington; WLEX-TV (MeTV, NBC) Lexington; WLJC-TV (TBN) Beattyville; WTVQ-DT (ABC, Antenna TV, Laff, MNT) Lexington; WUPX-TV (ION) Morehead.
Programming (via satellite): Discovery Channel; Georgia Highlands Television (GHTV); Pop; QVC; TBS; The Weather Channel; WGN America.
Fee: $30.00 installation; $12.66 monthly.
Expanded Basic Service 1
Subscribers: N.A.
Programming (via satellite): A&E; AMC; Animal Planet; BET; Bravo; BTN; Cartoon Network; CMT; CNBC; CNN; Comedy Central; C-SPAN; C-SPAN 2; Disney Channel; E! HD; ESPN; ESPN2; Food Network; Fox News Channel; Fox Sports 1; FOX Sports Ohio/Sports Time Ohio; Freeform; FX; Hallmark Channel; HGTV; History; HLN; Lifetime; MSNBC; MTV; Nickelodeon; Oxygen; Spike TV; Syfy; Telemundo; TLC; TNT; Travel Channel; truTV; TV Land; TVG Network; USA Network; VH1.
Fee: $40.00 monthly.
Digital Basic Service
Subscribers: N.A.
Programming (via satellite): AXS TV; BBC America; Bloomberg Television; CBS Sports Network; Cooking Channel; Discovery Digital Networks; Disney XD; DIY Network; DMX Music; ESPN Classic; ESPN HD; ESPNews; EWTN Global Catholic Network; FOX College Sports Central; FOX College Sports Pacific; Fuse; FXM; FYI; Golf Channel; Great American Country; GSN; HD Theater; History International; HITS (Headend In The Sky); IFC; LMN; Nat Geo WILD; National Geographic Channel; NBCSN; NFL Network; Nick 2; Nick Jr.; Nicktoons; Outdoor Channel; Ovation; Sprout; Starz Encore (multiplexed); Sundance TV (multiplexed); TeenNick; Trinity Broadcasting Network (TBN); Turner Classic Movies; Universal HD; WE tv.
Digital Pay Service 1
Pay Units: N.A.
Programming (via satellite): Cinemax (multiplexed); Flix; HBO (multiplexed); HBO HD; Showtime (multiplexed); Showtime HD; Starz (multiplexed); The Movie Channel (multiplexed).
Fee: $10.00 monthly (Cinemax or Starz), $13.00 monthly (HBO or Showtime/TMC).
Video-On-Demand: Yes
Pay-Per-View
iN DEMAND (delivered digitally); ESPN (delivered digitally); Fresh (delivered digitally); Shorteez (delivered digitally).

Internet Service
Operational: Yes. Began: March 1, 1999.
Subscribers: 77,754.
Fee: $99.95 installation; $44.95 monthly; $3.00 modem lease; $50.00 modem purchase.
Telephone Service
Digital: Operational
Subscribers: 30,067.
Fee: $40.00 monthly
Miles of Plant: 2,386.0 (coaxial); 936.0 (fiber optic). Homes passed: 151,286.
Chief Executive Officer: Glenn A. Britt. President & Chief Operations Officer: Robert D. Marcus.
Ownership: Time Warner Cable (MSO).

LIBERTY—Time Warner Cable. Now served by CORBIN, KY [KY0030]. ICA: KY0082.

LINCOLN COUNTY (eastern portion)—Mediacom, 90 Main St, Benton, KY 42025-1132. Phones: 845-695-2762; 417-875-5560 (Springfield regional office); 270-527-9939. Fax: 270-527-0813. Web Site: http://www.mediacomcable.com. Also serves Brodhead & Rockcastle County (western portion). ICA: KY0253.
TV Market Ranking: Below 100 (Brodhead, LINCOLN COUNTY (EASTERN PORTION), Rockcastle County (western portion)). Franchise award date: March 23, 1989. Franchise expiration date: N.A. Began: March 1, 1990.
Channel capacity: N.A. Channels available but not in use: N.A.
Basic Service
Subscribers: 36.
Programming (received off-air): WBKI-TV (CW, IND, Movies!) Campbellsville; WDKY-TV (FOX) Danville; WKSO-TV (PBS) Somerset; WKYT-TV (CBS, CW) Lexington; WLEX-TV (MeTV, NBC) Lexington; WLKY (CBS, MeTV) Louisville; WTVQ-DT (ABC, Antenna TV, Laff, MNT) Lexington.
Programming (via satellite): CMT; CNN; Discovery Channel; Disney Channel; E! HD; ESPN; Fox News Channel; Freeform; History; HLN; Lifetime; Nickelodeon; QVC; Spike TV; Syfy; TBS; The Weather Channel; TNT; Trinity Broadcasting Network (TBN); USA Network; WGN America.
Fee: $29.95 installation; $69.95 monthly; $3.95 converter.
Pay Service 1
Pay Units: N.A.
Programming (via satellite): Cinemax; HBO; Starz; Starz Encore.
Fee: $10.00 monthly.
Video-On-Demand: No
Internet Service
Operational: No.
Telephone Service
None
Miles of Plant: 65.0 (coaxial); None (fiber optic). Homes passed: 780.
Regional Vice President: Bill Copeland. Vice President, Financial Reporting: Kenneth J. Kohrs. General Manager: Dale Haney. Regional Technical Operations Director: Alan Freedman. Marketing Director: Will Kuebler.

Kentucky—Cable Systems

Technical Operations Manager: Jeff Brown. Marketing Manager: Melanie Westerman. Ownership: Mediacom LLC (MSO).

LIVERMORE—Time Warner Cable. Now served by OWENSBORO, KY [KY0004]. ICA: KY0093.

LONDON—Time Warner Cable, 7800 Crescent Executive Dr, Charlotte, NC 28217. Phones: 859-625-6600; 859-626-4800; 859-624-9666. Web Site: http://www.timewarnercable.com. Also serves Colony, East Bernstadt, Keavy & Laurel County (western portion). ICA: KY0015.

TV Market Ranking: Below 100 (East Bernstadt, Keavy, Laurel County (western portion) (portions)); Outside TV Markets (Colony, Laurel County (western portion) (portions), LONDON). Franchise award date: N.A. Franchise expiration date: N.A. Began: October 1, 1958.

Channel capacity: N.A. Channels available but not in use: N.A.

Basic Service
Subscribers: 4,487.
Programming (received off-air): WDKY-TV (FOX) Danville; WKLE (PBS) Lexington; WKMJ-TV (PBS) Louisville; WKYT-TV (CBS, CW) Lexington; WLEX-TV (MeTV, NBC) Lexington; WLJC-TV (TBN) Beattyville; WOBZ-LD (Retro TV, TNN) East Bernstadt; WTVQ-DT (ABC, Antenna TV, Laff, MNT) Lexington; WUPX-TV (ION) Morehead; WVTN-LP Corbin; WYMT-TV (CBS, CW) Hazard; allband FM.
Programming (via satellite): QVC; WGN America.
Fee: $49.99 installation; $24.50 monthly.

Expanded Basic Service 1
Subscribers: N.A.
Programming (via satellite): A&E; Animal Planet; BET; Bravo; Cartoon Network; CMT; CNBC; CNN; Comedy Central; C-SPAN; C-SPAN 2; Discovery Channel; Disney Channel; E! HD; ESPN; ESPN2; EWTN Global Catholic Network; Food Network; Fox News Channel; FOX Sports Ohio/Sports Time Ohio; FX; Hallmark Channel; HGTV; History; HLN; INSP; Lifetime; MSNBC; MTV; Nickelodeon; Oxygen; Pop; Spike TV; Syfy; TBS; The Weather Channel; TLC; TNT; Travel Channel; truTV; TV Land; USA Network; VH1.
Fee: $35.47 monthly.

Digital Basic Service
Subscribers: N.A.
Programming (via satellite): AXS TV; BBC America; Bloomberg Television; Boomerang; CBS Sports Network; Cloo; CMT; Cooking Channel; C-SPAN 3; Daystar TV Network; Discovery Digital Networks; Disney XD; DIY Network; ESPN Classic; ESPN HD; ESPN2 HD; ESPNews; EVINE Live; FamilyNet; Flix (multiplexed); FOX College Sports Central; FOX College Sports Pacific; Fox Sports 1; Fuse; FXM; FYI; Golf Channel; Great American Country; GSN; HD Theater; History International; HITS (Headend In The Sky); IFC; LMN; LOGO; MC; Nat Geo WILD; National Geographic Channel; NBA TV; NBCSN; Nick 2; Nick Jr.; Nicktoons; Outdoor Channel; Ovation; Reelz; Starz Encore (multiplexed); Sundance TV; TeenNick; Tennis Channel; The Word Network; TNT HD; Trinity Broadcasting Network (TBN); Turner Classic Movies; TVG Network; Universal HD; UP; WE tv.
Fee: $6.00 monthly (each tier).

Digital Pay Service 1
Pay Units: N.A.
Programming (via satellite): Cinemax (multiplexed); Cinemax HD; HBO (multiplexed); HBO HD; RAI Italia; RTN; Showtime (multiplexed); Showtime HD; Starz (multiplexed); Starz HD; TAC TV; The Filipino Channel; The Movie Channel (multiplexed); TV Asia; TV5, La Television International.
Fee: $14.00 monthly (each).

Video-On-Demand: No

Pay-Per-View
iN DEMAND (delivered digitally); Playboy TV (delivered digitally); Hot Choice (delivered digitally); Sports PPV (delivered digitally); Fresh (delivered digitally).

Internet Service
Operational: Yes.
Broadband Service: Road Runner.
Fee: $44.95 monthly.

Telephone Service
Digital: Operational
Fee: $44.95 monthly
Miles of Plant: 772.0 (coaxial); 306.0 (fiber optic). Homes passed: 6,407.
General Manager: Robert Trott. Senior Accounting Director: Karen Goodfellow. Marketing Director: Betrina Morse. Government & Public Affairs Manager: Carla Deaton. Technical Operations Manager: Dennis Lester. Office Manager: Laverne Farris.
Ownership: Time Warner Cable (MSO).

LOTHAIR—TVS Cable, PO Box 1410, Hindman, KY 41822-1410. Phones: 606-946-2600; 606-785-3450; 606-633-0778. Fax: 606-785-3110. E-mail: tvs@tvscable.com. Web Site: http://www.tvscable.com. Also serves Christopher, Jeff, Leatherwood & Viper. ICA: KY0335.

TV Market Ranking: Below 100 (Christopher, Jeff, Leatherwood, LOTHAIR, Viper).
Channel capacity: N.A. Channels available but not in use: N.A.

Basic Service
Subscribers: 1,477. Commercial subscribers: 28.
Fee: $50.00 installation; $23.50 monthly.

Internet Service
Operational: Yes.
Fee: $24.95-$79.95 monthly.
Vice President & General Manager: William K. Grigsby.
Ownership: TV Service Inc. (MSO).

LOUISA—Lycom Communications, 305 East Pike St, PO Box 1114, Louisa, KY 41230. Phones: 606-638-4278; 606-638-3600; 800-489-0640. Fax: 606-638-4278. E-mail: info@lycomonline.com. Web Site: http://lycomonline.com. ICA: KY0299.

TV Market Ranking: 36 (LOUISA). Franchise award date: N.A. Franchise expiration date: N.A. Began: January 1, 1991.
Channel capacity: N.A. Channels available but not in use: N.A.

Basic Service
Subscribers: 871.
Programming (received off-air): WCHS-TV (ABC, Antenna TV) Charleston; WKAS (PBS) Ashland; WKYT-TV (CBS, CW) Lexington; WLPX-TV (ION) Charleston; WOWK-TV (CBS) Huntington; WSAZ-TV (MNT, NBC, This TV) Huntington; WTSF (Daystar TV) Ashland; WVAH-TV (FOX, The Country Network) Charleston; WVPB-TV (PBS) Huntington; WYMT-TV (CBS, CW) Hazard.
Programming (via satellite): A&E; AMC; Animal Planet; Cartoon Network; CMT; CNBC; CNN; Comedy Central; C-SPAN; C-SPAN 2; CW PLUS; Discovery Channel; Disney Channel; E! HD; ESPN; ESPN Classic; ESPN2; Food Network; Fox News Channel; Fox Sports 1; FOX Sports Ohio/Sports Time Ohio; Freeform; FX; Great American Country; Hallmark Channel; HGTV; History; HLN; Lifetime; MTV; National Geographic Channel; Nickelodeon; Pop; QVC; RFD-TV; Spike TV; Syfy; TBS; The Weather Channel; TLC; TNT; Travel Channel; Trinity Broadcasting Network (TBN); truTV; Turner Classic Movies; TV Land; UP; USA Network; VH1; WGN America.
Fee: $23.25 monthly.

Expanded Basic Service 1
Subscribers: 809.
Fee: $26.70 monthly.

Digital Basic Service
Subscribers: 202.
Programming (via satellite): BBC America; Bloomberg Television; Boomerang; CMT; Destination America; Discovery Kids Channel; Discovery Life Channel; DIY Network; DMX Music; ESPN Classic; ESPN2; ESPNews; ESPNU; Fox Sports 1; FXM; Golf Channel; GSN; IFC; Investigation Discovery; MTV Classic; NBCSN; Nick Jr.; Nicktoons; OWN: Oprah Winfrey Network; Science Channel.
Fee: $13.75 monthly.

Digital Pay Service 1
Pay Units: N.A.
Programming (via satellite): Cinemax (multiplexed); Flix; HBO (multiplexed); Showtime (multiplexed); Starz (multiplexed); Starz Encore (multiplexed); The Movie Channel (multiplexed).
Fee: $11.95 monthly (Cinemax, HBO, Showtime/TMC/Flix or Starz/Encore).

Video-On-Demand: No

Internet Service
Operational: Yes. Began: August 1, 2001.
Broadband Service: Lycom Online.
Fee: $31.95 monthly.

Telephone Service
Digital: Operational
Miles of Plant: 25.0 (coaxial); None (fiber optic). Homes passed: 1,100.
President: Steven J. Lycans. Chief Technician: Aaron Lycans.
Ownership: Lycom Communications Inc. (MSO).

LOUISVILLE—No longer in operation. ICA: KY0304.

LOUISVILLE—Time Warner Cable, 60 Columbus Circle, 17th Fl, New York, NY 10023. Phones: 212-364-8200; 212-364-8200; 800-273-0144; 502-357-4400. Fax: 212-364-8252. Web Site: http://www.timewarnercable.com. Also serves Austin, Borden, Campbellsburg, Charlestown, Clark County (portions), Clarksville, Corydon, Crothersville, Floyd County (portions), Floyds Knobs, Georgetown, Greenville, Harrison County (portions), Jackson County (portions), Jeffersonville, Lanesville, Lexington, New Albany, New Pekin, Palmyra, Pekin, Salem, Saltillo, Scott County (portions), Scottsburg, Sellersburg, Utica, Vienna & Washington County (portions), IN; Anchorage, Audubon Park, Bancroft, Barbourmeade, Bedford, Beechwood Village, Bellemeade, Bellewood, Blue Ridge Manor, Brandenburg, Briarwood, Broad Fields, Broeck Pointe, Brownsboro Farm, Brownsboro Village, Buckner, Bullitt County (portions), Cambridge, Campbellsburg, Carroll County (portions), Carrollton, Cherrywood Village, Coldstream, Creekside, Crestwood, Crossgate, Doe Valley, Douglass Hills, Druid Hills, Eminence, Fairmeade, Fincastle, Forest Hills, Fort Knox, Ghent, Glenview, Glenview Hills, Glenview Manor, Goose Creek, Graymoor-Devondale, Green Spring, Hardin County (portions), Henry County (portions), Henryville, Heritage Creek, Hickory Hill, Hills and Dales, Hillview, Hollow Creek, Hollyvilla, Houston Acres, Hunters Hollow, Hurstbourne, Hurstbourne Acres, Indian Hills, Indian Hills-Cherokee, Jefferson County (portions), Jeffersontown, Jeffersonville (portions), Keeneland, Kingsley, La Grange, Langdon Place, Lebanon Junction, Lincolnshire, Lyndon, Lynnview, Manor Creek, Maryhill Estates, Meade County (portions), Meadow Vale, Meadowbrook Farm, Meadowview Estates, Middletown, Milton, Minor Lane Heights, Mockingbird Valley, Monroe, Moorland, Mount Washington, Muldraugh, Murray Hill, Naval Ordnance Station Louisville, New Castle, New Washington, Norbourne Estates, Northfield, Norwood, Old Brownsboro Place, Oldham County (portions), Orchard Grass Hills, Parkway Village, Pewee Valley, Pioneer Village, Plantation, Pleasureville, Plymouth Village, Prestonville, Prospect, Radcliff, Richlawn, River Bluff, Riverwood, Robinswood, Rolling Fields, Rolling Hills, Seneca Gardens, Shelby County (portions), Shelbyville, Shepherdsville, Shively, Simpsonville, Smithfield, South Park View, Spencer County (portions), Spring Valley, Springlee, St. Matthews, St. Regis Park, Strathmoor Gardens, Strathmoor Manor, Strathmoor Village, Sycamore, Taylorsville, Ten Broeck, Thornhill, Trimble County (portions), Watterson Park, Wellington, West Buechel, West Point, Whipps Millgate, Wildwood, Winding Falls, Windy Hills, Woodland Hills, Woodlawn Park, Worthington Hills & Worthville, KY. ICA: KY0001.

TV Market Ranking: 38 (Anchorage, Audubon Park, Bancroft, Barbourmeade, Bedford, Beechwood Village, Bellemeade, Bellewood, Blue Ridge Manor, Borden, Brandenburg, Briarwood, Broeck Pointe, Brownsboro Farm, Brownsboro Village, Buckner, Bullitt County (portions), Cambridge, Clarksville, Coldstream, Corydon, Creekside, Crossgate, Douglass Hills, Druid Hills, Eminence, Fincastle, Floyd County (portions), Floyds Knobs, Fort Knox, Georgetown, Glenview Hills, Glenview Manor, Goose Creek, Graymoor-Devondale, Green Spring, Greenville, Hardin County (portions), Harrison County (portions), Henry County (portions), Henryville, Hickory Hill, Hills and Dales, Hillview, Hollow Creek, Hollyvilla, Houston Acres, Hunters Hollow, Hurstbourne Acres, Indian Hills, Indian Hills-Cherokee, Jefferson County (portions), Jeffersontown, Jeffersonville (portions), Kingsley,

Cable Systems—Kentucky

Lanesville, Langdon Place, Lebanon Junction, Lexington, Lincolnshire, LOUISVILLE, Lyndon, Lynnview, Manor Creek, Maryhill Estates, Meade County (portions), Meadow Vale, Meadowbrook Farm, Meadowview Estates, Middletown, Minor Lane Heights, Mockingbird Valley, Moorland, Mount Washington, Muldraugh, Naval Ordnance Station Louisville, New Albany, New Castle, New Pekin, New Washington, Norbourne Estates, Northfield, Norwood, Old Brownsboro Place, Palmyra, Parkway Village, Pekin, Pewee Valley, Pioneer Village, Plantation, Pleasureville, Pleasureville, Pleasureville, Prospect, Radcliff, Richlawn, River Bluff, Riverwood, Rolling Fields, Rolling Hills, Salem, Scottsburg, Sellersburg, Seneca Gardens, Shelby County (portions), Shelbyville, Shepherdsville, Shively, Simpsonville, South Park View, Spencer County (portions), St. Matthews, St. Regis Park, Strathmoor Manor, Strathmoor Village, Sycamore, Taylorsville, Ten Broeck, Thornhill, Utica, Vienna, Washington County (portions), Watterson Park, West Buechel, West Point, Wildwood, Windy Hills, Woodland Hills, Woodlawn Park, Worthington Hills; Below 100 (Austin, Crothersville, Heritage Creek, Jackson County (portions), Henry County (portions), Shelby County (portions)); Outside TV Markets (Campbellsburg, Carrollton, Ghent, Trimble County (portions), Worthville, Henry County (portions) (portions), Washington County (portions)). Franchise award date: November 26, 1973. Franchise expiration date: N.A. Began: January 15, 1979.
Channel capacity: 58 (operating 2-way). Channels available but not in use: N.A.

Basic Service
Subscribers: 222,024.
Programming (received off-air): WAVE (Bounce TV, NBC, This TV) Louisville; WBKI-TV (CW, IND, Movies!) Campbellsville; WBNA (ION, Retro TV) Louisville; WDRB (Antenna TV, FOX) Louisville; WHAS-TV (ABC) Louisville; WKMJ-TV (PBS) Louisville; WKPC-TV (PBS) Louisville; WLKY (CBS, MeTV) Louisville; WMYO (MNT, My Family TV) Salem; 19 FMs.
Programming (via satellite): C-SPAN; C-SPAN 2; HSN; News 12 Interactive; QVC; The Weather Channel; TV One; Univision; WGN America.
Fee: $23.74 installation; $19.95 monthly.

Expanded Basic Service 1
Subscribers: N.A.
Programming (via satellite): A&E; AMC; Animal Planet; BET; Bravo; Cartoon Network; CMT; CNBC; CNN; Comedy Central; Discovery Channel; Disney Channel; E! HD; ESPN; ESPN2; Food Network; Fox News Channel; FOX Sports Ohio/Sports Time Ohio; Freeform; FX; Golf Channel; Hallmark Channel; HGTV; History; HLN; Lifetime; MSNBC; MTV; MTV2; Nickelodeon; Spike TV; Syfy; TBS; TLC; TNT; Travel Channel; Trinity Broadcasting Network (TBN); truTV; TV Land; TVG Network; USA Network; VH1.
Fee: $40.00 monthly.

Digital Basic Service
Subscribers: N.A.
Programming (via satellite): A&E; A&E HD; AMC; AMC HD; Animal Planet; Animal Planet HD; AXS TV; BBC America; BBC HD; BET; Bio HD; Bloomberg Television; Boomerang; Bravo; Bravo HD; BTN; Cartoon Network; Cartoon Network HD; CBS Sports Network; CBS Sports Network HD; Centric; Chiller; Cloo; CMT; CMT HD;

CNBC; CNBC HD+; CNN; CNN HD; Comedy Central; Comedy Central HD; Cooking Channel; C-SPAN; C-SPAN 2; C-SPAN 3; Daystar TV Network; Destination America; Destination America HD; Discovery Channel; Discovery Channel HD; Discovery Family; Discovery Life Channel; Disney Channel; Disney Channel HD; Disney XD; Disney XD HD; DIY Network; DIY Network HD; DMX Music; E! HD; ESPN; ESPN Classic; ESPN HD; ESPN2; ESPN2 HD; ESPNews; ESPNews HD; ESPNU; ESPNU HD; EVINE Live; EWTN Global Catholic Network; Food Network HD; Fox Business Network HD; Fox Business Network; Fox News Channel; Fox News HD; Fox Sports 1; Fox Sports 2; FOX Sports Ohio/Sports Time Ohio; Freeform; Freeform HD; FSN HD; Fuse; FX; FX HD; FXM; FYI; Golf Channel; Golf Channel HD; Great American Country; Hallmark Channel; Hallmark Channel HD; HD Theater; HGTV; HGTV HD; History; History HD; History International; HLN; HLN HD; HorseTV Channel; HSN; ID Investigation Discovery HD; IFC; Investigation Discovery; Jewelry Television; Lifetime; Lifetime HD; Lifetime Movie Network HD; LOGO; MGM HD; MSNBC; MTV; MTV Classic; MTV Hits; MTV Jams; MTV Live; MTV2; mtvU; Nat Geo WILD; National Geographic Channel; National Geographic Channel HD; NBCSN; NFL Network; NFL Network HD; Nick 2; Nick HD; Nick Jr.; Nickelodeon; Nicktoons; Outdoor Channel; Outdoor Channel HD; Ovation; OWN: Oprah Winfrey Network; Oxygen; Pop; QVC; Science Channel; Science HD; Smithsonian Channel HD; Spike TV; Spike TV HD; Sprout; Starz Encore (multiplexed); Starz Encore HD; Sundance TV; Syfy; Syfy HD; TBS; TBS HD; TeenNick; Tennis Channel; Tennis Channel HD; The Weather Channel; The Weather Channel HD; TLC; TLC HD; TNT; TNT HD; Tr3s; Travel Channel; Travel Channel HD; Trinity Broadcasting Network (TBN); truTV; truTV HD; Turner Classic Movies; Turner Classic Movies HD; TV Land; TV One; TVG Network; Universal HD; Univision; USA Network; USA Network HD; Versus HD; VH1; VH1 HD; VH1 Soul; WE tv; WE tv HD; WGN America; WGN America HD.

Digital Pay Service 1
Pay Units: N.A.
Programming (via satellite): Cinemax (multiplexed); Cinemax HD; Cinemax On Demand; Flix; HBO (multiplexed); HBO HD; HBO Latino; HBO on Demand; Showtime (multiplexed); Showtime HD; Showtime On Demand; Starz (multiplexed); Starz HD; The Movie Channel (multiplexed); The Movie Channel On Demand.
Fee: $10.00 monthly (Cinemax or Starz), $13.00 monthly (HBO or Showtime/TMC/Flix).

Video-On-Demand: Yes
Pay-Per-View
ESPN Now (delivered digitally); iN DEMAND (delivered digitally); Playboy TV (delivered digitally); Fresh (delivered digitally); Shorteez (delivered digitally).

Internet Service
Operational: Yes.
Subscribers: 258,087.
Fee: $99.95 installation; $44.95 monthly; $15.00 modem lease; $200.00 modem purchase.

Telephone Service
Digital: Operational
Subscribers: 138,262.
Miles of Plant: 12,120.0 (coaxial); 3,747.0 (fiber optic). Homes passed: 633,154.

Access the most current data instantly
FREE TRIAL @ ADVANCED TVFactbook
TELCO/IPTV • CABLE TV • TV STATIONS
www.warren-news.com/factbook.htm

Chief Executive Officer: Glenn A. Britt. President & Chief Operations Officer: Robert D. Marcus.
Ownership: Time Warner Cable (MSO).

LOWMANSVILLE—Tri-Wave Communications Inc, 109 Depot Rd, Paintsville, KY 41240-1325. Phone: 606-789-7603. Fax: 606-789-3391. ICA: KY0318.
TV Market Ranking: Outside TV Markets (LOWMANSVILLE).
Channel capacity: N.A. Channels available but not in use: N.A.

Basic Service
Subscribers: 30.
Programming (received off-air): WCHS-TV (ABC, Antenna TV) Charleston; WKMR (PBS) Morehead; WOWK-TV (CBS) Huntington; WSAZ-TV (MNT, NBC, This TV) Huntington; WVAH-TV (FOX, The Country Network) Charleston; WVPB-TV (PBS) Huntington; WYMT-TV (CBS, CW) Hazard.
Programming (via satellite): A&E; CNN; ESPN; ESPN2; Freeform; History; HLN; ION Television; Spike TV; TBS; TLC; TNT; USA Network; WGN America.
Fee: $28.80 monthly.

Pay Service 1
Pay Units: N.A.
Programming (via satellite): Showtime.

Video-On-Demand: No
Pay-Per-View
iN DEMAND (delivered digitally); Hot Choice (delivered digitally); Playboy TV (delivered digitally); Fresh (delivered digitally); Shorteez (delivered digitally).

Internet Service
Operational: Yes.
Fee: $24.95 monthly.

Telephone Service
Digital: Operational
Fee: $131.93 monthly
General Manager: Bart Ward.
Ownership: Tri-Wave Communications Inc. (MSO).

LYNCH—Formerly served by Tri-Star Communications. No longer in operation. ICA: KY0151.

MADISONVILLE—Time Warner Cable, 60 Columbus Circle, 17th Fl, New York, NY 10023. Phones: 859-431-0300; 212-364-8200. Fax: 203-328-0604. Web Site: http://www.timewarnercable.com. Also serves Beaver Dam, Centertown, Christian County (portions), Earlington, Hanson, Hartford, Hopkins County (unincorporated areas), Hopkinsville, McHenry, Mortons Gap, Ohio County (portions), Rockport, Sebree & White Plains. ICA: KY0013.
TV Market Ranking: 86 (Sebree); Below 100 (Beaver Dam, Centertown, Christian County (portions), Earlington, Hanson, Hartford, Hopkins County (unincorporated areas), Hopkinsville, MADISONVILLE, McHenry, Mortons Gap, Rockport, White Plains, Ohio County (portions)); Outside TV Markets (Ohio County (portions)). Fran-

chise award date: N.A. Franchise expiration date: N.A. Began: July 1, 1964.
Channel capacity: N.A. Channels available but not in use: N.A.

Basic Service
Subscribers: 13,714. Commercial subscribers: 924.
Programming (received off-air): WAZE-LP Evansville; WBKO (ABC, CW, FOX) Bowling Green; WEHT (ABC) Evansville; WEVV-TV (CBS, FOX) Evansville; WFIE (NBC, This TV) Evansville; WKMA-TV (PBS) Madisonville; WNIN (PBS) Evansville; WPSD-TV (Antenna TV, NBC) Paducah; WTVF (CBS, Laff, This TV) Nashville; WTVW (CW, MeTV) Evansville.
Programming (via satellite): C-SPAN; C-SPAN 2; EWTN Global Catholic Network; INSP; Pop; QVC; Trinity Broadcasting Network (TBN); WGN America.
Fee: $40.00 installation; $20.99 monthly.

Expanded Basic Service 1
Subscribers: N.A.
Programming (via satellite): A&E; AMC; Animal Planet; BET; Bravo; Cartoon Network; CMT; CNBC; CNN; Comedy Central; Discovery Channel; Disney Channel; Disney XD; E! HD; ESPN; ESPN Classic; ESPN2; Food Network; Fox News Channel; Fox Sports 1; Freeform; FX; Golf Channel; Great American Country; GSN; Hallmark Channel; Hallmark Movies & Mysteries; HGTV; History; HLN; Lifetime; MSNBC; MTV; National Geographic Channel; NBCSN; Nickelodeon; Outdoor Channel; Oxygen; Spike TV; Syfy; TBS; The Weather Channel; TLC; TNT; Travel Channel; truTV; Turner Classic Movies; TV Land; USA Network; VH1.

Digital Basic Service
Subscribers: N.A.
Programming (via satellite): A&E HD; AXS TV; BBC America; CMT; Cooking Channel; Destination America; Discovery Kids Channel; Discovery Life Channel; DIY Network; ESPN HD; ESPN2 HD; ESPNews; ESPNU; FSN HD; FXM; FYI; HD Theater; History HD; History International; HRTV; Investigation Discovery; Jewelry Television; LMN; MC; MTV Classic; MTV Hits; MTV Jams; MTV Live; MTV2; Nick 2; Nick Jr.; Nicktoons; OWN: Oprah Winfrey Network; RFD-TV; TeenNick; The Weather Channel HD; TNT HD; Universal HD; UP; USA Network HD; VH1 Soul.

Digital Pay Service 1
Pay Units: N.A.
Programming (via satellite): Cinemax (multiplexed); Cinemax HD; Flix; HBO (multiplexed); HBO HD; Showtime (multiplexed); Starz (multiplexed); Starz Encore (multiplexed); Starz HD; The Movie Channel (multiplexed).
Fee: $16.00 monthly (each).
Video-On-Demand: Planned
Pay-Per-View
iN DEMAND (delivered digitally); Playboy TV (delivered digitally); Fresh (delivered digitally); Shorteez (delivered digitally).

Kentucky—Cable Systems

Internet Service
Operational: Yes.
Subscribers: 3,439.
Fee: $40.00 installation; $31.99 monthly.

Telephone Service
Digital: Operational
Subscribers: 1,694.
Miles of Plant: 844.0 (coaxial); 385.0 (fiber optic). Homes passed: 13,941.
Chairman & Chief Executive Officer: Glenn A. Britt. President & Chief Operations Officer: Robert D. Marcus.
Ownership: Time Warner Cable (MSO).

MALONETON—Time Warner Cable. Now served by VANCEBURG, KY [KY0286]. ICA: KY0149.

MANCHESTER—Formerly served by C & W Cable. No longer in operation. ICA: KY0211.

MARION—Mediacom, 90 Main St, Benton, KY 42025-1132. Phones: 845-695-2762; 417-875-5560 (Springfield regional office); 270-527-9939. Fax: 270-527-0813. Web Site: http://www.mediacomcable.com. Also serves Caldwell County, Crittenden County, Fredonia, Princeton & Salem. ICA: KY0071.
TV Market Ranking: 69 (Crittenden County (portions), Fredonia, Salem; Below 100 (Caldwell County (portions), MARION, Princeton, Crittenden County (portions)); Outside TV Markets (Caldwell County (portions)). Franchise award date: N.A. Franchise expiration date: N.A. Began: September 1, 1982.
Channel capacity: N.A. Channels available but not in use: N.A.

Basic Service
Subscribers: 1,421.
Programming (received off-air): KFVS-TV (CBS, CW, MeTV) Cape Girardeau; WDKA (MNT, The Country Network) Paducah; WEHT (ABC) Evansville; WEVV-TV (CBS, FOX) Evansville; WKMA-TV (PBS) Madisonville; WPSD-TV (Antenna TV, NBC) Paducah; WSIL-TV (ABC) Harrisburg; WSMV-TV (COZI TV, NBC, TNN) Nashville; WTVF (CBS, Laff, This TV) Nashville; WTVW (CW, MeTV) Evansville.
Programming (via satellite): Pop; WGN America.
Fee: $36.95 installation; $40.00 monthly.

Expanded Basic Service 1
Subscribers: N.A.
Programming (via satellite): A&E; AMC; Animal Planet; BET; Bravo; Cartoon Network; CMT; CNBC; CNN; Comedy Central; C-SPAN; Discovery Channel; Discovery Life Channel; Disney Channel; E! HD; ESPN; ESPN2; Food Network; Fox News Channel; Fox Sports 1; Freeform; FX; Hallmark Channel; HGTV; History; HLN; INSP; Lifetime; MSNBC; MTV; Nickelodeon; Outdoor Channel; QVC; Spike TV; Syfy; TBS; The Weather Channel; TLC; Travel Channel; Trinity Broadcasting Network (TBN); Turner Classic Movies; TV Land; Univision Studios; USA Network; VH1; WE tv.

Digital Basic Service
Subscribers: N.A.
Programming (via satellite): BBC America; Bloomberg Television; Discovery Digital Networks; Fuse; FXM; FYI; Golf Channel; GSN; History International; IFC; LMN; MC; National Geographic Channel; NBCSN; Nick Jr.; Nicktoons; TeenNick; Turner Classic Movies.

Digital Pay Service 1
Pay Units: N.A.
Programming (via satellite): Cinemax (multiplexed); Flix; HBO (multiplexed); Showtime (multiplexed); Starz (multiplexed); Starz Encore (multiplexed); Sundance TV; The Movie Channel (multiplexed).

Video-On-Demand: No

Pay-Per-View
Mediacom PPV (delivered digitally); Playboy TV (delivered digitally); TEN Clips (delivered digitally); TEN Blox (delivered digitally).

Internet Service
Operational: Yes, DSL.
Broadband Service: Mediacom High Speed Internet.

Telephone Service
Digital: Operational
Miles of Plant: 128.0 (coaxial); None (fiber optic).
Regional Vice President: Bill Copeland. Vice President, Financial Reporting: Kenneth J. Kohrs. General Manager: Dale Haney. Regional Technical Operations Director: Alan Freedman. Marketing Director: Will Kuebler. Technical Operations Manager: Jeff Brown. Marketing Manager: Melanie Westerman.
Ownership: Mediacom LLC (MSO).

MARSHALL COUNTY—Mediacom, 90 Main St, Benton, KY 42025-1132. Phones: 845-695-2762; 417-875-5560 (Springfield regional office); 270-527-9939. Fax: 270-527-0813. Web Site: http://www.mediacomcable.com. Also serves Calloway County (portions), Dexter & Hardin. ICA: KY0035.
TV Market Ranking: 69 (Calloway County (portions), Dexter, Hardin, MARSHALL COUNTY); Below 100 (Calloway County (portions)); Outside TV Markets (Calloway County (portions)). Franchise award date: N.A. Franchise expiration date: N.A. Began: December 10, 1983.
Channel capacity: N.A. Channels available but not in use: N.A.

Basic Service
Subscribers: 3,562.
Programming (received off-air): KBSI (FOX) Cape Girardeau; KFVS-TV (CBS, CW, MeTV) Cape Girardeau; WDKA (MNT, The Country Network) Paducah; WKMU (PBS) Murray; WPSD-TV (Antenna TV, NBC) Paducah; WQTV-LP (CW) Murray; WSIL-TV (ABC) Harrisburg; WTCT (IND) Marion.
Programming (via satellite): Pop.
Fee: $36.95 installation; $40.00 monthly.

Expanded Basic Service 1
Subscribers: N.A.
Programming (via satellite): A&E; AMC; Animal Planet; Bravo; Cartoon Network; CMT; CNBC; CNN; Comedy Central; C-SPAN; Discovery Channel; Discovery Life Channel; Disney Channel; E! HD; ESPN; ESPN2; Food Network; Fox News Channel; Fox Sports 1; Freeform; FX; Golf Channel; Hallmark Channel; HGTV; History; HLN; INSP; Lifetime; MSNBC; MTV; Nickelodeon; Outdoor Channel; QVC; Spike TV; Syfy; TBS; The Weather Channel; TLC; TNT; Travel Channel; Trinity Broadcasting Network (TBN); TV Land; Univision Studios; USA Network; VH1; WE tv; WGN America.

Digital Basic Service
Subscribers: N.A.
Programming (via satellite): BBC America; Bloomberg Television; Destination America; Discovery Kids Channel; DMX Music; FXM; FYI; GSN; History; IFC; Investigation Discovery; LMN; National Geographic Channel; NBCSN; Nick Jr.; Nicktoons; OWN: Oprah Winfrey Network; TeenNick; Turner Classic Movies.

Digital Pay Service 1
Pay Units: N.A.
Programming (via satellite): Cinemax (multiplexed); Flix (multiplexed); HBO (multiplexed); Showtime (multiplexed); Starz (multiplexed); Starz Encore (multiplexed); Sundance TV (multiplexed); The Movie Channel.

Video-On-Demand: No

Internet Service
Operational: Yes.
Broadband Service: Mediacom High Speed Internet.

Telephone Service
Analog: Not Operational
Digital: Operational
Miles of Plant: 468.0 (coaxial); 23.0 (fiber optic). Homes passed: 5,412.
Regional Vice President: Bill Copeland. Vice President, Financial Reporting: Kenneth J. Kohrs. General Manager: Dale Haney. Regional Technical Operations Director: Alan Freedman. Marketing Director: Will Kuebler. Technical Operations Manager: Jeff Brown. Marketing Manager: Melanie Westerman.
Ownership: Mediacom LLC (MSO).

MARTINS FORK—Formerly served by Tri-State Cable TV. No longer in operation. ICA: KY0311.

MAYFIELD—Time Warner Cable, 13820 Sunrise Valley Dr, Herndon, VA 20171. Phones: 859-431-0300; 212-364-8200. Web Site: http://www.timewarnercable.com. Also serves Benton, Calloway County, Calvert City, Fulton, Graves County (portions) & Murray, KY; Bradford, Dyer, Gibson County, Hornbeak, Kenton, Lake County (portions), Obion County (portions), Ridgely, Rutherford, Samburg, South Fulton, Tiptonville & Wynnburg, TN. ICA: KY0037.
TV Market Ranking: 69 (Benton, Calloway County (portions), Calvert City, Graves County (portions), MAYFIELD); Below 100 (Bradford, Gibson County (portions), Dyer, Obion County (portions)); Outside TV Markets (Gibson County (portions), Hornbeak, Kenton, Lake County (portions), Ridgely, Rutherford, Samburg, Wynnburg, Fulton, Murray, Obion County (portions), South Fulton, Tiptonville, Calloway County (portions)). Franchise award date: N.A. Franchise expiration date: N.A. Began: January 1, 1966.
Channel capacity: N.A. Channels available but not in use: N.A.

Basic Service
Subscribers: 8,318. Commercial subscribers: 239.
Programming (received off-air): KBSI (FOX) Cape Girardeau; KFVS-TV (CBS, CW, MeTV) Cape Girardeau; WBBJ-TV (ABC, CBS, MeTV) Jackson; WDKA (MNT, The Country Network) Paducah; WKMU (PBS) Murray; WKRN-TV (ABC) Nashville; WNPT (PBS) Nashville; WPSD-TV (Antenna TV, NBC) Paducah; WQWQ-LP (CW, MeTV) Paducah; WSIL-TV (ABC) Harrisburg; WSMV-TV (COZI TV, NBC, TNN) Nashville; WTCT (IND) Marion; WTVF (CBS, Laff, This TV) Nashville; 17 FMs.
Programming (via satellite): INSP; QVC; WGN America.
Fee: $40.00 installation; $23.99 monthly.

Expanded Basic Service 1
Subscribers: N.A.
Programming (via satellite): A&E; AMC; Animal Planet; BET; Cartoon Network; CMT; CNBC; CNN; Comcast/Charter Sports Southeast (CSS); Comedy Central; C-SPAN; C-SPAN 2; Discovery Channel; Discovery Life Channel; Disney Channel; E! HD; ESPN; ESPN Classic; ESPN2; EWTN Global Catholic Network; Food Network; Fox News Channel; Fox Sports 1; Freeform; FX; Golf Channel; GSN; Hallmark Channel; HGTV; History; HLN; ION Television; Lifetime; MSNBC; MTV; National Geographic Channel; NBCSN; Nickelodeon; Outdoor Channel; Oxygen; Pop; Spike TV; Syfy; TBS; The Weather Channel; TLC; TNT; Travel Channel; truTV; Turner Classic Movies; TV Land; USA Network; VH1.

Digital Basic Service
Subscribers: N.A.
Programming (via satellite): A&E HD; AXS TV; BBC America; Bloomberg Television; Boomerang; Cloo; CMT; CNN en Espanol; Destination America; Discovery Kids Channel; Discovery Life Channel; Disney XD; DIY Network; ESPN Classic; ESPN HD; ESPN2 HD; ESPNews; ESPNU; FSN HD; FXM; FYI; Great American Country; HD Theater; History HD; History International; HRTV; Investigation Discovery; LMN; MC; MTV Classic; MTV Hits; MTV Jams; MTV Live; MTV2; Nick 2; Nick Jr.; Nicktoons; TeenNick; The Weather Channel HD; TNT HD; Tr3s; Universal HD; UP; Versus HD; VH1 Soul.

Digital Pay Service 1
Pay Units: N.A.
Programming (via satellite): Cinemax (multiplexed); Cinemax HD; Flix; HBO (multiplexed); HBO HD; Showtime (multiplexed); Starz (multiplexed); Starz Encore (multiplexed); Starz HD; The Movie Channel (multiplexed).

Video-On-Demand: No

Pay-Per-View
iN DEMAND (delivered digitally); SexSee (delivered digitally); VaVoom (delivered digitally); Juicy (delivered digitally).

Internet Service
Operational: Yes.
Fee: $40.00 installation; $31.99 monthly.

Telephone Service
Digital: Operational
Fee: $24.99 monthly
Miles of Plant: 141.0 (coaxial); None (fiber optic).
Chairman & Chief Executive Officer: Glenn A. Britt. Senior Technical Analyst: Cameron Miller.
Ownership: Time Warner Cable (MSO).

MAYKING—TVS Cable, PO Box 1410, Hindman, KY 41822-1410. Phones: 606-946-2600; 606-785-3450; 606-633-0778.

Cable Systems—Kentucky

Fax: 606-785-3110. E-mail: tvs@tvscable.com. Web Site: http://www.tvscable.com. Also serves Ermine & Thornton. ICA: KY0337.
TV Market Ranking: Below 100 (Ermine, MAYKING, Thornton).
Channel capacity: N.A. Channels available but not in use: N.A.
Basic Service
Subscribers: 715. Commercial subscribers: 8.
Fee: $50.00 installation; $23.50 monthly.
Internet Service
Operational: Yes.
Fee: $24.95–$79.95 monthly.
Vice President & General Manager: William K. Grigsby.
Ownership: TV Service Inc. (MSO).

MAYSVILLE—Limestone Bracken Cablevision, 626 Forest Ave, PO Box 100, Maysville, KY 41056. Phone: 606-564-9220. Fax: 606-564-4291. E-mail: limestone@maysvilleky.net. Web Site: http://www.limestonecable.com. Also serves Mason County. ICA: KY0033.
TV Market Ranking: Outside TV Markets (Mason County, MAYSVILLE). Franchise award date: January 1, 1960. Franchise expiration date: N.A. Began: January 1, 1960.
Channel capacity: N.A. Channels available but not in use: N.A.
Basic Service
Subscribers: 4,060.
Programming (received off-air): WCPO-TV (ABC, Escape) Cincinnati; WKMR (PBS) Morehead; WKRC-TV (CBS, CW) Cincinnati; WKYT-TV (CBS, CW) Lexington; WLEX-TV (MeTV, NBC) Lexington; WLWT (MeTV, NBC) Cincinnati; WSTR-TV (Antenna TV, MNT) Cincinnati; WTVQ-DT (ABC, Antenna TV, Laff, MNT) Lexington; WXIX-TV (Bounce TV, FOX) Newport; allband FM.
Programming (via satellite): QVC; WGN America.
Fee: $40.00 installation; $27.00 monthly.
Expanded Basic Service 1
Subscribers: N.A.
Programming (via satellite): A&E; AMC; Animal Planet; BET; CMT; CNBC; CNN; Comedy Central; C-SPAN; Discovery Channel; Disney Channel; E! HD; ESPN; ESPN2; EWTN Global Catholic Network; Food Network; Fox News Channel; Fox Sports 1; FOX Sports Ohio/Sports Time Ohio; Freeform; FX; Great American Country; History; HLN; Lifetime; LMN; MTV; National Geographic Channel; Nickelodeon; Outdoor Channel; Spike TV; Syfy; TBS; The Weather Channel; TLC; TNT; Travel Channel; Trinity Broadcasting Network (TBN); truTV; TV Land; USA Network; VH1.
Fee: $35.00 installation; $37.30 monthly.
Digital Basic Service
Subscribers: N.A.
Programming (via satellite): BBC America; Bloomberg Television; Bravo; Cloo; Discovery Life Channel; Disney XD; DMX Music; ESPN Classic; ESPNews; FXM; FYI; Golf Channel; GSN; HGTV; History International; IFC; Nick Jr.; Nicktoons; Starz Encore (multiplexed); TeenNick; Turner Classic Movies.
Pay Service 1
Pay Units: 333.
Programming (via satellite): HBO.
Fee: $12.95 monthly.
Pay Service 2
Pay Units: 143.
Programming (via satellite): Showtime.
Fee: $12.95 monthly.

Digital Pay Service 1
Pay Units: N.A.
Programming (via satellite): Cinemax (multiplexed); Flix; HBO (multiplexed); Showtime (multiplexed); Starz (multiplexed); The Movie Channel (multiplexed).
Fee: $12.95 monthly.
Video-On-Demand: No
Pay-Per-View
Special events, Addressable: No.
Internet Service
Operational: Yes.
Broadband Service: In-house.
Fee: $21.95–$64.95 monthly.
Telephone Service
None
Miles of Plant: 153.0 (coaxial); 30.0 (fiber optic). Homes passed: 6,500.
Vice President: Jeff Cracraft. General Manager: Ron Buerkley. Chief Technician: Jeff Mason. Customer Service Manager: Jean Black.
Ownership: Standard Tobacco Co. Inc. (MSO).

McCREARY COUNTY (portions)—Access Cable Television Inc, 302 Enterprise Dr, Somerset, KY 42501. Phone: 606-677-2444. Fax: 606-677-2443. E-mail: cable@accesshsd.net. Web Site: http://www.accesshsd.com. ICA: KY0331.
TV Market Ranking: Below 100 (MCCREARY COUNTY (PORTIONS)).
Channel capacity: N.A. Channels available but not in use: N.A.
Basic Service
Subscribers: 2,123.
Fee: $28.50 monthly.
President & General Manager: Roy Baker.
Ownership: Access Cable Television Inc. (MSO).

MCKINNEY—Time Warner Cable. Now served by CORBIN, KY [KY0030]. ICA: KY0297.

MIDDLESBORO—Time Warner Cable. Now served by CORBIN, KY [KY0030]. ICA: KY0034.

MIDWAY—Time Warner Cable. Now served by RICHMOND, KY [KY0008]. ICA: KY0154.

MILLVILLE—Formerly served by Chumley's Antenna Systems Inc. No longer in operation. ICA: KY0196.

MONTICELLO—Community Telecom Services, 49 Hardwood Dr, PO Box 579, Monticello, KY 42633. Phones: 606-348-0286 (Lisa Guinn, office mgr); 606-348-8416. Fax: 606-348-6397. E-mail: sales@ctsmediagroup.com. Web Site: http://www.ctsmediagroup.com. Also serves Wayne County. ICA: KY0047.
TV Market Ranking: Below 100 (Wayne County (portions)); Outside TV Markets (MONTICELLO, Wayne County (portions)). Franchise award date: May 12, 1980. Franchise expiration date: N.A. Began: November 1, 1960.
Channel capacity: N.A. Channels available but not in use: N.A.
Basic Service
Subscribers: 1,764. Commercial subscribers: 725.
Programming (received off-air): WBIR-TV (MeTV, NBC) Knoxville; WDKY-TV (FOX) Danville; WKSO-TV (PBS) Somerset; WKYT-TV (CBS, CW) Lexington; WLEX-TV (MeTV, NBC) Lexington; WTVQ-DT (ABC, Antenna TV, Laff, MNT) Lexington; 3 FMs.
Programming (via satellite): A&E; AMC; CMT; C-SPAN; CW PLUS; Discovery Channel; ESPN; ESPN2; Fox News Channel; FOX Sports Ohio/Sports Time Ohio; FX; HGTV; History; HLN; MTV; Nickelodeon; QVC; Syfy; Trinity Broadcasting Network (TBN); TV Land; VH1.
Fee: $19.50 monthly; $1.00 converter.
Expanded Basic Service 1
Subscribers: N.A.
Programming (via satellite): Lifetime; The Weather Channel; TNT; USA Network.
Fee: $2.58 monthly.
Expanded Basic Service 2
Subscribers: N.A.
Programming (via satellite): CNN; Disney Channel; Freeform; Spike TV; TBS; WGN America.
Fee: $7.12 monthly.
Pay Service 1
Pay Units: N.A.
Programming (via satellite): Cinemax; HBO; Showtime; The Movie Channel.
Fee: $15.00 installation; $10.95 monthly (Cinemax, Showtime or TMC), $11.95 monthly (HBO).
Video-On-Demand: No
Internet Service
Operational: Yes.
Fee: $34.95 monthly.
Telephone Service
None
Miles of Plant: 154.0 (coaxial); None (fiber optic). Homes passed: 4,209.
General Manager: Dale Hancock. Office Manager: Lisa Guinn.
Ownership: Community Telecom Services (MSO).

MOREHEAD—Time Warner Cable. Now served by RICHMOND, KY [KY0008]. ICA: KY0031.

MOREHEAD STATE UNIVERSITY—Morehead State University, 150 University Blvd, Dept. of Communications, Morehead, KY 40351. Phones: 800-585-6781; 606-783-2675. Fax: 606-783-5078. Web Site: http://www.moreheadstate.edu. ICA: KY0091.
TV Market Ranking: Below 100 (MOREHEAD STATE UNIVERSITY). Franchise award date: N.A. Franchise expiration date: N.A. Began: January 1, 1966.
Channel capacity: 64 (not 2-way capable). Channels available but not in use: N.A.
Basic Service
Subscribers: N.A.
Programming (received off-air): WDKY-TV (FOX) Danville; WKMR (PBS) Morehead; WKYT-TV (CBS, CW) Lexington; WTVQ-DT (ABC, Antenna TV, Laff, MNT) Lexington; WXIX-TV (Bounce TV, FOX) Newport; WYMT-TV (CBS, CW) Hazard.
Programming (via satellite): Bloomberg Television; Cartoon Network; CNBC; CNN; CNN International; C-SPAN; C-SPAN 2; Discovery Life Channel; HLN; MSNBC; Nickelodeon; The Weather Channel; TLC; USA Network.

Expanded Basic Service 1
Subscribers: N.A.
Programming (via satellite): A&E; AMC; Animal Planet; BET; CMT; Comedy Central; Discovery Channel; E! HD; ESPN; ESPN Classic; ESPN2; ESPNews; Freeform; GSN; History; Lifetime; MTV; MTV2; Spike TV; Syfy; TBS; TNT; truTV; Turner Classic Movies; VH1.
Fee: $10.00 monthly.
Video-On-Demand: Planned
Internet Service
Operational: No.
Telephone Service
None
Miles of Plant: 4.0 (coaxial); None (fiber optic). Homes passed: 1,664.
General Manager: Mike Hogge. Chief Technician: Jeff Smedley. Marketing Director: Taunya Jones.
Ownership: Morehead State U.

MORGANTOWN—Mediacom, 90 Main St, Benton, KY 42025-1132. Phones: 845-695-2762; 417-875-5560 (Springfield regional office); 270-527-9939. Fax: 270-527-0813. Web Site: http://www.mediacomcable.com. Also serves Brownsville, Butler County (portions) & Edmonson County. ICA: KY0096.
TV Market Ranking: Below 100 (Brownsville, Butler County (portions), Edmonson County, MORGANTOWN). Franchise award date: July 21, 1986. Franchise expiration date: N.A. Began: May 1, 1982.
Channel capacity: N.A. Channels available but not in use: N.A.
Basic Service
Subscribers: 531.
Programming (received off-air): WBKO (ABC, CW, FOX) Bowling Green; WKGB-TV (PBS) Bowling Green; WKYU-TV (PBS) Bowling Green; WNKY (CBS, NBC) Bowling Green; WPBM-CD (IND) Scottsville; WSMV-TV (COZI TV, NBC, TNN) Nashville; WTVF (CBS, Laff, This TV) Nashville; WZTV (Antenna TV, FOX, WeatherNation) Nashville.
Programming (via satellite): QVC; WGN America.
Fee: $46.75 installation; $39.95 monthly.
Expanded Basic Service 1
Subscribers: N.A.
Programming (via satellite): A&E; AMC; Animal Planet; Cartoon Network; CMT; CNBC; CNN; Comedy Central; C-SPAN; Discovery Channel; Disney Channel; E! HD; ESPN; ESPN2; EVINE Live; Food Network; Fox News Channel; Fox Sports 1; Freeform; FX; Great American Country; Hallmark Channel; HGTV; History; HLN; INSP; Lifetime; MSNBC; MTV; National Geographic Channel; Nickelodeon; Outdoor Channel; Spike TV; Syfy; TBS; The Weather Channel; TLC; TNT; Travel Channel; Trinity Broadcasting Network (TBN); Turner Classic Movies; TV Land; USA Network; VH1; WE tv.
Fee: $9.75 monthly.
Digital Basic Service
Subscribers: N.A.
Programming (via satellite): BBC America; Bloomberg Television; Discovery Digital Networks; DMX Music; ESPN Clas-

Kentucky—Cable Systems

sic; ESPNews; Fuse; FXM; FYI; Golf Channel; History International; IFC; LMN; National Geographic Channel; NBCSN; Nick Jr.; Nicktoons; TeenNick; Turner Classic Movies.
Digital Pay Service 1
Pay Units: N.A.
Programming (via satellite): Cinemax (multiplexed); HBO (multiplexed); Showtime (multiplexed); Starz (multiplexed); Starz Encore (multiplexed); The Movie Channel (multiplexed).
Video-On-Demand: No
Pay-Per-View
Playboy TV (delivered digitally); Fresh (delivered digitally); Shorteez (delivered digitally).
Internet Service
Operational: Yes.
Broadband Service: Mediacom High Speed Internet.
Telephone Service
None
Miles of Plant: 48.0 (coaxial); None (fiber optic).
Regional Vice President: Bill Copeland. Vice President, Financial Reporting: Kenneth J. Kohrs. General Manager: Dale Haney. Regional Technical Operations Director: Alan Freedman. Marketing Director: Will Kuebler. Technical Operations Manager: Jeff Brown. Marketing Manager: Melanie Westerman.
Ownership: Mediacom LLC (MSO).

MOUNT STERLING—Time Warner Cable. Now served by RICHMOND, KY [KY0008]. ICA: KY0046.

MOUNT VERNON—Formerly served by Charter Communications. Now served by Time Warner Cable, CORBIN, KY [KY0030]. ICA: KY0260.

MOUSIE—TVS Cable, PO Box 1410, Hindman, KY 41822-1410. Phones: 606-946-2600; 606-785-3450; 606-633-0778. Fax: 606-785-3110. E-mail: tvs@tvscable.com. Web Site: http://www.tvscable.com. ICA: KY0336.
TV Market Ranking: Below 100 (MOUSIE).
Channel capacity: N.A. Channels available but not in use: N.A.
Basic Service
Subscribers: 295.
Fee: $50.00 installation; $23.50 monthly.
Internet Service
Operational: Yes.
Fee: $24.95–$79.95 monthly.
Vice President & General Manager: William K. Grigsby.
Ownership: TV Service Inc. (MSO).

MOZELLE—Crystal Broadband Networks, PO Box 180336, Chicago, IL 60618. Phones: 817-685-9588; 630-200-0447. E-mail: sales@crystalbn.com. Web Site: http://crystalbn.com. Also serves Bledsoe & Helton. ICA: KY0261.
TV Market Ranking: Below 100 (Bledsoe, Helton, MOZELLE).
Channel capacity: N.A. Channels available but not in use: N.A.
Basic Service
Subscribers: 99.
Programming (received off-air): WAGV (IND) Harlan; WBIR-TV (MeTV, NBC) Knoxville; WCYB-TV (CW, Decades, NBC) Bristol; WEMT (FOX, Movies!, This TV) Greeneville; WJHL-TV (ABC, CBS, MeTV) Johnson City; WKHA (PBS) Hazard; WKPT-TV (COZI TV, Escape, MeTV, MNT) Kingsport; WLEX-TV (MeTV, NBC) Lexington; WTVQ-DT (ABC, Antenna TV, Laff, MNT) Lexington; WYMT-TV (CBS, CW) Hazard.
Programming (via satellite): INSP; WGN America.
Fee: $29.95 installation; $48.30 monthly; $2.00 converter.
Expanded Basic Service 1
Subscribers: N.A.
Programming (via satellite): A&E; AMC; CMT; CNN; Discovery Channel; Disney Channel; ESPN; ESPN2; Freeform; FX; Lifetime; Nickelodeon; QVC; Spike TV; TBS; TLC; TNT; Trinity Broadcasting Network (TBN); USA Network; VH1.
Fee: $26.65 monthly.
Digital Basic Service
Subscribers: N.A.
Programming (via satellite): BBC America; Bloomberg Television; Bravo; Discovery Life Channel; Disney XD; ESPN Classic; ESPNews; Fox Sports 1; Fuse; FXM; FYI; Golf Channel; Great American Country; GSN; HGTV; History; History International; IFC; LMN; MTV Classic; MTV2; National Geographic Channel; NBCSN; Nick Jr.; Nicktoons; Outdoor Channel; Syfy; TeenNick; The Word Network; Turner Classic Movies; VH1 Country; WE tv.
Digital Pay Service 1
Pay Units: N.A.
Programming (via satellite): Cinemax (multiplexed); HBO (multiplexed); Showtime (multiplexed); Starz (multiplexed); Starz Encore (multiplexed); The Movie Channel (multiplexed).
Fee: $15.95 monthly (each).
Video-On-Demand: No
Pay-Per-View
Playboy TV (delivered digitally); Fresh (delivered digitally).
Internet Service
Operational: No.
Telephone Service
None
Miles of Plant: 45.0 (coaxial); None (fiber optic). Homes passed: 981.
General Manager: Ron Page. Program Manager: Shawn Smith.
Ownership: Crystal Broadband Networks (MSO).

MURRAY—Murray Electric System, 401 Olive St, PO Box 1095, Murray, KY 42071. Phone: 270-753-5312. Fax: 270-761-5781. E-mail: murrayelectric@murray-ky.net. Web Site: http://www2.murray-ky.net. ICA: KY0321. **Note:** This system is an overbuild.
TV Market Ranking: 69 (MURRAY).
Channel capacity: 77 (operating 2-way). Channels available but not in use: N.A.

Basic Service
Subscribers: 2,899.
Programming (received off-air): KBSI (FOX) Cape Girardeau; KFVS-TV (CBS, CW, MeTV) Cape Girardeau; WBBJ-TV (ABC, CBS, MeTV) Jackson; WDKA (MNT, The Country Network) Paducah; WKMU (PBS) Murray; WKRN-TV (ABC) Nashville; WNPT (PBS) Nashville; WPSD-TV (Antenna TV, NBC) Paducah; WQWQ-LP (CW, MeTV) Paducah; WSIL-TV (ABC) Harrisburg; WSMV-TV (COZI TV, NBC, TNN) Nashville; WTVF (CBS, Laff, This TV) Nashville.
Fee: $13.00 monthly.
Expanded Basic Service 1
Subscribers: 2,219.
Programming (via satellite): A&E; AMC; Animal Planet; BET; Boomerang; Cartoon Network; CMT; CNBC; CNN; Comedy Central; C-SPAN; C-SPAN 2; Discovery Channel; Discovery Life Channel; Disney Channel; E! HD; ESPN; ESPN Classic; ESPN2; ESPNews; Food Network; Fox News Channel; Fox Sports 1; Freeform; FX; FXM; Golf Channel; Hallmark Channel; HGTV; History; HLN; INSP; ION Television; Lifetime; MSNBC; MTV; National Geographic Channel; Nickelodeon; Outdoor Channel; Ovation; Pop; Spike TV; Starz Encore; Syfy; TBS; The Weather Channel; TLC; TNT; Travel Channel; Trinity Broadcasting Network (TBN); truTV; Turner Classic Movies; TV Land; USA Network; VH1; WE tv; WGN America.
Fee: $27.45 monthly.
Digital Basic Service
Subscribers: N.A.
Programming (via satellite): BBC America; Bloomberg Television; Bravo; CMT; Discovery Digital Networks; Disney XD; DIY Network; DMX Music; ESPNU; Fuse; FYI; Great American Country; GSN; History International; LMN; NBCSN; Nick Jr.; Nicktoons; Oxygen; TeenNick.
Digital Pay Service 1
Pay Units: N.A.
Programming (via satellite): Cinemax (multiplexed); HBO (multiplexed); Showtime (multiplexed); Starz (multiplexed); Starz Encore (multiplexed).
Fee: $8.95 monthly (each).
Video-On-Demand: No
Pay-Per-View
iN DEMAND (delivered digitally); Hot Choice (delivered digitally); Playboy TV (delivered digitally).
Internet Service
Operational: Yes.
Broadband Service: In-house.
Fee: $22.45–$67.50 monthly.
Telephone Service
Digital: Operational
Fee: $29.99 monthly
Miles of Plant: 125.0 (coaxial); 18.0 (fiber optic). Homes passed: 7,100.
General Manager: Tony Thompson. Telecommunications Manager: David Richardson. Chief Technician: Joey Williams.
Ownership: Murray Electric System.

MURRAY—Time Warner Cable. Now served by MAYFIELD, KY [KY0037]. ICA: KY0025.

NEBO—Mediacom, 90 Main St, Benton, KY 42025-1132. Phones: 845-695-2762; 417-875-5560 (Springfield regional office); 270-527-9939. Fax: 270-527-0813. Web Site: http://www.mediacomcable.com. Also serves Hopkins County. ICA: KY0146.
TV Market Ranking: 86 (Hopkins County (portions)); Below 100 (NEBO, Hopkins County (portions)). Franchise award date: N.A. Franchise expiration date: N.A. Began: January 1, 1984.
Channel capacity: N.A. Channels available but not in use: N.A.
Basic Service
Subscribers: 50.
Programming (received off-air): WEHT (ABC) Evansville; WEVV-TV (CBS, FOX) Evansville; WFIE (NBC, This TV) Evansville; WKMA-TV (PBS) Madisonville; WTVW (CW, MeTV) Evansville.
Programming (via satellite): CMT; CNN; Discovery Channel; Disney Channel; ESPN; Freeform; Hallmark Channel; Nickelodeon; QVC; Spike TV; TBS; TNT; USA Network; WGN America.
Fee: $36.95 installation; $43.60 monthly.
Pay Service 1
Pay Units: N.A.
Programming (via satellite): Cinemax; HBO; Showtime; The Movie Channel.
Fee: $10.50 monthly (Cinemax, HBO or Showtime).
Video-On-Demand: No
Internet Service
Operational: No.
Telephone Service
None
Miles of Plant: 32.0 (coaxial); None (fiber optic). Homes passed: 600.
Regional Vice President: Bill Copeland. Vice President, Financial Reporting: Kenneth J. Kohrs. General Manager: Dale Haney. Regional Technical Operations Director: Alan Freedman. Marketing Director: Will Kuebler. Technical Operations Manager: Jeff Brown. Marketing Manager: Melanie Westerman.
Ownership: Mediacom LLC (MSO).

NELSON—Formerly served by Time Warner Cable. No longer in operation. ICA: KY0262.

NEW HAVEN—Formerly served by Adelphia Communications. Now served by Time Warner Cable, LEBANON, KY [KY0049]. ICA: KY0137.

NEWPORT—Formerly served by Insight Communications. Now served by Time Warner Cable, COVINGTON, KY [KY0002]. ICA: KY0264.

NICHOLASVILLE—Time Warner Cable. Now served by RICHMOND, KY [KY0008]. ICA: KY0036.

NORTH MIDDLETOWN—Time Warner Cable. Now served by RICHMOND, KY [KY0008]. ICA: KY0169.

NORTONVILLE—Mediacom, 90 Main St, Benton, KY 42025-1132. Phones: 845-695-2762; 417-875-5560 (Springfield regional office); 270-527-9939. Fax: 270-527-0813. Web Site: http://www.mediacomcable.com. Also serves Christian County, Crofton & Hopkins County (portions). ICA: KY0097.
TV Market Ranking: Below 100 (Christian County (portions), Crofton, Hopkins County (portions), NORTONVILLE); Outside TV Markets (Christian County (portions)). Franchise award date: N.A. Franchise expiration date: N.A. Began: May 1, 1983.
Channel capacity: N.A. Channels available but not in use: N.A.
Basic Service
Subscribers: 330.
Programming (received off-air): KFVS-TV (CBS, CW, MeTV) Cape Girardeau; WAZE-LP Evansville; WDKA (MNT, The Country Network) Paducah; WEHT (ABC) Evans-

Cable Systems—Kentucky

ville; WEVV-TV (CBS, FOX) Evansville; WFIE (NBC, This TV) Evansville; WKMA-TV (PBS) Madisonville; WPSD-TV (Antenna TV, NBC) Paducah; WSIL-TV (ABC) Harrisburg; WSMV-TV (COZI TV, NBC, TNN) Nashville; WTVF (CBS, Laff, This TV) Nashville; WTVW (CW, MeTV) Evansville. Programming (via satellite): Pop; WGN America.
Fee: $36.95 installation; $40.00 monthly.

Expanded Basic Service 1
Subscribers: N.A.
Programming (via satellite): A&E; AMC; Animal Planet; BET; Cartoon Network; CMT; CNBC; CNN; Comedy Central; C-SPAN; Discovery Channel; Discovery Life Channel; Disney Channel; E! HD; ESPN; ESPN2; Food Network; Fox News Channel; Fox Sports 1; Freeform; FX; Hallmark Channel; HGTV; History; HLN; INSP; Lifetime; MSNBC; MTV; Nickelodeon; Outdoor Channel; QVC; Spike TV; Syfy; TBS; The Weather Channel; TLC; TNT; Travel Channel; Trinity Broadcasting Network (TBN); TV Land; Univision Studios; USA Network; VH1; WE tv.

Digital Basic Service
Subscribers: N.A.
Programming (via satellite): BBC America; Bloomberg Television; Discovery Digital Networks; DMX Music; Fuse; FXM; FYI; Golf Channel; GSN; History International; IFC; LMN; MTV Classic; MTV Hits; MTV2; National Geographic Channel; NBCSN; Nick Jr.; Nicktoons; TeenNick; Turner Classic Movies.

Digital Pay Service 1
Pay Units: N.A.
Programming (via satellite): Cinemax (multiplexed); Flix (multiplexed); HBO (multiplexed); Showtime (multiplexed); Starz (multiplexed); Starz Encore (multiplexed); Sundance TV (multiplexed); The Movie Channel (multiplexed).

Video-On-Demand: No

Pay-Per-View
Playboy TV (delivered digitally); TEN Clips (delivered digitally); TEN Blox (delivered digitally).

Internet Service
Operational: Yes.
Broadband Service: Mediacom High Speed Internet.

Telephone Service
Digital: Operational
Miles of Plant: 50.0 (coaxial); None (fiber optic). Homes passed: 1,474.
Regional Vice President: Bill Copeland. Vice President, Financial Reporting: Kenneth J. Kohrs. General Manager: Dale Haney. Regional Technical Operations Director: Alan Freedman. Marketing Director: Will Kuebler. Technical Operations Manager: Jeff Brown. Marketing Manager: Melanie Westerman.
Ownership: Mediacom LLC (MSO).

OAK GROVE—Mediacom. Now served by TRENTON, KY [KY0101]. ICA: KY0105.

OLIVE HILL—Time Warner Cable. Now served by RICHMOND, KY [KY0008]. ICA: KY0099.

OWENSBORO—Time Warner Cable, 100 Industrial Dr, Owensboro, KY 42301-8711. Phone: 270-852-2000. Fax: 270-688-8378. Web Site: http://www.timewarnercable.com. Also serves Equality (village), Junction (village), Old Shawneetown (village), Ridgway (village) & Shawneetown, IL; Hatfield, Rockport & Spencer County (portions), IN; Baskett, Calhoun, Corydon, Daviess County (portions), Gallatin County (portions), Henderson (town), Henderson County (portions), Livermore, McLean County (portions), Morganfield, Robards, Sturgis, Union County (portions), Uniontown, Waverly & Webster County (portions), KY. ICA: KY0004.
TV Market Ranking: 69 (Equality (village), Gallatin County (portions), Junction (village), Old Shawneetown (village), Ridgway (village), Shawneetown); 86 (Baskett, Calhoun, Corydon, Daviess County (portions), Henderson (town), Henderson County (portions), McLean County (portions), Morganfield, OWENSBORO, Robards, Rockport, Spencer County (portions), Sturgis, Uniontown, Waverly); Below 100 (Webster County (portions), Livermore, Daviess County (portions), McLean County (portions)); Outside TV Markets (Daviess County (portions)). Franchise award date: N.A. Franchise expiration date: N.A. Began: January 1, 1967.
Channel capacity: N.A. Channels available but not in use: N.A.

Basic Service
Subscribers: 29,394.
Programming (received off-air): WDRB (Antenna TV, FOX) Louisville; WEHT (ABC) Evansville; WEVV-TV (CBS, FOX) Evansville; WFIE (NBC, This TV) Evansville; WKMU (PBS) Murray; WNIN (PBS) Evansville; WTVW (CW, MeTV) Evansville. Programming (via satellite): A&E; AMC; Animal Planet; BET; Bravo; Cartoon Network; CMT; CNBC; CNN; Comedy Central; C-SPAN; C-SPAN 2; Discovery Channel; E! HD; ESPN; ESPN2; EVINE Live; EWTN Global Catholic Network; Freeform; FX; Golf Channel; Hallmark Channel; HGTV; History; HLN; Lifetime; MSNBC; MTV; Nickelodeon; Oxygen; Pop; QVC; Spike TV; Syfy; The Weather Channel; TLC; TNT; Travel Channel; Trinity Broadcasting Network (TBN); truTV; TV Land; USA Network; VH1; WE tv; WGN America.
Fee: $29.99 installation; $20.99 monthly; $1.00 converter.

Expanded Basic Service 1
Subscribers: N.A.
Programming (via satellite): CNN; Disney Channel; Disney XD; ESPN Classic; Food Network; Fox News Channel; Fox Sports 1; NBCSN; TBS.
Fee: $12.54 monthly.

Digital Basic Service
Subscribers: N.A.
Programming (via satellite): BBC America; Bloomberg Television; Discovery Life Channel; DIY Network; ESPNews; FYI; Great American Country; GSN; History International; INSP; MC; Outdoor Channel.

Digital Expanded Basic Service
Subscribers: N.A.
Programming (via satellite): FOX College Sports Central; FOX College Sports Pacific; FXM; IFC; National Geographic Channel; Nick 2; Nick Jr.; Nicktoons; Sundance TV; TeenNick; Turner Classic Movies.
Fee: $6.00 monthly (per tier).

Digital Pay Service 1
Pay Units: N.A.
Programming (via satellite): Cinemax (multiplexed); Flix; HBO (multiplexed); HITS (Headend In The Sky); RAI Italia; RTN; Showtime (multiplexed); Starz (multiplexed); Starz Encore (multiplexed); TAC TV; The Filipino Channel; The Movie Channel (multiplexed); TV Asia; TV5; La Television International; Zee TV.
Fee: $14.00 monthly (each).

Video-On-Demand: Yes

Pay-Per-View
Playboy TV (delivered digitally); HITS PPV (delivered digitally); Hot Choice (delivered digitally); Shorteez (delivered digitally); Fresh (delivered digitally).

Internet Service
Operational: Yes.
Subscribers: 18,103.
Broadband Service: Road Runner.
Fee: $99.95 installation; $44.95 monthly.

Telephone Service
Digital: Operational
Subscribers: 4,806.
Fee: $44.95 monthly
Miles of Plant: 1,930.0 (coaxial); 910.0 (fiber optic). Homes passed: 73,992.
General Manager: Chris Poynter. Technical Operations Director: Don Collins. Marketing Manager: Don Rodgers.
Ownership: Time Warner Cable (MSO).

OWENTON—Inside Connect Cable (formerly Kentucky Ridge Country Communications), 4890 Knob Creek Rd, Brooks, KS 40109. Phone: 855-552-2253. Fax: 502-543-7553. E-mail: sales@insideconnect.net. Also serves Owen County (portions). ICA: KY0342.
Channel capacity: N.A. Channels available but not in use: N.A.

Basic Service
Subscribers: 379.
Fee: $40.00 installation; $55.56 monthly.
Ownership: Inside Connect Cable LLC.

OWINGSVILLE—Time Warner Cable. Now served by RICHMOND, KY [KY0008]. ICA: KY0139.

PADUCAH (town)—Comcast Cable. Now served by ELIZABETHTOWN, KY [KY0012]. ICA: KY0005.

PADUCAH (town)—Formerly served by NDW II Inc. No longer in operation. ICA: KY0305.

PAINTSVILLE—Formerly served by Charter Communications. Now served by Suddenlink Communications, KERMIT, WV [WV0038]. ICA: KY0266.

PARIS—Time Warner Cable. Now served by RICHMOND, KY [KY0008]. ICA: KY0043.

PARK CITY—Mediacom, 90 Main St, Benton, KY 42025-1132. Phones: 845-695-2762; 417-875-5560 (Springfield regional office); 270-527-9939. Fax: 270-527-0813. Web Site: http://www.mediacomcable.com. ICA: KY0324.
TV Market Ranking: Below 100 (PARK CITY).
Channel capacity: N.A. Channels available but not in use: N.A.

Basic Service
Subscribers: 1,012.
Programming (received off-air): WBKO (ABC, CW, FOX) Bowling Green; WKGB-TV (PBS) Bowling Green; WKYU-TV (PBS) Bowling Green; WNKY (CBS, NBC) Bowling Green; WSMV-TV (COZI TV, NBC, TNN) Nashville; WTVF (CBS, Laff, This TV) Nashville; WZTV (Antenna TV, FOX, WeatherNation) Nashville.
Programming (via satellite): A&E; AMC; Animal Planet; Cartoon Network; CMT; CNBC; CNN; Comedy Central; C-SPAN; Discovery Channel; Disney Channel; ESPN; ESPN2; EVINE Live; Food Network; Fox News Channel; Freeform; FX; HBO; HGTV; History; HLN; INSP; Lifetime; MSNBC; MTV; Nickelodeon; QVC; Spike TV; Syfy; TBS; The Weather Channel; TLC; TNT; Turner Classic Movies; USA Network; VH1; WGN America.
Fee: $41.90 monthly.

Pay Service 1
Pay Units: N.A.
Programming (via satellite): Showtime (multiplexed); The Movie Channel.

Internet Service
Operational: No.

Telephone Service
None

Regional Vice President: Bill Copeland. Vice President, Financial Reporting: Kenneth J. Kohrs. General Manager: Dale Haney. Regional Technical Operations Director: Alan Freedman. Marketing Director: Will Kuebler. Technical Operations Manager: Jeff Brown. Marketing Manager: Melanie Westerman.
Ownership: Mediacom LLC (MSO).

PARKSVILLE—Formerly served by Charter Communications. No longer in operation. ICA: KY0202.

PATHFORK—Formerly served by Suddenlink Communications. No longer in operation. ICA: KY0237.

PEOPLES—C & W Cable, 7920 Hwy 30 West, PO Box 490, Annville, KY 40402. Phone: 606-364-5357. Fax: 606-364-2138. Also serves Annville, Bond, Greenmount, Jackson County (portions), Laurel County (portions) & Tyner. ICA: KY0122.
TV Market Ranking: Below 100 (Bond, Greenmount, Jackson County (portions), PEOPLES, Tyner, Annville, Laurel County (portions)). Franchise award date: N.A. Franchise expiration date: N.A. Began: May 1, 1976.
Channel capacity: N.A. Channels available but not in use: N.A.

Basic Service
Subscribers: 165.
Programming (received off-air): WDKY-TV (FOX) Danville; WKLE (PBS) Lexington; WKYT-TV (CBS, CW) Lexington; WLEX-TV (MeTV, NBC) Lexington; WTVQ-DT (ABC, Antenna TV, Laff, MNT) Lexington; WYMT-TV (CBS, CW) Hazard.
Programming (via satellite): A&E; AMC; Animal Planet; Cartoon Network; CMT; CNN; CW PLUS; Discovery Channel; Disney Channel; Disney XD; ESPN; ESPN2; Food Network; Fox News Channel; Fox Sports 1; FOX Sports Networks; Freeform; FX; Golf Channel; Hallmark Channel; HGTV; History; ION Television; Lifetime; MTV; NBCSN; Nickelodeon; Outdoor Channel; QVC; RFD-TV; Spike TV; Starz Encore Westerns; Syfy; TBS; The Weather Chan-

Kentucky—Cable Systems

nel; TLC; TNT; Trinity Broadcasting Network (TBN); truTV; TV Land; UP; USA Network; VH1; WGN America.
Fee: $18.00 monthly.
Pay Service 1
Pay Units: N.A.
Programming (via satellite): HBO; Showtime; Starz Encore.
Fee: $23.00 monthly.
Video-On-Demand: No
Internet Service
Operational: No.
Telephone Service
None
Miles of Plant: 37.0 (coaxial); None (fiber optic). Homes passed: 890.
Vice President & General Manager: Veola Williams. Chief Technician: Brett Williams.
Ownership: C & W Cable Inc.

PERRYVILLE—Time Warner Cable. Now served by RICHMOND, KY [KY0008]. ICA: KY0170.

PIKEVILLE—Suddenlink Communications, 520 Maryville Centre Dr, Ste 300, St. Louis, MO 63141. Phones: 606-886-1363; 314-315-9400; 800-999-6845 (Customer service). Web Site: http://www.suddenlink.com. Also serves Elkhorn City, Pike County (portions) & South Pikeville. ICA: KY0045.
TV Market Ranking: Below 100 (Elkhorn City, Pike County (portions)); Outside TV Markets (PIKEVILLE, South Pikeville, Pike County (portions)). Franchise award date: December 28, 1987. Franchise expiration date: N.A. Began: September 1, 1951.
Channel capacity: N.A. Channels available but not in use: N.A.
Basic Service
Subscribers: 3,582. Commercial subscribers: 385.
Programming (received off-air): WCHS-TV (ABC, Antenna TV) Charleston; WKPI-TV (PBS) Pikeville; WLFG (IND, PBJ, Retro TV) Grundy; WLPX-TV (ION) Charleston; WOWK-TV (CBS) Huntington; WQCW (CW) Portsmouth; WSAZ-TV (MNT, NBC, This TV) Huntington; WVAH-TV (FOX, The Country Network) Charleston; WYMT-TV (CBS, CW) Hazard; allband FM.
Programming (via satellite): C-SPAN; QVC; WGN America.
Fee: $59.95 installation; $22.99 monthly.
Expanded Basic Service 1
Subscribers: N.A.
Programming (via satellite): A&E; AMC; Animal Planet; Cartoon Network; Celebrity Shopping Network; CMT; CNBC; CNN; Comedy Central; Discovery Channel; Disney Channel; E! HD; ESPN; ESPN Classic; ESPN2; Fox News Channel; Freeform; FX; HGTV; History; HLN; INSP; Lifetime; MTV; Nickelodeon; Spike TV; Syfy; TBS; The Weather Channel; TLC; TNT; Travel Channel; TV Land; USA Network; VH1.
Fee: $21.00 monthly.
Digital Basic Service
Subscribers: N.A.
Programming (via satellite): BBC America; Bloomberg Television; Cloo; CMT; Discovery Digital Networks; Disney XD; DMX Music; ESPNews; Fox Sports 1; Fuse; FXM; FYI; Golf Channel; GSN; History International; IFC; LMN; MTV Classic; MTV2; National Geographic Channel; NBCSN; Nick Jr.; Nicktoons; Outdoor Channel; TeenNick; Trinity Broadcasting Network (TBN); Turner Classic Movies; WE tv.
Pay Service 1
Pay Units: N.A.
Programming (via satellite): Cinemax; HBO; Showtime (multiplexed); The Movie Channel.
Fee: $25.00 installation; $10.00 monthly (Cinemax, HBO or TMC).
Digital Pay Service 1
Pay Units: N.A.
Programming (via satellite): Cinemax (multiplexed); HBO (multiplexed); Showtime (multiplexed); Starz (multiplexed); Starz Encore (multiplexed); The Movie Channel (multiplexed).
Video-On-Demand: No
Pay-Per-View
iN DEMAND (delivered digitally); Playboy TV (delivered digitally); Fresh (delivered digitally).
Internet Service
Operational: Yes.
Broadband Service: Suddenlink High Speed Internet.
Fee: $49.95 installation; $26.95 monthly.
Telephone Service
Digital: Operational
Miles of Plant: 401.0 (coaxial); 156.0 (fiber optic). Homes passed: 9,285.
Senior Vice President, Corporate Finance: Michael Pflantz. District Manager: Robert Herrald. General Manager: Patty Chapman. Chief Technician: David Carte.
Ownership: Cequel Communications Holdings I LLC (MSO).

PINE HILL—Time Warner Cable. Now served by RICHMOND, KY [KY0008]. ICA: KY0271.

PINEVILLE—Formerly served by NewWave Communications. Now served by Time Warner Cable, CORBIN, KY [KY0030]. ICA: KY0272.

PINEVILLE—Time Warner Cable. Now served by CORBIN, KY [KY0030]. ICA: KY0063.

PLEASANT RIDGE—Formerly served by Vital Communications. No longer in operation. ICA: KY0185.

PRESTONSBURG—Suddenlink Communications. Now served by KERMIT, WV [WV0038]. ICA: KY0273.

PRINCETON—Mediacom. Now served by MARION, KY [KY0071]. ICA: KY0274.

PROVIDENCE—Time Warner Cable, 60 Columbus Circle, 17th Fl, New York, NY 10023. Phones: 212-364-8200; 859-431-0300; 212-364-8200; 270-667-5545. Fax: 212-364-8252. Web Site: http://www.timewarnercable.com. Also serves Webster County (portions). ICA: KY0074.
TV Market Ranking: 86 (Webster County (portions) (portions)); Below 100 (PROVIDENCE, Webster County (portions) (portions)). Franchise award date: N.A. Franchise expiration date: N.A. Began: December 1, 1967.
Channel capacity: N.A. Channels available but not in use: N.A.
Basic Service
Subscribers: 408. Commercial subscribers: 5.
Programming (received off-air): WEHT (ABC) Evansville; WEVV-TV (CBS, FOX) Evansville; WFIE (NBC, This TV) Evansville; WKMA-TV (PBS) Madisonville; WNIN (PBS) Evansville; WPSD-TV (Antenna TV, NBC) Paducah; WTVW (CW, MeTV) Evansville; allband FM.
Programming (via satellite): Discovery Channel; QVC; TBS; WGN America.
Fee: $24.95 installation; $19.95 monthly; $2.00 converter.
Expanded Basic Service 1
Subscribers: N.A.
Programming (via satellite): A&E; AMC; Animal Planet; BET; CNBC; CNN; C-SPAN; Disney Channel; ESPN; ESPN2; Fox News Channel; Freeform; FX; HLN; Lifetime; MoviePlex; MTV; Nickelodeon; Spike TV; The Weather Channel; TLC; TNT; USA Network.
Fee: $21.45 monthly.
Digital Basic Service
Subscribers: N.A.
Programming (via satellite): BBC America; Bloomberg Television; Destination America; Discovery Kids Channel; Discovery Life Channel; Fox Sports 1; FXM; IFC; Investigation Discovery; National Geographic Channel; Outdoor Channel; OWN: Oprah Winfrey Network; Science Channel; Trinity Broadcasting Network (TBN); Turner Classic Movies.
Digital Pay Service 1
Pay Units: N.A.
Programming (via satellite): Cinemax (multiplexed); HBO (multiplexed); Showtime (multiplexed); Starz; Starz Encore (multiplexed); The Movie Channel.
Video-On-Demand: No
Pay-Per-View
Playboy TV (delivered digitally); Fresh (delivered digitally).
Internet Service
Operational: No.
Telephone Service
None
Miles of Plant: 44.0 (coaxial); None (fiber optic).
Chief Executive Officer: Glenn A. Britt. President & Chief Operations Officer: Robert D. Marcus.
Ownership: Time Warner Cable.

RICHMOND—Time Warner Cable, 1615 Foxhaven Dr, Richmond, KY 40475. Phones: 859-625-6600; 859-624-9666; 859-626-4800. Fax: 859-624-0060. Web Site: http://www.timewarnercable.com. Also serves Anderson County (eastern portion), Bath County (portions), Berea, Blue Bank, Bourbon County (portions), Boyle County (portions), Burgin, Burtonville, Camargo, Carlisle, Carter County (southwestern portion), Clark County (portions), Cynthiana, Danville, Elizaville, Enterprise, Epworth, Ewing, Fitch, Fleming County (portions), Flemingsburg, Foxport, Franklin County (southern portion), Garrard County (portions), Georgetown, Globe, Haldeman, Harrison County (portions), Harrodsburg, Hillsboro, Jeffersonville (portions), Jessamine County (portions), Junction City (Boyle County), Junction City (Lincoln County), Kingston, Kirksville, Lakeview Heights, Lancaster, LaRue County (portions), Lawrenceburg, Lawton, Lewis County (western portion), Limestone, Lincoln County (northern portion), Madison County (portions), Mercer County (portions), Midway, Millersburg, Montgomery County (portions), Morehead, Mount Carmel, Mount Sterling, Nepton, Nicholas County (portions), Nicholasville, North Middletown, Olive Hill, Owingsville, Paris, Perryville, Pine Hill, Ribolt, Ringos Mills, Rowan County (portions), Salt Lick, Scott County (portions), Sharkey, Sharpsburg, Soldier, Stamping Ground, Stanford, Tollesboro, Upper Tygart, Versailles, Waco, Wallingford, Washington County (portions), White Hall, Wilmore, Winchester & Woodford County (eastern portion). ICA: KY0008.
TV Market Ranking: Below 100 (Anderson County (eastern portion), Bath County (portions), Berea, Blue Bank, Bourbon County (portions), Boyle County (portions), Burgin, Burtonville, Camargo, Carlisle, Carter County (southwestern portion), Clark County (portions), Danville, Elizaville, Enterprise, Epworth, Ewing, Fitch, Flemingsburg, Foxport, Franklin County (southern portion), Garrard County (portions), Globe, Haldeman, Harrison County (portions), Hillsboro, Jeffersonville (portions), Jessamine County (portions), Junction City (Boyle County), Kingston, Kirksville, Lakeview Heights, Lancaster, LaRue County (portions), Lawrenceburg, Lawton, Lewis County (western portion), Limestone, Lincoln County (northern portion), Madison County (portions), Mercer County (portions), Midway, Millersburg, Montgomery County (portions), Mount Carmel, Mount Sterling, Nepton, Nicholas County (portions), North Middletown, Olive Hill, Owingsville, Paris, Perryville, Ribolt, RICHMOND, Ringos Mills, Salt Lick, Scott County (portions), Sharpsburg, Soldier, Stamping Ground, Stanford, Tollesboro, Upper Tygart, Versailles, Waco, Wallingford, Washington County (portions), White Hall, Wilmore, Winchester, Woodford County (eastern portion), Cynthiana, Georgetown, Harrodsburg, Morehead, Nicholasville); Outside TV Markets (Fleming County (portions), Pine Hill, Rowan County (portions), Sharkey). Franchise award date: N.A. Franchise expiration date: N.A. Began: January 28, 1965.
Channel capacity: N.A. Channels available but not in use: N.A.
Basic Service
Subscribers: 47,355.
Programming (received off-air): WDKY-TV (FOX) Danville; WKLE (PBS) Lexington; WKYT-TV (CBS, CW) Lexington; WLEX-TV (MeTV, NBC) Lexington; WLJC-TV (TBN) Beattyville; WTVQ-DT (ABC, Antenna TV, Laff, MNT) Lexington; WUPX-TV (ION) Morehead.
Programming (via satellite): QVC; WGN America.
Fee: $24.95-$61.55 installation; $24.50 monthly.
Expanded Basic Service 1
Subscribers: N.A.
Programming (via satellite): A&E; AMC; Animal Planet; BET; Bravo; Cartoon Network; CMT; CNBC; CNN; Comedy Central; C-SPAN; C-SPAN 2; Discovery Channel; Disney Channel; E! HD; ESPN; ESPN2; EVINE Live; EWTN Global Catholic Network; Food Network; Fox News Channel; FOX Sports Ohio/Sports Time Ohio; Freeform; FX; Hallmark Channel; HGTV; History; HLN;

Cable Systems—Kentucky

INSP; Lifetime; MSNBC; MTV; Nickelodeon; Oxygen; Pop; Spike TV; Syfy; TBS; The Weather Channel; TLC; TNT; Travel Channel; Trinity Broadcasting Network (TBN); truTV; TV Land; Univision Studios; USA Network; VH1.
Fee: $33.98 monthly.
Digital Basic Service
Subscribers: N.A.
Programming (via satellite): BBC America; Bloomberg Television; Discovery Life Channel; Disney XD; DIY Network; DMX Music; ESPN Classic; ESPNews; FOX College Sports Central; FOX College Sports Pacific; Fox Sports 1; Fuse; FXM; FYI; Golf Channel; Great American Country; GSN; History International; HITS (Headend In The Sky); IFC; LMN; MC; National Geographic Channel; NBCSN; Nick 2; Nick Jr.; Nicktoons; Outdoor Channel; Sundance TV; TeenNick; The Word Network; Turner Classic Movies; WE tv.
Fee: $6.00 monthly (each tier).
Digital Pay Service 1
Pay Units: N.A.
Programming (via satellite): ART America; Cinemax (multiplexed); Flix; HBO (multiplexed); RAI Italia; RTN; Showtime (multiplexed); Starz (multiplexed); Starz Encore (multiplexed); The Filipino Channel; The Movie Channel (multiplexed); TV Asia; TV5; La Television International; Zee TV.
Fee: $12.00 monthly (Cinemax, HBO, Showtime/TMC/Flix or Starz/Encore), $15.00 monthly (all others).
Video-On-Demand: Yes
Pay-Per-View
iN DEMAND (delivered digitally); Playboy TV (delivered digitally); Fresh (delivered digitally); Shorteez (delivered digitally); Hot Choice (delivered digitally); Urban Xtra (delivered digitally); Sports PPV (delivered digitally).
Internet Service
Operational: Yes.
Subscribers: 50,181.
Broadband Service: Road Runner.
Fee: $44.95 monthly.
Telephone Service
Digital: Operational
Subscribers: 17,845.
Fee: $44.95 monthly
Miles of Plant: 4,929.0 (coaxial); 2,218.0 (fiber optic). Homes passed: 180,977.
General Manager: Robert Trott. Technical Operations Manager: Dennis Lester. Marketing Director: Betrina Morse. Government & Public Affairs Manager: Carla Deaton. Office Manager: Laverne Farris.
Ownership: Time Warner Cable (MSO).

ROCHESTER—Formerly served by Vital Communications. No longer in operation. ICA: KY0309.

ROUGH RIVER DAM—Formerly served by Mediacom. No longer in operation. ICA: KY0276.

RUSSELL COUNTY (unincorporated areas)
—Mediacom, 90 Main St, Benton, KY 42025-1132. Phones: 845-695-2762; 417-875-5560 (Springfield regional office); 270-527-9939. Fax: 270-527-0813. Web Site: http://www.mediacomcable.com. Also serves Casey County (southern portion) & Windsor. ICA: KY0114.
TV Market Ranking: Below 100 (Casey County (southern portion), RUSSELL COUNTY (UNINCORPORATED AREAS), Windsor). Franchise award date: April 1, 1988. Franchise expiration date: N.A. Began: May 1, 1989.
Channel capacity: N.A. Channels available but not in use: N.A.
Basic Service
Subscribers: 37.
Programming (received off-air): WBIR-TV (MeTV, NBC) Knoxville; WBKO (ABC, CW, FOX) Bowling Green; WDKY-TV (FOX) Danville; WHAS-TV (ABC) Louisville; WKSO-TV (PBS) Somerset; WKYT-TV (CBS, CW) Lexington; WLEX-TV (MeTV, NBC) Lexington; WMYT-TV (Buzzr, IND, MNT) Rock Hill; WTVQ-DT (ABC, Antenna TV, Laff, MNT) Lexington.
Programming (via satellite): A&E; AMC; Animal Planet; Cartoon Network; CMT; CNBC; CNN; Comedy Central; C-SPAN 2; Discovery Channel; Disney Channel; E! HD; ESPN; ESPN2; Food Network; Fox News Channel; Fox Sports 1; FOX Sports Midwest; Freeform; FX; Great American Country; HGTV; History; HLN; INSP; Lifetime; MSNBC; MTV; National Geographic Channel; Nickelodeon; Outdoor Channel; QVC; Spike TV; Syfy; TBS; The Weather Channel; TLC; TNT; Travel Channel; Trinity Broadcasting Network (TBN); TV Land; USA Network; VH1; WGN America.
Fee: $29.95 installation; $69.95 monthly; $3.95 converter.
Pay Service 1
Pay Units: N.A.
Programming (via satellite): Cinemax; HBO; Starz; Starz Encore.
Fee: $9.00 monthly (Cinemax), $10.00 monthly (HBO).
Video-On-Demand: No
Internet Service
Operational: No.
Telephone Service
None
Miles of Plant: 70.0 (coaxial); None (fiber optic). Homes passed: 1,050.
Regional Vice President: Bill Copeland. Vice President, Financial Reporting: Kenneth J. Kohrs. General Manager: Dale Haney. Regional Technical Operations Director: Alan Freedman. Marketing Director: Will Kuebler. Technical Operations Manager: Jeff Brown. Marketing Manager: Melanie Westerman.
Ownership: Mediacom LLC (MSO).

RUSSELL SPRINGS—Duo County Telecom, 2150 North Main St, PO Box 80, Jamestown, KY 42629. Phones: 270-433-2121; 270-378-4141; 270-343-3131. Fax: 270-343-3800. E-mail: duotel@duo-county.com. Web Site: http://www.duocounty.com. Also serves Adair County (portions), Columbia (portions), Cumberland County (portions), Jamestown (portions) & Russell County (portions). ICA: KY0243.
TV Market Ranking: Below 100 (Adair County (portions), Columbia (portions), Jamestown (portions), Russell County (portions), RUSSELL SPRINGS). Franchise award date: February 23, 1988. Franchise expiration date: N.A. Began: January 10, 1971.
Channel capacity: N.A. Channels available but not in use: N.A.
Basic Service
Subscribers: 5,102 Includes cable & IPTV subscribers. Commercial subscribers: 295.
Programming (received off-air): WAVE (Bounce TV, NBC, This TV) Louisville; WBKI-TV (CW, IND, Movies!) Campbellsville; WBKO (ABC, CW, FOX) Bowling Green; WDKY-TV (FOX) Danville; WDRB (Antenna TV, FOX) Louisville; WHAS-TV (ABC) Louisville; WKRN-TV (ABC) Nashville; WKYT-TV (CBS, CW) Lexington; WLEX-TV (MeTV, NBC) Lexington; WLKY (CBS, MeTV) Louisville; WSMV-TV (COZI TV, NBC, TNN) Nashville; WTVF (CBS, Laff, This TV) Nashville; WTVQ-DT (ABC, Antenna TV, Laff, MNT) Lexington; 3 FMs.
Programming (via satellite): AMC; HLN; QVC; WGN America.
Fee: $35.00 installation; $27.18 monthly.
Expanded Basic Service 1
Subscribers: 2,518.
Programming (via satellite): A&E; Animal Planet; BET; Boomerang; Cartoon Network; CMT; CNBC; CNN; Comedy Central; C-SPAN; Discovery Channel; Disney Channel; E! HD; ESPN; ESPN Classic; ESPN2; Food Network; Fox News Channel; Freeform; FX; HGTV; History; ION Television; Lifetime; LMN; Local Cable Weather; MTV; Nickelodeon; OWN; Oprah Winfrey Network; Oxygen; RFD-TV; Spike TV; Syfy; The Weather Channel; TLC; TNT; Travel Channel; Trinity Broadcasting Network (TBN); truTV; TV Land; UP; USA Network; VH1.
Fee: $32.77 monthly.
Digital Basic Service
Subscribers: N.A.
Programming (via satellite): Bloomberg Television; C-SPAN 2; DIY Network; ESPNews; Fox Sports 1; Golf Channel; Hallmark Channel; MC; MSNBC; NBCSN; Outdoor Channel; Turner Classic Movies.
Digital Pay Service 1
Pay Units: N.A.
Programming (via satellite): Cinemax (multiplexed); Flix; HBO (multiplexed); Showtime; Sundance TV; The Movie Channel.
Fee: $13.95 monthly (Starz/Encore), $14.95 monthly (Cinemax or Showtime/TMC), $16.95 monthly (HBO).
Video-On-Demand: No
Pay-Per-View
Indemand (delivered digitally).
Internet Service
Operational: Yes.
Fee: $34.95-$59.95 monthly.
Telephone Service
Digital: Operational
Fee: $14.00 monthly
Miles of Plant: 127.0 (coaxial); None (fiber optic).
Chief Executive Officer & Executive Vice President: Tom Preston. Chief Financial Officer & Vice President: Daryl Hammond. Vice President, Operations: Mark Henry. Marketing Director: Eric West. Network Manager: Robert Lamb.
Ownership: Duo County Telephone Cooperative (MSO).

RUSSELLVILLE—Suddenlink Communications, 520 Maryville Centre Dr, Ste 300, St. Louis, MO 63141. Phones: 800-999-6845 (Customer service); 314-315-9400. Web Site: http://www.suddenlink.com. Also serves Auburn, Lewisburg & Logan County (portions). ICA: KY0032.
TV Market Ranking: Below 100 (Auburn, Lewisburg, Logan County (portions), RUSSELLVILLE). Franchise award date: March 27, 1986. Franchise expiration date: N.A. Began: April 1, 1980.
Channel capacity: N.A. Channels available but not in use: N.A.
Basic Service
Subscribers: 531. Commercial subscribers: 93.
Programming (received off-air): WBKO (ABC, CW, FOX) Bowling Green; WKLE (PBS) Lexington; WKYU-TV (PBS) Bowling Green; WNAB (CW, The Country Network) Nashville; WNKY (CBS, NBC) Bowling Green; WNPT (PBS) Nashville; WNPX-TV (ION) Cookeville; WPGD-TV (TBN) Hendersonville; WSMV-TV (COZI TV, NBC, TNN) Nashville; WTVF (CBS, Laff, This TV) Nashville; WUXP-TV (MNT) Nashville; WZTV (Antenna TV, FOX, WeatherNation) Nashville.
Programming (via satellite): Pop; WGN America.
Fee: $22.99 monthly.
Expanded Basic Service 1
Subscribers: N.A.
Programming (via satellite): A&E; AMC; Animal Planet; BET; Cartoon Network; CMT; CNBC; CNN; C-SPAN; Discovery Channel; Disney Channel; E! HD; ESPN; ESPN Classic; ESPN2; Food Network; Fox News Channel; Freeform; FX; HGTV; History; HLN; Lifetime; MTV; Nickelodeon; QVC; Spike TV; Syfy; TBS; The Weather Channel; TLC; TNT; Turner Classic Movies; TV Land; USA Network; VH1.
Fee: $22.00 monthly.
Digital Basic Service
Subscribers: N.A.
Programming (via satellite): BBC America; Bloomberg Television; CMT; Discovery Digital Networks; Disney XD; ESPNews; Fox Sports 1; Fuse; FXM; FYI; Golf Channel; GSN; History International; IFC; LMN; National Geographic Channel; NBCSN; Nick Jr.; Nicktoons; Outdoor Channel; TeenNick; Trinity Broadcasting Network (TBN); WE tv.
Digital Pay Service 1
Pay Units: N.A.
Programming (via satellite): Cinemax (multiplexed); HBO (multiplexed); Showtime (multiplexed); Starz (multiplexed); Starz Encore (multiplexed); The Movie Channel (multiplexed).
Fee: $7.95 monthly (Starz/Encore), $18.95 monthly (Cinemax, Showtime or TMC), $20.95 monthly (HBO).
Video-On-Demand: No
Pay-Per-View
iN DEMAND (delivered digitally); Playboy TV (delivered digitally); Fresh (delivered digitally).
Internet Service
Operational: Yes. Began: March 10, 2004.
Broadband Service: Suddenlink High Speed Internet.
Fee: $49.95 installation; $26.95 monthly.
Telephone Service
None
Miles of Plant: 96.0 (coaxial); None (fiber optic). Homes passed: 4,689.
President: Tom Kinley. Senior Vice President: Gerald Corman. Vice President: Robert Herrald. Vice President, Corporate Finance:

Access the most current data instantly
FREE TRIAL @ ADVANCED TVFactbook
TELCO/IPTV • CABLE TV • TV STATIONS
www.warren-news.com/factbook.htm

Kentucky—Cable Systems

Michael Pflantz. Chief Technician: Jim Adkins.
Ownership: Cequel Communications Holdings I LLC (MSO).

SALYERSVILLE—Howard's TV Cable, 911 East Maple St, PO Box 229, Salyersville, KY 41465. Phone: 606-349-3317. Fax: 606-349-3306. Also serves Falcon, Ivyton, Lickburg, Magoffin County & Pleasant Hill. ICA: KY0277.
TV Market Ranking: Below 100 (Ivyton, Magoffin County (portions), SALYERSVILLE); Outside TV Markets (Falcon, Lickburg, Magoffin County (portions), Pleasant Hill). Franchise award date: N.A. Franchise expiration date: N.A. Began: January 1, 1963.
Channel capacity: N.A. Channels available but not in use: N.A.
Basic Service
Subscribers: N.A.
Programming (received off-air): WCHS-TV (ABC, Antenna TV) Charleston; WDKY-TV (FOX) Danville; WFPX-TV (ION) Fayetteville; WKMR (PBS) Morehead; WKYT-TV (CBS, CW) Lexington; WLEX-TV (MeTV, NBC) Lexington; WLJC-TV (TBN) Beattyville; WOWK-TV (CBS) Huntington; WQCW (CW) Portsmouth; WSAZ-TV (MNT, NBC, This TV) Huntington; WTVQ-DT (ABC, Antenna TV, Laff, MNT) Lexington; WYMT-TV (CBS, CW) Hazard.
Programming (via satellite): AMC; Animal Planet; Cartoon Network; CMT; CNN; C-SPAN; C-SPAN 2; Discovery Channel; Disney Channel; E! HD; ESPN; ESPN2; Food Network; Fox Sports 1; Freeform; FX; Great American Country; Hallmark Channel; HGTV; HLN; HRTV; INSP; Lifetime; MTV; Nickelodeon; Outdoor Channel; Pop; QVC; Spike TV; Syfy; TBS; The Weather Channel; TLC; TNT; Travel Channel; Trinity Broadcasting Network (TBN); TV Land; USA Network; VH1; WE tv; WGN America.
Fee: $45.00 installation.
Digital Basic Service
Subscribers: N.A.
Programming (via satellite): BBC America; Discovery Digital Networks; ESPN Classic; Starz Encore (multiplexed).
Pay Service 1
Pay Units: N.A.
Programming (via satellite): Cinemax; HBO.
Fee: $10.00 monthly (Cinemax), $13.00 monthly (HBO).
Digital Pay Service 1
Pay Units: N.A.
Programming (via satellite): HBO (multiplexed); Showtime (multiplexed); Starz (multiplexed); The Movie Channel (multiplexed).
Video-On-Demand: No
Internet Service
Operational: Yes.
Broadband Service: AT&T.
Fee: $24.95 monthly.
Telephone Service
None
Miles of Plant: 200.0 (coaxial); None (fiber optic). Homes passed: 3,000.

Technical Manager: Rick Howard. Chief Technician: Greg Bowen. Office Manager: Frances Crace.
Ownership: Ruth & Rick Howard.

SANDY HOOK—Formerly served by Windjammer Cable. No longer in operation. ICA: KY0134.

SCOTTSVILLE—NCTC. Formerly [KY0073]. This cable system has converted to IPTV, 872 Hwy 52 Bypass East, PO Box 70, Lafayette, TN 37083. Phones: 270-622-7500 (Scottsville office); 615-644-6282 (Westmoreland); 615-666-2151. Fax: 615-666-6772. E-mail: help@blue.net. Web Site: http://www.nctc.com. Also serves Allen County (unincorporated areas), KY; Defeated, Lafayette, Red Boiling Springs, Siloam & Westmoreland, TN. ICA: KY5016.
TV Market Ranking: Below 100 (Lafayette, Red Boiling Springs, SCOTTSVILLE, Siloam, Westmoreland). Franchise award date: February 1, 1995. Franchise expiration date: N.A. Began: February 1, 1983.
Channel capacity: N.A. Channels available but not in use: N.A.
Basic
Subscribers: 6,247.
Programming (received off-air): WBKO (ABC, CW, FOX) Bowling Green; WHTN (Christian TV Network) Murfreesboro; WKRN-TV (ABC) Nashville; WNPT (PBS) Nashville; WPBM-CD (IND) Scottsville; WSMV-TV (COZI TV, NBC, TNN) Nashville; WTVF (CBS, Laff, This TV) Nashville; WUXP-TV (MNT) Nashville; WZTV (Antenna TV, FOX, WeatherNation) Nashville.
Programming (via satellite): C-SPAN; C-SPAN 2; Local Cable Weather; QVC; The Weather Channel; Trinity Broadcasting Network (TBN).
Fee: $19.95 monthly.
Deluxe
Subscribers: N.A.
Programming (via satellite): A&E; AMC; Animal Planet; BBC America; BET; Bloomberg Television; Boomerang; Bravo; Cartoon Network; CMT; CNBC; CNN; Comedy Central; Discovery Channel; Discovery Digital Networks; Disney Channel; DIY Network; E! HD; ESPN; ESPN Classic; ESPN2; ESPNews; Family Friendly Entertainment; Food Network; Fox News Channel; Fox Sports 1; Freeform; FX; Golf Channel; Great American Country; GSN; Hallmark Channel; HGTV; History; HLN; ION Television; Lifetime; LMN; MC; MSNBC; MTV; NBCSN; Nickelodeon; Outdoor Channel; OWN: Oprah Winfrey Network; Oxygen; RFD-TV; Spike TV; Syfy; TBS; TLC; TNT; Travel Channel; truTV; Turner Classic Movies; TV Land; USA Network; VH1; WGN America.
Cinemax
Subscribers: N.A.
Programming (via satellite): Cinemax (multiplexed).
HBO
Subscribers: N.A.
Programming (via satellite): HBO (multiplexed).

Showtime/TMC/Flix
Subscribers: N.A.
Programming (via satellite): Flix; Showtime (multiplexed); The Movie Channel (multiplexed).
Starz/Encore
Subscribers: N.A.
Programming (via satellite): Starz (multiplexed); Starz Encore (multiplexed).
Video-On-Demand: Yes
Pay-Per-View
iN DEMAND (delivered digitally).
Internet Service
Operational: Yes.
Fee: $29.95-$199.95 monthly.
Telephone Service
Digital: Operational
Chief Executive Officer: Nancy White. Vice President, Finance & Administrative Services: Johnny McClanahan.
Ownership: North Central Telephone Cooperative.

SCOTTSVILLE—NCTC. This cable system has converted to IPTV. See SCOTTSVILLE, KY [KY5016]. ICA: KY0073.

SEBREE—Time Warner Cable. Now served by MADISONVILLE, KY [KY0013]. ICA: KY0143.

SHARPSBURG—Formerly served by Adelphia Communications. Now served by Time Warner Cable, RICHMOND, KY [KY0008]. ICA: KY0279.

SHELBYVILLE—Formerly served by Insight Communications. Now served by Time Warner Cable, LOUISVILLE, KY [KY0001]. ICA: KY0022.

SHEPHERDSVILLE—Inside Connect Cable. Now served by BROOKS, KY [KY0199]. ICA: KY0327.

SITKA—Sitka TV Cable, 109 Depot Rd, Paintsville, KY 41240-1346. Phone: 606-789-7603. Fax: 606-789-3391. ICA: KY0320.
TV Market Ranking: Outside TV Markets (SITKA).
Channel capacity: N.A. Channels available but not in use: N.A.
Basic Service
Subscribers: N.A.
Programming (received off-air): WCHS-TV (ABC, Antenna TV) Charleston; WKPI-TV (PBS) Pikeville; WLPX-TV (ION) Charleston; WOWK-TV (CBS) Huntington; WQCW (CW) Portsmouth; WSAZ-TV (MNT, NBC, This TV) Huntington; WVAH-TV (FOX, The Country Network) Charleston; WVPB-TV (PBS) Huntington; WYMT-TV (CBS, CW) Hazard.
Programming (via satellite): Animal Planet; CMT; Discovery Channel; ESPN; Freeform; HGTV; MSNBC; Spike TV; Syfy; TBS; TNT; Trinity Broadcasting Network (TBN); TV Land; USA Network; WGN America.
Pay Service 1
Pay Units: N.A.
Programming (via satellite): The Movie Channel.
Fee: $7.00 monthly.
Video-On-Demand: No
Internet Service
Operational: No.
Telephone Service
None
Miles of Plant: 8.0 (coaxial); None (fiber optic).
General Manager: Bart Ward.
Ownership: Sitka TV Cable System.

SLAUGHTERS—Formerly served by Vital Communications. No longer in operation. ICA: KY0310.

SOLDIER—Time Warner Cable. Now served by RICHMOND, KY [KY0008]. ICA: KY0224.

SOMERSET (village)—Time Warner Cable. Now served by CORBIN, KY [KY0030]. ICA: KY0021.

STANFORD—Time Warner Cable. Now served by RICHMOND, KY [KY0008]. ICA: KY0283.

STANTON—Crystal Broadband Networks, PO Box 180336, Chicago, IL 60618. Phones: 877-319-0328; 630-206-0447. E-mail: helpdesk@crystalbn.com. Web Site: http://crystalbn.com. Also serves Clay City & Powell County (unincorporated areas). ICA: KY0095.
TV Market Ranking: Below 100 (Clay City, Powell County (unincorporated areas), STANTON). Franchise award date: N.A. Franchise expiration date: N.A. Began: January 1, 1970.
Channel capacity: N.A. Channels available but not in use: N.A.
Basic Service
Subscribers: 185.
Programming (received off-air): WDKY-TV (FOX) Danville; WKLE (PBS) Lexington; WKYT-TV (CBS, CW) Lexington; WLEX-TV (MeTV, NBC) Lexington; WLJC-TV (TBN) Beattyville; WTVQ-DT (ABC, Antenna TV, Laff, MNT) Lexington; WUPX-TV (ION) Morehead; WXIX-TV (Bounce TV, FOX) Newport.
Programming (via satellite): QVC; TBS; TV Land; WGN America.
Fee: $39.95 installation; $48.57 monthly.
Expanded Basic Service 1
Subscribers: N.A.
Programming (via satellite): A&E; AMC; CMT; CNN; C-SPAN; Discovery Channel; Disney Channel; E! HD; ESPN; ESPN2; Fox News Channel; Freeform; FX; HLN; Lifetime; MTV; Nickelodeon; Spike TV; Syfy; The Weather Channel; TLC; TNT; USA Network.
Fee: $23.20 monthly.
Digital Basic Service
Subscribers: N.A.
Programming (via satellite): BBC America; Bravo; CMT; Discovery Digital Networks; ESPN Classic; Fox Sports 1; FYI; Golf Channel; GSN; HGTV; History; History International; IFC; National Geographic Channel; NBCSN; Nick Jr.; TeenNick; Turner Classic Movies; WE tv.
Digital Pay Service 1
Pay Units: N.A.
Programming (via satellite): Cinemax (multiplexed); HBO (multiplexed); Showtime (multiplexed); Starz (multiplexed); Starz Encore; The Movie Channel (multiplexed).
Fee: $15.95 monthly (each).
Video-On-Demand: No
Pay-Per-View
iN DEMAND (delivered digitally); Playboy TV (delivered digitally).
Internet Service
Operational: No.
Telephone Service
None
Miles of Plant: 102.0 (coaxial); None (fiber optic). Homes passed: 2,278.
Ownership: Crystal Broadband Networks (MSO).

D-328 TV & Cable Factbook No. 85

Cable Systems—Kentucky

STURGIS—Time Warner Cable. Now served by OWENSBORO, KY [KY0004]. ICA: KY0102.

SUMMER SHADE—Mediacom, 90 Main St, Benton, KY 42025-1132. Phones: 845-695-2762; 417-875-5560 (Springfield regional office); 270-527-9939. Fax: 270-527-0813. Web Site: http://www.mediacomcable.com. Also serves Albany, Barren County (portions), Clinton County (portions), Edmonton, Eighty Eight, Gamaliel, Monroe County (portions) & Tompkinsville, KY; Pickett County (portions), TN. ICA: KY0092.
TV Market Ranking: Below 100 (Barren County (portions), Eighty Eight, Clinton County (portions), Edmonton, Pickett County (portions)); Outside TV Markets (Albany, Gamaliel, Monroe County (portions), Clinton County (portions), Pickett County (portions), SUMMER SHADE, Tompkinsville). Franchise award date: N.A. Franchise expiration date: N.A. Began: January 1, 1967.
Channel capacity: N.A. Channels available but not in use: N.A.
Basic Service
Subscribers: 240.
Programming (received off-air): WBKO (ABC, CW, FOX) Bowling Green; WKRN-TV (ABC) Nashville; WKSO-TV (PBS) Somerset; WKYT-TV (CBS, CW) Lexington; WKYU-TV (PBS) Bowling Green; WLKY (CBS, MeTV) Louisville; WPBM-CD (IND) Scottsville; WSMV-TV (COZI TV, NBC, TNN) Nashville; WTVF (CBS, Laff, This TV) Nashville; WUXP-TV (MNT) Nashville; WZTV (Antenna TV, FOX, WeatherNation) Nashville; allband FM.
Programming (via satellite): ION Television; Pop; WGN America.
Fee: $36.95 installation; $43.37 monthly.
Expanded Basic Service 1
Subscribers: N.A.
Programming (via satellite): A&E; AMC; Animal Planet; Bravo; Cartoon Network; CMT; CNBC; CNN; Comedy Central; C-SPAN; C-SPAN 2; Discovery Channel; Discovery Life Channel; Disney Channel; E! HD; ESPN; ESPN2; EVINE Live; Food Network; Fox News Channel; Fox Sports 1; FOX Sports Networks; Freeform; Fuse; FX; Great American Country; Hallmark Channel; HGTV; History; HLN; ION Television; Lifetime; MSNBC; MTV; National Geographic Channel; Nickelodeon; Outdoor Channel; QVC; RFD-TV; Spike TV; Syfy; TBS; Telemundo; The Weather Channel; TLC; TNT; Travel Channel; Trinity Broadcasting Network (TBN); truTV; TV Land; USA Network; VH1; WE tv.
Digital Basic Service
Subscribers: N.A.
Programming (via satellite): AXS TV; BBC America; Bloomberg Television; Cloo; CNN HD; Destination America; Discovery Kids Channel; ESPN HD; ESPN2 HD; ESPNews; Fuse; FXM; FYI; Golf Channel; GSN; HD Theater; History International; IFC; Investigation Discovery; LMN; MTV Classic; MTV Hits; MTV2; NBCSN; Nick Jr.; Nicktoons; OWN; Oprah Winfrey Network; Science Channel; TBS HD; TeenNick; TNT HD; Turner Classic Movies; TVG Network; Universal HD.
Digital Pay Service 1
Pay Units: N.A.
Programming (via satellite): Cinemax (multiplexed); Flix; HBO (multiplexed); Showtime (multiplexed); Showtime HD; Starz (multiplexed); Starz Encore (multiplexed); Starz HD; Sundance TV; The Movie Channel (multiplexed).
Video-On-Demand: No

Pay-Per-View
iN DEMAND (delivered digitally); Playgirl TV (delivered digitally); SexSee (delivered digitally); Juicy.
Internet Service
Operational: Yes.
Broadband Service: Mediacom High Speed Internet.
Telephone Service
Analog: Not Operational
Digital: Operational
Miles of Plant: 79.0 (coaxial); None (fiber optic).
Regional Vice President: Bill Copeland. Vice President, Financial Reporting: Kenneth J. Kohrs. General Manager: Dale Haney. Regional Technical Operations Director: Alan Freedman. Marketing Director: Will Kuebler. Marketing Manager: Melanie Westerman.
Ownership: Mediacom LLC (MSO).

SUMMER SHADE—Mediacom. Now served by SUMMER SHADE, KY [KY0092]. ICA: KY0103.

SUMMERSVILLE—Formerly served by NewWave Communications. No longer in operation. ICA: KY0295.

SYCAMORE CREEK—Formerly served by Inter Mountain Cable Inc. No longer in operation. ICA: KY0194.

TAYLORSVILLE—Formerly served by Insight Communications. Now served by Time Warner Cable, LOUISVILLE, KY [KY0001]. ICA: KY0140.

TOLLESBORO—Formerly served by Adelphia Communications. Now served by Time Warner Cable, RICHMOND, KY [KY0008]. ICA: KY0124.

TOPMOST—TVS Cable, PO Box 1410, Hindman, KY 41822-1410. Phones: 606-946-2600; 606-785-3450; 606-633-0778. Fax: 606-785-3110. E-mail: tvs@tvscable.com. Web Site: http://www.tvscable.com. Also serves Dema, Kite, Raven & Wayland. ICA: KY0338.
TV Market Ranking: Below 100 (Dema, Kite, Raven, TOPMOST, Wayland).
Channel capacity: N.A. Channels available but not in use: N.A.
Basic Service
Subscribers: 606.
Fee: $50.00 installation; $23.50 monthly.
Internet Service
Operational: Yes.
Fee: $24.95-$79.95 monthly.
Vice President & General Manager: William K. Grigsby.
Ownership: TV Service Inc. (MSO).

TRENTON—Mediacom, 90 Main St, Benton, KY 42025-1132. Phones: 845-695-2762; 417-875-5560; 270-527-9939. Fax: 270-527-0813. Web Site: http://www.mediacomcable.com. Also serves Christian County, Elkton, Guthrie, Hopkinsville, Oak Grove, Pembroke & Todd County, KY; Dover & Stewart County, TN. ICA: KY0101.
TV Market Ranking: Below 100 (Christian County (portions), Hopkinsville, Todd County (portions)); Outside TV Markets (Christian County (portions), Dover, Elkton, Guthrie, Oak Grove, Pembroke, Stewart County, Todd County (portions), TRENTON). Franchise award date: N.A.

Franchise expiration date: N.A. Began: September 1, 1983.
Channel capacity: N.A. Channels available but not in use: N.A.
Basic Service
Subscribers: 1,963.
Programming (received off-air): WBKO (ABC, CW, FOX) Bowling Green; WKMA-TV (PBS) Madisonville; WKRN-TV (ABC) Nashville; WNPT (PBS) Nashville; WSIL-TV (ABC) Harrisburg; WSMV-TV (COZI TV, NBC, TNN) Nashville; WTVF (CBS, Laff, This TV) Nashville.
Programming (via satellite): AMC; Pop; WGN America.
Fee: $36.95 installation; $44.95 monthly.
Expanded Basic Service 1
Subscribers: N.A.
Programming (via satellite): Animal Planet; BET; Cartoon Network; CNBC; CNN; Comedy Central; C-SPAN; Discovery Channel; Discovery Life Channel; E! HD; ESPN; ESPN Classic; ESPN2; Food Network; Fox News Channel; Fox Sports 1; FOX Sports Networks; Freeform; FX; Hallmark Channel; HGTV; History; INSP; Lifetime; MSNBC; MTV; Nickelodeon; Outdoor Channel; QVC; Spike TV; Syfy; TBS; The Weather Channel; TNT; Travel Channel; Trinity Broadcasting Network (TBN); TV Land; Univision Studios; USA Network; WE tv.
Digital Basic Service
Subscribers: N.A.
Programming (via satellite): BBC America; CBS Sports Network; CCTV-Documentary; Cloo; Discovery Kids Channel; ESPN2 HD; ESPNews; ESPNU; Golf Channel; GSN; IFC; NBCSN; OWN; Oprah Winfrey Network; Science Channel; Turner Classic Movies; TVG Network.
Digital Pay Service 1
Pay Units: N.A.
Programming (via satellite): Cinemax (multiplexed); HBO (multiplexed); Showtime (multiplexed); Starz (multiplexed); Starz Encore (multiplexed); The Movie Channel (multiplexed).
Video-On-Demand: No
Pay-Per-View
Hot Choice (delivered digitally); Playboy TV (delivered digitally); SexSee (delivered digitally).
Internet Service
Operational: Yes.
Subscribers: 3,877.
Broadband Service: Mediacom High Speed Internet.
Telephone Service
Analog: Not Operational
Digital: Operational
Subscribers: 1,255.
Miles of Plant: 406.0 (coaxial); 191.0 (fiber optic). Homes passed: 10,797.
Regional Vice President: Bill Copeland. Vice President, Financial Reporting: Kenneth J. Kohrs. General Manager: Dale Haney. Regional Technical Operations Director: Alan Freedman. Marketing Director: Will Kuebler. Marketing Manager: Melanie Westerman.
Ownership: Mediacom LLC (MSO).

TUTOR KEY—P & W TV Cable, 109 Depot Rd, Paintsville, KY 41240-1325. Phone: 606-789-7603. Fax: 606-789-3391. ICA: KY0319.
TV Market Ranking: Outside TV Markets (TUTOR KEY).
Channel capacity: 36 (not 2-way capable). Channels available but not in use: N.A.
Basic Service
Subscribers: N.A.
Programming (received off-air): WCHS-TV (ABC, Antenna TV) Charleston; WKPI-TV (PBS) Pikeville; WLPX-TV (ION) Charleston; WOWK-TV (CBS) Huntington; WQCW (CW) Portsmouth; WSAZ-TV (MNT, NBC, This TV) Huntington; WVAH-TV (FOX, The Country Network) Charleston; WVPB-TV (PBS) Huntington; WYMT-TV (CBS, CW) Hazard.
Programming (via satellite): A&E; Animal Planet; Cartoon Network; CMT; CNN; C-SPAN; Discovery Channel; ESPN; Freeform; HGTV; Lifetime; Outdoor Channel; Spike TV; Syfy; TBS; TLC; TNT; Trinity Broadcasting Network (TBN); Turner Classic Movies; TV Land; USA Network; WGN America.
Pay Service 1
Pay Units: N.A.
Programming (via satellite): The Movie Channel.
Fee: $6.00 monthly.
Video-On-Demand: No
Internet Service
Operational: No.
Telephone Service
None
Office Manager: Debbie Burton.
Ownership: P & W TV Cable Systems Inc.

UPTON—Mediacom, 90 Main St, Benton, KY 42025-1132. Phones: 845-695-2762; 417-875-5560 (Springfield regional office); 270-527-9939. Fax: 270-527-0813. Web Site: http://www.mediacomcable.com. Also serves Bonnieville, Hardin County (southeastern portion), Hart County, Larue County (western portion), Munfordville & Sonora. ICA: KY0086.
TV Market Ranking: Below 100 (Bonnieville, Hardin County (southeastern portion) (portions), Hart County, Larue County (western portion), Sonora, Munfordville, UPTON); Outside TV Markets (Hardin County (southeastern portion) (portions)). Franchise award date: N.A. Franchise expiration date: N.A. Began: January 1, 1965.
Channel capacity: N.A. Channels available but not in use: N.A.
Basic Service
Subscribers: 271.
Programming (received off-air): WAVE (Bounce TV, NBC, This TV) Louisville; WBKO (ABC, CW, FOX) Bowling Green; WDRB (Antenna TV, FOX) Louisville; WHAS-TV (ABC) Louisville; WKYU-TV (PBS) Bowling Green; WKZT-TV (PBS) Elizabethtown; WLKY (CBS, MeTV) Louisville; WNKY (CBS, NBC) Bowling Green; WSMV-TV (COZI TV, NBC, TNN) Nashville; WTVF (CBS, Laff, This TV) Nashville; allband FM.
Programming (via satellite): Pop; WGN America.
Fee: $36.95 installation; $71.95 monthly.

Kentucky—Cable Systems

CABLE & TV STATION COVERAGE
Atlas 2017
The perfect companion to the Television & Cable Factbook
To order call 800-771-9202 or visit www.warren-news.com

Expanded Basic Service 1
Subscribers: N.A.
Programming (via satellite): A&E; AMC; Animal Planet; Bravo; Cartoon Network; CMT; CNBC; CNN; Comedy Central; C-SPAN; C-SPAN 2; Discovery Channel; Discovery Life Channel; Disney Channel; E! HD; ESPN; ESPN2; EVINE Live; Food Network; Fox News Channel; Fox Sports 1; Freeform; Fuse; FX; Great American Country; Hallmark Channel; HGTV; History; HLN; INSP; ION Television; Lifetime; MSNBC; MTV; National Geographic Channel; Nickelodeon; Outdoor Channel; QVC; RFD-TV; Spike TV; Syfy; TBS; Telemundo; The Weather Channel; TLC; TNT; Travel Channel; Trinity Broadcasting Network (TBN); TV Land; USA Network; VH1; WE tv.

Digital Basic Service
Subscribers: N.A.
Programming (via satellite): BBC America; Bloomberg Television; Discovery Digital Networks; DMX Music; Fuse; FXM; FYI; Golf Channel; GSN; History International; IFC; LMN; NBCSN; Nick Jr.; Nicktoons; TeenNick; Turner Classic Movies.

Digital Pay Service 1
Pay Units: N.A.
Programming (via satellite): Cinemax (multiplexed); Flix (multiplexed); HBO (multiplexed); Showtime (multiplexed); Starz (multiplexed); Starz Encore (multiplexed); Sundance TV; The Movie Channel (multiplexed).

Video-On-Demand: No

Pay-Per-View
Barker (delivered digitally); Playboy TV (delivered digitally); TEN Clips (delivered digitally); TEN Blox (delivered digitally); Pleasure (delivered digitally).

Internet Service
Operational: Yes.
Subscribers: 206.
Broadband Service: Mediacom High Speed Internet.

Telephone Service
Digital: Operational
Miles of Plant: 140.0 (coaxial); 7.0 (fiber optic). Homes passed: 3,471.
Regional Vice President: Bill Copeland. Vice President, Financial Reporting: Kenneth J. Kohrs. General Manager: Dale Haney. Regional Technical Operations Director: Alan Freedman. Marketing Director: Will Kuebler. Technical Operations Manager: Jeff Brown. Marketing Manager: Melanie Westerman.
Ownership: Mediacom LLC (MSO).

UPTON/SONORA—Mediacom. Now served by UPTON (formerly Munfordville), KY [KY0086]. ICA: KY0048.

VAN LEAR—Big Sandy Broadband, 510 Rte 302 West, PO Box 586, West Van Lear, KY 41268-0586. Phones: 888-789-3455; 606-789-3455. Fax: 606-220-0405. E-mail: info@bigsandybb.com. Web Site: http://www.bigsandybb.com. Also serves Auxier, Boons Camp, Denver, East Point, Hagerhill, Meally, West Van Lear & Williamsport. ICA: KY0070.

TV Market Ranking: Outside TV Markets (Auxier, Boons Camp, Denver, East Point, Hagerhill, Meally, VAN LEAR, West Van Lear, Williamsport). Franchise award date: N.A. Franchise expiration date: N.A. Began: March 5, 1960.
Channel capacity: N.A. Channels available but not in use: N.A.

Basic Service
Subscribers: 2,130.
Programming (received off-air): WCHS-TV (ABC, Antenna TV) Charleston; WKPI-TV (PBS) Pikeville; WOWK-TV (CBS) Huntington; WQCW (CW) Portsmouth; WSAZ-TV (MNT, NBC, This TV) Huntington; WVAH-TV (FOX, The Country Network) Charleston; WVPB-TV (PBS) Huntington; WYMT-TV (CBS, CW) Hazard.
Programming (via satellite): ION Television; QVC; Trinity Broadcasting Network (TBN); WGN America.
Fee: $40.00 installation; $19.95 monthly.

Expanded Basic Service 1
Subscribers: N.A.
Programming (via satellite): A&E; AMC; Animal Planet; Cartoon Network; CMT; CNN; Comedy Central; C-SPAN; Discovery Channel; Disney Channel; E! HD; ESPN; ESPN2; Food Network; Fox News Channel; Fox Sports 1; FOX Sports Networks; Freeform; FX; Hallmark Channel; HGTV; History; Lifetime; MTV; National Geographic Channel; Nickelodeon; Outdoor Channel; Pop; Spike TV; Syfy; TBS; The Weather Channel; TLC; TNT; truTV; Turner Classic Movies; TV Land; USA Network; VH1; WE tv.
Fee: $30.00 installation; $41.95 monthly.

Digital Basic Service
Subscribers: N.A.
Programming (via satellite): BBC America; Destination America; Discovery Kids Channel; DMX Music; Investigation Discovery; PBS HD; Science Channel.
Fee: $7.50 installation.

Pay Service 1
Pay Units: 575.
Programming (via satellite): HBO.
Fee: $7.50 installation; $12.75 monthly.

Pay Service 2
Pay Units: N.A.
Programming (via satellite): Showtime; Starz Encore.

Digital Pay Service 1
Pay Units: N.A.
Programming (via satellite): HBO (multiplexed); Showtime (multiplexed); Starz (multiplexed); Starz Encore (multiplexed); The Movie Channel (multiplexed).
Fee: $14.95 monthly (each).

Video-On-Demand: No

Pay-Per-View
Playboy TV.

Internet Service
Operational: Yes. Began: March 1, 2003.
Broadband Service: In-house.
Fee: $24.95-$54.95 monthly; $4.00 modem lease.

Telephone Service
Analog: Not Operational
Digital: Operational
Fee: $34.95 monthly

Miles of Plant: 120.0 (coaxial); None (fiber optic). Homes passed: 4,000.
President & General Manager: Paul David Butcher. Chief Technician: Marty Wright. Customer Service Manager: Brian Marshall. Office Manager: Joy Music.
Ownership: Big Sandy Broadband.

VANCEBURG—Time Warner Cable, 7800 Crescent Executive Dr, Charlotte, NC 28217. Phones: 888-882-4604; 614-431-1280. Web Site: http://www.timewarnercable.com. Also serves Garrison & Maloneton. ICA: KY0286.
TV Market Ranking: Below 100 (Garrison, Maloneton, VANCEBURG). Franchise award date: N.A. Franchise expiration date: N.A. Began: January 1, 1965.
Channel capacity: N.A. Channels available but not in use: N.A.

Basic Service
Subscribers: 338.
Programming (received off-air): WCPO-TV (ABC, Escape) Cincinnati; WKMR (PBS) Morehead; WKYT-TV (CBS, CW) Lexington; WOWK-TV (CBS) Huntington; WQCW (CW) Portsmouth; WSAZ-TV (MNT, NBC, This TV) Huntington; WTVQ-DT (ABC, Antenna TV, Laff, MNT) Lexington; WVAH-TV (FOX, The Country Network) Charleston; WXIX-TV (Bounce TV, FOX) Newport.
Programming (via satellite): A&E; AMC; CMT; Discovery Channel; ESPN; ESPN2; Food Network; Fox News Channel; Freeform; FX; HGTV; HLN; Lifetime; Nickelodeon; QVC; Spike TV; The Weather Channel; TNT; Trinity Broadcasting Network (TBN); USA Network; VH1; WGN America.
Fee: $49.99 installation; $33.30 monthly.

Expanded Basic Service 1
Subscribers: N.A.
Programming (via satellite): CNN; Disney Channel; TBS.
Fee: $3.75 monthly.

Pay Service 1
Pay Units: N.A.
Programming (via satellite): Cinemax; HBO.
Fee: $12.99 monthly.

Video-On-Demand: No

Internet Service
Operational: Yes.
Broadband Service: RoadRunner.
Fee: $24.95 monthly.

Telephone Service
Digital: Operational
Fee: $24.99 monthly
Miles of Plant: 19.0 (coaxial); None (fiber optic). Homes passed: 4,300.
President: Rhonda Fraas. Vice President & General Manager: David Kreiman. Vice President, Government & Public Affairs: Mary Jo Green. Vice President, Engineering: Randy Hall. Vice President, Marketing: Mark Psigoda. Senior Accounting Director: Karen Goodfellow. Technical Operations Director: Jim Cavender. Government Affairs Director: Steve Cuckler.
Ownership: Time Warner Cable (MSO).

VANCLEVE—TVS Cable, PO Box 1410, Hindman, KY 41822-1410. Phones: 606-946-2600; 606-785-3450; 606-633-0778. Fax: 606-785-3110. E-mail: tvs@tvscable.com. Web Site: http://www.tvscable.com. Also serves Lee City. ICA: KY0325.
TV Market Ranking: Below 100 (Lee City, VANCLEVE).
Channel capacity: 60 (not 2-way capable). Channels available but not in use: N.A.

Basic Service
Subscribers: 249. Commercial subscribers: 1.
Programming (received off-air): WDKY-TV (FOX) Danville; WKPC-TV (PBS) Louisville; WKYT-TV (CBS, CW) Lexington; WLEX-TV (MeTV, NBC) Lexington; WLFG (IND, PBJ, Retro TV) Grundy; WLJC-TV (TBN) Beattyville; WTVQ-DT (ABC, Antenna TV, Laff, MNT) Lexington; WUPX-TV (ION) Morehead; WYMT-TV (CBS, CW) Hazard.
Programming (via satellite): WGN America.
Fee: $50.00 installation; $23.50 monthly.

Expanded Basic Service 1
Subscribers: N.A.
Programming (via satellite): A&E; Animal Planet; Bloomberg Television; Cartoon Network; CNN; Comedy Central; C-SPAN; CW PLUS; Discovery Channel; E! HD; ESPN; ESPN2; Food Network; Fox News Channel; Fox Sports 1; Freeform; FX; Great American Country; Hallmark Channel; HGTV; History; HLN; HRTV; Lifetime; MTV; National Geographic Channel; Nickelodeon; Outdoor Channel; QVC; Spike TV; Syfy; TBS; The Weather Channel; TLC; TNT; Travel Channel; truTV; Turner Classic Movies; TV Land; USA Network; VH1.
Fee: $34.05 monthly.

Digital Basic Service
Subscribers: N.A.
Programming (via satellite): BBC America; Church Channel; Cloo; CMT; Daystar TV Network; Discovery Digital Networks; Disney XD; DMX Music; ESPNews; EVINE Live; Fox Sports 1; FSN Digital Atlantic; FSN Digital Central; FSN Digital Pacific; Fuse; FYI; Golf Channel; GSN; History International; IFC; JUCE TV; LMN; NBCSN; Nick Jr.; Nicktoons; RFD-TV; TeenNick; The Word Network; Trinity Broadcasting Network (TBN); WE tv.

Pay Service 1
Pay Units: N.A.
Programming (via satellite): HBO.

Digital Pay Service 1
Pay Units: N.A.
Programming (via satellite): Cinemax (multiplexed); Flix; HBO (multiplexed); Showtime (multiplexed); Starz (multiplexed); Starz Encore (multiplexed); Sundance TV; The Movie Channel (multiplexed).

Video-On-Demand: No

Pay-Per-View
iN DEMAND (delivered digitally); Playboy TV (delivered digitally); Fresh (delivered digitally).

Internet Service
Operational: Yes.
Fee: $24.95-$79.95 monthly.

Telephone Service
Digital: Operational
Fee: $34.99-$59.99 monthly
Miles of Plant: 28.0 (coaxial); 12.0 (fiber optic).
Vice President & General Manager: William K. Grigsby. Assistant Manager: Kenny Salmons. Program Director: Betty Thomas. Chief Technician: Tony Everage.
Ownership: TV Service Inc. (MSO).

VARNEY—Inter Mountain Cable Inc. Now served by HAROLD, KY [KY0006]. ICA: KY0178.

VERSAILLES—Time Warner Cable. Now served by RICHMOND, KY [KY0008]. ICA: KY0040.

VICCO—TVS Cable, PO Box 1410, Hindman, KY 41822-1410. Phones: 606-946-2600; 606-785-3450; 606-633-0778. Fax: 606-

Cable Systems—Kentucky

785-3110. E-mail: tvs@tvscable.com. Web Site: http://www.tvscable.com. Also serves Allock, Cutshin & Sassafras. ICA: KY0339.
TV Market Ranking: Below 100 (Allock, Cutshin, Sassafras, VICCO).
Channel capacity: N.A. Channels available but not in use: N.A.
Basic Service
Subscribers: 386. Commercial subscribers: 4.
Fee: $50.00 installation; $23.50 monthly.
Internet Service
Operational: Yes.
Fee: $24.95-$79.95 monthly.
Vice President & General Manager: William K. Grigsby.
Ownership: TV Service Inc. (MSO).

WALKERTOWN—Walkertown Cable, 208 Cleveland Ave, Hazard, KY 41701-1156. Phone: 606-436-4593. Fax: 606-436-4593. ICA: KY0157.
TV Market Ranking: Below 100 (WALKERTOWN). Franchise award date: N.A. Franchise expiration date: N.A. Began: August 27, 1957.
Channel capacity: N.A. Channels available but not in use: N.A.
Basic Service
Subscribers: N.A.
Programming (received off-air): WKMR (PBS) Morehead; WKYT-TV (CBS, CW) Lexington; WLEX-TV (MeTV, NBC) Lexington; WTVQ-DT (ABC, Antenna TV, Laff, MNT) Lexington; WYMT-TV (CBS, CW) Hazard.
Programming (via satellite): Disney Channel.
Fee: $50.00 installation.
Pay Service 1
Pay Units: N.A.
Programming (via satellite): HBO; The Movie Channel.
Fee: $7.50 monthly (TMC), $9.00 monthly (HBO).
Internet Service
Operational: No.
Telephone Service
None
Miles of Plant: 4.0 (coaxial); None (fiber optic). Homes passed: 500.
General Manager: Brenda Caudell. Chief Technician: Roy Godsy.
Ownership: Community TV Inc.

WALLINS CREEK—Zito Media, 102 S Main St, PO Box 665, Coudersport, PA 16915. Phones: 814-260-9055; 800-365-6988. E-mail: info@zitomedia.com. Web Site: http://www.zitomedia.com. Also serves Coldiron, Dayhoit, Keith & Wallins. ICA: KY0317.
TV Market Ranking: Below 100 (Coldiron, Dayhoit, Keith, Wallins, WALLINS CREEK).
Channel capacity: N.A. Channels available but not in use: N.A.
Basic Service
Subscribers: 78.
Programming (received off-air): WAGV (IND) Harlan; WATE-TV (ABC, Laff) Knoxville; WBIR-TV (MeTV, NBC) Knoxville; WBXX-TV (CW, Escape) Crossville; WDKY-TV (FOX) Danville; WETP-TV (PBS) Sneedville; WKHA (PBS) Hazard; WKYT-TV (CBS, CW) Lexington; WLEX-TV (MeTV, NBC) Lexington; WYMT-TV (CBS, CW) Hazard.
Programming (via satellite): WGN America.
Fee: $49.95 installation; $18.95 monthly.
Expanded Basic Service 1
Subscribers: N.A.
Programming (via satellite): A&E; AMC; Cartoon Network; CMT; CNBC; CNN; Comedy Central; C-SPAN; Discovery Channel; Disney Channel; E! HD; ESPN; ESPN2; Fox News Channel; Fox Sports 1; Freeform; FX; Golf Channel; HGTV; History; HLN; Lifetime; MTV; Nickelodeon; Oxygen; Spike TV; Syfy; TBS; The Weather Channel; TLC; TNT; Trinity Broadcasting Network (TBN); Turner Classic Movies; TV Land; USA Network; VH1.
Fee: $17.48 monthly.
Digital Basic Service
Subscribers: N.A.
Programming (via satellite): BBC America; Bloomberg Television; Discovery Life Channel; Disney XD; DMX Music; ESPN Classic; ESPNews; Fuse; FXM; FYI; GSN; History International; IFC; LMN; NBCSN; Nick 2; Nick Jr.; Nicktoons; Sundance TV; TeenNick; TV Guide Interactive Inc.; WE tv.
Digital Pay Service 1
Pay Units: N.A.
Programming (via satellite): Cinemax (multiplexed); Flix; HBO (multiplexed); Showtime (multiplexed); Starz (multiplexed); Starz Encore; The Movie Channel (multiplexed).
Video-On-Demand: No
Pay-Per-View
iN DEMAND (delivered digitally); The Pleasure Network (delivered digitally); Fresh (delivered digitally); Shorteez (delivered digitally); Playboy TV (delivered digitally).
Internet Service
Operational: No.
Telephone Service
None
Miles of Plant: 43.0 (coaxial); None (fiber optic). Homes passed: 1,547.
President: James Rigas.
Ownership: Zito Media (MSO).

WANETA—Peoples Telecom, 1080 Main St South, McKee, KY 40447. Phones: 606-593-5000; 606-287-7101. E-mail: prtccs@prtcnet.org. Web Site: http://www.prtcnet.org. Also serves Gray Hawk, Jackson County & McKee. ICA: KY0113.
TV Market Ranking: Below 100 (Gray Hawk, Jackson County, WANETA, McKee). Franchise award date: N.A. Franchise expiration date: N.A. Began: May 1, 1954.
Channel capacity: N.A. Channels available but not in use: N.A.
Basic Service
Subscribers: 3,729.
Programming (received off-air): WDKY-TV (FOX) Danville; WDYL-LD (Daystar TV) Louisville; WKLE (PBS) Lexington; WKYT-TV (CBS, CW) Lexington; WLEX-TV (MeTV, NBC) Lexington; WLJC-TV (TBN) Beattyville; WTVQ-DT (ABC, Antenna TV, Laff, MNT) Lexington; WUPX-TV (ION) Morehead; WYMT-TV (CBS, CW) Hazard; allband FM.
Programming (via satellite): WGN America.
Fee: $100.00 installation; $17.95 monthly.
Expanded Basic Service 1
Subscribers: N.A.
Programming (via satellite): A&E; AMC; Animal Planet; Cartoon Network; CNN; Discovery Channel; Disney Channel; ESPN; ESPN2; Food Network; Fox News Channel; FOX Sports Ohio/Sports Time Ohio; Freeform; FX; History; Lifetime; Spike TV; Syfy; TBS; The Weather Channel; TLC; TNT; truTV; Turner Classic Movies; TV Land; USA Network; VH1.
Fee: $33.45 monthly.
Digital Basic Service
Subscribers: N.A.
Programming (via satellite): BBC America; Bloomberg Television; CMT; Destination America; Discovery Kids Channel; Discovery Life Channel; Disney XD; DMX Music; ESPN Classic; ESPN2; ESPNews; Fox Sports 1; Fuse; FXM; FYI; Golf Channel; HGTV; History; History International; Investigation Discovery; LMN; MTV Classic; MTV Hits; MTV2; Nick Jr.; Nicktoons; Outdoor Channel; Ovation; OWN: Oprah Winfrey Network; RFD-TV; Science Channel; TeenNick; Trinity Broadcasting Network (TBN); Turner Classic Movies; VH1 Soul.
Digital Pay Service 1
Pay Units: N.A.
Programming (via satellite): Cinemax; Flix; HBO (multiplexed); Showtime (multiplexed); Starz (multiplexed); Starz Encore (multiplexed); The Movie Channel (multiplexed).
Fee: $10.95 monthly (Cinemax or Starz/Encore), $12.95 monthly (HBO or Showtime).
Video-On-Demand: No
Internet Service
Operational: No, DSL.
Telephone Service
Analog: Operational
Miles of Plant: 82.0 (coaxial); None (fiber optic).
Chief Executive Officer & General Manager: Keith Grabbard. Chief Technician: Jeff Bingham.
Ownership: Peoples Rural Telephone Cooperative.

WARSAW—Time Warner Cable. Now served by COVINGTON, KY [KY0002]. ICA: KY0148.

WELCHS CREEK—Formerly served by Vital Communications. No longer in operation. ICA: KY0192.

WEST LIBERTY—MTTV. Formerly [KY0090]. This cable system has converted to IPTV, 425 Main St, PO Box 399, West Liberty, KY 41472. Phones: 800-939-3121; 606-743-3121. Fax: 606-743-3635. E-mail: service@mountaintelephone.com. Web Site: http://www.mrtc.com. Also serves Campton, Cannel City, Elliott County (unincorporated areas), Ezel, Frenchburg, Hazel Green, Index, Landsaw, Malone, Means, Menifee County (unincorporated areas), Mize, Morgan County (unincorporated areas), Sandy Hook & Wolfe County (unincorporated areas). ICA: KY5013.
TV Market Ranking: Below 100 (Campton (portions), Cannel City, Ezel, Frenchburg, Hazel Green, Landsaw, Malone, Means, Menifee County (unincorporated areas), Mize, Morgan County (unincorporated areas), WEST LIBERTY, Wolfe County (unincorporated areas)).
Channel capacity: N.A. Channels available but not in use: N.A.
Basic
Subscribers: 1,236.
Fee: $34.95 monthly. Includes 30+ channels & 1 STB.
Expanded Basic
Subscribers: N.A.
Fee: $64.95 monthly. Includes 145 channels & 1 STB.
Digital
Subscribers: N.A.
Fee: $77.95 monthly. Includes 250+ channels, all HD channels & 1 STB.
HD
Subscribers: N.A.
Fee: $5.95 monthly.
Hispanic
Subscribers: N.A.
Fee: $12.95 monthly. Includes 8 channels.
Cinemax
Subscribers: N.A.
Fee: $12.95 monthly. Includes 10 channels.
HBO
Subscribers: N.A.
Fee: $19.95 monthly. Includes 9 channels.
Showtime/TMC/Flix
Subscribers: N.A.
Fee: $13.95 monthly. Includes 13 channels.
Starz/Encore
Subscribers: N.A.
Fee: $12.95 monthly. Includes 15 channels.
Internet Service
Operational: Yes.
Fee: $39.95-$79.95 monthly.
Telephone Service
Digital: Operational
Fee: $24.00 monthly
General Manager: Shayne Ison. Marketing Director: Lisa Fannin. Central Office Manager: Richard Fraley. Office Manager: Angie Pennington.
Ownership: Mountain Rural Telephone Cooperative.

WEST LIBERTY—MTTV. This cable system has converted to IPTV. Now served by WEST LIBERTY, KY [KY5013]. ICA: KY0090.

WHITESBURG—Formerly served by Comcast Cable. No longer in operation. ICA: KY0123.

WHITESVILLE—Mediacom, 90 Main St, Benton, KY 42025-1132. Phones: 845-695-2762; 417-875-5560 (Springfield regional office); 270-527-9939. Fax: 270-527-0813. Web Site: http://www.mediacomcable.com. Also serves Daviess County (portions), Fordsville & Ohio County (portions). ICA: KY0290.
TV Market Ranking: Outside TV Markets (Daviess County (portions), Fordsville, Ohio County (portions), WHITESVILLE). Franchise award date: March 15, 1983. Franchise expiration date: N.A. Began: January 1, 1983.
Channel capacity: N.A. Channels available but not in use: N.A.
Basic Service
Subscribers: 77.
Programming (received off-air): WEHT (ABC) Evansville; WEVV-TV (CBS, FOX) Evansville; WFIE (NBC, This TV) Evansville; WKOH (PBS) Owensboro; WNIN (PBS) Evansville; WTVW (CW, MeTV) Evansville.
Programming (via satellite): A&E; AMC; Animal Planet; Cartoon Network; CMT; CNBC; CNN; Comedy Central; C-SPAN; Discovery Channel; Disney Channel; E! HD; ESPN; ESPN2; EWTN Global Catholic Net-

Kentucky—Cable Systems

work; Food Network; Fox News Channel; Fox Sports 1; Freeform; FX; Great American Country; Hallmark Channel; HGTV; History; HLN; Lifetime; MSNBC; MTV; National Geographic Channel; Nickelodeon; Outdoor Channel; QVC; Spike TV; Syfy; TBS; The Weather Channel; TLC; TNT; Travel Channel; Trinity Broadcasting Network (TBN); TV Land; USA Network; VH1; WE tv; WGN America.
Fee: $29.95 installation; $69.95 monthly; $3.95 converter.

Pay Service 1
Pay Units: N.A.
Programming (via satellite): Cinemax; HBO; Starz; Starz Encore.
Fee: $9.00 monthly (Cinemax), $10.00 monthly (HBO).

Video-On-Demand: No

Internet Service
Operational: No.

Telephone Service
None
Miles of Plant: 44.0 (coaxial); None (fiber optic). Homes passed: 930.
Regional Vice President: Bill Copeland. Vice President, Financial Reporting: Kenneth J. Kohrs. General Manager: Dale Haney. Regional Technical Operations Director: Alan Freedman. Marketing Director: Will Kuebler. Technical Operations Manager: Jeff Brown. Marketing Manager: Melanie Westerman.
Ownership: Mediacom LLC (MSO).

WHITLEY CITY—Access Cable Television Inc. Now served by McCREARY COUNTY, KY [KY0331]. ICA: KY0055.

WHITLEY COUNTY—Access Cable Television Inc, 302 Enterprise Dr, Somerset, KY 42501. Phone: 606-677-2444. Fax: 606-677-2443. E-mail: cable@accesshsd.net. Web Site: http://www.accesshsd.com. Also serves Williamsburg. ICA: KY0330.
TV Market Ranking: Below 100 (WHITLEY COUNTY, Williamsburg).
Channel capacity: N.A. Channels available but not in use: N.A.

Basic Service
Subscribers: 600.
Fee: $28.50 monthly.
President & General Manager: Roy Baker.
Ownership: Access Cable Television Inc. (MSO).

WHITLEY COUNTY (portions)—Zito Media, 102 S Main St, PO Box 665, Coudersport, PA 16915. Phones: 814-260-9055; 800-365-6988. E-mail: info@zitomedia.com. Web Site: http://www.zitomedia.com. Also serves Knox County (portions). ICA: KY0083.
TV Market Ranking: Below 100 (Knox County (portions), WHITLEY COUNTY (PORTIONS)). Franchise award date: December 1, 1995. Franchise expiration date: N.A. Began: March 1, 1980.
Channel capacity: 60 (2-way capable). Channels available but not in use: N.A.

Basic Service
Subscribers: 151.
Programming (received off-air): WATE-TV (ABC, Laff) Knoxville; WBIR-TV (MeTV, NBC) Knoxville; WBXX-TV (CW, Escape) Crossville; WDKY-TV (FOX) Danville; WKSO-TV (PBS) Somerset; WKYT-TV (CBS, CW) Lexington; WLEX-TV (MeTV, NBC) Lexington; WLJC-TV (TBN) Beattyville; WPXK-TV (ION) Jellico; WVLT-TV (CBS, MNT) Knoxville; WYMT-TV (CBS, CW) Hazard; allband FM.
Programming (via satellite): CMT; CNN; C-SPAN; Discovery Channel; Disney Channel; ESPN; ESPN2; Fox News Channel; Freeform; Hallmark Channel; HGTV; HLN; Lifetime; MTV; Nickelodeon; QVC; Spike TV; TBS; The Weather Channel; TNT; Travel Channel; Trinity Broadcasting Network (TBN); USA Network; VH1; WGN America.
Fee: $49.95 installation; $11.90 monthly; $3.95 converter.

Digital Basic Service
Subscribers: N.A.
Programming (via satellite): BBC America; Bloomberg Television; Cloo; Discovery Digital Networks; Disney XD; ESPN Classic; ESPNews; Fox Sports 1; Fuse; FXM; FYI; Golf Channel; GSN; History International; IFC; LMN; National Geographic Channel; NBCSN; Nick Jr.; Outdoor Channel; Syfy; TeenNick; Turner Classic Movies; WE tv.

Digital Pay Service 1
Pay Units: N.A.
Programming (via satellite): Cinemax (multiplexed); HBO (multiplexed); Showtime (multiplexed); Starz (multiplexed); Starz Encore (multiplexed); The Movie Channel (multiplexed).

Video-On-Demand: No

Pay-Per-View
iN DEMAND (delivered digitally); Playboy TV (delivered digitally); Fresh (delivered digitally).

Internet Service
Operational: No.

Telephone Service
None
Miles of Plant: 80.0 (coaxial); None (fiber optic). Homes passed: 1,300.
President: James Rigas.
Ownership: Zito Media (MSO).

WICKLIFFE—Zito Media, 102 S Main St, PO Box 665, Coudersport, PA 16915. Phones: 814-260-9055; 800-365-6988. E-mail: info@zitomedia.com. Web Site: http://www.zitomedia.com. Also serves Arlington, Bardwell, Barlow, Carlisle County, Clinton & La Center. ICA: KY0106.
TV Market Ranking: 69 (Arlington, Bardwell, Barlow, Carlisle County, Clinton, La Center, WICKLIFFE). Franchise award date: N.A. Franchise expiration date: N.A. Began: August 1, 1981.
Channel capacity: N.A. Channels available but not in use: N.A.

Basic Service
Subscribers: 631.
Programming (received off-air): KBSI (FOX) Cape Girardeau; KFVS-TV (CBS, CW, MeTV) Cape Girardeau; WDKA (MNT, The Country Network) Paducah; WKPD (PBS) Paducah; WPSD-TV (Antenna TV, NBC) Paducah; WQWQ-LP (CW, MeTV) Paducah; WSIL-TV (ABC) Harrisburg.
Programming (via satellite): A&E; AMC; Animal Planet; BET; Cartoon Network; CNBC; CNN; Comedy Central; C-SPAN; Discovery Channel; Disney Channel; Disney XD; ESPN; ESPN2; Fox News Channel; Freeform; Fuse; FX; Great American Country; Hallmark Channel; HGTV; History; HLN; Lifetime; National Geographic Channel; Outdoor Channel; Syfy; TBS; The Weather Channel; TLC; TNT; Trinity Broadcasting Network (TBN); Turner Classic Movies; USA Network; WGN America.
Fee: $49.95 installation; $17.20 monthly.

Digital Basic Service
Subscribers: N.A.
Programming (via satellite): BBC America; Bloomberg Television; Discovery Life Channel; DMX Music; E! HD; ESPN Classic; ESPNews; Fox Sports 1; FYI; Golf Channel; GSN; History International; WE tv.

Digital Expanded Basic Service
Subscribers: N.A.
Programming (via satellite): DMX Music; FXM; LMN; Starz Encore.
Fee: $13.95 monthly.

Pay Service 1
Pay Units: N.A.
Programming (via satellite): Cinemax; HBO; Showtime; Starz Encore; The Movie Channel.

Digital Pay Service 1
Pay Units: N.A.
Programming (via satellite): Cinemax (multiplexed); Flix; HBO (multiplexed); Showtime (multiplexed); The Movie Channel (multiplexed).
Fee: $10.00 monthly (each).

Video-On-Demand: Yes

Pay-Per-View
ESPN Now (delivered digitally); Hot Choice (delivered digitally); Playboy TV (delivered digitally); Fresh (delivered digitally); Shorteez (delivered digitally); Urban Xtra (delivered digitally).

Internet Service
Operational: Yes.
Fee: $49.95 installation; $44.95 monthly; $5.00 modem lease.

Telephone Service
Digital: Operational
Miles of Plant: 66.0 (coaxial); 55.0 (fiber optic). Homes passed: 3,144.
President: James Rigas.
Ownership: Zito Media (MSO).

WILLIAMSBURG—Time Warner Cable. Now served by CORBIN, KY [KY0030]. ICA: KY0053.

WILLIAMSTOWN—Williamstown Cable, 400 North Main St, PO Box 147, Williamstown, KY 41097. Phone: 859-824-3633. Fax: 859-824-6320. E-mail: rosborne@wtownky.org. Web Site: http://wkybb.net. ICA: KY0109. TV Market Ranking: 17 (WILLIAMSTOWN). Franchise award date: N.A. Franchise expiration date: N.A. Began: November 22, 1984.
Channel capacity: N.A. Channels available but not in use: N.A.

Basic Service
Subscribers: 899.
Programming (received off-air): WCET (PBS) Cincinnati; WCPO-TV (ABC, Escape) Cincinnati; WDRB (Antenna TV, FOX) Louisville; WHAS-TV (ABC) Louisville; WKON (PBS) Owenton; WKRC-TV (CBS, CW) Cincinnati; WKYT-TV (CBS, CW) Lexington; WLEX-TV (MeTV, NBC) Lexington; WLWT (MeTV, NBC) Cincinnati; WSTR-TV (Antenna TV, MNT) Cincinnati; WTVQ-DT (ABC, Antenna TV, Laff, MNT) Lexington; WXIX-TV (Bounce TV, FOX) Newport.
Programming (via satellite): A&E; AMC; Animal Planet; Boomerang; Cartoon Network; CMT; CNN; Comedy Central; C-SPAN; CW PLUS; Discovery Channel; Disney Channel; Disney XD; DIY Network; E! HD; ESPN; ESPN Classic; ESPN2; EWTN Global Catholic Network; Food Network; Fox News Channel; Fox Sports 1; FOX Sports Networks; Freeform; FX; Golf Channel; Hallmark Channel; HGTV; History; HLN; ION Television; Lifetime; MTV; National Geographic Channel; NFL Network; Nickelodeon; Outdoor Channel; Oxygen; Pop; QVC; RFD-TV; Spike TV; Syfy; TBS; The Weather Channel; TLC; TNT; Travel Channel; Trinity Broadcasting Network (TBN); truTV; Turner Classic Movies; TV Land; USA Network; VH1; WGN America.
Fee: $30.00 installation; $19.95 monthly; $5.00 converter.

Digital Basic Service
Subscribers: N.A.
Programming (via satellite): BBC America; CMT; Destination America; Discovery Kids Channel; Discovery Life Channel; ESPNews; FOX College Sports Central; FOX College Sports Pacific; FXM; FYI; Great American Country; GSN; History International; IFC; Investigation Discovery; MTV Classic; NBCSN; Nick Jr.; Nicktoons; OWN: Oprah Winfrey Network; Science Channel; Starz Encore; TeenNick; WE tv.

Digital Pay Service 1
Pay Units: N.A.
Programming (via satellite): Cinemax (multiplexed); Flix; HBO (multiplexed); Showtime (multiplexed); Starz; Sundance TV; The Movie Channel (multiplexed).

Video-On-Demand: Planned

Internet Service
Operational: Yes.
Fee: $75.00 installation; $39.95 monthly.

Telephone Service
None
Miles of Plant: 35.0 (coaxial); None (fiber optic). Homes passed: 1,500.
Treasurer & City Clerk: Vivian Link. General Manager: Chuck Hudson. Assistant Manager & Chief Technician: Roy Osborne. Program Director: Tony Penick. Marketing Manager: Dale Caskey.
Ownership: City of Williamstown Cable TV.

WILLISBURG—Formerly served by Windjammer Cable. No longer in operation. ICA: KY0322.

WINCHESTER—Time Warner Cable. Now served by RICHMOND, KY [KY0008]. ICA: KY0018.

LOUISIANA

Total Systems: 89	Communities with Applications: 0
Total Communities Served: 404	Number of Basic Subscribers: 575,842
Franchises Not Yet Operating: 0	Number of Expanded Basic Subscribers: 9,485
Applications Pending: 0	Number of Pay Units: 347

Top 100 Markets Represented: New Orleans (31); Texarkana, TX-Shreveport, LA (58); Baton Rouge (87); Beaumont-Port Arthur, TX (88); Monroe, LA-El Dorado, AR (99).

For a list of cable communities in this section, see the Cable Community Index located in the back of Cable Volume 2.
For explanation of terms used in cable system listings, see p. D-11.

ABBEVILLE—Cox Communications. Now served by BATON ROUGE, LA [LA0003]. ICA: LA0018.

ACADIA PARISH (portions)—Formerly served by Almega Cable. No longer in operation. ICA: LA0236.

ALEXANDRIA—Suddenlink Communications, 3250 Donahue Ferry Rd, Pineville, LA 71360. Phone: 314-315-9400. Fax: 318-640-6951. Web Site: http://www.suddenlink.com. Also serves Ball, Creola, Grant Parish (portions), Pineville, Pollock & Rapides Parish. ICA: LA0006.
TV Market Ranking: Below 100 (Ball, Creola, Grant Parish (portions), Pollock, Rapides Parish, ALEXANDRIA, Pineville). Franchise award date: August 23, 1957. Franchise expiration date: N.A. Began: October 20, 1958.
Channel capacity: 15 (operating 2-way). Channels available but not in use: N.A.
Basic Service
Subscribers: 21,810. Commercial subscribers: 2,460.
Programming (received off-air): KALB-TV (CBS, CW, NBC) Alexandria; KLAX-TV (ABC) Alexandria; KLFY-TV (CBS) Lafayette; KLPA-TV (PBS) Alexandria; WNTZ-TV (FOX, MNT) Natchez.
Programming (via satellite): ION Television; Pop; QVC; TBS; WGN America.
Fee: $40.00 installation; $12.31 monthly.
Expanded Basic Service 1
Subscribers: N.A.
Programming (via satellite): A&E; AMC; Animal Planet; BET; Bravo; Cartoon Network; CNBC; CNN; Comedy Central; C-SPAN; C-SPAN 2; Discovery Channel; Disney Channel; E! HD; ESPN; ESPN2; EWTN Global Catholic Network; Food Network; Fox News Channel; Fox Sports 1; FOX Sports Southwest; Freeform; FX; FXM; Great American Country; HGTV; History; HLN; Lifetime; LMN; MoviePlex; MSNBC; MTV; NBCSN; Nickelodeon; Outdoor Channel; Spike TV; Syfy; The Weather Channel; TLC; TNT; Travel Channel; Trinity Broadcasting Network (TBN); truTV; Turner Classic Movies; TV Land; USA Network; VH1.
Fee: $38.00 installation; $42.67 monthly.
Digital Basic Service
Subscribers: N.A.
Programming (via satellite): BBC America; Bloomberg Television; Discovery Digital Networks; Disney XD; ESPN Classic; ESPNews; Fuse; FYI; Golf Channel; GSN; Hallmark Channel; History International; IFC; MC; NBA TV; Nick Jr.; Nicktoons; Sundance TV; TeenNick.

Digital Pay Service 1
Pay Units: N.A.
Programming (via satellite): Cinemax (multiplexed); Flix; HBO (multiplexed); Showtime (multiplexed); Starz; The Movie Channel (multiplexed).
Video-On-Demand: No
Pay-Per-View
ESPN Now (delivered digitally); NBA TV (delivered digitally); MLB/NHL (delivered digitally); Fresh (delivered digitally); Hot Choice (delivered digitally); Shorteez (delivered digitally); Playboy TV (delivered digitally); iN DEMAND (delivered digitally).
Internet Service
Operational: Yes.
Subscribers: 20,343.
Broadband Service: Suddenlink High Speed Internet.
Fee: $45.00 installation; $29.95 monthly.
Telephone Service
Digital: Operational
Subscribers: 12,645.
Fee: $39.95 monthly
Miles of Plant: 1,594.0 (coaxial); 362.0 (fiber optic). Homes passed: 52,816.
Senior Vice President, Corporate Finance: Michael Pflantz. Vice President, Accounting: Sabrina Warr. General Manager: Diana DeVille. Chief Technician: Stephen Frye.
Ownership: Cequel Communications Holdings I LLC (MSO).

ANGOLA—Formerly served by Bailey Cable TV Inc. No longer in operation. ICA: LA0224.

ARCADIA—Alliance Communications, PO Box 9090, Tyler, TX 75711. Phones: 903-561-4411 (Tyler, TX office); 800-842-8160; 501-679-6619. E-mail: marketing@alliancecable.net. Web Site: http://www.alliancecable.net. Also serves Bienville Parish (portions). ICA: LA0073.
TV Market Ranking: Below 100 (ARCADIA, Bienville Parish (portions)). Franchise award date: May 23, 1979. Franchise expiration date: N.A. Began: January 1, 1981.
Channel capacity: N.A. Channels available but not in use: N.A.
Basic Service
Subscribers: 80.
Programming (received off-air): KLTM-TV (PBS) Monroe; KMSS-TV (FOX) Shreveport; KNOE-TV (ABC, CBS, CW) Monroe; KSLA (Bounce TV, CBS, Grit, This TV) Shreveport; KTAL-TV (NBC) Texarkana; KTBS-TV (ABC) Shreveport; KTVE (NBC) El Dorado.
Programming (via satellite): AMC; BET; CNN; Discovery Channel; ESPN; Freeform; HLN; ION Television; MTV; Nickelodeon; Pop; QVC; Spike TV; Syfy; The Weather Channel; Trinity Broadcasting Network (TBN); WE tv.
Fee: $45.00 installation; $22.45 monthly.

Expanded Basic Service 1
Subscribers: N.A.
Programming (via satellite): Animal Planet; CMT; Disney Channel; ESPN2; Fox News Channel; FOX Sports Southwest; History; TBS; TNT; truTV; USA Network; WGN America.
Fee: $16.00 monthly.
Digital Basic Service
Subscribers: N.A.
Programming (via satellite): BBC America; Bloomberg Television; Bravo; CMT; Destination America; Discovery Kids Channel; Discovery Life Channel; Disney XD; DMX Music; ESPN Classic; EVINE Live; Fox Sports 1; Fuse; FXM; FYI; Golf Channel; GSN; HGTV; History International; IFC; Investigation Discovery; LMN; MTV Classic; MTV Hits; MTV2; NBCSN; Nick Jr.; Outdoor Channel; OWN: Oprah Winfrey Network; Science Channel; TeenNick; Turner Classic Movies; VH1 Soul.
Digital Pay Service 1
Pay Units: N.A.
Programming (via satellite): Cinemax (multiplexed); Flix; HBO (multiplexed); Showtime (multiplexed); Starz (multiplexed); Starz Encore (multiplexed); The Movie Channel (multiplexed).
Video-On-Demand: No
Pay-Per-View
iN DEMAND (delivered digitally); Hot Choice (delivered digitally); Sports PPV (delivered digitally); ESPN Now (delivered digitally); Playboy TV (delivered digitally).
Internet Service
Operational: No.
Telephone Service
None
Miles of Plant: 36.0 (coaxial); None (fiber optic). Homes passed: 1,572.
Chief Financial Officer: David Starrett. Vice President & General Manager: John Brinker. Vice President, Programming: Julie Newman.
Ownership: Buford Media Group LLC (MSO).

ARNAUDVILLE—Allen's TV Cable Service Inc, 800 Victor II Blvd, PO Box 2643, Morgan City, LA 70380. Phone: 985-384-8335. E-mail: info@atvci.net. Web Site: http://www.atvc.net. Also serves St. Landry Parish (portions) & St. Martin Parish (portions). ICA: LA0239.
TV Market Ranking: 87 (St. Martin Parish (portions)); Below 100 (St. Landry Parish (portions), ARNAUDVILLE, St. Martin Parish (portions)).
Channel capacity: N.A. Channels available but not in use: N.A.
Basic Service
Subscribers: 348.
Fee: $66.90 installation; $18.65 monthly.
Miles of Plant: 187.0 (coaxial); 100.0 (fiber optic). Homes passed: 4,719.

President & General Manager: Gregory A. Price.
Ownership: Allen's TV Cable Service Inc. (MSO).

ASSUMPTION PARISH (portions)—Allen's TV Cable Service Inc, 800 Victor II Blvd, PO Box 2643, Morgan City, LA 70380. Phone: 985-384-8335. E-mail: info@atvci.net. Web Site: http://www.atvc.net. Also serves Belle River & Pierre Part. ICA: LA0240.
TV Market Ranking: 87 (ASSUMPTION PARISH (PORTIONS), Belle River, Pierre Part).
Channel capacity: N.A. Channels available but not in use: N.A.
Basic Service
Subscribers: 1,454.
Fee: $66.90 installation; $19.45 monthly.
President & General Manager: Gregory A. Price.
Ownership: Allen's TV Cable Service Inc. (MSO).

BASILE—Alliance Communications, PO Box 9090, Tyler, TX 75711. Phones: 903-561-4411 (Tyler, TX office); 800-842-8160; 501-679-6619. E-mail: marketing@alliancecable.net. Web Site: http://www.alliancecable.net. ICA: LA0094.
TV Market Ranking: Outside TV Markets (BASILE). Franchise award date: December 8, 1981. Franchise expiration date: N.A. Began: July 1, 1982.
Channel capacity: N.A. Channels available but not in use: N.A.
Basic Service
Subscribers: 87.
Programming (received off-air): KADN-TV (FOX, MNT) Lafayette; KALB-TV (CBS, CW, NBC) Alexandria; KATC (ABC, CW, Grit) Lafayette; KLFY-TV (CBS) Lafayette; KLTL-TV (PBS) Lake Charles; KPLC (Bounce TV, NBC, This TV) Lake Charles.
Programming (via satellite): EWTN Global Catholic Network; QVC; TBS; WGN America.
Fee: $45.00 installation; $25.45 monthly.
Expanded Basic Service 1
Subscribers: N.A.
Programming (via satellite): A&E; AMC; Animal Planet; BET; Cartoon Network; CMT; CNBC; CNN; Comedy Central; C-SPAN; Discovery Channel; Disney Channel; Disney XD; E! HD; ESPN; ESPN2; Fox News Channel; FOX Sports Networks; Freeform; HGTV; History; HLN; Lifetime; MTV; Nickelodeon; Outdoor Channel; Oxygen; Spike TV; Syfy; The Weather Channel; TLC; TNT; Travel Channel; TV Land; USA Network; VH1; WE tv.
Fee: $23.10 monthly.

2017 Edition   D-333

Louisiana—Cable Systems

Digital Basic Service
Subscribers: N.A.
Programming (via satellite): BBC America; Bloomberg Television; Bravo; CMT; Destination America; Discovery Kids Channel; Discovery Life Channel; Disney XD; DMX Music; EVINE Live; Fox Sports 1; Fuse; FXM; FYI; Golf Channel; GSN; History International; IFC; Investigation Discovery; LMN; MTV Classic; MTV Hits; MTV2; NBCSN; Nick Jr.; OWN: Oprah Winfrey Network; Science Channel; TeenNick; Trinity Broadcasting Network (TBN); Turner Classic Movies; VH1 Soul.

Pay Service 1
Pay Units: N.A.
Programming (via satellite): Cinemax; HBO.

Digital Pay Service 1
Pay Units: N.A.
Programming (via satellite): Cinemax (multiplexed); Flix; HBO (multiplexed); Showtime (multiplexed); Starz (multiplexed); Starz Encore (multiplexed); The Movie Channel (multiplexed).

Video-On-Demand: No

Pay-Per-View
iN DEMAND (delivered digitally); Hot Choice (delivered digitally); Club Jenna (delivered digitally); Playboy TV (delivered digitally).

Internet Service
Operational: No.

Telephone Service
None
Miles of Plant: 15.0 (coaxial); None (fiber optic). Homes passed: 808.
Chief Financial Officer: David Starrett. Vice President & General Manager: John Brinker. Vice President, Programming: Julie Newman.
Ownership: Buford Media Group LLC (MSO).

BASTROP—Suddenlink Communications, 1611 Park Loop Dr, Bastrop, LA 71220-3474. Phone: 314-315-9400. Fax: 318-283-1094. Web Site: http://www.suddenlink.com. Also serves Collinston, Mer Rouge & Morehouse Parish (portions). ICA: LA0027.
TV Market Ranking: 99 (BASTROP, Collinston, Mer Rouge). Franchise award date: N.A. Franchise expiration date: N.A. Began: December 1, 1964.
Channel capacity: 60 (operating 2-way). Channels available but not in use: N.A.

Basic Service
Subscribers: 3,659. Commercial subscribers: 313.
Programming (received off-air): KARD (Bounce TV, FOX) West Monroe; KLTM-TV (PBS) Monroe; KMCT-TV (IND) West Monroe; KMLU (MeTV) Columbia; KNOE-TV (ABC, CBS, CW) Monroe; KTVE (NBC) El Dorado.
Programming (via satellite): BET; CNN; C-SPAN; ESPN; FOX Sports Southwest; HLN; INSP; Pop; QVC; Spike TV; TBS; The Weather Channel; WGN America.
Fee: $40.00 installation; $33.50 monthly.

Expanded Basic Service 1
Subscribers: N.A.
Programming (via satellite): A&E; AMC; Animal Planet; Bravo; Cartoon Network; CNBC; Comedy Central; C-SPAN 2; Discovery Channel; Disney Channel; DMX Music; E! HD; ESPN2; Food Network; Fox News Channel; Fox Sports 1; Freeform; FX; Great American Country; HGTV; History; Lifetime; MSNBC; MTV; NBCSN; Nickelodeon; Oxygen; Syfy; TLC; TNT; Travel Channel; TV Land; USA Network; VH1.
Fee: $11.65 monthly.

Digital Basic Service
Subscribers: N.A.
Programming (via satellite): BBC America; Bloomberg Television; Discovery Digital Networks; Disney XD; ESPN Classic; ESPNews; FYI; Golf Channel; GSN; Hallmark Channel; History International; IFC; LMN; Outdoor Channel; Sundance TV; Trinity Broadcasting Network (TBN).

Pay Service 1
Pay Units: N.A.
Programming (via satellite): Cinemax; HBO; Showtime; Starz; Starz Encore; The Movie Channel.
Fee: $35.00 installation; $10.00 monthly (Cinemax), $12.00 monthly (HBO), $13.50 monthly (Showtime or Encore).

Digital Pay Service 1
Pay Units: N.A.
Programming (via satellite): Cinemax (multiplexed); HBO (multiplexed); Showtime (multiplexed); Starz (multiplexed); The Movie Channel (multiplexed).

Video-On-Demand: No

Pay-Per-View
Playboy TV (delivered digitally); Fresh (delivered digitally); NBA TV (delivered digitally); ESPN Now (delivered digitally); iN DEMAND (delivered digitally).

Internet Service
Operational: Yes.
Subscribers: 3,867.
Broadband Service: Suddenlink High Speed Internet.
Fee: $45.00 installation; $29.95 monthly.

Telephone Service
Digital: Operational
Subscribers: 2,751.
Fee: $39.95 monthly
Miles of Plant: 364.0 (coaxial); 66.0 (fiber optic). Homes passed: 10,202.
Senior Vice President, Corporate Finance: Michael Pflantz. Vice President, Accounting: Sabrina Warr. General Manager: Ron Watters. Chief Technician: Chris Parrott. District Technician: Robert Ingram.
Ownership: Cequel Communications Holdings I LLC (MSO).

BATON ROUGE—Cox Communications, 6205 Peachtree Dunwoody Rd, 12th Floor, Atlanta, GA 30328. Phone: 404-269-6590. Web Site: http://www.cox.com. Also serves Abbeville, Addis, Ascension Parish, Baker, Baldwin, Bayou Pigeon, Bayou Sorrel, Bayou Vista, Breaux Bridge, Broussard, Brusly, Carencro, Carville, Cecelia, Centerville, Central, Charenton, Crowley, Delcambre, Denham Springs, Donaldsonville, Duplessis, Duson, East Baton Rouge Parish, Erath, Erwinville, Franklin, Garden City, Gonzales, Gramercy, Grosse Tete, Henderson, Iberia Parish, Iberville, Iberville Parish, Jeanerette, Kaplan, Lafayette, Lafayette Parish, Loreauville, Lutcher, Maurice, Milton, New Iberia, Parks, Patterson, Plaquemine, Port Allen, Rayne, Rosedale, Scott, Slaughter, Sorrento, St. Gabriel, St. James Parish, St. Martin Parish, St. Martinville, St. Mary Parish, Sunshine, Verdunville, Vermilion Parish, Walker (portions), Watson, West Baton Rouge Parish, White Castle, Youngsville & Zachary. ICA: LA0003.
TV Market Ranking: 87 (Addis, Ascension Parish, Baker, BATON ROUGE, Bayou Pigeon, Bayou Sorrel, Brusly, Carville, Central, Denham Springs, Donaldsonville, Duplessis, East Baton Rouge Parish, Erwinville, Gonzales, Grosse Tete, Iberia Parish (portions), Iberville, Iberville Parish, Jeanerette, Loreauville, New Iberia, Plaquemine, Port Allen, Rosedale, Slaughter, Sorrento, St. Gabriel, St. Martin Parish (portions), Sunshine, Walker (portions), Watson, White Castle, Zachary); Below 100 (Abbeville, Breaux Bridge, Broussard, Carencro, Cecelia, Crowley, Delcambre, Duson, Erath, Henderson, Kaplan, Lafayette, Lafayette Parish, Maurice, Milton, Parks, Rayne, Scott, St. Martinville, Vermilion Parish, Youngsville, Iberia Parish (portions), St. Martin Parish (portions); Outside TV Markets (Baldwin, Bayou Vista, Centerville, Charenton, Franklin, Garden City, Gramercy, Lutcher, Patterson, St. Mary Parish, Verdunville). Franchise award date: January 1, 1974. Franchise expiration date: N.A. Began: April 21, 1975.
Channel capacity: N.A. Channels available but not in use: N.A.

Basic Service
Subscribers: 142,513. Commercial subscribers: 4,872.
Programming (received off-air): KPBN-LP (America One, IND, Untamed Sports TV) Baton Rouge; KZUP-CD (Retro TV) Baton Rouge; WAFB (Bounce TV, CBS) Baton Rouge; WBRZ-TV (ABC) Baton Rouge; WGMB-TV (FOX) Baton Rouge; WLFT-CD (MeTV, Soul of the South, The Country Network) Baton Rouge; WLPB-TV (PBS) Baton Rouge; WVLA-TV (NBC, This TV) Baton Rouge; 14 FMs.
Programming (via satellite): C-SPAN; C-SPAN 2; Discovery Channel; EWTN Global Catholic Network; Hallmark Channel; HLN; QVC; The Weather Channel; WGN America.
Fee: $54.95 installation; $21.99 monthly; $2.00 converter.

Expanded Basic Service 1
Subscribers: N.A.
Programming (via satellite): A&E; AMC; Animal Planet; BET; Bravo; Cartoon Network; CMT; CNBC; CNN; Comedy Central; Discovery Channel; Disney Channel; E! HD; ESPN; ESPN2; EVINE Live; Food Network; Fox News Channel; FOX Sports Networks; FOX Sports Southwest; Freeform; FX; Golf Channel; Great American Country; HGTV; History; Lifetime; MSNBC; MTV; MTV2; Nickelodeon; Oxygen; Pop; Spike TV; Syfy; TBS; TLC; TNT; Travel Channel; Trinity Broadcasting Network (TBN); truTV; TV Land; USA Network; VH1.
Fee: $26.02 monthly.

Digital Basic Service
Subscribers: N.A.
Programming (via satellite): BBC America; Bloomberg Television; Discovery Digital Networks; Disney XD; DMX Music; ESPN Classic; Fox Deportes; Fox Sports 1; FYI; GSN; History International; IFC; LMN; NBA TV; NBCSN; Nick Jr.; Outdoor Channel; Ovation; Sundance TV; Turner Classic Movies; WE tv.

Pay Service 1
Pay Units: N.A.
Programming (via satellite): Cinemax; HBO; Showtime; Starz; Starz Encore.
Fee: $5.25 installation; $1.75 monthly (Encore), $6.75 monthly (Starz), $11.75 monthly (Cinemax), $12.40 monthly (HBO or Showtime).

Digital Pay Service 1
Pay Units: N.A.
Programming (via satellite): Cinemax (multiplexed); HBO (multiplexed); Showtime (multiplexed); Starz (multiplexed); Starz Encore (multiplexed); The Movie Channel (multiplexed).
Fee: $12.99 monthly (each).

Video-On-Demand: No

Pay-Per-View
ESPN Now (delivered digitally); Hot Choice (delivered digitally); iN DEMAND (delivered digitally); Playboy TV (delivered digitally); Fresh (delivered digitally); Shorteez (delivered digitally); Sports PPV (delivered digitally).

Internet Service
Operational: Yes.
Subscribers: 207,859.
Broadband Service: Cox High Speed Internet.
Fee: $99.95 installation; $39.95 monthly; $10.00 modem lease.

Telephone Service
Digital: Operational
Subscribers: 132,256.
Fee: $38.95 monthly
Miles of Plant: 7,994.0 (coaxial); 1,839.0 (fiber optic). Homes passed: 353,437.
Senior Vice President & Regional Manager: Anthony Pope. Regional Vice President & General Manager: Jacqueline Vines. Vice President, Technical Operations: David Butler. Vice President, Cox Business Services: Leigh King. Vice President, Government & Public Affairs: Sharon Kleinpeter. Vice President, Tax: Mary Vickers. Vice President, Customer Care: Tom Makin. Vice President, Information Technology: Ramin Rastin. Vice President, Human Resources: Andy Rice.
Ownership: Cox Communications Inc. (MSO).

BAYOU L'OURSE—Allen's TV Cable Service Inc, 800 Victor II Blvd, PO Box 2643, Morgan City, LA 70380. Phone: 985-384-8335. E-mail: info@atvci.net. Web Site: http://www.atvc.net. Also serves Assumption Parish (portions). ICA: LA0138.
TV Market Ranking: Outside TV Markets (Assumption Parish (portions), BAYOU L'OURSE).
Channel capacity: N.A. Channels available but not in use: N.A.

Basic Service
Subscribers: 321.
Fee: $66.90 installation; $19.45 monthly.
President & General Manager: Gregory A. Price.
Ownership: Allen's TV Cable Service Inc. (MSO).

BELLE CHASSE—NewWave Communications, One Montgomery Plaza, 4th Floor, Sikeston, MO 63801. Phones: 573-472-9500; 888-863-9928. Fax: 573-472-9518. E-mail: info@newwave.com. Web Site: http://www.newwavecom.com. Also serves Naval Air Station Joint Reserve Base & Port Sulphur. ICA: LA0139.
TV Market Ranking: 31 (BELLE CHASSE, Naval Air Station Joint Reserve Base); Outside TV Markets (Port Sulphur).
Channel capacity: N.A. Channels available but not in use: N.A.

Basic Service
Subscribers: 1,373.
Programming (received off-air): WDSU (MeTV, NBC) New Orleans; WGNO (ABC, Antenna TV, Escape) New Orleans; WHNO (COZI TV, IND) New Orleans; WLAE-TV (PBS) New Orleans; WNOL-TV (CW, This TV) New Orleans; WPXL-TV (ION) New Orleans; WUPL (MNT) Slidell; WWL-TV (CBS) New Orleans; WYES-TV (PBS) New Orleans.
Programming (via satellite): BET; Pop; QVC; TBS; TLC; WGN America.
Fee: $35.00 installation; $34.78 monthly.

Expanded Basic Service 1
Subscribers: N.A.
Programming (via satellite): A&E; AMC; Animal Planet; Bravo; Cartoon Network; CMT; CNBC; CNN; Comedy Central; C-

Cable Systems—Louisiana

SPAN; Discovery Channel; Disney Channel; E! HD; ESPN; ESPN2; EWTN Global Catholic Network; Food Network; Fox News Channel; Freeform; FX; Hallmark Channel; History; HLN; INSP; Lifetime; MTV; Nickelodeon; Outdoor Channel; Spike TV; Syfy; The Weather Channel; TNT; Travel Channel; Trinity Broadcasting Network (TBN); truTV; Turner Classic Movies; TV Land; Univision; USA Network; VH1.
Fee: $26.50 monthly.
Digital Basic Service
Subscribers: N.A.
Programming (via satellite): BBC America; Cox Sports Television; Discovery Kids Channel; Disney XD; DMX Music; ESPN Classic; ESPNews; Fox Sports 1; FXM; FYI; Golf Channel; GSN; HGTV; History International; IFC; LMN; MTV Classic; MTV2; National Geographic Channel; Nick Jr.; Nicktoons; TeenNick; VH1 Country; WE tv.
Fee: $11.00 monthly.
Pay Service 1
Pay Units: N.A.
Programming (via satellite): HBO.
Fee: $14.95 installation; $13.95 monthly.
Digital Pay Service 1
Pay Units: N.A.
Programming (via satellite): Cinemax (multiplexed); HBO (multiplexed); Showtime (multiplexed); Starz (multiplexed); Starz Encore (multiplexed).
Fee: $8.00 monthly (Starz), $9.00 monthly (Cinemax), $11.00 monthly (Starz/Encore), $15.00 monthly (Showtime/TMC), $17.00 monthly (HBO) or $26.00 monthly (HBO/Cinemax).
Video-On-Demand: No
Pay-Per-View
iN DEMAND (delivered digitally); Playboy TV (delivered digitally).
Internet Service
Operational: Yes.
Fee: $39.99-$79.99 monthly; $6.00-$8.99 modem lease; $149.95 modem purchase.
Telephone Service
Digital: Operational
Fee: $39.95 monthly
Miles of Plant: 300.0 (coaxial); None (fiber optic).
General Manager: Staci Gowan.
Ownership: NewWave Communications LLC (MSO).

BENTON—Formerly served by Zoom Media. No longer in operation. ICA: LA0214.

BERNICE—Media3, PO Box 650, Milan, TX 38358. Phone: 866-257-2044. E-mail: customerservice@mymedia3.com. Web Site: http://www.mymedia3.com. Also serves Dubach, Lincoln Parish (portions) & Union Parish (portions). ICA: LA0081.
TV Market Ranking: 99 (BERNICE, Lincoln Parish (portions), Union Parish (portions)); Below 100 (Dubach, Lincoln Parish (portions)); Outside TV Markets (Lincoln Parish (portions)). Franchise award date: N.A. Franchise expiration date: N.A. Began: October 1, 1982.
Channel capacity: N.A. Channels available but not in use: N.A.
Basic Service
Subscribers: 114.
Programming (received off-air): KARD (Bounce TV, FOX) West Monroe; KKYK-CD (IND, WeatherNation) Little Rock; KLTM-TV (PBS) Monroe; KMLU (MeTV) Columbia; KMSS-TV (FOX) Shreveport; KNOE-TV (ABC, CBS, CW) Monroe; KPXJ (Antenna TV, CW, MeTV, Movies!) Minden; KSHV-

TV (MNT) Shreveport; KTBS-TV (ABC) Shreveport; KTVE (NBC) El Dorado.
Programming (via satellite): A&E; AMC; Animal Planet; BET; Cartoon Network; CNBC; CNN; Discovery Channel; Disney Channel; E! HD; ESPN; ESPN2; Food Network; Fox News Channel; FOX Sports Networks; Freeform; FX; Great American Country; HGTV; HLN; Lifetime; MTV; National Geographic Channel; Nickelodeon; Outdoor Channel; QVC; Spike TV; Syfy; TBS; The Weather Channel; TLC; TNT; Turner Classic Movies; USA Network.
Fee: $29.95 installation; $22.45 monthly.
Expanded Basic Service 1
Subscribers: N.A.
Fee: $28.50 monthly.
Digital Basic Service
Subscribers: N.A.
Programming (via satellite): BBC America; Bloomberg Television; Cloo; Destination America; Discovery Kids Channel; Disney XD; DMX Music; ESPN Classic; ESPNews; EVINE Live; FOX College Sports Central; FOX College Sports Pacific; Fox Sports 1; Fuse; FYI; Golf Channel; GSN; History; History International; IFC; Investigation Discovery; NBCSN; OWN; Oprah Winfrey Network; Science Channel; Sundance TV; Trinity Broadcasting Network (TBN); WE tv.
Pay Service 1
Pay Units: N.A.
Programming (via satellite): HBO; Showtime; The Movie Channel.
Fee: $12.95 monthly (each).
Digital Pay Service 1
Pay Units: N.A.
Programming (via satellite): Cinemax (multiplexed); Flix; HBO (multiplexed); Showtime (multiplexed); Starz (multiplexed); Starz Encore (multiplexed); The Movie Channel (multiplexed).
Video-On-Demand: No
Pay-Per-View
iN DEMAND (delivered digitally); Playboy TV (delivered digitally); Club Jenna (delivered digitally).
Internet Service
Operational: No.
Telephone Service
None
Miles of Plant: 35.0 (coaxial); None (fiber optic). Homes passed: 1,204.
Chief Financial Officer: Thomas Pate.
Ownership: CableSouth Media3 LLC (MSO).

BLANCHARD—NewWave Communications, One Montgomery Plaza, 4th Floor, Sikeston, MO 63801. Phones: 573-472-9500; 888-863-9928. Fax: 573-472-9518. E-mail: info@newwave.com. Web Site: http://www.newwavecom.com. Also serves Caddo Parish, Mooringsport, Oil City & Vivian. ICA: LA0038.
TV Market Ranking: 58 (BLANCHARD, Caddo Parish, Mooringsport, Oil City, Vivian). Franchise award date: July 22, 1981. Franchise expiration date: N.A. Began: January 1, 1982.
Channel capacity: N.A. Channels available but not in use: N.A.
Basic Service
Subscribers: 1,594.
Programming (received off-air): KLTS-TV (PBS) Shreveport; KMSS-TV (FOX) Shreveport; KPXJ (Antenna TV, CW, MeTV, Movies!) Minden; KSHV-TV (MNT) Shreveport; KSLA (Bounce TV, CBS, Grit, This TV) Shreveport; KTAL-TV (NBC) Texarkana; KTBS-TV (ABC) Shreveport; 2 FMs.
Fee: $35.00 installation; $34.39 monthly.

Expanded Basic Service 1
Subscribers: 1,550.
Programming (via satellite): A&E; Animal Planet; BET; Cartoon Network; CMT; CNN; Comedy Central; C-SPAN; Discovery Channel; ESPN; ESPN2; Food Network; Fox News Channel; Freeform; FX; Hallmark Channel; History; HLN; Lifetime; MTV; Nick Jr.; Nickelodeon; Outdoor Channel; Pop; Spike TV; Syfy; TBS; The Weather Channel; TLC; TNT; Travel Channel; Trinity Broadcasting Network (TBN); truTV; Turner Classic Movies; TV Land; USA Network; VH1; WGN America.
Fee: $48.70 monthly.
Digital Basic Service
Subscribers: N.A.
Programming (via satellite): BBC America; Bloomberg Television; Discovery Digital Networks; DMX Music; ESPN Classic; ESPNews; Fox Sports 1; FXM; FYI; Golf Channel; GSN; HGTV; History International; IFC; LMN; MTV2; Nicktoons; TeenNick; VH1 Country; WE tv.
Fee: $11.00 monthly.
Pay Service 1
Pay Units: N.A.
Programming (via satellite): HBO; Showtime.
Fee: $14.95 installation; $13.95 monthly (each).
Digital Pay Service 1
Pay Units: N.A.
Programming (via satellite): Cinemax (multiplexed); HBO (multiplexed); Showtime (multiplexed); Starz (multiplexed); Starz Encore (multiplexed).
Fee: $8.00 monthly (Starz), $9.00 monthly (Cinemax), $11.00 monthly (Starz/Encore), $15.00 monthly (Showtime/TMC), $17.00 monthly (HBO) or $26.00 monthly (HBO/Cinemax).
Video-On-Demand: No
Pay-Per-View
iN DEMAND (delivered digitally); Playboy TV (delivered digitally).
Internet Service
Operational: Yes. Began: February 1, 2003.
Fee: $39.95 installation; $39.99-$79.99 monthly; $6.00-$8.99 modem lease; $149.95 modem purchase.
Telephone Service
Digital: Operational
Fee: $39.95 monthly
Miles of Plant: 124.0 (coaxial); None (fiber optic). Homes passed: 6,700.
General Manager: Staci Gowan.
Ownership: NewWave Communications LLC (MSO).

BOGALUSA—Media3, PO Box 620, Milan, TN 38358. Phone: 866-257-2044 (Corporate office). E-mail: customerservice@mymedia3.com. Web Site: http://www.mymedia3.com. Also serves Franklinton & Washington Parish. ICA: LA0023.
TV Market Ranking: Below 100 (Franklinton, Washington Parish (portions)); Outside TV Markets (BOGALUSA, Washington Parish (portions)). Franchise award date: N.A. Franchise expiration date: N.A. Began: October 1, 1966.
Channel capacity: N.A. Channels available but not in use: N.A.
Basic Service
Subscribers: 388.
Programming (received off-air): WAFB (Bounce TV, CBS) Baton Rouge; WBRZ-TV (ABC) Baton Rouge; WDSU (MeTV, NBC) New Orleans; WGNO (ABC, Antenna TV, Escape) New Orleans; WHNO (COZI TV, IND) New Orleans; WLPB-TV (PBS) Ba-

ton Rouge; WNOL-TV (CW, This TV) New Orleans; WPXL-TV (ION) New Orleans; WSTY-LP (My Family TV) Hammond; WUPL (MNT) Slidell; WVLA-TV (NBC, This TV) Baton Rouge; WVUE-DT (Bounce TV, FOX) New Orleans; WWL-TV (CBS) New Orleans; WYES-TV (PBS) New Orleans; allband FM.
Programming (via satellite): C-SPAN; Pop; TBS; Trinity Broadcasting Network (TBN); WGN America.
Fee: $24.99 installation; $22.45 monthly.
Expanded Basic Service 1
Subscribers: N.A.
Programming (via satellite): A&E; AMC; Animal Planet; BET; Cartoon Network; CMT; CNBC; CNN; Discovery Channel; Disney Channel; E! HD; ESPN; ESPN2; EWTN Global Catholic Network; Fox News Channel; Fox Sports 1; FOX Sports Southwest; Freeform; FX; HGTV; HLN; Lifetime; MTV; Nickelodeon; Spike TV; Syfy; The Weather Channel; TLC; TNT; Travel Channel; truTV; Turner Classic Movies; TV Land; USA Network; VH1.
Fee: $42.99 monthly.
Digital Basic Service
Subscribers: N.A.
Programming (via satellite): BBC America; Discovery Digital Networks; DIY Network; FYI; Golf Channel; Great American Country; History International; IFC; LMN; MC; MTV2; NBCSN; Nick Jr.; Sundance TV; WE tv.
Pay Service 1
Pay Units: N.A.
Programming (via satellite): Flix; HBO; Showtime (multiplexed); Starz Encore; The Movie Channel.
Fee: $9.95 monthly (TMC), $10.95 monthly (HBO or Showtime).
Digital Pay Service 1
Pay Units: N.A.
Programming (via satellite): Cinemax (multiplexed); Starz (multiplexed); The Movie Channel.
Video-On-Demand: No
Internet Service
Operational: Yes.
Telephone Service
Digital: Operational
Miles of Plant: 140.0 (coaxial); None (fiber optic). Homes passed: 9,000.
Chief Financial Officer: Thomas Pate.
Ownership: CableSouth Media3 LLC (MSO).

BOSSIER CITY—Suddenlink Communications, 725 Benton Rd, Bossier City, LA 71111-3704. Phones: 314-315-9400; 888-822-5151 (Customer service); 318-747-1666 (Customer service). Fax: 318-746-2186. Web Site: http://www.suddenlink.com. Also serves Barksdale AFB, Bossier Parish, Fillmore, Haughton & Princeton. ICA: LA0008.
TV Market Ranking: 58 (Barksdale AFB, BOSSIER CITY, Bossier Parish, Fillmore, Haughton, Princeton). Franchise award date: August 8, 1979. Franchise expiration date: N.A. Began: August 1, 1978.
Channel capacity: N.A. Channels available but not in use: N.A.
Basic Service
Subscribers: 14,693. Commercial subscribers: 1,571.
Programming (received off-air): KLTS-TV (PBS) Shreveport; KMSS-TV (FOX) Shreveport; KPXJ (Antenna TV, CW, MeTV, Movies!) Minden; KSHV-TV (MNT) Shreveport; KSLA (Bounce TV, CBS, Grit, This TV) Shreveport; KTAL-TV (NBC) Texarkana; KTBS-TV (ABC) Shreveport; 12 FMs.
Programming (via satellite): BET; CNN; C-SPAN; Discovery Channel; EWTN Global

2017 Edition D-335

Louisiana—Cable Systems

Catholic Network; Hallmark Channel; INSP; Pop; QVC; TBS; WGN America.
Fee: $40.00 installation; $35.50 monthly; $1.10 converter.
Expanded Basic Service 1
Subscribers: N.A.
Programming (via satellite): A&E; AMC; Animal Planet; Cartoon Network; CNBC; CNN; Comedy Central; C-SPAN 2; Disney Channel; E! HD; ESPN; Fox News Channel; FOX Sports Southwest; Freeform; FX; Great American Country; History; HLN; Lifetime; MoviePlex; MTV; Nickelodeon; Spike TV; The Weather Channel; TLC; TNT; USA Network; VH1.
Fee: $42.00 installation; $15.56 monthly.
Digital Basic Service
Subscribers: N.A.
Programming (via satellite): BBC America; Bravo; Discovery Digital Networks; DMX Music; ESPN Classic; ESPN2; Fox Sports 1; Golf Channel; GSN; HGTV; IFC; NBCSN; Starz Encore; Syfy; Turner Classic Movies; TV Land; WE tv.
Pay Service 1
Pay Units: N.A.
Programming (via satellite): Cinemax; HBO; Showtime; Starz; Starz Encore.
Fee: $1.75 monthly (Encore), $6.75 monthly (Starz), $9.00 monthly (Cinemax), $10.95 monthly (HBO), $11.50 monthly (Showtime).
Digital Pay Service 1
Pay Units: N.A.
Programming (via satellite): HBO (multiplexed); Showtime (multiplexed); Starz (multiplexed); The Movie Channel.
Video-On-Demand: No
Pay-Per-View
iN DEMAND; iN DEMAND (delivered digitally); Spice.
Internet Service
Operational: Yes.
Subscribers: 17,129.
Broadband Service: Suddenlink High Speed Internet.
Fee: $45.00 installation; $29.95 monthly.
Telephone Service
Digital: Operational
Subscribers: 8,073.
Fee: $39.95 monthly
Miles of Plant: 1,026.0 (coaxial); 183.0 (fiber optic). Homes passed: 42,202.
Senior Vice President, Corporate Finance: Michael Pflantz. Vice President, Accounting: Sabrina Warr. General Manager: Jim Niswender. Marketing Director: Jon Hustmyre. Chief Technician: Lee Anderson.
Ownership: Cequel Communications Holdings I LLC (MSO).

BOURG—Charter Communications. Now served by THIBODAUX, LA [LA0011]. ICA: LA0013.

BOYCE—Suddenlink Communications, 520 Maryville Centre Dr, Ste 300, St. Louis, MO 63141. Phone: 314-315-9400. Web Site: http://www.suddenlink.com. Also serves Hotwells. ICA: LA0141.
TV Market Ranking: Below 100 (BOYCE, Hotwells). Franchise award date: N.A. Franchise expiration date: N.A. Began: October 1, 1982.
Channel capacity: N.A. Channels available but not in use: N.A.
Basic Service
Subscribers: 332.
Programming (received off-air): KALB-TV (CBS, CW, NBC) Alexandria; KATC (ABC, CW, Grit) Lafayette; KLAX-TV (ABC) Alexan-

dria; KLFY-TV (CBS) Lafayette; KLPA-TV (PBS) Alexandria; KLTM-TV (PBS) Monroe; KNOE-TV (ABC, CBS, CW) Monroe.
Programming (via satellite): CNN; ESPN; Freeform; Nickelodeon; TBS; The Weather Channel; USA Network; WGN America.
Fee: $40.00 installation; $38.50 monthly.
Pay Service 1
Pay Units: N.A.
Programming (via satellite): Flix; HBO; Showtime; The Movie Channel.
Fee: $1.95 monthly (Flix), $7.00 monthly (Showtime), $10.00 monthly (TMC), $12.00 monthly (HBO).
Video-On-Demand: No
Internet Service
Operational: Yes. Began: January 28, 2004.
Broadband Service: Suddenlink High Speed Internet.
Fee: $45.00 installation; $29.95 monthly.
Telephone Service
Digital: Operational
Fee: $39.95 monthly
Miles of Plant: 34.0 (coaxial); None (fiber optic). Homes passed: 1,101.
Senior Vice President, Corporate Finance: Michael Pflantz. Vice President, Accounting: Sabrina Warr. Regional Manager: Todd Cruthird. Area Manager: Mark Hood. Plant Manager: Dion Canaday.
Ownership: Cequel Communications Holdings I LLC (MSO).

BRAITHWAITE—Formerly served by CMA Cablevision. No longer in operation. ICA: LA0142.

BROUILLETTE—Formerly served by Almega Cable. No longer in operation. ICA: LA0143.

BUNKIE—Media3, PO Box 620, Milan, TN 38358. Phone: 866-257-2044. E-mail: customerservice@mymedia3.com. Web Site: http://www.mymedia3.com. Also serves Evergreen. ICA: LA0061.
TV Market Ranking: Below 100 (BUNKIE, Evergreen). Franchise award date: N.A. Franchise expiration date: N.A. Began: January 15, 1968.
Channel capacity: N.A. Channels available but not in use: N.A.
Basic Service
Subscribers: 594.
Programming (received off-air): KALB-TV (CBS, CW, NBC) Alexandria; KLAX-TV (ABC) Alexandria; KLFY-TV (CBS) Lafayette; KLPA-TV (PBS) Alexandria; KPLC (Bounce TV, NBC, This TV) Lake Charles; WAFB (Bounce TV, CBS) Baton Rouge; WBRZ-TV (ABC) Baton Rouge; WNTZ-TV (FOX, MNT) Natchez; WPXL-TV (ION) New Orleans; allband FM.
Programming (via satellite): QVC.
Fee: $24.95 installation; $22.45 monthly.
Expanded Basic Service 1
Subscribers: N.A.
Programming (via satellite): A&E; AMC; Animal Planet; BET; Cartoon Network; CMT; CNBC; CNN; Comedy Central; C-SPAN; Discovery Channel; Disney Channel; Disney XD; E! HD; ESPN; ESPN2; EWTN Global Catholic Network; Fox News Channel; FOX Sports Southwest; Freeform; Hallmark Channel; HGTV; History; HLN; Lifetime; MSNBC; MTV; Nickelodeon; Outdoor Channel; Oxygen; Spike TV; Syfy; TBS; The Weather Channel; TLC; TNT; Travel Channel; Trinity Broadcasting Network (TBN); Turner Classic Movies; TV Land; USA Network; VH1; WE tv; WGN America.
Fee: $42.99 monthly.

Pay Service 1
Pay Units: N.A.
Programming (via satellite): Cinemax; HBO; Showtime.
Fee: $10.00 installation; $11.50 monthly (each).
Video-On-Demand: No
Internet Service
Operational: Yes.
Telephone Service
Digital: Operational
Miles of Plant: 27.0 (coaxial); None (fiber optic).
President: G. Alan Taylor. Chief Financial Officer: Thomas Pate.
Ownership: CableSouth Media3 LLC (MSO).

BUTTE LA ROSE—Spillway Cablevision Inc, 10900 Hwy 77, PO Box 337, Maringouin, LA 70757. Phone: 225-625-2311. Fax: 225-625-3107. E-mail: cs@spillwaycable.com. Web Site: http://www.spillwaycable.com. ICA: LA0243.
TV Market Ranking: Below 100 (BUTTE LA ROSE).
Channel capacity: N.A. Channels available but not in use: N.A.
Basic Service
Subscribers: 63.
Fee: $26.00 installation; $30.95 monthly.
Manager: Sue Soileau.
Ownership: Spillway Cablevision Inc. (MSO).

CALHOUN—NewWave Communications, One Montgomery Plaza, 4th Floor, Sikeston, MO 63801. Phones: 573-472-9500; 888-863-9928. Fax: 573-472-9518. E-mail: info@newwave.com. Web Site: http://www.newwavecom.com. ICA: LA0104.
TV Market Ranking: 99 (CALHOUN). Franchise award date: January 12, 1979. Franchise expiration date: N.A. Began: May 1, 1983.
Channel capacity: N.A. Channels available but not in use: N.A.
Basic Service
Subscribers: 54.
Programming (received off-air): KARD (Bounce TV, FOX) West Monroe; KLTM-TV (PBS) Monroe; KMCT-TV (IND) West Monroe; KMLU (MeTV) Columbia; KNOE-TV (ABC, CBS, CW) Monroe; KTVE (NBC) El Dorado; KWMS-LP (MeTV, Retro TV) West Monroe.
Programming (via satellite): CNN; Discovery Channel; Fox News Channel; Freeform; HLN; Nickelodeon; TBS; The Weather Channel; TLC; WGN America; WPIX (Antenna TV, CW, This TV) New York.
Fee: $35.00 installation; $32.93 monthly.
Expanded Basic Service 1
Subscribers: N.A.
Programming (via satellite): A&E; Animal Planet; Cartoon Network; CMT; E! HD; ESPN; ESPN2; FOX Sports Southwest; FX; HGTV; History; Lifetime; MTV; Spike TV; TNT; Turner Classic Movies; TV Land; USA Network; VH1.
Fee: $47.70 monthly.
Pay Service 1
Pay Units: N.A.
Programming (via satellite): HBO; Starz; Starz Encore.
Fee: $14.95 installation; $7.00 monthly (Starz), $11.00 monthly (Starz/Encore) or $16.00 monthly (HBO).
Video-On-Demand: No
Pay-Per-View
iN DEMAND (delivered digitally); Playboy TV (delivered digitally); Club Jenna (delivered digitally).

Internet Service
Operational: No.
Telephone Service
None
Miles of Plant: 16.0 (coaxial); None (fiber optic). Homes passed: 600.
General Manager: Staci Gowan.
Ownership: NewWave Communications LLC (MSO).

CALVIN—Formerly served by Cebridge Connections. No longer in operation. ICA: LA0145.

CAMERON—Formerly served by Charter Communications. No longer in operation. ICA: LA0077.

CAMPTI—Red River Cable TV, 1813 Bessie St, PO Box 674, Coushatta, LA 71019-0674. Phone: 318-932-4991. Fax: 308-932-5123. ICA: LA0111.
TV Market Ranking: Outside TV Markets (CAMPTI). Franchise award date: N.A. Franchise expiration date: N.A. Began: March 1, 1983.
Channel capacity: N.A. Channels available but not in use: N.A.
Basic Service
Subscribers: N.A.
Programming (received off-air): KARD (Bounce TV, FOX) West Monroe; KLTS-TV (PBS) Shreveport; KMSS-TV (FOX) Shreveport; KNTS-LP (IND) Natchitoches; KSHV-TV (MNT) Shreveport; KSLA (Bounce TV, CBS, Grit, This TV) Shreveport; KTAL-TV (NBC) Texarkana; KTBS-TV (ABC) Shreveport.
Programming (via satellite): A&E; AMC; Animal Planet; BET; Cartoon Network; CNN; Discovery Channel; ESPN; ESPN2; Food Network; Fox News Channel; Fox Sports 1; FX; Great American Country; Hallmark Channel; HGTV; History; Lifetime; National Geographic Channel; Outdoor Channel; Syfy; TBS; The Weather Channel; TLC; TNT; Trinity Broadcasting Network (TBN); truTV; Turner Classic Movies; USA Network; WE tv; WGN America.
Pay Service 1
Pay Units: N.A.
Programming (via satellite): Cinemax; HBO; Starz Encore.
Video-On-Demand: No
Internet Service
Operational: Yes.
Telephone Service
None
Miles of Plant: 13.0 (coaxial); None (fiber optic). Homes passed: 550.
General Manager: Jimmy Hardy. Secretary: Stephanie Collier.
Ownership: Red River Cable TV (MSO).

CARLYSS—Cameron Communications. Formerly [LA0063]. This cable system has converted to IPTV, 153 West Dave Dugas Rd, PO Box 167, Sulphur, LA 70664-0167. Phones: 800-737-3900; 337-583-2111. Fax: 337-583-9474. Web Site: http://www.camtel.com. Also serves Cameron, Creole, Elizabeth, Grand Chenier, Grand Lake, Hackberry, Johnson Bayou, Moss Bluff, Pitkin & Sugartown, LA; Gilchrist, High Island & Nome, TX. ICA: LA5000.
TV Market Ranking: 88 (Hackberry); Below 100 (Cameron, CARLYSS, Creole, Grand Chenier); Outside TV Markets (Grand Lake).
Channel capacity: N.A. Channels available but not in use: N.A.
Basic
Subscribers: N.A.

Cable Systems—Louisiana

Expanded Basic
  Subscribers: 7,554.
  Fee: $49.95 installation; $73.95 monthly.
Family
  Subscribers: N.A.
  Fee: $6.95 monthly.
Sports & Information
  Subscribers: N.A.
  Fee: $8.95 monthly.
Cinemax
  Subscribers: N.A.
  Fee: $14.45 monthly.
HBO
  Subscribers: N.A.
  Fee: $15.70 monthly.
Showtime/TMC/Flix
  Subscribers: N.A.
  Fee: $14.45 monthly.
Starz/Encore
  Subscribers: N.A.
  Fee: $14.45 monthly.
Video-On-Demand: Yes
Internet Service
  Operational: Yes.
Telephone Service
  Digital: Operational
General Manager: Bruce Petry.
Ownership: American Broadband Communications Inc.

CARLYSS—Cameron Communications. This cable system has converted to IPTV. See CARLYSS, LA [LA5000]. ICA: LA0063.

CECILIA (northern portion)—Formerly served by Trust Cable. No longer in operation. ICA: LA0147.

CHATHAM—Formerly served by Chatham CATV. No longer in operation. ICA: LA0130.

CHOUDRANT—Formerly served by Almega Cable. No longer in operation. ICA: LA0215.

CLARENCE—Red River Cable TV, 1813 Bessie St, PO Box 674, Coushatta, LA 71019-0674. Phone: 318-932-4991. Fax: 318-932-5123. ICA: LA0133.
  TV Market Ranking: Outside TV Markets (CLARENCE). Franchise award date: N.A. Franchise expiration date: N.A. Began: August 1, 1985.
  Channel capacity: 12 (not 2-way capable). Channels available but not in use: N.A.
Basic Service
  Subscribers: N.A.
  Programming (received off-air): KALB-TV (CBS, CW, NBC) Alexandria; KLTM-TV (PBS) Monroe; KNOE-TV (ABC, CBS, CW) Monroe; KSLA (Bounce TV, CBS, Grit, This TV) Shreveport; KTAL-TV (NBC) Texarkana; KTBS-TV (ABC) Shreveport.
  Programming (via satellite): TBS; WGN America.
Video-On-Demand: No
Internet Service
  Operational: No.
Telephone Service
  None
Miles of Plant: 2.0 (coaxial); None (fiber optic). Homes passed: 160.
General Manager: Jimmy Hardy. Secretary: Stephanie Collier.
Ownership: Red River Cable TV (MSO).

CLAYTON (town)—Formerly served by Zoom Media. No longer in operation. ICA: LA0123.

CLINTON—Bailey Cable TV Inc, 807 Church St, Port Gibson, MS 39150-2413. Phone: 601-437-8300. Fax: 601-437-6860.
E-mail: cs@baileycable.net. Web Site: http://www.baileycable.net. ICA: LA0051.
TV Market Ranking: 87 (CLINTON).
Channel capacity: N.A. Channels available but not in use: N.A.
Basic Service
  Subscribers: 248.
  Fee: $15.00 installation; $42.95 monthly.
President: David A. Bailey.
Ownership: Bailey Cable TV Inc. (MSO).

CLOUTIERVILLE—Formerly served by Almega Cable. No longer in operation. ICA: LA0149.

COLFAX—Alliance Communications, PO Box 9090, Tyler, TX 75711. Phones: 903-561-4411 (Tyler, TX office); 501-679-6619; 800-842-8160. E-mail: marketing@alliancecable.net. Web Site: http://www.alliancecable.net. ICA: LA0097.
  TV Market Ranking: Below 100 (COLFAX). Franchise award date: N.A. Franchise expiration date: N.A. Began: November 1, 1982.
  Channel capacity: 54 (not 2-way capable). Channels available but not in use: N.A.
Basic Service
  Subscribers: 59.
  Programming (received off-air): KALB-TV (CBS, CW, NBC) Alexandria; KLAX-TV (ABC) Alexandria; KLFY-TV (CBS) Lafayette; KLPA-TV (PBS) Alexandria; KNOE-TV (ABC, CBS, CW) Monroe; WNTZ-TV (FOX, MNT) Natchez.
  Programming (via satellite): A&E; Animal Planet; BET; Cartoon Network; CNBC; CNN; C-SPAN; Discovery Channel; Disney Channel; ESPN; ESPN2; FOX Sports Networks; Freeform; FX; Great American Country; HGTV; HLN; Lifetime; MSNBC; MTV; National Geographic Channel; Nickelodeon; Outdoor Channel; Spike TV; TBS; The Weather Channel; TNT; Trinity Broadcasting Network (TBN); Turner Classic Movies; TV Land; USA Network.
  Fee: $45.00 installation; $25.45 monthly.
Digital Basic Service
  Subscribers: N.A.
  Programming (via satellite): BBC America; Bloomberg Television; Cloo; Destination America; Discovery Kids Channel; Disney XD; DMX Music; ESPN Classic; ESPNews; EVINE Live; FOX College Sports Central; FOX College Sports Pacific; Fox Sports 1; Fuse; FYI; Golf Channel; GSN; History; History International; IFC; Investigation Discovery; NBCSN; OWN; Oprah Winfrey Network; Science Channel; Sundance TV; WE tv.
Pay Service 1
  Pay Units: N.A.
  Programming (via satellite): Flix; HBO; Showtime; The Movie Channel.
  Fee: $1.95 monthly (Flix), $12.95 monthly (HBO, Showtime or TMC).
Digital Pay Service 1
  Pay Units: N.A.
  Programming (via satellite): Cinemax (multiplexed); Flix; HBO (multiplexed); Showtime (multiplexed); Starz (multiplexed); Starz Encore (multiplexed); The Movie Channel (multiplexed).
Video-On-Demand: No
Pay-Per-View
  iN DEMAND (delivered digitally); Playboy TV (delivered digitally); Club Jenna (delivered digitally).
Internet Service
  Operational: No.
Telephone Service
  None
Miles of Plant: 15.0 (coaxial); None (fiber optic). Homes passed: 704.
Chief Financial Officer: David Starrett. Vice President & General Manager: John Brinker. Vice President, Programming: Julie Newman.
Ownership: Buford Media Group LLC (MSO).

COLLINSTON—Northeast Tel, 6402 Howell St, PO Drawer 185, Collinston, LA 71229-0185. Phones: 318-823-2200; 888-318-1998; 318-874-7011. Fax: 318-874-2041. E-mail: info@ne-tel.com. Web Site: http://www.northeastnet.net. Also serves Bonita. ICA: LA0109.
  TV Market Ranking: 99 (COLLINSTON); Outside TV Markets (Bonita). Franchise award date: N.A. Franchise expiration date: N.A. Began: May 1, 1987.
  Channel capacity: N.A. Channels available but not in use: N.A.
Basic Service
  Subscribers: 285.
  Programming (received off-air): KARD (Bounce TV, FOX) West Monroe; KLTM-TV (PBS) Monroe; KMCT-TV (IND) West Monroe; KMLU (MeTV) Columbia; KNOE-TV (ABC, CBS, CW) Monroe; KTVE (NBC) El Dorado.
  Programming (via satellite): A&E; Animal Planet; BET; CMT; CNBC; CNN; C-SPAN; Discovery Channel; Disney Channel; ESPN; ESPN2; Food Network; Fox News Channel; Fox Sports 1; Freeform; FX; HGTV; History; Lifetime; NBCSN; Nickelodeon; Outdoor Channel; QVC; Spike TV; TBS; The Weather Channel; TLC; TNT; Travel Channel; Trinity Broadcasting Network (TBN); TV Land; USA Network; WGN America.
  Fee: $30.00 installation; $79.99 monthly.
Pay Service 1
  Pay Units: 83.
  Programming (via satellite): Cinemax.
  Fee: $15.00 installation; $12.00 monthly.
Pay Service 2
  Pay Units: 208.
  Programming (via satellite): HBO.
  Fee: $15.00 installation; $12.00 monthly.
Video-On-Demand: No
Internet Service
  Operational: Yes.
Telephone Service
  Digital: Operational
Miles of Plant: 25.0 (coaxial); None (fiber optic). Homes passed: 600.
President & General Manager: Mike George. Chief Technician: Tim Andrews. Communications Manager: Becky Darsey. Office Manager: Julia Lindsey.
Ownership: Northeast Louisiana Telephone Co. Inc.

COLUMBIA—NewWave Communications, One Montgomery Plaza, 4th Floor, Sikeston, MO 63801. Phones: 573-472-9500; 888-863-9928. Fax: 573-472-9518. E-mail: info@newwave.com. Web Site: http://www.newwavecom.com. Also serves Banks Springs, Clarks, Columbia Heights & Grayson. ICA: LA0074.
  TV Market Ranking: 99 (Banks Springs, Clarks, COLUMBIA, Columbia Heights, Grayson). Franchise award date: November 3, 1980. Franchise expiration date: N.A. Began: N.A.
  Channel capacity: N.A. Channels available but not in use: N.A.
Basic Service
  Subscribers: 164.
  Programming (received off-air): KARD (Bounce TV, FOX) West Monroe; KLTM-TV (PBS) Monroe; KMCT-TV (IND) West Monroe; KMLU (MeTV) Columbia; KNOE-TV (ABC, CBS, CW) Monroe; KTVE (NBC) El Dorado; KWMS-LP (MeTV, Retro TV) West Monroe.
  Programming (via satellite): CNN; ESPN; Fox News Channel; Freeform; TBS; TLC; WGN America.
  Fee: $35.00 installation; $32.93 monthly.
Expanded Basic Service 1
  Subscribers: N.A.
  Programming (via satellite): A&E; Animal Planet; BET; Cartoon Network; CMT; Discovery Channel; ESPN2; FX; HGTV; History; Lifetime; MTV; Nickelodeon; Spike TV; The Weather Channel; TNT; Turner Classic Movies; TV Land; USA Network.
  Fee: $47.70 monthly.
Digital Basic Service
  Subscribers: N.A.
  Programming (via satellite): BBC America; Discovery Kids Channel; ESPN Classic; ESPNews; FYI; Golf Channel; GSN; History International; LMN; MC; National Geographic Channel; Nick Jr.; TeenNick.
Pay Service 1
  Pay Units: N.A.
  Programming (via satellite): HBO.
  Fee: $14.95 installation; $13.95 monthly.
Digital Pay Service 1
  Pay Units: N.A.
  Programming (via satellite): Cinemax (multiplexed); HBO (multiplexed); Showtime (multiplexed); Starz (multiplexed); Starz Encore (multiplexed); The Movie Channel (multiplexed).
  Fee: $10.95 monthly (Cinemax or Starz/Encore), $13.95 monthly (HBO or Showtime).
Video-On-Demand: No
Internet Service
  Operational: No.
Telephone Service
  None
Miles of Plant: 44.0 (coaxial); None (fiber optic). Homes passed: 1,488.
General Manager: Staci Gowan.
Ownership: NewWave Communications LLC (MSO).

COTEAU HOLMES—Formerly served by Trust Cable. No longer in operation. ICA: LA0150.

COTTON VALLEY—Formerly served by Zoom Media. No longer in operation. ICA: LA0085.

Louisiana—Cable Systems

FULLY SEARCHABLE • CONTINUOUSLY UPDATED • DISCOUNT RATES FOR PRINT PURCHASERS
For more information call 800-771-9202 or visit www.warren-news.com

COUSHATTA—Red River Cable TV, 1813 Bessie St, PO Box 674, Coushatta, LA 71019-0674. Phone: 318-932-4991. Fax: 318-932-5123. ICA: LA0092.
TV Market Ranking: Outside TV Markets (COUSHATTA). Franchise award date: N.A. Franchise expiration date: N.A. Began: January 1, 1979.
Channel capacity: N.A. Channels available but not in use: N.A.
Basic Service
Subscribers: N.A.
Programming (received off-air): KARD (Bounce TV, FOX) West Monroe; KLTS-TV (PBS) Shreveport; KMSS-TV (FOX) Shreveport; KNTS-LP (IND) Natchitoches; KSHV-TV (MNT) Shreveport; KSLA (Bounce TV, CBS, Grit, This TV) Shreveport; KTAL-TV (NBC) Texarkana; KTBS-TV (ABC) Shreveport.
Programming (via satellite): A&E; AMC; Animal Planet; BET; Cartoon Network; CNN; Discovery Channel; ESPN; ESPN2; Food Network; Fox News Channel; Fox Sports 1; FX; Great American Country; Hallmark Channel; HGTV; History; Lifetime; National Geographic Channel; Outdoor Channel; Syfy; TBS; The Weather Channel; TLC; TNT; Trinity Broadcasting Network (TBN); truTV; Turner Classic Movies; USA Network; WE tv; WGN America.
Fee: $15.00 installation; $32.84 monthly.
Pay Service 1
Pay Units: N.A.
Programming (via satellite): Cinemax; HBO; Starz Encore.
Video-On-Demand: No
Internet Service
Operational: Yes.
Broadband Service: In-house.
Fee: $35.00 monthly; $50.00 modem purchase.
Telephone Service
None
Miles of Plant: 23.0 (coaxial); None (fiber optic). Homes passed: 800.
General Manager: Jimmy Hardy. Secretary: Stephanie Collier.
Ownership: Red River Cable TV (MSO).

CROWLEY—Cox Communications. Now served by BATON ROUGE, LA [LA0003]. ICA: LA0152.

DE QUINCY—Formerly served by Mediastream. No longer in operation. ICA: LA0047.

DE RIDDER—Suddenlink Communications, 1501 North Pine St, Deridder, LA 70634-2467. Phones: 888-822-5151; 314-315-9400. Fax: 337-463-7728. Web Site: http://www.suddenlink.com. Also serves Beauregard Parish (portions), Rosepine & Vernon Parish (portions). ICA: LA0031.
TV Market Ranking: Below 100 (Beauregard Parish (portions), Vernon Parish (portions)), Outside TV Markets (DE RIDDER, Rosepine, Beauregard Parish (portions), Vernon Parish (portions)). Franchise award date: N.A. Franchise expiration date: N.A. Began: September 1, 1965.
Channel capacity: 35 (operating 2-way). Channels available but not in use: N.A.
Basic Service
Subscribers: 3,250. Commercial subscribers: 258.
Programming (received off-air): KALB-TV (CBS, CW, NBC) Alexandria; KBMT (ABC) Beaumont; KLFY-TV (CBS) Lafayette; KLTL-TV (PBS) Lake Charles; KPLC (Bounce TV, NBC, This TV) Lake Charles; KVHP (FOX) Lake Charles; allband FM.
Programming (via satellite): C-SPAN; C-SPAN 2; Freeform; INSP; QVC; TBS; TNT; WGN America.
Fee: $40.00 installation; $33.50 monthly.
Expanded Basic Service 1
Subscribers: N.A.
Programming (via satellite): A&E; AMC; Animal Planet; BET; Cartoon Network; CNBC; CNN; Comedy Central; Discovery Channel; Disney Channel; E! HD; ESPN; ESPN2; Food Network; Fox News Channel; Fox Sports 1; FOX Sports Southwest; FX; Great American Country; HGTV; History; HLN; Lifetime; MSNBC; MTV; NBCSN; Nickelodeon; Spike TV; Syfy; The Weather Channel; TLC; Travel Channel; TV Land; USA Network; VH1.
Fee: $36.83 monthly.
Digital Basic Service
Subscribers: N.A.
Programming (via satellite): BBC America; Bloomberg Television; Discovery Digital Networks; Disney XD; ESPN Classic; ESPNews; Fuse; FYI; Golf Channel; GSN; Hallmark Channel; History International; IFC; LMN; NBA TV; Nicktoons; Outdoor Channel; Sundance TV; TeenNick; Turner Classic Movies.
Digital Pay Service 1
Pay Units: N.A.
Programming (via satellite): Cinemax (multiplexed); HBO (multiplexed); Showtime (multiplexed); Starz Encore (multiplexed); The Movie Channel.
Video-On-Demand: No
Pay-Per-View
Fresh (delivered digitally); Playboy TV (delivered digitally); iN DEMAND (delivered digitally).
Internet Service
Operational: Yes.
Subscribers: 3,799.
Broadband Service: Suddenlink High Speed Internet.
Fee: $45.00 installation; $39.95 monthly.
Telephone Service
Digital: Operational
Subscribers: 2,522.
Fee: $39.95 monthly
Miles of Plant: 96.0 (coaxial); 73.0 (fiber optic). Homes passed: 6,000.
Senior Vice President, Corporate Finance: Michael Pflantz. Vice President, Accounting: Sabrina Warr. General Manager: Mike Stidham. Chief Technician: Steve Shirley.
Ownership: Cequel Communications Holdings I LLC (MSO).

DELHI (town)—NewWave Communications. Now served by MONROE, LA [LA0049]. ICA: LA0082.

DIXIE INN—Formerly served by PC One Cable. No longer in operation. ICA: LA0216.

DODSON—Formerly served by Cebridge Connections. No longer in operation. ICA: LA0153.

DRY PRONG—Formerly served by Zoom Media. No longer in operation. ICA: LA0090.

EFFIE—Formerly served by Zoom Media. No longer in operation. ICA: LA0156.

EGAN—Formerly served by Trust Cable. No longer in operation. ICA: LA0157.

ESTHERWOOD—Formerly served by Alliance Communications Network. No longer in operation. ICA: LA0159.

ETHEL—Bailey Cable TV Inc, 807 Church St, Port Gibson, MS 39150-2413. Phone: 601-437-8300. Fax: 601-437-6860. E-mail: cs@baileycable.net. Web Site: http://www.baileycable.net. ICA: LA0160.
TV Market Ranking: 87 (ETHEL).
Channel capacity: N.A. Channels available but not in use: N.A.
Basic Service
Subscribers: 73.
Programming (received off-air): KLPB-TV (PBS) Lafayette; WAFB (Bounce TV, CBS) Baton Rouge; WBRZ-TV (ABC) Baton Rouge; WGMB-TV (FOX) Baton Rouge; WVLA-TV (NBC, This TV) Baton Rouge.
Programming (via satellite): A&E; Animal Planet; BET; Cartoon Network; CMT; CNN; Comedy Central; Cox Sports Television; C-SPAN; Discovery Channel; Disney Channel; ESPN; ESPN2; Food Network; Fox News Channel; Fox Sports 1; FOX Sports Networks; Freeform; FX; Golf Channel; Hallmark Channel; HGTV; History; INSP; KTLA (Antenna TV, CW, This TV) Los Angeles; Lifetime; MTV; Nickelodeon; Outdoor Channel; QVC; Spike TV; Syfy; TBS; The Weather Channel; TLC; TNT; Trinity Broadcasting Network (TBN); truTV; Turner Classic Movies; TV Land; USA Network; VH1; WGN America.
Fee: $15.00 installation; $42.95 monthly.
Pay Service 1
Pay Units: N.A.
Programming (via satellite): Cinemax; HBO (multiplexed).
Fee: $19.95 monthly.
Video-On-Demand: No
Internet Service
Operational: Yes.
Subscribers: 425.
Fee: $29.99 installation; $29.99 monthly; $6.95 modem lease; $69.95 modem purchase.
Telephone Service
None
President: David A. Bailey.
Ownership: Bailey Cable TV Inc. (MSO).

FARMERVILLE—NewWave Communications, One Montgomery Plaza, 4th Floor, Sikeston, MO 63801. Phones: 888-863-9928; 573-472-9500. Fax: 573-472-9518. E-mail: info@newwave.com. Web Site: http://www.newwavecom.com. ICA: LA0067.
TV Market Ranking: 99 (FARMERVILLE). Franchise award date: N.A. Franchise expiration date: N.A. Began: January 1, 1976.
Channel capacity: N.A. Channels available but not in use: N.A.
Basic Service
Subscribers: 371.
Programming (received off-air): KARD (Bounce TV, FOX) West Monroe; KLTM-TV (PBS) Monroe; KNOE-TV (ABC, CBS, CW) Monroe; KTVE (NBC) El Dorado.
Programming (via satellite): ESPN; Freeform; Hallmark Channel; TBS; WGN America.
Fee: $35.00 installation; $53.93 monthly.
Expanded Basic Service 1
Subscribers: N.A.
Programming (received off-air): KMCT-TV (IND) West Monroe.
Programming (via satellite): A&E; Animal Planet; BET; CMT; CNN; Discovery Channel; ESPN2; Fox News Channel; HGTV; History; Lifetime; MTV; Nickelodeon; Outdoor Channel; Spike TV; The Weather Channel; TLC; TNT; Turner Classic Movies; TV Land; USA Network; VH1.
Fee: $25.00 monthly.
Pay Service 1
Pay Units: N.A.
Programming (via satellite): HBO.
Fee: $14.95 installation; $16.00 monthly.
Video-On-Demand: No
Internet Service
Operational: No.
Telephone Service
None
Miles of Plant: 142.0 (coaxial); None (fiber optic). Homes passed: 1,600.
General Manager: Staci Gowan.
Ownership: NewWave Communications LLC (MSO).

FERRIDAY—Media3, PO Box 620, Milan, TN 38358. Phone: 866-257-2044. E-mail: customerservice@mymedia3.com. Web Site: http://www.mymedia3.com. Also serves Concordia Parish & Ridgecrest. ICA: LA0233.
TV Market Ranking: Below 100 (Concordia Parish, FERRIDAY, Ridgecrest).
Channel capacity: N.A. Channels available but not in use: N.A.
Basic Service
Subscribers: 661.
Programming (received off-air): KALB-TV (CBS, CW, NBC) Alexandria; KARD (Bounce TV, FOX) West Monroe; KLAX-TV (ABC) Alexandria; KLTM-TV (PBS) Monroe; KMLU (MeTV) Columbia; KNOE-TV (ABC, CBS, CW) Monroe; WAFB (Bounce TV, CBS) Baton Rouge; WNTZ-TV (FOX, MNT) Natchez.
Programming (via satellite): Pop; QVC; WGN America.
Fee: $24.95 installation; $22.45 monthly.
Expanded Basic Service 1
Subscribers: N.A.
Programming (via satellite): A&E; AMC; Animal Planet; BET; Bravo; Cartoon Network; CMT; CNBC; CNN; Comedy Central; C-SPAN; C-SPAN 2; Discovery Channel; Disney Channel; Disney XD; E! HD; ESPN; ESPN2; Food Network; Fox News Channel; Fox Sports 1; FOX Sports Southwest; Freeform; FX; Hallmark Channel; HGTV; History; HLN; INSP; ION Television; Lifetime; MSNBC; MTV; National Geographic Channel; NBCSN; Nickelodeon; Outdoor Channel; Oxygen; Spike TV; Syfy; TBS; The Weather Channel; TLC; TNT; Travel Channel; Trinity Broadcasting Network (TBN); truTV; Turner Classic Movies; TV Land; USA Network; VH1; WE tv.

Cable Systems—Louisiana

Pay Service 1
Pay Units: N.A.
Programming (via satellite): Cinemax; HBO.
Video-On-Demand: No
Internet Service
Operational: No.
Telephone Service
None
President: Alan Taylor. Chief Financial Officer: Thomas Pate. Business Manager: Glenda Elliott.
Ownership: CableSouth Media3 LLC (MSO).

FOLSOM—Charter Communications. Now served by SLIDELL, LA [LA0182]. ICA: LA0161.

FORKED ISLAND—Formerly served by Kaplan Telephone Co., KAPLAN, LA [LA0162]. No longer in operation. ICA: LA5020.

FORT POLK—Suddenlink Communications. Now served by LEESVILLE, LA [LA0035]. ICA: LA0163.

FOUR CORNERS—Formerly served by CableSouth Inc. No longer in operation. ICA: LA0164.

FRANKLIN—Cox Communications. Now served by BATON ROUGE, LA [LA0003]. ICA: LA0030.

GEORGETOWN—Formerly served by Almega Cable. No longer in operation. ICA: LA0132.

GIBSLAND—Alliance Communications, PO Box 9090, Tyler, TX 75711. Phones: 903-561-4411 (Tyler, TX office); 501-679-6619; 800-842-8160. E-mail: marketing@alliancecable.net. Web Site: http://www.alliancecable.net. ICA: LA0115.
TV Market Ranking: Below 100 (GIBSLAND). Franchise award date: N.A. Franchise expiration date: N.A. Began: December 1, 1982.
Channel capacity: 54 (not 2-way capable). Channels available but not in use: N.A.
Basic Service
Subscribers: 37.
Programming (received off-air): KLTS-TV (PBS) Shreveport; KPXJ (Antenna TV, CW, MeTV, Movies!) Minden; KSHV-TV (MNT) Shreveport; KSLA (Bounce TV, CBS, Grit, This TV) Shreveport; KTAL-TV (NBC) Texarkana; KTBS-TV (ABC) Shreveport.
Programming (via satellite): A&E; BET; Cartoon Network; CNN; Discovery Channel; Disney Channel; ESPN; Freeform; Great American Country; HGTV; HLN; Lifetime; National Geographic Channel; Nickelodeon; Spike TV; TBS; The Weather Channel; TLC; TNT; Trinity Broadcasting Network (TBN); Turner Classic Movies; USA Network.
Fee: $45.00 installation; $25.45 monthly.
Pay Service 1
Pay Units: N.A.
Programming (via satellite): HBO; Showtime; The Movie Channel.
Fee: $12.95 monthly (each).
Video-On-Demand: No
Internet Service
Operational: No.
Telephone Service
None
Miles of Plant: 10.0 (coaxial); None (fiber optic). Homes passed: 503.
Chief Financial Officer: David Starrett. Vice President & General Manager: John Brinker.

Vice President, Programming: Julie Newman.
Ownership: Buford Media Group LLC (MSO).

GOLDEN MEADOW—Vision Communications, 115 West 10th Blvd, PO Box 550, Larose, LA 70373. Phones: 985-693-4567; 800-256-5665; 985-693-0123. Fax: 985-693-3049. Web Site: http://www.viscom.net. Also serves Cut Off, Fourchon, Galliano, Gheens, Grand Isle, Lafourche Parish, Larose, Leeville, Lockport & Mathews. ICA: LA0014.
TV Market Ranking: 31 (Lafourche Parish (portions)); Outside TV Markets (Cut Off, Fourchon, Galliano, Gheens, GOLDEN MEADOW, Grand Isle, Larose, Leeville, Lockport, Mathews, Lafourche Parish (portions)). Franchise award date: N.A. Franchise expiration date: N.A. Began: April 1, 1969.
Channel capacity: N.A. Channels available but not in use: N.A.
Basic Service
Subscribers: 7,519. Commercial subscribers: 421.
Programming (received off-air): KFOL-CD (IND) Houma; WAFB (Bounce TV, CBS) Baton Rouge; WBRZ-TV (ABC) Baton Rouge; WDSU (MeTV, NBC) New Orleans; WGNO (ABC, Antenna TV, Escape) New Orleans; WHNO (COZI TV, IND) New Orleans; WLAE-TV (PBS) New Orleans; WNOL-TV (CW, This TV) New Orleans; WPXL-TV (ION) New Orleans; WUPL (MNT) Slidell; WVLA-TV (NBC, This TV) Baton Rouge; WVUE-DT (Bounce TV, FOX) New Orleans; WWL-TV (CBS) New Orleans; WYES-TV (PBS) New Orleans.
Programming (via satellite): A&E; AMC; Animal Planet; BET; Bravo; Cartoon Network; CMT; CNBC; CNN; Comedy Central; Cox Sports Television; C-SPAN; C-SPAN 2; Discovery Channel; Disney Channel; Disney XD; E! HD; ESPN; ESPN Classic; ESPN2; ESPNews; EWTN Global Catholic Network; Food Network; Fox News Channel; FOX Sports Southwest; Freeform; FX; Hallmark Channel; Hallmark Movies & Mysteries; HGTV; History; HLN; Lifetime; MSNBC; MTV; National Geographic Channel; Nickelodeon; Oxygen; Pop; QVC; Spike TV; Syfy; TBS; Telemundo; The Weather Channel; TLC; TNT; Travel Channel; Trinity Broadcasting Network (TBN); truTV; TV Land; USA Network; VH1; WGN America.
Fee: $15.00 installation; $64.99 monthly.
Digital Basic Service
Subscribers: N.A.
Programming (via satellite): BBC America; Bloomberg Television; Discovery Digital Networks; FOX College Sports Central; FOX College Sports Pacific; Fox Sports 1; Golf Channel; GSN; Nick Jr.; Outdoor Channel; Ovation.
Digital Pay Service 1
Pay Units: N.A.
Programming (via satellite): Cinemax (multiplexed); HBO (multiplexed); Showtime (multiplexed); Starz (multiplexed); Starz Encore (multiplexed); Sundance TV; The Movie Channel (multiplexed).
Fee: $12.95 monthly (Cinemax, HBO, Showtime/TMC or Starz/Encore).
Video-On-Demand: No
Internet Service
Operational: Yes, Dial-up.
Subscribers: 5,575.
Broadband Service: In-house.
Fee: $100.00 installation; $56.99-$66.99 monthly; $4.99 modem lease; $80.00 modem purchase.

Telephone Service
Analog: Operational
Miles of Plant: 560.0 (coaxial); 135.0 (fiber optic). Homes passed: 15,425.
Chief Executive Officer & Treasurer: A.G. Scanlan, II. President: Tony Duet. Chief Technician: Danny Landry. Marketing Director: Christie Duet.
Ownership: Vision Communications LLC (Louisiana) (MSO).

GRAMERCY—Cox Communications. Now served by BATON ROUGE, LA [LA0003]. ICA: LA0167.

GRAND CHENIER—Formerly served by CableSouth Inc. Now served by Cameron Communications, CARLYSS, LA [LA5000]. This cable system has converted to IPTV. ICA: LA0168.

GRAND COTEAU—Allen's TV Cable Service Inc, 800 Victor II Blvd, PO Box 2643, Morgan City, LA 70380. Phones: 985-384-8335 (Morgan City office); 337-662-5315. Fax: 985-384-5243. E-mail: info@atvci.net. Web Site: http://www.atvci.net. Also serves St. Landry Parish (portions) & Sunset. ICA: LA0207.
TV Market Ranking: Below 100 (GRAND COTEAU, St. Landry Parish (portions), Sunset). Franchise award date: N.A. Franchise expiration date: N.A. Began: January 1, 1980.
Channel capacity: N.A. Channels available but not in use: N.A.
Basic Service
Subscribers: 560.
Programming (received off-air): KADN-TV (FOX, MNT) Lafayette; KALB-TV (CBS, CW, NBC) Alexandria; KATC (ABC, CW, Grit) Lafayette; KDCG-CD (Antenna TV) Opelousas; KLFY-TV (CBS) Lafayette; KLWB (MeTV, This TV) New Iberia; WAFB (Bounce TV, CBS) Baton Rouge; WBRZ-TV (ABC) Baton Rouge; WLPB-TV (PBS) Baton Rouge; WVLA-TV (NBC, This TV) Baton Rouge.
Programming (via satellite): C-SPAN; QVC; WGN America.
Fee: $66.90 installation; $18.65 monthly; $3.95 converter.
Expanded Basic Service 1
Subscribers: N.A.
Programming (via satellite): A&E; AMC; Animal Planet; BET; Bravo; Cartoon Network; CatholicTV; CMT; CNBC; CNN; Comedy Central; Cox Sports Television; Discovery Channel; Disney Channel; E! HD; ESPN; ESPN Classic; ESPN2; EWTN Global Catholic Network; Food Network; Fox News Channel; FOX Sports Southwest; Freeform; FX; HGTV; History; HLN; Lifetime; MSNBC; MTV; Nickelodeon; Outdoor Channel; Spike TV; Syfy; TBS; The Weather Channel; TLC; TNT; Travel Channel; Trinity Broadcasting Network (TBN); TV Land; USA Network; WE tv.
Fee: $42.50 monthly.

Digital Basic Service
Subscribers: N.A.
Programming (via satellite): 3ABN; BBC America; Bloomberg Television; BYUtv; Church Channel; Classic Arts Showcase; Daystar TV Network; Destination America; Discovery Channel HD; Discovery Kids Channel (multiplexed); Discovery Life Channel; Discovery Times Channel; DIY Network; ESPN HD; ESPN2 HD; ESPNews; Family Friendly Entertainment; FamilyNet; Fox Sports 1; FSN Digital Atlantic; FSN Digital Central; FSN Digital Pacific; Fuse; FXM; FYI; GEB America; Golf Channel; GSN; Hallmark Channel; History International; IFC; JUCE TV; Louisiana Legislative Network; MTV Classic; MTV Hits; MTV Jams; MTV2; National Geographic Channel; National Geographic Channel HD; NBCSN; Nick 2; Nick Jr.; Nicktoons; OWN: Oprah Winfrey Network; Science Channel; TeenNick; Tennis Channel; TNT HD; Tr3s; Turner Classic Movies; Universal HD; VH1 Country; VH1 Soul.
Pay Service 1
Pay Units: N.A.
Programming (via satellite): HBO (multiplexed); Showtime (multiplexed); The Movie Channel (multiplexed).
Digital Pay Service 1
Pay Units: N.A.
Programming (via satellite): Cinemax (multiplexed); Flix; HBO (multiplexed); Playboy TV; Showtime (multiplexed); Starz (multiplexed); Starz Encore (multiplexed); The Movie Channel (multiplexed).
Fee: $7.95 monthly (Encore), $11.50 monthly (Starz or Cinemax), $12.50 monthly (TMC), $12.95 monthly (Playboy), $13.95 monthly (Showtime), $15.25 monthly (HBO).
Video-On-Demand: No
Pay-Per-View
iN DEMAND (delivered digitally); Hot Choice (delivered digitally); Playboy TV (delivered digitally); Fresh (delivered digitally); Shorteez (delivered digitally); Spice Xcess (delivered digitally); Club Jenna (delivered digitally); Tigervision (delivered digitally).
Internet Service
Operational: Yes.
Broadband Service: atvci.net.
Fee: $24.95-$69.95 monthly.
Telephone Service
None
Miles of Plant: 187.0 (coaxial); 100.0 (fiber optic). Homes passed: 4,719.
President & General Manager: Gregory A. Price. Vice President: David C. Price. Chief Technician: Chris A. Price. Office Manager: Cindy LaVergne.
Ownership: Allen's TV Cable Service Inc. (MSO).

GRAND LAKE—Formerly served by CableSouth Inc. Now served by Cameron Communications, CARLYSS, LA [LA5000]. This cable system has converted to IPTV. ICA: LA0169.

GREENSBURG—Formerly served by Almega Cable. No longer in operation. ICA: LA0129.

2017 Edition

D-339

Louisiana—Cable Systems

HACKBERRY—Formerly served by Charter Communications. No longer in operation. ICA: LA0105.

HALL SUMMIT—Formerly served by Red River Cable TV. No longer in operation. ICA: LA0134.

HAMMOND—Charter Communications. Now served by SLIDELL, LA [LA0182]. ICA: LA0016.

HAUGHTON—Formerly served by Cebridge Connections. No longer in operation. ICA: LA0227.

HAYNESVILLE—NewWave Communications, One Montgomery Plaza, 4th Floor, Sikeston, MO 63801. Phones: 573-472-9500; 888-863-9928. Fax: 573-472-9518. E-mail: info@newwave.com. Web Site: http://www.newwavecom.com. Also serves Homer. ICA: LA0076.
TV Market Ranking: 99 (HAYNESVILLE); Below 100 (Homer).
Channel capacity: N.A. Channels available but not in use: N.A.
Basic Service
Subscribers: 541.
Fee: $35.00 installation; $32.93 monthly.
Expanded Basic Service 1
Subscribers: 381.
Digital Basic Service
Subscribers: N.A.
Fee: $10.00 monthly.
Digital Pay Service 1
Pay Units: N.A.
Fee: $7.00 monthly (Starz), $9.00 monthly (Cinemax), $15.00 monthly (Showtime/TMC), $16.00 monthly (HBO) or $25.00 monthly (HBO/Cinemax).
Internet Service
Operational: Yes.
Fee: $36.99-$46.99 monthly; $6.00 modem lease.
Telephone Service
None
General Manager: Staci Gowan.
Ownership: NewWave Communications LLC (MSO).

HENRY—Formerly served by CableSouth Inc. No longer in operation. ICA: LA0170.

HOMER—NewWave Communications. Now served by HAYNESVILLE, LA [LA0076]. ICA: LA0062.

HOSSTON—Comcast Cable. Now served by SHREVEPORT, LA [LA0004]. ICA: LA0118.

HOUMA—Comcast Cable. Now served by MOBILE, AL [AL0002]. ICA: LA0010.

IBERIA PARISH (portions)—Suddenlink Communications, 520 Maryville Centre Dr, Ste 300, St. Louis, MO 63141. Phones: 888-822-5151; 314-315-9400. Fax: 314-965-0500. Web Site: http://www.suddenlink.com. Also serves New Iberia, St. Martin Parish (portions) & Vermilion Parish (portions). ICA: LA0072.
TV Market Ranking: Below 100 (St. Martin Parish (portions), Vermilion Parish (portions), IBERIA PARISH (PORTIONS), New Iberia).
Channel capacity: 62 (operating 2-way). Channels available but not in use: N.A.
Basic Service
Subscribers: 1,104.
Programming (received off-air): KADN-TV (FOX, MNT) Lafayette; KATC (ABC, CW, Grit) Lafayette; KLFY-TV (CBS) Lafayette; KLPB-TV (PBS) Lafayette; WVLA-TV (NBC, This TV) Baton Rouge.
Programming (via satellite): Pop; QVC.
Fee: $28.45 monthly; $2.00 converter.
Expanded Basic Service 1
Subscribers: N.A.
Programming (via satellite): A&E; AMC; Animal Planet; BET; Cartoon Network; CNBC; CNN; Comedy Central; C-SPAN; Discovery Channel; Disney Channel; E! HD; ESPN; ESPN2; EWTN Global Catholic Network; Food Network; Fox News Channel; Freeform; FX; Great American Country; HGTV; History; HLN; Lifetime; MSNBC; MTV; National Geographic Channel; Nickelodeon; Outdoor Channel; Spike TV; Syfy; TBS; The Weather Channel; TLC; TNT; Travel Channel; Trinity Broadcasting Network (TBN); Turner Classic Movies; TV Land; USA Network; VH1.
Fee: $25.00 monthly.
Digital Basic Service
Subscribers: N.A.
Programming (via satellite): BBC America; Bloomberg Television; Cloo; Discovery Digital Networks; Disney XD; DMX Music; ESPN Classic; ESPNews; Fox Sports 1; Fuse; FYI; Golf Channel; GSN; History International; IFC; NBCSN; WE tv.
Pay Service 1
Pay Units: N.A.
Programming (via satellite): Cinemax; HBO; Showtime; The Movie Channel.
Fee: $7.95 monthly (Cinemax), $10.95 monthly (HBO, Showtime or TMC).
Digital Pay Service 1
Pay Units: N.A.
Programming (via satellite): Cinemax (multiplexed); HBO (multiplexed); Showtime (multiplexed); Starz (multiplexed); Starz Encore (multiplexed); The Movie Channel (multiplexed).
Video-On-Demand: No
Pay-Per-View
iN DEMAND (delivered digitally); Playboy TV (delivered digitally); Fresh (delivered digitally).
Internet Service
Operational: Yes. Began: July 14, 2003.
Broadband Service: Suddenlink High Speed Internet.
Fee: $45.00 installation; $29.95 monthly.
Telephone Service
Digital: Operational
Fee: $39.95 monthly
Miles of Plant: 50.0 (coaxial); 20.0 (fiber optic).
Vice President, Corporate Finance: Michael Pflantz. Regional Manager: Todd Cruthird.
Ownership: Cequel Communications Holdings I LLC (MSO).

INNIS—Formerly served by Spillway Communications Inc. No longer in operation. ICA: LA0172.

IOTA—Charter Communications. Now served by OPELOUSAS, LA [LA0022]. ICA: LA0108.

IOWA—Suddenlink Communications, 520 Maryville Centre Dr, Ste 300, St. Louis, MO 63141. Phones: 888-822-5151; 314-315-9400. Web Site: http://www.suddenlink.com. Also serves Calcasieu Parish (portions) & Jefferson Davis Parish (portions). ICA: LA0060.
TV Market Ranking: Below 100 (Calcasieu Parish (portions), IOWA, Jefferson Davis Parish (portions)). Franchise award date: May 12, 1980. Franchise expiration date: N.A. Began: September 1, 1981.
Channel capacity: N.A. Channels available but not in use: N.A.
Basic Service
Subscribers: 1,287. Commercial subscribers: 38.
Programming (received off-air): KATC (ABC, CW, Grit) Lafayette; KFDM (CBS, CW) Beaumont; KLFY-TV (CBS) Lafayette; KLTL-TV (PBS) Lake Charles; KPLC (Bounce TV, NBC, This TV) Lake Charles; KVHP (FOX) Lake Charles.
Programming (via satellite): QVC; WGN America.
Fee: $40.00 installation; $27.99 monthly.
Expanded Basic Service 1
Subscribers: N.A.
Programming (via satellite): A&E; AMC; Animal Planet; BET; Cartoon Network; CMT; CNBC; CNN; C-SPAN; Discovery Channel; Disney Channel; Disney XD; ESPN; ESPN2; EWTN Global Catholic Network; Food Network; Fox News Channel; FOX Sports Southwest; Freeform; HGTV; History; HLN; ION Television; Lifetime; MTV; Nickelodeon; Outdoor Channel; Spike TV; Syfy; TBS; The Weather Channel; TLC; TNT; Travel Channel; Trinity Broadcasting Network (TBN); Turner Classic Movies; TV Land; USA Network; WE tv.
Fee: $42.99 monthly.
Pay Service 1
Pay Units: N.A.
Programming (via satellite): Cinemax; HBO; Showtime.
Fee: $20.00 installation; $10.40 monthly.
Video-On-Demand: No
Internet Service
Operational: No.
Telephone Service
None
Miles of Plant: 82.0 (coaxial); None (fiber optic). Homes passed: 2,012.
Senior Vice President, Corporate Finance: Michael Pflantz. Vice President, Accounting: Sabrina Warr. General Manager: Todd Cruthird. Corporate Communications Director: Gene Regan.
Ownership: Cequel Communications Holdings I LLC (MSO).

JACKSON—Bailey Cable TV Inc, 807 Church St, Port Gibson, MS 39150-2413. Phone: 601-437-8300. Fax: 601-437-6860. E-mail: cs@baileycable.net. Web Site: http://www.baileycable.net. ICA: LA0242.
TV Market Ranking: 87 (JACKSON).
Channel capacity: N.A. Channels available but not in use: N.A.
Basic Service
Subscribers: 319.
Fee: $15.00 installation; $42.95 monthly.
President: David A. Bailey.
Ownership: Bailey Cable TV Inc. (MSO).

JENA—Media3, PO Box 620, Milan, TN 38358. Phone: 866-257-2044. Fax: 731-723-7049. E-mail: customerservice@mymedia3.com. Web Site: http://www.mymedia3.com. Also serves Good Pine, La Salle Parish & Midway. ICA: LA0052.
TV Market Ranking: Below 100 (Good Pine, JENA, La Salle Parish, Midway). Franchise award date: N.A. Franchise expiration date: N.A. Began: January 1, 1964.
Channel capacity: N.A. Channels available but not in use: N.A.
Basic Service
Subscribers: 477.
Programming (received off-air): KALB-TV (CBS, CW, NBC) Alexandria; KARD (Bounce TV, FOX) West Monroe; KLAX-TV (ABC) Alexandria; KLTM-TV (PBS) Monroe; KMLU (MeTV) Columbia; KNOE-TV (ABC, CBS, CW) Monroe; 3 FMs.
Programming (via satellite): Freeform; HGTV; INSP; Outdoor Channel; QVC; Syfy; The Weather Channel; Trinity Broadcasting Network (TBN); VH1; WGN America.
Fee: $24.95 installation; $22.45 monthly; $1.19 converter.
Expanded Basic Service 1
Subscribers: N.A.
Programming (via satellite): A&E; AMC; Animal Planet; BET; Cartoon Network; CMT; CNBC; CNN; Comedy Central; Discovery Channel; Disney Channel; Disney XD; E! HD; ESPN; ESPN2; Food Network; FX; Hallmark Channel; History; HLN; Lifetime; MSNBC; MTV; National Geographic Channel; Nickelodeon; Oxygen; Spike TV; TBS; TLC; TNT; Travel Channel; truTV; TV Land; USA Network; WE tv.
Fee: $22.19 installation; $12.60 monthly.
Digital Basic Service
Subscribers: N.A.
Programming (via satellite): BBC America; Bloomberg Television; Bravo; Discovery Digital Networks; ESPN Classic; EVINE Live; Fox Sports 1; Fuse; FXM; FYI; Golf Channel; GSN; History International; IFC; INSP; LMN; MC; NBCSN; Nick Jr.; TeenNick; Turner Classic Movies.
Pay Service 1
Pay Units: N.A.
Programming (via satellite): HBO; Showtime; The Movie Channel.
Fee: $7.00 monthly.
Digital Pay Service 1
Pay Units: N.A.
Programming (via satellite): Cinemax (multiplexed); Flix; HBO (multiplexed); Showtime (multiplexed); Starz (multiplexed); Starz Encore (multiplexed); The Movie Channel (multiplexed).
Video-On-Demand: No
Pay-Per-View
Hot Choice (delivered digitally); Playboy TV (delivered digitally); Fresh (delivered digitally); Shorteez (delivered digitally).
Internet Service
Operational: No.
Telephone Service
None
Miles of Plant: 97.0 (coaxial); None (fiber optic). Homes passed: 3,385.
President: Alan Taylor. Chief Financial Officer: Thomas Pate. Business Manager: Glenda Elliott.
Ownership: CableSouth Media3 LLC (MSO).

JONESBORO—Suddenlink Communications, 208 Hudson Ave, Jonesboro, AR 72401. Phones: 870-935-3615; 888-822-5151; 314-315-9400. Fax: 318-259-4446. Web Site: http://www.suddenlink.com. Also serves East Hodge, Hodge, Jackson Parish (portions), North Hodge & Quitman. ICA: LA0173.
TV Market Ranking: 99 (Jackson Parish (portions)); Below 100 (Jackson Parish (portions)); Outside TV Markets (East Hodge, Hodge, JONESBORO, North Hodge, Quitman, Jackson Parish (portions)). Franchise award date: N.A. Franchise expiration date: N.A. Began: August 1, 1968.
Channel capacity: 42 (not 2-way capable). Channels available but not in use: N.A.
Basic Service
Subscribers: 636. Commercial subscribers: 88.
Programming (received off-air): KARD (Bounce TV, FOX) West Monroe; KLTM-TV

Cable Systems—Louisiana

(PBS) Monroe; KMLU (MeTV) Columbia; KNOE-TV (ABC, CBS, CW) Monroe; KSLA (Bounce TV, CBS, Grit, This TV) Shreveport; KTBS-TV (ABC) Shreveport; KTVE (NBC) El Dorado; allband FM.
Programming (via satellite): CNN; C-SPAN; ESPN; Great American Country; HLN; ION Television; TBS; The Weather Channel.
Fee: $40.00 installation; $36.50 monthly.

Expanded Basic Service 1
Subscribers: N.A.
Programming (via satellite): A&E; AMC; BET; Cartoon Network; Cox Sports Television; Discovery Channel; Disney Channel; ESPN2; FamilyNet; Freeform; HGTV; History; Lifetime; LMN; Nickelodeon; Outdoor Channel; Spike TV; TLC; TNT; TV Land; USA Network; VH1.
Fee: $43.72 monthly.

Digital Basic Service
Subscribers: N.A.
Programming (via satellite): BBC America; Bloomberg Television; Discovery Digital Networks; Disney XD; DMX Music; ESPNews; Fox Sports 1; Fuse; FYI; Golf Channel; GSN; History International; NBCSN; Sundance TV; The Word Network; Trinity Broadcasting Network (TBN).

Pay Service 1
Pay Units: N.A.
Programming (via satellite): HBO; Showtime; The Movie Channel.

Digital Pay Service 1
Pay Units: N.A.
Programming (via satellite): Cinemax; HBO (multiplexed); Showtime (multiplexed); Starz (multiplexed); Starz Encore; The Movie Channel (multiplexed).

Video-On-Demand: No

Pay-Per-View
ESPN Now (delivered digitally); Action PPV (delivered digitally); Shorteez (delivered digitally); Fresh (delivered digitally); Playboy TV (delivered digitally); iN DEMAND (delivered digitally).

Internet Service
Operational: Yes.
Broadband Service: Suddenlink High Speed Internet.

Telephone Service
Digital: Operational
Miles of Plant: 73.0 (coaxial); None (fiber optic).
Senior Vice President, Corporate Finance: Michael Pflantz. Vice President, Accounting: Sabrina Warr. General Manager: William R. Rogers. Chief Technician: Richard Woods.
Ownership: Cequel Communications Holdings I LLC (MSO).

JONESVILLE—Media3, PO Box 620, Milan, TN 38358. Phone: 866-257-2044. Fax: 731-723-7049. E-mail: customerservice@mymedia3.com. Web Site: http://www.mymedia3.com. Also serves Catahoula Parish (portions). ICA: LA0235.
TV Market Ranking: Below 100 (Catahoula Parish (portions), JONESVILLE).
Channel capacity: N.A. Channels available but not in use: N.A.

Basic Service
Subscribers: 72.
Programming (received off-air): KALB-TV (CBS, CW, NBC) Alexandria; KARD (Bounce TV, FOX) West Monroe; KLAX-TV (ABC) Alexandria; KLFY-TV (CBS) Lafayette; KLTM-TV (PBS) Monroe; KMLU (MeTV) Columbia; KNOE-TV (ABC, CBS, CW) Monroe; WNTZ-TV (FOX, MNT) Natchez.

Programming (via satellite): QVC; WGN America.
Fee: $24.95 installation; $22.45 monthly.

Expanded Basic Service 1
Subscribers: N.A.
Programming (via satellite): A&E; AMC; Animal Planet; BET; CMT; CNBC; CNN; C-SPAN; Discovery Channel; Disney Channel; Disney XD; E! HD; ESPN; ESPN2; Freeform; HGTV; History; Lifetime; MSNBC; MTV; National Geographic Channel; NBCSN; Nickelodeon; Oxygen; Spike TV; Syfy; TBS; The Weather Channel; TLC; TNT; Travel Channel; Trinity Broadcasting Network (TBN); TV Land; USA Network; VH1; WE tv.

Pay Service 1
Pay Units: N.A.
Programming (via satellite): Cinemax; HBO.

Video-On-Demand: No

Internet Service
Operational: No.

Telephone Service
None
President: Alan Taylor. Chief Financial Officer: Thomas Pate.
Ownership: CableSouth Media3 LLC (MSO).

KAPLAN—Kaplan Telephone Co. This cable system has converted to IPTV. See KAPLAN, LA [LA5021]. ICA: LA0162.

KAPLAN—KTC Pace. Formerly [LA0162]. This cable system has converted to IPTV. 220 North Cushing Ave, Kaplan, LA 70548. Phones: 337-643-7171; 866-643-7171; 337-643-2255. Fax: 337-643-6000. Web Site: http://ktcpace.com. Also serves Vermilion Parish (rural areas). ICA: LA5021.
TV Market Ranking: Below 100 (KAPLAN).
Channel capacity: N.A. Channels available but not in use: N.A.

Broadcast Basic
Subscribers: 1,642.
Fee: $17.90 monthly.

Silver
Subscribers: N.A.
Fee: $45.95 monthly. Includes 68 channels.

Gold
Subscribers: N.A.
Fee: $60.95 monthly. Includes 160 channels.

Cinemax
Subscribers: N.A.
Fee: $12.95 monthly. Includes 8 channels.

HBO
Subscribers: N.A.
Fee: $12.95 monthly. Includes 8 channels.

Showtime/TMC/Flix
Subscribers: N.A.
Fee: $12.95 monthly. Includes 11 channels.

Starz/Encore
Subscribers: N.A.
Fee: $12.95 monthly. Includes 7 channels.

Video-On-Demand: No

Pay-Per-View
Adult Programming (delivered digitally).

Internet Service
Operational: Yes.
Fee: $29.95-$99.95 monthly.

Telephone Service
Digital: Operational
Ownership: Kaplan Telephone Co. Inc. (MSO).

KENTWOOD—Media3, PO Box 650, Milan, TN 38358. Phone: 866-257-2044. E-mail: customerservice@mymedia3.com. Web Site: http://www.mymedia3.com. ICA: LA0098.
TV Market Ranking: Below 100 (KENTWOOD).
Franchise award date: N.A. Franchise expiration date: N.A. Began: September 1, 1981.
Channel capacity: N.A. Channels available but not in use: N.A.

Basic Service
Subscribers: 84.
Programming (received off-air): WAFB (Bounce TV, CBS) Baton Rouge; WBRZ-TV (ABC) Baton Rouge; WDSU (MeTV, NBC) New Orleans; WGNO (ABC, Antenna TV, Escape) New Orleans; WLPB-TV (PBS) Baton Rouge; WNOL-TV (CW, This TV) New Orleans; WPXL-TV (ION) New Orleans; WSTY-LP (My Family TV) Hammond; WVLA-TV (NBC, This TV) Baton Rouge; WVUE-DT (Bounce TV, FOX) New Orleans; WWL-TV (CBS) New Orleans.
Programming (via satellite): A&E; BET; Cartoon Network; CNBC; CNN; C-SPAN; Discovery Channel; Disney Channel; Disney XD; ESPN; ESPN2; Fox News Channel; Freeform; Fuse; FX; Great American Country; Hallmark Channel; HGTV; HLN; Lifetime; Outdoor Channel; QVC; TBS; The Weather Channel; TLC; TNT; Travel Channel; Trinity Broadcasting Network (TBN); Turner Classic Movies; USA Network; WGN America.
Fee: $24.95 installation; $22.45 monthly.

Digital Basic Service
Subscribers: N.A.
Programming (via satellite): BBC America; Bloomberg Television; Discovery Life Channel; DMX Music; ESPN Classic; ESPNews; FOX College Sports Central; FOX College Sports Pacific; Fox Sports 1; FYI; Golf Channel; GSN; History; History International; National Geographic Channel; WE tv.

Digital Expanded Basic Service
Subscribers: N.A.
Programming (via satellite): DMX Music; FXM; LMN; Starz Encore.
Fee: $13.95 monthly.

Pay Service 1
Pay Units: N.A.
Programming (via satellite): Cinemax; HBO.

Digital Pay Service 1
Pay Units: N.A.
Programming (via satellite): Cinemax (multiplexed); Flix; HBO (multiplexed); Showtime (multiplexed); The Movie Channel (multiplexed).
Fee: $13.26 monthly.

Pay-Per-View
ESPN Now (delivered digitally); Hot Choice (delivered digitally); Playboy TV (delivered digitally); Fresh (delivered digitally); Shorteez (delivered digitally); Urban Xtra (delivered digitally).

Internet Service
Operational: No.

Telephone Service
None
Miles of Plant: 20.0 (coaxial); None (fiber optic). Homes passed: 905.
Chief Financial Officer: Thomas Pate.
Ownership: CableSouth Media3 LLC (MSO).

KILBOURNE—Formerly served by Community Communications Co. No longer in operation. ICA: LA0135.

KINDER—Vyve Broadband, 2504 Westwood Dr, Westlake, LA 70669. Phones: 800-937-1397; 337-433-0892. Web Site: http://vyvebroadband.com. Also serves Allen Parish (portions), Elton & Oberlin. ICA: LA0054.
TV Market Ranking: Below 100 (KINDER, Allen Parish (portions)); Outside TV Markets (Elton, Oberlin, Allen Parish (portions)). Franchise award date: N.A. Franchise expiration date: N.A. Began: January 1, 1982.
Channel capacity: N.A. Channels available but not in use: N.A.

Basic Service
Subscribers: 377.
Programming (received off-air): KADN-TV (FOX, MNT) Lafayette; KALB-TV (CBS, CW, NBC) Alexandria; KATC (ABC, CW, Grit) Lafayette; KLFY-TV (CBS) Lafayette; KLTL-TV (PBS) Lake Charles; KPLC (Bounce TV, NBC, This TV) Lake Charles; KVHP (FOX) Lake Charles.
Programming (via satellite): A&E; AMC; Animal Planet; BET; Cartoon Network; CMT; CNBC; CNN; C-SPAN; C-SPAN 2; Discovery Channel; Disney Channel; ESPN; ESPN2; EWTN Global Catholic Network; Food Network; FOX Sports Networks; Freeform; HGTV; History; HLN; INSP; Lifetime; MSNBC; MTV; NBCSN; Nickelodeon; QVC; Spike TV; Syfy; TBS; The Weather Channel; TLC; TNT; TV Land; USA Network; VH1.
Fee: $59.99 installation; $25.00 monthly.

Digital Basic Service
Subscribers: N.A.
Programming (via satellite): BBC America; Bloomberg Television; Bravo; Discovery Digital Networks; DMX Music; Fox Sports 1; Fuse; Golf Channel; IFC; Outdoor Channel; Trinity Broadcasting Network (TBN); Turner Classic Movies; WE tv; Weatherscan.
Fee: $26.00 installation.

Pay Service 1
Pay Units: N.A.
Programming (via satellite): Cinemax; HBO (multiplexed); Starz; Starz Encore.
Fee: $10.00 installation.

Digital Pay Service 1
Pay Units: N.A.
Programming (via satellite): Cinemax (multiplexed); HBO (multiplexed); Showtime (multiplexed); Starz (multiplexed); Starz Encore (multiplexed); The Movie Channel (multiplexed).

Video-On-Demand: No

Pay-Per-View
Hot Choice (delivered digitally); Playboy TV (delivered digitally); Fresh (delivered digitally); Shorteez (delivered digitally); Sports PPV (delivered digitally).

Internet Service
Operational: Yes.
Broadband Service: Net Commander.

Telephone Service
None
Miles of Plant: 58.0 (coaxial); None (fiber optic). Homes passed included in Westlake.
President & Chief Executive Officer: Jeffrey DeMond. Senior Vice President, Financial Planning: Daniel White. Vice President, Mar-

Louisiana—Cable Systems

keting: Diane Quennoz. Vice President, Residential Services: Vin Zachariah.
Ownership: Vyve Broadband LLC (MSO).

KROTZ SPRINGS—Spillway Cablevision Inc, 10900 Hwy 77, PO Box 337, Maringouin, LA 70757. Phone: 225-625-2311. Fax: 225-625-3107. E-mail: cs@spillwaycable.com. Web Site: http://www.spillwaycable.com. Also serves St. Landry Parish (portions). ICA: LA0112.
TV Market Ranking: Below 100 (KROTZ SPRINGS, St. Landry Parish (portions)). Franchise award date: N.A. Franchise expiration date: N.A. Began: March 1, 1983.
Channel capacity: 54 (not 2-way capable). Channels available but not in use: N.A.
Basic Service
Subscribers: 63.
Programming (received off-air): KALB-TV (CBS, CW, NBC) Alexandria; KATC (ABC, CW, Grit) Lafayette; KLFY-TV (CBS) Lafayette; WAFB (Bounce TV, CBS) Baton Rouge; WBRZ-TV (ABC) Baton Rouge; WLPB-TV (PBS) Baton Rouge; WVLA-TV (NBC, This TV) Baton Rouge.
Programming (via satellite): TBS; TNT.
Fee: $26.00 installation; $30.95 monthly.
Pay Service 1
Pay Units: N.A.
Programming (via satellite): HBO; Showtime; The Movie Channel.
Fee: $12.95 monthly (each).
Video-On-Demand: No
Internet Service
Operational: Yes.
Telephone Service
None
Miles of Plant: 14.0 (coaxial); None (fiber optic). Homes passed: 558.
Manager: Sue Soileau.
Ownership: Spillway Cablevision Inc. (MSO).

LA PLACE—Comcast Cable. Now served by MOBILE, AL [AL0002]. ICA: LA0021.

LAFAYETTE—Cox Communications. Now served by BATON ROUGE, LA [LA0003]. ICA: LA0176.

LAKE ARTHUR—Vyve Broadband, 2504 Westwood Dr, Westlake, LA 70669. Phones: 800-937-1397; 337-433-0892. Web Site: http://vyvebroadband.com. Also serves Gueydan, Jefferson Davis Parish (portions), Roanoke & Welsh. ICA: LA0078.
TV Market Ranking: Below 100 (Gueydan, Jefferson Davis Parish (portions), LAKE ARTHUR, Roanoke, Welsh). Franchise award date: N.A. Franchise expiration date: N.A. Began: January 1, 1979.
Channel capacity: N.A. Channels available but not in use: N.A.
Basic Service
Subscribers: 440.
Programming (received off-air): KADN-TV (FOX, MNT) Lafayette; KALB-TV (CBS, CW, NBC) Alexandria; KATC (ABC, CW, Grit) Lafayette; KLFY-TV (CBS) Lafayette; KLTL-TV (PBS) Lake Charles; KPLC (Bounce TV, NBC, This TV) Lake Charles; KVHP (FOX) Lake Charles.
Programming (via satellite): CW PLUS; EWTN Global Catholic Network.
Fee: $59.99 installation; $25.00 monthly.
Expanded Basic Service 1
Subscribers: N.A.
Programming (via satellite): A&E; AMC; Animal Planet; BET; Bravo; Cartoon Network; CMT; CNBC; CNN; Comedy Central; C-SPAN; Discovery Channel; Disney Channel; DIY Network; E! HD; ESPN; ESPN2; Food Network; Fox News Channel; FOX Sports Southwest; Freeform; FX; FXM; Hallmark Channel; HGTV; History; HLN; INSP; Lifetime; MSNBC; MTV; NBCSN; Nick Jr.; Nickelodeon; QVC; Spike TV; Syfy; TBS; The Weather Channel; TLC; TNT; Travel Channel; truTV; TV Land; USA Network; VH1; WE tv.
Digital Basic Service
Subscribers: N.A.
Programming (via satellite): BBC America; Bloomberg Television; Bravo; Cloo; CMT; Destination America; Discovery Kids Channel; Discovery Life Channel; DMX Music; ESPN Classic; ESPN2; ESPNews; Fox Sports 1; Fuse; FXM; FYI; Golf Channel; Great American Country; GSN; HGTV; History; History International; IFC; Investigation Discovery; LMN; MTV Classic; MTV Hits; MTV Jams; MTV2; NBCSN; Nick Jr.; Nicktoons; Outdoor Channel; OWN: Oprah Winfrey Network; Science Channel; Sundance TV; Syfy; TeenNick; Trinity Broadcasting Network (TBN); Turner Classic Movies; UP; VH1 Soul; WE tv.
Fee: $20.00 installation.
Pay Service 1
Pay Units: N.A.
Programming (via satellite): Cinemax; HBO (multiplexed); Starz; Starz Encore.
Fee: $10.00 installation; $10.95 monthly (Showtime), $11.95 monthly (Cinemax), $12.95 monthly (Starz), $13.95 monthly (HBO).
Digital Pay Service 1
Pay Units: N.A.
Programming (via satellite): Cinemax (multiplexed); HBO (multiplexed); Showtime (multiplexed); Starz (multiplexed); Starz Encore (multiplexed); The Movie Channel (multiplexed).
Fee: $10.00 installation; $11.95 monthly (Cinemax), $12.95 monthly (Starz), $13.95 monthly (HBO).
Video-On-Demand: No
Pay-Per-View
iN DEMAND (delivered digitally); Hot Choice (delivered digitally); Playboy TV (delivered digitally); Fresh (delivered digitally); Shorteez (delivered digitally); Sports PPV (delivered digitally).
Internet Service
Operational: Yes.
Broadband Service: Net Commander.
Fee: $39.95 installation; $51.95 monthly.
Telephone Service
None
Miles of Plant: 25.0 (coaxial); None (fiber optic). Homes passed included in Westlake.
President & Chief Executive Officer: Jeffrey DeMond. Senior Vice President, Financial Planning: Daniel White. Vice President, Residential Services: Vin Zachariah. Vice President, Marketing: Diane Quennoz. Plant Manager: Marcus Edwards.
Ownership: Vyve Broadband LLC (MSO).

LAKE CHARLES—Suddenlink Communications, 1538 East Prien Lake Rd, Lake Charles, LA 70606-0830. Phones: 888-822-5151; 314-315-9400. Fax: 318-474-3436. Web Site: http://www.suddenlink.com. Also serves Calcasieu Parish & Sulphur. ICA: LA0007.
TV Market Ranking: Below 100 (Calcasieu Parish (portions), LAKE CHARLES, Sulphur). Franchise award date: N.A. Franchise expiration date: N.A. Began: September 1, 1967.
Channel capacity: N.A. Channels available but not in use: N.A.
Basic Service
Subscribers: 28,559.
Programming (received off-air): KATC (ABC, CW, Grit) Lafayette; KBMT (ABC) Beaumont; KBTV-TV (Bounce TV, FOX) Port Arthur; KFAM-CD (IND) Lake Charles; KFDM (CBS, CW) Beaumont; KLFY-TV (CBS) Lafayette; KLTL-TV (PBS) Lake Charles; KPLC (Bounce TV, NBC, This TV) Lake Charles; KVHP (FOX) Lake Charles; 14 FMs.
Programming (via satellite): BET; Discovery Channel; EWTN Global Catholic Network; INSP; ION Television; Pop; TBS.
Fee: $60.00 installation; $33.50 monthly; $.77 converter.
Expanded Basic Service 1
Subscribers: N.A.
Programming (via satellite): A&E; AMC; Animal Planet; Cartoon Network; CNBC; CNN; Comedy Central; C-SPAN; Disney Channel; E! HD; ESPN; ESPN Classic; ESPN2; Food Network; Fox News Channel; FOX Sports Southwest; Freeform; FX; Great American Country; HGTV; History; HLN; Lifetime; MoviePlex; MTV; Nickelodeon; Pop; QVC; Spike TV; The Weather Channel; TLC; TNT; Trinity Broadcasting Network (TBN); truTV; TV Land; USA Network.
Fee: $10.00 installation; $20.34 monthly.
Digital Basic Service
Subscribers: N.A.
Programming (via satellite): BBC America; Discovery Digital Networks; Golf Channel; GSN; IFC; NBCSN; Starz; Syfy; Turner Classic Movies; WE tv.
Pay Service 1
Pay Units: N.A.
Programming (via satellite): Cinemax; HBO; Showtime; Starz.
Fee: $10.00 installation; $1.75 monthly (Encore), $6.75 monthly (Starz), $8.00 monthly (Cinemax), $10.95 monthly (HBO), $11.50 monthly (Showtime).
Digital Pay Service 1
Pay Units: N.A.
Programming (via satellite): Cinemax (multiplexed); HBO (multiplexed); Showtime (multiplexed); Starz (multiplexed); The Movie Channel (multiplexed).
Fee: $6.75 monthly (Starz), $8.00 monthly (Cinemax), $10.95 monthly (HBO), $11.50 monthly (Showtime).
Video-On-Demand: No
Pay-Per-View
Fresh (delivered digitally); movies.
Internet Service
Operational: Yes.
Subscribers: 25,731.
Broadband Service: Suddenlink High Speed Internet.
Fee: $45.00 installation; $29.95 monthly.
Telephone Service
Digital: Operational
Subscribers: 14,751.
Fee: $39.95 monthly
Miles of Plant: 1,335.0 (coaxial); 268.0 (fiber optic). Homes passed: 66,397.
Senior Vice President, Corporate Finance: Michael Pflantz. Vice President, Accounting: Sabrina Warr. General Manager: Mike Ross. Chief Technician: Larry Stehr.
Ownership: Cequel Communications Holdings I LLC (MSO).

LAKE CLAIBORNE—Formerly served by Almega Cable. No longer in operation. ICA: LA0178.

LAKE PROVIDENCE—NewWave Communications, One Montgomery Plz, 4th Fl, Sikeston, MO 63801. Phones: 573-472-9500; 888-863-9928. Fax: 573-472-9518. E-mail: info@newwavecom.com. Web Site: http://www.newwavecom.com. Also serves Oak Grove. ICA: LA0053.
TV Market Ranking: Outside TV Markets (LAKE PROVIDENCE, Oak Grove). Franchise award date: November 28, 1979. Franchise expiration date: N.A. Began: January 1, 1980.
Channel capacity: N.A. Channels available but not in use: N.A.
Basic Service
Subscribers: 422.
Programming (received off-air): KARD (Bounce TV, FOX) West Monroe; KLTM-TV (PBS) Monroe; KMLU (MeTV) Columbia; KNOE-TV (ABC, CBS, CW) Monroe; KTVE (NBC) El Dorado.
Programming (via satellite): EWTN Global Catholic Network; INSP; QVC; TBS; The Weather Channel; WGN America.
Fee: $35.00 installation; $33.93 monthly.
Expanded Basic Service 1
Subscribers: N.A.
Programming (received off-air): WABG-TV (ABC, FOX) Greenwood.
Programming (via satellite): A&E; AMC; Animal Planet; BET; Cartoon Network; CMT; CNN; Discovery Channel; ESPN; ESPN2; Food Network; Fox News Channel; Freeform; FX; Hallmark Channel; HGTV; History; ION Television; Lifetime; MTV; Nickelodeon; Outdoor Channel; Pop; Spike TV; Syfy; TLC; TNT; Travel Channel; Trinity Broadcasting Network (TBN); Turner Classic Movies; TV Land; USA Network.
Fee: $50.20 monthly.
Digital Basic Service
Subscribers: N.A.
Programming (via satellite): Discovery Digital Networks; DMX Music; ESPN Classic; ESPNews; Fox Sports 1; FYI; Golf Channel; GSN; History International; LMN; National Geographic Channel; Nick Jr.; TeenNick.
Fee: $10.00 monthly.
Pay Service 1
Pay Units: N.A.
Programming (via satellite): HBO; Showtime.
Fee: $14.95 installation; $13.96 monthly (each).
Digital Pay Service 1
Pay Units: N.A.
Programming (via satellite): Cinemax (multiplexed); HBO (multiplexed); Showtime (multiplexed); Starz (multiplexed); Starz Encore (multiplexed); The Movie Channel (multiplexed).
Fee: $7.00 monthly (Starz), $9.00 monthly (Cinemax), $15.00 monthly (Showtime/TMC), $16.00 monthly (HBO) or $25.00 monthly (HBO/Cinemax).
Video-On-Demand: No
Pay-Per-View
iN DEMAND (delivered digitally); Playboy TV (delivered digitally); Shorteez (delivered digitally).
Internet Service
Operational: No.
Telephone Service
None
Homes passed: 2,400.
General Manager: Staci Gowan.
Ownership: NewWave Communications LLC (MSO).

LAKE ST. JOHN—Formerly served by Almega Cable. No longer in operation. ICA: LA0131.

LECOMPTE—Suddenlink Communications, 520 Maryville Centre Dr, Ste 300, St. Louis, MO 63141. Phones: 800-999-

Cable Systems—Louisiana

6845 (Customer service); 314-315-9400. Web Site: http://www.suddenlink.com. Also serves Cheneyville, Forest Hill, Glenmora, Kolin, McNary, Rapides Parish (portions) & Woodworth. ICA: LA0084.

TV Market Ranking: Below 100 (Cheneyville, Forest Hill, Glenmora, Kolin, LECOMPTE, McNary, Rapides Parish (portions), Woodworth). Franchise award date: N.A. Franchise expiration date: N.A. Began: March 1, 1983.

Channel capacity: N.A. Channels available but not in use: N.A.

Basic Service
Subscribers: 884. Commercial subscribers: 27.
Programming (received off-air): KALB-TV (CBS, CW, NBC) Alexandria; KATC (ABC, CW, Grit) Lafayette; KLAX-TV (ABC) Alexandria; KLFY-TV (CBS) Lafayette; KLPA-TV (PBS) Alexandria; KPLC (Bounce TV, NBC, This TV) Lake Charles.
Programming (via satellite): TBS; WGN America.
Fee: $28.45 monthly.

Pay Service 1
Pay Units: N.A.
Programming (via satellite): Cinemax; Flix; HBO; Showtime; The Movie Channel.
Fee: $1.95 monthly (Flix), $7.00 monthly (Cinemax or Showtime), $9.00 monthly (TMC), $12.00 monthly (HBO).

Video-On-Demand: No

Internet Service
Operational: Yes. Began: January 12, 2005.
Broadband Service: Suddenlink High Speed Internet.
Fee: $45.00 installation; $29.95 monthly.

Telephone Service
Digital: Operational
Fee: $39.95 monthly
Miles of Plant: 93.0 (coaxial); None (fiber optic). Homes passed: 2,871.
Regional Manager: Todd Cruthird. Area Manager: Mark Hood. Plant Manager: Dion Canaday.
Ownership: Cequel Communications Holdings I LLC (MSO).

LEESVILLE—Suddenlink Communications, 520 Maryville Centre Dr, Ste 300, St. Louis, MO 63141. Phones: 888-822-5151; 314-315-9400. Fax: 314-965-0500. Web Site: http://www.suddenlink.com. Also serves Anacoco, Fisher, Florien, Fort Polk, Hornbeck, New Llano, Sabine Parish (portions) & Vernon Parish (portions). ICA: LA0035.

TV Market Ranking: Below 100 (Vernon Parish (portions)); Outside TV Markets (Anacoco, Fisher, Florien, Fort Polk, Hornbeck, LEESVILLE, New Llano, Sabine Parish (portions), Vernon Parish (portions)). Franchise award date: N.A. Franchise expiration date: N.A. Began: August 8, 1963.

Channel capacity: 38 (operating 2-way). Channels available but not in use: N.A.

Basic Service
Subscribers: 4,323. Commercial subscribers: 412.
Programming (received off-air): KALB-TV (CBS, CW, NBC) Alexandria; KLAX-TV (ABC) Alexandria; KLFY-TV (CBS) Lafayette; KLPA-TV (PBS) Alexandria; WNTZ-TV (FOX, MNT) Natchez.
Programming (via satellite): EWTN Global Catholic Network; Pop; QVC.
Fee: $39.95 installation; $38.50 monthly; $2.95 converter.

Expanded Basic Service 1
Subscribers: N.A.
Programming (via satellite): A&E; AMC; Animal Planet; BET; Bravo; Cartoon Network; CNBC; CNN; Comedy Central; C-SPAN; Discovery Channel; Disney Channel; E! HD; ESPN; ESPN Classic; ESPN2; Food Network; Fox News Channel; Fox Sports 1; FOX Sports Southwest; Freeform; FX; Golf Channel; Great American Country; Hallmark Channel; HGTV; History; HLN; INSP; Lifetime; MSNBC; MTV; National Geographic Channel; Nickelodeon; Outdoor Channel; Spike TV; Syfy; TBS; Telemundo; The Weather Channel; TLC; TNT; Turner Classic Movies; TV Land; Univision Studios; USA Network; VH1.

Digital Basic Service
Subscribers: N.A.
Programming (via satellite): BBC America; Bloomberg Television; Cloo; C-SPAN 3; Discovery Digital Networks; Disney XD; DIY Network; ESPNews; FOX College Sports Central; FOX College Sports Pacific; Fuse; FXM; FYI; GSN; History International; HITS (Headend In The Sky); IFC; MC; NBCSN; Sundance TV; WE tv.

Pay Service 1
Pay Units: N.A.
Programming (via satellite): HBO; Showtime; Starz; The Movie Channel.
Fee: $24.95 installation; $10.95 monthly (each).

Digital Pay Service 1
Pay Units: N.A.
Programming (via satellite): Cinemax (multiplexed); Flix (multiplexed); HBO (multiplexed); Showtime (multiplexed); Starz (multiplexed); Starz Encore (multiplexed); The Movie Channel (multiplexed).

Pay-Per-View
iN DEMAND (delivered digitally); Playboy TV (delivered digitally).

Internet Service
Operational: Yes. Began: March 16, 2004.
Broadband Service: Suddenlink High Speed Internet.
Fee: $45.00 installation; $29.95 monthly.

Telephone Service
Digital: Operational
Fee: $39.95 monthly
Miles of Plant: 120.0 (coaxial); None (fiber optic). Homes passed: 7,528.
Senior Vice President, Corporate Finance: Michael Pflantz. Vice President, Accounting: Sabrina Warr. Regional Manager: Todd Cruthird. Marketing Director: Beverly Gambell. Technical Manager: Randy Berry.
Ownership: Cequel Communications Holdings I LLC (MSO).

LOGANSPORT—NewWave Communications, One Montgomery Plaza, 4th Floor, Sikeston, MO 63801. Phones: 888-863-9928; 573-472-9500. Fax: 573-472-9518. E-mail: info@newwave.com. Web Site: http://www.newwavecom.com. ICA: LA0096.

TV Market Ranking: Outside TV Markets (LOGANSPORT). Franchise award date: N.A. Franchise expiration date: N.A. Began: January 1, 1976.

Channel capacity: N.A. Channels available but not in use: N.A.

Basic Service
Subscribers: 110.
Programming (received off-air): KLTS-TV (PBS) Shreveport; KMSS-TV (FOX) Shreveport; KPXJ (Antenna TV, CW, MeTV, Movies!) Minden; KSHV-TV (MNT) Shreveport; KSLA (Bounce TV, CBS, Grit, This TV) Shreveport; KTAL-TV (NBC) Texarkana; KTBS-TV (ABC) Shreveport.
Programming (via satellite): A&E; BET; Cartoon Network; CMT; CNN; Discovery Channel; Disney Channel; ESPN; ESPN2; Freeform; HGTV; History; HLN; Lifetime; MTV; Nickelodeon; Outdoor Channel; Spike TV; Syfy; TBS; The Weather Channel; TLC; TNT; Trinity Broadcasting Network (TBN); Turner Classic Movies; TV Land; USA Network; VH1; WGN America.
Fee: $35.00 installation; $55.34 monthly.

Digital Basic Service
Subscribers: N.A.
Fee: $11.00 monthly.

Digital Pay Service 1
Pay Units: N.A.
Programming (via satellite): Cinemax; HBO; Showtime; Starz; Starz Encore; The Movie Channel.
Fee: $14.95 installation; $8.00 monthly (Starz), $9.00 monthly (Cinemax), $11.00 monthly (Starz/Encore), $15.00 monthly (Showtime/TMC), $17.00 monthly (HBO) or $26.00 monthly (HBO/Cinemax).

Video-On-Demand: No

Internet Service
Operational: Yes.
Fee: $39.99-$79.99 monthly; $6.00-$8.99 modem lease.

Telephone Service
Digital: Operational
Miles of Plant: 60.0 (coaxial); None (fiber optic).
General Manager: Staci Gowan.
Ownership: NewWave Communications LLC (MSO).

MANGHAM—Formerly served by Almega Cable. No longer in operation. ICA: LA0217.

MANSFIELD—NewWave Communications, One Montgomery Plaza, 4th Floor, Sikeston, MO 63801. Phones: 888-863-9928; 573-472-9500. Fax: 573-472-9518. E-mail: info@newwave.com. Web Site: http://www.newwavecom.com. ICA: LA0048.

TV Market Ranking: 58 (MANSFIELD). Franchise award date: N.A. Franchise expiration date: N.A. Began: January 1, 1976.

Channel capacity: N.A. Channels available but not in use: N.A.

Basic Service
Subscribers: 801.
Programming (received off-air): KLTS-TV (PBS) Shreveport; KMSS-TV (FOX) Shreveport; KPXJ (Antenna TV, CW, MeTV, Movies!) Minden; KSHV-TV (MNT) Shreveport; KSLA (Bounce TV, CBS, Grit, This TV) Shreveport; KTAL-TV (NBC) Texarkana; KTBS-TV (ABC) Shreveport.
Programming (via satellite): The Weather Channel.
Fee: $35.00 installation; $31.89 monthly.

Expanded Basic Service 1
Subscribers: N.A.
Programming (via satellite): A&E; BET; Cartoon Network; CMT; CNN; Comedy Central; Discovery Channel; ESPN; ESPN Classic; ESPN2; FamilyNet; Fox News Channel; Freeform; FX; Hallmark Channel; HGTV; History; HLN; Lifetime; MTV; Nickelodeon; Outdoor Channel; Spike TV; Syfy; TBS; TLC; TNT; Trinity Broadcasting Network (TBN); truTV; Turner Classic Movies; TV Land; USA Network; VH1; WGN America.
Fee: $48.40 monthly.

Digital Basic Service
Subscribers: N.A.
Programming (via satellite): BBC America; Discovery Digital Networks; DMX Music; ESPNews; Fox Sports 1; FXM; FYI; Golf Channel; GSN; History International; IFC; INSP; LMN; National Geographic Channel; Nick Jr.; TeenNick; WE tv.
Fee: $11.00 monthly.

Pay Service 1
Pay Units: N.A.
Programming (via satellite): HBO; Showtime.
Fee: $14.95 installation; $12.95 monthly (Showtime), $13.45 monthly (HBO).

Digital Pay Service 1
Pay Units: N.A.
Programming (via satellite): Cinemax (multiplexed); HBO (multiplexed); Showtime (multiplexed); Starz (multiplexed); Starz Encore (multiplexed); The Movie Channel.
Fee: $8.00 monthly (Starz), $9.00 monthly (Cinemax), $15.00 monthly (Showtime/TMC), $17.00 monthly (HBO) or $26.00 monthly (HBO/Cinemax).

Video-On-Demand: No

Pay-Per-View
iN DEMAND (delivered digitally); Playboy TV (delivered digitally); Fresh (delivered digitally); Shorteez (delivered digitally).

Internet Service
Operational: Yes.
Fee: $39.99-$79.99 monthly; $6.00-$8.99 modem lease.

Telephone Service
Digital: Operational
Miles of Plant: 100.0 (coaxial); None (fiber optic). Homes passed: 3,000.
General Manager: Staci Gowan.
Ownership: NewWave Communications LLC (MSO).

MANY—Suddenlink Communications, 520 Maryville Centre Dr, Ste 300, St. Louis, MO 63141. Phones: 888-822-5151; 314-315-9400. Web Site: http://www.suddenlink.com. Also serves Hemphill, Negreet, Sabine Parish (portions), Vernon Parish (portions) & Zwolle. ICA: LA0183.

TV Market Ranking: Outside TV Markets (MANY, Negreet, Sabine Parish (portions), Vernon Parish (portions), Zwolle). Franchise award date: N.A. Franchise expiration date: N.A. Began: November 1, 1963.

Channel capacity: N.A. Channels available but not in use: N.A.

Basic Service
Subscribers: 1,092. Commercial subscribers: 191.
Programming (received off-air): KALB-TV (CBS, CW, NBC) Alexandria; KLAX-TV (ABC) Alexandria; KLPA-TV (PBS) Alexandria; KMSS-TV (FOX) Shreveport; KNOE (ABC, CBS, CW) Monroe; KSHV-TV (MNT) Shreveport; KSLA (Bounce TV, CBS, Grit, This TV) Shreveport; KTBS-TV (ABC) Shreveport; KTRE (ABC, TMO) Lufkin; KYTX (CBS, COZI TV, CW) Nacogdoches; allband FM.

Louisiana—Cable Systems

Programming (via satellite): QVC; The Weather Channel.
Fee: $40.00 installation; $38.50 monthly.

Expanded Basic Service 1
Subscribers: N.A.
Programming (via satellite): A&E; BET; Cartoon Network; CNN; C-SPAN; Discovery Channel; Disney Channel; ESPN; ESPN2; EWTN Global Catholic Network; Fox News Channel; FOX Sports Southwest; Freeform; Great American Country; HGTV; History; HLN; Lifetime; Nickelodeon; Outdoor Channel; Pop; Spike TV; TBS; TLC; TNT; Turner Classic Movies; USA Network; WGN America.
Fee: $19.00 monthly.

Pay Service 1
Pay Units: N.A.
Programming (via satellite): HBO; Showtime.

Internet Service
Operational: Yes. Began: November 2, 2002.
Broadband Service: Suddenlink High Speed Internet.
Fee: $45.00 installation; $29.95 monthly.

Telephone Service
Digital: Operational
Fee: $39.95 monthly
Miles of Plant: 54.0 (coaxial); None (fiber optic). Homes passed: 1,662.
Senior Vice President, Corporate Finance: Michael Pflantz. Vice President, Accounting: Sabrina Warr. Regional Manager: Todd Cruthird.
Ownership: Cequel Communications Holdings I LLC (MSO).

MARINGOUIN—Spillway Cablevision Inc, 10900 Hwy 77, PO Box 337, Maringouin, LA 70757. Phone: 225-625-2311. Fax: 225-625-3107. E-mail: cs@spillwaycable.com. Web Site: http://www.spillwaycable.com. Also serves Fordoche, Iberville Parish (portions), Livonia & Pointe Coupee Parish. ICA: LA0059.
TV Market Ranking: 87 (Fordoche, Iberville Parish (portions), Livonia, MARINGOUIN, Pointe Coupee Parish (portions)); Outside TV Markets (Pointe Coupee Parish (portions)).
Channel capacity: N.A. Channels available but not in use: N.A.

Basic Service
Subscribers: 63.
Programming (received off-air): KLFY-TV (CBS) Lafayette; WAFB (Bounce TV, CBS) Baton Rouge; WBRL-CD (CW) Baton Rouge; WBRZ-TV (ABC) Baton Rouge; WGMB-TV (FOX) Baton Rouge; WLPB-TV (PBS) Baton Rouge; WVLA-TV (NBC, This TV) Baton Rouge.
Programming (via satellite): QVC; TBS.
Fee: $26.00 installation; $30.95 monthly.

Expanded Basic Service 1
Subscribers: N.A.
Programming (received off-air): KADN-TV (FOX, MNT) Lafayette.
Programming (via satellite): A&E; Animal Planet; BET; Bloomberg Television; CMT; CNN; Comedy Central; Cox Sports Television; Discovery Channel; Discovery Life Channel; Disney Channel; Disney XD; E! HD; ESPN; ESPN2; EWTN Global Catholic Network; Food Network; Fox News Channel; Freeform; FX; Great American Country; Hallmark Channel; HGTV; HLN; Lifetime; MTV; National Geographic Channel; Nickelodeon; Outdoor Channel; Spike TV; Syfy; The Weather Channel; TLC; TNT; Travel Channel; Trinity Broadcasting Network (TBN); Turner Classic Movies; TV Land; USA Network; VH1; WGN America.

Digital Basic Service
Subscribers: N.A.
Programming (via satellite): BBC America; CMT; Destination America; Discovery Kids Channel; DMX Music; ESPN Classic; ESPNews; EVINE Live; Fox Sports 1; Fuse; FXM; FYI; Golf Channel; GSN; History; History International; IFC; INSP; International Television (ITV); Investigation Discovery; LMN; MBC America; MTV Classic; MTV Hits; MTV Jams; MTV2; NBCSN; Nick Jr.; Nicktoons; Ovation; OWN; Oprah Winfrey Network; Science Channel; Sundance TV; TeenNick; The Word Network; VH1 Soul; WE tv.

Pay Service 1
Pay Units: N.A.
Programming (via satellite): Cinemax; HBO.
Fee: $10.00 monthly.

Digital Pay Service 1
Pay Units: N.A.
Programming (via satellite): Cinemax (multiplexed); Flix; HBO (multiplexed); Showtime (multiplexed); Starz (multiplexed); Starz Encore (multiplexed); The Movie Channel (multiplexed).

Video-On-Demand: No

Pay-Per-View
iN DEMAND (delivered digitally); Hot Choice (delivered digitally); Playboy TV (delivered digitally); Fresh (delivered digitally); Shorteez (delivered digitally); Club Jenna (delivered digitally); ESPN Now (delivered digitally); Sports PPV (delivered digitally).

Internet Service
Operational: Yes.
Broadband Service: In-house.
Fee: $50.00 installation; $32.95-$42.95 monthly.

Telephone Service
None
Miles of Plant: 70.0 (coaxial); None (fiber optic). Homes passed: 2,500.
Manager: Sue Soileau.
Ownership: Spillway Cablevision Inc.

MARION—Bayou Cable TV, 378 Main St, Marion, LA 71260. Phone: 318-292-4774. Fax: 318-292-4775. E-mail: admin@bayoucable.com. Web Site: http://www2.bayoucable.com. ICA: LA0119.
TV Market Ranking: 99 (MARION). Franchise award date: N.A. Franchise expiration date: N.A. Began: April 1, 1982.
Channel capacity: N.A. Channels available but not in use: N.A.

Basic Service
Subscribers: 104.
Programming (received off-air): KARD (Bounce TV, FOX) West Monroe; KLTM-TV (PBS) Monroe; KMCT-TV (IND) West Monroe; KMLU (MeTV) Columbia; KNOE-TV (ABC, CBS, CW) Monroe; KTVE (NBC) El Dorado.
Programming (via satellite): AMC; Hallmark Channel; Trinity Broadcasting Network (TBN); TV Land.
Fee: $25.00 installation; $54.99 monthly.

Expanded Basic Service 1
Subscribers: N.A.
Programming (via satellite): A&E; Animal Planet; BET; CMT; CNN; CW PLUS; Discovery Channel; ESPN; ESPN2; Food Network; Fox News Channel; Fox Sports 1; Freeform; FX; HGTV; History; Lifetime; MTV; National Geographic Channel; Nickelodeon; Outdoor Channel; Spike TV; TBS; The Weather Channel; TLC; TNT; USA Network; VH1; WGN America.
Fee: $20.00 monthly.

Pay Service 1
Pay Units: 9.
Programming (via satellite): HBO.
Fee: $10.95 monthly.

Pay Service 2
Pay Units: 3.
Programming (via satellite): Cinemax.
Fee: $8.95 monthly.

Video-On-Demand: No

Internet Service
Operational: No.

Telephone Service
None
Miles of Plant: 13.0 (coaxial); None (fiber optic). Homes passed: 450.
President & General Manager: Allen C. Booker. Chief Technician: Mark Andrews.
Ownership: Bayou Cable TV (MSO).

MARKSVILLE—Formerly served by Zoom Media. No longer in operation. ICA: LA0184.

MARKSVILLE—Media3, PO Box 650, Milan, TN 38358. Phone: 866-257-2044. E-mail: customerservice@mymedia3.com. Web Site: http://www.mymedia3.com. Also serves Avoyelles Parish (portions), Hessmer & Mansura. ICA: LA0040.
TV Market Ranking: Below 100 (Avoyelles Parish (portions), Hessmer, Mansura, MARKSVILLE). Franchise award date: N.A. Franchise expiration date: N.A. Began: March 1, 1969.
Channel capacity: N.A. Channels available but not in use: N.A.

Basic Service
Subscribers: 1,442.
Programming (received off-air): KADN-TV (FOX, MNT) Lafayette; KALB-TV (CBS, CW, NBC) Alexandria; KLAX-TV (ABC) Alexandria; KLFY-TV (CBS) Lafayette; KPLC (Bounce TV, NBC, This TV) Lake Charles; WAFB (Bounce TV, CBS) Baton Rouge; WBRZ-TV (ABC) Baton Rouge; WLPB-TV (PBS) Baton Rouge; WNTZ-TV (FOX, MNT) Natchez.
Programming (via satellite): QVC; WGN America.
Fee: $24.95 installation; $22.45 monthly.

Expanded Basic Service 1
Subscribers: N.A.
Programming (via satellite): A&E; AMC; Animal Planet; BET; Cartoon Network; CMT; CNBC; CNN; C-SPAN; Discovery Channel; Disney Channel; Disney XD; E! HD; ESPN; ESPN2; EWTN Global Catholic Network; Food Network; Fox News Channel; Fox Sports 1; FOX Sports Southwest; Freeform; FX; HGTV; History; HLN; Lifetime; MTV; National Geographic Channel; Nickelodeon; Outdoor Channel; Pop; Spike TV; Syfy; TBS; The Weather Channel; TLC; TNT; Trinity Broadcasting Network (TBN); Turner Classic Movies; TV Land; USA Network; VH1; WE tv.
Fee: $42.99 monthly.

Digital Basic Service
Subscribers: N.A.
Programming (via satellite): BBC America; Bloomberg Television; Comcast/Charter Sports Southeast (CSS); Discovery Digital Networks; DIY Network; Fox Sports 2; FXM; FYI; History International; IFC; LMN; MC; MTV2; Nick Jr.; Sundance TV; TV Guide Interactive Inc.

Digital Pay Service 1
Pay Units: N.A.
Programming (via satellite): Cinemax (multiplexed); Flix; HBO (multiplexed); Showtime (multiplexed); Starz (multiplexed); Starz Encore (multiplexed); The Movie Channel (multiplexed).

Fee: $9.00 monthly (Showtime or TMC), $11.00 monthly (HBO).

Video-On-Demand: Yes

Pay-Per-View
iN DEMAND (delivered digitally); Playboy TV (delivered digitally); Fresh (delivered digitally).

Internet Service
Operational: Yes.
Broadband Service: Charter Internet.

Telephone Service
Digital: Operational
Miles of Plant: 249.0 (coaxial); 55.0 (fiber optic). Homes passed: 6,200.
President: Alan Taylor. Chief Financial Officer: Thomas Pate.
Ownership: CableSouth Media3 LLC (MSO).

MCINTYRE—Formerly served by Almega Cable. No longer in operation. ICA: LA0226.

MELVILLE—Spillway Cablevision Inc, 10900 Hwy 77, PO Box 337, Maringouin, LA 70757. Phone: 225-625-2311. Fax: 225-625-3107. E-mail: cs@spillway.com. Web Site: http://www.spillwaycable.com. ICA: LA0113.
TV Market Ranking: Outside TV Markets (MELVILLE). Franchise award date: N.A. Franchise expiration date: N.A. Began: March 1, 1984.
Channel capacity: 54 (not 2-way capable). Channels available but not in use: N.A.

Basic Service
Subscribers: 76.
Programming (received off-air): KALB-TV (CBS, CW, NBC) Alexandria; KATC (ABC, CW, Grit) Lafayette; KLFY-TV (CBS) Lafayette; WAFB (Bounce TV, CBS) Baton Rouge; WBRZ-TV (ABC) Baton Rouge; WLPB-TV (PBS) Baton Rouge; WVLA-TV (NBC, This TV) Baton Rouge.
Programming (via satellite): Animal Planet; BET; CMT; CNN; Discovery Channel; ESPN; ESPN2; HGTV; Lifetime; NBCSN; Nickelodeon; Spike TV; TBS; The Weather Channel; TNT; Trinity Broadcasting Network (TBN); Turner Classic Movies; USA Network; WGN America.
Fee: $26.00 installation; $21.95 monthly.

Pay Service 1
Pay Units: N.A.
Programming (via satellite): HBO; Showtime; The Movie Channel.
Fee: $12.95 monthly (each).

Video-On-Demand: No

Internet Service
Operational: No.

Telephone Service
None
Miles of Plant: 12.0 (coaxial); None (fiber optic). Homes passed: 663.
Manager: Sue Soileau.
Ownership: Spillway Cablevision Inc. (MSO).

MERRYVILLE—Alliance Communications, PO Box 9090, Tyler, TX 75711. Phones: 903-561-4411 (Tyler, TX office); 501-679-6619; 800-842-8160. E-mail: marketing@alliancecable.net. Web Site: http://www.alliancecable.net. ICA: LA0120.
TV Market Ranking: Outside TV Markets (MERRYVILLE). Franchise award date: March 16, 1984. Franchise expiration date: N.A. Began: August 1, 1986.
Channel capacity: N.A. Channels available but not in use: N.A.

Basic Service
Subscribers: 20.
Programming (received off-air): KBMT (ABC) Beaumont; KBTV-TV (Bounce TV, FOX) Port Arthur; KFDM (CBS, CW) Beau-

Cable Systems—Louisiana

mont; KLTL-TV (PBS) Lake Charles; KPLC (Bounce TV, NBC, This TV) Lake Charles; KVHP (FOX) Lake Charles.
Programming (via satellite): EWTN Global Catholic Network; Freeform; QVC; TBS; WGN America.
Fee: $45.00 installation; $25.45 monthly.

Expanded Basic Service 1
Subscribers: N.A.
Programming (via satellite): A&E; AMC; CNBC; CNN; Discovery Channel; Disney Channel; ESPN; ESPN2; Nickelodeon; Outdoor Channel; Spike TV; The Weather Channel; TNT; USA Network.
Fee: $27.50 monthly.

Digital Basic Service
Subscribers: N.A.
Programming (via satellite): BBC America; Bloomberg Television; Bravo; CMT; Destination America; Discovery Kids Channel; Discovery Life Channel; Disney XD; DMX Music; Fox Sports 1; Fuse; FXM; FYI; Golf Channel; GSN; HGTV; History International; IFC; Investigation Discovery; LMN; MTV Classic; MTV Hits; MTV2; NBCSN; Nick Jr.; OWN: Oprah Winfrey Network; Science Channel; Syfy; TeenNick; Trinity Broadcasting Network (TBN); Turner Classic Movies; VH1 Soul; WE tv.

Pay Service 1
Pay Units: N.A.
Programming (via satellite): HBO.
Fee: $12.95 monthly.

Digital Pay Service 1
Pay Units: N.A.
Programming (via satellite): Cinemax (multiplexed); HBO (multiplexed); Showtime (multiplexed); Starz (multiplexed); Starz Encore (multiplexed); The Movie Channel.

Video-On-Demand: No

Pay-Per-View
iN DEMAND (delivered digitally).

Internet Service
Operational: No.

Telephone Service
None

Miles of Plant: 14.0 (coaxial); None (fiber optic). Homes passed: 446.
Chief Financial Officer: David Starrett. Vice President & General Manager: John Brinker. Vice President, Programming: Julie Newman.
Ownership: Buford Media Group LLC (MSO).

MINDEN—Suddenlink Communications, 726 Broadway St, Minden, LA 71055-3307. Phone: 314-315-9400. Web Site: http://www.suddenlink.com. Also serves Webster Parish. ICA: LA0032.
TV Market Ranking: 58 (MINDEN, Webster Parish (portions)); Below 100 (Webster Parish (portions)). Franchise award date: May 1, 1977. Franchise expiration date: N.A. Began: September 1, 1978.
Channel capacity: N.A. Channels available but not in use: N.A.

Basic Service
Subscribers: 2,309.
Programming (received off-air): KLTS-TV (PBS) Shreveport; KMSS-TV (FOX) Shreveport; KPXJ (Antenna TV, CW, MeTV, Movies!) Minden; KSHV-TV (MNT) Shreveport; KSLA (Bounce TV, CBS, Grit, This TV) Shreveport; KTAL-TV (NBC) Texarkana; KTBS-TV (ABC) Shreveport.
Programming (via satellite): C-SPAN; C-SPAN 2; Jewelry Television; Pop; QVC; TBS; The Weather Channel; Trinity Broadcasting Network (TBN); WGN America.
Fee: $35.00 installation; $35.50 monthly.

Expanded Basic Service 1
Subscribers: N.A.
Programming (via satellite): A&E; AMC; Animal Planet; BET; Bravo; Cartoon Network; CMT; CNBC; CNN; Comedy Central; Cox Sports Television; Discovery Channel; Disney Channel; ESPN; ESPN2; Food Network; Fox News Channel; Fox Sports 1; FOX Sports Southwest; Freeform; FX; Great American Country; HGTV; History; HLN; Lifetime; LMN; MTV; NBCSN; Nickelodeon; Outdoor Channel; OWN: Oprah Winfrey Network; Spike TV; Syfy; TLC; TNT; Travel Channel; truTV; TV Land; USA Network; VH1.
Fee: $10.17 monthly.

Digital Basic Service
Subscribers: N.A.
Programming (via satellite): BBC America; Bloomberg Television; CBS Sports Network; CMT; Cooking Channel; Destination America; Discovery Kids Channel; Disney XD; DIY Network; ESPN Classic; ESPNews; Fox Sports 2; Fuse; FYI; Golf Channel; GSN; Hallmark Channel; History International; IFC; Investigation Discovery; MC; MTV Classic; MTV Hits; MTV Jams; MTV2; Nat Geo WILD; National Geographic Channel; Nick Jr.; Nicktoons; Science Channel; Starz Encore (multiplexed); Sundance TV; TeenNick; Turner Classic Movies; TV One; VH1 Soul.

Digital Pay Service 1
Pay Units: N.A.
Programming (via satellite): Cinemax (multiplexed); HBO (multiplexed); Showtime (multiplexed); Starz (multiplexed); The Movie Channel (multiplexed).

Video-On-Demand: No

Pay-Per-View
iN DEMAND (delivered digitally); Fresh (delivered digitally); Playboy TV (delivered digitally).

Internet Service
Operational: Yes.
Broadband Service: Suddenlink High Speed Internet.
Fee: $45.00 installation; $29.95 monthly.

Telephone Service
Digital: Operational
Fee: $39.95 monthly
Miles of Plant: 80.0 (coaxial); None (fiber optic). Homes passed: 5,827.
Senior Vice President, Corporate Finance: Michael Pflantz. Vice President, Accounting: Sabrina Warr. General Manager: Roland Myers. Chief Technician: Brian Garland.
Ownership: Cequel Communications Holdings I LLC (MSO).

MIRE—Formerly served by Trust Cable. No longer in operation. ICA: LA0185.

MONROE—NewWave Communications, One Montgomery Plaza, 4th Floor, Sikeston, MO 63801. Phones: 573-472-9500; 888-863-9928. Fax: 573-472-9518. E-mail: info@newwave.com. Web Site: http://www.newwavecom.com. Also serves Delhi (town), Madison Parish (portions), Ouachita Parish (portions), Rayville & Tallulah. ICA: LA0049.
TV Market Ranking: 99 (Delhi (town), MONROE, Ouachita Parish (portions), Rayville); Outside TV Markets (Madison Parish (portions), Tallulah). Franchise award date: October 3, 1980. Franchise expiration date: N.A. Began: August 1, 1979.
Channel capacity: N.A. Channels available but not in use: N.A.

Access the most current data instantly
FREE TRIAL @ ADVANCED TVFactbook
TELCO/IPTV • CABLE TV • TV STATIONS
www.warren-news.com/factbook.htm

Basic Service
Subscribers: 4,416.
Programming (received off-air): KARD (Bounce TV, FOX) West Monroe; KLTM-TV (PBS) Monroe; KMCT-TV (IND) West Monroe; KMLU (MeTV) Columbia; KNOE-TV (ABC, CBS, CW) Monroe; KTVE (NBC) El Dorado.
Programming (via satellite): Freeform; HLN; ION Television; Pop; QVC; TBS; The Weather Channel; WGN America; WUCW (CW, The Country Network) Minneapolis.
Fee: $35.00 installation; $32.93 monthly.

Expanded Basic Service 1
Subscribers: N.A.
Programming (via satellite): A&E; AMC; Animal Planet; BET; CMT; CNBC; CNN; Comedy Central; C-SPAN; Discovery Channel; E! HD; ESPN; ESPN2; Food Network; Fox News Channel; FOX Sports Southwest; FX; Hallmark Channel; History; Lifetime; MTV; Nickelodeon; Spike TV; Syfy; TLC; TNT; Turner Classic Movies; TV Land; USA Network; VH1.

Digital Basic Service
Subscribers: N.A.
Programming (via satellite): BBC America; Discovery Digital Networks; DMX Music; ESPN Classic; ESPNews; Fox Sports 1; FXM; FYI; Golf Channel; GSN; HGTV; History International; IFC; LMN; National Geographic Channel; NBCSN; Nick Jr.; Outdoor Channel; TeenNick; WE tv.
Fee: $11.00 monthly.

Pay Service 1
Pay Units: N.A.
Programming (via satellite): HBO.
Fee: $14.95 installation; $13.95 monthly.

Digital Pay Service 1
Pay Units: N.A.
Programming (via satellite): Cinemax (multiplexed); HBO (multiplexed); Showtime (multiplexed); Starz (multiplexed); Starz Encore (multiplexed); The Movie Channel (multiplexed).
Fee: $8.00 monthly (Starz), $9.00 monthly (Cinemax), $11.00 monthly (Starz/Encore), $15.00 monthly (Showtime/TMC), $17.00 monthly (HBO) or $26.00 monthly (HBO/Cinemax).

Video-On-Demand: No

Pay-Per-View
iN DEMAND (delivered digitally); Playboy TV (delivered digitally); Fresh (delivered digitally).

Internet Service
Operational: Yes.
Fee: $49.95 installation; $39.99-$79.99 monthly; $6.00-$8.99 modem lease; $149.95 modem purchase.

Telephone Service
Digital: Operational
Fee: $39.95 monthly
Miles of Plant: 61.0 (coaxial); None (fiber optic). Homes passed: 4,542.
General Manager: Staci Gowan.
Ownership: NewWave Communications LLC (MSO).

MONTEREY—Formerly served by Almega Cable. No longer in operation. ICA: LA0186.

MONTGOMERY—Alliance Communications, PO Box 9090, Tyler, TX 75711. Phones: 903-561-4411 (Tyler, TX office); 501-679-6619; 800-842-8160. E-mail: marketing@alliancecable.net. Web Site: http://www.alliancecable.net. ICA: LA0116.
TV Market Ranking: Outside TV Markets (MONTGOMERY). Franchise award date: April 10, 1983. Franchise expiration date: N.A. Began: July 1, 1985.
Channel capacity: 54 (not 2-way capable). Channels available but not in use: N.A.

Basic Service
Subscribers: 19.
Programming (received off-air): KALB-TV (CBS, CW, NBC) Alexandria; KLAX-TV (ABC) Alexandria; KLPA-TV (PBS) Alexandria; KNOE-TV (ABC, CBS, CW) Monroe; KNTS-LP (IND) Natchitoches; WNTZ-TV (FOX, MNT) Natchez.
Programming (via satellite): A&E; Animal Planet; Cartoon Network; CNN; C-SPAN; Discovery Channel; Disney Channel; E! HD; ESPN; ESPN2; Freeform; FX; Great American Country; HGTV; HLN; Lifetime; National Geographic Channel; Nickelodeon; Outdoor Channel; Spike TV; TBS; The Weather Channel; TNT; Trinity Broadcasting Network (TBN); Turner Classic Movies; USA Network; VH1.
Fee: $45.00 installation; $22.45 monthly.

Pay Service 1
Pay Units: N.A.
Programming (via satellite): HBO; Showtime; The Movie Channel.
Fee: $12.95 monthly (each).

Video-On-Demand: No

Internet Service
Operational: No.

Telephone Service
None

Miles of Plant: 13.0 (coaxial); None (fiber optic). Homes passed: 430.
Chief Financial Officer: David Starrett. Vice President & General Manager: John Brinker. Vice President, Programming: Julie Newman.
Ownership: Buford Media Group LLC (MSO).

MOREAUVILLE—Suddenlink Communications, 520 Maryville Centre Dr, Ste 300, St. Louis, MO 63141. Phones: 888-822-5151; 314-315-9400. Web Site: http://www.suddenlink.com. Also serves Avoyelles Parish, Bordelonville, Cottonport, Echo, Plaucheville, Rapides Parish (portions) & Simmesport. ICA: LA0089.
TV Market Ranking: Below 100 (Avoyelles Parish (portions), Cottonport, Echo, MOREAUVILLE, Rapides Parish (portions)); Outside TV Markets (Avoyelles Parish (portions), Bordelonville, Plaucheville, Simmesport). Franchise award date: N.A. Franchise expiration date: N.A. Began: October 10, 1983.
Channel capacity: 54 (operating 2-way). Channels available but not in use: N.A.

2017 Edition   D-345

Louisiana—Cable Systems

Basic Service
Subscribers: 1,165. Commercial subscribers: 47.
Programming (received off-air): KALB-TV (CBS, CW, NBC) Alexandria; KLAX-TV (ABC) Alexandria; KLFY-TV (CBS) Lafayette; KLPA-TV (PBS) Alexandria; WAFB (Bounce TV, CBS) Baton Rouge; WBRZ-TV (ABC) Baton Rouge; WNTZ-TV (FOX, MNT) Natchez.
Programming (via satellite): C-SPAN; EWTN Global Catholic Network; Trinity Broadcasting Network (TBN).
Fee: $28.45 monthly.

Expanded Basic Service 1
Subscribers: N.A.
Programming (via satellite): A&E; AMC; Animal Planet; BET; Cartoon Network; CNBC; CNN; Discovery Channel; Disney Channel; E! HD; ESPN; ESPN2; Fox News Channel; FOX Sports Southwest; Freeform; FX; Great American Country; HGTV; History; HLN; Lifetime; MSNBC; MTV; National Geographic Channel; Nickelodeon; Outdoor Channel; Spike TV; TBS; The Weather Channel; TLC; TNT; Turner Classic Movies; TV Land; USA Network; VH1.
Fee: $24.00 monthly.

Digital Basic Service
Subscribers: N.A.
Programming (via satellite): BBC America; Cloo; Discovery Digital Networks; Disney XD; DMX Music; ESPN Classic; ESPNews; Fuse; FYI; Golf Channel; GSN; History International; IFC; NBCSN; WE tv.

Pay Service 1
Pay Units: N.A.
Programming (via satellite): Cinemax; HBO; Showtime; The Movie Channel.
Fee: $7.00 monthly (Cinemax or Showtime), $9.00 monthly (TMC), $12.00 monthly (HBO).

Digital Pay Service 1
Pay Units: N.A.
Programming (via satellite): Cinemax (multiplexed); HBO (multiplexed); Showtime (multiplexed); Starz; Starz Encore (multiplexed); The Movie Channel (multiplexed).

Video-On-Demand: No

Pay-Per-View
iN DEMAND (delivered digitally); Playboy TV (delivered digitally).

Internet Service
Operational: Yes. Began: January 5, 2006.
Broadband Service: Suddenlink High Speed Internet.
Fee: $45.00 installation; $29.95 monthly.

Telephone Service
Digital: Operational
Fee: $39.95 monthly
Miles of Plant: 103.0 (coaxial); None (fiber optic). Homes passed: 4,085.
Vice President, Corporate Finance: Michael Pflantz. Area Manager: Mark Hood. Regional Manager: Todd Cruthird. Plant Manager: Dion Canaday.
Ownership: Cequel Communications Holdings I LLC (MSO).

MORGAN CITY—Allen's TV Cable Service Inc, 800 Victor II Blvd, PO Box 2643, Morgan City, LA 70380. Phones: 337-662-5315; 985-384-8335. Fax: 985-384-5243. E-mail: info@atvci.net. Web Site: http://www.atvc.net. Also serves Berwick, St. Martin Parish (southern portion), St. Mary Parish (portions) & Stephensville. ICA: LA0188.
TV Market Ranking: 87 (St. Martin Parish (southern portion)); Below 100 (Stephensville, St. Mary Parish (portions), St. Martin Parish (southern portion)); Outside TV Markets (Berwick, MORGAN CITY, St. Mary Parish (portions)). Franchise award date: N.A. Franchise expiration date: N.A. Began: January 1, 1960.
Channel capacity: N.A. Channels available but not in use: N.A.

Basic Service
Subscribers: 3,449.
Programming (received off-air): KADN-TV (FOX, MNT) Lafayette; KATC (ABC, CW, Grit) Lafayette; KLFY-TV (CBS) Lafayette; WAFB (Bounce TV, CBS) Baton Rouge; WBRZ-TV (ABC) Baton Rouge; WDSU (MeTV, NBC) New Orleans; WGMB-TV (FOX) Baton Rouge; WLPB-TV (PBS) Baton Rouge; WPXL-TV (ION) New Orleans; WUPL (MNT) Slidell; WVLA-TV (NBC, This TV) Baton Rouge; WVUE-DT (Bounce TV, FOX) New Orleans; WWL-TV (CBS) New Orleans; WYES-TV (PBS) New Orleans.
Programming (via satellite): Cox Sports Television; C-SPAN; QVC; WGN America.
Fee: $66.90 installation; $19.45 monthly.

Expanded Basic Service 1
Subscribers: N.A.
Programming (via satellite): A&E; AMC; Animal Planet; BET; Bravo; Cartoon Network; CMT; CNBC; CNN; Comedy Central; Discovery Channel; Disney Channel; Disney XD; E! HD; ESPN; ESPN2; EWTN Global Catholic Network; Food Network; Fox News Channel; FOX Sports Southwest; Freeform; FX; HGTV; History; HLN; Lifetime; MSNBC; MTV; Nickelodeon; Outdoor Channel; Spike TV; Syfy; TBS; The Weather Channel; TLC; TNT; Travel Channel; Trinity Broadcasting Network (TBN); TV Land; Univision Studios; USA Network; VH1; WE tv.
Fee: $29.50 monthly.

Digital Basic Service
Subscribers: N.A.
Programming (via satellite): BBC America; Bloomberg Television; Discovery Digital Networks; DIY Network; ESPNews; FOX College Sports Central; FOX College Sports Pacific; Fox Sports 1; Fuse; FXM; FYI; GSN; Hallmark Channel; History International; IFC; MC; National Geographic Channel; Nick 2; Nick Jr.; Nicktoons; TeenNick.
Fee: $3.75 converter.

Digital Pay Service 1
Pay Units: N.A.
Programming (via satellite): Cinemax (multiplexed); HBO (multiplexed); Showtime (multiplexed); Starz (multiplexed); Starz Encore (multiplexed); The Movie Channel (multiplexed).
Fee: $3.75 converter.

Video-On-Demand: No

Pay-Per-View
iN DEMAND; Tigervision (delivered digitally); iN DEMAND (delivered digitally); Hot Choice (delivered digitally); Playboy TV (delivered digitally); Fresh (delivered digitally); Shorteez (delivered digitally).

Internet Service
Operational: Yes.
Broadband Service: atvci.net.
Fee: $24.95-$69.95 monthly; $6.75 modem lease; $75.00 modem purchase.

Telephone Service
None
Miles of Plant: 270.0 (coaxial); 60.0 (fiber optic). 750 /860 MHz
President & General Manager: Gregory A. Price. Vice President: David J. Price. Chief Technician: Chris A. Price. Office Manager: Cindy LaVergne.
Ownership: Allen's TV Cable Service Inc. (MSO).

NATCHEZ—Alliance Communications, PO Box 9090, Tyler, TX 75711. Phones: 903-561-4411 (Tyler, TX office); 501-679-6619; 800-842-8160. E-mail: marketing@alliancecable.net. Web Site: http://www.alliancecable.net. Also serves Point Place. ICA: LA0122.
TV Market Ranking: Outside TV Markets (NATCHEZ, Point Place). Franchise award date: N.A. Franchise expiration date: N.A. Began: May 1, 1985.
Channel capacity: 54 (not 2-way capable). Channels available but not in use: N.A.

Basic Service
Subscribers: 16.
Programming (received off-air): KALB-TV (CBS, CW, NBC) Alexandria; KARD (Bounce TV, FOX) West Monroe; KLAX-TV (ABC) Alexandria; KLPA-TV (PBS) Alexandria; KNOE-TV (ABC, CBS, CW) Monroe; KNTS-LP (IND) Natchitoches; KPXJ (Antenna TV, CW, MeTV, Movies!) Minden.
Programming (via satellite): A&E; BET; Cartoon Network; CNN; Discovery Channel; Disney Channel; ESPN; ESPN2; Freeform; Great American Country; HGTV; HLN; Lifetime; National Geographic Channel; Nickelodeon; Outdoor Channel; Spike TV; TBS; The Weather Channel; TNT; Trinity Broadcasting Network (TBN); Turner Classic Movies; USA Network.
Fee: $45.00 installation; $22.45 monthly.

Digital Basic Service
Subscribers: N.A.
Programming (via satellite): BBC America; Bloomberg Television; Cloo; Destination America; Discovery Kids Channel; DMX Music; ESPN Classic; ESPNews; EVINE Live; FOX College Sports Central; FOX College Sports Pacific; Fox Sports 1; Fuse; FYI; Golf Channel; GSN; History; Investigation Discovery; LMN; NBCSN; OWN; Oprah Winfrey Network; Science Channel; Syfy; WE tv.

Pay Service 1
Pay Units: N.A.
Programming (via satellite): Cinemax; HBO; Showtime.
Fee: $12.95 monthly (each).

Digital Pay Service 1
Pay Units: N.A.
Programming (via satellite): Cinemax (multiplexed); Flix; HBO (multiplexed); Showtime (multiplexed); Starz (multiplexed); Starz Encore (multiplexed); The Movie Channel (multiplexed).

Video-On-Demand: No

Pay-Per-View
iN DEMAND (delivered digitally); Playboy TV (delivered digitally); Club Jenna (delivered digitally).

Internet Service
Operational: No.

Telephone Service
None
Miles of Plant: 16.0 (coaxial); None (fiber optic). Homes passed: 415.
Chief Financial Officer: David Starrett. Vice President & General Manager: John Brinker. Vice President, Programming: Julie Newman.
Ownership: Buford Media Group LLC (MSO).

NATCHITOCHES—Suddenlink Communications, 321 Texas St, PO Box 698, Natchitoches, LA 71457. Phone: 314-315-9400. Fax: 318-352-4288. Web Site: http://www.suddenlink.com. Also serves Natchitoches Parish. ICA: LA0029.
TV Market Ranking: Below 100 (Natchitoches Parish (portions)); Outside TV Markets (NATCHITOCHES, Natchitoches Parish (portions)). Franchise award date: N.A. Franchise expiration date: N.A. Began: December 1, 1963.
Channel capacity: N.A. Channels available but not in use: N.A.

Basic Service
Subscribers: 4,088. Commercial subscribers: 444.
Programming (received off-air): KALB-TV (CBS, CW, NBC) Alexandria; KLAX-TV (ABC) Alexandria; KLPA-TV (PBS) Alexandria; KMSS-TV (FOX) Shreveport; KNTS-LP (IND) Natchitoches; KPXJ (Antenna TV, CW, MeTV, Movies!) Minden; KSHV-TV (MNT) Shreveport; KSLA (Bounce TV, CBS, Grit, This TV) Shreveport; KTBS-TV (ABC) Shreveport; allband FM.
Programming (via satellite): CNN; C-SPAN; C-SPAN 2; EWTN Global Catholic Network; FOX Sports Southwest; Freeform; Pop; QVC; TBS; The Weather Channel; WGN America.
Fee: $40.00 installation; $34.50 monthly.

Expanded Basic Service 1
Subscribers: N.A.
Programming (via satellite): A&E; AMC; Animal Planet; BET; Bravo; Cartoon Network; CNBC; Comedy Central; Discovery Channel; Disney Channel; E! HD; ESPN; ESPN2; Food Network; Fox News Channel; Fox Sports 1; FX; Great American Country; HGTV; History; HLN; Lifetime; MSNBC; MTV; Nickelodeon; Oxygen; Spike TV; Syfy; TLC; TNT; Travel Channel; TV Land; USA Network; VH1.
Fee: $14.85 monthly.

Digital Basic Service
Subscribers: N.A.
Programming (via satellite): BBC America; Bloomberg Television; Discovery Digital Networks; Disney XD; DMX Music; ESPN Classic; ESPNews; Fuse; FYI; Golf Channel; GSN; Hallmark Channel; History International; IFC; LMN; Nick Jr.; Nicktoons; Outdoor Channel; Sundance TV; TeenNick; Trinity Broadcasting Network (TBN).

Pay Service 1
Pay Units: N.A.
Programming (via satellite): Cinemax; HBO; Showtime; Starz; The Movie Channel.
Fee: $35.00 installation; $7.95 monthly (Starz or Encore), $14.00 monthly (HBO).

Digital Pay Service 1
Pay Units: N.A.
Programming (via satellite): Cinemax (multiplexed); HBO (multiplexed); Showtime (multiplexed); Starz (multiplexed); The Movie Channel (multiplexed).

Video-On-Demand: No

Pay-Per-View
Playboy TV (delivered digitally); Fresh (delivered digitally); NBA TV (delivered digitally); ESPN Now (delivered digitally); iN DEMAND (delivered digitally).

Internet Service
Operational: Yes.
Subscribers: 3,799.
Broadband Service: Suddenlink High Speed Internet.
Fee: $45.00 installation; $29.95 monthly; $10.00 modem lease.

Telephone Service
Digital: Operational
Subscribers: 2,522.
Fee: $39.95 monthly
Miles of Plant: 308.0 (coaxial); 73.0 (fiber optic). Homes passed: 12,464.
Senior Vice President, Corporate Finance: Michael Pflantz. Vice President, Accounting: Sabrina Warr. General Manager: Ronnie Waters.
Ownership: Cequel Communications Holdings I LLC (MSO).

Cable Systems—Louisiana

NATCHITOCHES (portions)—Formerly served by Rapid Cable. Now served by Suddenlink Communications, NATCHITOCHES, LA [LA0029]. ICA: LA0189.

NEW IBERIA—Cox Communications. Now served by BATON ROUGE, LA [LA0003]. ICA: LA0190.

NEW ORLEANS—Cox Communications, 6205 Peachtree Dunwoody Rd, 12th Floor, Atlanta, GA 30328. Phone: 404-269-6590. Web Site: http://www.cox.com. Also serves Ama, Arabi, Avondale, Barataria, Belle Chasse, Boutte, Braithwaite, Bridge City, Chalmette, Crown Point, Des Allemands, Destrehan, Gretna, Hahnville, Harahan, Harvey, Jean Lafitte, Jefferson Parish (portions), Kenner, Luling, Marrero, Meraux, Metairie, Orleans Parish, Plaquemines Parish (portions), Poydras, River Ridge, St. Bernard Parish, St. Charles Parish (portions), St. Rose, Terrytown, Violet & Westwego. ICA: LA0001.
TV Market Ranking: 31 (Arabi, Avondale, Barataria, Belle Chasse, Boutte, Bridge City, Chalmette, Crown Point, Des Allemands, Destrehan, Gretna, Hahnville, Harahan, Harvey, Jean Lafitte, Jefferson Parish (portions), Kenner, Luling, Marrero, Meraux, Metairie, NEW ORLEANS, Orleans Parish, Poydras, St. Bernard Parish, St. Charles Parish (portions), St. Rose, Violet, Westwego). Franchise award date: May 28, 1981. Franchise expiration date: N.A. Began: April 21, 1982.
Channel capacity: N.A. Channels available but not in use: N.A.
Basic Service
Subscribers: 155,526. Commercial subscribers: 6,680.
Programming (received off-air): WDSU (MeTV, NBC) New Orleans; WGNO (ABC, Antenna TV, Escape) New Orleans; WHNO (COZI TV, IND) New Orleans; WLAE-TV (PBS) New Orleans; WNOL-TV (CW, This TV) New Orleans; WPXL-TV (ION) New Orleans; WUPL (MNT) Slidell; WVUE-DT (Bounce TV, FOX) New Orleans; WWL-TV (CBS) New Orleans; WYES-TV (PBS) New Orleans; allband FM.
Programming (via satellite): BET; C-SPAN 2; EWTN Global Catholic Network; HLN; Pop; QVC; TBS; The Weather Channel; TLC; Trinity Broadcasting Network (TBN); WGN America.
Fee: $32.99 installation; $21.99 monthly.
Expanded Basic Service 1
Subscribers: N.A.
Programming (via satellite): A&E; AMC; Animal Planet; Bravo; Cartoon Network; CMT; CNBC; CNN; Comedy Central; C-SPAN; Discovery Channel; Disney Channel; E! HD; ESPN; ESPN Classic; ESPN2; Food Network; Fox News Channel; Fox Sports 1; FOX Sports Southwest; Freeform; FX; Hallmark Channel; HGTV; History; Lifetime; MSNBC; MTV; MTV2; NBCSN; Nickelodeon; Pop; Spike TV; Syfy; TNT; Travel Channel; truTV; Turner Classic Movies; TV Land; USA Network; VH1.
Fee: $27.44 monthly.
Digital Basic Service
Subscribers: N.A.
Programming (via satellite): BBC America; Bloomberg Television; Discovery Digital Networks; Disney XD; ESPNews; Flix; FYI; Golf Channel; GSN; History International; HITS (Headend In The Sky); LMN; MC; Oxygen; Sundance TV; The Word Network.

Pay Service 1
Pay Units: N.A.
Programming (via satellite): Cinemax; HBO; IFC; Showtime.
Fee: $8.95 monthly (IFC), $11.50 monthly (Cinemax, HBO or Showtime).
Digital Pay Service 1
Pay Units: N.A.
Programming (via satellite): Cinemax (multiplexed); HBO (multiplexed); Showtime (multiplexed); Starz (multiplexed); The Movie Channel (multiplexed).
Fee: $8.30 monthly (Starz/Encore), $12.50 monthly (Cinemax, HBO, Showtime or TMC).
Video-On-Demand: Yes
Pay-Per-View
Hot Choice; iN DEMAND; iN DEMAND (delivered digitally); Playboy TV (delivered digitally); Fresh (delivered digitally); Shorteez (delivered digitally).
Internet Service
Operational: Yes.
Subscribers: 161,264.
Broadband Service: Cox High Speed Internet.
Fee: $49.95 installation; $19.99-$53.99 monthly; $15.00 modem lease; $349.00 modem purchase.
Telephone Service
Digital: Operational
Subscribers: 90,434.
Fee: $9.95-$39.99 monthly
Miles of Plant: 5,878.0 (coaxial); 1,353.0 (fiber optic). Homes passed: 453,320.
Senior Vice President & Regional Manager: Anthony Pope. Vice President, Marketing: Ellen Lloyd. Vice President, Tax: Mary Vickers.
Ownership: Cox Communications Inc. (MSO).

NEW ROADS—Fidelity Communications, 3421 Ewing Rd, New Roads, LA 70760. Phones: 800-392-8070; 225-638-8057; 225-638-6801; 855-262-7434. E-mail: fidelityinfo@fidelitycommunications.com. Web Site: http://www.fidelitycommunications.com. Also serves Morganza (village) & Pointe Coupee Parish. ICA: LA0036.
TV Market Ranking: 87 (Morganza (village), NEW ROADS, Pointe Coupee Parish (portions)); Below 100 (Pointe Coupee Parish (portions)); Outside TV Markets (Pointe Coupee Parish (portions)). Franchise award date: October 15, 1979. Franchise expiration date: N.A. Began: February 1, 1981.
Channel capacity: N.A. Channels available but not in use: N.A.
Basic Service
Subscribers: 1,911. Commercial subscribers: 102.
Programming (received off-air): KLFY-TV (CBS) Lafayette; WAFB (Bounce TV, CBS) Baton Rouge; WBRZ-TV (ABC) Baton Rouge; WGMB-TV (FOX) Baton Rouge; WLPB-TV (PBS) Baton Rouge; WVLA-TV (NBC, This TV) Baton Rouge.
Programming (via satellite): QVC; Trinity Broadcasting Network (TBN); WGN America.
Fee: $29.99 installation; $28.99 monthly.
Digital Basic Service
Subscribers: N.A.
Programming (via satellite): BBC America; Bloomberg Television; Discovery Digital Networks; DIY Network; FYI; History International; IFC; LMN; MC; Nick 2; Nick Jr.; Nicktoons; Sundance LMN; TeenNick.

Digital Pay Service 1
Pay Units: N.A.
Programming (via satellite): Cinemax (multiplexed); Flix; HBO (multiplexed); Showtime (multiplexed); Starz (multiplexed); Starz Encore (multiplexed); The Movie Channel (multiplexed).
Video-On-Demand: No
Pay-Per-View
iN DEMAND (delivered digitally); Playboy TV (delivered digitally); Fresh (delivered digitally); Shorteez (delivered digitally).
Internet Service
Operational: Yes.
Subscribers: 1,599.
Fee: $29.99 monthly.
Telephone Service
Digital: Operational
Subscribers: 131.
Miles of Plant: 260.0 (coaxial); 97.0 (fiber optic). Homes passed: 7,784.
General Manager, AR/MO/LA/TX: Andy Davis.
Ownership: Fidelity Communications Co. (MSO).

NEWELLTON—Alliance Communications, PO Box 9090, Tyler, TX 75711. Phones: 903-561-4411 (Tyler, TX office); 501-679-6619; 800-842-8160. E-mail: marketing@alliancecable.net. Web Site: http://www.alliancecable.net. ICA: LA0114.
TV Market Ranking: Below 100 (NEWELLTON). Franchise award date: N.A. Franchise expiration date: N.A. Began: June 1, 1982.
Channel capacity: 54 (not 2-way capable). Channels available but not in use: N.A.
Basic Service
Subscribers: 41.
Programming (received off-air): KARD (Bounce TV, FOX) West Monroe; KLTM-TV (PBS) Monroe; KMLU (MeTV) Columbia; KNOE-TV (ABC, CBS, CW) Monroe; WJTV (Antenna TV, CBS) Jackson; WLBT (Bounce TV, NBC, This TV) Jackson.
Programming (via satellite): A&E; Animal Planet; BET; CNBC; CNN; C-SPAN; Discovery Channel; Disney Channel; ESPN; ESPN2; Fox News Channel; FOX Sports Networks; Freeform; FX; Golf Channel; Great American Country; HGTV; History; HLN; Lifetime; MSNBC; MTV; National Geographic Channel; Nickelodeon; Outdoor Channel; Spike TV; TBS; The Weather Channel; TNT; Trinity Broadcasting Network (TBN); Turner Classic Movies; USA Network.
Fee: $45.00 installation; $25.45 monthly.
Expanded Basic Service 1
Subscribers: N.A.
Fee: $27.50 monthly.
Digital Basic Service
Subscribers: N.A.
Programming (via satellite): BBC America; Bloomberg Television; Cloo; Destination America; Discovery Kids Channel; Disney XD; DMX Music; ESPN Classic; ESPNews; EVINE Live; FOX College Sports Central; FOX College Sports Pacific; Fox Sports 1; Fuse; FYI; GSN; History International; IFC;

Investigation Discovery; NBCSN; OWN: Oprah Winfrey Network; Science Channel; Sundance TV; WE tv.
Pay Service 1
Pay Units: N.A.
Programming (via satellite): Cinemax; HBO; Showtime.
Fee: $12.95 monthly (each).
Digital Pay Service 1
Pay Units: N.A.
Programming (via satellite): Cinemax (multiplexed); Flix; HBO (multiplexed); Showtime (multiplexed); Starz (multiplexed); Starz Encore (multiplexed); The Movie Channel (multiplexed).
Video-On-Demand: No
Pay-Per-View
iN DEMAND (delivered digitally); Playboy TV (delivered digitally); Club Jenna (delivered digitally).
Internet Service
Operational: No.
Telephone Service
None
Miles of Plant: 10.0 (coaxial); None (fiber optic). Homes passed: 731.
Chief Financial Officer: David Starrett. Vice President & General Manager: John Brinker. Vice President, Programming: Julie Newman.
Ownership: Buford Media Group LLC (MSO).

NORWOOD—Bailey Cable TV Inc, 807 Church St, Port Gibson, MS 39150-2413. Phone: 601-437-8300. Fax: 601-437-6860. E-mail: cs@baileycable.net. Web Site: http://www.baileycable.net. ICA: LA0191.
TV Market Ranking: Outside TV Markets (NORWOOD).
Channel capacity: N.A. Channels available but not in use: N.A.
Basic Service
Subscribers: 41.
Fee: $15.00 installation; $42.95 monthly.
President: David A. Bailey.
Ownership: Bailey Cable TV Inc. (MSO).

OAK GROVE—NewWave Communications. Now served by LAKE PROVIDENCE, LA [LA0053]. ICA: LA0086.

OAK RIDGE—Formerly served by Charter Communications. No longer in operation. ICA: LA0218.

OAKDALE—Media3, PO Box 650, Milan, TN 38358. Phone: 866-257-2044. E-mail: customerservice@mymedia3.com. Web Site: http://www.mymedia3.com. Also serves Allen Parish, Elizabeth & Pine Prairie. ICA: LA0241.
TV Market Ranking: Below 100 (Allen Parish (portions), OAKDALE); Outside TV Markets (Allen Parish (portions)).
Channel capacity: N.A. Channels available but not in use: N.A.
Basic Service
Subscribers: 728.
Fee: $24.95 installation; $22.45 monthly.
Miles of Plant: 114.0 (coaxial); None (fiber optic). Homes passed: 3,520.

2017 Edition

D-347

Louisiana—Cable Systems

President: Alan Taylor. Chief Financial Officer: Thomas Pate.
Ownership: CableSouth Media3 LLC (MSO).

OLLA—Alliance Communications, PO Box 9090, Tyler, TX 75711. Phones: 903-561-4411 (Tyler, TX office); 501-679-6619; 800-842-8160. E-mail: marketing@alliancecable.net. Web Site: http://www.alliancecable.net. Also serves La Salle Parish (portions), Tullos & Urania. ICA: LA0238.
TV Market Ranking: Outside TV Markets (OLLA, Tullos, Urania).
Channel capacity: N.A. Channels available but not in use: N.A.
Basic Service
Subscribers: 93.
Programming (received off-air): KALB-TV (CBS, CW, NBC) Alexandria; KARD (Bounce TV, FOX) West Monroe; KLAX-TV (ABC) Alexandria; KLTM-TV (PBS) Monroe; KMLU (MeTV) Columbia; KNOE-TV (ABC, CBS, CW) Monroe.
Programming (via satellite): A&E; AMC; Animal Planet; BET; Bravo; Cartoon Network; CMT; CNBC; CNN; Comedy Central; C-SPAN; C-SPAN 2; Discovery Channel; Disney Channel; Disney XD; E! HD; ESPN; ESPN2; EVINE Live; Food Network; Fox News Channel; Fox Sports 1; Freeform; FX; Golf Channel; Hallmark Channel; HGTV; History; HLN; INSP; ION Television; Lifetime; MSNBC; MTV; National Geographic Channel; Nickelodeon; Outdoor Channel; Oxygen; QVC; Spike TV; Syfy; TBS; The Weather Channel; TLC; TNT; Travel Channel; Trinity Broadcasting Network (TBN); truTV; Turner Classic Movies; TV Land; USA Network; VH1; WE tv; WGN America.
Fee: $45.00 installation; $22.45 monthly.
Digital Basic Service
Subscribers: N.A.
Programming (via satellite): BBC America; Bloomberg Television; CMT; Destination America; Discovery Kids Channel; DIY Network; Fuse; FXM; FYI; GSN; History International; IFC; Investigation Discovery; LMN; MC; MTV Classic; MTV Hits; MTV Jams; MTV2; Nick 2; Nick Jr.; Nicktoons; OWN: Oprah Winfrey Network; Science Channel; Sundance TV; TeenNick; Tr3s; VH1 Soul.
Digital Pay Service 1
Pay Units: N.A.
Programming (via satellite): Cinemax (multiplexed); Flix; HBO (multiplexed); LOGO; Showtime (multiplexed); Starz (multiplexed); Starz Encore; The Movie Channel (multiplexed).
Pay-Per-View
iN DEMAND (delivered digitally); Playboy TV (delivered digitally).
Internet Service
Operational: No.
Telephone Service
None
Chief Financial Officer: David Starrett. Vice President & General Manager: John Brinker. Vice President, Programming: Julie Newman.
Ownership: Buford Media Group LLC (MSO).

OPELOUSAS—Charter Communications, 12405 Powercourts Dr, St. Louis, MO 63131. Phones: 636-207-5100 (Corporate office); 337-582-3584; 985-446-4900 (Thibodaux office); 337-546-0087. Fax: 337-546-0038. Web Site: http://www.charter.com. Also serves Acadia Parish (portions), Chataignier, Church Point, Eunice, Evangeline Parish (portions), Iota, Jefferson Davis Parish (portions), Jennings, Leonville, St. Landry Parish (portions) & Washington. ICA: LA0022.
TV Market Ranking: Below 100 (Acadia Parish (portions), Chataignier, Church Point, Eunice, Evangeline Parish (portions), Iota, Jefferson Davis Parish (portions), Jennings, Leonville, OPELOUSAS, Washington, St. Landry Parish (portions)); Outside TV Markets (St. Landry Parish (portions)). Franchise award date: N.A. Franchise expiration date: N.A. Began: September 1, 1974.
Channel capacity: N.A. Channels available but not in use: N.A.
Digital Basic Service
Subscribers: 15,333.
Programming (via satellite): AXS TV; BBC America; Bloomberg Television; Discovery Digital Networks; DIY Network; ESPN; ESPN Classic; ESPNews; Fox Sports 2; FXM; FYI; Great American Country; HD Theater; IFC; LMN; MC; NFL Network; Nick 2; Nick Jr.; Nicktoons; Sundance TV; TeenNick; TV Guide Interactive Inc.; TVG Network.
Fee: $26.99 monthly.
Digital Expanded Basic Service
Subscribers: N.A.
Programming (via satellite): A&E; AMC; Animal Planet; BET; Bravo; Cartoon Network; CMT; CNBC; CNN; Comedy Central; C-SPAN; C-SPAN 2; Discovery Channel; Disney Channel; Disney XD; E! HD; ESPN; ESPN2; EWTN Global Catholic Network; Food Network; Fox News Channel; Fox Sports 1; FOX Sports Southwest; Freeform; FX; Golf Channel; GSN; Hallmark Channel; HGTV; History; HLN; INSP; Lifetime; MSNBC; MTV; National Geographic Channel; NBCSN; Nickelodeon; Outdoor Channel; Oxygen; Pop; Spike TV; Syfy; TBS; Telemundo; The Weather Channel; TLC; TNT; Travel Channel; Trinity Broadcasting Network (TBN); truTV; Turner Classic Movies; TV Land; USA Network; VH1; WE tv.
Fee: $42.99 monthly.
Digital Pay Service 1
Pay Units: N.A.
Programming (via satellite): Cinemax (multiplexed); Flix; HBO (multiplexed); HBO HD; Playboy TV; Showtime (multiplexed); Showtime HD; Starz (multiplexed); Starz Encore (multiplexed); The Movie Channel (multiplexed).
Fee: $9.95 monthly (Cinemax or Showtime/Showtime HD), $10.95 monthly (HBO/HBO HD or TMC).
Video-On-Demand: Yes
Pay-Per-View
iN DEMAND (delivered digitally); Playboy TV (delivered digitally); Fresh (delivered digitally); Shorteez (delivered digitally); NHL Center Ice (delivered digitally); MLB Extra Innings (delivered digitally).
Internet Service
Operational: Yes, DSL.
Subscribers: 9,851.
Broadband Service: Charter Internet.
Fee: $29.99 monthly.
Telephone Service
Digital: Operational
Subscribers: 5,582.
Fee: $29.99 monthly
Miles of Plant: 1,197.0 (coaxial); 471.0 (fiber optic). Homes passed: 40,394.
Vice President & General Manager: Kip Kraemer. Marketing Director: Lisa Brown. Government Relations Director: Jim Laurent. Technical Operations Director: Gary Savoie. Accounting Director: David Sovanski. Operations Manager: Blane Bercegeay. Plant Manager: Joe Semmes. Office Manager: Margaretta Frey.
Ownership: Charter Communications Inc. (MSO).

PALMETTO—Formerly served by Village Cable Co. No longer in operation. ICA: LA0136.

PECANIERE—Formerly served by CableSouth Inc. No longer in operation. ICA: LA0192.

PIERRE PART—Allen's TV Cable Service Inc. Now served by ASSUMPTION PARISH (portions), LA [LA0240]. ICA: LA0193.

PINE PRAIRIE—Formerly served by Charter Communications. Now served by Media3, OAKDALE, LA [LA0241]. ICA: LA0127.

PLAIN DEALING—Formerly served by Alliance Communications Network. No longer in operation. ICA: LA0100.

POINTE A LA HACHE—Formerly served by CMA Cablevision. No longer in operation. ICA: LA0195.

PORT BARRE—Allen's TV Cable Service Inc, 800 Victor II Blvd, PO Box 2643, Morgan City, LA 70380. Phone: 985-384-8335. E-mail: info@atvci.net. Web Site: http://www.atvc.net. Also serves St. Landry Parish (portions). ICA: LA0197.
TV Market Ranking: Below 100 (PORT BARRE, St. Landry Parish (portions)).
Channel capacity: N.A. Channels available but not in use: N.A.
Basic Service
Subscribers: 291.
Fee: $66.90 installation; $18.65 monthly.
Miles of Plant: 187.0 (coaxial); 100.0 (fiber optic). Homes passed: 4,719.
President & General Manager: Gregory A. Price.
Ownership: Allen's TV Cable Service Inc. (MSO).

RAYVILLE—Formerly served by Cotton Country Cable. No longer in operation. ICA: LA0219.

RESERVE—Reserve Telecommunications, 105 RTC Dr, Reserve, LA 70084. Phones: 888-611-6111; 985-536-1262. Web Site: http://www.rtconline.com. ICA: LA0244.
TV Market Ranking: 31 (RESERVE).
Channel capacity: N.A. Channels available but not in use: N.A.
Basic Service
Subscribers: 4,401.
Fee: $15.95 monthly.
Outside Plant Manager: Barry Firmin.
Ownership: Reserve Telecommunications (MSO).

ROBELINE—Formerly served by MARBAC Communications. No longer in operation. ICA: LA0199.

ROCKY BRANCH—Bayou Cable TV, 378 Main St, Marion, LA 71260. Phone: 318-292-4774. Fax: 318-292-4775. E-mail: admin@bayoucable.com. Web Site: http://www2.bayoucable.com. ICA: LA0228.
TV Market Ranking: 99 (ROCKY BRANCH).
Channel capacity: N.A. Channels available but not in use: N.A.
Basic Service
Subscribers: 81.
Programming (received off-air): KARD (Bounce TV, FOX) West Monroe; KLTM-TV (PBS) Monroe; KMCT-TV (IND) West Monroe; KMLU (MeTV) Columbia; KNOE-TV (ABC, CBS, CW) Monroe; KTVE (NBC) El Dorado.
Programming (via satellite): AMC; Hallmark Channel; QVC; Trinity Broadcasting Network (TBN); TV Land.
Fee: $25.00 installation; $54.99 monthly.
Expanded Basic Service 1
Subscribers: N.A.
Programming (via satellite): A&E; Animal Planet; CMT; CNN; CW PLUS; Discovery Channel; ESPN; ESPN2; FamilyNet; Food Network; Fox News Channel; Fox Sports 1; Freeform; FX; HGTV; History; Lifetime; MTV; National Geographic Channel; Nickelodeon; Outdoor Channel; Spike TV; TBS; The Weather Channel; TLC; TNT; USA Network; VH1; WGN America.
Fee: $20.00 monthly.
Pay Service 1
Pay Units: 3.
Programming (via satellite): HBO.
Fee: $10.95 monthly.
Pay Service 2
Pay Units: 4.
Programming (via satellite): Cinemax.
Fee: $8.95 monthly.
Video-On-Demand: No
Pay-Per-View
Playboy TV (delivered digitally); Fresh (delivered digitally); Shorteez (delivered digitally).
Internet Service
Operational: No.
Telephone Service
None
Miles of Plant: 15.0 (coaxial); None (fiber optic).
President & General Manager: Allen C. Booker. Chief Technician: Mark Andrews.
Ownership: Bayou Cable TV (MSO).

RODESSA—Formerly served by Almega Cable. No longer in operation. ICA: LA0110.

RUSTON—Suddenlink Communications, 1001 Cooktown Rd, Ruston, LA 71270-3113. Phone: 314-315-9400. Fax: 318-251-2711. Web Site: http://www.suddenlink.com. Also serves Grambling, Hilly, Lincoln Parish, Simsboro & Vienna. ICA: LA0201.
TV Market Ranking: 99 (Hilly, Lincoln Parish (portions), RUSTON, Vienna); Below 100 (Grambling, Simsboro, Lincoln Parish (portions)). Franchise award date: N.A. Franchise expiration date: N.A. Began: January 1, 1966.
Channel capacity: N.A. Channels available but not in use: N.A.
Basic Service
Subscribers: 5,410. Commercial subscribers: 525.
Programming (received off-air): KARD (Bounce TV, FOX) West Monroe; KLTM-TV (PBS) Monroe; KMCT-TV (IND) West Monroe; KMLU (MeTV) Columbia; KNOE-TV (ABC, CBS, CW) Monroe; KSLA (Bounce TV, CBS, Grit, This TV) Shreveport; KTBS-TV (ABC) Shreveport; KTVE (NBC) El Dorado; 1 FM.
Programming (via satellite): C-SPAN; C-SPAN 2; CW PLUS; FOX Sports Southwest; INSP; Pop; TBS; The Weather Channel; Trinity Broadcasting Network (TBN); WGN America.
Fee: $40.00 installation; $32.50 monthly.
Expanded Basic Service 1
Subscribers: N.A.
Programming (via satellite): A&E; AMC; Animal Planet; BET; Cartoon Network; CMT; CNBC; CNN; Comedy Central; Cox Sports Television; Discovery Channel; Disney Channel; ESPN; ESPN2; Food Network; Fox News Channel; Freeform; FX;

Cable Systems—Louisiana

Great American Country; HGTV; History; HLN; Lifetime; MTV; Nickelodeon; Outdoor Channel; Spike TV; Syfy; TLC; TNT; Travel Channel; truTV; Turner Classic Movies; TV Land; USA Network; VH1.
Fee: $16.60 monthly.

Digital Basic Service
Subscribers: N.A.
Programming (via satellite): AXS TV; BBC America; Bloomberg Television; Destination America; Discovery Kids Channel; Disney XD; ESPN HD; ESPNews; Fox Sports 1; Fuse; FXM; FYI; Golf Channel; GSN; HD Theater; History International; Investigation Discovery; LMN; MC; NBCSN; OWN: Oprah Winfrey Network; Science Channel; Starz Encore (multiplexed); Universal HD; WE tv.

Digital Pay Service 1
Pay Units: N.A.
Programming (via satellite): Cinemax (multiplexed); HBO (multiplexed); HBO HD; Showtime (multiplexed); Showtime HD; Starz (multiplexed); The Movie Channel (multiplexed).

Video-On-Demand: No

Pay-Per-View
ESPN Now (delivered digitally); iN DEMAND (delivered digitally); Playboy TV (delivered digitally); Fresh (delivered digitally).

Internet Service
Operational: Yes.
Broadband Service: Suddenlink High Speed Internet.
Fee: $45.00 installation; $29.95 monthly; $10.00 modem lease.

Telephone Service
None
Miles of Plant: 143.0 (coaxial); None (fiber optic).
Senior Vice President, Corporate Finance: Michael Pflantz. General Manager: J. Rex Holstead. Chief Technician: James C. Jennings.
Ownership: Cequel Communications Holdings I LLC (MSO).

SHREVEPORT—Comcast Cable, 6529 Quilen Rd, Shreveport, LA 71108-4438. Phones: 318-828-1152; 318-213-3322. Fax: 318-213-4225. Web Site: http://www.comcast.com. Also serves Belcher, Caddo Parish (portions), De Soto Parish (portions), Gilliam, Greenwood, Hosston & Stonewall, LA; Harrison County (portions), Panola County (portions) & Waskom, TX. ICA: LA0004.
TV Market Ranking: 58 (Belcher, Caddo Parish (portions), De Soto Parish (portions), Gilliam, Greenwood, Harrison County (portions), Hosston, Panola County (portions), SHREVEPORT, Stonewall, Waskom); Below 100 (Harrison County (portions), Panola County (portions)). Franchise award date: January 1, 1974. Franchise expiration date: N.A. Began: October 10, 1976.
Channel capacity: N.A. Channels available but not in use: N.A.

Basic Service
Subscribers: 35,591. Commercial subscribers: 2,722.
Programming (received off-air): KLTS-TV (PBS) Shreveport; KMSS-TV (FOX) Shreveport; KPXJ (Antenna TV, CW, MeTV, Movies!) Minden; KSHV-TV (MNT) Shreveport; KSLA (Bounce TV, CBS, Grit, This TV) Shreveport; KTAL-TV (NBC) Texarkana; KTBS-TV (ABC) Shreveport.
Programming (via satellite): Pop; QVC.
Fee: $52.95-$67.95 installation; $31.75 monthly.

Expanded Basic Service 1
Subscribers: N.A.
Programming (via satellite): A&E; AMC; Animal Planet; BET; Bravo; Cartoon Network; CMT; CNBC; CNN; Comcast/Charter Sports Southeast (CSS); Comedy Central; C-SPAN; C-SPAN 2; Discovery Channel; Discovery Life Channel; Disney Channel; E! HD; ESPN; ESPN2; Food Network; Fox News Channel; Fox Sports 1; FOX Sports Southwest; Freeform; FX; Golf Channel; Hallmark Channel; HGTV; History; HLN; Lifetime; MSNBC; MTV; National Geographic Channel; NBCSN; Nickelodeon; OWN: Oprah Winfrey Network; Oxygen; Spike TV; Syfy; TBS; The Weather Channel; TLC; TNT; Travel Channel; Trinity Broadcasting Network (TBN); truTV; Turner Classic Movies; TV Land; TV One; Univision Studios; USA Network; VH1; WE tv.
Fee: $34.33 monthly.

Digital Basic Service
Subscribers: N.A.
Programming (via satellite): A&E HD; BBC America; Bloomberg Television; Boomerang; CBS Sports Network HD; CMT; CNN HD; Cooking Channel; C-SPAN 3; Destination America; Discovery Kids Channel; Disney Channel; Disney XD; DIY Network; ESPN Classic; ESPN HD; ESPN2 HD; ESPNews; EVINE Live; EWTN Global Catholic Network; Food Network HD; Fox Business Network; FOX College Sports Central; FOX College Sports Pacific; Fox Sports 2; FSN HD; Fuse; FXM; FYI; Golf Channel HD; HD Theater; HGTV HD; History International; IFC; Investigation Discovery; Jewelry Television; LMN; MC; MTV Classic; MTV Hits; MTV Jams; MTV2; Nat Geo WILD; National Geographic Channel HD; NBA TV; NFL Network; NFL Network HD; NHL Network; Nick 2; Nick Jr.; Nicktoons; Outdoor Channel; Science Channel; Sprout; Starz Encore (multiplexed); Sundance TV; TBS HD; TeenNick; Tennis Channel; The Word Network; TNT HD; Tr3s; Universal HD; UP; USA Network HD; Versus HD; VH1 Soul; Weatherscan.

Digital Pay Service 1
Pay Units: N.A.
Programming (via satellite): Cinemax (multiplexed); Cinemax HD; HBO (multiplexed); HBO HD; MoviePlex; Showtime (multiplexed); Showtime HD; Starz (multiplexed); Starz HD; The Movie Channel (multiplexed).
Fee: $11.50 monthly (Cinemax, HBO, Showtime, TMC or Starz).

Video-On-Demand: Yes

Pay-Per-View
Hot Choice (delivered digitally); iN DEMAND (delivered digitally); MLB Extra Innings (delivered digitally); Spice (delivered digitally); Fresh (delivered digitally); Playboy TV (delivered digitally); Shorteez (delivered digitally); NBA League Pass (delivered digitally); MLS Direct Kick (delivered digitally); ESPN (delivered digitally); NHL Center Ice (delivered digitally).

Internet Service
Operational: Yes.
Subscribers: 32,812.
Broadband Service: Comcast High Speed Internet.
Fee: $99.95 installation; $49.95 monthly.

Telephone Service
Digital: Operational
Subscribers: 14,156.
Fee: $44.95 monthly
Miles of Plant: 2,775.0 (coaxial); 556.0 (fiber optic). Homes passed: 114,796.

Vice President, Government & Community Relations: Annette Hall. General Manager: Fred Fuller.
Ownership: Comcast Cable Communications Inc. (MSO).

SIBLEY—Suddenlink Communications, 520 Maryville Centre Dr, Ste 300, St. Louis, MO 63141. Phones: 888-822-5151; 314-315-9400. Web Site: http://www.suddenlink.com. Also serves Doyline, Dubberly, Heflin, Lake Bistineau, Ringgold & Webster Parish (southern portion). ICA: LA0121.
TV Market Ranking: 58 (Doyline, Dubberly, Heflin, Lake Bistineau, Ringgold, SIBLEY, Webster Parish (southern portion) (portions)); Below 100 (Webster Parish (southern portion) (portions)). Franchise award date: N.A. Franchise expiration date: N.A. Began: October 1, 1982.
Channel capacity: N.A. Channels available but not in use: N.A.

Basic Service
Subscribers: 748. Commercial subscribers: 42.
Programming (received off-air): KLTS-TV (PBS) Shreveport; KNOE-TV (ABC, CBS, CW) Monroe; KSLA (Bounce TV, CBS, Grit, This TV) Shreveport; KTAL-TV (NBC) Texarkana; KTBS-TV (ABC) Shreveport; KTVE (NBC) El Dorado.
Programming (via satellite): CNN; Disney Channel; ESPN; Freeform; Nickelodeon; TBS; The Weather Channel; USA Network; WGN America.
Fee: $28.45 monthly.

Pay Service 1
Pay Units: N.A.
Programming (via satellite): Cinemax; Flix; HBO; Showtime; The Movie Channel.
Fee: $4.95 monthly (Flix), $6.00 monthly (Showtime), $10.95 monthly (Cinemax, HBO or TMC).

Video-On-Demand: No

Internet Service
Operational: Yes. Began: May 5, 2005.
Broadband Service: Suddenlink High Speed Internet.
Fee: $45.00 installation; $29.95 monthly.

Telephone Service
Digital: Operational
Fee: $39.95 monthly
Miles of Plant: 108.0 (coaxial); None (fiber optic). Homes passed: 3,683.
Senior Vice President, Corporate Finance: Michael Pflantz. Regional Manager: Todd Cruthird. Area Manager: Russell Gaston.
Ownership: Cequel Communications Holdings I LLC (MSO).

SICILY ISLAND—Formerly served by Almega Cable. No longer in operation. ICA: LA0234.

SIMPSON—Formerly served by Zoom Media. No longer in operation. ICA: LA0202.

SLIDELL—Charter Communications, 12405 Powerscourt Dr, St. Louis, MO 63131. Phones: 636-207-5100 (Corporate office); 985-448-0688; 985-446-4900. Fax: 985-447-9541. Web Site: http://www.charter.com. Also serves Abita Springs, Albany, Amite City, Covington, Folsom, French Settlement, Hammond, Independence, Killian, Lacombe, Livingston, Livingston Parish (portions), Madisonville, Mandeville, Pearl River, Ponchatoula, Port Vincent, Roseland, Springfield, St. Tammany Parish (unincorporated areas), Tangipahoa Parish & Tickfaw, LA; Carrierre, McNeill, Pearl River County & Picayune, MS. ICA: LA0182.
TV Market Ranking: 31 (Abita Springs, Covington, Lacombe, Madisonville, Mandeville, Pearl River, SLIDELL, St. Tammany Parish (unincorporated areas) (portions), Tangipahoa Parish (portions)); 87 (Albany, French Settlement, Killian, Livingston, Livingston Parish (portions), Port Vincent, Springfield; Below 100 (Amite City, Folsom, Independence, McNeill, Pearl River County (portions), Ponchatoula, Roseland, Tickfaw, Hammond, Picayune, Abita Springs, St. Tammany Parish (unincorporated areas) (portions), Tangipahoa Parish (portions), Livingston Parish (portions)); Outside TV Markets (Carrierre, Pearl River County (portions)). Franchise award date: November 16, 1978. Franchise expiration date: N.A. Began: June 1, 1979.
Channel capacity: 68 (operating 2-way). Channels available but not in use: N.A.

Digital Basic Service
Subscribers: 62,075.
Programming (via satellite): AXS TV; BBC America; Bloomberg Television; Cooking Channel; Discovery Digital Networks; DIY Network; ESPN; ESPN Classic; ESPNews; Fox Sports 2; FXM; FYI; Great American Country; HD Theater; History International; IFC; LMN; MC; NFL Network; Nick 2; Nick Jr.; Nicktoons; Sundance TV; TeenNick; TVG Network.
Fee: $26.99 monthly.

Digital Expanded Basic Service
Subscribers: N.A.
Programming (via satellite): A&E; AMC; Animal Planet; BET; Bravo; Cartoon Network; CMT; CNBC; CNN; Comedy Central; C-SPAN; C-SPAN 2; Discovery Channel; Disney Channel; Disney XD; E! HD; ESPN; ESPN2; EWTN Global Catholic Network; Food Network; Fox News Channel; Fox Sports 1; FOX Sports Southwest; Freeform; FX; Golf Channel; GSN; Hallmark Channel; HGTV; History; HLN; Lifetime; MSNBC; MTV; National Geographic Channel; NBCSN; Nickelodeon; Oxygen; Spike TV; Syfy; TBS; Telemundo; The Weather Channel; TLC; TNT; Travel Channel; truTV; Turner Classic Movies; TV Land; USA Network; VH1; WE tv.
Fee: $42.99 monthly.

Digital Pay Service 1
Pay Units: N.A.
Programming (via satellite): Cinemax (multiplexed); HBO (multiplexed); Showtime (multiplexed); Starz (multiplexed); Starz Encore (multiplexed); The Movie Channel (multiplexed).

Video-On-Demand: Yes

Louisiana—Cable Systems

Pay-Per-View
Playboy TV (delivered digitally); Fresh (delivered digitally); Shorteez (delivered digitally).
Internet Service
Operational: Yes.
Subscribers: 53,451.
Broadband Service: Charter Internet.
Fee: $29.99 monthly.
Telephone Service
Digital: Operational
Subscribers: 24,050.
Fee: $29.99 monthly
Miles of Plant: 7,365.0 (coaxial); 1,805.0 (fiber optic). Homes passed: 186,543.
Vice President & General Manager: Kip Kraemer. Marketing Director: Lisa Brown. Government Relations Director: Jim Laurent. Technical Operations Director: Gary Savoie. Accounting Director: David Sovanski. Operations Manager: Dave Houghtlin.
Ownership: Charter Communications Inc. (MSO).

SPRINGHILL—NewWave Communications, One Montgomery Plaza, 4th Floor, Sikeston, MO 63801. Phones: 573-472-9500; 888-863-9928. Fax: 573-472-9518. E-mail: info@newwavecom.com. Web Site: http://www.newwavecom.com. Also serves Cullen & Porterville. ICA: LA0204.
TV Market Ranking: Below 100 (Cullen, Porterville, SPRINGHILL).
Channel capacity: N.A. Channels available but not in use: N.A.
Basic Service
Subscribers: 723.
Programming (received off-air): KLTS-TV (PBS) Shreveport; KMSS-TV (FOX) Shreveport; KPXJ (Antenna TV, CW, MeTV, Movies!) Minden; KSHV-TV (MNT) Shreveport; KSLA (Bounce TV, CBS, Grit, This TV) Shreveport; KTAL-TV (NBC) Texarkana; KTBS-TV (ABC) Shreveport; KTVE (NBC) El Dorado.
Programming (via satellite): C-SPAN; Hallmark Channel; Lifetime; QVC; TBS; Trinity Broadcasting Network (TBN); WGN America.
Fee: $35.00 installation; $31.27 monthly.
Expanded Basic Service 1
Subscribers: N.A.
Programming (via satellite): A&E; AMC; Animal Planet; BET; Cartoon Network; CMT; CNN; Comedy Central; Discovery Channel; ESPN; ESPN2; Food Network; Fox News Channel; Freeform; HGTV; History; HLN; Nickelodeon; Outdoor Channel; Pop; Spike TV; Syfy; The Weather Channel; TLC; TNT; Travel Channel; Turner Classic Movies; TV Land; USA Network; VH1.
Fee: $50.20 monthly.
Digital Basic Service
Subscribers: N.A.
Programming (via satellite): BBC America; Bloomberg Television; Bravo; Discovery Digital Networks; DMX Music; ESPN Classic; ESPNews; Fox Sports 1; FXM; FYI; Golf Channel; GSN; History International; IFC; LMN; NBCSN; Sundance TV; Trinity Broadcasting Network (TBN); WE tv.
Fee: $10.00 monthly.
Digital Pay Service 1
Pay Units: N.A.
Programming (via satellite): Cinemax (multiplexed); HBO (multiplexed); Showtime (multiplexed); Starz (multiplexed); Starz Encore (multiplexed); The Movie Channel.
Fee: $7.00 monthly (Starz), $9.00 monthly (Cinemax), $15.00 monthly (Showtime/TMC), $16.00 monthly (HBO) or $25.00 monthly (HBO/Cinemax).
Video-On-Demand: No

Pay-Per-View
iN DEMAND (delivered digitally); Hot Choice (delivered digitally); Playboy TV (delivered digitally); Fresh (delivered digitally); Shorteez (delivered digitally); ESPN Now (delivered digitally).
Internet Service
Operational: Yes.
Fee: $36.99-$46.99 monthly; $6.00 modem lease.
Telephone Service
None
General Manager: Staci Gowan.
Ownership: NewWave Communications LLC (MSO).

ST. BERNARD PARISH—Cox Communications. Now served by NEW ORLEANS, LA [LA0001]. ICA: LA0009.

ST. FRANCISVILLE—Bailey Cable TV Inc, 807 Church St, Port Gibson, MS 39150-2413. Phones: 601-437-8300; 601-437-8030; 601-849-4201; 601-892-5249. Fax: 601-437-6860. E-mail: cs@baileycable.net. Web Site: http://www.baileycable.net. Also serves West Feliciana Parish (portions). ICA: LA0056.
TV Market Ranking: 87 (ST. FRANCISVILLE, West Feliciana Parish (portions)). Franchise award date: N.A. Franchise expiration date: N.A. Began: January 1, 1982.
Channel capacity: N.A. Channels available but not in use: N.A.
Basic Service
Subscribers: 444.
Programming (received off-air): WAFB (Bounce TV, CBS) Baton Rouge; WBRZ-TV (ABC) Baton Rouge; WGMB-TV (FOX) Baton Rouge; WVLA-TV (NBC, This TV) Baton Rouge.
Programming (via satellite): A&E; AMC; Animal Planet; BET; Cartoon Network; CMT; CNN; C-SPAN; C-SPAN 2; Discovery Channel; ESPN; ESPN2; EWTN Global Catholic Network; Food Network; Fox News Channel; Freeform; HGTV; History; HLN; Lifetime; MTV; Nickelodeon; OWN; Oprah Winfrey Network; QVC; Spike TV; Syfy; TBS; The Weather Channel; TLC; TNT; Travel Channel; Trinity Broadcasting Network (TBN); TV Land; USA Network; VH1; WGN America.
Fee: $15.00 installation; $42.95 monthly; $2.00 converter.
Pay Service 1
Pay Units: N.A.
Programming (via satellite): Showtime; The Movie Channel.
Fee: $9.00 monthly (each).
Video-On-Demand: No
Internet Service
Operational: Yes.
Telephone Service
None
Miles of Plant: 78.0 (coaxial); 20.0 (fiber optic). Homes passed: 2,247.
President: David A. Bailey. Chief Technician: David Daigle. Office Manager: Connie Tillman.
Ownership: Bailey Cable TV Inc. (MSO).

ST. JAMES PARISH (portions)—Reserve Telecommunications, 105 RTC Dr, Reserve, LA 70084. Phones: 888-611-6111; 985-536-1111. Web Site: http://www.rtconline.com. Also serves Convent, Hester, Paulina & Vacherie. ICA: LA0245.
TV Market Ranking: Outside TV Markets (Convent, Hester, Paulina, ST. JAMES PARISH (PORTIONS), Vacherie.
Channel capacity: N.A. Channels available but not in use: N.A.

Outside Plant Manager: Barry Firmin.
Ownership: Reserve Telecommunications (MSO).

ST. JOSEPH—Suddenlink Communications, 520 Maryville Centre Dr, Ste 300, St. Louis, MO 63141. Phones: 888-822-5151; 314-315-9400. Web Site: http://www.suddenlink.com. Also serves Lake Bruin & Tensas Parish (portions). ICA: LA0206.
TV Market Ranking: Below 100 (Lake Bruin, ST. JOSEPH, Tensas Parish (portions)). Franchise award date: N.A. Franchise expiration date: N.A. Began: June 1, 1982.
Channel capacity: N.A. Channels available but not in use: N.A.
Basic Service
Subscribers: 235. Commercial subscribers: 10.
Programming (received off-air): KLTM-TV (PBS) Monroe; KNOE-TV (ABC, CBS, CW) Monroe; WAPT (ABC) Jackson; WJTV (Antenna TV, CBS) Jackson; WLBT (Bounce TV, NBC, This TV) Jackson.
Programming (via satellite): CNN; ESPN; Freeform; Nickelodeon; TBS; The Weather Channel; USA Network; WGN America.
Fee: $28.45 monthly.
Pay Service 1
Pay Units: N.A.
Programming (via satellite): Cinemax; HBO; Showtime.
Fee: $7.00 monthly (Cinemax or Showtime), $12.00 monthly (HBO).
Video-On-Demand: No
Internet Service
Operational: Yes. Began: April 22, 2004.
Broadband Service: Suddenlink High Speed Internet.
Fee: $45.00 installation; $29.95 monthly.
Telephone Service
Digital: Operational
Fee: $39.95 monthly
Miles of Plant: 45.0 (coaxial); None (fiber optic). Homes passed: 971.
Vice President, Corporate Finance: Michael Pflantz. Regional Manager: Todd Cruthird. Plant Manager: Dion Canaday.
Ownership: Cequel Communications Holdings I LLC (MSO).

ST. MARTINVILLE—Cox Communications. Now served by BATON ROUGE, LA [LA0003]. ICA: LA0019.

START—Formerly served by Almega Cable. No longer in operation. ICA: LA0126.

STERLINGTON—Bayou Cable TV, 378 Main St, Marion, LA 71260. Phone: 318-292-4774. Fax: 318-292-4775. E-mail: admin@bayoucable.com. Web Site: http://www2.bayoucable.com. ICA: LA0229.
TV Market Ranking: 99 (STERLINGTON).
Channel capacity: N.A. Channels available but not in use: N.A.
Basic Service
Subscribers: 281.
Programming (received off-air): KARD (Bounce TV, FOX) West Monroe; KLTM-TV (PBS) Monroe; KMCT-TV (IND) West Monroe; KMLU (MeTV) Columbia; KNOE-TV (ABC, CBS, CW) Monroe; KTVE (NBC) El Dorado.
Programming (via satellite): AMC; Hallmark Channel; QVC; Trinity Broadcasting Network (TBN); TV Land.
Fee: $25.00 installation; $54.99 monthly.
Expanded Basic Service 1
Subscribers: N.A.
Programming (via satellite): A&E; Animal Planet; BET; Cartoon Network; CMT; CNN;

CW PLUS; Discovery Channel; ESPN; ESPN2; FamilyNet; Food Network; Fox News Channel; Fox Sports 1; Freeform; FX; HGTV; History; Lifetime; MTV; National Geographic Channel; Nickelodeon; Outdoor Channel; Spike TV; TBS; The Weather Channel; TLC; TNT; USA Network; VH1; WGN America.
Fee: $20.00 monthly.
Pay Service 1
Pay Units: 31.
Programming (via satellite): HBO.
Fee: $10.95 monthly.
Pay Service 2
Pay Units: 6.
Programming (via satellite): Cinemax.
Fee: $8.95 monthly.
Video-On-Demand: No
Pay-Per-View
Playboy TV (delivered digitally); Fresh (delivered digitally); Shorteez (delivered digitally).
Internet Service
Operational: Yes.
Telephone Service
None
Miles of Plant: 12.0 (coaxial); None (fiber optic).
President & General Manager: Allen C. Booker. Chief Technician: Mark Andrews.
Ownership: Bayou Cable TV (MSO).

SULPHUR—Suddenlink Communications. Now served by LAKE CHARLES, LA [LA0007]. ICA: LA0024.

SWEETWATER—Formerly served by Charter Communications. No longer in operation. ICA: LA0209.

TALLULAH—NewWave Communications. Now served by MONROE, LA [LA0049]. ICA: LA0042.

TANGIPAHOA—Formerly served by Almega Cable. No longer in operation. ICA: LA0237.

THIBODAUX—Charter Communications, 12405 Powerscourt Dr, St. Louis, MO 63131. Phones: 636-207-5100 (Corporate office); 985-448-0688; 985-446-4900. Fax: 985-447-9541. Web Site: http://www.charter.com. Also serves Amelia, Assumption Parish (southern portion), Bourg, Chauvin, Donner, Gibson, Lafourche Parish (western portion), Napoleonville, St. Mary Parish, Terrebonne Parish (portions) & Vacherie. ICA: LA0011.
TV Market Ranking: Outside TV Markets (Amelia, Chauvin, Donner, Gibson, Lafourche Parish (western portion), Napoleonville, St. Mary Parish, Terrebonne Parish (portions), THIBODAUX, Vacherie, Bourg). Franchise award date: April 19, 1966. Franchise expiration date: N.A. Began: April 1, 1970.
Channel capacity: N.A. Channels available but not in use: N.A.
Digital Basic Service
Subscribers: 21,768.
Programming (via satellite): AXS TV; BBC America; Bloomberg Television; Discovery Digital Networks; DIY Network; ESPN Classic; ESPNews; Fox Sports 2; FXM; FYI; Great American Country; HBO; HD Theater; History International; IFC; LMN; MC; NFL Network; Nick 2; Nick Jr.; Nicktoons; Showtime; Sundance TV; TeenNick; TV Guide Interactive Inc.; TVG Network.
Fee: $26.99 monthly.

Cable Systems—Louisiana

Digital Expanded Basic Service
Subscribers: N.A.
Programming (via satellite): A&E; AMC; Animal Planet; BET; Bravo; Cartoon Network; CMT; CNN; Comedy Central; C-SPAN; C-SPAN 2; Discovery Channel; Disney Channel; Disney XD; E! HD; ESPN; ESPN2; Food Network; Fox News Channel; Fox Sports 1; FOX Sports Southwest; Freeform; FX; Golf Channel; GSN; Hallmark Channel; HGTV; History; HLN; Lifetime; MSNBC; MTV; National Geographic Channel; NBCSN; Nickelodeon; Outdoor Channel; Oxygen; Spike TV; Syfy; TBS; Telemundo; The Weather Channel; TLC; TNT; Travel Channel; truTV; Turner Classic Movies; TV Land; Univision Studios; USA Network; VH1; WE tv.
Fee: $42.99 monthly.

Digital Pay Service 1
Pay Units: N.A.
Programming (via satellite): Cinemax (multiplexed); Flix; HBO (multiplexed); Playboy TV; Showtime (multiplexed); Starz (multiplexed); Starz Encore (multiplexed); The Movie Channel (multiplexed).
Fee: $40.00 installation; $9.95 monthly (Cinemax, Showtime or TMC), $10.95 monthly (HBO).

Video-On-Demand: Yes

Pay-Per-View
iN DEMAND (delivered digitally); Playboy TV (delivered digitally); Fresh (delivered digitally); Shorteez (delivered digitally); NHL Center Ice (delivered digitally); MLB Extra Innings (delivered digitally).

Internet Service
Operational: Yes, DSL.
Subscribers: 22,828.
Broadband Service: Charter Internet.
Fee: $29.99 monthly.

Telephone Service
Digital: Operational
Subscribers: 8,621.
Fee: $29.99 monthly
Miles of Plant: 1,749.0 (coaxial); 785.0 (fiber optic). Homes passed: 54,938.
Vice President & General Manager: Kip Kraemer. Operations Manager: Ann Danos. Technical Operations Director: Gary Savoie. Accounting Director: David Sovanski. Marketing Director: Lisa Brown. Government Relations Director: Jim Laurent.
Ownership: Charter Communications Inc. (MSO).

TURKEY CREEK—Formerly served by Alliance Communications Network. No longer in operation. ICA: LA0095.

VARNADO—Formerly served by Charter Communications. No longer in operation. ICA: LA0232.

VILLE PLATTE—Suddenlink Communications, 520 Maryville Centre Dr, Ste 300, St. Louis, MO 63141. Phones: 337-363-0621; 314-315-9400. Web Site: http://www.suddenlink.com. Also serves Evangeline Parish & Mamou. ICA: LA0028.
TV Market Ranking: Below 100 (Evangeline Parish (portions)); Outside TV Markets (Evangeline Parish (portions), Mamou, VILLE PLATTE). Franchise award date: N.A. Franchise expiration date: N.A. Began: January 1, 1978.
Channel capacity: N.A. Channels available but not in use: N.A.

Basic Service
Subscribers: 1,427. Commercial subscribers: 93.
Programming (received off-air): KADN-TV (FOX, MNT) Lafayette; KALB (CBS, CW, NBC) Alexandria; KATC (ABC, CW, Grit) Lafayette; KDCG-CD (Antenna TV) Opelousas; KLFY-TV (CBS) Lafayette; KLPB-TV (PBS) Lafayette; WBRZ-TV (ABC) Baton Rouge.
Programming (via satellite): TBS; WGN America.
Fee: $28.45 monthly; $2.00 converter.

Expanded Basic Service 1
Subscribers: N.A.
Programming (via satellite): A&E; BET; Cartoon Network; CMT; CNN; C-SPAN; Discovery Channel; Disney Channel; ESPN; ESPN2; EWTN Global Catholic Network; Fox News Channel; FOX Sports Southwest; Freeform; HGTV; HLN; Lifetime; MTV; Nickelodeon; QVC; Spike TV; The Weather Channel; TLC; TNT; Trinity Broadcasting Network (TBN); Turner Classic Movies; TV Land; USA Network.
Fee: $25.00 monthly.

Pay Service 1
Pay Units: N.A.
Programming (via satellite): Cinemax; HBO; Showtime; The Movie Channel.
Fee: $10.00 installation; $7.95 monthly (Cinemax), $10.50 monthly (Showtime or TMC), $10.95 monthly (HBO).

Internet Service
Operational: Yes. Began: March 24, 2004.
Broadband Service: Suddenlink High Speed Internet.
Fee: $45.00 installation; $29.95 monthly.

Telephone Service
Digital: Operational
Fee: $39.95 monthly
Miles of Plant: 143.0 (coaxial); 25.0 (fiber optic). Homes passed: 7,506.
Vice President, Corporate Finance: Michael Pflantz. Regional Manager: Todd Cruthird.
Ownership: Cequel Communications Holdings I LLC (MSO).

VINTON—Formerly served by Allegiance Communications. Now served by Vyve Broadband, WESTLAKE, LA [LA0025]. ICA: LA0064.

WALLACE RIDGE—Formerly served by Zoom Media. No longer in operation. ICA: LA0211.

WATERPROOF—Alliance Communications, PO Box 9090, Tyler, TX 75711. Phones: 903-561-4411 (Tyler, TX office); 800-842-8160; 501-679-6619. E-mail: marketing@alliancecable.net. Web Site: http://www.alliancecable.net. ICA: LA0212.
TV Market Ranking: Below 100 (WATERPROOF). Franchise award date: N.A. Franchise expiration date: N.A. Began: August 1, 1983.
Channel capacity: 54 (not 2-way capable). Channels available but not in use: N.A.

Basic Service
Subscribers: 28.
Programming (received off-air): KARD (Bounce TV, FOX) West Monroe; KLTM-TV (PBS) Monroe; KMLU (MeTV) Columbia; KNOE-TV (ABC, CBS, CW) Monroe; WJTV (Antenna TV, CBS) Jackson; WLBT (Bounce TV, NBC, This TV) Jackson.
Programming (via satellite): A&E; Animal Planet; BET; Cartoon Network; CNN; Discovery Channel; Disney Channel; ESPN; ESPN2; Freeform; Great American Country; HGTV; History; HLN; Lifetime; MTV; National Geographic Channel; Nickelodeon; Outdoor Channel; Spike TV; TBS; The Weather Channel; TNT; Trinity Broadcasting Network (TBN); Turner Classic Movies; USA Network.
Fee: $45.00 installation; $22.45 monthly.

Pay Service 1
Pay Units: N.A.
Programming (via satellite): Cinemax; HBO; Showtime.
Fee: $12.95 monthly (each).

Video-On-Demand: No

Internet Service
Operational: No.

Telephone Service
None
Miles of Plant: 10.0 (coaxial); None (fiber optic). Homes passed: 417.
Chief Financial Officer: David Starrett.
Ownership: Buford Media Group LLC (MSO).

WELSH—Formerly served by Communi-Comm Services. Now served by Vyve Broadband, LAKE ARTHUR, LA [LA0078]. ICA: LA0079.

WEST MONROE—Comcast Cable. Now served by JACKSON, MS [MS0001]. ICA: LA0005.

WESTLAKE—Vyve Broadband, 4 International Dr, Ste 330, Rye Brook, NY 10573. Phones: 800-937-1397; 337-433-0892. Web Site: http://vyvebroadband.com. Also serves Calcasieu Parish (portions), De Quincy, Moss Bluff & Vinton. ICA: LA0025.
TV Market Ranking: 88 (Vinton); Below 100 (De Quincy, Moss Bluff, WESTLAKE). Franchise award date: N.A. Franchise expiration date: N.A. Began: January 1, 1980.
Channel capacity: N.A. Channels available but not in use: N.A.

Basic Service
Subscribers: 3,920.
Programming (received off-air): KATC (ABC, CW, Grit) Lafayette; KBMT (ABC) Beaumont; KBTV-TV (Bounce TV, FOX) Port Arthur; KFDM (CBS, CW) Beaumont; KLFY-TV (CBS) Lafayette; KPLC (Bounce TV, NBC, This TV) Lake Charles; WLPB-TV (PBS) Baton Rouge.
Programming (via satellite): Pop.
Fee: $25.00 monthly.

Expanded Basic Service 1
Subscribers: N.A.
Programming (via satellite): A&E; AMC; Animal Planet; BET; Cartoon Network; CMT; CNBC; CNN; C-SPAN; C-SPAN 2; Discovery Channel; Disney Channel; ESPN; ESPN2; Fox News Channel; FOX Sports Networks; Freeform; FX; HGTV; History; HLN; Lifetime; MSNBC; MTV; Nickelodeon; Outdoor Channel; QVC; Spike TV; Syfy; TBS; The Weather Channel; TLC; TNT; TV Land; USA Network; VH1.
Fee: $20.00 installation; $10.25 monthly.

Digital Basic Service
Subscribers: N.A.
Programming (via satellite): BBC America; Bloomberg Television; Bravo; Destination America; Discovery Kids Channel; DMX Music; ESPN Classic; ESPNews; Fox Sports 1; Golf Channel; GSN; IFC; Investigation Discovery; National Geographic Channel; NBCSN; OWN; Oprah Winfrey Network; Science Channel; Trinity Broadcasting Network (TBN); Turner Classic Movies; WE tv; Weatherscan.
Fee: $20.00 installation.

Digital Pay Service 1
Pay Units: N.A.
Programming (via satellite): Cinemax (multiplexed); HBO (multiplexed); Starz (multiplexed); Starz Encore (multiplexed).
Fee: $10.00 installation; $11.95 monthly (Cinemax), $12.95 monthly (Starz/Encore), $13.95 monthly (HBO).

Video-On-Demand: No

Internet Service
Operational: Yes.
Broadband Service: Net Commander.
Fee: $39.95 installation; $51.95 monthly.

Telephone Service
Digital: Operational
Miles of Plant: 174.0 (coaxial); None (fiber optic). Homes passed: 26,000. Homes passed includes Kinder & Lake Arthur.
President & Chief Executive Officer: Jeffrey DeMond. Vice President, Residential Services: Vin Zachariah. Vice President, Marketing: Diane Quennoz. Senior Vice President, Financial Planning: Daniel White.
Ownership: Vyve Broadband LLC (MSO).

WILSON—Formerly served by Trust Cable. No longer in operation. ICA: LA0213.

WINNFIELD—Suddenlink Communications, 701 West Court St, Winnfield, LA 71483-2635. Phone: 314-315-9400. Web Site: http://www.suddenlink.com. Also serves Joyce & Winn Parish. ICA: LA0046.
TV Market Ranking: 99 (Winn Parish (portions)); Below 100 (Joyce, Winn Parish (portions)); Outside TV Markets (WINNFIELD). Franchise award date: April 9, 1963. Franchise expiration date: N.A. Began: April 1, 1964.
Channel capacity: N.A. Channels available but not in use: N.A.

Basic Service
Subscribers: 1,134. Commercial subscribers: 122.
Programming (received off-air): KALB-TV (CBS, CW, NBC) Alexandria; KARD (Bounce TV, FOX) West Monroe; KLAX-TV (ABC) Alexandria; KLTM-TV (PBS) Monroe; KMLU (MeTV) Columbia; KNOE-TV (ABC, CBS, CW) Monroe; allband FM.
Programming (via satellite): A&E; AMC; Animal Planet; BET; Bravo; Cartoon Network; CMT; CNBC; CNN; Comedy Central; Cox Sports Television; C-SPAN; C-SPAN 2; CW PLUS; Discovery Channel; Disney Channel; E! HD; ESPN; ESPN2; Food Network; Fox News Channel; Fox Sports 1; FOX Sports Southwest; Freeform; FX; Great American Country; HGTV; History; HLN; Jewelry Television; Lifetime; LMN; MSNBC; MTV; NBCSN; Nickelodeon; Outdoor Channel; OWN: Oprah Winfrey Network; Oxygen; Pop; QVC; Spike TV; Syfy; TBS; The Weather Channel; TLC; TNT; Travel Channel; Trinity Broadcasting Network (TBN); truTV; Turner Classic Movies; TV Land; USA Network; VH1; WE tv.
Fee: $40.00 installation; $64.95 monthly; $2.74 converter.

Digital Basic Service
Subscribers: N.A.
Programming (via satellite): BBC America; Bloomberg Television; CBS Sports Network; CMT; Cooking Channel; Destination America; Discovery Kids Channel; Disney XD; DIY Network; ESPN Classic; ESPNews; Fox Sports 2; Fuse; FYI; Golf Channel; GSN; Hallmark Channel; History International; IFC; Investigation Discovery; MC; MTV Classic; MTV Hits; MTV Jams; MTV2; Nat Geo WILD; National Geographic Channel; Nick Jr.; Nicktoons; Science Channel; Starz Encore (multiplexed); Sundance TV; TeenNick; TV One; VH1 Soul.

Digital Pay Service 1
Pay Units: N.A.
Programming (via satellite): Cinemax (multiplexed); HBO (multiplexed); Showtime

2017 Edition

Louisiana—Cable Systems

(multiplexed); Starz (multiplexed); The Movie Channel (multiplexed).

Video-On-Demand: No

Pay-Per-View
iN DEMAND (delivered digitally); Playboy TV (delivered digitally); Fresh (delivered digitally).

Internet Service
Operational: Yes.
Broadband Service: Suddenlink High Speed Internet.

Telephone Service
Digital: Operational
Miles of Plant: 64.0 (coaxial); None (fiber optic). Homes passed: 3,200.
Senior Vice President, Corporate Finance: Michael Pflantz. General Manager: Ronnie Waters. Chief Technician: Leslie Alexander.
Ownership: Cequel Communications Holdings I LLC (MSO).

WINNSBORO—NewWave Communications, One Montgomery Plaza, 4th Floor, Sikeston, MO 63801. Phone: 877-794-2724. Web Site: http://www.newwavecom.com. Also serves Winnsboro Twp. ICA: LA0057.
TV Market Ranking: 99 (WINNSBORO, Winnsboro Twp.). Franchise award date: N.A. Franchise expiration date: N.A. Began: June 1, 1976.
Channel capacity: N.A. Channels available but not in use: N.A.

Basic Service
Subscribers: 436.
Programming (received off-air): KARD (Bounce TV, FOX) West Monroe; KLTM-TV (PBS) Monroe; KMCT-TV (IND) West Monroe; KNOE-TV (ABC, CBS, CW) Monroe; KTVE (NBC) El Dorado; WJTV (Antenna TV, CBS) Jackson; WLBT (Bounce TV, NBC, This TV) Jackson.
Programming (via satellite): Cartoon Network; Freeform; WGN America.
Fee: $29.99 installation; $23.97 monthly.

Expanded Basic Service 1
Subscribers: N.A.
Programming (via satellite): BET; CMT; CNN; C-SPAN; Disney Channel; ESPN; INSP; Lifetime; MTV; Nickelodeon; QVC; Spike TV; Syfy; The Weather Channel; USA Network.
Fee: $12.10 monthly.

Expanded Basic Service 2
Subscribers: N.A.
Programming (via satellite): AMC; Discovery Channel; TBS; TNT.
Fee: $21.13 installation; $3.20 monthly.

Pay Service 1
Pay Units: N.A.
Programming (via satellite): HBO; Showtime.
Fee: $8.00 monthly (Showtime), $10.00 monthly (HBO).

Video-On-Demand: No

Internet Service
Operational: No.

Telephone Service
None
Miles of Plant: 55.0 (coaxial); None (fiber optic). Homes passed: 2,548.
Chief Financial Officer: Randy McVay.
Ownership: NewWave Communications LLC (MSO).

WISNER—NewWave Communications, One Montgomery Plaza, 4th Floor, Sikeston, MO 63801. Phones: 573-472-9500; 888-863-9928. Fax: 573-472-9518. E-mail: info@newwave.com. Web Site: http://www.newwavecom.com. Also serves Gilbert. ICA: LA0093.
TV Market Ranking: Below 100 (Gilbert, WISNER). Franchise award date: March 11, 1982. Franchise expiration date: N.A. Began: December 1, 1982.
Channel capacity: N.A. Channels available but not in use: N.A.

Basic Service
Subscribers: 72.
Programming (received off-air): KARD (Bounce TV, FOX) West Monroe; KLAX-TV (ABC) Alexandria; KLTM-TV (PBS) Monroe; KNOE-TV (ABC, CBS, CW) Monroe; KTVE (NBC) El Dorado.
Programming (via satellite): CMT; CNN; Discovery Channel; ESPN; Freeform; Nickelodeon; Spike TV; TBS; The Weather Channel; TNT; Turner Classic Movies; USA Network; WGN America.
Fee: $35.00 installation; $65.78 monthly.

Pay Service 1
Pay Units: N.A.
Programming (via satellite): HBO; Showtime.
Fee: $14.95 installation; $13.95 monthly (each).

Video-On-Demand: No

Internet Service
Operational: No.

Telephone Service
None
Miles of Plant: 23.0 (coaxial); None (fiber optic). Homes passed: 800.
General Manager: Staci Gowan.
Ownership: NewWave Communications LLC (MSO).

MAINE

Total Systems: 23	Communities with Applications: 0
Total Communities Served: 367	Number of Basic Subscribers: 304,400
Franchises Not Yet Operating: 0	Number of Expanded Basic Subscribers: 0
Applications Pending: 0	Number of Pay Units: 1,812

Top 100 Markets Represented: Portland-Poland Spring (75).

For a list of cable communities in this section, see the Cable Community Index located in the back of Cable Volume 2.
For explanation of terms used in cable system listings, see p. D-11.

ADDISON (town)—Time Warner Cable. Now served by PORTLAND, ME [ME0001]. ICA: ME0044.

ASHLAND—Time Warner Cable. Now served by PRESQUE ISLE, ME [ME0008]. ICA: ME0052.

AUBURN—Formerly served by Oxford Networks. No longer in operation. ICA: ME5000.

AUGUSTA—Time Warner Cable. Now served by PORTLAND, ME [ME0001]. ICA: ME0004.

AVON—Time Warner Cable. Now served by PORTLAND, ME [ME0001]. ICA: ME0081.

BANGOR—Time Warner Cable. Now served by PORTLAND, ME [ME0001]. ICA: ME0002.

BELGRADE—Time Warner Cable. Now served by PORTLAND, ME [ME0001]. ICA: ME0088.

BETHEL—Formerly served by Adelphia Communications. Now served by Time Warner Cable, PORTLAND, ME [ME0001]. ICA: ME0029.

BINGHAM—Moosehead Enterprises, PO Box 526, Greenville, ME 04441. Phone: 207-695-3337. Fax: 207-695-3571. ICA: ME0116.
TV Market Ranking: Outside TV Markets (BINGHAM).
Channel capacity: N.A. Channels available but not in use: N.A.
Basic Service
Subscribers: 290.
Programming (received off-air): WABI-TV (CBS, CW) Bangor; WCSH (Antenna TV, NBC) Portland; WGME-TV (CBS) Portland; WMEB-TV (PBS) Orono; WMTW (ABC) Poland Spring; WVII-TV (ABC) Bangor.
Programming (via satellite): A&E; CNN; CW PLUS; Discovery Channel; ESPN; ESPN2; Freeform; Great American Country; Hallmark Channel; History; Lifetime; Outdoor Channel; QVC; TBS; TNT; Turner Classic Movies; USA Network; WGN America; WSBK-TV (MNT) Boston.
Fee: $30.00 installation; $37.50 monthly.
Pay Service 1
Pay Units: 52.
Programming (via satellite): HBO.
Fee: $12.00 monthly.
Video-On-Demand: No
Internet Service
Operational: No.
Telephone Service
None
President: Scott Richardson. Secretary: Sue Richardson. Treasurer: Earl Richardson.
Ownership: Moosehead Enterprises Inc.

BLUE HILL (town)—Formerly served by Adelphia Communications. Now served by Time Warner Cable, PORTLAND, ME [ME0001]. ICA: ME0060.

BOOTHBAY—Formerly served by Adelphia Communications. Now served by Time Warner Cable, PORTLAND, ME [ME0001]. ICA: ME0034.

BRIDGTON—Time Warner Cable. Now served by PORTLAND, ME [ME0001]. ICA: ME0022.

BRISTOL—Time Warner Cable. Now served by PORTLAND, ME [ME0001]. ICA: ME0039.

BRUNSWICK (town)—Comcast Cable. Now served by BOSTON, MA [MA0001]. ICA: ME0010.

BUCKFIELD—Time Warner Cable. Now served by PORTLAND, ME [ME0001]. ICA: ME0064.

BUXTON—Time Warner Cable. Now served by PORTLAND, ME [ME0001]. ICA: ME0011.

CALAIS—Time Warner Cable. Now served by PORTLAND, ME [ME0001]. ICA: ME0024.

CANTON (town)—Time Warner Cable. Now served by PORTLAND, ME [ME0001]. ICA: ME0077.

CARRABASSETT VALLEY—Time Warner Cable. Now served by PORTLAND, ME [ME0001]. ICA: ME0042.

CASTINE—Formerly served by Adelphia Communications. Now served by Time Warner Cable, PORTLAND, ME [ME0001]. ICA: ME0073.

CASTLE HILL—Time Warner Cable. Now served by PRESQUE ISLE, ME [ME0008]. ICA: ME0053.

CHERRYFIELD—Time Warner Cable. Now served by PORTLAND, ME [ME0001]. ICA: ME0111.

CORNISH (town)—Time Warner Cable. Now served by PORTLAND, ME [ME0001]. ICA: ME0041.

DANFORTH—Time Warner Cable, 1 Time Warner Ctr, New York, NY 10019. Phone: 212-484-8000. Web Site: http://www.timewarnercable.com. Also serves Weston. ICA: ME0090.
TV Market Ranking: Below 100 (Weston); Outside TV Markets (DANFORTH). Franchise award date: January 21, 1978. Franchise expiration date: N.A. Began: January 1, 1984.
Channel capacity: N.A. Channels available but not in use: N.A.
Basic Service
Subscribers: 29.
Programming (received off-air): WABI-TV (CBS, CW) Bangor; WAGM-TV (CBS, FOX) Presque Isle; WLBZ (NBC) Bangor; WMED-TV (PBS) Calais; WPFO (FOX) Waterville; WVII-TV (ABC) Bangor.
Programming (via satellite): A&E; AMC; Animal Planet; CMT; CNN; Comedy Central; Discovery Channel; E! HD; ESPN; Food Network; Fox News Channel; Freeform; Hallmark Channel; Hallmark Movies & Mysteries; Lifetime; New England Sports Network; Nickelodeon; QVC; Spike TV; Syfy; TBS; The Weather Channel; TLC; TNT; Trinity Broadcasting Network (TBN); truTV; USA Network; various Canadian stations; WGN America.
Fee: $60.00 installation; $52.75 monthly.
Video-On-Demand: No
Internet Service
Operational: No.
Telephone Service
None
Miles of Plant: 12.0 (coaxial); None (fiber optic). Homes passed: 225.
Ownership: Time Warner Cable.

DENMARK—Time Warner Cable. Now served by PORTLAND, ME [ME0001]. ICA: ME0085.

EAGLE LAKE—Formerly served by Adelphia Communications. Now served by Time Warner Cable, PRESQUE ISLE, ME [ME0008]. ICA: ME0079.

EAST MACHIAS—Formerly served by Pine Tree Cablevision. No longer in operation. ICA: ME0017.

EASTON—Time Warner Cable. Now served by PRESQUE ISLE, ME [ME0008]. ICA: ME0070.

FARMINGTON—Bee Line Cable TV, PO Box 431, Skowhegan, ME 04976. Phones: 207-474-2727 (Local); 800-439-4611. Fax: 207-474-0966. Web Site: http://www.getbeeline.com. Also serves Industry & Wilton. ICA: ME0028.
TV Market Ranking: Below 100 (Industry, Wilton, FARMINGTON).
Channel capacity: N.A. Channels available but not in use: N.A.
Basic Service
Subscribers: 1,512. Commercial subscribers: 7.
Fee: $20.00 installation; $30.34 monthly.
Internet Service
Operational: Yes.
Subscribers: 3,969.
Telephone Service
Digital: Operational
Subscribers: 1,364.
Miles of Plant: 873.0 (coaxial); 307.0 (fiber optic). Homes passed: 9,036.
Vice President & General Manager: George C. Allen.
Ownership: Bee Line Inc. (MSO).

FORT KENT—Formerly served by Adelphia Communications. Now served by Time Warner Cable, PRESQUE ISLE, ME [ME0008]. ICA: ME0031.

FRANKLIN (town)—Time Warner Cable. Now served by, PORTLAND, ME [ME0001]. ICA: ME0058.

FRIENDSHIP (town)—Time Warner Cable. Now served by PORTLAND, ME [ME0001]. ICA: ME0056.

GLENBURN—Time Warner Cable. Now served by PORTLAND, ME [ME0001]. ICA: ME0038.

GREENBUSH (town)—Formerly served by Argent Communications. No longer in operation. ICA: ME0061.

GREENE (town)—Time Warner Cable. Now served by PORTLAND, ME [ME0001]. ICA: ME0021.

GREENVILLE—Moosehead Enterprises, PO Box 526, Greenville, ME 04441. Phone: 207-695-3337. Fax: 207-695-3571. ICA: ME0113.
TV Market Ranking: Outside TV Markets (GREENVILLE).
Channel capacity: N.A. Channels available but not in use: N.A.
Basic Service
Subscribers: 520.
Programming (received off-air): WABI-TV (CBS, CW) Bangor; WLBZ (NBC) Bangor; WMEB-TV (PBS) Orono; WSBK-TV (MNT) Boston; WVII-TV (ABC) Bangor.
Programming (via satellite): A&E; CNN; Discovery Channel; ESPN; ESPN2; Freeform; FX; Great American Country; Hallmark Channel; HGTV; History; Lifetime; Outdoor Channel; QVC; TBS; TNT; Turner Classic Movies; USA Network; WGN America.
Fee: $30.00 installation; $37.50 monthly.
Pay Service 1
Pay Units: 80.
Programming (via satellite): HBO.
Fee: $12.00 monthly.
Video-On-Demand: No
Internet Service
Operational: No.

2017 Edition

D-353

Maine—Cable Systems

Telephone Service
None
President: Scott Richardson. Secretary: Sue Richardson. Treasurer: Earl Richardson.
Ownership: Moosehead Enterprises Inc. (MSO).

GUILFORD—Moosehead Enterprises, PO Box 526, Greenville, ME 04441. Phone: 207-695-3337. Fax: 207-695-3571. ICA: ME0057.
TV Market Ranking: Outside TV Markets (GUILFORD). Franchise award date: N.A. Franchise expiration date: N.A. Began: December 1, 1964.
Channel capacity: N.A. Channels available but not in use: N.A.
Basic Service
Subscribers: 257.
Programming (received off-air): WABI-TV (CBS, CW) Bangor; WLBZ (NBC) Bangor; WMEB-TV (PBS) Orono; WVII-TV (ABC) Bangor; allband FM.
Programming (via microwave): WSBK-TV (MNT) Boston.
Programming (via satellite): A&E; CNN; CW PLUS; Discovery Channel; ESPN; ESPN2; FX; Great American Country; Hallmark Channel; History; Lifetime; QVC; TBS; TNT; Turner Classic Movies; USA Network; WGN America.
Fee: $30.00 installation; $37.50 monthly.
Pay Service 1
Pay Units: 60.
Programming (via satellite): HBO.
Fee: $10.00 installation; $12.00 monthly.
Video-On-Demand: No
Internet Service
Operational: No.
Telephone Service
None
Miles of Plant: 23.0 (coaxial); None (fiber optic).
President: Scott Richardson. Secretary: Sue Richardson. Treasurer: Earl Richardson.
Ownership: Moosehead Enterprises Inc. (MSO).

HANCOCK—Time Warner Cable. Now served by PORTLAND, ME [ME0001]. ICA: ME0035.

HERMON—Time Warner Cable. Now served by PORTLAND, ME [ME0001]. ICA: ME0030.

HOULTON—Time Warner Cable, 1 Time Warner Ctr, New York, NY 10019. Phone: 212-484-8000. Web Site: http://www.timewarnercable.com. Also serves Aroostook County (portions), Bridgewater (town), Hodgdon, Littleton (town), Monticello & Monticello (town). ICA: ME0025.
TV Market Ranking: Below 100 (Bridgewater (town), Littleton (town), Monticello, Aroostook County (portions), Monticello (town)); Outside TV Markets (Hodgdon, HOULTON, Aroostook County (portions)). Franchise award date: N.A. Franchise expiration date: N.A. Began: December 18, 1954.
Channel capacity: N.A. Channels available but not in use: N.A.
Basic Service
Subscribers: 1,235.
Programming (received off-air): WAGM-TV (CBS, FOX) Presque Isle; WMEM-TV (PBS) Presque Isle; allband FM.
Programming (via microwave): WABI-TV (CBS, CW) Bangor; WLBZ (NBC) Bangor; WSBK-TV (MNT) Boston; WVII-TV (ABC) Bangor.
Programming (via satellite): A&E; Animal Planet; CMT; CNN; C-SPAN; Discovery Channel; DIY Network; ESPN; EWTN Global Catholic Network; Fox News Channel; Freeform; History; HLN; Lifetime; MTV; National Geographic Channel; New England Sports Network; Nickelodeon; QVC; Spike TV; Syfy; TBS; The Weather Channel; TLC; TNT; Travel Channel; Trinity Broadcasting Network (TBN); truTV; Turner Classic Movies; TV Land; USA Network; VH1.
Fee: $60.00 installation; $58.25 monthly; $25.00 converter.
Digital Basic Service
Subscribers: N.A.
Programming (via satellite): BBC America; Bloomberg Television; Discovery Kids Channel; Disney XD; DMX Music; ESPN Classic; ESPN2; ESPNews; EVINE Live; Fox Sports 1; FXM; FYI; Golf Channel; Great American Country; GSN; HGTV; History International; LMN; NBCSN; Nick Jr.; Nicktoons; Outdoor Channel; Starz Encore; TeenNick; WE tv.
Pay Service 1
Pay Units: 53.
Programming (via satellite): HBO.
Fee: $10.00 installation; $14.38 monthly.
Pay Service 2
Pay Units: 12.
Programming (via satellite): Showtime.
Fee: $10.00 installation; $12.38 monthly.
Pay Service 3
Pay Units: 15.
Programming (via satellite): The Movie Channel.
Fee: $10.00 installation; $12.38 monthly.
Pay Service 4
Pay Units: 2.
Programming (via satellite): Cinemax.
Fee: $12.38 monthly.
Pay Service 5
Pay Units: 29.
Programming (via satellite): Starz.
Fee: $12.38 monthly.
Digital Pay Service 1
Pay Units: 130.
Programming (via satellite): Cinemax (multiplexed); HBO (multiplexed); Showtime (multiplexed); Starz (multiplexed); Starz Encore (multiplexed); The Movie Channel (multiplexed).
Fee: $12.40 monthly (each).
Video-On-Demand: No
Pay-Per-View
iN DEMAND (delivered digitally); Hot Choice (delivered digitally); Playboy TV (delivered digitally); Fresh (delivered digitally); Shorteez (delivered digitally); ESPN Now (delivered digitally); Sports PPV (delivered digitally).
Internet Service
Operational: Yes. Began: January 1, 2002.
Fee: $19.95 monthly.
Telephone Service
Digital: Operational
Miles of Plant: 50.0 (coaxial); None (fiber optic). Homes passed: 2,500.
Ownership: Time Warner Cable (MSO).

HOWLAND—Time Warner Cable, 1 Time Warner Ctr, New York, NY 10019. Phone: 212-484-8000. Web Site: http://www.timewarnercable.com. Also serves Enfield, Passadumkeag & West Enfield. ICA: ME0092.
TV Market Ranking: Below 100 (Enfield, HOWLAND, Passadumkeag, West Enfield). Franchise award date: January 1, 1979. Franchise expiration date: N.A. Began: November 1, 1979.
Channel capacity: N.A. Channels available but not in use: N.A.
Basic Service
Subscribers: 337.
Programming (received off-air): WABI-TV (CBS, CW) Bangor; WLBZ (NBC) Bangor; WMEB-TV (PBS) Orono; WVII-TV (ABC) Bangor.
Programming (via microwave): WSBK-TV (MNT) Boston.
Programming (via satellite): A&E; Animal Planet; CMT; CNBC; CNN; Comedy Central; C-SPAN; Discovery Channel; Disney Channel; DIY Network; E! HD; ESPN; ESPN2; Food Network; Fox News Channel; Freeform; FXM; Hallmark Channel; Hallmark Movies & Mysteries; History; HLN; Lifetime; MSNBC; MTV; New England Sports Network; Nickelodeon; QVC; Spike TV; Syfy; TBS; The Weather Channel; TLC; TNT; Travel Channel; truTV; USA Network; VH1; WGN America; WPIX (Antenna TV, CW, This TV) New York.
Fee: $60.00 installation; $58.25 monthly; $25.00 converter.
Digital Basic Service
Subscribers: N.A.
Programming (via satellite): BBC America; Bloomberg Television; Cloo; CMT; Destination America; Discovery Kids Channel; Disney XD; ESPN Classic; ESPN2; ESPNews; Fox Sports 1; FXM; FYI; Golf Channel; GSN; HGTV; History International; LMN; MTV Classic; MTV2; National Geographic Channel; Nicktoons; Noggin; Outdoor Channel; OWN: Oprah Winfrey Network; Science Channel; TeenNick; Trinity Broadcasting Network (TBN); Turner Classic Movies.
Digital Pay Service 1
Pay Units: N.A.
Programming (via satellite): Cinemax (multiplexed); HBO; Showtime (multiplexed); Starz (multiplexed); Starz Encore (multiplexed); The Movie Channel (multiplexed).
Video-On-Demand: No
Internet Service
Operational: Yes.
Telephone Service
None
Miles of Plant: 11.0 (coaxial); None (fiber optic). Homes passed: 850.
Ownership: Time Warner Cable.

ISLAND FALLS—Time Warner Cable, 1 Time Warner Ctr, New York, NY 10019. Phone: 212-484-8000. Web Site: http://www.timewarnercable.com. Also serves Patten. ICA: ME0108.
TV Market Ranking: Outside TV Markets (ISLAND FALLS, Patten). Franchise award date: January 1, 1978. Franchise expiration date: N.A. Began: N.A.
Channel capacity: N.A. Channels available but not in use: N.A.
Basic Service
Subscribers: 107.
Programming (received off-air): WABI-TV (CBS, CW) Bangor; WAGM-TV (CBS, FOX) Presque Isle; WLBZ (NBC) Bangor; WMEM-TV (PBS) Presque Isle; WVII-TV (ABC) Bangor.
Programming (via satellite): Animal Planet; CMT; CNN; C-SPAN; Discovery Channel; Disney Channel; E! HD; ESPN; ESPN2; Food Network; Freeform; Hallmark Channel; History; HLN; Lifetime; MTV; New England Sports Network; Nickelodeon; QVC; Spike TV; Syfy; TBS; The Weather Channel; TLC; TNT; Travel Channel; Trinity Broadcasting Network (TBN); Turner Classic Movies; TV Land; USA Network; various Canadian stations; VH1.
Fee: $60.00 installation; $56.95 monthly; $25.00 converter.
Pay Service 1
Pay Units: 9.
Programming (via satellite): Cinemax; HBO.
Fee: $14.50 monthly (each).
Video-On-Demand: No
Internet Service
Operational: No.
Telephone Service
None
Miles of Plant: 15.0 (coaxial); None (fiber optic). Homes passed: 320.
Ownership: Time Warner Cable (MSO).

JACKMAN—Moosehead Enterprises, PO Box 526, Greenville, ME 04441. Phone: 207-695-3337. Fax: 207-695-3571. ICA: ME0065.
TV Market Ranking: Outside TV Markets (JACKMAN). Franchise award date: January 1, 1965. Franchise expiration date: N.A. Began: January 1, 1968.
Channel capacity: N.A. Channels available but not in use: N.A.
Basic Service
Subscribers: 276.
Programming (received off-air): WABI-TV (CBS, CW) Bangor; WCBB (PBS) Augusta; WMTW (ABC) Poland Spring; allband FM.
Programming (via microwave): WSBK-TV (MNT) Boston.
Programming (via satellite): ESPN; TBS; USA Network; WGN America; WXIA-TV (NBC) Atlanta.
Fee: $30.00 installation; $37.50 monthly.
Pay Service 1
Pay Units: 44.
Programming (via satellite): HBO.
Fee: $10.00 installation; $12.00 monthly.
Video-On-Demand: No
Internet Service
Operational: No.
Telephone Service
None
Miles of Plant: 23.0 (coaxial); None (fiber optic). Homes passed: 450.
President: Scott Richardson. Secretary: Sue Richardson. Treasurer: Earl Richardson.
Ownership: Moosehead Enterprises Inc. (MSO).

JAY—Time Warner Cable. Now served by PORTLAND, ME [ME0001]. ICA: ME0093.

JONESPORT—Time Warner Cable. Now served by PORTLAND, ME [ME0001]. ICA: ME0109.

KENDUSKEAG—Time Warner Cable. Now served by PORTLAND, ME [ME0001]. ICA: ME0040.

KENNEBUNK—Time Warner Cable. Now served by PORTLAND, ME [ME0001]. ICA: ME0014.

LEWISTON—Time Warner Cable. Now served by PORTLAND, ME [ME0001]. ICA: ME0003.

LINCOLN—Time Warner Cable. Now served by PORTLAND, ME [ME0001]. ICA: ME0117.

LINCOLNVILLE—Lincolnville Communications. Formerly [ME0094]. This cable system has converted to IPTV, 133 Back Meadow Rd, PO Box 179, Nobleboro, ME 04555-0179. Phones: 207-785-9911; 207-763-9911. Fax: 207-563-6740. E-mail: billing@tidewater.net. Web Site: http://www.lincolnvillecommunications.net. Also serves Alna, Appleton, Boothbay Harbor, Damariscotta, Edgecomb, Hope, Jefferson, Newcastle, Nobleboro, Searsmont & South Bristol. ICA: ME5003.
TV Market Ranking: Below 100 (Hope); Outside TV Markets (LINCOLNVILLE). Franchise award date: July 5, 1988. Franchise

Cable Systems—Maine

expiration date: N.A. Began: October 1, 1989.
Channel capacity: N.A. Channels available but not in use: N.A.

SD Basic
Subscribers: 138.
Programming (received off-air): WABI-TV (CBS, CW) Bangor; WFVX-LD Bangor; WGME-TV (CBS) Portland; WLBZ (NBC) Bangor; WMEB-TV (PBS) Orono; WPME (IND, MNT, Movies!) Lewiston; WPXT (CW, MeTV) Portland; WVII-TV (ABC) Bangor.
Programming (via satellite): A&E; AMC; Animal Planet; CNBC; CNN; Comcast SportsNet New England; C-SPAN; C-SPAN 2; Discovery Channel; Disney Channel; DIY Network; ESPN; ESPN2; Fox News Channel; Freeform; Great American Country; History; HLN; Lifetime; MTV; National Geographic Channel; New England Sports Network; Nickelodeon; Pop; QVC; Syfy; TBS; The Weather Channel; TLC; TNT; Travel Channel; Turner Classic Movies; USA Network; VH1.
Fee: $45.00 installation; $26.95 monthly.

Tier 1 SD
Subscribers: N.A.
Programming (via satellite): DMX Music; FYI; Golf Channel; NBCSN; Outdoor Channel; Science Channel.
Fee: $74.95 monthly.

Tier 2 SD
Subscribers: N.A.
Programming (via satellite): BBC America; Bloomberg Television; Cloo; CMT; Discovery Life Channel; GSN; LMN; MTV Classic; Nick Jr.; TeenNick.
Fee: $94.95 monthly.

Cinemax
Subscribers: N.A.
Fee: $9.00 monthly.

HBO
Subscribers: N.A.
Fee: $20.00 monthly.

Playboy
Subscribers: N.A.
Fee: $7.00 monthly.

Reality Kings
Subscribers: N.A.
Fee: $7.00 monthly.

Showtime/TMC
Subscribers: N.A.
Fee: $13.00 monthly.

Starz/Encore
Subscribers: N.A.
Fee: $12.00 monthly.
Video-On-Demand: No
Internet Service
Operational: No.
Telephone Service
None
President & General Manager: Shirley Manning. Vice President: Cathy Pelletier.
Ownership: Lincolnville Communications Inc.

LINCOLNVILLE—Lincolnville Communications. This cable system has converted to IPTV. See LINCOLNVILLE, ME [ME5003]. ICA: ME0094.

LOVELL (town)—Time Warner Cable. Now served by PORTLAND, ME [ME0001]. ICA: ME0066.

LUBEC—Formerly served by Pine Tree Cablevision. No longer in operation. ICA: ME0110.

MACHIAS—Formerly served by Pine Tree Cablevision. No longer in operation. ICA: ME0095.

MADAWASKA—Time Warner Cable. Now served by PRESQUE ISLE, ME [ME0008]. ICA: ME0026.

MARS HILL—Time Warner Cable. Now served by PRESQUE ISLE, ME [ME0008]. ICA: ME0096.

MATTAWAMKEAG (town)—Mattawamkeag Cablevision, 429 Court St, Houlton, ME 04730-1958. Phones: 207-521-5666; 800-532-4451 (Local only); 207-532-4451. Also serves Mattawamkeag & Winn. ICA: ME0071.
TV Market Ranking: Outside TV Markets (Mattawamkeag, MATTAWAMKEAG (TOWN), Winn). Franchise award date: January 1, 1987. Franchise expiration date: N.A. Began: September 1, 1989.
Channel capacity: N.A. Channels available but not in use: N.A.

Basic Service
Subscribers: N.A.
Programming (received off-air): WABI-TV (CBS, CW) Bangor; WBGR-LD (MeTV) Bangor; WLBZ (NBC) Bangor; WMEB-TV (PBS) Orono; WVII-TV (ABC) Bangor.
Programming (via satellite): AMC; CNN; Comedy Central; Discovery Channel; ESPN; Freeform; Great American Country; Lifetime; Nickelodeon; QVC; Spike TV; TBS; The Weather Channel; TLC; TNT; Trinity Broadcasting Network (TBN); TV Land; USA Network; WGN America; WPIX (Antenna TV, CW, This TV) New York; WSBK-TV (MNT) Boston.
Fee: $25.00 installation; $18.00 converter.

Pay Service 1
Pay Units: N.A.
Programming (via satellite): HBO.
Fee: $15.00 installation; $10.95 monthly.
Video-On-Demand: No
Internet Service
Operational: No.
Telephone Service
None
Miles of Plant: 20.0 (coaxial); None (fiber optic). Homes passed: 450.
General Manager: Donald Dee.
Ownership: Donald G. Dee.

MEDWAY—Time Warner Cable, 1 Time Warner Ctr, New York, NY 10019. Phone: 212-484-8000. Web Site: http://www.timewarnercable.com. ICA: ME0097.
TV Market Ranking: Outside TV Markets (MEDWAY). Franchise award date: January 1, 1978. Franchise expiration date: N.A. Began: November 1, 1979.
Channel capacity: N.A. Channels available but not in use: N.A.

Basic Service
Subscribers: 115.
Programming (received off-air): WABI-TV (CBS, CW) Bangor; WAGM-TV (CBS, FOX) Presque Isle; WFVX-LD Bangor; WLBZ (NBC) Bangor; WMEM-TV (PBS) Presque Isle; WVII-TV (ABC) Bangor.
Programming (via satellite): A&E; Animal Planet; CMT; CNN; CW PLUS; Discovery Channel; Disney Channel; DIY Network; E! HD; ESPN; ESPN2; EWTN Global Catholic Network; Fox News Channel; Freeform; History; HLN; Lifetime; MTV; New England Sports Network; Nickelodeon; Spike TV; Syfy; TBS; The Weather Channel; TLC; TNT; Travel Channel; Trinity Broadcasting Network (TBN); truTV; TV Land; USA Network; WGN America.
Fee: $60.00 installation; $56.95 monthly; $25.00 converter.

Pay Service 1
Pay Units: 9.
Programming (via satellite): HBO.
Fee: $35.00 installation; $14.50 monthly.

Pay Service 2
Pay Units: 3.
Programming (via satellite): Showtime.
Fee: $13.50 monthly.
Video-On-Demand: No
Internet Service
Operational: Yes.
Fee: $19.95 monthly.
Telephone Service
None
Miles of Plant: 18.0 (coaxial); None (fiber optic). Homes passed: 451.
Ownership: Time Warner Cable (MSO).

MILLINOCKET—Bee Line Cable TV, PO Box 431, Skowhegan, ME 04976. Phone: 207-474-2727. Fax: 207-723-2074. Web Site: http://www.getbeeline.com. Also serves East Millinocket. ICA: ME0015.
TV Market Ranking: Outside TV Markets (East Millinocket, MILLINOCKET). Franchise award date: N.A. Franchise expiration date: N.A. Began: March 4, 1966.
Channel capacity: N.A. Channels available but not in use: N.A.

Basic Service
Subscribers: 1,336. Commercial subscribers: 7.
Programming (received off-air): WABI-TV (CBS, CW) Bangor; WBGR-LD (MeTV) Bangor; WLBZ (NBC) Bangor; WMEB-TV (PBS) Orono; WVII-TV (ABC) Bangor; allband FM.
Programming (via satellite): A&E; AMC; CNBC; CNN; Comcast SportsNet New England; Comedy Central; C-SPAN; Discovery Channel; Disney Channel; Disney XD; ESPN; ESPN2; EWTN Global Catholic Network; Freeform; FX; Great American Country; HGTV; History; HLN; Lifetime; MTV; New England Sports Network; Nickelodeon; PIX11; Pop; QVC; Spike TV; Syfy; TBS; The Weather Channel; TLC; TNT; Trinity Broadcasting Network (TBN); Turner Classic Movies; TV Land; USA Network; VH1.
Fee: $20.00 installation; $27.58 monthly.

Digital Basic Service
Subscribers: N.A.
Programming (via satellite): Bloomberg Television; Bravo; Discovery Life Channel; ESPN Classic; FOX College Sports Central; FOX College Sports Pacific; Fox Sports 1; FXM; FYI; Golf Channel; GSN; History International; IFC; National Geographic Channel; Outdoor Channel; WE tv.

Pay Service 1
Pay Units: N.A.
Programming (via satellite): Cinemax; HBO; The Movie Channel.

Digital Pay Service 1
Pay Units: N.A.
Programming (via satellite): Cinemax (multiplexed); HBO (multiplexed); Showtime (multiplexed); Starz (multiplexed); Starz Encore (multiplexed); The Movie Channel (multiplexed).
Video-On-Demand: No

ADVANCED TVFactbook

FULLY SEARCHABLE • CONTINUOUSLY UPDATED • DISCOUNT RATES FOR PRINT PURCHASERS
For more information call **800-771-9202** or visit **www.warren-news.com**

Pay-Per-View
Playboy TV (delivered digitally); Fresh (delivered digitally); Hot Choice (delivered digitally); iN DEMAND (delivered digitally); Sports PPV (delivered digitally).
Internet Service
Operational: Yes.
Fee: $29.95 monthly.
Telephone Service
Digital: Operational
Fee: $34.95 monthly
Miles of Plant: 37.0 (coaxial); None (fiber optic). Homes passed: 4,650.
President: Paul Hannigan. Vice President & General Manager: George Allen. Marketing Director: Edythe May.
Ownership: Bee Line Inc. (MSO).

MILO—Time Warner Cable. Now served by PORTLAND, ME [ME0001]. ICA: ME0036.

MONSON—Moosehead Enterprises, PO Box 526, Greenville, ME 04441. Phone: 207-695-3337. Fax: 207-695-3571. ICA: ME0114.
TV Market Ranking: Outside TV Markets (MONSON).
Channel capacity: N.A. Channels available but not in use: N.A.

Basic Service
Subscribers: 65.
Programming (received off-air): WABI-TV (CBS, CW) Bangor; WLBZ (NBC) Bangor; WMEB-TV (PBS) Orono; WSBK-TV (MNT) Boston; WVII-TV (ABC) Bangor.
Programming (via satellite): A&E; CNN; CW PLUS; Discovery Channel; ESPN; Freeform; Great American Country; Hallmark Channel; QVC; TBS; TNT; Turner Classic Movies; USA Network; WGN America.
Fee: $30.00 installation; $34.50 monthly.

Pay Service 1
Pay Units: 15.
Programming (via satellite): HBO.
Fee: $12.00 monthly.
Video-On-Demand: No
Internet Service
Operational: No.
Telephone Service
None
President: Scott Richardson. Secretary: Sue Richardson. Treasurer: Earl Richardson.
Ownership: Moosehead Enterprises Inc. (MSO).

MONTICELLO (town)—Formerly served by Polaris Cable Services. Now served by Time Warner Cable, HOULTON, ME [ME0025]. ICA: ME0049.

MOUNT DESERT (town)—Time Warner Cable. Now served by PORTLAND, ME [ME0001]. ICA: ME0069.

NEW SHARON (town)—Formerly served by Argent Communications. No longer in operation. ICA: ME0055.

NEWCASTLE—Time Warner Cable. Now served by PORTLAND, ME [ME0001]. ICA: ME0016.

2017 Edition

Maine—Cable Systems

NORTH ANSON—Time Warner Cable. Now served by PORTLAND, ME [ME0001]. ICA: ME0062.

NORWAY—Time Warner Cable. Now served by PORTLAND, ME [ME0001]. ICA: ME0099.

OAKFIELD—Time Warner Cable, 1 Time Warner Ctr, New York, NY 10019. Phone: 212-484-8000. Web Site: http://www.timewarnercable.com. Also serves Dyer Brook, Merrill & Smyrna. ICA: ME0072.
TV Market Ranking: Outside TV Markets (Dyer Brook, Merrill, OAKFIELD, Smyrna). Franchise award date: January 1, 1976. Franchise expiration date: N.A. Began: January 1, 1978.
Channel capacity: N.A. Channels available but not in use: N.A.
Basic Service
Subscribers: 62.
Programming (received off-air): WAGM-TV (CBS, FOX) Presque Isle; WLBZ (NBC) Bangor; WMEM-TV (PBS) Presque Isle; WVII-TV (ABC) Bangor.
Programming (via satellite): A&E; AMC; Animal Planet; Bravo; CMT; CNN; Comedy Central; Discovery Channel; Disney Channel; E! HD; ESPN; ESPN2; Fox News Channel; Freeform; Hallmark Channel; History; HLN; Lifetime; National Geographic Channel; New England Sports Network; Nickelodeon; QVC; Spike TV; Syfy; TBS; The Weather Channel; TNT; Travel Channel; Trinity Broadcasting Network (TBN); truTV; USA Network; various Canadian stations; WGN America.
Fee: $60.00 installation; $54.85 monthly; $25.00 converter.
Pay Service 1
Pay Units: 6.
Programming (via satellite): HBO.
Fee: $35.00 installation; $14.50 monthly.
Video-On-Demand: No
Internet Service
Operational: Yes.
Telephone Service
None
Miles of Plant: 15.0 (coaxial); None (fiber optic). Homes passed: 250.
Ownership: Time Warner Cable (MSO).

PATTEN—Formerly served by Polaris Cable Services. Now served by Time Warner Cable, ISLAND FALLS, ME [ME0108]. ICA: ME0048.

PEMBROKE—Formerly served by Pine Tree Cablevision. No longer in operation. ICA: ME0100.

PITTSFIELD—Time Warner Cable. Now served by PORTLAND, ME [ME0001]. ICA: ME0032.

PLEASANT RIDGE PLANTATION—Formerly served by Pleasant Ridge Cablevision Inc. No longer in operation. ICA: ME0101.

POLAND—Formerly served by Adelphia Communications. No longer in operation. ICA: ME0033.

PORTAGE—Time Warner Cable. Now served by PRESQUE ISLE, ME [ME0008]. ICA: ME0080.

PORTLAND—Time Warner Cable, 118 Johnston Rd, Portland, ME 04102. Phones: 207-253-2200; 207-253-2385. Fax: 207-253-2404. Web Site: http://www.timewarnercable.com. Also serves Acton (town), Addison (town), Albion, Alfred, Alna, Andover, Arundel, Auburn, Augusta, Avon, Baileyville, Baldwin, Bangor, Bar Harbor, Bar Mills, Baring, Bass Harbor, Beals Island, Belfast, Belgrade (town), Belgrade Lakes, Belmont (town), Benton, Bernard, Bethel, Biddeford, Blue Hill (town), Boothbay, Boothbay Harbor, Bradley, Brewer, Bridgton, Bristol (town), Brownville, Bryant Pond, Buckfield (town), Bucksport, Burnham, Buxton, Calais, Camden, Canaan, Canton (town), Cape Elizabeth, Cape Porpoise, Carmel, Carrabassett Valley, Casco, Castine, Chelsea, Cherryfield, China, Clinton, Columbia Falls, Coplin, Corinna, Corinth (town), Cornish (town), Cumberland, Cushing (town), Cutler, Damariscotta, Dayton, Dedham (town), Deer Isle (town), Denmark (town), Dennysville, Detroit (town), Dexter, Dixfield, Dover-Foxcroft, Dresden, East Baldwin, East Boothbay, East Dixfield, East Machias, Eastport, Eddington, Edgecomb, Edmunds Twp., Ellsworth, Embden, Eustis, Fairfield, Falmouth, Farmingdale, Fayette, Franklin, Franklin (town), Friendship (town), Fryeburg, Gardiner, Glenburn, Gorham, Gouldsboro, Gray (town), Greene (town), Greenwood, Hallowell, Hampden, Hancock, Hanover (town), Harrington, Harrison, Hartland, Hermon, Hinkley, Hiram, Holden, Hollis, Jay, Jefferson (town), Jonesport, Kenduskeag, Kennebunk, Kennebunkport, Kezar Falls, Kingfield, Lamoine, Leeds, Levant, Lewiston, Limerick, Limington, Lincoln, Lisbon, Lisbon Falls, Litchfield, Livermore, Livermore Falls, Locke Mills, Lovell (town), Lubec, Lyman, Machias, Machiasport, Manchester, Manset, Marshfield, Mechanic Falls, Mexico, Milbridge, Milford, Milo, Minot, Monmouth, Moody, Mount Desert (town), Mount Vernon (town), Naples, New Gloucester (town), New Harbor, New Portland, New Vineyard, Newcastle, Newport, Newry, Nobleboro, Norridgewock, North Anson, North Berwick, North Haven, North Monmouth, North New Portland, North Vassalboro, North Yarmouth, Norway, Oakland, Ogunquit, Old Orchard Beach, Old Town, Orland, Orono, Orrington, Owls Head, Oxford, Palermo, Palmyra, Paris, Parsonfield, Peaks Island, Pemaquid, Pembroke, Penobscot Indian Island Reservation, Perry, Peru, Phillips, Pittsfield, Pittston, Poland, Port Clyde, Porter, Pownal, Princeton, Randolph, Raymond, Readfield (town), Richmond, Rockland, Rockport (town), Rome (town), Roque Bluffs, Round Pond, Roxbury (town), Rumford, Sabattus, Saco, Scarborough, Searsport, Sebago (town), Shawmut, Sidney (town), Smithfield (town), Solon, Sorrento, South Berwick, South Bristol (town), South Paris, South Portland, South Thomaston (town), Southport (town), Southwest Harbor, Spruce Head, St. Albans, St. George (town), Standish, Steep Falls, Stockton Springs, Stonington, Stratton, Strong, Sullivan, Surry, Tenants Harbor, Thomaston, Thorndike, Tremont, Trenton, Trevett, Turner, Union (town), Unity, Vassalboro, Veazie, Verona, Vinalhaven, Waldoboro, Wales, Warren (town), Waterboro, Waterford (town), Waterville, Wayne, Wells, West Baldwin, West Gardiner, West Paris, West Southport, Westbrook, Westport, Whitefield (town), Whiting, Whitneyville, Windham, Windsor (town), Winslow, Winter Harbor, Winterport, Winthrop, Wiscasset, Woodstock, Wyman, Yarmouth & York, ME; Albany, Bartlett, Brookfield (town), Center Ossipee, Conway, Eaton (town), Effingham, Freedom (town), Glen, Jackson, Jefferson, Kearsarge, Madison (town), Middleton (town), Moultonborough (town), North Conway, Ossipee (town), Sanbornville, Shelburne, Tamworth (town), Tuftonboro (town), Wakefield (town) & Waterville Valley, NH. ICA: ME0001.
TV Market Ranking: 75 (Alfred, Andover, Arundel, Auburn, Baldwin, Bar Mills, Bethel, Biddeford, Boothbay, Boothbay Harbor, Bridgton, Bryant Pond, Buckfield (town), Buxton, Canton (town), Cape Elizabeth, Cape Porpoise, Casco, Cornish (town), Cumberland, Dayton, Denmark (town), Dixfield, Dresden, East Baldwin, Effingham, Falmouth, Farmingdale, Freedom (town), Fryeburg, Gardiner, Gorham, Gray (town), Greene (town), Greenwood, Hallowell, Harrison, Hiram, Hollis, Jay, Kennebunk, Kennebunkport, Kezar Falls, Leeds, Lewiston, Limerick, Limington, Lisbon, Lisbon Falls, Litchfield, Livermore, Livermore Falls, Locke Mills, Lovell (town), Lyman, Manchester, Mechanic Falls, Monmouth, Moody, Naples, New Gloucester (town), North Monmouth, North Yarmouth, Norway, Ogunquit, Old Orchard Beach, Oxford, Paris, Peaks Island, Peru, Poland, Porter, PORTLAND, Pownal, Randolph, Raymond, Readfield (town), Richmond, Sabattus, Saco, Scarborough, Sebago (town), South Paris, South Portland, Southport (town), Standish, Steep Falls, Trevett, Turner, Wales, Waterboro, Waterford (town), Wayne, Wells, West Baldwin, West Gardiner, West Paris, Westbrook, Westport, Windham, Winthrop, Wiscasset, Woodstock, Yarmouth); Below 100 (Alna, Avon, Belfast, Belgrade (town), Belgrade Lakes, Belmont (town), Bradley, Brewer, Bristol (town), Brookfield (town), Bucksport, Burnham, Camden, Canaan, Carmel, Castine, Chelsea, Corinna, Corinth (town), Cushing (town), Damariscotta, Dedham (town), Detroit (town), Dexter, Dover-Foxcroft, East Boothbay, Eddington, Edgecomb, Ellsworth, Embden, Fairfield, Fayette, Franklin, Franklin (town), Friendship (town), Glenburn, Hampden, Hancock, Hartland, Hermon, Hinkley, Holden, Jefferson (town), Kenduskeag, Lamoine, Levant, Middleton (town), Milford, Mount Vernon (town), New Portland, New Vineyard, Newcastle, Newport, Nobleboro, Norridgewock, North Haven, North New Portland, Oakland, Old Town, Orono, Orrington, Owls Head, Palermo, Palmyra, Penobscot Indian Island Reservation, Pittsfield, Pittston, Rockland, Rockport (town), Rome (town), Sanbornville, Searsport, Shawmut, Sidney (town), Smithfield (town), Solon, South Bristol (town), South Thomaston (town), St. Albans, St. George (town), Stockton Springs, Strong, Sullivan, Surry, Thomaston, Thorndike, Trenton, Union (town), Unity, Veazie, Verona, Vinalhaven, Wakefield (town), Waldoboro, Warren (town), Whitefield (town), Whitneyville, Windsor (town), Winslow, Winterport, Wyman, Augusta, Bangor, Lincoln, Milo, North Anson, Waterville); Outside TV Markets (Acton (town), Albany, Baileyville, Bar Harbor, Baring, Bartlett, Bass Harbor, Beals Island, Bernard, Brownville, Carrabassett Valley, Center Ossipee, Columbia Falls, Coplin, Cutler, Deer Isle (town), Dennysville, East Machias, Eastport, Eaton (town), Edmunds Twp., Eustis, Glen, Gouldsboro, Hanover (town), Harrington, Jackson, Jefferson, Kearsarge, Kingfield, Lubec, Machias, Madison (town), Manset, Marshfield, Mexico, Milbridge, Moultonborough (town), Mount Desert (town), Newry, North Berwick, North Conway, Orland, Ossipee (town), Parsonfield, Pembroke, Perry, Phillips, Princeton, Roque Bluffs, Roxbury (town), Rumford, Shelburne, Sorrento, South Berwick, Southwest Harbor, Stonington, Stratton, Tamworth (town), Tremont, Tuftonboro (town), Waterville Valley, Whiting, Winter Harbor, Addison (town), Calais, Cherryfield, Conway, Jonesport, Machiasport, York). Franchise award date: June 27, 1974. Franchise expiration date: N.A. Began: February 1, 1975.
Channel capacity: 69 (operating 2-way). Channels available but not in use: N.A.
Basic Service
Subscribers: 275,991.
Programming (received off-air): WCBB (PBS) Augusta; WCSH (Antenna TV, NBC) Portland; WENH-TV (PBS) Durham; WGME-TV (CBS) Portland; WMTW (ABC) Poland Spring; WPFO (FOX) Waterville; WPME (IND, MNT, Movies!) Lewiston; WPXT (CW, MeTV) Portland.
Programming (via satellite): C-SPAN; EVINE Live; Pop; QVC.
Fee: $64.40 installation; $11.60 monthly.
Expanded Basic Service 1
Subscribers: N.A.
Programming (via satellite): A&E; AMC; Animal Planet; BET; Bravo; Cartoon Network; CMT; CNBC; CNN; Comcast SportsNet New England; Comedy Central; C-SPAN 2; Discovery Channel; Disney Channel; E! HD; ESPN; ESPN2; EWTN Global Catholic Network; Food Network; Fox News Channel; Freeform; FX; Golf Channel; Hallmark Channel; HGTV; History; HLN; Lifetime; LMN; MSNBC; MTV; National Geographic Channel; NBCSN; New England Cable News; New England Sports Network; Nickelodeon; Oxygen; Spike TV; Syfy; TBS; The Weather Channel; TLC; TNT; Travel Channel; truTV; TV Land; USA Network; VH1; WE tv.
Fee: $29.11 monthly.
Digital Basic Service
Subscribers: N.A.
Programming (via satellite): BBC America; Bloomberg Television; Boomerang; CNN International; Cooking Channel; C-SPAN 3; Discovery Digital Networks; Disney XD; DIY Network; ESPN Classic; ESPNews; FamilyNet; FOX College Sports Central; FOX College Sports Pacific; Fox Deportes; Fox Sports 1; Fuse; FXM; FYI; Great American Country; GSN; History International; MC; MTV Classic; MTV2; Nick 2; Nick Jr.; Outdoor Channel; Ovation; TeenNick; Tennis Channel; Trinity Broadcasting Network (TBN).
Digital Pay Service 1
Pay Units: N.A.
Programming (via satellite): Cinemax (multiplexed); HBO (multiplexed); Showtime (multiplexed); Starz (multiplexed); The Movie Channel (multiplexed); TV5MONDE USA.
Fee: $15.95 monthly (each).
Video-On-Demand: Yes
Pay-Per-View
iN DEMAND; Pleasure; iN DEMAND (delivered digitally); Playboy TV (delivered digitally); Fresh (delivered digitally); Hot Choice (delivered digitally); Pleasure (delivered digitally); Shorteez (delivered digitally); Sports PPV (delivered digitally).
Internet Service
Operational: Yes.
Subscribers: 276,159.
Broadband Service: EarthLink, Road Runner.
Fee: $38.45 installation; $44.95 monthly.
Telephone Service
Analog: Not Operational
Digital: Operational
Subscribers: 131,096.
Fee: $39.95 monthly

Cable Systems—Maine

Miles of Plant: 22,811.0 (coaxial); 1,060.0 (fiber optic). Homes passed: 602,766.
Area Vice President for Operations, New England: Paul Schonewolf. Vice President, Engineering: Scott Ducott. Vice President, Government & Public Affairs: Melinda Poore. Marketing Director: Gary Stack. Marketing Manager: Shanna Allen.
Ownership: Time Warner Cable (MSO).

PRESQUE ISLE—Time Warner Cable, 118 Johnston Rd, Portland, ME 04102. Phones: 207-253-2200; 207-253-2385. Fax: 207-253-2404. Web Site: http://www.timewarnercable.com. Also serves Allagash, Allagash (town), Aroostook County, Ashland, Blaine, Caribou, Castle Hill, Caswell (town), Connor (portions), Eagle Lake, Easton, Fort Fairfield, Fort Kent, Frenchville, Grand Isle, Hamlin (town), Limestone, Madawaska, Mapleton, Mars Hill, New Sweden (portions), Plantation St. John, Portage, Portage Lake, Sinclair, St. Agatha, St. Francis, St. Francis Twp., St. John, Van Buren, Wallagrass, Washburn, Westfield & Woodland. ICA: ME0008.
TV Market Ranking: Below 100 (Ashland, Blaine, Caribou, Castle Hill, Caswell (town), Connor (portions), Eagle Lake, Easton, Fort Fairfield, Hamlin (town), Limestone, Mapleton, Mars Hill, New Sweden (portions), Portage, Portage Lake, Sinclair, Van Buren, Washburn, Westfield, Woodland, Aroostook County, PRESQUE ISLE); Outside TV Markets (Allagash, Allagash (town), Fort Kent, Frenchville, Grand Isle, Plantation St. John, St. Agatha, St. Francis, St. Francis Twp., St. John, Wallagrass, Madawaska). Franchise award date: N.A. Franchise expiration date: N.A. Began: July 1, 1960.
Channel capacity: N.A. Channels available but not in use: N.A.
Basic Service
Subscribers: 12,375.
Programming (received off-air): WAGM-TV (CBS, FOX) Presque Isle; WMEM-TV (PBS) Presque Isle.
Programming (via microwave): WLBZ (NBC) Bangor; WVII-TV (ABC) Bangor.
Programming (via satellite): C-SPAN; C-SPAN 2; ION Television; Pop; QVC.
Fee: $61.40 installation; $21.99 monthly; $3.05 converter.
Expanded Basic Service 1
Subscribers: N.A.
Programming (via satellite): A&E; AMC; Animal Planet; Bravo; Cartoon Network; CMT; CNBC; CNN; Comcast SportsNet New England; Comedy Central; CW PLUS; Discovery Channel; Disney Channel; E! HD; ESPN; ESPN Classic; ESPN2; EVINE Live; EWTN Global Catholic Network; Food Network; Fox News Channel; Fox Sports 1; Freeform; FX; Golf Channel; GSN; Hallmark Channel; HGTV; History; HLN; INSP; Lifetime; MSNBC; MTV; National Geographic Channel; NBCSN; New England Sports Network; Nickelodeon; Outdoor Channel; Oxygen; Spike TV; Syfy; TBS; The Weather Channel; TLC; TNT; Travel Channel; truTV; Turner Classic Movies; TV Land; USA Network; VH1; WE tv.
Fee: $30.80 monthly.
Digital Basic Service
Subscribers: N.A.
Programming (via satellite): BBC America; Bloomberg Television; Boomerang; C-SPAN 3; Discovery Digital Networks; Disney XD; DIY Network; DMX Music; ESPNews; Fuse; FXM; FYI; Great American Country; History International; IFC; LMN; MTV Classic; MTV2; Nick Jr.; Ovation; TeenNick; Trinity Broadcasting Network (TBN).

Digital Expanded Basic Service
Subscribers: N.A.
Programming (via satellite): FOX College Sports Central; FOX College Sports Pacific; Fox Deportes.
Fee: $2.95 monthly.
Digital Pay Service 1
Pay Units: N.A.
Programming (via satellite): Cinemax (multiplexed); HBO (multiplexed); Showtime (multiplexed); Starz (multiplexed); The Movie Channel (multiplexed).
Fee: $12.95 monthly (each).
Video-On-Demand: Yes
Pay-Per-View
Hot Choice; iN DEMAND; Sports PPV (delivered digitally); Playboy TV (delivered digitally); Fresh; Pleasure; Hot Choice (delivered digitally); iN DEMAND (delivered digitally); Pleasure (delivered digitally); Fresh (delivered digitally); Shorteez (delivered digitally).
Internet Service
Operational: Yes.
Broadband Service: EarthLink, Road Runner.
Fee: $44.95 monthly.
Telephone Service
Analog: Not Operational
Digital: Operational
Fee: $39.99 monthly
Miles of Plant: 384.0 (coaxial); 170.0 (fiber optic). Homes passed: 14,059.
Area Vice President for Operations, New England: Paul Schonewolf. Vice President, Engineering: Scott Ducott. Vice President, Government & Public Affairs: Melinda Poore. Marketing Director: Gary Stack. Marketing Manager: Shanna Allen.
Ownership: Time Warner Cable (MSO).

RANGELEY (town)—Argent Communications, 10 Benning St., Ste 10, PO Box 235, Bristol, NH 03784. Phones: 877-295-1254; 603-295-1254. Fax: 206-202-1415. E-mail: service@argentcommunications.com. Web Site: http://www.argentcommunications.com. ICA: ME0059.
TV Market Ranking: Outside TV Markets (RANGELEY (TOWN)). Franchise award date: September 1, 1989. Franchise expiration date: N.A. Began: June 17, 1991.
Channel capacity: N.A. Channels available but not in use: N.A.
Basic Service
Subscribers: 311.
Programming (received off-air): WABI-TV (CBS, CW) Bangor; WCBB (PBS) Augusta; WCSH (Antenna TV, NBC) Portland; WMTW (ABC) Poland Spring.
Programming (via microwave): WSBK-TV (MNT) Boston.
Programming (via satellite): C-SPAN; C-SPAN 2; QVC; Trinity Broadcasting Network (TBN).
Fee: Free installation; $41.95 monthly.
Digital Basic Service
Subscribers: N.A.
Programming (via satellite): BBC America; Bloomberg Television; Discovery Life Channel; Disney XD; ESPN Classic; ESPNews; Fox Sports 1; Fuse; FXM; Golf Channel; Great American Country; GSN; LMN; MTV Classic; MTV2; National Geographic Channel; TeenNick; The Word Network; Turner Classic Movies; VH1 Country; WE tv.
Digital Expanded Basic Service
Subscribers: N.A.
Programming (via satellite): DMX Music; FOX College Sports Central; FOX College Sports Pacific; FYI; History International; IFC; NBCSN; Nick Jr.; Nicktoons; Outdoor Channel.
Digital Pay Service 1
Pay Units: N.A.
Programming (via satellite): Cinemax (multiplexed); HBO (multiplexed); Starz (multiplexed); Starz Encore (multiplexed).
Fee: $12.95 monthly (Cinemax or Starz/Encore), $14.95 monthly (HBO).
Video-On-Demand: No
Pay-Per-View
HITS (Headend In The Sky) (delivered digitally); Playboy TV (delivered digitally); Fresh (delivered digitally).
Internet Service
Operational: Yes.
Fee: $20.99-$49.99 monthly.
Telephone Service
Digital: Operational
Fee: $49.95 monthly
Miles of Plant: 15.0 (coaxial); None (fiber optic). Homes passed: 620.
Vice President, Business & Marketing: Andrew Bauer. General Manager: Shawn Bauer.
Ownership: Argent Communications LLC (MSO).

ROCKLAND—Time Warner Cable. Now served by PORTLAND, ME [ME0001]. ICA: ME0005.

ROCKWOOD—Moosehead Enterprises, PO Box 526, Greenville, ME 04441. Phone: 207-695-3337. Fax: 207-695-3571. ICA: ME0115.
TV Market Ranking: Below 100 (ROCKWOOD).
Channel capacity: N.A. Channels available but not in use: N.A.
Basic Service
Subscribers: 109.
Programming (received off-air): WABI-TV (CBS, CW) Bangor; WLBZ (NBC) Bangor; WMEB-TV (PBS) Orono; WVII-TV (ABC) Bangor.
Programming (via satellite): A&E; CNN; Discovery Channel; ESPN; ESPN2; Freeform; History; QVC; TBS; TNT; USA Network; WGN America; WPIX (Antenna TV, CW, This TV) New York.
Fee: $30.00 installation; $34.50 monthly.
Pay Service 1
Pay Units: 9.
Programming (via satellite): HBO.
Fee: $12.00 monthly.
Video-On-Demand: No
Internet Service
Operational: No.
Telephone Service
None
President: Scott Richardson. Secretary: Sue Richardson. Treasurer: Earl Richardson.
Ownership: Moosehead Enterprises Inc. (MSO).

RUMFORD—Formerly served by Adelphia Communications. Now served by Time Warner Cable, PORTLAND, ME [ME0001]. ICA: ME0102.

SANFORD—MetroCast Cablevision, 9 Apple Rd, Belmont, NH 03220-3251. Phones: 800-952-1001; 603-524-4425; 603-332-8629. Fax: 603-335-4106. Web Site: http://www.metrocast.com. Also serves Acton, East Lebanon, Newfield, Shapleigh & Springvale. ICA: ME0012.
TV Market Ranking: 75 (Newfield, SANFORD, Shapleigh, Springvale); Outside TV Markets (Acton, East Lebanon). Franchise award date: July 5, 1972. Franchise expiration date: N.A. Began: July 1, 1973.
Channel capacity: N.A. Channels available but not in use: N.A.
Basic Service
Subscribers: 6,720.
Programming (received off-air): WBZ-TV (CBS, Decades) Boston; WCBB (PBS) Augusta; WCSH (Antenna TV, NBC) Portland; WCVB-TV (ABC, MeTV) Boston; WENH-TV (PBS) Durham; WGBH-TV (PBS) Boston; WGME-TV (CBS) Portland; WHDH (NBC, This TV) Boston; WMTW (ABC) Poland Spring; WMUR-TV (ABC, MeTV) Manchester; WPFO (FOX) Waterville; WPME (IND, MNT, Movies!) Lewiston; WPXT (CW, MeTV) Portland.
Programming (via microwave): New England Cable News.
Programming (via satellite): C-SPAN; C-SPAN 2; EWTN Global Catholic Network; QVC; TBS; various Canadian stations.
Fee: $30.00 installation; $35.95 monthly.
Expanded Basic Service 1
Subscribers: N.A.
Programming (via satellite): A&E; AMC; Animal Planet; Bravo; Cartoon Network; CMT; CNBC; CNN; Comcast SportsNet New England; Comedy Central; Discovery Channel; Disney Channel; E! HD; ESPN; ESPN Classic; ESPN2; Food Network; Fox News Channel; Freeform; FX; Golf Channel; Great American Country; HGTV; History; HLN; Lifetime; MSNBC; MTV; National Geographic Channel; New England Sports Network; Nickelodeon; Spike TV; Syfy; The Weather Channel; TLC; TNT; Travel Channel; TV Land; USA Network; VH1.
Fee: $28.95 monthly.
Digital Basic Service
Subscribers: N.A.
Programming (via satellite): 3ABN; Anime Network; AWE; AXS TV; BBC America; Bloomberg Television; Boomerang; CBS Sports Network; CMT; Cooking Channel; Discovery Digital Networks; Disney XD; DIY Network; ESPN HD; ESPN2 HD; ESPNews; ESPNU; FamilyNet; FOX College Sports Central; FOX College Sports Pacific; Fox Sports 1; Fox Sports 2; Fuse; FYI; GSN; Hallmark Channel; Hallmark Movies & Mysteries; HD Theater; History International; IFC; INSP; LMN; MC; National Geographic Channel HD; NBCSN; NFL Network; Nick Jr.; Nicktoons; Outdoor Channel; Reelz; Sprout; TeenNick; TNT HD; Trinity Broadcasting Network (TBN); Universal HD; UP; WE tv; Weatherscan.
Digital Pay Service 1
Pay Units: N.A.
Programming (via satellite): Cinemax (multiplexed); Cinemax HD; Flix; HBO (multi-

Maine—Cable Systems

plexed); HBO HD; Showtime (multiplexed); Showtime HD; Starz (multiplexed); Starz Encore (multiplexed); Starz HD; Sundance TV; The Movie Channel (multiplexed); The Movie Channel HD.
Fee: $12.95 monthly (each).
Video-On-Demand: Yes
Pay-Per-View
ETC (delivered digitally); Hot Choice (delivered digitally); iN DEMAND; iN DEMAND (delivered digitally); Playboy TV; Playboy TV (delivered digitally); Pleasure (delivered digitally); Fresh (delivered digitally).
Internet Service
Operational: Yes.
Subscribers: 8,166.
Broadband Service: Great Works Internet.com.
Fee: $99.00 installation; $41.95 monthly; $5.00 modem lease; $149.50 modem purchase.
Telephone Service
Digital: Operational
Subscribers: 2,995.
Miles of Plant: 844.0 (coaxial); 289.0 (fiber optic). Homes passed: 16,768.
Vice President, Operations & General Manager: Steve Murdough. Corporate Director, Technical Operations: Jeff Drapeau. Vice President, Advanced Services: Josh Barstow. Regional Manager: Moira Campbell. Programming Director: Linda Stuchell.
Ownership: Harron Communications LP (MSO).

SEARSMONT—Formerly served by Argent Communications. No longer in operation. ICA: ME0087.

SEBAGO (town)—Time Warner Cable. Now served by PORTLAND, ME [ME0001]. ICA: ME0107.

SHERMAN—Pioneer Broadband, 37 North Street, Houlton, ME 04730. Phone: 207-532-1254. Fax: 207-532-7195. E-mail: info@PioneerBroadband.net. Web Site: http://www.pioneerbroadband.net. Also serves Sherman Mills & Stacyville. ICA: ME0074.
TV Market Ranking: Outside TV Markets (SHERMAN, Sherman Mills, Stacyville). Franchise award date: December 2, 1985. Franchise expiration date: N.A. Began: January 1, 1987.
Channel capacity: 34 (not 2-way capable). Channels available but not in use: N.A.
Basic Service
Subscribers: N.A.
Programming (received off-air): WABI-TV (CBS, CW) Bangor; WAGM-TV (CBS, FOX) Presque Isle; WLBZ (NBC) Bangor; WMEM-TV (PBS) Presque Isle; WVII-TV (ABC) Bangor.
Programming (via microwave): WSBK-TV (MNT) Boston.
Programming (via satellite): CNBC; Discovery Channel; ESPN; Freeform; Lifetime; Nickelodeon; QVC; Spike TV; TBS; TNT; Trinity Broadcasting Network (TBN); Turner Classic Movies; USA Network; WGN America; WNBC (COZI TV, NBC) New York; WPIX (Antenna TV, CW, This TV) New York; WWOR-TV (Bounce TV, Buzzr, Heroes & Icons, MNT) Secaucus.
Fee: $50.00 installation.
Pay Service 1
Pay Units: N.A.
Programming (via satellite): HBO.
Fee: $20.00 installation; $11.50 monthly.
Video-On-Demand: No

Internet Service
Operational: No.
Telephone Service
None
Miles of Plant: 15.0 (coaxial); None (fiber optic). Homes passed: 300.
Ownership: Pioneer Broadband.

SIDNEY (town)—Time Warner Cable. Now served by PORTLAND, ME [ME0001]. ICA: ME0045.

SKOWHEGAN—Bee Line Cable TV, PO Box 431, Skowhegan, ME 04976. Phones: 800-439-4611; 207-474-2727. Fax: 207-474-0966. Web Site: http://www.getbeeline.com. Also serves Anson & Madison. ICA: ME0018.
TV Market Ranking: Below 100 (Anson, Madison, SKOWHEGAN). Franchise award date: N.A. Franchise expiration date: N.A. Began: April 1, 1968.
Channel capacity: N.A. Channels available but not in use: N.A.
Basic Service
Subscribers: 2,615. Commercial subscribers: 7.
Programming (received off-air): WABI-TV (CBS, CW) Bangor; WCBB (PBS) Augusta; WCSH (Antenna TV, NBC) Portland; WGME-TV (CBS) Portland; WLBZ (NBC) Bangor; WMTW (ABC) Poland Spring; WPME (IND, MNT, Movies!) Lewiston; WPXT (CW, MeTV) Portland; WVII-TV (ABC) Bangor; 6 FMs.
Programming (via satellite): A&E; CNN; C-SPAN; Discovery Channel; Disney Channel; ESPN; EWTN Global Catholic Network; Freeform; History; HLN; Lifetime; MTV; New England Sports Network; Nickelodeon; Spike TV; TBS; TNT; Trinity Broadcasting Network (TBN); USA Network; VH1.
Fee: $20.00 installation; $28.94 monthly.
Digital Basic Service
Subscribers: N.A.
Programming (via satellite): Bloomberg Television; Bravo; Discovery Life Channel; DMX Music; ESPN Classic; FOX College Sports Central; FOX College Sports Pacific; Fox Sports 1; FXM; FYI; Golf Channel; GSN; History International; IFC; National Geographic Channel; Outdoor Channel; WE tv.
Pay Service 1
Pay Units: 346.
Programming (via satellite): HBO.
Fee: $11.00 monthly.
Pay Service 2
Pay Units: N.A.
Programming (via satellite): Cinemax; Showtime; Starz; Starz Encore; The Movie Channel.
Fee: $8.00 monthly (Cinemax or TMC), $10.00 monthly (Showtime), $11.00 monthly (Starz/Encore).
Digital Pay Service 1
Pay Units: 800.
Programming (via satellite): Cinemax (multiplexed); HBO (multiplexed); Showtime (multiplexed); Starz (multiplexed); Starz Encore (multiplexed); The Movie Channel (multiplexed).
Fee: $8.00 monthly (Cinemax or TMC); $11.00 monthly (HBO or Starz/Encore).
Video-On-Demand: No
Pay-Per-View
Hot Choice (delivered digitally); Playboy TV (delivered digitally); Fresh (delivered digitally); iN DEMAND (delivered digitally).

Internet Service
Operational: Yes.
Subscribers: 3,969.
Fee: $29.95 monthly.
Telephone Service
Digital: Operational
Subscribers: 1,364.
Fee: $34.95 monthly
Miles of Plant: 873.0 (coaxial); 307.0 (fiber optic). Homes passed: 9,036.
President: Paul Hannigan. Vice President & General Manager: George Allen. Marketing Director: Edythe May.
Ownership: Bee Line Inc. (MSO).

SMITHFIELD (town)—Time Warner Cable. Now served by PORTLAND, ME [ME0001]. ICA: ME0103.

SORRENTO—Time Warner Cable. Now served by PORTLAND, ME [ME0001]. ICA: ME0084.

ST. FRANCIS—Formerly served by Adelphia Communications. Now served by Time Warner Cable, PRESQUE ISLE, ME [ME0008]. ICA: ME0054.

STOCKHOLM (town)—Formerly served by Argent Communications. No longer in operations. ICA: ME0086.

STOCKTON SPRINGS—Time Warner Cable. Now served by PORTLAND, ME [ME0001]. ICA: ME0068.

STONINGTON—Formerly served by Adelphia Communications. Now served by Time Warner Cable, PORTLAND, ME [ME0001]. ICA: ME0046.

TEMPLE (town)—Argent Communications, 10 Benning St., Ste 10, PO Box 235, Bristol, NH 03784. Phones: 603-295-1254; 877-295-1254. Fax: 206-202-1415. E-mail: service@argentcommunications.com. Web Site: http://www.argentcommunications.com. ICA: ME0082.
TV Market Ranking: Below 100 (TEMPLE (TOWN)). Franchise award date: May 10, 1989. Franchise expiration date: N.A. Began: September 25, 1989.
Channel capacity: N.A. Channels available but not in use: N.A.
Basic Service
Subscribers: N.A.
Programming (received off-air): WCBB (PBS) Augusta; WCSH (Antenna TV, NBC) Portland; WGME-TV (CBS) Portland; WVII-TV (ABC) Bangor.
Programming (via microwave): WSBK-TV (MNT) Boston.
Programming (via satellite): C-SPAN; QVC; Trinity Broadcasting Network (TBN).
Fee: $56.63 installation; $12.25 monthly; $3.00 converter.
Expanded Basic Service 1
Subscribers: N.A.
Programming (via satellite): A&E; AMC; CNN; Comcast SportsNet New England; Discovery Channel; Disney Channel; ESPN; Freeform; FX; HGTV; History; HLN; Lifetime; MTV; New England Sports Network; Nickelodeon; Spike TV; Syfy; TBS; The Weather Channel; TLC; TNT; USA Network; VH1.
Fee: $20.22 monthly.

Digital Basic Service
Subscribers: N.A.
Programming (via satellite): BBC America; Bloomberg Television; Bravo; Discovery Life Channel; ESPN Classic; ESPNews; FXM; Golf Channel; GSN; Nick Jr.; Nicktoons; Turner Classic Movies; WE tv.
Digital Expanded Basic Service
Subscribers: N.A.
Programming (via satellite): IFC; MC; NBCSN; Outdoor Channel.
Digital Pay Service 1
Pay Units: N.A.
Programming (via satellite): Cinemax (multiplexed); Showtime (multiplexed); Starz (multiplexed); Starz Encore (multiplexed); The Movie Channel (multiplexed).
Fee: $12.95 monthly (each).
Video-On-Demand: No
Pay-Per-View
HITS (Headend In The Sky) (delivered digitally); Playboy TV (delivered digitally); Fresh (delivered digitally).
Internet Service
Operational: Yes.
Fee: $20.99-$49.99 installation.
Telephone Service
Digital: Operational
Fee: $49.95 monthly
Miles of Plant: 16.0 (coaxial); None (fiber optic). Homes passed: 223.
Vice President, Business & Marketing: Andrew Bauer. General Manager: Shawn Bauer.
Ownership: Argent Communications LLC (MSO).

TRENTON—Time Warner Cable. Now served by PORTLAND, ME [ME0001]. ICA: ME0063.

UNION (town)—Time Warner Cable. Now served by PORTLAND, ME [ME0001]. ICA: ME0051.

UNITY—Formerly served by FrontierVision. No longer in operation. ICA: ME0043.

VAN BUREN—Time Warner Cable. Now served by PRESQUE ISLE, ME [ME0008]. ICA: ME0037.

VINALHAVEN—Time Warner Cable. Now served by PORTLAND, ME [ME0001]. ICA: ME0067.

WARREN (town)—Time Warner Cable. Now served by PORTLAND, ME [ME0001]. ICA: ME0105.

WASHBURN—Time Warner Cable. Now served by PRESQUE ISLE, ME [ME0008]. ICA: ME0050.

WATERVILLE—Time Warner Cable. Now served by PORTLAND, ME [ME0001]. ICA: ME0006.

WELD—Formerly served by Argent Communications. No longer in operation. ICA: ME0083.

WINDHAM—Time Warner Cable. Now served by PORTLAND, ME [ME0001]. ICA: ME0019.

WINTER HARBOR—Formerly served by Pine Tree Cablevision. Now served by Time Warner Cable, PORTLAND, ME [ME0001]. ICA: ME0112.

YORK—Time Warner Cable. Now served by PORTLAND, ME [ME0001]. ICA: ME0009.

MARYLAND

Total Systems: 14	Communities with Applications: 0
Total Communities Served: 464	Number of Basic Subscribers: 1,250,512
Franchises Not Yet Operating: 0	Number of Expanded Basic Subscribers: 15,688
Applications Pending: 0	Number of Pay Units: 18,178

Top 100 Markets Represented: Baltimore (14); Harrisburg-Lancaster-York, PA (57); Washington, DC (9).

For a list of cable communities in this section, see the Cable Community Index located in the back of Cable Volume 2.
For explanation of terms used in cable system listings, see p. D-11.

ABINGDON—Armstrong Cable Services, 109 Jarrettsville Rd, Forest Hills, MD 21050. Phones: 410-658-3500; 410-658-5511; 724-283-0925. E-mail: info@zoominternet.net. Web Site: http://armstrongonewire.com/television. Also serves Bel Air, Cardiff, Castleton, Cecil County (portions), Darlington, Dublin, Forest Hill, Harford County (portions), Jarrettsville, Norrisville, Pylesville, Rising Sun, Street & Whiteford, MD; East Nottingham Twp., Elk Twp. (Chester County), Highland Twp. (Chester County), Londonderry Twp. (Chester County), Lower Oxford Twp., Oxford (town), Upper Oxford Twp., West Fallowfield Twp. & West Nottingham Twp., PA. ICA: MD0019. **Note:** This system is an overbuild.
TV Market Ranking: 14 (ABINGDON, Castleton, Dublin, Whiteford); 14,57 (Bel Air, Cardiff, Darlington, Forest Hill, Harford County (portions), Jarrettsville, Pylesville, Street); 57 (Cecil County (portions), East Nottingham Twp., Elk Twp. (Chester County), Highland Twp. (Chester County), Londonderry Twp. (Chester County), Lower Oxford Twp., Oxford (town), Rising Sun, Upper Oxford Twp., West Fallowfield Twp., West Nottingham Twp.). Franchise award date: June 14, 1988. Franchise expiration date: N.A. Began: October 1, 1989.
Channel capacity: 66 (operating 2-way). Channels available but not in use: N.A.
Digital Basic Service
Subscribers: 20,923.
Programming (received off-air): WBAL-TV (NBC) Baltimore; WBFF (FOX, The Country Network, This TV) Baltimore; WGAL (NBC, This TV) Lancaster; WJZ-TV (CBS, Decades) Baltimore; WMAR-TV (ABC, Bounce TV) Baltimore; WMPB (PBS) Baltimore; WNUV (Antenna TV, CW) Baltimore; WPMT (Antenna TV, FOX) York; WUTB (Bounce TV, MNT) Baltimore; WXBU (CW) Lancaster.
Programming (via satellite): A&E; AMC; Animal Planet; Cartoon Network; CMT; CNBC; CNN; Comedy Central; C-SPAN; Discovery Channel; Disney Channel; E! HD; ESPN; ESPN2; EWTN Global Catholic Network; Food Network; Fox News Channel; Freeform; FX; Hallmark Channel; HGTV; History; HLN; Lifetime; LMN; Mid-Atlantic Sports Network (MASN); MSNBC; MTV; Nickelodeon; Pop; QVC; Spike TV; Syfy; TBS; The Weather Channel; TLC; TNT; Trinity Broadcasting Network (TBN); Turner Classic Movies; TV Land; USA Network; VH1.
Fee: $35.00 installation; $23.95 monthly.
Digital Expanded Basic Service
Subscribers: N.A.
Programming (via satellite): BBC America; Bloomberg Television; Boomerang; Chiller; Cloo; CMT; Cooking Channel; Destination America; Discovery Kids Channel; Discovery Life Channel; Disney XD; DIY Network; ESPNews; ESPNU; Fox Sports 1; FYI; Golf Channel; Great American Country; GSN; Hallmark Movies & Mysteries; History International; HRTV; Investigation Discovery; Jewelry Television; LMN; MC; MTV Classic; MTV Hits; MTV Jams; MTV2; National Geographic Channel; NBC Universo; NBCSN; NFL Network; Nick 2; Nick Jr.; Outdoor Channel; OWN: Oprah Winfrey Network; Oxygen; RFD-TV; Science Channel; Sprout; TeenNick; Tennis Channel; Tr3s; VH1 Soul; WE tv.
Fee: $12.00 monthly.
Digital Expanded Basic Service 2
Subscribers: N.A.
Programming (via satellite): A&E HD; Animal Planet HD; CNN HD; Discovery Channel HD; ESPN HD; ESPN2 HD; Food Network HD; Fox News HD; FX HD; HD Theater; HGTV HD; History HD; NFL Network HD; NHL Network HD; Syfy HD; TBS HD; TLC HD; TNT HD; USA Network HD.
Fee: $9.00 monthly.
Digital Pay Service 1
Pay Units: N.A.
Programming (via satellite): Cinemax (multiplexed); Cinemax HD; Flix; HBO (multiplexed); HBO HD; Showtime (multiplexed); Showtime HD; Starz (multiplexed); Starz Encore (multiplexed); Starz HD; The Movie Channel (multiplexed).
Fee: $13.95 monthly (Cinemax, HBO, Showtime/TMC/Flix or Starz/Encore).
Video-On-Demand: No
Internet Service
Operational: Yes. Began: February 28, 2003.
Subscribers: 12,787.
Broadband Service: In-house.
Fee: $30.00 installation; $26.95-$39.95 monthly; $3.49 modem lease.
Telephone Service
Digital: Operational
Subscribers: 5,469.
Fee: $49.95 monthly
Miles of Plant: 1,172.0 (coaxial); 663.0 (fiber optic). Homes passed: 28,826.
Vice President, Financial Reporting: Mark Rankin. General Manager: James Culver. Technical Operations Director: Ken Goodman. Marketing Director: Jud Stewart.
Ownership: Armstrong Group of Companies (MSO).

ANNAPOLIS—Comcast Cable. Now served by TOWSON, MD [MD0003]. ICA: MD0006.

BALTIMORE—Comcast Cable. Now served by TOWSON, MD [MD0003]. ICA: MD0001.

BALTIMORE—Formerly served by Sprint Corp. No longer in operation. ICA: MD0051.

BALTIMORE (Inner Harbor)—Formerly served by Flight Systems Cablevision. No longer in operation. ICA: MD0040.

CAMBRIDGE—Comcast Cable. Now served by TOWSON, MD [MD0003]. ICA: MD0025.

CECILTON—Comcast Cable. Now served by TOWSON, MD [MD0003]. ICA: MD0055.

CHARLES COUNTY (portions)—Comcast Cable. Now served by TOWSON, MD [MD0003]. ICA: MD0012.

CHESAPEAKE BEACH—Comcast Cable. Now served by TOWSON, MD [MD0003]. ICA: MD0032.

CHESAPEAKE CITY—Atlantic Broadband, 330 Drummer Dr, Grasonville, MD 21638-1204. Phones: 888-536-9600 (Customer service); 302-376-7229; 800-441-7068 (Customer service); 800-559-1746; 302-378-0780; 302-378-7050. Fax: 302-378-1478. E-mail: info@atlanticbb.com. Web Site: http://atlanticbb.com. Also serves Delaware City, Middletown (town), New Castle County (portions), Odessa, St. Georges & Townsend, DE; Cecil County (portions), Kent County (portions) & Perry Point, MD. ICA: DE0005.
TV Market Ranking: 14 (Perry Point); Below 100 (Cecil County (portions), Delaware City, Kent County (portions), New Castle County (portions), Odessa, St. Georges, Townsend, CHESAPEAKE CITY, Middletown (town)). Franchise award date: N.A. Franchise expiration date: N.A. Began: September 17, 1980.
Channel capacity: 20 (operating 2-way). Channels available but not in use: N.A.
Basic Service
Subscribers: 3,328.
Programming (received off-air): KYW-TV (CBS, Decades) Philadelphia; WBAL-TV (NBC) Baltimore; WCAU (COZI TV, NBC) Philadelphia; WGTW-TV (TBN) Burlington; WHYY-TV (PBS) Wilmington; WJZ-TV (CBS, Decades) Baltimore; WMAR-TV (ABC, Bounce TV) Baltimore; WNUV (Antenna TV, CW) Baltimore; WPHL-TV (Antenna TV, MNT, This TV) Philadelphia; WPPX-TV (ION) Wilmington; WPSG (CW) Philadelphia; WPVI-TV (ABC, Live Well Network) Philadelphia; WTXF-TV (Buzzr, FOX, Movies!) Philadelphia.
Programming (via satellite): C-SPAN; C-SPAN 2; Mid-Atlantic Sports Network (MASN); QVC.
Fee: $40.00 installation; $21.16 monthly.
Expanded Basic Service 1
Subscribers: 3,200.
Programming (via satellite): A&E; AMC; Animal Planet; BET; Bravo; Cartoon Network; CMT; CNBC; CNN; Comcast SportsNet Philadelphia; Comedy Central; Discovery Channel; Disney Channel; E! HD; ESPN; ESPN2; Food Network; Fox News Channel; Fox Sports 1; Freeform; FX; HGTV; History; HLN; Lifetime; LMN; Mid-Atlantic Sports Network (MASN); MSNBC; MTV; National Geographic Channel; NBCSN; Nickelodeon; Nicktoons; OWN: Oprah Winfrey Network; Spike TV; Syfy; TBS; The Weather Channel; TLC; TNT; Travel Channel; TV Land; USA Network; VH1.
Fee: $51.33 monthly.
Digital Basic Service
Subscribers: N.A.
Programming (via satellite): A&E HD; Animal Planet HD; BBC America; Bloomberg Television; Cooking Channel; Destination America; Discovery Channel HD; Discovery Kids Channel; Disney XD; DIY Network; DMX Music; ESPN Classic; ESPN HD; ESPN2 HD; ESPNews; EWTN Global Catholic Network; Fox Sports 2; FYI; Golf Channel; Great American Country; GSN; Hallmark Channel; HD Theater; History International; IFC; Investigation Discovery; Jewelry Television; LOGO; Mid-Atlantic Sports Network (MASN); MTV Classic; MTV Hits; MTV Jams; MTV2; NFL Network; Nick 2; Nick Jr.; Oxygen; Science Channel; Starz (multiplexed); Starz Encore (multiplexed); Starz HD; TBS HD; TeenNick; TNT HD; Tr3s; Trinity Broadcasting Network (TBN); Turner Classic Movies; TVG Network; VH1 Country; VH1 Soul; WE tv; Weatherscan.
Digital Pay Service 1
Pay Units: N.A.
Programming (via satellite): Cinemax (multiplexed); Cinemax HD; Flix; HBO (multiplexed); HBO HD; Showtime (multiplexed); The Movie Channel (multiplexed).
Fee: $16.95 monthly (Cinemax, HBO or Showtime/TMC/Flix).
Video-On-Demand: Yes
Pay-Per-View
Hot Choice (delivered digitally); iN DEMAND (delivered digitally).
Internet Service
Operational: Yes. Began: January 1, 2004.
Subscribers: 10,181.
Broadband Service: Atlantic Broadband High-Speed Internet.
Fee: $25.00 installation; $22.95-$56.95 monthly.
Telephone Service
Digital: Operational
Subscribers: 3,293.
Fee: $49.95 monthly
Miles of Plant: 1,536.0 (coaxial); 482.0 (fiber optic). Homes passed: 13,523.
Senior Vice President & General Counsel: Bartlett Leber. Vice President & General Manager: Joseph DiJulio. Chief Financial Officer: Patrick Bratton. Marketing Director: Sam McGill. Plant Manager: Lenny Gilbert. Personnel Manager: Susan Gresh. Construction Manager: Rick Hudkins.
Ownership: Atlantic Broadband (MSO).

CRISFIELD—Charter Communications, 216 Moore Ave, PO Box 348, Suffolk, VA 23434. Phones: 314-543-2236; 636-207-5100

Maryland—Cable Systems

(Corporate office); 757-539-0713. Web Site: http://www.charter.com. Also serves Somerset County (portions). ICA: MD0031.
TV Market Ranking: Below 100 (CRISFIELD, Somerset County (portions)). Franchise award date: N.A. Franchise expiration date: N.A. Began: August 13, 1962.
Channel capacity: N.A. Channels available but not in use: N.A.
Digital Basic Service
Subscribers: 957.
Programming (via satellite): BBC America; Bloomberg Television; Discovery Digital Networks; Disney XD; DIY Network; ESPN Classic; ESPNews; FOX College Sports Central; FOX College Sports Pacific; Fuse; FXM; FYI; GSN; History International; IFC; LMN; MC; Mid-Atlantic Sports Network (MASN); National Geographic Channel; Nick 2; Nick Jr.; Nicktoons; Sundance TV; TeenNick; TV Guide Interactive Inc.
Fee: $49.99 installation; $26.99 monthly.
Digital Expanded Basic Service
Subscribers: N.A.
Programming (via satellite): A&E; AMC; Animal Planet; BET; Bravo; Cartoon Network; CMT; CNBC; CNN; Comcast SportsNet Mid-Atlantic; Comedy Central; C-SPAN; C-SPAN 2; Discovery Channel; Disney Channel; E! HD; ESPN; ESPN2; Fox News Channel; Fox Sports 1; Freeform; FX; Golf Channel; Hallmark Channel; HGTV; History; HLN; Lifetime; MTV; Nickelodeon; Oxygen; Spike TV; Syfy; TBS; The Weather Channel; TLC; TNT; Travel Channel; Turner Classic Movies; TV Land; USA Network; VH1; WE tv.
Fee: $47.99 monthly.
Digital Pay Service 1
Pay Units: N.A.
Programming (via satellite): Cinemax (multiplexed); Flix; HBO (multiplexed); Showtime (multiplexed); Starz (multiplexed); Starz Encore (multiplexed); The Movie Channel (multiplexed).
Fee: $10.95 monthly (Cinemax, Showtime or TMC), $11.95 monthly (HBO).
Video-On-Demand: Yes
Pay-Per-View
iN DEMAND (delivered digitally); Playboy TV (delivered digitally); Fresh (delivered digitally); Shorteez (delivered digitally).
Internet Service
Operational: Yes.
Broadband Service: Charter Internet.
Fee: $29.99 monthly.
Telephone Service
Digital: Operational
Miles of Plant: 69.0 (coaxial); None (fiber optic). Homes passed: 2,902.
Vice President & General Manager: Anthony Pope. Marketing Director: Brooke Sinclair. Accounting Director: David Sovanski. Operations Manager: Tom Ross. Marketing Manager: LaRisa Scales.
Ownership: Charter Communications Inc. (MSO).

CUMBERLAND—Atlantic Broadband, 201 South Mechanic St, Cumberland, MD 21502. Phones: 888-536-9600 (Customer service); 814-535-3506. Fax: 814-535-7749. E-mail: info@atlanticbb.com. Web Site: http://atlanticbb.com. Also serves Allegany County, MD; Cumberland Valley Twp., Londonderry Twp. (Bedford County) & Southampton Twp. (Bedford County), PA; Carpendale, Hampshire County, Mineral County, Ridgeley & Romney, WV. ICA: MD0014.
TV Market Ranking: Below 100 (Hampshire County (portions)); Outside TV Markets (Allegany County, Carpendale,

CUMBERLAND, Cumberland Valley Twp., Hampshire County (portions), Londonderry Twp. (Bedford County), Mineral County, Ridgeley, Romney, Southampton Twp. (Bedford County)). Franchise award date: N.A. Franchise expiration date: N.A. Began: December 1, 1951.
Channel capacity: N.A. Channels available but not in use: N.A.
Basic Service
Subscribers: 13,935.
Programming (received off-air): WDCA (Heroes & Icons, MNT, Movies!, Mundo-Max) Washington; WDCW (Antenna TV, CW, This TV) Washington; WHAG-TV (IND) Hagerstown; WJAC-TV (MeTV, NBC) Johnstown; WJAL (IND) Hagerstown; WJLA-TV (ABC, MeTV, Retro TV) Washington; WJZ-TV (CBS, Decades) Baltimore; WNPB-TV (PBS) Morgantown; WTAJ-TV (CBS) Altoona; WTTG (Buzzr, FOX) Washington; WUSA (Bounce TV, CBS, WeatherNation) Washington; WWCP-TV (FOX) Johnstown; WWPB (PBS) Hagerstown; 25 FMs.
Programming (via satellite): C-SPAN; C-SPAN 2; EWTN Global Catholic Network; INSP; ION Television; Jewelry Television; Pop; QVC.
Fee: $40.00 installation; $33.60 monthly; $3.95 converter.
Expanded Basic Service 1
Subscribers: N.A.
Programming (via satellite): A&E; AMC; Animal Planet; BET; Bravo; Cartoon Network; CMT; CNBC; CNN; Comcast SportsNet Mid-Atlantic; Comedy Central; Discovery Channel; Disney Channel; Disney XD; E! HD; ESPN; ESPN2; Food Network; Fox News Channel; Fox Sports 1; Freeform; FX; Golf Channel; GSN; Hallmark Channel; HGTV; History; HLN; Lifetime; Mid-Atlantic Sports Network (MASN); MSNBC; MTV; National Geographic Channel; NBCSN; Nickelodeon; Outdoor Channel; Oxygen; Root Sports Pittsburgh; Spike TV; Syfy; TBS; The Weather Channel; TLC; TNT; Travel Channel; Trinity Broadcasting Network (TBN); truTV; TV Land; USA Network; VH1.
Fee: $36.04 monthly.
Digital Basic Service
Subscribers: N.A.
Programming (via satellite): A&E HD; Animal Planet HD; BBC America; Bloomberg Television; BlueHighways TV; Boomerang; Chiller; CMT; Destination America; Discovery Channel HD; Discovery Life Channel; Disney Channel HD; DIY Network; ESPN Classic; ESPN HD; ESPN2 HD; ESPNews; ESPNU; Fox News HD; Fox Sports 2; FYI; Great American Country; HD Theater; History HD; History International; IFC; Investigation Discovery; LMN; MC; MTV Classic; MTV Hits; MTV Jams; MTV2; NFL Network; NFL Network HD; Nick 2; Nick Jr.; Nicktoons; Outdoor Channel 2 HD; OWN; Oprah Winfrey Network; Root Sports Pittsburgh; Science Channel; Science HD; Starz; Starz Encore; Starz HD; Syfy HD; TBS HD; TeenNick; TLC HD; TNT HD; Turner Classic Movies; TVG Network; USA Network HD; VH1 Soul; WE tv.
Digital Pay Service 1
Pay Units: N.A.
Programming (via satellite): Cinemax (multiplexed); Cinemax HD; Flix; HBO (multiplexed); HBO HD; Showtime (multiplexed); Showtime HD; The Movie Channel (multiplexed).
Fee: $20.00 installation; $15.95 monthly (Cinemax/Cinemax HD, HBO/HBO HD or Showtime/Showtime HD/TMC/Flix).
Video-On-Demand: Yes

Pay-Per-View
Club Jenna (delivered digitally); Hot Choice (delivered digitally); iN DEMAND (delivered digitally); Playboy TV (delivered digitally); Fresh (delivered digitally); Shorteez (delivered digitally); Spice: Xcess (delivered digitally).
Internet Service
Operational: Yes.
Broadband Service: Atlantic Broadband High-Speed Internet.
Fee: $24.95-$57.95 monthly.
Telephone Service
Digital: Operational
Fee: $44.95 monthly
Miles of Plant: 509.0 (coaxial); 54.0 (fiber optic). Homes passed: 29,968.
Senior Vice President & General Counsel: Bartlett Leber. Vice President: David Dane. General Manager: Don Feiertag. Technical Operations Director: Charles Sorchilla. Marketing & Customer Service Director: Dara Leslie. Marketing Manager: Natalie Kurchak.
Ownership: Atlantic Broadband (MSO).

DEEP CREEK LAKE—Formerly served by Comcast Cable. No longer in operation. ICA: MD0044.

DORCHESTER COUNTY (portions)—Bay Country Communications, 502 Maryland Ave, Cambridge, MD 21613. Phone: 410-901-2224. Fax: 410-901-9116. E-mail: questions@bcctv.net. Web Site: http://www.bcctv.com. Also serves Cambridge. ICA: MD0056.
TV Market Ranking: Below 100 (Cambridge, DORCHESTER COUNTY (PORTIONS)); Outside TV Markets (DORCHESTER COUNTY (PORTIONS)).
Channel capacity: N.A. Channels available but not in use: N.A.
Internet Service
Operational: Yes.
Fee: $50.00 installation; $34.95 monthly.
Telephone Service
Digital: Operational
Fee: $25.00 monthly
President: Todd Shilling. Vice President: Scott Shilling.
Ownership: Bay Country Communications.

EASTON—Easton Cable, 201 North Washington St, PO Box 1189, Easton, MD 21601. Phone: 410-822-6110. Fax: 410-822-0743. E-mail: info@eastonutilities.com. Web Site: http://www.eastonutilities.com. ICA: MD0026.
TV Market Ranking: Outside TV Markets (EASTON). Franchise award date: August 28, 1984. Franchise expiration date: N.A. Began: November 1, 1984.
Channel capacity: N.A. Channels available but not in use: N.A.
Basic Service
Subscribers: N.A.
Programming (received off-air): WBAL-TV (NBC) Baltimore; WBFF (FOX, The Country Network, This TV) Baltimore; WBOC-TV (CBS, FOX) Salisbury; WDCA (Heroes & Icons, MNT, Movies!, MundoMax) Washington; WETA-TV (PBS) Washington; WJLA-TV (ABC, MeTV, Retro TV) Washington; WJZ-TV (CBS, Decades) Baltimore; WMAR-TV (ABC, Bounce TV) Baltimore; WMDT (ABC, CW, MeTV) Salisbury; WMPT (PBS) Annapolis; WNUV (Antenna TV, CW) Baltimore; WRC-TV (COZI TV, NBC) Washington; WUSA (Bounce TV, CBS, WeatherNation) Washington; WUTB (Bounce TV, MNT) Baltimore.

Programming (via satellite): BET; CMT; CNN; C-SPAN; C-SPAN 2; Discovery Channel; Freeform; HLN; Lifetime; Pop; QVC; TBS; The Weather Channel; TLC; TNT; Travel Channel; Trinity Broadcasting Network (TBN).
Fee: $39.95 installation; $38.30 monthly.
Expanded Basic Service 1
Subscribers: N.A.
Programming (via satellite): A&E; AMC; Animal Planet; Bravo; Cartoon Network; CNBC; Comcast SportsNet Mid-Atlantic; Comedy Central; Disney Channel; E! HD; ESPN; ESPN2; Food Network; Fox News Channel; Fox Sports 1; FX; Golf Channel; HGTV; History; Mid-Atlantic Sports Network (MASN); MSNBC; MTV; NBCSN; Nickelodeon; Spike TV; Syfy; Turner Classic Movies; TV Land; USA Network; VH1.
Fee: $39.95 installation; $41.99 monthly.
Digital Basic Service
Subscribers: 3,691.
Fee: $77.05 monthly.
Digital Pay Service 1
Pay Units: N.A.
Programming (via satellite): Cinemax (multiplexed); HBO (multiplexed); Showtime; Starz; Starz Encore.
Fee: $12.95 monthly (Cinemax, HBO, Showtime or Starz/Encore).
Video-On-Demand: No
Pay-Per-View
iN DEMAND; Hot Choice.
Internet Service
Operational: Yes. Began: December 11, 1998.
Broadband Service: In-house.
Fee: $44.95 installation; $24.95-$145.00 monthly.
Telephone Service
Digital: Operational
Subscribers: 1,375.
Miles of Plant: 140.0 (coaxial); 60.0 (fiber optic). Homes passed: 11,121.
President & Chief Executive Officer: Hugh Grunden. Vice President, Operations: Geoffrey Oxnam. Chief Technician: Ted Book. Marketing Director: Terri Bennet. Communications Director: Theodore L. Book. Controller: Tracie Thomas.
Ownership: Easton Utilities Commission.

ELKTON—Comcast Cable. Now served by TOWSON, MD [MD0003]. ICA: MD0018.

FREDERICK COUNTY (portions)—Comcast Cable, 11800 Tech Rd, Silver Spring, MD 20904. Phones: 301-273-3418; 301-625-3402; 301-625-3500. Fax: 301-625-3474. Web Site: http://www.comcast.com. Also serves Bolling AFB, U.S. Soldiers' & Airmen's Home, Walter Reed Army Medical Center & Washington (portions), DC; Adamstown, Andrews AFB, Barnesville, Berwyn Heights, Bethesda, Bladensburg, Bowie, Boyds, Brentwood, Brookeville, Brunswick, Burkittsville, Burtonsville, Cabin John, Capitol Heights, Cheverly, Chevy Chase, College Park, Colmar Manor, Cottage City, Damascus, Derwood, District Heights, Edmondston, Emmitsburg, Fairmount Heights, Forest Heights, Fort Detrick, Frederick, Gaithersburg, Garrett Park, Germantown, Glen Echo, Glenarden, Greenbelt, Hancock, Hyattsville, Jefferson, Keedysville, Kensington, Landover Hills, Largo, Laurel (portions), Laytonsville, Libertytown, Middletown, Montgomery County (portions), Morningside, Mount Airy (Frederick County), Mount Rainier, Myersville, New Carrollton, New Market, North Brentwood, Olney, Oxon Hill, Point of Rocks, Poolesville, Potomac, Prince George's County (portions),

Cable Systems—Maryland

Riverdale, Rockville, Rosemont (village), Seat Pleasant, Sharpsburg, Silver Spring, Somerset, Takoma Park, Thurmont, University Park, Upper Marlboro, Walkersville, Washington County (portions), Washington Grove, West Bethesda, Wheaton & Woodsboro, MD; Fulton County (portions), PA; Alexandria, Arlington County (portions), Ashburn, Berryville (town), Boyce, Clarke County (portions), Fairfax County (portions), Frederick County (portions), Front Royal, Hamilton, Leesburg, Loudoun County (portions), Lovettsville, Middleburg, Middleton (town), Paeonien Springs, Purcellville, Rappahannock County (portions), Remington, Round Hill, South Riding, Stephens City, Stephenson, Sterling, Warren County (portions), Washington & Winchester, VA; Bath (town), Berkeley County (portions), Berkeley Springs, Bolivar, Charles Town, Great Cacapon, Harpers Ferry, Hedgesville, Jefferson County (portions), Martinsburg, Morgan County (portions), Ranson & Sheperdstown, WV. ICA: MD0009.

TV Market Ranking: 14 (Libertytown); 5 (Mount Rainier); 74 (Fulton County (portions)); 9 (Alexandria, Andrews AFB, Arlington County (portions), Ashburn, Barnesville, Berwyn Heights, Bladensburg, Bowie, Boyds, Brentwood, Cabin John, Cheverly, College Park, Colmar Manor, Cottage City, Edmondston, Forest Heights, Glen Echo, Glenarden, Greenbelt, Hyattsville, Landover Hills, Leesburg, Loudoun County (portions) (portions), Montgomery County (portions), New Carrollton, North Brentwood, Oxon Hill, Paeonien Springs, Poolesville, Potomac, Riverdale, South Riding, Sterling, University Park, Upper Marlboro, Walter Reed Army Medical Center, Washington (portions)); 9,14 (Bethesda, Brookeville, Burtonsville, Capitol Heights, Chevy Chase, Damascus, Derwood, District Heights, Fairmount Heights, FREDERICK COUNTY (PORTIONS), Gaithersburg, Garrett Park, Germantown, Kensington, Largo, Laurel (portions), Laytonsville, Morningside, Mount Airy (Frederick County), Olney, Prince George's County (portions), Rockville, Seat Pleasant, Silver Spring, Somerset, Takoma Park, Washington Grove, West Bethesda, Wheaton); Below 100 (Adamstown, Bath (town), Berkeley County (portions), Berkeley Springs, Berryville (town), Bolivar, Boyce, Brunswick, Burkittsville, Charles Town, Clarke County (portions), Emmitsburg, Fort Detrick, Frederick County (portions), Great Cacapon, Hamilton, Harpers Ferry, Hedgesville, Jefferson, Keedysville, Lovettsville, Martinsburg, Middleburg, Middleton, Morgan County (portions), Myersville, New Market, Point of Rocks, Purcellville, Ranson, Rappahannock County (portions) (portions), Remington, Rosemont (village), Round Hill, Sharpsburg, Stephenson, Thurmont, Walkersville, Washington County (portions), Woodsboro, Frederick, Hancock, Jefferson County (portions), Stephens City, Winchester, Fulton County (portions), Loudoun County (portions) (portions), FREDERICK COUNTY (PORTIONS)); Outside TV Markets (Middleton (town), Rappahannock County (portions) (portions), Warren County (portions), Washington, Front Royal). Franchise award date: N.A. Franchise expiration date: N.A. Began: July 1, 1967.

Channel capacity: 29 (operating 2-way). Channels available but not in use: N.A.

Basic Service
Subscribers: 547,623. Commercial subscribers: 26,345.
Programming (received off-air): WBAL-TV (NBC) Baltimore; WDCA (Heroes & Icons, MNT, Movies!, MundoMax) Washington; WDCW (Antenna TV, CW, This TV) Washington; WETA-TV (PBS) Washington; WHAG-TV (IND) Hagerstown; WJAL (IND) Hagerstown; WJLA-TV (ABC, MeTV, Retro TV) Washington; WJZ-TV (CBS, Decades) Baltimore; WMAR-TV (ABC, Bounce TV) Baltimore; WMPB (PBS) Baltimore; WNVC (ETV) Fairfax; WRC-TV (COZI TV, NBC) Washington; WTTG (Buzzr, FOX) Washington; WUSA (Bounce TV, CBS, WeatherNation) Washington; WWPX-TV (ION) Martinsburg.
Programming (via microwave): NewsChannel 8.
Programming (via satellite): C-SPAN; EWTN Global Catholic Network; Hallmark Channel; Pop; The Weather Channel; Trinity Broadcasting Network (TBN).
Fee: $29.50-$49.95 installation; $28.20 monthly.

Expanded Basic Service 1
Subscribers: N.A.
Programming (via satellite): A&E; AMC; Animal Planet; BET; CNBC; CNN; Comcast SportsNet Mid-Atlantic; Comedy Central; Discovery Channel; Disney Channel; E! HD; ESPN; ESPN2; Food Network; Fox News Channel; Freeform; FX; Great American Country; HGTV; History; HLN; Lifetime; MSNBC; MTV; Nickelodeon; Spike TV; Syfy; TBS; TLC; TNT; Travel Channel; truTV; TV Land; USA Network; VH1.
Fee: $18.49 monthly.

Digital Basic Service
Subscribers: N.A.
Programming (via satellite): BBC America; Bloomberg Television; Bravo; Discovery Digital Networks; DMX Music; ESPN Classic; Fox Sports 1; Golf Channel; GSN; Mid-Atlantic Sports Network (MASN); National Geographic Channel; NBCSN; Nick Jr.; Outdoor Channel; VH1; VH1 Country; WE tv.

Pay Service 1
Pay Units: N.A.
Programming (via satellite): Cinemax; HBO; Showtime.
Fee: $8.95 monthly (Cinemax or Showtime), $10.95 monthly (HBO).

Digital Pay Service 1
Pay Units: N.A.
Programming (via satellite): Cinemax (multiplexed); Fox Deportes; HBO (multiplexed); Showtime (multiplexed); Starz (multiplexed); Starz Encore (multiplexed); The Movie Channel (multiplexed).

Video-On-Demand: Yes

Pay-Per-View
Hot Choice (delivered digitally); Fresh (delivered digitally).

Internet Service
Operational: Yes. Began: March 1, 2000.
Subscribers: 358,937.
Broadband Service: Comcast High Speed Internet.
Fee: $42.95 monthly.

Telephone Service
Digital: Operational
Subscribers: 214,053.
Miles of Plant: 22,847.0 (coaxial); 6,659.0 (fiber optic). Homes passed: 1,555,272.
Vice President & General Manager: Sanford Ames, Jr. Technical Operations Director: Tom Kearny. Marketing Director: Kevin Oxedine.
Ownership: Comcast Cable Communications Inc. (MSO).

GRANTSVILLE—Comcast Cable. Now served by BLAIRSVILLE, PA [PA0320]. ICA: MD0045.

HAGERSTOWN—Antietam Cable Television Inc, 1000 Willow Cir, Hagerstown, MD 21740-6829. Phones: 301-797-5008 (Technical repair); 301-797-5000 (Customer service). Fax: 301-797-1835. Web Site: http://www.antietamcable.com. Also serves Bolivar, Boonsboro, Clear Spring, Foxville, Funkstown, Smithsburg, Washington County & Williamsport. ICA: MD0011.

TV Market Ranking: Below 100 (Bolivar, Boonsboro, Clear Spring, Foxville, Funkstown, HAGERSTOWN, Smithsburg, Washington County, Williamsport). Franchise award date: August 11, 1966. Franchise expiration date: N.A. Began: February 15, 1967.

Channel capacity: N.A. Channels available but not in use: N.A.

Basic Service
Subscribers: 28,942.
Programming (received off-air): WDCA (Heroes & Icons, MNT, Movies!, MundoMax) Washington; WDCW (Antenna TV, CW, This TV) Washington; WETA-TV (PBS) Washington; WHAG-TV (IND) Hagerstown; WJAL (IND) Hagerstown; WJLA-TV (ABC, MeTV, Retro TV) Washington; WJZ-TV (CBS, Decades) Baltimore; WMAR-TV (ABC, Bounce TV) Baltimore; WRC-TV (COZI TV, NBC) Washington; WTTG (Buzzr, FOX) Washington; WUSA (Bounce TV, CBS, WeatherNation) Washington; WWPB (PBS) Hagerstown; WWPX-TV (ION) Martinsburg; 28 FMs.
Programming (via satellite): C-SPAN; EWTN Global Catholic Network; Pop; Trinity Broadcasting Network (TBN).
Fee: $59.50 installation; $26.95 monthly; $1.57 converter.

Expanded Basic Service 1
Subscribers: N.A.
Programming (via satellite): A&E; AMC; Animal Planet; BET; Bravo; Cartoon Network; CMT; CNBC; CNN; Comcast SportsNet Mid-Atlantic; Comedy Central; C-SPAN 2; Discovery Channel; E! HD; ESPN; ESPN Classic; ESPN2; EVINE Live; Food Network; Fox News Channel; Fox Sports 1; Freeform; FX; Hallmark Channel; HGTV; History; HLN; Lifetime; Mid-Atlantic Sports Network (MASN); MSNBC; MTV; National Geographic Channel; Nickelodeon; QVC; Spike TV; Syfy; TBS; The Weather Channel; TLC; TNT; Travel Channel; truTV; Turner Classic Movies; TV Land; USA Network; VH1.
Fee: $35.75 monthly.

Digital Basic Service
Subscribers: 10,838.
Programming (via satellite): BBC America; Bloomberg Television; Cloo; Cooking Channel; Destination America; Discovery Kids Channel; Disney XD; DIY Network; DMX Music; ESPNews; FOX College Sports Central; FOX College Sports Pacific; Fox Sports 2; FXM; FYI; Golf Channel; Great American Country; GSN; History International; Investigation Discovery; MTV Classic; MTV Hits; MTV2; NBCSN; Nick Jr.; Nicktoons; Outdoor Channel; Ovation; OWN: Oprah Winfrey Network; Science Channel; Starz Encore (multiplexed); TeenNick.
Fee: $5.98 monthly.

Digital Expanded Basic Service
Subscribers: N.A.
Programming (via satellite): AXS TV; ESPN HD; Food Network HD; FX HD; HD Theater; HGTV HD; MGM HD; National Geographic Channel HD; TNT HD; Universal HD.
Fee: $9.95 monthly.

Pay Service 1
Pay Units: 3,102.
Programming (via satellite): Cinemax (multiplexed).
Fee: $20.00 installation; $9.00 monthly.

Pay Service 2
Pay Units: 5,394.
Programming (via satellite): HBO (multiplexed).
Fee: $14.95 monthly.

Pay Service 3
Pay Units: 4,428.
Programming (via satellite): Flix; Showtime.
Fee: $11.25 monthly.

Pay Service 4
Pay Units: 4,176.
Programming (via satellite): Sundance TV; The Movie Channel.
Fee: $20.00 installation; $11.25 monthly.

Digital Pay Service 1
Pay Units: N.A.
Programming (via satellite): Cinemax (multiplexed); Cinemax HD; HBO (multiplexed); HBO HD; Showtime (multiplexed); Showtime HD; Starz (multiplexed); Starz Encore (multiplexed); The Movie Channel.
Fee: $10.95 monthly (Showtime/TMC or Starz), $16.20 monthly (Cinemax/HBO).

Video-On-Demand: Yes

Pay-Per-View
iN DEMAND (delivered digitally); Playboy TV (delivered digitally); Fresh (delivered digitally); Spice: Xcess (delivered digitally).

Internet Service
Operational: Yes.
Subscribers: 27,405.
Broadband Service: Kiva Networking.
Fee: $40.00 installation; $39.95 monthly.

Telephone Service
Digital: Operational
Subscribers: 8,452.
Fee: $34.95 monthly
Miles of Plant: 1,995.0 (coaxial); 430.0 (fiber optic). Homes passed: 56,000.
President & General Manager: Brian Lynch. Chief Technician: Gary Davis. Marketing Director: Cynthia Garland. Ad Sales Manager: Tony Heaton.
Ownership: Schurz Communications Inc. (MSO).

HANCOCK—Comcast Cable. Now served by FREDERICK COUNTY (portions), MD [MD0009]. ICA: MD0028.

HARFORD COUNTY (portions)—Comcast Cable. Now served by TOWSON, MD [MD0003]. ICA: MD0046.

2017 Edition
D-361

Maryland—Cable Systems

HOWARD COUNTY (portions)—Formerly served by Mid-Atlantic Communications. Now served by Comcast Cable, TOWSON, MD [MD0003]. ICA: MD0047.

LEONARDTOWN—MetroCast Communications, 70 East Lancaster Ave, Frazier, PA 19355. Phones: 800-952-1001; 301-373-3201. Web Site: http://www.metrocast.com. Also serves Abell, Avenue, Bushwood, California, Callaway, Chaptico, Clements, Coltons Point, Compton, Dameron, Dryden, Great Mills, Helen, Hollywood, Lexington Park, Loveville, Mechanicsville, Morganza, Naval Air Station Patuxent River, Park Hall, Patuxent Heights, Patuxent River, Piney Point, Ridge, St. Inigoes, St. Mary's County, Tall Timbers & Valley Lee. ICA: MD0024.

TV Market Ranking: 9 (St. Mary's County (portions)); Outside TV Markets (Abell, Avenue, Bushwood, California, Callaway, Chaptico, Clements, Coltons Point, Compton, Dameron, Dryden, Great Mills, Helen, Hollywood, Lexington Park, Loveville, Mechanicsville, Morganza, Naval Air Station Patuxent River, Park Hall, Patuxent Heights, Patuxent River, Piney Point, Ridge, St. Inigoes, Tall Timbers, Valley Lee, LEONARDTOWN, St. Mary's County (portions)). Franchise award date: January 1, 1971. Franchise expiration date: N.A. Began: August 1, 1971.

Channel capacity: N.A. Channels available but not in use: N.A.

Basic Service
Subscribers: 13,599. Commercial subscribers: 1,150.
Programming (received off-air): WBAL-TV (NBC) Baltimore; WDCA (Heroes & Icons, MNT, Movies!, MundoMax) Washington; WDCW (Antenna TV, CW, This TV) Washington; WETA-TV (PBS) Washington; WJLA-TV (ABC, MeTV, Retro TV) Washington; WJZ-TV (CBS, Decades) Baltimore; WMAR-TV (ABC, Bounce TV) Baltimore; WMDO-CD (LATV, UniMas) Washington; WMPT (PBS) Annapolis; WRC-TV (COZI TV, NBC) Washington; WTTG (Buzzr, FOX) Washington; WUSA (Bounce TV, WeatherNation) Washington; allband FM.
Programming (via satellite): QVC.
Fee: $49.95 installation; $34.95 monthly.

Expanded Basic Service 1
Subscribers: N.A.
Programming (via satellite): A&E; AMC; Animal Planet; BET; Bloomberg Television; Bravo; Cartoon Network; CMT; CNBC; CNN; Comcast SportsNet Mid-Atlantic; Comedy Central; C-SPAN; C-SPAN 2; Discovery Channel; E! HD; ESPN; ESPN2; EWTN Global Catholic Network; Food Network; Fox News Channel; Fox Sports 1; Freeform; FX; FXM; Great American Country; HGTV; History; HLN; Lifetime; LMN; MSNBC; MTV; National Geographic Channel; NBCSN; Nickelodeon; Outdoor Channel; Spike TV; Syfy; TBS; The Weather Channel; TLC; TNT; Travel Channel; Trinity Broadcasting Network (TBN); truTV; TV Land; USA Network; VH1; WE tv.
Fee: $27.70 monthly.

Digital Basic Service
Subscribers: N.A.
Programming (via satellite): AWE; AXS TV; BBC America; CMT; Discovery Digital Networks; Disney XD; DMX Music; Fuse; FYI; GSN; HD Theater; History International; National Geographic Channel HD; Nick Jr.; Nicktoons; Outdoor Channel 2 HD; Sprout; TeenNick; TNT HD; Universal HD.

Digital Expanded Basic Service
Subscribers: 178.
Programming (via satellite): ESPN Classic; ESPNews; Golf Channel; IFC; NFL Network; Starz (multiplexed); Starz Encore (multiplexed); Turner Classic Movies.
Fee: $9.95 monthly.

Digital Pay Service 1
Pay Units: 1,078.
Programming (via satellite): Cinemax (multiplexed); HBO (multiplexed); Showtime (multiplexed); Showtime HD; Starz HD; The Movie Channel (multiplexed).
Fee: $9.95 monthly (Cinemax), $12.95 monthly (HBO or Showtime/TMC).

Video-On-Demand: No
Pay-Per-View
ESPN Now (delivered digitally); iN DEMAND (delivered digitally); Sports PPV (delivered digitally).

Internet Service
Operational: Yes. Began: January 1, 1998.
Broadband Service: MetroCast Internet.
Fee: $60.00 installation; $41.95 monthly; $2.95 modem lease; $99.00 modem purchase.

Telephone Service
None
Miles of Plant: 709.0 (coaxial); 65.0 (fiber optic). Homes passed: 34,471.
Chief Financial Officer: Shawn P. Flannery. Vice President, System Operations: Danny Jobe. General Manager: Bernard Hazelwood. Regional Marketing Manager: Kathleen MacLeod. Mid-Atlantic Regional Engineer: Jeff Shearer.
Ownership: Harron Communications LP (MSO).

LEXINGTON PARK—Formerly served by GMP Cable TV. Now served by MetroCast Communications, LEONARDTOWN, MD [MD0024]. ICA: MD0022.

LOTHIAN—Comcast Cable. Now served by TOWSON, MD [MD0003]. ICA: MD0053.

MILLERSVILLE—Broadstripe, 406 Headquarters Dr, Ste 201, Millersville, MD 21108-2554. Phone: 410-987-9300. Fax: 410-987-4890. Web Site: http://www.broadstripe.com. Also serves Annapolis Junction, Anne Arundel County (northern portion), Arnold, Gambrills, Glen Burnie, Hanover, Harmans, Jessup, Laurel, Linthicum, Odenton, Pasadena, Severn & Severna Park. ICA: MD0007. **Note:** This system is an overbuild.

TV Market Ranking: 9 (Annapolis Junction, Arnold, Gambrills, Glen Burnie, Hanover, Harmans, Jessup, Laurel, Linthicum, Odenton, Pasadena, Severn, Severna Park); 9,14 (Anne Arundel County (northern portion), MILLERSVILLE). Franchise award date: July 1, 1971. Franchise expiration date: N.A. Began: August 19, 1990.

Channel capacity: N.A. Channels available but not in use: N.A.

Basic Service
Subscribers: 11,461.
Programming (received off-air): WBAL-TV (NBC) Baltimore; WBFF (FOX, The Country Network, This TV) Baltimore; WETA-TV (PBS) Washington; WHUT-TV (PBS) Washington; WJLA-TV (ABC, MeTV, Retro TV) Washington; WJZ-TV (CBS, Decades) Baltimore; WMAR-TV (ABC, Bounce TV) Baltimore; WMPT (PBS) Annapolis; WNUV (Antenna TV, CW) Baltimore; WRC-TV (COZI TV, NBC) Washington; WTTG (Buzzr, FOX) Washington; WUSA (Bounce TV, CBS, WeatherNation) Washington; WUTB (Bounce TV, MNT) Baltimore.
Programming (via satellite): C-SPAN; Pop.
Fee: $49.95 installation; $21.95 monthly; $2.00 converter.

Expanded Basic Service 1
Subscribers: N.A.
Programming (via satellite): A&E; AMC; Animal Planet; BET; Bravo; Cartoon Network; CMT; CNBC; CNN; Comcast SportsNet Mid-Atlantic; Comedy Central; Cooking Channel; C-SPAN 2; Discovery Channel; Disney Channel; Disney XD; E! HD; ESPN; ESPN2; EVINE Live; Food Network; Fox News Channel; Fox Sports 1; Freeform; FX; Golf Channel; GSN; Hallmark Channel; HGTV; History; HLN; INSP; Lifetime; Mid-Atlantic Sports Network (MASN); MSNBC; MTV; National Geographic Channel; NBCSN; Nickelodeon; OWN: Oprah Winfrey Network; Oxygen; QVC; Spike TV; Syfy; TBS; The Weather Channel; TLC; TNT; Travel Channel; truTV; Turner Classic Movies; TV Land; Univision Studios; USA Network; VH1; WE tv; WGN America.
Fee: $50.00 installation; $37.65 monthly.

Digital Basic Service
Subscribers: N.A.
Programming (via satellite): 3ABN; BBC America; Bloomberg Television; BYUtv; Church Channel; Daystar TV Network; Discovery Digital Networks; DIY Network; ESPN; EWTN Global Catholic Network; FamilyNet; FYI; GEB America; History International; IFC; JUCE TV; LMN; MC; Nick 2; Nick Jr.; Nicktoons; TeenNick; Trinity Broadcasting Network (TBN); UP.

Digital Pay Service 1
Pay Units: N.A.
Programming (via satellite): Cinemax (multiplexed); Cinemax HD; Flix (multiplexed); HBO (multiplexed); HBO HD; Showtime (multiplexed); Showtime HD; Starz (multiplexed); Starz Encore (multiplexed); Starz HD; Sundance TV (multiplexed); The Movie Channel (multiplexed).
Fee: $12.00 monthly (each).

Video-On-Demand: No
Pay-Per-View
iN DEMAND (delivered digitally); Hot Choice (delivered digitally); Juicy (delivered digitally); VaVoom (delivered digitally); SexSee (delivered digitally); Pleasure (delivered digitally).

Internet Service
Operational: Yes.
Broadband Service: Millennium Cable-Speed.
Fee: $59.95 installation; $44.95 monthly; $5.00 modem lease; $300.00 modem purchase.

Telephone Service
Digital: Operational
Fee: $29.95 monthly

Miles of Plant: 1,200.0 (coaxial); None (fiber optic). Homes passed: 100,000.
Chief Executive Officer: John Bjorn. Chief Financial Officer: John Long. General Manager: Rick Oldenburg.
Ownership: Anne Arundel Broadband LLC.

MONTGOMERY COUNTY (portions)—Comcast Cable. Now served by FREDERICK COUNTY (portions), MD [MD0009]. ICA: MD0002.

MONTGOMERY COUNTY (portions)—RCN. This cable system has converted to IPTV. See WASHINGTON, DC (portions) [DC5001]. ICA: MD0054.

OAKLAND—Shentel, 500 Shentel Way, PO Box 459, Edinburg, VA 22824. Phones: 800-743-6835; 540-984-5224. Fax: 540-984-3438. E-mail: customer_service@shentel.net. Web Site: http://www.shentel.com. Also serves Deep Creek, Deer Park, Garrett County (portions), Gorman, Kitzmiller, Loch Lynn Heights & Mountain Lake Park, MD; Bayard, Blaine, Elk Garden, Gormania, Grant County (portions) & Mineral County (portions), WV. ICA: MD0029.

TV Market Ranking: Outside TV Markets (Bayard, Blaine, Deep Creek, Deer Park, Elk Garden, Garrett County (portions), Gorman, Gormania, Grant County (portions), Kitzmiller, Loch Lynn Heights, Mineral County (portions), Mountain Lake Park, OAKLAND). Franchise award date: January 1, 1985. Franchise expiration date: N.A. Began: January 1, 1952.

Channel capacity: 78 (operating 2-way). Channels available but not in use: N.A.

Basic Service
Subscribers: 253.
Programming (received off-air): KDKA-TV (CBS, Decades) Pittsburgh; WBOY-TV (ABC, NBC) Clarksburg; WDTV (CBS) Weston; WGPT (PBS) Oakland; WHAG-TV (IND) Hagerstown; WJAC-TV (MeTV, NBC) Johnstown; WPCB-TV (IND) Greensburg; WPGH-TV (Antenna TV, FOX, The Country Network) Pittsburgh; WPXI (MeTV, NBC) Pittsburgh; WQED (PBS) Pittsburgh; WTAE-TV (ABC, This TV) Pittsburgh.
Programming (via satellite): C-SPAN; Pop; The Weather Channel; Trinity Broadcasting Network (TBN); WGN America.
Fee: $99.95 installation; $34.78 monthly; $1.24 converter.

Expanded Basic Service 1
Subscribers: N.A.
Programming (via satellite): A&E; AMC; Animal Planet; Cartoon Network; CMT; CNBC; CNN; Comedy Central; Discovery Channel; Disney Channel; ESPN; ESPN Classic; ESPN2; Fox News Channel; Fox Sports 1; Freeform; FX; Golf Channel; Great American Country; GSN; Hallmark Channel; HGTV; History; HLN; Lifetime; MSNBC; MTV; National Geographic Channel; Nickelodeon; Outdoor Channel; Root Sports Pittsburgh; Spike TV; Syfy; TBS; TLC; TNT; TV Land; USA Network; VH1; WE tv.
Fee: $34.00 monthly.

Digital Basic Service
Subscribers: N.A.
Programming (via satellite): BBC America; Bloomberg Television; Discovery Digital Networks; Disney XD; DMX Music; ESPNews; EVINE Live; FOX College Sports Central; FOX College Sports Pacific; Fuse; FXM; FYI; History International; IFC; LMN; NBCSN; Turner Classic Movies.

Cable Systems—Maryland

Pay Service 1
Pay Units: N.A.
Programming (via satellite): Cinemax; HBO; Showtime; Starz; Starz Encore; The Movie Channel.
Fee: $17.50 installation; $14.95 -$16.95 monthly (each).
Digital Pay Service 1
Pay Units: N.A.
Programming (via satellite): Cinemax (multiplexed); HBO (multiplexed); Showtime (multiplexed); Starz (multiplexed); Starz Encore (multiplexed); The Movie Channel.
Video-On-Demand: No
Pay-Per-View
iN DEMAND (delivered digitally); Playboy TV (delivered digitally); Fresh (delivered digitally).
Internet Service
Operational: Yes. Began: June 7, 2004.
Broadband Service: Shentel High Speed Internet.
Fee: $45.00 installation; $29.95 monthly.
Telephone Service
Analog: Not Operational
Digital: Operational
Fee: $39.95 monthly
Miles of Plant: 125.0 (coaxial); None (fiber optic).
Vice President, Industry Affairs & Regulatory: Chris Kyle. Assistant Secretary, Associate General Counsel: Ann Flowers.
Ownership: Shentel (MSO).

OCEAN CITY—Comcast Cable. Now served by TOWSON, MD [MD0003]. ICA: MD0010.

OLDTOWN—Formerly served by Oldtown Community Systems Inc. No longer in operation. ICA: MD0035.

PERRYVILLE—Atlantic Broadband, 330 Drummer Dr, Grasonville, MD 21638-1204. Phones: 888-536-9600 (Customer service); 800-559-1746. Web Site: http://atlanticbb.com. Also serves Cecil County (portions) & Port Deposit. ICA: MD0058.
TV Market Ranking: 14 (Cecil County (portions), PERRYVILLE, Port Deposit); Below 100 (Cecil County (portions)).
Channel capacity: N.A. Channels available but not in use: N.A.
Basic Service
Subscribers: 1,311.
Fee: $40.00 installation; $27.06 monthly.
Expanded Basic Service 1
Subscribers: 1,119.
Fee: $45.33 monthly.
Chief Financial Officer: Patrick Bratton.
Ownership: Atlantic Broadband (MSO).

POCOMOKE—Comcast Cable. Now served by TOWSON, MD [MD0003]. ICA: MD0052.

PRINCE FREDERICK—Comcast Cable. Now served by TOWSON, MD [MD0003]. ICA: MD0016.

PRINCE GEORGE'S COUNTY (northern portion)—Comcast Cable. Now served by FREDERICK COUNTY (portions), MD [MD0009]. ICA: MD0004.

PRINCE GEORGE'S COUNTY (portions)—Comcast Cable. Now served by FREDERICK COUNTY (portions), MD [MD0009]. ICA: MD0005.

QUEENSTOWN—Atlantic Broadband, 330 Drummer Dr, Grasonville, MD 21638-1204. Phones: 888-536-9600 (Customer service); 800-559-1746; 410-827-6441. Fax: 410-827-4078. E-mail: info@atlanticbb.com. Web Site: http://atlanticbb.com. Also serves Barclay, Betterton, Caroline County (portions), Centreville, Chestertown, Church Hill, Crumpton, Fairlee, Grasonville, Kennedyville, Kent County (portions), Kent Island, Lynch, Millington, Oxford, Queen Anne's County (portions), Rio Vista, Rock Hall, St. Michaels, Stevensville, Still Pond, Sudlersville, Talbot County (portions), Templeville, Trappe & Warton. ICA: MD0050.
TV Market Ranking: 14 (Betterton, Centreville, Chestertown, Fairlee, Grasonville, Kennedyville, Kent Island, Lynch, Queen Anne's County (portions), QUEENSTOWN, Rock Hall, Stevensville, Still Pond); Below 100 (Trappe); Outside TV Markets (Barclay, Caroline County (portions), Church Hill, Crumpton, Millington, Oxford, Rio Vista, St. Michaels, Sudlersville, Templeville, Warton). Franchise award date: N.A. Franchise expiration date: N.A. Began: March 15, 1983.
Channel capacity: 20 (operating 2-way). Channels available but not in use: N.A.
Basic Service
Subscribers: 13,059.
Programming (received off-air): WBAL-TV (NBC) Baltimore; WBFF (FOX, The Country Network, This TV) Baltimore; WBOC-TV (CBS, FOX) Salisbury; WETA-TV (PBS) Washington; WJZ-TV (CBS, Decades) Baltimore; WMAR-TV (ABC, Bounce TV) Baltimore; WMPT (PBS) Annapolis; WNUV (Antenna TV, CW) Baltimore; WTTG (Buzzr, FOX) Washington; WUSA (Bounce TV, CBS, WeatherNation) Washington; WUTB (Bounce TV, MNT) Baltimore.
Programming (via satellite): C-SPAN; C-SPAN 2; Mid-Atlantic Sports Network (MASN); QVC.
Fee: $40.00 installation; $33.22 monthly.
Expanded Basic Service 1
Subscribers: 11,191.
Programming (via satellite): A&E; AMC; Animal Planet; BET; Bravo; Cartoon Network; CMT; CNBC; CNN; Comedy Central; Discovery Channel; Disney Channel; E! HD; ESPN; ESPN2; Food Network; Fox News Channel; Fox Sports 1; Freeform; FX; HGTV; History; HLN; Lifetime; LMN; Mid-Atlantic Sports Network (MASN); MSNBC; MTV; National Geographic Channel; NBCSN; Nickelodeon; Nicktoons; OWN: Oprah Winfrey Network; Spike TV; Syfy; TBS; The Weather Channel; TLC; TNT; Travel Channel; TV Land; USA Network; VH1.
Fee: $38.77 monthly.
Digital Basic Service
Subscribers: N.A.
Programming (via satellite): A&E HD; Animal Planet HD; BBC America; Bloomberg Television; Cooking Channel; Destination America; Discovery Channel HD; Discovery Kids Channel; Disney XD; DIY Network; ESPN Classic; ESPN HD; ESPN2 HD; ESPNews; EWTN Global Catholic Network; Fox Sports 2; FYI; Golf Channel; Great American Country; GSN; Hallmark Channel; HD Theater; History International; IFC; Investigation Discovery; Jewelry Television; LOGO; MC; Mid-Atlantic Sports Network (MASN); MTV Classic; MTV Hits; MTV Jams; MTV2; NFL Network; Nick 2; Nick Jr.; Oxygen; Science Channel; Starz; Starz Encore; Starz HD; TBS HD; TeenNick; TNT HD; Tr3s; Trinity Broadcasting Network (TBN); Turner Classic Movies; TVG Network; VH1 Country; VH1 Soul; WE tv; Weatherscan.

FULLY SEARCHABLE • CONTINUOUSLY UPDATED • DISCOUNT RATES FOR PRINT PURCHASERS
For more information call **800-771-9202** or visit **www.warren-news.com**

Digital Pay Service 1
Pay Units: N.A.
Programming (via satellite): Cinemax (multiplexed); Cinemax HD; Flix; HBO (multiplexed); HBO HD; Showtime (multiplexed); The Movie Channel (multiplexed).
Fee: $16.95 monthly (Cinemax/Cinemax HD, HBO/HBO HD or Showtime/TMC/Flix).
Video-On-Demand: Yes
Pay-Per-View
Hot Choice (delivered digitally); iN DEMAND (delivered digitally).
Internet Service
Operational: Yes.
Subscribers: 10,181.
Broadband Service: Atlantic Broadband High-Speed Internet.
Fee: $23.95-$57.95 monthly.
Telephone Service
Digital: Operational
Subscribers: 3,293.
Fee: $44.95 monthly
Miles of Plant: 1,479.0 (coaxial); 465.0 (fiber optic). Homes passed: 13,523.
Vice President & General Manager: Joseph Di Julio. Senior Vice President & General Counsel: Bartlett Leber. Marketing Director: Sam McGill. Personnel Manager: Susan Gresh. Construction Manager: Rick Hudkins.
Ownership: Atlantic Broadband (MSO).

RISING SUN—Armstrong Cable Services. Now served by ABINGDON, MD [MD0019]. ICA: MD0057.

SALISBURY—Comcast Cable. Now served by TOWSON, MD [MD0003]. ICA: MD0015.

TOWSON—Comcast Cable, 8031 Corporate Dr, Nottingham, MD 21236. Phone: 410-931-4600. Fax: 410-336-1619. Web Site: http://www.comcast.com. Also serves Bethel, Blades, Bowers Beach, Bridgeville, Broadkill Beach, Camden, Cheswold, Clayton, Delmar, Dewey Beach, Dover, Dover AFB, Ellendale, Farmington, Felton, Fenwick Island, Frederica, Georgetown, Greenwood, Harrington, Hartly, Henlopen Acres, Houston, Kent County (portions), Laurel, Leipsic, Lewes, Lincoln, Little Creek, Magnolia, Milford, Milton, New Castle County (portions), Rehoboth Beach, Seaford, Slaughter Beach, Smyrna, Sussex County (portions), Viola, Woodside & Wyoming, DE; Aberdeen, Aberdeen/Edgewood Proving Ground, Abingdon, Annapolis, Anne Arundel County (portions), Arbutus, Arnold, Baldwin, Baltimore, Baltimore County (unincorporated areas), Bel Air, Belcamp, Benedict, Berlin, Bethlehem, Bivalve, Brookview, Calvert Beach, Cambridge, Cape St. Claire, Caroline County (portions), Carroll County (portions), Catonsville, Cecil County (portions), Cecilton, Charles County (portions), Charlestown, Charlotte Hall, Chesapeake Beach, Chesapeake City, Church Creek, Churchville, Clarksville, Cobb Island, Cockeysville, Cold Spring, Columbia, Cooksville, Crofton, Crownsville, Curtis Bay, Davidsonville, Dayton, Deal Island, Deale, Delmar, Denton, Dorchester County (western portion), Dundalk, Dunkirk, Earleville, East New Market, Edgemere, Edgewood Arsenal, Elkridge, Elkton, Ellicott City, Essex, Fallston, Federalsburg, Forest Hill, Fort Meade, Fruitland, Fulton, Galena, Galestown, Galesville, Gambrills, Glen Burnie, Glenelg, Glenwood, Goldsboro, Greenhills, Greensboro, Hampstead, Hanover, Harford County (portions), Harmans, Harmony, Havre de Grace, Hebron, Henderson, Highland, Hillsboro, Howard County (portions), Hughesville, Hurlock, Indian Head, Jessup, Joppa, Kent County (portions), Kingsville, La Plata, Lansdowne, Laurel (portions), Linthicum, Lisbon, Lothian, Manchester (town), Mardela Springs, Marriottsville, Marydel, Maryland City, Mechanicsville, Middle River, Millersville, Mount Airy (Carroll County), Nanticoke, New Windsor, Newburg, North Beach, North East, Ocean City, Odenton, Overlea, Owings Mills, Parkville, Pasadena, Perry Hall, Perryman, Pikesville, Pocomoke, Pomfret, Preston, Prince Frederick, Princess Anne, Queen Anne, Randallstown, Reids Grove, Reisterstown, Ridgely, Rosedale, Salisbury, Savage, Secretary, Severn, Severna Park, Sharptown, Sherwood Forest, Simpsonville, Snow Hill, Somerset County (portions), St. Mary's City, Sykesville, Taneytown, Tanyard, Timonium-Lutherville, Union Bridge, Vienna, Waldorf, Warwick, West Friendship, Westminster, Wicomico County (portions), Wicomico County (southwestern portion), Woodbine, Woodlawn, Woodstock & Worcester County (portions), MD; Mount Joy, PA. ICA: MD0003.
TV Market Ranking: 14 (Aberdeen (portions), Aberdeen/Edgewood Proving Ground, Abingdon, Baldwin, Baltimore County (unincorporated areas), Belcamp, Cockeysville, Dundalk, Edgemere, Edgewood Arsenal, Essex, Fallston, Harford County (portions), Joppa, Kingsville, Manchester (town), Middle River, Overlea, Owings Mills, Parkville, Perry Hall, Perryman, Pikesville, Reisterstown, Rosedale, Timonium-Lutherville); 14,57 (Bel Air, Cecil County (portions), Churchville, Forest Hill, Hampstead, Havre de Grace, New Windsor, Westminster); 57 (Mount Joy, Taneytown); 57,9 (Union Bridge); 9 (Benedict, Charles County (portions), Charlotte Hall, Chesapeake Beach, Cooksville, Dayton, Deale, Dunkirk, Fulton, Galesville, Glenelg, Glenwood, Highland, Howard County (portions), Hughesville, Indian Head, Jessup, La Plata, Linthicum, Lisbon, Lothian, Mechanicsville, North Beach, Pomfret, Waldorf, West Friendship, Woodbine); 9,14 (Annapolis, Anne Arundel County (portions), Arbutus, Arnold, Baltimore, Cape St. Claire, Carroll County (portions), Catonsville, Clarksville, Cold Spring, Columbia, Crofton, Crownsville, Curtis Bay, Davidsonville, Elkridge, Ellicott City, Fort Meade, Gambrills, Glen Burnie, Greenhills, Hanover, Harmans, Lansdowne, Laurel (portions), Marriottsville, Maryland City, Millersville, Mount Airy (Carroll County), Odenton, Pasadena, Randallstown, Savage, Severn, Severna Park, Sherwood Forest, Simpsonville,

2017 Edition D-363

Maryland—Cable Systems

Sykesville, TOWSON (portions), Woodlawn, Woodstock); Below 100 (Berlin, Bethel, Bethlehem, Bivalve, Blades, Bowers Beach, Bridgeville, Broadkill Beach, Brookview, Charlestown, Chesapeake City, Church Creek, Clayton, Deal Island, Delmar, Delmar, Dewey Beach, Earleville, East New Market, Ellendale, Farmington, Federalsburg, Fenwick Island, Frederica, Fruitland, Galena, Galestown, Georgetown, Greenwood, Harmony, Hebron, Henlopen Acres, Hurlock, Kent County (portions), Laurel, Leipsic, Lewes, Lincoln, Little Creek, Mardela Springs, Milton, Nanticoke, Newburg, North East, Pocomoke, Preston, Princess Anne, Reids Grove, Seaford, Secretary, Sharptown, Slaughter Beach, Smyrna, Snow Hill, Somerset County (portions), Sussex County (portions), Tanyard, Vienna, Warwick, Wicomico County (portions), Wicomico County (southwestern portion), Worcester County (portions), Cambridge, Cecilton, Dorchester County (western portion), Dover, Elkton, Kent County (portions), Milford, Ocean City, Rehoboth Beach, Salisbury, Cecil County (portions), Mechanicsville, Carroll County (portions) (portions)); Outside TV Markets (Calvert Beach, Camden, Caroline County (portions), Cheswold, Cobb Island, Denton, Dover AFB, Felton, Goldsboro, Greensboro, Harrington, Hartly, Henderson, Hillsboro, Houston, Magnolia, Marydel, Prince Frederick, Queen Anne, Ridgely, St. Mary's City, Viola, Woodside, Wyoming, Dorchester County (western portion), Kent County (portions), Charles County (portions)). Franchise award date: N.A. Franchise expiration date: N.A. Began: October 1, 1978.
Channel capacity: N.A. Channels available but not in use: N.A.

Basic Service
Subscribers: 583,920. Commercial subscribers: 15,045.
Programming (received off-air): WBAL-TV (NBC) Baltimore; WBFF (FOX, The Country Network, This TV) Baltimore; WETA-TV (PBS) Washington; WFDC-DT (getTV, UNV) Arlington; WHUT-TV (PBS) Washington; WJZ-TV (CBS, Decades) Baltimore; WMAR-TV (ABC, Bounce TV) Baltimore; WMDO-CD (LATV, UniMas) Washington; WMPB (PBS) Baltimore; WNUV (Antenna TV, CW) Baltimore.
Programming (via satellite): A&E; AMC; Animal Planet; BET; Bravo; Cartoon Network; CMT; CNBC; CNN; Comcast Network Philadelphia; Comcast SportsNet Mid-Atlantic; Comedy Central; C-SPAN; C-SPAN 2; Discovery Channel; Disney Channel; E! HD; ESPN; ESPN2; EWTN Global Catholic Network; Food Network; Fox News Channel; Fox Sports 1; Freeform; FX; Golf Channel; Hallmark Channel; HGTV; History; HLN; ION Television; Lifetime; Mid-Atlantic Sports Network (MASN); MSNBC; MTV; NBCSN; Nickelodeon; OWN: Oprah Winfrey Network; Pop; QVC; Spike TV; Syfy; TBS; The Weather Channel; TLC; Travel Channel; Trinity Broadcasting Network (TBN); truTV; Turner Classic Movies; TV Land; TV One; USA Network; VH1; WGN America.
Fee: $39.95-$49.95 installation; $28.20 monthly; $2.34 converter.

Digital Basic Service
Subscribers: N.A.
Programming (via satellite): A&E HD; AMC; Animal Planet HD; BBC America; Bloomberg Television; BTN; CBS Sports Network; Cine Mexicano; Cinelatino; CMT; CNN en Espanol; CNN HD; Cooking Channel; C-SPAN 2; C-SPAN 3; Destination America; Discovery Channel HD; Discovery Kids Channel; Disney Channel HD; Disney XD; DIY Network; ESPN Classic; ESPN Deportes; ESPN HD; ESPN2 HD; ESPNews; Flix; Food Network HD; FOX College Sports Central; FOX College Sports Pacific; Fox Deportes; Freeform HD; Fuse; FYI; Golf Channel HD; GolTV; Great American Country; GSN; HD Theater; HGTV HD; History; History en Espanol; History HD; IFC; Investigation Discovery; ION Television; Jewelry Television; Korean Channel; LMN; LOGO; MC; MLB Network; MoviePlex; MTV Classic; MTV Hits; MTV Jams; MTV Live; MTV2; Nat Geo WILD; National Geographic Channel; National Geographic Channel HD; NBA TV; NBC Universo; NFL Network; NFL Network HD; NHL Network; Nick 2; Nick Jr.; Nicktoons; Oxygen; RTN; Science Channel; Science HD; Sprout; Starz Encore (multiplexed); Sundance TV; Syfy HD; TBS HD; TeenNick; Telemundo; Tennis Channel; The Word Network; TLC HD; TNT HD; TV Asia; TVG Network; UniMas; Universal HD; Univision; UP; USA Network HD; Versus HD; VH1 Soul; ViendoMovies; WE tv; Weatherscan; Zee TV.

Digital Pay Service 1
Pay Units: N.A.
Programming (via satellite): Cinemax (multiplexed); Cinemax HD; HBO (multiplexed); HBO HD; HBO on Demand; Playboy TV; Showtime (multiplexed); Showtime HD; Starz (multiplexed); Starz HD; The Movie Channel (multiplexed).
Fee: $15.99 monthly (Cinemax, Showtime/TMC or Starz), $17.99 monthly (HBO).

Video-On-Demand: Yes

Pay-Per-View
iN DEMAND (delivered digitally), Addressable: No; Playboy TV (delivered digitally); NHL Center Ice (delivered digitally); iN DEMAND; MLB Extra Innings (delivered digitally); Fresh (delivered digitally); Spice: Xcess (delivered digitally); NBA League Pass (delivered digitally); NBA TV (delivered digitally).

Internet Service
Operational: Yes.
Subscribers: 568,169.
Broadband Service: Comcast High Speed Internet.
Fee: $42.95 monthly; $199.00 modem purchase.

Telephone Service
Digital: Operational
Subscribers: 198,939.
Fee: $44.95 monthly

Miles of Plant: 28,792.0 (coaxial); 7,206.0 (fiber optic). Homes passed: 1,266,732.
Area Vice President & General Manager: Bryan Lynch. Regional Vice President, Marketing: Mark Watts. Technical Operations Director: Brady Hood. Engineering Director: Pete Sarkisian. Marketing Director: Chris Shea. Marketing Manager: Lisa Casper.; Michael Cuccurullo.
Ownership: Comcast Cable Communications Inc. (MSO).

WARWICK—Formerly served by Mid-Atlantic Communications. Now served by Comcast Cable, TOWSON, MD [MD0003]. ICA: MD0027.

WESTMINSTER—Comcast Cable. Now served by TOWSON, MD [MD0003]. ICA: MD0042.

MASSACHUSETTS

Total Systems: 10	Communities with Applications: 0
Total Communities Served: 368	Number of Basic Subscribers: 1,817,403
Franchises Not Yet Operating: 0	Number of Expanded Basic Subscribers: 0
Applications Pending: 0	Number of Pay Units: 0

Top 100 Markets Represented: Hartford-New Haven-New Britain-Waterbury-New London, CT (19); Providence, RI-New Bedford, MA (33); Albany-Schenectady-Troy, NY (34); Boston-Cambridge-Worcester-Lawrence (6).

For a list of cable communities in this section, see the Cable Community Index located in the back of Cable Volume 2.
For explanation of terms used in cable system listings, see p. D-11.

AMESBURY—Comcast Cable. Now served by BOSTON, MA [MA0001]. ICA: MA0052.

AMHERST—Comcast Cable. Now served by BURLINGTON, VT [VT0001]. ICA: MA0057.

ANDOVER—Comcast Cable. Now served by BOSTON, MA [MA0001]. ICA: MA0022.

ARLINGTON—Comcast Cable. Now served by BOSTON, MA [MA0001]. ICA: MA0009.

ATHOL—Time Warner Cable. Now served by KEENE, NH [NH0009]. ICA: MA0062.

BELCHERTOWN—Charter Communications. Now served by CHICOPEE, MA [MA0082]. ICA: MA0069.

BERNARDSTON—Comcast Cable. Now served by BURLINGTON, VT [VT0001]. ICA: MA0077.

BEVERLY—Comcast Cable. Now served by BOSTON, MA [MA0001]. ICA: MA0020.

BOSTON—Comcast Cable, 676 Island Pond Rd, Manchester, NH 03109. Phones: 413-730-4500 (Administrative office); 800-266-2278 (Customer service). Fax: 978-207-2312. Web Site: http://www.comcast.com. Also serves Bath, Berwick, Bowdoin (town), Bowdoinham (town), Brunswick (town), Durham (town), Eliot, Freeport (town), Harpswell, Kittery, Phippsburg (town), South Berwick, Topsham, West Bath & Woolwich, ME; Abington, Acton, Acushnet, Allston, Amesbury, Andover, Aquinnah, Arlington, Ashburnham, Ashby (town), Ashland, Attleboro, Avon, Ayer, Barnstable, Bedford, Bellingham, Belmont, Berkley, Beverly, Billerica, Blackstone, Bolton, Bourne, Boxborough, Boxford, Braintree, Brewster, Bridgewater, Brighton, Brockton, Brookline, Burlington, Cambridge, Canton, Carlisle (town), Carver, Charlestown, Chatham, Chelmsford, Chelsea, Chilmark, Clinton, Cohasset, Concord, Danvers, Dartmouth, Dedham, Dennis, Dighton, Dorchester, Dover, Dracut, Duxbury, East Boston, East Bridgewater, East Falmouth, Eastham, Easton, Edgartown, Essex, Everett, Fairhaven, Fall River, Falmouth, Fitchburg, Foxborough, Framingham, Franklin, Freetown, Gardner, Georgetown, Gloucester, Groveland, Halifax, Hamilton, Hanover, Hanscom AFB, Hanson, Harwich, Haverhill, Hingham, Holbrook, Holliston, Hopedale, Hopkinton, Hudson, Hull, Hyde Park, Ipswich, Jamaica Plain, Kingston, Lakeville, Lancaster, Lawrence, Leominster, Lexington, Lincoln (town), Littleton (town), Lowell, Lunenburg, Lynn, Lynnfield, Malden, Manchester-by-the-Sea (town), Mansfield, Marblehead, Marion, Marlborough, Marshfield, Mashpee, Mattapan, Mattapoisett, Maynard, Medfield, Medford, Medway, Melrose, Mendon, Merrimac, Methuen, Middleborough, Middleton, Milford, Millis, Milton, Nahant, Nantucket, Natick, Needham, New Bedford, Newbury, Newburyport, Newton, Norfolk, North Andover, North Attleboro, North Reading, Norton, Norwell, Norwood, Oak Bluffs, Orleans, Otis Air National Guard, Peabody, Pembroke, Phillipston, Plainville, Plymouth, Plympton, Provincetown, Quincy, Randolph, Raynham, Reading, Rehoboth, Revere, Rochester, Rockland, Rockport, Roslindale, Rowley, Roxbury, Salem, Salisbury, Sandwich, Saugus, Scituate, Seekonk, Sharon, Sherborn, Shirley (town), Somerset, Somerville, South Boston, South Yarmouth, Sterling, Stoneham, Stoughton, Stow, Sudbury, Swampscott, Swansea, Taunton, Templeton, Tewksbury, Tisbury, Topsfield, Townsend (town), Truro, Tyngsborough, Upton, Vineyard Haven, Wakefield, Walpole, Waltham, Wareham, Watertown, Wayland, Wellesley, Wellfleet, Wenham, West Bridgewater, West Newbury, West Roxbury, West Tisbury, Westford, Westminster, Weston, Westwood, Weymouth, Whitman, Wilmington, Winchendon, Winchester, Winthrop, Woburn, Wrentham, Yarmouth & Yarmouth (town), MA; Allenstown, Amherst, Antrim, Atkinson, Auburn, Bedford, Bennington, Boscawen, Bow, Brentwood, Candia, Canterbury, Chester, Chichester, Concord, Danville, Deering, Derry, Dover, Durham, East Kingston, Epping, Exeter, Francestown, Fremont, Goffstown, Greenland, Greenville, Hampstead, Hampton, Hampton Falls, Hancock, Henniker, Hillsborough, Hooksett, Hopkinton, Hudson, Jaffrey, Kensington, Kingston, Lee, Litchfield, Londonderry, Loudon, Madbury, Manchester, Merrimack, Milford, Mount Vernon, Nashua, New Boston, New Castle, New Ipswich, Newfields, Newington, Newmarket, Newton, North Hampton, Nottingham, Pelham, Pembroke, Peterborough, Plaistow, Portsmouth, Raymond, Rollinsford, Rye, Salem (town), Sandown, Seabrook, Somersworth, South Hampton, Stratham, Temple, Weare, Wilton & Windham, NH. ICA: MA0001.

TV Market Ranking: 33 (Acushnet, Aquinnah, Barnstable, Bourne, Chilmark, Dartmouth, Dighton, East Falmouth, Edgartown, Fairhaven, Fall River, Falmouth, Freetown, Mashpee, New Bedford, Oak Bluffs, Orleans, Otis Air National Guard, Rochester, Sandwich, Taunton, Tisbury, Vineyard Haven, Wareham, West Tisbury); 6 (Abington, Acton, Allston, Amesbury, Amherst, Andover, Arlington, Ashburnham, Ashby (town), Ashland, Atkinson, Auburn, Avon, Ayer, Bedford, Bedford, Bellingham, Belmont, Berkley, Beverly, Billerica, Blackstone, Bolton, BOSTON, Boxborough, Boxford, Braintree, Brentwood, Bridgewater, Brighton, Brookline, Burlington, Cambridge, Candia, Canton, Carlisle (town), Carver, Charlestown, Chelmsford, Chelsea, Chester, Clinton, Cohasset, Concord, Danvers, Dedham, Derry, Dorchester, Dover, Dracut, Duxbury, East Boston, East Bridgewater, East Kingston, Easton, Epping, Essex, Everett, Exeter, Fitchburg, Foxborough, Framingham, Franklin, Fremont, Gardner, Georgetown, Gloucester, Goffstown, Greenland, Greenville, Groveland, Halifax, Hamilton, Hampstead, Hampton, Hampton Falls, Hanover, Hanscom AFB, Hanson, Haverhill, Hingham, Holbrook, Holliston, Hooksett, Hopedale, Hopkinton, Hudson, Hudson, Hull, Hyde Park, Ipswich, Jamaica Plain, Kensington, Kingston, Kingston, Lakeville, Lancaster, Lawrence, Leominster, Lexington, Lincoln (town), Litchfield, Littleton (town), Londonderry, Lowell, Lunenburg, Lynn, Lynnfield, Malden, Manchester, Manchester-by-the-Sea (town), Marblehead, Marion, Marlborough, Marshfield, Mattapan, Maynard, Medfield, Medford, Melrose, Mendon, Merrimac, Merrimack, Methuen, Middleborough, Middleton, Milford, Millis, Milton, Mount Vernon, Nahant, Nashua, Natick, Needham, New Boston, New Castle, New Ipswich, Newbury, Newburyport, Newfields, Newington, Newmarket, Newton, Newton, Norfolk, North Andover, North Hampton, North Reading, Norwell, Norwood, Nottingham, Peabody, Pelham, Pembroke, Phillipston, Plaistow, Plymouth, Plympton, Portsmouth, Quincy, Randolph, Raymond, Raynham, Reading, Revere, Rockland, Rockport, Roslindale, Rowley, Roxbury, Rye, Salem, Salem (town), Salisbury, Sandown, Saugus, Scituate, Seabrook, Sharon, Sherborn, Shirley (town), Somerville, South Boston, South Hampton, Sterling, Stoneham, Stoughton, Stow, Stratham, Sudbury, Swampscott, Swansea, Templeton, Tewksbury, Topsfield, Townsend (town), Tyngsborough, Upton, Wakefield, Walpole, Waltham, Watertown, Wayland, Wellesley, Wenham, West Bridgewater, West Newbury, West Roxbury, Westford, Westminster, Weston, Westwood, Weymouth, Whitman, Wilmington, Wilton, Winchendon, Windham, Winthrop, Woburn, Wrentham); 6,33 (Attleboro, Mansfield, Milford, North Attleboro, Norton, Plainville, Seekonk, Somerset); 75 (Bath, Bowdoin (town), Bowdoinham (town), Brunswick (town), Freeport (town), Harpswell, Phippsburg (town), Topsham, West Bath, Woolwich); Below 100 (Allenstown, Antrim, Bennington, Boscawen, Bow, Brewster, Canterbury, Chichester, Deering, Dennis, Francestown, Hancock, Harwich, Henniker, Hillsborough, Hopkinton, Loudon, Nantucket, Pembroke, Peterborough, Provincetown, South Yarmouth, Temple, Weare, Yarmouth, Yarmouth (town), Concord); Outside TV Markets (Chatham, Eastham, Truro, Wellfleet). Franchise award date: August 12, 1981. Franchise expiration date: N.A. Began: December 29, 1982.

Channel capacity: N.A. Channels available but not in use: N.A.

Basic Service
Subscribers: 1,541,850. Commercial subscribers: 12,853.
Programming (received off-air): WBIN-TV (Antenna TV, IND, WeatherNation) Derry; WBPX-TV (ION) Boston; WBZ-TV (CBS, Decades) Boston; WCVB-TV (ABC, MeTV) Boston; WENH-TV (PBS) Durham; WFXT (FOX, Movies!) Boston; WGBH-TV (PBS) Boston; WGBX-TV (PBS) Boston; WHDH (NBC, This TV) Boston; WLVI (CW, The Country Network) Cambridge; WMFP (COZI TV, MeTV, Retro TV) Lawrence; WNEU (TMO) Merrimack; WSBK-TV (MNT) Boston; WUNI (Bounce TV, LATV, UNV) Worcester; WUTF-DT (getTV, UniMas) Marlborough; WWDP (IND) Norwell; WYDN (Daystar TV, ETV) Worcester.
Programming (via satellite): Comcast Network Philadelphia; Lifetime; Pop; TBS.
Fee: $29.00-$46.00 installation; $30.42 monthly; $1.21 converter.

Expanded Basic Service 1
Subscribers: N.A.
Programming (via satellite): A&E; AMC; Animal Planet; BET; Bravo; Brazzers TV; Cartoon Network; Catholic Television Network; CMT; CNBC; CNN; Comcast SportsNet New England; Comedy Central; C-SPAN; C-SPAN 2; Discovery Channel; Disney Channel; E! HD; ESPN; ESPN Classic; ESPN2; EWTN Global Catholic Network; Flix; Food Network; Fox News Channel; Freeform; Fuse; FX; Golf Channel; GSN; HGTV; History; HLN; Hot Choice; IFC; MSNBC; MTV; NBC Universo; New England Cable News; Nickelodeon; QVC; RTN; Spike TV; Syfy; The Weather Channel; TLC; TNT; Travel Channel; truTV; Turner Classic Movies; TV Land; TV5, La Television International; USA Network; VH1; WE tv.
Fee: $43.92 monthly.

Digital Basic Service
Subscribers: N.A.
Programming (via satellite): American's Youth Network; BBC America; Bloomberg Television; Cooking Channel; Discovery Life Channel; Disney XD; DIY Network; DMX Music; ESPNews; EWTN Global Catholic Network; Fox Sports 1; Fuse; FXM; FYI; Great American Country; History International; IFC; International Television (ITV); LMN; MC; National Geographic Channel; NBA TV; Nick Jr.; Nicktoons; Outdoor Channel; Oxygen; Sundance TV; TeenNick;

2017 Edition

D-365

Massachusetts—Cable Systems

The Word Network; Trinity Broadcasting Network (TBN); Turner Classic Movies; Weatherscan.

Digital Pay Service 1
Pay Units: N.A.
Programming (via satellite): Cinemax (multiplexed); Flix; HBO (multiplexed); Showtime (multiplexed); Starz Encore; The Movie Channel (multiplexed).
Fee: $14.00 monthly (each).

Video-On-Demand: Yes

Pay-Per-View
iN DEMAND; iN DEMAND (delivered digitally); Hot Choice (delivered digitally); Playboy TV (delivered digitally); Fresh (delivered digitally).

Internet Service
Operational: Yes.
Subscribers: 1,192,351.
Broadband Service: Comcast High Speed Internet.
Fee: $42.95 monthly; $10.00 modem lease.

Telephone Service
Analog: Not Operational
Digital: Operational
Subscribers: 832,155.
Miles of Plant: 50,468.0 (coaxial); 11,127.0 (fiber optic). Homes passed: 2,847,128.
Regional Vice President: Paul D'Arcangelo.
Marketing Director: Alan Clairmont. Public Relations Director: Jim Hughes.
Ownership: Comcast Cable Communications Inc. (MSO).

BOSTON—RCN Corp. Formerly [MA0105]. This cable system has converted to IPTV, 196 Van Buren St, Ste 300, Herndon, VA 20170. Phones: 800-746-4726; 609-681-2281. Web Site: http://www.rcn.com. Also serves Allston, Arlington, Auburndale, Back Bay, Bay Village, Beacon Hill, Brighton, Brookline, Burlington, Cambridge, Charlestown, Chestnut Hill, Dedham, Fenway-Kenmore, Framingham, Hyde Park, Jamaica Plain, Lexington, Mattapan, Medford, Milton, Mission Hill, Natick, Needham, Needham Heights, Newton, Newton Center, Newton Highlands, Newton Lower Falls, Newton Upper Falls, Newtonville, North End, Quincy, Roslindale, Roxbury, Somerville, South Boston, Stoneham, Waban, Wakefield, Waltham, Watertown, West Newton, West Roxbury, Westwood & Woburn. ICA: MA5096.
Channel capacity: N.A. Channels available but not in use: N.A.

Limited Basic
Subscribers: 55,029. Commercial subscribers: 5,360.
Fee: $28.76 monthly. Includes 47 channels - 34 in SD & 13 in HD. Additional $9.95 HD equipment fee for HD channels.

Signature Digital Cable
Subscribers: N.A.
Fee: $64.99 monthly. Includes 272 channels - 212 in SD & 60 in HD. Additional $9.95 HD equipment fee for HD channels.

HD Expanded Pack
Subscribers: N.A.
Fee: $8.99 monthly. Includes 6 additional HD channels.

Premiere Movies & Entertainment
Subscribers: N.A.
Fee: $10.99 monthly. Includes 30 channels - 27 in SD & 4 in HD. Additional $9.95 HD equipment fee for HD channels.

Premiere Family & Children
Subscribers: N.A.
Fee: $5.99 monthly. Includes 19 channels - 17 in SD & 2 in HD. Additional $9.95 HD equipment fee for HD channels.

Premiere News & Information
Subscribers: N.A.
Fee: $5.99 monthly. Includes 21 channels - 16 in SD & 5 in HD. Additional $9.95 HD equipment fee for HD channels.

Premiere Sports
Subscribers: N.A.
Fee: $9.99 monthly. Includes 36 channels - 28 in SD & 8 in HD. Additional $9.95 HD equipment fee for HD channels.

Premiere Total Pack
Subscribers: N.A.
Fee: $20.95 monthly. Includes 114 channels - 96 in SD & 18 in HD. Additional $9.95 HD equipment fee for HD channels.

MiVision Lite
Subscribers: N.A.
Fee: $12.00 monthly. Includes 40 channels in Spanish.

MiVision Plus
Subscribers: N.A.
Fee: $22.95 monthly. Includes 44 channels in Spanish.

Cinemax
Subscribers: N.A.
Fee: $9.99 monthly. Includes 16 channels - 8 in SD & 8 in HD plus Cinemax on Demand & MAXGo. Additional $9.95 HD equipment fee for HD channels.

HBO
Subscribers: N.A.
Fee: $15.95 monthly. Includes 14 channels - 7 in SD & 7 in HD plus HBO on Demand & HBO Go. Additional $9.95 HD equipment fee for HD channels.

Cinemax/HBO
Subscribers: N.A.
Fee: $19.95 monthly. Includes 16 channels of Cinemax - 8 in SD & 8 in HD & 14 channels of HBO - 7 in SD & 7 in HD plus Cinemax on Demand, HBO on Demand, MAXGo & HBO Go. Additional $9.95 HD equipment fee for HD channels.

Showtime/TMC
Subscribers: N.A.
Fee: $4.95 monthly. Includes 20 channels - 9 in SD & 11 in HD plus Showtime on Demand & The Movie Channel on Demand. Additional $9.95 HD equipment fee for HD channels.

Starz
Subscribers: N.A.
Fee: $5.00 monthly. Includes 13 channels - 9 in SD & 4 in HD plus Starz on Demand. Additional $9.95 HD equipment fee for HD channels.

Video-On-Demand: Yes

Internet Service
Operational: Yes.
Fee: $29.99-$79.99 monthly.

Telephone Service
Digital: Operational
Fee: $29.99 monthly
Miles of Plant: None (coaxial); 164,154.0 (fiber optic). Homes passed: 332,009.
Vice President & General Manager: Jamie Holanda.
Ownership: RCN Corp.

BOSTON—RCN Corp. This cable system has converted to IPTV. See BOSTON, MA [MA5096]. ICA: MA0105.

BRAINTREE—BELD Broadband, 150 Potter Rd, Braintree, MA 02184-1364. Phones: 781-848-1130; 781-348-2353. Fax: 781-348-1002. E-mail: cservice@beld.com. Web Site: http://www.beld.com. ICA: MA0106.
Note: This system is an overbuild.
TV Market Ranking: 6 (BRAINTREE). Franchise award date: August 25, 2000. Franchise expiration date: N.A. Began: August 25, 2000.
Channel capacity: N.A. Channels available but not in use: N.A.

Basic Service
Subscribers: 2,406.
Programming (received off-air): WBIN-TV (Antenna TV, IND, WeatherNation) Derry; WBPX-TV (ION) Boston; WBZ-TV (CBS, Decades) Boston; WCVB-TV (ABC, MeTV) Boston; WFXT (FOX, Movies!) Boston; WGBH-TV (PBS) Boston; WGBX-TV (PBS) Boston; WHDH (NBC, This TV) Boston; WLVI (CW, The Country Network) Cambridge; WMFP (COZI TV, MeTV, Retro TV) Lawrence; WSBK-TV (MNT) Boston; WUNI (Bounce TV, LATV, UNV) Worcester; WUTF-DT (getTV, UniMas) Marlborough; WWDP (IND) Norwell; WYDN (Daystar TV, ETV) Worcester.
Programming (via satellite): CatholicTV; C-SPAN; C-SPAN 2; New England Cable News; Pop; QVC.
Fee: $39.50 installation; $20.02 monthly.

Expanded Basic Service 1
Subscribers: N.A.
Programming (via satellite): A&E; AMC; Animal Planet; BET; Bravo; Cartoon Network; CMT; CNBC; CNN; Comcast SportsNet New England; Comedy Central; Discovery Channel; Disney Channel; E! HD; ESPN; Food Network; Fox News Channel; Freeform; FX; Great American Country; HGTV; HLN; Lifetime; MSNBC; MTV; New England Sports Network; Nickelodeon; Spike TV; TBS; The Weather Channel; TLC; TNT; Travel Channel; truTV; TV Land; USA Network; VH1; WGN America.
Fee: $46.00 installation; $42.25 monthly.

Digital Basic Service
Subscribers: N.A.
Programming (via satellite): BBC America; Bloomberg Television; Discovery Life Channel; Disney XD; ESPN Classic; ESPN2; ESPNews; Fox Sports 1; Fuse; FXM; FYI; Golf Channel; GSN; History; History International; IFC; LMN; MTV Classic; National Geographic Channel; NBCSN; NFL Network; Nick Jr.; Nicktoons; Outdoor Channel; Ovation; Syfy; TeenNick; Trinity Broadcasting Network (TBN); Turner Classic Movies; TV Guide Interactive Inc.; VH1 Country; VH1 Soul; WE tv.
Fee: $46.00 installation; $8.00 converter.

Digital Pay Service 1
Pay Units: N.A.
Programming (via satellite): Cinemax (multiplexed); Flix; HBO (multiplexed); Showtime (multiplexed); Starz (multiplexed); Starz Encore (multiplexed); The Movie Channel (multiplexed).

Video-On-Demand: Yes

Pay-Per-View
iN DEMAND (delivered digitally).

Internet Service
Operational: Yes. Began: December 1, 1999.
Broadband Service: BELD.net.
Fee: $50.00 installation; $43.25 monthly; $7.00 modem lease.

Telephone Service
Digital: Operational
Fee: $48.80 monthly
Miles of Plant: 170.0 (coaxial); None (fiber optic). Homes passed: 11,000.
General Manager: William Bottiggi. Chief Technician: Tom Bicica. Marketing & Programming Director: JoAnn Stak Bregnard. Broadband Division Manager: Jack Orpen.
Ownership: Braintree Electric Light Department.

BRAINTREE—Comcast Cable. Now served by BOSTON, MA [MA0001]. ICA: MA0048.

BROCKTON—Comcast Cable. Now served by BOSTON, MA [MA0001]. ICA: MA0012.

CHARLTON—Charter Communications. Now served by WORCESTER, MA [MA0002]. ICA: MA0066.

CHESTER—Comcast Cable. Now served by BURLINGTON, VT [VT0001]. ICA: MA0044.

CHICOPEE—Charter Communications, 355 Front St, Chicopee, MA 01013. Phones: 314-543-2236; 636-207-5100 (Corporate office); 508-853-1515. Web Site: http://www.charter.com. Also serves Belchertown, Brimfield, East Longmeadow, Easthampton, Hadley, Hampden, Ludlow, Southampton, Wales & Wilbraham. ICA: MA0082.
TV Market Ranking: 19 (Brimfield, CHICOPEE, East Longmeadow, Hampden, Ludlow, Southampton, Wales, Wilbraham); 6 (Belchertown); Below 100 (Easthampton, Hadley). Franchise award date: February 21, 1976. Franchise expiration date: N.A. Began: February 21, 1976.
Channel capacity: N.A. Channels available but not in use: N.A.

Digital Basic Service
Subscribers: 47,664.
Programming (via satellite): BBC America; Bloomberg Television; Discovery Digital Networks; DIY Network; ESPN Classic; ESPNews; Fox Deportes; Fox Sports 2; FSN Digital Atlantic; FSN Digital Central; FSN Digital Pacific; Fuse; FYI; Great American Country; History International; IFC; International Television (ITV); LMN; MC; NFL Network; Nick 2; Nick Jr.; Nicktoons; Sundance TV; TeenNick; TV Guide Interactive Inc.; TVG Network; WE tv.
Fee: $49.99 installation; $26.99 monthly.

Digital Expanded Basic Service
Subscribers: N.A.
Programming (via satellite): A&E; AMC; Animal Planet; Bravo; Cartoon Network; CMT; CNBC; CNN; Comedy Central; C-SPAN 2; Discovery Channel; Discovery Life Channel; Disney Channel; E! HD; ESPN; ESPN2; EWTN Global Catholic Network; Food Network; Fox News Channel; Fox Sports 1; Freeform; FX; Hallmark Channel; HGTV; History; HLN; Lifetime; MSNBC; MTV; National Geographic Channel; NBCSN; New England Cable News; New England Sports Network; Nickelodeon; Oxygen; Spike TV; Syfy; TBS; The Weather Channel; TLC; TNT; truTV; TV Land; Univision Studios; USA Network; VH1.
Fee: $53.00 monthly.

Digital Expanded Basic Service 2
Subscribers: N.A.
Programming (via satellite): Comcast SportsNet New England; Disney XD; Golf Channel; Travel Channel; Turner Classic Movies.
Fee: $2.25 monthly.

Digital Pay Service 1
Pay Units: N.A.
Programming (via satellite): Cinemax (multiplexed); Flix; HBO (multiplexed); Showtime (multiplexed); Starz (multiplexed); Starz Encore (multiplexed); The Movie Channel.
Fee: $1.99 installation; $9.95 monthly (Cinemax or TMC), $10.95 monthly (HBO or Showtime).

Video-On-Demand: Yes

Cable Systems—Massachusetts

Pay-Per-View
iN DEMAND (delivered digitally); Fresh (delivered digitally); Pleasure (delivered digitally); ETC (delivered digitally); Playboy TV (delivered digitally).
Internet Service
Operational: Yes.
Subscribers: 39,976.
Broadband Service: Charter Internet.
Fee: $29.99 monthly; $10.00 modem lease; $195.00 modem purchase.
Telephone Service
Digital: Operational
Subscribers: 26,577.
Fee: $29.99 monthly
Miles of Plant: 1,853.0 (coaxial); 1,296.0 (fiber optic). Homes passed: 74,497.
Vice President & General Manager: Greg Garabedian. Technical Operations Director: George Duffy. Marketing Director: Dennis Jerome. Accounting Director: David Sovanski. Marketing Manager: Paula Cecchetilli. Technical Operations Manager: Beatrice Welch.
Ownership: Charter Communications Inc. (MSO).

CONWAY—Comcast Cable. Now served by BURLINGTON, VT [VT0001]. ICA: MA0073.

DANVERS—Comcast Cable. Now served by BOSTON, MA [MA0001]. ICA: MA0058.

DEDHAM—Comcast Cable. Now served by BOSTON, MA [MA0001]. ICA: MA0061.

FAIRHAVEN—Comcast Cable. Now served by NEW BOSTON, MA [MA0001]. ICA: MA0084.

FORT DEVONS—Formerly served by Americable International. No longer in operation. ICA: MA0072.

FOXBOROUGH—Comcast Cable. Now served by BOSTON, MA [MA0001]. ICA: MA0004.

FRAMINGHAM—Comcast Cable. Now served by BOSTON, MA [MA0001]. ICA: MA0023.

GLOUCESTER—Comcast Cable. Now served by BOSTON, MA [MA0001]. ICA: MA0032.

HAVERHILL—Comcast Cable. Now served by BOSTON, MA [MA0001]. ICA: MA0085.

HINSDALE—Charter Communications. Now served by CHATHAM, NY [NY0088]. ICA: MA0096.

HOLLAND—Cox Communications. Now served by ENFIELD, CT [CT0011]. ICA: MA0097.

HOPKINTON—Comcast Cable. Now served by BOSTON, MA [MA0001]. ICA: MA0074.

LANESBORO—Formerly served by Charter Communications. No longer in operation. ICA: MA0086.

LAWRENCE—Comcast Cable. Now served by BOSTON, MA [MA0001]. ICA: MA0015.

LEE—Time Warner Cable. Now served by PITTSFIELD, MA [MA0090]. ICA: MA0059.

LEOMINSTER—Comcast Cable. Now served by BOSTON, MA [MA0001]. ICA: MA0017.

LEXINGTON—Comcast Cable. Now served by BOSTON, MA [MA0001]. ICA: MA0037.

LONGMEADOW—Comcast Cable. Now served by BURLINGTON, VT [VT0001]. ICA: MA0068.

LOWELL—Comcast Cable. Now served by BOSTON, MA [MA0001]. ICA: MA0008.

MALDEN—Comcast Cable. Now served by BOSTON, MA [MA0001]. ICA: MA0003.

MARION—Comcast Cable. Now served by BOSTON, MA [MA0001]. ICA: MA0043.

MARLBOROUGH—Comcast Cable. Now served by BOSTON, MA [MA0001]. ICA: MA0087.

MARSHFIELD—Comcast Cable. Now served by BOSTON, MA [MA0001]. ICA: MA0088.

MARTHA'S VINEYARD—Formerly served by Comcast Cable. No longer in operation. ICA: MA0056.

MASHPEE—Comcast Cable. Now served by BOSTON, MA [MA0001]. ICA: MA0064.

MAYNARD—Comcast Cable. Now served by BOSTON, MA [MA0001]. ICA: MA0026.

MIDDLEBOROUGH—Comcast Cable. Now served by BOSTON, MA [MA0001]. ICA: MA0042.

MILFORD—Comcast Cable. Now served by BOSTON, MA [MA0001]. ICA: MA0049.

NANTUCKET—Comcast Cable. Now served by BOSTON, MA [MA0001]. ICA: MA0067.

NATICK—Comcast Cable. Now served by BOSTON, MA [MA0001]. ICA: MA0045.

NEEDHAM—Comcast Cable. Now served by BOSTON, MA [MA0001]. ICA: MA0010.

NEW BEDFORD—Comcast Cable. Now served by BOSTON, MA [MA0001]. ICA: MA0013.

NEWBURYPORT—Comcast Cable. Now served by BOSTON, MA [MA0001]. ICA: MA0039.

NORTH ADAMS—Time Warner Cable. Now served by PITTSFIELD, MA [MA0090]. ICA: MA0036.

NORTH ANDOVER—Comcast Cable. Now served by BOSTON, MA [MA0001]. ICA: MA0060.

NORTHAMPTON—Comcast Communications. Now served by BURLINGTON, VT [VT0001]. ICA: MA0107.

NORWOOD—Comcast Cable. Now served by BOSTON, MA [MA0001]. ICA: MA0040.

NORWOOD—Norwood Light Broadband, 206 Central St, Norwood, MA 02062. Phone: 781-948-1150. E-mail: business@norwoodlight.com. Web Site: http://www.norwoodlight.com. ICA: MA0109.

TV Market Ranking: 6 (NORWOOD).
Channel capacity: N.A. Channels available but not in use: N.A.
Internet Service
Operational: Yes.
Fee: $29.95-$79.95 monthly.
Technical Operations Supervisor: Rick Durant.
Ownership: Norwood Light Broadband.

ORLEANS—Comcast Cable. Now served by BOSTON, MA [MA0001]. ICA: MA0030.

PEABODY—Comcast Cable. Now served by BOSTON, MA [MA0001]. ICA: MA0028.

PEMBROKE—Comcast Cable. Now served by BOSTON, MA [MA0001]. ICA: MA0095.

PEPPERELL—Charter Communications. Now served by WORCESTER, MA [MA0002]. ICA: MA0055.

PHILLIPSTON—Comcast Cable. Now served by BOSTON, MA [MA0001]. ICA: MA0079.

PITTSFIELD—Time Warner Cable, 1021 Highbridge Rd, Schenectady, NY 12303. Phones: 518-869-9587; 518-242-8890. Fax: 518-242-8948. Web Site: http://www.timewarnercable.com. Also serves Adams, Cheshire, Clarksburg, Dalton, Great Barrington, Housatonic, Lee, Lenox, North Adams, Richmond, Sheffield (town), Stockbridge & Williamstown. ICA: MA0090.
TV Market Ranking: 34 (Adams, Cheshire, Clarksburg, Dalton, Lenox, North Adams, PITTSFIELD, Richmond, Williamstown); Below 100 (Great Barrington, Housatonic, Lee, Sheffield (town), Stockbridge). Franchise award date: January 1, 1956. Franchise expiration date: N.A. Began: November 1, 1956.
Channel capacity: N.A. Channels available but not in use: N.A.
Basic Service
Subscribers: 32,884. Commercial subscribers: 547.
Programming (received off-air): WCWN (CW) Schenectady; WFSB (CBS, Escape, Laff) Hartford; WGBY-TV (PBS) Springfield; WMHT (PBS) Schenectady; WNYT (MeTV, NBC) Albany; WRGB (CBS, This TV) Schenectady; WTEN (ABC) Albany; WWLP (NBC, TheCoolTV) Springfield; WXXA-TV (FOX, Laff, The Country Network) Albany; WYPX-TV (ION) Amsterdam; 23 FMs.
Programming (via microwave): WCVB-TV (ABC, MeTV) Boston.
Programming (via satellite): Concert TV; C-SPAN 2; Pop; TBS.
Fee: $42.50 installation; $12.31 monthly.
Expanded Basic Service 1
Subscribers: N.A.
Programming (via satellite): A&E; AMC; Animal Planet; BET; Cartoon Network; CMT; CNBC; CNN; Comcast SportsNet New England; Comedy Central; C-SPAN; Discovery Channel; E! HD; ESPN; ESPN Classic; ESPN2; EVINE Live; EWTN Global Catholic Network; Food Network; Fox News Channel; Freeform; FX; Golf Channel; HGTV; History; HLN; Lifetime; LMN; MSNBC; MTV; National Geographic Channel; New England Cable News; Nickelodeon; Oxygen; QVC; Spike TV; The Weather Channel; TLC; TNT; Travel Channel; truTV; Turner Classic Movies; TV Land; Univision Studios; USA Network; VH1; WE tv.
Fee: $25.60 monthly.

Digital Basic Service
Subscribers: N.A.
Programming (via satellite): BBC America; Bloomberg Television; CMT; Cooking Channel; C-SPAN 3; Discovery Digital Networks; Disney Channel; Disney XD; DIY Network; DMX Music; ESPNews; Fox Sports 1; FSN Digital Atlantic; FSN Digital Central; FSN Digital Pacific; Great American Country; GSN; Hallmark Channel; History International; MSG; MSG Plus; NBCSN; Nick Jr.; Outdoor Channel; Ovation; Syfy; Time Warner Cable News NY1; Trinity Broadcasting Network (TBN); TV Asia; YES Network; Zee TV.
Digital Pay Service 1
Pay Units: N.A.
Programming (via satellite): Cinemax (multiplexed); Flix; FXM; HBO (multiplexed); IFC; Showtime (multiplexed); Starz (multiplexed); Starz Encore (multiplexed); Sundance TV; The Movie Channel (multiplexed).
Fee: $15.95 monthly (each).
Video-On-Demand: Yes
Pay-Per-View
iN DEMAND (delivered digitally); Playboy TV (delivered digitally); Fresh (delivered digitally); Shorteez (delivered digitally); Hot Choice (delivered digitally); Pleasure (delivered digitally); Adult PPV (delivered digitally).
Internet Service
Operational: Yes. Began: January 1, 1999.
Broadband Service: AOL for Broadband; EarthLink; Local.net; Road Runner.
Fee: $29.95 installation; $44.95 monthly.
Telephone Service
Digital: Operational
Vice President, Operations: Mark Loreno. Vice President, Marketing: Tricia Buhr. Vice President, Engineering: James Marchester. Vice President, Public Affairs: Peter Taubkin. Vice President, Customer Care: Paul Ventosa.
Ownership: Time Warner Cable (MSO).; Advance/Newhouse Partnership (MSO).

PLYMOUTH—Comcast Cable. Now served by BOSTON, MA [MA0001]. ICA: MA0050.

QUINCY—Comcast Cable. Now served by BOSTON, MA [MA0001]. ICA: MA0011.

REHOBOTH—Comcast Cable. Now served by BOSTON, MA [MA0001]. ICA: MA0108.

RUSSELL—Russell Municipal Cable TV, 65 Main St, PO Box 408, Russell, MA 01071-0408. Phones: 413-862-4400; 413-862-6204. Fax: 413-862-3103. E-mail: information@russellma.net. Web Site: http://www.townofrussell.us. ICA: MA0091.
TV Market Ranking: 19 (RUSSELL). Franchise award date: March 10, 1987. Franchise expiration date: N.A. Began: September 1, 1987.
Channel capacity: N.A. Channels available but not in use: N.A.
Basic Service
Subscribers: N.A.
Programming (received off-air): WGBY-TV (PBS) Springfield; WGGB-TV (ABC, FOX, MNT) Springfield; WSHM-LD (CBS, COZI TV) Springfield; WTIC-TV (Antenna TV, FOX) Hartford; WWLP (NBC, TheCoolTV) Springfield.
Programming (via satellite): A&E; AMC; Animal Planet; Cartoon Network; CMT; CNN; Comedy Central; C-SPAN; Discovery Channel; Disney Channel; DIY Network;

2017 Edition   D-367

Massachusetts—Cable Systems

E! HD; ESPN; ESPN2; Fox News Channel; Freeform; Hallmark Channel; HGTV; History; HLN; Lifetime; MTV; National Geographic Channel; NBCSN; New England Sports Network; Nickelodeon; Spike TV; Syfy; TBS; The Weather Channel; TLC; TNT; Travel Channel; truTV; Turner Classic Movies; TV Land; USA Network; VH1.
Fee: $30.00 installation.

Pay Service 1
Pay Units: N.A.
Programming (via satellite): HBO; Showtime; The Movie Channel.
Fee: $10.95 - $12.95 monthly (each).

Video-On-Demand: No

Internet Service
Operational: No, DSL.
Fee: $75.00 installation; $17.00-$35.00 monthly.

Telephone Service
None
Miles of Plant: None (coaxial); 20.0 (fiber optic). Homes passed: 585. Planning upgrade to 870 MHz.
General Manager: Sue Maxwell. Chief Technician: Richard Trusty.
Ownership: Russell Municipal Cable TV.

RUTLAND (town)—Charter Communications. Now served by WORCESTER, MA [MA0002]. ICA: MA0071.

SAUGUS—Comcast Cable. Now served by BOSTON, MA [MA0001]. ICA: MA0019.

SCITUATE—Comcast Cable. Now served by BOSTON, MA [MA0001]. ICA: MA0021.

SHREWSBURY—Shrewsbury's Community Cablevision, 100 Maple Ave, Shrewsbury, MA 01545-5347. Phones: 508-841-8502; 508-841-8500. Fax: 508-842-9419. E-mail: customerservice@ci.shrewsbury.ma.us. Web Site: http://www.selco.shrewsburyma.gov. ICA: MA0051.
TV Market Ranking: 6 (SHREWSBURY). Franchise award date: April 1, 1982. Franchise expiration date: N.A. Began: October 9, 1983.
Channel capacity: 80 (operating 2-way). Channels available but not in use: N.A.

Basic Service
Subscribers: 7,952.
Programming (received off-air): WBPX-TV (ION) Boston; WBZ-TV (CBS, Decades) Boston; WCVB-TV (ABC, MeTV) Boston; WFXT (FOX, Movies!) Boston; WGBH-TV (PBS) Boston; WGBX-TV (PBS) Boston; WHDH (NBC, This TV) Boston; WJAR (MeTV, NBC) Providence; WLVI (CW, The Country Network) Cambridge; WNEU (TMO) Merrimack; WSBE-TV (PBS) Providence; WSBK-TV (MNT) Boston; WUNI (Bounce TV, LATV, UNV) Worcester; WUTF-DT (getTV, UniMas) Marlborough; WWDP (IND) Norwell; WYDN (Daystar TV, ETV) Worcester.
Programming (via satellite): Bravo; Cartoon Network; C-SPAN; C-SPAN 2; Discovery Channel; EVINE Live; EWTN Global Catholic Network; Freeform; Hallmark Channel; MSNBC; MyNetworkTV; Pop; TBS; Travel Channel; Trinity Broadcasting Network (TBN); truTV.
Fee: $50.00 installation; $19.95 monthly.

Expanded Basic Service 1
Subscribers: N.A.
Programming (via satellite): A&E; AMC; Animal Planet; AZ TV; BET; CMT; CNBC; CNN; CNN International; Comcast SportsNet Mid-Atlantic; Comedy Central; Disney Channel; E! HD; ESPN; ESPN Classic; ESPN2; Food Network; Fox News Channel; FX; Golf Channel; HGTV; History; HLN; Lifetime; LMN; MTV; National Geographic Channel; New England Cable News; New England Sports Network; Nickelodeon; Spike TV; Syfy; The Weather Channel; TLC; TNT; TV Land; USA Network; VH1.
Fee: $35.00 installation; $33.55 monthly.

Digital Basic Service
Subscribers: N.A.
Programming (via satellite): AMC; Animal Planet HD; AXS TV; BBC America; Bloomberg Television; Boomerang; Bridges TV; Comcast SportsNet Mid-Atlantic; Cooking Channel; Destination America; Discovery Channel HD; Discovery Kids Channel; Discovery Life Channel; Disney XD; DIY Network; ESPN HD; ESPN2 HD; ESPNews; ESPNU; Fox Business Network; Fox Sports 1; Fox Sports 2; Fuse; FXM; Golf Channel; GSN; HD Theater; IFC; Investigation Discovery; MTV Classic; MTV2; Nat Geo WILD; National Geographic Channel HD; NBCSN; New England Sports Network; NFL Network; NHL Network; Nick Jr.; Nicktoons; Outdoor Channel; OWN: Oprah Winfrey Network; Oxygen; Science Channel; Science HD; Sprout; Sundance TV; TBS HD; TeenNick; Tennis Channel; TLC; TNT HD; Turner Classic Movies; Universal HD; Versus HD; WE tv.
Fee: $8.95 converter.

Digital Pay Service 1
Pay Units: N.A.
Programming (via satellite): Cinemax (multiplexed); Cinemax HD; Flix; HBO (multiplexed); HBO HD; Showtime (multiplexed); Showtime HD; Starz (multiplexed); Starz Encore (multiplexed); Starz HD; The Movie Channel (multiplexed); The Movie Channel HD; TV Asia; Zee TV.
Fee: $10.95 monthly (Cinemax, HBO, Starz/Encore, CCTV-4, TV Asia or Zee TV), $12.95 monthly (Showtime/TMC/Flix), $13.95 monthly (Playboy TV).

Video-On-Demand: Yes

Pay-Per-View
iN DEMAND (delivered digitally); MLB Extra Innings (delivered digitally); NHL Center Ice (delivered digitally); Playboy TV (delivered digitally).

Internet Service
Operational: Yes.
Subscribers: 11,019.
Broadband Service: In-house.
Fee: $50.00 installation; $19.95-$49.95 monthly.

Telephone Service
Digital: Operational
Subscribers: 3,814.
Miles of Plant: 599.0 (coaxial); 88.0 (fiber optic). Homes passed: 14,711.
General Manager: Thomas Josie. Operations Manager: Wayne Cullen. Marketing Manager: Jackie Pratt.
Ownership: Shrewsbury's Community Cablevision.

SOUTH YARMOUTH—Comcast Cable. Now served by BOSTON, MA [MA0001]. ICA: MA0031.

SPRINGFIELD—Comcast Cable. Now served by BURLINGTON, VT [VT0001]. ICA: MA0005.

STERLING—Comcast Cable. Now served by BOSTON, MA [MA0001]. ICA: MA0053.

STOUGHTON—Comcast Cable. Now served by BOSTON, MA [MA0001]. ICA: MA0025.

TAUNTON—Comcast Cable. Now served by BOSTON, MA [MA0001]. ICA: MA0033.

TISBURY—Comcast Cable. Now served by BOSTON, MA [MA0001]. ICA: MA0101.

UXBRIDGE—Charter Communications. Now served by WORCESTER, MA [MA0002]. ICA: MA0063.

WALES—Charter Communications. Now served by CHICOPEE, MA [MA0082]. ICA: MA0076.

WALTHAM—Comcast Cable. Now served by BOSTON, MA [MA0001]. ICA: MA0029.

WATERTOWN—Comcast Cable. Now served by BOSTON, MA [MA0001]. ICA: MA0047.

WEST STOCKBRIDGE—Charter Communications. Now served by CHATHAM, NY [NY0088]. ICA: MA0078.

WESTFIELD—Comcast Cable. Now served by BURLINGTON, VT [VT0001]. ICA: MA0006.

WESTFORD—Comcast Cable. Now served by BOSTON, MA [MA0001]. ICA: MA0093.

WESTPORT—Charter Communications, 12405 Powerscourt Dr, St. Louis, MO 63131. Phones: 636-207-5100 (Corporate office); 508-853-1515. Fax: 508-854-5086. Web Site: http://www.charter.com. ICA: MA0070.
TV Market Ranking: 33 (WESTPORT). Franchise award date: January 14, 1986. Franchise expiration date: N.A. Began: September 1, 1986.
Channel capacity: N.A. Channels available but not in use: N.A.

Digital Basic Service
Subscribers: 4,688.
Programming (via satellite): BBC America; Bloomberg Television; Discovery Digital Networks; Disney XD; DIY Network; ESPN Classic; ESPNews; Fuse; FYI; GSN; History International; IFC; LMN; Nick 2; Nick Jr.; Nicktoons; Sundance TV; TeenNick; TV Guide Interactive Inc.; WE tv.
Fee: $15.99 monthly.

Digital Expanded Basic Service
Subscribers: N.A.
Programming (via satellite): A&E; AMC; Animal Planet; Bravo; CNBC; CNN; Comcast SportsNet New England; Comedy Central; Discovery Channel; Disney Channel; E! HD; ESPN; ESPN2; Food Network; Freeform; HGTV; History; HLN; Lifetime; MTV; New England Sports Network; Nickelodeon; Spike TV; Syfy; TBS; The Weather Channel; TLC; TNT; Travel Channel; Turner Classic Movies; USA Network; VH1.
Fee: $53.00 monthly.

Digital Pay Service 1
Pay Units: N.A.
Programming (via satellite): Cinemax (multiplexed); Flix; HBO (multiplexed); Showtime (multiplexed); Starz (multiplexed); Starz Encore (multiplexed); The Movie Channel (multiplexed).
Fee: $4.95 monthly (Flix), $10.95 monthly (Cinemax or Showtime), $11.95 monthly (HBO).

Video-On-Demand: Yes

Pay-Per-View
iN DEMAND (delivered digitally) Playboy TV (delivered digitally); Fresh (delivered digitally); Shorteez (delivered digitally).

Internet Service
Operational: Yes.
Broadband Service: Charter Internet.
Fee: $29.99 monthly.

Telephone Service
Digital: Operational.
Miles of Plant: 131.0 (coaxial); None (fiber optic). Homes passed: 5,511.
Vice President & General Manager: Greg Garabedian. Technical Manager: Kevin Mailloux. Marketing Director: Dennis Jerome. Accounting Director: David Sovanski.
Ownership: Charter Communications Inc. (MSO).

WEYMOUTH—Comcast Cable. Now served by BOSTON, MA [MA0001]. ICA: MA0024.

WINCHENDON—Comcast Cable. Now served by BOSTON, MA [MA0001]. ICA: MA0075.

WOBURN—Comcast Cable. Now served by BOSTON, MA [MA0001]. ICA: MA0007.

WORCESTER—Charter Communications, 95 Higgins St, Worcester, MA 01606. Phones: 314-543-2236; 636-207-5100 (Corporate office); 508-853-1515. Web Site: http://www.charter.com. Also serves Auburn, Barre (town), Berlin, Boylston, Brookfield, Charlton, Douglas (town), Dudley, Dunstable, East Brookfield, East Brookfield (town), Grafton, Groton, Harvard, Holden, Hubbardston, Leicester, Millbury, Millville, North Brookfield, North Brookfield (town), Northborough, Northbridge, Oakham, Oxford, Paxton, Pepperell, Rutland (town), Southborough, Southbridge, Spencer, Sturbridge, Sutton, Upton, Uxbridge, Webster, West Boylston, West Brookfield & Westborough, MA; Brookline & Hollis, NH. ICA: MA0002.
TV Market Ranking: 6 (Barre (town), Berlin, Boylston, Brookfield, Brookline, Charlton, Dudley, Dunstable, East Brookfield, East Brookfield, Groton, Harvard, Holden, Hollis, Hubbardston, Leicester, North Brookfield, North Brookfield (town), Northborough, Oakham, Paxton, Pepperell, Rutland (town), Southbridge, Spencer, Sturbridge, West Boylston, West Brookfield); 6,33 (Auburn, Douglas (town), Grafton, Millbury, Millville, Northbridge, Oxford, Southborough, Sutton, Upton, Uxbridge, Webster, Westborough, WORCESTER). Franchise award date: January 1, 1972. Franchise expiration date: N.A. Began: May 1, 1969.
Channel capacity: N.A. Channels available but not in use: N.A.

Digital Basic Service
Subscribers: 124,930.
Programming (via satellite): BBC America; Bloomberg Television; Discovery Digital Networks; DIY Network; ESPN Classic; ESPNews; Fox Deportes; Fox Sports 2; FSN Digital Atlantic; FSN Digital Central; FSN Digital Pacific; FYI; Great American Country; History International; IFC; International Television (ITV); LMN; MC; NFL Network; Nick 2; Nick Jr.; Nicktoons; Sundance TV; TeenNick; TVG Network; WE tv.
Fee: $49.99 installation; $14.99 monthly.

Digital Expanded Basic Service
Subscribers: N.A.
Programming (via microwave): New England Cable News.
Programming (via satellite): A&E; AMC; Animal Planet; BET; Bravo; Cartoon Network; CNBC; CNN; Comcast SportsNet New England; Comedy Central; Discovery Channel; Discovery Life Channel; Dis-

ney Channel; Disney XD; E! HD; ESPN; ESPN2; Food Network; Fox News Channel; Fox Sports 1; Freeform; FX; Golf Channel; Hallmark Channel; HGTV; History; HLN; Lifetime; MSNBC; MTV; National Geographic Channel; NBCSN; New England Sports Network; Nickelodeon; Oxygen; Spike TV; Syfy; TBS; The Weather Channel; TLC; TNT; Travel Channel; truTV; Turner Classic Movies; TV Land; USA Network; VH1.

Fee: $55.00 monthly.

Digital Pay Service 1
Pay Units: N.A.
Programming (via satellite): Cinemax (multiplexed); Flix; HBO (multiplexed); Showtime (multiplexed); Starz (multiplexed); Starz Encore (multiplexed); The Movie Channel (multiplexed).

Video-On-Demand: Yes

Pay-Per-View
ETC (delivered digitally); iN DEMAND (delivered digitally); Playboy TV (delivered digitally); Pleasure (delivered digitally); Fresh (delivered digitally); NHL Center Ice (delivered digitally); MLB Extra Innings (delivered digitally).

Internet Service
Operational: Yes.
Subscribers: 111,396.
Broadband Service: Charter Internet.
Fee: $29.95 monthly; $10.00 modem lease; $195.00 modem purchase.

Telephone Service
Digital: Operational
Subscribers: 65,268.
Miles of Plant: 6,602.0 (coaxial); 2,656.0 (fiber optic). Homes passed: 241,179.
Vice President & General Manager: Greg Garabedian. Vice President, Technical Operations: Gregg Wood. Technical Operations Manager: Kevin Mailloux. Marketing Director: Dennis Jerome. Accounting Director: David Sovanski.
Ownership: Charter Communications Inc. (MSO).

MICHIGAN

Total Systems: 82	Communities with Applications: 0
Total Communities Served: 1,444	Number of Basic Subscribers: 1,723,565
Franchises Not Yet Operating: 0	Number of Expanded Basic Subscribers: 5,640
Applications Pending: 0	Number of Pay Units: 1,937

Top 100 Markets Represented: Kalamazoo-Grand Rapids-Battle Creek (37); Toledo, OH (52); Detroit (5); Flint-Bay City-Saginaw (61); South Bend-Elkhart, IN (80); Lansing-Onondaga (92).

For a list of cable communities in this section, see the Cable Community Index located in the back of Cable Volume 2. For explanation of terms used in cable system listings, see p. D-11.

ADDISON (village)—Comcast Cable. Now served by DETROIT, MI [MI0001]. ICA: MI0124.

ADRIAN—Comcast Cable. Now served by DETROIT, MI [MI0001]. ICA: MI0044.

AKRON/FAIRGROVE—Formerly served by Pine River Cable. No longer in operation. ICA: MI0212.

ALBA—Charter Communications. Now served by TRAVERSE CITY, MI [MI0026]. ICA: MI0241.

ALLEGAN—Charter Communications. Now served by ALLENDALE TWP., MI [MI0094]. ICA: MI0055.

ALLEN (village)—Formerly served by CableDirect. No longer in operation. ICA: MI0256.

ALLEN PARK—Comcast Cable. Now served by DETROIT, MI [MI0001]. ICA: MI0008.

ALLENDALE—AcenTek (formerly Allendale Communications). Now served by AcenTek, MESICK, MI [MI5074]. ICA: MI5000.

ALLENDALE TWP.—Charter Communications, 12405 Powerscourt Dr, St. Louis, MO 63131. Phones: 636-207-5100 (Corporate office); 231-947-5221. Web Site: http://www.charter.com. Also serves Aetna Twp. (Mecosta County), Alamo Twp., Algoma Twp., Allegan, Allegan County (portions), Allegan Twp., Alpine Twp., Amber Twp., Ashland Twp., Austin Twp. (Mecosta County), Belding, Berlin Twp. (Ionia County), Big Rapids, Blendon Twp., Blue Lake Twp. (Muskegon County), Bowne Twp., Brooks Twp. (portions), Caledonia, Caledonia Twp. (Kent County), Cannon, Cascade Twp., Casnovia (village), Cedar Springs, Coopersville, Country Acres Mobile Home Park, Courtland Twp., Crockery Twp., Dalton Twp. (portions), Day Twp., Deerfield Twp. (Mecosta County), Dorr Twp. (portions), Douglass Twp., Easton Twp., Edmore, Ensley Twp., Eureka Twp., Evart, Everett Twp., Evergreen Twp., Fillmore Twp. (northwest portion), Freeman Twp., Fruitland, Fruitport Charter Twp. (portions), Fruitport Village, Gaines Twp. (Kent County), Garfield Twp. (Newaygo County), Gobles City, Grand Haven, Grant, Grant Twp. (Newaygo County), Grant Twp. (Oceana County), Green Twp. (Mecosta County), Greenville, Gunplain Twp., Hamlin Twp. (Mason County), Hart, Hart Twp., Heath Twp., Hersey, Holland Twp., Home Twp., Hopkins, Howard City, Hudsonville, Ionia, Ionia Twp., Jamestown Twp. (portions), Kent City, Laketown Twp., Lakewood (village), Leighton Twp., Ludington, Lyons Twp., Lyons Village, Manlius Twp., Maple Valley Twp. (Montcalm County), Martin (village), Martin Twp., McBrides Village, Middleville, Montague, Montcalm Twp., Montcalm Twp. (northern portion), Morley, Muir, Nelson Twp. (portions), New Era (village), Newaygo, Olive Twp. (Ottawa County), Orangeville Twp., Orleans Twp. (Osceola County), Otisco Twp., Otsego City, Overisel Twp., Park Twp. (Ottawa County), Pentwater, Pere Marquette Twp., Pierson (village), Pine Grove Twp., Pine Twp., Plainfield Twp. (Kent County), Plainwell City, Polkton Twp., Port Sheldon Twp., Reed City, Reynolds Twp., Richmond Twp. (Osceola County), Robinson Twp., Rockford, Ronald Twp., Rothbury, Sand Lake, Scottville, Shelby (unincorporated areas), Sheridan, Sidney Twp., Solon Twp. (Kent County), Sparta, Sparta Twp., Spencer Twp., Spring Lake, Stanton, Stanwood, Summit Twp. (Mason Co.), Tallmadge Twp., Thornapple Twp., Trowbridge Twp., Tyrone Twp. (Kent County), Valley Twp., Watson Twp., Wayland, Weare Twp., White River Twp., Whitehall, Winfield Twp., Wright Twp. (portions), Yankee Springs Twp. & Zeeland Twp. ICA: MI0094.

TV Market Ranking: 37 (Alamo Twp., Algoma Twp., Allegan, Allegan County (portions), Allegan Twp., ALLENDALE TWP., Alpine Twp., Ashland Twp., Belding, Bowne Twp., Brooks Twp. (portions), Caledonia Twp. (Kent County), Cannon, Cascade Twp., Casnovia (village), Cedar Springs, Coopersville, Country Acres Mobile Home Park, Courtland Twp., Crockery Twp., Dorr Twp. (portions), Douglass Twp., Ensley Twp., Eureka Twp., Everett Twp., Evergreen Twp., Fillmore Twp. (northwest portion), Fruitport Charter Twp. (portions), Fruitport Village, Gaines Twp. (Kent County), Garfield Twp. (Newaygo County), Gobles City, Grand Haven, Grant, Grant Twp. (Newaygo County), Greenville, Gunplain Twp., Heath Twp., Holland Twp., Hopkins, Howard City, Jamestown Twp. (portions), Kent City, Laketown Twp., Leighton Twp., Lyons Twp., Lyons Village, Manlius Twp., Maple Valley Twp. (Montcalm County), Martin (village), Martin Twp., McBrides Village, Montcalm, Montcalm Twp. (northern portion), Muir, Nelson Twp. (portions), Newaygo, Olive Twp. (Ottawa County), Orangeville Twp., Orleans Twp., Otisco Twp., Otsego City, Overisel Twp., Park Twp. (Ottawa County), Pierson (village), Pine Grove Twp., Pine Twp., Plainfield Twp. (Kent County), Plainwell City, Polkton Twp., Port Sheldon Twp., Reynolds Twp., Robinson Twp., Rockford, Ronald Twp., Sand Lake, Sheridan, Sidney Twp., Solon Twp. (Kent County), Sparta, Sparta Twp., Spencer Twp., Spring Lake, Tallmadge Twp., Thornapple Twp., Trowbridge Twp., Tyrone Twp. (Kent County), Valley Twp., Watson Twp., Wayland, Wright Twp. (portions), Yankee Springs Twp., Zeeland Twp.); 37,92 (Berlin Twp. (Ionia County), Easton Twp., Ionia, Ionia Twp.); Below 100 (Blendon Twp., Blue Lake Twp. (Muskegon County), Dalton Twp. (portions), Freeman Twp., Fruitland, Grant Twp. (Oceana County), Hart Twp., Hersey, Hudsonville, Lakewood (village), New Era (village), Osceola Twp. (Osceola County), Richmond Twp. (Osceola County), Rothbury, Shelby (unincorporated areas), Weare Twp., White River Twp., Evart, Hart, Reed City, Whitehall); Outside TV Markets (Aetna Twp. (Mecosta County), Amber Twp., Austin Twp. (Mecosta County), Day Twp., Deerfield Twp. (Mecosta County), Edmore, Green Twp. (Mecosta County), Home Twp., Morley, Pere Marquette Twp., Scottville, Stanton, Stanwood, Summit Twp. (Mason Co.), Winfield Twp., Big Rapids, Ludington, Pentwater). Franchise award date: December 26, 1980. Franchise expiration date: N.A. Began: August 1, 1981.

Channel capacity: 64 (operating 2-way). Channels available but not in use: N.A.

Digital Basic Service
Subscribers: 92,058.
Programming (via satellite): AXS TV; BBC America; Boomerang; Cine Mexicano; CMT; CNN en Espanol; Destination America; Discovery Familia; Discovery Kids Channel; Discovery Life Channel; DIY Network; ESPN Deportes; ESPN HD; FOX College Sports Central; FOX College Sports Pacific; Fox Deportes; Fox Sports 2; Fuse; FXM; FYI; GolTV; Great American Country; HD Theater; History en Espanol; History International; IFC; Investigation Discovery; LMN; MC; MTV Classic; MTV Hits; MTV Jams; Nick 2; Nick Jr.; Nicktoons; Outdoor Channel; OWN; Oprah Winfrey Network; Science Channel; Sundance TV; TeenNick; TNT HD; Tr3s; UniMas; Universal HD; Univision; Univision Studios; VH1 Soul; VideoRola.
Fee: $14.99 monthly.

Digital Expanded Basic Service
Subscribers: N.A.
Programming (via satellite): A&E; AMC; Animal Planet; Bravo; Cartoon Network; CMT; CNBC; CNN; Comedy Central; Discovery Channel; Disney Channel; Disney XD; E! HD; ESPN; ESPN Classic; ESPN2; ESPNews; EWTN Global Catholic Network; Food Network; Fox News Channel; Fox Sports 1; FOX Sports Detroit; Freeform; FX; Golf Channel; GSN; Hallmark Channel; HGTV; History; HLN; INSP; Lifetime; MSNBC; MTV; MTV2; National Geographic Channel; NBCSN; Nickelodeon; Oxygen; Spike TV; Syfy; The Weather Channel; TLC; TNT; Travel Channel; Trinity Broadcasting Network (TBN); truTV; Turner Classic Movies; TV Land; Univision Studios; USA Network; VH1; WE tv.
Fee: $47.99 monthly.

Digital Pay Service 1
Pay Units: N.A.
Programming (via satellite): Cinemax (multiplexed); Cinemax HD; Flix; HBO (multiplexed); HBO HD; LOGO; Showtime (multiplexed); Showtime HD; Starz (multiplexed); Starz Encore (multiplexed); The Movie Channel (multiplexed).

Video-On-Demand: Yes

Pay-Per-View
iN DEMAND (delivered digitally); NHL Center Ice (delivered digitally); MLB Extra Innings (delivered digitally); ESPN (delivered digitally); Playboy TV (delivered digitally); Fresh (delivered digitally); Shorteez (delivered digitally).

Internet Service
Operational: Yes.
Subscribers: 90,924.
Broadband Service: Charter Internet.
Fee: $99.95 installation; $29.99 monthly; $3.95 modem lease.

Telephone Service
Digital: Operational.
Subscribers: 53,264.
Fee: $29.99 monthly
Miles of Plant: 7,520.0 (coaxial); 1,406.0 (fiber optic). Homes passed: 219,562.
Vice President & General Manager: Dan Spoelman. Marketing Director: Steve Schuh. Accounting Director: David Sovanski. Technical Operations Manager: Keith Schierbeek.
Ownership: Charter Communications Inc. (MSO).

ALMA—Charter Communications. Now served by MIDLAND, MI [MI0030]. ICA: MI0085.

ALMONT—Charter Communications. Now served by GOODRICH, MI [MI0290]. ICA: MI0257.

ALPENA—Charter Communications, 12405 Powerscourt Dr, St. Louis, MO 63131. Phones: 636-207-5100 (Corporate office); 989-340-0078; 989-356-4503; 231-947-5221 (Traverse City office). Fax: 989-356-3761. Web Site: http://www.charter.com. Also serves Alcona Twp., Alpena Twp., Caledonia Twp. (Alcona County), Green Twp. (Alpena County), Hawes Twp. (portions), Krakow Twp., Long Rapids Twp., Maple Ridge Twp. (Alpena County), Moltke Twp., Ossineke Twp., Rogers City, Rogers Twp., Sanborn Twp. & Wilson Twp. (Alpena County). ICA: MI0061.

TV Market Ranking: Below 100 (Alcona Twp., ALPENA, Alpena Twp., Green Twp. (Alpena County), Krakow Twp., Long Rapids Twp., Maple Ridge Twp. (Alpena County), Moltke Twp., Ossineke Twp., Rogers Twp., Sanborn

Cable Systems—Michigan

Twp., Wilson Twp. (Alpena County), Rogers City); Outside TV Markets (Caledonia Twp. (Alcona County), Hawes Twp. (portions)). Franchise award date: N.A. Franchise expiration date: N.A. Began: August 1, 1958.
Channel capacity: N.A. Channels available but not in use: N.A.

Digital Basic Service
Subscribers: 8,988.
Programming (via satellite): BBC America; Bloomberg Television; Discovery Digital Networks; DMX Music; ESPN Classic; ESPNews; Fuse; FXM; FYI; History International; IFC; LMN; Nick Jr.; Sundance TV; TeenNick.
Fee: $26.99 monthly.

Digital Expanded Basic Service
Subscribers: N.A.
Programming (via satellite): A&E; AMC; Animal Planet; BET; Bravo; Cartoon Network; CMT; CNBC; CNN; Comedy Central; Discovery Channel; Discovery Life Channel; Disney Channel; Disney XD; E! HD; ESPN; ESPN2; Food Network; Fox News Channel; Fox Sports 1; FOX Sports Detroit; Freeform; FX; Golf Channel; GSN; Hallmark Channel; HGTV; History; HLN; Lifetime; MSNBC; MTV; National Geographic Channel; NBCSN; Nickelodeon; Outdoor Channel; Oxygen; Spike TV; Syfy; Telemundo; The Weather Channel; TLC; TNT; Travel Channel; truTV; Turner Classic Movies; TV Land; Univision Studios; USA Network; VH1; WE tv.
Fee: $36.49 monthly.

Digital Pay Service 1
Pay Units: N.A.
Programming (via satellite): Cinemax (multiplexed); HBO (multiplexed); Showtime (multiplexed); Starz (multiplexed); The Movie Channel.
Fee: $10.00 monthly (Cinemax, HBO, Showtime/TMC or Starz).

Video-On-Demand: Yes
Pay-Per-View
ESPN Now (delivered digitally); Hot Choice (delivered digitally); iN DEMAND (delivered digitally); Playboy TV (delivered digitally); Fresh (delivered digitally); Shorteez (delivered digitally).

Internet Service
Operational: Yes.
Subscribers: 7,382.
Broadband Service: Charter Internet.
Fee: $49.95 installation; $29.99 monthly; $5.00 modem lease.

Telephone Service
Digital: Operational
Subscribers: 5,903.
Miles of Plant: 745.0 (coaxial); 342.0 (fiber optic). Homes passed: 19,402.
Vice President: Joe Boullion. General Manager: Ed Kavanaugh. Technical Operations Director: Rob Nowak. Accounting Director: David Sovanski. Marketing Manager: Brenda Auger.
Ownership: Charter Communications Inc. (MSO).

ALPHA (village)—Upper Peninsula Communications, 397 North US Hwy 41, Carney, MI 49812-9757. Phones: 906-639-2111; 906-639-2194. Fax: 906-639-9936. E-mail: louied@alphacomm.net. ICA: MI0258.
TV Market Ranking: Below 100 (ALPHA (VILLAGE)). Franchise award date: N.A. Franchise expiration date: N.A. Began: August 1, 1990.
Channel capacity: 40 (not 2-way capable). Channels available but not in use: N.A.

Basic Service
Subscribers: 24.
Programming (received off-air): WBKP (ABC, CW) Calumet; WJFW-TV (Antenna TV, NBC) Rhinelander; WJMN-TV (CBS) Escanaba; WLUC-TV (FOX, NBC) Marquette; WNMU (PBS) Marquette; WZMQ (Antenna TV, MeTV, MNT, This TV) Marquette.
Programming (via satellite): A&E; AMC; CMT; CNN; Discovery Channel; Disney Channel; ESPN; ESPN2; EWTN Global Catholic Network; Freeform; HGTV; History; HLN; ION Television; Lifetime; QVC; Spike TV; TBS; The Weather Channel; TLC; TNT; Turner Classic Movies; TV Land; USA Network; WGN America.
Fee: $50.00 installation; $32.00 monthly.

Pay Service 1
Pay Units: N.A.
Programming (via satellite): Showtime.

Video-On-Demand: No
Internet Service
Operational: No.
Telephone Service
None
Miles of Plant: 2.0 (coaxial); None (fiber optic). Homes passed: 114.
General Manager & Chief Technician: Louis Dupont.
Ownership: Upper Peninsula Communications Inc. (MSO).

AMASA—Upper Peninsula Communications, 397 North US Hwy 41, Carney, MI 49812-9757. Phones: 906-639-2111; 906-639-2194. Fax: 906-639-9936. E-mail: louied@alphacomm.net. ICA: MI0259.
TV Market Ranking: Outside TV Markets (AMASA). Franchise award date: N.A. Franchise expiration date: N.A. Began: August 1, 1990.
Channel capacity: 40 (not 2-way capable). Channels available but not in use: N.A.

Basic Service
Subscribers: 32.
Programming (received off-air): WBKP (ABC, CW) Calumet; WJFW-TV (Antenna TV, NBC) Rhinelander; WJMN-TV (CBS) Escanaba; WLUC-TV (FOX, NBC) Marquette; WNMU (PBS) Marquette; WZMQ (Antenna TV, MeTV, MNT, This TV) Marquette.
Programming (via satellite): A&E; AMC; CNN; C-SPAN; Discovery Channel; ESPN; ESPN2; Freeform; HGTV; History; HLN; ION Television; Lifetime; Spike TV; TBS; The Weather Channel; TLC; TNT; Trinity Broadcasting Network (TBN); Turner Classic Movies; TV Land; USA Network; WGN America.
Fee: $50.00 installation; $30.50 monthly.

Pay Service 1
Pay Units: N.A.
Programming (via satellite): Showtime.

Video-On-Demand: No
Internet Service
Operational: No.
Telephone Service
None
Miles of Plant: 3.0 (coaxial); None (fiber optic). Homes passed: 120.
General Manager & Chief Technician: Louis Dupont.
Ownership: Upper Peninsula Communications Inc. (MSO).

AMBOY TWP.—Formerly served by CableDirect. No longer in operation. ICA: MI0260.

ANN ARBOR—Comcast Cable. Now served by DETROIT, MI [MI0001]. ICA: MI0006.

APPLEGATE—Formerly served by Cablevision Systems Corp. No longer in operation. ICA: MI0262.

ARNOLD LAKE—Formerly served by Charter Communications. No longer in operation. ICA: MI0445.

ASHLEY—Formerly served by Pine River Cable. No longer in operation. ICA: MI0245.

ATLANTA—Formerly served by Northwoods Cable Inc. No longer in operation. ICA: MI0392.

ATTICA TWP.—Charter Communications. Now served by GOODRICH, MI [MI0290]. ICA: MI0263.

AU GRES—Charter Communications. Now served by MIDLAND, MI [MI0030]. ICA: MI0143.

AUBURN HILLS—Comcast Cable. Now served by DETROIT, MI [MI0001]. ICA: MI0005.

BAD AXE—Comcast Cable. Now served by DETROIT, MI [MI0001]. ICA: MI0108.

BAINBRIDGE TWP.—Michiana Supernet, 255B Bell Rd, Niles, MI 49120. Phone: 269-591-8798. Fax: 269-683-7453. E-mail: info@michianasupernet.com. Web Site: http://www.michianasupernet.com. Also serves Pipestone Twp. ICA: MI0449.
TV Market Ranking: 37 (BAINBRIDGE TWP., Pipestone Twp.).
Channel capacity: N.A. Channels available but not in use: N.A.
Vice President: Jack Brewer.
Ownership: SMR Communications Inc.

BALDWIN (village)—Mlcom, PO Box 100, Montague, MI 49437. Phone: 888-873-3353. Fax: 231-894-4960. E-mail: customerservice@micomcable.com. Web Site: http://www.micomcable.com. Also serves Big Prairie Twp., Croton Twp., Denver Twp., Everett Twp., Hesperia, Lilley Twp., Newfield Twp., Sherman Twp., White Cloud & Wilcox Twp. ICA: MI0214.
TV Market Ranking: 37 (Croton Twp.); Below 100 (BALDWIN (VILLAGE), Hesperia, Newfield Twp., White Cloud, Wilcox Twp.); Outside TV Markets (Big Prairie Twp.). Franchise award date: N.A. Franchise expiration date: N.A. Began: August 1, 1982.
Channel capacity: 36 (2-way capable). Channels available but not in use: N.A.

Basic Service
Subscribers: 642.
Programming (received off-air): WCMV (PBS) Cadillac; WFQX-TV (FOX) Cadillac; WPBN-TV (NBC) Traverse City; WTOM-TV (NBC) Cheboygan; WWTV (CBS) Cadillac; WZZM (ABC) Grand Rapids.
Programming (via satellite): Nickelodeon; Pop; QVC; WFUP (FOX) Vanderbilt.
Fee: $38.00 installation; $52.95 monthly.

Expanded Basic Service 1
Subscribers: N.A.
Programming (via satellite): A&E; AMC; Animal Planet; BET; BTN; Cartoon Network; CMT; CNBC; CNN; Comedy Central; C-SPAN; C-SPAN 2; Discovery Channel; Disney Channel; E! HD; ESPN; ESPN Classic; ESPN2; ESPNews; Food Network; Fox News Channel; Fox Sports 1; FOX Sports Detroit; Freeform; FX; Great American Country; GSN; Hallmark Channel; Hallmark Movies & Mysteries; HGTV; History; HLN; Lifetime; MSNBC; MTV; National Geographic Channel; NBCSN; Oxygen; Spike TV; Syfy; The Sportsman Channel; The Weather Channel; TLC; TNT; Travel Channel; Trinity Broadcasting Network (TBN); truTV; TV Land; USA Network; VH1; WE tv; WGN America.
Fee: $30.00 monthly.

Digital Basic Service
Subscribers: N.A.
Programming (via satellite): American Heroes Channel; BBC America; Bloomberg Television; Bravo; Centric; Chiller; Cloo; CMT; Cooking Channel; Destination America; Discovery Kids Channel; Discovery Life Channel; Disney XD; DMX Music; EVINE Live; Fuse; FXM; FYI; History; History International; Investigation Discovery; LMN; MTV Classic; MTV Hits; MTV2; Nick Jr.; Nicktoons; OWN: Oprah Winfrey Network; RFD-TV; Science Channel; Sprout; TeenNick; Turner Classic Movies; VH1 Soul; Youtoo America.

Digital Expanded Basic Service
Subscribers: N.A.
Programming (via satellite): Discovery Life Channel; ESPN Classic; ESPN2; ESPNews; FOX College Sports Central; FOX College Sports Pacific; Golf Channel; HorseTV Channel; Outdoor Channel; TVG Network.
Fee: $8.00 monthly.

Digital Pay Service 1
Pay Units: N.A.
Programming (via satellite): Cinemax (multiplexed); Flix; HBO (multiplexed); Showtime (multiplexed); Starz (multiplexed); Starz Encore (multiplexed); The Movie Channel.
Fee: $13.00 monthly (Starz/Encore), $14.00 monthly (Cinemax), $16.00 monthly (HBO or Showtime/TMC/Flix).

Video-On-Demand: No
Internet Service
Operational: Yes.
Telephone Service
None
Miles of Plant: 77.0 (coaxial); 19.0 (fiber optic). Homes passed: 1,000.
Ownership: Mlcom (MSO).

BARRYTON—Formerly served by Pine River Cable. No longer in operation. ICA: MI0264.

BARTON CITY—Formerly served by Pine River Cable. No longer in operation. ICA: MI0265.

BATTLE CREEK—Comcast Cable. Now served by DETROIT, MI [MI0001]. ICA: MI0020.

BAY CITY—Charter Communications. Now served by MIDLAND, MI [MI0030]. ICA: MI0018.

BEAR LAKE—Charter Communications. Now served by TRAVERSE CITY, MI [MI0026]. ICA: MI0149.

BEAVER ISLAND—Formerly served by Pine River Cable. No longer in operation. ICA: MI0352.

BEAVER TWP. (Bay County)—Charter Communications. Now served by MIDLAND, MI [MI0030]. ICA: MI0176.

BERGLAND—Charter Communications. Now served by IRONWOOD, MI [MI0064]. ICA: MI0269.

2017 Edition

Michigan—Cable Systems

BERLIN TWP. (St. Clair County)—Formerly served by Charter Communications. No longer in operation. ICA: MI0270.

BIG PRAIRIE TWP.—MIcom. Now served by BALDWIN (village), MI [MI0214]. ICA: MI0226.

BIG RAPIDS—Charter Communications. Now served by ALLENDALE TWP., MI [MI0094]. ICA: MI0083.

BIG STAR LAKE—Formerly served by MIcom. No longer in operation. ICA: MI0173.

BILLINGS TWP.—Charter Communications, 915 East Broomfield, Mt. Pleasant, MI 48858. Phones: 636-207-5100 (Corporate office); 314-543-2236; 231-947-5221 (Traverse City office); 989-356-4503. Web Site: http://www.charter.com. Also serves Hay Twp. & Tobacco Twp. ICA: MI0272.
TV Market Ranking: 61 (BILLINGS TWP.); Outside TV Markets (Hay Twp., Tobacco Twp.). Channel capacity: N.A. Channels available but not in use: N.A.
Digital Basic Service
Subscribers: 1,613.
Programming (received off-air): WCMU-TV (PBS) Mount Pleasant; WJRT-TV (ABC, MeTV) Flint; WNEM-TV (CBS, COZI TV, MNT) Bay City; WSMH (Antenna TV, FOX, The Country Network) Flint; WWTV (CBS) Cadillac.
Programming (via satellite): A&E; CMT; CNN; C-SPAN; Discovery Channel; ESPN; Freeform; HLN; Lifetime; MTV; Nickelodeon; Spike TV; TBS; The Weather Channel; USA Network; WGN America.
Fee: $49.99 installation; $14.99 monthly.
Pay Service 1
Pay Units: N.A.
Programming (via satellite): Showtime; The Movie Channel.
Fee: $20.00 installation; $7.00 monthly (each).
Video-On-Demand: No
Internet Service
Operational: No.
Telephone Service
None
Miles of Plant: 60.0 (coaxial); None (fiber optic). Homes passed: 3,332.
Vice President: Joe Boullion. General Manager: Ed Kavanaugh. Technical Operations Director: Rob Nowak. Accounting Director: David Sovanski. Marketing Manager: Brenda Auger.
Ownership: Charter Communications Inc. (MSO).

BIRMINGHAM—Comcast Cable. Now served by DETROIT, MI [MI0001]. ICA: MI0022.

BLOOMINGDALE TWP. (Van Buren County)—Bloomingdale Communications, 101 West Kalamazoo St, PO Box 187, Bloomingdale, MI 49026-0187. Phones: 269-415-0500 (Paw Paw office); 800-377-3130; 269-521-7300. Fax: 269-521-7373. E-mail: staff@bloomingdalecom.net. Web Site: http://www.bloomingdalecom.net. Also serves Arlington Twp., Bloomingdale (village), Cheshire Twp., Lee Twp. (Allegan County), Van Buren County (portions) & Waverly Twp. (Van Buren County). ICA: MI0177.
TV Market Ranking: 37 (Arlington Twp., BLOOMINGDALE TWP. (VAN BUREN COUNTY), Cheshire Twp., Lee Twp. (Allegan County), Van Buren County (portions), Waverly Twp. (Van Buren County)). Franchise award date: N.A. Franchise expiration date: N.A. Began: June 1, 1988.
Channel capacity: N.A. Channels available but not in use: N.A.
Basic Service
Subscribers: 1,213.
Programming (received off-air): WGVU-TV (PBS) Grand Rapids; WLLA (IND, MeTV) Kalamazoo; WOOD-TV (Laff, NBC) Grand Rapids; WOTV (ABC, Grit, TheCoolTV) Battle Creek; WSBT-TV (CBS, FOX) South Bend; WWMT (CBS, CW) Kalamazoo; WXMI (Antenna TV, FOX, This TV) Grand Rapids; WZPX-TV (ION) Battle Creek; WZZM (ABC) Grand Rapids.
Programming (via satellite): TBS; The Weather Channel.
Fee: $20.00 installation; $15.99 monthly.
Expanded Basic Service 1
Subscribers: N.A.
Programming (via satellite): A&E; AMC; CNBC; CNN; Discovery Channel; Disney Channel; ESPN; ESPN2; FOX Sports Networks; Freeform; History; HLN; Nickelodeon; QVC; Spike TV; Syfy; TLC; TNT; USA Network; WGN America.
Fee: $20.00 installation; $29.99 monthly.
Pay Service 1
Pay Units: 60.
Programming (via satellite): Cinemax; HBO; Starz Encore; The Movie Channel.
Fee: $3.00 monthly (Encore), $11.00 monthly (Cinemax), $13.00 monthly (TMC), $17.00 monthly (HBO).
Video-On-Demand: No
Internet Service
Operational: Yes, DSL.
Fee: $39.95-$69.95 monthly.
Telephone Service
Analog: Operational
Fee: $21.40 monthly
Miles of Plant: 73.0 (coaxial); None (fiber optic).
President: Robert Remington. General Manager: Mark Bahnson. Facilities Manager: Dan Key.
Ownership: Bloomingdale Communications.

BOARDMAN TWP. (southern portion)—ATI Networks Inc., 344 South Cedar St, PO Box 1558, Kalkaska, MI 49646. Phone: 231-518-0200. Fax: 231-518-0219. E-mail: info@atinetworks.net. Web Site: http://atinetworks.net. Also serves Kalkaska County (portions) & Orange Twp. (Kalkaska County). ICA: MI0221.
TV Market Ranking: Below 100 (BOARDMAN TWP. (SOUTHERN PORTION), Kalkaska County (portions), Orange Twp. (Kalkaska County)). Franchise award date: N.A. Franchise expiration date: N.A. Began: January 15, 1991.
Channel capacity: 54 (not 2-way capable). Channels available but not in use: N.A.
Basic Service
Subscribers: N.A.
Programming (received off-air): WCML (PBS) Alpena; WFQX-TV (FOX) Cadillac; WGTU (ABC, CW) Traverse City; WPBN-TV (NBC) Traverse City; WWTV (CBS) Cadillac.
Programming (via satellite): TBS.
Fee: $50.00 installation; $8.83 monthly; $1.00 converter.
Expanded Basic Service 1
Subscribers: N.A.
Programming (via satellite): A&E; Bravo; CMT; CNN; C-SPAN; Discovery Channel; ESPN; Freeform; HGTV; HLN; Spike TV; The Weather Channel; TNT; USA Network.
Fee: $14.10 monthly.
Pay Service 1
Pay Units: N.A.
Programming (via satellite): Cinemax; HBO.
Fee: $9.95 monthly (each).
Internet Service
Operational: No.
Telephone Service
None
Miles of Plant: 18.0 (coaxial); None (fiber optic). Homes passed: 422.
President & Managing Partner: Gary John. Office Manager: Shelly Narva.
Ownership: ATI Networks Inc. (MSO).

BRETHREN—Formerly served by Pine River Cable. No longer in operation. ICA: MI0274.

BRIDGEPORT TWP.—Charter Communications. Now served by MIDLAND, MI [MI0030]. ICA: MI0063.

BRIGHTON—Comcast Cable. Now served by DETROIT, MI [MI0001]. ICA: MI0046.

BRONSON TWP. (portions)—Formerly served by CableDirect. No longer in operation. ICA: MI0329.

BROOKLYN (IRISH HILLS)—Comcast Cable. Now served by SUMMIT TWP. (Jackson County), MI [MI0039]. ICA: MI0080.

BROOMFIELD TRAILER PARK—Charter Communications, 915 E Broomfield, Mt. Pleasant, MI 48858. Phones: 636-207-5100 (Corporate office); 314-543-2236. Web Site: http://www.charter.com. ICA: MI0275.
TV Market Ranking: Outside TV Markets (BROOMFIELD TRAILER PARK).
Channel capacity: N.A. Channels available but not in use: N.A.
Digital Basic Service
Subscribers: 17.
Programming (received off-air): WAQP (IND) Saginaw; WCMU-TV (PBS) Mount Pleasant; WJRT-TV (ABC, MeTV) Flint; WNEM-TV (CBS, COZI TV, MNT) Bay City; WWTV (CBS) Cadillac.
Programming (via satellite): CNN; Discovery Channel; ESPN; HLN; Spike TV; TBS; WGN America.
Fee: $49.99 installation; $32.99 monthly.
Pay Service 1
Pay Units: N.A.
Programming (via satellite): Showtime; The Movie Channel.
Fee: $20.00 installation; $7.00 monthly (each).
Internet Service
Operational: No.
Telephone Service
None
Miles of Plant: 2.0 (coaxial); None (fiber optic). Homes passed: 1,342.
Vice President & General Manager: Dan Spoelman. Accounting Director: David Sovanski. Operations Manager: Ed Bucao.
Ownership: Charter Communications Inc. (MSO).

BROWN CITY—Comcast Cable. Now served by DETROIT, MI [MI0001]. ICA: MI0370.

BRUTUS—Formerly served by CenturyLink. No longer in service. ICA: MI0444.

BURT—Charter Communications. Now served by TRAVERSE CITY, MI [MI0026]. ICA: MI0196.

BURTON—Comcast Cable. Now served by DETROIT, MI [MI0001]. ICA: MI0004.

BUTMAN TWP.—Charter Communications, 915 East Broomfield, Mt. Pleasant, MI 48858. Phones: 636-207-5100 (Corporate office); 989-340-0078; 231-947-5221 (Traverse City office); 989-356-4503. Web Site: http://www.charter.com. Also serves Bourret Twp., Clement Twp. & Secord Twp. ICA: MI0114.
TV Market Ranking: Below 100 (Bourret Twp.); Outside TV Markets (BUTMAN TWP, Clement Twp., Secord Twp.). Franchise award date: September 8, 1988. Franchise expiration date: N.A. Began: June 1, 1990.
Channel capacity: N.A. Channels available but not in use: N.A.
Digital Basic Service
Subscribers: 1,190.
Programming (received off-air): WAQP (IND) Saginaw; WCMU-TV (PBS) Mount Pleasant; WEYI-TV (Bounce TV, CW, NBC) Saginaw; WFQX-TV (FOX) Cadillac; WJRT-TV (ABC, MeTV) Flint; WNEM-TV (CBS, COZI TV, MNT) Bay City; WSMH (Antenna TV, FOX, The Country Network) Flint; WWTV (CBS) Cadillac.
Programming (via satellite): QVC; TBS.
Fee: $49.99 installation; $21.99 monthly; $1.00 converter.
Digital Expanded Basic Service
Subscribers: N.A.
Programming (via satellite): A&E; CNN; C-SPAN; C-SPAN 2; Discovery Channel; Disney Channel; ESPN; Fox News Channel; FOX Sports Detroit; Freeform; HGTV; History; HLN; Lifetime; MTV; Nickelodeon; Spike TV; Syfy; The Weather Channel; TLC; TNT; truTV; USA Network; VH1.
Fee: $36.49 monthly.
Digital Pay Service 1
Pay Units: N.A.
Programming (via satellite): Cinemax; HBO; Showtime.
Fee: $9.95 monthly (each).
Internet Service
Operational: Yes.
Subscribers: 9,995.
Broadband Service: Charter Internet.
Fee: $19.99 monthly.
Telephone Service
Digital: Operational
Subscribers: 8,710.
Fee: $14.99 monthly
Miles of Plant: 105.0 (coaxial); None (fiber optic). Homes passed: 3,393.
Vice President: Joe Boullion. General Manager: Ed Kavanaugh. Technical Operations Director: Rob Nowak. Accounting Director: David Sovanski. Marketing Manager: Brenda Auger.
Ownership: Charter Communications Inc. (MSO).

CADILLAC—Charter Communications. Now served by TRAVERSE CITY, MI [MI0026]. ICA: MI0082.

CAMBRIA TWP.—Formerly served by CableDirect. No longer in operation. ICA: MI0276.

CANADIAN LAKES—Formerly served by Charter Communications. No longer in operation. ICA: MI0164.

CARNEY/POWERS—Packerland Broadband, 105 Kent St., PO Box 885, Iron Mountain, MI 49801. Phone: 800-236-8434. Fax: 906-776-2811. E-mail: service@plbb.net; support@packerlandbroadband.com. Web Site: http://www.packerlandbroadband.com. Also serves Nadeau. ICA: MI0341.
TV Market Ranking: Below 100 (CARNEY/POWERS, Nadeau). Franchise award date:

Cable Systems—Michigan

October 1, 1985. Franchise expiration date: N.A. Began: November 1, 1986.
Channel capacity: 36 (not 2-way capable). Channels available but not in use: N.A.
Basic Service
Subscribers: 28.
Programming (received off-air): WBKB-TV (ABC, CBS, FOX) Alpena; WJFW-TV (Antenna TV, NBC) Rhinelander; WJMN-TV (CBS) Escanaba; WKRN-TV (ABC) Nashville; WLUC-TV (FOX, NBC) Marquette; WLUK-TV (Antenna TV, FOX) Green Bay; WNMU (PBS) Marquette.
Programming (via satellite): A&E; Cartoon Network; CMT; CNN; C-SPAN; Discovery Channel; Disney Channel; ESPN; ESPN2; EWTN Global Catholic Network; FOX Sports Networks; Freeform; HGTV; History; HLN; INSP; ION Television; Lifetime; MTV; Outdoor Channel; Spike TV; TBS; The Weather Channel; TNT; Turner Classic Movies; TV Land; USA Network; WGN America.
Fee: $75.00 installation; $26.95 monthly.
Pay Service 1
Pay Units: N.A.
Programming (via satellite): Cinemax.
Fee: $8.00 monthly.
Internet Service
Operational: No.
Telephone Service
None
Miles of Plant: 10.0 (coaxial); None (fiber optic).
General Manager: Cory Heigl. Marketing Director: Andy Datta. Billing/Sales Manager: Jessica Kuhn. Finance: Catherine Faccin.
Ownership: Packerland Broadband (MSO).

CARO—Charter Communications. Now served by GOODRICH, MI [MI0290]. ICA: MI0117.

CARPAC—Comcast Cable. Now served by DETROIT, MI [MI0001]. ICA: MI0371.

CARSON CITY—Formerly served by Pine River Cable. No longer in operation. ICA: MI0203.

CASEVILLE—Comcast Cable. Now served by DETROIT, MI [MI0001]. ICA: MI0038.

CASPIAN—Caspian Community TV Corp, PO Box 240, Caspian, MI 49915-0240. Phones: 906-265-3551 (Chief technician); 906-265-4747. Fax: 906-265-6688. Also serves Gaastra & Stambaugh. ICA: MI0163.
TV Market Ranking: Below 100 (CASPIAN, Gaastra, Stambaugh). Franchise award date: January 1, 1955. Franchise expiration date: N.A. Began: June 1, 1955.
Channel capacity: 50 (not 2-way capable). Channels available but not in use: N.A.
Basic Service
Subscribers: N.A.
Programming (received off-air): WFQX-TV (FOX) Cadillac; WJFW-TV (Antenna TV, NBC) Rhinelander; WLUC-TV (FOX, NBC) Marquette; WNMU (PBS) Marquette; WSAW-TV (CBS, MNT) Wausau; WXYZ-TV (ABC, Bounce TV) Detroit; allband FM.
Programming (via microwave): WJMN-TV (CBS) Escanaba; WLUK-TV (Antenna TV, FOX) Green Bay.
Programming (via satellite): A&E; Animal Planet; Cartoon Network; CNN; C-SPAN; CW PLUS; Discovery Channel; ESPN; EWTN Global Catholic Network; FOX Sports Detroit; Freeform; HGTV; History; Lifetime; TBS; The Weather Channel; TNT; Turner Classic Movies; TV Land; USA Network; WGN America.
Fee: $20.00 installation; $18.00 monthly.

Pay Service 1
Pay Units: N.A.
Programming (via satellite): The Movie Channel.
Fee: $20.00 installation; $8.00 monthly.
Internet Service
Operational: No.
Telephone Service
None
Miles of Plant: 27.0 (coaxial); None (fiber optic). Homes passed: 1,530.
General Manager: Victor Shepich. Chief Technician: Albert Melchiori.
Ownership: Caspian Community TV Corp.

CASS CITY—Charter Communications. Now served by GOODRICH, MI [MI0290]. ICA: MI0179.

CASSOPOLIS—Comcast Cable. Now served by CHAMPAIGN, IL [IL0019]. ICA: MI0168.

CHAMPION TWP.—Formerly served by Upper Peninsula Communications. Now served by Cable America Corp., REPUBLIC, MI [MI0216].. ICA: MI0278.

CHARLEVOIX—Charter Communications. Now served by TRAVERSE CITY, MI [MI0026]. ICA: MI0115.

CHEBOYGAN—Charter Communications. Now served by TRAVERSE CITY, MI [MI0026]. ICA: MI0101.

CHESANING—Charter Communications. Now served by MIDLAND, MI [MI0030]. ICA: MI0160.

CHESTER TWP. (Ottawa County)—Charter Communications, 315 Davis St, Grand Haven, MI 49417. Phones: 636-207-5100 (Corporate office); 616-647-6201. Web Site: http://www.charter.com. Also serves Ravenna & Ravenna Twp. ICA: MI0280.
TV Market Ranking: 37 (Ravenna). Franchise award date: N.A. Franchise expiration date: N.A. Began: July 1, 1991.
Channel capacity: 60 (not 2-way capable). Channels available but not in use: N.A.
Digital Basic Service
Subscribers: 417.
Programming (received off-air): WGVU-TV (PBS) Grand Rapids; WOOD-TV (Laff, NBC) Grand Rapids; WTLJ (IND) Muskegon; WWMT (CBS, CW) Kalamazoo; WXMI (Antenna TV, FOX, This TV) Grand Rapids; WZZM (ABC) Grand Rapids.
Programming (via satellite): CMT; C-SPAN; QVC; TBS; WGN America.
Fee: $49.99 installation; $14.99 monthly.
Digital Expanded Basic Service
Subscribers: N.A.
Programming (via satellite): A&E; AMC; CNBC; CNN; Comedy Central; Discovery Channel; Disney Channel; ESPN; ESPN2; Food Network; FOX Sports Detroit; Freeform; History; HLN; Lifetime; MTV; Nickelodeon; Spike TV; The Weather Channel; TLC; TNT; USA Network; VH1.
Fee: $45.99 monthly.
Digital Pay Service 1
Pay Units: N.A.
Programming (via satellite): Cinemax (multiplexed); HBO; Showtime; Starz; Starz Encore.
Fee: $6.95 monthly (Starz or Encore), $10.95 monthly (Cinemax), $11.95 monthly (HBO), $12.95 monthly (Showtime).
Internet Service
Operational: No.

Telephone Service
None
Homes passed: 873.
Vice President, Operations: Dan Spoelman. Marketing Director: Steve Schuh. Accounting Director: David Sovanski. Technical Operations Supervisor: Keith Schierbeek. Marketing Coordinator: Tracy Bruce.
Ownership: Charter Communications Inc. (MSO).

CHESTERFIELD TWP.—Comcast Cable. Now served by DETROIT, MI [MI0001]. ICA: MI0016.

CHIPPEWA TWP. (Isabella County)—Charter Communications. Now served by MIDLAND, MI [MI0030]. ICA: MI0156.

CLARE—Charter Communications. Now served by MIDLAND, MI [MI0030]. ICA: MI0355.

CLARK TWP.—Formerly served by Northwoods Cable Inc. No longer in operation. ICA: MI0282.

CLARKSTON—Comcast Cable. Now served by DETROIT, MI [MI0001]. ICA: MI0283.

CLEON TWP.—Ace Communications. Formerly served by THOMPSONVILLE, MI [MI0230]. This cable system has converted to IPTV. Now served by MESICK, MI [MI5074]. ICA: MI5024.

CLIMAX TWP.—Climax Telephone Co, Mail Stop Dept 3053, PO Box 30516, Lansing, MI 48909-8016. Phones: 800-627-5287; 269-746-4411. Fax: 269-746-9914. E-mail: info@ctstelecom.com. Web Site: http://www.ctstelecom.com. Also serves Charleston Twp. (portions), Comstock Twp. (portions), Pavilion Twp. (portions) & Scotts. ICA: MI0285.
TV Market Ranking: 37 (Charleston Twp. (portions), CLIMAX TWP., Comstock Twp. (portions), Pavilion Twp. (portions), Scotts). Franchise award date: N.A. Franchise expiration date: N.A. Began: June 1, 1985.
Channel capacity: N.A. Channels available but not in use: N.A.
Basic Service
Subscribers: 55.
Programming (received off-air): WGVU-TV (PBS) Grand Rapids; WLLA (IND, MeTV) Kalamazoo; WOOD-TV (Laff, NBC) Grand Rapids; WOTV (ABC, Grit, TheCoolTV) Battle Creek; WTLJ (IND) Muskegon; WWMT (CBS, CW) Kalamazoo; WXMI (Antenna TV, FOX, This TV) Grand Rapids.
Programming (via satellite): A&E; CNN; Disney Channel; FOX Sports Detroit; Freeform; FX; MTV; Nickelodeon; TLC; WGN America.
Fee: $40.00 installation; $24.00 monthly.
Expanded Basic Service 1
Subscribers: 40.
Programming (via satellite): AMC; CNBC; Discovery Channel; Disney XD; ESPN; Food Network; HGTV; History; HLN; Spike TV; TBS; The Weather Channel; TNT; USA Network; VH1.
Fee: $25.00 monthly.
Pay Service 1
Pay Units: N.A.
Programming (via satellite): HBO; Showtime.
Fee: $12.95 monthly (HBO) or $11.95 monthly (Showtime).
Video-On-Demand: No
Internet Service
Operational: No, DSL.

Telephone Service
Digital: Operational
Miles of Plant: 6.0 (coaxial); 6.0 (fiber optic). Homes passed: 800.
Chief Financial Officer: Kevin Doyle. General Manager: Bob Stewart. Sales Manager: Joe Vernon. Office Manager: Barb Payne.
Ownership: Climax Telephone Co.

COLDWATER—Charter Communications, 12405 Powerscourt Dr, St. Louis, MO 63131. Phones: 636-207-5100 (Corporate office); 810-653-0966; 810-652-1400. Web Site: http://www.charter.com. Also serves Algansee Twp., Allen Twp., Batavia Twp., Bethel Twp., Bronson, Burlington (village), Burr Oak, Colon, Fawn River Twp., Fredonia Twp., Girard Twp., Kinderhook Twp., Litchfield, Ovid Twp., Quincy, Reading, Sherman Twp. (St. Joseph County), Sturgis, Tekonsha & White Pigeon Twp. (eastern portion). ICA: MI0032.
TV Market Ranking: 37 (Allen Twp., Batavia Twp., Bethel Twp., Bronson, Burlington (village), Burr Oak, COLDWATER, Colon, Girard Twp., Ovid Twp., Quincy, Sherman Twp. (St. Joseph County)); 37,80 (Fawn River Twp., Sturgis, White Pigeon Twp. (eastern portion)); 37,92 (Fredonia Twp., Litchfield, Tekonsha); Below 100 (Reading); Outside TV Markets (Algansee Twp., Kinderhook Twp.). Franchise award date: N.A. Franchise expiration date: N.A. Began: July 1, 1966.
Channel capacity: 66 (operating 2-way). Channels available but not in use: N.A.
Digital Basic Service
Subscribers: 10,401.
Programming (via satellite): BBC America; Bloomberg Television; Discovery Digital Networks; Fuse; FXM; FYI; History International; IFC; LMN; MC; MTV Classic; MTV2; Nick Jr.; Nicktoons; TeenNick; TV Guide Interactive Inc.; VH1 Country.
Fee: $14.99 monthly.
Digital Expanded Basic Service
Subscribers: N.A.
Programming (via satellite): A&E; AMC; Animal Planet; Bravo; Cartoon Network; CMT; CNBC; CNN; Comedy Central; C-SPAN; Discovery Channel; Discovery Life Channel; Disney Channel; E! HD; ESPN; ESPN Classic; ESPN2; Food Network; Fox News Channel; Fox Sports 1; FOX Sports Detroit; Freeform; FX; Golf Channel; GSN; Hallmark Channel; HGTV; History; HLN; Lifetime; MSNBC; MTV; National Geographic Channel; NBCSN; Nickelodeon; Oxygen; Spike TV; Syfy; TBS; Telemundo; The Weather Channel; TLC; TNT; Travel Channel; truTV; Turner Classic Movies; TV Land; Univision Studios; USA Network; VH1; WE tv.
Fee: $47.99 monthly.
Digital Pay Service 1
Pay Units: N.A.
Programming (via satellite): Cinemax (multiplexed); HBO (multiplexed); Showtime (multiplexed); Starz (multiplexed); Starz Encore (multiplexed); The Movie Channel (multiplexed).
Fee: $25.00 installation.
Video-On-Demand: Yes
Pay-Per-View
iN DEMAND (delivered digitally); Playboy TV (delivered digitally); Fresh (delivered digitally).
Internet Service
Operational: Yes.
Subscribers: 9,233.
Broadband Service: Charter Internet.
Fee: $29.99 monthly.

2017 Edition D-373

Michigan—Cable Systems

Telephone Service
Digital: Operational
Subscribers: 5,977.
Miles of Plant: 820.0 (coaxial); 333.0 (fiber optic). Homes passed: 28,733.
Vice President & General Manager: Dave Slowick. Marketing Director: Steve Schuh. Accounting Director: David Sovanski. Technical Operations Manager: Frank Staley.
Ownership: Charter Communications Inc. (MSO).

COLDWATER—Coldwater Board of Public Utilities, 1 Grand St, Coldwater, MI 49036-1620. Phone: 517-279-9531. Fax: 517-279-0805. E-mail: cityone@cbpu.com. Web Site: http://www.coldwater.org/ProgramsAndServices/Cable_Internet_Phone_Menu.html. ICA: MI0436. **Note:** This system is an overbuild.
TV Market Ranking: 37 (COLDWATER).
Channel capacity: N.A. Channels available but not in use: N.A.
Basic Service
Subscribers: 1,949.
Programming (received off-air): WILX-TV (NBC, WeatherNation) Onondaga; WKAR-TV (PBS) East Lansing; WLLA (IND, MeTV) Kalamazoo; WLNS-TV (CBS) Lansing; WOOD-TV (Laff, NBC) Grand Rapids; WOTV (ABC, Grit, TheCoolTV) Battle Creek; WTLJ (IND) Muskegon; WWMT (CBS, CW) Kalamazoo; WXMI (Antenna TV, FOX, This TV) Grand Rapids; WXSP-CD (COZI TV, Escape, MNT) Grand Rapids; WZPX-TV (ION) Battle Creek.
Programming (via satellite): Cartoon Network; CMT; C-SPAN; C-SPAN 2; Discovery Channel; Food Network; INSP; QVC; The Weather Channel; TLC; Travel Channel.
Fee: $12.65 monthly.
Expanded Basic Service 1
Subscribers: N.A.
Programming (via satellite): A&E; AMC; Animal Planet; Bravo; CNBC; CNN; Comedy Central; Cooking Channel; Disney Channel; Disney XD; E! HD; ESPN; ESPN Classic; ESPN2; ESPNews; EWTN Global Catholic Network; Fox News Channel; Fox Sports 1; FOX Sports Detroit; Freeform; FX; FXM; Golf Channel; Great American Country; GSN; Hallmark Channel; History; HLN; Lifetime; MSNBC; MTV; National Geographic Channel; Nickelodeon; Outdoor Channel; OWN; Oprah Winfrey Network; Spike TV; Syfy; TBS; Telemundo; TNT; truTV; Turner Classic Movies; TV Land; USA Network; VH1; WE tv; WGN America.
Fee: $21.00 monthly.
Digital Basic Service
Subscribers: N.A.
Programming (via satellite): BBC America; Discovery Digital Networks; DIY Network; DMX Music; FYI; History International; IFC; International Television (ITV); LMN; NBCSN; Nick Jr.; Nicktoons; TeenNick.
Digital Pay Service 1
Pay Units: N.A.
Programming (via satellite): Cinemax (multiplexed); Flix; HBO (multiplexed); Showtime (multiplexed); Starz (multiplexed); Starz Encore (multiplexed); Sundance TV; The Movie Channel (multiplexed); WAM! America's Kidz Network.
Fee: $12.00 monthly (Cinemax), $14.25 monthly (HBO, Showtime/TMC/Flix/Sundance or Starz/Encore).
Video-On-Demand: No
Pay-Per-View
iN DEMAND (delivered digitally).

Internet Service
Operational: Yes.
Subscribers: 2,011.
Broadband Service: In-house.
Fee: $75.00 installation; $29.99-$39.99 monthly.
Telephone Service
Digital: Operational
Fee: $29.95 monthly
Miles of Plant: 89.0 (coaxial); 17.0 (fiber optic). Homes passed: 4,410.
Director: Paul H. Beckhusen. Chief Tech & Program Director: Jim Royer. Marketing Director & Ad Sales Manager: Jodi Shook. Communications Manager: Lindy Cox.
Ownership: Coldwater Board of Public Utilities.

COLEMAN—Charter Communications. Now served by MIDLAND, MI [MI0030]. ICA: MI0207.

COMMERCE TWP.—Comcast Cable. Now served by DETROIT, MI [MI0001]. ICA: MI0023.

COMSTOCK TWP.—Charter Communications, 4176 Commercial Ave, Kalamazoo, MI 49001. Phones: 314-543-2236; 636-207-5100 (Corporate office); 616-647-6201. Web Site: http://www.charter.com. Also serves Alamo Twp., Cooper Twp., Kalamazoo, Kalamazoo Twp. (western portion), Oshtemo Twp., Parchment, Pavilion Twp. & Portage (northeastern portion). ICA: MI0011.
TV Market Ranking: 37 (Alamo Twp., COMSTOCK TWP., Cooper Twp., Kalamazoo, Kalamazoo Twp. (western portion), Oshtemo Twp., Parchment, Pavilion Twp.); 37,80 (Portage (northeastern portion)). Franchise award date: N.A. Franchise expiration date: N.A. Began: October 1, 1966.
Channel capacity: N.A. Channels available but not in use: N.A.
Digital Basic Service
Subscribers: 32,087.
Programming (via satellite): BBC America; Boomerang; CNN en Espanol; CNN International; Discovery Digital Networks; DIY Network; Fox Sports 2; FSN Digital Atlantic; FSN Digital Central; FSN Digital Pacific; Fuse; FYI; Great American Country; History International; IFC; LMN; LWS Local Weather Station; MC; NFL Network; Nick 2; Nick Jr.; Outdoor Channel; Sundance TV; TeenNick; TV Guide Interactive Inc.
Fee: $49.99 installation; $14.99 monthly.
Digital Expanded Basic Service
Subscribers: N.A.
Programming (via satellite): A&E; AMC; Animal Planet; BET; Bravo; Cartoon Network; CMT; CNBC; CNN; Comedy Central; Discovery Channel; Discovery Life Channel; Disney Channel; Disney XD; DIY Network; E! HD; ESPN; ESPN Classic; ESPN2; Food Network; Fox News Channel; Fox Sports 1; FOX Sports Detroit; Freeform; FX; Golf Channel; GSN; Hallmark Channel; HGTV; History; HLN; Lifetime; MSNBC; MTV; National Geographic Channel; NBCSN; Nickelodeon; Oxygen; Spike TV; Syfy; TBS; Telemundo; The Weather Channel; TLC; TNT; Travel Channel; truTV; Turner Classic Movies; TV Land; USA Network; VH1; WE tv.
Fee: $47.99 monthly.
Digital Pay Service 1
Pay Units: N.A.
Programming (via satellite): Cinemax (multiplexed); Flix; HBO (multiplexed); Showtime (multiplexed); Starz (multiplexed); Starz Encore (multiplexed); The Movie Channel (multiplexed).
Fee: $11.05 monthly (Cinemax, HBO, Showtime or TMC/Flix), $14.95 monthly (Starz/Encore).
Video-On-Demand: Yes
Pay-Per-View
iN DEMAND (delivered digitally); Playboy TV (delivered digitally); Fresh (delivered digitally); Shorteez (delivered digitally); Sports PPV (delivered digitally); NHL Center Ice (delivered digitally); MLB Extra Innings (delivered digitally); ESPN Now (delivered digitally).
Internet Service
Operational: Yes.
Subscribers: 32,838.
Broadband Service: Charter Internet.
Fee: $29.99 monthly; $5.00 modem lease.
Telephone Service
Digital: Operational
Subscribers: 17,455.
Fee: $29.99 monthly
Miles of Plant: 1,816.0 (coaxial); 507.0 (fiber optic). Homes passed: 93,329.
Vice President & General Manager: Dan Spoelman. Marketing Director: Steve Schuh. Accounting Director: David Sovanski. Technical Operations Manager: Keith Schierbeek.
Ownership: Charter Communications Inc. (MSO).

COPEMISH—Ace Communications. Formerly served by THOMPSONVILLE, MI [MI0230]. This cable system has converted to IPTV. Now served by MESICK, MI [MI5074]. ICA: MI5025.

COUNTRY ACRES—Charter Communications. Now served by ALLENDALE TWP., MI [MI0094]. ICA: MI0252.

CROTON TWP.—MIcom. Now served by BALDWIN (village), MI [MI0214]. ICA: MI0446.

CRYSTAL FALLS—City of Crystal Falls, 401 Superior Ave, Crystal Falls, MI 49920-1424. Phone: 906-875-3012. E-mail: http://www.crystalfalls.org/utility.htm. Web Site: http://www.crystalfalls.org. ICA: MI0190.
TV Market Ranking: Below 100 (CRYSTAL FALLS). Franchise award date: April 1, 1959. Franchise expiration date: N.A. Began: April 1, 1959.
Channel capacity: N.A. Channels available but not in use: N.A.
Basic Service
Subscribers: 494.
Programming (received off-air): WJMN-TV (CBS) Escanaba; WLUC-TV (FOX, NBC) Marquette; WNMU (PBS) Marquette.
Programming (via satellite): A&E; CNN; Discovery Channel; Disney Channel; ESPN; FOX Sports Detroit; Hallmark Channel; HGTV; History; Nickelodeon; Spike TV; TBS; The Weather Channel; TNT; Turner Classic Movies; TV Land; USA Network; VH1; WGN America.
Fee: $30.00 installation; $38.00 monthly.
Pay Service 1
Pay Units: N.A.
Programming (via satellite): HBO.
Fee: $20.00 installation; $9.50 monthly.
Internet Service
Operational: No.
Telephone Service
None
Miles of Plant: 20.0 (coaxial); None (fiber optic). Homes passed: 900.

General Manager: Charles Nordeman. Chief Technician: Angelo Diqui. Billing Clerk: Tammy Hendrickson.
Ownership: City of Crystal Falls.

CRYSTAL TWP.—Formerly served by Great Lakes Communication. No longer in operation. ICA: MI0180.

CUSTER—Charter Communications, 1229 Manistee Hwy, Manistee, MI 49660. Phones: 314-543-2236; 636-207-5100 (Corporate office); 616-647-6201. Web Site: http://www.charter.com. Also serves Branch Twp. (Mason County), Fountain, Sherman Twp. (Mason County) & Sweetwater Twp. (Lake County). ICA: MI0167.
TV Market Ranking: Below 100 (Sweetwater Twp. (Lake County)); Outside TV Markets (Branch Twp. (Mason County), CUSTER, Fountain, Sherman Twp. (Mason County)). Franchise award date: N.A. Franchise expiration date: N.A. Began: October 19, 1990.
Channel capacity: 61 (2-way capable). Channels available but not in use: N.A.
Digital Basic Service
Subscribers: 461.
Programming (received off-air): WCMW (PBS) Manistee; WFQX-TV (FOX) Cadillac; WPBN-TV (NBC) Traverse City; WWTV (CBS) Cadillac; WZZM (ABC) Grand Rapids.
Programming (via satellite): C-SPAN; Freeform; QVC; TBS; TLC; VH1; WGN America.
Fee: $49.99 installation; $23.99 monthly.
Digital Expanded Basic Service
Subscribers: N.A.
Programming (via satellite): A&E; AMC; CMT; CNBC; CNN; Discovery Channel; Disney Channel; ESPN; ESPN2; Food Network; FOX Sports Detroit; HGTV; HLN; Lifetime; MSNBC; MTV; Nickelodeon; Spike TV; The Weather Channel; TNT; truTV; Turner Classic Movies; USA Network.
Digital Pay Service 1
Pay Units: N.A.
Programming (via satellite): Cinemax; HBO; Starz.
Fee: $6.95 monthly (Starz), $10.95 monthly (Cinemax), $11.95 monthly (HBO).
Video-On-Demand: No
Internet Service
Operational: No.
Telephone Service
None
Miles of Plant: 52.0 (coaxial); None (fiber optic). Homes passed: 1,546.
Vice President & General Manager: Dan Spoelman. Marketing Director: Steve Schuh. Accounting Director: David Sovanski. Technical Operations Manager: Keith Schierbeek.
Ownership: Charter Communications Inc. (MSO).

DAGGETT—Packerland Broadband, 105 Kent St., PO Box 885, Iron Mountain, MI 49801. Phones: 800-472-0576; 715-582-1141. Fax: 906-776-2811. E-mail: service@plbb.net; support@packerlandbroadband.com. Web Site: http://www.packerlandbroadband.com. ICA: MI0227.
TV Market Ranking: Below 100 (DAGGETT). Franchise award date: N.A. Franchise expiration date: N.A. Began: February 1, 1985.
Channel capacity: N.A. Channels available but not in use: N.A.
Basic Service
Subscribers: 14.
Programming (received off-air): WACY-TV (Escape, Grit, Laff, MNT) Appleton; WBAY-

Cable Systems—Michigan

TV (ABC) Green Bay; WCWF (CW) Suring; WFRV-TV (Bounce TV, CBS) Green Bay; WGBA-TV (MeTV, NBC) Green Bay; WLUK-TV (Antenna TV, FOX) Green Bay; WNMU (PBS) Marquette; WPNE-TV (PBS) Green Bay.

Fee: $75.00 installation; $17.50 monthly.

Expanded Basic Service 1

Subscribers: N.A.

Programming (via satellite): EWTN Global Catholic Network; Freeform; HGTV; Lifetime; Nickelodeon; Spike TV; TNT; USA Network.

Fee: $13.00 monthly.

Expanded Basic Service 2

Subscribers: N.A.

Programming (via satellite): A&E; AMC; Animal Planet; Bloomberg Television; Bravo; Classic Arts Showcase; CMT; CNN; Comedy Central; Discovery Channel; Disney Channel; Disney XD; DIY Network; E! HD; ESPN; ESPN2; Food Network; Fox News Channel; FX; FXM; Great American Country; Hallmark Channel; History; HLN; MTV; National Geographic Channel; Outdoor Channel; QVC; Syfy; TBS; TLC; Travel Channel; Trinity Broadcasting Network (TBN); truTV; Turner Classic Movies; TV Land; VH1; WGN America.

Fee: $10.00 monthly.

Pay Service 1

Pay Units: N.A.

Programming (via satellite): Cinemax.

Fee: $8.00 monthly.

Video-On-Demand: No

Internet Service

Operational: No.

Telephone Service

None

Miles of Plant: 6.0 (coaxial); None (fiber optic). Homes passed: 320.

General Manager & Chief Technician: Howard C. Lock.

Ownership: Packerland Broadband.

DE TOUR (village)—Formerly served by Upper Peninsula Communications. No longer in operation. ICA: MI0291.

DEARBORN—Comcast Cable. Now served by DETROIT, MI [MI0001]. ICA: MI0021.

DEARBORN HEIGHTS—Comcast Cable. Now served by DETROIT, MI [MI0001]. ICA: MI0010.

DECKERVILLE—Comcast Cable. Now served by DETROIT, MI [MI0001]. ICA: MI0372.

DELTON—Formerly served by MIcom. No longer in operation. ICA: MI0186.

DETROIT—Comcast Cable, 29777 Telegraph Rd, Ste 4400B, Southfield, MI 48034. Phones: 248-648-1971; 248-233-4871; 734-254-1500 (Plymouth office); 248-233-4712. Fax: 248-233-4719. Web Site: http://www.comcast.com. Also serves Elkhart County (portions) & LaGrange County, IN; Ada Twp., Adams Twp. (Hillsdale County), Addison (village), Adrian, Alaiedon Twp., Algonac, Allen Park, Allen Twp., Almena Twp., Alpine Twp., Ann Arbor, Ann Arbor Twp., Antwerp Twp., Arlington Twp., Armada (village), Armada Twp., Auburn Hills, Augusta, Augusta (village), Augusta Twp., Bad Axe, Bangor, Barry Twp., Barton Hills (village), Battle Creek, Bay Port Village, Bedford Twp. (Calhoun County), Belleville, Berkley, Berlin Twp. (Monroe County), Beverly Hills (village), Bingham Farms (village), Birmingham, Blackman Twp., Bloomfield Hills, Bloomfield Twp. (Oakland County), Brady Twp. (Kalamazoo County), Bridgehampton Twp., Brighton, Brighton Twp., Britton (village), Brockway Twp., Brookfield Twp., Brooklyn (Irish Hills), Brooks Twp., Brown City, Brownstown Twp., Bruce Twp. (Macomb County), Buel Twp., Burtchville Twp., Burton, Byron Twp., Caledonia, Calvin Twp., Cambria, Cambridge Twp., Cannon Twp., Canton Twp., Carpac, Carsonville, Cascade Twp., Casco Twp. (Allegan County), Casco Twp. (St. Clair County), Caseville, Cedar Creek Twp. (Muskegon County), Cement City, Center Line, Centreville, Charleston Twp. (portions), Chelsea, Chesterfield Twp., China Twp., Clarkston, Clawson, Clay Twp., Clinton, Clinton Twp., Clio, Clyde Twp. (Allegan County), Clyde Twp. (St. Clair County), Colfax Twp., Columbia Twp., Columbus Twp. (St. Clair County), Commerce Twp., Comstock Twp., Constantine, Cottrellville Twp., Covert Twp., Croswell, Dalton Twp., Dayton Twp. (Newaygo County), De Witt, De Witt Twp., Dearborn, Dearborn Heights, Decatur (village), Deckerville, Delta Twp., Dexter, Dorr Twp., Douglas (village), Dover Twp., Dundee, Dwight Twp., East China Twp., East Grand Rapids, East Lansing, Eastpointe, Eaton Rapids, Ecorse, Egelston Twp., Elk Twp., Elkton, Elmwood Twp., Emmett Twp., Exeter Twp., Fabius, Fairfield Twp., Fairhaven Twp., Fayette Twp., Fennville, Ferndale, Ferrysburg, Flat Rock, Flint, Flint Twp., Flowerfield, Flushing, Flushing Twp., Fort Gratiot Twp., Franklin (village), Franklin Twp., Fraser, Fremont, Frenchtown Twp., Fruitland Twp., Fruitport Charter Twp., Gagetown, Gaines Twp. (Genesee County), Gaines Twp. (Kent County), Galesburg, Ganges Twp., Garden City, Garfield Twp. (Newaygo County), Genesee Twp., Geneva Twp. (Van Buren County), Genoa Twp., Georgetown Twp., Gibraltar, Glenn, Gore Twp., Grand Blanc, Grand Blanc Twp., Grand Ledge, Grand Rapids, Grand Rapids Twp., Grandville, Grattan Twp., Green Oak Twp., Grosse Ile, Grosse Pointe, Grosse Pointe Farms, Grosse Pointe Park, Grosse Pointe Shores, Grosse Pointe Woods, Groveland Twp., Hamilton Twp. (Van Buren County), Hamlin Twp., Hamtramck, Harbor Beach, Harper Woods, Harrison Twp., Hartford, Hartland Twp., Hazel Park, Highland Twp. (Oakland County), Hillsdale, Holland, Holly Twp., Holly Village, Holton Twp., Howell, Hudson Twp., Hume Twp., Huntington Woods, Huron Twp., Independence Twp., Inkster, Ira Twp., Jackson, Jamestown Twp., Jefferson, Jefferson Twp. (Hillsdale County), Jones, Jonesville, Keego Harbor, Kentwood, Kimball Twp., Kinde, Lake Angelus, Lake Orion (village), Laketon Twp., Lansing, Lansing Twp., Lathrup Village, Lawrence, Lawrence Twp., Lawton, Lawton (village), Lenox Twp., Leoni Twp., Leroy Twp., Lexington (village), Lexington Twp., Liberty Twp. (Jackson County), Lima Twp., Lincoln Park, Lockport, Lodi Twp., London Twp., Lowell, Lowell Twp., Lyon Twp. (Oakland County), Macomb Twp., Madison Heights, Madison Twp., Manchester, Manlius Twp., Marcellus Twp., Marine City, Marion Twp. (Sanilac County), Marlette (village), Marshall, Marysville, McKinley Twp., Meade, Melvindale, Memphis, Mendon, Meridian Twp., Milford (village), Milford Twp., Monroe, Monroe Twp., Mottville, Mount Clemens, Mount Morris, Mount Morris Twp., Mundy Twp., Muskegon, Muskegon Heights, Napoleon Twp., New Baltimore, New Haven, Newberg Twp., Newton Twp., North Adams, North Muskegon, Northville, Northville Twp., Norton Shores, Norvell Twp., Nottawa, Novi, Oak Park, Oakland Twp., Oceola Twp., Oliver Twp., Oneida Twp., Onsted, Orchard Lake, Orion Twp., Oshtemo Twp., Owendale, Palmyra Twp., Pavilion, Paw Paw (village), Paw Paw Twp., Peck, Penn Twp. (portions), Pennfield Twp., Pigeon, Pittsfield Twp., Pittsford Twp., Plainfield Twp. (Kent County), Pleasant Ridge, Plymouth, Plymouth Twp., Pontiac, Port Austin, Port Hope, Port Huron, Port Huron Twp., Port Sanilac, Portage, Porter Twp. (Cass County), Porter Twp. (Van Buren County), Prairie Ronde, Prairieville, Raisin Twp., Raisinville Twp., Ray Twp., Richfield Twp. (Genesee County), Richland (village), Richland Twp., Richmond, Richmond Twp. (Macomb County), Ridgeway Twp., River Rouge, Riverview, Rives Junction, Rochester, Rochester Hills, Rockwood, Rollin, Romeo, Romulus, Roosevelt Park, Rose Twp. (Oakland County), Roseville, Ross Twp., Royal Oak, Royal Oak Twp., Rubicon Twp., Saline, Saline Twp., Sand Beach Twp., Sandstone Twp., Sandusky, Sanilac Twp., Saugatuck Twp., Schoolcraft, Schoolcraft Twp., Scio Twp., Scipio Twp., Sebewaing, Selfridge AFB, Shelby Twp., Sheridan Twp. (Newaygo County), Sherman Twp. (Newaygo County), Sherman Twp. (St. Joseph County), Somerset Twp., South Haven, South Haven Twp., South Rockwood, Southfield, Southgate, Sparta Twp., Speaker Twp., Spring Arbor Twp., Spring Lake Twp., Springfield, Springfield Twp., St. Clair, St. Clair Shores, St. Clair Twp., Sterling Heights, Sullivan Twp., Summit Twp. (Jackson County), Summit-Leoni, Sumpter Twp., Superior Twp. (Washtenaw County), Swartz Creek, Sylvan Lake, Sylvan Twp., Tallmadge Twp., Taylor, Tecumseh, Texas Twp., Three Rivers, Trenton, Troy, Ubly, Utica, Van Buren, Vandalia, Vergennes Twp., Verona Twp., Vicksburg, Vienna Twp. (Genesee County), Volinia Twp., Waldron, Walker, Walled Lake, Warren, Washington Twp. (Macomb County), Waterford Twp., Watertown Twp. (Clinton County), Watertown Twp. (Sanilac County), Waverly Twp. (Van Buren County), Wayne, West Bloomfield Twp., Westland, Wheatfield, White Lake Twp., White Pigeon, White Pigeon (village), Wildwood, Windsor Charter Twp., Winsor Twp., Wixom, Wolverine Lake (village), Woodhaven, Woodstock Twp., Worth Twp., Wright Twp. (Hillsdale County), Wright Twp. (Ottawa County), Wyoming, Yale, York Twp., Ypsilanti & Ypsilanti Twp., MI. ICA: MI0001.

TV Market Ranking: 37 (Ada Twp., Alpine Twp., Arlington Twp., Augusta, Augusta (village), Bangor, Barry Twp., Brady Twp. (Kalamazoo County), Brooks Twp., Byron Twp., Caledonia, Calvin Twp., Cannon Twp., Cascade Twp., Casco Twp. (Allegan County), Cedar Creek Twp. (Muskegon County), Charleston Twp. (portions), Clyde Twp. (Allegan County), Comstock Twp., Covert Twp., Dorr Twp., East Grand Rapids, Egelston Twp., Fennville, Ferrysburg, Fruitport Charter Twp., Gaines Twp. (Kent County), Galesburg, Garfield Twp. (Newaygo County), Geneva Twp. (Van Buren County), Georgetown Twp., Glenn, Grand Rapids, Grand Rapids Twp., Grandville, Grattan Twp., Hartford, Holland, Jamestown Twp., Jones, Kentwood, Laketon Twp., Lawrence, Leroy Twp., Lowell, Lowell Twp., Manlius Twp., Muskegon Heights, Newberg Twp., Norton Shores, Oshtemo Twp., Pavilion, Paw Paw Twp., Penn Twp. (portions), Plainfield Twp. (Kent County), Portage, Porter Twp. (Cass County), Prairie Ronde, Prairieville, Richland (village), Richland Twp., Ross Twp., Saugatuck Twp., Sheridan Twp. (Newaygo County), Sherman Twp. (Newaygo County), Sherman Twp. (St. Joseph County), Sparta Twp., Spring Lake Twp., Sullivan Twp., Tallmadge Twp., Texas Twp., Vandalia, Vergennes Twp., Vicksburg, Walker, Wright Twp. (Ottawa County), Wyoming); 37,80 (Almena Twp., Antwerp Twp., Centreville, Constantine, Decatur (village), Fabius, Flowerfield, Hamilton Twp. (Van Buren County), Lawrence Twp., Lawton, Lawton (village), Lockport, Marcellus Twp., Mendon, Mottville, Nottawa, Paw Paw (village), Porter Twp. (Van Buren County), Schoolcraft, Schoolcraft Twp., Three Rivers, Volinia Twp., Waverly Twp. (Van Buren County), White Pigeon, White Pigeon (village)); 37,92 (Battle Creek, Bedford Twp. (Calhoun County), Emmett Twp., Marshall, Newton Twp., Pennfield Twp., Spring Arbor Twp., Springfield); 5 (Allen Park, Ann Arbor, Ann Arbor Twp., Armada (village), Armada Twp., Auburn Hills, Augusta Twp., Barton Hills (village), Belleville, Berkley, Berlin Twp. (Monroe County), Beverly Hills (village), Bingham Farms (village), Birmingham, Bloomfield Hills, Bloomfield Twp. (Oakland County), Brownstown Twp., Bruce Twp. (Macomb County), Canton Twp., Casco Twp. (St. Clair County), Center Line, Chesterfield Twp., Clarkston, Clawson, Clay Twp., Clinton Twp., Cottrellville Twp., Dearborn, Dearborn Heights, DETROIT, Dundee, Eastpointe, Ecorse, Exeter Twp., Ferndale, Flat Rock, Franklin (village), Fraser, Frenchtown Twp., Garden City, Gibraltar, Grosse Ile, Grosse Pointe, Grosse Pointe Farms, Grosse Pointe Park, Grosse Pointe Woods, Groveland Twp., Hamtramck, Harper Woods, Harrison Twp., Hazel Park, Huntington Woods, Independence Twp., Inkster, Ira Twp., Lake Orion (village), Lathrup Village, Lenox Twp., Lima Twp., Lincoln Park, Lodi Twp., London Twp., Macomb Twp., Madison Heights, Melvindale, Monroe, Monroe Twp., Mount Clemens, New Baltimore, New Haven, Northville, Northville Twp., Novi, Oak Park, Oakland Twp., Orion Twp., Pittsfield Twp., Pleasant Ridge, Plymouth, Plymouth Twp., Raisinville Twp., Ray Twp., Richmond, Richmond Twp. (Macomb County) (portions), River Rouge, Riverview, Rockwood, Romeo, Romulus, Roseville, Royal Oak, Royal Oak Twp., Selfridge AFB, Shelby Twp., South Rockwood, Southfield, Southgate, Springfield Twp., St. Clair Shores, Sterling Heights, Sumpter Twp., Superior Twp. (Washtenaw County), Sylvan Twp., Taylor, Trenton, Troy, Utica, Van Buren, Warren, Washington Twp. (Macomb County), Wayne, West Bloomfield Twp., Westland, Woodhaven, York Twp., Ypsilanti, Ypsilanti Twp.); 5,61 (Commerce

ADVANCED TVFactbook

FULLY SEARCHABLE • CONTINUOUSLY UPDATED • DISCOUNT RATES FOR PRINT PURCHASERS

For more information call **800-771-9202** or visit **www.warren-news.com**

2017 Edition

D-375

Michigan—Cable Systems

CABLE & TV STATION COVERAGE

Atlas 2017

The perfect companion to the Television & Cable Factbook
To order call 800-771-9202 or visit www.warren-news.com

Twp., Highland Twp. (Oakland County), Keego Harbor, Lake Angelus, Lyon Twp. (Oakland County), Milford (village), Milford Twp., Orchard Lake, Pontiac, Rochester, Rochester Hills, Sylvan Lake, Walled Lake, Waterford Twp., White Lake Twp., Wixom, Wolverine Lake (village)); 52 (Addison (village), Adrian, Britton (village), Dover Twp., Fairfield Twp., Hudson Twp., Madison Twp., Palmyra Twp., Raisin Twp., Ridgeway Twp., Tecumseh, Woodstock Twp.); 61 (Bay Port Village, Brighton, Brighton Twp., Burton, Clio, Fairhaven Twp., Flint, Flint Twp., Flushing, Flushing Twp., Gagetown (portions), Genesee Twp., Genoa Twp., Grand Blanc, Grand Blanc Twp., Green Oak Twp., Hartland Twp., Holly Twp., Holly Village, Howell, Marlette (village), Mount Morris, Mount Morris Twp., Mundy Twp., Oceola Twp., Oliver Twp., Owendale, Richfield Twp. (Genesee County), Rose Twp. (Oakland County), Sebewaing, Swartz Creek, Vienna Twp. (Genesee County), Winsor Twp.); 61,92 (Gaines Twp. (Genesee County)); 80 (LaGrange County); 92 (Adams Twp. (Hillsdale County), Alaiedon Twp., Allen Twp., Blackman Twp., Brooklyn (Irish Hills), Cambridge Twp., Cement City, Chelsea, Columbia Twp., De Witt, De Witt Twp., Delta Twp., Dexter, East Lansing, Eaton Rapids, Franklin Twp., Grand Ledge, Hamlin Twp., Jackson, Jonesville, Lansing, Lansing Twp., Leoni Twp., Liberty Twp. (Jackson County), Meridian Twp., Napoleon Twp., North Adams, Norvell Twp., Oneida Twp., Rives Junction, Sandstone Twp., Scipio Twp., Somerset Twp., Summit Twp. (Jackson County), Summit-Leoni, Watertown Twp. (Clinton County), Wheatfield, Windsor Charter Twp.); Below 100 (Cambria, China Twp., Clinton, Clyde Twp. (St. Clair County), Columbus Twp. (St. Clair County), Dalton Twp., East China Twp., Fayette Twp., Fremont, Fruitland Twp., Holton Twp., Jefferson, Jefferson Twp. (Hillsdale County), Kimball Twp., Manchester, Marine City, Marysville, Memphis, North Muskegon, Onsted, Pittsford Twp., Rollin, Roosevelt Park, Saline, Saline Twp., Scio Twp., St. Clair, St. Clair Twp., Wright Twp. (Hillsdale County), Carpac, Hillsdale, Muskegon, Waldron, Richmond Twp. (Macomb County) (portions)); Outside TV Markets (Bad Axe, Bridgehampton Twp., Brockway Twp., Brookfield Twp., Buel Twp., Burtchville Twp., Carsonville, Caseville, Colfax Twp., Croswell, Douglas (village), Dwight Twp., Elk Twp., Elkton, Elmwood Twp., Fort Gratiot Twp., Ganges Twp., Gore Twp., Harbor Beach, Hume Twp., Huron Twp., Kinde, Lexington Twp., Marion Twp. (Sanilac County), McKinley Twp., Meade, Peck, Port Hope, Port Huron, Port Huron Twp., Port Sanilac, Rubicon Twp., Sand Beach Twp., Sanilac Twp., South Haven Twp., Speaker Twp., Ubly, Verona Twp., Watertown Twp. (Sanilac County), Wildwood, Worth Twp., Brown City, Deckerville, Lexington (village), Pigeon, Sandusky, South Haven, Yale, Gagetown (portions)). Franchise award date: August 31, 1983. Franchise expiration date: N.A. Began: December 18, 1986.

Channel capacity: N.A. Channels available but not in use: N.A.

Basic Service
Subscribers: 997,611. Commercial subscribers: 1,725.
Programming (received off-air): various Canadian stations; WADL (Antenna TV, getTV) Mount Clemens; WDIV-TV (NBC, This TV) Detroit; WJBK (Buzzr, FOX, Heroes & Icons, Movies!) Detroit; WKBD-TV (CW) Detroit; WMYD (Antenna TV, Escape, MNT) Detroit; WPXD-TV (ION) Ann Arbor; WTVS (PBS) Detroit; WWJ-TV (CBS, Decades) Detroit; WXYZ-TV (ABC, Bounce TV) Detroit; 20 FMs.
Programming (via satellite): A&E; AMC; Animal Planet; BET; Bravo; Cartoon Network; CNBC; CNN; Comedy Central; C-SPAN; C-SPAN 2; Discovery Channel; E! HD; ESPN; ESPN Classic; ESPN2; Food Network; Fox News Channel; Fox Sports 1; Freeform; Golf Channel; GSN; HGTV; History; HLN; INSP; Lifetime; MSNBC; MTV; Nickelodeon; Pop; QVC; Spike TV; Syfy; TBS; The Weather Channel; TLC; TNT; Trinity Broadcasting Network (TBN); truTV; Turner Classic Movies; TV Land; Univision Studios; USA Network; VH1; WGN America.
Fee: $50.00 installation; $25.20 monthly.

Digital Basic Service
Subscribers: N.A.
Programming (via satellite): BBC America; Catholic Television Network; Christian Television Network; C-SPAN 3; Discovery Digital Networks; Disney XD; DMX Music; ESPNews; EVINE Live; Flix; National Geographic Channel; Nick 2; Nick Jr.; Sundance TV; TeenNick; The Word Network; Weatherscan.

Pay Service 1
Pay Units: N.A.
Programming (via satellite): Cinemax; HBO; Showtime; The Movie Channel.
Fee: $15.00 installation; $9.00 monthly (each).

Digital Pay Service 1
Pay Units: N.A.
Programming (via satellite): Cinemax (multiplexed); HBO (multiplexed); Showtime (multiplexed); Starz (multiplexed); The Movie Channel (multiplexed).
Fee: $9.00 monthly (each).

Video-On-Demand: Yes

Pay-Per-View
iN DEMAND (delivered digitally); Playboy TV (delivered digitally); Fresh (delivered digitally); Shorteez (delivered digitally); Pleasure (delivered digitally).

Internet Service
Operational: Yes.
Subscribers: 987,170.
Broadband Service: Comcast High Speed Internet.
Fee: $42.95 monthly; $7.00 modem lease; $299.00 modem purchase.

Telephone Service
Analog: Not Operational
Digital: Operational
Subscribers: 561,972.

Fee: $44.95 monthly
Miles of Plant: 58,211.0 (coaxial); 16,894.0 (fiber optic). Homes passed: 2,906,514.
Vice President & General Manager: Mike Cleland. Vice President, Technical Operations: Steve Thomas. Vice President, Marketing: Tony Lent. Vice President, Communications: Jerome Espy.
Ownership: Comcast Cable Communications Inc. (MSO).

DETROIT—Formerly served by Sprint Corp. No longer in operation. ICA: MI0387.

DIMONDALE—WOW! Internet, Cable & Phone, 7887 East Belleview Ave, Ste 1000, Englewood, CO 80111. Phones: 866-496-9669; 720-479-3558. Fax: 720-479-3585. E-mail: wow_general@wideopenwest.com. Web Site: http://www.wowway.com. Also serves Alaiedon Twp., Albion, Albion Twp., Athens, Athens Twp., Aurelius Twp., Bath Twp., Bellevue, Benton Twp. (Eaton County), Berlin Twp. (Ionia County), Boston Twp., Bunker Hill Twp., Burlington Twp., Campbell Twp., Carlton Twp., Carmel Twp., Charlotte, Clarksville, Concord, Concord Twp., Convis Twp., Danby Twp., Dansville (village), Delhi Twp., Eagle (village), Eagle Twp., Eaton Rapids Twp., Eaton Twp., Eckford Twp., Fowlerville, Fredonia Twp., Freeport, Grass Lake, Grass Lake Twp., Green Oak Twp., Handy Twp., Hanover, Hanover Twp., Hastings, Hastings Twp., Henrietta Twp., Homer, Horton, Hubbardston, Ingham Twp., Laingsburg, Lake Odessa, Lebanon Twp., Leroy Twp., Leslie, Leslie Twp., Liberty Twp., Lyons Twp., Marengo Twp., Marshall, Marshall Twp., Mason, Matherton, Morrice, Mulliken, Munith, North Plains Twp., Odessa Twp., Olivet, Oneida Charter Twp., Onondaga Twp., Parma, Parma Twp., Perry, Perry Twp., Pewamo, Pleasant Lake, Portland, Portland Twp., Potterville, Pulaski Twp., Roxanne Twp., Saranac, Sciota Twp., Shaftsburg, Sheridan Twp., Sherwood, South Lyon, Spring Arbor Twp., Stockbridge, Stockbridge Twp., Sunfield, Sunfield Twp., Union City, Vevay Twp., Victor Twp., Walton Twp., Waterloo Twp., Watertown Twp. (Clinton County), Webberville, Westphalia, Wheatfield Twp., Williamston, Williamstown Twp., Windsor Twp., Woodhull Twp. & Woodland Twp. ICA: MI0136.

TV Market Ranking: 37 (Albion, Athens, Bellevue, Boston Twp., Burlington Twp., Campbell Twp., Charlotte, Clarksville, Convis Twp., Freeport, Hastings, Hastings Twp., Marengo Twp., Marshall, Olivet, Saranac, Sheridan Twp., Sherwood, Union City, Walton Twp., Woodland Twp.); 37,92 (Benton Twp. (Eaton County), Carlton Twp., Concord, DIMONDALE, Eaton Twp., Hanover, Homer, Horton, Lake Odessa, Liberty Twp., Mulliken, Odessa Twp., Parma, Potterville, Pulaski Twp., Roxanne Twp., Spring Arbor Twp., Sunfield); 5 (Green Oak Twp., South Lyon); 61 (Laingsburg, Morrice, Sciota Twp., Shaftsburg, Williamston); 61,92 (Fowlerville, Handy Twp., Perry, Victor Twp., Webberville, Wheatfield Twp., Williamstown Twp., Woodhull Twp.); 92 (Alaiedon Twp., Albion Twp., Athens Twp., Aurelius Twp., Bath Twp., Berlin Twp. (Ionia County), Bunker Hill Twp., Carmel Twp., Concord Twp., Danby Twp., Dansville (village), Delhi Twp., Eagle (village), Eagle Twp., Eaton Rapids Twp., Eckford Twp., Fredonia Twp., Grass Lake, Grass Lake Twp., Henrietta Twp., Hubbardston, Ingham Twp., Lebanon Twp., Leroy Twp., Leslie, Leslie Twp., Lyons Twp., Marshall Twp., Mason, Matherton, Munith, North Plains Twp., Oneida Charter Twp., Onondaga Twp., Parma Twp., Perry Twp., Pewamo, Pleasant Lake, Portland, Stockbridge, Stockbridge Twp., Sunfield Twp., Vevay Twp., Waterloo Twp., Watertown Twp. (Clinton County), Westphalia, Windsor Twp.); 92,37 (Portland Twp.); Below 100 (Hanover Twp.). Franchise award date: N.A. Franchise expiration date: N.A. Began: November 1, 1982.

Channel capacity: N.A. Channels available but not in use: N.A.

Basic Service
Subscribers: 20,349.
Programming (received off-air): WADL (Antenna TV, getTV) Mount Clemens; WDIV-TV (NBC, This TV) Detroit; WEYI-TV (Bounce TV, CW, NBC) Saginaw; WGVU-TV (PBS) Grand Rapids; WHTV (MNT) Jackson; WILX-TV (NBC, WeatherNation) Onondaga; WJBK (Buzzr, FOX, Heroes & Icons, Movies!) Detroit; WJRT-TV (ABC, MeTV) Flint; WKAR-TV (PBS) East Lansing; WKBD-TV (CW) Detroit; WLAJ (ABC, CW) Lansing; WLLA (IND, MeTV) Kalamazoo; WLNS-TV (CBS) Lansing; WMYD (Antenna TV, Escape, MNT) Detroit; WOOD-TV (Laff, NBC) Grand Rapids; WOTV (ABC, Grit, TheCoolTV) Battle Creek; WPXD-TV (ION) Ann Arbor; WSMH (Antenna TV, FOX, The Country Network) Flint; WSYM-TV (FOX, MeTV) Lansing; WTVS (PBS) Detroit; WWJ-TV (CBS, Decades) Detroit; WWMT (CBS, CW) Kalamazoo; WXMI (Antenna TV, FOX, This TV) Grand Rapids; WXYZ-TV (ABC, Bounce TV) Detroit; WZPX-TV (ION) Battle Creek; WZZM (ABC) Grand Rapids.
Programming (via satellite): C-SPAN; C-SPAN 2; EVINE Live; Pop; QVC; WGN America.
Fee: $50.00 installation; $32.00 monthly.

Expanded Basic Service 1
Subscribers: N.A.
Programming (via satellite): A&E; AMC; Animal Planet; Cartoon Network; CMT; CNBC; CNN; Comedy Central; Cooking Channel; Discovery Channel; Discovery Family; Disney Channel; Disney XD; E! HD; ESPN; ESPN2; Food Network; Fox News Channel; Fox Sports 1; FOX Sports Detroit; FOX Sports Networks; Freeform; FX; HGTV; History; HLN; Lifetime; MSNBC; MTV; National Geographic Channel; Nickelodeon; Spike TV; Syfy; TBS; The Weather Channel; TLC; TNT; Travel Channel; Trinity Broadcasting Network (TBN); truTV; TV Land; USA Network; VH1.
Fee: $32.74 monthly.

Digital Basic Service
Subscribers: N.A.
Programming (via satellite): BBC America; Bloomberg Television; Bravo; Discovery Digital Networks; Disney XD; DIY Network; DMX Music; ESPN Classic; ESPN HD; ESPNews; FSN Digital Atlantic; FSN Digital Central; FSN Digital Pacific; Fuse; FXM; FYI; Golf Channel; Great American Country; GSN; Hallmark Channel; HD Theater; History International; IFC; INSP; LMN; Nick Jr.; Nicktoons; Outdoor Channel; Syfy; TeenNick; Trinity Broadcasting Network (TBN); Turner Classic Movies; WE tv.

Digital Pay Service 1
Pay Units: N.A.
Programming (via satellite): Cinemax (multiplexed); HBO (multiplexed); HBO HD; Playboy TV; Showtime (multiplexed); Starz; Starz Encore (multiplexed); Starz HD; The Movie Channel (multiplexed).
Fee: $20.00 installation; $6.18 monthly (Starz/Encore), $7.26 monthly (Cinemax or Showtime/TMC), $8.77 monthly (HBO), $14.95 monthly (Playboy).

Video-On-Demand: No

Cable Systems—Michigan

FULLY SEARCHABLE • CONTINUOUSLY UPDATED • DISCOUNT RATES FOR PRINT PURCHASERS
For more information call **800-771-9202** or visit **www.warren-news.com**

Pay-Per-View
iN DEMAND (delivered digitally).
Internet Service
Operational: Yes. Began: January 1, 1997.
Subscribers: 22,359.
Broadband Service: Millennium Cable-Speed.
Fee: $49.95 installation; $27.95 monthly; $5.00 modem lease.
Telephone Service
Digital: Operational
Subscribers: 7,420.
Fee: $49.99 monthly
Miles of Plant: 3,048.0 (coaxial); 920.0 (fiber optic). Homes passed: 83,346.
Chief Executive Officer: Colleen Abdoulah. Chief Financial Officer: Rich Fish. General Manager: Mark Dineen.
Ownership: WideOpenWest LLC (MSO).

DOWAGIAC—Comcast Cable. Now served by CHAMPAIGN, IL [IL0019]. ICA: MI0292.

DRUMMOND ISLAND—Formerly served by Northwoods Cable Inc. No longer in operation. ICA: MI0210.

DURAND—Charter Communications. Now served by GOODRICH, MI [MI0290]. ICA: MI0075.

EAGLE HARBOR TWP.—Cable America Corp, 7822 East Gray Rd, Scottsdale, AZ 85260. Phones: 800-338-1808; 866-871-4492. E-mail: info@cableaz.com. Web Site: http://www.cableamerica.com. Also serves Agate Harbor & Keweenaw County (portions). ICA: MI0293.
TV Market Ranking: Below 100 (Agate Harbor, EAGLE HARBOR TWP., Keweenaw County (portions)). Franchise award date: September 1, 1992. Franchise expiration date: N.A. Began: N.A.
Channel capacity: N.A. Channels available but not in use: N.A.
Basic Service
Subscribers: 11.
Programming (received off-air): WBKP (ABC, CW) Calumet; WCCO-TV (CBS, Decades) Minneapolis; WDIV-TV (NBC, This TV) Detroit; WJMN-TV (CBS) Escanaba; WKBD-TV (CW) Detroit; WLUC-TV (FOX, NBC) Marquette; WNMU (PBS) Marquette; WTVS (PBS) Detroit; WWJ-TV (CBS, Decades) Detroit; WZMQ (Antenna TV, MeTV, MNT, This TV) Marquette.
Programming (via satellite): A&E; AMC; Animal Planet; BBC America; Cartoon Network; Classic Arts Showcase; CNBC; CNN; Comedy Central; C-SPAN; C-SPAN 2; Deutsche Welle TV; Discovery Channel; ESPN; ESPN2; Food Network; Fox News Channel; Fox Sports 1; FOX Sports Detroit; FX; Hallmark Channel; HGTV; History; HLN; ION Television; Lifetime; MSNBC; NASA TV; Nickelodeon; QVC; Syfy; TBS; The Weather Channel; TLC; TNT; truTV; Turner Classic Movies; TV Land; USA Network; VH1; WGN America.
Fee: $35.00 installation; $59.75 monthly.
Pay Service 1
Pay Units: 2.
Programming (via satellite): HBO.
Fee: $10.00 monthly.
Video-On-Demand: No
Internet Service
Operational: Yes.
Telephone Service
Digital: Operational
Miles of Plant: 9.0 (coaxial); None (fiber optic). Homes passed: 350.

Vice President, Engineering: Alan Jackson. Corporate Secretary: Gloria Jackson. General Manager: Debra Mefford. Chief Technician: James Grove. Marketing Director: John Mori. Controller: Walter G. Farak.
Ownership: CableAmerica Corp. (MSO).

EAST JORDAN—Charter Communications. Now served by TRAVERSE CITY, MI [MI0026]. ICA: MI0095.

EAST LANSING—Comcast Cable. Now served by DETROIT, MI [MI0001]. ICA: MI0024.

EATON RAPIDS—Comcast Cable. Now served by DETROIT, MI [MI0001]. ICA: MI0138.

EDWARDSBURG—Comcast Cable. Now served by CHAMPAIGN, IL [IL0019]. ICA: MI0296.

ELSIE—Charter Communications. Now served by MIDLAND, MI [MI0030]. ICA: MI0373.

ENGADINE—Lighthouse Computers Inc., 2972 West Eigth St, Ste A, Sault Ste Marie, MI 49783. Phones: 888-883-3393; 906-632-1820. Web Site: http://www.lighthouse.net. Also serves Naubinway & Portage Twp. (Mackinac County). ICA: MI0297.
TV Market Ranking: Outside TV Markets (ENGADINE, Naubinway, Portage Twp. (Mackinac County)). Franchise award date: April 1, 1988. Franchise expiration date: N.A. Began: March 24, 1989.
Channel capacity: N.A. Channels available but not in use: N.A.
Basic Service
Subscribers: 110.
Programming (received off-air): WCML (PBS) Alpena; WFQX-TV (FOX) Cadillac; WKRN-TV (ABC) Nashville; WTOM-TV (NBC) Cheboygan; WWUP-TV (CBS, FOX) Sault Ste. Marie.
Programming (via satellite): A&E; CNBC; CNN; C-SPAN; Discovery Channel; Disney Channel; ESPN; EWTN Global Catholic Network; Freeform; HGTV; History; ION Television; Lifetime; Outdoor Channel; QVC; Spike TV; TBS; The Weather Channel; TLC; TNT; Trinity Broadcasting Network (TBN); Turner Classic Movies; TV Land; USA Network; WGN America.
Fee: $25.00 installation; $34.50 monthly; $1.50 converter.
Pay Service 1
Pay Units: N.A.
Programming (via satellite): Cinemax.
Fee: $7.50 monthly.
Internet Service
Operational: No.
Telephone Service
None
Miles of Plant: 10.0 (coaxial); None (fiber optic).
General Manager & Chief Technician: Louis Dupont.
Ownership: Lighthouse Computers Inc. (MSO).

ESCANABA—Charter Communications. Now served by MARQUETTE, MI [MI0033]. ICA: MI0054.

EVART—Charter Communications. Now served by ALLENDALE TWP., MI [MI0094]. ICA: MI0187.

EWEN—Charter Communications. Now served by IRONWOOD, MI [MI0064]. ICA: MI0298.

FALMOUTH—Formerly served by Pine River Cable. No longer in operation. ICA: MI0443.

FARMINGTON—Bright House Networks. Now served by LIVONIA, MI [MI0019]. ICA: MI0015.

FENTON—Charter Communications. Now served by GOODRICH, MI [MI0290]. ICA: MI0035.

FIFE LAKE—Charter Communications. Now served by TRAVERSE CITY, MI [MI0026]. ICA: MI0224.

FINE LAKE—Formerly served by Pine River Cable. No longer in operation. ICA: MI0223.

FORESTER TWP.—Formerly served by Cablevision Systems Corp. No longer in operation. ICA: MI0254.

FORESTVILLE—Formerly served by Cablevision Systems Corp. No longer in operation. ICA: MI0391.

FOWLER—Charter Communications. Now served by MIDLAND, MI [MI0030]. ICA: MI0222.

FRASER TWP.—Formerly served by MIcom. No longer in operation. ICA: MI0197.

FRASER TWP.—Parish Communications, PO Box 10, Auburn, MI 48611. Phones: 800-466-6444; 989-662-6811. Web Site: http://www.parishonline.net. ICA: MI0450.
TV Market Ranking: 61 (FRASER TWP.).
Channel capacity: N.A. Channels available but not in use: N.A.
Basic Service
Subscribers: 147.
Fee: $55.00 installation; $52.85 monthly.
Internet Service
Operational: Yes.
Telephone Service
None
General Manager: Floyd Grocholski.
Ownership: Parish Communications.

FREDERIC TWP.—Formerly served by Charter Communications. No longer in operation. ICA: MI0300.

FREE SOIL—Formerly served by Charter Communications. No longer in operation. ICA: MI0301.

FREEPORT—Formerly served by Lewiston Communications. No longer in operation. ICA: MI0302.

FRENCHTOWN TWP.—Charter Communications, 1145 South Telegraph Rd, Monroe, MI 48161. Phones: 314-543-2236; 636-207-5100 (Corporate office); 810-653-0966;

810-652-1400. Web Site: http://www.charter.com. Also serves Ash Twp., Bedford Twp. (Monroe County), Berlin Twp. (Monroe County), Carleton (village), Dundee Twp., Erie Twp., Estral Beach, Exeter Twp., Huron Twp. (Wayne County), Ida Twp., La Salle Twp., London Twp., Luna Pier, Maybee, Monroe, Monroe Twp. (Monroe County), Raisinville Twp. & Summerfield Twp. (Monroe County). ICA: MI0027.
TV Market Ranking: 5,52 (Ash Twp., Bedford Twp. (Monroe County), Berlin Twp. (Monroe County), Carleton (village), Erie Twp., Estral Beach, Exeter Twp., FRENCHTOWN TWP., Huron Twp. (Wayne County), La Salle Twp., London Twp., Maybee, Monroe, Monroe Twp. (Monroe County), Raisinville Twp.); 52 (Dundee Twp., Ida Twp., Luna Pier, Summerfield Twp. (Monroe County)). Franchise award date: N.A. Franchise expiration date: N.A. Began: December 1, 1982.
Channel capacity: N.A. Channels available but not in use: N.A.

Digital Basic Service
Subscribers: 15,985.
Programming (via satellite): AXS TV; BBC America; Boomerang; CMT; CNN en Espanol; Discovery Channel HD; DIY Network; ESPN HD; ESPNews; FOX College Sports Central; FOX College Sports Pacific; Fox Sports 2; FOX Sports Detroit; FYI; History; History International; IFC; LMN; MC; Nick 2; Nick Jr.; Nicktoons; Outdoor Channel; Teen-Nick; TNT HD; Universal HD; Weatherscan; World.
Fee: $49.99 installation; $26.99 monthly.

Digital Expanded Basic Service
Subscribers: N.A.
Programming (via satellite): A&E; AMC; Animal Planet; BET; Bravo; Cartoon Network; CMT; CNBC; CNN; Comedy Central; C-SPAN; Discovery Channel; Discovery Life Channel; Disney Channel; Disney XD; E!; ESPN; ESPN Classic; ESPN2; EWTN Global Catholic Network; Food Network; Fox News Channel; Fox Sports 1; FOX Sports Detroit; Freeform; FX; Golf Channel; GSN; Hallmark Channel; HGTV; History; HLN; Jewelry Television; Lifetime; MSNBC; MTV; National Geographic Channel; NBCSN; Nickelodeon; Oxygen; Spike TV; Syfy; The Weather Channel; TLC; TNT; Travel Channel; truTV; Turner Classic Movies; TV Land; Univision Studios; USA Network; VH1; WE tv.
Fee: $36.49 monthly.

Digital Pay Service 1
Pay Units: N.A.
Programming (via satellite): Cinemax (multiplexed); Cinemax HD; Flix; HBO (multiplexed); HBO HD; LOGO; Showtime (multiplexed); Showtime HD; Starz (multiplexed); Starz Encore (multiplexed); The Movie Channel (multiplexed).
Video-On-Demand: Yes

Pay-Per-View
iN DEMAND (delivered digitally); NHL Center Ice (delivered digitally); MLB Extra Innings (delivered digitally); Playboy TV (delivered digitally); Club Jenna (delivered digi-

2017 Edition   D-377

Michigan—Cable Systems

tally); Fresh! (delivered digitally); Fresh (delivered digitally); Shorteez (delivered digitally).
Internet Service
Operational: Yes.
Subscribers: 15,662.
Broadband Service: Charter Internet.
Fee: $29.99 monthly.
Telephone Service
Digital: Operational
Subscribers: 8,298.
Fee: $29.99 monthly
Miles of Plant: 1,140.0 (coaxial); 378.0 (fiber optic). Homes passed: 35,771.
Vice President & General Manager: Dave Slowick. Technical Operations Director: Lloyd Collins. Marketing Director: Lisa Gayari. Accounting Director: David Sovanski.
Ownership: Charter Communications Inc. (MSO).

FROST TWP.—Charter Communications. Now served by MIDLAND, MI [MI0030]. ICA: MI0303.

GAGETOWN—Comcast Cable. Now served by DETROIT, MI [MI0001]. ICA: MI0427.

GARDEN TWP.—Upper Peninsula Communications, 397 North US Hwy 41, Carney, MI 49812-9757. Phones: 906-639-2111; 906-639-2194. Fax: 906-639-9936. E-mail: louied@alphacomm.net. ICA: MI0305.
TV Market Ranking: Below 100 (GARDEN TWP.). Franchise award date: N.A. Franchise expiration date: N.A. Began: March 1, 1992.
Channel capacity: N.A. Channels available but not in use: N.A.
Basic Service
Subscribers: 30.
Programming (received off-air): WJMN-TV (CBS) Escanaba; WKRN-TV (ABC) Nashville; WLUC-TV (FOX, NBC) Marquette; WNMU (PBS) Marquette; WZMQ (Antenna TV, MeTV, MNT, This TV) Marquette.
Programming (via satellite): A&E; CNBC; CNN; C-SPAN; Discovery Channel; ESPN; ESPN2; EWTN Global Catholic Network; FOX Sports Networks; Freeform; HGTV; History; ION Television; Outdoor Channel; Spike TV; Syfy; TBS; The Weather Channel; TNT; Trinity Broadcasting Network (TBN); Turner Classic Movies; USA Network; WGN America.
Fee: $26.00 installation; $30.50 monthly.
Pay Service 1
Pay Units: N.A.
Programming (via satellite): Cinemax.
Fee: $7.50 monthly.
Internet Service
Operational: No.
Telephone Service
None
General Manager & Chief Technician: Louis Dupont.
Ownership: Upper Peninsula Communications Inc. (MSO).

GARFIELD TWP. (Clare County)—Charter Communications. Now served by MIDLAND, MI [MI0030]. ICA: MI0306.

GAYLORD—Charter Communications. Now served by TRAVERSE CITY, MI [MI0026]. ICA: MI0093.

GERMFASK—Upper Peninsula Communications, 397 North US Hwy 41, Carney, MI 49812-9757. Phones: 906-639-2111; 906-639-2194. Fax: 906-639-9936. E-mail: louied@alphacomm.net. ICA: MI0307.
TV Market Ranking: Outside TV Markets (GERMFASK).
Channel capacity: 40 (not 2-way capable). Channels available but not in use: N.A.
Basic Service
Subscribers: 16.
Programming (received off-air): WKRN-TV (ABC) Nashville; WZMQ (Antenna TV, MeTV, MNT, This TV) Marquette.
Programming (via microwave): WJMN-TV (CBS) Escanaba; WTVS (PBS) Detroit.
Programming (via satellite): A&E; AMC; CNN; C-SPAN; Discovery Channel; ESPN; ESPN2; Hallmark Channel; HGTV; History; ION Television; Lifetime; Outdoor Channel; Spike TV; TBS; The Weather Channel; TLC; TNT; Turner Classic Movies; TV Land; USA Network; WGN America; WNBC (COZI TV, NBC) New York.
Fee: $31.00 monthly.
Pay Service 1
Pay Units: N.A.
Programming (via satellite): Showtime.
Internet Service
Operational: No.
Telephone Service
None
Miles of Plant: 5.0 (coaxial); None (fiber optic). Homes passed: 114.
General Manager & Chief Technician: Louis Dupont.
Ownership: Upper Peninsula Communications Inc. (MSO).

GILEAD—Formerly served by CableDirect. No longer in operation. ICA: MI0308.

GILMORE TWP. (Isabella County)—Charter Communications. Now served by MIDLAND, MI [MI0030]. ICA: MI0247.

GLENNIE (village)—Formerly served by CenturyLink. No longer in operation. ICA: MI0309.

GOODAR TWP.—Charter Communications, 345 South State St, Oscoda, MI 48750. Phones: 314-543-2236; 636-207-5100 (Corporate office); 989-340-0078; 989-356-4503. Web Site: http://www.charter.com. Also serves Cumming Twp., Hill Twp., Plainfield Twp. (Iosco County), Rose City & Rose Twp. (Ogemaw County). ICA: MI0127.
TV Market Ranking: Outside TV Markets (Cumming Twp., GOODAR TWP., Hill Twp., Plainfield Twp. (Iosco County), Rose Twp. (Ogemaw County), Rose City). Franchise award date: November 1, 1987. Franchise expiration date: N.A. Began: December 15, 1981.
Channel capacity: 70 (not 2-way capable). Channels available but not in use: N.A.
Digital Basic Service
Subscribers: 1,405.
Programming (received off-air): WBKB-TV (ABC, CBS, FOX) Alpena; WCML (PBS) Alpena; WEYI-TV (Bounce TV, CW, NBC) Saginaw; WFQX-TV (FOX) Cadillac; WJRT-TV (ABC, MeTV) Flint; WNEM-TV (CBS, COZI TV, MNT) Bay City; WWTV (CBS) Cadillac.
Programming (via satellite): A&E; Animal Planet; CMT; CNN; Comedy Central; Discovery Channel; Disney Channel; ESPN; Fox News Channel; Freeform; HLN; Lifetime; Nickelodeon; QVC; Spike TV; Syfy; TBS; The Weather Channel; TNT; Turner Classic Movies; USA Network; WGN America.
Fee: $49.99 installation; $12.99 monthly; $1.25 converter.
Digital Expanded Basic Service
Subscribers: N.A.
Programming (via satellite): CNN; Discovery Channel; ESPN; HLN; Nickelodeon; Syfy; The Weather Channel; TNT.
Fee: $36.49 monthly.
Digital Pay Service 1
Pay Units: N.A.
Programming (via satellite): Cinemax; HBO; Showtime.
Fee: $9.95 monthly (each).
Internet Service
Operational: No.
Telephone Service
None
Miles of Plant: 1,120.0 (coaxial); 278.0 (fiber optic). Homes passed: 33,931.
Vice President: Joe Boullion. General Manager: Ed Kavanaugh. Technical Operations Director: Rob Nowak. Accounting Director: David Sovanski. Marketing Manager: Brenda Auger.
Ownership: Charter Communications Inc. (MSO).

GOODELLS—Formerly served by Cablevision Systems Corp. No longer in operation. ICA: MI0310.

GOODRICH—Charter Communications, 12405 Powerscourt Dr, St. Louis, MO 63131. Phones: 636-207-5100 (Corporate office); 810-653-0966; 810-652-1400; 810-652-1430. Web Site: http://www.charter.com. Also serves Addison Twp., Almer Twp., Almont, Almont Twp., Arbela Twp., Arcadia Twp. (Lapeer County), Argentine Twp., Atlas Twp., Attica Twp., Bancroft, Brandon Twp., Burns Twp., Byron, Caro, Cass City, Clayton Twp. (Genesee County), Clifford, Columbiaville, Davison, Dayton Twp. (Tuscola County), Deerfield, Deerfield Twp. (Lapeer County), Dexter Twp., Dryden, Dryden Twp., Durand, Elba Twp. (Lapeer County), Elkland Twp., Ellington Twp., Fenton, Fenton Twp., Forest Twp. (Genesee County), Freemont Twp., Gaines, Gaines Twp. (Genesee County), Genesee County (portions), Green Oak Twp., Hadley Twp., Hamburg Twp., Howell, Imlay City, Imlay Twp., Indianfields Twp., Kingston (village), Kingston Twp., Koylton Twp., Lapeer, Lapeer Twp., Lennon, Leonard, Linden, Livingston County (portions), Marathon, Marathon Twp., Marion Twp. (Livingston County), Mayfield Twp. (Lapeer County), Mayville, Metamora, Metamora Twp., Millington, Millington Twp., North Branch (village), North Branch Twp., Northfield Twp., Novesta Twp., Oregon Twp., Ortonville, Otisville, Otter Lake, Oxford, Oxford (village), Oxford Twp., Pinckney, Putnam Twp., Richfield Twp. (Genesee County), Salem Twp. (Washtenaw County), Shiawassee Twp., Thetford Twp., Tuscola Twp., Tyrone Twp. (Livingston County), Unadilla Twp., Vassar, Vassar Twp., Venice Twp., Vernon (village), Vernon Twp. (Shiawassee County), Watertown Twp. (Tuscola County) & Webster Twp. ICA: MI0290.
TV Market Ranking: 37 (Deerfield Twp. (Lapeer County)); 5 (Salem Twp. (Washtenaw County)); 5,61 (Addison Twp., Leonard, Oxford, Oxford (village), Oxford Twp.); 61 (Almer Twp., Almont, Almont Twp., Arbela Twp., Argentine Twp., Atlas Twp., Attica Twp., Brandon Twp., Caro, Cass City, Clifford, Columbiaville, Davison, Dayton Twp. (Tuscola County), Deerfield, Dryden, Dryden Twp., Elba Twp. (Lapeer County), Elkland Twp., Ellington Twp., Fenton, Fenton Twp., Forest Twp. (Genesee County), Freemont Twp., Genesee County (portions), GOODRICH, Hadley Twp., Howell, Imlay City, Imlay Twp., Indianfields Twp., Kingston (village), Kingston Twp., Koylton Twp., Koylton Twp., Lapeer, Lapeer Twp., Linden, Marathon Twp., Mayfield Twp. (Lapeer County), Mayville, Metamora, Metamora Twp., Millington, Millington Twp., North Branch (village), North Branch Twp., Novesta Twp., Novesta Twp., Oregon Twp., Ortonville, Otisville, Otter Lake, Richfield Twp. (Genesee County), Thetford Twp., Tuscola Twp., Tyrone Twp. (Livingston County), Vassar, Vassar Twp.); 61,92 (Bancroft, Burns Twp., Byron, Clayton Twp. (Genesee County), Durand, Gaines, Gaines Twp. (Genesee County), Lennon, Shiawassee Twp., Venice Twp., Vernon (village), Vernon Twp. (Shiawassee County)); 92 (Green Oak Twp., Livingston County (portions) (portions), Marion Twp. (Livingston County), Northfield Twp., Pinckney, Unadilla Twp., Webster Twp.); Below 100 (Dexter Twp., Hamburg Twp., Putnam Twp., Livingston County (portions) (portions)); Outside TV Markets (Kingston Twp.). Franchise award date: N.A. Franchise expiration date: N.A. Began: July 1, 1979.
Channel capacity: 82 (operating 2-way). Channels available but not in use: N.A.
Digital Basic Service
Subscribers: 64,849.
Programming (via satellite): AXS TV; BBC America; CMT; Discovery Digital Networks; DIY Network; ESPN HD; ESPNews; Food Network; FOX College Sports Central; FOX College Sports Pacific; Fox Sports 2; Fuse; FXM; FYI; Great American Country; HD Theater; HGTV; History International; IFC; LMN; LOGO; MC; NBCSN; Nick 2; Nick Jr.; Nicktoons; Outdoor Channel; Sundance TV; TeenNick; Universal HD.
Fee: $14.99 monthly.
Digital Expanded Basic Service
Subscribers: N.A.
Programming (via satellite): A&E; AMC; Animal Planet; Bravo; Cartoon Network; CMT; CNBC; CNN; Comedy Central; C-SPAN; Discovery Channel; Disney Channel; Disney XD; E! HD; ESPN; ESPN Classic; ESPN2; Food Network; Fox News Channel; Fox Sports 1; FOX Sports Detroit; Freeform; FX; Golf Channel; GSN; Hallmark Channel; HGTV; History; HLN; Lifetime; MSNBC; MTV; MTV2; National Geographic Channel; NBCSN; Nickelodeon; Oxygen; Pop; Spike TV; Syfy; TBS; The Weather Channel; TLC; TNT; Travel Channel; truTV; Turner Classic Movies; TV Land; USA Network; VH1; WE tv.
Fee: $36.49 monthly.
Digital Pay Service 1
Pay Units: N.A.
Programming (via satellite): Cinemax (multiplexed); Cinemax HD; Cinemax On Demand; Flix; HBO (multiplexed); HBO HD; HBO on Demand; Showtime (multiplexed); Showtime HD; Showtime On Demand; Starz (multiplexed); Starz Encore (multiplexed); Starz On Demand; The Movie Channel (multiplexed).
Video-On-Demand: Yes
Pay-Per-View
Events & Movies (delivered digitally); ESPN (delivered digitally); NHL Center Ice (delivered digitally); MLB Extra Innings (delivered digitally); Playboy TV (delivered digitally); Fresh (delivered digitally); Shorteez (delivered digitally).

Cable Systems—Michigan

Internet Service
Operational: Yes.
Subscribers: 68,637.
Broadband Service: Charter Internet.
Fee: $29.99 monthly.
Telephone Service
Digital: Operational
Subscribers: 37,646.
Miles of Plant: 6,045.0 (coaxial); 672.0 (fiber optic). Homes passed: 142,007.
Vice President & General Manager: Dave Slowick. Technical Operations Director: Lloyd Collins. Marketing Director: Lisa Gayari. Accounting Director: David Sovanski.
Ownership: Charter Communications Inc. (MSO).

GRAND LAKE—Formerly served by Charter Communications. No longer in operation. ICA: MI0185.

GRAND MARAIS—Cable America Corp, 7822 East Gray Rd, Scottsdale, AZ 85260. Phones: 800-338-1808; 906-249-1057. Web Site: http://www.cableamerica.com. ICA: MI0215.
TV Market Ranking: Outside TV Markets (GRAND MARAIS). Franchise award date: N.A. Franchise expiration date: N.A. Began: January 1, 1986.
Channel capacity: 36 (not 2-way capable). Channels available but not in use: N.A.
Basic Service
Subscribers: 71.
Programming (received off-air): WJMN-TV (CBS) Escanaba; WLUC-TV (FOX, NBC) Marquette; WNMU (PBS) Marquette; WXYZ-TV (ABC, Bounce TV) Detroit; WZMQ (Antenna TV, MeTV, MNT, This TV) Marquette.
Programming (via satellite): A&E; AMC; Cartoon Network; CNBC; CNN; Discovery Channel; Disney Channel; ESPN; ESPN2; Fox News Channel; Fox Sports 1; FOX Sports Networks; Freeform; FX; Great American Country; Hallmark Channel; HGTV; History; ION Television; Lifetime; Syfy; TBS; The Weather Channel; TLC; TNT; Travel Channel; truTV; TV Land; USA Network; WGN America.
Fee: $35.00 installation; $59.75 monthly.
Pay Service 1
Pay Units: N.A.
Programming (via satellite): Showtime; The Movie Channel.
Fee: $15.00 installation; $6.95 monthly.
Video-On-Demand: No
Internet Service
Operational: No.
Telephone Service
None
Miles of Plant: 13.0 (coaxial); None (fiber optic). Homes passed: 420.
General Manager: Robert L. Grove. Controller: Walter G. Farak.
Ownership: CableAmerica Corp. (MSO).

GRAND RAPIDS—Comcast Cable. Now served by DETROIT, MI [MI0001]. ICA: MI0003.

GRANT—Charter Communications. Now served by ALLENDALE TWP., MI [MI0094]. ICA: MI0105.

GRASS LAKE—Formerly served by Millennium Digital Media. Now served by WOW! Internet Cable & Phone, DIMONDALE, MI [MI0136]. ICA: MI0191.

GRAYLING—Charter Communications. Now served by RICHFIELD TWP. (Roscommon County), MI [MI0116]. ICA: MI0129.

GREENVILLE—Charter Communications. Now served by ALLENDALE TWP., MI [MI0094]. ICA: MI0068.

HALE—Charter Communications, 236 W Huron Rd, PO Box 706, Augres, MI 48703. Phones: 314-543-2236; 636-207-5100 (Corporate office); 989-340-0078; 231-947-5221 (Traverse City office); 989-356-4503. Web Site: http://www.charter.com. ICA: MI0311.
TV Market Ranking: Outside TV Markets (HALE). Franchise award date: July 12, 1984. Franchise expiration date: N.A. Began: December 1, 1986.
Channel capacity: N.A. Channels available but not in use: N.A.
Digital Basic Service
Subscribers: 420.
Programming (received off-air): WBKB-TV (ABC, CBS, FOX) Alpena; WCML (PBS) Alpena; WEYI-TV (Bounce TV, CW, NBC) Saginaw; WJRT-TV (ABC, MeTV) Flint; WNEM-TV (CBS, COZI TV, MNT) Bay City.
Programming (via satellite): AMC; ESPN; Freeform; MTV; Nickelodeon; QVC; TBS; TLC; TNT; USA Network; VH1; WGN America.
Fee: $49.99 installation; $26.99 monthly.
Digital Expanded Basic Service
Subscribers: N.A.
Programming (via satellite): CNN; Discovery Channel; Disney Channel; Lifetime; Syfy; TNT.
Fee: $7.41 monthly.
Digital Pay Service 1
Pay Units: N.A.
Programming (via satellite): HBO; Showtime; The Movie Channel.
Fee: $10.95 monthly (Showtime or TMC), $11.95 monthly (HBO).
Internet Service
Operational: No.
Telephone Service
None
Miles of Plant: 52.0 (coaxial); None (fiber optic). Homes passed: 1,279.
Vice President: Joe Boullion. General Manager: Ed Kavanaugh. Technical Operations Director: Rob Nowak. Accounting Director: David Sovanski. Marketing Manager: Brenda Auger.
Ownership: Charter Communications Inc. (MSO).

HAMLIN TWP. (Mason County)—Charter Communications. Now served by ALLENDALE TWP., MI [MI0094]. ICA: MI0382.

HARBOR BEACH—Comcast Cable. Now served by DETROIT, MI [MI0001]. ICA: MI0428.

HART—Charter Communications. Now served by ALLENDALE TWP., MI [MI0094]. ICA: MI0268.

HARTLAND TWP.—Comcast Cable. Now served by DETROIT, MI [MI0001]. ICA: MI0367.

HAZEL PARK—Comcast Cable. Now served by DETROIT, MI [MI0001]. ICA: MI0079.

HESPERIA—MIcom. Now served by BALDWIN (village), MI [MI0214]. ICA: MI0434.

HIGGINS TWP.—Charter Communications. Now served by RICHFIELD TWP. (Roscommon County), MI [MI0116]. ICA: MI0077.

HIGHLAND PARK—MIcom, PO Box 100, Montague, MI 49437. Phone: 888-873-3353. Fax: 231-894-4960. E-mail: customerservice@micomcable.com. Web Site: http://www.micomcable.com. ICA: MI0066.
TV Market Ranking: 5 (HIGHLAND PARK). Franchise award date: July 12, 1982. Franchise expiration date: N.A. Began: July 13, 1984.
Channel capacity: 52 (not 2-way capable). Channels available but not in use: N.A.
Basic Service
Subscribers: 322.
Programming (received off-air): WADL (Antenna TV, getTV) Mount Clemens; WDIV-TV (NBC, This TV) Detroit; WJBK (Buzzr, FOX, Heroes & Icons, Movies!) Detroit; WKBD-TV (CW) Detroit; WMYD (Antenna TV, Escape, MNT) Detroit; WTVS (PBS) Detroit; WWJ-TV (CBS, Decades) Detroit; WXYZ-TV (ABC, Bounce TV) Detroit.
Programming (via satellite): TBS; WGN America.
Fee: $29.99 installation; $43.95 monthly.
Expanded Basic Service 1
Subscribers: N.A.
Programming (via satellite): A&E; BET; CNN; C-SPAN; C-SPAN 2; Discovery Channel; Disney Channel; ESPN; Freeform; Lifetime; Nickelodeon; The Weather Channel; TNT; USA Network.
Fee: $36.49 monthly.
Pay Service 1
Pay Units: N.A.
Programming (via satellite): Cinemax; HBO; Showtime; The Movie Channel.
Fee: $9.50 monthly (each).
Internet Service
Operational: No.
Telephone Service
None
Miles of Plant: 40.0 (coaxial); None (fiber optic).
Ownership: MIcom (MSO).

HILLMAN TWP.—Formerly served by Northwoods Cable Inc. No longer in operation. ICA: MI0235.

HILLSDALE—Comcast Cable. Now served by DETROIT, MI [MI0001]. ICA: MI0070.

HOLLAND—Comcast Cable. Now served by DETROIT, MI [MI0001]. ICA: MI0056.

HOPE—Parish Communications, PO Box 10, Auburn, MI 48611. Phones: 800-466-6444; 989-662-6811. Web Site: http://www.parishonline.net. ICA: MI0451.
TV Market Ranking: 61 (HOPE).
Channel capacity: N.A. Channels available but not in use: N.A.
Basic Service
Subscribers: 168.
Fee: $55.00 installation; $50.10 monthly.
Internet Service
Operational: Yes.
Telephone Service
None
General Manager: Floyd Grocholski.
Ownership: Parish Communications.

HOPE TWP. (Midland County)—Formerly served by MIcom. No longer in operation. ICA: MI0189.

HOUGHTON—Charter Communications. Now served by MARQUETTE, MI [MI0033]. ICA: MI0049.

HOUGHTON LAKE—Formerly served by Charter Communications. No longer in operation. ICA: MI0081.

HOWARD CITY—Charter Communications. Now served by ALLENDALE TWP., MI [MI0094]. ICA: MI0100.

HUDSON—Comcast Cable. Now served by DETROIT, MI [MI0001]. ICA: MI0182.

IMLAY CITY—Charter Communications. Now served by GOODRICH, MI [MI0290]. ICA: MI0313.

INDIAN RIVER—Charter Communications. Now served by TRAVERSE CITY, MI [MI0026]. ICA: MI0159.

IONIA—Charter Communications. Now served by ALLENDALE TWP., MI [MI0094]. ICA: MI0091.

IRON MOUNTAIN—Charter Communications. Now served by MARQUETTE, MI [MI0033]. ICA: MI0067.

IRON MOUNTAIN—Northside T.V. Corp, 521 Vulcan St, Iron Mountain, MI 49801-2333. Phone: 906-774-1351. Fax: 906-774-1393. E-mail: steve@upnorthcable.com. Web Site: http://www.upnorthcable.com. Also serves Austin Twp. (Mecosta County), Chippewa Twp. (Mecosta County), Martiny Twp. (southern portion) & Morton Twp. ICA: MI0194.
TV Market Ranking: Below 100 (IRON MOUNTAIN); Outside TV Markets (Austin Twp. (Mecosta County), Chippewa Twp. (Mecosta County), Martiny Twp. (southern portion), Morton Twp.). Franchise award date: N.A. Franchise expiration date: N.A. Began: October 1, 1955.
Channel capacity: N.A. Channels available but not in use: N.A.
Basic Service
Subscribers: N.A.
Programming (received off-air): WGBA-TV (MeTV, NBC) Green Bay; WJFW-TV (Antenna TV, NBC) Rhinelander; WLUC-TV (FOX, NBC) Marquette; WNMU (PBS) Marquette; WXYZ-TV (ABC, Bounce TV) Detroit; allband FM.
Programming (via microwave): WBAY-TV (ABC) Green Bay; WJMN-TV (CBS) Escanaba; WLUK-TV (Antenna TV, FOX) Green Bay.
Programming (via satellite): A&E; AMC; Cartoon Network; CNN; C-SPAN; Discovery Channel; ESPN; EWTN Global Catholic Network; Fox News Channel; Freeform; Hallmark Channel; HGTV; History; HLN; INSP; Lifetime; MTV; National Geographic Channel; Nickelodeon; Spike TV; TBS; The Weather Channel; TLC; TNT; TV Land; USA Network; VH1; WGN America.
Fee: $60.00 installation.
Pay Service 1
Pay Units: N.A.
Programming (via satellite): HBO.
Fee: $10.00 monthly.
Internet Service
Operational: Yes.
Broadband Service: In-house.
Fee: $30.00 monthly; $5.00 modem lease.
Telephone Service
Digital: Operational
Fee: $28.00 monthly

Michigan—Cable Systems

WARREN'S Washington Internet Daily
Covering the politics and policies of the internet.
FREE 30-DAY TRIAL—call 800-771-9202 or visit www.warren-news.com

Miles of Plant: 14.0 (coaxial); None (fiber optic).
Office Manager: Judy Short.
Ownership: Northside TV Corp.

IRON RIVER—Iron River Cable, 316 North 2nd Ave, Iron River, MI 49935-1418. Phone: 906-265-3810. Fax: 906-265-3020. E-mail: ircable@ironriver.tv. Web Site: http://www.ironriver.tv. Also serves Bates Twp. & Iron River Twp. ICA: MI0132.
TV Market Ranking: Below 100 (Bates Twp., IRON RIVER, Iron River Twp.). Franchise award date: May 27, 1957. Franchise expiration date: N.A. Began: November 1, 1957.
Channel capacity: N.A. Channels available but not in use: N.A.
Basic Service
Subscribers: 994. Commercial subscribers: 8.
Programming (received off-air): WBKP (ABC, CW) Calumet; WJMN-TV (CBS) Escanaba; WLUC-TV (FOX, NBC) Marquette; WLUK-TV (Antenna TV, FOX) Green Bay; WNMU (PBS) Marquette; WYOW (ABC, CW, This TV) Eagle River; WZMQ (Antenna TV, MeTV, MNT, This TV) Marquette; allband FM.
Programming (via satellite): AMC; Cartoon Network; CMT; C-SPAN; Discovery Channel; Discovery Life Channel; Disney Channel; ESPN; ESPN2; EWTN Global Catholic Network; Food Network; FOX Sports Detroit; FX; Golf Channel; HGTV; History; Lifetime; National Geographic Channel; Nickelodeon; Outdoor Channel; QVC; Syfy; TBS; The Weather Channel; TLC; TNT; Trinity Broadcasting Network (TBN); Turner Classic Movies; TV Land; USA Network; various Canadian stations; VH1; WGN America.
Fee: $50.00 installation; $32.00 monthly.
Expanded Basic Service 1
Subscribers: 850.
Programming (via satellite): A&E; Animal Planet; CNN; Comedy Central; Fox News Channel; Fox Sports 1; MTV; NBCSN; Spike TV.
Fee: $14.00 monthly.
Digital Basic Service
Subscribers: N.A.
Programming (via satellite): A&E HD; American Heroes Channel; Animal Planet HD; BBC America; Bravo; Bravo HD; Chiller; Cloo; CMT; Cooking Channel; Destination America; Destination America HD; Discovery Channel HD; Discovery Family; Discovery Life Channel; DIY Network; ESPN Classic; ESPN HD; ESPN2 HD; ESPNews; ESPNU; Food Network HD; FOX College Sports Central; FOX College Sports Pacific; FX HD; FXM; FYI; Golf Channel; Golf Channel HD; Great American Country; GSN; Hallmark Movies & Mysteries; HD Theater; HGTV HD; History HD; History International; IFC; Investigation Discovery; LMN; MC; MoviePlex; MTV Classic; MTV2; National Geographic Channel HD; NBCSN; Nick Jr.; Nicktoons; Outdoor Channel HD; OWN: Oprah Winfrey Network; PBS HD; Science Channel; Science HD; Syfy HD; TeenNick; The Sportsman Channel; TLC HD; TNT HD; Travel Channel HD; truTV HD; Turner Classic Movies HD; USA Network HD.
Fee: $5.00 converter.
Digital Pay Service 1
Pay Units: N.A.
Programming (via satellite): Cinemax (multiplexed); Flix; HBO (multiplexed); Showtime (multiplexed); Starz (multiplexed); Starz Encore (multiplexed); The Movie Channel (multiplexed).
Fee: $10.00 monthly (Cinemax), $13.00 monthly (Starz/Encore), $14.00 monthly (Showtime/TMC/Flix), $15.00 monthly (HBO).
Video-On-Demand: No
Internet Service
Operational: Yes.
Telephone Service
None
Miles of Plant: 52.0 (coaxial); 8.0 (fiber optic). Homes passed: 2,000.
President: Peter Nocerini. Chief Technician: Jerry Ward. Office Manager: Syndra Mottes.
Ownership: Iron River Cooperative TV Antenna Corp.

IRONWOOD—Charter Communications, 115 East McLeod Ave, Ironwood, MI 49938. Phones: 636-207-5100 (Corporate office); 314-543-2236; 231-947-5221 (Traverse City office); 906-475-0107 (Negaunee office). Web Site: http://www.charter.com. Also serves Bergland, Bergland Twp., Bessemer, Carp Lake, Erwin Twp., Ewen, Greenland Twp., Ontonagon, Rockland Twp., Stannard Twp., Wakefield & Watersmeet, MI; Hurley, Knight (town), Montreal & Pence, WI. ICA: MI0064.
TV Market Ranking: Below 100 (Watersmeet); Outside TV Markets (Bergland, Bergland Twp., Bessemer, Carp Lake, Erwin Twp., Ewen, Greenland Twp., Hurley, IRONWOOD, Knight (town), Montreal, Ontonagon, Pence, Rockland Twp., Stannard Twp., Wakefield). Franchise award date: January 1, 1958. Franchise expiration date: N.A. Began: January 1, 1958.
Channel capacity: N.A. Channels available but not in use: N.A.
Digital Basic Service
Subscribers: 5,708.
Programming (via satellite): BBC America; Cooking Channel; Discovery Digital Networks; DIY Network; ESPN Classic; FOX College Sports Central; FOX College Sports Pacific; Fox Sports 2; FXM; FYI; Great American Country; History International; IFC; LMN; NFL Network; Nick 2; Nick Jr.; Nicktoons; Outdoor Channel; Sundance TV; TeenNick.
Fee: $49.99 installation; $26.99 monthly.
Digital Expanded Basic Service
Subscribers: N.A.
Programming (via satellite): A&E; AMC; Animal Planet; Bravo; Cartoon Network; CMT; CNBC; CNN; Comedy Central; Discovery Channel; Discovery Life Channel; Disney Channel; Disney XD; E! HD; ESPN; ESPN2; Food Network; Fox News Channel; Fox Sports 1; FOX Sports Detroit; Freeform; FX; Golf Channel; GSN; HGTV; History; HLN; INSP; Lifetime; MSNBC; MTV; National Geographic Channel; NBCSN; Nickelodeon; Oxygen; Spike TV; Syfy; The Weather Channel; TNT; truTV; Turner Classic Movies; TV Land; USA Network; VH1; WE tv.
Fee: $36.49 monthly.
Digital Pay Service 1
Pay Units: N.A.
Programming (via satellite): Cinemax (multiplexed); DMX Music; HBO; Showtime (multiplexed); Starz (multiplexed); Starz Encore (multiplexed); The Movie Channel (multiplexed).
Video-On-Demand: Yes
Pay-Per-View
iN DEMAND; special events.
Internet Service
Operational: Yes.
Subscribers: 3,991.
Broadband Service: Charter Internet.
Fee: $39.99 monthly.
Telephone Service
Digital: Operational
Subscribers: 2,131.
Miles of Plant: 469.0 (coaxial); 405.0 (fiber optic). Homes passed: 13,812.
Vice President: Joe Boullion. General Manager: Rex Buettgenbach. Technical Operations Director: Rob Nowak. Accounting Director: David Sovanski. Government Relations Manager: Don Gladwell. Marketing Manager: Sandy Gottschalk.
Ownership: Charter Communications Inc. (MSO).

JACKSON—Comcast Cable. Now served by DETROIT, MI [MI0001]. ICA: MI0031.

JACKSON—Formerly served by Wireless Cable Systems Inc. No longer in operation. ICA: MI0390.

JAMESTOWN TWP.—Charter Communications. Now served by ALLENDALE TWP., MI [MI0094]. ICA: MI0109.

JONES—Comcast Cable. Now served by DETROIT, MI [MI0001]. ICA: MI0315.

KALEVA (village)—Formerly served by Pine River Cable. No longer in operation. ICA: MI0242.

KEELER TWP.—Sister Lakes Cable TV, PO Box 433, Dowagiac, MI 49047. Phone: 269-424-5737. E-mail: cs@sisterlakescable.com. Web Site: http://www.sisterlakescable.com. Also serves Silver Creek Twp. & Sister Lakes. ICA: MI0135.
TV Market Ranking: 37,80 (KEELER TWP., Silver Creek Twp., Sister Lakes). Franchise award date: May 1, 1986. Franchise expiration date: N.A. Began: July 1, 1987.
Channel capacity: N.A. Channels available but not in use: N.A.
Basic Service
Subscribers: N.A.
Programming (received off-air): WHME-TV (COZI TV, IND) South Bend; WNDU-TV (NBC) South Bend; WNIT (PBS) South Bend; WSBT-TV (CBS, FOX) South Bend; WSJV (Heroes & Icons) Elkhart; WWMT (CBS, CW) Kalamazoo; WXMI (Antenna TV, FOX, This TV) Grand Rapids.
Programming (via microwave): WGN-TV (IND) Chicago; WTTW (PBS) Chicago.
Programming (via satellite): A&E; AMC; Animal Planet; Cartoon Network; CMT; CNBC; CNN; Comedy Central; Concert TV; Discovery Channel; ESPN; ESPN2; Food Network; Fox News Channel; FX; Great American Country; Hallmark Channel; HGTV; History; HLN; Lifetime; MTV; National Geographic Channel; Nickelodeon; Outdoor Channel; QVC; Spike TV; Syfy; TBS; The Weather Channel; TLC; TNT; Travel Channel; TV Land; USA Network; VH1.
Fee: $30.00 installation.
Pay Service 1
Pay Units: N.A.
Programming (via satellite): Cinemax; HBO; Showtime.
Fee: $10.00 - $14.00 monthly (each).
Video-On-Demand: No
Internet Service
Operational: Yes.
Subscribers: 550.
Fee: $40.00 installation; $41.40 monthly; $60.00 modem lease.
Telephone Service
None
Miles of Plant: 40.0 (coaxial); 10.0 (fiber optic). Homes passed: 2,200.
Chief Technician: Tim Olmstead.
Ownership: Satellite Operations Inc.

KINCHELOE—Formerly served by Charter Communications. No longer in operation. ICA: MI0200.

KINDERHOOK TWP.—Formerly served by CableDirect. No longer in operation. ICA: MI0232.

KINGSTON TWP.—Charter Communications. Now served by GOODRICH, MI [MI0290]. ICA: MI0318.

LAKE GEORGE—Formerly served by Charter Communications. No longer in operation. ICA: MI0319.

LAKEVIEW—Charter Communications, 1202 West Benton, Greenville, MI 48838. Phones: 636-207-5100 (Corporate office); 616-647-6201. Web Site: http://www.charter.com. Also serves Belvidere Twp. & Cato Twp. ICA: MI0172.
TV Market Ranking: Outside TV Markets (Belvidere Twp., Cato Twp., LAKEVIEW). Channel capacity: 45 (not 2-way capable). Channels available but not in use: N.A.
Digital Basic Service
Subscribers: 434.
Programming (received off-air): WCMU-TV (PBS) Mount Pleasant; WGVU-TV (PBS) Grand Rapids; WOOD-TV (Laff, NBC) Grand Rapids; WTLJ (IND) Muskegon; WWTV (CBS) Cadillac; WXMI (Antenna TV, FOX, This TV) Grand Rapids; WZPX-TV (ION) Battle Creek; WZZM (ABC) Grand Rapids.
Programming (via satellite): C-SPAN; QVC; TBS; WGN America.
Fee: $49.99 installation; $14.99 monthly.
Digital Expanded Basic Service
Subscribers: N.A.
Programming (via satellite): A&E; AMC; CNBC; CNN; Comedy Central; Discovery Channel; Disney Channel; ESPN; ESPN2; Food Network; FOX Sports Detroit; Freeform; HGTV; History; HLN; Lifetime; MTV; Nickelodeon; Spike TV; The Weather Channel; TLC; TNT; USA Network; VH1.
Digital Pay Service 1
Pay Units: N.A.
Programming (via satellite): Cinemax; HBO; Starz.
Fee: $6.95 monthly (Starz), $10.95 monthly (Cinemax).
Internet Service
Operational: No.

D-380 TV & Cable Factbook No. 85

Cable Systems—Michigan

Telephone Service
None
Miles of Plant: 34.0 (coaxial); None (fiber optic). Homes passed: 1,347.
Vice President & General Manager: Dan Spoelman. Marketing Director: Steve Schuh. Accounting Director: David Sovanski. Technical Operations Manager: Keith Schierbeek.
Ownership: Charter Communications Inc. (MSO).

LANSING—Comcast Cable. Now served by DETROIT, MI [MI0001]. ICA: MI0007.

LANSING—Formerly served by Sprint Corp. No longer in operation. ICA: MI0394.

LAPEER—Charter Communications. Now served by GOODRICH, MI [MI0290]. ICA: MI0073.

LAWTON (village)—Comcast Cable. Now served by DETROIT, MI [MI0001]. ICA: MI0322.

LE ROY—Summit Digital, 107 West Bridge St, Portland, MI 48875. Phones: 231-825-2500; 888-600-5040. E-mail: info@summitdigital.net. Web Site: http://summitdigital.net. Also serves Ashton, Luther, Tustin & Wolf Lake. ICA: MI0198.
TV Market Ranking: Below 100 (Ashton, LE ROY, Luther, Tustin). Franchise award date: N.A. Franchise expiration date: N.A. Began: July 1, 1989.
Channel capacity: N.A. Channels available but not in use: N.A.
Basic Service
Subscribers: N.A.
Programming (received off-air): WCMV (PBS) Cadillac; WGTU (ABC, CW) Traverse City; WPBN-TV (NBC) Traverse City; WWTV (CBS) Cadillac; WZZM (ABC) Grand Rapids.
Programming (via satellite): A&E; Cartoon Network; CMT; CNN; Comedy Central; Discovery Channel; Disney Channel; ESPN; FOX Sports Networks; Freeform; HLN; Lifetime; MTV; Nickelodeon; QVC; Spike TV; Syfy; TBS; TNT; USA Network; VH1; WGN America.
Fee: $50.00 installation; $34.95 monthly.
Pay Service 1
Pay Units: N.A.
Programming (via satellite): Cinemax (multiplexed); HBO (multiplexed).
Fee: $11.00 - $13.00 monthly (each).
Video-On-Demand: No
Internet Service
Operational: Yes. Began: April 1, 2003.
Broadband Service: West Michigan Internet Service.
Fee: $19.95-$75.00 monthly.
Telephone Service
None
Miles of Plant: 69.0 (coaxial); None (fiber optic). Homes passed: 885.
Operations Manager: Patty Coleman.
Ownership: Summit Digital (MSO).

LEE TWP. (Midland County)—Parish Communications, PO Box 10, Auburn, MI 48611. Phones: 800-466-6444; 989-662-6811. Web Site: http://www.parishonline.net. ICA: MI0452.
TV Market Ranking: 61 (LEE TWP. (MIDLAND COUNTY)).
Channel capacity: N.A. Channels available but not in use: N.A.
Basic Service
Subscribers: 350.
Fee: $55.00 installation; $63.15 monthly.

Internet Service
Operational: Yes.
Telephone Service
None
General Manager: Floyd Grocholski.
Ownership: Parish Communications.

LEVERING—Charter Communications. Now served by TRAVERSE CITY, MI [MI0026]. ICA: MI0218.

LEWISTON—Lewiston Communications, 2 East Main St, PO Box 169, Fremont, MI 49412-0169. Phone: 989-786-0525. Also serves Albert Twp., Greenwood Twp. (Oscoda County) & Montmorency County. ICA: MI0323.
TV Market Ranking: Below 100 (Albert Twp., Greenwood Twp. (Oscoda County), LEWISTON, Montmorency County). Franchise award date: N.A. Franchise expiration date: N.A. Began: November 1, 1987.
Channel capacity: N.A. Channels available but not in use: N.A.
Basic Service
Subscribers: N.A.
Programming (received off-air): WBKB-TV (ABC, CBS, FOX) Alpena; WCML (PBS) Alpena; WFUP (FOX) Vanderbilt; WGTU (ABC, CW) Traverse City; WTOM-TV (NBC) Cheboygan; WWTV (CBS) Cadillac.
Programming (via satellite): A&E; AMC; Animal Planet; Cartoon Network; CMT; CNBC; CNN; Comedy Central; C-SPAN; Discovery Channel; E! HD; ESPN; ESPN2; Fox News Channel; Fox Sports 1; FOX Sports Detroit; Freeform; FX; Golf Channel; Hallmark Channel; HGTV; History; HLN; Lifetime; National Geographic Channel; Nickelodeon; Outdoor Channel; OWN: Oprah Winfrey Network; QVC; Spike TV; Syfy; TBS; The Weather Channel; TLC; TNT; Trinity Broadcasting Network (TBN); truTV; Turner Classic Movies; TV Land; USA Network; WGN America.
Fee: $55.00 installation.
Pay Service 1
Pay Units: N.A.
Programming (via satellite): Cinemax; HBO; Showtime.
Fee: $11.95 monthly (each).
Video-On-Demand: No
Internet Service
Operational: No.
Telephone Service
None
Miles of Plant: 71.0 (coaxial); None (fiber optic).
General Manager: Charles Lathrop. Chief Technician: Jim Batch.
Ownership: Lewiston Communications (MSO).

LEXINGTON (village)—Comcast Cable. Now served by DETROIT, MI [MI0001]. ICA: MI0128.

LILLEY TWP.—Formerly served by Charter Communications. No longer in operation. ICA: MI0192.

LIVINGSTON COUNTY (portions)—Charter Communications. Now served by GOODRICH, MI [MI0290]. ICA: MI0036.

LIVONIA—Bright House Networks, 14525 Farmington Rd, Livonia, MI 48154-5405. Phones: 734-422-3200 (Customer service); 734-422-2810. Fax: 734-422-2239. E-mail: bob.mccann@mybrighthouse.com. Web Site: http://brighthouse.com. Also serves Farmington, Farmington Hills, Novi, Novi Twp. & Redford. ICA: MI0019.
TV Market Ranking: 5 (Farmington, Farmington Hills, LIVONIA, Novi, Novi Twp., Redford). Franchise award date: January 1, 1983. Franchise expiration date: N.A. Began: February 6, 1984.
Channel capacity: N.A. Channels available but not in use: N.A.
Basic Service
Subscribers: 52,204. Commercial subscribers: 1,337.
Programming (received off-air): various Canadian stations; WADL (Antenna TV, getTV) Mount Clemens; WDIV-TV (NBC, This TV) Detroit; WJBK (Buzzr, FOX, Heroes & Icons, Movies!) Detroit; WKBD-TV (CW) Detroit; WMYD (Antenna TV, Escape, MNT) Detroit; WPXD-TV (ION) Ann Arbor; WTVS (PBS) Detroit; WWJ-TV (CBS, Decades) Detroit; WXYZ-TV (ABC, Bounce TV) Detroit.
Programming (via satellite): A&E; AMC; Animal Planet; BET; Bravo; Cartoon Network; CMT; CNBC; CNN; Comedy Central; C-SPAN; C-SPAN 2; Discovery Channel; Disney Channel; E! HD; ESPN; ESPN Classic; ESPN2; EVINE Live; EWTN Global Catholic Network; Food Network; Fox News Channel; Fox Sports 1; FOX Sports Detroit; Freeform; FX; Golf Channel; HGTV; History; HLN; Lifetime; MSNBC; MTV; National Geographic Channel; Nickelodeon; Oxygen; Pop; QVC; Spike TV; Syfy; TBS; The Weather Channel; TLC; TNT; Travel Channel; truTV; Turner Classic Movies; TV Land; USA Network; VH1; WE tv; WGN America.
Fee: $75.28 installation; $27.00 monthly; $2.50 converter.
Digital Basic Service
Subscribers: N.A.
Programming (via satellite): BBC America; Bloomberg Television; Discovery Digital Networks; Disney XD; DMX Music; ESPN Now; ESPNews; GSN; LMN; MTV Classic; MTV2; NBCSN; Nick Jr.; Outdoor Channel; Ovation; TeenNick; WAM! America's Kidz Network.
Digital Expanded Basic Service
Subscribers: N.A.
Programming (via satellite): FXM; IFC; Sundance TV.
Fee: $4.00 monthly (movie lovers), $4.95 monthly (sports package).
Digital Pay Service 1
Pay Units: N.A.
Programming (via satellite): Cinemax (multiplexed); Flix; HBO (multiplexed); Showtime (multiplexed); Starz (multiplexed); The Movie Channel (multiplexed).
Fee: $15.00 monthly (each).
Video-On-Demand: Yes
Pay-Per-View
iN DEMAND (delivered digitally); Fresh (delivered digitally); Shorteez (delivered digitally); Pleasure (delivered digitally); Hot Choice (delivered digitally).
Internet Service
Operational: Yes.
Subscribers: 57,555.
Broadband Service: Road Runner; EarthLink; AOL for Broadband.
Fee: $49.95 installation; $44.95 monthly.
Telephone Service
Analog: Operational
Digital: Operational
Subscribers: 34,320.
Fee: $39.95 monthly
Miles of Plant: 2,525.0 (coaxial); 478.0 (fiber optic). Homes passed: 124,312.
President: Bob McCann. Vice President, Engineering: Armis Baumanis. Vice President, Marketing: Dan Dinsmore. Chief Financial Officer: William Futera. Customer Service Manager: Mary Taylor.
Ownership: Bright House Networks LLC (MSO).

LOWELL—Comcast Cable. Now served by DETROIT, MI [MI0001]. ICA: MI0122.

LUDINGTON—Charter Communications. Now served by ALLENDALE TWP., MI [MI0094]. ICA: MI0324.

LUZERNE—Formerly served by Pine River Cable. No longer in operation. ICA: MI0325.

MACKINAC ISLAND—MIcom, PO Box 100, Montague, MI 49437. Phone: 888-873-3353. Fax: 231-894-4960. E-mail: customerservice@micomcable.com. Web Site: http://www.micomcable.com. ICA: MI0199.
TV Market Ranking: Below 100 (MACKINAC ISLAND). Franchise award date: July 11, 1990. Franchise expiration date: N.A. Began: July 15, 1991.
Channel capacity: 53 (not 2-way capable). Channels available but not in use: N.A.
Basic Service
Subscribers: 187.
Programming (received off-air): WCML (PBS) Alpena; WFQX-TV (FOX) Cadillac; WGTQ (ABC) Sault Ste. Marie; WTOM-TV (NBC) Cheboygan; WWUP-TV (CBS, FOX) Sault Ste. Marie.
Programming (via satellite): C-SPAN.
Fee: $29.99 installation; $34.70 monthly; $1.21 converter.
Expanded Basic Service 1
Subscribers: N.A.
Programming (via satellite): A&E; AMC; CNBC; CNN; Discovery Channel; Disney Channel; ESPN; ESPN2; FOX Sports Detroit; Freeform; HGTV; History; HLN; Nickelodeon; QVC; Spike TV; TBS; The Weather Channel; TNT; USA Network; WGN America.
Fee: $36.49 monthly.
Pay Service 1
Pay Units: N.A.
Programming (via satellite): HBO; Showtime; The Movie Channel.
Fee: $15.51 installation; $10.00 monthly (each).
Internet Service
Operational: Yes.
Subscribers: 99.
Telephone Service
None
Miles of Plant: 6.0 (coaxial); None (fiber optic). Homes passed: 400.
Ownership: MIcom (MSO).

MACKINAW CITY—Charter Communications. Now served by TRAVERSE CITY, MI [MI0026]. ICA: MI0326.

MADISON HEIGHTS—Comcast Cable. Now served by DETROIT, MI [MI0001]. ICA: MI0052.

MANCELONA—Charter Communications. Now served by TRAVERSE CITY, MI [MI0026]. ICA: MI0087.

MANISTEE—Charter Communications. Now served by TRAVERSE CITY, MI [MI0026]. ICA: MI0089.

MANTON—Charter Communications. Now served by TRAVERSE CITY, MI [MI0026]. ICA: MI0137.

Michigan—Cable Systems

MAPLE RAPIDS—Mutual Data Services, 319 North Clinton Ave, St. Johns, MI 48879. Phone: 989-224-6839. E-mail: mdsupport@mutualdata.com. Web Site: http://www.mutualdata.com. ICA: MI0234.
TV Market Ranking: 92 (MAPLE RAPIDS). Franchise award date: April 1, 1987. Franchise expiration date: N.A. Began: September 1, 1987.
Channel capacity: N.A. Channels available but not in use: N.A.

Basic Service
Subscribers: N.A.
Programming (received off-air): WILX-TV (NBC, WeatherNation) Onondaga; WJRT-TV (ABC, MeTV) Flint; WKAR-TV (PBS) East Lansing; WLNS-TV (CBS) Lansing; WOOD-TV (Laff, NBC) Grand Rapids; WSYM-TV (FOX, MeTV) Lansing; WWMT (CBS, CW) Kalamazoo.
Programming (via satellite): CNN; Discovery Channel; Disney Channel; ESPN; Freeform; HLN; TBS; TNT; USA Network; WGN America.
Fee: $30.00 installation; $19.95 monthly.

Pay Service 1
Pay Units: N.A.
Programming (via satellite): Showtime.
Fee: $20.00 installation; $7.00 monthly.

Internet Service
Operational: No.

Telephone Service
None
Miles of Plant: 4.0 (coaxial); None (fiber optic). Homes passed: 269.
Ownership: Mutual Data Services (MSO).

MARCELLUS—Mediacom, 109 East 5th St, Ste A, Auburn, IN 46706. Phones: 845-695-2762; 260-927-3015. Fax: 260-347-4433. Web Site: http://www.mediacomcable.com. Also serves Marcellus Twp. ICA: MI0431.
TV Market Ranking: 37,80 (MARCELLUS, Marcellus Twp.). Franchise award date: N.A. Franchise expiration date: N.A. Began: November 4, 1996.
Channel capacity: N.A. Channels available but not in use: N.A.

Basic Service
Subscribers: 39.
Programming (received off-air): WHME-TV (COZI TV, IND) South Bend; WNDU-TV (NBC) South Bend; WNIT (PBS) South Bend; WOOD-TV (Laff, NBC) Grand Rapids; WOTV (ABC, Grit, TheCoolTV) Battle Creek; WSBT-TV (CBS, FOX) South Bend; WSJV (Heroes & Icons) Elkhart; WWMT (CBS, CW) Kalamazoo; WXMI (Antenna TV, FOX, This TV) Grand Rapids.
Programming (via satellite): WGN America.
Fee: $45.00 installation; $40.00 monthly.

Expanded Basic Service 1
Subscribers: N.A.
Programming (via satellite): A&E; AMC; Animal Planet; Cartoon Network; CMT; CNN; Comedy Central; Discovery Channel; Disney Channel; ESPN; ESPN2; Food Network; FOX Sports Detroit; Freeform; HGTV; History; HLN; Lifetime; MTV; Nickelodeon; Radar Channel; Spike TV; Syfy; TBS; The Weather Channel; TLC; TNT; Travel Channel; Trinity Broadcasting Network (TBN); truTV; TV Land; USA Network; VH1.
Fee: $29.00 monthly.

Pay Service 1
Pay Units: N.A.
Programming (via satellite): Cinemax; HBO.
Fee: $7.99 monthly (Cinemax), $13.50 monthly (HBO).

Video-On-Demand: No

Internet Service
Operational: No.

Telephone Service
None
Miles of Plant: 14.0 (coaxial); None (fiber optic). Homes passed: 783.
Vice President, Financial Reporting: Kenneth J. Kohrs. Operations Director: Joe Poffenberger. Technical Operations Manager: Craig Grey.
Ownership: Mediacom LLC (MSO).

MARENISCO TWP.—Formerly served by Upper Peninsula Communications. No longer in operation. ICA: MI0249.

MARION—Formerly served by Pine River Cable. No longer in operation. ICA: MI0219.

MARQUETTE—Charter Communications, 359 US 41 East, Negaunee, MI 49866. Phones: 636-207-5100 (Corporate office); 314-543-2236; 231-947-5221 (Traverse City office); 906-475-0107. E-mail: jboullion@chartercom.com. Web Site: http://www.charter.com. Also serves Adams Twp. (Houghton County), Ahmeek, Allouez Twp., Au Train Twp., Baraga, Bark River Twp., Brampton Twp., Breitung Twp., Calumet, Chassell Twp., Chatham, Chocolay Twp., Christmas, Copper City, Dollar Bay, Eben Junction, Ely Twp., Escanaba, Ford River Twp., Forsyth Twp., Gladstone, Grand Island Twp., Gwinn, Hancock, Harris Twp., Harvey, Hermansville, Hiawatha Twp., Houghton, Iron Mountain, Ishpeming, Kingsford, Lake Linden, L'Anse, Laurium, Little Lake, Manistique, Masonville Twp. (southern portion), Meyer Twp., Munising, Negaunee, Osceola Twp. (Houghton County), Palmer, Princeton, Rock River Twp., Sagola Twp., Sands Twp., Skandia Twp., South Range, Thompson Twp., Tilden Twp., Torch Lake Twp. (Houghton County), Waucedah Twp., Wells Twp. & Wetmore, MI; Aurora, Commonwealth, Florence & Spread Eagle, WI. ICA: MI0033.
TV Market Ranking: Below 100 (Adams Twp. (Houghton County), Ahmeek, Allouez Twp., Au Train Twp., Aurora, Baraga, Brampton Twp., Breitung Twp., Calumet, Chassell Twp., Chatham, Chocolay Twp., Christmas, Commonwealth, Copper City, Dollar Bay, Eben Junction, Ely Twp., Florence, Ford River Twp., Forsyth Twp., Gladstone, Grand Island Twp., Gwinn, Hancock, Harris Twp., Harvey, Hermansville, Ishpeming, Kingsford, Lake Linden, L'Anse, Laurium, Little Lake, MARQUETTE, Masonville Twp. (southern portion), Meyer Twp., Negaunee, Osceola Twp. (Houghton County), Palmer, Princeton, Rock River Twp., Sands Twp., Skandia Twp., South Range, Spread Eagle, Tilden Twp., Torch Lake Twp. (Houghton County), Waucedah Twp., Wells Twp., Escanaba, Houghton, Iron Mountain); Outside TV Markets (Hiawatha Twp., Manistique, Munising, Thompson Twp., Wetmore). Franchise award date: October 1, 1960. Franchise expiration date: N.A. Began: October 1, 1960.
Channel capacity: N.A. Channels available but not in use: N.A.

Digital Basic Service
Subscribers: 34,952.
Programming (via satellite): AXS TV; BBC America; CMT; Cooking Channel; Discovery Digital Networks; DIY Network; ESPN Classic; ESPN HD; ESPNews; Food Network On Demand; FOX College Sports Central; FOX College Sports Pacific; Fox Sports 2; Fuse; FXM; FYI; Great American Country; HD Theater; HGTV On Demand; History International; IFC; LMN; MC; Nick 2; Nick Jr.; Outdoor Channel; Sundance TV; TeenNick; TNT HD; Universal HD; Versus On Demand.
Fee: $49.99 installation; $26.99 monthly.

Digital Expanded Basic Service
Subscribers: N.A.
Programming (via satellite): A&E; AMC; Animal Planet; Bravo; Cartoon Network; CMT; CNBC; CNN; Comedy Central; Discovery Channel; Discovery Life Channel; Disney Channel; Disney XD; E! HD; ESPN; ESPN2; Food Network; Fox News Channel; Fox Sports 1; FOX Sports Detroit; Freeform; FX; Golf Channel; GSN; Hallmark Channel; HGTV; History; HLN; Lifetime; MSNBC; MTV; National Geographic Channel; NBCSN; Nickelodeon; Oxygen; Spike TV; Syfy; TLC; TNT; Travel Channel; truTV; Turner Classic Movies; TV Land; USA Network; VH1; WE tv.
Fee: $36.49 monthly.

Digital Pay Service 1
Pay Units: N.A.
Programming (via satellite): Cinemax (multiplexed); Cinemax HD; Cinemax On Demand; Flix; HBO (multiplexed); HBO HD; HBO on Demand; LOGO; Showtime (multiplexed); Showtime HD; Showtime On Demand; Starz (multiplexed); Starz Encore (multiplexed); Starz On Demand; The Movie Channel (multiplexed).

Video-On-Demand: Yes

Pay-Per-View
iN DEMAND (delivered digitally); ESPN (delivered digitally); NHL Center Ice (delivered digitally); MLB Extra Innings (delivered digitally); Playboy TV (delivered digitally); Fresh (delivered digitally); Shorteez (delivered digitally).

Internet Service
Operational: Yes.
Subscribers: 31,443.
Broadband Service: Charter Internet.
Fee: $49.95 installation; $29.99 monthly.

Telephone Service
Digital: Operational
Subscribers: 18,952.
Fee: $29.99 monthly
Miles of Plant: 2,525.0 (coaxial); 1,059.0 (fiber optic). Homes passed: 82,888.
Vice President: Joe Boullion. General Manager: Rex Buettgenbach. Technical Operations Director: Rob Nowak. Accounting Director: David Sovanski. Government Relations Manager: Don Gladwell. Marketing Manager: Sandy Gottschalk.
Ownership: Charter Communications Inc. (MSO).

MASS CITY—Formerly served by Charter Communications. No longer in operation. ICA: MI0217.

MATTAWAN—Mediacom, 109 East 5th St, Ste A, Auburn, IN 46706. Phones: 845-695-2762; 260-927-3015. Fax: 260-347-4433. Web Site: http://www.mediacomcable.com. Also serves Almena Twp., Antwerp Twp. & Oshtemo Twp. ICA: MI0141.
TV Market Ranking: 37 (Almena Twp., Antwerp Twp., MATTAWAN, Oshtemo Twp). Franchise award date: N.A. Franchise expiration date: N.A. Began: April 1, 1974.
Channel capacity: N.A. Channels available but not in use: N.A.

Basic Service
Subscribers: 149.
Programming (received off-air): WGVU-TV (PBS) Grand Rapids; WLLA (IND, MeTV) Kalamazoo; WNDU-TV (NBC) South Bend; WOOD-TV (Laff, NBC) Grand Rapids; WOTV (ABC, Grit, TheCoolTV) Battle Creek; WWMT (CBS, CW) Kalamazoo; WXMI (Antenna TV, FOX, This TV) Grand Rapids; WZPX-TV (ION) Battle Creek.
Programming (via satellite): Trinity Broadcasting Network (TBN); WGN America.
Fee: $45.00 installation; $41.00 monthly.

Expanded Basic Service 1
Subscribers: N.A.
Programming (via satellite): A&E; AMC; Animal Planet; Cartoon Network; CMT; CNBC; CNN; Comedy Central; Discovery Channel; Disney Channel; E! HD; ESPN; ESPN Classic; ESPN2; EVINE Live; EWTN Global Catholic Network; Food Network; Fox Sports 1; FOX Sports Detroit; Freeform; Hallmark Channel; HGTV; History; HLN; Lifetime; MSNBC; MTV; MTV2; Nickelodeon; QVC; Radar Channel; Spike TV; Syfy; TBS; The Weather Channel; TLC; TNT; Travel Channel; truTV; Univision Studios; USA Network; VH1.
Fee: $29.00 monthly.

Digital Basic Service
Subscribers: N.A.
Programming (via satellite): BBC America; Bloomberg Television; Cloo; Discovery Digital Networks; ESPNews; Fuse; FXM; FYI; Golf Channel; History; History International; IFC; LMN; MC; MTV Classic; MTV Hits; National Geographic Channel; NBCSN; Nick Jr.; Nicktoons; Outdoor Channel; Science Channel; TeenNick; Turner Classic Movies; TVG Network.

Digital Pay Service 1
Pay Units: N.A.
Programming (via satellite): Cinemax (multiplexed); HBO (multiplexed); Showtime (multiplexed); Starz (multiplexed); Starz Encore (multiplexed); The Movie Channel (multiplexed).
Fee: $11.95 monthly (each).

Video-On-Demand: No

Pay-Per-View
iN DEMAND (delivered digitally); Club Jenna (delivered digitally); Playboy TV (delivered digitally); Fresh (delivered digitally); Spice: Xcess (delivered digitally).

Internet Service
Operational: No.

Telephone Service
None
Vice President, Financial Reporting: Kenneth J. Kohrs. Operations Director: Joe Poffenberger. Technical Operations Manager: Craig Grey.
Ownership: Mediacom LLC (MSO).

MAYVILLE—Charter Communications. Now served by GOODRICH, MI [MI0290]. ICA: MI0374.

Cable Systems—Michigan

McBAIN—Summit Digital, 107 West Bridge St, Portland, MI 48875. Phones: 231-825-2500; 888-600-5040. E-mail: info@summitdigital.net. Web Site: http://summitdigital.net. Also serves Riverside Twp. ICA: MI0240.
TV Market Ranking: Below 100 (MCBAIN, Riverside Twp.). Franchise award date: N.A. Franchise expiration date: N.A. Began: February 1, 1984.
Channel capacity: 36 (2-way capable). Channels available but not in use: N.A.
Basic Service
Subscribers: N.A.
Programming (received off-air): WCMV (PBS) Cadillac; WFQX-TV (FOX) Cadillac; WGTU (ABC, CW) Traverse City; WPBN-TV (NBC) Traverse City; WWTV (CBS) Cadillac.
Programming (via satellite): C-SPAN; Freeform; QVC; TBS; WGN America.
Fee: $50.00 installation; $29.95 monthly.
Expanded Basic Service 1
Subscribers: N.A.
Programming (via satellite): A&E; AMC; CMT; CNN; Discovery Channel; Disney Channel; E! HD; ESPN; ESPN2; Food Network; FOX Sports Detroit; HGTV; HLN; Lifetime; MTV; Nickelodeon; Spike TV; The Weather Channel; TLC; TNT; USA Network; VH1.
Pay Service 1
Pay Units: N.A.
Programming (via satellite): Cinemax; HBO.
Fee: $21.00 installation; $10.95 monthly (Cinemax), $11.95 monthly (HBO).
Internet Service
Operational: Yes.
Fee: $19.95-$75.00 monthly.
Miles of Plant: 6.0 (coaxial); None (fiber optic). Homes passed: 262.
Operations Manager: Patty Coleman.
Ownership: Summit Digital (MSO).

MEARS—Golden Communications, 8800 Ferry Street, Montague, MI 49437. Phone: 888-873-3353. Web Site: http://goldcommcable.com. Also serves Golden Twp. ICA: MI0395.
TV Market Ranking: Below 100 (Golden Twp., MEARS).
Channel capacity: N.A. Channels available but not in use: N.A.
Basic Service
Subscribers: N.A.
Programming (received off-air): WCMW (PBS) Manistee; WFQX-TV (FOX) Cadillac; WPBN-TV (NBC) Traverse City; WWTV (CBS) Cadillac; WZZM (ABC) Grand Rapids.
Programming (via satellite): A&E; AMC; Animal Planet; Cartoon Network; CMT; CNBC; CNN; Comedy Central; C-SPAN; Discovery Channel; E! HD; ESPN; ESPN2; Fox News Channel; Fox Sports 1; FOX Sports Detroit; Freeform; FX; Golf Channel; Hallmark Channel; HGTV; History; HLN; Lifetime; National Geographic Channel; Nickelodeon; Outdoor Channel; OWN: Oprah Winfrey Network; QVC; Spike TV; Syfy; TBS; The Weather Channel; TLC; TNT; Trinity Broadcasting Network (TBN); truTV; Turner Classic Movies; TV Land; USA Network; VH1; WGN America.
Fee: $55.00 installation.
Pay Service 1
Pay Units: N.A.
Programming (via satellite): HBO; Showtime.
Fee: $11.95 monthly (each).
Video-On-Demand: No
Internet Service
Operational: Yes.
Broadband Service: In-house.
Fee: $24.95 monthly.
Telephone Service
None
Miles of Plant: 30.0 (coaxial); None (fiber optic).
Ownership: Golden Communications (MSO).

MECOSTA—MIcom, PO Box 100, Montague, MI 49437. Phone: 888-873-3353. Fax: 231-894-4960. E-mail: customerservice@micomcable.com. Web Site: http://www.micomcable.com. Also serves Martiny Twp. ICA: MI0327.
TV Market Ranking: Outside TV Markets (Martiny Twp., MECOSTA). Franchise award date: N.A. Franchise expiration date: N.A. Began: October 1, 1989.
Channel capacity: N.A. Channels available but not in use: N.A.
Basic Service
Subscribers: 112.
Programming (received off-air): WCMU-TV (PBS) Mount Pleasant; WFQX-TV (FOX) Cadillac; WPBN-TV (NBC) Traverse City; WWTV (CBS) Cadillac; WZZM (ABC) Grand Rapids.
Programming (via satellite): CMT; CNN; Disney Channel; ESPN; Freeform; HLN; TBS; TNT; USA Network; WGN America.
Fee: $49.95 monthly.
Pay Service 1
Pay Units: N.A.
Programming (via satellite): Showtime.
Fee: $7.00 monthly.
Internet Service
Operational: No.
Telephone Service
None
Miles of Plant: 27.0 (coaxial); None (fiber optic). Homes passed: 1,174.
Ownership: MIcom (MSO).

MELLEN TWP.—Packerland Broadband, 105 Kent St., PO Box 885, Iron Mountain, MI 49801. Phones: 906-774-1291; 906-774-6621; 800-236-8434. Fax: 906-776-2811. E-mail: service@plbb.net; support@packerlandbroadband.com. Web Site: http://www.packerlandbroadband.com. ICA: MI0330.
TV Market Ranking: Below 100 (MELLEN TWP.).
Channel capacity: N.A. Channels available but not in use: N.A.
Basic Service
Subscribers: N.A.
Programming (received off-air): WBKP (ABC, CW) Calumet; WJMN-TV (CBS) Escanaba; WLUC-TV (FOX, NBC) Marquette; WNMU (PBS) Marquette; WZMQ (Antenna TV, MeTV, MNT, This TV) Marquette.
Programming (via satellite): A&E; AMC; CNBC; CNN; C-SPAN; Discovery Channel; Disney Channel; ESPN; ESPN2; Freeform; HGTV; History; ION Television; Lifetime; Outdoor Channel; Spike TV; TBS; The Weather Channel; TLC; TNT; Trinity Broadcasting Network (TBN); TV Land; USA Network; WGN America.
Fee: $26.00 installation.
Pay Service 1
Pay Units: N.A.
Programming (via satellite): Showtime.
Fee: $7.50 monthly.
Internet Service
Operational: No.
Telephone Service
None
Miles of Plant: 56.0 (coaxial); 8.0 (fiber optic). Homes passed: 1,109.
General Manager: Dan Plante. Technical Supervisor: Chad Kay.
Ownership: Packerland Broadband (MSO).

MENDON (village)—Mediacom, 109 East 5th St, Ste A, Auburn, IN 46706. Phones: 845-695-2762; 260-927-3015. Fax: 260-347-4433. Web Site: http://www.mediacomcable.com. Also serves Mendon Twp. ICA: MI0213.
TV Market Ranking: 37,80 (MENDON (VILLAGE), Mendon Twp.). Franchise award date: N.A. Franchise expiration date: N.A. Began: December 1, 1983.
Channel capacity: N.A. Channels available but not in use: N.A.
Basic Service
Subscribers: 30.
Programming (received off-air): WHME-TV (COZI TV, IND) South Bend; WLLA (IND, MeTV) Kalamazoo; WNDU-TV (NBC) South Bend; WOOD-TV (Laff, NBC) Grand Rapids; WOTV (ABC, Grit, TheCoolTV) Battle Creek; WSBT-TV (CBS, FOX) South Bend; WSJV (Heroes & Icons) Elkhart; WWMT (CBS, CW) Kalamazoo; WXMI (Antenna TV, FOX, This TV) Grand Rapids.
Programming (via satellite): WGN America.
Fee: $45.00 installation; $40.00 monthly.
Expanded Basic Service 1
Subscribers: N.A.
Programming (via satellite): A&E; AMC; Animal Planet; Cartoon Network; CMT; CNBC; CNN; C-SPAN; C-SPAN 2; Discovery Channel; Disney Channel; E! HD; ESPN; ESPN2; Food Network; Fox News Channel; Fox Sports 1; FOX Sports Networks; Freeform; Hallmark Channel; HGTV; History; HLN; Lifetime; MSNBC; MTV; Nickelodeon; Spike TV; Syfy; TBS; The Weather Channel; TLC; TNT; Travel Channel; Trinity Broadcasting Network (TBN); truTV; TV Land; Univision Studios; USA Network; VH1.
Fee: $29.00 monthly.
Pay Service 1
Pay Units: N.A.
Programming (via satellite): Cinemax; HBO.
Fee: $7.99 monthly (Cinemax), $13.50 monthly (HBO).
Video-On-Demand: No
Internet Service
Operational: No.
Telephone Service
None
Miles of Plant: 16.0 (coaxial); None (fiber optic). Homes passed: 724.
Vice President, Financial Reporting: Kenneth J. Kohrs. Operations Director: Joe Poffenberger. Technical Operations Manager: Craig Grey.
Ownership: Mediacom LLC (MSO).

MERRITT TWP.—Formerly served by Cablevision Systems Corp. No longer in operation. ICA: MI0384.

MESICK—AcenTek (formerly Ace Communications). This system has converted to IPTV, 207 East Cedar St, PO Box 360, Houston, MN 55943-0360. Phones: 888-404-4940; 507-896-6207; 507-896-4695. Fax: 507-896-2149; 507-896-3207. E-mail: info@acentek.net. Web Site: http://www.acentek.net. Also serves Allendale, Antioch Twp., Boardman Twp., Buckley, Cleon Twp., Colfax Twp., Coopersville, Copemish, Garfield, Georgetown, Grant Twp., Hanover Twp., Holland Charter Twp., Hoxeyville, Marilla, Mayfield, Olive, Orange Twp., Overisel, Park, Polkton, Robinson, Salem, Slagle Twp., South Boardman, South Branch Twp., Springdale Twp., Springfield Twp., Thompsonville, Weldon, Wexford Twp. & Zeeland Charter Twp. ICA: MI5074.
TV Market Ranking: 37 (Allendale, Coopersville, Georgetown, Holland Charter Twp., Olive, Overisel, Park, Polkton, Robinson, Zeeland Charter Twp.); Below 100 (Thompsonville); Outside TV Markets (Georgetown, Overisel, Park).
Channel capacity: N.A. Channels available but not in use: N.A.
Basic
Subscribers: 3,169. Commercial subscribers: 51.
Fee: $26.50 monthly. Includes 22 channels.
Basic Plus
Subscribers: N.A.
Fee: $55.95 monthly. Includes 98 channels plus 50 music channels.
Expanded Basic
Subscribers: N.A.
Fee: $69.95 monthly. Includes 186 channels plus 50 music channels.
Cinemax
Subscribers: N.A.
Fee: $12.95 monthly. Includes 8 channels.
HBO
Subscribers: N.A.
Fee: $16.95 monthly. Includes 10 channels.
Starz/Encore
Subscribers: N.A.
Fee: $10.95 monthly. Includes 15 channels.
Video-On-Demand: Yes
Internet Service
Operational: Yes.
Fee: $24.95-$59.95 monthly.
Telephone Service
Digital: Operational
Fee: $19.73 monthly
Chief Executive Officer: Todd Roesler.
Ownership: AcenTek.

MESICK—Formerly served by Pine River Cable. No longer in operation. ICA: MI0246.

MICHIGAMME—Formerly served by Upper Peninsula Communications. No longer in operation. ICA: MI0331.

MIDDLEVILLE/CALEDONIA—Charter Communications. Now served by ALLENDALE TWP., MI [MI0094]. ICA: MI0097.

MIDLAND—Charter Communications, 12405 Powerscourt Dr, St. Louis, MO 63131. Phones: 636-207-5100 (Corporate office); 810-653-0966; 810-652-1400. Web Site: http://www.charter.com. Also serves Alabaster Twp., Albee Twp., Alcona Twp., Alma, Arcada Twp., Arenac Twp., Au Gres, Au Sable Twp. (Iosco County), Auburn, Baldwin Twp. (Iosco County), Bangor Twp. (Bay County),

Michigan—Cable Systems

Bay City, Beaver Twp. (Bay County), Bennington Twp., Bethany Twp., Bingham Twp., Birch Run, Blumfield Twp., Brady Twp. (Saginaw County), Breckenridge, Bridgeport (portions), Bridgeport Twp., Buena Vista Twp., Burleigh Twp., Caledonia Twp. (Shiawassee County), Carrollton, Chesaning, Chippewa Twp. (Isabella County), Clare, Coe Twp., Coleman, Corunna, Deep River Twp., Denmark Twp., Denver Twp. (Isabella County), East Tawas, Edenville Twp., Elsie, Emerson Twp., Essexville, Farwell, Fowler, Frankenlust Twp., Frankenmuth, Freeland, Frost Twp., Garfield Twp., Garfield Twp. (Clare County), Geneva Twp. (Midland County), Gilmore Twp. (Isabella County), Grant Twp. (Iosco County), Grant Twp. (portions), Greenbush Twp. (Alcona County), Greendale Twp., Hampton Twp., Harrison, Harrisville, Hatton Twp., Hawes Twp. (portions), Hayes Twp. (Clare County), Ingersoll Twp., Isabella Twp., Ithaca, James Twp., Jonesfield Twp., Kawkawlin Twp. (southern portion), Kochville Twp. (portions), Larkin Twp., Lee Twp., Lincoln, Lincoln Twp., Maple Grove Twp., Mason Twp. (Arenac County), Merrill, Middlebury Twp., Midland Twp., Monitor Twp., Montrose, Montrose Twp., Mount Haley Twp., Mount Pleasant, Newark Twp., Oakley (village), Omer, Oscoda, Oscoda Twp., Ovid Village, Owosso, Owosso Twp., Pinconning, Pinconning Twp., Pine River Twp., Portsmouth Twp., Reese, Richland Twp. (Saginaw County), Rosebush, Rush Twp., Saginaw, Saginaw Twp., Shepherd, Sims Twp., Spaulding Twp., St. Charles (village), St. Charles Twp., St. Johns, St. Louis, Standish, Standish Twp., Sumner Twp. (portions), Surrey Twp., Swan Creek Twp., Tawas City, Tawas Twp., Taymouth Twp., Thomas Twp., Tittabawassee Twp., Turner Twp., Turner Village, Twining, Union Twp. (Isabella County), Vernon Twp., Warren Twp., Wheeler Twp., Whitney Twp., Whittemore, Wilber Twp., Williams Twp. (eastern portion), Williams Twp. (western portion), Wise Twp. & Zilwaukee. ICA: MI0030.

TV Market Ranking: 61 (Albee Twp., Arenac Twp., Au Gres, Auburn, Bangor Twp. (Bay County), Bay City, Beaver Twp. (Bay County), Birch Run, Blumfield Twp., Brady Twp. (Saginaw County), Breckenridge, Bridgeport (portions), Bridgeport Twp., Buena Vista Twp., Carrollton, Chesaning, Coe Twp., Deep River Twp., Denmark Twp., Edenville Twp., Essexville, Frankenlust Twp., Frankenmuth, Freeland, Garfield Twp., Geneva Twp. (Midland County), Greendale Twp., Hampton Twp., Ingersoll Twp., Ithaca, James Twp., Jonesfield Twp., Kawkawlin Twp. (southern portion), Kochville Twp. (portions), Larkin Twp., Lee Twp., Lincoln Twp., Maple Grove Twp., Mason Twp. (Arenac County), Merrill, MIDLAND, Midland Twp., Monitor Twp., Montrose, Montrose Twp., Mount Haley Twp., Oakley (village), Omer, Pinconning, Pinconning Twp., Portsmouth Twp., Reese, Richland Twp. (Saginaw County), Saginaw, Saginaw Twp., Sims Twp., Spaulding Twp., St. Charles (village), St. Charles Twp., St. Louis, Standish, Standish Twp., Swan Creek Twp., Taymouth Twp., Thomas Twp., Tittabawassee Twp., Wheeler Twp., Williams Twp. (eastern portion), Williams Twp. (western portion), Zilwaukee); 61,92 (Bennington Twp., Caledonia Twp. (Shiawassee County), Corunna, Elsie, Middlebury Twp., Ovid Village, Owosso, Owosso Twp., Rush Twp.); 92 (Bingham Twp., Fowler, St. Johns); Below 100 (Alcona Twp., Arcada Twp., Denver Twp. (Isabella County), Frost Twp., Garfield Twp. (Clare County), Greenbush Twp. (Alcona County), Harrison, Harrisville, Hatton Twp., Hayes Twp. (Clare County), Lincoln); Outside TV Markets (Alabaster Twp., Au Sable Twp. (Iosco County), Baldwin Twp. (Iosco County), Bethany Twp., Burleigh Twp., Clare, Denver Twp. (Isabella County), East Tawas, Emerson Twp., Farwell, Gilmore Twp. (Isabella County), Grant Twp. (Iosco County), Grant Twp. (portions), Hawes Twp. (portions), Isabella Twp., Newark Twp., Oscoda Twp., Pine River Twp., Rosebush, Shepherd, Sumner Twp. (portions), Surrey Twp., Tawas City, Tawas Twp., Turner Twp., Turner Village, Twining, Union Twp. (Isabella County), Vernon Twp., Warren Twp., Whitney Twp., Wilber Twp., Wise Twp., Alma, Coleman, Mount Pleasant, Oscoda, Whittemore).

Franchise award date: June 1, 1972. Franchise expiration date: N.A. Began: June 1, 1972.

Channel capacity: 61 (operating 2-way). Channels available but not in use: N.A.

Digital Basic Service
Subscribers: 109,746.
Programming (via satellite): AXS TV; BBC America; Discovery Digital Networks; DIY Network; ESPN Classic; ESPN HD; ESPN2 HD; ESPNews; ESPNU; Fox Business Network; FOX College Sports Central; FOX College Sports Pacific; Fox Sports 2; Fuse; FXM; FYI; Great American Country; HD Theater; History International; IFC; LMN; MC; Nick 2; Nick Jr.; Nicktoons; Outdoor Channel; Reelz; Sundance TV; TeenNick; TNT HD; TV Guide Interactive Inc.; Universal HD; WE tv.
Fee: $14.99 monthly.

Digital Expanded Basic Service
Subscribers: N.A.
Programming (via satellite): A&E; AMC; Animal Planet; Bravo; Cartoon Network; CMT; CNBC; CNN; Comedy Central; C-SPAN; Discovery Channel; Disney Channel; Disney XD; E! HD; ESPN; ESPN2; Food Network; Fox News Channel; Fox Sports 1; FOX Sports Detroit; Freeform; FX; Golf Channel; GSN; Hallmark Channel; HGTV; History; HLN; Lifetime; MSNBC; MTV; MTV2; National Geographic Channel; NBCSN; Nickelodeon; Oxygen; Pop; Spike TV; Syfy; The Weather Channel; TLC; TNT; Travel Channel; truTV; Turner Classic Movies; TV Land; USA Network; VH1.
Fee: $36.49 monthly.

Digital Pay Service 1
Pay Units: N.A.
Programming (via satellite): Cinemax (multiplexed); Cinemax HD; Flix; HBO (multiplexed); HBO HD; LOGO; Showtime (multiplexed); Showtime HD; Starz (multiplexed); Starz Encore (multiplexed); Starz HD; The Movie Channel (multiplexed).

Video-On-Demand: Yes

Pay-Per-View
iN DEMAND (delivered digitally); ESPN (delivered digitally); NHL Center Ice (delivered digitally); MLB Extra Innings (delivered digitally); Playboy TV (delivered digitally); Shorteez (delivered digitally); Fresh (delivered digitally).

Internet Service
Operational: Yes.
Subscribers: 95,648.
Broadband Service: Charter Internet.
Fee: $99.00 installation; $29.99 monthly.

Telephone Service
Digital: Operational
Subscribers: 52,731.
Fee: $29.99 monthly
Miles of Plant: 7,541.0 (coaxial); 2,312.0 (fiber optic). Homes passed: 274,043.

Vice President & General Manager: Dave Slowick. Technical Operations Director: Lloyd Collins. Marketing Director: Lisa Gayari. Accounting Director: David Sovanski.

Ownership: Charter Communications Inc. (MSO).

MIKADO TWP.—Formerly served by Pine River Cable. No longer in operation. ICA: MI0440.

MINDEN CITY—Formerly served by Cablevision Systems Corp. No longer in operation. ICA: MI0332.

MIO—MIcom, PO Box 100, Montague, MI 49437. Phone: 888-873-3353. Fax: 231-894-4960. E-mail: customerservice@micomcable.com. Web Site: http://www.micomcable.com. Also serves Big Creek Twp., Comins Twp., Elmer Twp., Fairview & Mentor Twp. ICA: MI0430.

TV Market Ranking: Outside TV Markets (Big Creek Twp., Comins Twp., Elmer Twp., Fairview, Mentor Twp., MIO).

Channel capacity: N.A. Channels available but not in use: N.A.

Basic Service
Subscribers: 303.
Programming (received off-air): WBKB-TV (ABC, CBS, FOX) Alpena; WCML (PBS) Alpena; WFUP (FOX) Vanderbilt; WGTU (ABC, CW) Traverse City; WTOM-TV (NBC) Cheboygan; WWTV (CBS) Cadillac.
Programming (via satellite): BTN; Disney Channel; Fox News Channel; QVC; TBS; Trinity Broadcasting Network (TBN); WGN America; WNBC (COZI TV, NBC) New York.
Fee: $48.95 monthly.

Expanded Basic Service 1
Subscribers: N.A.
Programming (via satellite): A&E; AMC; Animal Planet; Cartoon Network; CMT; CNBC; CNN; Comedy Central; C-SPAN; C-SPAN 2; Discovery Channel; Discovery Life Channel; Disney XD; DIY Network; E! HD; ESPN; ESPN2; EWTN Global Catholic Network; Food Network; Fox Sports 1; FOX Sports Detroit; Freeform; FX; Hallmark Channel; Hallmark Movies & Mysteries; HGTV; History; Lifetime; MTV; National Geographic Channel; NBCSN; Nickelodeon; Oxygen; Spike TV; Syfy; The Sportsman Channel; The Weather Channel; TNT; Travel Channel; truTV; Turner Classic Movies; TV Land; USA Network; VH1.
Fee: $23.40 monthly.

Digital Basic Service
Subscribers: N.A.
Programming (via satellite): American Heroes Channel; Bravo; Chiller; Cloo; CMT; Cooking Channel; Destination America; DMX Music; ESPN Classic; ESPN2; Fox Sports 1; Fuse; FYI; HGTV; History; History International; HorseTV Channel; Investigation Discovery; LMN; MTV Hits; MTV2; National Geographic Channel; RFD-TV; TeenNick; VH1; VH1 Soul.

Digital Pay Service 1
Pay Units: N.A.
Programming (via satellite): Cinemax (multiplexed); Flix; HBO (multiplexed); Showtime (multiplexed); Starz (multiplexed); Starz Encore (multiplexed); The Movie Channel (multiplexed).
Fee: $12.95 monthly (Starz/Encore), $13.95 monthly (Cinemax), $15.95 monthly (HBO or Showtime/TMC/Flix).

Internet Service
Operational: Yes.

Telephone Service
None
Ownership: MIcom (MSO).

MISSAUKEE COUNTY (unincorporated areas)—Formerly served by Pine River Cable. No longer in operation. ICA: MI0441.

MONROE—Comcast Cable. Now served by DETROIT, MI [MI0001]. ICA: MI0048.

MONTROSE—Charter Communications. Now served by MIDLAND, MI [MI0030]. ICA: MI0130.

MOUNT PLEASANT—Charter Communications. Now served by MIDLAND, MI [MI0030]. ICA: MI0069.

MULLETT TWP.—Formerly served by Northwoods Cable Inc. No longer in operation. ICA: MI0334.

MUSKEGON—Comcast Cable. Now served by DETROIT, MI [MI0001]. ICA: MI0014.

NASHVILLE—Martell Cable, 6625 Maple Ridge Rd, Alger, MI 48610. Phones: 888-642-0056; 248-960-5554. Web Site: http://martellcable.com. Also serves Vermontville. ICA: MI0211.

TV Market Ranking: 37,92 (NASHVILLE, Vermontville). Franchise award date: N.A. Franchise expiration date: N.A. Began: April 1, 1983.

Channel capacity: N.A. Channels available but not in use: N.A.

Basic Service
Subscribers: N.A.
Programming (received off-air): WILX-TV (NBC, WeatherNation) Onondaga; WKAR-TV (PBS) East Lansing; WLLA (IND, MeTV) Kalamazoo; WLNS-TV (CBS) Lansing; WOOD-TV (Laff, NBC) Grand Rapids; WOTV (ABC, Grit, TheCoolTV) Battle Creek; WSYM-TV (FOX, MeTV) Lansing; WWMT (CBS, CW) Kalamazoo; WXMI (Antenna TV, FOX, This TV) Grand Rapids; WZPX-TV (ION) Battle Creek.
Programming (via satellite): QVC; TBS; WGN America.
Fee: $41.99 installation.

Expanded Basic Service 1
Subscribers: N.A.
Programming (received off-air): WTLJ (IND) Muskegon.
Programming (via satellite): AMC; CMT; CNBC; CNN; Comedy Central; C-SPAN; Discovery Channel; Disney Channel; Disney XD; ESPN; ESPN2; Food Network; FOX Sports Detroit; Freeform; HLN; Lifetime; MTV; Nickelodeon; Spike TV; The Weather Channel; TNT; USA Network.
Fee: $21.45 monthly.

Pay Service 1
Pay Units: N.A.
Programming (via satellite): Cinemax; HBO; Starz.
Fee: $10.00 installation; $9.95 monthly (Starz), $11.45 monthly (Cinemax), $12.45 monthly (HBO).

Internet Service
Operational: No.
Miles of Plant: 11.0 (coaxial); None (fiber optic). Homes passed: 684.
Ownership: Martell Cable Service Inc. (MSO).

NEGAUNEE—City of Negaunee Cable TV, 225 North Pioneer Ave, PO Box 7, Negaunee, MI 49866. Phone: 906-464-6064. Fax: 906-475-9994. E-mail: sales@

Cable Systems—Michigan

negauneecable.com. Web Site: http://www.negauneecable.com. ICA: MI0145. **Note:** This system is an overbuild.
TV Market Ranking: Below 100 (NEGAUNEE). Franchise award date: N.A. Franchise expiration date: N.A. Began: March 1, 1985.
Channel capacity: N.A. Channels available but not in use: N.A.
Basic Service
Subscribers: N.A.
Programming (received off-air): WBKP (ABC, CW) Calumet; WFQX-TV (FOX) Cadillac; WJMN-TV (CBS) Escanaba; WLUC-TV (FOX, NBC) Marquette; WNMU (PBS) Marquette.
Programming (via microwave): WLUK-TV (Antenna TV, FOX) Green Bay.
Programming (via satellite): A&E; AMC; CNBC; CNN; C-SPAN; Discovery Channel; Disney Channel; ESPN; EWTN Global Catholic Network; FOX Sports Detroit; Freeform; Hallmark Channel; History; HLN; Lifetime; MTV; Nickelodeon; QVC; Spike TV; TBS; The Weather Channel; TLC; TNT; USA Network; VH1; WGN America.
Fee: $12.00 installation.
Pay Service 1
Pay Units: N.A.
Programming (via satellite): Cinemax; HBO.
Fee: $8.50 monthly.
Video-On-Demand: No
Internet Service
Operational: Yes.
Fee: $34.99 monthly.
Telephone Service
None
Miles of Plant: 27.0 (coaxial); None (fiber optic). Homes passed: 1,600.
General Manager: Gerald Peterson. Chief Technician: Dennis Howe. Marketing Director: Linda Nicholls.
Ownership: City of Negaunee Cable TV.

NEW LOTHROP—TVC Cable, 3095 Sheridan Rd, PO Box 369, Lennon, MI 48449. Phones: 810-621-3301; 810-621-3363. Fax: 810-621-9600. E-mail: customerserv@lentel.com. Web Site: http://www.lentel.com. Also serves Clayton Twp. (Genesee County), Durand, Gaines Twp. (Genesee County), Hazelton Twp., Lennon, Venice Twp. & Vernon Twp. ICA: MI0336. **Note:** This system is an overbuild.
TV Market Ranking: 61 (Clayton Twp. (Genesee County), Durand, Gaines Twp. (Genesee County), Hazelton Twp., LENNON, NEW LOTHROP, Venice Twp., Vernon Twp.). Franchise award date: N.A. Franchise expiration date: N.A. Began: June 1, 1989.
Channel capacity: 80 (operating 2-way). Channels available but not in use: N.A.
Basic Service
Subscribers: 1,979.
Programming (received off-air): WAQP (IND) Saginaw; WCMZ-TV (PBS) Flint; WEYI-TV (Bounce TV, CW, NBC) Saginaw; WILX-TV (NBC, WeatherNation) Onondaga; WJRT-TV (ABC, MeTV) Flint; WKAR-TV (PBS) East Lansing; WLNS-TV (CBS) Lansing; WNEM-TV (CBS, COZI TV, MNT) Bay City; WSMH (Antenna TV, FOX, The Country Network) Flint; WXYZ-TV (ABC, Bounce TV) Detroit.
Programming (via satellite): CW PLUS; ION Television; MyNetworkTV; Pop; QVC; The Weather Channel; WGN America.
Fee: $35.00 installation; $54.00 monthly.
Expanded Basic Service 1
Subscribers: N.A.
Programming (via satellite): A&E; AMC; Animal Planet; Bravo; BTN; Cartoon Network; CMT; CNBC; CNN; Comedy Central; C-SPAN; Discovery Channel; Disney Channel; Disney XD; DIY Network; E! HD; ESPN; ESPN Classic; ESPN2; Food Network; Fox News Channel; Fox Sports 1; FOX Sports Networks; Freeform; FX; Golf Channel; Hallmark Channel; HGTV; History; HLN; Lifetime; MTV; National Geographic Channel; NBCSN; NFL Network; Nickelodeon; Oxygen; RFD-TV; Spike TV; Syfy; TBS; TLC; TNT; Travel Channel; truTV; Turner Classic Movies; TV Land; USA Network; VH1; WE tv.
Digital Basic Service
Subscribers: N.A.
Programming (via satellite): BBC America; Bloomberg Television; Cloo; Daystar TV Network; Destination America; Discovery Kids Channel; Discovery Life Channel; DMX Music; ESPNews; FOX College Sports Central; FOX College Sports Pacific; FXM; FYI; Great American Country; GSN; History International; IFC; Investigation Discovery; LMN; MTV Classic; MTV Hits; MTV2; Nick Jr.; Nicktoons; Outdoor Channel; OWN; Oprah Winfrey Network; Science Channel; TeenNick; TVG Network; VH1 Country; VH1 Soul.
Fee: $25.00 installation.
Pay Service 1
Pay Units: N.A.
Programming (via satellite): Cinemax (multiplexed); HBO (multiplexed); Starz Encore.
Fee: $12.00 monthly.
Digital Pay Service 1
Pay Units: N.A.
Programming (via satellite): Cinemax (multiplexed); HBO (multiplexed); Showtime (multiplexed); Starz (multiplexed); Starz Encore (multiplexed); The Movie Channel (multiplexed).
Video-On-Demand: No
Pay-Per-View
Fresh (delivered digitally); Spice: Xcess (delivered digitally); Playboy TV (delivered digitally); Club Jenna (delivered digitally); Hot Choice (delivered digitally); iN DEMAND (delivered digitally).
Internet Service
Operational: Yes.
Broadband Service: In-house.
Fee: $31.99 monthly.
Telephone Service
None
Homes passed: 5,000.
President: Thomas Bowden. General Manager & Program Director: Randy Fletcher. Chief Technical Officer: Guy Wilson. Marketing Director & Ad Sales Manager: Sharon Patsey.
Ownership: TVC Inc.

NEWBERRY—Charter Communications, 2255 M-119, PO Box 849, Petoskey, MI 49770. Phones: 636-207-5100 (Corporate office); 906-635-1527; 231-947-5221 (Traverse City office). 314-543-2236. E-mail: jboullion@chartercom.com. Web Site: http://www.charter.com. Also serves McMillan Twp. (Luce County) & Pentland Twp. ICA: MI0166.
TV Market Ranking: Outside TV Markets (McMillan Twp. (Luce County), NEWBERRY, Pentland Twp.). Franchise award date: N.A. Franchise expiration date: N.A. Began: March 1, 1966.
Channel capacity: 42 (not 2-way capable). Channels available but not in use: N.A.
Digital Basic Service
Subscribers: 415.
Programming (received off-air): WFQX-TV (FOX) Cadillac; WGTQ (ABC) Sault Ste. Marie; WJMN-TV (CBS) Escanaba; WLUC-TV (FOX, NBC) Marquette; WNMU (PBS) Marquette; WTOM-TV (NBC) Cheboygan; WWUP-TV (CBS, FOX) Sault Ste. Marie.
Programming (via satellite): A&E; C-SPAN; C-SPAN 2; Discovery Channel; EWTN Global Catholic Network; FX; QVC; TBS; WGN America.
Fee: $49.99 installation; $23.99 monthly; $1.60 converter.
Digital Expanded Basic Service
Subscribers: N.A.
Programming (via satellite): AMC; Animal Planet; Cartoon Network; CNN; Discovery Life Channel; Disney Channel; Disney XD; ESPN; ESPN2; Fox News Channel; FOX Sports Detroit; Freeform; Hallmark Channel; HGTV; History; HLN; Lifetime; MTV; Nickelodeon; Spike TV; The Weather Channel; TLC; TNT; truTV; TV Land; USA Network; VH1.
Fee: $36.49 monthly.
Digital Pay Service 1
Pay Units: N.A.
Programming (via satellite): Cinemax; HBO; Starz; Starz Encore.
Fee: $1.75 monthly (Encore), $6.75 monthly (Starz), $12.85 monthly (Cinemax), $13.45 monthly (HBO).
Video-On-Demand: No
Internet Service
Operational: No.
Telephone Service
None
Miles of Plant: 32.0 (coaxial); None (fiber optic). Homes passed: 1,479.
Vice President: Joe Boullion. General Manager: John Badenski. Marketing Manager: Sandy Gottschalk. Chief Technician: John Randazzo. Accounting Director: David Sovanski.
Ownership: Charter Communications Inc. (MSO).

NILES—Comcast Cable. Now served by CHAMPAIGN, IL [IL0019]. ICA: MI0042.

NORTH BRANCH TWP.—Charter Communications. Now served by GOODRICH, MI [MI0290]. ICA: MI0337.

NORWAY—City of Norway CATV, 915 Main St, PO Box 99, Norway, MI 49870. Phone: 906-563-9961. Fax: 906-563-7502. E-mail: catv@norwaymi.com. Web Site: http://www.norwaymi.com. Also serves Norway Twp. ICA: MI0161.
TV Market Ranking: Below 100 (NORWAY, Norway Twp.). Franchise award date: N.A. Franchise expiration date: N.A. Began: January 1, 1954.
Channel capacity: N.A. Channels available but not in use: N.A.
Basic Service
Subscribers: N.A.
Programming (received off-air): WBUP (ABC) Ishpeming; WFQX-TV (FOX) Cadillac; WJMN-TV (CBS) Escanaba; WLUC-TV (FOX, NBC) Marquette; WLUK-TV (Antenna TV, FOX) Green Bay; WNMU (PBS) Marquette; allband FM.
Programming (via satellite): Cartoon Network; CNBC; C-SPAN; EWTN Global Catholic Network; Freeform; HGTV; HLN; Pop; Syfy; TBS; The Weather Channel; TLC; Travel Channel; TV Land; WGN America.
Fee: $35.00 installation.
Expanded Basic Service 1
Subscribers: N.A.
Programming (via satellite): A&E; Animal Planet; CMT; CNN; Comedy Central; Discovery Channel; Disney Channel; ESPN; ESPN2; Food Network; Fox News Channel; Fox Sports 1; FX; GSN; Hallmark Channel; History; Lifetime; Nickelodeon; Outdoor Channel; Spike TV; TNT; truTV; Turner Classic Movies; USA Network; VH1.
Fee: $14.00 monthly.
Pay Service 1
Pay Units: N.A.
Programming (via satellite): HBO.
Fee: $10.50 monthly.
Video-On-Demand: No
Internet Service
Operational: Yes.
Broadband Service: In-house.
Fee: $50.00 installation; $32.00 monthly.
Telephone Service
Digital: Operational
Miles of Plant: 53.0 (coaxial); None (fiber optic).
General Manager: Ray Anderson. Chief Technician: James Bryner.
Ownership: City of Norway CATV.

OLIVE TWP. (Ottawa County)—Charter Communications. Now served by ALLENDALE TWP., MI [MI0094]. ICA: MI0139.

OMER—Charter Communications. Now served by MIDLAND, MI [MI0030]. ICA: MI0209.

ONAWAY—Formerly served by Northwoods Cable Inc. No longer in operation. ICA: MI0201.

ONTONAGON—Charter Communications. Now served by IRONWOOD, MI [MI0064]. ICA: MI0181.

OSCODA—Charter Communications. Now served by MIDLAND, MI [MI0030]. ICA: MI0338.

OSHTEMO—Audrey Homes LLC, PO Box 3015, Kalamazoo, MI 49003. Phone: 269-321-7912. ICA: MI0447.
TV Market Ranking: 37 (OSHTEMO).
Channel capacity: N.A. Channels available but not in use: N.A.
Basic Service
Subscribers: 272.
Fee: $12.00 installation; $45.00 monthly.
Accounting Supervisor: Becki Patino.
Ownership: Audrey Homes LLC.

OSHTEMO TWP.—Comcast Cable. Now served by DETROIT, MI [MI0001]. ICA: MI0340.

Get the industry standard FREE —
For a no-obligation trial call 800-771-9202 or visit www.warren-news.com

2017 Edition D-385

Michigan—Cable Systems

OWOSSO—Charter Communications. Now served by MIDLAND, MI [MI0030]. ICA: MI0057.

OXFORD—Charter Communications. Now served by GOODRICH, MI [MI0290]. ICA: MI0059.

PELLSTON—Charter Communications. Now served by TRAVERSE CITY, MI [MI0026]. ICA: MI0236.

PENTWATER—Charter Communications. Now served by ALLENDALE TWP., MI [MI0094]. ICA: MI0158.

PERRINTON—Formerly served by Pine River Cable. No longer in operation. ICA: MI0229.

PETERSBURG—D & P Cable, 4200 Teal Rd, Petersburg, MI 49270. Phones: 734-279-1339; 800-311-7340. Fax: 734-279-2640. Web Site: http://d-pcommunications.com. Also serves Adrian, Blissfield, Britton, Deerfield, Dundee, Hudson, Ida Twp., Morenci, Palmyra Twp., Ridgeway Twp., Riga Twp., Seneca Twp., Summerfield Twp. & Tecumseh. ICA: MI0437. **Note**: This system is an overbuild.
 TV Market Ranking: 52 (Adrian, Blissfield, Britton, Deerfield, Dundee, Hudson, Ida Twp., Morenci, Palmyra Twp., PETERSBURG, Riga Twp., Seneca Twp., Summerfield Twp., Tecumseh).
 Channel capacity: 77 (operating 2-way). Channels available but not in use: N.A.
 Basic Service
  Subscribers: 5,091.
  Programming (received off-air): various Canadian stations; WDIV-TV (NBC, This TV) Detroit; WGTE-TV (PBS) Toledo; WJBK (Buzzr, FOX, Heroes & Icons, Movies!) Detroit; WKBD-TV (CW) Detroit; WLMB (IND) Toledo; WMYD (Antenna TV, Escape, MNT) Detroit; WNWO-TV (NBC, Retro TV) Toledo; WPXD-TV (ION) Ann Arbor; WTOL (CBS, MeTV) Toledo; WTVG (ABC, CW) Toledo; WTVS (PBS) Detroit; WUPW (FOX, TheCoolTV) Toledo; WWJ-TV (CBS, Decades) Detroit; WXYZ-TV (ABC, Bounce TV) Detroit.
  Programming (via satellite): C-SPAN; Pop; QVC; WGN America.
  Fee: $50.00 installation; $21.95 monthly.
 Expanded Basic Service 1
  Subscribers: 4,750.
  Programming (via satellite): A&E; AMC; Animal Planet; Cartoon Network; CMT; CNBC; CNN; Comedy Central; Discovery Channel; Disney Channel; Disney XD; E! HD; ESPN; ESPN Classic; ESPN2; ESPNews; EVINE Live; Food Network; Fox News Channel; FOX Sports Detroit; Freeform; FX; Golf Channel; Great American Country; Hallmark Channel; HGTV; History; HLN; INSP; Lifetime; MSNBC; MTV; National Geographic Channel; Nickelodeon; Outdoor Channel; Oxygen; RFD-TV; Spike TV; Syfy; TBS; The Weather Channel; TLC; TNT; Travel Channel; Trinity Broadcasting Network (TBN); truTV; Turner Classic Movies; TV Land; Univision Studios; USA Network; VH1; WE tv.
  Fee: $35.00 monthly.
 Digital Basic Service
  Subscribers: 1,370.
  Programming (via satellite): BBC America; Bloomberg Television; Bravo; Cloo; Cooking Channel; Discovery Digital Networks; DMX Music; Fox Sports 1; FXM; GSN; Hallmark Channel; NBCSN; Nick Jr.; Nicktoons; TeenNick.
  Fee: $15.00 monthly.
 Digital Pay Service 1
  Pay Units: N.A.
  Programming (via satellite): Cinemax (multiplexed); Flix (multiplexed); HBO (multiplexed); Showtime (multiplexed); Starz (multiplexed); Starz Encore (multiplexed); The Movie Channel (multiplexed).
  Fee: $12.95 monthly (Cinemax, Showtime/TMC or Starz/Encore), $16.00 monthly (HBO).
 Video-On-Demand: No
 Pay-Per-View
  iN DEMAND (delivered digitally); Fresh (delivered digitally); Playboy TV (delivered digitally).
 Internet Service
  Operational: Yes.
  Broadband Service: Cassnet.
  Fee: $29.95-$57.95 monthly.
 Telephone Service
  Digital: Operational
  Fee: $40.95 monthly
 Engineering Manager: Shane Bauman. Outside Plant Manager: Jamie LaRocca. Assistant Secretary: Theresa Holman.
 Ownership: D & P Communications Inc.

PETOSKEY—Charter Communications. Now served by TRAVERSE CITY, MI [MI0026]. ICA: MI0071.

PICKFORD TWP.—Sunrise Communications LLC, 20938 Washington Ave, PO Box 733, Onaway, MI 49765. Phones: 877-733-8101; 989-733-8100. Fax: 989-733-8155. E-mail: info@src-mi.com. Web Site: http://www.src-mi.com. ICA: MI0228.
 TV Market Ranking: Below 100 (PICKFORD TWP.). Franchise award date: November 23, 1988. Franchise expiration date: N.A. Began: January 1, 1990.
 Channel capacity: 57 (not 2-way capable). Channels available but not in use: N.A.
 Basic Service
  Subscribers: N.A.
  Programming (received off-air): WCML (PBS) Alpena; WFQX-TV (FOX) Cadillac; WGTQ (ABC) Sault Ste. Marie; WTOM-TV (NBC) Cheboygan; WWUP-TV (CBS, FOX) Sault Ste. Marie.
  Fee: $39.18 installation; $1.21 converter.
 Expanded Basic Service 1
  Subscribers: N.A.
  Programming (via satellite): A&E; AMC; CNN; Discovery Channel; Disney Channel; ESPN; ESPN2; FOX Sports Detroit; Freeform; HGTV; History; MTV; Nickelodeon; Spike TV; TBS; The Weather Channel; TNT; USA Network; WGN America.
  Fee: $39.18 installation; $39.95 monthly.
 Pay Service 1
  Pay Units: N.A.
  Programming (via satellite): HBO; Showtime.
 Internet Service
  Operational: Yes.
  Fee: $44.95 monthly.
 Telephone Service
  Digital: Operational
 Miles of Plant: 13.0 (coaxial); None (fiber optic). Homes passed: 311.
 General Manager: Rose Boyce.
 Ownership: Sunrise Communications LLC (MSO).

PIGEON—Comcast Cable. Now served by DETROIT, MI [MI0001]. ICA: MI0375.

PLYMOUTH—WOW! Internet, Cable & Phone, 7887 East Belleview Ave, Ste 1000, Englewood, CO 80111. Phones: 720-479-3558; 720-479-3500; 866-496-9669 (Customer service). Fax: 720-479-3585. E-mail: wow_general@wideopenwest.com. Web Site: http://www.wowway.com. Also serves Allen Park, Berkley, Beverly Hills, Birmingham, Canton Twp., Center Line, Clawson, Clinton, Dearborn, Dearborn Heights, Eastpointe, Ferndale, Fraser, Garden City, Grosse Ile, Harper Woods, Harrison Twp., Hazel Park, Huntington Woods, Lathrup Village, Lincoln Park, Madison Heights, Melvindale, Mount Clemens, Northville, Northville Twp., Pleasant Ridge, Plymouth Twp., Redford Twp., Riverview, Rochester, Rochester Hills, Roseville, Royal Oak, Shelby Twp., Southgate, St. Clair Shores, Sterling Heights, Taylor, Trenton, Troy, Utica, Warren, Wayne, Westland & Woodhaven. ICA: MI0422. **Note**: This system is an overbuild.
 TV Market Ranking: 5 (Allen Park, Berkley, Beverly Hills, Birmingham, Canton Twp., Center Line, Clawson, Clinton, Dearborn, Dearborn Heights, Eastpointe, Ferndale, Fraser, Garden City, Grosse Ile, Harper Woods, Harrison Twp., Hazel Park, Huntington Woods, Lathrup Village, Lincoln Park, Madison Heights, Melvindale, Mount Clemens, Northville, Northville Twp., Pleasant Ridge, PLYMOUTH, Plymouth Twp., Redford Twp., Riverview, Rochester, Rochester Hills, Roseville, Royal Oak, Shelby Twp., Southgate, St. Clair Shores, Sterling Heights, Taylor, Trenton, Troy, Utica, Warren, Wayne, Westland, Woodhaven). Franchise award date: June 1, 1995. Franchise expiration date: N.A. Began: N.A.
 Channel capacity: N.A. Channels available but not in use: N.A.
 Basic Service
  Subscribers: 150,949.
  Programming (received off-air): various Canadian stations; WADL (Antenna TV, getTV) Mount Clemens; WCMZ-TV (PBS) Flint; WDIV-TV (NBC, This TV) Detroit; WJBK (Buzzr, FOX, Heroes & Icons, Movies!) Detroit; WKBD-TV (CW) Detroit; WMYD (Antenna TV, Escape, MNT) Detroit; WPXD-TV (ION) Ann Arbor; WTVS (PBS) Detroit; WWJ-TV (CBS, Decades) Detroit; WXYZ-TV (ABC, Bounce TV) Detroit.
  Programming (via satellite): INSP; TBS; WGN America.
  Fee: $50.00 installation; $32.00 monthly.
 Expanded Basic Service 1
  Subscribers: N.A.
  Programming (via satellite): A&E; AMC; Animal Planet; BET; Bravo; BTN; Cartoon Network; CMT; CNBC; CNN; Comedy Central; C-SPAN; C-SPAN 2; Discovery Channel; Disney Channel; Disney XD; E! HD; ESPN; ESPN Classic; ESPN2; EVINE Live; EWTN Global Catholic Network; Food Network; Fox News Channel; Fox Sports 1; FOX Sports Detroit; Freeform; FX; Golf Channel; GSN; Hallmark Channel; HGTV; History; HLN; Lifetime; MSNBC; MTV; MTV2; National Geographic Channel; Nickelodeon; Nicktoons; OWN: Oprah Winfrey Network; QVC; Spike TV; Syfy; The Weather Channel; TLC; TNT; Travel Channel; truTV; Turner Classic Movies; TV Land; USA Network; VH1.
  Fee: $34.76 monthly.
 Digital Basic Service
  Subscribers: N.A.
  Programming (via satellite): AXS TV; BBC America; Bloomberg Television; Bridges TV; BTN; CMT; Cooking Channel; Destination America; Discovery Kids Channel; DIY Network; DMX Music; ESPNews; Fox Business Network; FOX College Sports Central; FOX College Sports Pacific; FXM; FYI; GemsTV; HD Theater; here! On Demand; History International; Investigation Discovery; Jewelry Television; LMN; MTV Classic; MTV Hits; Nat Geo WILD; NBCSN; NFL Network; NFL Network HD; Nick 2; Nick Jr.; Outdoor Channel; Oxygen; RTV; Science Channel; Sprout; Starz (multiplexed); Starz Encore (multiplexed); Sundance TV; TeenNick; Tennis Channel; The Word Network; Trinity Broadcasting Network (TBN); WE tv.
 Digital Expanded Basic Service
  Subscribers: N.A.
  Programming (via satellite): TAC TV.
  Fee: $4.99 monthly.
 Digital Pay Service 1
  Pay Units: N.A.
  Programming (via satellite): Cinemax (multiplexed); Cinemax On Demand; Flix; HBO (multiplexed); HBO On Demand; Showtime (multiplexed); Showtime On Demand; The Movie Channel (multiplexed); The Movie Channel On Demand.
  Fee: $15.00 monthly (Cinemax, HBO, Showtime/TMC/Flix or Starz).
 Video-On-Demand: Yes
 Pay-Per-View
  iN DEMAND (delivered digitally); Hot Choice (delivered digitally); XTSY (delivered digitally).
 Internet Service
  Operational: Yes.
  Subscribers: 196,290.
  Broadband Service: WOW! Internet.
  Fee: $40.99-$72.99 monthly; $2.50 modem lease.
 Telephone Service
  Digital: Operational
  Subscribers: 117,889.
 Miles of Plant: 9,181.0 (coaxial); 1,810.0 (fiber optic). Homes passed: 638,775.
 Chief Financial Officer: Rich Fish. Vice President & General Manager: Mark Dineen. Vice President, Sales & Marketing: Cathy Kuo. Chief Technical Officer: Cash Hagen.
 Ownership: WideOpenWest LLC (MSO).

PONTIAC—Comcast Cable. Now served by DETROIT, MI [MI0001]. ICA: MI0017.

PORT AUSTIN—Comcast Cable. Now served by DETROIT, MI [MI0001]. ICA: MI0376.

PORT HOPE—Comcast Cable. Now served by DETROIT, MI [MI0001]. ICA: MI0377.

PORTAGE TWP. (Mackinac County)—Formerly served by Upper Peninsula Communications. Now served by Lighthouse Computers Inc., ENGADINE, MI [MI0297]. ICA: MI0369.

POSEN—Sunrise Communications LLC, 20938 Washington Ave, PO Box 733, Onaway, MI 49765. Phones: 877-733-8101; 989-733-8100. Fax: 989-733-8155. E-mail: info@src-mi.com. Web Site: http://www.src-mi.com. Also serves Pulaski Twp. ICA: MI0250.
 TV Market Ranking: Below 100 (POSEN, Pulaski Twp.). Franchise award date: N.A. Franchise expiration date: N.A. Began: November 1, 1985.
 Channel capacity: 36 (2-way capable). Channels available but not in use: N.A.
 Basic Service
  Subscribers: N.A.
  Programming (received off-air): WBKB-TV (ABC, CBS, FOX) Alpena; WCML (PBS) Alpena; WGTQ (ABC) Sault Ste. Marie; WTOM-TV (NBC) Cheboygan; WWUP-TV (CBS, FOX) Sault Ste. Marie.

Cable Systems—Michigan

Programming (via satellite): C-SPAN; Freeform; HLN; QVC; TBS; TNT; WGN America.
Fee: $38.00 installation.
Expanded Basic Service 1
Subscribers: N.A.
Programming (via satellite): A&E; AMC; CMT; CNBC; CNN; Discovery Channel; Disney Channel; ESPN; ESPN2; Food Network; FOX Sports Detroit; Lifetime; MTV; Nickelodeon; Spike TV; The Weather Channel; TLC; USA Network; VH1.
Fee: $36.95 monthly.
Pay Service 1
Pay Units: N.A.
Programming (via satellite): Cinemax; HBO.
Fee: $10.95 monthly (Cinemax), $11.95 monthly (HBO).
Internet Service
Operational: No.
Telephone Service
None
Miles of Plant: 5.0 (coaxial); None (fiber optic). Homes passed: 199.
General Manager: Rose Boyce.
Ownership: Sunrise Communications LLC (MSO)

PRESCOTT (village)—Formerly served by Charter Communications. No longer in operation. ICA: MI0342.

REDFORD—Bright House Networks. Now served by LIVONIA, MI [MI0019]. ICA: MI0034.

REED CITY—Charter Communications. Now served by ALLENDALE TWP., MI [MI0094]. ICA: MI0165.

REESE—Charter Communications. Now served by MIDLAND, MI [MI0030]. ICA: MI0429.

REMUS—MIcom, PO Box 100, Montague, MI 49437. Phone: 888-873-3353. Fax: 231-894-4960. E-mail: customerservice@micomcable.com. Web Site: http://www.micomcable.com. Also serves Wheatland Twp. (Mecosta County). ICA: MI0344.
TV Market Ranking: Outside TV Markets (REMUS, Wheatland Twp. (Mecosta County)).
Channel capacity: N.A. Channels available but not in use: N.A.
Basic Service
Subscribers: N.A.
Programming (received off-air): WCMU-TV (PBS) Mount Pleasant; WJRT-TV (ABC, MeTV) Flint; WNEM-TV (CBS, COZI TV, MNT) Bay City; WPBN-TV (NBC) Traverse City; WWTV (CBS) Cadillac; WXMI (Antenna TV, FOX, This TV) Grand Rapids; WZZM (ABC) Grand Rapids.
Programming (via satellite): CMT; CNN; Discovery Channel; ESPN; Freeform; HLN; TBS; TNT; WGN America.
Fee: $30.00 installation; $32.00 monthly.
Pay Service 1
Pay Units: N.A.
Programming (via satellite): Showtime; The Movie Channel.
Fee: $20.00 installation; $7.00 monthly (each).
Internet Service
Operational: No.
Telephone Service
None
Miles of Plant: 3.0 (coaxial); None (fiber optic).
Vice President & General Manager: Dan Spoelman. Operations Manager: Ed Bucao.
Ownership: MIcom (MSO).

REPUBLIC TWP.—Cable America Corp, 7822 East Gray Rd, Scottsdale, AZ 85260. Phones: 800-338-1808; 906-249-1057. Web Site: http://www.cableamerica.com. Also serves Champion Twp., Humboldt Twp. & Michigamme. ICA: MI0216.
TV Market Ranking: Below 100 (Humboldt Twp., Michigamme, REPUBLIC TWP., Champion Twp.). Franchise award date: N.A. Franchise expiration date: N.A. Began: September 1, 1988.
Channel capacity: 36 (not 2-way capable). Channels available but not in use: N.A.
Basic Service
Subscribers: 207.
Programming (received off-air): WDIV-TV (NBC, This TV) Detroit; WJFW-TV (Antenna TV, NBC) Rhinelander; WJMN-TV (CBS) Escanaba; WLUC-TV (FOX, NBC) Marquette; WNMU (PBS) Marquette; WTOM-TV (NBC) Cheboygan; WXYZ-TV (ABC, Bounce TV) Detroit.
Programming (via satellite): A&E; CNN; Discovery Channel; ESPN; Freeform; Spike TV; TBS; TNT; USA Network; WGN America.
Fee: $59.75 monthly.
Pay Service 1
Pay Units: N.A.
Programming (via satellite): Showtime.
Fee: $15.00 installation; $6.95 monthly.
Video-On-Demand: No
Internet Service
Operational: No.
Telephone Service
None
Miles of Plant: 13.0 (coaxial); None (fiber optic). Homes passed: 420.
General Manager: Robert L. Grove. Controller: Walter G. Farak.
Ownership: CableAmerica Corp. (MSO).

RICHFIELD TWP. (Roscommon County)—Charter Communications, 236 W Huron Rd, PO Box 706, Augres, MI 48703. Phones: 636-207-5100 (Corporate office); 989-340-0078; 231-947-5221 (Traverse City office); 314-543-2236. Web Site: http://www.charter.com. Also serves Backus Twp., Beaver Creek Twp., Beaverton, Buckeye Twp., Churchill Twp., Denton Twp., Gerrish Twp., Gerrish Twp. (portions), Gladwin, Grayling, Higgins Twp., Lake Twp. (Roscommon County), Logan Twp., Lyon Twp. (Roscommon County), Markey Twp., Mills Twp. (Ogemaw County), Roscommon, Roscommon (village), South Branch Twp. & West Branch. ICA: MI0116.
TV Market Ranking: Below 100 (Backus Twp., Denton Twp., Markey Twp., Grayling); Outside TV Markets (Beaver Creek Twp., Beaverton, Buckeye Twp., Churchill Twp., Gerrish Twp., Gerrish Twp. (portions), Gladwin, Lake Twp. (Roscommon County), Logan Twp., Lyon Twp. (Roscommon County), Mills Twp. (Ogemaw County), Roscommon (village), South Branch Twp., Higgins Twp., RICHFIELD TWP. (ROSCOMMON COUNTY), Roscommon, West Branch).
Channel capacity: N.A. Channels available but not in use: N.A.
Digital Basic Service
Subscribers: 14,459.
Programming (via satellite): AXS TV; BBC America; Discovery Digital Networks; DIY Network; DMX Music; ESPNews; FOX College Sports Central; FOX College Sports Pacific; Fox Sports 2; Fuse; FXM; FYI; Great American Country; History International; IFC; LMN; NFL Network; Nick 2; Nick Jr.; Nicktoons; Pop; Sundance TV; TeenNick.
Fee: $49.99 installation; $26.99 monthly.

Digital Expanded Basic Service
Subscribers: N.A.
Programming (via satellite): A&E; AMC; Animal Planet; Bravo; Cartoon Network; CMT; CNBC; CNN; Comedy Central; Discovery Channel; Disney Channel; Disney XD; E! HD; ESPN; ESPN Classic; Food Network; Fox News Channel; Fox Sports 1; FOX Sports Detroit; Freeform; FX; Golf Channel; GSN; Hallmark Channel; HGTV; History; HLN; Lifetime; MSNBC; MTV; MTV2; National Geographic Channel; NBCSN; Nickelodeon; Outdoor Channel; Oxygen; Spike TV; Syfy; Telemundo; The Weather Channel; TLC; TNT; Travel Channel; truTV; Turner Classic Movies; TV Land; USA Network; VH1; WE tv.
Fee: $36.49 monthly.
Digital Pay Service 1
Pay Units: N.A.
Programming (via satellite): Cinemax (multiplexed); Flix; HBO (multiplexed); HBO HD; Showtime (multiplexed); Showtime HD; Starz (multiplexed); Starz Encore (multiplexed); The Movie Channel (multiplexed).
Fee: $1.95 installation; $6.95 monthly (Starz), $10.95 monthly (Cinemax), $11.95 monthly (HBO), $12.95 monthly (Showtime).
Video-On-Demand: Yes
Pay-Per-View
iN DEMAND (delivered digitally); ESPN Sports PPV (delivered digitally); NHL Center Ice/MLB Extra Innings (delivered digitally); Playboy TV (delivered digitally); Spice Live (delivered digitally); Spice Platinum (delivered digitally); Hot Net Plus (delivered digitally); Spice Hot (delivered digitally).
Internet Service
Operational: Yes.
Subscribers: 9,995.
Broadband Service: Charter Internet.
Fee: $29.99 monthly.
Telephone Service
Digital: Operational
Subscribers: 8,710.
Miles of Plant: 1,120.0 (coaxial); 278.0 (fiber optic). Homes passed: 33,931.
Vice President: Joe Boullion. General Manager: Ed Kavanaugh. Technical Operations Director: Rob Nowak. Accounting Director: David Sovanski. Marketing Manager: Brenda Auger.
Ownership: Charter Communications Inc. (MSO).

RICHLAND—Comcast Cable. Now served by DETROIT, MI [MI0001]. ICA: MI0316.

RICHLAND TWP.—Comcast Cable. Now served by DETROIT, MI [MI0001]. ICA: MI0439.

RIVES JUNCTION—Formerly served by Cablevision Systems Corp. No longer in operation. ICA: MI0345.

ROCKFORD—Charter Communications. Now served by ALLENDALE TWP., MI [MI0094]. ICA: MI0058.

ROGERS CITY—Charter Communications. Now served by ALPENA, MI [MI0061]. ICA: MI0154.

ROLLAND TWP.—Formerly served by Blanchard Cable Inc. No longer in operation. ICA: MI0448.

ROMULUS—Comcast Cable. Now served by DETROIT, MI [MI0001]. ICA: MI0047.

ROSCOMMON—Charter Communications. Now served by RICHFIELD TWP. (Roscommon County), MI [MI0116]. ICA: MI0193.

ROSEBUSH—Charter Communications. Now served by MIDLAND, MI [MI0030]. ICA: MI0231.

ROSEVILLE—Comcast Cable. Now served by DETROIT, MI [MI0001]. ICA: MI0037.

RUTLAND TWP.—MIcom, PO Box 100, Montague, MI 49437. Phone: 888-873-3353. Fax: 231-894-4960. E-mail: customerservice@micomcable.com. Web Site: http://www.micomcable.com. ICA: MI0220.
TV Market Ranking: 37 (RUTLAND TWP.). Franchise award date: N.A. Franchise expiration date: N.A. Began: November 1, 1983.
Channel capacity: 36 (not 2-way capable). Channels available but not in use: N.A.
Basic Service
Subscribers: 58.
Programming (received off-air): WGVU-TV (PBS) Grand Rapids; WILX-TV (NBC, WeatherNation) Onondaga; WLLA (IND, MeTV) Kalamazoo; WLNS-TV (CBS) Lansing; WOOD-TV (Laff, NBC) Grand Rapids; WOTV (ABC, Grit, TheCoolTV) Battle Creek; WTLJ (IND) Muskegon; WWMT (CBS, CW) Kalamazoo; WXMI (Antenna TV, FOX, This TV) Grand Rapids; WZPX-TV (ION) Battle Creek; WZZM (ABC) Grand Rapids.
Programming (via satellite): QVC; TBS; WGN America.
Fee: $36.00 installation; $38.95 monthly.
Expanded Basic Service 1
Subscribers: N.A.
Programming (via satellite): A&E; AMC; CMT; CNBC; CNN; C-SPAN; Discovery Channel; Disney Channel; ESPN; ESPN2; Food Network; FOX Sports Detroit; Freeform; HLN; Lifetime; Nickelodeon; Spike TV; The Weather Channel; TLC; TNT; USA Network.
Fee: $24.95 monthly.
Pay Service 1
Pay Units: N.A.
Programming (via satellite): Cinemax; HBO; Starz.
Fee: $10.00 installation; $5.95 monthly (Starz), $10.95 monthly (Cinemax), $11.95 monthly (HBO).
Internet Service
Operational: No.
Telephone Service
None
Homes passed: 300.
Ownership: MIcom (MSO).

SAGE TWP.—Charter Communications, 2304 South Mission, Mt. Pleasant, MI 48858. Phones: 314-543-2236; 636-207-5100 (Corporate office); 989-775-6846. Web Site: http://www.charter.com. Also serves Grout Twp. & Hamilton Twp. (Clare County). ICA: MI0133.
TV Market Ranking: Below 100 (Hamilton Twp. (Clare County)); Outside TV Markets (Grout Twp., SAGE TWP.). Franchise award date: January 22, 1988. Franchise expiration date: N.A. Began: December 1, 1988.
Channel capacity: N.A. Channels available but not in use: N.A.
Digital Basic Service
Subscribers: 581.
Programming (received off-air): WAQP (IND) Saginaw; WCMU-TV (PBS) Mount Pleasant; WEYI-TV (Bounce TV, CW, NBC)

Michigan—Cable Systems

Warren's Washington Internet Daily
Covering the politics and policies of the internet.
FREE 30-DAY TRIAL—call 800-771-9202 or visit www.warren-news.com

Saginaw; WFQX-TV (FOX) Cadillac; WJRT-TV (ABC, MeTV) Flint; WNEM-TV (CBS, COZI TV, MNT) Bay City; WSMH (Antenna TV, FOX, The Country Network) Flint; WWTV (CBS) Cadillac.
Fee: $49.99 installation; $19.99 monthly; $1.00 converter.
Digital Expanded Basic Service
Subscribers: N.A.
Programming (via satellite): A&E; CMT; CNN; C-SPAN; Discovery Channel; Disney Channel; ESPN; Fox News Channel; FOX Sports Detroit; Freeform; HGTV; History; HLN; Lifetime; MTV; Nickelodeon; Spike TV; Syfy; TBS; The Weather Channel; TLC; TNT; truTV; USA Network; WGN America.
Fee: $14.89 monthly.
Digital Pay Service 1
Pay Units: N.A.
Programming (via satellite): Cinemax; HBO.
Fee: $9.95 monthly (each).
Video-On-Demand: No
Internet Service
Operational: No.
Telephone Service
None
Miles of Plant: 71.0 (coaxial); None (fiber optic). Homes passed: 2,438.
Vice President & General Manager: Dan Spoelman. Accounting Director: David Sovanski. Operations Manager: Ed Bucao.
Ownership: Charter Communications Inc. (MSO).

SAGINAW—Charter Communications. Now served by MIDLAND, MI [MI0030]. ICA: MI0013.

SALINE—Comcast Cable. Now served by DETROIT, MI [MI0001]. ICA: MI0065.

SANDUSKY—Comcast Cable. Now served by DETROIT, MI [MI0001]. ICA: MI0162.

SANFORD—Formerly served by Charter Communications. No longer in operation. ICA: MI0088.

SAUGATUCK—Comcast Cable. Now served by DETROIT, MI [MI0001]. ICA: MI0110.

SAULT STE. MARIE—Charter Communications, 12405 Powerscourt Dr, St. Louis, MO 63131. Phones: 636-207-5100 (Corporate office); 906-635-1527; 231-947-5221 (Traverse City office); 906-632-8541. Fax: 906-635-1520. E-mail: jboullion@chartercom.com. Web Site: http://www.charter.com. Also serves Bay Mills Twp., Brimley, Dafter Twp., Kinross, Moran, Rudyard Twp., Soo Twp., St. Ignace & St. Ignace Twp. ICA: MI0090.
TV Market Ranking: Below 100 (Bay Mills Twp., Brimley, Dafter Twp., Kinross, Moran, Rudyard Twp., SAULT STE. MARIE, Soo Twp., St. Ignace, St. Ignace Twp.). Franchise award date: N.A. Franchise expiration date: N.A. Began: April 1, 1961.
Channel capacity: N.A. Channels available but not in use: N.A.

Digital Basic Service
Subscribers: 6,098.
Programming (via satellite): AXS TV; BBC America; Boomerang; Discovery Digital Networks; DIY Network; ESPN HD; FOX College Sports Central; FOX College Sports Pacific; Fox Sports 2; FXM; FYI; HD Theater; History International; IFC; LMN; MC; NFL Network; Nick 2; Nick Jr.; Nicktoons; Outdoor Channel; Sundance TV; TeenNick; TV Guide Interactive Inc.
Fee: $26.99 monthly.
Digital Expanded Basic Service
Subscribers: N.A.
Programming (via satellite): A&E; AMC; Animal Planet; Bravo; Cartoon Network; CMT; CNBC; CNN; Comedy Central; C-SPAN; C-SPAN 2; Discovery Channel; Discovery Life Channel; Disney Channel; Disney XD; E! HD; ESPN; ESPN Classic; ESPN2; EWTN Global Catholic Network; Food Network; Fox News Channel; Fox Sports 1; FOX Sports Detroit; Freeform; FX; Golf Channel; GSN; Hallmark Channel; HGTV; History; HLN; INSP; ION Television; Lifetime; MSNBC; MTV; National Geographic Channel; NBCSN; Nickelodeon; Oxygen; Spike TV; Syfy; TBS; The Weather Channel; TLC; TNT; Travel Channel; Trinity Broadcasting Network (TBN); truTV; Turner Classic Movies; TV Land; USA Network; VH1; WE tv.
Fee: $36.49 monthly.
Digital Pay Service 1
Pay Units: N.A.
Programming (via satellite): Cinemax (multiplexed); Flix; HBO (multiplexed); Showtime (multiplexed); Starz (multiplexed); Starz Encore (multiplexed); The Movie Channel (multiplexed).
Video-On-Demand: Yes
Pay-Per-View
Playboy TV (delivered digitally); Spice Live (delivered digitally); Spice Platinum (delivered digitally); Hot Net Plus (delivered digitally); Spice Hot (delivered digitally); iN DEMAND (delivered digitally); NHL Center Ice (delivered digitally); MLB Extra Innings (delivered digitally); Sports PPV (delivered digitally).
Internet Service
Operational: Yes.
Subscribers: 5,461.
Broadband Service: Charter Internet.
Fee: $29.99 monthly.
Telephone Service
Digital: Operational
Subscribers: 2,845.
Miles of Plant: 448.0 (coaxial); 150.0 (fiber optic). Homes passed: 15,173.
Vice President: Joe Boullion. General Manager: John Badenski. Accounting Director: David Sovanski. Chief Technician: John Randazzo. Marketing Manager: Sandy Gottschalk.
Ownership: Charter Communications Inc. (MSO).

SEBEWAING—Comcast Cable. Now served by DETROIT, MI [MI0001]. ICA: MI0184.

SENEY—Formerly served by Cable America Corp. No longer in operation. ICA: MI0253.

SEVILLE TWP.—Charter Communications, 1202 West Benton, Greenville, MI 48838. Phones: 314-543-2236; 636-207-5100 (Corporate office); 989-775-6846. Web Site: http://www.charter.com. Also serves Richland Twp. (Montcalm County), Riverdale & Sumner Twp. (portions). ICA: MI0175.
TV Market Ranking: Outside TV Markets (Richland Twp. (Montcalm County), SEVILLE TWP., Sumner Twp. (portions), Riverdale).
Channel capacity: N.A. Channels available but not in use: N.A.
Digital Basic Service
Subscribers: 363.
Programming (received off-air): WCMU-TV (PBS) Mount Pleasant; WEYI-TV (Bounce TV, CW, NBC) Saginaw; WJRT-TV (ABC, MeTV) Flint; WNEM-TV (CBS, COZI TV, MNT) Bay City; WOOD-TV (Laff, NBC) Grand Rapids; WSMH (Antenna TV, FOX, The Country Network) Flint; WWTV (CBS) Cadillac; WZPX-TV (ION) Battle Creek; WZZM (ABC) Grand Rapids.
Programming (via satellite): CMT; C-SPAN; Freeform; QVC; TBS; WGN America.
Fee: $49.99 installation; $14.99 monthly.
Digital Expanded Basic Service
Subscribers: N.A.
Programming (via satellite): A&E; AMC; CNBC; CNN; Comedy Central; Discovery Channel; Disney Channel; ESPN; ESPN2; Food Network; FOX Sports Detroit; History; HLN; Lifetime; MTV; Nickelodeon; Spike TV; The Weather Channel; TNT; USA Network; VH1.
Digital Pay Service 1
Pay Units: N.A.
Programming (via satellite): Cinemax; HBO; Starz.
Fee: $5.98 monthly (Starz), $10.95 monthly (Cinemax), $11.95 monthly (HBO).
Internet Service
Operational: No.
Miles of Plant: 31.0 (coaxial); None (fiber optic). Homes passed: 1,243.
Vice President & General Manager: Dan Spoelman. Accounting Director: David Sovanski. Operations Manager: Ed Bucao.
Ownership: Charter Communications Inc. (MSO).

SHERMAN TWP. (Isabella County)—Charter Communications, 1202 West Benton, Greenville, MI 48838. Phones: 314-543-2236; 636-207-5100 (Corporate office); 989-785-6846. Web Site: http://www.charter.com. Also serves Broomfield Twp., Deerfield Twp. (Isabella County) & Nottawa Twp. (Isabella County). ICA: MI0362.
TV Market Ranking: Outside TV Markets (Broomfield Twp., Nottawa Twp. (Isabella County), SHERMAN TWP. (ISABELLA COUNTY), Deerfield Twp. (Isabella County)).
Channel capacity: N.A. Channels available but not in use: N.A.
Digital Basic Service
Subscribers: 732.
Programming (received off-air): WCMU-TV (PBS) Mount Pleasant; WEYI-TV (Bounce TV, CW, NBC) Saginaw; WFQX-TV (FOX) Cadillac; WJRT-TV (ABC, MeTV) Flint; WNEM-TV (CBS, COZI TV, MNT) Bay City; WPBN-TV (NBC) Traverse City; WSMH (Antenna TV, FOX, The Country Network) Flint; WWTV (CBS) Cadillac; WZZM (ABC) Grand Rapids.
Programming (via satellite): A&E; Animal Planet; CMT; CNBC; CNN; C-SPAN; Discovery Channel; Disney Channel; ESPN; ESPN2; FOX Sports Detroit; Freeform; History; HLN; Lifetime; Nickelodeon; QVC; Spike TV; Syfy; TBS; The Weather Channel; TLC; TNT; Trinity Broadcasting Network (TBN); USA Network; WGN America.
Fee: $49.99 installation; $26.99 monthly.
Pay Service 1
Pay Units: N.A.
Programming (via satellite): Showtime (multiplexed).
Fee: $20.00 installation; $7.00 monthly.
Internet Service
Operational: No.
Telephone Service
None
Miles of Plant: 31.0 (coaxial); None (fiber optic). Homes passed: 1,735.
Vice President & General Manager: Dan Spoelman. Operations Manager: Ed Bucao. Accounting Director: David Sovanski.
Ownership: Charter Communications Inc. (MSO).

SHERWOOD TWP.—Formerly served by CableDirect. No longer in operation. ICA: MI0251.

SHINGLETON—Cable America Corp, 7822 East Gray Rd, Scottsdale, AZ 85260. Phones: 800-338-1808; 800-661-4169; 906-249-1057. Web Site: http://www.cableamerica.com. ICA: MI0383.
TV Market Ranking: Outside TV Markets (SHINGLETON). Franchise award date: N.A. Franchise expiration date: N.A. Began: January 1, 1992.
Channel capacity: 36 (not 2-way capable). Channels available but not in use: N.A.
Basic Service
Subscribers: 51.
Programming (received off-air): WJMN-TV (CBS) Escanaba; WLUC-TV (FOX, NBC) Marquette; WNMU (PBS) Marquette; WXYZ-TV (ABC, Bounce TV) Detroit; WZMQ (Antenna TV, MeTV, MNT, This TV) Marquette.
Programming (via satellite): A&E; AMC; Cartoon Network; CNBC; CNN; C-SPAN; Discovery Channel; Disney Channel; ESPN; ESPN2; Fox News Channel; Fox Sports 1; FOX Sports Networks; Freeform; FX; Great American Country; Hallmark Channel; HGTV; History; ION Television; Lifetime; QVC; Syfy; TBS; The Weather Channel; TLC; TNT; Travel Channel; truTV; TV Land; USA Network; WGN America.
Fee: $25.00 installation; $59.75 monthly.
Pay Service 1
Pay Units: N.A.
Programming (via satellite): Showtime; The Movie Channel.
Fee: $6.95 monthly.
Video-On-Demand: No
Internet Service
Operational: No.
Telephone Service
None
Miles of Plant: 2.0 (coaxial); None (fiber optic). Homes passed: 175.
General Manager: Robert L. Grove. Controller: Walter G. Farak.
Ownership: CableAmerica Corp.

SKIDWAY LAKE—Formerly served by Charter Communications. No longer in operation. ICA: MI0118.

SOUTH HAVEN—Comcast Cable. Now served by DETROIT, MI [MI0001]. ICA: MI0086.

Cable Systems—Michigan

SOUTHFIELD—Comcast Cable. Now served by DETROIT, MI [MI0001]. ICA: MI0009.

SPRINGDALE TWP.—Ace Communications. Formerly served by THOMPSONVILLE, MI [MI0230]. This cable system has converted to IPTV. Now served by MESICK, MI [MI5074]. ICA: MI5026.

SPRINGFIELD TWP. (Oakland County)—Comcast Cable. Now served by DETROIT, MI [MI0001]. ICA: MI0107.

SPRINGPORT TWP.—Springport Telephone Co, 400 East Main St, PO Box 208, Springport, MI 49284. Phones: 517-857-3100; 517-857-3500. Fax: 517-857-3329. E-mail: janet@springcom.com. Web Site: http://www3.springcom.com. Also serves Brookfield Twp. (Eaton County), Clarence Twp., Hamlin Twp. (Eaton County), Parma Twp., Sheridan Twp. (Calhoun County) & Springport (village). ICA: MI0350.
TV Market Ranking: 37,92 (Clarence Twp., Parma Twp., Sheridan Twp. (Calhoun County), Springport (village), SPRINGPORT TWP); 92 (Brookfield Twp. (Eaton County), Hamlin Twp. (Eaton County)). Franchise award date: N.A. Franchise expiration date: N.A. Began: August 1, 1989.
Channel capacity: N.A. Channels available but not in use: N.A.
Basic Service
Subscribers: 795.
Programming (received off-air): WILX-TV (NBC, WeatherNation) Onondaga; WKAR-TV (PBS) East Lansing; WLAJ (ABC, CW) Lansing; WLNS-TV (CBS) Lansing; WOOD-TV (Laff, NBC) Grand Rapids; WOTV (ABC, Grit, TheCoolTV) Battle Creek; WSYM-TV (FOX, MeTV) Lansing; WWMT (CBS, CW) Kalamazoo.
Fee: $35.00 installation; $19.00 monthly; $40.00 converter.
Expanded Basic Service 1
Subscribers: N.A.
Programming (received off-air): WHTV (MNT) Jackson; WXMI (Antenna TV, FOX, This TV) Grand Rapids.
Programming (via satellite): A&E; AMC; Animal Planet; Cartoon Network; CNBC; CNN; C-SPAN; C-SPAN 2; Discovery Channel; Disney Channel; Disney XD; E! HD; ESPN; ESPN2; Fox News Channel; Fox Sports 1; FOX Sports Networks; Freeform; FX; Golf Channel; Great American Country; HGTV; History; INSP; Lifetime; MTV; Nickelodeon; Outdoor Channel; QVC; Spike TV; Syfy; TBS; The Weather Channel; TLC; TNT; Travel Channel; Turner Classic Movies; TV Land; USA Network; VH1; WGN America.
Fee: $24.00 monthly.
Pay Service 1
Pay Units: N.A.
Programming (via satellite): Cinemax; HBO; Showtime; Starz Encore.
Fee: $2.00 monthly (Encore), $9.50 monthly (Cinemax), $9.00 monthly (Showtime), $11.70 monthly (HBO).
Video-On-Demand: No
Internet Service
Operational: Yes. Began: December 31, 1999.
Broadband Service: In-house.
Fee: $60.00 installation; $39.95 monthly.
Telephone Service
Analog: Operational
Miles of Plant: 50.0 (coaxial); None (fiber optic).
General Manager: Janet Beilfuss. Chief Technician: Jerry Riske.
Ownership: Springport Telephone Co.

SPRINGVALE TWP.—Parish Communications, PO Box 10, Auburn, MI 48611. Phones: 800-466-6444; 989-662-6811. Web Site: http://www.parishonline.net. ICA: MI0453.
TV Market Ranking: Below 100 (SPRINGVALE TWP.).
Channel capacity: N.A. Channels available but not in use: N.A.
Basic Service
Subscribers: 190.
Fee: $55.00 installation; $63.90 monthly.
Internet Service
Operational: Yes.
Telephone Service
None
General Manager: Floyd Grocholski.
Ownership: Parish Communications.

ST. IGNACE—Charter Communications. Now served by SAULT STE. MARIE, MI [MI0090]. ICA: MI0152.

ST. JOHNS—Charter Communications. Now served by MIDLAND, MI [MI0030]. ICA: MI0353.

ST. JOSEPH—Comcast Cable. Now served by CHAMPAIGN, IL [IL0019]. ICA: MI0045.

STANDISH—Charter Communications. Now served by MIDLAND, MI [MI0030]. ICA: MI0146.

STANTON—Charter Communications. Now served by ALLENDALE TWP., MI [MI0094]. ICA: MI0112.

STEPHENSON—Packerland Broadband, 105 Kent St., PO Box 885, Iron Mountain, MI 49801. Phones: 906-774-1291; 906-774-6621; 800-236-8434. Fax: 906-776-2811. E-mail: service@plbb.net; support@packerlandbroadband.com. Web Site: http://www.packerlandbroadband.com. Also serves Wallace. ICA: MI0433. **Note:** This system is an overbuild.
TV Market Ranking: Below 100 (STEPHENSON); Outside TV Markets (Wallace).
Channel capacity: N.A. Channels available but not in use: N.A.
Basic Service
Subscribers: N.A.
Programming (received off-air): WBAY-TV (ABC) Green Bay; WFRV-TV (Bounce TV, CBS) Green Bay; WGBA-TV (MeTV, NBC) Green Bay; WLUC-TV (FOX, NBC) Marquette; WLUK-TV (Antenna TV, FOX) Green Bay; WNMU (PBS) Marquette.
Programming (via satellite): CNN; CW PLUS; Discovery Channel; Freeform; TBS; TNT; WGN America.
Expanded Basic Service 1
Subscribers: N.A.
Programming (via satellite): A&E; CNBC; C-SPAN; Disney Channel; ESPN; ESPN2; EWTN Global Catholic Network; FOX Sports Detroit; HGTV; History; ION Television; Lifetime; Nickelodeon; Outdoor Channel; Spike TV; Syfy; The Weather Channel; TLC; Trinity Broadcasting Network (TBN); Turner Classic Movies; USA Network.
Pay Service 1
Pay Units: N.A.
Programming (via satellite): Cinemax; HBO.
Internet Service
Operational: Yes.
Fee: $26.95 monthly.
Telephone Service
Digital: Operational
Miles of Plant: 56.0 (coaxial); 8.0 (fiber optic). Homes passed: 1,109.
General Manager: Dan Plante. Technical Supervisor: Chad Kay.
Ownership: Packerland Broadband (MSO).

STERLING—Vogtmann Engineering Inc, 6625 Maple Ridge Rd, Alger, MI 48610. Phone: 989-836-8848. Web Site: http://www.veionline.com. Also serves Clayton, Deep River, Moffatt, Richland Twp. & Sterling Village. ICA: MI0244.
TV Market Ranking: 61 (STERLING, Sterling Village). Franchise award date: July 10, 1984. Franchise expiration date: N.A. Began: December 1, 1986.
Channel capacity: 35 (not 2-way capable). Channels available but not in use: N.A.
Basic Service
Subscribers: N.A.
Programming (received off-air): WEYI-TV (Bounce TV, CW, NBC) Saginaw; WJRT-TV (ABC, MeTV) Flint; WNEM-TV (CBS, COZI TV, MNT) Bay City; WWTV (CBS) Cadillac.
Programming (via satellite): ESPN; Freeform; Lifetime; Nickelodeon; QVC; Spike TV; Syfy; Travel Channel.
Fee: $50.00 installation; $17.64 monthly.
Expanded Basic Service 1
Subscribers: N.A.
Programming (via satellite): CNN; HLN; USA Network.
Fee: $2.60 monthly.
Expanded Basic Service 2
Subscribers: N.A.
Programming (via satellite): Discovery Channel; TBS; TNT; WGN America.
Fee: $4.95 monthly.
Pay Service 1
Pay Units: N.A.
Programming (via satellite): HBO; Showtime.
Fee: $10.95 monthly (Showtime), $11.95 monthly (HBO).
Internet Service
Operational: No.
Subscribers: 254.
Telephone Service
None
Miles of Plant: 70.0 (coaxial); 30.0 (fiber optic). Homes passed: 500.
Ownership: Vogtmann Engineering Inc.

STERLING HEIGHTS—Comcast Cable. Now served by DETROIT, MI [MI0001]. ICA: MI0002.

SUMMIT TWP. (Jackson County)—Comcast Cable. Now served by DETROIT, MI [MI0001]. ICA: MI0039.

THETFORD TWP.—Charter Communications. Now served by GOODRICH, MI [MI0290]. ICA: MI0378.

THOMAS TWP.—Charter Communications. Now served by MIDLAND, MI [MI0030]. ICA: MI0072.

THOMPSONVILLE—Ace Communications. This cable system has converted to IPTV. Now served by MESICK, MI [MI5074]. ICA: MI0230.

THREE OAKS—Comcast Cable. Now served by CHAMPAIGN, IL [IL0019]. ICA: MI0051.

THREE OAKS—Comcast Cable. Now served by CHAMPAIGN, IL [IL0019]. ICA: MI0078.

THREE RIVERS—Comcast Cable. Now served by DETROIT, MI [MI0001]. ICA: MI0050.

TRAVERSE CITY—Charter Communications, 12405 Powerscourt Dr, St. Louis, MO 63131. Phones: 636-207-5100 (Corporate office); 800-545-0994; 231-947-5221. Fax: 231-947-2004. Web Site: http://www.charter.com. Also serves Acadia Twp., Acme (village), Acme Twp., Alanson Twp., Alba, Almira Twp., Aloha Twp., Bagley Twp., Banks Twp., Bay Shore, Bay Twp., Bay View, Bear Creek Twp., Bear Lake, Bear Lake (village), Bear Lake Twp., Beaugrand (village), Bellaire (village), Benton Twp. (Cheboygan County), Benzie County (portions), Benzonia (village), Benzonia Twp., Beulah, Bingham Twp. (Leelanau County), Blair Twp., Blue Lake Twp., Boyne City, Boyne Falls (village), Boyne Valley Twp., Buckley (village), Burt Twp., Cadillac, Caldwell Twp., Carp Lake Twp., Cedar, Cedar Creek Twp., Centerville Twp., Central Lake (village), Central Lake Twp., Charlevoix, Charlevoix Twp., Cheboygan, Cherry Grove Twp., Chester Twp., Chestonia Twp., Clam Lake Twp., Clearwater Twp., Cleveland Twp., Cold Springs Twp., Conway, Corwith Twp., Crystal Lake, Dover Twp. (Otsego County), East Bay Twp., East Jordan, East Lake, Elberta, Elk Rapids (village), Elk Rapids Twp., Ellsworth, Elmira Twp., Elmwood Twp. (Leelanau County), Empire (village), Empire Twp., Evangeline Twp., Eveline Twp., Excelsior Twp., Fife Lake (village), Fife Lake Twp., Filer City Twp., Forest Home Twp., Forest Twp., Frankfort, Frederick, Friendship Twp., Garfield Twp. (Grand Traverse County), Gaylord, Gilmore Twp. (Benzie County), Glen Arbor Twp., Grant Twp. (Grand Traverse County), Green Lake Twp., Hanover Twp., Harbor Springs, Haring Twp., Hayes Twp., Helena Twp., Homestead Twp., Honor (village), Indian River, Inland Twp., Inverness Twp., Joyfield Twp., Kalkaska (village), Kalkaska Twp., Kasson Twp., Kearney Twp., Kingsley (village), Lake Ann (village), Lake City, Lake Twp., Leelanau Twp., Leland Twp., Levering, Liberty Twp., Little Traverse Twp., Littlefield Twp., Livingston Twp., Long Lake Twp., Mackinaw City, Mackinaw Twp., Mancelona, Mancelona Twp., Manistee, Manistee Twp., Manton, Maple City, Marion Twp., Mayfield, Mayfield Twp. (Grand Traverse County), McKinley Twp., Melrose Twp., Milton Twp. (Antrim County), Missaukee County (portions), Mullet Lake Twp., Northport (village), Norwood Twp., Nunda Twp., Oden, Onekama (village), Onekama Twp., Paradise Twp., Pellston, Peninsula Twp., Petoskey, Pleasanton Twp., Pleasantview Twp., Rapid River, Rapid River Twp., Reeder Twp., Resort Twp., Richland Twp. (Missaukee County), Selma Twp., Solon Twp. (Leelanau County), South Arm Twp., Springfield Twp., Springvale Twp., Star Twp., Stronach Twp., Suttons Bay, Suttons Bay Twp., The Homestead, Torch Lake Twp. (Antrim County), Tuscarora Twp., Vanderbilt, Wawatam Twp., West Traverse Twp., Whitewater Twp. & Wilson Twp. (Charlevoix County). ICA: MI0026.
TV Market Ranking: Below 100 (Acme (village), Acme Twp., Alanson Twp., Alba, Almira Twp., Aloha Twp., Bagley Twp., Banks Twp., Bay Shore, Bay Twp., Bay View, Bear Creek Twp., Beaugrand Twp., Bellaire (village), Benton Twp. (Cheboygan County), Benzie County (portions), Benzonia Twp., Beulah, Bingham Twp. (Leelanau County), Blair Twp., Blue Lake Twp., Boyne City, Boyne Falls (village), Boyne Valley Twp., Buckley (village), Burt Twp., Caldwell Twp., Carp Lake Twp., Cedar Creek

Michigan—Cable Systems

Twp., Centerville Twp., Central Lake Twp., Charlevoix, Charlevoix Twp., Cherry Grove Twp., Chester Twp., Chestonia Twp., Clam Lake Twp., Clearwater Twp., Cleveland Twp., Cold Springs Twp., Conway, Corwith Twp., Crystal Lake, East Bay Twp., East Jordan, Elberta, Elk Rapids (village), Elk Rapids Twp., Elmira Twp., Elmwood Twp. (Leelanau County), Empire (village), Empire Twp., Evangeline Twp., Eveline Twp., Excelsior Twp., Fife Lake (village), Fife Lake Twp., Forest Home Twp., Forest Twp., Frankfort, Frederick, Friendship Twp., Garfield Twp. (Grand Traverse County), Gaylord, Gilmore Twp. (Benzie County), Glen Arbor Twp., Grant Twp. (Grand Traverse County), Green Lake Twp., Hanover Twp., Harbor Springs, Haring Twp., Hayes Twp., Helena Twp., Homestead Twp., Honor (village), Inland Twp., Inverness Twp., Joyfield Twp., Kalkaska (village), Kalkaska Twp., Kasson Twp., Kearney Twp., Kingsley (village), Lake City, Lake Twp., Leelanau Twp., Leland Twp., Liberty Twp., Little Traverse Twp., Littlefield Twp., Livingston Twp., Long Lake Twp., Mackinaw City, Mackinaw Twp., Mancelona, Mancelona Twp., Manton, Maple City, Marion Twp., Mayfield, Mayfield Twp. (Grand Traverse County), McKinley Twp., Melrose Twp., Milton Twp. (Antrim County), Missaukee County (portions), Mullet Lake Twp., Northport (village), Norwood Twp., Nunda Twp., Oden, Onekama Twp., Paradise Twp., Peninsula Twp., Petoskey, Pleasanton Twp., Pleasantview Twp., Rapid River, Rapid River Twp., Reeder Twp., Resort Twp., Richland Twp. (Missaukee County), Selma Twp., Solon Twp. (Leelanau County), South Arm Twp., Springfield Twp., Springvale Twp., Star Twp., Suttons Bay, Suttons Bay Twp., The Homestead, Torch Lake Twp. (Antrim County), TRAVERSE CITY, Tuscarora Twp., Vanderbilt, Wawatam Twp., West Traverse Twp., Whitewater Twp., Wilson Twp. (Charlevoix County), Cadillac, Cheboygan, Indian River, Lake Ann (village), Levering, Pellston); Outside TV Markets (Acadia Twp., Bear Lake, Bear Lake (village), Bear Lake Twp., East Lake, Filer City Twp., Manistee, Manistee Twp., Onekama (village), Stronach Twp.). Franchise award date: January 1, 1965. Franchise expiration date: N.A. Began: January 1, 1966.
Channel capacity: N.A. Channels available but not in use: N.A.

Digital Basic Service
Subscribers: 71,951.
Programming (via satellite): AXS TV; BBC America; Boomerang; Discovery Digital Networks; DIY Network; ESPN HD; FOX College Sports Central; FOX College Sports Pacific; Fox Sports 2; FXM; FYI; HD Theater; History International; IFC; LMN; MC; NFL Network; Nick 2; Nick Jr.; Nicktoons; Outdoor Channel; Sundance TV; TeenNick.
Fee: $43.99 monthly.

Digital Expanded Basic Service
Subscribers: N.A.
Programming (via satellite): A&E; AMC; Animal Planet; Cartoon Network; CMT; CNBC; CNN; Comedy Central; C-SPAN; C-SPAN 2; Discovery Channel; Disney Channel; Disney XD; E! HD; ESPN; ESPN Classic; ESPN2; EWTN Global Catholic Network; Food Network; Fox News Channel; Fox Sports 1; FOX Sports Detroit; Freeform; FX; Golf Channel; GSN; Hallmark Channel; HGTV; History; INSP; ION Television; Lifetime; MSNBC; MTV; National Geographic Channel; NBCSN; Nickelodeon; Oxygen; Spike TV; Syfy; The Weather Channel; TLC; TNT; Travel Channel; Trinity Broadcasting Network (TBN); truTV; Turner Classic Movies; TV Land; USA Network; VH1; WE tv.
Fee: $12.24 monthly.

Digital Pay Service 1
Pay Units: N.A.
Programming (via satellite): Cinemax (multiplexed); Flix; HBO (multiplexed); Showtime (multiplexed); Starz (multiplexed); Starz Encore (multiplexed); The Movie Channel (multiplexed).

Video-On-Demand: Yes

Pay-Per-View
Hot Net Plus (delivered digitally); Playboy TV (delivered digitally); Spice Hot (delivered digitally); Spice Platinum (delivered digitally); Spice Live (delivered digitally); iN DEMAND (delivered digitally); NHL Center Ice/MLB Extra Innings (delivered digitally); ESPN Sports PPV (delivered digitally).

Internet Service
Operational: Yes.
Subscribers: 65,130.
Broadband Service: Charter Internet.
Fee: $99.95 installation; $29.99 monthly; $3.95 modem lease.

Telephone Service
Digital: Operational
Subscribers: 33,714.
Fee: $29.99 monthly
Miles of Plant: 6,482.0 (coaxial); 2,457.0 (fiber optic). Homes passed: 167,020.
Vice President & General Manager: Joe Boullion. Technical Operations Director: Rob Nowak. Marketing Manager: Tammy Reicha. Accounting Director: David Sovanski.
Ownership: Charter Communications Inc. (MSO).

UBLY—Comcast Cable. Now served by DETROIT, MI [MI0001]. ICA: MI0379.

UNION CITY—WOW! Internet, Cable & Phone. Now served by DIMONDALE, MI [MI0136]. ICA: MI0174.

UNIONVILLE—Formerly served by Pine River Cable. No longer in operation. ICA: MI0243.

VASSAR—Charter Communications. Now served by GOODRICH, MI [MI0290]. ICA: MI0131.

VERMONTVILLE—Formerly served by WOW! Internet, Cable & Phone. No longer in operation. ICA: MI0368.

WALDRON—Comcast Cable. Now served by DETROIT, MI [MI0001]. ICA: MI0438.

WATERSMEET—Charter Communications. Now served by IRONWOOD, MI [MI0064]. ICA: MI0358.

WATERVLIET—Comcast Cable. Now served by CHAMPAIGN, IL [IL0019]. ICA: MI0060.

WAYNE—Comcast Cable. Now served by CHAMPAIGN, IL [IL0019]. ICA: MI0084.

WELLSTON—Formerly served by Pine River Cable. No longer in operation. ICA: MI0237.

WEST BLOOMFIELD TWP.—Comcast Cable. Now served by DETROIT, MI [MI0001]. ICA: MI0028.

WEST BRANCH—Charter Communications. Now served by RICHFIELD TWP. (Roscommon County), MI [MI0116]. ICA: MI0148.

WESTLAND—Comcast Cable. Now served by DETROIT, MI [MI0001]. ICA: MI0012.

WHITE CLOUD—MIcom. Now served by BALDWIN (village), MI [MI0214]. ICA: MI0435.

WHITEHALL—Charter Communications. Now served by ALLENDALE TWP., MI [MI0094]. ICA: MI0092.

WHITTEMORE—Charter Communications. Now served by MIDLAND, MI [MI0030]. ICA: MI0233.

WISNER (village)—Formerly served by Northwoods Cable Inc. No longer in operation. ICA: MI0363.

WOLF LAKE—Summit Digital. Now served by LE ROY, MI [MI0198]. ICA: MI0442.

WOLVERINE (village)—Formerly served by Upper Peninsula Communications. No longer in operation. ICA: MI0364.

WOODHAVEN—Comcast Cable. Now served by DETROIT, MI [MI0001]. ICA: MI0365.

WOODLAND (village)—Formerly served by Pine River Cable. No longer in operation. ICA: MI0366.

WYANDOTTE—Wyandotte Municipal Services, 3200 Biddle Ave, Ste 100, Wyandotte, MI 48192-5901. Phones: 734-324-7100; 734-324-7190. Fax: 734-324-7130. E-mail: rlesko@wyan.org. Web Site: http://www.wyan.org. ICA: MI0053.
TV Market Ranking: 5 (WYANDOTTE). Franchise award date: N.A. Franchise expiration date: N.A. Began: January 4, 1983.
Channel capacity: N.A. Channels available but not in use: N.A.

Basic Service
Subscribers: 6,450.
Programming (received off-air): WADL (Antenna TV, getTV) Mount Clemens; WDIV-TV (NBC, This TV) Detroit; WGTE-TV (PBS) Toledo; WJBK (Buzzr, FOX, Heroes & Icons, Movies!) Detroit; WKBD-TV (CW) Detroit; WMYD (Antenna TV, Escape, MNT) Detroit; WTVS (PBS) Detroit; WWJ-TV (CBS, Decades) Detroit; WXYZ-TV (ABC, Bounce TV) Detroit.
Programming (via satellite): ION Television; Pop; The Weather Channel; various Canadian stations.
Fee: $18.49 monthly.

Expanded Basic Service 1
Subscribers: N.A.
Programming (via satellite): A&E; AMC; Animal Planet; Bravo; BTN; Cartoon Network; Catholic Television Network; CMT; CNBC; CNN; Comedy Central; C-SPAN; C-SPAN 2; Discovery Channel; Disney Channel; DIY Network; E! HD; ESPN; ESPN Classic; ESPN2; Food Network; Fox News Channel; Fox Sports 1; FOX Sports Detroit; Freeform; FX; FXM; Great American Country; Hallmark Channel; HGTV; History; HLN; Lifetime; MSNBC; MTV; National Geographic Channel; Nickelodeon; Outdoor Channel; QVC; Spike TV; Syfy; TBS; TLC; TNT; Travel Channel; Trinity Broadcasting Network (TBN); truTV; Turner Classic Movies; TV Land; USA Network; VH1; WE tv; WGN America.
Fee: $23.30 monthly.

Digital Basic Service
Subscribers: N.A.
Programming (via satellite): A&E HD; AXS TV; BBC America; BTN HD; CMT; Cooking Channel; Discovery Kids Channel; Disney XD; ESPN HD; ESPN2 HD; ESPNews; ESPNU; Fox Business Network; FSN HD; FYI; Golf Channel; GSN; HD Theater; History HD; History International; IFC; LMN; MC; MTV; MTV Classic; MTV Hits; MTV Jams; MTV2; Nat Geo WILD; National Geographic Channel HD; NBCSN; Nick 2; Nick Jr.; Nicktoons; OWN: Oprah Winfrey Network; Oxygen; Science Channel; Sprout; TeenNick; TNT HD; Universal HD; Versus HD; VH1 Soul.

Pay Service 1
Pay Units: 106.
Programming (via satellite): Cinemax.
Fee: $39.95 installation; $9.45 monthly.

Pay Service 2
Pay Units: 1,209.
Programming (via satellite): HBO.
Fee: $39.95 installation; $12.45 monthly.

Pay Service 3
Pay Units: 560.
Programming (via satellite): Showtime; The Movie Channel.
Fee: $11.45 monthly.

Digital Pay Service 1
Pay Units: N.A.
Programming (via satellite): Cinemax (multiplexed); Cinemax HD; Flix; HBO (multiplexed); HBO HD; Showtime (multiplexed); Showtime HD; Starz (multiplexed); Starz Encore (multiplexed); Sundance TV; The Movie Channel (multiplexed); The Movie Channel HD.
Fee: $9.45 monthly (Cinemax), $10.45 monthly (Starz/Encore), $11.45 monthly (Showtime/TMC), $12.45 monthly (HBO).

Video-On-Demand: No

Pay-Per-View
iN DEMAND (delivered digitally); Special events (delivered digitally).

Internet Service
Operational: Yes. Began: December 31, 2000.
Subscribers: 5,419.
Broadband Service: Cable Rocket.
Fee: $27.25-$59.95 monthly.

Telephone Service
Digital: Operational
Subscribers: 1,046.
Fee: $35.49 monthly
Miles of Plant: 118.0 (coaxial); 40.0 (fiber optic). Homes passed: 11,500.
General Manager: Rod Lesko. Assistant General Manager: James French. Cable Superintendent: Steve Timcoe. Program Director: Steve Colwell.
Ownership: Wyandotte Municipal Services.

YALE—Comcast Cable. Now served by DETROIT, MI [MI0001]. ICA: MI0381.

YORK TWP.—Comcast Cable. Now served by DETROIT, MI [MI0001]. ICA: MI0098.

MINNESOTA

Total Systems: 144	Communities with Applications: 0
Total Communities Served: 879	Number of Basic Subscribers: 839,199
Franchises Not Yet Operating: 0	Number of Expanded Basic Subscribers: 1,120
Applications Pending: 0	Number of Pay Units: 8,350

Top 100 Markets Represented: Minneapolis-St. Paul (13); Sioux Falls-Mitchell, SD (85); Duluth, MN-Superior, WI (89); Fargo-Valley City, ND (98).

For a list of cable communities in this section, see the Cable Community Index located in the back of Cable Volume 2.
For explanation of terms used in cable system listings, see p. D-11.

ADAMS—Mediacom. Now served by CHATFIELD, MN [MN0111]. ICA: MN0197.

ADRIAN—Clarity Telcom, 4850 Sugarloaf Pkwy, Ste 209-356, Lawrenceville, GA 30044. Phones: 720-479-3500; 866-399-8647. E-mail: sales@claritytel.com. Web Site: http://www.claritycomm.net. Also serves Edgerton, Ellsworth, Jasper, Lake Wilson, Luverne, Pipestone, Rushmore & Worthington. ICA: MN0158. **Note:** This system is an overbuild.
TV Market Ranking: 85 (Jasper, Luverne); Outside TV Markets (ADRIAN, Edgerton, Lake Wilson, Pipestone, Rushmore, Worthington, Ellsworth). Franchise award date: N.A. Franchise expiration date: N.A. Began: November 15, 1984.
Channel capacity: N.A. Channels available but not in use: N.A.
Basic Service
Subscribers: 3,759.
Programming (received off-air): KARE (NBC, WeatherNation) Minneapolis; KCAU-TV (ABC) Sioux City; KCSD-TV (PBS) Sioux Falls; KDLT-TV (Antenna TV, NBC) Sioux Falls; KELO-TV (CBS, MNT) Sioux Falls; KSFY-TV (ABC, CW) Sioux Falls; KSIN-TV (PBS) Sioux City; KSMN (PBS) Worthington; KTCA-TV (PBS) St. Paul; KTTW (FOX, This TV) Sioux Falls; KUSD-TV (PBS) Vermillion; WCCO-TV (CBS, Decades) Minneapolis; WFTC (MNT, Movies!) Minneapolis.
Programming (via satellite): A&E; AMC; Animal Planet; Bravo; Cartoon Network; CMT; CNBC; CNN; Comedy Central; C-SPAN; C-SPAN 2; Discovery Channel; Disney Channel; Disney XD; E! HD; ESPN; ESPN Classic; ESPN2; EWTN Global Catholic Network; Food Network; Fox News Channel; Fox Sports 1; FOX Sports North; Freeform; FX; FXM; Golf Channel; HGTV; History; HLN; ION Television; Lifetime; LMN; LWS Local Weather Station; MSNBC; MTV; National Geographic Channel; Nickelodeon; Outdoor Channel; Pop; QVC; Spike TV; Syfy; TBS; Telemundo; The Weather Channel; TLC; TNT; Travel Channel; Trinity Broadcasting Network (TBN); truTV; Turner Classic Movies; TV Land; Univision; Univision Studios; USA Network; VH1; WGN America.
Fee: $25.00 installation; $33.00 monthly.
Digital Basic Service
Subscribers: N.A.
Programming (via satellite): AXS TV; BBC America; Bloomberg Television; Cooking Channel; Discovery Life Channel; DIY Network; ESPN; ESPNews; Flix; FOX College Sports Central; FOX College Sports Pacific; Fuse; FYI; GSN; Hallmark Channel; HD Theater; History International; IFC; MC; National Geographic Channel; Nick Jr.; Nicktoons; Starz Encore Family; Sundance TV; TeenNick; WE tv.

Pay Service 1
Pay Units: N.A.
Programming (via satellite): HBO; Showtime.
Fee: $10.00 installation; $9.85 monthly.
Digital Pay Service 1
Pay Units: N.A.
Programming (via satellite): Cinemax; HBO (multiplexed); HITS (Headend In The Sky); Showtime (multiplexed); Starz (multiplexed); Starz Encore (multiplexed); The Movie Channel.
Video-On-Demand: Yes
Pay-Per-View
iN DEMAND (delivered digitally); Hot Choice (delivered digitally).
Internet Service
Operational: Yes.
Telephone Service
Analog: Not Operational
Digital: Operational
Miles of Plant: 21.0 (coaxial); None (fiber optic). Homes passed included in Viborg, SD.
Chief Executive Officer: Jim Gleason.
Ownership: Clarity Telecom (MSO).

AITKIN—Charter Communications. Now served by BRAINERD, MN [MN0022]. ICA: MN0103.

ALBANY—Charter Communications. Now served by ST. CLOUD, MN [MN0011]. ICA: MN0146.

ALBERT LEA—Charter Communications. Now served by AUSTIN, MN [MN0019]. ICA: MN0021.

ALEXANDRIA—Charter Communications, 1111 Hwy 29 North, PO Box 1116, Alexandria, MN 56308. Phones: 636-207-5100 (Corporate office); 507-289-8372 (Rochester administrative office); 320-763-6139 (Local office). E-mail: jon.melander@chartercom.com. Web Site: http://www.charter.com. Also serves Alexandria Twp., Carlos, Glenwood, La Grand Twp., Long Beach & Osakis. ICA: MN0031.
TV Market Ranking: Below 100 (ALEXANDRIA, Carlos, La Grand Twp., Long Beach, Osakis, Glenwood). Franchise award date: N.A. Franchise expiration date: N.A. Began: May 1, 1966.
Channel capacity: N.A. Channels available but not in use: N.A.
Digital Basic Service
Subscribers: 4,294. Commercial subscribers: 91.
Programming (via satellite): AXS TV; BBC America; Bloomberg Television; Boomerang; CBS Sports Network; CNN en Espanol; CNN International; Discovery Life Channel; DIY Network; ESPN; ESPN Classic; ESPNews; FOX College Sports Central; FOX College Sports Pacific; Fox Sports 2; Fuse; FXM; FYI; History International; IFC; LMN; MC; NFL Network; Nick 2; Nick Jr.; Nicktoons; Outdoor Channel; Sundance TV; TeenNick; TV Guide Interactive Inc.
Fee: $49.99 installation; $14.99 monthly.
Digital Expanded Basic Service
Subscribers: N.A.
Programming (via satellite): A&E; AMC; Animal Planet; Bravo; Cartoon Network; CMT; CNBC; CNN; Comedy Central; Discovery Channel; Disney Channel; Disney XD; E! HD; ESPN; ESPN2; Food Network; Fox News Channel; Fox Sports 1; FOX Sports North; Freeform; FX; Golf Channel; Hallmark Channel; HGTV; History; HLN; Lifetime; MSNBC; MTV; MTV2; National Geographic Channel; NBCSN; Nickelodeon; Oxygen; Spike TV; Syfy; The Weather Channel; TLC; TNT; Travel Channel; truTV; Turner Classic Movies; TV Land; Univision Studios; USA Network; VH1; WE tv.
Fee: $47.99 monthly.
Digital Pay Service 1
Pay Units: N.A.
Programming (via satellite): Cinemax (multiplexed); HBO (multiplexed); HBO HD; Showtime (multiplexed); Showtime HD; Starz (multiplexed); Starz Encore (multiplexed); The Movie Channel (multiplexed).
Video-On-Demand: Yes
Pay-Per-View
iN DEMAND (delivered digitally); NHL Center Ice (delivered digitally); MLB Extra Innings (delivered digitally); Playboy TV (delivered digitally); Spice Live (delivered digitally); Spice Platinum (delivered digitally); Hot Net Plus (delivered digitally); Spice Hot (delivered digitally).
Internet Service
Operational: Yes.
Broadband Service: Charter Internet.
Telephone Service
Digital: Operational
Fee: $29.99 monthly
Miles of Plant: 230.0 (coaxial); None (fiber optic). Homes passed: 8,199.
Vice President & General Manager: John Crowley. Chief Technician: Eric Cox. Marketing Director: Bill Haarstad. Accounting Director: David Sovanski. Operations Director: Craig Stensaas. Office Operations Manager: Jon Melander.
Ownership: Charter Communications Inc. (MSO).

ALEXANDRIA—Formerly served by Viking Vision. No longer in operation. ICA: MN0392.

ALTURA—Formerly served by Midcontinent Communications. Now served by Charter Communications, EAU CLAIRE, WI [WI0011]. ICA: MN0395.

ALVARADO—Wikstrom Cable LLC, PO Box 217, Karlstad, MN 56732. Phone: 218-436-2121. Fax: 218-436-3100. E-mail: service@wiktel.com. Web Site: http://www.wiktel.com. ICA: MN0237.
TV Market Ranking: Below 100 (ALVARADO). Franchise award date: June 1, 1981. Franchise expiration date: N.A. Began: November 1, 1981.
Channel capacity: N.A. Channels available but not in use: N.A.
Basic Service
Subscribers: 50.
Programming (received off-air): KBRR (FOX) Thief River Falls; KGFE (PBS) Grand Forks; KRDK-TV (CBS, Decades, Movies!) Valley City; KVLY-TV (MeTV, NBC, This TV) Fargo; WDAZ-TV (ABC, CW) Devils Lake.
Programming (via satellite): A&E; AMC; CNBC; CNN; Comedy Central; C-SPAN; Discovery Channel; Disney Channel; ESPN; ESPN2; FOX Sports Networks; Freeform; Great American Country; Hallmark Channel; HGTV; History; Lifetime; MTV; Nickelodeon; Spike TV; TBS; The Weather Channel; TLC; TNT; Trinity Broadcasting Network (TBN); TV Land; USA Network; VH1; WGN America.
Fee: $20.00 installation; $57.99 monthly.
Pay Service 1
Pay Units: 5.
Programming (via satellite): HBO.
Fee: $10.00 installation; $11.00 monthly.
Video-On-Demand: No
Internet Service
Operational: No.
Telephone Service
None
Miles of Plant: 4.0 (coaxial); None (fiber optic). Homes passed: 120.
General Manager: Bryan Wikstrom. Controller: Carrie Kern-Taggart.
Ownership: Wikstrom Systems LLC (MSO).

ANNANDALE—Formerly served by Heart of the Lakes Cable System Inc. No longer in operation. ICA: MN0085.

APPLETON—Mediacom, 1504 2nd St SE, PO Box 110, Waseca, MN 56093. Phones: 845-695-2762; 507-835-2356. Fax: 507-835-4567. Web Site: http://www.mediacomcable.com. Also serves Clinton, Dawson, Graceville, Lake Valley, Madison & Wheaton. ICA: MN0106.
TV Market Ranking: Outside TV Markets (APPLETON, Clinton, Dawson, Graceville, Lake Valley, Madison, Wheaton). Franchise award date: N.A. Franchise expiration date: N.A. Began: January 1, 1982.
Channel capacity: N.A. Channels available but not in use: N.A.
Basic Service
Subscribers: 1,426.
Programming (received off-air): KCCO-TV (CBS) Alexandria; KDLO-TV (CBS, MNT) Florence; KPXM-TV (ION) St. Cloud; KSAX (ABC) Alexandria; KSTC-TV (Antenna TV, This TV) Minneapolis; KTCI-TV (PBS) St.

2017 Edition   D-391

Minnesota—Cable Systems

Paul; KWCM-TV (PBS) Appleton; WUCW (CW, The Country Network) Minneapolis; allband FM.
Programming (via satellite): C-SPAN; Pop; The Weather Channel; WGN America.
Programming (via translator): KARE (NBC, WeatherNation) Minneapolis; KMSP-TV (Bounce TV, Buzzr, FOX) Minneapolis; WFTC (MNT, Movies!) Minneapolis.
Fee: $52.39 installation; $42.00 monthly; $2.00 converter.

Expanded Basic Service 1
Subscribers: N.A.
Programming (via satellite): A&E; AMC; Animal Planet; Bravo; Cartoon Network; CMT; CNBC; CNN; Comedy Central; C-SPAN 2; Discovery Channel; Discovery Life Channel; Disney Channel; E! HD; ESPN; ESPN2; EWTN Global Catholic Network; Fox News Channel; Fox Sports 1; FOX Sports North; Freeform; FX; FXM; Hallmark Channel; HGTV; History; HLN; INSP; ION Television; Lifetime; MSNBC; MTV; Nickelodeon; RFD-TV; Spike TV; Syfy; TBS; TLC; TNT; Travel Channel; Trinity Broadcasting Network (TBN); truTV; Turner Classic Movies; TV Land; Univision Studios; USA Network; VH1; WE tv.
Fee: $22.95 monthly.

Digital Basic Service
Subscribers: N.A.
Programming (via satellite): 52MX; AXS TV; BBC America; Bloomberg Television; Cinelatino; Cloo; CNN en Espanol; Destination America; Discovery Kids Channel; Discovery Life Channel; ESPN Deportes; ESPN HD; ESPN2 HD; ESPNews; Fox Deportes; Fox Sports 2; Fuse; FXM; FYI; Golf Channel; GSN; HD Theater; History en Espanol; History International; IFC; Investigation Discovery; LMN; MC; MTV Classic; MTV Hits; MTV2; Nat Geo WILD; National Geographic Channel; Nick Jr.; Nicktoons; Outdoor Channel; OWN: Oprah Winfrey Network; Reelz; Science Channel; TeenNick; Tr3s; Turner Classic Movies; TVG Network; ViendoMovies.

Pay Service 1
Pay Units: N.A.
Programming (via satellite): Showtime.

Digital Pay Service 1
Pay Units: N.A.
Programming (via satellite): Cinemax (multiplexed); Flix; HBO (multiplexed); HBO HD; Showtime (multiplexed); Showtime HD; Starz (multiplexed); Starz Encore (multiplexed); Sundance TV; The Movie Channel (multiplexed); The Movie Channel HD.
Fee: $7.00 monthly (Cinemax), $11.00 monthly each (all others).

Video-On-Demand: No

Pay-Per-View
iN DEMAND (delivered digitally); Spice: Xcess (delivered digitally); Pleasure (delivered digitally); Playboy TV (delivered digitally); Fresh (delivered digitally); SexSee (delivered digitally).

Internet Service
Operational: Yes.
Broadband Service: Mediacom High Speed Internet.

Telephone Service
Digital: Operational
Miles of Plant: 59.0 (coaxial); None (fiber optic). Homes passed: 3,971.
Vice President: Bill Jensen. Vice President, Financial Reporting: Kenneth J. Kohrs. Marketing & Sales Director: Lori Huberty. Engineering Manager: Kraig Kaiser.
Ownership: Mediacom LLC (MSO).

ARGYLE—Wikstrom Cable LLC, PO Box 217, Karlstad, MN 56732. Phone: 218-436-2121. Fax: 218-436-3100. E-mail: service@wiktel.com. Web Site: http://www.wiktel.com. ICA: MN0203.
TV Market Ranking: Below 100 (ARGYLE). Franchise award date: October 23, 1980. Franchise expiration date: N.A. Began: January 1, 1981.
Channel capacity: N.A. Channels available but not in use: N.A.

Basic Service
Subscribers: 169.
Programming (received off-air): KBRR (FOX) Thief River Falls; KGFE (PBS) Grand Forks; KRDK-TV (CBS, Decades, Movies!) Valley City; KVLY-TV (MeTV, NBC, This TV) Fargo; WDAZ-TV (ABC, CW) Devils Lake; allband FM.
Programming (via satellite): A&E; AMC; CMT; CNBC; CNN; Comedy Central; C-SPAN; Discovery Channel; Disney Channel; ESPN; ESPN2; Fox Sports 1; FOX Sports Networks; Freeform; FX; Great American Country; Hallmark Channel; HGTV; History; Lifetime; MTV; Nickelodeon; Outdoor Channel; Spike TV; TBS; The Weather Channel; TLC; TNT; Trinity Broadcasting Network (TBN); TV Land; USA Network; VH1; WGN America.
Fee: $20.00 installation; $57.99 monthly.

Pay Service 1
Pay Units: 7.
Programming (via satellite): HBO.
Fee: $10.00 installation; $11.00 monthly.

Video-On-Demand: No

Internet Service
Operational: No.

Telephone Service
None
Miles of Plant: 5.0 (coaxial); None (fiber optic). Homes passed: 250.
General Manager: Bryan Wikstrom. Controller: Carrie Kern-Taggart.
Ownership: Wikstrom Systems LLC (MSO).

AUSTIN—Charter Communications, 12405 Powerscourt Dr, St. Louis, MO 63131. Phones: 636-207-5100 (Corporate office); 507-289-8372 (Rochester administrative office); 314-543-2236. Fax: 507-437-7119. Web Site: http://www.charter.com. Also serves Albert Lea. ICA: MN0019.
TV Market Ranking: Below 100 (AUSTIN, Albert Lea). Franchise award date: January 1, 1971. Franchise expiration date: N.A. Began: March 1, 1973.
Channel capacity: N.A. Channels available but not in use: N.A.

Digital Basic Service
Subscribers: 8,892.
Programming (via satellite): AXS TV; BBC America; Bloomberg Television; Boomerang; CBS Sports Network; CNN en Espanol; CNN International; Discovery Digital Networks; DIY Network; ESPN Classic; ESPNews; FOX College Sports Central; FOX College Sports Pacific; Fox Sports 2; Fuse; FXM; FYI; History International; IFC; LMN; MC; NFL Network; Nick 2; Nick Jr.; Nicktoons; Outdoor Channel; Sundance TV; TeenNick; Turner Classic Movies.
Fee: $49.99 installation; $26.99 monthly.

Digital Expanded Basic Service
Subscribers: N.A.
Programming (via satellite): A&E; AMC; Animal Planet; BET; Bravo; Cartoon Network; CMT; CNBC; CNN; Comedy Central; Discovery Channel; Disney Channel; Disney XD; E! HD; ESPN; ESPN2; EVINE Live; EWTN Global Catholic Network; Food Network; Fox News Channel; Fox Sports 1; FOX Sports North; Freeform; FX; Golf Channel; GSN; Hallmark Channel; HGTV; History; HLN; INSP; Lifetime; MSNBC; MTV; MTV2; National Geographic Channel; NBCSN; Nickelodeon; Oxygen; Spike TV; Syfy; TBS; The Weather Channel; TLC; TNT; Travel Channel; truTV; TV Land; Univision Studios; USA Network; VH1; WE tv.
Fee: $47.99 monthly.

Digital Pay Service 1
Pay Units: N.A.
Programming (via satellite): Cinemax (multiplexed); Flix; HBO (multiplexed); HBO HD; Showtime (multiplexed); Showtime HD; Starz (multiplexed); Starz Encore (multiplexed); The Movie Channel.
Fee: $9.95 monthly (Cinemax or HBO), $11.95 monthly (Showtime).

Video-On-Demand: Yes

Pay-Per-View
iN DEMAND (delivered digitally); NHL Center Ice (delivered digitally); MLB Extra Innings (delivered digitally); Playboy TV (delivered digitally); Spice Live (delivered digitally); Spice Platinum (delivered digitally); Hot Net Plus (delivered digitally); Spice Hot (delivered digitally).

Internet Service
Operational: Yes.
Subscribers: 7,805.
Broadband Service: Charter Internet.
Fee: $29.99 monthly.

Telephone Service
Digital: Operational
Subscribers: 4,946.
Fee: $29.99 monthly.
Miles of Plant: 405.0 (coaxial); 169.0 (fiber optic). Homes passed: 22,368.
Vice President & General Manager: John Crowley. Marketing Director: Bill Haarstad. Technical Operations Director: Darin Helgeson. Accounting Director: David Sovanski. Operations Director: Craig Stensaas. Technical Supervisor: Ray Madrigal. Office Manager: Sherry Brown.
Ownership: Charter Communications Inc. (MSO).

AVON—Formerly served by US Cable of Coastal Texas LP. Now served by Midco, CAMBRIDGE, MN [MN0016]. ICA: MN0268.

BABBITT—Midcontinent Communications. Now served by ELY, MN [MN0060]. ICA: MN0116.

BADGER—Sjoberg's Cable TV Inc, 315 Main Ave North, Thief River Falls, MN 56701-1905. Phones: 800-828-8808; 218-681-3044. Fax: 218-681-6801. E-mail: office1@mncable.net; sjobergs@mncable.net. Web Site: http://trf.mncable.net. ICA: MN0269.
TV Market Ranking: Outside TV Markets (BADGER). Franchise award date: January 1, 1990. Franchise expiration date: N.A. Began: January 1, 1990.
Channel capacity: N.A. Channels available but not in use: N.A.

Basic Service
Subscribers: 98.
Programming (received off-air): KAWE (PBS) Bemidji; KBRR (FOX) Thief River Falls; KCPM (MNT) Grand Forks; KRDK-TV (CBS, Decades, Movies!) Valley City; KVLY-TV (MeTV, NBC, This TV) Fargo; WDAZ-TV (ABC, CW) Devils Lake.
Programming (via satellite): CNN; ESPN; TBS; various Canadian stations.
Fee: $25.00 installation; $55.92 monthly.

Expanded Basic Service 1
Subscribers: N.A.
Programming (via satellite): A&E; Animal Planet; Cartoon Network; CMT; CNBC; Comedy Central; CW PLUS; Discovery Channel; E! HD; ESPN2; Food Network; Fox News Channel; FOX Sports Networks; Freeform; FX; HGTV; History; Lifetime; MSNBC; MTV; Nickelodeon; Spike TV; Syfy; The Weather Channel; TLC; TNT; Turner Classic Movies; TV Land; USA Network; WGN America.
Fee: $23.71 monthly.

Digital Basic Service
Subscribers: N.A.
Programming (via satellite): A&E HD; AXS TV; BBC America; Bloomberg Television; Bravo; CBS Sports Network; Chiller; Cloo; CMT; CNN HD; Cooking Channel; Daystar TV Network; Destination America; Discovery Channel HD; Discovery Kids Channel; Disney XD; DIY Network; DMX Music; ESPN Classic; ESPN HD; ESPN2 HD; ESPNews; ESPNU; EVINE Live; EWTN Global Catholic Network; Food Network HD; Fox Business Network; FOX College Sports Central; FOX College Sports Pacific; Fox Sports 1; FSN HD; FXM; FYI; Golf Channel; Great American Country; GSN; Hallmark Channel; HGTV HD; History HD; History International; HLN; HRTV; IFC; Investigation Discovery; LMN; MTV Classic; MTV Hits; MTV2; Nat Geo WILD; National Geographic Channel; NBCSN; Nick Jr.; Nicktoons; Outdoor Channel; Outdoor Channel 2 HD; Ovation; OWN: Oprah Winfrey Network; Oxygen; RFD-TV; Science Channel; Sprout; Sundance TV; Syfy HD; TBS HD; TeenNick; Tennis Channel; The Word Network; TNT HD; TVG Network; Universal HD; UP; USA Network HD; Versus HD; VH1 Soul; WE tv.

Pay Service 1
Pay Units: N.A.
Programming (via satellite): HBO.
Fee: $11.00 monthly.

Digital Pay Service 1
Pay Units: N.A.
Programming (via satellite): Cinemax (multiplexed); Cinemax HD; HBO (multiplexed); HBO HD; Showtime (multiplexed); Starz (multiplexed); Starz Encore (multiplexed); The Movie Channel (multiplexed).
Fee: $8.00 monthly (Starz/Encore), $9.00 monthly (Cinemax or Showtime/TMC), $11.00 monthly (HBO).

Video-On-Demand: No

Internet Service
Operational: No.

Telephone Service
None
Miles of Plant: 4.0 (coaxial); None (fiber optic). Homes passed: 150.
President & General Manager: Richard J. Sjoberg. Chief Technician: Jerry Seim.
Ownership: Sjoberg's Cable TV Inc. (MSO).

BAGLEY—Bagley Public Utilities, 18 Main Ave South, PO Box M, Bagley, MN 56621. Phone: 218-694-2300. Fax: 218-694-6632. E-mail: vfletcher@bagleymn.us. Web Site: http://www.bagleymn.us. ICA: MN0133.
TV Market Ranking: Below 100 (BAGLEY). Franchise award date: February 1, 1976. Franchise expiration date: N.A. Began: February 1, 1976.
Channel capacity: N.A. Channels available but not in use: N.A.

Basic Service
Subscribers: 443.
Programming (received off-air): KAWE (PBS) Bemidji; KBRR (FOX) Thief River Falls; KCCW-TV (CBS) Walker; KRDK-TV

Cable Systems—Minnesota

(CBS, Decades, Movies!) Valley City; KVLY-TV (MeTV, NBC, This TV) Fargo; KVRR (Antenna TV, FOX) Fargo; WDAY-TV (ABC, CW) Fargo; allband FM.
Programming (via microwave): KMSP-TV (Bounce TV, Buzzr, FOX) Minneapolis.
Programming (via satellite): A&E; Bravo; CMT; CNN; Discovery Channel; Disney Channel; DIY Network; ESPN; FOX Sports North; Freeform; Hallmark Channel; HGTV; History; Lifetime; Outdoor Channel; QVC; Spike TV; TBS; The Weather Channel; TLC; TNT; Trinity Broadcasting Network (TBN); Turner Classic Movies; WGN America.
Fee: $50.00 installation; $48.00 monthly.
Pay Service 1
Pay Units: 42.
Programming (via satellite): HBO.
Fee: $13.00 monthly.
Internet Service
Operational: No.
Telephone Service
None
Miles of Plant: 15.0 (coaxial); None (fiber optic). Homes passed: 740.
General Manager: Michael Jensen. Business Manager: Vicky Fletcher. Chief Technician: Kraig Fontaine.
Ownership: Bagley Public Utilities.

BALATON—Midco, PO Box 5010, Sioux Falls, SD 57117. Phones: 800-888-1300; 605-229-1775. Fax: 605-229-0478. Web Site: http://www.midcocomm.com. ICA: MN0386.
TV Market Ranking: Outside TV Markets (BALATON).
Channel capacity: N.A. Channels available but not in use: N.A.
Basic Service
Subscribers: 95. Commercial subscribers: 6.
Programming (received off-air): KARE (NBC, WeatherNation) Minneapolis; KELO-TV (CBS, MNT) Sioux Falls; KMSP-TV (Bounce TV, Buzzr, FOX) Minneapolis; KRWF (ABC) Redwood Falls; KSFY-TV (ABC, CW) Sioux Falls; KWCM-TV (PBS) Appleton; WCCO-TV (CBS, Decades) Minneapolis; WFTC (MNT, Movies!) Minneapolis; WUCW (CW, The Country Network) Minneapolis.
Programming (via satellite): C-SPAN; C-SPAN 2; EWTN Global Catholic Network; INSP; QVC; WGN America.
Fee: $29.99 installation; $19.95 monthly.
Expanded Basic Service 1
Subscribers: N.A.
Programming (via satellite): A&E; AMC; Animal Planet; Bravo; Cartoon Network; CMT; CNBC; CNN; Comedy Central; Discovery Channel; Disney Channel; E! HD; ESPN; ESPN2; Food Network; Fox News Channel; FOX Sports North; Freeform; FX; Great American Country; HGTV; History; HLN; Lifetime; MSNBC; MTV; Nickelodeon; Oxygen; Spike TV; Syfy; TBS; The Weather Channel; TLC; TNT; Travel Channel; Turner Classic Movies; TV Land; USA Network; VH1.
Fee: $47.99 monthly.
Digital Basic Service
Subscribers: N.A.
Programming (via satellite): BBC America; Bloomberg Television; Discovery Digital Networks; DIY Network; Fuse; FYI; GSN; History International; IFC; MC; Nick 2; Nick Jr.; Nicktoons; Sundance TV; TeenNick; TV Guide Interactive Inc.; WE tv.
Digital Pay Service 1
Pay Units: N.A.
Programming (via satellite): Cinemax (multiplexed); HBO (multiplexed); Showtime (multiplexed); Starz (multiplexed); Starz Encore; The Movie Channel (multiplexed).
Video-On-Demand: No
Pay-Per-View
iN DEMAND (delivered digitally); Hot Choice (delivered digitally).
Internet Service
Operational: No.
Telephone Service
None
Miles of Plant: 5.0 (coaxial); None (fiber optic). Homes passed: 330.
Programming Director: Wynne Haakenstad.
Ownership: Midcontinent Communications (MSO).

BARNESVILLE—Barnesville Cable TV, 102 Front St North, PO Box 550, Barnesville, MN 56514-0550. Phones: 800-354-2292; 218-354-2292. Fax: 218-354-2472. E-mail: klauer@bvillemn.com. Web Site: http://www.barnesvillemn.com/solutions/city-utilities/cable. ICA: MN0107.
TV Market Ranking: 98 (BARNESVILLE). Franchise award date: N.A. Franchise expiration date: N.A. Began: January 1, 1981.
Channel capacity: N.A. Channels available but not in use: N.A.
Basic Service
Subscribers: N.A.
Programming (received off-air): KFME (PBS) Fargo; KMSP-TV (Bounce TV, Buzzr, FOX) Minneapolis; KRDK-TV (CBS, Decades, Movies!) Valley City; KVLY-TV (MeTV, NBC, This TV) Fargo; KVRR (Antenna TV, FOX) Fargo; WDAY-TV (ABC, CW) Fargo.
Programming (via satellite): Animal Planet; Bloomberg Television; Cartoon Network; CMT; CNN; Comedy Central; E! HD; ESPN Classic; ESPN2; ESPNews; Food Network; Fox News Channel; Fox Sports 1; FOX Sports North; FX; Golf Channel; GSN; Hallmark Channel; HGTV; HLN; MSNBC; MTV; Outdoor Channel; QVC; Spike TV; TBS; truTV; Turner Classic Movies; TV Land; VH1; WGN America.
Fee: $49.95 installation.
Expanded Basic Service 1
Subscribers: N.A.
Programming (via satellite): A&E; AMC; Discovery Channel; ESPN; Freeform; History; Lifetime; Nickelodeon; Syfy; The Weather Channel; TLC; TNT; USA Network.
Fee: $44.00 monthly.
Pay Service 1
Pay Units: N.A.
Programming (via satellite): Cinemax; HBO; Starz; Starz Encore (multiplexed).
Fee: $15.00 installation; $7.95 - $14.75 monthly (each).
Video-On-Demand: No
Internet Service
Operational: No, DSL.
Telephone Service
Analog: Operational
Miles of Plant: 24.0 (coaxial); 5.0 (fiber optic). Homes passed: 980.
General Manager: Guy Swenson. Chief Technician: Mike Pearson. Program Director: Ione Hammer. Marketing Director: Karen Lauer. Technical Assistant: Diane Hanson.
Ownership: City of Barnesville.

BARNESVILLE—Formerly served by Sprint Corp. No longer in operation. ICA: MN0271.

BARNUM—SCI Broadband, 111 Tobies Mill Pl, PO Box 810, Hinckley, MN 55037-0810. Phones: 800-222-9809; 320-384-7442. Fax: 320-279-8085. E-mail: sales@scibroadband.com. Web Site: http://www.scibroadband.com. ICA: MN0225.
TV Market Ranking: 89 (BARNUM). Franchise award date: April 10, 1989. Franchise expiration date: N.A. Began: April 1, 1990.
Channel capacity: N.A. Channels available but not in use: N.A.
Basic Service
Subscribers: 107.
Programming (received off-air): KBJR-TV (CBS, MNT, NBC) Superior; KDLH (CBS, CW) Duluth; KQDS-TV (Antenna TV, FOX) Duluth; WDIO-DT (ABC, MeTV) Duluth; WDSE (PBS) Duluth; WPIX (Antenna TV, CW, This TV) New York.
Programming (via satellite): A&E; Animal Planet; CNBC; CNN; Comedy Central; C-SPAN; Discovery Channel; Disney Channel; E! HD; ESPN; ESPN2; Fox News Channel; FOX Sports Networks; Freeform; Great American Country; HGTV; History; HLN; Lifetime; MTV; Nickelodeon; QVC; Spike TV; Syfy; TBS; The Weather Channel; TLC; TNT; Turner Classic Movies; TV Land; USA Network; VH1; WGN America.
Fee: $39.95 installation; $17.95 monthly.
Digital Basic Service
Subscribers: N.A.
Programming (via satellite): BBC America; Bloomberg Television; Cloo; Discovery Life Channel; DMX Music; ESPN Classic; ESPNews; Fox Sports 1; Fuse; FXM; FYI; Golf Channel; History International; INSP; National Geographic Channel; NBCSN; Outdoor Channel; Trinity Broadcasting Network (TBN); WE tv.
Digital Pay Service 1
Pay Units: N.A.
Programming (via satellite): Cinemax (multiplexed); Flix; HBO (multiplexed); Showtime (multiplexed); Starz (multiplexed); Starz Encore (multiplexed); Sundance TV; The Movie Channel (multiplexed).
Video-On-Demand: No
Pay-Per-View
ESPN Now (delivered digitally); Sports PPV (delivered digitally).
Internet Service
Operational: Yes. Began: April 1, 2004.
Broadband Service: SCI Broadband.
Fee: $24.95 monthly.
Telephone Service
Digital: Operational
Miles of Plant: 8.0 (coaxial); 1.0 (fiber optic). Homes passed: 299.
President: Ron Savage. General Manager: Mike Danielson. Chief Technician: Pat McCabe. Customer Service Manager: Donna Erickson.
Ownership: Savage Communications Inc. (MSO).

BARRETT—Runestone Cable TV, 100 Runestone Dr, PO Box 336, Hoffman, MN 56339. Phones: 218-458-6602; 320-986-2013; 800-986-6602. Fax: 320-986-2050. E-mail: help@runestone.net. Web Site: http://www.runestone.net. Also serves Cyrus, Donnelly, Elbow Lake, Erdahl, Herman, Hoffman, Kensington, Lowry, Norcross, Tintah & Wendell. ICA: MN0233.
TV Market Ranking: Below 100 (BARRETT, Cyrus, Donnelly, Elbow Lake, Erdahl, Hoffman, Kensington, Lowry, Norcross); Outside TV Markets (Herman, Tintah, Wendell). Franchise award date: N.A. Franchise expiration date: N.A. Began: December 1, 1984.
Channel capacity: N.A. Channels available but not in use: N.A.
Basic Service
Subscribers: 1,154.
Programming (received off-air): KARE (NBC, WeatherNation) Minneapolis; KCCO-TV (CBS) Alexandria; KMSP-TV (Bounce TV, Buzzr, FOX) Minneapolis; KSAX (ABC) Alexandria; KSTC-TV (Antenna TV, This TV) Minneapolis; KVLY-TV (MeTV, NBC, This TV) Fargo; KWCM-TV (PBS) Appleton; WFTC (MNT, Movies!) Minneapolis; WUCW (CW, The Country Network) Minneapolis.
Programming (via satellite): C-SPAN; QVC.
Fee: $35.00 installation; $50.98 monthly.
Expanded Basic Service 1
Subscribers: N.A.
Programming (via satellite): A&E; AMC; Animal Planet; Cartoon Network; CMT; CNN; Comedy Central; Discovery Channel; Disney Channel; ESPN; ESPN2; Fox News Channel; FOX Sports North; Freeform; FXM; Hallmark Channel; HGTV; History; HLN; ION Television; Lifetime; MTV; National Geographic Channel; Nickelodeon; Spike TV; Syfy; TBS; The Weather Channel; TLC; TNT; Travel Channel; Trinity Broadcasting Network (TBN); TV Land; USA Network; VH1; WGN America.
Fee: $33.74 monthly.
Digital Basic Service
Subscribers: N.A.
Programming (via satellite): Bloomberg Television; CMT; Destination America; Discovery Kids Channel; Discovery Life Channel; DMX Music; ESPN Classic; ESPNews; Fox Sports 1; Golf Channel; GSN; Investigation Discovery; MTV Classic; NBCSN; Nick Jr.; Nicktoons; Outdoor Channel; OWN; Oprah Winfrey Network; Science Channel; TeenNick; Turner Classic Movies.
Pay Service 1
Pay Units: 17.
Programming (via satellite): Cinemax; HBO; Showtime.
Fee: $15.00 installation; $8.00 monthly (Cinemax), $9.00 monthly (Showtime), $10.00 monthly (HBO).
Digital Pay Service 1
Pay Units: N.A.
Programming (via satellite): Cinemax (multiplexed); HBO (multiplexed); Showtime (multiplexed); Starz (multiplexed); Starz Encore (multiplexed); The Movie Channel (multiplexed).
Fee: $10.95 monthly (Starz/Encore), $12.95 monthly (Showtime/TMC), $13.95 monthly (Cinemax/HBO).
Video-On-Demand: No
Internet Service
Operational: No, DSL & dial-up.
Telephone Service
Analog: Operational
Miles of Plant: 36.0 (coaxial); None (fiber optic). Homes passed: 2,032.
Secretary-Treasurer: John M. Kapphahn. General Manager: Lee Maier. Plant Manager: Kent Hedstrom. Chief Technician: Dave Redepenning.
Ownership: Runestone Telecom Association (MSO).

BAUDETTE—Sjoberg's Cable TV Inc, 315 Main Ave North, Thief River Falls, MN 56701-1905. Phones: 800-828-8808; 218-681-3044. Fax: 218-681-6801. E-mail: office1@mncable.net; sjobergs@mncable.net. Web Site: http://trf.mncable.net. Also serves Spooner, Wabanica & Wheeler. ICA: MN0091.
TV Market Ranking: Outside TV Markets (BAUDETTE, Spooner, Wabanica, Wheeler). Franchise award date: April

Minnesota—Cable Systems

1, 1974. Franchise expiration date: N.A. Began: November 11, 1974.
Channel capacity: N.A. Channels available but not in use: N.A.

Basic Service
Subscribers: 714.
Programming (received off-air): KAWE (PBS) Bemidji; KRDK-TV (CBS, Decades, Movies!) Valley City; KVLY-TV (MeTV, NBC, This TV) Fargo; WDAZ-TV (ABC, CW) Devils Lake; allband FM.
Programming (via satellite): CNN; ESPN; Freeform; TBS; USA Network; various Canadian stations.
Fee: $25.00 installation; $53.33 monthly.

Expanded Basic Service 1
Subscribers: N.A.
Programming (received off-air): KCPM (MNT) Grand Forks; KVRR (Antenna TV, FOX) Fargo.
Programming (via satellite): A&E; Animal Planet; Cartoon Network; CMT; CNBC; Comedy Central; CW PLUS; Discovery Channel; E! HD; ESPN2; EWTN Global Catholic Network; Food Network; Fox News Channel; FOX Sports North; FX; HGTV; History; Lifetime; MSNBC; MTV; Nickelodeon; Spike TV; Syfy; The Weather Channel; TLC; TNT; Turner Classic Movies; TV Land; WGN America.
Fee: $21.12 monthly.

Digital Basic Service
Subscribers: N.A.
Programming (via satellite): BBC America; Bloomberg Television; Bravo; Cloo; CMT; Daystar TV Network; Destination America; Discovery Kids Channel; Discovery Life Channel; Disney XD; DMX Music; ESPN Classic; ESPNews; EVINE Live; Fox Business Network; FOX College Sports Central; FOX College Sports Pacific; Fox Sports 1; FXM; FYI; Golf Channel; Great American Country; GSN; History International; IFC; Investigation Discovery; LMN; MTV Classic; MTV Hits; MTV2; Nat Geo WILD; National Geographic Channel; NBCSN; Nick Jr.; Nicktoons; Outdoor Channel; Ovation; OWN: Oprah Winfrey Network; RFD-TV; Science Channel; Sprout; Sundance TV; TeenNick; The Word Network; Trinity Broadcasting Network (TBN); TVG Network; UP; VH1 Soul; WE tv.

Pay Service 1
Pay Units: N.A.
Programming (via satellite): HBO.
Fee: $11.00 monthly.

Digital Pay Service 1
Pay Units: N.A.
Programming (via satellite): Cinemax (multiplexed); HBO (multiplexed); Showtime (multiplexed); Starz (multiplexed); Starz Encore (multiplexed); The Movie Channel (multiplexed).
Fee: $8.00 monthly (Starz/Encore), $9.00 monthly (Cinemax or Showtime/TMC), $11.00 monthly (HBO).

Video-On-Demand: No

Pay-Per-View
iN DEMAND (delivered digitally).

Internet Service
Operational: Yes.
Broadband Service: Sjoberg's Cable TV.
Fee: $19.95 monthly; $10.65 modem lease; $69.99 modem purchase.

Telephone Service
None
Miles of Plant: 24.0 (coaxial); 7.0 (fiber optic). Homes passed: 1,050.
President & General Manager: Richard Sjoberg. Chief Technician: Jerry Seim.
Ownership: Sjoberg's Cable TV Inc. (MSO).

BELGRADE—Mediacom. Now served by MORRIS, MN [MN0210]. ICA: MN0176.

BELLE PLAINE—Mediacom. Now served by ST. PETER (formerly Waseca), MN [MN0043]. ICA: MN0102.

BELVIEW—Clara City Telephone Co, 227 South Main St, PO Box 800, Clara City, MN 56222. Phone: 320-847-2211. Fax: 320-847-2736. E-mail: bruce@hcinet.net. Web Site: http://www.hcinet.net. ICA: MN0238.
TV Market Ranking: Below 100 (BELVIEW). Franchise award date: July 12, 1984. Franchise expiration date: N.A. Began: July 1, 1985.
Channel capacity: N.A. Channels available but not in use: N.A.

Basic Service
Subscribers: 30.
Programming (received off-air): KEYC-TV (CBS, FOX) Mankato; KWCM-TV (PBS) Appleton; allband FM.
Programming (via satellite): A&E; AMC; CNN; Discovery Channel; ESPN; ESPN2; FOX Sports Networks; Freeform; Hallmark Channel; History; Lifetime; Nickelodeon; QVC; Spike TV; TBS; The Weather Channel; TLC; TNT; TV Land; USA Network; VH1.
Programming (via translator): KARE (NBC, WeatherNation) Minneapolis; KMSP-TV (Bounce TV, Buzzr, FOX) Minneapolis; KSTP-TV (ABC, MeTV) St. Paul; KTCA-TV (PBS) St. Paul; WCCO-TV (CBS, Decades) Minneapolis; WFTC (MNT, Movies!) Minneapolis; WUCW (CW, The Country Network) Minneapolis.
Fee: $20.00 installation; $48.50 monthly.

Pay Service 1
Pay Units: N.A.
Programming (via satellite): The Movie Channel.
Fee: $10.00 installation; $10.00 monthly.

Internet Service
Operational: No.

Telephone Service
None
Miles of Plant: 4.0 (coaxial); None (fiber optic). Homes passed: 150.
Treasurer & General Manager: Bruce Hanson.
Ownership: Hanson Communications Inc. (MSO).

BEMIDJI—Midco, PO Box 5010, Sioux Falls, SD 57117. Phones: 800-888-1300; 605-229-1775. Fax: 605-229-0478. Web Site: http://www.midcocomm.com. Also serves Beltrami County (portions), Cass Lake, Eckles, Frohn Twp., Grant Valley Twp., Northern Twp., Pike Bay Twp., Port Hope Twp., Turtle River & Wilton. ICA: MN0033.
TV Market Ranking: Below 100 (BEMIDJI, Cass Lake, Eckles, Frohn Twp., Northern Twp., Pike Bay Twp., Port Hope Twp., Turtle River, Wilton, Beltrami County (portions)); Outside TV Markets (Beltrami County (portions)). Franchise award date: January 1, 1968. Franchise expiration date: N.A. Began: January 1, 1971.
Channel capacity: N.A. Channels available but not in use: N.A.

Basic Service
Subscribers: 3,101.
Programming (received off-air): KARE (NBC, WeatherNation) Minneapolis; KAWE (PBS) Bemidji; KCCW-TV (CBS) Walker; KMSP-TV (Bounce TV, Buzzr, FOX) Minneapolis; KSAX (ABC) Alexandria; KSTC-TV (Antenna TV, This TV) Minneapolis; KVLY-TV (MeTV, NBC, This TV) Fargo; WDIO-DT (ABC, MeTV) Duluth; WFTC (MNT, Movies!) Minneapolis.
Programming (via satellite): C-SPAN; INSP; ION Television; Pop; QVC; WGN America.
Fee: $29.99 installation; $19.95 monthly.

Expanded Basic Service 1
Subscribers: N.A.
Programming (via satellite): A&E; AMC; Animal Planet; Bravo; Cartoon Network; CMT; CNBC; CNN; Comedy Central; C-SPAN 2; Discovery Channel; Disney Channel; Disney XD; E! HD; ESPN; ESPN Classic; ESPN2; Food Network; Fox News Channel; Fox Sports 1; FOX Sports North; Freeform; FX; Golf Channel; GSN; Hallmark Channel; HGTV; History; HLN; Lifetime; MSNBC; MTV; National Geographic Channel; NBCSN; Nickelodeon; Outdoor Channel; Oxygen; Spike TV; Syfy; TBS; The Weather Channel; TLC; TNT; Travel Channel; Trinity Broadcasting Network (TBN); truTV; Turner Classic Movies; TV Land; USA Network; VH1; WE tv.
Fee: $47.99 monthly.

Digital Basic Service
Subscribers: N.A.
Programming (via satellite): BBC America; Bloomberg Television; Boomerang; CNN en Espanol; CNN International; Discovery Digital Networks; DIY Network; ESPNews; FOX College Sports Central; FOX College Sports Pacific; Fox Sports 2; FXM; FYI; History International; IFC; LMN; MC; NFL Network; Nick 2; Nick Jr.; Nicktoons; Sundance TV; TeenNick; TV Guide Interactive Inc.

Digital Pay Service 1
Pay Units: N.A.
Programming (via satellite): Cinemax (multiplexed); Flix; HBO (multiplexed); Showtime (multiplexed); Starz (multiplexed); Starz Encore (multiplexed); The Movie Channel (multiplexed).

Video-On-Demand: No

Pay-Per-View
iN DEMAND (delivered digitally); Playboy TV (delivered digitally); Spice Live (delivered digitally); Spice Platinum (delivered digitally); Hot Net Plus (delivered digitally); Spice Hot (delivered digitally).

Internet Service
Operational: Yes. Began: March 1, 2002.
Broadband Service: Charter Internet.
Fee: $29.99 monthly.

Telephone Service
None
Miles of Plant: 327.0 (coaxial); None (fiber optic). Homes passed: 10,609.
Programming Director: Wynne Haakenstad.
Ownership: Midcontinent Communications (MSO).

BENSON—Charter Communications. Now served by WILLMAR, MN [MN0018]. ICA: MN0074.

BIG FALLS—Formerly served by Arvig. No longer in operation. ICA: MN0219.

BIGELOW—Formerly served by American Telecasting of America Inc. No longer in operation. ICA: MN0272.

BIGFORK—Arvig, 160 2nd Ave. SW, Perham, MN 56573. Phones: 888-992-7844; 218-743-3144 (Bigfork office); 218-346-4227. Fax: 218-338-3297. E-mail: answers@arvig.com. Web Site: http://arvig.com. ICA: MN0220.
TV Market Ranking: Outside TV Markets (BIGFORK). Franchise award date: N.A. Franchise expiration date: N.A. Began: October 15, 1990.
Channel capacity: N.A. Channels available but not in use: N.A.

Basic Service
Subscribers: 65.
Programming (received off-air): KAWE (PBS) Bemidji; KBJR-TV (CBS, MNT, NBC) Superior; KCCW-TV (CBS) Walker; KDLH (CBS, CW) Duluth; KVRR (Antenna TV, FOX) Fargo; WDIO-DT (ABC, MeTV) Duluth; WIRT-DT (ABC, MeTV) Hibbing.
Programming (via satellite): A&E; AMC; CNN; Discovery Channel; Disney Channel; ESPN; FOX Sports Midwest; Freeform; History; HLN; Lifetime; Nickelodeon; QVC; Spike TV; TBS; The Weather Channel; TNT; Trinity Broadcasting Network (TBN); TV Land; USA Network; WGN America.
Fee: $55.00 installation; $54.95 monthly; $2.00 converter.

Pay Service 1
Pay Units: 8.
Programming (via satellite): HBO; Showtime.
Fee: $12.95 monthly (Showtime), $17.95 monthly (HBO).

Video-On-Demand: No

Internet Service
Operational: Yes, DSL.
Fee: $42.95-$125.95 monthly.

Telephone Service
Analog: Operational
Fee: $19.20 monthly
Miles of Plant: None (coaxial); 1,748.0 (fiber optic). Homes passed: 2,996.
Chief Operating Officer & Vice President: David Arvig.
Ownership: Tekstar Communications Inc. (MSO).

BLACKDUCK—Paul Bunyan Communications. This cable system has converted to IPTV. Now served by SOLWAY, MN [MN5083]. ICA: MN0164.

BLOOMING PRAIRIE—Mediacom. Now served by CANNON FALLS, MN [MN0076]. ICA: MN0122.

BLOOMINGTON—Formerly served by Time Warner Cable. Now served by Comcast Cable, MINNEAPOLIS, MN [MN0001]. ICA: MN0273.

BLUE EARTH—BEVCOMM, 123 West Seventh St, Blue Earth, MN 56013. Phones: 800-473-1442; 507-526-2822. E-mail: info@bevcomm.net. Web Site: http://www.bevcomm.net. Also serves Elmore & Kiester. ICA: MN0058.
TV Market Ranking: Outside TV Markets (Elmore, Kiester).
Channel capacity: N.A. Channels available but not in use: N.A.

Basic Service
Subscribers: 726.
Fee: $35.95 monthly.

Expanded Basic Service 1
Subscribers: N.A.
Fee: $64.95 monthly.

Internet Service
Operational: Yes.
Fee: $9.95-$149.95 monthly.

Telephone Service
Digital: Operational
Fee: $29.83 monthly
Miles of Plant: 48.0 (coaxial); 56.0 (fiber optic). Homes passed: 2,000.
President & Chief Executive Officer: Bill Eckles.
Ownership: BEVCOMM.

BOVEY—SCI Broadband, 111 Tobies Mill Pl, PO Box 810, Hinckley, MN 55037-0810. Phones: 800-222-9809; 320-384-7442.

Fax: 320-279-8085. E-mail: sales@scibroadband.com. Web Site: http://www.scibroadband.com. Also serves Coleraine. ICA: MN0112.
TV Market Ranking: Below 100 (BOVEY, Coleraine). Franchise award date: N.A. Franchise expiration date: N.A. Began: July 10, 1965.
Channel capacity: N.A. Channels available but not in use: N.A.
Basic Service
Subscribers: 415.
Programming (received off-air): KAWE (PBS) Bemidji; KBJR-TV (CBS, MNT, NBC) Superior; KCCW-TV (CBS) Walker; KDLH (CBS, CW) Duluth; KMSP-TV (Bounce TV, Buzzr, FOX) Minneapolis; KVRR (Antenna TV, FOX) Fargo; WDIO-DT (ABC, MeTV) Duluth; WDSE (PBS) Duluth; WIRT-DT (ABC, MeTV) Hibbing; 1 FM.
Programming (via satellite): A&E; AMC; Animal Planet; Cartoon Network; CMT; CNBC; CNN; C-SPAN; Discovery Channel; Disney Channel; ESPN; ESPN2; EWTN Global Catholic Network; FOX Sports Midwest; Freeform; Hallmark Channel; HGTV; History; HLN; Lifetime; MTV; Nickelodeon; QVC; Spike TV; Syfy; TBS; The Weather Channel; TLC; TNT; TV Land; USA Network; VH1; WGN America.
Fee: $40.00 installation; $29.95 monthly; $3.95 converter.
Pay Service 1
Pay Units: N.A.
Programming (via satellite): HBO; Showtime.
Fee: $9.95 - $10.95 monthly (each).
Video-On-Demand: No
Internet Service
Operational: No, DSL.
Broadband Service: Offers dial-up and DSL only; no cable modem service.
Fee: $24.95 monthly.
Telephone Service
Analog: Operational
Fee: $34.95 monthly
Miles of Plant: 4.0 (coaxial); None (fiber optic). Homes passed: 790.
General Manager: Mike Danielson. President: Ron Savage. Chief Technician: Pat McCabe. Customer Service Manager: Donna Erickson.
Ownership: Savage Communications Inc. (MSO).

BOYD—FMTC/Acira, 301 Second St South, Bellingham, MN 56212. Phones: 800-692-0021; 320-568-2105. E-mail: farmers@farmerstel.net. Web Site: http://www.aciracoop.net. ICA: MN5376.
Channel capacity: N.A. Channels available but not in use: N.A.
Basic
Subscribers: 19.
Fee: $65.95 monthly.
Internet Service
Operational: Yes.
Telephone Service
Digital: Operational
General Manager, Acira: Kevin Beyer.
Ownership: Farmers Mutual Telephone Co. (Bellingham).

BRAINERD—Charter Communications, 12405 Powerscourt Dr, St. Louis, MO 63131. Phones: 636-207-5100 (Corporate office); 507-289-8372 (Rochester office); 218-829-9015 (Local office). Fax: 507-285-6162. Web Site: http://www.charter.com. Also serves Aitkin, Backus, Barclay Twp., Baxter, Bay Lake, Breezy Point, Browerville, Center Twp., Clarissa, Crosby, Crow Wing County (northern portion), Crow Wing County (unincorporated areas), Cuyuna, Deerwood, Hackensack, Hiram Twp., Ideal Twp., Irondale, Ironton, Jenkins, Lake Shore, Long Prairie, Nisswa, Oak Lawn Twp., Park Rapids, Pelican Twp. (Crow Wing County), Pequot Lakes, Perry Lake Twp., Pine River, Rabbit Lake Twp., Riverton, Staples, Wadena, Walden Twp. & Wolford. ICA: MN0022.
TV Market Ranking: Below 100 (Backus, Barclay Twp., Browerville, Clarissa, Crow Wing County (unincorporated areas) (portions), Hackensack, Hiram Twp., Jenkins, Long Prairie, Walden Twp., Park Rapids); Outside TV Markets (Aitkin, Baxter, Bay Lake, BRAINERD, Breezy Point, Center Twp., Crosby, Crow Wing County (unincorporated areas) (portions), Cuyuna, Deerwood, Ideal Twp., Irondale, Ironton, Lake Shore, Nisswa, Oak Lawn Twp., Pelican Twp. (Crow Wing County), Perry Lake Twp., Pine River, Rabbit Lake Twp., Riverton, Staples, Wolford, Pequot Lakes, Wadena). Franchise award date: December 18, 1955. Franchise expiration date: N.A. Began: November 1, 1956.
Channel capacity: N.A. Channels available but not in use: N.A.
Digital Basic Service
Subscribers: 13,007.
Programming (via satellite): BBC America; Boomerang; CNN en Espanol; Destination America; Discovery Kids Channel; Disney XD; DIY Network; ESPN Classic; ESPNews; FOX College Sports Central; FOX College Sports Pacific; Fox Sports 2; FYI; History International; IFC; Investigation Discovery; LMN; MC; NFL Network; Nick 2; Nick Jr.; Nicktoons; OWN: Oprah Winfrey Network; Sundance TV; TeenNick; Turner Classic Movies; WE tv.
Fee: $14.99 monthly.
Digital Expanded Basic Service
Subscribers: N.A.
Programming (via satellite): A&E; AMC; Animal Planet; Bravo; Cartoon Network; CMT; CNBC; CNN; Comedy Central; Discovery Channel; Disney Channel; E! HD; ESPN; ESPN2; Food Network; Fox News Channel; Fox Sports 1; FOX Sports North; Freeform; FX; Golf Channel; HGTV; History; HLN; Lifetime; MSNBC; MTV; NBCSN; Nickelodeon; Outdoor Channel; Spike TV; Syfy; TLC; TNT; Travel Channel; truTV; TV Land; USA Network; VH1.
Fee: $47.99 monthly.
Digital Pay Service 1
Pay Units: N.A.
Programming (via satellite): Cinemax (multiplexed); Flix; HBO (multiplexed); Showtime (multiplexed); Starz (multiplexed); Starz Encore; The Movie Channel (multiplexed).
Video-On-Demand: Yes
Pay-Per-View
Playboy TV (delivered digitally); Fresh (delivered digitally); Shorteez (delivered digitally).
Internet Service
Operational: Yes.
Subscribers: 10,174.
Broadband Service: Charter Internet.
Fee: $29.99 monthly.
Telephone Service
Digital: Operational
Subscribers: 5,331.
Miles of Plant: 1,723.0 (coaxial); 654.0 (fiber optic). Homes passed: 40,054.
Vice President & General Manager: John Crowley. Technical Operations Director: Mark Abramo. Marketing Director: Bill Haarstad. Accounting Director: David Sovanski. Operations Director: Craig Stensaas.
Ownership: Charter Communications Inc. (MSO).

BREWSTER—Midco, PO Box 5010, Sioux Falls, SD 57117. Phone: 800-888-1300. Web Site: http://www.midcocomm.com. ICA: MN0052.
TV Market Ranking: Outside TV Markets (BREWSTER). Franchise award date: N.A. Franchise expiration date: N.A. Began: September 1, 1983.
Channel capacity: N.A. Channels available but not in use: N.A.
Basic Service
Subscribers: 20.
Programming (received off-air): KARE (NBC, WeatherNation) Minneapolis; KDLT-TV (Antenna TV, NBC) Sioux Falls; KELO-TV (CBS, MNT) Sioux Falls; KEYC-TV (CBS, FOX) Mankato; KMSP-TV (Bounce TV, Buzzr, FOX) Minneapolis; KSFY-TV (ABC, CW) Sioux Falls; KSMN (PBS) Worthington; KSTP-TV (ABC, MeTV) St. Paul; WFTC (MNT, Movies!) Minneapolis.
Programming (via satellite): A&E; CMT; CNBC; CNN; Comedy Central; Discovery Channel; ESPN; ESPN2; FOX Sports North; Freeform; Hallmark Channel; HGTV; History; HLN; Lifetime; Nickelodeon; Outdoor Channel; Spike TV; TBS; The Weather Channel; TLC; TNT; Turner Classic Movies; TV Land; USA Network; VH1; WGN America.
Fee: $39.95 installation; $45.95 monthly.
Pay Service 1
Pay Units: N.A.
Programming (via satellite): HBO.
Fee: $11.95 monthly.
Video-On-Demand: No
Internet Service
Operational: Yes.
Telephone Service
None
Homes passed & miles of plant included in Cambridge.
President & Chief Executive Officer: Pat McAdaragh. Senior Vice President, Public Policy: Tom Simmons. Programming Director: Wynne Haakenstad.
Ownership: Midcontinent Communications (MSO).

BROOKLYN CENTER—Comcast Cable. Now served by MINNEAPOLIS, MI [MN0001]. ICA: MN0403.

BROOKLYN PARK—Comcast Cable. Now served by MINNEAPOLIS, MN [MN0001]. ICA: MN0004.

BROOTEN—Mediacom. Now served by MORRIS, MN [MN0210]. ICA: MN0187.

BROWERVILLE—Charter Communications. Now served by BRAINERD, MN [MN0022]. ICA: MN0276.

BROWNS VALLEY—Formerly served by Midcontinent Communications. No longer in operation. ICA: MN0169.

BROWNSVILLE—Mediacom. Now served by CALEDONIA, MN [MN0086]. ICA: MN0231.

BUFFALO—Charter Communications, 12405 Powerscourt Dr, St. Louis, MO 63131. Phones: 636-207-5100 (Corporate office); 507-289-8372 (Rochester administrative office); 763-682-5982 (Local office). Fax: 763-682-1645. Web Site: http://www.charter.com. Also serves Albertville, Big Lake, Chatham Twp., Cokato, Dassel, Dayton, Delano, Elk River, Franklin Twp., Hassan Twp., Maple Lake, Monticello, Otsego, Rockford, St. Michael & Watertown. ICA: MN0012.
TV Market Ranking: 13 (Albertville, Big Lake, BUFFALO, Chatham Twp., Dayton, Delano, Elk River, Franklin Twp., Hassan Twp., Otsego, Rockford, St. Michael, Watertown); Below 100 (Cokato, Dassel, Maple Lake, Monticello). Franchise award date: September 1, 1984. Franchise expiration date: N.A. Began: December 18, 1984.
Channel capacity: 64 (operating 2-way). Channels available but not in use: N.A.
Digital Basic Service
Subscribers: 19,625.
Programming (via satellite): AXS TV; BBC America; Bloomberg Television; Boomerang; CBS Sports Network; CNN en Espanol; CNN International; Discovery Life Channel; Disney XD; DIY Network; ESPN; ESPN Classic; ESPNews; FOX College Sports Central; FOX College Sports Pacific; Fox Sports 2; Fuse; FXM; FYI; History International; IFC; LMN; MC; NFL Network; Nick 2; Nick Jr.; Nicktoons; Outdoor Channel; Sundance TV; TeenNick; TV Guide Interactive Inc.
Fee: $26.99 monthly.
Digital Expanded Basic Service
Subscribers: N.A.
Programming (via satellite): A&E; AMC; Animal Planet; Bravo; Cartoon Network; CMT; CNBC; CNN; Comedy Central; C-SPAN; Discovery Channel; Disney Channel; E! HD; ESPN; ESPN2; Food Network; Fox News Channel; Fox Sports 1; FOX Sports North; Freeform; FX; Golf Channel; Great American Country; Hallmark Channel; HGTV; History; HLN; Lifetime; MSNBC; MTV; MTV2; National Geographic Channel; NBCSN; Nickelodeon; Oxygen; Spike TV; Syfy; The Weather Channel; TLC; TNT; Travel Channel; truTV; Turner Classic Movies; TV Land; Univision Studios; USA Network; VH1; WE tv.
Fee: $36.00 installation; $47.99 monthly.
Digital Pay Service 1
Pay Units: N.A.
Programming (via satellite): Cinemax (multiplexed); HBO (multiplexed); HBO HD; Showtime (multiplexed); Showtime HD; Starz (multiplexed); Starz Encore (multiplexed); The Movie Channel (multiplexed).
Video-On-Demand: Yes
Pay-Per-View
iN DEMAND (delivered digitally); NHL Center Ice (delivered digitally); MLB Extra Innings (delivered digitally); Playboy TV (delivered digitally); Spice Live (delivered digitally); Spice Platinum (delivered digitally); Hot Net Plus (delivered digitally); Spice Hot (delivered digitally).
Internet Service
Operational: Yes.
Subscribers: 22,089.
Broadband Service: Charter Internet.
Fee: $29.99 monthly.
Telephone Service
Digital: Operational
Subscribers: 10,368.
Fee: $29.99 monthly
Miles of Plant: 2,036.0 (coaxial); 390.0 (fiber optic). Homes passed: 56,537.
Vice President & General Manager: John Crowley. Marketing Director: Bill Haarstad. Accounting Director: David Sovanski. Operations Director: Craig Stensaas. Chief

Minnesota—Cable Systems

FULLY SEARCHABLE • CONTINUOUSLY UPDATED • DISCOUNT RATES FOR PRINT PURCHASERS
For more information call 800-771-9202 or visit www.warren-news.com

Technician: Jason Habiger. Office Manager: Sue Labelle.
Ownership: Charter Communications Inc. (MSO).

CALEDONIA—Mediacom, 4010 Alexandra Dr, Waterloo, IA 50702. Phones: 845-695-2762; 319-235-2197. Fax: 319-232-7841. Web Site: http://www.mediacomcable.com. Also serves Bloomfield Twp., Brownsville, Canton, Dakota, Dresbach, Hokah, Houston, Mabel, New Hartford Twp., Peterson & Spring Grove. ICA: MN0086.
TV Market Ranking: Below 100 (Brownsville, CALEDONIA, Dakota, Dresbach, Hokah, Houston, Mabel, New Hartford Twp., Peterson, Spring Grove); Outside TV Markets (Bloomfield Twp., Canton). Franchise award date: September 28, 1981. Franchise expiration date: N.A. Began: January 1, 1982.
Channel capacity: N.A. Channels available but not in use: N.A.

Basic Service
Subscribers: 489.
Programming (received off-air): KAAL (ABC, This TV) Austin; KIMT (CBS, MNT) Mason City; KPXM-TV (ION) St. Cloud; KTTC (CW, NBC) Rochester; KXLT-TV (FOX, MeTV) Rochester; WEAU (NBC) Eau Claire; WHLA-TV (PBS) La Crosse; WKBT-DT (CBS, MNT) La Crosse; WLAX (FOX, MeTV) La Crosse; WXOW (ABC, CW, This TV) La Crosse.
Programming (via satellite): C-SPAN; C-SPAN 2; QVC; WGN America.
Fee: $45.00 installation; $43.00 monthly.

Expanded Basic Service 1
Subscribers: N.A.
Programming (via satellite): A&E; AMC; Animal Planet; Bravo; Cartoon Network; CMT; CNBC; CNN; Comedy Central; Discovery Channel; Disney Channel; E! HD; ESPN; ESPN2; EWTN Global Catholic Network; Food Network; Fox News Channel; Fox Sports 1; FOX Sports North; Freeform; FX; Hallmark Channel; HGTV; History; HLN; Lifetime; MSNBC; MTV; National Geographic Channel; NBCSN; Nickelodeon; Pop; Spike TV; Syfy; TBS; The Weather Channel; TLC; TNT; Travel Channel; Trinity Broadcasting Network (TBN); truTV; Turner Classic Movies; TV Land; Univision Studios; USA Network; VH1; WE tv.
Fee: $20.96 monthly.

Digital Basic Service
Subscribers: N.A.
Programming (via satellite): BBC America; Bloomberg Television; Discovery Digital Networks; Disney XD; DMX Music; ESPNU; Fox Sports 2; FXM; FYI; Golf Channel; GSN; History International; IFC; LMN; Nat Geo WILD; Nick Jr.; Nicktoons; Outdoor Channel; Ovation; Turner Classic Movies.
Fee: $45.00 installation.

Digital Pay Service 1
Pay Units: N.A.
Programming (via satellite): Cinemax (multiplexed); Flix; HBO (multiplexed); Showtime (multiplexed); Starz (multiplexed); Starz Encore (multiplexed); Sundance TV; The Movie Channel (multiplexed).
Fee: $45.00 installation; $10.95 monthly (each).
Video-On-Demand: No
Pay-Per-View
Vubiquity Inc. (delivered digitally); ESPN Now (delivered digitally); Sports PPV (delivered digitally); Urban Xtra (delivered digitally); Fresh (delivered digitally); Shorteez (delivered digitally); Playboy TV (delivered digitally); Pleasure (delivered digitally).
Internet Service
Operational: Yes.
Broadband Service: Mediacom High Speed Internet.
Fee: $40.00 monthly.
Telephone Service
Digital: Operational
Miles of Plant: 74.0 (coaxial); None (fiber optic). Homes passed: 3,981.
Regional Vice President: Doug Frank. Vice President, Financial Reporting: Kenneth J. Kohrs. General Manager: Doug Nix. Marketing Director: Steve Schuh. Technical Operations Director: Greg Nank. Marketing Coordinator: Joni Lindauer.
Ownership: Mediacom LLC (MSO).

CALUMET—Mediacom, 1504 2nd St SE, PO Box 110, Waseca, MN 56093. Phones: 845-695-2762; 507-835-2356. Fax: 507-835-4567. Web Site: http://www.mediacomcable.com. Also serves Hibbing, Marble & Taconite. ICA: MN0027.
TV Market Ranking: Below 100 (CALUMET, Hibbing, Marble, Taconite). Franchise award date: January 1, 1965. Franchise expiration date: N.A. Began: March 10, 1966.
Channel capacity: N.A. Channels available but not in use: N.A.

Basic Service
Subscribers: 2,720.
Programming (received off-air): KBJR-TV (CBS, MNT, NBC) Superior; KDLH (CBS, CW) Duluth; KQDS-TV (Antenna TV, FOX) Duluth; WDIO-DT (ABC, MeTV) Duluth; WDSE (PBS) Duluth; allband FM.
Programming (via microwave): KMSP-TV (Bounce TV, Buzzr, FOX) Minneapolis.
Programming (via satellite): QVC; TBS; WGN America.
Fee: $59.75 installation; $42.00 monthly.

Expanded Basic Service 1
Subscribers: N.A.
Programming (via satellite): A&E; AMC; Animal Planet; Cartoon Network; Classic Arts Showcase; CMT; CNBC; CNN; Comedy Central; C-SPAN; C-SPAN 2; Discovery Channel; Disney Channel; ESPN; ESPN2; EWTN Global Catholic Network; Food Network; Fox News Channel; FOX Sports Midwest; Freeform; FX; FXM; GSN; Hallmark Channel; HGTV; History; HLN; ION Television; Lifetime; MTV; Nickelodeon; Outdoor Channel; Spike TV; Syfy; The Weather Channel; TLC; TNT; Travel Channel; truTV; TV Land; USA Network; VH1.
Fee: $50.00 installation; $48.05 monthly.

Digital Basic Service
Subscribers: N.A.
Programming (via satellite): BBC America; Bloomberg Television; Discovery Digital Networks; ESPN Classic; Fox Sports 1; FYI; Golf Channel; History International; IFC; LMN; NBCSN; Nick Jr.; Ovation; TeenNick; Trinity Broadcasting Network (TBN); Turner Classic Movies; WE tv.
Digital Pay Service 1
Pay Units: N.A.
Programming (via satellite): Cinemax (multiplexed); HBO (multiplexed); Showtime (multiplexed); Starz (multiplexed); Starz Encore (multiplexed); Sundance TV (multiplexed); The Movie Channel.
Fee: $7.95 monthly (Cinemax), $10.95 monthly (Showtime/TMC/Sundance or Starz/Encore), $11.95 monthly (HBO).
Video-On-Demand: No
Pay-Per-View
iN DEMAND (delivered digitally); Playboy TV (delivered digitally); Fresh (delivered digitally); Shorteez (delivered digitally); special events (delivered digitally).
Internet Service
Operational: Yes.
Subscribers: 3,445.
Broadband Service: Mediacom High Speed Internet.
Fee: $42.50 installation; $30.00 monthly.
Telephone Service
Digital: Operational
Subscribers: 1,803.
Miles of Plant: 90.0 (coaxial); None (fiber optic). Homes passed: 6,100.
Regional Vice President: Bill Jensen. Vice President, Financial Reporting: Kenneth J. Kohrs. Marketing & Sales Director: Lori Huberty. Engineering Manager: Kraig Kaiser.
Ownership: Mediacom LLC (MSO).

CAMBRIDGE—Midco, PO Box 5010, Sioux Falls, SD 57117. Phone: 800-888-1300. Web Site: http://www.midcocomm.com. Also serves Avon, Avon Twp., Baldwin Twp., Becker, Bethel, Blue Hill Twp., Bradford Twp., Braham, Cambridge Twp., Center City, Chisago City, Clear Lake, Clear Lake Twp., Clearwater, Cold Spring, Columbus Twp., East Bethel, Elgin, Elgin Twp., Foley, Forest Lake, Foreston, Greenfield Twp., Harris, Haven Twp., Holdingford, Isanti, Isanti Twp., Kellogg, Lent Twp., Lindstrom, Linwood, Linwood Twp., Livonia Twp., Marine on the St. Croix, May Twp., Milaca, Milaca Twp., Mora, Munson Twp., Nessel Twp., New Scandia Twp., North Branch, Ogilvie, Palmer Twp., Pierz, Pine City, Pine City Twp., Plainview, Pokegama Twp., Princeton, Reads Landing, Richmond, Rockville, Royalton, Rush City, Rush Lake, Scandia, Shafer, St. Augusta, St. Francis, St. Francis Twp., St. Joseph, St. Joseph Twp., St. Stephen, St. Wendel Twp., Stacy, Stanford Twp., Taylors Falls, Wabasha, Wakefield Twp., Wyoming & Zimmerman. ICA: MN0016.
TV Market Ranking: 13 (Bethel, Center City, Chisago City, Columbus Twp., East Bethel, Forest Lake, Foreston, Lent Twp., Lindstrom, Linwood, Linwood Twp., Marine on the St. Croix, May Twp., New Scandia Twp., Scandia, St. Francis, St. Francis Twp., Stacy, Stanford Twp., Wyoming); Below 100 (Avon, Baldwin Twp., Becker, Blue Hill Twp., Clear Lake, Clear Lake Twp., Clearwater, Cold Spring, Elgin, Elgin Twp., Foley, Greenfield Twp., Haven Twp., Holdingford, Kellogg, Livonia Twp., Milaca, Munson Twp., Palmer Twp., Pierz, Princeton, Reads Landing, Richmond, Rockville, Royalton, St. Augusta, St. Joseph, St. Joseph Twp., St. Stephen, St. Wendel Twp., Wakefield Twp., Zimmerman, Plainview, Wabasha); Outside TV Markets (Bradford Twp., Braham, CAMBRIDGE, Cambridge Twp., Harris, Isanti, Isanti Twp., Milaca, Mora, Nessel Twp., North Branch, Ogilvie, Pine City, Pine City Twp., Pokegama Twp., Rush City, Rush Lake, Shafer, Taylors Falls). Franchise award date: N.A. Franchise expiration date: N.A. Began: December 1, 1983.
Channel capacity: N.A. Channels available but not in use: N.A.

Basic Service
Subscribers: 22,338.
Programming (received off-air): KARE (NBC, WeatherNation) Minneapolis; KMSP-TV (Bounce TV, Buzzr, FOX) Minneapolis; KPXM-TV (ION) St. Cloud; KSTC-TV (Antenna TV, This TV) Minneapolis; KSTP-TV (ABC, MeTV) St. Paul; KTCA-TV (PBS) St. Paul; KTCI-TV (PBS) St. Paul; WCCO-TV (CBS, Decades) Minneapolis; WFTC (MNT, Movies!) Minneapolis; WUCW (CW, The Country Network) Minneapolis.
Programming (via satellite): EVINE Live; EWTN Global Catholic Network; Pop; QVC; Trinity Broadcasting Network (TBN); USA Network; WGN America.
Fee: $19.95 monthly.

Expanded Basic Service 1
Subscribers: N.A.
Programming (via satellite): A&E; AMC; Animal Planet; Bravo; Cartoon Network; CMT; CNBC; CNN; Comedy Central; C-SPAN; C-SPAN 2; Discovery Channel; Disney Channel; DIY Network; E! HD; ESPN; ESPN2; ESPNews; Food Network; Fox News Channel; Fox Sports 1; FOX Sports North; Freeform; FX; Great American Country; Hallmark Channel; HGTV; History; HLN; Lifetime; MSNBC; MTV; National Geographic Channel; Nickelodeon; Outdoor Channel; Oxygen; Spike TV; Syfy; TBS; The Weather Channel; TLC; TNT; Travel Channel; truTV; Turner Classic Movies; TV Land; VH1; WE tv.
Fee: $25.99 monthly.

Digital Basic Service
Subscribers: N.A.
Programming (via satellite): AWE; AZ TV; BBC America; Bloomberg Television; Cloo; Discovery Digital Networks; Disney XD; DMX Music; ESPN Classic; ESPN HD; Fuse; Golf Channel; GSN; HD Theater; IFC; LMN; NBCSN; Nick Jr.; Reelz; TeenNick.

Digital Expanded Basic Service
Subscribers: N.A.
Programming (via satellite): CMT; Discovery Life Channel; FXM; FYI; Hallmark Movies & Mysteries; History; History International; RFD-TV; Starz Encore.
Fee: $2.95 monthly.

Digital Expanded Basic Service 2
Subscribers: N.A.
Programming (via satellite): FOX College Sports Central; FOX College Sports Pacific; NFL Network.
Fee: $2.00 monthly.

Digital Pay Service 1
Pay Units: 4,760 Includes Minneota, Ellsworth WI & Pepin WI.
Programming (via satellite): Cinemax (multiplexed); Cinemax HD; HBO (multiplexed); HBO HD; Showtime (multiplexed); Showtime HD; Starz (multiplexed); Starz HD; The Movie Channel (multiplexed).
Fee: $6.95 monthly (Starz), $14.95 monthly (Cinemax, HBO, Showtime or TMC).
Video-On-Demand: No

Cable Systems—Minnesota

Pay-Per-View
iN DEMAND (delivered digitally); Playboy TV (delivered digitally); Fresh (delivered digitally).
Internet Service
Operational: Yes. Began: December 31, 2002.
Subscribers: 18,464.
Broadband Service: Warp Drive Online.
Telephone Service
Digital: Operational
Subscribers: 6,273.
Miles of Plant: 339.0 (coaxial); 91.0 (fiber optic). Homes passed: 62,274. Homes passed & miles of plant include Brewster, Ceylon, Dunnell, Heron Lake, Northrup, Round Lake, Storden, Wanamingo, & Ellsworth WI
President & Chief Executive Officer: Pat McAdaragh. Senior Vice President, Public Policy: Tom Simmons. Programming Director: Wynne Haakenstad.
Ownership: Midcontinent Communications (MSO).

CANBY—Midco, PO Box 5010, Sioux Falls, SD 57117. Phones: 800-888-1300; 605-229-1775. Fax: 605-229-0478. Web Site: http://www.midcocomm.com. ICA: MN0384.
TV Market Ranking: Outside TV Markets (CANBY).
Channel capacity: N.A. Channels available but not in use: N.A.
Basic Service
Subscribers: 263.
Programming (received off-air): KARE (NBC, WeatherNation) Minneapolis; KELO-TV (CBS, MNT) Sioux Falls; KMSP-TV (Bounce TV, Buzzr, FOX) Minneapolis; KRWF (ABC) Redwood Falls; KSFY-TV (ABC, CW) Sioux Falls; KWCM-TV (PBS) Appleton; WCCO-TV (CBS, Decades) Minneapolis; WFTC (MNT, Movies!) Minneapolis; WUCW (CW, The Country Network) Minneapolis.
Programming (via satellite): C-SPAN; C-SPAN 2; EWTN Global Catholic Network; INSP; QVC; WGN America.
Fee: $29.99 installation; $19.95 monthly.
Expanded Basic Service 1
Subscribers: N.A.
Programming (via satellite): A&E; AMC; Animal Planet; Bravo; Cartoon Network; CMT; CNBC; CNN; Comedy Central; Discovery Channel; Disney Channel; E! HD; ESPN; ESPN2; Food Network; Fox News Channel; FOX Sports North; Freeform; FX; Great American Country; HGTV; History; HLN; Lifetime; MSNBC; MTV; Nickelodeon; Oxygen; Spike TV; Syfy; TBS; The Weather Channel; TLC; TNT; Travel Channel; Turner Classic Movies; TV Land; USA Network; VH1.
Fee: $37.99 monthly.
Digital Basic Service
Subscribers: N.A.
Programming (via satellite): BBC America; Bloomberg Television; Discovery Digital Networks; DIY Network; Fuse; FYI; GSN; History International; IFC; MC; Nick 2; Nick Jr.; Nicktoons; Sundance TV; TeenNick; TV Guide Interactive Inc.; WE tv.
Digital Pay Service 1
Pay Units: N.A.
Programming (via satellite): Cinemax (multiplexed); HBO (multiplexed); Showtime (multiplexed); Starz (multiplexed); Starz Encore; The Movie Channel (multiplexed).
Video-On-Demand: No
Pay-Per-View
iN DEMAND (delivered digitally); Hot Choice (delivered digitally).

Internet Service
Operational: No.
Telephone Service
None
Miles of Plant: 13.0 (coaxial); None (fiber optic). Homes passed: 1,000.
Programming Director: Wynne Haakenstad.
Ownership: Midcontinent Communications (MSO).

CANNON FALLS—Mediacom, 1504 2nd St SE, PO Box 110, Waseca, MN 56093. Phones: 845-695-2762; 507-835-2356. Fax: 507-835-4567. Web Site: http://www.mediacomcable.com. Also serves Blooming Prairie, Brownsdale, Dodge Center, Hayfield, Kenyon, Mantorville, Waltham & West Concord. ICA: MN0076.
TV Market Ranking: 13 (CANNON FALLS); Below 100 (Blooming Prairie, Brownsdale, Hayfield, Kenyon, Mantorville, Waltham, West Concord, Dodge Center). Franchise award date: December 18, 1984. Franchise expiration date: N.A. Began: April 1, 1985.
Channel capacity: N.A. Channels available but not in use: N.A.
Basic Service
Subscribers: 1,340.
Programming (received off-air): KAAL (ABC, This TV) Austin; KARE (NBC, WeatherNation) Minneapolis; KIMT (CBS, MNT) Mason City; KMSP-TV (Bounce TV, Buzzr, FOX) Minneapolis; KPXM-TV (ION) St. Cloud; KSMQ-TV (PBS) Austin; KSTC-TV (Antenna TV, This TV) Minneapolis; KSTP-TV (ABC, MeTV) St. Paul; KTCA-TV (PBS) St. Paul; KTCI-TV (PBS) St. Paul; KTTC (CW, NBC) Rochester; WCCO-TV (CBS, Decades) Minneapolis; WFTC (MNT, Movies!) Minneapolis.
Programming (via satellite): C-SPAN 2; QVC; WGN America.
Fee: $30.00 installation; $43.00 monthly; $2.00 converter.
Expanded Basic Service 1
Subscribers: N.A.
Programming (via satellite): A&E; AMC; Animal Planet; BET; Bravo; CMT; CNBC; CNN; Comedy Central; C-SPAN; Discovery Channel; Discovery Life Channel; Disney Channel; E! HD; ESPN; ESPN Classic; ESPN2; EVINE Live; EWTN Global Catholic Network; Fox News Channel; Fox Sports 1; FOX Sports North; Freeform; FX; Hallmark Channel; HGTV; History; HLN; INSP; Lifetime; LMN; MSNBC; MTV; NBCSN; Nickelodeon; Pop; Spike TV; Syfy; TBS; The Weather Channel; TLC; TNT; Travel Channel; Trinity Broadcasting Network (TBN); truTV; Turner Classic Movies; TV Land; Univision Studios; USA Network; VH1; WE tv.
Digital Basic Service
Subscribers: N.A.
Programming (via satellite): AXS TV; BBC America; Bloomberg Television; Cloo; Destination America; Discovery Kids Channel; ESPN HD; ESPN2 HD; ESPNews; ESPNU; FOX College Sports Central; FOX College Sports Pacific; Fox Sports 2; Fuse; FYI; Golf Channel; GolTV; GSN; HD Theater; History International; IFC; Investigation Discovery; LMN; MC; MTV Classic; MTV Hits; MTV2; Nat Geo WILD; National Geographic Channel; Nick Jr.; Nicktoons; Outdoor Channel; OWN: Oprah Winfrey Network; Reelz; TeenNick; Tennis Channel; TVG Network; Universal HD.
Digital Pay Service 1
Pay Units: N.A.
Programming (via satellite): Cinemax (multiplexed); Flix; HBO; HBO HD; Showtime (multiplexed); Showtime HD;

Starz (multiplexed); Starz Encore (multiplexed); Starz HD; Sundance TV; The Movie Channel (multiplexed); The Movie Channel HD.
Fee: $15.00 installation; $8.95 monthly (TMC), $9.95 monthly (Cinemax or Showtime), $11.95 monthly (HBO).
Video-On-Demand: Yes
Pay-Per-View
iN DEMAND (delivered digitally); Fresh (delivered digitally); SexSee (delivered digitally); Playboy TV (delivered digitally).
Internet Service
Operational: Yes.
Broadband Service: Mediacom High Speed Internet.
Fee: $99.00 installation; $40.00 monthly.
Telephone Service
Digital: Operational
Miles of Plant: 32.0 (coaxial); None (fiber optic). Homes passed: 1,831.
Vice President: Bill Jensen. Vice President, Financial Reporting: Kenneth J. Kohrs. Marketing & Sales Director: Lori Huberty. Engineering Manager: Kraig Kaiser.
Ownership: Mediacom LLC (MSO).

CANNON FALLS TWP.—Midco, PO Box 5010, Sioux Falls, SD 57117. Phones: 800-888-1300; 605-274-3901. Web Site: http://www.midcocomm.com. Also serves Coates, Hampton, Hampton Twp., Marshan Twp., Nininger Twp., Randolph, Randolph Twp., Ravenna Twp., Rosemount, Stanton Twp., Vermillion & Vermillion Twp. ICA: MN0391.
TV Market Ranking: 13 (CANNON FALLS TWP., Coates, Hampton, Randolph, Randolph Twp., Vermillion). Franchise award date: January 1, 1990. Franchise expiration date: N.A. Began: January 1, 1991.
Channel capacity: N.A. Channels available but not in use: N.A.
Basic Service
Subscribers: 707. Commercial subscribers: 14.
Programming (received off-air): KARE (NBC, WeatherNation) Minneapolis; KMSP-TV (Bounce TV, Buzzr, FOX) Minneapolis; KSTC-TV (Antenna TV, This TV) Minneapolis; KSTP-TV (ABC, MeTV) St. Paul; KTCA-TV (PBS) St. Paul; KTCI-TV (PBS) St. Paul; WCCO-TV (CBS, Decades) Minneapolis; WFTC (MNT, Movies!) Minneapolis; WUCW (CW, The Country Network) Minneapolis.
Programming (via satellite): EWTN Global Catholic Network; ION Television; QVC; The Weather Channel; Trinity Broadcasting Network (TBN); WGN America.
Fee: $50.00 installation; $19.95 monthly.
Digital Basic Service
Subscribers: N.A.
Programming (via satellite): A&E; AMC; Animal Planet; Bravo; Cartoon Network; CNBC; CNN; Comedy Central; C-SPAN; Disney Channel; DMX Music; ESPN; ESPN2; ESPNews; Food Network; Fox News Channel; Fox Sports 1; FOX Sports North; Freeform; FX; GSN; Hallmark Channel; HGTV; History; MSNBC; MTV; National Geographic Channel; Nickelodeon; Outdoor Channel; Spike TV; Syfy; TBS; TLC; TNT; Travel Channel; truTV; Turner Classic Movies; TV Land; USA Network; VH1; WE tv.
Fee: $50.00 installation; $52.95 monthly.
Digital Expanded Basic Service
Subscribers: N.A.
Programming (via satellite): BBC America; Bloomberg Television; CMT; Discovery Channel; Discovery Digital Networks; Dis-

ney XD; Fuse; FYI; Golf Channel; GSN; IFC; Lifetime; NBCSN; Nick Jr.
Fee: $64.95 monthly.
Digital Pay Service 1
Pay Units: N.A.
Programming (via satellite): Cinemax (multiplexed); Flix; HBO (multiplexed); Showtime (multiplexed); Starz (multiplexed); Starz Encore (multiplexed); The Movie Channel (multiplexed).
Fee: $16.00 monthly (Cinemax, HBO, Showtime/TMC or Starz/Encore).
Video-On-Demand: No
Pay-Per-View
iN DEMAND (delivered digitally); Hot Choice (delivered digitally); Playboy TV (delivered digitally); Fresh (delivered digitally).
Internet Service
Operational: Yes.
Subscribers: 695.
Fee: $30.95-$41.95 monthly.
Telephone Service
Digital: Operational
Fee: $20.00 monthly
Miles of Plant: 135.0 (coaxial); 58.0 (fiber optic). Homes passed: 2,151.
President & Chief Executive Officer: Patrick McAdaragh. Chief Operating Officer: Dick Busch. Chief Financial Officer: Steven Grosser. Senior Vice President, Public Policy: W. Thomas Simmons. Programming Director: Wynne Haakenstad.
Ownership: Midcontinent Communications (MSO).

CANTON—Mediacom. Now served by CALEDONIA, MN [MN0086]. ICA: MN0221.

CARLOS—Arvig. Now served by PARKERS PRAIRIE, MN [MN0346]. ICA: MN0246.

CEYLON—Midco, PO Box 5010, Sioux Falls, SD 57117. Phone: 800-888-1300. Web Site: http://www.midcocomm.com. ICA: MN0222.
TV Market Ranking: Outside TV Markets (CEYLON). Franchise award date: N.A. Franchise expiration date: N.A. Began: November 1, 1980.
Channel capacity: N.A. Channels available but not in use: N.A.
Basic Service
Subscribers: 25.
Programming (received off-air): KAAL (ABC, This TV) Austin; KARE (NBC, WeatherNation) Minneapolis; KEYC-TV (CBS, FOX) Mankato; KMSP-TV (Bounce TV, Buzzr, FOX) Minneapolis; KSMN (PBS) Worthington; KSTC-TV (Antenna TV, This TV) Minneapolis; KSTP-TV (ABC, MeTV) St. Paul; KYIN (PBS) Mason City; WCCO-TV (CBS, Decades) Minneapolis; WFTC (MNT, Movies!) Minneapolis.
Programming (via satellite): A&E; CMT; CNBC; CNN; Comedy Central; Discovery Channel; ESPN; ESPN2; FOX Sports Networks; Freeform; HGTV; History; HLN; Lifetime; Nickelodeon; Outdoor Channel; Spike TV; TBS; The Weather Channel; TLC; TNT; Turner Classic Movies; TV Land; USA Network; VH1; WGN America.
Fee: $45.95 monthly.
Pay Service 1
Pay Units: N.A.
Programming (via satellite): HBO.
Fee: $11.95 monthly.
Internet Service
Operational: No.
Telephone Service
None
Homes passed & miles of plant included in Cambridge.

2017 Edition   D-397

Minnesota—Cable Systems

President & Chief Executive Officer: Pat McAdaragh. Senior Vice President, Public Policy: Tom Simmons. Programming Director: Wynne Haakenstad.
Ownership: Midcontinent Communications (MSO).

CHASKA—Formerly served by Time Warner Cable. Now served by Comcast Cable, MINNEAPOLIS, MN [MN0001]. ICA: MN0279.

CHATFIELD—Mediacom, 4010 Alexandra Dr, Waterloo, IA 50702. Phones: 845-695-2762; 319-235-2197. Fax: 319-232-7841. Web Site: http://www.mediacomcable.com. Also serves Adams, Dover, Dover Twp., Lanesboro, Le Roy, Lyle, Preston, Rushford, Rushford Village, Spring Valley & St. Charles. ICA: MN0111.
TV Market Ranking: Below 100 (Adams, CHATFIELD, Dover, Dover Twp., Lanesboro, Le Roy, Lyle, Preston, Rushford, Rushford Village, Spring Valley, St. Charles). Franchise award date: N.A. Franchise expiration date: N.A. Began: October 1, 1979.
Channel capacity: N.A. Channels available but not in use: N.A.
Basic Service
Subscribers: 1,704.
Programming (received off-air): KAAL (ABC, This TV) Austin; KIMT (CBS, MNT) Mason City; KPXM-TV (ION) St. Cloud; KSMQ-TV (PBS) Austin; KTCA-TV (PBS) St. Paul; KTTC (CW, NBC) Rochester; KXLT-TV (FOX, MeTV) Rochester; WCCO-TV (CBS, Decades) Minneapolis; WKBT-DT (CBS, MNT) La Crosse; WLAX (FOX, MeTV) La Crosse; WUCW (CW, The Country Network) Minneapolis; allband FM.
Programming (via microwave): KSTP-TV (ABC, MeTV) St. Paul.
Programming (via satellite): C-SPAN; C-SPAN 2; WGN America.
Fee: $35.16 installation; $48.00 monthly; $1.58 converter.
Expanded Basic Service 1
Subscribers: N.A.
Programming (via satellite): A&E; AMC; Animal Planet; BET; Bravo; Cartoon Network; CMT; CNBC; CNN; Comedy Central; Discovery Channel; Disney Channel; E! HD; ESPN; ESPN2; EVINE Live; EWTN Global Catholic Network; Food Network; Fox News Channel; Fox Sports 1; FOX Sports Midwest; Freeform; FX; Hallmark Channel; HGTV; History; HLN; INSP; Lifetime; MTV; National Geographic Channel; NBCSN; Nickelodeon; Pop; Spike TV; Syfy; TBS; The Weather Channel; TLC; TNT; Travel Channel; Trinity Broadcasting Network (TBN); truTV; Turner Classic Movies; TV Land; Univision Studios; USA Network; VH1; WE tv.
Fee: $16.22 monthly.
Digital Basic Service
Subscribers: N.A.
Programming (via satellite): BBC America; Bloomberg Television; Discovery Digital Networks; DMX Music; Fuse; FYI; Golf Channel; GSN; History International; IFC; LMN; Outdoor Channel.
Digital Pay Service 1
Pay Units: N.A.
Programming (via satellite): Cinemax (multiplexed); Flix; HBO (multiplexed); Showtime (multiplexed); Starz (multiplexed); Starz Encore (multiplexed); Sundance TV; The Movie Channel (multiplexed).
Fee: $5.95 monthly (Starz/Encore), $7.95 monthly (Cinemax), $11.95 monthly (HBO, Showtime or TMC).
Video-On-Demand: No

Pay-Per-View
Vubiquity Inc. (delivered digitally); ESPN Now (delivered digitally); Sports PPV (delivered digitally); Urban Xtra (delivered digitally); Fresh (delivered digitally); Shorteez (delivered digitally); Playboy TV (delivered digitally); Pleasure (delivered digitally).
Internet Service
Operational: Yes.
Broadband Service: Mediacom High Speed Internet.
Fee: $99.00 installation; $40.00 monthly.
Telephone Service
Digital: Operational
Miles of Plant: 95.0 (coaxial); None (fiber optic). Homes passed: 6,156.
Regional Vice President: Doug Frank. Vice President, Financial Reporting: Kenneth J. Kohrs. General Manager: Doug Nix. Technical Operations Director: Greg Nank. Marketing Director: Steve Schuh. Marketing Coordinator: Joni Lindauer.
Ownership: Mediacom LLC (MSO).

CHISAGO CITY—Midcontinent Communications. Now served by CAMBRIDGE, MN [MN0016]. ICA: MN0063.

CLEARBROOK—Garden Valley Telephone Co. Now served by McINTOSH, MN [MN0105]. ICA: MN0280.

CLEMENTS—Clara City Telephone Co, 227 South Main St, PO Box 800, Clara City, MN 56222. Phones: 888-283-7667; 320-847-2211. Fax: 320-847-2736. E-mail: bruce@hcinet.net. Web Site: http://www.hcinet.net. ICA: MN0393.
TV Market Ranking: Below 100 (CLEMENTS). Franchise award date: May 1, 1995. Franchise expiration date: N.A. Began: November 1, 1995.
Channel capacity: N.A. Channels available but not in use: N.A.
Basic Service
Subscribers: 15.
Programming (received off-air): KARE (NBC, WeatherNation) Minneapolis; KEYC-TV (CBS, FOX) Mankato; KMSP-TV (Bounce TV, Buzzr, FOX) Minneapolis; KSMN (PBS) Worthington; KSTP-TV (ABC, MeTV) St. Paul; WCCO-TV (CBS, Decades) Minneapolis; WFTC (MNT, Movies!) Minneapolis; WUCW (CW, The Country Network) Minneapolis.
Programming (via satellite): A&E; AMC; Discovery Channel; ESPN; Freeform; History; Lifetime; Nickelodeon; TLC; TNT; TV Land; USA Network; VH1.
Fee: $20.00 installation; $48.50 monthly.
Pay Service 1
Pay Units: N.A.
Programming (via satellite): Showtime.
Fee: $10.00 monthly.
Internet Service
Operational: No.
Telephone Service
None
Miles of Plant: 3.0 (coaxial); None (fiber optic). Homes passed: 80.
Treasurer & General Manager: Bruce Hanson.
Ownership: Hanson Communications Inc. (MSO).

CLINTON—Mediacom. Now served by APPLETON, MN [MN0106]. ICA: MN0193.

CLOQUET—Mediacom, 1504 2nd St SE, PO Box 110, Waseca, MN 56093. Phones: 845-695-2762; 507-835-2356. Fax: 507-835-4567. Web Site: http://www.mediacomcable.com. Also serves Beaver Bay, Carlton, Esko, Hermantown, Lake County, Midway Twp., Moose Lake, Moose Lake Twp., Proctor, Scanlon, Silver Bay, Silver Creek Twp., Sturgeon Lake, Thomson, Two Harbors & Windermere Twp. ICA: MN0042.
TV Market Ranking: 89 (Carlton, CLOQUET, Esko, Hermantown, Lake County (portions), Proctor, Scanlon, Thomson, Two Harbors); Below 100 (Midway Twp.); Outside TV Markets (Beaver Bay, Moose Lake Twp., Silver Creek Twp., Sturgeon Lake, Windermere Twp., Moose Lake, Silver Bay, Lake County (portions)). Franchise award date: November 29, 1979. Franchise expiration date: N.A. Began: March 1, 1981.
Channel capacity: N.A. Channels available but not in use: N.A.
Basic Service
Subscribers: 4,548.
Programming (received off-air): KBJR-TV (CBS, MNT, NBC) Superior; KDLH (CBS, CW) Duluth; KQDS-TV (Antenna TV, FOX) Duluth; WDIO-DT (ABC, MeTV) Duluth; WDSE (PBS) Duluth; allband FM.
Programming (via satellite): C-SPAN; C-SPAN 2; EWTN Global Catholic Network; INSP; ION Television; Pop; WGN America.
Fee: $10.00 installation; $42.00 monthly; $2.00 converter.
Expanded Basic Service 1
Subscribers: N.A.
Programming (via satellite): A&E; AMC; Animal Planet; Bravo; Cartoon Network; CMT; CNBC; CNN; Comedy Central; Discovery Channel; Disney Channel; E! HD; ESPN; ESPN2; Fox News Channel; Fox Sports 1; FOX Sports North; Freeform; FX; FXM; Hallmark Channel; HGTV; History; HLN; Lifetime; MSNBC; MTV; NBCSN; Nickelodeon; Spike TV; Syfy; TBS; The Weather Channel; TLC; TNT; Travel Channel; truTV; Turner Classic Movies; TV Land; USA Network; VH1; WE tv.
Digital Basic Service
Subscribers: N.A.
Programming (via satellite): BBC America; Bloomberg Television; Discovery Digital Networks; DMX Music; Fuse; FYI; Golf Channel; GSN; History International; HITS (Headend In The Sky); IFC; LMN; National Geographic Channel; Outdoor Channel.
Digital Pay Service 1
Pay Units: N.A.
Programming (via satellite): Cinemax (multiplexed); Flix; HBO (multiplexed); Showtime (multiplexed); Starz (multiplexed); Starz Encore (multiplexed); Sundance TV; The Movie Channel (multiplexed).
Fee: $15.00 installation; $8.95 monthly (Showtime), $9.95 monthly (Cinemax or TMC), $11.95 monthly (HBO).
Video-On-Demand: No
Pay-Per-View
Vubiquity Inc. (delivered digitally); ESPN Now (delivered digitally); Sports PPV (delivered digitally); Urban Xtra (delivered digitally); Fresh (delivered digitally); Shorteez (delivered digitally); Playboy TV (delivered digitally); Pleasure (delivered digitally).
Internet Service
Operational: Yes.
Broadband Service: Mediacom High Speed Internet.
Fee: $99.00 installation; $40.00 monthly.
Telephone Service
Analog: Not Operational
Digital: Operational
Miles of Plant: 104.0 (coaxial); None (fiber optic).
Vice President: Bill Jensen. Vice President, Financial Reporting: Kenneth J. Kohrs. Marketing & Sales Director: Lori Huberty. Engineering Manager: Kraig Kaiser.
Ownership: Mediacom LLC (MSO).

COLERAINE—Formerly served by North American Communications Corp. Now served by SCI Broadband, BOVEY, MN [MN0112]. ICA: MN0162.

COLOGNE—NU-Telecom, 2104 10th St East, Glencoe, MN 55336. Phones: 507-233-4259 (New Ulm office); 888-873-6853; 320-864-2818. Fax: 320-864-5612. E-mail: on-linecustservice@nu-telcom.net. Web Site: http://www.nutelecom.net. ICA: MN0282.
TV Market Ranking: 13 (COLOGNE).
Channel capacity: N.A. Channels available but not in use: N.A.
Digital Basic Service
Subscribers: 86.
Programming (received off-air): KARE (NBC, WeatherNation) Minneapolis; KMSP-TV (Bounce TV, Buzzr, FOX) Minneapolis; KSTP-TV (ABC, MeTV) St. Paul; KTCA-TV (PBS) St. Paul; KTCI-TV (PBS) St. Paul; WCCO-TV (CBS, Decades) Minneapolis; WFTC (MNT, Movies!) Minneapolis; WUCW (CW, The Country Network) Minneapolis.
Programming (via satellite): ION Television; QVC; TBS; Trinity Broadcasting Network (TBN); WGN America.
Fee: $50.00 installation; $21.95 monthly.
Digital Expanded Basic Service
Subscribers: N.A.
Programming (via satellite): A&E; AMC; CMT; CNN; Discovery Channel; Disney Channel; ESPN; ESPN2; FOX Sports Midwest; Freeform; Lifetime; Nickelodeon; Spike TV; Syfy; TLC; TNT; USA Network; VH1.
Fee: $49.95 monthly.
Digital Expanded Basic Service 2
Subscribers: N.A.
Fee: $62.95 monthly.
Digital Expanded Basic Service 3
Subscribers: N.A.
Fee: $10.95 monthly.
Digital Pay Service 1
Pay Units: N.A.
Programming (via satellite): Cinemax; HBO; Starz; Starz Encore; The Movie Channel.
Fee: $15.95 monthly (Cinemax, HBO, Showtime/TMC or Starz/Encore), $27.95 monthly (Cinemax/HBO).
Video-On-Demand: No
Internet Service
Operational: Yes, DSL.
Fee: $29.95-$64.95 monthly.
Telephone Service
None
Miles of Plant: 4.0 (coaxial); None (fiber optic).
President & Chief Executive Officer: Bill Otis. Chief Operating Officer & Vice President: Barbara Bornhoft. Chief Financial Officer & Treasurer: Curtis Kawlweski.
Ownership: New Ulm Telecom.

COMFREY—Clara City Telephone Co, 227 South Main St, PO Box 800, Clara City, MN 56222. Phones: 888-283-7667; 320-847-2211. Fax: 320-847-2736. E-mail: bruce@hcinet.net. Web Site: http://www.hcinet.net. ICA: MN0209.
TV Market Ranking: Below 100 (COMFREY). Franchise award date: N.A. Franchise expiration date: N.A. Began: September 1, 1984.
Channel capacity: N.A. Channels available but not in use: N.A.

Cable Systems—Minnesota

Basic Service
Subscribers: 40.
Programming (received off-air): KEYC-TV (CBS, FOX) Mankato; allband FM.
Programming (via satellite): A&E; AMC; CMT; CNN; Discovery Channel; ESPN; ESPN2; FOX Sports Networks; Freeform; Hallmark Channel; History; Lifetime; MTV; Nickelodeon; Spike TV; TBS; The Weather Channel; TLC; TNT; TV Land; USA Network; WGN America.
Programming (via translator): KARE (NBC, WeatherNation) Minneapolis; KMSP-TV (Bounce TV, Buzzr, FOX) Minneapolis; KSMN (PBS) Worthington; KSTP-TV (ABC, MeTV) St. Paul; WCCO-TV (CBS, Decades) Minneapolis; WFTC (MNT, Movies!) Minneapolis; WUCW (CW, The Country Network) Minneapolis.
Fee: $20.00 installation; $48.50 monthly; $2.00 converter.

Pay Service 1
Pay Units: N.A.
Programming (via satellite): Showtime.
Fee: $10.00 monthly.

Internet Service
Operational: No.

Telephone Service
None
Miles of Plant: 5.0 (coaxial); None (fiber optic). Homes passed: 250.
Treasurer & General Manager: Bruce Hanson. Chief Technician: Randy Maserek. Engineer: LaVerne Maserek.
Ownership: Hanson Communications Inc. (MSO).

CONCORD—Formerly served by Mediacom. No longer in operation. ICA: MN0191.

COOK—Mediacom, 1504 2nd St SE, PO Box 110, Waseca, MN 56093. Phones: 845-695-2762; 507-835-2356. Fax: 507-835-4567. E-mail: bjensen@mediacomcc.com. Web Site: http://www.mediacomcable.com. ICA: MN0283.
TV Market Ranking: Below 100 (COOK). Franchise award date: September 15, 1981. Franchise expiration date: N.A. Began: June 1, 1982.
Channel capacity: 52 (not 2-way capable). Channels available but not in use: N.A.

Basic Service
Subscribers: 9.
Programming (received off-air): KBJR-TV (CBS, MNT, NBC) Superior; KDLH (CBS, CW) Duluth; WDSE (PBS) Duluth; WIRT-DT (ABC, MeTV) Hibbing; allband FM.
Programming (via satellite): C-SPAN; C-SPAN 2; ION Television; QVC; WGN America.
Fee: $50.00 installation; $40.00 monthly.

Expanded Basic Service 1
Subscribers: N.A.
Programming (via satellite): A&E; AMC; Animal Planet; Bravo; CMT; CNN; Comedy Central; Discovery Channel; Disney Channel; E! HD; ESPN; ESPN2; Food Network; Fox Sports 1; FOX Sports North; Freeform; FX; Hallmark Channel; History; HLN; INSP; Lifetime; Nickelodeon; Spike TV; Syfy; TBS; The Weather Channel; TLC; TNT; Travel Channel; TV Land; USA Network; WE tv.

Pay Service 1
Pay Units: N.A.
Programming (via satellite): HBO.
Fee: $10.95 monthly.

Video-On-Demand: No

Internet Service
Operational: No.

Telephone Service
None
Miles of Plant: 5.0 (coaxial); None (fiber optic).
Vice President & General Manager: Bill Jensen. Vice President, Financial Reporting: Kenneth J. Kohrs. Marketing & Sales Director: Lori Huberty. Program Director: Barry Paden. Engineering Manager: Kraig Kaiser.
Ownership: Mediacom LLC (MSO).

COSMOS—Mediacom. Now served by PAYNESVILLE, MN [MN0125]. ICA: MN0284.

COTTONWOOD—Charter Communications. Now served by WILLMAR, MN [MN0018]. ICA: MN0385.

CROOKSTON—Midco. Now served by GRAND FORKS, ND [ND0003]. ICA: MN0047.

CROSSLAKE—Crosslake Communications, 35910 County Rd 66, Crosslake, MN 56442. Phones: 800-992-8220; 218-692-2777. Fax: 218-692-2410. Web Site: http://www.crosslake.net. Also serves Fifty Lakes & Manhattan Beach. ICA: MN0069.
TV Market Ranking: Below 100 (Manhattan Beach); Outside TV Markets (CROSSLAKE, Fifty Lakes). Franchise award date: N.A. Franchise expiration date: N.A. Began: January 1, 1985.
Channel capacity: N.A. Channels available but not in use: N.A.

Basic Service
Subscribers: 1,164.
Programming (received off-air): KARE (NBC, WeatherNation) Minneapolis; KAWB (PBS) Brainerd; KCCW-TV (CBS) Walker; KMSP-TV (Bounce TV, Buzzr, FOX) Minneapolis; KSTC-TV (Antenna TV, This TV) Minneapolis; KSTP-TV (ABC, MeTV) St. Paul; WFTC (MNT, Movies!) Minneapolis.
Programming (via satellite): A&E; AMC; Animal Planet; BTN; CMT; CNBC; CNN; Comedy Central; C-SPAN; Discovery Channel; Disney Channel; DIY Network; E! HD; ESPN; ESPN2; EWTN Global Catholic Network; Food Network; Fox News Channel; FOX Sports North; Freeform; FX; Great American Country; Hallmark Channel; HGTV; History; Lifetime; MSNBC; MTV; National Geographic Channel; NBCSN; Nickelodeon; Pop; QVC; Spike TV; Syfy; TBS; The Sportsman Channel; The Weather Channel; TLC; TNT; Travel Channel; Trinity Broadcasting Network (TBN); truTV; TV Land; USA Network; VH1; WGN America.
Fee: $37.49 monthly.

Digital Basic Service
Subscribers: N.A.
Programming (via satellite): A&E HD; AXS TV; Bloomberg Television; Bravo; BTN HD; Cloo; Cooking Channel; Destination America; Discovery Family; Discovery Life Channel; Disney XD; DMX Music; ESPN Classic; ESPN HD; ESPN2 HD; ESPNews; Food Network HD; Fox News HD; Fox Sports 1; FSN HD; FX HD; FXM; FYI; Golf Channel; GSN; HD Theater; HGTV HD; History HD; History International; IFC; Investigation Discovery; Lifetime Movie Network HD; LMN; National Geographic Channel; National Geographic Channel HD; Nick Jr.; Outdoor Channel; Outdoor Channel HD; OWN; Oprah Winfrey Network; Pivot; Science Channel; Travel Channel HD; Turner Classic Movies; Universal HD.

Digital Pay Service 1
Pay Units: N.A.
Programming (via satellite): Cinemax (multiplexed); Cinemax HD; Flix; HBO (multiplexed); HBO HD; Showtime (multiplexed); Showtime HD; Starz (multiplexed); Starz Encore; Starz HD; The Movie Channel (multiplexed); The Movie Channel HD.

Video-On-Demand: No

Internet Service
Operational: Yes.

Telephone Service
Analog: Operational
Miles of Plant: 100.0 (coaxial); None (fiber optic).
General Manager: Paul Hoge. Operations Manager: Jared Johnson. Marketing Director: Debbie Floerchinger.
Ownership: Crosslake Communications.

DAKOTA—Mediacom. Now served by CALEDONIA, MN [MN0086]. ICA: MN0201.

DALTON—Otter Tail Telcom, 100 Main St, PO Box 277, Underwood, MN 56586. Phones: 800-247-2706; 218-826-6161. Fax: 218-826-6298. Web Site: http://www.prtel.com. Also serves Ashby, Aurdal Twp., Elizabeth Twp., Erhard, Fergus Falls, Maine Twp., Oscar Twp., Rothsay & Underwood. ICA: MN0410.
TV Market Ranking: Outside TV Markets (Ashby, Aurdal Twp., DALTON, Elizabeth Twp., Elizabeth Twp., Erhard, Fergus Falls, Maine Twp., Oscar Twp., Rothsay, Underwood).
Channel capacity: N.A. Channels available but not in use: N.A.

Basic Service
Subscribers: 481.
Fee: $39.95 monthly.
Chief Executive Officer & General Manager: Dale Beckett. Business Operations Manager: Tim Brinkman.
Ownership: Otter Tail Telcom (MSO).

DAWSON—Mediacom. Now served by APPLETON, MN [MN0106]. ICA: MN0117.

DEER RIVER—Paul Bunyan Communications. This cable system has converted to IPTV. Now served by MORSE TWP, MN [MN5068]. ICA: MN0180.

DELAVAN—BEVCOMM. This cable system has converted to IPTV. Now served by NEW PRAGUE, MN [MN5366]. ICA: MN0289.

DEXTER—Formerly served by North American Communications Corp. This cable system has converted to IPTV. Now served by Jaguar Communications, OWATONNA, MN [MN5121]. ICA: MN0290.

DILWORTH—Formerly served by Loretel Cablevision. Now served by Cable One, FARGO, ND [ND0001]. ICA: MN0077.

DODGE CENTER—Mediacom. Now served by CANNON FALLS, MN [MN0076]. ICA: MN0093.

DULUTH—Charter Communications, 12405 Powerscourt Dr, St. Louis, MO 63131. Phones: 636-207-5100 (Corporate office); 218-529-8000; 715-831-8940. Fax: 507-285-6162. Web Site: http://www.charter.com. Also serves Rice Lake Twp., MN; Lake Nebagamon, Oliver, Parkland & Superior (village), WI. ICA: MN0006.
TV Market Ranking: 89 (DULUTH, Lake Nebagamon, Oliver, Parkland, Rice Lake Twp., Superior (village)). Franchise award date: June 22, 1968. Franchise expiration date: N.A. Began: August 15, 1973.
Channel capacity: N.A. Channels available but not in use: N.A.

Digital Basic Service
Subscribers: 18,677.
Programming (via satellite): AXS TV; BBC America; Discovery Digital Networks; ESPN; ESPNews; FOX College Sports Central; FOX College Sports Pacific; Fox Sports 2; Fuse; FYI; Great American Country; History International; IFC; LMN; MC; NFL Network; Nick 2; Nick Jr.; Nicktoons; Sundance TV; TeenNick; TV Guide Interactive Inc.
Fee: $26.99 monthly.

Digital Expanded Basic Service
Subscribers: N.A.
Programming (via satellite): A&E; AMC; Animal Planet; BET; Bravo; Cartoon Network; CMT; CNBC; CNN; Comedy Central; Discovery Channel; Disney Channel; Disney XD; DIY Network; E! HD; ESPN; ESPN Classic; ESPN2; EVINE Live; Food Network; Fox News Channel; Fox Sports 1; FOX Sports North; Freeform; FX; Golf Channel; GSN; Hallmark Channel; HGTV; History; HLN; Lifetime; MSNBC; MTV; MTV2; National Geographic Channel; NBCSN; Nickelodeon; Outdoor Channel; Oxygen; Spike TV; Syfy; TBS; The Weather Channel; TLC; TNT; Travel Channel; truTV; Turner Classic Movies; TV Land; USA Network; VH1; WE tv.
Fee: $25.48 installation; $47.99 monthly.

Digital Pay Service 1
Pay Units: N.A.
Programming (via satellite): Cinemax (multiplexed); HBO (multiplexed); HBO HD; Showtime (multiplexed); Showtime HD; Starz (multiplexed); Starz Encore (multiplexed); The Movie Channel (multiplexed).

Video-On-Demand: Yes

Pay-Per-View
iN DEMAND (delivered digitally); NHL Center Ice (delivered digitally); MLB Extra Innings (delivered digitally); Playboy TV (delivered digitally); Spice Live (delivered digitally); Spice Platinum (delivered digitally); Hot Network Plus (delivered digitally); Spice Hot (delivered digitally).

Internet Service
Operational: Yes.
Broadband Service: Charter Internet.
Fee: $29.99 monthly; $3.95 modem lease.

Telephone Service
Digital: Operational
Fee: $29.99 monthly
Miles of Plant: 515.0 (coaxial); 2.0 (fiber optic). Homes passed: 49,958.
Vice President & General Manager: John Crowley. Technical Operations Manager: Tom Gorsuch. Marketing Director: Bill Haarstad. Government Relations Director: Mike Hill. Accounting Director: David Sovanski.
Ownership: Charter Communications Inc. (MSO).

DUNDEE (village)—Formerly served by American Telecasting of America Inc. No longer in operation. ICA: MN0291.

DUNNELL—Midco, PO Box 5010, Sioux Falls, SD 57117. Phone: 800-888-1300. Web Site: http://www.midcocomm.com. ICA: MN0263.
TV Market Ranking: Outside TV Markets (DUNNELL). Franchise award date: N.A.

Minnesota—Cable Systems

FULLY SEARCHABLE • CONTINUOUSLY UPDATED • DISCOUNT RATES FOR PRINT PURCHASERS
For more information call 800-771-9202 or visit www.warren-news.com

Franchise expiration date: N.A. Began: November 1, 1980.
Channel capacity: N.A. Channels available but not in use: N.A.
Basic Service
Subscribers: 19.
Programming (received off-air): KARE (NBC, WeatherNation) Minneapolis; KEYC-TV (CBS, FOX) Mankato; KMSP-TV (Bounce TV, Buzzr, FOX) Minneapolis; KSMN (PBS) Worthington; KSTC-TV (Antenna TV, This TV) Minneapolis; KSTP-TV (ABC, MeTV) St. Paul; KYIN (PBS) Mason City; WCCO-TV (CBS, Decades) Minneapolis; WFTC (MNT, Movies!) Minneapolis.
Programming (via satellite): A&E; CMT; CNN; Comedy Central; ESPN; ESPN2; FOX Sports Networks; Freeform; HGTV; History; Lifetime; Nickelodeon; Outdoor Channel; Spike TV; TBS; The Weather Channel; TLC; TNT; Turner Classic Movies; TV Land; USA Network; WGN America.
Fee: $45.95 monthly.
Pay Service 1
Pay Units: N.A.
Programming (via satellite): HBO.
Fee: $11.95 monthly.
Internet Service
Operational: No.
Telephone Service
None
Homes passed & miles of plant included in Cambridge.
President & Chief Executive Officer: Pat McAdaragh. Senior Vice President, Public Policy: Tom Simmons. Programming Director: Wynne Haakenstad.
Ownership: Midcontinent Communications (MSO).

EAGAN—Comcast Cable. Now served by MINNEAPOLIS, MN [MN0001]. ICA: MN0405.

EAST GULL LAKE—SCI Broadband. Now served by PILLAGER, MN [MN0230]. ICA: MN0151.

EASTON—BEVCOMM. This cable system has converted to IPTV. Now served by NEW PRAGUE, MN [MN5366]. ICA: MN0292.

ECHO—Clara City Telephone Co, 227 South Main St, PO Box 800, Clara City, MN 56222. Phones: 888-283-7667; 320-847-2211. Fax: 320-847-2736. E-mail: bruce@hcinet.net. Web Site: http://www.hcinet.net. ICA: MN0239.
TV Market Ranking: Below 100 (ECHO). Franchise award date: January 1, 1988. Franchise expiration date: N.A. Began: December 26, 1988.
Channel capacity: N.A. Channels available but not in use: N.A.
Basic Service
Subscribers: 29.
Programming (received off-air): KEYC-TV (CBS, FOX) Mankato; KSFY-TV (ABC, CW) Sioux Falls; KWCM-TV (PBS) Appleton.
Programming (via satellite): A&E; AMC; CNN; Discovery Channel; ESPN; Freeform; History; Lifetime; Nickelodeon; Spike TV;

The Weather Channel; TLC; TNT; TV Land; USA Network; WGN America.
Programming (via translator): KARE (NBC, WeatherNation) Minneapolis; KMSP-TV (Bounce TV, Buzzr, FOX) Minneapolis; KSTP-TV (ABC, MeTV) St. Paul; KTCA-TV (PBS) St. Paul; WCCO-TV (CBS, Decades) Minneapolis; WFTC (MNT, Movies!) Minneapolis.
Fee: $20.00 installation; $48.50 monthly; $2.00 converter.
Pay Service 1
Pay Units: 4.
Programming (via satellite): Showtime.
Fee: $10.00 installation; $10.00 monthly.
Internet Service
Operational: No.
Telephone Service
None
Miles of Plant: 3.0 (coaxial); None (fiber optic). Homes passed: 150.
Treasurer & General Manager: Bruce Hanson.
Ownership: Hanson Communications Inc. (MSO).

EITZEN—Ace Communications. Formerly [MN0294]. This cable system has converted to IPTV. Now served by HOUSTON, MN [MN5105]. ICA: MN0294.

EITZEN—Ace Communications. Formerly [MN0294]. This cable system has converted to IPTV. Now served by HOUSTON, MN [MN5105]. ICA: MN5143.

ELBOW LAKE—Runestone Cable TV. Now served by BARRETT, MN [MN0233]. ICA: MN0135.

ELKO—Mediacom. Now served by PRIOR LAKE, MN [MN0039]. ICA: MN0295.

ELLSWORTH—Clarity Telcom. Now served by ADRIAN, MN [MN0158]. ICA: MN0296.

ELY—Midco, PO Box 5010, Sioux Falls, SD 57117. Phones: 800-888-1300; 605-229-1775. Fax: 605-229-0478. Web Site: http://www.midcocomm.com. Also serves Babbitt, Breitung Twp., Tower & Winton. ICA: MN0060.
TV Market Ranking: Outside TV Markets (Breitung Twp., ELY, Winton, Babbitt, Tower). Franchise award date: May 1, 1956. Franchise expiration date: N.A. Began: May 1, 1956.
Channel capacity: N.A. Channels available but not in use: N.A.
Basic Service
Subscribers: 1,306.
Programming (via microwave): KBJR-TV (CBS, MNT, NBC) Superior; KDLH (CBS, CW) Duluth; KQDS-TV (Antenna TV, FOX) Duluth; WDIO-DT (ABC, MeTV) Duluth; WDSE (PBS) Duluth.
Programming (via satellite): C-SPAN; EWTN Global Catholic Network; INSP; QVC; WGN America.
Fee: $29.99 installation; $19.95 monthly.

Expanded Basic Service 1
Subscribers: N.A.
Programming (via satellite): A&E; AMC; Animal Planet; Bravo; Cartoon Network; CMT; CNBC; CNN; Comedy Central; Discovery Channel; Disney Channel; E! HD; ESPN; ESPN2; Fox News Channel; Fox Sports 1; FOX Sports North; Freeform; FX; Hallmark Channel; HGTV; History; HLN; Lifetime; MSNBC; MTV; Nickelodeon; Oxygen; Spike TV; Syfy; TBS; The Weather Channel; TLC; TNT; Turner Classic Movies; TV Land; USA Network; VH1.
Fee: $47.99 monthly.
Digital Basic Service
Subscribers: N.A.
Programming (via satellite): BBC America; Discovery Digital Networks; Disney XD; DIY Network; FOX College Sports Central; FOX College Sports Pacific; FXM; FYI; History International; IFC; MC; Nick 2; Nick Jr.; Nicktoons; Sundance TV; TeenNick; TV Guide Interactive Inc.; WE tv.
Digital Pay Service 1
Pay Units: N.A.
Programming (via satellite): Cinemax (multiplexed); Flix; HBO (multiplexed); Showtime (multiplexed); Starz (multiplexed); Starz Encore; The Movie Channel (multiplexed).
Video-On-Demand: No
Pay-Per-View
iN DEMAND (delivered digitally); Hot Choice (delivered digitally).
Internet Service
Operational: Yes.
Fee: $29.99 monthly.
Telephone Service
None
Miles of Plant: 38.0 (coaxial); None (fiber optic). Homes passed: 1,890.
Programming Director: Wynne Haakenstad.
Ownership: Midcontinent Communications (MSO).

EMILY—Emily Cooperative Telephone. Formerly [MS0081]. This cable system has converted to IPTV, 40040 State Hwy 6, PO Box 100, Emily, MN 56447. Phones: 800-450-1036; 218-763-3000. Fax: 218-763-2042. E-mail: emilytel@emily.net. Web Site: http://www.emily.net. Also serves Beulah Twp., Crooked Lake Twp., Fairfield Twp., Fifty Lakes, Little Pine Twp. & Outing. ICA: MN5256.
TV Market Ranking: Below 100 (EMILY).
Channel capacity: N.A. Channels available but not in use: N.A.
Basic Digital
Subscribers: 70.
Fee: $32.45 monthly. Includes 20 channels.
Internet Service
Operational: Yes.
Fee: $19.95-$79.95 monthly.
Telephone Service
Digital: Operational
General Manager: Bob Olson. Business Manager: Charles Balk.
Ownership: Emily Cooperative Telephone Co.

EMILY—Emily Cooperative Telephone. This cable system has converted to IPTV. See EMILY, MN [MN5256]. ICA: MN0081.

EMMONS—Formerly served by Heck's TV & Cable. No longer in operation. ICA: MN0227.

EVELETH—Mediacom, 1504 2nd St SE, PO Box 110, Waseca, MN 56093. Phones: 845-695-2762; 507-835-2356. Fax: 507-835-4567. Web Site: http://www.

mediacomcable.com. Also serves Aurora, Biwabik, Buhl, Chisholm, Fayal Twp., Gilbert, Hoyt Lakes, Kinney, Lake County (western portion), Leonidas, Mountain Iron, Virginia & White Twp. ICA: MN0017.
TV Market Ranking: Below 100 (Aurora, Biwabik, Buhl, Chisholm, EVELETH, Fayal Twp., Gilbert, Kinney, Leonidas, Mountain Iron, Virginia, White Twp.); Outside TV Markets (Hoyt Lakes, Lake County (western portion)). Franchise award date: N.A. Franchise expiration date: N.A. Began: December 1, 1967.
Channel capacity: N.A. Channels available but not in use: N.A.
Basic Service
Subscribers: 4,889.
Programming (received off-air): KBJR-TV (CBS, MNT, NBC) Superior; KDLH (CBS, CW) Duluth; KQDS-TV (Antenna TV, FOX) Duluth; WDSE (PBS) Duluth; WIRT-DT (ABC, MeTV) Hibbing; allband FM.
Programming (via microwave): KMSP-TV (Bounce TV, Buzzr, FOX) Minneapolis.
Programming (via satellite): C-SPAN; C-SPAN 2; Pop; The Weather Channel; WGN America.
Fee: $15.00 installation; $42.00 monthly; $4.00 converter.
Expanded Basic Service 1
Subscribers: N.A.
Programming (via satellite): A&E; AMC; Animal Planet; Bravo; Cartoon Network; CMT; CNBC; CNN; Comedy Central; Discovery Channel; Disney Channel; E! HD; ESPN; ESPN2; EWTN Global Catholic Network; Food Network; FOX Sports North; Freeform; FX; Hallmark Channel; HGTV; History; HLN; ION Television; Lifetime; MSNBC; MTV; Nickelodeon; Spike TV; Syfy; TBS; TLC; TNT; Travel Channel; Trinity Broadcasting Network (TBN); truTV; USA Network; VH1; WE tv.
Fee: $26.45 monthly.
Digital Basic Service
Subscribers: N.A.
Programming (via satellite): BBC America; Bloomberg Television; Discovery Digital Networks; Fuse; FYI; Golf Channel; GSN; History International; IFC; LMN; MC; Outdoor Channel; WE tv.
Digital Pay Service 1
Pay Units: N.A.
Programming (via satellite): Cinemax (multiplexed); Flix; HBO (multiplexed); Showtime (multiplexed); Starz (multiplexed); Starz Encore (multiplexed); The Movie Channel (multiplexed).
Fee: $15.00 installation; $11.00 monthly (Cinemax, HBO, Showtime/TMC/Flix or Starz/Encore).
Video-On-Demand: No
Pay-Per-View
Playboy TV (delivered digitally); Fresh (delivered digitally); Shorteez (delivered digitally); Vubiquity Inc. (delivered digitally).
Internet Service
Operational: Yes.
Subscribers: 3,545.
Broadband Service: Mediacom High Speed Internet.
Fee: $69.95 installation; $40.95 monthly; $10.00 modem lease; $239.95 modem purchase.
Telephone Service
Digital: Operational
Subscribers: 2,537.
Miles of Plant: 345.0 (coaxial); 138.0 (fiber optic). Homes passed: 17,202.
Vice President: Bill Jensen. Vice President, Financial Reporting: Kenneth J. Kohrs. Mar-

Cable Systems—Minnesota

keting & Sales Director: Lori Huberty. Engineering Manager: Kraig Kaiser.
Ownership: Mediacom LLC (MSO).

FAIRMONT—Midco, PO Box 5010, Sioux Falls, SD 57117. Phones: 800-888-1300; 605-229-1775. Fax: 605-229-0478. Web Site: http://www.midcocomm.com. Also serves Sherburn. ICA: MN0040.
TV Market Ranking: Outside TV Markets (FAIRMONT, Sherburn). Franchise award date: January 1, 1957. Franchise expiration date: N.A. Began: January 1, 1957.
Channel capacity: N.A. Channels available but not in use: N.A.
Basic Service
Subscribers: 2,853.
Programming (received off-air): KAAL (ABC, This TV) Austin; KEYC-TV (CBS, FOX) Mankato; KTIN (PBS) Fort Dodge; KTTC (CW, NBC) Rochester; allband FM. Programming (via microwave): KARE (NBC, WeatherNation) Minneapolis; KMSP-TV (Bounce TV, Buzzr, FOX) Minneapolis; KSTP-TV (ABC, MeTV) St. Paul; KTCA-TV (PBS) St. Paul; WCCO-TV (CBS, Decades) Minneapolis; WFTC (MNT, Movies!) Minneapolis; WUCW (CW, The Country Network) Minneapolis.
Programming (via satellite): C-SPAN; C-SPAN 2; EWTN Global Catholic Network; Pop; QVC; TBS; WGN America.
Fee: $29.99 installation; $19.95 monthly.
Expanded Basic Service 1
Subscribers: N.A.
Programming (via satellite): A&E; AMC; Animal Planet; Bravo; Cartoon Network; CMT; CNBC; CNN; Comedy Central; Discovery Channel; Disney Channel; Disney XD; E! HD; ESPN; ESPN2; Food Network; Fox News Channel; Fox Sports 1; FOX Sports North; Freeform; FX; Golf Channel; GSN; Hallmark Channel; HGTV; History; HLN; Lifetime; MSNBC; MTV; MTV2; National Geographic Channel; NBCSN; Nickelodeon; Oxygen; Spike TV; Syfy; The Weather Channel; TLC; TNT; Travel Channel; Trinity Broadcasting Network (TBN); truTV; Turner Classic Movies; TV Land; USA Network; VH1; WE tv.
Fee: $47.99 monthly.
Digital Basic Service
Subscribers: N.A.
Programming (via satellite): BBC America; Bloomberg Television; Boomerang; CNN en Espanol; CNN International; Discovery Life Channel; DIY Network; FOX College Sports Central; FOX College Sports Pacific; Fox Sports 2; FXM; FYI; History International; IFC; MC; Nick 2; Nick Jr.; Nicktoons; Sundance TV; TeenNick; TV Guide Interactive Inc.
Digital Pay Service 1
Pay Units: N.A.
Programming (via satellite): Cinemax (multiplexed); Flix; HBO (multiplexed); Showtime (multiplexed); Starz (multiplexed); Starz Encore (multiplexed); The Movie Channel (multiplexed).
Video-On-Demand: No
Pay-Per-View
iN DEMAND (delivered digitally); Playboy TV (delivered digitally); Fresh (delivered digitally); Shorteez (delivered digitally).
Internet Service
Operational: Yes.
Broadband Service: Charter Internet.
Fee: $29.99 monthly.
Telephone Service
None
Miles of Plant: 99.0 (coaxial); None (fiber optic). Homes passed: 5,200.

Programming Director: Wynne Haakenstad.
Ownership: Midcontinent Communications (MSO).

FARIBAULT—Charter Communications. Now served by OWATONNA, MN [MN0023]. ICA: MN0026.

FERGUS FALLS—Charter Communications, 302 East Superior St, Duluth, MN 55802. Phones: 314-543-2236; 636-207-5100 (Corporate office); 507-289-8372 (Rochester office); 218-739-3464. Web Site: http://www.charter.com. Also serves Aurdal Twp., Buse Twp., Dane Prairie Twp. & Fergus Falls Twp. ICA: MN0032.
TV Market Ranking: Outside TV Markets (Aurdal Twp., Buse Twp., Dane Prairie Twp., FERGUS FALLS, Fergus Falls Twp.). Franchise award date: December 1, 1964. Franchise expiration date: N.A. Began: January 1, 1964.
Channel capacity: N.A. Channels available but not in use: N.A.
Digital Basic Service
Subscribers: 2,699.
Programming (via satellite): BBC America; Discovery Digital Networks; DIY Network; ESPNews; FOX College Sports Central; FOX College Sports Pacific; Fox Sports 2; FYI; History International; IFC; MC; NFL Network; Nick 2; Nick Jr.; Nicktoons; Sundance TV; TeenNick; TV Guide Interactive Inc.
Fee: $49.99 installation; $26.99 monthly.
Digital Expanded Basic Service
Subscribers: N.A.
Programming (via satellite): A&E; AMC; Animal Planet; Bravo; Cartoon Network; CMT; CNBC; CNN; Comedy Central; Discovery Channel; Disney Channel; Disney XD; E! HD; ESPN; ESPN2; Food Network; Fox News Channel; Fox Sports 1; FOX Sports North; Freeform; FX; Golf Channel; GSN; Hallmark Channel; HGTV; History; HLN; Lifetime; MSNBC; MTV; National Geographic Channel; NBCSN; Nickelodeon; Outdoor Channel; Oxygen; Spike TV; Syfy; TBS; The Weather Channel; TLC; TNT; Travel Channel; truTV; TV Land; USA Network; VH1; WE tv.
Fee: $47.99 monthly.
Digital Pay Service 1
Pay Units: N.A.
Programming (via satellite): Cinemax (multiplexed); Flix; HBO (multiplexed); Showtime (multiplexed); Starz (multiplexed); Starz Encore; The Movie Channel (multiplexed).
Video-On-Demand: Yes
Pay-Per-View
iN DEMAND; Playboy TV (delivered digitally); Spice Live (delivered digitally); Spice Platinum (delivered digitally); Hot Net Plus (delivered digitally); Spice Hot (delivered digitally).
Internet Service
Operational: Yes. Began: July 1, 2002.
Broadband Service: Charter Internet.
Fee: $29.99 monthly.
Telephone Service
Digital: Operational
Miles of Plant: 104.0 (coaxial); None (fiber optic).
Vice President & General Manager: John Crowley. Operations Director: Craig Stensaas. Technical Operations Director: Mark Abramo. Marketing Director: Bill Haarstad. Accounting Director: David Sovanski.
Ownership: Charter Communications Inc. (MSO).

FERTILE—Garden Valley Telephone Co. Now served by McINTOSH, MN [MN0105]. ICA: MN0297.

FINLAND—Formerly served by New Century Communications. No longer in operation. ICA: MN0298.

FLOODWOOD—SCI Broadband, 111 Tobies Mill Pl, PO Box 810, Hinckley, MN 55037-0810. Phones: 800-222-9809; 320-384-7442. Fax: 320-279-8085. E-mail: sales@scibroadband.com. Web Site: http://www.scibroadband.com. ICA: MN0175.
TV Market Ranking: Below 100 (FLOODWOOD). Franchise award date: July 28, 1984. Franchise expiration date: N.A. Began: June 1, 1985.
Channel capacity: N.A. Channels available but not in use: N.A.
Basic Service
Subscribers: 115.
Programming (received off-air): KBJR-TV (CBS, MNT, NBC) Superior; KCCW-TV (CBS) Walker; KDLH (CBS, CW) Duluth; KQDS-TV (Antenna TV, FOX) Duluth; WDIO-DT (ABC, MeTV) Duluth; WDSE (PBS) Duluth.
Programming (via satellite): A&E; Animal Planet; CNBC; CNN; Comedy Central; C-SPAN; Discovery Channel; Disney Channel; E! HD; ESPN; ESPN2; Fox News Channel; FOX Sports Networks; Freeform; Great American Country; HGTV; History; HLN; Lifetime; MTV; Nickelodeon; QVC; Spike TV; Syfy; TBS; The Weather Channel; TLC; TNT; Turner Classic Movies; TV Land; USA Network; VH1; WGN America; WPIX (Antenna TV, CW, This TV) New York.
Fee: $39.95 installation; $17.95 monthly.
Digital Basic Service
Subscribers: N.A.
Programming (via satellite): A&E; BBC America; Bloomberg Television; Cloo; Discovery Life Channel; DMX Music; ESPN Classic; ESPNews; Fox Sports 1; Fuse; FXM; Golf Channel; History International; INSP; National Geographic Channel; NBCSN; Outdoor Channel; Trinity Broadcasting Network (TBN); WE tv.
Digital Pay Service 1
Pay Units: N.A.
Programming (via satellite): Cinemax; Flix; HBO; Showtime; Starz; Starz Encore; Sundance TV; The Movie Channel.
Video-On-Demand: No
Pay-Per-View
ESPN Now (delivered digitally); Sports PPV (delivered digitally).
Internet Service
Operational: Yes.
Broadband Service: SCI Broadband.
Telephone Service
Digital: Operational
Miles of Plant: 4.0 (coaxial); None (fiber optic). Homes passed: 324.
President: Ron Savage. General Manager: Mike Danielson. Chief Technician: Pat Mc-

Cabe. Customer Service Manager: Donna Erickson.
Ownership: Savage Communications Inc. (MSO).

FOSSTON—City of Fosston Cable TV, 220 East 1st St, PO Box 239, Fosston, MN 56542. Phones: 218-435-1959; 218-435-1737. Fax: 218-435-1961. E-mail: dave.larson@fosston.com. Web Site: http://www.fosston.com. ICA: MN0123.
TV Market Ranking: Outside TV Markets (FOSSTON). Franchise award date: October 1, 1977. Franchise expiration date: N.A. Began: October 1, 1977.
Channel capacity: N.A. Channels available but not in use: N.A.
Basic Service
Subscribers: 242.
Programming (received off-air): KAWE (PBS) Bemidji; KBRR (FOX) Thief River Falls; KCCO-TV (CBS) Alexandria; KRDK-TV (CBS, Decades, Movies!) Valley City; KVLY-TV (MeTV, NBC, This TV) Fargo; WDAY-TV (ABC, CW) Fargo.
Programming (via satellite): A&E; AMC; Animal Planet; CMT; CNN; C-SPAN; Discovery Channel; Disney Channel; ESPN; ESPN2; Fox News Channel; FOX Sports Networks; Freeform; Hallmark Channel; HGTV; History; Lifetime; Nickelodeon; Outdoor Channel; Spike TV; Syfy; TBS; The Weather Channel; TLC; TNT; Travel Channel; Turner Classic Movies; TV Land; USA Network; VH1; WGN America.
Fee: $24.00 installation; $45.50 monthly.
Pay Service 1
Pay Units: N.A.
Programming (via satellite): Cinemax; HBO.
Fee: $12.50 installation; $7.00 monthly (Cinemax), $11.00 monthly (HBO).
Video-On-Demand: No
Internet Service
Operational: No.
Telephone Service
None
Miles of Plant: 11.0 (coaxial); None (fiber optic). Homes passed: 720.
General Manager: David Larson. Chief Technician: David K. Larson. Deputy City Administrator: Laurel Skala.
Ownership: City of Fosston Cable TV.

FOUNTAIN—Formerly served by Arvig. No longer in operation. ICA: MN0299.

FRANKLIN—Mediacom, 1504 2nd St SE, PO Box 110, Waseca, MN 56093. Phones: 845-695-2762; 507-835-2356. Fax: 507-835-4567. Web Site: http://www.mediacomcable.com. Also serves Arlington, Bird Island, Danube, Fairfax, Gaylord, Gibbon, Lower Sioux, Morton, North Redwood, Olivia, Redwood Falls, Sleepy Eye, Springfield & Winthrop. ICA: MN0057.
TV Market Ranking: Below 100 (Arlington, Bird Island, Danube, Fairfax, Gaylord, Gibbon, Lower Sioux, Morton, North Redwood, Sleepy Eye, Springfield, Winthrop, FRANKLIN, Olivia, Redwood Falls). Franchise award date: November 1, 1981. Fran-

2017 Edition
D-401

Minnesota—Cable Systems

CABLE & TV STATION COVERAGE
Atlas 2017
The perfect companion to the Television & Cable Factbook
To order call 800-771-9202 or visit www.warren-news.com

chise expiration date: N.A. Began: September 1, 1982.
Channel capacity: N.A. Channels available but not in use: N.A.
Basic Service
Subscribers: 3,683.
Programming (received off-air): KEYC-TV (CBS, FOX) Mankato; KPXM-TV (ION) St. Cloud; KSTC-TV (Antenna TV, This TV) Minneapolis; KTCI-TV (PBS) St. Paul; KWCM-TV (PBS) Appleton; WUCW (CW, The Country Network) Minneapolis; allband FM.
Programming (via satellite): C-SPAN; Pop; The Weather Channel; WGN America.
Programming (via translator): KARE (NBC, WeatherNation) Minneapolis; KMSP-TV (Bounce TV, Buzzr, FOX) Minneapolis; KSTP-TV (ABC, MeTV) St. Paul; KTCA-TV (PBS) St. Paul; WCCO-TV (CBS, Decades) Minneapolis; WFTC (MNT, Movies!) Minneapolis.
Fee: $52.39 installation; $43.00 monthly; $2.00 converter.
Expanded Basic Service 1
Subscribers: N.A.
Programming (via satellite): A&E; AMC; Animal Planet; BET; Bravo; Cartoon Network; CMT; CNBC; CNN; Comedy Central; Discovery Channel; Disney Channel; E! HD; ESPN; ESPN2; EWTN Global Catholic Network; Food Network; Fox News Channel; Fox Sports 1; FOX Sports North; Freeform; FX; FXM; Hallmark Channel; HGTV; History; HLN; INSP; Lifetime; MSNBC; MTV; Nickelodeon; QVC; Spike TV; Syfy; TBS; TLC; TNT; Travel Channel; Trinity Broadcasting Network (TBN); Turner Classic Movies; TV Land; Univision Studios; USA Network; VH1; WE tv.
Fee: $16.52 monthly.
Digital Basic Service
Subscribers: N.A.
Programming (via satellite): BBC America; Bloomberg Television; Discovery Digital Networks; DMX Music; Fuse; FYI; Golf Channel; GSN; History International; HITS (Headend In The Sky); IFC; LMN; National Geographic Channel; Outdoor Channel.
Digital Pay Service 1
Pay Units: N.A.
Programming (via satellite): Cinemax (multiplexed); Flix; HBO (multiplexed); Showtime (multiplexed); Starz (multiplexed); Starz Encore (multiplexed); Sundance TV; The Movie Channel (multiplexed).
Fee: $8.00 monthly (Starz/Encore), $9.95 monthly (Cinemax), $11.00 monthly (HBO, Showtime or TMC).
Video-On-Demand: Yes
Pay-Per-View
Vubiquity Inc. (delivered digitally); ESPN Now (delivered digitally); Sports PPV (delivered digitally); Urban Xtra (delivered digitally); Fresh (delivered digitally); Shorteez (delivered digitally); Playboy TV (delivered digitally); Pleasure (delivered digitally).
Internet Service
Operational: Yes.
Broadband Service: Mediacom High Speed Internet.
Fee: $40.00 monthly.

Telephone Service
Digital: Operational
Miles of Plant: 183.0 (coaxial); None (fiber optic). Homes passed: 9,242.
Vice President: Bill Jensen. Engineering Manager: Kraig Kaiser. Marketing & Sales Director: Lori Huberty. Vice President, Financial Reporting: Kenneth J. Kohrs.
Ownership: Mediacom LLC (MSO).

FRENCH RIVER TWP.—Formerly served by New Century Communications. No longer in operation. ICA: MN0300.

FRIDLEY—Formerly served by Time Warner Cable. Now served by Comcast Cable, MINNEAPOLIS, MN [MN0001]. ICA: MN0005.

FULDA—Mediacom. Now served by IVANHOE, MN [MN0189]. ICA: MN0142.

GARDEN CITY—Formerly served by North American Communications Corp. This cable system has converted to IPTV. Now served by Jaguar Communications, OWATONNA, MN [MN5121]. ICA: MN0301.

GARY—Formerly served by Loretel Cablevision. Now served by Arvig, PERHAM, MN [MN0050]. ICA: MN0264.

GAYLORD—Mediacom. Now served by FRANKLIN, MN [MN0057]. ICA: MN0053.

GLENCOE—NU-Telecom, 2104 10th St East, Glencoe, MN 55336. Phones: 888-873-6853; 320-864-2818. Fax: 320-864-5612. E-mail: on-linecustservice@nu-telcom.net. Web Site: http://www.nutelecom.net. Also serves Glencoe Twp. ICA: MN0065.
Channel capacity: N.A. Channels available but not in use: N.A.
Digital Basic Service
Subscribers: 758.
Programming (received off-air): KARE (NBC, WeatherNation) Minneapolis; KEYC-TV (CBS, FOX) Mankato; KMSP-TV (Bounce TV, Buzzr, FOX) Minneapolis; KPXM-TV (ION) St. Cloud; KSTC-TV (Antenna TV, This TV) Minneapolis; KSTP-TV (ABC, MeTV) St. Paul; KUCW (CW, Movies!, The Country Network) Ogden; WCCO-TV (CBS, Decades) Minneapolis; WFTC (MNT, Movies!) Minneapolis.
Programming (via satellite): Antenna TV; C-SPAN; EWTN Global Catholic Network; HSN; Live Well Network; MeTV; Pop; QVC; This TV; Trinity Broadcasting Network (TBN); WGN America.
Fee: $50.00 installation; $21.95 monthly.
Digital Expanded Basic Service
Subscribers: N.A.
Programming (via satellite): A&E; AMC; Animal Planet; Bravo; BTN; Cartoon Network; CMT; CNN; Comedy Central; Discovery Channel; Disney Channel; Disney Junior; Disney XD; E! HD; ESPN; ESPN2; Food Network; Fox Business Network; Fox News Channel; FOX Sports North; Freeform; FX; GSN; HGTV; History; HLN; Investigation Discovery; Lifetime; MSNBC; MTV; NASA TV; National Geographic Channel; NBCSN; Nickelodeon; OWN: Oprah Winfrey Network; Oxygen; Science Channel; Spike TV; Syfy; TBS; The Weather Channel; TLC; TNT; TV Land; Univision; USA Network; VH1; WE tv.
Fee: $51.95 monthly.
Digital Expanded Basic Service 2
Subscribers: N.A.
Programming (via satellite): American Heroes Channel; BBC America; Bloomberg Television; Centric; Chiller; Cloo; CMT; CNBC World; C-SPAN 2; C-SPAN 3; Destination America; Discovery Family; Discovery Life Channel; DIY Network; ESPNU; Fox Sports 1; FYI; Hallmark Channel; Hallmark Movies & Mysteries; MTV Classic; MTV Hits; MTV Jams; MTV2; Nat Geo WILD; NBC Universo; NFL Network; Nick Jr.; Nicktoons; Pursuit Channel; Reelz; RFD-TV; Sundance TV; Telemundo.
Fee: $65.95 monthly.
Digital Expanded Basic Service 3
Subscribers: N.A.
Fee: $10.95 monthly.
Digital Pay Service 1
Pay Units: N.A.
Programming (via satellite): Cinemax (multiplexed); Flix (multiplexed); HBO (multiplexed); Showtime (multiplexed); Starz; Starz Encore (multiplexed); The Movie Channel (multiplexed).
Fee: $15.95 monthly (Cinemax, HBO, Showtime/TMC or Starz/Encore), $27.95 monthly (Cinemax/HBO).
Internet Service
Operational: Yes.
Fee: $29.95-$64.95 monthly.
Telephone Service
None
President & Chief Executive Officer: Bill Otis. Chief Operating Officer & Vice President: Barbara Bornhoft. Chief Financial Officer & Treasurer: Curtis Kawlweski.
Ownership: New Ulm Telecom.

GLENVILLE—Midco. Now served by WASECA COUNTY (portions), MN [MN0266]. ICA: MN0183.

GLENWOOD—Charter Communications. Now served by ALEXANDRIA, MN [MN0031]. ICA: MN0082.

GOOD THUNDER—Formerly served by Woodstock LLC. No longer in operation. ICA: MN0173.

GOODHUE—Nu-Telecom (formerly Sleepy Eye Telephone). This cable system has converted to IPTV. See GOODHUE, MN [MN5120]. ICA: MN0208.

GOODHUE—NU-Telecom. Formerly [MN0208]. This cable system has converted to IPTV, 111 Second Ave, Goodhue, MN 55027. Phones: 844-354-4111; 888-742-8010; 651-923-5005. Fax: 651-923-4010. E-mail: on-linecustservice@nu-telecom.net. Web Site: http://www.nutelecom.net. Also serves Bellechester, Mazeppa & White Rock. ICA: MN5120.
TV Market Ranking: Below 100 (GOODHUE). Channel capacity: N.A. Channels available but not in use: N.A.
NU-Basic
Subscribers: 472.
Fee: $80.00 installation; $24.95 monthly.
Internet Service
Operational: Yes.
Fee: $39.95 monthly.

Telephone Service
Digital: Operational
Ownership: NU-Telecom.

GOODVIEW—Hiawatha Broadband. This cable system has converted to IPTV. Now served by WINONA, MN [MN5161]. ICA: MN5174.

GRACEVILLE—Mediacom. Now served by APPLETON, MN [MN0106]. ICA: MN0188.

GRANADA—Formerly served by Midcontinent Communications. Now served by BEVCOMM. This cable system has converted to IPTV. See NEW PRAGUE, MN [MN5366]. ICA: MN0257.

GRAND MARAIS—Mediacom, 1504 2nd St SE, PO Box 110, Waseca, MN 56093. Phones: 845-695-2762; 507-835-2356. Fax: 507-835-4567. E-mail: bjensen@mediacomcc.com. Web Site: http://www.mediacomcable.com. ICA: MN0303.
TV Market Ranking: Outside TV Markets (GRAND MARAIS). Franchise award date: N.A. Franchise expiration date: N.A. Began: August 1, 1984.
Channel capacity: 37 (not 2-way capable). Channels available but not in use: N.A.
Basic Service
Subscribers: 45.
Programming (via satellite): C-SPAN; C-SPAN 2; ION Television; QVC; WGN America.
Programming (via translator): KBJR-TV (CBS, MNT, NBC) Superior; KDLH (CBS, CW) Duluth; KQDS-TV (Antenna TV, FOX) Duluth; WDIO-DT (ABC, MeTV) Duluth; WDSE (PBS) Duluth.
Fee: $40.00 monthly.
Expanded Basic Service 1
Subscribers: N.A.
Programming (via satellite): A&E; AMC; Animal Planet; Bravo; CMT; CNBC; CNN; Comedy Central; Discovery Channel; Disney Channel; E! HD; ESPN; ESPN2; Food Network; Fox Sports 1; FOX Sports North; Freeform; FX; HGTV; History; HLN; INSP; Lifetime; MSNBC; MTV; Nickelodeon; Spike TV; TBS; The Weather Channel; TLC; TNT; Travel Channel; truTV; TV Land; USA Network; VH1; WE tv.
Pay Service 1
Pay Units: N.A.
Programming (via satellite): HBO; The Movie Channel.
Fee: $10.95 monthly (each).
Video-On-Demand: No
Internet Service
Operational: No.
Telephone Service
None
Miles of Plant: 14.0 (coaxial); None (fiber optic).
Vice President: Bill Jensen. Vice President, Financial Reporting: Kenneth J. Kohrs. Marketing & Sales Director: Lori Huberty. Program Director: Barry Paden. Engineering Manager: Kraig Kaiser.
Ownership: Mediacom LLC (MSO).

GRAND MEADOW—Arvig, 160 2nd Ave. SW, Perham, MN 56573. Phones: 888-992-7844; 218-346-4227; 507-754-5115 (Grand Meadow office). Fax: 218-338-3297. E-mail: answers@arvig.com. Web Site: http://arvig.com. Also serves Racine & Wykoff. ICA: MN0168.
TV Market Ranking: Below 100 (GRAND MEADOW, Racine). Franchise award date:

Cable Systems—Minnesota

August 5, 1984. Franchise expiration date: N.A. Began: October 1, 1984.
Channel capacity: N.A. Channels available but not in use: N.A.

Basic Service
Subscribers: 228.
Programming (received off-air): KAAL (ABC, This TV) Austin; KIMT (CBS, MNT) Mason City; KSMQ-TV (PBS) Austin; KTTC (CW, NBC) Rochester; KXLT-TV (FOX, MeTV) Rochester; KYIN (PBS) Mason City; WKBT-DT (CBS, MNT) La Crosse.
Programming (via satellite): A&E; AMC; CMT; CNN; Comedy Central; Discovery Channel; Disney Channel; ESPN; ESPN2; FOX Sports Midwest; Freeform; HGTV; History; Lifetime; Nickelodeon; Spike TV; TBS; TNT; USA Network; VH1; WGN America.
Fee: $55.00 installation; $47.95 monthly.

Pay Service 1
Pay Units: N.A.
Programming (via satellite): HBO; Showtime.
Fee: $12.95 monthly (Cinemax or Showtime), $17.95 monthly (HBO), $27.95 monthly (HBO/Showtime).

Video-On-Demand: No

Internet Service
Operational: No, DSL.
Fee: $42.95-$62.95 monthly.

Telephone Service
None
Miles of Plant: 7.0 (coaxial); None (fiber optic). Homes passed: 400.
Chief Operating Officer & Vice President: David Arvig. Video Director: David A. Pratt.
Ownership: Tekstar Communications Inc. (MSO).

GRAND RAPIDS—Mediacom, 1504 2nd St SE, PO Box 110, Waseca, MN 56093. Phones: 845-695-2762; 507-835-2356. Fax: 507-835-4567. Web Site: http://www.mediacomcable.com. Also serves Bass Brook Twp., Grand Prairie, Grand Rapids Twp., Harris Twp., Keewatin, La Prairie Twp. & Nashwauk. ICA: MN0038.
TV Market Ranking: Below 100 (Bass Brook Twp., Grand Prairie, GRAND RAPIDS, Grand Rapids Twp., Harris Twp., Keewatin, La Prairie Twp., Nashwauk). Franchise award date: N.A. Franchise expiration date: N.A. Began: March 1, 1965.
Channel capacity: N.A. Channels available but not in use: N.A.

Basic Service
Subscribers: 2,841.
Programming (received off-air): KAWE (PBS) Bemidji; KBJR-TV (CBS, MNT, NBC) Superior; KCCW-TV (CBS) Walker; KDLH (CBS, CW) Duluth; KQDS-TV (Antenna TV, FOX) Duluth; WDIO-DT (ABC, MeTV) Duluth; WDSE (PBS) Duluth; WIRT-DT (ABC, MeTV) Hibbing; allband FM.
Programming (via satellite): C-SPAN; C-SPAN 2; Pop; QVC; The Weather Channel; WGN America.
Fee: $15.00 installation; $45.00 monthly; $2.00 converter.

Expanded Basic Service 1
Subscribers: N.A.
Programming (via satellite): A&E; AMC; Animal Planet; Bravo; Cartoon Network; CMT; CNBC; CNN; Comedy Central; CW PLUS; Discovery Channel; Disney Channel; E! HD; ESPN; ESPN2; EWTN Global Catholic Network; Fox News Channel; Fox Sports 1; FOX Sports North; Freeform; FX; Hallmark Channel; HGTV; History; HLN; INSP; ION Television; Lifetime; MSNBC; MTV; Nickelodeon; Outdoor Channel; Spike TV; Syfy; TBS; TLC; TNT; Travel Channel; Trinity Broad-casting Network (TBN); truTV; Turner Classic Movies; TV Land; USA Network; VH1; WE tv.

Digital Basic Service
Subscribers: N.A.
Programming (via satellite): AXS TV; BBC America; Bloomberg Television; Cloo; CMT; Destination America; Discovery Kids Channel; Discovery Life Channel; ESPN Classic; ESPN HD; ESPN2 HD; ESPNews; Fuse; FXM; FYI; Golf Channel; GSN; HD Theater; History International; IFC; Investigation Discovery; LMN; MC; MTV Classic; MTV Hits; MTV2; National Geographic Channel; NBCSN; Nick Jr.; Nicktoons; Ovation; OWN: Oprah Winfrey Network; Science Channel; TeenNick; TVG Network; Universal HD; VH1 Soul.

Digital Pay Service 1
Pay Units: N.A.
Programming (via satellite): Cinemax (multiplexed); Flix; HBO (multiplexed); HBO HD; Showtime (multiplexed); Showtime HD; Starz (multiplexed); Starz Encore (multiplexed); Starz HD; Sundance TV; The Movie Channel (multiplexed); The Movie Channel HD.
Fee: $15.00 installation; $8.95 monthly (Showtime), $11.95 monthly (HBO).

Video-On-Demand: No

Pay-Per-View
iN DEMAND (delivered digitally); Spice: Xcess (delivered digitally); Playboy TV (delivered digitally); Fresh (delivered digitally); SexSee (delivered digitally).

Internet Service
Operational: Yes.
Subscribers: 3,445.
Broadband Service: Mediacom High Speed Internet.
Fee: $99.00 installation; $40.00 monthly.

Telephone Service
Digital: Operational
Subscribers: 1,803.
Miles of Plant: 343.0 (coaxial); 165.0 (fiber optic). Homes passed: 10,659.
Vice President: Bill Jensen. Vice President, Financial Reporting: Kenneth J. Kohrs. Engineering Manager: Kraig Kaiser. Marketing & Sales Director: Lori Huberty.
Ownership: Mediacom LLC (MSO).

GRANITE FALLS—Mediacom. Now served by PAYNESVILLE, MN [MN0125]. ICA: MN0070.

GREEN ISLE—Formerly served by North American Communications Corp. This cable system has converted to IPTV. Now served by Jaguar Communications, NEW MARKET, MN [MN5374]. ICA: MN0304.

GREENBUSH—Sjoberg's Cable TV Inc, 315 Main Ave North, Thief River Falls, MN 56701-1905. Phones: 800-828-8808; 218-681-3044. Fax: 218-681-6801. E-mail: office1@mncable.net; sjobergs@mncable.net. Web Site: http://trf.mncable.net. Also serves Hereim Twp. ICA: MN0186.
TV Market Ranking: Outside TV Markets (GREENBUSH, Hereim Twp.). Franchise award date: N.A. Franchise expiration date: N.A. Began: February 1, 1977.
Channel capacity: N.A. Channels available but not in use: N.A.

Basic Service
Subscribers: 198.
Programming (received off-air): KAWE (PBS) Bemidji; KBRR (FOX) Thief River Falls; KCPM (MNT) Grand Forks; various Canadian stations; WDAZ-TV (ABC, CW) Devils Lake; allband FM.
Programming (via microwave): KRDK-TV (CBS, Decades, Movies!) Valley City; KVLY-TV (MeTV, NBC, This TV) Fargo.
Programming (via satellite): CNN; ESPN; TBS.
Fee: $25.00 installation; $55.32 monthly.

Expanded Basic Service 1
Subscribers: N.A.
Programming (via satellite): A&E; Animal Planet; Cartoon Network; CMT; CNBC; Comedy Central; CW PLUS; Discovery Channel; E! HD; ESPN2; Food Network; Fox News Channel; FOX Sports Networks; Freeform; FX; HGTV; History; Lifetime; MSNBC; MTV; Nickelodeon; Spike TV; Syfy; The Weather Channel; TLC; TNT; Turner Classic Movies; TV Land; USA Network; WGN America.
Fee: $23.71 monthly.

Digital Basic Service
Subscribers: N.A.
Programming (via satellite): BBC America; Bloomberg Television; Bravo; CBS Sports Network; Chiller; Cloo; CMT; Cooking Channel; Daystar TV Network; Destination America; Discovery Kids Channel; Discovery Life Channel; Disney XD; DIY Network; DMX Music; ESPN Classic; ESPNews; ESPNU; EVINE Live; EWTN Global Catholic Network; Fox Business Network; FOX College Sports Central; FOX College Sports Pacific; Fox Sports 1; FXM; FYI; Golf Channel; Great American Country; GSN; Hallmark Channel; History International; HLN; HRTV; IFC; Investigation Discovery; LMN; MTV Classic; MTV Hits; MTV2; Nat Geo WILD; National Geographic Channel; NBCSN; Nick Jr.; Nicktoons; Outdoor Channel; Ovation; OWN: Oprah Winfrey Network; Oxygen; RFD-TV; Science Channel; Sprout; Sundance TV; TeenNick; Tennis Channel; The Word Network; TVG Network; UP; VH1 Soul; WE tv.

Digital Expanded Basic Service
Subscribers: N.A.
Programming (via satellite): A&E HD; AXS TV; CNN HD; Discovery Channel HD; ESPN HD; ESPN2 HD; Food Network HD; FSN HD; HGTV HD; History HD; Outdoor Channel 2 HD; Syfy HD; TBS HD; TNT HD; Universal HD; USA Network HD; Versus HD.
Fee: $5.00 monthly.

Pay Service 1
Pay Units: N.A.
Programming (via satellite): HBO.
Fee: $11.00 monthly.

Digital Pay Service 1
Pay Units: N.A.
Programming (via satellite): Cinemax (multiplexed); Cinemax HD; HBO (multiplexed); HBO HD; Showtime (multiplexed); Starz (multiplexed); Starz Encore (multiplexed); The Movie Channel (multiplexed).
Fee: $8.00 monthly (Starz/Encore), $9.00 monthly (Cinemax or Showtime/TMC), $11.00 monthly (HBO).

Video-On-Demand: No

Internet Service
Operational: No.

Telephone Service
None
Miles of Plant: 6.0 (coaxial); 17.0 (fiber optic). Homes passed: 322.
President & General Manager: Richard J. Sjoberg. Chief Technician: Jerry Seim.
Ownership: Sjoberg's Cable TV Inc. (MSO).

GREENWAY TWP.—SCI Broadband, 206 Power Ave N, PO Box 810, Hinckley, MN 55037-0810. Phones: 800-222-9809; 320-384-7442. Fax: 320-279-8085. E-mail: sales@scibroadband.com. Web Site: http://www.scibroadband.com. Also serves Lone Pine Twp. ICA: MN0411.
TV Market Ranking: Outside TV Markets (GREENWAY TWP., Lone Pine Twp.).
Channel capacity: N.A. Channels available but not in use: N.A.
Chief Technician: Keith Olson.
Ownership: Savage Communications Inc. (MSO).

GREY EAGLE—Arvig (formerly diversiCOM). This cable system has converted to IPTV. See MELROSE, MN [MN5017]. ICA: MN0232.

GROVE CITY—Mediacom. Now served by PAYNESVILLE, MN [MN0125]. ICA: MN0121.

GRYGLA—Garden Valley Telephone Co. Now served by McINTOSH, MN [MN0105]. ICA: MN0305.

HALLOCK—Wikstrom Cable LLC, PO Box 217, Karlstad, MN 56732. Phones: 218-436-2992; 800-436-1915. Fax: 218-436-3100. E-mail: service@wiktel.com. Web Site: http://www.wiktel.com. ICA: MN0134.
TV Market Ranking: Below 100 (HALLOCK). Franchise award date: May 1, 1990. Franchise expiration date: N.A. Began: May 12, 1973.
Channel capacity: N.A. Channels available but not in use: N.A.

Basic Service
Subscribers: 231.
Programming (received off-air): KGFE (PBS) Grand Forks; KNRR (FOX) Pembina; KRDK-TV (CBS, Decades, Movies!) Valley City; KVLY-TV (MeTV, NBC, This TV) Fargo; various Canadian stations; WDAZ-TV (ABC, CW) Devils Lake; allband FM.
Programming (via satellite): A&E; AMC; Cartoon Network; CMT; CNBC; CNN; C-SPAN; Discovery Channel; Disney Channel; ESPN; ESPN2; FOX Sports North; Freeform; HGTV; History; HLN; INSP; Lifetime; Nickelodeon; QVC; Spike TV; TBS; The Weather Channel; TLC; TNT; TV Land; USA Network; VH1; WGN America.
Fee: $51.23 monthly.

Pay Service 1
Pay Units: N.A.
Programming (via satellite): HBO; Showtime; The Movie Channel.
Fee: $20.00 installation; $10.95 monthly (HBO or Showtime).

Video-On-Demand: No

Internet Service
Operational: No.

2017 Edition

Minnesota—Cable Systems

FULLY SEARCHABLE • CONTINUOUSLY UPDATED • DISCOUNT RATES FOR PRINT PURCHASERS
For more information call 800-771-9202 or visit www.warren-news.com

Telephone Service
None
Miles of Plant: 11.0 (coaxial); None (fiber optic). Homes passed: 616.
Plant Manager: Al Lundeen.
Ownership: Wikstrom Systems LLC (MSO).

HAMPTON—Formerly served by Cannon Valley Cablevision. Now served by Midcontinent Communications, CANNON FALLS TWP., MN [MN0391]. ICA: MN0307.

HANCOCK—Mediacom. Now served by MORRIS, MN [MN0210]. ICA: MN0198.

HANLEY FALLS—Clara City Telephone Co, 227 South Main St, PO Box 800, Clara City, MN 56222. Phone: 320-847-2211. Fax: 320-847-2736. Web Site: http://www.hcinet.net. ICA: MN0308.
TV Market Ranking: Below 100 (HANLEY FALLS). Franchise award date: April 1, 1989. Franchise expiration date: N.A. Began: March 1, 1990.
Channel capacity: N.A. Channels available but not in use: N.A.
Basic Service
Subscribers: 42.
Programming (received off-air): KARE (NBC, WeatherNation) Minneapolis; KCCO-TV (CBS) Alexandria; KMSP-TV (Bounce TV, Buzzr, FOX) Minneapolis; KRWF (ABC) Redwood Falls; KSTC-TV (Antenna TV, This TV) Minneapolis; KWCM-TV (PBS) Appleton; WFTC (MNT, Movies!) Minneapolis.
Programming (via satellite): A&E; AMC; Animal Planet; Cartoon Network; CMT; CNN; Comedy Central; Discovery Channel; Disney Channel; ESPN; ESPN2; Food Network; FOX Sports North; Freeform; Hallmark Channel; HGTV; History; Lifetime; MTV; Nickelodeon; QVC; Spike TV; Syfy; TBS; The Weather Channel; TLC; TNT; Trinity Broadcasting Network (TBN); TV Land; Univision Studios; USA Network; VH1.
Fee: $20.00 installation; $38.95 monthly.
Pay Service 1
Pay Units: 10.
Programming (via satellite): Cinemax; HBO; Showtime.
Fee: $9.95 monthly (Cinemax), $10.95 monthly (Showtime), $11.95 monthly (HBO).
Video-On-Demand: No
Internet Service
Operational: Yes.
Telephone Service
Analog: Operational
Miles of Plant: 3.0 (coaxial); None (fiber optic). Homes passed: 125.
Treasurer & General Manager: Bruce Hanson.
Ownership: Hanson Communications Inc. (MSO).

HANSKA—Formerly served by Clara City Telephone Co. No longer in operation. ICA: MN0309.

HARMONY—Harmony Telephone Co, 35 1st Ave NE, PO Box 308, Harmony, MN 55939. Phone: 507-886-2525. Fax: 507-886-2500. E-mail: info@harmonytel.com; custserv@harmonytel.net. Web Site: http://www.harmonytel.com. ICA: MN0159.
TV Market Ranking: Outside TV Markets (HARMONY). Franchise award date: May 30, 1983. Franchise expiration date: N.A. Began: December 6, 1983.
Channel capacity: N.A. Channels available but not in use: N.A.
Basic Service
Subscribers: 283.
Programming (received off-air): KAAL (ABC, This TV) Austin; KIMT (CBS, MNT) Mason City; KTTC (CW, NBC) Rochester; KXLT-TV (FOX, MeTV) Rochester; KYIN (PBS) Mason City; WKBT-DT (CBS, MNT) La Crosse; WLAX (FOX, MeTV) La Crosse; WXOW (ABC, CW, This TV) La Crosse.
Programming (via satellite): A&E; AMC; Animal Planet; CMT; Disney Channel; ESPN; ESPN2; Fox News Channel; FOX Sports Networks; Freeform; HGTV; History; The Weather Channel; Trinity Broadcasting Network (TBN); TV Land; VH1; WGN America.
Fee: $20.00 installation; $41.00 monthly.
Pay Service 1
Pay Units: 90.
Programming (via satellite): HBO; Showtime.
Fee: $20.00 installation; $9.00 monthly (each).
Video-On-Demand: No
Internet Service
Operational: No.
Telephone Service
None
Miles of Plant: 12.0 (coaxial); None (fiber optic). Homes passed: 518.
Vice President, Operations: Jill Fishbaugher.
Co-Manager: C Otterness.; L Tingesdal.
Ownership: Harmony Telephone Co.

HAWLEY—Formerly served by Loretel Cablevision. Now served by Arvig, PERHAM, MN [MN0050]. ICA: MN0128.

HAYFIELD—Mediacom. Now served by CANNON FALLS, MN [MN0076]. ICA: MN0152.

HAYWARD—Formerly served by North American Communications Corp. This cable system has converted to IPTV. Now served by Jaguar Communications, OWATONNA, MN [MN5121]. ICA: MN0310.

HECTOR—Mediacom. Now served by HUTCHINSON, MN [MN0145]. ICA: MN0109.

HENDRICKS—Formerly served by US Cable of Coastal Texas LP. No longer in operation. ICA: MN0190.

HERON LAKE—Midco, PO Box 5010, Sioux Falls, SD 57117. Phone: 800-888-1300. Web Site: http://www.midcocomm.com. Also serves Okabena. ICA: MN0195.
TV Market Ranking: Outside TV Markets (HERON LAKE, Okabena). Franchise award date: N.A. Franchise expiration date: N.A. Began: February 1, 1984.
Channel capacity: N.A. Channels available but not in use: N.A.
Basic Service
Subscribers: 23. Commercial subscribers: 14.
Programming (received off-air): KELO-TV (CBS, MNT) Sioux Falls; KEYC-TV (CBS, FOX) Mankato; KSFY-TV (ABC, CW) Sioux Falls; KSMN (PBS) Worthington; KSTC-TV (Antenna TV, This TV) Minneapolis; WCCO-TV (CBS, Decades) Minneapolis; WFTC (MNT, Movies!) Minneapolis.
Programming (via satellite): A&E; Cartoon Network; CMT; CNBC; CNN; Comedy Central; Discovery Channel; ESPN; ESPN2; EWTN Global Catholic Network; Food Network; FOX Sports Networks; Freeform; HGTV; History; HLN; Lifetime; Nickelodeon; Outdoor Channel; Spike TV; TBS; The Weather Channel; TLC; TNT; Turner Classic Movies; TV Land; USA Network; VH1; WGN America.
Programming (via translator): KARE (NBC, WeatherNation) Minneapolis; KMSP-TV (Bounce TV, Buzzr, FOX) Minneapolis; KSTP-TV (ABC, MeTV) St. Paul.
Fee: $45.95 monthly.
Pay Service 1
Pay Units: N.A.
Programming (via satellite): Cinemax; HBO.
Fee: $11.95 monthly (each).
Internet Service
Operational: No.
Telephone Service
None
Homes passed & miles of plant included in Cambridge.
President & Chief Executive Officer: Pat McAdaragh. Senior Vice President, Public Policy: Tom Simmons. Programming Director: Wynne Haakenstad.
Ownership: Midcontinent Communications (MSO).

HILL CITY—SCI Broadband, 111 Tobies Mill Pl, PO Box 810, Hinckley, MN 55037-0810. Phones: 800-222-9809; 320-384-7442. Fax: 320-279-8085. E-mail: sales@scibroadband.com. Web Site: http://www.scibroadband.com. ICA: MN0153.
TV Market Ranking: Outside TV Markets (HILL CITY). Franchise award date: August 1, 1984. Franchise expiration date: N.A. Began: September 9, 1985.
Channel capacity: N.A. Channels available but not in use: N.A.
Basic Service
Subscribers: 161.
Programming (received off-air): KAWE (PBS) Bemidji; KBJR-TV (CBS, MNT, NBC) Superior; KCCW-TV (CBS) Walker; KDLH (CBS, CW) Duluth; KQDS-TV (Antenna TV, FOX) Duluth; WDIO-DT (ABC, MeTV) Duluth; WDSE (PBS) Duluth; WPIX (Antenna TV, CW, This TV) New York.
Programming (via satellite): A&E; Animal Planet; CNBC; CNN; Comedy Central; C-SPAN; Discovery Channel; Disney Channel; E! HD; ESPN; ESPN2; Fox News Channel; FOX Sports Networks; Freeform; Great American Country; HGTV; History; HLN; Lifetime; MTV; Nickelodeon; QVC; Spike TV; Syfy; TBS; The Weather Channel; TLC; TNT; Turner Classic Movies; TV Land; USA Network; VH1; WGN America.
Fee: $39.95 installation; $17.95 monthly.
Digital Basic Service
Subscribers: N.A.
Programming (via satellite): BBC America; Bloomberg Television; Cloo; Discovery Life Channel; DMX Music; ESPN Classic; ESPNews; Fox Sports 1; Fuse; FXM; FYI; Golf Channel; History International; INSP; National Geographic Channel; NBCSN; Outdoor Channel; Trinity Broadcasting Network (TBN); WE tv.
Digital Pay Service 1
Pay Units: N.A.
Programming (via satellite): Cinemax (multiplexed); Flix; HBO (multiplexed); Showtime (multiplexed); Starz (multiplexed); Starz Encore (multiplexed); Sundance TV; The Movie Channel (multiplexed).
Video-On-Demand: No
Pay-Per-View
ESPN Now (delivered digitally); Sports PPV (delivered digitally).
Internet Service
Operational: Yes.
Broadband Service: SCI Broadband.
Fee: $24.95 monthly.
Telephone Service
Digital: Operational
Miles of Plant: 9.0 (coaxial); None (fiber optic). Homes passed: 290.
General Manager: Mike Danielson. President: Ron Savage. Chief Technician: Pat McCabe. Customer Service Manager: Donna Erickson.
Ownership: Savage Communications Inc. (MSO).

HILLS—Alliance Communications. Now served by GARRETSON, SD [SD0016]. ICA: MN0215.

HOKAH—Mediacom. Now served by CALEDONIA, MN [MN0086]. ICA: MN0192.

HOMER—Hiawatha Broadband. This cable system has converted to IPTV. Now served by WINONA, MN [MN5161]. ICA: MN5172.

HOUSTON—AcenTek, 207 East Cedar St, PO Box 360, Houston, MN 55943-0360. Phones: 507-896-6207; 507-896-4695; 888-404-4940. Fax: 507-896-2149; 507-896-3207. E-mail: info@acentek.net. Web Site: http://www.acentek.net. Also serves Castalia, Clermont, Dorchester, Fort Atkinson, New Albin, Ossian & Waterville, IA; Bristol Twp., Brownsville, Caledonia, Canton, Dakota, Eitzen, Hokah, La Crescent, Lanesboro, Mound Prairie, Ostrander, Peterson, Rushford, Sheldon, Spring Grove & Yucatan, MN. ICA: MN5105.
TV Market Ranking: Below 100 (Eitzen, Ostrander, Spring Grove); Outside TV Markets (Spring Grove).
Channel capacity: N.A. Channels available but not in use: N.A.
Basic
Subscribers: 5,567. Commercial subscribers: 130.
Fee: $26.50 monthly. Includes 22 channels.
Basic Plus
Subscribers: 429.
Fee: $55.95 monthly. Includes 98 channels plus 50 music channels.
Expanded Basic
Subscribers: N.A.
Fee: $69.95 monthly. Includes 186 channels plus 50 music channels.
Cinemax
Subscribers: N.A.
Fee: $12.95 monthly. Includes 8 channels.
HBO
Subscribers: N.A.
Fee: $16.95 monthly. Includes 10 channels.

Cable Systems—Minnesota

Access the most current data instantly

www.warren-news.com/factbook.htm

Showtime/TMC
Subscribers: N.A.
Fee: $14.95 monthly. Includes 13 channels.
Starz/Encore
Subscribers: N.A.
Fee: $10.95 monthly. Includes 15 channels.
Video-On-Demand: Yes
Internet Service
Operational: Yes.
Fee: $39.95-$49.95 monthly.
Telephone Service
Digital: Operational
Fee: $17.00 monthly
Miles of Plant: None (coaxial); 589.0 (fiber optic). Fiber miles includes all Acentek systems.
Chief Executive Officer: Todd Roesler.
Ownership: AcenTek.

HOUSTON—Mediacom. Now served by CALEDONIA, MN [MN0086]. ICA: MN0138.

HOWARD LAKE—Mediacom. Now served by HUTCHINSON, MN [MN0145]. ICA: MN0143.

HUTCHINSON—Mediacom, 1504 2nd St SE, PO Box 110, Waseca, MN 56093. Phones: 845-695-2762; 507-835-2356. Fax: 507-835-4567. Web Site: http://www.mediacomcable.com. Also serves Brownton, Buffalo Lake, Collinwood Twp., Darwin, Dassel Twp., Ellsworth Twp., Hassen Valley Twp., Hector, Howard Lake, Lester Prairie, Litchfield, Litchfield Twp., Silver Lake, Stewart & Winsted. ICA: MN0145.
TV Market Ranking: Below 100 (Buffalo Lake, Darwin, Dassel Twp., Hector, Litchfield, Litchfield Twp., Stewart, Howard Lake); Outside TV Markets (Ellsworth Twp., Hassen Valley Twp., Lester Prairie, Silver Lake, Winsted, Brownton, HUTCHINSON). Franchise award date: N.A. Franchise expiration date: N.A. Began: November 1, 1985.
Channel capacity: N.A. Channels available but not in use: N.A.
Basic Service
Subscribers: 4,129.
Programming (received off-air): KARE (NBC, WeatherNation) Minneapolis; KEYC-TV (CBS, FOX) Mankato; KMSP-TV (Bounce TV, Buzzr, FOX) Minneapolis; KPXM-TV (ION) St. Cloud; KSTC-TV (Antenna TV, This TV) Minneapolis; KSTP-TV (ABC, MeTV) St. Paul; KTCA-TV (PBS) St. Paul; KTCI-TV (PBS) St. Paul; WCCO-TV (CBS, Decades) Minneapolis; WFTC (MNT, Movies!) Minneapolis; WUCW (CW, The Country Network) Minneapolis.
Programming (via satellite): C-SPAN; Pop; QVC; The Weather Channel; WGN America.
Fee: $43.00 monthly.
Expanded Basic Service 1
Subscribers: N.A.
Programming (via satellite): A&E; AMC; Animal Planet; BET; Bravo; Cartoon Network; CMT; CNBC; CNN; Comedy Central; Discovery Channel; Disney Channel; E! HD; ESPN; ESPN2; EWTN Global Catholic Network; Food Network; Fox News Channel; Fox Sports 1; FOX Sports North; Freeform; FX; FXM; Hallmark Channel; HGTV; History; HLN; INSP; Lifetime; MSNBC; MTV; Nickelodeon; Spike TV; Syfy; TBS; TLC; TNT; Travel Channel; Trinity Broadcasting Network (TBN); truTV; Turner Classic Movies; TV Land; Univision Studios; USA Network; VH1; WE tv.
Fee: $26.18 monthly.
Digital Basic Service
Subscribers: N.A.
Programming (via satellite): BBC America; Bloomberg Television; Discovery Digital Networks; DMX Music; Fuse; FYI; Golf Channel; GSN; History International; HITS (Headend In The Sky); IFC; LMN; NBCSN; Outdoor Channel.
Digital Pay Service 1
Pay Units: N.A.
Programming (via satellite): Cinemax (multiplexed); Flix; HBO (multiplexed); Showtime (multiplexed); Starz (multiplexed); Starz Encore (multiplexed); Sundance TV; The Movie Channel (multiplexed).
Fee: $9.95 monthly (each).
Video-On-Demand: No
Pay-Per-View
Vubiquity Inc. (delivered digitally); ESPN Now (delivered digitally); Sports PPV (delivered digitally); Urban Xtra (delivered digitally); Fresh (delivered digitally); Shorteez (delivered digitally); Playboy TV (delivered digitally); Pleasure (delivered digitally).
Internet Service
Operational: Yes.
Broadband Service: Mediacom High Speed Internet.
Fee: $99.00 installation; $40.95 monthly.
Telephone Service
Analog: Not Operational
Digital: Operational
Miles of Plant: 169.0 (coaxial); None (fiber optic). Homes passed: 10,663.
Vice President: Bill Jensen. Vice President, Financial Reporting: Kenneth J. Kohrs. Sales & Marketing Director: Lori Huberty. Engineering Manager: Kraig Kaiser.
Ownership: Mediacom LLC (MSO).

HUTCHINSON—Mediacom. Now served by HUTCHINSON, MN [MN0145]. ICA: MN0035.

INTERNATIONAL FALLS—Midco, PO Box 5010, Sioux Falls, SD 57117. Phones: 800-888-1300; 605-229-1775. Fax: 605-229-0478. Web Site: http://www.midcocomm.com. Also serves Koochiching County (portions), Ranier & South International Falls. ICA: MN0036.
TV Market Ranking: Below 100 (Ranier); Outside TV Markets (INTERNATIONAL FALLS, Koochiching County (portions), South International Falls). Franchise award date: N.A. Franchise expiration date: N.A. Began: October 1, 1957.
Channel capacity: N.A. Channels available but not in use: N.A.
Basic Service
Subscribers: 1,904. Commercial subscribers: 403.
Programming (via microwave): KBJR-TV (CBS, MNT, NBC) Superior; KDLH (CBS, CW) Duluth; KQDS-TV (Antenna TV, FOX) Duluth; WDIO-DT (ABC, MeTV) Duluth; WDSE (PBS) Duluth.
Programming (via satellite): C-SPAN; EWTN Global Catholic Network; INSP; Pop; QVC; TBS; WGN America.
Fee: $29.99 installation; $19.95 monthly; $2.00 converter.
Expanded Basic Service 1
Subscribers: N.A.
Programming (via satellite): A&E; AMC; Animal Planet; Bravo; Cartoon Network; CMT; CNBC; CNN; Comedy Central; Discovery Channel; Disney Channel; E! HD; ESPN; ESPN2; Food Network; Fox News Channel; Fox Sports 1; Freeform; FX; Golf Channel; Hallmark Channel; HGTV; History; HLN; Lifetime; MSNBC; MTV; National Geographic Channel; NBCSN; Nickelodeon; Outdoor Channel; Oxygen; Spike TV; Syfy; The Weather Channel; TLC; TNT; Travel Channel; truTV; TV Land; USA Network; VH1; WE tv.
Fee: $47.99 monthly.
Digital Basic Service
Subscribers: N.A.
Programming (via satellite): BBC America; Discovery Digital Networks; DIY Network; FXM; FYI; History International; IFC; LMN; MC; Nick Jr.; Sundance TV; TeenNick.
Digital Pay Service 1
Pay Units: N.A.
Programming (via satellite): Cinemax (multiplexed); Flix; HBO (multiplexed); Showtime (multiplexed); Starz (multiplexed); Starz Encore; The Movie Channel (multiplexed).
Fee: $25.00 installation; $9.65 monthly (Cinemax or HBO).
Video-On-Demand: No
Pay-Per-View
Hot Choice (delivered digitally); iN DEMAND (delivered digitally); Playboy TV (delivered digitally); Fresh (delivered digitally); Shorteez (delivered digitally); Sports PPV (delivered digitally).
Internet Service
Operational: Yes.
Fee: $29.99 monthly.
Telephone Service
None
Miles of Plant: 101.0 (coaxial); None (fiber optic). Homes passed: 4,819.
Programming Director: Wynne Haakenstad.
Ownership: Midcontinent Communications (MSO).

IONA—Formerly served by American Telecasting of America Inc. No longer in operation. ICA: MN0312.

ISLE—SCI Broadband, 111 Tobies Mill Pl, PO Box 810, Hinckley, MN 55037-0810. Phones: 800-222-9809; 320-384-7442. Fax: 320-279-8085. E-mail: sales@scibroadband.com. Web Site: http://www.scibroadband.com. Also serves East Side Twp., Isle Harbor, Kathio Twp., Lakeside Twp., Onamia, South Harbor & Wahkon. ICA: MN0313.
TV Market Ranking: Outside TV Markets (East Side Twp., ISLE, Isle Harbor, Kathio Twp., Lakeside Twp., South Harbor, Wahkon). Franchise award date: October 6, 1987. Franchise expiration date: N.A. Began: N.A.
Channel capacity: N.A. Channels available but not in use: N.A.
Basic Service
Subscribers: 1,282.
Programming (received off-air): KARE (NBC, WeatherNation) Minneapolis; KMSP-TV (Bounce TV, Buzzr, FOX) Minneapolis; KPXM-TV (ION) St. Cloud; KSTC-TV (Antenna TV, This TV) Minneapolis; KSTP-TV (ABC, MeTV) St. Paul; KTCA-TV (PBS) St. Paul; KTCI-TV (PBS) St. Paul; WCCO-TV (CBS, Decades) Minneapolis; WFTC (MNT, Movies!) Minneapolis; WUCW (CW, The Country Network) Minneapolis.
Programming (via satellite): A&E; Animal Planet; Cartoon Network; CNBC; CNN; Comedy Central; C-SPAN; Discovery Channel; Disney Channel; E! HD; ESPN; ESPN2; EWTN Global Catholic Network; Fox News Channel; FOX Sports Networks; Freeform; Great American Country; HGTV; History; HLN; Lifetime; MTV; National Geographic Channel; Nickelodeon; QVC; Spike TV; Syfy; TBS; The Weather Channel; TLC; TNT; Turner Classic Movies; TV Land; USA Network; VH1; WGN America.
Fee: $39.95 installation; $15.95 monthly.
Digital Basic Service
Subscribers: N.A.
Programming (via satellite): BBC America; Bloomberg Television; Cloo; Discovery Life Channel; DMX Music; ESPN Classic; ESP-News; Fox Sports 1; Fuse; FXM; FYI; Golf Channel; History International; INSP; National Geographic Channel; NBCSN; Outdoor Channel; Trinity Broadcasting Network (TBN); WE tv.
Pay Service 1
Pay Units: N.A.
Programming (via satellite): HBO.
Fee: $12.95 monthly.
Digital Pay Service 1
Pay Units: N.A.
Programming (via satellite): Cinemax (multiplexed); HBO (multiplexed); Showtime (multiplexed); Starz (multiplexed); Starz Encore (multiplexed); The Movie Channel (multiplexed).
Video-On-Demand: No
Pay-Per-View
ESPN Now (delivered digitally); Sports PPV (delivered digitally).
Internet Service
Operational: Yes.
Broadband Service: SCI Broadband.
Fee: $19.95 monthly.
Telephone Service
Digital: Operational
Miles of Plant: 97.0 (coaxial); None (fiber optic). Homes passed: 3,492.
General Manager: Mike Danielson. President: Ron Savage. Chief Technician: Pat McCabe. Customer Service Manager: Donna Erickson.
Ownership: Savage Communications Inc. (MSO).

IVANHOE—Mediacom, 1504 2nd St SE, PO Box 110, Waseca, MN 56093. Phones: 845-695-2762; 507-835-2356. Fax: 507-835-4567. Web Site: http://www.mediacomcable.com. Also serves Fulda, Hadley, Hope Twp., Lake Benton, Pipestone, Slayton & Tyler. ICA: MN0189.
TV Market Ranking: Outside TV Markets (Fulda, Hadley, Hope Twp., IVANHOE, Lake Benton, Slayton, Tyler, Pipestone). Franchise award date: October 30, 1975. Franchise expiration date: N.A. Began: December 1, 1976.
Channel capacity: N.A. Channels available but not in use: N.A.
Basic Service
Subscribers: 1,144.
Programming (received off-air): KARE (NBC, WeatherNation) Minneapolis; KDLT-TV (Antenna TV, NBC) Sioux Falls; KELO-TV (CBS, MNT) Sioux Falls; KESD-TV (PBS) Brookings; KSFY-TV (ABC, CW) Sioux Falls; KSMN (PBS) Worthington; KTCA-TV (PBS) St. Paul; KTTW (FOX, This TV) Sioux

2017 Edition   D-405

Minnesota—Cable Systems

Falls; KWSD (MeTV, Retro TV) Sioux Falls; allband FM.
Programming (via satellite): C-SPAN; C-SPAN 2; Pop; The Weather Channel; WGN America.
Programming (via translator): WCCO-TV (CBS, Decades) Minneapolis.
Fee: $52.39 installation; $42.00 monthly; $2.00 converter.

Expanded Basic Service 1
Subscribers: N.A.
Programming (via satellite): A&E; AMC; Animal Planet; Bravo; Cartoon Network; CMT; CNBC; CNN; Comedy Central; Discovery Channel; Disney Channel; E! HD; ESPN; ESPN2; EWTN Global Catholic Network; Food Network; Fox News Channel; Fox Sports 1; FOX Sports North; Freeform; FX; FXM; Hallmark Channel; HGTV; History; HLN; INSP; Lifetime; MSNBC; MTV; Nickelodeon; RFD-TV; Spike TV; Syfy; TBS; TLC; TNT; Travel Channel; Trinity Broadcasting Network (TBN); truTV; Turner Classic Movies; TV Land; Univision; Univision Studios; USA Network; VH1; WE tv.
Fee: $14.81 monthly.

Digital Basic Service
Subscribers: N.A.
Programming (via satellite): BBC America; Bloomberg Television; Discovery Digital Networks; DMX Music; Fuse; FYI; Golf Channel; GSN; History International; IFC; LMN; Outdoor Channel.

Digital Pay Service 1
Pay Units: N.A.
Programming (via satellite): Cinemax (multiplexed); Flix; HBO (multiplexed); Showtime (multiplexed); Starz (multiplexed); Starz Encore (multiplexed); Sundance TV; The Movie Channel (multiplexed).
Fee: $5.00 monthly (Starz/Encore), $7.00 monthly (Cinemax), $11.00 monthly (HBO, Showtime, TMC, Sundance or Flix).

Video-On-Demand: Yes
Pay-Per-View
Vubiquity Inc. (delivered digitally); Fresh (delivered digitally); Shorteez (delivered digitally); Playboy TV (delivered digitally); Hot Choice (delivered digitally).

Internet Service
Operational: Yes, DSL.
Broadband Service: Mediacom High Speed Internet.

Telephone Service
Digital: Operational
Miles of Plant: 49.0 (coaxial); None (fiber optic). Homes passed: 1,467.
Vice President: Bill Jensen. Vice President, Financial Reporting: Kenneth J. Kohrs. Marketing & Sales Manager: Lori Huberty. Engineering Manager: Kraig Kaiser.
Ownership: Mediacom LLC (MSO).

JACKSON—Jackson Municipal TV System, 80 West Ashley St, Jackson, MN 56143-1669. Phone: 507-847-3225. Fax: 507-847-5586. ICA: MN0314.
TV Market Ranking: Outside TV Markets (JACKSON). Franchise award date: June 1, 1957. Franchise expiration date: N.A. Began: July 1, 1957.
Channel capacity: N.A. Channels available but not in use: N.A.

Basic Service
Subscribers: 982.
Programming (received off-air): KARE (NBC, WeatherNation) Minneapolis; KEYC-TV (CBS, FOX) Mankato; KMSP-TV (Bounce TV, Buzzr, FOX) Minneapolis; KSFY-TV (ABC, CW) Sioux Falls; KSMN (PBS) Worthington; KSTC-TV (Antenna TV, This TV) Minneapolis; KSTP-TV (ABC, MeTV) St. Paul; KTIN (PBS) Fort Dodge; WCCO-TV (CBS, Decades) Minneapolis; WFTC (MNT, Movies!) Minneapolis; WUCW (CW, The Country Network) Minneapolis; allband FM.
Programming (via satellite): Freeform; TBS; The Weather Channel; TLC; USA Network; WGN America.
Fee: $30.00 installation; $11.28 monthly.

Expanded Basic Service 1
Subscribers: N.A.
Programming (via satellite): A&E; AMC; Animal Planet; Cartoon Network; CNN; Comedy Central; Discovery Channel; Disney Channel; DIY Network; E! HD; ESPN; ESPN2; Food Network; Fox News Channel; Fox Sports 1; FOX Sports Networks; FX; Great American Country; Hallmark Channel; HGTV; History; HLN; Lifetime; MTV; National Geographic Channel; Nickelodeon; Outdoor Channel; Spike TV; Syfy; TNT; Travel Channel; Turner Classic Movies; TV Land; VH1.
Fee: $15.00 installation; $27.75 monthly.

Pay Service 1
Pay Units: N.A.
Programming (via satellite): HBO.
Fee: $8.95 monthly.

Video-On-Demand: No
Internet Service
Operational: No.
Telephone Service
None
Miles of Plant: 37.0 (coaxial); None (fiber optic). Homes passed: 1,610.
General Manager: Curtis G. Egeland. City Administrator: Patrick Christopherson. Chief Technician: Steve Jenson.
Ownership: Jackson Municipal TV System.

JANESVILLE—Mediacom. Now served by ST. PETER (formerly Waseca), MN [MN0043]. ICA: MN0124.

JASPER—Clarity Telcom. Now served by ADRIAN, MN [MN0158]. Also serves JASPER. ICA: MN0315.

JEFFERS—NU-Telecom, 22 South Marshall, Springfield, MN 56087. Phones: 888-873-6853; 507-723-4211. Fax: 507-723-4377. E-mail: on-linecustservice@nu-telcom.net. Web Site: http://www.nutelecom.net. ICA: MN0316.
TV Market Ranking: Below 100 (JEFFERS). Channel capacity: 35 (operating 2-way). Channels available but not in use: N.A.

Basic Service
Subscribers: 29.
Programming (received off-air): KARE (NBC, WeatherNation) Minneapolis; KEYC-TV (CBS, FOX) Mankato; KMSP-TV (Bounce TV, Buzzr, FOX) Minneapolis; KSTP-TV (ABC, MeTV) St. Paul; KTCA-TV (PBS) St. Paul; WCCO-TV (CBS, Decades) Minneapolis; WFTC (MNT, Movies!) Minneapolis.
Programming (via satellite): AMC; CNN; Discovery Channel; Disney Channel; ESPN; FOX Sports Networks; Freeform; TBS; TNT; USA Network; WGN America.
Fee: $50.00 installation; $21.31 monthly.

Pay Service 1
Pay Units: 5.
Programming (via satellite): HBO.
Fee: $25.00 installation; $15.95 monthly.

Internet Service
Operational: No.

Telephone Service
None
Miles of Plant: 4.0 (coaxial); None (fiber optic).
President & Chief Executive Officer: Bill Otis. Chief Operating Officer & Vice President: Barbara Bornhoft. Chief Financial Officer & Treasurer: Curtis Kawlweski.
Ownership: New Ulm Telecom.

JORDAN—Formerly served by Time Warner Cable. Now served by Comcast Cable, MINNEAPOLIS, MN [MN0001]. ICA: MN0317.

KARLSTAD—Sjoberg's Cable TV Inc, 315 Main Ave North, Thief River Falls, MN 56701-1905. Phones: 800-828-8808; 218-681-3044. Fax: 218-681-6801. E-mail: office1@mncable.net; sjobergs@mncable.net. Web Site: http://trf.mncable.net. Also serves Deerwood Twp. ICA: MN0179.
TV Market Ranking: Outside TV Markets (Deerwood Twp., KARLSTAD). Franchise award date: N.A. Franchise expiration date: N.A. Began: September 1, 1978.
Channel capacity: N.A. Channels available but not in use: N.A.

Basic Service
Subscribers: 198.
Programming (received off-air): KBRR (FOX) Thief River Falls; KCPM (MNT) Grand Forks; KGFE (PBS) Grand Forks; WDAZ-TV (ABC, CW) Devils Lake; allband FM.
Programming (via microwave): KRDK-TV (CBS, Decades, Movies!) Valley City; KVLY-TV (MeTV, NBC, This TV) Fargo.
Programming (via satellite): CNN; ESPN; TBS; various Canadian stations.
Fee: $25.00 installation; $55.92 monthly.

Expanded Basic Service 1
Subscribers: N.A.
Programming (via satellite): A&E; Animal Planet; Cartoon Network; CMT; CNBC; Comedy Central; C-SPAN; CW PLUS; Discovery Channel; Disney Channel; E! HD; ESPN; Food Network; Fox News Channel; FOX Sports Networks; Freeform; FX; HGTV; History; Lifetime; MSNBC; MTV; Nickelodeon; Spike TV; Syfy; The Weather Channel; TLC; TNT; Turner Classic Movies; TV Land; USA Network; VH1; WGN America.
Fee: $23.71 monthly.

Digital Basic Service
Subscribers: N.A.
Programming (via satellite): BBC America; Bloomberg Television; Bravo; CBS Sports Network; Chiller; Cloo; CMT; Cooking Channel; Daystar TV Network; Destination America; Discovery Kids Channel; Discovery Life Channel; Disney XD; DIY Network; DMX Music; ESPN Classic; ESPNews; ESPNU; EVINE Live; EWTN Global Catholic Network; Fox Business Network; FOX College Sports Central; FOX College Sports Pacific; Fox Sports 1; FXM; FYI; Golf Channel; Great American Country; GSN; Hallmark Channel; History International; HLN; HRTV; IFC; Investigation Discovery; LMN; MTV Classic; MTV Hits; MTV2; Nat Geo WILD; National Geographic Channel; NBCSN; Nick Jr.; Nicktoons; Outdoor Channel; Ovation; OWN; Oprah Winfrey Network; Oxygen; Reelz; RFD-TV; Science Channel; Sprout; Sundance TV; TeenNick; Tennis Channel; The Word Network; Trinity Broadcasting Network (TBN); TVG Network; UP; VH1 Soul; WE tv.

Digital Expanded Basic Service
Subscribers: N.A.
Programming (via satellite): A&E HD; AXS TV; CNN HD; ESPN HD; ESPN2 HD; Food Network HD; FSN HD; HD Theater; HGTV HD; History HD; Outdoor Channel 2 HD; PBS HD; Syfy HD; TBS HD; TNT HD; Universal HD; USA Network HD; Versus HD.
Fee: $5.00 monthly.

Pay Service 1
Pay Units: N.A.
Programming (via satellite): Cinemax; HBO.
Fee: $9.00 monthly (Cinemax), $11.00 monthly (HBO).

Digital Pay Service 1
Pay Units: N.A.
Programming (via satellite): Cinemax (multiplexed); Cinemax HD; HBO (multiplexed); HBO HD; Showtime (multiplexed); Starz (multiplexed); Starz Encore (multiplexed); The Movie Channel (multiplexed).
Fee: $8.00 monthly (Starz/Encore), $9.00 monthly (Cinemax or Showtime/TMC), $11.00 monthly (HBO).

Video-On-Demand: No
Internet Service
Operational: No.
Telephone Service
None
Miles of Plant: 6.0 (coaxial); 17.0 (fiber optic). Homes passed: 348.
President & General Manager: Richard J. Sjoberg. Chief Technician: Jerry Seim.
Ownership: Sjoberg's Cable TV Inc. (MSO).

KEEWATIN—Mediacom. Now served by GRAND RAPIDS, MN [MN0038]. ICA: MN0078.

KELLIHER—Formerly served by North American Communications Corp. No longer in operation. ICA: MN0318.

KENNEDY—Wikstrom Cable LLC, PO Box 217, Karlstad, MN 56732. Phone: 218-436-2121. Fax: 218-436-3100. E-mail: service@wiktel.com. Web Site: http://www.wiktel.com. ICA: MN0234.
TV Market Ranking: Below 100 (KENNEDY). Franchise award date: June 7, 1982. Franchise expiration date: N.A. Began: November 1, 1982.
Channel capacity: N.A. Channels available but not in use: N.A.

Basic Service
Subscribers: 65.
Programming (received off-air): KBRR (FOX) Thief River Falls; KGFE (PBS) Grand Forks; KVLY-TV (MeTV, NBC, This TV) Fargo; WDAZ-TV (ABC, CW) Devils Lake.
Programming (via satellite): A&E; AMC; CNBC; CNN; Comedy Central; C-SPAN; Discovery Channel; Disney Channel; ESPN; ESPN2; Food Network; FOX Sports Networks; Freeform; Great American Country; HGTV; History; Lifetime; Nickelodeon; Spike TV; TBS; The Weather Channel; TLC; TNT; Trinity Broadcasting Network (TBN); TV Land; USA Network; various Canadian stations; VH1; WGN America.
Programming (via translator): KRDK-TV (CBS, Decades, Movies!) Valley City.
Fee: $20.00 installation; $57.99 monthly.

Pay Service 1
Pay Units: 5.
Programming (via satellite): HBO.
Fee: $10.00 installation; $11.00 monthly.

Video-On-Demand: No
Internet Service
Operational: No.
Telephone Service
None
Miles of Plant: 4.0 (coaxial); None (fiber optic). Homes passed: 141.
General Manager: Bryan Wikstrom. Controller: Carrie Kern-Taggart.
Ownership: Wikstrom Systems LLC (MSO).

Cable Systems—Minnesota

KENYON—Mediacom. Now served by CANNON FALLS, MN [MN0076]. ICA: MN0127.

KERKHOVEN—Charter Communications. Now served by WILLMAR, MN [MN0018]. ICA: MN0157.

KNIFE LAKE TWP.—Formerly served by New Century Communications. No longer in operation. ICA: MN0319.

KNIFE RIVER—Formerly served by Mediacom. No longer in operation. ICA: MN0320.

LAFAYETTE—Mediacom. Now served by ST. PETER (formerly Waseca), MN [MN0043]. ICA: MN0235.

LAKE BRONSON—Wikstrom Cable LLC, PO Box 217, Karlstad, MN 56732. Phone: 218-436-2121. Fax: 218-436-3100. E-mail: service@wiktel.com. Web Site: http://www.wiktel.com. ICA: MN0240.
TV Market Ranking: Below 100 (LAKE BRONSON). Franchise award date: August 18, 1985. Franchise expiration date: N.A. Began: September 1, 1985.
Channel capacity: N.A. Channels available but not in use: N.A.
Basic Service
Subscribers: 135.
Programming (received off-air): KGFE (PBS) Grand Forks; KNRR (FOX) Pembina; KRDK-TV (CBS, Decades, Movies!) Valley City; KVLY-TV (MeTV, NBC, This TV) Fargo; WDAZ-TV (ABC, CW) Devils Lake.
Programming (via satellite): A&E; AMC; CMT; CNBC; CNN; Comedy Central; Discovery Channel; Disney Channel; ESPN; ESPN2; FOX Sports Networks; Freeform; HGTV; History; Lifetime; Nickelodeon; Spike TV; Syfy; TBS; The Weather Channel; TLC; TNT; Trinity Broadcasting Network (TBN); TV Land; USA Network; various Canadian stations; VH1; WGN America.
Fee: $20.00 installation; $57.99 monthly.
Pay Service 1
Pay Units: 3.
Programming (via satellite): HBO.
Fee: $11.00 monthly.
Video-On-Demand: No
Internet Service
Operational: No.
Telephone Service
None
Miles of Plant: 5.0 (coaxial); None (fiber optic).
General Manager: Bryan Wikstrom. Controller: Carrie Kern-Taggart.
Ownership: Wikstrom Systems LLC (MSO).

LAKE CITY—Mediacom, 1504 2nd St SE, PO Box 110, Waseca, MN 56093. Phones: 845-695-2762; 507-835-2356. Fax: 507-835-4567. Web Site: http://www.mediacomcable.com. Also serves Florence Twp., Frontenac, Lake Twp. & Mount Pleasant Twp. ICA: MN0054.
TV Market Ranking: Below 100 (Florence Twp., Frontenac, LAKE CITY, Lake Twp., Mount Pleasant Twp.). Franchise award date: May 10, 1982. Franchise expiration date: N.A. Began: July 5, 1983.
Channel capacity: N.A. Channels available but not in use: N.A.
Basic Service
Subscribers: 741.
Programming (received off-air): KARE (NBC, WeatherNation) Minneapolis; KMSP-TV (Bounce TV, Buzzr, FOX) Minneapolis; KSTP-TV (ABC, MeTV) St. Paul; KTCA-TV (PBS) St. Paul; KTCI-TV (PBS) St. Paul;

KTTC (CW, NBC) Rochester; WCCO-TV (CBS, Decades) Minneapolis; WEAU (NBC) Eau Claire; WFTC (MNT, Movies!) Minneapolis; WKBT-DT (CBS, MNT) La Crosse; WLAX (FOX, MeTV) La Crosse; WUCW (CW, The Country Network) Minneapolis; 5 FMs.
Programming (via satellite): WGN America.
Fee: $25.00 installation; $42.00 monthly; $2.00 converter.
Expanded Basic Service 1
Subscribers: N.A.
Programming (via satellite): A&E; AMC; Animal Planet; Cartoon Network; CMT; CNBC; CNN; Comedy Central; C-SPAN; C-SPAN 2; Discovery Channel; Disney Channel; E! HD; ESPN; ESPN2; EWTN Global Catholic Network; Food Network; Fox News Channel; Fox Sports 1; FOX Sports North; Freeform; FX; Hallmark Channel; HGTV; History; HLN; INSP; Lifetime; MSNBC; MTV; Nickelodeon; QVC; Spike TV; Syfy; TBS; The Weather Channel; TLC; TNT; Travel Channel; TV Land; USA Network; VH1; WE tv.
Digital Basic Service
Subscribers: N.A.
Programming (via satellite): BBC America; Bloomberg Television; Discovery Digital Networks; DMX Music; Fuse; FYI; Golf Channel; GSN; History International; IFC; LMN; National Geographic Network; Outdoor Channel.
Digital Pay Service 1
Pay Units: N.A.
Programming (via satellite): Cinemax (multiplexed); Flix; HBO (multiplexed); Showtime (multiplexed); Starz (multiplexed); Starz Encore (multiplexed); Sundance TV; The Movie Channel (multiplexed).
Fee: $15.00 installation; $9.95 monthly (Cinemax, Showtime or TMC), $11.95 monthly (HBO).
Video-On-Demand: No
Pay-Per-View
Vubiquity Inc. (delivered digitally); ESPN Now (delivered digitally); Sports PPV (delivered digitally); Urban Xtra (delivered digitally); Fresh (delivered digitally); Shorteez (delivered digitally); Playboy TV (delivered digitally); Pleasure (delivered digitally).
Internet Service
Operational: Yes.
Broadband Service: Mediacom High Speed Internet.
Fee: $99.00 installation; $40.00 monthly.
Telephone Service
Digital: Operational
Miles of Plant: 50.0 (coaxial); None (fiber optic). Homes passed: 2,087.
Vice President: Bill Jensen. Vice President, Financial Reporting: Kenneth J. Kohrs. Marketing & Sales Director: Lori Huberty. Engineering Manager: Kraig Kaiser.
Ownership: Mediacom LLC (MSO).

LAKE CRYSTAL—Mediacom. Now served by ST. PETER (formerly Waseca), MN [MN0043]. ICA: MN0108.

LAKE LILLIAN—Clara City Telephone Co, 227 South Main St, PO Box 800, Clara City, MN 56222. Phone: 320-847-2211. Fax: 320-847-2736. Web Site: http://www.hcinet.net. ICA: MN0321.
TV Market Ranking: Below 100 (LAKE LILLIAN). Franchise award date: December 1, 1988. Franchise expiration date: N.A. Began: April 1, 1990.
Channel capacity: N.A. Channels available but not in use: N.A.

Basic Service
Subscribers: 47.
Programming (received off-air): KARE (NBC, WeatherNation) Minneapolis; KCCO-TV (CBS) Alexandria; KMSP-TV (Bounce TV, Buzzr, FOX) Minneapolis; KSAX (ABC) Alexandria; KSTC-TV (Antenna TV, This TV) Minneapolis; KWCM-TV (PBS) Appleton; WFTC (MNT, Movies!) Minneapolis; WUCW (CW, The Country Network) Minneapolis.
Programming (via satellite): A&E; AMC; Animal Planet; Cartoon Network; CMT; CNN; Comedy Central; Discovery Channel; Disney Channel; ESPN; ESPN2; Food Network; FOX Sports North; Freeform; Hallmark Channel; HGTV; History; Lifetime; MTV; Nickelodeon; Outdoor Channel; QVC; Spike TV; Syfy; TBS; The Weather Channel; TLC; TNT; Trinity Broadcasting Network (TBN); TV Land; USA Network; VH1.
Fee: $20.00 installation; $39.95 monthly.
Pay Service 1
Pay Units: 2.
Programming (via satellite): Cinemax; HBO; Showtime.
Fee: $9.95 monthly (Cinemax), $10.95 monthly (Showtime) or $11.95 monthly (HBO).
Video-On-Demand: No
Internet Service
Operational: Yes.
Telephone Service
Analog: Operational
Miles of Plant: 3.0 (coaxial); None (fiber optic). Homes passed: 130.
Treasurer & General Manager: Bruce Hanson.
Ownership: Hanson Communications Inc. (MSO).

LAKEFIELD—Formerly served by Lakefield Public TV. No longer in operation. ICA: MN0110.

LAMBERTON—Clara City Telephone Co, 227 South Main St, PO Box 800, Clara City, MN 56222. Phone: 320-847-2211. Fax: 320-847-2736. Web Site: http://www.hcinet.net. ICA: MN0171.
TV Market Ranking: Below 100 (LAMBERTON). Franchise award date: N.A. Franchise expiration date: N.A. Began: November 1, 1971.
Channel capacity: N.A. Channels available but not in use: N.A.
Basic Service
Subscribers: 73.
Programming (received off-air): KELO-TV (CBS, MNT) Sioux Falls; KEYC-TV (CBS, FOX) Mankato; KSFY-TV (ABC, CW) Sioux Falls; allband FM.
Programming (via satellite): CNN; Discovery Channel; ESPN; Freeform; HLN; Nickelodeon; Spike TV; TBS; The Weather Channel; TLC; TNT; USA Network; WGN America.
Programming (via translator): KARE (NBC, WeatherNation) Minneapolis; KMSP-TV (Bounce TV, Buzzr, FOX) Minneapolis; KSTP-TV (ABC, MeTV) St. Paul; KTCA-TV (PBS) St. Paul; KWCM-TV (PBS) Appleton; WCCO-TV (CBS, Decades) Minneapolis; WFTC (MNT, Movies!) Minneapolis; WUCW (CW, The Country Network) Minneapolis.
Fee: $20.00 installation; $48.50 monthly.
Pay Service 1
Pay Units: N.A.
Programming (via satellite): Showtime.
Fee: $15.00 installation; $15.00 monthly.
Video-On-Demand: No
Internet Service
Operational: No.

Telephone Service
None
Miles of Plant: 16.0 (coaxial); None (fiber optic). Homes passed: 398.
Treasurer & General Manager: Bruce Hanson.
Ownership: Hanson Communications Inc. (MSO).

LANCASTER—Wikstrom Cable LLC, PO Box 217, Karlstad, MN 56732. Phone: 218-436-2121. Fax: 218-436-3100. E-mail: service@wiktel.com. Web Site: http://www.wiktel.com. ICA: MN0228.
TV Market Ranking: Below 100 (LANCASTER). Franchise award date: June 13, 1984. Franchise expiration date: N.A. Began: August 1, 1984.
Channel capacity: N.A. Channels available but not in use: N.A.
Basic Service
Subscribers: 89.
Programming (received off-air): KGFE (PBS) Grand Forks; KNRR (FOX) Pembina; KRDK-TV (CBS, Decades, Movies!) Valley City; KVLY-TV (MeTV, NBC, This TV) Fargo; WDAZ-TV (ABC, CW) Devils Lake.
Programming (via satellite): A&E; AMC; CMT; CNBC; CNN; Comedy Central; Discovery Channel; Disney Channel; ESPN; ESPN2; FOX Sports Networks; Freeform; Hallmark Channel; HGTV; History; Lifetime; MTV; Nickelodeon; Spike TV; Syfy; TBS; The Weather Channel; TLC; TNT; Trinity Broadcasting Network (TBN); TV Land; USA Network; various Canadian stations; VH1; WGN America.
Fee: $20.00 installation; $57.99 monthly.
Pay Service 1
Pay Units: 5.
Programming (via satellite): HBO.
Fee: $10.00 installation; $11.00 monthly.
Video-On-Demand: No
Internet Service
Operational: No.
Telephone Service
None
Miles of Plant: 5.0 (coaxial); None (fiber optic). Homes passed: 160.
General Manager: Bryan Wikstrom. Controller: Carrie Kern-Taggart.
Ownership: Wikstrom Systems LLC (MSO).

LANESBORO—Mediacom. Now served by CHATFIELD, MN [MN0111]. ICA: MN0160.

LE ROY—Mediacom. Now served by CHATFIELD, MN [MN0111]. ICA: MN0174.

LE SUEUR—Mediacom. Now served by ST. PETER (formerly Waseca), MN [MN0043]. ICA: MN0068.

LEOTA—Formerly served by American Telecasting of America Inc. No longer in operation. ICA: MN0323.

LESTER PRAIRIE—Mediacom. Now served by HUTCHINSON, MN [MN0145]. ICA: MN0072.

LEWISTON—Hiawatha Broadband. This cable system has converted to IPTV. Now served by WINONA, MN [MN5161]. ICA: MN5155.

LEWISVILLE—Formerly served by North American Communications Corp. No longer in operation. ICA: MN0325.

LISMORE—Formerly served by K-Communications Inc. No longer in operation. ICA: MN0326.

2017 Edition

D-407

Minnesota—Cable Systems

ADVANCED TVFactbook

FULLY SEARCHABLE • CONTINUOUSLY UPDATED • DISCOUNT RATES FOR PRINT PURCHASERS
For more information call 800-771-9202 or visit www.warren-news.com

LITCHFIELD—Mediacom. Now served by HUTCHINSON, MN [MN0145]. ICA: MN0327.

LITTLE FALLS—Charter Communications. Now served by ST. CLOUD, MN [MN0011]. ICA: MN0044.

LITTLEFORK—Midco, PO Box 5010, Sioux Falls, SD 57117. Phones: 800-888-1300; 218-283-3409. Web Site: http://www.midcocomm.com. ICA: MN0200.
TV Market Ranking: Below 100 (LITTLEFORK). Franchise award date: N.A. Franchise expiration date: N.A. Began: October 1, 1970.
Channel capacity: N.A. Channels available but not in use: N.A.
Basic Service
Subscribers: 30. Commercial subscribers: 8.
Programming (via microwave): KBJR-TV (CBS, MNT, NBC) Superior; KDLH (CBS, CW) Duluth; WDIO-DT (ABC, MeTV) Duluth; WDSE (PBS) Duluth.
Programming (via satellite): AMC; Animal Planet; CNN; Discovery Channel; ESPN; Fox News Channel; Freeform; FX; MTV; Nickelodeon; Spike TV; TBS; TLC; TNT; USA Network; VH1.
Fee: $59.95 installation; $53.95 monthly.
Pay Service 1
Pay Units: N.A.
Programming (via satellite): HBO; Starz; Starz Encore.
Fee: $9.65 monthly (HBO).
Video-On-Demand: No
Internet Service
Operational: No.
Telephone Service
None
Miles of Plant: 9.0 (coaxial); None (fiber optic). Homes passed: 285.
Programming Director: Wynne Haakenstad.
Ownership: Midcontinent Communications (MSO).

LONG LAKE—Formerly served by New Century Communications. Now served by Mediacom, MOUND, MN [MN0010]. ICA: MN0245.

LONG PRAIRIE—Charter Communications. Now served by BRAINERD, MN [MN0022]. ICA: MN0329.

LOWRY—Formerly served by Lowry Telephone Co. Now served by Runestone Cable TV, BARRETT, MN [MN0233]. ICA: MN0330.

LUCAN—Clara City Telephone Co, 227 South Main St, PO Box 800, Clara City, MN 56222. Phone: 320-847-2211. Fax: 320-847-2736. Web Site: http://www.hcinet.net. ICA: MN0408.
TV Market Ranking: Below 100 (LUCAN). Channel capacity: N.A. Channels available but not in use: N.A.
Basic Service
Subscribers: 16.
Fee: $20.00 installation; $48.50 monthly.

Treasurer & General Manager: Bruce Hanson.
Ownership: Hanson Communications Inc. (MSO).

LUVERNE—Mediacom. Now served by WORTHINGTON, MN [MN0041]. ICA: MN0059.

LYLE—No longer in operation. ICA: MN0218.

MABEL—Mediacom. Now served by CALEDONIA, MN [MN0086]. ICA: MN0149.

MADELIA—Formerly served by Time Warner Cable. Now served by Comcast Cable, MINNEAPOLIS, MN [MN0001]. ICA: MN0101.

MADISON—Mediacom. Now served by APPLETON, MN [MN0106]. ICA: MN0096.

MADISON LAKE—Formerly served by North American Communications Corp. This cable system has converted to IPTV. Now served by Jaguar Communications, OWATONNA, MN [MN5121]. ICA: MN0331.

MAGNOLIA—Formerly served by American Telecasting of America Inc. No longer in operation. ICA: MN0332.

MAHNOMEN—Formerly served by Loretel Cablevision. Now served by Arvig, PERHAM, MN [MN0050]. ICA: MN0144.

MANKATO—Charter Communications, 12405 Powerscourt Dr, St. Louis, MO 63131. Phones: 636-207-5100 (Corporate office); 507-388-6973; 888-438-2427; 507-388-3930; 507-289-8372 (Rochester office). Fax: 507-388-4172. Web Site: http://www.charter.com. Also serves Belgrade Twp., Decoria Twp., Eagle Lake, Lime Twp., Mankato Twp., North Mankato, Skyline & South Bend Twp. ICA: MN0013.
TV Market Ranking: Below 100 (Belgrade Twp., Decoria Twp., Eagle Lake, Lime Twp., MANKATO, North Mankato, Skyline, South Bend Twp.). Franchise award date: November 1, 1956. Franchise expiration date: N.A. Began: April 1, 1957.
Channel capacity: 64 (operating 2-way). Channels available but not in use: N.A.
Digital Basic Service
Subscribers: 9,456.
Programming (via satellite): AXS TV; BBC America; Bloomberg Television; Boomerang; CBS Sports Network; CNN en Espanol; CNN International; Discovery Digital Networks; DIY Network; ESPN Classic; ESPN HD; ESPNews; FOX College Sports Central; FOX College Sports Pacific; Fox Sports 2; Fuse; FXM; FYI; History International; IFC; LMN; MC; NFL Network; Nick 2; Nick Jr.; Nicktoons; Outdoor Channel; Sundance TV; TeenNick; TV Guide Interactive Inc.
Fee: $14.57 monthly.
Digital Expanded Basic Service
Subscribers: N.A.
Programming (via satellite): A&E; AMC; Animal Planet; BET; Bravo; Cartoon Network; CMT; CNBC; CNN; Comedy Central; Discovery Channel; Disney Channel; Disney XD; E! HD; ESPN; ESPN2; EVINE Live; Food Network; Fox News Channel; Fox Sports 1; FOX Sports North; Freeform; FX; Golf Channel; GSN; Hallmark Channel; HGTV; History; HLN; Lifetime; MSNBC; MTV; MTV2; National Geographic Channel; NBCSN; Nickelodeon; Oxygen; Spike TV; Syfy; TBS; The Weather Channel; TLC; TNT; Travel Channel; truTV; Turner Classic Movies; TV Land; Univision Studios; USA Network; VH1; WE tv.
Fee: $49.99 monthly.
Digital Pay Service 1
Pay Units: N.A.
Programming (via satellite): Cinemax (multiplexed); Flix; HBO (multiplexed); HBO HD; Showtime (multiplexed); Showtime HD; Starz (multiplexed); Starz Encore (multiplexed); The Movie Channel (multiplexed).
Video-On-Demand: Yes
Pay-Per-View
iN DEMAND (delivered digitally); NHL Center Ice (delivered digitally); MLB Extra Innings (delivered digitally); Playboy TV (delivered digitally); Spice Live (delivered digitally); Spice Platinum (delivered digitally); Hot Net Plus (delivered digitally); Spice Hot (delivered digitally).
Internet Service
Operational: Yes.
Subscribers: 10,495.
Broadband Service: Charter Internet.
Telephone Service
Digital: Operational
Subscribers: 3,989.
Fee: $29.99 monthly
Miles of Plant: 480.0 (coaxial); 238.0 (fiber optic). Homes passed: 29,378.
Vice President & General Manager: Melissa Morris. Marketing Director: Bill Haarstad. Engineering Director: Darin Helgeson. Accounting Director: David Sovanski. Operations Director: Craig Stensaas. Customer Sales & Service Center Supervisor: Kristin Gardner. Technical Operations Supervisor: Tim Indrehus.
Ownership: Charter Communications Inc. (MSO).

MAPLEVIEW—Formerly served by North American Communications Corp. This cable system has converted to IPTV. Now served by Jaguar Communications, OWATONNA, MN [MN5121]. ICA: MN0333.

MARBLE—Formerly served by Marble Cable TV Systems. Now served by Mediacom, CALUMET, MN [MN0027]. ICA: MN0334.

MARSHALL—Charter Communications. Now served by WILLMAR, MN [MN0018]. ICA: MN0030.

MARSHALL—Clarity Telcom, 4850 Sugarloaf Pkwy, Ste 209-356, Lawrenceville, GA 30044. Phones: 720-479-3500; 866-399-8647. E-mail: sales@claritytel.com. Web Site: http://www.claritycomm.net. Also serves Currie, Slayton & Tracy. ICA: MN0288.
Note: This system is an overbuild.
TV Market Ranking: Below 100 (MARSHALL, Tracy); Outside TV Markets (Currie, Slayton). Franchise award date: N.A. Franchise expiration date: N.A. Began: August 1, 1984.
Channel capacity: N.A. Channels available but not in use: N.A.
Basic Service
Subscribers: 2,507.
Programming (received off-air): KARE (NBC, WeatherNation) Minneapolis; KDLT-TV (Antenna TV, NBC) Sioux Falls; KELO-TV (CBS, MNT) Sioux Falls; KEYC-TV (CBS, FOX) Mankato; KMSP-TV (Bounce TV, Buzzr, FOX) Minneapolis; KRWF (ABC) Redwood Falls; KSFY-TV (ABC, CW) Sioux Falls; KSTC-TV (Antenna TV, This TV) Minneapolis; KTCA-TV (PBS) St. Paul; KTTW (FOX, This TV) Sioux Falls; KWCM-TV (PBS) Appleton; WCCO-TV (CBS, Decades) Minneapolis; WFTC (MNT, Movies!) Minneapolis.
Programming (via satellite): A&E; AMC; Animal Planet; Bravo; Cartoon Network; CMT; CNBC; CNN; Comedy Central; C-SPAN; C-SPAN 2; CW PLUS; Discovery Channel; Disney Channel; Disney XD; E! HD; ESPN; ESPN Classic; ESPN2; Food Network; Fox News Channel; Fox Sports 1; FOX Sports North; Freeform; FX; Golf Channel; Hallmark Channel; HGTV; History; HLN; Lifetime; LMN; MSNBC; MTV; MyNetworkTV; National Geographic Channel; NFL Network; Nickelodeon; Pop; QVC; QVC HD; Spike TV; Syfy; TBS; The Weather Channel; TLC; TNT; Travel Channel; Trinity Broadcasting Network (TBN); truTV; Turner Classic Movies; TV Land; USA Network; VH1; WGN America.
Fee: $35.00 installation; $33.00 monthly.
Digital Basic Service
Subscribers: N.A.
Programming (via satellite): AXS TV; Bandamax; BBC America; Bloomberg Television; Boomerang; Cloo; Cloo on demand; CMT; Cooking Channel; De Pelicula; De Pelicula Clasico; Destination America; Discovery Kids Channel; Discovery Life Channel; DIY Network; ESPN Deportes; ESPN Deportes On Demand; ESPN HD; ESPN On Demand; ESPN2 HD; ESPNews; ESPNU; ESPNU On Demand; EWTN Global Catholic Network; Flix; FOX College Sports Central; FOX College Sports Pacific; Fox Deportes; Fuse; FXM; FYI; GSN; HD Theater; History International; IFC; Investigation Discovery; MC; MTV Classic; MTV Hits; MTV Jams; MTV2; Nat Geo WILD; National Geographic Channel; National Geographic Channel HD; National Geographic Channel On Demand; NBCSN; NFL Network HD; Nick Jr.; Nicktoons; Outdoor Channel; Outdoor Channel 2 HD; Outdoor Channel On Demand; OWN: Oprah Winfrey Network; RFD-TV; Ritmoson; Science Channel; Sundance TV; TBS HD; TeenNick; Telehit; TNT HD; TV Guide Network; Universal HD; UP; Versus HD; Versus On Demand; VH1 Soul; WAM! America's Kidz Network; WE tv.
Pay Service 1
Pay Units: N.A.
Programming (via satellite): HBO (multiplexed); Showtime (multiplexed).
Fee: $10.00 installation; $9.95 monthly (each).
Digital Pay Service 1
Pay Units: N.A.
Programming (via satellite): Cinemax (multiplexed); Cinemax HD; Cinemax On Demand; HBO (multiplexed); HBO GO; HBO HD; Showtime (multiplexed); Showtime HD; Showtime On Demand; Starz (multiplexed); Starz Encore (multiplexed); Starz HD; Starz On Demand; The Movie Channel (multiplexed); The Movie Channel On Demand.
Video-On-Demand: Yes
Pay-Per-View
iN DEMAND (delivered digitally); Hot Choice (delivered digitally).
Internet Service
Operational: Yes.
Fee: $29.95 installation; $39.95 monthly.

Cable Systems—Minnesota

Telephone Service
Analog: Not Operational
Digital: Operational
Miles of Plant: 3.0 (coaxial); None (fiber optic). Homes passed included in Viborg, SD.
Chief Executive Officer: Jim Gleason.
Ownership: Clarity Telecom (MSO).

MAYER—NU-Telecom, 2104 10th St East, Glencoe, MN 55336. Phones: 888-873-6853; 320-864-2818. Fax: 320-864-5612. E-mail: on-linecustservice@nu-telcom.net. Web Site: http://www.nutelecom.net. Also serves New Germany. ICA: MN0335.
TV Market Ranking: 13 (MAYER, New Germany). Franchise award date: June 1, 1988. Franchise expiration date: N.A. Began: January 1, 1989.
Channel capacity: N.A. Channels available but not in use: N.A.
Digital Basic Service
Subscribers: 134.
Programming (received off-air): KARE (NBC, WeatherNation) Minneapolis; KMSP-TV (Bounce TV, Buzzr, FOX) Minneapolis; KSTP-TV (ABC, MeTV) St. Paul; KTCA-TV (PBS) St. Paul; KTCI-TV (PBS) St. Paul; WCCO-TV (CBS, Decades) Minneapolis; WFTC (MNT, Movies!) Minneapolis; WUCW (CW, The Country Network) Minneapolis.
Programming (via satellite): TBS; WGN America.
Fee: $50.00 installation; $21.95 monthly; $3.50 converter.
Digital Expanded Basic Service
Subscribers: N.A.
Programming (via satellite): A&E; AMC; CMT; CNN; Discovery Channel; Disney Channel; ESPN; FOX Sports Midwest; Freeform; Lifetime; Nickelodeon; QVC; Spike TV; TNT; Trinity Broadcasting Network (TBN); USA Network.
Fee: $49.95 monthly.
Digital Expanded Basic Service 2
Subscribers: N.A.
Fee: $62.95 monthly.
Digital Expanded Basic Service 3
Subscribers: N.A.
Fee: $10.95 monthly.
Digital Pay Service 1
Pay Units: N.A.
Programming (via satellite): Cinemax; Flix; HBO; Showtime; Starz; Starz Encore; The Movie Channel.
Fee: $15.95 monthly (Cinemax, HBO, Showtime/TMC or Starz/Encore), $27.95 monthly (Cinemax/HBO).
Video-On-Demand: No
Internet Service
Operational: Yes.
Fee: $29.95-$64.95 monthly.
Telephone Service
None
Miles of Plant: 4.0 (coaxial); None (fiber optic). Homes passed: 337.
President & Chief Executive Officer: Bill Otis. Chief Operating Officer & Vice President: Barbara Bornhoft. Chief Financial Officer & Treasurer: Curtis Kawlweski.
Ownership: New Ulm Telecom.

MAZEPPA—Formerly served by US Cable of Coastal Texas L.P. No longer in operation. ICA: MN0204.

MCGREGOR—SCI Broadband, 111 Tobies Mill Pl, PO Box 810, Hinckley, MN 55037-0810. Phones: 800-222-9809; 320-384-7442. Fax: 320-279-8085. E-mail: sales@scibroadband.com. Web Site: http://www.scibroadband.com. ICA: MN0229.

TV Market Ranking: Outside TV Markets (MCGREGOR). Franchise award date: May 31, 1988. Franchise expiration date: N.A. Began: August 1, 1990.
Channel capacity: N.A. Channels available but not in use: N.A.
Basic Service
Subscribers: 104.
Programming (received off-air): KBJR-TV (CBS, MNT, NBC) Superior; KCCW-TV (CBS) Walker; KDLH (CBS, CW) Duluth; KQDS-TV (Antenna TV, FOX) Duluth; WDIO-DT (ABC, MeTV) Duluth; WDSE (PBS) Duluth.
Programming (via satellite): A&E; Animal Planet; CNBC; CNN; Comedy Central; C-SPAN; Discovery Channel; Disney Channel; E! HD; ESPN; ESPN2; Fox News Channel; FOX Sports Networks; Freeform; Great American Country; HGTV; History; HLN; Lifetime; MTV; Nickelodeon; QVC; Spike TV; Syfy; TBS; The Weather Channel; TLC; TNT; Turner Classic Movies; TV Land; USA Network; VH1; WGN America; WPIX (Antenna TV, CW, This TV) New York.
Fee: $39.95 installation; $17.95 monthly; $1.00 converter.
Pay Service 1
Pay Units: N.A.
Programming (via satellite): Cinemax; HBO.
Fee: $9.95 monthly (Cinemax), $10.95 monthly (HBO).
Video-On-Demand: No
Internet Service
Operational: No.
Telephone Service
None
Miles of Plant: 6.0 (coaxial); None (fiber optic). Homes passed: 197.
General Manager: Mike Danielson. President: Ron Savage. Chief Technician: Pat McCabe. Customer Service Manager: Donna Erickson.
Ownership: Savage Communications Inc. (MSO).

McINTOSH—Garden Valley Telephone Co, 201 Ross Ave, PO Box 259, Erskine, MN 56535-0259. Phones: 800-448-8260; 218-687-5251. Fax: 218-687-2454. E-mail: gvtc@gvtel.com. Web Site: http://www.gvtel.com. Also serves Badger Twp. (portions), Bransvold Twp. (portions), Clearbrook, Erskine, Erskine (village), Fertile, Godfrey Twp. (portions), Gonvick, Grove Park Twp. (portions), Grygla, Hill River Twp. (portions), King Twp. (portions), Knute Twp., Leon Twp. (portions), Lessor Twp. (portions), Mentor, Oklee, Pine Lake Twp. (portions), Plummer, Sletten Twp. (portions), St. Hilaire, Winger, Winger Twp. & Woodside Twp. (portions). ICA: MN0105.
TV Market Ranking: Below 100 (Badger Twp. (portions), Clearbrook, Erskine, Erskine (village), Godfrey Twp. (portions), Gonvick, Grove Park Twp. (portions), Grygla, Hill River Twp. (portions), Lessor Twp. (portions), Mentor, Oklee, Plummer, St. Hilaire, Woodside Twp. (portions)); Outside TV Markets (Bransvold Twp. (portions), Fertile, King Twp. (portions), Knute Twp., MCINTOSH, Sletten Twp. (portions), Winger, Winger Twp.). Franchise award date: March 12, 1979. Franchise expiration date: N.A. Began: N.A.
Channel capacity: N.A. Channels available but not in use: N.A.
Basic Service
Subscribers: 555. Commercial subscribers: 127.
Programming (received off-air): KAWE (PBS) Bemidji; KBRR (FOX) Thief River Falls; KFME (PBS) Fargo; KRDK-TV (CBS, Decades, Movies!) Valley City; KVLY-TV (MeTV, NBC, This TV) Fargo; WDAY-TV (ABC, CW) Fargo; WDAZ-TV (ABC, CW) Devils Lake.
Programming (via satellite): A&E; AMC; CNN; Discovery Channel; Disney Channel; ESPN; FOX Sports Networks; Freeform; History; Spike TV; TBS; TNT; TV Land; USA Network; WGN America.
Programming (via translator): KMSP-TV (Bounce TV, Buzzr, FOX) Minneapolis.
Fee: $50.00 installation; $53.25 monthly; $1.50 converter.
Pay Service 1
Pay Units: N.A.
Programming (via satellite): HBO.
Fee: $15.00 monthly.
Video-On-Demand: No
Internet Service
Operational: Yes.
Fee: $35.95-$119.95 monthly.
Telephone Service
Analog: Operational
Fee: $24.14-$26.15 monthly
Miles of Plant: 278.0 (coaxial); None (fiber optic). Homes passed: 1,813.
President: Vernon Hamnes. General Manager: George Fish. Service & Operations Manager: Dave Hamre. Facilities Manager & Safety Director: Randy Versdahl. Marketing & PR Supervisor: Julie Dahle.
Ownership: Garden Valley Telephone Co. (MSO).

McINTOSH—Garden Valley Telephone Co, 201 Ross Ave, PO Box 259, Erskine, MN 56535-0259. Phones: 218-687-5251; 800-448-8260. Fax: 218-687-2454. E-mail: gvtc@gvtel.com. Web Site: http://www.gvtel.com. Also serves Badger Twp. (portions), Bagley, Bear Creek, Bear Park Twp., Bejou Twp., Beltrami, Benville Twp., Black River Twp., Brandsvold Twp., Bray Twp., Brooks, Browns Creek Twp., Buzzle Twp., Chester Twp., Clearbrook, Clover Twp., Cloverleaf Twp., Columbia Twp., Copley Twp., Deer Park Twp., Dudley Twp., Eckvold Twp., Eddy Twp., Eden Twp., Emardville Twp., Equality Twp., Erskine, Erskine (village), Espelie Twp., Falk Twp., Fertile, Fosston, Garden Twp., Garfield Twp., Garnes Twp., Gatzke, Gentilly Twp., Gervais Twp., Godfrey Twp., Gonvick, Goodridge, Goodridge Twp., Grand Plain Twp., Greenwood Twp., Gregory Twp., Grove Park Twp., Grygla, Gully, Gully Twp., Hammond, Hamre Twp., Hangaard Twp., Heier Twp., Hickory Twp., High Landing Twp., Hill River Twp., Holst Twp., Island Lake Twp., Itasca Twp., Johnson Twp., Jones Twp., King Twp., Knute Twp., Kratka Twp., La Prairie Twp., Lake Pleasant Twp., Lambert Twp., Lammers Twp., Lee Twp., Lengby, Leon Twp., Leonard, Lessor Twp., Liberty Twp., Lockhart Twp., Louisville Twp., Mayfield Twp., Mentor, Minerva Twp., Minnie Twp., Moose Creek Twp., Moose River Twp., Moylan Twp., Nore Twp., Oklee, Onstad Twp., Pine Lake Twp., Plummer, Polk Centre Twp., Poplar River Twp., Popple Twp., Queen Twp., Red Lake Falls, Red Lake Falls Twp., Reiner Twp., Reis Twp., Rice Twp., River Falls Twp., River Twp., Rocksbury Twp., Rollis Twp., Roosevelt, Rosebud Twp., Russia Twp., Sanders Twp., Scandia Twp., Shevlin, Shevlin Twp., Sinclair Twp., Sletten Twp., Smiley Twp., Spring Creek Twp., Spruce Grove Twp., St. Hilaire, Star Twp., Steenerson Twp., Sundal Twp., Terrebonne Twp., Trail, Valley Twp., Veldt Twp., Winger, Winger Twp., Winsor Twp., Woodside Twp., Wyandotte Twp. & Wylie Twp. ICA: MN5241.
TV Market Ranking: Below 100 (Badger Twp. (portions), Clearbrook, Erskine, Erskine (village), Godfrey Twp., Gonvick, Grygla, Hill River Twp., Mentor, Oklee, Plummer, Shevlin, Shevlin Twp., St. Hilaire, Winger Twp.); Outside TV Markets (Bagley, Fertile, King Twp., Knute Twp., Mentor, Sletten Twp., Winger).
Channel capacity: N.A. Channels available but not in use: N.A.
Limited Basic
Subscribers: 1,126.
Fee: $50.00 installation; $27.95 monthly. Includes 24 channels.
Expanded Basic Lite
Subscribers: N.A.
Fee: $38.95 monthly. Includes 36 channels.
Expanded Basic
Subscribers: 1,083.
Fee: $68.50 monthly. Includes 96 channels plus music channels.
HD
Subscribers: N.A.
Fee: $9.95 monthly. Includes 64+ channels.
Hispanic
Subscribers: N.A.
Fee: $5.95 monthly. Includes 4 channels.
Sports/Variety
Subscribers: 77.
Fee: $8.50 monthly. Includes 31 channels.
Showtime/TMC
Subscribers: N.A.
Fee: $14.00 monthly. Includes 20 channels.
Starz/Encore
Subscribers: N.A.
Fee: $13.50 monthly. Includes 21 channels.
Video-On-Demand: No
Internet Service
Operational: Yes.
Fee: $35.95-$119.95 monthly.
Telephone Service
Digital: Operational
Fee: $24.95-$26.15 monthly
President: Vernon Hamnes. General Manager: George Fish. Service & Operations Manager: Dave Hamre. Facilities Manager & Safety Director: Randy Versdahl. Marketing & PR Supervisor: Julie Dahle.
Ownership: Garden Valley Telephone Co.

MELROSE—Arvig, 160 2nd Ave. SW, Perham, MN 56573. Phones: 218-346-4227; 320-256-7471 (Melrose office); 888-992-7844. Fax: 218-338-3297. E-mail: answers@arvig.com. Web Site: http://arvig.com. Also serves Birchdale Twp., Burnhamville Twp., Burtrum, Eden Lake Twp., Eden Valley, Fairhaven Twp., Farming Twp., Forest Prairie Twp., Getty Twp., Greenwald, Grey Eagle, Grove Twp., Kimball, Kingston, Kingston Twp., Luxemburg Twp., Maine Prairie Twp., Manannah Twp., Meire Grove, Melrose

2017 Edition

D-409

Minnesota—Cable Systems

Twp., Millwood Twp., Munson Twp., New Munich, Oak Twp., Richmond, Roscoe, Round Prairie Twp., Spring Hill, Spring Hill Twp., St. Martin, St. Martin Twp., St. Rosa, Wakefield Twp., Ward Springs, Watkins & Zion Twp. ICA: MN5017.
TV Market Ranking: Below 100 (Grey Eagle).
Channel capacity: N.A. Channels available but not in use: N.A.
Basic Entertainment
 Subscribers: 1,785.
 Fee: $55.00 installation; $22.95 monthly. Includes 20 channels.
Home Entertainment
 Subscribers: N.A.
 Fee: $53.95 monthly. Includes 74 channels plus music channels.
Life & Leisure Entertainment
 Subscribers: N.A.
 Fee: $64.95 monthly. Includes 109 channels plus music channels.
HD
 Subscribers: N.A.
 Fee: $9.95 monthly.
Cinemax
 Subscribers: N.A.
 Fee: $12.95 monthly. Includes 8 channels.
HBO
 Subscribers: N.A.
 Fee: $17.95 monthly. Includes 6 channels.
Cinemax/HBO
 Subscribers: N.A.
 Fee: $24.95 monthly. Includes 14 channels.
Encore
 Subscribers: N.A.
 Fee: $6.95 monthly. Includes 6 channels.
Showtime/TMC
 Subscribers: N.A.
 Fee: $13.95 monthly. Includes 11 channels.
Starz/Encore
 Subscribers: N.A.
 Fee: $13.95 monthly. Includes 11 channels.
Internet Service
 Operational: Yes.
 Fee: $52.95-$82.95 monthly.
Telephone Service
 Digital: Operational
 Fee: $14.00 monthly
Chief Operating Officer & Vice President: David Arvig.
Ownership: Tekstar Communications Inc.

MELROSE—Charter Communications. Now served by ST. CLOUD, MN [MN0011]. ICA: MN0095.

MENAHGA—West Central Telephone Assn. This cable system has converted to IPTV, 308 Frontage Rd, Sebeka, MN 56477. Phones: 800-945-2163; 218-837-5151. Fax: 218-837-5001. E-mail: wcphone@wcta.net. Web Site: http://www.wcta.net. Also serves Blueberry Twp., Nimrod, Red Eye Twp., Sebeka & Verndale. ICA: MN5130.
TV Market Ranking: Below 100 (Blueberry Twp., MENAHGA); Outside TV Markets (Sebeka, Red Eye Twp.).
Channel capacity: N.A. Channels available but not in use: N.A.

Networks Plus TV
 Subscribers: 1,231.
 Fee: $30.78 monthly. Includes 36 channels.
People's Choice TV
 Subscribers: N.A.
Complete TV
 Subscribers: N.A.
HD
 Subscribers: N.A.
 Fee: $9.95 monthly.
Cinemax
 Subscribers: N.A.
 Fee: $15.95 monthly. Includes 9 channels.
HBO
 Subscribers: N.A.
 Fee: $19.95 monthly. Includes 12 channels.
Cinemax/HBO
 Subscribers: N.A.
 Fee: $29.95 monthly. Includes 21 channels.
Playboy
 Subscribers: N.A.
 Fee: $12.95 monthly. Includes 1 channel.
Showtime/TMC/Flix
 Subscribers: N.A.
 Fee: $12.95 monthly. Includes 15 channels.
Starz/Encore
 Subscribers: N.A.
 Fee: $12.95 monthly. Includes 17 channels.
Internet Service
 Operational: Yes.
Telephone Service
 Digital: Operational
 Fee: $17.75 monthly
Chief Executive Officer & Manager: Anthony V. Mayer. President: Bruce Kinnunen. Vice President: Dave Pulji. Operations Director: Sheldon Sagedahl.
Ownership: West Central Telephone Association.

MENAHGA—West Central Telephone Assn. This cable system has converted to IPTV. See MENAHGA, MN [MN5130]. ICA: MN0118.

MIDDLE RIVER—Sjoberg's Cable TV Inc, 315 Main Ave North, Thief River Falls, MN 56701-1905. Phones: 800-828-8808; 218-681-3044. Fax: 218-681-6801. E-mail: office1@mncable.net; sjobergs@mncable.net. Web Site: http://trf.mncable.net. Also serves Spruce Valley Twp. ICA: MN0236.
TV Market Ranking: Below 100 (MIDDLE RIVER, Spruce Valley Twp.). Franchise award date: N.A. Franchise expiration date: N.A. Began: February 1, 1979.
Channel capacity: N.A. Channels available but not in use: N.A.
Basic Service
 Subscribers: 95.
 Programming (received off-air): KBRR (FOX) Thief River Falls; KCPM (MNT) Grand Forks; KGFE (PBS) Grand Forks; various Canadian stations; WDAZ-TV (ABC, CW) Devils Lake; allband FM.
 Programming (via microwave): KRDK-TV (CBS, Decades, Movies!) Valley City; KVLY-TV (MeTV, NBC, This TV) Fargo.
 Programming (via satellite): CNN; ESPN; TBS.
 Fee: $25.00 installation; $55.92 monthly.

Expanded Basic Service 1
 Subscribers: N.A.
 Programming (via satellite): A&E; Animal Planet; Cartoon Network; CMT; CNBC; Comedy Central; C-SPAN; CW PLUS; Discovery Channel; Disney Channel; E! HD; ESPN2; Food Network; Fox News Channel; FOX Sports Networks; Freeform; FX; HGTV; History; Lifetime; MSNBC; MTV; Nickelodeon; Spike TV; Syfy; The Weather Channel; TLC; TNT; Turner Classic Movies; TV Land; USA Network; VH1; WGN America.
 Fee: $23.71 monthly.
Digital Basic Service
 Subscribers: N.A.
 Programming (via satellite): BBC America; Bloomberg Television; Bravo; CBS Sports Network; Chiller; Cloo; CMT; Cooking Channel; Daystar TV Network; Destination America; Discovery Kids Channel; Discovery Life Channel; Disney XD; DIY Network; DMX Music; ESPN Classic; ESPNews; ESPNU; EVINE Live; EWTN Global Catholic Network; Fox Business Network; FOX College Sports Central; FOX College Sports Pacific; Fox Sports 1; FXM; FYI; Golf Channel; Great American Country; GSN; Hallmark Channel; History International; HLN; HRTV; IFC; Investigation Discovery; LMN; MTV Classic; MTV Hits; MTV2; Nat Geo WILD; National Geographic Channel; NBCSN; Nick Jr.; Nicktoons; Outdoor Channel; Ovation; OWN: Oprah Winfrey Network; Oxygen; Reelz; RFD-TV; Science Channel; Sprout; Sundance TV; TBS HD; TeenNick; Tennis Channel; The Word Network; Trinity Broadcasting Network (TBN); TVG Network; UP; VH1 Soul; WE tv.
Digital Expanded Basic Service
 Subscribers: N.A.
 Programming (via satellite): A&E HD; AXS TV; CNN HD; Discovery Channel HD; ESPN HD; ESPN2 HD; Food Network HD; FSN HD; HGTV HD; History HD; Outdoor Channel 2 HD; PBS HD; Syfy HD; TNT HD; Universal HD; USA Network HD; Versus HD.
 Fee: $5.00 monthly; $5.00 converter.
Pay Service 1
 Pay Units: N.A.
 Programming (via satellite): Cinemax; HBO.
 Fee: $9.00 monthly (Cinemax), $11.00 monthly (HBO).
Digital Pay Service 1
 Pay Units: N.A.
 Programming (via satellite): Cinemax (multiplexed); Cinemax HD; HBO (multiplexed); HBO HD; Showtime (multiplexed); Starz (multiplexed); Starz Encore (multiplexed); The Movie Channel (multiplexed).
 Fee: $8.00 monthly (Starz/Encore), $9.00 monthly (Cinemax or Showtime/TMC), $11.00 monthly (HBO).
Video-On-Demand: No
Pay-Per-View
 iN DEMAND.
Internet Service
 Operational: No.
Telephone Service
 None
Miles of Plant: 6.0 (coaxial); 11.0 (fiber optic). Homes passed: 159.
President & General Manager: Richard J. Sjoberg. Chief Technician: Jerry Seim.
Ownership: Sjoberg's Cable TV Inc. (MSO).

MINNEAPOLIS—Comcast Cable, 10 River Park Plz, St. Paul, MN 55107. Phone: 612-493-5000. Fax: 612-493-5837. Web Site: http://www.comcast.com. Also serves Afton, Andover, Anoka, Arden Hills, Bayport, Baytown Twp., Birchwood Village, Blaine, Bloomington, Brooklyn Center, Brooklyn Park, Burnsville, Carver, Centerville, Champlin, Chaska, Circle Pines, Columbia Heights, Coon Rapids, Corcoran, Cottage Grove, Crystal, Dellwood, Denmark Twp., Eagan, Eden Prairie, Edina, Falcon Heights, Fridley, Gem Lake, Golden Valley, Grant Twp., Grey Cloud Island Twp., Ham Lake, Hanover, Hastings, Helena Twp., Hilltop, Hopkins, Hugo, Inver Grove Heights, Jackson Twp., Jordan, Lake Elmo, Lake St. Croix Beach, Lakeland, Lakeland Shores, Landfall, Lanesburgh Twp., Lauderdale, Lexington, Lilydale, Lino Lakes, Little Canada, Louisville Twp. (Scott County), Madelia, Mahtomedi, Maple Grove, Maplewood, Medicine Lake, Mendota, Mendota Heights, Minnetonka, Montrose, Mounds View, New Brighton, New Hope, New Prague, New Ulm, Newport, North Oaks, North St. Paul, Oak Grove, Oak Park Heights, Oakdale, Osseo, Pine Springs, Plymouth, Ramsey, Richfield, Robbinsdale, Rogers, Roseville, Sand Creek Twp., Shakopee, Shoreview, South St. Paul, Spring Lake Park, St. Anthony, St. Louis Park, St. Marys Point, St. Paul, St. Paul Park, Stillwater, Stillwater Twp., Sunfish Lake, Vadnais Heights, Waverly, West Lakeland Twp., West St. Paul, White Bear Lake, White Bear Twp., Willernie & Woodbury, MN; Cato, Hudson, Manitowoc, Manitowoc (town), Manitowoc Rapids, Newton (town), North Hudson, Prescott, River Falls, Troy & Whitelaw, WI. ICA: MN0001.
TV Market Ranking: 13 (Afton, Andover, Anoka, Arden Hills, Bayport, Baytown Twp., Birchwood Village, Blaine, Bloomington, Brooklyn Center, Brooklyn Park, Burnsville, Carver, Centerville, Champlin, Chaska, Circle Pines, Columbia Heights, Coon Rapids, Corcoran, Cottage Grove, Crystal, Dellwood, Denmark Twp., Eagan, Eden Prairie, Edina, Falcon Heights, Fridley, Gem Lake, Golden Valley, Grant Twp., Grey Cloud Island Twp., Ham Lake, Hanover, Hastings, Helena Twp., Hilltop, Hopkins, Hudson, Hugo, Inver Grove Heights, Jackson Twp., Jordan, Lake Elmo, Lake St. Croix Beach, Lakeland, Lakeland Shores, Landfall, Lanesburgh Twp. (portions), Lauderdale, Lexington, Lilydale, Lino Lakes, Little Canada, Louisville Twp. (Scott County), Mahtomedi, Maple Grove, Maplewood, Medicine Lake, Mendota, Mendota Heights, MINNEAPOLIS, Minnetonka, Montrose, Mounds View, New Brighton, New Hope, New Prague, Newport, North Hudson, North Oaks, North St. Paul, Oak Grove, Oak Park Heights, Oakdale, Osseo, Pine Springs, Plymouth, Prescott, Ramsey, Richfield, River Falls, Robbinsdale, Rogers, Roseville, Sand Creek Twp., Shakopee, Shoreview, South St. Paul, Spring Lake Park, St. Anthony, St. Louis Park, St. Marys Point, St. Paul, St. Paul Park, Stillwater, Stillwater Twp., Sunfish Lake, Troy, Vadnais Heights, West Lakeland Twp., West St. Paul, White Bear Lake, White Bear Twp., Willernie, Woodbury); 62 (Cato, Manitowoc, Manitowoc (town), Manitowoc Rapids, Whitelaw); Below 100 (Madelia, New Ulm, Waverly, Lanesburgh Twp. (portions)); Outside TV Markets (Newton (town)). Franchise award date: January 1, 1982. Franchise expiration date: N.A. Began: December 1, 1983.
Channel capacity: N.A. Channels available but not in use: N.A.
Basic Service
 Subscribers: 493,123.
 Programming (received off-air): KARE (NBC, WeatherNation) Minneapolis; KMSP-TV (Bounce TV, Buzzr, FOX) Minneapolis;

Cable Systems—Minnesota

KPXM-TV (ION) St. Cloud; KSTC-TV (Antenna TV, This TV) Minneapolis; KSTP-TV (ABC, MeTV) St. Paul; KTCI-TV (PBS) St. Paul; WCCO-TV (CBS, Decades) Minneapolis; WFTC (MNT, Movies!) Minneapolis; WUCW (CW, The Country Network) Minneapolis.
Programming (via satellite): CNN; C-SPAN; EVINE Live; QVC; TBS; WGN America.
Fee: $40.00 installation; $25.34 monthly.

Expanded Basic Service 1
Subscribers: N.A.
Programming (via satellite): A&E; Animal Planet; BET; Bravo; BTN; Cartoon Network; CNBC; Comedy Central; Discovery Channel; Disney Channel; E! HD; ESPN; ESPN2; Food Network; Fox News Channel; FOX Sports North; Freeform; FX; Golf Channel; Hallmark Channel; HGTV; History; HLN; Jewelry Television; Lifetime; MSNBC; MTV; National Geographic Channel; NBCSN; Nickelodeon; Spike TV; Syfy; The Weather Channel; TLC; TNT; Travel Channel; truTV; Turner Classic Movies; TV Land; USA Network; VH1.
Fee: $36.38 monthly.

Digital Basic Service
Subscribers: N.A.
Programming (via satellite): A&E HD; AMC; AMC HD; Animal Planet HD; AXS TV; Azteca; BBC America; Bio HD; Bloomberg Television; Boomerang; Bravo HD; BTN; Cartoon Network HD; CBS Sports Network; CBS Sports Network HD; Centric; Cine Mexicano; Cinelatino; CMT; CMT HD; CNBC HD+; CNN en Espanol; CNN HD; Comedy Central HD; Cooking Channel; C-SPAN 2; C-SPAN 3; Destination America; Destination America HD; Discovery Channel HD; Discovery Family; Discovery Life Channel; Disney Channel HD; Disney XD; DIY Network; E! HD; ESPN Classic; ESPN Deportes; ESPN HD; ESPN2 HD; ESPNews; ESPNews HD; ESPNU; ESPNU HD; EWTN Global Catholic Network; Flix; Food Network HD; Fox Business Network; Fox Business Network HD; FOX College Sports Central; FOX College Sports Pacific; Fox Deportes; Fox Sports 1; Fox Sports 2; Freeform HD; FSN HD; Fuse; Fuse HD; FX HD; FXM; FYI; Golf Channel HD; Great American Country; GSN; Hallmark Channel HD; Hallmark Movie Channel HD; Hallmark Movies & Mysteries; HD Theater; HGTV HD; History en Espanol; History HD; History International; HLN HD; Home Shopping Network HD; ID Investigation Discovery HD; IFC; Investigation Discovery; Lifetime HD; Lifetime Movie Network HD; LMN; LOGO; MC; MGM HD; MLB Network; MoviePlex; MTV Classic; MTV Hits; MTV Jams; MTV Live; MTV2; Nat Geo WILD; National Geographic Channel; National Geographic Channel HD; NBA TV; NBC Universo; NFL Network; NFL Network HD; NFL RedZone; NHL Network; Nick 2; Nick HD; Nick Jr.; Nicktoons; Outdoor Channel; Outdoor Channel HD; Ovation; OWN: Oprah Winfrey Network; Oxygen; QVC HD; Reelz; Science Channel; Science HD; Spike TV HD; Sprout; Starz Encore (multiplexed); Starz Encore HD; Sundance TV; Syfy HD; TBS HD; TeenNick; Tennis Channel; The Sportsman Channel; The Weather Channel HD; TLC HD; TNT HD; Tr3s; Travel Channel HD; Trinity Broadcasting Network (TBN); truTV HD; Turner Classic Movies HD; TV One; TV One HD; UniMas; Universal HD; Univision; UP; USA Network HD; Versus HD; VH1 HD; ViendoMovies; WAM! America's Kidz Network; WE tv; WE tv HD; Weatherscan; WGN America HD.

Digital Pay Service 1
Pay Units: N.A.
Programming (via satellite): Cinemax (multiplexed); Cinemax HD; HBO (multiplexed); HBO HD; Saigon Broadcasting Television Network (SBTN); Showtime (multiplexed); Showtime HD; Starz (multiplexed); Starz HD; The Movie Channel (multiplexed); The Movie Channel HD; TV Asia; Zee TV.
Fee: $10.00 installation; $10.95 monthly (Cinemax/Cinemax HD, HBO/HBO HD, Showtime/Showtime HD, Starz/Starz HDTV or TMC/TMC HD).
Video-On-Demand: Yes
Pay-Per-View
iN DEMAND (delivered digitally); Shorteez (delivered digitally); Fresh (delivered digitally); Pleasure (delivered digitally); Playboy TV (delivered digitally).
Internet Service
Operational: Yes.
Subscribers: 516,853.
Broadband Service: Comcast High Speed Internet.
Fee: $100.00 installation; $42.95 monthly.
Telephone Service
Digital: Operational
Subscribers: 237,327.
Fee: $44.95 monthly
Miles of Plant: 18,924.0 (coaxial); 4,699.0 (fiber optic). Homes passed: 1,194,441.
Vice President: Bill Wright. Vice President, Sales & Marketing: Nick Kozel. Vice President, Government & Public Affairs: Kim Roden. Technical Operations Director: Mark Bisenius.
Ownership: Comcast Cable Communications Inc. (MSO).

MINNESOTA CITY—Hiawatha Broadband. This cable system has converted to IPTV. Now served by WINONA, MN [MN5161]. ICA: MN5173.

MINNESOTA LAKE—BEVCOMM. This cable system has converted to IPTV. Now served by NEW PRAGUE, MN [MN5366]. ICA: MN0337.

MISSION TWP.—Formerly served by Crosslake Communications, CROSSLAKE, MN [MN0069]. This cable system has converted to IPTV. Now served by Consolidated Telecommunications Co., RANDALL, MN [MN5026]. ICA: MN5299.

MONTEVIDEO—Charter Communications. Now served by WILLMAR, MN [MN0018]. ICA: MN0051.

MONTGOMERY—Mediacom. Now served by ST. PETER (formerly Waseca), MN [MN0043]. ICA: MN0338.

MONTROSE—Formerly served by Time Warner Cable. Now served by Comcast Cable, MINNEAPOLIS, MN [MN0001]. ICA: MN0339.

MOOSE LAKE—Mediacom. Now served by CLOQUET, MO [MN0042]. ICA: MN0136.

MORRIS—Mediacom, 1504 2nd St SE, PO Box 110, Waseca, MN 56093. Phones: 845-695-2762; 507-835-2356. Fax: 507-835-4567. Web Site: http://www.mediacomcable.com. Also serves Belgrade, Brooten, Chokio, Hancock & Starbuck. ICA: MN0210.
TV Market Ranking: Below 100 (Belgrade, Brooten, Hancock, Starbuck, MORRIS). Outside TV Markets (Chokio). Franchise award date: N.A. Franchise expiration date: N.A. Began: January 1, 1978.
Channel capacity: N.A. Channels available but not in use: N.A.

Basic Service
Subscribers: 903.
Programming (received off-air): KPXM-TV (ION) St. Cloud; KSTC-TV (Antenna TV, This TV) Minneapolis; KTCA-TV (PBS) St. Paul; KTCI-TV (PBS) St. Paul; WUCW (CW, The Country Network) Minneapolis; allband FM.
Programming (via satellite): C-SPAN; Pop; QVC; The Weather Channel; WGN America.
Programming (via translator): KARE (NBC, WeatherNation) Minneapolis; KCCO-TV (CBS) Alexandria; KMSP-TV (Bounce TV, Buzzr, FOX) Minneapolis; KSAX (ABC) Alexandria; KWCM-TV (PBS) Appleton; WFTC (MNT, Movies!) Minneapolis.
Fee: $52.39 installation; $42.00 monthly.

Expanded Basic Service 1
Subscribers: N.A.
Programming (via satellite): A&E; AMC; Animal Planet; Bravo; Cartoon Network; CMT; CNBC; CNN; Comedy Central; C-SPAN 2; Discovery Channel; Discovery Life Channel; Disney Channel; E! HD; ESPN; ESPN2; EWTN Global Catholic Network; Fox News Channel; Fox Sports 1; FOX Sports North; Freeform; FX; FXM; Hallmark Channel; HGTV; History; HLN; INSP; ION Television; Lifetime; MSNBC; MTV; Nickelodeon; RFD-TV; Spike TV; Syfy; TBS; TLC; TNT; Travel Channel; Trinity Broadcasting Network (TBN); truTV; Turner Classic Movies; TV Land; Univision Studios; USA Network; VH1; WE tv.
Fee: $16.38 monthly.

Digital Basic Service
Subscribers: N.A.
Programming (via satellite): 52MX; AXS TV; BBC America; Bloomberg Television; Cinelatino; Cloo; CNN en Espanol; Destination America; Discovery Kids Channel; Discovery Life Channel; ESPN Deportes; ESPN HD; ESPN2 HD; ESPNews; Fox Deportes; Fox Sports 2; Fuse; FXM; FYI; Golf Channel; GSN; HD Theater; History en Espanol; History International; IFC; Investigation Discovery; LMN; MC; MTV Classic; MTV Hits; MTV2; Nat Geo WILD; National Geographic Channel; Nick Jr.; Outdoor Channel; OWN: Oprah Winfrey Network; Reelz; Science Channel; Tr3s; Turner Classic Movies; TVG Network; ViendoMovies.

Pay Service 1
Pay Units: N.A.
Programming (via satellite): Showtime.

Digital Pay Service 1
Pay Units: N.A.
Programming (via satellite): Cinemax (multiplexed); Flix; HBO (multiplexed); HBO HD; Showtime (multiplexed); Showtime HD; Starz (multiplexed); Starz Encore (multiplexed); Starz HD; Sundance TV; The Movie Channel (multiplexed); The Movie Channel HD.
Fee: $11.00 monthly (each).
Video-On-Demand: No

Pay-Per-View
iN DEMAND (delivered digitally); SexSee (delivered digitally); Fresh (delivered digitally); Pleasure (delivered digitally); Playboy TV (delivered digitally).
Internet Service
Operational: Yes.
Broadband Service: Mediacom High Speed Internet.
Telephone Service
Digital: Operational
Miles of Plant: 56.0 (coaxial); None (fiber optic). Homes passed: 3,732.
Vice President: Bill Jensen. Vice President, Financial Reporting: Kenneth J. Kohrs. Marketing & Sales Manager: Lori Huberty. Engineering Manager: Kraig Kaiser.
Ownership: Mediacom LLC (MSO).

MORRIS—Mediacom. Now served by MORRIS, MN [MN0210]. ICA: MN0340.

MORRISTOWN—BEVCOMM, 100 2nd St SW, PO Box 86, Morristown, MN 55052. Phones: 800-473-1442; 507-685-4321; 800-390-6562. E-mail: info@bevcomm.net. Web Site: http://www.bevcomm.net. Also serves Warsaw. ICA: MN0167.
TV Market Ranking: Below 100 (MORRISTOWN, Warsaw). Franchise award date: N.A. Franchise expiration date: N.A. Began: August 1, 1984.
Channel capacity: N.A. Channels available but not in use: N.A.

Basic Service
Subscribers: 38.
Programming (received off-air): KARE (NBC, WeatherNation) Minneapolis; KEYC-TV (CBS, FOX) Mankato; KMSP-TV (Bounce TV, Buzzr, FOX) Minneapolis; KSTC-TV (Antenna TV, This TV) Minneapolis; KSTP-TV (ABC, MeTV) St. Paul; KTCA-TV (PBS) St. Paul; WCCO-TV (CBS, Decades) Minneapolis; WFTC (MNT, Movies!) Minneapolis; WUCW (CW, The Country Network) Minneapolis.
Programming (via satellite): C-SPAN; TBS; WGN America.
Fee: $35.00 installation; $36.95 monthly.

Expanded Basic Service 1
Subscribers: N.A.
Fee: $59.95 monthly.

Digital Basic Service
Subscribers: N.A.
Programming (via satellite): BBC America; Bloomberg Television; Bravo; Discovery Digital Networks; Disney XD; DMX Music; ESPN Classic; ESPN2; ESPNews; Fox Sports 1; Fuse; FYI; Golf Channel; GSN; HGTV; History; History International; IFC; National Geographic Channel; NBCSN; Nick Jr.; Nicktoons; Outdoor Channel; Syfy; TeenNick; Trinity Broadcasting Network (TBN); Turner Classic Movies; WE tv.
Fee: $63.95 monthly.

Digital Expanded Basic Service
Subscribers: 37.
Programming (via satellite): A&E; AMC; Animal Planet; CMT; CNBC; CNN; Comedy Central; Discovery Channel; Disney Channel; ESPN; ESPN Classic; ESPN2; Food Network; Fox News Channel; FOX Sports

2017 Edition D-411

Minnesota—Cable Systems

North; Freeform; FX; Hallmark Channel; HGTV; History; Lifetime; MSNBC; MTV; NBCSN; Nickelodeon; Spike TV; Syfy; The Weather Channel; TLC; TNT; truTV; Turner Classic Movies; TV Land; USA Network; VH1.
Fee: $68.95 monthly.

Digital Pay Service 1
Pay Units: N.A.
Programming (via satellite): Cinemax (multiplexed); Flix; HBO (multiplexed); Showtime (multiplexed); The Movie Channel (multiplexed).
Fee: $13.95 monthly (Cinemax), $14.95 monthly (HBO), $15.95 monthly (Showtime/TMC).

Video-On-Demand: No
Pay-Per-View
Fresh (delivered digitally); Playboy TV (delivered digitally); Hot Choice (delivered digitally); iN DEMAND (delivered digitally).

Internet Service
Operational: Yes.
Fee: $9.95-$79.95 monthly.

Telephone Service
Analog: Operational
Fee: $28.83 monthly
Miles of Plant: 18.0 (coaxial); None (fiber optic). Homes passed: 521.
President & Chief Executive Officer: Bill Eckles.
Ownership: BEVCOMM (MSO).

MORSE TWP.—Paul Bunyan Communications, 1831 Anne St NW, Ste 100, Bemidji, MN 56601. Phones: 218-999-1234; 888-586-3100; 218-444-1234. Fax: 214-444-1121. E-mail: tv@paulbunyan.net; info@paulbunyan.net. Web Site: http://www.paulbunyan.net. Also serves Alvwood Twp., Arbo Twp., Ardenhurst Twp., Ball Club, Cohasset, Deer River, Deer River Twp., Good Hope Twp., Grand Rapids, Grand Rapids Twp., Grattan Twp., Inger, Itasca County (Unorganized Townships), Kinghurst Twp., Koochiching County (Unorganized Townships), La Prairie, Max Twp., Mizpah Twp., Nore Twp., Northome, Oteneagen Twp., Pomroy Twp., Ponemah, Sand Lake Twp., Squaw Lake, Third River Twp., Wirt Twp. & Zemple. ICA: MN5068.
TV Market Ranking: Franchise award date: April 22, 2002. Franchise expiration date: N.A. Began: N.A.
Channel capacity: N.A. Channels available but not in use: N.A.

PBTV Lite
Subscribers: 4,053. Commercial subscribers: 22.
Fee: $75.00 installation; $7.95 monthly.

PBTV Fusion
Subscribers: N.A.

HD
Subscribers: N.A.
Fee: $9.99 monthly. 67 HD channels.

PBTV Extra
Subscribers: N.A.
Fee: $9.99 monthly. 33 channels.

PBTV Sports
Subscribers: N.A.
Fee: $6.99 monthly. 12 channels.

Cinemax
Subscribers: N.A.
Fee: $12.95 monthly. 9 channels.

HBO
Subscribers: N.A.
Fee: $15.95 monthly. 11 channels.

Cinemax/HBO
Subscribers: N.A.
Fee: $22.95 monthly. 9 channels of Cinemax & 11 channels of HBO.

Showtime/TMC
Subscribers: N.A.
Fee: $12.95 monthly. 13 channels.

Starz/Encore
Subscribers: N.A.
Fee: $12.95 monthly. 15 channels.

Movie Package
Subscribers: N.A.
Fee: $41.95 monthly. 48 channels of Cinemax, Encore, HBO, Showtime, Starz & TMC.

Video-On-Demand: Yes
Internet Service
Operational: Yes.
Fee: $44.95-$75.00 monthly.

Telephone Service
Digital: Operational
Fee: $20.95 monthly
Chief Executive Officer & General Manager: Gary Johnson. Video Services Coordinator: Keith Hunt.
Ownership: Paul Bunyan Communications.

MOTLEY—SCI Broadband. Now served by PILLAGER, MN [MN0230]. ICA: MN0217.

MOUND—Mediacom, 1504 2nd St SE, PO Box 110, Waseca, MN 56093. Phones: 845-695-2762; 507-835-2356. Fax: 507-835-4567. Web Site: http://www.mediacomcable.com. Also serves Chanhassen, Deephaven, Excelsior, Greenwood, Hamburg, Independence, Long Lake, Loretto, Maple Plain, Medina, Minnetonka Beach, Minnetrista, Norwood, Orono, Shorewood, Spring Park, St. Boniﬁcius, Tonka Bay, Victoria, Waconia, Wayzata, Woodland & Young America. ICA: MN0010.
TV Market Ranking: 13 (Chanhassen, Deephaven, Excelsior, Greenwood, Independence, Long Lake, Loretto, Maple Plain, Medina, Minnetonka Beach, Minnetrista, MOUND, Norwood, Orono, Shorewood, Spring Park, St. Boniﬁcius, Tonka Bay, Victoria, Waconia, Wayzata, Woodland, Young America); Outside TV Markets (Hamburg). Franchise award date: May 11, 1984. Franchise expiration date: N.A. Began: December 1, 1984.
Channel capacity: N.A. Channels available but not in use: N.A.

Basic Service
Subscribers: 15,654.
Programming (received off-air): KARE (NBC, WeatherNation) Minneapolis; KMSP-TV (Bounce TV, Buzzr, FOX) Minneapolis; KPXM-TV (ION) St. Cloud; KSTC-TV (Antenna TV, This TV) Minneapolis; KSTP-TV (ABC, MeTV) St. Paul; KTCA-TV (PBS) St. Paul; KTCI-TV (PBS) St. Paul; WCCO-TV (CBS, Decades) Minneapolis; WFTC (MNT, Movies!) Minneapolis; WUCW (CW, The Country Network) Minneapolis.
Programming (via satellite): C-SPAN; C-SPAN 2; QVC; The Weather Channel; WGN America.
Fee: $4.95 installation; $43.00 monthly.

Expanded Basic Service 1
Subscribers: N.A.
Programming (via satellite): A&E; AMC; Animal Planet; BET; Bravo; Cartoon Network; CMT; CNBC; CNN; Comedy Central; Discovery Channel; Disney Channel; E! HD; ESPN; ESPN2; EWTN Global Catholic Network; Food Network; Fox News Channel; Fox Sports 1; Freeform; FX; FXM; Hallmark Channel; HGTV; History; HLN; INSP; Lifetime; MSNBC; MTV; Nickelodeon; Pop; Spike TV; Syfy; TBS; TLC; TNT; Travel Channel; Trinity Broadcasting Network (TBN); truTV; Turner Classic Movies; TV Land; Univision Studios; USA Network; VH1; WE tv.
Fee: $26.45 monthly.

Digital Basic Service
Subscribers: N.A.
Programming (via satellite): BBC America; Bloomberg Television; Discovery Digital Networks; Fuse; FYI; Golf Channel; GSN; History International; HITS (Headend In The Sky); IFC; LMN; MC; NBCSN; Outdoor Channel.

Digital Pay Service 1
Pay Units: N.A.
Programming (via satellite): Cinemax (multiplexed); Flix; HBO (multiplexed); Showtime (multiplexed); Starz (multiplexed); Starz Encore (multiplexed); Sundance TV; The Movie Channel (multiplexed).
Fee: $10.00 monthly (each).

Video-On-Demand: Yes
Pay-Per-View
Pleasure (delivered digitally); ESPN Now (delivered digitally); ETC (delivered digitally); Playboy TV (delivered digitally); Fresh (delivered digitally); Shorteez (delivered digitally); Vubiquity Inc. (delivered digitally); Sports PPV (delivered digitally).

Internet Service
Operational: Yes.
Subscribers: 16,071.
Broadband Service: Mediacom High Speed Internet.
Fee: $69.95 installation; $40.95 monthly; $10.00 modem lease; $239.95 modem purchase.

Telephone Service
Analog: Not Operational
Digital: Operational
Subscribers: 8,043.
Miles of Plant: 1,124.0 (coaxial); 217.0 (fiber optic). Homes passed: 45,799.
Vice President: Bill Jensen. Vice President, Financial Reporting: Kenneth J. Kohrs. Engineering Manager: Kraig Kaiser. Marketing & Sales Director: Lori Huberty.
Ownership: Mediacom LLC (MSO).

MOUNTAIN LAKE—Mediacom. Now served by ST. PETER (formerly Waseca), MN [MN0043]. ICA: MN0126.

NEW AUBURN—Formerly served by North American Communications Corp. This cable system has converted to IPTV. Now served by Jaguar Communications, NEW MARKET, MN [MN5374]. ICA: MN0248.

NEW MARKET—Formerly served by North American Communications Corp. This cable system has converted to IPTV. Now served by Jaguar Communications. See NEW MARKET, MN [MN5374]. ICA: MN0223.

NEW MARKET—Jaguar Communications, 213 South Oak St, Owatonna, MN 55060. Phone: 507-214-1000. E-mail: support@jagcom.net. Web Site: http://www.jaguarcommunications.com. Also serves Dundas, Faribault, Green Isle, New Auburn, Northfield, Plato, Warsaw & Wells Twp. ICA: MN5374.
TV Market Ranking: Below 100 (Warsaw, Wells Twp.); Outside TV Markets (Green Isle, New Auburn, Plato).
Channel capacity: N.A. Channels available but not in use: N.A.

Internet Service
Operational: Yes.
Telephone Service
Digital: Operational
Ownership: Jaguar Communications.

NEW PRAGUE—BEVCOMM. Formerly [MN0337]. This cable system has converted to IPTV, 115 Main St West, New Prague,

MN 56071. Phones: 800-473-1442; 952-758-2501. E-mail: info@bevcomm.net. Web Site: http://www.bevcomm.net. Also serves Bricelyn, Delavan, Easton, Freeborn, Frost, Granada, Huntley, Minnesota Lake, Wells & Winnebago. ICA: MN5366.
TV Market Ranking: 13 (NEW PRAGUE); Below 100 (Delavan, Easton, Freeborn, Minnesota Lake, Wells, Winnebago); Outside TV Markets (Bricelyn, Frost).
Channel capacity: N.A. Channels available but not in use: N.A.

Digital Basic
Subscribers: 3,367.
Fee: $35.00 installation; $71.95 monthly. Includes 140+ channels.

HD
Subscribers: N.A.
Fee: $9.95 monthly.

EASE
Subscribers: N.A.
Fee: $7.95 monthly. Includes 33 sports & entertainment channels.

Cinemax
Subscribers: N.A.
Fee: $12.95 monthly. Includes 4 channels.

HBO
Subscribers: N.A.
Fee: $15.95 monthly. Includes 11 channels.

HBO/Starz/Encore
Subscribers: N.A.
Fee: $23.95 monthly. Includes 26 channels.

NFL RedZone
Subscribers: N.A.
Fee: $44.95 per season.

Playboy
Subscribers: N.A.
Fee: $14.95 monthly. Includes 1 channel.

Showtime/TMC/Flix
Subscribers: N.A.
Fee: $14.95 monthly. Includes 13 channels.

Starz/Encore
Subscribers: N.A.
Fee: $14.95 monthly. Includes 15 channels.

Video-On-Demand: Yes
Internet Service
Operational: Yes.
Fee: $9.95-$149.95 monthly.

Telephone Service
Digital: Operational
Fee: $29.83-$29.95 monthly
President & Chief Executive Officer: Bill Eckles.
Ownership: BEVCOMM.

NEW PRAGUE—Formerly served by Time Warner Cable. Now served by Comcast Cable, MINNEAPOLIS, MN [MN0001]. ICA: MN0341.

NEW ULM—Formerly served by Time Warner Cable. Now served by Comcast Cable, MINNEAPOLIS, MN [MN0001]. ICA: MN0034.

NEW ULM—NU-Telecom. Formerly [MN0285]. This cable system has converted to IPTV, 27 North Minnesota St, New Ulm, MN 56073. Phones: 888-873-6853; 507-354-4111. Fax: 507-233-4242. E-mail: on-linecustservice@nu-telcom.net. Web Site: http://www.nutelecom.net. Also serves Courtland, Essig, Klossner, Redwood Falls, Sanborn, Searles & Springfield. ICA: MN5117.
TV Market Ranking: Below 100 (Courtland, Essig, NEW ULM, Redwood Falls, Sanborn, Searles, Springfield).
Channel capacity: N.A. Channels available but not in use: N.A.

Cable Systems—Minnesota

NU-Basic
 Subscribers: 4,448.
 Fee: $50.00 installation; $18.95 monthly. Includes 33 channels plus 46 music channels.
NU-Entertainment
 Subscribers: N.A.
 Fee: $55.95 monthly. Includes 98 plus 46 music channels.
NU-Variety
 Subscribers: N.A.
 Fee: $62.95 monthly. Includes 124 channels plus 46 music channels.
HD Anywhere
 Subscribers: N.A.
 Fee: $9.95 monthly. Includes 64 channels.
NU-Premium
 Subscribers: N.A.
 Fee: $15.95 monthly (Cinemax, HBO, Playboy, Showtime/TMC or Starz/Encore), $26.95 monthly (HBO/Starz/Encore), $34.95 monthly (Cinemax/HBO/Starz/Encore), $44.95 monthly (all premium channels).
Video-On-Demand: No
Internet Service
 Operational: Yes.
 Fee: $44.95-$59.95 monthly.
Telephone Service
 Digital: Operational
 Fee: $15.23 monthly
President & Chief Executive Officer: Bill Otis.
Ownership: New Ulm Telecom (MSO).

NEW ULM—NU-Telecom. This cable system has converted to IPTV. See NEW ULM, MN [MN5117]. ICA: MN0285.

NEWFOLDEN—Sjoberg's Cable TV Inc, 315 Main Ave North, Thief River Falls, MN 56701-1905. Phones: 800-828-8808; 218-681-3044. Fax: 218-681-6801. E-mail: office1@mncable.net; sjobergs@mncable.net. Web Site: http://trf.mncable.net. ICA: MN0249.
 TV Market Ranking: Below 100 (NEWFOLDEN).
 Channel capacity: N.A. Channels available but not in use: N.A.
Basic Service
 Subscribers: 94.
 Programming (received off-air): KBRR (FOX) Thief River Falls; KCPM (MNT) Grand Forks; KGFE (PBS) Grand Forks; KRDK-TV (CBS, Decades, Movies!) Valley City; KVLY-TV (NBC, This TV) Fargo; WDAZ-TV (ABC, CW) Devils Lake.
 Programming (via satellite): CNN; ESPN; TBS; various Canadian stations.
 Fee: $25.00 installation; $55.92 monthly.
Expanded Basic Service 1
 Subscribers: N.A.
 Programming (via satellite): A&E; Animal Planet; Cartoon Network; CMT; CNBC; Comedy Central; C-SPAN; CW PLUS; Discovery Channel; Disney Channel; E! HD; ESPN2; Food Network; Fox News Channel; FOX Sports Networks; Freeform; FX; HGTV; History; Lifetime; MSNBC; MTV; Nickelodeon; Spike TV; Syfy; The Weather Channel; TBS; TNT; Turner Classic Movies; TV Land; USA Network; VH1; WGN America.
 Fee: $23.71 monthly.
Digital Basic Service
 Subscribers: N.A.
 Programming (via satellite): BBC America; Bloomberg Television; Bravo; CBS Sports Network; Chiller; Cloo; CMT; Cooking Channel; Daystar TV Network; Destination America; Discovery Kids Channel; Discovery Life Channel; Disney XD; DIY Network; DMX Music; ESPN Classic; ESPNews; ESPNU; EVINE Live; EWTN Global Catholic Network; Family Friendly Entertainment; Fox Business Network; FOX College Sports Central; FOX College Sports Pacific; Fox Sports 1; FXM; FYI; Golf Channel; Great American Country; GSN; Hallmark Channel; History International; HLN; HRTV; IFC; Investigation Discovery; LMN; MTV Classic; MTV Hits; MTV2; Nat Geo WILD; National Geographic Channel; NBCSN; Nick Jr.; Nicktoons; Outdoor Channel; Ovation; OWN: Oprah Winfrey Network; Oxygen; Reelz; RFD-TV; Science Channel; Sprout; Sundance TV; TeenNick; Tennis Channel; The Word Network; Trinity Broadcasting Network (TBN); TVG Network; VH1 Soul; WE tv.
Digital Expanded Basic Service
 Subscribers: N.A.
 Programming (via satellite): A&E HD; AXS TV; CNN HD; Discovery Channel HD; ESPN HD; ESPN2 HD; Food Network HD; FSN HD; HGTV HD; History HD; Outdoor Channel 2 HD; PBS HD; Syfy HD; TBS HD; TNT HD; Universal HD; USA Network HD; Versus HD.
 Fee: $5.00 monthly; $5.00 converter.
Pay Service 1
 Pay Units: N.A.
 Programming (via satellite): Cinemax; HBO.
 Fee: $9.00 monthly (Cinemax), $11.00 monthly (HBO).
Digital Pay Service 1
 Pay Units: N.A.
 Programming (via satellite): Cinemax (multiplexed); Cinemax HD; HBO (multiplexed); HBO HD; Showtime (multiplexed); Starz (multiplexed); Starz Encore (multiplexed); The Movie Channel (multiplexed).
 Fee: $8.00 monthly (Starz/Encore), $9.00 monthly (Cinemax or Showtime/TMC), $11.00 monthly (HBO).
Video-On-Demand: No
Internet Service
 Operational: No.
Telephone Service
 None
Miles of Plant: 4.0 (coaxial); 7.0 (fiber optic). Homes passed: 140.
President & General Manager: Richard J. Sjoberg. Chief Technician: Jerry Seim.
Ownership: Sjoberg's Cable TV Inc. (MSO).

NICOLLET—Clara City Telephone Co, 227 South Main St, PO Box 800, Clara City, MN 56222. Phones: 888-283-7667; 320-847-2211. Fax: 320-847-2736. E-mail: bruce@hcinet.net. Web Site: http://www.hcinet.net. ICA: MN0342.
 TV Market Ranking: Below 100 (NICOLLET). Franchise award date: June 1, 1991. Franchise expiration date: N.A. Began: N.A.
 Channel capacity: N.A. Channels available but not in use: N.A.
Basic Service
 Subscribers: 22.
 Programming (received off-air): KARE (NBC, WeatherNation) Minneapolis; KEYC-TV (CBS, FOX) Mankato; KMSP-TV (Bounce TV, Buzzr, FOX) Minneapolis; KSTP-TV (ABC, MeTV) St. Paul; KTCA-TV (PBS) St. Paul; KTCI-TV (PBS) St. Paul; WCCO-TV (CBS, Decades) Minneapolis; WFTC (MNT, Movies!) Minneapolis; WUCW (CW, The Country Network) Minneapolis.
 Programming (via satellite): A&E; AMC; CMT; CNN; Comedy Central; C-SPAN; Discovery Channel; ESPN; ESPN2; EWTN Global Catholic Network; FOX Sports Networks; Freeform; Hallmark Channel; HGTV; History; Lifetime; MTV; Nickelodeon; Spike TV; TBS; The Weather Channel; TLC; TNT; TV Land; USA Network; WGN America.
 Fee: $20.00 installation; $48.50 monthly; $2.00 converter.
Pay Service 1
 Pay Units: N.A.
 Programming (via satellite): The Movie Channel.
 Fee: $10.00 monthly.
Internet Service
 Operational: No.
Telephone Service
 None
Miles of Plant: 6.0 (coaxial); None (fiber optic).
General Manager & Treasurer: Bruce Hanson.
Ownership: Hanson Communications Inc. (MSO).

NORTHROP—Midco, PO Box 5010, Sioux Falls, SD 57117. Phone: 800-888-1300. Web Site: http://www.midcocomm.com. ICA: MN0401.
 TV Market Ranking: Outside TV Markets (NORTHROP).
 Channel capacity: N.A. Channels available but not in use: N.A.
Basic Service
 Subscribers: 23.
 Programming (received off-air): KAAL (ABC, This TV) Austin; KARE (NBC, WeatherNation) Minneapolis; KEYC-TV (CBS, FOX) Mankato; KMSP-TV (Bounce TV, Buzzr, FOX) Minneapolis; KSTC-TV (Antenna TV, This TV) Minneapolis; KSTP-TV (ABC, MeTV) St. Paul; KTCA-TV (PBS) St. Paul; WCCO-TV (CBS, Decades) Minneapolis; WFTC (MNT, Movies!) Minneapolis; WUCW (CW, The Country Network) Minneapolis.
 Programming (via satellite): A&E; CMT; CNN; Comedy Central; Discovery Channel; ESPN; ESPN2; FOX Sports North; Freeform; Hallmark Channel; HGTV; History; Lifetime; Nickelodeon; Outdoor Channel; Spike TV; TBS; The Weather Channel; TLC; TNT; Turner Classic Movies; TV Land; USA Network; WGN America.
 Fee: $45.95 monthly.
Pay Service 1
 Pay Units: N.A.
 Programming (via satellite): HBO.
 Fee: $11.95 monthly.
Internet Service
 Operational: No.
Homes passed & miles of plant included in Cambridge.
General Manager: Steve Johnson. Programming Director: Wynne Haakenstad. Customer Service Director: Jackie Torborg.
Ownership: Midcontinent Communications (MSO).

NORWOOD—Mediacom. Now served by MOUND, MN [MN0010]. ICA: MN0083.

OAKPORT—Formerly served by Loretel Cablevision. Now served by Cable One, FARGO, ND [ND0001]. ICA: MN0178.

Access the most current data instantly
www.warren-news.com/factbook.htm

OKLEE—Garden Valley Telephone Co. Now served by McINTOSH, MN [MN0105]. ICA: MN0344.

OLIVIA—Mediacom. Now served by FRANKLIN, MN [MN0057]. ICA: MN0062.

ONAMIA—SCI Broadband. Now served by ISLE, MN [MN0313]. ICA: MN0211.

ORTONVILLE—Midcontinent Communications. Now served by WATERTOWN, SD [SD0004]. ICA: MN0073.

OSAKIS—Charter Communications. Now served by ALEXANDRIA, MN [MN0031]. ICA: MN0155.

OSLO—Midcontinent Communications. Now served by GRAND FORKS, ND [ND0003]. ICA: MN0252.

OSTRANDER—Formerly served by Arvig. No longer on operation. ICA: MN0259.

OWATONNA—Charter Communications, 12405 Powerscourt Dr, St. Louis, MO 63131. Phones: 636-207-5100 (Corporate office); 507-455-2456; 507-289-8372 (Rochester administrative office). Fax: 507-437-7119. Web Site: http://www.charter.com. Also serves Faribault. ICA: MN0023.
 TV Market Ranking: Below 100 (Faribault, OWATONNA). Franchise award date: June 7, 1983. Franchise expiration date: N.A. Began: December 22, 1983.
 Channel capacity: N.A. Channels available but not in use: N.A.
Digital Basic Service
 Subscribers: 8,388.
 Programming (via satellite): AXS TV; BBC America; Bloomberg Television; Boomerang; CBS Sports Network; CNN en Espanol; CNN International; Discovery Digital Networks; DIY Network; ESPN; ESPN Classic; ESPNews; FOX College Sports Central; FOX College Sports Pacific; Fox Sports 2; Fuse; FXM; FYI; History International; IFC; LMN; MC; NFL Network; Nick 2; Nick Jr.; Nicktoons; Outdoor Channel; Sundance TV; TeenNick; Turner Classic Movies; TV Guide Interactive Inc.
 Fee: $14.99 monthly.
Digital Expanded Basic Service
 Subscribers: N.A.
 Programming (via satellite): A&E; AMC; Animal Planet; BET; Bravo; Cartoon Network; CMT; CNBC; CNN; Comedy Central; Discovery Channel; Disney Channel; Disney XD; E! HD; ESPN; ESPN2; EVINE Live; EWTN Global Catholic Network; Food Network; Fox News Channel; Fox Sports 1; FOX Sports North; Freeform; FX; Golf Channel; GSN; Hallmark Channel; HGTV; History; HLN; INSP; Lifetime; MSNBC; MTV; MTV2; National Geographic Channel; NBCSN; Nickelodeon; Oxygen; Spike TV; Syfy; TBS; The Weather Channel; TLC; TNT; Travel Channel; truTV; TV Land; Univision Studios; USA Network; VH1; WE tv.
 Fee: $47.99 monthly.

2017 Edition   D-413

Minnesota—Cable Systems

Digital Pay Service 1
  Pay Units: N.A.
  Programming (via satellite): Cinemax (multiplexed); Flix; HBO (multiplexed); HBO HD; Showtime (multiplexed); Showtime HD; Starz; Starz Encore; The Movie Channel (multiplexed).
Video-On-Demand: Yes
Pay-Per-View
  iN DEMAND (delivered digitally); NHL Center Ice (delivered digitally); MLB Extra Innings (delivered digitally); Playboy TV (delivered digitally); Spice Live (delivered digitally); Spice Platinum (delivered digitally); Hot Net Plus (delivered digitally); Spice Hot (delivered digitally).
Internet Service
  Operational: Yes.
  Subscribers: 8,061.
  Broadband Service: Charter Internet.
  Fee: $29.99 monthly.
Telephone Service
  Digital: Operational
  Subscribers: 4,566.
  Fee: $29.99 monthly
Miles of Plant: 448.0 (coaxial); 204.0 (fiber optic). Homes passed: 24,491.
Vice President & General Manager: John Crowley. Marketing Director: Bill Haarstad. Technical Operations Director: Darin Helgeson. Accounting Director: David Sovanski. Operations Director: Craig Stensaas. Chief Technician: Ray Madrigal. Office Manager: Sherry Brown.
Ownership: Charter Communications Inc. (MSO).

OWATONNA—Jaguar Communications, 213 South Oak St, Owatonna, MN 55060. Phones: 800-250-1517; 507-214-1000. E-mail: support@jagcom.net. Web Site: http://www.jaguarcommunications.com. Also serves Albert Lea, Austin, Blooming Prairie, Claremont, Clarks Grove, Dexter, Ellendale, Garden City, Hayfield, Hayward, Kasota, Lansing, Madison Lake, Mapleview, New Richland, Rose Creek, Vernon Center, Waseca & Washington Twp. ICA: MN5121.
TV Market Ranking: Below 100 (Dexter, Kasota, Lansing, Madison Lake, Mapleview, Rose Creek, Vernon Center, Washington Twp.).
Channel capacity: N.A. Channels available but not in use: N.A.
Internet Service
  Operational: Yes.
Telephone Service
  Digital: Operational
Ownership: Jaguar Communications.

PARK RAPIDS—Charter Communications. Now served by BRAINERD, MN [MN0022]. ICA: MN0345.

PARKERS PRAIRIE—Arvig, 160 2nd Ave. SW, Perham, MN 56573. Phones: 888-992-7844; 218-346-5500; 218-346-4227 (Parkers Prairie office). Fax: 218-338-3297. E-mail: answers@arvig.com. Web Site: http://arvig.com. Also serves Carlos, Miltona, Parkers Prairie Twp. & Urbank. ICA: MN0346.
TV Market Ranking: Below 100 (Miltona, Parkers Prairie Twp., Urbank, Carlos, PARKERS PRAIRIE). Franchise award date: December 1, 1983. Franchise expiration date: N.A. Began: December 1, 1983.
Channel capacity: N.A. Channels available but not in use: N.A.
Basic Service
  Subscribers: 210.
  Programming (received off-air): KARE (NBC, WeatherNation) Minneapolis; KMSP-TV (Bounce TV, Buzzr, FOX) Minneapolis; KVRR (Antenna TV, FOX) Fargo; KWCM-TV (PBS) Appleton; WCCO-TV (CBS, Decades) Minneapolis; WFTC (MNT, Movies!) Minneapolis.
  Programming (via microwave): KSAX (ABC) Alexandria.
  Programming (via satellite): A&E; AMC; CMT; CNN; Discovery Channel; Disney Channel; ESPN; ESPN2; Food Network; Fox News Channel; FOX Sports North; Freeform; FXM; Hallmark Channel; HGTV; History; Lifetime; MTV; Nickelodeon; Spike TV; TBS; The Weather Channel; TNT; TV Land; USA Network; VH1; WGN America.
  Fee: $40.00 installation; $57.95 monthly.
Pay Service 1
  Pay Units: N.A.
  Programming (via satellite): HBO.
  Fee: $17.95 monthly.
Internet Service
  Operational: Yes.
  Fee: $42.95-$125.95 monthly.
Telephone Service
  Analog: Operational
Miles of Plant: 25.0 (coaxial); None (fiber optic). Homes passed: 1,000.
Video Director: David Pratt.
Ownership: Tekstar Communications Inc. (MSO).

PAYNESVILLE—Mediacom, 1504 2nd St SE, PO Box 110, Waseca, MN 56093. Phones: 845-695-2762; 507-835-2356. Fax: 507-835-4567. Web Site: http://www.mediacomcable.com. Also serves Atwater, Clara City, Cosmos, Granite Falls, Grove City & Maynard. ICA: MN0125.
TV Market Ranking: Below 100 (Cosmos, Granite Falls, Maynard, Clara City, PAYNESVILLE); Outside TV Markets (Atwater, Grove City). Franchise award date: November 17, 1982. Franchise expiration date: N.A. Began: March 10, 1983.
Channel capacity: N.A. Channels available but not in use: N.A.
Basic Service
  Subscribers: 1,755.
  Programming (received off-air): KCCO-TV (CBS) Alexandria; KPXM-TV (ION) St. Cloud; KSAX (ABC) Alexandria; KTCA-TV (PBS) St. Paul; KTCI-TV (PBS) St. Paul; KWCM-TV (PBS) Appleton; allband FM.
  Programming (via satellite): C-SPAN; Pop; QVC; The Weather Channel; WGN America.
  Programming (via translator): KARE (NBC, WeatherNation) Minneapolis; KMSP-TV (Bounce TV, Buzzr, FOX) Minneapolis; KSTC-TV (Antenna TV, This TV) Minneapolis; WCCO-TV (CBS, Decades) Minneapolis; WFTC (MNT, Movies!) Minneapolis; WUCW (CW, The Country Network) Minneapolis.
  Fee: $52.39 installation; $42.00 monthly; $2.00 converter.
Expanded Basic Service 1
  Subscribers: N.A.
  Programming (via satellite): A&E; AMC; Animal Planet; Bravo; Cartoon Network; CMT; CNBC; CNN; Comedy Central; C-SPAN 2; Discovery Channel; Discovery Life Channel; Disney Channel; E! HD; ESPN; ESPN2; EWTN Global Catholic Network; Fox News Channel; Fox Sports 1; FOX Sports North; Freeform; FX; FXM; Hallmark Channel; HGTV; History; HLN; INSP; ION Television; Lifetime; MSNBC; MTV; Nickelodeon; RFD-TV; Spike TV; Syfy; TBS; TLC; TNT; Travel Channel; Trinity Broadcasting Network (TBN); truTV; Turner Classic Movies; TV Land; Univision Studios; USA Network; VH1; WE tv.
  Fee: $17.09 monthly.
Digital Basic Service
  Subscribers: N.A.
  Programming (via satellite): 52MX; AXS TV; BBC America; Bloomberg Television; Cinelatino; Cloo; CNN en Espanol; Destination America; Discovery Kids Channel; Discovery Life Channel; ESPN Deportes; ESPN HD; ESPN2 HD; ESPNews; Fox Deportes; Fox Sports 2; Fuse; FYI; Golf Channel; GSN; HD Theater; History en Espanol; History International; IFC; Investigation Discovery; LMN; MC; MTV Classic; MTV Hits; MTV2; Nat Geo WILD; National Geographic Channel; Nick Jr.; Nicktoons; Outdoor Channel; OWN: Oprah Winfrey Network; Reelz; Science Channel; TeenNick; Tr3s; Turner Classic Movies; TVG Network; ViendoMovies.
Pay Service 1
  Pay Units: N.A.
  Programming (via satellite): Showtime.
Digital Pay Service 1
  Pay Units: N.A.
  Programming (via satellite): Cinemax (multiplexed); Flix; HBO (multiplexed); HBO HD; Showtime (multiplexed); Showtime HD; Starz (multiplexed); Starz Encore (multiplexed); Starz HD; Sundance TV; The Movie Channel (multiplexed); The Movie Channel HD.
  Fee: $6.95 monthly (Starz/Starz HDTV/Encore), $7.00 monthly (Cinemax), $11.95 monthly (HBO/HBO HD), $12.95 monthly (Showtime/Showtime HD/TMC/TMC HD/Sundance/Flix).
Video-On-Demand: No
Pay-Per-View
  iN DEMAND (delivered digitally); Fresh (delivered digitally); Pleasure (delivered digitally); Playboy TV (delivered digitally); SexSee (delivered digitally).
Internet Service
  Operational: Yes.
  Broadband Service: Mediacom High Speed Internet.
  Fee: $40.00 monthly.
Telephone Service
  Analog: Not Operational
  Digital: Operational
Miles of Plant: 96.0 (coaxial); None (fiber optic). Homes passed: 4,463.
Vice President: Bill Jensen. Vice President, Financial Reporting: Kenneth J. Kohrs. Marketing & Sales Director: Lori Huberty. Engineering Manager: Kraig Kaiser.
Ownership: Mediacom LLC (MSO).

PAYNESVILLE—Mediacom. Now served by PAYNESVILLE, MN [MN0125]. ICA: MN0079.

PELICAN LAKE—Formerly served by Loretel Cablevision. Now served by Arvig, PELICAN RAPIDS, MN [MN0265]. ICA: MN0347.

PELICAN RAPIDS—Arvig, 160 2nd Ave. SW, Perham, MN 56573. Phones: 888-992-7844; 218-863-6451 (Pelican Rapids office); 218-346-4227. Fax: 218-338-3297. E-mail: answers@arvig.com. Web Site: http://arvig.com. Also serves Ada, Borup, Cormorant Twp., Dunn Twp., Glyndon, Glyndon Twp., Pelican Lake, Pelican Twp. & Scambler Twp. ICA: MN0265.
TV Market Ranking: 98 (Ada, Borup, Glyndon, Glyndon Twp.); Outside TV Markets (Cormorant Twp., Dunn Twp., Pelican Lake, Pelican Twp., Scambler Twp., PELICAN RAPIDS). Franchise award date: March 1, 1991. Franchise expiration date: N.A. Began: April 1, 1982.
Channel capacity: N.A. Channels available but not in use: N.A.
Basic Service
  Subscribers: 2,919.
  Programming (received off-air): KCPM (MNT) Grand Forks; KFME (PBS) Fargo; KRDK-TV (CBS, Decades, Movies!) Valley City; KVLY-TV (MeTV, NBC, This TV) Fargo; KVRR (Antenna TV, FOX) Fargo; WDAY-TV (ABC, CW) Fargo; WDAZ-TV (ABC, CW) Devils Lake.
  Programming (via satellite): C-SPAN; WGN America.
  Fee: $40.00 installation; $35.95 monthly; $2.50 converter.
Expanded Basic Service 1
  Subscribers: N.A.
  Programming (via satellite): A&E; Cartoon Network; CMT; CNBC; CNN; Comedy Central; Discovery Channel; Disney Channel; E! HD; ESPN; Food Network; Freeform; FX; Lifetime; MTV; National Geographic Channel; Nickelodeon; QVC; Spike TV; Syfy; TBS; The Weather Channel; TLC; TNT; TV Land; USA Network; VH1.
  Fee: $60.95 monthly.
Expanded Basic Service 2
  Subscribers: N.A.
  Programming (via satellite): FOX Sports Midwest; Turner Classic Movies.
  Fee: $76.95 monthly.
Pay Service 1
  Pay Units: 187.
  Programming (via satellite): HBO.
  Fee: $15.00 installation; $17.95 monthly.
Pay Service 2
  Pay Units: 155.
  Programming (via satellite): Cinemax.
  Fee: $15.00 installation; $12.95 monthly.
Pay Service 3
  Pay Units: 224.
  Programming (via satellite): Starz Encore.
  Fee: $15.00 installation; $6.95 monthly.
Pay Service 4
  Pay Units: N.A.
  Fee: $13.95 monthly (Showtime/TMC or Starz/Encore), $23.95 monthly (Cinemax/HBO).
Video-On-Demand: No
Pay-Per-View
  iN DEMAND (delivered digitally); Playboy TV (delivered digitally).
Internet Service
  Operational: Yes.
  Fee: $42.95-$69.95 monthly.
Telephone Service
  Analog: Operational
  Fee: $14.00 monthly
Miles of Plant: 14.0 (coaxial); 29.0 (fiber optic).
Chief Operating Officer & Vice President: David Arvig.
Ownership: Tekstar Communications Inc. (MSO).

PELICAN RAPIDS—Formerly served by Loretel Cablevision. Now served by Arvig, PELICAN RAPIDS, MN [MN0265]. ICA: MN0120.

PENGILLY—SCI Broadband, 111 Tobies Mill Pl, PO Box 810, Hinckley, MN 55037-0810. Phones: 800-222-9809; 320-384-7442. Fax: 320-279-8085. E-mail: sales@scibroadband.com. Web Site: http://www.scibroadband.com. ICA: MN0390.
TV Market Ranking: Below 100 (PENGILLY). Franchise award date: September 5, 1990. Franchise expiration date: N.A. Began: September 5, 1991.
Channel capacity: N.A. Channels available but not in use: N.A.

Cable Systems—Minnesota

Basic Service
Subscribers: N.A.
Programming (received off-air): KBJR-TV (CBS, MNT, NBC) Superior; KCCW-TV (CBS) Walker; KDLH (CBS, CW) Duluth; KQDS-TV (Antenna TV, FOX) Duluth; WDIO-DT (ABC, MeTV) Duluth; WDSE (PBS) Duluth.
Programming (via satellite): A&E; Animal Planet; CNBC; CNN; Comedy Central; C-SPAN; Discovery Channel; Disney Channel; E! HD; ESPN; ESPN2; EWTN Global Catholic Network; Fox News Channel; FOX Sports Networks; Freeform; Great American Country; HGTV; History; HLN; Lifetime; MTV; Nickelodeon; QVC; Spike TV; Syfy; TBS; The Weather Channel; TLC; TNT; Turner Classic Movies; TV Land; USA Network; VH1; WGN America; WPIX (Antenna TV, CW, This TV) New York.
Fee: $39.95 installation; $39.95 monthly.

Digital Basic Service
Subscribers: N.A.
Programming (via satellite): BBC America; Bloomberg Television; Cloo; Discovery Life Channel; DMX Music; ESPN Classic; ESPNews; Fox Sports 1; Fuse; FXM; FYI; Golf Channel; History International; INSP; National Geographic Channel; NBCSN; Outdoor Channel; Trinity Broadcasting Network (TBN); WE tv.

Digital Pay Service 1
Pay Units: N.A.
Programming (via satellite): Cinemax (multiplexed); Flix; HBO (multiplexed); Showtime (multiplexed); Starz (multiplexed); Starz Encore (multiplexed); Sundance TV; The Movie Channel (multiplexed).
Video-On-Demand: No
Pay-Per-View
ESPN Now (delivered digitally); Sports PPV (delivered digitally).
Internet Service
Operational: Yes.
Broadband Service: SCI Broadband.
Fee: $24.95 monthly.
Telephone Service
Digital: Operational
Miles of Plant: 21.0 (coaxial); None (fiber optic). Homes passed: 572.
General Manager: Mike Danielson. President: Ron Savage. Chief Technician: Pat McCabe. Customer Service Manager: Donna Erickson.
Ownership: Savage Communications Inc. (MSO).

PEQUOT LAKES—Charter Communications. Now served by BRAINERD, MN [MN0022]. ICA: MN0025.

PERHAM—Arvig, 160 2nd Ave. SW, Perham, MN 56573. Phones: 888-992-7844; 218-346-4227. Fax: 218-338-3297. E-mail: answers@arvig.com. Web Site: http://arvig.com. Also serves Akeley, Akeley Twp., Amor Twp., Atlanta Twp., Audubon, Audubon Twp., Badoura Twp., Battle Lake, Bertha Twp., Bluffton, Bluffton Twp., Boy Lake Twp., Burlington Twp., Butler Twp., Callaway, Candor Twp., Clay Twp., Clitherall, Clitherall Twp., Corliss Twp., Dead Lake Twp., Deer Creek, Dent, Detroit Lakes, Detroit Twp., Dora Twp., Edna Twp., Erie Twp., Everts Twp., Farden Twp., Frazee, Gary, Girard Twp., Goose Prairie Twp., Gorman Twp., Hawley, Henning, Henning Twp., Henrietta Twp., Hewitt, Hiram Twp., Hobart Twp., Holmesville Twp., Homestead Twp., Inguadona, Kego Twp., La Garde Twp., Lake Eunice Twp., Lake Grove Twp., Lake Park, Lake Park Twp., Lakeview Twp., Leaf Lake Twp., Leech Lake Twp., Lida Twp., Little Elbow Twp., Longville, Mahnomen, Maine Twp., Mantrap Twp., Nevis, Nevis Twp., New York Mills, Newton Twp., Nidaros Twp., Oak Valley Twp., Ogema, Osage Twp., Osakis, Ottertail, Ottertail Twp., Otto Twp., Park Rapids, Perham Twp., Pike Bay Twp., Pine Lake Twp., Pine Point Twp., Popple Grove Twp., Richville, Richwood Twp., Round Lake Twp., Rush Lake Twp., Shingobee, Star Lake Twp., Steamboat River Twp., Stowe Prairie Twp., Sugar Bush Twp., Sverdrup Twp., Ten Lake Twp., Thorpe Twp., Toad Lake Twp., Turtle Lake Twp., Twin Valley, Ulen, Ulen Twp., Vergas, Wabedo Twp., Walker, Waubun, Whipholt, White Oak Twp., Wilkinson Twp. & Wolf Lake Twp. ICA: MN0050. **Note:** This system is an overbuild.
TV Market Ranking: 98 (Hawley, Lake Park, Ulen); Below 100 (Akeley, Battle Lake, Clitherall, Clitherall Twp., Henning, Leech Lake Twp., Longville, Mantrap Twp., Nevis, Osage Twp., Shingobee, Walker); Outside TV Markets (Amor Twp., Audubon, Bertha Twp., Bluffton, Callaway, Dead Lake Twp., Deer Creek, Dent, Detroit Lakes, Detroit Twp., Everts Twp., Frazee, Gary, Holmesville Twp., Lake Eunice Twp., Lakeview Twp., Lida Twp., Mahnomen, Maine Twp., New York Mills, Nidaros Twp., Ottertail, PERHAM, Perham Twp., Richville, Richwood Twp., Sverdrup Twp., Waubun, Hawley, Ulen). Franchise award date: September 1, 1973. Franchise expiration date: N.A. Began: March 9, 1996.
Channel capacity: N.A. Channels available but not in use: N.A.

Digital Basic Service
Subscribers: 1,228.
Programming (received off-air): K49FA-D Fergus Falls; KCCO-TV (CBS) Alexandria; KCPM (MNT) Grand Forks; KFME (PBS) Fargo; KRDK-TV (CBS, Decades, Movies!) Valley City; KVLY-TV (MeTV, NBC, This TV) Fargo; KVRR (Antenna TV, FOX) Fargo; WDAY-TV (ABC, CW) Fargo.
Programming (via satellite): C-SPAN; WGN America.
Fee: $50.00 installation; $31.95 monthly.

Digital Expanded Basic Service
Subscribers: N.A.
Programming (via satellite): A&E; CMT; CNBC; CNN; Discovery Channel; ESPN; ESPN2; Fox News Channel; FOX Sports Networks; Freeform; FX; Hallmark Channel; History; Lifetime; MTV; Nickelodeon; QVC; Spike TV; TBS; The Weather Channel; TLC; TNT; USA Network; VH1.
Fee: $60.95 monthly.

Digital Expanded Basic Service 2
Subscribers: N.A.
Programming (via satellite): BBC America; Cooking Channel; Discovery Digital Networks; DIY Network; DMX Music; ESPN Classic; ESPNews; Fox Sports 1; FXM; Golf Channel; GSN; HGTV; IFC; LMN; National Geographic Channel; NBCSN; Nick Jr.; Outdoor Channel; Syfy; Turner Classic Movies; WE tv.

Digital Pay Service 1
Pay Units: 947.
Programming (via satellite): Cinemax (multiplexed); HBO (multiplexed).
Fee: $15.00 installation; $12.95 monthly (Cinemax), $17.95 monthly (HBO).

Digital Pay Service 2
Pay Units: 489.
Programming (via satellite): Showtime (multiplexed); Starz (multiplexed); Starz Encore (multiplexed); The Movie Channel (multiplexed).
Fee: $15.00 installation; $6.95 monthly (Encore), $13.95 monthly (Showtime/TMC or Starz/Encore).
Video-On-Demand: Yes
Pay-Per-View
iN DEMAND (delivered digitally); Playboy TV (delivered digitally).
Internet Service
Operational: Yes.
Subscribers: 1,800.
Fee: $42.95-$125.95 monthly.
Telephone Service
Digital: Operational
Fee: $19.20 monthly
Miles of Plant: 466.0 (coaxial); 64.0 (fiber optic). Homes passed: 10,910.
Chief Operating Officer & Vice President: David Arvig.
Ownership: Tekstar Communications Inc. (MSO).

PETERSON—Mediacom. Now served by CALEDONIA, MN [MN0086]. ICA: MN0251.

PILLAGER—SCI Broadband, 111 Tobies Mill Pl, PO Box 810, Hinckley, MN 55037-0810. Phones: 800-222-9809; 320-384-7442. Fax: 320-279-8085. E-mail: sales@scibroadband.com. Web Site: http://www.scibroadband.com. Also serves East Gull Lake & Motley. ICA: MN0230.
TV Market Ranking: Outside TV Markets (East Gull Lake, Motley, PILLAGER). Franchise award date: April 17, 1985. Franchise expiration date: N.A. Began: December 2, 1985.
Channel capacity: N.A. Channels available but not in use: N.A.

Basic Service
Subscribers: 724.
Programming (received off-air): KARE (NBC, WeatherNation) Minneapolis; KAWB (PBS) Brainerd; KCCO-TV (CBS) Alexandria; KMSP-TV (Bounce TV, Buzzr, FOX) Minneapolis; KSAX (ABC) Alexandria; KSTC-TV (Antenna TV, This TV) Minneapolis; WFTC (MNT, Movies!) Minneapolis.
Programming (via satellite): A&E; Animal Planet; Cartoon Network; CNBC; CNN; Comedy Central; C-SPAN; Discovery Channel; Disney Channel; E! HD; ESPN; ESPN2; Fox News Channel; FOX Sports Networks; Freeform; Golf Channel; Great American Country; HGTV; History; HLN; Lifetime; MTV; National Geographic Channel; Nickelodeon; QVC; Spike TV; Syfy; TBS; The Weather Channel; TLC; TNT; Turner Classic Movies; TV Land; USA Network; VH1; WGN America; WPIX (Antenna TV, CW, This TV) New York.
Fee: $50.00 installation; $15.95 monthly.

Digital Basic Service
Subscribers: N.A.
Programming (via satellite): BBC America; Bloomberg Television; Cloo; Discovery Life Channel; DMX Music; ESPN Classic; ESPNews; Fox Sports 1; Fuse; FXM; FYI; History International; INSP; National Geographic Channel; NBCSN; Outdoor Channel; Trinity Broadcasting Network (TBN); WE tv.

Pay Service 1
Pay Units: N.A.
Programming (via satellite): HBO.
Fee: $20.00 installation; $12.95 monthly.

Digital Pay Service 1
Pay Units: N.A.
Programming (via satellite): Cinemax; HBO; Showtime; Starz; Starz Encore; The Movie Channel.
Video-On-Demand: No
Pay-Per-View
ESPN Now (delivered digitally); Sports PPV (delivered digitally).

Internet Service
Operational: Yes.
Broadband Service: SCI Broadband.
Fee: $39.95 monthly.
Telephone Service
Digital: Operational
Miles of Plant: 66.0 (coaxial); None (fiber optic). Homes passed: 1,921.
General Manager: Mike Danielson. President: Ron Savage. Chief Technician: Pat McCabe. Customer Service Manager: Donna Erickson.
Ownership: Savage Communications Inc. (MSO).

PINE ISLAND—BEVCOMM (formerly Pine Island Telephone Co.) This cable system has converted to IPTV. See PINE ISLAND, MN [MN5365]. ICA: MN0089.

PINE ISLAND—BEVCOMM. Formerly [MN0089]. This cable system has converted to IPTV, 108 SW Second St, Pine Island, MN 55963. Phones: 800-473-1442; 507-356-8302. E-mail: info@bevcomm.net. Web Site: http://www.bevcomm.net. Also serves Oronoco, MN; Bay City & Hager City, WI. ICA: MN5365.
TV Market Ranking: Below 100 (Oronoco, PINE ISLAND).
Channel capacity: N.A. Channels available but not in use: N.A.

Digital Basic
Subscribers: 1,451.
Fee: $60.00 installation; $71.95 monthly. Includes 140+ channels.

HD
Subscribers: N.A.
Fee: $9.95 monthly.

EASE
Subscribers: N.A.
Fee: $7.95 monthly. Includes 33 sports & entertainment channels.

Cinemax
Subscribers: N.A.
Fee: $12.95 monthly. Includes 4 channels.

HBO
Subscribers: N.A.
Fee: $15.95 monthly. Includes 11 channels.

HBO/Starz/Encore
Subscribers: N.A.
Fee: $23.95 monthly. Includes 26 channels.

NFL RedZone
Subscribers: N.A.
Fee: $44.95 per season.

Playboy
Subscribers: N.A.
Fee: $14.95 monthly. Includes 1 channel.

Showtime/TMC/Flix
Subscribers: N.A.
Fee: $14.95 monthly. Includes 13 channels.

Starz/Encore
Subscribers: N.A.
Fee: $14.95 monthly. Includes 15 channels.

Video-On-Demand: Yes
Internet Service
Operational: Yes.
Fee: $9.95-$149.95 monthly.
Telephone Service
Digital: Operational
Fee: $28.83-$29.66 monthly
President & Chief Executive Officer: Bill Eckles.
Ownership: BEVCOMM.

PIPESTONE—Mediacom. Now served by IVANHOE, MN [MN0189]. ICA: MN0348.

PLAINVIEW—Midcontinent Communications. Now served by CAMBRIDGE, MN [MN0016]. ICA: MN0080.

Minnesota—Cable Systems

PLATO—Formerly served by North American Communications Corp. This cable system has converted to IPTV. Now served by Jaguar Communications, NEW MARKET, MN [MN5374]. ICA: MN0247.

PRIOR LAKE—Integra Telecom, 4960 Colorado St SE, Prior Lake, MN 55372. Phone: 952-226-7000. Web Site: http://www.integratelecom.com. Also serves Cedar Lake Twp., Credit River, Elko New Market, New Market Twp., Savage & Spring Lake. ICA: MN0406.
  TV Market Ranking: 13 (Cedar Lake Twp., Credit River, Elko New Market, New Market Twp., PRIOR LAKE, Savage, Spring Lake).
  Channel capacity: N.A. Channels available but not in use: N.A.
Basic Service
  Subscribers: 2,377.
  Fee: $99.99 installation; $20.00 monthly.
  Vice President & General Manager: Mary Korthour.
  Ownership: Integra Telecom.

PRIOR LAKE—Mediacom, 1504 2nd St SE, PO Box 110, Waseca, MN 56093. Phones: 845-695-2762; 507-835-2356. Fax: 507-835-4567. Web Site: http://www.mediacomcable.com. Also serves Canterbury Estates, Credit River Twp, Elko, New Market Twp., Savage, Spring Lake Twp., Veseli & Webster Twp. ICA: MN0039.
  TV Market Ranking: 13 (Canterbury Estates, Credit River Twp, Elko, New Market Twp., PRIOR LAKE, Savage, Spring Lake Twp., Veseli, Webster Twp.). Franchise award date: September 9, 1983. Franchise expiration date: N.A. Began: September 1, 1984.
  Channel capacity: 70 (operating 2-way). Channels available but not in use: N.A.
Basic Service
  Subscribers: 6,889.
  Programming (received off-air): KARE (NBC, WeatherNation) Minneapolis; KMSP-TV (Bounce TV, Buzzr, FOX) Minneapolis; KPXM-TV (ION) St. Cloud; KSTC-TV (Antenna TV, This TV) Minneapolis; KSTP-TV (ABC, MeTV) St. Paul; KTCA-TV (PBS) St. Paul; KTCI-TV (PBS) St. Paul; WCCO-TV (CBS, Decades) Minneapolis; WFTC (MNT, Movies!) Minneapolis; WUCW (CW, The Country Network) Minneapolis.
  Programming (via satellite): C-SPAN; The Weather Channel; WGN America.
  Fee: $30.00 installation; $43.00 monthly.
Expanded Basic Service 1
  Subscribers: N.A.
  Programming (via satellite): A&E; AMC; Animal Planet; BET; Bravo; Cartoon Network; CMT; CNBC; CNN; Comedy Central; C-SPAN 2; Discovery Channel; Disney Channel; E! HD; ESPN; ESPN2; EWTN Global Catholic Network; Food Network; Fox News Channel; Fox Sports 1; FOX Sports North; Freeform; FX; FXM; Hallmark Channel; HGTV; History; HLN; INSP; Lifetime; MSNBC; MTV; Nickelodeon; Pop; QVC; Spike TV; Syfy; TBS; TLC; TNT; Travel Channel; Trinity Broadcasting Network (TBN); truTV; Turner Classic Movies; TV Land; Univision Studios; USA Network; VH1; WE tv.
Digital Basic Service
  Subscribers: N.A.
  Programming (via satellite): BBC America; Bloomberg Television; Discovery Digital Networks; DMX Music; Fuse; FYI; Golf Channel; GSN; History International; HITS (Headend In The Sky); IFC; LMN; National Geographic Channel; Outdoor Channel.
Digital Pay Service 1
  Pay Units: N.A.
  Programming (via satellite): Cinemax (multiplexed); Flix; HBO (multiplexed); Showtime (multiplexed); Starz (multiplexed); Starz Encore (multiplexed); Sundance TV; The Movie Channel (multiplexed).
  Fee: $15.00 installation; $8.95 monthly (Showtime), $9.95 monthly (Cinemax or TMC), $11.95 monthly (HBO).
Video-On-Demand: Yes
Pay-Per-View
  Vubiquity Inc. (delivered digitally); ESPN Now (delivered digitally); Sports PPV (delivered digitally); Urban Xtra (delivered digitally); Fresh (delivered digitally); Shorteez (delivered digitally); Playboy TV (delivered digitally); Pleasure (delivered digitally).
Internet Service
  Operational: Yes.
  Subscribers: 7,469.
  Broadband Service: Mediacom High Speed Internet.
  Fee: $99.00 installation; $40.00 monthly.
Telephone Service
  Digital: Operational
  Subscribers: 3,808.
  Miles of Plant: 580.0 (coaxial); 182.0 (fiber optic). Homes passed: 22,296.
  Vice President: Bill Jensen. Vice President, Financial Reporting: Kenneth J. Kohrs. Engineering Manager: Kraig Kaiser. Marketing & Sales Director: Lori Huberty.
  Ownership: Mediacom LLC (MSO).

PROCTOR—Mediacom. Now served by CLOQUET, MN [MN0042]. ICA: MN0064.

RACINE—Arvig. Now served by GRAND MEADOW, MN [MN0168]. ICA: MN0258.

RANDALL—Consolidated Telecommunications Co. Formerly [MN0202]. This cable system has converted to IPTV, 1102 Madison St, PO Box 972, Brainerd, MN 56401. Phones: 800-753-9104; 218-454-1234. Fax: 218-829-6071. Web Site: http://www.connectctc.com. Also serves Baxter, Brainerd, Crosby, Freedhem, Ironton, Lincoln, Mission Twp., Motley, Nisswa, Nokay Lake Twp., Outing, Pillager & Sullivan Lake. ICA: MN5026.
  TV Market Ranking: Outside TV Markets (RANDALL, Brainerd).
  Channel capacity: N.A. Channels available but not in use: N.A.
Basic
  Subscribers: 4,287.
  Fee: $35.99 monthly.
Entertainment
  Subscribers: N.A.
  Fee: $69.59 monthly.
HD
  Subscribers: N.A.
  Fee: $9.95 monthly.
Big Value Tier
  Subscribers: N.A.
  Fee: $10.95 monthly.
Cinemax
  Subscribers: N.A.
  Fee: $13.95 monthly.
HBO
  Subscribers: N.A.
  Fee: $16.95 monthly.
Cinemax/HBO
  Subscribers: N.A.
  Fee: $22.95 monthly.
NFL RedZone
  Subscribers: N.A.
  Fee: $39.95 per season.
Playboy
  Subscribers: N.A.
  Fee: $15.95 monthly.
Showtime
  Subscribers: N.A.
  Fee: $14.95 monthly.
Showtime/TMC/Flix
  Subscribers: N.A.
  Fee: $17.95 monthly.
Starz/Encore
  Subscribers: N.A.
  Fee: $13.95 monthly.
Internet Service
  Operational: Yes.
  Fee: $44.95-$64.95 monthly.
Telephone Service
  Digital: Operational
  Fee: $14.95 monthly
  Chief Executive Officer & General Manager: Kevin Larson. Network Operations Manager: Steve Holmvig.
  Ownership: Consolidated Telecommunications Co. (MSO).

RANDALL—Consolidated Telecommunications Co. This cable system has converted to IPTV. See RANDALL, MN [MN5026]. ICA: MN0202.

RANDOLPH—Formerly served by Cannon Valley Cablevision. Now served by Midcontinent Communications, CANNON FALLS TWP., MN [MN0391]. ICA: MN0350.

RAVENNA—Formerly served by Cannon Valley Cablevision. Now served by Midcontinent Communications, CANNON FALLS TWP, MN [MN0391]. ICA: MN0351.

RAYMOND—Clara City Telephone Co, 227 South Main St, PO Box 800, Clara City, MN 56222. Phone: 320-847-2211. Fax: 320-847-2736. Web Site: http://www.hcinet.net. ICA: MN0352.
  TV Market Ranking: Below 100 (RAYMOND). Franchise award date: September 1, 1988. Franchise expiration date: N.A. Began: May 1, 1989.
  Channel capacity: N.A. Channels available but not in use: N.A.
Basic Service
  Subscribers: 133.
  Programming (received off-air): KARE (NBC, WeatherNation) Minneapolis; KCCO-TV (CBS) Alexandria; KMSP-TV (Bounce TV, Buzzr, FOX) Minneapolis; KSAX (ABC) Alexandria; KSTC-TV (Antenna TV, This TV) Minneapolis; KWCM-TV (PBS) Appleton; WFTC (MNT, Movies!) Minneapolis; WUCW (CW, The Country Network) Minneapolis.
  Programming (via satellite): A&E; AMC; Animal Planet; Cartoon Network; CMT; CNN; Comedy Central; Discovery Channel; Disney Channel; E! HD; ESPN; ESPN2; Food Network; Fox Sports 1; FOX Sports North; Freeform; Golf Channel; Hallmark Channel; Hallmark Movies & Mysteries; HGTV; History; Lifetime; MTV; Nickelodeon; Outdoor Channel; QVC; Spike TV; Syfy; TBS; The Weather Channel; TLC; TNT; Trinity Broadcasting Network (TBN); TV Land; USA Network; VH1; WGN America.
  Fee: $20.00 installation; $40.95 monthly.
Pay Service 1
  Pay Units: 15.
  Programming (via satellite): Cinemax; HBO; Showtime.
  Fee: $9.95 monthly (Cinemax), $10.95 monthly (Showtime), $11.95 monthly (HBO).
Video-On-Demand: No

Internet Service
  Operational: Yes.
Telephone Service
  Analog: Operational
  Miles of Plant: 5.0 (coaxial); None (fiber optic). Homes passed: 300.
  Treasurer & General Manager: Bruce Hanson.
  Ownership: Hanson Communications Inc. (MSO).

READING—Formerly served by American Telecasting of Minnesota Inc. No longer in operation. ICA: MN0353.

RED EYE TWP.—West Central Telephone Assn. Formerly served by MENAHGA, MN [MN0112]. This cable system has converted to IPTV. Now served by MENAHGA, MN [MN5130]. ICA: MN5250.

RED LAKE FALLS—Sjoberg's Cable TV Inc, 315 Main Ave North, Thief River Falls, MN 56701-1905. Phones: 218-681-3044; 800-828-8808. Fax: 218-681-6801. E-mail: office1@mncable.net; sjobergs@mncable.net. Web Site: http://trf.mncable.net. Also serves Red Lake Twp. ICA: MN0141.
  TV Market Ranking: Below 100 (RED LAKE FALLS, Red Lake Twp.). Franchise award date: N.A. Franchise expiration date: N.A. Began: October 1, 1977.
  Channel capacity: N.A. Channels available but not in use: N.A.
Basic Service
  Subscribers: 439.
  Programming (received off-air): KCPM (MNT) Grand Forks; KGFE (PBS) Grand Forks; KRDK-TV (CBS, Decades, Movies!) Valley City; KVLY-TV (MeTV, NBC, This TV) Fargo; various Canadian stations; WDAZ-TV (ABC, CW) Devils Lake; allband FM.
  Programming (via microwave): KBRR (FOX) Thief River Falls.
  Programming (via satellite): CNN; ESPN; TBS.
  Fee: $25.00 installation; $55.92 monthly.
Expanded Basic Service 1
  Subscribers: N.A.
  Programming (via satellite): A&E; Animal Planet; Cartoon Network; CMT; CNBC; Comedy Central; C-SPAN; CW PLUS; Discovery Channel; Discovery Channel HD; Disney Channel; E! HD; ESPN2; Food Network; Fox News Channel; FOX Sports Networks; Freeform; FX; HGTV; History; Lifetime; MSNBC; MTV; Nickelodeon; Spike TV; Syfy; The Weather Channel; TLC; TNT; Turner Classic Movies; TV Land; USA Network; VH1; WGN America.
  Fee: $23.71 monthly.
Digital Basic Service
  Subscribers: N.A.
  Programming (via satellite): BBC America; Bloomberg Television; Bravo; CBS Sports Network; Chiller; Cloo; CMT; Cooking Channel; Daystar TV Network; Destination America; Discovery Kids Channel; Discovery Life Channel; Disney XD; DIY Network; DMX Music; ESPN Classic; ESPNews; ESPNU; EVINE Live; EWTN Global Catholic Network; Fox Business Network; FOX College Sports Central; FOX College Sports Pacific; Fox Sports 1; FXM; FYI; Golf Channel; Great American Country; GSN; Hallmark Channel; History International; HLN; HRTV; IFC; Investigation Discovery; LMN; MTV Classic; MTV Hits; MTV2; Nat Geo WILD; National Geographic Channel; NBCSN; Nick Jr.; Nicktoons; Outdoor Channel; Ovation; OWN: Oprah Winfrey Network; Oxygen; Reelz; RFD-TV;

Cable Systems—Minnesota

Science Channel; Sprout; Sundance TV; TeenNick; Tennis Channel; The Word Network; Trinity Broadcasting Network (TBN); TVG Network; UP; VH1 Soul; WE tv.
Digital Expanded Basic Service
Subscribers: N.A.
Programming (via satellite): A&E HD; AXS TV; CNN HD; ESPN HD; ESPN2 HD; Food Network HD; FSN HD; HGTV HD; History HD; Outdoor Channel 2 HD; PBS HD; Syfy HD; TBS HD; TNT HD; Universal HD; USA Network HD; Versus HD.
Fee: $5.00 monthly; $5.00 converter.
Pay Service 1
Pay Units: N.A.
Programming (via satellite): Cinemax; HBO.
Fee: $9.00 monthly (Cinemax), $11.00 monthly (HBO).
Digital Pay Service 1
Pay Units: N.A.
Programming (via satellite): Cinemax (multiplexed); Cinemax HD; HBO (multiplexed); HBO HD; Showtime (multiplexed); Starz (multiplexed); Starz Encore (multiplexed); The Movie Channel (multiplexed).
Fee: $8.00 monthly (Starz/Encore), $9.00 monthly (Cinemax or Showtime/TMC), $11.00 monthly (HBO).
Video-On-Demand: No
Internet Service
Operational: Yes.
Telephone Service
None
Miles of Plant: 13.0 (coaxial); 19.0 (fiber optic). Homes passed: 555.
President & General Manager: Richard J. Sjoberg. Chief Technician: Jerry Seim.
Ownership: Sjoberg's Cable TV Inc. (MSO).

RED ROCK—Formerly served by North American Communications Corp. No longer in operation. ICA: MN0354.

RED WING—Charter Communications. Now served by ROSEMOUNT, MN [MN0009]. ICA: MN0028.

REMER—Eagle Cablevision Inc, 205 First Ave Northeast, PO Box 39, Remer, MN 56672-0039. Phone: 218-566-2302. Fax: 218-566-2166. ICA: MN0355.
TV Market Ranking: Below 100 (REMER). Franchise award date: N.A. Franchise expiration date: N.A. Began: January 1, 1971.
Channel capacity: 24 (not 2-way capable). Channels available but not in use: N.A.
Basic Service
Subscribers: N.A.
Programming (received off-air): KAWE (PBS) Bemidji; KCCW-TV (CBS) Walker; WIRT-DT (ABC, MeTV) Hibbing; allband FM.
Programming (via satellite): CNN; Discovery Channel; ESPN; Freeform; TBS; TNT; USA Network; WGN America; WNBC (COZI TV, NBC) New York.
Fee: $25.00 installation; $12.00 monthly.
Video-On-Demand: No
Internet Service
Operational: No, DSL & dial-up.
Broadband Service: Offers dial-up and DSL only; no cable modem service.
Telephone Service
None
Miles of Plant: 2.0 (coaxial); None (fiber optic).
President: Conrad Johnson. General Manager & Chief Technician: Dwayne Johnson.
Ownership: Eagle Cablevision Inc.

REVERE—Clara City Telephone Co, 227 South Main St, PO Box 200, Clara City, MN 56222. Phones: 320-847-2211; 507-831-4938. Fax: 320-847-2736. Web Site: http://www.hcinet.net. ICA: MN0356.
TV Market Ranking: Below 100 (REVERE). Franchise award date: N.A. Franchise expiration date: N.A. Began: January 1, 1972.
Channel capacity: N.A. Channels available but not in use: N.A.
Basic Service
Subscribers: 5.
Programming (received off-air): KELO-TV (CBS, MNT) Sioux Falls; KEYC-TV (CBS, FOX) Mankato; KSFY-TV (ABC, CW) Sioux Falls; KSMN (PBS) Worthington; KWCM-TV (PBS) Appleton; 1 FM.
Programming (via satellite): CMT; CNN; Discovery Channel; ESPN; FamilyNet; FOX Sports Networks; Freeform; HGTV; HLN; Lifetime; Nickelodeon; Spike TV; TBS; The Weather Channel; TLC; TNT; Turner Classic Movies; TV Land; USA Network; WGN America.
Programming (via translator): KARE (NBC, WeatherNation) Minneapolis; KMSP-TV (Bounce TV, Buzzr, FOX) Minneapolis; KSTP-TV (ABC, MeTV) St. Paul; WCCO-TV (CBS, Decades) Minneapolis; WFTC (MNT, Movies!) Minneapolis; WUCW (CW, The Country Network) Minneapolis.
Fee: $20.00 installation; $25.95 monthly.
Pay Service 1
Pay Units: N.A.
Programming (via satellite): Showtime.
Video-On-Demand: No
Internet Service
Operational: No.
Telephone Service
None
Miles of Plant: 1.0 (coaxial); None (fiber optic). Homes passed: 45.
Treasurer & General Manager: Bruce Hanson.
Ownership: Hanson Communications Inc. (MSO).

RICE—Benton Cooperative Telephone, 2220 125th St Northwest, Rice, MN 56367-9701. Phones: 800-683-0372; 320-393-2115. Fax: 320-393-2221. Web Site: http://www.bctelco.net. Also serves Milaca & Rice (village). ICA: MN0098.
TV Market Ranking: Below 100 (Milaca, RICE, Rice (village)). Franchise award date: N.A. Franchise expiration date: N.A. Began: November 1, 1984.
Channel capacity: N.A. Channels available but not in use: N.A.
Basic Service
Subscribers: 66.
Programming (received off-air): KARE (NBC, WeatherNation) Minneapolis; KCCO-TV (CBS) Alexandria; KMSP-TV (Bounce TV, Buzzr, FOX) Minneapolis; KPXM-TV (ION) St. Cloud; KSAX (ABC) Alexandria; KSTC-TV (Antenna TV, This TV) Minneapolis; KSTP-TV (ABC, MeTV) St. Paul; KTCA-TV (PBS) St. Paul; WCCO-TV (CBS, Decades) Minneapolis; WFTC (MNT, Movies!) Minneapolis; WUCW (CW, The Country Network) Minneapolis.
Programming (via satellite): A&E; AMC; Animal Planet; Bravo; CNN; Comedy Central; Discovery Channel; Disney Channel; Disney XD; E! HD; ESPN; EWTN Global Catholic Network; Food Network; Fox News Channel; FOX Sports Midwest; Freeform; FX; FXM; Great American Country; History; HLN; Lifetime; MTV; National Geographic Channel; Nickelodeon; Outdoor Channel; TBS; The Weather Channel; TLC; TNT; Travel Channel; Trinity Broadcasting Network (TBN); TV Land; USA Network; WGN America.
Fee: $25.00 installation; $19.95 monthly.

Communications Daily
Warren Communications News
Get the industry standard FREE —
For a no-obligation trial call 800-771-9202 or visit www.warren-news.com

Digital Basic Service
Subscribers: N.A.
Programming (via satellite): BBC America; Bravo; Cloo; Discovery Digital Networks; DMX Music; ESPN Classic; ESPN2; ESPNews; Fox Sports 1; FYI; Golf Channel; GSN; HGTV; History International; IFC; National Geographic Channel; NBCSN; Syfy; Turner Classic Movies.
Digital Pay Service 1
Pay Units: N.A.
Programming (via satellite): Cinemax (multiplexed); HBO; Showtime; Starz; Starz Encore; The Movie Channel.
Fee: $10.95 - $15.95 monthly (each).
Video-On-Demand: No
Pay-Per-View
iN DEMAND (delivered digitally); Adult movies (delivered digitally).
Internet Service
Operational: Yes, DSL.
Subscribers: 766.
Broadband Service: In-house.
Fee: $34.95 monthly.
Telephone Service
Analog: Operational
Miles of Plant: 19.0 (coaxial); None (fiber optic). Homes passed: 1,800.
General Manager: Cheryl Scapanski. Operations Manager: Duane Wentland. Office Manager: Tim Hayes.
Ownership: Benton Cooperative Telephone Co.

RICE—Benton Cooperative Telephone. IPTV service is no longer planned. ICA: MN5296.

ROCHESTER—Charter Communications, 12405 Powerscourt Dr, St. Louis, MO 63131. Phones: 636-207-5100 (Corporate office); 507-289-8372. Fax: 507-285-6162. Web Site: http://www.charter.com. Also serves Byron, Cascade Twp., Eyota, Haverhill Twp., Kasson, Marion Twp., Oronoco Twp., Stewartville & Zumbrota. ICA: MN0008.
TV Market Ranking: Below 100 (Byron, Cascade Twp., Eyota, Haverhill Twp., Kasson, Marion Twp., Oronoco Twp., ROCHESTER, Stewartville, Zumbrota). Franchise award date: May 19, 1958. Franchise expiration date: N.A. Began: October 1, 1958.
Channel capacity: N.A. Channels available but not in use: N.A.
Digital Basic Service
Subscribers: 29,657.
Programming (via satellite): BBC America; Bloomberg Television; Boomerang; CNN en Espanol; CNN International; Discovery Digital Networks; DIY Network; ESPN Classic; ESPNews; Fox Sports 2; FSN Digital Atlantic; FSN Digital Central; FSN Digital Pacific; Fuse; FXM; FYI; History International; IFC; LMN; MC; NFL Network; Nick 2; Nick Jr.; Nicktoons; Outdoor Channel; Sundance TV; TeenNick; Turner Classic Movies; TV Guide Interactive Inc.
Fee: $26.99 monthly.
Digital Expanded Basic Service
Subscribers: N.A.
Programming (via satellite): A&E; AMC; Animal Planet; BET; Bravo; Cartoon Network; CMT; CNBC; CNN; Comedy Central; Discovery Channel; Discovery Life Channel; Disney Channel; Disney XD; E! HD; ESPN; ESPN2; EVINE Live; EWTN Global Catholic Network; Food Network; Fox Sports 1; FOX Sports North; Freeform; FX; Golf Channel; GSN; Hallmark Channel; HGTV; History; HLN; INSP; Lifetime; MSNBC; MTV; National Geographic Channel; NBCSN; Nickelodeon; Oxygen; Spike TV; Syfy; TBS; The Weather Channel; TLC; TNT; Travel Channel; truTV; TV Land; Univision Studios; USA Network; VH1; WE tv.
Fee: $47.99 monthly.
Digital Pay Service 1
Pay Units: N.A.
Programming (via satellite): Cinemax (multiplexed); Flix; HBO (multiplexed); Showtime (multiplexed); Starz (multiplexed); Starz Encore (multiplexed); The Movie Channel (multiplexed).
Video-On-Demand: Yes
Pay-Per-View
Playboy TV (delivered digitally); Fresh (delivered digitally); Shorteez (delivered digitally); iN DEMAND (delivered digitally); Sports PPV (delivered digitally); iN DEMAND.
Internet Service
Operational: Yes.
Subscribers: 33,619.
Broadband Service: Charter Internet.
Fee: $29.99 monthly.
Telephone Service
Digital: Operational
Subscribers: 14,812.
Miles of Plant: 1,349.0 (coaxial); 437.0 (fiber optic). Homes passed: 70,577.
Vice President & General Manager: John Crowley. Technical Operations Director: Darin Helgeson. Marketing Director: Bill Haarstad. Accounting Director: David Sovanski. Operations Director: Craig Stensaas.
Ownership: Charter Communications Inc. (MSO).

ROLLINGSTONE—Charter Communications. Now served by EAU CLAIRE, WI [WI0011]. ICA: MN0213.

ROLLINGSTONE—Hiawatha Broadband. This cable system has converted to IPTV. Now served by WINONA, MN [MN5161]. ICA: MN5156.

ROSE CREEK—Formerly served by North American Communications Corp. This cable system has converted to IPTV. Now served by Jaguar Communications, OWATONNA, MN [MN5121]. ICA: MN0253.

ROSEAU—Sjoberg's Cable TV Inc, 315 Main Ave North, Thief River Falls, MN 56701-1905. Phones: 800-828-8808; 218-681-3044. Fax: 218-681-6801. E-mail: office1@mncable.net; sjobergs@mncable.net. Web Site: http://trf.mncable.net. Also serves Jadis Twp. ICA: MN0099.
TV Market Ranking: Outside TV Markets (Jadis Twp., ROSEAU). Franchise award date:

Minnesota—Cable Systems

CABLE & TV STATION COVERAGE
Atlas 2017
The perfect companion to the Television & Cable Factbook
To order call 800-771-9202 or visit www.warren-news.com

N.A. Franchise expiration date: N.A. Began: August 15, 1967.
Channel capacity: N.A. Channels available but not in use: N.A.
Basic Service
Subscribers: 1,009.
Programming (received off-air): KBRR (FOX) Thief River Falls; KCPM (MNT) Grand Forks; WDAZ-TV (ABC, CW) Devils Lake; allband FM.
Programming (via microwave): KAWE (PBS) Bemidji; KRDK-TV (CBS, Decades, Movies!) Valley City; KVLY-TV (MeTV, NBC, This TV) Fargo.
Programming (via satellite): CNN; ESPN; TBS.
Fee: $55.92 monthly.
Expanded Basic Service 1
Subscribers: N.A.
Programming (via satellite): A&E; Animal Planet; Cartoon Network; CMT; CNBC; Comedy Central; CW PLUS; Discovery Channel; E! HD; ESPN2; Food Network; Fox News Channel; FOX Sports Networks; Freeform; FX; HGTV; History; Lifetime; MSNBC; MTV; Nickelodeon; Spike TV; Syfy; The Weather Channel; TLC; TNT; Turner Classic Movies; TV Land; USA Network; WGN America.
Fee: $23.71 monthly.
Digital Basic Service
Subscribers: N.A.
Programming (via satellite): BBC America; Bloomberg Television; Bravo; CBS Sports Network; Chiller; Cloo; CMT; Cooking Channel; Daystar TV Network; Destination America; Discovery Kids Channel; Discovery Life Channel; Disney XD; DIY Network; DMX Music; ESPN Classic; ESPNews; ESPNU; EVINE Live; EWTN Global Catholic Network; Fox Business Network; FOX College Sports Central; FOX College Sports Pacific; Fox Sports 1; FXM; FYI; Golf Channel; Great American Country; GSN; Hallmark Channel; History International; HLN; HRTV; IFC; Investigation Discovery; LMN; MTV Classic; MTV Hits; MTV2; Nat Geo WILD; National Geographic Channel; NBCSN; Nick Jr.; Nicktoons; Outdoor Channel; Ovation; OWN: Oprah Winfrey Network; Oxygen; RFD-TV; Science Channel; Sprout; Sundance TV; TeenNick; Tennis Channel; The Word Network; TVG Network; UP; various Canadian stations; VH1 Soul; WE tv.
Digital Expanded Basic Service
Subscribers: N.A.
Programming (via satellite): A&E HD; AXS TV; CNN HD; Discovery Channel HD; ESPN HD; ESPN2 HD; Food Network HD; FSN HD; HGTV HD; History HD; Outdoor Channel 2 HD; PBS HD; Syfy HD; TBS HD; TNT HD; Universal HD; USA Network HD; Versus HD.
Fee: $5.00 monthly; $5.00 converter.
Pay Service 1
Pay Units: N.A.
Programming (via satellite): HBO.
Fee: $11.00 monthly.
Digital Pay Service 1
Pay Units: N.A.
Programming (via satellite): Cinemax (multiplexed); Cinemax HD; HBO; HBO HD;

Showtime (multiplexed); Starz (multiplexed); Starz Encore (multiplexed); The Movie Channel (multiplexed).
Fee: $8.00 monthly (Starz/Encore), $9.00 monthly (Cinemax or Showtime/TMC), $11.00 monthly (HBO).
Video-On-Demand: No
Internet Service
Operational: Yes. Began: October 1, 1999.
Broadband Service: Sjoberg's Cable TV.
Fee: $19.95 monthly; $10.00 modem lease; $129.00 modem purchase.
Telephone Service
None
Miles of Plant: 17.0 (coaxial); 7.0 (fiber optic). Homes passed: 1,100.
President & General Manager: Richard J. Sjoberg. Chief Technician: Jerry Seim.
Ownership: Sjoberg's Cable TV Inc. (MSO).

ROSEMOUNT—Charter Communications, 16900 Cedar Ave, Rosemount, MN 55068. Phones: 636-207-5100 (Corporate office); 314-543-2236; 507-289-8372 (Rochester office); 952-432-2575. Web Site: http://www.charter.com. Also serves Apple Valley, Dundas, Empire Twp., Farmington, Hay Creek Twp., Lakeville, Northfield & Red Wing. ICA: MN0009.
TV Market Ranking: 13 (Apple Valley, Empire Twp., Farmington, Lakeville, Northfield, ROSEMOUNT); Outside TV Markets (Dundas, Hay Creek Twp., Red Wing). Franchise award date: N.A. Franchise expiration date: N.A. Began: November 1, 1974.
Channel capacity: N.A. Channels available but not in use: N.A.
Digital Basic Service
Subscribers: 33,392.
Programming (via satellite): BBC America; Discovery Digital Networks; DIY Network; FYI; History International; LMN; MC; Nick Jr.; Sundance TV; TeenNick.
Fee: $49.99 installation; $14.99 monthly.
Digital Expanded Basic Service
Subscribers: N.A.
Programming (via satellite): A&E; AMC; Animal Planet; BET; Bravo; Cartoon Network; CMT; CNBC; CNN; Comedy Central; Discovery Channel; Disney Channel; Disney XD; E! HD; ESPN; ESPN2; Food Network; Fox News Channel; Fox Sports 1; Freeform; FX; Golf Channel; GSN; Hallmark Channel; HGTV; History; HLN; INSP; Lifetime; MSNBC; MTV; National Geographic Channel; NBCSN; Nickelodeon; Spike TV; Syfy; TBS; The Weather Channel; TLC; TNT; Travel Channel; truTV; Turner Classic Movies; TV Land; USA Network; VH1; WE tv.
Fee: $47.99 monthly.
Digital Pay Service 1
Pay Units: N.A.
Programming (via satellite): Cinemax (multiplexed); Flix; HBO (multiplexed); Showtime (multiplexed); Starz (multiplexed); Starz Encore (multiplexed); The Movie Channel (multiplexed).
Fee: $11.95 monthly (Cinemax, Showtime, Starz/Encore or TMC/Flix), $12.95 monthly (HBO).
Video-On-Demand: Yes

Pay-Per-View
iN DEMAND (delivered digitally); Playboy TV (delivered digitally); Fresh (delivered digitally); Shorteez (delivered digitally); sports.
Internet Service
Operational: Yes.
Subscribers: 41,435.
Broadband Service: Charter Internet.
Fee: $29.99 monthly; $9.95 modem lease.
Telephone Service
Digital: Operational
Subscribers: 21,138.
Miles of Plant: 1,870.0 (coaxial); 448.0 (fiber optic). Homes passed: 78,868.
Vice President & General Manager: John Crowley. Sales & Marketing Director: Bill Haarstad. Technical Operations Director: Darin Helgeson. Accounting Director: David Sovanski. Technical Operations Manager: Mark Harder. Office Manager: Linda Lindberg. Technical Operations Manager: Clayton Snyder.
Ownership: Charter Communications Inc. (MSO).

ROSEVILLE—Comcast Cable. Now served by MINNEAPOLIS, MN [MN0001]. ICA: MN0404.

ROUND LAKE—Midco, PO Box 5010, Sioux Falls, SD 57117. Phone: 800-888-1300. Web Site: http://www.midcocomm.com. ICA: MN0216.
TV Market Ranking: Outside TV Markets (ROUND LAKE). Franchise award date: N.A. Franchise expiration date: N.A. Began: November 1, 1983.
Channel capacity: N.A. Channels available but not in use: N.A.
Basic Service
Subscribers: 15. Commercial subscribers: 6.
Programming (received off-air): KDLT-TV (Antenna TV, NBC) Sioux Falls; KELO-TV (CBS, MNT) Sioux Falls; KEYC-TV (CBS, FOX) Mankato; KSFY-TV (ABC, CW) Sioux Falls; KSMN (PBS) Worthington; KSTC-TV (Antenna TV, This TV) Minneapolis; KSTP-TV (ABC, MeTV) St. Paul; KTIV (CW, MeTV, NBC) Sioux City; WFTC (MNT, Movies!) Minneapolis.
Programming (via satellite): A&E; CMT; CNBC; CNN; Comedy Central; Discovery Channel; ESPN; ESPN2; FOX Sports Networks; Freeform; HGTV; History; HLN; Lifetime; Nickelodeon; Outdoor Channel; Spike TV; TBS; The Weather Channel; TLC; TNT; Turner Classic Movies; TV Land; USA Network; VH1; WGN America.
Programming (via translator): KARE (NBC, WeatherNation) Minneapolis; KMSP-TV (Bounce TV, Buzzr, FOX) Minneapolis.
Fee: $45.95 monthly.
Pay Service 1
Pay Units: N.A.
Programming (via satellite): HBO.
Fee: $11.95 monthly.
Internet Service
Operational: No.
Homes passed & miles of plant included in Cambridge.
General Manager: Steve Johnson. Customer Service Director: Jackie Torberg. Programming Director: Wynne Haakenstad.
Ownership: Midcontinent Communications (MSO).

ROUND LAKE TWP.—New Century Communications, 3588 Kennebec Dr, Eagan, MN 55122-1001. Phone: 651-688-2623. Fax: 651-688-2624. Also serves Haugen

Twp. & McGregor (unincorporated areas). ICA: MN0357.
TV Market Ranking: Outside TV Markets (Haugen Twp., McGregor (unincorporated areas), ROUND LAKE TWP.).
Channel capacity: N.A. Channels available but not in use: N.A.
Basic Service
Subscribers: 64.
Programming (received off-air): KBJR-TV (CBS, MNT, NBC) Superior; KCCW-TV (CBS) Walker; KDLH (CBS, CW) Duluth; KQDS-TV (Antenna TV, FOX) Duluth; WDIO-DT (ABC, MeTV) Duluth; WDSE (PBS) Duluth.
Programming (via satellite): A&E; CMT; Discovery Channel; Disney Channel; ESPN; FOX Sports Networks; Freeform; History; HLN; Lifetime; Outdoor Channel; QVC; Showtime; Spike TV; TBS; TLC; TNT; Trinity Broadcasting Network (TBN); TV Land; USA Network; WGN America.
Fee: $30.00 installation; $36.85 monthly.
Video-On-Demand: No
Internet Service
Operational: No.
Telephone Service
None
Miles of Plant: 29.0 (coaxial); None (fiber optic). Homes passed: 700.
Executive Vice President: Marty Walch. General Manager & Chief Technician: Todd Anderson.
Ownership: New Century Communications (MSO).

RUSHMORE—Formerly served by K-Communications Inc. No longer in operation. ICA: MN0358.

RUTHTON—Woodstock Communications, 337 Aetna St, PO Box C, Ruthton, MN 56170-0018. Phones: 800-752-9397; 507-658-3830. Fax: 507-658-3914. E-mail: wtcinfo@woodstocktel.net. Web Site: http://www.woodstocktel.com. Also serves Holland & Woodstock. ICA: MN0359.
TV Market Ranking: Outside TV Markets (Holland, RUTHTON, Woodstock).
Channel capacity: N.A. Channels available but not in use: N.A.
Basic Service
Subscribers: N.A.
Programming (received off-air): KDLT-TV (Antenna TV, NBC) Sioux Falls; KELO-TV (CBS, MNT) Sioux Falls; KSFY-TV (ABC, CW) Sioux Falls; KSTP-TV (ABC, MeTV) St. Paul; KTTW (FOX, This TV) Sioux Falls; KWCM-TV (PBS) Appleton.
Programming (via microwave): KSMN (PBS) Worthington.
Programming (via satellite): A&E; Bravo; CNN; Comedy Central; CW PLUS; Discovery Channel; Disney Channel; ESPN; ESPN2; Food Network; FOX Sports Networks; Freeform; GSN; Hallmark Channel; Hallmark Movies & Mysteries; HGTV; History; HLN; Spike TV; TBS; TNT; Travel Channel; Trinity Broadcasting Network (TBN); WGN America.
Fee: $25.00 installation; $34.47 monthly.
Pay Service 1
Pay Units: 51.
Programming (via satellite): Showtime.
Fee: $10.50 monthly.
Video-On-Demand: No
Internet Service
Operational: No, DSL.
Telephone Service
Analog: Operational
Miles of Plant: 12.0 (coaxial); None (fiber optic).

Cable Systems—Minnesota

Chief Technician & Marketing Director: Dave Bukowski. Program Director: Terry Nelson. Ownership: Woodstock Telephone Co. (MSO).

RUTLEDGE (village)—Formerly served by New Century Communications. No longer in operation. ICA: MN0360.

SABIN—Midcontinent Communications. Now served by WEST FARGO, ND [ND0230]. ICA: MN0361.

SAGINAW—SCI Broadband, 111 Tobies Mill Pl, PO Box 810, Hinckley, MN 55037-0810. Phones: 320-384-7442; 800-222-9809. Web Site: http://www.scibroadband.com. Also serves Duluth (unincorporated areas). ICA: MN0277.
TV Market Ranking: 89 (Duluth (unincorporated areas), SAGINAW). Franchise award date: N.A. Franchise expiration date: N.A. Began: January 1, 1990.
Channel capacity: N.A. Channels available but not in use: N.A.
Basic Service
Subscribers: 79.
Programming (received off-air): KBJR-TV (CBS, MNT, NBC) Superior; KDLH (CBS, CW) Duluth; KQDS-TV (Antenna TV, FOX) Duluth; WDIO-DT (ABC, MeTV) Duluth; WDSE (PBS) Duluth.
Programming (via satellite): A&E; AMC; Animal Planet; CMT; CNN; Discovery Channel; Disney Channel; ESPN; ESPN2; Flix; Freeform; History; HLN; Lifetime; Nickelodeon; Showtime; Spike TV; Syfy; TBS; The Weather Channel; TLC; TNT; Trinity Broadcasting Network (TBN); TV Land; USA Network; WGN America.
Fee: $30.00 installation; $36.25 monthly.
Video-On-Demand: No
Internet Service
Operational: No.
Telephone Service
None
Miles of Plant: 43.0 (coaxial); None (fiber optic). Homes passed: 910.
Ownership: Savage Communications Inc. (MSO).

SANBORN—NU-Telecom. This cable system has converted to IPTV. Now served by NEW ULM, MN [MN5117]. ICA: MN0163.

SANDSTONE—SCI Broadband, 111 Tobies Mill Pl, PO Box 810, Hinckley, MN 55037-0810. Phones: 800-222-9809; 320-384-7442. Fax: 320-279-8085. E-mail: sales@scibroadband.com. Web Site: http://www.scibroadband.com. Also serves Askov, Finlayson, Hinckley, Rutledge & Willow Ridge. ICA: MN0166.
TV Market Ranking: Outside TV Markets (Askov, Finlayson, Hinckley, Rutledge, SANDSTONE, Willow Ridge). Franchise award date: August 1, 1984. Franchise expiration date: N.A. Began: January 1, 1985.
Channel capacity: N.A. Channels available but not in use: N.A.
Basic Service
Subscribers: 1,258.
Programming (received off-air): KARE (NBC, WeatherNation) Minneapolis; KBJR-TV (CBS, MNT, NBC) Superior; KDLH (CBS, CW) Duluth; KMSP-TV (Bounce TV, Buzzr, FOX) Minneapolis; KPXM-TV (ION) St. Cloud; KSTC-TV (Antenna TV, This TV) Minneapolis; KSTP-TV (ABC, MeTV) St. Paul; KTCA-TV (PBS) St. Paul; WCCO-TV (CBS, Decades) Minneapolis; WDIO-DT (ABC, MeTV) Duluth; WDSE (PBS) Duluth; WFTC (MNT, Movies!) Minneapolis; WUCW (CW, The Country Network) Minneapolis.
Programming (via satellite): A&E; Animal Planet; Cartoon Network; CNBC; CNN; Comedy Central; C-SPAN; Discovery Channel; Disney Channel; E! HD; ESPN; ESPN2; EWTN Global Catholic Network; Fox News Channel; FOX Sports Networks; Freeform; Great American Country; HGTV; History; HLN; Lifetime; MTV; National Geographic Channel; Nickelodeon; QVC; Spike TV; Syfy; TBS; The Weather Channel; TLC; TNT; Turner Classic Movies; TV Land; USA Network; VH1; WGN America.
Fee: $39.95 installation; $15.95 monthly.
Digital Basic Service
Subscribers: N.A.
Programming (via satellite): BBC America; Bloomberg Television; Cloo; Discovery Life Channel; DMX Music; ESPN Classic; ESPNews; Fox Sports 1; Fuse; FXM; FYI; Golf Channel; History International; INSP; National Geographic Channel; NBCSN; Outdoor Channel; Trinity Broadcasting Network (TBN); WE tv.
Pay Service 1
Pay Units: N.A.
Programming (via satellite): HBO.
Fee: $12.95 monthly.
Digital Pay Service 1
Pay Units: N.A.
Programming (via satellite): Cinemax (multiplexed); HBO (multiplexed); Showtime (multiplexed); Starz (multiplexed); Starz Encore (multiplexed); The Movie Channel (multiplexed).
Video-On-Demand: No
Pay-Per-View
ESPN Now (delivered digitally); Sports PPV (delivered digitally).
Internet Service
Operational: Yes.
Broadband Service: SCI Broadband.
Fee: $19.95 monthly.
Telephone Service
Digital: Operational
Miles of Plant: 65.0 (coaxial); None (fiber optic). Homes passed: 1,609.
General Manager: Mike Danielson. President: Ron Savage. Chief Technician: Pat McCabe. Customer Service Manager: Donna Erickson.
Ownership: Savage Communications Inc. (MSO).

SAUK CENTRE—Arvig, 160 2nd Ave. SW, Perham, MN 56573. Phones: 888-992-7844; 218-346-4227; 320-351-1460 (Sauk Centre office). Fax: 218-338-3297. E-mail: answers@arvig.com. Web Site: http://arvig.com. Also serves Kandota Twp. & Sauk Centre Twp. ICA: MN0407.
Channel capacity: N.A. Channels available but not in use: N.A.
Basic Service
Subscribers: 1,195.
Programming (received off-air): KARE (NBC, WeatherNation) Minneapolis; KMSP-TV (Bounce TV, Buzzr, FOX) Minneapolis; KSAX (ABC) Alexandria; KSTC-TV (Antenna TV, This TV) Minneapolis; WCCO-TV (CBS, Decades) Minneapolis; WFTC (MNT, Movies!) Minneapolis.
Programming (via satellite): C-SPAN; CW Television Network; EWTN Global Catholic Network; HSN; QVC; TBS; Trinity Broadcasting Network (TBN); WGN America.
Fee: $55.00 installation; $26.95 monthly.
Expanded Basic Service 1
Subscribers: N.A.
Fee: $46.95 monthly.
Expanded Basic Service 2
Subscribers: N.A.
Fee: $59.95 monthly.
Pay Service 1
Pay Units: N.A.
Programming (via satellite): Cinemax (multiplexed); HBO (multiplexed); Showtime (multiplexed); Starz (multiplexed); Starz Encore (multiplexed); The Movie Channel (multiplexed).
Fee: $6.95 monthly (Encore), $12.95 monthly (Cinemax), $13.95 monthly (Showtime/TMC or Starz/Encore), $17.95 monthly (HBO), $23.95 (Cinemax/HBO).
Internet Service
Operational: Yes.
Fee: $34.95-$59.95 monthly.
Telephone Service
Digital: Operational
Fee: $12.98 monthly
Chief Operating Officer & Vice President: David Arvig.
Ownership: Tekstar Communications Inc.

SAUK CENTRE—Formerly served by Charter Communications. No longer in operation. ICA: MN0071.

SHAKOPEE—Formerly served by Time Warner Cable. Now served by Comcast Cable, MINNEAPOLIS, MN [MN0001]. ICA: MN0024.

SHEVLIN—Garden Valley Telephone Co. This cable system has converted to IPTV. Now served by McINTOSH, MN [MN5241]. ICA: MN0363.

SHULTZ LAKE TWP.—Formerly served by New Century Communications. No longer in operation. ICA: MN0364.

SILVER BAY—Mediacom. Now served by CLOQUET, MN [MN0042]. ICA: MN0084.

SLAYTON—Mediacom. Now served by IVANHOE, MN [MN0189]. ICA: MN0092.

SLEEPY EYE—NU-Telecom (formerly Sleepy Eye Telephone). Formerly served by GOODHUE, MN [MN0208]. This cable system has converted to IPTV, 121 2nd Ave NW, Sleepy Eye, MN 56085. Phones: 844-354-4111; 800-235-5133; 507-794-3361. Fax: 507-794-2351. E-mail: onlinecustservice@nu-telcom.net. Web Site: http://www.nutelecom.net. ICA: MN5137.
Channel capacity: N.A. Channels available but not in use: N.A.
NU-Basic
Subscribers: 590.
Fee: $24.95 monthly.
Internet Service
Operational: Yes.
Fee: $44.95-$84.95 monthly.
Telephone Service
Digital: Operational
Fee: $14.00 monthly
Ownership: NU-Telecom.

SOLWAY—Paul Bunyan Communications, 1831 Anne St NW, Ste 100, Bemidji, MN 56601. Phones: 218-999-1234; 888-586-3100; 218-444-1234. Fax: 218-444-1121. E-mail: tv@paulbunyan.net; info@paulbunyan.net. Web Site: http://www.paulbunyan.net. Also serves Alaska Twp., Battle Twp., Becida, Bemidji, Bemidji Twp., Birch Twp., Blackduck, Buzzle Twp., Cass Lake, Cormant Twp., Durand Twp., Eckles Twp., Farden Twp., Fern Twp., Frohn Twp., Grant Valley Twp., Guthrie Twp., Hagali Twp., Hart Lake Twp., Helga Twp., Hendrickson Twp., Hines Twp., Hornet Twp., Itasca Twp., Jones Twp., Kelliher, Kelliher Twp., Lake Alice Twp., Lake George Twp., Lake Hattie Twp., Lakeport Twp., Lammers Twp., Langor Twp., Laporte, Liberty Twp., Maple Ridge Twp., Moose Lake, Nebish Twp., Northern Twp., O'Brien Twp., Ottertail Peninsula Twp., Pike Bay Twp., Port Hope Twp., Puposky, Quiring Twp., Red Lake Band of Chippewa Indian Reservation, Roosevelt Twp., Schoolcraft Twp., Shooks Twp., Shotley Twp., Steamboat River Twp., Sugar Bush Twp., Summit Twp., Taylor Twp., Ten Lakes Twp., Tenstrike, Third River Twp., Turtle Lake Twp., Turtle River, Turtle Rver Twp., Waskish, Wilkinson Twp., Wilton & Woodrow Twp. ICA: MN5083.
TV Market Ranking: Franchise award date: N.A. Franchise expiration date: N.A. Began: June 1, 2001.
Channel capacity: N.A. Channels available but not in use: N.A.
PBTV Lite
Subscribers: 10,497.
Fee: $75.00 installation; $7.95 monthly. 60 channels plus 69 music channels.
PBTV Fusion
Subscribers: N.A.
HD
Subscribers: N.A.
Fee: $9.99 monthly. 67 HD channels.
PBTV Extra
Subscribers: N.A.
Fee: $9.99 monthly. 33 channels.
PBTV Sports
Subscribers: N.A.
Fee: $6.99 monthly. 12 channels.
Cinemax
Subscribers: N.A.
Fee: $12.95 monthly. 9 channels.
HBO
Subscribers: N.A.
Fee: $15.95 monthly. 11 channels.
Cinemax/HBO
Subscribers: N.A.
Fee: $22.95 monthly. 9 channels of Cinemax & 11 channels of HBO.
Showtime/TMC
Subscribers: N.A.
Fee: $12.95 monthly. 13 channels.
Starz/Encore
Subscribers: N.A.
Fee: $12.95 monthly. 15 channels.
Movie Package
Subscribers: N.A.
Fee: $41.95 monthly. 48 channels of Cinemax, Encore, HBO, Showtime, Starz & TMC.
Video-On-Demand: Yes

Minnesota—Cable Systems

Internet Service
Operational: Yes.
Fee: $44.95-$75 monthly.
Telephone Service
Digital: Operational
Fee: $20.95 monthly
Chief Executive Officer & General Manager: Gary Johnson. Video Services Coordinator: Keith Hunt.
Ownership: Paul Bunyan Communications.

SPRING GROVE—Mediacom. Now served by CALEDONIA, MN [MN0086]. ICA: MN0137.

SPRINGFIELD—Mediacom. Now served by FRANKLIN, MN [MN0057]. ICA: MN0113.

SPRINGFIELD—NU-Telecom. This cable system has converted to IPTV. Now served by NEW ULM, MN [MN5117]. ICA: MN0396.

ST. CHARLES—Hiawatha Broadband. Formerly [MN0397]. This cable system has converted to IPTV. Now served by WINONA, MN [MN5161]. ICA: MN5158.

ST. CHARLES—Hiawatha Broadband. This cable system has converted to IPTV. Now served by WINONA, MN [MN5161]. ICA: MN0397.

ST. CLOUD—Charter Communications, 12405 Powerscourt Dr, St. Louis, MO 63131. Phones: 636-207-5100 (Corporate office); 507-289-8372 (Rochester administrative office); 320-252-0943; 800-581-0081. Fax: 507-285-6162. Web Site: http://www.charter.com. Also serves Albany, Belle Prairie Twp., Green Prairie Twp., Haven Twp., Le Sauk Twp., Little Falls, Little Falls Twp., Melrose, Minden Twp., Pike Creek Twp., Sartell, Sauk Rapids, St. Joseph Twp. & Waite Park. ICA: MN0011.
TV Market Ranking: Below 100 (Belle Prairie Twp., Green Prairie Twp., Haven Twp., Le Sauk Twp., Little Falls Twp., Minden Twp., Pike Creek Twp., Sartell, Sauk Rapids, ST. CLOUD, St. Joseph Twp., Waite Park, Albany, Little Falls, Melrose). Franchise award date: June 12, 1984. Franchise expiration date: N.A. Began: January 1, 1967.
Channel capacity: N.A. Channels available but not in use: N.A.
Digital Basic Service
Subscribers: 23,333.
Programming (via satellite): AXS TV; BBC America; Bloomberg Television; Boomerang; CBS Sports Network; CNN en Espanol; CNN International; Discovery Life Channel; DIY Network; ESPN; ESPN Classic; ESPNews; FOX College Sports Central; FOX College Sports Pacific; Fox Sports 2; Fuse; FXM; FYI; History International; IFC; LMN; MC; NFL Network; Nick 2; Nick Jr.; Nicktoons; Outdoor Channel; Sundance TV; TeenNick; TV Guide Interactive Inc.
Fee: $14.99 monthly.
Digital Expanded Basic Service
Subscribers: N.A.
Programming (via satellite): A&E; AMC; Animal Planet; BET; Bravo; Cartoon Network; CMT; CNBC; CNN; Comedy Central; Discovery Channel; Disney Channel; Disney XD; E! HD; ESPN; ESPN2; Food Network; Fox News Channel; Fox Sports 1; FOX Sports North; Freeform; FX; Golf Channel; Great American Country; GSN; Hallmark Channel; HGTV; History; HLN; Lifetime; MoviePlex; MSNBC; MTV; MTV2; National Geographic Channel; NBCSN; Nickelodeon; Oxygen; Spike TV; Syfy; TBS; The Weather Channel; TLC; TNT; Travel Channel; truTV; Turner Classic Movies; TV Land; Univision Studios; USA Network; VH1; WE tv.
Fee: $47.99 monthly.
Digital Pay Service 1
Pay Units: N.A.
Programming (via satellite): Cinemax (multiplexed); HBO (multiplexed); Showtime (multiplexed); Starz (multiplexed); Starz Encore (multiplexed); The Movie Channel (multiplexed).
Video-On-Demand: Yes
Pay-Per-View
iN DEMAND (delivered digitally); NHL Center Ice (delivered digitally); MLB Extra Innings (delivered digitally); Playboy TV (delivered digitally); Spice Live (delivered digitally); Spice Platinum (delivered digitally); Hot Net Plus (delivered digitally); Spice Hot (delivered digitally).
Internet Service
Operational: Yes.
Subscribers: 26,599.
Broadband Service: Charter Internet.
Fee: $29.99 monthly.
Telephone Service
Digital: Operational
Subscribers: 13,352.
Fee: $29.99 monthly
Miles of Plant: 1,098.0 (coaxial); 596.0 (fiber optic). Homes passed: 69,885.
Vice President & General Manager: John Crowley. Technical Operations Director: Mark Abramo. Operations Director: Craig Stensaas. Marketing Director: Bill Haarstad. Accounting Director: David Sovanski. Marketing Manager: Lisa Barton.
Ownership: Charter Communications Inc. (MSO).

ST. CLOUD—Formerly served by Astound Broadband. No longer in operation. ICA: MN0394.

ST. CROIX—Formerly served by Comcast Cable. No longer in operation. ICA: MN0007.

ST. HILAIRE—Garden Valley Telephone Co. Now served by McINTOSH, MN [MN0105]. ICA: MN0366.

ST. JAMES—Mediacom. Now served by ST. PETER (formerly Waseca), MN [MN0043]. ICA: MN0061.

ST. JOSEPH—Formerly served by Astound Communications. No longer in operation. ICA: MN0199.

ST. LOUIS PARK—Formerly served by Time Warner Cable. Now served by Comcast Cable, MINNEAPOLIS, MN [MN0001]. ICA: MN0367.

ST. PAUL—Comcast Cable. Now served by MINNEAPOLIS, MN [MN0001]. ICA: MN0003.

ST. PAUL—Comcast Cable. Now served by MINNEAPOLIS, MN [MN0001]. ICA: MN0002.

ST. PETER—Mediacom, 1504 2nd St SE, PO Box 110, Waseca, MN 56093. Phones: 845-695-2762; 507-835-2356. Fax: 507-835-4567. Web Site: http://www.mediacomcable.com. Also serves Belle Plaine, Butterfield, Cleveland, Henderson, Janesville, Kasota, Lafayette, Lake Crystal, Le Sueur, Lonsdale, Montgomery, Mountain Lake, Pemberton, St. James, Waldorf, Waseca, Wells & Winnebago. ICA: MN0043.
TV Market Ranking: 13 (Belle Plaine, Lonsdale); Below 100 (Cleveland, Henderson, Janesville, Kasota, Lafayette, Lake Crystal, Le Sueur, Pemberton, St. James, ST. PETER, Wells, Winnebago, Montgomery, Waseca); Outside TV Markets (Butterfield, Mountain Lake). Franchise award date: N.A. Franchise expiration date: N.A. Began: January 1, 1974.
Channel capacity: N.A. Channels available but not in use: N.A.
Basic Service
Subscribers: 6,478.
Programming (received off-air): KARE (NBC, WeatherNation) Minneapolis; KEYC-TV (CBS, FOX) Mankato; KMSP-TV (Bounce TV, Buzzr, FOX) Minneapolis; KSTC-TV (Antenna TV, This TV) Minneapolis; KSTP-TV (ABC, MeTV) St. Paul; KTCA-TV (PBS) St. Paul; KTCI-TV (PBS) St. Paul; WCCO-TV (CBS, Decades) Minneapolis; WFTC (MNT, Movies!) Minneapolis; WUCW (CW, The Country Network) Minneapolis; allband FM.
Programming (via satellite): C-SPAN; C-SPAN 2; Pop; The Weather Channel; WGN America.
Fee: $20.00 installation; $43.00 monthly.
Expanded Basic Service 1
Subscribers: N.A.
Programming (received off-air): KPXM-TV (ION) St. Cloud.
Programming (via satellite): A&E; AMC; Animal Planet; BET; Bravo; Cartoon Network; CMT; CNBC; CNN; Comedy Central; Discovery Channel; Disney Channel; E! HD; ESPN; ESPN2; EWTN Global Catholic Network; Food Network; Fox News Channel; Fox Sports 1; FOX Sports North; Freeform; FX; FXM; Hallmark Channel; HGTV; History; HLN; INSP; Lifetime; MSNBC; MTV; Nickelodeon; QVC; Spike TV; Syfy; TBS; TLC; TNT; Travel Channel; Trinity Broadcasting Network (TBN); truTV; Turner Classic Movies; TV Land; Univision Studios; USA Network; VH1; WE tv.
Fee: $15.06 monthly.
Digital Basic Service
Subscribers: N.A.
Programming (via satellite): BBC America; Bloomberg Television; Discovery Digital Networks; DMX Music; Fuse; FYI; Golf Channel; GSN; History International; HITS (Headend In The Sky); IFC; LMN; National Geographic Channel; NBCSN; Nick Jr.; Outdoor Channel; TeenNick.
Digital Pay Service 1
Pay Units: N.A.
Programming (via satellite): Cinemax (multiplexed); Flix; HBO (multiplexed); Showtime (multiplexed); Starz (multiplexed); Starz Encore (multiplexed); Sundance TV; The Movie Channel (multiplexed).
Fee: $7.00 monthly (Cinemax or Showtime), $9.00 monthly (HBO).
Video-On-Demand: Yes
Pay-Per-View
Vubiquity Inc. (delivered digitally); ESPN Now (delivered digitally); Sports PPV (delivered digitally); Urban Xtra (delivered digitally); Fresh (delivered digitally); Shorteez (delivered digitally); Playboy TV (delivered digitally); Pleasure (delivered digitally).
Internet Service
Operational: Yes.
Subscribers: 5,616.
Broadband Service: Mediacom High Speed Internet.
Fee: $99.00 installation; $40.00 monthly.

Telephone Service
Analog: Not Operational
Digital: Operational
Subscribers: 3,615.
Miles of Plant: 609.0 (coaxial); 449.0 (fiber optic). Homes passed: 29,303.
Regional Vice President: Bill Jensen. Vice President, Financial Reporting: Kenneth J. Kohrs. Marketing & Sales Director: Lori Huberty. Engineering Manager: Kraig Kaiser.
Ownership: Mediacom LLC (MSO).

ST. PETER—Mediacom. Now served by ST. PETER (formerly Waseca), MN [MN0043]. ICA: MN0049.

STACY—Midcontinent Communications. Now served by CAMBRIDGE, MN [MN0016]. ICA: MN0185.

STAPLES—Charter Communications. Now served by BRAINERD, MN [MN0022]. ICA: MN0368.

STARBUCK—Mediacom. Now served by MORRIS, MN [MN0210]. ICA: MN0131.

STEPHEN—Wikstrom Cable LLC, PO Box 217, Karlstad, MN 56732. Phone: 218-436-2121. Fax: 218-436-3100. E-mail: service@wiktel.com. Web Site: http://www.wiktel.com. ICA: MN0181.
TV Market Ranking: Outside TV Markets (STEPHEN). Franchise award date: July 6, 1978. Franchise expiration date: N.A. Began: January 1, 1979.
Channel capacity: N.A. Channels available but not in use: N.A.
Basic Service
Subscribers: 211.
Programming (received off-air): KBRR (FOX) Thief River Falls; KGFE (PBS) Grand Forks; KRDK-TV (CBS, Decades, Movies!) Valley City; KVLY-TV (MeTV, NBC, This TV) Fargo; WDAZ-TV (ABC, CW) Devils Lake; allband FM.
Programming (via satellite): A&E; AMC; CMT; CNBC; CNN; Comedy Central; C-SPAN; C-SPAN 2; Discovery Channel; Disney Channel; E! HD; ESPN; ESPN Classic; ESPN2; Food Network; Fox News Channel; Fox Sports 1; FOX Sports Networks; Freeform; FX; Golf Channel; Great American Country; Hallmark Channel; HGTV; History; Lifetime; MTV; Nickelodeon; Outdoor Channel; Spike TV; Syfy; TBS; The Weather Channel; TLC; TNT; Trinity Broadcasting Network (TBN); TV Land; USA Network; various Canadian stations; VH1; WGN America.
Fee: $20.00 installation; $57.99 monthly.
Pay Service 1
Pay Units: 11.
Programming (via satellite): HBO.
Fee: $10.00 installation; $11.00 monthly.
Video-On-Demand: No
Internet Service
Operational: No.
Telephone Service
None
Miles of Plant: 5.0 (coaxial); None (fiber optic). Homes passed: 320.
General Manager: Bryan Wikstrom. Controller: Carrie Kern-Taggart.
Ownership: Wikstrom Systems LLC (MSO).

STOCKTON—Formerly served by Midcontinent Communications. Now served by Charter Communications, EAU CLAIRE, WI [WI0011]. ICA: MN0369.

Cable Systems—Minnesota

STORDEN—Midco, PO Box 5010, Sioux Falls, SD 57117. Phone: 800-888-1300. Web Site: http://www.midcocomm.com. ICA: MN0244.
TV Market Ranking: Outside TV Markets (STORDEN).
Channel capacity: N.A. Channels available but not in use: N.A.
Basic Service
Subscribers: 29.
Programming (received off-air): KARE (NBC, WeatherNation) Minneapolis; KELO-TV (CBS, MNT) Sioux Falls; KEYC-TV (CBS, FOX) Mankato; KMSP-TV (Bounce TV, Buzzr, FOX) Minneapolis; KSFY-TV (ABC, CW) Sioux Falls; KSTC-TV (Antenna TV, This TV) Minneapolis; KSTP-TV (ABC, MeTV) St. Paul; KTCA-TV (PBS) St. Paul; WCCO-TV (CBS, Decades) Minneapolis; WFTC (MNT, Movies!) Minneapolis; WUCW (CW, The Country Network) Minneapolis.
Programming (via satellite): A&E; CMT; CNBC; CNN; Comedy Central; Discovery Channel; ESPN; ESPN2; FOX Sports North; Freeform; History; HLN; Lifetime; Nickelodeon; Outdoor Channel; Spike TV; TBS; The Weather Channel; TLC; TNT; Turner Classic Movies; USA Network; WGN America.
Fee: $45.95 monthly.
Pay Service 1
Pay Units: N.A.
Programming (via satellite): HBO.
Fee: $11.95 monthly.
Internet Service
Operational: No.
Telephone Service
None
Homes passed & miles of plant included in Cambridge.
President & Chief Executive Officer: Pat McAdaragh. Senior Vice President, Public Policy: Tom Simmons. Programming Director: Wynne Haakenstad.
Ownership: Midcontinent Communications (MSO).

SWANVILLE—Formerly served by 391 Satellite LLC. No longer in operation. ICA: MN0256.

TACONITE—Formerly served by City of Taconite Cable TV. Now served by Mediacom, CALUMET, MN [MN0027]. ICA: MN0370.

TAYLORS FALLS—Midcontinent Communications. Now served by CAMBRIDGE, MN [MN0016]. ICA: MN0371.

THIEF RIVER FALLS—Sjoberg's Cable TV Inc, 315 Main Ave North, Thief River Falls, MN 56701-1905. Phones: 800-828-8808; 218-681-3044. Fax: 218-681-6801. E-mail: office1@mncable.net; sjobergs@mncable.net. Web Site: http://trf.mncable.net. Also serves Holt, North Twp., Rocksbury Twp. & Viking. ICA: MN0045.
TV Market Ranking: Below 100 (Holt, North Twp., Rocksbury Twp., THIEF RIVER FALLS, Viking). Franchise award date: N.A. Franchise expiration date: N.A. Began: October 1, 1962.
Channel capacity: N.A. Channels available but not in use: N.A.
Basic Service
Subscribers: 3,297.
Programming (received off-air): KBRR (FOX) Thief River Falls; KCPM (MNT) Grand Forks; KGFE (PBS) Grand Forks; KRDK-TV (CBS, Decades, Movies!) Valley City; KVLY-TV (MeTV, NBC, This TV) Fargo; WDAZ-TV (ABC, CW) Devils Lake; 14 FMs.

Programming (via satellite): CNN; ESPN; PBS HD; TBS; various Canadian stations.
Fee: $25.00 installation; $17.95 monthly.
Expanded Basic Service 1
Subscribers: N.A.
Programming (via satellite): A&E; Animal Planet; Cartoon Network; CMT; CNBC; Comedy Central; C-SPAN; CW PLUS; Discovery Channel; Disney Channel; E! HD; ESPN2; Food Network; Fox News Channel; FOX Sports Networks; Freeform; FX; HGTV; History; Lifetime; MSNBC; MTV; Nickelodeon; Spike TV; Syfy; The Weather Channel; TLC; TNT; Turner Classic Movies; TV Land; USA Network; VH1; WGN America.
Fee: $23.71 monthly.
Digital Basic Service
Subscribers: N.A.
Programming (via satellite): A&E HD; AXS TV; BBC America; Bloomberg Television; Bravo; CBS Sports Network; Chiller; Cloo; CMT; CNN HD; Cooking Channel; Daystar TV Network; Destination America; Discovery Channel HD; Discovery Kids Channel; Discovery Life Channel; Disney XD; DIY Network; DMX Music; ESPN Classic; ESPN HD; ESPN2 HD; ESPNews; ESPNU; EVINE Live; EWTN Global Catholic Network; Food Network HD; Fox Business Network; FOX College Sports Central; FOX College Sports Pacific; Fox Sports 1; FSN HD; FXM; FYI; Golf Channel; Great American Country; GSN; Hallmark Channel; HGTV HD; History HD; History International; HLN; HRTV; IFC; Investigation Discovery; LMN; MTV Classic; MTV Hits; MTV2; Nat Geo WILD; National Geographic Channel; NBCSN; Nick Jr.; Nicktoons; Outdoor Channel; Outdoor Channel 2 HD; Ovation; OWN: Oprah Winfrey Network; Oxygen; Reelz; RFD-TV; Science Channel; Sprout; Sundance TV; Syfy HD; TBS HD; TeenNick; Tennis Channel; The Word Network; TNT HD; Trinity Broadcasting Network (TBN); TVG Network; Universal HD; UP; USA Network HD; Versus HD; VH1 Soul; WE tv.
Pay Service 1
Pay Units: N.A.
Programming (via satellite): Cinemax; HBO.
Fee: $9.00 monthly (Cinemax), $11.00 monthly (HBO).
Digital Pay Service 1
Pay Units: N.A.
Programming (via satellite): Cinemax (multiplexed); Cinemax HD; HBO (multiplexed); HBO HD; Showtime (multiplexed); Starz (multiplexed); Starz Encore (multiplexed); The Movie Channel (multiplexed).
Fee: $8.00 monthly (Starz/Encore), $9.00 monthly (Cinemax or Showtime/TMC), $11.00 monthly (HBO).
Video-On-Demand: No
Pay-Per-View
World Wrestling Entertainment Inc.
Internet Service
Operational: Yes. Began: March 1, 1999. Broadband Service: Sjoberg's Cable TV.
Fee: $19.95 monthly; $29.95 modem lease; $129.00 modem purchase.
Telephone Service
None
Miles of Plant: 48.0 (coaxial); 85.0 (fiber optic). Homes passed: 3,516.
President & General Manager: Richard J. Sjoberg. Chief Technician: Jerry Seim.
Ownership: Sjoberg's Cable TV Inc. (MSO).

TOWER—Midco. Now served by ELY, MN [MN0060]. ICA: MN0139.

Access the most current data instantly
FREE TRIAL @ ADVANCED TVFactbook
TELCO/IPTV • CABLE TV • TV STATIONS
www.warren-news.com/factbook.htm

TRACY—Charter Communications. Now served by WILLMAR, MN [MN0018]. ICA: MN0056.

TRIMONT—Formerly served by Clara City Telephone Co. No longer in operation. ICA: MN0372.

TRUMAN—Formerly served by Clara City Telephone Co. No longer in operation. ICA: MN0148.

TWO HARBORS—Mediacom. Now served by CLOQUET, MN [MN0042]. ICA: MN0067.

ULEN—Formerly served by Loretel Cablevision. Now served by Arvig, PERHAM, MN [MN0050]. ICA: MN0373.

VERNDALE—SCI Broadband, 111 Tobies Mill Pl, PO Box 810, Hinckley, MN 55037-0810. Phones: 800-222-9809; 320-384-7442. Fax: 320-279-8085. E-mail: sales@scibroadband.com. Web Site: http://www.scibroadband.com. ICA: MN0214.
TV Market Ranking: Outside TV Markets (VERNDALE). Franchise award date: July 15, 1985. Franchise expiration date: N.A. Began: July 18, 1985.
Channel capacity: N.A. Channels available but not in use: N.A.
Basic Service
Subscribers: 45.
Programming (received off-air): KARE (NBC, WeatherNation) Minneapolis; KAWB (PBS) Brainerd; KCCO-TV (CBS) Alexandria; KMSP-TV (Bounce TV, Buzzr, FOX) Minneapolis; KSAX (ABC) Alexandria; KVRR (Antenna TV, FOX) Fargo.
Programming (via satellite): A&E; Animal Planet; CNBC; CNN; Comedy Central; C-SPAN; Discovery Channel; Disney Channel; E! HD; ESPN; ESPN2; FOX Sports Networks; Freeform; Great American Country; HGTV; History; HLN; Lifetime; MTV; Nickelodeon; QVC; Spike TV; Syfy; TBS; The Weather Channel; TLC; TNT; Turner Classic Movies; TV Land; USA Network; VH1; WGN America; WPIX (Antenna TV, CW, This TV) New York.
Fee: $39.95 installation; $17.95 monthly.
Digital Basic Service
Subscribers: N.A.
Programming (via satellite): BBC America; Bloomberg Television; Cloo; Discovery Life Channel; DMX Music; ESPN Classic; ESPNews; Fox Sports 1; Fuse; FXM; FYI; Golf Channel; History International; INSP; National Geographic Channel; NBCSN; Outdoor Channel; Trinity Broadcasting Network (TBN); WE tv.
Digital Pay Service 1
Pay Units: N.A.
Programming (via satellite): Cinemax (multiplexed); Flix; HBO (multiplexed); Showtime (multiplexed); Starz (multiplexed); Starz Encore (multiplexed); Sundance TV; The Movie Channel (multiplexed).
Video-On-Demand: No

Pay-Per-View
ESPN Now (delivered digitally); Sports PPV (delivered digitally).
Internet Service
Operational: Yes.
Broadband Service: SCI Broadband.
Fee: $19.95 monthly.
Telephone Service
Digital: Operational
Miles of Plant: 8.0 (coaxial); 1.0 (fiber optic). Homes passed: 237.
General Manager: Mike Danielson. President: Ron Savage. Chief Technician: Pat McCabe. Customer Service Manager: Donna Erickson.
Ownership: Savage Communications Inc. (MSO).

VERNON CENTER—Formerly served by North American Communications Corp. This cable system has converted to IPTV. Now served by Jaguar Communications, OWATONNA, MN [MN5121]. ICA: MN0374.

WABASHA—Hiawatha Broadband. Formerly [MN0399]. This cable system has converted to IPTV. Now served by WINONA, MN [MN5161]. ICA: MN5160.

WABASHA—Hiawatha Broadband. This cable system has converted to IPTV. Now served by WINONA, MN [MN5161]. ICA: MN0399.

WABASHA—Midco. Now served by CAMBRIDGE, MN [MN0016]. ICA: MN0375.

WABASSO—Clara City Telephone Co, 227 South Main St, PO Box 8001, Clara City, MN 56222. Phones: 320-847-2211; 888-283-7667. Fax: 320-847-2736. E-mail: bruce@hcinet.net. Web Site: http://www.hcinet.net. ICA: MN0224.
TV Market Ranking: Below 100 (WABASSO). Franchise award date: June 1, 1984. Franchise expiration date: N.A. Began: July 1, 1984.
Channel capacity: N.A. Channels available but not in use: N.A.
Basic Service
Subscribers: 54.
Programming (received off-air): KEYC-TV (CBS, FOX) Mankato; KWCM-TV (PBS) Appleton.
Programming (via microwave): KARE (NBC, WeatherNation) Minneapolis; KMSP-TV (Bounce TV, Buzzr, FOX) Minneapolis; KSTP-TV (ABC, MeTV) St. Paul; KTCA-TV (PBS) St. Paul; WCCO-TV (CBS, Decades) Minneapolis.
Programming (via satellite): CMT; CNN; Discovery Channel; Disney Channel; ESPN; Freeform; TBS; TNT; USA Network; WGN America.
Fee: $20.00 installation; $48.50 monthly.
Pay Service 1
Pay Units: N.A.
Programming (via satellite): HBO.
Fee: $25.00 installation; $10.00 monthly.
Internet Service
Operational: No.

2017 Edition

Minnesota—Cable Systems

Telephone Service
None
Miles of Plant: 6.0 (coaxial); None (fiber optic). Homes passed: 265.
General Manager: Bruce Hanson.
Ownership: Hanson Communications Inc. (MSO).

WADENA—Charter Communications. Now served by BRAINERD, MN [MN0022]. ICA: MN0376.

WALDORF—Formerly served by Dynax Communications Inc. Now served by Mediacom, ST. PETER (formerly Waseca), MN [MN0043]. ICA: MN0260.

WALNUT GROVE—Clara City Telephone Co, 227 South Main St, PO Box 800, Clara City, MN 56222. Phone: 320-847-2211. Fax: 320-847-2736. Web Site: http://www.hcinet.net. ICA: MN0196.
TV Market Ranking: Below 100 (WALNUT GROVE). Franchise award date: N.A. Franchise expiration date: N.A. Began: April 10, 1973.
Channel capacity: N.A. Channels available but not in use: N.A.

Basic Service
Subscribers: 47.
Programming (received off-air): KELO-TV (CBS, MNT) Sioux Falls; KEYC-TV (CBS, FOX) Mankato; KSFY-TV (ABC, CW) Sioux Falls; KSMN (PBS) Worthington; WFTC (MNT, Movies!) Minneapolis; allband FM.
Programming (via satellite): CMT; CNN; Discovery Channel; ESPN; FamilyNet; FOX Sports Networks; Freeform; HGTV; HLN; Lifetime; Nickelodeon; Spike TV; TBS; The Weather Channel; TLC; TNT; Turner Classic Movies; TV Land; USA Network; WGN America.
Programming (via translator): KARE (NBC, WeatherNation) Minneapolis; KMSP-TV (Bounce TV, Buzzr, FOX) Minneapolis; KSTP-TV (ABC, MeTV) St. Paul; KTCA-TV (PBS) St. Paul; WCCO-TV (CBS, Decades) Minneapolis; WUCW (CW, The Country Network) Minneapolis.
Fee: $20.00 installation; $48.50 monthly.

Pay Service 1
Pay Units: N.A.
Programming (via satellite): Showtime.

Video-On-Demand: No

Internet Service
Operational: No.

Telephone Service
None
Miles of Plant: 6.0 (coaxial); None (fiber optic). Homes passed: 300.
Treasurer & General Manager: Bruce Hanson.
Ownership: Hanson Communications Inc. (MSO).

WANAMINGO—Midco, PO Box 5010, Sioux Falls, SD 57117. Phone: 800-888-1300. Web Site: http://www.midcocomm.com. ICA: MN0182.
TV Market Ranking: Below 100 (WANAMINGO). Franchise award date: N.A. Franchise expiration date: N.A. Began: December 1, 1988.
Channel capacity: N.A. Channels available but not in use: N.A.

Basic Service
Subscribers: 48. Commercial subscribers: 20.
Programming (received off-air): KARE (NBC, WeatherNation) Minneapolis; KMSP-TV (Bounce TV, Buzzr, FOX) Minneapolis; KSTC-TV (Antenna TV, This TV) Minneapolis; KSTP-TV (ABC, MeTV) St. Paul; KTCA-TV (PBS) St. Paul; KTCI-TV (PBS) St. Paul; KTTC (CW, NBC) Rochester; WCCO-TV (CBS, Decades) Minneapolis; WFTC (MNT, Movies!) Minneapolis.
Programming (via satellite): A&E; Animal Planet; CMT; CNBC; CNN; Comedy Central; C-SPAN; Discovery Channel; Disney Channel; ESPN; ESPN2; Food Network; FOX Sports Networks; Freeform; History; HLN; Lifetime; Nickelodeon; QVC; Syfy; TBS; The Weather Channel; TLC; TNT; Travel Channel; Turner Classic Movies; TV Land; USA Network; VH1; WGN America.
Fee: $53.95 monthly.

Pay Service 1
Pay Units: N.A.
Programming (via satellite): Cinemax; HBO.
Fee: $11.95 monthly (each).

Internet Service
Operational: No.

Telephone Service
None
Miles of Plant: 9.0 (coaxial); None (fiber optic). Homes passed: 407. Homes passed & miles of plant included in Cambridge.
President & Chief Executive Officer: Pat McAdaragh. Senior Vice President, Public Policy: Tom Simmons. Programming Director: Wynne Haakenstad.
Ownership: Midcontinent Communications (MSO).

WARREN—Sjoberg's Cable TV Inc, 315 Main Ave North, Thief River Falls, MN 56701-1905. Phones: 218-681-3044; 800-828-8808. Fax: 218-681-6801. E-mail: office1@mncable.net; sjobergs@mncable.net. Web Site: http://trf.mncable.net. Also serves McCrea Twp. ICA: MN0115.
TV Market Ranking: Below 100 (WARREN). Franchise award date: N.A. Franchise expiration date: N.A. Began: December 2, 1973.
Channel capacity: N.A. Channels available but not in use: N.A.

Basic Service
Subscribers: 453.
Programming (received off-air): KBRR (FOX) Thief River Falls; KCPM (MNT) Grand Forks; KGFE (PBS) Grand Forks; KRDK-TV (CBS, Decades, Movies!) Valley City; KVLY-TV (MeTV, NBC, This TV) Fargo; WDAZ-TV (ABC, NBC) Devils Lake; 9 FMs.
Programming (via satellite): CNN; ESPN; TBS; various Canadian stations.
Fee: $25.00 installation; $55.92 monthly.

Expanded Basic Service 1
Subscribers: N.A.
Programming (via satellite): A&E; Animal Planet; Cartoon Network; CMT; CNBC; Comedy Central; C-SPAN; CW PLUS; Discovery Channel; Disney Channel; E! HD; ESPN2; Food Network; Fox News Channel; FOX Sports Networks; Freeform; FX; HGTV; History; Lifetime; MSNBC; MTV; Nickelodeon; Spike TV; Syfy; The Weather Channel; TLC; TNT; Turner Classic Movies; TV Land; USA Network; VH1; WGN America.
Fee: $23.71 monthly.

Digital Basic Service
Subscribers: N.A.
Programming (via satellite): BBC America; Bloomberg Television; Bravo; CBS Sports Network; Chiller; Cloo; CMT; Cooking Channel; Daystar TV Network; Destination America; Discovery Kids Channel; Discovery Life Channel; Disney XD; DIY Network; DMX Music; ESPN Classic; ESPNews; ESPNU; EVINE Live; EWTN Global Catholic Network; Fox Business Network; FOX College Sports Central; FOX College Sports Pacific; Fox Sports 1; FXM; FYI; Golf Channel; Great American Country; GSN; Hallmark Channel; History International; HLN; HRTV; IFC; Investigation Discovery; LMN; MTV Classic; MTV Hits; MTV2; Nat Geo WILD; National Geographic Channel; NBCSN; Nick Jr.; Nicktoons; Outdoor Channel; Ovation; OWN: Oprah Winfrey Network; Oxygen; Reelz; RFD-TV; Science Channel; Sprout; Sundance TV; TeenNick; Tennis Channel; The Word Network; Trinity Broadcasting Network (TBN); TVG Network; UP; VH1 Soul; WE tv.

Digital Expanded Basic Service
Subscribers: N.A.
Programming (via satellite): A&E HD; AXS TV; CNN HD; Discovery Channel HD; ESPN HD; ESPN2 HD; Food Network HD; FSN HD; HGTV HD; History HD; Outdoor Channel 2 HD; PBS HD; Syfy HD; TBS HD; TNT HD; Universal HD; USA Network HD; Versus HD.
Fee: $5.00 monthly; $5.00 converter.

Pay Service 1
Pay Units: N.A.
Programming (via satellite): HBO.
Fee: $9.00 monthly (Cinemax), $11.00 monthly (HBO).

Digital Pay Service 1
Pay Units: N.A.
Programming (via satellite): Cinemax (multiplexed); Cinemax HD; HBO (multiplexed); HBO HD; Showtime (multiplexed); Starz (multiplexed); Starz Encore (multiplexed); The Movie Channel (multiplexed).
Fee: $8.00 monthly (Starz/Encore), $9.00 monthly (Cinemax or Showtime/TMC), $11.00 monthly (HBO).

Video-On-Demand: No

Internet Service
Operational: Yes. Began: December 31, 1999.
Broadband Service: Sjoberg's Cable TV.
Fee: $19.95 monthly; $10.00 modem lease; $129.00 modem purchase.

Telephone Service
None
Miles of Plant: 14.0 (coaxial); 2.0 (fiber optic). Homes passed: 784.
President & General Manager: Richard J. Sjoberg. Chief Technician: Jerry Seim.
Ownership: Sjoberg's Cable TV Inc. (MSO).

WARROAD—Sjoberg's Cable TV Inc, 315 Main Ave North, Thief River Falls, MN 56701-1905. Phones: 216-681-3044; 800-828-8808. Fax: 218-681-6801. E-mail: office1@mncable.net; sjobergs@mncable.net. Web Site: http://trf.mncable.net. Also serves Enstrom Twp., Lake Twp. & Moranville Twp. ICA: MN0129.
TV Market Ranking: Outside TV Markets (Enstrom Twp., Lake Twp., Moranville Twp., WARROAD). Franchise award date: N.A. Franchise expiration date: N.A. Began: February 1, 1972.
Channel capacity: N.A. Channels available but not in use: N.A.

Basic Service
Subscribers: 1,023.
Programming (received off-air): KAWE (PBS) Bemidji; KCPM (MNT) Grand Forks; KNRR (FOX) Pembina; WDAZ-TV (ABC, CW) Devils Lake; allband FM.
Programming (via microwave): KRDK-TV (CBS, Decades, Movies!) Valley City; KVLY-TV (MeTV, NBC, This TV) Fargo.
Programming (via satellite): CNN; ESPN; TBS; various Canadian stations.
Fee: $25.00 installation; $55.92 monthly.

Expanded Basic Service 1
Subscribers: N.A.
Programming (via satellite): A&E; Animal Planet; Cartoon Network; CMT; CNBC; Comedy Central; CW PLUS; Discovery Channel; E! HD; ESPN2; EWTN Global Catholic Network; Food Network; Fox News Channel; FOX Sports North; Freeform; FX; HGTV; History; Lifetime; MSNBC; MTV; Nickelodeon; Spike TV; Syfy; The Weather Channel; TLC; TNT; Turner Classic Movies; TV Land; USA Network; WGN America.
Fee: $23.71 monthly.

Digital Basic Service
Subscribers: N.A.
Programming (via satellite): BBC America; Bloomberg Television; Bravo; CBS Sports Network; Chiller; Cloo; CMT; Cooking Channel; Daystar TV Network; Destination America; Discovery Kids Channel; Discovery Life Channel; Disney XD; DIY Network; DMX Music; ESPN Classic; ESPNews; ESPNU; EVINE Live; EWTN Global Catholic Network; Fox Business Network; FOX College Sports Central; FOX College Sports Pacific; Fox Sports 1; FXM; FYI; Golf Channel; Great American Country; GSN; Hallmark Channel; History International; HLN; HRTV; IFC; Investigation Discovery; LMN; MTV Classic; MTV Hits; MTV2; Nat Geo WILD; National Geographic Channel; NBCSN; Nick Jr.; Nicktoons; Outdoor Channel; Ovation; OWN: Oprah Winfrey Network; Oxygen; RFD-TV; Science Channel; Sprout; Sundance TV; TeenNick; Tennis Channel; The Word Network; Trinity Broadcasting Network (TBN); TVG Network; UP; VH1 Soul; WE tv.

Digital Expanded Basic Service
Subscribers: N.A.
Programming (via satellite): A&E HD; AXS TV; CNN HD; Discovery Channel HD; ESPN HD; ESPN2 HD; Food Network HD; FSN HD; HGTV HD; History HD; Outdoor Channel 2 HD; PBS HD; Syfy HD; TBS HD; TNT HD; Universal HD; USA Network HD; Versus HD.
Fee: $5.00 monthly; $5.00 converter.

Pay Service 1
Pay Units: N.A.
Programming (via satellite): Cinemax; HBO.
Fee: $11.00 monthly.

Digital Pay Service 1
Pay Units: N.A.
Programming (via satellite): Cinemax (multiplexed); Cinemax HD; HBO (multiplexed); HBO HD; Showtime (multiplexed); Starz (multiplexed); Starz Encore (multiplexed); The Movie Channel (multiplexed).
Fee: $8.00 monthly (Starz/Encore), $9.00 monthly (Cinemax or Showtime/TMC), $11.00 monthly (HBO).

Video-On-Demand: No

Internet Service
Operational: Yes. Began: December 31, 1999.
Broadband Service: Sjoberg's Cable TV.
Fee: $19.95 monthly; $10.00 modem lease; $29.00 modem purchase.

Telephone Service
None
Miles of Plant: 14.0 (coaxial); 3.0 (fiber optic).
President & General Manager: Richard J. Sjoberg. Chief Technician: Jerry Seim.
Ownership: Sjoberg's Cable TV Inc. (MSO).

WARSAW—Formerly served by North American Communications Corp. This cable system has converted to IPTV. Now served by Jaguar Communications, NEW MARKET, MN [MN5374]. ICA: MN0377.

WASECA COUNTY (portions)—Midco, PO Box 5010, Sioux Falls, SD 57117. Phone: 800-888-1300. Web Site: http://www.midcocomm.com. Also serves Alden,

Claremont, Clarks Grove, Ellendale, Elysian, Freeborn, Geneva, Glenville, Hartland, Hollandale, Le Center, Mapleton, Medford, New Richland, St. Clair & Waterville. ICA: MN0266.
TV Market Ranking: Below 100 (Claremont, Clarks Grove, Ellendale, Elysian, Freeborn, Geneva, Hartland, Hollandale, Le Center, Mapleton, New Richland, St. Clair, WASECA COUNTY (PORTIONS), Waterville, Alden, Glenville); Outside TV Markets (Medford). Franchise award date: N.A. Franchise expiration date: N.A. Began: March 1, 1985.
Channel capacity: N.A. Channels available but not in use: N.A.

Basic Service
Subscribers: 1,211.
Programming (received off-air): KAAL (ABC, This TV) Austin; KARE (NBC, WeatherNation) Minneapolis; KEYC-TV (CBS, FOX) Mankato; KMSP-TV (Bounce TV, Buzzr, FOX) Minneapolis; KSMQ-TV (PBS) Austin; KSTC-TV (Antenna TV, This TV) Minneapolis; KSTP-TV (ABC, MeTV) St. Paul; KTCA-TV (PBS) St. Paul; KTTC (CW, MeTV) Rochester; WCCO-TV (CBS, Decades) Minneapolis; WFTC (MNT, Movies!) Minneapolis; allband FM.
Programming (via satellite): Food Network; TBS; Travel Channel.
Fee: $19.95 monthly.

Expanded Basic Service 1
Subscribers: N.A.
Programming (via satellite): A&E; Animal Planet; BTN; Cartoon Network; CMT; CNBC; CNN; Comedy Central; C-SPAN; Discovery Channel; Disney Channel; ESPN; ESPN2; EVINE Live; EWTN Global Catholic Network; FOX Sports North; Freeform; FX; HGTV; History; Lifetime; MTV; Nickelodeon; Outdoor Channel; Spike TV; Syfy; The Weather Channel; TLC; TNT; Turner Classic Movies; TV Land; USA Network; VH1.
Fee: $24.95 monthly.

Digital Basic Service
Subscribers: N.A.
Programming (via satellite): BBC America; Bloomberg Television; Bravo; Cloo; Discovery Kids Channel; Disney XD; DMX Music; ESPN Classic; ESPNews; Fox Sports 1; Fuse; Golf Channel; GSN; IFC; LMN; MTV Classic; MTV2; NBCSN; Nick Jr.; OWN: Oprah Winfrey Network; Science Channel; TeenNick; Trinity Broadcasting Network (TBN); WE tv.

Digital Expanded Basic Service
Subscribers: N.A.
Programming (via satellite): CMT; Destination America; Discovery Life Channel; FXM; FYI; History International; Investigation Discovery; Starz Encore (multiplexed).
Fee: $2.95 monthly.

Digital Expanded Basic Service 2
Subscribers: N.A.
Programming (via satellite): NFL Network; Outdoor Channel.
Fee: $3.95 monthly.

Digital Pay Service 1
Pay Units: N.A.
Programming (via satellite): Cinemax (multiplexed); HBO (multiplexed); Showtime (multiplexed); Starz (multiplexed); The Movie Channel (multiplexed).
Fee: $14.95 monthly (each).
Video-On-Demand: No
Pay-Per-View
iN DEMAND (delivered digitally); Fresh (delivered digitally); Playboy TV (delivered digitally); Club Jenna.
Internet Service
Operational: No.

Telephone Service
None
President & Chief Executive Officer: Pat McAdaragh. Senior Vice President, Public Policy: Tom Simmons. Programming Director: Wynne Haakenstad.
Ownership: Midcontinent Communications (MSO).

WATSON—Formerly served by Farmers Mutual Telephone. No longer in operation. ICA: MN0379.

WELCOME—Clara City Telephone Co, 227 South Main St, PO Box 800, Clara City, MN 56222. Phone: 320-847-2211. Fax: 320-847-2736. Web Site: http://www.hcinet.net. ICA: MN0380.
TV Market Ranking: Outside TV Markets (WELCOME). Franchise award date: N.A. Franchise expiration date: N.A. Began: September 1, 1986.
Channel capacity: 35 (operating 2-way). Channels available but not in use: N.A.

Basic Service
Subscribers: 92.
Programming (received off-air): KARE (NBC, WeatherNation) Minneapolis; KEYC-TV (CBS, FOX) Mankato; KMSP-TV (Bounce TV, Buzzr, FOX) Minneapolis; KSTC-TV (Antenna TV, This TV) Minneapolis; KSTP-TV (ABC, MeTV) St. Paul; KTCA-TV (PBS) St. Paul; WCCO-TV (CBS, Decades) Minneapolis; WFTC (MNT, Movies!) Minneapolis; WUCW (CW, The Country Network) Minneapolis.
Programming (via satellite): A&E; Animal Planet; CMT; CNBC; CNN; Discovery Channel; Disney Channel; ESPN; ESPN2; FOX Sports North; Freeform; History; Lifetime; National Geographic Channel; Nickelodeon; Spike TV; TBS; The Weather Channel; TLC; TNT; Turner Classic Movies; TV Land; USA Network; VH1; WGN America.
Fee: $20.00 installation; $52.14 monthly.

Digital Basic Service
Subscribers: N.A.
Programming (via satellite): BBC America; Bloomberg Television; Bravo; CMT; Destination America; Discovery Kids Channel; Discovery Life Channel; Disney XD; ESPN Classic; ESPN2; ESPNews; EVINE Live; FOX College Sports Central; FOX College Sports Pacific; Fox Sports 1; Fuse; FXM; FYI; Golf Channel; Great American Country; GSN; HGTV; History International; IFC; Investigation Discovery; MTV Classic; MTV2; NBCSN; Nick Jr.; Nicktoons; Outdoor Channel; Ovation; OWN: Oprah Winfrey Network; Science Channel; TeenNick; Trinity Broadcasting Network (TBN); WE tv.
Fee: $7.00 monthly (per package).

Digital Pay Service 1
Pay Units: N.A.
Programming (via satellite): Cinemax (multiplexed); Flix; HBO (multiplexed); Showtime (multiplexed); Starz (multiplexed); Starz Encore (multiplexed); Sundance TV; The Movie Channel (multiplexed).
Fee: $11.00 monthly (each).
Video-On-Demand: No

Pay-Per-View
iN DEMAND (delivered digitally); Hot Choice (delivered digitally); Spice (delivered digitally); Spice 2 (delivered digitally); Playboy TV (delivered digitally).

Internet Service
Operational: No.

Telephone Service
None
Treasurer & General Manager: Bruce Hanson.
Ownership: Hanson Communications Inc. (MSO).

WELLS—Mediacom. Now served by ST. PETER (formerly Waseca), MN [MN0043]. ICA: MN0088.

WESTBROOK—Formerly served by US Cable of Coastal Texas LP. No longer in operation. ICA: MN0154.

WESTBROOK—Westbrook Public Utilities, 556 First Ave, PO Box 308, Westbrook, MN 56183-0308. Phone: 507-274-6712. Fax: 507-274-5569. Web Site: http://www.cityofwestbrookmn.com/page10.html. ICA: MN0400.
TV Market Ranking: Outside TV Markets (WESTBROOK). Franchise award date: N.A. Franchise expiration date: N.A. Began: December 31, 1992.
Channel capacity: N.A. Channels available but not in use: N.A.

Basic Service
Subscribers: 170.
Programming (received off-air): KARE (NBC, WeatherNation) Minneapolis; KELO-TV (CBS, MNT) Sioux Falls; KEYC-TV (CBS, FOX) Mankato; KMSP-TV (Bounce TV, Buzzr, FOX) Minneapolis; KSFY-TV (ABC, CW) Sioux Falls; KSTP-TV (ABC, MeTV) St. Paul; WCCO-TV (CBS, Decades) Minneapolis; WFTC (MNT, Movies!) Minneapolis.
Programming (via satellite): A&E; CMT; CNN; Discovery Channel; Disney Channel; ESPN; ESPN2; Fox Sports 1; FOX Sports Networks; Freeform; Hallmark Channel; HGTV; History; Lifetime; Nickelodeon; Spike TV; TBS; The Weather Channel; TLC; TNT; Turner Classic Movies; USA Network; WGN America.
Fee: $15.00 installation; $45.00 monthly.

Pay Service 1
Pay Units: N.A.
Programming (via satellite): HBO.
Fee: $12.50 monthly.
Internet Service
Operational: No.
Telephone Service
None
Miles of Plant: 7.0 (coaxial); None (fiber optic). Homes passed: 400.
Superintendent: Carl Conrad. Office Manager: Kelly Beaty.
Ownership: City of Westbrook.

WHEATON—Mediacom. Now served by APPLETON, MN [MN0106]. ICA: MN0104.

WILLMAR—Charter Communications, 12405 Powerscourt Dr, St. Louis, MO 63131. Phones: 636-207-5100 (Corporate office); 320-235-1535 (Local office); 507-289-8372 (Rochester administrative office). Fax: 320-235-1462. E-mail: jmelander@chartercom.com. Web Site: http://www.charter.com. Also serves Benson, Cottonwood, Green Lake Twp., Harrison Twp., Irving Twp., Kandiyohi, Kerkhoven, Marshall, Merdock, Montevideo, New London, New London Twp., Pennock, Spicer, St. Johns Twp. & Tracy. ICA: MN0018.
TV Market Ranking: Below 100 (Cottonwood, Marshall, Tracy); Outside TV Markets (Benson, Green Lake Twp., Harrison Twp., Irving Twp., Kandiyohi, Kerkhoven, Pennock, New London, New London Twp., Spicer, St. Johns Twp., WILLMAR, Montev-

ideo). Franchise award date: December 1, 1957. Franchise expiration date: N.A. Began: November 1, 1957.
Channel capacity: N.A. Channels available but not in use: N.A.

Digital Basic Service
Subscribers: 11,008.
Programming (via satellite): AXS TV; BBC America; Bloomberg Television; Boomerang; CBS Sports Network; CNN en Espanol; CNN International; Discovery Life Channel; Disney XD; DIY Network; ESPN; ESPN Classic; ESPNews; FOX College Sports Central; FOX College Sports Pacific; Fox Sports 2; Fuse; FXM; FYI; History International; IFC; LMN; MC; NFL Network; Nick 2; Nick Jr.; Nicktoons; Outdoor Channel; Sundance TV; TeenNick; TV Guide Interactive Inc.
Fee: $14.99 monthly.

Digital Expanded Basic Service
Subscribers: N.A.
Programming (received off-air): WCMN-LP St. Cloud-Sartell.
Programming (via satellite): A&E; AMC; Animal Planet; BET; Bravo; Cartoon Network; CMT; CNBC; CNN; Comedy Central; Discovery Channel; Disney Channel; E! HD; ESPN; ESPN2; Food Network; Fox News Channel; Fox Sports 1; FOX Sports North; Freeform; FX; Golf Channel; GSN; Hallmark Channel; HGTV; History; HLN; Lifetime; MoviePlex; MSNBC; MTV; MTV2; National Geographic Channel; NBCSN; Nickelodeon; Oxygen; Spike TV; Syfy; The Weather Channel; TLC; TNT; Travel Channel; truTV; Turner Classic Movies; TV Land; Univision; Univision Studios; USA Network; VH1; WE tv.
Fee: $47.99 monthly.

Digital Pay Service 1
Pay Units: N.A.
Programming (via satellite): Cinemax (multiplexed); HBO (multiplexed); HBO HD; Showtime (multiplexed); Showtime HD; Starz (multiplexed); Starz Encore (multiplexed); The Movie Channel (multiplexed).
Video-On-Demand: Yes
Pay-Per-View
iN DEMAND (delivered digitally); NHL Center Ice (delivered digitally); MLB Extra Innings (delivered digitally); Playboy TV (delivered digitally); Spice Live (delivered digitally); Spice Platinum (delivered digitally); Hot Net Plus (delivered digitally); Spice Hot (delivered digitally).

Internet Service
Operational: Yes.
Subscribers: 9,144.
Broadband Service: Charter Internet.
Fee: $29.99 monthly.
Telephone Service
Digital: Operational
Subscribers: 5,442.
Miles of Plant: 737.0 (coaxial); 532.0 (fiber optic). Homes passed: 29,927.
Vice President & General Manager: John Crowley. Technical Operations Director: Mark Abramo. Marketing Director: Bill Haarstad. Accounting Director: David Sovanski. Operations Director: Craig Stensaas. Office Manager: Jon Melander.
Ownership: Charter Communications Inc. (MSO).

WILLOW RIVER—Formerly served by New Century Communications. No longer in operation. ICA: MN0250.

WILMONT—Formerly served by K-Communications Inc. No longer in operation. ICA: MN0242.

Minnesota—Cable Systems

WINDOM—Windom Telecomm, 443 10th St, Windom, MN 56101. Phones: 507-832-8000; 507-831-6129. Fax: 507-832-8010. E-mail: support@windomnet.com. Web Site: http://www.windomnet.com. ICA: MN0066. Channel capacity: N.A. Channels available but not in use: N.A.

Basic Service
Subscribers: 1,154.
Programming (received off-air): KARE (NBC, WeatherNation) Minneapolis; KELO-TV (CBS, MNT) Sioux Falls; KEYC-TV (CBS, FOX) Mankato; KMSP-TV (Bounce TV, Buzzr, FOX) Minneapolis; KSFY-TV (ABC, CW) Sioux Falls; KSMN (PBS) Worthington; KSTC-TV (Antenna TV, This TV) Minneapolis; KSTP-TV (ABC, MeTV) St. Paul; KTTW (FOX, This TV) Sioux Falls; WCCO-TV (CBS, Decades) Minneapolis; WFTC (MNT, Movies!) Minneapolis.
Programming (via satellite): C-SPAN; C-SPAN 2; The Weather Channel.
Fee: $40.00 monthly.

Expanded Basic Service 1
Subscribers: N.A.
Programming (via satellite): A&E; AMC; Animal Planet; Bloomberg Television; Blue Highways TV; Bravo; BTN; CMT; CNN; Comedy Central; Discovery Channel; Disney Channel; ESPN; ESPN Classic; ESPN2; EWTN Global Catholic Network; Food Network; Fox News Channel; FOX Sports Networks; Freeform; FX; Hallmark Channel; HGTV; History; HLN; Lifetime; MSNBC; MTV; National Geographic Channel; Nickelodeon; RFD-TV; Spike TV; Syfy; TBS; TLC; TNT; Travel Channel; Trinity Broadcasting Network (TBN); Turner Classic Movies; TV Land; USA Network; VH1; WGN America.
Fee: $54.90 monthly.

Digital Basic Service
Subscribers: N.A.
Fee: $15.00 monthly.

Digital Expanded Basic Service
Subscribers: N.A.
Fee: $12.95 monthly.

Pay Service 1
Pay Units: N.A.
Programming (via satellite): Flix; HBO (multiplexed); Showtime (multiplexed); Starz (multiplexed); Starz Encore (multiplexed); The Movie Channel (multiplexed).
Fee: $12.95 monthly (Showtime/TMC/Flix or Starz/Encore), $14.99 monthly (HBO).

Internet Service
Operational: Yes.
Fee: $31.95-$89.95 monthly.

Telephone Service
Digital: Operational
Fee: $14.45 monthly
General Manager: Dan Olsen.
Ownership: Windom Telecommunications.

WINNEBAGO—Mediacom. Now served by ST. PETER (formerly Waseca), MN [MN0043]. ICA: MN0114.

WINONA—Charter Communications. Now served by EAU CLAIRE, WI [WI0011]. ICA: MN0014.

WINONA—Hiawatha Broadband. Formerly Winona, MN [MN0398]. This cable system has converted to IPTV, 58 Johnson St, Winona, MN 55987. Phones: 507-454-8881; 888-474-9995. Fax: 507-474-4000. E-mail: info@hbci.com. Web Site: http://www.hbci.com. Also serves Dover, Elgin, Eyota, Goodview, Hillsdale, Homer, Lake City, Lewiston, Minneiska, Minnesota City, Plainview, Red Wing, Rollingstone, St. Charles, Stockton, Utica, Wabasha & Wilson (town), MN; Buffalo City & Cochrane, WI. ICA: MN5161.
TV Market Ranking: Below 100 (St. Charles). Channel capacity: N.A. Channels available but not in use: N.A.

Basic
Subscribers: 6,242.
Fee: $19.95 monthly.

Internet Service
Operational: Yes.

Telephone Service
Digital: Operational
Ownership: Hiawatha Broadband Communications Inc.

WINONA—Hiawatha Broadband. This cable system has converted to IPTV. Now served by WINONA, MN [MN5161]. ICA: MN0398.

WOOD LAKE—Clara City Telephone Co, 227 South Main St, PO Box 800, Clara City, MN 56222. Phones: 888-283-7667; 320-847-2211. Fax: 320-847-2736. E-mail: bruce@hcinet.net. Web Site: http://www.hcinet.net. ICA: MN0381.
TV Market Ranking: Below 100 (WOOD LAKE). Franchise award date: N.A. Franchise expiration date: N.A. Began: October 1, 1988.
Channel capacity: N.A. Channels available but not in use: N.A.

Basic Service
Subscribers: 29.
Programming (received off-air): KEYC-TV (CBS, FOX) Mankato; KSFY-TV (ABC, CW) Sioux Falls; KWCM-TV (PBS) Appleton.
Programming (via satellite): A&E; AMC; CMT; CNN; Discovery Channel; ESPN; ESPN2; FOX Sports Networks; Freeform; History; Lifetime; Nickelodeon; Spike TV; The Weather Channel; TLC; TNT; TV Land; USA Network.
Programming (via translator): KARE (NBC, WeatherNation) Minneapolis; KMSP-TV (Bounce TV, Buzzr, FOX) Minneapolis; KSTP-TV (ABC, MeTV) St. Paul; KTCA-TV (PBS) St. Paul; WCCO-TV (CBS, Decades) Minneapolis; WFTC (MNT, Movies!) Minneapolis.
Fee: $20.00 installation; $48.50 monthly; $2.00 converter.

Pay Service 1
Pay Units: N.A.
Programming (via satellite): The Movie Channel.
Fee: $10.00 monthly.

Internet Service
Operational: No.

Telephone Service
None
Miles of Plant: 4.0 (coaxial); None (fiber optic). Homes passed: 165.
Treasurer & General Manager: Bruce Hanson.
Ownership: Hanson Communications Inc. (MSO).

WOOD LAKE—Midco, PO Box 5010, Sioux Falls, SD 57117. Phone: 800-888-1300. Web Site: http://www.midcocomm.com. Also serves Clarkfield, Ghent, Lynd, Milroy, Minneota, Morgan, Porter, Renville, Russell, Sacred Heart & Taunton. ICA: MN0336.
TV Market Ranking: Below 100 (Milroy, Morgan, Renville, Sacred Heart). Outside TV Markets (Clarkfield, Ghent, Lynd, Porter, Russell, Taunton, Minneota, WOOD LAKE). Franchise award date: N.A. Franchise expiration date: N.A. Began: February 1, 1973.
Channel capacity: N.A. Channels available but not in use: N.A.

Basic Service
Subscribers: N.A.
Programming (received off-air): KEYC-TV (CBS, FOX) Mankato; KSFY-TV (ABC, CW) Sioux Falls; KWCM-TV (PBS) Appleton; all-band FM.
Programming (via satellite): A&E; Animal Planet; CMT; CNBC; CNN; C-SPAN; Discovery Channel; ESPN; ESPN2; EVINE Live; EWTN Global Catholic Network; Food Network; FOX Sports Networks; Freeform; FX; HGTV; History; HLN; Lifetime; MSNBC; MTV; Nickelodeon; Outdoor Channel; Spike TV; TBS; The Weather Channel; TLC; TNT; Trinity Broadcasting Network (TBN); Turner Classic Movies; TV Land; USA Network; VH1; WGN America.
Programming (via translator): KARE (NBC, WeatherNation) Minneapolis; KMSP-TV (Bounce TV, Buzzr, FOX) Minneapolis; KSTC-TV (Antenna TV, This TV) Minneapolis; KSTP-TV (ABC, MeTV) St. Paul; KTCA-TV (PBS) St. Paul; WCCO-TV (CBS, Decades) Minneapolis; WFTC (MNT, Movies!) Minneapolis.
Fee: $56.95 monthly.

Digital Basic Service
Subscribers: 599. Commercial subscribers: 180.
Programming (via satellite): BBC America; Bloomberg Television; Bravo; Cloo; Discovery Digital Networks; Disney XD; DMX Music; ESPN Classic; ESPNews; Fox Sports 1; Fuse; Golf Channel; GSN; IFC; LMN; NBCSN; Nick Jr.; Syfy; TeenNick; WE tv.
Fee: $60.95 monthly.

Digital Expanded Basic Service
Subscribers: N.A.
Programming (via satellite): CMT; Discovery Life Channel; FXM; FYI; History; Starz Encore (multiplexed).
Fee: $2.95 monthly.

Pay Service 1
Pay Units: N.A.
Programming (via satellite): Cinemax; HBO.
Fee: $12.95 monthly (each).

Digital Pay Service 1
Pay Units: N.A.
Programming (via satellite): Cinemax (multiplexed); HBO (multiplexed); Showtime (multiplexed); Starz (multiplexed); The Movie Channel (multiplexed).
Fee: $6.95 monthly (Starz), $14.95 monthly (Cinemax, HBO, Showtime or TMC).

Video-On-Demand: No

Pay-Per-View
Fresh (delivered digitally); Playboy TV (delivered digitally); iN DEMAND (delivered digitally).

Internet Service
Operational: No.

Telephone Service
None
President & Chairman of the Board: Pat McAdaragh. Senior Vice President, Public Policy: Tom Simmons. Programming Director: Wynne Haakenstad.
Ownership: Midcontinent Communications (MSO).

WORTHINGTON—Mediacom, 1504 2nd St SE, PO Box 110, Waseca, MN 56093. Phones: 845-695-2762; 507-835-2356. Fax: 507-835-4567. Web Site: http://www.mediacomcable.com. Also serves Luverne. ICA: MN0041.
TV Market Ranking: 85 (Luverne); Outside TV Markets (WORTHINGTON). Franchise award date: January 26, 1981. Franchise expiration date: N.A. Began: December 1, 1981.
Channel capacity: N.A. Channels available but not in use: N.A.

Basic Service
Subscribers: 1,250.
Programming (received off-air): KDLT-TV (Antenna TV, NBC) Sioux Falls; KELO-TV (CBS, MNT) Sioux Falls; KESD-TV (PBS) Brookings; KSFY-TV (ABC, CW) Sioux Falls; KSMN (PBS) Worthington; KTTW (FOX, This TV) Sioux Falls; KWSD (MeTV, Retro TV) Sioux Falls; allband FM.
Programming (via microwave): KARE (NBC, WeatherNation) Minneapolis; KTCA-TV (PBS) St. Paul; WCCO-TV (CBS, Decades) Minneapolis.
Programming (via satellite): C-SPAN; C-SPAN 2; Pop; The Weather Channel; WGN America.
Fee: $20.00 installation; $42.00 monthly.

Expanded Basic Service 1
Subscribers: N.A.
Programming (via satellite): A&E; AMC; Animal Planet; Bravo; Cartoon Network; CMT; CNBC; CNN; Comedy Central; Discovery Channel; Disney Channel; E! HD; ESPN; ESPN2; EWTN Global Catholic Network; Fox News Channel; Fox Sports 1; FOX Sports North; Freeform; FX; FXM; Hallmark Channel; HGTV; History; HLN; INSP; Lifetime; MSNBC; MTV; Nickelodeon; RFD-TV; Spike TV; Syfy; TBS; TLC; TNT; Travel Channel; Trinity Broadcasting Network (TBN); truTV; Turner Classic Movies; TV Land; Univision; Univision Studios; USA Network; VH1; WE tv.
Fee: $24.68 monthly.

Digital Basic Service
Subscribers: N.A.
Programming (via satellite): 52MX; AXS TV; BBC America; Bloomberg Television; CBS Sports Network; CCTV-Documentary; Cinelatino; Cloo; CNN en Espanol; CNN HD; Destination America; Discovery Kids Channel; Discovery Life Channel; ESPN Deportes; ESPN HD; ESPN2 HD; ESPNews; ESPNU; FOX College Sports Central; FOX College Sports Pacific; Fox Deportes; Fox Sports 2; FSN HD; Fuse; FYI; Golf Channel; GolTV; GSN; HD Theater; History en Espanol; History International; IFC; Investigation Discovery; ION Television; LMN; MC; MTV Classic; MTV Hits; MTV2; Nat Geo WILD; National Geographic Channel; Nick Jr.; Nicktoons; Outdoor Channel; OWN; Oprah Winfrey Network; Qubo; Reelz; Science Channel; TBS HD; TeenNick; Tennis Channel; TNT HD; Tr3s; TVG Network; Universal HD; ViendoMovies.

Digital Pay Service 1
Pay Units: N.A.
Programming (via satellite): Cinemax (multiplexed); Flix; HBO (multiplexed); HBO HD; Showtime (multiplexed); Showtime HD; Starz (multiplexed); Starz Encore (multiplexed); Starz HD; Sundance TV; The Movie Channel (multiplexed); The Movie Channel HD.
Fee: $12.50 installation; $10.00 monthly (each).

Video-On-Demand: No

Pay-Per-View
iN DEMAND (delivered digitally); Playboy TV (delivered digitally); Spice: Xcess (delivered digitally); Fresh (delivered digitally); SexSee (delivered digitally).

Internet Service
Operational: Yes.
Broadband Service: Mediacom High Speed Internet.
Fee: $40.00 monthly.

Cable Systems—Minnesota

Telephone Service
Digital: Operational
Miles of Plant: 82.0 (coaxial); None (fiber optic). Homes passed: 6,792.
Vice President: Bill Jensen. Vice President, Financial Reporting: Kenneth J. Kohrs. Engineering Manager: Kraig Kaiser. Marketing & Sales Director: Lori Huberty.
Ownership: Mediacom LLC (MSO).

WRENSHALL—Formerly served by New Century Communications. No longer in operation. ICA: MN0261.

WYKOFF—Formerly served by North American Communications Corp. Now served by Arvig, GRAND MEADOW, MN [MN0168]. ICA: MN0383.

Communications Daily
Warren Communications News

Get the industry standard FREE —
For a no-obligation trial call 800-771-9202 or visit www.warren-news.com

MISSISSIPPI

Total Systems: 66	Communities with Applications: 0
Total Communities Served: 338	Number of Basic Subscribers: 380,682
Franchises Not Yet Operating: 0	Number of Expanded Basic Subscribers: 1,522
Applications Pending: 0	Number of Pay Units: 20

Top 100 Markets Represented: Memphis, TN (26); New Orleans, LA (31); Mobile, AL-Pensacola, FL (59); Jackson (77).

For a list of cable communities in this section, see the Cable Community Index located in the back of Cable Volume 2.
For explanation of terms used in cable system listings, see p. D-11.

ABERDEEN TWP.—MetroCast Mississippi. Now served by PONTOTOC, MS [MS0045]. ICA: MS0035.

ACKERMAN—Formerly served by Delta Telephone (Telapex). Now served by Franklin Telephone, MEADVILLE, MS [MS5012]. ICA: MS5017.

AMORY—MetroCast Mississippi. Now served by PONTOTOC, MS [MS0045]. ICA: MS0127.

ANGUILLA—NewWave Communications, One Montgomery Plaza, 4th Floor, Sikeston, MO 63801. Phones: 573-472-9500; 888-863-9928. Fax: 573-472-9518. E-mail: info@newwave.com. Web Site: http://www.newwavecom.com. ICA: MS0128.
TV Market Ranking: Below 100 (ANGUILLA). Channel capacity: N.A. Channels available but not in use: N.A.
Basic Service
Subscribers: 39.
Programming (received off-air): WABG-TV (ABC, FOX) Greenwood; WDBD (FOX, Grit) Jackson; WJTV (Antenna TV, CBS) Jackson; WLBT (Bounce TV, NBC, This TV) Jackson; WXVT (CBS) Greenville.
Programming (via satellite): BET; Cartoon Network; CNN; Discovery Channel; ESPN; EVINE Live; Freeform; HLN; INSP; Nickelodeon; Spike TV; TBS; The Weather Channel; TNT; Turner Classic Movies; TV Land; USA Network; WGN America.
Fee: $35.00 installation; $42.99 monthly.
Pay Service 1
Pay Units: N.A.
Programming (via satellite): Cinemax; HBO.
Fee: $14.95 installation; $13.95 monthly (each).
Video-On-Demand: No
Internet Service
Operational: No.
Telephone Service
None
Miles of Plant: 9.0 (coaxial); None (fiber optic).
General Manager: Staci Gowan.
Ownership: NewWave Communications LLC (MSO).

ARCOLA—NewWave Communications, One Montgomery Plaza, 4th Floor, Sikeston, MO 63801. Phones: 573-472-9500; 888-863-9928. Fax: 573-472-9518. E-mail: info@newwave.com. Web Site: http://www.newwavecom.com. ICA: MS0129.
TV Market Ranking: Below 100 (ARCOLA). Channel capacity: N.A. Channels available but not in use: N.A.
Basic Service
Subscribers: 24.
Programming (received off-air): WABG-TV (ABC, FOX) Greenwood; WDBD (FOX, Grit) Jackson; WLBT (Bounce TV, NBC, This TV) Jackson; WMAO-TV (PBS) Greenwood; WXVT (CBS) Greenville.
Programming (via satellite): A&E; BET; Cartoon Network; CNN; Discovery Channel; ESPN; EVINE Live; Freeform; Spike TV; Syfy; TBS; TNT; Trinity Broadcasting Network (TBN); Turner Classic Movies; USA Network; WGN America.
Fee: $35.00 installation; $44.30 monthly.
Pay Service 1
Pay Units: N.A.
Programming (via satellite): Cinemax; HBO.
Fee: $14.95 installation; $10.95 monthly (Cinemax), $13.95 monthly (HBO).
Video-On-Demand: No
Internet Service
Operational: No.
Telephone Service
None
Miles of Plant: 5.0 (coaxial); None (fiber optic). Homes passed: 200.
General Manager: Staci Gowan.
Ownership: NewWave Communications LLC (MSO).

ARTESIA—Formerly served by Cable TV Inc. No longer in operation. ICA: MS0119.

ARTESIA—Franklin Telephone (Telapex). Now served by MEADVILLE, MS [MS5012]. ICA: MS5018.

ASHLAND—MetroCast Mississippi. Now served by PONTOTOC, MS [MS0045]. ICA: MS0078.

BALDWYN—MetroCast Mississippi. Now served by PONTOTOC, MS [MS0045]. ICA: MS0037.

BASSFIELD—Alliance Communications, PO Box 9090, Tyler, TX 75711. Phones: 903-561-4411; 501-679-6619 (Greenbrier, AR office); 800-842-8160. Web Site: http://www.alliancecable.net. ICA: MS0130.
TV Market Ranking: Below 100 (BASSFIELD). Franchise award date: N.A. Franchise expiration date: N.A. Began: April 1, 1982.
Channel capacity: N.A. Channels available but not in use: N.A.
Basic Service
Subscribers: 21.
Programming (received off-air): WDAM-TV (ABC, Bounce TV, NBC, This TV) Laurel; WHLT (CBS) Hattiesburg; WLOX (ABC, Bounce TV, CBS) Biloxi; WMAH-TV (PBS) Biloxi; WXXV-TV (FOX, MNT, NBC) Gulfport.
Programming (via satellite): A&E; AMC; BET; Cartoon Network; CNN; Discovery Channel; Disney Channel; E! HD; ESPN; ESPN2; Fox News Channel; Fox Sports 1; Freeform; Great American Country; HLN; Lifetime; Outdoor Channel; QVC; TBS; The Weather Channel; TLC; TNT; Trinity Broadcasting Network (TBN); USA Network; WGN America.
Fee: $45.00 installation; $22.45 monthly.
Pay Service 1
Pay Units: N.A.
Programming (via satellite): Showtime; The Movie Channel.
Fee: $25.00 installation; $11.95 monthly (each).
Internet Service
Operational: No.
Telephone Service
None
Miles of Plant: 11.0 (coaxial); None (fiber optic). Homes passed: 238.
Chief Financial Officer: David Starrett. Vice President & General Manager: John Brinker. Vice President, Programming: Julie Newman.
Ownership: Buford Media Group LLC (MSO).

BAY SPRINGS—TEC (formerly Bay Springs Telephone) This cable system has converted to IPTV. See BAY SPRINGS, MS [MS5034]. ICA: MS0227.

BAY SPRINGS—TEC (formerly Video Inc.) This cable system has converted to IPTV. See BAY SPRINGS, MS [MS5034]. ICA: MS0063.

BAY SPRINGS—TEC. This cable system has converted to IPTV, 236 East Capitol St, Jackson, MS 39201. Phones: 800-832-2515; 601-353-9118. Fax: 601-355-9746. E-mail: request@tec.com. Web Site: http://tec.com. Also serves Laurel, Louin, Soso & Stringer. ICA: MS5034.
TV Market Ranking: Below 100 (BAY SPRINGS, Laurel, Soso). Franchise award date: N.A. Franchise expiration date: N.A. Began: March 1, 1982.
Channel capacity: N.A. Channels available but not in use: N.A.
Basic
Subscribers: 1,734.
Programming (received off-air): WDAM-TV (ABC, Bounce TV, NBC, This TV) Laurel; WHLT (CBS) Hattiesburg; WJTV (Antenna TV, CBS) Jackson; WTOK-TV (ABC, CW, FOX, MNT) Meridian; WXXV-TV (FOX, MNT, NBC) Gulfport.
Programming (via satellite): QVC; The Weather Channel.
Fee: $25.00 installation; $14.95 monthly.
Expanded Basic
Subscribers: 1,522.
Programming (via satellite): A&E; AMC; Animal Planet; Bloomberg Television; Boomerang; Bravo; Cartoon Network; Cloo; CMT; CNN; Discovery Channel; Discovery Kids Channel; Disney Channel; DMX Music; ESPN; ESPN2; ESPNews; Fox News Channel; Fox Sports 1; Freeform; FXM; FYI; Golf Channel; GSN; Hallmark Channel; HGTV; History; History International; Lifetime; LMN; MSNBC; National Geographic Channel; Nickelodeon; Nicktoons; Outdoor Channel; Spike TV; Syfy; TBS; TLC; TNT; Travel Channel; Trinity Broadcasting Network (TBN); Turner Classic Movies; USA Network; WE tv; WGN America.
Fee: $24.00 monthly.
Cinemax
Subscribers: N.A.
Programming (via satellite): Cinemax.
HBO
Subscribers: N.A.
Programming (via satellite): HBO.
TMC
Subscribers: N.A.
Programming (via satellite): The Movie Channel.
Video-On-Demand: No
Pay-Per-View
iN DEMAND (delivered digitally); ESPN Now (delivered digitally).
Internet Service
Operational: Yes.
Fee: $39.95-$69.95 monthly.
Telephone Service
Analog: Operational
Secretary-Treasurer: Wayne Skelton.
Ownership: Telephone Electronics Corp. (TEC).

BAY ST. LOUIS—Mediacom. Now served by WAVELAND, MS [MS0022]. ICA: MS0152.

BEAUMONT—Mediacom, 760 Middle St, PO Box 1009, Fairhope, AL 36532. Phones: 251-928-0374; 850-934-7700 (Gulf Breeze regional office). Fax: 251-928-3804. Web Site: http://www.mediacomcable.com. ICA: MS0093.
TV Market Ranking: Below 100 (BEAUMONT). Franchise award date: October 1, 1983. Franchise expiration date: N.A. Began: February 1, 1986.
Channel capacity: N.A. Channels available but not in use: N.A.
Basic Service
Subscribers: 50.
Programming (received off-air): WDAM-TV (ABC, Bounce TV, NBC, This TV) Laurel; WHLT (CBS) Hattiesburg; WKRG-TV (CBS, MeTV) Mobile; WLOX (ABC, Bounce TV, CBS) Biloxi; WMAH-TV (PBS) Biloxi; WXXV-TV (FOX, MNT, NBC) Gulfport.
Programming (via satellite): A&E; AMC; Animal Planet; BET; Cartoon Network; CMT; CNBC; CNN; Comedy Central; C-SPAN; CW PLUS; Discovery Channel; Discovery Life Channel; Disney Channel; E! HD; ESPN; ESPN2; Fox News Channel; Fox Sports 1; FOX Sports South/SportSouth; FX; Hallmark Channel; HGTV; History; HLN; INSP; MSNBC; MTV; Nickelodeon; QVC; Spike TV; Syfy; TBS; The Weather Channel; TLC; TNT; Turner Classic Movies; TV Land; USA Network.
Fee: $29.50 installation; $40.00 monthly.

D-426   TV & Cable Factbook No. 85

Cable Systems—Mississippi

Pay Service 1
Pay Units: N.A.
Programming (via satellite): Cinemax; Flix; HBO (multiplexed); Showtime; The Movie Channel.
Fee: $2.95 monthly (Flix), $10.45 monthly (Cinemax, Showtime or TMC), $12.45 monthly (HBO).
Video-On-Demand: No
Internet Service
Operational: No.
Telephone Service
None
Miles of Plant: 10.0 (coaxial); None (fiber optic). Homes passed: 433.
Vice President: David Servies. Operations Director: Gene Wuchner. Technical Operations Manager: Mike Sneary. Sales & Marketing Manager: Joey Nagem.
Ownership: Mediacom LLC (MSO).

BELMONT—Formerly served by Almega Cable. No longer in operation. ICA: MS0131.

BELMONT—MetroCast Mississippi. Now served by PONTOTOC, MS [MS0045]. ICA: MS0224.

BELZONI—Cable TV of Belzoni Inc, 102 South Hayden St, Belzoni, MS 39038-3914. Phone: 662-247-1834. Fax: 662-247-3237. E-mail: office@belzonicable.com; stephen@belzonicable.com. Web Site: http://www.belzonicable.com. ICA: MS0073.
TV Market Ranking: Below 100 (BELZONI). Franchise award date: N.A. Franchise expiration date: N.A. Began: December 1, 1970.
Channel capacity: N.A. Channels available but not in use: N.A.
Basic Service
Subscribers: 800.
Programming (received off-air): WABG-TV (ABC, FOX) Greenwood; WAPT (ABC) Jackson; WJTV (Antenna TV, CBS) Jackson; WLBT (Bounce TV, NBC, This TV) Jackson; WXVT (CBS) Greenville.
Programming (via satellite): A&E; Animal Planet; BET; Cartoon Network; CMT; CNN; Comedy Central; C-SPAN; Discovery Channel; Disney Channel; E! HD; ESPN; ESPN2; ESPNews; Food Network; Fox News Channel; Fox Sports 1; FOX Sports South/SportSouth; FX; Hallmark Channel; HGTV; History; HLN; ION Television; Lifetime; MTV; National Geographic Channel; Nickelodeon; Outdoor Channel; QVC; Syfy; TBS; The Movie Channel; The Weather Channel; TLC; TNT; Trinity Broadcasting Network (TBN); Turner Classic Movies; TV Land; USA Network; VH1; WGN America.
Fee: $38.00 installation; $48.50 monthly.
Pay Service 1
Pay Units: N.A.
Programming (via satellite): Cinemax; HBO; Showtime.
Fee: $11.77 monthly (each).
Internet Service
Operational: Yes. Began: January 1, 2002.
Broadband Service: Worldcom.
Fee: $32.00 installation; $32.05 monthly.
Telephone Service
None
Miles of Plant: 31.0 (coaxial); None (fiber optic). Homes passed: 826.
General Manager: Del Lott. Technician: Les Vance.
Ownership: Del Lott.

BENOIT—Formerly served by J & L Cable. No longer in operation. ICA: MS0101.

BENTONIA—Formerly served by Comcast Cable. No longer in operation. ICA: MS0132.

BILOXI—Cable One. Now served by GULFPORT, MS [MS0008]. ICA: MS0002.

BILOXI—Formerly served by Prime Time Communications. No longer in operation. ICA: MS5010.

BOONEVILLE—MetroCast Mississippi. Now served by PONTOTOC, MS [MS0045]. ICA: MS0133.

BROOKHAVEN—Cable One, 230 5th Ave, McComb, MS 39648. Phones: 601-835-2752; 601-833-9199; 601-833-7991. Web Site: http://www.cableone.net. Also serves Lincoln County (portions), Magnolia, McComb, New Sight, Pike County, Summit & Wesson. ICA: MS0024.
TV Market Ranking: Outside TV Markets (BROOKHAVEN, Lincoln County (portions), Magnolia, McComb, New Sight, Pike County, Summit, Wesson). Franchise award date: April 1, 1964. Franchise expiration date: N.A. Began: April 1, 1964.
Channel capacity: N.A. Channels available but not in use: N.A.
Basic Service
Subscribers: 4,266.
Programming (received off-air): WAPT (ABC) Jackson; WBRZ-TV (ABC) Baton Rouge; WDAM-TV (ABC, Bounce TV, NBC, This TV) Laurel; WDBD (FOX, Grit) Jackson; WJTV (Antenna TV, CBS) Jackson; WLBT (Bounce TV, NBC, This TV) Jackson; WLOO (MNT) Vicksburg; WMAU-TV (PBS) Bude; WWL-TV (CBS) New Orleans; allband FM.
Programming (via satellite): A&E; AMC; Animal Planet; BET; Bravo; Cartoon Network; CMT; CNBC; CNN; Comedy Central; C-SPAN; C-SPAN 2; Discovery Channel; Disney Channel; ESPN; ESPN2; Food Network; Fox News Channel; Freeform; FX; HGTV; History; HLN; Lifetime; MSNBC; MTV; Nickelodeon; Pop; QVC; Spike TV; Syfy; TBS; The Weather Channel; TLC; TNT; Travel Channel; Trinity Broadcasting Network (TBN); Turner Classic Movies; TV Land; USA Network; VH1; WGN America.
Fee: $90.00 installation; $29.00 monthly.
Digital Basic Service
Subscribers: N.A.
Programming (via satellite): 3ABN; Boomerang; BYUtv; Discovery Digital Networks; Disney XD; DMX Music; ESPN Classic; ESPNews; FamilyNet; FOX College Sports Central; FOX College Sports Pacific; Fox Sports 1; Fox Sports 2; FXM; FYI; Golf Channel; Great American Country (multiplexed); Hallmark Channel; History International; HITS (Headend In The Sky); INSP; National Geographic Channel; Outdoor Channel; TNT HD; Trinity Broadcasting Network (TBN); truTV; TVG Network; Universal HD.
Digital Pay Service 1
Pay Units: N.A.
Programming (via satellite): Cinemax (multiplexed); Flix; HBO (multiplexed); Showtime (multiplexed); Showtime HD; Starz; Starz Encore (multiplexed); Sundance TV; The Movie Channel (multiplexed); The Movie Channel HD.
Fee: $15.00 monthly (each package).
Video-On-Demand: No
Pay-Per-View
iN DEMAND (delivered digitally); Pleasure (delivered digitally); SexSee (delivered digitally); Juicy (delivered digitally); VaVoom (delivered digitally).

Internet Service
Operational: Yes.
Subscribers: 4,466.
Broadband Service: CableONE.net.
Fee: $75.00 installation; $43.00 monthly.
Telephone Service
Digital: Operational
Subscribers: 2,150.
Fee: $39.95 monthly
Miles of Plant: 712.0 (coaxial), 482.0 (fiber optic). Homes passed: 19,738.
Vice President: Patrick A. Dolohanty. General Manager: Bobby McCool. Technical Operations Manager: John Hilbert. Marketing Director: Jullia Ivey.
Ownership: Cable ONE Inc. (MSO).

BRUCE—MetroCast Mississippi. Now served by PONTOTOC, MS [MS0045]. ICA: MS0075.

BURNSVILLE—Formerly served by Almega Cable. No longer in operation. ICA: MS0099.

BURNSVILLE—Formerly served by MetroCast Mississippi. Now served by MaxxSouth Broadband, PONTOTOC, MS [MS0045]. ICA: MS0255.

CALHOUN CITY—MetroCast Mississippi. Now served by PONTOTOC, MS [MS0045]. ICA: MS0025.

CANTON—Comcast Cable. Now served by JACKSON, MS [MS0001]. ICA: MS0026.

CARRIERRE—Charter Communications. Now served by SLIDELL, LA [LA0182]. ICA: MS0135.

CARTHAGE—MaxxSouth Broadband, 911 Hwy 12 West, Ste 202-B, Starkville, MS 39759. Phone: 800-457-5351. Web Site: http://www.maxxsouth.com. Also serves Leake County (portions). ICA: MS0054.
TV Market Ranking: Outside TV Markets (CARTHAGE). Franchise award date: March 1, 1978. Franchise expiration date: N.A. Began: November 1, 1979.
Channel capacity: N.A. Channels available but not in use: N.A.
Basic Service
Subscribers: 437.
Programming (received off-air): WAPT (ABC) Jackson; WDBD (FOX, Grit) Jackson; WJTV (Antenna TV, CBS) Jackson; WLBT (Bounce TV, NBC, This TV) Jackson; WMPN-TV (PBS) Jackson; WTVA (ABC, NBC) Tupelo.
Programming (via satellite): C-SPAN; Hallmark Channel; QVC; Trinity Broadcasting Network (TBN); WGN America.
Fee: $55.00 installation; $35.95 monthly.
Expanded Basic Service 1
Subscribers: N.A.
Programming (via satellite): A&E; Animal Planet; BET; Cartoon Network; CNBC; CNN; Discovery Channel; ESPN; ESPN2; Food Network; Fox News Channel; FX; FXM; Great American Country; HGTV; History; HLN; Lifetime; National Geographic Channel; Nickelodeon; Outdoor Channel; Spike TV; Syfy; TBS; The Weather Channel; TLC; TNT; Travel Channel; Turner Classic Movies; TV Land; USA Network; VH1.
Fee: $31.00 monthly.
Digital Basic Service
Subscribers: N.A.
Programming (via satellite): BBC America; Destination America; Discovery Kids Channel; Discovery Life Channel; DMX Music;

ESPNews; Fox Sports 1; Golf Channel; Investigation Discovery; LMN; OWN: Oprah Winfrey Network; Science Channel; WE tv.
Pay Service 1
Pay Units: N.A.
Programming (via satellite): Cinemax; HBO.
Digital Pay Service 1
Pay Units: N.A.
Programming (via satellite): Cinemax (multiplexed); Flix; HBO (multiplexed); Showtime (multiplexed); Starz (multiplexed); Starz Encore (multiplexed); The Movie Channel (multiplexed).
Fee: $10.00 monthly (each).
Video-On-Demand: No
Pay-Per-View
iN DEMAND (delivered digitally); Hot Choice (delivered digitally); Playboy TV (delivered digitally); Fresh (delivered digitally).
Internet Service
Operational: Yes.
Fee: $79.99 installation; $35.99 monthly.
Telephone Service
None
Miles of Plant: 26.0 (coaxial); None (fiber optic). Homes passed: 1,510.
General Manager: Rick Ferrall.
Ownership: MaxxSouth Broadband (MSO).

CARY—Formerly served by J & L Cable. No longer in operation. ICA: MS0110.

CENTREVILLE—Bailey Cable TV Inc, 807 Church St, Port Gibson, MS 39150-2413. Phone: 601-437-8300. Fax: 601-437-6860. E-mail: cs@baileycable.net. Web Site: http://www.baileycable.net. ICA: MS0048.
TV Market Ranking: Outside TV Markets (CENTREVILLE). Franchise award date: N.A. Franchise expiration date: N.A. Began: February 1, 1982.
Channel capacity: N.A. Channels available but not in use: N.A.
Basic Service
Subscribers: 196.
Programming (received off-air): WAFB (Bounce TV, CBS) Baton Rouge; WBRZ-TV (ABC) Baton Rouge; WGMB-TV (FOX) Baton Rouge; WJTV (Antenna TV, CBS) Jackson; WLBT (Bounce TV, NBC, This TV) Jackson; WMAU-TV (PBS) Bude; WVLA-TV (NBC, This TV) Baton Rouge.
Programming (via satellite): A&E; AMC; Animal Planet; BET; Cartoon Network; CMT; CNN; Comedy Central; C-SPAN; Discovery Channel; ESPN; ESPN Classic; ESPN2; Food Network; Fox News Channel; Fox Sports 1; FOX Sports Networks; FOX Sports South/SportSouth; Freeform; Great American Country; Hallmark Channel; Hallmark Movies & Mysteries; HGTV; History; HLN; INSP; Lifetime; LMN; MSNBC; Nickelodeon; Outdoor Channel; QVC; RFD-TV; Spike TV; Syfy; TBS; The Weather Channel; TLC; TNT; Travel Channel; Trinity Broadcasting Network (TBN); Turner Classic Movies; TV Land; USA Network; VH1; WGN America.
Fee: $15.00 installation; $42.95 monthly.
Pay Service 1
Pay Units: N.A.
Programming (via satellite): Cinemax; HBO (multiplexed).
Fee: $19.95 monthly.
Video-On-Demand: No
Internet Service
Operational: Yes.
Broadband Service: In-house.
Fee: $29.99 installation; $29.99 monthly; $6.95 modem lease; $69.95 modem purchase.

Mississippi—Cable Systems

Telephone Service
None
Miles of Plant: 43.0 (coaxial); None (fiber optic). Homes passed: 1,805.
President: David A. Bailey.
Ownership: Bailey Cable TV Inc. (MSO).

CHARLESTON—Cable One. Now served by GRENADA, MS [MS0021]. ICA: MS0053.

CHUNKY—Formerly served by Zoom Media. No longer in operation. ICA: MS0136.

CLARKSDALE—Cable One, 221 South Sharpe Ave, PO Box 1200, Cleveland, MS 38732. Phone: 662-627-4747. E-mail: sstevenson@cableone.net. Web Site: http://www.cableone.net. Also serves Batesville, Coahoma County, Courtland, Duncan, Lambert, Lyon, Marks, Panola County (portions), Pope & Quitman County (portions). ICA: MS0017.
TV Market Ranking: Outside TV Markets (Batesville, CLARKSDALE, Coahoma County, Courtland, Duncan, Lambert, Lyon, Marks, Panola County (portions), Pope, Quitman County (portions)). Franchise award date: May 7, 1957. Franchise expiration date: N.A. Began: April 1, 1958. Channel capacity: N.A. Channels available but not in use: N.A.
Basic Service
Subscribers: 3,283.
Programming (received off-air): KATV (ABC, Retro TV) Little Rock; WABG-TV (ABC, FOX) Greenwood; WATN-TV (ABC) Memphis; WHBQ-TV (Decades, FOX, Movies!) Memphis; WKNO (PBS) Memphis; WLMT (CW, MeTV, MNT) Memphis; WMC-TV (Bounce TV, NBC, This TV) Memphis; WMPN-TV (PBS) Jackson; WREG-TV (Antenna TV, CBS) Memphis; WTVA (ABC, NBC) Tupelo; WXVT (CBS) Greenville; 6 FMs.
Programming (via satellite): A&E; AMC; Animal Planet; BET; Cartoon Network; CMT; CNBC; CNN; Comedy Central; C-SPAN; Discovery Channel; Disney Channel; ESPN; ESPN2; Food Network; Fox News Channel; Freeform; FX; HGTV; History; HLN; INSP; Lifetime; MSNBC; MTV; Nickelodeon; Pop; QVC; Spike TV; Syfy; The Weather Channel; TLC; TNT; Turner Classic Movies; TV Land; USA Network; VH1; WGN America.
Fee: $90.00 installation; $29.00 monthly.
Digital Basic Service
Subscribers: N.A.
Programming (via satellite): 3ABN; Boomerang; BYUtv; Discovery Digital Networks; Disney XD; ESPN Classic; ESPN HD; FamilyNet; FOX College Sports Central; FOX College Sports Pacific; Fox Sports 1; Fox Sports 2; FXM; FYI; Golf Channel; Great American Country; GSN; Hallmark Channel; History International; HITS (Headend In The Sky); INSP; MC; National Geographic Channel; Outdoor Channel; TNT HD; Trinity Broadcasting Network (TBN); truTV; TVG Network; Universal HD; WE tv.
Digital Pay Service 1
Pay Units: N.A.
Programming (via satellite): Cinemax (multiplexed); HBO (multiplexed); HBO HD; Showtime; Showtime HD; Starz In Black; Sundance TV; The Movie Channel (multiplexed); The Movie Channel HD.
Fee: $15.00 monthly (each).
Video-On-Demand: No
Pay-Per-View
Hot Choice; iN DEMAND; Playboy TV; iN DEMAND (delivered digitally); Adult PPV (delivered digitally); Sports PPV (delivered digitally).

Internet Service
Operational: Yes. Began: January 1, 2001.
Subscribers: 3,431.
Broadband Service: CableONE.net.
Fee: $75.00 installation; $43.00 monthly; $5.00 modem lease.
Telephone Service
Digital: Operational
Subscribers: 1,607.
Fee: $39.95 monthly
Miles of Plant: 620.0 (coaxial); 169.0 (fiber optic). Homes passed: 19,402.
Vice President: Patrick A. Dolohanty. General Manager: John Busby. Chief Technician: Elvis Brown. Marketing Director: Sharon Stevenson.
Ownership: Cable ONE Inc. (MSO).

CLEVELAND—Cable One, 221 South Sharpe Ave, PO Box 1200, Cleveland, MS 38732. Phone: 662-843-4016. Fax: 662-843-6114. Web Site: http://www.cableone.net. Also serves Bolivar County (portions), Boyle, Drew, Merigold, Mound Bayou, Pace, Renova, Ruleville, Shaw (portions), Shelby & Sunflower County (portions). ICA: MS0019.
TV Market Ranking: Below 100 (Bolivar County (portions), Boyle, CLEVELAND, Drew, Pace, Renova, Ruleville, Shaw (portions), Sunflower County (portions)); Outside TV Markets (Merigold, Mound Bayou, Shelby). Franchise award date: September 1, 1987. Franchise expiration date: N.A. Began: January 1, 1957.
Channel capacity: N.A. Channels available but not in use: N.A.
Basic Service
Subscribers: 3,256.
Programming (received off-air): KATV (ABC, Retro TV) Little Rock; WABG-TV (ABC, FOX) Greenwood; WHCQ-LD (America One, COZI TV, ION) Cleveland; WJTV (Antenna TV, CBS) Jackson; WMC-TV (Bounce TV, NBC, This TV) Memphis; WMPN-TV (PBS) Jackson; WREG-TV (Antenna TV, CBS) Memphis; WXVT (CBS) Greenville.
Programming (via satellite): A&E; AMC; Animal Planet; BET; Cartoon Network; CMT; CNBC; CNN; Comedy Central; C-SPAN; C-SPAN 2; CW PLUS; Discovery Channel; Disney Channel; E! HD; ESPN; ESPN2; Food Network; Fox News Channel; Freeform; FX; HGTV; History; HLN; INSP; Lifetime; MSNBC; MTV; Nickelodeon; Pop; QVC; Spike TV; Syfy; TBS; The Weather Channel; TLC; TNT; Turner Classic Movies; TV Land; USA Network; VH1.
Fee: $90.00 installation; $29.00 monthly.
Digital Basic Service
Subscribers: N.A.
Programming (via satellite): 3ABN; Boomerang; BYUtv; Discovery Digital Networks; Disney XD; ESPN Classic; ESPNews; FamilyNet; FOX College Sports Central; FOX College Sports Pacific; Fox Sports 1; Fox Sports 2; FXM; FYI; Golf Channel; Great American Country; Hallmark Channel; History International; HITS (Headend In The Sky); INSP; National Geographic Channel; Outdoor Channel; TNT HD; Trinity Broadcasting Network (TBN); truTV; Universal HD.
Digital Pay Service 1
Pay Units: N.A.
Programming (via satellite): Cinemax (multiplexed); DMX Music; Flix; HBO (multiplexed); Showtime (multiplexed); Showtime HD; Starz (multiplexed); Starz Encore (multiplexed); Sundance TV; The Movie Channel (multiplexed); The Movie Channel HD.

Fee: $15.00 monthly (each).
Video-On-Demand: No
Pay-Per-View
iN DEMAND (delivered digitally); Pleasure (delivered digitally); SexSee (delivered digitally); Juicy (delivered digitally); VaVoom (delivered digitally).
Internet Service
Operational: Yes. Began: June 1, 2002.
Broadband Service: CableONE.net.
Fee: $75.00 installation; $43.00 monthly.
Telephone Service
Digital: Operational
Fee: $39.95 monthly
Miles of Plant: 166.0 (coaxial); 60.0 (fiber optic). Homes passed: 37,000.
Vice President: Patrick A. Dolohanty. General Manager: Pete Peden. Technical Manager: Charlie Marshall. Marketing Director: Kay Bullock.
Ownership: Cable ONE Inc. (MSO).

COAHOMA—Media3, PO Box 650, Milan, TN 38358. Phone: 866-257-2044. E-mail: customerservice@mymedia3.com. Web Site: http://www.mymedia3.com. Also serves Friars Point, Jonestown & Lula. ICA: MS0092.
TV Market Ranking: Outside TV Markets (COAHOMA, Friars Point, Jonestown, Lula). Franchise award date: N.A. Franchise expiration date: N.A. Began: December 1, 1984.
Channel capacity: N.A. Channels available but not in use: N.A.
Basic Service
Subscribers: 165.
Programming (received off-air): KATV (ABC, Retro TV) Little Rock; WABG-TV (ABC, FOX) Greenwood; WATN-TV (ABC) Memphis; WHBQ-TV (Decades, FOX, Movies!) Memphis; WLMT (CW, MeTV, MNT) Memphis; WMAV-TV (PBS) Oxford; WMC-TV (Bounce TV, NBC, This TV) Memphis; WREG-TV (Antenna TV, CBS) Memphis; WXVT (CBS) Greenville.
Programming (via satellite): BET; CNN; ESPN; Freeform; TBS; TNT; USA Network; WGN America.
Fee: $29.95 installation; $22.45 monthly.
Expanded Basic Service 1
Subscribers: N.A.
Programming (via satellite): A&E; AMC; Animal Planet; Cartoon Network; C-SPAN; Discovery Channel; ESPN2; FX; Hallmark Channel; History; HLN; Lifetime; MTV; Nickelodeon; Outdoor Channel; Spike TV; Syfy; The Weather Channel; TLC; Trinity Broadcasting Network (TBN); truTV; Turner Classic Movies; TV Land; VH1.
Digital Basic Service
Subscribers: N.A.
Programming (via satellite): BBC America; Bloomberg Television; Discovery Digital Networks; ESPN Classic; ESPNews; Fox Sports 1; FXM; FYI; Golf Channel; GSN; HGTV; History International; IFC; MC; National Geographic Channel; NBCSN; Nick Jr.; Nicktoons; Ovation; Sundance TV; TeenNick; WE tv.
Pay Service 1
Pay Units: N.A.
Programming (via satellite): Cinemax; HBO.
Fee: $10.95 monthly (each).
Digital Pay Service 1
Pay Units: N.A.
Programming (via satellite): Cinemax (multiplexed); Flix; HBO (multiplexed); Showtime (multiplexed); Starz (multiplexed); Starz Encore (multiplexed); The Movie Channel (multiplexed).

Pay-Per-View
Hot Choice (delivered digitally); Playboy TV (delivered digitally); Fresh (delivered digitally); Shorteez (delivered digitally).
Internet Service
Operational: No.
Telephone Service
None
Miles of Plant: 28.0 (coaxial); None (fiber optic). Homes passed: 1,164.
Chief Financial Officer: Thomas Pate.
Ownership: CableSouth Media3 LLC (MSO).

COFFEEVILLE—Formerly served by MetroCast Mississippi. Now served by MaxxSouth Broadband, PONTOTOC, MS [MS0045]. ICA: MS0137.

COLES POINT—Formerly served by Foster Communications Inc. No longer in operation. ICA: MS0105.

COLLINS—Media3, PO Box 650, Milan, TN 38358. Phone: 866-257-2044. E-mail: customerservice@mymedia3.com. Web Site: http://www.mymedia3.com. Also serves Covington County (portions). ICA: MS0076.
TV Market Ranking: Below 100 (COLLINS, Covington County (portions)). Franchise award date: N.A. Franchise expiration date: N.A. Began: February 1, 1982.
Channel capacity: N.A. Channels available but not in use: N.A.
Basic Service
Subscribers: 547.
Programming (received off-air): WAPT (ABC) Jackson; WDAM-TV (ABC, Bounce TV, NBC, This TV) Hattiesburg; WHLT (CBS) Hattiesburg; WLOX (ABC, Bounce TV, CBS) Biloxi; WMAH-TV (PBS) Biloxi; WXXV-TV (FOX, MNT, NBC) Gulfport.
Programming (via satellite): A&E; Animal Planet; BET; Cartoon Network; CMT; CNBC; CNN; Comedy Central; C-SPAN; Discovery Channel; Disney Channel; ESPN; ESPN2; Food Network; Fox News Channel; FOX Sports Networks; Freeform; Hallmark Channel; HGTV; History; HLN; Lifetime; MTV; Nickelodeon; Spike TV; TBS; The Weather Channel; TLC; TNT; Travel Channel; Trinity Broadcasting Network (TBN); Turner Classic Movies; USA Network; VH1; WGN America.
Fee: $29.95 installation; $22.95 monthly.
Pay Service 1
Pay Units: N.A.
Programming (via satellite): HBO; The Movie Channel.
Fee: $11.24 monthly (each).
Internet Service
Operational: No.
Telephone Service
None
Miles of Plant: 25.0 (coaxial); None (fiber optic). Homes passed: 1,200.
Chief Financial Officer: Thomas Pate.
Ownership: CableSouth Media3 LLC (MSO).

COLUMBIA—Media3, PO Box 620, Milan, TN 38358. Phone: 866-257-2044. E-mail: customerservice@mymedia3.com. Web Site: http://www.mymedia3.com. Also serves Foxworth & Marion County (portions). ICA: MS0036.
TV Market Ranking: Below 100 (COLUMBIA, Foxworth, Marion County (portions)). Franchise award date: N.A. Franchise expiration date: N.A. Began: March 1, 1959.
Channel capacity: N.A. Channels available but not in use: N.A.

Cable Systems—Mississippi

Basic Service
Subscribers: 1,106.
Programming (received off-air): W45AA-D Columbia; WDAM-TV (ABC, Bounce TV, NBC, This TV) Laurel; WHLT (CBS) Hattiesburg; WLBT (Bounce TV, NBC, This TV) Jackson; WLOX (ABC, Bounce TV, CBS) Biloxi; WXXV-TV (FOX, MNT, NBC) Gulfport; 1 FM.
Programming (via satellite): C-SPAN; CW PLUS; INSP; ION Television; QVC.
Fee: $24.95 installation; $22.49 monthly.

Expanded Basic Service 1
Subscribers: N.A.
Programming (via satellite): A&E; AMC; Animal Planet; BET; Bravo; Cartoon Network; CMT; CNBC; CNN; Comedy Central; C-SPAN 2; Discovery Channel; Disney Channel; Disney XD; E! HD; ESPN; ESPN2; Food Network; Fox News Channel; Freeform; Golf Channel; Hallmark Channel; HGTV; History; HLN; Lifetime; MSNBC; MTV; National Geographic Channel; NBCSN; Nickelodeon; Outdoor Channel; Oxygen; Spike TV; Syfy; TBS; The Weather Channel; TLC; TNT; Travel Channel; Trinity Broadcasting Network (TBN); truTV; Turner Classic Movies; TV Land; USA Network; VH1; WE tv.
Fee: $42.99 monthly.

Digital Basic Service
Subscribers: N.A.
Programming (via satellite): BBC America; Bloomberg Television; Discovery Digital Networks; DIY Network; ESPN Classic; Fuse; FYI; History International; IFC; LMN; MC; Nick 2; Nick Jr.; Nicktoons; Sundance TV; TeenNick; TV Guide Interactive Inc.

Digital Pay Service 1
Pay Units: N.A.
Programming (via satellite): Cinemax (multiplexed); Flix; HBO (multiplexed); Showtime (multiplexed); Starz (multiplexed); Starz Encore (multiplexed); The Movie Channel (multiplexed).

Pay-Per-View
iN DEMAND (delivered digitally); Playboy TV (delivered digitally); Fresh (delivered digitally); Shorteez (delivered digitally).

Internet Service
Operational: Yes.

Telephone Service
Digital: Operational
Miles of Plant: 81.0 (coaxial); None (fiber optic). Homes passed: 4,304.
President: Alan Taylor. Chief Financial Officer: Thomas Pate. Business Manager: Glenda Elliott.
Ownership: CableSouth Media3 LLC (MSO).

COLUMBUS—Cable One, 319 College St, PO Box 1468, Columbus, MS 39703. Phone: 662-328-1781. Fax: 662-329-8484. E-mail: dlusby@cableone.net. Web Site: http://www.cableone.net. Also serves Caledonia, Columbus AFB, Hamilton, Lowndes County, New Hope, Rural Hill & Steens. ICA: MS0138.
TV Market Ranking: Below 100 (Caledonia, COLUMBUS, Columbus AFB, Hamilton, Lowndes County, New Hope, Rural Hill, Steens). Franchise award date: N.A. Franchise expiration date: N.A. Began: September 1, 1954.
Channel capacity: N.A. Channels available but not in use: N.A.

Basic Service
Subscribers: 7,174.
Programming (received off-air): WCBI-TV (CBS, CW, MNT) Columbus; WLOV-TV (FOX, MeTV, This TV) West Point; WMAB-TV (PBS) Mississippi State; WSES (ABC, TNN) Tuscaloosa; WTVA (ABC, NBC) Tupelo.
Programming (via satellite): A&E; AMC; Animal Planet; BET; Cartoon Network; CMT; CNBC; CNN; Comedy Central; C-SPAN; CW PLUS; Discovery Channel; Disney Channel; ESPN; ESPN2; Food Network; Fox News Channel; Freeform; FX; HGTV; History; HLN; Lifetime; MSNBC; MTV; Nickelodeon; Pop; QVC; Spike TV; SportSouth; Syfy; TBS; The Weather Channel; TLC; TNT; Travel Channel; Turner Classic Movies; TV Land; USA Network; VH1; WGN America.
Fee: $90.00 installation; $24.00 monthly.

Digital Basic Service
Subscribers: N.A.
Programming (via satellite): 3ABN; Boomerang; BYUtv; Discovery Digital Networks; Disney XD; DMX Music; ESPN Classic; ESPNews; FamilyNet; FOX College Sports Central; FOX College Sports Pacific; Fox Sports 1; Fox Sports 2; FXM; FYI; Golf Channel; Hallmark Channel; History International; INSP; National Geographic Channel; Outdoor Channel; TNT HD; Trinity Broadcasting Network (TBN); truTV; Universal HD.
Fee: $8.95 monthly.

Digital Pay Service 1
Pay Units: N.A.
Programming (via satellite): Cinemax (multiplexed); Flix; HBO (multiplexed); HITS (Headend In The Sky); Showtime (multiplexed); Showtime HD; Starz (multiplexed); Starz Encore; Sundance TV; The Movie Channel (multiplexed); The Movie Channel HD.
Fee: $15.00 monthly (each package).

Video-On-Demand: No

Pay-Per-View
VaVoom (delivered digitally); Pleasure (delivered digitally); SexSee (delivered digitally); Juicy (delivered digitally).

Internet Service
Operational: Yes. Began: February 1, 2001.
Subscribers: 9,248.
Broadband Service: CableONE.net.
Fee: $75.00 installation; $43.00 monthly.

Telephone Service
Digital: Operational
Subscribers: 3,497.
Fee: $39.95 monthly
Miles of Plant: 1,022.0 (coaxial); 179.0 (fiber optic). Homes passed: 25,794.
Vice President: Patrick A. Dolohanty. General Manager: David Lusby. Technical Operations Manager: Greg Youngblood. Office Manager: Peggy Chittem.
Ownership: Cable ONE Inc. (MSO).

CORINTH—Comcast Cable, One Comcast Center, Philadelphia, PA 19103. Phone: 215-286-1700. Fax: 215-286-7790. E-mail: info@comcast.com. Web Site: http://www.comcast.com. Also serves Alcorn County (portions), Farmington & Glen, MS; Guys, McNairy County (portions) & Michie, TN. ICA: MS0226.
TV Market Ranking: Below 100 (McNairy County (portions) (portions)); Outside TV Markets (Alcorn County (portions), CORINTH, Farmington, Glen, McNairy County (portions) (portions), Michie, Guys).
Channel capacity: N.A. Channels available but not in use: N.A.

Basic Service
Subscribers: 4,412. Commercial subscribers: 205.
Fee: $29.57-$42.00 installation; $14.35 monthly.

Internet Service
Operational: Yes.
Subscribers: 3,088.

Telephone Service
Digital: Operational
Subscribers: 969.
Miles of Plant: 652.0 (coaxial); 142.0 (fiber optic). Homes passed: 12,760.
Ownership: Comcast Cable Communications Inc.

CORINTH—Formerly served by Zoom Media. No longer in operation. ICA: MS0016.

CRAWFORD—Formerly served by Cable TV Inc. No longer in operation. ICA: MS0216.

CROSBY—Franklin Telephone (Telapex). This cable system has converted to IPTV. Now served by MEADVILLE, MS [MS5012]. ICA: MS0141.

CROWDER—Alliance Communications, PO Box 9090, Tyler, TX 75711. Phones: 903-561-4411; 800-842-8160; 501-679-6619 (Greenbrier, AR office). Web Site: http://www.alliancecable.net. ICA: MS0109.
TV Market Ranking: Outside TV Markets (CROWDER). Franchise award date: N.A. Franchise expiration date: N.A. Began: December 1, 1984.
Channel capacity: N.A. Channels available but not in use: N.A.

Basic Service
Subscribers: 35.
Programming (received off-air): WABG-TV (ABC, FOX) Greenwood; WATN-TV (ABC) Memphis; WHBQ-TV (Decades, FOX, Movies!) Memphis; WMAV-TV (PBS) Oxford; WMC-TV (Bounce TV, NBC, This TV) Memphis; WXVT (CBS) Greenville.
Programming (via satellite): BET; CNN; Discovery Channel; ESPN; TBS; TNT; USA Network; WGN America.
Fee: $45.00 installation; $25.45 monthly.

Pay Service 1
Pay Units: N.A.
Programming (via satellite): Cinemax; HBO; Showtime; The Movie Channel.
Fee: $11.95 monthly (each).

Internet Service
Operational: No.

Telephone Service
None
Miles of Plant: 5.0 (coaxial); None (fiber optic). Homes passed: 252.
Chief Financial Officer: David Starrett. Vice President & General Manager: John Brinker. Vice President, Programming: Julie Newman.
Ownership: Buford Media Group LLC (MSO).

CRYSTAL SPRINGS—Bailey Cable TV Inc, 807 Church St, Port Gibson, MS 39150-2413. Phones: 601-437-8300; 601-849-4201; 601-892-5249. Fax: 601-437-6860. E-mail: cs@baileycable.net. Web Site: http://www.baileycable.net. Also serves Copiah County. ICA: MS0143.
TV Market Ranking: 77 (Copiah County (portions), CRYSTAL SPRINGS); Outside TV Markets (Copiah County (portions)).
Channel capacity: N.A. Channels available but not in use: N.A.

Basic Service
Subscribers: 253.
Programming (received off-air): WAPT (ABC) Jackson; WDBD (FOX, Grit) Jackson; WJTV (Antenna TV, CBS) Jackson; WLBT (Bounce TV, NBC, This TV) Jackson.
Programming (via satellite): A&E; Cartoon Network; CMT; CNN; C-SPAN; Discovery Channel; ESPN; ESPN2; Freeform; History; MTV; Nickelodeon; QVC; Spike TV; Syfy; TBS; The Weather Channel; TLC; TNT; Trinity Broadcasting Network (TBN); TV Land; USA Network; VH1; WGN America.
Fee: $15.00 installation; $42.95 monthly.

Pay Service 1
Pay Units: N.A.
Programming (via satellite): Showtime; The Movie Channel.
Fee: $9.00 monthly (each).

Video-On-Demand: No

Internet Service
Operational: Yes.
Fee: $39.99 monthly.

Telephone Service
None
President: David A. Bailey. General Manager: Dwight Bailey. Chief Technician: John Portertaen.
Ownership: Bailey Cable TV Inc. (MSO).

CRYSTAL SPRINGS—Telepak Networks (Telapex). Now served by MEADVILLE, MS [MS5012]. ICA: MS5005.

DE KALB—Formerly served by Zoom Media. No longer in operation. ICA: MS0144.

DECATUR—Formerly served by Mediacom. Now served by MaxxSouth Broadband, PONTOTOC, MS [MS0045]. ICA: MS0196.

EAGLE LAKE—Franklin Telephone (Telapex). This cable system has converted to IPTV. Now served by MEADVILLE, MS [MS5012]. ICA: MS0211.

EUPORA—Cable TV Inc, 612 Hwy 82 West, PO Box 2598, Starkville, MS 39760. Phone: 662-324-5121. Fax: 662-324-5121. Also serves Webster County. ICA: MS0147.
TV Market Ranking: Below 100 (EUPORA, Webster County); Outside TV Markets (Webster County). Franchise award date: March 16, 1965. Franchise expiration date: N.A. Began: November 1, 1965.
Channel capacity: N.A. Channels available but not in use: N.A.

Basic Service
Subscribers: N.A.
Programming (received off-air): WABG-TV (ABC, FOX) Greenwood; WCBI-TV (CBS, CW, MNT) Columbus; WLOV-TV (FOX, MeTV, This TV) West Point; WMAB-TV (PBS) Mississippi State; WTVA (ABC, NBC) Tupelo.
Programming (via satellite): A&E; AMC; BET; Cartoon Network; CNBC; CNN; C-SPAN; Discovery Channel; Disney Channel; Disney XD; E! HD; ESPN; ESPN2; Fox News Channel; Fox Sports 1; Freeform; Fuse; FX; Great American Country; GSN; HGTV; History; HLN; Lifetime; Outdoor Channel; QVC; TBS; The Weather Channel; TLC; TNT; Trinity Broadcasting Network (TBN); USA Network; WGN America.
Fee: $40.00 installation.

Pay Service 1
Pay Units: N.A.
Programming (via satellite): HBO; Showtime.
Fee: $9.95 - $14.95 monthly (each).

Internet Service
Operational: No.

Telephone Service
None
Miles of Plant: 23.0 (coaxial); None (fiber optic). Homes passed: 1,393.
General Manager: Andy Williams.
Ownership: Andy Williams (MSO).

2017 Edition D-429

Mississippi—Cable Systems

EVERGREEN—Formerly served by SouthTel Communications L.P. No longer in operation. ICA: MS0111.

FAYETTE—Formerly served by Almega Cable. No longer in operation. ICA: MS0071.

FLORA—Franklin Telephone (Telapex). Formerly [MS0148]. This cable system has converted to IPTV, 1018 Highland Colony Pkwy, Ste 700, Ridgeland, MS 39157. Phones: 601-355-1522 (Telapex); 877-835-3725 (Telepak Networks). Fax: 601-353-0950. Web Site: http://www.telapex.com. Also serves Lost Rabbit. ICA: MS5019.
Channel capacity: N.A. Channels available but not in use: N.A.
Basic
Subscribers: 546.
Fee: $43.99 monthly. Includes 120+ channels plus music channels.
Internet Service
Operational: Yes.
Telephone Service
Digital: Operational
Vice President: Brooks Derryberry.
Ownership: Telapex Inc.

FLORA—Franklin Telephone (Telepax). This cable system has converted to IPTV. See FLORA, MS [MS5019]. ICA: MS0148.

FOREST—MaxxSouth Broadband, 911 Hwy 12 West, Ste 202-B, Starkville, MS 39759. Phone: 800-457-5351. Web Site: http://www.maxxsouth.com. Also serves Morton & Scott County (unincorporated areas). ICA: MS0032.
TV Market Ranking: 77 (Morton, Scott County (unincorporated areas) (portions)); Outside TV Markets (FOREST, Scott County (unincorporated areas) (portions)). Franchise award date: January 1, 1969. Franchise expiration date: N.A. Began: December 1, 1970.
Channel capacity: N.A. Channels available but not in use: N.A.
Basic Service
Subscribers: 601. Commercial subscribers: 93.
Programming (received off-air): WAPT (ABC) Jackson; WDBD (FOX, Grit) Jackson; WJTV (Antenna TV, CBS) Jackson; WLBT (Bounce TV, NBC, This TV) Jackson; WLOO (MNT) Vicksburg; WMPN-TV (PBS) Jackson; WTOK-TV (ABC, CW, FOX, MNT) Meridian.
Programming (via satellite): QVC; The Weather Channel; WGN America.
Fee: $55.00 installation; $35.95 monthly.
Expanded Basic Service 1
Subscribers: N.A.
Programming (via satellite): A&E; Animal Planet; BET; Cartoon Network; CNBC; CNN; Comedy Central; C-SPAN; Discovery Channel; ESPN; ESPN2; Food Network; Fox News Channel; FX; FXM; Great American Country; Hallmark Channel; HGTV; History; HLN; Lifetime; MTV; Nickelodeon; Outdoor Channel; Spike TV; Syfy; TBS; TLC; TNT; Travel Channel; Turner Classic Movies; TV Land; USA Network; WE tv.
Fee: $30.00 installation; $31.00 monthly.
Digital Basic Service
Subscribers: N.A.
Programming (via satellite): 52MX; BBC America; Cine Mexicano; CNN en Espanol; Destination America; Discovery Kids Channel; DMX Music; ESPN Deportes; ESPNews; Fox Deportes; Fox Sports 1; Golf Channel; History en Espanol; Investigation Discovery; LMN; National Geographic Channel; OWN: Oprah Winfrey Network; Science Channel; Trinity Broadcasting Network (TBN).
Pay Service 1
Pay Units: N.A.
Programming (via satellite): Cinemax; HBO.
Fee: $7.00 monthly (Cinemax), $14.00 monthly (HBO).
Digital Pay Service 1
Pay Units: N.A.
Programming (via satellite): Cinemax (multiplexed); Flix; HBO (multiplexed); HBO Latino; Showtime (multiplexed); Starz (multiplexed); Starz Encore (multiplexed); The Movie Channel (multiplexed).
Fee: $11.00 monthly (HBO, Showtime or TMC), $14.00 monthly (Cinemax).
Video-On-Demand: No
Pay-Per-View
iN DEMAND (delivered digitally); Hot Choice (delivered digitally); Playboy TV (delivered digitally); Fresh (delivered digitally).
Internet Service
Operational: Yes.
Fee: $79.99 installation; $35.99 monthly.
Telephone Service
None
Miles of Plant: 137.0 (coaxial); None (fiber optic). Homes passed: 3,380.
General Manager: Rick Ferrall.
Ownership: MaxxSouth Broadband (MSO).

FRANKLIN CREEK—Formerly served by CableSouth Inc. No longer in operation. ICA: MS0149.

FULTON—Comcast Cable. Now served by TUPELO, MS [MS0009]. ICA: MS0033.

GLOSTER—Bailey Cable TV Inc, 807 Church St, Port Gibson, MS 39150-2413. Phone: 601-437-8300. Fax: 601-437-6860. E-mail: cs@baileycable.net. Web Site: http://www.baileycable.net. ICA: MS0219.
TV Market Ranking: Below 100 (GLOSTER). Channel capacity: N.A. Channels available but not in use: N.A.
Basic Service
Subscribers: 194.
Fee: $15.00 installation; $42.95 monthly.
President: David A. Bailey.
Ownership: Bailey Cable TV Inc. (MSO).

GREENVILLE—Suddenlink Communications, 318 Main St, Greenville, MS 38701. Phones: 800-999-6845 (Customer service); 314-315-9400. Web Site: http://www.suddenlink.com. Also serves Metcalfe & Swiftwater. ICA: MS0010.
TV Market Ranking: Below 100 (GREENVILLE, Metcalfe, Swiftwater). Franchise award date: May 4, 1954. Franchise expiration date: N.A. Began: October 1, 1954.
Channel capacity: 78 (operating 2-way). Channels available but not in use: N.A.
Basic Service
Subscribers: 6,110. Commercial subscribers: 686.
Programming (received off-air): KATV (ABC, Retro TV) Little Rock; KTVE (NBC) El Dorado; WABG-TV (ABC, FOX) Greenwood; WJTV (Antenna TV, CBS) Jackson; WLBT (Bounce TV, NBC, This TV) Jackson; WMAO-TV (PBS) Greenwood; WXVT (CBS) Greenville.
Programming (via satellite): C-SPAN; CW PLUS; INSP; ION Television; Pop; The Weather Channel.
Fee: $40.00 installation; $35.50 monthly.
Expanded Basic Service 1
Subscribers: N.A.
Programming (via satellite): A&E; AMC; BET; CNN; C-SPAN 2; Discovery Channel; Disney Channel; E! HD; ESPN; Fox News Channel; Freeform; Great American Country; GSN; HGTV; HLN; Lifetime; Nickelodeon; Spike TV; TLC; TNT; TV Land; USA Network.
Fee: $17.43 monthly.
Expanded Basic Service 2
Subscribers: N.A.
Programming (via satellite): Cartoon Network; CNBC; Comedy Central; ESPN2; History; MoviePlex; MTV; Syfy; Travel Channel; truTV; Turner Classic Movies; VH1.
Expanded Basic Service 3
Subscribers: N.A.
Programming (via satellite): TBS; WGN America.
Fee: $.65 monthly.
Digital Basic Service
Subscribers: N.A.
Programming (via satellite): BBC America; Bloomberg Television; Discovery Digital Networks; Disney XD; DMX Music; ESPN Classic; ESPNews; Fox Sports 1; FXM; Golf Channel; LMN; NBCSN; Outdoor Channel; Trinity Broadcasting Network (TBN); WE tv.
Pay Service 1
Pay Units: N.A.
Programming (via satellite): Cinemax (multiplexed); Flix; HBO (multiplexed); Showtime (multiplexed); The Movie Channel (multiplexed).
Fee: $9.71 monthly (Cinemax or HBO), $11.60 monthly (Flix, Showtime or TMC).
Digital Pay Service 1
Pay Units: N.A.
Programming (via satellite): Cinemax (multiplexed); HBO (multiplexed); Showtime (multiplexed); Starz (multiplexed); The Movie Channel.
Video-On-Demand: No
Pay-Per-View
iN DEMAND (delivered digitally); Playboy TV (delivered digitally); Fresh (delivered digitally); ESPN Now (delivered digitally); iN DEMAND.
Internet Service
Operational: Yes. Began: March 1, 2002.
Broadband Service: Suddenlink High Speed Internet.
Fee: $29.95 monthly.
Telephone Service
Digital: Operational
Miles of Plant: 233.0 (coaxial); 50.0 (fiber optic). Homes passed: 18,500.
Senior Vice President, Corporate Finance: Michael Pflantz. Vice President, Accounting: Sabrina Warr. General Manager: John Marshall. Chief Technician: Steve Bennett.
Ownership: Cequel Communications Holdings I LLC (MSO).

GREENWOOD—Suddenlink Communications, 801 West Park Ave, Ste B, Greenwood, MS 38930. Phone: 314-315-9400. Web Site: http://www.suddenlink.com. Also serves Carroll County (portions), Indianola, Leflore County, Moorhead, Sidon & Sunflower County. ICA: MS0151.
TV Market Ranking: Below 100 (Carroll County (portions), GREENWOOD, Indianola, Leflore County, Moorhead, Sidon, Sunflower County (portions)); Outside TV Markets (Sunflower County (portions)). Franchise award date: N.A. Franchise expiration date: N.A. Began: October 1, 1955.
Channel capacity: N.A. Channels available but not in use: N.A.
Basic Service
Subscribers: 5,036. Commercial subscribers: 548.
Programming (received off-air): WABG-TV (ABC, FOX) Greenwood; WJTV (Antenna TV, CBS) Jackson; WLBT (Bounce TV, NBC, This TV) Jackson; WMAO-TV (PBS) Greenwood; WTVA (ABC, NBC) Tupelo; WXVT (CBS) Greenville; 10 FMs.
Programming (via microwave): WMC-TV (Bounce TV, NBC, This TV) Memphis.
Programming (via satellite): A&E; BET; Cartoon Network; CMT; CNBC; Comedy Central; C-SPAN; C-SPAN 2; CW PLUS; Discovery Channel; Discovery Life Channel; E! HD; ESPN; ESPN Classic; EVINE Live; Food Network; Freeform; FX; Golf Channel; HGTV; History; HLN; INSP; ION Television; Lifetime; MSNBC; MTV; Nickelodeon; Pop; QVC; Spike TV; Syfy; TBS; The Weather Channel; TLC; Travel Channel; Trinity Broadcasting Network (TBN); Turner Classic Movies; TV Land; USA Network; VH1; WGN America.
Fee: $40.00 installation; $30.95 monthly; $.56 converter.
Expanded Basic Service 1
Subscribers: N.A.
Programming (via satellite): AMC; Bravo; CNN; Disney Channel; Disney XD; ESPN2; Fox News Channel; Hallmark Channel; Oxygen; TNT; truTV.
Fee: $8.00 monthly.
Digital Basic Service
Subscribers: N.A.
Programming (via satellite): Animal Planet; AXS TV; BBC America; Bloomberg Television; Discovery Digital Networks; DIY Network; ESPN HD; ESPNews; Fox Sports 1; Fuse; FXM; FYI; GSN; HD Theater; History International; IFC; LMN; LOGO; MC; National Geographic Channel; NBCSN; Nick 2; Nick Jr.; Nicktoons; Outdoor Channel; SportSouth; TeenNick; TNT HD; Universal HD; WE tv.
Digital Pay Service 1
Pay Units: N.A.
Programming (via satellite): Cinemax (multiplexed); HBO (multiplexed); HBO HD; Showtime (multiplexed); Showtime HD; Starz (multiplexed); Starz Encore (multiplexed); The Movie Channel (multiplexed).
Fee: $12.00 monthly (each).
Video-On-Demand: Planned
Pay-Per-View
Playboy TV (delivered digitally); Hot Choice (delivered digitally); Fresh (delivered digitally); iN DEMAND (delivered digitally).
Internet Service
Operational: Yes.
Subscribers: 3,623.
Broadband Service: Suddenlink High Speed Internet.
Fee: $20.99 installation; $44.95 monthly.
Telephone Service
Digital: Operational
Subscribers: 2,089.
Fee: $49.95 monthly
Miles of Plant: 384.0 (coaxial); 186.0 (fiber optic). Homes passed: 19,579.
Senior Vice President, Corporate Finance: Michael Pflantz. Vice President, Accounting: Sabrina Warr. General Manager: John Marshall. Corporate Communications Director: Gene Regan.
Ownership: Cequel Communications Holdings I LLC (MSO).

GRENADA—Cable One, 2247 South Commerce St, PO Box 1210, Grenada, MS 38901. Phone: 662-843-4016. Web Site: http://www.cableone.net. Also serves Carrollton,

Cable Systems—Mississippi

Charleston, Duck Hill, Durant, Goodman, Grenada County, Itta Bena, Kilmichael, Leflore County, Lexington, Montgomery County (portions), North Carrollton, Pickens, Sumner, Tallahatchie County, Tchula, Tutwiler, Vaiden, Webb, Winona & Yazoo City. ICA: MS0021.
TV Market Ranking: Below 100 (Carrollton, Charleston, Duck Hill, GRENADA, Grenada County (portions), Itta Bena, Leflore County, Lexington, Montgomery County (portions), North Carrollton, Sumner, Tallahatchie County, Tchula, Vaiden, Webb, Winona); Outside TV Markets (Durant, Goodman, Grenada County (portions), Kilmichael, Pickens, Tutwiler, Yazoo City).
Channel capacity: N.A. Channels available but not in use: N.A.
Basic Service
Subscribers: 5,561.
Fee: $90.00 installation; $72.00 monthly.
Vice President: Patrick A. Dolohanty.
Ownership: Cable ONE Inc. (MSO).

GULFPORT—Cable One, 19201 Pineville Rd, Long Beach, MS 39560-3315. Phones: 228-575-6786; 228-864-1506. Fax: 228-867-6992. E-mail: jwhite@cableone.net. Web Site: http://www.cableone.net. Also serves Biloxi, Diamondhead, D'Iberville, Escatawpa, Gautier, Hancock County (portions), Harrison County (portions), Jackson County (portions), Keesler AFB, Long Beach, Moss Point, Ocean Springs, Pascagoula, Pass Christian & Van Cleave. ICA: MS0008.
TV Market Ranking: 59 (Escatawpa, Jackson County (portions) (portions), Moss Point, Pascagoula); Below 100 (Diamondhead, D'Iberville, Gautier, GULFPORT, Hancock County (portions), Keesler AFB, Ocean Springs, Pass Christian, Van Cleave, Biloxi, Long Beach, Jackson County (portions) (portions)). Franchise award date: N.A. Franchise expiration date: N.A. Began: February 1, 1968.
Channel capacity: N.A. Channels available but not in use: N.A.
Basic Service
Subscribers: 48,145.
Programming (received off-air): WDSU (MeTV, NBC) New Orleans; WGNO (ABC, Antenna TV, Escape) New Orleans; WKRG-TV (CBS, MeTV) Mobile; WLOX (ABC, Bounce TV, CBS) Biloxi; WMAH-TV (PBS) Biloxi; WNOL-TV (CW, This TV) New Orleans; WVUE-DT (Bounce TV, FOX) New Orleans; WWL-TV (CBS) New Orleans; WXXV-TV (FOX, MNT, NBC) Gulfport; WYES-TV (PBS) New Orleans; 4 FMs.
Programming (via satellite): A&E; AMC; Animal Planet; BET; Cartoon Network; CMT; CNBC; CNN; C-SPAN; C-SPAN 2; Discovery Channel; Disney Channel; E! HD; ESPN; ESPN2; EVINE Live; EWTN Global Catholic Network; Food Network; Fox News Channel; Freeform; FX; HGTV; History; HLN; Lifetime; MSNBC; MTV; NASA TV; Nickelodeon; Pop; QVC; Spike TV; Syfy; TBS; The Weather Channel; TLC; TNT; Trinity Broadcasting Network (TBN); Turner Classic Movies; TV Land; USA Network; VH1; WGN America.
Fee: $72.00 monthly; $1.50 converter.
Digital Basic Service
Subscribers: N.A.
Programming (via satellite): 3ABN; Boomerang; BYUtv; Discovery Digital Networks; Disney XD; ESPN Classic; ESPNews; FamilyNet; FOX College Sports Central; FOX College Sports Pacific; Fox Sports 1; Fox Sports 2; FXM; FYI; Golf Channel; Great American Country; Hallmark Channel; History International; INSP; National Geographic Channel; Outdoor Channel; Telemundo; TNT HD; Trinity Broadcasting Network (TBN); truTV; TVG Network; Universal HD.
Digital Pay Service 1
Pay Units: N.A.
Programming (via satellite): Cinemax; Showtime HD; Starz (multiplexed); Starz Encore (multiplexed); The Movie Channel HD.
Fee: $15.00 monthly (each).
Video-On-Demand: No
Pay-Per-View
iN DEMAND (delivered digitally); Pleasure (delivered digitally); SexSee (delivered digitally); Juicy (delivered digitally); VaVoom (delivered digitally).
Internet Service
Operational: Yes. Began: September 1, 2001.
Subscribers: 46,687.
Broadband Service: CableONE.net.
Fee: $75.00 installation; $43.00 monthly; $170.00 modem purchase.
Telephone Service
Digital: Operational
Subscribers: 18,418.
Fee: $39.95 monthly
Miles of Plant: 4,378.0 (coaxial); 1,421.0 (fiber optic). Homes passed: 98,673.
Vice President: Patrick A. Dolohanty. General Manager: Jim Perry. Chief Technician: Mike Thompson. Marketing Director: Carol Lucas.
Ownership: Cable ONE Inc. (MSO).

GUNNISON—Formerly served by J & L Cable. No longer in operation. ICA: MS0108.

HATTIESBURG—Comcast Cable, 1827 Joiner Rd, Sandersville, GA 31089. Phones: 601-268-1188; 601-579-3960. Web Site: http://www.comcast.com. Also serves Clarke County (portions), Ellisville, Forrest County (portions), Heidelberg, Jasper County (portions), Jones County (portions), Lamar County (portions), Lauderdale, Lauderdale County (portions), Laurel, Marion, Meridian, Pachuta, Paulding, Petal, Purvis, Russell, Sandersville & Toomsuba. ICA: MS0005.
TV Market Ranking: Below 100 (Clarke County (portions), Ellisville, Forrest County (portions), HATTIESBURG, Heidelberg, Jasper County (portions), Jones County (portions), Lamar County (portions), Lauderdale, Lauderdale County (portions), Marion, Pachuta, Petal, Purvis, Russell, Sandersville, Toomsuba, Laurel, Meridian, Paulding). Franchise award date: N.A. Franchise expiration date: N.A. Began: January 1, 1954.
Channel capacity: N.A. Channels available but not in use: N.A.
Basic Service
Subscribers: 45,741. Commercial subscribers: 2,931.
Programming (received off-air): WDAM-TV (ABC, Bounce TV, NBC, This TV) Laurel; WHLT (CBS) Hattiesburg; WLOX (ABC, Bounce TV, CBS) Biloxi; WMAH-TV (PBS) Biloxi; WXXV-TV (FOX, MNT, NBC) Gulfport.
Programming (via satellite): A&E; AMC; Animal Planet; BET; Bravo; Cartoon Network; CMT; CNBC; CNN; Comcast/Charter Sports Southeast (CSS); Comedy Central; C-SPAN; C-SPAN 2; CW PLUS; Discovery Channel; E! HD; ESPN; ESPN Classic; ESPN2; EWTN Global Catholic Network; Food Network; Fox News Channel; Fox Sports 1; Freeform; FX; Golf Channel; Great American Country; GSN; HGTV; History; HLN; INSP; ION Television; Lifetime; MSNBC; MTV; NBCSN; Nickelodeon; Outdoor Channel; OWN: Oprah Winfrey Network; Pop; QVC; Spike TV; Syfy; TBS; The Weather Channel; TLC; TNT; Trinity Broadcasting Network (TBN); truTV; Turner Classic Movies; TV Land; USA Network; VH1; WGN America.
Fee: $52.95-$67.95 installation; $20.70 monthly.
Digital Basic Service
Subscribers: N.A.
Programming (via satellite): BBC America; C-SPAN 3; Discovery Digital Networks; Disney Channel; Disney XD; DMX Music; ESPNews; National Geographic Channel; Nick 2; Nick Jr.; TeenNick; WAM! America's Kidz Network; Weatherscan.
Pay Service 1
Pay Units: N.A.
Programming (via satellite): Cinemax; HBO; Showtime.
Fee: $14.50 monthly (each).
Digital Pay Service 1
Pay Units: N.A.
Programming (via satellite): Cinemax (multiplexed); HBO (multiplexed); Showtime (multiplexed); Starz (multiplexed); Starz Encore (multiplexed); Sundance TV (multiplexed); The Movie Channel (multiplexed).
Fee: $14.50 monthly (each).
Video-On-Demand: Yes
Pay-Per-View
iN DEMAND (delivered digitally); Hot Choice (delivered digitally); Playboy TV (delivered digitally); Fresh (delivered digitally); Shorteez (delivered digitally); Pleasure (delivered digitally).
Internet Service
Operational: Yes.
Subscribers: 38,042.
Broadband Service: Comcast High Speed Internet.
Fee: $42.95 monthly; $5.00 modem lease.
Telephone Service
Digital: Operational
Subscribers: 17,010.
Miles of Plant: 3,560.0 (coaxial); 1,200.0 (fiber optic). Homes passed: 145,459.
General Manager: Farrel Ryder. Operations Manager: Mike Boez. Marketing Manager: Dan Carleton.
Ownership: Comcast Cable Communications Inc. (MSO).

HAZLEHURST—Bailey Cable TV Inc, 807 Church St, Port Gibson, MS 39150-2413. Phones: 601-437-8300; 601-849-4201; 601-892-5249. Fax: 601-437-6860. E-mail: cs@baileycable.net. Web Site: http://www.baileycable.net. ICA: MS0153.
TV Market Ranking: 77 (HAZLEHURST).
Channel capacity: N.A. Channels available but not in use: N.A.
Basic Service
Subscribers: 244.
Fee: $15.00 installation; $42.95 monthly.
Internet Service
Operational: Yes.
President: David A. Bailey. General Manager: Dwight Bailey. Chief Technician: Jim Morton.
Ownership: Bailey Cable TV Inc. (MSO).

HICKORY FLAT—Formerly served by MetroCast Mississippi. Now served by MaxxSouth Broadband, PONTOTOC, MS [MS0045]. ICA: MS0154.

HOLLANDALE—NewWave Communications, One Montgomery Plaza, 4th Floor, Sikeston, MO 63801. Phones: 800-753-2465; 888-863-9928. Fax: 573-472-9518. E-mail: info@newwave.com. Web Site: http://www.newwavecom.com. ICA: MS0060.
TV Market Ranking: Below 100 (HOLLANDALE). Franchise award date: August 20, 1974. Franchise expiration date: N.A. Began: January 1, 1976.
Channel capacity: N.A. Channels available but not in use: N.A.
Basic Service
Subscribers: 247.
Programming (received off-air): WABG-TV (ABC, FOX) Greenwood; WDBD (FOX, Grit) Jackson; WJTV (Antenna TV, CBS) Jackson; WLBT (Bounce TV, NBC, This TV) Jackson; WMAO-TV (PBS) Greenwood; WXVT (CBS) Greenville.
Programming (via satellite): BET; CNN; ESPN; Freeform; Hallmark Channel; MTV; Spike TV; TBS; Turner Classic Movies; USA Network; WGN America.
Fee: $35.00 installation; $35.78 monthly.
Expanded Basic Service 1
Subscribers: N.A.
Programming (via satellite): A&E; CMT; CW PLUS; Discovery Channel; E! HD; ESPN2; Fox News Channel; HGTV; History; HLN; Lifetime; Nickelodeon; Syfy; The Weather Channel; TLC; TNT; Trinity Broadcasting Network (TBN); TV Land; VH1.
Fee: $45.45 monthly.
Digital Basic Service
Subscribers: N.A.
Fee: $11.00 monthly.
Digital Pay Service 1
Pay Units: N.A.
Programming (via satellite): Cinemax; HBO; Showtime; Starz; Starz Encore; The Movie Channel.
Fee: $14.95 installation; $8.00 monthly (Starz), $9.00 monthly (Cinemax), $11.00 monthly (Starz/Encore), $15.00 monthly (Showtime/TMC), $17.00 monthly (HBO) or $26.00 monthly (HBO/Cinemax).
Video-On-Demand: No
Internet Service
Operational: No.
Telephone Service
Digital: Operational
Miles of Plant: 17.0 (coaxial); None (fiber optic). Homes passed: 1,400.
General Manager: Staci Gowan.
Ownership: NewWave Communications LLC (MSO).

HOLLY SPRINGS—Formerly served by MetroCast Mississippi. Now served by MaxxSouth Broadband, PONTOTOC, MS [MS0045]. ICA: MS0040.

HOUSTON—Formerly served by MetroCast Mississippi. Now served by MaxxSouth Broadband, PONTOTOC, MS [MS0045]. ICA: MS0044.

INDIANOLA—Formerly served by Adelphia Communications. Now served by Suddenlink Communications, GREENWOOD, MS [MS0151]. ICA: MS0155.

INVERNESS—Franklin Telephone (Telapex). Formerly [MS0080]. This cable system has converted to IPTV. Now served by MEADVILLE, MS [MS5012]. ICA: MS5007.

ISOLA—Delta Telephone (Telapex). Formerly [MS0080]. This cable system has converted to IPTV. Now served by MEADVILLE, MS [MS5012]. ICA: MS5011.

2017 Edition   D-431

Mississippi—Cable Systems

ISOLA-INVERNESS—Franklin Telephone (Telapex). This cable system has converted to IPTV. Now served by MEADVILLE, MS [MS5012]. ICA: MS0080.

ITTA BENA—Cable One. Now served by GRENADA, MS [MS0021]. ICA: MS0156.

IUKA—MetroCast Mississippi. Now served by PONTOTOC, MS [MS0045]. ICA: MS0043.

JACKSON—Comcast Cable, 5375 Executive Pl, Jackson, MS 39206. Phones: 601-982-0922; 601-982-1187. Fax: 601-321-3888. Web Site: http://www.comcast.com. Also serves Calhoun, Lakeshore, Monroe, Ouachita Parish (northern portion), Richwood, Swartz & West Monroe, LA; Bolton, Brandon, Canton, Cleary Heights, Clinton, Deerfield, Edwards, Fannin, Florence, Flowood, Hinds County (portions), Johns, Lake Ridgelea, Madison, Madison County (portions), Pearl, Pelahatchie, Puckett, Rankin, Rankin County (portions), Raymond, Richland, Ridgeland & Star, MS. ICA: MS0001.

TV Market Ranking: 77 (Bolton, Brandon, Canton, Cleary Heights, Clinton, Deerfield, Edwards, Fannin, Florence, Flowood, Hinds County (portions), JACKSON, Johns, Lake Ridgelea, Madison, Madison County (portions), Pearl, Pelahatchie, Puckett, Rankin, Rankin County (portions), Raymond, Richland, Ridgeland, Star); 99 (Calhoun, Lakeshore, Monroe, Ouachita Parish (northern portion), Richwood, Swartz, West Monroe); Outside TV Markets (Madison County (portions)). Franchise award date: March 3, 1970. Franchise expiration date: N.A. Began: September 2, 1972.

Channel capacity: N.A. Channels available but not in use: N.A.

Basic Service
Subscribers: 92,069. Commercial subscribers: 7,853.
Programming (received off-air): WAPT (ABC) Jackson; WDBD (FOX, Grit) Jackson; WJTV (Antenna TV, CBS) Jackson; WLBT (Bounce TV, NBC, This TV) Jackson; WLOO (MNT) Vicksburg; WMPN-TV (PBS) Jackson.
Programming (via satellite): Comcast Network Philadelphia; C-SPAN; QVC; The Weather Channel; WGN America.
Fee: $52.95-$67.95 installation; $31.74 monthly.

Expanded Basic Service 1
Subscribers: N.A.
Programming (via satellite): A&E; AMC; Animal Planet; BET; Bravo; Cartoon Network; CMT; CNBC; CNN; Comcast/Charter Sports Southeast (CSS); Comedy Central; C-SPAN 2; Discovery Channel; Disney Channel; E! HD; ESPN; ESPN2; Food Network; Fox News Channel; FOX Sports South/SportSouth; Freeform; FX; Golf Channel; Hallmark Channel; HGTV; History; HLN; ION Television; Lifetime; LMN; MSNBC; MTV; NBCSN; Nickelodeon; OWN; Oprah Winfrey Network; Pop; Spike TV; Syfy; TBS; TLC; TNT; Travel Channel; Trinity Broadcasting Network (TBN); truTV; Turner Classic Movies; TV Land; USA Network; VH1.
Fee: $31.56 monthly.

Digital Basic Service
Subscribers: N.A.
Programming (via satellite): A&E HD; Animal Planet HD; BBC America; Bloomberg Television; Boomerang; BTN; CBS Sports Network; CMT; CNN HD; Cooking Channel; C-SPAN 3; Daystar TV Network; Destination America; Discovery Channel HD; Discovery Kids Channel; Discovery Life Channel; Disney Channel HD; Disney XD; DIY Network; ESPN Classic; ESPN HD; ESPN2 HD; ESPNews; EVINE Live; EWTN Global Catholic Network; FamilyNet; Flix; Food Network HD; Fox Business Network; FOX College Sports Central; FOX College Sports Pacific; Fox News HD; Fox Sports 1; Fox Sports 2; Freeform HD; FSN HD; Fuse; FX HD; FXM; FYI; Golf Channel HD; GolTV; Great American Country; HD Theater; HGTV HD; History HD; History International; IFC; INSP; Investigation Discovery; MC; MLB Network; MoviePlex; MTV Classic; MTV Hits; MTV Jams; MTV Live; MTV2; Nat Geo WILD; National Geographic Channel; National Geographic Channel HD; NBA TV; NFL Network; NFL Network HD; Nick 2; Nick Jr.; Nicktoons; Outdoor Channel; RTV; Science Channel; Sprout; Starz Encore (multiplexed); Sundance TV; Syfy HD; TBS HD; TeenNick; Tennis Channel; The Word Network; TNT HD; Tr3s; Trinity Broadcasting Network (TBN); TV One; Universal HD; Univision Studios; UP; USA Network HD; Versus HD; VH1 Soul; WE tv.

Digital Pay Service 1
Pay Units: N.A.
Programming (via satellite): Cinemax (multiplexed); Cinemax HD; HBO (multiplexed); HBO HD; MoviePlex; Playboy TV; Showtime (multiplexed); Showtime HD; Starz (multiplexed); Starz HD; The Movie Channel (multiplexed).
Fee: $11.95 monthly (each).

Video-On-Demand: Yes

Pay-Per-View
iN DEMAND (delivered digitally); NBA League Pass; MLS Direct Kick (delivered digitally); NHL Center Ice (delivered digitally); MLB Extra Innings (delivered digitally); Sports PPV delivered digitally (delivered digitally); Playboy TV (delivered digitally); Fresh (delivered digitally); Juicy (delivered digitally).

Internet Service
Operational: Yes. Began: June 1, 2000.
Subscribers: 86,093.
Broadband Service: Comcast High Speed Internet.
Fee: $79.95 installation; $42.95 monthly.

Telephone Service
Digital: Operational
Subscribers: 43,746.
Fee: $44.95 monthly
Miles of Plant: 5,416.0 (coaxial); 957.0 (fiber optic). Homes passed: 295,360.
Vice President & General Manager: Ronnie Colvini. Engineering Director: Sandy McKnight. Chief Technician: Clifton Callahan. Marketing Director: Wesley Dowling. Public Affairs Director: Frances Smith.
Ownership: Comcast Cable Communications Inc. (MSO).

JUMPERTOWN—Formerly served by Vista III Media. Now served by MaxxSouth Broadband, PONTOTOC, MS [MS0045]. ICA: MS0114.

KILN—Formerly served by Trust Cable. No longer in operation. ICA: MS0157.

KOSCIUSKO—MaxxSouth Broadband, 911 Hwy 12 West, Ste 202-B, Starkville, MS 39759. Phone: 800-457-5351. Web Site: http://www.maxxsouth.com. Also serves Attala County (unincorporated areas) & McAdams. ICA: MS0158.
TV Market Ranking: Below 100 (Attala County (unincorporated areas) (portions)); Outside TV Markets (Attala County (unincorporated areas) (portions), KOSCIUSKO, McAdams). Franchise award date: January 1, 1966. Franchise expiration date: N.A. Began: April 1, 1967.
Channel capacity: N.A. Channels available but not in use: N.A.

Basic Service
Subscribers: 1,095. Commercial subscribers: 111.
Programming (received off-air): WABG-TV (ABC, FOX) Greenwood; WAPT (ABC) Jackson; WDBD (FOX, Grit) Jackson; WJTV (Antenna TV, CBS) Jackson; WLBT (Bounce TV, NBC, This TV) Jackson; WMAB-TV (PBS) Mississippi State; WTVA (ABC, NBC) Tupelo.
Programming (via satellite): C-SPAN; QVC; Trinity Broadcasting Network (TBN); WGN America.
Fee: $55.00 installation; $35.95 monthly; $2.50 converter.

Expanded Basic Service 1
Subscribers: N.A.
Programming (via satellite): A&E; Animal Planet; BET; Cartoon Network; CMT; CNBC; CNN; Discovery Channel; ESPN; ESPN2; Food Network; Fox News Channel; Fox Sports 1; Freeform; FX; FXM; Great American Country; Hallmark Channel; HGTV; History; HLN; Lifetime; National Geographic Channel; Nickelodeon; Outdoor Channel; Spike TV; Syfy; TBS; The Weather Channel; TLC; TNT; Travel Channel; Turner Classic Movies; TV Land; USA Network; VH1.
Fee: $31.00 monthly.

Digital Basic Service
Subscribers: N.A.
Programming (via satellite): BBC America; Bravo; Destination America; Discovery Kids Channel; Discovery Life Channel; DMX Music; ESPN HD; ESPN2 HD; ESPNews; Golf Channel; HD Theater; IFC; Investigation Discovery; TNT HD; WE tv.
Fee: $5.95 monthly.

Pay Service 1
Pay Units: N.A.
Programming (via satellite): Cinemax; HBO.
Fee: $13.50 monthly.

Digital Pay Service 1
Pay Units: N.A.
Programming (via satellite): Cinemax (multiplexed); Flix; HBO (multiplexed); Showtime (multiplexed); Starz (multiplexed); Starz Encore (multiplexed); The Movie Channel (multiplexed).
Fee: $10.00 monthly (each).

Video-On-Demand: No

Pay-Per-View
Playboy TV (delivered digitally); iN DEMAND (delivered digitally); Fresh (delivered digitally); Hot Choice (delivered digitally).

Internet Service
Operational: Yes.
Fee: $79.99 installation; $35.99 monthly.

Telephone Service
Analog: Not Operational
Digital: Operational
Fee: $29.99 monthly
Miles of Plant: 120.0 (coaxial); None (fiber optic).
General Manager: Rick Ferrall.
Ownership: MaxxSouth Broadband (MSO).

KOSSUTH—Formerly served by Zoom Media. No longer in operation. ICA: MS0046.

LAKE—Formerly served by Zoom Media. No longer in operation. ICA: MS0159.

LAUDERDALE—Comcast Cable. Now served by HATTIESBURG, MS [MS0005]. ICA: MS0160.

LAUREL—Comcast Cable. Now served by HATTIESBURG, MS [MS0005]. ICA: MS0013.

LEAKESVILLE—Alliance Communications, PO Box 9090, Tyler, TX 75711. Phones: 903-561-4411; 501-679-6619 (Greenbrier, AR office); 800-842-8160. Web Site: http://www.alliancecable.net. ICA: MS0095.
TV Market Ranking: Outside TV Markets (LEAKESVILLE). Franchise award date: N.A. Franchise expiration date: N.A. Began: July 14, 1989.
Channel capacity: N.A. Channels available but not in use: N.A.

Basic Service
Subscribers: 59.
Programming (received off-air): WDAM-TV (ABC, Bounce TV, NBC, This TV) Laurel; WKRG-TV (CBS, MeTV) Mobile; WLOX (ABC, Bounce TV, CBS) Biloxi; WMAH-TV (PBS) Biloxi; WXXV-TV (FOX, MNT, NBC) Gulfport.
Programming (via satellite): A&E; AMC; Cartoon Network; CNBC; CNN; Comedy Central; Discovery Channel; Disney Channel; ESPN; ESPN2; Fox News Channel; Fox Sports 1; FOX Sports South/SportSouth; Freeform; FX; Great American Country; HLN; Lifetime; Outdoor Channel; QVC; TBS; The Weather Channel; TNT; Travel Channel; Trinity Broadcasting Network (TBN); USA Network; WGN America.
Fee: $35.00 installation; $22.45 monthly.

Pay Service 1
Pay Units: N.A.
Programming (via satellite): HBO.
Fee: $9.42 monthly.

Internet Service
Operational: No.

Telephone Service
None
Miles of Plant: 11.0 (coaxial); None (fiber optic). Homes passed: 588.
Chief Financial Officer: David Starrett. Vice President & General Manager: John Brinker. Vice President, Programming: Julie Newman.
Ownership: Buford Media Group LLC (MSO).

LELAND—NewWave Communications, One Montgomery Plaza, 4th Floor, Sikeston, MO 63801. Phones: 573-472-9500; 888-863-9928. Fax: 573-472-9518. E-mail: info@newwave.com. Web Site: http://www.newwavecom.com. ICA: MS0039.
TV Market Ranking: Below 100 (LELAND). Franchise award date: N.A. Franchise expiration date: N.A. Began: February 1, 1957.
Channel capacity: N.A. Channels available but not in use: N.A.

Basic Service
Subscribers: 643.
Programming (received off-air): WABG-TV (ABC, FOX) Greenwood; WDBD (FOX, Grit) Jackson; WJTV (Antenna TV, CBS) Jackson; WLBT (Bounce TV, NBC, This TV) Jackson; WMAO-TV (PBS) Greenwood; WXVT (CBS) Greenville.
Programming (via satellite): C-SPAN; CW PLUS; FOX Sports Networks; ION Television; MTV; TBS; The Weather Channel; Travel Channel; Trinity Broadcasting Network (TBN); WGN America.
Fee: $35.00 installation; $34.78 monthly.

Expanded Basic Service 1
Subscribers: N.A.
Programming (via satellite): A&E; AMC; Animal Planet; BET; Cartoon Network; CMT; CNN; C-SPAN 2; Discovery Channel; E! HD; ESPN; ESPN2; Fox News Channel; FX; Hallmark Channel; HGTV; History; Lifetime;

Cable Systems—Mississippi

MSNBC; MTV; Nickelodeon; Spike TV; Syfy; TLC; TNT; Turner Classic Movies; TV Land; USA Network; VH1.
Fee: $48.20 monthly.
Digital Basic Service
Subscribers: N.A.
Fee: $11.00 monthly.
Digital Pay Service 1
Pay Units: N.A.
Programming (via satellite): Cinemax; HBO; Showtime; Starz; Starz Encore; The Movie Channel.
Fee: $14.95 installation; $8.00 monthly (Starz), $9.00 monthly (Cinemax), $11.00 monthly (Starz/Encore), $15.00 (Showtime/TMC), $17.00 monthly (HBO) or $26.00 monthly (HBO/Cinemax).
Video-On-Demand: No
Internet Service
Operational: Yes.
Fee: $36.99-$46.99 monthly; $6.00 modem lease.
Telephone Service
Digital: Operational
Miles of Plant: 25.0 (coaxial); None (fiber optic). Homes passed: 2,600.
General Manager: Staci Gowan.
Ownership: NewWave Communications LLC (MSO).

LEXINGTON—Formerly served by CableSouth Media. Now served by Cable One, GRENADA, MS [MS0021]. ICA: MS0161.

LIBERTY—Bailey Cable TV Inc, 807 Church St, Port Gibson, MS 39150-2413. Phone: 601-437-8300. Fax: 601-437-6860. E-mail: cs@baileycable.net. Web Site: http://www.baileycable.net. ICA: MS0221.
TV Market Ranking: Outside TV Markets (LIBERTY).
Channel capacity: N.A. Channels available but not in use: N.A.
Basic Service
Subscribers: 65.
Fee: $15.00 installation; $42.95 monthly.
President: David A. Bailey.
Ownership: Bailey Cable TV Inc. (MSO).

LOUISE—Franklin Telephone (Telapex). This cable system has converted to IPTV. Now served by MEADVILLE, MS [MS5012]. ICA: MS0121.

LOUISE—Franklin Telephone (Telapex). This cable system has converted to IPTV. Now served by MEADVILLE, MS [MS5012]. ICA: MS5029.

LOUISVILLE—Formerly served by Mediacom. Now served by MaxxSouth Broadband, PONTOTOC, MS [MS0045]. ICA: MS0228.

LUCEDALE—Mediacom, 760 Middle St, PO Box 1009, Fairhope, AL 36532. Phones: 850-934-7700 (Gulf Breeze regional office); 251-928-0374. Fax: 251-928-3804. Web Site: http://www.mediacomcable.com. Also serves George County. ICA: MS0065.
TV Market Ranking: 59 (George County (portions), LUCEDALE); Below 100 (George County (portions)); Outside TV Markets (George County (portions)). Franchise award date: May 20, 1980. Franchise expiration date: N.A. Began: August 1, 1981.
Channel capacity: N.A. Channels available but not in use: N.A.
Basic Service
Subscribers: 260.
Programming (received off-air): WALA-TV (FOX) Mobile; WDAM-TV (ABC, Bounce TV, NBC, This TV) Laurel; WEAR-TV (ABC, The Country Network) Pensacola; WFNA (Bounce TV, CW) Gulf Shores; WJTC (IND) Pensacola; WKRG-TV (CBS, MeTV) Mobile; WLOX (ABC, Bounce TV, CBS) Biloxi; WMAH-TV (PBS) Biloxi; WMPV-TV (TBN) Mobile; WPMI-TV (NBC) Mobile.
Programming (via satellite): A&E; AMC; Animal Planet; BET; Cartoon Network; CMT; CNBC; CNN; Comedy Central; C-SPAN; Discovery Channel; Disney Channel; Disney XD; E! HD; ESPN; ESPN2; Food Network; Fox News Channel; Fox Sports 1; FOX Sports South/SportSouth; Freeform; FX; Golf Channel; Hallmark Channel; HGTV; History; HLN; INSP; ION Television; Lifetime; MSNBC; MTV; Nickelodeon; Outdoor Channel; Pop; QVC; Spike TV; Syfy; TBS; The Weather Channel; TLC; TNT; Travel Channel; truTV; Turner Classic Movies; TV Land; USA Network; VH1; WE tv; WGN America.
Fee: $29.50 installation; $46.42 monthly; $3.35 converter.
Digital Basic Service
Subscribers: N.A.
Programming (via satellite): BBC America; Discovery Digital Networks; DMX Music; GSN; IFC.
Fee: $5.00 converter.
Digital Pay Service 1
Pay Units: N.A.
Programming (via satellite): Cinemax (multiplexed); Flix; HBO (multiplexed); Showtime (multiplexed); Starz (multiplexed); Starz Encore (multiplexed); Sundance TV; The Movie Channel (multiplexed).
Fee: $9.95 monthly (Cinemax, Starz/Encore or Showtime/TMC/Flix/Sundance), $11.95 monthly (HBO).
Video-On-Demand: Yes
Pay-Per-View
special events (delivered digitally); Sports PPV (delivered digitally).
Internet Service
Operational: Yes.
Subscribers: 158.
Broadband Service: Mediacom High Speed Internet.
Fee: $49.95 installation; $40.95 monthly.
Telephone Service
Digital: Operational
Subscribers: 29.
Miles of Plant: 42.0 (coaxial); 48.0 (fiber optic). Homes passed: 1,777.
Vice President: David Servies. Operations Director: Gene Wuchner. Technical Operations Manager: Mike Sneary. Sales & Marketing Manager: Joey Nagem.
Ownership: Mediacom LLC (MSO).

LUMBERTON—Media3, PO Box 620, Milan, TN 38358. Phone: 866-257-2044. E-mail: customerservice@mymedia3.com. Web Site: http://www.mymedia3.com. ICA: MS0055.
TV Market Ranking: Below 100 (LUMBERTON). Franchise award date: April 15, 1980. Franchise expiration date: N.A. Began: January 1, 1981.
Channel capacity: N.A. Channels available but not in use: N.A.
Basic Service
Subscribers: 140.
Programming (received off-air): WDAM-TV (ABC, Bounce TV, NBC, This TV) Laurel; WHLT (CBS) Hattiesburg; WLOX (ABC, Bounce TV, CBS) Biloxi; WMAH-TV (PBS) Biloxi; WXXV-TV (FOX, MNT, NBC) Gulfport.
Programming (via satellite): A&E; AMC; BET; Bravo; Cartoon Network; CNBC; CNN; Comedy Central; C-SPAN; Discovery Channel; Disney Channel; E! HD; ESPN; ESPN2; Fox News Channel; Fox Sports 1; Freeform; Fuse; FX; Great American Country; HGTV; History; HLN; Lifetime; Outdoor Channel; QVC; TBS; The Weather Channel; TLC; TNT; Travel Channel; Trinity Broadcasting Network (TBN); USA Network; WGN America.
Fee: $24.95 installation; $22.45 monthly.
Digital Basic Service
Subscribers: N.A.
Pay Service 1
Pay Units: N.A.
Programming (via satellite): HBO; Starz; Starz Encore.
Fee: $25.00 installation; $9.42 monthly (HBO).
Internet Service
Operational: No.
Telephone Service
None
Miles of Plant: 17.0 (coaxial); 3.0 (fiber optic). Homes passed: 896.
Chief Financial Officer: Thomas Pate. President: Alan Taylor. General Manager: Drew Cannon. Chief Technician: Brian Malley. Marketing Director: Glenda C. Elliott.
Ownership: CableSouth Media3 LLC (MSO).

MABEN—Formerly served by MetroCast Mississippi. Now served by MaxxSouth Broadband, PONTOTOC, MS [MS0045]. ICA: MS0094.

MACEDONIA—Formerly served by Zoom Media. No longer in operation. ICA: MS0163.

MACON—Cable TV Inc, 612 Hwy 82 West, PO Box 2598, Starkville, MS 39760. Phone: 662-324-5121. Fax: 662-324-0233. Also serves Brooksville & Shuqualak. ICA: MS0217.
TV Market Ranking: Below 100 (Brooksville, MACON, Shuqualak).
Channel capacity: N.A. Channels available but not in use: N.A.
Basic Service
Subscribers: N.A.
Programming (received off-air): WCBI-TV (CBS, CW, MNT) Columbus; WLOV-TV (FOX, MeTV, This TV) West Point; WMAB-TV (PBS) Mississippi State; WSES (ABC, TNN) Tuscaloosa; WTOK-TV (ABC, CW, FOX, MNT) Meridian; WTVA (ABC, NBC) Tupelo.
Programming (via satellite): A&E; AMC; Animal Planet; BET; Cartoon Network; CMT; CNBC; CNN; C-SPAN; C-SPAN 2; Discovery Channel; ESPN; ESPN2; Food Network; Fox News Channel; FOX Sports South/SportSouth; Freeform; Hallmark Channel; HGTV; History; HLN; HSN; Lifetime; Nickelodeon; QVC; Spike TV; Syfy; TBS; The Weather Channel; TLC; TNT; Travel Channel; Trinity Broadcasting Network (TBN); truTV; TV Land; USA Network; WGN America.
Fee: $40.00 installation.
Pay Service 1
Pay Units: N.A.
Programming (via satellite): Cinemax; HBO; Showtime; Starz; Starz Encore; The Movie Channel.
Fee: $9.95 - $12.75 monthly (each).

Access the most current data instantly
FREE TRIAL @ ADVANCED TVFactbook
TELCO/IPTV • CABLE TV • TV STATIONS
www.warren-news.com/factbook.htm

Internet Service
Operational: No.
Telephone Service
None
General Manager: Andy Williams.
Ownership: Andy Williams (MSO).

MAGEE—Bailey Cable TV Inc, 807 Church St, Port Gibson, MS 39150-2413. Phones: 601-437-8300; 601-849-4201; 601-892-5249. Fax: 601-437-6860. E-mail: cs@baileycable.net. Web Site: http://www.baileycable.net. ICA: MS0051.
TV Market Ranking: Below 100 (MAGEE). Franchise award date: N.A. Franchise expiration date: N.A. Began: July 1, 1981.
Channel capacity: N.A. Channels available but not in use: N.A.
Basic Service
Subscribers: 438.
Programming (received off-air): WAPT (ABC) Jackson; WDAM-TV (ABC, Bounce TV, NBC, This TV) Laurel; WDBD (FOX, Grit) Jackson; WJTV (Antenna TV, CBS) Jackson; WLBT (Bounce TV, NBC, This TV) Jackson.
Programming (via satellite): A&E; BET; Cartoon Network; CMT; CNN; C-SPAN; Discovery Channel; ESPN; ESPN2; Freeform; History; MTV; Nickelodeon; QVC; Spike TV; Syfy; TBS; The Weather Channel; TLC; TNT; Trinity Broadcasting Network (TBN); TV Land; USA Network; VH1; WGN America.
Fee: $15.00 installation; $42.95 monthly; $2.00 converter.
Pay Service 1
Pay Units: N.A.
Programming (via satellite): Showtime; The Movie Channel.
Fee: $9.00 monthly (each).
Video-On-Demand: No
Internet Service
Operational: Yes.
Fee: $29.99 monthly.
Telephone Service
None
Miles of Plant: 40.0 (coaxial); None (fiber optic). Homes passed: 1,750.
President: David A. Bailey. General Manager: Dwight Bailey. Chief Technician: Jim Morton.
Ownership: Bailey Cable TV Inc. (MSO).

MAYERSVILLE—Formerly served by J & L Cable. No longer in operation. ICA: MS0122.

MCLAURIN—Formerly served by Home Cable Entertainment. No longer in operation. ICA: MS0165.

MEADVILLE—Franklin Telephone. Formerly [MS0069]. This cable system has converted to IPTV, 154 Main St East, PO Box 278, Meadville, MS 39653. Phones: 601-964-8311 (New Augusta office); 601-384-5855 (Bude office); 601-384-5851. E-mail: comments@FTBweb.net. Web Site: http://www.ftcweb.net. Also serves Ackerman, Artesia, Barlow, Benndale, Brookhaven, Brooksville, Bude, Chester, Choctaw County (portions), Crawford, Crosby, Crys-

2017 Edition   D-433

Mississippi—Cable Systems

tal Springs, Eagle Lake, Eddiceton, Franklin County (portions), Hazelhurst, Hermanville, Holly Bluff, Humphrey's County (portions), Inverness, Isola, Janice, Lawrence, Louise, McLain, New Augusta, New Hebron, Pattison, Roxie, Sunflower County (portions) & Union Church. ICA: MS5012.
TV Market Ranking: Below 100 (Bude, Crosby, Humphrey's County (portions), New Augusta); Outside TV Markets (Eagle Lake, Louise).
Channel capacity: N.A. Channels available but not in use: N.A.
Basic
Subscribers: 2,864.
Fee: $95.65 installation; $18.92 monthly.
Internet Service
Operational: Yes.
Telephone Service
Digital: Operational
General Manager: Tom Griffin.
Ownership: Telapex Inc.

MEADVILLE-BUDE—Franklin Telephone (Telapex). This cable system has converted to IPTV. Now served by MEADVILLE, MS [MS5012]. ICA: MS0069.

MENDENHALL—Bailey Cable TV Inc, 807 Church St, Port Gibson, MS 39150-2413. Phones: 601-437-8300; 601-849-4201; 601-892-5249. Fax: 601-437-6860. E-mail: cs@baileycable.net. Web Site: http://www.baileycable.net. Also serves Braxton, D'Lo, Mount Olive & Simpson County. ICA: MS0081.
TV Market Ranking: 77 (D'Lo, MENDENHALL, Simpson County (portions)); Below 100 (Braxton, Mount Olive, Simpson County (portions)); Outside TV Markets (Simpson County (portions)). Franchise award date: N.A. Franchise expiration date: N.A. Began: July 1, 1981.
Channel capacity: N.A. Channels available but not in use: N.A.
Basic Service
Subscribers: 228.
Programming (received off-air): WAPT (ABC) Jackson; WDBD (FOX, Grit) Jackson; WJTV (Antenna TV, CBS) Jackson; WLBT (Bounce TV, NBC, This TV) Jackson. Programming (via satellite): A&E; BET; Cartoon Network; CMT; CNN; C-SPAN; Discovery Channel; ESPN; ESPN2; Freeform; History; MTV; Nickelodeon; QVC; Spike TV; Syfy; TBS; The Weather Channel; TLC; TNT; Trinity Broadcasting Network (TBN); TV Land; USA Network; VH1; WGN America.
Fee: $15.00 installation; $42.95 monthly.
Pay Service 1
Pay Units: N.A.
Programming (via satellite): Showtime; The Movie Channel.
Fee: $10.00 installation; $9.00 monthly (each).
Video-On-Demand: No
Internet Service
Operational: No.

Telephone Service
None
Miles of Plant: 20.0 (coaxial); None (fiber optic). Homes passed: 750.
President: David A. Bailey. General Manager: Dwight Bailey. Chief Technician: Jim Morton.
Ownership: Bailey Cable TV Inc. (MSO).

MERIDIAN—Comcast Cable. Now served by HATTIESBURG, MS [MS0005]. ICA: MS0007.

MERIDIAN NAVAL AIR STATION—Media3, PO Box 650, Milan, TN 38358. Phone: 866-257-2044. E-mail: customerservice@mymedia3.com. Web Site: http://www.mymedia3.com. ICA: MS0215.
TV Market Ranking: Below 100 (MERIDIAN NAVAL AIR STATION).
Channel capacity: N.A. Channels available but not in use: N.A.
Basic Service
Subscribers: 11.
Programming (received off-air): WGBC (FOX, NBC) Meridian; WMAW-TV (PBS) Meridian; WMDN (CBS) Meridian; WTOK-TV (ABC, CW, FOX, MNT) Meridian.
Programming (via satellite): A&E; Animal Planet; BET; Cartoon Network; CNN; Comedy Central; C-SPAN; Discovery Channel; Disney Channel; Disney XD; DIY Network; E! HD; ESPN; ESPN2; Food Network; Fox News Channel; Fox Sports 1; Freeform; Fuse; FX; Golf Channel; Great American Country; GSN; HGTV; History; HLN; INSP; Lifetime; MSNBC; Outdoor Channel; QVC; Syfy; TBS; The Weather Channel; TLC; TNT; Travel Channel; Turner Classic Movies; USA Network; WGN America.
Fee: $24.95 installation; $22.45 monthly.
Pay Service 1
Pay Units: N.A.
Programming (via satellite): HBO; Showtime.
Internet Service
Operational: No.
Telephone Service
None
Miles of Plant: 8.0 (coaxial); None (fiber optic). Homes passed: 519.
Chief Financial Officer: Thomas Pate.
Ownership: CableSouth Media3 LLC (MSO).

MONTICELLO—Formerly served by Zoom Media. No longer in operation. ICA: MS0072.

MOOREVILLE—Formerly served by Foster Communications Inc. No longer in operation. ICA: MS0085.

MOOREVILLE—Formerly served by SouthTel Communications LP. No longer in operation. ICA: MS0166.

MOUND BAYOU—Formerly served by Galaxy Cablevision. Now served by Cable One, CLEVELAND, MS [MS0019]. ICA: MS0061.

NATCHEZ—Cable One, 107 North Dr. M.L. King St, Natchez, MS 39120. Phone: 601-442-5418. Fax: 601-442-1466. Web Site: http://www.cableone.net. Also serves Concordia Parish (portions) & Vidalia, LA; Adams County, MS. ICA: MS0012.
TV Market Ranking: Below 100 (Adams County, Concordia Parish (portions), NATCHEZ, Vidalia). Franchise award date: September 1, 1958. Franchise expiration date: N.A. Began: September 1, 1958.
Channel capacity: N.A. Channels available but not in use: N.A.
Basic Service
Subscribers: 2,595.
Programming (received off-air): KALB-TV (CBS, CW, NBC) Alexandria; KLAX-TV (ABC) Alexandria; KNOE-TV (ABC, CBS, CW) Monroe; WAPT (ABC) Jackson; WBRZ-TV (ABC) Baton Rouge; WJTV (Antenna TV, CBS) Jackson; WLBT (Bounce TV, NBC, This TV) Jackson; WMAU-TV (PBS) Bude; WNTZ-TV (FOX, MNT) Natchez; allband FM.
Programming (via satellite): C-SPAN; CW PLUS; Pop.
Fee: $90.00 installation; $29.00 monthly; $2.00 converter.
Expanded Basic Service 1
Subscribers: N.A.
Programming (via satellite): A&E; AMC; Animal Planet; BET; Cartoon Network; CMT; CNBC; CNN; C-SPAN 2; Discovery Channel; Disney Channel; ESPN; ESPN2; Food Network; Fox News Channel; Freeform; FX; HGTV; History; HLN; INSP; Lifetime; MSNBC; MTV; Nickelodeon; QVC; Spike TV; Syfy; TBS; The Weather Channel; TLC; TNT; Travel Channel; Turner Classic Movies; TV Land; USA Network; VH1.
Digital Basic Service
Subscribers: N.A.
Programming (via satellite): 3ABN; A&E HD; Boomerang; BYUtv; Cine Mexicano; CNN en Espanol; Discovery Kids Channel; Disney XD; ESPN Classic; ESPN Deportes; ESPN HD; ESPN2 HD; ESPNews; FamilyNet; Food Network HD; FOX College Sports Central; FOX College Sports Pacific; Fox Deportes; Fox Sports 1; Fox Sports 2; FXM; FYI; Golf Channel; Great American Country; GSN; Hallmark Channel; HD Theater; HGTV HD; History International; INSP; La Familia Cosmovision; MC; National Geographic Channel; National Geographic Channel HD; NBC Universo; Outdoor Channel; OWN; Oprah Winfrey Network; Science Channel; Telemundo; Toon Disney en Espanol; Trinity Broadcasting Network (TBN); TVG Network; Universal HD; WE tv.
Digital Pay Service 1
Pay Units: N.A.
Programming (via satellite): Cinemax (multiplexed); Flix; HBO (multiplexed); HBO HD; Showtime (multiplexed); Showtime HD; Starz (multiplexed); Starz Encore (multiplexed); Sundance TV; The Movie Channel (multiplexed); The Movie Channel HD.
Fee: $15.00 monthly (Cinemax, HBO, Showtime/TMC/Flix/Sundance or Starz/Encore).
Video-On-Demand: No
Pay-Per-View
iN DEMAND (delivered digitally); SexSee (delivered digitally); Juicy (delivered digitally); VaVoom (delivered digitally).
Internet Service
Operational: Yes.
Subscribers: 2,978.
Broadband Service: CableONE.net.
Fee: $75.00 installation; $43.00 monthly.

Telephone Service
Digital: Operational
Subscribers: 1,434.
Fee: $39.95 monthly
Miles of Plant: 471.0 (coaxial); 69.0 (fiber optic). Homes passed: 15,250.
Vice President: Patrick A. Dolohanty. General Manager: Bobby McCool. Chief Technician: Kenny Wright. Office Manager: Dorothy Champion. Marketing Director: Jullia Ivey.
Ownership: Cable ONE Inc. (MSO).

NETTLETON—Formerly served by Metro-Cast Mississippi. Now served by MaxxSouth Broadband, PONTOTOC, MS [MS0045]. ICA: MS0170.

NEW ALBANY—Formerly served by Metro-Cast Mississippi. Now served by MaxxSouth Broadband, PONTOTOC, MS [MS0045]. ICA: MS0027.

NEW AUGUSTA—Franklin Telephone (Telapex). This cable system has converted to IPTV. Now served by MEADVILLE, MS [MS5012]. ICA: MS5030.

NEW AUGUSTA—Telapex. This cable system has converted to IPTV. Now served by Franklin Telephone (Telapex), MEADVILLE, MS [MS5012]. ICA: MS0117.

NEW HEBRON—Franklin Telephone (Telapex). This cable system has converted to IPTV. Now served by MEADVILLE, MS [MS5012]. ICA: MS5014.

NEW HEBRON—Franklin Telephone (Telapex). This cable system has converted to IPTV. Now served by MEADVILLE, MS [MS5012]. ICA: MS0171.

NEWTON—Formerly served by MetroCast Mississippi. Now served by MaxxSouth Broadband, PONTOTOC, MS [MS0045]. ICA: MS0059.

OAKLAND—Formerly served by L & J Cable. No longer in operation. ICA: MS0208.

OKTIBBEHA COUNTY—Dixie Cablevision Inc, 612 Hwy 82 West, PO Box 2598, Starkville, MS 39760. Phone: 662-324-5121. Fax: 662-324-0233. ICA: MS0218.
TV Market Ranking: Below 100 (OKTIBBEHA COUNTY (portions)); Outside TV Markets (OKTIBBEHA COUNTY (portions)).
Channel capacity: N.A. Channels available but not in use: N.A.
Basic Service
Subscribers: N.A.
Fee: $40.00 installation.
Internet Service
Operational: No.
Telephone Service
None
General Manager: Andy Williams.
Ownership: Andy Williams (MSO).

OSYKA—Formerly served by Almega Cable. No longer in operation. ICA: MS0120.

OXFORD—Formerly served by MetroCast Mississippi. Now served by MaxxSouth Broadband, PONTOTOC, MS [MS0045]. ICA: MS0020.

PACHUTA—Formerly served by Galaxy Cablevision. No longer in operation. ICA: MS0173.

Cable Systems—Mississippi

PASCAGOULA—Cable One. Now served by GULFPORT, MS [MS0008]. ICA: MS0003.

PAULDING—Comcast Cable. Now served by HATTIESBURG, MS [MS0005]. ICA: MS0210.

PEARL—Comcast Cable. Now served by JACKSON, MS [MS0001]. ICA: MS0006.

PEARLINGTON—Mediacom. Now served by WAVELAND, MS [MS0022]. ICA: MS0088.

PHILADELPHIA—MaxxSouth Broadband, 911 Hwy 12 West, Ste 202-B, Starkville, MS 39759. Phone: 800-457-5351. Web Site: http://www.maxxsouth.com. Also serves Choctaw Indian Reservation & Neshoba County (unincorporated areas). ICA: MS0029.
TV Market Ranking: Below 100 (Neshoba County (unincorporated areas) (portions)); Outside TV Markets (Choctaw Indian Reservation, Neshoba County (unincorporated areas) (portions), PHILADELPHIA). Franchise award date: March 20, 1967. Franchise expiration date: N.A. Began: December 10, 1967.
Channel capacity: N.A. Channels available but not in use: N.A.
Basic Service
Subscribers: 1,775.
Programming (received off-air): WGBC (FOX, NBC) Meridian; WHTV (MNT) Jackson; WJTV (Antenna TV, CBS) Jackson; WMAB-TV (PBS) Mississippi State; WMDN (CBS) Meridian; WTOK-TV (ABC, CW, FOX, MNT) Meridian; WTVA (ABC, NBC) Tupelo. Programming (via satellite): CW PLUS; Hallmark Channel; Trinity Broadcasting Network (TBN); WGN America.
Fee: $55.00 installation; $30.95 monthly.
Expanded Basic Service 1
Subscribers: N.A.
Programming (via satellite): A&E; BET; Cartoon Network; CMT; CNBC; CNN; Comcast/Charter Sports Southeast (CSS); Comedy Central; C-SPAN; Discovery Channel; Disney Channel; ESPN; ESPN2; Food Network; Fox News Channel; FOX Sports South/SportSouth; Freeform; FX; FXM; Golf Channel; Great American Country; HGTV; History; HLN; Lifetime; MTV; National Geographic Channel; Nickelodeon; Outdoor Channel; QVC; RFD-TV; Spike TV; Syfy; TBS; The Weather Channel; TNT; Travel Channel; Turner Classic Movies; TV Land; UP; USA Network; VH1.
Fee: $30.00 installation; $31.00 monthly.
Digital Basic Service
Subscribers: N.A.
Programming (via satellite): Animal Planet HD; BBC America; Bravo; CMT; Destination America; Discovery Channel HD; Discovery Kids Channel; Discovery Life Channel; DMX Music; ESPN HD; ESPN2 HD; ESPNews; Fox Sports1; HD Theater; IFC; Investigation Discovery; MTV Classic; Nick Jr.; Nicktoons; Outdoor Channel 2 HD; OWN: Oprah Winfrey Network; Science Channel; Science HD; TLC HD; TNT HD; WE tv.
Digital Pay Service 1
Pay Units: N.A.
Programming (via satellite): Cinemax (multiplexed); Cinemax HD; Flix; HBO (multiplexed); HBO HD; Showtime; Starz (multiplexed); Starz Encore (multiplexed); The Movie Channel.
Video-On-Demand: No
Pay-Per-View
iN DEMAND (delivered digitally); Hot Choice (delivered digitally).

Internet Service
Operational: Yes.
Fee: $79.99 installation; $35.99 monthly.
Telephone Service
Analog: Not Operational
Digital: Operational
Fee: $29.95 monthly
Miles of Plant: 155.0 (coaxial); 16.0 (fiber optic). Homes passed: 3,975.
General Manager: Rick Ferrall.
Ownership: MaxxSouth Broadband (MSO).

PICAYUNE—Charter Communications. Now served by SLIDELL, LA [LA0182]. ICA: MS0023.

PONTOTOC—Formerly served by Zoom Media. No longer in operation. ICA: MS0041.

PONTOTOC—MaxxSouth Broadband, 911 Hwy 12 West, Ste 202-B, Starkville, MS 39759. Phone: 800-457-5351. Web Site: http://www.maxxsouth.com. Also serves Red Bay, AL; Abbeville, Aberdeen Twp., Amory, Ashland, Baldwyn, Becker, Belmont, Booneville, Bruce, Burnsville, Calhoun City, Coffeeville, Decatur, Dennis, Derma, Ecru, Golden, Guntown, Hatley, Hickory Flat, Holly Springs, Houston, Ingomar, Iuka, Jumpertown, Lafayette County (unincorporated areas), Lee County (unincorporated areas), Louisville, Maben, Mathiston, Myrtle, Nettleton, New Albany, Newton, Noxapater, Oktibbeha County (unincorporated areas), Oxford, Pittsboro, Potts Camp, Saltillo, Shannon, Smithville, Snow Lake Shores, Starkville, Tishomingo County, Union (town), Union County, University of Mississippi, Vardaman, Water Valley, Wheeler & Winston County, MS. ICA: MS0045.
TV Market Ranking: Below 100 (Abbeville, Becker, Derma, Ecru, Guntown, Hatley, Houston, Ingomar, Jumpertown, Lafayette County (unincorporated areas), Lee County (unincorporated areas), Mathiston, Myrtle, Newton, Oktibbeha County (unincorporated areas), Pittsboro, PONTOTOC, Saltillo, Shannon, Smithville, Snow Lake Shores, Tishomingo County, Union County (portions), University of Mississippi, Vardaman, Aberdeen Twp., Amory, Ashland, Baldwyn, Belmont, Booneville, Bruce, Calhoun City, Hickory Flat, Holly Springs, Iuka, Maben, Nettleton, New Albany, Oxford, Potts Camp, Starkville, Union (town)); Outside TV Markets (Water Valley, Burnsville, Coffeeville). Franchise award date: May 10, 1966. Franchise expiration date: N.A. Began: November 1, 1968.
Channel capacity: N.A. Channels available but not in use: N.A.
Basic Service
Subscribers: 22,641.
Programming (received off-air): W15CG Pontotoc; WATN-TV (ABC) Memphis; WCBI-TV (CBS, CW, MNT) Columbus; WHBQ-TV (Decades, FOX, Movies!) Memphis; WLMT (CW, MeTV, MNT) Memphis; WLOV-TV (FOX, MeTV, This TV) West Point; WMAV-TV (PBS) Oxford; WMC-TV (Bounce TV, NBC, This TV) Memphis; WREG-TV (Antenna TV, CBS) Memphis; WTVA (ABC, NBC) Tupelo; allband FM. Programming (via satellite): WGN America.
Fee: $49.95 installation; $35.95 monthly; $3.35 converter.
Expanded Basic Service 1
Subscribers: N.A.
Programming (via satellite): A&E; AMC; Animal Planet; BET; Bravo; Cartoon Network; CMT; CNBC; CNN; Comedy Central; C-SPAN; C-SPAN 2; Discovery Channel; Discovery Life Channel; Disney Channel; E! HD; ESPN; ESPN Classic; ESPN2; Food Network; Fox News Channel; Fox Sports 1; Freeform; FX; Golf Channel; Great American Country; Hallmark Channel; HGTV; History; HLN; INSP; ION Television; Lifetime; MSNBC; MTV; Nickelodeon; Outdoor Channel; QVC; Spike TV; SportSouth; Syfy; TBS; The Weather Channel; TLC; TNT; Travel Channel; Trinity Broadcasting Network (TBN); TV Land; USA Network; VH1; WE tv.
Fee: $33.00 monthly; $3.35 converter.
Digital Basic Service
Subscribers: N.A.
Programming (via satellite): BBC America; Bloomberg Television; Cloo; Discovery Digital Networks; Disney XD; DMX Music; ESPN Classic; ESPNews; Fox Sports 1; Fuse; FXM; FYI; Golf Channel; GSN; HD Theater; History International; IFC; LMN; National Geographic Channel; NBCSN; NFL Network; Nick Jr.; Nicktoons; Outdoor Channel; TeenNick; TNT HD; Turner Classic Movies; Universal HD.
Fee: $5.00 converter.
Digital Pay Service 1
Pay Units: N.A.
Programming (via satellite): Cinemax (multiplexed); Flix; HBO (multiplexed); Showtime (multiplexed); Starz (multiplexed); Sundance TV; The Movie Channel (multiplexed).
Fee: $6.00 monthly (Encore), $13.00 monthly (Cinemax, HBO, Starz or Showtime/TMC/Flix/Sundance).
Video-On-Demand: Yes
Pay-Per-View
Fresh (delivered digitally); Hot Choice (delivered digitally); Playboy TV (delivered digitally); ESPN (delivered digitally); MLB Extra Innings (delivered digitally).
Internet Service
Operational: Yes.
Subscribers: 21,418.
Fee: $79.99 installation; $43.95 monthly.
Telephone Service
Digital: Operational
Subscribers: 3,644.
Miles of Plant: 3,381.0 (coaxial); 1,092.0 (fiber optic). Homes passed: 80,208.
General Manager: Rick Ferrall.
Ownership: MaxxSouth Broadband (MSO).

POPLARVILLE—Media3, PO Box 650, Milan, TN 38358. Phone: 866-257-2044. E-mail: customerservice@mymedia3.com. Web Site: http://www.mymedia3.com. ICA: MS0068.
TV Market Ranking: Below 100 (POPLARVILLE). Franchise award date: N.A. Franchise expiration date: N.A. Began: January 1, 1981.
Channel capacity: N.A. Channels available but not in use: N.A.
Basic Service
Subscribers: 204.
Programming (received off-air): WDAM-TV (ABC, Bounce TV, NBC, This TV) Laurel; WGNO (ABC, Antenna TV, Escape) New Orleans; WHLT (CBS) Hattiesburg; WLOX (ABC, Bounce TV, CBS) Biloxi; WMAH-TV (PBS) Biloxi; WWL-TV (CBS) New Orleans; WXXV-TV (FOX, MNT, NBC) Gulfport. Programming (via satellite): A&E; AMC; BET; Cartoon Network; CNBC; CNN; Comedy Central; C-SPAN; Discovery Channel; Disney Channel; ESPN; ESPN2; Fox News Channel; Freeform; Fuse; FX; Great American Country; Hallmark Channel; HGTV; History; HLN; Lifetime; Outdoor Channel; QVC; TBS; The Weather Channel; TLC; TNT; Trinity Broadcasting Network (TBN); USA Network; WGN America.
Fee: $24.95 installation; $22.45 monthly.
Pay Service 1
Pay Units: N.A.
Programming (via satellite): HBO; Starz; Starz Encore.
Fee: $25.00 installation; $9.42 monthly (HBO).
Internet Service
Operational: No.
Telephone Service
None
Miles of Plant: 43.0 (coaxial); None (fiber optic). Homes passed: 1,048.
Chief Financial Officer: Thomas Pate. President: Alan Taylor. General Manager: Drew Cannon. Chief Technician: Brian Malley. Marketing Director: Glenda C. Elliott.
Ownership: CableSouth Media3 LLC (MSO).

PORT GIBSON—Bailey Cable TV Inc, 807 Church St, Port Gibson, MS 39150-2413. Phones: 601-437-8300; 601-892-5249. Fax: 601-437-6860. E-mail: cs@baileycable.net. Web Site: http://www.baileycable.net. ICA: MS0212.
TV Market Ranking: Below 100 (PORT GIBSON).
Channel capacity: N.A. Channels available but not in use: N.A.
Basic Service
Subscribers: 201.
Programming (received off-air): WAPT (ABC) Jackson; WDBD (FOX, Grit) Jackson; WJTV (Antenna TV, CBS) Jackson; WLBT (Bounce TV, NBC, This TV) Jackson. Programming (via satellite): A&E; BET; Cartoon Network; CMT; CNBC; CNN; C-SPAN; Discovery Channel; ESPN; ESPN2; Freeform; History; MTV; Nickelodeon; QVC; Spike TV; Syfy; TBS; The Movie Channel; The Weather Channel; TLC; TNT; Trinity Broadcasting Network (TBN); TV Land; USA Network; VH1; WGN America.
Fee: $15.00 installation; $42.95 monthly.
Pay Service 1
Pay Units: N.A.
Programming (via satellite): Showtime.
Fee: $9.00 monthly.
Video-On-Demand: No
Internet Service
Operational: Yes.
Fee: $39.99 monthly.
Telephone Service
None
President: David A. Bailey. General Manager: Dwight Bailey. Chief Technician: Jim Morton.
Ownership: Bailey Cable TV Inc.

Mississippi—Cable Systems

POTTS CAMP—Formerly served by Metro-Cast Mississippi. Now served by MaxxSouth Broadband, PONTOTOC, MS [MS0045]. ICA: MS0214.

PRENTISS—Formerly served by Zoom Media. No longer in operation. ICA: MS0086.

PUCKETT—Comcast Cable. Now served by JACKSON, MS [MS0001]. ICA: MS0199.

QUITMAN—NewWave Communications, One Montgomery Plaza, 4th Floor, Sikeston, MO 63801. Phones: 573-472-9500; 888-863-9928. Fax: 573-472-9518. E-mail: info@newwave.com. Web Site: http://www.newwavecom.com. Also serves Enterprise & Stonewall. ICA: MS0176.
- TV Market Ranking: Below 100 (Enterprise, QUITMAN, Stonewall). Franchise award date: July 1, 1987. Franchise expiration date: N.A. Began: July 1, 1967.
- Channel capacity: N.A. Channels available but not in use: N.A.

Basic Service
- Subscribers: 424.
- Programming (received off-air): WGBC (FOX, NBC) Meridian; WMAW-TV (PBS) Meridian; WMDN (CBS) Meridian; WTOK-TV (ABC, CW, FOX, MNT) Meridian. Programming (via satellite): C-SPAN.
- Fee: $35.00 installation; $35.78 monthly.

Expanded Basic Service 1
- Subscribers: N.A.
- Programming (via satellite): A&E; Animal Planet; BET; Cartoon Network; CMT; CNBC; CNN; Comedy Central; Discovery Channel; E! HD; ESPN; ESPN2; Family Friendly Entertainment; Food Network; Fox News Channel; Freeform; FX; GSN; Hallmark Channel; HGTV; History; HLN; INSP; Lifetime; MTV; Nickelodeon; Outdoor Channel; QVC; Spike TV; Syfy; TBS; The Weather Channel; TLC; TNT; Travel Channel; Trinity Broadcasting Network (TBN); Turner Classic Movies; TV Land; Univision Studios; USA Network; VH1; WGN America.
- Fee: $49.20 monthly.

Digital Basic Service
- Subscribers: N.A.
- Programming (via satellite): BBC America; Bloomberg Television; Discovery Kids Channel; DMX Music; ESPN Classic; ESPNews; Fox Sports 1; FXM; FYI; Golf Channel; History International; IFC; LMN; National Geographic Channel; Nick Jr.; Nicktoons; TeenNick; WE tv.
- Fee: $11.00 monthly.

Digital Pay Service 1
- Pay Units: N.A.
- Programming (via satellite): Cinemax (multiplexed); HBO (multiplexed); Showtime (multiplexed); Starz (multiplexed); Starz Encore (multiplexed); The Movie Channel (multiplexed).
- Fee: $8.00 monthly (Starz), $9.00 monthly (Cinemax), $11.00 monthly (Starz/Encore), $15.00 monthly (Showtime/TMC), $17.00 monthly (HBO) or $26.00 monthly (HBO/Cinemax).

Video-On-Demand: No

Pay-Per-View
- iN DEMAND (delivered digitally); Hot Choice (delivered digitally); Playboy TV (delivered digitally); Fresh (delivered digitally); Shorteez (delivered digitally).

Internet Service
- Operational: Yes.
- Fee: $36.99-$46.99 monthly; $6.00 modem lease.

Telephone Service
- Digital: Operational
- Miles of Plant: 97.0 (coaxial); None (fiber optic).
- General Manager: Staci Gowan.
- Ownership: NewWave Communications LLC (MSO).

RALEIGH—MaxxSouth Broadband, 911 Hwy 12 West, Ste 202-B, Starkville, MS 39759. Phone: 800-457-5351. Web Site: http://www.maxxsouth.com. ICA: MS0177.
- TV Market Ranking: Below 100 (RALEIGH). Franchise award date: March 1, 1982. Franchise expiration date: N.A. Began: August 1, 1983.
- Channel capacity: N.A. Channels available but not in use: N.A.

Basic Service
- Subscribers: 90.
- Programming (received off-air): WAPT (ABC) Jackson; WDAM-TV (ABC, Bounce TV, NBC, This TV) Laurel; WDBD (FOX, Grit) Jackson; WJTV (Antenna TV, CBS) Jackson; WLBT (Bounce TV, NBC, This TV) Jackson; WMPN-TV (PBS) Jackson. Programming (via satellite): A&E; CMT; CNN; Discovery Channel; ESPN; Freeform; HLN; TBS; TNT; WGN America.
- Fee: $55.00 installation; $55.95 monthly.

Pay Service 1
- Pay Units: 20.
- Programming (via satellite): HBO.
- Fee: $13.95 monthly.

Internet Service
- Operational: No.

Telephone Service
- None
- Miles of Plant: 18.0 (coaxial); None (fiber optic).
- General Manager: Rick Ferrall.
- Ownership: MaxxSouth Broadband (MSO).

RICHTON—Alliance Communications, PO Box 9090, Tyler, TX 75711. Phones: 903-561-4411; 501-679-6619 (Greenbrier, AR office); 800-842-8160. Web Site: http://www.alliancecable.net. ICA: MS0089.
- TV Market Ranking: Below 100 (RICHTON). Franchise award date: N.A. Franchise expiration date: N.A. Began: July 14, 1989.
- Channel capacity: N.A. Channels available but not in use: N.A.

Basic Service
- Subscribers: 46.
- Programming (received off-air): WDAM-TV (ABC, Bounce TV, NBC, This TV) Laurel; WHLT (CBS) Hattiesburg; WLOX (ABC, Bounce TV, CBS) Biloxi; WMAH-TV (PBS) Biloxi; WXXV-TV (FOX, MNT, NBC) Gulfport. Programming (via satellite): A&E; BET; Cartoon Network; CNBC; CNN; Comedy Central; Discovery Channel; Disney Channel; ESPN; ESPN2; Fox News Channel; Fox Sports 1; Freeform; Great American Country; HGTV; History; HLN; Lifetime; Outdoor Channel; QVC; TBS; The Weather Channel; TLC; TNT; Trinity Broadcasting Network (TBN); USA Network; WGN America.
- Fee: $35.00 installation; $25.45 monthly.

Pay Service 1
- Pay Units: N.A.
- Programming (via satellite): Cinemax; HBO.
- Fee: $9.42 monthly (HBO).

Internet Service
- Operational: No.

Telephone Service
- None
- Miles of Plant: 11.0 (coaxial); None (fiber optic). Homes passed: 525.
- Chief Financial Officer: David Starrett. Vice President & General Manager: John Brinker.

Vice President, Programming: Julie Newman.
- Ownership: Buford Media Group LLC (MSO).

RIENZI—Formerly served by Zoom Media. No longer in operation. ICA: MS0097.

RIPLEY—Ripley Video Cable Co. Inc, 115 North Main St, PO Box 368, Ripley, MS 38663. Phone: 662-837-4881. E-mail: leon@ripleycable.net; dbailey@ripleycable.net. Web Site: http://www.ripleycable.net. Also serves Blue Mountain. ICA: MS0179.
- TV Market Ranking: Below 100 (Blue Mountain, RIPLEY). Franchise award date: June 1, 1969. Franchise expiration date: N.A. Began: January 1, 1969.
- Channel capacity: N.A. Channels available but not in use: N.A.

Basic Service
- Subscribers: 2,959.
- Programming (received off-air): WATN-TV (ABC) Memphis; WBII-CD (PBJ, Retro TV) Holly Springs; WCBI-TV (CBS, CW, MNT) Columbus; WFLI-TV (CW, MeTV) Cleveland; WHBQ-TV (Decades, FOX, Movies!) Memphis; WLMT (CW, MeTV, MNT) Memphis; WMAE-TV (PBS) Booneville; WMC-TV (Bounce TV, NBC, This TV) Memphis; WPXX-TV (ION, MNT) Memphis; WREG-TV (Antenna TV, CBS) Memphis; WTVA (ABC, NBC) Tupelo.
- Programming (via satellite): A&E; AMC; Animal Planet; BET; Boomerang; Cartoon Network; CMT; CNN; Comcast/Charter Sports Southeast (CSS); Comedy Central; C-SPAN; Discovery Channel; Disney Channel; E! HD; ESPN; ESPN Classic; ESPN2; Food Network; FOX Sports Networks; FOX Sports South/SportSouth; Freeform; FX; Great American Country; Hallmark Channel; HGTV; History; HLN; Lifetime; MTV; National Geographic Channel; Nickelodeon; Outdoor Channel; Pop; Spike TV; SportSouth; Syfy; TBS; The Weather Channel; TLC; TNT; truTV; Turner Classic Movies; TV Land; USA Network; VH1; WGN America.
- Fee: $50.00 installation; $26.99 monthly.

Digital Basic Service
- Subscribers: N.A.
- Programming (via satellite): BBC America; Bloomberg Television; Destination America; Discovery Kids Channel; Discovery Life Channel; DMX Music; ESPN Classic; ESPNews; Fox Sports 1; FYI; Golf Channel; GSN; History International; IFC; Investigation Discovery; LMN; National Geographic Channel; NBCSN; OWN: Oprah Winfrey Network; RFD-TV; Science Channel; Starz (multiplexed); Starz Encore (multiplexed); Trinity Broadcasting Network (TBN); WE tv.

Pay Service 1
- Pay Units: N.A.
- Programming (via satellite): Cinemax; HBO.
- Fee: $10.95 monthly (each).

Digital Pay Service 1
- Pay Units: N.A.
- Programming (via satellite): Cinemax (multiplexed); HBO (multiplexed); Showtime (multiplexed); The Movie Channel (multiplexed).
- Fee: $13.95 monthly (each).

Video-On-Demand: No

Pay-Per-View
- iN DEMAND (delivered digitally); Playboy TV (delivered digitally).

Internet Service
- Operational: Yes.
- Broadband Service: In-house.
- Fee: $50.00 installation; $29.95-$59.95 monthly.

Telephone Service
- Digital: Operational
- Miles of Plant: 127.0 (coaxial); None (fiber optic). Homes passed: 4,250.
- General Manager: Leon M. Bailey Jr. Chief Financial Officer: Diane Bailey. Chief Technician: Daniel F. Alsup. Business Development Manager: Jody Steverson.
- Ownership: Leon M. Bailey Jr.

ROLLING FORK—RF Cable LLC, 19999 Hwy 61, Rolling Fork, MS 39159. Phone: 662-873-4027. Fax: 662-873-6090. E-mail: rfcable@msdeltawireless.com. ICA: MS0083.
- TV Market Ranking: Below 100 (ROLLING FORK). Franchise award date: N.A. Franchise expiration date: N.A. Began: August 1, 1980.
- Channel capacity: N.A. Channels available but not in use: N.A.

Basic Service
- Subscribers: N.A.
- Programming (received off-air): WABG-TV (ABC, FOX) Greenwood; WAPT (ABC) Jackson; WJTV (Antenna TV, CBS) Jackson; WLBT (Bounce TV, NBC, This TV) Jackson; WMPN-TV (PBS) Jackson. Programming (via satellite): CNN; Freeform; TBS; WGN America.
- Fee: $45.00 installation.

Pay Service 1
- Pay Units: N.A.
- Programming (via satellite): HBO.
- Fee: $45.00 installation; $15.00 monthly.

Internet Service
- Operational: No.

Telephone Service
- None
- Miles of Plant: 12.0 (coaxial); None (fiber optic). Homes passed: 675.
- General Manager: George Martin.
- Ownership: RF Cable LLC.

ROSEDALE—Cablevision of Rosedale, 1920 Hwy 425 North, Monticello, AR 71655-4463. Phones: 870-367-7300; 870-367-3166. Fax: 870-367-9770. E-mail: cccaccounts@ccc-cable.net. Web Site: http://ccc-cable.com. ICA: MS0052.
- TV Market Ranking: Below 100 (ROSEDALE). Franchise award date: N.A. Franchise expiration date: N.A. Began: April 1, 1980.
- Channel capacity: N.A. Channels available but not in use: N.A.

Basic Service
- Subscribers: 373.
- Programming (received off-air): KARZ-TV (Bounce TV, MNT) Little Rock; KASN (CW, The Country Network) Pine Bluff; KATV (ABC, Retro TV) Little Rock; KKYK-CD (IND, WeatherNation) Little Rock; KTVE (NBC) El Dorado; WABG-TV (ABC, FOX) Greenwood; WMAO-TV (PBS) Greenwood; WXVT (CBS) Greenville.
- Programming (via satellite): A&E; AMC; BET; CNN; Comedy Central; Discovery Channel; Disney Channel; ESPN; ESPN2; EWTN Global Catholic Network; FOX Sports Networks; Freeform; Lifetime; National Geographic Channel; Nickelodeon; Outdoor Channel; QVC; Spike TV; Syfy; TBS; The Weather Channel; TLC; TNT; Trinity Broadcasting Network (TBN); Turner Classic Movies; USA Network; VH1; WGN America.
- Fee: $30.00 installation; $49.90 monthly.

Digital Pay Service 1
- Pay Units: N.A.
- Programming (via satellite): Cinemax; HBO; Showtime; Starz; Starz Encore.
- Fee: $12.00 monthly (each).

Cable Systems—Mississippi

Internet Service
Operational: Yes.
Fee: $30.00 installation; $29.95 monthly.
Telephone Service
Digital: Operational
Fee: $29.95 monthly
Miles of Plant: 34.0 (coaxial); None (fiber optic). Homes passed: 741.
President: Bill Copeland.
Ownership: Community Communications Co. (MSO).

ROXIE—Franklin Telephone (Telapex). This cable system has converted to IPTV. Now served by MEADVILLE, MS [MS5012]. ICA: MS0180.

SANFORD—Formerly served by Home Cable Entertainment. No longer in operation. ICA: MS0118.

SCOOBA—Cable TV Inc, 612 Hwy 82 West, PO Box 2598, Starkville, MS 39760. Phone: 662-324-5121. Fax: 662-324-0233. ICA: MS0213.
TV Market Ranking: Below 100 (SCOOBA).
Channel capacity: N.A. Channels available but not in use: N.A.
Basic Service
Subscribers: N.A.
Programming (received off-air): WCBI-TV (CBS, CW, MNT) Columbus; WDBB (CW) Bessemer; WGBC (FOX, NBC) Meridian; WMAB-TV (PBS) Mississippi State; WTOK-TV (ABC, CW, FOX, MNT) Meridian; WTVA (ABC, NBC) Tupelo.
Programming (via satellite): Cartoon Network; CNN; Discovery Channel; ESPN; Freeform; HLN; MTV; Spike TV; TBS; USA Network.
Fee: $40.00 installation.
Pay Service 1
Pay Units: N.A.
Programming (via satellite): Cinemax; HBO.
Fee: $10.28 monthly (each).
Internet Service
Operational: No.
Telephone Service
None
Miles of Plant: 17.0 (coaxial); None (fiber optic). Homes passed: 51.
General Manager: Andy Williams.
Ownership: Andy Williams (MSO).

SEMINARY—Formerly served by Home Cable Entertainment. No longer in operation. ICA: MS0183.

SHELBY—Formerly served by Galaxy Cablevision. Now served by Cable One, CLEVELAND, MS [MS0019]. ICA: MS0070.

SHUBUTA—Alliance Communications, PO Box 9090, Tyler, TX 75711. Phones: 903-561-4411; 501-679-6619 (Greenbrier, AR office); 800-842-8160. Web Site: http://www.alliancecable.net. ICA: MS0184.
TV Market Ranking: Below 100 (SHUBUTA). Franchise award date: N.A. Franchise expiration date: N.A. Began: N.A.
Channel capacity: N.A. Channels available but not in use: N.A.
Basic Service
Subscribers: 23.
Programming (received off-air): WDAM-TV (ABC, Bounce TV, NBC, This TV) Laurel; WGBC (FOX, NBC) Meridian; WMAW-TV (PBS) Meridian; WMDN (CBS) Meridian; WTOK-TV (ABC, CW, FOX, MNT) Meridian.
Programming (via satellite): A&E; AMC; Animal Planet; BET; Cartoon Network; CNBC; CNN; C-SPAN; Discovery Channel; Disney Channel; E! HD; ESPN; ESPN2; FOX Sports South/SportSouth; Freeform; FX; Great American Country; Hallmark Channel; HGTV; HLN; Lifetime; Outdoor Channel; TBS; The Weather Channel; TLC; TNT; USA Network; WGN America.
Fee: $35.00 installation; $25.45 monthly.
Pay Service 1
Pay Units: N.A.
Programming (via satellite): HBO.
Fee: $25.00 installation; $11.00 monthly.
Internet Service
Operational: No.
Telephone Service
None
Miles of Plant: 8.0 (coaxial); None (fiber optic). Homes passed: 260.
Chief Financial Officer: David Starrett. Vice President & General Manager: John Brinker. Vice President, Programming: Julie Newman.
Ownership: Buford Media Group LLC (MSO).

ST. ANDREWS—Mediacom, 760 Middle St, PO Box 1009, Fairhope, AL 36532. Phones: 850-934-7700 (Gulf Breeze regional office); 251-928-0374. Fax: 251-928-3804. Web Site: http://www.mediacomcable.com. Also serves Ocean Springs. ICA: MS0100.
TV Market Ranking: Below 100 (Ocean Springs, ST. ANDREWS). Franchise award date: May 13, 1982. Franchise expiration date: N.A. Began: March 1, 1983.
Channel capacity: N.A. Channels available but not in use: N.A.
Basic Service
Subscribers: 13.
Programming (received off-air): WALA-TV (FOX) Mobile; WKRG-TV (CBS, MeTV) Mobile; WLOX (ABC, Bounce TV, CBS) Biloxi; WMAH-TV (PBS) Biloxi; WPMI-TV (NBC) Mobile; WXXV-TV (FOX, MNT, NBC) Gulfport.
Programming (via satellite): A&E; AMC; Animal Planet; CMT; CNBC; CNN; Comedy Central; CW PLUS; Discovery Channel; Disney Channel; E! HD; ESPN; ESPN2; Fox News Channel; Fox Sports 1; FOX Sports South/SportSouth; Freeform; FX; Hallmark Channel; HGTV; History; HLN; MSNBC; MTV; Nickelodeon; Spike TV; Syfy; TBS; The Weather Channel; TLC; TNT; Turner Classic Movies; TV Land; USA Network; VH1; WGN America.
Fee: $29.50 installation; $40.00 monthly; $3.35 converter.
Pay Service 1
Pay Units: N.A.
Programming (via satellite): Cinemax; Flix; HBO (multiplexed); Showtime; The Movie Channel.
Fee: $2.95 monthly (Flix), $10.45 monthly (Cinemax, Showtime or TMC), $12.45 monthly (HBO).
Video-On-Demand: No
Internet Service
Operational: No.
Telephone Service
None
Miles of Plant: 16.0 (coaxial); None (fiber optic). Homes passed: 430.
Vice President: David Servies. Operations Director: Gene Wuchner. Technical Operations Manager: Mike Sneary. Sales & Marketing Manager: Joey Nagem.
Ownership: Mediacom LLC (MSO).

STARKVILLE—Formerly served by Metro-Cast Mississippi. Now served by MaxxSouth Broadband, PONTOTOC, MS [MS0045]. ICA: MS0018.

STATE LINE—Formerly served by Zoom Media. No longer in operation. ICA: MS0186.

SUMNER—Cable One. Now served by GRENADA, MS [MS0021]. ICA: MS0066.

SUMRALL—Media3, PO Box 650, Milan, TN 38358. Phone: 866-257-2044. E-mail: customerservice@mymedia3.com. Web Site: http://www.mymedia3.com. ICA: MS0098.
TV Market Ranking: Below 100 (SUMRALL). Franchise award date: N.A. Franchise expiration date: N.A. Began: July 14, 1989.
Channel capacity: N.A. Channels available but not in use: N.A.
Basic Service
Subscribers: 31.
Programming (received off-air): WDAM-TV (ABC, Bounce TV, NBC, This TV) Laurel; WHLT (CBS) Hattiesburg; WLOX (ABC, Bounce TV, CBS) Biloxi; WMAH-TV (PBS) Biloxi; WXXV-TV (FOX, MNT, NBC) Gulfport.
Programming (via satellite): A&E; AMC; BET; CNBC; CNN; Comedy Central; Discovery Channel; Disney Channel; Disney XD; ESPN; ESPN2; Fox News Channel; Fox Sports 1; Freeform; Great American Country; Lifetime; Outdoor Channel; QVC; TBS; The Weather Channel; TNT; Trinity Broadcasting Network (TBN); USA Network; WGN America.
Fee: $24.95 installation; $22.45 monthly.
Pay Service 1
Pay Units: N.A.
Programming (via satellite): Cinemax; HBO.
Fee: $9.42 monthly (HBO).
Internet Service
Operational: No.
Telephone Service
None
Miles of Plant: 13.0 (coaxial); None (fiber optic). Homes passed: 395.
Chief Financial Officer: Thomas Pate.
Ownership: CableSouth Media3 LLC (MSO).

SUNFLOWER—Sledge Cable. Formerly [MS0195]. This cable system has converted to IPTV, 124 Delta Ave, PO Box 68, Sunflower, MS 38778. Phones: 662-569-3311; 888-655-7707. E-mail: rsledge@deltaland.net. Web Site: http://www.deltaland.net. ICA: MS5031.
Channel capacity: N.A. Channels available but not in use: N.A.
Internet Service
Operational: Yes.
Telephone Service
Digital: Operational
President: Robert O. Sledge Jr.
Ownership: Sledge Telephone Co.

SUNFLOWER—Sledge Cable. This cable system has converted to IPTV. See SUNFLOWER, MS [MS5031]. ICA: MS0195.

SUNRISE—Formerly served by Home Cable Entertainment. No longer in operation. ICA: MS0107.

TAYLORSVILLE—Formerly served by Zoom Media. No longer in operation. ICA: MS0087.

TERRY—Bailey Cable TV Inc, 807 Church St, Port Gibson, MS 39150-2413. Phones: 601-437-8300; 601-849-4201; 601-892-5249. Fax: 601-437-6860. E-mail: cs@baileycable.net. Web Site: http://www.baileycable.net. ICA: MS0223.
TV Market Ranking: 77 (TERRY).
Channel capacity: N.A. Channels available but not in use: N.A.
Basic Service
Subscribers: 80.
Fee: $15.00 installation; $42.95 monthly.
Internet Service
Operational: Yes.
President: David A. Bailey. Manager: Dwight Bailey. Chief Technician: Jim Morton.
Ownership: Bailey Cable TV Inc. (MSO).

TUPELO—Comcast Cable, 353 North Gloster St, Tupelo, MS 38804. Phones: 662-842-5625; 256-859-7828; 662-844-8694. Fax: 662-844-0940. Web Site: http://www.comcast.com. Also serves Altoona, Attalla, Big Cove, Brownsboro, Cherokee County (portions), Cloverdale, Colbert County (portions), Cottondale (Tuscaloosa County), Etowah County (portions), Florence, Gadsden, Glencoe, Hampton Cove, Hawk Pride Mountain, Hokes Bluff, Holt, Huntsville, Jefferson County (portions), Lakeview, Lauderdale County (portions), Madison, Madison County (portions), Meridianville, Muscle Shoals, Northport, Owens Cross Roads, Rainbow City, Reece City, Ridgeville, Sheffield, St. Clair County (portions), St. Florian, Toney, Tuscaloosa, Tuscaloosa County (portions), Tuscumbia & Walnut Grove, AL; Belden, Bissell, Chickasaw County (portions), Clay County (portions), Fulton, Itawamba County (portions), Lee County (portions), Manatachie, Marietta, Mooreville, Okolona, Plantersville, Pontotoc County (portions), Prentiss County (portions), Saltillo, Sherman, Tremont, Union County (portions), Verona & West Point, MS. ICA: MS0009.
TV Market Ranking: 18 (Cherokee County (portions)); 40 (Jefferson County (portions), St. Clair County (portions)); 96 (Big Cove, Brownsboro, Hampton Cove, Huntsville, Lauderdale County (portions), Madison, Madison County (portions), Meridianville, Owens Cross Roads, Toney); Below 100 (Altoona, Belden, Bissell, Chickasaw County (portions), Clay County (portions), Cloverdale, Colbert County (portions), Cottondale (Tuscaloosa County), Etowah County (portions), Fulton, Glencoe, Hawk Pride Mountain, Hokes Bluff, Holt, Itawamba County (portions), Lakeview, Lee County (portions), Manatachie, Marietta, Muscle Shoals, Northport, Okolona, Plantersville, Pontotoc County (portions), Rainbow City, Reece City, Ridgeville, Saltillo, Sheffield, Sherman, St. Florian, Tremont, TUPELO, Tuscaloosa County (portions), Tuscumbia, Union County (portions), Verona, Walnut Grove, West Point, Attalla, Florence, Gadsden, Prentiss County (portions), Tuscaloosa, St. Clair County (portions), Lauderdale County (portions)); Outside TV Markets (Prentiss County (portions)). Franchise

Mississippi—Cable Systems

award date: N.A. Franchise expiration date: N.A. Began: May 1, 1955.
Channel capacity: N.A. Channels available but not in use: N.A.

Basic Service
Subscribers: 104,037. Commercial subscribers: 8,741.
Programming (received off-air): WAFF (Bounce TV, NBC, This TV) Huntsville; WCBI-TV (CBS, CW, MNT) Columbus; WFIQ (PBS) Florence; WHBQ-TV (Decades, FOX, Movies!) Memphis; WHDF (CW) Florence; WHNT-TV (Antenna TV, CBS) Huntsville; WMAE-TV (PBS) Booneville; WMC-TV (Bounce TV, NBC, This TV) Memphis; WTVA (ABC, NBC) Tupelo; allband FM.
Programming (via satellite): A&E; AMC; Animal Planet; BET; Cartoon Network; CMT; CNBC; CNN; Comcast/Charter Sports Southeast (CSS); Comedy Central; Discovery Channel; Disney Channel; E! HD; ESPN; ESPN2; Food Network; Fox News Channel; Fox Sports 1; FX; Golf Channel; HGTV; History; HLN; Lifetime; LWS Local Weather Station; MTV; MyNetworkTV; NBCSN; Nickelodeon; Outdoor Channel; OWN; Oprah Winfrey Network; QVC; Spike TV; TBS; The Weather Channel; TLC; TNT; Turner Classic Movies; TV Land; USA Network; VH1.
Fee: $42.91-$67.95 installation; $24.50 monthly.

Digital Basic Service
Subscribers: N.A.
Programming (via satellite): BBC America; CMT; Cooking Channel; C-SPAN 2; C-SPAN 3; Daystar TV Network; Destination America; Discovery Channel HD; Discovery Kids Channel; Disney Channel; Disney XD; DIY Network; ESPN HD; ESPN2 HD; ESPNews; Flix; FOX College Sports Central; FOX College Sports Pacific; FYI; GolTV; GSN; History International; Investigation Discovery; Jewelry Television; LMN; MC; MoviePlex; MTV Classic; MTV Jams; MTV2; National Geographic Channel; NBA TV; NFL Network; Nick 2; Nick Jr.; Science Channel; Sprout; Starz Encore (multiplexed); Sundance TV; TeenNick; TNT HD; Tr3s; TV Guide Interactive Inc.; VH1 Soul; WAM! America's Kidz Network.

Digital Pay Service 1
Pay Units: N.A.
Programming (via satellite): Cinemax (multiplexed); Cinemax HD; HBO (multiplexed); HBO HD; Showtime (multiplexed); Showtime HD; Starz (multiplexed); Starz HD; The Movie Channel (multiplexed).

Video-On-Demand: Yes

Pay-Per-View
iN DEMAND (delivered digitally); Hot Choice (delivered digitally); Special events (delivered digitally).

Internet Service
Operational: Yes.
Subscribers: 89,326.
Broadband Service: Comcast High Speed Internet.
Fee: $42.95 monthly.

Telephone Service
Digital: Operational
Subscribers: 41,088.
Miles of Plant: 7,427.0 (coaxial); 2,175.0 (fiber optic). Homes passed: 312,894.
Vice President & General Manager: Ellen Rosson. Chief Technician: Frank Newsome. Office Manager: Pete Clark.
Ownership: Comcast Cable Communications Inc. (MSO).

TYLERTOWN—Media3, PO Box 650, Milan, TN 38358. Phone: 866-257-2044. E-mail: customerservice@mymedia3.com. Web Site: http://www.mymedia3.com. ICA: MS0077.
TV Market Ranking: Outside TV Markets (TYLERTOWN). Franchise award date: N.A. Franchise expiration date: N.A. Began: February 1, 1974.
Channel capacity: N.A. Channels available but not in use: N.A.

Basic Service
Subscribers: 104.
Programming (received off-air): WAFB (Bounce TV, CBS) Baton Rouge; WDAM-TV (ABC, Bounce TV, NBC, This TV) Laurel; WDBD (FOX, Grit) Jackson; WJTV (Antenna TV, CBS) Jackson; WLBT (Bounce TV, NBC, This TV) Jackson; WLOX (ABC, Bounce TV, CBS) Biloxi; WMAU-TV (PBS) Bude; WVUE-DT (Bounce TV, FOX) New Orleans; WWL-TV (CBS) New Orleans.
Programming (via satellite): A&E; BET; Cartoon Network; CNBC; CNN; Comedy Central; C-SPAN; C-SPAN 2; Discovery Channel; Disney Channel; Disney XD; ESPN; ESPN2; Fox News Channel; Freeform; Fuse; FX; Great American Country; Hallmark Channel; HLN; INSP; Outdoor Channel; QVC; TBS; The Weather Channel; TLC; TNT; Trinity Broadcasting Network (TBN); Turner Classic Movies; USA Network; WGN America.
Fee: $24.95 installation; $22.45 monthly.

Digital Basic Service
Subscribers: N.A.
Programming (via satellite): BBC America; Bloomberg Television; Discovery Life Channel; DMX Music; ESPN Classic; ESPNews; FYI; Golf Channel; GSN; History International; National Geographic Channel; WE tv.

Digital Expanded Basic Service
Subscribers: N.A.
Programming (via satellite): DMX Music; FXM; LMN; Starz Encore; Turner Classic Movies.
Fee: $13.96 monthly.

Pay Service 1
Pay Units: N.A.
Programming (via satellite): Cinemax; HBO.
Fee: $25.00 installation.

Digital Pay Service 1
Pay Units: N.A.
Programming (via satellite): Cinemax (multiplexed); Flix; HBO (multiplexed); Showtime (multiplexed); The Movie Channel (multiplexed).
Fee: $15.50 monthly.

Pay-Per-View
ESPN Now (delivered digitally); Hot Choice (delivered digitally); Playboy TV (delivered digitally); Fresh (delivered digitally); Shorteez (delivered digitally); Urban Xtra (delivered digitally).

Internet Service
Operational: No.

Telephone Service
None
Miles of Plant: 26.0 (coaxial); None (fiber optic). Homes passed: 849.
Chief Financial Officer: Thomas Pate. President: Alan Taylor. General Manager: Drew Cannon. Chief Technician: Brian Malley. Marketing Director: Glenda C. Elliott.
Ownership: CableSouth Media3 LLC (MSO).

UNION (town)—Formerly served by Mediacom. Now served by MaxxSouth Broadband, PONTOTOC, MS [MS0045]. ICA: MS0038.

UNION (town)—Formerly served by Mediacom. Now served by MaxxSouth Broadband, PONTOTOC, MS [MS0045]. ICA: MS0067.

VICKSBURG—Vicksburg Video Inc, 900 Hwy 61 North, PO Box 1276, Vicksburg, MS 39183. Phones: 601-636-1370; 601-636-1351. Fax: 601-636-3791. E-mail: vicksburgvideocs@cablelynx.com. Web Site: http://www.vicksburgvideo.com. ICA: MS0011.
TV Market Ranking: Below 100 (VICKSBURG). Franchise award date: June 1, 1965. Franchise expiration date: N.A. Began: February 1, 1971.
Channel capacity: N.A. Channels available but not in use: N.A.

Basic Service
Subscribers: 2,930. Commercial subscribers: 12.
Programming (received off-air): WAPT (ABC) Jackson; WDBD (FOX, Grit) Jackson; WJTV (Antenna TV, CBS) Jackson; WLBT (Bounce TV, NBC, This TV) Jackson; WLOO (MNT) Vicksburg; WMPN-TV (PBS) Jackson.
Programming (via satellite): A&E; AMC; Animal Planet; BET; Cartoon Network; CMT; CNBC; CNN; C-SPAN; C-SPAN 2; Discovery Channel; Disney Channel; ESPN; ESPN Classic; ESPN2; EVINE Live; EWTN Global Catholic Network; Food Network; Fox News Channel; FOX Sports Southwest; Freeform; FX; HGTV; History; HLN; ION Television; Lifetime; LMN; MSNBC; MTV; Nickelodeon; Pop; QVC; Spike TV; Syfy; TBS; Telemundo; The Weather Channel; TLC; TNT; Travel Channel; Trinity Broadcasting Network (TBN); truTV; Turner Classic Movies; TV Land; USA Network; VH1; WGN America.
Fee: $49.95 installation; $31.90 monthly.

Digital Basic Service
Subscribers: N.A.
Programming (via satellite): BBC America; CMT; Destination America; Discovery Kids Channel; Discovery Life Channel; Disney XD; DMX Music; ESPNews; Fox Sports 1; FSN Digital Atlantic; FSN Digital Central; FSN Digital Pacific; FYI; Golf Channel; Great American Country; GSN; History International; Investigation Discovery; LMN; MTV Classic; MTV Hits; MTV Jams; MTV2; National Geographic Channel; Nick 2; Nick Jr.; Nicktoons; Outdoor Channel; OWN: Oprah Winfrey Network; Science Channel; TeenNick; Tr3s; VH1 Soul; WE tv.

Digital Expanded Basic Service
Subscribers: N.A.
Programming (via satellite): AXS TV; CNN HD; Discovery Channel HD; ESPN HD; Outdoor Channel 2 HD; TBS HD; TNT HD.
Fee: $5.00 monthly.

Digital Pay Service 1
Pay Units: N.A.
Programming (via satellite): Cinemax (multiplexed); Cinemax HD; HBO (multiplexed); HBO HD; Starz (multiplexed); Starz Encore (multiplexed); Starz HD.
Fee: $12.95 monthly (Cinemax, HBO or Starz/Encore).

Video-On-Demand: No

Pay-Per-View
iN DEMAND (delivered digitally).

Internet Service
Operational: Yes. Began: December 31, 2000.
Subscribers: 2,717.
Broadband Service: Cablelynx.
Fee: $24.95-$44.95 monthly.

Telephone Service
Analog: Not Operational
Digital: Operational
Subscribers: 715.
Fee: $45.70 monthly.
Miles of Plant: 652.0 (coaxial); 163.0 (fiber optic). Homes passed: 20,045.

Vice President, Administration: Charlotte A. Dial. General Manager: Beau Balch. Plant Manager: Henry Harris. Office Manager: Dee Dee Sumner.
Ownership: WEHCO Video Inc. (MSO).

WATER VALLEY—Formerly served by MetroCast Mississippi. Now served by MaxxSouth Broadband, PONTOTOC, MS [MS0045]. ICA: MS0050.

WAVELAND—Mediacom, 5973 Hwy 90 West, Theodore, AL 36582. Phones: 845-695-2762; 251-928-0374; 850-934-7700 (Gulf Breeze regional office). Fax: 251-928-3804. Web Site: http://www.mediacomcable.com. Also serves Bay St. Louis, Hancock County (portions), Pearlington, Stone County (portions) & Wiggins. ICA: MS0022.
TV Market Ranking: 31 (Pearlington); Below 100 (Bay St. Louis, Stone County (portions), WAVELAND, Wiggins). Franchise award date: June 22, 1978. Franchise expiration date: N.A. Began: July 1, 1979.
Channel capacity: N.A. Channels available but not in use: N.A.

Basic Service
Subscribers: 2,765. Commercial subscribers: 387.
Programming (received off-air): WDSU (MeTV, NBC) New Orleans; WGNO (ABC, Antenna TV, Escape) New Orleans; WLOX (ABC, Bounce TV, CBS) Biloxi; WMPN-TV (PBS) Jackson; WNOL-TV (CW, This TV) New Orleans; WPXL-TV (ION) New Orleans; WUPL (MNT) Slidell; WVUE-DT (Bounce TV, FOX) New Orleans; WWL-TV (CBS) New Orleans; WXXV-TV (FOX, MNT, NBC) Gulfport; WYES-TV (PBS) New Orleans.
Programming (via satellite): A&E; AMC; Animal Planet; BET; Bravo; Cartoon Network; CMT; CNBC; CNN; Comedy Central; C-SPAN; C-SPAN 2; Discovery Channel; Discovery Life Channel; Disney Channel; E! HD; ESPN; ESPN2; EWTN Global Catholic Network; Food Network; Fox News Channel; Fox Sports 1; FOX Sports South/SportSouth; Freeform; FX; Golf Channel; Hallmark Channel; HGTV; History; HLN; Lifetime; MSNBC; MTV; Nickelodeon; Outdoor Channel; Pop; QVC; Spike TV; Syfy; TBS; The Weather Channel; TLC; TNT; Travel Channel; Trinity Broadcasting Network (TBN); truTV; Turner Classic Movies; TV Land; USA Network; VH1; WE tv; WGN America.
Fee: $44.25 installation; $41.00 monthly; $3.35 converter.

Digital Basic Service
Subscribers: N.A.
Programming (via satellite): BBC America; Cloo; Destination America; Discovery Kids Channel; DMX Music; ESPNews; Fuse; FXM; FYI; GSN; History International; IFC; Investigation Discovery; LMN; MTV Classic; MTV Hits; MTV2; National Geographic Channel; NBCSN; Nick Jr.; Nicktoons; OWN: Oprah Winfrey Network; Science Channel; TeenNick.
Fee: $5.00 converter.

Digital Pay Service 1
Pay Units: N.A.
Programming (via satellite): Cinemax (multiplexed); Flix; HBO (multiplexed); Showtime (multiplexed); Starz (multiplexed); Starz Encore (multiplexed); Sundance TV; The Movie Channel (multiplexed).
Fee: $9.95 monthly (Starz/Encore or Showtime/TMC/Flix/Sundance), $11.95 monthly (HBO).

Video-On-Demand: No

Cable Systems—Mississippi

Access the most current data instantly

FREE TRIAL @ ADVANCED TVFactbook — TELCO/IPTV • CABLE TV • TV STATIONS

www.warren-news.com/factbook.htm

Pay-Per-View
Sports PPV (delivered digitally); Urban Xtra (delivered digitally); special events (delivered digitally).

Internet Service
Operational: Yes.
Broadband Service: Mediacom High Speed Internet.
Fee: $49.95 installation; $40.95 monthly.

Telephone Service
None
Miles of Plant: 208.0 (coaxial); None (fiber optic). Homes passed: 7,642.
Vice President: David Servies. Operations Director: Gene Wuchner. Technical Operations Manager: Mike Sneary. Sales & Marketing Manager: Joey Nagem. Vice President, Financial Reporting: Kenneth J. Kohrs.
Ownership: Mediacom LLC (MSO).

WAYNESBORO—NewWave Communications, One Montgomery Plaza, 4th Floor, Sikeston, MO 63801. Phones: 573-472-9500; 888-863-9928. Fax: 573-472-9518. E-mail: info@newwave.com. Web Site: http://www.newwavecom.com. Also serves Buckatunna. ICA: MS0188.
TV Market Ranking: Below 100 (WAYNESBORO); Outside TV Markets (Buckatunna). Franchise award date: March 3, 1964. Franchise expiration date: N.A. Began: July 1, 1965.
Channel capacity: N.A. Channels available but not in use: N.A.

Basic Service
Subscribers: 946.
Programming (received off-air): WDAM-TV (ABC, Bounce TV, NBC, This TV) Laurel; WHLT (CBS) Hattiesburg; WKRG-TV (CBS, MeTV) Mobile; WLOX (ABC, Bounce TV, CBS) Biloxi; WMAW-TV (PBS) Meridian; WTOK-TV (ABC, CW, FOX, MNT) Meridian; WXXV-TV (FOX, MNT, NBC) Gulfport; all-band FM.
Programming (via satellite): QVC; TBS.
Fee: $35.00 installation; $35.78 monthly.

Expanded Basic Service 1
Subscribers: N.A.
Programming (via satellite): A&E; AMC; Animal Planet; BET; Cartoon Network; CMT; CNBC; CNN; Comedy Central; C-SPAN; CW PLUS; Discovery Channel; E! HD; ESPN; ESPN2; Family Friendly Entertainment; Food Network; Fox News Channel; Freeform; FX; GSN; HGTV; History; HLN; INSP; Lifetime; MTV; Nickelodeon; Outdoor Channel; Spike TV; Syfy; The Weather Channel; TLC; TNT; Travel Channel; Trinity Broadcasting Network (TBN); TV Land; Univision Studios; USA Network; VH1; WGN America.
Fee: $49.20 monthly.

Digital Basic Service
Subscribers: N.A.
Programming (via satellite): BBC America; Bloomberg Television; Discovery Digital Networks; DMX Music; ESPN Classic; ESPNews; Fox Sports 1; FXM; FYI; Golf Channel; History International; IFC; LMN; National Geographic Channel; Nick Jr.; Nicktoons; TeenNick; WE tv.
Fee: $11.00 monthly.

Digital Pay Service 1
Pay Units: N.A.
Programming (via satellite): Cinemax (multiplexed); HBO (multiplexed); Showtime (multiplexed); Starz (multiplexed); Starz Encore (multiplexed); The Movie Channel (multiplexed).
Fee: $8.00 monthly (Starz), $9.00 monthly (Cinemax), $11.00 monthly (Starz/Encore), $15.00 monthly (Showtime/TMC), $17.00 monthly (HBO) or $26.00 monthly (HBO/Cinemax).

Video-On-Demand: No

Pay-Per-View
iN DEMAND (delivered digitally); Hot Choice (delivered digitally); Playboy TV (delivered digitally); Fresh (delivered digitally); Shorteez (delivered digitally).

Internet Service
Operational: Yes.
Fee: $36.99-$46.99 monthly; $6.00 modem lease.

Telephone Service
Digital: Operational
Miles of Plant: 43.0 (coaxial); None (fiber optic).
General Manager: Staci Gowan.
Ownership: NewWave Communications LLC (MSO).

WEIR—Delta Telephone (Telapex). Formerly [MS0126]. This cable system has converted to IPTV, 1018 Highland Colony Pkwy, Ste 700, Ridgeland, MS 39157. Phones: 877-433-7878 (Delta Telephone); 601-355-1522 (Telapex). Fax: 601-353-0950. E-mail: comments@dtcweb.com. Web Site: http://www.telapex.com. ICA: MS5013.
Channel capacity: N.A. Channels available but not in use: N.A.

Basic
Subscribers: 53.
Fee: $30.00 installation; $27.18 monthly. Includes 110+ channels.

Internet Service
Operational: Yes.

Telephone Service
Digital: Operational
Vice President, Telapex & General Manager, Delta Telephone: L. Brooks Derryberry.
Ownership: Telapex Inc.

WEIR—Delta Telephone (Telapex). This cable system has converted to IPTV. See WEIR, MS [MS5013]. ICA: MS0126.

WIGGINS—Mediacom. Now served by WAVELAND, MS [MS0022]. ICA: MS0058.

WINONA—Cable One. Now served by GRENADA, MS [MS0021]. ICA: MS0014.

WINSTONVILLE—Formerly served by J & L Cable. No longer in operation. ICA: MS0209.

WOODVILLE—Bailey Cable TV Inc, 807 Church St, Port Gibson, MS 39150-2413. Phone: 601-437-8300. Fax: 601-437-6860. E-mail: cs@baileycable.net. Web Site: http://www.baileycable.net. ICA: MS0220.
TV Market Ranking: Below 100 (WOODVILLE).
Channel capacity: N.A. Channels available but not in use: N.A.

Basic Service
Subscribers: 297.
Fee: $15.00 installation; $42.95 monthly.
President: David A. Bailey.
Ownership: Bailey Cable TV Inc. (MSO).

MISSOURI

Total Systems: 86	Communities with Applications: 0
Total Communities Served: 704	Number of Basic Subscribers: 798,681
Franchises Not Yet Operating: 0	Number of Expanded Basic Subscribers: 5,242
Applications Pending: 0	Number of Pay Units: 130,517

Top 100 Markets Represented: St. Louis (11); Kansas City (22); Cape Girardeau, MO-Paducah, KY-Harrisburg, IL (69).

For a list of cable communities in this section, see the Cable Community Index located in the back of Cable Volume 2.
For explanation of terms used in cable system listings, see p. D-11.

ADRIAN—Provincial Cable & Data, 123A West Main St, Odessa, MO 64076. Phones: 816-633-1626; 866-284-3346. E-mail: customercare@provincial-cable.net. Web Site: http://www.provincialcable.com. ICA: MO0175.
TV Market Ranking: Outside TV Markets (ADRIAN). Franchise award date: N.A. Franchise expiration date: N.A. Began: December 1, 1973.
Channel capacity: N.A. Channels available but not in use: N.A.
Basic Service
Subscribers: 92.
Programming (received off-air): KCPT (PBS) Kansas City; KCTV (CBS) Kansas City; KCWE (CW, Movies!, This TV) Kansas City; KMBC-TV (ABC, MeTV) Kansas City; KMCI-TV (Bounce TV, Escape, IND) Lawrence; KPXE-TV (ION) Kansas City; KSHB-TV (COZI TV, Grit, NBC) Kansas City; KSMO-TV (Bounce TV, MNT) Kansas City; WDAF-TV (Antenna TV, FOX) Kansas City; allband FM.
Programming (via satellite): INSP; QVC; Trinity Broadcasting Network (TBN).
Fee: $15.00 installation; $19.98 monthly.
Expanded Basic Service 1
Subscribers: N.A.
Programming (via satellite): A&E; AMC; Animal Planet; Cartoon Network; Classic Arts Showcase; CNN; Discovery Channel; Disney Channel; ESPN; ESPN2; Fox Sports 1; Freeform; FX; Great American Country; HGTV; HLN; Lifetime; Nickelodeon; TBS; The Weather Channel; TLC; TNT; Travel Channel; USA Network.
Fee: $48.45 monthly.
Pay Service 1
Pay Units: N.A.
Programming (via satellite): Showtime; The Movie Channel.
Fee: $8.95 monthly (TMC), $10.95 monthly (Showtime).
Video-On-Demand: No
Internet Service
Operational: Yes.
Fee: $49.95 installation; $24.95-$44.95 monthly.
Telephone Service
None
Miles of Plant: 13.0 (coaxial); None (fiber optic). Homes passed: 686.
General Manager: Perry Scarborough. Office Manager: Misti Runyan.
Ownership: Provincial Cable & Data (MSO).

ADVANCE—Formerly served by Cebridge Connections. Now served by Semo Communications Corp., ADVANCE, MO [MO0171]. ICA: MO0178.

ADVANCE—Semo Communications Corp, 107 Semo Ln, PO Box C, Sikeston, MO 63801-0937. Phones: 800-635-8230; 573-471-6594; 573-471-6599. Fax: 573-471-6878. E-mail: semosupport@cablerocket.com. Web Site: http://www.semocommunications.com. Also serves Anniston, Bell City, Blodgett, Brownwood, Canalou, Delta, Fruitland, Haywood City, Matthews, Morehouse Colony, Morley, New Madrid County (northern portion), Pocahontas, Scott County (southern portion), Vanduser, Wilson City & Wyatt. ICA: MO0171.
TV Market Ranking: 69 (ADVANCE, Bell City, Blodgett, Brownwood, Delta, Fruitland, Haywood City, Morehouse Colony, Morley, New Madrid County (northern portion), Pocahontas, Scott County (southern portion), Vanduser, Wilson City, Wyatt); Outside TV Markets (Anniston, Canalou, Matthews). Franchise award date: November 1, 1981. Franchise expiration date: N.A. Began: January 1, 1982.
Channel capacity: N.A. Channels available but not in use: N.A.
Basic Service
Subscribers: 1,422.
Programming (received off-air): KBSI (FOX) Cape Girardeau; KFVS-TV (CBS, CW, MeTV) Cape Girardeau; WDKA (MNT, The Country Network) Paducah; WKMU (PBS) Murray; WPSD-TV (Antenna TV, NBC) Paducah; WSIL-TV (ABC) Harrisburg; WTCT (IND) Marion.
Programming (via satellite): ION Television; QVC.
Fee: $35.00 installation; $25.62 monthly; $1.00 converter.
Expanded Basic Service 1
Subscribers: N.A.
Programming (via satellite): A&E; AMC; Animal Planet; BET; Cartoon Network; CNBC; CNN; Comedy Central; Cooking Channel; C-SPAN; C-SPAN 2; CW PLUS; Discovery Channel; Disney Channel; DIY Network; E! HD; ESPN; ESPN Classic; ESPN2; Food Network; Fox News Channel; Fox Sports 1; FOX Sports Midwest; Freeform; FX; Great American Country; Hallmark Channel; HGTV; History; HLN; Lifetime; MTV; National Geographic Channel; Nickelodeon; Outdoor Channel; Oxygen; Spike TV; Syfy; TBS; The Weather Channel; TLC; TNT; Travel Channel; truTV; Turner Classic Movies; TV Land; USA Network; VH1; WGN America.
Fee: $47.95 monthly.
Digital Basic Service
Subscribers: N.A.
Programming (via satellite): BBC America; Bloomberg Television; Bravo; Cloo; CMT; Destination America; Discovery Kids Channel; Discovery Life Channel; Disney XD; DMX Music; ESPN HD; ESPNews; EVINE Live; FOX College Sports Central; FOX College Sports Pacific; Fuse; FXM; FYI; Golf Channel; GSN; History International; IFC; Investigation Discovery; LMN; MTV Classic; MTV2; National Geographic Channel HD; NBCSN; Nick Jr.; Nicktoons; Outdoor Channel 2 HD; OWN: Oprah Winfrey Network; RFD-TV; Science Channel; Starz Encore; Starz Encore Classic; Starz Encore Family; Starz Encore Suspense; Starz Encore Westerns; TeenNick; TNT HD; Trinity Broadcasting Network (TBN); TVG Network; Universal HD; VH1 Soul; WE tv; Weatherscan.
Digital Pay Service 1
Pay Units: N.A.
Programming (via satellite): Cinemax (multiplexed); Flix; HBO (multiplexed); Showtime (multiplexed); Starz (multiplexed); The Movie Channel (multiplexed).
Video-On-Demand: No
Pay-Per-View
Spice: Xcess (delivered digitally); Hot Choice (delivered digitally); iN DEMAND (delivered digitally); Playboy TV (delivered digitally); Fresh (delivered digitally); Club Jenna (delivered digitally).
Internet Service
Operational: Yes.
Telephone Service
Digital: Operational
Fee: $29.99 monthly
Miles of Plant: 150.0 (coaxial); 100.0 (fiber optic). Homes passed: 4,197.
President: Tyrone Garrett. Vice President: Shannon Garrett. Chief Technician: Jim Crittenden.
Ownership: Semo Communications Inc.

ALBA—Mediacom. Now served by CARL JUNCTION, MO [MO0094]. ICA: MO0237.

ALBANY—Mediacom. Now served by EXCELSIOR SPRINGS, MO [MO0040]. ICA: MO0144.

ALTON—Formerly served by Boycom Cablevision Inc. No longer in operation. ICA: MO0382.

AMAZONIA—Formerly served by CableDirect. No longer in operation. ICA: MO0356.

AMSTERDAM—Craw-Kan. Now served by GIRARD, KS [KS0446]. ICA: MO0383.

ANDERSON—Mediacom. Now served by DIAMOND, MO [MO0156]. ICA: MO0193.

ANNAPOLIS—Formerly served by Charter Communications. No longer in operation. ICA: MO0432.

APPLETON CITY—Mediacom, 1533 South Enterprise Ave, Springfield, MO 65804. Phones: 845-695-2762; 417-875-5500; 417-875-5560. Fax: 417-883-0265. Web Site: http://www.mediacomcable.com. ICA: MO0184.
TV Market Ranking: Outside TV Markets (APPLETON CITY). Franchise award date: June 7, 1973. Franchise expiration date: N.A. Began: June 1, 1975.
Channel capacity: N.A. Channels available but not in use: N.A.
Basic Service
Subscribers: 110.
Programming (received off-air): KCPT (PBS) Kansas City; KCWE (CW, Movies!, This TV) Kansas City; KMBC-TV (ABC, MeTV) Kansas City; KMOS-TV (PBS) Sedalia; KOAM-TV (CBS) Pittsburg; KODE-TV (ABC) Joplin; KOLR (CBS) Springfield; KPXE-TV (ION) Kansas City; KSHB-TV (COZI TV, Grit, NBC) Kansas City; KSNF (NBC) Joplin; WDAF-TV (Antenna TV, FOX) Kansas City.
Programming (via satellite): A&E; AMC; CMT; CNN; Disney Channel; ESPN; Freeform; HLN; Lifetime; QVC; Spike TV; Syfy; TBS; The Weather Channel; TLC; TNT; USA Network; WGN America.
Fee: $35.00 installation; $37.05 monthly.
Pay Service 1
Pay Units: N.A.
Programming (via satellite): HBO; Showtime; The Movie Channel.
Fee: $10.50 monthly (each).
Video-On-Demand: No
Internet Service
Operational: No.
Telephone Service
None
Miles of Plant: 9.0 (coaxial); None (fiber optic). Homes passed: 691.
Regional Vice President: Bill Copeland. Vice President, Financial Reporting: Kenneth J. Kohrs. Regional Technical Operations Director: Alan Freedman. Marketing Director: Will Kuebler.
Ownership: Mediacom LLC (MSO).

ARCHIE—Mediacom, 901 North College Ave, Columbia, MO 65201. Phones: 845-695-2762; 573-443-1536. Fax: 417-883-0265. Web Site: http://www.mediacomcable.com. ICA: MO0246.
TV Market Ranking: Outside TV Markets (ARCHIE).
Channel capacity: N.A. Channels available but not in use: N.A.
Basic Service
Subscribers: 30.
Fee: $42.00 monthly.
Vice President, Financial Reporting: Kenneth J. Kohrs.
Ownership: Mediacom LLC (MSO).

ARGYLE—Formerly served by First Cable of Missouri Inc. No longer in operation. ICA: MO0377.

ARMSTRONG—Formerly served by Cebridge Connections. No longer in operation. ICA: MO0325.

Cable Systems—Missouri

ATLANTA—Formerly served by CableDirect. No longer in operation. ICA: MO0330.

AVA—Mediacom. Now served by SEYMOUR, MO [MO0172]. ICA: MO0116.

AVALON—Green Hills Communications. This cable system has converted to IPTV, 7926 Northeast State Rte M, PO Box 227, Breckenridge, MO 64625. Phones: 800-846-3426; 660-644-5411. Fax: 660-644-5464. E-mail: comments@greenhills.net. Web Site: http://www.greenhills.net. Also serves Bogard, Breckenridge, Chillicothe, Cowgill, Dawn, Knoxville, Lock Springs, Ludlow, Mooresville, Norborne, Polo, Stet, Tina & Wheeling. ICA: MO5156.
TV Market Ranking: Outside TV Markets (Norborne, Tina). Franchise award date: September 27, 2007. Franchise expiration date: N.A. Began: N.A.
Channel capacity: N.A. Channels available but not in use: N.A.
Tier One
Subscribers: N.A.
Tier Two
Subscribers: 1,049.
Fee: $57.53 monthly.
Internet Service
Operational: Yes.
Fee: $39.99-$94.99 monthly.
Telephone Service
Digital: Operational
Fee: $16.00 monthly
General Manager: Steve Gann.
Ownership: Green Hills Companies.

BARING—Formerly served by CableDirect. No longer in operation. ICA: MO0440.

BARNARD—Formerly served by CableDirect. No longer in operation. ICA: MO0384.

BARNHART—Formerly served by Charter Communications. No longer in operation. ICA: MO0385.

BELL CITY—Semo Communications Corporation. Now served by ADVANCE, MO [MO0171]. ICA: MO0311.

BELLE—Formerly served by Almega Cable. No longer in operation. ICA: MO0076.

BENTON—Charter Communications. Now served by ST. LOUIS, MO [MO0009]. ICA: MO0200.

BERNIE—Formerly served by Cebridge Connections. Now served by NewWave Communications, DEXTER, MO [MO0039]. ICA: MO0143.

BETHANY—Mediacom. Now served by EXCELSIOR SPRINGS, MO [MO0040]. ICA: MO0386.

BEVIER—Chariton Valley Cablevision. Now served by MACON, MO [MO0071]. ICA: MO0203.

BILLINGS—Mediacom. Now served by SEYMOUR, MO [MO0172]. ICA: MO0242.

BIRCH TREE—Formerly served by Boycom Cablevision Inc. No longer in operation. ICA: MO0235.

BISMARCK—Charter Communications. Now served by ST. LOUIS, MO [MO0009]. ICA: MO0174.

BOGARD—Formerly served by CableDirect. No longer in operation. ICA: MO0388.

BOLCKOW—Formerly served by CableDirect. No longer in operation. ICA: MO0363.

BOLIVAR (town)—Windstream, 4001 Rodney Parham Rd, Little Rock, AR 72212. Phones: 877-759-9020; 866-971-9463; 501-748-7000. Fax: 501-748-6392. E-mail: support@windstream.net. Web Site: http://www.windstream.com. Also serves Polk County. ICA: MO0055.
TV Market Ranking: Below 100 (BOLIVAR (TOWN), Polk County (portions)); Outside TV Markets (Polk County (portions)). Franchise award date: May 8, 1980. Franchise expiration date: N.A. Began: November 1, 1981.
Channel capacity: N.A. Channels available but not in use: N.A.
Basic Service
Subscribers: 1,002.
Programming (received off-air): KOLR (CBS) Springfield; KOZK (PBS) Springfield; KSPR (ABC) Springfield; KWBM (Retro TV) Harrison; KYTV (CW, NBC, WeatherNation) Springfield.
Programming (via satellite): A&E; Animal Planet; CMT; CNN; Discovery Channel; Disney Channel; ESPN; ESPN2; Fox News Channel; Fox Sports 1; FOX Sports Midwest; Freeform; FX; FXM; HGTV; History; HLN; Lifetime; National Geographic Channel; Nickelodeon; Spike TV; TBS; The Weather Channel; TLC; TNT; Trinity Broadcasting Network (TBN); Turner Classic Movies; USA Network; WGN America.
Fee: $50.00 monthly.
Pay Service 1
Pay Units: 302.
Programming (via satellite): HBO (multiplexed).
Fee: $12.95 monthly.
Video-On-Demand: No
Internet Service
Operational: Yes, DSL & dial-up.
Telephone Service
Digital: Operational
Miles of Plant: 75.0 (coaxial); None (fiber optic). Homes passed: 4,000.
President & Chief Executive Officer: Tony Thomas. Chief Financial Officer & Treasurer: Bob Gunderman. Executive Vice President, Operations: Mark Farriss. Executive Vice President, Engineering & Chief Technology Officer: Randy Nicklas.
Ownership: Windstream Communications Inc. (MSO).

BOONVILLE—Suddenlink Communications, 520 Maryville Centre Dr, Ste 300, St. Louis, MO 63141. Phones: 660-359-2677; 660-882-7681; 314-315-9400. Web Site: http://www.suddenlink.com. Also serves Cooper County (portions). ICA: MO0062.
TV Market Ranking: Below 100 (BOONVILLE, Cooper County (portions)). Franchise award date: November 5, 1964. Franchise expiration date: N.A. Began: April 1, 1965.
Channel capacity: 61 (operating 2-way). Channels available but not in use: N.A.
Basic Service
Subscribers: 961. Commercial subscribers: 139.
Programming (received off-air): KCTV (CBS) Kansas City; KMIZ (ABC, MeTV, MNT) Columbia; KMOS-TV (PBS) Sedalia; KOMU-TV (CW, NBC) Columbia; KQFX-LD Columbia; KRCG (CBS) Jefferson City.
Programming (via satellite): C-SPAN; QVC.
Fee: $28.45 monthly.
Expanded Basic Service 1
Subscribers: N.A.
Programming (via satellite): A&E; AMC; Animal Planet; BET; Cartoon Network; CNBC; CNN; Comedy Central; Discovery Channel; Disney Channel; E! HD; ESPN; ESPN2; Food Network; Fox News Channel; Fox Sports 1; FOX Sports Midwest; Freeform; FX; Great American Country; Hallmark Channel; HGTV; History; HLN; Lifetime; MSNBC; MTV; National Geographic Channel; Nickelodeon; Outdoor Channel; Spike TV; Syfy; TBS; The Weather Channel; TLC; TNT; Travel Channel; Trinity Broadcasting Network (TBN); Turner Classic Movies; TV Land; USA Network; VH1.
Fee: $25.00 monthly.
Digital Basic Service
Subscribers: N.A.
Programming (via satellite): BBC America; Bloomberg Television; Cloo; Discovery Digital Networks; Disney XD; DMX Music; ESPN Classic; ESPNews; Fuse; FYI; Golf Channel; GSN; History; History International; IFC; NBCSN; WE tv.
Pay Service 1
Pay Units: N.A.
Programming (via satellite): HBO; Showtime; The Movie Channel.
Fee: $7.95 monthly (TMC), $9.95 monthly (Showtime), $10.95 monthly (HBO).
Digital Pay Service 1
Pay Units: N.A.
Programming (via satellite): Cinemax (multiplexed); HBO (multiplexed); Showtime (multiplexed); Starz; Starz Encore (multiplexed); The Movie Channel (multiplexed).
Video-On-Demand: No
Pay-Per-View
iN DEMAND (delivered digitally); Playboy TV (delivered digitally); Fresh (delivered digitally).
Internet Service
Operational: Yes. Began: June 23, 2002.
Broadband Service: Suddenlink High Speed Internet.
Fee: $29.95 monthly.
Telephone Service
Digital: Operational
Fee: $49.95 monthly
Miles of Plant: 45.0 (coaxial); None (fiber optic). Homes passed: 2,988.
Senior Vice President, Corporate Finance: Michael Pflantz. Regional Manager: Todd Cruthird. Plant Manager: Brent Lowell. Regional Marketing Manager: Beverly Gambell.
Ownership: Cequel Communications Holdings I LLC (MSO).

BOSWORTH—Formerly served by CableDirect. No longer in operation. ICA: MO0389.

BOWLING GREEN—Formerly served by Crystal Broadband Networks. No longer in operation. ICA: MO0107.

BRANSON—Suddenlink Communications, 310 Walnut Ext, PO Box 1109, Branson, MO 65616. Phones: 877-869-7897; 314-315-9400. Fax: 417-335-8262. Web Site: http://www.suddenlink.com. Also serves Branson View Estates, Bull Creek, Hollister, Indian Point, Merriam Woods, Rockaway Beach, Stone County (portions), Taney County (portions) & Venice on the Lake. ICA: MO0038.
TV Market Ranking: Below 100 (BRANSON, Branson View Estates, Bull Creek, Hollister, Indian Point, Merriam Woods, Rockaway Beach, Stone County (portions), Venice on the Lake); Outside TV Markets (Taney County (portions)). Franchise award date: February 28, 1994. Franchise expiration date: N.A. Began: December 1, 1969.
Channel capacity: 40 (2-way capable). Channels available but not in use: N.A.
Basic Service
Subscribers: 7,417. Commercial subscribers: 3,680.
Programming (received off-air): KOLR (CBS) Springfield; KOZK (PBS) Springfield; KOZL-TV (IND) Springfield; KSPR (ABC) Springfield; KWBM (Retro TV) Harrison; KYTV (CW, NBC, WeatherNation) Springfield.
Programming (via satellite): CNN; C-SPAN; C-SPAN 2; QVC; TBS; Trinity Broadcasting Network (TBN); WGN America.
Fee: $40.00 installation; $61.95 monthly; $3.95 converter.
Expanded Basic Service 1
Subscribers: N.A.
Programming (via satellite): A&E; AMC; Animal Planet; Bravo; Cartoon Network; CMT; CNBC; Comedy Central; Discovery Channel; Disney Channel; E! HD; ESPN; ESPN2; Food Network; Fox News Channel; Fox Sports 1; FOX Sports Midwest; Freeform; FX; Great American Country; HGTV; History; HLN; INSP; Lifetime; MSNBC; MTV; NBCSN; Nickelodeon; Oxygen; Pop; Spike TV; Syfy; The Weather Channel; TLC; TNT; Travel Channel; TV Land; USA Network; VH1.
Digital Basic Service
Subscribers: N.A.
Programming (via satellite): BBC America; Bloomberg Television; Cooking Channel; Discovery Life Channel; Disney XD; DIY Network; ESPN Classic; ESPNews; Fox Sports 2; FYI; Golf Channel; GSN; Hallmark Channel; History International; IFC; LMN; MC; National Geographic Channel; NBA TV; Nick Jr.; Nicktoons; Outdoor Channel; Starz Encore (multiplexed); Sundance TV; TeenNick.
Digital Pay Service 1
Pay Units: N.A.
Programming (via satellite): Cinemax (multiplexed); HBO (multiplexed); Showtime (multiplexed); Starz (multiplexed); The Movie Channel (multiplexed).
Video-On-Demand: No
Pay-Per-View
Playboy TV (delivered digitally); Fresh (delivered digitally); NBA League Pass (delivered digitally); iN DEMAND (delivered digitally).
Internet Service
Operational: Yes.
Subscribers: 6,954.
Broadband Service: Suddenlink High Speed Internet.
Telephone Service
Digital: Operational
Subscribers: 2,915.
Miles of Plant: 911.0 (coaxial); 166.0 (fiber optic). Homes passed: 29,554.
Senior Vice President, Corporate Finance: Michael Pflantz. Vice President, Accounting: Sabrina Warr. General Manager: Terrill Bradley. Chief Engineer: Tim Crotti.
Ownership: Cequel Communications Holdings I LLC (MSO).

BRAYMER—Formerly served by Allegiance Communications. No longer in operation. ICA: MO0232.

BROOKFIELD—Suddenlink Communications, 520 Maryville Centre Dr, Ste 300, St. Louis, MO 63141. Phones: 314-315-9400; 660-258-2472. Web Site: http://

2017 Edition D-441

Missouri—Cable Systems

www.suddenlink.com. Also serves Linn County (portions). ICA: MO0073.
TV Market Ranking: Below 100 (Linn County (portions)); Outside TV Markets (BROOKFIELD, Linn County (portions)). Franchise award date: May 1, 1963. Franchise expiration date: N.A. Began: January 1, 1964.
Channel capacity: 62 (operating 2-way). Channels available but not in use: N.A.

Basic Service
Subscribers: 497.
Programming (received off-air): KOMU-TV (CW, NBC) Columbia; KTVO (ABC) Kirksville.
Programming (via microwave): KCPT (PBS) Kansas City; KCTV (CBS) Kansas City; KMBC-TV (ABC, MeTV) Kansas City; KSHB-TV (COZI TV, Grit, NBC) Kansas City; KSMO-TV (Bounce TV, MNT) Kansas City; WDAF-TV (Antenna TV, FOX) Kansas City.
Programming (via satellite): C-SPAN; QVC.
Fee: $28.45 monthly.

Expanded Basic Service 1
Subscribers: N.A.
Programming (via satellite): A&E; AMC; Animal Planet; BET; Cartoon Network; CNBC; CNN; Comedy Central; Discovery Channel; Disney Channel; E! HD; ESPN; ESPN2; Food Network; Fox News Channel; FOX Sports Midwest; Freeform; FX; Great American Country; Hallmark Channel; HGTV; History; HLN; Lifetime; MSNBC; MTV; National Geographic Channel; Nickelodeon; Spike TV; Syfy; TBS; The Weather Channel; TLC; TNT; Travel Channel; Trinity Broadcasting Network (TBN); Turner Classic Movies; TV Land; USA Network; VH1.
Fee: $25.00 monthly.

Digital Basic Service
Subscribers: N.A.
Programming (via satellite): BBC America; Bloomberg Television; Cloo; Discovery Digital Networks; Disney XD; DMX Music; ESPN Classic; ESPNews; Fox Sports 1; Fuse; FYI; Golf Channel; GSN; History International; IFC; NBCSN; Outdoor Channel; WE tv.

Pay Service 1
Pay Units: N.A.
Programming (via satellite): Cinemax (multiplexed); HBO (multiplexed); Showtime (multiplexed); The Movie Channel.

Digital Pay Service 1
Pay Units: N.A.
Programming (via satellite): Cinemax (multiplexed); HBO (multiplexed); Showtime (multiplexed); Starz; Starz Encore (multiplexed); The Movie Channel (multiplexed).

Video-On-Demand: No

Pay-Per-View
iN DEMAND (delivered digitally); Playboy TV (delivered digitally); Fresh (delivered digitally).

Internet Service
Operational: Yes. Began: January 1, 2003.
Broadband Service: Suddenlink High Speed Internet.
Fee: $29.95 monthly.

Telephone Service
Digital: Operational
Miles of Plant: 39.0 (coaxial); 2.0 (fiber optic). Homes passed: 2,600.
Senior Vice President, Corporate Finance: Michael Pflantz. Regional Manager: Todd Cruthird.
Ownership: Cequel Communications Holdings I LLC (MSO).

BROWNING—Formerly served by CableDirect. No longer in operation. ICA: MO0281.

BRUNSWICK—Mediacom, 1533 South Enterprise Ave, Springfield, MO 65804. Phones: 845-695-2762; 417-875-5500; 417-875-5560 (Springfield regional office); 816-637-4500. Fax: 417-883-0265. Web Site: http://www.mediacomcable.com. Also serves Salisbury. ICA: MO0155.
TV Market Ranking: Outside TV Markets (BRUNSWICK, Salisbury). Franchise award date: N.A. Franchise expiration date: N.A. Began: June 1, 1976.
Channel capacity: N.A. Channels available but not in use: N.A.

Basic Service
Subscribers: 240.
Programming (received off-air): KCPT (PBS) Kansas City; KCTV (CBS) Kansas City; KCWE (CW, Movies!, This TV) Kansas City; KMBC-TV (ABC, MeTV) Kansas City; KMCI-TV (Bounce TV, Escape, IND) Lawrence; KMIZ (ABC, MeTV, MNT) Columbia; KMOS-TV (PBS) Sedalia; KOMU-TV (CW, NBC) Columbia; KRCG (CBS) Jefferson City; KSHB-TV (COZI TV, Grit, NBC) Kansas City; WDAF-TV (Antenna TV, FOX) Kansas City.
Programming (via satellite): WGN America.
Fee: $35.00 installation; $42.00 monthly; $1.70 converter.

Expanded Basic Service 1
Subscribers: N.A.
Programming (via satellite): A&E; AMC; Animal Planet; Bravo; Cartoon Network; CMT; CNBC; CNN; Comedy Central; C-SPAN; Discovery Channel; Disney Channel; E! HD; ESPN; ESPN2; EVINE Live; EWTN Global Catholic Network; Food Network; Fox News Channel; Fox Sports 1; FOX Sports Midwest; Freeform; FX; Hallmark Channel; HGTV; History; HLN; INSP; Lifetime; MSNBC; MTV; Nickelodeon; Outdoor Channel; Pop; QVC; Spike TV; Syfy; TBS; The Weather Channel; TLC; TNT; Travel Channel; Trinity Broadcasting Network (TBN); truTV; TV Land; USA Network; VH1; WE tv.

Digital Basic Service
Subscribers: N.A.
Programming (via satellite): BBC America; Bloomberg Television; Discovery Life Channel; Fuse; FXM; FYI; Golf Channel; GSN; History International; IFC; LMN; MC; National Geographic Channel; NBCSN; Nick Jr.; Nicktoons; TeenNick; Turner Classic Movies.

Digital Pay Service 1
Pay Units: N.A.
Programming (via satellite): Cinemax (multiplexed); Flix (multiplexed); HBO (multiplexed); Showtime (multiplexed); Starz (multiplexed); Starz Encore (multiplexed); Sundance TV (multiplexed); The Movie Channel (multiplexed).

Video-On-Demand: No

Pay-Per-View
Mediacom PPV & Events PPV (delivered digitally); Playboy TV (delivered digitally); SexSee (delivered digitally); Pleasure (delivered digitally); Hot Body (delivered digitally).

Internet Service
Operational: Yes.
Broadband Service: Mediacom High Speed Internet.
Fee: $55.95 monthly.

Telephone Service
Digital: Operational
Miles of Plant: 25.0 (coaxial); None (fiber optic). Homes passed: 1,496.
Regional Vice President: Bill Copeland. Vice President, Financial Reporting: Kenneth J. Kohrs. Regional Technical Operations Director: Alan Freedman. Operations Director: Bryan Gann. Marketing Director: Will Kuebler. Technical Operations Manager: Roger Shearer.
Ownership: Mediacom LLC (MSO).

BRUNSWICK—Mediacom. Now served by BRUNSWICK (formerly Salisbury), MO [MO0155]. ICA: MO0213.

BUFFALO—Provincial Cable & Data, 123A West Main St, Odessa, MO 64076. Phones: 816-633-1626; 866-284-3346. E-mail: customercare@provincial-cable.net. Web Site: http://www.provincialcable.com. ICA: MO0127.
TV Market Ranking: Below 100 (BUFFALO). Franchise award date: N.A. Franchise expiration date: N.A. Began: November 1, 1982.
Channel capacity: N.A. Channels available but not in use: N.A.

Basic Service
Subscribers: 151.
Programming (received off-air): KOLR (CBS) Springfield; KOZK (PBS) Springfield; KOZL-TV (IND) Springfield; KSMO-TV (Bounce TV, MNT) Kansas City; KSPR (ABC) Springfield; KYTV (CW, NBC, WeatherNation) Springfield.
Programming (via satellite): C-SPAN; ESPN2; INSP; QVC.
Fee: $35.95 installation; $18.98 monthly.

Expanded Basic Service 1
Subscribers: N.A.
Programming (via satellite): A&E; AMC; Animal Planet; Bravo; Cartoon Network; CBS Sports Network; CNBC; CNN; Comedy Central; Discovery Channel; Disney Channel; E! HD; ESPN; Food Network; Fox News Channel; Freeform; FX; Great American Country; Hallmark Channel; HGTV; History; HLN; Lifetime; MSNBC; National Geographic Channel; Nickelodeon; Syfy; TBS; The Weather Channel; TLC; TNT; Travel Channel; Trinity Broadcasting Network (TBN); truTV; USA Network; WE tv; WGN America.
Fee: $48.45 monthly.

Digital Basic Service
Subscribers: N.A.
Programming (via satellite): BBC America; Bloomberg Television; Destination America; Discovery Kids Channel; Discovery Life Channel; Disney XD; ESPN Classic; ESPNews; Fox Sports 1; FXM; FYI; Golf Channel; GSN; History International; IFC; Investigation Discovery; LMN; Outdoor Channel; OWN: Oprah Winfrey Network; Science Channel; Starz Encore (multiplexed); Turner Classic Movies.

Pay Service 1
Pay Units: N.A.
Programming (via satellite): Cinemax; HBO; Showtime; The Movie Channel.
Fee: $8.95 monthly (TMC), $10.95 monthly (Cinemax or Showtime), $12.95 monthly (HBO).

Digital Pay Service 1
Pay Units: N.A.
Programming (via satellite): Cinemax (multiplexed); Flix; HBO (multiplexed); Showtime (multiplexed); Starz (multiplexed); The Movie Channel (multiplexed).
Fee: $8.95 monthly (TMC), $10.95 monthly (Cinemax or Showtime), $12.95 monthly (HBO).

Video-On-Demand: No

Pay-Per-View
iN DEMAND (delivered digitally); Hot Choice (delivered digitally); Playboy TV (delivered digitally); Fresh (delivered digitally); Shorteez (delivered digitally).

Internet Service
Operational: Yes.
Broadband Service: In-house.
Fee: $24.95-$44.95 monthly.

Telephone Service
None
Miles of Plant: 14.0 (coaxial); None (fiber optic). Homes passed: 1,200.
General Manager: Perry Scarborough. Office Manager: Misti Runyan.
Ownership: Provincial Cable & Data (MSO).

BUNCETON—Formerly served by OTELCO. No longer in operation. ICA: MO0295.

BUNKER—Formerly served by Cebridge Connections. No longer in operation. ICA: MO0278.

BURLINGTON JUNCTION—Formerly served by B & L Technologies LLC. No longer in operation. ICA: MO0258.

BUTLER—Mediacom, 901 North College Ave, Columbia, MO 65201. Phones: 845-695-2762; 417-875-5500; 417-875-5560 (Springfield regional office); 573-443-1536. Fax: 417-883-0265. Web Site: http://www.mediacomcable.com. ICA: MO0097.
TV Market Ranking: Outside TV Markets (BUTLER). Franchise award date: January 1, 1985. Franchise expiration date: N.A. Began: October 1, 1971.
Channel capacity: N.A. Channels available but not in use: N.A.

Basic Service
Subscribers: 328.
Programming (received off-air): KCPT (PBS) Kansas City; KCTV (CBS) Kansas City; KCWE (CW, Movies!, This TV) Kansas City; KMBC-TV (ABC, MeTV) Kansas City; KOAM-TV (CBS) Pittsburg; KPXE-TV (ION) Kansas City; KSHB-TV (COZI TV, Grit, NBC) Kansas City; KSMO-TV (Bounce TV, MNT) Kansas City; KSNF (NBC) Joplin; WDAF-TV (Antenna TV, FOX) Kansas City.
Programming (via satellite): A&E; AMC; Animal Planet; Cartoon Network; CMT; CNBC; CNN; Comedy Central; C-SPAN; Discovery Channel; Disney Channel; E! HD; ESPN; ESPN2; Food Network; Fox Sports 1; Freeform; HGTV; History; HLN; INSP; Lifetime; MSNBC; Nickelodeon; Pop; QVC; Spike TV; Syfy; TBS; The Weather Channel; TLC; TNT; Travel Channel; Trinity Broadcasting Network (TBN); truTV; TV Land; USA Network; VH1; WE tv; WGN America.
Fee: $35.00 installation; $42.00 monthly.

Digital Basic Service
Subscribers: N.A.
Programming (via satellite): BBC America; Bloomberg Television; Discovery Life Channel; DMX Music; Fuse; FXM; FYI; Golf Channel; GSN; History International; IFC; LMN; National Geographic Channel; NBCSN; Nick Jr.; Nicktoons; TeenNick; Turner Classic Movies.

Digital Pay Service 1
Pay Units: N.A.
Programming (via satellite): Cinemax (multiplexed); Flix (multiplexed); HBO (multiplexed); Showtime (multiplexed); Starz (multiplexed); Starz Encore (multiplexed); Sundance TV (multiplexed); The Movie Channel (multiplexed).

Video-On-Demand: No

Pay-Per-View
Playboy TV (delivered digitally); Ten Clips (delivered digitally); Pleasure (delivered digitally); Hot Body (delivered digitally); Events (delivered digitally).

Cable Systems—Missouri

Internet Service
Operational: Yes.
Broadband Service: Mediacom High Speed Internet.
Telephone Service
Digital: Operational
Miles of Plant: 42.0 (coaxial); None (fiber optic). Homes passed: 2,633.
Regional Vice President: Bill Copeland. Vice President, Financial Reporting: Kenneth J. Kohrs. Regional Technical Operations Director: Alan Freedman. Operations Director: Bryan Gann. Marketing Director: Will Kuebler. Technical Operations Manager: Roger Shearer.
Ownership: Mediacom LLC (MSO).

CABOOL—Mediacom. Now served by SEYMOUR, MO [M00172]. ICA: M00163.

CAINSVILLE—Formerly served by Longview Communications. No longer in operation. ICA: M00277.

CAIRO—Formerly served by Almega Cable. No longer in operation. ICA: M00390.

CALIFORNIA—Formerly served by Crystal Broadband Networks. No longer in operation. ICA: M00103.

CAMDEN POINT—Formerly served by Allegiance Communications. No longer in operation. ICA: M00176.

CAMERON—Mediacom. Now served by EXCELSIOR SPRINGS, MO [M00040]. ICA: M00089.

CANTON—Formerly served by Westcom. No longer in operation. ICA: M00391.

CAPE GIRARDEAU—Charter Communications. Now served by ST. LOUIS, MO [M00009]. ICA: M00018.

CARL JUNCTION—Mediacom, 1533 South Enterprise Ave, Springfield, MO 65804. Phones: 845-695-2762; 417-875-5500; 417-875-5560. Fax: 417-883-0265. Web Site: http://www.mediacomcable.com. Also serves Galena, KS; Airport Drive Village, Alba, Duenweg, Duquesne, Jasper County, Neck City, Oronogo & Purcell, MO. ICA: M00094.
TV Market Ranking: Below 100 (Airport Drive Village, Alba, CARL JUNCTION, Duenweg, Duquesne, Galena, Jasper County, Neck City, Oronogo, Purcell). Franchise award date: August 1, 1979. Franchise expiration date: N.A. Began: December 21, 1982.
Channel capacity: N.A. Channels available but not in use: N.A.
Basic Service
Subscribers: 1,646.
Programming (received off-air): KCLJ-LP Joplin-Carthage; KFJX (FOX) Pittsburg; KGCS-LD (America One, IND) Joplin; KJPX-LP (Retro TV) Joplin; KOAM-TV (CBS) Pittsburg; KODE-TV (ABC) Joplin; KOZJ (PBS) Joplin; KSNF (NBC) Joplin.
Programming (via satellite): CW PLUS; INSP; Pop; WGN America.
Fee: $35.00 installation; $42.00 monthly.
Expanded Basic Service 1
Subscribers: N.A.
Programming (via satellite): A&E; AMC; Animal Planet; Bravo; Cartoon Network; CMT; CNBC; CNN; Comedy Central; C-SPAN; Discovery Channel; Discovery Life Channel; Disney Channel; ESPN; ESPN2; EVINE Live; Food Network; Fox Sports 1; FOX Sports Midwest; Freeform; FX; Hallmark Channel; HGTV; History; HLN; Lifetime; MSNBC; MTV; Nickelodeon; Outdoor Channel; QVC; Spike TV; Syfy; TBS; The Weather Channel; TLC; TNT; Travel Channel; truTV; TV Land; USA Network; VH1; WE tv.
Digital Basic Service
Subscribers: N.A.
Programming (via satellite): BBC America; Bloomberg Television; Cloo; Discovery Digital Networks; ESPNews; Fuse; FXM; FYI; Golf Channel; GSN; History International; IFC; LMN; MC; National Geographic Channel; NBCSN; Nick Jr.; Nicktoons; TeenNick; Turner Classic Movies.
Digital Pay Service 1
Pay Units: N.A.
Programming (via satellite): Cinemax (multiplexed); Flix (multiplexed); HBO (multiplexed); Showtime (multiplexed); Starz (multiplexed); Starz Encore (multiplexed); Sundance TV (multiplexed); The Movie Channel (multiplexed).
Video-On-Demand: Yes
Pay-Per-View
Special events (delivered digitally); Playboy TV (delivered digitally); SexSee (delivered digitally); Juicy (delivered digitally).
Internet Service
Operational: Yes.
Broadband Service: Mediacom High Speed Internet.
Telephone Service
Digital: Operational
Miles of Plant: 86.0 (coaxial); None (fiber optic). Homes passed: 5,903.
Regional Vice President: Bill Copeland. Vice President, Financial Reporting: Kenneth J. Kohrs. Regional Technical Operations Director: Alan Freedman. Marketing Director: Will Kuebler.
Ownership: Mediacom LLC (MSO).

CARROLLTON—Mediacom, 1533 South Enterprise Ave, Springfield, MO 65804. Phones: 845-695-2762; 417-875-5500; 417-875-5560 (Springfield regional office); 816-637-4500 (Excelsior Springs office). Fax: 417-883-0265. Web Site: http://www.mediacomcable.com. ICA: M00095.
TV Market Ranking: Outside TV Markets (CARROLLTON). Franchise award date: N.A. Franchise expiration date: N.A. Began: December 1, 1976.
Channel capacity: N.A. Channels available but not in use: N.A.
Basic Service
Subscribers: 413.
Programming (received off-air): KCTV (CBS) Kansas City; KCWE (CW, Movies!, This TV) Kansas City; KMBC-TV (ABC, MeTV) Kansas City; KMIZ (ABC, MeTV, MNT) Columbia; KMOS-TV (PBS) Sedalia; KOMU-TV (CW, NBC) Columbia; KPXE-TV (ION) Kansas City; KSHB-TV (COZI TV, Grit, NBC) Kansas City; KSMO-TV (Bounce TV, MNT) Kansas City; WDAF-TV (Antenna TV, FOX) Kansas City; 1 FM.
Programming (via satellite): Pop; WGN America.
Fee: $35.00 installation; $42.00 monthly.
Expanded Basic Service 1
Subscribers: N.A.
Programming (via satellite): A&E; AMC; Animal Planet; Bravo; Cartoon Network; CMT; CNBC; CNN; Comedy Central; C-SPAN; Discovery Channel; E! HD; ESPN; ESPN2; EVINE Live; Food Network; Fox News Channel; Fox Sports 1; FOX Sports Midwest; Freeform; FX; Hallmark Channel; HGTV; History; HLN; INSP; Lifetime; MSNBC; MTV; Nickelodeon; Outdoor Channel; QVC; Spike TV; Syfy; TBS; The Weather Channel; TLC; TNT; Travel Channel; Trinity Broadcasting Network (TBN); truTV; TV Land; USA Network; VH1; WE tv.
Fee: $3.95 monthly.
Digital Basic Service
Subscribers: N.A.
Programming (via satellite): BBC America; Bloomberg Television; Discovery Life Channel; Fuse; FXM; FYI; Golf Channel; GSN; History International; IFC; LMN; MC; National Geographic Channel; NBCSN; Nick Jr.; Nicktoons; TeenNick; Turner Classic Movies.
Digital Pay Service 1
Pay Units: N.A.
Programming (via satellite): Cinemax (multiplexed); Flix (multiplexed); HBO (multiplexed); Showtime (multiplexed); Starz (multiplexed); Starz Encore (multiplexed); Sundance TV (multiplexed); The Movie Channel (multiplexed).
Video-On-Demand: No
Pay-Per-View
Mediacom PPB & Events PPV (delivered digitally); Playboy TV (delivered digitally); TEN Clips (delivered digitally); Pleasure (delivered digitally); Hot Body (delivered digitally).
Internet Service
Operational: Yes.
Broadband Service: Mediacom High Speed Internet.
Telephone Service
Digital: Operational
Miles of Plant: 31.0 (coaxial); None (fiber optic). Homes passed: 2,214.
Regional Vice President: Bill Copeland. Vice President, Financial Reporting: Kenneth J. Kohrs. Regional Technical Operations Director: Alan Freedman. Marketing Director: Will Kuebler. Operations Director: Bryan Gann. Technical Operations Manager: Roger Shearer.
Ownership: Mediacom LLC (MSO).

CARTHAGE—Suddenlink Communications, 231 East 4th St, Carthage, MO 64836-1629. Phone: 314-315-9400. Fax: 417-359-5373. Web Site: http://www.suddenlink.com. Also serves Brooklyn Heights & Fidelity. ICA: M00034.
TV Market Ranking: Below 100 (Brooklyn Heights, CARTHAGE, Fidelity). Franchise award date: N.A. Franchise expiration date: N.A. Began: March 1, 1967.
Channel capacity: N.A. Channels available but not in use: N.A.
Basic Service
Subscribers: 2,428. Commercial subscribers: 262.
Programming (received off-air): KFJX (FOX) Pittsburg; KOAM-TV (CBS) Pittsburg; KODE-TV (ABC) Joplin; KOZJ (PBS) Joplin; KSNF (NBC) Joplin; allband FM.
Programming (via satellite): TBS; WGN America.
Fee: $40.00 installation; $34.50 monthly; $1.27 converter.
Expanded Basic Service 1
Subscribers: N.A.
Programming (via satellite): A&E; AMC; Animal Planet; Cartoon Network; CMT; CNBC; CNN; Comedy Central; C-SPAN; C-SPAN 2; CW PLUS; Discovery Channel; Discovery Life Channel; Disney Channel; ESPN; ESPN2; Food Network; Fox News Channel; FOX Sports Midwest; Freeform; FX; Hallmark Channel; HGTV; History; HLN; Lifetime; Nickelodeon; Outdoor Channel; QVC; Spike TV; Syfy; The Weather Channel; TLC; TNT; Travel Channel; TV Land; Univision Studios; USA Network; VH1.
Fee: $15.71 monthly.
Digital Basic Service
Subscribers: N.A.
Programming (via satellite): BBC America; Bloomberg Television; Discovery Digital Networks; DMX Music; ESPN Classic; ESPNews; Fox Sports 1; Golf Channel; GSN; INSP; Trinity Broadcasting Network (TBN); Turner Classic Movies.
Digital Pay Service 1
Pay Units: N.A.
Programming (via satellite): HBO (multiplexed); HITS (Headend In The Sky); Showtime (multiplexed); Starz (multiplexed); Starz Encore (multiplexed); Sundance TV; The Movie Channel (multiplexed).
Pay-Per-View
iN DEMAND (delivered digitally); Fresh (delivered digitally); Playboy TV (delivered digitally); Hot Choice (delivered digitally).
Internet Service
Operational: Yes.
Broadband Service: Suddenlink High Speed Internet.
Fee: $29.95 monthly.
Telephone Service
Digital: Operational
Miles of Plant: 121.0 (coaxial); 26.0 (fiber optic). Homes passed: 7,239.
Senior Vice President, Corporate Finance: Michael Pflantz. Vice President, Accounting: Sabrina Warr. General Manager: Terrill Bradley. Chief Engineer: Tim Crotti.
Ownership: Cequel Communications Holdings I LLC (MSO).

CARUTHERSVILLE—Mediacom, 1533 South Enterprise Ave, Springfield, MO 65804. Phones: 845-695-2762; 417-875-5500; 417-875-5560 (Springfield regional office); 573-333-1148 (Caruthersville office). Fax: 417-883-0265. Web Site: http://www.mediacomcable.com. Also serves Hayti & Hayti Heights. ICA: M00041.
TV Market Ranking: Outside TV Markets (CARUTHERSVILLE, Hayti, Hayti Heights). Franchise award date: May 14, 1964. Franchise expiration date: N.A. Began: January 22, 1966.
Channel capacity: N.A. Channels available but not in use: N.A.
Basic Service
Subscribers: 1,275.
Programming (received off-air): KAIT (ABC, NBC) Jonesboro; KBSI (FOX) Cape Girardeau; KFVS-TV (CBS, CW, MeTV) Cape Girardeau; WATN-TV (ABC) Mem-

Missouri—Cable Systems

phis; WHBQ-TV (Decades, FOX, Movies!) Memphis; WKNO (PBS) Memphis; WMC-TV (Bounce TV, NBC, This TV) Memphis; WREG-TV (Antenna TV, CBS) Memphis. Programming (via satellite): WGN America.
Fee: $40.16 installation; $42.00 monthly; $1.05 converter.
Expanded Basic Service 1
Subscribers: N.A.
Programming (via satellite): A&E; AMC; Animal Planet; BET; Bravo; Cartoon Network; CMT; CNBC; CNN; Comedy Central; C-SPAN; C-SPAN 2; Discovery Channel; Discovery Life Channel; Disney Channel; E! HD; ESPN; ESPN2; Food Network; Fox News Channel; Fox Sports 1; FOX Sports Midwest; Freeform; FX; Hallmark Channel; HGTV; History; HLN; INSP; Lifetime; MSNBC; MTV; Nickelodeon; Outdoor Channel; Pop; QVC; TBS; The Weather Channel; TLC; TNT; Travel Channel; Trinity Broadcasting Network (TBN); truTV; TV Land; USA Network; VH1.
Fee: $23.37 monthly.
Digital Basic Service
Subscribers: N.A.
Programming (via satellite): BBC America; Bloomberg Television; Discovery Digital Networks; DMX Music; Fuse; FXM; Golf Channel; GSN; IFC; LMN; MTV Classic; MTV Hits; MTV2; National Geographic Channel; NBCSN; Nick Jr.; Nicktoons; TeenNick; Turner Classic Movies.
Digital Pay Service 1
Pay Units: N.A.
Programming (via satellite): Cinemax (multiplexed); Flix (multiplexed); HBO (multiplexed); Showtime (multiplexed); Starz (multiplexed); Starz Encore (multiplexed); Sundance TV (multiplexed); The Movie Channel (multiplexed).
Video-On-Demand: No
Pay-Per-View
special events; Mediacom PPV (delivered digitally); Playboy TV (delivered digitally); TEN Clips (delivered digitally); TEN (delivered digitally); TEN Blox (delivered digitally).
Internet Service
Operational: Yes.
Broadband Service: Mediacom High Speed Internet.
Telephone Service
None
Miles of Plant: 72.0 (coaxial); 10.0 (fiber optic). Homes passed: 4,721.
Regional Vice President: Bill Copeland. Vice President, Financial Reporting: Kenneth J. Kohrs. Regional Technical Operations Director: Alan Freedman. Operations Director: Bryan Gann. Marketing Director: Will Kuebler. Technical Operations Director: Roger Shearer. Chief Technician: Randall Waldrop.
Ownership: Mediacom LLC (MSO).

CASS COUNTY—Formerly served by Longview Communications. No longer in operation. ICA: MO0470.

CASS COUNTY (northwestern portion)—Formerly served by Cass County Cable. No longer in operation. ICA: MO0348.

CASSVILLE—Mediacom, 1533 South Enterprise Ave, Springfield, MO 65804. Phones: 845-695-2762; 417-875-5500; 417-875-5560. Fax: 417-883-0265. Web Site: http://www.mediacomcable.com. Also serves Exeter & Purdy. ICA: MO0118.
TV Market Ranking: Below 100 (CASSVILLE, Exeter, Purdy). Franchise award date: January 12, 1983. Franchise expiration date: N.A. Began: July 1, 1983.
Channel capacity: N.A. Channels available but not in use: N.A.
Basic Service
Subscribers: 458.
Programming (received off-air): KODE-TV (ABC) Joplin; KOLR (CBS) Springfield; KOZK (PBS) Springfield; KSPR (ABC) Springfield; KWBM (Retro TV) Harrison; KYTV (CW, NBC, WeatherNation) Springfield.
Programming (via satellite): A&E; AMC; Animal Planet; Bravo; Cartoon Network; CMT; CNBC; CNN; Comedy Central; C-SPAN; Discovery Channel; Discovery Life Channel; Disney Channel; ESPN; ESPN2; EVINE Live; Food Network; Fox News Channel; Fox Sports 1; FOX Sports Midwest; Freeform; FX; Hallmark Channel; HGTV; History; HLN; INSP; Lifetime; MSNBC; MTV; Nickelodeon; Outdoor Channel; Pop; QVC; Spike TV; Syfy; TBS; The Weather Channel; TLC; TNT; Travel Channel; Trinity Broadcasting Network (TBN); truTV; TV Land; USA Network; VH1; WE tv; WGN America.
Fee: $35.00 installation; $42.00 monthly.
Digital Basic Service
Subscribers: N.A.
Programming (via satellite): BBC America; Bloomberg Television; Discovery Digital Networks; DMX Music; Fuse; FXM; FYI; Golf Channel; GSN; History International; IFC; LMN; National Geographic Channel; NBCSN; Nick Jr.; Nicktoons; TeenNick; Turner Classic Movies.
Pay Service 1
Pay Units: N.A.
Programming (via satellite): Cinemax; Flix; HBO (multiplexed); Showtime (multiplexed); The Movie Channel.
Fee: $2.95 monthly (Flix), $7.50 monthly (TMC), $10.50 monthly (Cinemax, HBO or Showtime).
Digital Pay Service 1
Pay Units: N.A.
Programming (via satellite): Cinemax (multiplexed); Flix (multiplexed); HBO (multiplexed); Showtime (multiplexed); Starz (multiplexed); Starz Encore (multiplexed); Sundance TV (multiplexed); The Movie Channel (multiplexed).
Video-On-Demand: Yes
Pay-Per-View
Playboy TV (delivered digitally); TEN Clips (delivered digitally); Pleasure (delivered digitally); Hot Body (delivered digitally); Events (delivered digitally).
Internet Service
Operational: Yes.
Broadband Service: Mediacom High Speed Internet.
Telephone Service
Digital: Operational
Miles of Plant: 45.0 (coaxial); None (fiber optic). Homes passed: 2,787.
Vice President: Bill Copeland. Vice President, Financial Reporting: Kenneth J. Kohrs. Regional Technical Operations Director: Alan Freedman. Marketing Director: Will Kuebler.
Ownership: Mediacom LLC (MSO).

CENTERVIEW—Formerly served by CableDirect. No longer in operation. ICA: MO0393.

CENTRALIA—Formerly served by US Cable. Now served by Charter Communications, ST. LOUIS, MO [MO0009]. ICA: MO0104.

CHAMOIS—Formerly served by Mid Missouri Broadband. No longer in operation. ICA: MO0284.

CHARLESTON—Charter Communications. Now served by ST. LOUIS, MO [MO0009]. ICA: MO0043.

CHESTERFIELD—Charter Communications. Now served by ST. LOUIS, MO [MO0009]. ICA: MO0015.

CHILHOWEE—Formerly served by National Cable Inc. No longer in operation. ICA: MO0333.

CHILLICOTHE—Zito Media, 102 S Main St, PO Box 665, Coudersport, PA 16915. Phones: 814-260-9055; 800-365-6988. E-mail: info@zitomedia.com. Web Site: http://www.zitomedia.com. Also serves Livingston County (portions). ICA: MO0046.
TV Market Ranking: Outside TV Markets (CHILLICOTHE, Livingston County (portions)). Franchise award date: June 4, 1963. Franchise expiration date: N.A. Began: June 4, 1963.
Channel capacity: N.A. Channels available but not in use: N.A.
Basic Service
Subscribers: 1,761.
Programming (received off-air): KCPT (PBS) Kansas City; KCTV (CBS) Kansas City; KCWE (CW, Movies!, This TV) Kansas City; KMBC-TV (ABC, MeTV) Kansas City; KMCI-TV (Bounce TV, Escape, IND) Lawrence; KPXE-TV (ION) Kansas City; KQTV (ABC) St. Joseph; KSHB-TV (COZI TV, Grit, NBC) Kansas City; KSMO-TV (Bounce TV, MNT) Kansas City; WDAF-TV (Antenna TV, FOX) Kansas City; 23 FMs.
Programming (via satellite): C-SPAN; C-SPAN 2; EVINE Live; QVC; TBS; Trinity Broadcasting Network (TBN); WGN America.
Fee: $49.95 installation; $19.50 monthly; $.57 converter.
Expanded Basic Service 1
Subscribers: N.A.
Programming (via satellite): A&E; AMC; Animal Planet; Bravo; Cartoon Network; CMT; CNBC; CNN; Comedy Central; Discovery Channel; Discovery Life Channel; Disney Channel; E! HD; ESPN; ESPN Classic; ESPN2; EWTN Global Catholic Network; Food Network; Fox News Channel; FOX Sports Midwest; Freeform; FX; Great American Country; Hallmark Channel; HGTV; History; HLN; INSP; Lifetime; LMN; MSNBC; MTV; National Geographic Channel; Nickelodeon; OWN: Oprah Winfrey Network; Oxygen; Spike TV; Syfy; The Weather Channel; TLC; TNT; Travel Channel; truTV; Turner Classic Movies; TV Land; USA Network; VH1; WE tv.
Fee: $31.66 monthly.
Digital Basic Service
Subscribers: N.A.
Programming (via satellite): AXS TV; BBC America; Bloomberg Television; Discovery Digital Networks; Disney XD; ESPN; ESPNews; Fox Sports 1; Fuse; FXM; FYI; Golf Channel; GSN; HD Theater; History International; MC; MTV Classic; MTV Hits; MTV2; NBCSN; Nick Jr.; Nicktoons; Outdoor Channel; Ovation; Sundance TV; TeenNick; TNT.
Digital Pay Service 1
Pay Units: N.A.
Programming (via satellite): Cinemax (multiplexed); HBO; IFC; Showtime; Starz (multiplexed); Starz Encore (multiplexed); The Movie Channel (multiplexed).
Fee: $12.00 monthly (each).
Video-On-Demand: No
Pay-Per-View
iN DEMAND (delivered digitally); Fresh (delivered digitally); Shorteez (delivered digitally); Playboy TV (delivered digitally); Pleasure (delivered digitally); Hot Choice (delivered digitally); TEN Blue (delivered digitally); TEN Clips (delivered digitally); TEN Blox (delivered digitally).
Internet Service
Operational: Yes.
Broadband Service: In-house.
Fee: $19.95-$49.99 installation; $49.95 monthly.
Telephone Service
Digital: Operational
Fee: $49.95 monthly
Miles of Plant: 84.0 (coaxial); None (fiber optic).
President: James Rigas.
Ownership: Zito Media (MSO).

CHULA—Formerly served by CableDirect. No longer in operation. ICA: MO0370.

CLARENCE—Milan Interactive Communications, 312 South Main St, PO Box 240, Milan, MO 63556. Phone: 660-265-7174. Fax: 660-256-7174. ICA: MO0394.
TV Market Ranking: Outside TV Markets (CLARENCE). Franchise award date: N.A. Franchise expiration date: N.A. Began: January 1, 1988.
Channel capacity: N.A. Channels available but not in use: N.A.
Basic Service
Subscribers: 54.
Programming (received off-air): KHQA-TV (ABC, CBS) Hannibal; KTVO (ABC) Kirksville; WGEM-TV (CW, FOX, NBC) Quincy; WTJR (Christian TV Network) Quincy.
Programming (via satellite): CNN; C-SPAN; TBS; WGN America.
Fee: $29.95 installation; $40.77 monthly.
Video-On-Demand: No
Pay-Per-View
iN DEMAND (delivered digitally).
Internet Service
Operational: No.
Telephone Service
None
Miles of Plant: 20.0 (coaxial); None (fiber optic). Homes passed: 566.
President & General Manager: Rick Gardener.
Ownership: Milan Interactive Communications (MSO).

CLARKSBURG—Formerly served by First Cable of Missouri Inc. No longer in operation. ICA: MO0339.

CLARKSDALE—Formerly served by CableDirect. No longer in operation. ICA: MO0355.

CLARKSVILLE—Formerly served by First Cable of Missouri Inc. No longer in operation. ICA: MO0456.

CLARKTON—NewWave Communications. Now served by DEXTER, MO [MO0039]. ICA: MO0110.

CLEARMONT—Formerly served by Longview Communications. No longer in operation. ICA: MO0467.

CLEVER—Formerly served by Suddenlink Communications. No longer in operation. ICA: MO0288.

CLINTON—Charter Communications. Now served by ST. LOUIS, MO [MO0009]. ICA: MO0050.

COFFMAN BEND—Formerly served by Almega Cable. No longer in operation. ICA: MO0124.

COLE CAMP—Provincial Cable & Data, 123A West Main St, Odessa, MO 64076. Phones: 816-633-1626; 866-284-3346. E-mail: customercare@provincial-cable.net. Web Site: http://www.provincialcable.com. ICA: MO0201.
TV Market Ranking: Below 100 (COLE CAMP). Franchise award date: N.A. Franchise expiration date: N.A. Began: March 1, 1983.
Channel capacity: N.A. Channels available but not in use: N.A.
Basic Service
  Subscribers: 121.
  Programming (received off-air): KCWE (CW, Movies!, This TV) Kansas City; KMBC-TV (ABC, MeTV) Kansas City; KMIZ (ABC, MeTV, MNT) Columbia; KMOS-TV (PBS) Sedalia; KOMU-TV (CW, NBC) Columbia; KRCG (CBS) Jefferson City; KSMO-TV (Bounce TV, MNT) Kansas City; WDAF-TV (Antenna TV, FOX) Kansas City.
  Programming (via satellite): C-SPAN; QVC; Trinity Broadcasting Network (TBN).
  Fee: $35.95 installation; $15.98 monthly.
Expanded Basic Service 1
  Subscribers: N.A.
  Programming (via satellite): A&E; AMC; Animal Planet; Cartoon Network; CBS Sports Network; CNN; Comedy Central; Discovery Channel; Disney Channel; DIY Network; E! HD; ESPN; ESPN Classic; ESPN2; Food Network; Fox News Channel; Freeform; FX; Great American Country; Hallmark Channel; Hallmark Movies & Mysteries; HGTV; History; HLN; Lifetime; MSNBC; Syfy; TBS; The Weather Channel; TLC; TNT; Travel Channel; USA Network; WGN America.
  Fee: $48.45 monthly.
Digital Basic Service
  Subscribers: N.A.
  Programming (via satellite): BBC America; Bloomberg Television; Discovery Digital Networks; Disney XD; ESPNews; Fox Sports 1; Fuse; FXM; FYI; Golf Channel; GSN; History International; IFC; LMN; NBCSN; Outdoor Channel; Starz Encore (multiplexed); Sundance TV; Turner Classic Movies.
Pay Service 1
  Pay Units: N.A.
  Programming (via satellite): Cinemax; HBO; Showtime; The Movie Channel.
  Fee: $8.95 monthly (TMC), $10.95 monthly (Cinemax or Showtime), $12.95 monthly (HBO).
Digital Pay Service 1
  Pay Units: N.A.
  Programming (via satellite): Cinemax (multiplexed); Flix; HBO (multiplexed); Showtime (multiplexed); Starz (multiplexed); The Movie Channel (multiplexed).
  Fee: $8.95 monthly (TMC), $10.95 monthly (Showtime or Cinemax), $12.95 monthly (HBO).
Video-On-Demand: No
Internet Service
  Operational: Yes.
  Broadband Service: In-house.
  Fee: $49.95 installation; $19.95-$49.95 monthly.
Telephone Service
  None
Miles of Plant: 6.0 (coaxial); None (fiber optic). Homes passed: 540.
General Manager: Perry Scarborough. Office Manager: Misti Runyan.
Ownership: Provincial Cable & Data (MSO).

COLE COUNTY (portions)—Suddenlink Communications, 520 Maryville Centre Dr, Ste 300, St. Louis, MO 63141. Phones: 800-999-6845; 314-315-9400. Web Site: http://www.suddenlink.com. Also serves Centertown, Lohman, St. Martins & Wardsville. ICA: MO0060.
TV Market Ranking: Below 100 (Centertown, COLE COUNTY (PORTIONS), Lohman, St. Martins, Wardsville). Franchise award date: July 1, 1986. Franchise expiration date: N.A. Began: October 1, 1986.
Channel capacity: N.A. Channels available but not in use: N.A.
Basic Service
  Subscribers: 329. Commercial subscribers: 28.
  Programming (received off-air): KMIZ (ABC, MeTV, MNT) Columbia; KMOS-TV (PBS) Sedalia; KNLJ (Christian TV Network) Jefferson City; KOMU-TV (CW, NBC) Columbia; KRCG (CBS) Jefferson City.
  Programming (via satellite): A&E; AMC; Cartoon Network; CMT; CNBC; CNN; C-SPAN; Discovery Channel; Disney Channel; E! HD; ESPN; FOX Sports Midwest; Freeform; HLN; Lifetime; Nickelodeon; QVC; Spike TV; TBS; The Weather Channel; TNT; Travel Channel; Turner Classic Movies; TV Land; USA Network; WGN America.
  Fee: $28.45 monthly.
Pay Service 1
  Pay Units: N.A.
  Programming (via satellite): HBO; Showtime; The Movie Channel.
  Fee: $5.95 monthly (TMC), $9.95 monthly (Showtime), $10.95 monthly (HBO).
Internet Service
  Operational: Yes. Began: November 29, 2004.
  Broadband Service: Suddenlink High Speed Internet.
  Fee: $29.95 monthly.
Telephone Service
  None
Miles of Plant: 125.0 (coaxial); None (fiber optic). Homes passed: 3,075.
Senior Vice President, Corporate Finance: Michael Pflantz. Regional Manager: Todd Cruthird. Regional Marketing Manager: Beverly Gambell.
Ownership: Cequel Communications Holdings I LLC (MSO).

COLUMBIA—Charter Communications. Now served by ST. LOUIS, MO [MO0009]. ICA: MO0037.

COLUMBIA—Mediacom, 901 North College Ave, Columbia, MO 65201. Phones: 845-695-2762; 573-443-1536; 417-875-5560 (Springfield regional office). Fax: 417-883-0265. Web Site: http://www.mediacomcable.com. Also serves Boone County (portions) & University of Missouri. ICA: MO0005.
TV Market Ranking: Below 100 (Boone County (portions), COLUMBIA, University of Missouri). Franchise award date: July 22, 1977. Franchise expiration date: N.A. Began: July 1, 1977.
Channel capacity: N.A. Channels available but not in use: N.A.
Basic Service
  Subscribers: 11,273.
  Programming (received off-air): KETC (PBS) St. Louis; KMIZ (ABC, MeTV, MNT) Columbia; KMOS-TV (PBS) Sedalia; KNLJ (Christian TV Network) Jefferson City; KOMU-TV (CW, NBC) Columbia; KQFX-LD Columbia; KRCG (CBS) Jefferson City; KSDK (Bounce TV, NBC) St. Louis.
  Programming (via satellite): C-SPAN 2; Discovery Channel; EVINE Live; LWS Local Weather Station; Pop; QVC; TBS; WGN America.
  Fee: $50.00 installation; $45.00 monthly; $1.94 converter.
Expanded Basic Service 1
  Subscribers: N.A.
  Programming (via satellite): A&E; AMC; Animal Planet; BET; Bravo; Cartoon Network; CMT; CNBC; CNN; Comedy Central; C-SPAN; Disney Channel; E! HD; ESPN; ESPN2; EWTN Global Catholic Network; Food Network; Fox News Channel; FOX Sports Midwest; Freeform; FX; Hallmark Channel; HGTV; History; HLN; ION Television; Lifetime; MSNBC; MTV; Nickelodeon; Oxygen; Spike TV; Syfy; Telemundo; The Weather Channel; TLC; TNT; Travel Channel; truTV; TV Land; USA Network; VH1; WE tv.
  Fee: $9.85 installation; $16.55 monthly.
Digital Basic Service
  Subscribers: N.A.
  Programming (via satellite): AXS TV; BBC America; Bloomberg Television; Discovery Life Channel; Disney XD; ESPN; Fox Sports 1; Fuse; FXM; FYI; Golf Channel; GSN; HD Theater; History International; IFC; LMN; MC; MTV2; National Geographic Channel; NBCSN; Nick Jr.; Nicktoons; Outdoor Channel; Ovation; TeenNick; Trinity Broadcasting Network (TBN); Turner Classic Movies; Universal HD.
Digital Pay Service 1
  Pay Units: N.A.
  Programming (via satellite): Cinemax (multiplexed); Flix; HBO (multiplexed); Showtime; Starz (multiplexed); Starz Encore (multiplexed); Sundance TV; The Movie Channel (multiplexed).
Video-On-Demand: Yes
Pay-Per-View
  ESPN (delivered digitally); Fresh (delivered digitally); Shorteez (delivered digitally); Playboy TV (delivered digitally).
Internet Service
  Operational: Yes.
  Subscribers: 14,397.
  Broadband Service: Mediacom High Speed Internet.
  Fee: $150.00 installation; $39.95 monthly.
Telephone Service
  Digital: Operational
  Subscribers: 4,632.
Miles of Plant: 1,034.0 (coaxial); 123.0 (fiber optic). Homes passed: 57,042.
Regional Vice President: Bill Copeland. Vice President, Financial Reporting: Kenneth J. Kohrs. Regional Technical Operations Director: Alan Freedman. Operations Director: Bryan Gann. Marketing Director: Will Kuebler. Technical Operations Manager: Roger Shearer. Marketing Coordinator: Brad Koetters.
Ownership: Mediacom LLC (MSO).

CONCEPTION JUNCTION—Formerly served by B & L Technologies LLC. No longer in operation. ICA: MO0433.

CONWAY—Formerly served by Fidelity Communications. No longer in operation. ICA: MO0274.

COWGILL—Green Hills Communications. This cable system has converted to IPTV. Now served by AVALON, MO [MO5156]. ICA: MO0445.

CRAIG—Formerly served by CableDirect. No longer in operation. ICA: MO0397.

CRANE—Mediacom. Now served by SEYMOUR, MO [MO0172]. ICA: MO0198.

CREIGHTON—Formerly served by CableDirect. No longer in operation. ICA: MO0343.

CROCKER—Formerly served by Longview Communications. No longer in operation. ICA: MO0234.

CUBA—Formerly served by Charter Communications. No longer in operation. ICA: MO0080.

CURRYVILLE—Formerly served by First Cable of Missouri Inc. No longer in operation. ICA: MO0366.

DE KALB—Formerly served by CableDirect. No longer in operation. ICA: MO0368.

DEXTER—NewWave Communications, One Montgomery Plaza, 4th Floor, Sikeston, MO 63801. Phone: 888-863-9928 (Customer service). Fax: 573-614-4802. E-mail: info@newwavecom.com. Web Site: http://www.newwavecom.com. Also serves Clay County (portions), Greene County (portions), Greenway, Lafe, Marmaduke, Piggott, Pollard, Rector & St. Francis, AR; Bernie, Bloomfield, Campbell, Clarkton, Dunklin County (portions), Essex, Frisbee, Gibson, Gideon, Holcomb, Homestown, Kennett, Malden, New Madrid, North Wardell, Parma, Pemiscot County (portions), Portageville, Risco, Senath, Steele, Stoddard County (portions), Tallapoosa & Wardell, MO. ICA: MO0039.
TV Market Ranking: 69 (Stoddard County (portions)); Below 100 (Bernie, Bloomfield, Campbell, Clay County (portions), DEXTER, Dunklin County (portions), Essex, Gibson, Gideon, Greene County (portions), Greenway, Holcomb, Lafe, Malden, Marmaduke, New Madrid, Piggott, Pollard, St. Francis, Clarkton, Parma, Pemiscot County (portions), Rector, Stoddard County (portions)); Outside TV Markets (Frisbee, Homestown, North Wardell, Risco, Senath, Tallapoosa, Wardell, Kennett, Pemiscot County (portions), Portageville, Steele, Stoddard County (portions)). Franchise award date: January 1, 1956. Franchise expiration date: N.A. Began: June 1, 1957.
Channel capacity: N.A. Channels available but not in use: N.A.
Basic Service
  Subscribers: 9,525.
  Programming (received off-air): KAIT (ABC, NBC) Jonesboro; KBSI (FOX) Cape

Missouri—Cable Systems

Girardeau; KFVS-TV (CBS, CW, MeTV) Cape Girardeau; KPOB-TV (ABC) Poplar Bluff; WKMU (PBS) Murray; WPSD-TV (Antenna TV, NBC) Paducah; WQWQ-LP (CW, MeTV) Paducah.
Programming (via microwave): WDKA (MNT, The Country Network) Paducah; WTCT (IND) Marion.
Programming (via satellite): C-SPAN; C-SPAN 2; EVINE Live; INSP; QVC; Trinity Broadcasting Network (TBN).
Fee: $29.95 installation; $34.78 monthly.

Expanded Basic Service 1
Subscribers: 5,242.
Programming (via satellite): A&E; AMC; Animal Planet; Bravo; Cartoon Network; CMT; CNBC; CNN; Comedy Central; Discovery Channel; Disney Channel; E! HD; ESPN; ESPN Classic; ESPN2; Food Network; Fox News Channel; Fox Sports 1; FOX Sports Midwest; Freeform; FX; Golf Channel; Great American Country; GSN; Hallmark Channel; HGTV; History; HLN; Jewelry Television; Lifetime; MSNBC; MTV; Nickelodeon; Outdoor Channel; Oxygen; Spike TV; Syfy; TBS; The Weather Channel; TLC; TNT; Travel Channel; truTV; TV Land; USA Network; VH1.
Fee: $42.95 monthly.

Digital Basic Service
Subscribers: N.A.
Programming (via satellite): A&E HD; AXS TV; BBC America; Bloomberg Television; Cloo; CMT; Destination America; Discovery Kids Channel; Disney XD; DIY Network; ESPN Classic; ESPN HD; ESPN2 HD; ESPNews; FSN HD; FXM; FYI; HD Theater; History HD; History International; IFC; Investigation Discovery; LMN; MC; MTV Classic; MTV Hits; MTV Live; MTV2; NBCSN; Nick Jr.; Nicktoons; OWN; Oprah Winfrey Network; RFD-TV; Science Channel; TeenNick; The Weather Channel HD; TNT HD; Turner Classic Movies; USA Network HD; Versus HD; VH1 Soul.

Digital Pay Service 1
Pay Units: 1,298.
Programming (via satellite): Cinemax (multiplexed); Cinemax HD; Flix; HBO (multiplexed); HBO HD; Showtime (multiplexed); Starz (multiplexed); Starz Encore; Starz HD; The Movie Channel (multiplexed).

Video-On-Demand: No
Pay-Per-View
iN DEMAND (delivered digitally); Hot Choice (delivered digitally); Playboy TV (delivered digitally); Fresh (delivered digitally); Shorteez (delivered digitally).

Internet Service
Operational: Yes.
Fee: $40.00 installation; $23.95 monthly.

Telephone Service
None
Miles of Plant: 102.0 (coaxial); 10.0 (fiber optic).
General Manager: John Helmers.
Ownership: NewWave Communications LLC (MSO).

DIAMOND—Mediacom, 1533 South Enterprise Ave, Springfield, MO 65804. Phones: 417-875-5500; 417-875-5588; 845-695-2762. Fax: 417-883-0265. Web Site: http://www.mediacomcable.com. Also serves Anderson, Goodman, Granby, Newtonia, Sarcoxie & Stark City. ICA: M00156.
TV Market Ranking: Below 100 (Anderson, Goodman, Newtonia, Sarcoxie, Stark City, DIAMOND, Granby). Franchise award date: October 14, 1981. Franchise expiration date: N.A. Began: November 1, 1983.
Channel capacity: N.A. Channels available but not in use: N.A.

Basic Service
Subscribers: 617.
Programming (received off-air): KCLJ-LP Joplin-Carthage; KFJX (FOX) Pittsburg; KGCS-LD (America One, IND) Joplin; KJPX-LP (Retro TV) Joplin; KOAM-TV (CBS) Pittsburg; KODE-TV (ABC) Joplin; KOZK (PBS) Springfield; KSNF (NBC) Joplin.
Programming (via satellite): CW PLUS; Pop; WGN America.
Fee: $35.00 installation; $42.00 monthly.

Expanded Basic Service 1
Subscribers: N.A.
Programming (via satellite): A&E; AMC; Animal Planet; Bravo; Cartoon Network; CMT; CNBC; CNN; Comedy Central; C-SPAN; Discovery Channel; Discovery Life Channel; Disney Channel; ESPN; ESPN2; EVINE Live; Food Network; Fox News Channel; Fox Sports 1; FOX Sports Midwest; Freeform; FX; Hallmark Channel; HGTV; History; HLN; Lifetime; MSNBC; MTV; Nickelodeon; Outdoor Channel; QVC; Spike TV; Syfy; TBS; The Weather Channel; TLC; TNT; Travel Channel; truTV; TV Land; USA Network; VH1.

Digital Basic Service
Subscribers: N.A.
Programming (via satellite): BBC America; Bloomberg Television; Cloo; Discovery Digital Networks; ESPNews; Fuse; FXM; FYI; Golf Channel; GSN; History International; IFC; LMN; MC; National Geographic Channel; NBCSN; Nick Jr.; Nicktoons; TeenNick; Turner Classic Movies.

Pay Service 1
Pay Units: N.A.
Programming (via satellite): Cinemax; Flix; HBO; Showtime (multiplexed); The Movie Channel.
Fee: $10.00 installation; $9.00 monthly (Cinemax or HBO); $10.50 monthly (Showtime/TMC/Flix).

Digital Pay Service 1
Pay Units: N.A.
Programming (via satellite): Cinemax (multiplexed); Flix (multiplexed); HBO (multiplexed); Showtime (multiplexed); Starz (multiplexed); Starz Encore (multiplexed); Sundance TV (multiplexed); The Movie Channel (multiplexed).

Video-On-Demand: Yes
Pay-Per-View
Special events (delivered digitally); Playboy TV (delivered digitally); SexSee (delivered digitally); Juicy (delivered digitally).

Internet Service
Operational: Yes.
Broadband Service: Mediacom High Speed Internet.

Telephone Service
Digital: Operational
Miles of Plant: 93.0 (coaxial); None (fiber optic). Homes passed: 4,802.
Vice President: Bill Copeland. Vice President, Financial Reporting: Kenneth J. Kohrs. Regional Technical Operations Director: Alan Freedman. Marketing Director: Will Kuebler.
Ownership: Mediacom LLC (MSO).

DIAMOND—Mediacom. Now served by DIAMOND, MO [M00156]. ICA: M00266.

DIXON—Cable America Corp. Now served by ST. ROBERT, MO [M00023]. ICA: M00125.

DONIPHAN—Boycom Cablevision Inc, 3467 Township Line Rd, Poplar Bluff, MO 63901. Phones: 800-890-6620; 573-686-9101. Fax: 573-686-4722. Web Site: http://www.boycom.com. ICA: M00063.

TV Market Ranking: Below 100 (DONIPHAN). Franchise award date: June 6, 1986. Franchise expiration date: N.A. Began: January 1, 1960.
Channel capacity: N.A. Channels available but not in use: N.A.

Basic Service
Subscribers: N.A.
Programming (received off-air): KAIT (ABC, NBC) Jonesboro; KFVS-TV (CBS, CW, MeTV) Cape Girardeau; KTEJ (PBS) Jonesboro; allband FM.
Programming (via satellite): CNN; C-SPAN; CW PLUS; Discovery Channel; TBS; TLC; TNT; Trinity Broadcasting Network (TBN); USA Network; WGN America.
Fee: $29.95 installation; $39.95 monthly.

Expanded Basic Service 1
Subscribers: N.A.
Programming (via satellite): A&E; AMC; C-SPAN 2; Disney Channel; Disney XD; E! HD; ESPN; ESPN2; FOX Sports Midwest; Freeform; FX; Great American Country; HGTV; History; HLN; INSP; Lifetime; MSNBC; National Geographic Channel; Nickelodeon; Outdoor Channel; Spike TV; Syfy; The Weather Channel; Turner Classic Movies; TV Land; WE tv.
Fee: $20.00 monthly.

Pay Service 1
Pay Units: N.A.
Programming (via satellite): Cinemax; HBO; Showtime; Starz; Starz Encore; The Movie Channel.
Fee: $8.99 monthly (Cinemax), $12.00 monthly (HBO), $13.99 monthly (Showtime/TMC).

Video-On-Demand: No
Internet Service
Operational: No.
Telephone Service
None
Miles of Plant: 128.0 (coaxial); None (fiber optic). Homes passed: 2,931.
President: Steven Boyers. General Manager: Shelly Batton. Chief Technician: Phil Huett.
Ownership: Boycom Cablevision Inc. (MSO).

DOOLITTLE—Cable America Corp. Now served by ST. ROBERT, MO [M00023]. ICA: M00265.

DOWNING—Formerly served by Longview Communications. No longer in operation. ICA: M00398.

DREXEL—Formerly served by Almega Cable. No longer in operation. ICA: M00217.

DUDLEY—Formerly served by Boycom Cablevision Inc. No longer in operation. ICA: M00342.

DUQUESNE—Mediacom. Now served by CARL JUNCTION, MO [M00094]. ICA: M00131.

DURHAM—Formerly served by CableDirect. No longer in operation. ICA: M00439.

EAGLEVILLE—Formerly served by Longview Communications. No longer in operation. ICA: M00268.

EAST LYNNE—Formerly served by CableDirect. No longer in operation. ICA: M00364.

EASTON—Formerly served by First Cable of Missouri Inc. No longer in operation. ICA: M00446.

EDINA—Formerly served by Charter Communications. No longer in operation. ICA: M00189.

EL DORADO SPRINGS—Fidelity Communications, 64 North Clark St, Sullivan, MO 63080. Phones: 573-468-8081; 417-667-2857 (Nevada office); 800-392-8070. Fax: 573-468-5440. E-mail: custserv@fidelitycommunications.com. Web Site: http://www.fidelitycommunications.com. ICA: M00112.
TV Market Ranking: Outside TV Markets (EL DORADO SPRINGS). Franchise award date: October 1, 1964. Franchise expiration date: N.A. Began: February 1, 1965.
Channel capacity: 49 (not 2-way capable). Channels available but not in use: N.A.

Basic Service
Subscribers: 294. Commercial subscribers: 42.
Programming (received off-air): KOAM-TV (CBS) Pittsburg; KODE-TV (ABC) Joplin; KOLR (CBS) Springfield; KOZK (PBS) Springfield; KOZL-TV (IND) Springfield; KPXE-TV (ION) Kansas City; KSMO-TV (Bounce TV, MNT) Kansas City; KSPR (ABC) Springfield; KYTV (CW, NBC, WeatherNation) Springfield; WDAF-TV (Antenna TV, FOX) Kansas City; allband FM.
Programming (via satellite): INSP; QVC; WGN America.
Fee: $29.99 installation; $28.99 monthly.

Expanded Basic Service 1
Subscribers: N.A.
Programming (via satellite): A&E; AMC; Bravo; Cartoon Network; CMT; CNBC; CNN; Comedy Central; Discovery Channel; Disney Channel; E! HD; ESPN; ESPN2; Fox News Channel; Freeform; FX; HGTV; History; HLN; Lifetime; MTV; Nickelodeon; Oxygen; Spike TV; Syfy; TBS; The Weather Channel; TLC; TNT; TV Land; USA Network; VH1.
Fee: $49.99 monthly.

Digital Basic Service
Subscribers: N.A.
Programming (via satellite): BBC America; Bloomberg Television; Discovery Digital Networks; Disney XD; DIY Network; FYI; GSN; History International; IFC; MC; Nick 2; Nick Jr.; Nicktoons; Sundance TV; TeenNick; WE tv.

Digital Pay Service 1
Pay Units: N.A.
Programming (via satellite): Cinemax (multiplexed); HBO (multiplexed); Showtime (multiplexed); Starz (multiplexed); Starz Encore (multiplexed); The Movie Channel (multiplexed).
Fee: $11.95 monthly (each).

Video-On-Demand: No
Pay-Per-View
iN DEMAND (delivered digitally); Pleasure (delivered digitally); ETC (delivered digitally); The Erotic Network (delivered digitally).

Internet Service
Operational: Yes.
Fee: $54.99-$99.99 monthly.

Telephone Service
None
Miles of Plant: 25.0 (coaxial); None (fiber optic). Homes passed: 2,519.
General Manager, Missouri: Don Knight. Video Product Manager: Loren King.
Ownership: Fidelity Communications Co. (MSO).

ELDON—Charter Communications. Now served by ST. LOUIS, MO [M00009]. ICA: M00085.

Cable Systems—Missouri

ELLINGTON—Formerly served by Boycom Cablevision Inc. No longer in operation. ICA: MO0164.

ELMO—Formerly served by CableDirect. No longer in operation. ICA: MO0468.

ELSBERRY—Formerly served by Crystal Broadband Networks. No longer in operation. ICA: MO0142.

EMINENCE—Formerly served by Boycom Cablevision Inc. No longer in operation. ICA: MO0195.

EOLIA—Formerly served by First Cable of Missouri Inc. No longer in operation. ICA: MO0312.

ESSEX—Formerly served by Cebridge Connections. Now served by NewWave Communications, DEXTER, MO [MO0039]. ICA: MO0263.

EUGENE—Formerly served by First Cable of Missouri Inc. No longer in operation. ICA: MO0376.

EVERTON—Mediacom, 1533 South Enterprise Ave, Springfield, MO 65804. Phones: 845-695-2762; 417-875-5500; 417-875-5560. Fax: 417-883-0265. Web Site: http://www.mediacomcable.com. Also serves Ash Grove, Golden City, Greene County (unincorporated areas), Greenfield, Lockwood, Miller, Mount Vernon, Walnut Grove & Willard. ICA: MO0400.
TV Market Ranking: Below 100 (Ash Grove, EVERTON, Golden City, Greene County (unincorporated areas), Greenfield, Miller, Mount Vernon, Walnut Grove, Willard); Outside TV Markets (Lockwood).
Channel capacity: N.A. Channels available but not in use: N.A.
Basic Service
Subscribers: 1,905.
Programming (received off-air): KOLR (CBS) Springfield; KOZK (PBS) Springfield; KOZL-TV (IND) Springfield; KSNF (NBC) Joplin; KSPR (ABC) Springfield; KWBM (Retro TV) Harrison; KYCW-LD (CW) Springfield; KYTV (CW, NBC, WeatherNation) Springfield.
Programming (via satellite): EVINE Live; Pop; WGN America.
Fee: $35.00 installation; $42.00 monthly.
Expanded Basic Service 1
Subscribers: N.A.
Programming (via satellite): A&E; AMC; Animal Planet; Bravo; Cartoon Network; CMT; CNBC; CNN; Comedy Central; C-SPAN; Discovery Channel; Disney Channel; E! HD; ESPN; ESPN2; Food Network; Fox News Channel; Fox Sports 1; FOX Sports Midwest; Freeform; FX; FXM; Hallmark Channel; HGTV; History; HLN; INSP; Lifetime; MSNBC; MTV; Nickelodeon; Outdoor Channel; QVC; Spike TV; Syfy; TBS; The Weather Channel; TLC; TNT; Travel Channel; Trinity Broadcasting Network (TBN); truTV; TV Land; USA Network; VH1; WE tv.
Digital Basic Service
Subscribers: N.A.
Programming (via satellite): AXS TV; BBC America; Bloomberg Television; Cloo; Discovery Digital Networks; ESPN; ESPNews; Fuse; FYI; Golf Channel; GSN; HD Theater; History International; HITS (Headend In The Sky); IFC; LMN; MC; National Geographic Channel; NBCSN; Nick Jr.; Nicktoons; TeenNick; Turner Classic Movies; Universal HD.

Digital Pay Service 1
Pay Units: N.A.
Programming (via satellite): Cinemax (multiplexed); Flix (multiplexed); HBO (multiplexed); HBO HD; Showtime (multiplexed); Showtime HD; Starz (multiplexed); Starz Encore (multiplexed); Starz HD; Sundance TV (multiplexed); The Movie Channel (multiplexed).
Video-On-Demand: Yes
Pay-Per-View
Special events (delivered digitally); Playboy TV (delivered digitally); SexSee (delivered digitally); Juicy (delivered digitally).
Internet Service
Operational: Yes.
Broadband Service: Mediacom High Speed Internet.
Telephone Service
Analog: Not Operational
Digital: Operational
Miles of Plant: 5.0 (coaxial); None (fiber optic).
Regional Vice President: Bill Copeland. Vice President, Financial Reporting: Kenneth J. Kohrs. Regional Technical Operations Director: Alan Freedman. Marketing Director: Will Kuebler.
Ownership: Mediacom LLC (MSO).

EWING—Formerly served by CableDirect. No longer in operation. ICA: MO0296.

EXCELSIOR SPRINGS—Mediacom, 901 North College Ave, Columbia, MO 65201. Phones: 845-695-2762; 573-443-1536; 816-637-4500 (Local office). Fax: 573-449-8492. Web Site: http://www.mediacomcable.com. Also serves Albany, Bethany, Cameron, Crystal Lakes, Excelsior Estates, Henrietta, Homestead Village, Lawson, Norborne, Richmond & Wood Heights. ICA: MO0040.
TV Market Ranking: 22 (Crystal Lakes, Excelsior Estates, EXCELSIOR SPRINGS, Henrietta, Homestead Village, Lawson, Richmond, Wood Heights); Below 100 (Cameron); Outside TV Markets (Albany, Bethany, Norborne). Franchise award date: February 16, 1981. Franchise expiration date: N.A. Began: January 1, 1982.
Channel capacity: N.A. Channels available but not in use: N.A.
Basic Service
Subscribers: 3,856.
Programming (received off-air): KCPT (PBS) Kansas City; KCTV (CBS) Kansas City; KCWE (CW, Movies!, This TV) Kansas City; KMBC-TV (ABC, MeTV) Kansas City; KMCI-TV (Bounce TV, Escape, IND) Lawrence; KPXE-TV (ION) Kansas City; KQTV (ABC) St. Joseph; KSHB-TV (COZI TV, Grit, NBC) Kansas City; KSMO-TV (Bounce TV, MNT) Kansas City; WDAF-TV (Antenna TV, FOX) Kansas City; allband FM.
Programming (via satellite): WGN America.
Fee: $35.00 installation; $45.70 monthly; $2.20 converter.
Expanded Basic Service 1
Subscribers: N.A.
Programming (via satellite): A&E; AMC; Animal Planet; Bravo; Cartoon Network; CMT; CNBC; CNN; Comedy Central; C-SPAN; Discovery Channel; Disney Channel; E! HD; ESPN; ESPN2; EVINE Live; Food Network; Fox News Channel; Fox Sports 1; FOX Sports Midwest; Freeform; FX; Hallmark Channel; HGTV; History; HLN; INSP; Lifetime; MSNBC; MTV; Nickelodeon; Pop; QVC; Spike TV; Syfy; TBS; The Weather Channel; TLC; TNT; Travel Channel; Trinity Broadcasting Network (TBN); truTV; TV Land; USA Network; VH1; WE tv.
Digital Basic Service
Subscribers: N.A.
Programming (via satellite): BBC America; Bloomberg Television; Discovery Life Channel; Fuse; FXM; FYI; Golf Channel; GSN; History International; IFC; LMN; MC; National Geographic Channel; NBCSN; Nick Jr.; Nicktoons; TeenNick; Turner Classic Movies.
Digital Pay Service 1
Pay Units: N.A.
Programming (via satellite): Cinemax (multiplexed); Flix (multiplexed); HBO (multiplexed); Showtime (multiplexed); Starz (multiplexed); Starz Encore (multiplexed); Sundance TV (multiplexed); The Movie Channel (multiplexed).
Video-On-Demand: No
Pay-Per-View
Mediacom PPV (delivered digitally); Playboy TV (delivered digitally); TEN Clips (delivered digitally); TEN Blox (delivered digitally).
Internet Service
Operational: Yes.
Broadband Service: Mediacom High Speed Internet.
Telephone Service
Digital: Operational
Miles of Plant: 94.0 (coaxial); None (fiber optic). Homes passed: 6,074.
Vice President, Financial Reporting: Kenneth J. Kohrs. General Manager: Gary Baugh. Marketing Director: Wes Shaver. Technical Operations Manager: Tom Evans.
Ownership: Mediacom LLC (MSO).

FAIR GROVE—Formerly served by Fidelity Communications. No longer in operation. ICA: MO0461.

FAIR PLAY—Formerly served by Cebridge Connections. No longer in operation. ICA: MO0286.

FAIRDEALING—Boycom Cablevision Inc, 3467 Township Line Rd, Poplar Bluff, MO 63901. Phones: 800-890-6620; 800-935-0255; 573-686-9101. Fax: 573-686-4722. E-mail: customer_service@boycomonline.com. Web Site: http://www.boycom.com. Also serves Butler County (portions). ICA: MO0444.
TV Market Ranking: Below 100 (FAIRDEALING). Franchise award date: N.A. Franchise expiration date: N.A. Began: May 5, 1993.
Channel capacity: N.A. Channels available but not in use: N.A.
Digital Basic Service
Subscribers: N.A.
Programming (received off-air): KAIT (ABC, NBC) Jonesboro; KBSI (FOX) Cape Girardeau; KFVS-TV (CBS, CW, MeTV) Cape Girardeau; KPOB-TV (ABC) Poplar Bluff; KTEJ (PBS) Jonesboro; WPSD-TV (Antenna TV, NBC) Paducah.
Programming (via satellite): 3ABN; A&E; AMC; Animal Planet; BBC America; Bloomberg Television; Bravo; Cartoon Network; Cinemax (multiplexed); CNBC; CNN; Comedy Central; C-SPAN; C-SPAN 2; Discovery Channel; Discovery Digital Networks; Disney Channel; Disney XD; DMX Music; E! HD; ESPN; ESPN Classic; ESPN2; ESPNews; Food Network; Fox News Channel; Fox Sports 1; FOX Sports Midwest; Freeform; Fuse; FX; FXM; FYI; Golf Channel; Great American Country; GSN; Hallmark Channel; HGTV; History; History International; HLN; IFC; Lifetime; LMN; MTV; NBCSN; Nick Jr.; Nickelodeon; Outdoor Channel; Pop; QVC; Spike TV; Syfy; TBS; TeenNick; The Weather Channel; TLC; TNT; Travel Channel; Trinity Broadcasting Network (TBN); truTV; TV Land; USA Network; VH1; WE tv; WGN America.
Fee: $32.12 monthly.
Digital Pay Service 1
Pay Units: N.A.
Programming (via satellite): Cinemax; HBO (multiplexed); Showtime (multiplexed); Starz (multiplexed); Starz Encore (multiplexed); The Movie Channel (multiplexed).
Fee: $4.19 monthly (Encore), $10.00 monthly (Cinemax or Starz), $12.00 monthly (Showtime/TMC), $15.00 monthly (HBO).
Video-On-Demand: No
Pay-Per-View
iN DEMAND (delivered digitally); ESPN Now (delivered digitally); Sports PPV (delivered digitally).
Internet Service
Operational: Yes. Began: September 1, 2003.
Broadband Service: ParaSun Technologies (ISP & Tech support) and SBC to Net.
Fee: $29.95 monthly.
Telephone Service
None
Miles of Plant: 80.0 (coaxial); None (fiber optic).
President: Steven Boyers. General Manager: Shelly Batton. Chief Technician: Phil Huett.
Ownership: Boycom Cablevision Inc.

FARBER—Formerly served by US Cable. Now served by Charter Communications, ST. LOUIS, MO [MO0009]. ICA: MO0109.

FARMINGTON—Charter Communications. Now served by ST. LOUIS, MO [MO0009]. ICA: MO0035.

FAUCETT—Formerly served by CableDirect. No longer in operation. ICA: MO0323.

FAYETTE—Suddenlink Communications. No longer in operation. ICA: MO0122.

FERGUSON—Charter Communications. Now served by ST. LOUIS, MO [MO0009]. ICA: MO0014.

FISK—Boycom Cablevision Inc. Now served by ELLSINORE, MO [MO0196]. ICA: MO0318.

Missouri—Cable Systems

Access the most current data instantly
FREE TRIAL @ www.warren-news.com/factbook.htm

FLAT RIVER—Formerly served by Charter Communications. No longer in operation. ICA: MO0026.

FORDLAND—Formerly served by Cebridge Connections. No longer in operation. ICA: MO0289.

FORSYTH—Mediacom. Now served by SEYMOUR, MO [MO0172]. ICA: MO0126.

FRANKFORD—Formerly served by Westcom. No longer in operation. ICA: MO0326.

FREDERICKTOWN (village)—Charter Communications. Now served by ST. LOUIS, MO [MO0009]. ICA: MO0074.

FREEBURG—Formerly served by CableDirect. No longer in operation. ICA: MO0282.

FREMONT—Formerly served by Cebridge Connections. No longer in operation. ICA: MO0378.

FULTON—Charter Communications. Now served by ST. LOUIS, MO [MO0009]. ICA: MO0045.

GAINESVILLE—Formerly served by Almega Cable. No longer in operation. ICA: MO0229.

GALENA—Formerly served by Almega Cable. No longer in operation. ICA: MO0314.

GALLATIN—Formerly served by Longview Communications. No longer in operation. ICA: MO0147.

GALT—Formerly served by CableDirect. No longer in operation. ICA: MO0402.

GARDEN CITY—Formerly served by Longview Communications. No longer in operation. ICA: MO0211.

GASCONADE—Formerly served by First Cable of Missouri Inc. No longer in operation. ICA: MO0331.

GERALD—Fidelity Communications. Now served by PHELPS COUNTY (portions), MO [MO0475]. ICA: MO0206.

GLASGOW—Suddenlink Communications. No longer in operation. ICA: MO0199.

GOODMAN—Mediacom. Now served by DIAMOND, MO [MO0156]. ICA: MO0223.

GOWER—Formerly served by Allegiance Communications. No longer in operation. ICA: MO0208.

GRANT CITY—Formerly served by B & L Technologies LLC. No longer in operation. ICA: MO0204.

GRAVOIS MILLS—Formerly served by Lake Communications. No longer in operation. ICA: MO0087.

GREEN CASTLE—Formerly served by Longview Communications. No longer in operation. ICA: MO0324.

GREEN RIDGE—Formerly served by CableDirect. No longer in operation. ICA: MO0316.

GREENTOP—Formerly served by Longview Communications. No longer in operation. ICA: MO0280.

GREENVILLE—Formerly served by Almega Cable. No longer in operation. ICA: MO0247.

HALLSVILLE—Formerly served by Longview Communications. Now served by Provincial Cable & Data, STURGEON, MO [MO0395]. ICA: MO0255.

HAMILTON—Formerly served by Allegiance Communications. No longer in operation. ICA: MO0160.

HANNIBAL—Charter Communications. Now served by ST. LOUIS, MO [MO0009]. ICA: MO0021.

HARRISBURG—Formerly served by First Cable of Missouri Inc. No longer in operation. ICA: MO0338.

HARRISONVILLE—Fidelity Communications, 64 North Clark St, Sullivan, MO 63080. Phones: 800-392-8070; 417-667-2857 (Nevada office); 573-468-8081. Fax: 573-468-5440. E-mail: custserv@fidelitycommunications.com. Web Site: http://www.fidelitycommunications.com. ICA: MO0070.
TV Market Ranking: 22 (HARRISONVILLE). Franchise award date: March 5, 1980. Franchise expiration date: N.A. Began: July 19, 1980.
Channel capacity: N.A. Channels available but not in use: N.A.
Basic Service
  Subscribers: 893. Commercial subscribers: 52.
  Programming (received off-air): KCPT (PBS) Kansas City; KCTV (CBS) Kansas City; KCWE (CW, Movies!, This TV) Kansas City; KMBC-TV (ABC, MeTV) Kansas City; KMCI-TV (Bounce TV, Escape, IND) Lawrence; KMOS-TV (PBS) Sedalia; KPXE-TV (ION) Kansas City; KSHB-TV (COZI TV, Grit, NBC) Kansas City; KSMO-TV (Bounce TV, MNT) Kansas City; WDAF-TV (Antenna TV, FOX) Kansas City; allband FM.
  Programming (via satellite): A&E; CNN; Comedy Central; C-SPAN; E! HD; Freeform; Hallmark Channel; HLN; Lifetime; MTV; Nickelodeon; Pop; QVC; TNT; Trinity Broadcasting Network (TBN); USA Network; VH1; WGN America.
  Fee: $29.99 installation; $28.99 monthly.

Expanded Basic Service 1
  Subscribers: N.A.
  Programming (via satellite): AMC; Animal Planet; Bravo; Cartoon Network; CMT; CNBC; Discovery Channel; Discovery Life Channel; Disney Channel; ESPN; ESPN2; Food Network; Fox News Channel; Fox Sports 1; FOX Sports Midwest; FX; Golf Channel; HGTV; History; MSNBC; National Geographic Channel; NBCSN; Oxygen; Spike TV; Syfy; TBS; The Weather Channel; TLC; Travel Channel; truTV; Turner Classic Movies; TV Land.
  Fee: $49.99 monthly.
Digital Basic Service
  Subscribers: N.A.
  Programming (via satellite): BBC America; Bloomberg Television; Discovery Digital Networks; Disney XD; DIY Network; FYI; GSN; History International; IFC; LMN; MC; Nick 2; Nick Jr.; Nicktoons; Sundance TV; TeenNick; TV Guide Interactive Inc.; WE tv.
Digital Pay Service 1
  Pay Units: N.A.
  Programming (via satellite): Cinemax (multiplexed); Flix; HBO (multiplexed); Showtime (multiplexed); Starz (multiplexed); Starz Encore (multiplexed); The Movie Channel (multiplexed).
  Fee: $14.00 monthly (each).
Video-On-Demand: Yes
Pay-Per-View
  iN DEMAND (delivered digitally); ETC (delivered digitally); Pleasure (delivered digitally).
Internet Service
  Operational: Yes.
  Fee: $54.99-$99.99 monthly.
Telephone Service
  Digital: Operational
  Fee: $29.99 monthly
Miles of Plant: 43.0 (coaxial); None (fiber optic). Homes passed: 4,906.
General Manager, Missouri: Don Knight. Video Product Manager: Loren King.
Ownership: Fidelity Communications Co. (MSO).

HARTVILLE—Formerly served by Cebridge Connections. No longer in operation. ICA: MO0279.

HAWK POINT—Formerly served by First Cable of Missouri Inc. No longer in operation. ICA: MO0285.

HERMANN—Mediacom, 901 North College Ave, Columbia, MO 65201. Phones: 845-695-2762; 573-443-1536; 417-875-5560 (Springfield regional office). Fax: 417-883-0265. Web Site: http://www.mediacomcable.com. ICA: MO0105.
TV Market Ranking: Outside TV Markets (HERMANN). Franchise award date: N.A. Franchise expiration date: N.A. Began: February 1, 1981.
Channel capacity: N.A. Channels available but not in use: N.A.
Basic Service
  Subscribers: 265.
  Programming (received off-air): KDNL-TV (ABC, The Country Network) St. Louis; KETC (PBS) St. Louis; KMIZ (ABC, MeTV, MNT) Columbia; KMOV (CBS) St. Louis; KOMU-TV (CW, NBC) Columbia; KPLR-TV (CW, This TV) St. Louis; KRCG (CBS) Jefferson City; KSDK (Bounce TV, NBC) St. Louis; KTVI (Antenna TV, Escape, FOX) St. Louis.
  Programming (via satellite): A&E; CNN; C-SPAN; Discovery Channel; Disney Channel; Freeform; HLN; Lifetime; MTV; Nickelodeon; QVC; TBS; TNT; WGN America.
  Fee: $60.00 installation; $43.20 monthly.
Expanded Basic Service 1
  Subscribers: N.A.
  Programming (via satellite): AMC; ESPN; FOX Sports Networks; Spike TV; truTV; USA Network.
  Fee: $11.27 installation; $2.18 monthly.
Pay Service 1
  Pay Units: N.A.
  Programming (via satellite): HBO; Starz Encore.
Video-On-Demand: No
Internet Service
  Operational: Yes.
  Broadband Service: Mediacom High Speed Internet.
Telephone Service
  None
Miles of Plant: 19.0 (coaxial); None (fiber optic). Homes passed: 1,522.
Regional Vice President: Bill Copeland. Vice President, Financial Reporting: Kenneth J. Kohrs. Regional Technical Operations Director: Alan Freedman. Operations Director: Bryan Gann. Marketing Director: Will Kuebler. Technical Operations Manager: Roger Shearer.
Ownership: Mediacom LLC (MSO).

HIGBEE—Formerly served by Longview Communications. No longer in operation. ICA: MO0260.

HIGGINSVILLE—Citizens CableVision, 1905 Walnut St., PO Box 737, Higginsville, MO 64037. Phones: 800-321-4282; 660-584-2288; 888-845-5201. E-mail: customerservice@ctcis.net. Web Site: http://www.myccvtv.net. Also serves Alma, Blackburn, Concordia, Corder, Emma, Gilliam, Houstonia, Malta Bend, Slater, Sweet Springs & Waverly. ICA: MO0313.
TV Market Ranking: Below 100 (Concordia, Corder, Emma, Houstonia, Sweet Springs, Alma); Outside TV Markets (Blackburn, Gilliam, HIGGINSVILLE, Malta Bend, Slater, Waverly). Franchise award date: N.A. Franchise expiration date: N.A. Began: November 1, 1984.
Channel capacity: N.A. Channels available but not in use: N.A.
Basic Service
  Subscribers: 1,605.
  Programming (received off-air): KCPT (PBS) Kansas City; KCTV (CBS) Kansas City; KCWE (CW, Movies!, This TV) Kansas City; KMBC-TV (ABC, MeTV) Kansas City; KMCI-TV (Bounce TV, Escape, IND) Lawrence; KMIZ (ABC, MeTV, MNT) Columbia; KMOS-TV (PBS) Sedalia; KOMU-TV (CW, NBC) Columbia; KPXE-TV (ION) Kansas City; KQFX-LD Columbia; KSHB-TV (COZI TV, Grit, NBC) Kansas City; KSMO-TV (Bounce TV, MNT) Kansas City; WDAF-TV (Antenna TV, FOX) Kansas City.
  Programming (via satellite): A&E; AMC; Animal Planet; Boomerang; Cartoon Network; CNN; Comedy Central; Cooking Channel; C-SPAN; Discovery Channel; Disney Channel; Disney XD; E! HD; ESPN; ESPN Classic; ESPN2; EVINE Live; Food Network; Fox News Channel; Fox Sports 1; FOX Sports Midwest; Fuse; FX; Great American Country; Hallmark Channel; HGTV; History; HLN; INSP; Lifetime; MSNBC; National Geographic Channel; Outdoor Channel; Pop; QVC; Syfy; TBS; The Weather Channel; TLC; TNT; Turner Classic Movies; TV Land; USA Network; WGN America.
  Fee: $39.95 installation; $38.95 monthly.

Cable Systems—Missouri

Digital Basic Service
Subscribers: N.A.
Programming (via satellite): BBC America; Bloomberg Television; Cloo; Discovery Digital Networks; DMX Music; ESPN Classic; ESPNews; FOX College Sports Central; FOX College Sports Pacific; Fox Sports 1; Fuse; FXM; FYI; Golf Channel; GSN; History International; IFC; LMN; National Geographic Channel; Outdoor Channel; Turner Classic Movies; WE tv.

Pay Service 1
Pay Units: N.A.
Programming (via satellite): Cinemax; HBO; Showtime; The Movie Channel.
Fee: $9.95 monthly (Showtime or TMC), $10.95 monthly (Cinemax), $14.95 monthly (HBO).

Digital Pay Service 1
Pay Units: N.A.
Programming (via satellite): Cinemax (multiplexed); Flix; HBO (multiplexed); Showtime (multiplexed); Starz (multiplexed); Starz Encore (multiplexed); The Movie Channel (multiplexed).
Fee: $9.95 monthly (Showtime or TMC), $10.95 monthly (Cinemax), $14.95 monthly (HBO).

Video-On-Demand: No
Pay-Per-View
iN DEMAND (delivered digitally); Hot Choice (delivered digitally); Playboy TV (delivered digitally); Fresh (delivered digitally).
Internet Service
Operational: No.
Telephone Service
None
Miles of Plant: 137.0 (coaxial); None (fiber optic). Homes passed: 6,991.
President: Brian Cornelius.
Ownership: Citizens Telephone Co. (Missouri) (MSO).

HIGHWAY DD—Formerly served by Cebridge Connections. Now served by Suddenlink Communications, NIXA, MO [MO0068]. ICA: MO0092.

HOLDEN—Formerly served by Crystal Broadband Networks. No longer in operation. ICA: MO0145.

HOLT—Formerly served by CableDirect. No longer in operation. ICA: MO0248.

HOLTS SUMMIT—Mediacom. Now served by JEFFERSON CITY, MO [MO0020]. ICA: MO0108.

HOPKINS—Formerly served by B & L Technologies LLC. No longer in operation. ICA: MO0261.

HORNERSVILLE—Formerly served by Base Cablevision. No longer in operation. ICA: MO0429.

HOUSTON—Formerly served by Houston Cable Inc. Now served by Cable America Corp., ST. ROBERT, MO [MO0023]. ICA: MO0146.

HUME—Formerly served by Midwest Cable Inc. No longer in operation. ICA: MO0335.

HURDLAND—Formerly served by CableDirect. No longer in operation. ICA: MO0435.

IBERIA—Formerly served by Longview Communications. No longer in operation. ICA: MO0245.

IMPERIAL—Charter Communications. Now served by ST. LOUIS, MO [MO0009]. ICA: MO0012.

INDEPENDENCE—Comcast Cable, 4700 Little Blue Pkwy, PO Box 2000, Independence, MO 64057. Phones: 816-795-1100; 816-795-8377. Fax: 816-795-0946. Web Site: http://www.comcast.com. Also serves Johnson County (portions) & Olathe, KS; Baldwin Park, Bates City, Blue Springs, Buckner, Cass County (portions), Grain Valley, Greenwood, Jackson County, Kansas City (portions), Lafayette County (portions), Lake Lotawano, Lake Tapawingo, Lake Winnebago, Lees Summit, Oak Grove, Odessa, Peculiar, Pleasant Hill, Raymore, Raytown, Sibley & Sugar Creek, MO. ICA: MO0004.
TV Market Ranking: 22 (Baldwin Park, Bates City, Blue Springs, Buckner, Cass County (portions), Grain Valley, Greenwood, INDEPENDENCE, Jackson County, Johnson County (portions), Kansas City (portions), Lafayette County (portions), Lake Lotawano, Lake Tapawingo, Lake Winnebago, Lees Summit, Oak Grove, Odessa, Olathe, Peculiar, Pleasant Hill, Raymore, Raytown, Sibley, Sugar Creek); Outside TV Markets (Cass County (portions), Lafayette County (portions)). Franchise award date: N.A. Franchise expiration date: N.A. Began: November 1, 1971.
Channel capacity: N.A. Channels available but not in use: N.A.

Basic Service
Subscribers: 59,999.
Programming (received off-air): KCPT (PBS) Kansas City; KCTV (CBS) Kansas City; KCWE (CW, Movies!, This TV) Kansas City; KMBC-TV (ABC, MeTV) Kansas City; KMCI-TV (Bounce TV, Escape, IND) Lawrence; KPXE-TV (ION) Kansas City; KSHB-TV (COZI TV, Grit, NBC) Kansas City; KSMO-TV (Bounce TV, MNT) Kansas City; WDAF-TV (Antenna TV, FOX) Kansas City; allband FM.
Programming (via satellite): C-SPAN; OWN: Oprah Winfrey Network; QVC; WGN America.
Fee: $50.00 installation; $23.53 monthly.

Expanded Basic Service 1
Subscribers: N.A.
Programming (via satellite): A&E; AMC; Animal Planet; BET; Bravo; Cartoon Network; CNBC; CNN; Comedy Central; Discovery Channel; Disney Channel; E! HD; ESPN; ESPN2; Food Network; Fox News Channel; Fox Sports 1; FOX Sports Midwest; Freeform; FX; Golf Channel; HGTV; History; HLN; Lifetime; MSNBC; MTV; Nickelodeon; Spike TV; Syfy; TBS; The Weather Channel; TLC; TNT; Travel Channel; truTV; Turner Classic Movies; TV Land; USA Network; VH1.
Fee: $20.00 installation.

Digital Basic Service
Subscribers: N.A.
Programming (via satellite): 3ABN; A&E HD; Animal Planet HD; BBC America; BTN; BYUtv; CBS Sports Network; Cine Mexicano; Cinelatino; CMT; CNN en Espanol; CNN HD; Cooking Channel; C-SPAN 2; C-SPAN 3; Daystar TV Network; Destination America; Discovery Channel HD; Discovery Kids Channel; Disney Channel HD; Disney XD; DIY Network; ESPN Classic; ESPN Deportes; ESPN HD; ESPN2 HD; ESPNews; FamilyNet; Flix; Food Network HD; Fox Business Network; FOX College Sports Central; FOX College Sports Pacific; Fox Deportes; Fox News HD; Freeform HD; FSN HD; Fuse; FYI; Golf Channel HD; GolTV; Great American Country; GSN; Hallmark Movies & Mysteries; HD Theater; HGTV HD; History en Espanol; History HD; History International; IFC; INSP; Investigation Discovery; LMN; LOGO; MC; MLB Network; MTV Classic; MTV Hits; MTV Jams; MTV Live; MTV2; Nat Geo WILD; National Geographic Channel; National Geographic Channel HD; NBA TV; NBC Universo; NFL Network; NFL Network HD; NHL Network; Nick 2; Nick Jr.; Nicktoons; Outdoor Channel; Oxygen; RLTV; Science Channel; Science HD; Sprout; Starz Encore (multiplexed); Sundance TV; Syfy HD; TBS HD; TeenNick; Tennis Channel; TLC HD; TNT HD; Tr3s; Trinity Broadcasting Network (TBN); TV Guide Interactive Inc.; TV One; UniMas; Universal HD; Univision; USA Network HD; Versus HD; VH1 Soul; ViendoMovies; WE tv; Weatherscan.

Digital Pay Service 1
Pay Units: N.A.
Programming (via satellite): Cinemax (multiplexed); Cinemax On Demand; HBO (multiplexed); HBO HD; HBO on Demand; Playboy TV; Showtime (multiplexed); Showtime HD; Starz (multiplexed); Starz HD; The Movie Channel (multiplexed).
Fee: $9.95 monthly (Cinemax, HBO, Showtime/TMC, Starz or Playboy).

Video-On-Demand: Yes
Pay-Per-View
Playboy TV (delivered digitally); iN DEMAND (delivered digitally); Spice: Xcess (delivered digitally); iN DEMAND; ESPN Now (delivered digitally); NBA TV (delivered digitally).
Internet Service
Operational: Yes.
Subscribers: 55,382.
Broadband Service: Comcast High Speed Internet.
Fee: $149.00 installation; $42.95 monthly; $7.00 modem lease; $299.00 modem purchase.
Telephone Service
Digital: Operational
Subscribers: 27,128.
Fee: $44.95 monthly
Miles of Plant: 3,832.0 (coaxial); 782.0 (fiber optic). Homes passed: 205,167.
General Manager: Kimberly Wepler. Chief Technician: Ken Covey. Marketing Director: Bill Rougdly. Customer Service Manager: Dana Price.
Ownership: Comcast Cable Communications Inc. (MSO).

IRONTON—Charter Communications. Now served by ST. LOUIS, MO [MO0009]. ICA: MO0084.

IVY BEND—Formerly served by Almega Cable. No longer in operation. ICA: MO0169.

JACKSONVILLE—Formerly served by First Cable of Missouri Inc. No longer in operation. ICA: MO0379.

JAMESPORT—Formerly served by CableDirect. No longer in operation. ICA: MO0292.

JASPER—Mediacom. Now served by LIBERAL, MO [MO0187]. ICA: MO0218.

JEFFERSON CITY—Mediacom, 901 North College Ave, Columbia, MO 65201. Phones: 845-695-2762; 573-443-1536; 417-875-5560 (Springfield regional office). Fax: 417-883-0265. Web Site: http://www.mediacomcable.com. Also serves Callaway County, Cole County (portions) & Holts Summit. ICA: MO0020.
TV Market Ranking: Below 100 (Callaway County, Cole County (portions), Holts Summit, JEFFERSON CITY). Franchise award date: April 20, 1971. Franchise expiration date: N.A. Began: May 1, 1970.
Channel capacity: N.A. Channels available but not in use: N.A.

Basic Service
Subscribers: 6,892.
Programming (received off-air): KMIZ (ABC, MeTV, MNT) Columbia; KMOS-TV (PBS) Sedalia; KNLJ (Christian TV Network) Jefferson City; KOMU-TV (CW, NBC) Columbia; KRCG (CBS) Jefferson City.
Programming (via microwave): KETC (PBS) St. Louis; KMBC-TV (ABC, MeTV) Kansas City; KMOV (CBS) St. Louis; KPLR-TV (CW, This TV) St. Louis.
Programming (via satellite): C-SPAN 2; Discovery Channel; EVINE Live; LWS Local Weather Station; Pop; QVC; TBS; WGN America.
Fee: $60.00 installation; $42.00 monthly; $1.18 converter.

Expanded Basic Service 1
Subscribers: N.A.
Programming (via satellite): A&E; AMC; Animal Planet; BET; Bravo; Cartoon Network; CMT; CNBC; CNN; Comedy Central; C-SPAN; Disney Channel; E! HD; ESPN; ESPN2; EWTN Global Catholic Network; Food Network; Fox News Channel; FOX Sports Midwest; Freeform; FX; Hallmark Channel; HGTV; History; HLN; ION Television; Lifetime; MSNBC; MTV; Nickelodeon; Oxygen; Spike TV; Syfy; The Weather Channel; TLC; TNT; Travel Channel; truTV; TV Land; USA Network; VH1; WE tv.
Fee: $45.95 monthly.

Digital Basic Service
Subscribers: N.A.
Programming (via satellite): AXS TV; BBC America; Bloomberg Television; Discovery Life Channel; Disney XD; ESPN; Fox Sports 1; Fuse; FXM; FYI; Golf Channel; GSN; HD Theater; History International; IFC; LMN; MC; MTV2; National Geographic Channel; NBCSN; Nick Jr.; Nicktoons; Outdoor Channel; Ovation; TeenNick; Trinity Broadcasting Network (TBN); Turner Classic Movies; Universal HD.

Digital Pay Service 1
Pay Units: N.A.
Programming (via satellite): Cinemax (multiplexed); Flix; HBO (multiplexed); Showtime (multiplexed); Starz (multiplexed); Starz Encore (multiplexed); Sundance TV; The Movie Channel (multiplexed).
Video-On-Demand: Yes

2017 Edition

Missouri—Cable Systems

Pay-Per-View
ESPN (delivered digitally); Fresh (delivered digitally); Shorteez (delivered digitally); Playboy TV (delivered digitally).
Internet Service
Operational: Yes.
Broadband Service: Mediacom High Speed Internet.
Fee: $49.95 monthly.
Telephone Service
Digital: Operational
Miles of Plant: 290.0 (coaxial); 71.0 (fiber optic).
Regional Vice President: Bill Copeland. Vice President, Financial Reporting: Kenneth J. Kohrs. Regional Technical Operations Director: Alan Freedman. Operations Director: Bryan Gann. Marketing Director: Will Kuebler. Technical Operations Manager: Roger Shearer.
Ownership: Mediacom LLC (MSO).

JONESBURG—Formerly served by Charter Communications. No longer in operation. ICA: MO0463.

JOPLIN—Cable One, 2600 Davis Blvd, Joplin, MO 64804. Phones: 417-781-3333; 417-624-6340. Fax: 417-623-5413. E-mail: webmaster@cableone.net. Web Site: http://www.cableone.net. Also serves Carterville, Cliff Village, Leawood, Newton Town, Redings Mill, Saginaw, Shoal Creek Drive, Silver Creek & Webb City. ICA: MO0016.
TV Market Ranking: Below 100 (Carterville, Cliff Village, JOPLIN, Leawood, Redings Mill, Saginaw, Shoal Creek Drive, Silver Creek, Webb City). Franchise award date: N.A. Franchise expiration date: N.A. Began: March 1, 1967.
Channel capacity: N.A. Channels available but not in use: N.A.
Basic Service
Subscribers: 7,650.
Programming (received off-air): KFJX (FOX) Pittsburg; KOAM-TV (CBS) Pittsburg; KODE-TV (ABC) Joplin; KOZJ (PBS) Joplin; KSNF (NBC) Joplin; 4 FMs.
Programming (via satellite): A&E; AMC; Animal Planet; BET; Bravo; Cartoon Network; CMT; CNBC; CNN; Comedy Central; C-SPAN; C-SPAN 2; CW PLUS; Discovery Channel; Disney Channel; E! HD; ESPN; ESPN Classic; ESPN2; EVINE Live; Food Network; Fox News Channel; FOX Sports Midwest; Freeform; FX; HGTV; History; HLN; ION Television; Lifetime; MSNBC; MTV; Nickelodeon; Pop; QVC; Spike TV; Syfy; TBS; The Weather Channel; TLC; TNT; Travel Channel; Trinity Broadcasting Network (TBN); Turner Classic Movies; TV Land; USA Network; VH1; WGN America.
Fee: $90.00 installation; $35.00 monthly.
Digital Basic Service
Subscribers: N.A.
Programming (via satellite): 3ABN; Boomerang; BYUtv; Discovery Digital Networks; Disney XD; ESPN Classic; ESPN HD; ESPNews; FamilyNet; FOX College Sports Central; FOX College Sports Pacific; Fox Sports 1; Fox Sports 2; FXM; FYI; Golf Channel; Great American Country; Hallmark Channel; History International; HITS (Headend In The Sky); INSP; MC; National Geographic Channel; Outdoor Channel; TNT HD; Trinity Broadcasting Network (TBN); truTV; Universal HD.
Fee: $30.00 installation.
Digital Pay Service 1
Pay Units: N.A.
Programming (via satellite): Cinemax (multiplexed); Flix; HBO (multiplexed); HBO HD;

Showtime (multiplexed); Showtime HD; Starz (multiplexed); Starz Encore (multiplexed); Sundance TV; The Movie Channel (multiplexed); The Movie Channel HD.
Fee: $15.00 monthly (each package).
Video-On-Demand: No
Pay-Per-View
Pleasure (delivered digitally); ESPN Now (delivered digitally); SexSee (delivered digitally); Juicy (delivered digitally); VaVoom (delivered digitally).
Internet Service
Operational: Yes. Began: September 1, 2002.
Subscribers: 10,965.
Broadband Service: CableONE.net.
Fee: $75.00 installation; $43.00 monthly.
Telephone Service
Digital: Operational
Subscribers: 3,633.
Fee: $39.95 monthly
Miles of Plant: 737.0 (coaxial); 510.0 (fiber optic). Homes passed: 36,669.
Vice President: Patrick A. Dolohanty. General Manager: Charlotte McClure. Marketing Director: Jeff Denefrio. Plant Manager: Terry Peacock.
Ownership: Cable ONE Inc. (MSO).

JOPLIN (northwest)—Formerly served by Almega Cable. No longer in operation. ICA: MO0205.

KAHOKA—Kahoka Cable, 250 North Morgan St, Kahoka, MO 63445-1433. Phone: 660-727-3711. Fax: 660-727-7891. E-mail: cs@cablerocket.tv. Web Site: http://www.kahokamo.com. ICA: MO0150.
TV Market Ranking: Outside TV Markets (KAHOKA). Franchise award date: April 1, 1984. Franchise expiration date: N.A. Began: September 1, 1984.
Channel capacity: N.A. Channels available but not in use: N.A.
Basic Service
Subscribers: 518.
Programming (received off-air): KHQA-TV (ABC, CBS) Hannibal; KTVO (ABC) Kirksville; KYOU-TV (FOX) Ottumwa; WGEM-TV (CW, FOX, NBC) Quincy; WTJR (Christian TV Network) Quincy.
Programming (via satellite): A&E; AMC; Animal Planet; Cartoon Network; CMT; CNN; Comedy Central; C-SPAN; Discovery Channel; Disney Channel; ESPN; ESPN Classic; ESPN2; Fox Sports 1; FOX Sports Networks; Freeform; FX; Great American Country; HGTV; History; HLN; INSP; Lifetime; MSNBC; MTV; Nickelodeon; Outdoor Channel; QVC; Spike TV; Syfy; TBS; The Weather Channel; TLC; TNT; truTV; Turner Classic Movies; TV Land; USA Network; VH1; WGN America.
Fee: $20.00 installation; $53.00 monthly.
Pay Service 1
Pay Units: 89.
Programming (via satellite): Cinemax (multiplexed).
Fee: $15.00 installation; $12.95 monthly.
Pay Service 2
Pay Units: 118.
Programming (via satellite): HBO (multiplexed).
Fee: $15.00 installation; $12.95 monthly.
Pay Service 3
Pay Units: 55.
Programming (via satellite): Flix; Showtime; The Movie Channel.
Fee: $15.00 installation; $12.95 monthly.
Video-On-Demand: No
Internet Service
Operational: Yes.
Fee: $24.95 monthly.

Telephone Service
None
Miles of Plant: 22.0 (coaxial); None (fiber optic). Homes passed: 1,100.
General Manager: Sandie Hopp. Chief Technician: Scott Goben.
Ownership: City of Kahoka.

KANSAS CITY—Formerly served by People's Choice TV. No longer in operation. ICA: MO0453.

KANSAS CITY—Time Warner Cable, 6550 Winchester Ave, Kansas City, MO 64133-4660. Phones: 816-569-6694; 816-358-5360. Fax: 816-358-7987. Web Site: http://www.timewarnercable.com. Also serves Bonner Springs, Countryside, De Soto, Edwardsville, Edwardsville Park, Fairway, Fort Leavenworth, Gardner, Johnson County (northeastern portion), Kansas City (south of Kaw River), Lake of the Forest, Lake Quivera, Lansing, Leavenworth, Leavenworth County (portions), Leawood, Lenexa, Merriam, Mission, Mission Hills, Mission Woods, Olathe (portions), Overland Park, Prairie Village, Roeland Park, Shawnee, Westwood, Westwood Hills & Wyandotte County (portions), KS; Avondale, Belton, Clay County (portions), Claycomo, Ferrelview, Gladstone, Glenaire, Grandview, Houston Lake, Independence, Jackson County (portions), John Knox Village, Kearney, Lake Lotawana, Lake Waukomis, Lee's Summit, Liberty, Loch Lloyd, Lone Jack, North Kansas City, Northmoor, Oaks Village, Oakview, Oakwood, Oakwood Park, Parkville, Platte City, Platte County (portions), Platte Woods, Pleasant Valley, Richards-Gebaur AFB, Riverside, Smithville, Tracy, Weatherby Lake & Weston, MO. ICA: MO0001.
TV Market Ranking: 22 (Avondale, Belton, Bonner Springs, Clay County (portions), Claycomo, Countryside, De Soto, Edwardsville, Edwardsville Park, Fairway, Ferrelview, Fort Leavenworth, Gardner, Gladstone, Glenaire, Grandview, Houston Lake, Independence, Jackson County (portions), John Knox Village, Johnson County (northeastern portion), KANSAS CITY, Kansas City (south of Kaw River), Kearney, Lake Lotawana, Lake of the Forest, Lake Waukomis, Lansing, Leavenworth, Leawood, Lee's Summit, Lenexa, Liberty, Loch Lloyd, Lone Jack, Merriam, Mission, Mission Hills, Mission Woods, North Kansas City, Northmoor, Oaks Village, Oakview, Oakwood, Oakwood Park, Olathe (portions), Overland Park, Parkville, Platte City, Platte Woods, Pleasant Valley, Prairie Village, Richards-Gebaur AFB, Riverside, Roeland Park, Shawnee, Smithville, Tracy, Weatherby Lake, Weston, Westwood, Westwood Hills, Wyandotte County (portions). Franchise award date: January 1, 1979. Franchise expiration date: N.A. Began: May 19, 1980.
Channel capacity: N.A. Channels available but not in use: N.A.
Basic Service
Subscribers: 172,267.
Programming (received off-air): KCPT (PBS) Kansas City; KCTV (CBS) Kansas City; KCWE (CW, Movies!, This TV) Kansas City; KMBC-TV (ABC, MeTV) Kansas City; KMCI-TV (Bounce TV, Escape, IND) Lawrence; KPXE-TV (ION) Kansas City; KSHB-TV (COZI TV, Grit, NBC) Kansas City; KSMO-TV (Bounce TV, MNT) Kansas City; KTWU (PBS) Topeka; WDAF-TV (Antenna TV, FOX) Kansas City.

Programming (via satellite): TBS; WGN America.
Fee: $29.95 installation; $20.95 monthly.
Expanded Basic Service 1
Subscribers: N.A.
Programming (via satellite): A&E; AMC; Animal Planet; BET; Bravo; Cartoon Network; CMT; CNBC; CNN; Comedy Central; C-SPAN; C-SPAN 2; Discovery Channel; Disney Channel; E! HD; ESPN; ESPN Classic; ESPN2; ESPNews; EVINE Live; Food Network; Fox News Channel; FOX Sports Midwest; Freeform; FX; Golf Channel; Hallmark Channel; HGTV; History; HLN; Lifetime; MoviePlex; MSNBC; MTV; National Geographic Channel; NBCSN; Nickelodeon; Oxygen; Pop; QVC; Spike TV; Syfy; The Weather Channel; TLC; TNT; Travel Channel; truTV; Turner Classic Movies; TV Land; USA Network; VH1; WE tv.
Fee: $38.47 monthly.
Digital Basic Service
Subscribers: N.A.
Programming (via satellite): ART America; BBC America; Bloomberg Television; Boomerang; Cooking Channel; C-SPAN 3; Discovery Digital Networks; Disney XD; DIY Network; ESPNews; EWTN Global Catholic Network; Flix; Fox Sports 1; FSN Digital Atlantic; FSN Digital Central; FSN Digital Pacific; FXM; FYI; Great American Country; GSN; History International; HITS (Headend In The Sky); IFC; LMN; MC; MTV Classic; MTV2; NBA TV; Nick Jr.; Outdoor Channel; Ovation; RTN; Sundance TV; TeenNick; The Filipino Channel; The Word Network; Trinity Broadcasting Network (TBN); TV Asia; TV5MONDE USA.
Digital Pay Service 1
Pay Units: 116,000.
Programming (via satellite): Cinemax (multiplexed); HBO (multiplexed); Showtime (multiplexed); Starz (multiplexed); The Movie Channel (multiplexed).
Video-On-Demand: Yes
Pay-Per-View
Hot Choice (delivered digitally); iN DEMAND (delivered digitally); Playboy TV (delivered digitally); Pleasure (delivered digitally); Fresh (delivered digitally); Shorteez (delivered digitally).
Internet Service
Operational: Yes.
Subscribers: 222,113.
Broadband Service: Road Runner.
Fee: $39.95 installation; $44.95 monthly.
Telephone Service
Digital: Operational
Subscribers: 105,668.
Fee: $39.95 monthly
Miles of Plant: 10,585.0 (coaxial); 3,010.0 (fiber optic). Homes passed: 643,676.
President: Roger Ponder. Vice President, Marketing: Dennis Narciso. Vice President, Engineering: Bob Porter. General Manager: Dale Fox. Public Affairs Director: Damon Shelby Porter. Public Affairs Manager: Lori Hanson.
Ownership: Time Warner Cable (MSO).

KENNETT—NewWave Communications. Now served by DEXTER, MO [MO0039]. ICA: MO0032.

KEYTESVILLE—Formerly served by Longview Communications. No longer in operation. ICA: MO0230.

KIMBERLING CITY—Mediacom. Now served by SEYMOUR, MO [MO0172]. ICA: MO0407.

Cable Systems—Missouri

KING CITY—Formerly served by Longview Communications. No longer in operation. ICA: MO0214.

KINGSTON—Formerly served by First Cable of Missouri Inc. No longer in operation. ICA: MO0334.

KINLOCH—Formerly served by Data Cablevision. No longer in operation. ICA: MO0153.

KIRKSVILLE—Cable One, 402 North Main St, PO Box D, Kirksville, MO 63501. Phone: 660-665-7066. Fax: 660-627-2603. Web Site: http://www.cableone.net. Also serves Adair County & La Plata. ICA: MO0027.
TV Market Ranking: Below 100 (Adair County, KIRKSVILLE, La Plata). Franchise award date: September 8, 1964. Franchise expiration date: N.A. Began: N.A.
Channel capacity: N.A. Channels available but not in use: N.A.
Basic Service
Subscribers: 2,615.
Programming (received off-air): KHQA-TV (ABC, CBS) Hannibal; KTVO (ABC) Kirksville; KYOU-TV (FOX) Ottumwa; WGEM-TV (CW, FOX, NBC) Quincy; 1 FM.
Programming (via microwave): KCPT (PBS) Kansas City; KCTV (CBS) Kansas City; KSHB-TV (COZI TV, Grit, NBC) Kansas City.
Programming (via satellite): C-SPAN; C-SPAN 2; Pop; QVC; TBS; WGN America.
Fee: $90.00 installation; $35.00 monthly.
Expanded Basic Service 1
Subscribers: N.A.
Programming (via satellite): A&E; AMC; Animal Planet; BET; Cartoon Network; CMT; CNBC; CNN; Comedy Central; Discovery Channel; Disney Channel; ESPN; ESPN2; Food Network; Fox News Channel; FOX Sports Midwest; Freeform; FX; HGTV; History; HLN; Lifetime; MSNBC; MTV; Nickelodeon; Spike TV; Syfy; The Weather Channel; TLC; TNT; Turner Classic Movies; TV Land; USA Network; VH1.
Fee: $42.50 monthly.
Digital Basic Service
Subscribers: N.A.
Programming (via satellite): 3ABN; Boomerang; BYUtv; Discovery Digital Networks; Disney XD; DMX Music; ESPN Classic; ESPNews; FamilyNet; FOX College Sports Central; FOX College Sports Pacific; Fox HD; Fox Sports 1; Fox Sports 2; FXM; FYI; Golf Channel; Great American Country; Hallmark Channel; History International; HITS (Headend In The Sky); INSP; National Geographic Channel; Outdoor Channel; TNT HD; Trinity Broadcasting Network (TBN); truTV; TVG Network; Universal HD.
Digital Pay Service 1
Pay Units: N.A.
Programming (via satellite): Cinemax (multiplexed); Flix; HBO (multiplexed); Showtime (multiplexed); Showtime HD; Starz (multiplexed); Starz Encore (multiplexed); Sundance TV; The Movie Channel (multiplexed); The Movie Channel HD.
Fee: $15.00 monthly (Cinemax, HBO, Showtime/TMC/Flix/Sundance or Starz/Encore).
Video-On-Demand: No
Pay-Per-View
iN Demand; iN DEMAND (delivered digitally); Pleasure (delivered digitally); Sports PPV (delivered digitally); SexSee (delivered digitally); Juicy (delivered digitally); VaVoom (delivered digitally).
Internet Service
Operational: Yes. Began: January 1, 1988.
Subscribers: 3,010.

Broadband Service: CableONE.net.
Fee: $75.00 installation; $43.00 monthly.
Telephone Service
Digital: Operational
Subscribers: 1,117.
Fee: $39.95 monthly
Miles of Plant: 245.0 (coaxial); 71.0 (fiber optic). Homes passed: 10,047.
Vice President: Patrick A. Dolohanty. General Manager: Joann King. Chief Technician: Martin Stitzer.
Ownership: Cable ONE Inc. (MSO).

KNOB NOSTER—Charter Communications. Now served by ST. LOUIS, MO [MO0009]. ICA: MO0061.

KNOX CITY—Formerly served by CableDirect. No longer in operation. ICA: MO0408.

LA BELLE—Formerly served by Westcom. No longer in operation. ICA: MO0219.

LA MONTE—Formerly served by Provincial Cable & Data. No longer in operation. ICA: MO0224.

LA PLATA—Formerly served by Almega Cable. No longer in operation. ICA: MO0162.

LACLEDE—Formerly served by Longview Communications. No longer in operation. ICA: MO0307.

LAKE SHERWOOD—Cable America Corp, 7822 East Gray Rd, Scottsdale, AZ 85260. Phones: 800-338-1808; 314-739-0444. Web Site: http://www.cableamerica.com. Also serves Marthasville, New Melle, St. Charles County & Warren County. ICA: MO0458.
TV Market Ranking: 11 (New Melle, St. Charles County (portions)); Outside TV Markets (LAKE SHERWOOD, Marthasville, Warren County, St. Charles County (portions)). Franchise award date: January 1, 1988. Franchise expiration date: N.A. Began: N.A.
Channel capacity: 40 (not 2-way capable). Channels available but not in use: N.A.
Basic Service
Subscribers: 234.
Programming (received off-air): KDNL-TV (ABC, The Country Network) St. Louis; KETC (PBS) St. Louis; KMOV (CBS) St. Louis; KNLC (IND, My Family TV) St. Louis; KPLR-TV (CW, This TV) St. Louis; KSDK (Bounce TV, NBC) St. Louis; KTVI (Antenna TV, Escape, FOX) St. Louis; WRBU (ION) East St. Louis.
Programming (via satellite): A&E; AMC; CNN; C-SPAN; Discovery Channel; Disney Channel; ESPN; Freeform; HLN; Lifetime; Nickelodeon; Spike TV; Syfy; TBS; The Weather Channel; TLC; TNT; USA Network; VH1; WGN America.
Fee: $9.95 installation; $21.99 monthly; $1.55 converter.
Pay Service 1
Pay Units: N.A.
Programming (via satellite): Cinemax; HBO.
Fee: $11.00 monthly (each).
Internet Service
Operational: Yes.
Telephone Service
Digital: Operational
Miles of Plant: 52.0 (coaxial); None (fiber optic). Homes passed: 2,500.
Vice President, Engineering: Alan Jackson. General Manager: Debra Mefford. Market-

ing Director: John Mori. Chief Technician: James Grove. Controller: Walter G. Farak.
Ownership: CableAmerica Corp. (MSO).

LAKE ST. LOUIS—Charter Communications. Now served by ST. LOUIS, MO [MO0009]. ICA: MO0028.

LAKE VIKING—Formerly served by First Cable of Missouri Inc. No longer in operation. ICA: MO0447.

LAMAR—Suddenlink Communications, 231 East 4th St, Carthage, MO 64836-1629. Phone: 314-315-9400. Fax: 417-359-5373. Web Site: http://www.suddenlink.com. Also serves Lamar Heights. ICA: MO0086.
TV Market Ranking: Below 100 (LAMAR, Lamar Heights). Franchise award date: July 16, 1979. Franchise expiration date: N.A. Began: June 23, 1980.
Channel capacity: N.A. Channels available but not in use: N.A.
Basic Service
Subscribers: 315. Commercial subscribers: 59.
Programming (received off-air): KFJX (FOX) Pittsburg; KOAM-TV (CBS) Pittsburg; KODE-TV (ABC) Joplin; KOZK (PBS) Springfield; KSNF (NBC) Joplin.
Programming (via satellite): C-SPAN; QVC; TBS; WGN America.
Fee: $40.00 installation; $34.50 monthly.
Expanded Basic Service 1
Subscribers: N.A.
Programming (via satellite): A&E; AMC; Animal Planet; CMT; CNBC; CNN; Comedy Central; C-SPAN 2; CW PLUS; Discovery Channel; Discovery Life Channel; Disney Channel; ESPN; ESPN2; Food Network; Fox News Channel; FOX Sports Midwest; Freeform; FX; Hallmark Channel; HGTV; History; HLN; Lifetime; Nickelodeon; Outdoor Channel; Spike TV; Syfy; The Weather Channel; TLC; TNT; Travel Channel; TV Land; USA Network; VH1.
Fee: $15.10 monthly.
Digital Basic Service
Subscribers: N.A.
Programming (via satellite): BBC America; Bloomberg Television; Discovery Digital Networks; DMX Music; ESPN Classic; ESPNews; Fox Sports 1; Golf Channel; Starz Encore (multiplexed); Trinity Broadcasting Network (TBN); Turner Classic Movies.
Digital Pay Service 1
Pay Units: N.A.
Programming (via satellite): Cinemax (multiplexed); HBO (multiplexed); Showtime (multiplexed); Starz (multiplexed); Sundance TV; The Movie Channel (multiplexed).
Video-On-Demand: Yes
Pay-Per-View
iN DEMAND (delivered digitally); Fresh (delivered digitally); Playboy TV (delivered digitally); Hot Choice (delivered digitally).
Internet Service
Operational: Yes.
Broadband Service: Suddenlink High Speed Internet.
Fee: $29.95 monthly.

Telephone Service
Digital: Operational
Miles of Plant: 71.0 (coaxial); 8.0 (fiber optic). Homes passed: 2,396.
Senior Vice President, Corporate Finance: Michael Pflantz. Vice President, Accounting: Sabrina Warr. General Manager: Terrill Bradley. Chief Engineer: Tim Crotti.
Ownership: Cequel Communications Holdings I LLC (MSO).

LAMPE—Formerly served by Crystal Broadband Networks. No longer in operation. ICA: MO0133.

LANCASTER—Formerly served by Longview Communications. No longer in operation. ICA: MO0212.

LATHROP—Formerly served by Allegiance Communications. No longer in operation. ICA: MO0410.

LEBANON—Fidelity Communications. Now served by PHELPS COUNTY (portions), MO [MO0475]. ICA: MO0051.

LEETON—Formerly served by CableDirect. No longer in operation. ICA: MO0309.

LESTERVILLE—Formerly served by Almega Cable. No longer in operation. ICA: MO0231.

LEXINGTON—Suddenlink Communications, 520 Maryville Centre Dr, Ste 300, St. Louis, MO 63141. Phones: 800-999-6845 (Customer service); 314-315-9400. Web Site: http://www.suddenlink.com. Also serves Napoleon & Wellington. ICA: MO0083.
TV Market Ranking: 22 (Napoleon, Wellington); Outside TV Markets (LEXINGTON). Franchise award date: N.A. Franchise expiration date: N.A. Began: May 1, 1974.
Channel capacity: 36 (operating 2-way). Channels available but not in use: N.A.
Basic Service
Subscribers: 501.
Programming (received off-air): KCPT (PBS) Kansas City; KCTV (CBS) Kansas City; KCWE (CW, Movies!, This TV) Kansas City; KMBC-TV (ABC, MeTV) Kansas City; KMOS-TV (PBS) Sedalia; KPXE-TV (ION) Kansas City; KSHB-TV (COZI TV, Grit, NBC) Kansas City; KSMO-TV (Bounce TV, MNT) Kansas City; WDAF-TV (Antenna TV, FOX) Kansas City; allband FM.
Programming (via satellite): QVC; The Weather Channel.
Fee: $28.45 monthly.
Expanded Basic Service 1
Subscribers: N.A.
Programming (via satellite): A&E; AMC; Animal Planet; BET; Bravo; Cartoon Network; Celebrity Shopping Network; CNBC; CNN; Comedy Central; C-SPAN; Discovery Channel; Disney Channel; E! HD; ESPN; ESPN2; Food Network; Fox News Channel; Fox Sports 1; FOX Sports Midwest; Freeform; FX; Great American Country; Hallmark Channel; HGTV; History; HLN; Lifetime; MSNBC; MTV; National Geo-

Missouri—Cable Systems

graphic Channel; Nickelodeon; Outdoor Channel; Spike TV; Syfy; TBS; TLC; TNT; Travel Channel; Turner Classic Movies; TV Land; Univision Studios; USA Network; VH1.
Fee: $23.00 monthly.
Digital Basic Service
Subscribers: N.A.
Programming (via satellite): BBC America; Bloomberg Television; Cloo; Discovery Digital Networks; Disney XD; DMX Music; ESPN Classic; ESPNews; EVINE Live; FOX College Sports Central; FOX College Sports Pacific; Fuse; FYI; Golf Channel; GSN; History International; IFC; NBCSN; Sundance TV; Trinity Broadcasting Network (TBN); WE tv.
Pay Service 1
Pay Units: N.A.
Programming (via satellite): HBO; Showtime; The Movie Channel.
Fee: $7.95 monthly (TMC), $9.95 monthly (Showtime), $10.95 monthly (HBO).
Digital Pay Service 1
Pay Units: N.A.
Programming (via satellite): Cinemax (multiplexed); Flix; HBO (multiplexed); Showtime (multiplexed); Starz (multiplexed); Starz Encore (multiplexed); The Movie Channel (multiplexed).
Video-On-Demand: No
Pay-Per-View
iN DEMAND (delivered digitally); Playboy TV (delivered digitally); Fresh (delivered digitally); Shorteez (delivered digitally).
Internet Service
Operational: Yes. Began: March 1, 2002.
Broadband Service: Suddenlink High Speed Internet.
Fee: $29.95 monthly.
Telephone Service
None
Miles of Plant: 88.0 (coaxial); None (fiber optic). Homes passed: 2,259.
Vice President, Corporate Finance: Michael Pflantz. Regional Manager: Todd Cruthird. Regional Marketing Manager: Beverly Gambell.
Ownership: Cequel Communications Holdings I LLC (MSO).

LIBERAL—Mediacom, 1533 South Enterprise Ave, Springfield, MO 65804. Phones: 845-695-2762; 417-875-5500. Fax: 417-883-0265. Web Site: http://www.mediacomcable.com. Also serves Mulberry, KS; Jasper, MO. ICA: MO0187.
TV Market Ranking: Below 100 (Jasper, LIBERAL, Mulberry).
Channel capacity: N.A. Channels available but not in use: N.A.
Basic Service
Subscribers: 146.
Fee: $42.00 monthly.
Vice President, Financial Reporting: Kenneth J. Kohrs.
Ownership: Mediacom LLC (MSO).

LICKING—Formerly served by Licking Cable. Now served by Cable America Corp., ST. ROBERT, MO [MO0023]. ICA: MO0170.

LINCOLN—Formerly served by Provincial Cable & Data. No longer in operation. ICA: MO0221.

LINN—Cable America Corp, 7822 East Gray Rd, Scottsdale, AZ 85260. Phone: 800-338-1808. Web Site: http://www.cableamerica.com. Also serves Loose Creek. ICA: MO0411.

TV Market Ranking: Below 100 (LINN, Loose Creek).
Channel capacity: N.A. Channels available but not in use: N.A.
Basic Service
Subscribers: 183.
Programming (received off-air): KETC (PBS) St. Louis; KMIZ (ABC, MeTV, MNT) Columbia; KNLJ (Christian TV Network) Jefferson City; KOMU-TV (CW, NBC) Columbia; KPLR-TV (CW, This TV) St. Louis; KRCG (CBS) Jefferson City.
Fee: $9.95 installation; $22.99 monthly.
Expanded Basic Service 1
Subscribers: N.A.
Programming (via satellite): A&E; AMC; Cartoon Network; CMT; CNN; Comedy Central; Discovery Channel; Disney Channel; ESPN; ESPN2; Fox News Channel; FOX Sports Midwest; Freeform; FX; HGTV; HLN; Lifetime; Nickelodeon; QVC; Spike TV; Syfy; TBS; The Weather Channel; TNT; truTV; TV Land; USA Network; WGN America.
Fee: $59.95 monthly.
Digital Basic Service
Subscribers: N.A.
Programming (via satellite): BBC America; Bloomberg Television; Bravo; Discovery Kids Channel; Discovery Life Channel; Disney XD; DMX Music; EVINE Live; Fox Sports 1; Fuse; FXM; FYI; Golf Channel; GSN; History; History International; IFC; LMN; NBCSN; Nick Jr.; Outdoor Channel; TeenNick; Trinity Broadcasting Network (TBN); Turner Classic Movies; WE tv.
Fee: $64.99 monthly.
Pay Service 1
Pay Units: N.A.
Programming (via satellite): Cinemax; HBO.
Digital Pay Service 1
Pay Units: N.A.
Programming (via satellite): Cinemax (multiplexed); HBO (multiplexed); Showtime (multiplexed); Starz (multiplexed); Starz Encore (multiplexed); The Movie Channel (multiplexed).
Internet Service
Operational: Yes.
Fee: $19.95-$54.95 monthly.
Telephone Service
Digital: Operational
Fee: $19.95 monthly
Controller: Walter G. Farak.
Ownership: CableAmerica Corp.

LOOSE CREEK—Formerly served by Mid Missouri Broadband. Now served by Cable America, LINN, MO [MO0411]. ICA: MO0303.

LOUISIANA—Charter Communications, 12405 Powerscourt Dr, St. Louis, MO 63131. Phones: 575-437-3101; 636-207-5100 (Corporate office); 573-560-3059; 888-438-2427. Web Site: http://www.charter.com. ICA: MO0081.
TV Market Ranking: Below 100 (LOUISIANA). Franchise award date: N.A. Franchise expiration date: N.A. Began: April 15, 1985.
Channel capacity: N.A. Channels available but not in use: N.A.
Digital Basic Service
Subscribers: 441.
Programming (via satellite): A&E; AMC; Animal Planet; AWE; BBC America; BET; Bloomberg Television; Cartoon Network; Cloo; CMT; CNN; Comedy Central; Discovery Digital Networks; Disney XD; E! HD; ESPN; EVINE Live; Food Network; Fox News Channel; FOX Sports Midwest; Freeform; Fuse; FX; FYI; GSN; HGTV; History; History International; Lifetime; LMN; MSNBC;

MTV; Nat Geo WILD; Nick Jr.; Nickelodeon; Oxygen; QVC; Spike TV; Starz Encore (multiplexed); Syfy; The Weather Channel; TLC; Travel Channel; Trinity Broadcasting Network (TBN); truTV; TV Land; USA Network.
Fee: $26.99 monthly; $8.00 converter.
Digital Expanded Basic Service
Subscribers: N.A.
Programming (via satellite): DMX Music; FXM; IFC; LMN; Starz Encore; Turner Classic Movies; WE tv.
Digital Expanded Basic Service 2
Subscribers: N.A.
Programming (via satellite): ESPN Classic; ESPNews; Golf Channel; NBCSN; NFL Network; Outdoor Channel; TeenNick.
Digital Pay Service 1
Pay Units: N.A.
Programming (via satellite): HBO (multiplexed); Showtime (multiplexed); Starz (multiplexed); The Movie Channel (multiplexed).
Fee: $8.95 monthly (Starz), $11.95 monthly (Cinemax, HBO, Showtime or TMC).
Pay-Per-View
iN DEMAND (delivered digitally); Playboy TV (delivered digitally); Fresh (delivered digitally).
Internet Service
Operational: Yes.
Broadband Service: Charter Internet.
Telephone Service
None
Accounting Director: David Sovanski.
Ownership: Charter Communications Inc. (MSO).

LOWRY CITY—Mediacom, 1533 South Enterprise Ave, Springfield, MO 65804. Phones: 845-695-2762; 417-875-5500; 417-875-5560. Fax: 417-883-0265. Web Site: http://www.mediacomcable.com. ICA: MO0252.
TV Market Ranking: Outside TV Markets (LOWRY CITY). Franchise award date: N.A. Franchise expiration date: N.A. Began: July 1, 1986.
Channel capacity: N.A. Channels available but not in use: N.A.
Basic Service
Subscribers: 37.
Programming (received off-air): KMBC-TV (ABC, MeTV) Kansas City; KMOS-TV (PBS) Sedalia; KOLR (CBS) Springfield; KPXE-TV (ION) Kansas City; KSHB-TV (COZI TV, Grit, NBC) Kansas City; KYTV (CW, NBC, WeatherNation) Springfield; WDAF-TV (Antenna TV, FOX) Kansas City.
Programming (via satellite): AMC; CMT; CNN; Discovery Channel; ESPN; ESPN2; Freeform; HLN; Lifetime; Nickelodeon; QVC; Spike TV; TBS; The Weather Channel; TNT; USA Network; WGN America.
Fee: $35.00 installation; $45.05 monthly.
Pay Service 1
Pay Units: N.A.
Programming (via satellite): Showtime; The Movie Channel.
Fee: $10.50 monthly (each).
Video-On-Demand: No
Internet Service
Operational: No.
Telephone Service
None
Miles of Plant: 4.0 (coaxial); None (fiber optic). Homes passed: 348.
Regional Vice President: Bill Copeland. Vice President, Financial Reporting: Kenneth J. Kohrs. Regional Technical Operations Manager: Alan Freedman. Marketing Director: Will Kuebler.
Ownership: Mediacom LLC (MSO).

MACKS CREEK—Formerly served by Almega Cable. No longer in operation. ICA: MO0361.

MACON—Chariton Valley Cablevision, 1213 East Briggs Dr, Macon, MO 63552. Phone: 660-395-9600. Fax: 660-395-4403. E-mail: feedback@cvalley.net. Web Site: http://www.cvalley.net. Also serves Bevier, Callao & New Cambria. ICA: MO0071.
TV Market Ranking: Below 100 (Bevier, Callao, MACON, New Cambria). Franchise award date: December 1, 1984. Franchise expiration date: N.A. Began: September 1, 1979.
Channel capacity: N.A. Channels available but not in use: N.A.
Basic Service
Subscribers: 2,188.
Programming (received off-air): KHQA-TV (ABC, CBS) Hannibal; KOMU-TV (CW, NBC) Columbia; KTVO (ABC) Kirksville; KYOU-TV (FOX) Ottumwa; WGEM-TV (CW, FOX, NBC) Quincy.
Programming (via satellite): A&E; AMC; Animal Planet; BET; Cartoon Network; CMT; CNBC; CNN; Comedy Central; C-SPAN; C-SPAN 2; Discovery Channel; Disney Channel; E! HD; ESPN; ESPN Classic; ESPN2; Food Network; Fox News Channel; Fox Sports 1; FOX Sports Networks; Freeform; Golf Channel; Great American Country; Hallmark Channel; HGTV; History; HLN; ION Television; KRMA-TV (PBS) Denver; Lifetime; MSNBC; MTV; National Geographic Channel; NBCSN; Nickelodeon; OWN: Oprah Winfrey Network; Pop; QVC; Spike TV; Syfy; TBS; The Weather Channel; TLC; TNT; Travel Channel; Trinity Broadcasting Network (TBN); truTV; Turner Classic Movies; TV Land; USA Network; VH1; WGN America.
Fee: $35.00 installation; $45.99 monthly.
Digital Basic Service
Subscribers: N.A.
Programming (via satellite): Bloomberg Television; DMX Music; FXM; FYI; History International; Outdoor Channel; WE tv.
Digital Pay Service 1
Pay Units: N.A.
Programming (via satellite): Cinemax; HBO (multiplexed); Showtime; Starz; Starz Encore; The Movie Channel.
Video-On-Demand: No
Pay-Per-View
iN DEMAND (delivered digitally); Fresh (delivered digitally); Hot Choice (delivered digitally); ESPN On Demand (delivered digitally); ESPN Now (delivered digitally).
Internet Service
Operational: Yes.
Fee: $29.99-$59.99 monthly.
Telephone Service
Digital: Operational
Subscribers: 1,726.
Fee: 14.00-$18.75 monthly
Miles of Plant: None (coaxial); 4,636.0 (fiber optic). Homes passed: 6,648.
General Manager: Jim Simon. Network Operations Director: Jesse Estevez. Plant Operations Director: Jerry Grauel. Sales & Marketing Director: Ryan Johnson. Finance Director: Tina Jordan.
Ownership: Chariton Valley Telecom.

MADISON—Charter Communications. No longer in operation. ICA: MO0275.

MAITLAND—American Broadband Missouri, 208 Ash St., PO Box 112, Maitland, MO 64466. Phones: 888-438-4490; 660-935-2211. Fax: 417-395-2120. Web Site: http://www.abbmissouri.com. Also serves Graham & Skidmore. ICA: MO0473.

Cable Systems—Missouri

TV Market Ranking: Below 100 (MAITLAND); Outside TV Markets (Graham, Skidmore).
Channel capacity: N.A. Channels available but not in use: N.A.

Basic Service
Subscribers: 187.
Programming (received off-air): KCPT (PBS) Kansas City; KCTV (CBS) Kansas City; KCWE (CW, Movies!, This TV) Kansas City; KMBC-TV (ABC, MeTV) Kansas City; KMCI-TV (Bounce TV, Escape, IND) Lawrence; KODE-TV (ABC) Joplin; KSHB-TV (COZI TV, Grit, NBC) Kansas City; KSMO-TV (Bounce TV, MNT) Kansas City; WDAF-TV (Antenna TV, FOX) Kansas City.
Programming (via satellite): A&E; CNN; Comedy Central; Discovery Channel; Disney Channel; ESPN; ESPN2; Freeform; Great American Country; Hallmark Channel; HGTV; History; Lifetime; Nickelodeon; Outdoor Channel; QVC; Spike TV; Syfy; TBS; TLC; TNT; Travel Channel; Trinity Broadcasting Network (TBN); TV Land; USA Network; VH1; WGN America.
Fee: $42.95 monthly.

Pay Service 1
Pay Units: N.A.
Programming (via satellite): Cinemax; HBO.

Internet Service
Operational: No, DSL.

Telephone Service
Analog: Operational
General Manager & Chief Technician: Reese Copsey.
Ownership: American Broadband Communications Inc. (MSO).

MAITLAND—Formerly served by Holway Telephone Co. Now served by American Broadband Missouri, MAITLAND, MO [MO0473]. ICA: MO0336.

MALDEN—NewWave Communications. Now served by DEXTER, MO [MO0039]. ICA: MO0053.

MANSFIELD—Mediacom. Now served by SEYMOUR, MO [MO0172]. ICA: MO0190.

MARBLE HILL—Formerly served by Boycom Cablevision Inc. No longer in operation. ICA: MO0123.

MARCELINE—Mediacom, 1533 South Enterprise Ave, Springfield, MO 65804. Phones: 845-695-2762; 417-875-5500; 417-875-5560 (Springfield regional office); 816-637-4500 (Excelsior Springs office). Fax: 417-883-0265. Web Site: http://www.mediacomcable.com. ICA: MO0129.
TV Market Ranking: Outside TV Markets (MARCELINE). Franchise award date: November 4, 1980. Franchise expiration date: N.A. Began: January 1, 1976.
Channel capacity: N.A. Channels available but not in use: N.A.

Basic Service
Subscribers: 143.
Programming (received off-air): KCPT (PBS) Kansas City; KCTV (CBS) Kansas City; KCWE (CW, Movies!, This TV) Kansas City; KMBC-TV (ABC, MeTV) Kansas City; KOMU-TV (CW, NBC) Columbia; KRCG (CBS) Jefferson City; KSHB-TV (COZI TV, Grit, NBC) Kansas City; KSMQ-TV (PBS) Austin; KTVO (ABC) Kirksville; WDAF-TV (Antenna TV, FOX) Kansas City; allband FM.
Programming (via satellite): Pop; WGN America.
Fee: $35.00 installation; $42.00 monthly; $1.70 converter.

Expanded Basic Service 1
Subscribers: N.A.
Programming (via satellite): A&E; AMC; Animal Planet; Bravo; Cartoon Network; CMT; CNBC; CNN; Comedy Central; C-SPAN; Discovery Channel; Disney Channel; E! HD; ESPN; ESPN2; EVINE Live; EWTN Global Catholic Network; Food Network; Fox News Channel; Fox Sports 1; FOX Sports Midwest; Freeform; FX; Hallmark Channel; HGTV; History; HLN; INSP; Lifetime; MSNBC; MTV; Nickelodeon; Outdoor Channel; QVC; Spike TV; Syfy; TBS; The Weather Channel; TLC; TNT; Travel Channel; Trinity Broadcasting Network (TBN); truTV; TV Land; USA Network; VH1; WE tv.

Digital Basic Service
Subscribers: N.A.
Programming (via satellite): BBC America; Bloomberg Television; Discovery Life Channel; Fuse; FXM; FYI; Golf Channel; GSN; History International; IFC; LMN; MC; National Geographic Channel; NBCSN; Nick Jr.; Nicktoons; TeenNick; Turner Classic Movies.

Digital Pay Service 1
Pay Units: N.A.
Programming (via satellite): Cinemax (multiplexed); Flix (multiplexed); HBO (multiplexed); Showtime (multiplexed); Starz (multiplexed); Starz Encore (multiplexed); Sundance TV (multiplexed); The Movie Channel (multiplexed).

Video-On-Demand: No

Pay-Per-View
Mediacom PPV & Events PPV (delivered digitally); Playboy TV (delivered digitally); TEN Clips (delivered digitally); Pleasure (delivered digitally); Hot Body (delivered digitally).

Internet Service
Operational: Yes.
Broadband Service: Mediacom High Speed Internet.

Telephone Service
Digital: Operational
Miles of Plant: 25.0 (coaxial); None (fiber optic). Homes passed: 1,522.
Regional Vice President: Bill Copeland. Vice President, Financial Reporting: Kenneth J. Kohrs. Regional Technical Operations Director: Alan Freedman. Operations Director: Bryan Gann. Marketing Director: Will Kuebler. Technical Operations Manager: Roger Shearer.
Ownership: Mediacom LLC (MSO).

MARSHALL—Zito Media, 102 S Main St, PO Box 665, Coudersport, PA 16915. Phones: 814-260-9055; 800-365-6988. E-mail: info@zitomedia.com. Web Site: http://www.zitomedia.com. ICA: MO0036.
TV Market Ranking: Below 100 (MARSHALL). Franchise award date: April 15, 1963. Franchise expiration date: N.A. Began: September 23, 1965.
Channel capacity: N.A. Channels available but not in use: N.A.

Basic Service
Subscribers: 1,589.
Programming (received off-air): KCPT (PBS) Kansas City; KCTV (CBS) Kansas City; KCWE (CW, Movies!, This TV) Kansas City; KMBC-TV (ABC, MeTV) Kansas City; KMCI-TV (Bounce TV, Escape, IND) Lawrence; KMIZ (ABC, MeTV, MNT) Columbia; KMOS-TV (PBS) Sedalia; KOMU-TV (CW, NBC) Columbia; KPXE-TV (ION) Kansas City; KRCG (CBS) Jefferson City; KSHB-TV (COZI TV, Grit, NBC) Kansas City; KSMO-TV (Bounce TV, MNT) Kansas City;
WDAF-TV (Antenna TV, FOX) Kansas City; 22 FMs.
Programming (via satellite): C-SPAN; C-SPAN 2; EVINE Live; QVC; TBS.
Fee: $49.95 installation; $18.60 monthly; $.57 converter.

Expanded Basic Service 1
Subscribers: N.A.
Programming (via satellite): A&E; AMC; Animal Planet; BET; Bravo; Cartoon Network; CMT; CNBC; CNN; Comedy Central; Discovery Channel; Discovery Life Channel; Disney Channel; E! HD; ESPN; ESPN Classic; ESPN2; Food Network; Fox News Channel; FOX Sports Midwest; Freeform; FX; Great American Country; Hallmark Channel; HGTV; History; HLN; INSP; Lifetime; LMN; MSNBC; MTV; National Geographic Channel; Nickelodeon; OWN: Oprah Winfrey Network; Oxygen; Spike TV; Syfy; The Weather Channel; TLC; TNT; Travel Channel; Trinity Broadcasting Network (TBN); truTV; TV Land; Univision Studios; USA Network; VH1; WE tv.
Fee: $34.40 monthly.

Digital Basic Service
Subscribers: N.A.
Programming (via satellite): AXS TV; BBC America; Bloomberg Television; Discovery Digital Networks; Disney XD; ESPN; ESPNews; Fox Sports 1; Fuse; FYI; Golf Channel; GSN; HD Theater; History International; MC; MTV Classic; MTV Hits; MTV2; NBCSN; Nick Jr.; Nicktoons; Outdoor Channel; Ovation; TeenNick; TNT HD; Turner Classic Movies.

Digital Pay Service 1
Pay Units: N.A.
Programming (via satellite): Cinemax (multiplexed); FXM; HBO; IFC; Showtime; Starz (multiplexed); Starz Encore (multiplexed); Sundance TV; The Movie Channel (multiplexed).
Fee: $12.00 monthly (each).

Video-On-Demand: No

Pay-Per-View
iN DEMAND (delivered digitally); Fresh (delivered digitally); Shorteez (delivered digitally); Playboy TV (delivered digitally); Pleasure (delivered digitally); Hot Choice (delivered digitally); TEN, TEN Blue, TEN Clips, TEN Blox (delivered digitally).

Internet Service
Operational: Yes.

Telephone Service
Digital: Operational
Fee: $49.95 monthly
Miles of Plant: 81.0 (coaxial); None (fiber optic). Homes passed: 6,054.
President: James Rigas.
Ownership: Zito Media (MSO).

MARSHFIELD—Mediacom. Now served by SEYMOUR, MO [MO0172]. ICA: MO0096.

MARYLAND HEIGHTS—Cable America Corp, 7822 East Gray Rd, Scottsdale, AZ 85260. Phones: 800-338-1808; 314-739-0444; 314-291-1970. E-mail: helpdesk@cablemo.net. Web Site: http://www.cableamerica.com. ICA: MO0464. **Note:** This system is an overbuild.

TV Market Ranking: 11 (MARYLAND HEIGHTS). Franchise award date: October 24, 1995. Franchise expiration date: N.A. Began: January 1, 1997.
Channel capacity: N.A. Channels available but not in use: N.A.

Basic Service
Subscribers: 696.
Programming (received off-air): KDNL-TV (ABC, The Country Network) St. Louis; KETC (PBS) St. Louis; KMOV (CBS) St. Louis; KNLC (IND, My Family TV) St. Louis; KPLR-TV (CW, This TV) St. Louis; KSDK (Bounce TV, NBC) St. Louis; KTVI (Antenna TV, Escape, FOX) St. Louis; WRBU (ION) East St. Louis.
Programming (via satellite): Pop.
Fee: $9.95 installation; $21.99 monthly.

Expanded Basic Service 1
Subscribers: N.A.
Programming (via satellite): A&E; AMC; Animal Planet; BBC America; BET; Bravo; Cartoon Network; CMT; CNBC; CNN; Comedy Central; C-SPAN; C-SPAN 2; Discovery Channel; Disney Channel; E! HD; ESPN; ESPN Classic; ESPN2; EWTN Global Catholic Network; Food Network; Fox News Channel; Fox Sports 1; FOX Sports Networks; Freeform; FX; Golf Channel; Great American Country; GSN; Hallmark Channel; HGTV; History; HLN; INSP; ION Television; Lifetime; MTV; National Geographic Channel; Nickelodeon; OWN: Oprah Winfrey Network; Oxygen; QVC; Spike TV; Syfy; TBS; The Weather Channel; TLC; TNT; Travel Channel; truTV; Turner Classic Movies; TV Land; Univision; Univision Studios; USA Network; VH1; WGN America.
Fee: $33.50 monthly.

Digital Basic Service
Subscribers: N.A.
Programming (via satellite): Bloomberg Television; Discovery Digital Networks; Disney XD; DMX Music; Fuse; FXM; FYI; History International; LMN; MTV2; Nicktoons; Outdoor Channel; Starz Encore (multiplexed); TeenNick; Trinity Broadcasting Network (TBN).

Digital Pay Service 1
Pay Units: N.A.
Programming (via satellite): Cinemax (multiplexed); Flix; HBO (multiplexed); Showtime (multiplexed); Starz (multiplexed); Sundance TV; The Movie Channel (multiplexed).
Fee: $11.95 monthly (Cinemax, HBO, Showtime/TMC/Flix/Sundance or Starz).

Video-On-Demand: No

Pay-Per-View
iN DEMAND; adult PPV (delivered digitally); Special events (delivered digitally).

Internet Service
Operational: Yes. Began: March 1, 2000.
Broadband Service: CableAmerica.
Fee: $15.70 installation; $45.95 monthly; $9.95 modem lease; $199.95 modem purchase.

Telephone Service
Digital: Operational
Miles of Plant: 94.0 (coaxial); None (fiber optic). Homes passed: 7,230.

2017 Edition   D-453

Missouri—Cable Systems

Access the most current data instantly
www.warren-news.com/factbook.htm

Vice President, Engineering: Alan Jackson. General Manager: Debra Mefford. Controller: Walter G. Farak. Marketing Director: John Mori. Chief Technician: James Grove. Ownership: CableAmerica Corp. (MSO).

MARYVILLE—Suddenlink Communications, 520 Maryville Centre Dr, Ste 300, St. Louis, MO 63141. Phones: 800-999-6845 (Customer service); 314-315-9400. Web Site: http://www.suddenlink.com. Also serves Nodaway County (portions) & Northwest Missouri State University. ICA: MO0413.
TV Market Ranking: Outside TV Markets (MARYVILLE, Northwest Missouri State University). Franchise award date: N.A. Franchise expiration date: N.A. Began: April 1, 1964.
Channel capacity: 41 (operating 2-way). Channels available but not in use: N.A.

Basic Service
Subscribers: 1,795.
Programming (received off-air): KCPT (PBS) Kansas City; KCTV (CBS) Kansas City; KCWE (CW, Movies!, This TV) Kansas City; KMBC-TV (ABC, MeTV) Kansas City; KMTV-TV (Antenna TV, CBS, Escape) Omaha; KQTV (ABC) St. Joseph; KSHB-TV (COZI TV, Grit, NBC) Kansas City; KSMO-TV (Bounce TV, MNT) Kansas City; KTAJ-TV (TBN) St. Joseph; WDAF-TV (Antenna TV, FOX) Kansas City; WOWT (IND, NBC) Omaha.
Programming (via satellite): A&E; INSP; Pop; QVC.
Fee: $40.00 installation; $32.95 monthly.

Expanded Basic Service 1
Subscribers: N.A.
Programming (via satellite): A&E; AMC; Animal Planet; BET; Bravo; Cartoon Network; CNBC; CNN; Comedy Central; C-SPAN; Discovery Channel; Disney Channel; E! HD; ESPN; ESPN Classic; ESPN2; EWTN Global Catholic Network; Food Network; Fox News Channel; Fox Sports 1; FOX Sports Midwest; Freeform; FX; Golf Channel; Great American Country; Hallmark Channel; HGTV; History; HLN; Lifetime; MSNBC; MTV; National Geographic Channel; Nickelodeon; Outdoor Channel; Spike TV; Syfy; TBS; The Weather Channel; TLC; TNT; Travel Channel; truTV; Turner Classic Movies; TV Land; Univision Studios; USA Network; VH1.
Fee: $23.00 monthly.

Digital Basic Service
Subscribers: N.A.
Programming (via satellite): BBC America; Bloomberg Television; Cloo; Discovery Digital Networks; Disney XD; DMX Music; ESPNews; Fuse; FXM; FYI; GSN; History; History International; IFC; NBCSN; Sundance TV; WE tv.

Pay Service 1
Pay Units: N.A.
Programming (via satellite): Cinemax; HBO; Showtime; The Movie Channel.
Fee: $10.00 installation; $7.95 monthly (TMC), $9.95 monthly (Showtime), $10.95 monthly (Cinemax/HBO).

Digital Pay Service 1
Pay Units: N.A.
Programming (via satellite): Cinemax (multiplexed); HBO (multiplexed); Showtime (multiplexed); Starz (multiplexed); Starz Encore (multiplexed); The Movie Channel (multiplexed).
Video-On-Demand: No
Pay-Per-View
iN DEMAND (delivered digitally); Playboy TV (delivered digitally); Fresh (delivered digitally); Shorteez (delivered digitally).
Internet Service
Operational: Yes. Began: June 3, 2004.
Broadband Service: Suddenlink High Speed Internet.
Fee: $29.95 monthly.
Telephone Service
None
Miles of Plant: 87.0 (coaxial); None (fiber optic). Homes passed: 4,741.
Senior Vice President, Corporate Finance: Michael Pflantz. Regional Manager: Todd Cruthird. Regional Marketing Manager: Beverly Gambell. Ownership: Cequel Communications Holdings I LLC (MSO).

MAYSVILLE—Formerly served by Allegiance Communications. No longer in operation. ICA: MO0209.

MAYVIEW—Formerly served by CableDirect. No longer in operation. ICA: MO0353.

MEADVILLE—Formerly served by Longview Communications. No longer in operation. ICA: MO0434.

MEMPHIS—Formerly served by Longview Communications. No longer in operation. ICA: MO0149.

MERCER—Formerly served by Telnet South LC. No longer in operation. ICA: MO0271.

META—Formerly served by CableDirect. No longer in operation. ICA: MO0362.

MEXICO—Charter Communications. Now served by ST. LOUIS, MO [MO0009]. ICA: MO0033.

MIDDLETOWN (town)—Formerly served by First Cable of Missouri Inc. No longer in operation. ICA: MO0344.

MILAN—Milan Interactive Communications, 312 South Main St, PO Box 240, Milan, MO 63556. Phone: 660-265-7174. ICA: MO0148.
TV Market Ranking: Below 100 (MILAN). Franchise award date: March 7, 1985. Franchise expiration date: N.A. Began: June 1, 1965.
Channel capacity: N.A. Channels available but not in use: N.A.

Basic Service
Subscribers: 160.
Programming (received off-air): KHQA-TV (ABC, CBS) Hannibal; KMBC-TV (ABC, MeTV) Kansas City; KTVO (ABC) Kirksville; KYOU-TV (FOX) Ottumwa; WGEM-TV (CW, FOX, NBC) Quincy; WTVS (PBS) Detroit.
Programming (via satellite): INSP; QVC; WGN America.
Fee: $29.95 installation; $39.95 monthly.
Video-On-Demand: No
Internet Service
Operational: No.
Telephone Service
None
Miles of Plant: 16.0 (coaxial); None (fiber optic). Homes passed: 880.
President & General Manager: Rick Gardener. Ownership: Milan Interactive Communications (MSO).

MINDENMINES—Formerly served by Cebridge Connections. No longer in operation. ICA: MO0329.

MISSIONARY—Formerly served by Crystal Broadband Networks. No longer in operation. ICA: MO0180.

MOBERLY—Charter Communications. Now served by ST. LOUIS, MO [MO0009]. ICA: MO0031.

MOKANE—Formerly served by First Cable of Missouri Inc. No longer in operation. ICA: MO0349.

MONETT—Suddenlink Communications, 231 East 4th St, Carthage, MO 64836-1629. Phones: 800-743-0285 (Customer service); 314-315-9400. Web Site: http://www.suddenlink.com. Also serves Aurora, Marionville, Pierce City & Verona. ICA: MO0052.
TV Market Ranking: Below 100 (Aurora, Marionville, MONETT, Pierce City, Verona). Franchise award date: April 7, 1981. Franchise expiration date: N.A. Began: July 1, 1982.
Channel capacity: N.A. Channels available but not in use: N.A.

Basic Service
Subscribers: 2,981. Commercial subscribers: 232.
Programming (received off-air): KOAM-TV (CBS) Pittsburg; KODE-TV (ABC) Joplin; KOLR (CBS) Springfield; KOZK (PBS) Springfield; KOZL-TV (IND) Springfield; KSNF (NBC) Joplin; KSPR (ABC) Springfield; KYTV (CW, NBC, WeatherNation) Springfield.
Programming (via satellite): TBS; WGN America.
Fee: $40.00 installation; $33.50 monthly.

Expanded Basic Service 1
Subscribers: N.A.
Programming (via satellite): A&E; Animal Planet; Cartoon Network; CMT; CNBC; CNN; Comedy Central; C-SPAN; Discovery Channel; Disney Channel; ESPN; Food Network; Fox News Channel; FOX Sports Midwest; Freeform; FX; Hallmark Channel; HGTV; History; HLN; Lifetime; Nickelodeon; Outdoor Channel; QVC; Spike TV; Syfy; The Weather Channel; TLC; TNT; Travel Channel; TV Land; USA Network; VH1.
Fee: $16.44 monthly.

Expanded Basic Service 2
Subscribers: N.A.
Programming (via satellite): AMC; ESPN2; MTV; Turner Classic Movies.
Fee: $3.95 monthly.

Digital Basic Service
Subscribers: N.A.
Programming (via satellite): Bloomberg Television; Discovery Digital Networks; DMX Music; ESPN Classic; Fox Sports 1; Golf Channel; INSP; Trinity Broadcasting Network (TBN).

Pay Service 1
Pay Units: N.A.
Programming (via satellite): Cinemax; HBO.
Fee: $10.60 installation; $8.95 monthly (Cinemax), $10.95 monthly (HBO).

Digital Pay Service 1
Pay Units: N.A.
Programming (via satellite): Cinemax (multiplexed); HBO (multiplexed); Showtime (multiplexed); Starz (multiplexed); Starz Encore (multiplexed); Sundance TV; The Movie Channel (multiplexed).
Video-On-Demand: Yes
Pay-Per-View
iN DEMAND (delivered digitally).
Internet Service
Operational: Yes.
Broadband Service: Suddenlink High Speed Internet.
Fee: $39.95 monthly.
Telephone Service
Digital: Operational.
Miles of Plant: 114.0 (coaxial); 35.0 (fiber optic).
Senior Vice President, Corporate Finance: Michael Pflantz. Vice President, Accounting: Sabrina Warr. General Manager: Terrill Bradley. Chief Engineer: Tim Crotti. Ownership: Cequel Communications Holdings I LLC (MSO).

MONROE CITY—Formerly served by US Cable of Coastal Texas LP. Now served by Charter Communications, ST. LOUIS, MO [MO0009]. ICA: MO0058.

MONTGOMERY CITY—Formerly served by US Cable. Now served by Charter Communications, ST. LOUIS, MO [MO0009]. ICA: MO0057.

MONTICELLO—Formerly served by CableDirect. No longer in operation. ICA: MO0443.

MOUND CITY—Rock Port Cablevision, 107 West Opp St, PO Box 147, Rock Port, MO 64482. Phones: 877-202-1764; 660-744-5311. Web Site: http://www.rptel.net. ICA: MO0183.
TV Market Ranking: Below 100 (MOUND CITY).
Channel capacity: N.A. Channels available but not in use: N.A.

Basic Service
Subscribers: 82.
Fee: $48.00 monthly.
Chief Technician: Gary McGuire. Ownership: Rock Port Telephone Co. (MSO).

MOUNTAIN GROVE—Formerly served by Almega Cable. Now served by Cable America Corp., ST. ROBERT, MO [MO0023]. ICA: MO0093.

MOUNTAIN VIEW—Formerly served by Boycom Cablevision Inc. No longer in operation. ICA: MO0128.

NAYLOR—Formerly served by Boycom Cablevision Inc. No longer in operation. ICA: MO0181.

NEOSHO—Suddenlink Communications, 520 Maryville Centre Dr, Ste 300, St. Louis, MO 63141. Phones: 800-999-6845; 314-315-9400. Web Site: http://www.suddenlink.com. Also serves Newton County (portions). ICA: MO0047.

Cable Systems—Missouri

TV Market Ranking: Below 100 (NEOSHO, Newton County (portions)). Franchise award date: January 28, 1966. Franchise expiration date: N.A. Began: January 28, 1966.
Channel capacity: N.A. Channels available but not in use: N.A.
Basic Service
Subscribers: 1,240.
Programming (received off-air): KOAM-TV (CBS) Pittsburg; KODE-TV (ABC) Joplin; KOZJ (PBS) Joplin; KSNF (NBC) Joplin; KYTV (CW, NBC, WeatherNation) Springfield.
Programming (via satellite): A&E; AMC; Animal Planet; CMT; CNBC; CNN; C-SPAN; Discovery Channel; Disney Channel; ESPN; FOX Sports Midwest; Freeform; HGTV; History; HLN; Lifetime; Nickelodeon; QVC; Spike TV; Syfy; TBS; The Weather Channel; TLC; TNT; TV Land; USA Network; WGN America.
Fee: $28.45 monthly.
Pay Service 1
Pay Units: N.A.
Programming (via satellite): HBO; Showtime; The Movie Channel.
Fee: $15.00 installation; $7.95 monthly (TMC), $9.95 monthly (Showtime), $10.95 monthly (HBO).
Internet Service
Operational: Yes. Began: October 17, 2003.
Broadband Service: Suddenlink High Speed Internet.
Fee: $29.95 monthly.
Telephone Service
None
Miles of Plant: 83.0 (coaxial); None (fiber optic).
Senior Vice President, Corporate Finance: Michael Pflantz. Regional Manager: Todd Cruthird. Regional Marketing Manager: Beverly Gambell.
Ownership: Cequel Communications Holdings I LLC (MSO).

NEVADA—Fidelity Communications, 64 North Clark St, Sullivan, MO 63080. Phones: 573-468-8081; 417-667-2857 (Nevada office); 800-392-8070. Fax: 573-468-5440. E-mail: custserv@fidelitycommunications.com. Web Site: http://www.fidelitycommunications.com. Also serves Vernon County (southwestern portions). ICA: MO0048.
TV Market Ranking: Below 100 (Vernon County (southwestern portions)); Outside TV Markets (NEVADA). Franchise award date: N.A. Franchise expiration date: N.A. Began: October 1, 1964.
Channel capacity: 55 (not 2-way capable). Channels available but not in use: N.A.
Basic Service
Subscribers: 1,561. Commercial subscribers: 164.
Programming (received off-air): KCPT (PBS) Kansas City; KCTV (CBS) Kansas City; KFJX (FOX) Pittsburg; KOAM-TV (CBS) Pittsburg; KODE-TV (ABC) Joplin; KOLR (CBS) Springfield; KSHB-TV (COZI TV, Grit, NBC) Kansas City; KSNF (NBC) Joplin; 14 FMs.
Programming (via satellite): C-SPAN; INSP; QVC; The Weather Channel.
Fee: $29.99 installation; $28.99 monthly; $2.00 converter.
Digital Basic Service
Subscribers: N.A.
Programming (via satellite): BBC America; Bloomberg Television; Discovery Digital Networks; Disney XD; DIY Network; FYI; GSN; History International; IFC; MC;
NBCSN; Nick 2; Nick Jr.; Nicktoons; Sundance TV; TeenNick; TV Guide Interactive Inc.; WE tv.
Digital Pay Service 1
Pay Units: N.A.
Programming (via satellite): Cinemax (multiplexed); Flix; HBO (multiplexed); Showtime (multiplexed); Starz (multiplexed); Starz Encore (multiplexed); The Movie Channel (multiplexed).
Fee: $10.00 installation; $11.50 monthly (each).
Video-On-Demand: No
Pay-Per-View
iN DEMAND (delivered digitally); Pleasure (delivered digitally); ETC (delivered digitally).
Internet Service
Operational: Yes.
Fee: $54.99-$99.99 monthly.
Telephone Service
Digital: Operational
Fee: $29.99 monthly
Miles of Plant: 81.0 (coaxial); None (fiber optic). Homes passed: 5,808.
General Manager, Missouri: Don Knight. Video Product Manager: Loren King.
Ownership: Fidelity Communications Co. (MSO).

NEW BLOOMFIELD—Formerly served by Longview Communications. No longer in operation. ICA: MO0415.

NEW CAMBRIA—Chariton Valley Cablevision. Now served by MACON, MO [MO0071]. ICA: MO0337.

NEW FRANKLIN—Formerly served by Longview Communications. No longer in operation. ICA: MO0215.

NEW HAVEN—Fidelity Communications. Now served by PHELPS COUNTY, MO [MO0045]. ICA: MO0197.

NEW MADRID—Charter Communications. Now served by ST. LOUIS, MO [MO0009]. ICA: MO0056.

NEWBURG—Cable America Corp. Now served by ST. ROBERT, MO [MO0023]. ICA: MO0240.

NEWTON—Formerly served by Midwest Cable Inc. No longer in operation. ICA: MO0357.

NIANGUA—Formerly served by Almega Cable. No longer in operation. ICA: MO0192.

NIANGUA—Formerly served by Cebridge Connections. No longer in operation. ICA: MO0310.

NIXA—Suddenlink Communications, 520 Maryville Centre Dr, Ste 300, St. Louis, MO 63141. Phones: 417-581-7875; 800-999-6845 (Customer service); 314-315-9346; 314-315-9400. Web Site: http://www.suddenlink.com. Also serves Aunt's Creek, Branson West, Christian County, Highlandville, Kimberling City, Lakeview, Ozark, Reeds Spring & Stone County (portions). ICA: MO0068.
TV Market Ranking: Below 100 (Aunt's Creek, Branson West, Christian County, Highlandville, Kimberling City, Lakeview, NIXA, Ozark, Reeds Spring, Stone County (portions)). Franchise award date: December 1, 1981. Franchise expiration date: N.A. Began: November 10, 1982.
Channel capacity: 41 (operating 2-way). Channels available but not in use: N.A.
Basic Service
Subscribers: 6,885. Commercial subscribers: 396.
Programming (received off-air): KOLR (CBS) Springfield; KOZK (PBS) Springfield; KOZL-TV (IND) Springfield; KSPR (ABC) Springfield; KWBM (Retro TV) Harrison; KYTV (CW, NBC, WeatherNation) Springfield.
Programming (via satellite): KYCW-LD (CW) Springfield; QVC; The Weather Channel; Trinity Broadcasting Network (TBN).
Fee: $40.00 installation; $38.50 monthly.
Expanded Basic Service 1
Subscribers: N.A.
Programming (via satellite): A&E; AMC; Animal Planet; Bravo; Cartoon Network; CNBC; CNN; Comedy Central; C-SPAN; Discovery Channel; Disney Channel; E! HD; ESPN; Food Network; Fox News Channel; Fox Sports 1; FOX Sports Midwest; Freeform; FX; Golf Channel; Great American Country; Hallmark Channel; HGTV; History; HLN; INSP; Lifetime; MSNBC; MTV; National Geographic Channel; Nickelodeon; Outdoor Channel; Spike TV; Syfy; TBS; TLC; TNT; Travel Channel; Turner Classic Movies; TV Land; USA Network; VH1.
Digital Basic Service
Subscribers: N.A.
Programming (via satellite): BBC America; Bloomberg Television; Cloo; CMT; Discovery Digital Networks; Disney XD; DMX Music; ESPN Classic; ESPNews; Fuse; FYI; GSN; History International; IFC; LMN; NBCSN; Nick Jr.; Nicktoons; TeenNick; WE tv.
Pay Service 1
Pay Units: N.A.
Programming (via satellite): HBO; Showtime; The Movie Channel.
Fee: $5.95 monthly (TMC), $9.95 monthly (Showtime), $10.95 monthly (Showtime).
Digital Pay Service 1
Pay Units: N.A.
Programming (via satellite): Cinemax (multiplexed); HBO (multiplexed); Showtime (multiplexed); Starz (multiplexed); Starz Encore (multiplexed); The Movie Channel (multiplexed).
Video-On-Demand: No
Pay-Per-View
iN DEMAND (delivered digitally); Playboy TV (delivered digitally); Fresh (delivered digitally).
Internet Service
Operational: Yes. Began: November 29, 2004.
Subscribers: 9,424.
Broadband Service: Suddenlink High Speed Internet.
Fee: $29.95 monthly.
Telephone Service
Digital: Operational
Subscribers: 3,331.
Miles of Plant: 1,019.0 (coaxial); 213.0 (fiber optic). Homes passed: 26,726.
Senior Vice President, Corporate Finance: Michael Pflantz. Regional Manager: Todd Cruthird. Regional Marketing Manager: Beverly Gambell.
Ownership: Cequel Communications Holdings I LLC (MSO).

NOEL—Formerly served by Crystal Broadband Networks. No longer in operation. ICA: MO0416.

NORBORNE—Green Hills Communications. This cable system has converted to IPTV. Now served by AVALON, MO [MO5156]. ICA: MO0469.

NORBORNE—Mediacom. Now served by EXCELSIOR SPRINGS, MO [MO0040]. ICA: MO0241.

NORTHSHORE—Formerly served by Almega Cable. No longer in operation. ICA: MO0159.

NORWOOD—Formerly served by Cebridge Connections. No longer in operation. ICA: MO0299.

NOVINGER—Formerly served by Longview Communications. No longer in operation. ICA: MO0233.

OREGON—South Holt Cablevision Inc, PO Box 227, Oregon, MO 64473-0227. Phone: 660-446-2900. Fax: 660-446-2800. E-mail: ottman@ofmlive.net. Also serves Forest City. ICA: MO0191.
TV Market Ranking: Below 100 (Forest City, OREGON). Franchise award date: N.A. Franchise expiration date: N.A. Began: September 1, 1982.
Channel capacity: N.A. Channels available but not in use: N.A.
Basic Service
Subscribers: 282.
Programming (received off-air): KCTV (CBS) Kansas City; KCWE (CW, Movies!, This TV) Kansas City; KMBC-TV (ABC, MeTV) Kansas City; KQTV (ABC) St. Joseph; KSHB-TV (COZI TV, Grit, NBC) Kansas City; KSMO-TV (Bounce TV, MNT) Kansas City; KTWU (PBS) Topeka; WDAF-TV (Antenna TV, FOX) Kansas City; WIBW-TV (CBS, MeTV, MNT) Topeka.
Programming (via satellite): CNN; Discovery Channel; Disney Channel; ESPN; ESPN2; Freeform; Lifetime; MTV; Nickelodeon; Spike TV; TBS; TNT; USA Network; VH1; WGN America.
Fee: $59.50 monthly.
Pay Service 1
Pay Units: 182.
Programming (via satellite): HBO.
Fee: $10.00 monthly.
Video-On-Demand: No
Internet Service
Operational: No.
Telephone Service
None
Miles of Plant: 10.0 (coaxial); None (fiber optic). Homes passed: 598.

Missouri—Cable Systems

Assistant General Manager: Wendy Ottman. Technician: Steve Rogers. Ownership: South Holt Cablevision Inc.

OSAGE BEACH—Charter Communications. Now served by ST. LOUIS, MO [MO0009]. ICA: MO0017.

OSCEOLA—Mediacom, 1533 South Enterprise Ave, Springfield, MO 65804. Phones: 845-695-2762; 417-875-5500; 417-875-5560. Fax: 417-883-0265. Web Site: http://www.mediacomcable.com. ICA: MO0216.
TV Market Ranking: Outside TV Markets (OSCEOLA). Franchise award date: August 1, 1982. Franchise expiration date: N.A. Began: August 1, 1982.
Channel capacity: N.A. Channels available but not in use: N.A.
Basic Service
  Subscribers: 51.
  Programming (received off-air): KMBC-TV (ABC, MeTV) Kansas City; KMOS-TV (PBS) Sedalia; KOLR (CBS) Springfield; KOZK (PBS) Springfield; KOZL-TV (IND) Springfield; KPXE-TV (ION) Kansas City; KSHB-TV (COZI TV, Grit, NBC) Kansas City; KSPR (ABC) Springfield; KYTV (CW, NBC, WeatherNation) Springfield.
  Programming (via satellite): A&E; AMC; Animal Planet; Cartoon Network; CMT; CNBC; CNN; Comedy Central; C-SPAN; Discovery Channel; ESPN; ESPN2; Food Network; Fox Sports 1; Freeform; FX; HGTV; History; HLN; INSP; ION Television; Lifetime; MSNBC; Nickelodeon; QVC; Spike TV; Syfy; TBS; The Weather Channel; TLC; TNT; Travel Channel; Trinity Broadcasting Network (TBN); truTV; TV Land; USA Network; VH1; WE tv; WGN America.
  Fee: $35.00 installation; $47.68 monthly.
Pay Service 1
  Pay Units: N.A.
  Programming (via satellite): Flix; HBO (multiplexed); Showtime; The Movie Channel.
  Fee: $10.50 monthly (HBO, Showtime or TMC).
Video-On-Demand: No
Internet Service
  Operational: No.
Telephone Service
  None
Miles of Plant: 8.0 (coaxial); None (fiber optic). Homes passed: 679.
Regional Vice President: Bill Copeland. Vice President, Financial Reporting: Kenneth J. Kohrs. Regional Technical Operations Director: Alan Freedman. Marketing Director: Will Kuebler.
Ownership: Mediacom LLC (MSO).

OTTERVILLE—Formerly served by CableDirect. No longer in operation. ICA: MO0304.

OVERLAND—Charter Communications. Now served by ST. LOUIS, MO [MO0009]. ICA: MO0013.

PACIFIC—Charter Communications. Now served by ST. LOUIS, MO [MO0009]. ICA: MO0078.

PALMYRA—Formerly served by Cass Cable TV Inc. Now served by Charter Communications, ST. LOUIS, MO [MO0009]. ICA: MO0101.

PARIS—Formerly served by US Cable. Now served by Charter Communications, ST. LOUIS, MO [MO0009]. ICA: MO0157.

PARMA—NewWave Communications. Now served by DEXTER, MO [MO0039]. ICA: MO0167.

PARNELL—Formerly served by B & L Technologies LLC. No longer in operation. ICA: MO0442.

PERRY—Formerly served by Charter Communications. No longer in operation. ICA: MO0250.

PERRYVILLE—Charter Communications, 12405 Powerscourt Dr, St. Louis, MO 63131. Phones: 636-207-5100 (Corporate office); 636-207-7044 (St. Louis office); 573-335-4424. Fax: 573-334-9265. Web Site: http://www.charter.com. Also serves Perry County (portions). ICA: MO0054.
TV Market Ranking: 69 (Perry County (portions), PERRYVILLE). Franchise award date: N.A. Franchise expiration date: N.A. Began: June 1, 1982.
Channel capacity: N.A. Channels available but not in use: N.A.
Digital Basic Service
  Subscribers: 1,144.
  Programming (via satellite): BBC America; Discovery Digital Networks; DIY Network; FYI; History International; IFC; MC; National Geographic Channel; Nick 2; Nick Jr.; Nicktoons; Sundance TV; TeenNick; TV Guide Interactive Inc.
  Fee: $26.99 monthly.
Digital Expanded Basic Service
  Subscribers: N.A.
  Programming (via satellite): A&E; Animal Planet; Bravo; Cartoon Network; CNBC; CNN; Comedy Central; Discovery Channel; Disney Channel; Disney XD; E! HD; ESPN2; Food Network; Fox News Channel; Fox Sports 1; FOX Sports Midwest; Freeform; FX; FXM; Golf Channel; Hallmark Channel; HGTV; History; HLN; Lifetime; MSNBC; NBCSN; Oxygen; Spike TV; TBS; The Weather Channel; TLC; TNT; truTV; Turner Classic Movies; TV Land; USA Network; VH1.
  Fee: $49.99 monthly.
Digital Pay Service 1
  Pay Units: N.A.
  Programming (via satellite): Cinemax (multiplexed); Flix; HBO (multiplexed); Showtime (multiplexed); Starz (multiplexed); Starz Encore (multiplexed); The Movie Channel (multiplexed).
  Fee: $12.50 monthly (each).
Video-On-Demand: No
Pay-Per-View
  Hot Choice (delivered digitally); ETC (delivered digitally); Pleasure (delivered digitally); iN DEMAND (delivered digitally).
Internet Service
  Operational: Yes. Began: July 1, 2002.
  Broadband Service: Charter Internet.
  Fee: $49.95 installation; $29.99 monthly.
Telephone Service
  None
Homes passed: 3,667.
Vice President & General Manager: Steve Trippe. Operations Director: Dave Miller. Accounting Director: David Sovanski. Marketing Director: Beverly Wall. Plant Manager: Kevin Goetz. Operations Manager: Dave Huntsman. Technical Operations Manager: Barry Moore. Office Manager: Sheila Tuschoff.
Ownership: Charter Communications Inc. (MSO).

PHELPS COUNTY (portions)—Cable America Corp, 7822 East Gray Rd, Scottsdale, AZ 85260. Phone: 800-338-1808. Web Site: http://www.cableamerica.com. Also serves Rolla. ICA: MO0476.
TV Market Ranking: Outside TV Markets (PHELPS COUNTY (portions), Rolla).
Channel capacity: N.A. Channels available but not in use: N.A.
Basic Service
  Subscribers: 108.
  Fee: $9.95 installation; $55.00 monthly.
Controller: Walter G. Farak.
Ownership: CableAmerica Corp. (MSO).

PHELPS COUNTY (portions)—Fidelity Communications, 64 North Clark St, Sullivan, MO 63080. Phones: 800-392-8070; 573-336-8081. Fax: 573-468-5440. E-mail: custserv@fidelitycommunications.com. Web Site: http://www.fidelitycommunications.com.
Also serves Crawford County (portions), Dent County (portions), Franklin County (portions), Gasconade County (portions), Gerald, Laclede County (portions), Lebanon, New Haven, Owensville, Rolla, Rosebud, Salem, Sullivan & Washington County (portions). ICA: MO0475.
TV Market Ranking: Below 100 (Laclede County (portions) (portions)); Outside TV Markets (Dent County (portions), Gerald, Laclede County (portions) (portions), Lebanon, PHELPS COUNTY (PORTIONS), Rolla, Rosebud, Salem, New Haven, Sullivan).
Channel capacity: N.A. Channels available but not in use: N.A.
Basic Service
  Subscribers: 10,250.
  Fee: $9.95 installation; $28.99 monthly.
Internet Service
  Operational: Yes.
  Subscribers: 6,500.
  Fee: $46.99-$89.99 monthly.
Telephone Service
  Digital: Operational
  Subscribers: 7,752.
  Fee: $16.00 monthly
Miles of Plant: 489.0 (coaxial); 97.0 (fiber optic). Homes passed: 22,010.
General Manager, Missouri: Don Knight. Video Product Manager: Loren King.
Ownership: Fidelity Communications Co. (MSO).

PIEDMONT—Boycom Cablevision Inc, 3467 Township Line Rd, Poplar Bluff, MO 63901. Phones: 800-890-6620; 573-686-9101. Fax: 573-686-4722. Web Site: http://www.boycom.com. Also serves Leeper, Mill Spring, Patterson & Wayne County (portions). ICA: MO0075.
TV Market Ranking: Below 100 (Leeper, Mill Spring, Patterson, PIEDMONT, Wayne County (portions)); Outside TV Markets (Wayne County (portions)). Franchise award date: July 7, 1964. Franchise expiration date: N.A. Began: January 1, 1965.
Channel capacity: N.A. Channels available but not in use: N.A.
Basic Service
  Subscribers: 643.
  Programming (received off-air): KBSI (FOX) Cape Girardeau; KETC (PBS) St. Louis; KFVS-TV (CBS, CW, MeTV) Cape Girardeau; KMOV (CBS) St. Louis; KPLR-TV (CW, This TV) St. Louis; KPOB-TV (ABC) Poplar Bluff; KSDK (Bounce TV, NBC) St. Louis; KTVI (Antenna TV, Escape, FOX) St. Louis; WPSD-TV (Antenna TV, NBC) Paducah.
  Programming (via satellite): C-SPAN; The Weather Channel; TLC; TNT; Trinity Broadcasting Network (TBN); USA Network; WGN America.
  Fee: $61.50 installation.
Expanded Basic Service 1
  Subscribers: N.A.
  Programming (via satellite): A&E; AMC; Animal Planet; Cartoon Network; CNBC; CNN; Comedy Central; Discovery Channel; Disney Channel; E! HD; ESPN; ESPN Classic; ESPN2; Food Network; Fox News Channel; Fox Sports 1; FOX Sports Midwest; Freeform; Great American Country; Hallmark Channel; HGTV; History; HLN; Lifetime; MSNBC; MTV; Nickelodeon; Outdoor Channel; Spike TV; Syfy; TBS; Travel Channel; TV Land; VH1; WE tv.
  Fee: $20.00 monthly.
Digital Basic Service
  Subscribers: N.A.
  Programming (via satellite): BBC America; Bloomberg Television; C-SPAN 3; Discovery Digital Networks; Disney XD; DIY Network; DMX Music; ESPNews; FOX College Sports Central; FOX College Sports Pacific; Fuse; FXM; FYI; GSN; History International; IFC; LMN; Sundance TV.
Pay Service 1
  Pay Units: N.A.
  Programming (via satellite): Cinemax; HBO; Showtime; Starz; Starz Encore; The Movie Channel.
  Fee: $5.99 monthly (Encore), $8.99 monthly (Cinemax), $12.99 monthly (HBO), $13.99 monthly (Showtime/TMC).
Digital Pay Service 1
  Pay Units: N.A.
  Programming (via satellite): Cinemax (multiplexed); Flix; HBO (multiplexed); Showtime (multiplexed); Starz (multiplexed); Starz Encore (multiplexed); The Movie Channel (multiplexed).
Video-On-Demand: No
Pay-Per-View
  iN DEMAND (delivered digitally); Playboy TV (delivered digitally); Fresh (delivered digitally).
Internet Service
  Operational: Yes.
  Subscribers: 168.
Telephone Service
  None
Miles of Plant: 126.0 (coaxial); 25.0 (fiber optic). Homes passed: 2,432.
President: Steven Boyers. General Manager: Shelly Batton. Chief Technician: Phil Huett.
Ownership: Boycom Cablevision Inc. (MSO).

PILOT GROVE—Formerly served by Otelco. No longer in operation. ICA: MO0238.

PLATTSBURG—Formerly served by Allegiance Communications. No longer in operation. ICA: MO0158.

PLEASANT HOPE—Formerly served by Fidelity Communications. No longer in operation. ICA: MO0328.

POCAHONTAS—Semo Communications Corp. Now served by ADVANCE, MO [MO0171]. ICA: MO0225.

POMME DE TERRE—American Broadband Missouri, 153 W Dave Dugas Rd, PO Box 167, Sulphur, LA 70664-0167. Phones: 800-737-3900; 337-583-2111. Fax: 704-845-2299. Web Site: http://www.camtel.com. Also serves Hermitage, Hickory County, Humansville, Pittsburg, Weaubleau & Wheatland. ICA: MO0066.
TV Market Ranking: Outside TV Markets (Hermitage, Hickory County, Humansville,

Cable Systems—Missouri

Pittsburg, POMME DE TERRE, Weaubleau, Wheatland). Franchise award date: January 14, 1985. Franchise expiration date: N.A. Began: July 1, 1987.
Channel capacity: N.A. Channels available but not in use: N.A.
Basic Service
Subscribers: N.A.
Programming (received off-air): KOLR (CBS) Springfield; KOZK (PBS) Springfield; KOZL-TV (IND) Springfield; KSPR (ABC) Springfield; KYTV (CW, NBC, WeatherNation) Springfield.
Programming (via satellite): C-SPAN; INSP; QVC; WGN America.
Fee: $29.95 installation.
Expanded Basic Service 1
Subscribers: N.A.
Programming (via satellite): A&E; AMC; Animal Planet; Cartoon Network; CMT; CNN; Comedy Central; Discovery Channel; Disney Channel; E! HD; ESPN; ESPN Classic; ESPN2; Food Network; Fox News Channel; Fox Sports 1; Freeform; Golf Channel; Hallmark Channel; HGTV; History; HLN; Lifetime; MTV; Nickelodeon; Outdoor Channel; Spike TV; Syfy; TBS; The Weather Channel; TLC; TNT; Travel Channel; Trinity Broadcasting Network (TBN); truTV; TV Land; USA Network; VH1.
Fee: $39.95 monthly.
Digital Basic Service
Subscribers: N.A.
Programming (via satellite): BBC America; Bloomberg Television; Cloo; Discovery Digital Networks; Disney XD; DMX Music; ESPNews; EVINE Live; FXM; FYI; Great American Country; GSN; History International; IFC; LMN; NBCSN; Nick Jr.; Nicktoons; TeenNick; Turner Classic Movies.
Digital Pay Service 1
Pay Units: N.A.
Programming (via satellite): Cinemax (multiplexed); Flix; HBO (multiplexed); Showtime (multiplexed); Starz (multiplexed); Starz Encore (multiplexed).
Fee: $11.95 monthly.
Pay-Per-View
Hot Choice (delivered digitally); Shorteez (delivered digitally); Fresh (delivered digitally); Playboy TV (delivered digitally); iN DEMAND (delivered digitally).
Internet Service
Operational: Yes.
Fee: $40.00 installation; $31.99 monthly.
Telephone Service
Digital: Operational
Miles of Plant: 88.0 (coaxial); None (fiber optic). Homes passed: 3,285.
President: Pat Eudy.
Ownership: American Broadband Communications Inc. (MSO).

POPLAR BLUFF—Boycom Cablevision Inc, 3467 Township Line Rd, Poplar Bluff, MO 63901. Phones: 800-890-6620; 573-686-9101. Fax: 573-686-4722. Web Site: http://www.boycom.com. Also serves Carter County (southeast portion), Ellsinore, Fisk, Grandin, Hunter & Oxly. ICA: MO0196.
TV Market Ranking: Below 100 (Carter County (southeast portion), Fisk, Grandin, Hunter, POPLAR BLUFF, Ellsinore). Franchise award date: February 2, 1971. Franchise expiration date: N.A. Began: February 1, 1979.
Channel capacity: N.A. Channels available but not in use: N.A.
Basic Service
Subscribers: N.A.
Programming (received off-air): KAIT (ABC, NBC) Jonesboro; KBSI (FOX) Cape Girardeau; KFVS-TV (CBS, CW, MeTV) Cape Girardeau; KTEJ (PBS) Jonesboro; WPSD-TV (Antenna TV, NBC) Paducah.
Programming (via satellite): C-SPAN; INSP; The Weather Channel; WGN America.
Fee: $29.95 installation; $19.95 monthly.
Expanded Basic Service 1
Subscribers: N.A.
Programming (via satellite): A&E; AMC; Animal Planet; CMT; CNN; Discovery Channel; Disney Channel; ESPN; ESPN2; EVINE Live; Fox News Channel; Fox Sports 1; FOX Sports Midwest; Freeform; FX; Golf Channel; Great American Country; Hallmark Channel; HGTV; History; Lifetime; LMN; MTV; National Geographic Channel; Nickelodeon; Outdoor Channel; Spike TV; Syfy; TBS; TLC; TNT; Trinity Broadcasting Network (TBN); Turner Classic Movies; TV Land; USA Network; VH1.
Fee: $20.00 monthly.
Video-On-Demand: No
Internet Service
Operational: No.
Telephone Service
None
Miles of Plant: 28.0 (coaxial); None (fiber optic). Homes passed: 568.
President: Steven Boyers. General Manager: Shelly Batton. Chief Technician: Phil Huett.
Ownership: Boycom Cablevision Inc. (MSO).

POPLAR BLUFF—NewWave Communications, One Montgomery Plaza, 4th Floor, Sikeston, MO 63801. Phone: 888-863-9928. Web Site: http://www.newwavecom.com. Also serves Butler County (portions). ICA: MO0024.
TV Market Ranking: Below 100 (Butler County (portions), POPLAR BLUFF). Franchise award date: November 3, 1957. Franchise expiration date: N.A. Began: August 23, 1957.
Channel capacity: N.A. Channels available but not in use: N.A.
Basic Service
Subscribers: 3,451.
Programming (received off-air): KAIT (ABC, NBC) Jonesboro; KBSI (FOX) Cape Girardeau; KFVS-TV (CBS, CW, MeTV) Cape Girardeau; KPOB-TV (ABC) Poplar Bluff; KSDK (Bounce TV, NBC) St. Louis; KTEJ (PBS) Jonesboro; WPSD-TV (Antenna TV, NBC) Paducah; WQWQ-LP (CW, MeTV) Paducah.
Programming (via microwave): KMOV (CBS) St. Louis; WDKA (MNT, The Country Network) Paducah.
Programming (via satellite): HLN; ION Television; Pop; The Weather Channel; WGN America.
Fee: $40.00 installation; $27.78 monthly.
Expanded Basic Service 1
Subscribers: N.A.
Programming (via satellite): A&E; AMC; Animal Planet; BET; Cartoon Network; CMT; CNBC; CNN; Comedy Central; C-SPAN; C-SPAN 2; Discovery Channel; Disney Channel; DIY Network; E! HD; ESPN; ESPN Classic; ESPN2; ESPNews; Family Friendly Entertainment; Food Network; Fox News Channel; Fox Sports 1; FOX Sports Midwest; Freeform; FX; Golf Channel; Great American Country; Hallmark Channel; HGTV; History; INSP; Lifetime; MSNBC; MTV; National Geographic Channel; NBCSN; Nickelodeon; Outdoor Channel; QVC; Spike TV; Syfy; TBS; TLC; TNT; Travel Channel; Trinity Broadcasting Network (TBN); truTV; Turner Classic Movies; TV Land; USA Network; VH1; WE tv.
Fee: $31.02 monthly.
Digital Basic Service
Subscribers: 1,093.
Programming (via satellite): 3ABN; A&E HD; AWE; AXS TV; BBC America; Bloomberg Television; Boomerang; CNN International; Colours; Destination America; Discovery Channel HD; Discovery Kids Channel; Discovery Life Channel; Disney XD; Enlace USA; ESPN HD; ESPN2 HD; ESPNU; Fox Business Network; FSN Digital Atlantic; FSN Digital Central; FSN Digital Pacific; FSN HD; Fuse; FX HD; FXM; FYI; Hallmark Movies & Mysteries; History HD; History International; IFC; Investigation Discovery; LMN; MC; MTV Classic; MTV Hits; MTV2; National Geographic Channel HD; Nick Jr.; Nicktoons; Outdoor Channel 2 HD; OWN: Oprah Winfrey Network; RFD-TV; Science Channel; TeenNick; UP; Versus HD.
Fee: $11.00 monthly.
Digital Expanded Basic Service
Subscribers: N.A.
Programming (via satellite): Cinelatino; ESPN Deportes; La Familia Cosmovision; ULTRA HDPlex.
Fee: $4.00 monthly.
Pay Service 1
Pay Units: 420.
Programming (via satellite): Cinemax.
Fee: $10.90 monthly.
Pay Service 2
Pay Units: 1,633.
Programming (via satellite): HBO.
Fee: $12.25 monthly.
Pay Service 3
Pay Units: 442.
Programming (via satellite): Showtime.
Fee: $10.00 monthly.
Digital Pay Service 1
Pay Units: 1,107.
Programming (via satellite): Cinemax (multiplexed); Cinemax HD; Flix; HBO (multiplexed); HBO HD; Showtime (multiplexed); Showtime HD; Starz (multiplexed); Starz Encore (multiplexed); Starz HD; The Movie Channel (multiplexed); The Movie Channel HD.
Fee: $8.90 monthly (Starz/Encore), $8.95 monthly (Cinemax), $9.95 monthly (Showtime/TMC/Flix/Sundance), $10.95 monthly (HBO).
Video-On-Demand: No
Pay-Per-View
Hot Choice (delivered digitally); iN DEMAND (delivered digitally), Addressable: No.
Internet Service
Operational: Yes.
Subscribers: 3,809.
Broadband Service: imsinternet.net, semo.net, tcmax.net.
Fee: $29.95 monthly.
Telephone Service
None
Miles of Plant: 428.0 (coaxial); 123.0 (fiber optic). Homes passed: 15,500.
Chief Financial Officer: Rod Siemers.
Ownership: NewWave Communications LLC (MSO).

PORTAGE DES SIOUX—Formerly served by Cable America Corp. No longer in operation. ICA: MO0418.

PORTAGEVILLE—NewWave Communications. Now served by DEXTER, MO [MO0039]. ICA: MO0099.

PORTER MILLS—Formerly served by Lake Communications. No longer in operation. ICA: MO0090.

POTOSI—Formerly served by Crystal Broadband Networks. No longer in operation. ICA: MO0106.

POWERSITE—Formerly served by Almega Cable. No longer in operation. ICA: MO0452.

PRINCETON—Formerly served by Longview Communications. No longer in operation. ICA: MO0185.

PURDY—Mediacom. Now served by CASSVILLE, MO [MO0118]. ICA: MO0227.

PUXICO—Boycom Cablevision Inc, 3467 Township Line Rd, Poplar Bluff, MO 63901. Phones: 800-890-6620; 573-686-9101. Fax: 573-686-4722. Web Site: http://www.boycom.com. ICA: MO0202.
TV Market Ranking: Below 100 (PUXICO). Franchise award date: January 20, 1982. Franchise expiration date: N.A. Began: August 1, 1982.
Channel capacity: N.A. Channels available but not in use: N.A.
Basic Service
Subscribers: N.A.
Programming (received off-air): KAIT (ABC, NBC) Jonesboro; KBSI (FOX) Cape Girardeau; KFVS-TV (CBS, CW, MeTV) Cape Girardeau; KTEJ (PBS) Jonesboro; WPSD-TV (Antenna TV, NBC) Paducah.
Programming (via satellite): A&E; Animal Planet; CNN; Discovery Channel; Disney Channel; ESPN; FOX Sports Midwest; Freeform; Great American Country; History; Lifetime; MTV; Nickelodeon; Spike TV; TBS; The Weather Channel; TNT; Trinity Broadcasting Network (TBN); USA Network; WGN America.
Fee: $61.50 installation.
Pay Service 1
Pay Units: N.A.
Programming (via satellite): Cinemax; HBO; Showtime; The Movie Channel.
Fee: $9.49 monthly (Cinemax), $13.49 monthly (HBO, Showtime or TMC).
Video-On-Demand: No
Internet Service
Operational: Yes.
Telephone Service
None
Miles of Plant: 27.0 (coaxial); None (fiber optic). Homes passed: 540.
President: Steven Boyers. General Manager: Shelly Batton. Chief Technician: Phil Huett.
Ownership: Boycom Cablevision Inc. (MSO).

Missouri—Cable Systems

QULIN—Formerly served by Boycom Cablevision Inc. No longer in operation. ICA: MO0291.

RAVENWOOD—Formerly served by B & L Technologies LLC. No longer in operation. ICA: MO0320.

RENICK—Formerly served by Charter Communications. No longer in operation. ICA: MO0419.

RENICK—Milan Interactive Communications, 312 South Main St, PO Box 240, Milan, MO 63556. Phone: 660-265-7174. ICA: MO0471.
TV Market Ranking: Below 100 (RENICK).
Channel capacity: N.A. Channels available but not in use: N.A.
Basic Service
Subscribers: 10.
Programming (received off-air): KMIZ (ABC, MeTV, MNT) Columbia; KOMU-TV (CW, NBC) Columbia; KRCG (CBS) Jefferson City.
Programming (via satellite): CNN; Discovery Channel; ESPN; TBS; TNT; USA Network; WGN America.
Fee: $29.95 installation; $40.77 monthly.
Video-On-Demand: No
Internet Service
Operational: No.
Telephone Service
None
President & General Manager: Rick Gardener.
Ownership: Milan Interactive Communications (MSO).

REPUBLIC—Cable America Corp, 7822 East Gray Rd, Scottsdale, AZ 85260. Phones: 800-338-1808; 417-732-7242. Web Site: http://www.cableamerica.com. Also serves Clever & Greene County (southwestern portion). ICA: MO0069.
TV Market Ranking: Below 100 (Clever, Greene County (southwestern portion), REPUBLIC). Franchise award date: March 25, 1995. Franchise expiration date: N.A. Began: July 1, 1981.
Channel capacity: N.A. Channels available but not in use: N.A.
Basic Service
Subscribers: 742.
Programming (received off-air): KETC (PBS) St. Louis; KOLR (CBS) Springfield; KOZK (PBS) Springfield; KOZL-TV (IND) Springfield; KSDK (Bounce TV, NBC) St. Louis; KSPR (ABC) Springfield; KWBM (Retro TV) Harrison; WRBU (ION) East St. Louis.
Programming (via satellite): C-SPAN; C-SPAN 2; Pop; The Weather Channel; WGN America.
Fee: $9.95 installation; $22.99 monthly.
Expanded Basic Service 1
Subscribers: N.A.
Programming (via satellite): A&E; AMC; Animal Planet; Cartoon Network; CNBC; CNN; Comedy Central; Discovery Channel; Disney Channel; ESPN; ESPN2; Food Network; Fox News Channel; Fox Sports 1; FOX Sports Midwest; Freeform; FX; Golf Channel; Great American Country; Hallmark Channel; HGTV; History; HLN; INSP; Lifetime; MTV; NBCSN; Nickelodeon; QVC; Spike TV; Syfy; TBS; TLC; TNT; Travel Channel; Trinity Broadcasting Network (TBN); truTV; Turner Classic Movies; TV Land; USA Network; VH1; WE tv.
Fee: $30.95 monthly.

Digital Basic Service
Subscribers: 452.
Programming (via satellite): BBC America; Bloomberg Television; Bravo; Discovery Digital Networks; Disney XD; DMX Music; ESPN Classic; ESPN2; ESPNews; Fox Sports 1; Fuse; FXM; FYI; Golf Channel; GSN; HGTV; History; History International; IFC; LMN; Nick Jr.; Nicktoons; Starz Encore (multiplexed); Syfy; TeenNick; Trinity Broadcasting Network (TBN); Turner Classic Movies; WE tv.
Fee: $14.00 monthly.
Digital Pay Service 1
Pay Units: N.A.
Programming (via satellite): Cinemax (multiplexed); HBO (multiplexed); Showtime (multiplexed); Starz (multiplexed); The Movie Channel (multiplexed).
Video-On-Demand: No
Internet Service
Operational: Yes.
Fee: $14.95 installation; $25.95 monthly.
Telephone Service
Digital: Operational
Miles of Plant: 74.0 (coaxial); None (fiber optic). Homes passed: 4,570.
Vice President, Engineering: Alan Jackson. General Manager: Debra Mefford. Chief Technician: James Grove. Controller: Walter G. Farak. Marketing Director: John Mori.
Ownership: CableAmerica Corp. (MSO).

RICH HILL—American Broadband Missouri, PO Box 39, Blair, NE 68008. Phones: 888-438-4490; 417-395-2121. Fax: 417-395-2120. Web Site: http://www.abbmissouri.com. ICA: MO0177.
TV Market Ranking: Outside TV Markets (RICH HILL). Franchise award date: N.A. Franchise expiration date: N.A. Began: July 1, 1976.
Channel capacity: N.A. Channels available but not in use: N.A.
Basic Service
Subscribers: 294.
Programming (received off-air): KCPT (PBS) Kansas City; KCTV (CBS) Kansas City; KCWE (CW, Movies!, This TV) Kansas City; KMBC-TV (ABC, MeTV) Kansas City; KMCI-TV (Bounce TV, Escape, IND) Lawrence; KODE-TV (ABC) Joplin; KPXE-TV (ION) Kansas City; KSHB-TV (COZI TV, Grit, NBC) Kansas City; KSMO-TV (Bounce TV, MNT) Kansas City; WDAF-TV (Antenna TV, FOX) Kansas City; allband FM.
Programming (via satellite): A&E; CNN; Comedy Central; Discovery Channel; Disney Channel; ESPN; ESPN2; Freeform; Great American Country; Hallmark Channel; HGTV; History; Lifetime; Nickelodeon; Outdoor Channel; QVC; Spike TV; Syfy; TBS; TLC; TNT; Travel Channel; Trinity Broadcasting Network (TBN); Turner Classic Movies; TV Land; USA Network; VH1; WGN America.
Fee: $27.50 installation; $42.95 monthly.
Pay Service 1
Pay Units: 92.
Programming (via satellite): Cinemax; Flix; HBO; Showtime; The Movie Channel.
Fee: $12.95 monthly (each).
Internet Service
Operational: No, DSL & dial-up.
Telephone Service
Analog: Operational
Miles of Plant: 30.0 (coaxial); None (fiber optic). Homes passed: 807.
General Manager & Chief Technician: Reese Copsey.
Ownership: American Broadband Communications Inc. (MSO).

RICHLAND—Cable America Corp. Now served by ST. ROBERT, MO [MO0023]. ICA: MO0139.

RICHMOND—Mediacom. Now served by EXCELSIOR SPRINGS, MO [MO0040]. ICA: MO0077.

ROCK PORT—Rock Port Cablevision, 107 West Opp St, PO Box 147, Rock Port, MO 64482. Phones: 660-744-5314; 877-202-1764; 660-744-5311. Fax: 660-744-2120. Web Site: http://www.rptel.net. Also serves Atchison County, Fairfax & Tarkio. ICA: MO0186.
TV Market Ranking: Outside TV Markets (Atchison County, Fairfax, ROCK PORT, Tarkio). Franchise award date: March 1, 1984. Franchise expiration date: N.A. Began: November 1, 1984.
Channel capacity: 36 (not 2-way capable). Channels available but not in use: N.A.
Basic Service
Subscribers: 653.
Programming (received off-air): KCTV (CBS) Kansas City; KETV (ABC, MeTV) Omaha; KMBC-TV (ABC, MeTV) Kansas City; KMTV-TV (Antenna TV, CBS, Escape) Omaha; KPTM (Estrella TV, FOX, MNT, This TV) Omaha; KQTV (ABC) St. Joseph; KSHB-TV (COZI TV, Grit, NBC) Kansas City; KXVO (Azteca America, CW) Omaha; KYNE-TV (PBS) Omaha; WDAF-TV (Antenna TV, FOX) Kansas City; WOWT (IND, NBC) Omaha.
Programming (via satellite): A&E; AMC; Animal Planet; Cartoon Network; CMT; CNBC; CNN; Comedy Central; C-SPAN; Discovery Channel; Discovery Life Channel; Disney Channel; DIY Network; ESPN; ESPN Classic; ESPN2; Food Network; Fox News Channel; Fox Sports 1; FOX Sports Networks; Freeform; FX; Golf Channel; Great American Country; Hallmark Channel; HGTV; History; HLN; Lifetime; MoviePlex; MTV; National Geographic Channel; Nickelodeon; Outdoor Channel; QVC; RFD-TV; Spike TV; TBS; The Weather Channel; TLC; TNT; Travel Channel; Trinity Broadcasting Network (TBN); TV Land; USA Network; VH1; WGN America.
Fee: $35.00 installation; $48.00 monthly.
Digital Basic Service
Subscribers: N.A.
Programming (via satellite): BBC America; Bravo; Discovery Digital Networks; DMX Music; ESPNews; IFC; NBCSN; Nick Jr.; Syfy; Turner Classic Movies; WE tv.
Fee: $35.00 installation.
Pay Service 1
Pay Units: N.A.
Programming (via satellite): Cinemax; HBO; Starz; Starz Encore.
Fee: $25.00 installation; $3.50 monthly (Encore), $8.00 monthly (Starz), $9.00 monthly (Cinemax), $11.00 monthly (HBO).
Digital Pay Service 1
Pay Units: N.A.
Programming (via satellite): HBO (multiplexed); Starz; Starz Encore (multiplexed); The Movie Channel.
Fee: $6.50 monthly (Cinemax or HBO), $6.95 monthly (TMC).
Video-On-Demand: No
Pay-Per-View
iN DEMAND (delivered digitally); Playboy TV (delivered digitally).
Internet Service
Operational: No, DSL.
Telephone Service
None
Miles of Plant: 69.0 (coaxial); None (fiber optic). Homes passed: 3,462.

General Manager: Raymond Henagan. Chief Technician: Gary McGuire.
Ownership: Rock Port Telephone Co.

ROCKAWAY BEACH—Formerly served by Cox Communications. Now served by Suddenlink Communications, BRANSON, MO [MO0038]. ICA: MO0420.

ROCKVILLE—Formerly served by N.W. Communications. No longer in operation. ICA: MO0358.

ROGERSVILLE—Mediacom. Now served by SEYMOUR, MO [MO0172]. ICA: MO0272.

ROLLA—Formerly served by Phelps County Cable. Now served by Cable America Corp., PHELPS COUNTY (portions), MO [MO0475]. ICA: MO0421.

RUSSELLVILLE—Formerly served by Longview Communications. No longer in operation. ICA: MO0262.

SALEM—Fidelity Communications. Now served by PHELPS COUNTY (portions), MO [MO0475]. ICA: MO0059.

SARCOXIE—Mediacom. Now served by DIAMOND, MO [MO0156]. ICA: MO0179.

SCHELL CITY—American Broadband Missouri, 616 East Park, PO Box 30, Rich Hill, MO 64779-0030. Phones: 888-438-4490; 417-395-2121. Web Site: http://www.klmtel.net. ICA: MO0472.
TV Market Ranking: Outside TV Markets (SCHELL CITY).
Channel capacity: N.A. Channels available but not in use: N.A.
Basic Service
Subscribers: 60.
Programming (received off-air): KCTV (CBS) Kansas City; KCWE (CW, Movies!, This TV) Kansas City; KMBC-TV (ABC, MeTV) Kansas City; KOAM-TV (CBS) Pittsburg; KOLR (CBS) Springfield; KOZK (PBS) Springfield; KOZL-TV (IND) Springfield; KSHB-TV (COZI TV, Grit, NBC) Kansas City; KSMO-TV (Bounce TV, MNT) Kansas City; KSPR (ABC) Springfield; KYTV (CW, NBC, WeatherNation) Springfield; WDAF-TV (Antenna TV, FOX) Kansas City.
Programming (via satellite): A&E; CMT; CNN; Discovery Channel; Disney Channel; ESPN; ESPN2; Fox Sports 1; HGTV; History; HLN; Lifetime; Nickelodeon; Outdoor Channel; QVC; Spike TV; TBS; TLC; TNT; truTV; Turner Classic Movies; USA Network.
Fee: $42.95 monthly.
Pay Service 1
Pay Units: N.A.
Programming (via satellite): Flix; HBO; Showtime; Sundance TV; The Movie Channel.
Internet Service
Operational: No, DSL & dial-up.
Telephone Service
Analog: Operational
General Manager & Chief Technician: Reese Copsey.
Ownership: American Broadband Communications Inc. (MSO).

SEDALIA—Charter Communications. Now served by ST. LOUIS, MO [MO0009]. ICA: MO0025.

SELIGMAN—Formerly served by Allegiance Communications. No longer in operation. ICA: MO0457.

Cable Systems—Missouri

SENECA—Formerly served by Crystal Broadband Networks. No longer in operation. ICA: MO0152.

SENECA—Formerly served by S-Go Video. IPTV service no longer in operation. ICA: MO5032.

SEYMOUR—Mediacom, 1533 South Enterprise Ave, Springfield, MO 65804. Phones: 845-695-2762; 417-875-5500; 417-875-5560. Fax: 417-883-0265. Web Site: http://www.mediacomcable.com. Also serves Ava, Billings, Cabool, Crane, Forsyth, Kimberling City, Mansfield, Marshfield, Rogersville & Strafford. ICA: MO0172.
TV Market Ranking: Below 100 (Billings, Crane, Kimberling City, Marshfield, Rogersville, SEYMOUR, Strafford, Forsyth); Outside TV Markets (Ava, Cabool, Mansfield). Franchise award date: July 3, 1979. Franchise expiration date: N.A. Began: N.A.
Channel capacity: N.A. Channels available but not in use: N.A.
Basic Service
Subscribers: 2,525.
Programming (received off-air): KOLR (CBS) Springfield; KOZK (PBS) Springfield; KSPR (ABC) Springfield; KWBM (Retro TV) Harrison; KYTV (CW, NBC, WeatherNation) Springfield.
Programming (via satellite): A&E; AMC; Animal Planet; Bravo; Cartoon Network; CMT; CNBC; CNN; Comedy Central; C-SPAN; Discovery Channel; Disney Channel; E! HD; Enlace USA; ESPN; ESPN2; Food Network; Fox News Channel; Fox Sports 1; FOX Sports Networks; Freeform; FX; FXM; Hallmark Channel; HGTV; History; HLN; INSP; Lifetime; MSNBC; MTV; Nickelodeon; Outdoor Channel; Pop; QVC; Spike TV; Syfy; TBS; The Weather Channel; TLC; TNT; Travel Channel; truTV; TV Land; USA Network; VH1; WGN America.
Fee: $35.00 installation; $42.00 monthly.
Digital Basic Service
Subscribers: N.A.
Programming (via satellite): AXS TV; BBC America; Bloomberg Television; Bravo HD; Cine Mexicano; CNN en Espanol; Discovery Life Channel; Disney XD; ESPN; Fox Deportes; Fuse; FYI; Golf Channel; GSN; HD Theater; History en Espanol; History International; IFC; International Television (ITV); LMN; MTV Classic; MTV Hits; MTV2; National Geographic Channel; NBCSN; Nick Jr.; Showtime HD; Starz HD; TeenNick; Turner Classic Movies; Worship Network.
Digital Pay Service 1
Pay Units: N.A.
Programming (via satellite): Cinemax (multiplexed); HBO (multiplexed); Showtime (multiplexed); Starz (multiplexed).
Video-On-Demand: Yes
Internet Service
Operational: Yes.
Broadband Service: Mediacom High Speed Internet.
Fee: $55.95 monthly.
Telephone Service
Analog: Not Operational
Digital: Operational
Miles of Plant: 110.0 (coaxial); None (fiber optic). Homes passed: 6,912.
Regional Vice President: Bill Copeland. Vice President, Financial Reporting: Kenneth J. Kohrs. Regional Technical Operations Director: Alan Freedman. Marketing Director: Will Kuebler. Customer Service Manager: Cindy Reese.
Ownership: Mediacom LLC (MSO).

SHELBINA—Formerly served by US Cable. Now served by Charter Communications, ST. LOUIS, MO [MO0009]. ICA: MO0098.

SHELDON—Formerly served by Cebridge Connections. No longer in operation. ICA: MO0297.

SHERIDAN—Formerly served by B & L Technologies LLC. No longer in operation. ICA: MO0354.

SILEX—Formerly served by First Cable of Missouri Inc. No longer in operation. ICA: MO0373.

SKIDMORE—Holway Telephone Co. Now served by MAITLAND, MO [MO0336]. ICA: MO0350.

SMITHTON—Provincial Cable & Data, 123A West Main St, Odessa, MO 64076. Phones: 816-633-1626; 866-284-3346. E-mail: customercare@provincial-cable.net. Web Site: http://www.provincialcable.com. Also serves Brooking Park. ICA: MO0298.
TV Market Ranking: Below 100 (Brooking Park, SMITHTON). Franchise award date: N.A. Franchise expiration date: N.A. Began: June 1, 1985.
Channel capacity: N.A. Channels available but not in use: N.A.
Basic Service
Subscribers: 115.
Programming (received off-air): KMIZ (ABC, MeTV, MNT) Columbia; KMOS-TV (PBS) Sedalia; KOMU-TV (CW, NBC) Columbia; KRCG (CBS) Jefferson City.
Programming (via satellite): A&E; AMC; Animal Planet; Cartoon Network; CNN; C-SPAN; Discovery Channel; Disney Channel; E! HD; ESPN; ESPN2; Fox News Channel; Freeform; Fuse; FX; Great American Country; HGTV; History; HLN; Lifetime; Outdoor Channel; TBS; The Weather Channel; TLC; TNT; Turner Classic Movies; USA Network; WGN America.
Fee: $40.45 monthly.
Pay Service 1
Pay Units: N.A.
Programming (via satellite): Cinemax; HBO; Showtime; Starz; Starz Encore; The Movie Channel.
Fee: $9.95 monthly (Showtime, TMC or Starz/Encore), $10.95 monthly (Cinemax), $14.95 monthly (HBO).
Video-On-Demand: No
Internet Service
Operational: No.
Telephone Service
None
Miles of Plant: 18.0 (coaxial); None (fiber optic). Homes passed: 889.
General Manager: Perry Scarborough. Office Manager: Misti Runyan.
Ownership: Provincial Cable & Data (MSO).

SPARTA—Formerly served by Almega Cable. No longer in operation. ICA: MO0257.

SPRING CITY—Formerly served by Almega Cable. No longer in operation. ICA: MO0134.

SPRINGFIELD—Mediacom, 1533 South Enterprise Ave, Springfield, MO 65804. Phones: 845-695-2762; 417-875-5500; 417-875-5560. Fax: 417-883-0265. Web Site: http://www.mediacomcable.com. Also serves Battlefield & Greene County (portions). ICA: MO0006.
TV Market Ranking: Below 100 (Battlefield, Greene County (portions), SPRINGFIELD). Franchise award date: N.A. Franchise expiration date: N.A. Began: December 1, 1979.
Channel capacity: N.A. Channels available but not in use: N.A.
Basic Service
Subscribers: 21,234.
Programming (received off-air): KOLR (CBS) Springfield; KOZK (PBS) Springfield; KOZL-TV (IND) Springfield; KSPR (ABC) Springfield; KYTV (CW, NBC, WeatherNation) Springfield; allband FM.
Programming (via satellite): C-SPAN; C-SPAN 2; Discovery Channel; TBS; The Weather Channel; WGN America.
Fee: $39.95 installation; $42.00 monthly.
Expanded Basic Service 1
Subscribers: N.A.
Programming (via satellite): A&E; AMC; Animal Planet; BET; Bravo; Cartoon Network; CMT; CNBC; CNN; Comedy Central; Disney Channel; E! HD; ESPN; ESPN2; EWTN Global Catholic Network; Fox News Channel; FOX Sports Midwest; Freeform; FX; Hallmark Channel; HLN; ION Television; Lifetime; MSNBC; MTV; Nickelodeon; Pop; QVC; Spike TV; Syfy; TLC; TNT; Travel Channel; Trinity Broadcasting Network (TBN); truTV; USA Network; VH1.
Fee: $12.95 installation; $21.84 monthly.
Expanded Basic Service 2
Subscribers: N.A.
Programming (via satellite): Disney XD; DMX Music; Fox Deportes; HITS (Headend In The Sky).
Fee: $6.99 monthly.
Digital Basic Service
Subscribers: N.A.
Programming (via satellite): BBC America; Discovery Digital Networks; ESPN Classic; Fox Sports 1; Golf Channel; GSN; HGTV; History; IFC; NBCSN; Nick Jr.; Outdoor Channel; Turner Classic Movies; TV Land; VH1 Country; WE tv.
Fee: $3.50 converter.
Pay Service 1
Pay Units: N.A.
Programming (via satellite): Cinemax (multiplexed); HBO (multiplexed); Showtime (multiplexed); Starz; Starz Encore; The Movie Channel.
Fee: $12.95 installation; $1.75 monthly (Encore), $6.75 monthly (Starz), $12.40 monthly (Cinemax, HBO, Showtime or TMC).
Digital Pay Service 1
Pay Units: N.A.
Programming (via satellite): Cinemax (multiplexed); DMX Music; HBO (multiplexed); Showtime (multiplexed); Starz (multiplexed); The Movie Channel (multiplexed).
Fee: $7.95 monthly (DMX).
Video-On-Demand: Yes
Pay-Per-View
Hot Choice (delivered digitally); iN DEMAND; Playboy TV (delivered digitally); Fresh (delivered digitally); special events (delivered digitally).
Internet Service
Operational: Yes.
Subscribers: 21,628.
Broadband Service: Mediacom High Speed Internet.
Fee: $99.95 installation; $45.95 monthly.
Telephone Service
Digital: Operational
Subscribers: 10,478.
Miles of Plant: 2,003.0 (coaxial); 494.0 (fiber optic). Homes passed: 125,243.
Regional Vice President: Bill Copeland. Vice President, Financial Reporting: Kenneth J. Kohrs. Regional Technical Operations Director: Alan Freedman. Marketing Director: Will Kuebler. Senior Government & Community Relations Manager: Randy Hollis. Customer Service Manager: Cindy Reese. Marketing Coordinator: Brad Koetters.
Ownership: Mediacom LLC (MSO).

ST. CHARLES—Charter Communications. Now served by ST. LOUIS, MO [MO0009]. ICA: MO0007.

ST. CLAIR—Charter Communications. Now served by ST. LOUIS, MO [MO0009]. ICA: MO0140.

ST. JAMES—Charter Communications. Now served by ST. LOUIS, MO [MO0009]. ICA: MO0113.

ST. JOSEPH—Suddenlink Communications, 520 Maryville Centre Dr, Ste 300, St. Louis, MO 63141. Phones: 314-315-9400; 816-279-1234 (Customer service). Web Site: http://www.suddenlink.com. Also serves Agency, Country Club Village & Savannah. ICA: MO0011.
TV Market Ranking: Below 100 (Agency, Country Club Village, Savannah, ST. JOSEPH). Franchise award date: April 1, 1965. Franchise expiration date: N.A. Began: December 21, 1965.
Channel capacity: N.A. Channels available but not in use: N.A.
Basic Service
Subscribers: 14,982. Commercial subscribers: 1,028.
Programming (received off-air): KCPT (PBS) Kansas City; KCTV (CBS) Kansas City; KCWE (CW, Movies!, This TV) Kansas City; KMBC-TV (ABC, MeTV) Kansas City; KQTV (ABC) St. Joseph; KSHB-TV (COZI TV, Grit, NBC) Kansas City; KTAJ-TV (TBN) St. Joseph; KTWU (PBS) Topeka; WDAF-TV (Antenna TV, FOX) Kansas City; 13 FMs.
Programming (via satellite): Animal Planet; BET; CMT; CNBC; CNN; C-SPAN; C-SPAN 2; Discovery Channel; Disney Channel; E! HD; ESPN; ESPN2; EWTN Global Catholic Network; Fox News Channel; FOX Sports Midwest; Freeform; Great American Country; HGTV; HLN; Lifetime; MoviePlex; MTV; National Geographic Channel; Nickelodeon; OWN: Oprah Winfrey Network; Pop; QVC; Spike TV; Syfy; TBS; The Weather Channel; TLC; TNT; truTV; TV Land; USA Network; VH1; WGN America.
Fee: $35.00 installation; $65.48 monthly; $3.75 converter.

2017 Edition

D-459

Missouri—Cable Systems

FREE TRIAL @
Access the most current data instantly
ADVANCED TVFactbook
TELCO/IPTV • CABLE TV • TV STATIONS
www.warren-news.com/factbook.htm

Expanded Basic Service 1
Subscribers: N.A.
Programming (via satellite): A&E; Cartoon Network; Comedy Central; Food Network; Fox Sports 1; Golf Channel; GSN; Hallmark Channel; History; LMN; MSNBC; NBCSN; Travel Channel; Turner Classic Movies.
Fee: $10.00 installation; $4.70 monthly.

Digital Basic Service
Subscribers: N.A.
Programming (via satellite): AXS TV; BBC America; Bloomberg Television; Boomerang; Discovery Digital Networks; DIY Network; ESPN; ESPN Classic; ESPNews; EVINE Live; Fuse; FYI; HD Theater; History International; LOGO; MC; Nick 2; Nick Jr.; Nicktoons; Outdoor Channel; TeenNick; Trinity Broadcasting Network (TBN); WE tv.

Digital Pay Service 1
Pay Units: 892.
Programming (via satellite): Cinemax.
Fee: $10.20 monthly.

Digital Pay Service 2
Pay Units: 2,663.
Programming (via satellite): HBO (multiplexed).
Fee: $9.00 monthly.

Digital Pay Service 3
Pay Units: 160.
Programming (via satellite): Playboy TV.
Fee: $8.00 monthly.

Digital Pay Service 4
Pay Units: 1,976.
Programming (via satellite): Showtime (multiplexed); The Movie Channel (multiplexed).
Fee: $10.20 monthly.

Digital Pay Service 5
Pay Units: 1,977.
Programming (via satellite): Starz (multiplexed); Starz Encore (multiplexed).
Fee: $10.20 monthly.

Video-On-Demand: No

Pay-Per-View
Hot Choice (delivered digitally); Fresh (delivered digitally).

Internet Service
Operational: Yes.
Subscribers: 16,718.
Broadband Service: Suddenlink High Speed Internet.
Fee: $99.00 installation; $39.95 monthly; $5.00 modem lease; $60.00 modem purchase.

Telephone Service
Digital: Operational
Subscribers: 6,400.
Fee: $44.95 monthly

Miles of Plant: 623.0 (coaxial); 265.0 (fiber optic). Homes passed: 37,000.

Senior Vice President, Corporate Finance: Michael Pflantz. Regional Manager: Todd Cruthird.

Ownership: Cequel Communications Holdings I LLC (MSO).

ST. LOUIS—Charter Communications, 941 Charter Commons, St. Louis, MO 63017. Phones: 314-543-2236; 636-207-5100 (Corporate office); 636-207-7044. Web Site: http://www.charter.com. Also serves Addieville, Albers, Alorton, Alton, Ashley, Aviston, Beaucoup, Beckemeyer, Belleville, Bethalto, Breese, Cahokia, Carlyle, Caseyville, Central City, Centralia, Centreville, Chouteau Twp., Clinton County (portions), Collinsville, Columbia, Cottage Hills, Damiansville, Dupo, East Alton, East St. Louis, Edwardsville, Fairview Heights, Freeburg, Germantown, Glen Carbon, Godfrey, Granite City, Hartford, Highland, Jefferson County (portions), Junction City, Lebanon, Madison, Madison County, Madison County (portions), Marine, Marion County (portions), Maryville, Mascoutah, Millstadt (portions), Monroe County (portions), Moro Twp., Mount Vernon, Nashville, New Baden, Odin, O'Fallon, Okawville, Pontoon Beach, Roxana, Salem, Sandoval, Scott AFB, Shiloh, South Roxana, St. Clair County (portions), St. Jacob, Summerfield, Swansea, Trenton, Troy, Venice, Wamac, Washington County (portions), Waterloo, Wood River & Woodlawn, IL; Affton, Arcadia, Arnold, Audrain County (portions), Ballwin, Bella Villa, Bellerive, Bel-Nor, Bel-Ridge, Benton, Berkeley, Beverly Hills, Bismarck, Black Jack, Bonne Terre, Bourbon, Breckenridge Hills, Brentwood, Bridgeton, Bridgeton Terrace, Callaway County (portions), Calverton Park, Camden County, Camdenton, Cape Girardeau, Cedar Hill, Cedar Hill Lakes, Centralia, Charlack, Charleston, Chesterfield, Clarkson Valley, Clayton, Clinton, Cobalt Village, Columbia, Cool Valley, Cottleville, Country Club Hills, Country Life Acres, Crawford County (portions), Crestwood, Creve Coeur, Crystal City, Crystal Lake Park, Dardenne Prairie, De Soto, Dellwood, Des Peres, Desloge, Doe Run, East Prairie, Edmundson, Eldon, Ellisville, Eureka, Farber, Farmington, Fenton, Ferguson, Festus, Flint Hill, Flordell Hills, Florissant, Fountain N' Lakes, Franklin County (northeastern portion), Franklin County (southwestern portion), Fredericktown, Frontenac, Fulton, Glen Echo Park, Glendale, Grantwood Village, Green Park, Greendale, Hanley Hills, Hannibal, Hazelwood, Henry County, Herculaneum, High Ridge, Hillsboro, Hillsdale, House Springs, Howardville, Huntleigh, Huntsville, Imperial, Iron Mountain Lake, Ironton, Jackson, Jefferson County (portions), Jefferson County (unincorporated areas), Jennings, Johnson County (portions), Junction City, Kelso, Kimmswick, Kingdom City, Kinloch, Kirkwood, Knob Noster, Labadie, Laddonia, Ladue, Lake Ozark, Lake St. Louis, Lakeland, Lakeshire, Lambert, Laurie, Leadington, Leadwood, Lemay, Lilbourn, Lincoln County, Linn Creek, Mackenzie, Manchester, Maplewood, Marlborough, Marston, Martinsburg, Maryland Heights, Mehlville, Mexico, Miller County (portions), Miner, Moberly, Moline Acres, Monroe City, Montgomery City, Morehouse, Morgan County (portions), Moscow Mills, Nameoki, New Florence, New Madrid, New Madrid County (portions), Normandy, Northwoods, Norwood Court, Oakland, Oakville, O'Fallon, Olivette, Olympian Village, Oran, Osage Beach, Overland, Pacific, Pagedale, Palmyra, Paris, Park Hills, Parkway, Pasadena Hills, Pasadena Park, Pettis County (portions), Pevely, Phelps County (portions), Pilot Knob, Pine Lawn, Randolph County (portions), Richmond Heights, Riverview, Rock Hill, Sappington, Scott City, Scott County, Sedalia, Shelbina, Shelby County (portions), Shelbyville, Shrewsbury, Sikeston, Spanish Lake, St. Ann, St. Charles, St. Charles County (portions), St. Clair, St. Francois County (portions), St. George, St. James, St. John, St. Louis County, St. Paul, St. Peters, Steelville, Sullivan, Sunrise Beach, Sunset Hills, Sycamore Hills, Terre du Lac, Times Beach, Town & Country, Troy, Truesdale, Twin Oaks, Union, University City, Uplands Park, Valley Park, Vandiver, Velda City, Velda Village Hills, Villa Ridge, Village of Four Seasons, Vinita Park, Vinita Terrace, Walnut Hills, Warrensburg, Warrenton, Warson Woods, Washington, Webster Groves, Weldon Spring, Wellsville, Wentzville, Westwood, Whiteman AFB, Wilbur Park, Wildwood, Winchester, Woodson Terrace & Wright City, MO. ICA: MO0009.

TV Market Ranking: 11 (Affton, Albers, Alorton, Alton, Arnold, Aviston, Ballwin, Bella Villa, Bellerive, Belleville, Bel-Nor, Bel-Ridge, Berkeley, Bethalto, Beverly Hills, Black Jack, Breckenridge Hills, Brentwood, Bridgeton, Bridgeton Terrace, Cahokia, Calverton Park, Caseyville, Cedar Hill, Cedar Hill Lakes, Centreville, Charlack, Chesterfield, Chouteau Twp., Clarkson Valley, Clayton, Collinsville, Columbia, Cool Valley, Cottage Hills, Cottleville, Country Club Hills, Country Life Acres, Crestwood, Creve Coeur, Crystal City, Crystal Lake Park, Damiansville, Dardenne Prairie, Dellwood, Des Peres, Dupo, East Alton, East St. Louis, Edmundson, Edwardsville, Ellisville, Eureka, Fairview Heights, Fenton, Ferguson, Festus, Flordell Hills, Florissant, Franklin County (northeastern portion), Franklin County (southwestern portion) (portions), Freeburg, Frontenac, Glen Carbon, Glen Echo Park, Glendale, Godfrey, Granite City, Grantwood Village, Green Park, Greendale, Hanley Hills, Hartford, Hazelwood, Herculaneum, High Ridge, Highland, Hillsboro, Hillsdale, House Springs, Huntleigh, Imperial, Jefferson County (portions), Jefferson County (unincorporated areas) (portions), Jennings, Kimmswick, Kinloch, Kirkwood, Labadie, Ladue, Lake St. Louis, Lakeshire, Lebanon, Lemay, Mackenzie, Madison, Madison County (portions), Madison County (portions), Manchester, Maplewood, Marine, Marlborough, Maryland Heights, Maryville, Mascoutah, Mehlville, Millstadt (portions), Moline Acres, Monroe County (portions), Moro Twp., Nameoki, New Baden, Normandy, Northwoods, Norwood Court, Oakland, Oakville, O'Fallon, O'Fallon, Olivette, Olympian Village, Overland, Pacific, Pagedale, Pasadena Hills, Pasadena Park, Pevely, Pine Lawn, Pontoon Beach, Richmond Heights, Riverview, Rock Hill, Roxana, Sappington, Scott AFB, Shiloh, Shrewsbury, South Roxana, Spanish Lake, St. Ann, St. Charles, St. Charles County (portions), St. Clair County (portions), St. George, St. Jacob, St. John, ST. LOUIS, St. Louis County, St. Paul, St. Peters, Summerfield, Sunset Hills, Swansea, Sycamore Hills, Times Beach, Town & Country, Trenton, Troy, Twin Oaks, University City, Uplands Park, Valley Park, Velda City, Velda Village Hills, Venice, Vinita Park, Vinita Terrace, Warson Woods, Waterloo, Webster Groves, Weldon Spring, Westwood, Wilbur Park, Wildwood, Winchester, Wood River, Woodson Terrace); 22 (Johnson County (portions)); 69 (Cape Girardeau, Charleston, Jackson, Jefferson County (portions), Kelso, Lambert, Miner, Morehouse, New Madrid County (portions), Oran, Scott City, Scott County, Sikeston); Below 100 (Addieville, Ashley, Beaucoup, Beckemeyer, Callaway County (portions), Camden County (portions), Central City, Centralia, Centralia, Clinton County (portions), Columbia, Eldon, Farber, Junction City, Kingdom City, Knob Noster, Lakeland, Laurie, Lilbourn, Marion County (portions), Marston, Monroe City, Mount Vernon, Nashville, Odin, Palmyra, Pettis County (portions), Sandoval, Sedalia, Shelbina, Vandiver, Walnut Hills, Wamac, Washington County (portions), Whiteman AFB, Audrain County (portions), Carlyle, Fulton, Hannibal, Mexico, Miller County (portions), Moberly, Morgan County (portions), New Madrid, Randolph County (portions), Salem, Shelby County (portions), Warrensburg, Woodlawn, Madison County (portions), Monroe County (portions), Jefferson County (portions), New Madrid County (portions)); Outside TV Markets (Arcadia, Bismarck, Bonne Terre, Bourbon, Camden County (portions), Camdenton, Cobalt Village, De Soto, Desloge, Doe Run, East Prairie, Flint Hill, Fountain N' Lakes, Fredericktown, Germantown, Henry County, Howardville, Huntsville, Iron Mountain Lake, Ironton, Junction City, Laddonia, Lake Ozark, Leadington, Leadwood, Lincoln County, Linn Creek, Martinsburg, Montgomery City, Moscow Mills, New Florence, Paris, Park Hills, Parkway, Phelps County (portions), Pilot Knob, Shelbyville, St. Clair, St. Francois County (portions), St. James, Steelville, Sunrise Beach, Terre du Lac, Troy, Truesdale, Union, Villa Ridge, Village of Four Seasons, Washington, Wellsville, Wentzville, Wright City, Audrain County (portions), Breese, Clinton, Farmington, Miller County (portions), Morgan County (portions), Okawville, Osage Beach, Randolph County (portions), Shelby County (portions), Sullivan, Warrensburg, Warrenton, Franklin County (southwestern portion) (portions), Jefferson County (portions), Jefferson County (unincorporated areas) (portions), St. Charles County (portions), Johnson County (portions), New Madrid County (portions)). Franchise award date: January 1, 1980. Franchise expiration date: N.A. Began: April 1, 1981.

Channel capacity: 61 (operating 2-way). Channels available but not in use: N.A.

Digital Basic Service
Subscribers: 407,772.
Programming (via satellite): BBC America; Bloomberg Television; Cooking Channel; Discovery Life Channel; DIY Network; ESPN Classic; ESPNews; Fox Sports 2; FSN Digital Atlantic; FSN Digital Central; FSN Digital Pacific; Fuse; FYI; Great American Country; History International; IFC; International Television (ITV); LMN; MC; NFL Network; Nick 2; Nick Jr.; Nicktoons; Outdoor Channel; Showtime (multiplexed); Sundance TV; TeenNick; The Movie Channel (multiplexed); TV One; Weatherscan.
Fee: $49.99 installation; $14.99 monthly.

Digital Expanded Basic Service
Subscribers: N.A.
Programming (via satellite): A&E; AMC; Animal Planet; AXS TV; BET; Bravo; Cartoon Network; CMT; CNBC; CNN; Comedy Central; Discovery Channel; Disney Channel; Disney XD; E! HD; ESPN; ESPN2; Food Network; Fox News Channel; Fox Sports 1; FOX Sports Midwest; Freeform; FX; FXM; Golf Channel; GSN; Hallmark Channel; HGTV; History; HLN; Lifetime; MSNBC;

D-460 TV & Cable Factbook No. 85

Cable Systems—Missouri

MTV; MTV2; National Geographic Channel; NBCSN; Nickelodeon; Oxygen; Spike TV; Syfy; TLC; TNT; Travel Channel; truTV; Turner Classic Movies; TV Land; USA Network; VH1; WE tv.
Fee: $49.99 monthly.
Digital Pay Service 1
Pay Units: N.A.
Programming (via satellite): Cinemax (multiplexed); HBO (multiplexed); Playboy TV; Starz (multiplexed).
Fee: $10.00 installation; $11.75 monthly (each).
Video-On-Demand: Yes
Pay-Per-View
iN DEMAND (delivered digitally); Sports PPV (delivered digitally); ESPN Now (delivered digitally); Playboy TV (delivered digitally); Fresh (delivered digitally); Shorteez (delivered digitally).
Internet Service
Operational: Yes.
Subscribers: 388,771.
Broadband Service: Charter Internet.
Fee: $29.99 monthly; $5.00 modem lease.
Telephone Service
Digital: Operational
Subscribers: 196,818.
Fee: $29.99 monthly
Miles of Plant: 26,689.0 (coaxial); 6,228.0 (fiber optic). Homes passed: 1,396,118.
General Manager: Sean O'Donnell. Marketing Director: Aaron Geisel. Operations Director: Tom Williams. Chief Technician: Rob Burton. Ad Sales Manager: Kevin Shannon. Accounting Director: Steve Lottmann.
Ownership: Charter Communications Inc. (MSO).

ST. LOUIS—Charter Communications. Now served by ST. LOUIS, MO [MO0009]. ICA: MO0002.

ST. LOUIS—Formerly served by Sprint Corp. No longer in operation. ICA: MO0454.

ST. ROBERT—Cable America Corp, 7822 East Gray Rd, Scottsdale, AZ 85260. Phones: 800-338-1808; 573-336-5284. Web Site: http://www.cableamerica.com. Also serves Dixon, Doolittle, Fort Leonard Wood, Houston, Licking, Mountain Grove, Newburg, Pulaski County (portions), Richland, Waynesville & Willow Springs. ICA: MO0023.
TV Market Ranking: Outside TV Markets (Dixon, DOOLITTLE, Fort Leonard Wood, Houston, Licking, Mountain Grove, Newburg, Pulaski County (portions), Richland, ST. ROBERT, Waynesville, Willow Springs). Franchise award date: September 18, 1999. Franchise expiration date: N.A. Began: December 1, 1984.
Channel capacity: N.A. Channels available but not in use: N.A.
Basic Service
Subscribers: 3,817.
Programming (received off-air): KOLR (CBS) Springfield; KOZK (PBS) Springfield; KOZL-TV (IND) Springfield; KRCG (CBS) Jefferson City; KSPR (ABC) Springfield; KWBM (Retro TV) Harrison; KYCW-LD (CW) Springfield; KYTV (CW, NBC, WeatherNation) Springfield; allband FM.
Programming (via satellite): Pop; WGN America.
Fee: $9.95 installation; $22.99 monthly.
Expanded Basic Service 1
Subscribers: N.A.
Programming (via satellite): A&E; AMC; Animal Planet; BET; Bravo; Cartoon Network; CMT; CNBC; CNN; Comedy Central; C-SPAN; C-SPAN 2; Discovery Channel; Disney Channel; E! HD; ESPN; ESPN Classic; ESPN2; Food Network; Fox News Channel; FOX Sports Midwest; Freeform; FX; Great American Country; Hallmark Channel; HGTV; History; HLN; Lifetime; MSNBC; MTV; NFL Network; Nickelodeon; Spike TV; Syfy; TBS; The Weather Channel; TLC; TNT; Travel Channel; Trinity Broadcasting Network (TBN); truTV; TV Land; Univision Studios; USA Network; VH1.
Fee: $27.70 monthly.
Digital Basic Service
Subscribers: 3,675.
Programming (via satellite): BBC America; Bloomberg Television; CMT; Destination America; Discovery Kids Channel; Discovery Life Channel; Disney XD; ESPN2; ESPNews; ESPNU; Fox Sports 1; Fuse; FXM; FYI; Golf Channel; GSN; History International; IFC; Investigation Discovery; LMN; MC; MTV Classic; MTV2; Nick Jr.; Nicktoons; Outdoor Channel; OWN; Oprah Winfrey Network; Science Channel; Starz Encore (multiplexed); TeenNick; Trinity Broadcasting Network (TBN); Turner Classic Movies.
Fee: $12.00 monthly.
Digital Expanded Basic Service
Subscribers: N.A.
Programming (via satellite): AXS TV; Bravo HD; CNBC HD+; Discovery Channel HD; ESPN HD; ESPN2 HD; Syfy HD; TBS HD; TNT HD; Universal HD; USA Network HD.
Fee: $6.95 monthly.
Digital Pay Service 1
Pay Units: N.A.
Programming (via satellite): Cinemax (multiplexed); Cinemax HD; Flix; HBO (multiplexed); HBO HD; Showtime (multiplexed); Showtime HD; Starz (multiplexed); Starz HD; Sundance TV; The Movie Channel (multiplexed).
Fee: $11.95 monthly (Cinemax, HBO, Showtime/TMC/Flix/Sundance or Starz/Encore).
Video-On-Demand: No
Pay-Per-View
Hot Choice.
Internet Service
Operational: Yes.
Subscribers: 5,155.
Broadband Service: CableAmerica.
Fee: $14.95 installation; $40.95 monthly; $9.95 modem lease; $199.00 modem purchase.
Telephone Service
Digital: Operational
Subscribers: 823.
Miles of Plant: 543.0 (coaxial); 232.0 (fiber optic). Homes passed: 20,738.
Vice President, Engineering: Alan Jackson. General Manager: Debra Mefford. Chief Technician: James Grove. Controller: Walter G. Farak. Marketing Director: John Mori.
Ownership: CableAmerica Corp. (MSO).

ST. THOMAS—Formerly served by First Cable of Missouri Inc. No longer in operation. ICA: MO0365.

STANBERRY—Formerly served by Longview Communications. No longer in operation. ICA: MO0173.

STE. GENEVIEVE—Formerly served by Charter Communications. No longer in operation. ICA: MO0091.

STE. GENEVIEVE—Formerly served by Charter Communications. No longer in operation. ICA: MO0422.

STEELE—NewWave Communications. Now served by DEXTER, MO [MO0039]. ICA: MO0135.

STEELVILLE—Charter Communications. Now served by ST. LOUIS, MO [MO0009]. ICA: MO0151.

STOCKTON—Windstream, 4001 Rodney Parham Rd, Little Rock, AR 72212. Phones: 877-759-9020; 866-971-9463; 501-748-7000. Fax: 501-748-6392. E-mail: support@windstream.net. Web Site: http://www.windstream.com. ICA: MO0166.
TV Market Ranking: Outside TV Markets (STOCKTON). Franchise award date: November 9, 1981. Franchise expiration date: N.A. Began: September 1, 1982.
Channel capacity: N.A. Channels available but not in use: N.A.
Basic Service
Subscribers: 212.
Programming (received off-air): KOLR (CBS) Springfield; KOZK (PBS) Springfield; KSPR (ABC) Springfield; KWBM (Retro TV) Harrison; KYTV (CW, NBC, WeatherNation) Springfield.
Programming (via satellite): A&E; Animal Planet; CMT; CNN; Discovery Channel; Disney Channel; ESPN; ESPN2; Fox News Channel; Fox Sports 1; FOX Sports Midwest; Freeform; FX; FXM; HGTV; History; HLN; Lifetime; National Geographic Channel; Nickelodeon; QVC; Spike TV; TBS; The Weather Channel; TLC; TNT; Trinity Broadcasting Network (TBN); Turner Classic Movies; USA Network; WGN America.
Fee: $50.00 monthly.
Pay Service 1
Pay Units: 62.
Programming (via satellite): HBO.
Fee: $12.95 monthly.
Video-On-Demand: No
Internet Service
Operational: Yes.
Telephone Service
Digital: Operational
Miles of Plant: 25.0 (coaxial); None (fiber optic). Homes passed: 1,000.
President & Chief Executive Officer: Tony Thomas. Chief Financial Officer & Treasurer: Bob Gunderman. Executive Vice President, Operations: Mark Farris. Executive Vice President, Engineering & Chief Technology Officer: Randy Nicklas.
Ownership: Windstream Communications Inc. (MSO).

STOTTS CITY—Formerly served by Cebridge Connections. No longer in operation. ICA: MO0367.

STOVER—Formerly served by Provincial Cable & Data. No longer in operation. ICA: MO0226.

STRAFFORD—Mediacom. Now served by SEYMOUR, MO [MO0172]. ICA: MO0222.

STURGEON—Provincial Cable & Data, 123A West Main St, Odessa, MO 64076. Phones: 866-284-3346 (Customer service); 816-633-1626. E-mail: customercare@provincial-cable.net. Web Site: http://www.provincialcable.com. Also serves Clark & Hallsville. ICA: MO0395.
TV Market Ranking: Below 100 (Clark, STURGEON, Hallsville). Franchise award date: N.A. Franchise expiration date: N.A. Began: September 1, 1984.
Channel capacity: N.A. Channels available but not in use: N.A.
Basic Service
Subscribers: 46.
Programming (received off-air): KMIZ (ABC, MeTV, MNT) Columbia; KMOS-TV (PBS) Sedalia; KNLJ (Christian TV Network) Jefferson City; KOMU-TV (CW, NBC) Columbia; KRCG (CBS) Jefferson City.
Programming (via satellite): A&E; AMC; Animal Planet; Cartoon Network; CNN; C-SPAN; Discovery Channel; Disney Channel; Disney XD; ESPN; ESPN2; Fox News Channel; Freeform; Fuse; FX; HLN; Lifetime; MSNBC; Outdoor Channel; QVC; TBS; The Weather Channel; TLC; TNT; USA Network; WGN America.
Fee: $37.45 monthly.
Pay Service 1
Pay Units: N.A.
Programming (via satellite): Cinemax; HBO; Showtime; The Movie Channel.
Fee: $9.95 monthly (Showtime or TMC), $10.95 monthly (Cinemax), $14.95 monthly (HBO).
Video-On-Demand: No
Internet Service
Operational: Yes.
Fee: $49.95 installation; $24.95-$44.95 monthly.
Telephone Service
None
Miles of Plant: 12.0 (coaxial); None (fiber optic). Homes passed: 428.
General Manager: Perry Scarborough. Office Manager: Misti Runyan.
Ownership: Provincial Cable & Data (MSO).

SULLIVAN—Charter Communications. Now served by ST. LOUIS, MO [MO0009]. ICA: MO0030.

SULLIVAN—Charter Communications. Now served by SULLIVAN (formerly WASHINGTON), MO [MO0030]. ICA: MO0072.

SULLIVAN—Fidelity Communications. Now served by PHELPS COUNTY (portions), MO [MO0475]. ICA: MO0042.

SUMMERSVILLE—Formerly served by Almega Cable. No longer in operation. ICA: MO0259.

SYRACUSE—Formerly served by First Cable of Missouri Inc. No longer in operation. ICA: MO0374.

TAOS—Formerly served by Longview Communications. No longer in operation. ICA: MO0270.

Missouri—Cable Systems

TERRE DU LAC—Charter Communications. Now served by ST. LOUIS, MO [MO0009]. ICA: MO0194.

THAYER—Fidelity Communications, 64 North Clark St, Sullivan, MO 63080. Phones: 417-256-5245 (West Plains office); 573-468-8081; 800-392-8070. Fax: 573-468-5440. E-mail: custserv@fidelitycommunications.com. Web Site: http://www.fidelitycommunications.com. Also serves Fulton County (portions) & Mammoth Spring. ICA: MO0423.
TV Market Ranking: Outside TV Markets (Fulton County (portions), Mammoth Spring, THAYER). Franchise award date: N.A. Franchise expiration date: N.A. Began: July 1, 1959.
Channel capacity: N.A. Channels available but not in use: N.A.
Basic Service
Subscribers: 267. Commercial subscribers: 103.
Programming (received off-air): KAIT (ABC, NBC) Jonesboro; KOLR (CBS) Springfield; KOZK (PBS) Springfield; KOZL-TV (IND) Springfield; KSPR (ABC) Springfield; KXNW (Antenna TV, MNT) Eureka Springs; KYTV (CW, NBC, WeatherNation) Springfield.
Programming (via satellite): C-SPAN; QVC; Trinity Broadcasting Network (TBN); WGN America.
Fee: $29.99 installation; $28.99 monthly; $3.45 converter.
Expanded Basic Service 1
Subscribers: N.A.
Programming (via satellite): A&E; AMC; Comedy Central; Lifetime; MTV; Syfy; TBS; TLC; Travel Channel; USA Network; VH1.
Video-On-Demand: No
Pay-Per-View
iN DEMAND.
Internet Service
Operational: Yes.
Fee: $54.99-$99.99 monthly.
Telephone Service
None
Miles of Plant: 50.0 (coaxial); None (fiber optic). Homes passed: 2,093.
General Manager, Missouri: Don Knight. Video Product Manager: Loren King.
Ownership: Fidelity Communications Co. (MSO).

TINA—Green Hills Communications. This cable system has converted to IPTV. Now served by AVALON, MO [MO5156]. ICA: MO0375.

TIPTON—Formerly served by Charter Communications. No longer in operation. ICA: MO0141.

TIPTON—Formerly served by Crystal Broadband Networks. No longer in operation. ICA: MO0474.

TRENTON—Suddenlink Communications, 520 Maryville Centre Dr, Ste 300, St. Louis, MO 63141. Phones: 660-359-2677; 314-315-9400. Web Site: http://www.suddenlink.com. Also serves Grundy County (portions). ICA: MO0064.
TV Market Ranking: Outside TV Markets (Grundy County (portions), TRENTON). Franchise award date: January 1, 1957. Franchise expiration date: N.A. Began: January 1, 1965.
Channel capacity: 61 (operating 2-way). Channels available but not in use: N.A.

Basic Service
Subscribers: 776. Commercial subscribers: 106.
Programming (received off-air): KCPT (PBS) Kansas City; KCTV (CBS) Kansas City; KMBC-TV (ABC, MeTV) Kansas City; KQTV (ABC) St. Joseph; KSHB-TV (COZI TV, Grit, NBC) Kansas City; KSMO-TV (Bounce TV, MNT) Kansas City; WDAF-TV (Antenna TV, FOX) Kansas City.
Programming (via satellite): C-SPAN; Pop; QVC; Trinity Broadcasting Network (TBN).
Fee: $28.45 monthly.
Expanded Basic Service 1
Subscribers: N.A.
Programming (via satellite): A&E; AMC; Animal Planet; BET; Bravo; Cartoon Network; CNBC; CNN; Comedy Central; Discovery Channel; Disney Channel; E! HD; ESPN; ESPN2; Food Network; Fox News Channel; FOX Sports Midwest; Freeform; FX; Great American Country; Hallmark Channel; HGTV; History; HLN; Lifetime; MSNBC; MTV; National Geographic Channel; Nickelodeon; Spike TV; Syfy; TBS; The Weather Channel; TLC; TNT; Travel Channel; Turner Classic Movies; TV Land; USA Network; VH1.
Fee: $24.00 monthly.
Digital Basic Service
Subscribers: N.A.
Programming (via satellite): BBC America; Bloomberg Television; Cloo; Discovery Digital Networks; Disney XD; DMX Music; ESPN Classic; ESPNews; Fox Sports 1; Fuse; FYI; Golf Channel; GSN; History; History International; IFC; NBCSN; Outdoor Channel; WE tv.
Pay Service 1
Pay Units: N.A.
Programming (via satellite): Cinemax; HBO; Showtime; The Movie Channel.
Fee: $10.95 monthly (Showtime or TMC), $13.95 monthly (Cinemax or HBO).
Digital Pay Service 1
Pay Units: N.A.
Programming (via satellite): Cinemax (multiplexed); HBO (multiplexed); Showtime (multiplexed); Starz; Starz Encore (multiplexed); The Movie Channel (multiplexed).
Video-On-Demand: No
Pay-Per-View
iN DEMAND (delivered digitally); Playboy TV (delivered digitally); Fresh (delivered digitally).
Internet Service
Operational: Yes. Began: June 2, 2006.
Broadband Service: Cebridge High Speed Cable Internet.
Fee: $29.95 monthly.
Telephone Service
Digital: Operational
Miles of Plant: 51.0 (coaxial); None (fiber optic). Homes passed: 2,996.
Vice President, Corporate Finance: Michael Pflantz. Regional Manager: Todd Cruthird.
Ownership: Cequel Communications Holdings I LLC (MSO).

TRIMBLE—Formerly served by Time Warner Cable. No longer in operation. ICA: MO0424.

TROY—Charter Communications. Now served by ST. LOUIS, MO [MO0009]. ICA: MO0100.

UNIONVILLE—Unionville Missouri CATV, 1611 Grant St, PO Box 255, Unionville, MO 63565. Phone: 660-947-3818. Fax: 660-947-7756. Web Site: http://www.unionvillemo.org. ICA: MO0120.
TV Market Ranking: Below 100 (UNIONVILLE). Franchise award date: N.A. Franchise expiration date: N.A. Began: September 1, 1980.
Channel capacity: N.A. Channels available but not in use: N.A.
Basic Service
Subscribers: 750.
Programming (received off-air): KCCI (CBS, MeTV) Des Moines; KDIN-TV (PBS) Des Moines; KTVO (ABC) Kirksville; KYOU-TV (FOX) Ottumwa; WHO-DT (Antenna TV, NBC) Des Moines; WOI-DT (ABC) Ames; allband FM.
Programming (via satellite): A&E; Cartoon Network; CMT; CNN; Discovery Channel; Disney Channel; ESPN; ESPN2; Fox News Channel; FOX Sports Midwest; Freeform; Great American Country; HGTV; History; Lifetime; LMN; MTV; Nickelodeon; Outdoor Channel; QVC; Spike TV; Syfy; TBS; The Weather Channel; TLC; TNT; Trinity Broadcasting Network (TBN); Turner Classic Movies; TV Land; USA Network; VH1; WGN America.
Fee: $15.00 installation; $27.50 monthly; $10.00 converter.
Pay Service 1
Pay Units: N.A.
Programming (via satellite): Cinemax; Showtime; The Movie Channel.
Fee: $15.00 installation; $7.50 monthly (each).
Video-On-Demand: No
Internet Service
Operational: No.
Telephone Service
None
Miles of Plant: 28.0 (coaxial); None (fiber optic). Homes passed: 1,200.
General Manager: Doug Hurley. Cable Clerk: Melinda Haines.
Ownership: City of Unionville Cable TV.

URBANA—Formerly served by Cebridge Connections. No longer in operation. ICA: MO0380.

URICH—Formerly served by CableDirect. No longer in operation. ICA: MO0276.

UTICA (village)—Formerly served by Green Hills Communications Inc. No longer in operation. ICA: MO0448.

VAN BUREN—Boycom Cablevision Inc, 3467 Township Line Rd, Poplar Bluff, MO 63901. Phones: 800-890-6620; 573-686-9101. Fax: 573-686-4722. Web Site: http://www.boycom.com. ICA: MO0165.
TV Market Ranking: Outside TV Markets (VAN BUREN). Franchise award date: February 5, 1987. Franchise expiration date: N.A. Began: N.A.
Channel capacity: N.A. Channels available but not in use: N.A.
Basic Service
Subscribers: N.A.
Programming (received off-air): KAIT (ABC, NBC) Jonesboro; KBSI (FOX) Cape Girardeau; KFVS-TV (CBS, CW, MeTV) Cape Girardeau; KTEJ (PBS) Jonesboro; KYTV (CW, NBC, WeatherNation) Springfield; WNBC (COZI TV, NBC) New York.
Programming (via satellite): C-SPAN; The Weather Channel; Trinity Broadcasting Network (TBN); WGN America.
Fee: $29.95 installation; $19.95 monthly.
Expanded Basic Service 1
Subscribers: N.A.
Programming (via satellite): A&E; AMC; CNN; Discovery Channel; Disney Channel; Disney XD; ESPN; ESPN2; FOX Sports Midwest; Freeform; Great American Country; HGTV; History; Lifetime; MTV; National Geographic Channel; Nickelodeon; Spike TV; TBS; TNT; TV Land; USA Network; VH1.
Fee: $20.00 monthly.
Pay Service 1
Pay Units: N.A.
Programming (via satellite): Cinemax; HBO; Showtime; The Movie Channel.
Fee: $9.49 monthly (Cinemax), $13.49 monthly (HBO, Showtime, or TMC).
Video-On-Demand: No
Internet Service
Operational: Yes.
Telephone Service
None
Miles of Plant: 25.0 (coaxial); None (fiber optic). Homes passed: 717.
President: Steven Boyers. General Manager: Shelly Batton. Chief Technician: Phil Huett.
Ownership: Boycom Cablevision Inc. (MSO).

VANDALIA—Formerly served by Crystal Broadband Networks. No longer in operation. ICA: MO0114.

VERSAILLES—Formerly served by Crystal Broadband Networks. No longer in operation. ICA: MO0132.

VIBURNUM—Formerly served by Crystal Broadband Networks. No longer in operation. ICA: MO0243.

VIENNA—Formerly served by Longview Communications. No longer in operation. ICA: MO0317.

VILLA RIDGE—Charter Communications. Now served by ST. LOUIS, MO [MO0009]. ICA: MO0401.

WAPPAPELLO—Boycom Cablevision Inc, 3467 Township Line Rd, Poplar Bluff, MO 63901. Phones: 800-890-6620; 573-686-9101. Fax: 573-686-4722. Web Site: http://www.boycom.com. Also serves Butler County (northern portion) & Wayne County (southern portion). ICA: MO0332.
TV Market Ranking: Below 100 (Butler County (northern portion), WAPPAPELLO, Wayne County (southern portion)).
Channel capacity: N.A. Channels available but not in use: N.A.
Basic Service
Subscribers: N.A.
Programming (received off-air): KAIT (ABC, NBC) Jonesboro; KBSI (FOX) Cape Girardeau; KFVS-TV (CBS, CW, MeTV) Cape Girardeau; KPOB-TV (ABC) Poplar Bluff; KTEJ (PBS) Jonesboro; WPSD-TV (Antenna TV, NBC) Paducah; WRBU (ION) East St. Louis.
Programming (via satellite): A&E; AMC; Animal Planet; Cartoon Network; CNBC; CNN; C-SPAN; Discovery Channel; Disney Channel; ESPN; ESPN2; Fox News Channel; FOX Sports Midwest; Freeform; Fuse; Golf Channel; Great American Country; Hallmark Channel; HGTV; History; HLN; Lifetime; Nickelodeon; Outdoor Channel; QVC; Spike TV; Syfy; TBS; The Weather Channel; TLC; TNT; Travel Channel; Trinity Broadcasting Network (TBN); TV Land; USA Network; WGN America.
Fee: $38.75 monthly.
Pay Service 1
Pay Units: N.A.
Programming (via satellite): Cinemax; HBO.
Fee: $10.00 monthly (each).
Video-On-Demand: No
Internet Service
Operational: Yes.

Cable Systems—Missouri

Telephone Service
None
Miles of Plant: 6.0 (coaxial); None (fiber optic).
President: Steven Boyers. General Manager: Shelly Batton. Chief Technician: Phil Huett. Ownership: Boycom Cablevision Inc. (MSO).

WARDELL—Formerly served by Almega Cable. No longer in operation. ICA: MO0228.

WARRENSBURG—Charter Communications. Now served by ST. LOUIS, MO [MO0009]. ICA: MO0425.

WARRENTON—Charter Communications. Now served by ST. LOUIS, MO [MO0009]. ICA: MO0065.

WARSAW—Formerly served by Crystal Broadband Networks. No longer in operation. ICA: MO0426.

WELLSTON—Formerly served by Data Cablevision. No longer in operation. ICA: MO0121.

WEST PLAINS—Fidelity Communications, 64 North Clark St, Sullivan, MO 63080. Phones: 417-256-5245 (West Plains office); 573-468-8081; 800-392-8070. Fax: 573-468-5440. E-mail: custserv@fidelitycommunications.com. Web Site: http://www.fidelitycommunications.com. Also serves Howell County (portions). ICA: MO0044.

TV Market Ranking: Outside TV Markets (Howell County (portions), WEST PLAINS). Franchise award date: N.A. Franchise expiration date: N.A. Began: October 1, 1956.
Channel capacity: N.A. Channels available but not in use: N.A.
Basic Service
Subscribers: 1,004. Commercial subscribers: 250.
Programming (received off-air): K38HE-D West Plains; KAIT (ABC, NBC) Jonesboro; KKYK-CD (IND, WeatherNation) Little Rock; KOLR (CBS) Springfield; KOZK (PBS) Springfield; KOZL-TV (IND) Springfield; KSPR (ABC) Springfield; KWBM (Retro TV) Harrison; KYCW-LD (CW) Springfield; KYTV (CW, NBC, WeatherNation) Springfield.
Programming (via satellite): C-SPAN; QVC; The Weather Channel; Trinity Broadcasting Network (TBN); WGN America.
Fee: $29.99 installation; $28.99 monthly.
Digital Basic Service
Subscribers: N.A.
Programming (via satellite): BBC America; Bloomberg Television; CMT; Disney XD; DIY Network; ESPN Classic; ESPNews; FYI; GSN; History International; IFC; Investigation Discovery; LMN; MC; Nick 2; Nick Jr.; Nicktoons; Sundance TV; TeenNick; WE tv.
Digital Pay Service 1
Pay Units: N.A.
Programming (via satellite): Cinemax (multiplexed); Flix; HBO (multiplexed); LOGO; Showtime (multiplexed); Starz (multiplexed); Starz Encore; The Movie Channel (multiplexed).

Fee: $10.95 monthly (each).
Video-On-Demand: Yes
Pay-Per-View
iN Demand (delivered digitally); SexSee (delivered digitally).
Internet Service
Operational: Yes.
Fee: $54.99-$99.99 monthly.
Telephone Service
Digital: Operational
Fee: $29.99 monthly
Miles of Plant: 125.0 (coaxial); None (fiber optic). Homes passed: 5,699.
General Manager, Missouri: Don Knight. Video Product Manager: Loren King. Ownership: Fidelity Communications Co. (MSO).

WESTBORO—Formerly served by CableDirect. No longer in operation. ICA: MO0427.

WESTPHALIA—Formerly served by CableDirect. No longer in operation. ICA: MO0340.

WHEELING—Formerly served by Longview Communications. No longer in operation. ICA: MO0436.

WILLIAMSVILLE—Formerly served by Almega Cable. No longer in operation. ICA: MO0267.

WILLOW SPRINGS—Formerly served by Almega Cable. Now served by Cable America Corp., ST. ROBERT, MO [MO0023]. ICA: MO0154.

WILSON BEND—Formerly served by Almega Cable. No longer in operation. ICA: MO0220.

WINDSOR—Formerly served by Crystal Broadband Networks. No longer in operation. ICA: MO0119.

WINFIELD—Formerly served by Charter Communications. No longer in operation. ICA: MO0115.

WINONA—Formerly served by Boycom Cablevision Inc. No longer in operation. ICA: MO0207.

WYACONDA—Formerly served by CableDirect. No longer in operation. ICA: MO0428.

MONTANA

Total Systems: 63	Communities with Applications: 0
Total Communities Served: 128	Number of Basic Subscribers: 124,500
Franchises Not Yet Operating: 0	Number of Expanded Basic Subscribers: 45,221
Applications Pending: 0	Number of Pay Units: 1,200

Top 100 Markets Represented: N.A.

For a list of cable communities in this section, see the Cable Community Index located in the back of Cable Volume 2.
For explanation of terms used in cable system listings, see p. D-11.

ABSAROKEE—Formerly served by USA Communications. No longer in operation. ICA: MT0079.

ALBERTON—Formerly served by Optimum. No longer in operation. ICA: MT0100.

ANACONDA—Charter Communications, 12405 Powerscourt Dr, St. Louis, MO 63131. Phones: 636-207-5100 (Corporate office); 406-782-1616; 877-273-7626 (Customer service). Web Site: http://www.charter.com. Also serves Deer Lodge County. ICA: MT0014.
TV Market Ranking: Below 100 (ANACONDA, Deer Lodge County (portions)); Outside TV Markets (Deer Lodge County (portions)). Franchise award date: N.A. Franchise expiration date: N.A. Began: September 1, 1962.
Channel capacity: N.A. Channels available but not in use: N.A.

Digital Basic Service
Subscribers: 1,464.
Programming (via satellite): A&E HD; Animal Planet HD; BBC America; Bloomberg Television; Bravo; CBS Sports Network; CMT; Cooking Channel; Destination America; Discovery Channel HD; Discovery Kids Channel; Discovery Life Channel; Disney Channel HD; Disney XD; DIY Network; DMX Music; ESPN Classic; ESPN HD; ESPNews; Food Network HD; FOX College Sports Central; FOX College Sports Pacific; Fox Sports 1; Freeform HD; Fuse; FXM; FYI; Golf Channel; GSN; HD Theater; HGTV HD; History HD; History International; HorseTV Channel; IFC; Investigation Discovery; ION Television; LMN; MTV Classic; MTV Hits; MTV Jams; MTV2; Nat Geo WILD; National Geographic Channel; National Geographic Channel HD; NBCSN; NFL Network; Nick 2; Nick Jr.; Nicktoons; Outdoor Channel; OWN: Oprah Winfrey Network; RFD-TV; Science Channel; Science HD; Sprout; Syfy HD; TeenNick; Tr3s; Trinity Broadcasting Network (TBN); Universal HD; UP; USA Network HD; VH1 Soul.
Fee: $26.99 monthly.

Digital Expanded Basic Service
Subscribers: N.A.
Programming (via satellite): A&E; AMC; Animal Planet; Cartoon Network; CMT; CNBC; CNN; Comedy Central; Discovery Channel; Disney Channel; E! HD; ESPN; ESPN2; Food Network; Fox News Channel; Freeform; FX; Hallmark Channel; HGTV; History; HLN; INSP; ION Television; MSNBC; MTV; Nickelodeon; Oxygen; Root Sports Rocky Mountain; Spike TV; Syfy; The Weather Channel; TLC; TNT; Travel Channel; truTV; Turner Classic Movies; TV Land; USA Network; VH1.
Fee: $28.99 monthly.

Digital Pay Service 1
Pay Units: N.A.
Programming (via satellite): Cinemax (multiplexed); Flix; HBO (multiplexed); HBO HD; Showtime (multiplexed); Starz (multiplexed); Starz Encore (multiplexed); Starz HD; The Movie Channel (multiplexed).

Video-On-Demand: No

Pay-Per-View
iN DEMAND (delivered digitally).

Internet Service
Operational: Yes.
Broadband Service: Charter Internet.
Fee: $39.95 monthly; $3.00 modem lease.

Telephone Service
Digital: Operational
Fee: $49.99 monthly
Miles of Plant: 34.0 (coaxial); 5.0 (fiber optic). Homes passed: 4,007.
Accounting Director: David Sovanski. President & Chief Executive Officer: Tom Rutledge. General Manager: Mike Oswald. Chief Technician: Todd Hawke.
Ownership: Charter Communications Inc. (MSO).

ARLEE—Formerly served by Bresnan Communications. No longer in operation. ICA: MT0092.

BAKER—Mid-Rivers Communications, 904 C Ave, PO Box 280, Circle, MT 59215. Phones: 406-535-3336; 406-485-3301. Fax: 406-485-2924. E-mail: customerservices@midrivers.coop. Web Site: http://www.midrivers.com. Also serves Ekalaka. ICA: MT0041.
TV Market Ranking: Outside TV Markets (BAKER, Ekalaka). Franchise award date: September 1, 1976. Franchise expiration date: N.A. Began: November 1, 1977.
Channel capacity: N.A. Channels available but not in use: N.A.

Basic Service
Subscribers: 552. Commercial subscribers: 6.
Programming (received off-air): KHME (MeTV, This TV) Rapid City; KOTA-TV (ABC, FOX) Rapid City.
Programming (via microwave): KQCD-TV (FOX, NBC) Dickinson; KUSM-TV (PBS) Bozeman; KXGN-TV (CBS, NBC) Glendive; KXMA-TV (CBS) Dickinson.
Programming (via satellite): A&E; AMC; Animal Planet; Bloomberg Television; Cartoon Network; CMT; CNN; C-SPAN; CW PLUS; Discovery Channel; Disney Channel; E! HD; ESPN; ESPN2; EWTN Global Catholic Network; Food Network; Fox News Channel; Fox Sports 1; Freeform; FX; Great American Country; Hallmark Channel; HGTV; History; HLN; ION Television; KMGH-TV (ABC, Azteca America) Denver; KUSA (NBC, WeatherNation) Denver; Lifetime; MSNBC; MTV; National Geographic Channel; Nickelodeon; Outdoor Channel; RFD-TV; Spike TV; Syfy; TBS; The Weather Channel; TNT; Travel Channel; Trinity Broadcasting Network (TBN); truTV; Turner Classic Movies; TV Land; USA Network; VH1; WE tv; WGN America.
Fee: $49.95 installation; $28.15 monthly.

Digital Basic Service
Subscribers: N.A.
Programming (via satellite): BBC America; Bravo; CMT; Destination America; Discovery Kids Channel; Disney XD; ESPN Classic; ESPN2; ESPNews; Golf Channel; GSN; HGTV; History; IFC; Investigation Discovery; MTV Classic; National Geographic Channel; NBCSN; Nick Jr.; OWN: Oprah Winfrey Network; Science Channel; Syfy; Turner Classic Movies; WE tv.

Pay Service 1
Pay Units: 138.
Programming (via satellite): Cinemax; HBO.
Fee: $12.00 monthly.

Digital Pay Service 1
Pay Units: N.A.
Programming (via satellite): Cinemax (multiplexed); HBO (multiplexed); Showtime (multiplexed); Starz (multiplexed); Starz Encore (multiplexed); The Movie Channel (multiplexed).

Internet Service
Operational: No, DSL.
Subscribers: 346.

Telephone Service
Analog: Operational
Miles of Plant: 31.0 (coaxial); 155.0 (fiber optic). Homes passed: 996.
President: Mark Robbins. General Manager: Bill Wade. Chief Technician: Mike Sokoloski. Customer Service Manager: Deb Wagner.
Ownership: Mid-Rivers Telephone Cooperative Inc. (MSO).

BELFRY—Formerly served by Belfry Cable TV. No longer in operation. ICA: MT0106.

BELT—Formerly served by KLiP Interactive. No longer in operation. ICA: MT0073.

BIG FLAT—Formerly served by Bresnan Communications. No longer in operation. ICA: MT0093.

BIG SKY—Bulldog Cable, 455 Gees Mill Business Ct, Conyers, GA 30013. Phones: 706-997-9003; 800-388-6577. Web Site: http://www.bulldogcable.com. Also serves Big Sky Resort. ICA: MT0033.
TV Market Ranking: Below 100 (BIG SKY). Franchise award date: N.A. Franchise expiration date: N.A. Began: October 1, 1981.
Channel capacity: N.A. Channels available but not in use: N.A.

Basic Service
Subscribers: 134.
Programming (received off-air): KTVM-TV (MeTV, Movies!, NBC, This TV) Butte; KUSM-TV (PBS) Bozeman; KXLF-TV (CBS, CW, Grit) Butte.
Programming (via satellite): A&E; AMC; Animal Planet; CMT; CNBC; CNN; Comedy Central; Discovery Channel; Disney Channel; E! HD; ESPN; ESPN2; Fox News Channel; Freeform; FX; Golf Channel; History; HLN; KCNC-TV (CBS, Decades) Denver; KDVR (Antenna TV, FOX) Denver; KTVX (ABC, MeTV) Salt Lake City; KWGN-TV (CW, This TV) Denver; Lifetime; National Geographic Channel; NBCSN; Outdoor Channel; Pop; QVC; Root Sports Rocky Mountain; Spike TV; TBS; The Weather Channel; TLC; TNT; truTV; TV Land; USA Network; WGN America.
Fee: $44.95 installation; $46.00 monthly.

Pay Service 1
Pay Units: N.A.
Programming (via satellite): HBO; Showtime.
Fee: $12.00 monthly (each).

Video-On-Demand: No

Internet Service
Operational: No.

Telephone Service
None
Miles of Plant: 12.0 (coaxial); None (fiber optic). Homes passed: 859.
President: Mark Wilson. General Manager East: Mark Miller. General Manager West: Vance Johnson. Controller: Ashley Hull.
Ownership: Bulldog Cable (MSO).

BIG TIMBER—Charter Communications, 12405 Powerscourt Dr, St. Louis, MO 63131. Phones: 636-207-5100 (Corporate office); 877-273-7626. Web Site: http://www.charter.com. ICA: MT0042.
TV Market Ranking: Outside TV Markets (BIG TIMBER). Franchise award date: N.A. Franchise expiration date: N.A. Began: November 1, 1954.
Channel capacity: N.A. Channels available but not in use: N.A.

Digital Basic Service
Subscribers: 385.
Programming (via satellite): BBC America; Bloomberg Television; Cloo; CMT; Destination America; Discovery Kids Channel; Discovery Life Channel; DMX Music; ESPN Classic; ESPN2; ESPNews; EVINE Live; FOX College Sports Central; FOX College Sports Pacific; Fox Sports 1; FXM; FYI; Golf Channel; GSN; History; History International; Investigation Discovery; LMN; MTV Classic; MTV Hits; MTV2; National Geographic Channel; NBCSN; Nick Jr.; Outdoor Channel; Ovation; OWN: Oprah Winfrey Network; Science Channel; TeenNick; Trinity Broadcasting Network (TBN); VH1 Soul; WE tv.
Fee: $26.99 monthly.

Cable Systems—Montana

Digital Expanded Basic Service
Subscribers: N.A.
Programming (via satellite): A&E; Altitude Sports & Entertainment; AMC; Animal Planet; CMT; CNBC; CNN; Comedy Central; Discovery Channel; Discovery Life Channel; E! HD; ESPN; ESPN Classic; ESPN2; ESPNews; Food Network; FOX Sports Networks; FX; Golf Channel; Great American Country; Hallmark Channel; HGTV; History; HLN; Lifetime; MSNBC; MTV; National Geographic Channel; NBCSN; Nickelodeon; OWN: Oprah Winfrey Network; Spike TV; Syfy; TLC; TNT; Travel Channel; TV Land; USA Network; VH1; WE tv.
Fee: $18.04 monthly.

Digital Pay Service 1
Pay Units: N.A.
Programming (via satellite): Cinemax (multiplexed); HBO (multiplexed); Showtime (multiplexed); Starz (multiplexed); Starz Encore (multiplexed); The Movie Channel (multiplexed).
Fee: $13.00 monthly (Cinemax, HBO, Showtime/TMC/Flix or Starz/Encore).

Video-On-Demand: No

Pay-Per-View
iN DEMAND (delivered digitally); Hot Choice (delivered digitally); Playboy TV (delivered digitally); Fresh (delivered digitally); Shorteez (delivered digitally); Club Jenna (delivered digitally).

Internet Service
Operational: Yes.
Broadband Service: Charter Internet.
Fee: $35.95 monthly.

Telephone Service
None
Miles of Plant: 13.0 (coaxial); None (fiber optic). Homes passed: 750.
President & Chief Executive Officer: Tom Rutledge. Programming Director: E. McRae Budill. Accounting Director: David Sovanski.
Ownership: Charter Communications Inc. (MSO).

BILLINGS—Charter Communications, 12405 Powerscourt Dr, St. Louis, MO 63131. Phones: 636-207-5100 (Corporate office); 406-238-7700; 877-273-7626. Fax: 406-238-7777. Web Site: http://www.charter.com. Also serves Columbus, Laurel, Park City & Yellowstone County. ICA: MT0001.
TV Market Ranking: Below 100 (BILLINGS, Yellowstone County (portions), Laurel; Outside TV Markets (Yellowstone County (portions)). Franchise award date: N.A. Franchise expiration date: N.A. Began: December 1, 1968.
Channel capacity: N.A. Channels available but not in use: N.A.

Digital Basic Service
Subscribers: 28,141.
Programming (via satellite): 3ABN; A&E HD; Animal Planet HD; AXS TV; BBC America; Bloomberg Television; BlueHighways TV; Bravo; CBS Sports Network; CMT; CNN HD; Cooking Channel; C-SPAN 3; Destination America; Discovery Channel HD; Discovery Kids Channel; Discovery Life Channel; Disney Channel HD; Disney XD; DIY Network; DMX Music; ESPN Classic; ESPN HD; ESPN2 HD; ESPNews; Food Network HD; FOX College Sports Central; FOX College Sports Pacific; Fox Sports 1; Freeform HD; Fuse; FXM; FYI; Golf Channel; GSN; HD Theater; HGTV HD; History HD; History International; IFC; INSP; Investigation Discovery; ION Television; Lifetime Movie Network HD; LMN; MTV Classic; MTV Hits; MTV2; Nat Geo WILD; National Geographic Channel; National Geographic Channel HD; NBCSN; NFL Network; NFL Network HD; NHL Network; Nick Jr.; Nicktoons; Outdoor Channel; OWN: Oprah Winfrey Network; RFD-TV; Science Channel; Science HD; Sprout; Syfy HD; TBS HD; TeenNick; The Weather Channel HD; TLC HD; TNT HD; Trinity Broadcasting Network (TBN); TV Guide Network; Universal HD; UP; USA Network HD; Versus HD; VH1 Soul.
Fee: $26.99 monthly; $4.05 converter.

Digital Expanded Basic Service
Subscribers: 21,900.
Programming (via satellite): A&E; Altitude Sports & Entertainment; AMC; Animal Planet; Cartoon Network; CMT; CNBC; CNN; Comedy Central; Disney Channel; E! HD; ESPN; ESPN2; Food Network; Fox News Channel; Freeform; FX; Great American Country; Hallmark Channel; HGTV; History; HLN; ION Television; Lifetime; MSNBC; MTV; Nickelodeon; Oxygen; Pop; Root Sports Rocky Mountain; Spike TV; Syfy; TLC; TNT; Travel Channel; truTV; Turner Classic Movies; TV Land; Univision Studios; USA Network; VH1.
Fee: $22.50 installation; $18.99 monthly; $4.05 converter.

Digital Pay Service 1
Pay Units: N.A.
Programming (via satellite): Cinemax (multiplexed); Cinemax HD; Cinemax On Demand; Flix; HBO (multiplexed); HBO HD; HBO on Demand; Showtime (multiplexed); Showtime HD; Starz (multiplexed); Starz Encore (multiplexed); Starz HD; Starz On Demand; The Movie Channel (multiplexed); The Movie Channel HD.
Fee: $11.00 monthly (Cinemax, HBO, Showtime/TMC/Flix or Starz/Encore).

Video-On-Demand: Yes

Pay-Per-View
ESPN Now (delivered digitally); NBA League Pass (delivered digitally); MLS Direct Kick (delivered digitally); iN DEMAND (delivered digitally); MLB Extra Innings (delivered digitally); NHL Center Ice (delivered digitally).

Internet Service
Operational: Yes. Began: March 1, 2000.
Subscribers: 33,351.
Broadband Service: Charter Internet.
Fee: $99.95 installation; $39.95 monthly; $3.00 modem lease; $59.95 modem purchase.

Telephone Service
Digital: Operational
Subscribers: 20,662.
Fee: $49.99 monthly
Miles of Plant: 1,142.0 (coaxial); 295.0 (fiber optic). Homes passed: 64,522.
President & Chief Executive Officer: Tom Rutledge. Vice President & General Manager: Sean O'Donnell. Technical Operations Manager: Tom Campbell. Business Operations Manager: Randi Friez. Marketing Director: Jackie Heitman. Accounting Director: David Sovanski.
Ownership: Charter Communications Inc. (MSO).

BILLINGS—Formerly served by USA Digital TV. No longer in operation. ICA: MT0120.

BILLINGS (western portion)—USA Communications, 920 East 56th St, Ste B, Kearney, NE 68847. Phones: 800-628-6060; 406-628-2100; 406-628-6336. Web Site: http://usacommunications.tv. ICA: MT0067.
TV Market Ranking: Franchise award date: N.A. Franchise expiration date: N.A. Began: November 1, 1988.
Channel capacity: N.A. Channels available but not in use: N.A.

Basic Service
Subscribers: 497.
Programming (received off-air): KHMT (FOX) Hardin; KSVI (ABC) Billings; KTVQ (CBS, CW, Grit) Billings; KULR-TV (NBC) Billings; KUSM-TV (PBS) Bozeman.
Programming (via satellite): A&E; Cartoon Network; CNBC; CNN; Discovery Channel; ESPN; ESPN2; Fox News Channel; Freeform; Great American Country; Hallmark Channel; HGTV; History; HLN; KWGN-TV (CW, This TV) Denver; Lifetime; Nickelodeon; Pop; Spike TV; Syfy; TBS; The Weather Channel; TLC; TNT; Turner Classic Movies; USA Network; VH1; WGN America.
Fee: $39.95 installation; $22.00 monthly.

Digital Basic Service
Subscribers: N.A.
Programming (via satellite): BBC America; BET; Bloomberg Television; Bravo; Destination America; Discovery Kids Channel; Discovery Life Channel; Fox Sports 1; Fuse; FYI; Golf Channel; GSN; History International; IFC; Investigation Discovery; LMN; NBCSN; Outdoor Channel; Ovation; OWN: Oprah Winfrey Network; Science Channel; The Weather Channel; WE tv.

Pay Service 1
Pay Units: N.A.
Programming (via satellite): HBO; Showtime.
Fee: $10.95 monthly (each).

Digital Pay Service 1
Pay Units: N.A.
Programming (via satellite): Cinemax (multiplexed); Flix; HBO (multiplexed); Showtime (multiplexed); Starz (multiplexed); Starz Encore (multiplexed); The Movie Channel (multiplexed).

Video-On-Demand: No

Pay-Per-View
iN DEMAND (delivered digitally).

Internet Service
Operational: Yes, Dial-up.

Telephone Service
Analog: Not Operational
Digital: Operational
Miles of Plant: 10.0 (coaxial); None (fiber optic).
Chief Financial Officer: Amber Reineke. General Manager: Doug Wayne. Operations Manager: Stuart Gilbertson.
Ownership: USA Companies LP (MSO).

BOULDER—Charter Communications, 12405 Powerscourt Dr, St. Louis, MO 63131. Phones: 636-207-5100 (Corporate office); 877-273-7626; 516-803-2300 (Corporate office). Web Site: http://www.charter.com. ICA: MT0051.
TV Market Ranking: Below 100 (BOULDER). Franchise award date: N.A. Franchise expiration date: N.A. Began: February 1, 1982.
Channel capacity: N.A. Channels available but not in use: N.A.

Digital Basic Service
Subscribers: 38. Commercial subscribers: 5.
Programming (received off-air): KTVH-DT (CW, NBC) Helena; KTVM-TV (MeTV, Movies!, NBC, This TV) Butte; KUSM-TV (PBS) Bozeman; KXLF-TV (CBS, CW, Grit) Butte.
Programming (via satellite): C-SPAN; Discovery Channel; KDVR (Antenna TV, FOX) Denver; KMGH-TV (ABC, Azteca America) Denver; Lifetime; QVC; TBS.
Fee: $34.95 installation; $26.99 monthly.

Digital Expanded Basic Service
Subscribers: 29.
Programming (via satellite): A&E; AMC; Animal Planet; Cartoon Network; CNBC; CNN; Disney Channel; ESPN; ESPN2; Fox News Channel; Freeform; HGTV; MoviePlex; Nickelodeon; Root Sports Rocky Mountain; Spike TV; The Weather Channel; TLC; TNT; truTV; USA Network.
Fee: $39.00 monthly.

Pay Service 1
Pay Units: N.A.
Programming (via satellite): HBO; Showtime; Starz; Starz Encore.

Video-On-Demand: No

Internet Service
Operational: Yes.
Broadband Service: Charter Internet.
Fee: $39.95 monthly.

Telephone Service
Analog: Not Operational
Digital: Operational
Fee: $49.99 monthly
Miles of Plant: 8.0 (coaxial); None (fiber optic). Homes passed: 678.
President & Chief Executive Officer: Tom Rutledge. General Manager: Mike Oswald. Chief Technician: Ed McFadden. Accounting Director: David Sovanski.
Ownership: Charter Communications Inc. (MSO).

BOZEMAN—Charter Communications, 12405 Powerscourt Dr, St. Louis, MO 63131. Phones: 636-207-5100 (Corporate office); 406-587-8922; 406-782-9383 (Butte office). Fax: 406-782-9020. Web Site: http://www.charter.com. Also serves Belgrade, Gallatin County & Manhattan. ICA: MT0007.
TV Market Ranking: Below 100 (Belgrade, BOZEMAN, Gallatin County (portions), Manhattan); Outside TV Markets (Gallatin County (portions)). Franchise award date: N.A. Franchise expiration date: N.A. Began: June 1, 1954.
Channel capacity: N.A. Channels available but not in use: N.A.

Digital Basic Service
Subscribers: 10,150.
Programming (via satellite): A&E HD; Animal Planet HD; AXS TV; BBC America; Bloomberg Television; BlueHighways TV; Bravo HD; BYUtv; CBS Sports Network; CMT; CNBC HD+; CNN HD; Cooking Channel; C-SPAN 3; Destination America; Discovery Channel HD; Discovery Kids Channel; Discovery Life Channel; Disney Channel HD; Disney XD; DIY Network; DMX Music; ESPN Classic; ESPN HD; ESPN2 HD; ESPNews; Food Network HD; FOX College Sports Central; FOX College Sports Pacific; Fox Sports 1; Freeform HD; Fuse; FXM; FYI; Golf Channel; GSN; HD Theater; HGTV HD; History HD; History International; HRTV; IFC; Investigation Discovery; ION Television; Lifetime Movie Network HD; LMN; MTV Classic; MTV Hits; MTV Jams; MTV2; Nat Geo WILD; National Geographic Channel; National Geographic Channel HD; NBCSN; NFL Network; NFL Network HD; NHL Network; Nick 2; Nick Jr.; Nicktoons; Outdoor Channel; Outdoor Channel 2 HD; OWN: Oprah Winfrey Network; Qubo; RFD-TV; Science Channel; Science HD; Sprout; Syfy HD; TBS HD; TeenNick; The Weather Channel HD; TLC HD; TNT HD; Tr3s; Trinity Broadcasting Network (TBN); TV Guide Network; Universal HD; UP; USA Network HD; Versus HD; VH1 Soul.
Fee: $20.99 monthly.

Montana—Cable Systems

Digital Expanded Basic Service
Subscribers: 8,143.
Programming (via satellite): Altitude Sports & Entertainment; AMC; Animal Planet; Bravo; Cartoon Network; CMT; CNBC; CNN; Comedy Central; Discovery Channel; Disney Channel; E! HD; ESPN; ESPN2; Food Network; Fox News Channel; Freeform; FX; Hallmark Channel; HGTV; History; HLN; INSP; ION Television; MSNBC; MTV; Nickelodeon; Oxygen; Root Sports Rocky Mountain; Spike TV; Syfy; The Weather Channel; TLC; TNT; Travel Channel; truTV; Turner Classic Movies; TV Land; USA Network; VH1.

Digital Pay Service 1
Pay Units: N.A.
Programming (via satellite): Cinemax (multiplexed); Cinemax HD; Cinemax On Demand; Flix; HBO (multiplexed); HBO HD; HBO on Demand; Showtime (multiplexed); Showtime HD; Showtime On Demand; Starz (multiplexed); Starz Encore (multiplexed); Starz HD; Starz On Demand; The Movie Channel (multiplexed); The Movie Channel HD.

Video-On-Demand: Yes

Pay-Per-View
ESPN (delivered digitally); MLB Extra Innings (delivered digitally); NHL Center Ice (delivered digitally); iN DEMAND (delivered digitally).

Internet Service
Operational: Yes.
Broadband Service: Charter Internet.
Fee: $39.95 monthly; $3.00 modem lease.

Telephone Service
Analog: Not Operational
Digital: Operational
Subscribers: 7,051.
Fee: $39.95 monthly
Miles of Plant: 709.0 (coaxial); 241.0 (fiber optic). Homes passed: 31,646.
President & Chief Executive Officer: Tom Rutledge. General Manager: Mike Oswald. Chief Technician: Scott Riss. Accounting Director: David Sovanski.
Ownership: Charter Communications Inc. (MSO).

BRIDGER—Bridger Cable TV, 215 North B St, PO Box 561, Bridger, MT 59014. Phone: 406-662-3516. Fax: 406-662-3516. E-mail: randy@brmt.net. Web Site: http://www.brmt.net. ICA: MT0121.
TV Market Ranking: Outside TV Markets (BRIDGER).
Channel capacity: N.A. Channels available but not in use: N.A.

Basic Service
Subscribers: 125.
Programming (received off-air): KHMT (FOX) Hardin; KSVI (ABC) Billings; KTVQ (CBS, CW, Grit) Billings; KULR-TV (NBC) Billings; KUSM-TV (PBS) Bozeman.
Programming (via satellite): Discovery Channel; Freeform; History; KWGN-TV (CW, This TV) Denver; The Weather Channel; TLC; TNT; WGN America.
Fee: $18.00 monthly.

Expanded Basic Service 1
Subscribers: N.A.
Programming (via satellite): A&E; AMC; Animal Planet; CMT; CNN; Disney Channel; Disney XD; ESPN; ESPN2; Fox News Channel; HGTV; Lifetime; MTV; Nickelodeon; Root Sports Rocky Mountain; Spike TV; Syfy; TV Land; USA Network; VH1.
Fee: $18.00 monthly.

Pay Service 1
Pay Units: N.A.
Programming (via satellite): Cinemax; HBO; Starz Encore.
Fee: $1.50 monthly (Encore), $12.00 monthly (Cinemax or HBO).

Video-On-Demand: No

Internet Service
Operational: Yes.
Fee: free installation; $30.00 monthly.

Telephone Service
None
General Manager: Randy Novakovich. Office Manager: Deb Novakovich.
Ownership: Randy Novakovich (MSO).

BROADUS—Skyview TV Inc, 105 North Wilbur, PO Box 445, Broadus, MT 59317. Phone: 406-436-2820. Fax: 406-436-2820. ICA: MT0075.
TV Market Ranking: Outside TV Markets (BROADUS). Franchise award date: N.A. Franchise expiration date: N.A. Began: August 1, 1981.
Channel capacity: 45 (not 2-way capable). Channels available but not in use: N.A.

Basic Service
Subscribers: 150.
Programming (received off-air): KUSM-TV (PBS) Bozeman.
Programming (via satellite): A&E; AMC; Animal Planet; Cartoon Network; CMT; CNN; C-SPAN; C-SPAN 2; Discovery Channel; Disney Channel; ESPN; ESPN2; Fox News Channel; FOX Sports Networks; Freeform; Hallmark Channel; HGTV; History; HLN; Lifetime; MTV; Nickelodeon; Outdoor Channel; Spike TV; Syfy; TBS; The Weather Channel; TLC; TNT; Trinity Broadcasting Network (TBN); TV Land; USA Network; VH1; WGN America.
Programming (via translator): KHME (MeTV, This TV) Rapid City; KTVQ (CBS, CW, Grit) Billings; KULR-TV (NBC) Billings.
Fee: $20.00 installation; $46.00 monthly.

Pay Service 1
Pay Units: 40.
Programming (via satellite): HBO.
Fee: $10.00 installation; $10.00 monthly.

Internet Service
Operational: No.

Telephone Service
None
Miles of Plant: 7.0 (coaxial); None (fiber optic). Homes passed: 350.
Secretary-Treasurer: Mary Sturtz. General Manager: Richard Sturtz.
Ownership: Richard Sturtz.; Gali Estate.; Comcast Cable Communications Inc. (MSO).

BUTTE—Charter Communications, 12405 Powerscourt Dr, St. Louis, MO 63131. Phones: 636-207-5100 (Corporate office); 877-273-7626 (Customer service); 406-782-1616. Fax: 406-782-9020. Web Site: http://www.charter.com. Also serves Silver Bow County & Walkerville. ICA: MT0005.
TV Market Ranking: Below 100 (BUTTE, Silver Bow County, Walkerville). Franchise award date: N.A. Franchise expiration date: N.A. Began: June 1, 1962.
Channel capacity: N.A. Channels available but not in use: N.A.

Digital Basic Service
Subscribers: 6,207.
Programming (via satellite): A&E HD; Animal Planet HD; AXS TV; BBC America; Bloomberg Television; Bravo; Bravo HD; CBS Sports Network; CMT; CNBC HD+; CNN HD; Cooking Channel; Destination America; Discovery Channel HD; Discovery Kids Channel; Discovery Life Channel; Disney Channel HD; Disney XD; DIY Network; DMX Music; ESPN Classic; ESPN HD; ESPN2 HD; ESPNews; Food Network HD; FOX College Sports Central; FOX College Sports Pacific; Fox Sports 1; Freeform HD; Fuse; FXM; FYI; Golf Channel; GSN; HD Theater; HGTV HD; History HD; History International; HRTV; IFC; Investigation Discovery; ION Television; Lifetime Movie Network HD; LMN; MTV Classic; MTV Hits; MTV Jams; MTV Live; MTV2; Nat Geo WILD; National Geographic Channel; National Geographic Channel HD; NBCSN; NFL Network; NFL Network HD; NHL Network; Nick 2; Nick Jr.; Nicktoons; Outdoor Channel; Outdoor Channel 2 HD; OWN: Oprah Winfrey Network; Qubo; RFD-TV; Science Channel; Science HD; Sprout; Syfy HD; TBS HD; TeenNick; The Weather Channel HD; TLC HD; TNT HD; Tr3s; Trinity Broadcasting Network (TBN); TV Guide Network; Universal HD; UP; USA Network HD; Versus HD; VH1 Soul.
Fee: $26.99 monthly.

Digital Expanded Basic Service
Subscribers: N.A.
Programming (via satellite): A&E; Altitude Sports & Entertainment; AMC; Animal Planet; Cartoon Network; CNBC; CNN; Comedy Central; Discovery Channel; Disney Channel; E! HD; ESPN; ESPN2; Food Network; Fox News Channel; Freeform; FX; Hallmark Channel; HGTV; History; INSP; ION Television; MSNBC; MTV; Nickelodeon; Oxygen; Root Sports Rocky Mountain; Spike TV; Syfy; TBS; The Weather Channel; TLC; TNT; Travel Channel; truTV; Turner Classic Movies; TV Land; USA Network; VH1.
Fee: $28.99 monthly.

Digital Pay Service 1
Pay Units: N.A.
Programming (via satellite): Cinemax (multiplexed); Cinemax HD; Cinemax On Demand; Flix; HBO (multiplexed); HBO HD; HBO on Demand; Showtime (multiplexed); Showtime HD; Showtime On Demand; Starz (multiplexed); Starz Encore (multiplexed); Starz HD; Starz On Demand; The Movie Channel (multiplexed); The Movie Channel HD.

Video-On-Demand: Yes

Pay-Per-View
ESPN (delivered digitally); iN DEMAND (delivered digitally); MLB Extra Innings (delivered digitally); NHL Center Ice (delivered digitally).

Internet Service
Operational: Yes.
Subscribers: 6,496.
Broadband Service: Charter Internet.
Fee: $39.95 monthly; $3.00 modem lease.

Telephone Service
Analog: Not Operational
Digital: Operational
Subscribers: 4,202.
Fee: $49.99 monthly
Miles of Plant: 236.0 (coaxial); 145.0 (fiber optic). Homes passed: 17,402.
President & Chief Executive Officer: Tom Rutledge. General Manager: Mike Oswald. Chief Technician: Todd Hawke. Accounting Director: David Sovanski.
Ownership: Charter Communications Inc. (MSO).

CASCADE—Charter Communications, 12405 Powerscourt Dr, St. Louis, MO 63131. Phones: 636-207-5100 (Corporate office); 406-452-4111; 877-273-7626; 406-727-8881. Web Site: http://www.charter.com. ICA: MT0074.
TV Market Ranking: Below 100 (CASCADE). Franchise award date: N.A. Franchise expiration date: N.A. Began: January 1, 1982.
Channel capacity: N.A. Channels available but not in use: N.A.

Digital Basic Service
Subscribers: 34. Commercial subscribers: 3.
Programming (received off-air): KFBB-TV (ABC, FOX) Great Falls; KRTV (CBS, CW, Grit) Great Falls; KTGF (IND) Great Falls; KUSM-TV (PBS) Bozeman.
Programming (via satellite): C-SPAN; Fox News Channel; KUSA (NBC, WeatherNation) Denver; Lifetime; QVC; TLC; truTV.
Fee: $34.95 installation; $24.99 monthly.

Digital Expanded Basic Service
Subscribers: N.A.
Programming (via satellite): A&E; AMC; Animal Planet; Cartoon Network; CNBC; CNN; Discovery Channel; Disney Channel; ESPN; ESPN2; Freeform; HGTV; History; MoviePlex; Nickelodeon; Root Sports Rocky Mountain; Spike TV; The Weather Channel; TNT; USA Network.
Fee: $18.99 monthly.

Pay Service 1
Pay Units: N.A.
Programming (via satellite): HBO; Showtime; Starz; Starz Encore.
Fee: $6.99 monthly (Starz/Encore), $14.15 monthly (HBO).

Video-On-Demand: No

Internet Service
Operational: Yes.
Broadband Service: Charter Internet.
Fee: $39.95 monthly.

Telephone Service
Digital: Operational
Fee: $49.99 monthly
Miles of Plant: 5.0 (coaxial); None (fiber optic). Homes passed: 380.
President & Chief Executive Officer: Tom Rutledge. Vice President & General Manager: Sean O'Donnell. General Manager: Patty Faloon. Technical Operations Manager: Doug Sappington. Accounting Director: David Sovanski.
Ownership: Charter Communications Inc. (MSO).

CHARLO—Formerly served by KLiP Interactive. No longer in operation. ICA: MT0103.

CHESTER—Formerly served by KLiP Interactive. No longer in operation. ICA: MT0054.

CHINOOK—Charter Communications, 12405 Powerscourt Dr, St. Louis, MO 63131. Phones: 636-207-5100 (Corporate office); 406-727-8881; 516-803-2300 (Corporate office); 877-273-7626. Web Site: http://www.charter.com. Also serves Blaine County (northern portion). ICA: MT0044.
TV Market Ranking: Below 100 (Blaine County (northern portion), CHINOOK). Franchise award date: July 1, 1991. Franchise expiration date: N.A. Began: February 1, 1981.
Channel capacity: N.A. Channels available but not in use: N.A.

Digital Basic Service
Subscribers: 82.
Programming (via satellite): AMC; Animal Planet; BBC America; Bloomberg Television; Bravo; BYUtv; Cartoon Network; CBS Sports Network; CMT; CNBC; Cooking Channel; Destination America; Discovery Channel; Discovery Kids Channel; Discovery Life Channel; Disney Channel; Disney XD; ESPN; ESPN Classic; ESPN2; ESPNews; Food Network; Fox News Chan-

Cable Systems—Montana

FULLY SEARCHABLE • CONTINUOUSLY UPDATED • DISCOUNT RATES FOR PRINT PURCHASERS
For more information call **800-771-9202** or visit **www.warren-news.com**

nel; Fox Sports 1; Freeform; Fuse; FXM; FYI; Golf Channel; GSN; Hallmark Channel; HGTV; History; History International; IFC; Investigation Discovery; Lifetime; LMN; MoviePlex; MTV Classic; MTV Hits; MTV2; Nat Geo WILD; National Geographic Channel; NBCSN; Nick Jr.; Nickelodeon; Nicktoons; Outdoor Channel; OWN: Oprah Winfrey Network; RFD-TV; Root Sports Rocky Mountain; Science Channel; Spike TV; Sprout; Syfy; TeenNick; The Weather Channel; TLC; TNT; Trinity Broadcasting Network (TBN); Turner Classic Movies; TV Land; UP; USA Network; VH1 Soul.
Fee: $26.99 monthly.
Digital Expanded Basic Service
Subscribers: N.A.
Programming (via satellite): FOX College Sports Central; FOX College Sports Pacific; HRTV; NFL Network.
Digital Pay Service 1
Pay Units: N.A.
Programming (via satellite): Cinemax (multiplexed); Flix; HBO (multiplexed); Showtime (multiplexed); Starz (multiplexed); Starz Encore (multiplexed); The Movie Channel (multiplexed).
Video-On-Demand: No
Internet Service
Operational: Yes.
Broadband Service: Charter Internet.
Fee: $39.95 monthly.
Telephone Service
Digital: Operational
Fee: $49.99 monthly
Miles of Plant: 9.0 (coaxial); None (fiber optic). Homes passed: 820.
President & Chief Executive Officer: Tom Rutledge. Accounting Director: David Sovanski. Chief Technician: Jim Passon.
Ownership: Charter Communications Inc. (MSO).

CHOTEAU—3 Rivers Communications, 202 5th St South, PO Box 429, Fairfield, MT 59436. Phones: 800-796-4567; 406-467-2535. Fax: 406-467-3490. E-mail: 3rt@3rivers.net. Web Site: http://www.3rivers.net. ICA: MT0034.
TV Market Ranking: Outside TV Markets (CHOTEAU). Franchise award date: N.A. Franchise expiration date: N.A. Began: July 1, 1979.
Channel capacity: N.A. Channels available but not in use: N.A.
Basic Service
Subscribers: 192.
Programming (received off-air): KFBB-TV (ABC, FOX) Great Falls; KRTV (CBS, CW, Grit) Great Falls; KTGF (IND) Great Falls; KUSM-TV (PBS) Bozeman; allband FM.
Programming (via satellite): C-SPAN; C-SPAN 2; FX; Lifetime; QVC; TBS; TLC.
Fee: $39.99 installation; $20.49 monthly.
Expanded Basic Service 1
Subscribers: N.A.
Programming (via satellite): A&E; Altitude Sports & Entertainment; AMC; Animal Planet; Cartoon Network; CMT; CNBC; CNN; Comedy Central; Discovery Channel; Disney Channel; E! HD; ESPN; ESPN2; Food Network; Fox News Channel; Freeform; Hallmark Channel; HGTV; HLN; INSP; MoviePlex; MSNBC; MTV; Nickelodeon; Pop; Root Sports Rocky Mountain; Spike TV; The Weather Channel; TNT; Travel Channel; truTV; USA Network; VH1.
Fee: $33.00 monthly.
Digital Basic Service
Subscribers: N.A.
Programming (via satellite): BBC America; BET; Bloomberg Television; Bravo; CBS Sports Network; CMT; Destination America; Discovery Kids Channel; Discovery Life Channel; Disney XD; DMX Music; ESPN Classic; ESPNews; Fox Sports 1; Fuse; FXM; FYI; Golf Channel; GSN; History; History International; IFC; Investigation Discovery; LMN; MTV Classic; MTV Hits; MTV2; National Geographic Channel; NBCSN; Nick Jr.; Nicktoons; Outdoor Channel; OWN: Oprah Winfrey Network; RFD-TV; Science Channel; Sprout; Syfy; TeenNick; Trinity Broadcasting Network (TBN); Turner Classic Movies; TV Land; VH1 Soul.
Fee: $24.99 monthly.
Digital Pay Service 1
Pay Units: N.A.
Programming (via satellite): HBO (multiplexed); Showtime (multiplexed); Starz (multiplexed); Starz Encore (multiplexed); The Movie Channel.
Video-On-Demand: No
Internet Service
Operational: Yes, DSL & dial-up.
Telephone Service
Digital: Operational
Miles of Plant: 16.0 (coaxial); None (fiber optic). Homes passed: 1,500.
Chief Financial Officer: Bradley C. Veis. General Manager: Mike Henning. Sales & Marketing Director: Terry Noyd. Customer Operations Director: Sandi Oveson.
Ownership: 3 Rivers Communications (MSO).

CIRCLE—Mid-Rivers Communications. Now served by GLENDIVE, MT [MT0013]. ICA: MT0096.

COLSTRIP—USA Communications, 920 East 56th St, Ste B, Kearney, NE 68847. Phones: 800-628-6060; 406-628-2100; 308-236-1412 (Kearney corporate office); 406-628-6336. Fax: 406-628-8181. Web Site: http://usacommunications.tv. ICA: MT0110.
TV Market Ranking: Outside TV Markets (COLSTRIP). Franchise award date: N.A. Franchise expiration date: N.A. Began: January 1, 1981.
Channel capacity: N.A. Channels available but not in use: N.A.
Basic Service
Subscribers: 130.
Programming (received off-air): KBZK (CBS, Grit) Bozeman; KSVI (ABC) Billings; KTVQ (CBS, CW, Grit) Billings; KULR-TV (NBC) Billings; KUSM-TV (PBS) Bozeman.
Programming (via satellite): A&E; AMC; Animal Planet; Bloomberg Television; CMT; CNN; C-SPAN; Discovery Channel; Disney Channel; ESPN; Freeform; MTV; Nickelodeon; Outdoor Channel; QVC; TBS; TNT; Turner Classic Movies; USA Network; VH1; WGN America.
Fee: $29.95 installation; $24.95 monthly.
Expanded Basic Service 1
Subscribers: N.A.
Programming (via satellite): HLN; INSP; Spike TV; Syfy; TLC.
Fee: $30.00 monthly.
Pay Service 1
Pay Units: 20.
Programming (via satellite): HBO.
Fee: $13.00 monthly.
Pay Service 2
Pay Units: 20.
Programming (via satellite): Starz.
Fee: $9.00 monthly.
Video-On-Demand: No
Internet Service
Operational: Yes.
Fee: $24.95 installation; $19.95 monthly.

Telephone Service
Digital: Operational
Miles of Plant: 20.0 (coaxial); None (fiber optic).
Chief Financial Officer: Amber Reineke. General Manager: Doug Lane. Operations Manager: Stuart Gilbertson.
Ownership: USA Companies LP (MSO).

COLUMBUS—Formerly served by Cable Montana. No longer in operation. ICA: MT0048.

CONRAD—3 Rivers Communications, 202 5th St South, PO Box 429, Fairfield, MT 59436. Phones: 406-271-2535 (Conrad office); 406-467-2535 (Fairfield office); 800-796-4567. Fax: 406-467-3490. E-mail: 3rt@3rivers.net. Web Site: http://www.3rivers.net. Also serves Pondera County. ICA: MT0031.
TV Market Ranking: Outside TV Markets (CONRAD, Pondera County). Franchise award date: N.A. Franchise expiration date: N.A. Began: June 1, 1979.
Channel capacity: N.A. Channels available but not in use: N.A.
Basic Service
Subscribers: 219.
Programming (received off-air): KFBB-TV (ABC, FOX) Great Falls; KRTV (CBS, CW, Grit) Great Falls; KTGF (IND) Great Falls; KUSM-TV (PBS) Bozeman.
Programming (via satellite): CW PLUS; ION Television; Lifetime; Pop; QVC; TBS.
Fee: $39.99 installation; $20.49 monthly.
Expanded Basic Service 1
Subscribers: N.A.
Programming (via satellite): A&E; Altitude Sports & Entertainment; AMC; Animal Planet; Cartoon Network; CMT; CNBC; CNN; Comedy Central; C-SPAN; Discovery Channel; Disney Channel; E! HD; ESPN; ESPN2; Food Network; Fox News Channel; Freeform; FX; Hallmark Channel; HGTV; HLN; MSNBC; Nickelodeon; Oxygen; Root Sports Rocky Mountain; Spike TV; The Weather Channel; TLC; TNT; Travel Channel; truTV; USA Network; VH1.
Fee: $33.00 monthly.
Digital Basic Service
Subscribers: N.A.
Programming (via satellite): BBC America; Bloomberg Television; Bravo; CBS Sports Network; CMT; Destination America; Discovery Kids Channel; Discovery Life Channel; Disney XD; DMX Music; ESPN Classic; ESPNews; Fox Sports 1; Fuse; FXM; FYI; Golf Channel; GSN; History; History International; IFC; Investigation Discovery; ION Television; LMN; MTV Classic; MTV Hits; MTV2; National Geographic Channel; NBCSN; Nick Jr.; Nicktoons; Outdoor Channel; OWN: Oprah Winfrey Network; RFD-TV; Science Channel; Sprout; Syfy; TeenNick; Trinity Broadcasting Network (TBN); TV Land; VH1 Soul.
Fee: $24.99 monthly.
Digital Pay Service 1
Pay Units: N.A.
Programming (via satellite): Cinemax (multiplexed); Flix; HBO (multiplexed); Showtime (multiplexed); Starz (multiplexed); Starz Encore (multiplexed); The Movie Channel (multiplexed).
Video-On-Demand: No
Pay-Per-View
Hot Choice (delivered digitally); iN DEMAND (delivered digitally); Fresh (delivered digitally).
Internet Service
Operational: Yes.
Telephone Service
Digital: Operational
Miles of Plant: 17.0 (coaxial); None (fiber optic). Homes passed: 1,415.
General Manager: David Gibson. Human Resources Director: Bonnie Mayer. Customer Operations Director: Sandi Oveson. Finance Director: Brad Veis. Technical & Network Operations Director: Ron Warnick.
Ownership: 3 Rivers Communications (MSO).

CROW AGENCY—Crow Cable TV, 1119 North Custer Ave, PO Box 338, Hardin, MT 59034-0338. Phones: 406-665-1531; 406-855-7056. Fax: 406-665-1531. Also serves Crow Indian Reservation. ICA: MT0097.
TV Market Ranking: Below 100 (CROW AGENCY, Crow Indian Reservation). Franchise award date: N.A. Franchise expiration date: N.A. Began: January 1, 1964.
Channel capacity: N.A. Channels available but not in use: N.A.
Basic Service
Subscribers: 90.
Programming (received off-air): KHMT (FOX) Hardin; KSVI (ABC) Billings; KTVQ (CBS, CW, Grit) Billings; KULR-TV (NBC) Billings.
Programming (via satellite): A&E; CMT; CNN; C-SPAN; Discovery Channel; Disney Channel; Disney XD; ESPN; ESPN2; EWTN Global Catholic Network; Freeform; History; KRMA-TV (PBS) Denver; Lifetime; Nickelodeon; Spike TV; Syfy; TBS; The Weather Channel; TLC; TNT; Trinity Broadcasting Network (TBN); Turner Classic Movies; USA Network; WGN America.
Fee: $40.00 installation; $35.50 monthly.
Pay Service 1
Pay Units: N.A.
Programming (via satellite): Cinemax; HBO.
Fee: $11.50 monthly (each).
Internet Service
Operational: No.
Telephone Service
None
Miles of Plant: 5.0 (coaxial); None (fiber optic). Homes passed: 270.
General Manager: Tom Zelka.; Rose Marie Zelka.
Ownership: Tom Zelka.

CULBERTSON—Formerly served by Bulldog Cable. No longer in operation. ICA: MT0072.

CUT BANK—Charter Communications, 2910 10th Ave South, Great Falls, MT 59405. Phones: 636-207-5100 (Corporate office); 406-452-4111; 877-273-7626; 406-727-8881. Web Site: http://www.charter.com. Also serves Blackfeet Indian Reservation & Glacier County (portions). ICA: MT0020.

2017 Edition   D-467

Montana—Cable Systems

TV Market Ranking: Outside TV Markets (Blackfeet Indian Reservation, CUT BANK, Glacier County (portions)). Franchise award date: N.A. Franchise expiration date: N.A. Began: July 1, 1955.
Channel capacity: N.A. Channels available but not in use: N.A.
Digital Basic Service
Subscribers: 605.
Programming (via satellite): BBC America; Bloomberg Television; Bravo; CBS Sports Network; CMT; Destination America; Discovery Kids Channel; Discovery Life Channel; Disney XD; DMX Music; ESPN Classic; ESPNews; FOX College Sports Central; FOX College Sports Pacific; Fox Sports 1; Fuse; FXM; FYI; Golf Channel; Great American Country; GSN; History International; HRTV; IFC; Investigation Discovery; ION Television; LMN; MTV Classic; MTV Hits; MTV2; Nat Geo WILD; National Geographic Channel; NBCSN; NFL Network; Nick Jr.; Nicktoons; Outdoor Channel; OWN: Oprah Winfrey Network; RFD-TV; Science Channel; Sprout; TeenNick; Trinity Broadcasting Network (TBN); UP; VH1 Soul.
Fee: $26.99 monthly.
Digital Expanded Basic Service
Subscribers: 485.
Programming (via satellite): A&E; Altitude Sports & Entertainment; AMC; Animal Planet; Cartoon Network; CMT; CNBC; CNN; Comedy Central; CW PLUS; Discovery Channel; Disney Channel; E! HD; ESPN; ESPN2; Food Network; Fox News Channel; Freeform; FX; Hallmark Channel; HGTV; History; HLN; INSP; ION Television; Lifetime; MSNBC; MTV; Nickelodeon; Oxygen; Root Sports Rocky Mountain; Spike TV; Syfy; The Weather Channel; TLC; TNT; Travel Channel; truTV; TV Land; USA Network; VH1.
Fee: $28.99 monthly.
Digital Pay Service 1
Pay Units: N.A.
Programming (via satellite): Cinemax (multiplexed); Flix; HBO (multiplexed); Showtime (multiplexed); Starz (multiplexed); Starz Encore (multiplexed); The Movie Channel (multiplexed).
Video-On-Demand: No
Pay-Per-View
Hot Choice (delivered digitally); iN DEMAND; iN DEMAND (delivered digitally); Fresh (delivered digitally).
Internet Service
Operational: Yes.
Broadband Service: Charter Internet.
Fee: $39.95 monthly.
Telephone Service
Digital: Operational
Fee: $49.99 monthly
Miles of Plant: 30.0 (coaxial); None (fiber optic). Homes passed: 2,202.
President & Chief Executive Officer: Tom Rutledge. Vice President & General Manager: Sean O'Donnell. General Manager: Patty Faloon. Technical Operations Manager: Doug Sappington. Accounting Director: David Sovanski.
Ownership: Charter Communications Inc. (MSO).

DARBY (town)—Formerly served by KLiP Interactive. No longer in operation. ICA: MT0085.

DEER LODGE—Charter Communications, 201 East Front St, Butte, MT 63131. Phones: 636-207-5100 (Corporate office); 406-782-1616; 877-273-7626 (Customer service). Web Site: http://www.charter.com. Also serves Powell County. ICA: MT0025.

TV Market Ranking: Below 100 (Powell County (portions)); Outside TV Markets (DEER LODGE, Powell County (portions)). Franchise award date: N.A. Franchise expiration date: N.A. Began: December 1, 1966.
Channel capacity: N.A. Channels available but not in use: N.A.
Digital Basic Service
Subscribers: 625.
Programming (via satellite): A&E HD; Animal Planet HD; BBC America; Bloomberg Television; Bravo; CBS Sports Network; CMT; Cooking Channel; Destination America; Discovery Kids Channel; Discovery Life Channel; Disney XD; DIY Network; DMX Music; ESPN Classic; ESPNews; Food Network HD; Fox Sports 1; Fuse; FXM; FYI; Golf Channel; GSN; HD Theater; HGTV HD; History HD; History International; IFC; Investigation Discovery; LMN; MTV Classic; MTV Hits; MTV Jams; MTV2; Nat Geo WILD; National Geographic Channel; National Geographic Channel HD; NBCSN; NFL Network; Nick 2; Nick Jr.; Nicktoons; Outdoor Channel; OWN: Oprah Winfrey Network; RFD-TV; Science Channel; Science HD; Sprout; TeenNick; Tr3s; Trinity Broadcasting Network (TBN); Universal HD; UP; USA Network HD; VH1 Soul.
Fee: $34.99 installation; $26.99 monthly.
Digital Expanded Basic Service
Subscribers: N.A.
Programming (via satellite): A&E; Altitude Sports & Entertainment; AMC; Animal Planet; Cartoon Network; CMT; CNBC; CNN; Comedy Central; Discovery Channel; Disney Channel; E! HD; ESPN; ESPN2; Food Network; Fox News Channel; Freeform; FX; Hallmark Channel; HGTV; History; HLN; INSP; ION Television; MSNBC; MTV; Nickelodeon; Oxygen; Root Sports Rocky Mountain; Spike TV; Syfy; The Weather Channel; TLC; TNT; Travel Channel; truTV; Turner Classic Movies; TV Land; USA Network; VH1.
Fee: $48.99 monthly.
Digital Pay Service 1
Pay Units: N.A.
Programming (via satellite): Cinemax (multiplexed); Flix; HBO (multiplexed); HBO HD; Showtime (multiplexed); Starz (multiplexed); Starz Encore (multiplexed); Starz HD; The Movie Channel (multiplexed).
Video-On-Demand: No
Pay-Per-View
iN DEMAND (delivered digitally); FOX College Sports Central (delivered digitally); FOX College Sports Pacific (delivered digitally); HRTV (delivered digitally).
Internet Service
Operational: Yes.
Broadband Service: Charter Internet.
Fee: $39.95 monthly.
Telephone Service
Digital: Operational
Fee: $49.99 monthly
Miles of Plant: 18.0 (coaxial); 2.0 (fiber optic). Homes passed: 1,988.
President & Chief Executive Officer: Tom Rutledge. General Manager: Mike Oswald. Chief Technician: Todd Hawke. Accounting Director: David Sovanski.
Ownership: Charter Communications Inc. (MSO).

DILLON—Charter Communications, 12405 Powerscourt Dr, St. Louis, MO 63131. Phones: 636-207-5100 (Corporate office); 877-273-7626 (Customer service); 406-782-1616. Web Site: http://www.charter.com. Also serves Beaverhead County (portions). ICA: MT0019.

TV Market Ranking: Outside TV Markets (DILLON). Franchise award date: N.A. Franchise expiration date: N.A. Began: January 1, 1961.
Channel capacity: N.A. Channels available but not in use: N.A.
Digital Basic Service
Subscribers: 841.
Programming (via satellite): A&E HD; Animal Planet HD; BBC America; Bloomberg Television; Bravo; CBS Sports Network; CMT; Cooking Channel; Destination America; Discovery Channel HD; Discovery Kids Channel; Discovery Life Channel; Disney Channel HD; Disney XD; DIY Network; DMX Music; ESPN Classic; ESPN HD; ESPNews; Food Network HD; Fox Sports 1; Freeform HD; Fuse; FXM; FYI; Golf Channel; GSN; HD Theater; HGTV HD; History HD; History International; IFC; Investigation Discovery; LMN; MTV Classic; MTV Hits; MTV Jams; MTV2; Nat Geo WILD; National Geographic Channel; National Geographic Channel HD; NBCSN; Nick 2; Nick Jr.; Nicktoons; Outdoor Channel; OWN: Oprah Winfrey Network; RFD-TV; Science Channel; Science HD; Sprout; Syfy HD; TeenNick; Tr3s; Trinity Broadcasting Network (TBN); Universal HD; UP; USA Network HD; VH1 Soul.
Fee: $34.99 installation; $26.99 monthly.
Digital Expanded Basic Service
Subscribers: N.A.
Programming (via satellite): A&E; Altitude Sports & Entertainment; AMC; Animal Planet; Cartoon Network; CMT; CNBC; CNN; Comedy Central; Discovery Channel; Disney Channel; E! HD; ESPN; ESPN2; Food Network; Fox News Channel; Freeform; FX; Hallmark Channel; HGTV; History; HLN; INSP; ION Television; MSNBC; MTV; Nickelodeon; Oxygen; Root Sports Rocky Mountain; Spike TV; Syfy; The Weather Channel; TLC; TNT; Travel Channel; truTV; Turner Classic Movies; TV Land; USA Network; VH1.
Fee: $48.99 monthly.
Digital Pay Service 1
Pay Units: N.A.
Programming (via satellite): Cinemax (multiplexed); Flix; HBO (multiplexed); HBO HD; Showtime (multiplexed); Starz (multiplexed); Starz Encore (multiplexed); Starz HD; The Movie Channel (multiplexed).
Video-On-Demand: No
Pay-Per-View
iN DEMAND (delivered digitally); NFL Network (delivered digitally); FOX College Sports Central (delivered digitally); FOX College Sports Pacific (delivered digitally); HRTV (delivered digitally).
Internet Service
Operational: Yes.
Subscribers: 1,013.
Broadband Service: Charter Internet.
Fee: $39.95 monthly.
Telephone Service
Analog: Not Operational
Digital: Operational
Subscribers: 608.
Fee: $49.99 monthly
Miles of Plant: 71.0 (coaxial); 14.0 (fiber optic). Homes passed: 3,318.
President & Chief Executive Officer: Tom Rutledge. General Manager: Mike Oswald. Chief Technician: Todd Hawke. Accounting Director: David Sovanski.
Ownership: Charter Communications Inc. (MSO).

DRUMMOND—Formerly served by Cowley Telecable. No longer in operation. ICA: MT0107.

DUTTON—Formerly served by KLiP Interactive. No longer in operation. ICA: MT0089.

EKALAKA—Mid-Rivers Communications. Now served by BAKER, MT [MT0041]. ICA: MT0098.

ENNIS—Formerly served by Bulldog Cable. No longer in operation. ICA: MT0062.

EUREKA—Tobacco Valley Cable, 300 Dewey Ave, PO Box 648, Eureka, MT 59917-0648. Phones: 406-889-3311; 406-889-3099. Fax: 406-889-3787. Web Site: http://interbel.com. ICA: MT0119.

TV Market Ranking: Outside TV Markets (EUREKA).
Channel capacity: N.A. Channels available but not in use: N.A.
Basic Service
Subscribers: 356.
Programming (received off-air): KAYU-TV (FOX, This TV) Spokane; KCFW-TV (MeTV, NBC, This TV) Kalispell; KHQ-TV (NBC) Spokane; KPAX-TV (CBS, CW, Grit) Missoula; KREM (CBS, TheCoolTV) Spokane; KSPS-TV (PBS) Spokane; KXLY-TV (ABC, MeTV) Spokane; various Canadian stations; 4 FMs.
Programming (via satellite): A&E; Animal Planet; Boomerang; Cartoon Network; CNBC; CNN; Discovery Channel; ESPN; ESPN2; FamilyNet; Fox News Channel; Freeform; Great American Country; Hallmark Channel; History; HLN; National Geographic Channel; Outdoor Channel; RFD-TV; Syfy; TBS; TLC; TNT; USA Network; WGN America.
Fee: $25.00 installation; $22.95 monthly.
Digital Basic Service
Subscribers: N.A.
Programming (via satellite): Bloomberg Television; Bravo; Cloo; Discovery Life Channel; DMX Music; ESPN Classic; ESPN2; ESPNews; Fox Sports 1; FXM; FYI; Golf Channel; GSN; HGTV; History International; IFC; NBCSN; Science Channel; Trinity Broadcasting Network (TBN); Turner Classic Movies; WE tv.
Digital Pay Service 1
Pay Units: N.A.
Programming (via satellite): Cinemax (multiplexed); HBO (multiplexed); Showtime (multiplexed); Starz (multiplexed); Starz Encore (multiplexed); The Movie Channel (multiplexed).
Internet Service
Operational: No, DSL.
Telephone Service
Analog: Operational
Miles of Plant: 15.0 (coaxial); None (fiber optic). Homes passed: 700.
General Manager: Randy Wilson. Chief Technician: Robert Little. Comptroller: Virginia Henke.
Ownership: InterBel Telephone Cooperative Inc.

FAIRVIEW—Mid-Rivers Communications. Now served by SIDNEY (town), MT [MT0018]. ICA: MT0059.

FORSYTH—USA Communications, 920 East 56th St, Ste B, Kearney, NE 68847. Phones: 406-628-2100; 308-236-1512 (Kearney corporate office); 800-628-6060; 406-628-6336. Fax: 406-628-8181. Web Site: http://usacommunications.tv. ICA: MT0036.
TV Market Ranking: Outside TV Markets (FORSYTH). Franchise award date: N.A.

Cable Systems—Montana

Franchise expiration date: N.A. Began: December 1, 1975.
Channel capacity: N.A. Channels available but not in use: N.A.

Basic Service
Subscribers: 265.
Programming (received off-air): KHMT (FOX) Hardin; KSVI (ABC) Billings; KTVQ (CBS, CW, Grit) Billings; KULR-TV (NBC) Billings; KUSM-TV (PBS) Bozeman.
Programming (via satellite): A&E; CNBC; CW PLUS; Freeform; Outdoor Channel; Pop; QVC; Spike TV; TBS; The Weather Channel; TLC; WGN America.
Fee: $29.95 installation; $24.95 monthly.

Expanded Basic Service 1
Subscribers: N.A.
Programming (via satellite): Altitude Sports & Entertainment; AMC; Animal Planet; Cartoon Network; CMT; CNN; Discovery Channel; E! HD; ESPN; ESPN2; ESPNews; Food Network; Fox News Channel; FOX Sports Networks; FX; Hallmark Channel; HGTV; History; HLN; Lifetime; MSNBC; MTV; Nickelodeon; Syfy; TNT; TV Land; USA Network; VH1.
Fee: $18.04 monthly.

Digital Basic Service
Subscribers: N.A.
Programming (via satellite): BBC America; Bloomberg Television; Cloo; CMT; Destination America; Discovery Kids Channel; Discovery Life Channel; DMX Music; ESPN Classic; ESPN2; ESPNews; EVINE Live; FOX College Sports Central; FOX College Sports Pacific; Fox Sports 1; FXM; FYI; Golf Channel; GSN; History; History International; Investigation Discovery; LMN; MTV Classic; MTV Hits; MTV2; National Geographic Channel; NBCSN; Nick Jr.; Ovation; OWN; Oprah Winfrey Network; Science Channel; TeenNick; Trinity Broadcasting Network (TBN); VH1 Soul; WE tv.
Fee: $13.00 monthly.

Digital Pay Service 1
Pay Units: N.A.
Programming (via satellite): Cinemax (multiplexed); Flix; HBO (multiplexed); Showtime (multiplexed); Starz (multiplexed); Starz Encore (multiplexed); The Movie Channel (multiplexed).
Fee: $13.00 monthly (Cinemax, HBO, Showtime/TMC/Flix or Starz/Encore).

Video-On-Demand: No

Pay-Per-View
iN DEMAND (delivered digitally); Hot Choice (delivered digitally); Playboy TV (delivered digitally); Fresh (delivered digitally); Shorteez (delivered digitally); Club Jenna (delivered digitally).

Internet Service
Operational: Yes.
Broadband Service: Cable Montana.
Fee: $35.95 monthly.

Telephone Service
Digital: Operational
Miles of Plant: 20.0 (coaxial); None (fiber optic). Homes passed: 850.
Chief Financial Officer: Amber Reineke. Operations Manager: Stuart Gilbertson. General Manager: Doug Lane.
Ownership: USA Companies LP (MSO).

FORT BENTON—Charter Communications, 2910 10th Ave South, Great Falls, MT 59405. Phones: 636-207-5100 (Corporate office); 406-452-4111; 877-273-7626; 406-727-8881. Web Site: http://www.charter.com. ICA: MT0035.
TV Market Ranking: Outside TV Markets (FORT BENTON). Franchise award date: N.A. Franchise expiration date: N.A. Began: March 1, 1980.
Channel capacity: N.A. Channels available but not in use: N.A.

Digital Basic Service
Subscribers: 119.
Programming (via satellite): BBC America; Bloomberg Television; Bravo; CBS Sports Network; CMT; Destination America; Discovery Kids Channel; Discovery Life Channel; Disney XD; DMX Music; ESPN Classic; ESPNews; Fox Sports 1; Fuse; FXM; FYI; Golf Channel; GSN; History International; IFC; Investigation Discovery; LMN; MTV Classic; MTV Hits; MTV2; National Geographic Channel; NBCSN; Nick Jr.; Nicktoons; Outdoor Channel; OWN; Oprah Winfrey Network; RFD-TV; Science Channel; Syfy; TeenNick; Trinity Broadcasting Network (TBN); VH1 Soul.
Fee: $34.99 installation; $26.99 monthly.

Digital Expanded Basic Service
Subscribers: N.A.
Programming (via satellite): A&E; AMC; Animal Planet; Cartoon Network; CMT; CNBC; CNN; Comedy Central; C-SPAN 2; Discovery Channel; Disney Channel; E! HD; ESPN; ESPN2; Food Network; Fox News Channel; Freeform; Hallmark Channel; HGTV; History; HLN; MSNBC; MTV; Nickelodeon; Oxygen; Root Sports Rocky Mountain; Spike TV; The Weather Channel; TNT; Travel Channel; truTV; Turner Classic Movies; TV Land; USA Network; VH1.
Fee: $28.99 monthly.

Digital Pay Service 1
Pay Units: N.A.
Programming (via satellite): Cinemax (multiplexed); Flix; HBO (multiplexed); Showtime (multiplexed); Starz (multiplexed); Starz Encore (multiplexed); The Movie Channel (multiplexed).

Video-On-Demand: No

Internet Service
Operational: Yes.
Broadband Service: Charter Internet.
Fee: $39.95 monthly.

Telephone Service
Analog: Not Operational
Digital: Operational
Fee: $49.99 monthly
Miles of Plant: 12.0 (coaxial); None (fiber optic). Homes passed: 880.
President & Chief Executive Officer: Tom Rutledge. Vice President & General Manager: Sean O'Donnell. General Manager: Patty Faloon. Technical Operations Manager: Doug Sappington. Accounting Director: David Sovanski.
Ownership: Charter Communications Inc. (MSO).

FOUR CORNERS—Formerly served by Northwestern Communications Corp. No longer in operation. ICA: MT0111.

FROMBERG—Formerly served by USA Communications. No longer in operation. ICA: MT0088.

GARDINER—Formerly served by North Yellowstone Cable TV. No longer in operation. ICA: MT0112.

GLASGOW—Nemont Communications, 61 Hwy 13 South, PO Box 600, Scobey, MT 59263-0600. Phones: 406-967-2311; 800-636-6680. Fax: 406-783-5283. E-mail: nemont@nemont.coop. Web Site: http://www.nemont.net. Also serves Valley County. ICA: MT0022.

FULLY SEARCHABLE • CONTINUOUSLY UPDATED • DISCOUNT RATES FOR PRINT PURCHASERS
For more information call **800-771-9202** or visit **www.warren-news.com**

TV Market Ranking: Outside TV Markets (GLASGOW, Valley County). Franchise award date: October 1, 1993. Franchise expiration date: N.A. Began: January 1, 1961.
Channel capacity: N.A. Channels available but not in use: N.A.

Basic Service
Subscribers: 166. Commercial subscribers: 8.
Programming (via microwave): KFBB-TV (ABC, FOX) Great Falls; KRTV (CBS, CW, Grit) Great Falls; KTGF (IND) Great Falls; KUSM-TV (PBS) Bozeman.
Programming (via satellite): A&E; C-SPAN; C-SPAN 2; CW PLUS; Pop; QVC; TBS; truTV.
Fee: $25.00 installation; $20.99 monthly.

Expanded Basic Service 1
Subscribers: N.A.
Programming (via satellite): Altitude Sports & Entertainment; AMC; Animal Planet; Cartoon Network; CMT; CNBC; CNN; Comedy Central; Discovery Channel; Disney Channel; E! HD; ESPN; ESPN2; EWTN Global Catholic Network; Food Network; Fox News Channel; Freeform; FX; Hallmark Channel; HLN; INSP; Lifetime; MSNBC; MTV; Nickelodeon; Oxygen; Root Sports Rocky Mountain; Spike TV; The Weather Channel; TLC; TNT; Travel Channel; USA Network; VH1.
Fee: $30.00 monthly.

Digital Basic Service
Subscribers: N.A.
Programming (via satellite): BBC America; Bloomberg Television; Bravo; CBS Sports Network; CMT; Destination America; Discovery Kids Channel; Discovery Life Channel; Disney XD; DMX Music; ESPN Classic; ESPNews; Fox Sports 1; Fuse; FXM; FYI; Golf Channel; GSN; HGTV; History; History International; IFC; Investigation Discovery; LMN; MTV Classic; MTV Hits; MTV2; National Geographic Channel; NBCSN; Nick Jr.; Nicktoons; Outdoor Channel; OWN; Oprah Winfrey Network; RFD-TV; Science Channel; Syfy; TeenNick; Trinity Broadcasting Network (TBN); Turner Classic Movies; TV Land; VH1 Soul.
Fee: $18.00 monthly; $4.40 converter.

Digital Pay Service 1
Pay Units: N.A.
Programming (via satellite): Cinemax (multiplexed); Flix; HBO (multiplexed); Showtime (multiplexed); Starz (multiplexed); Starz Encore (multiplexed); The Movie Channel (multiplexed).
Fee: $5.00 monthly (Encore), $9.00 monthly (Starz), $16.00 monthly (Cinemax, HBO or Showtime/TMC).

Video-On-Demand: No

Pay-Per-View
iN DEMAND (delivered digitally).

Internet Service
Operational: Yes.
Fee: $43.95-$65.00 monthly.

Telephone Service
Digital: Operational
Miles of Plant: 24.0 (coaxial); 3.0 (fiber optic).

Chief Executive Officer: Mike Kilgore. Chief Financial Officer: Remi Sun.
Ownership: Nemont Telephone Coop (MSO).

GLENDIVE—Mid-Rivers Communications, 904 C Ave, PO Box 280, Circle, MT 59215. Phones: 406-485-3301; 406-377-3336; 406-238-7706; 406-238-7700. Fax: 406-485-2924. E-mail: customerservices@midrivers.coop. Web Site: http://www.midrivers.com. Also serves Bloomfield, Brockway, Circle, Dawson County, Fallon, Richey & Terry. ICA: MT0013.
TV Market Ranking: Below 100 (Bloomfield, Dawson County (portions), GLENDIVE); Outside TV Markets (Brockway, Dawson County (portions), Fallon, Circle, Richey, Terry). Franchise award date: N.A. Franchise expiration date: N.A. Began: May 1, 1967.
Channel capacity: N.A. Channels available but not in use: N.A.

Basic Service
Subscribers: 2,038.
Programming (received off-air): KUMV-TV (FOX, NBC) Williston; KXGN-TV (CBS, NBC) Glendive.
Programming (via microwave): KUSM-TV (PBS) Bozeman.
Programming (via satellite): A&E; CNBC; CNN; C-SPAN; CW PLUS; Discovery Channel; Freeform; HLN; KDVR (Antenna TV, FOX) Denver; KMGH-TV (ABC, Azteca America) Denver; Lifetime; MTV; Nickelodeon; TBS; The Weather Channel; TNT; WGN America.
Fee: $60.00 installation; $26.60 monthly; $.64 converter.

Expanded Basic Service 1
Subscribers: N.A.
Programming (via satellite): AMC; Animal Planet; Bravo; Cartoon Network; CMT; Comedy Central; C-SPAN 2; Discovery Life Channel; Disney Channel; Disney XD; E! HD; ESPN; ESPN Classic; ESPN2; ESPNU; EWTN Global Catholic Network; Food Network; Fox News Channel; Fox Sports 1; FX; Great American Country; GSN; Hallmark Channel; HGTV; History; ION Television; MSNBC; National Geographic Channel; Outdoor Channel; Oxygen; RFD-TV; Root Sports Rocky Mountain; Spike TV; Syfy; TLC; Travel Channel; Trinity Broadcasting Network (TBN); truTV; Turner Classic Movies; TV Land; USA Network; VH1.
Fee: $11.39 monthly.

Digital Basic Service
Subscribers: N.A.
Programming (via satellite): A&E HD; AXS TV; BBC America; Bloomberg Television; Bravo; CMT; Destination America; Discovery Channel HD; Discovery Kids Channel; Disney XD; ESPN Classic; ESPN HD; ESPN2 HD; ESPNews; Food Network HD; Fuse; FXM; FYI; Golf Channel; GSN; HGTV HD; History International; IFC; Investigation Discovery; LMN; MTV Classic; MTV2; National Geographic Channel; National Geographic Channel HD; NBCSN; Nick Jr.; Nicktoons; Outdoor Channel 2 HD; OWN; Oprah

Montana—Cable Systems

Winfrey Network; Science Channel; TeenNick; TNT HD; Trinity Broadcasting Network (TBN); Universal HD; VH1 Soul; WE tv.
Pay Service 1
Pay Units: N.A.
Programming (via satellite): Cinemax; HBO; Showtime; Starz; Starz Encore; The Movie Channel.
Fee: $11.95 monthly (Cinemax, HBO or Showtime).
Digital Pay Service 1
Pay Units: N.A.
Programming (via satellite): Cinemax (multiplexed); Cinemax HD; Flix; HBO (multiplexed); HBO HD; Showtime (multiplexed); Starz (multiplexed); Starz Encore (multiplexed); The Movie Channel (multiplexed).
Video-On-Demand: No
Pay-Per-View
iN DEMAND (delivered digitally).
Internet Service
Operational: Yes, DSL & dial-up.
Telephone Service
Analog: Operational
Miles of Plant: 43.0 (coaxial); None (fiber optic). Homes passed: 3,339.
President: Mark Robbins. General Manager: Bill Wade. Chief Technician: Mike Sokoloski. Customer Service Manager: Deb Wagner.
Ownership: Mid-Rivers Telephone Cooperative Inc. (MSO).

GRANT CREEK—Formerly served by Charter Communications. No longer in operation. ICA: MT0094.

GREAT FALLS—Charter Communications, 12405 Powerscourt Dr, St. Louis, MO 63131. Phones: 636-207-5100 (Corporate office); 406-452-4111; 877-273-7626; 406-727-8881. Fax: 406-727-6433. Web Site: http://www.charter.com. Also serves Black Eagle, Cascade County & Malmstrom AFB. ICA: MT0003.
TV Market Ranking: Below 100 (Black Eagle, Cascade County, GREAT FALLS, Malmstrom AFB). Franchise award date: N.A. Franchise expiration date: N.A. Began: June 1, 1958.
Channel capacity: N.A. Channels available but not in use: N.A.
Digital Basic Service
Subscribers: 12,905.
Programming (via satellite): A&E HD; Animal Planet HD; AXS TV; BBC America; Bloomberg Television; Bravo; BYUtv; CBS Sports Network; CMT; CNN HD; Cooking Channel; C-SPAN 3; Destination America; Discovery Channel HD; Discovery Kids Channel; Discovery Life Channel; Disney Channel HD; Disney XD; DIY Network; DMX Music; ESPN HD; ESPN2 HD; ESPNews; Food Network HD; FOX College Sports Central; FOX College Sports Pacific; Fox Sports 1; Freeform HD; Fuse; FXM; FYI; Golf Channel; Great American Country; GSN; HD Theater; HGTV HD; History HD; History International; HRTV; IFC; Investigation Discovery; ION Television; Lifetime Movie Network HD; LMN; MTV Classic; MTV Hits; MTV Jams; MTV2; Nat Geo WILD; National Geographic Channel; National Geographic Channel HD; NBCSN; NFL Network; NFL Network HD; NHL Network; Nick 2; Nick Jr.; Nicktoons; Outdoor Channel; Outdoor Channel 2 HD; OWN: Oprah Winfrey Network; Qubo; RFD-TV; Science Channel; Science HD; Sprout; Syfy HD; TBS HD; TeenNick; The Weather Channel HD; TLC HD; TNT HD; Tr3s; Trinity Broadcasting Network (TBN); Universal HD; UP; USA Network HD; Versus HD; VH1 Soul.
Fee: $26.99 monthly.
Digital Expanded Basic Service
Subscribers: N.A.
Programming (via satellite): A&E; Altitude Sports & Entertainment; AMC; Animal Planet; BET; Cartoon Network; CMT; CNBC; CNN; Comedy Central; Discovery Channel; Disney Channel; E! HD; ESPN; ESPN Classic; ESPN2; Food Network; Fox News Channel; Freeform; FX; Hallmark Channel; HGTV; History; HLN; INSP; ION Television; MSNBC; MTV; Nickelodeon; Oxygen; Root Sports Rocky Mountain; Spike TV; Syfy; The Weather Channel; TLC; TNT; Travel Channel; truTV; Turner Classic Movies; TV Land; USA Network; VH1.
Fee: $28.99 monthly.
Digital Pay Service 1
Pay Units: N.A.
Programming (via satellite): Cinemax (multiplexed); Cinemax HD; Flix; HBO (multiplexed); HBO HD; HBO on Demand; Showtime (multiplexed); Showtime HD; Showtime On Demand; Starz (multiplexed); Starz Encore (multiplexed); Starz HD; Starz On Demand; The Movie Channel (multiplexed); The Movie Channel HD.
Video-On-Demand: Yes
Pay-Per-View
Hot Choice (delivered digitally); iN DEMAND (delivered digitally); Playboy TV (delivered digitally); Fresh (delivered digitally); ESPN (delivered digitally); MLB Extra Innings (delivered digitally); NHL Center Ice (delivered digitally).
Internet Service
Operational: Yes. Began: March 1, 2000.
Subscribers: 17,445.
Broadband Service: Charter Internet.
Fee: $99.95 installation; $52.95 monthly; $10.00 modem lease.
Telephone Service
Analog: Not Operational
Digital: Operational
Subscribers: 10,457.
Fee: $49.99 monthly
Miles of Plant: 497.0 (coaxial); 133.0 (fiber optic). Homes passed: 34,875.
President & Chief Executive Officer: Tom Rutledge. Vice President & General Manager: Sean O'Donnell. Technical Operations Manager: Doug Sappington. Accounting Director: David Sovanski.
Ownership: Charter Communications Inc. (MSO).

HAMILTON—Charter Communications, 924 South 3rd West, Missoula, MT 59810. Phones: 636-207-5100 (Corporate office); 406-728-4869; 516-803-2300 (Corporate office); 877-273-7626. Web Site: http://www.charter.com. Also serves Corvallis & Ravalli County (portions). ICA: MT0015.
TV Market Ranking: Below 100 (Ravalli County (portions)); Outside TV Markets (Corvallis, HAMILTON, Ravalli County (portions)). Franchise award date: N.A. Franchise expiration date: N.A. Began: September 1, 1964.
Channel capacity: N.A. Channels available but not in use: N.A.
Digital Basic Service
Subscribers: 1,183.
Programming (via satellite): A&E HD; Animal Planet HD; BBC America; Bloomberg Television; Bravo; CMT; Destination America; Discovery Channel HD; Discovery Kids Channel; Discovery Life Channel; Disney Channel HD; Disney XD; DMX Music; ESPN Classic; ESPN HD; ESPNews; Food Network HD; FOX College Sports Central; FOX College Sports Pacific; Fox Sports 1; Freeform HD; Fuse; FXM; FYI; Golf Channel; GSN; HD Theater; HGTV HD; History HD; History International; HorseTV Channel; IFC; Investigation Discovery; ION Television; LMN; MTV Classic; MTV Hits; MTV2; Nat Geo WILD; National Geographic Channel; National Geographic Channel HD; NBCSN; NFL Network; Nick Jr.; Nicktoons; Outdoor Channel; OWN: Oprah Winfrey Network; RFD-TV; Science Channel; Science HD; Sprout; Syfy HD; TeenNick; Trinity Broadcasting Network (TBN); Universal HD; UP; USA Network HD; VH1 Soul.
Fee: $34.95 installation; $26.99 monthly.
Digital Expanded Basic Service
Subscribers: N.A.
Programming (via satellite): A&E; Altitude Sports & Entertainment; AMC; Animal Planet; Cartoon Network; CMT; CNBC; CNN; Comedy Central; Discovery Channel; Disney Channel; E! HD; ESPN; ESPN2; Food Network; Fox News Channel; Freeform; FX; Great American Country; Hallmark Channel; HGTV; History; HLN; INSP; ION Television; Lifetime; MSNBC; MTV; Nickelodeon; Oxygen; Root Sports Rocky Mountain; Spike TV; Syfy; The Weather Channel; TLC; TNT; Travel Channel; truTV; Turner Classic Movies; TV Land; USA Network; VH1.
Fee: $4.00 monthly.
Digital Pay Service 1
Pay Units: N.A.
Programming (via satellite): Cinemax (multiplexed); Flix; HBO (multiplexed); HBO HD; Showtime (multiplexed); Starz (multiplexed); Starz Encore (multiplexed); Starz HD; The Movie Channel (multiplexed).
Video-On-Demand: No
Internet Service
Operational: Yes.
Subscribers: 1,145.
Broadband Service: Charter Internet.
Fee: $39.95 monthly.
Telephone Service
Digital: Operational
Subscribers: 626.
Fee: $49.99 monthly
Miles of Plant: 130.0 (coaxial); 26.0 (fiber optic). Homes passed: 4,805.
President & Chief Executive Officer: Tom Rutledge. General Manager: Mike Oswald. Technical Operations Manager: Alan White. Accounting Director: David Sovanski.
Ownership: Charter Communications Inc. (MSO).

HARDIN—USA Communications, 920 East 56th St, Ste B, Kearney, NE 68847. Phones: 406-628-2100; 800-628-6060; 406-628-6336; 308-236-1512 (Kearney corporate office). Fax: 406-628-8181. Web Site: http://usacommunications.tv. ICA: MT0030.
TV Market Ranking: Below 100 (HARDIN). Franchise award date: N.A. Franchise expiration date: N.A. Began: January 1, 1968.
Channel capacity: N.A. Channels available but not in use: N.A.
Basic Service
Subscribers: 426.
Programming (received off-air): KHMT (FOX) Hardin; KSVI (ABC) Billings; KTVQ (CBS, CW, Grit) Billings; KULR-TV (NBC) Billings; KWBM (Retro TV) Harrison.
Programming (via satellite): 3ABN; A&E; Food Network; FOX Sports Networks; Freeform; Hallmark Channel; HLN; KRMA-TV (PBS) Denver; Pop; QVC; TBS; The Weather Channel; WGN America.
Fee: $29.95 installation; $24.95 monthly.
Expanded Basic Service 1
Subscribers: N.A.
Programming (via satellite): Altitude Sports & Entertainment; AMC; Animal Planet; Cartoon Network; CMT; CNBC; CNN; Discovery Channel; E! HD; ESPN; ESPN2; ESPNews; Fox News Channel; FX; HGTV; History; Lifetime; MSNBC; MTV; Nickelodeon; Outdoor Channel; Spike TV; Syfy; TLC; TNT; Trinity Broadcasting Network (TBN); TV Land; USA Network; VH1.
Fee: $18.04 monthly.
Digital Basic Service
Subscribers: N.A.
Programming (via satellite): BBC America; Bloomberg Television; Cloo; CMT; Daystar TV Network; Destination America; Discovery Kids Channel; Discovery Life Channel; DMX Music; ESPN Classic; ESPN2; ESPNews; EVINE Live; FOX College Sports Central; FOX College Sports Pacific; Fox Sports 1; FXM; FYI; Golf Channel; GSN; History; History International; LMN; MTV Classic; MTV Hits; MTV2; National Geographic Channel; NBCSN; Nick Jr.; Outdoor Channel; Ovation; OWN: Oprah Winfrey Network; Science Channel; TeenNick; Trinity Broadcasting Network (TBN); VH1 Soul; WE tv.
Fee: $13.00 monthly.
Digital Pay Service 1
Pay Units: N.A.
Programming (via satellite): Cinemax (multiplexed); Flix; HBO (multiplexed); Showtime (multiplexed); Starz (multiplexed); Starz Encore (multiplexed); The Movie Channel (multiplexed).
Fee: $13.00 monthly (Cinemax, HBO, Showtime/TMC/Flix or Starz/Encore).
Video-On-Demand: No
Internet Service
Operational: Yes.
Broadband Service: Cable Montana.
Fee: $35.95 monthly.
Telephone Service
Digital: Operational
Fee: $39.95 monthly
Miles of Plant: 18.0 (coaxial); None (fiber optic). Homes passed: 1,326.
Chief Financial Officer: Amber Reineke. Operations Manager: Stuart Gilbertson. General Manager: Doug Lane.
Ownership: USA Companies LP (MSO).

HARLEM—Charter Communications, 12405 Powerscourt Dr, St. Louis, MO 63131. Phones: 636-207-5100 (Corporate office); 516-803-2300 (Corporate office); 877-273-7626; 406-727-8881. Web Site: http://www.charter.com. ICA: MT0071.
TV Market Ranking: Outside TV Markets (HARLEM). Franchise award date: Jan-

Cable Systems—Montana

uary 1, 1992. Franchise expiration date: N.A. Began: July 1, 1981.
Channel capacity: N.A. Channels available but not in use: N.A.

Digital Basic Service
Subscribers: 35. Commercial subscribers: 4.
Programming (via microwave): KFBB-TV (ABC, FOX) Great Falls; KRTV (CBS, CW, Grit) Great Falls; KTGF (IND) Great Falls; KUSM-TV (PBS) Bozeman.
Programming (via satellite): A&E; CMT; CNN; C-SPAN; Lifetime; QVC; TBS; truTV.
Fee: $34.95 installation; $26.99 monthly.

Digital Expanded Basic Service
Subscribers: N.A.
Programming (via satellite): AMC; Animal Planet; Cartoon Network; CNBC; CNN; Discovery Channel; Disney Channel; E! HD; ESPN; ESPN2; Fox News Channel; Freeform; HGTV; History; Nickelodeon; Spike TV; The Weather Channel; TLC; TNT; USA Network.
Fee: $28.99 monthly.

Pay Service 1
Pay Units: N.A.
Programming (via satellite): HBO; Showtime; Starz; Starz Encore.
Video-On-Demand: No
Internet Service
Operational: Yes.
Broadband Service: Charter Internet.
Fee: $52.95 monthly.
Telephone Service
Digital: Operational
Fee: $49.99 monthly
Miles of Plant: 5.0 (coaxial); None (fiber optic). Homes passed: 435.
President & Chief Executive Officer: Tom Rutledge. Vice President: Sean O'Donnell. General Manager: Patty Faloon. Chief Technician: Jim Passon. Accounting Director: David Sovanski.
Ownership: Charter Communications Inc. (MSO).

HARLOWTON—Mid-Rivers Communications, 904 C Ave, PO Box 280, Circle, MT 59215. Phones: 406-535-3336; 406-485-3301. Fax: 406-485-2924. E-mail: customerservices@midrivers.coop. Web Site: http://www.midrivers.com. ICA: MT0061.
TV Market Ranking: Outside TV Markets (HARLOWTON). Franchise award date: N.A. Franchise expiration date: N.A. Began: June 1, 1980.
Channel capacity: 65 (not 2-way capable). Channels available but not in use: N.A.

Basic Service
Subscribers: 98.
Programming (received off-air): KUSM-TV (PBS) Bozeman.
Programming (via satellite): A&E; AMC; Animal Planet; Cartoon Network; CMT; CNBC; CNN; C-SPAN; Discovery Channel; Disney Channel; DIY Network; E! HD; ESPN; ESPN2; Food Network; Fox News Channel; Freeform; Hallmark Channel; HGTV; History; KWGN-TV (CW, This TV) Denver; Lifetime; MTV; Nickelodeon; Outdoor Channel; RFD-TV; Root Sports Rocky Mountain; Spike TV; Syfy; TBS; The Weather Channel; TLC; TNT; Travel Channel; Turner Classic Movies; TV Land; USA Network; VH1; WE tv; WGN America.
Programming (via translator): KSVI (ABC) Billings; KTVQ (CBS, CW, Grit) Billings; KULR-TV (NBC) Billings.
Fee: $49.95 installation; $45.70 monthly; $3.00 converter.

Pay Service 1
Pay Units: N.A.
Programming (via satellite): HBO; The Movie Channel.
Fee: $15.00 installation; $12.00 monthly.
Internet Service
Operational: No.
Telephone Service
None
Miles of Plant: 11.0 (coaxial); None (fiber optic). Homes passed: 500.
President: Mark Robbins. General Manager: Bill Wade. Central Office Supervisor: Mike Sokoloski. Customer Service Manager: Deb Wagner.
Ownership: Mid-Rivers Telephone Cooperative Inc. (MSO).

HAVRE—Charter Communications, 1770 2nd St West, Havre, MT 59501. Phones: 636-207-5100 (Corporate office); 516-803-2300 (Corporate office); 877-273-7626; 406-727-8881. Web Site: http://www.charter.com. Also serves Hill County. ICA: MT0008.
TV Market Ranking: Below 100 (HAVRE, Hill County). Franchise award date: October 3, 1988. Franchise expiration date: N.A. Began: January 1, 1954.
Channel capacity: N.A. Channels available but not in use: N.A.

Digital Basic Service
Subscribers: 2,188.
Programming (via satellite): A&E HD; Animal Planet HD; AXS TV; BBC America; Bloomberg Television; Bravo; Bravo HD; BYUtv; CBS Sports Network; CMT; CNBC HD+; CNN HD; Cooking Channel; Destination America; Discovery Channel HD; Discovery Kids Channel; Discovery Life Channel; Disney Channel HD; Disney XD; DIY Network; DMX Music; ESPN Classic; ESPN HD; ESPN2 HD; ESPNews; Food Network HD; FOX College Sports Central; FOX College Sports Pacific; Fox Sports 1; Freeform HD; Fuse; FXM; FYI; Golf Channel; GSN; HD Theater; HGTV HD; History HD; History International; HRTV; IFC; Investigation Discovery; ION Television; Lifetime Movie Network HD; LMN; MTV Classic; MTV Hits; MTV Jams; MTV2; Nat Geo WILD; National Geographic Channel; National Geographic Channel HD; NBCSN; NFL Network; NFL Network HD; Nick 2; Nick Jr.; Nicktoons; Outdoor Channel; OWN: Oprah Winfrey Network; RFD-TV; Science Channel; Science HD; Syfy HD; TBS HD; TeenNick; TLC HD; TNT HD; Tr3s; Trinity Broadcasting Network (TBN); Universal HD; UP; USA Network HD; Versus HD; VH1 Soul.
Fee: $34.95 installation; $26.99 monthly; $4.05 converter.

Digital Expanded Basic Service
Subscribers: N.A.
Programming (via satellite): A&E; Altitude Sports & Entertainment; AMC; Animal Planet; Cartoon Network; CMT; CNBC; CNN; Comedy Central; Discovery Channel; Disney Channel; E! HD; ESPN; ESPN2; EWTN Global Catholic Network; Food Network; Fox News Channel; Freeform; FX; Hallmark Channel; HGTV; History; HLN; INSP; Lifetime; MSNBC; MTV; Nickelodeon; Oxygen; Root Sports Rocky Mountain; Spike TV; Syfy; The Weather Channel; TLC; TNT; truTV; Turner Classic Movies; TV Land; USA Network; VH1.
Fee: $28.99 monthly.

Digital Pay Service 1
Pay Units: N.A.
Programming (via satellite): Cinemax (multiplexed); Cinemax HD; Flix; HBO (multiplexed); HBO HD; Showtime (multiplexed); Showtime HD; Starz (multiplexed); Starz Encore (multiplexed); Starz HD; The Movie Channel (multiplexed); The Movie Channel HD.
Video-On-Demand: No
Pay-Per-View
iN DEMAND (delivered digitally); Fresh (delivered digitally).
Internet Service
Operational: Yes.
Broadband Service: Charter Internet.
Fee: $52.95 monthly.
Telephone Service
Analog: Not Operational
Digital: Operational
Fee: $49.99 monthly
Miles of Plant: 65.0 (coaxial); 10.0 (fiber optic). Homes passed: 5,593.
Vice President: Sean O'Donnell. President & Chief Executive Officer: Tom Rutledge. General Manager: Patty Faloon. Chief Technician: Jim Passon. Accounting Director: David Sovanski.
Ownership: Charter Communications Inc. (MSO).

HELENA—Charter Communications, 12405 Powerscourt Dr, St. Louis, MO 63131. Phones: 636-207-5100 (Corporate office); 516-803-2300 (Corporate office); 877-273-7626. Fax: 406-443-5843. Web Site: http://www.charter.com. Also serves Clancy, East Helena, Jefferson County (unincorporated areas), Lewis & Clark County (portions) & Montana City. ICA: MT0004.
TV Market Ranking: Below 100 (Clancy, East Helena, HELENA, Jefferson County (unincorporated areas), Montana City, Lewis & Clark County (portions)); Outside TV Markets (Lewis & Clark County (portions)). Franchise award date: N.A. Franchise expiration date: N.A. Began: January 1, 1955.
Channel capacity: N.A. Channels available but not in use: N.A.

Digital Basic Service
Subscribers: 11,725.
Programming (via satellite): A&E HD; Animal Planet HD; AXS TV; BBC America; Bloomberg Television; BlueHighways TV; Bravo; Bravo HD; BYUtv; CBS Sports Network; CMT; CNBC HD+; CNN HD; Cooking Channel; C-SPAN 3; Destination America; Discovery Channel HD; Discovery Kids Channel; Disney Channel HD; Disney XD; DIY Network; DMX Music; ESPN Classic; ESPN HD; ESPN2 HD; ESPNews; Food Network HD; FOX College Sports Central; FOX College Sports Pacific; Fox Sports 1; Freeform HD; Fuse; FXM; FYI; Golf Channel; Great American Country; GSN; HD Theater; HGTV HD; History HD; History International; HRTV; IFC; Investigation Discovery; ION Television; Lifetime Movie Network HD; LMN; MTV Classic; MTV Hits; MTV Live; MTV2; Nat Geo WILD; National Geographic Channel; National Geographic Channel HD; NBCSN; NFL Network; NFL Network HD; NHL Network; Nick Jr.; Nicktoons; Outdoor Channel; Outdoor Channel 2 HD; OWN: Oprah Winfrey Network; Qubo; RFD-TV; Science Channel; Science HD; Sprout; Syfy HD; TBS HD; TeenNick; The Weather Channel HD; TLC HD; TNT HD; Trinity Broadcasting Network (TBN); Universal HD; UP; USA Network HD; Versus HD; VH1 Soul.
Fee: $26.99 monthly.

Digital Expanded Basic Service
Subscribers: N.A.
Programming (via satellite): A&E; Altitude Sports & Entertainment; AMC; Animal Planet; Cartoon Network; CMT; CNBC; CNN; Comedy Central; Discovery Channel; Disney Channel; E! HD; ESPN;

Encore (multiplexed); Starz HD; The Movie Channel (multiplexed); The Movie Channel HD.

ESPN2; Food Network; Fox News Channel; Freeform; FX; Hallmark Channel; HGTV; History; HLN; INSP; MSNBC; MTV; Nickelodeon; Oxygen; Root Sports Rocky Mountain; Spike TV; Syfy; The Weather Channel; TLC; TNT; Travel Channel; truTV; TV Land; USA Network; VH1.
Fee: $28.99 monthly.

Digital Pay Service 1
Pay Units: N.A.
Programming (via satellite): Cinemax (multiplexed); Cinemax HD; Cinemax On Demand; Flix; HBO (multiplexed); HBO HD; HBO on Demand; Showtime (multiplexed); Showtime HD; Showtime On Demand; Starz (multiplexed); Starz Encore (multiplexed); Starz HD; Starz On Demand; The Movie Channel (multiplexed); The Movie Channel HD.
Video-On-Demand: Yes
Pay-Per-View
ESPN Now (delivered digitally); Sports PPV (delivered digitally); iN DEMAND (delivered digitally); Urban Xtra (delivered digitally); Fresh (delivered digitally); Shorteez (delivered digitally); Playboy TV (delivered digitally); Hot Choice (delivered digitally).
Internet Service
Operational: Yes. Began: January 1, 2001.
Broadband Service: Charter Internet.
Fee: $99.95 installation; $52.95 monthly; $10.00 modem lease.
Telephone Service
Analog: Not Operational
Digital: Operational
Fee: $49.99 monthly
Miles of Plant: 335.0 (coaxial); 86.0 (fiber optic). Homes passed: 23,556.
President & Chief Executive Officer: Tom Rutledge. General Manager: Mike Oswald. Chief Technician: Ed McFadden. Accounting Director: David Sovanski.
Ownership: Charter Communications Inc. (MSO).

HOT SPRINGS—Hot Springs Telephone Co, 216 Main St, PO Box 627, Hot Springs, MT 59845. Phones: 406-741-2662; 406-741-2751. Web Site: http://www.hotsprgs.net. ICA: MT0078.
TV Market Ranking: Outside TV Markets (HOT SPRINGS). Franchise award date: N.A. Franchise expiration date: N.A. Began: April 1, 1984.
Channel capacity: N.A. Channels available but not in use: N.A.

Basic Service
Subscribers: N.A.
Programming (received off-air): KECI-TV (MeTV, Movies!, NBC, This TV) Missoula; KPAX-TV (CBS, CW, Grit) Missoula; KTMF (ABC, FOX) Missoula.
Programming (via satellite): A&E; Cartoon Network; CNBC; CNN; Discovery Channel; Disney Channel; ESPN; ESPN2; Freeform; History; KDVR (Antenna TV, FOX) Denver; Nickelodeon; Outdoor Channel; Spike TV; TBS; The Weather Channel; TLC; TNT; Travel Channel; Trinity Broadcasting Network (TBN); Turner Classic Movies; TV Land; VH1; WGN America.
Fee: $31.45 installation.

Pay Service 1
Pay Units: N.A.
Programming (via satellite): HBO; Showtime; The Movie Channel.
Fee: $10.95 monthly (each).
Video-On-Demand: No
Internet Service
Operational: Yes, DSL.

2017 Edition
D-471

Montana—Cable Systems

Telephone Service
Analog: Operational
Miles of Plant: 3.0 (coaxial); None (fiber optic). Homes passed: 81.
General Manager: Laurence Walchuk.
Ownership: Hot Springs Telephone Co. (MSO).

HYSHAM—Mid-Rivers Communications, 904 C Ave, PO Box 280, Circle, MT 59215. Phones: 406-535-3336; 406-485-3301. Fax: 406-485-2924. E-mail: customerservices@midrivers.coop. Web Site: http://www.midrivers.com. ICA: MT0086.
TV Market Ranking: Outside TV Markets (HYSHAM). Franchise award date: June 14, 1982. Franchise expiration date: N.A. Began: October 1, 1982.
Channel capacity: N.A. Channels available but not in use: N.A.
Basic Service
Subscribers: 31.
Programming (received off-air): KHMT (FOX) Hardin; KSVI (ABC) Billings; KTVQ (CBS, CW, Grit) Billings; KULR-TV (NBC) Billings.
Programming (via satellite): Cartoon Network; CNN; Discovery Channel; Disney Channel; ESPN; Freeform; HGTV; Spike TV; TBS; TNT; Turner Classic Movies; USA Network; WGN America.
Fee: $49.95 installation; $37.70 monthly.
Pay Service 1
Pay Units: 22.
Programming (via satellite): HBO.
Fee: $15.00 installation; $12.00 monthly.
Internet Service
Operational: No.
Telephone Service
None
Miles of Plant: 5.0 (coaxial); None (fiber optic). Homes passed: 230.
President: Mark Robbins. General Manager: Bill Wade. Chief Technician: Mike Sokoloski. Customer Service Manager: Deb Wagner.
Ownership: Mid-Rivers Telephone Cooperative Inc. (MSO).

JOLIET—Formerly served by USA Communications. No longer in operation. ICA: MT0113.

JORDAN—Mid-Rivers Communications, 904 C Ave, PO Box 280, Circle, MT 59215. Phones: 406-535-3336; 406-485-3301. Fax: 406-485-2924. E-mail: customerservices@midrivers.coop. Web Site: http://www.midrivers.com. ICA: MT0114.
TV Market Ranking: Outside TV Markets (JORDAN). Franchise award date: N.A. Franchise expiration date: N.A. Began: January 1, 1983.
Channel capacity: N.A. Channels available but not in use: N.A.
Basic Service
Subscribers: 139.
Programming (received off-air): KFBB-TV (ABC, FOX) Great Falls; KHMT (FOX) Hardin; KTVQ (CBS, CW, Grit) Billings; KULR-TV (NBC) Billings; KUSM-TV (PBS) Bozeman.
Programming (via satellite): A&E; AMC; CNBC; CNN; C-SPAN; Discovery Channel; Disney Channel; DIY Network; ESPN; ESPN2; EWTN Global Catholic Network; Fox News Channel; Freeform; FXM; Great American Country; HGTV; History; HLN; ION Television; Lifetime; Nickelodeon; Outdoor Channel; QVC; RFD-TV; Spike TV; Syfy; TBS; The Weather Channel; TLC; TNT; Travel Channel; TV Land; WE tv; WGN America.
Fee: $49.95 installation; $26.95 monthly.

Pay Service 1
Pay Units: N.A.
Programming (via satellite): HBO; The Movie Channel.
Fee: $8.00 monthly (TMC), $10 monthly (HBO).
Video-On-Demand: No
Internet Service
Operational: Yes.
Broadband Service: MegaSpeed.
Fee: $25.00 installation; $49.95 monthly.
Telephone Service
Analog: Operational
Miles of Plant: 18.0 (coaxial); None (fiber optic). Homes passed: 200.
President: Mark Robbins. General Manager: Bill Wade. Chief Technician: Mike Sokolosky. Customer Service Manager: Deb Wagner.
Ownership: Mid-Rivers Telephone Cooperative Inc. (MSO).

KALISPELL—Charter Communications, 12405 Powerscourt Dr, St. Louis, MO 63131. Phones: 636-207-5100 (Corporate office); 516-803-2300 (Corporate office); 877-273-7626. Fax: 406-755-7204. Web Site: http://www.charter.com. Also serves Bigfork, Columbia Falls, Flathead County, Lakeside, Somers & Whitefish. ICA: MT0006.
TV Market Ranking: Below 100 (Bigfork, Columbia Falls, Flathead County (portions), KALISPELL, Lakeside, Somers, Whitefish); Outside TV Markets (Flathead County (portions)). Franchise award date: N.A. Franchise expiration date: N.A. Began: May 1, 1983.
Channel capacity: N.A. Channels available but not in use: N.A.
Digital Basic Service
Subscribers: 13,100.
Programming (via satellite): A&E HD; Animal Planet HD; AXS TV; BBC America; Bloomberg Television; Bravo; Bravo HD; CBS Sports Network; CMT; CNBC HD+; CNN HD; Cooking Channel; C-SPAN 3; Destination America; Discovery Channel HD; Discovery Kids Channel; Discovery Life Channel; Disney Channel HD; Disney XD; DIY Network; DMX Music; ESPN Classic; ESPN HD; ESPN2 HD; ESPNews; Food Network HD; FOX College Sports Central; FOX College Sports Pacific; Fox Sports 1; Freeform HD; Fuse; FXM; FYI; Golf Channel; GSN; HD Theater; HGTV HD; History HD; History International; HRTV; IFC; Investigation Discovery; ION Television; Lifetime Movie Network HD; LMN; MTV Classic; MTV Hits; MTV Jams; MTV Live; MTV2; Nat Geo WILD; National Geographic Channel; National Geographic Channel HD; NBCSN; NFL Network HD; NFL Network HD; NHL Network; Nick 2; Nick Jr.; Nicktoons; Outdoor Channel; Outdoor Channel 2 HD; OWN; Oprah Winfrey Network; Qubo; RFD-TV; Science Channel; Science HD; Sprout; Syfy HD; TBS HD; TeenNick; The Weather Channel HD; TLC HD; TNT HD; Tr3s; Trinity Broadcasting Network (TBN); Universal HD; UP; USA Network HD; Versus HD; VH1 Soul.
Fee: $26.99 monthly.
Digital Expanded Basic Service
Subscribers: N.A.
Programming (via satellite): A&E; Altitude Sports & Entertainment; AMC; Animal Planet; BYUtv; Cartoon Network; CMT; CNBC; CNN; Comedy Central; Discovery Channel; Disney Channel; E! HD; ESPN; ESPN2; EWTN Global Catholic Network; Food Network; Fox News Channel; Freeform; FX; Hallmark Channel; HGTV; History; HLN; INSP; ION Television; Life-

time; MSNBC; MTV; Nickelodeon; Oxygen; QVC; Spike TV; Syfy; The Weather Channel; TLC; TNT; Travel Channel; truTV; Turner Classic Movies; TV Land; USA Network; VH1.
Fee: $28.99 monthly.
Digital Pay Service 1
Pay Units: N.A.
Programming (via satellite): Cinemax (multiplexed); Cinemax HD; Cinemax On Demand; Flix; HBO (multiplexed); HBO HD; HBO on Demand; Showtime (multiplexed); Showtime HD; Showtime On Demand; Starz (multiplexed); Starz Encore (multiplexed); Starz HD; Starz On Demand; The Movie Channel (multiplexed).
Video-On-Demand: Yes
Pay-Per-View
iN DEMAND (delivered digitally); ESPN (delivered digitally); MLB Extra Innings (delivered digitally); NHL Center Ice (delivered digitally).
Internet Service
Operational: Yes.
Subscribers: 13,618.
Broadband Service: Charter Internet.
Fee: $52.95 monthly.
Telephone Service
Digital: Operational
Subscribers: 8,296.
Fee: $49.99 monthly
Miles of Plant: 1,304.0 (coaxial); 356.0 (fiber optic). Homes passed: 32,318.
President & Chief Executive Officer: Tom Rutledge. Vice President: Sean O'Donnell. Chief Technician: Weldon Plympton. General Manager: Patty Faloon. Accounting Director: David Sovanski.
Ownership: Charter Communications Inc. (MSO).

LAME DEER—Formerly served by Eagle Cablevision Inc. No longer in operation. ICA: MT0058.

LAUREL—Charter Communications. Now served by BILLINGS, MT [MT0001]. ICA: MT0023.

LAVINA—Mid-Rivers Communications. Now served by ROUNDUP, MT [MT0043]. ICA: Mt0109.

LEWISTOWN—Mid-Rivers Communications, 904 C Ave, PO Box 280, Circle, MT 59215. Phones: 406-485-3301; 406-535-3336. Fax: 406-485-2924. E-mail: customerservices@midrivers.coop. Web Site: http://www.midrivers.com. Also serves Fergus County. ICA: MT0012.
TV Market Ranking: Below 100 (Fergus County, LEWISTOWN). Franchise award date: July 1, 1998. Franchise expiration date: N.A. Began: March 1, 1955.
Channel capacity: N.A. Channels available but not in use: N.A.
Basic Service
Subscribers: 1,798.
Programming (via microwave): KFBB-TV (ABC, FOX) Great Falls; KRTV (CBS, CW, Grit) Great Falls; KTGF (IND) Great Falls; KUSM-TV (PBS) Bozeman.
Programming (via satellite): A&E; CNN; C-SPAN; Discovery Channel; FX; Lifetime; QVC; TBS.
Fee: $49.95 installation; $26.95 monthly.
Expanded Basic Service 1
Subscribers: N.A.
Programming (via satellite): AMC; Animal Planet; Cartoon Network; CNBC; Destination America; Disney Channel; Disney XD; ESPN; Fox News Channel; Freeform; Hall-

mark Channel; History; HLN; MSNBC; MTV; Nickelodeon; Ovation; Oxygen; Root Sports Rocky Mountain; Spike TV; TeenNick; The Weather Channel; TLC; TNT; Travel Channel; Trinity Broadcasting Network (TBN); TV Land; USA Network.
Fee: $16.97 monthly.
Digital Basic Service
Subscribers: N.A.
Programming (via satellite): BBC America; Bravo; Discovery Digital Networks; DMX Music; ESPN Classic; ESPN2; Golf Channel; GSN; HGTV; IFC; National Geographic Channel; NBCSN; Nick Jr.; Syfy; Turner Classic Movies; WE tv.
Fee: $12.00 monthly.
Digital Expanded Basic Service
Subscribers: N.A.
Programming (via satellite): Bloomberg Television; Fox Sports 1; FYI; History International; Outdoor Channel.
Fee: $5.99 monthly.
Pay Service 1
Pay Units: N.A.
Programming (via satellite): Cinemax; HBO; Showtime; Starz; Starz Encore.
Fee: $1.75 monthly (Encore), $6.75 monthly (Starz), $13.20 monthly (Cinemax), $14.15 monthly (HBO or Showtime).
Digital Pay Service 1
Pay Units: N.A.
Programming (via satellite): Cinemax (multiplexed); HBO (multiplexed); Showtime (multiplexed); Starz (multiplexed); Starz Encore (multiplexed); The Movie Channel (multiplexed).
Fee: $1.75 monthly (Encore), $6.75 monthly (Starz), $13.20 monthly (Cinemax), $14.15 monthly (HBO, Showtime & TMC).
Video-On-Demand: No
Pay-Per-View
iN DEMAND (delivered digitally); Playboy TV (delivered digitally); Fresh (delivered digitally); Shorteez (delivered digitally).
Internet Service
Operational: Yes.
Subscribers: 1,776.
Telephone Service
Digital: Operational
Subscribers: 2,548.
Miles of Plant: 66.0 (coaxial); 263.0 (fiber optic). Homes passed: 3,468.
President: Mark Robbins. General Manager: Bill Wade. Chief Technician: Mike Sokolosky. Customer Service Manager: Deb Wagner.
Ownership: Mid-Rivers Telephone Cooperative Inc. (MSO).

LIBBY—MontanaSky West, 1286 Burns Way, Kalispell, MT 59901. Phone: 406-293-4335. Web Site: http://www.montanasky.tv. Also serves Lincoln County (portions). ICA: MT0010.
TV Market Ranking: Below 100 (Lincoln County (portions) (portions)); Outside TV Markets (LIBBY, Lincoln County (portions) (portions)). Franchise award date: N.A. Franchise expiration date: N.A. Began: March 1, 1981.
Channel capacity: N.A. Channels available but not in use: N.A.
Basic Service
Subscribers: 754.
Programming (received off-air): KPAX-TV (CBS, CW, Grit) Missoula; KQUP (IND) Pullman; 7 FMs.
Programming (via microwave): KAYU-TV (FOX, This TV) Spokane; KCFW-TV (MeTV, NBC, This TV) Kalispell; KHQ-TV (NBC) Spokane; KREM (CBS, TheCoolTV)

Cable Systems—Montana

Spokane; KSPS-TV (PBS) Spokane; KXLY-TV (ABC, MeTV) Spokane.
Programming (via satellite): C-SPAN; C-SPAN 2; Discovery Channel; MSNBC; Northwest Cable News; QVC; TBS; WGN America.
Fee: $29.99 installation; $30.95 monthly.

Expanded Basic Service 1
Subscribers: N.A.
Programming (via satellite): A&E; AMC; Animal Planet; Cartoon Network; CMT; CNBC; CNN; Comedy Central; Disney Channel; E! HD; ESPN; ESPN2; Food Network; Fox News Channel; Freeform; FX; Hallmark Channel; HGTV; History; HLN; Lifetime; MTV; Nickelodeon; Oxygen; Spike TV; Syfy; The Weather Channel; TLC; TNT; Travel Channel; truTV; TV Land; USA Network; VH1.
Fee: $28.88 monthly.

Digital Basic Service
Subscribers: N.A.
Programming (via satellite): BBC America; Bloomberg Television; Bravo; Discovery Life Channel; Disney XD; FXM; FYI; Great American Country; GSN; History International; International Television (ITV); LMN; MBC America; TeenNick; The Word Network; Trinity Broadcasting Network (TBN); Turner Classic Movies; WE tv.
Fee: $11.99 monthly.

Digital Expanded Basic Service
Subscribers: N.A.
Programming (via satellite): ESPN Classic; ESPNews; Fox Sports 1; Golf Channel; IFC; MC; National Geographic Channel; NBCSN; Nick Jr.; Nicktoons; Outdoor Channel; Sundance TV.
Fee: $12.49 monthly.

Digital Pay Service 1
Pay Units: N.A.
Programming (via satellite): Cinemax (multiplexed); HBO (multiplexed); Showtime (multiplexed); Starz (multiplexed).
Fee: $15.95 monthly (Cinemax, HBO, Showtime or Starz).

Video-On-Demand: No

Pay-Per-View
Shorteez (delivered digitally); Hot Choice (delivered digitally); Fresh (delivered digitally); Playboy TV (delivered digitally).

Internet Service
Operational: Yes. Began: December 1, 2001.
Fee: $24.95 installation; $45.95 monthly.

Telephone Service
None
Chief Executive Officer & General Manager: Frederick Weber.
Ownership: MontanaSky West LLC (MSO).

LINCOLN—Lincoln Cable TV, 111 Stemple Pass Rd, Lincoln, MT 59639-9509. Phones: 406-362-4452; 406-362-4216. Fax: 406-362-4606. E-mail: ltc@linctel.net. Web Site: http://www.linctel.net. ICA: MT0115.
TV Market Ranking: Outside TV Markets (LINCOLN). Franchise award date: N.A. Franchise expiration date: N.A. Began: April 1, 1987.
Channel capacity: 36 (not 2-way capable). Channels available but not in use: N.A.

Basic Service
Subscribers: 373.
Programming (received off-air): KTVH-DT (CW, NBC) Helena; KXLF-TV (CBS, CW, Grit) Butte.
Programming (via satellite): A&E; AMC; CNN; Discovery Channel; ESPN; ESPN2; Freeform; FXM; History; KRMA-TV (PBS) Denver; KWGN-TV (CW, This TV) Denver; Outdoor Channel; Spike TV; TBS; The Weather Channel; TNT; USA Network; WGN America.
Fee: $20.00 installation; $37.90 monthly; $1.50 converter.

Pay Service 1
Pay Units: 200.
Programming (via satellite): Flix; Showtime; The Movie Channel.
Fee: $11.50 monthly.

Internet Service
Operational: No.

Telephone Service
None
Miles of Plant: 29.0 (coaxial); None (fiber optic). Homes passed: 550.
General Manager: Ken Lumpkin. Chief Technician: Arron Daniel.
Ownership: Lincoln Telephone Co.

LIVINGSTON (town)—Charter Communications, 511 West Mendenhall Dr, Bozeman, MT 59715. Phones: 636-207-5100 (Corporate office); 877-273-7626 (Customer service); 406-782-1616 (Butte office). Web Site: http://www.charter.com. Also serves Park County. ICA: MT0011.
TV Market Ranking: Below 100 (LIVINGSTON (TOWN), Park County (portions)); Outside TV Markets (Park County (portions)). Franchise award date: N.A. Franchise expiration date: N.A. Began: May 1, 1954.
Channel capacity: N.A. Channels available but not in use: N.A.

Digital Basic Service
Subscribers: 1,593.
Programming (via satellite): A&E HD; Animal Planet HD; BBC America; Bloomberg Television; Bravo; CBS Sports Network; CMT; Cooking Channel; Destination America; Discovery Channel HD; Discovery Kids Channel; Discovery Life Channel; Disney Channel HD; Disney XD; DIY Network; DMX Music; ESPN Classic; ESPN HD; ESPNews; Food Network HD; FOX College Sports Central; FOX College Sports Pacific; Fox Sports 1; Freeform HD; Fuse; FXM; FYI; Golf Channel; GSN; HD Theater; HGTV HD; History HD; History International; HRTV; IFC; Investigation Discovery; ION Television; LMN; MTV Classic; MTV Hits; MTV2; Nat Geo WILD; National Geographic Channel; National Geographic Channel HD; NBCSN; NFL Network; Nick Jr.; Nicktoons; Outdoor Channel; OWN: Oprah Winfrey Network; RFD-TV; Science Channel; Science HD; Sprout; Syfy HD; TeenNick; Trinity Broadcasting Network (TBN); Universal HD; UP; USA Network HD; VH1 Soul.
Fee: $34.95 installation; $26.99 monthly.

Digital Expanded Basic Service
Subscribers: N.A.
Programming (via satellite): A&E; Altitude Sports & Entertainment; AMC; Animal Planet; Cartoon Network; CMT; CNBC; CNN; Comedy Central; Discovery Channel; Disney Channel; E! HD; ESPN; ESPN2; Food Network; Fox News Channel; Freeform; FX; Hallmark Channel; HGTV; History; HLN; INSP; ION Television; MSNBC; MTV; Nickelodeon; Oxygen; Root Sports Rocky Mountain; Spike TV; Syfy; The Weather Channel; TLC; TNT; Travel Channel; truTV; Turner Classic Movies; TV Land; USA Network; VH1.
Fee: $28.99 monthly.

Digital Pay Service 1
Pay Units: N.A.
Programming (via satellite): Cinemax (multiplexed); Flix; HBO (multiplexed); HBO HD; Showtime (multiplexed); Starz (multiplexed); Starz Encore (multiplexed); Starz HD; The Movie Channel (multiplexed).

Video-On-Demand: No

Internet Service
Operational: Yes.
Subscribers: 1,647.
Broadband Service: Charter Internet.
Fee: $52.95 monthly.

Telephone Service
Analog: Not Operational
Digital: Operational
Subscribers: 993.
Fee: $49.99 monthly
Miles of Plant: 76.0 (coaxial); 2,464.0 (fiber optic). Homes passed: 4,942.
President & Chief Executive Officer: Tom Rutledge. General Manager: Mike Oswald. Chief Technician: Todd Hawke. Accounting Director: David Sovanski.
Ownership: Charter Communications Inc. (MSO).

LODGE GRASS—Formerly served by Eagle Cablevision Inc. No longer in operation. ICA: MT0083.

LOLO—Formerly served by Bresnan Communications. Now served by Charter Communications, MISSOULA, MT [MT0002]. ICA: MT0017.

MALTA—Charter Communications, 12405 Powerscourt Dr, St. Louis, MO 63131. Phones: 636-207-5100 (Corporate office); 516-803-2300 (Corporate office); 877-273-7626; 406-727-8881. Web Site: http://www.charter.com. Also serves Phillips County (portions). ICA: MT0032.
TV Market Ranking: Outside TV Markets (MALTA). Franchise award date: N.A. Franchise expiration date: N.A. Began: March 1, 1980.
Channel capacity: N.A. Channels available but not in use: N.A.

Digital Basic Service
Subscribers: 163.
Programming (via satellite): BBC America; Bloomberg Television; Bravo; CBS Sports Network; CMT; Destination America; Discovery Kids Channel; Disney XD; DMX Music; ESPN Classic; ESPNews; Fox Sports 1; Fuse; FXM; FYI; Golf Channel; GSN; HGTV; History International; IFC; Investigation Discovery; LMN; MTV Classic; MTV Hits; MTV2; National Geographic Channel; NBCSN; Nick Jr.; Nicktoons; Outdoor Channel; OWN: Oprah Winfrey Network; RFD-TV; Science Channel; Sprout; Syfy; TeenNick; Trinity Broadcasting Network (TBN); Turner Classic Movies; TV Land; UP; VH1 Soul.
Fee: $34.95 installation; $26.99 monthly.

Digital Expanded Basic Service
Subscribers: N.A.
Programming (via satellite): A&E; Altitude Sports & Entertainment; AMC; Animal Planet; Cartoon Network; CMT; CNBC; Comedy Central; Discovery Channel; Disney Channel; E! HD; ESPN; ESPN2; Food Network; Fox News Channel; Freeform; Hallmark Channel; History; HLN; INSP; MSNBC; MTV; Nickelodeon; Oxygen; Root Sports Rocky Mountain; Spike TV; The Weather Channel; TLC; TNT; Travel Channel; USA Network; VH1.
Fee: $28.99 monthly.

Digital Pay Service 1
Pay Units: N.A.
Programming (via satellite): Cinemax (multiplexed); Flix; HBO (multiplexed); Showtime (multiplexed); Starz (multiplexed); Starz Encore (multiplexed); The Movie Channel (multiplexed).

Video-On-Demand: No

Pay-Per-View
iN DEMAND (delivered digitally).

Internet Service
Operational: Yes.
Broadband Service: Charter Internet.
Fee: $52.95 monthly.

Telephone Service
Digital: Operational
Fee: $49.99 monthly
Miles of Plant: 17.0 (coaxial); None (fiber optic). Homes passed: 1,098.
President & Chief Executive Officer: Tom Rutledge. Vice President: Sean O'Donnell. General Manager: Patty Faloon. Chief Technician: Jim Passon. Accounting Director: David Sovanski.
Ownership: Charter Communications Inc. (MSO).

MANHATTAN—Formerly served by Bresnan Communications. Now served by Charter Communications, BOZEMAN, MT [MT0007]. ICA: MT0052.

MARION—Formerly served by Mallard Cablevision. No longer in operation. ICA: MT0101.

MELSTONE—Formerly served by Mel-View Cable TV. No longer in operation. ICA: MT0108.

MILES CITY—Mid-Rivers Communications, 904 C Ave, PO Box 280, Circle, MT 59215. Phone: 406-485-3301. Fax: 406-485-2924. E-mail: customerservices@midrivers.coop. Web Site: http://www.midrivers.com. Also serves Custer County (portions). ICA: MT0009.
TV Market Ranking: Below 100 (MILES CITY, Custer County (portions)); Outside TV Markets (Custer County (portions)). Franchise award date: N.A. Franchise expiration date: N.A. Began: June 1, 1962.
Channel capacity: 36 (not 2-way capable). Channels available but not in use: N.A.

Basic Service
Subscribers: 2,761.
Programming (received off-air): KULR-TV (NBC) Billings; KYUS-TV (NBC) Miles City.
Programming (via microwave): KTVQ (CBS, CW, Grit) Billings; KUSM-TV (PBS) Bozeman.
Programming (via satellite): A&E; CNBC; CNN; C-SPAN; C-SPAN 2; Discovery Channel; Freeform; HLN; Lifetime; MTV; Nickelodeon; QVC; TBS; The Weather Channel; TNT.
Fee: $49.95 installation; $27.40 monthly; $.69 converter.

Expanded Basic Service 1
Subscribers: N.A.
Programming (via satellite): AMC; Disney Channel; ESPN; FOX Sports Networks; Spike TV; truTV; USA Network.
Fee: $11.39 monthly.

Pay Service 1
Pay Units: N.A.
Programming (via satellite): Cinemax; HBO; Showtime; Starz; Starz Encore.

Video-On-Demand: No

Internet Service
Operational: Yes, DSL & dial-up.

Telephone Service
Analog: Operational
Miles of Plant: 47.0 (coaxial); None (fiber optic). Homes passed: 4,561.
President: Mark Robbins. General Manager: Bill Wade. Chief Technician: Mike Sokoloski. Customer Service Manager: Deb Wagner.
Ownership: Mid-Rivers Telephone Cooperative Inc. (MSO).

Montana—Cable Systems

MILLTOWN—Formerly served by Bresnan Communications. Now served by Charter Communications, MISSOULA, MT [MT0002]. ICA: MT0027.

MISSOULA—Charter Communications, 12405 Powerscourt Dr, St. Louis, MO 63131. Phones: 636-207-5100 (Corporate office); 406-728-4869; 877-273-7626; 406-727-8881. Fax: 406-727-6433. Web Site: http://www.charter.com. Also serves Bonner, Clinton, Florence, Lolo, Milltown, Missoula County & Missoula South. ICA: MT0002.
TV Market Ranking: Below 100 (Bonner, Clinton, Florence, Lolo, Milltown, MISSOULA, Missoula County (portions), Missoula South); Outside TV Markets (Missoula County (portions)). Franchise award date: N.A. Franchise expiration date: N.A. Began: September 1, 1956.
Channel capacity: N.A. Channels available but not in use: N.A.

Digital Basic Service
Subscribers: 14,986.
Programming (via satellite): A&E HD; Animal Planet HD; AXS TV; BBC America; Bloomberg Television; BlueHighways TV; Bravo HD; BYUtv; CBS Sports Network; CMT; CNBC HD+; CNN HD; Cooking Channel; C-SPAN 3; Destination America; Discovery Channel HD; Discovery Life Channel; Disney Channel HD; Disney XD; DIY Network; DMX Music; ESPN Classic; ESPN HD; ESPN2 HD; ESPNews; Food Network HD; FOX College Sports Central; FOX College Sports Pacific; Fox Sports 1; Freeform HD; Fuse; FXM; FYI; Golf Channel; GSN; HD Theater; HGTV HD; History HD; History International; HRTV; IFC; Investigation Discovery; ION Television; Lifetime Movie Network HD; LMN; MTV Classic; MTV Hits; MTV Jams; MTV Live; MTV2; Nat Geo WILD; National Geographic Channel; National Geographic Channel HD; NBCSN; NFL Network; NFL Network HD; NHL Network; Nick 2; Nick Jr.; Nicktoons; Outdoor Channel; Outdoor Channel 2 HD; OWN; Oprah Winfrey Network; Qubo; RFD-TV; Science Channel; Science HD; Sprout; Syfy HD; TBS HD; TeenNick; The Weather Channel HD; TLC HD; TNT HD; Tr3s; Trinity Broadcasting Network (TBN); Universal HD; UP; USA Network HD; Versus HD; VH1 Soul.
Fee: $19.99 monthly.

Digital Expanded Basic Service
Subscribers: 14,142.
Programming (via satellite): A&E; Altitude Sports & Entertainment; AMC; Animal Planet; Bravo; Cartoon Network; CMT; CNBC; CNN; Comedy Central; Discovery Channel; Disney Channel; E! HD; ESPN; ESPN2; Food Network; Fox News Channel; Freeform; FX; Great American Country; Hallmark Channel; HGTV; History; HLN; INSP; MSNBC; MTV; Nickelodeon; Oxygen; Root Sports Rocky Mountain; Spike TV; Syfy; The Weather Channel; TLC; TNT; Travel Channel; truTV; Turner Classic Movies; TV Land; USA Network; VH1.
Fee: $29.95 installation; $28.99 monthly.

Digital Pay Service 1
Pay Units: N.A.
Programming (via satellite): Cinemax (multiplexed); Cinemax On Demand; Flix; HBO (multiplexed); HBO HD; HBO on Demand; Showtime (multiplexed); Showtime HD; Showtime On Demand; Starz (multiplexed); Starz Encore (multiplexed); Starz HD; Starz On Demand; The Movie Channel (multiplexed); The Movie Channel HD.
Video-On-Demand: Yes

Pay-Per-View
iN DEMAND (delivered digitally); ESPN (delivered digitally); MLB Network (delivered digitally); NHL Center Ice (delivered digitally).

Internet Service
Operational: Yes.
Subscribers: 22,213.
Broadband Service: Charter Internet.
Fee: $52.95 monthly.

Telephone Service
Analog: Not Operational
Digital: Operational
Subscribers: 10,773.
Fee: $49.99 monthly
Miles of Plant: 1,037.0 (coaxial); 251.0 (fiber optic). Homes passed: 55,337.
President & Chief Executive Officer: Tom Rutledge. General Manager: Mike Oswald. Technical Operations Manager: Alan White. Accounting Director: David Sovanski.
Ownership: Charter Communications Inc. (MSO).

MISSOULA—Formerly served by Cable Montana. Now served by Charter Communications, MISSOULA, MT [MT0002]. ICA: MT0021.

NINE MILE—Formerly served by Bresnan Communications. No longer in operation. ICA: MT0077.

OPPORTUNITY—Formerly served by Western Cable TV. No longer in operation. ICA: MT0076.

PARADISE—Formerly served by KLiP Interactive. No longer in operation. ICA: MT0116.

PARK CITY—Formerly served by Optimum. No longer in operation. ICA: MT0091.

PHILIPSBURG—Formerly served by Eagle Cablevision Inc. No longer in operation. ICA: MT0056.

PLAINS—Access Montana, 300 Main St SW, Ronan, MT 59864. Phone: 406-676-3300. Fax: 406-676-8889. E-mail: support@ronan.net. Web Site: http://www.accessmontana.com. ICA: MT0063.
TV Market Ranking: Outside TV Markets (PLAINS). Franchise award date: N.A. Franchise expiration date: N.A. Began: May 1, 1982.
Channel capacity: N.A. Channels available but not in use: N.A.

Basic Service
Subscribers: 91.
Programming (received off-air): KSPS-TV (PBS) Spokane.
Programming (via microwave): KECI-TV (MeTV, Movies!, NBC, This TV) Missoula; KPAX-TV (CBS, CW, Grit) Missoula; KXLY-TV (ABC, MeTV) Spokane.
Programming (via satellite): A&E; Animal Planet; Cartoon Network; CNN; Discovery Channel; Disney Channel; E! HD; ESPN; ESPN2; Fox News Channel; Freeform; HGTV; History; HLN; KDVR (Antenna TV, FOX) Denver; Nickelodeon; Outdoor Channel; Root Sports Rocky Mountain; Spike TV; TBS; The Weather Channel; TLC; TNT; Trinity Broadcasting Network (TBN); Turner Classic Movies; USA Network; VH1; WGN America.
Fee: $44.95 installation; $48.95 monthly.

Pay Service 1
Pay Units: N.A.
Programming (via satellite): Cinemax; HBO; Showtime.
Fee: $8.25 monthly (Cinemax or Showtime) or $11.75 monthly (HBO).
Video-On-Demand: No

Internet Service
Operational: No.

Telephone Service
None
Miles of Plant: 19.0 (coaxial); None (fiber optic). Homes passed: 134.
Ownership: Western Montana Community Telephone (MSO).

PLENTYWOOD—Bulldog Cable, 455 Gees Mill Business Ct, Conyers, GA 30013. Phones: 706-997-9003; 800-388-6577. Web Site: http://www.bulldogcable.com. ICA: MT0039.
TV Market Ranking: Outside TV Markets (PLENTYWOOD). Franchise award date: May 16, 1978. Franchise expiration date: N.A. Began: June 20, 1979.
Channel capacity: N.A. Channels available but not in use: N.A.

Basic Service
Subscribers: 80.
Programming (received off-air): KUMV-TV (FOX, NBC) Williston; KWSE (PBS) Williston; KXGN-TV (CBS, NBC) Glendive; KXMD-TV (CBS) Williston; 1 FM.
Programming (via satellite): A&E; CMT; CNN; Discovery Channel; Disney Channel; E! HD; ESPN; ESPN2; Fox News Channel; Freeform; FX; HGTV; History; KDVR (Antenna TV, FOX) Denver; KMGH-TV (ABC, Azteca America) Denver; Lifetime; National Geographic Channel; Root Sports Rocky Mountain; Spike TV; TBS; The Weather Channel; TLC; TNT; Trinity Broadcasting Network (TBN); Turner Classic Movies; TV Land; USA Network; WGN America.
Fee: $44.95 installation; $43.26 monthly.

Pay Service 1
Pay Units: 30.
Programming (via satellite): HBO.
Fee: $12.00 monthly.
Video-On-Demand: No

Internet Service
Operational: No.

Telephone Service
None
Miles of Plant: 16.0 (coaxial); None (fiber optic). Homes passed: 495.
President: Mark Wilson. General Manager East: Mark Miller. General Manager West: Vance Johnson. Controller: Ashley Hull.
Ownership: Bulldog Cable (MSO).

POLSON—Charter Communications, 12405 Powerscourt Dr, St. Louis, MO 63131. Phones: 636-207-5100 (Corporate office); 516-803-2300 (Corporate office); 877-273-7626. Web Site: http://www.charter.com. Also serves Lake County, Pablo & Ronan. ICA: MT0016.
TV Market Ranking: Below 100 (Lake County (portions), POLSON); Outside TV Markets (Lake County (portions), Pablo, Ronan). Franchise award date: N.A. Franchise expiration date: N.A. Began: October 1, 1966.
Channel capacity: N.A. Channels available but not in use: N.A.

Digital Basic Service
Subscribers: 1,528.
Programming (via satellite): A&E HD; Animal Planet HD; AXS TV; BBC America; Bloomberg Television; Bravo; Bravo HD; CBS Sports Network; CMT; CNBC HD+; CNN HD; Cooking Channel; Destination America; Discovery Channel HD; Discovery Kids Channel; Discovery Life Channel; Disney Channel HD; Disney XD; DIY Network; DMX Music; ESPN Classic; ESPN HD; ESPN2 HD; ESPNews; Food Network HD; FOX College Sports Central; FOX College Sports Pacific; Fox Sports 1; Freeform HD; Fuse; FXM; FYI; Golf Channel; Great American Country; GSN; HD Theater; HGTV HD; History HD; History International; HRTV; IFC; Investigation Discovery; ION Television; Lifetime Movie Network HD; LMN; MTV Classic; MTV Hits; MTV Jams; MTV Live; MTV2; Nat Geo WILD; National Geographic Channel; National Geographic Channel HD; NBCSN; NFL Network; NFL Network HD; Nick 2; Nick Jr.; Nicktoons; Outdoor Channel; Outdoor Channel 2 HD; OWN; Oprah Winfrey Network; RFD-TV; Science Channel; Science HD; Sprout; Syfy HD; TBS HD; TeenNick; The Weather Channel HD; TLC HD; TNT HD; Tr3s; Trinity Broadcasting Network (TBN); Universal HD; UP; USA Network HD; Versus HD; VH1 Soul.
Fee: $26.99 monthly.

Digital Expanded Basic Service
Subscribers: N.A.
Programming (via satellite): A&E; Altitude Sports & Entertainment; AMC; Animal Planet; Cartoon Network; CMT; CNBC; CNN; Comedy Central; Discovery Channel; Disney Channel; E! HD; ESPN; ESPN2; Food Network; Fox News Channel; Freeform; FX; Hallmark Channel; HGTV; History; HLN; INSP; ION Television; MSNBC; MTV; Nickelodeon; Oxygen; Pop; Spike TV; Syfy; The Weather Channel; TLC; TNT; Travel Channel; truTV; Turner Classic Movies; TV Land; USA Network; VH1.
Fee: $10.95 monthly.

Digital Pay Service 1
Pay Units: 710.
Programming (via satellite): Cinemax (multiplexed); Cinemax HD; Flix; HBO (multiplexed); HBO HD; Showtime (multiplexed); Showtime HD; Starz (multiplexed); Starz Encore (multiplexed); Starz HD; The Movie Channel (multiplexed); The Movie Channel HD.
Video-On-Demand: No

Pay-Per-View
iN DEMAND (delivered digitally).

Internet Service
Operational: Yes.
Broadband Service: Charter Internet.
Fee: $52.95 monthly.

Telephone Service
Digital: Operational
Fee: $49.99 monthly
Miles of Plant: 130.0 (coaxial); 42.0 (fiber optic). Homes passed: 5,492.
President & Chief Executive Officer: Tom Rutledge. Vice President: Sean O'Donnell. General Manager: Patty Faloon. Chief Technician: Weldon Plympton. Accounting Director: David Sovanski.
Ownership: Charter Communications Inc. (MSO).

POPLAR—Bulldog Cable, 455 Gees Mill Business Ct, Conyers, GA 30013. Phones: 706-997-9003; 800-388-6577; 706-215-1385. Web Site: http://www.bulldogcable.com. ICA: MT0040.
TV Market Ranking: Outside TV Markets (POPLAR). Franchise award date: N.A. Franchise expiration date: N.A. Began: October 1, 1982.
Channel capacity: N.A. Channels available but not in use: N.A.

Basic Service
Subscribers: 54.
Programming (received off-air): KFBB-TV (ABC, FOX) Great Falls; KUMV-TV (FOX, NBC) Williston; KWSE (PBS) Williston;

Cable Systems—Montana

Access the most current data instantly
FREE TRIAL @ ADVANCED TVFactbook
TELCO/IPTV • CABLE TV • TV STATIONS
www.warren-news.com/factbook.htm

KXGN-TV (CBS, NBC) Glendive; KXMD-TV (CBS) Williston.
Programming (via satellite): A&E; Cartoon Network; CNN; Comedy Central; Discovery Channel; Disney Channel; ESPN; ESPN2; Fox News Channel; Freeform; HGTV; HLN; INSP; KDVR (Antenna TV, FOX) Denver; KMGH-TV (ABC, Azteca America) Denver; QVC; Root Sports Rocky Mountain; Spike TV; TBS; TNT; Trinity Broadcasting Network (TBN); Turner Classic Movies; USA Network; WGN America.
Fee: $44.95 installation; $36.35 monthly.
Pay Service 1
Pay Units: N.A.
Programming (via satellite): Cinemax; HBO.
Fee: $10.00 installation; $12.00 monthly (each).
Video-On-Demand: No
Internet Service
Operational: No.
Telephone Service
None
Miles of Plant: 14.0 (coaxial); None (fiber optic). Homes passed: 771.
President: Mark Wilson. General Manager West: Vance Johnson. General Manager East: Mark Miller. Controller: Ashley Hull.
Ownership: Bulldog Cable (MSO).

RED LODGE—Charter Communications, 12405 Powerscourt Dr, St. Louis, MO 63131. Phones: 636-207-5100 (Corporate office); 877.273.7626. Web Site: http://www.charter.com. ICA: MT0037.
TV Market Ranking: Outside TV Markets (RED LODGE). Franchise award date: N.A. Franchise expiration date: N.A. Began: July 2, 1984.
Channel capacity: N.A. Channels available but not in use: N.A.
Digital Basic Service
Subscribers: 705.
Programming (via satellite): BBC America; Bloomberg Television; Cloo; CMT; Destination America; Discovery Kids Channel; Discovery Life Channel; DMX Music; ESPN Classic; ESPNews; EVINE Live; FOX College Sports Central; FOX College Sports Pacific; Fox Sports 1; FXM; FYI; Golf Channel; GSN; History; History International; Investigation Discovery; LMN; MTV Classic; MTV Hits; MTV2; National Geographic Channel; NBCSN; Nick Jr.; Outdoor Channel; Ovation; OWN: Oprah Winfrey Network; Science Channel; TeenNick; Trinity Broadcasting Network (TBN); VH1 Soul; WE tv.
Fee: $26.99 monthly.
Digital Expanded Basic Service
Subscribers: N.A.
Programming (via satellite): Altitude Sports & Entertainment; AMC; Cartoon Network; CMT; CNBC; CNN; Comedy Central; C-SPAN; Discovery Channel; E! HD; ESPN; ESPN Classic; ESPN2; Fox News Channel; FX; Hallmark Channel; HGTV; History; HLN; MSNBC; MTV; Nickelodeon; Outdoor Channel; Root Sports Rocky Mountain; Spike TV; Syfy; The Weather Channel; TNT; truTV; TV Land; USA Network; VH1.
Fee: $18.04 monthly.
Digital Pay Service 1
Pay Units: N.A.
Programming (via satellite): Cinemax (multiplexed); Flix; HBO (multiplexed); Showtime (multiplexed); Starz (multiplexed); Starz Encore (multiplexed); The Movie Channel (multiplexed).
Fee: $13.00 monthly (Cinemax, HBO, Showtime/TMC/Flix or Starz/Encore).
Video-On-Demand: No

Pay-Per-View
iN DEMAND (delivered digitally); Hot Choice (delivered digitally); Playboy TV (delivered digitally); Fresh (delivered digitally); Shorteez (delivered digitally); Club Jenna (delivered digitally).
Internet Service
Operational: Yes.
Broadband Service: Charter Internet.
Fee: $35.95 monthly.
Telephone Service
Digital: Operational
Fee: $39.95 monthly
Miles of Plant: 14.0 (coaxial); None (fiber optic).
President & Chief Executive Officer: Tom Rutledge.; James L. Dolan. Programming Director: E. McRae Budill. Accounting Director: David Sovanski.
Ownership: Charter Communications Inc. (MSO).

RICHEY—Mid-Rivers Communications. Now served by GLENDIVE, MT [MT0013]. ICA: MT0104.

RIVERSIDE GREENS—Formerly served by Northwestern Communications Corp. No longer in operation. ICA: MT0117.

RONAN—Formerly served by Bresnan Communications. Now served by Charter Communications, POLSON, MT [MT0016]. ICA: MT0029.

ROUNDUP—Mid-Rivers Communications, 904 C Ave, PO Box 280, Circle, MT 59215. Phones: 406-535-3336; 406-485-3301. Fax: 406-485-2924. E-mail: customerservices@midrivers.coop. Web Site: http://www.midrivers.com. Also serves Grass Range, Lavina, Ryegate & Winnett. ICA: MT0043.
TV Market Ranking: Outside TV Markets (Lavina, ROUNDUP, Winnett, Ryegate). Franchise award date: N.A. Franchise expiration date: N.A. Began: July 1, 1981.
Channel capacity: N.A. Channels available but not in use: N.A.
Basic Service
Subscribers: 403.
Programming (received off-air): KSVI (ABC) Billings; KTVQ (CBS, CW, Grit) Billings; KULR-TV (NBC) Billings.
Programming (via microwave): KUSM-TV (PBS) Bozeman.
Programming (via satellite): A&E; CNBC; CNN; C-SPAN; Discovery Channel; Disney Channel; ESPN; Freeform; FXM; HGTV; History; HLN; INSP; Lifetime; Nickelodeon; Outdoor Channel; QVC; Spike TV; Syfy; TBS; TLC; TNT; Travel Channel; TV Land; WE tv; WGN America.
Fee: $49.95 installation; $27.60 monthly.
Expanded Basic Service 1
Subscribers: N.A.
Programming (via satellite): ESPN2; The Weather Channel.
Fee: $2.50 monthly.
Digital Basic Service
Subscribers: N.A.
Programming (via satellite): BBC America; Bravo; Discovery Digital Networks; DMX Music; ESPN Classic; ESPN2; ESPNews; Golf Channel; GSN; HGTV; History; IFC; MTV Classic; National Geographic Channel; NBCSN; Nick Jr.; Syfy; Turner Classic Movies; VH1 Country; WE tv.
Pay Service 1
Pay Units: N.A.
Programming (via satellite): Showtime; The Movie Channel.
Fee: $5.95 monthly (Showtime), $8.00 monthly (TMC).

Digital Pay Service 1
Pay Units: N.A.
Programming (via satellite): Cinemax (multiplexed); Flix; HBO (multiplexed); Showtime (multiplexed); Starz (multiplexed); Starz Encore (multiplexed); The Movie Channel (multiplexed).
Video-On-Demand: No
Pay-Per-View
iN DEMAND (delivered digitally); ESPN Now (delivered digitally); Sports PPV (delivered digitally).
Internet Service
Operational: Yes, DSL.
Telephone Service
Analog: Operational
Miles of Plant: 5.0 (coaxial); 258.0 (fiber optic). Homes passed: 1,102.
President: Mark Robbins. General Manager: Bill Wade. Chief Technician: Mike Sokolosky. Customer Service Manager: Deb Wagner.
Ownership: Mid-Rivers Telephone Cooperative Inc. (MSO).

RYEGATE—Mid-Rivers Communications. Now served by ROUNDUP, MT [MT0043]. ICA: MT0102.

SAVAGE—Mid-Rivers Communications. Now served by SIDNEY (town), MT [MT0018]. ICA: MT0105.

SCOBEY—Bulldog Cable, 455 Gees Mill Business Ct, Conyers, GA 30013. Phones: 706-997-9003; 800-388-6577. Web Site: http://www.bulldogcable.com. ICA: MT0047.
TV Market Ranking: Outside TV Markets (SCOBEY). Franchise award date: N.A. Franchise expiration date: N.A. Began: December 1, 1980.
Channel capacity: N.A. Channels available but not in use: N.A.
Basic Service
Subscribers: 33.
Programming (received off-air): KUMV-TV (FOX, NBC) Williston; KXMD-TV (CBS) Williston.
Programming (via satellite): A&E; Cartoon Network; CNN; Discovery Channel; Disney Channel; ESPN; ESPN2; Fox News Channel; Freeform; HGTV; INSP; KDVR (Antenna TV, FOX) Denver; KMGH-TV (ABC, Azteca America) Denver; Root Sports Rocky Mountain; Spike TV; TBS; TNT; Turner Classic Movies; USA Network; WGN America.
Fee: $44.95 installation; $36.00 monthly.
Pay Service 1
Pay Units: 20.
Programming (via satellite): HBO.
Fee: $15.00 installation; $12.00 monthly.
Video-On-Demand: No
Internet Service
Operational: No.
Telephone Service
None
Miles of Plant: 22.0 (coaxial); None (fiber optic). Homes passed: 570.

President: Mark Wilson. General Manager East: Mark Miller. General Manager West: Vance Johnson. Controller: Ashley Hull.
Ownership: Bulldog Cable (MSO).

SEELEY LAKE—Access Montana, 300 Main St SW, Ronan, MT 59864. Phone: 406-676-3300. Fax: 406-676-8889. E-mail: support@ronan.net. Web Site: http://www.accessmontana.com. ICA: MT0060.
TV Market Ranking: Below 100 (SEELEY LAKE). Franchise award date: N.A. Franchise expiration date: N.A. Began: July 1, 1983.
Channel capacity: N.A. Channels available but not in use: N.A.
Basic Service
Subscribers: 40.
Programming (received off-air): KTVM-TV (MeTV, Movies!, NBC, This TV) Butte; KXLF-TV (CBS, CW, Grit) Butte.
Programming (via satellite): A&E; AMC; Animal Planet; CMT; CNN; Discovery Channel; Disney Channel; ESPN; ESPN2; Freeform; KDVR (Antenna TV, FOX) Denver; KMGH-TV (ABC, Azteca America) Denver; KRMA-TV (PBS) Denver; Nickelodeon; Spike TV; Syfy; TBS; TNT; USA Network; VH1; WGN America.
Fee: $45.00 installation; $45.95 monthly.
Pay Service 1
Pay Units: N.A.
Programming (via satellite): HBO; Showtime.
Internet Service
Operational: No.
Telephone Service
None
Miles of Plant: 16.0 (coaxial); None (fiber optic). Homes passed: 493.
Treasurer: Robert Erickson.
Ownership: Western Montana Community Telephone (MSO).

SHELBY—3 Rivers Communications, 202 5th St South, PO Box 429, Fairfield, MT 59436. Phones: 406-424-8535 (Shelby office); 800-796-4567; 406-467-2535 (Fairfield office). Fax: 406-467-3490. E-mail: 3rt@3rivers.net. Web Site: http://www.3rivers.net. ICA: MT0024.
TV Market Ranking: Outside TV Markets (SHELBY). Franchise award date: N.A. Franchise expiration date: N.A. Began: July 1, 1955.
Channel capacity: N.A. Channels available but not in use: N.A.
Basic Service
Subscribers: 191.
Programming (received off-air): KFBB-TV (ABC, FOX) Great Falls; KRTV (CBS, CW, Grit) Great Falls; KTGF (IND) Great Falls.
Programming (via microwave): KHQ-TV (NBC) Spokane; KUSM-TV (PBS) Bozeman; KXLY-TV (ABC, MeTV) Spokane.
Programming (via satellite): C-SPAN; C-SPAN 2; FX; Lifetime; QVC; TBS.
Fee: $39.99 installation; $20.49 monthly.

2017 Edition   D-475

Montana—Cable Systems

Communications Daily
Warren Communications News

Get the industry standard FREE —
For a no-obligation trial call 800-771-9202 or visit www.warren-news.com

Expanded Basic Service 1
Subscribers: N.A.
Programming (via satellite): A&E; Altitude Sports & Entertainment; AMC; Animal Planet; Cartoon Network; CMT; CNBC; CNN; Comedy Central; Discovery Channel; Disney Channel; ESPN; ESPN2; Food Network; Fox News Channel; Freeform; Hallmark Channel; HGTV; History; HLN; Nickelodeon; Oxygen; Root Sports Rocky Mountain; Spike TV; The Weather Channel; TLC; TNT; Travel Channel; truTV; Turner Classic Movies; USA Network.
Fee: $33.00 monthly.
Digital Basic Service
Subscribers: N.A.
Programming (via satellite): BBC America; Bloomberg Television; Bravo; CBS Sports Network; CMT; Destination America; Discovery Kids Channel; Discovery Life Channel; Disney XD; DMX Music; ESPN Classic; ESPNews; Fox Sports 1; Fuse; FXM; FYI; Golf Channel; Great American Country; GSN; History International; IFC; Investigation Discovery; LMN; MTV Classic; MTV Hits; MTV2; National Geographic Channel; NBCSN; Nick Jr.; Nicktoons; Outdoor Channel; OWN: Oprah Winfrey Network; RFD-TV; Science Channel; Sprout; Syfy; Teen-Nick; Trinity Broadcasting Network (TBN); TV Land; VH1 Soul.
Fee: $24.99 monthly.
Digital Pay Service 1
Pay Units: N.A.
Programming (via satellite): Cinemax (multiplexed); Flix; HBO (multiplexed); Showtime (multiplexed); Starz (multiplexed); Starz Encore (multiplexed); The Movie Channel (multiplexed).
Video-On-Demand: No
Pay-Per-View
Hot Choice (delivered digitally); iN DEMAND; iN DEMAND (delivered digitally); Fresh (delivered digitally).
Internet Service
Operational: Yes, DSL & dial-up.
Telephone Service
Digital: Operational
Miles of Plant: 26.0 (coaxial); None (fiber optic). Homes passed: 1,500.
General Manager: David Gibson. Human Resources Director: Bonnie Mayer. Customer Operations Director: Sandi Oveson. Finance Director: Brad Veis. Technical & Network Operations Director: Rom Warnick.
Ownership: 3 Rivers Communications (MSO).

SHERIDAN—Formerly served by Ruby Valley Cable Co. Inc. No longer in operation. ICA: MT0084.

SIDNEY (town)—Mid-Rivers Communications, 904 C Ave, PO Box 280, Circle, MT 59215. Phones: 406-535-3336; 406-485-3301. Fax: 406-485-2924. E-mail: customerservices@midrivers.coop. Web Site: http://www.midrivers.com. Also serves Crane, Fairview, Lambert, Richland County (portions) & Savage. ICA: MT0018.
TV Market Ranking: Below 100 (Fairview, Richland County (portions), Savage; Outside TV Markets (Crane, Lambert, SIDNEY (TOWN), Richland County (portions)). Franchise award date: N.A. Franchise expiration date: N.A. Began: May 1, 1967.
Channel capacity: 37 (2-way capable). Channels available but not in use: N.A.
Basic Service
Subscribers: 1,957.
Programming (received off-air): KUMV-TV (FOX, NBC) Williston; KWSE (PBS) Williston; KXMD-TV (CBS) Williston.
Programming (via microwave): KUSM-TV (PBS) Bozeman; KXGN-TV (CBS, NBC) Glendive.
Programming (via satellite): CW PLUS; HLN; KDVR (Antenna TV, FOX) Denver; KMGH-TV (ABC, Azteca America) Denver; TBS; WGN America.
Fee: $49.95 installation; $26.95 monthly.
Expanded Basic Service 1
Subscribers: N.A.
Programming (via satellite): A&E; AMC; Animal Planet; Bravo; Cartoon Network; CMT; CNBC; CNN; Comedy Central; C-SPAN; C-SPAN 2; Discovery Channel; Discovery Life Channel; Disney Channel; Disney XD; E! HD; ESPN; ESPN Classic; ESPN2; ES-PNU; EWTN Global Catholic Network; Food Network; Fox News Channel; Fox Sports 1; Freeform; FX; Great American Country; GSN; Hallmark Channel; HGTV; History; ION Television; Lifetime; MSNBC; MTV; National Geographic Channel; Nickelodeon; Outdoor Channel; Oxygen; RFD-TV; Root Sports Rocky Mountain; Spike TV; Syfy; The Weather Channel; TLC; TNT; Travel Channel; Trinity Broadcasting Network (TBN); truTV; Turner Classic Movies; TV Land; USA Network; VH1.
Fee: $15.00 monthly.
Digital Basic Service
Subscribers: N.A.
Programming (via satellite): A&E HD; AXS TV; BBC America; Bloomberg Television; Bravo; CMT; Destination America; Discovery Channel HD; Discovery Kids Channel; Disney XD; ESPN Classic; ESPN HD; ESPN2 HD; ESPNews; Food Network HD; Fuse; FXM; FYI; Golf Channel; GSN; HGTV HD; History International; IFC; Investigation Discovery; LMN; MTV Classic; MTV2; National Geographic Channel; National Geographic Channel HD; NBCSN; Nick Jr.; Nicktoons; Outdoor Channel 2 HD; OWN: Oprah Winfrey Network; Science Channel; Teen-Nick; TNT HD; Trinity Broadcasting Network (TBN); Universal HD; VH1 Soul; WE tv.
Pay Service 1
Pay Units: N.A.
Programming (via satellite): Cinemax; HBO; Showtime; Starz; Starz Encore; The Movie Channel.
Fee: $15.00 installation; $1.75 monthly (Encore), $6.75 monthly (Starz), $10.00 monthly (Cinemax, HBO or Showtime).
Digital Pay Service 1
Pay Units: N.A.
Programming (via satellite): Cinemax (multiplexed); Cinemax HD; Flix; HBO HD; Showtime (multiplexed); Starz (multiplexed); Starz Encore (multiplexed); The Movie Channel (multiplexed).
Video-On-Demand: No
Pay-Per-View
iN DEMAND (delivered digitally).
Internet Service
Operational: Yes, DSL & dial-up.
Telephone Service
Analog: Operational
Miles of Plant: 33.0 (coaxial); None (fiber optic).
President: Mark Robbins. General Manager: Bill Wade. Chief Technician: Mike Sokoloski. Customer Service Manager: Deb Wagner.
Ownership: Mid-Rivers Telephone Cooperative Inc. (MSO).

ST. IGNATIUS—Access Montana, 300 Main St SW, Ronan, MT 59864. Phone: 406-676-3300. Fax: 406-676-8889. E-mail: support@ronan.net. Web Site: http://www.accessmontana.com. ICA: MT0055.
TV Market Ranking: Below 100 (ST. IGNATIUS). Franchise award date: N.A. Franchise expiration date: N.A. Began: April 4, 1985.
Channel capacity: N.A. Channels available but not in use: N.A.
Basic Service
Subscribers: 72.
Programming (received off-air): KECI-TV (MeTV, Movies!, NBC, This TV) Missoula; KPAX-TV (CBS, CW, Grit) Missoula; KTMF (ABC, FOX) Missoula.
Programming (via satellite): A&E; Animal Planet; Cartoon Network; CNN; Discovery Channel; Disney Channel; ESPN; ESPN2; Fox News Channel; Freeform; History; HLN; KDVR (Antenna TV, FOX) Denver; Lifetime; MTV; Nickelodeon; Outdoor Channel; Root Sports Rocky Mountain; Spike TV; TBS; The Weather Channel; TLC; TNT; Trinity Broadcasting Network (TBN); Turner Classic Movies; USA Network; VH1; WGN America.
Fee: $44.95 installation; $48.95 monthly.
Pay Service 1
Pay Units: N.A.
Programming (via satellite): Cinemax; HBO; Showtime.
Fee: $8.95 - $11.75 monthly (each).
Video-On-Demand: No
Internet Service
Operational: Yes.
Fee: $19.95 monthly.
Telephone Service
None
Miles of Plant: 4.0 (coaxial); None (fiber optic).
Treasurer: Robert Erickson.
Ownership: Western Montana Community Telephone (MSO).

ST. REGIS—Formerly served by KLiP Interactive. No longer in operation. ICA: MT0090.

STANFORD—Formerly served by B.E.K. Inc. No longer in operation. ICA: MT0069.

STEVENSVILLE—Charter Communications, 12405 Powerscourt Dr, St. Louis, MO 63131. Phones: 636-207-5100 (Corporate office); 406-728-4869; 516-803-2300 (Corporate office); 877-273-7626. Web Site: http://www.charter.com. Also serves Ravalli County (portions). ICA: MT0065.
TV Market Ranking: Below 100 (STEVENSVILLE, Ravalli County (portions); Outside TV Markets (Ravalli County (portions)). Franchise award date: N.A. Franchise expiration date: N.A. Began: September 1, 1982.
Channel capacity: N.A. Channels available but not in use: N.A.
Digital Basic Service
Subscribers: 98. Commercial subscribers: 8.
Programming (received off-air): KECI-TV (MeTV, Movies!, NBC, This TV) Missoula; KPAX-TV (CBS, CW, Grit) Missoula; KTMF (ABC, FOX) Missoula.
Programming (via microwave): KSPS-TV (PBS) Spokane.
Programming (via satellite): A&E; Altitude Sports & Entertainment; C-SPAN; CW PLUS; Discovery Channel; Lifetime; QVC; TBS; truTV.
Fee: $26.99 installation; $24.99 monthly.
Digital Expanded Basic Service
Subscribers: N.A.
Programming (via satellite): AMC; Animal Planet; Cartoon Network; CNBC; CNN; Disney Channel; ESPN; Fox News Channel; Freeform; HGTV; HLN; Nickelodeon; Root Sports Rocky Mountain; Spike TV; The Weather Channel; TLC; TNT; USA Network.
Fee: $47.99 monthly.
Pay Service 1
Pay Units: N.A.
Programming (via satellite): HBO; Showtime; Starz; Starz Encore.
Fee: $1.75 monthly (Encore), $6.75 monthly (Starz), $14.15 monthly (HBO or Showtime).
Video-On-Demand: No
Internet Service
Operational: Yes.
Broadband Service: Charter Internet.
Fee: $36.95 monthly.
Telephone Service
Analog: Not Operational
Digital: Operational
Fee: $46.99 monthly
Miles of Plant: 10.0 (coaxial); None (fiber optic). Homes passed: 1,071.
President & Chief Executive Officer: Tom Rutledge. General Manager: Mike Oswald. Technical Operations Manager: Alan White. Accounting Director: David Sovanski.
Ownership: Charter Communications Inc. (MSO).

SUN PRAIRIE—Formerly served by Charter Communications. No longer in operation. ICA: MT0046.

SUPERIOR—Access Montana, 300 Main St SW, Ronan, MT 59864. Phone: 406-676-3300. Fax: 406-676-8889. E-mail: support@ronan.net. Web Site: http://www.accessmontana.com. ICA: MT0049.
TV Market Ranking: Outside TV Markets (SUPERIOR). Franchise award date: N.A. Franchise expiration date: N.A. Began: March 1, 1963.
Channel capacity: N.A. Channels available but not in use: N.A.
Basic Service
Subscribers: 85.
Programming (received off-air): KECI-TV (MeTV, Movies!, NBC, This TV) Missoula; KPAX-TV (CBS, CW, Grit) Missoula; allband FM.
Programming (via satellite): A&E; Altitude Sports & Entertainment; AMC; Animal Planet; CMT; CNN; Discovery Channel; Disney Channel; ESPN; ESPN2; Freeform; History; HLN; KDVR (Antenna TV, FOX) Denver; KMGH-TV (ABC, Azteca America) Denver; KRMA-TV (PBS) Denver; Lifetime; Nickelodeon; QVC; Spike TV; TBS; The

Cable Systems—Montana

Weather Channel; TLC; TNT; TV Land; USA Network; VH1; WGN America.
Fee: $44.95 installation; $84.95 monthly.
Pay Service 1
Pay Units: N.A.
Programming (via satellite): HBO; Showtime.
Fee: $8.25 monthly (Showtime), $11.75 monthly (HBO).
Video-On-Demand: No
Internet Service
Operational: No.
Telephone Service
None
Miles of Plant: 28.0 (coaxial); None (fiber optic). Homes passed: 807.
Treasurer: Robert Erickson. General Manager: Mike Oswald. Technical Operations Manager: Alan White.
Ownership: Western Montana Community Telephone (MSO).

TERRY—Mid-Rivers Communications. Now served by GLENDIVE, MT [MT0013]. ICA: MT0070.

THOMPSON FALLS—Access Montana, 300 Main St SW, Ronan, MT 59864. Phone: 406-676-3300. Fax: 406-676-8889. E-mail: support@ronan.net. Web Site: http://www.accessmontana.com. ICA: MT0053.
TV Market Ranking: Outside TV Markets (THOMPSON FALLS). Franchise award date: N.A. Franchise expiration date: N.A. Began: July 1, 1982.
Channel capacity: N.A. Channels available but not in use: N.A.
Basic Service
Subscribers: 41.
Programming (received off-air): KECI-TV (MeTV, Movies!, NBC, This TV) Missoula; KREM (CBS, TheCoolTV) Spokane; KUFM-TV (PBS) Missoula; KXLY-TV (ABC, MeTV) Spokane.
Programming (via satellite): C-SPAN; Discovery Channel; KDVR (Antenna TV, FOX) Denver; Lifetime; QVC; TBS; truTV.
Fee: $44.95 installation; $48.95 monthly.
Expanded Basic Service 1
Subscribers: N.A.
Programming (via satellite): Altitude Sports & Entertainment; AMC; Animal Planet; Cartoon Network; CNBC; CNN; Disney Channel; ESPN; ESPN2; Fox News Channel; Freeform; HGTV; HLN; MoviePlex; Root Sports Rocky Mountain; Spike TV; The Weather Channel; TLC; TNT; USA Network.
Pay Service 1
Pay Units: N.A.
Programming (via satellite): HBO; Showtime; Starz; Starz Encore.
Fee: $8.25 monthly (Showtime or Starz/Encore), $11.75 monthly (HBO).
Video-On-Demand: No
Internet Service
Operational: No.
Telephone Service
None
Miles of Plant: 12.0 (coaxial); None (fiber optic). Homes passed: 685.
Treasurer: Robert Erickson.
Ownership: Western Montana Community Telephone (MSO).

TOWNSEND—Charter Communications, 12405 Powerscourt Dr, St. Louis, MO 63131. Phones: 636-207-5100 (Corporate office); 877-273-7626; 516-803-2300 (Corporate office). Web Site: http://www.charter.com. Also serves Broadwater County. ICA: MT0045.
TV Market Ranking: Below 100 (Broadwater County (portions), TOWNSEND); Outside TV Markets (Broadwater County (portions)). Franchise award date: N.A. Franchise expiration date: N.A. Began: October 1, 1979.
Channel capacity: N.A. Channels available but not in use: N.A.
Digital Basic Service
Subscribers: 101.
Programming (via satellite): BBC America; Bravo; CMT; Destination America; Discovery Kids Channel; DMX Music; ESPN Classic; ESPNews; Fox Sports 1; Golf Channel; GSN; History; IFC; Investigation Discovery; MTV Classic; National Geographic Channel; NBCSN; Nick Jr.; OWN: Oprah Winfrey Network; Science Channel; Syfy; Turner Classic Movies; TV Land.
Fee: $26.99 monthly.
Digital Expanded Basic Service
Subscribers: N.A.
Programming (via satellite): A&E; Altitude Sports & Entertainment; AMC; Animal Planet; Cartoon Network; CNBC; CNN; Disney Channel; ESPN; ESPN2; Fox News Channel; Freeform; HGTV; Lifetime; MoviePlex; Nickelodeon; Root Sports Utah; Spike TV; The Weather Channel; TLC; TNT; USA Network.
Fee: $28.99 monthly.
Digital Pay Service 1
Pay Units: N.A.
Programming (via satellite): HBO (multiplexed); Showtime 2; Starz Edge; Starz Encore (multiplexed); The Movie Channel.
Video-On-Demand: No
Internet Service
Operational: Yes.
Broadband Service: Charter Internet.
Fee: $52.95 monthly.
Telephone Service
Digital: Operational
Fee: $49.99 monthly
Miles of Plant: 12.0 (coaxial); None (fiber optic). Homes passed: 956.
President & Chief Executive Officer: Tom Rutledge. General Manager: Mike Oswald. Chief Technician: Ed McFadden. Accounting Director: David Sovanski.
Ownership: Charter Communications Inc. (MSO).

TROY—MontanaSky West, 1286 Burns Way, Kalispell, MT 59901. Phone: 406-293-4335. Web Site: http://www.montanasky.tv. ICA: MT0122.
TV Market Ranking: Outside TV Markets (TROY).
Channel capacity: N.A. Channels available but not in use: N.A.
Basic Service
Subscribers: 46.
Programming (received off-air): KAYU-TV (FOX, This TV) Spokane; KCFW-TV (MeTV, NBC, This TV) Kalispell; KHQ-TV (NBC) Spokane; KQUP (IND) Pullman; KREM (CBS, TheCoolTV) Spokane; KSPS-TV (PBS) Spokane; KXLY-TV (ABC, MeTV) Spokane.
Programming (via satellite): C-SPAN; C-SPAN 2; Discovery Channel; MSNBC; Northwest Cable News; QVC; TBS; WGN America.
Fee: $29.99 installation; $30.95 monthly.
Expanded Basic Service 1
Subscribers: N.A.
Programming (via satellite): A&E; AMC; Animal Planet; Cartoon Network; CMT; CNBC; CNN; Comedy Central; Disney Channel; E! HD; ESPN; ESPN2; Food Network; Fox News Channel; Fox Sports 1; Freeform; FX; Hallmark Channel; HGTV; History; HLN; Lifetime; MTV; MTV2; Nickelodeon; Oxygen; Spike TV; Syfy; The Weather Channel; TLC; TNT; Travel Channel; truTV; TV Land; USA Network; VH1.
Fee: $35.80 installation; $28.88 monthly.
Digital Basic Service
Subscribers: N.A.
Programming (via satellite): BBC America; Bloomberg Television; Bravo; Discovery Life Channel; Disney XD; ESPN Classic; ESPNews; FXM; GSN; LMN; MC; National Geographic Channel; Nick Jr.; Nicktoons; TeenNick; Trinity Broadcasting Network (TBN); Turner Classic Movies; WE tv.
Fee: $11.99 monthly.
Digital Expanded Basic Service
Subscribers: N.A.
Programming (via satellite): FYI; Golf Channel; History International; IFC; NBCSN; Outdoor Channel.
Fee: $12.49 monthly.
Digital Pay Service 1
Pay Units: N.A.
Programming (via satellite): Cinemax (multiplexed); Flix; HBO (multiplexed); Showtime (multiplexed); Starz (multiplexed); Starz Encore (multiplexed); The Movie Channel (multiplexed).
Fee: $15.95 monthly (each).
Video-On-Demand: No
Pay-Per-View
HITS (Headend In The Sky) (delivered digitally); Playboy TV (delivered digitally); Fresh (delivered digitally).
Internet Service
Operational: Yes.
Subscribers: 82.
Fee: $19.95 installation; $45.95 monthly; $3.00 modem lease; $99.00 modem purchase.
Telephone Service
None
Miles of Plant: 23.0 (coaxial); None (fiber optic). Homes passed: 600.
Chief Executive Officer & General Manager: Frederick Weber.
Ownership: MontanaSky West LLC (MSO).

TWIN BRIDGES—Formerly served by Twin Bridges Cable TV Inc. No longer in operation. ICA: MT0118.

VALIER—Formerly served by KLiP Interactive. No longer in operation. ICA: MT0081.

VICTOR—Formerly served by Bresnan Communications. No longer in operation. ICA: MT0082.

WEST YELLOWSTONE—Bulldog Cable, 455 Gees Mill Business Ct, Conyers, GA 30013. Phones: 706-997-9003; 800-388-6577. Web Site: http://www.bulldogcable.com. ICA: MT0050.
TV Market Ranking: Outside TV Markets (WEST YELLOWSTONE). Franchise award date: N.A. Franchise expiration date: N.A. Began: November 1, 1979.
Channel capacity: 45 (not 2-way capable). Channels available but not in use: N.A.
Basic Service
Subscribers: 103.
Programming (received off-air): KISU-TV (PBS) Pocatello; KPVI-DT (Antenna TV, NBC, This TV) Pocatello; KXLF-TV (CBS, CW, Grit) Butte.
Programming (via microwave): KSL-TV (NBC) Salt Lake City; KTVX (ABC, MeTV) Salt Lake City; KUTV (CBS, This TV) Salt Lake City.
Programming (via satellite): A&E; Animal Planet; CMT; CNN; Discovery Channel; Disney Channel; ESPN; ESPN2; Fox News Channel; Freeform; HGTV; History; HLN; KDVR (Antenna TV, FOX) Denver; Nickelodeon; Outdoor Channel; Pop; QVC; Root Sports Rocky Mountain; Spike TV; Syfy; TBS; The Weather Channel; TLC; TNT; Travel Channel; Turner Classic Movies; USA Network; VH1; WGN America.
Programming (via translator): KIFI-TV (ABC, CW, UniMas) Idaho Falls.
Fee: $44.95 installation; $46.00 monthly.
Pay Service 1
Pay Units: N.A.
Programming (via satellite): HBO; Showtime; The Movie Channel.
Fee: $12.00 monthly (each).
Video-On-Demand: No
Internet Service
Operational: No.
Telephone Service
None
Miles of Plant: 10.0 (coaxial); None (fiber optic). Homes passed: 550.
President: Mark Wilson. General Manager East: Mark Miller. General Manager West: Vance Johnson. Controller: Ashley Hull.
Ownership: Bulldog Cable (MSO).

WHITE SULPHUR SPRINGS—Formerly served by Eagle Cablevision Inc. No longer in operation. ICA: MT0057.

WHITEHALL—Whitehall Cable TV, 33 Sowden Ln, PO Box 1075, Whitehall, MT 59759-1075. Phone: 406-287-7800. ICA: MT0064.
TV Market Ranking: Below 100 (WHITEHALL). Franchise award date: June 1, 1981. Franchise expiration date: N.A. Began: N.A.
Channel capacity: N.A. Channels available but not in use: N.A.
Basic Service
Subscribers: N.A.
Programming (received off-air): KTVM-TV (MeTV, Movies!, NBC, This TV) Butte; KWYB (ABC, FOX) Butte; KXLF-TV (CBS, CW, Grit) Butte.
Programming (via satellite): Animal Planet; Cartoon Network; CMT; CNN; C-SPAN 2; Discovery Channel; ESPN; ESPN2; Freeform; MTV; Nickelodeon; Outdoor Channel; QVC; Root Sports Rocky Mountain; Spike TV; TBS; The Weather Channel; TLC; TNT; truTV; Turner Classic Movies; TV Land; VH1; WGN America.
Fee: $22.50 installation.
Pay Service 1
Pay Units: N.A.
Programming (via satellite): The Movie Channel.
Fee: $8.50 monthly.
Internet Service
Operational: No.
Telephone Service
None
Miles of Plant: 5.0 (coaxial); None (fiber optic). Homes passed: 425.
General Manager & Chief Technician: Scott Mercer.
Ownership: Scott Mercer.

WIBAUX—Mid-Rivers Communications, 904 C Ave, PO Box 280, Circle, MT 59215. Phones: 406-535-3336; 406-485-3301. Fax: 406-485-2924. E-mail: lcedar@midrivers.com. Web Site: http://www.midrivers.com. ICA: MT0087.
TV Market Ranking: Below 100 (WIBAUX). Franchise award date: N.A. Franchise expiration date: N.A. Began: January 1, 1975.
Channel capacity: N.A. Channels available but not in use: N.A.

Montana—Cable Systems

Basic Service
Subscribers: 173.
Programming (received off-air): KDSE (PBS) Dickinson; KQCD-TV (FOX, NBC) Dickinson; KXGN-TV (CBS, NBC) Glendive.
Programming (via satellite): CNN; C-SPAN; C-SPAN 2; Discovery Channel; Disney Channel; HLN; KMGH-TV (ABC, Azteca America) Denver; QVC; Spike TV; TBS; The Weather Channel; WGN America.
Fee: $49.95 installation; $22.40 monthly.

Expanded Basic Service 1
Subscribers: N.A.
Programming (via satellite): A&E; AMC; Animal Planet; Cartoon Network; CMT; CNBC; Comedy Central; Concert TV; E! HD; ESPN; ESPN2; EWTN Global Catholic Network; Food Network; Fox Sports 1; Freeform; Hallmark Channel; HGTV; History; Lifetime; Nickelodeon; Outdoor Channel; Starz Encore; Syfy; TLC; TNT; Travel Channel; Trinity Broadcasting Network (TBN); TV Land; USA Network.
Fee: $12.00 monthly.

Pay Service 1
Pay Units: N.A.
Programming (via satellite): Cinemax; HBO; Showtime; The Movie Channel.
Fee: $8.00 monthly (Cinemax, Showtime or TMC), $10.00 monthly (HBO).

Internet Service
Operational: No.

Telephone Service
Analog: Operational
Miles of Plant: 7.0 (coaxial); None (fiber optic). Homes passed: 250.
President: Mark Robbins. General Manager: Bill Wade. Chief Technician: Mike Sokolosky. Customer Service Manager: Deb Wagner.
Ownership: Mid-Rivers Telephone Cooperative Inc. (MSO).

WOLF POINT—Nemont Communications, 61 Hwy 13 South, PO Box 600, Scobey, MT 59263-0600. Phones: 406-967-2311; 800-636-6680. Fax: 406-783-5283. E-mail: nemont@nemont.coop. Web Site: http://www.nemont.net. Also serves Roosevelt County. ICA: MT0028.
TV Market Ranking: Below 100 (Roosevelt County (portions)); Outside TV Markets (Roosevelt County (portions), WOLF POINT). Franchise award date: February 16, 1981. Franchise expiration date: N.A. Began: June 1, 1979.
Channel capacity: N.A. Channels available but not in use: N.A.

Basic Service
Subscribers: 549. Commercial subscribers: 10.
Programming (via microwave): KFBB-TV (ABC, FOX) Great Falls; KUMV-TV (FOX, NBC) Williston; KUSM-TV (PBS) Bozeman; KXMD-TV (CBS) Williston.
Programming (via satellite): C-SPAN; C-SPAN 2; CW PLUS; KMGH-TV (ABC, Azteca America) Denver; KUSA (NBC, WeatherNation) Denver; Pop; QVC; TBS; WGN America.
Fee: $25.00 installation; $20.99 monthly.

Expanded Basic Service 1
Subscribers: 522.
Programming (via satellite): A&E; Altitude Sports & Entertainment; AMC; Animal Planet; Cartoon Network; CMT; CNBC; CNN; Comedy Central; Discovery Channel; Disney Channel; E! HD; ESPN; ESPN2; Food Network; Fox News Channel; Freeform; FX; Hallmark Channel; HGTV; History; HLN; INSP; Lifetime; MSNBC; MTV; Nickelodeon; Oxygen; Root Sports Rocky Mountain; Spike TV; Syfy; The Weather Channel; TLC; TNT; Travel Channel; truTV; Turner Classic Movies; TV Land; USA Network; VH1.
Fee: $30.00 monthly.

Digital Basic Service
Subscribers: 287.
Programming (via satellite): BBC America; Bloomberg Television; Bravo; CBS Sports Network; CMT; Destination America; Discovery Kids Channel; Disney XD; DMX Music; ESPN Classic; ESPNews; Fox Sports 1; Fuse; FXM; FYI; Golf Channel; Great American Country; GSN; History International; IFC; Investigation Discovery; LMN; MTV Classic; MTV Hits; MTV2; Nat Geo WILD; National Geographic Channel; NBCSN; Nick Jr.; Nicktoons; Outdoor Channel; OWN: Oprah Winfrey Network; RFD-TV; Science Channel; Sprout; TeenNick; Trinity Broadcasting Network (TBN); UP; VH1 Soul.
Fee: $18.00 monthly.

Digital Pay Service 1
Pay Units: N.A.
Programming (via satellite): Cinemax (multiplexed); Flix; HBO (multiplexed); Showtime (multiplexed); Starz (multiplexed); Starz Encore (multiplexed); The Movie Channel (multiplexed).
Fee: $5.00 monthly (Encore), $9.00 monthly (Starz), $16.00 monthly (Cinemax, HBO or Showtime/TMC).

Video-On-Demand: No

Pay-Per-View
iN DEMAND (delivered digitally); HRTV (delivered digitally); NFL Network (delivered digitally); FOX College Sports Central (delivered digitally); FOX College Sports Pacific (delivered digitally).

Internet Service
Operational: Yes.
Fee: $43.95-65.00 monthly.

Telephone Service
Digital: Operational
Miles of Plant: 18.0 (coaxial); None (fiber optic). Homes passed: 1,617.
Chief Executive Officer: Mike Kilgore. Chief Financial Officer: Remi Sun.
Ownership: Nemont Telephone Coop (MSO).

NEBRASKA

Total Systems: 99	Communities with Applications: 0
Total Communities Served: 337	Number of Basic Subscribers: 318,883
Franchises Not Yet Operating: 0	Number of Expanded Basic Subscribers: 1,747
Applications Pending: 0	Number of Pay Units: 54,465

Top 100 Markets Represented: Omaha (53); Lincoln-Hastings-Kearney (91).

For a list of cable communities in this section, see the Cable Community Index located in the back of Cable Volume 2.
For explanation of terms used in cable system listings, see p. D-11.

AINSWORTH—Three River Digital Cable, PO Box 66, Lynch, NE 68746. Phones: 402-569-2666 (Lynch office); 402-387-1353. E-mail: info@threeriver.net. Web Site: http://www.threeriver.net. Also serves Long Pine, Naper, O'Neill, Springview & Valentine. ICA: NE0049.
TV Market Ranking: Outside TV Markets (AINSWORTH, Long Pine, Springview, Naper, O'Neill, Valentine). Franchise award date: May 14, 1990. Franchise expiration date: N.A. Began: January 1, 1978.
Channel capacity: N.A. Channels available but not in use: N.A.
Basic Service
Subscribers: 1,783.
Programming (received off-air): KMNE-TV (PBS) Bassett; KOLN (CBS, MNT, NBC) Lincoln; KPLO-TV (CBS, MNT) Reliance; all-band FM.
Programming (via satellite): A&E; AMC; Cartoon Network; CMT; CNBC; CNN; C-SPAN; Discovery Channel; Disney Channel; ESPN; Freeform; HLN; INSP; KMGH-TV (ABC, Azteca America) Denver; KUSA (NBC, WeatherNation) Denver; Lifetime; MTV; Nickelodeon; Pop; QVC; Root Sports Rocky Mountain; Spike TV; TBS; The Weather Channel; TLC; TNT; TV Land; USA Network; VH1; WGN America.
Fee: $17.95 monthly.
Pay Service 1
Pay Units: N.A.
Programming (via satellite): Cinemax; HBO; Showtime; Starz Encore; The Movie Channel.
Fee: $20.00 installation; $11.00 monthly (Showtime), $12.00 monthly (Cinemax, Encore, HBO or TMC).
Video-On-Demand: No
Internet Service
Operational: No.
Telephone Service
None
Miles of Plant: 28.0 (coaxial); None (fiber optic).
General Manager: Neil K. Classen.
Ownership: Three River Digital Cable LLC (MSO).

ALBION (town)—Eagle Communications, 2703 Hall St, Ste 15, PO Box 817, Hays, KS 67601. Phone: 785-625-4000. Fax: 785-625-8030. Web Site: http://www.eaglecom.net. ICA: NE0040.
TV Market Ranking: Outside TV Markets (ALBION (TOWN)). Franchise award date: N.A. Franchise expiration date: N.A. Began: January 1, 1970.
Channel capacity: N.A. Channels available but not in use: N.A.
Basic Service
Subscribers: 322.
Programming (received off-air): KGIN (CBS, MNT, NBC) Grand Island; KHGI-TV (ABC) Kearney; KHNE-TV (PBS) Hastings; KLKN (ABC) Lincoln; KNHL (IND) Hastings; KTVG-TV (FOX) Grand Island.
Programming (via satellite): C-SPAN; C-SPAN 2; EWTN Global Catholic Network; Freeform; Hallmark Channel; HLN; Pop; QVC; TBS; The Weather Channel; Trinity Broadcasting Network (TBN); WGN America.
Fee: $24.95 installation; $64.95 monthly.
Expanded Basic Service 1
Subscribers: N.A.
Programming (via satellite): A&E; AMC; Animal Planet; Cartoon Network; CMT; CNBC; CNN; Comedy Central; Discovery Channel; E! HD; ESPN; ESPN2; Food Network; Fox News Channel; FOX Sports Midwest; FX; Great American Country; HGTV; History; ION Television; Lifetime; MSNBC; MTV; Nickelodeon; Outdoor Channel; Spike TV; Syfy; TLC; TNT; Travel Channel; truTV; Turner Classic Movies; TV Land; Univision Studios; USA Network; VH1.
Digital Basic Service
Subscribers: N.A.
Programming (via satellite): BBC America; Bloomberg Television; Discovery Kids Channel; Discovery Life Channel; DMX Music; ESPN Classic; ESPNews; EVINE Live; Fox Sports 1; FSN Digital Atlantic; FSN Digital Central; FSN Digital Pacific; FXM; FYI; Golf Channel; GSN; History; History International; HITS (Headend In The Sky); International Television (ITV); MBC America; National Geographic Channel; NBCSN; Nick Jr.; Outdoor Channel; Ovation; Syfy; Teen-Nick; Trinity Broadcasting Network (TBN).
Fee: $14.00 monthly.
Digital Pay Service 1
Pay Units: N.A.
Programming (via satellite): Cinemax (multiplexed); Flix; FXM; HBO (multiplexed); IFC; Showtime (multiplexed); Starz (multiplexed); Starz Encore (multiplexed); Sundance TV; The Movie Channel (multiplexed); WE tv.
Video-On-Demand: No
Pay-Per-View
iN DEMAND (delivered digitally); Hot Choice (delivered digitally); Playboy TV (delivered digitally); Fresh (delivered digitally); Shorteez (delivered digitally); ESPN Now (delivered digitally).
Internet Service
Operational: Yes.
Broadband Service: Cable Nebraska.
Telephone Service
Digital: Operational
Miles of Plant: 16.0 (coaxial); None (fiber optic). Homes passed: 1,145.
President & Chief Executive Officer: Gary Shorman. Chief Operating Officer: Kurt K. David. General Manager: Travis Kohlrus. Marketing Manager: Elizabeth Jaeger.
Ownership: Eagle Communications Inc. (MSO).

ALEXANDRIA—Formerly served by Comstar Cable TV Inc. No longer in operation. ICA: NE0226.

ALLEN (village)—CenCom NNTV. This cable system has converted to IPTV. See JACKSON, NE [NE5019]. ICA: NE0258.

ALLIANCE—Charter Communications. Now served by SCOTTSBLUFF, NE [NE0008]. ICA: NE0017.

ALMA—Eagle Communications, 2703 Hall St, Ste 15, PO Box 817, Hays, KS 67601. Phone: 785-625-4000. Fax: 785-625-8030. E-mail: support@eaglecom.net. Web Site: http://www.eaglecom.net. ICA: NE0059.
TV Market Ranking: Outside TV Markets (ALMA).
Channel capacity: N.A. Channels available but not in use: N.A.
Basic Service
Subscribers: 97.
Programming (received off-air): KGIN (CBS, MNT, NBC) Grand Island; KHGI-TV (ABC) Kearney; KLNE-TV (PBS) Lexington; KNHL (IND) Hastings; KSNB-TV (MeTV, MNT, NBC) Superior.
Programming (via satellite): A&E; CNN; Discovery Channel; Disney Channel; Disney XD; ESPN; EWTN Global Catholic Network; Food Network; Fox News Channel; FOX Sports Midwest; FOX Sports Networks; Freeform; Great American Country; HGTV; History; HLN; INSP; MTV; National Geographic Channel; Nickelodeon; QVC; Spike TV; TBS; The Weather Channel; TLC; TNT; TV Land; USA Network; VH1; WGN America.
Fee: $24.95 installation; $49.95 monthly.
Pay Service 1
Pay Units: N.A.
Programming (via satellite): HBO; Showtime; The Movie Channel.
Fee: $11.95 monthly (each).
Video-On-Demand: No
Internet Service
Operational: Yes.
Subscribers: 39.
Fee: $30.00 installation.
Telephone Service
None
Miles of Plant: 10.0 (coaxial); None (fiber optic). Homes passed: 700.
President & Chief Executive Officer: Gary Shorman. Chief Operating Officer: Kurt K. David. General Manager: Travis Kohlrus. Marketing Manager: Elizabeth Jaeger.
Ownership: Eagle Communications Inc. (MSO).

ANSLEY—NCTC Cable. Now served by BURWELL, NE [NE0045]. ICA: NE0150.

ARAPAHOE—ATC Communications, 524 Nebraska Ave, PO Box 300, Arapahoe, NE 68922. Phones: 866-222-7873; 308-962-7298. Fax: 308-962-5373. E-mail: support@atcjet.net. Web Site: http://www.atcjet.net. Also serves Elwood, Farnam & Holbrook. ICA: NE0260.
TV Market Ranking: Below 100 (Holbrook); Outside TV Markets (ARAPAHOE, Elwood, Farnam). Franchise award date: N.A. Franchise expiration date: N.A. Began: January 1, 1983.
Channel capacity: N.A. Channels available but not in use: N.A.
Basic Service
Subscribers: 499.
Programming (received off-air): KGIN (CBS, MNT, NBC) Grand Island; KHGI-TV (ABC) Kearney; KLNE-TV (PBS) Lexington; KSNK (NBC) McCook.
Programming (via satellite): A&E; Animal Planet; Cartoon Network; CMT; CNN; Comedy Central; Discovery Channel; Disney Channel; DIY Network; ESPN; ESPN2; Food Network; Fox News Channel; Fox Sports 1; FOX Sports Midwest; Freeform; FX; Golf Channel; GSN; Hallmark Channel; HGTV; History; INSP; Nickelodeon; Outdoor Channel; QVC; Spike TV; Syfy; TBS; The Weather Channel; TLC; TNT; Travel Channel; Turner Classic Movies; TV Land; USA Network; VH1; WGN America.
Fee: $20.00 installation; $39.95 monthly.
Expanded Basic Service 1
Subscribers: 242.
Programming (via satellite): FXM; MTV; Starz; Starz Encore; Starz Encore Classic; Starz Encore Suspense; Starz Encore Westerns.
Fee: $20.00 installation; $10.95 monthly.
Pay Service 1
Pay Units: 55.
Programming (via satellite): Cinemax.
Fee: $20.00 installation; $9.95 monthly.
Pay Service 2
Pay Units: 40.
Programming (via satellite): HBO.
Fee: $20.00 installation; $9.95 monthly.
Video-On-Demand: No
Internet Service
Operational: Yes.
Fee: $29.95-$99.95 monthly.
Telephone Service
None
Miles of Plant: None (coaxial); 25.0 (fiber optic). Homes passed: 855.
President: John M. Koller. Vice President, Regulatory Affairs: Steven T. Koller. General Manager: Rich Redman. Operations Manager: Jim Meyers. Chief Technician: Michael G Monie.
Ownership: Applied Communications Technology.

2017 Edition   D-479

Nebraska—Cable Systems

ARCADIA—NCTC Cable. Now served by BURWELL, NE [NE0045]. ICA: NE0206.

ARNOLD—Great Plains Cablevision. Now served by BROKEN BOW, NE [NE0031]. ICA: NE0114.

ASHLAND—Charter Communications. Now served by SPRINGFIELD (formerly Plattsmouth), NE [NE0020]. ICA: NE0047.

ASHTON—NCTC Cable. Now served by BURWELL, NE [NE0045]. ICA: NE0227.

ATKINSON—Formerly served by Fort Randall Cable. No longer in operation. ICA: NE0261.

AUBURN—Time Warner Cable. Now served by LINCOLN, NE [NE0002]. ICA: NE0013.

AURORA—Mid-State Community TV, 1001 12th St, Aurora, NE 68818-2004. Phones: 800-821-1831; 402-694-5101. Fax: 402-694-2848. E-mail: midstate@midstatetv.com. Web Site: http://www.midstatetv.com. Also serves Hampton & Phillips. ICA: NE0033.
TV Market Ranking: 91 (AURORA, Hampton, Phillips). Franchise award date: N.A. Franchise expiration date: N.A. Began: February 1, 1968.
Channel capacity: N.A. Channels available but not in use: N.A.
Basic Service
Subscribers: 848.
Programming (received off-air): KHGI-TV (ABC) Kearney; KHNE-TV (PBS) Hastings; KNHL (IND) Hastings; KOLN (CBS, MNT, NBC) Lincoln; KTVG-TV (FOX) Grand Island.
Programming (via satellite): A&E; AMC; Animal Planet; Cartoon Network; CMT; CNN; Comedy Central; C-SPAN; Discovery Channel; Disney Channel; DIY Network; E! HD; ESPN; ESPN2; Food Network; Fox News Channel; Fox Sports 1; FOX Sports Midwest; Freeform; FX; Hallmark Channel; HLN; ION Television; Lifetime; MSNBC; MTV; National Geographic Channel; Nickelodeon; Oxygen; Pop; QVC; Spike TV; TBS; The Weather Channel; TLC; TNT; Travel Channel; truTV; TV Land; USA Network; VH1; WGN America; WPIX (Antenna TV, CW, This TV) New York.
Fee: $20.00 installation; $49.95 monthly; $2.00 converter.
Digital Basic Service
Subscribers: N.A.
Programming (via satellite): BBC America; Bloomberg Television; Bravo; Discovery Life Channel; DMX Music; ESPN Classic; ESPNews; FXM; Golf Channel; GSN; HGTV; History; IFC; NBCSN; Nick Jr.; Nicktoons; Outdoor Channel; Syfy; Trinity Broadcasting Network (TBN); Turner Classic Movies; WE tv.
Pay Service 1
Pay Units: N.A.
Programming (via satellite): HBO.
Fee: $20.00 installation; $10.50 monthly.
Pay Service 2
Pay Units: 150.
Programming (via satellite): Cinemax.
Fee: $20.00 installation; $7.50 monthly.
Digital Pay Service 1
Pay Units: N.A.
Programming (via satellite): Cinemax (multiplexed); HBO (multiplexed); Showtime (multiplexed); Starz (multiplexed); Starz Encore (multiplexed); The Movie Channel (multiplexed).
Fee: $6.50 monthly (Starz/Encore), $8.50 monthly (Cinemax), $12.50 monthly (HBO), $12.95 monthly (Showtime/TMC).
Video-On-Demand: No
Pay-Per-View
Hot Choice (delivered digitally).
Internet Service
Operational: No, DSL.
Telephone Service
None
Miles of Plant: 62.0 (coaxial); None (fiber optic). Homes passed: 2,654. Miles of plant (coax) includes miles of plant (fiber).
President & General Manager: Phillip C. Nelson. Chief Technician: Pat Shaw. Marketing Director: Tina Hunt. Customer Service Manager: Pat Phillips.
Ownership: Mid-State Community TV Inc.

AVOCA (town)—Formerly served by CableDirect. No longer in operation. ICA: NE0123.

BANCROFT—Great Plains Communications, 1600 Great Plains Ctr, PO Box 500, Blair, NE 68008-0500. Phones: 402-426-9511; 888-343-8014. Fax: 402-456-6550. E-mail: lquist@gpcom.com. Web Site: http://www.gpcom.com. ICA: NE0151.
TV Market Ranking: Outside TV Markets (BANCROFT). Franchise award date: December 1, 1983. Franchise expiration date: N.A. Began: N.A.
Channel capacity: N.A. Channels available but not in use: N.A.
Basic Service
Subscribers: 85.
Programming (received off-air): KCAU-TV (ABC) Sioux City; KETV (ABC, MeTV) Omaha; KMTV-TV (Antenna TV, CBS, Escape) Omaha; KPTM (Estrella TV, FOX, MNT, This TV) Omaha; KTIV (CW, MeTV, NBC) Sioux City; KXNE-TV (PBS) Norfolk; KXVO (Azteca America, CW) Omaha.
Programming (via satellite): A&E; AMC; Animal Planet; CNN; Discovery Channel; Disney Channel; ESPN; ESPN2; Fox News Channel; Freeform; Great American Country; Hallmark Channel; HGTV; History; HLN; Lifetime; Nickelodeon; QVC; Spike TV; TBS; The Weather Channel; TLC; TNT; Travel Channel; TV Land; USA Network; WGN America.
Fee: $45.00 installation; $41.99 monthly.
Expanded Basic Service 1
Subscribers: N.A.
Fee: $47.99 monthly.
Digital Basic Service
Subscribers: N.A.
Programming (via satellite): BBC America; Bravo; Discovery Digital Networks; DMX Music; ESPN Classic; ESPNews; Fox Sports 1; FYI; Golf Channel; GSN; History International; IFC; LMN; National Geographic Channel; NBCSN; Outdoor Channel; Syfy; Turner Classic Movies; WE tv.
Fee: $47.95 monthly.
Pay Service 1
Pay Units: 20.
Programming (via satellite): HBO; Showtime.
Fee: $9.95 monthly (Showtime), $10.95 monthly (HBO).
Digital Pay Service 1
Pay Units: 10.
Programming (via satellite): Cinemax (multiplexed); Flix; HBO (multiplexed); Showtime (multiplexed); Starz Encore (multiplexed); The Movie Channel (multiplexed); WAM! America's Kidz Network.
Fee: $12.00 monthly.
Video-On-Demand: No
Pay-Per-View
iN DEMAND (delivered digitally); ESPN (delivered digitally).
Internet Service
Operational: Yes, DSL & dial-up.
Broadband Service: In-house.
Fee: $49.95 installation; $39.95 monthly.
Telephone Service
Digital: Operational
Miles of Plant: 4.0 (coaxial); None (fiber optic).
Senior Director: Lea Ann Quist. Chief Technician: Mark Stottler. Marketing Manager: Casey Carrigan.
Ownership: Great Plains Communications Inc. (MSO).

BASSETT—American Broadband, 1605 Washington St, Blair, NE 68008-0400. Phones: 402-533-1000; 401-426-6200. Fax: 402-533-1111. Web Site: http://www.americanbroadband.com. Also serves Rock County. ICA: NE0094.
TV Market Ranking: Outside TV Markets (BASSETT, Rock County). Franchise award date: N.A. Franchise expiration date: N.A. Began: August 1, 1982.
Channel capacity: N.A. Channels available but not in use: N.A.
Basic Service
Subscribers: 125 Included in Blair.
Programming (received off-air): KLKN (ABC) Lincoln; KMNE-TV (PBS) Bassett; KOLN (CBS, MNT, NBC) Lincoln; allband FM.
Programming (via satellite): A&E; AMC; Cartoon Network; CMT; CNN; Comedy Central; C-SPAN; Discovery Channel; E! HD; ESPN; ESPN2; FOX Sports Midwest; Freeform; FX; HGTV; History; HLN; KUSA (NBC, WeatherNation) Denver; Lifetime; Nickelodeon; Spike TV; TBS; The Weather Channel; TLC; TNT; USA Network; VH1; WGN America; WXYZ-TV (ABC, Bounce TV) Detroit.
Fee: $25.00 installation; $42.95 monthly.
Pay Service 1
Pay Units: N.A.
Programming (via satellite): Cinemax; HBO; Showtime.
Fee: $10.00 monthly (Cinemax or Showtime), $12.00 monthly (HBO).
Video-On-Demand: No
Internet Service
Operational: Yes.
Telephone Service
Digital: Operational
Miles of Plant: 10.0 (coaxial); None (fiber optic). Total homes in area & homes passed included in Blair.
President, State Operations: Mike Jacobsen. General Manager, Cable Television: Mike Storjohann. Program Director: Kay Peterson.
Ownership: American Broadband Communications Inc. (MSO).

BAYARD—Charter Communications. Now served by SCOTTSBLUFF, NE [NE0008]. ICA: NE0056.

BEATRICE—Charter Communications, 12405 Powerscourt Dr, St. Louis, MO 63131. Phones: 636-207-5100 (Corporate office); 308-234-6428; 507-289-8372 (Rochester administrative office); 308-236-1500. Fax: 308-234-6452. Web Site: http://www.charter.com. ICA: NE0016.
TV Market Ranking: Outside TV Markets (BEATRICE). Franchise award date: N.A. Franchise expiration date: N.A. Began: August 1, 1963.
Channel capacity: N.A. Channels available but not in use: N.A.
Digital Basic Service
Subscribers: 2,722.
Programming (via satellite): BBC America; Bravo; Discovery Kids Channel; DMX Music; ESPN Classic; ESPNews; FYI; GSN; History International; IFC; LMN; MTV2; NBCSN; Nick Jr.; Nicktoons; OWN: Oprah Winfrey Network; Syfy; TeenNick; Trinity Broadcasting Network (TBN); Turner Classic Movies; TV Guide Interactive Inc.; WE tv.
Fee: $26.99 monthly.
Digital Expanded Basic Service
Subscribers: N.A.
Programming (via satellite): A&E; AMC; Animal Planet; Cartoon Network; CMT; CNBC; CNN; Comedy Central; Discovery Channel; Disney Channel; Disney XD; E! HD; ESPN; ESPN2; Food Network; Fox News Channel; Fox Sports 1; FOX Sports Networks; Freeform; FX; Golf Channel; Hallmark Channel; HGTV; History; HLN; Lifetime; MSNBC; MTV; Nickelodeon; Oxygen; Spike TV; TBS; The Weather Channel; TLC; TNT; Travel Channel; truTV; TV Land; USA Network; VH1.
Fee: $47.99 monthly.
Digital Pay Service 1
Pay Units: N.A.
Programming (via satellite): Cinemax (multiplexed); Flix; HBO (multiplexed); Showtime (multiplexed); Starz (multiplexed); Starz Encore (multiplexed); The Movie Channel (multiplexed).
Video-On-Demand: Yes
Pay-Per-View
iN DEMAND (delivered digitally); Playboy TV (delivered digitally); Fresh (delivered digitally); Shorteez (delivered digitally).
Internet Service
Operational: Yes.
Broadband Service: Charter Internet.
Fee: $29.99 monthly.
Telephone Service
Digital: Operational
Miles of Plant: 81.0 (coaxial); None (fiber optic). Homes passed: 6,873.
Vice President & General Manager: John Crowley. Technical Operations Director: Marty Kovarik. Technical Operations Manager: Terry Petzoldt. Office Manager: Dawn Harmon. Accounting Director: David Sovanski.
Ownership: Charter Communications Inc. (MSO).

BEAVER CITY—PinPoint Cable TV. Now served by CAMBRIDGE, NE [NE0269]. ICA: NE0100.

BEAVER CROSSING—Formerly served by Zito Media. No longer in operation. ICA: NE0155.

BEAVER LAKE—Formerly served by Our Cable. No longer in operation. ICA: NE0262.

BEE (village)—Formerly served by TelePartners. No longer in operation. ICA: NE0263.

BEEMER—Formerly served by TelePartners. Now served by Cable One, NORFOLK, NE [NE0006]. ICA: NE0165.

BELLWOOD—Eagle Communications, 2703 Hall St, Ste 15, PO Box 817, Hays, KS 67601. Phone: 308-236-1512. Web Site: http://www.eaglecom.net. ICA: NE0265.

Cable Systems—Nebraska

TV Market Ranking: Outside TV Markets (BELLWOOD). Franchise award date: N.A. Franchise expiration date: N.A. Began: May 1, 1983.
Channel capacity: N.A. Channels available but not in use: N.A.
Basic Service
Subscribers: 30.
Programming (received off-air): KETV (ABC, MeTV) Omaha; KLKN (ABC) Lincoln; KMTV-TV (Antenna TV, CBS, Escape) Omaha; KOLN (CBS, MNT, NBC) Lincoln; KPTM (Estrella TV, FOX, MNT, This TV) Omaha; KUON-TV (PBS) Lincoln; KXVO (Azteca America, CW) Omaha; WOWT (IND, NBC) Omaha.
Programming (via satellite): A&E; CNN; Discovery Channel; ESPN; ESPN2; FOX Sports Midwest; Freeform; HGTV; Lifetime; Nickelodeon; Outdoor Channel; QVC; TBS; The Weather Channel; TLC; TNT; Turner Classic Movies; USA Network; WGN America.
Fee: $24.95 installation; $49.95 monthly.
Pay Service 1
Pay Units: N.A.
Programming (via satellite): HBO; Showtime; The Movie Channel.
Fee: $7.95 monthly (TMC), $8.95 monthly (Showtime), $13.95 monthly (HBO).
Internet Service
Operational: Yes.
Telephone Service
None
Miles of Plant: 3.0 (coaxial); None (fiber optic). Homes passed: 192.
Operations Manager: Stuart Gilbertson. Chief Operating Officer: Kurt K. David. Chief Financial Officer: Amber Reineke.
Ownership: Eagle Communications Inc. (MSO).

BENEDICT—Formerly served by Galaxy Cablevision. No longer in operation. ICA: NE0231.

BENKELMAN—BWTelcom, 607 Chief St, PO Box 684, Benkelman, NE 69021. Phones: 308-423-8950; 800-835-0053; 308-394-6000; 308-423-2000. Fax: 308-423-5618. E-mail: bwtelcom@bwtelcom.net. Web Site: http://www.bwtelcom.net. ICA: NE0051.
TV Market Ranking: Outside TV Markets (BENKELMAN). Franchise award date: November 1, 1982. Franchise expiration date: N.A. Began: November 1, 1982.
Channel capacity: N.A. Channels available but not in use: N.A.
Basic Service
Subscribers: 255.
Programming (received off-air): KBSL-DT (CBS) Goodland; KPNE-TV (PBS) North Platte; KSNK (NBC) McCook; KWNB-TV (ABC) Hayes Center.
Programming (via satellite): A&E; CMT; CNBC; CNN; Discovery Channel; ESPN; ESPN Classic; ESPN2; Fox News Channel; Freeform; FX; KCNC-TV (CBS, Decades) Denver; KWGN-TV (CW, This TV) Denver; Lifetime; Nickelodeon; Outdoor Channel; Root Sports Rocky Mountain; Spike TV; Syfy; TBS; The Weather Channel; TLC; TNT; Travel Channel; Turner Classic Movies; USA Network; VH1; WGN America.
Fee: $27.85 installation; $47.25 monthly.
Expanded Basic Service 1
Subscribers: 187.
Programming (via satellite): AMC; Animal Planet; Bloomberg Television; Cartoon Network; Comedy Central; Disney Channel; Food Network; Fox Sports 1; Great American Country; Hallmark Channel; HGTV; History; HLN; MTV; National Geographic Channel; NBCSN; TV Land.
Fee: $45.00 installation; $22.00 monthly.
Pay Service 1
Pay Units: 35.
Programming (via satellite): HBO; Showtime; The Movie Channel.
Fee: $18.51 monthly (Showtime/TMC), $19.15 monthly (HBO).
Video-On-Demand: No
Internet Service
Operational: Yes.
Telephone Service
None
Miles of Plant: 28.0 (coaxial); None (fiber optic). Homes passed: 500.
Vice President: Kacey L. Harper. General Manager & Chief Technician: Randall Raile. Marketing Director: Loretta Raile. Bookkeeper: Jenna Edwards.
Ownership: BWTelcom (MSO).

BENNINGTON—Cox Communications. Now served by OMAHA, NE [NE0001]. ICA: NE0110.

BIG SPRINGS—Eagle Communications, 2703 Hall St, Ste 15, PO Box 817, Hays, KS 67601. Phone: 785-625-4000. Fax: 785-625-8030. E-mail: support@eaglecom.net. Web Site: http://www.eaglecom.net. ICA: NE0148.
TV Market Ranking: Outside TV Markets (BIG SPRINGS).
Channel capacity: N.A. Channels available but not in use: N.A.
Basic Service
Subscribers: 47.
Fee: $24.95 installation; $39.95 monthly.
President & Chief Executive Officer: Gary Shorman. Chief Operating Officer: Kurt K. David. General Manager: Travis Kohlrus. Marketing Manager: Elizabeth Jaeger.
Ownership: Eagle Communications Inc. (MSO).

BLAIR—American Broadband, 1605 Washington St, Blair, NE 68008-0400. Phones: 402-533-1000; 402-426-6200. Fax: 402-533-1111. Web Site: http://www.americanbroadband.com. Also serves Arlington, Fort Calhoun, Herman, Kennard & Washington County. ICA: NE0027.
TV Market Ranking: 53 (Arlington, BLAIR, Fort Calhoun, Herman, Kennard, Washington County). Franchise award date: N.A. Franchise expiration date: N.A. Began: November 1, 1980.
Channel capacity: N.A. Channels available but not in use: N.A.
Basic Service
Subscribers: 3,213.
Programming (received off-air): KETV (ABC, MeTV) Omaha; KHIN (PBS) Red Oak; KMTV-TV (Antenna TV, CBS, Escape) Omaha; KPTM (Estrella TV, FOX, MNT, This TV) Omaha; KXVO (Azteca America, CW) Omaha; KYNE-TV (PBS) Omaha; WOWT (IND, NBC) Omaha.
Programming (via satellite): C-SPAN; Pop; QVC; The Weather Channel; WGN America.
Fee: $25.00 installation; $19.00 monthly.
Expanded Basic Service 1
Subscribers: N.A.
Programming (via satellite): A&E; AMC; Animal Planet; CMT; CNBC; CNN; Comedy Central; Discovery Channel; Disney Channel; ESPN; ESPN2; Food Network; Fox News Channel; FOX Sports Networks; Freeform; FX; Hallmark Channel; HGTV; History; HLN; Lifetime; MSNBC; MTV; Nickelodeon; Spike TV; Syfy; TBS; TLC; TNT; truTV; USA Network; VH1.
Fee: $19.95 monthly.
Digital Basic Service
Subscribers: N.A. Includes Lyons, Oakland, Tekamah, & Wayne
Programming (via satellite): Animal Planet HD; AXS TV; Cloo; Destination America; Discovery Channel HD; Discovery Kids Channel; Disney XD; DMX Music; ESPN HD; ESPN2 HD; ESPNews; ESPNU; EWTN Global Catholic Network; Fox Sports 1; Fox Sports 2; FSN Digital Atlantic; FSN Digital Central; FSN Digital Pacific; Fuse; FYI; Golf Channel; GSN; HD Theater; Investigation Discovery; LMN; MyNetworkTV; National Geographic Channel; National Geographic Channel HD; NBCSN; Outdoor Channel; OWN: Oprah Winfrey Network; RFD-TV; Science Channel; Science HD; TLC HD; Turner Classic Movies; Universal HD; WE tv.
Fee: $12.94 monthly.
Digital Pay Service 1
Pay Units: N.A.
Programming (via satellite): Cinemax (multiplexed); Cinemax HD; HBO (multiplexed); HBO HD; Showtime (multiplexed); Showtime HD; Starz (multiplexed); Starz Encore (multiplexed); Starz HD; The Movie Channel (multiplexed); The Movie Channel HD.
Fee: $11.10 monthly (Cinemax), $12.00 monthly (Starz/Encore or Showtime/TMC), $13.35 monthly (HBO).
Video-On-Demand: No
Pay-Per-View
iN DEMAND (delivered digitally); Playboy TV (delivered digitally); Club Jenna (delivered digitally).
Internet Service
Operational: Yes.
Telephone Service
Digital: Operational
Miles of Plant: 31.0 (coaxial); None (fiber optic). Homes passed: 10,900. Homes passed includes Bassett, Laurel, Lyons, Oakland, Tekamah & Wayne
President, State Operations: Mike Jacobsen. General Manager, Cable Television: Mike Storjohann. Programming Manager: Kay Petersen.
Ownership: American Broadband Communications Inc. (MSO).

BLOOMFIELD—Great Plains Communications, 1600 Great Plains Ctr, PO Box 500, Blair, NE 68008-0500. Phone: 855-853-1483. Fax: 402-456-6550. E-mail: contactus@gpcom.com. Web Site: http://www.gpcom.com. Also serves Center, Creighton, Crofton, Niobrara, Plainview, Verdigre, Wausa, Winneetoon & Wynot. ICA: NE0065.
TV Market Ranking: Outside TV Markets (BLOOMFIELD, Center, Creighton, Crofton, Niobrara, Plainview, Verdigre, Wausa, Winnetoon). Franchise award date: N.A. Franchise expiration date: N.A. Began: August 1, 1983.
Channel capacity: N.A. Channels available but not in use: N.A.

FULLY SEARCHABLE • CONTINUOUSLY UPDATED • DISCOUNT RATES FOR PRINT PURCHASERS
For more information call **800-771-9202** or visit **www.warren-news.com**

Basic Service
Subscribers: 1,506.
Programming (received off-air): KCAU-TV (ABC) Sioux City; KELO-TV (CBS, MNT) Sioux Falls; KLKN (ABC) Lincoln; KOLN (CBS, MNT, NBC) Lincoln; KPTH (FOX, MNT, This TV) Sioux City; KTIV (CW, MeTV, NBC) Sioux City; KXNE-TV (PBS) Norfolk.
Programming (via satellite): A&E; AMC; Animal Planet; CMT; CNBC; CNN; C-SPAN; Discovery Channel; Disney Channel; ESPN; Fox News Channel; Freeform; Hallmark Channel; HLN; Lifetime; MTV; Nickelodeon; Pop; QVC; Root Sports Rocky Mountain; Spike TV; Syfy; TBS; The Weather Channel; TLC; TNT; Travel Channel; TV Land; USA Network; VH1; WGN America.
Fee: $45.00 installation; $23.49 monthly.
Expanded Basic Service 1
Subscribers: N.A.
Programming (via satellite): Cartoon Network; Comedy Central; ESPN2; Food Network; HGTV; History; NBCSN; Turner Classic Movies.
Fee: $6.50 monthly.
Digital Basic Service
Subscribers: N.A.
Programming (via satellite): BBC America; Bravo; Discovery Digital Networks; DMX Music; ESPN Classic; Fox Sports 1; FYI; Golf Channel; History International; IFC; LMN; Nick Jr.; TeenNick; Turner Classic Movies; WE tv.
Fee: $43.95 monthly.
Pay Service 1
Pay Units: 90.
Programming (via satellite): Showtime.
Fee: $9.95 monthly.
Pay Service 2
Pay Units: 270.
Programming (via satellite): HBO.
Fee: $10.75 monthly.
Digital Pay Service 1
Pay Units: 195.
Programming (via satellite): Cinemax (multiplexed); HBO (multiplexed); Showtime (multiplexed); Starz (multiplexed); Starz Encore (multiplexed); The Movie Channel (multiplexed).
Fee: $12.00 monthly.
Video-On-Demand: No
Pay-Per-View
iN DEMAND (delivered digitally).
Internet Service
Operational: Yes, DSL & dial-up.
Broadband Service: In-house.
Fee: $49.95 installation; $39.95 monthly.
Telephone Service
Digital: Operational
Miles of Plant: 18.0 (coaxial); None (fiber optic).
Senior Director of Product Management: LeaAnn Quist.
Ownership: Great Plains Communications Inc. (MSO).

BLUE HILL—Glenwood Telecommunications, 510 West Gage St, Blue Hill, NE 68930. Phone: 402-756-3131. Fax: 402-756-3134. E-mail: info@shopglenwood.net. Web Site: http://shopglenwood.net. Also serves Bladen, Campbell, Funk, Holstein,

2017 Edition   D-481

Nebraska—Cable Systems

Lawrence, Roseland, Superior & Upland. ICA: NE0093.
TV Market Ranking: 91 (Bladen, BLUE HILL, Campbell, Funk, Holstein, Lawrence, Roseland, Upland); Below 100 (Superior). Franchise award date: March 1, 1982. Franchise expiration date: N.A. Began: August 1, 1982.
Channel capacity: N.A. Channels available but not in use: N.A.

Basic Service
Subscribers: 1,270.
Programming (received off-air): KFXL-TV (FOX) Lincoln; KGIN (CBS, MNT, NBC) Grand Island; KHGI-TV (ABC) Kearney; KHNE-TV (PBS) Hastings; KNHL (IND) Hastings; KTVG-TV (FOX) Grand Island; allband FM.
Programming (via satellite): C-SPAN; EWTN Global Catholic Network; QVC; The Weather Channel; Trinity Broadcasting Network (TBN); WGN America.
Fee: $55.00 installation; $18.95 monthly; $1.00 converter.

Expanded Basic Service 1
Subscribers: 883.
Programming (via satellite): A&E; AMC; Animal Planet; Cartoon Network; CMT; CNN; Comedy Central; Discovery Channel; Disney Channel; DIY Network; ESPN; ESPN Classic; ESPN2; ESPNU; Food Network; Fox News Channel; FOX Sports Midwest; Freeform; FX; Golf Channel; Hallmark Channel; HGTV; History; HLN; Lifetime; MTV; National Geographic Channel; Nickelodeon; Spike TV; Syfy; TBS; TLC; TNT; Turner Classic Movies; TV Land; USA Network; VH1.
Fee: $55.00 monthly.

Digital Basic Service
Subscribers: 298.
Programming (via satellite): BBC America; Bloomberg Television; Bravo; Cloo; CMT; Daystar TV Network; Discovery Digital Networks; Disney XD; DMX Music; ESPNews; EVINE Live; Fox Sports 1; FSN Digital Atlantic; FSN Digital Central; FSN Digital Pacific; Fuse; FXM; FYI; Great American Country; GSN; History International; IFC; LMN; NBCSN; Nick Jr.; Nicktoons; Outdoor Channel; RFD-TV; Sprout; TeenNick; WE tv.
Fee: $67.00 monthly.

Pay Service 1
Pay Units: 151.
Programming (via satellite): Showtime.
Fee: $10.00 installation; $9.50 monthly.

Pay Service 2
Pay Units: 116.
Programming (via satellite): HBO.
Fee: $10.00 installation; $10.95 monthly.

Digital Pay Service 1
Pay Units: N.A.
Programming (via satellite): Cinemax (multiplexed); Flix; HBO (multiplexed); Showtime (multiplexed); Starz (multiplexed); Starz Encore (multiplexed); The Movie Channel (multiplexed).
Fee: $12.95 monthly (Showtime/TMC or Starz/Encore), $16.95 monthly (HBO/Cinemax).

Video-On-Demand: No
Pay-Per-View
iN DEMAND (delivered digitally); Playboy TV (delivered digitally); Fresh (delivered digitally); Hot Choice (delivered digitally).

Internet Service
Operational: No, DSL.

Telephone Service
Digital: Operational
Miles of Plant: 7.0 (coaxial); None (fiber optic).
Chief Executive Officer & General Manager: Stanley Rouse. Operations Director: Alan Selby. Plant Supervisor: Kurt Allen. Marketing Manager: Troy Stickels.
Ownership: Glenwood Telecommunications (MSO).

BOELUS—NCTC Cable. Now served by BURWELL, NE [NE0045]. ICA: NE0378.

BRADSHAW—Zito Media, 102 S Main St, PO Box 665, Coudersport, PA 16915. Phones: 814-260-9055; 800-365-6988. E-mail: info@zitomedia.com. Web Site: http://www.zitomedia.com. ICA: NE0193.
TV Market Ranking: Below 100 (BRADSHAW). Franchise award date: N.A. Franchise expiration date: N.A. Began: September 1, 1984.
Channel capacity: N.A. Channels available but not in use: N.A.

Basic Service
Subscribers: N.A.
Programming (received off-air): KHGI-TV (ABC) Kearney; KHNE-TV (PBS) Hastings; KLKN (ABC) Lincoln; KNHL (IND) Hastings; KOLN (CBS, MNT, NBC) Lincoln; KSNB-TV (MeTV, MNT, NBC) Superior.
Programming (via satellite): Cartoon Network; CNN; Disney Channel; ESPN; Freeform; Lifetime; Outdoor Channel; TBS; WGN America.
Fee: $35.00 installation.

Pay Service 1
Pay Units: N.A.
Programming (via satellite): Cinemax; HBO.
Fee: $11.95 monthly (Cinemax), $12.95 monthly (HBO).

Internet Service
Operational: No.

Telephone Service
None
Miles of Plant: 4.0 (coaxial); None (fiber optic). Homes passed: 135.
President: James Rigas.
Ownership: Zito Media (MSO).

BRAINARD—Formerly served by Zito Media. No longer in operation. ICA: NE0191.

BRIDGEPORT—Charter Communications. Now served by SCOTTSBLUFF, NE [NE0008]. ICA: NE0048.

BRISTOW TWP.—Formerly served by Sky Scan Cable Co. No longer in operation. ICA: NE0267.

BROCK—Formerly served by CableDirect. No longer in operation. ICA: NE0245.

BROKEN BOW—Great Plains Communications, 1600 Great Plains Ctr, PO Box 500, Blair, NE 68008-0500. Phones: 402-426-9511; 888-343-8014. Fax: 402-456-6550. E-mail: lquist@gpcom.com. Web Site: http://www.gpcom.com. Also serves Arnold, Callaway, Oconto & Stapleton. ICA: NE0031.
TV Market Ranking: Below 100 (Stapleton); Outside TV Markets (Callaway, Oconto, Arnold, BROKEN BOW).
Channel capacity: N.A. Channels available but not in use: N.A.

Basic Service
Subscribers: 911.
Programming (received off-air): KGIN (CBS, MNT, NBC) Grand Island; KNOP-TV (NBC) North Platte; KPNE-TV (PBS) North Platte; KWNB-TV (ABC) Hayes Center.
Programming (via microwave): KCNC-TV (CBS, Decades) Denver.
Programming (via satellite): A&E; Animal Planet; CNBC; CNN; Discovery Channel; Disney Channel; ESPN; Fox News Channel; Freeform; FX; Great American Country; HLN; KMGH-TV (ABC, Azteca America) Denver; Lifetime; MTV; Nickelodeon; Pop; QVC; Root Sports Rocky Mountain; Spike TV; TBS; The Weather Channel; TLC; TNT; Travel Channel; TV Land; USA Network; VH1; WGN America.
Fee: $45.00 installation; $24.95 monthly.

Expanded Basic Service 1
Subscribers: N.A.
Programming (via satellite): Cartoon Network; Comedy Central; ESPN2; HGTV; History; KWGN-TV (CW, This TV) Denver; NBCSN; Turner Classic Movies.
Fee: $47.99 monthly.

Digital Basic Service
Subscribers: N.A.
Programming (via satellite): BBC America; Bravo; Discovery Digital Networks; DMX Music; ESPN Classic; Fox Sports 1; FYI; Golf Channel; History International; IFC; LMN; National Geographic Channel; Nick Jr.; Outdoor Channel; Syfy; TeenNick; Turner Classic Movies; WE tv.
Fee: $47.95 monthly.

Pay Service 1
Pay Units: 65.
Programming (via satellite): Cinemax; Flix; HBO; Showtime; Sundance TV; The Movie Channel.
Fee: $9.95 monthly (Showtime), $10.95 monthly (HBO).

Digital Pay Service 1
Pay Units: N.A.
Programming (via satellite): Cinemax (multiplexed); HBO (multiplexed); Showtime (multiplexed); Starz Encore (multiplexed); The Movie Channel (multiplexed).
Fee: $12.00 monthly.

Video-On-Demand: No
Pay-Per-View
iN DEMAND (delivered digitally); Sports PPV.

Internet Service
Operational: Yes, DSL & dial-up.
Subscribers: 263.
Broadband Service: In-house.
Fee: $49.95 installation; $39.95 monthly.

Telephone Service
Digital: Operational
Miles of Plant: 49.0 (coaxial); 11.0 (fiber optic). Homes passed: 1,500.
Senior Director: Lea Ann Quist. Chief Technician: Mark Stottler. Marketing Manager: Casey Garrigan.
Ownership: Great Plains Communications Inc. (MSO).

BRULE—Eagle Communications, 2703 Hall St, Ste 15, PO Box 817, Hays, KS 67601. Phone: 877-234-0102. Web Site: http://www.eaglecom.net. ICA: NE0174.
TV Market Ranking: Outside TV Markets (BRULE). Franchise award date: N.A. Franchise expiration date: N.A. Began: February 1, 1984.
Channel capacity: N.A. Channels available but not in use: N.A.

Basic Service
Subscribers: 50.
Programming (received off-air): KETV (ABC, MeTV) Omaha; KNOP-TV (NBC) North Platte; KOLN (CBS, MNT, NBC) Lincoln.
Programming (via satellite): CNN; Discovery Channel; Disney Channel; ESPN; Freeform; KDVR (Antenna TV, FOX) Denver; KWGN-TV (CW, This TV) Denver; Spike TV; TBS; TNT; USA Network; WGN America.
Fee: $24.95 installation; $47.95 monthly.

Pay Service 1
Pay Units: N.A.
Programming (via satellite): HBO.
Fee: $14.00 monthly.

Video-On-Demand: No
Internet Service
Operational: No.

Telephone Service
None
Homes passed: 186.
Chief Financial Officer: Amber Reineke. Chief Operating Officer: Kurt K. David.
Ownership: Eagle Communications Inc. (MSO).

BRUNSWICK (village)—Formerly served by Sky Scan Cable Co. No longer in operation. ICA: NE0268.

BURWELL—NCTC Cable, 22 LaBarre St, PO Box 700, Gibbon, NE 68840. Phones: 888-873-6282; 308-468-6341. Fax: 308-468-9929. E-mail: nctc@nctc.net. Web Site: http://www.nctc.net. Also serves Ansley, Arcadia, Ashton, Boelus, Dannebrog, Elba, Mason City, North Loup, Sargent, Scotia & Taylor. ICA: NE0045.
TV Market Ranking: 91 (Ashton, Boelus); Below 100 (Dannebrog, Elba, Ashton); Outside TV Markets (BURWELL, Ansley, Arcadia, Mason City, North Loup, Sargent, Scotia, Taylor). Franchise award date: N.A. Franchise expiration date: N.A. Began: March 1, 1970.
Channel capacity: N.A. Channels available but not in use: N.A.

Basic Service
Subscribers: 593.
Programming (received off-air): KGIN (CBS, MNT, NBC) Grand Island; KHGI-TV (ABC) Kearney; KMNE-TV (PBS) Bassett; KNHL (IND) Hastings; KTVG-TV (FOX) Grand Island; allband FM.
Programming (via satellite): A&E; AMC; Animal Planet; Cartoon Network; CMT; CNBC; CNN; Comedy Central; C-SPAN; CW PLUS; Discovery Channel; E! HD; ESPN; ESPN Classic; EWTN Global Catholic Network; Food Network; Fox News Channel; FOX Sports Midwest; Freeform; FX; Great American Country; Hallmark Channel; HGTV; History; HLN; ION Television; Lifetime; MSNBC; MTV; NBCSN; Nickelodeon; Outdoor Channel; QVC; Spike TV; Syfy; TBS; The Weather Channel; TLC; TNT; Travel Channel; Trinity Broadcasting Network (TBN); truTV; Turner Classic Movies; TV Land; USA Network; VH1; WGN America.
Fee: $45.00 installation; $47.45 monthly.

Digital Basic Service
Subscribers: N.A.
Programming (via satellite): BBC America; Bloomberg Television; Cloo; Daystar TV Network; Discovery Life Channel; DMX Music; ESPNews; EVINE Live; FOX College Sports Central; FOX College Sports Pacific; Fox Sports 1; FXM; FYI; Golf Channel; GSN; History International; LMN; Nick Jr.; Ovation; RFD-TV; TeenNick; UP; WE tv.

Pay Service 1
Pay Units: N.A.
Programming (via satellite): HBO.
Fee: $10.95 monthly.

Digital Pay Service 1
Pay Units: N.A.
Programming (via satellite): Cinemax (multiplexed); Flix; HBO (multiplexed); Showtime (multiplexed); Starz (multiplexed); Starz Encore (multiplexed); The Movie Channel (multiplexed).

Cable Systems—Nebraska

Fee: $10.95 monthly (Cinemax), $12.95 monthly (HBO or Showtime/TMC/Flix), $13.95 monthly (Starz/Encore).
Video-On-Demand: No
Internet Service
Operational: No, DSL & dial-up.
Telephone Service
Analog: Operational
Miles of Plant: 13.0 (coaxial); None (fiber optic). Homes passed: 1,600.
Vice President, Engineering: Kevin McGregor. Vice President & General Manager: Andrew D. Jader. Assistant Manager: Terry Erickson. Technical Operations Manager: Nick Jeffres.
Ownership: Nebraska Central Telecom Inc. (MSO).

BUTTE—CenCom NNTV. This cable system has converted to IPTV. See JACKSON, NE [NE5019]. ICA: NE0157.

BYRON—Formerly served by Zito Media. No longer in operation. ICA: NE0249.

CAMBRIDGE—PinPoint Communications, 611 Patterson St, PO Box 490, Cambridge, NE 69022-0490. Phones: 308-697-7678; 800-793-2788. Fax: 308-697-3631. E-mail: info@pnpt.com. Web Site: http://www.pnpt.com. Also serves Bartley, Beaver City, Culbertson, Indianola & Oxford. ICA: NE0269.
TV Market Ranking: Below 100 (Bartley, CAMBRIDGE, Indianola, Culbertson); Outside TV Markets (Beaver City). Franchise award date: N.A. Franchise expiration date: N.A. Began: January 1, 1983.
Channel capacity: N.A. Channels available but not in use: N.A.
Basic Service
Subscribers: 129.
Programming (received off-air): KGIN (CBS, MNT, NBC) Grand Island; KHGI-TV (ABC) Kearney; KLNE-TV (PBS) Lexington; KSNK (NBC) McCook; KTVG-TV (FOX) Grand Island.
Programming (via satellite): A&E; Animal Planet; CMT; CNBC; CNN; Discovery Channel; Disney Channel; ESPN; ESPN2; EWTN Global Catholic Network; FOX Sports Networks; Freeform; Golf Channel; HGTV; History; Lifetime; Nickelodeon; Spike TV; TBS; The Weather Channel; TLC; TNT; USA Network; VH1; WGN America.
Fee: $15.00 installation; $37.95 monthly.
Pay Service 1
Pay Units: 85.
Programming (via satellite): HBO; Showtime.
Fee: $17.95 monthly (each).
Video-On-Demand: No
Internet Service
Operational: Yes. Began: January 1, 2003.
Broadband Service: PinPoint Internet.
Fee: $15.00 installation; $59.95-$79.95 monthly.
Telephone Service
Analog: Not Operational
Digital: Operational
Fee: $17.50 monthly
Miles of Plant: 11.0 (coaxial); None (fiber optic). Homes passed: 348.
Executive Vice President: J. Thomas Shoemaker.
Ownership: PinPoint Communications Inc.

CEDAR BLUFFS—Formerly served by TelePartners. No longer in operation. ICA: NE0175.

CEDAR CREEK—Formerly served by Westcom. No longer in operation. ICA: NE0271.

CEDAR RAPIDS—Eagle Communications, 2703 Hall St, Ste 15, PO Box 817, Hays, KS 67601. Phone: 785-625-4000. Fax: 785-625-8030. E-mail: support@eaglecom.net. Web Site: http://www.eaglecom.net. ICA: NE0154.
TV Market Ranking: Below 100 (CEDAR RAPIDS). Franchise award date: N.A. Franchise expiration date: N.A. Began: January 1, 1985.
Channel capacity: N.A. Channels available but not in use: N.A.
Basic Service
Subscribers: 84.
Programming (received off-air): KGIN (CBS, MNT, NBC) Grand Island; KHGI-TV (ABC) Kearney; KHNE-TV (PBS) Hastings; KLKN (ABC) Lincoln; KNHL (IND) Hastings; KTVG-TV (FOX) Grand Island.
Programming (via satellite): C-SPAN; C-SPAN 2; CW PLUS; EWTN Global Catholic Network; MyNetworkTV; QVC; TBS; The Weather Channel; Trinity Broadcasting Network (TBN); Univision Studios; WGN America.
Fee: $24.95 installation; $64.95 monthly.
Expanded Basic Service 1
Subscribers: N.A.
Programming (via satellite): A&E; AMC; Animal Planet; Cartoon Network; CMT; CNBC; CNN; Comedy Central; Discovery Channel; E! HD; ESPN; ESPN Classic; ESPN2; Food Network; Fox News Channel; FOX Sports Midwest; Freeform; FX; Great American Country; Hallmark Channel; HGTV; History; HLN; ION Television; Lifetime; MSNBC; MTV; NBCSN; Nickelodeon; Outdoor Channel; RFD-TV; Spike TV; Syfy; TLC; TNT; Travel Channel; truTV; Turner Classic Movies; TV Land; USA Network; VH1.
Digital Basic Service
Subscribers: N.A.
Programming (via satellite): BBC America; Bloomberg Television; Cine Mexicano; Cinelatino; Cloo; CMT; CNN en Espanol; Daystar TV Network; Destination America; Discovery Channel HD; Discovery Kids Channel; Discovery Life Channel; DMX Music; ESPN Classic; ESPN Deportes; ESPN HD; ESPN2; ESPNews; EVINE Live; FOX College Sports Central; FOX College Sports Pacific; Fox Deportes; Fox Sports 1; FXM; FYI; Golf Channel; GSN; History; History en Espanol; History International; Investigation Discovery; LMN; MTV Classic; MTV Hits; MTV2; NBCSN; Nick Jr.; Outdoor Channel; Ovation; OWN: Oprah Winfrey Network; Science Channel; Syfy; TBS HD; TeenNick; TNT HD; Tr3s; Trinity Broadcasting Network (TBN); VH1 Soul; ViendoMovies; WE tv.
Fee: $14.00 monthly.
Digital Pay Service 1
Pay Units: N.A.
Programming (via satellite): Cinemax (multiplexed); Flix; HBO (multiplexed); HBO Latino; Showtime (multiplexed); Starz (multiplexed); Starz Encore (multiplexed); The Movie Channel (multiplexed).
Video-On-Demand: No
Pay-Per-View
iN DEMAND (delivered digitally); Hot Choice (delivered digitally); Playboy TV (delivered digitally); Fresh (delivered digitally); Spice: Xcess (delivered digitally); Club Jenna (delivered digitally).
Internet Service
Operational: Yes.
Broadband Service: Cable Nebraska.

FULLY SEARCHABLE • CONTINUOUSLY UPDATED • DISCOUNT RATES FOR PRINT PURCHASERS
For more information call **800-771-9202** or visit **www.warren-news.com**

Telephone Service
None
Miles of Plant: 4.0 (coaxial); None (fiber optic). Homes passed: 225.
President & Chief Executive Officer: Gary Shorman. Chief Operating Officer: Kurt K. David. General Manager: Travis Kohlrus. Marketing Manager: Elizabeth Jaeger.
Ownership: Eagle Communications Inc. (MSO).

CENTRAL CITY—Eagle Communications, 2703 Hall St, Ste 15, PO Box 817, Hays, KS 67601. Phones: 877-613-2453; 785-625-4000 (Corporate office). Fax: 785-625-8030. Web Site: http://www.eaglecom.net. ICA: NE0044.
TV Market Ranking: Below 100 (CENTRAL CITY). Franchise award date: N.A. Franchise expiration date: N.A. Began: October 12, 1979.
Channel capacity: N.A. Channels available but not in use: N.A.
Basic Service
Subscribers: 520.
Programming (received off-air): KGIN (CBS, MNT, NBC) Grand Island; KHGI-TV (ABC) Kearney; KHNE-TV (PBS) Hastings; KLKN (ABC) Lincoln; KNHL (IND) Hastings; KTVG-TV (FOX) Grand Island.
Programming (via satellite): C-SPAN; C-SPAN 2; EWTN Global Catholic Network; Freeform; Hallmark Channel; HLN; Pop; QVC; TBS; The Weather Channel; Trinity Broadcasting Network (TBN); WGN America.
Fee: $24.95 installation; $64.95 monthly.
Expanded Basic Service 1
Subscribers: N.A.
Programming (via satellite): A&E; AMC; Animal Planet; Cartoon Network; CMT; CNBC; CNN; Comedy Central; Discovery Channel; E! HD; ESPN; ESPN2; Food Network; Fox News Channel; FOX Sports Networks; FX; Great American Country; HGTV; History; ION Television; Lifetime; MSNBC; MTV; Nickelodeon; Outdoor Channel; Spike TV; Syfy; TLC; TNT; Travel Channel; truTV; Turner Classic Movies; TV Land; Univision Studios; USA Network; VH1.
Digital Basic Service
Subscribers: N.A.
Programming (via satellite): BBC America; Bloomberg Television; Discovery Life Channel; DMX Music; ESPN Classic; ESPN2; ESPNews; EVINE Live; FSN Digital Atlantic; FSN Digital Central; FSN Digital Pacific; FXM; FYI; Golf Channel; GSN; History; History International; HITS (Headend In The Sky); International Television (ITV); MBC America; National Geographic Channel; NBCSN; Nick Jr.; Outdoor Channel; Ovation; TeenNick.
Fee: $14.00 monthly.
Digital Pay Service 1
Pay Units: N.A.
Programming (via satellite): Cinemax (multiplexed); Daystar TV Network; Flix; FXM; HBO (multiplexed); IFC; Showtime (multiplexed); Starz (multiplexed); Sundance TV;

The Movie Channel (multiplexed); WAM! America's Kidz Network; WE tv.
Fee: $5.00 monthly.
Video-On-Demand: No
Pay-Per-View
iN DEMAND (delivered digitally); Hot Choice (delivered digitally); Playboy TV (delivered digitally); Fresh (delivered digitally); Shorteez (delivered digitally).
Internet Service
Operational: Yes.
Broadband Service: Cable Nebraska.
Telephone Service
Digital: Operational
Miles of Plant: 28.0 (coaxial); None (fiber optic). Homes passed: 1,222.
Chief Operating Officer: Kurt K. David.
Ownership: Eagle Communications Inc. (MSO).

CERESCO—Zito Media, 102 S Main St, PO Box 665, Coudersport, PA 16915. Phones: 814-260-9055; 800-365-6988. E-mail: info@zitomedia.com. Web Site: http://www.zitomedia.com. ICA: NE0116.
TV Market Ranking: 91 (CERESCO). Franchise award date: N.A. Franchise expiration date: N.A. Began: June 1, 1983.
Channel capacity: N.A. Channels available but not in use: N.A.
Basic Service
Subscribers: 23.
Programming (received off-air): KETV (ABC, MeTV) Omaha; KMTV-TV (Antenna TV, CBS, Escape) Omaha; KOLN (CBS, MNT, NBC) Lincoln; KPTM (Estrella TV, FOX, MNT, This TV) Omaha; KUON-TV (PBS) Lincoln; KXVO (Azteca America, CW) Omaha; WOWT (IND, NBC) Omaha.
Programming (via satellite): Cartoon Network; CNN; Discovery Channel; Disney Channel; ESPN; ESPN2; Fox News Channel; FOX Sports Midwest; Freeform; HGTV; HLN; Lifetime; Outdoor Channel; TBS; The Weather Channel; TLC; TNT; USA Network; WGN America.
Fee: $49.95 installation; $48.30 monthly.
Pay Service 1
Pay Units: N.A.
Programming (via satellite): Cinemax; HBO; Showtime; The Movie Channel.
Fee: $7.95 monthly (TMC), $8.95 monthly (Showtime), $9.95 monthly (Cinemax), $13.95 monthly (HBO).
Internet Service
Operational: No.
Telephone Service
None
Miles of Plant: 6.0 (coaxial); None (fiber optic). Homes passed: 316.
President: James Rigas.
Ownership: Zito Media (MSO).

CHADRON—Great Plains Communications, 1600 Great Plains Ctr, PO Box 500, Blair, NE 68008-0500. Phones: 402-426-9511; 888-343-8014. Fax: 402-426-6550. E-mail: lquist@gpcom.com. Web Site: http://www.gpcom.com. Also serves Gordon, Hay Springs & Rushville. ICA: NE0024.
TV Market Ranking: Outside TV Markets (CHADRON, Gordon, Hay Springs,

2017 Edition
D-483

Nebraska—Cable Systems

Rushville). Franchise award date: N.A. Franchise expiration date: N.A. Began: December 1, 1965.
Channel capacity: N.A. Channels available but not in use: N.A.

Basic Service
Subscribers: 1,709.
Programming (received off-air): KNEP (ABC) Scottsbluff; KTNE-TV (PBS) Alliance.
Programming (via microwave): KCNC-TV (CBS, Decades) Denver; KDVR (Antenna TV, FOX) Denver; KMGH-TV (ABC, Azteca America) Denver; KTVD (MeTV, MNT) Denver; KUSA (NBC, WeatherNation) Denver; KWGN-TV (CW, This TV) Denver.
Programming (via satellite): C-SPAN; INSP; Pop; QVC; Trinity Broadcasting Network (TBN); WGN America.
Fee: $45.00 installation; $24.95 monthly; $1.13 converter.

Expanded Basic Service 1
Subscribers: N.A.
Programming (via satellite): A&E; Altitude Sports & Entertainment; AMC; Animal Planet; Bravo; Cartoon Network; CMT; CNBC; CNN; Comedy Central; Discovery Channel; Disney Channel; Disney XD; E! HD; ESPN; ESPN Classic; ESPN2; Food Network; Fox News Channel; Fox Sports 1; Freeform; FX; Golf Channel; Great American Country; Hallmark Channel; HGTV; History; HLN; Lifetime; LMN; MSNBC; MTV; National Geographic Channel; NBCSN; Nickelodeon; Outdoor Channel; Root Sports Rocky Mountain; Spike TV; Syfy; TBS; The Weather Channel; TLC; TNT; Travel Channel; truTV; Turner Classic Movies; TV Land; USA Network; VH1.
Fee: $47.99 monthly.

Digital Basic Service
Subscribers: N.A.
Programming (via satellite): BBC America; Bloomberg Television; CMT; Destination America; Discovery Kids Channel; Discovery Life Channel; DIY Network; FM; FYI; GSN; Hallmark Movies & Mysteries; History International; IFC; Investigation Discovery; MC; MTV Classic; MTV Hits; MTV Jams; MTV2; Nick 2; Nick Jr.; Nicktoons; OWN: Oprah Winfrey Network; RFD-TV; Science Channel; TeenNick; Tr3s; VH1 Soul; WE tv.

Digital Pay Service 1
Pay Units: N.A.
Programming (via satellite): Cinemax (multiplexed); Flix; HBO (multiplexed); Showtime (multiplexed); Starz (multiplexed); Starz Encore (multiplexed); The Movie Channel (multiplexed).
Fee: $12.00 monthly (Cinemax/Starz/Encore, HBO or Showtime/TMC/Flix).

Video-On-Demand: No

Pay-Per-View
iN DEMAND (delivered digitally); Pleasure (delivered digitally); ETC (delivered digitally).

Internet Service
Operational: Yes, DSL & dial-up.
Broadband Service: In-house.
Fee: $49.95 installation; $39.95 monthly.

Telephone Service
Analog: Not Operational
Digital: Operational
Miles of Plant: 63.0 (coaxial); None (fiber optic).
Senior Director: Lea Ann Quist. Chief Technician: Mark Stottler. Marketing Manager: Casey Garrigan.
Ownership: Great Plains Communications Inc. (MSO).

CHAMBERS—Formerly served by Sky Scan Cable Co. No longer in operation. ICA: NE0272.

CHAPMAN—Great Plains Communications, 1600 Great Plains Ctr, PO Box 500, Blair, NE 68008-0500. Phones: 402-426-9511; 888-343-8014. Fax: 402-426-6550. E-mail: lquist@gpcom.com. Web Site: http://www.gpcom.com. ICA: NE0273.
TV Market Ranking: 91 (CHAPMAN). Franchise award date: October 1, 1988. Franchise expiration date: N.A. Began: October 1, 1988.
Channel capacity: N.A. Channels available but not in use: N.A.

Basic Service
Subscribers: 32.
Programming (received off-air): KGIN (CBS, MNT, NBC) Grand Island; KHGI-TV (ABC) Kearney; KHNE-TV (PBS) Hastings; KLKN (ABC) Lincoln; KNHL (IND) Hastings; KTVG-TV (FOX) Grand Island.
Programming (via satellite): A&E; AMC; Animal Planet; CNN; Discovery Channel; Disney Channel; ESPN; ESPN2; Fox News Channel; Freeform; Great American Country; Hallmark Channel; HGTV; History; HLN; Lifetime; Nickelodeon; QVC; Root Sports Rocky Mountain; Spike TV; TBS; The Weather Channel; TLC; TNT; Travel Channel; TV Land; USA Network; WGN America.
Fee: $45.00 installation; $41.99 monthly.

Pay Service 1
Pay Units: 15.
Programming (via satellite): HBO.
Fee: $10.95 monthly.

Pay Service 2
Pay Units: N.A.
Programming (via satellite): Showtime.
Fee: $9.95 monthly.

Video-On-Demand: No

Pay-Per-View
iN DEMAND (delivered digitally); ESPN (delivered digitally).

Internet Service
Operational: Yes, DSL.
Broadband Service: In-house.

Telephone Service
Digital: Operational
Senior Director: Lea Ann Quist. Chief Technician: Mark Stottler. Marketing Manager: Casey Garrigan.
Ownership: Great Plains Communications Inc. (MSO).

CHAPPELL—PC Telcom. Now served by HOLYOKE, CO [CO0065]. ICA: NE0084.

CHESTER—Zito Media, 102 S Main St, PO Box 665, Coudersport, PA 16915. Phones: 814-260-9055; 800-365-6988. E-mail: info@zitomedia.com. Web Site: http://www.zitomedia.com. ICA: NE0158.
TV Market Ranking: Below 100 (CHESTER). Franchise award date: N.A. Franchise expiration date: N.A. Began: February 1, 1984.
Channel capacity: N.A. Channels available but not in use: N.A.

Basic Service
Subscribers: 2.
Programming (received off-air): KHNE-TV (PBS) Hastings; KLKN (ABC) Lincoln; KNHL (IND) Hastings; KOLN (CBS, MNT, NBC) Lincoln; KSNB-TV (MeTV, MNT, NBC) Superior.
Programming (via satellite): A&E; AMC; Cartoon Network; CNN; Discovery Channel; Disney Channel; ESPN; FOX Sports Midwest; Freeform; HGTV; History; Lifetime; Outdoor Channel; QVC; TBS; The Weather Channel; TLC; TNT; Trinity Broadcasting Network (TBN); Turner Classic Movies; USA Network; WGN America.
Fee: $49.95 installation; $48.30 monthly.

Pay Service 1
Pay Units: N.A.
Programming (via satellite): Cinemax; HBO.
Fee: $9.95 monthly (Cinemax), $13.95 monthly (HBO).

Internet Service
Operational: No.

Telephone Service
None
Miles of Plant: 5.0 (coaxial); None (fiber optic). Homes passed: 198.
President: James Rigas.
Ownership: Zito Media (MSO).

CLARKS—CenCom Inc., PO Box 66, Jackson, NE 68743. Phone: 402-632-4811. E-mail: nntc@nntc.net. Web Site: http://www.nntc.net. ICA: NE0189.
Channel capacity: N.A. Channels available but not in use: N.A.

Basic Service
Subscribers: 4.
Programming (received off-air): KFXL-TV (FOX) Lincoln; KHGI-TV (ABC) Kearney; KHNE-TV (PBS) Hastings; KLKN (ABC) Lincoln; KNHL (IND) Hastings; KOLN (CBS, MNT, NBC) Lincoln.
Programming (via satellite): A&E; AMC; Animal Planet; Cartoon Network; CMT; CNBC; CNN; Comedy Central; C-SPAN; C-SPAN 2; Discovery Channel; E! HD; ESPN; ESPN Classic; ESPN2; EWTN Global Catholic Network; Food Network; Fox News Channel; Freeform; FX; Great American Country; Hallmark Channel; HGTV; HSN; MSNBC; MTV; Nickelodeon; Outdoor Channel; QVC; Spike TV; Syfy; TBS; The Weather Channel; TLC; TNT; Travel Channel; Trinity Broadcasting Network (TBN); TV Land; USA Network; VH1; WB Television Network (WBN); WGN America.
Fee: $8.75 installation; $37.50 monthly.

Internet Service
Operational: Yes.

Telephone Service
Digital: Operational
Fee: $17.50 monthly
Manager: Emory Graffis.
Ownership: Northeast Nebraska Telephone Co.

CLARKSON—Formerly served by TelePartners. No longer in operation. ICA: NE0166.

CLAY CENTER—Zito Media, 102 S Main St, PO Box 665, Coudersport, PA 16915. Phones: 814-260-9055; 800-365-6988. E-mail: info@zitomedia.com. Web Site: http://www.zitomedia.com. Also serves Edgar, Fairfield, Harvard & Sutton. ICA: NE0085.
TV Market Ranking: 91 (CLAY CENTER, Edgar, Fairfield, Harvard, Sutton). Franchise award date: N.A. Franchise expiration date: N.A. Began: June 1, 1982.
Channel capacity: N.A. Channels available but not in use: N.A.

Basic Service
Subscribers: 379.
Programming (received off-air): KHGI-TV (ABC) Kearney; KHNE-TV (PBS) Hastings; KLKN (ABC) Lincoln; KNHL (IND) Hastings; KOLN (CBS, MNT, NBC) Lincoln; KPTM (Estrella TV, FOX, MNT, This TV) Omaha; KSNB-TV (MeTV, MNT, NBC) Superior; KXVO (Azteca America, CW) Omaha.
Programming (via satellite): A&E; AMC; Animal Planet; Boomerang; Cartoon Network; CNN; Comedy Central; C-SPAN; Discovery Channel; Disney Channel; Disney XD; E! HD; ESPN; ESPN2; EWTN Global Catholic Network; Food Network; Fox News Channel; FOX Sports Midwest; Freeform; Fuse; FX; Great American Country; Hallmark Channel; HGTV; History; HLN; INSP; Lifetime; MSNBC; National Geographic Channel; Outdoor Channel; Pop; QVC; Syfy; TBS; The Weather Channel; TLC; TNT; Travel Channel; Trinity Broadcasting Network (TBN); Turner Classic Movies; TV Land; USA Network; WGN America.
Fee: $49.95 installation; $16.51 monthly.

Digital Basic Service
Subscribers: N.A.
Programming (via satellite): BBC America; Bloomberg Television; Discovery Life Channel; DMX Music; ESPN Classic; ESPNews; Fox Sports 1; FSN Digital Atlantic; FSN Digital Central; FSN Digital Pacific; FYI; Golf Channel; GSN; History International; Outdoor Channel; WE tv.
Fee: $12.95 monthly.

Digital Expanded Basic Service
Subscribers: N.A.
Programming (via satellite): DMX Music; FXM; IFC; LMN; Starz Encore.
Fee: $12.95 monthly.

Pay Service 1
Pay Units: N.A.
Programming (via satellite): Cinemax; HBO; Showtime; The Movie Channel.
Fee: $7.95 monthly (TMC), $9.95 monthly (Showtime), $10.95 monthly (Cinemax), $13.95 monthly (HBO).

Digital Pay Service 1
Pay Units: N.A.
Programming (via satellite): Cinemax (multiplexed); Flix; HBO (multiplexed); Showtime (multiplexed); The Movie Channel (multiplexed).
Fee: $15.60 monthly.

Pay-Per-View
ESPN Now (delivered digitally); Hot Choice (delivered digitally); Playboy TV (delivered digitally); Fresh (delivered digitally).

Internet Service
Operational: Yes.
Broadband Service: Galaxy Cable Internet.
Fee: $49.95 installation; $44.95 monthly; $5.00 modem lease.

Telephone Service
None
Miles of Plant: 39.0 (coaxial); None (fiber optic). Homes passed: 1,875.
President: James Rigas.
Ownership: Zito Media (MSO).

CLEARWATER—CenCom NNTV. This cable system has converted to IPTV. See JACKSON, NE [NE5019]. ICA: NE0144.

CODY—Formerly served by Midcontinent Communications. No longer in operation. ICA: NE0274.

COLERIDGE—CenCom NNTV. This cable system has converted to IPTV. See JACKSON, NE [NE5019]. ICA: NE0113.

COLUMBUS—Eagle Communications, 2703 Hall St, Ste 15, PO Box 817, Hays, KS 67601. Phone: 877-234-0102. Web Site: http://www.eaglecom.net. ICA: NE0395.
TV Market Ranking: Outside TV Markets (COLUMBUS).
Channel capacity: N.A. Channels available but not in use: N.A.

Cable Systems—Nebraska

Basic Service
Subscribers: 211.
Fee: $24.95 installation; $64.95 monthly.
Chief Operating Officer: Kurt K. David. Chief Financial Officer: Amber Reineke.
Ownership: Eagle Communications Inc. (MSO).

COLUMBUS—Time Warner Cable. Now served by LINCOLN, NE [NE0002]. ICA: NE0015.

COLUMBUS (portions)—Formerly served by Sky Scan Cable Co. No longer in operation. ICA: NE0275.

COMSTOCK—Formerly served by Consolidated Cable Inc. No longer in operation. ICA: NE0247.

CORTLAND—Formerly served by Great Plains Communications. No longer in operation. ICA: NE0169.

COZAD—Charter Communications. Now served by KEARNEY, NE [NE0011]. ICA: NE0029.

CRAWFORD—Mobius Communications Co, 523 Niobrara Ave, PO Box 246, Hemingford, NE 69348. Phones: 308-487-5500; 877-266-2487. Web Site: http://bbc.net. ICA: NE0042.
TV Market Ranking: Outside TV Markets (CRAWFORD).
Channel capacity: N.A. Channels available but not in use: N.A.
Basic Service
Subscribers: 124.
Fee: $21.99 monthly.
General Manager: Tonya Mayer.
Ownership: Mobius Communications Co. (MSO).

CRESTON—Formerly served by Sky Scan Cable Co. No longer in operation. ICA: NE0251.

CULBERTSON—PinPoint Cable TV. Now served by CAMBRIDGE, NE [NE0269]. ICA: NE0120.

CURTIS—Formerly served by Consolidated Cable Inc. No longer in operation. ICA: NE0071.

DALTON—Dalton Telephone Co, PO Box 19817, Colorado City, CO 81019. Phones: 308-377-2222; 866-542-6779. E-mail: dtc@daltontel.net; support@daltontel.net. Web Site: http://www.daltontel.net. Also serves Dix, Gurley, Lodgepole & Potter. ICA: NE0240.
TV Market Ranking: Outside TV Markets (DALTON, Dix, Gurley, Lodgepole, Potter).
Channel capacity: N.A. Channels available but not in use: N.A.
Basic Service
Subscribers: 135.
Programming (received off-air): KNEP (ABC) Scottsbluff; KSTF (CBS, CW) Scottsbluff; KTNE-TV (PBS) Alliance.
Programming (via satellite): A&E; AMC; Animal Planet; Bravo; Cartoon Network; CMT; CNBC; CNN; Comedy Central; C-SPAN; C-SPAN 2; Discovery Channel; Discovery Life Channel; Disney Channel; ESPN; ESPN Classic; ESPN2; EWTN Global Catholic Network; Food Network; Fox News Channel; Fox Sports 1; FOX Sports Networks; Freeform; FX; Great American Country; Hallmark Channel; HGTV; HLN; INSP; KCNC-TV (CBS, Decades) Denver; KDVR (Antenna TV, FOX) Denver; KMGH-TV (ABC, Azteca America) Denver; KUSA (NBC, WeatherNation) Denver; Lifetime; MTV; National Geographic Channel; Nickelodeon; QVC; Spike TV; Syfy; TBS; The Weather Channel; TLC; TNT; Travel Channel; truTV; Turner Classic Movies; TV Land; USA Network; VH1; WGN America.
Fee: $50.00 installation; $49.95 monthly.
Digital Basic Service
Subscribers: 40.
Programming (via satellite): BBC America; Bravo; Destination America; Discovery Kids Channel; Disney XD; DMX Music; Fox Sports 1; FYI; History; History International; IFC; Investigation Discovery; LMN; MTV Classic; MTV Hits; MTV2; NBCSN; Nick Jr.; Nicktoons; OWN: Oprah Winfrey Network; Science Channel; TeenNick; VH1 Country; VH1 Soul; WE tv.
Fee: $50.00 installation; $65.95 monthly.
Digital Expanded Basic Service
Subscribers: N.A.
Programming (via satellite): Wisdom TV; Bloomberg Television; ESPNews; FOX College Sports Central; FOX College Sports Pacific; Fuse; FXM; Golf Channel; GSN; International Television (ITV); Outdoor Channel; Ovation; Trinity Broadcasting Network (TBN).
Fee: $6.00 monthly.
Pay Service 1
Pay Units: N.A.
Programming (via satellite): Cinemax; HBO; Showtime; The Movie Channel.
Fee: $3.00 monthly (TMC), $7.95 monthly (Showtime), $12.95 monthly (HBO or Cinemax).
Digital Pay Service 1
Pay Units: N.A.
Programming (via satellite): Cinemax (multiplexed); Flix; HBO (multiplexed); Showtime (multiplexed); Starz (multiplexed); Starz Encore (multiplexed); The Movie Channel (multiplexed).
Fee: $10.95 monthly (Cinemax), $12.95 monthly (Showtime/TMC or Starz/Encore), $14.95 monthly (HBO).
Video-On-Demand: No
Pay-Per-View
iN DEMAND (delivered digitally).
Internet Service
Operational: Yes.
Fee: $19.28 monthly.
Telephone Service
Digital: Operational
Fee: $49.95-$109.95 monthly
Miles of Plant: 15.0 (coaxial); None (fiber optic). Homes passed: 750.
General Manager: David Shipley.
Ownership: Dalton Telephone Co.

DANNEBROG—NCTC Cable. Now served by BURWELL, NE [NE0045]. ICA: NE0277.

DAVEY (village)—Formerly served by TelePartners. No longer in operation. ICA: NE0278.

DAVID CITY—Time Warner Cable. Now served by LINCOLN, NE [NE0002]. ICA: NE0360.

DAWSON—Formerly served by CableDirect. No longer in operation. ICA: NE0225.

DAYKIN—Formerly served by Comstar Cable TV Inc. No longer in operation. ICA: NE0279.

DECATUR—CenCom NNTV. This cable system has converted to IPTV. See JACKSON, NE [NE5019]. ICA: NE0145.

DESHLER—Zito Media, 102 S Main St, PO Box 665, Coudersport, PA 16915. Phones: 814-260-9055; 800-365-6988. E-mail: info@zitomedia.com. Web Site: http://www.zitomedia.com. ICA: NE0086.
TV Market Ranking: Below 100 (DESHLER).
Franchise award date: N.A. Franchise expiration date: N.A. Began: November 1, 1982.
Channel capacity: N.A. Channels available but not in use: N.A.
Basic Service
Subscribers: 49.
Programming (received off-air): KHNE-TV (PBS) Hastings; KLKN (ABC) Lincoln; KNHL (IND) Hastings; KOLN (CBS, MNT, NBC) Lincoln; KSNB-TV (MeTV, MNT, NBC) Superior.
Programming (via satellite): A&E; AMC; Animal Planet; Cartoon Network; CNN; C-SPAN; Discovery Channel; Disney Channel; E! HD; ESPN; ESPN2; Fox News Channel; FOX Sports Midwest; Freeform; FX; Great American Country; HGTV; History; Lifetime; Outdoor Channel; TBS; The Weather Channel; TLC; TNT; Turner Classic Movies; USA Network; WGN America.
Fee: $49.95 installation; $44.00 monthly.
Pay Service 1
Pay Units: N.A.
Programming (via satellite): Cinemax; HBO; Showtime; Starz Encore; The Movie Channel.
Fee: $7.95 monthly (TMC), $8.95 monthly (Showtime), $9.95 monthly (Cinemax), $13.95 monthly (HBO).
Internet Service
Operational: No.
Telephone Service
None
Miles of Plant: 6.0 (coaxial); None (fiber optic). Homes passed: 425.
President: James Rigas.
Ownership: Zito Media (MSO).

DILLER—Diode Cable, 300 Commercial St, PO Box 236, Diller, NE 68342. Phones: 402-793-5124; 402-793-5124; 877-668-9749. Fax: 402-793-5139. E-mail: customerservice@diodecom.net; diodetech@diodecom.net. Web Site: http://diodecom.net. Also serves Odell. ICA: NE0137.
TV Market Ranking: Outside TV Markets (DILLER, Odell). Franchise award date: N.A. Franchise expiration date: N.A. Began: January 1, 1983.
Channel capacity: N.A. Channels available but not in use: N.A.
Basic Service
Subscribers: 114.
Programming (received off-air): KLKN (ABC) Lincoln; KOLN (CBS, MNT, NBC) Lincoln; KPTM (Estrella TV, FOX, MNT, This TV) Omaha; KSNB-TV (MeTV, MNT, NBC) Superior; KXVO (Azteca America, CW) Omaha.
Programming (via satellite): CMT; CNN; Discovery Channel; ESPN; FOX Sports Midwest; Freeform; FX; Nickelodeon; Outdoor Channel; Spike TV; TBS; The Weather Channel; TLC; TNT; TV Land; USA Network; WGN America; WNBC (COZI TV, NBC) New York.
Fee: $25.00 installation; $35.00 monthly.
Expanded Basic Service 1
Subscribers: 16.
Fee: $15.50 monthly.
Pay Service 1
Pay Units: N.A.
Programming (via satellite): HBO.
Fee: $8.44 monthly.
Video-On-Demand: No
Internet Service
Operational: Yes.
Telephone Service
Analog: Operational
Miles of Plant: 30.0 (coaxial); 10.0 (fiber optic). Homes passed: 400.
President: Randy Sandman. General Manager: Loren Duerksen. Chief Technician: J. D. Anderson. Marketing Director: Danni Stark.
Ownership: Diode Cable Co. Inc. (MSO).

DIX—Formerly served by HunTel Cablevision. Now served by Dalton Telephone Co., DALTON, NE [NE0240]. ICA: NE0223.

DIXON/CONCORD—CenCom NNTV. This cable system has converted to IPTV. See JACKSON, NE [NE5019]. ICA: NE0385.

DODGE—Great Plains Communications. Now served by NORTH BEND, NE [NE0080]. ICA: NE0170.

DONIPHAN—Mid-State Community TV, 1001 12th St, Aurora, NE 68818-2004. Phones: 800-821-1831; 402-694-5101. Fax: 402-694-2848. E-mail: midstate@midstatetv.com. Web Site: http://www.midstatetv.com. ICA: NE0108.
TV Market Ranking: 91 (DONIPHAN).
Channel capacity: N.A. Channels available but not in use: N.A.
Basic Service
Subscribers: 3.
Fee: $29.95 monthly.
President & General Manager: Phillip C. Nelson.
Ownership: Mid-State Community TV Inc. (MSO).

DUBOIS—Formerly served by CableDirect. No longer in operation. ICA: NE0244.

DUNCAN—Formerly served by Cable Nebraska. No longer in operation. ICA: NE0177.

DUNNING—Formerly served by Consolidated Cable Inc. No longer in operation. ICA: NE0254.

DWIGHT (village)—Formerly served by TelePartners. No longer in operation. ICA: NE0280.

ELBA—NCTC Cable. Now served by BURWELL, NE [NE0045]. ICA: NE0281.

ELGIN—Great Plains Communications, 1600 Great Plains Ctr, PO Box 500, Blair, NE 68008-0500. Phones: 402-426-9511; 888-343-8014. Fax: 402-456-6550. E-mail: lquist@gpcom.com. Web Site: http://www.gpcom.com. Also serves Ewing, Neligh, Oakdale & Petersburg. ICA: NE0282.
TV Market Ranking: Outside TV Markets (ELGIN, Ewing, Neligh, Oakdale, Petersburg). Franchise award date: January 1, 1983. Franchise expiration date: N.A. Began: March 1, 1984.
Channel capacity: N.A. Channels available but not in use: N.A.
Basic Service
Subscribers: 634.
Programming (received off-air): KLKN (ABC) Lincoln; KOLN (CBS, MNT, NBC)

Nebraska—Cable Systems

Lincoln; KTIV (CW, MeTV, NBC) Sioux City; KUSA (NBC, WeatherNation) Denver; KXNE-TV (PBS) Norfolk.
Programming (via satellite): A&E; AMC; Animal Planet; Bravo; Cartoon Network; CMT; CNBC; CNN; Comedy Central; C-SPAN; Discovery Channel; Disney Channel; E! HD; ESPN; ESPN2; EWTN Global Catholic Network; Fox News Channel; Freeform; HGTV; History; HLN; Lifetime; MSNBC; MTV; NBCSN; Nickelodeon; Pop; QVC; Root Sports Rocky Mountain; Spike TV; Syfy; TBS; The Weather Channel; TNT; Travel Channel; Turner Classic Movies; TV Land; USA Network; VH1; WGN America.
Fee: $45.00 installation; $23.49 monthly.

Expanded Basic Service 1
Subscribers: N.A.
Fee: $47.99 monthly.

Digital Basic Service
Subscribers: N.A.
Programming (via satellite): BBC America; Bravo; Discovery Digital Networks; DMX Music; ESPN Classic; ESPNews; Fox Sports 1; FYI; Golf Channel; History International; IFC; LMN; Nick Jr.; TeenNick; Turner Classic Movies; WE tv.
Fee: $47.95 monthly.

Pay Service 1
Pay Units: N.A.
Programming (via satellite): HBO; Showtime; Starz Encore.
Fee: $9.95 monthly (Showtime), $10.95 monthly (HBO).

Digital Pay Service 1
Pay Units: N.A.
Programming (via satellite): Cinemax (multiplexed); HBO (multiplexed); Showtime (multiplexed); Starz (multiplexed); Starz Encore (multiplexed); The Movie Channel (multiplexed).
Fee: $12.00 monthly (each).

Video-On-Demand: No

Pay-Per-View
iN DEMAND (delivered digitally).

Internet Service
Operational: Yes, DSL & dial-up.
Broadband Service: Netlink.
Fee: $49.95 installation; $39.95 monthly.

Telephone Service
Digital: Operational
Senior Director: Lea Ann Quist. Chief Technician: Mark Stottler. Marketing Manager: Casey Garrigan.
Ownership: Great Plains Communications Inc. (MSO).

ELSIE—Elsie Communications. No longer in operation. ICA: NE0257.

ENDICOTT—Formerly served by Westcom. No longer in operation. ICA: NE0211.

EWING—Great Plains Cable TV. Now served by ELGIN, NE [NE0282]. ICA: NE0283.

FAIRBURY—Time Warner Cable. Now served by LINCOLN, NE [NE0002]. ICA: NE0018.

FALLS CITY—Time Warner Cable. Now served by LINCOLN, NE [NE0002]. ICA: NE0351.

FARNHAM—Formerly served by Consolidated Cable Inc. No longer in operation. ICA: NE0229.

FAWN HEIGHTS—Formerly served by TelePartners. No longer in operation. ICA: NE0381.

FILLEY—Formerly served by Comstar Cable TV Inc. No longer in operation. ICA: NE0284.

FRANKLIN—Eagle Communications, 2703 Hall St, Ste 15, PO Box 817, Hays, KS 67601. Phone: 785-625-4000. Fax: 785-625-8030. E-mail: support@eaglecom.net. Web Site: http://www.eaglecom.net. ICA: NE0396.
TV Market Ranking: Outside TV Markets (FRANKLIN).
Channel capacity: N.A. Channels available but not in use: N.A.

Basic Service
Subscribers: 64.
Fee: $24.95 installation; $49.95 monthly.
President & Chief Executive Officer: Gary Shorman. Chief Operating Officer: Kurt K. David. General Manager: Travis Kohlrus. Marketing Manager: Elizabeth Jaeger.
Ownership: Eagle Communications Inc. (MSO).

FRANKLIN—Formerly served by PinPoint Cable TV. No longer in operation. ICA: NE0073.

FREMONT—Time Warner Cable. Now served by LINCOLN, NE [NE0002]. ICA: NE0007.

FULLERTON—Eagle Communications, 2703 Hall St, Ste 15, PO Box 817, Hays, KS 67601. Phone: 785-625-4000. Fax: 785-625-8030. E-mail: support@eaglecom.net. Web Site: http://www.eaglecom.net. ICA: NE0058.
TV Market Ranking: Outside TV Markets (FULLERTON). Franchise award date: N.A. Franchise expiration date: N.A. Began: November 1, 1968.
Channel capacity: N.A. Channels available but not in use: N.A.

Basic Service
Subscribers: 224.
Programming (received off-air): KGIN (CBS, MNT, NBC) Grand Island; KHGI-TV (ABC) Kearney; KHNE-TV (PBS) Hastings; KLKN (ABC) Lincoln; KNHL (IND) Hastings; KTVG-TV (FOX) Grand Island; allband FM.
Programming (via satellite): C-SPAN; C-SPAN 2; EWTN Global Catholic Network; Freeform; Hallmark Channel; HLN; Pop; QVC; TBS; The Weather Channel; Trinity Broadcasting Network (TBN); WGN America.
Fee: $24.95 installation; $64.95 monthly.

Expanded Basic Service 1
Subscribers: N.A.
Programming (via satellite): A&E; AMC; Animal Planet; Cartoon Network; CMT; CNBC; CNN; Comedy Central; Discovery Channel; E! HD; ESPN; ESPN2; Food Network; Fox News Channel; FOX Sports Midwest; FX; Great American Country; HGTV; History; ION Television; Lifetime; MSNBC; Outdoor Channel; Spike TV; Syfy; TLC; TNT; Travel Channel; truTV; Turner Classic Movies; TV Land; Univision Studios; USA Network.

Digital Basic Service
Subscribers: N.A.
Programming (via satellite): BBC America; Bloomberg Television; Discovery Life Channel; DMX Music; ESPN Classic; ESPN2; ESPNews; EVINE Live; Fox Sports 1; FSN Digital Atlantic; FSN Digital Central; FSN Digital Pacific; FXM; FYI; Golf Channel; GSN; History; History International; HITS (Headend In The Sky); International Television (ITV); MBC America; MTV; National Geographic Channel; NBCSN; Nick Jr.; Nickelodeon; Outdoor Channel; Ovation; Syfy; TeenNick; Trinity Broadcasting Network (TBN); VH1.
Fee: $14.00 monthly.

Digital Pay Service 1
Pay Units: N.A.
Programming (via satellite): Cinemax (multiplexed); Flix; FXM; HBO (multiplexed); IFC; LMN; Showtime (multiplexed); Starz (multiplexed); Starz Encore (multiplexed); The Movie Channel (multiplexed); WAM! America's Kidz Network; WE tv.
Fee: $15.00 monthly.

Video-On-Demand: No

Pay-Per-View
iN DEMAND (delivered digitally); Playboy TV (delivered digitally).

Internet Service
Operational: Yes.
Broadband Service: Cable Nebraska.

Telephone Service
Digital: Operational
Miles of Plant: 12.0 (coaxial); None (fiber optic). Homes passed: 635.
President & Chief Executive Officer: Gary Shorman. Chief Operating Officer: Kurt K. David. General Manager: Travis Kohlrus. Marketing Manager: Elizabeth Jaeger.
Ownership: Eagle Communications Inc. (MSO).

FUNK—Glenwood Telecommunications. Now served by BLUE HILL, NE [NE0093]. ICA: NE0285.

GARLAND—Formerly served by Zito Media. No longer in operation. ICA: NE0214.

GENEVA—Formerly served by Sprint Corp. No longer in operation. ICA: NE0352.

GENEVA—Zito Media, 102 S Main St, PO Box 665, Coudersport, PA 16915. Phones: 814-260-9055; 800-365-6988. E-mail: info@zitomedia.com. Web Site: http://www.zitomedia.com. Also serves Bruning, Davenport, Exeter, Fairmont, McCool Junction, Milligan & Shickley. ICA: NE0043.
TV Market Ranking: Below 100 (Bruning, Davenport, Shickley); Outside TV Markets (Exeter, Fairmont, GENEVA, McCool Junction, Milligan). Franchise award date: N.A. Franchise expiration date: N.A. Began: March 1, 1981.
Channel capacity: N.A. Channels available but not in use: N.A.

Basic Service
Subscribers: 587.
Programming (received off-air): KHGI-TV (ABC) Kearney; KHNE-TV (PBS) Hastings; KLKN (ABC) Lincoln; KNHL (IND) Hastings; KOLN (CBS, MNT, NBC) Lincoln; KPTM (Estrella TV, FOX, MNT, This TV) Omaha; KSNB-TV (MeTV, MNT, NBC) Superior; KXVO (Azteca America, CW) Omaha.
Programming (via satellite): A&E; AMC; Animal Planet; Boomerang; Cartoon Network; CNN; Comedy Central; C-SPAN; Discovery Channel; Disney Channel; Disney XD; E! HD; ESPN; ESPN2; EWTN Global Catholic Network; Food Network; Fox News Channel; FOX Sports Midwest; Freeform; Fuse; FX; Great American Country; Hallmark Channel; HGTV; History; HLN; INSP; Lifetime; MSNBC; National Geographic Channel; Outdoor Channel; Pop; QVC; Syfy; TBS; The Weather Channel; TLC; TNT; Travel Channel; Trinity Broadcasting Network (TBN); Turner Classic Movies; TV Land; USA Network; WGN America.
Fee: $49.95 installation; $17.31 monthly.

Digital Basic Service
Subscribers: N.A.
Programming (via satellite): BBC America; Bloomberg Television; Discovery Life Channel; DMX Music; ESPN Classic; ESPNews; Fox Sports 1; FSN Digital Atlantic; FSN Digital Central; FSN Digital Pacific; FYI; Golf Channel; GSN; History International; WE tv.
Fee: $12.95 monthly.

Digital Expanded Basic Service
Subscribers: N.A.
Programming (via satellite): FXM; IFC; LMN; Starz Encore.
Fee: $12.95 monthly.

Pay Service 1
Pay Units: N.A.
Programming (via satellite): Cinemax; HBO; Showtime; The Movie Channel.
Fee: $7.95 monthly (TMC), $9.95 monthly (Showtime), $10.95 monthly (Cinemax), $13.95 monthly (HBO).

Digital Pay Service 1
Pay Units: N.A.
Programming (via satellite): Cinemax (multiplexed); Flix; HBO (multiplexed); Showtime (multiplexed); The Movie Channel (multiplexed).
Fee: $15.60 monthly.

Video-On-Demand: No; No

Pay-Per-View
ESPN Now (delivered digitally); Hot Choice (delivered digitally); Playboy TV (delivered digitally); Fresh (delivered digitally).

Internet Service
Operational: Yes.
Fee: $49.95 installation; $44.95 monthly; $5.00 modem lease.

Telephone Service
Digital: Planned
Miles of Plant: 47.0 (coaxial); None (fiber optic). Homes passed: 2,628.
President: James Rigas.
Ownership: Zito Media (MSO).

GENOA—Eagle Communications, 2703 Hall St, Ste 15, PO Box 817, Hays, KS 67601. Phone: 785-625-4000. Fax: 785-625-8030. E-mail: support@eaglecom.net. Web Site: http://www.eaglecom.net. ICA: NE0083.
TV Market Ranking: Outside TV Markets (GENOA). Franchise award date: February 1, 1980. Franchise expiration date: N.A. Began: January 1, 1982.
Channel capacity: N.A. Channels available but not in use: N.A.

Basic Service
Subscribers: 150.
Programming (received off-air): KGIN (CBS, MNT, NBC) Grand Island; KHGI-TV (ABC) Kearney; KHNE-TV (PBS) Hastings; KLKN (ABC) Lincoln; KNHL (IND) Hastings; KTVG-TV (FOX) Grand Island.
Programming (via satellite): C-SPAN; C-SPAN 2; EWTN Global Catholic Network; MyNetworkTV; Pop; QVC; TBS; The Weather Channel; Trinity Broadcasting Network (TBN); Univision Studios; WGN America.
Fee: $24.95 installation; $64.95 monthly.

Expanded Basic Service 1
Subscribers: N.A.
Programming (via satellite): A&E; AMC; Animal Planet; Cartoon Network; CMT; CNBC; CNN; Comedy Central; Discovery Channel; E! HD; ESPN; ESPN Classic; ESPN2; Food Network; Fox News Channel; FOX Sports Midwest; Freeform; FX; Great American Country; Hallmark Channel; HGTV; History; HLN; ION Television; Lifetime; MSNBC; MTV; NBCSN; Nickelodeon; Outdoor Channel; RFD-TV; Spike TV; Syfy;

Cable Systems—Nebraska

TLC; TNT; Travel Channel; truTV; Turner Classic Movies; TV Land; USA Network; VH1.
Digital Basic Service
Subscribers: N.A.
Programming (via satellite): AZ TV; BBC America; Bloomberg Television; Cloo; CMT; Destination America; Discovery Channel HD; Discovery Kids Channel; Discovery Life Channel; DMX Music; ESPN HD; ESPNews; EVINE Live; FOX College Sports Central; FOX College Sports Pacific; Fox Sports 1; FXM; FYI; Golf Channel; GSN; History International; HITS (Headend In The Sky); Investigation Discovery; MTV Classic; MTV Hits; MTV2; MyNetworkTV; Nick Jr.; Ovation; OWN; Oprah Winfrey Network; Science Channel; TBS HD; TeenNick; TNT HD; VH1 Soul; WE tv.
Fee: $14.00 monthly.
Digital Pay Service 1
Pay Units: N.A.
Programming (via satellite): Cinemax (multiplexed); Flix; HBO (multiplexed); LMN; Showtime (multiplexed); Starz (multiplexed); Starz Encore (multiplexed); The Movie Channel (multiplexed).
Fee: $10.00 monthly.
Video-On-Demand: No
Pay-Per-View
iN DEMAND (delivered digitally); Playboy TV (delivered digitally); Hot Choice (delivered digitally); Fresh (delivered digitally); Spice Xcess (delivered digitally); Club Jenna (delivered digitally).
Internet Service
Operational: Yes.
Broadband Service: Cable Nebraska.
Telephone Service
Digital: Operational
Miles of Plant: 8.0 (coaxial); None (fiber optic). Homes passed: 485.
President & Chief Executive Officer: Gary Shorman. Chief Operating Officer: Kurt K. David. General Manager: Travis Kohlrus. Marketing Manager: Elizabeth Jaeger.
Ownership: Eagle Communications Inc. (MSO).

GILTNER—Mid-State Community TV, 1001 12th St, Aurora, NE 68818-2004. Phones: 800-821-1831; 402-694-5101. Fax: 402-694-2848. E-mail: midstate@midstatetv.com. Web Site: http://www.midstatetv.com. ICA: NE0210.
TV Market Ranking: 91 (GILTNER).
Channel capacity: N.A. Channels available but not in use: N.A.
Basic Service
Subscribers: 3.
Fee: $29.95 monthly.
President & General Manager: Phillip C. Nelson.
Ownership: Mid-State Community TV Inc. (MSO).

GINGER COVE—Formerly served by TelePartners. No longer in operation. ICA: NE0362.

GLENVIL—Formerly served by Zito Media. No longer in operation. ICA: NE0178.

GOEHNER (village)—Formerly served by TelePartners. No longer in operation. ICA: NE0286.

GORDON—Great Plains Communications. Now served by CHADRON, NE [NE0024]. ICA: NE0287.

GOTHENBURG—Charter Communications. Now served by KEARNEY, NE [NE0011]. ICA: NE0034.

GRAND ISLAND—Charter Communications. Now served by KEARNEY, NE [NE0011]. ICA: NE0005.

GRAND ISLAND—Zito Media, 102 S Main St, PO Box 665, Coudersport, PA 16915. Phones: 814-260-9055; 800-365-6988. E-mail: info@zitomedia.com. Web Site: http://www.zitomedia.com. ICA: NE0101.
TV Market Ranking: 91 (GRAND ISLAND). Franchise award date: N.A. Franchise expiration date: N.A. Began: March 1, 1988.
Channel capacity: N.A. Channels available but not in use: N.A.
Basic Service
Subscribers: 28.
Programming (received off-air): KGIN (CBS, MNT, NBC) Grand Island; KHGI-TV (ABC) Kearney; KHNE-TV (PBS) Hastings; KLKN (ABC) Lincoln; KNHL (IND) Hastings; KTVG-TV (FOX) Grand Island.
Programming (via satellite): A&E; AMC; Animal Planet; Cartoon Network; CNN; Discovery Channel; Disney Channel; Disney XD; E! HD; ESPN; ESPN2; Fox News Channel; FOX Sports Midwest; Freeform; Fuse; FX; Great American Country; HGTV; History; HLN; Lifetime; MSNBC; Outdoor Channel; QVC; TBS; The Weather Channel; TLC; TNT; Turner Classic Movies; USA Network; WGN America.
Fee: $49.95 installation; $45.85 monthly.
Pay Service 1
Pay Units: N.A.
Programming (via satellite): Cinemax; HBO; Showtime; The Movie Channel.
Fee: $6.95 monthly (TMC), $7.95 monthly (Showtime), $11.95 monthly (Cinemax), $12.95 monthly (HBO).
Internet Service
Operational: No.
Telephone Service
None
Miles of Plant: 16.0 (coaxial); None (fiber optic). Homes passed: 712.
President: James Rigas.
Ownership: Zito Media (MSO).

GRANT—Great Plains Communications, 1600 Great Plains Ctr, PO Box 500, Blair, NE 68008-0500. Phones: 402-426-9511; 888-343-8014. Fax: 402-456-6550. E-mail: lquist@gpcom.com. Web Site: http://www.gpcom.com. Also serves Hayes Center, Imperial, Palisade & Venango. ICA: NE0070.
TV Market Ranking: Below 100 (Hayes Center, Imperial, Palisade); Outside TV Markets (GRANT, Venango). Franchise award date: N.A. Franchise expiration date: N.A. Began: September 30, 1976.
Channel capacity: N.A. Channels available but not in use: N.A.
Basic Service
Subscribers: 1,001.
Programming (received off-air): KNOP-TV (NBC) North Platte; KOLN (CBS, MNT, NBC) Lincoln; KPNE-TV (PBS) North Platte; KWNB-TV (ABC) Hayes Center; allband FM.
Programming (via satellite): A&E; Animal Planet; CMT; CNBC; CNN; C-SPAN; Discovery Channel; Disney Channel; E! HD; ESPN; Food Network; Fox News Channel; Freeform; FX; Hallmark Channel; History; HLN; KCNC-TV (CBS, Decades) Denver; KUSA (NBC, WeatherNation) Denver; KWGN-TV (CW, This TV) Denver; Lifetime; MSNBC; Pop; QVC; Root Sports Rocky Mountain; TBS; The Weather Channel; TLC; TNT; Travel Channel; TV Land; USA Network; WGN America.
Fee: $45.00 installation; $23.49 monthly.
Digital Basic Service
Subscribers: N.A.
Programming (via satellite): BBC America; Bravo; Discovery Digital Networks; DMX Music; ESPN Classic; Fox Sports 1; FYI; History International; IFC; LMN; National Geographic Channel; NBCSN; Nick Jr.; Starz Encore; Syfy; TeenNick; Turner Classic Movies; WE tv.
Fee: $47.95 monthly.
Pay Service 1
Pay Units: 302 Includes Digital Pay Service 1.
Programming (via satellite): HBO; Showtime.
Fee: $20.00 installation; $9.00 monthly (each).
Digital Pay Service 1
Pay Units: N.A. Included in Pay Service 1
Programming (via satellite): Cinemax (multiplexed); HBO (multiplexed); Showtime (multiplexed); Starz (multiplexed); Starz Encore (multiplexed); The Movie Channel (multiplexed).
Fee: $12.00 monthly (HBO, Cinemax, Starz/Encore or Showtime/TMC).
Video-On-Demand: No
Pay-Per-View
iN DEMAND (delivered digitally); Sports PPV.
Internet Service
Operational: Yes, DSL & dial-up.
Broadband Service: In-house.
Fee: $49.95 installation; $39.95 monthly.
Telephone Service
Digital: Operational
Miles of Plant: 35.0 (coaxial); None (fiber optic).
Senior Director: Lea Ann Quist. Chief Technician: Mark Stottler. Marketing Manager: Casey Garrigan.
Ownership: Great Plains Communications Inc. (MSO).

GREELEY—Center Cable Co, PO Box 117, Greeley, NE 68842-0117. Phones: 308-428-2915 (Office); 308-428-5925 (home). Fax: 308-428-5585. ICA: NE0179.
TV Market Ranking: Outside TV Markets (GREELEY). Franchise award date: N.A. Franchise expiration date: N.A. Began: April 1, 1982.
Channel capacity: 35 (operating 2-way). Channels available but not in use: N.A.
Basic Service
Subscribers: N.A.
Programming (received off-air): KGIN (CBS, MNT, NBC) Grand Island; KHGI-TV (ABC) Kearney; KNHL (IND) Hastings; KOLN (CBS, MNT, NBC) Lincoln.
Programming (via satellite): TBS; WGN America.
Pay Service 1
Pay Units: N.A.
Programming (via satellite): Cinemax; HBO.
Fee: $11.95 monthly (each).
Video-On-Demand: No

Internet Service
Operational: Yes.
Broadband Service: In-house.
Fee: $24.95 monthly.
Telephone Service
None
Miles of Plant: 5.0 (coaxial); None (fiber optic). Homes passed: 180.
General Manager: Martin Callahan.
Ownership: Center Cable TV.

GREENWOOD—Charter Communications. Now served by SPRINGFIELD (formerly Plattsmouth), NE [NE0020]. ICA: NE0159.

GRESHAM—Formerly served by Zito Media. No longer in operation. ICA: NE0195.

GRETNA—Zito Media, 102 S Main St, PO Box 665, Coudersport, PA 16915. Phones: 814-260-9055; 800-365-6988. E-mail: info@zitomedia.com. Web Site: http://www.zitomedia.com. Also serves Douglas County (portions), Elkhorn, Sarpy County (portions), Valley & Waterloo. ICA: NE0060.
TV Market Ranking: 53,91 (Douglas County (portions), Elkhorn, GRETNA, Sarpy County (portions), Valley, Waterloo). Franchise award date: N.A. Franchise expiration date: N.A. Began: September 1, 1981.
Channel capacity: N.A. Channels available but not in use: N.A.
Basic Service
Subscribers: 153.
Programming (received off-air): KETV (ABC, MeTV) Omaha; KMTV-TV (Antenna TV, CBS, Escape) Omaha; KOLN (CBS, MNT, NBC) Lincoln; KPTM (Estrella TV, FOX, MNT, This TV) Omaha; KUON-TV (PBS) Lincoln; KXVO (Azteca America, CW) Omaha; KYNE-TV (PBS) Omaha; WOWT (IND, NBC) Omaha.
Programming (via satellite): A&E; AMC; Cartoon Network; CNBC; CNN; Comedy Central; Discovery Channel; Disney Channel; Disney XD; ESPN; ESPN2; Fox News Channel; FOX Sports Midwest; Freeform; Fuse; FX; Great American Country; History; HLN; INSP; Lifetime; Outdoor Channel; QVC; Syfy; TBS; The Weather Channel; TNT; Travel Channel; Turner Classic Movies; TV Land; USA Network; WGN America.
Fee: $49.95 installation; $17.79 monthly.
Digital Basic Service
Subscribers: N.A.
Programming (via satellite): BBC America; Bloomberg Television; Discovery Life Channel; DMX Music; ESPN Classic; ESPNews; Fox Sports 1; FSN Digital Atlantic; FSN Digital Central; FSN Digital Pacific; FYI; Golf Channel; GSN; History International; National Geographic Channel; WE tv.
Fee: $13.95 monthly.
Digital Expanded Basic Service
Subscribers: N.A.
Programming (via satellite): DMX Music; FXM; LMN; Starz Encore.
Fee: $13.95 monthly.

Nebraska—Cable Systems

Pay Service 1
Pay Units: N.A.
Programming (via satellite): Cinemax; HBO; Showtime; Starz Encore.
Fee: $3.95 monthly (Encore), $7.95 monthly (Showtime), $11.95 monthly (Cinemax), $12.95 monthly (HBO).
Digital Pay Service 1
Pay Units: N.A.
Programming (via satellite): Cinemax (multiplexed); Flix; HBO (multiplexed); Showtime (multiplexed); The Movie Channel (multiplexed).
Fee: $10.00 monthly.
Video-On-Demand: No
Pay-Per-View
ESPN Now (delivered digitally); Hot Choice (delivered digitally); Playboy TV (delivered digitally); Fresh (delivered digitally); Shorteez (delivered digitally); Urban Xtra (delivered digitally).
Internet Service
Operational: No.
Telephone Service
None
Miles of Plant: 51.0 (coaxial); None (fiber optic). Homes passed: 3,662.
President: James Rigas.
Ownership: Zito Media (MSO).

GUIDE ROCK—Formerly served by Glenwood Telecommunications. No longer in operation. ICA: NE0192.

HADAR—Formerly served by Sky Scan Cable Co. Now served by Cable One, NORFOLK, NE [NE0006]. ICA: NE0288.

HAIGLER—BWTelcom, 607 Chief St, PO Box 684, Benkelman, NE 69021. Phones: 308-423-8950; 800-835-0053; 308-394-6000; 308-423-2000. Fax: 308-423-5818. E-mail: bwtelcom@bwtelcom.net. Web Site: http://www.bwtelcom.net. ICA: NE0232.
TV Market Ranking: Outside TV Markets (HAIGLER). Franchise award date: N.A. Franchise expiration date: N.A. Began: September 1, 1989.
Channel capacity: N.A. Channels available but not in use: N.A.
Basic Service
Subscribers: 44.
Programming (received off-air): KBSL-DT (CBS) Goodland; KPNE-TV (PBS) North Platte; KSNK (NBC) McCook; KWNB-TV (ABC) Hayes Center.
Programming (via satellite): A&E; CMT; CNBC; CNN; Discovery Channel; Disney Channel; ESPN; ESPN2; Freeform; KCNC-TV (CBS, Decades) Denver; KWGN-TV (CW, This TV) Denver; Lifetime; MTV; Nickelodeon; Outdoor Channel; Root Sports Rocky Mountain; Spike TV; Syfy; TBS; The Weather Channel; TLC; TNT; TV Land; USA Network; VH1; WGN America.
Fee: $27.85 installation; $47.25 monthly.
Expanded Basic Service 1
Subscribers: 25.
Fee: $22.00 monthly.
Pay Service 1
Pay Units: 18.
Programming (via satellite): HBO; Showtime; The Movie Channel.
Fee: $10.00 installation; $18.15 monthly (Showtime/TMC), $19.15 monthly (HBO).
Video-On-Demand: No
Internet Service
Operational: Yes.
Telephone Service
None
Miles of Plant: 3.0 (coaxial); None (fiber optic). Homes passed: 120.

Vice President: Kacey L. Harper. General Manager & Chief Technician: Randall Raile. Marketing Director: Loretta Raile. Bookkeeper: Jenna Edwards.
Ownership: BWTelcom (MSO).

HARDY—Formerly served by Diode Cable Co. No longer in operation. ICA: NE0230.

HARRISON—WinDBreak Cable, 1140 10th St, Gering, NE 69341-3239. Phone: 308-436-4650. Fax: 308-436-4779. E-mail: bill@intertech.net. Web Site: http://www.windbreak.com. ICA: NE0380.
TV Market Ranking: Outside TV Markets (HARRISON).
Channel capacity: N.A. Channels available but not in use: N.A.
Basic Service
Subscribers: N.A.
Programming (received off-air): KLWY (FOX) Cheyenne; KNEP (ABC) Scottsbluff; KSTF (CBS, CW) Scottsbluff; KTNE-TV (PBS) Alliance.
Programming (via satellite): CNN; Discovery Channel; Freeform; Hallmark Channel; KUSA (NBC, WeatherNation) Denver; KWGN-TV (CW, This TV) Denver; Spike TV; TBS; The Weather Channel; USA Network.
Fee: $20.20 installation.
Pay Service 1
Pay Units: N.A.
Programming (via satellite): Showtime; The Movie Channel.
Fee: $20.00 installation; $7.95 monthly (each).
Video-On-Demand: No
Internet Service
Operational: Yes. Began: January 1, 1998.
Broadband Service: In-house.
Fee: $24.95 monthly.
Telephone Service
None
Miles of Plant: 32.0 (coaxial); None (fiber optic). Homes passed: 170.
General Manager & Chief Technician: Bill Bauer. Office Manager: Aubrey Luevano.
Ownership: WinDBreak Cable (MSO).

HARTINGTON—Cedarvision, 103 West Centre St, PO Box 157, Hartington, NE 68739. Phone: 402-254-3901. Fax: 402-254-2453. E-mail: htc@hartel.net. Web Site: http://www.hartel.net. ICA: NE0063.
TV Market Ranking: Outside TV Markets (HARTINGTON). Franchise award date: December 18, 1979. Franchise expiration date: N.A. Began: May 1, 1981.
Channel capacity: 14 (not 2-way capable). Channels available but not in use: N.A.
Basic Service
Subscribers: 32.
Programming (received off-air): KCAU-TV (ABC) Sioux City; KELO-TV (CBS, MNT) Sioux Falls; KMEG (Azteca America, CBS, Decades) Sioux City; KPTH (FOX, MNT, This TV) Sioux City; KSFY-TV (ABC, CW) Sioux Falls; KTIV (CW, MeTV, NBC) Sioux City; KUSD-TV (PBS) Vermillion; KXNE-TV (PBS) Norfolk.
Programming (via satellite): A&E; AMC; Animal Planet; CNN; Comedy Central; Discovery Channel; Disney Channel; ESPN; ESPN2; EWTN Global Catholic Network; Freeform; Great American Country; Hallmark Channel; HGTV; History; Lifetime; Nickelodeon; Spike TV; TBS; The Weather Channel; TLC; TNT; Turner Classic Movies; USA Network; WGN America.
Fee: $25.00 installation; $29.95 monthly.
Pay Service 1
Pay Units: N.A.
Programming (via satellite): Cinemax; HBO.

Fee: $9.50 monthly.
Video-On-Demand: No
Internet Service
Operational: No, DSL.
Telephone Service
Analog: Operational
Miles of Plant: 3.0 (coaxial); None (fiber optic). Homes passed: 688.
Chief Executive Officer & General Manager: William Dendinger. Marketing Manager: Mike Becker. Chief Technician: Bill Noecker. Controller: John Mines.
Ownership: Hartington Telephone Co.

HASTINGS—Charter Communications. Now served by KEARNEY, NE [NE0011]. ICA: NE0010.

HAY SPRINGS—Great Plains Communications. Now served by CHADRON, NE [NE0024]. ICA: NE0095.

HEBRON—Diode Cable, 300 Commercial St, PO Box 236, Diller, NE 68342. Phones: 877-668-9749; 402-793-5124; 877-668-9749; 402-793-2532; 402-793-5124. Fax: 402-793-5139. E-mail: customerservice@diodecom.net; diodetech@diodecom.net. Web Site: http://diodecom.net. ICA: NE0068.
TV Market Ranking: Below 100 (HEBRON). Franchise award date: N.A. Franchise expiration date: N.A. Began: December 1, 1980.
Channel capacity: N.A. Channels available but not in use: N.A.
Basic Service
Subscribers: 293.
Programming (received off-air): KHNE-TV (PBS) Hastings; KLKN (ABC) Lincoln; KNHL (IND) Hastings; KOLN (CBS, MNT, NBC) Lincoln; KSNB-TV (MeTV, MNT, NBC) Superior.
Programming (via satellite): C-SPAN; EWTN Global Catholic Network; QVC; The Weather Channel; Trinity Broadcasting Network (TBN).
Fee: $20.00 installation; $46.00 monthly.
Expanded Basic Service 1
Subscribers: 12.
Programming (via satellite): A&E; AMC; Animal Planet; Cartoon Network; CMT; CNBC; CNN; Comedy Central; Discovery Channel; Disney Channel; E! HD; ESPN; ESPN Classic; ESPN2; Food Network; Fox News Channel; Fox Sports 1; FOX Sports Midwest; Freeform; FX; Great American Country; GSN; Hallmark Channel; HGTV; History; HLN; Lifetime; MTV; National Geographic Channel; Nickelodeon; Outdoor Channel; Spike TV; Syfy; TBS; TLC; TNT; Travel Channel; truTV; Turner Classic Movies; TV Land; USA Network; VH1; WGN America.
Fee: $31.80 monthly.
Digital Basic Service
Subscribers: 17.
Programming (via satellite): BBC America; Bloomberg Television; Bravo; Destination America; Discovery Kids Channel; Discovery Life Channel; Disney XD; DMX Music; ESPN Classic; ESPNews; Fuse; FXM; FYI; Golf Channel; History International; IFC; Investigation Discovery; LMN; MTV Classic; MTV2; National Geographic Channel; NBCSN; Nick Jr.; Nicktoons; OWN: Oprah Winfrey Network; Science Channel; TeenNick; VH1 Country; WE tv.
Fee: $12.55 monthly.
Pay Service 1
Pay Units: N.A.
Programming (via satellite): Cinemax; HBO.
Fee: $7.50 monthly (Cinemax), $10.25 monthly (HBO).

Digital Pay Service 1
Pay Units: N.A.
Programming (via satellite): Cinemax (multiplexed); HBO (multiplexed); Showtime (multiplexed); Starz (multiplexed).
Video-On-Demand: No
Internet Service
Operational: Yes.
Subscribers: 170.
Broadband Service: In-house.
Fee: $24.95-$46.95 monthly.
Telephone Service
Analog: Operational
Miles of Plant: 80.0 (coaxial); 4.0 (fiber optic). Homes passed: 650.
President: Randy Sandman. General Manager: Loren Duerksen. Chief Technician: J. D. Anderson. Marketing Director: Danni Stark.
Ownership: Diode Cable Co. Inc. (MSO).

HEMINGFORD—Mobius Communications Co, 523 Niobrara Ave, PO Box 246, Hemingford, NE 69348. Phones: 308-487-5500; 877-266-2487. Web Site: http://bbc.net. ICA: NE0389.
TV Market Ranking: Outside TV Markets (HEMINGFORD, HEMINGFORD).
Channel capacity: N.A. Channels available but not in use: N.A.
Basic Service
Subscribers: 51.
Fee: $21.99 monthly.
General Manager: Tonya Mayer.
Ownership: Mobius Communications Co. (MSO).

HENDERSON—Mainstay Cable TV, 1000 North Main St, PO Box 487, Henderson, NE 68371. Phone: 402-723-4448. Fax: 402-723-4451. E-mail: mainstay@mainstaycomm.net. Web Site: http://www.mainstaycomm.net. ICA: NE0087.
TV Market Ranking: 91 (HENDERSON). Franchise award date: August 9, 1982. Franchise expiration date: N.A. Began: December 1, 1982.
Channel capacity: N.A. Channels available but not in use: N.A.
Basic Service
Subscribers: 185.
Programming (received off-air): KHGI-TV (ABC) Kearney; KNHL (IND) Hastings; KOLN (CBS, MNT, NBC) Lincoln; KSNB-TV (MeTV, MNT, NBC) Superior; KUON-TV (PBS) Lincoln.
Programming (via satellite): A&E; Cartoon Network; CNN; Discovery Channel; Disney Channel; ESPN; ESPN2; Fox News Channel; FOX Sports Networks; Freeform; Hallmark Channel; HGTV; History; INSP; National Geographic Channel; Nickelodeon; Spike TV; TBS; The Weather Channel; TLC; TNT; Turner Classic Movies; TV Land; USA Network; WGN America.
Fee: $25.00 installation; $42.50 monthly.
Pay Service 1
Pay Units: 35.
Programming (via satellite): HBO.
Fee: $16.50 monthly.
Video-On-Demand: No
Internet Service
Operational: Yes, DSL.
Broadband Service: In-house.
Fee: $34.95-$129.95 monthly.
Telephone Service
Analog: Operational
Fee: $17.50 monthly
Miles of Plant: 13.0 (coaxial); None (fiber optic). Homes passed: 450.
General Manager: Matt Friesen.
Ownership: Mainstay Communications.

Cable Systems—Nebraska

HOLDREGE—Charter Communications. Now served by KEARNEY, NE [NE0011]. ICA: NE0028.

HOMER—Formerly served by HunTel Cablevision. Now served by American Broadband, WAYNE, NE [NE0374]. ICA: NE0372.

HOOPER—WesTel Systems, 012 East 3rd St, PO Box 330, Remsen, IA 51050. Phones: 712-786-1181; 402-654-3344; 800-628-5989. Fax: 712-786-2400. E-mail: acctinfo@westelsystems.com. Web Site: http://www.westelsystems.com. Also serves Uehling & Winslow. ICA: NE0131.
TV Market Ranking: Outside TV Markets (HOOPER, Uehling, Winslow). Franchise award date: N.A. Franchise expiration date: N.A. Began: January 1, 1984.
Channel capacity: 40 (not 2-way capable). Channels available but not in use: N.A.
Basic Service
Subscribers: 183.
Programming (received off-air): KETV (ABC, MeTV) Omaha; KLKN (ABC) Lincoln; KMTV-TV (Antenna TV, CBS, Escape) Omaha; KOLN (CBS, MNT, NBC) Lincoln; KPTM (Estrella TV, FOX, MNT, This TV) Omaha; KUON-TV (PBS) Lincoln; KXVO (Azteca America, CW) Omaha; WOWT (IND, NBC) Omaha.
Programming (via satellite): A&E; AMC; Cartoon Network; CMT; CNN; Discovery Channel; Disney Channel; DIY Network; ESPN; ESPN2; Food Network; Fox News Channel; Fox Sports 1; FOX Sports Networks; Freeform; FX; Great American Country; HGTV; History; HLN; Lifetime; MSNBC; MTV; NBCSN; Nickelodeon; QVC; Spike TV; Syfy; TBS; The Weather Channel; TLC; TNT; Travel Channel; Turner Classic Movies; TV Land; USA Network; VH1; WE tv; WGN America.
Fee: $20.00 installation; $39.95 monthly.
Digital Basic Service
Subscribers: N.A.
Programming (via satellite): BBC America; Bloomberg Television; CMT; Destination America; Discovery Kids Channel; Discovery Life Channel; Disney XD; DMX Music; ESPN Classic; ESPNews; EVINE Live; Fuse; FXM; FYI; Golf Channel; GSN; History International; Investigation Discovery; LMN; MTV Classic; MTV Hits; MTV2; Nick Jr.; Nicktoons; Outdoor Channel; OWN; Oprah Winfrey Network; RFD-TV; Science Channel; TeenNick; The Word Network; Trinity Broadcasting Network (TBN); Turner Classic Movies; VH1 Soul.
Pay Service 1
Pay Units: N.A.
Programming (via satellite): Cinemax; HBO.
Fee: $12.95 monthly.
Digital Pay Service 1
Pay Units: N.A.
Programming (via satellite): Cinemax (multiplexed); Flix; HBO (multiplexed); Showtime (multiplexed); Starz (multiplexed); Starz Encore (multiplexed); The Movie Channel (multiplexed).
Internet Service
Operational: No.
Telephone Service
Analog: Operational
Miles of Plant: 6.0 (coaxial); None (fiber optic). Homes passed: 392.
Chief Executive Officer: Robert Gannon. General Manager: William Daubendiek II.
Ownership: WesTel Systems (MSO).

HORDVILLE—Mid-State Community TV, 1001 12th St, Aurora, NE 68818-2004. Phones: 800-821-1831; 402-694-5101. Fax: 402-694-2848. E-mail: midstate@midstatetv.com. Web Site: http://www.midstatetv.com. ICA: NE0293.
TV Market Ranking: Below 100 (HORDVILLE). Channel capacity: N.A. Channels available but not in use: N.A.
Basic Service
Subscribers: 1.
Fee: $29.95 monthly.
President & General Manager: Phillip C. Nelson.
Ownership: Mid-State Community TV Inc. (MSO).

HOWELLS—Formerly served by TelePartners. No longer in operation. ICA: NE0363.

HUBBARD—CenCom NNTV. This cable system has converted to IPTV. See JACKSON, NE [NE5019]. ICA: NE0375.

HUMPHREY—Eagle Communications, 2703 Hall St, Ste 15, PO Box 817, Hays, KS 67601. Phone: 785-625-4000. Fax: 785-625-8030. E-mail: support@eaglecom.net. Web Site: http://www.eaglecom.net. ICA: NE0142.
TV Market Ranking: Outside TV Markets (HUMPHREY). Franchise award date: N.A. Franchise expiration date: N.A. Began: January 1, 1984.
Channel capacity: N.A. Channels available but not in use: N.A.
Basic Service
Subscribers: 92.
Programming (received off-air): KLKN (ABC) Lincoln; KOLN (CBS, MNT, NBC) Lincoln; KPTM (Estrella TV, FOX, MNT, This TV) Omaha; KXNE-TV (PBS) Norfolk; KXVO (Azteca America, CW) Omaha; WOWT (IND, NBC) Omaha.
Programming (via satellite): A&E; AMC; Animal Planet; Cartoon Network; CNBC; CNN; C-SPAN; Discovery Channel; E! HD; ESPN; ESPN2; EWTN Global Catholic Network; Food Network; Fox News Channel; FOX Sports Midwest; Freeform; FX; Great American Country; HGTV; History; HLN; Lifetime; MSNBC; Nickelodeon; Outdoor Channel; QVC; TBS; The Weather Channel; TLC; TNT; USA Network; VH1; WGN America.
Fee: $24.95 installation; $64.95 monthly.
Pay Service 1
Pay Units: N.A.
Programming (via satellite): Cinemax; HBO.
Internet Service
Operational: Yes.
Telephone Service
Digital: Operational
Miles of Plant: 8.0 (coaxial); None (fiber optic). Homes passed: 342.
President & Chief Executive Officer: Gary Shorman. Chief Operating Officer: Kurt K. David. General Manager: Travis Kohlrus. Marketing Manager: Elizabeth Jaeger.
Ownership: Eagle Communications Inc. (MSO).

HYANNIS—Formerly served by Consolidated Cable Inc. No longer in operation. ICA: NE0099.

INDIANOLA—PinPoint Cable TV. Now served by CAMBRIDGE, NE [NE0269]. ICA: NE0109.

JANSEN—Formerly served by Diode Cable Co. No longer in operation. ICA: NE0248.

JOHNSON LAKE—Charter Communications. Now served by KEARNEY, NE [NE0011]. ICA: NE0295.

JUNIATA—Charter Communications. Now served by KEARNEY, NE [NE0011]. ICA: NE0125.

KEARNEY—Charter Communications, 809 Central Ave, Kearney, NE 68847. Phones: 636-207-5100 (Corporate office); 308-234-6428; 507-289-8372 (Rochester administrative office); 314-543-2236. Web Site: http://www.charter.com. Also serves Adams County (portions), Alda, Amherst, Axtell, Bertrand, Cairo, Cozad, Dawson County (portions), Elm Creek, Gibbon, Gothenburg, Grand Island, Hall County (portions), Hastings, Hildreth, Holdrege, Johnson Lake, Juniata, Lexington, Litchfield, Loomis, Loup City, Miller (unincorporated areas), Minden, Odessa, Ord, Overton, Phillips, Pleasanton, Ravenna, Riverdale (village), Shelton, St. Libory, St. Paul, Sumner, Wilcox & Wood River. ICA: NE0011.
TV Market Ranking: 91 (Adams County (portions), Alda, Amherst, Axtell, Bertrand, Cairo, Elm Creek, Gibbon, Grand Island, Hall County (portions), Hastings, Hildreth, Juniata, KEARNEY, Lexington, Litchfield, Loomis, Miller (unincorporated areas), Minden, Odessa, Overton, Phillips, Pleasanton, Ravenna, Riverdale (village), Shelton, St. Libory, Sumner, Wilcox, Wood River; Below 100 (Gothenburg, St. Paul, Lexington (portions)); Outside TV Markets (Cozad, Johnson Lake, Loup City, Ord, Lexington (portions)). Franchise award date: N.A. Franchise expiration date: N.A. Began: May 16, 1983.
Channel capacity: N.A. Channels available but not in use: N.A.
Digital Basic Service
Subscribers: 26,297.
Programming (via satellite): BBC America; Bloomberg Television; Bravo; Discovery Digital Networks; DMX Music; ESPNews; FYI; GSN; History International; IFC; LMN; Nick Jr.; Outdoor Channel; Sundance TV; TeenNick; Turner Classic Movies; WE tv.
Fee: $49.99 installation; $26.99 monthly.
Digital Expanded Basic Service
Subscribers: N.A.
Programming (via satellite): A&E; AMC; Animal Planet; Cartoon Network; CMT; CNBC; CNN; Comedy Central; Discovery Channel; Discovery Life Channel; Disney Channel; Disney XD; ESPN; ESPN Classic; ESPN2; Food Network; Fox News Channel; Fox Sports 1; FOX Sports Midwest; Freeform; FX; Golf Channel; Hallmark Channel; HGTV; History; HLN; Lifetime; MSNBC; MTV; National Geographic Channel; NBCSN; Nickelodeon; Oxygen; Pop; Spike TV; Syfy; TBS; The Weather Channel; TLC; TNT; Travel Channel; Trinity Broadcasting Network (TBN); TV Land; Univision; USA Network; VH1; WGN America.
Fee: $47.99 monthly.
Digital Pay Service 1
Pay Units: N.A.
Programming (via satellite): Cinemax (multiplexed); HBO (multiplexed); Showtime (multiplexed); Starz (multiplexed); The Movie Channel.
Fee: $6.00 monthly (Showtime), $7.00 monthly (Cinemax), $10.34 monthly (HBO).
Video-On-Demand: Yes
Pay-Per-View
iN DEMAND (delivered digitally); Fresh (delivered digitally); Shorteez (delivered digitally); Playboy TV (delivered digitally).
Internet Service
Operational: Yes.
Subscribers: 25,747.
Broadband Service: Charter Internet.
Fee: $29.99 monthly.
Telephone Service
Digital: Operational
Subscribers: 10,427.
Miles of Plant: 1,615.0 (coaxial); 1,121.0 (fiber optic). Homes passed: 76,110.
Vice President & General Manager: John Crowley. Technical Operations Director: Marty Kovarik. Technical Operations Manager: Terry Petzoldt. Marketing Director: Bill Haarstad. Business Manager: Chuck Haase. Office Manager: Dawn Harmon. Accounting Director: David Sovanski.
Ownership: Charter Communications Inc. (MSO).

KENESAW—Charter Communications, 12405 Powerscourt Dr, St. Louis, MO 63131. Phones: 636-207-5100 (Corporate office); 507-289-8372 (Rochester administrative office); 308-389-4070. Fax: 308-382-2047. Web Site: http://www.charter.com. ICA: NE0379.
TV Market Ranking: 91 (KENESAW). Channel capacity: N.A. Channels available but not in use: N.A.
Digital Basic Service
Subscribers: 29.
Programming (received off-air): KHGI-TV (ABC) Kearney; KHNE-TV (PBS) Hastings; KNHL (IND) Hastings; KOLN (CBS, MNT, NBC) Lincoln; KTVG-TV (FOX) Grand Island.
Programming (via satellite): A&E; AMC; CNBC; CNN; Discovery Channel; Disney Channel; E! HD; ESPN; ESPN2; FOX Sports Midwest; Freeform; Great American Country; History; Lifetime; Nickelodeon; Outdoor Channel; Spike TV; Syfy; TBS; The Weather Channel; TLC; TNT; Trinity Broadcasting Network (TBN); TV Land; USA Network; VH1; WGN America.
Fee: $39.99 monthly.
Pay Service 1
Pay Units: N.A.
Programming (via satellite): Cinemax (multiplexed); HBO (multiplexed).
Fee: $10.00 monthly (each).
Video-On-Demand: No
Internet Service
Operational: No.
Telephone Service
None
Miles of Plant: 8.0 (coaxial); None (fiber optic).
Vice President & General Manager: John Crowley. Technical Operations Director: Marty Kovarik. Technical Operations Manager: Terry Petzoldt. Office Manager: Mary Ivers. Accounting Director: David Sovanski.
Ownership: Charter Communications Inc. (MSO).

KIMBALL—Charter Communications. Now served by SIDNEY (town), NE [NE0021]. ICA: NE0032.

LAKE CUNNINGHAM—Formerly served by TelePartners. No longer in operation. ICA: NE0079.

LAKE MALONEY—Formerly served by Charter Communications. No longer in operation. ICA: NE0297.

LAKE VENTURA—Formerly served by Charter Communications. No longer in operation. ICA: NE0298.

LAKE WACONDA—Formerly served by Westcom. No longer in operation. ICA: NE0343.

2017 Edition

Nebraska—Cable Systems

Access the most current data instantly
FREE TRIAL @ www.warren-news.com/factbook.htm

LAUREL—American Broadband. Now served by BLAIR, NE [NE0027]. ICA: NE0121.

LEIGH—Formerly served by TelePartners. No longer in operation. ICA: NE0365.

LEWELLEN—Formerly served by Consolidated Cable Inc. No longer in operation. ICA: NE0156.

LEXINGTON—Charter Communications. Now served by KEARNEY, NE [NE0011]. ICA: NE0022.

LINCOLN—Formerly served by Sprint Corp. No longer in operation. ICA: NE0350.

LINCOLN—Time Warner Cable, 5400 South 16th St, Lincoln, NE 68512-1278. Phones: 402-421-0300 (Customer service); 402-421-0330. Fax: 402-421-0310. Web Site: http://www.timewarnercable.com. Also serves Auburn, Cedar Bluffs, Columbus, Crete, David City, Denton (village), Dodge County, Fairbury, Falls City, Fremont, Humboldt, Inglewood (village), Lancaster County, Nebraska City, Pawnee City, Platte County, Saunders County, Seward, Seward County, Table Rock (village), Tecumseh & York. ICA: NE0002.
TV Market Ranking: 53 (Cedar Bluffs, Dodge County (portions), Fremont, Inglewood (village), Saunders County (portions)); 91 (Crete, Denton (village), Lancaster County, LINCOLN, Seward, Seward County); Outside TV Markets (David City, Nebraska City, Pawnee City, Platte County, Table Rock (village), Tecumseh, Auburn, Columbus, Fairbury, Falls City, York, Dodge County (portions), Saunders County (portions)). Franchise award date: N.A. Franchise expiration date: N.A. Began: September 1, 1968.
Channel capacity: N.A. Channels available but not in use: N.A.
Basic Service
Subscribers: 66,788.
Programming (received off-air): KETV (ABC, MeTV) Omaha; KLKN (ABC) Lincoln; KMTV-TV (Antenna TV, CBS, Escape) Omaha; KOLN (CBS, MNT, NBC) Lincoln; KPTM (Estrella TV, FOX, MNT, This TV) Omaha; KSNB-TV (MeTV, MNT, NBC) Superior; KUON-TV (PBS) Lincoln; KXVO (Azteca America, CW) Omaha; WOWT (IND, NBC) Omaha.
Programming (via satellite): CNN; C-SPAN; C-SPAN 2; Pop; TBS; TLC; WGN America.
Fee: $39.99 installation; $21.99 monthly; $.68 converter.
Expanded Basic Service 1
Subscribers: N.A.
Programming (via satellite): A&E; AMC; Animal Planet; BET; Bravo; Cartoon Network; CMT; CNBC; Comedy Central; Discovery Channel; Disney Channel; E! HD; ESPN; ESPN Classic; ESPN2; EVINE Live; EWTN Global Catholic Network; Food Network; Fox News Channel; FOX Sports Midwest; Freeform; FX; Golf Channel; Hallmark Channel; HGTV; History; HLN; ION Television; Lifetime; LMN; MSNBC; MTV; National Geographic Channel; Nickelodeon; OWN: Oprah Winfrey Network; Oxygen; QVC; Spike TV; Syfy; The Weather Channel; TNT; Travel Channel; truTV; Turner Classic Movies; TV Land; Univision Studios; USA Network; VH1; WE tv.
Fee: $32.05 monthly.
Digital Basic Service
Subscribers: N.A.
Programming (via satellite): BBC America; Bloomberg Television; Boomerang; CNN International; Cooking Channel; C-SPAN 3; Discovery Life Channel; Disney XD; DIY Network; DMX Music; ESPNews; Fox Sports 1; FSN Digital Atlantic; FSN Digital Central; FSN Digital Pacific; Fuse; FXM; FYI; Great American Country; GSN; History International; HITS (Headend In The Sky); IFC; MTV Classic; MTV2; NASA TV; NBA TV; NBCSN; Nick Jr.; Nicktoons; Outdoor Channel; Ovation; TeenNick; Tennis Channel; Trinity Broadcasting Network (TBN).
Digital Pay Service 1
Pay Units: 37,728.
Programming (via satellite): Cinemax (multiplexed); HBO (multiplexed); Showtime (multiplexed); Starz (multiplexed); Starz Encore (multiplexed); The Movie Channel (multiplexed).
Fee: $12.99 monthly (each).
Video-On-Demand: Yes
Pay-Per-View
NBA League Pass (delivered digitally); WNBA Season Pass; NHL Center Ice (delivered digitally); MLB Extra Innings (delivered digitally); iN DEMAND (delivered digitally); Pleasure (delivered digitally); Playboy TV (delivered digitally); Fresh (delivered digitally); Shorteez (delivered digitally); NBA TV (delivered digitally); Hot Choice (delivered digitally).
Internet Service
Operational: Yes, DSL.
Subscribers: 69,253.
Broadband Service: Road Runner.
Fee: $39.95 installation; $44.95 monthly.
Telephone Service
Digital: Operational
Subscribers: 27,262.
Fee: $39.95 monthly
Miles of Plant: 2,860.0 (coaxial); 775.0 (fiber optic). Homes passed: 184,194.
Group Vice President: Beth Scarborough. Vice President, Operations: Dick Cassidy. Senior Engineering Director: John Pokojski. Technical Operations Manager: Rick Hollman. Area Marketing Manager: Sean Heyen. Public Affairs Director: Ann Shrewsbury.
Ownership: Time Warner Cable (MSO).; Advance/Newhouse Partnership (MSO).

LINDSAY—Formerly served by TelePartners. No longer in operation. ICA: NE0366.

LOCHLAND—Formerly served by Glenwood Telecommunications. No longer in operation. ICA: NE0384.

LYMAN—WinDBreak Cable, 1140 10th St, Gering, NE 69341-3239. Phone: 308-436-4650. Fax: 308-436-4779. E-mail: bill@intertech.net. Web Site: http://www.windbreak.com. ICA: NE0180.
TV Market Ranking: Below 100 (LYMAN).
Channel capacity: N.A. Channels available but not in use: N.A.
Basic Service
Subscribers: 2,700.
Programming (received off-air): KGWN-TV (CBS, CW) Cheyenne; KNEP (ABC) Scottsbluff; KSTF (CBS, CW) Scottsbluff; KTNE-TV (PBS) Alliance.
Programming (via satellite): CNN; C-SPAN; Discovery Channel; Fox News Channel; Freeform; Hallmark Channel; KUSA (NBC, WeatherNation) Denver; Spike TV; TBS; The Weather Channel; USA Network.
Fee: $20.20 installation; $49.88 monthly.
Pay Service 1
Pay Units: N.A.
Programming (via satellite): Showtime; The Movie Channel.
Fee: $20.00 installation; $7.95 monthly (each).
Internet Service
Operational: No.
Telephone Service
None
Miles of Plant: 6.0 (coaxial); None (fiber optic).
General Manager & Chief Technician: Bill Bauer. Office Manager: Aubrey Luevano.
Ownership: WinDBreak Cable.

LYNCH—Formerly served by TelePartners. No longer in operation. ICA: NE0367.

LYONS—American Broadband. Now served by BLAIR, NE [NE0027]. ICA: NE0112.

MADRID—Formerly served by Consolidated Cable Inc. No longer in operation. ICA: NE0205.

MALCOLM—Zito Media, 102 S Main St, PO Box 665, Coudersport, PA 16915. Phones: 814-260-9055; 800-365-6988. E-mail: info@zitomedia.com. Web Site: http://www.zitomedia.com. ICA: NE0208.
TV Market Ranking: 91 (MALCOLM). Franchise award date: N.A. Franchise expiration date: N.A. Began: July 1, 1984.
Channel capacity: N.A. Channels available but not in use: N.A.
Basic Service
Subscribers: 4.
Programming (received off-air): KETV (ABC, MeTV) Omaha; KLKN (ABC) Lincoln; KMTV-TV (Antenna TV, CBS, Escape) Omaha; KOLN (CBS, MNT, NBC) Lincoln; KPTM (Estrella TV, FOX, MNT, This TV) Omaha; KUON-TV (PBS) Lincoln; KXVO (Azteca America, CW) Omaha; WOWT (IND, NBC) Omaha.
Programming (via satellite): A&E; Animal Planet; Cartoon Network; CNN; Discovery Channel; Disney Channel; ESPN; FOX Sports Midwest; Freeform; History; Spike TV; TBS; TLC; TNT; USA Network; WGN America.
Fee: $49.95 installation; $41.55 monthly.
Pay Service 1
Pay Units: N.A.
Programming (via satellite): Cinemax; HBO.
Fee: $11.95 monthly (Cinemax), $12.95 monthly (HBO).
Internet Service
Operational: No.
Telephone Service
None
Miles of Plant: 2.0 (coaxial); None (fiber optic). Homes passed: 114.
President: James Rigas.
Ownership: Zito Media (MSO).

MARQUETTE—Mid-State Community TV, 1001 12th St, Aurora, NE 68818-2004. Phones: 800-821-1831; 402-694-5101. Fax: 402-694-2848. E-mail: midstate@midstatetv.com. Web Site: http://www.midstatetv.com. ICA: NE0301.
TV Market Ranking: Below 100 (MARQUETTE).
Channel capacity: N.A. Channels available but not in use: N.A.
Basic Service
Subscribers: 1.
Fee: $29.95 monthly.
President & General Manager: Phillip C. Nelson.
Ownership: Mid-State Community TV Inc. (MSO).

MARTINSBURG (village)—CenCom NNTV. This cable system has converted to IPTV. See JACKSON, NE [NE5019]. ICA: NE0388.

MASON CITY—NCTC Cable. Now served by BURWELL, NE [NE0045]. ICA: NE0302.

MAXWELL—Formerly served by Consolidated Cable Inc. No longer in operation. ICA: NE0303.

McCOOK—Great Plains Communications, 1600 Great Plains Ctr, PO Box 500, Blair, NE 68008-0500. Phones: 888-343-8014; 402-426-9511. Fax: 402-456-6550. E-mail: lquist@gpcom.com. Web Site: http://www.gpcom.com. Also serves Red Willow County (portions). ICA: NE0019.
TV Market Ranking: Below 100 (MCCOOK, Red Willow County (portions)). Franchise award date: N.A. Franchise expiration date: N.A. Began: November 1, 1970.
Channel capacity: N.A. Channels available but not in use: N.A.
Basic Service
Subscribers: 912.
Programming (received off-air): KGIN (CBS, MNT, NBC) Grand Island; KHGI-TV (ABC) Kearney; KLNE-TV (PBS) Lexington; KSNK (NBC) McCook; 4 FMs.
Programming (via satellite): C-SPAN; Discovery Channel; FX; Hallmark Channel; INSP; Lifetime; Pop; QVC; TBS; The Weather Channel; truTV; WGN America.
Fee: $45.00 installation; $23.49 monthly.
Expanded Basic Service 1
Subscribers: 248.
Fee: $45.95 monthly.
Digital Basic Service
Subscribers: N.A.
Programming (via satellite): BBC America; Bloomberg Television; Discovery Digital Networks; DMX Music; EVINE Live; FXM; FYI; GSN; History International; IFC; LMN; NBCSN; Nick Jr.; Outdoor Channel; TeenNick; Trinity Broadcasting Network (TBN); Turner Classic Movies.
Fee: $12.83 monthly.
Digital Pay Service 1
Pay Units: N.A.
Programming (via satellite): Cinemax (multiplexed); HBO (multiplexed); Showtime (multiplexed); Starz (multiplexed); Starz Encore (multiplexed); The Movie Channel (multiplexed).
Video-On-Demand: No

Cable Systems—Nebraska

Pay-Per-View
Hot Choice (delivered digitally); iN DEMAND; iN DEMAND (delivered digitally); Playboy TV (delivered digitally); Fresh (delivered digitally); Shorteez (delivered digitally); sports.
Internet Service
Operational: Yes. Began: February 1, 2003. Fee: $29.99 monthly.
Telephone Service
None
Miles of Plant: 44.0 (coaxial); None (fiber optic). Homes passed: 3,608.
Senior Director: Lea Ann Quist. Chief Technician: Mark Stottler. Marketing Manager: Casey Garrigan.
Ownership: Great Plains Communications Inc. (MSO).

MEAD—Formerly served by TelePartners. No longer in operation. ICA: NE0185.

MEADOW GROVE—Formerly served by USA Communications. No longer in operation. ICA: NE0186.

MINATARE—Charter Communications. Now served by SCOTTSBLUFF, NE [NE0008]. ICA: NE0077.

MINDEN—Charter Communications. Now served by KEARNEY, NE [NE0011]. ICA: NE0037.

MITCHELL—Charter Communications. Now served by SCOTTSBLUFF, NE [NE0008]. ICA: NE0041.

MONROE—Eagle Communications, 2703 Hall St, Ste 15, PO Box 817, Hays, KS 67601. Phone: 785-625-4000. Fax: 785-625-8030. E-mail: support@eaglecom.net. Web Site: http://www.eaglecom.net. ICA: NE0368.
TV Market Ranking: Outside TV Markets (MONROE).
Channel capacity: N.A. Channels available but not in use: N.A.
Basic Service
Subscribers: 24.
Programming (received off-air): KGIN (CBS, MNT, NBC) Grand Island; KHGI-TV (ABC) Kearney; KHNE-TV (PBS) Hastings; KLKN (ABC) Lincoln; KNHL (IND) Hastings; KTVG-TV (FOX) Grand Island; KUON-TV (PBS) Lincoln.
Programming (via satellite): A&E; AMC; Animal Planet; Cartoon Network; CMT; CNBC; CNN; Comedy Central; C-SPAN; C-SPAN 2; Discovery Channel; E! HD; ESPN; ESPN Classic; ESPN2; EWTN Global Catholic Network; Food Network; Fox News Channel; Freeform; FX; Great American Country; Hallmark Channel; HGTV; History; HLN; Lifetime; MSNBC; MTV; NBCSN; Nickelodeon; Outdoor Channel; QVC; Root Sports Rocky Mountain; Spike TV; Syfy; TBS; The Weather Channel; TLC; TNT; Travel Channel; Trinity Broadcasting Network (TBN); truTV; Turner Classic Movies; TV Land; Univision Studios; USA Network; VH1; WGN America.
Fee: $24.99 installation; $64.95 monthly.
Pay Service 1
Pay Units: N.A.
Fee: $10.95 monthly.
Video-On-Demand: No
Internet Service
Operational: Yes.
Telephone Service
None
Miles of Plant: 3.0 (coaxial); None (fiber optic). Homes passed: 122.

President & Chief Executive Officer: Gary Shorman. Chief Operating Officer: Kurt K. David. General Manager: Travis Kohlrus. Marketing Manager: Elizabeth Jaeger.
Ownership: Eagle Communications Inc. (MSO).

MORRILL—Charter Communications. Now served by SCOTTSBLUFF, NE [NE0008]. ICA: NE0076.

NAPER—Three Rivers Digital Cable (formerly Cable Nebraska). Now served by AINSWORTH, NE [NE0049]. ICA: NE0256.

NEHAWKA—Formerly served by Westcom. No longer in operation. ICA: NE0305.

NELSON—Zito Media, 102 S Main St, PO Box 665, Coudersport, PA 16915. Phones: 814-260-9055; 800-365-6988. E-mail: info@zitomedia.com. Web Site: http://www.zitomedia.com. ICA: NE0306.
TV Market Ranking: 91 (NELSON). Franchise award date: May 1, 1999. Franchise expiration date: N.A. Began: N.A.
Channel capacity: N.A. Channels available but not in use: N.A.
Basic Service
Subscribers: 26.
Programming (received off-air): KHGI-TV (ABC) Kearney; KHNE-TV (PBS) Hastings; KNHL (IND) Hastings; KOLN (CBS, MNT, NBC) Lincoln; KSNB-TV (MeTV, MNT, NBC) Superior.
Programming (via satellite): A&E; AMC; Animal Planet; Cartoon Network; CNBC; CNN; C-SPAN; Discovery Channel; Disney Channel; ESPN; ESPN2; FOX Sports Midwest; Freeform; Fuse; FX; Great American Country; HGTV; History; HLN; INSP; Lifetime; Outdoor Channel; QVC; TBS; The Weather Channel; TLC; TNT; USA Network; WGN America.
Fee: $45.80 monthly.
Pay Service 1
Pay Units: N.A.
Programming (via satellite): Cinemax.
Pay Service 2
Pay Units: 24.
Programming (via satellite): Showtime.
Internet Service
Operational: No.
Telephone Service
None
Miles of Plant: 9.0 (coaxial); None (fiber optic). Homes passed: 250.
President: James Rigas.
Ownership: Zito Media (MSO).

NEWCASTLE—CenCom NNTV. This cable system has converted to IPTV. See JACKSON, NE [NE5019]. ICA: NE0198.

NEWMAN GROVE—Eagle Communications, 2703 Hall St, Ste 15, PO Box 817, Hays, KS 67601. Phone: 785-625-4000. Fax: 785-625-8030. E-mail: support@eaglecom.net. Web Site: http://www.eaglecom.net. ICA: NE0097.
TV Market Ranking: Outside TV Markets (NEWMAN GROVE). Franchise award date: N.A. Franchise expiration date: N.A. Began: December 1, 1983.
Channel capacity: N.A. Channels available but not in use: N.A.
Basic Service
Subscribers: 128.
Programming (received off-air): KGIN (CBS, MNT, NBC) Grand Island; KHGI-TV (ABC) Kearney; KHNE-TV (PBS) Hastings; KLKN (ABC) Lincoln; KNHL (IND) Hastings; KTVG-TV (FOX) Grand Island.
Programming (via satellite): C-SPAN; C-SPAN 2; EWTN Global Catholic Network; Freeform; Hallmark Channel; HLN; Pop; QVC; TBS; The Weather Channel; Trinity Broadcasting Network (TBN); WGN America.
Fee: $24.95 installation; $64.95 monthly.
Expanded Basic Service 1
Subscribers: N.A.
Programming (via satellite): A&E; AMC; Animal Planet; Cartoon Network; CMT; CNBC; CNN; Comedy Central; Discovery Channel; E! HD; ESPN; ESPN2; Food Network; Fox News Channel; FOX Sports Midwest; FX; Great American Country; HGTV; History; ION Television; Lifetime; MSNBC; MTV; Nickelodeon; Outdoor Channel; Spike TV; Syfy; TLC; TNT; Travel Channel; truTV; Turner Classic Movies; TV Land; Univision Studios; USA Network; VH1; WE tv.
Digital Basic Service
Subscribers: N.A.
Programming (via satellite): BBC America; Bloomberg Television; Discovery Life Channel; DMX Music; ESPN Classic; ESPNews; EVINE Live; Fox Sports 1; FSN Digital Atlantic; FSN Digital Central; FSN Digital Pacific; FXM; FYI; Golf Channel; GSN; History; History International; HITS (Headend In The Sky); International Television (ITV); MBC America; National Geographic Channel; NBCSN; Nick Jr.; Outdoor Channel; Ovation; Syfy; TeenNick; Trinity Broadcasting Network (TBN).
Fee: $14.00 monthly.
Digital Pay Service 1
Pay Units: N.A.
Programming (via satellite): Cinemax (multiplexed); Flix; FXM; HBO (multiplexed); IFC; LMN; Showtime (multiplexed); Starz (multiplexed); Sundance TV; The Movie Channel (multiplexed); WAM! America's Kidz Network.
Fee: $17.00 monthly.
Video-On-Demand: No
Pay-Per-View
iN DEMAND (delivered digitally); ESPN Now (delivered digitally); Hot Choice (delivered digitally); Playboy TV (delivered digitally); Shorteez (delivered digitally).
Internet Service
Operational: Yes.
Broadband Service: Cable Nebraska.
Telephone Service
Digital: Operational
Miles of Plant: 6.0 (coaxial); None (fiber optic). Homes passed: 412.
President & Chief Executive Officer: Gary Shorman. Chief Operating Officer: Kurt K. David. General Manager: Travis Kohlrus. Marketing Manager: Elizabeth Jaeger.
Ownership: Eagle Communications Inc. (MSO).

NICKERSON—Formerly served by TelePartners. No longer in operation. ICA: NE0369.

NORFOLK—Cable One, 100 North Victory Rd, Norfolk, NE 68701-6800. Phone: 402-379-2330. Fax: 402-379-4224. E-mail: mdrahota@cableone.net. Web Site: http://www.cableone.net. Also serves Battle Creek, Beemer, Hadar, Hoskins, Madison, Pierce, Pilger, Randolph, Tilden, West Point, Wisner & Woodland Park. ICA: NE0006.
TV Market Ranking: Outside TV Markets (Battle Creek, Beemer, Hadar, Hoskins, Madison, NORFOLK, Pierce, Pilger, Randolph, Tilden, West Point, Wisner, Woodland Park). Franchise award date: July 16, 1979. Franchise expiration date: N.A. Began: April 1, 1980.
Channel capacity: N.A. Channels available but not in use: N.A.
Basic Service
Subscribers: 6,704.
Programming (received off-air): KCAU-TV (ABC) Sioux City; KETV (ABC, MeTV) Omaha; KMEG (Azteca America, CBS, Decades) Sioux City; KMTV-TV (Antenna TV, CBS, Escape) Omaha; KPTH (FOX, MNT, This TV) Sioux City; KTIV (CW, MeTV, NBC) Sioux City; KXVO (Azteca America, CW) Omaha; KYNE-TV (PBS) Omaha; WOWT (IND, NBC) Omaha; 25 FMs.
Programming (via satellite): C-SPAN; C-SPAN 2; EWTN Global Catholic Network; Pop; QVC; WGN America.
Fee: $55.00 installation; $20.00 monthly.
Expanded Basic Service 1
Subscribers: N.A.
Programming (via satellite): A&E; AMC; Animal Planet; Cartoon Network; CMT; CNBC; CNN; Comedy Central; Discovery Channel; Disney Channel; ESPN; ESPN2; Food Network; Fox News Channel; FOX Sports Midwest; Freeform; FX; HGTV; History; HLN; Lifetime; MSNBC; MTV; Nickelodeon; Spike TV; Syfy; TBS; The Weather Channel; TLC; TNT; Turner Classic Movies; TV Land; Univision Studios; USA Network; VH1.
Digital Basic Service
Subscribers: N.A.
Programming (via satellite): 3ABN; A&E HD; Boomerang; BYUtv; Cine Mexicano; CNN en Espanol; Discovery Kids Channel; Disney XD; ESPN Classic; ESPN Deportes; ESPN HD; ESPN2 HD; ESPNews; FamilyNet; Food Network HD; FOX College Sports Central; FOX College Sports Pacific; Fox Deportes; Fox Sports 1; Fox Sports 2; FXM; FYI; Golf Channel; Great American Country; GSN; Hallmark Channel; HD Theater; HGTV HD; History International; INSP; La Familia Cosmovision; MC; National Geographic Channel; National Geographic Channel HD; NBC Universo; Outdoor Channel; OWN: Oprah Winfrey Network; Science Channel; TBS HD; Telemundo; TNT HD; Toon Disney en Espanol; Trinity Broadcasting Network (TBN); TVG Network; Universal HD; WE tv.
Fee: $9.95 monthly.
Digital Pay Service 1
Pay Units: N.A.
Programming (via satellite): Cinemax (multiplexed); HBO (multiplexed); HBO HD; Showtime (multiplexed); Showtime HD; Starz; Starz Encore (multiplexed); Sundance TV; The Movie Channel (multiplexed); The Movie Channel HD.
Fee: $7.00 monthly (each).
Video-On-Demand: No
Pay-Per-View
iN DEMAND (delivered digitally); SexSee (delivered digitally); Juicy; VaVoom (delivered digitally).
Internet Service
Operational: Yes. Began: July 29, 2003.
Subscribers: 6,068.
Broadband Service: CableONE.net.
Fee: $75.00 installation; $43.00 monthly.
Telephone Service
Digital: Operational
Subscribers: 2,231.
Fee: $39.95 monthly
Miles of Plant: 628.0 (coaxial); 225.0 (fiber optic). Homes passed: 20,070.
General Manager: Mike Drahota. Chief Technician: Scott Owens.
Ownership: Cable ONE Inc. (MSO).

Nebraska—Cable Systems

NORTH BEND—Great Plains Communications, 1600 Great Plains Ctr, PO Box 500, Blair, NE 68008-0500. Phones: 402-426-9511; 888-343-8014. Fax: 402-456-6550. E-mail: lquist@gpcom.com. Web Site: http://www.gpcom.com. Also serves Dodge, Scribner & Snyder. ICA: NE0080.

TV Market Ranking: Outside TV Markets (Dodge, NORTH BEND, Scribner, Snyder). Franchise award date: November 1, 1984. Franchise expiration date: N.A. Began: N.A.

Channel capacity: N.A. Channels available but not in use: N.A.

Basic Service
Subscribers: 546.
Programming (received off-air): KETV (ABC, MeTV) Omaha; KLKN (ABC) Lincoln; KMTV-TV (Antenna TV, CBS, Escape) Omaha; KOLN (CBS, MNT, NBC) Lincoln; KPTM (Estrella TV, FOX, MNT, This TV) Omaha; KUON-TV (PBS) Lincoln; KXVO (Azteca America, CW) Omaha; WOWT (IND, NBC) Omaha.
Programming (via satellite): A&E; AMC; Animal Planet; CMT; CNN; Discovery Channel; Disney Channel; ESPN; Freeform; HLN; Lifetime; Nickelodeon; QVC; Root Sports Rocky Mountain; Spike TV; Syfy; TBS; The Weather Channel; TLC; TNT; Travel Channel; TV Land; USA Network; WGN America.
Fee: $45.00 installation; $23.49 monthly.

Expanded Basic Service 1
Subscribers: N.A.
Programming (via satellite): Cartoon Network; Comedy Central; ESPN2; HGTV; History; NBCSN; Turner Classic Movies; VH1.
Fee: $47.99 monthly.

Digital Basic Service
Subscribers: N.A.
Programming (via satellite): BBC America; Bravo; Discovery Digital Networks; DMX Music; ESPN Classic; Fox Sports 1; FYI; Golf Channel; History International; IFC; LMN; Nick Jr.; TeenNick; Turner Classic Movies; WE tv.
Fee: $47.95 monthly.

Pay Service 1
Pay Units: N.A.
Programming (via satellite): HBO; Showtime.
Fee: $9.95 monthly (Showtime), $10.95 monthly (HBO).

Digital Pay Service 1
Pay Units: N.A.
Programming (via satellite): Cinemax (multiplexed); HBO (multiplexed); Showtime (multiplexed); Starz (multiplexed); Starz Encore (multiplexed); The Movie Channel (multiplexed).
Fee: $12.00 monthly.

Video-On-Demand: No

Pay-Per-View
iN DEMAND (delivered digitally).

Internet Service
Operational: Yes, DSL & dial-up.
Broadband Service: In-house.
Fee: $49.95 installation; $39.95 monthly.

Telephone Service
Digital: Operational
Miles of Plant: 13.0 (coaxial); None (fiber optic).
Senior Director: Lea Ann Quist. Chief Technician: Mark Stottler. Marketing Manager: Casey Garrigan.
Ownership: Great Plains Communications Inc. (MSO).

NORTH LOUP—NCTC Cable. Now served by BURWELL, NE [NE0045]. ICA: NE0209.

NORTH PLATTE—Charter Communications, 1510 East 4th St, North Platte, NE 69101. Phones: 636-207-5100 (Corporate office); 308-696-1222; 314-543-2236; 507-289-8372 (Rochester administrative office). Web Site: http://www.charter.com. Also serves Keith County (portions), Lincoln County (portions) & Ogallala. ICA: NE0009.

TV Market Ranking: Below 100 (Lincoln County (portions) (portions), NORTH PLATTE); Outside TV Markets (Keith County (portions), Lincoln County (portions) (portions), Ogallala). Franchise award date: N.A. Franchise expiration date: N.A. Began: August 1, 1970.

Channel capacity: N.A. Channels available but not in use: N.A.

Digital Basic Service
Subscribers: 5,355.
Programming (via satellite): BBC America; Bloomberg Television; Bravo; Discovery Digital Networks; DMX Music; ESPN Classic; FXM; FYI; Golf Channel; GSN; History; History International; IFC; LMN; Nick Jr.; Outdoor Channel; Ovation; Sundance TV; Syfy; TeenNick; Trinity Broadcasting Network (TBN); Turner Classic Movies; WE tv.
Fee: $49.99 installation; $26.99 monthly.

Digital Expanded Basic Service
Subscribers: N.A.
Programming (via satellite): A&E; AMC; Animal Planet; Cartoon Network; CMT; CNBC; CNN; Comedy Central; Disney Channel; Disney XD; E! HD; ESPN; ESPN2; Food Network; Fox News Channel; Fox Sports 1; FOX Sports Midwest; Freeform; FX; Great American Country; Hallmark Channel; HGTV; HLN; INSP; Lifetime; MSNBC; MTV; National Geographic Channel; NBCSN; Nickelodeon; Spike TV; TBS; Telemundo; The Weather Channel; TLC; TNT; Travel Channel; truTV; TV Land; USA Network; VH1.
Fee: $47.99 monthly.

Digital Pay Service 1
Pay Units: N.A.
Programming (via satellite): Cinemax (multiplexed); HBO (multiplexed); Showtime (multiplexed); Starz (multiplexed); Starz Encore (multiplexed); The Movie Channel (multiplexed).

Video-On-Demand: Yes

Pay-Per-View
Hot Choice (delivered digitally); iN DEMAND (delivered digitally); Playboy TV (delivered digitally); Fresh (delivered digitally); Shorteez (delivered digitally); sports.

Internet Service
Operational: Yes.
Subscribers: 5,913.
Broadband Service: Charter Internet.
Fee: $29.99 monthly.

Telephone Service
Digital: Operational
Subscribers: 2,289.
Miles of Plant: 114.0 (coaxial); None (fiber optic). Homes passed: 9,892.
Vice President & General Manager: John Crowley. Technical Operations Director: Marty Kovarik. Technical Operations Manager: Joel Saunders. Office Manager: Cathi Wentink. Accounting Director: David Sovanski.
Ownership: Charter Communications Inc. (MSO).

OAKLAND—American Broadband. Now served by BLAIR, NE [NE0027]. ICA: NE0074.

OBERT/MASKELL—CenCom NNTV. This cable system has converted to IPTV. See JACKSON, NE [NE5019]. ICA: NE0387.

OCONTO—Great Plains Cable TV. Now served by BROKEN BOW, NE [NE0031]. ICA: NE0309.

OGALLALA—Charter Communications. Now served by NORTH PLATTE, NE [NE0009]. ICA: NE0025.

OMAHA—CenturyLink Prism. Formerly Qwest [NE0377]. This cable system has converted to IPTV., 125 South Dakota Ave, Sioux Falls, SD 57104. Phones: 800-475-7526; 605-334-0044. E-mail: prismtveverywhere@centurylink.net. Web Site: http://www.centurylink.com/prismtv. Also serves Carter Lake, Council Bluffs & Pottawattamie County (portions), IA; Bellevue, Douglas County (unincorporated areas), Gretna, La Vista, Papillion, Ralston, Sarpy County (unincorporated areas) & Springfield, NE. ICA: NE5000.

TV Market Ranking: 53 (Bellevue, Carter Lake, Council Bluffs, Douglas County (unincorporated areas), Gretna, La Vista, OMAHA, Papillion, Sarpy County (unincorporated areas)); 91 (Springfield).

Channel capacity: N.A. Channels available but not in use: N.A.

Prism Essential
Subscribers: 15,042. Commercial subscribers: 16.
Fee: $34.99 monthly. Includes 140+ channels including music channels.

Prism Complete
Subscribers: N.A.
Fee: $39.99 monthly. Includes 190+ channels including music channels.

Prism Preferred
Subscribers: N.A.
Fee: $49.99 monthly. Includes 290+ channels including Showtime/TMC & Starz/Encore.

Prism Premium
Subscribers: N.A.
Fee: $79.99 monthly. Includes 320+ channels including all premium movie channels.

Prism Paquette Latino
Subscribers: N.A.
Fee: $8.49 monthly.

Cinemax
Subscribers: N.A.
Fee: $12.99 monthly.

HBO
Subscribers: N.A.
Fee: $14.99 monthly.

Showtime
Subscribers: N.A.
Fee: $14.99 monthly.

Starz/Encore
Subscribers: N.A.
Fee: $12.99 monthly.

Video-On-Demand: Yes

Internet Service
Operational: Yes.
Fee: $29.95 monthly.

Telephone Service
Digital: Operational
Vice President, Operations: Julie Darlington.
Ownership: CenturyLink (MSO).

OMAHA—Cox Communications, 6205 Peachtree Dunwoody Rd, 12th Floor, Atlanta, GA 30328. Phone: 402-933-2000. Web Site: http://www.cox.com. Also serves Carter Lake & Council Bluffs, IA; Bellevue, Bennington, Douglas County, Elkhorn, Gretna, La Vista, Papillion, Ralston, Sarpy County (unincorporated areas), Valley & Waterloo, NE. ICA: NE0001. **Note:** This system is an overbuild.

TV Market Ranking: 53 (Bellevue, Bennington, Carter Lake, Council Bluffs, Elkhorn, La Vista, OMAHA, Papillion, Ralston, Valley, Waterloo); 53,91 (Douglas County, Gretna, Sarpy County (unincorporated areas)). Franchise award date: September 4, 1981. Franchise expiration date: N.A. Began: September 4, 1981.

Channel capacity: 61 (operating 2-way). Channels available but not in use: N.A.

Basic Service
Subscribers: 169,045.
Programming (received off-air): KETV (ABC, MeTV) Omaha; KHIN (PBS) Red Oak; KMTV-TV (Antenna TV, CBS, Escape) Omaha; KPTM (Estrella TV, FOX, MNT, This TV) Omaha; KXVO (Azteca America, CW) Omaha; KYNE-TV (PBS) Omaha; WOWT (IND, NBC) Omaha.
Programming (via satellite): Cox Sports Television; C-SPAN; C-SPAN 2; EWTN Global Catholic Network; Jewelry Television; Pop; QVC; TBS; TLC; Univision Studios; WGN America; WOWT 6 News.
Fee: $38.95 installation; $21.99 monthly.

Expanded Basic Service 1
Subscribers: N.A.
Programming (via satellite): A&E; AMC; Animal Planet; BET; Bravo; Cartoon Network; CMT; CNBC; CNN; Comedy Central; Discovery Channel; Disney Channel; E! HD; ESPN; ESPN2; Food Network; Fox News Channel; Freeform; FX; Golf Channel; HGTV; History; HLN; ION Television; Lifetime; MSNBC; MTV; Nickelodeon; Root Sports Rocky Mountain; Spike TV; Syfy; Telemundo; The Weather Channel; TNT; Travel Channel; Turner Classic Movies; TV Land; USA Network; VH1.
Fee: $30.79 monthly.

Digital Basic Service
Subscribers: N.A.
Programming (via satellite): A&E HD; AMC HD; Animal Planet HD; Azteca; Bandamax; BBC America; Bloomberg Television; Boomerang; Bravo HD; Chiller; Cinelatino; CMT; CMT HD; CNBC HD+; CNN en Espanol; CNN HD; Cooking Channel; De Pelicula; De Pelicula Clasico; Destination America; Destination America HD; Discovery Channel HD; Discovery Kids Channel; Discovery Life Channel; Disney XD; DIY Network; ESPN Classic; ESPN Deportes; ESPN HD; ESPN2 HD; ESPNews; ESPNU; Flix; Food Network HD; Fox Deportes; Fox Sports 1; Fox Sports 2; Fuse; FYI; Golf Channel HD; GolTV; Great American Country; GSN; Hallmark Channel; Hallmark Movie Channel HD; HD Theater; HGTV HD; History en Espanol; History HD; History International; IFC; INSP; Investigation Discovery; Lifetime HD; Lifetime Movie Network HD; LMN; MC; MTV Classic; MTV Hits; MTV Jams; MTV Live; MTV2; mtvU; Nat Geo WILD; National Geographic Channel; National Geographic Channel HD; NBA TV; NBC Universo; NBCSN; NFL Network; NFL Network HD; NHL Network; Nick HD; Nick Jr.; Nicktoons; NickToons en Espanol; Outdoor Channel; OWN: Oprah Winfrey Network; Oxygen; Ritmoson; Root Sports Rocky Mountain; Science Channel; Science HD; Spike TV HD; Sprout; Starz Encore; Starz Encore Family; Sundance TV; Syfy HD; TBS HD; TeenNick; Telehit; Telemundo; TLC HD; TNT HD; Tr3s; Travel Channel HD; Trinity Broadcasting Network (TBN); truTV; TV One; UniMas; Universal HD; Univision; UP; USA Network HD; Versus HD; VH1 HD; WGN America.

Cable Systems—Nebraska

Pay Service 1
Pay Units: N.A.
Programming (via satellite): HBO.
Fee: $16.99 monthly.

Digital Pay Service 1
Pay Units: N.A.
Programming (via satellite): Cinemax (multiplexed); Cinemax HD; HBO (multiplexed); HBO HD; Showtime (multiplexed); Showtime HD; Starz (multiplexed); Starz HD; The Movie Channel (multiplexed).
Fee: $8.95 monthly (Cinemax/Cinemax HD, Starz/Starz HDTV or Showtime/Showtime HD), $10.95 monthly (HBO/HBO HD or TMC).

Video-On-Demand: Yes

Pay-Per-View
iN DEMAND (delivered digitally); Playboy TV (delivered digitally); Club Jenna (delivered digitally); Spice: Xcess (delivered digitally); Juicy (delivered digitally); SexSee (delivered digitally).

Internet Service
Operational: Yes. Began: September 1, 1997.
Subscribers: 189,330.
Broadband Service: Cox High Speed Internet.
Fee: $149.95 installation; $29.99-$59.99 monthly; $15.00 modem lease; $219.00 modem purchase.

Telephone Service
Digital: Operational
Subscribers: 127,553.
Fee: $15.89 monthly
Miles of Plant: 7,751.0 (coaxial); 2,328.0 (fiber optic). Homes passed: 362,356.
Vice President & General Manager: Percy Kirk. Vice President, Network Operations: Joe Seda. Vice President, Public & Government Affairs: Kristin Pec. Vice President, Tax: Mary Vickers.
Ownership: Cox Communications Inc. (MSO).

OMAHA—Formerly served by Digital Broadcast Corp. No longer in operation. ICA: NE0354.

OMAHA (western portion)—CenturyLink (formerly Qwest Choice TV.) This cable system has converted to IPTV. See Omaha, NE [NE5000]. ICA: NE0377.

O'NEILL—Three Rivers Digital Cable (formerly Cable Nebraska). Now served by AINSWORTH, NE [NE0049]. ICA: NE0030.

ORCHARD—Formerly served by TelePartners. No longer in operation. ICA: NE0370.

ORD—Charter Communications. Now served by KEARNEY, NE [NE0011]. ICA: NE0310.

ORLEANS—Formerly served by PinPoint Cable TV. No longer in operation. ICA: NE0143.

OSCEOLA—Eagle Communications, 2703 Hall St, Ste 15, PO Box 817, Hays, KS 67601. Phone: 785-625-4000. Fax: 785-625-8030. E-mail: support@eaglecom.net. Web Site: http://www.eaglecom.net. ICA: NE0089.
TV Market Ranking: Outside TV Markets (OSCEOLA). Franchise award date: N.A. Franchise expiration date: N.A. Began: April 1, 1982.
Channel capacity: N.A. Channels available but not in use: N.A.

Basic Service
Subscribers: 102.
Programming (received off-air): KGIN (CBS, MNT, NBC) Grand Island; KHGI-TV (ABC) Kearney; KHNE-TV (PBS) Hastings; KLKN (ABC) Lincoln; KNHL (IND) Hastings; KTVG-TV (FOX) Grand Island.
Programming (via satellite): C-SPAN; C-SPAN 2; CW PLUS; EWTN Global Catholic Network; MyNetworkTV; QVC; TBS; The Weather Channel; Trinity Broadcasting Network (TBN); Univision Studios; WGN America.
Fee: $24.95 installation; $64.95 monthly.

Expanded Basic Service 1
Subscribers: N.A.
Programming (via satellite): A&E; AMC; Animal Planet; Cartoon Network; CMT; CNBC; CNN; Comedy Central; Discovery Channel; E! HD; ESPN; ESPN Classic; ESPN2; Food Network; Fox News Channel; FOX Sports Midwest; Freeform; FX; Great American Country; Hallmark Channel; HGTV; History; HLN; ION Television; Lifetime; MSNBC; MTV; NBCSN; Nickelodeon; Outdoor Channel; RFD-TV; Spike TV; Syfy; TLC; TNT; Travel Channel; truTV; Turner Classic Movies; TV Land; USA Network; VH1.

Digital Basic Service
Subscribers: N.A.
Programming (via satellite): BBC America; Bloomberg Television; Cine Mexicano; Cinelatino; Cloo; CMT; CNN en Espanol; Daystar TV Network; Destination America; Discovery Channel HD; Discovery Kids Channel; Discovery Life Channel; DMX Music; ESPN Classic; ESPN Deportes; ESPN HD; ESPN2; ESPNews; EVINE Live; FOX College Sports Central; FOX College Sports Pacific; Fox Deportes; Fox Sports 1; FXM; FYI; Golf Channel; GSN; History; History en Espanol; History International; Investigation Discovery; LMN; MTV Classic; MTV Hits; MTV2; NBCSN; Nick Jr.; Outdoor Channel; Ovation; OWN: Oprah Winfrey Network; Science Channel; Syfy; TBS HD; TeenNick; TNT HD; Tr3s; Trinity Broadcasting Network (TBN); VH1 Soul; ViendoMovies; WE tv.
Fee: $14.00 monthly.

Digital Pay Service 1
Pay Units: N.A.
Programming (via satellite): Cinemax (multiplexed); Flix; HBO (multiplexed); HBO Latino; Showtime (multiplexed); Starz (multiplexed); Starz Encore (multiplexed); The Movie Channel (multiplexed).

Video-On-Demand: No

Pay-Per-View
iN DEMAND (delivered digitally); Hot Choice (delivered digitally); Playboy TV (delivered digitally); Fresh (delivered digitally); Spice: Xcess (delivered digitally); Club Jenna (delivered digitally).

Internet Service
Operational: Yes.
Broadband Service: Cable Nebraska.

Telephone Service
Digital: Operational
Miles of Plant: 9.0 (coaxial); None (fiber optic). Homes passed: 429.
President & Chief Executive Officer: Gary Shorman. Chief Operating Officer: Kurt K. David. General Manager: Travis Kohlrus. Marketing Manager: Elizabeth Jaeger.
Ownership: Eagle Communications Inc. (MSO).

OSHKOSH—WinDBreak Cable, 1140 10th St, Gering, NE 69341-3239. Phone: 308-436-4650. Web Site: http://www.windbreak.com. ICA: NE0090.
TV Market Ranking: Outside TV Markets (OSHKOSH). Franchise award date: N.A. Franchise expiration date: N.A. Began: January 1, 1968.
Channel capacity: N.A. Channels available but not in use: N.A.

Basic Service
Subscribers: N.A.
Programming (received off-air): KNEP (ABC) Scottsbluff; KRNE-TV (PBS) Merriman; allband FM.
Programming (via satellite): C-SPAN; EWTN Global Catholic Network; INSP; KCNC-TV (CBS, Decades) Denver; KTVD (MeTV, MNT) Denver; KUSA (NBC, WeatherNation) Denver; KWGN-TV (CW, This TV) Denver; QVC; Trinity Broadcasting Network (TBN); WGN America.
Fee: $39.24 installation; $30.95 monthly.

Expanded Basic Service 1
Subscribers: N.A.
Programming (via satellite): A&E; AMC; Animal Planet; Bravo; Cartoon Network; CMT; CNBC; CNN; Comedy Central; Discovery Channel; Disney Channel; Disney XD; E! HD; ESPN; ESPN2; Food Network; Fox News Channel; Fox Sports 1; Freeform; FX; Golf Channel; Hallmark Channel; HGTV; History; HLN; Lifetime; MSNBC; MTV; National Geographic Channel; NBCSN; Nickelodeon; Outdoor Channel; Oxygen; Root Sports Rocky Mountain; Spike TV; Syfy; TBS; The Weather Channel; TLC; TNT; Travel Channel; truTV; Turner Classic Movies; TV Land; USA Network; VH1.
Fee: $15.86 monthly.

Digital Basic Service
Subscribers: N.A.
Programming (via satellite): BBC America; Bloomberg Television; Discovery Digital Networks; DIY Network; FYI; GSN; History International; IFC; LMN; MC; Nick 2; Nick Jr.; Sundance TV; TeenNick; TV Guide Interactive Inc.; WE tv.

Pay Service 1
Pay Units: N.A.
Programming (via satellite): Cinemax; Showtime; Starz Encore.
Fee: $3.65 monthly (Encore), $9.70 monthly (Showtime), $11.66 monthly (Cinemax).

Digital Pay Service 1
Pay Units: N.A.
Programming (via satellite): Cinemax (multiplexed); Flix; HBO (multiplexed); Showtime (multiplexed); Starz (multiplexed); Starz Encore (multiplexed); The Movie Channel (multiplexed).

Video-On-Demand: No

Pay-Per-View
iN DEMAND (delivered digitally); Pleasure (delivered digitally); ETC (delivered digitally).

Internet Service
Operational: Yes, DSL & dial-up.
Fee: $49.95 installation; $39.95 monthly.

Telephone Service
None
Miles of Plant: 15.0 (coaxial); None (fiber optic).
General Manager & Chief Technician: Bill Bauer. Office Manager: Cheryl McLean.
Ownership: WinDBreak Cable (MSO).

OSMOND—Formerly served by HunTel Cablevision. Now served by American Broadband, WAYNE, NE [NE0374]. ICA: NE0119.

OTOE—Formerly served by CableDirect. No longer in operation. ICA: NE0237.

OXFORD—PinPoint Cable TV. Now served by CAMBRIDGE, NE [NE0269]. ICA: NE0092.

PAGE (village)—Formerly served by Sky Scan Cable Co. No longer in operation. ICA: NE0311.

PALMER—Eagle Communications, 2703 Hall St, Ste 15, PO Box 817, Hays, KS 67601. Phone: 785-625-4000. Fax: 785-625-8030. E-mail: support@eaglecom.net. Web Site: http://www.eaglecom.net. ICA: NE0313.
TV Market Ranking: Below 100 (PALMER). Franchise award date: N.A. Franchise expiration date: N.A. Began: January 1, 1988.
Channel capacity: N.A. Channels available but not in use: N.A.

Basic Service
Subscribers: 59.
Programming (received off-air): KGIN (CBS, MNT, NBC) Grand Island; KHGI-TV (ABC) Kearney; KHNE-TV (PBS) Hastings; KLKN (ABC) Lincoln; KNHL (IND) Hastings; KTVG-TV (FOX) Grand Island.
Programming (via satellite): C-SPAN; C-SPAN 2; EWTN Global Catholic Network; MyNetworkTV; QVC; TBS; The Weather Channel; Trinity Broadcasting Network (TBN); Univision Studios; WGN America; WPIX (Antenna TV, CW, This TV) New York.
Fee: $24.95 installation; $64.95 monthly.

Expanded Basic Service 1
Subscribers: N.A.
Programming (via satellite): A&E; AMC; Animal Planet; Cartoon Network; CMT; CNBC; CNN; Comedy Central; Discovery Channel; E! HD; ESPN; ESPN Classic; ESPN2; Food Network; Fox News Channel; FOX Sports Networks; Freeform; FX; Great American Country; Hallmark Channel; HGTV; History; HLN; ION Television; Lifetime; MSNBC; MTV; NBCSN; Nickelodeon; Outdoor Channel; RFD-TV; Spike TV; Syfy; TLC; TNT; Travel Channel; truTV; Turner Classic Movies; TV Land; USA Network; VH1.

Digital Basic Service
Subscribers: N.A.
Programming (via satellite): BBC America; Bloomberg Television; Cine Mexicano; Cinelatino; Cloo; CMT; CNN en Espanol; Daystar TV Network; Destination America; Discovery Channel HD; Discovery Kids Channel; Discovery Life Channel; DMX Music; ESPN Classic; ESPN Deportes; ESPN HD; ESPN2; ESPNews; EVINE Live; FOX College Sports Central; FOX College Sports Pacific; Fox Deportes; Fox Sports 1; FXM; FYI; Golf Channel; GSN; History; History en Espanol; History International; Investigation Discovery; LMN; MTV Classic; MTV Hits; MTV2; NBCSN; Nick Jr.; Outdoor Channel; Ovation; OWN: Oprah Winfrey Network; Science Channel; Syfy; TBS HD; TeenNick; TNT HD; Tr3s; Trinity

Nebraska—Cable Systems

Broadcasting Network (TBN); VH1 Soul; ViendoMovies; WE tv.
Fee: $14.00 monthly.
Digital Pay Service 1
Pay Units: N.A.
Programming (via satellite): Cinemax (multiplexed); Flix; HBO (multiplexed); HBO Latino; Showtime (multiplexed); Starz (multiplexed); Starz Encore (multiplexed); The Movie Channel (multiplexed).
Video-On-Demand: No
Pay-Per-View
iN DEMAND (delivered digitally); Hot Choice (delivered digitally); Playboy TV (delivered digitally); Fresh (delivered digitally); Spice; Xcess (delivered digitally); Club Jenna (delivered digitally).
Internet Service
Operational: Yes.
Broadband Service: Cable Nebraska.
Fee: $35.95 monthly.
Telephone Service
Digital: Operational
President & Chief Executive Officer: Gary Shorman. Chief Operating Officer: Kurt K. David. General Manager: Travis Kohlrus. Marketing Manager: Elizabeth Jaeger.
Ownership: Eagle Communications Inc. (MSO).

PAXTON—Eagle Communications, 2703 Hall St, Ste 15, PO Box 817, Hays, KS 67601. Phone: 785-625-4000. Fax: 785-625-8030. E-mail: support@eaglecom.net. Web Site: http://www.eaglecom.net. ICA: NE0162.
TV Market Ranking: Below 100 (PAXTON).
Franchise award date: N.A. Franchise expiration date: N.A. Began: February 1, 1985.
Channel capacity: N.A. Channels available but not in use: N.A.
Basic Service
Subscribers: 66.
Programming (received off-air): KETV (ABC, MeTV) Omaha; KNOP-TV (NBC) North Platte; KOLN (CBS, MNT, NBC) Lincoln; KPNE-TV (PBS) North Platte; KWNB-TV (ABC) Hayes Center.
Programming (via satellite): A&E; AMC; CNN; Discovery Channel; Disney Channel; ESPN; Freeform; Lifetime; QVC; Spike TV; TBS; TNT; USA Network; WGN America.
Fee: $24.95 installation; $47.95 monthly.
Pay Service 1
Pay Units: N.A.
Programming (via satellite): HBO.
Fee: $14.00 monthly.
Video-On-Demand: No
Internet Service
Operational: No.
Telephone Service
None
Homes passed: 206.
President & Chief Executive Officer: Gary Shorman. Chief Operating Officer: Kurt K. David. General Manager: Travis Kohlrus. Marketing Manager: Elizabeth Jaeger.
Ownership: Eagle Communications Inc. (MSO).

PENDER—Formerly served by HunTel Cablevision. Now served by American Broadband, WAYNE, NE [NE0374]. ICA: NE0096.

PERU—Zito Media, 102 S Main St, PO Box 665, Coudersport, PA 16915. Phones: 814-260-9055; 800-365-6988. E-mail: info@zitomedia.com. Web Site: http://www.zitomedia.com. ICA: NE0103.
TV Market Ranking: Outside TV Markets (PERU). Franchise award date: N.A. Franchise expiration date: N.A. Began: N.A.
Channel capacity: N.A. Channels available but not in use: N.A.
Basic Service
Subscribers: 11.
Programming (received off-air): KETV (ABC, MeTV) Omaha; KMTV-TV (Antenna TV, CBS, Escape) Omaha; KOLN (CBS, MNT, NBC) Lincoln; KPTM (Estrella TV, FOX, MNT, This TV) Omaha; KUON-TV (PBS) Lincoln; KXVO (Azteca America, CW) Omaha; WOWT (IND, NBC) Omaha.
Programming (via satellite): A&E; Cartoon Network; CNN; Comedy Central; Discovery Channel; Disney Channel; Disney XD; E! HD; ESPN; ESPN2; Fox News Channel; FOX Sports Midwest; Freeform; Fuse; Great American Country; HGTV; HLN; Lifetime; Outdoor Channel; TBS; The Weather Channel; TNT; Travel Channel; USA Network.
Fee: $49.95 installation; $44.20 monthly.
Pay Service 1
Pay Units: N.A.
Programming (via satellite): Cinemax; HBO.
Fee: $11.95 monthly (Cinemax), $12.95 monthly (HBO).
Internet Service
Operational: No.
Telephone Service
None
Miles of Plant: 6.0 (coaxial); None (fiber optic). Homes passed: 320.
President: James Rigas.
Ownership: Zito Media (MSO).

PICKRELL—Formerly served by Comstar Cable TV Inc. No longer in operation. ICA: NE0315.

PILGER—Formerly served by Sky Scan Cable Co. Now served by Cable One, NORFOLK, NE [NE0006]. ICA: NE0316.

PLATTE CENTER—Eagle Communications, 2703 Hall St, Ste 15, PO Box 817, Hays, KS 67601. Phone: 785-625-4000. Fax: 785-625-8030. E-mail: support@eaglecom.net. Web Site: http://www.eaglecom.net. ICA: NE0391.
TV Market Ranking: Outside TV Markets (PLATTE CENTER).
Channel capacity: N.A. Channels available but not in use: N.A.
Basic Service
Subscribers: 24.
Programming (received off-air): KLKN (ABC) Lincoln; KOLN (CBS, MNT, NBC) Lincoln; KPTM (Estrella TV, FOX, MNT, This TV) Omaha; KUON-TV (PBS) Lincoln; KXVO (Azteca America, CW) Omaha; WOWT (IND, NBC) Omaha.
Programming (via satellite): A&E; AMC; Cartoon Network; CNN; Discovery Channel; ESPN; ESPN2; Fox News Channel; Freeform; Great American Country; Hallmark Channel; HGTV; History; HLN; Lifetime; NBCSN; Nickelodeon; Outdoor Channel; QVC; Spike TV; TBS; The Weather Channel; TLC; TNT; USA Network; WGN America.
Fee: $24.95 installation; $64.95 monthly.
Pay Service 1
Pay Units: N.A.
Programming (via satellite): HBO.
Internet Service
Operational: No.
Telephone Service
None
President & Chief Executive Officer: Gary Shorman. Chief Operating Officer: Kurt K. David. General Manager: Travis Kohlrus. Marketing Manager: Elizabeth Jaeger.
Ownership: Eagle Communications Inc. (MSO).

PLATTE CENTER—Formerly served by TelePartners. No longer in operation. ICA: NE0371.

POLK—Eagle Communications, 2703 Hall St, Ste 15, PO Box 817, Hays, KS 67601. Phone: 785-625-4000. Fax: 785-625-8030. E-mail: support@eaglecom.net. Web Site: http://www.eaglecom.net. ICA: NE0140.
TV Market Ranking: Below 100 (POLK). Franchise award date: N.A. Franchise expiration date: N.A. Began: February 1, 1983.
Channel capacity: N.A. Channels available but not in use: N.A.
Basic Service
Subscribers: 29.
Programming (received off-air): KGIN (CBS, MNT, NBC) Grand Island; KHGI-TV (ABC) Kearney; KHNE-TV (PBS) Hastings; KLKN (ABC) Lincoln; KNHL (IND) Hastings; KTVG-TV (FOX) Grand Island.
Programming (via satellite): C-SPAN; C-SPAN 2; EWTN Global Catholic Network; MyNetworkTV; QVC; TBS; The Weather Channel; Trinity Broadcasting Network (TBN); Univision Studios; WGN America.
Fee: $24.95 installation; $64.95 monthly.
Expanded Basic Service 1
Subscribers: N.A.
Programming (via satellite): A&E; AMC; Animal Planet; Cartoon Network; CMT; CNBC; CNN; Comedy Central; Discovery Channel; E! HD; ESPN; ESPN Classic; ESPN2; Food Network; Fox News Channel; FOX Sports Midwest; Freeform; FX; Great American Country; Hallmark Channel; HGTV; History; HLN; ION Television; Lifetime; MSNBC; MTV; NBCSN; Nickelodeon; Outdoor Channel; RFD-TV; Spike TV; Syfy; TLC; TNT; Travel Channel; truTV; Turner Classic Movies; TV Land; USA Network; VH1.
Digital Basic Service
Subscribers: N.A.
Programming (via satellite): BBC America; Bloomberg Television; Cine Mexicano; Cinelatino; Cloo; CMT; CNN en Espanol; Daystar TV Network; Destination America; Discovery Channel HD; Discovery Kids Channel; Discovery Life Channel; DMX Music; ESPN Classic; ESPN Deportes; ESPN HD; ESPNews; EVINE Live; FOX College Sports Central; FOX College Sports Pacific; Fox Deportes; Fox Sports 1; FXM; FYI; Golf Channel; GSN; History; History en Espanol; History International; Investigation Discovery; LMN; MTV Classic; MTV Hits; MTV2; NBCSN; Nick Jr.; Outdoor Channel; Ovation; OWN: Oprah Winfrey Network; Science Channel; Syfy; TBS HD; TeenNick; TNT HD; Tr3s; Trinity Broadcasting Network (TBN); VH1 Soul; ViendoMovies; WE tv.
Fee: $14.00 monthly.
Digital Pay Service 1
Pay Units: N.A.
Programming (via satellite): Cinemax (multiplexed); Flix; HBO (multiplexed); HBO Latino; Showtime (multiplexed); Starz (multiplexed); Starz Encore (multiplexed); The Movie Channel.
Video-On-Demand: No
Pay-Per-View
iN DEMAND (delivered digitally); Hot Choice (delivered digitally); Playboy TV (delivered digitally); Fresh (delivered digitally); Spice; Xcess (delivered digitally); Club Jenna (delivered digitally).
Internet Service
Operational: Yes.
Broadband Service: Cable Nebraska.
Telephone Service
Digital: Operational
Miles of Plant: 4.0 (coaxial); None (fiber optic). Homes passed: 194.
President & Chief Executive Officer: Gary Shorman. Chief Operating Officer: Kurt K. David. General Manager: Travis Kohlrus. Marketing Manager: Elizabeth Jaeger.
Ownership: Eagle Communications Inc. (MSO).

PONCA—Great Plains Communications, 1600 Great Plains Ctr, PO Box 500, Blair, NE 68008-0500. Phone: 855-853-1483. Fax: 402-426-6099. E-mail: lquist@gpcom.com. Web Site: http://www.gpcom.com. ICA: NE0318.
Channel capacity: N.A. Channels available but not in use: N.A.
Basic Service
Subscribers: 251.
Fee: $45.00 installation; $23.49 monthly.
Expanded Basic Service 1
Subscribers: N.A.
Fee: $47.95 monthly.
Senior Director: Lea Ann Quist.
Ownership: Great Plains Communications Inc. (MSO).

PRAGUE (village)—Formerly served by Westcom. No longer in operation. ICA: NE0221.

RAYMOND—Formerly served by Zito Media. No longer in operation. ICA: NE0250.

RED CLOUD—Eagle Communications, 2703 Hall St, Ste 15, PO Box 817, Hays, KS 67601. Phone: 785-625-4000. Fax: 785-625-8030. E-mail: support@eaglecom.net. Web Site: http://www.eaglecom.net. ICA: NE0393.
TV Market Ranking: Outside TV Markets (RED CLOUD).
Channel capacity: N.A. Channels available but not in use: N.A.
Basic Service
Subscribers: 115.
Fee: $24.95 installation; $49.95 monthly.
President & Chief Executive Officer: Gary Shorman. Chief Operating Officer: Kurt K. David. General Manager: Travis Kohlrus. Marketing Manager: Elizabeth Jaeger.
Ownership: Eagle Communications Inc. (MSO).

RED CLOUD—Formerly served by PinPoint Cable TV. No longer in operation. ICA: NE0321.

REPUBLICAN CITY—Formerly served by PinPoint Cable TV. No longer in operation. ICA: NE0234.

RICHLAND—Formerly served by Eagle Communications. No longer in operation. ICA: NE0390.

RISING CITY—Eagle Communications, 2703 Hall St, Ste 15, PO Box 817, Hays, KS 67601. Phone: 785-625-4000. Fax: 785-625-8030. E-mail: support@eaglecom.net. Web Site: http://www.eaglecom.net. ICA: NE0394.
TV Market Ranking: Below 100 (RISING CITY).
Channel capacity: N.A. Channels available but not in use: N.A.
Basic Service
Subscribers: 67.
Fee: $24.95 installation; $64.95 monthly.

Cable Systems—Nebraska

President & Chief Executive Officer: Gary Shorman. Chief Operating Officer: Kurt K. David. General Manager: Travis Kohlrus. Marketing Manager: Elizabeth Jaeger. Ownership: Eagle Communications Inc. (MSO).

RULO—Formerly served by CableDirect. No longer in operation. ICA: NE0207.

RUSKIN—Formerly served by Diode Cable Co. No longer in operation. ICA: NE0246.

SALEM—Formerly served by CableDirect. No longer in operation. ICA: NE0242.

SARGENT—NCTC Cable. Now served by BURWELL, NE [NE0045]. ICA: NE0081.

SCHUYLER—Eagle Communications, 2703 Hall St, Ste 15, PO Box 817, Hays, KS 67601. Phone: 785-625-4000. Fax: 785-625-8030. E-mail: support@eaglecom.net. Web Site: http://www.eaglecom.net. ICA: NE0039.
TV Market Ranking: Outside TV Markets (SCHUYLER). Franchise award date: N.A. Franchise expiration date: N.A. Began: November 1, 1980.
Channel capacity: N.A. Channels available but not in use: N.A.

Basic Service
Subscribers: 287.
Programming (received off-air): KETV (ABC, MeTV) Omaha; KLKN (ABC) Lincoln; KMTV-TV (Antenna TV, CBS, Escape) Omaha; KOLN (CBS, MNT, NBC) Lincoln; KPTM (Estrella TV, FOX, MNT, This TV) Omaha; KUON-TV (PBS) Lincoln; KXVO (Azteca America, CW) Omaha; WOWT (IND, NBC) Omaha.
Programming (via satellite): EWTN Global Catholic Network; MyNetworkTV; QVC; TBS; Telemundo; The Weather Channel; UniMas; Univision; Univision Studios; WGN America; WPIX (Antenna TV, CW, This TV) New York.
Fee: $24.95 installation; $64.95 monthly.

Expanded Basic Service 1
Subscribers: N.A.
Programming (via satellite): A&E; Animal Planet; Cartoon Network; CMT; CNBC; CNN; Comedy Central; Discovery Channel; E! HD; ESPN; ESPN Classic; ESPN2; Food Network; Fox News Channel; FOX Sports Midwest; Freeform; FX; Great American Country; Hallmark Channel; HGTV; History; HLN; ION Television; Lifetime; MSNBC; MTV; NBCSN; Nickelodeon; Outdoor Channel; RFD-TV; Spike TV; Syfy; TLC; TNT; Travel Channel; truTV; Turner Classic Movies; TV Land; USA Network; VH1.

Digital Basic Service
Subscribers: N.A.
Programming (via satellite): Alterna'TV; AZ TV; BBC America; Bloomberg Television; Cloo; CMT; Daystar TV Network; Destination America; Discovery Channel HD; Discovery Kids Channel; Discovery Life Channel; DMX Music; ESPN HD; ESPNews; EVINE Live; FOX College Sports Central; FOX College Sports Pacific; Fox Sports 1; FXM; FYI; Golf Channel; GSN; History International; Investigation Discovery; MBC America; MTV Classic; MTV Hits; MTV2; MyNetworkTV; Nick Jr.; Outdoor Channel; Ovation; OWN: Oprah Winfrey Network; Science Channel; TBS HD; TeenNick; TNT HD; Trinity Broadcasting Network (TBN); VH1 Soul; WE tv.
Fee: $14.00 monthly.

Pay Service 1
Pay Units: N.A.
Programming (via satellite): HBO Latino.

Digital Pay Service 1
Pay Units: N.A.
Programming (via satellite): Cinemax (multiplexed); Flix; HBO (multiplexed); LMN; Showtime (multiplexed); Starz (multiplexed); Starz Encore (multiplexed); The Movie Channel (multiplexed).
Fee: $3.00 monthly (Cinemax/HBO), $10 monthly (Showtime/TMC/Flix).

Video-On-Demand: No

Pay-Per-View
iN DEMAND (delivered digitally); Hot Choice (delivered digitally); Playboy TV (delivered digitally); Fresh (delivered digitally); Spice: Xcess (delivered digitally); Club Jenna (delivered digitally).

Internet Service
Operational: Yes.
Broadband Service: Cable Nebraska.
Fee: $42.95 monthly.

Telephone Service
Digital: Operational
Miles of Plant: 32.0 (coaxial); None (fiber optic). Homes passed: 1,778.
President & Chief Executive Officer: Gary Shorman. Chief Operating Officer: Kurt K. David. General Manager: Travis Kohlrus. Marketing Manager: Elizabeth Jaeger. Ownership: Eagle Communications Inc. (MSO).

SCOTIA—NCTC Cable. Now served by BURWELL, NE [NE0045]. ICA: NE0217.

SCOTTSBLUFF—Charter Communications, 1602 Ave A, Scottsbluff, NE 69361. Phones: 314-543-2236; 636-207-5100 (Corporate office); 308-632-5700 (Scottsbluff office); 507-289-8372 (Rochester administrative office). Web Site: http://www.charter.com. Also serves Alliance, Bayard, Box Butte County (portions), Bridgeport, Gering, Melbeta, Minatare, Mitchell, Morrill, Scotts Bluff County (portions) & Terrytown. ICA: NE0008.
TV Market Ranking: Below 100 (Bayard, Box Butte County (portions), Bridgeport, Gering, Melbeta, Minatare, Mitchell, Morrill, Scotts Bluff County (portions), SCOTTSBLUFF, Terrytown). Outside TV Markets (Box Butte County (portions), Alliance). Franchise award date: N.A. Franchise expiration date: N.A. Began: February 1, 1960.
Channel capacity: N.A. Channels available but not in use: N.A.

Digital Basic Service
Subscribers: 7,124.
Programming (via satellite): BBC America; Bloomberg Television; Discovery Life Channel; Disney XD; DIY Network; ESPN Classic; ESPNews; Fox Deportes; Fox Sports 2; Fuse; FXM; FYI; GSN; History International; IFC; LMN; MC; Nick 2; Nick Jr.; Nicktoons; Outdoor Channel; Sundance TV; TeenNick; Trinity Broadcasting Network (TBN); TV Guide Interactive Inc.; WE tv.
Fee: $49.99 installation; $26.99 monthly.

Digital Expanded Basic Service
Subscribers: N.A.
Programming (via satellite): A&E; AMC; Animal Planet; Bravo; Cartoon Network; CMT; CNBC; CNN; Comedy Central; Discovery Channel; Disney Channel; E! HD; ESPN; ESPN2; Food Network; Fox News Channel; Fox Sports 1; Freeform; FX; Golf Channel; Great American Country; Hallmark Channel; HGTV; History; HLN; Lifetime; MSNBC; MTV; National Geographic Channel; NBCSN; Nickelodeon; Oxygen; Root Sports Rocky Mountain; Spike TV; Syfy; TBS; Telemundo; The Weather Channel; TLC; TNT; Travel Channel; truTV; Turner Classic Movies; TV Land; Univision; Univision Studios; USA Network; VH1.
Fee: $47.99 monthly.

Digital Pay Service 1
Pay Units: N.A.
Programming (via satellite): Cinemax (multiplexed); Flix; HBO (multiplexed); Showtime (multiplexed); Starz (multiplexed); Starz Encore (multiplexed); The Movie Channel (multiplexed).
Fee: $20.00 installation.

Video-On-Demand: Yes

Pay-Per-View
iN DEMAND (delivered digitally); Hot Choice (delivered digitally); Playboy TV (delivered digitally); Fresh (delivered digitally); Shorteez (delivered digitally).

Internet Service
Operational: Yes.
Subscribers: 6,158.
Broadband Service: Charter Internet.
Fee: $29.99 monthly.

Telephone Service
Digital: Operational
Subscribers: 2,657.
Miles of Plant: 486.0 (coaxial); 430.0 (fiber optic). Homes passed: 22,744.
Vice President & General Manager: John Crowley. Technical Operations Director: Marty Kovarik. Technical Operations Manager: Joel Saunders. Marketing Director: Bill Haarstad. Accounting Director: David Sovanski.
Ownership: Charter Communications Inc. (MSO).

SHELBY—Eagle Communications, 2703 Hall St, Ste 15, PO Box 817, Hays, KS 67601. Phone: 785-625-4000. Fax: 785-625-8030. E-mail: support@eaglecom.net. Web Site: http://www.eaglecom.net. ICA: NE0118.
TV Market Ranking: Outside TV Markets (SHELBY). Franchise award date: N.A. Franchise expiration date: N.A. Began: April 1, 1982.
Channel capacity: N.A. Channels available but not in use: N.A.

Basic Service
Subscribers: 91.
Programming (received off-air): KGIN (CBS, MNT, NBC) Grand Island; KHGI-TV (ABC) Kearney; KHNE-TV (PBS) Hastings; KLKN (ABC) Lincoln; KNHL (IND) Hastings; KTVG-TV (FOX) Grand Island.
Programming (via satellite): C-SPAN; C-SPAN 2; EWTN Global Catholic Network; MyNetworkTV; QVC; TBS; The Weather Channel; Trinity Broadcasting Network (TBN); Univision Studios; WGN America.
Fee: $24.95 installation; $64.95 monthly.

Expanded Basic Service 1
Subscribers: N.A.
Programming (via satellite): A&E; AMC; Animal Planet; Cartoon Network; CMT; CNBC; CNN; Comedy Central; Discovery Channel; E! HD; ESPN; ESPN Classic; ESPN2; Food Network; Fox News Channel; FOX Sports Midwest; Freeform; FX; Great American Country; Hallmark Channel; HGTV; History; HLN; ION Television; Lifetime; MSNBC; MTV; NBCSN; Nickelodeon; Outdoor Channel; RFD-TV; Spike TV; Syfy; TLC; TNT; Travel Channel; truTV; Turner Classic Movies; TV Land; USA Network; VH1.

Digital Basic Service
Subscribers: N.A.
Programming (via satellite): BBC America; Bloomberg Television; Cine Mexicano; Cinelatino; Cloo; CMT; CNN en Espanol; Daystar TV Network; Destination America; Discovery Channel HD; Discovery Kids Channel; Discovery Life Channel; DMX Music; ESPN Classic; ESPN Deportes; ESPN HD; ESPN2; EVINE Live; FOX College Sports Central; FOX College Sports Pacific; Fox Deportes; Fox Sports 1; FXM; FYI; Golf Channel; GSN; History; History en Espanol; History International; Investigation Discovery; LMN; MTV Classic; MTV Hits; MTV2; NBCSN; Nick Jr.; Outdoor Channel; Ovation; OWN: Oprah Winfrey Network; Science Channel; Syfy; TBS HD; TeenNick; TNT HD; Tr3s; Trinity Broadcasting Network (TBN); VH1 Soul; ViendoMovies; WE tv.
Fee: $14.00 monthly.

Digital Pay Service 1
Pay Units: N.A.
Programming (via satellite): Cinemax (multiplexed); Flix; HBO (multiplexed); HBO Latino; Showtime (multiplexed); Starz (multiplexed); Starz Encore (multiplexed); The Movie Channel (multiplexed).

Video-On-Demand: No

Pay-Per-View
iN DEMAND (delivered digitally); Hot Choice (delivered digitally); Playboy TV (delivered digitally); Fresh (delivered digitally); Spice: Xcess (delivered digitally); Club Jenna (delivered digitally).

Internet Service
Operational: Yes.
Broadband Service: Cable Nebraska.

Telephone Service
Digital: Operational
Miles of Plant: 6.0 (coaxial); None (fiber optic). Homes passed: 325.
President & Chief Executive Officer: Gary Shorman. Chief Operating Officer: Kurt K. David. General Manager: Travis Kohlrus. Marketing Manager: Elizabeth Jaeger.
Ownership: Eagle Communications Inc. (MSO).

SHUBERT—Formerly served by CableDirect. No longer in operation. ICA: NE0224.

SIDNEY (town)—Charter Communications, PO Box 298, Sidney, NE 69149. Phones: 314-543-2236; 636-207-5100 (Corporate office); 507-289-8372 (Rochester administrative office). Web Site: http://www.charter.com. Also serves Cheyenne County (portions), Kimball & Kimball County (portions). ICA: NE0021.
TV Market Ranking: Below 100 (Cheyenne County (portions) (portions), Kimball County (portions) (portions), SIDNEY (TOWN)); Outside TV Markets (Cheyenne County (portions) (portions), Kimball County (portions) (portions), Kimball). Franchise award date: N.A. Franchise expiration date: N.A. Began: September 1, 1958.
Channel capacity: N.A. Channels available but not in use: N.A.

Digital Basic Service
Subscribers: 1,673.
Programming (via satellite): BBC America; Bloomberg Television; Bravo; Discovery Digital Networks; DMX Music; ESPN Classic; Fox Sports 1; Fuse; FXM; FYI; Golf Channel; GSN; History International; IFC; LMN; NBCSN; Nick Jr.; Outdoor Channel; TeenNick; Trinity Broadcasting Network (TBN); Turner Classic Movies; TV Guide Interactive Inc.; WE tv.
Fee: $49.99 installation; $26.99 monthly.

2017 Edition — D-495

Nebraska—Cable Systems

Digital Expanded Basic Service
Subscribers: N.A.
Programming (via satellite): A&E; AMC; Animal Planet; Cartoon Network; CMT; CNBC; CNN; Comedy Central; Discovery Channel; Discovery Life Channel; Disney Channel; Disney XD; E! HD; ESPN; ESPN2; Food Network; Fox News Channel; Freeform; FX; Great American Country; Hallmark Channel; HGTV; History; HLN; Lifetime; MSNBC; MTV; National Geographic Channel; Nickelodeon; Oxygen; Root Sports Rocky Mountain; Spike TV; Syfy; TBS; The Weather Channel; TLC; TNT; Travel Channel; truTV; TV Land; USA Network; VH1.
Fee: $47.99 monthly.

Digital Pay Service 1
Pay Units: N.A.
Programming (via satellite): Cinemax (multiplexed); Flix; HBO (multiplexed); Showtime (multiplexed); Starz (multiplexed); Starz Encore (multiplexed); The Movie Channel (multiplexed).

Video-On-Demand: Yes

Pay-Per-View
iN DEMAND (delivered digitally); Hot Choice (delivered digitally); Playboy TV (delivered digitally); Fresh (delivered digitally); Shorteez (delivered digitally).

Internet Service
Operational: Yes.
Broadband Service: Charter Internet.
Fee: $29.99 monthly.

Telephone Service
Digital: Operational
Miles of Plant: 54.0 (coaxial); None (fiber optic). Homes passed: 2,926.
Vice President & General Manager: John Crowley. Technical Operations Director: Marty Kovarik. Technical Operations Manager: Joel Saunders. Marketing Director: Bill Haarstad. Accounting Director: David Sovanski.
Ownership: Charter Communications Inc. (MSO).

SILVER CREEK (village)—Eagle Communications, 2703 Hall St, Ste 15, PO Box 817, Hays, KS 67601. Phone: 785-625-4000. Fax: 785-625-8030. E-mail: support@eaglecom.net. Web Site: http://www.eaglecom.net. ICA: NE0324.
TV Market Ranking: Outside TV Markets (SILVER CREEK (VILLAGE)). Franchise award date: N.A. Franchise expiration date: N.A. Began: N.A.
Channel capacity: N.A. Channels available but not in use: N.A.

Basic Service
Subscribers: 28.
Programming (received off-air): KHGI-TV (ABC) Kearney; KHNE-TV (PBS) Hastings; KLKN (ABC) Lincoln; KNHL (IND) Hastings; KOLN (CBS, MNT, NBC) Lincoln; KPTM (Estrella TV, FOX, MNT, This TV) Omaha.
Programming (via satellite): A&E; AMC; Animal Planet; Cartoon Network; CNN; Discovery Channel; ESPN; FOX Sports Midwest; Freeform; HGTV; History; Lifetime; Nickelodeon; Outdoor Channel; QVC; TBS; The Weather Channel; TLC; TNT; USA Network; WGN America.
Fee: $24.95 installation; $64.95 monthly.

Pay Service 1
Pay Units: N.A.
Programming (via satellite): HBO; Showtime; The Movie Channel.
Fee: $6.95 monthly (TMC), $7.95 monthly (Showtime), $12.95 monthly (HBO).

Internet Service
Operational: Yes.

Telephone Service
None
Miles of Plant: 4.0 (coaxial); None (fiber optic). Homes passed: 197.
President & Chief Executive Officer: Gary Shorman. Chief Operating Officer: Kurt K. David. General Manager: Travis Kohlrus. Marketing Manager: Elizabeth Jaeger.
Ownership: Eagle Communications Inc. (MSO).

SPALDING—Eagle Communications, 2703 Hall St, Ste 15, PO Box 817, Hays, KS 67601. Phone: 785-625-4000. Fax: 785-625-8030. E-mail: support@eaglecom.net. Web Site: http://www.eaglecom.net. ICA: NE0326.
TV Market Ranking: Outside TV Markets (SPALDING). Franchise award date: October 1, 1989. Franchise expiration date: N.A. Began: N.A.
Channel capacity: N.A. Channels available but not in use: N.A.

Basic Service
Subscribers: 88.
Programming (received off-air): KGIN (CBS, MNT, NBC) Grand Island; KHGI-TV (ABC) Kearney; KHNE-TV (PBS) Hastings; KLKN (ABC) Lincoln; KNHL (IND) Hastings.
Programming (via satellite): C-SPAN; C-SPAN 2; EWTN Global Catholic Network; Freeform; Hallmark Channel; HLN; Pop; QVC; TBS; The Weather Channel; Trinity Broadcasting Network (TBN); WGN America.
Fee: $24.95 installation; $64.95 monthly.

Expanded Basic Service 1
Subscribers: N.A.
Programming (via satellite): A&E; AMC; Animal Planet; Cartoon Network; CMT; CNBC; CNN; Comedy Central; Discovery Channel; E! HD; ESPN; ESPN2; Fox News Channel; FOX Sports Networks; FX; Great American Country; HGTV; History; ION Television; Lifetime; MSNBC; MTV; Nickelodeon; Outdoor Channel; Spike TV; TLC; TNT; Travel Channel; truTV; Turner Classic Movies; TV Land; Univision Studios; USA Network; VH1.
Fee: $19.25 monthly.

Digital Basic Service
Subscribers: N.A.
Programming (via satellite): BBC America; Bloomberg Television; Discovery Life Channel; DMX Music; ESPN Classic; ESPN2; ESPNews; EVINE Live; Fox Sports 1; FSN Digital Atlantic; FSN Digital Central; FSN Digital Pacific; FXM; FYI; Golf Channel; GSN; History; History International; HITS (Head-end In The Sky); International Television (ITV); MBC America; National Geographic Channel; NBCSN; Nick Jr.; Outdoor Channel; Ovation; Syfy; TeenNick; Trinity Broadcasting Network (TBN).
Fee: $14.00 monthly.

Digital Pay Service 1
Pay Units: N.A.
Programming (via satellite): Cinemax (multiplexed); Flix; FXM; HBO (multiplexed); IFC; Showtime (multiplexed); Starz (multiplexed); Starz Encore (multiplexed); Sundance TV; The Movie Channel (multiplexed); WE tv.
Fee: $13.00 monthly (each).

Video-On-Demand: No

Pay-Per-View
iN DEMAND (delivered digitally); Hot Choice (delivered digitally); Playboy TV (delivered digitally); Fresh (delivered digitally); Shorteez (delivered digitally); ESPN Now (delivered digitally); Sports PPV (delivered digitally).

Internet Service
Operational: Yes.
Broadband Service: Cable Nebraska.
Fee: $35.95 monthly.

Telephone Service
None
President & Chief Executive Officer: Gary Shorman. Chief Operating Officer: Kurt K. David. General Manager: Travis Kohlrus. Marketing Manager: Elizabeth Jaeger.
Ownership: Eagle Communications Inc. (MSO).

SPENCER—CenCom NNTV. This cable system has converted to IPTV. See JACKSON, NE [NE5019]. ICA: NE0147.

SPRINGFIELD—Charter Communications, PO Box 1448, Kearney, NE 68848. Phones: 636-207-5100 (Corporate office); 314-543-2236; 507-289-8372 (Rochester administrative office); 308-236-1500. Web Site: http://www.charter.com. Also serves Ashland, Cass County (portions), Greenwood, Louisville, Plattsmouth, Wahoo & Waverly. ICA: NE0020.
TV Market Ranking: 53 (Ashland, Louisville, Plattsmouth, Wahoo, Waverly); 53,91 (Cass County (portions) (portions)); 91 (SPRINGFIELD). Franchise award date: January 20, 1981. Franchise expiration date: N.A. Began: January 20, 1981.
Channel capacity: N.A. Channels available but not in use: N.A.

Digital Basic Service
Subscribers: 2,738.
Programming (via satellite): BBC America; Bravo; Discovery Digital Networks; DMX Music; ESPN Classic; ESPNews; Fox Sports 1; FYI; Golf Channel; GSN; History International; IFC; LMN; NBCSN; Starz Encore; WE tv.
Fee: $49.99 installation; $26.99 monthly.

Digital Expanded Basic Service
Subscribers: N.A.
Programming (via satellite): A&E; AMC; Animal Planet; Cartoon Network; CNBC; CNN; Comedy Central; Discovery Channel; Disney Channel; E! HD; ESPN; ESPN2; FOX Sports Midwest; Freeform; FX; Great American Country; HGTV; History; HLN; INSP; Lifetime; MSNBC; MTV; Nickelodeon; QVC; Spike TV; Syfy; TBS; The Weather Channel; TLC; TNT; Turner Classic Movies; TV Land; USA Network; VH1.
Fee: $47.99 monthly.

Digital Pay Service 1
Pay Units: N.A.
Programming (via satellite): Cinemax (multiplexed); HBO (multiplexed); Showtime (multiplexed); Starz (multiplexed); The Movie Channel (multiplexed).
Fee: $10.50 monthly (each).

Video-On-Demand: Yes

Pay-Per-View
iN DEMAND (delivered digitally); Playboy TV (delivered digitally).

Internet Service
Operational: Yes.
Broadband Service: Charter Internet.
Fee: $29.99 monthly.

Telephone Service
Digital: Operational
Miles of Plant: 62.0 (coaxial); 22.0 (fiber optic). Homes passed: 4,608.
Vice President & General Manager: John Crowley. Technical Operations Director: Marty Kovarik. Technical Operations Manager: Terry Petzoldt. Office Manager: Dawn Harmon. Accounting Director: David Sovanski.
Ownership: Charter Communications Inc. (MSO).

SPRINGFIELD (portions)—Formerly served by TelePartners. No longer in operation. ICA: NE0382.

ST. EDWARD—Eagle Communications, 2703 Hall St, Ste 15, PO Box 817, Hays, KS 67601. Phone: 785-625-4000. Fax: 785-625-8030. E-mail: support@eaglecom.net. Web Site: http://www.eaglecom.net. ICA: NE0104.
TV Market Ranking: Outside TV Markets (ST. EDWARD).
Channel capacity: N.A. Channels available but not in use: N.A.

Basic Service
Subscribers: 139.
Fee: $24.95 installation; $64.95 monthly.
President & Chief Executive Officer: Gary Shorman. Chief Operating Officer: Kurt K. David. General Manager: Travis Kohlrus. Marketing Manager: Elizabeth Jaeger.
Ownership: Eagle Communications Inc. (MSO).

STAMFORD (town)—Formerly served by PinPoint Cable TV. No longer in operation. ICA: NE0239.

STANTON—Stanton Telecom, 1004 Ivy St., PO Box 716, Stanton, NE 68779. Phones: 800-411-2264; 402-439-2264; 402-439-5000. Fax: 402-439-7777. E-mail: info@stanton.net. Web Site: http://www.stantontelecom.com. ICA: NE0066.
TV Market Ranking: Outside TV Markets (STANTON). Franchise award date: N.A. Franchise expiration date: N.A. Began: February 15, 1982.
Channel capacity: N.A. Channels available but not in use: N.A.

Basic Service
Subscribers: 445.
Programming (received off-air): KETV (ABC, MeTV) Omaha; KLKN (ABC) Lincoln; KMEG (Azteca America, CBS, Decades) Sioux City; KMTV-TV (Antenna TV, CBS, Escape) Omaha; KPTM (Estrella TV, FOX, MNT, This TV) Omaha; KTIV (CW, MeTV, NBC) Sioux City.
Programming (via satellite): A&E; AMC; Animal Planet; Cartoon Network; CMT; CNBC; CNN; Comedy Central; CW PLUS; Discovery Channel; Disney Channel; ESPN; ESPN Classic; ESPN2; Food Network; Fox News Channel; FOX Sports Midwest; Freeform; FX; Golf Channel; Great American Country; HGTV; History International; Lifetime; MSNBC; MTV; National Geographic Channel; Nickelodeon; Outdoor Channel; Spike TV; Syfy; TBS; The Weather Channel; TLC; TNT; Travel Channel; Turner Classic Movies; TV Land; USA Network; VH1; WGN America.
Fee: $50.00 installation; $48.99 monthly.

Pay Service 1
Pay Units: N.A.
Programming (via satellite): HBO; The Movie Channel.
Fee: $12.50 installation; $9.50 monthly (TMC), $10.50 monthly (HBO).

Video-On-Demand: No

Internet Service
Operational: Yes.

Telephone Service
Digital: Operational
Miles of Plant: 18.0 (coaxial); None (fiber optic). Homes passed: 630.
President: Leona Paden. Vice President & General Manager: Bob Paden. Marketing & Public Relations Director: Judy Throener. Outside Plant Manager: Steve Hansen. Office Manager: Colleen Paden.
Ownership: Cable TV of Stanton.

Cable Systems—Nebraska

STAPLEHURST (village)—Formerly served by Zito Media. No longer in operation. ICA: NE0222.

STEINAUER—Formerly served by CableDirect. No longer in operation. ICA: NE0376.

STELLA (town)—Formerly served by StellaVision. No longer in operation. ICA: NE0216.

STRATTON—Peregrine Communications, 14818 West 6th Ave, Ste 16A, Golden, CO 80401-6585. Phones: 303-278-9660; 800-359-9660. Fax: 303-278-9685. E-mail: peregrine.info@perecom.com. Web Site: http://www.perecom.com. ICA: NE0328.
TV Market Ranking: Below 100 (STRATTON). Franchise award date: N.A. Franchise expiration date: N.A. Began: July 1, 1985.
Channel capacity: 12 (not 2-way capable). Channels available but not in use: N.A.
Basic Service
  Subscribers: 40.
  Programming (received off-air): KBSL-DT (CBS) Goodland; KHGI-TV (ABC) Kearney; KLNE-TV (PBS) Lexington; KSNK (NBC) McCook; KWNB-TV (ABC) Hayes Center.
  Programming (via satellite): A&E; AMC; CNN; Discovery Channel; Disney Channel; ESPN; Freeform; Lifetime; Nickelodeon; QVC; Spike TV; TBS; TNT; USA Network; WGN America.
  Fee: $36.90 monthly.
Pay Service 1
  Pay Units: N.A.
  Programming (via satellite): HBO.
  Fee: $14.00 monthly.
Video-On-Demand: No
Internet Service
  Operational: No.
Telephone Service
  None
General Manager: Patty Hyyppa. Chief Technician: Don Green.
Ownership: Peregrine Communications (MSO).

STROMSBURG—Eagle Communications, 2703 Hall St, Ste 15, PO Box 817, Hays, KS 67601. Phone: 785-625-4000. Fax: 785-625-8030. E-mail: support@eaglecom.net. Web Site: http://www.eaglecom.net. ICA: NE0075.
TV Market Ranking: Outside TV Markets (STROMSBURG). Franchise award date: N.A. Franchise expiration date: N.A. Began: April 1, 1981.
Channel capacity: N.A. Channels available but not in use: N.A.
Basic Service
  Subscribers: 127.
  Programming (received off-air): KGIN (CBS, MNT, NBC) Grand Island; KHGI-TV (ABC) Kearney; KHNE-TV (PBS) Hastings; KLKN (ABC) Lincoln; KNHL (IND) Hastings; KTVG-TV (FOX) Grand Island.
  Programming (via satellite): C-SPAN; C-SPAN 2; CW PLUS; EWTN Global Catholic Network; MyNetworkTV; QVC; TBS; The Weather Channel; Trinity Broadcasting Network (TBN); Univision Studios; WGN America.
  Fee: $24.95 installation; $64.95 monthly.
Expanded Basic Service 1
  Subscribers: N.A.
  Programming (via satellite): A&E; AMC; Animal Planet; Cartoon Network; CMT; CNBC; CNN; Comedy Central; Discovery Channel; E! HD; ESPN; ESPN Classic; ESPN2; Food Network; Fox News Channel; FOX Sports Midwest; Freeform; FX; Great American Country; Hallmark Channel; HGTV; History; HLN; ION Television; Lifetime; MSNBC; MTV; NBCSN; Nickelodeon; Outdoor Channel; RFD-TV; Spike TV; Syfy; TLC; TNT; Travel Channel; truTV; Turner Classic Movies; TV Land; USA Network; VH1.
Digital Basic Service
  Subscribers: N.A.
  Programming (via satellite): BBC America; Bloomberg Television; Cine Mexicano; Cinelatino; Cloo; CMT; CNN en Espanol; Daystar TV Network; Destination America; Discovery Channel HD; Discovery Kids Channel; Discovery Life Channel; DMX Music; ESPN Classic; ESPN Deportes; ESPN HD; ESPN2; ESPNews; EVINE Live; FOX College Sports Central; FOX College Sports Pacific; Fox Deportes; Fox Sports 1; FXM; FYI; Golf Channel; GSN; History; History en Espanol; History International; Investigation Discovery; MTV Classic; MTV Hits; MTV2; NBCSN; Outdoor Channel; Ovation; OWN; Oprah Winfrey Network; Science Channel; Syfy; TBS HD; TeenNick; TNT HD; Tr3s; Trinity Broadcasting Network (TBN); VH1 Soul; ViendoMovies; WE tv.
  Fee: $14.00 monthly.
Digital Pay Service 1
  Pay Units: N.A.
  Programming (via satellite): Cinemax (multiplexed); Flix; HBO (multiplexed); HBO Latino; LMN; Showtime (multiplexed); Starz (multiplexed); Starz Encore (multiplexed); The Movie Channel (multiplexed).
Video-On-Demand: No
Pay-Per-View
  iN DEMAND (delivered digitally); Hot Choice (delivered digitally); Playboy TV (delivered digitally); Fresh (delivered digitally); Club Jenna (delivered digitally); Spice: Xcess (delivered digitally).
Internet Service
  Operational: Yes.
  Broadband Service: Cable Nebraska.
Telephone Service
  Digital: Operational
Miles of Plant: 9.0 (coaxial); None (fiber optic). Homes passed: 530.
President & Chief Executive Officer: Gary Shorman. Chief Operating Officer: Kurt K. David. General Manager: Travis Kohlrus. Marketing Manager: Elizabeth Jaeger.
Ownership: Eagle Communications Inc. (MSO).

STUART—CenCom NNTV. This cable system has converted to IPTV. See JACKSON, NE [NE5019]. ICA: NE0135.

SUPERIOR—Glenwood Telecommunications. Now served by BLUE HILL, NE [NE0093]. ICA: NE0383.

SUTHERLAND—Great Plains Communications, 1600 Great Plains Ctr, PO Box 500, Blair, NE 68008-0500. Phones: 402-426-9511; 888-343-8014. Fax: 402-456-6550. E-mail: lquist@gpcom.com. Web Site: http://www.gpcom.com. Also serves Hershey. ICA: NE0330.
TV Market Ranking: Below 100 (Hershey, SUTHERLAND). Franchise award date: March 1, 1982. Franchise expiration date: N.A. Began: April 1, 1983.
Channel capacity: N.A. Channels available but not in use: N.A.
Basic Service
  Subscribers: 308.
  Programming (received off-air): KGIN (CBS, MNT, NBC) Grand Island; KNOP-TV (NBC) North Platte; KPNE-TV (PBS) North Platte; KWNB-TV (ABC) Hayes Center.
  Programming (via satellite): A&E; AMC; Animal Planet; CNN; Discovery Channel; Disney Channel; ESPN; Fox News Channel; Freeform; Great American Country; HLN; KCNC-TV (CBS, Decades) Denver; KMGH-TV (ABC, Azteca America) Denver; Lifetime; Nickelodeon; Pop; QVC; Root Sports Rocky Mountain; Spike TV; TBS; The Weather Channel; TLC; TNT; Travel Channel; USA Network; VH1; WGN America.
  Fee: $45.00 installation; $23.49 monthly.
Expanded Basic Service 1
  Subscribers: N.A.
  Programming (via satellite): Cartoon Network; Comedy Central; ESPN2; Food Network; HGTV; History; NBCSN; Turner Classic Movies; TV Land.
  Fee: $47.99 monthly.
Digital Basic Service
  Subscribers: N.A.
  Programming (via satellite): BBC America; Bravo; Discovery Digital Networks; DMX Music; ESPN Classic; Fox Sports 1; FYI; Golf Channel; History International; IFC; LMN; National Geographic Channel; Outdoor Channel; Syfy; TeenNick; Turner Classic Movies; WE tv.
  Fee: $11.50 monthly.
Pay Service 1
  Pay Units: N.A.
  Programming (via satellite): Cinemax; Flix; HBO; Showtime (multiplexed); Sundance TV; The Movie Channel.
  Fee: $10.00 installation; $9.95 monthly (each).
Digital Pay Service 1
  Pay Units: N.A.
  Programming (via satellite): Cinemax (multiplexed); HBO (multiplexed); Showtime (multiplexed); Starz (multiplexed); Starz Encore (multiplexed); The Movie Channel (multiplexed).
Video-On-Demand: No
Pay-Per-View
  iN DEMAND (delivered digitally); Sports PPV.
Internet Service
  Operational: Yes, DSL & dial-up.
  Broadband Service: In-house.
  Fee: $49.95 installation; $39.95 monthly.
Telephone Service
  Digital: Operational
Senior Director: Lea Ann Quist. Chief Technician: Mark Stottler. Marketing Manager: Casey Garrigan.
Ownership: Great Plains Communications Inc. (MSO).

SWANTON—Formerly served by Comstar Cable TV Inc. No longer in operation. ICA: NE0342.

SYRACUSE—Zito Media, 102 S Main St, PO Box 665, Coudersport, PA 16915. Phones: 814-260-9055; 800-365-6988. E-mail: info@zitomedia.com. Web Site: http://www.zitomedia.com. Also serves Bennet, Cass County (portions), Cook, Eagle, Elmwood, Johnson, Murdock, Murray, Nemaha County (portions), Palmyra, Sterling, Unadilla & Weeping Water. ICA: NE0053.
TV Market Ranking: 53,91 (Eagle, Elmwood, Murdock, Weeping Water); 91 (Bennet, Cass County (portions), Cook, Murray, Nemaha County (portions), Palmyra, Sterling, SYRACUSE, Unadilla); Outside TV Markets (Johnson). Franchise award date: N.A. Franchise expiration date: N.A. Began: October 1, 1981.
Channel capacity: N.A. Channels available but not in use: N.A.
Basic Service
  Subscribers: 797.
  Programming (received off-air): KETV (ABC, MeTV) Omaha; KLKN (ABC) Lincoln; KMTV-TV (Antenna TV, CBS, Escape) Omaha; KOLN (CBS, MNT, NBC) Lincoln; KPTM (Estrella TV, FOX, MNT, This TV) Omaha; KSNB-TV (MeTV, MNT, NBC) Superior; KUON-TV (PBS) Lincoln; KXVO (Azteca America, CW) Omaha; WOWT (IND, NBC) Omaha.
  Programming (via satellite): A&E; AMC; Animal Planet; Boomerang; Cartoon Network; CNN; Comedy Central; C-SPAN; Discovery Channel; Disney Channel; Disney XD; E! HD; ESPN; ESPN2; EWTN Global Catholic Network; Food Network; Fox News Channel; FOX Sports Midwest; Freeform; Fuse; FX; Great American Country; Hallmark Channel; HGTV; History; HLN; INSP; Lifetime; MSNBC; National Geographic Channel; Outdoor Channel; Pop; QVC; Syfy; TBS; The Weather Channel; TLC; TNT; Travel Channel; Trinity Broadcasting Network (TBN); Turner Classic Movies; TV Land; USA Network; WGN America.
  Fee: $49.95 installation; $18.65 monthly.
Digital Basic Service
  Subscribers: N.A.
  Programming (via satellite): BBC America; Bloomberg Television; Discovery Life Channel; ESPN Classic; ESPNews; FSN Digital Atlantic; FSN Digital Central; FSN Digital Pacific; FYI; Golf Channel; GSN; History International; WE tv.
  Fee: $12.95 monthly.
Digital Expanded Basic Service
  Subscribers: N.A.
  Programming (via satellite): DMX Music; FXM; IFC; LMN; Starz Encore.
  Fee: $12.95 monthly.
Pay Service 1
  Pay Units: N.A.
  Programming (via satellite): Cinemax; HBO; Showtime; The Movie Channel.
  Fee: $11.95 installation; $6.95 monthly (TMC), $7.95 monthly (Showtime), $11.00 monthly (Cinemax), $12.95 monthly (HBO).
Digital Pay Service 1
  Pay Units: N.A.
  Programming (via satellite): Cinemax (multiplexed); Flix; HBO (multiplexed); Showtime (multiplexed); The Movie Channel (multiplexed).
  Fee: $15.60 monthly.
Video-On-Demand: No
Pay-Per-View
  ESPN Now (delivered digitally); Hot Choice (delivered digitally); Playboy TV (delivered digitally); Fresh (delivered digitally).
Internet Service
  Operational: Yes.
  Fee: $49.95 installation; $44.95 monthly; $5.00 modem lease.
Telephone Service
  None
Miles of Plant: 59.0 (coaxial); None (fiber optic). Homes passed: 3,280.
President: James Rigas.
Ownership: Zito Media (MSO).

TALMAGE—Formerly served by Great Plains Communications. No longer in operation. ICA: NE0252.

TAYLOR—NCTC Cable. Now served by BURWELL, NE [NE0045]. ICA: NE0235.

TEKAMAH—American Broadband. Now served by BLAIR, NE [NE0027]. ICA: NE0061.

Nebraska—Cable Systems

TOBIAS—Formerly served by CableDirect. No longer in operation. ICA: NE0253.

TRENTON—Great Plains Communications, 1600 Great Plains Ctr, PO Box 500, Blair, NE 68008-0500. Phones: 888-343-8014; 402-426-9511. Fax: 402-456-6550. Web Site: http://www.gpcom.com. ICA: NE0141.
TV Market Ranking: Below 100 (TRENTON). Franchise award date: August 17, 1983. Franchise expiration date: N.A. Began: February 1, 1984.
Channel capacity: N.A. Channels available but not in use: N.A.
Basic Service
Subscribers: 78.
Programming (received off-air): KBSL-DT (CBS) Goodland; KSNK (NBC) McCook; KWNB-TV (ABC) Hayes Center.
Programming (via satellite): C-SPAN; QVC; WGN America.
Fee: $45.00 installation; $19.95 monthly; $.57 converter.
Expanded Basic Service 1
Subscribers: N.A.
Programming (via satellite): A&E; AMC; Animal Planet; Cartoon Network; CMT; CNBC; CNN; Comedy Central; C-SPAN; Discovery Channel; Disney Channel; E! HD; ESPN; ESPN2; EVINE Live; EWTN Global Catholic Network; Food Network; Fox News Channel; Fox Sports 1; FOX Sports Networks; Freeform; FX; Hallmark Channel; HGTV; History; HLN; Lifetime; LMN; MSNBC; MTV; Nickelodeon; Oxygen; Spike TV; Syfy; TBS; The Weather Channel; TLC; TNT; Travel Channel; Trinity Broadcasting Network (TBN); truTV; Turner Classic Movies; TV Land; USA Network; VH1; WE tv.
Fee: $30.18 installation; $47.99 monthly.
Pay Service 1
Pay Units: N.A.
Programming (via satellite): Cinemax; HBO; The Movie Channel.
Fee: $10.95 monthly (Cinemax or HBO), $11.00 monthly (TMC).
Video-On-Demand: No
Pay-Per-View
Hot Choice, Addressable: No.
Internet Service
Operational: Yes.
Telephone Service
Digital: Operational
Miles of Plant: 6.0 (coaxial); None (fiber optic).
Senior Director: Lea Ann Quist. Chief Technician: Mark Stottler. Marketing Manager: Casey Garrigan.
Ownership: Great Plains Communications Inc. (MSO).

TRUMBULL—Mid-State Community TV, 1001 12th St, Aurora, NE 68818-2004. Phones: 800-821-1831; 402-694-5101. Fax: 402-694-2848. E-mail: midstate@midstatetv.com. Web Site: http://www.midstatetv.com. ICA: NE0331.
TV Market Ranking: 91 (TRUMBULL).
Channel capacity: N.A. Channels available but not in use: N.A.
Basic Service
Subscribers: 14.
Fee: $61.95 monthly.
President & General Manager: Phillip C. Nelson.
Ownership: Mid-State Community TV Inc. (MSO).

ULYSSES—Formerly served by Zito Media. No longer in operation. ICA: NE0183.

UNION—Formerly served by Westcom. No longer in operation. ICA: NE0334.

VALENTINE—Three Rivers Digital Cable (formerly Cable Nebraska). Now served by AINSWORTH, NE [NE0049]. ICA: NE0036.

VALPARAISO—Zito Media, 102 S Main St, PO Box 665, Coudersport, PA 16915. Phones: 814-260-9055; 800-365-6988. E-mail: info@zitomedia.com. Web Site: http://www.zitomedia.com. ICA: NE0168.
TV Market Ranking: 91 (VALPARAISO). Franchise award date: N.A. Franchise expiration date: N.A. Began: December 1, 1983.
Channel capacity: N.A. Channels available but not in use: N.A.
Basic Service
Subscribers: 40.
Programming (received off-air): KETV (ABC, MeTV) Omaha; KMTV-TV (Antenna TV, CBS, Escape) Omaha; KOLN (CBS, MNT, NBC) Lincoln; KPTM (Estrella TV, FOX, MNT, This TV) Omaha; KUON-TV (PBS) Lincoln; KXVO (Azteca America, CW) Omaha; WOWT (IND, NBC) Omaha.
Programming (via satellite): A&E; Cartoon Network; CNN; Discovery Channel; Disney Channel; E! HD; ESPN; ESPN2; EWTN Global Catholic Network; Fox News Channel; FOX Sports Midwest; Freeform; History; HLN; Lifetime; Outdoor Channel; TBS; The Weather Channel; TLC; TNT; Turner Classic Movies; USA Network; WGN America.
Fee: $49.95 installation; $45.95 monthly.
Pay Service 1
Pay Units: N.A.
Programming (via satellite): Cinemax; HBO.
Fee: $11.95 monthly (Cinemax), $12.95 monthly (HBO).
Internet Service
Operational: No.
Telephone Service
None
Miles of Plant: 5.0 (coaxial); None (fiber optic). Homes passed: 180.
President: James Rigas.
Ownership: Zito Media (MSO).

VERDON—Formerly served by CableDirect. No longer in operation. ICA: NE0218.

WACO—Zito Media, 102 S Main St, PO Box 665, Coudersport, PA 16915. Phones: 814-260-9055; 800-365-6988. E-mail: info@zitomedia.com. Web Site: http://www.zitomedia.com. Also serves Utica. ICA: NE0212.
TV Market Ranking: 91 (Utica); Outside TV Markets (WACO). Franchise award date: January 8, 1984. Franchise expiration date: N.A. Began: October 1, 1985.
Channel capacity: N.A. Channels available but not in use: N.A.
Basic Service
Subscribers: 37.
Programming (received off-air): KETV (ABC, MeTV) Omaha; KLKN (ABC) Lincoln; KMTV-TV (Antenna TV, CBS, Escape) Omaha; KNHL (IND) Hastings; KOLN (CBS, MNT, NBC) Lincoln; KPTM (Estrella TV, FOX, MNT, This TV) Omaha; KUON-TV (PBS) Lincoln; KXVO (Azteca America, CW) Omaha; WOWT (IND, NBC) Omaha.
Programming (via satellite): A&E; AMC; Cartoon Network; CNN; C-SPAN; Discovery Channel; Disney Channel; ESPN; Fox News Channel; FOX Sports Midwest; Freeform; Fuse; FX; HGTV; HLN; Lifetime; Outdoor Channel; QVC; TBS; The Weather Channel; TNT; Travel Channel; USA Network; WGN America.
Fee: $49.95 installation; $45.86 monthly.
Pay Service 1
Pay Units: N.A.
Programming (via satellite): Cinemax; HBO; Showtime; The Movie Channel.
Fee: $7.95 monthly (TMC), $8.95 monthly (Showtime), $9.95 monthly (Cinemax), $13.95 monthly (HBO).
Internet Service
Operational: No.
Telephone Service
None
Miles of Plant: 8.0 (coaxial); None (fiber optic). Homes passed: 498.
President: James Rigas.
Ownership: Zito Media (MSO).

WAHOO—Charter Communications. Now served by SPRINGFIELD (formerly Plattsmouth), NE [NE0020]. ICA: NE0035.

WALLACE—Formerly served by Consolidated Cable Inc. No longer in operation. ICA: NE0336.

WALTHILL—Formerly served by HunTel Cablevision. Now served by American Broadband, WAYNE, NE [NE0374]. ICA: NE0373.

WASHINGTON (village)—Formerly served by TelePartners. No longer in operation. ICA: NE0337.

WAUNETA—BWTelcom, 607 Chief St, PO Box 684, Benkelman, NE 69021. Phones: 308-423-8950; 800-835-0053; 308-394-6000; 308-423-2000. Fax: 308-423-5818. E-mail: bwtelcom@bwtelcom.net. Web Site: http://www.bwtelcom.net. Also serves Chase County (portions). ICA: NE0338.
TV Market Ranking: Below 100 (Chase County (portions), WAUNETA).
Channel capacity: N.A. Channels available but not in use: N.A.
Basic Service
Subscribers: 162.
Programming (received off-air): KBSL-DT (CBS) Goodland; KPNE-TV (PBS) North Platte; KSNK (NBC) McCook; KWNB-TV (ABC) Hayes Center.
Programming (via satellite): A&E; CMT; CNBC; CNN; Discovery Channel; ESPN; ESPN Classic; ESPN2; Fox News Channel; Freeform; FX; KCNC-TV (CBS, Decades) Denver; KWGN-TV (CW, This TV) Denver; Lifetime; Nickelodeon; Outdoor Channel; Root Sports Rocky Mountain; Spike TV; Syfy; TBS; The Weather Channel; TLC; TNT; Travel Channel; Turner Classic Movies; USA Network; VH1; WGN America.
Fee: $27.85 installation; $47.25 monthly.
Expanded Basic Service 1
Subscribers: 113.
Programming (via satellite): AMC; Animal Planet; Bloomberg Television; Cartoon Network; Comedy Central; Disney Channel; Food Network; Fox Sports 1; Great American Country; Hallmark Channel; HGTV; History; HLN; MTV; National Geographic Channel; NBCSN; TV Land.
Fee: $22.00 monthly.
Pay Service 1
Pay Units: 19.
Programming (via satellite): HBO; Showtime; The Movie Channel.
Fee: $18.15 monthly (Showtime/TMC), $19.15 monthly (HBO).
Video-On-Demand: No

Internet Service
Operational: Yes.
Telephone Service
None
Vice President: Kacey L. Harper. General Manager & Chief Technician: Randall Raile. Marketing Director: Loretta Raile. Bookkeeper: Jenna Edwards.
Ownership: BWTelcom (MSO).

WAYNE—American Broadband, 1605 Washington St, Blair, NE 68008-0400. Phones: 402-426-6200; 402-533-1100. Fax: 402-375-4077. Web Site: http://www.americanbroadband.com. Also serves Belden, Carroll, Emerson, Homer, Osmond, Pender, Pierce County (portions), Wakefield & Walthill. ICA: NE0374.
TV Market Ranking: Below 100 (Emerson, Homer, Pender, Wakefield, Walthill); Outside TV Markets (Belden, Carroll, Osmond, Pierce County (portions), WAYNE).
Channel capacity: N.A. Channels available but not in use: N.A.
Basic Service
Subscribers: 2,481.
Programming (received off-air): KCAU-TV (ABC) Sioux City; KETV (ABC, MeTV) Omaha; KMEG (Azteca America, CBS, Decades) Sioux City; KMTV-TV (Antenna TV, CBS, Escape) Omaha; KPTH (FOX, MNT, This TV) Sioux City; KTIV (CW, MeTV, NBC) Sioux City; KXNE-TV (PBS) Norfolk; WOWT (IND, NBC) Omaha.
Programming (via satellite): CW PLUS; EWTN Global Catholic Network; FX; National Geographic Channel; Pop; QVC; WGN America.
Fee: $30.00 installation; $19.00 monthly.
Expanded Basic Service 1
Subscribers: N.A.
Programming (via satellite): A&E; AMC; Cartoon Network; CNBC; CNN; Comedy Central; C-SPAN; Discovery Channel; Disney Channel; Disney XD; E! HD; ESPN; ESPN2; Food Network; Fox News Channel; FOX Sports Midwest; Freeform; Great American Country; HGTV; History; Lifetime; MSNBC; MTV; Nickelodeon; Spike TV; Syfy; TBS; The Weather Channel; TLC; TNT; TV Land; USA Network; VH1.
Fee: $19.99 monthly.
Digital Basic Service
Subscribers: N.A. Included in Blair
Programming (via satellite): BBC America; Bloomberg Television; Discovery Kids Channel; Discovery Life Channel; DMX Music; ESPN Classic; ESPNews; FXM; Golf Channel; GSN; NBCSN; Nicktoons; Outdoor Channel; OWN: Oprah Winfrey Network; Science Channel; Trinity Broadcasting Network (TBN); Turner Classic Movies; WE tv.
Fee: $7.95 monthly.
Pay Service 1
Pay Units: N.A.
Programming (via satellite): Cinemax; HBO; Showtime.
Fee: $11.10 monthly (Cinemax), $12.00 monthly (Showtime), $13.35 monthly (HBO).
Digital Pay Service 1
Pay Units: N.A.
Programming (via satellite): Bravo; Cinemax (multiplexed); HBO (multiplexed); IFC; Showtime (multiplexed); Starz (multiplexed); Starz Encore (multiplexed); The Movie Channel (multiplexed).
Fee: $11.10 monthly (Cinemax), $12.00 monthly (Starz/Encore/Bravo/IFC or Showtime/TMC), $13.55 monthly (HBO).
Video-On-Demand: No

Cable Systems—Nebraska

Pay-Per-View
iN DEMAND (delivered digitally).
Internet Service
Operational: Yes.
Broadband Service: In-house.
Fee: $30.00 monthly; $180.00 modem purchase.
Telephone Service
Digital: Operational
Miles of Plant: 35.0 (coaxial); None (fiber optic). Homes passed included in Blair.
President, State Operations: Mike Jacobsen.
Cable Television Manager: Mike Storjohann.
General Manager: Joe Jedensky. Programming Manager: Kay Petersen.
Ownership: American Broadband Communications Inc. (MSO).

WESTERN—Zito Media, 102 S Main St, PO Box 665, Coudersport, PA 16915. Phones: 814-260-9055; 800-365-6988. E-mail: info@zitomedia.com. Web Site: http://www.zitomedia.com. ICA: NE0202.
TV Market Ranking: Outside TV Markets (WESTERN). Franchise award date: N.A. Franchise expiration date: N.A. Began: September 10, 1984.
Channel capacity: N.A. Channels available but not in use: N.A.
Basic Service
Subscribers: 3.
Programming (received off-air): KHNE-TV (PBS) Hastings; KLKN (ABC) Lincoln; KOLN (CBS, MNT, NBC) Lincoln; KPTM (Estrella TV, FOX, MNT, This TV) Omaha; KSNB-TV (MeTV, MNT, NBC) Superior; KXVO (Azteca America, CW) Omaha.
Programming (via satellite): Cartoon Network; CNN; Discovery Channel; Disney Channel; ESPN; FOX Sports Midwest; Freeform; KUSA (NBC, WeatherNation) Denver; Outdoor Channel; TBS; TNT; USA Network; WGN America.
Fee: $49.95 installation; $41.55 monthly.
Pay Service 1
Pay Units: N.A.
Programming (via satellite): Cinemax; HBO.
Fee: $11.95 monthly (Cinemax), $12.95 monthly (HBO).
Internet Service
Operational: No.
Telephone Service
None
Miles of Plant: 5.0 (coaxial); None (fiber optic). Homes passed: 168.

President: James Rigas.
Ownership: Zito Media (MSO).

WESTON (village)—Formerly served by Westcom. No longer in operation. ICA: NE0238.

WILBER—Zito Media, 102 S Main St, PO Box 665, Coudersport, PA 16915. Phones: 814-260-9055; 800-365-6988. E-mail: info@zitomedia.com. Web Site: http://www.zitomedia.com. Also serves Blue Springs, Clatonia, De Witt, Dorchester, Friend, Hallam, Hickman, Milford, Pleasant Dale, Plymouth & Wymore. ICA: NE0055.
TV Market Ranking: 91 (Clatonia, De Witt, Dorchester, Friend, Hallam, Hickman, Milford, Pleasant Dale, WILBER); Outside TV Markets (Blue Springs, Plymouth, Wymore). Franchise award date: N.A. Franchise expiration date: N.A. Began: June 1, 1981.
Channel capacity: N.A. Channels available but not in use: N.A.
Basic Service
Subscribers: 905.
Programming (received off-air): KETV (ABC, MeTV) Omaha; KLKN (ABC) Lincoln; KMTV-TV (Antenna TV, CBS, Escape) Omaha; KOLN (CBS, MNT, NBC) Lincoln; KPTM (Estrella TV, FOX, MNT, This TV) Omaha; KSNB-TV (MeTV, MNT, NBC) Superior; KUON-TV (PBS) Lincoln; KXVO (Azteca America, CW) Omaha; WOWT (IND, NBC) Omaha.
Programming (via satellite): A&E; AMC; Animal Planet; Boomerang; Cartoon Network; CNN; Comedy Central; C-SPAN; Discovery Channel; Disney Channel; Disney XD; E! HD; ESPN; ESPN2; EWTN Global Catholic Network; Food Network; Fox News Channel; FOX Sports Midwest; Freeform; Fuse; FX; Great American Country; Hallmark Channel; HGTV; History; HLN; Lifetime; MSNBC; National Geographic Channel; Outdoor Channel; Pop; QVC; Syfy; TBS; The Weather Channel; TLC; TNT; Travel Channel; Trinity Broadcasting Network (TBN); Turner Classic Movies; TV Land; USA Network; WGN America.
Fee: $49.95 installation; $17.45 monthly.
Digital Basic Service
Subscribers: N.A.
Programming (via satellite): BBC America; Bloomberg Television; Discovery Life Channel; ESPN Classic; ESPNews; Fox Sports 1; FSN Digital Atlantic; FSN Digital Central; FSN Digital Pacific; FYI; Golf Channel; GSN; History International; WE tv.
Fee: $12.95 monthly.
Digital Expanded Basic Service
Subscribers: N.A.
Programming (via satellite): DMX Music; FXM; IFC; LMN; Starz Encore.
Fee: $12.95 monthly.
Pay Service 1
Pay Units: N.A.
Programming (via satellite): Cinemax; HBO; Showtime; The Movie Channel.
Fee: $7.95 monthly (TMC), $9.95 monthly (Showtime), $10.95 monthly (Cinemax), $14.95 monthly (HBO).
Digital Pay Service 1
Pay Units: N.A.
Programming (via satellite): Cinemax (multiplexed); Flix; HBO (multiplexed); Showtime (multiplexed); The Movie Channel (multiplexed).
Fee: $15.60 monthly.
Video-On-Demand: No
Pay-Per-View
ESPN Now (delivered digitally); Hot Choice (delivered digitally); Playboy TV (delivered digitally); Fresh (delivered digitally).
Internet Service
Operational: Yes. Began: March 1, 1999.
Broadband Service: Galaxy Cable Internet.
Fee: $49.95 installation; $44.95 monthly; $5.00 modem lease.
Telephone Service
None
Miles of Plant: 80.0 (coaxial); 1,015.0 (fiber optic). Homes passed: 4,491.
President: James Rigas.
Ownership: Zito Media (MSO).

WINSIDE—CenCom NNTV. This cable system has converted to IPTV. See JACKSON, NE [NE5019]. ICA: NE0386.

WINSIDE (village)—Formerly served by Sky Scan Cable Co. No longer in operation. ICA: NE0340.

WOLBACH—Great Plains Communications, 1600 Great Plains Ctr, PO Box 500, Blair, NE 68008-0500. Phones: 888-343-8014; 402-426-9511. Fax: 402-426-6550. E-mail: lquist@gpcom.com. Web Site: http://www.gpcom.com. ICA: NE0392.
TV Market Ranking: Below 100 (WOLBACH).
Channel capacity: N.A. Channels available but not in use: N.A.
Basic Service
Subscribers: 41.
Programming (received off-air): KGIN (CBS, MNT, NBC) Grand Island; KHGI-TV (ABC) Kearney; KHNE-TV (PBS) Hastings; KLKN (ABC) Lincoln; KNHL (IND) Hastings; KTVG-TV (FOX) Grand Island.
Programming (via satellite): A&E; AMC; Animal Planet; CNN; Discovery Channel; Disney Channel; ESPN; ESPN2; Fox News Channel; Freeform; Great American Country; Hallmark Channel; HGTV; History; HLN; Lifetime; Nickelodeon; QVC; Root Sports Rocky Mountain; Spike TV; TBS; The Weather Channel; TLC; TNT; Travel Channel; TV Land; USA Network; WGN America.
Fee: $45.00 installation; $41.99 monthly.
Expanded Basic Service 1
Subscribers: 21.
Fee: $47.99 monthly.
Pay Service 1
Pay Units: N.A.
Programming (via satellite): HBO; Showtime.
Fee: $9.95 monthly (Showtime), $10.95 monthly (HBO).
Video-On-Demand: No
Internet Service
Operational: Yes.
Telephone Service
Digital: Operational
Senior Director: Lea Ann Quist.
Ownership: Great Plains Communications Inc. (MSO).

WOODCLIFF LAKES—Formerly served by Time Warner Cable. No longer in operation. ICA: NE0364.

WYNOT—Formerly served by CenCom Inc. No longer in operation. ICA: NE0236.

YORK—Time Warner Cable. Now served by LINCOLN, NE [NE0002]. ICA: NE0012.

YUTAN—Formerly served by TelePartners. No longer in operation. ICA: NE0102.

NEVADA

Total Systems: 21	Communities with Applications: 0
Total Communities Served: 61	Number of Basic Subscribers: 406,477
Franchises Not Yet Operating: 0	Number of Expanded Basic Subscribers: 54,558
Applications Pending: 0	Number of Pay Units: 115

Top 100 Markets Represented: N.A.

For a list of cable communities in this section, see the Cable Community Index located in the back of Cable Volume 2.
For explanation of terms used in cable system listings, see p. D-11.

ALAMO—Rainbow Cable, 27 Main St, PO Box 300, Pioche, NV 89043-0300. Phone: 775-962-5111. Fax: 775-962-5193. ICA: NV0032.
TV Market Ranking: Outside TV Markets (ALAMO).
Channel capacity: N.A. Channels available but not in use: N.A.
Basic Service
Subscribers: N.A.
Programming (via microwave): KCNC-TV (CBS, Decades) Denver; KMGH-TV (ABC, Azteca America) Denver; KUSA (NBC, WeatherNation) Denver.
Programming (via satellite): CMT; Discovery Channel; Disney Channel; ESPN; Freeform; HLN; MTV; Nickelodeon; Spike TV; TBS; TLC; TNT; USA Network; WGN America.
Fee: $43.00 installation.
Pay Service 1
Pay Units: N.A.
Programming (via satellite): Cinemax; HBO; Showtime.
Fee: $7.90 monthly (Showtime), $7.95 monthly (Cinemax), $9.95 monthly (HBO).
Video-On-Demand: No
Internet Service
Operational: No.
Telephone Service
None
General Manager: Paul Christian. Chief Technician: Paul Donohue. Office Manager: Valinda Woodworth.
Ownership: Christian Enterprises (MSO).

BATTLE MOUNTAIN—Satview Broadband, 3550 Barron Way, Ste 13A, Reno, NV 89511. Phones: 775-324-2198 (Reno office); 775-333-6626; 877-538 2662. Fax: 775-333-0225. E-mail: satviewreno@yahoo.com. Web Site: http://www.satview.net. ICA: NV0016.
TV Market Ranking: Outside TV Markets (BATTLE MOUNTAIN). Franchise award date: N.A. Franchise expiration date: N.A. Began: January 1, 1987.
Channel capacity: N.A. Channels available but not in use: N.A.
Basic Service
Subscribers: N.A.
Programming (via microwave): K32CA-D Battle Mountain; KCNC-TV (CBS, Decades) Denver; KCWY-DT (CW, NBC) Casper; KOLO-TV (ABC, IND, Movies!) Reno; KSTU (Antenna TV, FOX) Salt Lake City; KTVN (Antenna TV, CBS) Reno; KUSA (NBC, WeatherNation) Denver.
Programming (via satellite): C-SPAN; C-SPAN 2; CW PLUS; ION Television; Pop; QVC.
Fee: $62.00 installation; $15.01 monthly.
Expanded Basic Service 1
Subscribers: N.A.
Programming (via satellite): A&E; AMC; Animal Planet; Cartoon Network; CNBC; CNN; Comedy Central; Discovery Channel; Disney Channel; E! HD; ESPN; ESPN2; Food Network; Fox News Channel; Freeform; FX; Great American Country; Hallmark Channel; HGTV; HLN; Lifetime; MSNBC; MTV; Nickelodeon; Root Sports Rocky Mountain; Spike TV; TBS; The Weather Channel; TLC; TNT; Travel Channel; TV Land; Univision; Univision Studios; USA Network; VH1.
Fee: $24.98 installation; $24.98 monthly.
Digital Basic Service
Subscribers: N.A.
Programming (via satellite): BBC America; Bloomberg Television; CMT; Destination America; Discovery Kids Channel; Discovery Life Channel; Disney XD; DMX Music; Fuse; FXM; FYI; GSN; History; History International; IFC; Investigation Discovery; LMN; MTV Classic; MTV2; National Geographic Channel; Nick Jr.; Nicktoons; OWN; Oprah Winfrey Network; Science Channel; Syfy; TeenNick; Tr3s; Trinity Broadcasting Network (TBN); Turner Classic Movies; WE tv.
Fee: $11.95 monthly.
Digital Expanded Basic Service
Subscribers: N.A.
Programming (via satellite): ESPN Classic; ESPNews; Fox Sports 1; Golf Channel; NBCSN; Outdoor Channel.
Digital Pay Service 1
Pay Units: N.A.
Programming (via satellite): Cinemax (multiplexed); HBO (multiplexed); Showtime (multiplexed); Starz (multiplexed); Starz Encore (multiplexed); The Movie Channel (multiplexed).
Video-On-Demand: No
Pay-Per-View
iN DEMAND (delivered digitally); Club Jenna (delivered digitally); Playboy TV (delivered digitally); Fresh (delivered digitally).
Internet Service
Operational: No.
Telephone Service
None
Miles of Plant: 18.0 (coaxial); None (fiber optic). Homes passed: 1,481.
President: Tariq Ahmad.
Ownership: Satview Broadband Ltd. (MSO).

BEATTY—Formerly served by Eagle West Communications Inc. No longer in operation. ICA: NV0024.

BLUE DIAMOND—Formerly served by Eagle West Communications Inc. No longer in operation. ICA: NV0031.

BOULDER CITY (northern portion)—Formerly served by Eagle West Communications Inc. No longer in operation. ICA: NV0033.

CALIENTE—Rainbow Cable. Now served by PIOCHE, NV [NV0047]. ICA: NV0035.

CALLVILLE BAY—Formerly served by Eagle West Communications Inc. No longer in operation. ICA: NV0036.

CARLIN—Satview Broadband, 3550 Barron Way, Ste 13A, Reno, NV 89511. Phones: 775-324-2198 (Reno office); 877-538 2662; 775-333-6626. Fax: 775-333-0225. E-mail: satviewreno@yahoo.com. Web Site: http://www.satview.net. ICA: NV0020.
TV Market Ranking: Below 100 (CARLIN). Franchise award date: July 1, 1986. Franchise expiration date: N.A. Began: November 1, 1986.
Channel capacity: N.A. Channels available but not in use: N.A.
Basic Service
Subscribers: N.A.
Programming (received off-air): K15EE-D Elko; KENV-DT (NBC) Elko; KSTU (Antenna TV, FOX) Salt Lake City; KUCW (CW, Movies!, The Country Network) Ogden.
Programming (via satellite): C-SPAN; C-SPAN 2; ION Television; QVC.
Programming (via translator): KOLO-TV (ABC, IND, Movies!) Reno; KTVN (Antenna TV, CBS) Reno.
Fee: $62.00 installation; $15.01 monthly.
Expanded Basic Service 1
Subscribers: N.A.
Programming (via satellite): A&E; AMC; Animal Planet; Cartoon Network; CNBC; CNN; Comedy Central; Discovery Channel; Disney Channel; E! HD; ESPN; ESPN2; Fox News Channel; Freeform; FX; Great American Country; Hallmark Channel; HLN; Lifetime; MSNBC; MTV; Nickelodeon; Root Sports Rocky Mountain; Spike TV; TBS; The Weather Channel; TLC; TNT; TV Land; Univision; USA Network; VH1.
Fee: $13.35 installation; $24.98 monthly.
Digital Basic Service
Subscribers: N.A.
Programming (via satellite): BBC America; Bloomberg Television; Bravo; CMT; Destination America; Discovery Kids Channel; Discovery Life Channel; Disney XD; ESPN Classic; Fox Sports 1; Fuse; FXM; FYI; GSN; HGTV; History; History International; IFC; Investigation Discovery; LMN; MC; MTV Classic; MTV2; National Geographic Channel; Nick Jr.; Nicktoons; OWN; Oprah Winfrey Network; Science Channel; Syfy; TeenNick; Trinity Broadcasting Network (TBN); Turner Classic Movies; WE tv.
Fee: $11.95 monthly.
Digital Expanded Basic Service
Subscribers: N.A.
Programming (via satellite): ESPNews; Golf Channel; NBCSN; Outdoor Channel.
Digital Pay Service 1
Pay Units: N.A.
Programming (via satellite): Cinemax (multiplexed); HBO (multiplexed); Showtime (multiplexed); Starz (multiplexed); Starz Encore (multiplexed); The Movie Channel (multiplexed).
Video-On-Demand: No
Pay-Per-View
iN DEMAND (delivered digitally); Playboy TV (delivered digitally); Fresh (delivered digitally); Club Jenna (delivered digitally).
Internet Service
Operational: No.
Telephone Service
None
Miles of Plant: 9.0 (coaxial); None (fiber optic). Homes passed: 763.
President: Tariq Ahmad.
Ownership: Satview Broadband Ltd. (MSO).

CARSON CITY—Charter Communications. Now served by RENO, NV [NV0002]. ICA: NV0004.

CARSON CITY—Formerly served by Quadravision. No longer in operation. ICA: NV0051.

CRYSTAL BAY—Formerly served by Charter Communications. No longer in operation. ICA: NV0005.

ELKO—Satview Broadband, 3550 Barron Way, Ste 13A, Reno, NV 89511. Phones: 775-324-2198 (Reno office); 775-333-6626; 877-538 2662. Fax: 775-333-0225. E-mail: satviewreno@yahoo.com. Web Site: http://www.satview.net. Also serves Elko County (portions) & Spring Creek. ICA: NV0009.
TV Market Ranking: Below 100 (ELKO, Elko County (portions), Spring Creek). Franchise award date: N.A. Franchise expiration date: N.A. Began: October 1, 1956.
Channel capacity: N.A. Channels available but not in use: N.A.
Basic Service
Subscribers: N.A.
Programming (received off-air): KENV-DT (NBC) Elko.
Programming (via microwave): KNPB (PBS) Reno; KSL-TV (NBC) Salt Lake City; KSTU (Antenna TV, FOX) Salt Lake City; KTVN (Antenna TV, CBS) Reno; KTVX (ABC, MeTV) Salt Lake City; KUCW (CW, Movies!, The Country Network) Ogden; KUED (PBS) Salt Lake City; KUTH-DT (getTV, UNV) Provo; KUTV (CBS, This TV) Salt Lake City.
Programming (via satellite): C-SPAN; C-SPAN 2; Pop; QVC.
Fee: $62.00 installation; $15.01 monthly; $.85 converter.
Expanded Basic Service 1
Subscribers: N.A.
Programming (via satellite): A&E; AMC; Animal Planet; Cartoon Network; CNBC; CNN; Comedy Central; Discovery Channel; Disney Channel; E! HD; ESPN;

Cable Systems—Nevada

ESPN2; Food Network; Fox News Channel; Freeform; FX; Great American Country; Hallmark Channel; HGTV; History; HLN; Lifetime; MSNBC; MTV; Nickelodeon; Root Sports Rocky Mountain; Spike TV; Syfy; TBS; The Weather Channel; TLC; TNT; Travel Channel; TV Land; Univision; USA Network; VH1.
Fee: $25.98 monthly.

Digital Basic Service
Subscribers: N.A.
Programming (via satellite): AWE; BBC America; Bravo; CMT; Destination America; Discovery Kids Channel; Discovery Life Channel; Disney XD; DMX Music; Fuse; FXM; FYI; GSN; History International; IFC; Investigation Discovery; LMN; MTV Classic; MTV2; National Geographic Channel; Nick Jr.; Nicktoons; OWN; Oprah Winfrey Network; Science Channel; TeenNick; Tr3s; Trinity Broadcasting Network (TBN); Turner Classic Movies; WE tv.

Digital Expanded Basic Service
Subscribers: N.A.
Programming (via satellite): ESPN Classic; ESPN Deportes; ESPNews; Fox Sports 1; Golf Channel; NBCSN; Outdoor Channel.

Digital Expanded Basic Service 2
Subscribers: N.A.
Programming (via satellite): Cinelatino; CNN en Espanol; ESPN Deportes; Fox Deportes; History en Espanol; NBC Universo; Tr3s; ViendoMovies.

Digital Pay Service 1
Pay Units: N.A.
Programming (via satellite): Cinemax (multiplexed); HBO (multiplexed); Showtime (multiplexed); Starz (multiplexed); Starz Encore (multiplexed); The Movie Channel (multiplexed).

Video-On-Demand: No

Pay-Per-View
iN DEMAND (delivered digitally); Club Jenna (delivered digitally); Fresh (delivered digitally); Playboy TV (delivered digitally).

Internet Service
Operational: No.

Telephone Service
None

Miles of Plant: 137.0 (coaxial); None (fiber optic).
President: Tariq Ahmad.
Ownership: Satview Broadband Ltd. (MSO).

ELY—Beehive Broadband, 2000 Sunset Rd, Lake Point, UT 84074. Phones: 800-615-8021; 435-837-6000. Fax: 435-837-6109. E-mail: support@wirelessbeehive.com. Web Site: http://www.beehivebroadband.com. ICA: NV0013.
TV Market Ranking: Below 100 (ELY). Franchise award date: N.A. Franchise expiration date: N.A. Began: August 1, 1983.
Channel capacity: 57 (operating 2-way). Channels available but not in use: N.A.

Basic Service
Subscribers: 234. Commercial subscribers: 7.
Programming (received off-air): KBYU-TV (PBS) Provo; KJZZ-TV (IND) Salt Lake City; KPNZ (Estrella TV) Ogden; KSL-TV (NBC) Salt Lake City; KSTU (Antenna TV, FOX) Salt Lake City; KTVX (ABC, MeTV) Salt Lake City; KUCW (CW, Movies!, The Country Network) Ogden; KUED (PBS) Salt Lake City; KUEN (ETV) Ogden; KUPX-TV (ION) Provo; KUTV (CBS, This TV) Salt Lake City; 4 FMs.
Programming (via satellite): EWTN Global Catholic Network.
Fee: $79.00 installation; $20.38 monthly; $1.50 converter.

Expanded Basic Service 1
Subscribers: N.A.
Programming (received off-air): KHSV (Antenna TV, MNT) Las Vegas; KLAS-TV (CBS, MeTV, Movies!) Las Vegas; KLVX (PBS) Las Vegas; KOLO-TV (ABC, IND, Movies!) Reno; KVVU-TV (Escape, FOX) Henderson.
Programming (via satellite): A&E; AMC; Animal Planet; Cartoon Network; CMT; CNBC; Comedy Central; Discovery Channel; Disney Channel; ESPN; Fox News Channel; Freeform; FX; Hallmark Channel; HLN; Lifetime; MTV; Nickelodeon; Outdoor Channel; QVC; Root Sports Rocky Mountain; Spike TV; TBS; The Weather Channel; TLC; TNT; TV Land; UniMas; Univision; Univision Studios; USA Network; VH1; WGN America.
Fee: $26.25 monthly.

Digital Basic Service
Subscribers: N.A.
Programming (via satellite): BBC America; Bravo; Discovery Digital Networks; Disney XD; DMX Music; ESPN Classic; ESPN2; ESPNews; EVINE Live; FOX College Sports Central; FOX College Sports Pacific; Fox Sports 1; Fuse; FYI; Golf Channel; Great American Country; GSN; HGTV; History; History International; IFC; LMN; National Geographic Channel; NBCSN; Nick Jr.; TeenNick; The Word Network; Turner Classic Movies; WE tv.

Video-On-Demand: No

Pay-Per-View
iN DEMAND (delivered digitally); Playboy TV (delivered digitally).

Internet Service
Operational: No.

Telephone Service
None

Homes passed: 2,500.
President: Scott Wilson. Manager: Wayne A. McCulley.
Ownership: Beehive Broadband LLC (MSO).

EMPIRE—Formerly served by United States Gypsum Co. No longer in operation. ICA: NV0030.

EUREKA—Beehive Broadband, 2000 Sunset Rd, Lake Point, UT 84074. Phones: 800-615-8021; 435-837-6000. Fax: 435-837-6109. E-mail: support@wirelessbeehive.com. Web Site: http://www.centracom.com. ICA: NV0027.
TV Market Ranking: Outside TV Markets (EUREKA). Franchise award date: February 1, 1988. Franchise expiration date: N.A. Began: July 25, 1988.
Channel capacity: N.A. Channels available but not in use: N.A.

Basic Service
Subscribers: 9. Commercial subscribers: 5.
Programming (via satellite): A&E; AMC; Animal Planet; CMT; CNN; Comedy Central; Discovery Channel; Disney Channel; ESPN; Fox News Channel; Freeform; FX; Lifetime; Nickelodeon; QVC; Root Sports Rocky Mountain; Spike TV; TBS; The Weather Channel; TLC; TNT; USA Network; WGN America.
Programming (via translator): KBYU-TV (PBS) Provo; KJZZ-TV (IND) Salt Lake City; KNPB (PBS) Reno; KPNZ (Estrella TV) Ogden; KSL-TV (NBC) Salt Lake City; KSTU (Antenna TV, FOX) Salt Lake City; KTVX (ABC, MeTV) Salt Lake City; KUCW (CW, Movies!, The Country Network) Ogden; KUED (PBS) Salt Lake City; KUEN (ETV) Ogden; KUTV (CBS, This TV) Salt Lake City.
Fee: $79.00 installation; $20.38 monthly; $1.50 converter.

Pay Service 1
Pay Units: N.A.
Programming (via satellite): Cinemax; HBO; Showtime; Starz; Starz Encore.
Fee: $1.75 monthly (Encore), $13.95 monthly (Cinemax, HBO, Showtime or Starz).

Video-On-Demand: No

Internet Service
Operational: No.

Telephone Service
None

Miles of Plant: 7.0 (coaxial); None (fiber optic). Homes passed: 350.
President: Scott Wilson. Manager: Wayne A. McCulley.
Ownership: Beehive Broadband LLC (MSO).

FERNLEY—Charter Communications. Now served by RENO, NV [NV0002]. ICA: NV0012.

GARDNERVILLE—Charter Communications. Now served by RENO, NV [NV0002]. ICA: NV0007.

GOLDFIELD—Formerly served by Eagle West Communications Inc. No longer in operation. ICA: NV0039.

HAWTHORNE—Charter Communications, 12405 Powerscourt Dr, St. Louis, MO 63131. Phones: 636-207-5100 (Corporate office); 775-348-2772; 775-850-1200. Fax: 775-850-1279. Web Site: http://www.charter.com. ICA: NV0015.
TV Market Ranking: Outside TV Markets (HAWTHORNE). Franchise award date: N.A. Franchise expiration date: N.A. Began: June 1, 1982.
Channel capacity: N.A. Channels available but not in use: N.A.

Digital Basic Service
Subscribers: 132.
Programming (via satellite): BBC America; Bloomberg Television; Bravo; Discovery Digital Networks; Discovery Life Channel; Disney XD; DMX Music; ESPN Classic; Fox Sports 1; Fuse; FXM; FYI; Golf Channel; GSN; History; History International; IFC; LMN; NBCSN; Nick Jr.; Outdoor Channel; Pop; Syfy; TeenNick; Trinity Broadcasting Network (TBN); Turner Classic Movies; WE tv.
Fee: $26.99 monthly.

Digital Expanded Basic Service
Subscribers: N.A.
Programming (via satellite): A&E; AMC; Animal Planet; BET; Cartoon Network; CNBC; CNN; Comcast SportsNet Bay Area; Discovery Channel; Disney Channel; E! HD; ESPN; ESPN2; Fox News Channel; Freeform; FX; Hallmark Channel; HGTV; HLN; Lifetime; MoviePlex; MSNBC; MTV; Nickelodeon; Spike TV; TBS; The Weather Channel; TLC; TNT; Univision; USA Network; VH1.
Fee: $32.58 monthly.

Digital Pay Service 1
Pay Units: N.A.
Programming (via satellite): Cinemax (multiplexed); Flix; HBO (multiplexed); Showtime (multiplexed); Starz (multiplexed); Starz Encore; The Movie Channel (multiplexed).

Video-On-Demand: No

Pay-Per-View
iN DEMAND (delivered digitally); ESPN Now (delivered digitally); ESPN Sports PPV (delivered digitally); Hot Choice (delivered digitally); Playboy TV (delivered digitally); Fresh (delivered digitally); Shorteez (delivered digitally).

Internet Service
Operational: No.

Telephone Service
None

Miles of Plant: 22.0 (coaxial); None (fiber optic). Homes passed: 1,602.
Vice President & General Manager: Manny Martinez. Technical Operations Manager: Carol Eure. Accounting Director: David Sovanski.
Ownership: Charter Communications Inc. (MSO).

HENDERSON (portions)—Formerly served by Prime Time Communications. No longer in operation. ICA: NV5000.

INDIAN SPRINGS—Formerly served by United Cable Management. No longer in operation. ICA: NV0041.

INDIAN SPRINGS AFB—Formerly served by United Cable Management. No longer in operation. ICA: NV0042.

JACKPOT—Satview Broadband, 3550 Barron Way, Ste 13A, Reno, NV 89511. Phones: 775-324-2198 (Reno office); 877-538-2662; 775-333-6626. Fax: 775-333-0225. E-mail: satviewreno@yahoo.com. Web Site: http://www.satview.net. ICA: NV0026.
TV Market Ranking: Outside TV Markets (JACKPOT). Franchise award date: January 1, 1974. Franchise expiration date: N.A. Began: January 15, 1976.
Channel capacity: N.A. Channels available but not in use: N.A.

Basic Service
Subscribers: 322.
Programming (received off-air): KAID (PBS) Boise; KBOI-TV (CBS, CW) Boise; KIVI-TV (ABC, Escape, FOX) Nampa; KMVT (CBS, CW) Twin Falls; KSTU (Antenna TV, FOX) Salt Lake City; KTVB (NBC) Boise; allband FM.
Programming (via satellite): A&E; CNN; Discovery Channel; Disney Channel; ESPN; ESPN2; History; MTV; Nickelodeon; QVC; Root Sports Rocky Mountain; Spike TV; Syfy; TBS; TNT; truTV; Turner Classic Movies; UniMas; Univision; Univision Studios; USA Network; WGN America.
Fee: $30.00 installation; $33.49 monthly.

Pay Service 1
Pay Units: 115.
Programming (via satellite): Cinemax; HBO.
Fee: $8.00 monthly (Cinemax), $9.50 monthly (HBO).

Internet Service
Operational: No.

Telephone Service
None

Miles of Plant: 6.0 (coaxial); None (fiber optic). Homes passed: 500.
President: Tariq Ahmad.
Ownership: Satview Broadband Ltd. (MSO).

LAS VEGAS—Cox Communications, 6205 Peachtree Dunwoody Rd, 12th Floor, Atlanta, GA 30328. Phone: 404-269-6590. Web Site: http://www.cox.com. Also serves Boulder City, Clark County, Green Valley, Henderson & North Las Vegas. ICA: NV0001.
TV Market Ranking: Below 100 (Boulder City, Clark County (portions), Henderson, LAS VEGAS, North Las Vegas); Outside TV Markets (Clark County (portions), Green Valley). Franchise award date: January 1,

Nevada—Cable Systems

1979. Franchise expiration date: N.A. Began: March 1, 1980.
Channel capacity: N.A. Channels available but not in use: N.A.

Basic Service
Subscribers: 306,936.
Programming (received off-air): KBLR (TMO) Paradise; KHSV (Antenna TV, MNT) Las Vegas; KINC (UNV) Las Vegas; KLAS-TV (CBS, MeTV, Movies!) Las Vegas; KLVX (PBS) Las Vegas; KSNV (NBC) Las Vegas; KTNV-TV (ABC, Grit, Laff) Las Vegas; KVCW (CW, The Country Network) Las Vegas; KVVU-TV (Escape, FOX) Henderson.
Programming (via satellite): QVC; TBS; WGN America.
Fee: $39.95 installation; $24.99 monthly.

Expanded Basic Service 1
Subscribers: N.A.
Programming (via satellite): A&E; AMC; Animal Planet; Azteca; BET; Bravo; Cartoon Network; CMT; CNBC; CNN; Comedy Central; Cox Sports Television; C-SPAN; C-SPAN 2; Discovery Channel; Disney Channel; E! HD; ESPN; ESPN2; Food Network; Fox News Channel; FOX Sports West/Prime Ticket; Freeform; FX; Golf Channel; Hallmark Channel; HGTV; History; HLN; ION Television; Lifetime; MSNBC; MTV; MTV2; NBCSN; Nickelodeon; OWN: Oprah Winfrey Network; Pop; Spike TV; Syfy; The Weather Channel; TLC; TNT; Travel Channel; truTV; Turner Classic Movies; TV Land; UniMas; Univision; USA Network; VH1.
Fee: $37.95 monthly.

Digital Basic Service
Subscribers: N.A.
Programming (via satellite): A&E HD; AMC HD; Animal Planet HD; BBC America; Bloomberg Television; Boomerang; Bravo HD; BYUtv; Cartoon Network HD; CBS Sports Network; Chiller; CMT; CNBC HD+; CNN HD; Comedy Central; Cooking Channel; Destination America; Destination America HD; Discovery Channel HD; Discovery Kids Channel; Discovery Life Channel; Disney XD; DIY Network; E! HD; ESPN Classic; ESPN HD; ESPN2 HD; ESPNews; ESPNU; EWTN Global Catholic Network; Food Network HD; Fox Business Network; FOX College Sports Central; FOX College Sports Pacific; Fox News HD; Fox Sports 1; Fox Sports 2; Fuse; FX HD; FYI; GemsTV; Golf Channel HD; GSN; Hallmark Movie Channel HD; HD Theater; HGTV HD; History HD; History International; IFC; INSP; Investigation Discovery; Jewelry Television; LATV; Lifetime HD; Lifetime Movie Network HD; LMN; LOGO; MC; Mexicanal; MLB Network; MTV Classic; MTV Hits; MTV Live; mtvU; Nat Geo WILD; National Geographic Channel; National Geographic Channel HD; NBA TV; NBC Universo; NFL Network; NFL Network HD; NHL Network; Nick HD; Nick Jr.; Nicktoons; Oxygen; Science Channel; Science HD; Spike TV HD; Sprout; Starz Encore (multiplexed); Starz Encore Family; Sundance TV; Syfy HD; TBS HD; TeenNick; Tennis Channel; TLC HD; TNT HD; Tr3s; Travel Channel HD; Trinity Broadcasting Network (TBN); TV One; TVG Network; Universal HD; USA Network HD; Versus HD; VH1 HD; Vme TV; WE tv; Weatherscan; World.
Fee: $49.95 installation; $10.45 monthly.

Digital Expanded Basic Service
Subscribers: N.A.
Programming (via satellite): Bandamax; Cartoon Network en Espanol; CNN en Espanol; De Pelicula; De Pelicula Clasico; Disney XD; ESPN Deportes; Fox Deportes; GolTV; History en Espanol; Nick-Toons en Espanol; Ritmoson; Telehit; Tr3s; ViendoMovies.
Fee: $4.00 monthly.

Digital Pay Service 1
Pay Units: N.A.
Programming (via satellite): Cinemax (multiplexed); Cinemax HD; Flix; GMA Pinoy TV; HBO (multiplexed); HBO HD; Showtime (multiplexed); Showtime HD; Starz (multiplexed); Starz HD; The Filipino Channel; The Movie Channel (multiplexed).

Video-On-Demand: Yes

Pay-Per-View
Playboy TV (delivered digitally); MLB Extra Innings (delivered digitally); NHL Center Ice (delivered digitally); Spice: Xcess (delivered digitally); Club Jenna (delivered digitally); Juicy (delivered digitally); Sports PPV (delivered digitally); SexSee (delivered digitally); NBA League Pass (delivered digitally); MLS Direct Kick (delivered digitally); special events.

Internet Service
Operational: Yes. Began: August 1, 1997.
Subscribers: 375,163.
Broadband Service: Cox High Speed Internet.
Fee: $99.95 installation; $29.95-$57.99 monthly; $10.00 modem lease; $199.00 modem purchase.

Telephone Service
Digital: Operational
Subscribers: 210,751.
Fee: $10.40 monthly
Miles of Plant: 13,212.0 (coaxial); 2,996.0 (fiber optic). Homes passed: 858,898.
Senior Vice President & General Manager: Marilyn Burrows. Vice President, Sales & Marketing: Ellen Lloyd. Vice President, Network Development: Henry Schwab. Vice President, Business Operations: Tina Denicole. Vice President, Public Affairs & Government Operations: Steve Schorr. Vice President, Tax: Mary Vickers.
Ownership: Cox Communications Inc. (MSO).

LAS VEGAS—Formerly served by Sprint Corp. No longer in operation. ICA: NV0055.

LAUGHLIN—Suddenlink Communications, 520 Maryville Centre Dr, Ste 300, St. Louis, MO 63141. Phone: 314-315-9400. Web Site: http://www.suddenlink.com. ICA: NV0043.
TV Market Ranking: Below 100 (LAUGHLIN). Franchise award date: January 1, 1985. Franchise expiration date: N.A. Began: April 15, 1985.
Channel capacity: N.A. Channels available but not in use: N.A.

Basic Service
Subscribers: 1,302.
Programming (received off-air): KAET (PBS) Phoenix; KFTR-DT (getTV, UniMas) Ontario; KHSV (Antenna TV, MNT) Las Vegas; KINC (UNV) Las Vegas; KLAS-TV (CBS, MeTV, Movies!) Las Vegas; KLVX (PBS) Las Vegas; KSNV (NBC) Las Vegas; KTNV-TV (ABC, Grit, Laff) Las Vegas; KVVU-TV (Escape, FOX) Henderson.
Programming (via satellite): C-SPAN; C-SPAN 2; WGN America.
Fee: $35.00 installation; $23.45 monthly.

Expanded Basic Service 1
Subscribers: N.A.
Programming (via satellite): A&E; AMC; Animal Planet; CMT; CNBC; CNN; Comedy Central; Discovery Channel; Disney XD; E! HD; ESPN; ESPN2; ESPNews; Fox News Channel; Freeform; FX; History; HLN; Lifetime; MTV; Nickelodeon; Pop; QVC; Spike TV; Syfy; TBS; The Weather Channel; TLC; TNT; Travel Channel; Trinity Broadcasting Network (TBN); truTV; Turner Classic Movies; TV Land; USA Network; VH1.
Fee: $51.20 monthly.

Digital Basic Service
Subscribers: N.A.
Programming (via satellite): BBC America; Discovery Digital Networks; ESPN Classic; Fox Sports 1; FYI; Golf Channel; GSN; HGTV; History International; IFC; LMN; National Geographic Channel; NBCSN; WE tv.
Fee: $13.95 monthly.

Digital Pay Service 1
Pay Units: N.A.
Programming (via satellite): Cinemax (multiplexed); DMX Music; HBO (multiplexed); Showtime (multiplexed); Starz (multiplexed); Starz Encore (multiplexed); The Movie Channel (multiplexed).
Fee: $12.95 monthly (HBO), $13.95 monthly (Showtime, Cinemax, or Starz & Encore).

Video-On-Demand: No

Pay-Per-View
Hot Choice; iN DEMAND; Playboy TV; Spice.

Internet Service
Operational: Yes.
Broadband Service: CMA.
Fee: $39.95 installation; $44.95 monthly; $2.95 modem lease; $39.95 modem purchase.

Telephone Service
Digital: Operational
Fee: $39.95 monthly
Miles of Plant: 32.0 (coaxial); None (fiber optic). Homes passed: 4,282.
Senior Vice President, Corporate Finance: Michael Pflantz. Vice President: Dave Beasley. General Manager: Jerry Smith. Chief Technician: Daniel Coenen. Marketing Director: Julie Ferguson.
Ownership: Cequel Communications Holdings I LLC (MSO).

LOCKWOOD—Charter Communications. Now served by RENO, NV [NV0002]. ICA: NV0028.

LOGANDALE—Formerly served by Baja Broadband. No longer in operation. ICA: NV0046.

LOVELOCK—Formerly served by Lovelock Cable TV. No longer in operation. ICA: NV0044.

McGILL—Beehive Broadband, 2000 Sunset Rd, Lake Point, UT 84074. Phones: 800-615-8021; 435-837-6000. Fax: 435-837-6109.
E-mail: support@wirelessbeehive.com. Web Site: http://www.beehivebroadband.com. ICA: NV0021.
TV Market Ranking: Below 100 (MCGILL). Franchise award date: February 1, 1988. Franchise expiration date: N.A. Began: May 23, 1988.
Channel capacity: 40 (not 2-way capable). Channels available but not in use: N.A.

Basic Service
Subscribers: 17. Commercial subscribers: 2.
Programming (via translator): KBYU-TV (PBS) Provo; KJZZ-TV (IND) Salt Lake City; KLAS-TV (CBS, MeTV, Movies!) Las Vegas; KPNZ (Estrella TV) Ogden; KSL-TV (NBC) Salt Lake City; KSTU (Antenna TV, FOX) Salt Lake City; KTVX (ABC, MeTV) Salt Lake City; KUCW (CW, Movies!, The Country Network) Ogden; KUED (PBS) Salt Lake City; KUEN (ETV) Ogden; KUPX-TV (ION) Provo; KUTV (CBS, This TV) Salt Lake City.
Fee: $79.00 installation; $20.38 monthly.

Expanded Basic Service 1
Subscribers: N.A.
Programming (via satellite): A&E; AMC; Animal Planet; CMT; CNN; Comedy Central; Discovery Channel; Disney Channel; ESPN; Fox News Channel; Freeform; FX; Lifetime; Nickelodeon; QVC; Root Sports Rocky Mountain; Spike TV; TBS; The Weather Channel; TLC; TNT; USA Network; WGN America.
Fee: $25.00 monthly.

Digital Basic Service
Subscribers: N.A.
Programming (via satellite): BBC America; Bravo; Discovery Digital Networks; Disney XD; DMX Music; ESPN Classic; ESPN2; ESPNews; EVINE Live; FOX College Sports Central; FOX College Sports Pacific; Fox Sports 1; Fuse; FYI; Golf Channel; Great American Country; GSN; HGTV; History; History International; IFC; LMN; National Geographic Channel; NBCSN; The Word Network; Turner Classic Movies; WE tv.

Digital Pay Service 1
Pay Units: N.A.
Programming (via satellite): Cinemax (multiplexed); Flix; HBO (multiplexed); Showtime (multiplexed); Starz (multiplexed); Starz Encore (multiplexed); The Movie Channel (multiplexed).
Fee: $12.95 monthly (HBO, Cinemax, Showtime/TMC/Flix or Starz/Encore).

Video-On-Demand: No

Pay-Per-View
iN DEMAND (delivered digitally); Playboy TV (delivered digitally).

Internet Service
Operational: No.

Telephone Service
None
Miles of Plant: 12.0 (coaxial); None (fiber optic). Homes passed: 500.
President: Scott Wilson. Manager: Wayne A. McCulley.
Ownership: Beehive Broadband LLC (MSO).

MESQUITE—Baja Broadband. Now served by ST. GEORGE, UT [UT0007]. ICA: NV0045.

MESQUITE—Reliance Connects, 61 West Mesquite Blvd, PO Box 299, Mesquite, NV 89027. Phone: 702-346-5211. Fax: 702-346-5216. E-mail: info@rconnects.com. Web Site: http://relianceconnects.com. Also serves Beaverdam, Littlefield & Scenic, AZ; Bunkerville, NV. ICA: NV0058.

Cable Systems—Nevada

TV Market Ranking: Below 100 (Beaverdam, Bunkerville, Littlefield, MESQUITE, Scenic). Channel capacity: N.A. Channels available but not in use: N.A.
Basic Service
Subscribers: 1,477.
Fee: $23.70 monthly.
General Manager: Harold Oster.
Ownership: Reliance Connects (MSO).

NELLIS AFB—Formerly served by Bluebird Communications. No longer in operation. ICA: NV0011.

PAHRUMP—Suddenlink Communications, 520 Maryville Centre Dr, Ste 300, St. Louis, MO 63141. Phone: 314-315-9400. Web Site: http://www.suddenlink.com. ICA: NV0014.
TV Market Ranking: Outside TV Markets (PAHRUMP). Franchise award date: January 1, 1989. Franchise expiration date: N.A. Began: January 1, 1985.
Channel capacity: N.A. Channels available but not in use: N.A.
Basic Service
Subscribers: 573.
Programming (received off-air): KHSV (Antenna TV, MNT) Las Vegas; KINC (UNV) Las Vegas; KLAS-TV (CBS, MeTV, Movies!) Las Vegas; KLVX (PBS) Las Vegas; KPVM-LP (ION) Pahrump; KPVT-LP (Retro TV) Pahrump; KSNV (NBC) Las Vegas; KTNV-TV (ABC, Grit, Laff) Las Vegas; KVVU-TV (Escape, FOX) Henderson.
Programming (via satellite): Animal Planet; CNN; C-SPAN; ESPN; Fox News Channel; FX; Lifetime; Nickelodeon; TBS; The Weather Channel; TNT; TV Land; USA Network; WGN America.
Fee: $35.00 installation; $29.45 monthly.
Expanded Basic Service 1
Subscribers: N.A.
Programming (received off-air): KHMP-LD (America One) Las Vegas.
Programming (via satellite): A&E; AMC; Cartoon Network; CMT; Comedy Central; C-SPAN 2; Discovery Channel; E! HD; ESPN Classic; ESPN2; EWTN Global Catholic Network; Food Network; FOX Sports West/Prime Ticket; Freeform; GSN; Hallmark Channel; HGTV; History; HLN; INSP; MSNBC; MTV; National Geographic Channel; Pop; QVC; Spike TV; Syfy; TLC; Travel Channel; Trinity Broadcasting Network (TBN); Turner Classic Movies; VH1.
Fee: $47.70 monthly.
Digital Basic Service
Subscribers: N.A.
Programming (via satellite): Discovery Digital Networks; ESPNews; Fox Sports 1; FXM; FYI; Golf Channel; History International; IFC; LMN; MTV Classic; MTV2; Nick Jr.; Nicktoons; Outdoor Channel; TeenNick; VH1 Country.
Fee: $12.00 monthly.
Digital Pay Service 1
Pay Units: N.A.
Programming (via satellite): Cinemax (multiplexed); DMX Music; HBO (multiplexed); Showtime (multiplexed); Starz (multiplexed); Starz Encore (multiplexed); The Movie Channel (multiplexed).
Fee: $10.95 monthly (Cinemax or Starz/Encore), $13.95 monthly (HBO or Showtime).
Pay-Per-View
Hot Network (delivered digitally); Spice (delivered digitally); special events (delivered digitally).

Internet Service
Operational: Yes.
Broadband Service: CMA.
Fee: $39.95 installation; $37.95 monthly; $2.95 modem lease; $39.95 modem purchase.
Telephone Service
Digital: Operational
Fee: $39.95 monthly
Miles of Plant: 270.0 (coaxial); None (fiber optic). Homes passed: 2,000.
Senior Vice President, Corporate Finance: Michael Pflantz. General Manager: Jerry Smith. Chief Technician: Greg Petras. Marketing Director: Julie Ferguson.
Ownership: Cequel Communications Holdings I LLC (MSO).

PIOCHE—Rainbow Cable, 27 Main St, PO Box 300, Pioche, NV 89043-0300. Phones: 775-962-5200; 775-962-5111. Fax: 775-962-5193. Also serves Caliente & Panaca. ICA: NV0047.
TV Market Ranking: Outside TV Markets (Caliente, Panaca, PIOCHE).
Channel capacity: N.A. Channels available but not in use: N.A.
Basic Service
Subscribers: 457.
Programming (via microwave): KCNC-TV (CBS, Decades) Denver; KMGH-TV (ABC, Azteca America) Denver; KUSA (NBC, WeatherNation) Denver.
Programming (via satellite): CMT; Discovery Channel; Disney Channel; ESPN; Freeform; HLN; MTV; Nickelodeon; Spike TV; TBS; TLC; TNT; USA Network; WGN America.
Fee: $43.00 installation; $41.95 monthly.
Pay Service 1
Pay Units: N.A.
Programming (via satellite): Cinemax; HBO; Showtime.
Fee: $7.90 monthly (Showtime), $7.95 monthly (Cinemax), $9.95 monthly (HBO).
Video-On-Demand: No
Internet Service
Operational: No.
Telephone Service
None
Vice President & General Manager: Paul Christian. Chief Technician: Paul Donohue. Office Manager: Valinda Woodworth.
Ownership: Christian Enterprises (MSO).

PIOCHE—Rainbow Cable. Now served by PIOCHE, NV [NV0047]. ICA: NV0048.

RENO—Charter Communications, 12405 Powerscourt Dr, St. Louis, MO 63131. Phones: 636-207-5100 (Corporate office); 775-348-2772; 775-850-1200. Fax: 775-850-1279. Web Site: http://www.charter.com. Also serves El Dorado County (portions), Meyers, North Lake Tahoe & South Lake Tahoe, CA; Carson City, Churchill County (portions), Dayton, Douglas County (portions), Fallon, Fallon Station, Fernley, Gardnerville, Glenbrook, Lyon County (northern portion), Lyon County (northwestern portion), Minden, Silver Springs, Sparks, Stateline, Storey County (southern portion), Wadsworth & Washoe County, NV. ICA: NV0002.
TV Market Ranking: Below 100 (Dayton, Douglas County (portions) (portions), Glenbrook, Lyon County (northern portion) (portions), Lyon County (northwestern portion), RENO, Sparks, Storey County (southern portion), Wadsworth, Washoe County, Carson City, Fernley, Silver Springs); Outside TV Markets (Churchill County (portions), Douglas County (portions) (portions), El Dorado County (portions), Fallon Station, Lyon County (northern portion) (portions), Minden, Stateline, Fallon, Gardnerville, Meyers, South Lake Tahoe). Franchise award date: N.A. Franchise expiration date: N.A. Began: September 1, 1953.
Channel capacity: N.A. Channels available but not in use: N.A.
Digital Basic Service
Subscribers: 93,822.
Programming (via satellite): BBC America; Bravo; Discovery Digital Networks; DMX Music; ESPN Classic; Golf Channel; GSN; History; IFC; NBCSN; Turner Classic Movies; WE tv.
Fee: $26.99 monthly.
Digital Expanded Basic Service
Subscribers: 54,558.
Programming (via satellite): A&E; AMC; Animal Planet; BET; Cartoon Network; CNBC; CNN; Comcast SportsNet Bay Area; Comedy Central; Disney Channel; E! HD; ESPN; ESPN2; Food Network; Fox News Channel; FX; Great American Country; Hallmark Channel; HGTV; HLN; ION Television; Lifetime; MSNBC; MTV; NBC Universo; Nickelodeon; Spike TV; Syfy; TLC; TNT; TV Land; Univision; USA Network; VH1.
Fee: $30.30 monthly.
Digital Pay Service 1
Pay Units: N.A.
Programming (via satellite): Cinemax (multiplexed); HBO (multiplexed); Showtime (multiplexed); Starz (multiplexed); Starz Encore (multiplexed); The Movie Channel (multiplexed).
Video-On-Demand: Yes
Pay-Per-View
Hot Choice (delivered digitally); iN DEMAND; iN DEMAND (delivered digitally); Fresh (delivered digitally); Shorteez (delivered digitally).
Internet Service
Operational: Yes. Began: November 1, 2000.
Broadband Service: Charter Internet.
Fee: $29.99 monthly; $10.00 modem lease; $300.00 modem purchase.
Telephone Service
Digital: Operational
Subscribers: 27,541.
Fee: $34.99 monthly
Miles of Plant: 6,023.0 (coaxial); 2,143.0 (fiber optic). Homes passed: 314,534.
Vice President & General Manager: Manny Martinez. Technical Operations Manager: Carol Eure. Accounting Director: David Sovanski.
Ownership: Charter Communications Inc. (MSO).

RENO—Formerly served by Quadravision. No longer in operation. ICA: NV0053.

RUTH—Formerly served by Central Telecom Services (CUTV). No longer in operation. ICA: NV0029.

ADVANCED TVFactbook
FULLY SEARCHABLE • CONTINUOUSLY UPDATED • DISCOUNT RATES FOR PRINT PURCHASERS
For more information call **800-771-9202** or visit **www.warren-news.com**

SILVER SPRINGS—Charter Communications. Now served by RENO, NV [NV0002]. ICA: NV0017.

TONOPAH—Formerly served by RealStar Communications. No longer in operation. ICA: NV0050.

TOPAZ LAKE—Satview Broadband, 3550 Barron Way, Ste 13A, Reno, NV 89511. Phones: 775-333-6626 (Customer care); 775-324-2198. Fax: 775-333-0225. E-mail: satviewreno@yahoo.com. Web Site: http://www.satview.net. Also serves Walker, CA; Holbrook Junction & Topaz Ranch Estates, NV. ICA: NV0019.
TV Market Ranking: Outside TV Markets (Holbrook Junction, TOPAZ LAKE, Topaz Ranch Estates, Walker). Franchise award date: March 1, 1980. Franchise expiration date: N.A. Began: June 5, 1979.
Channel capacity: N.A. Channels available but not in use: N.A.
Basic Service
Subscribers: 200.
Programming (received off-air): KAME-TV (MeTV, MNT) Reno; KNPB (PBS) Reno; KOLO-TV (ABC, IND, Movies!) Reno; KREN-TV (CW, UNV) Reno; KRNS-CD (IND) Reno; KRNV-DT (NBC, This TV) Reno; KRXI-TV (FOX, Retro TV) Reno; KTVN (Antenna TV, CBS) Reno; allband FM.
Programming (via satellite): A&E; AMC; Animal Planet; Cartoon Network; CMT; CNBC; CNN; Comcast SportsNet California; C-SPAN; Discovery Channel; Disney Channel; E! HD; ESPN; ESPN2; Food Network; Fox News Channel; Fox Sports 1; Freeform; FX; Hallmark Channel; HGTV; History; HLN; ION Television; Lifetime; MSNBC; MTV; National Geographic Channel; Nickelodeon; QVC; Spike TV; TBS; The Weather Channel; TLC; TNT; Travel Channel; truTV; Turner Classic Movies; Univision Studios; USA Network; VH1.
Fee: $40.00 installation; $26.25 monthly.
Digital Basic Service
Subscribers: N.A.
Programming (via satellite): A&E HD; AWE; AXS TV; AYM Sports; Bandamax; BBC America; Bloomberg Television; Bravo; BYUtv; Cartoon Network; CBS Sports Network; Cinelatino; CMT; CNN en Espanol; Comedy Central; Cooking Channel; C-SPAN 2; Daystar TV Network; Destination America; Discovery Familia; Discovery Kids Channel; Discovery Life Channel; Disney XD; DIY Network; ESPN Classic; ESPN Deportes; ESPN HD; ESPN2 HD; ESPNews; ESPNU; Fox Business Network; FOX College Sports Central; FOX College Sports Pacific; Fox Deportes; Fuse; FXM; FYI; Golf Channel; GolTV; Great American Country; GSN; Hallmark Movies & Mysteries; HD Theater; History en Espanol; History International; HITN; IFC; Infinito; Investigation Discovery; Jewelry Television; LMN; MTV Classic; MTV Hits; MTV Jams; MTV Live; MTV2; NBC Universo; NBCSN; Nick Jr.; Outdoor Channel; OWN; Oprah Winfrey Network; Pop; Science Channel; Starz Encore (multiplexed); Sundance TV; Syfy;

Nevada—Cable Systems

FULLY SEARCHABLE • CONTINUOUSLY UPDATED • DISCOUNT RATES FOR PRINT PURCHASERS
For more information call 800-771-9202 or visit www.warren-news.com

TeenNick; Tennis Channel; TNT HD; Tr3s; Trinity Broadcasting Network (TBN); TV Land; UP; VH1 Soul; VideoRola; Vubiquity Inc.; WE tv.
Digital Pay Service 1
Pay Units: N.A.
Programming (via satellite): Cinemax (multiplexed); Cinemax HD; HBO (multiplexed); HBO HD; Showtime (multiplexed); Showtime HD; Starz (multiplexed); Starz HD; The Movie Channel.
Internet Service
Operational: No.
Telephone Service
None
Miles of Plant: 30.0 (coaxial); None (fiber optic). Homes passed: 3,000.
President: Tariq Ahmad.
Ownership: Satview Broadband Ltd.

VERDI—Formerly served by Suddenlink Communications. No longer in operation. ICA: NV0056.

VIRGINIA CITY—Comstock Community TV Inc, PO Box 9, Virginia City, NV 89440-0009. Phone: 775-847-0572. Also serves Gold Hill. ICA: NV0025.
TV Market Ranking: Below 100 (Gold Hill, VIRGINIA CITY). Franchise award date: N.A. Franchise expiration date: N.A. Began: November 1, 1957.
Channel capacity: 27 (not 2-way capable). Channels available but not in use: N.A.
Basic Service
Subscribers: N.A.
Programming (received off-air): KAME-TV (MeTV, MNT) Reno; KNPB (PBS) Reno; KOLO-TV (ABC, IND, Movies!) Reno; KREN-TV (CW, UNV) Reno; KRNV-DT (NBC, This TV) Reno; KRXI-TV (FOX, Retro TV) Reno; KTVN (Antenna TV, CBS) Reno.
Programming (via satellite): A&E; Animal Planet; CNN; Comedy Central; Discovery Channel; ESPN; Food Network; Fox News Channel; FXM; Hallmark Channel; HGTV; History; HLN; Lifetime; National Geographic Channel; Outdoor Channel; QVC; Spike TV; Syfy; TBS; TLC; TNT; Travel Channel; Turner Classic Movies; WGN America.
Fee: $65.00 installation; $15.00 monthly.
Video-On-Demand: No
Internet Service
Operational: No.
Telephone Service
None
Miles of Plant: 5.0 (coaxial); None (fiber optic).
General Manager & Program Director: Barbara Bowers. Chief Technician: Gary Greenlund.
Ownership: Comstock Community TV Inc.

WELLINGTON—Satview Broadband, 3550 Barron Way, Ste 13A, Reno, NV 89511. Phones: 775-333-6626 (Customer care); 775-324-2198. Fax: 775-333-0225. E-mail: satviewreno@yahoo.com. Web Site: http://www.satview.net. ICA: NV0057.
TV Market Ranking: Outside TV Markets (WELLINGTON).
Channel capacity: N.A. Channels available but not in use: N.A.

Digital Basic Service
Subscribers: N.A.
Programming (received off-air): KAME-TV (MeTV, MNT) Reno; KNPB (PBS) Reno; KOLO-TV (ABC, IND, Movies!) Reno; KRNV-DT (NBC, This TV) Reno; KRXI-TV (FOX, Retro TV) Reno; KTVN (Antenna TV, CBS) Reno.
Programming (via satellite): A&E; AMC; BBC America; Bloomberg Television; Bravo; Classic Arts Showcase; Destination America; Discovery Channel; Discovery Kids Channel; Discovery Life Channel; Disney Channel; ESPN; ESPN2; Fox News Channel; Fox Sports 1; Freeform; FXM; FYI; Golf Channel; Great American Country; HGTV; History; Investigation Discovery; MSNBC; Nickelodeon; Outdoor Channel; OWN: Oprah Winfrey Network; QVC; Science Channel; Spike TV; Syfy; TBS; TNT; Trinity Broadcasting Network (TBN); Turner Classic Movies; Univision Studios; USA Network; WE tv; WGN America.
Fee: $38.00 monthly.
Digital Pay Service 1
Pay Units: N.A.
Programming (via satellite): Cinemax (multiplexed); HBO (multiplexed); Starz (multiplexed); Starz Encore (multiplexed); The Movie Channel.
Pay-Per-View
XTSY (delivered digitally).
Internet Service
Operational: No.
Telephone Service
None
President: Tariq Ahmad.
Ownership: Satview Broadband Ltd. (MSO).

WELLS—Satview Broadband, 3550 Barron Way, Ste 13A, Reno, NV 89511. Phones: 775-324-2198 (Reno office); 877-538-2662; 775-333-6626. Fax: 775-333-0225. E-mail: satviewreno@yahoo.com. Web Site: http://www.satview.net. ICA: NV0023.
TV Market Ranking: Outside TV Markets (WELLS). Franchise award date: N.A. Franchise expiration date: N.A. Began: April 1, 1957.
Channel capacity: N.A. Channels available but not in use: N.A.
Basic Service
Subscribers: 395.
Programming (via microwave): KENV-DT (NBC) Elko; KSL-TV (NBC) Salt Lake City; KSTU (Antenna TV, FOX) Salt Lake City; KTVN (Antenna TV, CBS) Reno; KTVX (ABC, MeTV) Salt Lake City; KUCW (CW, Movies!, The Country Network) Ogden; KUED (PBS) Salt Lake City; KUTV (CBS, This TV) Salt Lake City.
Programming (via satellite): C-SPAN; Hallmark Channel; QVC.
Fee: $45.47 installation; $11.11 monthly.
Expanded Basic Service 1
Subscribers: N.A.
Programming (via satellite): A&E; AMC; Animal Planet; Cartoon Network; CNBC; CNN; Comedy Central; Discovery Channel; Disney Channel; E! HD; ESPN; ESPN2; Fox News Channel; FOX Sports Networks; Freeform; FX; HLN; Lifetime; MSNBC; MTV; Nickelodeon; Spike TV; TBS; The Weather Channel; TLC; TNT; TV Land; Univision; USA Network; VH1.
Fee: $12.67 installation; $1.91 monthly.
Digital Basic Service
Subscribers: N.A.
Programming (via satellite): BBC America; Bloomberg Television; Bravo; Discovery Life Channel; Disney XD; DMX Music; ESPN Classic; ESPNews; Fox Sports 1; Fuse; FXM; FYI; Golf Channel; GSN; HGTV; History; History International; IFC; LMN; NBCSN; Nick Jr.; Outdoor Channel; Syfy; TeenNick; Trinity Broadcasting Network (TBN); Turner Classic Movies; WE tv.
Digital Pay Service 1
Pay Units: N.A.
Programming (via satellite): Cinemax (multiplexed); Flix; HBO (multiplexed); Showtime (multiplexed); Starz (multiplexed); Starz Encore (multiplexed); The Movie Channel (multiplexed).
Video-On-Demand: No
Pay-Per-View
iN DEMAND (delivered digitally); ESPN Now (delivered digitally); Sports PPV (delivered digitally); Hot Choice (delivered digitally); Playboy TV (delivered digitally); Fresh (delivered digitally); Shorteez (delivered digitally).
Internet Service
Operational: No.
Telephone Service
None
Miles of Plant: 20.0 (coaxial); None (fiber optic). Homes passed: 1,500.
President: Tariq Ahmad.
Ownership: Satview Broadband Ltd. (MSO).

WINNEMUCCA—CalNeva Broadband, 322 Ash St, PO Box 1470, Westwood, CA 96137. Phones: 530-256-2028; 866-330-2028; 775-625-1138; 775-625-1120. Web Site: http://blog.calneva.org. Also serves Humboldt County (portions). ICA: NV0010.
TV Market Ranking: Below 100 (Humboldt County (portions), WINNEMUCCA); Outside TV Markets (Humboldt County (portions)). Franchise award date: March 1, 1982. Franchise expiration date: N.A. Began: August 6, 1982.
Channel capacity: N.A. Channels available but not in use: N.A.
Basic Service
Subscribers: 403.
Programming (received off-air): KAME-TV (MeTV, MNT) Reno; KNPB (PBS) Reno; KOLO-TV (ABC, IND, Movies!) Reno; KREN-TV (CW, UNV) Reno; KRNV-DT (NBC, This TV) Reno; KRXI-TV (FOX, Retro TV) Reno; KTVN (Antenna TV, CBS) Reno; KTVX (ABC, MeTV) Salt Lake City; KUTV (CBS, This TV) Salt Lake City.
Programming (via satellite): ION Television; NASA TV; QVC; WGN America.
Fee: $65.00 installation; $31.00 monthly.
Expanded Basic Service 1
Subscribers: N.A.
Programming (via satellite): 3ABN; A&E; AMC; Animal Planet; Boomerang; Cartoon Network; CMT; CNBC; CNN; Comcast SportsNet Bay Area; Comedy Central; C-SPAN; C-SPAN 2; Discovery Channel; DIY Network; E! HD; ESPN; ESPN Classic; ESPN2; Food Network; Fox News Channel; Fox Sports 1; Freeform; FX; Great American Country; Hallmark Channel; HGTV; History; HLN; Lifetime; MSNBC; MTV; National Geographic Channel; Nickelodeon; Outdoor Channel; Pop; Spike TV; Syfy; TBS; The Weather Channel; TLC; TNT; Travel Channel; truTV; Turner Classic Movies; TV Land; Univision; Univision Studios; USA Network; VH1.
Fee: $19.00 monthly.
Digital Basic Service
Subscribers: N.A.
Programming (via satellite): BBC America; Bloomberg Television; CMT; Destination America; Discovery Kids Channel; DMX Music; ESPNews; Fox Sports 1; FYI; Golf Channel; GSN; History International; Investigation Discovery; LMN; MTV Classic; MTV Jams; MTV2; Nick Jr.; Nicktoons; Outdoor Channel; Ovation; OWN: Oprah Winfrey Network; Science Channel; TeenNick; VH1 Soul.
Fee: $12.95 monthly.
Digital Expanded Basic Service
Subscribers: N.A.
Programming (via satellite): FXM; Sundance TV.
Fee: $4.65 monthly.
Pay Service 1
Pay Units: N.A.
Programming (via satellite): HBO.
Digital Pay Service 1
Pay Units: N.A.
Programming (via satellite): Cinemax (multiplexed); HBO (multiplexed); Showtime (multiplexed); Starz (multiplexed); Starz Encore (multiplexed); The Movie Channel (multiplexed).
Fee: $8.35 monthly (Starz), $13.00 monthly (HBO or Cinemax), $20.30 monthly (Showtime/TMC).
Video-On-Demand: No
Pay-Per-View
Pay-per-view 1 (delivered digitally); Pay-per-view 2 (delivered digitally); Pay-per-view 3 (delivered digitally); Pay-per-view 4 (delivered digitally).
Internet Service
Operational: Yes.
Broadband Service: Rapid High Speed Internet.
Fee: $29.95 installation; $24.95 monthly.
Telephone Service
None
Miles of Plant: 89.0 (coaxial); None (fiber optic). Homes passed: 3,703.
General Manager: Tom Gelardi.
Ownership: CalNeva Broadband LLC (MSO).

YERINGTON—Charter Communications, 12405 Powerscourt Dr, St. Louis, MO 63131. Phones: 636-207-5100 (Corporate office); 775-348-2772; 775-850-1200. Fax: 775-850-1279. Web Site: http://www.charter.com. Also serves Lyon County (portions). ICA: NV0008.
TV Market Ranking: Outside TV Markets (Lyon County (portions), YERINGTON). Franchise award date: N.A. Franchise expiration date: N.A. Began: August 1, 1964.
Channel capacity: N.A. Channels available but not in use: N.A.
Digital Basic Service
Subscribers: 198.
Programming (via satellite): AWE; AXS TV; BBC America; Bloomberg Television; BYUtv; CBS Sports Network; CMT; Cooking Channel; Daystar TV Network; Discovery Digital Networks; Disney XD; DIY Network; ESPN HD; ESPNews; FOX College Sports Central; FOX College Sports Pacific; Fox Sports 2; Fuse; FXM; FYI; GolTV; Great American Country; GSN; Hallmark Movies & Mysteries; HD Theater; History International; HITS (Headend In The Sky); IFC; INSP; Jewelry Television; LMN; MC; MTV Live; NBCSN; Nick Jr.; Nicktoons; Outdoor Channel; Sundance TV; TeenNick; Tennis Channel; TNT HD; Trinity Broadcasting

Cable Systems—Nevada

Network (TBN); Universal HD; Versus On Demand; WE tv.
Fee: $35.99 monthly.

Digital Expanded Basic Service
Subscribers: N.A.
Programming (via satellite): A&E; AMC; Animal Planet; BET; Bravo; Cartoon Network; CMT; CNBC; CNN; Comcast SportsNet Bay Area; Comedy Central; Discovery Channel; Disney Channel; E! HD; ESPN; ESPN Classic; ESPN2; Food Network; Fox Deportes; Fox Sports 1; Freeform; FX; Golf Channel; Hallmark Channel; HGTV; History; HLN; Lifetime; MSNBC; MTV; MTV2; National Geographic Channel; Nickelodeon; Oxygen; Spike TV; Syfy; The Weather Channel; TLC; TNT; Travel Channel; truTV; Turner Classic Movies; TV Land; USA Network; VH1.
Fee: $32.58 monthly.

Digital Pay Service 1
Pay Units: N.A.
Programming (via satellite): Cinemax (multiplexed); Cinemax HD; Cinemax On Demand; HBO (multiplexed); HBO HD; HBO on Demand; Showtime (multiplexed); Showtime HD; Showtime On Demand; Starz (multiplexed); Starz Encore (multiplexed); Starz HD; Starz On Demand; The Filipino Channel; The Movie Channel (multiplexed).
Video-On-Demand: Yes

Pay-Per-View
iN DEMAND (delivered digitally); NHL Center Ice (delivered digitally); Sports PPV (delivered digitally); Playboy TV (delivered digitally); SexSee (delivered digitally); MLB Extra Innings (delivered digitally).

Internet Service
Operational: Yes.
Broadband Service: Charter Internet.
Fee: $29.99 monthly; $10.00 modem lease.

Telephone Service
Digital: Operational
Miles of Plant: 49.0 (coaxial); None (fiber optic). Homes passed: 7,266.

Vice President & General Manager: Manny Martinez. Technical Operations Manager: Carol Eure. Accounting Director: David Sovanski.
Ownership: Charter Communications Inc. (MSO).

NEW HAMPSHIRE

Total Systems: 11
Total Communities Served: 89
Franchises Not Yet Operating: 0
Applications Pending: 0

Communities with Applications: 0
Number of Basic Subscribers: 102,428
Number of Expanded Basic Subscribers: 0
Number of Pay Units: 360

Top 100 Markets Represented: Boston-Cambridge-Worcester-Lawrence, MA (6); Portland-Poland Spring, ME (75).

For a list of cable communities in this section, see the Cable Community Index located in the back of Cable Volume 2.
For explanation of terms used in cable system listings, see p. D-11.

ALSTEAD—Formerly served by Adelphia Communications. Now served by Comcast Cable, BURLINGTON, VT [VT0001]. ICA: NH0025.

ANDOVER (town)—Formerly served by Adelphia Communications. Now served by Comcast Cable, BURLINGTON, VT [VT0001]. ICA: NH0028.

BATH (village)—Formerly served by Adelphia Communications. Now served by Time Warner Cable, BERLIN, NH [NH0012]. ICA: NH0035.

BELMONT—MetroCast Cablevision, 9 Apple Rd, Belmont, NH 03220-3251. Phones: 800-952-1001; 603-524-3767 (Administrative office). Fax: 603-524-5190. Web Site: http://www.metrocast.com. Also serves Alexandria, Alton, Barnstead, Bridgewater, Bristol, Center Harbor, Deerfield, Epsom, Franklin, Gilford, Gilmanton, Hebron, Laconia, Meredith, New Durham, New Hampton, Northfield, Northfield (town), Northwood, Pittsfield, Sanbornton (town), Strafford (town-portions), Tilton & Wolfeboro. ICA: NH0044.
TV Market Ranking: 6 (Alton, Barnstead, Deerfield, Epsom, Franklin, Gilmanton, Laconia, New Durham, Northfield, Northwood, Pittsfield, Strafford (town-portions), Tilton, Wolfeboro); Below 100 (Alexandria, BELMONT, Bridgewater, Bristol, Center Harbor, Gilford, Hebron, Meredith, New Hampton, Northfield, Sanbornton (town), Alton, Barnstead, Epsom, Franklin, Gilmanton, Laconia, New Durham, Northfield, Pittsfield, Strafford (town-portions), Tilton, Wolfeboro). Franchise award date: N.A. Franchise expiration date: N.A. Began: July 1, 1952.
Channel capacity: N.A. Channels available but not in use: N.A.
Basic Service
Subscribers: 27,119.
Programming (received off-air): WBIN-TV (Antenna TV, IND, WeatherNation) Derry; WENH-TV (PBS) Durham; WMFP (COZI TV, MeTV, Retro TV) Lawrence; WMTW (ABC) Poland Spring; WMUR-TV (ABC, MeTV) Manchester; WNEU (TMO) Merrimack; WPXG-TV (ION) Concord; allband FM. Programming (via microwave): New England Cable News; WBZ-TV (CBS, Decades) Boston; WCSH (Antenna TV, NBC) Portland; WCVB-TV (ABC, MeTV) Boston; WFXT (FOX, Movies!) Boston; WGBH-TV (PBS) Boston; WGME-TV (CBS) Portland; WHDH (NBC, This TV) Boston; WLVI (CW, The Country Network) Cambridge; WSBK-TV (MNT) Boston. Programming (via satellite): C-SPAN; Pop; TBS.
Fee: $30.00 installation; $35.95 monthly.

Expanded Basic Service 1
Subscribers: N.A.
Programming (via satellite): Fox Sports Net New Englan; A&E; AMC; Animal Planet; Bravo; Cartoon Network; CNBC; CNN; Comedy Central; C-SPAN; Discovery Channel; Disney Channel; E! HD; ESPN; ESPN2; EWTN Global Catholic Network; Fox News Channel; Freeform; FX; Golf Channel; HGTV; History; HLN; Lifetime; MSNBC; MTV; New England Sports Network; Nickelodeon; QVC; Spike TV; Syfy; The Weather Channel; TLC; TNT; USA Network; VH1.
Fee: $28.95 monthly.
Digital Basic Service
Subscribers: N.A.
Programming (via satellite): BBC America; Bloomberg Television; Boomerang; Discovery Digital Networks; DIY Network; ESPN Classic; Fox Sports 1; FXM; FYI; GSN; History International; IFC; LMN; MC; NBCSN; Nick Jr.; Outdoor Channel; truTV; Turner Classic Movies; WE tv.
Fee: $6.95 monthly.
Digital Pay Service 1
Pay Units: N.A.
Programming (via satellite): Cinemax (multiplexed); HBO (multiplexed); Showtime (multiplexed); Starz (multiplexed); The Movie Channel (multiplexed).
Fee: $12.95 monthly (each).
Video-On-Demand: Yes
Pay-Per-View
iN DEMAND; iN DEMAND (delivered digitally); ETC; Pleasure (delivered digitally); TEN-The Erotic Network.
Internet Service
Operational: Yes. Began: January 1, 2001.
Subscribers: 28,961.
Broadband Service: Great Works Internet.
Fee: $99.00 installation; $41.95 monthly; $5.00 modem lease; $149.50 modem purchase.
Telephone Service
Digital: Operational
Subscribers: 12,601.
Miles of Plant: 3,293.0 (coaxial); 1,038.0 (fiber optic). Homes passed: 64,266.
Vice President, Advanced Services: Josh Barstow. Technical Operations Corporate Director: Jeff Drapeau. Regional General Manager: Moira Campbell.
Ownership: Harron Communications LP (MSO).

BERLIN—Time Warner Cable, 118 Johnston Rd, Portland, ME 04102. Phones: 207-253-2400; 207-253-2200. Fax: 207-253-2405. Web Site: http://www.timewarnercable.com. Also serves Ashland, Bath (village), Bethlehem (town), Campton, Carroll, Dalton, Dorchester (town), Franconia, Gorham, Groton (town), Groveton, Holderness (portions), Lancaster, Lincoln, Lisbon, Littleton, Monroe (town), North Woodstock, Northumberland (town), Plymouth, Randolph, Rumney (town), Sugar Hill (town), Thornton, Warren (town), Wentworth (town), Whitefield & Woodstock. ICA: NH0012.
TV Market Ranking: Below 100 (Ashland, Dorchester (town), Groton (town), Rumney (town), Warren (town), Wentworth (town), Plymouth), Outside TV Markets (Bath (village), BERLIN, Bethlehem (town), Campton, Carroll, Dalton, Franconia, Gorham, Groveton, Holderness (portions), Lancaster, Lincoln, Lisbon, Monroe (town), North Woodstock, Northumberland (town), Randolph, Sugar Hill (town), Thornton, Whitefield, Woodstock, Littleton). Franchise award date: N.A. Franchise expiration date: N.A. Began: December 4, 1954.
Channel capacity: N.A. Channels available but not in use: N.A.

Basic Service
Subscribers: 15,309.
Programming (received off-air): W27BL Berlin; WCAX-TV (CBS, Movies!) Burlington; WCBB (PBS) Augusta; WCSH (Antenna TV, NBC) Portland; WGME-TV (CBS) Portland; WLED-TV (PBS) Littleton; WMTW (ABC) Poland Spring; 16 FMs. Programming (via microwave): WSBK-TV (MNT) Boston.
Programming (via satellite): C-SPAN; C-SPAN 2; Jewelry Television; Pop; QVC; TBS.
Fee: $61.40 installation; $20.99 monthly.

Expanded Basic Service 1
Subscribers: N.A.
Programming (via satellite): A&E; AMC; Animal Planet; BBC America; Bravo; Cartoon Network; CMT; CNBC; CNN; Comedy Central; Discovery Channel; Discovery Life Channel; Disney Channel; E! HD; ESPN; ESPN2; EVINE Live; EWTN Global Catholic Network; Food Network; Fox News Channel; Fox Sports 1; Freeform; FX; Great American Country; Hallmark Channel; HGTV; History; HLN; INSP; ION Television; Lifetime; LMN; MSNBC; MTV; National Geographic Channel; New England Sports Network; Nickelodeon; OWN: Oprah Winfrey Network; Oxygen; Spike TV; Syfy; The Weather Channel; TLC; TNT; Travel Channel; truTV; TV Land; USA Network; VH1; WE tv.
Fee: $15.00 installation; $41.82 monthly.

Digital Basic Service
Subscribers: N.A.
Programming (via satellite): Bloomberg Television; Boomerang; CNN International; C-SPAN 3; Discovery Digital Networks; Disney XD; DIY Network; DMX Music; ESPN Classic; ESPNews; FamilyNet; Fuse; Golf Channel; GSN; IFC; MTV Classic; MTV2; NBCSN; Nick Jr.; Nicktoons; Outdoor Channel; Ovation; TeenNick; Trinity Broadcasting Network (TBN); Turner Classic Movies.

Digital Expanded Basic Service
Subscribers: N.A.
Programming (via satellite): Fox Sports 2; FSN Digital Atlantic; FSN Digital Central; FSN Digital Pacific; NBA TV; Tennis Channel.
Fee: $7.00 monthly.
Digital Pay Service 1
Pay Units: N.A.
Programming (via satellite): Cinemax (multiplexed); HBO (multiplexed); Showtime (multiplexed); Starz (multiplexed); The Movie Channel (multiplexed).
Fee: $15.95 monthly (each).
Video-On-Demand: No
Pay-Per-View
iN DEMAND (delivered digitally); MLB Extra Innings (delivered digitally); TeN Clips (delivered digitally); TeN Blue (delivered digitally).
Internet Service
Operational: Yes.
Broadband Service: EarthLink, Road Runner.
Fee: $99.95 installation; $44.95 monthly.
Telephone Service
Analog: Not Operational
Digital: Operational
Fee: $39.95 monthly
President: Keith Burkley. Vice President, Marketing & Sales: David Leopold. Vice President, Engineering: Scott Ducott. Vice President, Government & Public Affairs: Melinda Poore.
Ownership: Time Warner Cable (MSO).

CAMPTON—Formerly served by Adelphia Communications. Now served by Time Warner Cable, BERLIN, NH [NH0012]. ICA: NH0036.

CARROLL—Formerly served by Adelphia Communications. Now served by Time Warner Cable, BERLIN, NH [NH0012]. ICA: NH0037.

CLAREMONT—Comcast Cable. Now served by BURLINGTON, VT [VT0001]. ICA: NH0011.

CONCORD—Comcast Cable. Now served by BOSTON, MA [MA0001]. ICA: NH0001.

CONWAY—Time Warner Cable. Now served by PORTLAND, ME [ME0001]. ICA: NH0038.

CORNISH—Formerly served by Adelphia Communications. Now served by Comcast Cable, BURLINGTON, VT [VT0001]. ICA: NH0065.

DERRY—Comcast Cable. Now served by BOSTON, MA [MA0001]. ICA: NH0005.

EXETER—Comcast Cable. Now served by BOSTON, MA [MA0001]. ICA: NH0068.

Cable Systems—New Hampshire

FREEDOM (town)—Formerly served by Adelphia Communications. Now served by Time Warner Cable, PORTLAND, ME [ME0001]. ICA: NH0024.

GRANTHAM—Formerly served by Adelphia Communications. Now served by Comcast Cable, BURLINGTON, VT [VT0001]. ICA: NH0066.

GREENVILLE—Formerly served by Adelphia Communications. Now served by Comcast Cable, BOSTON, MA [MA0001]. ICA: NH0064.

HILL (town)—Formerly served by Adelphia Communications. Now served by Comcast Cable, BURLINGTON, VT [VT0001]. ICA: NH0042.

HINSDALE—Formerly served by Adelphia Communications. No longer in operation. ICA: NH0019.

KEENE—Time Warner Cable, 118 Johnston Rd, Portland, ME 04102. Phones: 207-253-2400; 207-253-2200. Fax: 207-253-2404. Web Site: http://www.timewarnercable.com. Also serves Athol & Orange, MA; Marlborough, Richmond (town), Roxbury (town), Surry & Swanzey, NH. ICA: NH0009.
 TV Market Ranking: 6 (Athol, Orange); Outside TV Markets (KEENE, Marlborough, Richmond (town), Roxbury (town), Surry, Swanzey). Franchise award date: N.A. Franchise expiration date: N.A. Began: December 1, 1955.
 Channel capacity: N.A. Channels available but not in use: N.A.
Basic Service
 Subscribers: 13,468.
 Programming (received off-air): WBIN-TV (Antenna TV, IND, WeatherNation) Derry; WBZ-TV (CBS, Decades) Boston; WCVB-TV (ABC, MeTV) Boston; WEKW-TV (PBS) Keene; WFXT (FOX, Movies!) Boston; WGBH-TV (PBS) Boston; WHDH (NBC, This TV) Boston; WMUR-TV (ABC, MeTV) Manchester; WNNE (NBC) Hartford; WSBK-TV (MNT) Boston; WVTA (PBS) Windsor; 30 FMs.
 Programming (via microwave): WLVI (CW, The Country Network) Cambridge.
 Programming (via satellite): C-SPAN; C-SPAN 2; ION Television; Pop; Telemundo.
 Fee: $61.40 installation; $17.99 monthly.
Expanded Basic Service 1
 Subscribers: N.A.
 Programming (via satellite): A&E; AMC; Animal Planet; BBC America; Bravo; CMT; CNBC; CNN; Comcast SportsNet New England; Discovery Channel; Discovery Life Channel; Disney Channel; E! HD; ESPN; EVINE Live; EWTN Global Catholic Network; Food Network; Fox News Channel; Freeform; FX; Great American Country; Hallmark Channel; HLN; INSP; Jewelry Television; Lifetime; MSNBC; MTV; New England Sports Network; Nickelodeon; OWN: Oprah Winfrey Network; Oxygen; QVC; Spike TV; TBS; The Weather Channel; TLC; TNT; Travel Channel; truTV; TV Land; USA Network; VH1; WE tv.
 Fee: $46.29 monthly.
Expanded Basic Service 2
 Subscribers: N.A.
 Programming (via satellite): Cartoon Network; Comedy Central; ESPN2; HGTV; History; Syfy.
 Fee: $6.95 monthly.

Digital Basic Service
 Subscribers: N.A.
 Programming (via satellite): BBC America; Bloomberg Television; Boomerang; CNN International; C-SPAN 3; Discovery Digital Networks; Disney XD; DMX Music; ESPN Classic; ESPNews; FamilyNet; Fox Sports 1; Golf Channel; GSN; IFC; MTV Classic; MTV2; NBCSN; Nick Jr.; Nicktoons; Outdoor Channel; Ovation; TeenNick; Trinity Broadcasting Network (TBN); Turner Classic Movies.
Digital Pay Service 1
 Pay Units: N.A.
 Programming (via satellite): Cinemax; HBO (multiplexed); Showtime (multiplexed); Starz (multiplexed); The Movie Channel (multiplexed).
 Fee: $15.95 monthly (each).
Video-On-Demand: No
Pay-Per-View
 MLB Extra Innings (delivered digitally); iN DEMAND.
Internet Service
 Operational: Yes.
 Subscribers: 12,145.
 Broadband Service: EarthLink, Road Runner.
 Fee: $99.95 installation; $44.95 monthly.
Telephone Service
 Analog: Not Operational
 Digital: Operational
 Subscribers: 6,499.
 Fee: $39.95 monthly
 Miles of Plant: 510.0 (coaxial); 256.0 (fiber optic). Homes passed: 26,997.
 President: Keith Burkley. Vice President, Engineering: Scott Ducott. Vice President, Marketing & Sales: David Leopold. Vice President, Government & Public Affairs: Melinda Poore.
 Ownership: Time Warner Cable (MSO).

LEBANON—Comcast Cable. Now served by BURLINGTON, VT [VT0001]. ICA: NH0045.

LINCOLN—Formerly served by Adelphia Communications. Now served by Time Warner Cable, BERLIN, NH [NH0012]. ICA: NH0046.

LITTLETON—Time Warner Cable. Now served by BERLIN, NH [NH0012]. ICA: NH0020.

LONDONDERRY—Comcast Cable. Now served by BOSTON, MA [MA0001]. ICA: NH0008.

MADISON (town)—Formerly served by Adelphia Communications. Now served by Time Warner Cable, PORTLAND, ME [ME0001]. ICA: NH0047.

MANCHESTER—Comcast Cable. Now served by BOSTON, MA [MA0001]. ICA: NH0048.

MERRIMACK—Formerly served by Adelphia Communications. Now served by Comcast Cable, BOSTON, MA [MA0001]. ICA: NH0049.

MILAN (town)—Argent Communications, 10 Benning St., Ste 10, PO Box 235, Bristol, NH 03784. Phones: 877-295-1254; 603-895-1254. Fax: 206-202-1415. E-mail: service@argentcommunications.com. Web Site: http://www.argentcommunications.com. ICA: NH0029.
 TV Market Ranking: Outside TV Markets (MILAN (TOWN)). Franchise award date: June 26, 1989. Franchise expiration date: N.A. Began: November 5, 1990.
 Channel capacity: N.A. Channels available but not in use: N.A.
Basic Service
 Subscribers: 268.
 Programming (received off-air): W27BL Berlin; WCBB (PBS) Augusta; WCSH (Antenna TV, NBC) Portland; WENH-TV (PBS) Durham; WGME-TV (CBS) Portland; WMTW (ABC) Poland Spring; WMUR-TV (ABC, MeTV) Manchester; WSBK-TV (MNT) Boston.
 Programming (via satellite): A&E; Animal Planet; CMT; C-SPAN; Freeform; ION Television; QVC; TBS; Travel Channel.
 Fee: Free installation; $41.95 monthly; $.89 converter.
Expanded Basic Service 1
 Subscribers: N.A.
 Programming (via satellite): CNN; Comcast SportsNet New England; Discovery Channel; Disney Channel; ESPN; ESPN2; HLN; Lifetime; MTV; New England Sports Network; Nickelodeon; The Weather Channel; TNT; USA Network.
Digital Basic Service
 Subscribers: N.A.
 Programming (via satellite): BBC America; Bloomberg Television; Bravo; Discovery Life Channel; ESPN Classic; Fox Sports 1; FXM; Golf Channel; GSN; IFC; MC; National Geographic Channel; NBCSN; Nick Jr.; Outdoor Channel; Trinity Broadcasting Network (TBN); VH1 Country; WE tv.
 Fee: $18.95 monthly.
Digital Pay Service 1
 Pay Units: N.A.
 Programming (via satellite): Cinemax (multiplexed); HBO (multiplexed); Starz (multiplexed); Starz Encore (multiplexed).
 Fee: $12.95 monthly (Cinemax or Starz/Encore), $14.95 monthly (HBO).
Video-On-Demand: No
Pay-Per-View
 Fresh (delivered digitally); Playboy TV (delivered digitally).
Internet Service
 Operational: Yes.
 Fee: $39.95 monthly.
Telephone Service
 Digital: Operational
 Miles of Plant: 43.0 (coaxial); None (fiber optic). Homes passed: 648.
 Vice President, Business & Marketing: Andrew Bauer. General Manager: Shawn Bauer.
 Ownership: Argent Communications LLC (MSO).

MONROE (town)—Formerly served by Adelphia Communications. Now served by Time Warner Cable, BERLIN, NH [NH0012]. ICA: NH0050.

MOULTONBOROUGH (town)—Formerly served by Adelphia Communications. Now served by Time Warner Cable, PORTLAND, ME [ME0001]. ICA: NH0015.

NASHUA—Comcast Cable. Now served by BOSTON, MA [MA0001]. ICA: NH0002.

ADVANCED TVFactbook

FULLY SEARCHABLE • CONTINUOUSLY UPDATED • DISCOUNT RATES FOR PRINT PURCHASERS

For more information call **800-771-9202** or visit **www.warren-news.com**

NELSON (town)—FiberCast Cable, 25 South Maple St, Manchester, NH 03103. Phone: 603-689-0000. E-mail: support@fibercast.net. Web Site: http://www.fibercastcable.com. Also serves Harrisville (town) & Sullivan (town). ICA: NH0032.
 TV Market Ranking: Below 100 (Harrisville (town), NELSON (TOWN), Sullivan (town)). Franchise award date: February 22, 1990. Franchise expiration date: N.A. Began: August 22, 1990.
 Channel capacity: N.A. Channels available but not in use: N.A.
Basic Service
 Subscribers: 290.
 Programming (received off-air): WBIN-TV (Antenna TV, IND, WeatherNation) Derry; WBPX-TV (ION) Boston; WBZ-TV (CBS, Decades) Boston; WCVB-TV (ABC, MeTV) Boston; WENH-TV (PBS) Durham; WFXT (FOX, Movies!) Boston; WGBH-TV (PBS) Boston; WHDH (NBC, This TV) Boston; WLVI (CW, The Country Network) Cambridge; WMUR-TV (ABC, MeTV) Manchester; WNNE (NBC) Hartford; WSBK-TV (MNT) Boston.
 Programming (via satellite): A&E; Animal Planet; Cartoon Network; CNBC; CNN; C-SPAN; Discovery Channel; Disney Channel; ESPN; ESPN2; EVINE Live; Freeform; History; HLN; Lifetime; MTV; Nickelodeon; QVC; Spike TV; Syfy; TBS; The Weather Channel; TLC; TNT; Travel Channel; Trinity Broadcasting Network (TBN); Turner Classic Movies; USA Network.
 Fee: Free installation; $41.95 monthly.
Pay Service 1
 Pay Units: 15.
 Programming (via satellite): Cinemax; HBO; Showtime; The Movie Channel.
 Fee: $15.00 installation; $9.95 monthly (Starz & Encore), $11.95 monthly (Cinemax), $14.95 monthly (HBO), $14.95 monthly (Showtime & TMC).
Video-On-Demand: No
Internet Service
 Operational: Yes.
 Fee: $21.00 monthly.
Telephone Service
 None
 Miles of Plant: 5.0 (coaxial); None (fiber optic).
 President: Gent Khav.
 Ownership: FiberCast Cable (MSO).

NEW BOSTON—Formerly served by Adelphia Communications. Now served by Comcast Cable, BOSTON, MA [MA0001]. ICA: NH0051.

NEW LONDON—Formerly served by Adelphia Communications. Now served by Comcast Cable, BURLINGTON, VT [VT0001]. ICA: NH0023.

NEWPORT—Formerly served by Adelphia Communications. Now served by Comcast Cable, BURLINGTON, VT [VT0001]. ICA: NH0017.

2017 Edition   D-507

New Hampshire—Cable Systems

CABLE & TV STATION COVERAGE
Atlas 2017
The perfect companion to the Television & Cable Factbook
To order call 800-771-9202 or visit www.warren-news.com

PETERBOROUGH—Formerly served by Adelphia Communications. Now served by Comcast Cable, BOSTON, MA [MA0001]. ICA: NH0013.

PLAINFIELD (town)—Formerly served by Adelphia Communications. Now served by Comcast Cable, BURLINGTON, VT [VT0001]. ICA: NH0054.

PLYMOUTH—Time Warner Cable. Now served by BERLIN, NH [NH0012]. ICA: NH0055.

PORTSMOUTH—Comcast Cable. Now served by BOSTON, MA [MA0001]. ICA: NH0003.

ROCHESTER—MetroCast Communications, 70 East Lancaster Ave, Frazer, PA 19355. Phones: 800-952-1001; 603-332-5466; 603-524-3767. Web Site: http://www.metrocast.com. Also serves Lebanon (portions), ME; Barrington, East Rochester, Farmington, Milton, Milton Mills & Strafford (town-portions), NH. ICA: NH0007.
TV Market Ranking: Below 100 (Barrington, East Rochester, Farmington, ROCHESTER, Strafford (town-portions)); Outside TV Markets (Lebanon (portions), Milton). Franchise award date: April 1, 1979. Franchise expiration date: N.A. Began: November 1, 1980.
Channel capacity: N.A. Channels available but not in use: N.A.
Basic Service
Subscribers: 43,420.
Programming (received off-air): WBIN-TV (Antenna TV, IND, WeatherNation) Derry; WBZ-TV (CBS, Decades) Boston; WCSH (Antenna TV, NBC) Portland; WCVB-TV (ABC, MeTV) Boston; WENH-TV (PBS) Durham; WFXT (FOX, Movies!) Boston; WGME-TV (CBS) Portland; WHDH (NBC, This TV) Boston; WLVI (CW, The Country Network) Cambridge; WMEA-TV (PBS) Biddeford; WMFP (COZI TV, MeTV, Retro TV) Lawrence; WMTW (ABC) Poland Spring; WMUR-TV (ABC, MeTV) Manchester; WNEU (TMO) Merrimack; WPXG-TV (ION) Concord; WSBK-TV (MNT) Boston; allband FM.
Programming (via satellite): C-SPAN; QVC.
Fee: $30.00 installation; $35.95 monthly.
Expanded Basic Service 1
Subscribers: N.A.
Programming (via microwave): New England Cable News.
Programming (via satellite): A&E; AMC; Animal Planet; Cartoon Network; CNBC; CNN; Comcast SportsNet New England; Comedy Central; Discovery Channel; Disney Channel; Disney XD; E! HD; ESPN; ESPN2; EWTN Global Catholic Network; Fox News Channel; Freeform; FX; Great American Country; HGTV; History; HLN; Lifetime; MSNBC; MTV; NBCSN; New England Sports Network; Nickelodeon; Pop; Spike TV; Starz Encore; Syfy; TBS; The Weather Channel; TLC; TNT; Trinity Broadcasting Network (TBN); truTV; USA Network; VH1.
Fee: $28.95 monthly.

Digital Basic Service
Subscribers: N.A.
Programming (via satellite): BBC America; Bloomberg Television; Boomerang; Discovery Digital Networks; DIY Network; ESPN Classic; FamilyNet; Fox Sports 1; FXM; FYI; GSN; History International; IFC; LMN; MC; National Geographic Channel; NBCSN; Nick Jr.; Outdoor Channel; Ovation; truTV; Turner Classic Movies; WE tv.
Fee: $6.95 monthly; $4.00 converter.
Digital Pay Service 1
Pay Units: N.A.
Programming (via satellite): Cinemax (multiplexed); HBO (multiplexed); Showtime (multiplexed); Starz (multiplexed); The Movie Channel (multiplexed).
Fee: $12.95 monthly (each).
Video-On-Demand: Yes
Pay-Per-View
Hot Choice (delivered digitally); iN DEMAND; iN DEMAND (delivered digitally); Playboy TV; Playboy TV (delivered digitally); Fresh (delivered digitally).
Internet Service
Operational: Yes.
Broadband Service: Great Works Internet.
Fee: $99.00 installation; $41.95 monthly; $5.00 modem lease; $149.50 modem purchase.
Telephone Service
Digital: Operational
Miles of Plant: 1,070.0 (coaxial); 394.0 (fiber optic).
Vice President, Advanced Services: Josh Barstow. Vice President & Corporate Controller: Brian W. Earnshaw. Technical Operations Corporate Director: Jeff Drapeau. Regional General Manager: Moira Campbell.
Ownership: Harron Communications LP (MSO).

SPOFFORD—Argent Communications, 10 Benning St., Ste 10, PO Box 235, Bristol, NH 03784. Phones: 603-922-7025; 877-295-1254. Fax: 206-202-1415. E-mail: service@argentcommunications.com. Web Site: http://www.argentcommunications.com. Also serves Chesterfield, East Westmoreland, West Chesterfield & Westmoreland. ICA: NH0057.
TV Market Ranking: Outside TV Markets (Chesterfield, East Westmoreland, SPOFFORD, West Chesterfield, Westmoreland). Franchise award date: October 1, 1971. Franchise expiration date: N.A. Began: November 1, 1971.
Channel capacity: N.A. Channels available but not in use: N.A.
Basic Service
Subscribers: 685.
Programming (received off-air): WBZ-TV (CBS, Decades) Boston; WCVB-TV (ABC, MeTV) Boston; WENH-TV (PBS) Durham; WFXT (FOX, Movies!) Boston; WHDH (NBC, This TV) Boston; WLVI (CW, The Country Network) Cambridge; WMUR-TV (ABC, MeTV) Manchester; WNNE (NBC) Hartford; WSBK-TV (MNT) Boston; allband FM.
Programming (via satellite): A&E; Animal Planet; Cartoon Network; CNBC; CNN; Comcast SportsNet Philadelphia; C-SPAN; Discovery Channel; Disney Channel; ESPN; ESPN2; EVINE Live; Freeform; History; HLN; ION Television; Lifetime; MTV; Nickelodeon; Spike TV; Syfy; TBS; The Weather Channel; TLC; TNT; Travel Channel; Trinity Broadcasting Network (TBN); Turner Classic Movies; USA Network.
Fee: Free installation; $41.95 monthly; $2.50 converter.
Pay Service 1
Pay Units: N.A.
Programming (via satellite): HBO; Showtime; The Movie Channel.
Fee: $10.00 monthly (HBO).
Video-On-Demand: No
Internet Service
Operational: Yes. Began: January 1, 2003.
Fee: $21.00 monthly.
Telephone Service
Digital: Operational
Miles of Plant: 32.0 (coaxial); None (fiber optic).
Vice President, Business & Marketing: Andrew Bauer. General Manager: Shawn Bauer.
Ownership: Argent Communications LLC (MSO).

STODDARD—FiberCast Cable, 25 South Maple St, Manchester, NH 03103. Phones: 603-689-0000; 603-689-0010. E-mail: support@fibercast.net. Web Site: http://www.fibercastcable.com. Also serves Marlow. ICA: NH0067.
TV Market Ranking: Below 100 (Marlow, STODDARD).
Channel capacity: N.A. Channels available but not in use: N.A.
Basic Service
Subscribers: 115.
Programming (received off-air): WBIN-TV (Antenna TV, IND, WeatherNation) Derry; WBPX-TV (ION) Boston; WBZ-TV (CBS, Decades) Boston; WCVB-TV (ABC, MeTV) Boston; WENH-TV (PBS) Durham; WFXT (FOX, Movies!) Boston; WGBH-TV (PBS) Boston; WHDH (NBC, This TV) Boston; WLVI (CW, The Country Network) Cambridge; WMUR-TV (ABC, MeTV) Manchester; WSBK-TV (MNT) Boston.
Programming (via satellite): A&E; Animal Planet; Cartoon Network; CNBC; CNN; C-SPAN; Discovery Channel; Disney Channel; ESPN; ESPN2; EVINE Live; Freeform; History; HLN; Lifetime; MTV; Nickelodeon; Spike TV; Syfy; TBS; The Weather Channel; TLC; TNT; Travel Channel; Trinity Broadcasting Network (TBN); Turner Classic Movies; USA Network.
Fee: $50.00 installation; $35.95 monthly.
Pay Service 1
Pay Units: N.A.
Programming (via satellite): Cinemax; HBO; Showtime; The Movie Channel.
Fee: $15.00 installation; $11.95 monthly (Cinemax), $12.95 monthly (HBO), $14.95 monthly (Showtime & TMC).
Video-On-Demand: No
Internet Service
Operational: No.
Telephone Service
None
President: Gent Khav.
Ownership: FiberCast Cable (MSO).

STRATFORD (town)—FiberCast Cable, 25 South Maple St, Manchester, NH 03103. Phone: 603-689-0000. E-mail: support@fibercast.net. Web Site: http://www.fibercastcable.com. Also serves Groveton. ICA: NH0058.
TV Market Ranking: Outside TV Markets (Groveton, STRATFORD (TOWN)). Franchise award date: June 8, 1989. Franchise expiration date: N.A. Began: January 1, 1990.
Channel capacity: N.A. Channels available but not in use: N.A.
Basic Service
Subscribers: 150.
Programming (received off-air): WCAX-TV (CBS, Movies!) Burlington; WMUR-TV (ABC, MeTV) Manchester; WPFO (FOX) Waterville; WVTB (PBS) St. Johnsbury.
Programming (via satellite): A&E; AMC; CNN; Comcast SportsNet New England; C-SPAN; Discovery Channel; Disney Channel; ESPN; ESPN2; Fox News Channel; Freeform; HGTV; History; ION Television; Lifetime; MSNBC; MTV; MyNetworkTV; New England Sports Network; Nickelodeon; Spike TV; Syfy; TBS; The Weather Channel; TLC; TNT; USA Network; VH1; WNBC (COZI TV, NBC) New York.
Fee: Free installation; $41.95 monthly.
Digital Basic Service
Subscribers: N.A.
Programming (via satellite): BBC America; Bloomberg Television; Bravo; CMT; Discovery Digital Networks; Disney XD; DMX Music; ESPN Classic; ESPNews; FOX College Sports Central; FOX College Sports Pacific; Fox Sports 1; Fuse; FXM; FYI; Golf Channel; Great American Country; History International; IFC; LMN; National Geographic Channel; NBCSN; Nick Jr.; Nicktoons; Outdoor Channel; TeenNick; The Word Network; Trinity Broadcasting Network (TBN); WE tv.
Digital Pay Service 1
Pay Units: N.A.
Programming (via satellite): Cinemax (multiplexed); HBO (multiplexed); Starz (multiplexed); Starz Encore (multiplexed).
Fee: $12.95 monthly (Cinemax or Starz/Encore), $14.95 monthly (HBO).
Video-On-Demand: No
Pay-Per-View
Hits Movies & Events (delivered digitally); Fresh (delivered digitally); Playboy TV (delivered digitally).
Internet Service
Operational: No.
Telephone Service
None
Miles of Plant: 20.0 (coaxial); None (fiber optic). Homes passed: 342.
Vice President, Business & Marketing: Andrew Bauer. General Manager: Shawn Bauer.
Ownership: FiberCast Cable (MSO).

SUGAR HILL (town)—Formerly served by Adelphia Communications. Now served by Time Warner Cable, BERLIN, NH [NH0012]. ICA: NH0059.

TROY—Argent Communications, 10 Benning St., Ste 10, PO Box 235, Bristol, NH 03784. Phones: 877-295-1254; 603-295-1254. Fax: 206-202-1415. E-mail: service@argentcommunications.com. Web Site: http://www.argentcommunications.com. Also serves Fitzwilliam & Rindge. ICA: NH0060.
TV Market Ranking: Below 100 (Fitzwilliam, Rindge, TROY). Franchise award date: July 21, 1984. Franchise expiration date: N.A. Began: February 28, 1985.
Channel capacity: N.A. Channels available but not in use: N.A.

D-508   TV & Cable Factbook No. 85

Cable Systems—New Hampshire

Basic Service
Subscribers: 1,025.
Programming (received off-air): WBZ-TV (CBS, Decades) Boston; WCVB-TV (ABC, MeTV) Boston; WENH-TV (PBS) Durham; WFXT (FOX, Movies!) Boston; WGBH-TV (PBS) Boston; WHDH (NBC, This TV) Boston; WLVI (CW, The Country Network) Cambridge; WMUR-TV (ABC, MeTV) Manchester; WSBK-TV (MNT) Boston; allband FM.
Programming (via satellite): A&E; Animal Planet; Cartoon Network; CNBC; CNN; Comcast SportsNet New England; C-SPAN; C-SPAN 2; C-SPAN 3; Discovery Channel; Disney Channel; ESPN; ESPN2; EVINE Live; Fox News Channel; Freeform; FX; Great American Country; History; HLN; ION Television; Lifetime; MTV; National Geographic Channel; New England Sports Network; Nickelodeon; Pop; Spike TV; Syfy; TBS; The Weather Channel; TLC; TNT; Travel Channel; Trinity Broadcasting Network (TBN); Turner Classic Movies; TV Land; USA Network.
Fee: Free installation; $41.95 monthly.

Digital Basic Service
Subscribers: N.A.
Programming (via satellite): Bloomberg Television; Bravo; CNN International; Destination America; Discovery Kids Channel; Discovery Life Channel; ESPN Classic; ESPNews; Fox Sports 1; FXM; FYI; Golf Channel; GSN; HGTV; History; IFC; Investigation Discovery; LMN; Nick Jr.; Outdoor Channel; Ovation; OWN; Oprah Winfrey Network; Science Channel; Sundance TV; Turner Classic Movies; WE tv.
Fee: $18.95 monthly.

Pay Service 1
Pay Units: N.A.
Programming (via satellite): HBO.
Fee: $12.95 monthly.

Digital Pay Service 1
Pay Units: N.A.
Programming (via satellite): Cinemax (multiplexed); HBO (multiplexed); Showtime (multiplexed); Starz (multiplexed); Starz Encore (multiplexed); The Movie Channel (multiplexed).
Fee: $12.95 monthly (Cinemax or Starz/Encore), $14.95 monthly (HBO).

Video-On-Demand: No

Pay-Per-View
Special events (delivered digitally); Pleasure (delivered digitally); Fresh (delivered digitally); Shorteez (delivered digitally); Playboy TV (delivered digitally).

Internet Service
Operational: Yes. Began: September 1, 2002.
Fee: $21.00 monthly; $4.00 modem lease; $50.00 modem purchase.

Telephone Service
Digital: Operational
Miles of Plant: 35.0 (coaxial); None (fiber optic).
Vice President, Business & Marketing: Andrew Bauer. General Manager: Shawn Bauer.
Ownership: Argent Communications LLC (MSO).

WAKEFIELD (town)—Formerly served by Adelphia Communications. Now served by Time Warner Cable, PORTLAND, ME [ME0001]. ICA: NH0030.

WARNER—TDS Cable, 525 Junction Rd, Madison, WI 53717. Phones: 888-225-5837; 603-746-3000; 603-746-9911. Fax: 608-830-5519. E-mail: comments@tdstelecom.com. Web Site: http://www.tdstelecom.com. Also serves Bradford, Newbury & Sutton (town). ICA: NH0018.

TV Market Ranking: Below 100 (Bradford, Newbury, Sutton (town), WARNER). Franchise award date: June 2, 1984. Franchise expiration date: N.A. Began: November 1, 1984.
Channel capacity: N.A. Channels available but not in use: N.A.

Basic Service
Subscribers: 579.
Programming (received off-air): WBIN-TV (Antenna TV, IND, WeatherNation) Derry; WBZ-TV (CBS, Decades) Boston; WCVB-TV (ABC, MeTV) Boston; WENH-TV (PBS) Durham; WFXT (FOX, Movies!) Boston; WGBH-TV (PBS) Boston; WHDH (NBC, This TV) Boston; WLVI (CW, The Country Network) Cambridge; WMTW (ABC) Poland Spring; WMUR-TV (ABC, MeTV) Manchester; WNEU (TMO) Merrimack; WNNE (NBC) Hartford; WPXG-TV (ION) Concord; WSBK-TV (MNT) Boston; WVTA (PBS) Windsor; allband FM.
Programming (via satellite): A&E; AMC; CNBC; CNN; C-SPAN; Discovery Channel; Disney Channel; ESPN; ESPN2; Freeform; FX; HGTV; History; HLN; Lifetime; MTV; New England Sports Network; Nickelodeon; Pop; Spike TV; TBS; The Weather Channel; TNT; USA Network; VH1; WGN America.
Fee: $29.00 installation; $42.90 monthly.

Pay Service 1
Pay Units: 77.
Programming (via satellite): Cinemax.
Fee: $13.00 monthly.

Pay Service 2
Pay Units: 208.
Programming (via satellite): HBO.
Fee: $16.00 monthly.

Pay Service 3
Pay Units: 60.
Programming (via satellite): Showtime.
Fee: $9.95 monthly.

Video-On-Demand: No

Internet Service
Operational: Yes.

Telephone Service
Analog: Operational
Miles of Plant: 150.0 (coaxial); None (fiber optic). Homes passed: 3,100.
General Manager: Marc Violette. Assistant Treasurer: Sharon Tisdale.
Ownership: TDS Telecom.

WENTWORTH (town)—Formerly served by Adelphia Communications. Now served by Time Warner Cable, BERLIN, NH [NH0012]. ICA: NH0062.

WEST STEWARTSTOWN—Formerly served by White Mountain Cablevision. No longer in operation. ICA: NH0021.

NEW JERSEY

Total Systems: 19	Communities with Applications: 0
Total Communities Served: 701	Number of Basic Subscribers: 2,124,455
Franchises Not Yet Operating: 0	Number of Expanded Basic Subscribers: 10,232
Applications Pending: 0	Number of Pay Units: 194,734

Top 100 Markets Represented: New York, NY-Linden-Paterson-Newark, NJ (1); Philadelphia, PA-Burlington, NJ (4).

For a list of cable communities in this section, see the Cable Community Index located in the back of Cable Volume 2.
For explanation of terms used in cable system listings, see p. D-11.

ALLAMUCHY TWP.—Cablevision. Now served by MORRIS TWP., NJ [NJ0005]. ICA: NJ0046.

ATLANTIC CITY—Formerly served by OrionVision. No longer in operation. ICA: NJ0064.

AUDUBON—Comcast Cable, 401 White Horse Rd, Voorhees, NJ 08043. Phone: 856-821-6100. Fax: 856-821-6108. Web Site: http://www.comcast.com. Also serves Absecon, Alloway Twp., Atlantic City, Audubon Park, Avalon Borough, Barnegat Light Borough, Barnegat Twp., Barrington, Bass River, Beach Haven Borough, Beachwood Borough, Bellmawr, Berkeley Twp., Berlin Borough, Beverly, Bordentown, Bordentown Twp., Bridgeton, Brigantine, Brooklawn Borough, Buena, Buena Vista Twp., Burlington City, Burlington County (portions), Burlington Twp., Camden, Cape May, Cape May Borough, Cape May Point, Carneys Point, Cedar Bonnet, Cherry Hill Twp., Chesilhurst Borough, Chesterfield Twp., Cinnaminson, Clayton, Clementon, Collingswood, Commercial Twp., Corbin City, Crestwood Village, Deerfield Twp., Delanco, Delaware Twp., Delran Twp., Dennis Twp., Deptford Twp., Dover Twp., Downe Twp., Eaglewood Twp., East Greenwich Twp., Eastampton Twp., Edgewater Park, Egg Harbor City, Egg Harbor Twp., Elk Twp., Elmer Borough, Elsinboro Twp., Evesham Twp., Fairfield Twp. (Cumberland County), Fieldsboro, Florence Twp., Folsom Borough, Fort Dix, Franklin Twp. (Gloucester County), Galloway Twp., Gibbsboro, Glassboro, Gloucester, Gloucester County (portions), Gloucester Twp., Greenwich, Haddon Heights, Haddon Twp., Haddonfield, Hainesport Twp., Hamilton Twp., Hammonton, Harrison Twp. (Gloucester County), Harvey Cedars Borough, Hi-Nella, Hopewell, Hopewell Twp. (Cumberland County), Island Heights Borough, Lacey Twp., Lakehurst Borough, Laurel Lake, Laurel Springs, Lawnside, Lawrence Twp. (Cumberland County), Lindenwold, Linwood, Little Egg Harbor Twp., Logan Twp., Long Beach Twp., Longport, Lower Alloways Creek Twp., Lower Twp., Lumberton, Magnolia, Mannington Twp., Mansfield Twp. (Burlington County), Mantua Twp., Maple Shade, Maple Shade Twp., Margate City, Maurice River, McGuire AFB, Medford Lakes, Medford Twp., Merchantville, Middle Twp., Millville, Monroe Twp. (Gloucester County), Moorestown Twp., Mount Ephraim Borough, Mount Holly Twp., Mount Laurel Twp., Mullica Twp., National Park, New Hanover Twp., Newfield, North Hanover Twp., North Wildwood, Northfield, Oaklyn, Ocean City, Ocean Gate Borough, Ocean Twp., Oldmans Twp., Palmyra, Paulsboro, Pemberton Borough, Pemberton Twp., Penns Grove, Pennsauken Twp., Pennsville Twp., Pilesgrove Twp., Pine Beach Borough, Pine Hill, Pine Valley, Pitman, Pittsgrove Twp., Pleasantville, Plumsted Twp., Port Republic, Quinton Twp., Riverside, Riverton, Runnemede, Salem, Sea Isle City, Seaview Harbor, Shamong Twp., Shiloh Borough, Ship Bottom Borough, Somerdale, Somers Point, South Harrison Twp., South Toms River Borough, Southampton Twp., Springfield Twp. (Burlington County), Stone Harbor Borough, Stratford, Surf City Borough, Swainton, Swedesboro, Tabernacle Twp., Tavistock, Titusville, Upper Deerfield Twp., Upper Pittsgrove Twp., Upper Twp., Ventnor City, Vineland, Voorhees Twp., Washington Twp. (Gloucester County), Waterford Twp., Wenonah, West Amwell Twp., West Berlin, West Cape May Borough, West Deptford Twp., West Trenton, West Wildwood Borough, Westampton Twp., Westville, Weymouth City, Wildwood, Wildwood Crest Borough, Willingboro, Winslow Twp., Woodbine, Woodbury, Woodbury Heights, Woodland Twp., Woodlynne, Woodstown Borough, Woolwich Twp. & Wrightstown. ICA: NJ0003.

TV Market Ranking: 1,4 (Delaware Twp., Hopewell); 4 (Alloway Twp., AUDUBON, Audubon Park, Barrington, Bellmawr, Berkeley Twp., Berlin Borough, Beverly, Bordentown, Bordentown Twp., Brooklawn Borough, Buena, Buena Vista Twp., Burlington City, Burlington County (portions), Burlington Twp., Camden, Cherry Hill Twp., Chesilhurst Borough, Chesterfield Twp., Cinnaminson, Clayton, Clementon, Collingswood, Crestwood Village, Deerfield Twp., Delanco, Delran Twp., Deptford Twp., East Greenwich Twp., Eastampton Twp., Edgewater Park, Elk Twp., Elmer Borough, Elsinboro Twp., Evesham Twp., Fieldsboro, Florence Twp., Folsom Borough, Fort Dix, Franklin Twp. (Gloucester County), Gibbsboro, Glassboro, Gloucester, Gloucester County (portions), Gloucester Twp., Greenwich, Haddon Heights, Haddon Twp., Haddonfield, Hainesport Twp., Hammonton, Harrison Twp. (Gloucester County), Hi-Nella, Lakehurst Borough, Laurel Springs, Lawnside, Lindenwold, Logan Twp., Lower Alloways Creek Twp., Lumberton, Magnolia, Mansfield Twp. (Burlington County), Mantua Twp., Maple Shade, Maple Shade Twp., McGuire AFB, Medford Lakes, Medford Twp., Merchantville, Monroe Twp. (Gloucester County), Moorestown Twp., Mount Ephraim Borough, Mount Laurel Twp., National Park, New Hanover Twp., Newfield, North Hanover Twp., Oaklyn, Oldmans Twp., Palmyra, Paulsboro, Pemberton Borough, Pemberton Twp., Penns Grove, Pennsauken Twp., Pennsville Twp., Pilesgrove Twp., Pine Hill, Pine Valley, Pitman, Pittsgrove Twp., Plumsted Twp., Riverside, Riverton, Runnemede, Shamong Twp., Somerdale, South Harrison Twp., South Toms River Borough, Southampton Twp., Springfield Twp. (Burlington County), Stratford, Swedesboro, Tabernacle Twp., Tavistock, Titusville, Upper Pittsgrove Twp., Voorhees Twp., Washington Twp. (Gloucester County), Waterford Twp., Wenonah, West Amwell Twp., West Berlin, West Deptford Twp., West Trenton, Westampton Twp., Westville, Willingboro, Winslow Twp., Woodbury, Woodbury Heights, Woodland Twp., Woodlynne, Woodstown Borough, Woolwich Twp., Wrightstown); Below 100 (Absecon, Atlantic City, Barnegat Light Borough, Barnegat Twp., Beach Haven Borough, Bridgeton, Brigantine, Cape May, Cape May Borough, Cape May Point, Cedar Bonnet, Commercial Twp., Corbin City, Dennis Twp., Downe Twp., Egg Harbor City, Egg Harbor Twp., Fairfield Twp. (Cumberland County), Galloway Twp., Hamilton Twp., Harvey Cedars Borough, Hopewell Twp. (Cumberland County), Lacey Twp., Laurel Lake, Lawrence Twp. (Cumberland County), Linwood, Little Egg Harbor Twp., Longport, Lower Twp., Mannington Twp., Margate City, Maurice River, Middle Twp., Millville, Mullica Twp., North Wildwood, Northfield, Ocean City, Ocean Twp., Pleasantville, Port Republic, Quinton Twp., Salem, Sea Isle City, Seaview Harbor, Shiloh Borough, Ship Bottom Borough, Somers Point, Stone Harbor Borough, Surf City Borough, Swainton, Upper Deerfield Twp., Upper Twp., Ventnor City, West Cape May Borough, West Wildwood Borough, Wildwood Crest Borough, Woodbine, Avalon Borough, Long Beach Twp., Vineland, Wildwood); Outside TV Markets (Beachwood Borough, Dover Twp., Eaglewood Twp., Island Heights Borough, Ocean Gate Borough, Pine Beach Borough). Franchise award date: March 21, 1975. Franchise expiration date: N.A. Began: April 15, 1975.

Channel capacity: N.A. Channels available but not in use: N.A.

Basic Service
Subscribers: 589,016. Commercial subscribers: 11,412.
Programming (received off-air): KYW-TV (CBS, Decades) Philadelphia; WCAU (COZI TV, NBC) Philadelphia; WFMZ-TV (Retro TV) Allentown; WFPA-CD (UniMas) Philadelphia; WGTW-TV (TBN) Burlington; WHYY-TV (PBS) Wilmington; WMCN-TV (Bounce TV, Tuff TV) Atlantic City; WPHL-TV (Antenna TV, MNT, This TV) Philadelphia; WPPX-TV (ION) Wilmington; WPSG (CW) Philadelphia; WPVI-TV (ABC, Live Well Network) Philadelphia; WTVE (IND) Reading; WTXF-TV (Buzzr, FOX, Movies!) Philadelphia; WUVP-DT (getTV, UNV) Vineland; WWSI (TMO) Atlantic City; WYBE (ETV, IND) Philadelphia; 5 FMs.
Programming (via satellite): Cable TV Network of New Jersey; Comcast Network Philadelphia; C-SPAN; EWTN Global Catholic Network; HSN; QVC.
Fee: $42.90 installation; $17.90 monthly.

Expanded Basic Service 1
Subscribers: N.A.
Programming (via satellite): A&E; AMC; Animal Planet; BET; Bravo; Cartoon Network; CNBC; CNN; Comcast SportsNet Philadelphia; Comedy Central; Discovery Channel; E! HD; ESPN; ESPN2; EVINE Live; Food Network; Fox News Channel; Fox Sports 1; Freeform; FX; Golf Channel; GSN; Hallmark Channel; HGTV; History; HLN; Lifetime; MSNBC; MTV; NBCSN; Nickelodeon; OWN: Oprah Winfrey Network; Pop; Spike TV; Syfy; TBS; The Weather Channel; TLC; TNT; truTV; Turner Classic Movies; TV Land; USA Network; VH1.
Fee: $23.45 monthly.

Digital Basic Service
Subscribers: N.A.
Programming (via satellite): 52MX; A&E HD; AMC HD; Animal Planet HD; Bandamax; BBC America; Bio HD; Bloomberg Television; Bravo HD; Canal 22 Internacional; Cartoon Network HD; CB Tu Television Michoacan; CBS Sports Network; CBS Sports Network HD; Centric; Cine Mexicano; Cinelatino; CMT; CMT HD; CNBC HD+; CNN en Espanol; CNN HD; Comcast Network Philadelphia; Comcast SportsNet Plus HD; Comedy Central HD; Cooking Channel; C-SPAN 2; C-SPAN 3; Daystar TV Network; De Pelicula; De Pelicula Clasico; Destination America; Destination America HD; Discovery Channel HD; Discovery Family; Discovery Life Channel; Disney Channel; Disney Channel HD; Disney XD; Disney XD HD; DIY Network; E! HD; Enlace USA; ESPN Classic; ESPN Deportes; ESPN HD; ESPN2 HD; ESPNews; ESPNews HD; ESPNU; ESPNU HD; EVINE Live; Flix; Food Network HD; Fox Business Network; Fox Business Network HD; FOX College Sports Central; FOX College Sports Pacific; Fox Deportes; Fox News HD; Freeform HD; Fuse; Fuse HD; FX HD; FYI; gmcHD; Golf Channel HD; GolTV; Gran Cine; Great American Country; GSN; Hallmark Channel; Hallmark Channel HD; Hallmark Movie Channel HD; Hallmark Movies & Mysteries; HD Theater; HGTV HD; History en Espanol; History HD; History International; HLN HD; Home Shopping Network HD; HTV; ID Investigation Discovery HD; IFC; IFC HD; Infinito; Investigation Discovery; Jewelry Television; La Familia Cosmovision; Lifetime HD; Lifetime Movie Network HD; LMN; LOGO; MC; Mexicanal; MGM HD; MLB Network; MLB Network HD; MoviePlex; MTV Classic; MTV Hits; MTV Jams; MTV Live; MTV2; Multimedios Television; Nat Geo WILD; National Geographic Channel; National Geographic Channel HD; NBA TV; NBA TV HD; NBC Universo; NFL Net-

Cable Systems—New Jersey

work; NFL Network HD; NFL RedZone; NHL Network; NHL Network HD; Nick 2; Nick HD; Nick Jr.; Nicktoons; Oxygen; QVC HD; Reelz; Ritmoson; RLTV; Science Channel; Science HD; Spike TV HD; Sprout; Starz Encore (multiplexed); Starz Encore HD; Sundance TV; Syfy HD; TBS HD; TeenNick; TeleFormula; Telehit; Tennis Channel; Tennis Channel HD; The Weather Channel HD; TLC HD; TNT HD; Tr3s; Travel Channel; Travel Channel HD; truTV; truTV HD; Turner Classic Movies; Turner Classic Movies HD; TV One; TV One HD; TVG Network; Universal HD; Univision; UP; USA Network HD; Versus HD; VH1 HD; VH1 Soul; VideoRola; ViendoMovies; WE tv; WE tv HD; Weatherscan; YES HD.
Fee: $14.95 monthly.

Digital Pay Service 1
Pay Units: N.A.
Programming (via satellite): Cinemax (multiplexed); Cinemax HD; HBO (multiplexed); HBO HD; Showtime (multiplexed); Showtime HD; Starz (multiplexed); Starz HD; The Movie Channel (multiplexed).
Fee: $18.05 monthly (each).

Video-On-Demand: Yes

Pay-Per-View
Sports PPV (delivered digitally); ESPN Now (delivered digitally); iN DEMAND; iN DEMAND (delivered digitally); Playboy TV (delivered digitally); Fresh (delivered digitally); Shorteez (delivered digitally); Pleasure (delivered digitally).

Internet Service
Operational: Yes.
Subscribers: 543,876.
Broadband Service: Comcast High Speed Internet.
Fee: $42.95 monthly; $10.00 modem lease; $290.00 modem purchase.

Telephone Service
Digital: Operational
Subscribers: 370,070.
Miles of Plant: 28,988.0 (coaxial); 7,230.0 (fiber optic). Homes passed: 1,352,681.
Regional Senior Vice President: Greg Arnold. Area Vice President: John Del Viscio. Vice President, Engineering: John Cody. Vice President, Technical Operations: Mike Taylor. Public Relations Director: Fred DeAndrea. Government Affairs Director: Kathy Farinaccio. Marketing Director: Aaron Geisel.
Ownership: Comcast Cable Communications Inc. (MSO).

AVALON—Comcast Cable. Now served by AUDUBON, NJ [NJ0003]. ICA: NJ0033.

AVALON—Comcast Cable. Now served by AUDUBON, NJ [NJ0003]. ICA: NJ0018.

AVON-BY-THE-SEA—Cablevision, 1501 18th Ave, Wall, NJ 07719. Phones: 516-803-2300 (Corporate office); 973-659-2200. Web Site: http://www.cablevision.com. Also serves Asbury Park, Belmar, Bradley Beach, Brielle, Farmingdale, Interlaken, Lake Como, Manasquan, Monmouth County (portions), Neptune, Neptune Twp., Ocean Beach, Ocean Twp., Sea Girt, Spring Lake, Spring Lake Heights, Wall & Wall Twp. ICA: NJ0012.
TV Market Ranking: 1 (Asbury Park, AVON-BY-THE-SEA, Belmar, Bradley Beach, Farmingdale, Interlaken, Lake Como, Neptune, Ocean Twp., Spring Lake, Spring Lake Heights); 1,4 (Monmouth County (portions), Wall). Outside TV Markets (Brielle, Manasquan, Ocean Beach, Sea Girt, Monmouth County (portions), Wall). Franchise award date: N.A. Franchise expiration date: N.A. Began: November 1, 1979.
Channel capacity: 43 (operating 2-way). Channels available but not in use: N.A.

Basic Service
Subscribers: 89,704.
Programming (received off-air): WABC-TV (ABC, Live Well Network) New York; WCAU (COZI TV, NBC) Philadelphia; WCBS-TV (CBS, Decades) New York; WFUT-DT (getTV, UniMas) Newark; WHYY-TV (PBS) Wilmington; WNBC (COZI TV, NBC) New York; WNET (PBS) Newark; WNJT (PBS) Trenton; WNJU (TMO) Linden; WNYW (FOX, Movies!) New York; WPHL-TV (Antenna TV, MNT, This TV) Philadelphia; WPIX (Antenna TV, CW, This TV) New York; WPVI-TV (ABC, Live Well Network) Philadelphia; WPXN-TV (ION) New York; WTXF-TV (Buzzr, FOX, Movies!) Philadelphia; WWOR-TV (Bounce TV, Buzzr, Heroes & Icons, MNT) Secaucus; WXTV-DT (UNV) Paterson.
Programming (via microwave): News 12 New Jersey.
Programming (via satellite): The Weather Channel.
Fee: $39.95 installation; $12.72 monthly; $2.28 converter.

Expanded Basic Service 1
Subscribers: N.A.
Programming (via satellite): A&E; AMC; Animal Planet; BET; Bravo; Cartoon Network; CNBC; CNN; Comedy Central; C-SPAN; C-SPAN 2; Discovery Channel; Disney Channel; E! HD; ESPN; ESPN2; EVINE Live; Flix; Food Network; Fox News Channel; Fox Sports 1; Freeform; Fuse; FX; GSN; HGTV; History; HLN; IFC; Lifetime; MSG; MSG Plus; MSNBC; MTV; MTV2; News 12 Traffic & Weather; Nickelodeon; QVC; Spike TV; SportsNet New York; Syfy; TBS; TLC; TNT; Travel Channel; truTV; Turner Classic Movies; TV Land; USA Network; VH1; WE tv; YES Network.
Fee: $37.03 monthly.

Digital Basic Service
Subscribers: N.A.
Programming (via satellite): Azteca; BBC World News; Bloomberg Television; Canal Sur; Caracol TV; Cartoon Network en Espanol; Cinelatino; CMT; CNN en Espanol; CNN HD; C-SPAN 3; Destination America; Discovery Kids Channel; Disney XD; Docu TVE; Ecuavisa Internacional; ESPN Classic; ESPN Deportes; ESPN HD; ESPN2 HD; ESPNews; EuroNews; Food Network HD; FOX College Sports Central; FOX College Sports Pacific; Fox Deportes; Fox Life; Fox Sports 2; FXM; FYI; Golf Channel; GolTV; Great American Country; Hallmark Channel; HD Theater; here! On Demand; HGTV HD; History en Espanol; History International; HTV; iN DEMAND; Infinito; Investigation Discovery; Jewelry Television; La Familia Cosmovision; LOGO; Mariavision; MC; Momentum; MTV Classic; MTV Hits; National Geographic Channel; National Geographic Channel HD; NBA TV; NBC Universo; NBCSN; NHL Network; Nick Jr.; Nicktoons; Outdoor Channel; Oxygen; Science Channel; Sundance TV; TBS HD; TeenNick; Telefe Internacional; TNT HD; Toon Disney en Espanol; Tr3s; TVG Network; ULTRA HD-Plex; Universal HD; Versus HD; VH1 Soul; ViendoMovies; Vme TV; YES HD.
Fee: $10.95 monthly.

Pay Service 1
Pay Units: N.A.
Programming (via satellite): Cinemax; HBO (multiplexed); Showtime (multiplexed); The Movie Channel.

Digital Pay Service 1
Pay Units: N.A.
Programming (via satellite): Cinemax (multiplexed); Cinemax HD; Cinemax On Demand; HBO (multiplexed); HBO HD; HBO on Demand; International Television (ITV); Korean Channel; MBC America; Playboy TV; Portuguese Channel; RAI Italia; RTN; Showtime (multiplexed); Showtime HD; Showtime On Demand; Starz; Starz Encore (multiplexed); Starz HD; The Movie Channel (multiplexed); The Movie Channel HD; TV Asia; TV Polonia; TV5, La Television International; Zee TV.
Fee: $10.00 installation; $9.95 monthly (Cinemax, Showtime, Starz/Encore, Playboy, TMC, RAI, SPT, TV5 or TV Polonia), $11.95 monthly (HBO), $24.95 monthly (TV Japan).

Video-On-Demand: Yes

Internet Service
Operational: Yes.
Subscribers: 37,441.
Broadband Service: Optimum Online.
Fee: $46.95 installation; $34.95 monthly; $299.00 modem purchase.

Telephone Service
Digital: Operational
Subscribers: 31,198.
Fee: $34.95 monthly
Miles of Plant: 1,214.0 (coaxial); 307.0 (fiber optic).
Executive Vice President, Programming: Tom Montemagno. Vice President, Field Operations: Frank Dagliere. Vice President, Government Affairs: Adam Falk.
Ownership: Altice USA (MSO).

BAYONNE—Cablevision, 685 Broadway, Bayonne, NJ 11714. Phones: 201-405-8222; 201-651-4000; 516-803-2300 (Corporate office). Web Site: http://www.cablevision.com. ICA: NJ0028.
TV Market Ranking: 1 (BAYONNE). Franchise award date: October 24, 1979. Franchise expiration date: N.A. Began: January 1, 1980.
Channel capacity: 87 (operating 2-way). Channels available but not in use: N.A.

Basic Service
Subscribers: 12,186.
Programming (received off-air): WABC-TV (ABC, Live Well Network) New York; WCBS-TV (CBS, Decades) New York; WFUT-DT (getTV, UniMas) Newark; WLIW (PBS) Garden City; WMBC-TV (Azteca America) Newton; WNBC (COZI TV, NBC) New York; WNET (PBS) Newark; WNJN (PBS) Montclair; WNJU (TMO) Linden; WNYW (FOX, Movies!) New York; WPIX (Antenna TV, CW, This TV) New York; WPXN-TV (ION) New York; WWOR-TV (Bounce TV, Buzzr, Heroes & Icons, MNT) Secaucus; WXTV-DT (UNV) Paterson.
Programming (via microwave): News 12 New Jersey.
Programming (via satellite): QVC.
Fee: $39.95 installation; $12.79 monthly.

Expanded Basic Service 1
Subscribers: N.A.
Programming (via satellite): A&E; AMC; Animal Planet; BET; Bravo; Cartoon Network; CMT; CNBC; Comedy Central; C-SPAN; C-SPAN 2; Discovery Channel; Discovery Life Channel; E! HD; ESPN; ESPN2; Food Network; Fox News Channel; Fox Sports 1; Freeform; FX; GSN; HGTV; History; HLN; Lifetime; MSNBC; MTV; MTV2; News 12 Traffic & Weather; Nickelodeon; Spike TV; Syfy; TBS; The Weather Channel; TLC; TNT; Travel Channel; truTV; TV Land; USA Network; VH1; WE tv.
Fee: $37.16 monthly.

Digital Basic Service
Subscribers: N.A.
Programming (via satellite): Bloomberg Television; CMT; C-SPAN 3; Discovery Digital Networks; Disney Channel; Disney XD; ESPN Classic; ESPNews; EuroNews; Flix; FXM; FYI; Hallmark Channel; History International; IFC; MC; MSG; MSG Plus; MTV; MTV Classic; National Geographic Channel; NBC Universo; Nick Jr.; Nicktoons; Oxygen; TeenNick.
Fee: $10.95 monthly.

Digital Pay Service 1
Pay Units: N.A.
Programming (via satellite): Cinemax (multiplexed); HBO (multiplexed); Showtime (multiplexed); Starz; Starz Encore; The Movie Channel (multiplexed).

Video-On-Demand: Yes

Pay-Per-View
Special events.

Internet Service
Operational: Yes.
Subscribers: 14,194.
Broadband Service: Optimum Online.
Fee: $46.95 installation; $34.95 monthly.

Telephone Service
Digital: Operational
Subscribers: 11,184.
Fee: $34.95 monthly
Miles of Plant: 166.0 (coaxial); 44.0 (fiber optic). Homes passed: 30,252.
Executive Vice President, Programming: Tom Montemagno. Vice President, Field Operations: Christopher Fulton.
Ownership: Altice USA (MSO).

BERGENFIELD—Cablevision, 5 Legion Dr, Cresskill, NJ 07626. Phones: 201-405-8222; 201-651-4000; 516-803-2300 (Corporate office). Web Site: http://www.cablevision.com. Also serves Closter, Cresskill, Demarest, Dumont, Emerson, Fair Lawn, Harrington Park, Haworth, Hillsdale, New Milford, Northvale, Norwood, Old Tappan, Oradell, Paramus, River Vale Twp., Rockleigh, Saddle River, Tenafly & Woodcliff Lake. ICA: NJ0013.
TV Market Ranking: 1 (BERGENFIELD, Closter, Cresskill, Dumont, Emerson, Fair Lawn, Harrington Park, Haworth, Hillsdale, New Milford, Northvale, Norwood, Old Tappan, Oradell, Paramus, River Vale Twp., Rockleigh, Saddle River, Tenafly, Woodcliff Lake); 7 (Demarest). Franchise award date: July 18, 1974. Franchise expiration date: N.A. Began: November 1, 1976.
Channel capacity: N.A. Channels available but not in use: N.A.

Basic Service
Subscribers: 43,065.
Programming (received off-air): WABC-TV (ABC, Live Well Network) New York; WCBS-TV (CBS, Decades) New York; WFUT-DT (getTV, UniMas) Newark; WLIW (PBS) Garden City; WLNY-TV (IND) Riverhead; WMBC-TV (Azteca America) Newton; WNBC (COZI TV, NBC) New York; WNET (PBS) Newark; WNJN (PBS) Montclair; WNJU (TMO) Linden; WNYJ-TV (ETV) West Milford; WNYW (FOX, Movies!) New York; WPIX (Antenna TV, CW, This TV) New York; WPXN-TV (ION) New York; WRNN-TV (IND) Kingston; WWOR-TV (Bounce TV, Buzzr, Heroes & Icons, MNT) Secaucus; WXTV-DT (UNV) Paterson.
Programming (via satellite): News 12 New Jersey.
Fee: $39.95 installation; $14.58 monthly; $2.72 converter.

Expanded Basic Service 1
Subscribers: N.A.
Programming (via satellite): A&E; AMC; Animal Planet; BET; Bravo; Cartoon Network; CNBC; CNN; Comcast Network Philadelphia; Comedy Central; C-SPAN; C-SPAN 2; Discovery Channel; Disney Channel; DMX Music; E! HD; ESPN; ESPN2; EVINE Live; Food Network; Fox News Channel; Fox Sports 1; Freeform; Fuse; FX; Golf Channel; GSN; HGTV; History; HLN; IFC; Lifetime; MSG; MSG Plus; MSNBC; MTV; MTV2; News 12 Traffic & Weather; Nickelodeon; QVC; Spike TV; SportsNet New York; Syfy; TBS; The Weather Channel; TLC; TNT; Travel Channel; truTV; Turner Classic Movies; TV Land; USA Network; VH1; WE tv; YES Network.
Fee: $34.43 monthly.
Digital Basic Service
Subscribers: N.A.
Programming (via satellite): Azteca; Bloomberg Television; CMT; C-SPAN 3; Discovery Digital Networks; Disney XD; ESPN Classic; ESPN HD; ESPNews; EuroNews; FOX College Sports Central; FOX College Sports Pacific; Fox HD; Fox Sports 2; FXM; FYI; Golf Channel; GolTV; Hallmark Channel; History International; HITS (Headend In The Sky); Jewelry Television; Korean Channel; LOGO; MBC America; MC; MSG; National Geographic Channel; NBA TV; NBCSN; Nick Jr.; Nicktoons; Outdoor Channel; Oxygen; Portuguese Channel; RAI Italia; RTN; Sundance TV; TeenNick; TNT HD; TV Asia; TV Polonia; TVG Network; Universal HD; Zee TV.
Fee: $10.95 monthly, $9.95-$14.95 monthly (International Channels).
Pay Service 1
Pay Units: N.A.
Programming (via satellite): Cinemax; Flix; HBO (multiplexed); Showtime (multiplexed); Starz; Starz Encore; The Movie Channel.
Digital Pay Service 1
Pay Units: N.A.
Programming (via satellite): Cinemax (multiplexed); Cinemax HD; Cinemax On Demand; HBO (multiplexed); HBO HD; HBO on Demand; Showtime (multiplexed); Showtime HD; Showtime On Demand; Starz (multiplexed); Starz Encore (multiplexed); Starz HD; The Movie Channel (multiplexed); The Movie Channel HD.
Fee: $9.95 monthly (Cinemax, Showtime/TMC, or Starz/Encore), $11.95 monthly (HBO).
Video-On-Demand: Yes
Pay-Per-View
Pleasure (delivered digitally); Playboy TV (delivered digitally); Fresh (delivered digitally); iN DEMAND (delivered digitally); ESPN Now (delivered digitally); NBA (delivered digitally); NHL/MLB (delivered digitally).
Internet Service
Operational: Yes.
Subscribers: 48,275.
Broadband Service: Optimum Online.
Fee: $46.95 installation; $34.95 monthly; $299.00 modem purchase.
Telephone Service
Digital: Operational
Subscribers: 40,145.
Fee: $34.95 monthly
Miles of Plant: 1,616.0 (coaxial); 444.0 (fiber optic). Homes passed: 91,181.
Executive Vice President, Programming: Tom Montemagno. Vice President, Field Operations: Christopher Fulton.
Ownership: Altice USA (MSO).

BURLINGTON COUNTY—Comcast Cable. Now served by AUDUBON, NJ [NJ0003]. ICA: NJ0017.

CARLSTADT BOROUGH—Comcast Cable. Now served by WEST ORANGE TWP., NJ [NJ0001]. ICA: NJ0019.

EAST WINDSOR—Comcast Cable. Now served by EATONTOWN BOROUGH, NJ [NJ0009]. ICA: NJ0051.

EATONTOWN BOROUGH—Comcast Cable, 403 South St, Eatontown, NJ 07724-1878. Phones: 732-602-7444 (Union office); 732-542-8107. Fax: 732-935-5572. Web Site: http://www.comcast.com. Also serves Allenhurst Borough, Atlantic Highlands Borough, Bay Head, Bedminster, Bernardsville, Bethlehem Twp., Branchburg Twp., Brick Twp., Chatham Twp., Chester, Clinton, Cranbury Twp., Deal Borough, Delaware Twp., East Amwell Twp., East Brunswick, East Windsor Twp., Ewing, Fair Haven Borough, Far Hills Borough, Flemington, Fort Monmouth, Franklin Park, Franklin Twp. (Hunterdon County), Franklin Twp. (Somerset County), Freehold Borough, Harding Twp., Hazlet Twp., Helmetta, Highlands Borough, Hightstown, Hillsborough, Holmdel Twp., Jamesburg, Lambertville, Lawrence, Lawrenceville, Lebanon Borough, Little Silver Borough, Loch Arbour (village), Long Branch, Long Hill Twp., Manahawkin, Manchester Twp., Mantoloking, Mendham, Middletown Twp., Millington, Millstone, Monmouth Beach Borough, Monroe Twp., Montgomery Twp., Ocean County (portions), Oceanport Borough, Peapack-Gladstone, Pennington Borough, Plainsboro, Point Pleasant, Point Pleasant Beach, Princeton Borough, Princeton Junction, Princeton Twp., Raritan Twp., Readington Twp., Red Bank Borough, Rocky Hill Borough, Roosevelt, Rumson Borough, Sea Bright Borough, Shrewsbury Borough, Shrewsbury Twp., South Brunswick Twp., Spotswood, Stockton Borough, Tewksbury Twp., Tinton Falls Borough, Trenton, Tuckerton Borough, Union Twp., West Long Branch & West Windsor Twp., NJ; Ambler Borough, Amity, Amity (Bucks County), Bally, Bechtelsville, Bedminster Twp., Bensalem, Boyertown, Bridgeport, Bristol Borough, Bristol Twp., Buckingham Twp. (Bucks County), Chalfont, Charlestown Twp., Colebrookdale, Collegeville, Conshohocken, Douglass (Berks County), Douglass Twp. (Montgomery County), Doylestown Borough, Doylestown Twp., Dublin, Earl Twp. (Berks County), East Coventry Twp., East Greenville, East Norriton, East Pikeland Twp., East Rockhill Twp., East Vincent Twp., Falls Twp. (Bucks County), Franconia, Green Lane, Hatboro Borough, Hatfield Borough, Hatfield Twp., Hereford, Hilltown Twp., Horsham Twp., Hulmeville, Ivyland, King of Prussia, Langhorne Borough, Langhorne Manor Borough, Lansdale (borough), Limerick, Lower Frederick, Lower Gwynedd Twp. (Montgomery County), Lower Makefield Twp., Lower Pottsgrove Twp., Lower Providence Twp., Lower Salford, Lower Southampton, Marlborough Twp., Middletown Twp. (Bucks County), Milford Square, Morrisville, New Britain Borough, New Britain Twp., New Hanover (Montgomery County), New Hope (Bucks County), Newtown Borough, Newtown Twp. (Bucks County), Norristown, North Coventry Twp., Northampton, Oley, Oley Twp., Penndel Borough, Pennsburg, Perkasie, Perkiomen, Phoenixville, Plumstead, Plymouth Twp. (Montgomery County), Pottstown, Quakertown, Red Hill, Richlandtown, Royersford, Salford, Schwenksville, Sellersville, Silverdale, Skippack, Solebury, Souderton, South Coventry Twp., Spring City, Springfield Twp. (Delaware County), Telford, Tinicum Twp. (Delaware County), Towamencin Twp., Trappe, Trumbauersville, Tullytown, Upper Dublin, Upper Frederick Twp., Upper Gwynedd Twp., Upper Hanover Twp., Upper Makefield Twp., Upper Merion Twp., Upper Pottsgrove, Upper Providence (Delaware County), Upper Salford, Upper Southampton, Warminster, Warrington Twp. (Bucks County), Warwick Twp. (Bucks County), Washington, West Conshohocken, West Norriton, West Pottsgrove, West Rockhill Twp., Whitemarsh Twp., Whitpain Twp., Worcester Twp. (Montgomery County), Wrightstown & Yardley Borough, PA. ICA: NJ0009.
TV Market Ranking: 1 (Allenhurst Borough, Atlantic Highlands Borough, Bedminster, Bernardsville, Chatham Twp., Chester, Deal Borough, East Windsor Twp., EATONTOWN BOROUGH, Fair Haven Borough, Fort Monmouth, Franklin Twp. (Hunterdon County), Franklin Twp. (Somerset County), Harding Twp., Hazlet Twp., Highlands Borough, Holmdel Twp., Little Silver Borough, Loch Arbour (village), Long Branch, Long Hill Twp., Mendham, Middletown Twp., Millington, Monmouth Beach Borough, Oceanport Borough, Peapack-Gladstone, Red Bank Borough, Rumson Borough, Sea Bright Borough, Shrewsbury Borough, Shrewsbury Twp., Tewksbury Twp., Tinton Falls Borough, West Long Branch); 1,4 (Bethlehem Twp., Branchburg Twp., Cranbury Twp., East Amwell Twp., East Brunswick, Flemington, Franklin Park, Freehold Borough, Helmetta, Hightstown, Hillsborough, Jamesburg, Lawrence, Lawrenceville, Lebanon Borough, Millstone, Monroe Twp., Montgomery Twp., Plainsboro, Princeton Borough, Princeton Junction, Princeton Twp., Raritan Twp., Readington Twp., Rocky Hill Borough, Roosevelt, South Brunswick Twp., Spotswood, Union Twp., West Windsor Twp.); 10 (Amity); 4 (Ambler Borough, Amity (Bucks County), Bedminster Twp., Bensalem, Boyertown, Bridgeport, Bristol Borough, Bristol Twp., Buckingham Twp. (Bucks County), Chalfont, Charlestown Twp., Colebrookdale, Collegeville, Conshohocken, Douglass Twp. (Montgomery County), Doylestown Borough, Doylestown Twp., Dublin, East Coventry Twp., East Greenville, East Norriton, East Pikeland Twp., East Rockhill Twp., East Vincent Twp., Ewing, Falls Twp. (Bucks County), Far Hills Borough, Franconia, Green Lane, Hatboro Borough, Hatfield Borough, Hatfield Twp., Hilltown Twp., Horsham Twp., Hulmeville, Ivyland, King of Prussia, Lambertville, Langhorne Borough, Langhorne Manor Borough, Lansdale (borough), Limerick, Lower Frederick, Lower Gwynedd Twp. (Montgomery County), Lower Makefield Twp., Lower Pottsgrove Twp., Lower Providence Twp., Lower Salford, Lower Southampton, Manchester Twp., Marlborough Twp., Middletown Twp. (Bucks County), Milford Square, Morrisville, New Britain Borough, New Britain Twp., New Hanover (Montgomery County), New Hope (Bucks County), Newtown Borough, Newtown Twp. (Bucks County), Norristown, North Coventry Twp., Northampton, Oley, Penndel Borough, Pennington Borough, Pennsburg, Perkasie, Perkiomen, Phoenixville, Plumstead, Plymouth Twp. (Montgomery County), Pottstown, Quakertown, Red Hill, Richlandtown, Royersford, Salford, Schwenksville, Sellersville, Silverdale, Skippack, Solebury, Souderton, South Coventry Twp., Spring City, Springfield Twp. (Delaware County), Stockton Borough, Telford, Tinicum Twp. (Delaware County), Towamencin Twp., Trappe, Trenton, Trumbauersville, Tullytown, Upper Dublin, Upper Frederick Twp., Upper Gwynedd Twp., Upper Hanover Twp., Upper Makefield Twp., Upper Merion Twp., Upper Pottsgrove, Upper Providence (Delaware County), Upper Salford, Upper Southampton, Warminster, Warrington Twp. (Bucks County), Warwick Twp. (Bucks County), West Conshohocken, West Norriton, West Pottsgrove, West Rockhill Twp., Whitemarsh Twp., Whitpain Twp., Worcester Twp. (Montgomery County), Wrightstown, Yardley Borough); 57 (Washington); Below 100 (Bally, Bechtelsville, Earl Twp. (Berks County), Hereford, Manahawkin, Oley Twp., Tuckerton Borough, Clinton); Outside TV Markets (Bay Head, Brick Twp., Mantoloking, Ocean County (portions), Point Pleasant, Point Pleasant Beach). Franchise award date: N.A. Franchise expiration date: N.A. Began: March 1, 1972.
Channel capacity: 50 (operating 2-way). Channels available but not in use: N.A.
Basic Service
Subscribers: 418,966. Commercial subscribers: 12,392.
Programming (received off-air): WABC-TV (ABC, Live Well Network) New York; WCAU (COZI TV, NBC) Philadelphia; WCBS-TV (CBS, Decades) New York; WFUT-DT (getTV, UniMas) Newark; WMBC-TV (Azteca America) Newton; WNBC (COZI TV, NBC) New York; WNET (PBS) Newark; WNJN (PBS) Montclair; WNJU (TMO) Linden; WNYE-TV (PBS) New York; WNYW (FOX, Movies!) New York; WPIX (Antenna TV, CW, This TV) New York; WPXN-TV (ION) New York; WWOR-TV (Bounce TV, Buzzr, Heroes & Icons, MNT) Secaucus; WXTV-DT (UNV) Paterson.
Programming (via satellite): AMC; Cartoon Network; Comcast Network Philadelphia; C-SPAN; EWTN Global Catholic Network; Fox News Channel; QVC; Syfy; TBS; TNT; WGN America.
Fee: $42.90 installation; $23.00 monthly.
Expanded Basic Service 1
Subscribers: N.A.
Programming (via satellite): A&E; Animal Planet; BET; Bravo; CMT; CNBC; CNN; Comedy Central; C-SPAN 2; Discovery Channel; E! HD; ESPN; ESPN2; Food Network; Fox Sports 1; Freeform; FX; Golf Channel; HGTV; History; HLN; Lifetime; MoviePlex; MSG; MSG Plus; MSNBC; MTV; NBCSN; News 12 New Jersey; Nickelodeon; OWN: Oprah Winfrey Network; Pop; Spike TV; SportsNet New York; The Weather Channel; TLC; truTV; Turner Classic Movies; TV Land; USA Network; VH1; YES Network.
Fee: $44.25 monthly.
Digital Basic Service
Subscribers: N.A.
Programming (via satellite): BBC America; Bloomberg Television; CBS Sports Network; Cooking Channel; C-SPAN 3; Discovery Digital Networks; Disney Channel; DIY Network; ESPN Classic; ESPN HD; ESPN2 HD; ESPNews; EVINE Live; Flix; FOX College Sports Central; FOX College Sports Pacific; FYI; GolTV; Great American Country; GSN; Hallmark Channel; HD Theater; History International; HITS (Headend In The Sky); Jewelry Television; LMN; MC; MTV Live; Nat Geo WILD; National Geographic Channel; NBA TV; NFL Network; Nick 2; Nick

Cable Systems—New Jersey

Jr.; Nicktoons; Oxygen; Pop; Sprout; Starz Encore (multiplexed); Sundance TV; TeenNick; Tennis Channel; TNT HD; Travel Channel; Trinity Broadcasting Network (TBN); TV One; Universal HD; Versus HD; WAM! America's Kidz Network; Weatherscan.
Fee: $14.95 monthly.

Digital Pay Service 1
Pay Units: 30,703.
Programming (via satellite): Cinemax (multiplexed); Cinemax HD; Cinemax On Demand; HBO (multiplexed); HBO HD; HBO on Demand; Showtime (multiplexed); Showtime HD; Showtime On Demand; Starz (multiplexed); Starz HD; Starz On Demand; The Movie Channel (multiplexed); The Movie Channel On Demand.
Fee: $16.25 monthly (each).

Video-On-Demand: Yes

Pay-Per-View
Fresh (delivered digitally); Sports PPV (delivered digitally); iN DEMAND (delivered digitally); Playgirl TV (delivered digitally); ESPN (delivered digitally).

Internet Service
Operational: Yes.
Subscribers: 523,557.
Broadband Service: Comcast High Speed Internet.
Fee: $42.95 monthly; $7.00 modem lease; $299.00 modem purchase.

Telephone Service
Digital: Operational
Subscribers: 338,049.
Miles of Plant: 30,170.0 (coaxial); 5,100.0 (fiber optic). Homes passed: 1,298,685.
Area Vice President: Keith Taub. Vice President, Marketing: Marge Jackson. Vice President, Technical Operations: Bob Kennedy. Public Relations Director: Fred DeAndrea.
Ownership: Comcast Cable Communications Inc. (MSO).

ELIZABETH—Cablevision, 536 Broad St, Elizabeth, NJ 07208. Phones: 201-405-8222; 201-651-4000; 516-803-2300 (Corporate office). Web Site: http://www.cablevision.com. ICA: NJ0023.
TV Market Ranking: 1 (ELIZABETH). Franchise award date: N.A. Franchise expiration date: N.A. Began: March 31, 1972.
Channel capacity: N.A. Channels available but not in use: N.A.

Basic Service
Subscribers: 21,916.
Programming (received off-air): WABC-TV (ABC, Live Well Network) New York; WCBS-TV (CBS, Decades) New York; WFUT-DT (getTV, UniMas) Newark; WLIW (PBS) Garden City; WMBC-TV (Azteca America) Newton; WNBC (COZI TV, NBC) New York; WNET (PBS) Newark; WNJN (PBS) Montclair; WNJU (TMO) Linden; WNYJ-TV (ETV) West Milford; WNYW (FOX, Movies!) New York; WPIX (Antenna TV, CW, This TV) New York; WPXN-TV (ION) New York; WWOR-TV (Bounce TV, Buzzr, Heroes & Icons, MNT) Secaucus; WXTV-DT (UNV) Paterson; 27 FMs.
Programming (via satellite): News 12 New Jersey; QVC.
Fee: $39.95 installation; $12.25 monthly.

Expanded Basic Service 1
Subscribers: N.A.
Programming (via satellite): A&E; AMC; Animal Planet; BET; Bravo; Cartoon Network; CNBC; CNN; Comcast Network Philadelphia; Comedy Central; C-SPAN; C-SPAN 2; Discovery Channel; Disney Channel; E! HD; ESPN; ESPN2; EVINE Live; Food Network; Fox News Channel; Fox Sports 1; Freeform; Fuse; FX; GSN; HGTV; History;

HLN; IFC; Lifetime; MSG; MSNBC; MTV; MTV2; NBC Universo; News 12 Traffic & Weather; Nickelodeon; Spike TV; SportsNet New York; Syfy; TBS; The Weather Channel; TLC; TNT; Travel Channel; truTV; Turner Classic Movies; TV Land; Univision; USA Network; VH1; WE tv; YES Network.
Fee: $37.70 monthly.

Digital Basic Service
Subscribers: N.A.
Programming (via satellite): Azteca; BBC World News; Bloomberg Television; Canal Sur; Caracol TV; Cartoon Network en Espanol; Cinelatino; CMT; CNN en Espanol; CNN HD; C-SPAN 3; Destination America; Discovery Kids Channel; Disney XD; Docu TVE; Ecuavisa Internacional; ESPN Classic; ESPN Deportes; ESPN HD; ESPN2 HD; ESPNews; EuroNews; Food Network HD; FOX College Sports Central; FOX College Sports Pacific; Fox Deportes; Fox Life; Fox Sports 2; FXM; FYI; Golf Channel; GolTV; Great American Country; Hallmark Channel; HD Theater; here! On Demand; HGTV HD; History en Espanol; History International; HTV; iN DEMAND; Infinito; Investigation Discovery; Jewelry Television; La Familia Cosmovision; LOGO; Mariavision; MC; Momentum; MTV Classic; MTV Hits; National Geographic Channel; National Geographic Channel HD; NBA TV; NBC Universo; NBCSN; NHL Network; Nick Jr.; Nicktoons; Outdoor Channel; Oxygen; Science Channel; Sundance TV; TBS HD; TeenNick; Telefe Internacional; TNT HD; Toon Disney en Espanol; Tr3s; TVG Network; ULTRA HD-Plex; Universal HD; Versus HD; VH1 Soul; ViendoMovies; Vme TV; YES HD.
Fee: $10.95 monthly.

Pay Service 1
Pay Units: N.A.
Programming (via satellite): Cinemax; Flix; HBO (multiplexed); Portuguese Channel; Showtime (multiplexed); The Movie Channel.

Digital Pay Service 1
Pay Units: N.A.
Programming (via satellite): Cinemax (multiplexed); Cinemax HD; Cinemax On Demand; HBO (multiplexed); HBO on Demand; Korean Channel; Playboy TV; Portuguese Channel; RAI Italia; RTN; Showtime (multiplexed); Showtime HD; Showtime On Demand; Starz (multiplexed); Starz Encore (multiplexed); Starz HD; The Movie Channel (multiplexed); The Movie Channel HD; TV Asia; TV Polonia; TV5, La Television International.
Fee: $9.95 monthly (Cinemax, Encore/ Starz/Starz HDTV, Showtime/Showtime HD/Showtime On Demand, TMC/TMC HD, RAI, TV5, TV Polonia or Playboy), $11.95 monthly (HBO), $24.95 monthly (TV Japan).

Video-On-Demand: Yes

Pay-Per-View
Movies; special events; Playboy TV; Spice2.

Internet Service
Operational: Yes.
Subscribers: 24,252.
Broadband Service: Optimum Online.
Fee: $34.95 monthly; $299.00 modem purchase.

Telephone Service
Digital: Operational
Subscribers: 19,130.
Fee: $34.95 monthly.
Miles of Plant: 294.0 (coaxial); 74.0 (fiber optic). Homes passed: 50,169.

FULLY SEARCHABLE • CONTINUOUSLY UPDATED • DISCOUNT RATES FOR PRINT PURCHASERS
For more information call 800-771-9202 or visit **www.warren-news.com**

Executive Vice President, Programming: Tom Montemagno. Vice President, Field Operations: Christopher Fulton.
Ownership: Altice USA (MSO).

FORT LEE BOROUGH—Time Warner Cable, 120 East 23rd St, New York, NY 10010. Phone: 201-598-7200. Fax: 212-420-4803. Web Site: http://www.timewarnercable.com. Also serves Cliffside Park Borough, Edgewater Borough, Englewood, Englewood Cliffs Borough, Fairview Borough, Guttenberg (town), Leonia Borough, Little Ferry Borough, Moonachie Borough, Palisades Park, Ridgefield Borough, Ridgefield Park (village) & Teterboro Borough. ICA: NJ0010.
TV Market Ranking: 1 (Cliffside Park Borough, Edgewater Borough, Englewood, Englewood Cliffs Borough, Fairview Borough, FORT LEE BOROUGH, Guttenberg (town), Leonia Borough, Little Ferry Borough, Moonachie Borough, Palisades Park, Ridgefield Borough, Ridgefield Park (village), Teterboro Borough). Franchise award date: N.A. Franchise expiration date: N.A. Began: November 1, 1971.
Channel capacity: N.A. Channels available but not in use: N.A.

Basic Service
Subscribers: 28,405. Commercial subscribers: 805.
Programming (received off-air): WABC-TV (ABC, Live Well Network) New York; WCBS-TV (CBS, Decades) New York; WFUT-DT (getTV, UniMas) Newark; WLIW (PBS) Garden City; WMBC-TV (Azteca America) Newton; WNBC (COZI TV, NBC) New York; WNET (PBS) Newark; WNJB (PBS) New Brunswick; WNJU (TMO) Linden; WNYE-TV (PBS) New York; WNYW (FOX, Movies!) New York; WPIX (Antenna TV, CW, This TV) New York; WPXN-TV (ION) New York; WWOR-TV (Bounce TV, Buzzr, Heroes & Icons, MNT) Secaucus; WXTV-DT (UNV) Paterson; 28 FMs.
Programming (via microwave): News 12 New Jersey.
Fee: $30.30 installation; $12.75 monthly.

Expanded Basic Service 1
Subscribers: N.A.
Programming (via microwave): Time Warner Cable News NY1.
Programming (via satellite): A&E; AMC; Animal Planet; BET; Bravo; Cartoon Network; CNBC; CNN; Comedy Central; C-SPAN; C-SPAN 2; Discovery Channel; Disney Channel; E! HD; ESPN; ESPN Classic; ESPN2; EVINE Live; EWTN Global Catholic Network; Food Network; Fox News Channel; Freeform; FX; Golf Channel; GSN; HGTV; History; HLN; IFC; Lifetime; MSG; MSG Plus; MSNBC; MTV; National Geographic Channel; Nickelodeon; Oxygen; Pop; QVC; Spike TV; Syfy; TBS; The Weather Channel; TLC; TNT; Travel Channel; truTV; Turner Classic Movies; TV Land; Univision; USA Network; VH1; WE tv; Yesterday USA.
Fee: $37.08 monthly.

Digital Basic Service
Subscribers: N.A.
Programming (via satellite): BBC America; Bloomberg Television; Boomerang; CMT;

Discovery Digital Networks; Disney XD; Fox Deportes; Fox Sports 1; Fuse; Great American Country; Hallmark Channel; LMN; MTV Classic; MTV2; NBC Universo; NBCSN; Nick Jr.; Sundance TV; TeenNick.
Fee: $9.95 monthly.

Digital Pay Service 1
Pay Units: N.A.
Programming (via satellite): Cinemax (multiplexed); Deutsche Welle TV; HBO (multiplexed); New Greek TV; RAI Italia; RTN; Showtime (multiplexed); Starz (multiplexed); Starz Encore (multiplexed); The Movie Channel (multiplexed); TV Asia; TV Polonia; TV5, La Television International; Zee TV.
Fee: $9.95 monthly (CCTV, RTN, RAI, Deutsche Welle or TV5), $12.95 monthly (HBO, Showtime, Cinemax, TMC, Starz or Encore), $14.95 monthly (TV Asia, Antenna or Zee TV), $17.95 monthly (TV Polonia), $24.95 monthly (TV Japan).

Video-On-Demand: Yes

Pay-Per-View
ESPN Now (delivered digitally); Hot Choice (delivered digitally); iN DEMAND; iN DEMAND (delivered digitally); Playboy TV (delivered digitally); Fresh (delivered digitally); Shorteez (delivered digitally); Sports PPV (delivered digitally).

Internet Service
Operational: Yes. Began: March 1, 2001.
Subscribers: 36,951.
Broadband Service: EarthLink, LocalNet, Road Runner.
Fee: $30.50 installation; $44.95 monthly.

Telephone Service
Digital: Operational
Subscribers: 18,213.
Fee: $39.95 monthly
Miles of Plant: 719.0 (coaxial); 279.0 (fiber optic). Homes passed: 94,058.
President: Howard Szarfarc. Vice President, Sales: Ken Fluger. Vice President, Marketing: David Goldberg. Vice President, Public Affairs: Harriet Novet. Vice President, Engineering: Larry Pestana. Vice President, Technical Operations: Norberto Rivera. General Manager: Brien Kelly.
Ownership: Time Warner Cable (MSO).

FREEHOLD—Cablevision, 1501 18th Ave, Wall, NJ 07719. Phone: 516-803-2300. Web Site: http://www.cablevision.com. Also serves Colts Neck, Englishtown, Freehold Twp., Howell, Howell Twp., Jackson, Jackson Twp., Lakewood, Lakewood Twp., Manalapan Twp., Marlboro Twp., Millstone Twp. & Upper Freehold Twp. ICA: NJ0063.
TV Market Ranking: 1 (Colts Neck, Englishtown, FREEHOLD, Howell, Jackson, Lakewood, Manalapan Twp., Marlboro Twp., Millstone Twp.); 1,4 (Freehold Twp.); 4 (Howell Twp., Jackson Twp., Lakewood Twp.).
Channel capacity: N.A. Channels available but not in use: N.A.

Basic Service
Subscribers: 77,523.
Fee: $39.95 installation; $16.72 monthly.

2017 Edition   D-513

New Jersey—Cable Systems

Internet Service
Operational: Yes.
Subscribers: 80,468.
Telephone Service
Digital: Operational
Subscribers: 66,665.
Miles of Plant: 3,553.0 (coaxial); 876.0 (fiber optic). Homes passed: 125,411.
Executive Vice President, Programming: Tom Montemagno.
Ownership: Altice USA (MSO).

GLOUCESTER COUNTY—Comcast Cable. Now served by AUDUBON, NJ [NJ0003]. ICA: NJ0022.

HAMILTON TWP. (Mercer County)—Cablevision, 2137 Hamilton Ave, Hamilton, NJ 08619. Phones: 516-803-2300 (Corporate office); 973-659-2200. Web Site: http://www.cablevision.com. Also serves Allentown & Washington Twp. (Mercer County). ICA: NJ0024.
TV Market Ranking: 4 (Allentown, HAMILTON TWP. (MERCER COUNTY), Washington Twp. (Mercer County)). Franchise award date: October 1, 1980. Franchise expiration date: N.A. Began: December 31, 1980.
Channel capacity: N.A. Channels available but not in use: N.A.
Basic Service
Subscribers: 24,012.
Programming (received off-air): KYW-TV (CBS, Decades) Philadelphia; WABC-TV (ABC, Live Well Network) New York; WCAU (COZI TV, NBC) Philadelphia; WCBS-TV (CBS, Decades) New York; WFMZ-TV (Retro TV) Allentown; WFUT-DT (getTV, UniMas) Newark; WGTW-TV (TBN) Burlington; WHYY-TV (PBS) Wilmington; WNBC (COZI TV, NBC) New York; WNET (PBS) Newark; WNJT (PBS) Trenton; WNYW (FOX, Movies!) New York; WPHL-TV (Antenna TV, MNT, This TV) Philadelphia; WPIX (Antenna TV, CW, This TV) New York; WPPX-TV (ION) Wilmington; WPSG (CW) Philadelphia; WPVI-TV (ABC, Live Well Network) Philadelphia; WPXN-TV (ION) New York; WTXF-TV (Buzzr, FOX, Movies!) Philadelphia; WUVP-DT (getTV, UNV) Vineland; WWOR-TV (Bounce TV, Buzzr, Heroes & Icons, MNT) Secaucus; WXTV-DT (UNV) Paterson; WYBE (ETV, IND) Philadelphia.
Programming (via microwave): News 12 New Jersey.
Fee: $39.95 installation; $16.13 monthly; $1.75 converter.
Expanded Basic Service 1
Subscribers: N.A.
Programming (via satellite): A&E; AMC; Animal Planet; BET; Bravo; Cartoon Network; CNBC; CNN; Comcast SportsNet Mid-Atlantic; Comedy Central; C-SPAN; C-SPAN 2; Discovery Channel; Disney Channel; E! HD; ESPN; ESPN2; Food Network; Fox News Channel; Fox Sports 1; Freeform; Fuse; FX; HGTV; History; HLN; IFC; Lifetime; MSG; MSG Plus; MSNBC; MTV; MTV2; News 12 Traffic & Weather; Nickelodeon; QVC; Spike TV; SportsNet New York; Syfy; TBS; The Weather Channel; TLC; TNT; Travel Channel; truTV; Turner Classic Movies; TV Land; USA Network; VH1; WE tv; YES Network.
Fee: $33.23 monthly.
Digital Basic Service
Subscribers: N.A.
Programming (via satellite): Azteca; BBC World News; Bloomberg Television; Canal Sur; Caracol TV; Cartoon Network; Cinelatino; CMT; CNN en Espanol; CNN HD; C-SPAN 3; Destination America; Discovery Kids Channel; Disney XD; Docu TVE; Ecuavisa Internacional; ESPN Classic; ESPN Deportes; ESPN HD; ESPN2 HD; ESPNews; EuroNews; EVINE Live; Food Network HD; FOX College Sports Central; FOX College Sports Pacific; Fox Deportes; Fox Life; Fox Sports 2; FXM; FYI; Golf Channel; GolTV; Great American Country; Hallmark Channel; HD Theater; here! On Demand; HGTV HD; History en Espanol; History International; HTV; iN DEMAND; Infinito; Investigation Discovery; Jewelry Television; La Familia Cosmovision; LOGO; Mariavision; MC; Momentum; MTV Classic; MTV Hits; National Geographic Channel; National Geographic Channel HD; NBA TV; NBC Universo; NBCSN; NHL Network; Nick Jr.; Nicktoons; Outdoor Channel; Oxygen; Science Channel; Sundance TV; TBS HD; TeenNick; Telefe Internacional; TNT HD; Toon Disney en Espanol; Tr3s; TVG Network; ULTRA HDPlex; Universal HD; Versus HD; VH1 Soul; ViendoMovies; Vme TV; YES HD.
Fee: $10.95 monthly.
Pay Service 1
Pay Units: N.A.
Programming (via satellite): Cinemax; Flix; HBO (multiplexed); Showtime (multiplexed); The Movie Channel.
Digital Pay Service 1
Pay Units: N.A.
Programming (via satellite): Cinemax (multiplexed); Cinemax HD; Cinemax On Demand; HBO (multiplexed); HBO HD; HBO on Demand; Korean Channel; MBC America; Portuguese Channel; RAI Italia; RTN; Showtime (multiplexed); Showtime HD; Showtime On Demand; Starz (multiplexed); Starz Encore; Starz HD; The Movie Channel (multiplexed); The Movie Channel HD; TV Asia; TV Polonia; TV5, La Television International.
Fee: $9.95 monthly (Cinemax, Showtime, Starz/Encore, Playboy, TMC, RAI, SPT, TV5 or TV Polonia), $11.95 monthly (HBO), $24.95 monthly (TV Japan).
Video-On-Demand: Yes
Pay-Per-View
Fresh (delivered digitally); special events (delivered digitally).
Internet Service
Operational: Yes.
Subscribers: 23,996.
Broadband Service: Optimum Online.
Fee: $46.95 installation; $34.95 monthly; $299.00 modem purchase.
Telephone Service
Digital: Operational
Subscribers: 19,901.
Fee: $34.95 monthly
Miles of Plant: 933.0 (coaxial); 234.0 (fiber optic). Homes passed: 46,772.
Executive Vice President, Programming: Tom Montemagno. Vice President, Field Operations: Frank Dagliere. Vice President, Government Affairs: Adam Falk.
Ownership: Altice USA (MSO).

HILLSBOROUGH—Comcast Cable. Now served by EATONTOWN BOROUGH, NJ [NJ0009]. ICA: NJ0025.

HOBOKEN—Cablevision, 360 First St, Hoboken, NJ 07030. Phones: 201-405-8222; 201-651-4000; 516-803-2300 (Corporate office). Web Site: http://www.cablevision.com. Also serves North Bergen, Union City, Weehawken & West New York. ICA: NJ0008.
TV Market Ranking: 1 (HOBOKEN, North Bergen, Union City, Weehawken, West New York). Franchise award date: N.A. Franchise expiration date: N.A. Began: September 1, 1970.
Channel capacity: N.A. Channels available but not in use: N.A.
Basic Service
Subscribers: 44,527.
Programming (received off-air): WABC-TV (ABC, Live Well Network) New York; WCBS-TV (CBS, Decades) New York; WFUT-DT (getTV, UniMas) Newark; WLIW (PBS) Garden City; WMBC-TV (Azteca America) Newton; WNBC (COZI TV, NBC) New York; WNET (PBS) Newark; WNJN (PBS) Montclair; WNJU (TMO) Linden; WNYJ-TV (ETV) West Milford; WNYW (FOX, Movies!) New York; WPIX (Antenna TV, CW, This TV) New York; WPXN-TV (ION) New York; WWOR-TV (Bounce TV, Buzzr, Heroes & Icons, MNT) Secaucus; WXTV-DT (UNV) Paterson.
Programming (via satellite): News 12 New Jersey; QVC.
Fee: $39.95 installation; $13.26 monthly; $1.76 converter.
Expanded Basic Service 1
Subscribers: N.A.
Programming (via satellite): A&E; AMC; Animal Planet; BET; Bravo; Cartoon Network; CNBC; CNN; Comcast Network Philadelphia; Comedy Central; C-SPAN; C-SPAN 2; Discovery Channel; Disney Channel; E! HD; ESPN; ESPN2; Food Network; Fox News Channel; Fox Sports 1; Freeform; Fuse; FX; GSN; HGTV; History; HLN; Lifetime; MSNBC; MTV; MTV2; NBC Universo; News 12 Traffic & Weather; Nickelodeon; Spike TV; Syfy; TBS; The Weather Channel; TLC; TNT; Travel Channel; truTV; TV Land; Univision; USA Network; VH1; WE tv.
Fee: $36.69 monthly.
Digital Basic Service
Subscribers: N.A.
Programming (via satellite): Azteca; BBC World News; Bloomberg Television; Canal Sur; Caracol TV; Cartoon Network en Espanol; Cinelatino; CMT; CNN en Espanol; CNN HD; C-SPAN 3; Destination America; Discovery Kids Channel; Disney XD; Docu TVE; Ecuavisa Internacional; ESPN Classic; ESPN Deportes; ESPN HD; ESPN2 HD; ESPNews; EuroNews; EVINE Live; Food Network HD; FOX College Sports Central; FOX College Sports Pacific; Fox Deportes; Fox Life; Fox Sports 2; FXM; FYI; Golf Channel; GolTV; Great American Country; Hallmark Channel; HD Theater; here! On Demand; HGTV HD; History en Espanol; History International; HTV; iN DEMAND; Infinito; Investigation Discovery; Jewelry Television; La Familia Cosmovision; LOGO; Mariavision; MC; Momentum; MTV Classic; MTV Hits; National Geographic Channel; National Geographic Channel HD; NBA TV; NBC Universo; NBCSN; NHL Network; Nick Jr.; Nicktoons; Outdoor Channel; Oxygen; Science Channel; Sundance TV; TBS HD; TeenNick; Telefe Internacional; The Word Network; TNT HD; Toon Disney en Espanol; Tr3s; TVG Network; ULTRA HDPlex; Universal HD; Versus HD; VH1 Soul; ViendoMovies; YES HD.
Fee: $10.95 monthly.
Pay Service 1
Pay Units: N.A.
Programming (via satellite): Cinemax; Flix; HBO (multiplexed); IFC; MSG; MSG Plus; Playboy TV; Showtime (multiplexed); The Movie Channel; Turner Classic Movies; YES Network.
Fee: $20.00 installation; $9.95 monthly (Cinemax or TMC), $11.95 monthly (Showtime).
Digital Pay Service 1
Pay Units: N.A.
Programming (via satellite): Cinemax (multiplexed); Cinemax HD; Cinemax On Demand; HBO (multiplexed); HBO HD; HBO on Demand; International Television (ITV); Korean Channel; MBC America; Playboy TV; Portuguese Channel; RAI Italia; RTN; Showtime (multiplexed); Showtime HD; Showtime On Demand; Starz (multiplexed); Starz Encore; Starz HD; The Movie Channel (multiplexed); The Movie Channel HD; TV Asia; TV Polonia; TV5, La Television International; Zee TV.
Fee: $9.95 monthly (Cinemax, Showtime, Starz/Encore, Playboy, TMC, RAI, SPT, TV5 or TV Polonia), $11.95 monthly (HBO), $24.95 monthly (TV Japan).
Video-On-Demand: Yes
Pay-Per-View
Anime Network (delivered digitally); Disney Channel (delivered digitally); iN DEMAND (delivered digitally); NBA TV (delivered digitally); Sports PPV (delivered digitally); Playboy TV; iN DEMAND (delivered digitally); Playboy TV (delivered digitally).
Internet Service
Operational: Yes.
Subscribers: 54,604.
Broadband Service: Optimum Online.
Fee: $46.95 installation; $34.95 monthly; $299.00 modem purchase.
Telephone Service
Digital: Operational
Subscribers: 41,364.
Fee: $34.95 monthly
Miles of Plant: 324.0 (coaxial); 82.0 (fiber optic). Homes passed: 119,690.
Executive Vice President, Programming: Tom Montemagno. Vice President, Field Operations: Christopher Fulton.
Ownership: Altice USA (MSO).

HUNTERDON COUNTY—Service Electric Cable TV of Hunterdon Inc., PO Box 20151, Lehigh Valley, PA 18002. Phones: 800-225-9102; 610-865-9100. Fax: 610-865-7888. E-mail: office@sectv.com. Web Site: http://www.sectv.com. Also serves Alexandria Twp., Alpha Boro, Bloomsbury, Frenchtown Boro, Greenwich Twp., Harmony Twp., Holland Twp., Kingwood Twp., Lopatcong Twp., Milford Boro, Phillipsburg & Pohatcong Twp. ICA: NJ0067.
TV Market Ranking: 4 (Alexandria Twp., Holland Twp., HUNTERDON COUNTY, Kingwood Twp.); Below 100 (Bloomsbury, Frenchtown Boro, Greenwich Twp., Harmony Twp., Lopatcong Twp., Milford Boro, PHILLIPSBURG, Pohatcong Twp.).
Channel capacity: N.A. Channels available but not in use: N.A.
Basic Service
Subscribers: 11,132.
Programming (received off-air): KYW-TV (CBS, Decades) Philadelphia; WABC-TV (ABC, Live Well Network) New York; WBPH-TV (IND) Bethlehem; WCAU (COZI TV, NBC) Philadelphia; WCBS-TV (CBS, Decades) New York; WFMZ-TV (Retro TV) Allentown; WHYY-TV (PBS) Wilmington; WLVT-TV (PBS) Allentown; WMBC-TV (Azteca America) Newton; WNBC (COZI TV, NBC) New York; WNJT (PBS) Trenton; WNYW (FOX, Movies!) New York; WPHL-TV (Antenna TV, MNT, This TV) Philadelphia; WPIX (Antenna TV, CW, This TV) New York; WPSG (CW) Philadelphia; WPVI-TV (ABC, Live Well Network) Philadelphia; WPXN-TV (ION) New York; WTXF-TV (Buzzr, FOX, Movies!) Philadelphia; WWOR-TV (Bounce TV, Buzzr, Heroes & Icons, MNT) Secaucus; WXTV-DT (UNV) Paterson.

Cable Systems—New Jersey

Programming (via satellite): AccuWeather Inc.; Antenna TV; BBC America; Bravo; Comcast Network Philadelphia; Cooking Channel; C-SPAN; C-SPAN 2; EVINE Live; EWTN Global Catholic Network; HSN; INSP; NASA TV; OWN: Oprah Winfrey Network; Oxygen; QVC; RTV; Telemundo; The Weather Channel; truTV.
Fee: $49.95 installation; $19.49 monthly; $2.95 converter.

Expanded Basic Service 1
Subscribers: 10,221.
Programming (via satellite): A&E; AMC; Animal Planet; BET; BTN; Cartoon Network; CMT; CNBC; CNN; Comcast SportsNet Philadelphia; Comedy Central; Discovery Channel; Disney Channel; Disney XD; E! HD; ESPN; ESPN2; Food Network; Fox News Channel; Fox Sports 1; Freeform; FX; Golf Channel; GSN; Hallmark Channel; HGTV; History; HLN; Lifetime; LMN; MLB Network; MSG; MSNBC; MTV; National Geographic Channel; NBCSN; NFL Network; Nickelodeon; Outdoor Channel; Spike TV; SportsNet New York; Syfy; TBS; TLC; TNT; Travel Channel; Turner Classic Movies; TV Land; USA Network; VH1; WE tv; YES Network.
Fee: $69.24 monthly.

Digital Basic Service
Subscribers: 2,187.
Programming (via satellite): Bloomberg Television; Boomerang; BTN; CBS Sports Network; Chiller; Destination America; Discovery Family; DIY Network; ESPNews; ESPNU; Fox Business Network; Fox Sports 2; FSN Digital Atlantic; FSN Digital Central; FSN Digital Pacific; FXM; FYI; History International; IFC; MC; NBA TV; NHL Network; Nick 2; Nick Jr.; Nicktoons; Sprout; TeenNick; Tennis Channel; TVG Network.
Fee: $12.99 monthly; $4.95 converter.

Digital Expanded Basic Service
Subscribers: 11.
Programming (via satellite): Cine Mexicano; Enlace USA; ESPN Deportes; La Familia Cosmovision; Telemundo; Time Warner Cable News NY1; Tr3s; Univision; Vme TV.
Fee: $5.95 monthly.

Digital Pay Service 1
Pay Units: 1,597.
Programming (via microwave): RTP-USA.
Programming (via satellite): Cinemax (multiplexed); Cinemax HD; Flix; HBO (multiplexed); HBO HD; HBO Latino; Playboy TV; RAI Italia; Showtime (multiplexed); Showtime HD; Starz (multiplexed); Starz Encore (multiplexed); The Filipino Channel; The Movie Channel (multiplexed); Zee TV.
Fee: $10.49 monthly (Portuguese Channel/ RAI), $12.45 monthly (Filipino), $12.99 monthly (Cinemax), $13.49 monthly (Starz/Encore), $13.99 monthly (Playboy), $14.99 monthly (HBO), $15.49 monthly (Showtime/TMC or Zee TV).

Video-On-Demand: Yes

Pay-Per-View
Movies, Special Events (delivered digitally).

Internet Service
Operational: Yes. Began: January 1, 1995.
Subscribers: 3,363.
Fee: $39.95 installation; $29.95-$39.95 monthly.

Telephone Service
Digital: Operational
Subscribers: 558.
Miles of Plant: 480.0 (coaxial); None (fiber optic). Homes passed: 22,141.
General Manager: John Capparell. Chief Engineer: Jeff Kelly. Program Director: Andy Himmelwright. Marketing Director: Steve Salash. Regulatory Affairs Director: Arlean Lilly. Customer Service Manager: John Ritter.
Ownership: Service Electric Cable TV Inc. (MSO).

JERSEY CITY—Comcast Cable. Now served by WEST ORANGE TWP., NJ [NJ0001]. ICA: NJ0007.

LAMBERTVILLE—Comcast Cable. Now served by EATONTOWN BOROUGH, NJ [NJ0009]. ICA: NJ0042.

LONG BEACH TWP.—Comcast Cable. Now served by AUDUBON, NJ [NJ0003]. ICA: NJ0030.

LONG HILL—Comcast Cable. Now served by EATONTOWN BOROUGH, NJ [NJ0009]. ICA: NJ0036.

MAPLE SHADE—Comcast Cable. Now served by AUDUBON, NJ [NJ0003]. ICA: NJ0041.

MILLSTONE TWP.—Cablevision Systems Corp. Now served by FREEHOLD, NJ [NJ0063]. ICA: NJ0047.

MORRIS TWP.—Cablevision, 683 New Jersey 10, Randolph, NJ 07869. Phones: 973-659-2200; 516-803-2300 (Corporate office). Fax: 973-659-2266. Web Site: http://www.cablevision.com. Also serves Allamuchy Twp., Boonton, Boonton Twp., Chatham, Denville, Dover, East Hanover Twp., Florham Park, Hanover Twp., Hopatcong, Jefferson Twp., Madison, Mine Hill Twp., Montville Twp., Morris Plains, Morristown, Mount Arlington, Mount Olive Twp., Mountain Lakes, Netcong, Parsippany, Parsippany-Troy Hills Twp., Picatinny Arsenal, Randolph Twp., Rockaway, Rockaway Twp., Roxbury Twp., Stanhope, Victory Gardens & Wharton. ICA: NJ0005.
TV Market Ranking: 1 (Allamuchy Twp. (portions), Boonton, Boonton, Chatham, Denville, Dover, East Hanover Twp., Florham Park, Hanover Twp., Hopatcong, Jefferson Twp., Madison, Mine Hill Twp., Montville Twp., Morris Plains, MORRIS TWP., Morristown, Mount Arlington, Mount Olive Twp., Mountain Lakes, Netcong, Parsippany, Parsippany-Troy Hills Twp., Picatinny Arsenal, Randolph Twp., Rockaway, Rockaway Twp., Roxbury Twp., Stanhope, Victory Gardens, Wharton); Below 100 (Allamuchy Twp. (portions)).
Franchise award date: February 1, 1972.
Franchise expiration date: N.A. Began: February 1, 1972.
Channel capacity: 41 (operating 2-way). Channels available but not in use: N.A.

Basic Service
Subscribers: 102,310.
Programming (received off-air): WABC-TV (ABC, Live Well Network) New York; WCBS-TV (CBS, Decades) New York; WFUT-DT (getTV, UniMas) Newark; WLNY-TV (IND) Riverhead; WMBC-TV (Azteca America) Newton; WNBC (COZI TV, NBC) New York; WNET (PBS) Newark; WNJN (PBS) Montclair; WNJU (TMO) Linden; WNYJ-TV (ETV) West Milford; WNYW (FOX, Movies!) New York; WPIX (Antenna TV, CW, This TV) New York; WPXN-TV (ION) New York; WRNN-TV (IND) Kingston; WWOR-TV (Bounce TV, Buzzr, Heroes & Icons, MNT) Secaucus; WXTV-DT (UNV) Paterson.
Programming (via microwave): News 12 New Jersey.
Programming (via satellite): QVC.
Fee: $39.95 installation; $11.75 monthly; $1.50 converter.

Expanded Basic Service 1
Subscribers: N.A.
Programming (via satellite): A&E; AMC; Animal Planet; BET; Bravo; Cartoon Network; CNBC; CNN; Comedy Central; C-SPAN; C-SPAN 2; Discovery Channel; Disney Channel; E! HD; ESPN; ESPN2; Food Network; Fox News Channel; Fox Sports 1; Freeform; Fuse; FX; GSN; HGTV; History; HLN; Lifetime; MSG; MSG Plus; MSNBC; MTV; MTV2; News 12 Traffic & Weather; Nickelodeon; Spike TV; SportsNet New York; Syfy; TBS; The Weather Channel; TLC; TNT; Travel Channel; truTV; TV Land; USA Network; VH1; WE tv; YES Network.
Fee: $38.06 monthly.

Digital Basic Service
Subscribers: N.A.
Programming (via satellite): Azteca; BBC World News; Bloomberg Television; Canal Sur; Caracol TV; Cartoon Network en Espanol; Cinelatino; CMT; CNN en Espanol; CNN HD; C-SPAN 3; Destination America; Discovery Kids Channel; Disney XD; Docu TVE; Ecuavisa Internacional; ESPN Classic; ESPN Deportes; ESPN HD; ESPN2 HD; ESPNews; EuroNews; EVINE Live; Food Network HD; FOX College Sports Central; FOX College Sports Pacific; Fox Deportes; Fox Life; Fox Sports 2; FXM; FYI; Golf Channel; GolTV; Great American Country; Hallmark Channel; HD Theater; here! On Demand; HGTV HD; History en Espanol; History International; HTV; iN DEMAND; Infinito; Investigation Discovery; Jewelry Television; La Familia Cosmovision; LOGO; Mariavision; MC; Momentum; MTV Classic; MTV Hits; National Geographic Channel; National Geographic Channel HD; NBA TV; NBC Universo; NBCSN; NHL Network; Nick Jr.; Nicktoons; Outdoor Channel; Oxygen; Science Channel; Sundance TV; TBS HD; TeenNick; Telefe Internacional; TNT HD; Toon Disney en Espanol; Tr3s; TVG Network; ULTRA HD-Plex; Universal HD; Versus HD; VH1 Soul; ViendoMovies; Vme TV; YES HD.
Fee: $10.95 monthly; $2.95 converter.

Pay Service 1
Pay Units: N.A.
Programming (via satellite): Cinemax; Flix; HBO (multiplexed); IFC; Showtime (multiplexed); The Movie Channel; Turner Classic Movies.

Digital Pay Service 1
Pay Units: N.A.
Programming (via satellite): Cinemax (multiplexed); Cinemax HD; Cinemax On Demand; HBO (multiplexed); HBO HD; HBO on Demand; International Television (ITV); Korean Channel; MBC America; Playboy TV; RAI Italia; RTN; Showtime (multiplexed); Showtime HD; Showtime On Demand; Starz (multiplexed); Starz Encore (multiplexed); Starz HD; The Movie Channel (multiplexed); The Movie Channel HD; TV Asia; TV Polonia; TV5, La Television International; Zee TV.
Fee: $9.95 monthly (Cinemax, Showtime, Starz/Encore, Playboy, TMC, RAI, SPT, TV5 or TV Polonia), $11.95 monthly (HBO), $24.95 monthly (TV Japan).

Video-On-Demand: Yes

Pay-Per-View
Hot Choice; iN DEMAND; Spice; special events.

Internet Service
Operational: Yes.
Subscribers: 109,961.
Broadband Service: Optimum Online.
Fee: $46.95 installation; $34.95 monthly; $299.00 modem purchase.

Telephone Service
Digital: Operational
Subscribers: 89,557.
Fee: $34.95 monthly
Miles of Plant: 3,923.0 (coaxial); 987.0 (fiber optic). Homes passed: 174,006.
Executive Vice President, Programming: Tom Montemagno. Vice President, Field Operations: Frank Dagliere. Vice President, Government Affairs: Adam Falk.
Ownership: Altice USA (MSO).

NEWARK—Cablevision, 360 Central Ave, Newark, NJ 07103. Phones: 201-405-8222; 516-803-2300 (Corporate office); 201-651-4000. Web Site: http://www.cablevision.com. Also serves South Orange Twp. ICA: NJ0011.
TV Market Ranking: 1 (NEWARK, South Orange Twp.). Franchise award date: N.A. Franchise expiration date: N.A. Began: June 19, 1982.
Channel capacity: N.A. Channels available but not in use: N.A.

Basic Service
Subscribers: 46,403. Commercial subscribers: 2,249.
Programming (received off-air): WABC-TV (ABC, Live Well Network) New York; WCBS-TV (CBS, Decades) New York; WFUT-DT (getTV, UniMas) Newark; WLIW (PBS) Garden City; WMBC-TV (Azteca America) Newton; WNBC (COZI TV, NBC) New York; WNET (PBS) Newark; WNJN (PBS) Montclair; WNJU (TMO) Linden; WNYJ-TV (ETV) West Milford; WNYW (FOX, Movies!) New York; WPIX (Antenna TV, CW, This TV) New York; WPXN-TV (ION) New York; WWOR-TV (Bounce TV, Buzzr, Heroes & Icons, MNT) Secaucus; WXTV-DT (UNV) Paterson; 2 FMs.
Programming (via microwave): News 12 New Jersey.
Programming (via satellite): CNN HD.
Fee: $39.95 installation; $9.32 monthly; $2.80 converter.

Expanded Basic Service 1
Subscribers: N.A.
Programming (via satellite): A&E; AMC; Animal Planet; BET; Bravo; Cartoon Network; CNBC; CNN; Comedy Central; C-SPAN; C-SPAN 2; Discovery Channel; Disney Channel; E! HD; ESPN; ESPN2; EVINE Live; Food Network; Fox News Channel; Fox Sports 1; Freeform; Fuse; FX; GSN; HGTV; History; HLN; Lifetime; MSNBC; MTV; MTV2; NBC Universo; News 12 Traffic & Weather; Nickelodeon; QVC; Spike TV; SportsNet New York; Syfy; TBS; The Weather Channel; TLC;

New Jersey—Cable Systems

TNT; Travel Channel; truTV; TV Land; Univision; USA Network; VH1; WE tv.
Fee: $40.63 monthly.

Digital Basic Service
Subscribers: N.A.
Programming (via satellite): Azteca; BBC World News; Bloomberg Television; Canal Sur; Caracol TV; Cartoon Network en Espanol; Cinelatino; CMT; CNN en Espanol; C-SPAN 3; Destination America; Discovery Kids Channel; Disney XD; Docu TVE; Ecuavisa Internacional; ESPN Classic; ESPN Deportes; ESPN HD; ESPN2 HD; ESPNews; EuroNews; Food Network HD; FOX College Sports Central; FOX College Sports Pacific; Fox Deportes; Fox Life; Fox Sports 2; FXM; FYI; Golf Channel; GolTV; Great American Country; Hallmark Channel; HD Theater; here! On Demand; HGTV HD; History en Espanol; History International; HTV; iN DEMAND; Infinito; Investigation Discovery; Jewelry Television; La Familia Cosmovision; LOGO; Mariavision; MC; Momentum; MSG Plus; MTV Classic; MTV Hits; National Geographic Channel; National Geographic Channel HD; NBA TV; NBC Universo; NBCSN; NHL Network; Nick Jr.; Nicktoons; Outdoor Channel; Oxygen; Science Channel; Sundance TV; TBS HD; TeenNick; Telefe Internacional; The Word Network; TNT HD; Toon Disney en Espanol; Tr3s; TVG Network; ULTRA HDPlex; Universal HD; Versus HD; VH1 Soul; ViendoMovies; Vme TV; YES HD.
Fee: $10.95 monthly.

Pay Service 1
Pay Units: N.A.
Programming (via satellite): Cinemax; Flix; HBO (multiplexed); IFC; MSG; MSG Plus; Playboy TV; Portuguese Channel; Showtime (multiplexed); The Movie Channel; Turner Classic Movies; YES Network.

Digital Pay Service 1
Pay Units: N.A.
Programming (via satellite): Cinemax (multiplexed); Cinemax HD; Cinemax On Demand; HBO (multiplexed); HBO HD; HBO on Demand; International Television (ITV); Korean Channel; MBC America; Playboy TV; Portuguese Channel; RTN; Showtime (multiplexed); Showtime HD; Showtime On Demand; Starz (multiplexed); Starz Encore (multiplexed); Starz HD; The Movie Channel (multiplexed); The Movie Channel HD; TV Asia; TV Polonia; Zee TV.
Fee: $9.95 monthly (Cinemax, Showtime, Starz/Encore, Playboy, TMC, RAI, SPT, TV5 or TV Polonia), $11.95 monthly (HBO), $24.95 monthly (TV Japan).

Video-On-Demand: Yes

Pay-Per-View
Playboy TV (delivered digitally); iN DEMAND (delivered digitally); NBA TV (delivered digitally); Sports PPV (delivered digitally); Playboy TV.

Internet Service
Operational: Yes.
Subscribers: 53,095.
Broadband Service: Optimum Online.
Fee: $46.95 installation; $34.95 monthly; $299.00 modem purchase.

Telephone Service
Digital: Operational
Subscribers: 43,900.
Fee: $34.95 monthly
Miles of Plant: 619.0 (coaxial); 179.0 (fiber optic). Homes passed: 132,550.
Executive Vice President, Programming: Tom Montemagno. Vice President, Field Operations: Christopher Fulton.
Ownership: Altice USA (MSO).

OAKLAND—Cablevision, 40 Potash Rd, Oakland, NJ 07436-3100. Phones: 201-405-8222; 516-803-2300 (Corporate office); 201-651-4000. Fax: 516-803-1183. Web Site: http://www.cablevision.com. Also serves Allendale, Alpine, Bloomingdale, Bogota, Butler, Cedar Grove Twp., Clifton, Elmwood Park, Franklin Lakes, Garfield, Glen Rock, Hackensack, Haledon, Hasbrouck Heights, Hawthorne, Ho-Ho-Kus, Kinnelon, Lincoln Park, Little Falls Twp., Lodi, Maywood, Midland Park, Montville Twp. (northeastern portion), North Caldwell, North Haledon, Nutley Twp., Park Ridge, Passaic, Pequannock Twp., Pompton Lakes, Prospect Park, Ramsey, Ridgewood, Ringwood, River Edge, Riverdale, Rochelle Park, Saddle Brook Twp., South Hackensack Twp., Teaneck, Totowa, Upper Saddle River, Waldwick, Wanaque, Washington Twp. (Bergen County), Wayne, West Paterson, Westwood, Wood-Ridge & Wyckoff. ICA: NJ0002.
TV Market Ranking: 1 (Allendale, Alpine, Bloomingdale, Bogota, Butler, Cedar Grove Twp., Clifton, Elmwood Park, Franklin Lakes, Garfield, Glen Rock, Hackensack, Haledon, Hasbrouck Heights, Hawthorne, Ho-Ho-Kus, Kinnelon, Lincoln Park, Little Falls Twp., Lodi, Maywood, Midland Park, Montville Twp. (northeastern portion), North Caldwell, North Haledon, Nutley Twp., OAKLAND, Park Ridge, Passaic, Pequannock Twp., Pompton Lakes, Prospect Park, Ramsey, Ridgewood, Ringwood, River Edge, Riverdale, Rochelle Park, Saddle Brook Twp., South Hackensack Twp., Teaneck, Totowa, Upper Saddle River, Waldwick, Wanaque, Washington Twp. (Bergen County), Wayne, West Paterson, Westwood, Wood-Ridge, Wyckoff).
Franchise award date: N.A. Franchise expiration date: N.A. Began: September 1, 1966.
Channel capacity: N.A. Channels available but not in use: N.A.

Basic Service
Subscribers: 177,037. Commercial subscribers: 10,428.
Programming (received off-air): WABC-TV (ABC, Live Well Network) New York; WCBS-TV (CBS, Decades) New York; WFUT-DT (getTV, UniMas) Newark; WLIW (PBS) Garden City; WLNY-TV (IND) Riverhead; WMBC-TV (Azteca America) Newton; WNBC (COZI TV, NBC) New York; WNET (PBS) Newark; WNJN (PBS) Montclair; WNJU (TMO) Linden; WNYJ-TV (ETV) West Milford; WNYW (FOX, Movies!) New York; WPIX (Antenna TV, CW, This TV) New York; WPXN-TV (ION) New York; WRNN-TV (IND) Kingston; WWOR-TV (Bounce TV, Buzzr, Heroes & Icons, MNT) Secaucus; WXTV-DT (UNV) Paterson, 15 FMs.
Programming (via microwave): News 12 New Jersey.
Programming (via satellite): QVC.
Fee: $39.95 installation; $12.18 monthly; $1.00 converter.

Expanded Basic Service 1
Subscribers: N.A.
Programming (via satellite): A&E; AMC; Animal Planet; BET; Bravo; Cartoon Network; CNBC; CNN; Comcast Network Philadelphia; Comedy Central; C-SPAN; C-SPAN 2; Discovery Channel; Disney Channel; E! HD; ESPN; ESPN2; EVINE Live; Food Network; Fox News Channel; Fox Sports 1; Freeform; Fuse; FX; GSN; HGTV; History; HLN; Lifetime; MSG; MSG Plus; MSNBC; MTV; MTV2; News 12 Traffic & Weather; Nickelodeon; Spike TV; SportsNet New York; Syfy; TBS; The Weather Channel; TLC; TNT; Travel Channel; truTV; Turner Classic Movies; TV Land; USA Network; VH1; WE tv; YES Network.
Fee: $37.77 monthly.

Digital Basic Service
Subscribers: N.A.
Programming (via satellite): Azteca; BBC World News; Bloomberg Television; Canal Sur; Caracol TV; Cartoon Network en Espanol; Cinelatino; CMT; CNN en Espanol; CNN HD; C-SPAN 3; Destination America; Disney XD; Docu TVE; Ecuavisa Internacional; ESPN Classic; ESPN Deportes; ESPN HD; ESPN2 HD; ESPNews; EuroNews; Food Network HD; FOX College Sports Central; FOX College Sports Pacific; Fox Deportes; Fox Life; Fox Sports 2; FXM; FYI; Golf Channel; GolTV; Great American Country; Hallmark Channel; HD Theater; here! On Demand; HGTV HD; History en Espanol; History International; HTV; iN DEMAND; Infinito; Investigation Discovery; Jewelry Television; La Familia Cosmovision; LOGO; Mariavision; MC; Momentum; MTV Classic; MTV Hits; National Geographic Channel; National Geographic Channel HD; NBA TV; NBC Universo; NBCSN; NHL Network; Nick Jr.; Nicktoons; Outdoor Channel; Oxygen; Science Channel; Sundance TV; TBS HD; TeenNick; Telefe Internacional; TNT HD; Toon Disney en Espanol; Tr3s; TVG Network; ULTRA HDPlex; Universal HD; Versus HD; VH1 Soul; ViendoMovies; Vme TV; YES HD.
Fee: $10.95 monthly.

Pay Service 1
Pay Units: N.A.
Programming (via satellite): Cinemax; Flix; HBO (multiplexed); IFC; Showtime (multiplexed); The Movie Channel.

Digital Pay Service 1
Pay Units: N.A.
Programming (via satellite): Cinemax (multiplexed); Cinemax HD; Cinemax On Demand; HBO (multiplexed); HBO HD; HBO on Demand; International Television (ITV); Korean Channel; MBC America; Playboy TV; RTN; Showtime (multiplexed); Showtime HD; Showtime On Demand; Starz; Starz Encore (multiplexed); Starz HD; The Movie Channel (multiplexed); The Movie Channel HD; TV Asia; TV Polonia; TV5, La Television International; Zee TV.
Fee: $9.95 monthly (Cinemax, Showtime, Starz/Encore, Playboy, TMC, RAI, SPT, TV5 or TV Polonia), $11.95 monthly (HBO), $24.95 monthly (TV Japan).

Video-On-Demand: Yes

Pay-Per-View
iN DEMAND; Playboy TV; Fresh; Shorteez.

Internet Service
Operational: Yes.
Subscribers: 192,208.
Broadband Service: Optimum Online.
Fee: $46.95 installation; $34.95 monthly; $299.00 modem purchase.

Telephone Service
Digital: Operational
Subscribers: 161,367.
Fee: $34.95 monthly
Miles of Plant: 4,620.0 (coaxial); 1,209.0 (fiber optic). Homes passed: 342,879.
Executive Vice President, Programming: Tom Montemagno. Vice President, Field Operations: Christopher Fulton. Government Affairs Manager: Gary Shaw.
Ownership: Altice USA (MSO).

OCEAN COUNTY—Comcast Cable. Now served by EATONTOWN BOROUGH, NJ [NJ0009]. ICA: NJ0020.

PARAMUS—Cablevision. Now served by BERGENFIELD, NJ [NJ0013]. ICA: NJ0066.

PATERSON—Cablevision, 100 Hamilton Plaza, Paterson, NJ 07505. Phones: 201-405-8222; 516-803-2300 (Corporate office); 201-651-4000. Web Site: http://www.cablevision.com. ICA: NJ0059.
TV Market Ranking: 1 (PATERSON). Franchise award date: May 16, 1986. Franchise expiration date: N.A. Began: March 16, 1987.
Channel capacity: N.A. Channels available but not in use: N.A.

Basic Service
Subscribers: 24,119. Commercial subscribers: 1,308.
Programming (received off-air): WABC-TV (ABC, Live Well Network) New York; WCBS-TV (CBS, Decades) New York; WFUT-DT (getTV, UniMas) Newark; WLIW (PBS) Garden City; WLNY-TV (IND) Riverhead; WMBC-TV (Azteca America) Newton; WNBC (COZI TV, NBC) New York; WNET (PBS) Newark; WNJN (PBS) Montclair; WNJU (TMO) Linden; WNYJ-TV (ETV) West Milford; WNYW (FOX, Movies!) New York; WPIX (Antenna TV, CW, This TV) New York; WPXN-TV (ION) New York; WRNN-TV (IND) Kingston; WWOR-TV (Bounce TV, Buzzr, Heroes & Icons, MNT) Secaucus; WXTV-DT (UNV) Paterson.
Programming (via microwave): News 12 New Jersey.
Programming (via satellite): QVC.
Fee: $39.95 installation; $12.22 monthly.

Expanded Basic Service 1
Subscribers: N.A.
Programming (via satellite): A&E; AMC; Animal Planet; BET; Bravo; Cartoon Network; CNBC; CNN; Comcast Network Philadelphia; Comedy Central; C-SPAN; C-SPAN 2; Discovery Channel; Disney Channel; E! HD; ESPN; ESPN2; EVINE Live; Food Network; Fox News Channel; Fox Sports 1; Freeform; Fuse; FX; GSN; HGTV; History; HLN; INSP; Lifetime; MSG; MSG Plus; MSNBC; MTV; MTV2; News 12 Traffic & Weather; Nickelodeon; Spike TV; SportsNet New York; Syfy; TBS; The Weather Channel; TLC; TNT; Travel Channel; Trinity Broadcasting Network (TBN); truTV; Turner Classic Movies; TV Land; Univision; USA Network; VH1; WE tv; YES Network.
Fee: $37.77 monthly.

Digital Basic Service
Subscribers: N.A.
Programming (via satellite): Azteca; BBC World News; Bloomberg Television; Canal Sur; Caracol TV; Cartoon Network en Espanol; Cinelatino; CMT; CNN en Espanol; CNN HD; C-SPAN 3; Destination America; Discovery Kids Channel; Disney XD; Docu TVE; Ecuavisa Internacional; ESPN Classic; ESPN Deportes; ESPN HD; ESPN2 HD; ESPNews; EuroNews; EVINE Live; Food Network HD; FOX College Sports Central; FOX College Sports Pacific; Fox Deportes; Fox Life; Fox Sports 2; FXM; FYI; Golf Channel; GolTV; Great American Country; Hallmark Channel; HD Theater; here! On Demand; HGTV HD; History en Espanol; History International; HTV; iN DEMAND; Infinito; Investigation Discovery; Jewelry Television; La Familia Cosmovision; LOGO; Mariavision; MC; Momentum; MTV Classic; MTV Hits; National Geographic Channel; National Geographic Channel HD; NBA TV; NBC Universo; NBCSN; NHL Network; Nick Jr.; Nicktoons; Outdoor Channel; Oxygen; Science Channel; Sundance TV; TBS HD; TeenNick; Telefe Internacional; TNT HD; Toon Disney en Espanol; Tr3s; TVG Network; ULTRA HD-

Cable Systems—New Jersey

Plex; Universal HD; Versus HD; VH1 Soul; ViendoMovies; Vme TV; YES HD.
Fee: $10.95 monthly.
Pay Service 1
Pay Units: N.A.
Programming (via satellite): Cinemax; Flix; HBO (multiplexed); IFC; Showtime (multiplexed); The Movie Channel.
Digital Pay Service 1
Pay Units: N.A.
Programming (via satellite): Cinemax (multiplexed); Cinemax HD; Cinemax On Demand; HBO (multiplexed); HBO HD; HBO on Demand; International Television (ITV); Korean Channel; MBC America; Playboy TV; RTN; Showtime (multiplexed); Showtime HD; Showtime On Demand; Starz (multiplexed); Starz Encore (multiplexed); Starz HD; The Movie Channel (multiplexed); The Movie Channel HD; TV Asia; TV Polonia; TV5, La Television International; Zee TV.
Fee: $9.95 monthly (Cinemax, Showtime, Starz/Encore, Playboy, TMC, RAI, SPT, TV5 or TV Polonia), $11.95 monthly (HBO), $24.95 monthly (TV Japan).
Video-On-Demand: Yes
Pay-Per-View
Playboy TV (delivered digitally); Sports PPV (delivered digitally); NBA TV (delivered digitally); iN DEMAND (delivered digitally).
Internet Service
Operational: Yes.
Subscribers: 26,814.
Broadband Service: Optimum Online.
Fee: $46.95 installation; $34.95 monthly; $299.00 modem purchase.
Telephone Service
Digital: Operational
Subscribers: 22,745.
Fee: $34.95 monthly
Miles of Plant: 260.0 (coaxial); 64.0 (fiber optic). Homes passed: 57,659.
Executive Vice President, Programming: Tom Montemagno. Vice President, Field Operations: Christoper Fulton.
Ownership: Altice USA (MSO).

PHILLIPSBURG—Service Electric Cable TV of Hunterdon Inc. Now served by HUNTERDON COUNTY, NJ [NJ0067]. ICA: NJ0065.

PLAINFIELD—Comcast Cable. Now served by WEST ORANGE TWP, NJ [NJ0001]. ICA: NJ0026.

PLEASANTVILLE—Comcast Cable. Now served by AUDUBON, NJ [NJ0003]. ICA: NJ0006.

PORT MURRAY—Comcast Cable. Now served by WEST ORANGE TWP., NJ [NJ0001]. ICA: NJ0027.

PRINCETON—Comcast Cable. Now served by EATONTOWN BOROUGH, NJ [NJ0009]. ICA: NJ0040.

RARITAN—Cablevision, 275 Centennial Ave, Piscataway, NJ 08854. Phones: 973-659-2200; 516-803-2300 (Corporate office). Fax: 973-659-2266. Web Site: http://www.cablevision.com. Also serves Aberdeen Twp., Bedminster (portions), Bernards Twp., Bound Brook, Bridgewater, Dunellen, Edison, Green Brook, Highland Park, Keansburg, Keyport, Manville, Matawan, Metuchen, Middlesex, Milltown, New Brunswick, North Brunswick Twp., Old Bridge, Piscataway, Sayreville, Somerville, South Amboy, South Bound Brook, Union Beach, Warren Twp. & Watchung. ICA: NJ0004.
TV Market Ranking: 1 (Aberdeen Twp., Bedminster (portions), Bernards Twp., Bound Brook, Bridgewater, Dunellen, Edison, Green Brook, Highland Park, Keansburg, Keyport, Manville, Matawan, Metuchen, Middlesex, Milltown, New Brunswick, North Brunswick Twp., Old Bridge, Piscataway, RARITAN, Sayreville, Somerville, South Amboy, South Bound Brook, Union Beach, Warren Twp., Watchung). Franchise award date: N.A. Franchise expiration date: N.A. Began: August 12, 1977.
Channel capacity: N.A. Channels available but not in use: N.A.
Basic Service
Subscribers: 143,990.
Programming (received off-air): WABC-TV (ABC, Live Well Network) New York; WCAU (COZI TV, NBC) Philadelphia; WCBS-TV (CBS, Decades) New York; WFUT-DT (getTV, UniMas) Newark; WHYY-TV (PBS) Wilmington; WNBC (COZI TV, NBC) New York; WNET (PBS) Newark; WNJT (PBS) Trenton; WNJU (TMO) Linden; WNYW (FOX, Movies!) New York; WPHL-TV (Antenna TV, MNT, This TV) Philadelphia; WPIX (Antenna TV, CW, This TV) New York; WPVI-TV (ABC, Live Well Network) Philadelphia; WPXN-TV (ION) New York; WTXF-TV (Buzzr, FOX, Movies!) Philadelphia; WWOR-TV (Bounce TV, Buzzr, Heroes & Icons, MNT) Secaucus; WXTV-DT (UNV) Paterson.
Programming (via satellite): News 12 New Jersey.
Fee: $39.95 installation; $10.14 monthly.
Expanded Basic Service 1
Subscribers: N.A.
Programming (via microwave): News 12 Traffic & Weather.
Programming (via satellite): A&E; AMC; Animal Planet; BET; Bravo; Cartoon Network; CNBC; CNN; Comcast Network Philadelphia; Comedy Central; C-SPAN; C-SPAN 2; Discovery Channel; Disney Channel; E! HD; ESPN; ESPN2; Food Network; Fox News Channel; Fox Sports 1; Freeform; Fuse; FX; GSN; HGTV; History; HLN; IFC; Lifetime; MSG; MSG Plus; MSNBC; MTV; MTV2; Nickelodeon; QVC; Spike TV; SportsNet New York; Syfy; TBS; The Weather Channel; TLC; TNT; Travel Channel; truTV; TV Land; USA Network; VH1; WE tv; YES Network.
Fee: $32.66 monthly.
Digital Basic Service
Subscribers: N.A.
Programming (via satellite): Azteca; BBC World News; Bloomberg Television; Canal Sur; Caracol TV; Cartoon Network en Espanol; Cinelatino; CMT; CNN en Espanol; CNN HD; C-SPAN 3; Destination America; Discovery Kids Channel; Disney XD; Docu TVE; Ecuavisa Internacional; ESPN Classic; ESPN Deportes; ESPN HD; ESPN2 HD; ESPNews; EuroNews; EVINE Live; Food Network HD; FOX College Sports Central; FOX College Sports Pacific; Fox Deportes; Fox Life; Fox Sports 2; FXM; FYI; Golf Channel; GolTV; Great American Country; Hallmark Channel; HD Theater; here! On Demand; HGTV HD; History en Espanol; History International; HTV; iN DEMAND; Infinito; Investigation Discovery; Jewelry Television; La Familia Cosmovision; LOGO; Mariavision; MC; Momentum; MTV Classic; MTV Hits; National Geographic Channel; National Geographic Channel HD; NBA TV; NBC Universo; NBCSN; NHL Network; Nick Jr.; Nicktoons; Outdoor Channel; Oxygen; Science Channel; Sundance TV; TBS HD; TeenNick; Telefe Internacional; TNT HD; Toon Disney en Espanol; Tr3s; Turner Classic Movies; TVG Network; ULTRA HDPlex; Universal HD; Versus HD; VH1 Soul; ViendoMovies; Vme TV; YES HD.
Fee: $10.95 monthly.
Pay Service 1
Pay Units: N.A.
Programming (via satellite): Cinemax; Flix; HBO (multiplexed); Showtime (multiplexed); The Movie Channel.
Digital Pay Service 1
Pay Units: N.A.
Programming (via satellite): Cinemax (multiplexed); Cinemax HD; Cinemax On Demand; HBO (multiplexed); HBO HD; HBO on Demand; International Television (ITV); Korean Channel; MBC America; RAI Italia; RTN; Showtime (multiplexed); Showtime HD; Showtime On Demand; Starz; Starz Encore (multiplexed); Starz HD; The Movie Channel (multiplexed); The Movie Channel HD; TV Asia; TV Polonia; TV5, La Television International; Zee TV.
Fee: $9.95 monthly (Cinemax, Showtime, Starz/Encore, Playboy, TMC, RAI, SPT, TV5 or TV Polonia), $11.95 monthly (HBO), $24.95 monthly (TV Japan).
Video-On-Demand: Yes
Pay-Per-View
Hot Choice; Fresh; Shorteez; Playboy TV.
Internet Service
Operational: Yes.
Subscribers: 157,568.
Broadband Service: Optimum Online.
Fee: $46.95 installation; $34.95 monthly; $299.00 modem purchase.
Telephone Service
Digital: Operational
Subscribers: 120,396.
Fee: $34.95 monthly.
Miles of Plant: 4,265.0 (coaxial); 1,078.0 (fiber optic). Homes passed: 247,000.
Executive Vice President, Programming: Tom Montemagno. Vice President, Field Operations: Frank Dagliere. Vice President, Government Affairs: Adam Falk.
Ownership: Altice USA (MSO).

SEASIDE HEIGHTS—Cablevision, 1501 18th Ave, Wall, NJ 07719. Phone: 516-364-8400. Web Site: http://www.cablevision.com. Also serves Berkeley Twp., Dover Twp. (portions), Lavallette & Seaside Park. ICA: NJ0069.
TV Market Ranking: 1 (Berkeley Twp.); Outside TV Markets (Dover Twp. (portions) (portions), Lavallette, SEASIDE HEIGHTS, Seaside Park).
Channel capacity: N.A. Channels available but not in use: N.A.
Basic Service
Subscribers: 9,475. Commercial subscribers: 256.
Fee: $39.95 installation; $13.96 monthly.
Internet Service
Operational: Yes.
Subscribers: 5,786.
Telephone Service
Digital: Operational
Subscribers: 3,845.
Miles of Plant: 236.0 (coaxial); 58.0 (fiber optic). Homes passed: 19,909.
Executive Vice President, Programming: Tom Montemagno.
Ownership: Altice USA (MSO).

SPARTA—Service Electric Cable Company, 320 Sparta Ave, PO Box 853, Sparta, NJ 07871. Phones: 800-992-0132 (Customer service); 973-729-7653 (Administrative office); 973-729-7642. Fax: 973-729-5635. E-mail: seconj@ptd.net. Web Site: http://www.sectv.com. Also serves Andover Borough, Andover Twp., Blairstown Twp., Branchville, Byram Twp., Frankford Twp., Franklin, Fredon, Frelinghyusen Twp., Green Twp., Hamburg, Hampton Twp., Hardwick Twp., Hardyston Twp., Hope, Jefferson Twp., Knowlton, Lafayette Twp., Newton, Ogdensburg, Sandyston Twp., Sparta Twp., Stillwater Twp., Sussex, Vernon Twp. & Wantage Twp. ICA: NJ0061.
TV Market Ranking: 1 (Andover Borough, Andover Twp., Branchville, Byram Twp., Frankford Twp., Franklin, Fredon, Green Twp., Hamburg, Hampton Twp., Hardyston Twp., Jefferson Twp., Lafayette Twp., Newton, Ogdensburg, SPARTA, Sparta Twp., Sussex, Vernon Twp., Wantage Twp.); Below 100 (Blairstown Twp., Frelinghyusen Twp., Hardwick Twp., Hope, Sandyston Twp., Stillwater Twp., Knowlton). Franchise award date: N.A. Franchise expiration date: N.A. Began: January 1, 1963.
Channel capacity: N.A. Channels available but not in use: N.A.
Basic Service
Subscribers: 23,692.
Programming (received off-air): WABC-TV (ABC, Live Well Network) New York; WCBS-TV (CBS, Decades) New York; WMBC-TV (Azteca America) Newton; WNBC (COZI TV, NBC) New York; WNET (PBS) Newark; WNJN (PBS) Montclair; WNYE-TV (PBS) New York; WNYW (FOX, Movies!) New York; WPIX (Antenna TV, CW, This TV) New York; WPXN-TV (ION) New York; WTBY-TV (TBN) Poughkeepsie; WWOR-TV (Bounce TV, Buzzr, Heroes & Icons, MNT) Secaucus; WXTV-DT (UNV) Paterson; allband FM.
Programming (via satellite): C-SPAN; EWTN Global Catholic Network; News 12 New Jersey; Pop; QVC; WGN America.
Fee: $36.00 installation; $22.99 monthly.
Expanded Basic Service 1
Subscribers: N.A.
Programming (via satellite): A&E; AMC; Animal Planet; Cartoon Network; CMT; CNBC; CNN; Comedy Central; Discovery Channel; Discovery Life Channel; E! HD; ESPN; ESPN Classic; ESPN2; EVINE Live; Food Network; Fox News Channel; Fox Sports 1; Freeform; FX; FXM; Hallmark Channel; HGTV; History; HLN; Lifetime; MSG; MSG Plus; MSNBC; MTV; National Geographic Channel; NBCSN; NFL Network; Nickelodeon; Spike TV; SportsNet New York; Syfy; TBS; The Weather Channel; TLC; TNT; Travel Channel; truTV; Turner Classic Movies; TV Land; USA Network; VH1; WE tv; YES Network.
Fee: $33.13 monthly.

New Jersey—Cable Systems

Digital Basic Service
Subscribers: N.A.
Programming (via satellite): AXS TV; BBC America; Boomerang; Bravo; CMT; C-SPAN 2; Discovery Digital Networks; DIY Network; ESPNews; ESPNU; Fox Sports 2; FSN Digital Atlantic; FSN Digital Central; FSN Digital Pacific; FYI; Golf Channel; Hallmark Channel; HD Theater; History International; IFC; LMN; MC; NASA TV; Nick 2; Nick Jr.; Outdoor Channel; Sprout; TeenNick; TNT HD; TVG Network; WALN Cable Radio.
Fee: $5.99 monthly.

Digital Pay Service 1
Pay Units: N.A.
Programming (via satellite): Cinemax (multiplexed); HBO (multiplexed); Showtime (multiplexed); Showtime HD; Starz (multiplexed); Starz Encore (multiplexed); Starz HD; The Movie Channel (multiplexed); The Movie Channel HD.
Fee: $13.00 monthly (HBO), $11.00 monthly (Cinemax).

Video-On-Demand: Planned

Pay-Per-View
iN DEMAND.

Internet Service
Operational: Yes. Began: January 1, 1996.
Subscribers: 14,013.
Broadband Service: ProLog Express.
Fee: $50.00 installation; $21.95-$89.95 monthly; $9.95 modem lease; $100.00 modem purchase.

Telephone Service
Digital: Operational
Subscribers: 4,672.
Miles of Plant: 2,640.0 (coaxial); 1,164.0 (fiber optic). Homes passed: 45,000.
General Manager: William Brayford. Chief Technician: Robert Jais. Regulatory Affairs Director: Arlean Lilly.
Ownership: Service Electric Cable TV Inc. (MSO).

TOMS RIVER—Comcast Cable. Now served by AUDUBON, NJ [NJ0003]. ICA: NJ0049.

TRENTON—Comcast Cable. Now served by AUDUBON, NJ [NJ0003]. ICA: NJ0015.

VINELAND—Comcast Cable. Now served by AUDUBON, NJ [NJ0003]. ICA: NJ0034.

WEST ORANGE TWP.—Comcast Cable, 800 Rahway Ave, Union, NJ 07083.
Phones: 908-349-8504; 732-602-7444.
Fax: 908-851-8888. Web Site: http://www.comcast.com. Also serves Belleville Twp., Belvidere, Berkeley Heights Twp., Bloomfield Twp., Caldwell Borough, Califon, Carlstadt, Carteret, Clark Twp., Cranford Twp., East Newark, East Orange, East Rutherford, Edison, Essex Fells Borough, Fairfield Twp. (Essex County), Fanwood, Franklin (Hunterdon County), Garwood Borough, Glen Gardner, Glen Ridge Twp., Hackettstown, Hampton, Harrison (town), High Bridge, Hillside Twp., Independence Twp., Irvington Twp., Jersey City, Kearny, Kenilworth Borough, Lebanon, Liberty Twp., Linden, Livingston Twp., Lyndhurst, Mansfield Twp. (Warren County), Maplewood Twp., Millburn Twp., Montclair Twp., Mount Olive, Mountainside Borough, New Providence, North Arlington, North Plainfield, Orange, Oxford, Perth Amboy, Piscataway, Plainfield, Port Murray, Rahway, Roseland Borough, Roselle Borough, Roselle Park Borough, Rutherford, Scotch Plains Twp., Secaucus (town), Short Hills, South Plainfield, South River Borough, Springfield Twp. (Union County), Summit, Union Twp., Verona Twp., Wallington, Washington Borough, Washington Twp. (Morris County), Washington Twp. (Warren County), West Caldwell Twp., Westfield (town), White Twp., Winfield Twp. & Woodbridge Twp. ICA: NJ0001.
TV Market Ranking: 1 (Belleville Twp., Berkeley Heights Twp., Bloomfield Twp., Caldwell Borough, Califon, Carlstadt, Carteret, Clark Twp., Cranford Twp., East Newark, East Orange, East Rutherford, Edison, Essex Fells Borough, Fairfield Twp. (Essex County), Fanwood, Franklin (Hunterdon County), Garwood Borough, Glen Ridge Twp., Hackettstown, Harrison (town), High Bridge, Hillside Twp., Irvington Twp., Jersey City, Kearny, Kenilworth Borough, Lebanon, Linden, Livingston Twp., Lyndhurst, Maplewood Twp., Millburn Twp., Montclair Twp., Mount Olive, Mountainside Borough, New Providence, North Arlington, North Plainfield, Orange, Perth Amboy, Plainfield, Rahway, Roseland Borough, Roselle Borough, Roselle Park Borough, Rutherford, Scotch Plains Twp., Secaucus (town), Short Hills, South Plainfield, South River Borough, Springfield Twp. (Union County), Summit, Union Twp., Verona Twp., Wallington, Washington Twp. (Morris County), West Caldwell Twp., WEST ORANGE TWP., Westfield (town), Winfield Twp., Woodbridge Twp.); Below 100 (Belvidere, Glen Gardner, Hampton, Independence Twp., Liberty Twp., Mansfield Twp. (Warren County), Oxford, Washington Borough, Washington Twp. (Warren County), White Twp., Port Murray). Franchise award date: N.A. Franchise expiration date: N.A. Began: September 1, 1975.
Channel capacity: 29 (operating 2-way). Channels available but not in use: N.A.

Basic Service
Subscribers: 234,790. Commercial subscribers: 10,842.
Programming (received off-air): WABC-TV (ABC, Live Well Network) New York; WCBS-TV (CBS, Decades) New York; WFUT-DT (getTV, UniMas) Newark; WLIW (PBS) Garden City; WLNY-TV (IND) Riverhead; WMBC-TV (Azteca America) Newton; WNBC (COZI TV, NBC) New York; WNET (PBS) Newark; WNJN (PBS) Montclair; WNJU (TMO) Linden; WNYE-TV (PBS) New York; WNYW (FOX, Movies!) New York; WPIX (Antenna TV, CW, This TV) New York; WPXN-TV (ION) New York; WWOR-TV (Bounce TV, Buzzr, Heroes & Icons, MNT) Secaucus; WXTV-DT (UNV) Paterson; WYXN-LD New York.
Programming (via satellite): Comcast Network Philadelphia; C-SPAN; EWTN Global Catholic Network; MSG Plus; Pop; QVC; TBS; WGN America.
Fee: $42.90 installation; $18.40 monthly.

Expanded Basic Service 1
Subscribers: N.A.
Programming (via microwave): News 12 New Jersey.
Programming (via satellite): A&E; AMC; Animal Planet; BET; Cartoon Network; CNBC; CNN; Comedy Central; Discovery Channel; E! HD; ESPN; ESPN2; Food Network; Fox News Channel; Fox Sports 1; Freeform; FX; Golf Channel; HGTV; History; HLN; Lifetime; MSG; MSNBC; MTV; NBCSN; Nickelodeon; OWN: Oprah Winfrey Network; Spike TV; SportsNet New York; Syfy; The Weather Channel; TLC; TNT; truTV; Turner Classic Movies; TV Land; USA Network; VH1; YES Network.
Fee: $19.40 monthly.

Digital Basic Service
Subscribers: N.A.
Programming (via satellite): BBC America; CBS Sports Network; CMT; Cooking Channel; C-SPAN 3; Discovery Digital Networks; Disney Channel; Disney XD; DIY Network; ESPN HD; ESPN2 HD; ESPNews; Flix; FOX College Sports Central; FOX College Sports Pacific; FYI; GolTV; Great American Country; GSN; Hallmark Channel; HD Theater; History International; HITS (Headend In The Sky); Jewelry Television; LMN; LOGO; MC; MoviePlex; MTV Live; National Geographic Channel; NBA TV; NFL Network; Nick 2; Nick Jr.; Nicktoons; Oxygen; Sprout; Starz Encore (multiplexed); Sundance TV; Teen-Nick; Tennis Channel; The Word Network; TNT HD; Travel Channel; Trinity Broadcasting Network (TBN); TV One; Weatherscan.
Fee: $14.95 monthly.

Pay Service 1
Pay Units: N.A.
Programming (via satellite): HBO.
Fee: $12.00 installation; $11.00 monthly.

Digital Pay Service 1
Pay Units: 162,434.
Programming (via satellite): ART America; Cinemax (multiplexed); Cinemax HD; HBO (multiplexed); HBO HD; RAI Italia; Showtime (multiplexed); Showtime HD; Starz (multiplexed); Starz HD; The Filipino Channel; The Movie Channel (multiplexed); TV Asia; TV Polonia; TV5, La Television International; Zee TV.
Fee: $20.25 monthly (each).

Video-On-Demand: Yes

Pay-Per-View
iN DEMAND (delivered digitally); Playboy TV (delivered digitally); Fresh (delivered digitally); Pleasure (delivered digitally); ESPN (delivered digitally); NBA (delivered digitally); NHL/MLB (delivered digitally).

Internet Service
Operational: Yes.
Subscribers: 288,858.
Broadband Service: Comcast High Speed Internet.
Fee: $42.95 monthly; $7.00 modem lease; $299.00 modem purchase.

Telephone Service
Digital: Operational
Subscribers: 177,981.
Fee: $44.95 monthly
Miles of Plant: 11,658.0 (coaxial); 2,856.0 (fiber optic). Homes passed: 807,660.
Area Vice President: Keith Taub. Vice President, Marketing: Marge Jackson. Vice President, Technical Operations: Bob Kennedy. Public Relations Director: Fred DeAndrea.
Ownership: Comcast Cable Communications Inc. (MSO).

WILDWOOD—Comcast Cable. Now served by AUDUBON, NJ [NJ0003]. ICA: NJ0068.

NEW MEXICO

Total Systems:	37	**Communities with Applications:**	0
Total Communities Served:	122	**Number of Basic Subscribers:**	182,958
Franchises Not Yet Operating:	0	**Number of Expanded Basic Subscribers:**	107
Applications Pending:	0	**Number of Pay Units:**	3,564

Top 100 Markets Represented: Albuquerque (81).

For a list of cable communities in this section, see the Cable Community Index located in the back of Cable Volume 2.
For explanation of terms used in cable system listings, see p. D-11.

ALAMOGORDO—Baja Broadband, 525 Junction Rd, Madison, WI 53717. Phones: 866-622-8848; 575-437-3101. Fax: 608-830-5519. Web Site: http://www.bajabroadband.com. Also serves Boles Acres, Holloman AFB, La Luz, Otero County (portions) & Tularosa. ICA: NM0076.
TV Market Ranking: Outside TV Markets (ALAMOGORDO, Boles Acres, Holloman AFB, La Luz, Otero County (portions), Tularosa). Franchise award date: January 1, 1964. Franchise expiration date: N.A. Began: June 1, 1964.
Channel capacity: N.A. Channels available but not in use: N.A.

Basic Service
Subscribers: 2,617.
Programming (received off-air): KVBA-LP Alamogordo; 15 FMs.
Programming (via microwave): KASA-TV (COZI TV, FOX) Santa Fe; KASY-TV (MNT) Albuquerque; KBIM-TV (CBS, The Country Network) Roswell; KCHF (IND, WeatherNation) Santa Fe; KDBC-TV (CBS, MNT, This TV) El Paso; KFOX-TV (FOX, Retro TV) El Paso; KLUZ-TV (LATV, UNV) Albuquerque; KOAT-TV (ABC, Estrella TV) Albuquerque; KOBR (NBC, This TV) Roswell; KRPV-DT (GLC) Roswell; KRWG-TV (PBS) Las Cruces; KTEL-TV (TMO) Carlsbad; KVIA-TV (ABC, Azteca America, CW) El Paso; KWBQ (CW, Grit, Laff) Santa Fe.
Programming (via satellite): C-SPAN; C-SPAN 2; Pop; QVC; TBS; The Weather Channel; WGN America.
Fee: $54.95 installation; $36.95 monthly; $3.43 converter.

Expanded Basic Service 1
Subscribers: N.A.
Programming (via satellite): A&E; AMC; Animal Planet; BET; Bravo; Cartoon Network; CMT; CNBC; CNN; Comedy Central; Discovery Channel; Discovery Life Channel; Disney Channel; E! HD; ESPN; ESPN2; Food Network; Fox News Channel; Fox Sports 1; FOX Sports Arizona; Freeform; FX; Golf Channel; Great American Country; GSN; Hallmark Channel; HGTV; History; HLN; Lifetime; MSNBC; MTV; National Geographic Channel; NBCSN; Nickelodeon; Spike TV; Syfy; TLC; TNT; Travel Channel; TV Land; Univision; USA Network; VH1; WE tv.
Fee: $27.85 monthly.

Digital Basic Service
Subscribers: N.A.
Programming (via satellite): BBC America; Bloomberg Television; CMT; Destination America; Discovery Kids Channel; Disney XD; DIY Network; ESPN Classic; Fox Business Network; FOX College Sports Central; FOX College Sports Pacific; FYI; History International; IFC; Investigation Discovery; LMN; LOGO; MC; MTV Classic; MTV Hits; MTV Jams; MTV2; Nat Geo WILD; Nick 2; Nick Jr.; Nicktoons; OWN; Oprah Winfrey Network; Science Channel; TeenNick; Tr3s; VH1 Soul.
Fee: $7.95 monthly.

Digital Expanded Basic Service
Subscribers: N.A.
Programming (via satellite): A&E HD; ESPN HD; Food Network HD; FSN HD; FX HD; Golf Channel HD; HGTV HD; History HD; KWGN-TV (CW, This TV) Denver; National Geographic Channel HD; TBS HD; TNT HD; Versus HD.

Digital Expanded Basic Service 2
Subscribers: N.A.
Programming (via satellite): AXS TV; Universal HD.

Digital Pay Service 1
Pay Units: N.A.
Programming (via satellite): Cinemax (multiplexed); Cinemax HD; Deutsche Welle TV; Flix; HBO (multiplexed); HBO HD; Showtime (multiplexed); Showtime HD; Starz (multiplexed); Starz Encore (multiplexed); Starz HD; The Movie Channel (multiplexed); The Movie Channel HD.
Fee: $4.00 monthly (Encore), $5.00 monthly (Deutsche Welle), $7.00 monthly (Cinemax), $8.00 monthly (Starz), $13.00 monthly (HBO or Showtime).

Video-On-Demand: No

Pay-Per-View
iN DEMAND (delivered digitally); Playboy TV (delivered digitally); Spice: Xcess (delivered digitally); Club Jenna (delivered digitally); Hot Choice (delivered digitally); Fresh (delivered digitally); Shorteez (delivered digitally).

Internet Service
Operational: Yes.
Broadband Service: In-house.
Fee: $49.95 installation; $34.99 monthly; $4.96 modem lease; $69.95 modem purchase.

Telephone Service
Analog: Operational
Miles of Plant: 298.0 (coaxial); 31.0 (fiber optic). Homes passed: 23,650.
Chief Executive Officer: William A. Schuler. Area Vice President & General Manager: Tom Jaskiewicz. Chief Operating Officer: Phillip Klein. Vice President, Corporate Finance: Carl Shapiro. Assistant Treasurer: Noel Hutton. Technical Operations Manager: Harold Vilas. Office Manager: Barbara Mick.
Ownership: TDS Telecom (MSO).

ALBUQUERQUE—Comcast Cable, 4611 Montbel Pl Northeast, Albuquerque, NM 87107-6821. Phones: 505-344-0690; 505-761-6200. Fax: 505-334-7301. Web Site: http://www.comcast.com. Also serves Aztec, Bayard, Belen, Bernalillo, Bernalillo County (portions), Bloomfield, Bosque Farms, Corrales, Dona Ana, Edgewood, Eldorado, Farmington, Grant County (portions), Hurley (town), Isleta, Kirtland, Kirtland AFB, Las Cruces, Los Lunas, Los Ranchos de Albuquerque, Mesilla, Moriarty, Peralta, Placitas, San Juan County (portions), Sandoval County (portions), Santa Clara (village), Santa Fe, Santa Fe County (portions), Silver City, Silver City (unincorporated areas), South Santa Fe, Teusque, Teusque Pueblo, Tijeras, Tyrone & White Sands. ICA: NM0001.
TV Market Ranking: 81 (ALBUQUERQUE, Belen, Bernalillo, Bosque Farms, Corrales, Edgewood, Isleta, Kirtland AFB, Los Lunas, Los Ranchos de Albuquerque, Moriarty, Peralta, Placitas, Sandoval County (portions), Santa Fe County (portions), Tijeras; Below 100 (Aztec, Bayard, Bloomfield, Dona Ana, Eldorado, Grant County (portions) (portions), Hurley (town), Kirtland, Mesilla, San Juan County (portions), Santa Clara (village), Silver City (unincorporated areas), South Santa Fe, Tyrone, White Sands, Farmington, Las Cruces, Santa Fe, Silver City); Outside TV Markets (Grant County (portions) (portions), San Juan County (portions)). Franchise award date: September 1, 1977. Franchise expiration date: N.A. Began: June 1, 1978.
Channel capacity: N.A. Channels available but not in use: N.A.

Basic Service
Subscribers: 135,909.
Programming (received off-air): KASA-TV (COZI TV, FOX) Santa Fe; KASY-TV (MNT) Albuquerque; KAZQ (ETV) Albuquerque; KCHF (IND, WeatherNation) Santa Fe; KLUZ-TV (LATV, UNV) Albuquerque; KNAT-TV (TBN) Albuquerque; KNME-TV (PBS) Albuquerque; KOAT-TV (ABC, Estrella TV) Albuquerque; KOB (NBC, This TV) Albuquerque; KRQE (CBS) Albuquerque; KWBQ (CW, Grit, Laff) Santa Fe; 8 FMs.
Programming (via satellite): C-SPAN; EWTN Global Catholic Network; ION Television; National Geographic Channel; NBCSN; Pop; QVC; Telemundo; Univision; WGN America.
Fee: $42.00 installation; $42.04 monthly; $3.40 converter.

Expanded Basic Service 1
Subscribers: N.A.
Programming (via satellite): A&E; AMC; Animal Planet; BET; Bravo; Cartoon Network; CMT; CNBC; CNN; Comedy Central; C-SPAN 2; Discovery Channel; Disney Channel; E! HD; ESPN; ESPN2; Food Network; Fox News Channel; Fox Sports 1; FOX Sports Southwest; Freeform; FX; Golf Channel; Great American Country; Hallmark Channel; HGTV; History; HLN; Lifetime; MSNBC; MTV; Nickelodeon; OWN: Oprah Winfrey Network; Spike TV; Syfy; TBS; The Weather Channel; TLC; TNT; truTV; Turner Classic Movies; TV Land; USA Network; VH1.
Fee: $39.09 monthly.

Digital Basic Service
Subscribers: N.A.
Programming (via satellite): BBC America; C-SPAN 3; Discovery Digital Networks; Disney XD; DMX Music; ESPNews; HITS (Headend In The Sky); Nick 2; Nick Jr.; Starz Encore (multiplexed); TeenNick; WAM! America's Kidz Network; Weatherscan.
Fee: $10.95 monthly.

Digital Pay Service 1
Pay Units: N.A.
Programming (via satellite): Cinemax (multiplexed); HBO (multiplexed); Showtime (multiplexed); Starz (multiplexed); The Movie Channel (multiplexed).
Fee: $15.95 monthly (Cinemax, Showtime, TMC or Starz), $16.95 monthly (HBO).

Video-On-Demand: Yes

Pay-Per-View
iN DEMAND; Hot Choice (delivered digitally); EVINE Live (delivered digitally); ESPN Now (delivered digitally); iN DEMAND (delivered digitally); Playboy TV (delivered digitally); Pleasure (delivered digitally); Fresh (delivered digitally); Shorteez (delivered digitally).

Internet Service
Operational: Yes. Began: December 1, 2000.
Subscribers: 131,245.
Broadband Service: Comcast High Speed Internet.
Fee: $150.00 installation; $42.95 monthly; $5.00 modem lease.

Telephone Service
Digital: Operational
Subscribers: 51,929.
Miles of Plant: 9,310.0 (coaxial); 1,353.0 (fiber optic). Homes passed: 475,523.
Area Vice President: Scott Westerman. Vice President & General Manager: Chris Dunkeson. Marketing Director: Richard Brehm. Engineering Director: Ken Hamilton. Public Relations Director: Eilene Vaughn-Pickrell. Marketing Coordinator: P.J. Ruble.
Ownership: Comcast Cable Communications Inc. (MSO).

ALBUQUERQUE—Formerly served by Multimedia Development Corp. No longer in operation. ICA: NM0100.

ANGEL FIRE (village)—Comcast Cable, 1546 Paseo Del Pueblo Sur, PO Box 1854, Taos, NM 87571-1854. Phones: 505-758-3569; 505-758-3207. Fax: 505-758-4441. Web Site: http://www.comcast.com. Also serves Angel Fire (unincorporated areas). ICA: NM0048.
TV Market Ranking: Outside TV Markets (Angel Fire (unincorporated areas), ANGEL FIRE (VILLAGE)). Franchise award date: January 1, 1980. Franchise expiration date: N.A. Began: January 1, 1981.
Channel capacity: N.A. Channels available but not in use: N.A.

2017 Edition D-519

New Mexico—Cable Systems

Basic Service
Subscribers: 44.
Programming (via microwave): KRPV-DT (GLC) Roswell.
Programming (via satellite): A&E; AMC; CMT; CNBC; C-SPAN; Disney Channel; E! HD; ESPN; ESPN Classic; ESPN2; Fox News Channel; FOX Sports Southwest; Freeform; Golf Channel; HGTV; History; HLN; Lifetime; MTV; Nickelodeon; The Weather Channel; TLC; Turner Classic Movies; TV Land; USA Network; WGN America.
Programming (via translator): KASA-TV (COZI TV, FOX) Santa Fe; KASY-TV (MNT) Albuquerque; KNME-TV (PBS) Albuquerque; KOAT-TV (ABC, Estrella TV) Albuquerque; KOB (NBC, This TV) Albuquerque; KRQE (CBS) Albuquerque; KWBQ (CW, Grit, Laff) Santa Fe.
Fee: $42.00 installation; $46.98 monthly.

Expanded Basic Service 1
Subscribers: N.A.
Programming (via satellite): CNN; Comedy Central; Discovery Channel; Outdoor Channel; QVC; TBS; TNT; VH1.
Fee: $10.55 monthly.

Pay Service 1
Pay Units: N.A.
Programming (via satellite): Cinemax; HBO (multiplexed).
Fee: $10.45 monthly (each).

Pay-Per-View
Movies; special events.

Telephone Service
Digital: Operational
Miles of Plant: 20.0 (coaxial); None (fiber optic).
Vice President & General Manager: Chris Dunkesen. Operations Manager: David Quintana.
Ownership: Comcast Cable Communications Inc. (MSO).

ARTESIA—PVT, 4011 West Main St, Artesia, NM 88210-9566. Phone: 800-505-4844. Fax: 505-746-4142. E-mail: pvtcsrs@pvt.com. Web Site: http://www.pvt.com. Also serves Cloudcroft, Dexter, Eddy County (portions), Hagerman & Twin Forks. ICA: NM0016.
TV Market Ranking: Below 100 (ARTESIA, Dexter, Eddy County (portions), Hagerman); Outside TV Markets (Cloudcroft, Eddy County (portions), Twin Forks). Franchise award date: September 1, 1993. Franchise expiration date: N.A. Began: March 1, 1961.
Channel capacity: N.A. Channels available but not in use: N.A.

Basic Service
Subscribers: 2,677.
Programming (received off-air): KBIM-TV (CBS, The Country Network) Roswell; KOBR (NBC, This TV) Roswell; KRPV-DT (GLC) Roswell; KTEL-TV (TMO) Carlsbad.
Programming (via microwave): KASA-TV (COZI TV, FOX) Santa Fe; KENW (PBS) Portales; KLUZ-TV (LATV, UNV) Albuquerque; KOAT-TV (ABC, Estrella TV) Albuquerque; KWBQ (CW, Grit, Laff) Santa Fe.
Programming (via satellite): C-SPAN; C-SPAN 2; EVINE Live; EWTN Global Catholic Network; Pop; QVC; The Weather Channel; Univision; WGN America.
Fee: $37.05 installation; $35.44 monthly; $.66 converter.

Expanded Basic Service 1
Subscribers: N.A.
Programming (via satellite): A&E; AMC; Animal Planet; Boomerang; Cartoon Network; CMT; CNBC; CNN; Comedy Central; Discovery Channel; Disney Channel; E! HD; ESPN; ESPN Classic; ESPN2; Food Network; Fox News Channel; FOX Sports Networks; Freeform; FX; Hallmark Channel; HLN; Lifetime; MTV; National Geographic Channel; Nickelodeon; RFD-TV; Spike TV; Starz Encore; Syfy; TBS; TLC; TNT; Travel Channel; truTV; Turner Classic Movies; TV Land; USA Network; VH1.
Fee: $23.00 monthly.

Digital Basic Service
Subscribers: N.A.
Programming (via satellite): BBC America; Bloomberg Television; Cloo; Daystar TV Network; Destination America; Discovery Kids Channel; Discovery Life Channel; Disney XD; DMX Music; Fuse; FYI; Great American Country; GSN; HGTV; History; History International; HITS (Headend In The Sky); Investigation Discovery; MTV Classic; MTV2; Nick Jr.; Nicktoons; OWN: Oprah Winfrey Network; Science Channel; Syfy; Trinity Broadcasting Network (TBN); VH1 Country.
Fee: $8.35 monthly.

Digital Expanded Basic Service
Subscribers: 49.
Programming (via satellite): Bravo; E! HD; FXM; IFC; LMN; Starz Encore (multiplexed); Turner Classic Movies; WE tv.
Fee: $11.43 monthly.

Digital Expanded Basic Service 2
Subscribers: 58.
Programming (via satellite): ESPNews; FOX College Sports Central; FOX College Sports Pacific; Fox Sports 1; Golf Channel; NBCSN; Outdoor Channel; TeenNick.
Fee: $9.38 monthly.

Digital Pay Service 1
Pay Units: 393 Includes Elephant Butte.
Programming (via satellite): Cinemax (multiplexed); HBO (multiplexed); Showtime (multiplexed); Starz (multiplexed); The Movie Channel (multiplexed).

Video-On-Demand: No

Pay-Per-View
Playboy TV (delivered digitally); Fresh (delivered digitally); iN DEMAND (delivered digitally).

Internet Service
Operational: Yes.
Broadband Service: In-house.
Fee: $99.95 installation; $39.95-$59.95 monthly.

Telephone Service
Analog: Not Operational
Digital: Operational
Fee: $36.95 monthly
Miles of Plant: 182.0 (coaxial); 75.0 (fiber optic). Homes passed: 6,300. Miles of plant (fiber) includes Elephant Butte.
Chief Executive Officer: Glenn Lovelace. Vice President, Marketing & Sales: Terry Mullins. Vice President, Plant & Operations: Sammy Reno.
Ownership: Penasco Valley Telecommunications (MSO).

BRAZOS—Formerly served by US Cable of Coastal Texas LP. No longer in operation. ICA: NM0073.

CARLSBAD—Baja Broadband, 525 Junction Rd, Madison, WI 53717. Phones: 575-437-3101; 800-996-8788; 877-422-5282. Fax: 608-830-5519. E-mail: customersupportnm@bajabb.tv. Web Site: http://www.bajabroadband.com. Also serves Eddy County (southern portions) & Loving. ICA: NM0008.
TV Market Ranking: Below 100 (CARLSBAD, Eddy County (southern portions) (portions), Loving); Outside TV Markets (Eddy County (southern portions) (portions)). Franchise award date: February 10, 1992. Franchise expiration date: N.A. Began: March 1, 1961.
Channel capacity: N.A. Channels available but not in use: N.A.

Basic Service
Subscribers: 3,613.
Programming (via satellite): C-SPAN; Discovery Channel; Hallmark Channel; Pop; QVC; Starz Encore; The Weather Channel; TNT.
Programming (via translator): KASA-TV (COZI TV, FOX) Santa Fe; KASY-TV (MNT) Albuquerque; KBIM-TV (CBS, The Country Network) Roswell; KCHF (IND, Weather-Nation) Santa Fe; KENW (PBS) Portales; KLUZ-TV (LATV, UNV) Albuquerque; KOAT-TV (ABC, Estrella TV) Albuquerque; KOBR (NBC, This TV) Roswell; KRPV-DT (GLC) Roswell; KTEL-TV (TMO) Carlsbad; KWBQ (CW, Grit, Laff) Santa Fe.
Fee: $28.84 installation; $34.62 monthly; $1.85 converter.

Expanded Basic Service 1
Subscribers: N.A.
Programming (via satellite): A&E; AMC; Animal Planet; Boomerang; Cartoon Network; CMT; CNBC; CNN; Comedy Central; C-SPAN 2; Disney Channel; E! HD; ESPN; ESPN2; EWTN Global Catholic Network; Food Network; Fox News Channel; Fox Sports 1; FOX Sports Arizona; Freeform; FX; Great American Country; History; HLN; INSP; MTV; National Geographic Channel; NBC Universo; Nickelodeon; Oxygen; Spike TV; Syfy; TBS; TLC; truTV; TV Land; UniMas; Univision; USA Network; VH1.
Fee: $23.35 monthly.

Digital Basic Service
Subscribers: N.A.
Programming (via satellite): A&E HD; Animal Planet HD; AWE; AXS TV; BBC America; Bloomberg Television; Bravo; Cloo; CMT; Destination America; Discovery Channel HD; Discovery Kids Channel; Discovery Life Channel; Disney XD; DMX Music; ESPN Classic; ESPN HD; ESPNews; Food Network HD; FOX College Sports Central; FOX College Sports Pacific; Fox Sports 1; FSN HD; Fuse; FXM; FYI; Golf Channel; GSN; HGTV; HGTV HD; History HD; History International; IFC; Investigation Discovery; LMN; MTV Classic; MTV2; Nat Geo WILD; National Geographic Channel HD; NBCSN; NFL Network; Nick Jr.; Outdoor Channel; OWN: Oprah Winfrey Network; Science Channel; Starz Encore (multiplexed); Syfy; Syfy HD; TeenNick; Trinity Broadcasting Network (TBN); Turner Classic Movies; Universal HD; USA Network HD; WE tv.
Fee: $19.40 monthly; $8.00 converter.

Digital Expanded Basic Service
Subscribers: N.A.
Programming (via satellite): Cine Mexicano; Cinelatino; CNN en Espanol; ESPN Deportes; Fox Deportes; History en Espanol; NBC Universo; Tr3s; ViendoMovies.
Fee: $4.95 monthly.

Digital Expanded Basic Service 2
Subscribers: N.A.
Programming (via satellite): HD Theater.
Fee: $4.95 monthly.

Pay Service 1
Pay Units: N.A.
Programming (via satellite): Cinemax; HBO.
Fee: $14.50 monthly (each).

Digital Pay Service 1
Pay Units: N.A.
Programming (via satellite): Cinemax (multiplexed); HBO (multiplexed); Showtime (multiplexed); Starz (multiplexed); The Movie Channel (multiplexed).
Fee: $8.95 monthly (Starz), $11.95 monthly (Cinemax, HBO, Showtime or TMC).

Video-On-Demand: No

Pay-Per-View
iN DEMAND (delivered digitally), Addressable: No; Fresh (delivered digitally); Playboy TV (delivered digitally); Club Jenna.

Internet Service
Operational: Yes.
Subscribers: 4,813.
Broadband Service: Warp Drive Online.
Fee: $27.95-$54.95 monthly.

Telephone Service
Digital: Operational
Subscribers: 1,188.
Fee: $24.95-$39.95 monthly
Miles of Plant: 398.0 (coaxial); 398.0 (fiber optic). Homes passed: 16,066. Homes passed & miles of plant included in Seminole, TX.
Vice President, Corporate Finance: Carl Shapiro. Assistant Treasurer: Noel Hutton.
Ownership: TDS Telecom (MSO).

CARRIZOZO—Baja Broadband, 525 Junction Rd, Madison, WI 53717. Phones: 877-422-5282; 575-257-5121. Fax: 608-830-5519. E-mail: customersupportnm@bajabb.tv. Web Site: http://www.bajabroadband.com. ICA: NM0051.
TV Market Ranking: Outside TV Markets (CARRIZOZO). Franchise award date: N.A. Franchise expiration date: N.A. Began: January 1, 1977.
Channel capacity: N.A. Channels available but not in use: N.A.

Basic Service
Subscribers: 39.
Programming (received off-air): KRPV-DT (GLC) Roswell; KTEL-TV (TMO) Carlsbad.
Programming (via satellite): Freeform; Spike TV; TBS; Univision Studios; WGN America.
Programming (via translator): KASA-TV (COZI TV, FOX) Santa Fe; KNME-TV (PBS) Albuquerque; KOAT-TV (ABC, Estrella TV) Albuquerque; KOB (NBC, This TV) Albuquerque; KRQE (CBS) Albuquerque.
Fee: $29.95-$54.95 installation; $29.60 monthly.

Expanded Basic Service 1
Subscribers: N.A.
Programming (via satellite): A&E; AMC; Animal Planet; CMT; CNN; Discovery Channel; E! HD; ESPN; Fox News Channel; Fox Sports 1; HGTV; HLN; Lifetime; Nickelodeon; Syfy; TLC; TNT; Travel Channel; TV Land; USA Network; WE tv.
Fee: $20.00 monthly.

Video-On-Demand: No

Internet Service
Operational: Yes.

Telephone Service
None
Miles of Plant: 12.0 (coaxial); None (fiber optic). Homes passed: 557.
Vice President, Corporate Finance: Carl Shapiro. Assistant Treasurer: Noel Hutton. General Manager: Gary Massaglia. Technical Operations Manager: Harold Vilas. Office Manager: Barbara Mick.
Ownership: TDS Telecom (MSO).

CHAMA—Satview Broadband, 3550 Barron Way, Ste 13A, Reno, NV 89511. Phones: 575-437-3101; 775-738 2662; 775-333-6626 (Elko, NV office); 877-538 2662. E-mail: satviewreno@yahoo.com. Web Site: http://www.satview.net. Also serves Rio Arriba County. ICA: NM0055.

TV Market Ranking: Below 100 (Rio Arriba County (portions)); Outside TV Markets (CHAMA, Rio Arriba County (portions)). Franchise award date: N.A. Franchise expiration date: N.A. Began: April 1, 1965.
Channel capacity: N.A. Channels available but not in use: N.A.
Basic Service
Subscribers: 22.
Programming (received off-air): KASA-TV (COZI TV, FOX) Santa Fe; KASY-TV (MNT) Albuquerque; KLUZ-TV (LATV, UNV) Albuquerque; KNME-TV (PBS) Albuquerque; KOAT-TV (ABC, Estrella TV) Albuquerque; KOB (NBC, This TV) Albuquerque; KRQE (CBS) Albuquerque; KTEL-TV (TMO) Carlsbad.
Programming (via satellite): A&E; Animal Planet; CMT; CNN; C-SPAN; Discovery Channel; Disney Channel; E! HD; ESPN; EWTN Global Catholic Network; Food Network; Fox News Channel; Freeform; HGTV; History; HLN; KMGH-TV (ABC, Azteca America) Denver; Lifetime; MTV; Nickelodeon; Outdoor Channel; Spike TV; Syfy; TBS; The Weather Channel; TLC; TNT; Turner Classic Movies; TV Land; UniMas; USA Network; VH1; WGN America.
Fee: $46.01 monthly.
Pay Service 1
Pay Units: N.A.
Programming (via satellite): HBO.
Fee: $11.95 monthly.
Pay-Per-View
Shorteez (delivered digitally); Fresh (delivered digitally); Playboy TV (delivered digitally); iN DEMAND (delivered digitally).
Internet Service
Operational: No.
Telephone Service
None
Miles of Plant: 264.0 (coaxial); None (fiber optic). Homes passed: 333. Homes passed & miles of plant included in Seminole, TX.
President: Tariq Ahmad.
Ownership: Satview Broadband Ltd. (MSO).

CHAPARRAL—Chaparral Cable Company, 320 McCombs Rd, Ste A, Chaparral, NM 88081. Phone: 575-824-4099. Fax: 575-824-1465. Web Site: http://www.chaparralcable.com. ICA: NM0409.
TV Market Ranking: Below 100 (CHAPARRAL).
Channel capacity: N.A. Channels available but not in use: N.A.
Basic Service
Subscribers: 711.
Fee: $35.49 monthly.
President: Ben Mossa. Vice President, Secutary Treasurer: Gregory A. Groth. Chief Technician: Adrian Valerio.
Ownership: Chaparral Cable Co.

CIMARRON—Comcast Cable, 1026 South 2nd St, Raton, NM 87740. Phone: 575-445-5553. Fax: 575-445-2835. Web Site: http://www.comcast.com. ICA: NM0058.
TV Market Ranking: Outside TV Markets (CIMARRON). Franchise award date: N.A. Franchise expiration date: N.A. Began: May 1, 1982.
Channel capacity: N.A. Channels available but not in use: N.A.
Basic Service
Subscribers: 41.
Programming (received off-air): KASA-TV (COZI TV, FOX) Santa Fe; KWBQ (CW, Grit, Laff) Santa Fe.
Programming (via satellite): Animal Planet; Cartoon Network; CMT; CNBC; CNN; Discovery Channel; Disney Channel; E! HD;

ESPN; ESPN2; EWTN Global Catholic Network; Food Network; Freeform; Hallmark Channel; HGTV; Lifetime; MTV; NBCSN; Nickelodeon; QVC; Spike TV; TBS; TLC; TNT; Univision Studios; USA Network; VH1.
Programming (via translator): KASY-TV (MNT) Albuquerque; KNME-TV (PBS) Albuquerque; KOAT-TV (ABC, Estrella TV) Albuquerque; KOB (NBC, This TV) Albuquerque; KRQE (CBS) Albuquerque.
Fee: $42.00 installation; $51.74 monthly.
Pay Service 1
Pay Units: N.A.
Programming (via satellite): Cinemax; HBO; Starz Encore.
Video-On-Demand: No
Internet Service
Operational: Yes.
Telephone Service
None
Miles of Plant: 6.0 (coaxial); None (fiber optic). Homes passed: 321.
Vice President & General Manager: Chris Dunkeson. Operations Manager: Ricky Armijo. Office Manager: Tammy Trujillo.
Ownership: Comcast Cable Communications Inc. (MSO).

CLAYTON (town)—Formerly served by Baja Broadband. No longer in operation. ICA: NM0027.

CLOUDCROFT—PVT Cable Services. Now served by ARTESIA, NM [NM0016]. ICA: NM0038.

CLOVIS—Suddenlink Communications, 1106 Main St, Clovis, NM 88101-5935. Phone: 314-315-9400. Fax: 505-769-3140. Web Site: http://www.suddenlink.com. Also serves Cannon AFB & Texico, NM; Farwell, TX. ICA: NM0007.
TV Market Ranking: Below 100 (Cannon AFB, CLOVIS, Farwell, Texico). Franchise award date: February 1, 1954. Franchise expiration date: N.A. Began: November 9, 1954.
Channel capacity: 41 (operating 2-way). Channels available but not in use: N.A.
Basic Service
Subscribers: 5,851. Commercial subscribers: 414.
Programming (received off-air): KAMR-TV (IND, NBC) Amarillo; KBIM-TV (CBS, The Country Network) Roswell; KCIT (FOX, This TV) Amarillo; KENW (PBS) Portales; KFDA-TV (CBS, TMO) Amarillo; KOBR (NBC, This TV) Roswell; KVIH-TV (ABC, CW) Clovis; 16 FMs.
Programming (via satellite): CNBC; C-SPAN; C-SPAN 2; Freeform; HLN; Pop; TBS; The Weather Channel; TLC; TNT; Trinity Broadcasting Network (TBN).
Fee: $40.00 installation; $33.94 monthly; $2.25 converter.
Expanded Basic Service 1
Subscribers: N.A.
Programming (via satellite): A&E; AMC; Animal Planet; BET; Cartoon Network; CMT; CNN; Comedy Central; Discovery Channel; Disney Channel; E! HD; ESPN; ESPN2; Food Network; Fox News Channel; Fox Sports 1; FOX Sports Southwest; FX; HGTV; History; Lifetime; MSNBC; MTV; NBCSN; Nickelodeon; OWN: Oprah Winfrey Network; Spike TV; Syfy; Telemundo; Travel Channel; truTV; TV Land; Univision; Univision Studios; USA Network; VH1.
Fee: $26.45 monthly.
Digital Basic Service
Subscribers: N.A.
Programming (via satellite): BBC America; Bloomberg Television; Discovery Digi-

tal Networks; Disney XD; DMX Music; ESPN Classic; ESPNews; EWTN Global Catholic Network; Fuse; FYI; Golf Channel; Great American Country; GSN; Hallmark Channel; History International; HITS (Headend In The Sky); IFC; LMN; Outdoor Channel; Oxygen; Sundance TV.
Pay Service 1
Pay Units: N.A.
Programming (via satellite): Cinemax; HBO; Showtime; Starz.
Fee: $30.00 installation; $10.95 monthly (each).
Digital Pay Service 1
Pay Units: N.A.
Programming (via satellite): Cinemax (multiplexed); HBO (multiplexed); Showtime (multiplexed); Starz (multiplexed); The Movie Channel (multiplexed).
Video-On-Demand: No
Pay-Per-View
Sports PPV (delivered digitally); iN DEMAND (delivered digitally); ESPN Now (delivered digitally); NBA TV (delivered digitally).
Internet Service
Operational: Yes.
Subscribers: 7,836.
Broadband Service: Suddenlink High Speed Internet.
Fee: $100.00 installation; $24.95 monthly.
Telephone Service
Digital: Operational
Subscribers: 2,825.
Fee: $49.95 monthly
Miles of Plant: 484.0 (coaxial); 73.0 (fiber optic). Homes passed: 20,657.
Senior Vice President, Corporate Finance: Michael Pflantz. Vice President, Accounting: Sabrina Warr. General Manager: Gordon Smith. Chief Technician: Bob Baker.
Ownership: Cequel Communications Holdings I LLC (MSO).

CROWNPOINT—Formerly served by Crownpoint Cable TV Inc. No longer in operation. ICA: NM0054.

CUBA—Formerly served by Sun Valley Cable Inc. No longer in operation. ICA: NM0094.

DEMING—Comcast Cable, 109 North Silver Ave, Deming, NM 88030-3711. Phone: 575-546-0417. Fax: 575-546-6718. Web Site: http://www.comcast.com. Also serves Luna County (portions). ICA: NM0077.
TV Market Ranking: Below 100 (Luna County (portions)); Outside TV Markets (DEMING, Luna County (portions)). Franchise award date: N.A. Franchise expiration date: N.A. Began: February 1, 1967.
Channel capacity: N.A. Channels available but not in use: N.A.
Basic Service
Subscribers: 1,252.
Programming (via satellite): A&E; AMC; Animal Network; Cartoon Network; CNBC; CNN; Comedy Central; C-SPAN; Discovery Channel; Disney Channel; E! HD; ESPN; ESPN2; Fox News Channel; FOX Sports West/Prime Ticket; Freeform; FX; Golf Channel; HGTV; History; HSN2; Lifetime; MTV; NBCSN; Nickelodeon; OWN: Oprah Winfrey Network; QVC; Spike TV; TBS; Telemundo; The Weather Channel; TLC; TNT; Trinity Broadcasting Network (TBN); TV Land; Univision; USA Network; VH1; WGN America.
Programming (via translator): KASA-TV (COZI TV, FOX) Santa Fe; KASY-TV (MNT) Albuquerque; KCHF (IND, WeatherNa-

tion) Santa Fe; KLUZ-TV (LATV, UNV) Albuquerque; KOAT-TV (ABC, Estrella TV) Albuquerque; KOB (NBC, This TV) Albuquerque; KRPV-DT (GLC) Roswell; KRQE (CBS) Albuquerque; KRWG-TV (PBS) Las Cruces; KTSM-TV (Estrella TV, NBC) El Paso; KVIA-TV (ABC, Azteca America, CW) El Paso; KWBQ (CW, Grit, Laff) Santa Fe.
Fee: $42.00 installation; $51.36 monthly.
Digital Basic Service
Subscribers: N.A.
Programming (via satellite): BBC America; CBS Sports Network; Cine Mexicano; Cinelatino; CMT; CNN en Espanol; C-SPAN 3; Destination America; Discovery Kids Channel; Disney XD; ESPN Deportes; ESPNews; EWTN Global Catholic Network; Flix; Food Network; Fox Deportes; FYI; GSN; Hallmark Channel; History en Espanol; History International; Investigation Discovery; LMN; LOGO; MC; MoviePlex; MTV Classic; MTV Hits; MTV Jams; MTV2; National Geographic Channel; NBC Universo; NFL Network; Nick 2; Nick Jr.; Science Channel; Sprout; Starz Encore (multiplexed); Sundance TV; Syfy; TeenNick; Tr3s; Travel Channel; truTV; Turner Classic Movies; VH1 Soul; ViendoMovies.
Fee: $11.95 monthly.
Digital Pay Service 1
Pay Units: N.A.
Programming (via satellite): Cinemax (multiplexed); HBO (multiplexed); Showtime (multiplexed); Starz (multiplexed); The Movie Channel (multiplexed).
Fee: $14.95 monthly (each).
Pay-Per-View
iN DEMAND (delivered digitally); Hot Choice (delivered digitally); Playboy TV (delivered digitally); Fresh (delivered digitally); Spice: Xcess (delivered digitally).
Internet Service
Operational: Yes.
Telephone Service
None
Miles of Plant: 80.0 (coaxial); None (fiber optic).
Area Vice President: John Christopher. General Manager: Manny Orquiz. Chief Technician: Donnie Hall. Office Manager: Amelia Munoz.
Ownership: Comcast Cable Communications Inc. (MSO).

DIXON—Satview Broadband, 3550 Barron Way, Ste 13A, Reno, NV 89511. Phones: 575-437-3101; 775-333-6626; 877-538-2662. Web Site: http://www.satview.net. ICA: NM0063.
TV Market Ranking: Outside TV Markets (DIXON).
Channel capacity: N.A. Channels available but not in use: N.A.
Basic Service
Subscribers: 43.
Programming (received off-air): KASA-TV (COZI TV, FOX) Santa Fe; KASY-TV (MNT) Albuquerque; KNME-TV (PBS) Albuquerque; KOAT-TV (ABC, Estrella TV) Albuquerque; KOB (NBC, This TV) Albuquerque; KRQE (CBS) Albuquerque.
Programming (via satellite): A&E; Animal Planet; CMT; CNN; C-SPAN; Discovery Channel; Disney Channel; E! HD; ESPN; EWTN Global Catholic Network; Food Network; Fox News Channel; Freeform; HGTV; History; HLN; KMGH-TV (ABC, Azteca America) Denver; Lifetime; MTV; Nickelodeon; Outdoor Channel; Spike TV; Syfy; TBS; The Weather Channel; TLC; TNT; Turner Classic Movies; TV Land; UniMas; USA Network; VH1; WGN America.

2017 Edition

Cable Systems—New Mexico

D-521

New Mexico—Cable Systems

Programming (via translator): KLUZ-TV (LATV, UNV) Albuquerque; KTEL-TV (TMO) Carlsbad.
Fee: $19.00 installation; $44.45 monthly.
Pay Service 1
Pay Units: N.A.
Programming (via satellite): HBO.
Fee: $11.95 monthly.
Pay-Per-View
Shorteez (delivered digitally); Fresh (delivered digitally); Playboy TV (delivered digitally); iN DEMAND (delivered digitally).
Internet Service
Operational: No.
Telephone Service
None
President: Ahmad Tariq.
Ownership: Satview Broadband Ltd. (MSO).

ELEPHANT BUTTE—PVT, 4011 West Main St, Artesia, NM 88210-9566. Phones: 575-748-1241; 800-505-4844. Fax: 505-746-4142. Web Site: http://www.pvt.com. ICA: NM0049.
TV Market Ranking: Outside TV Markets (ELEPHANT BUTTE). Franchise award date: N.A. Franchise expiration date: N.A. Began: June 1, 1988.
Channel capacity: 56 (not 2-way capable). Channels available but not in use: N.A.
Basic Service
Subscribers: N.A.
Programming (received off-air): KOBR (NBC, This TV) Roswell; KRWG-TV (PBS) Las Cruces.
Programming (via satellite): A&E; AMC; CMT; CNBC; CNN; Comedy Central; Discovery Channel; Disney Channel; E! HD; ESPN; ESPN2; Fox News Channel; FOX Sports Networks; Freeform; FX; HGTV; History; HLN; INSP; Lifetime; Outdoor Channel; Spike TV; TBS; The Weather Channel; TLC; TNT; Travel Channel; TV Land; USA Network; WGN America.
Programming (via translator): KASA-TV (COZI TV, FOX) Santa Fe; KLUZ-TV (LATV, UNV) Albuquerque; KOAT-TV (ABC, Estrella TV) Albuquerque; KRQE (CBS) Albuquerque.
Fee: $25.00 installation.
Digital Basic Service
Subscribers: N.A.
Programming (via satellite): Disney XD; DMX Music; ESPNews; Fox Sports 1; FSN Digital Atlantic; FSN Digital Central; FSN Digital Pacific; Golf Channel; LMN; NBCSN; Turner Classic Movies; WE tv.
Fee: $12.00 monthly.
Pay Service 1
Pay Units: N.A.
Programming (via satellite): HBO.
Fee: $11.00 monthly.
Digital Pay Service 1
Pay Units: N.A. Included in Artesia.
Programming (via satellite): Cinemax (multiplexed); HBO (multiplexed); Showtime (multiplexed); Starz; Starz Encore (multiplexed).
Fee: $10.00 monthly (Cinemax,Showtime/TMC or Starz/Encore), $11.00 monthly (HBO).
Video-On-Demand: No
Internet Service
Operational: No.
Telephone Service
None
Miles of Plant: 78.0 (coaxial); 15.0 (fiber optic). Homes passed: 5,055. Miles of plant included in Artesia.
Chief Executive Officer: Glenn Lovelace. Vice President, Plant & Operations: Sammy Reno. Vice President, Sales & Marketing: Terry Mullins.
Ownership: Penasco Valley Telecommunications (MSO).

ESPANOLA—Satview Broadband, 3550 Barron Way, Ste 13A, Reno, NV 89511. Phones: 575-437-3101; 775-333-6626 (Elko, NV office); 775-324-2198; 877-538 2662. E-mail: satviewreno@yahoo.com. Web Site: http://www.satview.net. Also serves Rio Arriba, San Juan Pueblo, Santa Clara Indian Reservation & Santa Fe. ICA: NM0014.
TV Market Ranking: Below 100 (ESPANOLA, Rio Arriba, San Juan Pueblo, Santa Clara Indian Reservation, Santa Fe). Franchise award date: N.A. Franchise expiration date: N.A. Began: August 1, 1978.
Channel capacity: N.A. Channels available but not in use: N.A.
Basic Service
Subscribers: 1,843.
Programming (received off-air): KASA-TV (COZI TV, FOX) Santa Fe; KASY-TV (MNT) Albuquerque; KCHF (IND, WeatherNation) Santa Fe; KLUZ-TV (LATV, UNV) Albuquerque; KNAT-TV (TBN) Albuquerque; KNME-TV (PBS) Albuquerque; KOAT-TV (ABC, Estrella TV) Albuquerque; KOB (NBC, This TV) Albuquerque; KRPV-DT (GLC) Roswell; KRQE (CBS) Albuquerque; KTEL-TV (TMO) Carlsbad; KWBQ (CW, Grit, Laff) Santa Fe; allband FM.
Programming (via satellite): CNBC; CNN; Comedy Central; C-SPAN; ESPN Deportes; Food Network; Fox Deportes; HGTV; Lifetime; National Geographic Channel; Pop; Root Sports Rocky Mountain; TNT; USA Network; WGN America.
Fee: $59.90 installation; $36.28 monthly.
Expanded Basic Service 1
Subscribers: N.A.
Programming (via satellite): A&E; Animal Planet; Cartoon Network; CMT; C-SPAN 2; Discovery Channel; Disney Channel; E! HD; ESPN; ESPN2; EVINE Live; EWTN Global Catholic Network; Fox News Channel; Fox Sports 1; Freeform; FX; Great American Country; History; HLN; MTV; Nickelodeon; Outdoor Channel; QVC; Spike TV; Syfy; TBS; The Weather Channel; TLC; Travel Channel; truTV; Turner Classic Movies; TV Land; UniMas; VH1.
Fee: $10.36 monthly.
Digital Basic Service
Subscribers: N.A.
Programming (via satellite): BBC America; Bloomberg Television; Bravo; Cloo; Discovery Digital Networks; Disney XD; DMX Music; ESPN Classic; ESPNews; Fox Sports 1; Fuse; FYI; Golf Channel; GSN; History International; HITS (Headend In The Sky); IFC; LMN; NBCSN; Nick Jr.; Starz Encore (multiplexed); TeenNick; Trinity Broadcasting Network (TBN); WE tv.
Fee: $20.90 monthly; $8.00 converter.
Digital Pay Service 1
Pay Units: N.A.
Programming (via satellite): Cinemax (multiplexed); HBO (multiplexed); Showtime (multiplexed); Starz (multiplexed); The Movie Channel (multiplexed).
Fee: $8.95 monthly (Starz), $11.95 monthly (Cinemax, HBO, Showtime or TMC).
Video-On-Demand: No
Pay-Per-View
Playboy TV (delivered digitally); Fresh (delivered digitally); iN DEMAND (delivered digitally).
Internet Service
Operational: No.
Telephone Service
None
President: Tariq Ahmad.
Ownership: Satview Broadband Ltd. (MSO).

ESTANCIA—Formerly served by Chamisa Futurevision. No longer in operation. ICA: NM0052.

EUNICE—Formerly served by US Cable of Coastal Texas L.P. Now served by Baja Broadband, LEA COUNTY (southern portion), NM [NM0006]. ICA: NM0033.

FARMINGTON—Comcast Cable. Now served by ALBUQUERQUE, NM [NM0001]. ICA: NM0004.

FORT SUMNER—Formerly served by Reach Broadband. No longer in operation. ICA: NM0040.

FOUR HILLS—Formerly served by JRC Telecommunications. No longer in operation. ICA: NM0032.

GALLUP—Comcast Cable, 201 South 1st St, Gallup, NM 87301-6209. Phone: 505-863-9334. Fax: 505-722-7327. Web Site: http://www.comcast.com. Also serves Gamerco. ICA: NM0010.
TV Market Ranking: Outside TV Markets (GALLUP, Gamerco). Franchise award date: January 1, 1954. Franchise expiration date: N.A. Began: June 1, 1954.
Channel capacity: 56 (operating 2-way). Channels available but not in use: N.A.
Basic Service
Subscribers: 2,498.
Programming (received off-air): KASA-TV (COZI TV, FOX) Santa Fe; KASY-TV (MNT) Albuquerque; KCHF (IND, WeatherNation) Santa Fe; KLUZ-TV (LATV, UNV) Albuquerque; KNAT-TV (TBN) Albuquerque; KNME-TV (PBS) Albuquerque; KOAT-TV (ABC, Estrella TV) Albuquerque; KOBF (NBC, This TV) Farmington; KRQE (CBS) Albuquerque; KTEL-TV (TMO) Carlsbad; KWBQ (CW, Grit, Laff) Santa Fe.
Programming (via satellite): C-SPAN; C-SPAN 2; Discovery Channel; Pop; QVC; TBS; The Weather Channel; WGN America.
Fee: $42.00 installation; $27.57 monthly.
Expanded Basic Service 1
Subscribers: N.A.
Programming (via satellite): A&E; AMC; Animal Planet; Cartoon Network; CMT; CNBC; CNN; Comedy Central; Disney Channel; E! HD; ESPN; ESPN2; EWTN Global Catholic Network; Food Network; Fox News Channel; Freeform; FX; Golf Channel; Hallmark Channel; HGTV; History; HLN; Lifetime; MTV; NBCSN; Nickelodeon; OWN: Oprah Winfrey Network; Root Sports Rocky Mountain; Spike TV; Syfy; TLC; TNT; truTV; TV Land; USA Network; VH1.
Fee: $29.53 monthly.
Digital Basic Service
Subscribers: N.A.
Programming (via satellite): BBC America; Bravo; Discovery Digital Networks; Disney XD; DMX Music; ESPN Classic; ESPNews; Fox Sports 1; Fuse; FXM; FYI; GSN; History International; IFC; LMN; MTV Classic; MTV2; National Geographic Channel; NFL Network; Nick Jr.; Outdoor Channel; TeenNick; Turner Classic Movies; VH1 Country; WE tv.
Fee: $10.20 monthly.
Digital Pay Service 1
Pay Units: N.A.
Programming (via satellite): Cinemax (multiplexed); HBO (multiplexed); Showtime (multiplexed); Starz (multiplexed); Starz Encore (multiplexed); The Movie Channel (multiplexed).
Fee: $10.74 monthly (each).
Video-On-Demand: No
Pay-Per-View
iN DEMAND (delivered digitally); Fresh (delivered digitally); Playboy TV (delivered digitally); Shorteez (delivered digitally); Pleasure (delivered digitally).
Internet Service
Operational: Yes.
Telephone Service
None
Miles of Plant: 111.0 (coaxial); None (fiber optic). Homes passed: 19,600.
Vice President & General Manager: Chris Dunkeson. Operations Manager: Mark Johnson. Chief Technician: Pat Gonzales. Office Manager: Mary Gonzales.
Ownership: Comcast Cable Communications Inc. (MSO).

GRANTS—Comcast Cable, 216 North 2nd St, Grants, NM 87020-2504. Phone: 505-287-9451. Fax: 505-287-7474. Web Site: http://www.comcast.com. Also serves Bluewater, Cibola County (portions), Milan, San Rafael & Valencia County (portions). ICA: NM0012.
TV Market Ranking: Outside TV Markets (Bluewater, Cibola County (portions), GRANTS, Milan, San Rafael). Franchise award date: N.A. Franchise expiration date: N.A. Began: September 1, 1972.
Channel capacity: N.A. Channels available but not in use: N.A.
Basic Service
Subscribers: 609.
Programming (received off-air): KASA-TV (COZI TV, FOX) Santa Fe; KASY-TV (MNT) Albuquerque; KCHF (IND, WeatherNation) Santa Fe; KLUZ-TV (LATV, UNV) Albuquerque; KNME-TV (PBS) Albuquerque; KOAT-TV (ABC, Estrella TV) Albuquerque; KOB (NBC, This TV) Albuquerque; KRQE (CBS) Albuquerque; KTEL-CD (TMO) Albuquerque; KWBQ (CW, Grit, Laff) Santa Fe; 1 FM.
Programming (via satellite): A&E; AMC; Animal Planet; Cartoon Network; CNBC; CNN; Comedy Central; Discovery Channel; Disney Channel; E! HD; ESPN; EWTN Global Catholic Network; Food Network; Fox News Channel; FOX Sports Networks; Freeform; Golf Channel; Great American Country; Hallmark Channel; HGTV; History; Lifetime; MSNBC; MTV; NBCSN; Nickelodeon; Outdoor Channel; Pop; QVC; Spike TV; TBS; The Weather Channel; TLC; TNT; Trinity Broadcasting Network (TBN); Univision; USA Network; VH1; WGN America.
Fee: $42.00 installation; $61.24 monthly.
Digital Basic Service
Subscribers: N.A. Includes Socorro.
Programming (via satellite): BBC America; CBS Sports Network; CMT; C-SPAN 3; Destination America; Discovery Kids Channel; Disney XD; ESPNews; Flix; FYI; History International; Investigation Discovery; MC; MTV Classic; MTV Jams; MTV2; National Geographic Channel; Nick 2; Nick Jr.; Science Channel; Starz Encore (multiplexed); Sundance TV; TeenNick; Tr3s; TV One; VH1 Soul; WAM! America's Kidz Network.
Fee: $11.95 monthly.
Digital Pay Service 1
Pay Units: N.A.
Programming (via satellite): Cinemax (multiplexed); HBO (multiplexed); Showtime (multiplexed); Starz (multiplexed); The Movie Channel (multiplexed).

Cable Systems—New Mexico

Fee: $14.95 monthly (each).
Video-On-Demand: No
Pay-Per-View
iN DEMAND (delivered digitally); Hot Choice (delivered digitally); Playboy TV (delivered digitally); Fresh (delivered digitally); Pleasure (delivered digitally).
Internet Service
Operational: Yes.
Telephone Service
None
Miles of Plant: 110.0 (coaxial); None (fiber optic). Homes passed: 7,060.
Vice President & General Manager: Chris Dunkeson. Operations Manager: Earl Chavez. Chief Technician: Tommy Chavez.
Ownership: Comcast Cable Communications Inc. (MSO).

HATCH—Comcast Cable, 109 North Silver Ave, Deming, NM 88030-3711. Phones: 505-546-0417; 505-546-7909. Fax: 505-546-6718. Web Site: http://www.comcast.com. Also serves Dona Ana County (portions). ICA: NM0078.
TV Market Ranking: Below 100 (Dona Ana County (portions), HATCH); Outside TV Markets (Dona Ana County (portions)). Franchise award date: N.A. Franchise expiration date: N.A. Began: March 1, 1965.
Channel capacity: N.A. Channels available but not in use: N.A.
Basic Service
Subscribers: 37.
Programming (received off-air): KASA-TV (COZI TV, FOX) Santa Fe; KOAT-TV (ABC, Estrella TV) Albuquerque; KOB (NBC, This TV) Albuquerque; KRPV-DT (GLC) Roswell; KRQE (CBS) Albuquerque; KRWG-TV (PBS) Las Cruces; KTEL-CD (TMO) Albuquerque; KTSM-TV (Estrella TV, NBC) El Paso; KVIA-TV (ABC, Azteca America, CW) El Paso; various Mexican stations; allband FM.
Programming (via satellite): A&E; Animal Planet; Cartoon Network; CMT; CNBC; CNN; Comedy Central; C-SPAN; Discovery Channel; Disney Channel; E! HD; ESPN; Food Network; Fox News Channel; FOX Sports Southwest; Freeform; Hallmark Channel; HGTV; History; Lifetime; MTV; NBCSN; Nickelodeon; Outdoor Channel; OWN: Oprah Winfrey Network; QVC; Spike TV; Syfy; TBS; The Weather Channel; TLC; TNT; Trinity Broadcasting Network (TBN); truTV; Turner Classic Movies; TV Land; Univision; Univision Studios; USA Network; WGN America.
Fee: $42.00 installation; $46.98 monthly.
Pay Service 1
Pay Units: N.A.
Programming (via satellite): HBO.
Fee: $15.00 installation; $9.00 monthly.
Internet Service
Operational: Yes.
Telephone Service
None
Miles of Plant: 26.0 (coaxial); 8.0 (fiber optic). Homes passed: 574.
Vice President: John Christopher. General Manager: Manny Orquiz. Chief Technician: Donnie Hall. Office Manager: Amelia Munoz.
Ownership: Comcast Cable Communications Inc. (MSO).

HIGH ROLLS MOUNTAIN PARK—Formerly served by Baja Broadband. No longer in operation. ICA: NM0079.

JAL—Baja Broadband, 525 Junction Rd, Madison, WI 53717. Phones: 575-437-3101; 877-422-5282; 800-996-8788. Fax: 608-830-5519. Web Site: http://www.bajabroadband.com. ICA: NM0037.
TV Market Ranking: Outside TV Markets (JAL). Franchise award date: N.A. Franchise expiration date: N.A. Began: February 1, 1978.
Channel capacity: N.A. Channels available but not in use: N.A.
Basic Service
Subscribers: 88.
Programming (received off-air): KENW (PBS) Portales; KMID (ABC) Midland; KMLM-DT (GLC) Odessa; KOSA-TV (CBS, MNT) Odessa; KPEJ-TV (FOX) Odessa; KRQE (CBS) Albuquerque; KUPB (UNV) Midland; KWES-TV (CW, NBC, TMO) Odessa.
Programming (via satellite): A&E; AMC; Animal Planet; Cartoon Network; CMT; CNBC; CNN; Comedy Central; C-SPAN; Discovery Channel; Disney Channel; E! HD; ESPN; ESPN2; EVINE Live; Food Network; Fox News Channel; FOX Sports Networks; Freeform; FX; Hallmark Channel; HLN; KTLA (Antenna TV, CW, This TV) Los Angeles; Lifetime; MoviePlex; MTV; National Geographic Channel; Nickelodeon; QVC; Spike TV; TBS; The Weather Channel; TLC; TNT; truTV; TV Land; UniMas; USA Network; VH1; WGN America.
Fee: $19.99 installation; $58.75 monthly; $1.00 converter.
Pay Service 1
Pay Units: N.A.
Programming (via satellite): HBO; Starz; Starz Encore.
Fee: $3.00 monthly (Encore), $7.75 monthly (Starz), $14.50 monthly (HBO).
Digital Pay Service 1
Pay Units: N.A.
Programming (via satellite): Cinemax; HBO (multiplexed); Showtime (multiplexed); Starz (multiplexed); The Movie Channel (multiplexed).
Fee: $8.95 monthly (Starz), $11.95 monthly (Cinemax, HBO, Showtime or TMC).
Video-On-Demand: No
Pay-Per-View
iN DEMAND (delivered digitally); Playboy TV (delivered digitally); Fresh (delivered digitally); Club Jenna (delivered digitally).
Internet Service
Operational: Yes.
Fee: $27.95-$54.95 monthly.
Telephone Service
Digital: Operational
Fee: $24.95-$39.95 monthly
Homes passed & miles of plant included in Seminole, TX.
Vice President, Corporate Finance: Carl Shapiro. Assistant Treasurer: Noel Hutton.
Ownership: TDS Telecom (MSO).

LA MESA—Formerly served by Windjammer Cable. No longer in operation. ICA: NM0102.

LAS CRUCES—Comcast Cable. Now served by ALBUQUERQUE, NM [NM0001]. ICA: NM0002.

LAS CRUCES—Formerly served by Santa Fe Wireless Cable TV. No longer in operation. ICA: NM0097.

LAS VEGAS—Comcast Cable, 2530 Hot Springs Blvd, Las Vegas, NM 87701-3739. Phone: 505-425-7531. Fax: 505-425-6822. Web Site: http://www.comcast.com. Also serves San Miguel County (portions). ICA: NM0080.
TV Market Ranking: Below 100 (San Miguel County (portions) (portions)); Outside TV Markets (LAS VEGAS, San Miguel County (portions) (portions)). Franchise award date: N.A. Franchise expiration date: N.A. Began: May 7, 1967.
Channel capacity: N.A. Channels available but not in use: N.A.
Basic Service
Subscribers: 1,307.
Programming (received off-air): KASA-TV (COZI TV, FOX) Santa Fe; KASY-TV (MNT) Albuquerque; KCHF (IND, WeatherNation) Santa Fe; KLUZ-TV (LATV, UNV) Albuquerque; KNME-TV (PBS) Albuquerque; KOAT-TV (ABC, Estrella TV) Albuquerque; KOB (NBC, This TV) Albuquerque; KRPV-DT (GLC) Roswell; KRQE (CBS) Albuquerque; KTEL-TV (TMO) Carlsbad; KWBQ (CW, Grit, Laff) Santa Fe; 10 FMs.
Programming (via satellite): A&E; AMC; Bravo; C-SPAN; Disney Channel; E! HD; ESPN; EWTN Global Catholic Network; Fox News Channel; FOX Sports Southwest; Freeform; MTV; Nickelodeon; QVC; Spike TV; TBS; The Weather Channel; TNT; UniMas; USA Network; WGN America.
Fee: $42.00 installation; $47.16 monthly.
Expanded Basic Service 1
Subscribers: N.A.
Programming (via satellite): Animal Planet; Cartoon Network; CMT; CNBC; CNN; Comedy Central; Discovery Channel; ESPN2; Food Network; Golf Channel; Hallmark Channel; HGTV; History; Lifetime; NBCSN; OWN: Oprah Winfrey Network; Syfy; The Weather Channel; TLC; Travel Channel; TV Land; VH1.
Fee: $12.55 monthly.
Digital Basic Service
Subscribers: N.A.
Programming (via satellite): BBC America; CBS Sports Network; CMT; C-SPAN 3; Destination America; Discovery Kids Channel; Disney XD; ESPNews; Flix; FYI; History International; Investigation Discovery; LMN; LOGO; MC; MoviePlex; MTV Classic; MTV Jams; MTV2; National Geographic Channel; NFL Network; Nick 2; Nick Jr.; RFD-TV; Science Channel; Sprout; Starz Encore (multiplexed); Sundance TV; TeenNick; Tr3s; TV One; VH1 Soul.
Fee: $10.20 monthly.
Digital Pay Service 1
Pay Units: N.A.
Programming (via satellite): Cinemax (multiplexed); HBO (multiplexed); Showtime (multiplexed); Starz (multiplexed); The Movie Channel (multiplexed).
Fee: $11.49 monthly (each).
Video-On-Demand: No
Pay-Per-View
iN DEMAND (delivered digitally); Playboy TV (delivered digitally); Fresh (delivered digitally); Spice: Xcess (delivered digitally); Hot Choice (delivered digitally).
Internet Service
Operational: Yes.
Telephone Service
None
Miles of Plant: 198.0 (coaxial); 12.0 (fiber optic). Homes passed: 6,401.
Vice President & General Manager: Chris Dunkeson. Operations Manager: Ricky Armijo. Chief Technician: Henry Garcia.
Ownership: Comcast Cable Communications Inc. (MSO).

LEA COUNTY (southern portion)—Baja Broadband, 525 Junction Rd, Madison, WI 53717. Phones: 575-437-3101; 877-422-5282; 800-996-8788. Fax: 608-830-5519. E-mail: customersupportnm@bajabb.tv. Web Site: http://www.bajabroadband.com. Also serves Eunice & Hobbs. ICA: NM0006.
TV Market Ranking: Below 100 (LEA COUNTY (SOUTHERN PORTION) (portions), Eunice, Hobbs); Outside TV Markets (LEA COUNTY (SOUTHERN PORTION) (portions)). Franchise award date: N.A. Franchise expiration date: N.A. Began: January 1, 1955.
Channel capacity: N.A. Channels available but not in use: N.A.
Basic Service
Subscribers: 4,209.
Programming (received off-air): KASA-TV (COZI TV, FOX) Santa Fe; KCHF (IND, WeatherNation) Santa Fe; KENW (PBS) Portales; KJTV-TV (FOX) Lubbock; KMID (ABC) Midland; KOSA-TV (CBS, MNT) Odessa; KRPV-DT (GLC) Roswell; KTEL-TV (TMO) Carlsbad; KWBQ (CW, Grit, Laff) Santa Fe; KWES-TV (CW, NBC, TMO) Odessa.
Programming (via microwave): KBIM-TV (CBS, The Country Network) Roswell; KOBR (NBC, This TV) Roswell.
Programming (via satellite): C-SPAN; EVINE Live; Pop; QVC; TBS.
Programming (via translator): KASY-TV (MNT) Albuquerque; KLUZ-TV (LATV, UNV) Albuquerque; KOAT-TV (ABC, Estrella TV) Albuquerque.
Fee: $59.94 installation; $32.02 monthly; $3.55 converter.
Expanded Basic Service 1
Subscribers: N.A.
Programming (via satellite): A&E; AMC; Animal Planet; BET; Cartoon Network; CMT; CNBC; CNN; Comedy Central; Discovery Channel; Disney Channel; E! HD; ESPN; ESPN2; EWTN Global Catholic Network; Food Network; Fox News Channel; Fox Sports 1; FOX Sports Southwest; Freeform; FX; Hallmark Channel; History; HLN; Lifetime; MoviePlex; MSNBC; MTV; National Geographic Channel; Nickelodeon; Oxygen; Spike TV; The Weather Channel; TLC; TNT; TV Land; USA Network; VH1.
Fee: $24.94 monthly.
Digital Basic Service
Subscribers: N.A.
Programming (via satellite): BBC America; Bloomberg Television; Bravo; Cloo; CMT; Destination America; Discovery Kids Channel; Discovery Life Channel; Disney XD; DMX Music; ESPN Classic; ESPNews; Fox Sports 1; Fuse; FYI; Golf Channel; GSN; HGTV; History International; IFC; Investigation Discovery; LMN; MTV Classic; MTV2; Nat Geo WILD; NBC Universo; NBCSN; Nick Jr.; Outdoor Channel; OWN: Oprah Winfrey Network; Science Channel; Starz En-

New Mexico—Cable Systems

core (multiplexed); Syfy; TeenNick; Trinity Broadcasting Network (TBN); Turner Classic Movies; WE tv.
Fee: $17.85 monthly; $8.00 converter.
Digital Expanded Basic Service
Subscribers: N.A.
Programming (via satellite): Cine Mexicano; Cinelatino; CNN en Espanol; ESPN Deportes; Fox Deportes; History en Espanol; NBC Universo; Tr3s; ViendoMovies.
Fee: $4.99 monthly.
Digital Expanded Basic Service 2
Subscribers: N.A.
Programming (via satellite): A&E HD; Animal Planet HD; AXS TV; Discovery Channel HD; ESPN HD; Food Network HD; FSN HD; HD Theater; HGTV HD; History HD; National Geographic Channel HD; PBS HD; Syfy HD; Universal HD; USA Network HD.
Fee: $16.95 monthly.
Pay Service 1
Pay Units: N.A.
Programming (via satellite): Cinemax; HBO; Starz Encore.
Fee: $3.00 monthly (Encore), $14.50 monthly (Cinemax/HBO).
Digital Pay Service 1
Pay Units: N.A.
Programming (via satellite): Cinemax (multiplexed); HBO (multiplexed); Showtime (multiplexed); Starz (multiplexed); The Movie Channel (multiplexed).
Fee: $8.95 monthly (Starz), $11.95 monthly (Cinemax, HBO, Showtime or TMC).
Video-On-Demand: No
Pay-Per-View
iN DEMAND (delivered digitally); Fresh (delivered digitally); Playboy TV (delivered digitally); Club Jenna (delivered digitally).
Internet Service
Operational: Yes.
Subscribers: 5,109.
Broadband Service: Warp Drive Online.
Fee: $27.95 monthly.
Telephone Service
Digital: Operational
Subscribers: 1,182.
Miles of Plant: 3,970.0 (coaxial); 1,442.0 (fiber optic). Homes passed: 18,687. Homes passed & miles of plant included in Seminole, TX.
Vice President, Corporate Finance: Carl Shapiro. Assistant Treasurer: Noel Hutton.
Ownership: TDS Telecom (MSO).

LOGAN—Formerly served by Baja Broadband. No longer in operation. ICA: NM0053.

LORDSBURG—Formerly served by City TV Cable. No longer in operation. ICA: NM0024.

LOS ALAMOS—Comcast Cable, 2534 Camino Entrada, Santa Fe, NM 87507-4807. Phones: 505-438-2600; 505-474-7886. Fax: 505-474-7986. Web Site: http://www.comcast.com. Also serves White Rock. ICA: NM0015.
TV Market Ranking: Below 100 (LOS ALAMOS, White Rock). Franchise award date: N.A. Franchise expiration date: N.A. Began: March 1, 1980.
Channel capacity: N.A. Channels available but not in use: N.A.
Basic Service
Subscribers: 2,013.
Programming (received off-air): KASA-TV (COZI TV, FOX) Santa Fe; KASY-TV (MNT) Albuquerque; KCHF (IND, WeatherNation) Santa Fe; KLUZ-TV (LATV, UNV) Albuquerque; KNAT-TV (TBN) Albuquerque; KNME-TV (PBS) Albuquerque; KOAT-TV

(ABC, Estrella TV) Albuquerque; KOB (NBC, This TV) Albuquerque; KPAX-TV (CBS, CW, Grit) Missoula; KRQE (CBS) Albuquerque; KWBQ (CW, Grit, Laff) Santa Fe; allband FM.
Programming (via satellite): Freeform; Nickelodeon; QVC; Spike TV; Telemundo; TV Land; WGN America.
Fee: $42.00 installation; $51.36 monthly.
Expanded Basic Service 1
Subscribers: N.A.
Programming (via satellite): A&E; AMC; Animal Planet; Bravo; Cartoon Network; CMT; CNBC; CNN; Comedy Central; C-SPAN; C-SPAN 2; Discovery Channel; Disney Channel; E! HD; ESPN; ESPN2; EWTN Global Catholic Network; Food Network; Fox News Channel; Fox Sports 1; FOX Sports Southwest; FX; Golf Channel; Great American Country; Hallmark Channel; HGTV; History; HLN; Lifetime; MSNBC; MTV; NBCSN; OWN: Oprah Winfrey Network; Syfy; TBS; The Weather Channel; TLC; TNT; truTV; USA Network; VH1.
Fee: $6.04 monthly.
Digital Basic Service
Subscribers: N.A.
Programming (via satellite): BBC America; C-SPAN 3; Discovery Digital Networks; Disney XD; DMX Music; ESPNews; Flix; Nick 2; Nick Jr.; Sundance TV; TeenNick.
Fee: $18.58 monthly.
Digital Pay Service 1
Pay Units: N.A.
Programming (via satellite): Cinemax (multiplexed); HBO (multiplexed); Showtime (multiplexed); Starz; The Movie Channel (multiplexed).
Fee: $14.95 monthly (each).
Video-On-Demand: No
Pay-Per-View
iN DEMAND (delivered digitally); Playboy TV (delivered digitally); Fresh (delivered digitally); Shorteez (delivered digitally).
Internet Service
Operational: Yes.
Broadband Service: Comcast High Speed Internet.
Fee: $42.95 monthly; $5.00 modem lease.
Telephone Service
Digital: Operational
Miles of Plant: 129.0 (coaxial); 32.0 (fiber optic). Homes passed: 7,521.
Vice President & General Manager: Chris Dunkeson. Operations Director: Carmen Valadez. Chief Technician: Chris Ciak.
Ownership: Comcast Cable Communications Inc. (MSO).

LOS LUNAS—Comcast Cable. Now served by ALBUQUERQUE, NM [NM0001]. ICA: NM0013.

LOS OJOS—Formerly served by US Cable of Coastal Texas L.P. No longer in operation. ICA: NM0081.

LOVINGTON—Baja Broadband, 525 Junction Rd, Madison, WI 53717. Phone: 877-422-5282. Fax: 608-830-5519. Web Site: http://www.bajabroadband.com. Also serves Lea County (portions). ICA: NM0020.
TV Market Ranking: Below 100 (LOVINGTON, Lea County (portions)); Outside TV Markets (Lea County (portions)). Franchise award date: N.A. Franchise expiration date: N.A. Began: December 1, 1954.
Channel capacity: 52 (operating 2-way). Channels available but not in use: N.A.
Basic Service
Subscribers: 617.
Programming (received off-air): KUPT (MNT) Hobbs [Licensed & silent]; 1 FM.

Programming (via satellite): CNBC; CNN; C-SPAN; C-SPAN 2; ESPN; ESPN2; FOX Sports Southwest; HLN; MSNBC; QVC; Spike TV; Telemundo; The Weather Channel; Univision.
Programming (via translator): KASA-TV (COZI TV, FOX) Santa Fe; KASY-TV (MNT) Albuquerque; KBIM-TV (CBS, The Country Network) Roswell; KENW (PBS) Portales; KJTV-TV (FOX) Lubbock; KLUZ-TV (LATV, UNV) Albuquerque; KOAT-TV (ABC, Estrella TV) Albuquerque; KOBR (NBC, This TV) Roswell; KRPV-DT (GLC) Roswell; KWBQ (CW, Grit, Laff) Santa Fe; KWES-TV (CW, NBC, TMO) Odessa.
Fee: $42.00 installation; $42.99 monthly; $.73 converter.
Expanded Basic Service 1
Subscribers: N.A.
Programming (via satellite): A&E; AMC; Animal Planet; BET; Cartoon Network; CMT; Discovery Channel; Disney Channel; E! HD; Fox News Channel; Freeform; Golf Channel; HGTV; History; Lifetime; MTV; Nickelodeon; Outdoor Channel; OWN: Oprah Winfrey Network; Syfy; TBS; TLC; TNT; USA Network; VH1; WGN America.
Fee: $9.30 monthly.
Digital Basic Service
Subscribers: N.A.
Programming (via satellite): BBC America; CMT; C-SPAN 3; Discovery Digital Networks; Disney XD; ESPNews; Flix; FYI; History International; HITS (Headend In The Sky); LMN; LOGO; MC; MoviePlex; National Geographic Channel; NFL Network; Nick 2; Nick Jr.; Sprout; Starz Encore (multiplexed); Sundance TV; TeenNick; TV One.
Fee: $11.20 monthly.
Digital Pay Service 1
Pay Units: N.A.
Programming (via satellite): Cinemax (multiplexed); HBO (multiplexed); Showtime (multiplexed); Starz (multiplexed); The Movie Channel (multiplexed).
Fee: $10.22 monthly (each).
Video-On-Demand: No
Pay-Per-View
iN DEMAND (delivered digitally); Hot Choice (delivered digitally); Playboy TV (delivered digitally).
Internet Service
Operational: Yes.
Telephone Service
None
Miles of Plant: 51.0 (coaxial); None (fiber optic). Homes passed: 3,410.
President & Chief Executive Officer: David Wittwer. Vice President, Cable Operations: Mark Barber. Assistant Treasurer: Noel Hutton.
Ownership: TDS Telecom (MSO).

MAXWELL—Formerly served by Rocky Mountain Cable. No longer in operation. ICA: NM0070.

MELROSE—Formerly served by Rapid Cable. No longer in operation. ICA: NM0061.

MORA—Formerly served by Rocky Mountain Cable. No longer in operation. ICA: NM0050.

MOUNTAINAIR—Formerly served by Chamisa Futurevision. No longer in operation. ICA: NM0046.

NAVAJO—Formerly served by Frontier Communications. No longer in operation. ICA: NM0083.

PECOS—Comcast Cable, 2534 Camino Entrada, Santa Fe, NM 87507-4807. Phones: 505-438-2600; 505-474-7886. Fax: 505-474-7986. Web Site: http://www.comcast.com. Also serves San Miguel County (portions). ICA: NM0042.
TV Market Ranking: Below 100 (PECOS, San Miguel County (portions)). Franchise award date: July 14, 1981. Franchise expiration date: N.A. Began: April 1, 1983.
Channel capacity: N.A. Channels available but not in use: N.A.
Basic Service
Subscribers: 37.
Programming (received off-air): KASA-TV (COZI TV, FOX) Santa Fe; KASY-TV (MNT) Albuquerque; KLUZ-TV (LATV, UNV) Albuquerque; KNME-TV (PBS) Albuquerque; KOAT-TV (ABC, Estrella TV) Albuquerque; KOB (NBC, This TV) Albuquerque; KRPV-DT (GLC) Roswell; KRQE (CBS) Albuquerque; KTEL-TV (TMO) Carlsbad; KWBQ (CW, Grit, Laff) Santa Fe.
Programming (via satellite): A&E; AMC; Bravo; C-SPAN; Disney Channel; E! HD; ESPN; ESPN2; EWTN Global Catholic Network; Fox News Channel; FOX Sports Southwest; Freeform; Great American Country; HGTV; MTV; NBCSN; Nickelodeon; QVC; Spike TV; Syfy; TBS; The Weather Channel; TLC; Turner Classic Movies; TV Land; Univision; USA Network; WGN America.
Fee: $42.00 installation; $47.53 monthly.
Expanded Basic Service 1
Subscribers: N.A.
Programming (via satellite): Cartoon Network; CMT; CNN; Comedy Central; Discovery Channel; TNT.
Fee: $10.20 monthly.
Pay Service 1
Pay Units: N.A.
Programming (via satellite): Cinemax; HBO (multiplexed).
Fee: $16.80 installation; $8.44 monthly (each).
Internet Service
Operational: Yes.
Telephone Service
None
Miles of Plant: 16.0 (coaxial); None (fiber optic). Homes passed: 506.
Vice President & General Manager: Chris Dunkeson. Operations Director: Carmen Valadez. Chief Technician: Chris Ciak.
Ownership: Comcast Cable Communications Inc. (MSO).

PENASCO—Satview Broadband, 3550 Barron Way, Ste 13A, Reno, NV 89511. Phones: 575-437-3101; 775-333-6626 (Elko, NV office); 877-538 2662; 775-324-2198. E-mail: satviewreno@yahoo.com. Web Site: http://www.satview.net. Also serves Picuris. ICA: NM0105.
TV Market Ranking: Outside TV Markets (PENASCO, Picuris). Franchise award date: N.A. Franchise expiration date: N.A.
Channel capacity: N.A. Channels available but not in use: N.A.
Basic Service
Subscribers: 42.
Programming (received off-air): KASA-TV (COZI TV, FOX) Santa Fe; KASY-TV (MNT) Albuquerque; KCHF (IND, WeatherNation) Santa Fe; KLUZ-TV (LATV, UNV) Albuquerque; KNME-TV (PBS) Albuquerque; KOAT-TV (ABC, Estrella TV) Albuquerque; KOB (NBC, This TV) Albuquerque; KRQE (CBS) Albuquerque; KTEL-TV (TMO) Carlsbad; KWBQ (CW, Grit, Laff) Santa Fe.
Programming (via satellite): A&E; Animal Planet; CMT; CNN; C-SPAN; Discovery

Cable Systems—New Mexico

Channel; Disney Channel; ESPN; EWTN Global Catholic Network; Food Network; Fox News Channel; Freeform; HGTV; History; HLN; Lifetime; MTV; Nickelodeon; Spike TV; Syfy; TBS; The Weather Channel; TLC; TNT; Turner Classic Movies; TV Land; UniMas; USA Network; VH1; WGN America.
Fee: $19.95 installation; $44.45 monthly.

Digital Basic Service
Subscribers: N.A.
Programming (via satellite): BBC America; Bloomberg Television; Bravo; Cloo; Discovery Kids Channel; Disney XD; ESPN Classic; ESPNews; FOX College Sports Central; FOX College Sports Pacific; Fox Sports 1; Fuse; Golf Channel; Great American Country; GSN; IFC; LMN; MTV Classic; MTV2; NBCSN; Nick Jr.; OWN: Oprah Winfrey Network; Science Channel; Starz Encore; TeenNick; The Word Network; Trinity Broadcasting Network (TBN); VH1 Soul; WE tv.
Fee: $12.95 monthly.

Digital Expanded Basic Service
Subscribers: N.A.
Programming (via satellite): CMT; Destination America; Discovery Life Channel; FXM; FYI; History International; Investigation Discovery; MTV Hits; Ovation; Starz Encore (multiplexed).
Fee: $4.95 monthly.

Pay Service 1
Pay Units: N.A.
Programming (via satellite): HBO.
Fee: $11.95 monthly.

Digital Pay Service 1
Pay Units: N.A.
Programming (via satellite): Cinemax (multiplexed); HBO (multiplexed); Showtime (multiplexed); Starz (multiplexed); The Movie Channel (multiplexed).

Pay-Per-View
iN DEMAND (delivered digitally); Playboy TV (delivered digitally); Fresh (delivered digitally).

Internet Service
Operational: No.

Telephone Service
None
President: Tariq Ahmad.
Ownership: Satview Broadband Ltd. (MSO).

PLAYAS—Formerly served by Playas CATV. No longer in operation. ICA: NM0084.

POJOAQUE—Formerly served by Comcast Cable. No longer in operation. ICA: NM0104.

PORTALES—Comcast Cable, 708 East 2nd St, Portales, NM 88130-6006. Phones: 575-356-8571; 800-266-2278. Fax: 505-359-0958. Web Site: http://www.comcast.com. Also serves Roosevelt County (portions). ICA: NM0018.
TV Market Ranking: Below 100 (PORTALES, Roosevelt County (portions)); Outside TV Markets (Roosevelt County (portions)). Franchise award date: N.A. Franchise expiration date: N.A. Began: January 1, 1963.
Channel capacity: 62 (not 2-way capable). Channels available but not in use: N.A.

Basic Service
Subscribers: 972.
Programming (received off-air): KENW (PBS) Portales; 5 FMs.
Programming (via microwave): KAMR-TV (IND, NBC) Amarillo; KASA-TV (COZI TV, FOX) Santa Fe; KBIM-TV (CBS, The Country Network) Roswell; KCIT (FOX, This TV) Amarillo; KFDA-TV (CBS, TMO) Amarillo; KOAT-TV (ABC, Estrella TV) Albuquerque; KOBR (NBC, This TV) Roswell; KRPV-DT (GLC) Roswell; KVII-TV (ABC, CW) Amarillo.
Programming (via satellite): Disney Channel; ESPN2; Freeform; Spike TV.
Fee: $42.00 installation; $53.00 monthly; $.81 converter.

Expanded Basic Service 1
Subscribers: N.A.
Programming (via satellite): A&E; AMC; Animal Planet; BET; Cartoon Network; CMT; CNBC; CNN; Comedy Central; C-SPAN; C-SPAN 2; Discovery Channel; E! HD; ESPN; Food Network; Fox News Channel; FOX Sports Southwest; FX; Golf Channel; Hallmark Channel; HGTV; History; HLN; Lifetime; MSNBC; MTV; NBCSN; Nickelodeon; Outdoor Channel; OWN: Oprah Winfrey Network; QVC; Syfy; TBS; Telemundo; The Weather Channel; TLC; TNT; Travel Channel; Trinity Broadcasting Network (TBN); truTV; TV Land; Univision; Univision Studios; USA Network; VH1.
Fee: $5.45 monthly.

Digital Basic Service
Subscribers: N.A.
Programming (via satellite): BBC America; CMT; C-SPAN 3; Discovery Digital Networks; Disney XD; ESPNews; Flix; FYI; History International; LMN; LOGO; MC; Nat Geo WILD; National Geographic Channel; NFL Network; Nick 2; Nick Jr.; Nicktoons; Sprout; Starz Encore (multiplexed); Sundance TV; TeenNick; TV One.
Fee: $11.20 monthly.

Digital Pay Service 1
Pay Units: N.A.
Programming (via satellite): Cinemax (multiplexed); HBO (multiplexed); Showtime (multiplexed); Starz (multiplexed); The Movie Channel (multiplexed).
Fee: $5.00 installation; $9.95 monthly (each).

Video-On-Demand: No

Pay-Per-View
iN DEMAND (delivered digitally); Hot Choice (delivered digitally); Playboy TV (delivered digitally).

Internet Service
Operational: Yes.

Telephone Service
None
Miles of Plant: 55.0 (coaxial); None (fiber optic). Homes passed: 4,196.
Area Vice President: John Christopher. General Manager: Dennis Jones. Chief Technician: Spencer DeBord. Office Manager: Frederick Dominguez.
Ownership: Comcast Cable Communications Inc. (MSO).

QUESTA—Comcast Cable, 1546 Paseo Del Pueblo Sur, PO Box 1854, Taos, NM 87571-1854. Phones: 505-758-3569; 505-758-3207. Fax: 505-758-4441. Web Site: http://www.comcast.com. Also serves Cerro. ICA: NM0047.
TV Market Ranking: Outside TV Markets (Cerro, QUESTA). Franchise award date: January 1, 2001. Franchise expiration date: N.A. Began: June 1, 1981.
Channel capacity: N.A. Channels available but not in use: N.A.

Basic Service
Subscribers: 60.
Programming (received off-air): KLUZ-TV (LATV, UNV) Albuquerque; KNME-TV (PBS) Albuquerque; KOAT-TV (ABC, Estrella TV) Albuquerque; KOB (NBC, This TV) Albuquerque; KRQE (CBS) Albuquerque.
Programming (via satellite): A&E; AMC; CMT; CNN; Comedy Central; C-SPAN; Discovery Channel; Disney Channel; ESPN; ESPN2; EWTN Global Catholic Network; Food Network; Fox News Channel; FOX Sports Networks; FOX Sports Southwest; Freeform; FX; History; HLN; HSN2; Lifetime; MSNBC; MTV; NBCSN; Nickelodeon; The Weather Channel; TLC; TNT; TV Land; Univision; USA Network; WGN America.
Fee: $42.00 installation; $49.72 monthly.

Expanded Basic Service 1
Subscribers: N.A.
Programming (via satellite): Cartoon Network; E! HD; Golf Channel; QVC; Spike TV; Syfy; TBS; VH1.
Fee: $14.43 monthly.

Pay Service 1
Pay Units: N.A.
Programming (via satellite): Cinemax; HBO (multiplexed).
Fee: $16.00 installation; $10.45 monthly (each).

Pay-Per-View
Movies; special events.

Internet Service
Operational: Yes.

Telephone Service
None
Miles of Plant: 32.0 (coaxial); None (fiber optic). Homes passed: 428.
Vice President & General Manager: Chris Dunkeson. Operations Manager: David Quintana.
Ownership: Comcast Cable Communications Inc. (MSO).

RAMAH—Formerly served by Navajo Communications. No longer in operation. ICA: NM0085.

RATON—Comcast Cable, 1026 South 2nd St, Raton, NM 87740. Phone: 505-445-5553. Fax: 505-445-2835. Web Site: http://www.comcast.com. ICA: NM0019.
TV Market Ranking: Outside TV Markets (RATON). Franchise award date: N.A. Franchise expiration date: N.A. Began: November 1, 1954.
Channel capacity: N.A. Channels available but not in use: N.A.

Basic Service
Subscribers: 674.
Programming (via satellite): Discovery Channel; Hallmark Channel; QVC; TBS; Telemundo; The Weather Channel.
Programming (via translator): KASA-TV (COZI TV, FOX) Santa Fe; KLUZ-TV (LATV, UNV) Albuquerque; KNME-TV (PBS) Albuquerque; KOAT-TV (ABC, Estrella TV) Albuquerque; KOB (NBC, This TV) Albuquerque; KRDO-TV (ABC, TMO) Colorado Springs; KRQE (CBS) Albuquerque.
Fee: $42.00 installation; $27.57 monthly; $3.00 converter.

Expanded Basic Service 1
Subscribers: N.A.
Programming (via satellite): A&E; AMC; Animal Planet; Cartoon Network; CMT; CNBC; CNN; Comedy Central; Disney Channel; E! HD; ESPN; ESPN2; EWTN Global Catholic Network; Fox News Channel; Freeform; FX; Golf Channel; HGTV; History; HLN; Lifetime; MTV; NBCSN; Nickelodeon; Outdoor Channel; OWN: Oprah Winfrey Network; Root Sports Rocky Mountain; Spike TV; TLC; TNT; TV Land; USA Network; VH1.
Fee: $26.86 monthly.

Digital Basic Service
Subscribers: N.A.
Programming (via satellite): BBC America; Bravo; Discovery Digital Networks; DMX Music; ESPN Classic; ESPNews; Fox Sports 1; GSN; IFC; MTV Classic; Nick Jr.; Syfy; Turner Classic Movies; VH1 Country; WE tv.
Fee: $14.95 monthly.

Pay Service 1
Pay Units: N.A.
Programming (via satellite): Cinemax; HBO; Showtime.

Digital Pay Service 1
Pay Units: N.A.
Programming (via satellite): Cinemax (multiplexed); HBO (multiplexed); Showtime (multiplexed); Starz (multiplexed); Starz Encore (multiplexed); The Movie Channel (multiplexed).
Fee: $11.03 monthly (each).

Video-On-Demand: No

Pay-Per-View
iN DEMAND (delivered digitally); Playboy TV (delivered digitally); Fresh (delivered digitally); Shorteez (delivered digitally).

Internet Service
Operational: Yes.

Telephone Service
None
Miles of Plant: 68.0 (coaxial); None (fiber optic). Homes passed: 3,666.
Vice President & General Manager: Chris Dunkeson. Operations Manager: Ricky Armijo. Office Manager: Tammy Trujillo.
Ownership: Comcast Cable Communications Inc. (MSO).

RED RIVER—Comcast Cable, 1546 Paseo Del Pueblo Sur, PO Box 1854, Taos, NM 87571-1854. Phones: 505-758-3569; 505-758-3207. Fax: 505-758-4441. Web Site: http://www.comcast.com. Also serves Taos County (portions). ICA: NM0086.
TV Market Ranking: Outside TV Markets (RED RIVER, Taos County (portions)). Franchise award date: N.A. Franchise expiration date: N.A. Began: February 1, 1968.
Channel capacity: N.A. Channels available but not in use: N.A.

Basic Service
Subscribers: 90.
Programming (received off-air): KASA-TV (COZI TV, FOX) Santa Fe; KNME-TV (PBS) Albuquerque; KOAT-TV (ABC, Estrella TV) Albuquerque; KOB (NBC, This TV) Albuquerque; KRQE (CBS) Albuquerque; 1 FM.
Programming (via satellite): A&E; Animal Planet; Cartoon Network; CMT; CNBC; CNN; C-SPAN; Discovery Channel; Disney Channel; E! HD; ESPN; ESPN2; Freeform; HGTV; Lifetime; MTV; Nickelodeon; QVC; Spike TV; TBS; The Weather Channel; TLC; TNT; USA Network; VH1.
Fee: $42.00 installation; $51.74 monthly.

Access the most current data instantly
FREE TRIAL @ ADVANCED TVFactbook
TELCO/IPTV • CABLE TV • TV STATIONS
www.warren-news.com/factbook.htm

2017 Edition D-525

New Mexico—Cable Systems

Pay Service 1
Pay Units: N.A.
Programming (via satellite): HBO.
Fee: $13.68 monthly.
Internet Service
Operational: Yes.
Telephone Service
None
Miles of Plant: 11.0 (coaxial); None (fiber optic).
Vice President & General Manager: Chris Dunkeson. Operations Manager: David Quintana.
Ownership: Comcast Cable Communications Inc. (MSO).

RESERVE TWP.—Formerly served by Eagle West Communications Inc. No longer in operation. ICA: NM0065.

RIO RANCHO—Cable One, 7501 Nita Pl NE, Rio Rancho, NM 87124. Phone: 505-892-5114. Fax: 505-892-0748. Web Site: http://www.cableone.net. Also serves Sandoval County (portions). ICA: NM0009.
TV Market Ranking: 81 (RIO RANCHO, Sandoval County (portions)). Franchise award date: N.A. Franchise expiration date: N.A. Began: March 15, 1981.
Channel capacity: N.A. Channels available but not in use: N.A.
Basic Service
Subscribers: 4,252.
Programming (received off-air): KASA-TV (COZI TV, FOX) Santa Fe; KASY-TV (MNT) Albuquerque; KAZQ (ETV) Albuquerque; KCHF (IND, WeatherNation) Santa Fe; KLUZ-TV (LATV, UNV) Albuquerque; KNAT-TV (TBN) Albuquerque; KNME-TV (PBS) Albuquerque; KOAT-TV (ABC, Estrella TV) Albuquerque; KOB (NBC, This TV) Albuquerque; KRQE (CBS) Albuquerque; KWBQ (CW, Grit, Laff) Santa Fe; 2 FMs.
Programming (via satellite): Pop; QVC; Telemundo; UniMas; WGN America.
Fee: $90.00 installation; $35.00 monthly; $45.62 converter.
Expanded Basic Service 1
Subscribers: N.A.
Programming (via satellite): A&E; AMC; Animal Planet; Cartoon Network; CMT; CNBC; CNN; Comedy Central; C-SPAN; C-SPAN 2; Discovery Channel; Disney Channel; ESPN; ESPN2; EWTN Global Catholic Network; Food Network; Fox News Channel; FOX Sports Midwest; Freeform; FX; HGTV; History; HLN; Lifetime; MSNBC; MTV; Nickelodeon; Spike TV; Syfy; TBS; The Weather Channel; TLC; TNT; Travel Channel; Turner Classic Movies; TV Land; USA Network; VH1.
Digital Basic Service
Subscribers: N.A.
Programming (via satellite): 3ABN; A&E HD; Boomerang; BYUtv; Cine Mexicano; CNN en Espanol; Discovery Kids Channel; Disney XD; ESPN Classic; ESPN Deportes; ESPN HD; ESPNews; FamilyNet; Food Network HD; FOX College Sports Central; FOX College Sports Pacific; Fox Deportes; Fox Sports 1; Fox Sports 2; FXM; FYI; Golf Channel; Great American Country; GSN; Hallmark Channel; HD Theater; HGTV HD; History International; INSP; La Familia Cosmovision; MC; National Geographic Channel; National Geographic Channel HD; Outdoor Channel; OWN: Oprah Winfrey Network; Science Channel; TBS HD; TNT HD; Toon Disney en Espanol; Trinity Broadcasting Network (TBN); TVG Network; Universal HD; WE tv.

Digital Pay Service 1
Pay Units: N.A.
Programming (via satellite): Cinemax (multiplexed); Flix (multiplexed); HBO (multiplexed); HBO HD; Showtime (multiplexed); Showtime HD; Starz (multiplexed); Starz Encore (multiplexed); Sundance TV; The Movie Channel (multiplexed); The Movie Channel HD.
Fee: $9.95 installation; $13.95 monthly (Cinemax, HBO/HBO HD or Showtime/Showtime HD/TMC/TMC HD/Flix/Sundance).
Video-On-Demand: No
Pay-Per-View
iN DEMAND (delivered digitally); SexSee (delivered digitally); Juicy (delivered digitally); VaVoom (delivered digitally).
Internet Service
Operational: Yes.
Broadband Service: CableONE.net.
Fee: $75.00 installation; $43.00 monthly.
Telephone Service
Digital: Operational
Subscribers: 3,235.
Fee: $39.95 monthly
Miles of Plant: 827.0 (coaxial); 200.0 (fiber optic). Homes passed: 34,339.
Vice President: Patrick A. Dolohanty. General Manager: Dan Hernandez. Marketing Director: Joan Gunn. Customer Service Manager: Sarah Schuetz.
Ownership: Cable ONE Inc. (MSO).

ROSWELL—Cable One, 2005 South Main St, Roswell, NM 88203-2508. Phone: 575-623-2391. Fax: 505-624-9569. E-mail: cindilucero@cableone.net. Web Site: http://www.cableone.net. Also serves Chaves County. ICA: NM0005.
TV Market Ranking: Below 100 (Chaves County (portions), ROSWELL); Outside TV Markets (Chaves County (portions)). Franchise award date: N.A. Franchise expiration date: N.A. Began: January 1, 1958.
Channel capacity: N.A. Channels available but not in use: N.A.
Basic Service
Subscribers: 5,640.
Programming (received off-air): KASA-TV (COZI TV, FOX) Santa Fe; KASY-TV (MNT) Albuquerque; KBIM-TV (CBS, The Country Network) Roswell; KENW (PBS) Portales; KLUZ-TV (LATV, UNV) Albuquerque; KOAT-TV (ABC, Estrella TV) Albuquerque; KOBR (NBC, This TV) Roswell; KRPV-DT (GLC) Roswell; KTEL-TV (TMO) Carlsbad; KWBQ (CW, Grit, Laff) Santa Fe; 3 FMs.
Programming (via satellite): A&E; AMC; Animal Planet; BET; Cartoon Network; CMT; CNBC; CNN; C-SPAN; C-SPAN 2; Discovery Channel; Disney Channel; E! HD; ESPN; ESPN Classic; ESPN2; EVINE Live; EWTN Global Catholic Network; Food Network; Fox News Channel; FOX Sports Arizona; Freeform; FX; HGTV; History; HLN; Lifetime; MSNBC; MTV; Nickelodeon; Pop; QVC; Spike TV; Syfy; TBS; The Weather Channel; TLC; TNT; Turner Classic Movies; TV Land; USA Network; VH1.
Fee: $90.00 installation; $24.00 monthly; $10.00 converter.
Digital Basic Service
Subscribers: N.A.
Programming (via satellite): 3ABN; Boomerang; BYUtv; Discovery Digital Networks; Disney XD; ESPN Classic; ESPNews; FamilyNet; FOX College Sports Central; FOX College Sports Pacific; Fox Sports 1; Fox Sports 2; FXM; FYI; Golf Channel; Hallmark Channel; History International; HITS (Headend In The Sky); INSP; MC; National Geographic Channel; Outdoor Channel; TNT HD; Trinity Broadcasting Network (TBN); truTV; TVG Network; Universal HD.
Digital Pay Service 1
Pay Units: 3,171.
Programming (via satellite): Cinemax (multiplexed); Flix; HBO (multiplexed); Showtime (multiplexed); Showtime HD; Starz Encore (multiplexed); Sundance TV; The Movie Channel (multiplexed); The Movie Channel HD.
Fee: $16.00 monthly (each package).
Video-On-Demand: No
Pay-Per-View
Pleasure (delivered digitally); SexSee (delivered digitally); Juicy (delivered digitally); VaVoom (delivered digitally).
Internet Service
Operational: Yes.
Subscribers: 6,646.
Broadband Service: CableONE.net.
Fee: $75.00 installation; $43.00 monthly.
Telephone Service
Digital: Operational
Subscribers: 3,155.
Fee: $39.95 monthly
Miles of Plant: 642.0 (coaxial); 130.0 (fiber optic). Homes passed: 22,158.
Vice President: Patrick A. Dolohanty. General Manager: David Gonzalez. Technical Operations Manager: Dave Ashlyn. Marketing Manager: Cindi Lucero. Office Manager: April Avitia.
Ownership: Cable ONE Inc. (MSO).

ROSWELL—Formerly served by Microwave Communication Services. No longer in operation. ICA: NM0098.

RUIDOSO—Baja Broadband, 525 Junction Rd, Madison, WI 53717. Phones: 877-422-5282; 575-257-5121. Fax: 608-830-5519. E-mail: customersupportnm@bajabb.tv. Web Site: http://www.bajabroadband.com. Also serves Alto, Capitan, Lincoln & Ruidoso Downs. ICA: NM0011.
TV Market Ranking: Outside TV Markets (Alto, Capitan, Lincoln, RUIDOSO, Ruidoso Downs). Franchise award date: N.A. Franchise expiration date: N.A. Began: January 1, 1965.
Channel capacity: N.A. Channels available but not in use: N.A.
Basic Service
Subscribers: 2,941.
Programming (received off-air): KASA-TV (COZI TV, FOX) Santa Fe; KASY-TV (MNT) Albuquerque; KBIM-TV (CBS, The Country Network) Roswell; KCHF (IND, Weather-Nation) Santa Fe; KENW (PBS) Portales; KFOX-TV (FOX, Retro TV) El Paso; KLUZ-TV (LATV, UNV) Albuquerque; KOAT-TV (ABC, Estrella TV) Albuquerque; KOBR (NBC, This TV) Roswell; KRPV-DT (GLC) Roswell; KTEL-TV (TMO) Carlsbad; KVBA-LP Alamogordo; KVIA-TV (ABC, Azteca America, CW) El Paso.
Programming (via satellite): C-SPAN; C-SPAN 2; Pop; QVC; The Weather Channel; WGN America.
Fee: $54.95 installation; $36.95 monthly.
Expanded Basic Service 1
Subscribers: N.A.
Programming (via satellite): A&E; AMC; Animal Planet; Bravo; Cartoon Network; CMT; CNBC; CNN; Comedy Central; Discovery Channel; Disney Channel; Disney XD; E! HD; ESPN; ESPN Classic; ESPN2; Food Network; Fox News Channel; Fox Sports 1; FOX Sports Arizona; Freeform; FX; Golf Channel; Great American Country; GSN; Hallmark Channel; HGTV; History; HLN; Lifetime; LMN; MSNBC; MTV; National Geographic Channel; NBCSN; Nickelodeon; Spike TV; Syfy; TBS; TLC; TNT; Travel Channel; truTV; Turner Classic Movies; TV Land; USA Network; VH1.
Digital Basic Service
Subscribers: N.A.
Programming (via satellite): BBC America; Bloomberg Television; CMT; Destination America; Discovery Kids Channel; Discovery Life Channel; DIY Network; Fox Business Network; FOX College Sports Central; FOX College Sports Pacific; FYI; History International; IFC; Investigation Discovery; LOGO; MC; MTV Classic; MTV Hits; MTV Jams; MTV2; Nick 2; Nick Jr.; Nicktoons; OWN: Oprah Winfrey Network; Science Channel; Sundance TV; TeenNick; Tr3s; VH1 Soul; WE tv.
Fee: $7.95 monthly.
Digital Expanded Basic Service
Subscribers: N.A.
Programming (via satellite): A&E HD; ESPN HD; Food Network HD; FSN HD; FX HD; Golf Channel HD; HGTV HD; History HD; National Geographic Channel HD; TBS HD; TNT HD; Versus HD.
Digital Expanded Basic Service 2
Subscribers: N.A.
Programming (via satellite): AXS TV; Universal HD.
Digital Pay Service 1
Pay Units: N.A.
Programming (via satellite): Cinemax (multiplexed); Cinemax HD; Flix; HBO (multiplexed); HBO HD; Showtime (multiplexed); Showtime HD; Starz (multiplexed); Starz Encore (multiplexed); Starz HD; The Movie Channel (multiplexed); The Movie Channel HD.
Video-On-Demand: No
Pay-Per-View
iN DEMAND (delivered digitally); Hot Choice (delivered digitally); Fresh (delivered digitally); Shorteez (delivered digitally); Playboy TV (delivered digitally); Club Jenna (delivered digitally); Spice: Xcess (delivered digitally).
Internet Service
Operational: Yes.
Broadband Service: In-house.
Fee: $49.99 installation; $34.99 monthly; $4.95 modem lease; $65.95 modem purchase.
Telephone Service
Analog: Operational
Miles of Plant: 350.0 (coaxial); None (fiber optic).
Area Vice President & General Manager: Tom Jaskiewicz. Vice President, Corporate Finance: Carl Shapiro. Assistant Treasurer: Noel Hutton. Technical Operations Manager: Harold Vilas. Office Manager: Barbara Mick.
Ownership: TDS Telecom (MSO).

SAN ANTONIO—Formerly served by Sun Valley Cable Inc. No longer in operation. ICA: NM0095.

SAN JON—Formerly served by Elk River TV Cable Co. No longer in operation. ICA: NM0103.

SANTA BARBARA—Formerly served by JRC Telecommunications. No longer in operation. ICA: NM0072.

SANTA CLARA INDIAN RESERVATION—Formerly served by Baja Broadband. Now served by Satview Broadband, ESPANOLA, NM [NM0014]. ICA: NM0087.

Cable Systems—New Mexico

SANTA FE—Comcast Cable. Now served by ALBUQUERQUE, NM [NM0001]. ICA: NM0003.

SANTA FE—Formerly served by Santa Fe Wireless Cable TV. No longer in operation. ICA: NM0099.

SANTA ROSA—Reach Broadband, PO Box 507, Arp, TX 75750. Phones: 903-859-3789; 800-687-1258. Web Site: http://www.reachbroadband.net. ICA: NM0030.
TV Market Ranking: Outside TV Markets (SANTA ROSA). Franchise award date: March 11, 1980. Franchise expiration date: N.A. Began: January 1, 1981.
Channel capacity: N.A. Channels available but not in use: N.A.
Basic Service
Subscribers: 140.
Programming (received off-air): KASA-TV (COZI TV, FOX) Santa Fe; KLUZ-TV (LATV, UNV) Albuquerque; KNME-TV (PBS) Albuquerque; KOAT-TV (ABC, Estrella TV) Albuquerque; KOB (NBC, This TV) Albuquerque; KRPV-DT (GLC) Roswell; KRQE (CBS) Albuquerque; KTEL-TV (TMO) Carlsbad.
Programming (via satellite): A&E; Animal Planet; Cartoon Network; CNN; C-SPAN; Discovery Channel; Disney Channel; ESPN; ESPN2; EWTN Global Catholic Network; Fox News Channel; FOX Sports Networks; Freeform; FX; Great American Country; History; HLN; Lifetime; National Geographic Channel; Nickelodeon; QVC; Root Sports Rocky Mountain; Spike TV; TBS; The Weather Channel; TLC; TNT; Turner Classic Movies; TV Land; Univision; USA Network; VH1.
Fee: $49.95 installation; $18.81 monthly.
Digital Basic Service
Subscribers: N.A.
Programming (via satellite): BBC America; Bloomberg Television; Cloo; Destination America; Discovery Kids Channel; Disney XD; DMX Music; ESPN Classic; ESPN2; ESPNews; EVINE Live; FOX College Sports Central; FOX College Sports Pacific; Fox Sports 1; Fuse; FYI; Golf Channel; GSN; HGTV; History International; IFC; Investigation Discovery; NBCSN; Outdoor Channel; OWN: Oprah Winfrey Network; Science Channel; Sundance TV; WE tv.
Pay Service 1
Pay Units: N.A.
Programming (via satellite): HBO; Showtime; The Movie Channel.
Fee: $5.95 monthly (TMC), $9.95 monthly (Showtime), $10.95 monthly (HBO).
Digital Pay Service 1
Pay Units: N.A.
Programming (via satellite): Cinemax (multiplexed); Flix; HBO (multiplexed); Showtime (multiplexed); Starz (multiplexed); Starz Encore (multiplexed); The Movie Channel (multiplexed).
Video-On-Demand: No
Pay-Per-View
iN DEMAND (delivered digitally); Playboy TV (delivered digitally).
Internet Service
Operational: No.
Telephone Service
None
Miles of Plant: 17.0 (coaxial); None (fiber optic). Homes passed: 1,130.
Controller: Jeffrey Lowe.
Ownership: RB3 LLC (MSO).

SHIPROCK—Formerly served by Frontier Communications. No longer in operation. ICA: NM0101.

SILVER CITY—Comcast Cable. Now served by ALBUQUERQUE, NM [NM0001]. ICA: NM0017.

SOCORRO—Baja Broadband, 525 Junction Rd, Madison, WI 53717. Phone: 505-835-2424. Web Site: http://www.bajabroadband.com. ICA: NM0023.
TV Market Ranking: Outside TV Markets (SOCORRO). Franchise award date: N.A. Franchise expiration date: N.A. Began: January 1, 1977.
Channel capacity: N.A. Channels available but not in use: N.A.
Basic Service
Subscribers: 398.
Programming (received off-air): KASA-TV (COZI TV, FOX) Santa Fe; KNAT-TV (TBN) Albuquerque; KNME-TV (PBS) Albuquerque; KOAT-TV (ABC, Estrella TV) Albuquerque; KOB (NBC, This TV) Albuquerque; KRQE (CBS) Albuquerque.
Programming (via satellite): A&E; AMC; Animal Planet; Cartoon Network; CNN; Comedy Central; C-SPAN; Discovery Channel; Disney Channel; E! HD; ESPN; ESPN2; EWTN Global Catholic Network; FOX Sports Southwest; Freeform; Golf Channel; Great American Country; Hallmark Channel; HGTV; History; MSNBC; MTV; OWN: Oprah Winfrey Network; QVC; Spike TV; Syfy; TBS; The Weather Channel; TNT; TV Land; Univision; USA Network; WGN America.
Fee: $50.00 installation; $46.49 monthly.
Digital Basic Service
Subscribers: N.A. Included in Grants.
Programming (via satellite): BBC America; C-SPAN 3; Discovery Digital Networks; Disney XD; DMX Music; ESPNews; Flix; Nick 2; Nick Jr.; Sundance TV; TeenNick; WAM! America's Kidz Network.
Fee: $12.95 monthly.
Pay Service 1
Pay Units: N.A.
Programming (via satellite): Cinemax; HBO (multiplexed); Showtime.
Fee: $10.00 installation; $8.00 monthly (Cinemax), $9.95 monthly (HBO, Showtime or TMC).
Digital Pay Service 1
Pay Units: N.A.
Programming (via satellite): Cinemax (multiplexed); HBO (multiplexed); Showtime (multiplexed); Starz (multiplexed); The Movie Channel (multiplexed).
Fee: $15.00 monthly (each).
Video-On-Demand: No
Pay-Per-View
iN DEMAND (delivered digitally); Playboy TV (delivered digitally); Fresh (delivered digitally); Shorteez (delivered digitally); Pleasure (delivered digitally).
Internet Service
Operational: Yes.
Telephone Service
None
Miles of Plant: 84.0 (coaxial); None (fiber optic). Homes passed: 4,518.
President & Chief Executive Officer: David Wittwer. Vice President, Cable Operations: Mark Barber. Assistant Treasurer: Noel Hutton.
Ownership: TDS Telecom (MSO).

SPRINGER—Comcast Cable, 2530 Hot Springs Blvd, Las Vegas, NM 87701-3739. Phone: 505-425-7531. Fax: 505-445-6822. Web Site: http://www.comcast.com. ICA: NM0039.
TV Market Ranking: Outside TV Markets (SPRINGER). Franchise award date: N.A. Franchise expiration date: N.A. Began: May 1, 1976.
Channel capacity: N.A. Channels available but not in use: N.A.
Basic Service
Subscribers: 72.
Programming (received off-air): KASA-TV (COZI TV, FOX) Santa Fe; 1 FM.
Programming (via satellite): Animal Planet; Cartoon Network; CMT; CNBC; CNN; Discovery Channel; Disney Channel; E! HD; ESPN; ESPN2; Freeform; HGTV; Lifetime; MTV; Nickelodeon; QVC; Spike TV; TBS; The Weather Channel; TLC; TNT; Univision Studios; USA Network; VH1.
Programming (via translator): KNME-TV (PBS) Albuquerque; KOAT-TV (ABC, Estrella TV) Albuquerque; KOB (NBC, This TV) Albuquerque; KRQE (CBS) Albuquerque.
Fee: $42.00 installation; $51.74 monthly.
Pay Service 1
Pay Units: N.A.
Programming (via satellite): HBO; Starz Encore.
Video-On-Demand: No
Internet Service
Operational: Yes.
Telephone Service
None
Homes passed: 501.
Vice President & General Manager: Chris Dunkeson. Operations Manager: Ricky Armijo. Chief Technician: Henry Garcia.
Ownership: Comcast Cable Communications Inc. (MSO).

TAOS—Comcast Cable, 1546 Paseo Del Pueblo Sur, PO Box 1854, Taos, NM 87571-1854. Phones: 505-758-3569; 505-758-3207; 545-445-5553. Fax: 505-758-4441. Web Site: http://www.comcast.com. Also serves El Prado, Ranchos de Taos & Taos County (portions). ICA: NM0090.
TV Market Ranking: Below 100 (Taos County (portions)); Outside TV Markets (El Prado, Ranchos de Taos, TAOS, Taos County (portions)). Franchise award date: January 1, 1972. Franchise expiration date: N.A. Began: August 1, 1972.
Channel capacity: N.A. Channels available but not in use: N.A.
Basic Service
Subscribers: 856.
Programming (received off-air): KASA-TV (COZI TV, FOX) Santa Fe; KASY-TV (MNT) Albuquerque; KCHF (IND, WeatherNation) Santa Fe; KLUZ-TV (LATV, UNV) Albuquerque; KNME-TV (PBS) Albuquerque; KOAT-TV (ABC, Estrella TV) Albuquerque; KOB (NBC, This TV) Albuquerque; KRPV-DT (GLC) Roswell; KRQE (CBS) Albuquerque; KTEL-TV (TMO) Carlsbad; KWBQ (CW, Grit, Laff) Santa Fe; 13 FMs.
Programming (via satellite): AMC; Cartoon Network; CMT; C-SPAN; C-SPAN 2; Disney Channel; EWTN Global Catholic Network; Fox News Channel; FOX Sports Southwest; Freeform; FX; Hallmark Channel; History; HLN; Lifetime; MTV; Nickelodeon; QVC; Spike TV; Sundance TV; The Weather Channel; TLC; TV Land; WGN America.
Fee: $42.00 installation; $46.44 monthly; $.62 converter.
Expanded Basic Service 1
Subscribers: N.A.
Programming (via satellite): A&E; Animal Planet; Bravo; CNBC; CNN; Comedy Central; Discovery Channel; E! HD; ESPN; ESPN2; Food Network; Fox Sports 1; Golf Channel; HGTV; OWN: Oprah Winfrey Network; TBS; TNT; Travel Channel; truTV; USA Network.
Fee: $14.43 monthly.
Digital Basic Service
Subscribers: N.A.
Programming (via satellite): BBC America; CBS Sports Network; CMT; C-SPAN 3; Discovery Digital Networks; Disney XD; ESPNews; Flix; FYI; History International; HITS (Headend In The Sky); LMN; LOGO; MC; MoviePlex; Nat Geo WILD; National Geographic Channel; NFL Network; Nick 2; Nick Jr.; Nicktoons; Sprout; Starz Encore (multiplexed); Syfy; TeenNick; TV One.
Fee: $11.95 monthly.
Digital Pay Service 1
Pay Units: N.A.
Programming (via satellite): Cinemax (multiplexed); HBO (multiplexed); Showtime (multiplexed); Starz (multiplexed).
Fee: $12.87 monthly (each).
Video-On-Demand: No
Pay-Per-View
iN DEMAND; iN DEMAND (delivered digitally); Playboy TV (delivered digitally); Hot Choice (delivered digitally).
Internet Service
Operational: Yes.
Telephone Service
None
Miles of Plant: 90.0 (coaxial); 25.0 (fiber optic).
Vice President & General Manager: Chris Dunkeson. Operations Manager: David Quintana.
Ownership: Comcast Cable Communications Inc. (MSO).

TATUM—Formerly served by Rapid Cable. No longer in operation. ICA: NM0057.

THOREAU—Formerly served by Comcast Cable. No longer in operation. ICA: NM0060.

TOHATCHI—Formerly served by Frontier Communications. No longer in operation. ICA: NM0066.

TRUTH OR CONSEQUENCES—Baja Broadband, 525 Junction Rd, Madison, WI 53717. Phones: 877-422-5282; 575-894-6636. Fax: 608-830-5519. E-mail: customersupportnm@bajabb.tv. Web Site: http://www.bajabroadband.com. Also serves Elephant Butte, Sierra County (unincorporated areas) & Williamsburg. ICA: NM0022.
TV Market Ranking: Below 100 (Sierra County (unincorporated areas) (portions)); Outside TV Markets (Elephant Butte, Sierra County (unincorporated areas) (portions),

New Mexico—Cable Systems

TRUTH OR CONSEQUENCES, Williamsburg). Franchise award date: July 1, 1974. Franchise expiration date: N.A. Began: July 1, 1974.
Channel capacity: N.A. Channels available but not in use: N.A.

Basic Service
Subscribers: 389.
Programming (via microwave): KASA-TV (COZI TV, FOX) Santa Fe; KASY-TV (MNT) Albuquerque; KFOX-TV (FOX, Retro TV) El Paso; KLUZ-TV (LATV, UNV) Albuquerque; KNME-TV (PBS) Albuquerque; KOAT-TV (ABC, Estrella TV) Albuquerque; KOB (NBC, This TV) Albuquerque; KRPV-DT (GLC) Roswell; KRQE (CBS) Albuquerque; KRWG-TV (PBS) Las Cruces; KTEL-TV (TMO) Carlsbad.
Programming (via satellite): Pop; QVC; TBS; The Weather Channel; Trinity Broadcasting Network (TBN); WGN America.
Fee: $29.95 installation; $36.95 monthly.

Expanded Basic Service 1
Subscribers: N.A.
Programming (via satellite): A&E; AMC; Animal Planet; Cartoon Network; CMT; CNBC; CNN; Comedy Central; Discovery Channel; Disney Channel; DIY Network; E! HD; ESPN; ESPN2; Food Network; Fox News Channel; Freeform; FX; Great American Country; GSN; Hallmark Channel; History; HLN; Lifetime; MSNBC; MTV; Nickelodeon; Spike TV; Syfy; TLC; TNT; Travel Channel; truTV; TV Land; USA Network; VH1.
Fee: $27.95 monthly.

Digital Basic Service
Subscribers: N.A.
Programming (via satellite): BBC America; Bloomberg Television; Bravo; CMT; Destination America; Discovery Kids Channel; Discovery Life Channel; Disney XD; ESPN Classic; Fox Sports 1; Fuse; FXM; FYI; Golf Channel; HGTV; History International; IFC; Investigation Discovery; LMN; MC; MTV Classic; MTV Hits; MTV2; NBCSN; Nick Jr.; Outdoor Channel; OWN: Oprah Winfrey Network; Science Channel; TeenNick; Turner Classic Movies; VH1 Soul; WE tv.
Fee: $9.95 monthly.

Digital Expanded Basic Service
Subscribers: N.A.
Programming (via satellite): A&E HD; ESPN HD; Food Network HD; HGTV HD; History HD; TBS HD; TNT HD.

Digital Expanded Basic Service 2
Subscribers: N.A.
Programming (via satellite): AXS TV; Universal HD.

Digital Pay Service 1
Pay Units: N.A.
Programming (via satellite): Cinemax (multiplexed); Cinemax HD; Flix; HBO (multiplexed); HBO HD; Showtime (multiplexed); Showtime HD; Starz (multiplexed); Starz Encore (multiplexed); Starz HD; The Movie Channel (multiplexed); The Movie Channel HD.

Video-On-Demand: No

Pay-Per-View
iN DEMAND (delivered digitally); Hot Choice (delivered digitally); Playboy TV (delivered digitally); Fresh (delivered digitally); Spice: Xcess (delivered digitally); SexSee (delivered digitally); Juicy (delivered digitally); XTSY (delivered digitally).

Internet Service
Operational: Yes. Began: August 1, 2003.
Subscribers: 588.
Broadband Service: In-house.
Fee: $49.99 installation; $34.99 monthly; $4.95 modem lease; $69.95 modem purchase.

Telephone Service
Analog: Operational
Subscribers: 201.
Miles of Plant: 49.0 (coaxial); None (fiber optic). Homes passed: 3,397.
Vice President, Corporate Finance: Carl Shapiro. Assistant Treasurer: Noel Hutton. General Manager: Tom Jaskiewicz. Technical Operations Manager: Harold Vilas. Office Manager: Barbara Mick.
Ownership: TDS Telecom (MSO).

TUCUMCARI—Comcast Cable, 1808 South 1st St, Tucumcari, NM 88401-3506. Phones: 505-461-4410; 505-461-3160. Fax: 505-461-0116. Web Site: http://www.comcast.com. Also serves Quay County (portions). ICA: NM0021.
TV Market Ranking: Below 100 (Quay County (portions)); Outside TV Markets (TUCUMCARI, Quay County (portions)). Franchise award date: January 1, 1956. Franchise expiration date: N.A. Began: October 1, 1956.
Channel capacity: 37 (not 2-way capable). Channels available but not in use: N.A.

Basic Service
Subscribers: 355.
Programming (received off-air): KASA-TV (COZI TV, FOX) Santa Fe; KENW (PBS) Portales; KRQE (CBS) Albuquerque.
Programming (via satellite): A&E; AMC; Cartoon Network; CMT; CNBC; CNN; C-SPAN; CW PLUS; Discovery Channel; Disney Channel; E! HD; ESPN; EWTN Global Catholic Network; FOX Sports Southwest; Freeform; Hallmark Channel; History; HLN; Lifetime; MSNBC; MTV; NBCSN; Nickelodeon; QVC; Spike TV; Syfy; TBS; The Weather Channel; TLC; TNT; Trinity Broadcasting Network (TBN); Univision; Univision Studios; USA Network; VH1; WGN America.
Programming (via translator): KAMR-TV (IND, NBC) Amarillo; KCIT (FOX, This TV) Amarillo; KFDA-TV (CBS, TMO) Amarillo; KOAT-TV (ABC, Estrella TV) Albuquerque; KOB (NBC, This TV) Albuquerque; KVII-TV (ABC, CW) Amarillo.
Fee: $42.00 installation; $49.17 monthly.

Pay Service 1
Pay Units: N.A.
Programming (via satellite): Cinemax; HBO.
Fee: $19.95 installation; $9.00 monthly (Cinemax), $12.95 monthly (HBO).

Video-On-Demand: No

Internet Service
Operational: Yes.

Telephone Service
None
Miles of Plant: 55.0 (coaxial); None (fiber optic). Homes passed: 3,200.
Area Vice President: John Christopher. General Manager: Dennis Jones. Chief Technician: Spencer DeBord. Office Manager: Frederick Dominguez.
Ownership: Comcast Cable Communications Inc. (MSO).

TWIN FORKS—PVT Cable Services. Now served by ARTESIA, NM [NM0016]. ICA: NM0056.

VAUGHN—Formerly served by Cebridge Connections. No longer in operation. ICA: NM0062.

WAGON MOUND—Formerly served by Rocky Mountain Cable. No longer in operation. ICA: NM0071.

YAH-TA-HEY—Formerly served by Frontier Communications. No longer in operation. ICA: NM0092.

ZUNI—Formerly served by Frontier Communications. No longer in operation. ICA: NM0093.

Index to Sections
Television & Cable Factbook No. 85

TV STATIONS VOLUME

Section A

Call Letters of U.S. Television Stations A-9

Ownership of U.S. Commercial Television Stations A-1560

Television Market Rankings (Nielsen) A-1

Television Stations, Commercial A-20

Television Stations, Public/Educational. A-1489

Section B

Low Power Television/Translator Stations B-1

Low Power Television/Translator Station Ownership B-189

Section C – Charts

Nielsen Geographic Regions Summary. C-9

Nielsen TV Household Estimates ranked by DMA C-10

Nielsen TV Households by States and Counties C-12

Parent/Satellite Television Stations C-3

Total Television Stations On Air. C-1

TV Station Affiliations by Market C-5

CABLE SYSTEMS VOLUME

Section D

Call Letters of U.S. Television Stations D-1

Cable Systems. D-14

Cable Community Index . . . . (Back of Cable Volume 2)

Cable Owners. D-887

Section E

Brokerage & Financing Services E-133

Management & Technical Consulting Services E-139

Pay TV & Satellite Services E-1

Program Sources & Services E-105

Section F – Charts

Abbreviations F-8

Cable Penetration by State F-7

Estimated Growth of the Cable Industry F-1

Glossary of Cable Terms F-13

Largest U.S. Cable Systems F-2

Nielsen Cable TV Household Estimates Alphabetical by DMA F-4

Nielsen Cable TV Household Estimates by State F-6

Cable Systems State Index

Alabama	D-15	Nevada	D-500
Alaska	D-37	New Hampshire	D-506
Arizona	D-44	New Jersey	D-510
Arkansas	D-54	New Mexico	D-519
California	D-82	New York	D-529
Colorado	D-111	North Carolina	D-550
Connecticut	D-127	North Dakota	D-568
Delaware	D-132	Ohio	D-577
District of Columbia	D-133	Oklahoma	D-607
Florida	D-134	Oregon	D-637
Georgia	D-151	Pennsylvania	D-648
Hawaii	D-177	Rhode Island	D-683
Idaho	D-179	South Carolina	D-684
Illinois	D-186	South Dakota	D-694
Indiana	D-225	Tennessee	D-705
Iowa	D-240	Texas	D-718
Kansas	D-278	Utah	D-790
Kentucky	D-306	Vermont	D-797
Louisiana	D-333	Virginia	D-801
Maine	D-353	Washington	D-814
Maryland	D-359	West Virginia	D-833
Massachusetts	D-365	Wisconsin	D-848
Michigan	D-370	Wyoming	D-871
Minnesota	D-391	Other U.S. Territories and Possessions	D-881
Mississippi	D-426		
Missouri	D-440	Cable Owners	D-887
Montana	D-464	Cable Community Index	(end of Cable Volume 2)
Nebraska	D-479		

TELEVISION & CABLE FACTBOOK
VOLUME 85

Albert Warren
Editor & Publisher 1961-2006

Paul L. Warren, Chairman & Publisher
Daniel Y. Warren, President & Editor

EDITORIAL & BUSINESS HEADQUARTERS
2115 Ward Court, N.W., Washington, DC 20037
Phones: 202-872-9200; 800-771-9202
Fax: 202-318-8350
E-mail: factbook-info@warren-news.com
Web site: http://www.warren-news.com

Editorial-Factbook/Directories
Michael C. Taliaferro, Managing Editor & Assistant Publisher—Directories
Kari M. Osel, Senior Editor & Editorial Supvr.
Colleen M. Crosby, Sr. Editor & Editorial Supvr.
Robert T. Dwyer, Senior Research Editor

Advertising – Factbook/Directories
Richard Nordin, Director of Advertising
Phone: 703-819-7976
Fax: 202-478-5135

Editorial-News
Jonathan Make, Executive Editor
Paul Gluckman, Executive Senior Editor
Howard Buskirk, Executive Senior Editor
Rebecca Day, Senior Editor
David Kaut, Senior Editor
Matt Daneman, Senior Editor
Dibya Sarkar, Senior Editor
Monty Tayloe, Associate Editor
John Hendel, Associate Editor
Adam Bender, Associate Editor
Jimm Phillips, Assistant Editor
R. Michael Feazel, Consulting Editor

Business
Brig Easley, Executive Vice President & Controller
Sheran Fernando, Chief Operating Officer
Annette Munroe, Director, Marketing & Circulation
Katrina McCray, Senior Sales & Marketing Support Specialist
Loraine Taylor, Sales & Marketing Support Assistant

Information Systems
Deborah Jacobs, Information Systems Manager
Gregory E. Jones, Database/Network Manager

Sales
William R. Benton, Sales Director
Agnes Mannarelli, National Accounts Manager
Jim Sharp, Account Manager
Bruce Ryan, Account Manager
Matt Long, Account Manager

Publications & Services of Warren Communications News

TELEVISION & CABLE FACTBOOK: ONLINE

CABLE & STATION COVERAGE ATLAS
Published Annually

COMMUNICATIONS DAILY

CONSUMER ELECTRONICS DAILY

INTERNATIONAL TRADE TODAY

WARREN'S WASHINGTON INTERNET DAILY

Copyright © 2017 by Warren Communications News.

All Rights Reserved
ISBN: 978-1-57696-010-3
ISSN: 0732-8648

It is against the law to make a copy of this publication or any portion of its content without our explicit permission. Federal copyright law (17 USC 504) makes it illegal, punishable with fines up to $100,000 per violation plus attorney's fees. It is also illegal to input any of this publication into any computer or data retrieval system without our permission. Warren Communications News frequently has taken action against individuals and firms that violated our copyright, or other rights, and we will continue to do so. We request that subscribers advise their staffs of the law and the financial penalties that will result from the copying or improper use of this publication. We welcome inquiries about additional subscriptions and we are prepared to grant authorization for certain occasional reproduction of portions of this publication, but only upon formal request to the publisher. For additional subscriptions, please contact our Sales Dept. at 800-771-9202.

Index to Sections
Television & Cable Factbook No. 85

TV STATIONS VOLUME

Section A

Call Letters of U.S. Television Stations A-9

Ownership of U.S. Commercial Television Stations A-1560

Television Market Rankings (Nielsen) A-1

Television Stations, Commercial A-20

Television Stations, Public/Educational A-1489

Section B

Low Power Television/Translator Stations B-1

Low Power Television/Translator Station Ownership B-189

Section C – Charts

Nielsen Geographic Regions Summary C-9

Nielsen TV Household Estimates ranked by DMA C-10

Nielsen TV Households by States and Counties C-12

Parent/Satellite Television Stations C-3

Total Television Stations On Air C-1

TV Station Affiliations by Market C-5

CABLE SYSTEMS VOLUME

Section D

Call Letters of U.S. Television Stations D-1

Cable Systems D-14

Cable Community Index . . . . (Back of Cable Volume 2)

Cable Owners D-887

Section E

Brokerage & Financing Services E-133

Management & Technical Consulting Services E-139

Pay TV & Satellite Services E-1

Program Sources & Services E-105

Section F – Charts

Abbreviations F-8

Cable Penetration by State F-7

Estimated Growth of the Cable Industry F-1

Glossary of Cable Terms F-13

Largest U.S. Cable Systems F-2

Nielsen Cable TV Household Estimates Alphabetical by DMA F-4

Nielsen Cable TV Household Estimates by State F-6

Index to Contents
Television & Cable Factbook No. 85

A

@Radical Media Inc.	E-105
@Max	E-5
@Max (See also Max Latino)	E-57
1-World LLC	E-105
3ABN	E-5
3ABN Latino (See also 3ABN)	E-5
3 Ball Entertainment	E-105
3DGO!	E-5
4SD	E-5
4SD (See also Channel 4 San Diego)	E-19
5 News	E-5
5 Star Max	E-5
5 Star Max (See also Cinemax)	E-20
6 News	E-6
10 News 2	E-6
10 News Channel	E-6
24/7 News Channel	E-6
52MX	E-6
54 Broadcasting Inc.	A-1560
62nd Street Productions	E-105
89 Edit	E-105
101 Network	E-6
101 Network (See also Audience Network)	E-11
A&E	E-6
Aapka Colors	E-6
AARP TV	E-105
AAT Television	E-6
Abbreviations	1
ABC Family Channel	E-6
ABC Family Channel (See also Freeform)	E-40
ABC News	E-105
ABC News/Univision Network	E-6
ABC News/Univision Network (See also Fusion)	E-41
ABC Studios	E-105
ABI Research	E-139
ABP Ananda	E-6
ABP Ananda (See also ABP News)	E-6
ABP News	E-6
David Abraham & Co. LLC	E-133
ACC Digital Network	E-6
Accenthealth	E-105
Accent Media	E-105
ACC Network	E-7
AccuWeather Inc.	E-105
AccuWeather Network	E-7
Action Max	E-7
Action Max (See also Cinemax)	E-20
ActiveVideo	E-139
Adell Broadcasting Corp.	A-1560
Admiralty Properties LLC	A-1560
Adult Swim	E-7
Adventist Television Network	E-7
Adventist Television Network (See also Hope Channel)	E-48
Aerco Broadcasting Corp.	A-1560
The Africa Channel	E-7
African Box Office	E-7
African Box Office (See also Afrotainment Plus)	E-7
African TV Network (ATVN)	E-7
Afrique Music Television	E-7
Afrotainment Music	E-7
Afrotainment Plus	E-7
Afrotainment Music (See also Afrotainment Plus)	E-7
Agency for Instructional Technology	E-105
Aircraft Music Library	E-105
The Aker Partners Inc.	E-139
Alden Films/Films Of The Nations	E-105
Aliento Vision	E-7
Al Karma TV	E-7
Allegro Productions Inc.	E-106
The Allen Broadcasting Corp.	A-1560
Alliance for Christian Media	E-106
Allied Vaughn	E-106
Allison Payment Systems LLC	E-139
All Mobile Video	E-106
Almavision	E-7
Alpha Broadcasting Corp.	A-1560
Alta Communications	E-133
Alterna'TV	E-106
Altitude Sports & Entertainment	E-7
Amazon Inc.	E-106
AmberWatch TV	E-8
AMC	E-8
Amdocs, Broadband Cable & Satellite Division	E-139
America One Television	E-8
America One Television (See also Youtoo America)	E-103
America teve	E-8
America CV Network LLC	E-106
America-CV Station Group Inc.	A-1560
American Christian Television Services Inc.	A-1560
American Desi	E-8
American ED TV	E-8
American European Consulting Co. Inc.	E-139
American Heroes Channel	E-8
American Heroes Channel (See also Discovery Channel)	E-27
American ICN TV Network	E-8
American Jewish Committee	E-106
AmericanLife TV Network	E-8
AmericanLife TV Network (See also Youtoo America)	E-103
American Movie Classics	E-9
American Movie Classics (See also AMC)	E-8
American Public Television (APTV)	E-106
American Religious Town Hall Meeting Inc.	E-106
American Sports Network	E-9
America's Auction Network	E-9
AMGTV	E-9
AMIT	E-106
Amrita TV	E-9
ANA Television Network	E-9
Anchor Pacific Corp.	E-139
Angel One	E-9
Angel Two	E-9
Angel Two (See also Angel One)	E-9

2017 Edition   iii

Index to Contents

CABLE & TV STATION COVERAGE
Atlas 2017
The perfect companion to the Television & Cable Factbook
To order call 800-771-9202 or visit www.warren-news.com

Anhui TV International	E-9
Animal Planet	E-9
Animal Planet (See also Discovery Channel)	E-27
Animal Planet HD	E-9
Animal Planet HD (See also Animal Planet)	E-9
Anime Network	E-9
Annenberg Channel	E-106
Another Country	E-106
Antena 3 Internacional	E-9
Antenna Satellite TV	E-9
Antenna TV	E-9
APA International Film Distributors Inc.	E-106
AP ENPS	E-106
Aperio Communications LLC	A-1560
Aplauso TV	E-10
AP Radio Network (APRN)	E-106
AP Television News	E-107
Aptinet Inc.	E-107
Arabic Channel	E-10
Arabic Channel (See also TAC TV)	E-84
Archdiocese of Baltimore	E-107
Neal Ardman	A-1560
ARENAS	E-107
Ariana Afghanistan TV	E-10
Ariana TV	E-10
Arirang DTV	E-10
Arizona News Channel	E-10
ARCTEK Satellite Productions	E-107
Armenian Film Foundation	E-107
Armenian Public Channel	E-10
Armenian Russian Television Network (ARTN)	E-10
Army & Air Force Hometown News Service	E-107
Army & Air Force Hometown News Service (See also Joint Hometown News Service)	E-118
Philip A Arno	A-1560
ART America	E-10
Artbeats Software Inc.	E-107
Ascent Media Group	E-107, E-139
ASC-TV	E-10
Asianet	E-10
Asianet Movies	E-10
Asianet Movies (See also Asianet)	E-10
Asianet News	E-10
Asianet News (See also Asianet)	E-10
Asianet Plus	E-10
Asianet Plus (See also Asianet)	E-10
Asia Travel TV	E-10
Asia TV USA Ltd.	E-107
Asociacion Evangelistica Cristo Viene Inc.	A-1560
Aspire	E-10
Associated Christian Television System Inc.	A-1560
Associated Press	E-107
Associated Television International	E-107
AssyriaSat	E-11
Atlanta Interfaith Broadcasters	E-11
ATLX (Athletics Training Lifestyle)	E-11
Atres Series	E-11
ATV Broadcast LLC	E-139
ATV Home Channel (America)	E-11
Audience Network	E-11
Audience Research & Development LLC	E-139
AUS Consultants	E-133
The Austin Co.	E-139
The Auto Channel	E-11
Automotive.TV	E-11
Aviva TV	E-11
AWE	E-11
Awesomeness Films	E-107
AwesomenessTV	E-107
AXA Equitable	E-133
AXS TV	E-11
AYM Sports	E-11
AZ Clic	E-11
AZCAR USA Inc.	E-139
AZ Corazon	E-11
Azteca	E-12
AZ TV	E-12

B

B4U Movies	E-13
B4U Music	E-13
B4U Music (See B4U Movies)	E-13
BabyFirst Americas	E-12
BabyFirstTV	E-12
Baby TV	E-12
Backchannelmedia Inc.	E-139
Bahakel Communications Ltd.	A-1560
Bruce R Baker	A-1561
Baker Scott & Co.	E-140
Balboa Capital	E-133
Bandamax	E-12
Bandamax (See also Univision)	E-96
Band Internacional	E-12
Bang U	E-12
Bank of America	E-133
BNY Mellon, Media & Technology Division	E-133
Barbary Post	E-107
Barca TV	E-12
Barclays Capital	E-133
Barger Broadcast Services Inc.	E-133
Barker Capital LLC	E-133
Baron Services Inc.	E-107
Batjac Productions Inc.	E-107
Bay News 9	E-12
Bay News 9 en Espanol	E-12
Bay News 9 en Espanol (See also InfoMas)	E-50
Bayou City Broadcasting Evansville Inc.	A-1561
BBC America	E-12
BBC America On Demand	E-12
BBC America On Demand (See also BBC America)	E-12
BBC Arabic	E-13
BBC Arabic (See also BBC World News)	E-13
BBC World News	E-13
BBC Worldwide Ltd.	E-107
BeachTV	E-13
Beach TV Properties Inc.	A-1561
Beamly	E-108
Beast	E-108
Beauty & Fashion Channel	E-13
Beijing TV	E-13
beIN SPORT	E-13
beIN SPORT En Espanol	E-13
beIN SPORT En Espanol (See also BeIN Sport)	E-13
Dave Bell Associates Inc.	E-108

iv TV & Cable Factbook No. 85

Index to Contents

Bellum Entertainment	E-108
Thomas Benson Jr.	A-1561
BET	E-13
BET Gospel	E-13
BET Gospel (See also BET)	E-13
BET Hip Hop	E-13
BET Hip Hop (See also BET)	E-13
BET J	E-13
BET J (See also Centric)	E-19
BET Play	E-13
BET Play (See also BET)	E-13
BET Soul	E-13
BET Soul (See also BET)	E-13
Better Life Media	E-108
Better Life Television Inc.	A-1561
BIA Capital Strategies LLC	E-133
BIA Digital Partnership LP	E-133
The BIA Kelsey Group	E-133, E-140
Big Shoulders Digital Video Productions	E-108
Big Sky Edit	E-108
Big Ten Network	E-13
Big Ten Network (See also BTN)	E-16
Bikini Edit	E-108
BIO	E-13
BIO (See also FYI)	E-42
BitCentral	E-140
BiteSizeTV	E-108
Biz TV	E-13
Blackburn & Co. Inc.	E-134
Blackhawk Broadcasting LLC	A-1561
Black Heritage Network	E-14
Blackmagic Design USA	E-140
Black Network Television	E-14
Black Television News Channel	E-14
Blast Digital	E-108
Blockbuster On Demand	E-14
Block Communications Inc.	A-1561
Bloomberg Television	E-14
BlueHighways TV	E-14
Blue Ocean Network	E-14
BlueRock	E-108
BMO Capital Markets, Media & Communications Group	E-134
Boerner Communications Inc.	E-140
Boise Telecasters LP	A-1561
Bolivia TV	E-14
Bollywood Hits On Demand	E-14
Bond & Pecaro Inc.	E-134, E-140
Bonded Services	E-108
Bonjour America TV	E-14
Bonneville International	E-108
Bonneville International Corp.	A-1561
Bonten Media Group LLC	A-1561
Book TV	E-14
Boomerang	E-14
Boosey & Hawkes Music Publishers Ltd.	E-108
Booz, Allen & Hamilton Inc.	E-140
Bortz Media & Sports Group	E-140
Bosco Productions	E-108
BosTel	E-15
Boston Catholic Television	E-15
Boston Catholic Television (See also CatholicTV)	E-18
Boston Kids & Family	E-15
Bounce TV	E-15
Bowman Valuation Services LLC	E-134
Box	E-15
BoxTV: The Boxing Channel	E-15
Frank Boyle & Co. LLC	E-134

Access the most current data instantly

FREE TRIAL @ ADVANCED TVFactbook
TELCO/IPTV • CABLE TV • TV STATIONS
www.warren-news.com/factbook.htm

Bravo	E-15
Brazzers TV	E-15
Brean Murray, Carret & Co. LLC	E-134
Breathe Editing Inc.	E-108
Bridges TV	E-15
Bright House Sports Network	E-15
Bright House Travel Weather Now	E-16
Bright House Travel Weather Now (See also Bay News 9)	E-12
Stephen C Brissette	A-1561
Bristlecone Broadcasting LLC	A-1562
Broadcasting Licenses LP	A-1562
Broadcast Media Group Inc.	E-108
Broadcast Music Inc. (BMI)	E-108
Broadcast Services Inc.	E-140
Broadcast Trust	A-1562
Broad Green Pictures	E-109
BroadView Software Inc.	E-140
Broadway Television Network	E-109
Broadway Video Entertainment	E-109
Brokerage & Financing Services	E-133
Stuart N. Brotman Communications	E-140
Eugene J. Brown	A-1562
BTN	E-16
BTN2Go	E-16
BTN2Go (See also BTN)	E-16
Buckalew Media Inc	A-1562
BuenaVision TV	E-16
Bug Editorial Inc.	E-109
Bulkley Capital LP	E-134
Bunim-Murray Productions	E-109
Burrud Productions Inc.	E-109
Buzzco Associates Inc.	E-109
BuzzFeed Motion Pictures	E-109
BUZZR TV	E-16
Buzztime	E-16
Buzztime (See also NTN Buzztime)	E-67
BV Investment Partners LLC	E-134
Byrne Acquisition Group LLC	A-1562
BYUtv	E-16

C

C7 Jalisco	E-16
C13 de Chile	E-26
C13 de Chile (See also Canal 13 de Chile)	E-16
Cable Systems	**D-14**
Cable Community Index	(Back of Cable Volume 2)
Cable Ownership	D-887
Alabama	D-15
Alaska	D-37
Arizona	D-44
Arkansas	D-54
California	D-82
Colorado	D-111
Connecticut	D-127
Delaware	D-132
District of Columbia	D-133
Florida	D-134
Georgia	D-151

2017 Edition   v

Index to Contents

Communications Daily
Warren Communications News

Get the industry standard FREE —
For a no-obligation trial call 800-771-9202 or visit www.warren-news.com

Hawaii	D-177
Idaho	D-179
Illinois	D-186
Indiana	D-225
Iowa	D-240
Kansas	D-278
Kentucky	D-306
Louisiana	D-333
Maine	D-353
Maryland	D-359
Massachusetts	D-365
Michigan	D-370
Minnesota	D-391
Mississippi	D-426
Missouri	D-440
Montana	D-464
Nebraska	D-479
Nevada	D-500
New Hampshire	D-506
New Jersey	D-510
New Mexico	D-519
New York	D-529
North Carolina	D-550
North Dakota	D-568
Ohio	D-577
Oklahoma	D-607
Oregon	D-637
Pennsylvania	D-648
Puerto Rico	D-884
Rhode Island	D-683
South Carolina	D-684
South Dakota	D-694
Tennessee	D-705
Texas	D-718
Utah	D-790
Vermont	D-797
Virginia	D-801
Washington	D-814
West Virginia	D-833
Wisconsin	D-848
Wyoming	D-871
Cuba	D-881
Guam	D-882
Mariana Islands	D-883
Virgin Islands	D-886
Cable Audit Associates Inc.	E-140
Cable Noticias	E-16
Cable Ownership	D-887
Cable Penetration by State	F-1
Cable System Services	E-140
Cable TV Network of New Jersey	E-16
CAD Drafting Services Inc.	E-140
Cadent Network	E-140
Cadillac Telecasting Co.	A-1562
Cala Broadcast Partners LLC	A-1562
California Channel	E-16
California-Oregon Broadcasting Inc.	A-1562
Call Letters (U.S.)	A-9, D-1
Campus Group Companies	E-109
Camrac Studios	E-109
Canal 10 de Cancun	E-16
Canal 10 de Honduras	E-16
Canal 13 de Chile	E-16
Canal 22 Internacional	E-16
Canal 24 Horas	E-17
Canal 24 Horas (See also TVE International)	E-93
Canal 44 (XHIJ-TV)	E-16
Canal Once	E-17
Canal Sur	E-17
Canal Sur (See also Sur)	E-83
Candid Camera Inc.	E-109
Cannell Studios	E-109
CAN TV	E-17
Capgemini, Telecom, Media & Entertainment Group	E-140
Capital News 9	E-17
Capital Off Track Betting Television Network	E-17
Capitol Broadcasting Co. Inc.	A-1562
Caption Colorado	E-109
CaptionMax	E-109
Caracol TV	E-17
Career Entertainment Television	E-17
Caribbean Broadcasting Network LLC	A-1562
Carolina Christian Broadcasting Inc.	A-1562
Carousel	E-17
William B. Carr & Associates Inc.	E-141
Cars.TV	E-17
Cartoon Network	E-17
Cartoon Network en Espanol (See also Cartoon Network)	E-17
Cartoon Network en Espanol	E-17
Casa Club TV	E-17
Casa Club TV (See also MasChic)	E-56
Casa en Denver, Debtor-in-Possession	A-1562
Castle Rock Entertainment	E-109
Catch 47	E-18
Catch 47 (See also Bright House Sports Network)	E-15
The Catholic, Apostolic & Roman Church In Puerto Rico	A-1562
Catholic Communication Campaign	E-109
Catholic Television Network	E-18
CatholicTV	E-18
CB24	E-18
CB Communications Inc.	E-141
CBC/Radio-Canada	E-18, E-109
C.B. Distribution Co.	E-110
C.B. Distribution Co. (See also listing for Jess S. Morgan & Co)	E-121
CBeebies	E-18
CBS All Access	E-18
CBS Sports Network	E-18
CBS Corp.	A-1562
CBS News Inc.	E-110
CBS Television Distribution	E-110
CBS Television Studios	E-110
CB Tu Television Michoacan	E-18
CCI Systems	E-141
CCTV-4	E-18
CCTV-4 (See also CCTV America)	E-18
CCTV-6	E-18
CCTV-6 (See also China Movie Channel)	E-19
CCTV-9	E-18
CCTV-9 (See also CCTV-Documentary)	E-18
CCTV-11	E-18
CCTV-11 (See also CCTV-Opera)	E-18
CCTV-13	E-18
CCTV-13 (See also CCTV-News)	E-18
CCTV America	E-18
CCTV-Documentary	E-18
CCTV-Entertainment	E-18

Index to Contents

CCTV-Entertainment (See also CCTV-Documentary)	E-18
CCTV-News	E-18
CCTV-News (See also CCTV-Documentary)	E-18
CCTV-Opera	E-18
CCTV-Opera (See also CCTV-Documentary)	E-18
Celebrity Shopping Network	E-18
Central Florida News 13	E-18
Centric	E-19
Centric (See also BET)	E-13
Centroamerica TV	E-19
CET: Comcast Entertainment Television	E-19
CGNTV USA	E-19
Chadbourn Marcath Inc.	E-141
Chaisson & Co. Inc.	E-134
Jeff Chang	A-1563
Channel 3 TV Co LLC	A-1563
Channel 4 San Diego	E-19
Channel One Russia	E-19
Channel Z Edit	E-110
Chapman/Leonard Studio Equipment Inc.	E-110
Chase	E-134
Chena Broadcasting LLC	A-1563
Chernin Entertainment	E-110
Chicago Access Network Television	E-19
Chicago Access Network Television (See also CAN TV)	E-17
Chiller	E-19
China Movie Channel	E-19
China Movie Channel (See also CCTV-Documentary)	E-18
Chinese Entertainment Television (CETV)	E-19
Chinese Television Network	E-19
Chinese Television Network (See also CTI-Zhong Tian)	E-26
Christian Church (Disciples of Christ), Communication Ministries	E-110
Christian Faith Broadcast Inc.	A-1563
Christian Television Network	E-19, E-110
Christian Television Network Inc.	A-1563
The Christophers	E-110
CHR Solutions Inc.	E-141
Church Channel	E-19
Church Federation of Greater Indianapolis Inc.	E-110
The Church of Jesus Christ of Latter-Day Saints	E-110
Church World Service	E-110
Cine Mexicano	E-20
Cine Nostalgia	E-20
Cine Sony Television	E-20
Cine Clasico	E-20
Cinecraft Productions Inc.	E-110
Cinedigm	E-110
Cine Estelar	E-20
CineGroupe	E-110
Cinelan	E-110
Cinelatino	E-20
Cinema Arts Inc.	E-111
Cine Magnetics Digital & Video Laboratories	E-111
Cinemax	E-20
Cinemax On Demand	E-20
Cinemax On Demand (See also Cinemax)	E-20
Cinemoi North America	E-111
Cisneros Media Distribution	A-1563
Citadel Communications LLC	E-134
Citibank N.A.	E-134
Dick Clark Productions Inc.	E-111
Clasico TV	E-20
Classic Arts Showcase	E-20
Cloo	E-21
CLTV	E-21
Club Jenna	E-21
Club Jenna (See also Reality Kings TV (RKTV))	E-74
CMS Station Brokerage	E-134
CMT	E-21
CMT Loaded	E-21
CMT Loaded (See also CMT)	E-21
CMT Pure Country	E-21
CMT Pure Country (See also CMT)	E-21
cn/2	E-21
CN8	E-21
CN8 (See also Comcast Network Philadelphia)	E-22
CN100	E-21
CNBC	E-21
CNBC Pro	E-21
CNBC Pro (See also CNBC)	E-21
CNBC World	E-21
CNBC World (See also CNBC)	E-21
CNET Networks Inc.	E-111
CNN	E-21
CNN en Espanol	E-22
CNN en Espanol (See also CNN)	E-21
CNNGo	E-22
CNNGo (See also CNN)	E-21
CNN International	E-22
CNN International (See also CNN)	E-21
CNN Newsource Sales Inc.	E-111, E-141
CNZ Communications SE LLC	A-1563
Coastal Television Network	E-22
Coastal Television Broadcasting Co. LLC	A-1564
Coastline Community College Center	E-111
CobbCorp LLC	E-134
Cocola Broadcasting Companies LLC	A-1564
College & School Network	E-111
College Bowl Co.	E-111
College Sports Television	E-22
College Sports Television (See also CBS Sports Network)	E-18
Colors Kannada	E-22
Colors Marathi	E-22
Colors Marathi (See also Colors Kannada)	E-22
Colours	E-22
Columbia Telecommunications Corp./CTC Technology & Energy	E-141
Columbia Tristar Television Group	E-111
Columbia Tristar Television Group (See also listing for Sony Pictures Television)	E-126
Comcast/Charter Sports Southeast (CSS)	E-22
Comcast Entertainment Television	E-22
Comcast Entertainment Television (See also CET: Comcast Entertainment Television)	E-19
Comcast Hometown Network	E-22
Comcast Network Philadelphia	E-22
Comcast SportsNet Bay Area	E-23
Comcast SportsNet California	E-23
Comcast SportsNet Chicago	E-23
Comcast SportsNet Houston	E-23
Comcast SportsNet Houston (See also Root Sports Southwest)	E-76
Comcast SportsNet Mid-Atlantic	E-23
Comcast SportsNet New England	E-23
Comcast SportsNet Northwest	E-23
Comcast SportsNet Philadelphia	E-23
Comcast SportsNet Washington	E-24
Comcast SportsNet West	E-24
Comcast SportsNet West (See also Comcast SportsNet California)	E-23

2017 Edition — vii

Index to Contents

CABLE & TV STATION COVERAGE Atlas 2017
The perfect companion to the Television & Cable Factbook
To order call 800-771-9202 or visit www.warren-news.com

Comcast Sports Southwest (CSS) E-24
Comcast Sports Southwest (CSS) (See also Root Sports Southwest) E-76
Comcast Television 2 . . . . E-24
Comcast Television 2 (See also Comcast Television (Michigan)) E-24
Comcast Television (Michigan) E-24
Comedy Central E-24
Comedy Time E-24
Comedy.TV E-24
Comet E-24
Communications Engineering Inc. E-141
Communications Equity Associates E-134, E-141
Compro Productions Inc. E-111
Comsearch E-141
Comsonics Inc. E-141
Comtel Video Services Inc. E-111, E-141
Concert TV E-24
Concordia Publishing House E-111
Conde Nast Entertainment E-111
Conley & Associates LLC E-134, E-141
Connecticut Network E-24
Connecticut Network (See also CT-N) E-26
Connecticut Public Broadcasting Inc. E-111
Consulate E-111
Contec E-141
Content Media Corp. Ltd. E-111
Continental Film Productions Corp. E-112
Contradiction Films E-112
Cookie Jar Entertainment Inc. E-112
Cooking Channel E-24
Corgan Media Lab E-112
Cornerstone Television E-24
Cornerstone Television Inc. A-1564
Cornwall Associates E-141
Corridor Television LLP A-1564
Cosmo Street E-112
Costa de Oro Television Inc. A-1564
Country Music Television E-24
Country Music Television (See also CMT) E-21
The Country Network E-24
County Television Network San Diego E-25
Court TV E-25
Court TV (See also truTV) E-92
Cowles Co. A-1564
Cox & Cox LLC E-134
Cox Enterprises Inc. A-1564
Cox Sports Television E-25
COZI TV E-25
Crackle E-25, E-112
Cranston Acquisition LLC A-1564
Craven Film E-112
Create TV E-25
CreaTV San Jose E-25
Credit Protection Association Inc. E-142
Credit Suisse E-134
Crew Cuts E-112
CrewStar Inc. E-142
Crime & Investigation Network E-25
Crime & Investigation Network (See also A&E) E-6
Crime Channel E-25

Critical Mention Inc. (Clip Syndicate) E-142
Critical Content E-112
CRN Digital Talk Radio E-112
Cross Hill Communications LLC A-1565
Crossings TV E-25
Crosspoint E-112
Crossroads Christian Communications Inc. E-112
Crown International Pictures Inc. E-112
Crystal Cathedral Ministries E-112
Crystal Computer Corp. E-142
Crystal Pictures Inc. E-112
CSG Systems Inc. E-142
CSN+ E-25
CSN+ (See also regional Comcast SportsNet listings) E-23
C-SPAN E-25
C-SPAN 2 . . . . E-26
C-SPAN 2 (See also C-SPAN) E-25
C-SPAN 3 . . . . E-26
C-SPAN 3 (See also C-SPAN) E-25
C-SPAN Extra E-26
C-SPAN Extra (See also C-SPAN 3) E-26
CTC International E-26
CTI-Zhong Tian E-26
CT-N E-26
CTNi E-26
CTNi (See also Christian Television Network) E-19, E-110
CTV Inc. E-112
Cubamax TV E-26
CubaNetwork E-26
CubaPlay Television E-26
Cumbia Entertainment LLC A-1565
Cunningham Broadcasting Corp. A-1565
Cut & Run E-112
Cutters E-112
CVC Capital Corp. E-135
CW11 New York E-26
CW11 New York (See also PIX11) E-72
CWK Network Inc. E-112
CW PLUS E-26
Cyclones.tv E-26
CYR TV (Chinese Yellow River TV) E-26

D

Damas TV E-26
dapTV associates E-112
Dare to Dream Network E-26
Dare to Dream Network (See also 3ABN) E-5
Dataworld E-142
Dennis J Davis A-1565
Day 1 . . . . E-113
Day of Discovery (RBC Ministries) E-113
Daystar TV Network E-27
Debmar-Mercury E-113
Decades E-27
Deep Dish TV E-113
Defense Media Activity E-113
DeLaHoyaTV E-27
Deloitte & Touche LLP E-135
Deluxe Advertising Services E-113
Deluxe Laboratories Inc. E-113
De Pelicula E-27
De Pelicula (See also Univision) E-96
De Pelicula Clasico E-27
De Pelicula Clasico (See also De Pelicula) E-27
Destination America E-27

Index to Contents

Destination America (See also Discovery Channel)	E-27
Destination Education	E-113
Deutsche Welle TV	E-27
DeWolfe Music	E-113
DG FastChannel Inc.	E-142
DG FastChannel Inc. (See also Extreme Reach Inc)	E-142
Digimation Inc.	E-113
Digital Force	E-113
Digital Juice Inc.	E-113
Digital Post Services	E-113
Diligent Systems Inc.	E-113
DIRECTV Cinema	E-27
Discovery Channel	E-27
Discovery Digital Networks	E-113
Discovery Education	E-113
Discovery en Espanol	E-28
Discovery en Espanol (See also Discovery Channel)	E-27
Discovery Familia	E-28
Discovery Familia (See also Discovery Channel)	E-27
Discovery Family	E-28
Discovery Fit & Health (See also Discovery Life Channel)	E-28
Discovery Fit & Health	E-28
Discovery Health Channel	E-28
Discovery Health Channel (See also OWN: Oprah Winfrey Network)	E-70
Discovery Home Channel	E-28
Discovery Home Channel (See also Destination America)	E-27
Discovery Kids Channel	E-28
Discovery Kids Channel (See also Discovery Family)	E-28
Discovery Kids en Espanol	E-28
Discovery Kids en Espanol (See also Discovery Familia)	E-28
Discovery Life Channel	E-28
Discovery Life Channel (See also Discovery Channel)	E-27
Discovery Times Channel	E-28
Discovery Times Channel (See also Investigation Discovery)	E-51
Discovery Travel & Living (Viajar y Vivir)	E-28
Discovery Travel & Living (Viajar y Vivir) (See also Discovery Familia)	E-28
Disney Channel	E-28
Disney Enterprises Inc.	A-1565
Disney Family Movies	E-29
Disney Family Movies (See also Disney Channel)	E-28
Disney Junior	E-29
Disney Junior (See also Disney Channel)	E-28
Disney XD	E-29
Disney XD (See also Disney XD)	E-29
Disney XD en Espanol	E-29
Disney XD en Espanol (See also Disney Channel)	E-28
Dispatch Broadcast Group	A-1565
Diversified Communications	A-1565
Diversified Systems Inc.	E-142
Diya TV	E-29
DIY Network	E-29
DJM Films Inc.	E-113
DLT Entertainment Ltd.	E-113
DMTV7	E-29
DMX Music	E-29, E-113
Doctor Television Channel (DrTV)	E-30
Documentary Channel	E-30
Documentary Channel (See also Pivot)	E-72
Docurama Films	E-114
Docu TVE	E-30
Docu TVE (See also TVE Internacional)	E-93
Dodgers On Demand	E-30
DogTV	E-30
Dolphins Television Network	E-30
Dom Kino	E-30
Dominican View	E-30
Dominican View (See also ULTRA HDPlex)	E-95
Dominion Broadcasting Inc.	A-1565
Dominion Sky Angel	E-30
Dominion Sky Angel (See also Angel One)	E-9
Dove Broadcasting Inc.	A-1565, E-114
Dow Jones Newswires	E-114
DragonTV	E-30
Draper Holdings Business Trust	A-1565
Dreamcatcher Broadcasting LLC	A-1566
DreamWorks Animation SKG	E-114
DreamWorks Studios SKG	E-114
Drew Associates Inc.	E-114
Driver	E-114
DriverTV	E-30
DuArt Film & Video	E-114
Dubai TV	E-30
Paul H. Dujardin	A-1566

E

E!	E-30
Eastern Television Corp.	A-1566
Ebenezer Broadcasting Group Inc.	A-1566
EBRU TV	E-30
EBS International (Entertainment Business Services)	E-142
Ecology Cable Service	E-31
ECTV	E-31
Ecuador TV	E-31
Ecuador TV (See also ECTV)	E-31
Ecuavisa Internacional	E-31
Ecumenical TV Channel	E-31
Editbar	E-114
Ralph Edwards Productions	E-114
EDX Wireless LLC	E-142
E! Entertainment Television	E-31
E! Entertainment Television (See also E!)	E-30
Effros Communications	E-142
EJTV	E-31
El Garage TV USA	E-31
elgourmet	E-31
Bert Elliott Sound	E-114
Ellis Communications Group LLC	A-1566
Ellis Entertainment Corp.	E-114
El Rey	E-31
Emirates Dubai Television	E-31
Emirates Dubai Television (See also Dubai TV)	E-30
Employment & Career Channel	E-31
Encore	E-31
Encore (See also Starz Encore)	E-82
Encore Action	E-31
Encore Action (See also Starz Encore Action)	E-82
Encore Black	E-31
Encore Black (See also Starz Encore Black)	E-82
Encore Classic	E-31
Encore Classic (See also Starz Encore Classic)	E-82
Encore Drama	E-31
Encore Drama (See also Starz Encore Black)	E-82
Encore Espanol	E-31
Encore Espanol (See also Starz Encore Espanol)	E-82
Encore Family	E-31

2017 Edition

Index to Contents

Encore Family (See also Starz Encore Family)	E-83
Encore Love	E-31
Encore Love (See also Starz Encore Classic)	E-82
Encore Mystery	E-31
Encore Mystery (See also Starz Encore Suspense)	E-83
Encore Play	E-31
Encore Play (See also Starz Encore)	E-82
Encore Suspense	E-31
Encore Suspense (See also Starz Encore Suspense)	E-83
Encore Wam	E-31
Encore Wam (See also Starz Encore Family)	E-83
Encore Westerns	E-31
Encore Westerns (See also Starz Encore Westerns)	E-83
Encuentro Christian Network Corp.	A-1566
Encyclopaedia Britannica Inc.	E-114
Endemol Shine North America	E-114
English Club	E-31
English On Demand	E-32
Enlace Juvenil	E-32
Enlace Juvenil (See also EJTV)	E-31
Enlace USA	E-32
Enoki Films USA Inc.	E-115
Entravision Communications Corp.	A-1566
EnVest Media LLC	E-135
Envision TV	E-32
Envoy Productions	E-115
EPI Group LLC.	A-1566
EPIX	E-32
EPIX 2	E-32
EPIX 2 (See also EPIX)	E-32
EPIX 3	E-32
EPIX 3 (See also EPIX Hits)	E-32
EPIX Drive-In	E-32
EPIX Drive-In (See also EPIX)	E-32
EPIX Hits	E-32
EPIX Hits (See also EPIX)	E-32
Equidata	E-142
The Erotic Network	E-32
Escape	E-32
eScapes Network	E-32
Espiritu Santo y Fuego Network	E-32
ESPN	E-32
ESPN2	E-33
ESPN2 (See also ESPN)	E-32
ESPN3	E-33
ESPN3 (See also WATCH ESPN)	E-100
ESPN360.com	E-33
ESPN360.com (See also ESPN3)	E-33
ESPN Bases Loaded	E-33
ESPN Bases Loaded (See also ESPN)	E-32
ESPN Buzzer Beater	E-33
ESPN Buzzer Beater (See also ESPN)	E-32
ESPN Classic	E-33
ESPN Classic (See also ESPN)	E-32
ESPN College Extra	E-33
ESPN College Extra (See also ESPN)	E-32
ESPN Deportes	E-33
ESPN Deportes (See also ESPN)	E-32
ESPN Deportes + por ESPN3	E-33
ESPN Deportes + por ESPN3 (See also ESPN Deportes)	E-33
ESPNews	E-33
ESPNews (See also ESPN)	E-32
ESPN Full Court	E-33
ESPN Full Court (See also ESPN College Extra)	E-33
ESPN Game Plan	E-33
ESPN Game Plan (See also ESPN College Extra)	E-33
ESPN Goal Line	E-33
ESPN Goal Line (See also ESPN)	E-32
ESPN Now	E-33
ESPN Now (See also WATCH ESPN)	E-100
ESPNU	E-33
ESPNU (See also ESPN)	E-32
Esquire Network	E-33
Esquire TV Now	E-33
Esquire TV Now (See also Esquire Network)	E-33
Esteem Broadcasting LLC	A-1566
Estimated Growth of the Cable Industry	F-1
Estrella TV	E-33
estudio5	E-34
ES.TV	E-34
ETC	E-115
Eternal Word TV Network	E-34
Eternal Word TV Network (See also EWTN Global Catholic Network)	E-34
ET-Global	E-34
ET-News	E-34
ET-News (See also ET-GLOBAL)	E-34
ETV Kannada	E-34
ETV Kannada (See also Colors Kannada)	E-22
ETV Marathi	E-34
ETV Marathi (See also Colors Marathi)	E-22
EUE/Screen Gems Studios	E-115
Eurochannel	E-34
Eurocinema	E-34
EuroNews	E-34
Evangelistic Alaska Missionary Fellowship	A-1567
EVINE Live	E-34
EWTN en Espanol	E-34
EWTN en Espanol (See also EWTN Global Catholic Network)	E-34
EWTN Global Catholic Network	E-34
EXFO	E-142
The Exline Co.	E-135, E-142
Expo TV	E-34
Extreme Reach Inc.	E-142
Exxxotica	E-34

F

Faith Broadcasting Network Inc.	A-1567
Faith For Today	E-115
Faith Television Network	E-35
Faith Television Network (See also The Family Channel)	E-35
Familia TV	E-35
The Family Channel	E-35
Family Friendly Entertainment	E-35
FamilyNet	E-35
Family Theater Productions	E-115
Farm Journal Media	E-115
Fashion One 4K	E-35
Fashion One Television Ltd.	E-35
FashionTV	E-35
Fast Cuts	E-115
FBR Capital Markets, Technology, Media & Telecommunications Group	E-135
Festival Direct	E-35
Festival Direct (See also Independent Film Channel)	E-50
FidoTV	E-35

Index to Contents

The Field	E-115
Fight Network	E-35
Fight Now TV	E-35
Fil Am TV	E-35
Gregory P. Filandrinos	A-1567
The Filipino Channel	E-36
Filmack Studios	E-115
FilmCore	E-115
FilmCore (See also Deluxe Advertising Services)	E-113
Film Festival Channel	E-36
FilmRise	E-115
Films Around the World Inc.	E-115
Films of India	E-115
Films of India (See also listing for 1-World LLC)	E-105
Final Cut Ltd.	E-115
Find it on Demand	E-36
Fine Art Productions, Richie Suraci Pictures MultiMedia, InterActive	E-115
Fine Living Network	E-36
Fine Living Network (See also Cooking Channel)	E-24
Michael Fiore Films	E-115
FiOS1 Dallas	E-36
FiOS1 High School Sports Widget	E-36
FiOS1 Long Island	E-36
FiOS1 New Jersey	E-36
FiOS1 New Jersey (See also FiOS Long Island)	E-36
FiOS1 Potomac	E-36
FiOS1 Potomac (See also FiOS Long Island)	E-36
Firestone Communications Inc.	E-115
Fireworks International	E-115
First Assembly of God of West Monroe	A-1567
First Light Video Publishing	E-115
Fischer Edit	E-116
FitTV	E-36
FitTV (See also Discovery Life Channel)	E-28
Fix & Foxi	E-36
Flatiron Film Co.	E-116
Flinn Broadcasting Corp.	A-1567
George S. Flinn III	A-1567
George S. Flinn Jr.	A-1567
Flix	E-36
Florida Channel	E-36
Fluid	E-116
FMX Cable FM System	E-36
FNTSY Sports Network	E-36
Follow Productions	E-116
Food Network	E-36
Paul Dean Ford	E-142
Richard A. Foreman Associates Inc.	E-135
FOROtv	E-37
FOROtv (See also Univision)	E-96
Forrester Research Inc.	E-143
Fort Myers Broadcasting Co.	A-1567
Forum Communications Co.	A-1567
Foundation	E-116
Fox 21 Television Studios	E-116
Fox Business Go	E-37
Fox Business Go (See also Fox Business Network)	E-37
Fox Business Network	E-37
FOX College Sports Atlantic	E-37
FOX College Sports Central	E-37
FOX College Sports Central (See also FOX College Sports Atlantic)	E-37
FOX College Sports Pacific	E-37
FOX College Sports Pacific (See also FOX College Sports Atlantic)	E-37
Fox Deportes	E-37
Fox Life	E-37
Fox Movie Channel	E-37
Fox Movie Channel (See also FXM)	E-42
Fox News Channel	E-37
Fox News Go	E-37
Fox News Go (See also Fox News Channel)	E-37
Fox Reality Channel	E-37
Fox Reality Channel (See also Nat Geo WILD)	E-62
Fox Soccer	E-38
Fox Soccer (See also Fox Soccer Plus)	E-38
Fox Soccer 2Go	E-38
Fox Soccer 2Go (See also Fox Soccer Plus)	E-38
Fox Soccer Plus	E-38
FOX Sports 1	E-38
FOX Sports 2	E-38
FOX Sports 2 (See also FOX Sports 1)	E-38
FOX Sports Arizona	E-38
FOX Sports Arizona Plus	E-38
FOX Sports Arizona Plus (See also FOX Sports Arizona)	E-38
FOX Sports Carolinas	E-38
FOX Sports Detroit	E-38
FOX Sports Detroit Plus	E-38
FOX Sports Detroit Plus (See also FOX Sports Detroit)	E-38
FOX Sports Florida/Sun Sports	E-38
FOX Sports Florida Plus	E-38
FOX Sports Florida Plus (See also FOX Sports Florida/Sun Sports)	E-38
FOX Sports Go	E-38
FOX Sports Go (See also Fox Sports Networks)	E-39
FOX Sports Houston	E-38
FOX Sports Indiana	E-39
FOX Sports Indiana Plus	E-39
FOX Sports Indiana Plus (See also FOX Sports Indiana)	E-39
FOX Sports Kansas City	E-39
FOX Sports Kansas City (See also FOX Sports Midwest)	E-39
FOX Sports Kansas City Plus	E-39
FOX Sports Kansas City Plus (See also FOX Sports Kansas City)	E-39
FOX Sports Midwest	E-39
FOX Sports Midwest Plus	E-39
FOX Sports Midwest Plus (See also FOX Sports Midwest)	E-39
FOX Sports Net New York	E-39
FOX Sports Net New York (See also MSG Plus)	E-60
FOX Sports Net Northwest	E-39
FOX Sports Net Northwest (See also Root Sports Northwest)	E-76
FOX Sports Net Pittsburgh	E-39
FOX Sports Net Pittsburgh (See also Root Sports Pittsburgh)	E-76
FOX Sports Net Rocky Mountain	E-39
FOX Sports Net Rocky Mountain (See also Root Sports Rocky Mountain)	E-76
FOX Sports Net Utah	E-39
FOX Sports Net Utah (See also Root Sports Rocky Mountain)	E-76
FOX Sports Net West 2	E-39
FOX Sports Net West 2 (See also FOX Sports West/Prime Ticket)	E-40
FOX Sports Networks	E-39
FOX Sports Networks (See also regional FOX Sports Networks)	E-39
FOX Sports New Orleans	E-39
FOX Sports New Orleans (See also FOX Sports Southwest)	E-40
FOX Sports North	E-39
FOX Sports North Plus	E-39
FOX Sports North Plus (See also FOX Sports North)	E-39
FOX Sports Ohio/Sports Time Ohio	E-39
FOX Sports Ohio Plus	E-39
FOX Sports Ohio Plus (See also FOX Sports Ohio/Sports Time Ohio)	E-39
FOX Sports Oklahoma	E-40
FOX Sports Oklahoma (See also FOX Sports Southwest)	E-40

2017 Edition xi

Index to Contents

Communications Daily
Warren Communications News
Get the industry standard FREE —
For a no-obligation trial call 800-771-9202 or visit www.warren-news.com

FOX Sports Oklahoma Plus	E-40
FOX Sports Oklahoma Plus (See also FOX Sports Oklahoma)	E-40
FOX Sports San Diego	E-40
FOX Sports South/SportSouth	E-40
FOX Sports South Plus	E-40
FOX Sports South Plus (See also FOX Sports South/SportSouth)	E-40
FOX Sports Southwest	E-40
FOX Sports Southwest Plus	E-40
FOX Sports Southwest Plus (See also FOX Sports Southwest)	E-40
FOX Sports Tennessee	E-40
FOX Sports Tennessee (See also FOX Sports South/SportSouth)	E-40
FOX Sports West/Prime Ticket	E-40
FOX Sports West Plus	E-40
FOX Sports West Plus (See also FOX Sports West/Prime Ticket)	E-40
FOX Sports Wisconsin	E-40
FOX Sports Wisconsin (See also FOX Sports North)	E-39
FOX Sports Wisconsin Plus	E-40
FOX Sports Wisconsin Plus (See also FOX Sports Wisconsin)	E-40
FOX Sports World	E-40
FOX Sports World (See also FOX Soccer PLUS)	E-38
Fox Studios Australia	E-116
Fox Studios Australia (See also listing for Granada Media)	E-117
Fox Television Holdings LLC	A-1567
France 24	E-40
Sandy Frank Entertainment Inc.	E-116
Frederator Studios	E-116
Freeform	E-40
Freeman Corp.	E-143
Free Speech TV	E-41
Free To Choose Network	E-41
Fremantle Corp.	E-116
FremantleMedia Ltd.	E-116
Jim French Design Shop	E-143
Fresh	E-41
Fresh (See also Brazzers TV)	E-15
Chuck Fries Productions	E-116
Peter Froehlich & Co.	E-143
Frost Great Outdoors	E-41
FSZ TV (Fantasy Sports Zone TV)	E-41
Fuel TV	E-41
Fuel TV (See also Fox Sports 2)	E-38
Fujian Straits TV	E-41
FUMC Television Ministries	E-116
FUNimation Channel	E-41
Funny or Die	E-116
Fuse	E-41
Fusion	E-41
Future is Now (FIN)	E-116
FX	E-42
FXM	E-42
FXM (See also FX)	E-42
FXNOW	E-42
FXNOW (See also FX)	E-42
FXX	E-42
FXX (See also FX)	E-42
FYI	E-42

G

Gabba Media LLC	E-116
Gaiam TV Fit & Yoga	E-42
GalaVision	E-42
GalaVision (See also Univision)	E-96
GameHD	E-42
GameHD (See also iN DEMAND)	E-50
Game Show Network	E-42
Game Show Network (See also GSN)	E-44
Gammon Miller LLC	E-135
Clifton Gardiner & Co. LLC	E-135
Gari Media Group	E-116
GAS	E-42
GAS (See also TeenNick)	E-85
Gateway Films/Vision Video	E-116
Gavel to Gavel Alaska	E-42
GBTV	E-42
GBTV (See also TheBlaze)	E-87
GCN	E-42
GEB America	E-42
GE Capital Solutions	E-135
Geller Media International	E-143
Gem Shopping Network	E-43
GemsTV	E-43
General Communication Inc.	A-1568
GeoMart	E-143
Georgia Highlands Television (GHTV)	E-43
Georgia Public Broadcasting	E-43
Georgia U.S. Data Services Inc.	E-143
Gerren Entertainment Productions	E-116
getTV	E-43
G.I.G. of North Dakota LLC	A-1568
GLC	E-43
Glendive Broadcasting Corp.	A-1568
Global Christian Network	E-43
Global Christian Network (See also GCN)	E-42
GlobeCast America	E-116
Globo International NY Ltd.	E-117
Glossary of Cable Terms	F-13
GMA Life TV	E-43
GMA Life TV (See also GMA Pinoy TV)	E-43
GMA Pinoy TV	E-43
gmc	E-43
gmc (See also UP)	E-97
gMovies	E-43
GOCOM Media of Illinois LLC	A-1568
God TV	E-43
Golf Channel	E-43
GolTV	E-43
Gabriela Gomez	A-1568
Good Life Broadcasting Inc.	E-117
Mark Gordon Co	E-117
Gorman & Associates	E-143
GoScout Homes	E-44
Gospel Music Channel	E-44
Gospel Music Channel (See also UP)	E-97
Gospel Music TV	E-44
Gospel Music TV (See also Family Friendly Entertainment)	E-35
Gracenote	E-117
Graham Brock Inc.	E-143
Graham Media Group Inc.	A-1568
Granada Media	E-117
Gran Cine	E-44
Granite Broadcasting LLC	A-1568
Sherry Grant Enterprises Inc.	E-117
Gray Television Inc.	A-1568

Index to Contents

GRB Entertainment	E-117
Great American Country	E-44
Great Lakes Data Systems Inc.	E-143
Greek Channel	E-44
Greek Channel (See also New Greek TV)	E-62
Ross Greenburg Productions	E-117
Griffin Communications LLC	A-1569
W.B. Grimes & Co.	E-135
Grit	E-44
GSN	E-44
GTN	E-44
GTN (See also Guardian Television Network)	E-44
Guangdong Southern Television (TVS)	E-44
Guardian Television Network	E-44

H

H2	E-44
H2 (See also Viceland)	E-98
Alfred Haber Distribution Inc.	E-117
Hadden & Associates	E-135
Hallmark Channel	E-44
Hallmark Movies & Mysteries	E-45
Hallmark Movies & Mysteries (See also Hallmark Channel)	E-44
Halogen TV	E-45
Halogen TV (See also Pivot)	E-72
Harmony Gold USA Inc.	E-117
Harpo Productions Inc.	E-117
Hartley Film Foundation Inc.	E-117
Havoc TV	E-45
Hawaii Catholic TV Inc.	A-1569
Hawkeye Network	E-45
Hazardous	E-45
Hazardous (See also NBCSN)	E-63
HBO	E-45
HBO 2	E-45
HBO 2 (See also HBO)	E-45
HBO Comedy	E-45
HBO Comedy (See also HBO)	E-45
HBO en Espanol	E-45
HBO en Espanol (See also HBO Latino)	E-45
HBO Enterprises	E-117
HBO Family	E-45
HBO Family (See also HBO)	E-45
HBO GO	E-45
HBO GO (See also HBO)	E-45
HBO Latino	E-45
HBO Latino (See also HBO)	E-45
HBO Now	E-45
HBO Now (See also HBO)	E-45
HBO on Broadband	E-45
HBO Signature	E-46
HBO Signature (See also HBO)	E-45
HBO Studio Productions	E-117
HBO Zone	E-46
HBO Zone (See also HBO)	E-45
HDNet	E-46
HDNet (See also AXS TV)	E-11
HDNet Movies	E-46
HDNet Movies (See also AXS TV)	E-11
HD Theater	E-46
HD Theater (See also Velocity)	E-98
Headline News	E-46
Headline News (See also HLN)	E-47
Health & Wellness Channel	E-46
HealthiNation	E-46
Health on Demand	E-46
F.P. Healy & Co. Inc.	E-143
Hearst Entertainment Inc.	E-117
Hearst Television Inc.	A-1569, E-117
Hearst Television Inc. (See also Hearst Entertainment Inc)	E-117
Heartland	E-46
Heartland Media LLC	A-1569
Norman Hecht Research Inc.	E-143
Helena Civic Television (HCT)	E-46
Hellerstein & Associates	E-143
Hemisphere Media Holdings LLC	A-1569
Henninger Media Services	E-117
Henson Media Inc.	E-135
Thomas B Henson	A-1569
here! TV	E-46
Heritage Broadcasting Group	A-1569
HERO Broadcasting LLC	A-1569
Heroes & Icons	E-46
HGTV	E-46
R. Miller Hicks & Co.	E-135, E-143
High 4K TV	E-47
High Noon Entertainment	E-117
H. Dean Hinson	A-1569
Hispanic Pay TV Channel	E-47
History	E-47
History en Espanol	E-47
History en Espanol (See also History)	E-47
History International	E-47
History International (See also Viceland)	E-98
The HistoryMakers	E-118
HITN	E-47
HITS (Headend In The Sky)	E-47
HITV Operating Co. Inc.	A-1569
HLN	E-47
HLW International LLP	E-143
Hmong TV Network	E-47
HmongUSA TV	E-47
HMX, El Canal del Hombre	E-47
Hoffman Communications Inc.	E-118
Hoffman-Schutz Media Capital	E-135
Hola! TV	E-47
Hollywood Vaults Inc.	E-118
Holston Valley Broadcasting Corp.	A-1570
Holt Media Group	E-135
Home & Garden Television	E-48
Home & Garden Television (See also HGTV)	E-46
Home Box Office	E-48
Home Box Office (See also HBO)	E-45
Home Shopping Network	E-48
Home Shopping Network (See also HSN)	E-48
Home Shopping Network 2	E-48
Home Shopping Network 2 (See also HSN2)	E-48
Homestead Editorial Inc.	E-118
Homestead Films	E-118
Hope Channel	E-48
Horizon Media Inc.	E-143
Horseshoe Curve Communications LLC	A-1570
HorseTV Channel	E-48
Hot Choice	E-48

2017 Edition   xiii

Index to Contents

HOT TV (History of Television)	E-48
Hour of Harvest Inc.	A-1570
HPC Puckett & Co.	E-135
HRTV	E-48
HSN	E-48
HSN2	E-48
HSN2 (See also HSN)	E-48
HTV	E-48
Hubbard Broadcasting Inc.	A-1570
Hub Network	E-48
Hub Network (See also Discovery Family)	E-28
Hulu	E-48
Hulu Latino	E-48
Hulu Latino (See also Hulu)	E-48
J.C. Humke & Associates Inc.	E-144
Hunan Satellite TV (HTV)	E-48
Hunt Channel	E-49
Hunt Channel (See also Angel Two)	E-9
Hurricane Vision	E-49
Hustler TV	E-49
Hwazan TV	E-49
Hyena Editorial Inc.	E-118

I

IAVC	E-49
ICTV	E-49
ICTV (See also ActiveVideo)	E-139
i-cubed HYPERMEDIA	E-118
IDC Services Inc.	E-144
Idea Channel	E-49
Idea Channel (See also Free To Choose Network)	E-41
iDriveTV	E-49
IFC	E-49
IFC Films	E-118
Iglesia JEMIR	E-49
i-Health	E-49
i-Health (See also ION Life)	E-51
i-Lifetv	E-49
i-Lifetv (See also Pivot)	E-72
Illinois Channel	E-49
iMetro	E-49
iMetro (See also ION Television)	E-51
IMG World	E-118
Impact	E-49
The Impact Network	E-49
Impact Productions	E-118
iN DEMAND	E-50
Independent Communications Inc.	A-1570
Independent Film Channel	E-50
Independent Film Channel (See also IFC)	E-49
Independent Music Network	E-50
Indianapolis Community Television Inc.	A-1570
IndiePlex	E-50
iND PPV en Espanol	E-50
iND PPV en Espanol (See also iN DEMAND)	E-50
Infinito	E-50
InfoMas	E-50
Infonetics Research	E-144

Informa Telecoms & Media	E-144
Infosys Technologies Ltd.	E-144
ING Investment Management	E-135
Initiative Media Worldwide Inc.	E-144
Inmigrante TV	E-50
Insight Research Corp.	E-144
INSP	E-50
Integrated Alliance LP	E-144
Intellicast	E-50
Intellicast (See also The Weather Channel)	E-100
Intermountain West Communications LLC	A-1570
International Contact Inc.	E-118
International Creative Management Inc.	E-144
International Family Television	E-50
International Media Distribution (IMD)	E-118
International Program Consultants Inc.	E-118
International Technology & Trade Associates Inc.	E-144
International Tele-Film	E-118
International Television (ITV)	E-50
IntiNetwork	E-50
Investigation Discovery	E-51
Investigation Discovery (See also Discovery Channel)	E-27
ION Life	E-51
ION Life (See also ION Television)	E-51
ION Media Stations LLC	A-1570
ION Television	E-51
Iowa Communications Network	E-51
I-Play	E-51
I Square Media LLC	A-1571
The Israeli Network	E-51
iSuppli	E-144
Italianation	E-51
It Is Written International Television	E-118
Ivanhoe Broadcast News Inc.	E-118

J

Jade Channel	E-51
Jane.TV	E-51
Janus Films Co.	E-118
JB Broadcasting Inc.	A-1571
JCTV	E-51
JCTV (See also JUCE TV)	E-52
Jewelry Television	E-51
Jewish Broadcasting Service	E-52
The Jewish Channel	E-52
Jewish Life TV	E-52
Jiangsu International Channel	E-52
Jia Yu Channel	E-52
The Jim Henson Company	E-118
JK Investments LLC	A-1571
Johnson Publishing Co. Inc.	E-118
Joint Hometown News Service	E-118
Jones Group Ltd.	E-135
Jones/NCTI	E-144
Jones/NCTI (See also NCTI)	E-146
Jorgenson Broadcast Brokerage Inc.	E-135
David J Joseph	A-1571
JTV	E-52
JTV Direct	E-52
JTV Direct (See also Jewelry Television)	E-51
JUCE TV	E-52
Juicy	E-52
Jump TV	E-119
Jupiter Entertainment	E-119

Index to Contents

Justice Central.TV E-52
Justice Network E-52

K

Kabillion E-52
Kabillion Girls Rule E-52
Kabillion Girls Rule (See also Kabillion) E-52
kaBOOM! Entertainment Inc. E-119
Kalba International Inc. E-144
Kalil & Co. Inc. E-136
Kamen Entertainment Group Inc. E-119
Kane Reece Associates Inc. E-136, E-144
Kansas Now 22 . . . . E-52
Karaoke Channel E-52
KAZT LLC A-1571
KBS America E-53
Kelso Longview Television E-53
KEMS E-53
Kentucky Educational Television (KET) E-53
Kepper, Tupper & Co. E-136
KET2 . . . . E-53
KET2 (See also Kentucky Educational Television (KET)) E-53
Ketchikan TV LLC A-1571
KETKY E-53
KETKY (See also Kentucky Educational Television (KET)) E-53
KeyCorp. E-136
Killer Tracks: Network Music E-119
Kinetic Content E-119
King World Productions Inc. E-119
King World Productions Inc. (See also listing for CBS Television Distribution) . . E-110
KITV Inc. A-1571
Klavo E-53
Klein & E-119
KLRU Create E-53
KLRU Create (See also KLRU-Q) E-53
KLRU Q E-53
KLRU-TOO E-53
KLRU-TOO (See also KLRU Q) E-53
KLTV E-53
KLTV (See also Kelso Longview Television) E-53
KM Communications Inc. A-1571
K-MTN Television E-53
Knowles Media Brokerage Services E-136
Knoxville TV LLC A-1571
Edward J. Koplar A-1571
Paul H. Koplin A-1571
Korean EverRock Multi-Media Service E-53
Korean Channel E-53
Korean EverRock Multi-Media Service (See also KEMS) E-53
Korea One: Chicagoland Korean TV E-53
Korea One: Chicagoland Korean TV (See also Washington Korean TV) E-99
Kozacko Media Services E-136
KSQA LLC A-1571
KStateHD.TV E-53
KTBS LLC A-1571
KTGF License Corp. A-1571
KTLA Los Angeles E-53
KTV - Kids & Teens Television E-54
Kultur International Films Inc. E-119
Lara Kunkler A-1571
Kunlun Drama E-54
KUSA Productions E-119
Kushner Locke Co. Inc. E-119
KyLinTV E-119

Communications Daily
Warren Communications News

Get the industry standard FREE —
For a no-obligation trial call 800-771-9202 or visit www.warren-news.com

L

LA1 . . . . E-54
La Cadena del Milagro Inc. A-1571
La Familia Cosmovision E-54
LAFF E-54
Lake Superior Community Broadcasting Corp. A-1571
Largest U.S. Cable Systems (chart) F-2
Latele Novela Network E-54
Latham Foundation E-119
Latin American Sports E-54
Latinoamerica Television E-54
Latin World Entertainment E-145
LATV E-54
Lazard E-136
Leftfield Pictures E-119
Legacy Broadcasting LLC A-1571
Legendary Entertainment E-119
Legislative Counsel Bureau - Broadcast and Production Services . . . E-54
Lehmann Strobel PC E-145
Lyle Leimkuhler A-1572
H. Chase Lenfest A-1572
LeSEA Broadcasting Corp. A-1572
LeSEA Broadcasting Network E-54, E-119
LeSEA Broadcasting Network (See also World Harvest Television) . . E-102
Lear Levin Productions Inc. E-119
Liberman Broadcasting Inc. A-1572
Liberty U. A-1572
Life Design TV E-54
Life OK. E-54
Lifestyle Family Television E-54
Lifestyle Magazine E-119
Lifestyle Network E-54
Lifetime E-54
Lifetime Movie Network E-55
Lifetime Movie Network (See also LMN) E-55
Lifetime Real Women E-55
Lifetime Real Women (See also LRW) E-56
Lilly Broadcasting Holdings LLC A-1572
Kevin T. Lilly A-1572
Lincoln Broadcasting Co. A-1572
Lincoln Square Productions E-119
Link TV E-55
Linsman Film E-119
Lionsgate Entertainment E-119
Liquidation Channel E-55
Arthur D. Little Inc. E-145
Litton Entertainment E-120
Live Well Network E-55
Living Faith Ministries Inc. A-1572
Living Faith Television E-55
LMN E-55
LMN (See also Lifetime) E-54
LNS Captioning E-120
Local Cable Weather E-55
James L. Lockwood Jr. A-1572
LocusPoint Networks LLC A-1572
Logic General Inc. E-120

2017 Edition   XV

Index to Contents

CABLE & TV STATION COVERAGE
Atlas 2017
The perfect companion to the Television & Cable Factbook
To order call 800-771-9202 or visit www.warren-news.com

LOGO	E-55
Lo Mejor On Demand	E-55
London Broadcasting Co. LP	A-1572
Long Communications LLC	A-1572
Longhorn Network	E-55
Look & Co.	E-120
Lottery Channel	E-56
Loud TV	E-120
Louisiana Legislative Network	E-56
Louisiana Television Broadcasting LLC	A-1572
Low Power Television Stations	B-1
Low Power Television Stations Ownership	B-189
LRW	E-56
LRW (See also Lifetime)	E-54
Paul Lucci	A-1573
Luxe.TV	E-56
LVES-TV	E-56
LWS Local Weather Station	E-56
LX.TV	E-120
Lynx Images Inc.	E-120

M

Macau Asia Satellite TV (MASTV)	E-56
MAC TV	E-56
Madison Dearborn Partners LLC	E-136
Madison Square Garden Network	E-56
Madison Square Garden Network (See also MSG)	E-60
Frank N. Magid Associates Inc.	E-145
Maginglia Media	E-120
Magnetic Image Video	E-145
Mag Rack	E-56
The Mahlman Co.	E-136
Major Market Broadcasting of North Dakota Inc.	A-1573
Maker Studios Inc.	E-120
Malibu Broadcasting LLC	A-1573
Management & Technical Consulting Services	E-139
Manavision3	E-56
Manhan Media Inc.	A-1573
Maranatha Broadcasting Co. Inc.	A-1573
M/A/R/C Research	E-145
Mariavision	E-56
Market Strategies	E-145
Guenter Marksteiner	A-1573
Mark III Media Inc.	A-1573
Marquee Broadcasting Inc.	A-1573
Pluria Marshall Jr.	A-1573
Marsh & McLennan Cos. (MMC)	E-145
Lynn M Martin	A-1573
Maryknoll World Productions	E-120
MasChic	E-56
MasMusica TeVe Network	E-56
Massachusetts Spanish TV Network (MASTV)	E-56
Mauck & Associates Inc.	E-145
Mauna Kea Broadcasting Co Inc.	A-1573
MavTV	E-56
Max GO	E-56
Max GO (See also Cinemax)	E-20
Max Latino	E-57
Max Latino (See also Cinemax)	E-20
Max Media X LLC	A-1573
MaxxSouth Sports	E-57
Maysles Films Inc.	E-120
MBC Action	E-57
MBC Action (See also MBC TV)	E-57
MBC America	E-57
MBCD	E-57
MBC Drama	E-57
MBC Drama (See also MBC America)	E-57
MBC Drama (See also MBC TV)	E-57
MBC Kids	E-57
MBC Kids (See also MBC TV)	E-57
MBC Masr	E-57
MBC Masr (See also MBC TV)	E-57
MBC TV	E-57
MB Revolution LLC	A-1573
MC	E-57
MC-TV	E-57
MCG Capital Corp.	E-136
McGuane Studio Inc.	E-120
MCH Enterprises Inc.	E-136
B.K. McIntyre & Associates	E-145
MC Play	E-57
MC Play (See also MC)	E-57
M/C Venture Partners	E-136
MDTV: Medical News Now	E-57
R.E. Meador & Associates Inc.	E-136
Meadowlane Enterprises Inc.	E-120
Meadows Racing Network	E-57
Meadows Racing Network (See also HRTV)	E-48
Media General Inc.	A-1573
Medialink Worldwide Inc.	E-120
Media Services Group Inc.	E-136
Mediaset Italia	E-57
MediaSpan Online Services	E-145
Media Venture Partners LLC	E-136
Medstar Television Inc.	E-120
Mega TV	E-57
Melli TV	E-58
Melli TV (See also MTC Persian Television)	E-60
Lee Mendelson Film Productions Inc.	E-120
Mercury Broadcasting Co. Inc.	A-1574
Meredith Corp.	A-1574
Meridian Design Associates Architects	E-145
Meruelo Media Holdings	A-1574
MetroChannels	E-58
MetroChannels (See also News 12 Interactive)	E-64
Metro Sports	E-58
Metro Sports (See also Time Warner Cable SportsChannel (Kansas City))	E-90
Metro Sports 2	E-58
Metro Sports 2 (See also Time Warner Cable SportsChannel 2 (Kansas City))	E-89
MeTV	E-58
Mexicanal	E-58
Mexico TV	E-58
MGM Channel	E-58
MGM Television Entertainment Inc.	E-120
MHz Networks	E-58
MHz Worldview	E-58
MHz Worldview (See also MHz Networks)	E-58
Mi Musica	E-58
Miami Station Split Co.	A-1574
Miami TeVe	E-58
Mi Cine	E-58
Micronesia Broadcasting LLC	A-1574
Mid-Atlantic Sports Network (MASN)	E-58
Midco Sports Network	E-58

Index to Contents

Midhudsonmedia	E-145
Mid-State Television Inc.	A-1574
Midwest Christian Television	E-58
Midwest Christian Television (See also MC-TV)	E-57
Midwest Television Inc.	A-1574
Milenio Television	E-58
Milestone Communications Inc.	E-137
Military Channel	E-59
Military Channel (See also American Heroes Channel)	E-8
Military History	E-59
Military History (See also History)	E-47
Warren Miller Entertainment	E-121
Milner-Fenwick Inc.	E-121
Milwaukee Media LLC	A-1574
Minnesota House & Senate Television	E-59
Miramax	E-121
Mira TV	E-59
Mission TV	E-59
Mission Broadcasting Inc.	A-1575
Mississippi TV LLC	A-1575
The Curators of the U. of Missouri	A-1575
Mitts Telecasting Co. LLC	A-1575
MLB Extra Innings	E-59
MLB Extra Innings (See also MLB Network)	E-59
MLB Network	E-59
MLB Network Strike Zone	E-59
MLB Network Strike Zone (See also MLB Network)	E-59
MLS Direct Kick	E-59
MMMRC LLC	A-1575
MMTC Media & Telecom Brokers	E-137
Mnet	E-59
Mobile Video Tapes Inc.	A-1575
MobiTV Inc.	E-145
Modern Sound Pictures Inc.	E-121
Dan Modisett	A-1575
Moffitt-Lee Productions	E-121
MOFOS	E-59
Mojo HD	E-59
Mojo HD (See also iN DEMAND)	E-50
Mokupuni Television Co. Inc.	A-1575
Momentum	E-59
Monkeyland Audio Inc.	E-121
More MAX	E-59
More MAX (See also Cinemax)	E-20
Jess S. Morgan & Co.	E-121
Morgan Murphy Media	A-1575
Morris Multimedia Inc.	A-1575
Motors TV	E-59
Mountain Broadcasting Corp.	A-1575
Mountain Licenses LP	A-1575
Mount Mansfield Television Inc.	A-1575
The Movie Channel	E-59
The Movie Channel Xtra	E-59
Moviecraft Inc.	E-121
Movie Max	E-59
Movie Max (See also Cinemax)	E-20
MoviePlex	E-60
Movies!	E-60
Movies! Carolina	E-60
MSG	E-60
MSG 3D	E-60
MSG 3D (See also MSG)	E-60
MSG Plus	E-60
MSNBC	E-60
MTC Persian Television	E-60
MTV	E-60
MTV2	E-61
MTV2 (See also MTV)	E-60
MTV Classic	E-61
MTV Classic (See also MTV)	E-60
MTV Hits	E-61
MTV Hits (See also NickMusic)	E-67
MTV Jams	E-61
MTV Jams (See also MTV)	E-60
MTV Live	E-61
MTV Live (See also MTV)	E-60
mtvU	E-61
mtvU (See also MTV)	E-60
Multicom Entertainment Group Inc.	E-121
Multicomm Sciences International Inc.	E-146
Multimedios Television	E-61
Stephen P Mumblow	A-1575
mun2	E-61
mun2 (See also NBC Universo)	E-63
MundoFOX	E-61
MundoFOX (See also MundoMax)	E-61
MundoMax	E-61
Muscular Dystrophy Association	E-121
Music Choice	E-61
Music Choice (See also MC)	E-57
Muzika Pervogo	E-61
My Combat Channel	E-61
My Damn Channel	E-121
MyDestination.TV	E-61
My Family TV	E-61
My Family TV (See also The Family Channel)	E-35
MyFootage.com	E-121
MyMediaBroker.com	E-137
MyNetworkTV	E-61
MYX TV	E-61

N

Nacion TV	E-61
Narrative Television Network	E-61
NASA TV	E-61
NASA TV UHD	E-62
Nat Geo Mundo	E-62
Nat Geo WILD	E-62
Nathan Associates Inc.	E-146
National Captioning Institute	E-121
National City Corp.	E-137
National Council of Churches USA (NCC)	E-121
National Economic Research Associates Inc. (NERA)	E-146
National Film Board of Canada	E-121
National Geographic Channel	E-62
National Geographic Television	E-121
New Greek TV	E-62
National Iranian Television	E-62
National Jewish TV (NJT)	E-62
National Lampoon College Television	E-62
National Technical Information Service	E-121
National TeleConsultants Inc.	E-146
Native American Television	E-146
Navy Office of Information (OI-03)	E-122
NBA League Pass	E-62

2017 Edition xvii

Index to Contents

Communications Daily
Warren Communications News

Get the industry standard FREE —
For a no-obligation trial call 800-771-9202 or visit www.warren-news.com

NBA League Pass (See also NBA TV)	E-63
NBA TV	E-63
NBC Deportes	E-63
NBC Deportes (See also Telemundo Deportes)	E-86
NBC News	E-122
NBCSN	E-63
NBC Sports Network	E-63
NBC Sports Network (See also NBCSN)	E-63
NBCUniversal LLC	A-1575
NBC Universo	E-63
NBI Holdings LLC	A-1576
NCTI	E-146
NEO Cricket	E-63
NEON	E-63
NEON (See also Time Warner Cable SportsChannel Ohio)	E-90
NESN	E-63
NESN (See also New England Sports Network)	E-63
NESN National	E-63
NESN National (See also New England Sports Network)	E-63
NESNPlus	E-63
NESNPlus (See also New England Sports Network)	E-63
Netflix	E-63, E-122
Netherlands Consulate General	E-122
New Age Media	A-1576
New Commerce Communications (NCC)	E-137
New England Cable News	E-63
New England Sports Network	E-63
New Evangelization TV	E-64
New Form Digital	E-122
New Life Evangelistic Center Inc.	A-1577
News 8 Austin	E-64
News 8 Austin (See also Time Warner Cable News (Austin))	E-88
News 10 Now	E-64
News 10 Now (See also Time Warner Cable News (Central NY))	E-88
News 12 Bronx	E-64
News 12 Bronx (See also News 12 Interactive)	E-64
News 12 Brooklyn	E-64
News 12 Brooklyn (See also News 12 Interactive)	E-64
News 12 Connecticut	E-64
News 12 Connecticut (See also News 12 Interactive)	E-64
News 12 Hudson Valley	E-64
News 12 Hudson Valley (See also News 12 Interactive)	E-64
News 12 Interactive	E-64
News 12 Long Island	E-64
News 12 New Jersey	E-64
News 12 New Jersey (See also News 12 Interactive)	E-64
News 12 New Jersey en Espanol	E-64
News 12 New Jersey en Espanol (See also News 12 New Jersey)	E-64
News 12 the Bronx en Espanol	E-64
News 12 the Bronx en Espanol (See also News 12 Bronx)	E-64
News 12 Traffic & Weather	E-64
News 12 Traffic & Weather (See also News 12 Interactive)	E-64
News 12 Westchester	E-64
News 12 Westchester (See also News 12 Interactive)	E-64
News 14 Carolina	E-64
News Broadcast Network	E-122
News Channel 3 Anytime	E-64
News Channel 5+	E-65
NewsChannel 8	E-65
Newsday TV	E-65
Newsmax TV	E-65
NewsON	E-65
News on One - WOWT	E-65
News on One - WOWT (See also WOWT 6 News)	E-102
News Plus	E-65
News-Press & Gazette Co.	A-1577
Newswatch 15	E-65
Newsy	E-65
New Tang Dynasty TV	E-65
Newton Media Associates Inc.	E-122
New Visions Syndication	E-122
New York 1 Noticias	E-65
New York 1 Noticias (See also Time Warner Cable News NY1)	E-89
New York Network	E-65
New York Racing Channel	E-65
New York State Assembly Radio Television	E-65
Nexstar Broadcasting Group Inc.	A-1577
NFL Films Inc.	E-122
NFL Network	E-66
NFL RedZone	E-66
NFL RedZone (See also NFL Network)	E-66
NHK World Premium	E-66
NHK World Premium (See also NHK World TV)	E-66
NHK World TV	E-66
NHL Center Ice	E-66
NHL Center Ice (See also NHL Network)	E-66
NHL Network	E-66
Nick 2	E-66
Nick 2 (See also Nickelodeon)	E-66
Nick At Nite	E-66
Nick At Nite (See also Nickelodeon)	E-66
Nickelodeon	E-66
Nick en Espanol	E-67
Nick en Espanol (See also Nickelodeon)	E-66
Nick Jr.	E-67
Nick Jr. (See also Nickelodeon)	E-66
NickMusic	E-67
NickMusic (See also Nickelodeon)	E-66
Nicktoons	E-67
Nicktoons (See also Nickelodeon)	E-66
NickToons en Espanol	E-67
NickToons en Espanol (See also Nicktoons)	E-67
Nielsen Cable TV Household Estimates (chart)	C-10, F-4
Nielsen Geographic Regions Summary (chart)	C-9
Nippon Golden Network	E-67
Nippon Golden Network 2	E-67
Nippon Golden Network 2 (See also Nippon Golden Network)	E-67
Nippon Golden Network 3	E-67
Nippon Golden Network 3 (See also Nippon Golden Network)	E-67
NJTV	E-67
Noggin	E-67
Noggin (See also Nick Jr)	E-67
NoireTV Africa	E-67
Nonstop Network	E-67
Nonstop Network (See also COZI TV)	E-25
Norflicks Productions Ltd.	E-122
Norman Fischer & Associates Inc. (NFA Inc.)	E-137, E-146
Northeast Ohio Network	E-67
Northeast Ohio Network (See also Time Warner Cable SportsChannel (Northeast Ohio))	E-90
Northeast Video Productions	E-122
North Shore-LIJ Health TV	E-67
Northstar Media LLC	A-1577
NorthStar Telesolutions	E-146

Index to Contents

Northwest Broadcasting Inc.	A-1577
Northwest Cable News	E-67
Norwell Television LLC	A-1577
The NOW Network	E-67
NPM Inc.	A-1578
NRB Network	E-67
NRJ Holdings LLC	A-1578
NRT Communications Group LLC	A-1578
N.S. Bienstock Inc.	E-146
NTDTV	E-67
NTDTV (See also New Tang Dynasty TV)	E-65
NTN24	E-67
NTN Buzztime	E-67
NTV America	E-68
NTV International Corp.	E-122
NUVOtv	E-68
NUVOtv (See also Fuse)	E-41
NW Media	E-122
NY1	E-68
NY1 (See also Time Warner Cable News NY1)	E-89
NY1 Noticias	E-68
NY1 Noticias (See also Time Warner Cable News NY1 Noticias)	E-89
NY1 Rail & Road	E-68

O

Oasis TV	E-68
OC 16	E-68
Ocean Park Pictures Inc.	E-122
Ocean State Networks	E-68
OC Sports	E-68
ODU-TV	E-68
The Office of Communication of The Episcopal Church	E-122
Ogletree Productions	E-122
OGM Production Music	E-122
Ohio Channel	E-68
OKState.TV	E-68
Olelo	E-68
Ole TV	E-68
Olympusat Inc.	E-122
Once TV Mexico	E-68
Once TV Mexico (See also Canal Once)	E-17
One America News Network	E-68
One Caribbean Television	E-68
OneSportsPLUS	E-68
One World Sports	E-69
On The Air Studios	E-122
Open Student Television Network (OSTN)	E-123
Oppenheimer & Co. Inc.	E-137
Opus1 Music Library	E-123
Oral Roberts University	A-1578
Orbita TV	E-69
ORC International	E-146
Oregon Public Affairs Network	E-69
Oregon TV LLC	A-1578
Orion Television	E-123
Orion Television (See also listing for MGM Television Entertainment Inc)	E-120
OTA Broadcasting LLC	A-1578
Oui TV	E-69
Oui TV (See also Afrotainment Plus)	E-7
Outdoor Channel	E-69
Outer Max	E-69
Outer Max (See also Cinemax)	E-20
Outpost Entertainment	E-123
Outside Television	E-69
OUTV	E-69

ADVANCED TVFactbook

FULLY SEARCHABLE • CONTINUOUSLY UPDATED • DISCOUNT RATES FOR PRINT PURCHASERS
For more information call **800-771-9202** or visit **www.warren-news.com**

Ovation	E-69
Ovation Data Services Inc.	E-146
Earl Owensby Studios	E-123
Jim Owens Entertainment Inc.	E-123
Ownership of U.S. Commercial Television Stations	A-1560
OWN: Oprah Winfrey Network	E-70
Oxford Media Group Inc.	A-1578
Oxygen	E-70

P

PAC-12 Arizona	E-70
PAC-12 Arizona (See also PAC-12 Networks)	E-70
PAC-12 Bay Area	E-70
PAC-12 Bay Area (See also PAC-12 Networks)	E-70
PAC-12 Los Angeles	E-70
PAC-12 Los Angeles (See also PAC-12 Networks)	E-70
PAC-12 Mountain	E-70
PAC-12 Mountain (See also PAC-12 Networks)	E-70
PAC-12 Networks	E-70
PAC-12 Now	E-70
PAC-12 Now (See also PAC-12 Networks)	E-70
PAC-12 Oregon	E-70
PAC-12 Oregon (See also PAC-12 Networks)	E-70
PAC-12 Washington	E-70
PAC-12 Washington (See also PAC-12 Networks)	E-70
Pacvia TV	E-70
Raul & Consuelo Palazuelos	A-1578
Palladia	E-70
Palladia (See also MTV Live)	E-61
Pantomime Pictures Inc.	E-123
Parables Television Network	E-70
Paramount Licensing	E-123
Paramount Studios Group	E-123
Paramount Studios Group (See also listing for The Studios at Paramount)	E-127
Paramount Television Group	E-123
Paramount Television Group (See also listing for CBS Television Studios)	E-110
Parent & Satellite TV Stations	C-3
Parker Broadcasting of Colorado Holdco LLC	A-1578
Pasiones	E-70
Pathe News Inc.	E-123
Patrick Communications LLC	E-137, E-146
Patriots On Demand	E-70
Patterson Studios Inc.	E-123
Paulist Productions	E-123
Paxton Media Group Inc.	A-1578
Pay TV & Satellite Services	E-1
PBJ	E-70
PBS HD	E-71
PBS International	E-123
PBS Kids	E-71
PCTV	E-71
PDI Construction	E-146
PeaceTV	E-71
Peacock Productions	E-123
Peckham Productions Inc.	E-123
PegasusTV	E-71
Pennebaker Associates Inc.	E-123
Penn National Racing Alive	E-71

2017 Edition xix

Index to Contents

Communications Daily
Warren Communications News
Get the industry standard FREE —
For a no-obligation trial call 800-771-9202 or visit www.warren-news.com

Pennsylvania Cable Network	E-71
Penthouse TV	E-71
Peregrine Communications	E-146
Perennial Pictures Film Corp.	E-123
Peru Magico	E-71
Pets.TV	E-71
PFC - O Canal do Futebol	E-71
Phoenix Communications Group Inc.	E-123
Phoenix Entertainment Group	E-123
Phoenix Films & Video	E-123
Phoenix InfoNews	E-71
Phoenix Movies Channel	E-71
Phoenix Movies Channel (See also Phoenix Infonews)	E-71
Phoenix North America Chinese Channel	E-71
Phoenix North America Chinese Channel (See also Phoenix Infonews)	E-71
John Pierce & Co. LLC	E-137
Pikes Peak Community College	E-71
Pilot Productions Inc.	E-123
Pinnacle Media Worldwide	E-147
Pittsburgh Cable News Channel	E-71
Pivot	E-72
PIX11	E-72
Pixar Animation Studios	E-123
Planet Green	E-72
Planet Green (See also Destination America)	E-27
Playboy en Espanol	E-72
Playboy en Espanol (See also Playboy TV)	E-72
Playboy Entertainment Group Inc.	E-123
Playboy TV	E-72
Players Network (PNTV)	E-72
Playgirl TV	E-72
Play-It Productions	E-124
PlayOn! Sports	E-124
Pleasure	E-72
PMCM TV LLC	A-1578
PNC Financial Services Group	E-137
Pohly Co.	E-147
Point of View Productions	E-124, E-147
Poker Central	E-72
PokerTV Network	E-72
Kenneth D. Polin	A-1578
Pollack/Belz Broadcasting Co. LLC	A-1578
Pop	E-72
Popcornflix.com	E-73
Portuguese Channel	E-73
Pottstown Community TV	E-73
Pottstown Community TV (See also PCTV)	E-71
Power Television International LLC	A-1579
PPV En Espanol	E-73
PPV En Espanol (See also iN DEMAND)	E-50
Praise Television	E-73
Presbyterian Church (U.S.A.)	E-124
PriceWaterhouseCoopers (PWC)	E-147
PrideVision TV	E-73
PrideVision TV (See also OutTV)	E-69
Prime Ticket	E-73
Prime Ticket (See also FOX Sports West)	E-40
Prime Time Christian Broadcasting Inc.	A-1579
Production Studio Inc.	E-124
Program Sources & Services	E-105
Promark Television Inc.	E-124
Providence Equity Partners Inc.	E-137
PSSI Global Services/Strategic Television	E-124
Public Interest Video Network	E-73
Puerto Rico Network	E-73
Pulse Films	E-124
Punch TV Network	E-73
Pursuit Channel	E-73
PX TV	E-73
Pyramid Media	E-124

Q

The Quad	E-73
Quality Cable Services Inc.	E-147
Quartet International Inc.	E-124
Qubo	E-73
Que Huong	E-73
Quincy Newspapers Inc.	A-1579
QVC	E-73
QVC Plus	E-74
QVC Plus (See also QVC)	E-73

R

Radar Channel	E-74
Radiant Life Ministries Inc.	A-1579
RAI Italia	E-74
Raleigh Studios	E-124
Ramar Communications Inc.	A-1579
Rancho Palos Verde Broadcasters Inc.	A-1579
R & F Broadcasting	A-1579
Rang-A-Rang Television	E-74
Rapid Broadcasting Co.	A-1579
Raycom Sports Inc.	E-124
Raycom Media Inc.	A-1579
Dana Christian Raymant	A-1579
Stan Raymond & Associates Inc.	E-137
RBC Daniels	E-137
RCH Cable	E-147
RCN Novelas	E-74
RCN Nuestra Tele	E-74
RCN TV	E-74
RCTV International	E-124
RCW Associates	E-147
ReacTV	E-74
Real	E-74
Real Hip-Hop Network	E-74
Reality Kings TV (RKTV)	E-74
Realtor.com Channel	E-74
Recipe.TV	E-74
Red ADvenir	E-74
Red Ryder Enterprises Inc.	E-124
Red River Broadcast Co. LLC	A-1580
Michael Reed	A-1580
Reel Media International	E-124
Reeltime Distributing Corp.	E-124
Reelz	E-75
Regional Music Television	E-75
Regional News Network	E-75
Register Communications Inc., Debtor in Possession	A-1580
Reino Unido TV	E-75
Relativity Media	E-124
Rembrandt Films	E-124
Renegade	E-124

Index to Contents

RetroPlex	E-75
Retro TV Network	E-75
Retro TV Network (See also RTV)	E-77
Revelations Entertainment	E-125
Rev'n	E-75
Revolt TV	E-75
REZN8	E-125
RFD-TV	E-75
RFK Engineering Solutions LLC	E-147
Rhode Island News Channel	E-75
Rhode Island Statewide Interconnect	E-75
Ride TV	E-76
RingSide Creative	E-125
Riot Creative	E-125
Ritmoson	E-76
Ritmoson (See also Univision)	E-96
RKO Pictures	E-125
RLTV	E-76
R News	E-76
R News (See also Time Warner Cable News (Rochester))	E-89
RNL	E-147
Roberts Media LLC	A-1580
Robinson/Jeffrey Associates Inc.	E-137
Rockfleet Broadcasting LP.	A-1580
Peter Rodgers Organization	E-125
Roku Channel Store	E-125
Roland Company Inc.	E-125
Root Sports Northwest	E-76
Root Sports Pittsburgh	E-76
Root Sports Rocky Mountain	E-76
Root Sports Southwest	E-76
Root Sports Utah	E-76
Root Sports Utah (See also Root Sports Rocky Mountain)	E-76
Robert Rosenheim Associates	E-125
RSN Resort TV	E-76
RSN Resort TV (See also Outside Television)	E-69
RT America	E-76
RTN	E-76
RTN+	E-76
RTN+ (See also RTN)	E-76
RTP Internacional	E-77
RTP-USA	E-125
RTR Planeta	E-77
RTV	E-77
RTVI	E-77
Rumba TV	E-77
Rumbaut & Company	E-137
Rural TV	E-77
Russian Kino	E-77
Russian Kino (See also TV 1000 Russian Kino)	E-94
Russian Media Group LLC	E-125
Russia Today	E-77
Thomas D. Rutherford	A-1580
RW Productions Inc.	E-125

S

S2One Inc.	E-148
SAB TV	E-77
Safe TV	E-77
Saga Communications Inc.	A-1580
SagamoreHill Broadcasting LLC	A-1580
SagamoreHill Midwest LLC	A-1580
SagamoreHill of Columbus GA LLC	A-1580
Saigon Broadcasting Television Network (SBTN)	E-77
Saigon TV	E-77

Access the most current data instantly
FREE TRIAL @ ADVANCED TVFactbook
TELCO/IPTV • CABLE TV • TV STATIONS
www.warren-news.com/factbook.htm

Saint Cloud State University Channel	E-77
Saint Johns County Government Television	E-77
Salaam TV	E-77
San Diego News Channel 10	E-78
San Diego News Channel 10 (See also 10 News Channel)	E-6
Sandler Capital Management	E-137
Santiago ROI	E-147
Satterfield & Perry Inc.	E-137
SATV 10 LLC	A-1580
SaudiTV	E-78
SBTN	E-78
SBTN (See also Saigon Broadcasting Television Network)	E-77
Scenic Cable Network & Production	E-125
Schurz Communications Inc.	A-1580
Ernesto Schweikert III	A-1580
Science Channel	E-78
Sci-Fi Channel	E-78
Sci-Fi Channel (See also Syfy)	E-84
Scream Factory	E-125
The E. W. Scripps Co.	A-1580
Seal Rock Broadcasters LLC	A-1581
Seals Entertainment Co. Inc.	E-125
Sear Sound	E-125
SEC Network	E-78
SEC Network+	E-78
SEC Network+ (See also SEC Network)	E-78
Second Generation of Iowa Ltd.	A-1581
Seeso	E-78
Semillitas	E-78
Senal de Vida	E-78
Senal de Vida (See also ULTRA HDPlex)	E-95
SendtoNews	E-125
September Productions	E-125
Serestar Communications Corp.	A-1581
Sesame Workshop	E-125
Setanta Sports USA	E-78
Seventh-Day Adventist Church, Communications Department	E-126
SexSee	E-78
SFM Entertainment	E-126
Shalom TV	E-78
Shalom TV (See also Jewish Broadcasting Service)	E-52
Shanghai Dragon TV	E-78
Shanghai Dragon TV (See also DragonTV)	E-30
SharjahTV	E-78
Timothy G. Sheehan	A-1581
Shenzhen Satellite TV	E-78
Shepherd's Chapel Network	E-78
Burt Sherwood & Associates Inc.	E-138
Shield Media LLC	A-1581
SHO2	E-78
SHO2 (See also Showtime)	E-79
SHO Beyond	E-78
SHO Beyond (See also Showtime)	E-79
SHO Extreme	E-78
SHO Extreme (See also Showtime)	E-79
SHO Next	E-78
SHO Next (See also Showtime)	E-79
Shop at Home	E-78
ShopHQ	E-78

2017 Edition

Index to Contents

FULLY SEARCHABLE • CONTINUOUSLY UPDATED • DISCOUNT RATES FOR PRINT PURCHASERS
For more information call **800-771-9202** or visit **www.warren-news.com**

ShopHQ (See also EVINE Live)	E-34
ShopNBC	E-78
ShopNBC (See also EVINE Live)	E-34
ShopTV	E-78
Shorteez	E-78
Shorteez (See also Bang U)	E-12
ShortsHD	E-78
Showcase Productions Inc.	E-126
Showcase Productions Inc. (See also Films Around the World Inc)	E-115
SHO Women	E-79
SHO Women (See also Showtime)	E-79
Showplace Television Syndication	E-126
Showtime	E-79
Showtime 2	E-78
Showtime 2 (See also SHO2)	E-78
Showtime Beyond	E-79
Showtime Beyond (See also SHO Beyond)	E-78
Showtime en Espanol	E-79
Showtime en Espanol (See also Showtime)	E-79
Showtime Extreme	E-79
Showtime Extreme (See also SHO Extreme)	E-78
Showtime FamilyZone	E-79
Showtime FamilyZone (See also Showtime)	E-79
Showtime Next	E-79
Showtime Next (See also SHO Next)	E-78
Showtime Showcase	E-79
Showtime Showcase (See also Showtime)	E-79
Showtime Women	E-79
Showtime Women (See also SHO Women)	E-79
Si TV	E-79
Siemens Power Technologies Intl.	E-147
Silverton Broadcasting Co. LLC	A-1581
James F. Simpson	A-1581
Sinclair Broadcast Group Inc.	A-1581
SignaSys Inc.	E-147
Sino TV	E-79
SinoVision	E-79
Sirens Media	E-126
Si TV (See also Fuse)	E-41
Six News Now	E-79
Six News Now (See also SNN: Suncoast News Network)	E-80
SJL of Pennsylvania Inc.	A-1582
The Ski Channel	E-79
Skotleski Productions	E-126
Sky Angel US LLC	E-126
Sky Link TV	E-79
Sky Television LLC	A-1582
Sleuth	E-79
Sleuth (See also cloo)	E-21
Slice	E-79
Smile of a Child TV	E-79
Smith	E-126
Smith & Fisher	E-147
Smithsonian Channel	E-79
Sneak Prevue (See also Pop)	E-72
Sneak Prevue	E-79
SNJ Today	E-79
SNL Financial	E-138
SNN Local News	E-80
SNN Local News (See also SNN: Suncoast News Network)	E-80
SNN: Suncoast News Network	E-80
Snowden Associates	E-138
Softwright LLC	E-147
Somat Publishing Ltd.	E-126
Son Broadcasting	E-80
Son Broadcasting Inc.	A-1582
SonLife Broadcasting Network	E-80
Sonshine Family TV Inc.	A-1582
Sony BMG Music Entertainment	E-126
Sony Entertainment Television Asia	E-80
Sony Movie Channel	E-80
Sony Movie Channel Everywhere	E-80
Sony Movie Channel Everywhere (See also Sony Movie Channel)	E-80
Sony Pictures Television	E-126
SoonerVision	E-80
Sorpresa!	E-80
Sorensen Media Group Inc.	A-1582
Soul of the South Network	E-80
Soundtrack Channel	E-80
The South Carolina Channel	E-80
Southeastern Channel	E-80
Southeastern Ohio Television System	A-1583
Southern Broadcast Corp. of Sarasota	A-1583
Southern TV Corp.	A-1583
Spanish Independent Broadcast Network	E-80
Spanish Broadcasting System (SBS)	E-126
Spanish Broadcasting System Inc.	A-1583
SpanPro Inc.	E-147
Speed	E-80
Speed (See also Fox Sports 1)	E-38
Spice 2	E-80
Spice 2 (See also Bang U)	E-12
Spice	E-80
Spice (See also Brazzers TV)	E-15
Spice Hot	E-81
Spice Hot (See also Reality Kings TV (RKTV))	E-74
Spice: Xcess	E-81
Spice: Xcess (See also MOFOS)	E-59
Spike TV	E-81
Sporting Channel	E-81
SportsChoice	E-81
Sportskool	E-81
The Sportsman Channel	E-81
SportsNet New York	E-81
SportSouth	E-81
SportSouth (See also FOX Sports South)	E-40
Sports PPV	E-81
SportsTime Ohio	E-81
SportsTime Ohio (See also FOX Sports Ohio)	E-39
Sports View Plus	E-81
Sprout	E-81
STAR One	E-82
STAR Chinese Channel	E-82
STAR Gold	E-82
STAR Gold (See also STAR Plus)	E-82
STAR India NEWS	E-82
STAR India NEWS (See also ABP News)	E-6
Star News	E-82
Star News (See also ABP News)	E-6
STAR One (See also Life OK)	E-54
STAR Plus	E-82
Starz	E-82
Starz Cinema	E-82
Starz Cinema (See also Starz)	E-82
Starz Comedy	E-82
Starz Comedy (See also Starz)	E-82

Index to Contents

Starz Edge	E-82
Starz Edge (See also Starz)	E-82
Starz Encore	E-82
Starz Encore Action	E-82
Starz Encore Action (See also Starz Encore)	E-82
Starz Encore Black	E-82
Starz Encore Black (See also Starz Encore)	E-82
Starz Encore Classic	E-82
Starz Encore Classic (See also Starz Encore)	E-82
Starz Encore Espanol	E-82
Starz Encore Espanol (See also Starz Encore)	E-82
Starz Encore Family	E-83
Starz Encore Family (See also Starz Encore)	E-82
Starz Encore Suspense	E-83
Starz Encore Suspense (See also Starz Encore)	E-82
Starz Encore Westerns	E-83
Starz Encore Westerns (See also Starz Encore)	E-82
Starz In Black	E-83
Starz In Black (See also Starz)	E-82
Starz Kids & Family	E-83
Starz Kids & Family (See also Starz)	E-82
Starz Play	E-83
Starz Play (See also Starz)	E-82
State Street Corp.	E-138
Sterling Institute Inc.	E-147
James A. Stern	A-1583
Stevens Design & Animation LLC	E-126
Howard Stirk Holdings LLC	A-1583
Stonegate Capital Group LLC	E-138
Marty Stouffer Productions Ltd.	E-126
Strata Marketing Inc.	E-147
Streampix	E-83
Structural Systems Technology Inc.	E-148
The Studios at Paramount	E-127
STX Entertainment	E-127
Style Network	E-83
Style Network (See also Esquire Network)	E-33
Suddenlink2GO	E-83
Sunbeam Television Corp.	A-1583
Sunbelt-South Telecommunications Ltd.	A-1583
Sunbelt Television Inc.	A-1583
Sun Broadcasting Inc.	A-1583
Sun Channel	E-83
Sundance Select	E-127
Sundance TV	E-83
Sunrise Media LLC	E-127
Sun Sports	E-83
Sun Sports (See also FOX Sports Florida/Sun Sports)	E-38
Super Canal	E-83
Super Canal (See also ULTRA HDPlex)	E-95
Superene	E-83
Superstation WGN	E-83
Superstation WGN (See also WGN America)	E-101
Sur	E-83
The Surf Channel	E-83
Sur Peru	E-83
Sur Peru (See also Sur)	E-83
Swain Film & Video Inc.	E-127
SWRV TV	E-84
SWRV TV (See also MC)	E-57
Syfy	E-84
Syntellect Inc.	E-148
The Syzygy Network	E-84
Szabo Associates Inc.	E-148

T

TAC TV	E-84
TACH-TV	E-84
Taiwan Macroview TV	E-84
Taiwan Macroview TV (See also MAC TV)	E-56
Talkline Communications TV Network	E-84
Tamer Media LLC	A-1583
Tanana Valley Television Co.	A-1583
Tango Traffic	E-84
Tapesh TV	E-84
Sarkes Tarzian Inc.	A-1583
Tavsir Iran	E-84
TBN Enlace USA	E-84
TBN Enlace USA (See also Enlace USA)	E-32
TBN Salsa	E-84
TBS	E-84
TC Specialties	E-148
TCT	E-85
TCT Family	E-85
TCT Family (See also TCT)	E-85
TCT La Fuente	E-85
TCT La Fuente (See also TCT)	E-85
TCT of Michigan Inc.	A-1584
TD Bank	E-138
TeamHD	E-85
TeamHD (See also iN DEMAND)	E-50
Technicolor Inc./CFI	E-127
TeenNick	E-85
TEGNA Inc.	A-1584
Tele Vida Abudante	E-85
Teleadoracion Christian Network Inc.	A-1584
Teleamazonas	E-85
Telecafe	E-85
Telecare	E-85
TeleCentro	E-85
TeleCentro (See also ULTRA HDPlex)	E-95
Telecinco Inc.	A-1584
TeleCom Productions	E-127
Tele El Salvador	E-85
Tele El Salvador (See also ULTRA HDPlex)	E-95
Telefe Internacional	E-85
Telefilm Canada	E-127
TeleFormula	E-85
TeleFutura	E-85
TeleFutura (See also UniMas)	E-96
Telegenic Programs Inc.	E-127
Telehit	E-85
Telehit (See also Univision)	E-96
Telekaribe	E-85
Telemiami	E-85
Telemicro Internacional	E-86
Telemundo	E-86
Telemundo Deportes	E-86
Telemundo Internacional	E-86
Telemundo Internacional (See also Telemundo)	E-86
Telemundo Network Group	E-127
Telemundo Puerto Rico	E-86

2017 Edition   xxiii

Index to Contents

CABLE & TV STATION COVERAGE
Atlas 2017
The perfect companion to the Television & Cable Factbook
To order call 800-771-9202 or visit www.warren-news.com

Telemundo Puerto Rico (See also Telemundo)	E-86
Tele N	E-86
Telenostalgia	E-86
Telephone and Data Systems	A-1584
Telepictures Productions	E-127
TeleRitmo	E-86
Tele-Romantica	E-86
Telestrategies Inc.	E-148
Teletech Communications	E-127
Teletech Inc.	E-148
Televen America	E-86
Televisa	E-127
Television Stations (Commercial)	A-20
Television Station Owners	A-1560
Alabama	A-21
Alaska	A-57
Arizona	A-71
Arkansas	A-99
California	A-122
Colorado	A-215
Connecticut	A-244
Delaware	A-254
District of Columbia	A-258
Florida	A-265
Georgia	A-342
Hawaii	A-380
Idaho	A-404
Illinois	A-419
Indiana	A-458
Iowa	A-492
Kansas	A-517
Kentucky	A-542
Louisiana	A-564
Maine	A-597
Maryland	A-608
Massachusetts	A-619
Michigan	A-638
Minnesota	A-681
Mississippi	A-707
Missouri	A-731
Montana	A-764
Nebraska	A-783
Nevada	A-802
New Hampshire	A-819
New Jersey	A-824
New Mexico	A-837
New York	A-857
North Carolina	A-908
North Dakota	A-948
Ohio	A-969
Oklahoma	A-1011
Oregon	A-1037
Pennsylvania	A-1066
Puerto Rico	A-1456
Rhode Island	A-1107
South Carolina	A-1112
South Dakota	A-1136
Tennessee	A-1154
Texas	A-1190
Utah	A-1310
Vermont	A-1324
Virginia	A-1329
Washington	A-1358
West Virginia	A-1387
Wisconsin	A-1404
Wyoming	A-1441
Guam	A-1454
Virgin Islands	A-1484
Television Korea 24	E-86
Television Market Rankings (Nielsen)	A-1
Television Representatives Inc.	E-127
Television Station Owners	A-1560
Television Stations on Air (Chart)	C-1
Television Stations Public & Educational	A-1492
The Television Syndication Co. Inc.	E-127
TeleXitos	E-87
Telvue Corp.	E-148
Tempo	E-87
TEN	E-87
Ten Cricket	E-87
Tennessee Broadcasting LLC	A-1584
Tennis Channel	E-87
Tennis Channel Plus	E-87
Tennis Channel Plus (See also Tennis Channel)	E-87
TERRITORY	E-127
Texas Channel	E-87
Texas House of Representatives Video/Audio Services	E-87
Texas Television Inc.	A-1584
TFC	E-87
TFC (See also The Filipino Channel)	E-36
The Auto Channel (See also TACH-TV)	E-84
TheBlaze	E-87
TheCoolTV	E-87
The Erotic Network (See also TEN)	E-87
The Learning Channel	E-87
The Learning Channel (See also TLC)	E-90
The Movie Channel (See also Showtime)	E-79
The Movie Channel Xtra (See also The Movie Channel)	E-59
The N	E-87
The N (See also TeenNick)	E-85
The New Encore	E-63
The New Encore (See also Starz Encore)	E-82
Thirteen/WNET	E-127
This TV	E-87
Thomas Broadcasting Co.	A-1584
Thomson Reuters Corp.	E-127
Three Angels Broadcasting Network	E-88
Three Angels Broadcasting Network (See also 3ABN)	E-5
Three Thousand Eight	E-128
Thriller Max	E-88
Thriller Max (See also Cinemax)	E-20
Thunder Bay Broadcasting Corp.	A-1584
TiBA Solutions	E-148
Tigervision	E-88
Timeless Media Group	E-128
Time Warner Cable Community (Socal)	E-88
Time Warner Cable Deportes	E-88
Time Warner Cable News (Antelope Valley)	E-88
Time Warner Cable News (Austin)	E-88
Time Warner Cable News (Brooklyn)	E-88
Time Warner Cable News (Brooklyn) (See also Time Warner Cable News NY1)	E-89
Time Warner Cable News (Buffalo)	E-88
Time Warner Cable News (Capital Region NY)	E-88
Time Warner Cable News (Central NC)	E-88
Time Warner Cable News (Central NY)	E-88
Time Warner Cable News (Charlotte)	E-88

Index to Contents

Time Warner Cable News (Coastal NC)	E-88
Time Warner Cable News (Hudson Valley)	E-88
Time Warner Cable News (Hudson Valley) (See also Time Warner Cable News (Capital Region NY)	E-88
Time Warner Cable News (Jamestown)	E-88
Time Warner Cable News (Manhattan)	E-89
Time Warner Cable News (Manhattan) (See also Time Warner Cable News NY1)	E-89
Time Warner Cable News (Northern NY)	E-89
Time Warner Cable News (Northern NY) (See also Time Warner Cable News (Central NY)	E-88
Time Warner Cable News (Queens)	E-89
Time Warner Cable News (Queens) (See also Time Warner Cable News NY1)	E-89
Time Warner Cable News (Rochester)	E-89
Time Warner Cable News (San Antonio)	E-89
Time Warner Cable News (Southern Tier NY)	E-89
Time Warner Cable News (Southern Tier NY) (See also Time Warner Cable News (Central NY)	E-88
Time Warner Cable News (Staten Island)	E-89
Time Warner Cable News (Staten Island) (See also Time Warner Cable News NY1)	E-89
Time Warner Cable News (The Bronx)	E-88
Time Warner Cable News (The Bronx) (See also Time Warner Cable News NY1)	E-89
Time Warner Cable News (Triad NC)	E-89
Time Warner Cable News NY1 Noticias	E-89
Time Warner Cable News NY1 Noticias (See also Time Warner Cable News NY1)	E-89
Time Warner Cable News NY1	E-89
Time Warner Cable Sports 3 Albany	E-89
Time Warner Cable Sports 3 Albany (See also Time Warner Cable SportsChannel (Albany)	E-89
Time Warner Cable Sports Central New York	E-89
Time Warner Cable Sports Central New York (See also Time Warner Cable SportsChannel (Syracuse)	E-90
Time Warner Cable SportsChannel (Albany)	E-89
Time Warner Cable SportsChannel (Austin)	E-89
Time Warner Cable SportsChannel (Buffalo)	E-89
Time Warner Cable SportsChannel (Columbia)	E-89
Time Warner Cable SportsChannel (Columbia) (See also Time Warner Cable SportsChannel (Eastern North Carolina)	E-89
Time Warner Cable SportsChannel (Dallas)	E-89
Time Warner Cable SportsChannel (Eastern North Carolina)	E-89
Time Warner Cable SportsChannel (Green Bay)	E-89
Time Warner Cable SportsChannel (Green Bay) (See also Time Warner Cable SportsChannel (Milwaukee)	E-90
Time Warner Cable SportsChannel (Kansas City)	E-90
Time Warner Cable SportsChannel (Lincoln)	E-90
Time Warner Cable SportsChannel (Mid Ohio)	E-90
Time Warner Cable SportsChannel (Mid Ohio) (See also Time Warner Cable SportsChannel (Northeast Ohio)	E-90
Time Warner Cable SportsChannel (Milwaukee)	E-90
Time Warner Cable SportsChannel (Northeast Ohio)	E-90
Time Warner Cable SportsChannel (Rochester)	E-90
Time Warner Cable SportsChannel (Southwest Ohio)	E-90
Time Warner Cable SportsChannel (Southwest Ohio) (See also Time Warner Cable SportsChannel (Northeast Ohio)	E-90
Time Warner Cable SportsChannel (Syracuse)	E-90
Time Warner Cable SportsChannel (Western North Carolina)	E-90
Time Warner Cable SportsChannel (Western North Carolina) (See also Time Warner Cable SportsChannel (Eastern North Carolina)	E-89
Time Warner Cable SportsChannel Wisconsin	E-90
Time Warner Cable SportsChannel Wisconsin (See also Time Warner Cable SportsChannel (Milwaukee)	E-90
Time Warner Cable SportsChannel 2 (Kansas City)	E-89
Time Warner Cable SportsNet	E-90
Time Warner Cable SportsNet Buffalo	E-90
Time Warner Cable SportsNet Buffalo (See also Time Warner Cable SportsChannel (Buffalo)	E-89
Time Warner Cable SportsNet LA	E-90
Time Warner Cable SportsNet Rochester	E-90
Time Warner Cable SportsNet Rochester (See also Time Warner Cable SportsChannel (Rochester)	E-90
Time Warner Inc.	A-1584
Tivi5MONDE	E-90
TKMI Broadcasting	E-90
TLC	E-90
Total Living Network	E-91
TMC	E-91
TMC (See also The Movie Channel)	E-59
TMC Xtra	E-91
TMC Xtra (See also The Movie Channel Xtra)	E-59
TM Studios	E-128
TNN (The Nashville Network)	E-91
TNN (The Nashville Network) (See also Heartland)	E-46
Turner Network Television	E-91
Today Video	E-128
Tokyo TV	E-91
Too Much for TV On Demand	E-91
Too Much for TV On Demand (See also iN DEMAND)	E-50
Toon Disney	E-91
Toon Disney (See also Disney XD)	E-29
TOP Channel TV	E-91
Top Kopy	E-128
Torstar Media Group Television (Toronto Star TV)	E-91
Touchstone Pictures/Walt Disney	E-128
Touchstone Television	E-128
Touchstone Television (See also listing for ABC Studios)	E-105
Tougaloo College	A-1585
Towers Watson	E-148
Tr3s	E-91
Tr3s (See also MTV)	E-60
Trace Sport Stars	E-91
Transcomm Inc.	E-148
Trans World International	E-128
Trans World International (See also listing for IMG World)	E-118
Travel Channel	E-91
Travel Channel Beyond	E-91
Travel Channel Beyond (See also Travel Channel)	E-91
Travel on Demand	E-91
Travelview International	E-128
Travel Weather Now	E-91
Travel Weather Now (See also Bright House Travel Weather Now)	E-16
Triangle Inc.	E-128
Tribeca Film Center	E-128
Tribune Broadcasting Co.	A-1585
Tribune Media Services Inc.	E-128
Tribune Media Services Inc. (See also Gracenote)	E-117
Trimark Television	E-128
Trimark Television (See also listing for Lionsgate Entertainment)	E-119
Trinity Broadcasting Network (TBN)	E-91
Trinity Broadcasting Network Inc.	A-1585
Tristar Television	E-128
Tristar Television (See also listing for Sony Pictures Television)	E-126
Tri-State Christian Television	E-92
Tri-State Christian Television (See also TCT)	E-85
Tri-State Christian TV Inc.	A-1585
Tri-State Family Broadcasting Inc.	A-1585
Trojan Vision	E-92
Troma Entertainment Inc.	E-128
True Blue	E-92
truTV	E-92

2017 Edition

Index to Contents

FULLY SEARCHABLE • CONTINUOUSLY UPDATED • DISCOUNT RATES FOR PRINT PURCHASERS

For more information call **800-771-9202** or visit **www.warren-news.com**

TTV Capital	E-138
Benjamin A Tucker	A-1585
TUFF TV	E-92
Tu Ingles TV	E-92
John B Tupper	A-1585
Turner Broadcasting System Inc.	E-128
Turner Classic Movies	E-92
Turner Network Television (See also TNT)	E-92
TNT	E-92
Turner South	E-93
Turner South (See also SportSouth)	E-81
Turner Sports	E-128
TV2	E-93
TV5, La Television International	E-93
TV5MONDE USA	E-93
TV 1000 Russian Kino	E-94
TV Agro	E-93
TV Asia	E-93
TVC+ Latino	E-93
TV Chile	E-93
TV Chile (See also ULTRA HDPlex)	E-95
TV Colombia	E-93
TV Colombia (See also RCN Nuestra Tele)	E-74
Television Dominicana	E-93
TVE Internacional	E-93
TV Globo Internacional	E-93
TVGN	E-93
TVGN (See also Pop)	E-72
TVG Network	E-93
TV Guide Interactive Inc.	E-93
TV Guide Network	E-93
TV Guide Network (See also Pop)	E-72
TV Households by State and County (chart)	C-12
TVHS	E-93
Tvidavision	E-94
TV Japan	E-94
TVK2	E-94
TVK2 (See also TVK (Korean)	E-94
TVK (Korean)	E-94
TVK Pop on Demand	E-94
TVK Pop on Demand (See also TVK (Korean)	E-94
TV Land	E-94
TV Mex	E-94
TVO	E-128
TV One	E-94
TV Orient	E-95
TVP Info	E-95
TVP Info (See also TV Polonia)	E-95
TV Polonia	E-95
TV Record	E-95
TV Romania International	E-95
TV Venezuela	E-95
TVW	E-95
TW3	E-95
TW3 (See also Time Warner Cable Sports 3 Albany)	E-89
TWC TV New England	E-95
Twentieth Century Fox Film Corp.	E-128
Twentieth Century Fox Home Entertainment	E-129
Twentieth Century Fox Television	E-129
Twentieth Television	E-129
TyC Sports	E-95
Tyler Media LLC	A-1585

U

UBC-TV Network	E-95
UCTV	E-95
UHD-1	E-95
Ronald Ulloa	A-1585
Ultra Cine	E-95
Ultra Cine (See also ULTRA HDPlex)	E-95
Ultra Clasico	E-95
Ultra Clasico (See also ULTRA HDPlex)	E-95
Ultra Docu	E-95
Ultra Docu (See also ULTRA HDPlex)	E-95
Ultra Familia	E-95
Ultra Familia (See also ULTRA HDPlex)	E-95
Ultra Fiesta	E-95
Ultra Fiesta (See also ULTRA HDPlex)	E-95
Ultra Film	E-95
Ultra Film (See also ULTRA HDPlex)	E-95
ULTRA HDPlex	E-95
Ultra Kidz	E-95
Ultra Kidz (See also ULTRA HDPlex)	E-95
Ultra Luna	E-95
Ultra Luna (See also ULTRA HDPlex)	E-95
Ultra Macho	E-96
Ultra Macho (See also ULTRA HDPlex)	E-95
Ultra Mex	E-96
Ultra Mex (See also ULTRA HDPlex)	E-95
Ultra Tainment	E-96
Ultra Tainment (See also ULTRA HDPlex)	E-95
UniMas	E-96
UniMas (See also Univision)	E-96
Unique Business News	E-96
Unique Satellite TV	E-96
United Church of Christ, Office of Communications	E-129
United Communications Corp.	A-1585
United Film Enterprises Inc.	E-129
United Methodist Communications	E-129
United Nations	E-129
United Nations (See also listing for UN Multimedia)	E-130
United Press International	E-129
United Recovery Systems	E-148
Universal Cable Productions	E-129
Universal HD	E-96
Universal Music Publishing Group (UMPG)	E-129
Universal Television	E-129
Board of Trustees, U. of Alabama	A-1586
University of California TV (UCTV)	E-96
University of Southern California: Hugh M. Hefner Moving Image Archive	E-129
Univision	E-96
Univision Communications Inc.	A-1586
Univision Deportes	E-96
Univision Deportes (See also Univision)	E-96
Univision Deportes Dos	E-96
Univision Deportes Dos (See also Univision Deportes)	E-96
Univision Story House	E-130
Univision Studios	E-130
Univision tdn	E-96
Univision tdn (See also Univision Deportes)	E-96
Univision tlnovelas	E-96
Univision tlnovelas (See also Univision)	E-96
UN Multimedia	E-130
Untamed Sports TV	E-96

Index to Contents

Unum Provident Corp.	E-138
Unusual Films	E-130
UP	E-97
UPA Productions of America	E-130
Upliftv	E-97
Urban Movie Channel	E-97
USA 800 Inc.	E-148
USA Network	E-97
USA Now	E-97
USA Now (See also USA Network)	E-97
USA Television Holdings LLC	A-1587
U.S. Department of Agriculture, Office of Communications	E-130
U.S. Department of Commerce	E-148
U.S. Military TV Network	E-97
Utilisima	E-97
Utilisima (See also Fox Life)	E-37
UVideos	E-97
Valuation Research Corp.	E-138
VAN-TV	E-97
Varvid Inc.	E-148
VasalloVision Network	E-98

V

Thomas J Vaughan	A-1587
T.J. Vaughan & Associates	E-148
VaVoom	E-98
VCY America Inc.	A-1587
Velocity	E-98
VeneMovies	E-98
VeneMovies (See also ViendoMovies)	E-98
Venevision International Inc.	E-130
Venevision International Inc. (See also Cisneros Media Distribution)	E-111
Venevision Productions	E-130
Venture Technologies Group LLC	A-1587
Veria Living	E-98
Veria Living (See also Z Living)	E-104
Veritas Productions Inc.	E-130
Veronis Suhler Stevenson	E-138
Versus	E-98
Versus (See also NBCSN)	E-63
Vertigo Productions	E-130
VH1	E-98
VH1 Classic	E-98
VH1 Classic (See also MTV)	E-60
VH1 Country	E-98
VH1 Country (See also CMT Pure Country)	E-21
VH1 Soul	E-98
VH1 Soul (See also BET)	E-13
Viacom Inc.	E-130
Vice	E-130
Viceland	E-98
Victory Studios	E-130
Victory Television Network Inc.	A-1587
Vida Vision	E-98
VidCAD	E-148
Video Mix TV	E-98
Video Zona TV	E-98
Video-Cinema Films Inc.	E-130
Video Enterprises Inc.	E-130
Video Express Productions	E-130
Video/Fashion Network	E-98
Video Music Club	E-98
Video Music Club (See also VMC)	E-99
VideoRola	E-98
ViendoMovies	E-98

Communications Daily
Warren Communications News

Get the industry standard FREE —
For a no-obligation trial call 800-771-9202 or visit www.warren-news.com

Vietnamese American Network Television	E-98
Vietnamese American Network Television (See also VAN-TV)	E-97
VIP 2000	E-130
Viratech.org	E-130
Vision Communications LLC (New York)	A-1587
VisLink Services	E-148
Vista Street Entertainment	E-130
VITAC	E-130
Viva Television Network	E-98
Viva Television Network (See also Vme TV)	E-99
VividTV	E-98
VMC	E-99
Vme Kids	E-99
Vme TV	E-99
Vozzcom Inc.	E-149
Vremya	E-99
VRV	E-99
V-Soft Communications	E-149
VStv	E-99
Vubiquity Inc.	E-130
VUDU	E-99
VU Television Network	E-99

W

Wachovia Corp.	E-138
Waitt Broadcasting Inc.	A-1587
TheWalktv	E-99
Wallach Entertainment	E-131
Waller Capital Partners	E-138
WALN Cable Radio	E-99
Walt Disney Animation Studios	E-131
Walt Disney Pictures	E-131
Walt Disney Studios	E-131
Walters-Storyk Design Group Inc.	E-149
WAM! America's Kidz Network	E-99
WAM! America's Kidz Network (See also Starz Encore Family)	E-83
WAPA America	E-99
Warner Bros. Animation Inc.	E-131
Warner Bros. Digital Networks	E-131
Warner Bros. Domestic Television Distribution	E-131
Warner Bros. International Television Distribution	E-131
Warner Bros. Pictures	E-131
Warner Bros. Pictures Domestic Distribution	E-131
Warner Bros. Pictures International	E-131
Warner Bros. Television Group	E-131
Warner Home Video	E-131
Warner Independent Pictures	E-131
Warren & Morris Ltd.	E-149
Frank Washington	A-1587
Washington Korean TV	E-99
WATCH ABC Family	E-99
WATCH ABC Family (See also WATCH Freeform)	E-100
WATCH Disney Channel	E-99
WATCH Disney Channel (See also Disney Channel)	E-28
WATCH Disney Junior	E-99
WATCH Disney Junior (See also Disney Channel)	E-28
WATCH Disney XD	E-100
WATCH Disney XD (See also Disney Channel)	E-28

2017 Edition xxvii

Index to Contents

WATCH ESPN	E-100
WATCH ESPN (See also ESPN)	E-32
WATCH Food Network	E-100
WATCH Food Network (See also Food Network)	E-36
WATCH Freeform	E-100
WATCH Freeform (See also Freeform)	E-40
WATCH TBS	E-100
WATCH TBS (See also TBS)	E-84
WATCH TCM	E-100
WATCH TCM (See also Turner Classic Movies)	E-92
WATCH TNT	E-100
WATCH TNT (See also TNT)	E-92
WATCH truTV	E-100
WATCH truTV (See also truTV)	E-92
Waterman Broadcasting Corp.	A-1587
Waypoint Media	A-1587
WBHQ Columbia LLC	A-1587
WBIN Inc.	A-1587
WCTY Channel 16	E-100
The Weather Channel	E-100
WeatherNation	E-100
Weather Network	E-100
Weathernews Inc.	E-131
Weatherscan	E-100
WeatherVision	E-131
Weber Shandwick	E-149
Weigel Broadcasting Co.	A-1587
Evan Weiner Productions	E-131
Wells Fargo Securities LLC	E-138
West American Finance Corp.	A-1587
Westchester Films	E-132
Western Broadcasting Corp. of Puerto Rico.	A-1587
Western New Life Inc.	A-1588
Western Pacific Broadcast LLC	A-1588
Weston Woods Studios Inc.	E-132
West Virginia Media Holdings LLC	A-1588
WETA UK	E-101
WE tv	E-101
WGN	E-101
WGN America	E-101
WGN (See also WGN America)	E-101
WHDH LLC	A-1588
Wheeler Broadcasting LLC	A-1588
WheelsTV	E-101
White Knight Holdings Inc.	A-1588
Wicked On Demand	E-101
WideOrbit	E-149
Wilderness Communications LLC	A-1588
Wild TV	E-101
William Morris Endeavor Entertainment	E-149
Williams Communications Inc.	E-149
Willow	E-101
WINK News Now 24/7	E-101
Winston Broadcasting Network Inc.	A-1588
WisconsinEye	E-101
Dana R. Withers	A-1588
WizeBuys TV	E-101
WKTV	E-102
WKYT-TV	E-102
Jason Wolff	A-1588
Woods Communications Corp.	A-1588
Word Broadcasting Network Inc.	A-1588
The Word Network	E-102
Word of God Fellowship Inc.	A-1588
The Works	E-102
World	E-102
World Class Video	E-132
World Fishing Network	E-102
World Harvest Television	E-102
World of Wonder Productions	E-132
World Picks On Demand (Hindi, Latino, Mandarin, Russian)	E-102
World Property Channel	E-132
Worldwide Entertainment Corp.	E-132
World Wrestling Entertainment Inc.	E-132
Worship Network	E-102
WOWT 6 News	E-102
WPA Film Library	E-132
WQED Multimedia	E-132
WRNN-TV Associates LP	A-1589
WRS Motion Picture & Video Laboratory	E-132
WSI Corp.	E-149
WTTW Local Productions	E-132
WTTW National Productions	E-132
WWE Network	E-102
Wyomedia Corp.	A-1589

X

Xfinity on Demand	E-102
XHIJ-TV	E-102
XHIJ-TV (See also Canal 44 (XHIJ-TV))	E-16
Xiamen TV	E-102
XTSY	E-103
XTV	E-103

Y

Yangtse River Drama	E-103
Yankees Entertainment & Sports	E-103
Yankees Entertainment & Sports (See also YES Network)	E-103
YES2	E-103
YES2 (See also YES Network)	E-103
YES Network	E-103
Yesterday USA	E-103
YNN (Capital Region & Hudson Valley, NY) (See also Time Warner Cable News (Capital Region) & Time Warner Cable News (Hudson Valley)	E-88
YNN (Central, Northern & Southern Tier, NY) (See also Time Warner Cable News (Central NY), (Northern NY) & (Southern Tier NY)	E-88
YNN Austin	E-103
YNN Austin (See also Time Warner Cable News (Austin)	E-88
YNN (Capital Region & Hudson Valley, NY)	E-103
YNN (Central, Northern & Southern Tier, NY)	E-103
YNN Rochester	E-103
YNN Rochester (See also Time Warner Cable News (Rochester))	E-89
Jim Young & Associates Inc.	E-149
Youtoo America	E-103
YouTube	E-132
Yuma 77	E-103

Z

Zeebox	E-132
Zeebox (See also Beamly)	E-108
Zee Business	E-103
Zee Business (See also Zee TV)	E-103

Index to Contents

Zee Cinema	E-103
Zee Cinema (See also Zee TV)	E-103
Zee Kannada	E-103
Zee Marathi	E-103
Zee Marathi (See also Zee TV)	E-103
Zee Punjabi	E-103
Zee Smile	E-103
Zee Smile (See also Zee TV)	E-103
Zee TV	E-103
ZGS Broadcasting Holdings Inc.	A-1589
Zhejiang TV	E-104
Zhong Tian Channel	E-104
Zhong Tian Channel (See also CTI-Zhong Tian)	E-26
Zing Networks Ltd.	E-104
Z Living	E-104
Z Living Go	E-104
Z Living Go (See also Z Living)	E-104
ZoneTV	E-104
ZUUS Country	E-104
ZUUS Country (See also The Country Network)	E-24

Communications Daily

Warren Communications News

Get the industry standard FREE —
For a no-obligation trial call 800-771-9202 or visit www.warren-news.com

2017 Edition

Cable Systems State Index

Alabama	D-15	Nevada	D-500
Alaska	D-37	New Hampshire	D-506
Arizona	D-44	New Jersey	D-510
Arkansas	D-54	New Mexico	D-519
California	D-82	New York	D-529
Colorado	D-111	North Carolina	D-550
Connecticut	D-127	North Dakota	D-568
Delaware	D-132	Ohio	D-577
District of Columbia	D-133	Oklahoma	D-607
Florida	D-134	Oregon	D-637
Georgia	D-151	Pennsylvania	D-648
Hawaii	D-177	Rhode Island	D-683
Idaho	D-179	South Carolina	D-684
Illinois	D-186	South Dakota	D-694
Indiana	D-225	Tennessee	D-705
Iowa	D-240	Texas	D-718
Kansas	D-278	Utah	D-790
Kentucky	D-306	Vermont	D-797
Louisiana	D-333	Virginia	D-801
Maine	D-353	Washington	D-814
Maryland	D-359	West Virginia	D-833
Massachusetts	D-365	Wisconsin	D-848
Michigan	D-370	Wyoming	D-871
Minnesota	D-391	Other U.S. Territories and Possessions	D-881
Mississippi	D-426		
Missouri	D-440	Cable Owners	D-887
Montana	D-464	Cable Community Index	(end of Cable Volume 2)
Nebraska	D-479		

NEW YORK

Total Systems: 54	Communities with Applications: 0
Total Communities Served: 1,700	Number of Basic Subscribers: 3,875,643
Franchises Not Yet Operating: 0	Number of Expanded Basic Subscribers: 1,784
Applications Pending: 0	Number of Pay Units: 2,613

Top 100 Markets Represented: Hartford-New Haven-New Britain-Waterbury-New London, CT (19); New York, NY-Linden-Paterson-Newark, NJ (1); Buffalo (24); Albany-Schenectady-Troy (34); Syracuse (35); Rochester (56).

For a list of cable communities in this section, see the Cable Community Index located in the back of Cable Volume 2.
For explanation of terms used in cable system listings, see p. D-11.

ADAMS (town)—Formerly served by Time Warner Cable. No longer in operation. ICA: NY0119.

AFTON—Adams Cable Service, 19 North Main St, Carbondale, PA 18407. Phones: 888-222-0077; 570-282-6121. Fax: 570-282-3787. E-mail: frontdesk@echoes.net. Web Site: http://www.adamscable.com. Also serves Colesville, Deposit, Kirkwood, Sanford & Windsor (town). ICA: NY0100.
TV Market Ranking: Below 100 (AFTON, Colesville, Deposit, Kirkwood, Sanford, Windsor (town)).
Channel capacity: 78 (not 2-way capable).
Channels available but not in use: N.A.
Basic Service
Subscribers: 2,387.
Fee: $40.00 installation; $23.99 monthly.
Miles of Plant: 1,600.0 (coaxial); 532.0 (fiber optic). Homes passed: 30,000.
President: Douglas V.R. Adams.
Ownership: Adams CATV Inc. (MSO).

ALBANY—Time Warner Cable, 1021 Highbridge Rd, Schenectady, NY 12303. Phones: 518-869-9587; 518-869-5500; 866-321-2225. Fax: 518-869-1007. Web Site: http://www.timewarnercable.com. Also serves Alplaus, Altamont (village), Ames (village), Amsterdam, Amsterdam (town), Argyle (town), Argyle (village), Averill Park, Ballston (town), Ballston Lake, Ballston Spa (village), Berne (town), Bethlehem (town), Bleecker (town), Bolton (town), Broadalbin (town), Broadalbin (village), Brunswick (town), Burnt Hills, Cambridge (town), Cambridge (village), Canajoharie (town), Canajoharie (village), Caroga (town), Castleton (village), Charlton (town), Cherry Valley (town), Cherry Valley (village), Chester (town), Clifton Park (town), Cobleskill (town), Cobleskill (village), Coeymans (town), Cohoes, Colonie (town), Colonie (village), Corinth (town), Corinth (village), Crown Point (town), Day (town), Defreestville, Delanson (village), Delmar, Duanesburg, East Greenbush (town), Easton (town), Edinburg (town), Esperance (town), Esperance (village), Florida (town), Fonda (village), Fort Ann (town), Fort Ann (village), Fort Edward (town), Fort Edward (village), Fort Johnson (village), Fort Plain (village), Fulton (town), Fultonville (village), Galway (town), Galway (village), Glen (town), Glens Falls, Glenville (town), Gloversville, Granville (town), Green Island (village), Greenfield (town), Greenwich (town), Greenwich (village), Guilderland (town), Hadley (town), Hagaman (village), Hague (town), Halfmoon (town), Hampton (town), Hartford (town), Hoosick (town), Hoosick Falls (village), Horicon (town), Hudson Falls (village), Jackson (town), Johnstown (city), Johnstown (town), Kinderhook (town), Kinderhook (village), Kingsbury (town), Knox (town), Lake George (town), Lake George (village), Lake Luzerne (town), Malta (town), Mariaville, Mayfield, Mayfield (town), Mayfield (village), Mechanicville, Menands (village), Middle Granville, Middleburgh (town), Middleburgh (village), Milton (town), Minden (town), Mohawk (town), Moreau (town), Moriah (town), Nassau (town), Nassau (village), Nelliston (village), New Scotland (town), Niskayuna (town), Northampton (town), Northumberland (town), Northville (village), Palatine (town), Palatine Bridge (town), Perth (town), Pittstown (town), Poestenkill (town), Port Henry (village), Princetown, Princetown (town), Providence (town), Putnam (town), Queensbury (town), Rensselaer (town), Richmondville (town), Richmondville (village), Root (town), Rotterdam (portions), Rotterdam (town), Round Lake (village), Salem (village), Sand Lake (town), Saratoga (town), Saratoga Springs, Schaghticoke (town), Schaghticoke (village), Schenectady, Schodack (town), Schoharie (town), Schoharie (village), Schroon (town), Schroon Lake, Schuylerville (village), Scotia (village), Seward (town), Sharon (town), Sharon Springs (village), South Glens Falls (village), St. Johnsville (town), St. Johnsville (village), Stillwater (town), Stillwater (village), Stuyvesant (town), Ticonderoga (town), Troy, Valatie (village), Valley Falls (village), Victory Mills (village), Voorheesville (village), Warrensburg (town), Waterford (town), Waterford (village), Watervliet, Watervliet Arsenal, Whitehall (town), Whitehall (village), Wilton (town) & Wright (town). ICA: NY0014.
TV Market Ranking: 1 (Chester (town)); 34 (ALBANY, Alplaus, Altamont (village), Ames (village), Amsterdam, Amsterdam (town), Averill Park, Ballston (town), Ballston Lake, Ballston Spa (village), Berne (town), Bethlehem (town), Broadalbin (town), Broadalbin (village), Brunswick (town), Burnt Hills, Cambridge (town), Cambridge (village), Canajoharie (town), Canajoharie (village), Castleton (village), Charlton (town), Clifton Park (town), Cobleskill (town), Cobleskill (village), Coeymans (town), Cohoes, Colonie (town), Colonie (village), Corinth (town), Corinth (village), Day (town), Defreestville, Delanson (village), Delmar, Duanesburg, East Greenbush (town), Easton (town), Esperance (town), Esperance (village), Florida (town), Fonda (village), Fort Johnson (village), Fulton (town), Fultonville (village), Galway (town), Galway (village), Glen (town), Glenville (town), Gloversville, Green Island (village), Greenfield (town), Greenwich (town), Greenwich (village), Guilderland (town), Hagaman (village), Halfmoon (town), Hoosick (town), Hoosick Falls (village), Jackson (town), Johnstown (city), Johnstown (town), Kinderhook (town), Kinderhook (village), Knox (town), Malta (town), Mariaville, Mayfield, Mayfield (town), Mayfield (village), Mechanicville, Menands (village), Middleburgh (town), Middleburgh (village), Milton (town), Mohawk (town), Nassau (town), Nassau (village), New Scotland (town), Niskayuna (town), North Greenbush (town), Northampton (town), Northville (village), Palatine Bridge (town), Perth (town), Pittstown (town), Poestenkill (town), Princetown (town), Providence (town), Rensselaer (town), Richmondville (town), Richmondville (village), Root (town), Rotterdam (portions), Rotterdam (town), Round Lake (village), Sand Lake (town), Saratoga (town), Saratoga Springs, Schaghticoke (town), Schaghticoke (village), Schenectady, Schodack (town), Schoharie (town), Schoharie (village), Scotia (village), Seward (town), Sharon (town), Sharon Springs (village), Stillwater (town), Stillwater (village), Stuyvesant (town), Troy, Valatie (village), Valley Falls (village), Voorheesville (village), Waterford (town), Waterford (village), Watervliet, Watervliet Arsenal, Wilton (town), Wright (town)); 50 (Edinburg (town), Northumberland (town)); Below 100 (Bleecker (town), Caroga (town), Cherry Valley (town), Cherry Valley (village), Crown Point (town), Fort Plain (village), Hadley (town), Lake Luzerne (town), Minden (town), Moriah (town), Nelliston (village), Palatine (town), St. Johnsville (town), St. Johnsville (village), Port Henry (village)); Outside TV Markets (Argyle (town), Argyle (village), Bolton (town), Fort Ann (town), Fort Ann (village), Fort Edward (town), Fort Edward (village), Glens Falls, Granville (town), Hague (town), Hampton (town), Hartford (town), Horicon (town), Hudson Falls (village), Kingsbury (town), Lake George (town), Lake George (village), Middle Granville, Moreau (town), Putnam (town), Queensbury (town), Salem (town), Salem (village), Schroon (town), Schroon Lake, South Glens Falls (village), Ticonderoga (town), Warrensburg (town), Whitehall (town), Whitehall (village)). Franchise award date: N.A. Franchise expiration date: N.A. Began: July 1, 1974.
Channel capacity: 72 (operating 2-way).
Channels available but not in use: N.A.
Basic Service
Subscribers: 281,325.
Programming (received off-air): WCWN (CW) Schenectady; WMHT (PBS) Schenectady; WNYA (Antenna TV, MNT) Pittsfield; WNYT (MeTV, NBC) Albany; WRGB (CBS, This TV) Schenectady; WTEN (ABC) Albany; WXXA-TV (FOX, Laff, The Country Network) Albany; WYPX-TV (ION) Amsterdam.
Programming (via satellite): Capital News 9; C-SPAN; Pop; QVC; TBS.
Fee: $42.50 installation; $9.99 monthly.
Expanded Basic Service 1
Subscribers: N.A.
Programming (via satellite): A&E; AMC; Animal Planet; BET; Cartoon Network; CMT; CNBC; CNN; Comedy Central; C-SPAN 2; Discovery Channel; Disney Channel; E! HD; ESPN; ESPN Classic; ESPN2; EVINE Live; EWTN Global Catholic Network; Food Network; Fox News Channel; Freeform; FX; Golf Channel; HGTV; History; HLN; Lifetime; LMN; MSG; MSG Plus; MSNBC; MTV; National Geographic Channel; NBCSN; Nickelodeon; OWN: Oprah Winfrey Network; Oxygen; Spike TV; SportsNet New York; Syfy; The Weather Channel; TLC; TNT; Travel Channel; truTV; Turner Classic Movies; TV Land; Univision Studios; USA Network; VH1; WE tv; YES Network.
Fee: $10.00 installation; $31.18 monthly.
Digital Basic Service
Subscribers: N.A.
Programming (via satellite): BBC America; Bloomberg Television; Cooking Channel; C-SPAN 3; Discovery Digital Networks; Disney XD; DIY Network; DMX Music; ESPNews; Fox Sports 1; FSN Digital Atlantic; FSN Digital Central; FSN Digital Pacific; Great American Country; GSN; Hallmark Channel; History; National Geographic Channel; NBCSN; Nick Jr.; Outdoor Channel; Ovation; Time Warner Cable News NY1; Trinity Broadcasting Network (TBN); TV Asia; Zee TV.
Digital Pay Service 1
Pay Units: N.A.
Programming (via satellite): Cinemax; Flix; FXM; HBO (multiplexed); Showtime (multiplexed); Starz (multiplexed); Starz Encore (multiplexed); The Movie Channel (multiplexed).
Fee: $15.95 monthly (each).
Video-On-Demand: Yes
Pay-Per-View
iN DEMAND; Playboy TV; NBA/WNBA League Pass (delivered digitally); NHL Center Ice/MLB Extra Innings (delivered digitally); Fresh; iN DEMAND (delivered digitally); Playboy TV (delivered digitally); Fresh (delivered digitally); Shorteez (delivered digitally); Hot Choice (delivered digitally); Pleasure (delivered digitally); Adult PPV (delivered digitally).
Internet Service
Operational: Yes. Began: July 22, 1997.
Subscribers: 312,629.
Broadband Service: AOL for Broadband; EarthLink; Local.net; Road Runner.
Fee: $24.95 installation; $44.95 monthly.
Telephone Service
Digital: Operational
Subscribers: 198,438.
Fee: $44.95 monthly

New York—Cable Systems

Miles of Plant: 14,552.0 (coaxial); 4,889.0 (fiber optic). Homes passed: 638,664.
Vice President, Operations: Mark Loreno. Vice President, Marketing: Tricia Buhr. Vice President, Public Affairs: Peter Taubkin. Vice President, Engineering: James Marchester. Vice President, Customer Care: Paul Ventosa. General Manager, Ad Sales: Kevin Bartlett.
Ownership: Time Warner Cable (MSO).; Advance/Newhouse Partnership (MSO).

ALBION (town)—Time Warner Cable. Now served by BUFFALO (formerly Lackawanna), NY [NY0216]. ICA: NY0196.

ALDEN (town)—Time Warner Cable. Now served by BUFFALO (formerly Lackawanna), NY [NY0216]. ICA: NY0197.

ALEXANDRIA BAY—Castle Cable TV, 26 South Main St, PO Box 339, Hammond, NY 13646. Phone: 315-482-9975. Fax: 315-324-5917. E-mail: castlecable@cit-tele.com. Web Site: http://www.castlecabletv.com. ICA: NY0137.
TV Market Ranking: Below 100 (ALEXANDRIA BAY). Franchise award date: August 21, 1984. Franchise expiration date: N.A. Began: May 31, 1985.
Channel capacity: N.A. Channels available but not in use: N.A.
Basic Service
Subscribers: 1,015.
Programming (received off-air): WWNY-TV (CBS) Carthage; WWTI (ABC, CW) Watertown.
Programming (via satellite): A&E; CMT; CNN; CNN International; C-SPAN; C-SPAN 2; Discovery Channel; Discovery Life Channel; Disney Channel; Disney XD; DIY Network; ESPN; ESPN2; EWTN Global Catholic Network; Food Network; Fox News Channel; Freeform; FX; Golf Channel; Hallmark Channel; HGTV; History; HLN; Lifetime; MTV; National Geographic Channel; Nickelodeon; Outdoor Channel; Pop; QVC; Spike TV; Syfy; TBS; The Weather Channel; TLC; TNT; truTV; Turner Classic Movies; TV Land; USA Network; VH1; WDIV-TV (NBC, This TV) Detroit; WGN America; WSBK-TV (MNT) Boston; YES Network.
Fee: $70.00 installation; $58.95 monthly.
Pay Service 1
Pay Units: 246.
Programming (via satellite): Cinemax.
Fee: $12.95 monthly.
Pay Service 2
Pay Units: 316.
Programming (via satellite): HBO.
Fee: $12.95 monthly.
Video-On-Demand: No
Internet Service
Operational: Yes.
Broadband Service: In-house.
Fee: $45.00 installation; $34.95 monthly.
Telephone Service
None
Miles of Plant: 110.0 (coaxial); 83.0 (fiber optic). Homes passed: 3,000.
General Manager: Beverly Morley. Accounting Supervisor: Shelly L. Cole.
Ownership: Castle Cable TV Inc.

ALFRED—Formerly served by Alfred Cable System Inc. No longer in operation. ICA: NY0154.

AMITYVILLE—Cablevision, 1111 Stewart Ave, Bethpage, NY 11714. Phone: 516-803-2300. Fax: 516-803-1183. Web Site: http://www.cablevision.com. Also serves Asharoken, Atlantic Beach, Babylon, Babylon (village), Baxter Estates, Bayville, Bellerose (Nassau County), Brookville (village), Cedarhurst, Centre Island, Cove Neck, East Hills, East Rockaway, East Williston, Farmingdale, Floral Park, Flower Hill, Freeport, Garden City, Glen Cove, Great Neck, Great Neck Estates, Great Neck Plaza (village), Hempstead (village), Hewlett Bay Park, Hewlett Harbor, Hewlett Neck, Huntington, Huntington Bay, Huntington Station, Island Park, Kensington (village), Kings Point, Lake Success (village), Lattingtown, Laurel Hollow, Lawrence, Lindenhurst, Lloyd Harbor, Long Beach, Lynbrook, Malverne, Manhasset, Manorhaven, Massapequa, Massapequa Park, Matinecock, Mill Neck, Mineola, Munsey Park (village), Muttontown, New Hyde Park, North Hempstead, North Hills (village), Northport, Old Brookville, Old Westbury, Oyster Bay, Oyster Bay Cove, Plainedge, Plainview, Plandome (village), Plandome Heights (village), Plandome Manor, Port Washington, Rockville Centre, Roslyn, Roslyn Estates, Roslyn Harbor (village), Russell Gardens (village), Saddle Rock (village), Sands Point, Sea Cliff, Seaford, South Floral Park, Stewart Manor, Thomaston (village), Upper Brookville, Valley Stream, Westbury, Williston Park & Woodsburgh. ICA: NY0001.
TV Market Ranking: 1 (AMITYVILLE, Asharoken, Atlantic Beach, Babylon, Babylon (village), Baxter Estates, Bayville, Bellerose (Nassau County), Brookville (village), Cedarhurst, Centre Island (portions), Cove Neck, East Hills, East Rockaway, East Williston, Farmingdale, Floral Park, Flower Hill, Freeport, Garden City, Glen Cove, Great Neck, Great Neck Estates, Great Neck Plaza (village), Hempstead (village), Hewlett Bay Park, Hewlett Harbor, Hewlett Neck, Huntington, Huntington, Huntington Bay, Huntington Station, Island Park, Kensington (village), Kings Point, Lake Success (village), Lattingtown, Laurel Hollow, Lawrence, Lindenhurst, Lloyd Harbor, Long Beach, Lynbrook, Malverne, Manhasset, Manorhaven, Massapequa, Massapequa Park, Matinecock, Mill Neck, Mineola, Munsey Park (village), Muttontown, New Hyde Park, North Hempstead, North Hills (village), Old Brookville, Old Westbury, Oyster Bay, Oyster Bay Cove, Plainedge, Plandome (village), Plandome Heights (village), Plandome Manor, Port Washington, Rockville Centre, ROSLYN, Roslyn, Roslyn Estates, Roslyn Harbor (village), Russell Gardens (village), Saddle Rock (village), Sands Point, Sea Cliff, Seaford, South Floral Park, Stewart Manor, Thomaston (village), Upper Brookville, Valley Stream, Westbury, Williston Park, Woodsburgh); Below 100 (Northport, Plainview); Outside TV Markets (Centre Island (portions)). Franchise award date: N.A. Franchise expiration date: N.A. Began: November 1, 1973.
Channel capacity: N.A. Channels available but not in use: N.A.
Basic Service
Subscribers: 355,262.
Programming (received off-air): WABC-TV (ABC, Live Well Network) New York; WCBS-TV (CBS, Decades) New York; WFTY-DT (UniMas) Smithtown; WLIW (PBS) Garden City; WLNY-TV (IND) Riverhead; WNBC (COZI TV, NBC) New York; WNET (PBS) Newark; WNJU (TMO) Linden; WNYW (FOX, Movies!) New York; WPIX (Antenna TV, CW, This TV) New York; WPXN-TV (ION) New York; WWOR-TV (Bounce TV, Buzzr, Heroes & Icons, MNT) Secaucus; WXTV-DT (UNV) Paterson.
Programming (via satellite): EVINE Live; News 12 Long Island; QVC.
Fee: $39.95 installation; $16.13 monthly.
Expanded Basic Service 1
Subscribers: N.A.
Programming (via satellite): A&E; AMC; Animal Planet; BET; Bravo; Cartoon Network; CNBC; CNN; Comedy Central; C-SPAN; C-SPAN 2; Discovery Channel; Disney Channel; E! HD; ESPN; ESPN2; Food Network; Fox News Channel; Fox Sports 1; Freeform; Fuse; FX; GSN; HGTV; History; HLN; IFC; Jewelry Television; Lifetime; MSG; MSG Plus; MSNBC; MTV; MTV2; News 12 Traffic & Weather; Nickelodeon; Spike TV; SportsNet New York; Syfy; TBS; Telecare; The Weather Channel; TLC; TNT; Travel Channel; truTV; Turner Classic Movies; TV Land; Univision; USA Network; VH1; WE tv; YES Network.
Fee: $34.53 monthly.
Digital Basic Service
Subscribers: N.A.
Programming (via satellite): Animal Planet HD; Azteca; BBC World News; Bloomberg Television; Canal Sur; Caracol TV; Cartoon Network en Espanol; CBS Sports Network; Cinelatino; CMT; CMT HD; CNN en Espanol; CNN HD; C-SPAN 3; Destination America; Discovery Channel HD; Discovery Kids Channel; Disney XD; Docu TVE; Ecuavisa Internacional; ESPN Classic; ESPN Deportes; ESPN HD; ESPN2 HD; ESPNews; EuroNews; Food Network HD; FOX College Sports Central; FOX College Sports Pacific; Fox Deportes; Fox Life; Fox News HD; Fox Sports 2; FX HD; FXM; FYI; GMA Pinoy TV; Golf Channel; GolTV; Great American Country; Hallmark Channel; Hallmark Movie Channel HD; Hallmark Movies & Mysteries; HD Theater; here! On Demand; HGTV HD; History en Espanol; History International; HTV; iN DEMAND; Infinito; Investigation Discovery; Jewelry Television; Korean Channel; La Familia Cosmovision; LATV; LOGO; Mariavision; MBC America; MC; Momentum; MTV Classic; MTV Hits; National Geographic Channel; National Geographic Channel HD; NBA TV; NBC Universo; NBCSN; NHL Network; Nick HD; Nick Jr.; Nicktoons; NTV America; Outdoor Channel; Oxygen; RTN; Science Channel; Science HD; Spike TV HD; Sundance TV; TBS HD; TeenNick; Telefe Internacional; Telemicro Internacional; The Filipino Channel; The Jewish Channel; The Weather Channel HD; TLC HD; TNT HD; Toon Disney en Espanol; Tr3s; Travel Channel HD; TV Asia; TV Polonia; TV5MONDE USA; TVG Network; ULTRA HDPlex; Universal HD; Versus HD; VH1 HD; VH1 Soul; ViendoMovies; Vme TV; YES HD; Zee TV.
Fee: $10.95 monthly.
Pay Service 1
Pay Units: N.A.
Programming (via satellite): Cinemax; Flix; HBO (multiplexed); Showtime (multiplexed); The Movie Channel.
Digital Pay Service 1
Pay Units: N.A.
Programming (via satellite): Cinemax (multiplexed); Cinemax HD; Cinemax On Demand; HBO (multiplexed); HBO HD; HBO on Demand; Playboy TV; Showtime (multiplexed); Showtime HD; Showtime On Demand; Starz Encore; Starz HD; Starz On Demand; The Movie Channel (multiplexed); The Movie Channel HD.
Fee: $9.95 monthly (Cinemax, Playboy, Showtime/TMC or Starz/Encore), $11.95 monthly (HBO).
Video-On-Demand: Yes
Internet Service
Operational: Yes.
Subscribers: 389,823.
Broadband Service: Optimum Online.
Fee: $46.95 installation; $34.95 monthly; $299.00 modem purchase.
Telephone Service
Digital: Operational
Subscribers: 339,610.
Fee: $34.95 monthly
Miles of Plant: 9,680.0 (coaxial); 2,464.0 (fiber optic). Homes passed: 587,756.
Executive Vice President, Programming: Tom Montemagno. Senior Vice President, Field Operations: Christopher Coffey. Senior Vice President, Media Relations: Charles Schueler. Vice President, Government Affairs: Dan Ahouse. Corporate Communications Manager: Kristen Blank.
Ownership: Altice USA (MSO).

AMSTERDAM—Time Warner Cable. Now served by ALBANY, NY [NY0014]. ICA: NY0047.

ANDES—MTC Cable. Now served by MARGARETVILLE, NY [NY0155]. ICA: NY0192.

ANGELICA (town)—Time Warner Cable. Now served by DEWITT, NY [NY0013]. ICA: NY0198.

ARGYLE—Time Warner Cable. Now served by ALBANY, NY [NY0014]. ICA: NY0271.

AUBURN—Time Warner Cable. Now served by DEWITT, NY [NY0013]. ICA: NY0049.

AUGUSTA (town)—Formerly served by Chain Lakes Cablevision. Now served by Time Warner Cable, DEWITT, NY [NY0013]. ICA: NY0199.

AVOCA (town)—Time Warner Cable. Now served by DEWITT, NY [NY0013]. ICA: NY0200.

BAINBRIDGE—Time Warner Cable. Now served by DEWITT, NY [NY0013]. ICA: NY0120.

BALDWINSVILLE—Time Warner Cable. Now served by DEWITT, NY [NY0013]. ICA: NY0074.

BATAVIA—Time Warner Cable. Now served by BUFFALO (formerly Lackawanna), NY [NY0216]. ICA: NY0249.

BATH (town)—Time Warner Cable. Now served by DEWITT, NY [NY0013]. ICA: NY0093.

BERKSHIRE—Haefele TV Inc, 24 East Tioga St, PO Box 312, Spencer, NY 14883. Phone: 607-589-6235. Fax: 607-589-7211. E-mail: htv@htva.net. Web Site: http://www.htva.net. Also serves Berkshire (town), Candor (portions), Caroline (town), Harford (town), Newark Valley (town), Richford (town) & Virgil (town). ICA: NY0139.
TV Market Ranking: Below 100 (BERKSHIRE, Berkshire (town), Candor (portions), Caroline (town), Harford (town), Newark Valley (town), Richford (town), Virgil (town)).
Channel capacity: N.A. Channels available but not in use: N.A.

Cable Systems—New York

Basic Service
Subscribers: 583.
Fee: $30.00 installation; $24.95 monthly.
Vice President: Denise A. Laue.
Ownership: Haefele TV Inc. (MSO).

BERLIN (town)—Charter Communications. Now served by CHATHAM, NY [NY0088]. ICA: NY0187.

BETHEL (town)—Time Warner Cable, 2 Industrial Dr, PO Box 887, Middletown, NY 10941-0887. Phones: 845-692-6796; 845-692-5339; 212-598-7200 (New York office). Fax: 845-692-0901. Web Site: http://www.timewarnercable.com. Also serves Andes, Barryville, Big Indian, Blooming Grove (town), Bloomingburg (village), Bloomington, Boiceville, Cairo, Callicoon (town), Catskill (town), Chester (village), Chichester, Cochecton, Colchester Twp., Cornwall (town), Cornwall-on-Hudson (village), Cottekill, Crawford (town), Deerpark (town), Delaware (town), Denning, Denver, Eldred, Ellenville (town), Esopus (town), Fallsburg (town), Fleischmanns, Forestburgh (town), Fremont (town) (Sullivan County), Gardiner (town), Glen Spey, Goshen (town), Goshen (village), Grahamsville (town), Grand Gorge, Hamptonburgh (town), Hardenburgh, High Falls, Highland (town), Highland Falls (village), Hortonville, Hudson Valley, Hunter (town), Hunter (village), Hurley (town), Jeffersonville (village), Jewett (town), Kingston, Kingston (town), La Grange (town), Lexington, Liberty (town), Liberty (village), Lloyd (town), Lumberland (town), Mamakating (town), Marbletown (town), Marlboro (town), Maybrook (village), Middletown, Montgomery (town), Montgomery (village), Monticello (village), Mount Hope (town), Mount Tremper, Napanoch, Narrowsburg, Neversink (town), New Paltz (town), New Paltz (village), New Windsor (town), Newburgh, Newburgh (town), North Branch, Olive (town), Oliverea, Otisville (village), Phoenicia, Plattekill (town), Pleasant Valley (town), Pond Eddy, Port Jervis, Poughkeepsie, Poughkeepsie (town), Red Hook (town), Red Hook (village), Rhinebeck (town), Rhinebeck (village), Rhinecliff, Rochester (town), Rockland (town), Rosendale (town), Saugerties (town), Saugerties (village), Shandaken (town), Shawangunk (town), Shokan, Stone Ridge, Sullivan County (portions), Tannersville (village), Thompson (town), Tillson, Tivoli (town), Tusten (town), Ulster (town), Walden (village), Wallkill (town), Washingtonville (village), Wawarsing (town), Wawayanda (town), West Hurley (town), West Point, West Point Military Academy, West Shokan, Woodridge (village), Woodstock (town), Wurtsboro (village) & Yulan. ICA: NY0231.
TV Market Ranking: 1 (Blooming Grove (town), Chester (village), Cornwall-on-Hudson (village), Deerpark (town), Goshen (town), Goshen (village), Highland (town), Highland Falls (village), Highland Falls (village), Plattekill (town), Rochester (town), West Point, West Point Military Academy); 34 (Cairo, Catskill (town)); Below 100 (Barryville, Big Indian, Bloomingburg (village), Bloomington, Boiceville, Chichester, Cornwall (town), Cottekill, Crawford (town), Denning, Eldred, Ellenville (town), Esopus (town), Fallsburg (town), Fallsburg (town), Fleischmanns, Gardiner (town), Glen Spey, Grahamsville (town), Hamptonburgh (town), Hardenburgh, High Falls, Hunter (town), Hunter (village), Hurley (town), Jewett (town), Kingston, Kingston (town), La Grange (town), Lexington, Lloyd (town), Mamakating (town), Marbletown (town), Marbletown (town), Marlboro (town), Maybrook (village), Middletown, Montgomery (town), Montgomery (village), Mount Hope (town), Mount Tremper, Napanoch, Neversink (town), New Paltz (village), New Windsor (town), Newburgh, Newburgh (town), Olive (town), Oliverea, Otisville (village), Phoenicia, Pleasant Valley (town), Pond Eddy, Port Jervis, Poughkeepsie, Poughkeepsie (town), Red Hook (town), Red Hook (village), Rhinebeck (village), Rhinecliff, Rosendale (town), Saugerties (town), Saugerties (village), Shandaken (town), Shawangunk (town), Shokan, Stone Ridge, Tannersville (village), Tillson, Tivoli (village), Tusten (town), Ulster (town), Walden (village), Wallkill (town), Washingtonville (village), Wawarsing (town), Wawayanda (town), West Shokan, Woodridge (village), Woodstock (town), Wurtsboro (village), Yulan, Hudson Valley); Outside TV Markets (Andes, Callicoon (town), Cochecton, Colchester Twp., Deerpark (town), Delaware (town), Denver, Fallsburg (town), Forestburgh (town), Fremont (town) (Sullivan County), Grand Gorge, Hortonville, Jeffersonville (village), Liberty (town), Liberty (village), Lumberland (town), Monticello (village), Narrowsburg, North Branch, Rockland (town), Sullivan County (portions), Thompson (town), BETHEL (TOWN)). Franchise award date: June 1, 1966. Franchise expiration date: N.A. Began: February 2, 1956.
Channel capacity: N.A. Channels available but not in use: N.A.

Basic Service
Subscribers: 130,877.
Programming (received off-air): WABC-TV (ABC, Live Well Network) New York; WCBS-TV (CBS, Decades) New York; WMBC-TV (Azteca America) Newton; WNBC (COZI TV, NBC) New York; WNET (PBS) Newark; WNYW (FOX, Movies!) New York; WPIX (Antenna TV, CW, This TV) New York; WPXN-TV (ION) New York; WRNN-TV (IND) Kingston; WTBY-TV (TBN) Poughkeepsie; WTEN (ABC) Albany; WWOR-TV (Bounce TV, Buzzr, Heroes & Icons, MNT) Secaucus; WXTV-DT (UNV) Paterson; 20 FMs.
Programming (via satellite): CNN; Discovery Channel; ESPN; FX; PIX11; QVC; TNT.
Fee: $40.95 installation; $19.75 monthly.

Expanded Basic Service 1
Subscribers: N.A.
Programming (via satellite): A&E; AMC; Animal Planet; BET; Bravo; Cartoon Network; CMT; CNBC; Comedy Central; C-SPAN; Discovery Life Channel; Disney Channel; E! HD; ESPN2; EVINE Live; EWTN Global Catholic Network; Food Network; Fox News Channel; Freeform; Fuse; Golf Channel; Hallmark Channel; HGTV; History; HLN; Lifetime; LMN; MSG; MSG Plus; MSNBC; MTV; National Geographic Channel; NBCSN; Nickelodeon; Oxygen; Pop; Spike TV; SportsNet New York; Syfy; TBS; Telemundo; The Weather Channel; TLC; Travel Channel; truTV; Turner Classic Movies; TV Land; TV One; Univision; USA Network; VH1; YES Network.

Digital Basic Service
Subscribers: N.A.
Programming (via satellite): AXS TV; BBC America; BBC America On Demand; Bloomberg Television; Boomerang; CBS Sports Network; CCTV-Documentary; CNN International; Cooking Channel; C-SPAN; C-SPAN 2; C-SPAN 3; Destination America; Discovery Kids Channel; Disney XD; DIY Network; ESPN Classic; ESPN HD; ESPN2 HD; ESPNews; Fox Business Network; FOX College Sports Central; FOX College Sports Pacific; Fox Deportes; Fox Sports 1; Fox Sports 2; FXM; FYI; Great American Country; Great American Country On Demand; GSN; HD Theater; History International; IFC; Investigation Discovery; LOGO; MC; MTV Classic; MTV2; National Geographic Channel HD; National Geographic Channel On Demand; NBA TV; Nick 2; Nick Jr.; Outdoor Channel; Ovation; OWN; Oprah Winfrey Network; Science Channel; Starz Encore Family; Sundance TV; TBN HD; TeenNick; Tennis Channel; The Word Network; TNT HD; Universal HD; UP; YES HD.

Pay Service 1
Pay Units: N.A.
Programming (via satellite): HBO.

Digital Pay Service 1
Pay Units: N.A.
Programming (via satellite): ART America; Cinemax (multiplexed); Cinemax HD; Cinemax On Demand; CT-N; HBO (multiplexed); HBO HD; HBO on Demand; International Television (ITV); MBC America; RTN; Showtime (multiplexed); Showtime HD; Showtime On Demand; Starz (multiplexed); Starz Encore (multiplexed); Starz HD; The Movie Channel (multiplexed); The Movie Channel On Demand; TV Polonia; TV5MONDE USA; Zee TV.
Fee: $14.95 monthly (Cinemax, HBO, Starz/Encore or Showtime/TMC).

Video-On-Demand: Yes

Pay-Per-View
Playboy TV; Spice.

Internet Service
Operational: Yes.
Subscribers: 135,159.
Broadband Service: EarthLink, LocalNet, Road Runner.
Fee: $44.95 monthly.

Telephone Service
Digital: Operational
Subscribers: 86,846.
Fee: $39.95 monthly
Miles of Plant: 10,369.0 (coaxial); 8,144.0 (fiber optic). Homes passed: 288,287.
President: Howard Szarfarc. Vice President, Technical Operations: John Brown. Vice President, Marketing: David Goldberg. General Manager: Roger Wells. Public Affairs Director: Brenda Parks.
Ownership: Time Warner Cable (MSO).

BINGHAMTON—Time Warner Cable. Now served by DEWITT, NY [NY0013]. ICA: NY0016.

BLENHEIM—MidTel Cable TV, 103 Cliff St, PO Box 191, Middleburgh, NY 12122. Phones: 877-827-5211; 518-827-5211. Fax: 518-817-7600. E-mail: info@midtel.net. Web Site: http://www.midtel.net. Also serves Broome, Fulton, Middleburg (village), Middleburgh (town), Schoharie (town), Schoharie (village) & Summit. ICA: NY0291.
Channel capacity: N.A. Channels available but not in use: N.A.

Basic Service
Subscribers: 448. Commercial subscribers: 5.
Fee: $21.95 monthly.

Expanded Basic Service 1
Subscribers: 267.
Fee: $70.95 monthly.

Digital Basic Service
Subscribers: 408.
Fee: $75.95 monthly.

Digital Pay Service 1
Pay Units: N.A.
Fee: $12.95 monthly (Cinemax), $14.95 monthly (Showtime or Starz/Encore), $15.95 monthly (HBO), $17.95 monthly (Playboy), $19.95 monthly (Bang U, Brazzers TV or Reality Kings), $24.95 monthly (Hustler).

Internet Service
Operational: Yes.
Fee: $35.95-$66.95 monthly.

Telephone Service
Digital: Operational
Fee: $14.44 monthly
President: Jason S. Becker.
Ownership: Middleburgh Telephone Co.

BLOOMVILLE—DTC Cable, 107 Main St, PO Box 271, Delhi, NY 13753-0271. Phones: 888-898-8006; 607-746-1500. Fax: 607-746-7991. E-mail: custserv@delhitel.com. Web Site: http://www.delhitel.com. Also serves Kortright. ICA: NY0201.
TV Market Ranking: Outside TV Markets (BLOOMVILLE). Franchise award date: N.A. Franchise expiration date: N.A. Began: January 1, 1957.
Channel capacity: 30 (not 2-way capable). Channels available but not in use: N.A.

Basic Service
Subscribers: 13.
Programming (received off-air): WBNG-TV (CBS, CW) Binghamton; WICZ-TV (FOX) Binghamton; WIVT (ABC) Binghamton; WNBC (COZI TV, NBC) New York; WSKG-TV (PBS) Binghamton; WSYR-TV (ABC, IND, MeTV) Syracuse.
Programming (via satellite): C-SPAN; The Weather Channel; Trinity Broadcasting Network (TBN).
Fee: $40.95 installation; $35.95 monthly.

Expanded Basic Service 1
Subscribers: N.A.
Programming (via satellite): A&E; AMC; Animal Planet; CMT; CNN; Discovery Channel; Disney Channel; ESPN; Freeform; FX; History; QVC; Spike TV; TBS; TNT; USA Network; WGN America; YES Network.
Fee: $40.00 monthly.

Pay Service 1
Pay Units: N.A.
Programming (via satellite): HBO.
Fee: $14.95 monthly.

Video-On-Demand: No

Internet Service
Operational: Yes.
Fee: $29.95-$149.95 monthly.

New York—Cable Systems

Telephone Service
Analog: Operational
Fee: $15.27 monthly
Miles of Plant: 15.0 (coaxial); None (fiber optic).
General Manager: Jason Miller. Business Manager: Steve Oles.
Ownership: DTC Cable Inc. (MSO).

BOLIVAR (town)—Time Warner Cable. Now served by DEWITT, NY [NY0013]. ICA: NY0202.

BOVINA (town)—DTC Cable. Formerly [NY0284]. This cable system has converted to IPTV, 107 Main St, PO Box 271, Delhi, NY 13753-0271. Phones: 888-898-8006; 607-746-1500. Fax: 607-746-7991. E-mail: custserv@delhitel.com. Web Site: http://www.delhitel.com. ICA: NY5382.
TV Market Ranking: Outside TV Markets (BOVINA (TOWN)).
Channel capacity: N.A. Channels available but not in use: N.A.
Lifeline
Subscribers: 67.
Programming (received off-air): WBGH-CD (NBC) Binghamton; WBNG-TV (CBS, CW) Binghamton; WICZ-TV (FOX) Binghamton; WIVT (ABC) Binghamton; WSKG-TV (PBS) Binghamton; WSYR-TV (ABC, IND, MeTV) Syracuse.
Programming (via satellite): Bloomberg Television; C-SPAN; C-SPAN 2; The Weather Channel; Trinity Broadcasting Network (TBN); WGN America.
Fee: $40.95 installation; $21.95 monthly. Includes 14 channels.
Basic
Subscribers: 49.
Programming (received off-air): WPIX (Antenna TV, CW, This TV) New York.
Programming (via satellite): A&E; AMC; American Heroes Channel; Animal Planet; BBC America; BET; Bravo; Cartoon Network; Centric; Church Channel; CMT; CNBC; CNN; Comedy Central; Destination America; Discovery Channel; Discovery Family; Disney Channel; Disney XD; DMX Music; E! HD; Enlace USA; ESPN; ESPN Classic; ESPN2; ESPNews; ESPNU; EWTN Global Catholic Network; Food Network; Fox Business Network; Fox News Channel; Freeform; Fuse; FX; FYI; Golf Channel; Great American Country; GSN; Hallmark Channel; Hallmark Movies & Mysteries; HGTV; History; History International; HLN; HSN; IFC; INSP; JUCE TV; Lifetime; LMN; MLB Network; MSG; MSG Plus; MSNBC; MTV; MTV Classic; MTV Hits; MTV Jams; MTV2; National Geographic Channel; NBCSN; Nick Jr.; Nickelodeon; Nicktoons; Outdoor Channel; OWN: Oprah Winfrey Network; Oxygen; QVC; RFD-TV; Science Channel; Smile of a Child TV; Spike TV; Syfy; TBS; TeenNick; TLC; TNT; Travel Channel; Trinity Broadcasting Network (TBN); truTV; Turner Classic Movies; TV Land; USA Network; Velocity; VH1; VH1 Soul; WE tv; YES Network.
Fee: $61.95 monthly. Includes 153 channels plus music.
Expanded Basic
Subscribers: N.A.
Programming (via satellite): Chiller; Cloo; Cooking Channel; Fox Sports 1; FSN Digital Atlantic; FSN Digital Central; FSN Digital Pacific; FXM; NFL Network; Starz Encore; Starz Encore Black; Starz Encore Classic; Starz Encore Family; Starz Encore Suspense; Starz Encore Westerns.
Fee: $69.95 monthly. Includes 171 channels plus music.

HD
Subscribers: N.A.
Fee: $9.95 monthly.
Premium Packages
Subscribers: N.A.
Programming (via satellite): Cinemax (multiplexed); Flix; HBO; Playboy TV; Showtime (multiplexed); Starz (multiplexed); The Movie Channel (multiplexed).
Fee: $14.95 monthly/one movie package, $24.95/two movie packages, $33.95/three movie packages or $42.95/all movie packages. Packages include Cinemax (4 channels), HBO (6 channels), Showtime/TMC (10 channels), Starz (5 channels) or Playboy (1 channel).
Video-On-Demand: Yes
Internet Service
Operational: Yes.
Fee: $29.95-$149.95 monthly.
Telephone Service
Digital: Operational
Fee: $15.72 monthly
General Manager: Jason Miller. Business Manager: Steve Oles.
Ownership: DTC Cable Inc. (MSO).

BOVINA (town)—DTC Cable. This cable system has converted to IPTV. See BOVINA (town), NY [NY5382]. ICA: NY0284.

BRONX—Cablevision, 930 Soundview Ave, Bronx, NY 10473. Phones: 516-803-2300 (Corporate office); 718-991-6000. Web Site: http://www.cablevision.com. ICA: NY0011.
TV Market Ranking: 1 (BRONX). Franchise award date: June 1, 1968. Franchise expiration date: N.A. Began: October 1, 1988.
Channel capacity: N.A. Channels available but not in use: N.A.
Basic Service
Subscribers: 289,019.
Programming (received off-air): WABC-TV (ABC, Live Well Network) New York; WCBS-TV (CBS, Decades) New York; WFUT-DT (getTV, UniMas) Newark; WLIW (PBS) Garden City; WLNY-TV (IND) Riverhead; WMBC-TV (Azteca America) Newton; WNBC (COZI TV, NBC) New York; WNET (PBS) Newark; WNJU (TMO) Linden; WNYE-TV (PBS) New York; WNYW (FOX, Movies!) New York; WPIX (Antenna TV, CW, This TV) New York; WPXN-TV (ION) New York; WWOR-TV (Bounce TV, Buzzr, Heroes & Icons, MNT) Secaucus; WXTV-DT (UNV) Paterson.
Programming (via satellite): ESPN; QVC.
Fee: $39.95 installation; $15.52 monthly.
Expanded Basic Service 1
Subscribers: N.A.
Programming (via satellite): AMC; Animal Planet; BET; Bravo; Cartoon Network; CNBC; CNN; Comedy Central; C-SPAN; C-SPAN 2; Discovery Channel; Discovery Life Channel; E! HD; ESPN2; Fox News Channel; Freeform; History; Lifetime; MSG; MSG Plus; MSNBC; MTV; MTV2; News 12 Traffic & Weather; Nickelodeon; Spike TV; Syfy; TBS; The Weather Channel; Time Warner Cable News NY1; TLC; TNT; truTV; TV Land; Univision; USA Network; VH1; WE tv.
Fee: $34.43 monthly.
Digital Basic Service
Subscribers: N.A.
Programming (via satellite): Bloomberg Television; CMT; C-SPAN 3; Discovery Digital Networks; Disney Channel; Disney XD; ESPN Classic; ESPNews; EuroNews; Fox Deportes; FXM; FYI; Hallmark Channel; History International; IFC; National

Geographic Channel; Nick Jr.; Nicktoons; Oxygen; TeenNick.
Fee: $10.95 monthly; $2.95 converter.
Digital Pay Service 1
Pay Units: N.A.
Programming (via satellite): Cinemax (multiplexed); HBO (multiplexed); Showtime (multiplexed); Starz (multiplexed); Starz Encore (multiplexed); The Movie Channel (multiplexed).
Video-On-Demand: Yes
Pay-Per-View
Special events; Playboy TV.
Internet Service
Operational: Yes.
Subscribers: 284,562.
Broadband Service: Optimum Online.
Fee: $46.95 installation; $34.95 monthly.
Telephone Service
Digital: Operational
Subscribers: 244,172.
Fee: $34.95 monthly
Miles of Plant: 974.0 (coaxial); 291.0 (fiber optic). Homes passed: 515,611.
Executive Vice President, Programming: Tom Montemagno. Vice President, Field Operations: Thomas Monaghan.
Ownership: Altice USA (MSO).

BROOKHAVEN—Cablevision, 1111 Stewart Ave, Bethpage, NY 11714. Phone: 516-803-2300. Web Site: http://www.cablevision.com. Also serves Bellport, Lake Grove (village), Patchogue (village) & Poquott (village). ICA: NY0290.
TV Market Ranking: 19 (Bellport, BROOKHAVEN, Lake Grove (village), Poquott (village)).
Channel capacity: N.A. Channels available but not in use: N.A.
Basic Service
Subscribers: 76,779.
Fee: $39.95 installation; $13.41 monthly.
Internet Service
Operational: Yes.
Subscribers: 78,481.
Telephone Service
Digital: Operational
Subscribers: 67,302.
Miles of Plant: 2,126.0 (coaxial); 523.0 (fiber optic). Homes passed: 101,559.
Executive Vice President, Programming: Tom Montemagno.
Ownership: Altice USA (MSO).

BROOKHAVEN—Cablevision Systems Corp. Now served by BROOKHAVEN, NY [NY0290]. ICA: NY0015.

BROOKLYN—Cablevision, 1111 Stewart Ave, Bethpage, NY 11714. Phones: 914-762-8717; 718-951-2082; 718-617-3500. Web Site: http://www.cablevision.com. Also serves Kings County. ICA: NY0009.
TV Market Ranking: 1 (BROOKLYN, Kings County). Franchise award date: June 1, 1983. Franchise expiration date: N.A. Began: August 23, 1988.
Channel capacity: N.A. Channels available but not in use: N.A.
Basic Service
Subscribers: 298,436.
Programming (received off-air): WABC-TV (ABC, Live Well Network) New York; WCBS-TV (CBS, Decades) New York; WFTY-DT (UniMas) Smithtown; WLIW (PBS) Garden City; WLNY-TV (IND) Riverhead; WMBC-TV (Azteca America) Newton; WNBC (COZI TV, NBC) New York; WNET (PBS) Newark; WNJU (TMO) Linden; WNYW (FOX, Movies!) New York; WPIX (Antenna TV, CW, This TV) New York;

WPXN-TV (ION) New York; WRNN-TV (IND) Kingston; WWOR-TV (Bounce TV, Buzzr, Heroes & Icons, MNT) Secaucus; 30 FMs.
Programming (via satellite): ESPN; ESPN2; News 12 Brooklyn; QVC; Time Warner Cable News NY1.
Fee: $49.95 installation; $15.52 monthly.
Expanded Basic Service 1
Subscribers: N.A.
Programming (via satellite): A&E; AMC; Animal Planet; BET; Bravo; Cartoon Network; CNBC; CNN; Comedy Central; C-SPAN; C-SPAN 2; Discovery Channel; Disney Channel; E! HD; ESPN2; Food Network; Fox News Channel; Fox Sports 1; Freeform; Fuse; FX; GSN; HGTV; History; HLN; IFC; Lifetime; MSG; MSG Plus; MSNBC; MTV; MTV2; New Evangelization TV; News 12 Traffic & Weather; Nickelodeon; Spike TV; SportsNet New York; Syfy; TBS; The Weather Channel; TLC; TNT; Travel Channel; truTV; Turner Classic Movies; TV Land; Univision; USA Network; VH1; WE tv; YES Network.
Fee: $34.43 monthly.
Digital Basic Service
Subscribers: N.A.
Programming (via satellite): Azteca; BBC World News; Bloomberg Television; Canal Sur; Caracol TV; Cartoon Network en Espanol; Cinelatino; CMT; CNN en Espanol; CNN HD; C-SPAN 3; Destination America; Discovery Kids Channel; Disney XD; Docu TVE; Ecuavisa Internacional; ESPN Classic; ESPN Deportes; ESPN HD; ESPN2 HD; ESPNews; EuroNews; EVINE Live; Food Network HD; FOX College Sports Central; FOX College Sports Pacific; Fox Deportes; Fox Life; Fox Sports 2; FSN HD; FXM; FYI; Golf Channel; GolTV; Great American Country; Hallmark Channel; HD Theater; here! On Demand; HGTV HD; History en Espanol; History International; HTV; iN DEMAND; Infinito; Investigation Discovery; Jewelry Television; La Familia Cosmovision; LOGO; Mariavision; MC; Momentum; MTV Classic; MTV Hits; National Geographic Channel; National Geographic Channel HD; NBA TV; NBC Universo; NBCSN; NHL Network; Nick Jr.; Nicktoons; Outdoor Channel; Oxygen; Science Channel; Sundance TV; TBS HD; TeenNick; Telefe Internacional; TNT HD; Toon Disney en Espanol; Tr3s; TVG Network; ULTRA HDPlex; Universal HD; Versus HD; VH1 Soul; ViendoMovies; Vme TV; YES HD.
Fee: $10.95 monthly; $2.95 converter.
Pay Service 1
Pay Units: N.A.
Programming (via satellite): Cinemax; Flix; HBO (multiplexed); Showtime (multiplexed); The Movie Channel.
Fee: $9.95 monthly (Cinemax, Showtime or TMC), $11.95 monthly (HBO).
Digital Pay Service 1
Pay Units: N.A.
Programming (via satellite): Cinemax (multiplexed); Cinemax HD; Cinemax On Demand; HBO (multiplexed); HBO HD; HBO on Demand; Korean Channel; MBC America; Playboy TV; RAI Italia; RTN; Showtime (multiplexed); Showtime HD; Showtime On Demand; Starz (multiplexed); Starz Encore (multiplexed); Starz HD; The Movie Channel (multiplexed); The Movie Channel HD; TV Asia; TV Polonia; TV5, La Television International.
Fee: $9.95 monthly (Cinemax, Showtime, Starz/Encore, TMC, RAI, SPT, TV5 or TV Polinia), $11.95 monthly (HBO), $24.95 monthly (TV Japan).
Video-On-Demand: Yes
Pay-Per-View
iN DEMAND; Playboy TV; Club Jenna.

Internet Service

Operational: Yes.

Subscribers: 358,784.

Broadband Service: Optimum Online.

Fee: $46.95 installation; $34.95 monthly.

Telephone Service

Digital: Operational

Subscribers: 264,194.

Fee: $34.95 monthly

Miles of Plant: 1,510.0 (coaxial); 440.0 (fiber optic). Homes passed: 698,993.

Executive Vice President, Programming: Tom Montemagno. Vice President, Field Operations: Samuel Magliaro.

Ownership: Altice USA (MSO).

BROOKLYN—Formerly served by Cellularvision of New York. No longer in operation. ICA: NY0276.

BUFFALO—Time Warner Cable, 355 Chicago St, Buffalo, NY 14204-2069. Phone: 716-558-8881. Fax: 716-558-8855. Web Site: http://www.timewarnercable.com. Also serves Akron (village), Alabama (town), Albion (town), Albion (village), Alden (town), Alden (village), Alexander (town), Alexander (village), Allegany (town), Allegany (village), Amherst (town), Amity (town), Andover (town), Andover (village), Angola, Arcade (town), Arcade (village), Arcadia (town), Attica (town), Attica (village), Aurelius (town), Aurora (town), Aurora (village), Avon (town), Avon (village), Barker (village), Barre (town), Barrington (town), Batavia, Batavia (town), Belmont (village), Bennington (town), Benton (town), Bergen (town), Bergen (village), Bethany (town), Blasdell (village), Bloomfield (village), Boston (town), Branchport, Brant (town), Bristol (town), Brockport (village), Butler (town), Byron (town), Caledonia (town), Caledonia (village), Cambria (town), Canadice (town), Canandaigua, Canandaigua (town), Caneadea (town), Carlton (town), Castile (town), Castile (village), Cattaraugus (village), Cayuga (village), Chaffee (town), Chautauqua (town), Cheektowaga (town), Chili (town), Churchville (village), Clarence (town), Clarendon (town), Clarkson (town), Clifton Springs (village), Clyde (village), Colden, Coldspring (town), Collins (town), Concord (town), Conesus (town), Conewango (town), Corfu (village), Covert (town), Covington (town), Cuba (town), Cuba (village), Darien (town), Delevan (village), Depew, Dresden (village), Dunkirk, Dunkirk (town), Eagle (town), East Aurora (village), East Bloomfield (town), East Concord Twp., East Randolph (village), East Rochester (village), Eden (town), Elba (town), Elba (village), Ellicottville (town), Ellicottville (village), Elma (town), Evans (town), Fairport (village), Farmington (town), Farnham (village), Fayette (town), Fillmore, Forestville (village), Franklinville (town), Franklinville (village), Freedom (town), Gaines (town), Gainesville (town), Gainesville (village), Galen (town), Gates (town), Genesee Falls (town), Geneseo (town), Geneseo (village), Geneva, Geneva (town), Gorham (town), Gowanda (village), Grand Island (town), Great Valley (town), Greece (town), Groveland (portions), Hamburg (town), Hamburg (village), Hamlin (town), Hammondsport (village), Hanover (town), Hartland (town), Helmuth (town), Henrietta (town), Hilton (village), Hinsdale (town), Holland (town), Holley (village), Honeoye, Honeoye Falls (village), Hopewell (town), Hume (town), Huron (town), Interlaken (village), Irondequoit (town), Ischua (town), Italy (town), Java (town), Jerusalem (town), Junius, Kendall (town), Kenmore (village), Lackawanna, Lancaster (town), Lancaster (village), Lawtons (town), Le Roy (town), Le Roy (village), Ledyard (town), Leicester (town), Leicester (village), Lewiston (town), Lewiston (village), Lima (town), Lima (village), Livonia (town), Livonia (village), Lockport, Lockport (town), Lodi (town), Lodi (village), Lyndonville (village), Lyons (town), Lyons (village), Macedon (town), Macedon (village), Machias (town), Manchester (town), Manchester (village), Mansfield (town), Marilla (town), Marion (town), Mayville (village), Medina (village), Mendon (town), Middlebury (town), Middleport (village), Middlesex (town), Milo (town), Montour (town), Montour Falls (village), Mount Morris (town), Mount Morris (village), Murray (town), Naples (town), Naples (village), New Albion (town), Newark (village), Newfane (town), Newstead (town), Niagara (town), Niagara Falls, North Collins (town), North Collins (village), North Tonawanda, Nunda (town), Nunda (village), Oakfield (town), Oakfield (village), Odessa (village), Ogden (town), Olean, Olean (town), Ontario (town), Orangeville (town), Orchard Park (town), Orchard Park (village), Ovid (town), Ovid (village), Palmyra (town), Palmyra (village), Parma (town), Pavilion (town), Pembroke (town), Pendleton (town), Penfield (town), Penn Yan (village), Perinton (town), Perry (town), Perry (village), Perrysburg (town), Perrysburg (village), Persia (town), Phelps (town), Phelps (village), Pike (town), Pike (village), Pittsford (town), Pittsford (village), Pomfret (portions), Portage (town), Porter, Portland (portions), Portville (town), Portville (village), Prattsburgh (town), Pulteney (town), Randolph (town), Randolph (village), Ransomville, Reading (town), Red Creek (village), Richmond (town), Ridgeway (town), Riga (town), Ripley (town), Rochester, Romulus (town), Rose (town), Royalton (town), Rush (town), Rushville (village) (Ontario County), Rushville (village) (Yates County), Sanborn, Sandusky (town), Sardinia (town), Savannah (town), Scio (portions), Scottsville (village), Seneca (town), Seneca Falls (town), Seneca Falls (village), Shelby (town), Sheldon (town), Sheridan (town), Sherman (town), Sherman (village), Shortsville (village), Silver Creek (village), Silver Springs (village), Sloan (village), Sodus (town), Sodus (village), Sodus Point (village), Somerset (town), South Bristol (town), Spencerport (village), Springport (town), Springville (village), Stafford (town), Sweden (town), Tonawanda, Tonawanda (town), Torrey, Tyrone (town), Union Springs (village), Urbana (town), Varick (town), Victor (town), Victor (village), Wales (town), Walworth (town), Warsaw (town), Warsaw (village), Waterloo (town), Waterloo (village), Wayne (town), Webster (town), Webster (village), Wellsville (town), Wellsville (village), West Bloomfield (town), West Seneca (town), Westfield (town), Westfield (village), Wheatfield (town), Wheatland (town), Wheeler (portions), Williamson (town), Williamsville (village), Willing (town), Wilson (town), Wilson (village), Wolcott (town), Wolcott (village), Wyoming, Yates (town), York (town), Yorkshire (town) & Youngstown (village), NY; Ceres Twp., Eldred Borough, Eldred Twp. & Ulysses Borough, PA. ICA: NY0216.

TV Market Ranking: 24 (Akron (village), Alabama (town), Alden (town), Alden (village), Alexander (town), Alexander (village), Amherst (town), Angola, Arcade (town), Arcade (village), Attica (town), Attica (village), Barker (village), Barre (town), Bennington (town), Blasdell (village), Boston (town), Brant (town), BUFFALO, Cambria (town), Chaffee (town), Cheektowaga (town), Clarence (town), Colden, Collins (town), Concord (town), Corfu (village), Darien (town), Delevan (village), Depew, Dunkirk, Dunkirk (town), East Aurora (village), East Concord Twp., Eden (town), Elma (town), Evans (town), Farnham (village), Forestville (village), Gowanda (village), Grand Island (town), Hamburg (town), Hamburg (village), Hanover (town), Hartland (town), Helmuth (town), Holland (town), Honeoye Falls (village), Java (town), Kenmore (village), Lackawanna, Lancaster (town), Lancaster (village), Lawtons (town), Lewiston (town), Lewiston (village), Lockport, Lockport (town), Marilla (town), Medina (village), Middleport (village), Newfane (town), Newstead (town), Niagara (town), Niagara Falls, North Collins (town), North Collins (village), North Tonawanda, Orangeville (town), Orchard Park (town), Orchard Park (village), Pembroke (town), Pendleton (town), Perrysburg (town), Perrysburg (village), Persia (town), Porter, Ransomville, Ridgeway (town), Royalton (town), Rush (town), Sanborn, Sardinia (town), Scottsville (village), Shelby (town), Sheldon (town), Sheridan (town), Silver Creek (village), Sloan (village), Somerset (town), Springville (village), Tonawanda, Wales (town), West Bloomfield (town), West Seneca (town), Westfield (town), Wheatfield (town), Wheatland (town), Williamsville (village), Wilson (town), Wilson (village), York (town), Yorkshire (town), Youngstown (village)); 24,56 (Batavia, Oakfield (town), Oakfield (village)); 34 (Tonawanda (town)); 35 (Aurelius (town), Aurora (town), Aurora (village), Butler (town), Cayuga (village), Ledyard (town), Savannah (town), Seneca (town), Seneca Falls (town), Seneca Falls (village), Springport (town), Union Springs (village)); 56 (Albion (town), Albion (village), Arcadia (town), Avon (town), Avon (village), Batavia (town), Bergen (town), Bergen (village), Bethany (town), Bloomfield (village), Bristol (town), Brockport (village), Byron (town), Caledonia (town), Caledonia (village), Canadice (town), Canandaigua, Canandaigua (town), Carlton (town), Chili (town), Churchville (village), Clarendon (town), Clarkson (town), Clifton Springs (village), Conesus (town), Covington (town), East Bloomfield (town), East Rochester (village), Elba (town), Elba (village), Fairport (village), Farmington (town), Gaines (town), Gates (town), Geneseo (town), Geneseo (village), Greece (town), Groveland (portions), Hamlin (town), Henrietta (town), Hilton (village), Holley (village), Honeoye, Hopewell (town), Irondequoit (town), Kendall (town), Le Roy (town), Le Roy (village), Leicester (town), Leicester (village), Lima (town), Lima (village), Livonia (town), Livonia (village), Lyons (town), Lyons (village), Macedon (town), Macedon (village), Manchester (town), Manchester (village), Marion (town), Mendon (town), Middlebury (town), Mount Morris (town), Mount Morris (village), Murray (town), Newark (village), Ogden (town), Ontario (town), Palmyra (town), Palmyra (village), Parma (town), Pavilion (town), Penfield (town), Perinton (town), Phelps (town), Phelps (village), Pittsford (village), Red Creek (village), Richmond (town), Riga (town), Rochester, Rushville (village) (Ontario County), Rushville (village) (Yates County), Shortsville (village), Sodus (town), Sodus (village), Sodus Point (village), South Bristol (town), Spencerport (village), Stafford (town), Sweden (town), Victor (town), Victor (village), Walworth (town), Webster (town), Webster (village), Williamson (town), Wyoming); Below 100 (Allegany (town), Allegany (village), Barrington (town), Benton (town), Caneadea (town), Castile (town), Castile (village), Cattaraugus (village), Chautauqua (town), Coldspring (town), Conewango (town), Covert (town), Cuba (town), Cuba (village), Dresden (village), Eagle (town), East Randolph (village), Ellicottville (town), Ellicottville (village), Fayette (town), Fillmore, Franklinville (town), Franklinville (village), Freedom (town), Gainesville (town), Gainesville (village), Genesee Falls (town), Gorham (town), Great Valley (town), Hammondsport (village), Hinsdale (town), Hume (town), Interlaken (village), Ischua (town), Italy (town), Jerusalem (town), Junius, Lodi (town), Lodi (village), Lyndonville (village), Machias (town), Mansfield (town), Mayville (village), Milo (town), Montour (town), Montour Falls (village), Naples (village), New Albion (town), Nunda (town), Nunda (village), Odessa (village), Olean (town), Ovid (town), Penn Yan (village), Perry (town), Perry (village), Pike (town), Pike (village), Pittsford (town), Pomfret (portions), Portage (town), Portland (portions), Prattsburgh (town), Pulteney (town), Randolph (town), Randolph (village), Reading (town), Ripley (town), Romulus (town), Sandusky (town), Sherman (town), Sherman (village), Silver Springs (village), Torrey, Tyrone (town), Urbana (town), Warsaw (town), Warsaw (village), Westfield (village), Wheeler (portions), Yates (town), Olean); Outside TV Markets (Amity (town), Andover (town), Andover (village), Belmont (village), Ceres Twp., Clyde (village), Eldred Borough, Eldred Twp., Galen (town), Geneva (town), Huron (town), Middlesex (town), Naples (town), Ovid (village), Portville (town), Portville (village), Rose (town), Scio (portions), Varick (town), Waterloo (town), Waterloo (village), Wayne (town), Wellsville (town), Wellsville (village), Willing (town), Wolcott (town), Wolcott (village), Geneva, Ulysses Borough, Red Creek (village)). Franchise award date: N.A. Franchise expiration date: N.A. Began: May 1, 1965.

Channel capacity: N.A. Channels available but not in use: N.A.

Basic Service

Subscribers: 489,148.

Programming (received off-air): WBBZ-TV (MeTV, This TV) Springville; WGRZ (An-

New York—Cable Systems

tenna TV, NBC, WeatherNation) Buffalo; WIVB-TV (CBS) Buffalo; WKBW-TV (ABC, Escape) Buffalo; WNED-TV (PBS) Buffalo; WNLO (CW) Buffalo; WNYB (IND) Jamestown; WNYO-TV (MNT) Buffalo; WPXJ-TV (ION) Batavia; WUTV (FOX, The Country Network) Buffalo.
Programming (via satellite): C-SPAN; C-SPAN 2; EWTN Global Catholic Network; Pop; QVC; various Canadian stations.
Fee: $7.52 monthly.

Expanded Basic Service 1
Subscribers: N.A.
Programming (via satellite): A&E; AMC; Animal Planet; BET; Bravo; Cartoon Network; CMT; CNBC; CNN; Comedy Central; Discovery Channel; Disney Channel; E! HD; ESPN; ESPN2; Food Network; Fox News Channel; Freeform; FX; Hallmark Channel; HGTV; History; HLN; Lifetime; MSG; MSNBC; MTV; NBCSN; Nickelodeon; Oxygen; Spike TV; SportsNet New York; Syfy; TBS; The Weather Channel; TLC; TNT; Travel Channel; truTV; Turner Classic Movies; TV Land; USA Network; VH1; YES Network.

Digital Basic Service
Subscribers: N.A.
Programming (via satellite): 52MX; A&E HD; AXS TV; BBC America; BBC America On Demand; Bloomberg Television; Boomerang; Bridges TV; CBS Sports Network; Cinelatino; CMT; CNN en Espanol; Cooking Channel; Daystar TV Network; Destination America; Discovery Kids Channel; Discovery Life Channel; Disney XD; DIY Network; ESPN Classic; ESPN Deportes; ESPN HD; ESPN2 HD; ESPNews; ESPNU; Fox Business Network; FOX College Sports Central; FOX College Sports Pacific; Fox Deportes; Fox Sports 1; Fox Sports 2; Fuse; FXM; FYI; Golf Channel; Great American Country; GSN; HD Theater; History en Espanol; History International; IFC; Investigation Discovery; LMN; LOGO; MC; MTV Classic; MTV Hits; MTV Jams; MTV Live; MTV2; Nat Geo WILD; National Geographic Channel; National Geographic Channel On Demand; NBA TV; NHL Network; Nick 2; Nick Jr.; Nicktoons; Outdoor Channel; OWN: Oprah Winfrey Network; Oxygen On Demand; Reelz; Science Channel; Sundance TV; TeenNick; Tennis Channel; The Word Network; TNT HD; Toon Disney en Espanol; Tr3s; Trinity Broadcasting Network (TBN); TV Guide Network; TV One; Universal HD; UP; Versus HD; VH1 Soul; WE tv; YES HD.
Fee: $57.95 monthly.

Digital Pay Service 1
Pay Units: N.A.
Programming (via satellite): Cinemax (multiplexed); Cinemax HD; Cinemax On Demand; HBO (multiplexed); HBO HD; HBO on Demand; Showtime (multiplexed); Showtime HD; Showtime On Demand; Starz (multiplexed); Starz Encore (multiplexed); Starz HD; Starz On Demand; The Movie Channel (multiplexed); The Movie Channel On Demand.
Fee: $11.95 monthly (each).

Video-On-Demand: Yes

Pay-Per-View
Playboy TV (delivered digitally); Fresh (delivered digitally); SexSee (delivered digitally); Juicy (delivered digitally); VaVoom (delivered digitally); Sports PPV (delivered digitally); NBA League Pass (delivered digitally).

Internet Service
Operational: Yes.
Subscribers: 522,732.

Broadband Service: Road Runner.
Fee: $44.95 monthly; $3.00 modem lease.
Telephone Service
Digital: Operational
Subscribers: 254,135.
Fee: $39.95 monthly
Miles of Plant: 23,613.0 (coaxial); 8,859.0 (fiber optic). Homes passed: 1,164,379.
President: Gordon Harp. Vice President, Customer Operations: David Fraass. Vice President, Marketing: Steve Jaworowski. Vice President, Public & Government Affairs: Robin Wolfgang. Marketing Manager: Jean Calabrese. Technical Operations Manager: Steve Pawlik.
Ownership: Time Warner Cable (MSO).

BUFFALO—Time Warner Cable. Now served by BUFFALO, NY [NY0216]. ICA: NY0008.

BURDETT—Haefele TV Inc, 24 East Tioga St, PO Box 312, Spencer, NY 14883. Phone: 607-589-6235. Fax: 607-589-7211. E-mail: htv@htva.net. Web Site: http://www.htva.net. Also serves Bradford (town), Burdett (village), Hector (town - portions), Milo (town), Orange (town) & Reading. ICA: NY0158.
TV Market Ranking: Below 100 (Bradford (town), BURDETT, Burdett (village), Hector (town - portions), Milo (town), Orange (town), Reading).
Channel capacity: N.A. Channels available but not in use: N.A.
Basic Service
Subscribers: 969.
Fee: $30.00 installation; $24.95 monthly.
President: Denise A. Laue.
Ownership: Haefele TV Inc. (MSO).

BURLINGTON (town)—Formerly served by Chain Lakes Cablevision. Now served by Time Warner Cable, DEWITT, NY [NY0013]. ICA: NY0173.

CANAJOHARIE (village)—Time Warner Cable. Now served by ALBANY, NY [NY0014]. ICA: NY0103.

CARMEL—Comcast Cable. Now served by NEW BRITAIN, CT [CT0037]. ICA: NY0051.

CATO (town)—Formerly served by Time Warner Cable. Now served by Time Warner Cable, DEWITT, NY [NY0013]. ICA: NY0207.

CATSKILL—Mid-Hudson Cablevision Inc., 200 Jefferson Hts, PO Box 399, Catskill, NY 12414-0399. Phones: 518-943-6600; 800-342-5400. Fax: 518-943-6603. E-mail: cable@mid-hudson.com. Web Site: http://www2.mhcable.com. Also serves Athens (town), Athens (village), Bethlehem (town), Cairo (town), Catskill (town), Catskill (village), Claverack, Coeymans, Columbiaville, Coxsackie (town), Coxsackie (village), Gallatin, Greenport (Columbia County), Greenville, Hudson, Livingston (town), New Baltimore, Philmont, Ravena (village), Stockport, Stockport (town), Stottville, Taghkanic & Westerlo. ICA: NY0039.
TV Market Ranking: 34 (Athens (town), Athens (village), Bethlehem (town), Cairo (town), CATSKILL, Catskill (town), Catskill (village), Claverack, Coeymans, Columbiaville, Coxsackie (town), Coxsackie (village), Greenport (Columbia County), Greenville, Hudson, New Baltimore, Philmont, Ravena (village), Stockport, Stockport (town), Stottville, Taghkanic, Taghkanic, Westerlo), Below 100 (Gallatin, Livingston (town)). Franchise award date:

January 1, 1970. Franchise expiration date: N.A. Began: September 1, 1971.
Channel capacity: N.A. Channels available but not in use: N.A.
Basic Service
Subscribers: 12,128.
Programming (received off-air): WCWN (CW) Schenectady; WMHT (PBS) Schenectady; WNYT (MeTV, NBC) Albany; WRGB (CBS, This TV) Schenectady; WRNN-TV (IND) Kingston; WTEN (ABC) Albany; WXXA-TV (FOX, Laff, The Country Network) Albany; 21 FMs.
Programming (via satellite): C-SPAN; C-SPAN 2; EWTN Global Catholic Network; Fox News Channel; FX; MSNBC; MyNetworkTV; Pop; QVC.
Fee: $71.95 monthly.
Digital Basic Service
Subscribers: N.A.
Programming (via satellite): BBC America; Bloomberg Television; Chiller; Cloo; CMT; Cooking Channel; Destination America; Discovery Kids Channel; Discovery Life Channel; Disney XD; DMX Music; ESPNews; EVINE Live; Fox Business Network; FOX College Sports Central; FOX College Sports Pacific; Great American Country; GSN; History International; IFC; Investigation Discovery; LMN; MTV Classic; MTV Hits; MTV2; Nick Jr.; Nicktoons; Outdoor Channel; Ovation; OWN: Oprah Winfrey Network; RFD-TV; RTV; Science Channel; Sprout; Sundance TV; TeenNick; The Word Network; Trinity Broadcasting Network (TBN); TVG Network; VH1 Soul.
Fee: $6.95 monthly; $5.95 converter.
Digital Expanded Basic Service
Subscribers: N.A.
Programming (via satellite): A&E HD; Animal Planet HD; AXS TV; Bravo HD; Discovery Channel HD; ESPN HD; Food Network HD; FX HD; HD Theater; HGTV HD; History HD; National Geographic Channel HD; Outdoor Channel 2 HD; QVC HD; Science HD; Syfy HD; TBS HD; TLC HD; TNT HD; Universal HD; USA Network HD; YES HD.
Fee: $7.50 monthly; $7.95 converter.
Pay Service 1
Pay Units: N.A.
Programming (via satellite): Cinemax; HBO (multiplexed); Showtime.
Fee: $9.95 monthly (Cinemax), $11.95 monthly (HBO or Showtime/TMC).
Digital Pay Service 1
Pay Units: N.A.
Programming (via satellite): Cinemax (multiplexed); Cinemax HD; HBO (multiplexed); HBO HD; HBO on Demand; Showtime (multiplexed); Starz (multiplexed); Starz Encore (multiplexed); Starz HD; The Movie Channel (multiplexed).
Fee: $13.40 monthly (Cinemax), $13.95 monthly (HBO, Showtime/TMC or Starz/Encore).
Video-On-Demand: Yes
Pay-Per-View
iN DEMAND (delivered digitally); Playboy TV (delivered digitally); Fresh (delivered digitally); Spice: Xcess (delivered digitally); Club Jenna (delivered digitally).
Internet Service
Operational: Yes.
Subscribers: 12,403.
Broadband Service: In-house.
Fee: $49.95 monthly; $10.00 modem lease.
Telephone Service
Digital: Operational
Subscribers: 4,881.
Fee: $29.95 monthly
Miles of Plant: 2,587.0 (coaxial); 594.0 (fiber optic). Homes passed: 38,000.

President: James M. Reynolds. Chief Technician: Edward Harter. Chief Engineer: David Fingar.
Ownership: Mid-Hudson Cablevision Inc.

CENTRAL SQUARE (village)—Time Warner Cable. Now served by DEWITT, NY [NY0013]. ICA: NY0091.

CHAMPLAIN (town)—Time Warner Cable. Now served by DEWITT, NY [NY0013]. ICA: NY0101.

CHATHAM—Charter Communications, 12405 Powerscourt Dr, St. Louis, MO 63131. Phones: 636-207-5100 (Corporate office); 508-853-1515. Fax: 508-854-5042. Web Site: http://www.charter.com. Also serves Hinsdale, Lanesborough & West Stockbridge, MA; Ancram (town), Austerlitz (town), Berlin (town), Canaan (town), Copake (town), Ghent (town), Hillsdale (town), New Lebanon (town) & Petersburg, NY. ICA: NY0088.
TV Market Ranking: 34 (Austerlitz (town), Berlin (town), Canaan (town), CHATHAM, Ghent (town), Hillsdale (town), Hinsdale, Lanesborough, New Lebanon (town), Petersburg, West Stockbridge), Below 100 (Ancram (town), Copake (town)). Franchise award date: July 1, 1983. Franchise expiration date: N.A. Began: June 1, 1993.
Channel capacity: N.A. Channels available but not in use: N.A.
Digital Basic Service
Subscribers: 2,941.
Programming (via satellite): BBC America; Discovery Digital Networks; DMX Music; ESPNews; Fuse; FYI; Golf Channel; IFC; LMN; MTV2; Nick Jr.; TeenNick; Turner Classic Movies; TV Guide Interactive Inc.; WE tv.
Fee: $18.99 monthly.
Digital Expanded Basic Service
Subscribers: N.A.
Programming (via satellite): A&E; AMC; Animal Planet; Bravo; Cartoon Network; CMT; CNBC; CNN; Comedy Central; C-SPAN 2; Discovery Channel; Disney Channel; Disney XD; E! HD; ESPN; ESPN Classic; ESPN2; Food Network; Fox News Channel; Fox Sports 1; Freeform; FX; GSN; HGTV; History; HLN; HRTV; Lifetime; MSG; MSG Plus; MTV; NBCSN; Nickelodeon; Spike TV; Syfy; TBS; The Weather Channel; TLC; TNT; Travel Channel; TV Land; USA Network; VH1; Yesterday USA.
Fee: $55.00 monthly.
Digital Pay Service 1
Pay Units: N.A.
Programming (via satellite): Cinemax (multiplexed); Flix; HBO (multiplexed); Showtime (multiplexed); Starz (multiplexed); Starz Encore (multiplexed); The Movie Channel (multiplexed).
Video-On-Demand: Yes
Pay-Per-View
iN DEMAND (delivered digitally); Playboy TV (delivered digitally).
Internet Service
Operational: Yes.
Broadband Service: Charter Internet.
Telephone Service
Digital: Operational
Miles of Plant: 300.0 (coaxial); None (fiber optic). Homes passed: 5,500.
Vice President & General Manager: Greg Garabedian. Technical Operations Director: George Duffy. Marketing Director: Dennis Jerome. Accounting Director: David Sovanski. Marketing Manager: Paula

Cucchetelli. Operations Manager: Kevin Maillous.
Ownership: Charter Communications Inc. (MSO).

CINCINNATUS—Formerly served by Chain Lakes Cablevision. Now served by Time Warner Cable, DEWITT, NY [NY0013]. ICA: NY0279.

CLYMER (town)—Time Warner Cable. Now served by JAMESTOWN, NY [NY0030]. ICA: NY0185.

COBLESKILL (town)—Time Warner Cable. Now served by ALBANY, NY [NY0014]. ICA: NY0082.

COHOCTON (town)—Time Warner Cable. Now served by DEWITT, NY [NY0013]. ICA: NY0177.

CONSTANTIA (town)—Time Warner Cable. Now served by DEWITT, NY [NY0013]. ICA: NY0117.

COOPERSTOWN (village)—Time Warner Cable. Now served by DEWITT, NY [NY0013]. ICA: NY0105.

CORTLAND—Time Warner Cable. Now served by DEWITT, NY [NY0013]. ICA: NY0062.

CUYLER—Formerly served by Chain Lakes Cablevision. Now served by Time Warner Cable, DEWITT, NY [NY0013]. ICA: NY0157.

DANSVILLE (town)—Time Warner Cable. Now served by DEWITT, NY [NY0013]. ICA: NY0208.

DE RUYTER—Formerly served by Chain Lakes Cablevision. No longer in operation. ICA: NY0165.

DELHI (town)—DTC Cable. This cable system has converted to IPTV. Now served by DELHI (village), NY [NY5141]. ICA: NY0285.

DELHI (town)—Time Warner Cable. Now served by DEWITT, NY [NY0013]. ICA: NY0140.

DELHI (village)—DTC Cable. Formerly [NY0140]. This cable system has converted to IPTV, 107 Main St, PO Box 271, Delhi, NY 13753-0271. Phones: 607-746-1500; 888-898-8006. Fax: 607-746-7991. E-mail: custserv@delhitel.com. Web Site: http://www.delhitel.com. Also serves Delhi (town) & Fraser. ICA: NY5141.
TV Market Ranking: Outside TV Markets (DELHI (VILLAGE)).
Channel capacity: N.A. Channels available but not in use: N.A.
Lifeline
Subscribers: 494.
Programming (received off-air): WBNG-TV (CBS, CW) Binghamton; WICZ-TV (FOX) Binghamton; WIVT (ABC) Binghamton; WNYT (MeTV, NBC) Albany; WNYW (FOX, Movies!) New York; WSKG-TV (PBS) Binghamton; WSYR-TV (ABC, IND, MeTV) Syracuse.
Programming (via satellite): Bloomberg Television; C-SPAN; C-SPAN 2; The Weather Channel; WBGH-CD (NBC) Binghamton; WGN America; WIVT (ABC) Binghamton.
Fee: $40.95 installation; $21.95 monthly. 14 channels.
Basic
Subscribers: N.A.
Programming (received off-air): WPIX (Antenna TV, CW, This TV) New York.
Programming (via satellite): A&E; AMC; American Heroes Channel; Animal Planet; BBC America; BET; Bravo; Cartoon Network; Centric; Church Channel; CMT; CNBC; CNN; Comedy Central; Destination America; Discovery Channel; Discovery Family; Disney Channel; Disney XD; DMX Music; E! HD; Enlace USA; ESPN; ESPN Classic; ESPN2; ESPNews; ESPNU; EWTN Global Catholic Network; Food Network; Fox Business Network; Fox News Channel; Freeform; Fuse; FX; FYI; Golf Channel; Great American Country; GSN; Hallmark Channel; HGTV; History; History International; HLN; HSN; IFC; INSP; JUCE TV; Lifetime; LMN; MLB Network; MSG; MSG Plus; MSNBC; MTV; MTV Classic; MTV Hits; MTV Jams; MTV2; National Geographic Channel; NBCSN; Nick Jr.; Nickelodeon; Nicktoons; Outdoor Channel; OWN: Oprah Winfrey Network; QVC; RFD-TV; Science Channel; Smile of a Child TV; Spike TV; Syfy; TBS; TeenNick; TLC; TNT; Travel Channel; Trinity Broadcasting Network (TBN); truTV; Turner Classic Movies; TV Land; USA Network; Velocity; VH1; VH1 Soul; WE tv; YES Network.
Fee: $61.95 monthly. Includes 153 channels plus music.
Expanded Basic
Subscribers: 445.
Programming (via satellite): Chiller; Cloo; Cooking Channel; Fox Sports 1; FSN Digital Atlantic; FSN Digital Central; FSN Digital Pacific; FXM; NFL Network; Starz Encore (multiplexed); Starz Encore Black; Starz Encore Classic; Starz Encore Family; Starz Encore Suspense; Starz Encore Westerns.
Fee: $69.95 monthly. Includes 171 channels plus music.
HD
Subscribers: N.A.
Fee: $9.95 monthly.
Premium Packages
Subscribers: N.A.
Programming (via satellite): Cinemax (multiplexed); Flix; HBO (multiplexed); Playboy TV; Showtime (multiplexed); Starz (multiplexed); The Movie Channel (multiplexed).
Fee: $14.95 monthly/1 movie package, $24.95/2 movie packages, $33.95/3 movie packages or $42.95/all movie packages. Packages include Cinemax (4 channels), HBO (6 channels), Showtime/TMC (10 channels), Starz (5 channels) or Playboy (1 channel).
Video-On-Demand: Yes
Pay-Per-View
Playboy TV (delivered digitally).
Internet Service
Operational: Yes.
Fee: $29.95-$149.95 monthly.
Telephone Service
Digital: Operational
Fee: $15.72 monthly
General Manager: Jason Miller. Business Manager: Steve Oles.
Ownership: DTC Cable Inc. (MSO).

DEPOSIT—Adams Cable Service. Now served by AFTON, NY [NY0100]. ICA: NY0148.

DEWITT—Time Warner Cable, 6005 Fair Lakes Rd, East Syracuse, NY 13057. Phones: 315-634-6000; 315-634-6100. Fax: 315-634-6219. Web Site: http://www.timewarnercable.com. Also serves Adams (town), Adams (village), Adams Center, Addison (town), Addison (village), Afton (town), Afton (village), Albion Center (town), Alexandria (town), Alfred (town), Alfred (village), Alma (town), Almond (town), Almond (village), Altmar (village), Altona (town), Amboy, Angelica (town), Angelica (village), Annsville (town), Antwerp (town), Antwerp (village), Apulia Station, Arkport (village), Ashland (town), Auburn, Augusta (town), Ava (town), Avoca (town), Avoca (village), Bainbridge (town), Bainbridge (village), Baldwinsville (village), Bangor (town), Barker (town), Barneveld (village), Barton (town), Bath (town), Bath (village), Belfast (town), Belleville, Big Flats (town), Binghamton, Binghamton (town), Black River (village), Bloomingdale, Bolivar (town), Bolivar (village), Bombay (town), Boonville (town), Boonville (village), Brasher (town), Bridgewater (town), Bridgewater (village), Brighton (town), Brookfield (town), Brownville (town), Brownville (village), Brushton (village), Brutus (town), Burke (town), Burke (village), Burlington (town), Burns (town), Butternuts (town), Camden (town), Camden (village), Cameron, Camillus (town), Camillus (village), Campbell (town), Canaseraga (village), Canastota (village), Candor (town), Candor (village), Canisteo (town), Canisteo (village), Canton (town), Canton (village), Cape Vincent (town), Cape Vincent (village), Caroline (town), Castorland (village), Catlin (town), Cato (town), Cato (village), Caton (town), Cayuga Heights (village), Cazenovia (town), Cazenovia (village), Central Square (village), Champion (town), Champlain (town), Champlain (village), Chateaugay (town), Chateaugay (village), Chaumont (village), Chazy (town), Chemung (town), Chenango (town), Chittenango (village), Cicero (town), Cincinnatus (town), Clarksville (town), Clay (town), Clayton (town), Clayton (village), Clayville (village), Cleveland (village), Clinton (village), Cohocton (town), Cohocton (village), Cold Brook (village), Colton (town), Columbia (town), Columbus (town), Conklin (town), Constable (town), Constableville (village), Constantia (town), Cooperstown (village), Copenhagen (village), Corning, Corning (town), Cortland (town), Cortlandville (village), Coventry (town), Covert (town), Croghan (town), Croghan (village), Cuyler (town), Danby (town), Dansville (town), Dansville (village), Danube (town), Davenport (town), De Kalb (town), Deansboro, Decatur (town), Deerfield, Deferiet (village), Delhi (town), Delhi (village), Denmark (town), Deruyter (town), Deruyter (village), Dexter (village), Diana (town), Dickinson (town), Dix, Dolgeville (village), Dryden (town), Dryden (village), Dundee (village), Eagle Bay, Earlville (village), East Carthage (village), East Syracuse (village), Eaton (town), Edmeston (town), Elbridge (town), Elbridge (village), Ellenburg (town), Ellisburg (town), Ellisburg (village), Elmira, Elmira (town), Elmira Heights (village), Endicott (village), Erin (town), Erwin (town), Evans Mills (village), Exeter (town), Fabius (town), Fabius (village), Fair Haven (village), Fairfield (town), Fayetteville (village), Fenner (town), Fenton (town), Fleming (town), Floyd (town), Forestport (town), Fort Covington (town), Fort Drum (town), Fowler (town), Frankfort (town), Frankfort (village), Franklin (town), Franklin (village), Freeville (town), Fremont (town) (Steuben County), Friendship (town), Fulton, Garrattsville, Geddes (town), Genesee (town), Georgetown (town), German Flatts (town), Gilbertsville (village), Glen Park (village), Glenfield (village), Gouverneur (village), Granby (town), Greene (town), Greene (village), Greig (town), Griffiss AFB, Groton (town), Groton (village), Groveland (portions), Guilford (town), Hamden, Hamilton (town), Hamilton (village), Hancock Field AFB, Hannibal (town), Hannibal (village), Harpersfield (town), Harrietstown (town), Harrisville (town), Hartsville (town), Hartwick (town), Hastings (town), Henderson (town), Herkimer (town), Herkimer (village), Hermon (village), Herrings (village), Heuvelton (village), Hobart (village), Holland Patent (village), Homer (town), Homer (village), Hopkinton (town), Hornby (town), Hornell, Hornellsville (town), Horseheads (town), Horseheads (village), Hounsfield (town), Ilion (village), Indian River, Ingraham, Inlet (town), Ira (town), Ithaca, Ithaca (town), Jasper (town), Jefferson (town), Johnson City (village), Jordan (village), Killawog, Kirkland (town), Kirkwood (town), Kortright (town), Lacona (village), Lafayette (town), Lake Placid (village), Lansing (town), Lansing (village), Laurens (town), Laurens (village), Lawrence (town), Le Ray (town), Lebanon (town), Lee (town), Lenox (town), Lewis (town), Leyden (town), Lincoln (town), Lindley (town), Lisbon (town), Lisle (town), Lisle (village), Litchfield (town), Little Falls, Little Falls (town), Liverpool (village), Lorraine (town), Louisville (town), Lowville (town), Lowville (village), Lyme (town), Lyons Falls (village), Lyonsdale (town), Lysander (town), Madison (town), Madison (village), Madrid (town), Maine (town), Malone (town), Malone (village), Mandana, Manheim (town), Manlius (town), Manlius (village), Mannsville (village), Marathon (town), Marathon (village), Marcellus (town), Marcellus (village), Marcy, Marcy (town), Marshall (town), Martinsburg (town), Maryland (town), Masonville (town), Massena, Massena (village), McGraw (village), Mentz (town), Meredith (town), Meridian (village), Mexico (town), Mexico (village), Middlefield (town), Middleville (village), Milford (town), Milford (village), Millport (village), Minetto (town), Minoa (village), Mohawk (village), Moira (town), Mooers (town), Mooers (village), Morris (town), Morris (village), Morristown (town), Morristown (village), Morrisville (village), Mount Upton, Munnsville (village), Nanticoke (town), Nelson (town), New Berlin (town), New Berlin (village), New Bremen (town), New Hartford (town), New Hartford (village), New Haven (town), New Haven (village), New Lisbon (town), New York Mills (village), Newark Valley (town), Newark Valley (village), Newfield (town), Newport (town), Newport (village), Nichols (town), Nichols (village), Niles (town), Norfolk (town), North Dansville (town), North Elba (town), North Hornell (village), North Norwich (town), North Pitcher, North Syracuse (village), Norwich, Norwich (town), Norwood (village), Ogdensburg, Oneida, Oneida Castle (village), Oneonta, Oneonta (town), Onondaga (town), Oriskany (village), Oriskany Falls (village), Orleans (town), Orwell (town), Oswegatchie (town), Oswego, Oswego (town), Otego (town), Otego (village), Otisco (town), Otsego (town), Otselic (town), Owasco (town), Owego (town), Owego (village), Oxford (town), Oxford (village), Painted Post (village), Palermo (town), Pamelia (town), Paris (town), Parish (town), Parish (village), Parishville (town), Pennellville, Perkinsville, Peterboro, Pharsalia (town), Philadelphia (town), Philadelphia (village), Phoenix (vil-

New York—Cable Systems

lage), Pierrepont (town), Pierrepont Manor, Pitcairn (town), Pitcher (town), Pittsfield (town), Plainfield (town), Plymouth (town), Poland (village), Pompey (town), Port Byron (village), Port Dickinson (village), Port Leyden (village), Potsdam (town), Potsdam (village), Pratts Hollow, Preble (town), Prospect (village), Pulaski (village), Rathbone, Remsen (town), Remsen (village), Rensselaer Falls (village), Richburg (village), Richfield (town), Richfield Springs (village), Richland (town), Richville (village), Riverside (village), Rockdale, Rodman (town), Rome, Rouses Point (village), Russell (town), Russia (town), Rutland (town), Sackets Harbor (village), Salina (town), Salisbury (town), Sandy Creek (town), Sandy Creek (village), Sangerfield (town), Santa Clara (town), Saranac Lake (village), Savona (village), Schroeppel (town), Schuyler (town), Scio (portions), Scott (town), Scriba (town), Sempronius (town), Sennett (town), Sherburne (town), Sherburne (village), Sherrill, Sidney (town), Sidney (village), Skaneateles (town), Skaneateles (village), Smithfield (town), Smyrna (town), Smyrna (village), Solvay (village), South Corning (village), Southport (town), Spafford (town), Sparta (town), Springfield (town), Springwater (town), St. Armand (town), Stamford (town), Stamford (village), Stark, Starkey (town), Sterling (town), Stockbridge (town), Stockholm (town), Sullivan (town), Summitt (town), Sylvan Beach (village), Syracuse, Taylor (town), Thendara, Theresa (town), Theresa (village), Throop (town), Thurston (town), Tioga (town), Trenton (town), Triangle (town), Troupsburg (town), Trumansburg (village), Truxton (town), Tully (town), Tully (village), Tupper Lake (town), Tupper Lake (village), Turin (town), Turin (village), Tuscarora (town), Ulysses (town), Unadilla (town), Unadilla (village), Union (town), Utica, Van Buren (town), Vermontville, Vernon (town), Vernon (village), Verona (town), Vestal (town), Veteran (town), Vienna (town), Virgil (town), Volney (town), Waddington (town), Waddington (village), Walton (town), Walton (village), Wampsville (village), Warren, Watertown, Watertown (town), Waterville (village), Watkins Glen (village), Watson (town), Waverly (town), Waverly (village), Wayland (town), Wayland (village), Webb (town), Weedsport (village), Wellesley Island, Wellsburg (village), West Carthage (village), West Chazy, West Leyden, West Monroe (town), West Sparta (town), West Turin (town), West Winfield (village), Western (town), Westmoreland (town), Westville (town), Wheeler (portions), Whitesboro, Whitestown (town), Whitestown (village), Whitney Point (village), Willet (town), Wilna (town), Winfield (town), Wirt (town), Wolcott (town), Woodhull (town), Worcester (town) & Yorkville (village), NY; Athens Borough, Athens Twp., Bridgewater Twp., Ceres Twp., Choconut Twp., Deerfield Twp., Dimock Twp., Elkland, Franklin Twp., Lawrence Twp., Lawrenceville Borough, Liberty Twp., Litchfield Twp., Montrose Borough, Nelson Twp., Osceola Twp., Sayre Borough, Sciota, Shinglehouse, Silver Lake Twp., South Waverly, Springville Twp., Tioga Borough & Ulster Twp., PA. ICA: NY0013.

TV Market Ranking: 34 (Summitt (town)); 35 (Albion Center (town), Altmar (village), Amboy, Annsville (town), Apulia Station, Auburn, Augusta (town), Baldwinsville (village), Brutus (town), Camden (town), Camden (village), Camillus (town), Camillus (village), Canastota (village), Cato (town), Cato (village), Caton (town), Cazenovia (town), Cazenovia (village), Central Square (village), Chittenango (village), Cicero (town), Clay (town), Cleveland (village), Constantia (town), Cortland, Cortlandville (town), Cuyler (town), Deruyter (town), Deruyter (village), DEWITT, East Syracuse (village), Eaton (town), Elbridge (town), Elbridge (village), Fabius (town), Fabius (village), Fair Haven (village), Fayetteville (village), Fenner (town), Fleming (town), Fulton, Geddes (town), Georgetown (town), Granby (town), Groton (town), Groton (village), Hamilton (town), Hamilton (village), Hancock Field AFB, Hannibal (town), Hannibal (village), Hastings (town), Homer (town), Homer (village), Ira (town), Jordan (village), Lafayette (town), Lebanon (town), Lee (town), Lenox (town), Lincoln (town), Liverpool (village), Lysander (town), Madison (town), Madison (village), Mandana, Manlius (town), Manlius (village), Marcellus (town), Marcellus (village), McGraw (village), Mentz (town), Meridian (village), Mexico (town), Mexico (village), Minetto (town), Minoa (village), Morrisville (village), Munnsville (village), Nelson (town), New Haven (town), New Haven (village), Niles (town), North Pitcher, North Syracuse (village), Oneida, Oneida Castle (village), Onondaga (town), Oswego, Otisco (town), Otselic (town), Owasco (town), Palermo (town), Parish (town), Parish (village), Pennellville, Peterboro, Phoenix (village), Pitcher (town), Pompey (town), Port Byron (village), Pratts Hollow, Preble (town), Salina (town), Schroeppel (town), Scott (town), Scriba (town), Sempronius (town), Sennett (town), Sherrill, Skaneateles (town), Skaneateles (village), Smithfield (town), Smyrna (village), Solvay (village), Spafford (town), Sterling (town), Stockbridge (town), Sullivan (town), Sylvan Beach (village), Syracuse, Taylor (town), Throop (town), Truxton (town), Tully (town), Tully (village), Van Buren (town), Vernon (town), Vernon (village), Verona (town), Vienna (town), Volney (town), Wampsville (village), Weedsport (village), West Monroe (town), Western (town), Whitesboro); 49 (Bridgewater Twp., Dimock Twp., Montrose Borough, Silver Lake Twp., Springville Twp.); Below 100 (Adams (town), Adams (village), Adams Center, Addison (town), Addison (village), Afton (town), Afton (village), Alexandria (town), Alfred (village), Almond (town), Altona (town), Antwerp (town), Antwerp (village), Arkport (village), Ashland (town), Athens Borough, Athens Twp., Ava (town), Avoca (town), Avoca (village), Bainbridge (town), Bainbridge (village), Barker (town), Barneveld (village), Barton (town), Bath (town), Bath (village), Belfast (town), Belleville, Big Flats (town), Binghamton (town), Black River (village), Bloomingdale, Bolivar (town), Boonville (town), Boonville (village), Bridgewater (town), Bridgewater (village), Brighton (town), Brookfield (town), Brownville (town), Brownville (village), Burlington (town), Burns (town), Cameron, Campbell (town), Candor (town), Candor (village), Canisteo (town), Canisteo (village), Canton (town), Cape Vincent (town), Cape Vincent (village), Caroline (town), Castorland (village), Catlin (town), Cayuga Heights (village), Champion (town), Champlain (village), Chateaugay (village), Chaumont (village), Chazy (town), Chemung (town), Chenango (town), Choconut Twp., Cincinnatus (town), Clayton (town), Clayton (village), Clayville (village), Clinton (village), Cohocton (town), Cohocton (village), Cold Brook (village), Columbia (town), Columbus (town), Conklin (town), Constableville (village), Cooperstown (village), Copenhagen (village), Corning, Coventry (town), Covert (town), Croghan (town), Croghan (village), Danby (town), Dansville (village), Danube (town), Deansboro, Decatur (town), Deerfield, Deerfield Twp., Deferiet (village), Denmark (town), Dexter (village), Diana (town), Dickinson (town), Dix, Dolgeville (village), Dryden (town), Dryden (village), Dundee (village), Earlville (village), East Carthage (village), Edmeston (town), Elkland, Ellenburg (town), Ellisburg (town), Ellisburg (village), Elmira (town), Elmira Heights (village), Endicott (village), Erin (town), Erwin (town), Evans Mills (village), Exeter (town), Fairfield (town), Fenton (town), Floyd (town), Forestport (town), Fort Drum, Fowler (town), Frankfort (town), Frankfort (village), Freeville (village), Fremont (town) (Steuben County), Friendship (town), Garrattsville, German Flatts (town), Glen Park (village), Glenfield, Gouverneur (town), Gouverneur (village), Greene (town), Greene (village), Greig (town), Griffiss AFB, Guilford (town), Harrietstown (town), Hartsville (town), Hartwick (town), Henderson (town), Herkimer (town), Herkimer (village), Herrings (village), Holland Patent (village), Hornby (town), Hornellsville (town), Horseheads (town), Horseheads (village), Hounsfield (town), Hounsfield (town), Indian River, Ingraham, Ithaca (town), Jasper (town), Johnson City (village), Killawog, Kirkland (town), Kirkwood (town), Lacona (village), Lake Placid (village), Lansing (town), Lansing (village), Lawrence (town), Lawrence Twp., Lawrenceville Borough, Le Ray (town), Lewis (town), Leyden (town), Liberty Twp., Lindley (town), Lisle (village), Lisle (village), Litchfield (town), Litchfield Twp., Little Falls, Little Falls (town), Lorraine (town), Lowville (town), Lowville (village), Lyme (town), Lyons Falls (village), Lyonsdale (town), Maine (town), Manheim (town), Mannsville (village), Marathon (village), Marcy, Marcy (town), Marshall (town), Martinsburg (town), Masonville (town), Middlefield (town), Middleville (village), Millport (village), Mohawk (village), Mooers (town), Mount Upton, Nanticoke (town), Nelson Twp., New Berlin (town), New Berlin (village), New Bremen (town), New Hartford (town), New Hartford (village), New York Mills (village), Newark Valley (town), Newfield (town), Newport (town), Newport (village), Nichols (town), Nichols (village), North Elba (town), North Hornell (village), Oriskany (village), Oriskany Falls (village), Orleans (town), Orwell (town), Osceola Twp., Oswegatchie (town), Oswego (town), Otsego (town), Owego (town), Owego (village), Oxford (town), Oxford (village), Painted Post (village), Pamelia (town), Paris (town), Philadelphia (town), Philadelphia (village), Pierrepont Manor, Pitcairn (town), Pittsfield (town), Plainfield (town), Poland (village), Port Dickinson (village), Port Leyden (village), Prospect (village), Pulaski (village), Rathbone, Remsen (town), Remsen (village), Richfield (town), Richfield Springs (village), Richland (town), Richville (village), Riverside (village), Rockdale, Rodman (town), Rome, Rouses Point (village), Russia (town), Rutland (town), Sackets Harbor (village), Salisbury (town), Sandy Creek (town), Sandy Creek (village), Sangerfield (town), Santa Clara (town), Savona (village), Schuyler (town), Scio (portions), Sciota, Sherburne (town), Sherburne (village), Sidney (town), Sidney (village), Smyrna (town), South Corning (village), South Waverly, Southport (town), Springfield (town), St. Armand (town), Stark, Starkey (town), Thendara, Theresa (town), Theresa (village), Thurston (town), Tioga (town), Tioga Borough, Trenton (town), Triangle (town), Troupsburg (town), Trumansburg (village), Tupper Lake (town), Tupper Lake (village), Turin (town), Turin (village), Tuscarora (town), Ulster Twp., Ulysses (town), Unadilla (town), Unadilla (village), Union (town), Vermontville, Vestal (town), Veteran (town), Virgil (town), Watertown (town), Waterville (village), Watkins Glen (village), Watson (town), Waverly (town), Waverly (village), Wayland (village), Webb (town), Wellesley Island, Wellsburg (village), West Carthage (village), West Chazy, West Leyden, West Turin (town), West Winfield (village), Westmoreland (town), Wheeler (portions), Whitestown (town), Whitestown (village), Whitney Point (village), Willet (town), Wilna (town), Winfield (town), Woodhull (town), Yorkville (village), Almond (village), Binghamton, Champlain (town), Corning (town), Hornell, Ilion (village), Ithaca, Saranac Lake (village), Sayre Borough, Utica, Watertown); Outside TV Markets (Alfred (town), Alma (town), Angelica (town), Angelica (village), Bangor (town), Bolivar (village), Bombay (town), Brasher (town), Brushton (village), Burke (town), Burke (village), Butternuts (town), Canaseraga (village), Canton (village), Ceres Twp., Chateaugay (town), Clarksville (town), Colton (town), Constable (town), Dansville (town), Davenport (town), De Kalb (town), Delhi (town), Delhi (village), Eagle Bay, Fort Covington (town), Franklin (town), Franklin (village), Franklin Twp., Genesee (town), Gilbertsville (village), Groveland (portions), Hamden, Harpersfield (town), Harrisville (town), Hermon (village), Heuvelton (village), Hobart (village), Hopkinton (town), Inlet (town), Jefferson (town), Kortright (town), Laurens (town), Laurens (village), Lisbon (town), Louisville (town), Madrid (town), Malone (town), Malone (village), Maryland (town), Massena (village), Meredith (town), Milford (town), Milford (village), Moira (town), Mooers (village), Morris (town), Morris (village), Morristown (town), Morristown (village), New Lisbon (town), Newark Valley (village), Norfolk (town), North Dansville (town), North Norwich (town), Norwich, Norwich (town), Norwood (village), Ogdensburg, Oneonta (town), Otego (town), Otego (village), Parishville (town), Perkinsville, Pharsalia (town), Pierrepont (town), Plymouth (town), Potsdam (town), Potsdam (village), Rensselaer Falls (village), Richburg (village), Russell (town), Shinglehouse, Sparta (town), Springwater (town), Stamford (town), Stamford (village), Stockholm (town), Waddington (town), Waddington (village), Walton (town), Walton (village), Wayland (town), West Sparta (town), Westville (town), Wirt (town), Wolcott (town), Worcester (town), Massena, Oneonta). Franchise award date: April 1, 1974. Franchise expiration date: N.A. Began: April 1, 1974.

Channel capacity: 70 (operating 2-way). Channels available but not in use: N.A.

Basic Service

Subscribers: 438,766. Commercial subscribers: 10,628.

Programming (received off-air): WCNY-TV (PBS) Syracuse; WNYS-TV (MNT) Syracuse; WSPX-TV (ION) Syracuse; WSTM-

Cable Systems—New York

TV (NBC) Syracuse; WSTQ-LP (CW) Syracuse; WSYR-TV (ABC, IND, MeTV) Syracuse; WSYT (FOX, The Country Network) Syracuse; WTVH (CBS) Syracuse.
Programming (via satellite): Jewelry Television; TBS; WGN America.
Fee: $75.54 installation; $9.60 monthly; $2.00 converter.

Expanded Basic Service 1
Subscribers: N.A.
Programming (via satellite): A&E; BET; Cartoon Network; CNBC; CNN; Comedy Central; C-SPAN; C-SPAN 2; Discovery Channel; Discovery Life Channel; E! HD; ESPN; ESPN2; EVINE Live; EWTN Global Catholic Network; Food Network; Fox News Channel; Freeform; FX; Hallmark Channel; HGTV; HLN; Lifetime; LMN; MSG Plus; MSNBC; MTV; NBCSN; Nickelodeon; Oxygen; QVC; Spike TV; Syfy; The Weather Channel; TLC; TNT; Travel Channel; TV Land; Univision Studios; USA Network; VH1; WE tv; YES Network.
Fee: $37.00 installation; $36.07 monthly.

Digital Basic Service
Subscribers: N.A.
Programming (via satellite): AMC; BBC America; Bloomberg Television; Boomerang; Bravo; CMT; Cooking Channel; C-SPAN 3; Discovery Digital Networks; Disney Channel; Disney XD; DIY Network; ESPN Classic; ESPNews; Fox Sports 1; Fuse; FXM; FYI; Golf Channel; Great American Country; GSN; History; History International; IFC; MSG; MTV Classic; MTV2; National Geographic Channel; Nick 2; Nick Jr.; Outdoor Channel; Ovation; Sundance TV; TeenNick; Trinity Broadcasting Network (TBN); truTV; Turner Classic Movies; Weatherscan.

Digital Expanded Basic Service
Subscribers: N.A.
Programming (via satellite): Fox Sports 2; FSN Digital Atlantic; FSN Digital Central; FSN Digital Pacific; NBA TV; Tennis Channel.
Fee: $4.95 monthly.

Digital Pay Service 1
Pay Units: N.A.
Programming (via satellite): Cinemax (multiplexed); HBO (multiplexed); Showtime (multiplexed); Starz (multiplexed); The Movie Channel (multiplexed).
Fee: $8.00 monthly (Cinemax), $9.50 monthly (Showtime, Starz or TMC), $10.95 monthly (HBO).
Video-On-Demand: Yes

Pay-Per-View
iN DEMAND (delivered digitally); Playboy TV (delivered digitally); Fresh (delivered digitally).

Internet Service
Operational: Yes.
Subscribers: 498,449.
Broadband Service: EarthLink, LocalNet, Road Runner.
Fee: $39.95 installation; $44.95 monthly.

Telephone Service
Digital: Operational
Subscribers: 303,052.
Fee: $39.95 monthly
Miles of Plant: 27,506.0 (coaxial); 10,737.0 (fiber optic). Homes passed: 1,016,059.
President: Mary Cotter. Vice President, Engineering: Henry Hryckiewicz. Vice President, Marketing: John Melvany. Vice President, Public Affairs: Jeff Unaitis. Technical Operations Director: Bruce Tompkns.
Ownership: Time Warner Cable (MSO).; Advance/Newhouse Partnership (MSO).

2017 Edition

DOVER PLAINS—Cablevision, 1 Van Cortland Ave, Ossining, NY 10562-3309. Phones: 914-762-8717; 516-803-2300 (Corporate office). Fax: 516-803-1183. Web Site: http://www.cablevision.com. Also serves Verbank & Wingdale. ICA: NY0209.
TV Market Ranking: 19 (DOVER PLAINS, Wingdale); Below 100 (Verbank). Franchise award date: N.A. Franchise expiration date: N.A. Began: January 1, 1964.
Channel capacity: N.A. Channels available but not in use: N.A.

Basic Service
Subscribers: N.A.
Programming (received off-air): W42AE Poughkeepsie; WABC-TV (ABC, Live Well Network) New York; WCBS-TV (CBS, Decades) New York; WFUT-DT (getTV, UniMas) Newark; WMBC-TV (Azteca America) Newton; WNBC (COZI TV, NBC) New York; WNET (PBS) Newark; WNJN (PBS) Montclair; WNJU (TMO) Linden; WNYW (FOX, Movies!) New York; WPIX (Antenna TV, CW, This TV) New York; WPXN-TV (ION) New York; WRNN-TV (IND) Kingston; WTBY-TV (TBN) Poughkeepsie; WWOR-TV (Bounce TV, Buzzr, Heroes & Icons, MNT) Secaucus; WXTV-DT (UNV) Paterson.
Programming (via satellite): Disney Channel.
Fee: $49.95 installation; $15.11 monthly.

Expanded Basic Service 1
Subscribers: N.A.
Programming (via satellite): A&E; AMC; Animal Planet; BET; Bravo; Cartoon Network; CMT; CNBC; CNN; Comedy Central; C-SPAN; C-SPAN 2; Discovery Channel; E! HD; ESPN; ESPN2; Food Network; Fox News Channel; Fox Sports 1; Freeform; Fuse; FX; GSN; HGTV; History; HLN; IFC; Lifetime; MSG; MSG Plus; MSNBC; MTV; MTV2; News 12 Traffic & Weather; Nickelodeon; QVC; Spike TV; SportsNet New York; Syfy; TBS; The Weather Channel; TLC; TNT; Travel Channel; truTV; Turner Classic Movies; TV Land; USA Network; VH1; WE tv; YES Network.
Fee: $34.84 monthly.

Digital Basic Service
Subscribers: N.A.
Programming (via satellite): Azteca; BBC World News; Bloomberg Television; Canal Sur; Caracol TV; Cartoon Network en Espanol; Cinelatino; CMT; CNN en Espanol; CNN HD; C-SPAN 3; Destination America; Discovery Kids Channel; Disney XD; Docu TVE; Ecuavisa Internacional; ESPN Classic; ESPN Deportes; ESPN HD; ESPN2 HD; ESPNews; EuroNews; EVINE Live; Food Network HD; FOX College Sports Central; FOX College Sports Pacific; Fox Deportes; Fox Life; Fox Sports 2; FXM; FYI; Golf Channel; GolTV; Great American Country; Hallmark Channel; HD Theater; here! On Demand; HGTV HD; History en Espanol; History International; HTV; Infinito; Investigation Discovery; Jewelry Television; La Familia Cosmovision; LOGO; Mariavision; MC; Momentum; MTV Classic; MTV Hits; National Geographic Channel; National Geographic Channel HD; NBA TV; NBC Universo; NBCSN; NHL Network; Nick Jr.; Nicktoons; Outdoor Channel; Oxygen; Science Channel; Sundance TV; TBS HD; TeenNick; Telefe Internacional; TNT HD; Toon Disney en Espanol; Tr3s; TVG Network; ULTRA HD-Plex; Universal HD; Versus HD; VH1 Soul; ViendoMovies; Vme TV; YES HD.
Fee: $10.95 monthly.

Access the most current data instantly
ADVANCED TVFactbook
TELCO/IPTV • CABLE TV • TV STATIONS
www.warren-news.com/factbook.htm

Pay Service 1
Pay Units: N.A.
Programming (via satellite): Cinemax; Flix; HBO (multiplexed); Showtime (multiplexed); Starz; The Movie Channel.
Fee: $10.45 monthly.

Digital Pay Service 1
Pay Units: N.A.
Programming (via satellite): Cinemax (multiplexed); Cinemax HD; Cinemax On Demand; HBO (multiplexed); HBO HD; HBO on Demand; Korean Channel; MBC America; Portuguese Channel; RAI Italia; RTN; Showtime (multiplexed); Showtime HD; Showtime On Demand; Starz (multiplexed); Starz Encore (multiplexed); Starz HD; The Movie Channel (multiplexed); The Movie Channel HD; TV Asia; TV Polonia; TV5, La Television International; Zee TV.
Fee: $9.95 monthly (Cinemax, Playboy, Showtime, Starz/Encore, TMC, RAI, SPT, TV5 or TV Polonia), $11.95 monthly (HBO), $14.95 monthly (Chinese or Korean package), $19.95 monthly (South Asian package), $24.95 monthly (TV Japan), $29.95 monthly (Russian package).
Video-On-Demand: Yes

Pay-Per-View
Playboy TV; Sports PPV (delivered digitally); NBA TV (delivered digitally); iN DEMAND (delivered digitally); Playboy TV (delivered digitally).

Internet Service
Operational: Yes.
Broadband Service: Optimum Online.
Fee: $46.95 installation; $34.95 monthly.

Telephone Service
Digital: Operational
Fee: $34.95 monthly
Miles of Plant: 377.0 (coaxial); 42.0 (fiber optic). Homes passed: 10,615.
Vice President, Field Operations: Mark Fitchett. Area Operations Manager: Gary Kirkland. Chief Technician: Steve Wrisley. Media Relations Director: Patrick Macelro.
Ownership: Altice USA (MSO).

DOWNSVILLE—Formerly served by Downsville Community Antenna. No longer in operation. ICA: NY0210.

DRESDEN (village)—Time Warner Cable. Now served by BUFFALO (formerly Lackawanna), NY [NY0216]. ICA: NY0211.

DUNDEE (village)—Time Warner Cable. Now served by DEWITT, NY [NY0013]. ICA: NY0212.

DUNKIRK—Time Warner Cable. Now served by BUFFALO (formerly Lackawanna), NY [NY0216]. ICA: NY0064.

EAST HAMPTON—Formerly served by Cablevision Systems Corp. Now served by Optimum, RIVERHEAD, NY [NY0024]. ICA: NY0060.

EDINBURG (town)—Formerly served by Adelphia Communications. Now served by Time Warner Cable, ALBANY, NY [NY0014]. ICA: NY0143.

ELLENVILLE (town)—Time Warner Cable. Now served by BETHEL (town), NY [NY0231]. ICA: NY0087.

ELMIRA—Time Warner Cable. Now served by DEWITT, NY [NY0013]. ICA: NY0215.

ELMIRA/CORNING—Time Warner Cable. Now served by DEWITT, NY [NY0013]. ICA: NY0057.

ENFIELD—Haefele TV Inc, 24 East Tioga St, PO Box 312, Spencer, NY 14883. Phone: 607-589-6235. Fax: 607-589-7211. E-mail: htv@htva.net. Web Site: http://www.htva.net. Also serves Catharine (town), Enfield (town) & Hector (town - portions). ICA: NY0152.
TV Market Ranking: Below 100 (Catharine (town), ENFIELD, Enfield (town), Hector (town - portions). Franchise award date: December 27, 1984. Franchise expiration date: N.A. Began: April 1, 1985.
Channel capacity: N.A. Channels available but not in use: N.A.

Basic Service
Subscribers: 550.
Programming (received off-air): WBNG-TV (CBS, CW) Binghamton; WCNY-TV (PBS) Syracuse; WICZ-TV (FOX) Binghamton; WNYS-TV (MNT) Syracuse; WSKG-TV (PBS) Binghamton; WSYR-TV (ABC, IND, MeTV) Syracuse; WSYT (FOX, The Country Network) Syracuse; WTVH (CBS) Syracuse.
Programming (via satellite): A&E; AMC; Animal Planet; Cartoon Network; CMT; CNBC; CNN; Comedy Central; C-SPAN; Discovery Channel; Disney Channel; DIY Network; E! HD; ESPN; ESPN Classic; ESPN2; EWTN Global Catholic Network; Food Network; Fox News Channel; Fox Sports 1; Freeform; FX; Great American Country; Hallmark Channel; HGTV; History; HLN; ION Television; Lifetime; MSG; MSG Plus; MSNBC; MTV; Nickelodeon; Pop; QVC; Spike TV; Syfy; TBS; The Weather Channel; TLC; TNT; Travel Channel; truTV; TV Land; USA Network; VH1; WE tv; WPIX (Antenna TV, CW, This TV) New York; YES Network.
Fee: $30.00 installation; $24.95 monthly; $1.00 converter.

Digital Basic Service
Subscribers: N.A.
Programming (via satellite): BBC America; Bloomberg Television; Bravo; Discovery Life Channel; Disney XD; DMX Music; ESPN Classic; ESPNews; FXM; FYI; Golf Channel; GSN; History International; IFC; INSP; LMN; MTV2; Nick Jr.; Nicktoons; Outdoor Channel; TeenNick; Turner Classic Movies.
Fee: $12.95 monthly.

Pay Service 1
Pay Units: N.A.
Programming (via satellite): Cinemax.
Fee: $9.00 monthly.

D-537

New York—Cable Systems

Pay Service 2
Pay Units: 221.
Programming (via satellite): HBO (multiplexed).
Fee: $10.00 monthly.
Digital Pay Service 1
Pay Units: N.A.
Programming (via satellite): Cinemax (multiplexed); HBO (multiplexed); Showtime (multiplexed); Starz (multiplexed); Starz Encore.
Fee: $9.95 monthly (Starz/Encore), $12.95 monthly (Showtime/TMC), $17.00 monthly (Cinemax/HBO).
Video-On-Demand: No
Internet Service
Operational: Yes. Began: October 1, 1999. Broadband Service: In-house.
Fee: $34.50-$51.95 monthly; $9.95 modem lease; $89.00 modem purchase.
Telephone Service
Digital: Operational
Miles of Plant: 87.0 (coaxial); None (fiber optic).
President & Manager: Lee Haefele. Vice President: Denise A. Laue. Chief Technician: Michael McNamara.
Ownership: Haefele TV Inc. (MSO).

FORESTPORT (town)—Time Warner Cable. Now served by DEWITT, NY [NY0013]. ICA: NY0217.

FREDONIA (village)—Time Warner Cable. Now served by JAMESTOWN, NY [NY0030]. ICA: NY0090.

FRIENDSHIP (town)—Time Warner Cable. Now served by DEWITT, NY [NY0013]. ICA: NY0166.

FULTON—Time Warner Cable. Now served by DEWITT, NY [NY0013]. ICA: NY0063.

GENEVA—Time Warner Cable. Now served by BUFFALO (formerly Lackawanna), NY [NY0216]. ICA: NY0218.

GERMANTOWN—GTel. This cable system has converted to IPTV, 210 Main St, PO Box 188, Germantown, NY 12526. Phones: 518-537-6255; 518-537-4835. Fax: 518-537-6700. E-mail: questions@gtel.net. Web Site: http://www.gtel.net. Also serves Clermont. ICA: NY5178.
TV Market Ranking: 34 (GERMANTOWN); Below 100 (Clermont). Franchise award date: September 1, 1984. Franchise expiration date: N.A. Began: September 1, 1984.
Channel capacity: N.A. Channels available but not in use: N.A.
Basic
Subscribers: 757.
Programming (received off-air): WCWN (CW) Schenectady; WMHT (PBS) Schenectady; WNYT (MeTV, NBC) Albany; WRGB (CBS, This TV) Schenectady; WTEN (ABC) Albany; WXXA-TV (FOX, Laff, The Country Network) Albany.
Programming (via satellite): A&E; Animal Planet; CMT; CNBC; CNN; Comedy Central; C-SPAN; Discovery Channel; ESPN; ESPN2; EWTN Global Catholic Network; Food Network; Fox News Channel; Freeform; History; Lifetime; MSG; MSG Plus; MTV; Nickelodeon; Outdoor Channel; Pop; QVC; Spike TV; SportsNet New York; Syfy; TBS; The Weather Channel; TLC; TNT; Turner Classic Movies; USA Network; VH1; YES Network.
Fee: $50.00 installation; $57.99 monthly. Includes 148+ channels.

Expanded
Subscribers: N.A.
Programming (via satellite): BBC America; Destination America; Discovery Kids Channel; Investigation Discovery; MC; OWN: Oprah Winfrey Network; Science Channel; Starz Encore.
Fee: $72.99 monthly. Includes 191+ channels.
HD
Subscribers: N.A.
Fee: $10.00 monthly. Includes 47 channels.
Cinemax
Subscribers: N.A.
Fee: $12.95 monthly. Includes 10 channels - 5 in SD & 5 in HD.
HBO
Subscribers: N.A.
Fee: $17.95 monthly. Includes 14 channels - 7 in SD & 7 in HD.
Showtime/TMC
Subscribers: N.A.
Fee: $14.95 monthly. Includes 15 channels - 11 in SD & 4 in HD.
Starz/Encore
Subscribers: N.A.
Fee: $7.95 monthly. Includes 8 channels - 6 in SD & 2 in HD.
Video-On-Demand: No
Pay-Per-View
Playboy TV (delivered digitally); Fresh (delivered digitally); special events (delivered digitally).
Internet Service
Operational: Yes.
Telephone Service
Digital: Operational
Fee: $21.43 monthly
President: Bruce Bohnsack. Controller: Karen Borovich. General Manager: Peter Mercer. Broadband Manager: Jim Castle. Marketing Manager: Brittany Dufresne. Customer Service Manager: Tammy Holmes.
Ownership: GTel Teleconnections.

GERMANTOWN—GTel. This cable system has converted to IPTV. See GERMANTOWN, NY [NY5178]. ICA: NY0141.

GLENS FALLS—Time Warner Cable. Now served by ALBANY, NY [NY0014]. ICA: NY0044.

GREENE (town)—Time Warner Cable. Now served by DEWITT, NY [NY0013]. ICA: NY0150.

GREIG (town)—Time Warner Cable. Now served by DEWITT, NY [NY0013]. ICA: NY0222.

HAMDEN—DTC Cable. Formerly [NY0223]. This cable system has converted to IPTV, 107 Main St, PO Box 271, Delhi, NY 13753-0271. Phones: 607-746-1500; 888-898-8006. Fax: 607-746-7991. E-mail: custserv@delhitel.com. Web Site: http://www.delhitel.com. Also serves Delancey. ICA: NY5383.
TV Market Ranking: Outside TV Markets (Delancey, HAMDEN). Franchise award date: N.A. Franchise expiration date: N.A. Began: April 1, 1958.
Channel capacity: N.A. Channels available but not in use: N.A.
Lifeline
Subscribers: 91.
Programming (received off-air): WBGH-CD (NBC) Binghamton; WBNG-TV (CBS, CW) Binghamton; WICZ-TV (FOX) Binghamton; WIVT (ABC) Binghamton; WRGB (CBS, This TV) Schenectady; WSKG-TV (PBS)

Binghamton; WSYR-TV (ABC, IND, MeTV) Syracuse.
Programming (via satellite): Bloomberg Television; C-SPAN; C-SPAN 2; The Weather Channel; WGN America.
Fee: $40.95 installation; $21.95 monthly. Includes 14 channels.
Basic
Subscribers: 86.
Programming (received off-air): WPIX (Antenna TV, CW, This TV) New York.
Programming (via satellite): A&E; AMC; American Heroes Channel; Animal Planet; BBC America; BET; Bravo; Cartoon Network; Centric; Church Channel; CMT; CNBC; CNN; Comedy Central; Destination America; Discovery Channel; Discovery Family; Disney Channel; Disney XD; E! HD; Enlace USA; ESPN; ESPN Classic; ESPN2; ESPNews; ESPNU; EWTN Global Catholic Network; Food Network; Fox Business Network; Fox News Channel; Freeform; Fuse; FX; FYI; Golf Channel; Great American Country; GSN; Hallmark Channel; Hallmark Movies & Mysteries; HGTV; History; History International; HLN; HSN; IFC Free; INSP; JUCE TV; Lifetime; LMN; MLB Network; MSG; MSG Plus; MSNBC; MTV; MTV Classic; MTV Hits; MTV Jams; MTV2; National Geographic Channel; NBCSN; Nick Jr.; Nickelodeon; Nicktoons; Outdoor Channel; OWN: Oprah Winfrey Network; Oxygen; QVC; RFD-TV; Science Channel; Smile of a Child TV; Spike TV; Syfy; TBS; TeenNick; TLC; TNT; Travel Channel; Trinity Broadcasting Network (TBN); truTV; Turner Classic Movies; TV Land; USA Network; Velocity; VH1; VH1 Soul; WE tv; YES Network.
Fee: $61.95 monthly. Includes 153 channels plus music.
Expanded Basic
Subscribers: N.A.
Programming (via satellite): Chiller; Cloo; Cooking Channel; Fox Sports 1; FSN Digital Atlantic; FSN Digital Central; FSN Digital Pacific; FXM; NFL Network; Starz Encore; Starz Encore Black; Starz Encore Classic; Starz Encore Family; Starz Encore Suspense; Starz Encore Westerns.
Fee: $69.95 monthly. Includes 171 channels plus music.
HD
Subscribers: N.A.
Fee: $9.95 monthly.
Premium Packages
Subscribers: N.A.
Programming (via satellite): Cinemax (multiplexed); Flix; HBO (multiplexed); Playboy TV; Showtime (multiplexed); Starz; The Movie Channel (multiplexed).
Fee: $14.95 monthly/one movie package, $24.95/two movie packages, $33.95/three movie packages or $42.95/all movie packages. Packages include Cinemax (4 channels), HBO (6 channels), Showtime/TMC (10 channels), Starz (5 channels) or Playboy (1 channel).
Video-On-Demand: Yes
Internet Service
Operational: Yes.
Fee: $29.95-$149.95 monthly.
Telephone Service
Digital: Operational
Fee: $15.72 monthly
General Manager: Jason Miller. Business Manager: Steve Oles.
Ownership: DTC Cable Inc. (MSO).

HAMDEN—DTC Cable. This cable system has converted to IPTV. See HAMDEN, NY [NY5383]. ICA: NY0223.

HAMMOND—Citizens Cablevision. This cable system has converted to IPTV. See HAMMOND (town), NY [NY5403]. ICA: NY0289.

HAMMOND (town)—Citizens Cablevision. Formerly [NY0289]. This cable system has converted to IPTV, 26 South Main St, PO Box 217, Hammond, NY 13646. Phone: 315-324-5911. Fax: 315-324-5917. Web Site: http://www.cit-tele.com. ICA: NY5403.
TV Market Ranking: Below 100 (HAMMOND (TOWN)).
Channel capacity: N.A. Channels available but not in use: N.A.
Lifeline
Subscribers: 302.
Fee: $99.99 installation; $35.50 monthly. Includes 15 channels.
Basic Value
Subscribers: N.A.
Fee: $65.75 monthly. Includes 64 channels.
Extended Basic
Subscribers: N.A.
Fee: $85.25 monthly. Includes 129 channels.
HD
Subscribers: N.A.
Fee: $5.95 monthly.
Cinemax
Subscribers: N.A.
Fee: $10.95 monthly. Includes 3 channels.
HBO
Subscribers: N.A.
Fee: $13.95 monthly. Includes 4 channels.
Starz/Encore
Subscribers: N.A.
Fee: $10.95 monthly. Includes 10 channels.
Internet Service
Operational: Yes.
Fee: $52.95 installation; $40.95-$89.95 monthly.
Telephone Service
Analog: Operational
Fee: $14.60 monthly
Chairman: Donald A. Ceresoli Sr. President: Donald A. Ceresoli Jr. Secretary-Treasurer: Mary Trukowski. Accounting Supervisor: Shelly L. Cole.
Ownership: Citizens Cablevision Inc. (MSO).

HANCOCK—Hancock Video, 34 Read St, PO Box 608, Hancock, NY 13783-0608. Phones: 607-637-2568; 800-360-4664. Fax: 607-637-9999. Also serves Cadosia, East Branch, Fishs Eddy, Hancock Twp. & Tompkins (town), NY; Lake Como (village), Lakewood, Preston Park (village) & Starlight (village), PA. ICA: NY0147.
TV Market Ranking: 49 (Lake Como (village), Lakewood, Preston Park (village), Starlight (village)); Below 100 (Cadosia, HANCOCK, Hancock Twp., Tompkins (town)); Outside TV Markets (East Branch, Fishs Eddy). Franchise award date: N.A. Franchise expiration date: N.A. Began: January 2, 1959.
Channel capacity: 31 (not 2-way capable). Channels available but not in use: N.A.
Basic Service
Subscribers: 508.
Programming (received off-air): WBNG-TV (CBS, CW) Binghamton; WICZ-TV (FOX) Binghamton; WIVT (ABC) Binghamton; WNEP-TV (ABC, Antenna TV) Scranton; WSKG-TV (PBS) Binghamton; WVIA-TV (PBS) Scranton; allband FM.
Programming (via satellite): A&E; AMC; CNBC; CNN; Discovery Channel; Disney Channel; Disney XD; ESPN; ESPN2; Freeform; History; Nickelodeon; QVC; Spike TV; Syfy; TBS; The Weather Channel;

Cable Systems—New York

TNT; USA Network; WGN America; WPIX (Antenna TV, CW, This TV) New York.
Fee: $50.00 installation; $62.95 monthly.
Pay Service 1
Pay Units: N.A.
Programming (via satellite): Cinemax.
Fee: $7.00 monthly.
Pay Service 2
Pay Units: 320.
Programming (via satellite): HBO.
Fee: $10.00 installation; $10.50 monthly.
Video-On-Demand: No
Internet Service
Operational: No, DSL & dial-up.
Telephone Service
None
Miles of Plant: 30.0 (coaxial); None (fiber optic). Homes passed: 1,200.
President: Robert C. Wrighter, Sr. Vice President & Treasurer: Donald C. Wrighter, Sr. General Manager: Beth Miller. Chief Technician: Gary Schoonmaker. Customer Service Manager: Mary Lynn Smith.
Ownership: Hancel Inc. (MSO).

HARTFORD (town)—Time Warner Cable. Now served by ALBANY, NY [NY0014]. ICA: NY0183.

HENDERSON (town)—Time Warner Cable. Now served by DEWITT, NY [NY0013]. ICA: NY0129.

HIGHLAND FALLS (village)—Time Warner Cable. Now served by BETHEL (town), NY [NY0231]. ICA: NY0261.

HORNELL—Time Warner Cable. Now served by DEWITT, NY [NY0013]. ICA: NY0076.

HUNTER (town)—Time Warner Cable. Now served by BETHEL (town), NY [NY0231]. ICA: NY0130.

ILION (village)—Time Warner Cable. Now served by DEWITT, NY [NY0013]. ICA: NY0036.

INDIAN LAKE (town)—Hamilton County Cable TV Inc, 1330 State Rt. 30, PO Box 275, Wells, NY 12190. Phones: 518-924-2013; 800-562-1560. Web Site: http://www.hcctelevision.com. ICA: NY0168.
TV Market Ranking: Outside TV Markets (INDIAN LAKE (TOWN)). Franchise award date: January 1, 1987. Franchise expiration date: N.A. Began: December 1, 1987.
Channel capacity: N.A. Channels available but not in use: N.A.
Basic Service
Subscribers: 105.
Programming (received off-air): WMHT (PBS) Schenectady; WNYT (MeTV, NBC) Albany; WRGB (CBS, This TV) Schenectady; WTEN (ABC) Albany; WXXA-TV (FOX, Laff, The Country Network) Albany.
Programming (via satellite): A&E; AMC; Animal Planet; Cartoon Network; CNN; Cooking Channel; Discovery Channel; DIY Network; ESPN; Food Network; Fox News Channel; Freeform; Great American Country; HGTV; History; Lifetime; QVC; TBS; The Weather Channel; TNT; USA Network.
Fee: $80.00 installation; $42.00 monthly.
Digital Basic Service
Subscribers: 34.
Programming (via satellite): American Heroes Channel; BBC America; Bloomberg Television; Bravo; Destination America; Discovery Family; Discovery Life Channel; Disney XD; ESPN Classic; ESPN2; Fox Sports 1; FXM; FYI; Golf Channel; History International; Investigation Discovery; MC; National Geographic Channel; NBCSN; Outdoor Channel; OWN; Oprah Winfrey Network; Science Channel; Syfy; Trinity Broadcasting Network (TBN); Turner Classic Movies; WE tv.
Fee: $44.75 monthly.
Pay Service 1
Pay Units: N.A.
Programming (via satellite): HBO.
Fee: $10.00 monthly.
Digital Pay Service 1
Pay Units: N.A.
Programming (via satellite): Cinemax (multiplexed); HBO (multiplexed).
Video-On-Demand: No
Internet Service
Operational: No.
Telephone Service
None
Miles of Plant: 17.0 (coaxial); None (fiber optic). Homes passed: 650.
President: Paul F. Schonewolf.
Ownership: Hamilton County/Gore Mountain Cable TV Inc. (MSO).

ISLIP—Cablevision. Now served by SUFFOLK COUNTY, NY [NY0006]. ICA: NY0225.

ITHACA—Time Warner Cable. Now served by DEWITT, NY [NY0013]. ICA: NY0028.

JAMESTOWN—Time Warner Cable, 120 Plaza Dr, Vestal, NY 13850-3658. Phones: 607-644-1646; 716-664-7315 (Jamestown office). Fax: 607-644-1501. Web Site: http://www.timewarnercable.com. Also serves Bemus Point (village), Brocton (village), Busti (town), Carroll (town), Cassadaga (village), Celoron (village), Cherry Creek (village), Clymer (town), Ellery (town), Ellicott (town), Ellington (town), Falconer (village), Fredonia (village), French Creek (town), Gerry (town), Harmony (town), Kiantone (town), Lakewood (village), Maple Springs, Mina (town), North Harmony (town), Panama (village), Poland (town), Pomfret (portions), Portland (portions), Sinclairville (village), South Dayton (village), Stockton (town) & Villenova (town), NY; Wayne Twp. (Erie County), PA. ICA: NY0030.
TV Market Ranking: Below 100 (Bemus Point (village), Brocton (village), Busti (town), Carroll (town), Cassadaga (village), Celoron (village), Cherry Creek (village), Clymer (town), Ellery (town), Ellicott (town), Ellington (town), Falconer (village), Fredonia (village), French Creek (town), Gerry (town), Harmony (town), JAMESTOWN, Kiantone (town), Lakewood (village), Maple Springs, Mina (town), North Harmony (town), Panama (village), Poland (town), Pomfret (portions), Portland (portions), Sinclairville (village), South Dayton (village), Stockton (town), Villenova (town), Wayne Twp. (Erie County)). Franchise award date: January 1, 1965. Franchise expiration date: N.A. Began: January 1, 1965.
Channel capacity: N.A. Channels available but not in use: N.A.
Basic Service
Subscribers: 18,068.
Programming (received off-air): WGRZ (Antenna TV, NBC, WeatherNation) Buffalo; WICU-TV (NBC) Erie; WIVB-TV (CBS) Buffalo; WJET-TV (ABC) Erie; WKBW-TV (ABC, Escape) Buffalo; WNED-TV (PBS) Buffalo; WNYB (IND) Jamestown; WNYO-TV (MNT) Buffalo; WPIX (Antenna TV, CW, This TV) New York; WSEE-TV (CBS, CW) Erie; WUTV (FOX, The Country Network) Buffalo; allband FM.
Programming (via satellite): BET; ION Television; NewsChannel 8; Pop; TBS; Telemundo; TLC; WGN America.
Fee: $47.91-$75.54 installation; $18.99 monthly; $2.87 converter.
Expanded Basic Service 1
Subscribers: N.A.
Programming (via satellite): A&E; AMC; Animal Planet; Bravo; Cartoon Network; CMT; CNN; Comedy Central; C-SPAN; C-SPAN 2; Discovery Channel; Discovery Life Channel; Disney Channel; E! HD; ESPN; ESPN Classic; ESPN2; EVINE Live; EWTN Global Catholic Network; Food Network; Fox News Channel; Fox Sports 1; Freeform; Fuse; FX; Golf Channel; HGTV; History; HLN; Lifetime; LMN; MSNBC; MTV; Nickelodeon; QVC; Spike TV; Syfy; The Weather Channel; TNT; Travel Channel; truTV; Turner Classic Movies; TV Land; USA Network; VH1; WE tv; YES Network.
Fee: $29.97 monthly.
Digital Basic Service
Subscribers: N.A.
Programming (via satellite): BBC America; Bloomberg Television; Cooking Channel; C-SPAN 3; Discovery Digital Networks; Disney XD; DIY Network; ESPNews; FXM; FYI; Great American Country; History International; IFC; MC; MTV Classic; Nick Jr.; Outdoor Channel; Ovation; Sundance TV; TeenNick; Trinity Broadcasting Network (TBN).
Digital Expanded Basic Service
Subscribers: N.A.
Programming (via satellite): Fox Deportes; Fox Sports 2; FSN Digital Atlantic; FSN Digital Central; FSN Digital Pacific; NBA TV; Tennis Channel.
Fee: $4.95 monthly.
Digital Pay Service 1
Pay Units: N.A.
Programming (via satellite): Cinemax (multiplexed); Flix; HBO (multiplexed); HITS (Headend In The Sky); Showtime (multiplexed); Starz; The Movie Channel (multiplexed); TV Asia; Zee TV.
Fee: $13.95 monthly (each).
Video-On-Demand: Yes
Pay-Per-View
iN DEMAND (delivered digitally); Hot Choice (delivered digitally); Playboy TV (delivered digitally); Fresh (delivered digitally); Shorteez (delivered digitally); Pleasure (delivered digitally); Sports PPV (delivered digitally).
Internet Service
Operational: Yes.
Subscribers: 13,855.
Broadband Service: Road Runner.
Fee: $39.95 installation; $44.95 monthly.
Telephone Service
Digital: Operational
Subscribers: 8,084.
Fee: $39.95 monthly
Miles of Plant: 862.0 (coaxial); 180.0 (fiber optic). Homes passed: 40,211.
President: Mary Cotter. Vice President & General Manager: Chris Stramm. Vice President, Marketing: John Melvany. Vice President, Public Affairs: Dave Whalen. Technical Operations Director: Bruce Tomkins.
Ownership: Time Warner Cable (MSO).; Advance/Newhouse Partnership (MSO).

JASPER (town)—Time Warner Cable. Now served by DEWITT, NY [NY0013]. ICA: NY0226.

JOHNSBURG (town)—Hamilton County Cable TV Inc, 1330 State Rt. 30, PO Box 275, Wells, NY 12190. Phones: 518-924-2013; 800-562-1560. Web Site: http://www.hcctelevision.com. ICA: NY0156.
TV Market Ranking: Outside TV Markets (JOHNSBURG (TOWN)). Franchise award date: January 1, 1988. Franchise expiration date: N.A. Began: June 1, 1988.
Channel capacity: N.A. Channels available but not in use: N.A.
Basic Service
Subscribers: 201.
Programming (received off-air): WMHT (PBS) Schenectady; WNYT (MeTV, NBC) Albany; WRGB (CBS, This TV) Schenectady; WTEN (ABC) Albany; WXXA-TV (FOX, Laff, The Country Network) Albany.
Programming (via satellite): A&E; AMC; CNN; C-SPAN; Discovery Channel; ESPN; ESPN2; Freeform; QVC; Spike TV; TBS; TNT; USA Network; WABC-TV (ABC, Live Well Network) New York; WGN America.
Fee: $80.00 installation; $42.00 monthly.
Digital Basic Service
Subscribers: 65.
Fee: $44.75 monthly.
Pay Service 1
Pay Units: N.A.
Programming (via satellite): Cinemax; HBO.
Fee: $9.00 monthly (Cinemax), $10.00 monthly (HBO).
Video-On-Demand: No
Internet Service
Operational: No.
Telephone Service
None
Miles of Plant: 31.0 (coaxial); None (fiber optic). Homes passed: 800.
President: Paul F. Schonewolf.
Ownership: Hamilton County/Gore Mountain Cable TV Inc. (MSO).

JOHNSTOWN (city)—Time Warner Cable. Now served by ALBANY, NY [NY0014]. ICA: NY0054.

KEENE VALLEY—Keene Valley Video Inc, 1948 State Route 73, PO Box 47, Keene Valley, NY 12943. Phone: 518-576-4510. E-mail: info@kvvi.net. Web Site: http://www.kvvi.net. Also serves Keene (town). ICA: NY0171.
TV Market Ranking: Below 100 (Keene (town), KEENE VALLEY). Franchise award date: N.A. Franchise expiration date: N.A. Began: June 15, 1982.
Channel capacity: N.A. Channels available but not in use: N.A.

2017 Edition
D-539

New York—Cable Systems

CABLE & TV STATION COVERAGE
Atlas 2017
The perfect companion to the Television & Cable Factbook
To order call 800-771-9202 or visit www.warren-news.com

Basic Service
Subscribers: 303. Commercial subscribers: 12.
Programming (received off-air): WCAX-TV (CBS, Movies!) Burlington; WETK (PBS) Burlington; WFFF-TV (FOX, IND) Burlington; WPTZ (MeTV, NBC, This TV) Plattsburgh; WVNY (ABC) Burlington.
Programming (via satellite): A&E; AMC; CMT; CNN; C-SPAN; C-SPAN 2; Discovery Channel; Disney Channel; ESPN; ESPN2; Fox Sports 1; Freeform; History; HLN; Lifetime; MTV; Nickelodeon; Outdoor Channel; QVC; Spike TV; TBS; The Weather Channel; TLC; TNT; USA Network; VH1.
Fee: $50.00 installation; $40.00 monthly.
Pay Service 1
Pay Units: 25.
Programming (via satellite): Showtime.
Fee: $5.00 monthly.
Video-On-Demand: No
Internet Service
Operational: Yes.
Broadband Service: In-house.
Fee: $60.00-$100.00 monthly.
Telephone Service
None
Miles of Plant: 24.0 (coaxial); None (fiber optic). Homes passed: 400.
President & General Manager: Timothy Whitney. Office Manager: Anita Hall.
Ownership: Timothy A. Whitney.

KINDERHOOK—Berkshire Cable Corporation, 908 W Frontview St, Dodge City, KS 67801. Phones: 800-400-5568; 518-758-9951. Web Site: http://www.fairpoint.com. Also serves Niverville, Stuyvesant, Stuyvesant Falls & Valatie (village). ICA: NY0287.
TV Market Ranking: 34 (KINDERHOOK, Niverville, Stuyvesant, Stuyvesant Falls, Valatie (village)).
Channel capacity: N.A. Channels available but not in use: N.A.
Basic Service
Subscribers: N.A.
Programming (received off-air): Pop; WCWN (CW) Schenectady; WMHT (PBS) Schenectady; WNYA (Antenna TV, MNT) Pittsfield; WNYT (MeTV, NBC) Albany; WRGB (CBS, This TV) Schenectady; WTEN (ABC) Albany; WXXA-TV (FOX, Laff, The Country Network) Albany.
Programming (via satellite): C-SPAN.
Fee: $56.00 installation; $29.45 monthly.
Expanded Basic Service 1
Subscribers: N.A.
Programming (via satellite): A&E; AMC; Animal Planet; Bravo; Capital Off Track Betting Television Network; Cartoon Network; CMT; CNBC; CNN; Comedy Central; Discovery Channel; Disney Channel; E! HD; ESPN; ESPN Classic; ESPN2; Food Network; Fox News Channel; Fox Sports 1; Freeform; FX; Golf Channel; Hallmark Channel; HGTV; History; HLN; HSN; Lifetime; MSG; MSG Plus; MSNBC; MTV; National Geographic Channel; Nickelodeon; Outdoor Channel; Oxygen; QVC; Spike TV; SportsNet New York; Syfy; TBS; The Weather Channel; TLC; TNT; Travel Channel; Trinity Broadcasting Network (TBN); truTV; Turner Classic Movies; TV Land; USA Network; VH1; WE tv.
Fee: $23.95 monthly.
Digital Basic Service
Subscribers: 46.
Programming (via satellite): American Heroes Channel; BBC America; Bloomberg Television; Bravo; Centric; Chiller; Church Channel; cloo; Destination America; Discovery Family; Discovery Life Channel; Disney XD; DMX Music; ESPN Classic; ESPN2; ESPNews; ESPNU; EVINE Live; FOX College Sports Central; FOX College Sports Pacific; Fox Sports 1; Fuse; FXM; FYI; Golf Channel; Great American Country; GSN; HGTV; History; History International; IFC; Investigation Discovery; JUCE TV; LMN; MTV; MTV Classic; MTV Hits; MTV2; National Geographic Channel; NBCSN; Nick Jr.; Nicktoons; Outdoor Channel; OWN: Oprah Winfrey Network; RetroPlex; RFD-TV; Science Channel; Sprout; Syfy; TeenNick; The Word Network; TheCoolTV; This TV; Trinity Broadcasting Network (TBN); Turner Classic Movies; VH1 Country; VH1 Soul; WE tv.
Fee: $26.45 monthly.
Digital Pay Service 1
Pay Units: N.A.
Programming (via satellite): Cinemax (multiplexed); Cinemax HD; Flix; HBO (multiplexed); HBO HD; Showtime (multiplexed); Showtime HD; Starz (multiplexed); Starz Encore (multiplexed); Starz HD; The Movie Channel (multiplexed).
Fee: $10.00 monthly (Cinemax or Starz/Encore), $12.00 monthly (Showtime/TMC/Flix), $14.00 monthly (HBO).
Internet Service
Operational: Yes.
Fee: $39.95 monthly.
Telephone Service
Digital: Operational
Senior Vice President, Governmental Affairs: Pat Morse. General Manager: Robert Holmes. Accounting Director: Angela Unruh.
Ownership: FairPoint Communications Inc. (MSO).

KINGSTON—Time Warner Cable. Now served by BETHEL (town), NY [NY0231]. ICA: NY0038.

LANCASTER (town)—Time Warner Cable. Now served by BUFFALO, NY [NY0216]. ICA: NY0043.

LIMESTONE—Atlantic Broadband. Now served by BRADFORD, PA [PA0085]. ICA: NY0228.

LONG LAKE—C H Comm LLC, 9507 Cherokee Trail, Crossville, TN 38572. Phone: 866-788-5261. Fax: 931-788-0489. ICA: NY0172.
TV Market Ranking: Outside TV Markets (LONG LAKE). Franchise award date: N.A. Franchise expiration date: N.A. Began: January 1, 1954.
Channel capacity: N.A. Channels available but not in use: N.A.
Basic Service
Subscribers: N.A.
Programming (received off-air): WNPI-DT (PBS) Norwood; WRGB (CBS, This TV) Schenectady; WTEN (ABC) Albany; WWNY-TV (CBS) Carthage; allband FM.
Programming (via satellite): Bravo; ESPN; EWTN Global Catholic Network; HGTV; Nickelodeon; QVC; Spike TV; TNT; WNBC (COZI TV, NBC) New York.
Fee: $45.00 installation; $16.67 monthly.
Expanded Basic Service 1
Subscribers: N.A.
Programming (via satellite): CNN; Discovery Channel; USA Network.
Fee: $3.33 monthly.
Expanded Basic Service 2
Subscribers: N.A.
Programming (via satellite): TBS; WGN America.
Fee: $2.95 monthly.
Pay Service 1
Pay Units: N.A.
Programming (via satellite): The Movie Channel.
Fee: $25.00 installation; $10.95 monthly.
Video-On-Demand: No
Internet Service
Operational: No.
Telephone Service
None
Miles of Plant: 25.0 (coaxial); None (fiber optic). Homes passed: 715.
General Manager & Chief Technician: Charles Himelrick. Assistant Manager: Diane Bowles. Marketing Director: Sean Feeney.
Ownership: C H Comm LLC (MSO).

LYNBROOK—Cablevision Systems Corp. Now served by AMITYVILLE, NY [NY0001]. ICA: NY0069.

MALONE (town)—Time Warner Cable. Now served by DEWITT, NY [NY0013]. ICA: NY0079.

MAMARONECK—Cablevision, 609 Center Ave, Mamaroneck, NY 10543. Phones: 914-762-8717; 516-803-2300 (Corporate office). Web Site: http://www.cablevision.com. Also serves Ardsley, Bronxville, Dobbs Ferry, Eastchester, Elmsford, Greenburgh, Hastings-on-Hudson, Irvington (village), Larchmont (village), New Rochelle, Pelham, Pelham Manor, Rye (city), Rye Brook (village), Scarsdale, Tuckahoe & White Plains. ICA: NY0012.
TV Market Ranking: 1 (Ardsley, Bronxville, Dobbs Ferry, Eastchester, Elmsford, Greenburgh, Hastings-on-Hudson, Irvington (village), Larchmont (village), MAMARONECK, New Rochelle, Pelham, Pelham Manor, Rye (city), Rye Brook (village), Scarsdale, Tuckahoe, White Plains). Franchise award date: N.A. Franchise expiration date: N.A. Began: November 1, 1977.
Channel capacity: N.A. Channels available but not in use: N.A.
Basic Service
Subscribers: 74,605.
Programming (received off-air): WABC-TV (ABC, Live Well Network) New York; WCBS-TV (CBS, Decades) New York; WFTY-DT (UniMas) Smithtown; WLIW (PBS) Garden City; WLNY-TV (IND) Riverhead; WNBC (COZI TV, NBC) New York; WNET (PBS) Newark; WNJU (TMO) Linden; WNYW (FOX, Movies!) New York; WPIX (Antenna TV, CW, This TV) New York; WPXN-TV (ION) New York; WWOR-TV (Bounce TV, Buzzr, Heroes & Icons, MNT) Secaucus; WXTV-DT (UNV) Paterson; 28 FMs.
Programming (via satellite): EVINE Live; News 12 Long Island; QVC.
Fee: $39.95 installation; $11.18 monthly; $3.00 converter.
Expanded Basic Service 1
Subscribers: N.A.
Programming (via satellite): A&E; AMC; Animal Planet; BET; Bravo; Cartoon Network; CNBC; CNN; Comedy Central; C-SPAN; C-SPAN 2; Discovery Channel; Disney Channel; E! HD; ESPN; ESPN2; Food Network; Fox News Channel; Fox Sports 1; Freeform; Fuse; FX; Golf Channel; HGTV; History; HLN; Lifetime; MSG; MSG Plus; MSNBC; MTV; MTV2; News 12 Traffic & Weather; Nickelodeon; Spike TV; SportsNet New York; Syfy; TBS; Telecare; The Weather Channel; TLC; TNT; Travel Channel; truTV; Turner Classic Movies; TV Land; Univision; USA Network; VH1; WE tv; YES Network.
Fee: $39.37 monthly.
Digital Basic Service
Subscribers: N.A.
Programming (via satellite): Azteca; BBC World News; Bloomberg Television; Canal Sur; Caracol TV; Cartoon Network en Espanol; Cinelatino; CMT; CNN en Espanol; CNN HD; C-SPAN 3; Destination America; Discovery Kids Channel; Disney XD; Docu TVE; Ecuavisa Internacional; ESPN Classic; ESPN Deportes; ESPN HD; ESPN2 HD; ESPNews; EuroNews; Food Network HD; FOX College Sports Central; FOX College Sports Pacific; Fox Deportes; Fox Life; Fox Sports 2; FSN HD; FXM; FYI; Golf Channel; GolTV; Great American Country; Hallmark Channel; HD Theater; HGTV HD; History en Espanol; History International; HTV; iN DEMAND; Infinito; Investigation Discovery; Jewelry Television; La Familia Cosmovision; LOGO; Mariavision; MC; Momentum; MTV Classic; MTV Hits; National Geographic Channel; National Geographic Channel HD; NBA TV; NBC Universo; NBCSN; NHL Network; Nick Jr.; Nicktoons; Outdoor Channel; Science Channel; Sundance TV; TBS HD; TeenNick; Telefe Internacional; TNT HD; Toon Disney en Espanol; Tr3s; TVG Network; ULTRA HDPlex; Universal HD; Versus HD; VH1 Soul; ViendoMovies; Vme TV; YES HD.
Fee: $10.95 monthly.
Pay Service 1
Pay Units: N.A.
Programming (via satellite): Cinemax; HBO (multiplexed); Showtime (multiplexed); The Movie Channel.
Digital Pay Service 1
Pay Units: N.A.
Programming (via satellite): Cinemax (multiplexed); Cinemax HD; HBO (multiplexed); HBO HD; Korean Channel; RAI Italia; RTN; Showtime (multiplexed); Showtime HD; Starz (multiplexed); Starz Encore (multiplexed); Starz HD; The Movie Channel (multiplexed); The Movie Channel HD; TV Asia; TV Polonia; TV5, La Television International; Zee TV.
Fee: $9.95 monthly (Cinemax, Playboy, Showtime, Starz/Encore, TMC, RAI, SPT, TV5 Monde or TV Polonia), $11.95 monthly (HBO), $24.95 monthly (TV Japan).
Video-On-Demand: Yes
Pay-Per-View
iN DEMAND; Club Jenna; Playboy TV; special events.
Internet Service
Operational: Yes.
Subscribers: 79,165.
Broadband Service: Optimum Online.
Fee: $46.95 installation; $34.95 monthly.

D-540

TV & Cable Factbook No. 85

Cable Systems—New York

Telephone Service
Digital: Operational
Subscribers: 65,825.
Fee: $34.95 monthly
Miles of Plant: 1,716.0 (coaxial); 442.0 (fiber optic). Homes passed: 150,159.
Executive Vice President, Programming: Tom Montemagno. Vice President, Field Operations: Mark Fitchett. Vice President, Local Ad Sales: John Oleynick. Operations Manager: Jeff Stiggers.
Ownership: Altice USA (MSO).

MANHATTAN—RCN Corp. This cable system has converted to IPTV. See NEW YORK CITY, NY [NY5312]. ICA: NY0282.

MANHATTAN—Time Warner Cable, 120 East 23rd St, New York, NY 10010. Phone: 212-598-7200. Fax: 212-420-4803. Web Site: http://www.timewarnercable.com. Also serves Astoria, Bayside, Beechhurst, Bellerose (Queens County), Brooklyn, Brooklyn Heights, Cambria Heights, College Point, Corona, Douglaston, East Elmhurst, Floral Park, Flushing, Forest Hills, Fresh Meadows, Glen Oaks, Glendale, Hollis, Howard Beach, Jackson Heights, Jamaica, Kew Garden Hills, Laurelton, Linden Hill, Little Neck, Long Island City, Malba, Maspeth, Middle Village, New York, Oakland Gardens, Ozone Park, Pomonok, Queens, Queens Village, Rego Park, Richmond Hill, Ridgewood, Rockaway Beach, Rockaway Park, Rockaway Point, Roosevelt Island, Rosedale, Springfield Gardens, Utopia, Whitestone & Woodside. ICA: NY0235.
TV Market Ranking: 1 (Astoria, Bayside, Beechhurst, Bellerose (Queens County), Brooklyn, Brooklyn Heights, Cambria Heights, College Point, Corona, Douglaston, East Elmhurst, Floral Park, Flushing, Forest Hills, Fresh Meadows, Glen Oaks, Glendale, Hollis, Howard Beach, Jackson Heights, Jamaica, Kew Garden Hills, Laurelton, Linden Hill, Little Neck, Long Island City, Malba, MANHATTAN, Maspeth, Middle Village, New York, Oakland Gardens, Ozone Park, Pomonok, Queens, Queens Village, Rego Park, Richmond Hill, Ridgewood, Rockaway Beach, Rockaway Park, Rockaway Point, Roosevelt Island, Rosedale, Springfield Gardens, Utopia, Whitestone, Woodside). Franchise award date: August 1, 1970. Franchise expiration date: N.A. Began: January 1, 1967.
Channel capacity: N.A. Channels available but not in use: N.A.
Basic Service
Subscribers: 751,966.
Programming (received off-air): WABC-TV (ABC, Live Well Network) New York; WCBS-TV (CBS, Decades) New York; WFUT-DT (getTV, UniMas) Newark; WLIW (PBS) Garden City; WMBC-TV (Azteca America) Newton; WNBC (COZI TV, NBC) New York; WNET (PBS) Newark; WNJU (TMO) Linden; WNYE-TV (PBS) New York; WNYW (FOX, Movies!) New York; WPIX (Antenna TV, CW, This TV) New York; WPXN-TV (ION) New York; WWOR-TV (Bounce TV, Buzzr, Heroes & Icons, MNT) Secaucus; WXTV-DT (UNV) Paterson; 24 FMs.
Programming (via satellite): C-SPAN; C-SPAN 2; EVINE Live; Food Network; Pop; QVC; TBS; Time Warner Cable News NY1.
Fee: $19.95-$40.95 installation; $22.75 monthly.
Expanded Basic Service 1
Subscribers: N.A.
Programming (via satellite): A&E; AMC; BET; Bravo; Cartoon Network; CNBC; CNN; Comedy Central; Discovery Channel; Disney Channel; E! HD; ESPN; ESPN2; Fox News Channel; Freeform; FX; Hallmark Channel; History; HLN; Lifetime; LMN; MSG; MSG Plus; MSNBC; MTV; Nickelodeon; Oxygen; Spike TV; Syfy; The Weather Channel; TLC; TNT; truTV; Univision; USA Network; VH1; WE tv; YES Network.
Fee: $29.03 monthly.
Digital Basic Service
Subscribers: N.A.
Programming (via satellite): Animal Planet; BBC America; Bloomberg Television; Boomerang; CMT; CNBC; C-SPAN 3; Discovery Life Channel; Disney XD; DMX Music; ESPN Classic; ESPNews; Fox Deportes; Fox Sports 1; Fuse; Golf Channel; GSN; Hallmark Channel; HGTV; IFC; MTV Classic; MTV2; NBC Universo; NBCSN; Nick 2; Nick Jr.; Ovation; Sundance TV; TeenNick; Travel Channel; Turner Classic Movies; TV Land; WAM! America's Kidz Network.
Fee: $9.95 monthly.
Digital Pay Service 1
Pay Units: N.A.
Programming (via satellite): Cinemax (multiplexed); Deutsche Welle TV; HBO (multiplexed); New Greek TV; RTN; Showtime (multiplexed); Starz (multiplexed); Starz Encore (multiplexed); The Movie Channel (multiplexed); TV Asia; TV Polonia; TV5, La Television International; Zee TV.
Fee: $9.95 monthly (CCTV, Deutsche Welle, RTN, RAI or TV5), $12.95 monthly (Cinemax, Encore, HBO, Showtime, Starz or TMC), $14.95 monthly (Antenna, TV Asia or Zee TV), $17.95 monthly (TV Polonia), $24.95 monthly (TV Japan).
Video-On-Demand: Yes
Pay-Per-View
WNBA Season Pass (delivered digitally); MLB Extra Innings (delivered digitally); NHL Center Ice (delivered digitally); NBA League Pass (delivered digitally); special events (delivered digitally); Playboy TV (delivered digitally).
Internet Service
Operational: Yes.
Subscribers: 840,104.
Broadband Service: EarthLink, LocalNet, Road Runner.
Fee: $30.50 installation; $44.95 monthly.
Telephone Service
Digital: Operational
Subscribers: 369,202.
Fee: $39.95 monthly
Miles of Plant: 3,267.0 (coaxial); 1,154.0 (fiber optic). Homes passed: 1,803,922.
President: Howard Szarfarc. Vice President, Sales: Ken Fluger. Vice President, Marketing: David Goldberg. Vice President & General Manager: Barbara Kelly. Vice President, Public Affairs: Harriet Novet. Vice President, Engineering: Larry Pestana. Vice President, Technical Operations: Norberto Rivera. Public Relations Director: Suzanne Giuliani.
Ownership: Time Warner Cable (MSO).

MARGARETVILLE—MTC Cable, 50 Swart Street, PO Box 260, Margaretville, NY 12455. Phones: 845-586-2288; 800-586-4050; 845-586-3311. Fax: 845-586-4050. E-mail: mtc@catskill.net. Web Site: http://www.mtctelcom.com. Also serves Andes, Arkville, Colchester, Conesville, Downsville, Fleischmanns, Gilboa, Halcott, Middletown & Roxbury. ICA: NY0155.
TV Market Ranking: Outside TV Markets (Andes, Arkville, Colchester, Conesville, Fleischmanns, Halcott, MARGARETVILLE, Middletown, Roxbury, Downsville). Franchise award date: N.A. Franchise expiration date: N.A. Began: January 1, 1953.
Channel capacity: N.A. Channels available but not in use: N.A.
Basic Service
Subscribers: 2,596.
Programming (received off-air): WABC-TV (ABC, Live Well Network) New York; WBNG-TV (CBS, CW) Binghamton; WBXI-CA (CBS) Indianapolis; WICZ-TV (FOX) Binghamton; WIVT (ABC) Binghamton; WNBC (COZI TV, NBC) New York; WNET (PBS) Newark; WNYT (MeTV, NBC) Albany; WNYW (FOX, Movies!) New York; WPIX (Antenna TV, CW, This TV) New York; WRGB (CBS, This TV) Schenectady; WSKG-TV (PBS) Binghamton; WWOR-TV (Bounce TV, Buzzr, Heroes & Icons, MNT) Secaucus; allband FM.
Programming (via satellite): QVC; The Weather Channel.
Fee: $39.00 installation; $27.95 monthly.
Digital Basic Service
Subscribers: N.A.
Programming (via satellite): AXS TV; BBC America; Bravo; CBS Sports Network; Discovery Digital Networks; DIY Network; ESPN; ESPN Classic; ESPNews; FOX College Sports Central; FOX College Sports Pacific; Fuse; FXM; FYI; Great American Country; GSN; History; Lifetime; MC; National Geographic Channel; Nick 2; Nick Jr.; Nicktoons; TeenNick.
Fee: $51.15 monthly.
Pay Service 1
Pay Units: N.A.
Programming (via satellite): HBO.
Fee: $10.00 monthly.
Digital Pay Service 1
Pay Units: N.A.
Programming (via satellite): HBO (multiplexed); Showtime (multiplexed); Starz (multiplexed); Starz Encore (multiplexed); The Movie Channel (multiplexed).
Fee: $9.00 monthly (each).
Video-On-Demand: No
Pay-Per-View
iN DEMAND (delivered digitally); Pleasure (delivered digitally); Hot Choice (delivered digitally).
Internet Service
Operational: Yes, DSL.
Subscribers: 1,000.
Broadband Service: In-house.
Fee: $41.95-$49.95 monthly.
Telephone Service
Digital: Operational
Fee: $39.95 monthly
Miles of Plant: 23.0 (coaxial); None (fiber optic). Homes passed: 3,500.
Operations Manager: Glen Faulkner.
Ownership: Margaretville Telephone Co. (MSO).

MASSENA—Time Warner Cable. Now served by DEWITT, NY [NY0013]. ICA: NY0072.

McDONOUGH—Formerly served by Haefele TV Inc. No longer in operation. ICA: NY0230.

MINERVA (town)—C H Comm LLC, 9507 Cherokee Trail, Crossville, TN 38572. Phone: 866-788-5261. Fax: 931-788-0489. ICA: NY0178.
TV Market Ranking: Outside TV Markets (MINERVA (TOWN)).
Channel capacity: N.A. Channels available but not in use: N.A.
Basic Service
Subscribers: 50.
Programming (received off-air): WCAX-TV (CBS, Movies!) Burlington; WCDC-TV (ABC) Adams; WETK (PBS) Burlington; WFFF-TV (FOX, IND) Burlington; WPIX (Antenna TV, CW, This TV) New York; WPTZ (MeTV, NBC, This TV) Plattsburgh; WVNY (ABC) Burlington.
Programming (via satellite): A&E; AMC; Cartoon Network; CMT; CNN; C-SPAN; Discovery Channel; E! HD; ESPN; ESPN2; Food Network; Freeform; Hallmark Channel; HGTV; History; HLN; Lifetime; MSNBC; Outdoor Channel; OWN; Oprah Winfrey Network; QVC; Spike TV; Syfy; TBS; The Weather Channel; TLC; TNT; Trinity Broadcasting Network (TBN); TV Land; USA Network; WGN America.
Fee: $43.15 installation; $41.95 monthly; $25.00 converter.
Digital Basic Service
Subscribers: N.A.
Programming (via satellite): BBC America; Bloomberg Television; Bravo; Cloo; Destination America; Discovery Kids Channel; DMX Music; ESPN Classic; ESPNews; Fox Sports 1; Fuse; FYI; Golf Channel; GSN; History International; IFC; Investigation Discovery; NBCSN; Science Channel; Turner Classic Movies; WE tv.
Fee: $12.95 monthly.
Digital Pay Service 1
Pay Units: N.A.
Programming (via satellite): Cinemax (multiplexed); HBO (multiplexed); Showtime (multiplexed); Starz (multiplexed); Starz Encore (multiplexed).
Fee: $10.95 monthly (Cinemax), $12.95 monthly (HBO, Showtime or Starz/Encore).
Internet Service
Operational: No.
Telephone Service
None
Miles of Plant: 16.0 (coaxial); None (fiber optic).
General Manager & Chief Technician: Charles Himelrick. Assistant Manager: Diane Bowles. Marketing Director: Sean Feeney.
Ownership: C H Comm LLC (MSO).

MINISINK—Cablevision. Now served by WARWICK, NY [NY0045]. ICA: NY0232.

MORAVIA—Southern Cayuga County Cablevision, PO Box 157, Locke, NY 13092-0157. Phone: 315-497-0444. Fax: 315-497-7653. Also serves Genoa Twp., King Ferry, Locke Twp. & Moravia (village). ICA: NY0233.
TV Market Ranking: 35 (Locke Twp., MORAVIA, Moravia (village)); Below 100 (Genoa Twp., King Ferry). Franchise award date: N.A. Franchise expiration date: N.A. Began: November 1, 1952.
Channel capacity: N.A. Channels available but not in use: N.A.
Basic Service
Subscribers: 5,273.
Programming (received off-air): WBNG-TV (CBS, CW) Binghamton; WCNY-TV (PBS) Syracuse; WENY-TV (ABC, CW) Elmira; WHAM-TV (ABC, CW) Rochester; WHEC-TV (MeTV, NBC) Rochester; WNYS-TV (MNT) Syracuse; WPIX (Antenna TV, CW, This TV) New York; WSTM-TV (NBC) Syracuse; WSYR-TV (ABC, IND, MeTV) Syracuse; WSYT (FOX, The Country Network) Syracuse; WTVH (CBS) Syracuse; WUHF (Antenna TV, FOX) Rochester; allband FM.
Programming (via satellite): A&E; Animal Planet; CMT; CNN; C-SPAN; Discovery

2017 Edition

D-541

New York—Cable Systems

Channel; ESPN; ESPN2; Freeform; History; HLN; KTLA (Antenna TV, CW, This TV) Los Angeles; MSG; MTV; Nickelodeon; QVC; Spike TV; Syfy; TBS; The Weather Channel; TLC; TNT; TV Land; USA Network; VH1; WGN America; WSBK-TV (MNT) Boston.
Fee: $30.00 installation; $50.00 monthly.

Pay Service 1
Pay Units: N.A.
Programming (via satellite): Cinemax; HBO; Showtime; The Movie Channel.
Fee: $9.50 monthly (each).

Video-On-Demand: Planned

Internet Service
Operational: Yes.
Broadband Service: Netlink.
Fee: $54.00 installation; $34.95 monthly.

Telephone Service
None
Miles of Plant: 16.0 (coaxial); None (fiber optic).
General Manager: Ray S. Dyer Jr.
Ownership: Ray S. Dyer Jr.

MORRIS (town)—Time Warner Cable. Now served by DEWITT, NY [NY0013]. ICA: NY0179.

MOUNT KISCO—Cablevision. Now served by YORKTOWN, NY [NY0050]. ICA: NY0067.

MOUNT TREMPER—Time Warner Cable. Now served by BETHEL (town), NY [NY0231]. ICA: NY0193.

MOUNT VERNON—Time Warner Cable, 701 North MacQuesten Pkwy, Mount Vernon, NY 10552. Phones: 914-662-3100; 914-699-8080. Fax: 914-699-8131. Web Site: http://www.timewarnercable.com. ICA: NY0032.
TV Market Ranking: 1 (MOUNT VERNON).
Franchise award date: August 1, 1971.
Franchise expiration date: N.A. Began: August 1, 1971.
Channel capacity: N.A. Channels available but not in use: N.A.

Basic Service
Subscribers: 9,221.
Programming (received off-air): WABC-TV (ABC, Live Well Network) New York; WCBS-TV (CBS, Decades) New York; WEDW (PBS) Bridgeport; WFUT-DT (getTV, UniMas) Newark; WLIW (PBS) Garden City; WLNY-TV (IND) Riverhead; WMBC-TV (Azteca America) Newton; WNBC (COZI TV, NBC) New York; WNET (PBS) Newark; WNJU (TMO) Linden; WNYE-TV (PBS) New York; WNYW (FOX, Movies!) New York; WPIX (Antenna TV, CW, This TV) New York; WPXN-TV (ION) New York; WWOR-TV (Bounce TV, Buzzr, Heroes & Icons, MNT) Secaucus; WXTV-DT (UNV) Paterson; WYXN-LD New York; allband FM.
Programming (via satellite): Bravo; C-SPAN; Disney Channel; Food Network; News 12 Westchester; Time Warner Cable News NY1.
Fee: $19.95-$40.95 installation; $20.50 monthly.

Expanded Basic Service 1
Subscribers: N.A.
Programming (via satellite): A&E; AMC; BET; Bloomberg Television; Cartoon Network; CNBC; CNN; Comedy Central; Discovery Channel; E! HD; ESPN; ESPN Classic; ESPN2; EWTN Global Catholic Network; Freeform; HGTV; History; HLN; Lifetime; LMN; MSG; MSG Plus; MSNBC; MTV; National Geographic Channel; Nickelodeon; Oxygen; Pop; QVC; Spike TV; Syfy; TBS; The Weather Channel; TLC; TNT; Travel Channel; truTV; Univision; USA Network; VH1; WE tv; Yesterday USA.
Fee: $28.26 monthly.

Digital Basic Service
Subscribers: N.A.
Programming (via satellite): AXS TV; BBC America; Bloomberg Television; Boomerang; CBS Sports Network; CMT; CNN International; Cooking Channel; C-SPAN 3; Discovery Life Channel; Disney XD; DIY Network; ESPN; ESPNews; FOX College Sports Central; FOX College Sports Pacific; Fox Sports 2; Fuse; Great American Country; GSN; Hallmark Channel; HD Theater; LOGO; MC; MTV Classic; MTV2; NBC Universo; Nick 2; Nick Jr.; TeenNick; Tennis Channel; The Word Network; TNT HD.
Fee: $9.95 monthly.

Digital Pay Service 1
Pay Units: N.A.
Programming (via satellite): Cinemax (multiplexed); Deutsche Welle TV; HBO (multiplexed); HBO HD; New Greek TV; RAI Italia; RTN; Showtime (multiplexed); Showtime HD; Starz (multiplexed); Starz Encore (multiplexed); The Movie Channel (multiplcxcd); TV Asia; TV Polonia; TV5, La Television International; Zee TV.
Fee: $14.95 monthly (each).

Video-On-Demand: Yes

Pay-Per-View
iN DEMAND (delivered digitally); Playboy TV (delivered digitally); Special events (delivered digitally); Sports PPV (delivered digitally); NBA TV (delivered digitally).

Internet Service
Operational: Yes.
Subscribers: 8,017.
Broadband Service: EarthLink, LocalNet, Road Runner.
Fee: $30.50 installation; $44.95 monthly.

Telephone Service
Digital: Operational
Subscribers: 6,070.
Fee: $39.95 monthly
Miles of Plant: 148.0 (coaxial); 75.0 (fiber optic). Homes passed: 33,069.
President: Howard Szarfarc. Senior Vice President & General Manager: Barbara Kelly. Vice President, Sales: Ken Fluger. Vice President, Marketing: David Goldberg. Vice President, Public Affairs: Harriet Novet. Vice President, Engineering: Larry Pestana. Vice President, Technical Operations: Norberto Rivera. General Manager: Brien Kelley.
Ownership: Time Warner Cable (MSO).

NAPLES (town)—Time Warner Cable. Now served by BUFFALO (formerly Lackawanna), NY [NY0216]. ICA: NY0161.

NEW BERLIN (town)—Time Warner Cable. Now served by DEWITT, NY [NY0013]. ICA: NY0133.

NEW PALTZ (village)—Time Warner Cable. Now served by BETHEL (town), NY [NY0231]. ICA: NY0234.

NEW YORK CITY—RCN. Formerly served by MANHATTAN, NY [NY0282]. This cable system has converted to IPTV, 196 Van Buren St, Ste 300, Herndon, VA 20170. Phones: 800-746-4726; 609-681-2281. Web Site: http://www.rcn.com. Also serves Astoria, Brighton Beach, Brooklyn, Corona, East Elmhurst, Elmhurst, Flushing, Forest Hills, Fresh Meadows, Harlem, Jackson Heights, Jamaica, Kew Gardens, Long Island City, Manhattan, Maspeth, Middle Village, Oakland Gardens, Queens, Rego Park, Sunnyside & Woodside. ICA: NY5312.
TV Market Ranking: 1 (East Elmhurst, Elmhurst, Flushing, Forest Hills, Fresh Meadows, Jackson Heights, Kew Gardens, Long Island City, Middle Village, NEW YORK CITY, Rego Park, Sunnyside, Woodside).
Channel capacity: N.A. Channels available but not in use: N.A.

Limited Basic
Subscribers: 64,165. Commercial subscribers: 5,134.
Fee: $29.08 monthly. Includes 54 channels - 40 in SD & 14 in HD. Additional $9.95 HD equipment fee for HD channels.

Signature Digital Cable
Subscribers: N.A.
Fee: $60.00 monthly. Includes 298 channels - 231 in SD & 67 in HD. Additional $9.95 HD equipment fee for HD channels.

HD Expanded Pack
Subscribers: N.A.
Fee: $8.99 monthly. Includes 6 additional HD channels. Additional $9.95 HD equipment fee for HD channels.

Premiere Movies & Entertainment
Subscribers: N.A.
Fee: $10.99 monthly. Includes 30 channels - 27 in SD & 4 in HD. Additional $9.95 HD equipment fee for HD channels.

Premiere Family & Children
Subscribers: N.A.
Fee: $5.99 monthly. Includes 20 channels - 18 in SD & 2 in HD. Additional $9.95 HD equipment fee for HD channels.

Premiere News & Information
Subscribers: N.A.
Fee: $5.99 monthly. Includes 20 channels - 15 in SD & 5 in HD. Additional $9.95 HD equipment fee for HD channels.

Premiere Sports
Subscribers: N.A.
Fee: $9.99 monthly. Includes 35 channels - 27 in SD & 8 in HD. Additional $9.95 HD equipment fee for HD channels.

Premiere Total Pack
Subscribers: N.A.
Fee: $20.95 monthly. Includes 113 channels - 95 in SD & 18 in HD. Additional $9.95 HD equipment fee for HD channels.

MiVision Lite
Subscribers: N.A.
Fee: $12.00 monthly. Includes 40 channels in Spanish.

MiVision Plus
Subscribers: N.A.
Fee: $22.95 monthly. Includes 44 channels in Spanish.

Cinemax
Subscribers: N.A.
Fee: $11.95 monthly. Includes 16 channels - 8 in SD & 8 in HD plus Cinemax on Demand & MAXGo. Additional $9.95 HD equipment fee for HD channels.

HBO
Subscribers: N.A.
Fee: $15.95 monthly. Includes 14 channels - 7 in SD & 7 in HD plus HBO on Demand & HBO Go. Additional $9.95 HD equipment fee for HD channels.

Cinemax/HBO
Subscribers: N.A.
Fee: $19.95 monthly. Includes 16 channels - 8 in SD & 8 in HD & 14 channels of HBO - 7 in SD 7 & 7 in HD plus Cinemax on Demand, HBO on Demand, MAXGo & HBO Go. Additional $9.95 HD equipment fee for HD channels.

Showtime/TMC
Subscribers: N.A.
Fee: $4.95 monthly. Includes 20 channels - 9 in SD & 11 in HD plus Showtime on Demand & The Movie Channel on Demand. Additional $9.95 HD equipment fee for HD channels.

Starz
Subscribers: N.A.
Fee: $5.00 monthly. Includes 13 channels - 9 in SD & 4 in HD plus Starz on Demand. Additional $9.95 HD equipment fee for HD channels.

Video-On-Demand: Yes

Internet Service
Operational: Yes.
Fee: $49.99-$59.99 monthly.

Telephone Service
Digital: Operational
Fee: $25.00 monthly
Vice President & General Manager: Jamie Hill.
Ownership: RCN Corp.

NEWARK VALLEY (town)—Time Warner Binghamton. Now served by DEWITT, NY [NY0013]. ICA: NY0275.

NEWBURGH—Time Warner Cable. Now served by BETHEL (town), NY [NY0231]. ICA: NY0029.

NEWCOMB—Formerly served by C H Comm LLC. No longer in operation. ICA: NY0236.

NIAGARA FALLS—Time Warner Cable. Now served by BUFFALO (formerly Lackawanna), NY [NY0216]. ICA: NY0026.

NORTH SALEM—Formerly served by Cablevision Systems Corp. Now served by Optimum, YORKTOWN, NY [NY0050]. ICA: NY0077.

NORTHVILLE—Formerly served by Adelphia Communications. Now served by Time Warner Cable, ALBANY, NY [NY0014]. ICA: NY0270.

NORWICH (town)—Time Warner Cable. Now served by DEWITT, NY [NY0013]. ICA: NY0095.

OGDENSBURG—Time Warner Cable. Now served by DEWITT, NY [NY0013]. ICA: NY0081.

OLD FORGE—Formerly served by Adelphia Communications. No longer in operation. ICA: NY0136.

OLEAN—Time Warner Cable. Now served by BUFFALO (formerly Lackawanna), NY [NY0216]. ICA: NY0056.

OLIVE (town)—Time Warner Cable. Now served by BETHEL (town), NY [NY0231]. ICA: NY0138.

ONEIDA—Time Warner Cable. Now served by DEWITT, NY [NY0013]. ICA: NY0237.

ONEONTA—Time Warner Cable. Now served by DEWITT, NY [NY0013]. ICA: NY0065.

OSSINING—Cablevision, 1 Van Cortland Ave, Ossining, NY 10562-3309. Phones: 914-762-8717; 516-803-2300 (Corporate office); 914-762-8684. Fax: 516-803-1183. Web Site: http://www.cablevision.com. Also serves Bedford Hills, Briarcliff Manor, Buchanan, Cortlandt, Croton-on-Hudson,

Haverstraw, Mount Pleasant (Westchester County), New Castle, North Tarrytown, Peekskill, Philipstown, Pleasantville, Pomona, Ramapo (town), Sleepy Hollow, Stony Point, Tarrytown & West Haverstraw. ICA: NY0018.
TV Market Ranking: 1 (Bedford Hills, Briarcliff Manor, Buchanan, Cortlandt, Croton-Hudson, Haverstraw, Mount Pleasant (Westchester County), New Castle, North Tarrytown, OSSINING, Peekskill, Pleasantville, Pomona, Ramapo (town), Sleepy Hollow, Stony Point, Tarrytown, West Haverstraw); Below 100 (Philipstown).
Channel capacity: 42 (operating 2-way). Channels available but not in use: N.A.

Basic Service
Subscribers: 49,819. Commercial subscribers: 2,607.
Programming (received off-air): WABC-TV (ABC, Live Well Network) New York; WCBS-TV (CBS, Decades) New York; WFUT-DT (getTV, UniMas) Newark; WLIW (PBS) Garden City; WMBC-TV (Azteca America) Newton; WNBC (COZI TV, NBC) New York; WNET (PBS) Newark; WNJN (PBS) Montclair; WNJU (TMO) Linden; WNYW (FOX, Movies!) New York; WPIX (Antenna TV, CW, This TV) New York; WPXN-TV (ION) New York; WRNN-TV (IND) Kingston; WTBY-TV (TBN) Poughkeepsie; WWOR-TV (Bounce TV, Buzzr, Heroes & Icons, MNT) Secaucus; WXTV-DT (UNV) Paterson.
Fee: $39.95 installation; $18.00 monthly.

Expanded Basic Service 1
Subscribers: N.A.
Programming (via satellite): A&E; AMC; Animal Planet; BET; Bravo; Cartoon Network; CNBC; CNN; Comedy Central; C-SPAN; C-SPAN 2; Discovery Channel; Disney Channel; E! HD; ESPN; ESPN2; Food Network; Fox News Channel; Fox Sports 1; Freeform; Fuse; FX; GSN; HGTV; History; HLN; Lifetime; MSNBC; MTV; News 12 Traffic & Weather; Nickelodeon; QVC; Spike TV; SportsNet New York; Syfy; TBS; The Weather Channel; TLC; TNT; Travel Channel; truTV; Turner Classic Movies; TV Land; USA Network; VH1; WE tv.
Fee: $31.95 monthly.

Digital Basic Service
Subscribers: N.A.
Programming (via satellite): Animal Planet HD; Azteca; Bloomberg Television; Bollywood Hits On Demand; Bravo HD; Canal Sur; Caracol TV; Cartoon Network en Espanol; CBS Sports Network; Chiller; Cinelatino; Cloo; CMT; CMT HD; CNBC HD+; CNN en Espanol; CNN HD; C-SPAN 3; Destination America; Discovery Channel HD; Discovery Kids Channel; Disney XD; Docu TVE; Ecuavisa Internacional; ESPN Classic; ESPN Deportes; ESPN HD; ESPN2 HD; ESPNews; EuroNews; EVINE Live; Food Network HD; FOX College Sports Central; FOX College Sports Pacific; Fox Deportes; Fox Life; Fox News HD; Fox Sports 2; FX HD; FXM; FYI; GMA Pinoy TV; Golf Channel; GolTV; Great American Country; Hallmark Channel; Hallmark Movie Channel HD; Hallmark Movies & Mysteries; HD Theater; here! On Demand; HGTV HD; History en Espanol; History International; HTV; Infinito; Investigation Discovery; Jewelry Television; Korean Channel; La Familia Cosmovision; LATV; LOGO; Mariavision; MC; Momentum; MTV Classic; MTV Hits; National Geographic Channel; National Geographic Channel HD; NBA TV; NBC Universo; NBCSN; NHL Network; NHL Network HD; Nick HD; Nick Jr.; Nicktoons; Outdoor Channel; Oxygen; RTN; Science Channel; Science HD; Sino TV; Spike TV HD; Sundance TV; Syfy HD; TBS HD; TeenNick; Telefe Internacional; Telemicro Internacional; The Filipino Channel; The Jewish Channel; The Weather Channel HD; TLC HD; TNT HD; Toon Disney en Espanol; Tr3s; Travel Channel HD; TV Asia; TV Polonia; TV5MONDE USA; TVG Network; ULTRA HDPlex; Universal HD; USA Network HD; Versus HD; VH1 HD; ViendoMovies; Vme TV; YES HD; Zee TV.
Fee: $10.95 monthly.

Pay Service 1
Pay Units: N.A.
Programming (via satellite): Cinemax; Flix; HBO (multiplexed); IFC; MSG; MSG Plus; Showtime (multiplexed); The Movie Channel; YES Network.

Digital Pay Service 1
Pay Units: N.A.
Programming (via satellite): Cinemax (multiplexed); Cinemax HD; Cinemax On Demand; HBO (multiplexed); HBO HD; HBO on Demand; Showtime (multiplexed); Showtime HD; Showtime On Demand; Starz (multiplexed); Starz Encore (multiplexed); Starz HD; Starz On Demand; The Movie Channel (multiplexed); The Movie Channel HD.

Video-On-Demand: Yes

Pay-Per-View
iN DEMAND; Playboy TV; Club Jenna; Sports PPV (delivered digitally); NBA TV (delivered digitally); iN DEMAND (delivered digitally); Playboy TV (delivered digitally).

Internet Service
Operational: Yes. Began: December 31, 2002.
Subscribers: 52,787.
Broadband Service: Optimum Online.
Fee: $46.95 installation; $34.95 monthly.

Telephone Service
Digital: Operational
Subscribers: 44,900.
Fee: $34.95 monthly
Miles of Plant: 1,967.0 (coaxial); 470.0 (fiber optic). Homes passed: 84,653.
Executive Vice President, Programming: Tom Montemagno. Vice President, Field Operations: Mark Fitchett. Vice President, Local Ad Sales: John Oleynicki.
Ownership: Altice USA (MSO).

OSWEGO—Time Warner Cable. Now served by DEWITT, NY [NY0013]. ICA: NY0061.

OTSELIC—Formerly served by Chain Lakes Cablevision. Now served by Time Warner Cable, DEWITT, NY [NY0013]. ICA: NY0160.

OWEGO (village)—Time Warner Cable. Now served by DEWITT, NY [NY0013]. ICA: NY0104.

OXFORD (town)—Time Warner Cable. Now served by DEWITT, NY [NY0013]. ICA: NY0142.

PENN YAN (village)—Time Warner Cable. Now served by BUFFALO (formerly Lackawanna), NY [NY0216]. ICA: NY0108.

PETERBORO—Formerly served by Chain Lakes Cablevision. Now served by Time Warner Cable, DEWITT, NY [NY0013]. ICA: NY0238.

PHOENICIA—Time Warner Cable. Now served by BETHEL (town), NY [NY0231]. ICA: NY0239.

PINE HILL—Formerly served by Time Warner Cable. No longer in operation. ICA: NY0106.

PLATTSBURGH—Charter Communications, 68 Bridge St, Plattsburgh, NY 12901. Phones: 636-207-5100 (Corporate office); 508-853-1515. Web Site: http://www.charter.com. Also serves Au Sable (town), Beekmantown, Black Brook (town), Chesterfield (town), Clinton County (portions), Dannemora (village), Elizabethtown, Essex, Jay, Keeseville (village), Lewis, Peru (town), Saranac (town), Schuyler Falls (town), Westport (town) & Wilmington. ICA: NY0263.
TV Market Ranking: Below 100 (Au Sable (town), Beekmantown, Black Brook (town), Chesterfield (town), Clinton County (portions), Dannemora (village), Elizabethtown, Essex, Jay, Keeseville (village), Lewis, Peru (town), PLATTSBURGH, Saranac (town), Schuyler Falls (town), Westport (town), Wilmington). Franchise award date: January 1, 1967. Franchise expiration date: N.A. Began: December 1, 1967.
Channel capacity: 68 (operating 2-way). Channels available but not in use: N.A.

Digital Basic Service
Subscribers: 13,568.
Programming (via satellite): BBC America; Bloomberg Television; Discovery Digital Networks; Disney XD; DIY Network; ESPN Classic; FYI; History International; IFC; LMN; MC; Nick Jr.; Sundance TV; TeenNick; WE tv.
Fee: $49.99 installation; $26.99 monthly.

Digital Expanded Basic Service
Subscribers: N.A.
Programming (via satellite): A&E; AMC; Animal Planet; BET; Cartoon Network; CMT; CNBC; CNN; Comedy Central; Discovery Channel; Disney Channel; E! HD; ESPN; ESPN2; Food Network; Fox News Channel; Fox Sports 1; Freeform; FX; Golf Channel; Hallmark Channel; HGTV; History; HLN; Lifetime; MSG; MSG Plus; MSNBC; MTV; National Geographic Channel; NBCSN; Nickelodeon; Oxygen; Spike TV; Syfy; TBS; The Weather Channel; TLC; TNT; Travel Channel; truTV; Turner Classic Movies; TV Land; USA Network; VH1; YES Network.
Fee: $55.00 monthly.

Digital Pay Service 1
Pay Units: N.A.
Programming (via satellite): Cinemax (multiplexed); HBO (multiplexed); Showtime (multiplexed); Starz (multiplexed); Starz Encore (multiplexed); The Movie Channel (multiplexed).
Fee: $13.95 monthly (Cinemax, HBO, Showtime, Starz/Encore or TMC).

Video-On-Demand: Yes

Pay-Per-View
iN DEMAND (delivered digitally); Playboy TV (delivered digitally); Fresh (delivered digitally); Shorteez (delivered digitally).

Internet Service
Operational: Yes.
Subscribers: 13,525.
Broadband Service: Charter Internet.
Fee: $29.99 monthly.

Telephone Service
Digital: Operational
Subscribers: 4,007.

Miles of Plant: 1,042.0 (coaxial); 450.0 (fiber optic). Homes passed: 29,065.
Vice President & General Manager: Greg Garabedian. Technical Operations Director: George Duffy. Chief Technician: Dan Rushford. Marketing Director: Dennis Jerome. Senior Accounting Director: Steve Lottmann. Operations Manager: Kevin Maillous.
Ownership: Charter Communications Inc. (MSO).

PORT CHESTER—Cablevision, 6 Executive Plaza, Yonkers, NY 11714. Phones: 914-762-8717; 516-803-2300 (Corporate office). Web Site: http://www.cablevision.com. Also serves Harrison. ICA: NY0048.
TV Market Ranking: 1 (Harrison, PORT CHESTER). Franchise award date: January 25, 1979. Franchise expiration date: N.A. Began: March 1, 1980.
Channel capacity: 44 (operating 2-way). Channels available but not in use: N.A.

Basic Service
Subscribers: 12,341.
Programming (received off-air): WABC-TV (ABC, Live Well Network) New York; WCBS-TV (CBS, Decades) New York; WFUT-DT (getTV, UniMas) Newark; WLIW (PBS) Garden City; WLNY-TV (IND) Riverhead; WMBC-TV (Azteca America) Newton; WNBC (COZI TV, NBC) New York; WNET (PBS) Newark; WNJU (TMO) Linden; WNYE-TV (PBS) New York; WNYW (FOX, Movies!) New York; WPIX (Antenna TV, CW, This TV) New York; WPXN-TV (ION) New York; WRNN-TV (IND) Kingston; WWOR-TV (Bounce TV, Buzzr, Heroes & Icons, MNT) Secaucus; WXTV-DT (UNV) Paterson; WZME (Retro TV) Bridgeport; 30 FMs.
Fee: $39.95 installation; $16.58 monthly.

Expanded Basic Service 1
Subscribers: N.A.
Programming (via satellite): A&E; AMC; Animal Planet; BET; Bravo; Cartoon Network; CNBC; CNN; Comedy Central; C-SPAN; C-SPAN 2; Discovery Channel; Disney Channel; E! HD; ESPN; ESPN2; EVINE Live; EWTN Global Catholic Network; Food Network; Fox News Channel; Fox Sports 1; Freeform; Fuse; FX; GSN; HGTV; History; HLN; IFC; Lifetime; MSG; MSG Plus; MSNBC; MTV; MTV2; NBC Universo; News 12 Traffic & Weather; News 12 Westchester; Nickelodeon; QVC; Spike TV; SportsNet New York; Syfy; TBS; The Weather Channel; TLC; TNT; Travel Channel; truTV; Turner Classic Movies; TV Land; Univision; USA Network; VH1; WE tv; YES Network.
Fee: $39.37 monthly.

Digital Basic Service
Subscribers: N.A.
Programming (via microwave): Docu TVE.
Programming (via satellite): Azteca; Bloomberg Television; Caracol TV; Cartoon Network en Espanol; Cinelatino; CMT; CNN en Espanol; CNN HD; C-SPAN 3; Destination America; Discovery Kids Channel; Disney XD; Ecuavisa Internacional; ESPN Classic; ESPN Deportes; ESPN HD; ESPNews; EuroNews; FOX College Sports

New York—Cable Systems

Central; FOX College Sports Pacific; Fox Deportes; Fox Sports 2; FXM; FYI; Golf Channel; Hallmark Channel; HD Theater; History en Espanol; History International; HTV; Infinito; Investigation Discovery; Jewelry Television; La Familia Cosmovision; LOGO; Mariavision; MC; MTV Classic; MTV Hits; National Geographic Channel; National Geographic Channel HD; NBA TV; NBC Universo; NBCSN; NHL Network; Nick Jr.; Nicktoons; Outdoor Channel; Oxygen; Science Channel; Sundance TV; Sur; TBS HD; TeenNick; Telefe Internacional; TNT HD; Toon Disney en Espanol; Tr3s; TVG Network; ULTRA HDPlex; Universal HD; Versus HD; VH1 Soul; ViendoMovies; Vme TV.
Fee: $10.95 monthly.

Pay Service 1
Pay Units: N.A.
Programming (via satellite): Cinemax; Flix; HBO (multiplexed); Showtime (multiplexed); The Movie Channel.

Digital Pay Service 1
Pay Units: N.A.
Programming (via satellite): Cinemax (multiplexed); Cinemax HD; Cinemax On Demand; HBO (multiplexed); HBO HD; HBO on Demand; MBC America; RAI Italia; RTN; Showtime (multiplexed); Showtime HD; Showtime On Demand; Starz Encore (multiplexed); Starz HD; The Movie Channel (multiplexed); The Movie Channel HD; TV Asia; TV Polonia; TV5, La Television International; Zee TV.
Fee: $9.95 monthly (Cinemax, Playboy, Showtime, Starz/Encore, TMC, CCTV, MCB, RAI, TV5, TV Asia, TV Japan, TV Polonia or Zee TV), $11.95 monthly (HBO), $14.95 monthly (RTN).

Video-On-Demand: Yes

Pay-Per-View
iN DEMAND (delivered digitally); Playboy TV (delivered digitally); iN DEMAND (delivered digitally); NBA League Pass (delivered digitally).

Internet Service
Operational: Yes.
Subscribers: 13,065.
Broadband Service: Optimum Online.
Fee: $46.95 installation; $34.95 monthly.

Telephone Service
Digital: Operational
Subscribers: 10,860.
Fee: $34.95 monthly
Miles of Plant: 311.0 (coaxial); 79.0 (fiber optic). Homes passed: 18,716.
Executive Vice President, Programming: Tom Montemagno. Vice President, Field Operations: Mark Fitchett.
Ownership: Altice USA (MSO).

PORT HENRY (village)—Time Warner Cable. Now served by ALBANY, NY [NY0014]. ICA: NY0123.

PORT JERVIS—Time Warner Cable. Now served by BETHEL (town), NY [NY0231]. ICA: NY0240.

POTSDAM (town)—Time Warner Cable. Now served by DEWITT, NY [NY0013]. ICA: NY0053.

POUGHKEEPSIE—Time Warner Cable. Now served by BETHEL (town), NY [NY0231]. ICA: NY0035.

PRINCETOWN (town)—Formerly served by Princetown Cable Co. Now served by Time Warner Cable, ALBANY, NY [NY0151]. ICA: NY0151.

QUEENS—RCN Corp. This cable system has converted to IPTV. See NEW YORK CITY, NY [NY5312]. ICA: NY0283.

QUEENSBURY—Formerly served by Adelphia Communications. No longer in operation. ICA: NY0042.

RAMAPO (town)—Now served by Cablevision, ROCKLAND, NY [NY0017]. ICA: NY0059.

RENSSELAER (town)—Time Warner Cable. Now served by ALBANY, NY [NY0014]. ICA: NY0034.

RHINEBECK (town)—Time Warner Cable. Now served by BETHEL (town), NY [NY0231]. ICA: NY0094.

RIVERHEAD—Cablevision, 254 Old Country Rd, Riverhead, NY 11714. Phone: 516-803-2300. Web Site: http://www.cablevision.com. Also serves Dering Harbor, East Hampton, Greenport, North Haven, Quogue, Sag Harbor, Sagaponack, Shelter Island, Southampton, Southampton (village), Southold, West Hampton Dunes, Westhampton & Westhampton Beach. ICA: NY0024.
TV Market Ranking: 19 (Dering Harbor, East Hampton, Greenport, North Haven, RIVERHEAD, Sag Harbor, Sagaponack, Shelter Island, Southampton (village), Southold, West Hampton Dunes); Below 100 (Quogue, Southampton, Westhampton, Westhampton Beach). Franchise award date: N.A. Franchise expiration date: N.A. Began: May 9, 1984.
Channel capacity: 42 (operating 2-way). Channels available but not in use: N.A.

Basic Service
Subscribers: 77,841.
Programming (received off-air): WFTY-DT (UniMas) Smithtown; WLIW (PBS) Garden City; WLNY-TV (IND) Riverhead; WNJU (TMO) Linden; WVVH-CD (IND) Southampton; WWOR-TV (Bounce TV, Buzzr, Heroes & Icons, MNT) Secaucus; WXTV-DT (UNV) Paterson; allband FM.
Programming (via microwave): WABC-TV (ABC, Live Well Network) New York; WCBS-TV (CBS, Decades) New York; WNBC (COZI TV, NBC) New York; WNET (PBS) Newark; WNYW (FOX, Movies!) New York; WPIX (Antenna TV, CW, This TV) New York; WPXN-TV (ION) New York.
Programming (via satellite): EVINE Live; News 12 Long Island; QVC.
Fee: $39.95 installation; $17.64 monthly; $2.95 converter.

Expanded Basic Service 1
Subscribers: N.A.
Programming (via satellite): A&E; AMC; Animal Planet; BET; Bravo; Cartoon Network; CNBC; CNN; Comedy Central; C-SPAN; C-SPAN 2; Discovery Channel; Disney Channel; E! HD; ESPN; ESPN2; Food Network; Fox News Channel; Fox Sports 1; Freeform; Fuse; FX; GSN; HGTV; History; HLN; Lifetime; MSG; MSG Plus; MSNBC; MTV; MTV2; News 12 Traffic & Weather; Nickelodeon; Spike TV; SportsNet New York; Syfy; TBS; Telecare; The Weather Channel; TLC; TNT; Travel Channel; truTV; Turner Classic Movies; TV Land; Univision; USA Network; VH1; WE tv; YES Network.
Fee: $32.31 monthly.

Digital Basic Service
Subscribers: N.A.
Programming (via satellite): Azteca; BBC World News; Bloomberg Television; Canal Sur; Caracol TV; Cartoon Network en Espanol; Cinelatino; CMT; CNN en Espanol; CNN HD; C-SPAN 3; Destination America; Discovery Kids Channel; Disney XD; Docu TVE; Ecuavisa Internacional; ESPN Classic; ESPN Deportes; ESPN HD; ESPN2 HD; ESPNews; EuroNews; Food Network HD; FOX College Sports Central; FOX College Sports Pacific; Fox Deportes; Fox Life; Fox Sports 2; FSN HD; FXM; FYI; Golf Channel; GolTV; Great American Country; Hallmark Channel; HD Theater; here! On Demand; HGTV HD; History en Espanol; History International; HTV; iN DEMAND; Infinito; Investigation Discovery; Jewelry Television; La Familia Cosmovision; LOGO; Mariavision; MC; Momentum; MTV Classic; MTV Hits; National Geographic Channel; National Geographic Channel HD; NBA TV; NBC Universo; NBCSN; Nick Jr.; Nicktoons; Outdoor Channel; Oxygen; Science Channel; Sundance TV; TBS HD; TeenNick; Telefe Internacional; TNT HD; Toon Disney en Espanol; Tr3s; TVG Network; ULTRA HDPlex; Universal HD; Versus HD; VH1 Soul; ViendoMovies; Vme TV; YES HD.
Fee: $10.95 monthly; $2.95 converter.

Pay Service 1
Pay Units: N.A.
Programming (via satellite): Cinemax; Flix; HBO (multiplexed); IFC; Showtime; The Movie Channel.

Digital Pay Service 1
Pay Units: N.A.
Programming (via satellite): Cinemax (multiplexed); Cinemax HD; Cinemax On Demand; HBO (multiplexed); HBO HD; HBO on Demand; Korean Channel; RAI Italia; RTN; Showtime (multiplexed); Showtime HD; Showtime On Demand; Starz (multiplexed); Starz Encore (multiplexed); The Movie Channel (multiplexed); TV Asia; TV Polonia; TV5, La Television International; Zee TV.
Fee: $9.95 monthly (Cinemax/Cinemax HD/Cinemax On Demand, Showtime/ Showtime HD/Showtime On Demand, RAI, TV5 or TV Polonia), $11.95 monthly (HBO/HBO HD/HBO On Demand), $24.95 monthly (TV Japan).

Video-On-Demand: Yes

Pay-Per-View
iN DEMAND; Playboy TV; Club Jenna.

Internet Service
Operational: Yes.
Subscribers: 73,259.
Broadband Service: Optimum Online.
Fee: $46.95 installation; $34.95 monthly; $299.00 modem purchase.

Telephone Service
Digital: Operational
Subscribers: 54,906.
Fee: $34.95 monthly
Miles of Plant: 3,343.0 (coaxial); 807.0 (fiber optic). Homes passed: 96,030.
Senior Vice President, Field Operations: Christopher Coffee. Executive Vice President, Programming: Tom Montemagno. Corporate Communications Manager: Kristen Blank.
Ownership: Altice USA (MSO).

ROCHESTER—Time Warner Cable. Now served by BUFFALO (formerly Lackawanna), NY [NY0216]. ICA: NY0003.

ROCKLAND—Cablevision, 235 West Nyack Rd, West Nyack, NY 10994. Phones: 201-405-8222; 516-803-2300 (Corporate office); 201-651-4000. Web Site: http://www.cablevision.com. Also serves Mahwah Twp. & Montvale, NJ; Airmont (village), Chestnut Ridge, Clarkstown, Grand View-on-Hudson, Hillburn, Montebello, Nanuet, New Hempstead, Nyack, Orangetown (town), Piermont, Ramapo, Ramapo Corridor, Rockland County (unincorporated areas), Sloatsburg, South Nyack, Spring Valley, Suffern, Tuxedo, Tuxedo Park, Upper Nyack, Wesley Hills & West Nyack, NY. ICA: NY0017.
TV Market Ranking: 1 (Airmont (village), Chestnut Ridge, Clarkstown, Grand View-on-Hudson, Hillburn, Mahwah Twp., Montebello, Montvale, Nanuet, New Hempstead, Nyack, Orangetown (town), Piermont, Ramapo, Ramapo Corridor, ROCKLAND, Rockland County (unincorporated areas), Sloatsburg, South Nyack, Spring Valley, Suffern, Tuxedo, Tuxedo Park, Upper Nyack, Wesley Hills, West Nyack). Franchise award date: N.A. Franchise expiration date: N.A. Began: November 8, 1980.
Channel capacity: 42 (operating 2-way). Channels available but not in use: N.A.

Basic Service
Subscribers: 50,519.
Programming (received off-air): WABC-TV (ABC, Live Well Network) New York; WCBS-TV (CBS, Decades) New York; WFUT-DT (getTV, UniMas) Newark; WLIW (PBS) Garden City; WLNY-TV (IND) Riverhead; WMBC-TV (Azteca America) Newton; WNBC (COZI TV, NBC) New York; WNET (PBS) Newark; WNJN (PBS) Montclair; WNJU (TMO) Linden; WNYJ-TV (ETV) West Milford; WNYW (FOX, Movies!) New York; WPIX (Antenna TV, CW, This TV) New York; WPXN-TV (ION) New York; WRNN-TV (IND) Kingston; WWOR-TV (Bounce TV, Buzzr, Heroes & Icons, MNT) Secaucus; WXTV-DT (UNV) Paterson; 23 FMs.
Programming (via satellite): News 12 New Jersey.
Fee: $39.95 installation; $17.10 monthly; $2.95 converter.

Expanded Basic Service 1
Subscribers: N.A.
Programming (via satellite): A&E; AMC; Animal Planet; BET; Bravo; Cartoon Network; CNBC; CNN; Comedy Central; C-SPAN; C-SPAN 2; Discovery Channel; Disney Channel; E! HD; ESPN; ESPN2; Food Network; Fox News Channel; Fox Sports 1; Freeform; Fuse; FX; GSN; HGTV; History; HLN; IFC; Lifetime; MSG; MSG Plus; MSNBC; MTV; MTV2; News 12 Traffic & Weather; Nickelodeon; QVC; Spike TV; SportsNet New York; Syfy; TBS; The Weather Channel; TLC; TNT; Travel Channel; truTV; Turner Classic Movies; TV Land; USA Network; VH1; WE tv; YES Network.
Fee: $31.95 monthly.

Digital Basic Service
Subscribers: N.A.
Programming (via satellite): Animal Planet HD; Azteca; BBC World News; Bloomberg Television; Canal Sur; Caracol TV; Cartoon Network en Espanol; CMT; CNN en Espanol; CNN HD; C-SPAN 3; Destination America; Discovery Kids Channel; Disney XD; Docu TVE; Ecuavisa Internacional; ESPN Classic; ESPN Deportes; ESPN HD; ESPN2 HD; ESPNews; EuroNews; EVINE Live; Food Network HD; FOX College Sports Central; FOX College Sports Pacific; Fox Deportes; Fox Life; Fox Sports 2; FSN HD; FXM; FYI; Golf Channel; GolTV; Great American Country; Hallmark Channel; HD Theater; here! On Demand; HGTV HD; History en Espanol; History International; HTV; iN DEMAND; Infinito; Investigation Discovery; Jewelry Television; La Familia Cosmovision; LOGO; Mariavision; MC; Momentum; MTV Classic; MTV Hits; National Geographic Chan-

Cable Systems—New York

nel; National Geographic Channel HD; NBA TV; NBC Universo; NBCSN; NHL Network; Nick Jr.; Nicktoons; Outdoor Channel; Oxygen; Science Channel; Sundance TV; TBS HD; TeenNick; Telefe Internacional; TNT HD; Toon Disney en Espanol; Tr3s; TVG Network; ULTRA HDPlex; Universal HD; Versus HD; VH1 Soul; ViendoMovies; Vme TV; YES HD.
Fee: $10.95 monthly; $2.95 converter.
Pay Service 1
Pay Units: N.A.
Programming (via satellite): Cinemax; Flix; HBO (multiplexed); Showtime (multiplexed); The Movie Channel.
Digital Pay Service 1
Pay Units: N.A.
Programming (via satellite): Cinemax (multiplexed); Cinemax HD; Cinemax On Demand; HBO (multiplexed); HBO HD; HBO on Demand; Korean Channel; RAI Italia; RTN; Showtime (multiplexed); Showtime HD; Showtime On Demand; Starz (multiplexed); Starz Encore (multiplexed); Starz HD; The Movie Channel (multiplexed); The Movie Channel HD; TV Asia; TV Polonia; TV5, La Television International; Zee TV.
Fee: $9.95 monthly (Cinemax, Showtime, Starz/Encore, TMC, RAI, SPT, TV5 or TV Polinia), $11.95 monthly (HBO) & $24.95 monthly (TV Japan).
Video-On-Demand: Yes
Pay-Per-View
iN DEMAND (delivered digitally); Playboy TV (delivered digitally); Club Jenna (delivered digitally).
Internet Service
Operational: Yes.
Subscribers: 58,458.
Broadband Service: Optimum Online.
Fee: $46.95 installation; $34.95 monthly; $299.00 modem purchase.
Telephone Service
Digital: Operational
Subscribers: 48,746.
Fee: $34.95 monthly
Miles of Plant: 2,792.0 (coaxial); 714.0 (fiber optic). Homes passed: 106,253.
Executive Vice President, Programming: Tom Montemagno. Vice President, Field Operations: Christopher Fulton. Operations Manager: Mark Quirk.
Ownership: Altice USA (MSO).

ROME—Time Warner Cable. Now served by DEWITT, NY [NY0013]. ICA: NY0037.

ROSENDALE (town)—Time Warner Cable. Now served by BETHEL (town), NY [NY0231]. ICA: NY0112.

SALAMANCA—Atlantic Broadband, 24 Main St, Bradford, PA 16701. Phones: 888-536-9600; 814-539-8971. Fax: 814-362-2190. E-mail: info@atlanticbb.com. Web Site: http://atlanticbb.com. Also serves Great Valley, Little Valley (town), Little Valley (village) & Salamanca (town). ICA: NY0099.
TV Market Ranking: Below 100 (Great Valley, Little Valley (town), Little Valley (village), SALAMANCA, Salamanca (town)). Franchise award date: December 13, 1965. Franchise expiration date: N.A. Began: January 1, 1965.
Channel capacity: N.A. Channels available but not in use: N.A.
Basic Service
Subscribers: 1,265. Commercial subscribers: 83.
Programming (received off-air): WGRZ (Antenna TV, NBC, WeatherNation) Buffalo; WIVB-TV (CBS) Buffalo; WKBW-TV (ABC, Escape) Buffalo; WNED-TV (PBS) Buffalo; WNYB (IND) Jamestown; WSEE-TV (CBS, CW) Erie; WUTV (FOX, The Country Network) Buffalo.
Programming (via satellite): C-SPAN; INSP; Pop; QVC; various Canadian stations; WGN America.
Fee: $40.00 installation; $34.63 monthly.
Expanded Basic Service 1
Subscribers: 1,072.
Programming (via satellite): A&E; AMC; Animal Planet; Bravo; Cartoon Network; CMT; CNBC; CNN; Comedy Central; Discovery Channel; Disney Channel; E! HD; ESPN; ESPN Classic; ESPN2; Food Network; Fox News Channel; Fox Sports 1; Freeform; FX; Golf Channel; Hallmark Channel; HGTV; History; Lifetime; LMN; MSG; MSNBC; MTV; National Geographic Channel; Nickelodeon; Outdoor Channel; OWN: Oprah Winfrey Network; Oxygen; Spike TV; Syfy; TBS; The Weather Channel; TLC; TNT; Travel Channel; truTV; Turner Classic Movies; TV Land; USA Network; VH1.
Fee: $45.91 monthly.
Digital Basic Service
Subscribers: 306.
Programming (via satellite): A&E HD; Animal Planet HD; BBC America; Bloomberg Television; Boomerang; Chiller; CMT; Destination America; Discovery Channel HD; Discovery Kids Channel; Disney Channel HD; Disney XD; DIY Network; DMX Music; ESPN HD; ESPN2 HD; ESPNews; ESPNU; Fox Sports 2; FYI; GSN; HD Theater; History International; IFC; Investigation Discovery; MTV Classic; MTV Hits; MTV Jams; MTV2; NFL Network; NFL Network HD; Nick 2; Nick Jr.; Nicktoons; Science Channel; Starz (multiplexed); Starz Encore (multiplexed); Syfy HD; TBS HD; TeenNick; TLC HD; TNT HD; Tr3s; USA Network HD; VH1 Soul; WE tv; Weatherscan.
Fee: $74.99 monthly.
Digital Pay Service 1
Pay Units: 210.
Programming (via satellite): HBO (multiplexed).
Fee: $15.95 monthly.
Digital Pay Service 2
Pay Units: 120.
Programming (via satellite): Cinemax (multiplexed).
Fee: $15.95 monthly.
Digital Pay Service 3
Pay Units: N.A.
Programming (via satellite): Flix; Showtime (multiplexed); The Movie Channel (multiplexed).
Fee: $15.95 monthly.
Video-On-Demand: No
Pay-Per-View
iN DEMAND (delivered digitally); Hot Choice (delivered digitally); Spice: Xcess (delivered digitally); Club Jenna (delivered digitally); Fresh (delivered digitally); Shorteez (delivered digitally); Playboy TV (delivered digitally).
Internet Service
Operational: Yes.
Broadband Service: Atlantic Broadband High-Speed Internet.
Fee: $24.95-$57.95 monthly.
Telephone Service
Digital: Operational
Fee: $44.95 monthly
Miles of Plant: 74.0 (coaxial); 16.0 (fiber optic). Homes passed: 4,800.
Chief Financial Officer: Patrick Bratton. Senior Vice President & General Counsel: Leslie Brown. Vice President: David Dane. General Manager: Mike Papasergi. Marketing & Customer Service Director: Dara Leslie.

Access the most current data instantly
FREE TRIAL @
www.warren-news.com/factbook.htm

Technical Operations Director: Charles Sorchillo. Marketing Manager: Natalie Kurchak.
Ownership: Atlantic Broadband (MSO).

SARANAC LAKE (village)—Time Warner Cable. Now served by DEWITT, NY [NY0013]. Also serves Saranac Lake (village). ICA: NY0243.

SARATOGA SPRINGS—Time Warner Cable. Now served by ALBANY, NY [NY0014]. ICA: NY0027.

SAUGERTIES (town)—Time Warner Cable. Now served by BETHEL (town), NY [NY0231]. ICA: NY0244.

SCHENECTADY—Time Warner Cable. Now served by ALBANY, NY [NY0014]. ICA: NY0025.

SCHROEPPEL (town)—Time Warner Cable. Now served by DEWITT, NY [NY0013]. ICA: NY0128.

SCHROON (town)—Time Warner Cable. Now served by ALBANY, NY [NY0014]. ICA: NY0159.

SIDNEY (town)—Time Warner Cable. Now served by DEWITT, NY [NY0013]. ICA: NY0109.

SILVER CREEK (village)—Time Warner Cable. Now served by BUFFALO (formerly Lackawanna), NY [NY0216]. ICA: NY0111.

SMITHVILLE—Haefele TV Inc, 24 East Tioga St, PO Box 312, Spencer, NY 14883. Phone: 607-589-6235. Fax: 607-589-7211. E-mail: htv@htva.net. Web Site: http://www.htva.net. Also serves Greene (town). ICA: NY0174.
TV Market Ranking: Below 100 (Greene (town), SMITHVILLE). Franchise award date: October 18, 1990. Franchise expiration date: N.A. Began: January 1, 1991.
Channel capacity: N.A. Channels available but not in use: N.A.
Basic Service
Subscribers: 132.
Programming (received off-air): WBNG-TV (CBS, CW) Binghamton; WBPN-LP Binghamton; WCNY-TV (PBS) Syracuse; WETM-TV (IND, NBC) Elmira; WICZ-TV (FOX) Binghamton; WIVT (ABC) Binghamton; WSKG-TV (PBS) Binghamton; WSTM-TV (NBC) Syracuse.
Programming (via satellite): A&E; AMC; Animal Planet; Cartoon Network; CMT; CNBC; CNN; Discovery Channel; Disney Channel; ESPN; ESPN2; Food Network; Fox Sports 1; Freeform; Great American Country; HGTV; History; HLN; Lifetime; MSNBC; Nick At Nite; Nickelodeon; QVC; Spike TV; Syfy; TBS; The Weather Channel; TLC; TNT; Travel Channel; Turner Classic Movies; USA Network; VH1.
Fee: $30.00 installation; $24.95 monthly; $1.00 converter.

Pay Service 1
Pay Units: 10.
Programming (via satellite): Cinemax.
Fee: $9.00 monthly.
Pay Service 2
Pay Units: 29.
Programming (via satellite): HBO.
Fee: $9.50 monthly.
Video-On-Demand: No
Internet Service
Operational: Yes.
Fee: $34.50-$51.95 monthly.
Telephone Service
Digital: Operational
Miles of Plant: 12.0 (coaxial); None (fiber optic). Homes passed: 365.
President & General Manager: Lee Haefele. Vice President: Denise A. Laue. Chief Technician: Michael McNamara.
Ownership: Haefele TV Inc. (MSO).

SPENCER—Haefele TV Inc, 24 East Tioga St, PO Box 312, Spencer, NY 14883. Phone: 607-589-6235. Fax: 607-589-7211. E-mail: htv@htva.net. Web Site: http://www.htva.net. Also serves Barton (town), Candor (portions), Cayuta (town), Smithboro, Spencer (town), Tioga & Van Etten (village). ICA: NY0145.
TV Market Ranking: Below 100 (Barton (town), Candor (portions), Cayuta (town), Smithboro, SPENCER, Spencer (town), Tioga, Van Etten (village)). Franchise award date: July 11, 1983. Franchise expiration date: N.A. Began: September 1, 1983.
Channel capacity: N.A. Channels available but not in use: N.A.
Basic Service
Subscribers: 1,258.
Programming (received off-air): WBNG-TV (CBS, CW) Binghamton; WETM-TV (IND, NBC) Elmira; WICZ-TV (FOX) Binghamton; WIVT (ABC) Binghamton; WSKG-TV (PBS) Binghamton; WSYT (FOX, The Country Network) Syracuse; WVIA-TV (PBS) Scranton.
Programming (via satellite): A&E; AMC; Animal Planet; Cartoon Network; CMT; CNBC; CNN; Comedy Central; C-SPAN; Discovery Channel; Disney Channel; DIY Network; E! HD; ESPN; ESPN Classic; ESPN2; Food Network; Fox News Channel; Fox Sports 1; Freeform; FX; Great American Country; Hallmark Channel; HGTV; History; ION Television; Lifetime; MSG; MSG Plus; MSNBC; MTV; Nickelodeon; Pop; QVC; Spike TV; Syfy; TBS; The Weather Channel; TLC; TNT; Travel Channel; Trinity Broadcasting Network (TBN); truTV; TV Land; USA Network; VH1; WBXI-CA (CBS) Indianapolis; WE tv; WGN America; WPIX (Antenna TV, CW, This TV) New York; YES Network.
Fee: $30.00 installation; $24.95 monthly; $1.00 converter.
Digital Basic Service
Subscribers: N.A.
Programming (via satellite): BBC America; Bloomberg Television; Bravo; Discovery Life Channel; Disney XD; DMX Music; ESPN Classic; ESPNews; FXM; FYI; Golf Channel; GSN; History International; IFC; INSP; LMN; MTV2; Nick Jr.; Nicktoons;

2017 Edition D-545

New York—Cable Systems

Outdoor Channel; TeenNick; Turner Classic Movies.
Fee: $12.95 monthly.

Pay Service 1
Pay Units: N.A.
Programming (via satellite): Cinemax; HBO.
Fee: $9.00 monthly (Cinemax), $10.00 monthly (HBO).

Digital Pay Service 1
Pay Units: N.A.
Programming (via satellite): Cinemax; HBO; Showtime (multiplexed); Starz (multiplexed); Starz Encore (multiplexed); The Movie Channel (multiplexed).
Fee: $3.99 monthly (Encore), $9.00 monthly (Cinemax), $9.95 monthly (Starz/Encore), $12.95 monthly (Showtime/TMC), $14.95 monthly (HBO), $20.00 monthly (Cinemax/HBO), $33.50 monthly (all pay channels).

Video-On-Demand: No

Pay-Per-View
Fresh (delivered digitally); Vubiquity Inc. (delivered digitally).

Internet Service
Operational: Yes. Began: October 1, 1999.
Broadband Service: In-house.
Fee: $34.50-$51.95 monthly; $9.95 modem lease; $89.00 modem purchase.

Telephone Service
Digital: Operational
Miles of Plant: 137.0 (coaxial); None (fiber optic). Homes passed: 3,069.
President & Manager: Lee Haefele. Vice President: Denise Laue. Chief Technician: Michael McNamara.
Ownership: Haefele TV Inc. (MSO).

SPRINGVILLE (village)—Time Warner Cable. Now served by BUFFALO, NY [NY0216]. ICA: NY0052.

STAMFORD (town)—Time Warner Cable. Now served by DEWITT, NY [NY0013]. ICA: NY0146.

STATEN ISLAND—Time Warner Cable, 100 Cable Way, Staten Island, NY 10303. Phones: 718-816-8686; 718-447-7000. Fax: 718-816-8433. Web Site: http://www.timewarnercable.com. ICA: NY0010.
TV Market Ranking: 1 (STATEN ISLAND). Franchise award date: July 19, 1983. Franchise expiration date: N.A. Began: August 1, 1986.
Channel capacity: N.A. Channels available but not in use: N.A.

Basic Service
Subscribers: 44,427.
Programming (received off-air): WABC-TV (ABC, Live Well Network) New York; WCBS-TV (CBS, Decades) New York; WFUT-DT (getTV, UniMas) Newark; WLIW (PBS) Garden City; WLNY-TV (IND) Riverhead; WMBC-TV (Azteca America) Newton; WNBC (COZI TV, NBC) New York; WNET (PBS) Newark; WNJU (TMO) Linden; WNYE-TV (PBS) New York; WNYW (FOX, Movies!) New York; WPIX (Antenna TV, CW, This TV) New York; WPXN-TV (ION) New York; WWOR-TV (Bounce TV, Buzzr, Heroes & Icons, MNT) Secaucus; WXTV-DT (UNV) Paterson; WYXN-LD New York; 4 FMs.
Programming (via satellite): A&E; AMC; BET; Bravo; Cartoon Network; CNBC; CNN; Comedy Central; C-SPAN; C-SPAN 2; Discovery Channel; Disney Channel; E! HD; ESPN; ESPN2; EVINE Live; Food Network; Fox News Channel; Freeform; FX; HGTV; History; HLN; Lifetime; LMN; MSG; MSG Plus; MSNBC; MTV; National Geographic Channel; Nickelodeon; Oxygen; Pop; QVC; Spike TV; Syfy; TBS; The Weather Channel; Time Warner Cable News NY1; TLC; TNT; truTV; Univision; USA Network; VH1; WE tv; Yesterday USA.
Fee: $20.00 installation; $21.00 monthly; $2.86 converter.

Expanded Basic Service 1
Subscribers: N.A.
Programming (via satellite): Animal Planet; ESPN Classic; EWTN Global Catholic Network; Flix; IFC; Starz Encore Family; Travel Channel; Turner Classic Movies; TV Land.
Fee: $17.84 monthly.

Digital Basic Service
Subscribers: N.A.
Programming (via satellite): AXS TV; BBC America; Bloomberg Television; Boomerang; CMT; CNN International; Cooking Channel; C-SPAN 3; Discovery Life Channel; Disney XD; DIY Network; ESPN HD; ESPNews; Fox Sports 1; Fuse; FXM; Golf Channel; Great American Country; GSN; Hallmark Channel; HD Theater; LOGO; MC; MTV Classic; MTV2; NBC Universo; NBCSN; Nick 2; Nick Jr.; Sundance TV; TeenNick; The Word Network; TNT HD.
Fee: $9.95 monthly.

Digital Pay Service 1
Pay Units: N.A.
Programming (via satellite): Cinemax (multiplexed); Deutsche Welle TV; HBO (multiplexed); HBO HD; New Greek TV; RAI Italia; RTN; Showtime (multiplexed); Showtime HD; Starz (multiplexed); Starz Encore (multiplexed); The Movie Channel (multiplexed); TV Asia; TV Polonia; TV5, La Television International; Zee TV.
Fee: $14.95 monthly (each).

Video-On-Demand: Yes

Pay-Per-View
Movies & Events (delivered digitally); Playboy TV (delivered digitally); Sports PPV (delivered digitally).

Internet Service
Operational: Yes.
Subscribers: 48,965.
Broadband Service: Road Runner.
Fee: $44.95 monthly.

Telephone Service
Digital: Operational
Subscribers: 33,599.
Fee: $39.95 monthly
Miles of Plant: 1,156.0 (coaxial); 598.0 (fiber optic). Homes passed: 190,842.
President: Howard Szarfarc. Area Vice President: Brien Kelly. Vice President, Sales: Ken Fluger. Vice President, Marketing: David Goldberg. Vice President, Public Affairs: Harriet Novet. Vice President, Engineering: Larry Pestana. Vice President, Technical Operations: Norberto Rivera. Marketing & Public Affairs Director: Gina Gutman.
Ownership: Time Warner Cable (MSO).

SUFFOLK COUNTY—Cablevision, 1111 Stewart Ave, Bethpage, NY 11714. Phone: 516-803-2300. Fax: 516-803-1183. Web Site: http://www.cablevision.com. Also serves Belle Terre, Brightwaters, Head of the Harbor, Islandia, Islip, Nissequogue, Old Field, Port Jefferson, Shoreham, Smithtown & Village of the Branch. ICA: NY0006.
TV Market Ranking: 1 (Head of the Harbor); 1,19 (SUFFOLK COUNTY (portions)); 19 (Belle Terre, Nissequogue, Old Field, Port Jefferson, Shoreham, Smithtown, Village of the Branch); Below 100 (Brightwaters, Islandia, Islip, Port Jefferson, SUFFOLK COUNTY (portions); Outside TV Markets (SUFFOLK COUNTY (portions)). Franchise award date: N.A. Franchise expiration date: N.A. Began: January 1, 1966.
Channel capacity: 119 (operating 2-way). Channels available but not in use: N.A.

Basic Service
Subscribers: 146,625.
Programming (received off-air): WABC-TV (ABC, Live Well Network) New York; WCBS-TV (CBS, Decades) New York; WFTY-DT (UniMas) Smithtown; WLIW (PBS) Garden City; WLNY-TV (IND) Riverhead; WNBC (COZI TV, NBC) New York; WNET (PBS) Newark; WNJU (TMO) Linden; WNYW (FOX, Movies!) New York; WPIX (Antenna TV, CW, This TV) New York; WPXN-TV (ION) New York; WWOR-TV (Bounce TV, Buzzr, Heroes & Icons, MNT) Secaucus; WXTV-DT (UNV) Paterson.
Programming (via satellite): EVINE Live; News 12 Long Island; QVC.
Fee: $39.95 installation; $16.22 monthly; $2.95 converter.

Expanded Basic Service 1
Subscribers: N.A.
Programming (via satellite): A&E; AMC; Animal Planet; BET; Bravo; Cartoon Network; CNBC; CNN; Comedy Central; C-SPAN; C-SPAN 2; Discovery Channel; Disney Channel; E! HD; ESPN; ESPN2; Food Network; Fox News Channel; Fox Sports 1; Freeform; Fuse; FX; GSN; HGTV; History; HLN; IFC; Lifetime; MSG; MSG Plus; MSNBC; MTV; MTV2; News 12 Traffic & Weather; Nickelodeon; Spike TV; Syfy; TBS; Telecare; The Weather Channel; TLC; TNT; Travel Channel; truTV; Turner Classic Movies; TV Land; USA Network; VH1; WE tv; YES Network.
Fee: $33.73 monthly; $2.95 converter.

Digital Basic Service
Subscribers: N.A.
Programming (via satellite): Animal Planet HD; Azteca; BBC World News; Bloomberg Television; Canal Sur; Caracol TV; Cartoon Network en Espanol; CBS Sports Network; Cinelatino; CMT; CMT HD; CNN en Espanol; CNN HD; C-SPAN 3; Destination America; Discovery Channel HD; Discovery Kids Channel; Disney XD; Docu TVE; Ecuavisa Internacional; ESPN Classic; ESPN Deportes; ESPN HD; ESPN2 HD; ESPNews; EuroNews; Food Network HD; FOX College Sports Central; FOX College Sports Pacific; Fox Deportes; Fox Life; Fox News HD; Fox Sports 2; FX HD; FXM; FYI; GMA Pinoy TV; Golf Channel; GolTV; Great American Country; Hallmark Channel; Hallmark Movie Channel HD; Hallmark Movies & Mysteries; HD Theater; here! On Demand; HGTV HD; History en Espanol; History International; HTV; Infinito; Investigation Discovery; Jewelry Television; Korean Channel; La Familia Cosmovision; LATV; LOGO; Mariavision; MBC America; MC; Momentum; MTV Classic; MTV Hits; National Geographic Channel; National Geographic Channel HD; NBA TV; NBC Universo; NBCSN; NHL Network; NHL Network HD; Nick HD; Nick Jr.; Nicktoons; NTV America; Outdoor Channel; Oxygen; RTN; Science Channel; Science HD; Spike TV HD; Sundance TV; TBS HD; TeenNick; Telefe Internacional; Telemicro Internacional; The Filipino Channel; The Jewish Channel; The Weather Channel HD; TLC HD; TNT HD; Toon Disney en Espanol; Tr3s; Travel Channel HD; TV Asia; TV Polonia; TV5MONDE USA; TVG Network; ULTRA HDPlex; Universal HD; Versus HD; VH1 HD; VH1 Soul; ViendoMovies; Vme TV; YES HD; Zee TV.
Fee: $10.95 monthly; $2.95 converter.

Pay Service 1
Pay Units: N.A.
Programming (via satellite): Flix; HBO (multiplexed); Showtime (multiplexed); The Movie Channel.

Digital Pay Service 1
Pay Units: N.A.
Programming (via satellite): Cinemax (multiplexed); Cinemax HD; Cinemax On Demand; HBO (multiplexed); HBO HD; HBO on Demand; Playboy TV; Showtime (multiplexed); Showtime HD; Showtime On Demand; Starz Encore (multiplexed); Starz HD; Starz On Demand; The Movie Channel (multiplexed); The Movie Channel HD.
Fee: $9.95 monthly (Cinemax/Cinemax HD/Cinemax On Demand/Showtime HD/TMC HD/HBO HD/Starz HDTV, Playboy, Starz On Demand/Encore, TMC or Showtime/Showtime On Demand), $11.95 monthly (HBO/HBO On Demand).

Video-On-Demand: Yes

Pay-Per-View
Playboy TV; Club Jenna.

Internet Service
Operational: Yes.
Subscribers: 153,994.
Broadband Service: Optimum Online.
Fee: $46.95 installation; $34.95 monthly; $299.00 modem purchase.

Telephone Service
Digital: Operational
Subscribers: 134,020.
Fee: $34.95 monthly
Miles of Plant: 4,692.0 (coaxial); 1,183.0 (fiber optic). Homes passed: 233,803.
Executive Vice President, Programming: Tom Montemagno. Senior Vice President, Field Operations: Christopher Coffey. Corporate Communications Manager: Kristin Blank.
Ownership: Altice USA (MSO).

SULLIVAN (town)—Time Warner Cable. Now served by DEWITT, NY [NY0013]. ICA: NY0096.

SULLIVAN COUNTY—Time Warner Cable. Now served by BETHEL (town), NY [NY0231]. ICA: NY0251.

SUMMIT (town)—Formerly served by C H Comm LLC. No longer in operation. ICA: NY0180.

SYRACUSE—Time Warner Cable. Now served by DEWITT, NY [NY0013]. ICA: NY0021.

TOMPKINS COUNTY—Formerly served by Time Warner Cable. No longer in operation. ICA: NY0280.

TROUPSBURG (town)—Time Warner Cable. Now served by DEWITT, NY [NY0013]. ICA: NY0253.

TROY—Time Warner Cable. Now served by ALBANY, NY [NY0014]. ICA: NY0020.

TURIN (town)—Formerly served by Turin Cable TV. Now served by Time Warner Cable, DEWITT, NY [NY0013]. ICA: NY0254.

TUSTEN—Time Warner Cable. Now served by BETHEL (town), NY [NY0231]. ICA: NY0255.

UTICA—Time Warner Cable. Now served by DEWITT, NY [NY0013]. ICA: NY0022.

Cable Systems—New York

WALDEN (village)—Time Warner Cable. Now served by BETHEL (town), NY [NY0231]. ICA: NY0256.

WALTON (village)—Time Warner Cable. Now served by DEWITT, NY [NY0013]. ICA: NY0121.

WAPPINGERS FALLS—Cablevision, 719 Old Rt 9N, Wappingers Falls, NY 12590. Phone: 845-297-3333. Web Site: http://www.cablevision.com. Also serves Amenia (town), Beacon, Blooming Grove, Clinton (town), Cold Spring, Dover (town), East Fishkill, Esopus, Fishkill (village), Harriman, Hyde Park, Kent, La Grange, Lloyd, Marlboro, Milan, Millbrook, Millerton, Monroe (village), Nelsonville, North East (town), Pine Plains (town), Plattekill, Poughkeepsie, South Blooming Grove, Stanford (town), Union Vale (town), Wappinger (town), Washington (town) & Woodbury. ICA: NY0288.

TV Market Ranking: 1 (Blooming Grove, Harriman, Lloyd, Marlboro, Monroe (village), Plattekill, Poughkeepsie, South Blooming Grove, Woodbury (portions)); 19 (Amenia (town), Cold Spring, Dover (town), Union Vale (town)); Below 100 (Beacon, Clinton (town), East Fishkill, Esopus, Fishkill (village), Hyde Park, Kent, La Grange, Milan, Millbrook, Millerton, Nelsonville, North East (town), Pine Plains (town), Stanford (town), Wappinger (town), Washington (town), WAPPINGERS FALLS).

Channel capacity: 42 (not 2-way capable). Channels available but not in use: N.A.

Basic Service
Subscribers: 65,199. Commercial subscribers: 3,135.
Programming (received off-air): W42AE Poughkeepsie; WABC-TV (ABC, Live Well Network) New York; WCBS-TV (CBS, Decades) New York; WLIW (PBS) Garden City; WMBC-TV (Azteca America) Newton; WNBC (COZI TV, NBC) New York; WNET (PBS) Newark; WNJU (TMO) Linden; WNYW (FOX, Movies!) New York; WPIX (Antenna TV, CW, This TV) New York; WPXN-TV (ION) New York; WRNN-TV (IND) Kingston; WTBY-TV (TBN) Poughkeepsie; WWOR-TV (Bounce TV, Buzzr, Heroes & Icons, MNT) Secaucus.
Programming (via satellite): Antenna TV; C-SPAN; Estrella TV; HSN; Live Well Network; NJTV; QVC; QVC HD; UniMas; UniMas HD; Univision; Univision HD; Vme TV.
Fee: $39.95 installation; $17.46 monthly.

Expanded Basic Service 1
Subscribers: N.A.
Programming (via satellite): A&E; AMC; Animal Planet; BET; Bravo; Cartoon Network; CNBC; CNN; Comedy Central; C-SPAN 2; Discovery Channel; Disney Channel; E! HD; ESPN; ESPN2; EWTN Global Catholic Network; Food Network; Fox News Channel; Fox Sports 1; Freeform; Fuse; FX; GSN; HGTV; History; HLN; Lifetime; MSG; MSG Plus; MSNBC; MTV; MTV2; News 12 Traffic & Weather; Nickelodeon; Oxygen; Spike TV; SportsNet New York; Syfy; TBS; Telecare; The Weather Channel; TLC; TNT; Travel Channel; truTV; Turner Classic Movies; TV Land; USA Network; VH1; WE tv.
Fee: $40.95 monthly.

Digital Basic Service
Subscribers: N.A.
Programming (via satellite): A&E HD; AMC HD; American Heroes Channel; Animal Planet HD; BBC America; BBC HD; BBC World News; Bio HD; Bloomberg Television; Boomerang; Bravo HD; Cartoon Network HD; CBS Sports Network; CBS Sports Network HD; Centric; CMT; CMT HD; CNBC HD+; CNN HD; Comedy Central HD; C-SPAN 3; Daystar TV Network; Destination America; Destination America HD; Discovery Channel HD; Discovery Family; Disney Channel HD; Disney XD; Disney XD HD; E! HD; ESPN HD; ESPN2 HD; ESPNews; ESPNews HD; ESPNU; ESPNU HD; EuroNews; EVINE Live; Food Network HD; Fox Business Network; Fox Business Network HD; Fox Deportes; Fox News HD; Freeform HD; Fuse HD; FX HD; FXM; FYI; Golf Channel; Golf Channel HD; Great American Country; Hallmark Channel; Hallmark Movie Channel HD; Hallmark Movies & Mysteries; HD Theater; HGTV HD; History HD; History International; IFC; IFC HD; Investigation Discovery; Jewelry Television; LOGO; MLB Network; MLB Network HD; MSNBC HD; MTV Classic; MTV Hits; MTV Live; Nat Geo WILD; Nat Geo WILD HD; National Geographic Channel; National Geographic Channel HD; NBA TV; NBA TV HD; NBC Universo; NBCSN; Nick HD; Nick Jr.; Nicktoons; OWN: Oprah Winfrey Network; Oxygen HD; Reelz; Science Channel; Science HD; Spike TV HD; Syfy HD; TBS HD; TeenNick; The Weather Channel HD; TLC HD; TNT HD; Tr3s; Travel Channel HD; truTV HD; Turner Classic Movies HD; TV One; Universal HD; USA Network HD; Versus HD; VH1 HD; VH1 Soul; WE tv HD; YES HD.
Fee: $11.95 monthly.

Digital Expanded Basic Service
Subscribers: N.A.
Programming (via satellite): Azteca; Canal Sur; Caracol TV; Cartoon Network en Espanol; Cinelatino; CNN en Espanol; Dominican View; Ecuavisa Internacional; ESPN Deportes; Fox Deportes; Fox Life; GolTV; History en Espanol; HTV; Infinito; Latele Novela Network; Mariavision; Momentum; NBC Universo; RCN Nuestra Tele; Telefe Internacional; Telemicro Internacional; Tr3s; ULTRA HDPlex; VeneMovies.
Fee: $14.95 monthly.

Digital Expanded Basic Service 2
Subscribers: N.A.
Programming (via satellite): Antenna Satellite TV; ART America; Channel One Russia; Deutsche Welle TV; GMA Pinoy TV; International Television (ITV); Korean Channel; MBC America; Mega TV; NEO Cricket; NTV America; Portuguese Channel; RTP-USA; RTV; RTVI; Sino TV; The Filipino Channel; TV Asia; TV Polonia; TV5, La Television International; Zee TV.
Fee: $4.95 monthly (Deutsche Welle or RTPi), $9.95 monthly (ART, Jus Punjabi, SPT, Rai Tialia or TV5 Monde), $10.95 monthly (Portuguese package), $14.94 monthly (Chinese, Filipino, Greek or Korean package), $19.95 monthly (Brazilian or Polish package), $24.95 monthly (South Asian package or TV Japan) $29.95 monthly (Russian package).

Digital Pay Service 1
Pay Units: N.A.
Programming (via satellite): Cinemax (multiplexed); Cinemax HD (multiplexed); HBO (multiplexed); HBO HD (multiplexed); Playboy TV; Showtime (multiplexed); Showtime HD (multiplexed); Smithsonian Channel; Smithsonian Channel HD; Starz (multiplexed); Starz Encore (multiplexed); Starz Encore HD; Starz HD (multiplexed); Sundance TV; The Movie Channel (multiplexed); The Movie Channel HD (multiplexed).
Fee: $5.95 monthly (Sundance), $11.95 monthly (Cinemax, Playboy, Showtime, Starz/Encore or TMC), $14.95 monthly (HBO).

Internet Service
Operational: Yes.
Subscribers: 69,317.
Fee: $29.95 monthly.

Telephone Service
Digital: Operational
Subscribers: 57,363.
Miles of Plant: 3,983.0 (coaxial); 922.0 (fiber optic). Homes passed: 101,838.
Executive Vice President, Programming: Tom Montemagno. Vice President, Field Operations: Mark Fitchett. Vice President, Local Ad Sales: John Oleynick. Operations Manager: Roger Ferriera.
Ownership: Altice USA (MSO).

WARSAW (village)—Time Warner Cable. Now served by BUFFALO (formerly Lackawanna), NY [NY0216]. ICA: NY0126.

WARWICK—Cablevision, 19 South St, Warwick, NY 10990. Phones: 845-986-6060; 516-803-2300 (Corporate office); 845-986-0221. Fax: 845-986-0031. Web Site: http://www.cablevision.com. Also serves Montague Twp., Sandyston Twp. & West Milford, NJ; Chester (town) (Orange County), Chester (village), Florida (village), Greenville, Greenwood Lake, Greenwood Lake (village), Minisink, Unionville, Warwick (village) & Warwick Twp., NY; Matamoras & Westfall Twp., PA. ICA: NY0045.

TV Market Ranking: 1 (Chester (town) (Orange County), Chester (village), Florida (village), Greenville, Greenwood Lake, Unionville, WARWICK, Warwick (village), Warwick Twp., West Milford); 8 (Greenwood Lake); Below 100 (Minisink, Montague Twp., Sandyston Twp., Westfall Twp., Matamoras). Franchise award date: March 1, 1977. Franchise expiration date: N.A. Began: December 2, 1978.

Channel capacity: 41 (operating 2-way). Channels available but not in use: N.A.

Basic Service
Subscribers: 25,820. Commercial subscribers: 1,102.
Programming (received off-air): WABC-TV (ABC, Live Well Network) New York; WCBS-TV (CBS, Decades) New York; WFUT-DT (getTV, UniMas) Newark; WMBC-TV (Azteca America) Newton; WNBC (COZI TV, NBC) New York; WNET (PBS) Newark; WNJN (PBS) Montclair; WNJU (TMO) Linden; WNYJ-TV (ETV) West Milford; WNYW (FOX, Movies!) New York; WPIX (Antenna TV, CW, This TV) New York; WPXN-TV (ION) New York; WRNN-TV (IND) Kingston; WTBY-TV (TBN) Poughkeepsie; WWOR-TV (Bounce TV, Buzzr, Heroes & Icons, MNT) Secaucus; WXTV-DT (UNV) Paterson.
Programming (via satellite): EVINE Live; News 12 New Jersey; QVC.
Fee: $49.95 installation; $12.60 monthly; $3.00 converter.

Expanded Basic Service 1
Subscribers: N.A.
Programming (via satellite): A&E; AMC; Animal Planet; BET; Bravo; Cartoon Network; CNBC; CNN; Comedy Central; C-SPAN 2; Discovery Channel; Disney Channel; E! HD; ESPN; ESPN2; Food Network; Fox News Channel; Fox Sports 1; Freeform; Fuse; FX; GSN; HGTV; History; HLN; IFC; Lifetime; MSG; MSG Plus; MSNBC; MTV; MTV2; News 12 Traffic & Weather; Nickelodeon; Spike TV; SportsNet New York; Syfy; TBS; The Weather Channel; TLC; TNT; Travel Channel; truTV; Turner Classic Movies; TV Land; USA Network; VH1; WE tv; YES Network.
Fee: $35.99 monthly.

Digital Basic Service
Subscribers: N.A.
Programming (via satellite): BBC World News; Bloomberg Television; Canal Sur; Cartoon Network en Espanol; Cinelatino; CMT; CNN en Espanol; CNN HD; C-SPAN 3; Destination America; Discovery Kids Channel; Disney XD; Docu TVE; ESPN Classic; ESPN Deportes; ESPN HD; ESPN2 HD; ESPNews; EuroNews; EVINE Live; Food Network HD; FOX College Sports Central; FOX College Sports Pacific; Fox Deportes; Fox Life; Fox Sports 2; FSN HD; FXM; FYI; Golf Channel; GolTV; Great American Country; Hallmark Channel; HD Theater; HGTV HD; History en Espanol; History International; iN DEMAND; Infinito; Investigation Discovery; Jewelry Television; La Familia Cosmovision; LOGO; Mariavision; MC; Momentum; MTV Classic; MTV Hits; National Geographic Channel; National Geographic Channel HD; NBA TV; NBC Universo; NBCSN; NHL Network; Nick Jr.; Nicktoons; Outdoor Channel; Oxygen; Science Channel; Sundance TV; TBS HD; TeenNick; Telefe Internacional; TNT HD; Toon Disney en Espanol; Tr3s; TVG Network; ULTRA HDPlex; Universal HD; Versus HD; VH1 Soul; Vme TV; YES HD.
Fee: $9.95 monthly; $2.95 converter.

Pay Service 1
Pay Units: N.A.
Programming (via satellite): Cinemax; Flix; HBO (multiplexed); Showtime (multiplexed); The Movie Channel.

Digital Pay Service 1
Pay Units: N.A.
Programming (via satellite): Azteca; Caracol TV; Cinemax (multiplexed); Cinemax HD; Ecuavisa Internacional; HBO (multiplexed); HBO HD; Korean Channel; MBC America; Portuguese Channel; RAI Italia; RTN; Showtime (multiplexed); Showtime HD; Starz (multiplexed); Starz Encore (multiplexed); Starz HD; The Movie Channel (multiplexed); The Movie Channel HD; TV Asia; TV Polonia; TV5, La Television International; ViendoMovies; Zee TV.
Fee: $10.00 installation; $9.95 monthly (Cinemax/Cinemax HD, Showtime/Showtime HD, Starz/Starz HDTV/Encore, RAI, TV5 or TV Polonia), $11.95 monthly (HBO/HBO HD), $24.95 monthly (TV Japan).

Video-On-Demand: Yes

New York—Cable Systems

CABLE & TV STATION COVERAGE
Atlas 2017
The perfect companion to the Television & Cable Factbook
To order call 800-771-9202 or visit www.warren-news.com

Pay-Per-View
iN DEMAND (delivered digitally); Playboy TV (delivered digitally); Club Jenna (delivered digitally).
Internet Service
Operational: Yes.
Subscribers: 24,693.
Broadband Service: Optimum Online.
Fee: $46.95 installation; $34.95 monthly; $299.00 modem purchase.
Telephone Service
Digital: Operational
Subscribers: 18,751.
Fee: $34.95 monthly
Miles of Plant: 1,668.0 (coaxial); 414.0 (fiber optic). Homes passed: 35,759.
Executive Vice President, Programming: Tom Montemagno. Vice President, Field Operations: Christopher Fulton. Operations Manager: Mark Quirk.
Ownership: Altice USA (MSO).

WARWICK—Formerly served by Alteva (formerly WVT). No longer in operation. ICA: NY5173.

WASHINGTONVILLE (village)—Time Warner Cable. Now served by BETHEL (town), NY [NY0231]. ICA: NY0258.

WATERTOWN—Time Warner Cable. Now served by DEWITT, NY [NY0013]. ICA: NY0206.

WATERTOWN—Time Warner Cable. Now served by DEWITT, NY [NY0013]. ICA: NY0040.

WELLESLEY ISLAND—Time Warner Cable. Now served by DEWITT, NY [NY0013]. ICA: NY0281.

WELLS—Hamilton County Cable TV Inc, 1330 State Rt. 30, PO Box 275, Wells, NY 12190. Phones: 518-924-2013; 800-562-1560. Web Site: http://www.hcctelevision.com. ICA: NY0260.
TV Market Ranking: Below 100 (WELLS). Franchise award date: November 1, 1984. Franchise expiration date: N.A. Began: July 1, 1985.
Channel capacity: N.A. Channels available but not in use: N.A.
Basic Service
Subscribers: 271.
Programming (received off-air): WMHT (PBS) Schenectady; WNYT (MeTV, NBC) Albany; WRGB (CBS, This TV) Schenectady; WTEN (ABC) Albany; WXXA-TV (FOX, Laff, The Country Network) Albany.
Programming (via satellite): A&E; AMC; Animal Planet; CNN; C-SPAN; Discovery Channel; ESPN; Freeform; History; Lifetime; QVC; Spike TV; TBS; TNT; USA Network; WGN America.
Fee: $80.00 installation; $42.00 monthly.
Digital Basic Service
Subscribers: 86.
Fee: $44.75 monthly.
Pay Service 1
Pay Units: N.A.
Programming (via satellite): Cinemax; HBO.
Fee: $9.00 monthly (Cinemax), $10.00 monthly (HBO).
Video-On-Demand: No
Internet Service
Operational: No.
Telephone Service
None
Miles of Plant: 27.0 (coaxial); None (fiber optic).
President: Paul F. Schonewolf.
Ownership: Hamilton County/Gore Mountain Cable TV Inc. (MSO).

WELLSVILLE (town)—Time Warner Cable. Now served by BUFFALO, NY [NY0216]. ICA: NY0086.

WESTFIELD (town)—Time Warner Cable. Now served by BUFFALO (formerly Lackawanna), NY [NY0216]. ICA: NY0286.

WHITEHALL (town)—Time Warner Cable. Now served by ALBANY, NY [NY0014]. ICA: NY0134.

WHITESVILLE—Formerly served by Fitzgerald Cable TV. No longer in operation. ICA: NY0191.

WHITNEY POINT (village)—Time Warner Cable. Now served by DEWITT, NY [NY0013]. ICA: NY0135.

WILLSBORO (town)—Cable Communications of Willsboro, 3669 Essex Rd, PO Box 625, Willsboro, NY 12996. Phone: 518-963-4116. Fax: 518-963-7405. E-mail: herb@willex.com. Also serves Essex. ICA: NY0162.
TV Market Ranking: Below 100 (Essex, WILLSBORO (TOWN)). Franchise award date: July 27, 1987. Franchise expiration date: N.A. Began: July 5, 1988.
Channel capacity: N.A. Channels available but not in use: N.A.
Basic Service
Subscribers: 453.
Programming (received off-air): various Canadian stations; WCAX-TV (CBS, Movies!) Burlington; WCFE-TV (PBS) Plattsburgh; WETK (PBS) Burlington; WFFF-TV (FOX, IND) Burlington; WPTZ (MeTV, NBC, This TV) Plattsburgh; WVNY (ABC) Burlington; WWOR-TV (Bounce TV, Buzzr, Heroes & Icons, MNT) Secaucus.
Programming (via satellite): Cartoon Network; CMT; Comedy Central; ESPN2; FX; WGN America.
Fee: $34.95 installation; $48.95 monthly.
Expanded Basic Service 1
Subscribers: N.A.
Programming (via satellite): A&E; AMC; Animal Planet; Bravo; CNBC; CNN; Discovery Channel; Disney Channel; ESPN; Food Network; Fox News Channel; Hallmark Channel; HGTV; History; Lifetime; MTV; National Geographic Channel; Nickelodeon; QVC; Spike TV; Syfy; TBS; The Weather Channel; TLC; TNT; Turner Classic Movies; TV Land; USA Network; WPIX (Antenna TV, CW, This TV) New York.
Digital Basic Service
Subscribers: N.A.
Programming (via satellite): BBC America; Bloomberg Television; CMT; Discovery Digital Networks; Disney XD; DMX Music; E! HD; ESPN Classic; ESPNews; Fox Sports 1; FXM; FYI; Golf Channel; GSN; History International; IFC; LMN; NBCSN; Nick Jr.; Nicktoons; Outdoor Channel; Ovation; TeenNick; WE tv.
Pay Service 1
Pay Units: 59.
Programming (via satellite): HBO.
Fee: $9.95 monthly.
Pay Service 2
Pay Units: 103.
Programming (via satellite): Cinemax.
Fee: $8.95 monthly.
Digital Pay Service 1
Pay Units: N.A.
Programming (via satellite): Cinemax (multiplexed); Flix; HBO (multiplexed); Showtime (multiplexed); Starz (multiplexed); Starz Encore (multiplexed); Sundance TV; The Movie Channel (multiplexed).
Internet Service
Operational: Yes.
Broadband Service: In-house.
Fee: $49.95 installation; $39.95 monthly; $5.00 modem lease.
Miles of Plant: 32.0 (coaxial); None (fiber optic). Homes passed: 1,000.
President & General Manager: Herb Longware.
Ownership: Cable Communications of Willsboro Inc.

WINDHAM—Mid-Hudson Cablevision Inc., 200 Jefferson Hts, PO Box 399, Catskill, NY 12414-0399. Phones: 800-342-5400; 518-943-6600; 518-943-6653. Fax: 518-943-6603. E-mail: cable@mid-hudson.com. Web Site: http://www2.mhcable.com. Also serves Ashland (town) (Greene County), Durham, Prattsville (town), Rensselaerville & Roxbury. ICA: NY0149.
TV Market Ranking: 34 (Ashland (town) (Greene County), Durham, Rensselaerville, WINDHAM); Below 100 (Prattsville (town)); Outside TV Markets (Roxbury). Franchise award date: N.A. Franchise expiration date: N.A. Began: June 1, 1990.
Channel capacity: N.A. Channels available but not in use: N.A.
Basic Service
Subscribers: 295.
Programming (received off-air): WCWN (CW) Schenectady; WMHT (PBS) Schenectady; WNYT (MeTV, NBC) Albany; WRGB (CBS, This TV) Schenectady; WTEN (ABC) Albany; WXXA-TV (FOX, Laff, The Country Network) Albany.
Programming (via satellite): Fox News Channel; FX; MyNetworkTV; Pop; QVC.
Fee: $50.00 installation; $24.95 monthly; $2.00 converter.
Expanded Basic Service 1
Subscribers: N.A.
Programming (received off-air): WYXN-LD New York.
Programming (via satellite): A&E; AMC; Animal Planet; Bravo; Cartoon Network; Cinemax; CMT; CNBC; CNN; Comedy Central; C-SPAN; C-SPAN 2; Discovery Channel; Disney Channel; E! HD; ESPN; ESPN Classic; ESPN2; EWTN Global Catholic Network; Food Network; Fox Sports 1; Freeform; Fuse; FXM; FYI; Golf Channel; GSN; Hallmark Channel; HGTV; History; HLN; Lifetime; MSG; MSG Plus; MSNBC; MTV; National Geographic Channel; NBCSN; Nickelodeon; Spike TV; SportsNet New York; Syfy; TBS; The Weather Channel; TLC; TNT; Travel Channel; truTV; Turner Classic Movies; TV Land; USA Network; VH1; WE tv; YES Network.
Fee: $32.50 monthly.
Digital Basic Service
Subscribers: N.A.
Programming (via satellite): BBC America; Bloomberg Television; Chiller; Cloo; CMT; Cooking Channel; Destination America; Discovery Kids Channel; Discovery Life Channel; Disney XD; DMX Music; ESPNews; EVINE Live; Fox Business Network; FOX College Sports Central; FOX College Sports Pacific; Great American Country; GSN; History International; IFC; Investigation Discovery; LMN; MTV Classic; MTV Hits; MTV2; Nick Jr.; Nicktoons; Outdoor Channel; Ovation; OWN: Oprah Winfrey Network; RFD-TV; RTV; Science Channel; Sprout; Sundance TV; TeenNick; The Word Network; Trinity Broadcasting Network (TBN); TVG Network; VH1 Soul.
Fee: $6.95 monthly; $6.95 converter.
Digital Expanded Basic Service
Subscribers: N.A.
Programming (via satellite): A&E HD; Animal Planet HD; AXS TV; Bravo HD; ESPN HD; Food Network HD; FX HD; HD Theater; HGTV HD; History HD; National Geographic Channel HD; Outdoor Channel 2 HD; QVC HD; Science HD; Syfy HD; TBS HD; TLC HD; TNT HD; Universal HD; USA Network HD; YES HD.
Fee: $7.50 monthly; $7.95 converter.
Digital Pay Service 1
Pay Units: N.A.
Programming (via satellite): Cinemax HD (multiplexed); Cinemax On Demand; HBO (multiplexed); HBO HD; HBO on Demand; Showtime; Starz (multiplexed); Starz Encore (multiplexed); Starz HD; The Movie Channel (multiplexed).
Fee: $11.95 monthly (Showtime/TMC), $13.40 monthly (Cinemax), $13.95 monthly (HBO or Starz/Encore).
Pay-Per-View
iN DEMAND (delivered digitally); Playboy TV (delivered digitally); Club Jenna (delivered digitally).
Internet Service
Operational: Yes.
Fee: $49.95 monthly.
Telephone Service
Analog: Not Operational
Digital: Operational
Fee: $29.95 monthly
Miles of Plant: 53.0 (coaxial); None (fiber optic). Homes passed: 1,375.
President: James M. Reynolds. Chief Engineer: David Fingar. Chief Technician: Edward Harter.
Ownership: Mid-Hudson Cablevision Inc. (MSO).

WOODHULL (town)—Time Warner Cable. Now served by DEWITT, NY [NY0013]. ICA: NY0262.

WOODRIDGE (village)—Time Warner Cable. Now served by BETHEL (town), NY [NY0231]. ICA: NY0153.

WOODSTOCK (town)—Time Warner Cable. Now served by BETHEL (town), NY [NY0231]. ICA: NY0098.

YONKERS—Cablevision, 6 Executive Plaza, Yonkers, NY 11714. Phones: 914-762-8717; 516-803-2300 (Corporate office). Web Site: http://www.cablevision.com. ICA: NY0019.

Cable Systems—New York

TV Market Ranking: 1 (YONKERS). Franchise award date: December 16, 1976. Franchise expiration date: N.A. Began: October 1, 1977.
Channel capacity: N.A. Channels available but not in use: N.A.

Basic Service
Subscribers: 44,997.
Programming (received off-air): WABC-TV (ABC, Live Well Network) New York; WCBS-TV (CBS, Decades) New York; WFUT-DT (getTV, UniMas) Newark; WLIW (PBS) Garden City; WLNY-TV (IND) Riverhead; WMBC-TV (Azteca America) Newton; WNBC (COZI TV, NBC) New York; WNET (PBS) Newark; WNJU (TMO) Linden; WNYW (FOX, Movies!) New York; WPIX (Antenna TV, CW, This TV) New York; WPXN-TV (ION) New York; WRNN-TV (IND) Kingston; WWOR-TV (Bounce TV, Buzzr, Heroes & Icons, MNT) Secaucus; WXTV-DT (UNV) Paterson.
Programming (via satellite): News 12 Westchester; Pop.
Fee: $39.95 installation; $17.80 monthly.

Expanded Basic Service 1
Subscribers: N.A.
Programming (via satellite): A&E; AMC; Animal Planet; BET; Bravo; Cartoon Network; CMT; CNBC; CNN; Comedy Central; C-SPAN; C-SPAN 2; Discovery Channel; Discovery Life Channel; Disney Channel; E! HD; ESPN; ESPN2; Food Network; Fox News Channel; Fox Sports 1; Freeform; Fuse; FX; GSN; HGTV; History; HLN; Lifetime; MSNBC; MTV; MTV2; NBC Universo; News 12 Traffic & Weather; Nickelodeon; QVC; Spike TV; Syfy; TBS; The Weather Channel; TLC; TNT; Travel Channel; truTV; TV Land; Univision; USA Network; VH1; WE tv.
Fee: $32.15 monthly.

Digital Basic Service
Subscribers: N.A.
Programming (via satellite): Bloomberg Television; CMT; C-SPAN 3; Discovery Digital Networks; Disney XD; ESPN Classic; ESPNews; EuroNews; Fox Deportes; FXM; FYI; Hallmark Channel; History International; Mag Rack; MC; MSG; MSG Plus; MTV Classic; National Geographic Channel; NBA TV; NBC Universo; Nick Jr.; Oxygen; TeenNick.
Fee: $10.95 monthly.

Pay Service 1
Pay Units: N.A.
Programming (via satellite): Cinemax; Flix; HBO (multiplexed); IFC; MSG; MSG Plus; Showtime; Starz; Starz Encore; The Movie Channel; Turner Classic Movies; YES Network.

Digital Pay Service 1
Pay Units: N.A.
Programming (via satellite): Cinemax (multiplexed); HBO (multiplexed); Showtime (multiplexed); Starz (multiplexed); Starz Encore (multiplexed); The Movie Channel (multiplexed).
Fee: $9.95 monthly (Cinemax, Showtime, TMC or Starz/Encore), $11.95 monthly (HBO).

Video-On-Demand: Yes

Pay-Per-View
Playboy TV (delivered digitally); iN DEMAND (delivered digitally); NBA TV (delivered digitally); Sports PPV (delivered digitally); Playboy TV; iN DEMAND.

Internet Service
Operational: Yes.
Subscribers: 46,408.
Broadband Service: Optimum Online.
Fee: $46.95 installation; $34.95 monthly; $299.00 modem purchase.

Telephone Service
Digital: Operational
Subscribers: 40,825.
Fee: $34.95 monthly
Miles of Plant: 1,266.0 (coaxial); 313.0 (fiber optic). Homes passed: 70,034.
Executive Vice President, Programming: Tom Montemagno. Vice President, Field Operations: Mark Fitchett.
Ownership: Altice USA (MSO).

YORKTOWN—Cablevision, 2013 Crompond Rd, Yorktown, NY 10598. Phone: 516-803-2300 (Corporate office). Fax: 516-803-1183. Web Site: http://www.cablevision.com. Also serves Bedford, Lewisboro, Mount Kisco, North Castle, North Salem, Pound Ridge, Putnam Valley & Somers. ICA: NY0050.
TV Market Ranking: 1 (Bedford, Mount Kisco, North Castle, Putnam Valley, YORKTOWN); 19 (Lewisboro, North Salem, Pound Ridge, Somers). Franchise award date: September 17, 1980. Franchise expiration date: N.A. Began: January 1, 1981.
Channel capacity: N.A. Channels available but not in use: N.A.

Basic Service
Subscribers: 31,269.
Programming (received off-air): WABC-TV (ABC, Live Well Network) New York; WCBS-TV (CBS, Decades) New York; WFUT-DT (getTV, UniMas) Newark; WLIW (PBS) Garden City; WNBC (COZI TV, NBC) New York; WNET (PBS) Newark; WNJU (TMO) Linden; WNYW (FOX, Movies!) New York; WPIX (Antenna TV, CW, This TV) New York; WPXN-TV (ION) New York; WRNN-TV (IND) Kingston; WTBY-TV (TBN) Poughkeepsie; WWOR-TV (Bounce TV, Buzzr, Heroes & Icons, MNT) Secaucus; WXTV-DT (UNV) Paterson; WZME (Retro TV) Bridgeport.
Programming (via satellite): News 12 Westchester.
Fee: $39.95 installation; $18.00 monthly; $2.08 converter.

Expanded Basic Service 1
Subscribers: N.A.
Programming (via satellite): A&E; AMC; Animal Planet; BET; Bravo; Cartoon Network; CNBC; CNN; Comedy Central; C-SPAN; C-SPAN 2; Discovery Channel; Disney Channel; E! HD; ESPN; ESPN2; EVINE Live; Food Network; Fox News Channel; Fox Sports 1; Freeform; Fuse; FX; GSN; HGTV; History; HLN; Life; Lifetime; MSG; MSG Plus; MSNBC; MTV; MTV2; News 12 Traffic & Weather; Nickelodeon; QVC; Spike TV; SportsNet New York; Syfy; TBS; The Weather Channel; TLC; TNT; Travel Channel; truTV; Turner Classic Movies; TV Land; USA Network; VH1; WE tv; YES Network.
Fee: $21.95 monthly.

Digital Basic Service
Subscribers: N.A.
Programming (via satellite): Animal Planet HD; Azteca; BBC World News; Bloomberg Television; Bravo HD; Canal Sur; Caracol TV; Cartoon Network en Espanol; CBS Sports Network; Chiller; Cinelatino; Cloo; CMT; CMT HD; CNBC HD+; CNN en Espanol; CNN HD; C-SPAN 3; Destination America; Discovery Channel HD; Discovery Kids Channel; Disney XD; Docu TVE; Ecuavisa Internacional; ESPN Classic; ESPN Deportes; ESPN HD; ESPN2 HD; ESPNews; EuroNews; Food Network HD; FOX College Sports Central; FOX College Sports Pacific; Fox Deportes; Fox Life; Fox News HD; Fox Sports 2; FX HD; FXM; FYI; Golf Channel; GolTV; Great American Country; Hallmark Channel; Hallmark Movie Channel HD; Hallmark Movies & Mysteries; HD Theater; here! On Demand; HGTV HD; History en Espanol; History International; HTV; iN DEMAND; Infinito; Investigation Discovery; Jewelry Television; La Familia Cosmovision; LATV; LOGO; Mariavision; MC; Momentum; MTV Classic; MTV Hits; National Geographic Channel; National Geographic Channel HD; NBA TV; NBC Universo; NBCSN; NHL Network; NHL Network HD; Nick HD; Nick Jr.; Nicktoons; Outdoor Channel; Oxygen; Science Channel; Science HD; Spike TV HD; Sundance TV; Syfy HD; TBS HD; TeenNick; Telefe Internacional; The Movie Channel (multiplexed); The Weather Channel HD; TLC HD; TNT HD; Toon Disney en Espanol; Tr3s; Travel Channel HD; TVG Network; ULTRA HDPlex; Universal HD; USA Network HD; Versus HD; VH1 HD; VH1 Soul; ViendoMovies; Vme TV; YES HD.
Fee: $10.95 monthly.

Pay Service 1
Pay Units: N.A.
Programming (via satellite): Cinemax; Flix; HBO (multiplexed); Showtime (multiplexed); The Movie Channel.

Digital Pay Service 1
Pay Units: N.A.
Programming (via satellite): Bollywood Hits On Demand; Cinemax (multiplexed); Cinemax HD; Cinemax On Demand; GMA Pinoy TV; HBO (multiplexed); HBO HD; HBO on Demand; Korean Channel; MBC America; Playboy TV; RAI Italia; RTN; Showtime (multiplexed); Showtime HD; Showtime On Demand; Starz (multiplexed); Starz Encore (multiplexed); Starz HD; Starz On Demand; Telemicro Internacional; The Filipino Channel; The Movie Channel HD; TV Asia; TV Polonia; TV5MONDE USA; Zee TV.
Fee: $9.95 monthly (Cinemax, Playboy, Showtime, Starz/Encore, TMC, RAI, SPT, TV5 or TV Polonia), $11.95 monthly (HBO), $24.95 monthly (TV Japan).

Video-On-Demand: Yes

Pay-Per-View
Playboy TV; Club Jenna.

Internet Service
Operational: Yes.
Subscribers: 32,776.
Broadband Service: Optimum Online.
Fee: $46.95 installation; $34.95 monthly.

Telephone Service
Digital: Operational
Subscribers: 26,683.
Fee: $34.95 monthly
Miles of Plant: 1,993.0 (coaxial); 454.0 (fiber optic). Homes passed: 49,717.
Executive Vice President, Programming: Tom Montemagno. Vice President, Field Operations: Mark Fitchett. Operations Manager: Frank Turco.
Ownership: Altice USA (MSO).

NORTH CAROLINA

Total Systems: 62	Communities with Applications: 0
Total Communities Served: 742	Number of Basic Subscribers: 1,556,813
Franchises Not Yet Operating: 0	Number of Expanded Basic Subscribers: 424
Applications Pending: 0	Number of Pay Units: 1,570

Top 100 Markets Represented: Charlotte (42); Norfolk-Newport News-Portsmouth-Hampton, VA (44); Greenville-Spartanburg-Anderson, SC-Asheville, NC (46); Greensboro-High Point-Winston-Salem (47); Raleigh-Durham-Goldsboro-Fayetteville (73); Greenville-Washington-New Bern (84).

For a list of cable communities in this section, see the Cable Community Index located in the back of Cable Volume 2.
For explanation of terms used in cable system listings, see p. D-11.

AHOSKIE—Formerly served by Adelphia Communications. Now served by Time Warner Cable, MURFREESBORO, NC [NC0144]. ICA: NC0081.

ALBEMARLE—Time Warner Cable. Now served by CHARLOTTE, NC [NC0001]. ICA: NC0030.

ANDERSON CREEK TWP.—Charter Communications. Now served by ANGIER, NC [NC0194]. ICA: NC0188.

ANDREWS—Cable TV of Cherokee County, 1421 Creekside Dr, PO Box 1000, Murphy, NC 28906-1000. Phone: 828-837-7118. Fax: 828-837-3820. E-mail: murphycabletv@cabletvonline.net. Web Site: http://www.cabletvonline.net. ICA: NC0254.
TV Market Ranking: Outside TV Markets (ANDREWS).
Channel capacity: N.A. Channels available but not in use: N.A.
Basic Service
Subscribers: 349.
Fee: $45.00 installation; $9.95 monthly.
Chief Executive Officer: William J. Cooke.
President: David P. Daniel.
Ownership: CND Acquisition Co. LLC (MSO).

ANDREWS—Formerly served by Cable TV of Andrews. Now served by Cable TV of Cherokee County, ANDREWS, NC [NC0254]. ICA: NC0189.

ANGIER—Charter Communications, 109 South 13th St, Erwin, NC 28339. Phones: 314-543-2236; 636-207-5100 (Corporate office); 919-708-5902. Web Site: http://www.charter.com. Also serves Anderson Creek Twp., Benson, Beulaville, Broadway, Calypso, Cameron, Camp Lejeune, Carolina Beach, Chatham County (unincorporated areas), Coats, Dunn, Duplin County, Erwin, Faison, Fort Fisher AFB, Harnett County (portions), Holly Ridge, Johnston County (portions), Kenansville, Kure Beach, Lee County (portions), Lillington, Magnolia, Moore County (portions), New Hanover County (unincorporated areas), Newton Grove, North Topsail Beach, Onslow County, Pender County (portions), Richlands, Rose Hill, Sanford, Siler City, Sneads Ferry, Surf City, Topsail Beach, Vass, Wallace, Warsaw & Whispering Pines. ICA: NC0194.
TV Market Ranking: 47 (Chatham County (unincorporated areas), Siler City); 73 (Anderson Creek Twp., ANGIER, Benson, Beulaville, Broadway, Calypso, Cameron, Coats, Dunn, Duplin County (portions), Erwin, Harnett County (portions), Johnston County (portions), Kenansville, Lee County (portions), Lillington, Newton Grove, Plainview, Sanford, Vass, Warsaw, Whispering Pines); 84 (Camp Lejeune, Onslow County (portions), Richlands); Below 100 (Carolina Beach, Faison, Fort Fisher AFB, Kure Beach, New Hanover County (unincorporated areas), North Topsail Beach, Pender County (portions), Sneads Ferry, Surf City, Topsail Beach, Wallace, Holly Ridge, Chatham County (unincorporated areas), Duplin County (portions), Lee County (portions), Onslow County (portions)); Outside TV Markets (Magnolia, Rose Hill, Chatham County (unincorporated areas), Duplin County (portions), Lee County (portions)). Franchise award date: N.A. Franchise expiration date: N.A. Began: May 1, 1984.
Channel capacity: N.A. Channels available but not in use: N.A.
Digital Basic Service
Subscribers: 43,996.
Programming (received off-air): WFPX-TV (ION) Fayetteville; WLFL (CW, The Country Network) Raleigh; WNCN (Antenna TV, CBS) Goldsboro; WRAL-TV (NBC, This TV) Raleigh; WRAY-TV (IND) Wilson; WRAZ (FOX, MeTV) Raleigh; WRDC (MNT) Durham; WTVD (ABC, Live Well Network) Durham; WUNC-TV (PBS) Chapel Hill; WUVC-DT (Bounce TV, getTV, UNV) Fayetteville.
Programming (via satellite): BBC America; Boomerang; CNN International; C-SPAN; C-SPAN 2; Discovery Digital Networks; Disney XD; DIY Network; FOX College Sports Central; FOX College Sports Pacific; Fox Sports 2; FXM; FYI; History International; HITS (Headend In The Sky); IFC; LMN; MC; Nick 2; Nick Jr.; Nicktoons; Pop; QVC; Sundance TV; TeenNick; Trinity Broadcasting Network (TBN); TV Guide Interactive Inc.; WGN America.
Fee: $49.99 installation; $26.99 monthly; $1.43 converter.
Digital Expanded Basic Service
Subscribers: N.A.
Programming (via satellite): A&E; AMC; Animal Planet; BET; Bravo; Cartoon Network; CMT; CNBC; CNN; Comedy Central; Discovery Channel; Disney Channel; E! HD; ESPN; ESPN2; Food Network; Fox Sports 1; Freeform; FX; Golf Channel; Hallmark Channel; HGTV; History; HLN; Lifetime; MSNBC; MTV; National Geographic Channel; NBCSN; Nickelodeon; Oxygen; Spike TV; Syfy; TBS; Telemundo; The Weather Channel; TLC; TNT; Travel Channel; truTV; TV Land; Univision; USA Network; VH1; WE tv.
Fee: $35.00 installation; $12.97 monthly.
Digital Pay Service 1
Pay Units: N.A.
Programming (via satellite): Cinemax (multiplexed); Flix; HBO (multiplexed); Showtime (multiplexed); Starz (multiplexed); Starz Encore (multiplexed); The Movie Channel (multiplexed).

Fee: $9.95 monthly (Cinemax, HBO, Showtime or TMC).
Video-On-Demand: Yes
Pay-Per-View
iN DEMAND (delivered digitally); Playboy TV (delivered digitally); Fresh (delivered digitally); Shorteez (delivered digitally).
Internet Service
Operational: Yes.
Subscribers: 13,916.
Broadband Service: Charter Internet.
Fee: $29.99 monthly.
Telephone Service
Digital: Operational
Subscribers: 4,327.
Miles of Plant: 2,730.0 (coaxial); 844.0 (fiber optic). Homes passed: 56,402. Miles of plant (coax & fiber) includes Kenly & Troy.
Vice President & General Manager: Anthony Pope. Marketing Director: Brooke Sinclair. Accounting Director: David Sovanski. Office Manager: Brenda Brinson. Marketing Manager: LaRisa Scales. Operations Manager: Doug Underwood.
Ownership: Charter Communications Inc. (MSO).

ARROWHEAD BEACH—Mediacom. Now served by EDENTON, NC [NC0076]. ICA: NC0161.

ASHEBORO—Time Warner Cable. Now served by GREENSBORO, NC [NC0006]. ICA: NC0052.

ASHEVILLE—Charter Communications, 1670 Hendersonville Rd, Asheville, NC 28803. Phones: 314-543-2236; 636-207-5100 (Corporate office); 828-209-2200. Web Site: http://www.charter.com. Also serves Biltmore Forest, Black Mountain, Buncombe County (northern portion), Canton, Clyde, Fletcher, Haywood County, Maggie Valley, Marion, Mars Hill, Marshall, McDowell County (central portion), Montreat, Old Fort, Waynesville, Weaverville & Woodfin. ICA: NC0012.
TV Market Ranking: 46 (ASHEVILLE, Biltmore Forest, Black Mountain, Canton, Clyde, Fletcher, Haywood County, Maggie Valley, Marion, Mars Hill, Marshall, McDowell County (central portion), Montreat, Old Fort, Waynesville, Weaverville, Woodfin); Below 100 (McDowell County (central portion)). Franchise award date: January 1, 1969. Franchise expiration date: N.A. Began: October 3, 1968.
Channel capacity: N.A. Channels available but not in use: N.A.
Digital Basic Service
Subscribers: 60,329.
Programming (via satellite): AXS TV; BBC America; Bloomberg Television; Boomerang; CNN en Espanol; CNN International; Cooking Channel; Discovery Life Channel; DIY Network; ESPN; ESPN Classic; FOX College Sports Central; FOX College Sports Pacific; Fox Sports 2; FXM; FYI; HD Theater; History International; IFC; LMN; MC; NFL Network; Nick 2; Nick Jr.; Nicktoons; Outdoor Channel; Sundance TV; TeenNick; Trinity Broadcasting Network (TBN); WE tv.
Fee: $49.99 installation; $26.99 monthly.
Digital Expanded Basic Service
Subscribers: N.A.
Programming (via satellite): A&E; AMC; Animal Planet; BET; Bravo; Cartoon Network; CMT; CNBC; CNN; Comcast/Charter Sports Southeast (CSS); Comedy Central; Discovery Channel; Disney Channel; Disney XD; E! HD; ESPN; ESPN2; Food Network; Fox News Channel; Fox Sports 1; FOX Sports South/SportSouth; Freeform; FX; Golf Channel; GSN; Hallmark Channel; HGTV; History; HLN; Lifetime; MSNBC; MTV; National Geographic Channel; NBCSN; Nickelodeon; Oxygen; QVC; Spike TV; Syfy; TBS; Telemundo; The Weather Channel; TLC; TNT; Travel Channel; truTV; Turner Classic Movies; TV Land; Univision Studios; USA Network; VH1.
Fee: $47.99 monthly.
Digital Pay Service 1
Pay Units: N.A.
Programming (via satellite): Cinemax (multiplexed); HBO (multiplexed); HBO HD; Showtime HD; Starz (multiplexed).
Video-On-Demand: Yes
Pay-Per-View
Playboy TV (delivered digitally); Fresh (delivered digitally); Spice Live (delivered digitally).
Internet Service
Operational: Yes.
Subscribers: 62,506.
Broadband Service: Charter Internet.
Fee: $29.99 monthly; $9.95 modem lease; $199.95 modem purchase.
Telephone Service
Digital: Operational
Subscribers: 32,899.
Fee: $29.95 monthly
Miles of Plant: 5,066.0 (coaxial); 1,470.0 (fiber optic). Homes passed: 151,303.
Vice President & General Manager: Anthony Pope. Marketing Director: Brooke Sinclair. Accounting Director: David Sovanski. Operations Manager: Janet Cloyde. Engineering Manager: Dean McCracken. Sales & Marketing Manager: Karen Sims.
Ownership: Charter Communications Inc. (MSO).

AULANDER—Formerly served by Adelphia Communications. Now served by Time Warner Cable, MURFREESBORO, NC [NC0144]. ICA: NC0190.

Cable Systems—North Carolina

BAILEY—Time Warner Cable. Now served by RALEIGH, NC [NC0003]. ICA: NC0117.

BALD HEAD ISLAND—Tele-Media, 804 Jacksonville Rd, PO Box 39, Bellefonte, PA 16823-0039. Phones: 814-353-2025; 800-704-4254. Fax: 910-842-2821. Web Site: http://www.tele-media.com. ICA: NC0238.
TV Market Ranking: Below 100 (BALD HEAD ISLAND). Franchise award date: July 1, 1991. Franchise expiration date: N.A. Began: September 1, 1991.
Channel capacity: N.A. Channels available but not in use: N.A.

Basic Service
Subscribers: 721.
Programming (received off-air): WBTW (Antenna TV, CBS, MNT) Florence; WECT (Bounce TV, NBC) Wilmington; WSFX-TV (FOX, This TV) Wilmington; WUNJ-TV (PBS) Wilmington; WWAY (ABC, CBS, CW, Retro TV) Wilmington.
Programming (via satellite): A&E; AMC; Animal Planet; Cartoon Network; CNBC; CNN; Comedy Central; C-SPAN; C-SPAN 2; CW PLUS; Discovery Channel; Disney Channel; E! HD; ESPN; ESPN2; Food Network; Fox News Channel; Freeform; FX; Golf Channel; GSN; Hallmark Channel; HGTV; History; HLN; Lifetime; MTV; Nickelodeon; QVC; Spike TV; Syfy; TBS; The Weather Channel; TLC; TNT; Travel Channel; Trinity Broadcasting Network (TBN); TV Land; USA Network; VH1; WGN America.
Fee: $75.00 installation; $69.25 monthly.

Digital Basic Service
Subscribers: N.A.
Programming (via satellite): BBC America; Bloomberg Television; Bravo; CMT; Destination America; Discovery Kids Channel; Discovery Life Channel; DMX Music; ESPN Classic; ESPNews; Fuse; FYI; Great American Country; History International; IFC; Investigation Discovery; LMN; MBC America; MTV Classic; MTV2; National Geographic Channel; Nick Jr.; Nicktoons; OWN; Oprah Winfrey Network; Science Channel; TeenNick; The Word Network; Turner Classic Movies; WE tv.
Fee: $18.90 monthly.

Digital Expanded Basic Service
Subscribers: N.A.
Programming (via satellite): FOX College Sports Central; FOX College Sports Pacific; Fox Sports 1; FXM; NBCSN; Outdoor Channel.
Fee: $2.95 monthly.

Digital Pay Service 1
Pay Units: N.A.
Programming (via satellite): Cinemax (multiplexed); Flix; HBO (multiplexed); Showtime (multiplexed); Starz (multiplexed); Starz Encore (multiplexed); The Movie Channel (multiplexed).
Fee: $7.00 monthly (Cinemax), $9.00 monthly (Starz/Encore), $11.00 monthly (Showtime/TMC/Flix), $12.00 monthly (HBO).

Video-On-Demand: No

Internet Service
Operational: Yes.
Subscribers: 118.
Fee: $46.95 monthly.

Telephone Service
Digital: Operational
Miles of Plant: 28.0 (coaxial); None (fiber optic). Homes passed: 803.
President: Robert Stemler. Station Manager & Chief Technician: John Hockenberry.
Ownership: Tele-Media Corp. (MSO).

BATH (town)—Red's TV Cable Inc, PO Box 202, Farmville, NC 27828-0202. Phone: 252-753-3074. E-mail: cable@redcable.com. Web Site: http://www.redscable.com. Also serves Beaufort County (unincorporated areas). ICA: NC0173.
TV Market Ranking: 84 (BATH (TOWN), Beaufort County (unincorporated areas)).
Channel capacity: N.A. Channels available but not in use: N.A.

Basic Service
Subscribers: N.A.
Programming (received off-air): WFXI (Bounce TV, FOX, MNT) Morehead City; WNCT-TV (CBS, CW) Greenville; WRAL-TV (NBC, This TV) Raleigh; WUNK-TV (PBS) Greenville.
Programming (via satellite): Electronic Program Guide; CNN; Comcast SportsNet Mid-Atlantic; ESPN; Freeform; Lifetime; QVC; TBS; The Weather Channel; TNT; Turner Classic Movies; USA Network; WGN America.
Fee: $50.00 installation.

Expanded Basic Service 1
Subscribers: N.A.
Programming (via satellite): CNBC; C-SPAN; Spike TV.
Fee: $45.00 installation; $13.00 monthly.

Digital Basic Service
Subscribers: N.A.
Fee: $50.00 installation; $4.95 monthly.

Pay Service 1
Pay Units: N.A.
Programming (via satellite): Cinemax; HBO; Showtime; Starz Encore; The Movie Channel.
Fee: $8.00 - $11.00 monthly (each).

Internet Service
Operational: Yes.
Broadband Service: In-house.
Fee: $39.95 monthly.

Telephone Service
None
Miles of Plant: 16.0 (coaxial); None (fiber optic).
General Manager: Frank Styers.
Ownership: Red's TV Cable Inc.

BELHAVEN—Belhaven Cable TV, 235 Pamlico St, PO Box 8, Belhaven, NC 27810. Phone: 252-943-3736. Fax: 252-943-3738. E-mail: bctv@beaufortco.com. Web Site: http://www.belhavencabletv.com. ICA: NC0130.
TV Market Ranking: 84 (BELHAVEN). Franchise award date: N.A. Franchise expiration date: N.A. Began: February 1, 1983.
Channel capacity: 41 (operating 2-way). Channels available but not in use: N.A.

Basic Service
Subscribers: 227.
Programming (received off-air): WCTI-TV (ABC, Decades, Movies!) New Bern; WFXI (Bounce TV, FOX, MNT) Morehead City; WITN-TV (MeTV, MNT, NBC) Washington; WNCT-TV (CBS, CW) Greenville; WUND-TV (PBS) Edenton.
Programming (via satellite): A&E; BET; Cartoon Network; CNBC; CNN; Comedy Central; C-SPAN; Discovery Channel; Disney Channel; ESPN; Fox News Channel; Freeform; Golf Channel; HGTV; History; HLN; Lifetime; MTV; Nickelodeon; Outdoor Channel; QVC; TBS; The Weather Channel; TLC; Trinity Broadcasting Network (TBN); WGN America.
Fee: $35.95 installation; $42.45 monthly.

Expanded Basic Service 1
Subscribers: 50.
Programming (via satellite): AMC; CMT; ESPN2; FX; Spike TV; Syfy; Turner Classic Movies; USA Network.
Fee: $6.00 monthly.

Digital Basic Service
Subscribers: N.A.
Programming (via satellite): BBC America; Discovery Digital Networks; DMX Music; Nick 2; Nick Jr.; TeenNick.
Fee: $9.95 monthly.

Pay Service 1
Pay Units: N.A.
Programming (via satellite): Cinemax; HBO; Showtime.
Fee: $10.00 monthly (Cinemax or Showtime), $12.00 monthly (HBO).

Digital Pay Service 1
Pay Units: N.A.
Programming (via satellite): Cinemax (multiplexed); Flix; HBO (multiplexed); Showtime (multiplexed); Starz (multiplexed); Starz Encore (multiplexed); Sundance TV; The Movie Channel (multiplexed).

Video-On-Demand: Yes

Internet Service
Operational: Yes, DSL & dial-up.
Fee: $50.00 installation; $39.95 monthly; $5.00 modem lease; $99.99 modem purchase.

Telephone Service
Analog: Operational
Fee: $51.94 monthly
Digital: Not Operational
Miles of Plant: 20.0 (coaxial); None (fiber optic). Homes passed: 900.
General Manager: Ben Johnson. Chief Technologist: Tim Fields. Marketing Director: Pleasant Sanders. Corporate Secretary: Corki Leverett.
Ownership: Belhaven Cable TV Inc.

BELHAVEN—TriCounty Telecom, 2193 NC 99 Hwy South, PO Box 520, Belhaven, NC 27810-0520. Phones: 252-927-8000; 252-964-8000. Fax: 252-964-2211. E-mail: questions@gotricounty.com. Web Site: http://www.gotricounty.biz. Also serves Camp Leach, Douglas Crossroads, Hyde County (portions), Pamlico Beach, Pantego, Pike Road, Pinetown, Smithton, Terra Ceia & White Post. ICA: NC0182.
TV Market Ranking: 84 (BELHAVEN, Camp Leach, Douglas Crossroads, Pamlico Beach, Pantego, Pike Road, Pinetown, Smithton, Terra Ceia, White Post); Outside TV Markets (Hyde County (portions)). Franchise award date: September 9, 2007. Franchise expiration date: N.A. Began: April 19, 1993.
Channel capacity: N.A. Channels available but not in use: N.A.

Digital Basic Service
Subscribers: N.A.
Programming (via satellite): C-SPAN; C-SPAN 2; CW PLUS; DMX Music; INSP; Trinity Broadcasting Network (TBN); WGN America.
Fee: $50.00 installation; $22.45 monthly; $5.95 converter.

Digital Expanded Basic Service
Subscribers: N.A.
Programming (via satellite): A&E; AMC; Animal Planet; BET; Boomerang; Bravo; Cartoon Network; CMT; CNBC; CNN; Comedy Central; Destination America; Discovery Channel; Disney Channel; E! HD; ESPN; ESPN Classic; ESPN2; EVINE Live; Food Network; Fox News Channel; FOX Sports Carolinas; Freeform; FX; HGTV; History; HLN; Lifetime; LMN; Mid-Atlantic Sports Network (MASN); MTV; National Geographic Channel; Nickelodeon; Oxygen; QVC; Science Channel; Spike TV; Sprout; Syfy; TBS; The Weather Channel; TLC; TNT; Travel Channel; TV Land; USA Network; VH1.
Fee: $37.50 monthly.

Digital Expanded Basic Service 2
Subscribers: N.A.
Programming (via satellite): A&E HD; Animal Planet HD; BBC America; Bloomberg Television; CBS Sports Network; Chiller; Cloo; CMT; Cooking Channel; Destination America; Discovery Channel HD; Discovery Kids Channel; Discovery Life Channel; Disney Channel HD; Disney XD; DIY Network; ESPN HD; ESPN2 HD; ESPNews; ESPNU; FamilyNet; Food Network HD; Fox Business Network; FOX College Sports Central; FOX College Sports Pacific; Fox News HD; Fox Sports 1; Freeform HD; Fuse; FX HD; FXM; FYI; Golf Channel; Great American Country; GSN; Hallmark Channel; Hallmark Movie Channel HD; Hallmark Movies & Mysteries; HD Theater; HGTV HD; History HD; History International; IFC; Investigation Discovery; LMN; MSNBC; MTV Classic; MTV Hits; MTV2; Nat Geo WILD; National Geographic Channel HD; NBCSN; Nick Jr.; Nicktoons; Outdoor Channel; Outdoor Channel 2 HD; OWN; Oprah Winfrey Network; RFD-TV; Science HD; Syfy HD; TeenNick; TLC HD; Travel Channel HD; truTV; Turner Classic Movies; Universal HD; UP; USA Network HD; VH1 Soul; WE tv.
Fee: $20.00 monthly.

Digital Pay Service 1
Pay Units: N.A.
Programming (via satellite): Cinemax (multiplexed); Cinemax HD; HBO (multiplexed); HBO HD; Showtime (multiplexed); Showtime HD; Starz (multiplexed); Starz Encore (multiplexed); Starz HD; The Movie Channel (multiplexed).
Fee: $7.75 - $14.50 monthly (each); $5.95 converter.

Video-On-Demand: No

Pay-Per-View
Fresh (delivered digitally); iN DEMAND (delivered digitally); Playboy TV (delivered digitally).

Internet Service
Operational: No, DSL & dial-up.

Telephone Service
Analog: Operational
Miles of Plant: 277.0 (coaxial); 65.0 (fiber optic). Homes passed: 3,878.
Chief Executive Officer & General Manager: Greg Coltrain. Plant Manager: Fred Smith. Marketing & Media Relations Manager: Terry Raupe.
Ownership: Tri-County Communications Inc.

BENSON—Charter Communications. Now served by ANGIER, NC [NC0194]. ICA: NC0141.

BLACK MOUNTAIN—Formerly served by Tri-Star Communications. No longer in operation. ICA: NC0067.

BOONE—Charter Communications. Now served by HICKORY, NC [NC0009]. ICA: NC0023.

BREVARD—Comporium Communications, 190 East Main St, PO Box 1177, Brevard, NC 28712. Phones: 828-884-3950; 828-884-2671. Fax: 828-885-2300. Web Site: http://www.comporium.com. Also serves

2017 Edition
D-551

North Carolina—Cable Systems

Lake Toxaway, Pisgah Forest, Rosman & Transylvania County. ICA: NC0053.

TV Market Ranking: 46 (BREVARD, Lake Toxaway, Rosman, Transylvania County (portions)); Outside TV Markets (Transylvania County (portions)). Franchise award date: January 1, 1979. Franchise expiration date: N.A. Began: February 19, 1980.

Channel capacity: 22 (not 2-way capable). Channels available but not in use: N.A.

Basic Service
Subscribers: 4,882.
Programming (received off-air): WHNS (COZI TV, Escape, FOX) Greenville; WLOS (ABC, Antenna TV) Asheville; WMYA-TV (MNT, The Country Network) Anderson; WSPA-TV (CBS, MeTV) Spartanburg; WUNF-TV (PBS) Asheville; WYCW (CW) Asheville; WYFF (NBC, Movies!) Greenville; allband FM.
Programming (via satellite): C-SPAN; Freeform; Lifetime; The Weather Channel.
Fee: $25.00 installation; $15.95 monthly.

Expanded Basic Service 1
Subscribers: N.A.
Programming (via satellite): A&E; AMC; Animal Planet; BET; Cartoon Network; CMT; CNBC; CNN; C-SPAN 2; Discovery Channel; Disney Channel; E! HD; ESPN; ESPN2; Fox News Channel; Fox Sports 1; Golf Channel; HGTV; History; HLN; MTV; Nickelodeon; Spike TV; Syfy; TBS; TLC; TNT; Travel Channel; Trinity Broadcasting Network (TBN); USA Network; VH1; WGN America.
Fee: $30.70 monthly.

Pay Service 1
Pay Units: 161.
Programming (via satellite): Cinemax (multiplexed).
Fee: $10.95 monthly.

Pay Service 2
Pay Units: 493.
Programming (via satellite): HBO (multiplexed).
Fee: $11.95 monthly.

Pay Service 3
Pay Units: 68.
Programming (via satellite): Showtime (multiplexed).
Fee: $10.95 monthly.

Pay Service 4
Pay Units: 54.
Programming (via satellite): The Movie Channel (multiplexed).
Fee: $10.95 monthly.

Video-On-Demand: No

Internet Service
Operational: Yes.

Telephone Service
Analog: Operational
Miles of Plant: 866.0 (coaxial); 174.0 (fiber optic). Homes passed: 14,227.
Executive Vice President, Marketing: John Barnes Jr. Executive Vice President, Cable TV & Affiliate Relations: William C. Beaty Jr. Chief Technician: Gary Butler. Broadband Engineering Manager: Brian Bendt. Customer Service Manager: Lorretta Sanders.
Ownership: Comporium Communications (MSO).

BRYSON CITY—Zito Media, 102 S Main St, PO Box 665, Coudersport, PA 16915. Phones: 814-260-9055; 800-365-6988. E-mail: info@zitomedia.com. Web Site: http://www.zitomedia.com. Also serves Swain County (portions). ICA: NC0193.

TV Market Ranking: Outside TV Markets (BRYSON CITY, Swain County (portions)). Franchise award date: February 10, 1981.

Franchise expiration date: N.A. Began: October 1, 1981.
Channel capacity: N.A. Channels available but not in use: N.A.

Basic Service
Subscribers: 651.
Programming (received off-air): WHNS (COZI TV, Escape, FOX) Greenville; WLOS (ABC, Antenna TV) Asheville; WSPA-TV (CBS, MeTV) Spartanburg; WUNE-TV (PBS) Linville; WYFF (NBC, Movies!) Greenville.
Programming (via satellite): Comedy Central; C-SPAN; QVC; TBS; TLC; WGN America.
Fee: $49.95 installation; $20.72 monthly; $1.78 converter.

Expanded Basic Service 1
Subscribers: N.A.
Programming (via satellite): A&E; AMC; Animal Planet; Cartoon Network; CMT; CNN; Discovery Channel; Disney Channel; ESPN; ESPN2; Freeform; FX; HGTV; History; HLN; Lifetime; MTV; Nickelodeon; Spike TV; The Weather Channel; TNT; Turner Classic Movies; TV Land; USA Network; VH1.
Fee: $18.00 monthly.

Digital Basic Service
Subscribers: N.A.
Programming (via satellite): BBC America; Bloomberg Television; Discovery Digital Networks; DMX Music; ESPN Classic; Golf Channel; GSN; ION Television; Outdoor Channel; Syfy; Trinity Broadcasting Network (TBN).
Fee: $13.95 monthly.

Pay Service 1
Pay Units: N.A.
Programming (via satellite): HBO (multiplexed); Showtime (multiplexed); The Movie Channel (multiplexed).
Fee: $11.95 monthly (HBO), $12.96 monthly (Showtime/TMC).

Digital Pay Service 1
Pay Units: N.A.
Programming (via satellite): Cinemax (multiplexed); HBO (multiplexed); Showtime (multiplexed); Starz (multiplexed); Starz Encore (multiplexed); The Movie Channel (multiplexed).
Fee: $7.95 monthly (Starz/Encore), $18.95 monthly (Cinemax or Showtime/TMC), $20.95 monthly (HBO).

Video-On-Demand: No

Pay-Per-View
special events (delivered digitally); Sports PPV (delivered digitally).

Internet Service
Operational: Yes. Began: November 1, 2004.
Broadband Service: Rapid High Speed Internet.
Fee: $50.00 installation; $39.95 monthly.

Telephone Service
Digital: Operational
Miles of Plant: 87.0 (coaxial); 12.0 (fiber optic). Homes passed: 2,974.
President: James Rigas.
Ownership: Zito Media (MSO).

BUNCOMBE COUNTY (northern portion)—Charter Communications. Now served by ASHEVILLE, NC [NC0012]. ICA: NC0179.

BUNN—Formerly served by Adelphia Communications. Now served by Time Warner Cable, RALEIGH, NC [NC0003]. ICA: NC0114.

BUNNLEVEL—Formerly served by Carolina Cable Partnership. No longer in operation. ICA: NC0160.

BURKE COUNTY—Charter Communications. Now served by HICKORY, NC [NC0009]. ICA: NC0028.

BURLINGTON—Time Warner Cable. Now served by GREENSBORO, NC [NC0006]. ICA: NC0015.

BURNSVILLE—Charter Communications. Now served by HICKORY, NC [NC0009]. ICA: NC0128.

BURNSVILLE—Country Cablevision Inc, 9449 State Hwy 197 South, Burnsville, NC 28714-9633. Phones: 800-722-4074; 828-682-4074. Fax: 828-682-6895. Web Site: http://ccvn.com. Also serves Little Switzerland, Madison County, Mitchell County, Spruce Pine & Yancey County. ICA: NC0099.

TV Market Ranking: 46 (BURNSVILLE, Little Switzerland, Madison County, Mitchell County (portions), Yancey County (portions)); Below 100 (Spruce Pine, Mitchell County (portions)). Franchise award date: N.A. Franchise expiration date: N.A. Began: September 1, 1990.

Channel capacity: N.A. Channels available but not in use: N.A.

Basic Service
Subscribers: 2,965.
Programming (received off-air): WBTV (Bounce TV, CBS) Charlotte; WCYB-TV (CW, Decades, NBC) Bristol; WHNS (COZI TV, Escape, FOX) Greenville; WJHL-TV (ABC, CBS, MeTV) Johnson City; WKPT-TV (COZI TV, Escape, MeTV, MNT) Kingsport; WLOS (ABC, Antenna TV) Asheville; WMYA-TV (MNT, The Country Network) Anderson; WSPA-TV (CBS, MeTV) Spartanburg; WUNC-TV (PBS) Chapel Hill; WYCW (CW) Asheville; WYFF (NBC, Movies!) Greenville.
Programming (via satellite): A&E; AMC; Animal Planet; Cartoon Network; CMT; CNBC; CNN; Comedy Central; C-SPAN; C-SPAN 2; Discovery Channel; Disney Channel; E! HD; ESPN; ESPN Classic; ESPN2; EVINE Live; Food Network; Fox News Channel; FOX Sports South/SportSouth; Freeform; FX; Great American Country; Hallmark Channel; HGTV; History; HLN; ION Television; Lifetime; MTV; National Geographic Channel; Nickelodeon; Outdoor Channel; Pop; QVC; Spike TV; Syfy; TBS; The Weather Channel; TLC; TNT; Travel Channel; Trinity Broadcasting Network (TBN); Turner Classic Movies; TV Land; USA Network; VH1; WGN America.
Fee: $39.00 installation; $53.99 monthly.

Digital Basic Service
Subscribers: N.A.
Programming (via satellite): BBC America; Bloomberg Television; Bravo; Discovery Life Channel; Disney XD; DMX Music; ESPN Classic; ESPN2; ESPNews; Fox Sports 1; FSN Digital Atlantic; FSN Digital Central; FSN Digital Pacific; Fuse; FXM; FYI; Golf Channel; Great American Country; GSN; HGTV; History; History International; IFC; International Television (ITV); National Geographic Channel; NBCSN; Nick Jr.; Nicktoons; Outdoor Channel; Ovation; Syfy; TeenNick; Trinity Broadcasting Network (TBN); Turner Classic Movies; WE tv.

Digital Pay Service 1
Pay Units: 101.
Programming (via satellite): Cinemax (multiplexed).
Fee: $13.00 monthly.

Digital Pay Service 2
Pay Units: 201.
Programming (via satellite): HBO (multiplexed).
Fee: $13.00 monthly.

Digital Pay Service 3
Pay Units: 183.
Programming (via satellite): Starz (multiplexed); Starz Encore (multiplexed).
Fee: $13.00 monthly.

Digital Pay Service 4
Pay Units: 114.
Programming (via satellite): Showtime; The Movie Channel (multiplexed).
Fee: $13.00 monthly.

Video-On-Demand: No

Pay-Per-View
iN DEMAND (delivered digitally); Hot Choice (delivered digitally); Playboy TV (delivered digitally); Fresh (delivered digitally); Shorteez (delivered digitally).

Internet Service
Operational: Yes.
Broadband Service: In-house.
Fee: $29.99-$49.99 monthly; $9.95 modem lease.

Telephone Service
Analog: Not Operational
Digital: Operational
Fee: $29.99-$39.99 monthly
Miles of Plant: 600.0 (coaxial); 40.0 (fiber optic). Homes passed: 12,000.
President: Randall Miller. Secretary-Treasurer: Bryan Hyder. Chief Technician: James McPeters.
Ownership: Ray V. Miller Group.

BUXTON—Charter Communications, PO Box 1996, Kill Devil Hills, NC 27948. Phones: 314-543-2236; 636-207-5100 (Corporate office); 757-539-0713 (Suffolk office); 252-441-1582. Web Site: http://www.charter.com. Also serves Avon, Dare County (portions), Frisco, Hatteras, Rodanthe, Salvo & Waves. ICA: NC0118.

TV Market Ranking: Below 100 (Avon, Dare County (portions), Rodanthe, Salvo, Waves); Outside TV Markets (BUXTON, Frisco, Hatteras). Franchise award date: N.A. Franchise expiration date: N.A. Began: May 1, 1974.

Channel capacity: N.A. Channels available but not in use: N.A.

Digital Basic Service
Subscribers: 2,993.
Programming (via satellite): BBC America; Bloomberg Television; Discovery Digital Networks; DIY Network; ESPN Classic; ESPNews; FOX College Sports Central; FOX College Sports Pacific; Fox Deportes; Fox Sports 2; FXM; FYI; Great American Country; History International; HITS (Headend In The Sky); IFC; LMN; MC; Mid-Atlantic Sports Network (MASN); Nick 2; Nick Jr.; Nicktoons; Sundance TV; TeenNick; TV Guide Interactive Inc.
Fee: $49.99 installation; $34.99 monthly.

Digital Expanded Basic Service
Subscribers: N.A.
Programming (via satellite): Animal Planet; BET; Bravo; Cartoon Network; CMT; Disney Channel; Disney XD; E! HD; ESPN; ESPN2; Food Network; Fox News Channel; Fox Sports 1; Freeform; Golf Channel; Hallmark Channel; HGTV; History; Lifetime; MSNBC; National Geographic Channel; Oxygen; Syfy; TBS; TLC; TNT; Travel Channel; truTV; TV Land; WE tv.
Fee: $47.99 monthly.

Digital Pay Service 1
Pay Units: N.A.
Programming (via satellite): Cinemax (multiplexed); Flix; HBO (multiplexed);

Cable Systems—North Carolina

Access the most current data instantly
www.warren-news.com/factbook.htm

Showtime (multiplexed); Starz (multiplexed); Starz Encore (multiplexed); The Movie Channel (multiplexed).
Fee: $5.00 installation; $11.95 monthly (Cinemax, HBO, Showtime or TMC).
Video-On-Demand: No
Pay-Per-View
iN DEMAND (delivered digitally); Playboy TV (delivered digitally); Fresh (delivered digitally); Shorteez (delivered digitally).
Internet Service
Operational: Yes.
Subscribers: 12,481.
Broadband Service: Charter Internet.
Fee: $29.99 monthly.
Telephone Service
Digital: Operational
Subscribers: 7,541.
Miles of Plant: 198.0 (coaxial); 39.0 (fiber optic). Homes passed: 7,516.
Vice President & General Manager: Anthony Pope. Marketing Director: Brooke Sinclair. Accounting Director: David Sovanski. Technical Operations Director: Joel Sprout. Operations Manager: Tom Ross. Marketing Manager: LaRisa Scales.
Ownership: Charter Communications Inc. (MSO).

BUXTON—Charter Communications. Now served by BUXTON, NC [NC0118]. ICA: NC0110.

CAMDEN COUNTY—Mediacom. Now served by CURRITUCK, NC [NC0083]. ICA: NC0133.

CAMP LEJEUNE—Charter Communications. Now served by ANGIER, NC [NC0194]. ICA: NC0044.

CAMP WESLEY—Time Warner Cable. Now served by CHARLOTTE, NC [NC0001]. ICA: NC0159.

CAROLINA BEACH—Charter Communications. Now served by ANGIER, NC [NC0194]. ICA: NC0041.

CARRBORO—Time Warner Cable. Now served by RALEIGH, NC [NC0003]. ICA: NC0250.

CARY—Time Warner Cable. Now served by RALEIGH, NC [NC0003]. ICA: NC0196.

CEDAR ISLAND—Time Warner Cable. Now served by JACKSONVILLE, NC [NC0025]. ICA: NC0249.

CHAPEL HILL—Time Warner Cable. Now served by RALEIGH, NC [NC0003]. ICA: NC0017.

CHARLOTTE—Time Warner Cable, 3140 West Arrowood Rd, Charlotte, NC 28273. Phones: 704-938-5144; 704-378-2500. Fax: 704-504-1997. Web Site: http://www.timewarnercable.com. Also serves Albemarle, Anson County, Ansonville, Badin, Belmont, Belwood, Bessemer City, Boiling Springs, Cabarrus County, Camp Wesley, Casar, Cherryville, China Grove, Cleveland, Cleveland County, Concord, Cornelius, Cramerton, Dallas, Davidson, Dobbins Heights, Earl, East Spencer, Ellerbe, Fairview (town), Faith, Fallston, Gaston County, Gastonia, Gold Hill, Granite Quarry, Grover, Hamlet, Harmony, Harrisburg, Hemby Bridge, Hoffman, Huntersville, Indian Trail, Iredell County, Kannapolis, Kings Mountain, Kingstown, Lake Park, Landis, Lattimore, Lawndale, Lilesville, Locust, Lowell, Marshville, Marvin (village), Matthews, McAdenville, Mecklenburg County (unincorporated areas), Midland, Mineral Springs (town), Mint Hill, Misenheimer, Monroe, Montgomery County (portions), Mooresboro, Mooresville, Mount Gilead, Mount Holly, Mount Pleasant, New London, Norwood, Oakboro, Patterson Springs, Pineville, Polkville, Ranlo, Red Cross, Richfield, Richmond County, Rockingham, Rockwell, Rowan County, Salisbury, Shelby, Spencer, Spencer Mountain, Stallings, Stanfield, Stanley, Stanly County, Statesville, Troutman, Union County, Unionville (town), Waco, Wadesboro, Waxhaw, Weddington, Wesley Chapel & Wingate, NC; Clover, Fort Mill, Lancaster County (portions), McBee, Patrick, York & York County (portions), SC. ICA: NC0001.
TV Market Ranking: 42 (Anson County (portions), Belmont, Bessemer City, Cabarrus County, CHARLOTTE, Cherryville, China Grove, Cleveland, Clover, Concord, Cornelius, Cramerton, Dallas, Davidson, Fairview (town), Faith, Fort Mill, Gaston County, Gastonia, Harrisburg, Huntersville, Indian Trail, Kannapolis, Kings Mountain, Kingstown, Lake Park, Lancaster County (portions), Landis, Locust, Lowell, Marshville, Marvin (village), Matthews, McAdenville, Mecklenburg County (unincorporated areas), Midland, Mineral Springs (town), Mint Hill, MONROE, Mooresville, Mount Holly, Mount Pleasant, Oakboro, Pineville, Ranlo, Rockwell, Shelby, Spencer Mountain, Stallings, Stanfield, Stanley, Stanly County (portions), Union County, Unionville (town), Waxhaw, Weddington, Wesley Chapel, Wingate, York, York County (portions)); 42,46 (Cleveland County (portions), Grover, Patterson Springs); 42,47 (East Spencer, Rowan County (portions), Salisbury); 46 (Boiling Springs, Earl, Lattimore, Mooresboro); 47 (Camp Wesley, Gold Hill, Harmony, Spencer); 73 (Richmond County (portions)); Below 100 (Badin, Belwood, Casar, Fallston, Granite Quarry, Hemby Bridge, Iredell County (portions), Lawndale, Misenheimer, New London, Polkville, Red Cross, Richfield, Troutman, Waco, Albemarle, Statesville, York County (portions), Cleveland County (portions)); Outside TV Markets (Ansonville, Dobbins Heights, Ellerbe, Hamlet, Hoffman, Iredell County (portions), Lilesville, McBee, Montgomery County (portions), Mount Gilead, Norwood, Patrick, Rockingham, Wadesboro, Anson County (portions), Stanly County (portions), Richmond County (portions)). Franchise award date: February 1, 1967. Franchise expiration date: N.A. Began: February 1, 1967.
Channel capacity: 75 (operating 2-way). Channels available but not in use: N.A.
Basic Service
Subscribers: 339,334.
Programming (received off-air): WAXN-TV (getTV, IND) Kannapolis; WBTV (Bounce TV, CBS) Charlotte; WCCB (CW, MeTV) Charlotte; WCNC-TV (NBC) Charlotte; WHKY-TV (IND, PBJ, Retro TV, Tuff TV) Hickory; WJZY (Antenna TV, FOX, Heroes & Icons, Movies!, The Country Network) Belmont; WMYT-TV (Buzzr, IND, MNT) Rock Hill; WNSC-TV (PBS) Rock Hill; WSOC-TV (ABC) Charlotte; WTVI (PBS) Charlotte; WUNG-TV (PBS) Concord.
Programming (via satellite): WGN America.
Fee: $42.50 installation; $12.99 monthly; $3.35 converter.

Expanded Basic Service 1
Subscribers: N.A.
Programming (via satellite): A&E; AMC; Animal Planet; BET; Bravo; Cartoon Network; CMT; CNBC; CNN; Comedy Central; C-SPAN; C-SPAN 2; Discovery Channel; Disney Channel; E! HD; ESPN; ESPN Classic; ESPN2; EVINE Live; EWTN Global Catholic Network; Food Network; Fox News Channel; Fox Sports 1; FOX Sports South/SportSouth; Freeform; FX; Golf Channel; Hallmark Channel; HGTV; History; HLN; INSP; Lifetime; LMN; MSNBC; MTV; National Geographic Channel; NBCSN; Nickelodeon; OWN: Oprah Winfrey Network; Oxygen; Pop; QVC; Spike TV; Syfy; TBS; The Weather Channel; TLC; TNT; Travel Channel; truTV; Turner Classic Movies; TV Land; Univision Studios; USA Network; WE tv.
Fee: $39.95 monthly.
Digital Basic Service
Subscribers: N.A.
Programming (via satellite): BBC America; Bloomberg Television; Boomerang; Cooking Channel; C-SPAN 3; Discovery Life Channel; Disney Channel; Disney XD; DIY Network; FamilyNet; Fuse; FYI; Great American Country; GSN; History International; IFC; INSP; MC; MTV Classic; MTV2; Nick Jr.; Nicktoons; Ovation; TeenNick.
Fee: $6.42 converter.
Digital Expanded Basic Service
Subscribers: N.A.
Programming (via satellite): ESPNews; Fox Sports 2; FSN Digital Atlantic; FSN Digital Central; FSN Digital Pacific; NBA TV; Outdoor Channel; Tennis Channel.
Digital Pay Service 1
Pay Units: N.A.
Programming (via satellite): Cinemax (multiplexed); Deutsche Welle TV; Flix; FXM; HBO (multiplexed); HITS (Headend In The Sky); RAI Italia; Saigon Broadcasting Television Network (SBTN); Showtime (multiplexed); Starz (multiplexed); Starz Encore (multiplexed); Sundance TV; The Movie Channel (multiplexed); TV5, La Television International; WAM! America's Kidz Network; Zee TV.
Fee: $11.95 monthly (Cinemax, HBO, Showtime/TMC or Starz), $9.95 or $14.95 monthly (international channels).
Video-On-Demand: Yes
Pay-Per-View
iN DEMAND (delivered digitally); ESPN Now (delivered digitally); Adult (delivered digitally); Sports PPV (delivered digitally).
Internet Service
Operational: Yes.
Subscribers: 376,889.
Broadband Service: Road Runner, AOL, EarthLink.
Fee: $39.95 installation; $46.95 monthly.
Telephone Service
Digital: Operational
Subscribers: 191,804.
Fee: $39.95 monthly
Miles of Plant: 25,757.0 (coaxial); 1,476.0 (fiber optic). Homes passed: 904,061.

President, Time Warner Cable Charlotte: Mike Munley. Vice President, Technical Operations: Mike Cullim. Vice President, Marketing & Sales: Eric Franey. Vice President, Engineering: Richard Newcomb. Public Affairs Director: Jessica Graham. Technical Operations Director: Donnie Stone. Government Affairs Director: Michael Tanck.
Ownership: Time Warner Cable (MSO).; Advance/Newhouse Partnership (MSO).

CHEROKEE INDIAN RESERVATION—Cherokee Cablevision, 55 John Crowe Rd, PO Box 487, Cherokee, NC 28719-0487. Phone: 828-497-4861. Fax: 828-497-4983. Also serves Qualla. ICA: NC0106.
TV Market Ranking: Outside TV Markets (CHEROKEE INDIAN RESERVATION, Qualla). Franchise award date: N.A. Franchise expiration date: N.A. Began: March 1, 1980.
Channel capacity: 24 (not 2-way capable). Channels available but not in use: N.A.
Basic Service
Subscribers: N.A.
Programming (received off-air): WDEF-TV (Bounce TV, CBS, Escape) Chattanooga; WETP-TV (PBS) Sneedville; WLOS (ABC, Antenna TV) Asheville; WUNE-TV (PBS) Linville; WYFF (NBC, Movies!) Greenville.
Programming (via satellite): CMT; CNN; C-SPAN; Discovery Channel; Disney Channel; ESPN; MTV; Nickelodeon; Spike TV; TBS; The Weather Channel; TLC; TNT; USA Network; WGN America.
Fee: $25.00 installation.
Pay Service 1
Pay Units: N.A.
Programming (via satellite): Cinemax; Showtime.
Fee: $10.00 monthly (each).
Video-On-Demand: No
Internet Service
Operational: Yes.
Broadband Service: IBBS.
Telephone Service
None
Miles of Plant: 200.0 (coaxial); None (fiber optic).
General Manager: Delores Murphy.
Ownership: Cherokee Cablevision Inc.

CHERRY POINT—Time Warner Cable. Now served by JACKSONVILLE, NC [NC0025]. ICA: NC0077.

CHINQUAPIN—Formerly served by Charter Communications. No longer in operation. ICA: NC0223.

CHURCHLAND—Piedmont Communications Services, Inc, 191 Reeds Baptist Church Rd, Lexington, NC 27295. Phone: 336-787-5433. E-mail: ptmc@ptmc.net. Web Site: http://ptmc.net. Also serves Davidson County (western portion), Reeds Cross Roads & Tyro. ICA: NC0212.
TV Market Ranking: 47 (CHURCHLAND, Davidson County (western portion), Reeds Cross Roads, Tyro). Franchise award

2017 Edition

D-553

North Carolina—Cable Systems

date: N.A. Franchise expiration date: N.A. Began: January 1, 1989.
Channel capacity: 65 (operating 2-way). Channels available but not in use: N.A.

Basic Service
Subscribers: 2,547.
Programming (received off-air): WBTV (Bounce TV, CBS) Charlotte; WCWG (Bounce TV, CW, Estrella TV, IND) Lexington; WFMY-TV (CBS) Greensboro; WGHP (Antenna TV, FOX) High Point; WGPX-TV (ION) Burlington; WLXI (IND) Greensboro; WMYV (MNT) Greensboro; WUNL-TV (PBS) Winston-Salem; WXII-TV (MeTV, NBC) Winston-Salem; WXLV-TV (ABC, The Country Network) Winston-Salem.
Programming (via satellite): WGN America.
Fee: $62.95 monthly.

Expanded Basic Service 1
Subscribers: N.A.
Programming (via satellite): A&E; AMC; Animal Planet; BET; Cartoon Network; CMT; CNBC; CNN; Comedy Central; C-SPAN; Discovery Channel; Disney Channel; Disney XD; ESPN; ESPN Classic; ESPN2; Food Network; Fox News Channel; Fox Sports 1; FOX Sports South/SportSouth; Freeform; FX; Golf Channel; Great American Country; Hallmark Channel; HGTV; History; HLN; INSP; Lifetime; LMN; MSNBC; MTV; National Geographic Channel; NBCSN; Nickelodeon; Outdoor Channel; Pop; QVC; Spike TV; Syfy; TBS; The Weather Channel; TLC; TNT; Travel Channel; truTV; TV Land; USA Network; VH1.
Fee: $32.00 monthly.

Digital Basic Service
Subscribers: N.A.
Programming (via satellite): BBC America; Bloomberg Television; Bravo; Cloo; CMT; C-SPAN 2; Discovery Life Channel; DMX Music; ESPNews; Flix; FSN Digital Atlantic; FSN Digital Central; FSN Digital Pacific; Fuse; FXM; FYI; GSN; History International; HITS (Headend In The Sky); IFC; MTV Classic; MTV2; Nick Jr.; Nicktoons; TeenNick; Turner Classic Movies; WE tv.
Fee: $10.00 monthly, $8.95 monthly (Spanish Tier).

Pay Service 1
Pay Units: N.A.
Programming (via satellite): Cinemax; HBO.
Fee: $8.95 monthly (Cinemax), $9.95 monthly (HBO).

Digital Pay Service 1
Pay Units: N.A.
Programming (via satellite): Cinemax (multiplexed); HBO (multiplexed); Showtime (multiplexed); Starz (multiplexed); Starz Encore (multiplexed); The Movie Channel (multiplexed).
Fee: $8.95 monthly (Cinemax, Showtime or TMC), $9.95 monthly (HBO), $12.95 monthly (Starz /Encore).

Video-On-Demand: No

Pay-Per-View
Playboy TV (delivered digitally); Fresh (delivered digitally); iN DEMAND.

Internet Service
Operational: Yes, DSL & dial-up. Began: January 31, 2003.
Broadband Service: InfoAve.net.
Fee: $19.95-$39.95 monthly.

Telephone Service
None
Miles of Plant: 250.0 (coaxial); None (fiber optic). Homes passed: 4,160.
President: Gary L. Brown. Chief Operating Officer: Amy R. Hanson. General Manager: Mike Stanley. Chief Technician: Bill Purcell.
Ownership: Piedmont Telephone Membership Corp.

COLERAIN—Mediacom, 910 NC Highway 32 South, PO Box 580, Plymouth, NC 27962. Phones: 845-695-2762; 252-793-1570. Fax: 252-793-6135. Web Site: http://www.mediacomcable.com. Also serves Bertie County (eastern portion), Merry Hill, Powellsville & Windsor. ICA: NC0255.
TV Market Ranking: 84 (Bertie County (eastern portion), Windsor); Below 100 (Bertie County (eastern portion)); Outside TV Markets (COLERAIN, Merry Hill, Powellsville, Bertie County (eastern portion)).
Channel capacity: N.A. Channels available but not in use: N.A.

Basic Service
Subscribers: 526.
Fee: $41.00 monthly.
Vice President, Financial Reporting: Kenneth J. Kohrs.
Ownership: Mediacom LLC (MSO).

COLUMBIA—Mediacom. Now served by PLYMOUTH (town), NC [NC0085]. ICA: NC0154.

COLUMBUS COUNTY (central portion)—Formerly served by Carolina Cable Partnership. No longer in operation. ICA: NC0197.

COLUMBUS COUNTY (unincorporated areas)—Time Warner Cable. Now served by WILMINGTON, NC [NC0007]. ICA: NC0155.

CONWAY—Mediacom, 910 NC Highway 32 South, PO Box 580, Plymouth, NC 27962. Phones: 845-695-2762; 252-793-1570. Fax: 252-793-6135. Web Site: http://www.mediacomcable.com. Also serves Bertie County (westhern portion), Jackson, Kelford, Lewiston, Milwaukee, Northampton County (portions), Rich Square, Roxobel, Seaboard, Severn & Woodland. ICA: NC0115.
TV Market Ranking: 84 (Bertie County (westhern portion)); Below 100 (Lewiston, Northampton County (portions), Bertie County (westhern portion)); Outside TV Markets (Jackson, Kelford, Milwaukee, Northampton County (portions), Roxobel, Seaboard, Severn, Woodland, CONWAY, Rich Square, Bertie County (westhern portion)). Franchise award date: March 1, 1984. Franchise expiration date: N.A. Began: January 23, 1985.
Channel capacity: N.A. Channels available but not in use: N.A.

Basic Service
Subscribers: 1,014.
Programming (received off-air): WAVY-TV (Bounce TV, NBC) Portsmouth; WCTI-TV (ABC, Decades, Movies!) New Bern; WGNT (Antenna TV, CW) Portsmouth; WHRO-TV (PBS) Hampton-Norfolk; WITN-TV (MeTV, MNT, NBC) Washington; WPXV-TV (ION) Norfolk; WSKY-TV (Escape, IND, Laff) Manteo; WTKR (CBS) Norfolk; WTVZ-TV (MNT, The Country Network) Norfolk; WUND-TV (PBS) Edenton; WVBT (FOX) Virginia Beach; WVEC (ABC) Hampton.
Programming (via satellite): History; Pop.
Fee: $45.00 installation; $41.00 monthly.

Expanded Basic Service 1
Subscribers: N.A.
Programming (via satellite): A&E; AMC; Animal Planet; AXS TV; BET; Bravo; Cartoon Network; CMT; CNBC; CNN; Comedy Central; C-SPAN; Discovery Channel; Disney Channel; Disney XD; ESPN; ESPN2; Food Network; Fox News Channel; Fox Sports 1; Freeform; FX; Hallmark Channel; HD Theater; HGTV; HLN; INSP; Lifetime; MSNBC; MTV; Nickelodeon; Outdoor Channel; QVC; Spike TV; Syfy; TBS; The Weather Channel; TLC; TNT; Travel Channel; TV Land; Universal HD; USA Network; VH1; WE tv; WGN America.
Fee: $33.49 monthly.

Digital Basic Service
Subscribers: N.A.
Programming (via satellite): BBC America; Bloomberg Television; Discovery Digital Networks; Fuse; FXM; FYI; Golf Channel; GSN; History International; IFC; LMN; MC; MTV2; National Geographic Channel; NBCSN; Nick Jr.; TeenNick; The Word Network; truTV; Turner Classic Movies; Weatherscan.
Fee: $8.00 monthly.

Digital Pay Service 1
Pay Units: N.A.
Programming (via satellite): Cinemax (multiplexed); Flix (multiplexed); HBO (multiplexed); HBO HD; Showtime (multiplexed); Showtime HD; Starz (multiplexed); Starz Encore (multiplexed); Starz HD; Sundance TV (multiplexed); The Movie Channel (multiplexed); The Movie Channel HD.
Fee: $8.00 monthly (Starz/Encore), $9.95 monthly (Cinemax or Showtime/TMC/Flix/Sundance), $13.95 monthly (HBO).

Video-On-Demand: No

Pay-Per-View
ESPN (delivered digitally).

Internet Service
Operational: Yes. Began: January 1, 2002.
Broadband Service: Mediacom High Speed Internet.
Fee: $40.95 monthly; $3.00 modem lease.

Telephone Service
Digital: Operational
Fee: $39.95 monthly
Homes passed: 2,748. Miles of plant included in Plymouth (town).
Vice President, Financial Reporting: Kenneth J. Kohrs. General Manager: Wayne Holiday. Office Manager: Wendy White. Marketing Analyst: Renette Ruffin.
Ownership: Mediacom LLC (MSO).

CONWAY—Mediacom. Now served by CONWAY (formerly Rich Square), NC [NC0115]. ICA: NC0198.

COROLLA—Charter Communications. Now served by KILL DEVIL HILLS, NC [NC0256]. ICA: NC0139.

CRAVEN—Formerly served by Time Warner Cable. No longer in operation. ICA: NC0165.

CRESTON (southern portion)—Zito Media, 102 S Main St, PO Box 665, Coudersport, PA 16915. Phones: 814-260-9055; 800-365-6988. E-mail: info@zitomedia.com. Web Site: http://www.zitomedia.com. ICA: NC0199.
Channel capacity: N.A. Channels available but not in use: N.A.

Basic Service
Subscribers: 2.
Programming (received off-air): WBTV (Bounce TV, CBS) Charlotte; WCYB-TV (CW, Decades, NBC) Bristol; WGHP (Antenna TV, FOX) High Point; WJHL-TV (ABC, CBS, MeTV) Johnson City; WKPT-TV (COZI TV, Escape, MeTV, MNT) Kingsport; WUNL-TV (PBS) Winston-Salem; WXII-TV (MeTV, NBC) Winston-Salem.
Programming (via satellite): CNN; Discovery Channel; ESPN; Freeform; Spike TV; TBS; The Weather Channel; USA Network.
Fee: $49.95 installation; $37.05 monthly.

Digital Basic Service
Subscribers: N.A.
Programming (via satellite): BBC America; Bloomberg Television; Bravo; CMT; Discovery Life Channel; Disney XD; DMX Music; Fox Sports 1; Fuse; FXM; FYI; Golf Channel; GSN; HGTV; History; History International; IFC; INSP; LMN; NBCSN; Nick Jr.; Outdoor Channel; Syfy; TeenNick; Trinity Broadcasting Network (TBN); Turner Classic Movies; WE tv.

Pay Service 1
Pay Units: N.A.
Programming (via satellite): HBO.
Fee: $12.00 monthly.

Digital Pay Service 1
Pay Units: N.A.
Programming (via satellite): Cinemax (multiplexed); HBO (multiplexed); Showtime (multiplexed); Starz (multiplexed); Starz Encore (multiplexed); The Movie Channel (multiplexed).

Video-On-Demand: No

Pay-Per-View
iN DEMAND (delivered digitally); Hot Choice (delivered digitally); Playboy TV (delivered digitally).

Internet Service
Operational: No.

Telephone Service
None
Miles of Plant: 15.0 (coaxial); None (fiber optic). Homes passed: 300.
President: James Rigas.
Ownership: Zito Media (MSO).

CRUSO—Carolina Mountain Cable. Now served by HAYWOOD COUNTY (portions), NC [NC0127]. ICA: NC0158.

CURRITUCK—Mediacom, 910 NC Highway 32 South, PO Box 580, Plymouth, NC 27962. Phones: 845-695-2762; 252-793-1570. Fax: 252-793-6135. Web Site: http://www.mediacomcable.com. Also serves Camden, Camden County, Currituck County (southern portion) & South Mills. ICA: NC0083.
TV Market Ranking: 44 (Camden County (portions)); Below 100 (Currituck County (southern portion), South Mills, Camden, Camden County (portions)). Franchise award date: November 5, 1984. Franchise expiration date: N.A. Began: July 1, 1985.
Channel capacity: N.A. Channels available but not in use: N.A.

Basic Service
Subscribers: 2,205.
Programming (received off-air): WAVY-TV (Bounce TV, NBC) Portsmouth; WGNT (Antenna TV, CW) Portsmouth; WHRO-TV (PBS) Hampton-Norfolk; WITN-TV (MeTV, MNT, NBC) Washington; WNCT-TV (CBS, CW) Greenville; WSKY-TV (Escape, IND, Laff) Manteo; WTKR (CBS) Norfolk; WTVZ-TV (MNT, The Country Network) Norfolk; WUND-TV (PBS) Edenton; WVBT (FOX) Virginia Beach; WVEC (ABC) Hampton.
Programming (via satellite): History; ION Television; Pop; WGN America.
Fee: $29.50 installation; $48.07 monthly.

Expanded Basic Service 1
Subscribers: N.A.
Programming (via satellite): A&E; AMC; Animal Planet; BET; Bravo; Cartoon Network; CMT; CNBC; CNN; Comedy Central; C-SPAN; Discovery Channel; Discovery Life Channel; Disney Channel; Disney XD; ESPN; ESPN2; Food Network; Fox News Channel; Fox Sports 1; FOX Sports Networks; Freeform; FX; Hallmark Channel; HGTV; HLN; INSP; Lifetime; MSNBC; MTV; Nickelodeon; Outdoor Channel; QVC; Spike TV; Syfy; TBS; The Weather Channel; TLC; TNT; Travel Channel; TV Land; USA Network; VH1; WE tv.
Fee: $34.70 monthly.

Cable Systems—North Carolina

Digital Basic Service
Subscribers: N.A.
Programming (via satellite): BBC America; Discovery Digital Networks; Fuse; FYI; Golf Channel; GSN; History International; IFC; LMN; NBCSN; Turner Classic Movies.

Digital Pay Service 1
Pay Units: N.A.
Programming (via satellite): Cinemax (multiplexed); Flix; HBO (multiplexed); Showtime (multiplexed); Starz (multiplexed); Starz Encore; Sundance TV; The Movie Channel (multiplexed).

Video-On-Demand: No

Internet Service
Operational: Yes. Began: January 1, 2002.
Broadband Service: Mediacom High Speed Internet.
Fee: $40.95 monthly.

Telephone Service
Analog: Operational
Homes passed: 5,612. Miles of plant included in Plymouth (town).
Vice President, Financial Reporting: Kenneth J. Kohrs. General Manager: Wayne Holiday. Office Manager: Wendy White. Marketing Analyst: Renette Ruffin.
Ownership: Mediacom LLC (MSO).

DAVIDSON COUNTY—Time Warner Cable. Now served by GREENSBORO, NC [NC0006]. ICA: NC0040.

DOBSON—Time Warner Cable. Now served by GREENSBORO, NC [NC0006]. ICA: NC0091.

DOVER—Formerly served by Johnston County Cable LP. No longer in operation. ICA: NC0185.

DUNCAN—Formerly served by Carolina Cable Partnership. No longer in operation. ICA: NC0149.

DURHAM—Time Warner Cable. Now served by RALEIGH, NC [NC0003]. ICA: NC0005.

EDENTON—Mediacom, 910 NC Highway 32 South, PO Box 580, Plymouth, NC 27962. Phones: 845-695-2762; 252-793-1570. Fax: 252-793-6135. Web Site: http://www.mediacomcable.com. Also serves Arrowhead Beach, Chowan Beach, Chowan County, Hertford, Perquimans County & Winfall. ICA: NC0076.
TV Market Ranking: Outside TV Markets (Arrowhead Beach, Chowan Beach, Chowan County, EDENTON, Hertford, Perquimans County, Winfall). Franchise award date: December 8, 1980. Franchise expiration date: N.A. Began: August 1, 1981.
Channel capacity: N.A. Channels available but not in use: N.A.

Basic Service
Subscribers: 2,502.
Programming (received off-air): WAVY-TV (Bounce TV, NBC) Portsmouth; WCTI-TV (ABC, Decades, Movies!) New Bern; WGNT (Antenna TV, CW) Portsmouth; WHRO-TV (PBS) Hampton-Norfolk; WITN-TV (MeTV, MNT, NBC) Washington; WPXV-TV (ION) Norfolk; WSKY-TV (Escape, IND, Laff) Manteo; WTKR (CBS) Norfolk; WTVZ-TV (MNT, The Country Network) Norfolk; WUND-TV (PBS) Edenton; WVBT (FOX) Virginia Beach; WVEC (ABC) Hampton; allband FM.
Programming (via satellite): History; Pop; WGN America.
Fee: $45.00 installation; $41.00 monthly.

Expanded Basic Service 1
Subscribers: N.A.
Programming (via satellite): A&E; AMC; Animal Planet; BET; Bravo; Cartoon Network; CMT; CNBC; CNN; Comedy Central; C-SPAN; Discovery Channel; Discovery Life Channel; Disney Channel; Disney XD; ESPN; ESPN2; Food Network; Fox News Channel; Fox Sports 1; Freeform; FX; Hallmark Channel; HGTV; HLN; INSP; Lifetime; MSNBC; MTV; Nickelodeon; Outdoor Channel; QVC; Spike TV; Syfy; TBS; The Weather Channel; TLC; TNT; Travel Channel; TV Land; USA Network; VH1; WE tv.
Fee: $33.49 monthly.

Digital Basic Service
Subscribers: N.A.
Programming (via satellite): AXS TV; BBC America; Bloomberg Television; Discovery Digital Networks; DMX Music; ESPN; ESPNews; Fuse; FXM; FYI; Golf Channel; GSN; HD Theater; History International; IFC; LMN; MTV2; National Geographic Channel; NBCSN; Nick Jr.; TeenNick; The Word Network; truTV; Turner Classic Movies; Weatherscan.
Fee: $8.00 monthly.

Digital Pay Service 1
Pay Units: N.A.
Programming (via satellite): Cinemax (multiplexed); Flix (multiplexed); HBO (multiplexed); HBO HD; Showtime (multiplexed); Showtime HD; Starz (multiplexed); Starz Encore (multiplexed); Starz HD; Sundance TV (multiplexed); The Movie Channel (multiplexed); The Movie Channel HD.
Fee: $8.00 monthly (Starz), $9.95 monthly (Cinemax or Showtime), $13.95 monthly (HBO).

Video-On-Demand: Planned

Pay-Per-View
iN DEMAND (delivered digitally); ESPN Sports PPV (delivered digitally).

Internet Service
Operational: Yes. Began: January 1, 2002.
Broadband Service: Mediacom High Speed Internet.
Fee: $59.95 installation; $40.95 monthly; $3.00 modem lease.

Telephone Service
Digital: Operational
Fee: $39.95 monthly
Homes passed: 5,444. Miles of plant (coax & fiber) included in Plymouth (town).
General Manager: Wayne Holiday. Vice President, Financial Reporting: Kenneth J. Kohrs. Marketing Analyst: Renette Ruffin. Office Manager: Wendy White.
Ownership: Mediacom LLC (MSO).

ELIZABETH CITY—Time Warner Cable, 7800 Crescent Executive Dr, Charlotte, NC 28217. Phones: 919-573-7029; 919-573-7000. Web Site: http://www.timewarnercable.com. Also serves Pasquotank County. ICA: NC0043.
TV Market Ranking: 44 (Pasquotank County (portions)); Outside TV Markets (ELIZABETH CITY, Pasquotank County (portions)). Franchise award date: November 1, 1973. Franchise expiration date: N.A. Began: March 1, 1976.
Channel capacity: N.A. Channels available but not in use: N.A.

Basic Service
Subscribers: 10,049.
Programming (received off-air): W18BB-D (America One) Elizabeth City; WAVY-TV (Bounce TV, NBC) Portsmouth; WGNT (Antenna TV, CW) Portsmouth; WHRO-TV (PBS) Hampton-Norfolk; WNCT-TV (CBS, CW) Greenville; WPXV-TV (ION) Norfolk; WSKY-TV (Escape, IND, Laff) Manteo; WTKR (CBS) Norfolk; WTVZ-TV (MNT, The Country Network) Norfolk; WUND-TV (PBS) Edenton; WVBT (FOX) Virginia Beach; WVEC (ABC) Hampton; allband FM.
Programming (via satellite): Pop; QVC; TBS.
Fee: $47.99 installation; $11.99 monthly.

Expanded Basic Service 1
Subscribers: N.A.
Programming (via satellite): A&E; AMC; Animal Planet; BET; Cartoon Network; CMT; CNBC; CNN; Comedy Central; C-SPAN 2; Discovery Channel; Disney Channel; E! HD; ESPN; ESPN2; EWTN Global Catholic Network; Food Network; Fox News Channel; Freeform; FX; HGTV; History; HLN; INSP; Lifetime; LWS Local Weather Station; MSNBC; MTV; Nickelodeon; Spike TV; Syfy; The Weather Channel; TLC; TNT; Travel Channel; truTV; TV Land; USA Network; VH1.
Fee: $34.18 monthly.

Digital Basic Service
Subscribers: N.A.
Programming (via satellite): BBC America; Bloomberg Television; C-SPAN 3; Discovery Digital Networks; Disney XD; ESPN Classic; ESPNews; Fox Sports 1; FXM; FYI; Golf Channel; GSN; History International; HITS (Headend In The Sky); IFC; MC; National Geographic Channel; NBCSN; Nick Jr; Outdoor Channel; TeenNick; Trinity Broadcasting Network (TBN); Turner Classic Movies; WE tv.
Fee: $10.00 monthly.

Digital Pay Service 1
Pay Units: N.A.
Programming (via satellite): Cinemax (multiplexed); Flix; HBO (multiplexed); Showtime (multiplexed); Starz (multiplexed); Starz Encore (multiplexed); The Movie Channel (multiplexed).
Fee: $15.95 monthly (HBO, Cinemax, Showtime, TMC or Starz), $19.95 monthly (Playboy).

Video-On-Demand: No

Pay-Per-View
Urban Extra (delivered digitally); Fresh (delivered digitally); Playboy TV (delivered digitally); Hot Choice (delivered digitally).

Internet Service
Operational: Yes. Began: September 1, 2000.
Subscribers: 6,095.
Broadband Service: Road Runner.
Fee: $44.95 monthly.

Telephone Service
Digital: Operational
Subscribers: 3,198.
Miles of Plant: 1,077.0 (coaxial); 52.0 (fiber optic). Homes passed: 28,196.
Vice President & General Manager: Chris Whitaker. Vice President, Technical Operations: Gary Frederick. Vice President, Government & Public Affairs: Brad Phillips. Vice President, Sales & Marketing: Tom Smith. Senior Accounting Director: Karen Goodfellow.
Ownership: Time Warner Cable (MSO).

Access the most current data instantly
FREE TRIAL @
www.warren-news.com/factbook.htm

ELIZABETHTOWN—Time Warner Cable. Now served by WILMINGTON, NC [NC0007]. ICA: NC0071.

ELKIN—Time Warner Cable. Now served by GREENSBORO, NC [NC0006]. ICA: NC0095.

ENFIELD—Suddenlink Communications. Now served by ROCKY MOUNT, NC [NC0016]. ICA: NC0126.

FAIR BLUFF—Formerly served by MIM Cable. No longer in operation. ICA: NC0178.

FAISON—Charter Communications. Now served by ANGIER, NC [NC0194]. ICA: NC0236.

FARMINGTON—Yadtel, PO Box 368, Yadkinville, NC 27055. Phone: 336-463-5023. E-mail: yadtel@yadtel.com; cstservice@yadtel.com. Web Site: http://www.yadtel.com. Also serves Cooleemee, Davie County (portions), Harmony, Iredell County (portions), Mocksville, Yadkin County (portions) & Yadkinville. ICA: NC0253.
Channel capacity: N.A. Channels available but not in use: N.A.

Digital Basic Service
Subscribers: 2,908.
Fee: $22.99 monthly.

Digital Expanded Basic Service
Subscribers: 185.
Fee: $28.35 monthly.

Digital Expanded Basic Service 2
Subscribers: 63.
Fee: $5.25 monthly.

Digital Pay Service 1
Pay Units: N.A.
Fee: $12.55 monthly (Cinemax, Showtime or Starz), $13.60 monthly (HBO).

Internet Service
Operational: Yes.
Fee: $20.99-$49.99 monthly.

Telephone Service
Digital: Operational
Miles of Plant: None (coaxial); 3,399.0 (fiber optic). Homes passed: 19,712.
Chief Executive Officer & General Manager: Mitzie S. Branon.
Ownership: Yadkin Valley Telephone Membership Corp. Inc.

FARMVILLE—Time Warner Cable, 7800 Crescent Executive Dr, Charlotte, NC 28217. Phones: 919-573-7029; 919-573-7000. Web Site: http://www.timewarnercable.com. Also serves Pitt County. ICA: NC0096.
TV Market Ranking: 84 (FARMVILLE); 84,73 (Pitt County). Franchise award date: N.A. Franchise expiration date: N.A. Began: December 22, 1981.
Channel capacity: N.A. Channels available but not in use: N.A.

Basic Service
Subscribers: 1,355.
Programming (received off-air): WCTI-TV (ABC, Decades, Movies!) New Bern; WLFL (CW, The Country Network) Raleigh; WNCT-TV (CBS, CW) Greenville; WRAL-TV (NBC, This TV) Raleigh; WTVD (ABC,

2017 Edition   D-555

North Carolina—Cable Systems

Live Well Network) Durham; WUNK-TV (PBS) Greenville; WYDO (Bounce TV, FOX) Greenville.
Programming (via satellite): Pop; TBS; WGN America.
Fee: $47.99 installation; $21.49 monthly; $3.00 converter.

Expanded Basic Service 1
Subscribers: N.A.
Programming (via satellite): A&E; AMC; Animal Planet; BET; Bravo; Cartoon Network; CMT; CNBC; CNN; Comedy Central; C-SPAN; C-SPAN 2; Disney Channel; E! HD; ESPN; ESPN Classic; ESPN2; EWTN Global Catholic Network; Food Network; Fox News Channel; FOX Sports Networks; Freeform; FX; Golf Channel; Hallmark Channel; HGTV; History; HLN; INSP; Lifetime; LMN; MSNBC; MTV; Nickelodeon; Oxygen; QVC; Spike TV; Syfy; The Weather Channel; TLC; TNT; Travel Channel; Trinity Broadcasting Network (TBN); truTV; Turner Classic Movies; TV Land; USA Network; VH1; WE tv.
Fee: $33.00 monthly.

Digital Basic Service
Subscribers: N.A.
Programming (via satellite): BBC America; Bloomberg Television; Cooking Channel; C-SPAN 3; Discovery Digital Networks; Disney XD; DIY Network; ESPNews; Fox Sports 1; FSN Digital Atlantic; FSN Digital Central; FSN Digital Pacific; Fuse; Great American Country; GSN; HITS (Headend In The Sky); MC; MTV Classic; MTV2; NBCSN; Nick Jr.; Outdoor Channel; Ovation; TeenNick.

Digital Pay Service 1
Pay Units: N.A.
Programming (via satellite): Cinemax (multiplexed); Flix; FXM; HBO (multiplexed); IFC; Showtime (multiplexed); Starz (multiplexed); Sundance TV; The Movie Channel (multiplexed).
Fee: $14.50 monthly (each).

Video-On-Demand: Yes

Pay-Per-View
iN DEMAND (delivered digitally); Hot Choice (delivered digitally); Playboy TV (delivered digitally); Fresh (delivered digitally); Shorteez (delivered digitally); Pleasure (delivered digitally); ESPN Now (delivered digitally).

Internet Service
Operational: Yes. Began: December 31, 2002.
Broadband Service: Road Runner.
Fee: $99.95 installation; $44.95 monthly; $3.00 modem lease.

Telephone Service
Digital: Operational
Fee: $44.95 monthly
Miles of Plant: 92.0 (coaxial); None (fiber optic). Homes passed: 2,962.
President: Tom Adams. Vice President, Technical Operations: Gary Frederick. Vice President, Government & Public Affairs: Brad Phillips. Vice President, Sales & Marketing: Tom Smith. Senior Accounting Director: Karen Goodfellow.
Ownership: Time Warner Cable (MSO).; Advance/Newhouse Partnership (MSO).

FAYETTEVILLE—Time Warner Cable. Now served by RALEIGH, NC [NC0003]. ICA: NC0004.

FOREST CITY—Northland Cable Television, 1108 West Main St, Forest City, NC 28043. Phones: 888-667-8452; 828-625-8012 (Lake Lure); 828-245-1633 (Forest City). Fax: 828-245-8850. E-mail: forestcity@northlandcabletv.com. Web Site: http://www.yournorthland.com. Also serves Bostic, Chimney Rock, Ellenboro, Gilkey Twp., Harris, Henderson County (northeastern portion), Lake Lure, Polk County (northern portion), Ruth, Rutherford County (portions), Rutherfordton, Sandy Mush & Spindale. ICA: NC0054.
TV Market Ranking: 46 (Bostic, Chimney Rock, Ellenboro, FOREST CITY, Gilkey Twp., Harris, Henderson County (northeastern portion), Lake Lure, Polk County (northern portion), Ruth, Rutherford County (portions), Rutherfordton, Sandy Mush, Spindale)); Below 100 (Rutherford County (portions)). Franchise award date: February 7, 1977. Franchise expiration date: N.A. Began: August 1, 1979.
Channel capacity: N.A. Channels available but not in use: N.A.

Basic Service
Subscribers: 2,712.
Programming (received off-air): WBTV (Bounce TV, CBS) Charlotte; WGGS-TV (IND) Greenville; WHNS (COZI TV, Escape, FOX) Greenville; WLOS (ABC, Antenna TV) Asheville; WMYA-TV (MNT, The Country Network) Anderson; WRET-TV (PBS) Spartanburg; WSPA-TV (CBS, MeTV) Spartanburg; WUNF-TV (PBS) Asheville; WYCW (CW) Asheville; WYFF (NBC, Movies!) Greenville.
Programming (via satellite): A&E; BET; Cartoon Network; CNBC; CNN; Discovery Channel; ESPN; Food Network; Fox News Channel; FOX Sports South/SportSouth; Great American Country; Hallmark Channel; HGTV; Pop; QVC; TBS; The Weather Channel; TLC; TNT; USA Network; WGN America.
Fee: $55.00 installation; $47.64 monthly; $3.00 converter.

Expanded Basic Service 1
Subscribers: N.A.
Programming (via satellite): Animal Planet; Comedy Central; C-SPAN; ESPN2; FX; FXM; History; HLN; Lifetime; MTV; Nickelodeon; Outdoor Channel; Spike TV; Syfy; Turner Classic Movies.
Fee: $20.00 monthly.

Digital Basic Service
Subscribers: N.A.
Programming (via satellite): BBC America; Bloomberg Television; Bravo; Discovery Digital Networks; DMX Music; Fox Sports 1; Golf Channel; GSN; IFC; National Geographic Channel; NBCSN; Trinity Broadcasting Network (TBN); WE tv.
Fee: $9.50 monthly.

Pay Service 1
Pay Units: N.A.
Programming (via satellite): HBO.
Fee: $15.00 installation; $10.00 monthly.

Digital Pay Service 1
Pay Units: N.A.
Programming (via satellite): Cinemax (multiplexed); Flix; HBO (multiplexed); Showtime (multiplexed); Starz (multiplexed); Starz Encore (multiplexed); The Movie Channel (multiplexed).
Fee: $14.75 monthly (Cinemax, HBO, Showtime/TMC/Flix or Starz/Encore).

Video-On-Demand: No

Pay-Per-View
Special events, Addressable: No; Playboy TV (delivered digitally); Fresh (delivered digitally).

Internet Service
Operational: Yes.
Subscribers: 1,952.
Fee: $42.99 monthly.

Telephone Service
Analog: Not Operational
Digital: Operational
Subscribers: 874.
Fee: $29.99 monthly
Miles of Plant: 888.0 (coaxial); 179.0 (fiber optic). Homes passed: 21,825.
Executive Vice President: Richard I. Clark. General Manager: Ronnie Parker. Marketing Director: Donna McCann. Office Manager: Patty Crowder.
Ownership: Northland Communications Corp. (MSO).

FOUNTAIN—Formerly served by Vital Communications. No longer in operation. ICA: NC0184.

FRANKLIN/SYLVA—Morris Broadband. Now served by HENDERSONVILLE, NC [NC0033]. ICA: NC0087.

GASTONIA—Time Warner Cable. Now served by CHARLOTTE, NC [NC0001]. ICA: NC0020.

GATES COUNTY (portions)—Charter Communications. Now served by SUFFOLK, VA [VA0025]. ICA: NC0226.

GOLD HILL—Time Warner Cable. Now served by CHARLOTTE, NC [NC0001]. ICA: NC0140.

GOLDSBORO—Time Warner Cable. Now served by RALEIGH, NC [NC0003]. ICA: NC0021.

GOLDSTON—Formerly served by Main Street Broadband. No longer in operation. ICA: NC0229.

GREENSBORO—Time Warner Cable, PO Box 35568, Greensboro, NC 27425. Phones: 919-283-2877; 336-665-0160. Fax: 336-665-9979. Web Site: http://www.timewarnercable.com. Also serves Alamance (village), Alamance County, Archdale, Asheboro, Bermuda Run (town), Bethania (town), Biscoe (town), Booneville (town), Burlington, Candor, Carroll, Caswell County (portions), Clemmons (village), Cooleemee (town), Danbury (town), Davidson County, Davie County (portions), Denton (town), Dobson (town), East Bend (town), Eden (town), Elkin (town), Elon (town), Forsyth County, Franklinville (town), Gibsonville, Graham, Green Level (town), Guilford County, Haw River (town), High Point, Jamestown (town), Jonesville (town), Kernersville (town), King, Lewisville (town), Lexington (town), Liberty, Madison, Mayodan, Mebane, Midway, Mocksville (town), Mount Airy, Oak Ridge (town), Ossipee (town), Pilot Mountain (town), Pleasant Garden (town), Ramseur (town), Randleman, Randolph County (portions), Reidsville, Rockingham County (portions), Rural Hall (town), Seagrove (town), Sedalia, Star (town), Stokes County (portions), Stokesdale (town), Stoneville, Summerfield (town), Surry County, Swepsonville (town), Thomasville, Tobaccoville (village), Trinity, Walkertown (town), Wallburg (town), Walnut Cove (town), Wentworth (town), White Plains, Whitsett (town), Wilkes County, Winston-Salem, Yadkin County & Yadkinville (town), NC; Carroll County (portions), VA. ICA: NC0006.
TV Market Ranking: 47 (Alamance (village), Alamance County, Archdale, Asheboro, Bermuda Run (town), Bethania (town), Booneville (town), Burlington, Carroll, Carroll County (portions), Clemmons (village), Cooleemee (town), Danbury (town), Davidson County, Davie County (portions), Denton (town), Dobson (town), East Bend (town), Eden (town), Elkin (town), Elon (town), Forsyth County, Franklinville (town), Gibsonville, Graham, Green Level (town), GREENSBORO, Guilford County, Haw River (town), High Point, Jamestown (town), Jonesville (town), Kernersville (town), King, Lewisville (town), Lexington (town), Liberty, Madison, Mayodan, Mebane, Midway, Mocksville (town), Mount Airy, Oak Ridge (town), Ossipee (town), Pilot Mountain (town), Pleasant Garden (town), Ramseur (town), Randleman, Randolph County (portions), Reidsville, Rockingham County (portions), Rural Hall (town), Seagrove (town), Sedalia, Stokes County (portions), Stokesdale (town), Stoneville, Summerfield (town), Surry County (portions), Swepsonville (town), Thomasville, Tobaccoville (village), Trinity, Walkertown (town), Wallburg (town), Walnut Cove (town), Wentworth (town), White Plains, Whitsett (town), Wilkes County (portions), Winston-Salem, Yadkin County, Yadkinville (town)); 73,47 (Caswell County (portions)); Below 100 (Caswell County (portions)); Outside TV Markets (Biscoe (town), Candor, Star (town), Carroll County (portions), Surry County (portions), Wilkes County (portions), Caswell County (portions)). Franchise award date: January 1, 1968. Franchise expiration date: N.A. Began: January 1, 1968.
Channel capacity: N.A. Channels available but not in use: N.A.

Basic Service
Subscribers: 271,244.
Programming (received off-air): WCWG (Bounce TV, CW, Estrella TV, IND) Lexington; WFMY-TV (CBS) Greensboro; WGHP (Antenna TV, FOX) High Point; WGPX-TV (ION) Burlington; WLXI (IND) Greensboro; WMYV (MNT) Greensboro; WUNL-TV (PBS) Winston-Salem; WXII-TV (MeTV, NBC) Winston-Salem; WXLV-TV (ABC, The Country Network) Winston-Salem.
Programming (via satellite): WGN America.
Fee: $42.50 installation; $11.30 monthly.

Expanded Basic Service 1
Subscribers: N.A.
Programming (via satellite): A&E; AMC; Animal Planet; BET; Bravo; Cartoon Network; CMT; CNBC; CNN; Comedy Central; C-SPAN; C-SPAN 2; Discovery Channel; Discovery Life Channel; Disney Channel; E! HD; ESPN; ESPN2; EVINE Live; EWTN Global Catholic Network; Food Network; Fox News Channel; FOX Sports Networks; FOX Sports South/SportSouth; Freeform; FX; Golf Channel; Hallmark Channel; HGTV; History; HLN; INSP; Lifetime; LMN; MoviePlex; MSNBC; MTV; National Geographic Channel; NBCSN; Nickelodeon; Oxygen; Pop; QVC; Spike TV; Syfy; TBS; The Weather Channel; TLC; TNT; Travel Channel; truTV; Turner Classic Movies; TV Land; Univision Studios; USA Network; VH1; WE tv.
Fee: $42.75 monthly.

Digital Basic Service
Subscribers: N.A.
Programming (via satellite): BBC America; Bloomberg Television; Boomerang; C-SPAN 3; Discovery Digital Networks; Disney XD; DIY Network; ESPN Classic; ESPNews; Flix; Fox Sports 1; FSN Digital Atlantic; FSN Digital Central; FSN Digital Pacific; Fuse; FXM; FYI; GSN; History International; HITS (Headend In The Sky); IFC; MC; Nick Jr.; Outdoor Channel; Ovation; Starz Encore (multiplexed); Sundance TV; Tennis Channel.

Cable Systems—North Carolina

Pay Service 1
 Pay Units: N.A.
 Programming (via satellite): Cinemax; HBO; Showtime; The Movie Channel.
 Fee: $8.00 monthly (each).
Digital Pay Service 1
 Pay Units: N.A.
 Programming (via satellite): Cinemax (multiplexed); HBO (multiplexed); Showtime (multiplexed); Starz (multiplexed); The Movie Channel (multiplexed).
 Fee: $8.00 monthly (each).
Video-On-Demand: Yes
Pay-Per-View
 iN DEMAND (delivered digitally); Sports PPV (delivered digitally).
Internet Service
 Operational: Yes.
 Subscribers: 277,285.
 Broadband Service: AOL for Broadband, EarthLink, Road Runner.
 Fee: $49.95 installation; $46.95 monthly.
Telephone Service
 Digital: Operational
 Subscribers: 138,129.
 Fee: $44.95 monthly
Miles of Plant: 23,177.0 (coaxial); 505.0 (fiber optic). Homes passed: 749,040.
Regional Vice President, Government Relations: Jack Stanley. Area Vice President, Operations: Dianne Blackwood. Vice President, Marketing & Sales: David Marshall. Marketing Director: Beth Alphin. Technical Operations Director: Anthony Siero.
Ownership: Time Warner Cable (MSO).; Advance/Newhouse Partnership (MSO).

GREENVILLE—Suddenlink Communications, 520 Maryville Centre Dr, Ste 300, St. Louis, MO 63141. Phones: 252-757-2200 (Administrative office); 866-999-3278; 314-315-9400. Web Site: http://www.suddenlink.com. Also serves Ayden, Grimesland, Pitt County, Simpson & Winterville. ICA: NC0014.
TV Market Ranking: 84 (Ayden, Grimesland, Pitt County, Simpson, Winterville); 84,73 (GREENVILLE). Franchise award date: August 5, 1976. Franchise expiration date: N.A. Began: June 1, 1978.
Channel capacity: 66 (operating 2-way). Channels available but not in use: N.A.
Basic Service
 Subscribers: 23,543. Commercial subscribers: 4,568.
 Programming (received off-air): WCTI-TV (ABC, Decades, Movies!) New Bern; WEPX-TV (ION) Greenville; WNCT-TV (CBS, CW) Greenville; WRAL-TV (NBC, This TV) Raleigh; WUNK-TV (PBS) Greenville; WYDO (Bounce TV, FOX) Greenville.
 Programming (via satellite): QVC; WGN America.
 Fee: $25.00 monthly.
Expanded Basic Service 2
 Subscribers: N.A.
 Programming (via satellite): CNN; Comedy Central; Disney Channel; Golf Channel; HLN; Spike TV; Turner Classic Movies; TV Land.
 Fee: $6.46 monthly.
Digital Basic Service
 Subscribers: N.A.
 Programming (via satellite): BBC America; Bloomberg Television; Daystar TV Network; Discovery Digital Networks; Disney XD; ESPN Classic; ESPNews; EWTN Global Catholic Network; FamilyNet; Fox Sports 1; Fuse; GSN; Hallmark Channel; LMN; MC; NBA TV; NBCSN; Nick Jr.; Nicktoons; Outdoor Channel; Sundance TV; TeenNick; The Word Network; truTV.
 Fee: $7.95 monthly.

Pay Service 1
 Pay Units: N.A.
 Programming (via satellite): Cinemax; HBO (multiplexed); Showtime; The Movie Channel.
 Fee: $13.33 installation; $10.25 monthly (Showtime), $10.75 monthly (Cinemax or TMC), $11.50 monthly (HBO).
Digital Pay Service 1
 Pay Units: N.A.
 Programming (via satellite): Cinemax (multiplexed); HBO (multiplexed); Showtime (multiplexed); Starz Encore (multiplexed); The Movie Channel (multiplexed).
 Fee: $10.95 monthly (Cinemax, Showtime/TMC or Starz/Encore), $11.50 monthly (HBO).
Video-On-Demand: No
Pay-Per-View
 iN DEMAND; Playboy TV (delivered digitally); Fresh (delivered digitally); Shorteez (delivered digitally); iN DEMAND (delivered digitally); Hot Choice (delivered digitally); ESPN (delivered digitally).
Internet Service
 Operational: Yes.
 Subscribers: 27,761.
 Broadband Service: Suddenlink High Speed Internet.
 Fee: $99.95 installation; $39.95 monthly; $15.00 modem lease; $199.95 modem purchase.
Telephone Service
 Digital: Operational
 Subscribers: 12,194.
 Fee: $39.95 monthly
Miles of Plant: 1,441.0 (coaxial); 364.0 (fiber optic). Homes passed: 64,744.
Vice President & General Manager: Phil Ahlschlager. Senior Vice President, Corporate Finance: Michael Pflantz. Field Operations Director: Bill Paramore. Field Operations Manager: Ken Willard.
Ownership: Cequel Communications Holdings I LLC (MSO).

HALIFAX—Crystal Broadband Networks. Now served by WHITAKERS, NC [NC0164]. ICA: NC0183.

HALLS TWP.—StarVision, PO Box 319, Clinton, NC 28328. Phones: 910-564-4194; 910-564-7888. Fax: 910-564-5410. Web Site: http://www.starvision.tv. Also serves Beaverdam, Clinton, Garland, Honeycutt Twp., Mingo, Rockfish, Roseboro, Salemburg, Sampson County, Tar Heel, Turkey & Western Prong Twp. ICA: NC0070.
TV Market Ranking: 73 (Clinton, Garland, Roseboro, Salemburg, Sampson County (portions)); Outside TV Markets (Sampson County (portions)). Franchise award date: May 1, 1980. Franchise expiration date: N.A. Began: May 8, 1981.
Channel capacity: N.A. Channels available but not in use: N.A.
Basic Service
 Subscribers: N.A.
 Programming (received off-air): WECT (Bounce TV, NBC) Wilmington; WFPX-TV (ION) Fayetteville; WLFL (CW, The Country Network) Raleigh; WNCN (Antenna TV, CBS) Goldsboro; WRAL-TV (NBC, This TV) Raleigh; WRAZ (FOX, MeTV) Raleigh; WRDC (MNT) Durham; WTVD (ABC, Live Well Network) Durham; WUNU (PBS) Lumberton; WUVC-DT (Bounce TV, getTV, UNV) Fayetteville.
 Programming (via satellite): C-SPAN; INSP; Pop; QVC; Trinity Broadcasting Network (TBN); WGN America.
 Fee: $22.95 monthly.

Expanded Basic Service 1
 Subscribers: N.A.
 Programming (via satellite): A&E; AMC; Animal Planet; BET; Bravo; Cartoon Network; CMT; CNBC; CNN; Comedy Central; Discovery Channel; Disney Channel; DIY Network; E! HD; ESPN; ESPN Classic; ESPN2; ESPNU; Family Friendly Entertainment; Food Network; Fox News Channel; Freeform; FX; Hallmark Channel; HGTV; History; HLN; Lifetime; MSNBC; MTV; National Geographic Channel; Nickelodeon; OWN: Oprah Winfrey Network; RFD-TV; Spike TV; Syfy; TBS; The Weather Channel; TLC; TNT; Travel Channel; TV Land; USA Network; VH1.
 Fee: $39.99 monthly.
Digital Basic Service
 Subscribers: N.A.
 Programming (via satellite): AXS TV; BBC America; Bloomberg Television; CMT; Destination America; Discovery Channel HD; Discovery Kids Channel; Discovery Life Channel; Disney XD; ESPN Deportes; ESPN HD; ESPNews; Fox Sports 1; FXM; FYI; Golf Channel; Great American Country; GSN; History International; Investigation Discovery; LMN; MC; MTV Classic; MTV Hits; MTV2; NBCSN; Nick Jr.; Nicktoons; Outdoor Channel; Oxygen; Science Channel; Sundance TV; TeenNick; truTV; Universal HD; UP; VH1 Soul; WE tv.
Digital Expanded Basic Service
 Subscribers: N.A.
 Programming (via satellite): Cine Mexicano; Enlace USA; La Familia Cosmovision; Tr3s; ULTRA HDPlex.
 Fee: $45.11 monthly.
Digital Expanded Basic Service 2
 Subscribers: N.A.
 Fee: $88.73 monthly.
Digital Expanded Basic Service 3
 Subscribers: N.A.
 Fee: $8.39 monthly.
Digital Pay Service 1
 Pay Units: N.A.
 Programming (via satellite): Cinemax (multiplexed); Flix; HBO (multiplexed); Playboy TV; Showtime; Starz (multiplexed); Starz Encore; The Movie Channel (multiplexed).
 Fee: $13.12 monthly (Playboy), $13.22 monthly (Cinemax), $15.22 monthly (Starz/Encore), $16.01 monthly (Showtime/TMC/Flix), $16.12 monthly (HBO).
Video-On-Demand: No
Pay-Per-View
 Hot Choice (delivered digitally); iN DEMAND (delivered digitally); Fresh (delivered digitally); Spice: Xcess (delivered digitally).
Internet Service
 Operational: Yes.
 Fee: $79.95 installation; $49.95 monthly.
Telephone Service
 None
Miles of Plant: None (coaxial); 94.0 (fiber optic). Homes passed: 6,491.
President: Robert G. Hester. Executive Vice President & Chief Operating Officer: Lyman M. Horne.
Ownership: StarVision Inc.

HARRIS—Northland Cable Television. Now served by FOREST CITY, NC [NC0054]. ICA: NC0246.

HAYWOOD COUNTY (portions)—Carolina Mountain Cablevision Inc, 4930 Jonathan Creek Rd, Waynesville, NC 28785. Phones: 866-571-8671; 828-926-2288 (Main Office). Fax: 828-377-0006. E-mail: cmc@cbvnol.com. Web Site: http://www.cbvnol.com. Also serves Cruso & Waynesville. ICA: NC0127.
TV Market Ranking: 46 (Cruso, HAYWOOD COUNTY (PORTIONS), Waynesville). Franchise award date: N.A. Franchise expiration date: N.A. Began: May 15, 1990.
Channel capacity: N.A. Channels available but not in use: N.A.
Basic Service
 Subscribers: 1,105.
 Programming (received off-air): WHNS (COZI TV, Escape, FOX) Greenville; WLOS (ABC, Antenna TV) Asheville; WSPA-TV (CBS, MeTV) Spartanburg; WUNC-TV (PBS) Chapel Hill; WUNF-TV (PBS) Asheville; WYFF (NBC, Movies!) Greenville.
 Programming (via satellite): A&E; AMC; Animal Planet; Cartoon Network; CMT; CNBC; CNN; Comedy Central; Cooking Channel; C-SPAN; C-SPAN 2; CW PLUS; Discovery Channel; Disney Channel; DIY Network; E! HD; ESPN; ESPN Classic; ESPN2; ESPNU; EVINE Live; EWTN Global Catholic Network; Food Network; Fox News Channel; FOX Sports South/SportSouth; Freeform; FX; Great American Country; Hallmark Channel; HGTV; History; HLN; INSP; ION Television; Lifetime; MSNBC; MTV; MyNetworkTV; National Geographic Channel; Nickelodeon; Outdoor Channel; Pop; QVC; RFD-TV; Spike TV; Syfy; TBS; The Weather Channel; TLC; TNT; Travel Channel; Trinity Broadcasting Network (TBN); truTV; Turner Classic Movies; TV Land; USA Network; VH1; WGN America.
 Fee: $39.00 installation; $53.99 monthly.
Digital Basic Service
 Subscribers: N.A.
 Programming (via satellite): A&E HD; BBC America; Bloomberg Television; Bravo; Cloo; CMT; Destination America; Discovery Kids Channel; Discovery Life Channel; Disney Channel HD; Disney XD; DMX Music; ESPN HD; ESPN2 HD; ESPNews; ESPNews HD; ESPNU HD; Food Network HD; Fox Business Network; Fox News HD; Fox Sports 1; Freeform HD; Fuse; FXM; FYI; Golf Channel; GSN; Hallmark Movies & Mysteries; HGTV HD; History HD; History International; IFC; Investigation Discovery; Lifetime Movie Network HD; MTV Classic; MTV Hits; MTV Jams; MTV2; National Geographic Channel HD; NBCSN; Nick Jr.; Nicktoons; Outdoor Channel 2 HD; OWN: Oprah Winfrey Network; Science Channel; TeenNick; Travel Channel HD; Universal HD; UP; VH1 Soul; WE tv; Weatherscan.
 Fee: $39.00 installation; $5.00 converter.
Digital Pay Service 1
 Pay Units: N.A.
 Programming (via satellite): Cinemax (multiplexed); Flix; HBO (multiplexed); Showtime (multiplexed); Starz (multiplexed); Starz Encore (multiplexed); Starz HD; The Movie Channel (multiplexed).
Video-On-Demand: No
Pay-Per-View
 iN DEMAND (delivered digitally); Hot Choice (delivered digitally); Club Jenna (delivered digitally); Playboy TV (delivered digitally); Fresh (delivered digitally); Spice: Xcess (delivered digitally).
Internet Service
 Operational: Yes.
 Subscribers: 624.
 Fee: $39.00 installation; $29.99-$49.99 monthly; $69.00 modem purchase.
Telephone Service
 Digital: Operational
Miles of Plant: 379.0 (coaxial); 67.0 (fiber optic). Homes passed: 5,000.

2017 Edition D-557

North Carolina—Cable Systems

Secretary-Treasurer & General Manager: Bryan Hyder. Chief Technician: Terry Sersland.
Ownership: Carolina Mountain Cablevision Inc. (MSO).

HENDERSON (portions)—Time Warner Cable. Now served by RALEIGH, NC [NC0003]. ICA: NC0062.

HENDERSONVILLE—Morris Broadband, 719 South Grove St, Hendersonville, NC 28792. Phones: 888-855-9036; 828-692-3278; 828-692-3278. Web Site: http://morrisbroadband.com. Also serves Dana, Dillsboro, Dysartsville Twp., East Flat Rock, Flat Rock, Fletcher, Forest Hills, Franklin, Glenwood, Henderson County, Jackson County (unincorporated areas), Laurel Park, Macon County, Mills River, Nebo, Sylva & Webster. ICA: NC0033.
TV Market Ranking: 46 (Dana, Dysartsville Twp., East Flat Rock, Flat Rock, Fletcher, Glenwood, Henderson County, HENDERSONVILLE, Jackson County (unincorporated areas), Laurel Park, Mills River, Nebo); Below 100 (Macon County (portions), Franklin); Outside TV Markets (Dillsboro, Forest Hills, Macon County (portions), Sylva, Webster, Jackson County (unincorporated areas)). Franchise award date: June 10, 1976. Franchise expiration date: N.A. Began: February 1, 1970.
Channel capacity: N.A. Channels available but not in use: N.A.

Basic Service
Subscribers: 14,334.
Programming (received off-air): WGGS-TV (IND) Greenville; WHNS (COZI TV, Escape, FOX) Greenville; WLOS (ABC, Antenna TV) Asheville; WMYA-TV (MNT, The Country Network) Anderson; WSPA-TV (CBS, MeTV) Spartanburg; WUNF-TV (PBS) Asheville; WYCW (CW) Asheville; WYFF (NBC, Movies!) Greenville; allband FM.
Programming (via satellite): QVC; WGN America.
Fee: $45.00 installation; $28.24 monthly; $1.00 converter.

Expanded Basic Service 1
Subscribers: N.A.
Programming (via satellite): A&E; AMC; Animal Planet; BET; Bravo; Cartoon Network; CMT; CNBC; CNN; Comedy Central; C-SPAN; C-SPAN 2; Discovery Channel; Disney Channel; ESPN; ESPN2; EVINE Live; EWTN Global Catholic Network; Food Network; Fox News Channel; Fox Sports 1; FOX Sports South/SportSouth; Freeform; FX; Golf Channel; HGTV; History; HLN; INSP; Lifetime; MSNBC; MTV; Nickelodeon; Pop; Spike TV; Syfy; TBS; The Weather Channel; TLC; TNT; Travel Channel; truTV; TV Land; Univision Studios; USA Network; VH1; WE tv.
Fee: $25.00 installation; $18.62 monthly.

Digital Basic Service
Subscribers: N.A.
Programming (via satellite): AXS TV; BBC America; Bloomberg Television; Bravo; Discovery Digital Networks; DMX Music; ESPN; ESPNews; Fuse; FXM; FYI; GSN; HD Theater; History International; IFC; LMN; MTV Classic; MTV2; National Geographic Channel; NBCSN; Nick Jr.; Nicktoons; Outdoor Channel; TeenNick; Turner Classic Movies; Weatherscan.

Digital Pay Service 1
Pay Units: N.A.
Programming (via satellite): Cinemax (multiplexed); Flix (multiplexed); HBO (multiplexed); Showtime (multiplexed); Showtime HD; Starz (multiplexed); Starz Encore (multiplexed); Starz HD; Sundance TV (multiplexed); The Movie Channel (multiplexed).
Fee: $13.95 monthly (HBO), $9.95 monthly (Cinemax or Showtime), $8.00 monthly (Starz/Encore).

Video-On-Demand: No

Pay-Per-View
ESPN (delivered digitally); iN DEMAND (delivered digitally).

Internet Service
Operational: Yes.
Subscribers: 14,867.
Broadband Service: In-house.
Fee: $59.95 installation; $29.95-$59.95 monthly; $3.00 modem lease.

Telephone Service
Digital: Operational
Subscribers: 3,344.
Fee: $49.95 monthly
Miles of Plant: 2,818.0 (coaxial); 2,670.0 (fiber optic). Homes passed: 63,874.
Chairman & Chief Executive Officer: William S. Morris III. Senior Vice President, Finance: Craig Mitchell. Vice President: Susie Morris Baker.
Ownership: Morris Communications Co LLC (MSO).

HICKORY—Charter Communications, 12405 Powerscourt Dr, St. Louis, MO 63131. Phones: 636-207-5100 (Corporate office); 828-322-2288. Fax: 828-322-5492. Web Site: http://www.charter.com. Also serves Alexander County, Alleghany County (portions), Ashe County, Avery County, Bakersville, Banner Elk, Beech Mountain, Blowing Rock, Boone, Brookford, Burke County, Burnsville, Cajah's Mountain, Caldwell County, Catawba (northern portion), Catawba County, Cedar Rock, Claremont, Connelly Springs, Conover, Crossnore, Dallas, Drexel, Elk Park, Gaston County, Glen Alpine, Granite Falls, High Shoals, Hildebran, Hudson, Lenoir, Lincoln County, Lincolnton, Longview, Maiden, Mitchell County (portions), Newland, Newton, North Hickory, North Wilkesboro, Rhodhiss, Roaring Gap, Ronda, Rutherford College, Sawmills, Seven Devils, Spruce Pine, Sugar Mountain, Taylorsville, Thurmond, Valdese, Vale, Watauga County, Wilkes County (portions), Wilkesboro & Yancey County (portions), NC; Carter County, Johnson County (portions), Mountain City & Trade, TN. ICA: NC0009.
TV Market Ranking: 42 (Catawba County (portions), Dallas, Gaston County, High Shoals, Lincoln County (portions), Lincolnton, Maiden); 46 (Burnsville, Mitchell County (portions) (portions), Spruce Pine, Yancey County (portions)); Below 100 (Alexander County, Ashe County (portions), Avery County, Bakersville, Banner Elk, Beech Mountain, Blowing Rock, Brookford, Burke County, Cajah's Mountain, Caldwell County, Carter County, Catawba (northern portion), Cedar Rock, Claremont, Connelly Springs, Conover, Crossnore, Drexel, Elk Park, Glen Alpine, Granite Falls, HICKORY, Hildebran, Hudson, Johnson County (portions), Lenoir, Longview, Newland, Newton, North Hickory, Rhodhiss, Rutherford College, Sawmills, Seven Devils, Sugar Mountain, Taylorsville, Trade, Valdese, Vale, Watauga County (portions), Wilkesboro, Mountain City, North Wilkesboro, Wilkes County (portions), Catawba County (portions), Lincoln County (portions), Mitchell County (portions) (portions)); Outside TV Markets (Alleghany County (portions) (portions), Ashe County (portions), Roaring Gap, Ronda, Thurmond, Watauga County (portions), Boone, Wilkes County (portions)). Franchise award date: N.A. Franchise expiration date: N.A. Began: November 15, 1976.
Channel capacity: 61 (operating 2-way). Channels available but not in use: N.A.

Digital Basic Service
Subscribers: 91,183.
Programming (via satellite): AXS TV; BBC America; Bloomberg Television; Boomerang; CNN International; Discovery Digital Networks; DIY Network; ESPN; ESPN Classic; ESPNews; FOX College Sports Central; FOX College Sports Pacific; Fox Deportes; Fox Sports 2; FXM; FYI; Great American Country; History International; HITS (Headend In The Sky); IFC; LMN; MC; NFL Network; Nick 2; Nick Jr.; Nicktoons; Sundance TV; TeenNick; TV Guide Interactive Inc.
Fee: $26.99 monthly.

Digital Expanded Basic Service
Subscribers: N.A.
Programming (via satellite): A&E; AMC; Animal Planet; BET; Bravo; Cartoon Network; CMT; CNBC; CNN; Comedy Central; C-SPAN; Discovery Channel; Disney Channel; Disney XD; E! HD; ESPN; ESPN2; Food Network; Fox News Channel; Fox Sports 1; FOX Sports South/SportSouth; Freeform; FX; Golf Channel; GSN; Hallmark Channel; HGTV; History; HLN; Lifetime; MSNBC; MTV; National Geographic Channel; NBCSN; Nickelodeon; Oxygen; Spike TV; Syfy; TBS; Telemundo; The Weather Channel; TLC; TNT; Travel Channel; truTV; Turner Classic Movies; TV Land; USA Network; VH1; WE tv.
Fee: $47.99 monthly.

Digital Pay Service 1
Pay Units: N.A.
Programming (via satellite): Cinemax (multiplexed); Flix; HBO (multiplexed); HBO HD; Showtime (multiplexed); Showtime HD; Starz (multiplexed); Starz Encore (multiplexed); The Movie Channel (multiplexed).

Video-On-Demand: Yes

Pay-Per-View
iN DEMAND (delivered digitally); NHL Center Ice (delivered digitally); MLB Extra Innings (delivered digitally); Pleasure (delivered digitally); Playboy TV (delivered digitally); Fresh (delivered digitally); Shorteez (delivered digitally).

Internet Service
Operational: Yes. Began: September 1, 2000.
Subscribers: 61,307.
Broadband Service: Charter Internet.
Fee: $29.99 monthly; $10.00 modem lease; $220.00 modem purchase.

Telephone Service
Digital: Operational
Subscribers: 39,282.
Fee: $29.99 monthly
Miles of Plant: 9,574.0 (coaxial); 3,053.0 (fiber optic). Homes passed: 220,394.
Vice President & General Manager: Anthony Pope. Accounting Director: David Sovanski. Marketing Director: Brooke Sinclair. Operations Manager: Sam Scialabba. Sales & Marketing Manager: Karen Sims.
Ownership: Charter Communications Inc. (MSO).

HIGH POINT—Time Warner Cable. Now served by GREENSBORO, NC [NC0006]. ICA: NC0024.

HIGHLANDS—Northland Cable Television, 4160 Cashiers Rd, PO Box 1087, Highlands, NC 28741. Phones: 888-667-8452; 828-526-5675. Fax: 828-526-9266. E-mail: highlands@northlandcabletv.com. Web Site: http://www.yournorthland.com. Also serves Jackson County (portions), Macon County (eastern portion) & Sapphire Valley. ICA: NC0094.
TV Market Ranking: 46 (Sapphire Valley); Below 100 (HIGHLANDS, Macon County (eastern portion)); Outside TV Markets (Macon County (eastern portion)). Franchise award date: October 3, 1979. Franchise expiration date: N.A. Began: July 2, 1982.
Channel capacity: N.A. Channels available but not in use: N.A.

Basic Service
Subscribers: 1,461.
Programming (received off-air): WAGA-TV (Buzzr, FOX, Movies!) Atlanta; WGTV (PBS) Athens; WHNS (COZI TV, Escape, FOX) Greenville; WLOS (ABC, Antenna TV) Asheville; WMYA-TV (MNT, The Country Network) Anderson; WSB-TV (ABC, MeTV) Atlanta; WSPA-TV (CBS, MeTV) Spartanburg; WUNC-TV (PBS) Chapel Hill; WYCW (CW) Asheville; WYFF (NBC, Movies!) Greenville; allband FM.
Programming (via satellite): A&E; Animal Planet; Cartoon Network; CNBC; CNN; Comedy Central; C-SPAN; Discovery Channel; E! HD; ESPN; ESPN2; Food Network; Fox News Channel; FX; FXM; Golf Channel; Great American Country; Hallmark Channel; HGTV; History; HLN; Lifetime; MSNBC; National Geographic Channel; Nickelodeon; Outdoor Channel; QVC; Spike TV; SportSouth; Syfy; TBS; The Weather Channel; TLC; TNT; Trinity Broadcasting Network (TBN); TV Land; USA Network.
Fee: $75.00 installation; $47.64 monthly.

Digital Basic Service
Subscribers: N.A.
Programming (via satellite): BBC America; Discovery Kids Channel; DMX Music; ESPNews; Fox Sports 1; IFC; LMN; NBCSN; OWN: Oprah Winfrey Network; Science Channel; WE tv.

Digital Expanded Basic Service
Subscribers: N.A.
Programming (via satellite): ESPN HD; ESPN2 HD; HD Theater; TNT HD.
Fee: $5.99 monthly.

Pay Service 1
Pay Units: N.A.
Programming (via satellite): HBO.
Fee: $13.50 monthly.

Digital Pay Service 1
Pay Units: N.A.
Programming (via satellite): Cinemax (multiplexed); Flix; HBO (multiplexed); Showtime (multiplexed); Starz (multiplexed); Starz Encore (multiplexed); The Movie Channel (multiplexed).
Fee: $14.75 monthly (Cinemax, HBO, Showtime/TMC/Flix or Starz/Encore).

Pay-Per-View
iN DEMAND (delivered digitally); Playboy TV (delivered digitally).

Internet Service
Operational: Yes. Began: May 1, 2004.
Broadband Service: Northland Express.
Fee: $44.99 monthly.

Telephone Service
Digital: Operational
Fee: $29.99 monthly
Miles of Plant: 113.0 (coaxial); None (fiber optic). Homes passed: 5,000.
Executive Vice President: Richard I. Clark. Regional Manager: Bill Staley. Plant Manager: Alan Boggs. Marketing Manager: Melinda

Cable Systems—North Carolina

Harbin. Technical Manager: Marty Mashburn.
Ownership: Northland Communications Corp. (MSO).

HOLLISTER—Crystal Broadband Networks, PO Box 180336, Chicago, IL 60618. Phones: 630-206-0447; 877-319-0328. E-mail: helpdesk@crystalbn.com. Web Site: http://crystalbn.com. ICA: NC0200.
TV Market Ranking: Below 100 (HOLLISTER).
Channel capacity: N.A. Channels available but not in use: N.A.
Basic Service
 Subscribers: 89.
 Programming (received off-air): WITN-TV (MeTV, MNT, NBC) Washington; WLFL (CW, The Country Network) Raleigh; WNCN (Antenna TV, CBS) Goldsboro; WNCT-TV (CBS, CW) Greenville; WRAL-TV (NBC, This TV) Raleigh; WRAY-TV (IND) Wilson; WRAZ (FOX, MeTV) Raleigh; WRDC (MNT) Durham; WTVD (ABC, Live Well Network) Durham; WUNP-TV (PBS) Roanoke Rapids.
 Programming (via satellite): QVC; Trinity Broadcasting Network (TBN).
 Fee: $39.95 installation; $44.27 monthly; $2.00 converter.
Expanded Basic Service 1
 Subscribers: N.A.
 Programming (via satellite): AMC; BET; CMT; CNN; C-SPAN; Discovery Channel; Disney Channel; Disney XD; ESPN; ESPN2; Fox News Channel; Freeform; HLN; Lifetime; MSNBC; MTV; Nickelodeon; Spike TV; Syfy; TBS; The Weather Channel; TLC; TNT; USA Network; VH1.
 Fee: $19.69 monthly.
Digital Basic Service
 Subscribers: N.A.
 Programming (via satellite): BBC America; Bravo; Discovery Digital Networks; ESPN Classic; ESPNews; Golf Channel; GSN; History; IFC; MC; NBCSN; Nick Jr.; WE tv.
 Fee: $10.11 monthly.
Pay Service 1
 Pay Units: N.A.
 Programming (via satellite): HBO.
 Fee: $15.95 monthly.
Digital Pay Service 1
 Pay Units: N.A.
 Programming (via satellite): Cinemax (multiplexed); HBO (multiplexed); Showtime (multiplexed); Starz (multiplexed); Starz Encore (multiplexed); The Movie Channel (multiplexed).
 Fee: $15.95 monthly (each).
Video-On-Demand: No
Pay-Per-View
 HITS Movies & Events (delivered digitally).
Internet Service
 Operational: No.
Telephone Service
 None
Miles of Plant: 68.0 (coaxial); None (fiber optic). Homes passed: 1,529.
Ownership: Crystal Broadband Networks (MSO).

HOLLY RIDGE—Charter Communications. Now served by ANGIER, NC [NC0194]. ICA: NC0069.

IRON DUFF—Formerly served by Carolina Mountain Cable. No longer in operation. ICA: NC0124.

JACKSONVILLE—Time Warner Cable, 101 Innovation Ave, Ste 100, Morrisville, NC 27560. Phones: 919-573-7029; 910-763-0004 (Wilmington office): 919-573-7000.
Web Site: http://www.timewarnercable.com. Also serves Alliance (town), Arapahoe (town), Atlantic Beach (town), Aurora (town), Bayboro (town), Beaufort (town), Beaufort County, Bogue, Cape Carteret (town), Carteret County, Cedar Island, Cedar Point (town), Cherry Point (town), Craven County, Duplin County (portions), Emerald Isle (town), Grantsboro (town), Harkers Island, Havelock, Indian Beach (town), Jones County (portions), Lenoir County, Maysville (town), Mesic (town), Minnesott (town), Morehead City, Newport (town), Onslow County, Oriental, Pamlico County, Peletier, Pine Knoll Shores (town), Pink Hill, Pollocksville (town), Stonewall, Swansboro (town) & Vandemere. ICA: NC0025.
TV Market Ranking: 73 (Duplin County (portions) (portions)); 73,84 (Lenoir County, Pink Hill); 84 (Alliance (town), Arapahoe (town), Atlantic Beach (town), Aurora (town), Bayboro (town), Beaufort County, Bogue, Cape Carteret (town), Carteret County (portions), Cedar Point (town), Cherry Point (town), Craven County, Emerald Isle (town), Grantsboro (town), Havelock, Indian Beach (town), JACKSONVILLE, Jones County (portions), Maysville (town), Mesic (town), Minnesott (town), Morehead City, Newport (town), Onslow County, Oriental, Pamlico County, Peletier, Pine Knoll Shores (town), Pollocksville (town), Stonewall, Swansboro (town), Vandemere); Below 100 (Beaufort (town), Harkers Island, Cedar Island, Duplin County (portions) (portions), Carteret County (portions) (portions); Outside TV Markets (Duplin County (portions) (portions)).
Franchise award date: December 1, 1973. Franchise expiration date: N.A. Began: July 20, 1965.
Channel capacity: N.A. Channels available but not in use: N.A.
Basic Service
 Subscribers: 58,519.
 Programming (received off-air): WCTI-TV (ABC, Decades, Movies!) New Bern; WECT (Bounce TV, NBC) Wilmington; WFXI (Bounce TV, FOX, MNT) Morehead City; WNCT-TV (CBS, CW) Greenville; WUNM-TV (PBS) Jacksonville; WWAY (ABC, CBS, CW, Retro TV) Wilmington.
 Programming (via satellite): Animal Planet; Bravo; Cartoon Network; C-SPAN 2; Disney Channel; E! HD; ESPN Classic; ESPN2; EVINE Live; Food Network; Fox News Channel; Fox Sports 1; Fuse; Golf Channel; HGTV; ION Television; Jewelry Television; LMN; National Geographic Channel; NBCSN; Oxygen; Pop; Travel Channel; Turner Classic Movies; WE tv.
 Fee: $42.50 installation; $13.99 monthly.
Expanded Basic Service 1
 Subscribers: N.A.
 Programming (via satellite): A&E; AMC; BET; CMT; CNBC; CNN; Comedy Central; Discovery Channel; ESPN; Freeform; FX; Hallmark Channel; History; HLN; Lifetime; MSNBC; MTV; Nickelodeon; QVC; Spike TV; Syfy; TBS; The Weather Channel; TLC; TNT; Trinity Broadcasting Network (TBN); truTV; USA Network; VH1; WGN America.
 Fee: $44.16 monthly.
Digital Basic Service
 Subscribers: N.A.
 Programming (via satellite): BBC America; Bloomberg Television; Cooking Channel; C-SPAN 3; Discovery Digital Networks; Disney Channel; Disney XD; DIY Network; ESPNews; Flix; Fox Sports 2; FOX Sports Networks (multiplexed); FYI; GSN; History International; IFC; INSP; MC; NBA TV; Nick Jr.; Outdoor Channel; Ovation; Tennis Channel; The Word Network; TV Land.
Digital Pay Service 1
 Pay Units: N.A.
 Programming (via satellite): Cinemax (multiplexed); FXM; HBO (multiplexed); Showtime (multiplexed); Starz Encore (multiplexed); Sundance TV; The Movie Channel (multiplexed).
 Fee: $10.50 monthly (each).
Video-On-Demand: Yes
Pay-Per-View
 Hot Choice (delivered digitally); Pleasure (delivered digitally); iN DEMAND (delivered digitally); Fresh (delivered digitally); Shorteez (delivered digitally); Playboy TV (delivered digitally); ESPN Now (delivered digitally).
Internet Service
 Operational: Yes.
 Subscribers: 35,688.
 Broadband Service: Road Runner.
 Fee: $69.95 installation; $44.95 monthly.
Telephone Service
 Digital: Operational
 Subscribers: 17,430.
 Fee: $44.95 monthly
Miles of Plant: 2,212.0 (coaxial); 259.0 (fiber optic). Homes passed: 69,071.
Vice President & General Manager: Kim Cannon. Vice President, Sales & Marketing: Tom Smith. Public Affairs Director: Marty Feurer. Technical Operations Director: Joe Pell. Customer Care Manager: Linda Bell.
Ownership: Time Warner Cable (MSO).; Advance/Newhouse Partnership (MSO).

KANNAPOLIS—Time Warner Cable. Now served by CHARLOTTE, NC [NC0001]. ICA: NC0010.

KENLY—Charter Communications, 12405 Powerscourt Dr, St. Louis, MO 63131. Phones: 636-207-5100 (Corporate office); 919-708-5902. Fax: 919-774-6126. Web Site: http://www.charter.com. Also serves Johnston County (portions), Lucama, Micro & Princeton. ICA: NC0148.
TV Market Ranking: 73 (Johnston County (portions), KENLY, Lucama, Micro, Princeton). Franchise award date: N.A. Franchise expiration date: N.A. Began: January 1, 1983.
Channel capacity: N.A. Channels available but not in use: N.A.
Digital Basic Service
 Subscribers: 233.
 Programming (via satellite): BBC America; Bloomberg Television; Discovery Life Channel; Disney XD; DIY Network; ESPN Classic; ESPNews; FOX College Sports Central; FOX College Sports Pacific; Fuse; FXM; FYI; GSN; History International; IFC; LMN; MC; National Geographic Channel; Nick 2; Nick Jr.; Sundance TV; TeenNick; TV Guide Interactive Inc.; WE tv.
 Fee: $26.99 monthly.
Digital Expanded Basic Service
 Subscribers: N.A.
 Programming (via satellite): A&E; AMC; BET; Bravo; Cartoon Network; CMT; CNBC; CNN; Comedy Central; Discovery Channel; Disney Channel; E! HD; ESPN; ESPN2; Food Network; Fox News Channel; Fox Sports 1; Freeform; FX; Golf Channel; HGTV; History; HLN; Lifetime; MSNBC; MTV; Nickelodeon; Oxygen; Spike TV; Syfy; TBS; Telemundo; The Weather Channel; TLC; TNT; Trinity Broadcasting Network (TBN); Turner Classic Movies; TV Land; USA Network; VH1.
 Fee: $47.99 monthly.
Digital Pay Service 1
 Pay Units: N.A.
 Programming (via satellite): Cinemax (multiplexed); Flix; HBO (multiplexed); Showtime (multiplexed); Starz (multiplexed); Starz Encore; The Movie Channel (multiplexed).
Video-On-Demand: No
Pay-Per-View
 iN DEMAND (delivered digitally); Playboy TV (delivered digitally); Fresh (delivered digitally).
Internet Service
 Operational: Yes.
 Broadband Service: Charter Internet.
 Fee: $29.99 monthly.
Telephone Service
 None
Homes passed: 1,116. Miles of plant (coax & fiber) included in Angier.
Vice President & General Manager: Anthony Pope. Marketing Director: Brooke Sinclair. Accounting Director: David Sovanski. Office Manager: Brenda Brinson. Marketing Manager: LaRisa Scales. Operations Manager: Doug Underwood.
Ownership: Charter Communications Inc. (MSO).

KILL DEVIL HILLS—Charter Communications, PO Box 1996, Kill Devil Hills, NC 27948. Phones: 314-543-2236; 636-207-5100 (Corporate office). Web Site: http://www.charter.com. Also serves Colington, Corolla, Dare County (portions), Duck, Kitty Hawk, Manns Harbor, Manteo, Nags Head, Southern Shores, Stumpy Point & Wanchese. ICA: NC0256.
TV Market Ranking: Below 100 (Colington, Corolla, Dare County (portions), Duck, Kitty Hawk, Manns Harbor, Nags Head, Southern Shores, Stumpy Point, Wanchese, Manteo).
Channel capacity: N.A. Channels available but not in use: N.A.
Digital Basic Service
 Subscribers: 18,079.
 Fee: $49.99 installation; $34.99 monthly.
Internet Service
 Operational: Yes.
 Subscribers: 12,481.
Telephone Service
 Digital: Operational
 Subscribers: 7,541.
Miles of Plant: 804.0 (coaxial); 186.0 (fiber optic). Homes passed: 34,864.
Accounting Director: David Sovanski.
Ownership: Charter Communications Inc. (MSO).

KING—Time Warner Cable. Now served by GREENSBORO, NC [NC0006]. ICA: NC0064.

KINSTON—Suddenlink Communications, 520 Maryville Centre Dr, Ste 300, St. Louis, MO 63141. Phones: 314-315-9400; 877-694-9474. Web Site: http://www.suddenlink.com. Also serves La Grange, Lenoir County (portions), Walnut Creek & Wayne County (portions). ICA: NC0034.
TV Market Ranking: 73 (Walnut Creek, Wayne County (portions)); 84 (KINSTON, La Grange, Lenoir County (portions)).
Channel capacity: N.A. Channels available but not in use: N.A.
Basic Service
 Subscribers: 7,567.
 Fee: $25.00 monthly.
Internet Service
 Operational: Yes.
 Subscribers: 6,532.
Telephone Service
 Digital: Operational
 Subscribers: 4,769.

2017 Edition

North Carolina—Cable Systems

Miles of Plant: 714.0 (coaxial); 211.0 (fiber optic). Homes passed: 23,771.
Senior Vice President, Corporate Finance: Michael Pflantz. Vice President, Accounting: Sabrina Warr.
Ownership: Cequel Communications Holdings I LLC (MSO).

LAKE GASTON—Time Warner Cable. Now served by MURFREESBORO, NC [NC0144]. ICA: NC0121.

LAKE NORMAN—Formerly served by MI-Connection. No longer in operation. ICA: NC0103.

LAKE TOXAWAY—Comporium Communications. Now served by BREVARD, NC [NC0053]. ICA: NC0156.

LAKE WACCAMAW—Time Warner Cable. Now served by WILMINGTON, NC [NC0007]. ICA: NC0201.

LANSING—Formerly served by Mediacom. Now served by Morris Broadband, WEST JEFFERSON, NC [NC0098]. ICA: NC0169.

LAURINBURG—Time Warner Cable. Now served by COLUMBIA, SC [SC0002]. ICA: NC0061.

LEXINGTON—Windstream, 4001 Rodney Parham Rd, Little Rock, AR 72212. Phones: 877-759-9020; 866-971-9463; 501-748-7000. Fax: 501-748-6392. E-mail: support@windstream.net. Web Site: http://www.windstream.com. Also serves Denton, High Point, Linwood, Thomasville & Welcome. ICA: NC0247. **Note:** This system is an overbuild.
TV Market Ranking: 47 (High Point, LEXINGTON). Franchise award date: January 1, 1997. Franchise expiration date: N.A. Began: October 1, 1997.
Channel capacity: N.A. Channels available but not in use: N.A.
Basic Service
Subscribers: 6,219.
Programming (received off-air): WBTV (Bounce TV, CBS) Charlotte; WCWG (Bounce TV, CW, Estrella TV, IND) Lexington; WFMY-TV (CBS) Greensboro; WGHP (Antenna TV, FOX) High Point; WGPX-TV (ION) Burlington; WLXI (IND) Greensboro; WMYV (MNT) Greensboro; WUNL-TV (PBS) Winston-Salem; WXII-TV (MeTV, NBC) Winston-Salem; WXLV-TV (ABC, The Country Network) Winston-Salem.
Programming (via satellite): C-SPAN; C-SPAN 2; INSP; News 14 Carolina; Pop; QVC; WGN America.
Fee: $50.00 installation; $25.00 monthly.
Expanded Basic Service 1
Subscribers: N.A.
Programming (via satellite): A&E; AMC; Animal Planet; BET; Bravo; Cartoon Network; CMT; CNBC; CNN; Comedy Central; Discovery Channel; Discovery Life Channel; Disney Channel; Disney XD; E! HD; ESPN; ESPN Classic; ESPN2; Food Network; Fox News Channel; Fox Sports 1; FOX Sports South/SportSouth; Freeform; FX; Golf Channel; Great American Country; GSN; Hallmark Channel; HGTV; History; HLN; Lifetime; LMN; MoviePlex; MSNBC; MTV; National Geographic Channel; Nickelodeon; Outdoor Channel; OWN: Oprah Winfrey Network; Spike TV; Syfy; TBS; The Weather Channel; TLC; TNT; Travel Channel; truTV; Turner Classic Movies; TV Land; Univision Studios; USA Network; VH1; WE tv.
Fee: $45.89 monthly.
Digital Basic Service
Subscribers: N.A.
Programming (via satellite): A&E HD; Animal Planet HD; AXS TV; BBC America; Boomerang; CMT; CNBC World; CNN HD; Cooking Channel; Destination America; Discovery Channel HD; Discovery Kids Channel; Disney Channel HD; DIY Network; DMX Music; E! HD; ESPN HD; ESPN2 HD; ESPNews; ESPNU; Food Network HD; Fox Business Network; Fox Sports 2; Freeform HD; FX HD; FXM; FYI; Golf Channel HD; Hallmark Movies & Mysteries; HD Theater; HGTV HD; History International; Investigation Discovery; Lifetime HD; Lifetime Movie Network HD; MTV Classic; MTV Hits; MTV Jams; MTV2; Nat Geo WILD; National Geographic Channel HD; NBCSN; Nick 2; Nick Jr.; Nicktoons; OWN: Oprah Winfrey Network; Oxygen; RFD-TV; Science Channel; Science HD; TBS HD; TeenNick; TLC HD; TNT HD; Travel Channel HD; Universal HD; UP; Versus HD; VH1 Soul.
Digital Expanded Basic Service
Subscribers: N.A.
Programming (via satellite): FOX College Sports Central; FOX College Sports Pacific; Tennis Channel.
Fee: $1.99 monthly.
Digital Expanded Basic Service 2
Subscribers: N.A.
Programming (via satellite): Cine Mexicano; Cinelatino; CNN en Espanol; ESPN Deportes; Fox Deportes; History en Espanol; NBC Universo; Tr3s; ViendoMovies.
Fee: $4.19 monthly.
Digital Pay Service 1
Pay Units: N.A.
Programming (via satellite): Cinemax (multiplexed); Flix; HBO (multiplexed); HBO HD; Showtime (multiplexed); Showtime HD; Starz; Starz Encore (multiplexed); Sundance TV; The Movie Channel (multiplexed).
Fee: $6.39 monthly (Encore), $10.29 monthly (Starz), $10.99 monthly (Cinemax or HBO), $13.99 monthly (Showtime/TMC).
Video-On-Demand: Yes
Pay-Per-View
iN DEMAND (delivered digitally); Hot Choice (delivered digitally); Pleasure (delivered digitally).
Internet Service
Operational: Yes.
Broadband Service: TURBOconnect.
Fee: $21.99-$59.99 monthly.
Telephone Service
Analog: Not Operational
Digital: Operational
Fee: $39.95-$49.95 monthly
Miles of Plant: 855.0 (coaxial); None (fiber optic). Homes passed: 28,500.
President & Chief Executive Officer: Tony Thomas. Chief Financial Officer & Treasurer: Bob Gunderman. Executive Vice President, Operations: Mark Farriss. Executive Vice President, Engineering & Chief Technology Officer: Randy Nicklas.
Ownership: Windstream Communications Inc.

LIBERTY—Randolph Telephone. Formerly [NC0258]. This cable system has converted to IPTV, 317 East Dixie Dr, Asheboro, NC 27203. Phones: 336-622-7900; 336-879-5684. E-mail: csrep@rtmc.net. Web Site: http://www.rtmc.net. Also serves Badin Lake, Bennett, Coleridge, Farmer, High Falls, Jackson Creek, Liberty (Alamance County), Liberty (Randolph County), Liberty (town), Pisgah, Randolph County (portions) & Staley. ICA: NC5022.
Channel capacity: N.A. Channels available but not in use: N.A.
Essential
Subscribers: 2,067.
Fee: $199.00 installation; $15.95 monthly. Includes 27 channels.
Classic
Subscribers: 1,882.
Fee: $64.95 monthly. Includes 64 channels plus music channels.
HD
Subscribers: N.A.
Fee: $7.95 monthly. Includes 78 channels.
Variety
Subscribers: N.A.
Fee: $8.95 monthly. Includes 37 channels.
Cinemax
Subscribers: N.A.
Fee: $10.95 monthly. Includes 8 channels.
HBO
Subscribers: N.A.
Fee: $17.95 monthly. Includes 7 channels.
NFL RedZone
Subscribers: N.A.
Fee: $44.95 per season.
Showtime/TMC
Subscribers: N.A.
Fee: $15.95 monthly. Includes 15 channels.
Starz/Encore
Subscribers: N.A.
Fee: $11.95 monthly. Includes 17 channels.
Internet Service
Operational: Yes.
Fee: $29.95-$97.95 monthly.
Telephone Service
Digital: Operational
Fee: $16.00 monthly
General Manager & Chief Executive Officer: Frankie Cagle.
Ownership: Randolph Telephone Membership Corp.

LIBERTY—Randolph Telephone. This cable system has converted to IPTV. See LIBERTY, NC [NC5022]. ICA: NC0258.

LITTLETON—Time Warner Cable. Now served by RALEIGH, NC [NC0003]. ICA: NC0123.

LUMBERTON—Time Warner Cable. Now served by RALEIGH, NC [NC0003]. ICA: NC0055.

MARION—Charter Communications. Now served by ASHEVILLE, NC [NC0012]. ICA: NC0068.

MARTIN COUNTY (central portion)—Suddenlink Communications, 520 Maryville Centre Dr, Ste 300, St. Louis, MO 63141. Phones: 877-804-6501 (Customer service); 314-315-9400. Web Site: http://www.suddenlink.com. Also serves Beargrass, Bethel, Everetts, Parmele, Robersonville & Williamston. ICA: NC0101.
TV Market Ranking: 84 (Beargrass, Bethel, Everetts, MARTIN COUNTY (CENTRAL PORTION), Parmele, Robersonville, Williamston). Franchise award date: January 4, 1983. Franchise expiration date: N.A. Began: December 1, 1983.
Channel capacity: 35 (operating 2-way). Channels available but not in use: N.A.
Basic Service
Subscribers: 2,750.
Programming (received off-air): WCTI-TV (ABC, Decades, Movies!) New Bern; WEPX-TV (ION) Greenville; WFXI (Bounce TV, FOX, MNT) Morehead City; WITN-TV (MeTV, MNT, NBC) Washington; WNCT-TV (CBS, CW) Greenville; WRAL-TV (NBC, This TV) Raleigh; WUNC-TV (PBS) Chapel Hill; WUNK-TV (PBS) Greenville; 1 FM.
Programming (via satellite): C-SPAN 2; QVC; WGN America.
Fee: $25.00 monthly.
Expanded Basic Service 1
Subscribers: N.A.
Programming (via satellite): A&E; AMC; Animal Planet; BET; Bravo; Cartoon Network; CMT; CNBC; CNN; Comedy Central; C-SPAN; C-SPAN 2; Discovery Channel; Disney Channel; E! HD; ESPN; ESPN2; EVINE Live; Food Network; Fox News Channel; Freeform; FX; Golf Channel; HGTV; History; HLN; INSP; Lifetime; MSNBC; MTV; Nickelodeon; Pop; Spike TV; Syfy; TBS; Telemundo; The Weather Channel; TLC; TNT; Travel Channel; Trinity Broadcasting Network (TBN); Turner Classic Movies; TV Land; USA Network; VH1.
Fee: $2.85 monthly.
Digital Basic Service
Subscribers: N.A.
Programming (via satellite): AXS TV; BBC America; Bloomberg Television; CBS Sports Network; Cooking Channel; Daystar TV Network; Discovery Digital Networks; Disney XD; DIY Network; ESPN Classic; ESPN HD; ESPNews; EWTN Global Catholic Network; FamilyNet; Food Network HD; Fox Sports 1; Fox Sports 2; Fuse; Great American Country; GSN; Hallmark Channel; HD Theater; HGTV HD; HITS (Headend In The Sky); LMN; MC; National Geographic Channel; NBCSN; Nick Jr.; Nicktoons; Outdoor Channel; Oxygen; Starz Encore (multiplexed); Sundance TV; TeenNick; Tennis Channel; The Word Network; TNT HD; truTV; TV One.
Digital Pay Service 1
Pay Units: N.A.
Programming (via satellite): Cinemax (multiplexed); HBO (multiplexed); HBO HD; Showtime (multiplexed); Showtime HD; Starz (multiplexed); Starz HD; The Movie Channel (multiplexed).
Video-On-Demand: No
Pay-Per-View
iN DEMAND (delivered digitally); Playboy TV (delivered digitally); Fresh (delivered digitally); Shorteez (delivered digitally); Hot Choice (delivered digitally); ESPN (delivered digitally).
Internet Service
Operational: Yes.
Broadband Service: Suddenlink High Speed Internet.
Fee: $100.00 installation; $39.95 monthly.
Telephone Service
Digital: Operational
Fee: $49.95 monthly
Miles of Plant: 40.0 (coaxial); None (fiber optic). Homes passed: 5,942.
Vice President, Corporate Finance: Michael Pflantz. General Manager: Bill Paramore. Chief Technician: Ed Diehl.
Ownership: Cequel Communications Holdings I LLC (MSO).

MEBANE—Time Warner Cable. Now served by GREENSBORO, NC [NC0006]. ICA: NC0074.

Cable Systems—North Carolina

MID LAKES TRAILER PARK—Crystal Broadband Networks, PO Box 180336, Chicago, IL 60618. Phones: 817-685-9588; 630-206-0447. Web site: http://crystalbn.com. Also serves Edgecombe County (portions). ICA: NC0206.
TV Market Ranking: 84 (Edgecombe County (portions), MID LAKES TRAILER PARK).
Channel capacity: N.A. Channels available but not in use: N.A.
Basic Service
Subscribers: 41.
Programming (received off-air): WLFL (CW, The Country Network) Raleigh; WNCN (Antenna TV, CBS) Goldsboro; WNCT-TV (CBS, CW) Greenville; WRAL-TV (NBC, This TV) Raleigh; WRAY-TV (IND) Wilson; WRDC (MNT) Durham; WTVD (ABC, Live Well Network) Durham; WUNP-TV (PBS) Roanoke Rapids; WYDO (Bounce TV, FOX) Greenville.
Programming (via satellite): Freeform; Trinity Broadcasting Network (TBN).
Fee: $39.95 installation; $41.82 monthly; $2.00 converter.
Expanded Basic Service 1
Subscribers: N.A.
Programming (via satellite): AMC; Animal Planet; BET; CMT; CNN; C-SPAN; Discovery Channel; Disney Channel; ESPN; ESPN2; Fox News Channel; HGTV; HLN; Lifetime; MSNBC; MTV; Nickelodeon; QVC; Spike TV; Syfy; TBS; The Weather Channel; TLC; TNT; USA Network; VH1.
Fee: $19.69 monthly.
Digital Basic Service
Subscribers: N.A.
Programming (via satellite): Bravo; ESPN Classic; History; NBCSN; WE tv.
Fee: $11.00 monthly.
Pay Service 1
Pay Units: N.A.
Programming (via satellite): HBO.
Fee: $11.95 monthly.
Digital Pay Service 1
Pay Units: N.A.
Programming (via satellite): Cinemax (multiplexed); HBO (multiplexed); Showtime (multiplexed); Starz Encore; The Movie Channel (multiplexed).
Fee: $15.95 monthly (each).
Video-On-Demand: No
Pay-Per-View
Hits Movies & Events (delivered digitally).
Internet Service
Operational: No.
Telephone Service
None
Miles of Plant: 46.0 (coaxial); None (fiber optic). Homes passed: 1,127.
General Manager: Ron Page. Program Manager: Shawn Smith.
Ownership: Crystal Broadband Networks (MSO).

MOCKSVILLE—Time Warner Cable. Now served by GREENSBORO, NC [NC0006]. ICA: NC0080.

MONROE—Time Warner Cable. Now served by CHARLOTTE, NC [NC0001]. ICA: NC0031.

MOORESVILLE—MI-Connection, 435 South Broad St, PO Box 90, Mooresville, NC 28115. Phones: 704-660-3840; 704-662-3255. E-mail: ahall@mi-connection.com. Web Site: http://www.mi-connection.com. Also serves Cornelius, Davidson & Mecklenburg County (unincorporated areas). ICA: NC0207.
TV Market Ranking: 42 (Cornelius, Davidson, MOORESVILLE). Franchise award date:

N.A. Franchise expiration date: N.A. Began: January 1, 1982.
Channel capacity: N.A. Channels available but not in use: N.A.
Basic Service
Subscribers: 9,268.
Programming (received off-air): WAXN-TV (getTV, IND) Kannapolis; WBTV (Bounce TV, CBS) Charlotte; WCCB (CW, MeTV) Charlotte; WCNC-TV (NBC) Charlotte; WHKY-TV (IND, PBJ, Retro TV, Tuff TV) Hickory; WJZY (Antenna TV, FOX, Heroes & Icons, Movies!, The Country Network) Belmont; WMYT-TV (Buzzr, IND, MNT) Rock Hill; WSOC-TV (ABC) Charlotte; WTVI (PBS) Charlotte; WUNG-TV (PBS) Concord.
Programming (via satellite): C-SPAN; EVINE Live; INSP; Pop; QVC; WGN America.
Fee: $35.00 installation; $22.48 monthly.
Expanded Basic Service 1
Subscribers: N.A.
Programming (via satellite): A&E; AMC; Animal Planet; BET; Cartoon Network; CMT; CNBC; CNN; Comedy Central; C-SPAN 2; Discovery Channel; Disney Channel; E! HD; ESPN; ESPN2; Food Network; Fox News Channel; Fox Sports 1; FOX Sports South/SportSouth; Freeform; FX; Hallmark Channel; HGTV; History; HLN; ION Television; Lifetime; MSNBC; MTV; Nickelodeon; Spike TV; Syfy; TBS; The Weather Channel; TLC; TNT; Travel Channel; truTV; TV Land; Univision Studios; USA Network; VH1.
Fee: $32.99 monthly.
Digital Basic Service
Subscribers: N.A.
Programming (via satellite): 52MX; AXS TV; BBC America; Bloomberg Television; Bravo; Cine Mexicano; Cinelatino; CMT; CNN en Espanol; Destination America; Discovery Kids Channel; Discovery Life Channel; ESPN Classic; ESPN HD; ESPN2 HD; ESPNews; Fox Deportes; FXM; Golf Channel; GSN; HD Theater; History en Espanol; Investigation Discovery; La Familia Cosmovision; MC; MTV Classic; NBCSN; Nick Jr.; Nicktoons; Outdoor Channel; OWN: Oprah Winfrey Network; Science Channel; Tr3s; Trinity Broadcasting Network (TBN); ULTRA HDPlex; WE tv.
Digital Pay Service 1
Pay Units: N.A.
Programming (via satellite): Cinemax (multiplexed); HBO (multiplexed); HBO HD; Playboy TV; Showtime (multiplexed); Showtime HD; Starz (multiplexed); Starz Encore (multiplexed); Starz HD; The Movie Channel (multiplexed).
Fee: $12.95 monthly (Cinemax, HBO, Showtime/TMC or Starz/Encore), $19.95 monthly (Playboy).
Video-On-Demand: Planned
Pay-Per-View
iN DEMAND (delivered digitally); Playboy TV (delivered digitally); Club Jenna (delivered digitally); Fresh (delivered digitally); Hot Choice (delivered digitally).
Internet Service
Operational: Yes.
Subscribers: 10,268.
Broadband Service: In-house.
Fee: $44.95 monthly.
Telephone Service
Digital: Operational
Subscribers: 2,947.
Miles of Plant: 789.0 (coaxial); 971.0 (fiber optic). Homes passed: 39,296.
General Manager: Alan Hall. Technical Operations Manager: Robert Lackey. Operations Manager: James R. Miller, Jr. Marketing Coordinator: Sandra Munsey.
Ownership: MI-Connection (MSO).

MORGANTON—CoMPAS-City of Morganton Public Antenna System, 305 East Union St, Ste A100, Morganton, NC 28655. Phones: 828-438-5228; 828-438-5353. Fax: 828-432-2532. E-mail: compas@ci.morganton.nc.us. Web Site: http://compas.compascable.net. ICA: NC0065.
TV Market Ranking: Below 100 (MORGANTON). Franchise award date: N.A. Franchise expiration date: N.A. Began: January 15, 1993.
Channel capacity: N.A. Channels available but not in use: N.A.
Basic Service
Subscribers: 2,896.
Programming (received off-air): WAXN-TV (getTV, IND) Kannapolis; WBTV (Bounce TV, CBS) Charlotte; WCCB (CW, MeTV) Charlotte; WCNC-TV (NBC) Charlotte; WHKY-TV (IND, PBJ, Retro TV, Tuff TV) Hickory; WJZY (Antenna TV, FOX, Heroes & Icons, Movies!, The Country Network) Belmont; WLOS (ABC, Antenna TV) Asheville; WMYT-TV (Buzzr, IND, MNT) Rock Hill; WSOC-TV (ABC) Charlotte; WSPA-TV (CBS, MeTV) Spartanburg; WUNE-TV (PBS) Linville; WYFF (NBC, Movies!) Greenville.
Programming (via satellite): Freeform; Pop; QVC; TBS; The Weather Channel; TLC; TNT.
Fee: $35.00 installation; $25.45 monthly.
Expanded Basic Service 1
Subscribers: N.A.
Programming (via satellite): A&E; AMC; Animal Planet; BET; Bravo; Cartoon Network; CMT; CNBC; CNN; Comedy Central; C-SPAN; Discovery Channel; Disney Channel; Disney XD; E! HD; ESPN; ESPN Classic; ESPN2; Food Network; Fox News Channel; Fox Sports 1; FOX Sports South/SportSouth; FX; Golf Channel; GSN; Hallmark Channel; HGTV; History; HLN; LMN; MSNBC; MTV; National Geographic Channel; NBCSN; Nickelodeon; Outdoor Channel; OWN: Oprah Winfrey Network; Oxygen; Spike TV; Syfy; Travel Channel; Trinity Broadcasting Network (TBN); truTV; Turner Classic Movies; TV Land; Univision Studios; USA Network; VH1; WE tv; WGN America.
Fee: $40.95 monthly.
Digital Basic Service
Subscribers: N.A.
Programming (via satellite): AXS TV; BBC America; Bloomberg Television; Boomerang; Cloo; Cooking Channel; C-SPAN 3; Discovery Digital Networks; DIY Network; Fuse; FXM; FYI; GSN; HD Theater; History International; IFC; Mag Rack; National Geographic Channel HD; Nick 2; Nick Jr.; Nicktoons; Outdoor Channel 2 HD; Sportskool; TeenNick.
Fee: $5.00 converter.
Digital Pay Service 1
Pay Units: N.A.
Programming (via satellite): Cinemax (multiplexed); HBO (multiplexed); Showtime (multiplexed); Starz (multiplexed); Starz Encore; The Movie Channel.
Fee: $7.00 monthly (Cinemax, Showtime/TMC or Starz/Encore), $12.95 monthly (HBO).

FULLY SEARCHABLE • CONTINUOUSLY UPDATED • DISCOUNT RATES FOR PRINT PURCHASERS
For more information call **800-771-9202** or visit **www.warren-news.com**

Digital Pay Service 2
Pay Units: 7.
Programming (via satellite): HITS (Headend In The Sky).
Fee: $7.00 monthly.
Video-On-Demand: Yes
Pay-Per-View
iN DEMAND (delivered digitally).
Internet Service
Operational: Yes.
Fee: $23.95-$69.95 monthly.
Telephone Service
Digital: Operational
Miles of Plant: 66.0 (coaxial); 112.0 (fiber optic). Homes passed: 6,200.
General Manager: Bill Harkins. Chief Tech Engineer: Randy Loop. City Manager: Sally Sandy.
Ownership: City of Morganton.

MORVEN—Formerly served by WFL Cable Television Associates Inc. No longer in operation. ICA: NC0166.

MOUNT AIRY—Time Warner Cable. Now served by GREENSBORO, NC [NC0006]. ICA: NC0075.

MURFREESBORO—Time Warner Cable, 7800 Crescent Executive Dr, Charlotte, NC 28217. Phones: 919-573-7029; 919-573-7000. Web Site: http://www.timewarnercable.com. Also serves Ahoskie (town), Aulander (town), Bertie County (portions), Cofield (village), Hertford County (portions), Lake Gaston & Winton (town). ICA: NC0144.
TV Market Ranking: Outside TV Markets (Ahoskie (town), Aulander (town), Bertie County (portions), Cofield (village), Hertford County (portions), MURFREESBORO, Winton (town), Lake Gaston). Franchise award date: May 16, 1966. Franchise expiration date: N.A. Began: December 1, 1967.
Channel capacity: N.A. Channels available but not in use: N.A.
Basic Service
Subscribers: 2,849.
Programming (received off-air): WAVY-TV (Bounce TV, NBC) Portsmouth; WGNT (Antenna TV, CW) Portsmouth; WHRO-TV (PBS) Hampton-Norfolk; WNCT-TV (CBS, CW) Greenville; WPXV-TV (ION) Norfolk; WRAL-TV (NBC, This TV) Raleigh; WSKY-TV (Escape, IND, Laff) Manteo; WTKR (CBS) Norfolk; WTVZ-TV (MNT, The Country Network) Norfolk; WUND-TV (PBS) Edenton; WVBT (FOX) Virginia Beach; WVEC (ABC) Hampton; allband FM.
Programming (via satellite): EVINE Live; QVC; WGN America.
Fee: $47.99 installation; $15.99 monthly; $3.25 converter.
Expanded Basic Service 1
Subscribers: N.A.
Programming (via satellite): A&E; AMC; Animal Planet; BET; Bravo; Cartoon Network; CMT; CNBC; CNN; Comedy Central; C-SPAN; C-SPAN 2; Discovery Channel; Disney Channel; E! HD; ESPN; ESPN2; Food Network; Fox News Channel; Freeform; FX;

2017 Edition   D-561

North Carolina—Cable Systems

Hallmark Channel; HGTV; History; HLN; Lifetime; MSNBC; MTV; Nickelodeon; Oxygen; Pop; Spike TV; Syfy; TBS; The Weather Channel; TLC; TNT; Travel Channel; truTV; TV Land; USA Network; VH1.
Fee: $36.10 monthly.

Digital Basic Service
Subscribers: N.A.
Programming (via satellite): BBC America; Bloomberg Television; Discovery Digital Networks; Disney XD; DIY Network; DMX Music; ESPN Classic; ESPNews; Fox Sports 1; Fuse; FXM; FYI; Golf Channel; Great American Country; GSN; History International; IFC; LMN; MC; National Geographic Channel; NBCSN; Nick 2; Nick Jr.; Outdoor Channel; Sundance TV; TeenNick; Trinity Broadcasting Network (TBN); Turner Classic Movies; WE tv.
Fee: $11.00 monthly; $4.69 converter.

Digital Pay Service 1
Pay Units: N.A.
Programming (via satellite): ART America; Cinemax (multiplexed); Flix; HBO (multiplexed); HITS (Headend In The Sky); RAI Italia; RTN; Showtime (multiplexed); Starz (multiplexed); Starz Encore (multiplexed); The Filipino Channel; The Movie Channel (multiplexed); TV5, La Television International.
Fee: $10.00 monthly (ART, CCTV, Filipino, RAI, TV5 or TV Japan), $15.00 monthly (TV Russia), $15.95 monthly (Cinemax, HBO, Showtime/TMC/Flix or Starz/Encore).

Video-On-Demand: No

Pay-Per-View
Sports PPV (delivered digitally); iN DEMAND (delivered digitally); Playboy TV (delivered digitally); Fresh (delivered digitally); Shorteez (delivered digitally); Hot Choice (delivered digitally); Urban Xtra (delivered digitally).

Internet Service
Operational: Yes.
Broadband Service: Road Runner.
Fee: $44.95 monthly.

Telephone Service
Digital: Operational
Miles of Plant: 138.0 (coaxial); None (fiber optic). Homes passed: 7,823.
Vice President & General Manager: Chris Whitaker. Vice President, Technical Operations: Gary Frederick. Vice President, Government & Public Affairs: Brad Phillips. Vice President, Sales & Marketing: Tom Smith. Senior Accounting Director: Karen Goodfellow.
Ownership: Time Warner Cable (MSO).

MURPHY—Cable TV of Cherokee County, 1421 Creekside Dr, PO Box 1000, Murphy, NC 28906-1000. Phones: 828-837-9704; 828-837-7118. Fax: 828-837-3820. E-mail: murphycabletv@cabletvonline.net. Web Site: http://www.cabletvonline.net. Also serves Cherokee County (portions). ICA: NC0079.
TV Market Ranking: Outside TV Markets (Cherokee County (portions), MURPHY). Franchise award date: N.A. Franchise expiration date: N.A. Began: March 15, 1972.
Channel capacity: N.A. Channels available but not in use: N.A.

Basic Service
Subscribers: 288.
Programming (received off-air): WAGA-TV (Buzzr, FOX, Movies!) Atlanta; WDEF-TV (Bounce TV, CBS, Escape) Chattanooga; WDSI-TV (FOX, MNT) Chattanooga; WLOS (ABC, Antenna TV) Asheville; WRCB (Antenna TV, NBC) Chattanooga; WSB-TV (ABC, MeTV) Atlanta; WTCI (PBS) Chattanooga; WTVC (ABC, This TV, WeatherNation) Chattanooga; WUNE-TV (PBS) Linville; WYFF (NBC, Movies!) Greenville; allband FM.
Fee: $45.00 installation; $9.95 monthly.

Expanded Basic Service 1
Subscribers: N.A.
Programming (via satellite): 3ABN; A&E; Animal Planet; Cartoon Network; CMT; CNBC; CNN; Discovery Channel; Disney Channel; Disney XD; ESPN; ESPN2; EWTN Global Catholic Network; Family Friendly Entertainment; Food Network; Fox News Channel; Fox Sports 1; FOX Sports South/SportSouth; Freeform; Golf Channel; Hallmark Channel; HGTV; History; HLN; ION Television; Lifetime; MSNBC; Nickelodeon; Outdoor Channel; QVC; Spike TV; SportSouth; Syfy; TBS; The Weather Channel; TLC; TNT; Travel Channel; Trinity Broadcasting Network (TBN); truTV; Turner Classic Movies; TV Land; USA Network; VH1; WGN America; WPIX (Antenna TV, CW, This TV) New York.
Fee: $69.00 installation; $42.08 monthly.

Pay Service 1
Pay Units: 140.
Programming (via satellite): HBO; Showtime.
Fee: $9.95 monthly (each).

Video-On-Demand: No

Internet Service
Operational: Yes.
Fee: $69.95 installation.

Telephone Service
None
Miles of Plant: 342.0 (coaxial); None (fiber optic). Homes passed: 6,800.
Chief Executive Officer: William Cook. President: David P. Daniel. Chief Technician: Dean Hensley.
Ownership: CND Acquisition Co. LLC (MSO).

NASH COUNTY—Crystal Broadband Networks, PO Box 180336, Chicago, IL 60618. Phones: 877-319-0328; 630-206-0447. E-mail: helpdesk@crystalbn.com. Web Site: http://crystalbn.com. Also serves Castalia, Dortches, Edgecombe County (portions) & Red Oak. ICA: NC0105.
TV Market Ranking: 84 (Edgecombe County (portions)); Below 100 (Castalia, Dortches, NASH COUNTY, Red Oak, Edgecombe County (portions)). Franchise award date: October 1, 1986. Franchise expiration date: N.A. Began: January 1, 1986.
Channel capacity: N.A. Channels available but not in use: N.A.

Basic Service
Subscribers: 151.
Programming (received off-air): WLFL (CW, The Country Network) Raleigh; WNCN (Antenna TV, CBS) Goldsboro; WNCT-TV (CBS, CW) Greenville; WRAL-TV (NBC, This TV) Raleigh; WRAZ (FOX, MeTV) Raleigh; WRDC (MNT) Durham; WRPX-TV (ION) Rocky Mount; WTVD (ABC, Live Well Network) Durham; WUNK-TV (PBS) Greenville.
Programming (via satellite): QVC; WGN America.
Fee: $39.95 installation; $45.25 monthly; $1.86 converter.

Expanded Basic Service 1
Subscribers: N.A.
Programming (via satellite): A&E; AMC; Animal Planet; BET; Bravo; Cartoon Network; CMT; CNBC; CNN; Comedy Central; C-SPAN; C-SPAN 2; Discovery Channel; Disney Channel; E! HD; ESPN; ESPN2; Food Network; Fox News Channel; Freeform; FX; Hallmark Channel; HGTV; History; HLN; Lifetime; MSNBC; MTV; Nickelodeon; Oxygen; Pop; Spike TV; Syfy; TBS; The Weather Channel; TLC; TNT; Travel Channel; truTV; TV Land; USA Network; VH1.
Fee: $22.45 monthly.

Digital Basic Service
Subscribers: N.A.
Programming (via satellite): BBC America; Bloomberg Television; Discovery Digital Networks; Disney XD; DIY Network; ESPN Classic; ESPNews; Fox Sports 1; Fuse; FXM; FYI; Golf Channel; Great American Country; GSN; History International; HITS (Headend In The Sky); IFC; LMN; MC; National Geographic Channel; NBCSN; Nick 2; Nick Jr.; Outdoor Channel; Starz Encore (multiplexed); Sundance TV; TeenNick; Trinity Broadcasting Network (TBN); Turner Classic Movies; WE tv.
Fee: $11.00 monthly.

Digital Pay Service 1
Pay Units: N.A.
Programming (via satellite): Cinemax (multiplexed); HBO (multiplexed); Showtime (multiplexed); Starz (multiplexed); The Movie Channel (multiplexed).
Fee: $15.95 monthly (each).

Video-On-Demand: No

Pay-Per-View
Hot Choice (delivered digitally); Playboy TV (delivered digitally); Fresh (delivered digitally); Shorteez (delivered digitally).

Internet Service
Operational: No.

Telephone Service
None
Miles of Plant: 162.0 (coaxial); None (fiber optic). Homes passed: 4,022.
Ownership: Crystal Broadband Networks (MSO).

NEBO—Morris Broadband. Now served by HENDERSONVILLE, NC [NC0033]. ICA: NC0113.

NEW BERN—Suddenlink Communications, 520 Maryville Centre Dr, Ste 300, St. Louis, MO 63141. Phones: 314-315-9400; 877-694-9474. Web Site: http://www.suddenlink.com. Also serves Bridgeton, Craven County, River Bend, Trent Woods & Vanceboro. ICA: NC0029.
TV Market Ranking: 84 (Bridgeton, Craven County, NEW BERN, River Bend, Trent Woods, Vanceboro).
Channel capacity: N.A. Channels available but not in use: N.A.

Basic Service
Subscribers: 13,094.
Fee: $25.00 monthly.

Internet Service
Operational: Yes.
Subscribers: 12,975.

Telephone Service
Digital: Operational
Subscribers: 7,807.
Miles of Plant: 831.0 (coaxial); 254.0 (fiber optic). Homes passed: 31,527.
Senior Vice President, Corporate Finance: Michael Pflantz.
Ownership: Cequel Communications Holdings I LLC (MSO).

NEWPORT—Time Warner Cable. Now served by JACKSONVILLE, NC [NC0025]. ICA: NC0013.

NEWTON GROVE—Charter Communications. Now served by ANGIER, NC [NC0194]. ICA: NC0218.

NORTH WILKESBORO—Charter Communications. Now served by HICKORY, NC [NC0009]. ICA: NC0046.

OAK CITY—Crystal Broadband Networks, PO Box 180336, Chicago, IL 60618. Phones: 877-319-0328; 630-206-0447. E-mail: helpdesk@crystalbn.com. Web Site: http://crystalbn.com. Also serves Edgecombe County (portions), Halifax County (portions), Hamilton, Hassel, Hobgood & Martin County (unincorporated areas). ICA: NC0147.
TV Market Ranking: 84 (Edgecombe County (portions), Halifax County (portions), Hamilton, Hassel, Hobgood, Martin County (unincorporated areas), OAK CITY). Franchise award date: July 1, 1985. Franchise expiration date: N.A. Began: April 1, 1986.
Channel capacity: N.A. Channels available but not in use: N.A.

Basic Service
Subscribers: 58.
Programming (received off-air): WCTI-TV (ABC, Decades, Movies!) New Bern; WEPX-TV (ION) Greenville; WNCN (Antenna TV, CBS) Goldsboro; WNCT-TV (CBS, CW) Greenville; WRAL-TV (NBC, This TV) Raleigh; WTVD (ABC, Live Well Network) Durham; WUNK-TV (PBS) Greenville; WYDO (Bounce TV, FOX) Greenville.
Programming (via satellite): Freeform; QVC; Trinity Broadcasting Network (TBN).
Fee: $39.95 installation; $44.17 monthly; $2.00 converter.

Expanded Basic Service 1
Subscribers: N.A.
Programming (via satellite): AMC; BET; CMT; CNN; C-SPAN; Discovery Channel; Disney Channel; ESPN; ESPN2; Fox News Channel; HGTV; HLN; Lifetime; MSNBC; MTV; Nickelodeon; Spike TV; Syfy; TBS; The Weather Channel; TLC; TNT; USA Network; VH1.
Fee: $19.69 monthly.

Digital Basic Service
Subscribers: N.A.
Programming (via satellite): BBC America; Bravo; Discovery Digital Networks; ESPNews; Golf Channel; GSN; History International; IFC; NBCSN; WE tv.
Fee: $10.21 monthly; $5.00 converter.

Pay Service 1
Pay Units: N.A.
Programming (via satellite): HBO.
Fee: $15.95 monthly.

Digital Pay Service 1
Pay Units: N.A.
Programming (via satellite): Cinemax (multiplexed); HBO (multiplexed); Starz (multiplexed); Starz Encore (multiplexed); The Movie Channel (multiplexed).
Fee: $15.95 monthly (each).

Video-On-Demand: No

Pay-Per-View
Playboy TV (delivered digitally).

Internet Service
Operational: No.

Telephone Service
None
Miles of Plant: 29.0 (coaxial); None (fiber optic). Homes passed: 1,389.
Ownership: Crystal Broadband Networks (MSO).

OCEAN ISLE BEACH/BRICK LANDING—Formerly served by Tele-Media. Now served by Time Warner Cable, WILMINGTON, NC [NC0007]. ICA: NC0244.

Cable Systems—North Carolina

OCRACOKE—Belhaven Cable TV, 235 Pamlico St, PO Box 8, Belhaven, NC 27810. Phone: 252-943-3736. Web Site: http://www.belhavencabletv.com. ICA: NC0257.
TV Market Ranking: Below 100 (OCRACOKE).
Channel capacity: N.A. Channels available but not in use: N.A.
Basic Service
Subscribers: 58.
Fee: $33.45 monthly.
Ownership: Belhaven Cable TV Inc. (MSO).

OLDE POINTE—Formerly served by Charter Communications. No longer in operation. ICA: NC0224.

ORRUM—Formerly served by Carolina Cable Partnership. No longer in operation. ICA: NC0208.

PAMLICO COUNTY—Time Warner Cable. Now served by JACKSONVILLE, NC [NC0025]. ICA: NC0192.

PEMBROKE—Formerly served by Carolina Cable Partnership. No longer in operation. ICA: NC0251.

PINETOPS—Crystal Broadband Networks, PO Box 180336, Chicago, IL 60618. Phones: 877-319-0328; 630-206-0447. E-mail: helpdesk@crystalbn.com. Web Site: http://crystalbn.com. Also serves Edgecombe County (portions) & Macclesfield. ICA: NC0204.
TV Market Ranking: 84 (Edgecombe County (portions), Macclesfield, PINETOPS).
Channel capacity: N.A. Channels available but not in use: N.A.
Basic Service
Subscribers: 144.
Programming (received off-air): WCTI-TV (ABC, Decades, Movies!) New Bern; WLFL (CW, The Country Network) Raleigh; WNCN (Antenna TV, CBS) Goldsboro; WNCT-TV (CBS, CW) Greenville; WRAL-TV (NBC, This TV) Raleigh; WRAY-TV (IND) Wilson; WRAZ (FOX, MeTV) Raleigh; WRDC (MNT) Durham; WRPX-TV (ION) Rocky Mount; WTVD (ABC, Live Well Network) Durham; WUNK-TV (PBS) Greenville.
Programming (via satellite): QVC.
Fee: $39.95 installation; $36.57 monthly.
Expanded Basic Service 1
Subscribers: N.A.
Programming (via satellite): AMC; Animal Planet; BET; CMT; CNN; Discovery Channel; Disney Channel; ESPN; ESPN2; Fox News Channel; Freeform; FX; HLN; Lifetime; MSNBC; Nickelodeon; Spike TV; Syfy; TBS; The Weather Channel; TLC; TNT; Trinity Broadcasting Network (TBN); USA Network; WPIX (Antenna TV, CW, This TV) New York.
Fee: $19.69 monthly.
Digital Basic Service
Subscribers: N.A.
Programming (via satellite): BBC America; Bravo; Discovery Digital Networks; DMX Music; ESPN Classic; ESPNews; Golf Channel; GSN; HGTV; History; IFC; NBCSN; Nick Jr.; Starz Encore (multiplexed); WE tv.
Fee: $11.00 monthly.
Pay Service 1
Pay Units: N.A.
Programming (via satellite): HBO.
Fee: $14.99 monthly.
Digital Pay Service 1
Pay Units: N.A.
Programming (via satellite): Cinemax (multiplexed); HBO (multiplexed); Showtime (multiplexed); Starz.

Fee: $15.95 monthly (each).
Video-On-Demand: No
Pay-Per-View
Playboy TV (delivered digitally); Hits Movies & Events (delivered digitally).
Internet Service
Operational: No.
Telephone Service
None
Miles of Plant: 41.0 (coaxial); None (fiber optic). Homes passed: 2,424.
Ownership: Crystal Broadband Networks (MSO).

PINK HILL—Time Warner Cable. Now served by JACKSONVILLE, NC [NC0025]. ICA: NC0210.

PLYMOUTH (town)—Mediacom, 910 NC Highway 32 South, PO Box 580, Plymouth, NC 27962. Phones: 845-695-2762; 252-793-1570. Fax: 252-793-6135. Web Site: http://www.mediacomcable.com. Also serves Columbia, Creswell, Jamesville, Martin County (portions), Roper, Tyrrell County (portions) & Washington County. ICA: NC0085.
TV Market Ranking: 84 (Jamesville, Martin County (portions), PLYMOUTH (TOWN), Roper, Washington County (portions)); Below 100 (Columbia, Tyrrell County (portions)); Outside TV Markets (Creswell, Washington County (portions)). Franchise award date: December 12, 1972. Franchise expiration date: N.A. Began: June 12, 1973.
Channel capacity: N.A. Channels available but not in use: N.A.
Basic Service
Subscribers: 1,266.
Programming (received off-air): WAVY-TV (Bounce TV, NBC) Portsmouth; WCTI-TV (ABC, Decades, Movies!) New Bern; WEPX-TV (ION) Greenville; WGNT (Antenna TV, CW) Portsmouth; WHRO-TV (PBS) Hampton-Norfolk; WITN-TV (MeTV, MNT, NBC) Washington; WNCT-TV (CBS, CW) Greenville; WSKY-TV (Escape, IND, Laff) Manteo; WTKR (CBS) Norfolk; WUND-TV (PBS) Edenton; WVEC (ABC) Hampton; WYDO (Bounce TV, FOX) Greenville.
Programming (via satellite): History; Pop; WGN America.
Fee: $45.00 installation; $41.00 monthly; $3.00 converter.
Expanded Basic Service 1
Subscribers: N.A.
Programming (via satellite): A&E; AMC; Animal Planet; BET; Bravo; Cartoon Network; CMT; CNBC; CNN; Comedy Central; C-SPAN; Discovery Channel; Discovery Life Channel; Disney Channel; Disney XD; ESPN; ESPN2; Food Network; Fox News Channel; Fox Sports 1; Freeform; FX; Hallmark Channel; HGTV; HLN; INSP; Lifetime; MSNBC; MTV; Nickelodeon; Outdoor Channel; QVC; Spike TV; Syfy; TBS; The Weather Channel; TLC; TNT; Travel Channel; TV Land; USA Network; VH1; WE tv.
Fee: $33.49 monthly.
Digital Basic Service
Subscribers: N.A.
Programming (via satellite): AXS TV; BBC America; Bloomberg Television; Discovery Digital Networks; DMX Music; ESPN; ESPNews; Fuse; FXM; FYI; Golf Channel; GSN; HD Theater; History International; IFC; LMN; MTV2; National Geographic Channel; NBCSN; Nick Jr.; TeenNick; The Word Network; truTV; Turner Classic Movies; Weatherscan.
Fee: $8.00 monthly.

Digital Pay Service 1
Pay Units: N.A.
Programming (via satellite): Cinemax (multiplexed); Flix (multiplexed); HBO (multiplexed); HBO HD; Showtime (multiplexed); Showtime HD; Starz (multiplexed); Starz Encore (multiplexed); Starz HD; Sundance TV (multiplexed); The Movie Channel (multiplexed); The Movie Channel HD.
Fee: $8.00 monthly (Starz), $9.95 monthly (Cinemax or Showtime), $13.95 monthly (HBO).
Video-On-Demand: No
Pay-Per-View
iN DEMAND (delivered digitally); ESPN Sports PPV (delivered digitally).
Internet Service
Operational: Yes. Began: January 1, 2002.
Broadband Service: Mediacom High Speed Internet.
Fee: $59.95 installation; $40.95 monthly; $3.00 modem lease.
Telephone Service
Analog: Not Operational
Digital: Operational
Fee: $39.95 monthly
Miles of Plant: 1,100.0 (coaxial); None (fiber optic). Homes passed: 7,609. Miles of plant (coax and fiber) includes Conway, Currituck & Edenton.
Vice President, Financial Reporting: Kenneth J. Kohrs. General Manager: Wayne Holiday. Office Manager: Wendy White. Marketing Analyst: Renette Ruffin.
Ownership: Mediacom LLC (MSO).

POWELLSVILLE—Mediacom. Now served by COLERAIN, NC [NC0255]. ICA: NC0180.

PRINCETON—Formerly served by Southern Cablevision. Now served by Charter Communications, KENLY, NC [NC0148]. ICA: NC0177.

RAEFORD—Time Warner Cable. Now served by RALEIGH, NC [NC0003]. ICA: NC0108.

RALEIGH—Time Warner Cable, 101 Innovation Ave, Ste 100, Morrisville, NC 27560. Phones: 919-573-7029; 919-573-7000. Fax: 919-573-7042. Web Site: http://www.timewarnercable.com. Also serves Aberdeen (town), Apex (town), Archer Lodge, Autryville, Bailey, Beacon Ridge (town), Black Creek (town), Bunn (town), Butner (town), Carrboro, Carthage (town), Cary (town), Chapel Hill, Chatham County, Clayton (town), Creedmoor (town), Cumberland County, Dunn, Durham, Durham County, Eastover, Elm City, Erwin (town), Eureka, Fairmont (town), Falcon, Fayetteville, Fort Bragg, Four Oaks (town), Foxfire (village), Franklin County (portions), Franklinton (town), Fremont (town), Fuquay-Varina (town), Garner (town), Godwin (town), Goldsboro, Granville County (portions), Halifax County (portions), Henderson, Hillsborough (town), Hoke County (portions), Holly Springs (town), Hope Mills (town), Johnston County (portions), Kittrell (village), Knightdale (town), Linden, Littleton, Louisburg, Lumber Bridge (town), Lumberton, Middleburg (town), Middlesex (town), Momeyer, Moore County (portions), Morrisville (town), Mount Olive (town), Nash County, Norlina, Northampton County (portions), Orange County, Oxford, Parkton (town), Pembroke (town), Pikeville (town), Pine Level (town), Pinebluff (town), Pinehurst (town), Pinewild (town), Pittsboro (town), Pope AFB, Princeton (town), Raeford (town), RALEIGH, Red Springs (town), Rennert (town), Robeson County (portions), Rolesville (town), Saratoga (town), Selma (town), Seven Lakes (town), Seymour Johnson AFB, Sims (town), Smithfield (town), Southern Pines (town), Spring Hope (town), Spring Lake (town), St. Pauls (town), Stantonsburg (town), Stedman (town), Stem, Stovall (town), Taylortown (town), Vance County, Wade (town), Wake County (portions), Wake Forest, Warren County (portions), Warrenton, Wayne County, Wendell (town), West End (town), Wilson (town), Wilson County, Youngsville (town) & Zebulon (town). ICA: NC0003.
TV Market Ranking: 47,73 (Chatham County (portions)); 73 (Aberdeen (town), Apex (town), Archer Lodge, Autryville, Bailey, Beacon Ridge (town), Bunn (town), Butner (town), Carrboro, Cary (town), Chapel Hill, Clayton (town), Creedmoor (town), Cumberland County, Dunn, Durham, Durham County, Eastover, Erwin (town), Falcon, Fayetteville, Fort Bragg, Four Oaks (town), Franklin County (portions), Franklinton (town), Fuquay-Varina (town), Garner (town), Godwin (town), Goldsboro, Granville County (portions), Hillsborough (town), Hoke County (portions), Holly Springs (town), Hope Mills (town), Johnston County (portions), Kittrell (village), Knightdale (town), Linden, Louisburg, Lumber Bridge (town) (portions), Lumberton, Middlesex (town), Momeyer, Moore County (portions), Morrisville (town), Mount Olive (town), Nash County (portions), Orange County, Oxford, Parkton (town), Pembroke (town), Pikeville (town), Pine Level (town), Pinebluff (town), Pinehurst (town), Pinewild (town), Pittsboro (town), Pope AFB, Princeton (town), Raeford (town), RALEIGH, Red Springs (town), Rennert (town), Robeson County (portions), Rolesville (town), Selma (town), Seymour Johnson AFB, Sims (town), Smithfield (town), Southern Pines (town), Spring Hope (town), Spring Lake (town), St. Pauls (town), Stedman (town), Stem, Taylortown (town), Vance County (portions), Wade (town), Wake County (portions), Wake Forest, Wendell (town), Youngsville (town)); 73,84 (Black Creek (town), Elm City, Eureka, Fremont (town), Saratoga (town), Stantonsburg (town), Wayne County, Wilson (town), Wilson County (portions)); 84 (Halifax County (portions)); Below 100 (Northampton County (portions), Warren County (portions), Littleton, Chatham County (portions), Moore County (portions), Robeson County (portions), Halifax County (portions)); Outside TV Markets (Carthage (town), Fairmont (town), Foxfire (village), Middleburg (town), Norlina, Northampton County (portions), Seven Lakes (town), Stovall (town), Warren County (portions), Warrenton, West End (town), Zebulon (town), Henderson, Chatham County (portions), Moore County (portions), Robeson County (portions), Vance County (portions)). Franchise award date: June 1, 1983. Franchise expiration date: N.A. Began: September 14, 1968.
Channel capacity: N.A. Channels available but not in use: N.A.
Basic Service
Subscribers: 407,967.
Programming (received off-air): WLFL (CW, The Country Network) Raleigh; WNCN (Antenna TV, CBS) Goldsboro; WRAL-TV (NBC, This TV) Raleigh; WRAY-TV (IND) Wilson; WRAZ (FOX, MeTV) Raleigh; WRDC (MNT) Durham; WRPX-TV (ION) Rocky Mount; WTVD (ABC, Live Well Network) Durham; WUNC-TV (PBS) Chapel Hill; WUVC-DT

North Carolina—Cable Systems

(Bounce TV, getTV, UNV) Fayetteville; 2 FMs.
Programming (via satellite): Pop; TBS; WGN America.
Fee: $42.50 installation; $14.99 monthly; $2.88 converter.

Expanded Basic Service 1
Subscribers: N.A.
Programming (via satellite): A&E; AMC; Animal Planet; BET; Cartoon Network; CMT; CNBC; CNN; Comedy Central; C-SPAN; C-SPAN 2; Discovery Channel; Discovery Life Channel; Disney Channel; E! HD; ESPN; ESPN Classic; ESPN2; EVINE Live; EWTN Global Catholic Network; Food Network; Fox News Channel; FOX Sports Networks; Freeform; FX; Golf Channel; Hallmark Channel; HGTV; History; HLN; INSP; Lifetime; MSNBC; MTV; National Geographic Channel; NBCSN; Nickelodeon; Oxygen; QVC; Spike TV; Syfy; The Weather Channel; TLC; TNT; Travel Channel; truTV; Turner Classic Movies; TV Land; USA Network; VH1; WE tv.
Fee: $36.05 monthly.

Digital Basic Service
Subscribers: N.A.
Programming (via satellite): BBC America; Bloomberg Television; Boomerang; Cooking Channel; C-SPAN 3; C-SPAN Extra; Discovery Digital Networks; Disney Channel; Disney XD; DIY Network; ESPNews; Fox Sports 1; FSN Digital Atlantic; FSN Digital Central; FSN Digital Pacific; Fuse; FYI; Great American Country; GSN; History International; HITS (Headend In The Sky); IFC; MBC America; MC; MTV Classic; MTV Hits; MTV2; NBA TV; Nick Jr.; Outdoor Channel; Ovation; TeenNick; Tennis Channel; Trinity Broadcasting Network (TBN); WAM! America's Kidz Network.
Fee: $16.25 monthly.

Digital Pay Service 1
Pay Units: N.A.
Programming (via satellite): Cinemax (multiplexed); Flix (multiplexed); FXM; HBO (multiplexed); Showtime (multiplexed); Starz Encore (multiplexed); Sundance TV; The Movie Channel (multiplexed).
Fee: $14.50 monthly (each).

Video-On-Demand: Yes

Pay-Per-View
Pleasure (delivered digitally); ESPN Now (delivered digitally); Playboy TV (delivered digitally); Fresh (delivered digitally); Shorteez (delivered digitally); Hot Choice (delivered digitally); Sports PPV (delivered digitally).

Internet Service
Operational: Yes. Began: October 1, 2003.
Subscribers: 138,805.
Broadband Service: EarthLink, Road Runner, AOL.
Fee: $99.95 installation; $44.95 monthly; $3.00 modem lease.

Telephone Service
Digital: Operational
Subscribers: 68,336.
Fee: $44.95 monthly
Miles of Plant: 8,446.0 (coaxial); 1,938.0 (fiber optic).
Vice President & General Manager: Chris Whitaker. Vice President, Finance: Rick Bennett. Vice President, Human Resources: Ann Burford. Vice President, Technical Services: Gary Frederick. Vice President, Voice: Margie Fry. Vice President, Marketing & Sales: Tom Smith. Vice President, Government & Public Affairs: Jack Stanley. Vice President, Customer Care: Michele Varsano.
Ownership: Time Warner Cable (MSO).; Advance/Newhouse Partnership (MSO).

RANGER—Formerly served by Cable TV of Cherokee County. No longer in operation. ICA: NC0116.

REIDSVILLE—Time Warner Cable. Now served by GREENSBORO, NC [NC0006]. ICA: NC0045.

RIEGELWOOD—Time Warner Cable. Now served by WILMINGTON, NC [NC0007]. ICA: NC0217.

ROANOKE RAPIDS—Charter Communications, 12405 Powerscourt Dr, St. Louis, MO 63131. Phones: 636-207-5100 (Corporate office); 757-539-0713 (Suffolk office); 252-441-1582. Fax: 252-441-1581. Web Site: http://www.charter.com. Also serves Garysburg, Gaston, Halifax County, Northampton County & Weldon. ICA: NC0214.
TV Market Ranking: Below 100 (Halifax County (portions), Northampton County (portions), Weldon); Outside TV Markets (Garysburg, Gaston, Halifax County (portions), Northampton County (portions), ROANOKE RAPIDS). Franchise award date: N.A. Franchise expiration date: N.A. Began: March 1, 1965.
Channel capacity: N.A. Channels available but not in use: N.A.

Digital Basic Service
Subscribers: 6,403.
Programming (via satellite): BBC America; Bloomberg Television; Boomerang; CNN en Espanol; CNN International; Discovery Digital Networks; DIY Network; ESPN Classic; ESPNews; FOX College Sports Central; FOX College Sports Pacific; Fox Deportes; Fox Sports 2; Fuse; FXM; FYI; Great American Country; History International; IFC; LMN; MC; Mid-Atlantic Sports Network (MASN); Nick 2; Nick Jr.; Nicktoons; Sundance TV; TeenNick; Turner Classic Movies; TV Guide Interactive Inc.
Fee: $26.99 monthly.

Digital Expanded Basic Service
Subscribers: N.A.
Programming (via satellite): A&E; AMC; Animal Planet; BET; Bravo; Cartoon Network; CMT; CNBC; CNN; Comedy Central; Discovery Channel; Disney Channel; Disney XD; E! HD; ESPN; ESPN2; Food Network; Fox News Channel; Fox Sports 1; Freeform; FX; Golf Channel; GSN; Hallmark Channel; HGTV; History; HLN; Lifetime; MSNBC; MTV; MTV2; National Geographic Channel; NBCSN; Nickelodeon; Oxygen; Spike TV; TBS; The Weather Channel; TLC; TNT; Travel Channel; truTV; TV Land; USA Network; VH1; WE tv.
Fee: $47.99 monthly.

Digital Pay Service 1
Pay Units: N.A.
Programming (via satellite): Cinemax (multiplexed); HBO (multiplexed); Showtime (multiplexed); Starz (multiplexed); Starz Encore (multiplexed).

Video-On-Demand: No

Pay-Per-View
iN DEMAND (delivered digitally); Playboy TV (delivered digitally); Fresh (delivered digitally); Shorteez (delivered digitally).

Internet Service
Operational: Yes.
Subscribers: 3,698.
Broadband Service: Charter Internet.
Fee: $29.99 monthly.

Telephone Service
Digital: Operational
Subscribers: 2,638.
Miles of Plant: 495.0 (coaxial); 104.0 (fiber optic). Homes passed: 16,255.

Vice President & General Manager: Anthony Pope. Marketing Director: Brooke Sinclair. Accounting Director: David Sovanski. Marketing Manager: LaRisa Scales. Technical Operations Manager: Joel Sprout. Operations Manager: Doug Underwood.
Ownership: Charter Communications Inc. (MSO).

ROARING FORK—Formerly served by Almega Cable. No longer in operation. ICA: NC0213.

ROBBINS—Formerly served by Vital Communications. No longer in operation. ICA: NC0153.

ROBBINSVILLE—Zito Media, 102 S Main St, PO Box 665, Coudersport, PA 16915. Phones: 814-260-9055; 800-365-6988. E-mail: info@zitomedia.com. Web Site: http://www.zitomedia.com. Also serves Graham County (central portion) & Santeetlah. ICA: NC0231.
TV Market Ranking: Outside TV Markets (Graham County (central portion), ROBBINSVILLE, Santeetlah). Franchise award date: September 25, 1980. Franchise expiration date: N.A. Began: October 1, 1981.
Channel capacity: N.A. Channels available but not in use: N.A.

Basic Service
Subscribers: 202.
Programming (received off-air): WLOS (ABC, Antenna TV) Asheville; WUNE-TV (PBS) Linville; WYFF (NBC, Movies!) Greenville.
Programming (via satellite): C-SPAN; QVC; The Weather Channel; TLC; WGN America; WSEE-TV (CBS, CW) Erie.
Fee: $49.95 installation; $22.20 monthly; $1.78 converter.

Expanded Basic Service 1
Subscribers: N.A.
Programming (via satellite): A&E; AMC; Cartoon Network; CMT; CNN; Comedy Central; Discovery Channel; Disney Channel; ESPN; ESPN2; FOX Sports South/SportSouth; Freeform; FX; HLN; Lifetime; MTV; Nickelodeon; Spike TV; TBS; TNT; Turner Classic Movies; USA Network.
Fee: $20.00 monthly.

Digital Basic Service
Subscribers: N.A.
Programming (via satellite): BBC America; Cloo; Discovery Digital Networks; Disney XD; DMX Music; ESPN Classic; ESPNews; Fox Sports 1; Fuse; FYI; Golf Channel; GSN; History International; IFC; LMN; MTV2; National Geographic Channel; NBCSN; Nick Jr.; Syfy; TeenNick; WE tv.

Digital Pay Service 1
Pay Units: N.A.
Programming (via satellite): Cinemax (multiplexed); HBO (multiplexed); Showtime (multiplexed); Starz (multiplexed); Starz Encore (multiplexed); The Movie Channel (multiplexed).

Video-On-Demand: No

Pay-Per-View
iN DEMAND (delivered digitally); Playboy TV (delivered digitally).

Internet Service
Operational: Yes.

Telephone Service
Digital: Operational
Miles of Plant: 69.0 (coaxial); None (fiber optic). Homes passed: 1,951.
President: James Rigas.
Ownership: Zito Media (MSO).

ROBESON COUNTY (western portion)—Formerly served by Carolina Cable Partnership. No longer in operation. ICA: NC0215.

ROCKINGHAM—Time Warner Cable. Now served by CHARLOTTE, NC [NC0001]. ICA: NC0038.

ROCKY MOUNT—Suddenlink Communications, 520 Maryville Centre Dr, Ste 300, St. Louis, MO 63141. Phones: 314-315-9400; 877-694-9474. Web Site: http://www.suddenlink.com. Also serves Conetoe, Edgecombe County (eastern portion), Enfield, Halifax County (portions), Nash County, Nashville, Princeville, Red Oak, Scotland Neck, Sharpsburg & Tarboro. ICA: NC0016.
TV Market Ranking: 73 (Nash County (portions)); 84 (Conetoe, Edgecombe County (eastern portion), Princeville, ROCKY MOUNT, Sharpsburg, Tarboro); Below 100 (Halifax County (portions), Nashville, Red Oak, Enfield, Scotland Neck, Nash County (portions), Edgecombe County (eastern portion)).
Channel capacity: N.A. Channels available but not in use: N.A.

Basic Service
Subscribers: 17,063.
Fee: $25.00 monthly.
Senior Vice President, Corporate Finance: Michael Pflantz.
Ownership: Cequel Communications Holdings I LLC.

ROSEBORO—StarVision. Now served by HALLS TWP., NC [NC0070]. ICA: NC0216.

ROWLAND—Time Warner Cable. Now served by COLUMBIA, SC [SC0002]. ICA: NC0174.

ROXBORO—Charter Communications, 12405 Powerscourt Dr, St. Louis, MO 63131. Phones: 636-207-5100 (Corporate office); 336-599-2042. Fax: 336-599-1792. Web Site: http://www.charter.com. Also serves Caswell County (portions), Milton & Person County (portions). ICA: NC0059.
TV Market Ranking: 73 (Caswell County (portions), Person County (portions), ROXBORO); Below 100 (Milton); Outside TV Markets (Caswell County (portions), Person County (portions)). Franchise award date: December 1, 1979. Franchise expiration date: N.A. Began: May 26, 1980.
Channel capacity: N.A. Channels available but not in use: N.A.

Digital Basic Service
Subscribers: 3,328.
Programming (via satellite): Discovery Digital Networks; DIY Network; FYI; History International; LMN; MC; MTV2; Nick Jr.; Sundance TV; TeenNick; TV Guide Interactive Inc.
Fee: $26.99 monthly.

Digital Expanded Basic Service
Subscribers: N.A.
Programming (via satellite): A&E; AMC; Animal Planet; BET; Cartoon Network; CMT; CNBC; CNN; Comedy Central; C-SPAN; Discovery Channel; Disney Channel; E! HD; ESPN; ESPN2; Fox News Channel; Fox Sports 1; Freeform; FX; Golf Channel; HGTV; History; HLN; Lifetime; MSNBC; MTV; National Geographic Channel; NBCSN; Nickelodeon; Spike TV; Syfy; TBS; The Weather Channel; TLC; TNT; Travel Channel; truTV; TV Land; USA Network; VH1.
Fee: $47.99 monthly.

D-564   TV & Cable Factbook No. 85

Cable Systems—North Carolina

Digital Pay Service 1
Pay Units: N.A.
Programming (via satellite): Cinemax (multiplexed); Flix; HBO (multiplexed); Showtime (multiplexed); Starz (multiplexed); Starz Encore (multiplexed); The Movie Channel (multiplexed).
Fee: $11.00 monthly (Cinemax or HBO).
Video-On-Demand: No
Pay-Per-View
iN DEMAND (delivered digitally), Addressable: No; Playboy TV (delivered digitally); Fresh (delivered digitally); Shorteez (delivered digitally).
Internet Service
Operational: Yes, DSL.
Broadband Service: Charter Internet.
Fee: $29.99 monthly.
Telephone Service
None
Miles of Plant: 328.0 (coaxial); 21.0 (fiber optic).
Vice President & General Manager: Anthony Pope. Marketing Director: Brooke Sinclair. Accounting Director: David Sovanski. Chief Technician: Steve Folly. Office Manager: Brenda Brinson. Plant Manager: Barry Creasy. Marketing Manager: LaRisa Scales. Operations Manager: Doug Underwood.
Ownership: Charter Communications Inc. (MSO).

SALISBURY—Time Warner Cable. Now served by CHARLOTTE, NC [NC0001]. ICA: NC0022.

SANFORD—Charter Communications. Now served by ANGIER, NC [NC0194]. ICA: NC0219.

SANTREE MOBILE HOME PARK—Formerly served by Adelphia Communications. No longer in operation. ICA: NC0220.

SCOTLAND NECK—Suddenlink Communications. Now served by ROCKY MOUNT, NC [NC0016]. ICA: NC0146.

SELMA/GARNER—Time Warner Cable. Now served by RALEIGH, NC [NC0003]. ICA: NC0032.

SHALLOTTE—ATMC. Formerly [NC0050]. This cable system has been converted to IPTV, 640 Whiteville Rd NW, PO Box 3198, Shallotte, NC 28459-3198. Phones: 888-367-2862; 910-754-4311. Fax: 910-754-5499. E-mail: contact@atlantictelephone.org. Web Site: http://www.atmc.net. Also serves Bolivia, Brick Landing, Brunswick County (portions), Brunswick County (unincorporated areas), Calabash, Carolina Shores, Holden Beach, Longwood, Ocean Isle Beach, Sunset Beach, Sunset Harbor, Supply, Tabor City, Varnamtown & Whiteville. ICA: NC5004.
TV Market Ranking: Below 100 (Bolivia, Brick Landing, Brunswick County (unincorporated areas), Calabash, Carolina Shores, Holden Beach, Longwood, Ocean Isle Beach, SHALLOTTE, Sunset Beach, Sunset Harbor, Supply). Franchise award date: May 26, 1980. Franchise expiration date: N.A. Began: October 1, 1982.
Channel capacity: N.A. Channels available but not in use: N.A.
Broadcast Basic
Subscribers: 28,158.
Programming (received off-air): WBTW (Antenna TV, CBS, MNT) Florence; WECT (Bounce TV, NBC) Wilmington; WILM-LD (MeTV) Wilmington; WSFX-TV (FOX, This TV) Wilmington; WWAY (ABC, CBS, CW, Retro TV) Wilmington.
Programming (via satellite): C-SPAN; C-SPAN 2; MyNetworkTV; PBS HD; QVC; TBS HD; WGN America.
Fee: $27.50 installation; $14.50 monthly. Includes 26 channels - 18 in SD & 8 in HD, 45 music channels & one digital adapter.
Expanded Basic
Subscribers: N.A.
Programming (received off-air): WECT (Bounce TV, NBC) Wilmington.
Programming (via satellite): A&E; A&E HD; AMC; AMC HD; Animal Planet HD; BET; Bravo HD; Cartoon Network; CMT; CNBC; CNBC HD+; CNN HD; Comedy Central; Daystar TV Network; Discovery Channel; Discovery Channel HD; Disney Channel; Disney Channel HD; E! HD; ESPN; ESPN Classic; ESPN HD; ESPN2; ESPN2 HD; EWTN Global Catholic Network; FamilyNet; Food Network HD; Fox News HD; Fox Sports 1; Freeform; Freeform HD; FX; FX HD; Golf Channel; Great American Country; Hallmark Channel; Hallmark Movies & Mysteries; HGTV HD; History; History HD; HLN; INSP; Investigation Discovery; Lifetime HD; MLB Network HD; MSNBC; MTV; National Geographic Channel; National Geographic Channel HD; Nickelodeon; Spike TV; Spike TV HD; Syfy HD; The Weather Channel HD; The Word Network; TLC; TNT; TNT HD; Travel Channel HD; truTV; Turner Classic Movies; Turner Classic Movies HD; TV Land; USA Network HD; VH1.
Fee: $55.75 monthly. Includes 80 channels - 30 in SD & 50 in HD, 45 music channels & one digital box.
Bronze Plus
Subscribers: N.A.
Programming (via satellite): AXS TV; BBC America; Bio HD; Boomerang; Chiller; Cooking Channel; Crime & Investigation Network; Destination America; Discovery Life Channel; Disney XD; DIY Network; ESPNews; ESPNU HD; Fox Business Network; Fox Business Network HD; FOX College Sports Central; FOX College Sports Pacific; FXM; FYI; GSN; Hallmark Movie Channel HD; History; History International; Lifetime Movie Network HD; LMN; MTV Classic; MTV Hits; MTV2; NBCSN; Nick Jr.; Nicktoons; Outdoor Channel; Ovation; Oxygen; RFD-TV; RTV; Science Channel; Science HD; TeenNick; Tennis Channel.
Fee: $67.75 monthly. Includes 127 channels - 57 in SD & 70 in HD, 45 music channels & one digital box.
Gold Plus
Subscribers: N.A.
Fee: $93.75 monthly. Includes 127 channels - 54 in SD & 73 in HD, 45 music channels, two premium channel suites & one digital box.
Platinum Plus
Subscribers: N.A.
Fee: $112.50 monthly. Includes 127 channels - 52 in SD & 75 in HD, 45 music channels four premium channel suites & one digital box.
Cinemax
Subscribers: N.A.
Programming (via satellite): Cinemax (multiplexed); Cinemax HD.
Fee: $15.50 monthly. Includes 7 channels plus Cinemax on Demand.
HBO
Subscribers: N.A.
Programming (via satellite): HBO (multiplexed); HBO HD.
Fee: $17.25 monthly. Includes 8 channels plus HBO on Demand.
Cinemax/HBO
Subscribers: N.A.
Programming (via satellite): Cinemax (multiplexed); Cinemax HD (multiplexed); HBO (multiplexed); HBO HD (multiplexed).
Fee: $26.95 monthly. Includes 15 channels (7 Cinemax channels & 8 HBO channels) plus Cinemax on Demand & HBO on Demand.
Encore Movie Pak
Subscribers: N.A.
Programming (via satellite): Starz Encore (multiplexed).
Fee: $6.75 monthly. Includes 7 channels plus Encore on Demand.
Showtime Unlimited
Subscribers: N.A.
Programming (via satellite): Flix; Showtime (multiplexed); Showtime HD; The Movie Channel (multiplexed).
Fee: $14.20 monthly. Includes 9 channels (5 Showtime channels, 2 TMC channels & 1 Flix channel) plus Showtime on Demand.
Starz Super Pak
Subscribers: N.A.
Programming (via satellite): Starz (multiplexed); Starz HD.
Fee: $15.25 monthly. Includes 15 channels (7 Encore channels & 6 Starz channels) plus Encore on Demand & Starz on Demand.
Video-On-Demand: Yes
Pay-Per-View
iN DEMAND; Club Jenna (delivered digitally); ESPN (delivered digitally); MLB Extra Innings (delivered digitally).
Internet Service
Operational: Yes.
Fee: $57.45-$103.45 monthly.
Telephone Service
Digital: Operational
Fee: $18.71 monthly
Miles of Plant: None (coaxial); 5,784.0 (fiber optic).
President: Lyle Ray King. Chief Executive Officer & General Manager: Allen Russ. Chief Financial Officer: Roger A. Cox. Engineering Director: Jackson Canady. Marketing & Programming Director: Percy Woodard. Cable Operations Manager: Brent Brinson.
Ownership: Atlantic Telephone Membership Corp.

SHALLOTTE—ATMC. This cable system has converted to IPTV. See SHALLOTTE, NC [NC5004]. ICA: NC0050.

SHELBY—Time Warner Cable. Now served by CHARLOTTE, NC [NC0001]. ICA: NC0027.

SIMPSON—Suddenlink Communications. Now served by GREENVILLE, NC [NC0014]. ICA: NC0221.

SMITHFIELD—Formerly served by Johnston County Cable LP. Now served by Time Warner Cable, RALEIGH, NC [NC0003]. ICA: NC0072.

SNOW HILL—MediaCast, 1121 Southeast 2nd St, PO Box 368, Snow Hill, NC 28580-0368. Phone: 252-747-5682. Fax: 252-747-3061. E-mail: dhancock@windstream.net. Also serves Greene County (portions), Grifton, Hookerton, Lenoir County (portions), Maury, Pitt County (portions) & Walstonburg. ICA: NC0073.
TV Market Ranking: 84,73 (Greene County (portions), Grifton, Hookerton, Lenoir County (portions), Maury, Pitt County (portions), SNOW HILL, Walstonburg). Franchise award date: N.A. Franchise expiration date: N.A. Began: October 1, 1983.
Channel capacity: N.A. Channels available but not in use: N.A.
Basic Service
Subscribers: N.A.
Programming (received off-air): WCTI-TV (ABC, Decades, Movies!) New Bern; WEPX-TV (ION) Greenville; WITN-TV (MeTV, MNT, NBC) Washington; WLFL (CW, The Country Network) Raleigh; WNCT-TV (CBS, CW) Greenville; WRAL-TV (NBC, This TV) Raleigh; WTVD (ABC, Live Well Network) Durham; WUNK-TV (PBS) Greenville; WYDO (Bounce TV, FOX) Greenville.
Programming (via satellite): C-SPAN; WGN America.
Fee: $29.95 installation.
Expanded Basic Service 1
Subscribers: N.A.
Programming (via satellite): AMC; BET; CNN; Discovery Channel; Disney Channel; ESPN; ESPN2; Freeform; FX; HLN; INSP; Lifetime; MTV; Nickelodeon; Spike TV; TBS; The Weather Channel; TNT; USA Network.
Fee: $38.95 monthly.
Digital Basic Service
Subscribers: N.A.
Programming (via satellite): BBC America; Bloomberg Television; Discovery Digital Networks; Disney XD; DMX Music; ESPN Classic; ESPNews; Fox Sports 1; FXM; Golf Channel; GSN; LMN; NBCSN; Nick Jr.; Nicktoons; Outdoor Channel; TeenNick; Trinity Broadcasting Network (TBN); Turner Classic Movies.
Digital Pay Service 1
Pay Units: N.A.
Programming (via satellite): Cinemax (multiplexed); Flix; HBO (multiplexed); Showtime (multiplexed); Starz; Starz Encore; The Movie Channel (multiplexed).
Video-On-Demand: No
Pay-Per-View
Shorteez (delivered digitally); Playboy TV (delivered digitally); Fresh (delivered digitally); iN DEMAND (delivered digitally).
Internet Service
Operational: No.
Telephone Service
None
Miles of Plant: 232.0 (coaxial); None (fiber optic). Homes passed: 5,325.
General Manager: Mark Bookout. Chief Technician: Bobby Thurman. Office Manager: Michelle Price.
Ownership: Dale-Media Inc.

SOUTHERN PINES—Time Warner Cable. Now served by RALEIGH, NC [NC0003]. ICA: NC0048.

SPARTA—Alleghany Cablevision Inc, 115 Atwood St., Suite B, Sparta, NC 28675. Phone: 336-372-5801. Fax: 336-372-5801. E-mail: alleghanycablevision@yahoo.com. Web Site: http://www.alleghanycommunitytelevision.com. ICA: NC0152.
TV Market Ranking: Outside TV Markets (SPARTA). Franchise award date: March 1, 1990. Franchise expiration date: N.A. Began: August 1, 1990.
Channel capacity: N.A. Channels available but not in use: N.A.
Basic Service
Subscribers: 306.
Programming (received off-air): WBTV (Bounce TV, CBS) Charlotte; WCCB (CW, MeTV) Charlotte; WJZY (Antenna TV, FOX,

2017 Edition

D-565

North Carolina—Cable Systems

Heroes & Icons, Movies!, The Country Network) Belmont; WSOC-TV (ABC) Charlotte; WUNL-TV (PBS) Winston-Salem; WXII-TV (MeTV, NBC) Winston-Salem.
Programming (via satellite): A&E; CMT; CNN; Comedy Central; C-SPAN; Discovery Channel; Disney Channel; ESPN; Freeform; HLN; INSP; Lifetime; MTV; Nickelodeon; QVC; TBS; TLC; TNT; USA Network; VH1; WGN America.
Fee: $25.00 installation; $30.00 monthly.

Expanded Basic Service 1
Subscribers: 126.
Fee: $27.85 monthly.

Pay Service 1
Pay Units: 19.
Programming (via satellite): Cinemax.
Fee: $8.95 monthly.

Pay Service 2
Pay Units: 14.
Programming (via satellite): HBO.
Fee: $10.95 monthly.

Pay Service 3
Pay Units: 15.
Programming (via satellite): Showtime.
Fee: $5.95 monthly.

Video-On-Demand: No

Internet Service
Operational: No.

Telephone Service
None

Miles of Plant: 70.0 (coaxial); None (fiber optic). Homes passed: 1,500.
President & General Manager: George Sheets. Chief Technician: Steve Rose. Office Manager: Jennie Andrews.
Ownership: Alleghany Cablevision Inc.

SPRING HOPE—Time Warner Cable. Now served by RALEIGH, NC [NC0003]. ICA: NC0122.

STATESVILLE—Formerly served by Adelphia Communications. No longer in operation. ICA: NC0035.

STATESVILLE—Time Warner Cable. Now served by CHARLOTTE, NC [NC0001]. ICA: NC0252.

SUNSET HARBOR—Formerly served by Tele-Media. Now served by ATMC, SHALLOTTE, NC [NC5004]. ICA: NC0245.

SUPPLY—Formerly served by Tele-Media. Now served by ATMC, SHALLOTTE, NC [NC5004]. ICA: NC0243.

SYLVA—Formerly served by Mediacom. Now served by Morris Broadband, HENDERSONVILLE, NC [NC0033]. ICA: NC0078.

TROY—Charter Communications, 12405 Powerscourt Dr, St. Louis, MO 63131. Phones: 636-207-5100 (Corporate office); 919-708-5902. Fax: 919-708-6126. Web Site: http://www.charter.com. ICA: NC0248.
TV Market Ranking: Outside TV Markets (TROY).
Channel capacity: N.A. Channels available but not in use: N.A.

Digital Basic Service
Subscribers: 119.
Programming (via satellite): BBC America; Bloomberg Television; Discovery Life Channel; Disney XD; DIY Network; ESPN Classic; ESPNews; FOX College Sports Central; FOX College Sports Pacific; Fuse; FXM; FYI; GSN; History International; IFC; LMN; MC; National Geographic Channel; Nick 2; Nick Jr.; Nicktoons; Sundance TV; TeenNick; TV Guide Interactive Inc.; WE tv.
Fee: $26.99 monthly.

Digital Expanded Basic Service
Subscribers: N.A.
Programming (via satellite): A&E; AMC; BET; Bravo; Cartoon Network; CMT; CNBC; CNN; Comedy Central; Discovery Channel; Disney Channel; E! HD; ESPN; ESPN2; Food Network; Fox News Channel; Fox Sports 1; Freeform; FX; Golf Channel; HGTV; History; HLN; INSP; Lifetime; MSNBC; MTV; Nickelodeon; Oxygen; Spike TV; Syfy; TBS; Telemundo; The Weather Channel; TLC; TNT; Turner Classic Movies; TV Land; USA Network; VH1.

Digital Pay Service 1
Pay Units: N.A.
Programming (via satellite): Cinemax (multiplexed); Flix; HBO (multiplexed); Showtime (multiplexed); Starz (multiplexed); Starz Encore; The Movie Channel (multiplexed).

Video-On-Demand: No

Pay-Per-View
iN DEMAND (delivered digitally); Playboy TV (delivered digitally); Fresh (delivered digitally).

Internet Service
Operational: No.

Telephone Service
None

Miles of plant (coax & fiber) included in Angier.
Vice President & General Manager: Anthony Pope. Marketing Director: Brooke Sinclair. Accounting Director: David Sovanski. Office Manager: Brenda Brinson. Marketing Manager: Larissa Scales. Operations Manager: Doug Underwood.
Ownership: Charter Communications Inc. (MSO).

TRYON—Charter Communications. Now served by SPARTANBURG, SC [SC0003]. ICA: NC0211.

VASS—Charter Communications. Now served by ANGIER, NC [NC0194]. ICA: NC0222.

WADESBORO—Time Warner Cable. Now served by CHARLOTTE, NC [NC0001]. ICA: NC0082.

WAGRAM—Formerly served by Wagram Cable TV. No longer in operation. ICA: NC0186.

WARSAW—Charter Communications. Now served by ANGIER, NC [NC0194]. ICA: NC0151.

WASHINGTON (portions)—Suddenlink Communications, 520 Maryville Centre Dr, Ste 300, St. Louis, MO 63141. Phones: 877-804-6501 (Customer service); 314-315-9400. Web Site: http://www.suddenlink.com. Also serves Beaufort County (portions), Chocowinity & Washington Park. ICA: NC0057.
TV Market Ranking: 84 (Beaufort County (portions), Chocowinity, WASHINGTON (PORTIONS), Washington Park). Franchise award date: March 13, 1978. Franchise expiration date: N.A. Began: May 1, 1979.
Channel capacity: 61 (operating 2-way). Channels available but not in use: N.A.

Basic Service
Subscribers: 6,021. Commercial subscribers: 308.
Programming (received off-air): WCTI-TV (ABC, Decades, Movies!) New Bern; WEPX-TV (ION) Greenville; WNCT-TV (CBS, CW) Greenville; WUNK-TV (PBS) Greenville; WYDO (Bounce TV, FOX) Greenville; 1 FM.
Programming (via satellite): QVC; WGN America.
Fee: $25.00 monthly.

Expanded Basic Service 1
Subscribers: N.A.
Programming (via satellite): A&E; AMC; Animal Planet; BET; Cartoon Network; CMT; CNBC; CNN; Comedy Central; C-SPAN; C-SPAN 2; Discovery Channel; Disney Channel; E! HD; ESPN; ESPN2; Food Network; Fox News Channel; Freeform; FX; Golf Channel; History; HLN; Lifetime; MSNBC; MTV; Nickelodeon; Pop; Spike TV; Syfy; TBS; Telemundo; The Weather Channel; TLC; TNT; Travel Channel; Trinity Broadcasting Network (TBN); Turner Classic Movies; TV Land; USA Network; VH1; Weatherscan.
Fee: $3.15 monthly.

Digital Basic Service
Subscribers: N.A.
Programming (via satellite): BBC America; Bloomberg Television; Daystar TV Network; Discovery Digital Networks; Disney XD; ESPN Classic; ESPNews; EWTN Global Catholic Network; FamilyNet; Fox Sports 1; Fuse; GSN; Hallmark Channel; LMN; MC; NBA TV; NBCSN; Nick Jr.; Nicktoons; Outdoor Channel; Sundance TV; TeenNick; The Word Network; truTV.

Pay Service 1
Pay Units: N.A.
Programming (via satellite): Cinemax; HBO (multiplexed); Showtime.
Fee: $9.75 monthly (Showtime), $10.75 monthly (Cinemax or HBO).

Digital Pay Service 1
Pay Units: N.A.
Programming (via satellite): Cinemax (multiplexed); HBO (multiplexed); Showtime (multiplexed); Starz (multiplexed); The Movie Channel (multiplexed).

Video-On-Demand: No

Pay-Per-View
iN DEMAND (delivered digitally); Playboy TV (delivered digitally); Fresh (delivered digitally); Shorteez (delivered digitally); Hot Choice (delivered digitally); ESPN (delivered digitally).

Internet Service
Operational: Yes. Began: January 1, 2001. Broadband Service: Suddenlink High Speed Internet.
Fee: $100.00 installation; $39.95 monthly.

Telephone Service
Digital: Operational
Fee: $49.95 monthly

Miles of Plant: 286.0 (coaxial); 42.0 (fiber optic). Homes passed: 11,483.
Senior Vice President, Corporate Finance: Michael Pflantz. General Manager & Chief Technician: Hugh Worsley.
Ownership: Cequel Communications Holdings I LLC (MSO).

WAYNE COUNTY (northern portion)—Time Warner Cable. Now served by RALEIGH, NC [NC0003]. ICA: NC0227.

WAYNESVILLE—Charter Communications. Now served by ASHEVILLE, NC [NC0012]. ICA: NC0042.

WEST JEFFERSON—Morris Broadband, 719 South Grove St, Hendersonville, NC 28792. Phones: 888-855-9036; 888-855-9276; 828-692-3278; 828-692-3278. Web Site: http://morrisbroadband.com. Also serves Ashe County (portions), Jefferson & Lansing. ICA: NC0098.
TV Market Ranking: Below 100 (Ashe County (portions)); Outside TV Markets (Jefferson, Lansing, WEST JEFFERSON, Ashe County (portions)). Franchise award date: N.A. Franchise expiration date: N.A. Began: March 1, 1966.
Channel capacity: N.A. Channels available but not in use: N.A.

Basic Service
Subscribers: 812.
Programming (received off-air): WBTV (Bounce TV, CBS) Charlotte; WCCB (CW, MeTV) Charlotte; WCYB-TV (CW, Decades, NBC) Bristol; WGHP (Antenna TV, FOX) High Point; WJZY (Antenna TV, FOX, Heroes & Icons, Movies!, The Country Network) Belmont; WSOC-TV (ABC) Charlotte; WUNL-TV (PBS) Winston-Salem; WXII-TV (MeTV, NBC) Winston-Salem; allband FM.
Programming (via satellite): Pop; WGN America.
Fee: $45.00 installation; $25.94 monthly; $1.00 converter.

Expanded Basic Service 1
Subscribers: N.A.
Programming (via satellite): A&E; AMC; Animal Planet; Bravo; Cartoon Network; CMT; CNBC; CNN; Comedy Central; C-SPAN; C-SPAN 2; Discovery Channel; Disney Channel; E! HD; ESPN; ESPN2; EVINE Live; Food Network; Fox News Channel; Freeform; FX; History; HLN; INSP; Lifetime; MTV; Nickelodeon; Outdoor Channel; QVC; Spike TV; Syfy; TBS; The Weather Channel; TLC; TNT; Travel Channel; Trinity Broadcasting Network (TBN); truTV; TV Land; USA Network; VH1; WE tv.
Fee: $35.02 monthly.

Digital Basic Service
Subscribers: N.A.
Programming (via satellite): BBC America; Bloomberg Television; Discovery Digital Networks; Fox Sports 1; Fuse; FXM; FYI; Golf Channel; GSN; History International; IFC; LMN; MC; National Geographic Channel; NBCSN; Nick Jr.; Nicktoons; TeenNick; Turner Classic Movies; Weatherscan.

Digital Pay Service 1
Pay Units: N.A.
Programming (via satellite): Cinemax (multiplexed); Flix; HBO (multiplexed); Showtime (multiplexed); Starz (multiplexed); Starz Encore (multiplexed); Sundance TV; The Movie Channel (multiplexed).
Fee: $8.00 monthly (Starz/Encore), $9.95 monthly (Cinemax or Showtime/TMC/Flix/Sundance), $13.95 monthly (HBO).

Video-On-Demand: No

Internet Service
Operational: Yes.
Broadband Service: In-house.
Fee: $29.95-$59.95 monthly.

Telephone Service
Digital: Operational
Fee: $49.95 monthly

Miles of Plant: 115.0 (coaxial); None (fiber optic).
Chairman & Chief Executive Officer: William K. Morris III. Senior Vice President, Finance: Craig Mitchell. Vice President: Susie Morris Baker.
Ownership: Morris Communications Co LLC (MSO).

WHITAKERS—Crystal Broadband Networks, PO Box 180336, Chicago, IL 60618. Phones: 630-206-0447; 877-319-0328. E-mail: helpdesk@crystalbn.com. Web Site: http://crystalbn.com. Also serves Edge-

Cable Systems—North Carolina

combe County (portions), Halifax & Nash County (portions). ICA: NC0164.
TV Market Ranking: Below 100 (WHITAKERS, Halifax). Franchise award date: June 1, 1985. Franchise expiration date: N.A. Began: November 1, 1985.
Channel capacity: N.A. Channels available but not in use: N.A.

Basic Service
Subscribers: 40.
Programming (received off-air): WLFL (CW, The Country Network) Raleigh; WNCN (Antenna TV, CBS) Goldsboro; WNCT-TV (CBS, CW) Greenville; WRAL-TV (NBC, This TV) Raleigh; WRAY-TV (IND) Wilson; WRAZ (FOX, MeTV) Raleigh; WRDC (MNT) Durham; WRPX-TV (ION) Rocky Mount; WTVD (ABC, Live Well Network) Durham; WUNP-TV (PBS) Roanoke Rapids.
Fee: $39.95 installation; $41.82 monthly; $2.00 converter.

Expanded Basic Service 1
Subscribers: N.A.
Programming (via satellite): A&E; AMC; BET; CMT; CNN; C-SPAN; Discovery Channel; Disney Channel; ESPN; ESPN2; Freeform; HGTV; HLN; Lifetime; MSNBC; MTV; Nickelodeon; Spike TV; Syfy; TBS; TNT; Trinity Broadcasting Network (TBN); USA Network; VH1.
Fee: $22.45 monthly.

Digital Basic Service
Subscribers: N.A.
Programming (via satellite): Bravo; ESPN Classic; History International; NBCSN; WE tv.
Fee: $11.00 monthly.

Digital Pay Service 1
Pay Units: N.A.
Programming (via satellite): Cinemax (multiplexed); HBO (multiplexed); Showtime (multiplexed); Starz (multiplexed); Starz Encore (multiplexed); The Movie Channel (multiplexed).
Fee: $15.95 monthly (each).
Video-On-Demand: No
Internet Service
Operational: No.
Telephone Service
None
Miles of Plant: 27.0 (coaxial); None (fiber optic). Homes passed: 1,017.
Ownership: Crystal Broadband Networks (MSO).

WHITEVILLE—Time Warner Cable. Now served by WILMINGTON, NC [NC0007]. ICA: NC0088.

WILMINGTON—Formerly served by Microwave Communication Services. No longer in operation. ICA: NC0228.

WILMINGTON—Time Warner Cable, 101 Innovation Ave, Ste 100, Morrisville, NC 27560. Phones: 919-573-7029; 910-763-0004 (Wilmington office); 919-573-7000 (Morrisville office). Fax: 919-573-7042. Web Site: http://www.timewarnercable.com. Also serves Bladen County (portions), Bladenboro (town), Bolling Spring Lakes (town), Bolton (town), Brunswick (town), Brunswick County (portions), Burgaw (town), Caswell Beach (town), Chadbourn (town), Clarkton (town), Columbus County, Dublin (town), East Arcadia (town), Elizabethtown, Holden Beach, Holden Beach (town), Lake Waccamaw, Leland (town), Long Beach (town), Navassa (town), New Hanover County, Northwest (town), Oak Island, Ocean Isle Beach (town), Pender County, Riegelwood, Sandy Creek (town), Southport (town), St. Helena (town), St. James (town), Tabor City (town), Watha (town), White Lake (town), Whiteville, Wrightsville Beach (town) & Yaupon Beach (town). ICA: NC0007.
TV Market Ranking: 73 (Bladen County (portions), Dublin (town), Elizabethtown); Below 100 (Bolling Spring Lakes (town), Bolton (town), Brunswick County (portions), Burgaw (town), Caswell Beach (town), East Arcadia (town), Holden Beach (town), Leland (town), Long Beach (town), Navassa (town), New Hanover County, Northwest (town), Oak Island, Ocean Isle Beach (town), Pender County, Sandy Creek (town), Southport (town), St. Helena (town), Tabor City (town), Watha (town), WILMINGTON, Wrightsville Beach (town), Yaupon Beach (town), Columbus County, Riegelwood, St. James (town)); Outside TV Markets (Bladenboro (town), Brunswick (town), Chadbourn (town), Clarkton (town), White Lake (town), Whiteville, Lake Waccamaw, Bladen County (portions)). Franchise award date: N.A. Franchise expiration date: N.A. Began: April 1, 1962.
Channel capacity: N.A. Channels available but not in use: N.A.

Basic Service
Subscribers: 77,688.
Programming (received off-air): WECT (Bounce TV, NBC) Wilmington; WSFX-TV (FOX, This TV) Wilmington; WUNJ-TV (PBS) Wilmington; WWAY (ABC, CBS, CW, Retro TV) Wilmington; allband FM.
Programming (via satellite): AMC; Animal Planet; Bravo; Cartoon Network; CMT; Comedy Central; C-SPAN 2; CW PLUS; Disney Channel; E! HD; ESPN Classic; ESPN2; EVINE Live; EWTN Global Catholic Network; Food Network; Fox News Channel; Fox Sports 1; FX; Golf Channel; HGTV; History; INSP; ION Television; LMN; MSNBC; National Geographic Channel; NBCSN; Oxygen; Pop; Syfy; TBS; Travel Channel; truTV; Turner Classic Movies; TV Land; WE tv; WGN America.
Fee: $42.50 installation; $14.99 monthly.

Expanded Basic Service 1
Subscribers: N.A.
Programming (via satellite): A&E; BET; CNBC; CNN; C-SPAN; Discovery Channel; ESPN; Freeform; Hallmark Channel; HLN; Lifetime; MTV; Nickelodeon; QVC; Spike TV; The Weather Channel; TLC; TNT; Trinity Broadcasting Network (TBN); USA Network; VH1.
Fee: $36.25 monthly.

Digital Basic Service
Subscribers: N.A.
Programming (via satellite): BBC America; Bloomberg Television; Cooking Channel; C-SPAN 3; Discovery Digital Networks; Disney XD; DIY Network; ESPNews; Fox Sports 2; FOX Sports Networks (multiplexed); Fuse; FYI; Great American Country; GSN; History International; IFC; INSP; Jewelry Television; MC; MTV Classic; MTV2; NBA TV; Nick Jr.; Outdoor Channel; Ovation; Tennis Channel; The Word Network; WAM! America's Kidz Network.

Digital Pay Service 1
Pay Units: N.A.
Programming (via satellite): Cinemax (multiplexed); Flix (multiplexed); FXM; HBO (multiplexed); MoviePlex; Showtime (multiplexed); Starz Encore; Sundance TV; The Movie Channel.
Fee: $14.00 monthly (each).
Video-On-Demand: Yes
Pay-Per-View
Hot Choice (delivered digitally); Pleasure (delivered digitally); Fresh (delivered digitally); Shorteez (delivered digitally); Playboy TV (delivered digitally); iN DEMAND (delivered digitally).
Internet Service
Operational: Yes. Began: May 1, 2000.
Subscribers: 71,326.
Broadband Service: Road Runner.
Fee: $69.95 installation; $46.95 monthly.
Telephone Service
Digital: Operational
Subscribers: 31,787.
Fee: $44.95 monthly
Miles of Plant: 4,506.0 (coaxial); 528.0 (fiber optic). Homes passed: 140,688.
President: Tom Adams. Vice President, Technical Services: Gary Frederick. Vice President, Sales & Marketing: Tom Smith. General Manager: Kim Cannon. Government & Public Affairs Director: Marty Feurer.
Ownership: Time Warner Cable (MSO).; Advance/Newhouse Partnership (MSO).

WILSON—Time Warner Cable. Now served by RALEIGH, NC [NC0003]. ICA: NC0026.

WINDSOR—Mediacom. Now served by COLERAIN, NC [NC0255]. ICA: NC0111.

WINSTON-SALEM—Time Warner Cable. Now served by GREENSBORO, NC [NC0006]. ICA: NC0002.

Communications Daily
Warren Communications News

Get the industry standard FREE —
For a no-obligation trial call 800-771-9202 or visit www.warren-news.com

---

2017 Edition
D-567

NORTH DAKOTA

Total Systems: 35	Communities with Applications: 0
Total Communities Served: 208	Number of Basic Subscribers: 149,432
Franchises Not Yet Operating: 0	Number of Expanded Basic Subscribers: 20,849
Applications Pending: 0	Number of Pay Units: 11,376

Top 100 Markets Represented: Fargo-Valley City (98).

For a list of cable communities in this section, see the Cable Community Index located in the back of Cable Volume 2.
For explanation of terms used in cable system listings, see p. D-11.

ARVILLA—Formerly served by Midcontinent Communications. No longer in operation. ICA: ND0171.

BEACH—Beach Cable TV, 105 2nd St NE, PO Box 868, Beach, ND 58621. Phone: 701-629-1112. ICA: ND0231.
TV Market Ranking: Below 100 (BEACH).
Channel capacity: N.A. Channels available but not in use: N.A.
Basic Service
Subscribers: 373.
Fee: $47.00 monthly.
Ownership: Tom Wilhelmi.

BEACH—Formerly served by Midcontinent Conunications. No longer in operation. ICA: ND0041.

BERTHOLD—SRT Communications. Now served by VELVA, ND [ND0059]. ICA: ND0100.

BEULAH—Midco, PO Box 5010, Sioux Falls, SD 57117. Phones: 800-888-1300; 605-229-1775. Fax: 605-229-0478. E-mail: darrell_wrege@mmi.net. Web Site: http://www.midcocomm.com. Also serves Center, Dodge, Gladstone, Golden Valley, Halliday, Hazen, Killdeer, Pick City, Richardton, Riverdale, Stanton, Turtle Lake, Underwood & Zap. ICA: ND0017.
TV Market Ranking: Below 100 (Center, Gladstone, Killdeer, Richardton); Outside TV Markets (BEULAH, Dodge, Golden Valley, Halliday, Hazen, Pick City, Riverdale, Stanton, Turtle Lake, Underwood, Zap).
Franchise award date: December 23, 1986. Franchise expiration date: N.A. Began: June 1, 1978.
Channel capacity: N.A. Channels available but not in use: N.A.
Basic Service
Subscribers: 2,855.
Programming (received off-air): KBMY (ABC) Bismarck; KFYR-TV (FOX, MeTV, NBC) Bismarck; KNDB (Heroes & Icons) Bismarck; KSRE (PBS) Minot; KXMB-TV (CBS) Bismarck.
Programming (via satellite): A&E; CNN; C-SPAN; Discovery Channel; ESPN; Freeform; Lifetime; MTV; Nickelodeon; Pop; QVC; Spike TV; TBS; The Weather Channel; TNT; USA Network; VH1; WGN America.
Fee: $25.00 installation; $19.95 monthly.
Expanded Basic Service 1
Subscribers: N.A.
Programming (via satellite): AMC; Animal Planet; Cartoon Network; CMT; CNBC; Comedy Central; C-SPAN 2; Disney Channel; E! HD; ESPN Classic; ESPN2; EWTN Global Catholic Network; Food Network; Fox News Channel; Fox Sports 1; FOX Sports North; FX; Hallmark Channel; HGTV; History; HLN; INSP; MSNBC; NBCSN; NFL Network; Outdoor Channel; OWN; Oprah Winfrey Network; Syfy; TLC; Travel Channel; Turner Classic Movies; TV Land; WE tv.
Digital Basic Service
Subscribers: N.A.
Programming (via satellite): BBC America; Boomerang; CBS Sports Network; Cooking Channel; C-SPAN 3; Destination America; Discovery Kids Channel; Discovery Life Channel; Disney XD; DIY Network; DMX Music; ESPN Classic; ESPNews; FOX College Sports Central; FOX College Sports Pacific; FYI; Golf Channel; GolTV; Great American Country; GSN; History International; IFC; Investigation Discovery; LMN; National Geographic Channel; NBCSN; NFL Network; Nick 2; Nick Jr.; Nicktoons; Outdoor Channel; OWN: Oprah Winfrey Network; Sundance TV; TeenNick; Tennis Channel; Trinity Broadcasting Network (TBN); Turner Classic Movies; TV One; TVG Network; WE tv.
Digital Pay Service 1
Pay Units: N.A.
Programming (via satellite): Cinemax (multiplexed); HBO (multiplexed); HITS (Headend In The Sky); Showtime (multiplexed); Starz (multiplexed); Starz Encore; The Movie Channel (multiplexed).
Video-On-Demand: No
Internet Service
Operational: Yes.
Broadband Service: Midcontinent.
Fee: $35.00 installation; $19.95 monthly; $8.00 modem lease; $39.00 modem purchase.
Telephone Service
Digital: Operational
Fee: $18.00 monthly
Miles of Plant: 140.0 (coaxial); 16.0 (fiber optic). Homes passed: 8,395.
General Manager: Darrell Wrege. Programming Director: Wynne Haakenstad. Marketing Director: Fred Jamieson. Customer Service Manager: Kathy Fuhrmann.
Ownership: Midcontinent Communications (MSO).; Comcast Cable Communications Inc. (MSO).

BISMARCK—Midco, PO Box 5010, Sioux Falls, SD 57117. Phones: 701-224-0897; 800-888-1300; 605-229-1775 (Administrative office). Web Site: http://www.midcocomm.com. Also serves Glen Ullin, Hebron, Lincoln, Mandan, New Salem & Washburn. ICA: ND0002.
TV Market Ranking: Below 100 (BISMARCK, Hebron, Lincoln, New Salem, Mandan); Outside TV Markets (Glen Ullin, Washburn).
Franchise award date: January 1, 1967. Franchise expiration date: N.A. Began: December 1, 1967.
Channel capacity: N.A. Channels available but not in use: N.A.
Basic Service
Subscribers: 30,526.
Programming (received off-air): KBME-TV (PBS) Bismarck; KBMY (ABC) Bismarck; KFYR-TV (FOX, MeTV, NBC) Bismarck; KNDB (Heroes & Icons) Bismarck; KXMB-TV (CBS) Bismarck.
Programming (via satellite): A&E; AMC; Animal Planet; BET; Bravo; Cartoon Network; Celebrity Shopping Network; CMT; CNBC; CNN; Comedy Central; C-SPAN; C-SPAN 2; CW PLUS; Discovery Channel; Disney Channel; E! HD; ESPN; ESPN2; EWTN Global Catholic Network; Food Network; Fox News Channel; Fox Sports 1; FOX Sports North; Freeform; FX; Hallmark Channel; HGTV; History; HLN; INSP; Lifetime; MSNBC; MTV; NBCSN; Nickelodeon; Outdoor Channel; OWN: Oprah Winfrey Network; Oxygen; Pop; QVC; Radar Channel; Spike TV; Syfy; TBS; The Weather Channel; TLC; TNT; Travel Channel; Trinity Broadcasting Network (TBN); truTV; Turner Classic Movies; TV Land; USA Network; VH1; WE tv; WGN America.
Fee: $19.95 monthly.
Digital Basic Service
Subscribers: N.A.
Programming (via satellite): 3ABN; A&E HD; Animal Planet HD; AXS TV; BBC America; Bloomberg Television; Boomerang; BTN; Canal Sur; CBS Sports Network; Cine Mexicano; Cinelatino; CMT; CNN en Espanol; CNN HD; Cooking Channel; C-SPAN 3; Destination America; Discovery Channel HD; Discovery Kids Channel; Discovery Life Channel; Disney Channel HD; Disney XD; DIY Network; ESPN Classic; ESPN Deportes; ESPN HD; ESPN2 HD; ESPNews; Food Network HD; Fox Business Network; FOX College Sports Central; FOX College Sports Pacific; Fox Deportes; Freeform HD; FSN HD; Fuse; FYI; Golf Channel; GolTV; Great American Country; GSN; HD Theater; HGTV HD; History en Espanol; History HD; History International; IFC; Investigation Discovery; ION Television; JUCE TV; LMN; MC; MTV Classic; MTV Hits; MTV Jams; MTV Live; MTV2; National Geographic Channel; National Geographic Channel HD; NBC Universo; NBCSN; NFL Network; NHL Network; Nick 2; Nick Jr.; Nicktoons; Outdoor Channel; OWN: Oprah Winfrey Network; Qubo; Reelz; RFD-TV; Science Channel; Sprout; Sundance TV; Syfy HD; TBS HD; TeenNick; Telemundo; Tennis Channel; TLC HD; TNT HD; Toon Disney en Espanol; Tr3s; Trinity Broadcasting Network (TBN); Turner Classic Movies; TV One; TVG Network; Universal HD; Versus HD; VH1 Soul; WE tv.
Digital Pay Service 1
Pay Units: N.A.
Programming (via satellite): Cinemax (multiplexed); Cinemax HD; Flix; HBO (multiplexed); HBO HD; HBO Latino; Showtime (multiplexed); Showtime HD; Starz (multiplexed); Starz Encore (multiplexed); Starz HD; The Movie Channel (multiplexed); The Movie Channel HD.
Video-On-Demand: No
Pay-Per-View
iN DEMAND (delivered digitally); Sports PPV (delivered digitally).
Internet Service
Operational: Yes. Began: January 1, 1996.
Subscribers: 29,187.
Broadband Service: MidcoNet.
Fee: $35.00 installation; $19.95 monthly; $10.00 modem lease; $50.00 modem purchase.
Telephone Service
Digital: Operational
Subscribers: 15,019.
Fee: $18.00 monthly
Miles of Plant: 870.0 (coaxial); 154.0 (fiber optic). Homes passed: 51,638.
General Manager: Darrel Wrege. Programming Director: Wynne Haakenstad.
Ownership: Midcontinent Communications (MSO).; Comcast Cable Communications Inc. (MSO).

BOWDON—DCT. This cable system has converted to IPTV. Now served by JAMESTOWN, ND [ND5005]. ICA: ND0139.

BOWMAN—Midco, PO Box 5010, Sioux Falls, SD 57117. Phones: 605-229-1775; 800-888-1300. Fax: 605-229-0478. Web Site: http://www.midcocomm.com. Also serves Hettinger, Reeder, Rhame & Scranton. ICA: ND0030.
TV Market Ranking: Outside TV Markets (BOWMAN, Hettinger, Reeder, Rhame, Scranton). Franchise award date: May 6, 1986. Franchise expiration date: N.A. Began: May 1, 1980.
Channel capacity: N.A. Channels available but not in use: N.A.
Basic Service
Subscribers: 392. Commercial subscribers: 48.
Programming (received off-air): KDSE (PBS) Dickinson; KHSD-TV (ABC, FOX) Lead; KQCD-TV (FOX, NBC) Dickinson; KQME (MeTV, This TV) Lead; KXMA-TV (CBS) Dickinson.
Programming (via satellite): A&E; AMC; Animal Planet; Cartoon Network; CMT; CNBC; CNN; C-SPAN; CW PLUS; Discovery Channel; Disney Channel; ESPN; ESPN2; Food Network; Fox News Channel; FOX Sports North; Freeform; FX; HGTV; History; HLN; INSP; Lifetime; MTV; Nickelodeon; Pop; QVC; Spike TV; Syfy; TBS; The Weather Channel; TLC; TNT; TV Land; USA Network; VH1; WE tv; WGN America.
Fee: $50.00 installation; $19.95 monthly.
Digital Basic Service
Subscribers: N.A.
Programming (via satellite): 3ABN; A&E HD; AMC HD; Animal Planet HD; BBC Amer-

Cable Systems—North Dakota

ica; Bloomberg Television; Boomerang; BTN; BTN HD; Canal Sur; CBS Sports Network; Centric; Cine Mexicano; Cinelatino; Cloo; CMT; CNN en Espanol; CNN HD; Cooking Channel; C-SPAN 2; C-SPAN 3; Destination America; Discovery Channel HD; Discovery Family; Discovery Life Channel; Disney Channel HD; Disney XD; DIY Network; ESPN Classic; ESPN Deportes; ESPN HD; ESPN2 HD; ESPNews; ESPNU; Food Network HD; Fox Business Network; FOX College Sports Central; FOX College Sports Pacific; Fox Deportes; Fox News HD; Freeform HD; Fuse; FX HD; FXM; FYI; Golf Channel; Golf Channel HD; GolTV; Great American Country; GSN; Hallmark Channel; HD Theater; HGTV HD; History en Espanol; History HD; History International; IFC; Investigation Discovery; ION Television; JUCE TV; Lifetime; MC; MLB Network; MLB Network HD; MTV Classic; MTV Hits; MTV Jams; MTV Live; MTV2; National Geographic Channel; National Geographic Channel HD; NBC Universo; NBCSN; NFL Network; NFL Network HD; NHL Network; Nick 2; Nick Jr.; Nicktoons; Outdoor Channel; OWN; Oprah Winfrey Network; Qubo; Reelz; RFD-TV; Science Channel; Science HD; Spike TV HD; Sprout; Sundance TV; Syfy HD; TBS HD; TeenNick; Telemundo; Tennis Channel; The Weather Channel HD; TLC HD; TNT HD; Toon Disney en Espanol; Tr3s; Trinity Broadcasting Network (TBN); Turner Classic Movies; TV One; TVG Network; Universal HD; USA Network HD; Versus HD; ViendoMovies; WE tv.

Digital Pay Service 1
Pay Units: N.A.
Programming (via satellite): Cinemax (multiplexed); Cinemax HD; Flix; HBO (multiplexed); HBO HD; HBO Latino; Showtime (multiplexed); Showtime HD; Starz (multiplexed); Starz Encore (multiplexed); Starz HD; The Movie Channel (multiplexed); The Movie Channel HD.

Video-On-Demand: No

Pay-Per-View
iN DEMAND (delivered digitally); MLS Direct Kick (delivered digitally); NBA League Pass (delivered digitally); NHL Center Ice (delivered digitally); MLB Extra Innings (delivered digitally).

Internet Service
Operational: Yes.
Subscribers: 108.
Fee: $35.00 installation; $19.95 monthly.

Telephone Service
Digital: Operational
Subscribers: 95.
Fee: $18.00 monthly
Miles of Plant: 27.0 (coaxial); 13.0 (fiber optic). Homes passed: 1,042.
General Manager: Darrell Wrege. Programming Director: Wynne Haakenstad. Marketing Director: Trish McCann. Customer Service Manager: Kris Virggves.
Ownership: Midcontinent Communications (MSO).; Comcast Cable Communications Inc. (MSO).

CARPIO—SRT Communications. Now served by VELVA, ND [ND0059]. ICA: ND0154.

CARRINGTON—Midcontinent Communications. Now served by COOPERSTOWN (village), ND [ND0054]. ICA: ND0015.

CARSON—Formerly served by Northland Communications. No longer in operation. ICA: ND0104.

CASSELTON—Midcontinent Communications. Now served by WEST FARGO, ND [ND0230]. ICA: ND0039.

CAVALIER COUNTY (portions)—United Communications, 411 7th Ave, PO Box 729, Langdon, ND 58249. Phones: 800-844-9708; 701-256-5156. Fax: 701-256-5150. E-mail: info@utma.com. Web Site: http://www.utma.com. ICA: ND0228.
Channel capacity: N.A. Channels available but not in use: N.A.

Basic Service
Subscribers: 53.
Programming (received off-air): KNRR (FOX) Pembina; KRDK-TV (CBS, Decades, Movies!) Valley City; KVLY-TV (MeTV, NBC, This TV) Fargo; WDAZ-TV (ABC, CW) Devils Lake.
Programming (via satellite): WGN America.
Fee: $15.00 monthly.

Internet Service
Operational: Yes.

Telephone Service
Digital: Operational
General Manager: Perry Oyster. Assistant General Manager: Dennis Hansel. Facilities Manager: Ross Feil. Customer Service Manager: Kirsten Gendron.
Ownership: United Telephone Mutual Aid Corp.

CLEVELAND—DCT. This cable system has converted to IPTV. Now served by JAMESTOWN, ND [ND5005]. ICA: ND0162.

COOPERSTOWN (village)—Midco, PO Box 5010, Sioux Falls, SD 57117. Phones: 605-229-1775; 800-888-1300. Fax: 605-229-0478. Web Site: http://www.midcocomm.com. Also serves Aneta, Binford, Carrington, Hannaford, Hope, Kensal, New Rockford, Page & Wimbledon. ICA: ND0054.
TV Market Ranking: 98 (Hannaford, Hope, Page, Wimbledon); Below 100 (Kensal, New Rockford); Outside TV Markets (Aneta, Binford, COOPERSTOWN (VILLAGE), Carrington). Franchise award date: January 13, 1988. Franchise expiration date: N.A. Began: February 1, 1981.
Channel capacity: N.A. Channels available but not in use: N.A.

Basic Service
Subscribers: 975.
Programming (received off-air): KGFE (PBS) Grand Forks; KJRR (FOX) Jamestown; KRDK-TV (CBS, Decades, Movies!) Valley City; KVLY-TV (MeTV, NBC, This TV) Fargo; WDAZ-TV (ABC, CW) Devils Lake; 1 FM.
Programming (via satellite): A&E; AMC; Cartoon Network; CMT; CNBC; CNN; C-SPAN; Discovery Channel; Disney Channel; ESPN; ESPN2; ESPNews; EWTN Global Catholic Network; FOX Sports North; Freeform; FX; Hallmark Channel; HGTV; History; HLN; INSP; Lifetime; NFL Network; Nickelodeon; Pop; QVC; Spike TV; TBS; The Weather Channel; TLC; TNT; TV Land; USA Network; VH1; WGN America.
Fee: $50.00 installation; $19.95 monthly.

Pay Service 1
Pay Units: N.A.
Programming (via satellite): HBO; Showtime; The Movie Channel.
Fee: $20.00 installation; $11.00 monthly (Showtime or TMC), $12.00 monthly (HBO).

Video-On-Demand: No

Internet Service
Operational: No.

Telephone Service
None
Miles of Plant: 31.0 (coaxial); None (fiber optic). Homes passed: 1,637.
General Manager: Darrell Wrege. Marketing Director: Fred Jamieson. Programming Director: Wynne Haakenstad. Customer Service Manager: Kathy Fuhrmann.
Ownership: Midcontinent Communications (MSO).; Comcast Cable Communications Inc. (MSO).

DEVILS LAKE—Midco, PO Box 5010, Sioux Falls, SD 57117. Phones: 800-888-1300 (Customer service); 800-456-0564; 605-229-1775. Fax: 605-229-0478. Web Site: http://www.midcocomm.com. Also serves Bisbee, Cando, Edmore, Langdon, Starkweather & Walhalla. ICA: ND0009.
TV Market Ranking: Below 100 (Cando, DEVILS LAKE, Edmore, Starkweather, Walhalla); Outside TV Markets (Bisbee, Langdon). Franchise award date: December 1, 1986. Franchise expiration date: N.A. Began: April 1, 1964.
Channel capacity: N.A. Channels available but not in use: N.A.

Basic Service
Subscribers: 2,777.
Programming (received off-air): KGFE (PBS) Grand Forks; KNRR (FOX) Pembina; KRDK-TV (CBS, Decades, Movies!) Valley City; KVLY-TV (MeTV, NBC, This TV) Fargo; WDAZ-TV (ABC, CW) Devils Lake; 5 FMs.
Programming (via satellite): A&E; AMC; Animal Planet; Cartoon Network; CMT; CNBC; CNN; Comedy Central; C-SPAN; C-SPAN 2; Discovery Channel; Discovery Life Channel; Disney Channel; E! HD; ESPN; ESPN Classic; ESPN2; ESPNews; EWTN Global Catholic Network; Food Network; Fox News Channel; Fox Sports 1; FOX Sports North; Freeform; FX; HGTV; History; HLN; INSP; ION Television; Lifetime; MSNBC; MTV; NBCSN; Nickelodeon; Outdoor Channel; OWN; Oprah Winfrey Network; Pop; QVC; Spike TV; Syfy; TBS; The Weather Channel; TLC; TNT; Travel Channel; truTV; Turner Classic Movies; TV Land; USA Network; VH1; WE tv; WGN America.
Fee: $50.00 installation; $19.95 monthly.

Digital Basic Service
Subscribers: N.A.
Programming (via satellite): BBC America; Bravo; Discovery Digital Networks; Disney XD; DMX Music; Fuse; FXM; FYI; Golf Channel; GSN; History International; IFC; LMN; Nick Jr.; Nicktoons; TeenNick; Trinity Broadcasting Network (TBN).

Digital Pay Service 1
Pay Units: N.A.
Programming (via satellite): Cinemax (multiplexed); Flix; HBO (multiplexed); Showtime (multiplexed); Starz Encore; The Movie Channel (multiplexed).

Video-On-Demand: No

Pay-Per-View
iN DEMAND (delivered digitally).

Internet Service
Operational: Yes.
Broadband Service: MidcoNet.
Fee: $35.00 installation; $19.95 monthly.

Telephone Service
Digital: Operational
Fee: $18.00 monthly
Miles of Plant: 76.0 (coaxial); None (fiber optic). Homes passed: 5,789.
General Manager: Darrell Wrege. Programming Director: Wynne Haakenstad. Marketing Director: Fred Jamieson. Customer Service Manager: Kathy Fuhrmann.
Ownership: Midcontinent Communications (MSO).; Comcast Cable Communications Inc. (MSO).

DICKINSON—Consolidated Telecom, 507 South Main, PO Box 1408, Dickinson, ND 58602. Phones: 888-225-5282; 701-483-4000. Fax: 701-483-0001. Web Site: http://www.ctctel.com. ICA: ND0005.
TV Market Ranking: Below 100 (DICKINSON). Franchise award date: N.A. Franchise expiration date: N.A. Began: January 1, 1965.
Channel capacity: N.A. Channels available but not in use: N.A.

Basic Service
Subscribers: 10,298 Includes IPTV subscribers.
Programming (received off-air): KDSE (PBS) Dickinson; KQCD-TV (FOX, NBC) Dickinson; KXMA-TV (CBS) Dickinson.
Programming (via satellite): C-SPAN; ESPN; EWTN Global Catholic Network; Freeform; KMGH-TV (ABC, Azteca America) Denver; Pop; QVC; TBS; The Weather Channel; VH1; WGN America.
Fee: $24.00 installation; $15.99 monthly.

Expanded Basic Service 1
Subscribers: N.A.
Programming (via satellite): A&E; AMC; Animal Planet; Cartoon Network; CNBC; CNN; Discovery Channel; Disney Channel; ESPN2; Fox Sports 1; Great American Country; HGTV; History; HLN; Lifetime; MTV; NBCSN; Nickelodeon; Oxygen; Spike TV; Syfy; TLC; TNT; TV Land; USA Network; WE tv.
Fee: $37.50 monthly.

Digital Basic Service
Subscribers: N.A.
Programming (via satellite): BBC America; Bloomberg Television; Discovery Digital Networks; Disney XD; DIY Network; DMX Music; ESPN Classic; FYI; History International; IFC.
Fee: $12.00 monthly.

Digital Pay Service 1
Pay Units: N.A.
Programming (via satellite): Cinemax (multiplexed); Flix; HBO (multiplexed); Showtime (multiplexed); Starz; Starz Encore; The Movie Channel (multiplexed).
Fee: $15.75 monthly (each).

Video-On-Demand: Planned

Pay-Per-View
iN DEMAND.

Internet Service
Operational: Yes.
Broadband Service: In-house.
Fee: $48.00 installation; $29.95-$59.95 monthly; $10.00 modem lease; $300.00 modem purchase.

Telephone Service
Analog: Operational
Fee: $24.95 monthly
Miles of Plant: 77.0 (coaxial); None (fiber optic).
Chief Operating Officer: Bryan Personne.
Ownership: Consolidated Telcom.

DUNN CENTER—Formerly served by Eagle Cablevision Inc. No longer in operation. ICA: ND0174.

EDGELEY—DRN. This cable system has converted to IPTV. Now served by OAKES, ND [ND5032]. ICA: ND0182.

ELGIN—Formerly served by Northland Communications. No longer in operation. ICA: ND0183.

North Dakota—Cable Systems

ENDERLIN—MLGC. Formerly [ND0222]. This cable system has converted to IPTV, 301 Dewey St, PO Box 66, Enderlin, ND 58027. Phones: 877-893-6542; 701-437-3300. Fax: 701-437-3022. E-mail: mandl@mlgc.com. Web Site: http://www.mlgc.com. Also serves Finley, Kindred, Northwood & Sheldon. ICA: ND5000.
TV Market Ranking: 98 (ENDERLIN, Kindred); Outside TV Markets (Finley, Northwood).
Channel capacity: N.A. Channels available but not in use: N.A.
E-Basic
Subscribers: 959.
Programming (received off-air): KFME (PBS) Fargo; KRDK-TV (CBS, Decades, Movies!) Valley City; KVLY-TV (MeTV, NBC, This TV) Fargo; KVRR (Antenna TV, FOX) Fargo; WDAY-TV (ABC, CW) Fargo.
Programming (via satellite): A&E; CMT; CNN; Discovery Channel; Disney Channel; ESPN; ESPN2; FOX Sports Networks; Freeform; History; Nickelodeon; QVC; Spike TV; Syfy; TBS; The Weather Channel; TNT; USA Network; WGN America.
Fee: $40.00 installation; $50.93 monthly.
Digital
Subscribers: N.A.
Fee: $70.88 monthly.
Cinemax
Subscribers: N.A.
Programming (via satellite): Cinemax.
Fee: $10.00 monthly.
HBO
Subscribers: N.A.
Programming (via satellite): HBO.
Fee: $18.00 monthly.
Showtime/TMC
Subscribers: N.A.
Programming (via satellite): Showtime.
Fee: $16.00 monthly.
Starz/Encore
Subscribers: N.A.
Programming (via satellite): Starz; Starz Encore.
Fee: $16.00 monthly.
Video-On-Demand: No
Internet Service
Operational: Yes.
Fee: $99.00 installation; $65.99-$123.99 monthly.
Telephone Service
Digital: Operational
Fee: $18.25 monthly
Vice President: Tyler Kilde.
Ownership: MLGC (MSO).

ENDERLIN—MLGC. This cable system has converted to IPTV. Now served by ENDERLIN, ND [ND5000]. ICA: ND0222.

ESMOND—Formerly served by Midco. No longer in operation. ICA: ND0132.

FARGO—Cable One, 1024 Page Dr, PO Box 10757, Fargo, ND 58103-2336. Phones: 701-540-5727; 701-280-0033. Fax: 701-461-7005. Web Site: http://www.cableone.net. Also serves Dilworth, Moorhead & Oakport, MN; Briarwood, Cass County (portions), Frontier, Horace, Prairie Rose, Reed, Reile's Acres & West Fargo, ND. ICA: ND0001.
TV Market Ranking: 98 (Briarwood, Cass County (portions), Dilworth, FARGO, Frontier, Horace, Moorhead, Oakport, Prairie Rose, Reed, Reile's Acres, West Fargo). Franchise award date: July 2, 1979. Franchise expiration date: N.A. Began: November 29, 1979.
Channel capacity: N.A. Channels available but not in use: N.A.

Basic Service
Subscribers: 22,449.
Programming (received off-air): KCPM (MNT) Grand Forks; KFME (PBS) Fargo; KRDK-TV (CBS, Decades, Movies!) Valley City; KVLY-TV (MeTV, NBC, This TV) Fargo; KVRR (Antenna TV, FOX) Fargo; WDAY-TV (ABC, CW) Fargo.
Programming (via satellite): C-SPAN; C-SPAN 2; Pop; QVC; WGN America.
Fee: $90.00 installation; $35.00 monthly; $1.75 converter.

Expanded Basic Service 1
Subscribers: N.A.
Programming (via satellite): A&E; AMC; Animal Planet; Bravo; Cartoon Network; CMT; CNBC; CNN; Comedy Central; Discovery Channel; Disney Channel; E! HD; ESPN; ESPN2; EWTN Global Catholic Network; Food Network; Fox News Channel; Fox Sports 1; Freeform; FX; Hallmark Channel; HGTV; History; HLN; HSN; INSP; Lifetime; MSNBC; MTV; Nickelodeon; Oxygen; Spike TV; Syfy; TBS; The Weather Channel; This TV; TLC; TNT; Travel Channel; truTV; Turner Classic Movies; TV Land; USA Network; VH1.

Digital Basic Service
Subscribers: N.A.
Programming (via satellite): 3ABN; A&E HD; AMC HD; Animal Planet HD; BBC America; Bloomberg Television; Boomerang; BTN; BTN HD; Canal Sur; CBS Sports Network; Centric; Cine Mexicano; Cinelatino; Cloo; CMT; CNN en Espanol; CNN HD; Cooking Channel; C-SPAN 2; C-SPAN 3; Destination America; Discovery Channel HD; Discovery Family; Discovery Life Channel; Disney Channel HD; Disney XD; DIY Network; ESPN Classic; ESPN Deportes; ESPN HD; ESPN2 HD; ESPNews; ESPNU; Food Network HD; Fox Business Network; FOX College Sports Central (multiplexed); FOX College Sports Pacific (multiplexed); Fox Deportes; Fox News HD; Freeform HD; FSN HD; Fuse; FX HD; FXM; FYI; Golf Channel; Golf Channel HD; GolTV; Great American Country; HD Theater; HGTV HD; History en Espanol; History HD; History International; IFC; Investigation Discovery (multiplexed); ION Television; JUCE TV; LMN; MC; MLB Network; MLB Network HD; MTV Classic; MTV Hits; MTV Jams; MTV Live; MTV2; National Geographic Channel; National Geographic Channel HD; NBC Universo; NBCSN; NFL Network; NFL Network HD; NFL RedZone; NHL Network; NHL Network HD; Nick 2; Nick Jr.; Nicktoons; Outdoor Channel; OWN: Oprah Winfrey Network; Qubo; Reelz; RFD-TV; Science Channel; Science HD; Spike TV HD; Sprout; Sundance TV; Syfy HD; TBS HD; TeenNick; Telemundo; Tennis Channel; The Sportsman Channel; The Weather Channel; TLC HD; TNT HD; Tr3s; Trinity Broadcasting Network (TBN); Turner Classic Movies; TVG Network; Universal HD; USA Network HD; Versus HD; ViendoMovies; WE tv.
Fee: $75.00 installation; $9.95 monthly; $10.00 converter.

Digital Pay Service 1
Pay Units: 3,162.
Programming (via satellite): Cinemax (multiplexed); Cinemax HD; Flix; HBO (multiplexed); HBO HD; Showtime (multiplexed); Showtime HD; Starz (multiplexed); Starz Encore (multiplexed); Starz HD; The Movie Channel (multiplexed); The Movie Channel HD.

Video-On-Demand: No

Pay-Per-View
Movies/Specials (delivered digitally); Adult (delivered digitally); Adult (delivered digitally); Adult (delivered digitally).
Internet Service
Operational: Yes. Began: April 30, 2000.
Subscribers: 29,129.
Broadband Service: CableONE.net.
Fee: $75.00 installation; $43.00 monthly; $6.00 modem lease.
Telephone Service
Analog: Not Operational
Digital: Operational
Subscribers: 9,588.
Fee: $39.95 monthly
Miles of Plant: 1,389.0 (coaxial); 364.0 (fiber optic). Homes passed: 91,066.
Vice President: Patrick A. Dolohanty. General Manager: Scott Geston. Marketing Director: Laurie Nicholson. Program Director: Tamara Rostad. Internet Manager: Dave Barge. Technical Operations Manager: Bryon Brenneman. Office Manager: Laureen Nyborg. Ad Sales Manager: Shereen Stark.
Ownership: Cable ONE Inc. (MSO).

FINLEY—MLGC. This cable system has converted to IPTV. Now served by ENDERLIN, ND [ND5000]. ICA: ND0184.

FLASHER—Formerly served by Flasher Cablevision Inc. No longer in operation. ICA: ND0114.

FOREST RIVER—Formerly served by Midcontinent Communications. No longer in operation. ICA: ND0160.

FORMAN—DRN. This cable system has converted to IPTV. Now served by OAKES, ND [ND5032]. ICA: ND0080.

GACKLE—Formerly served by Midcontinent Communications. No longer in operation. ICA: ND0093.

GARRISON—RTC. Now served by PARSHALL, ND [ND0020]. ICA: ND0033.

GILBY—Formerly served by Midcontinent Communications. No longer in operation. ICA: ND0142.

GLENFIELD—DCTV, 630 5th St North, PO Box 299, Carrington, ND 58421. Phones: 800-771-0974; 701-952-1001 (Jamestown office); 701-652-3184. E-mail: customerservice@daktel.com. Web Site: http://www.daktel.com. Also serves Sheyenne. ICA: ND0130.
TV Market Ranking: Below 100 (Sheyenne); Outside TV Markets (GLENFIELD). Franchise award date: N.A. Franchise expiration date: N.A. Began: December 1, 1984.
Channel capacity: 28 (not 2-way capable). Channels available but not in use: N.A.
Digital Basic Service
Subscribers: 12.
Programming (received off-air): KFME (PBS) Fargo; KFYR-TV (FOX, MeTV, NBC) Bismarck; KJRR (FOX) Jamestown; KRDK-TV (CBS, Decades, Movies!) Valley City; KVLY-TV (MeTV, NBC, This TV) Fargo; WDAY-TV (ABC, CW) Fargo; WDAZ-TV (ABC, CW) Devils Lake.
Programming (via satellite): CW PLUS; ION Television; JUCE TV; TBS; This TV; WGN America.
Fee: $21.00 monthly.

Digital Expanded Basic Service
Subscribers: N.A.
Programming (via satellite): 3ABN; A&E; A&E HD; AMC; Animal Planet; Animal Planet HD; AXS TV; BBC America; Bloomberg Television; Boomerang; Bravo; Bravo HD; BTN; Cartoon Network; CBS Sports Network; Chiller; CMT; CNBC; CNBC HD+; CNN; CNN International; Comedy Central; Cooking Channel; C-SPAN; C-SPAN 2; C-SPAN 3; Destination America; Destination America HD; Discovery Channel; Discovery Channel HD; Discovery Kids Channel; Discovery Life Channel; Disney Channel; Disney XD; DIY Network; E! HD; ESPN; ESPN Classic; ESPN HD; ESPN2; ESPN2 HD; ESPNews; ESPNews HD; ESPNU; ESPNU HD; EWTN Global Catholic Network; Food Network; Food Network HD; FOX College Sports Central; FOX College Sports Pacific; Fox News Channel; Fox Sports 1; Fox Sports 2; Freeform; FSN Digital; FSN HD; Fuse; FX; FXM; FYI; Golf Channel; Golf Channel HD; GolTV; Great American Country; GSN; Hallmark Channel; HD Theater; HGTV; HGTV HD; History; History International; HLN; HorseTV Channel; HSN; INSP; Investigation Discovery; Jewelry Television; Lifetime; Lifetime HD; LMN; MC; MSNBC; MTV; MTV Classic; MTV Hits; MTV Live; MTV2; National Geographic Channel; National Geographic Channel HD; NBCSN; NFL Network; NFL Network HD; NFL RedZone; Nick Jr.; Nickelodeon; Nicktoons; Outdoor Channel; Ovation; OWN: Oprah Winfrey Network; Oxygen; QVC; RFD-TV; Science Channel; Science HD; Spike TV; Syfy; Syfy HD; TeenNick; Tennis Channel; The Sportsman Channel; The Weather Channel; TLC; TLC HD; TNT; Travel Channel; Trinity Broadcasting Network (TBN); truTV; Turner Classic Movies; TV Land; TVG Network; Universal HD; USA Network; USA Network HD; VH1; VH1 Country; WE tv; World Fishing Network.
Digital Pay Service 1
Pay Units: N.A.
Programming (via satellite): Cinemax (multiplexed); Flix; HBO (multiplexed); Showtime (multiplexed); Showtime HD; Starz (multiplexed); Starz Encore (multiplexed); Starz HD; Sundance TV; The Movie Channel (multiplexed).
Video-On-Demand: No
Internet Service
Operational: Yes.
Telephone Service
Digital: Operational
Miles of Plant: 3.0 (coaxial); None (fiber optic). Homes passed: 140.
Chief Executive Officer & General Manager: Keith Larson. Chief Plant Officer: Paul Berg. Chief Financial Officer: Cindy Hewitt. Chief Marketing Officer & Internal Operations Officer: Holly Utke. Business Account Executive: Lori Soldberg.
Ownership: Dakota Central Telecommunications.

GLENFIELD—Formerly served by Dakota Central Telecommunications. Now served by GLENFIELD, ND [ND0130]. ICA: ND0173.

GRAFTON—Midcontinent Communications. Now served by GRAND FORKS, ND [ND0003]. ICA: ND0014.

GRAND FORKS—Formerly served by Microwave Communication Services. No longer in operation. ICA: ND0215.

Cable Systems—North Dakota

GRAND FORKS—Midco, PO Box 5010, Sioux Falls, SD 57117. Phones: 701-772-6411 (Local office); 800-888-1300. Web Site: http://www.midcocomm.com. Also serves Crookston, East Grand Forks & Oslo, MN; Buxton, Drayton, Emerado, Galesburg, Grafton, Grand Forks AFB, Grandin, Hatton, Hillsboro, Larimore, Manvel, Mayville, Minto, Portland, Reynolds & Thompson, ND. ICA: ND0003.

TV Market Ranking: 98 (Galesburg, Grandin); Below 100 (Buxton, Crookston, Drayton, East Grand Forks, Emerado, GRAND FORKS, Grand Forks AFB, Hatton, Mayville, Portland, Reynolds, Thompson, Larimore, Manvel, Minto, Oslo); Outside TV Markets (Hillsboro, Grafton). Franchise award date: N.A. Franchise expiration date: N.A. Began: November 1, 1970.

Channel capacity: N.A. Channels available but not in use: N.A.

Basic Service
Subscribers: 23,112.
Programming (received off-air): KBRR (FOX) Thief River Falls; KGFE (PBS) Grand Forks; KRDK-TV (CBS, Decades, Movies!) Valley City; KVLY-TV (MeTV, NBC, This TV) Fargo; WDAZ-TV (ABC, CW) Devils Lake.
Programming (via satellite): CNN; CW PLUS; Freeform; Pop; QVC; The Weather Channel; various Canadian stations; WGN America.
Fee: $25.00 installation; $19.95 monthly; $1.50 converter.

Expanded Basic Service 1
Subscribers: 18,212.
Programming (via satellite): A&E; AMC; Animal Planet; BET; Bravo; Cartoon Network; Celebrity Shopping Network; CMT; CNBC; Comedy Central; C-SPAN; C-SPAN 2; Discovery Channel; Disney Channel; E! HD; ESPN; ESPN2; EWTN Global Catholic Network; Food Network; Fox News Channel; Fox Sports 1; FOX Sports North; FX; Hallmark Channel; HGTV; History; HLN; INSP; Lifetime; MSNBC; MTV; NBCSN; Nickelodeon; Outdoor Channel; Oxygen; Spike TV; Syfy; TBS; TLC; TNT; Travel Channel; Trinity Broadcasting Network (TBN); truTV; Turner Classic Movies; TV Land; USA Network; VH1; WE tv.
Fee: $25.00 installation; $19.97 monthly.

Digital Basic Service
Subscribers: N.A.
Programming (via satellite): 3ABN; A&E HD; Animal Planet HD; AXS TV; BBC America; Bloomberg Television; Boomerang; BTN; Canal Sur; CBS Sports Network; Cine Mexicano; Cinelatino; CMT; CNN en Espanol; CNN HD; Cooking Channel; C-SPAN 3; Destination America; Discovery Channel HD; Discovery Kids Channel; Discovery Life Channel; Disney Channel HD; Disney XD; DIY Network; ESPN Classic; ESPN Deportes; ESPN HD; ESPN2 HD; ESPNews; Food Network HD; Fox Business Network; FOX College Sports Central; FOX College Sports Pacific; Fox Deportes; Freeform HD; FSN HD; Fuse; FYI; Golf Channel; GolTV; Great American Country; GSN; HD Theater; HGTV HD; History en Espanol; History HD; History International; IFC; Investigation Discovery; ION Television; JUCE TV; LMN; MC; MTV Classic; MTV Hits; MTV Jams; MTV Live; MTV2; National Geographic Channel; National Geographic Channel HD; NBC Universo; NBCSN; NFL Network; NHL Network; Nick 2; Nick Jr.; Nicktoons; Outdoor Channel; OWN; Oprah Winfrey Network; Qubo; Reelz; RFD-TV; Science Channel; Sprout; Sundance TV; Syfy HD; TBS HD; TeenNick; Telemundo; Tennis Channel; TLC HD; TNT HD; Toon Disney en Espanol; Tr3s; Trinity Broadcasting Network (TBN); Turner Classic Movies; TV One; TVG Network; Universal HD; USA Network HD; Versus HD; VH1 Soul; WE tv.

Digital Pay Service 1
Pay Units: 2,107.
Programming (via satellite): Cinemax (multiplexed); Cinemax HD; HBO (multiplexed); HBO HD; Showtime (multiplexed); Showtime HD; Starz (multiplexed); Starz Encore (multiplexed); Starz HD; The Movie Channel (multiplexed); The Movie Channel HD.
Fee: $12.90 monthly (each).

Video-On-Demand: No

Pay-Per-View
ESPN Now (delivered digitally); Hot Choice (delivered digitally); iN DEMAND (delivered digitally); Playboy TV (delivered digitally); Fresh (delivered digitally).

Internet Service
Operational: Yes.
Subscribers: 22,771.
Broadband Service: MidcoNet.
Fee: $35.00 installation; $19.95 monthly.

Telephone Service
Digital: Operational
Subscribers: 9,011.
Fee: $18.00 monthly
Miles of Plant: 333.0 (coaxial); 130.0 (fiber optic). Homes passed: 53,428.
General Manager: Butch Motenburg. Chief Technician: Mark Jensen. Programming Director: Wynne Haakenstad.
Ownership: Midcontinent Communications (MSO).; Comcast Cable Communications Inc. (MSO).

GRANVILLE—SRT Communications. Now served by VELVA, ND [ND0059]. ICA: ND0111.

GWINNER—DRN. This cable system has converted to IPTV. Now served by OAKES, ND [ND5032]. ICA: ND0073.

HANKINSON—Midco. Now served by WAHPETON, ND [ND0007]. ICA: ND0025.

HARVEY—Midco. Now served by MINOT, ND [ND0004]. ICA: ND0019.

JAMESTOWN—Cable Services Inc, PO Box 1995, Jamestown, ND 58402. Phones: 701-252-2225; 701-252-2225. Fax: 701-252-1105. Web Site: http://csicable.com. ICA: ND0191.
TV Market Ranking: 98 (JAMESTOWN). Franchise award date: N.A. Franchise expiration date: N.A. Began: December 24, 1964.
Channel capacity: N.A. Channels available but not in use: N.A.

Basic Service
Subscribers: 2,329.
Programming (received off-air): KFME (PBS) Fargo; KJRR (FOX) Jamestown; KRDK-TV (CBS, Decades, Movies!) Valley City; KVLY-TV (MeTV, NBC, This TV) Fargo; various Canadian stations; WDAY-TV (ABC, CW) Fargo; 7 FMs.
Programming (via satellite): A&E; Animal Planet; Cartoon Network; CNBC; CNN; Comedy Central; C-SPAN; C-SPAN 2; C-SPAN 3; Discovery Channel; Disney Channel; E! HD; ESPN; ESPN2; Food Network; Fox News Channel; FOX Sports Networks; Freeform; FX; Great American Country; Hallmark Channel; HGTV; History; HLN; INSP; Lifetime; MSNBC; MTV; NASA TV; Nickelodeon; Pop; QVC; Spike TV; Syfy; TBS; The Weather Channel; TLC; TNT; Trinity Broadcasting Network (TBN); Turner Classic Movies; USA Network; VH1; WGN America.
Fee: $22.00 installation; $25.00 monthly.

Pay Service 1
Pay Units: 800.
Programming (via satellite): Showtime; The Movie Channel.
Fee: $10.00 installation; $7.95 monthly.

Video-On-Demand: No

Internet Service
Operational: Yes. Began: September 1, 1999.
Broadband Service: In-house.
Fee: $30.00 installation; $29.99 monthly; $4.00 modem lease; $56.56 modem purchase.

Telephone Service
Digital: Operational
Miles of Plant: 125.0 (coaxial); 100.0 (fiber optic).
President & General Manager: Roy Sheppard. Chief Technician: Roger Nelson. Marketing Manager: Chris Sheppard.
Ownership: Cable Services Inc. (MSO).

JAMESTOWN—DCT. This cable system has converted to IPTV, 630 5th St North, PO Box 299, Carrington, ND 58421. Phones: 701-952-1001 (Jamestown office); 800-771-0974; 701-652-3184. Fax: 701-674-8121. E-mail: customerservice@daktel.com. Web Site: http://www.daktel.com. Also serves Bordulac, Bowdon, Carrington, Cleveland, Edmunds, Gackle, Grace City, Hurdsfield, Kensal, Medina, Montpelier, Streeter, Sykeston, Wimbledon, Woodworth & Ypsilanti. ICA: ND5005.
TV Market Ranking: 98 (Ypsilanti); Below 100 (Cleveland, Woodworth); Outside TV Markets (Sykeston).
Channel capacity: N.A. Channels available but not in use: N.A.

Local
Subscribers: 332.
Fee: $17.95 monthly. Includes 24 channels.

Digital
Subscribers: N.A.
Fee: $58.75 monthly. Includes 123 channels.

Sports
Subscribers: N.A.
Fee: $5.95 monthly. Includes 13 channels.

Cinemax
Subscribers: N.A.
Fee: $9.95 monthly. Includes 3 channels.

HBO
Subscribers: N.A.
Fee: $15.95 monthly. Includes 6 channels.

Cinemax/HBO
Subscribers: N.A.
Fee: $23.95 monthly. Includes 9 channels.

Playboy
Subscribers: N.A.
Fee: $12.95 monthly. Includes 1 channel.

Showtime
Subscribers: N.A.
Fee: $10.95 monthly. Includes 8 channels.

Starz/Encore
Subscribers: N.A.
Fee: $12.95 monthly. Includes 13 channels.

Internet Service
Operational: Yes.
Fee: $44.95-$94.95 monthly.

Telephone Service
Digital: Operational
Chief Executive Officer & General Manager: Keith A. Larson. Chief Plant Officer: Paul Berg. Chief Financial Officer: Cindy Hewitt. Chief Marketing Officer & Internal Operations Officer: Holly Utke. Business Account Executive: Lori Soldberg.
Ownership: Dakota Central Telecommunications.

KENMARE—RTC. Now served by PARSHALL, ND [ND0020]. ICA: ND0043.

KINDRED—MLGC. Now served by ENDERLIN, ND [ND5000]. ICA: ND0223.

KULM—Formerly served by Cable Services Inc. No longer in operation. ICA: ND0108.

LA MOURE—Formerly served by Midcontinent Communications. No longer in operation. ICA: ND0051.

LAKOTA—Polar Cablevision. This cable system has converted to IPTV. Now served by PARK RIVER, ND [ND5106]. ICA: ND0058.

LANGDON—Midcontinent Communications. Now served by DEVILS LAKE, ND [ND0009]. ICA: ND0022.

LARIMORE—Midcontinent Communications. Now served by GRAND FORKS, ND [ND0003]. ICA: ND0048.

LEEDS—Midco, PO Box 5010, Sioux Falls, SD 57117. Phones: 605-229-1775; 800-888-1300. Fax: 605-229-0478. Web Site: http://www.midcocomm.com. ICA: ND0081.
TV Market Ranking: Below 100 (LEEDS). Franchise award date: December 1, 1986. Franchise expiration date: N.A. Began: October 1, 1974.
Channel capacity: N.A. Channels available but not in use: N.A.

Basic Service
Subscribers: 22. Commercial subscribers: 5.
Programming (received off-air): KGFE (PBS) Grand Forks; KMOT (FOX, NBC) Minot; KVLY-TV (MeTV, NBC, This TV) Fargo; KXMC-TV (CBS) Minot; WDAZ-TV (ABC, CW) Devils Lake.
Programming (via satellite): A&E; AMC; Cartoon Network; CMT; CNBC; CNN; C-SPAN; Discovery Channel; Disney Channel; ESPN; ESPN2; Freeform; FX; HLN; INSP; Lifetime; Nickelodeon; Pop; QVC; Spike TV; TBS; The Weather Channel; TLC; TNT; TV Land; USA Network; VH1; WGN America.
Fee: $50.00 installation; $45.95 monthly.

Pay Service 1
Pay Units: N.A.
Programming (via satellite): HBO; Showtime; The Movie Channel.
Fee: $20.00 installation; $11.00 monthly (Showtime or TMC), $12.00 monthly (HBO).

North Dakota—Cable Systems

Internet Service
Operational: No.
Telephone Service
None
Miles of Plant: 6.0 (coaxial); None (fiber optic). Homes passed: 314.
General Manager: Darrell Wrege. Programming Director: Wynne Haakenstad. Marketing Director: Fred Jamieson. Customer Service Manager: Kathy Fuhrmann.
Ownership: Midcontinent Communications (MSO).; Comcast Cable Communications Inc. (MSO).

LISBON—DRN. This cable system has converted to IPTV. Now served by OAKES, ND [ND5032]. ICA: ND0225.

LISBON (village)—Formerly served by Cable Services Inc. No longer in operation, PO Box 1995, Jamestown, ND 58402. Web Site: http://csicable.com. ICA: ND0040.
Channel capacity: N.A. Channels available but not in use: N.A.

LITCHVILLE—DRN. This cable system has converted to IPTV. Now served by OAKES, ND [ND5032]. ICA: ND0135.

MADDOCK—Maddock Cable TV, 306 2nd St, PO Box 368, Maddock, ND 58348. Phone: 701-438-2541. ICA: ND0087.
TV Market Ranking: Below 100 (MADDOCK). Franchise award date: N.A. Franchise expiration date: N.A. Began: February 1, 1983.
Channel capacity: N.A. Channels available but not in use: N.A.
Basic Service
Subscribers: 140.
Programming (received off-air): KARE (NBC, WeatherNation) Minneapolis; KMOT (FOX, NBC) Minot; KNRR (FOX) Pembina; KXMC-TV (CBS) Minot; WDAZ-TV (ABC, CW) Devils Lake; allband FM.
Programming (via satellite): A&E; CMT; CNN; C-SPAN; Discovery Channel; Disney Channel; ESPN; ESPN2; Fox News Channel; FOX Sports Networks; Freeform; Hallmark Channel; Hallmark Movies & Mysteries; History; MTV; National Geographic Channel; Nickelodeon; TBS; TLC; TNT; TV Land; VH1; WGN America.
Programming (via translator): KGFE (PBS) Grand Forks.
Fee: $28.00 monthly.
Digital Basic Service
Subscribers: N.A.
Programming (via satellite): BBC America; Bloomberg Television; Cloo; CMT; Destination America; Discovery Kids Channel; Discovery Life Channel; Disney XD; ESPN Classic; ESPN2; ESPNews; FOX College Sports Central; FOX College Sports Pacific; Fox Sports 1; Fuse; FXM; FYI; Golf Channel; Great American Country; GSN; HGTV; History; History International; IFC; Investigation Discovery; MTV Classic; MTV Hits; MTV2; National Geographic Channel; Nick Jr.; Nicktoons; Outdoor Channel; Ovation; OWN: Oprah Winfrey Network; Science Channel; Sundance TV; TeenNick; The Word Network; Trinity Broadcasting Network (TBN); Turner Classic Movies; UP; VH1 Soul; WE tv.
Pay Service 1
Pay Units: 127.
Programming (via satellite): HBO.
Fee: $7.00 monthly.
Digital Pay Service 1
Pay Units: N.A.
Programming (via satellite): Flix; Showtime (multiplexed); Starz (multiplexed); Starz Encore (multiplexed); The Movie Channel (multiplexed).
Video-On-Demand: No
Internet Service
Operational: No.
Telephone Service
None
Miles of Plant: 5.0 (coaxial); None (fiber optic). Homes passed: 253.
General Manager: Byron Ellingson.
Ownership: Maddock Area Development Corp.

MANVEL—Midcontinent Communications. Now served by GRAND FORKS, ND [ND0003]. ICA: ND0127.

MARION—DRN. This cable system has converted to IPTV. Now served by OAKES, ND [ND5032]. ICA: ND0116.

MAX—RTC. Now served by PARSHALL, ND [ND0020]. ICA: ND0109.

MCCLUSKY—Midco, PO Box 5010, Sioux Falls, SD 57117. Phones: 605-229-1775; 800-888-1300. Fax: 605-229-0478. Web Site: http://www.midcocomm.com. Also serves Goodrich. ICA: ND0092.
TV Market Ranking: Outside TV Markets (Goodrich, MCCLUSKY). Franchise award date: April 5, 1988. Franchise expiration date: N.A. Began: January 15, 1983.
Channel capacity: N.A. Channels available but not in use: N.A.
Basic Service
Subscribers: 91. Commercial subscribers: 6.
Programming (received off-air): KBME-TV (PBS) Bismarck; KBMY (ABC) Bismarck; KFYR-TV (FOX, MeTV, NBC) Bismarck; KNDB (Heroes & Icons) Bismarck; KXMC-TV (CBS) Minot.
Programming (via satellite): A&E; AMC; Animal Planet; Cartoon Network; CMT; CNBC; CNN; C-SPAN; Discovery Channel; Disney Channel; ESPN; ESPN2; FOX Sports North; Freeform; HGTV; History; HLN; INSP; Lifetime; Nickelodeon; QVC; Spike TV; Syfy; TBS; The Weather Channel; TLC; TNT; TV Land; USA Network; VH1; WE tv; WGN America.
Fee: $50.00 installation; $45.95 monthly.
Pay Service 1
Pay Units: N.A.
Programming (via satellite): HBO; Showtime; The Movie Channel.
Fee: $20.00 installation; $11.00 monthly (Showtime or TMC), $12.00 monthly (HBO).
Video-On-Demand: No
Internet Service
Operational: Yes.
Fee: $35.00 installation; $19.95 monthly.
Telephone Service
Digital: Operational
Fee: $18.00 monthly
Miles of Plant: 5.0 (coaxial); None (fiber optic). Homes passed: 365.
General Manager: Darrell Wrege. Marketing Director: Fred Jamieson. Customer Service Manager: Kathy Fuhrmann. Programming Director: Wynne Haakenstad.
Ownership: Midcontinent Communications (MSO).; Comcast Cable Communications Inc. (MSO).

MEDINA—Formerly served by Cable Services Inc. No longer in operation. ICA: ND0101.

METIGOSHE—SRT Communications. Now served by VELVA, ND [ND0059]. ICA: ND0198.

MILNOR—Formerly served by Dickey Rural Networks. No longer in operation. ICA: ND0067.

MINNEWAUKAN—Midco, PO Box 5010, Sioux Falls, SD 57117. Phones: 605-229-1775; 800-888-1300. Fax: 605-229-0478. Web Site: http://www.midcocomm.com. ICA: ND0102.
TV Market Ranking: Below 100 (MINNEWAUKAN). Franchise award date: January 1, 1987. Franchise expiration date: N.A. Began: January 10, 1975.
Channel capacity: N.A. Channels available but not in use: N.A.
Basic Service
Subscribers: 25. Commercial subscribers: 8.
Programming (received off-air): KGFE (PBS) Grand Forks; KNRR (FOX) Pembina; KRDK-TV (CBS, Decades, Movies!) Valley City; KVLY-TV (MeTV, NBC, This TV) Fargo; WDAZ-TV (ABC, CW) Devils Lake; allband FM.
Programming (via satellite): A&E; AMC; Animal Planet; Cartoon Network; CMT; CNBC; CNN; C-SPAN; Discovery Channel; Disney Channel; ESPN; ESPN2; FOX Sports North; Freeform; HGTV; History; HLN; INSP; Lifetime; Nickelodeon; QVC; Spike TV; Syfy; TBS; The Weather Channel; TLC; TNT; Turner Classic Movies; TV Land; USA Network; VH1; WE tv; WGN America.
Fee: $50.00 installation; $45.95 monthly.
Pay Service 1
Pay Units: N.A.
Programming (via satellite): HBO; Showtime; The Movie Channel.
Fee: $20.00 installation; $11.00 monthly (Showtime or TMC), $12.00 monthly (HBO).
Video-On-Demand: No
Internet Service
Operational: No.
Telephone Service
None
Miles of Plant: 3.0 (coaxial); None (fiber optic). Homes passed: 232.
General Manager: Darrell Wrege. Programming Director: Wynne Haakenstad. Marketing Director: Fred Jamieson. Customer Service Manager: Kathy Fuhrmann.
Ownership: Midcontinent Communications (MSO).; Comcast Cable Communications Inc. (MSO).

MINOT—Formerly served by Microwave Communication Services. No longer in operation. ICA: ND0219.

MINOT—Formerly served by Vision Systems. No longer in operation. ICA: ND0210.

MINOT—Midco, PO Box 5010, Sioux Falls, SD 57117. Phones: 701-852-0376; 800-888-1300 (Customer service); 605-229-1775 (Administrative office). Web Site: http://www.midcocomm.com. Also serves Anamoose, Bottineau, Burlington, Drake, Dunseith, Fessenden, Glenburn, Harvey, Lansford, Minot AFB, Mohall, Rolette, Rolla, Rugby, Ruthville, St. John, Surrey, Towner, Ward County (portions) & Willow City. ICA: ND0004.
TV Market Ranking: Below 100 (Burlington, Glenburn, Lansford, MINOT, Minot AFB, Ruthville, Surrey); Outside TV Markets (Anamoose, Bottineau, Drake, Dunseith, Fessenden, Mohall, Rolla, St. John, Towner, Willow City, Harvey, Rolette, Rugby). Franchise award date: N.A. Franchise expiration date: N.A. Began: December 1, 1974.
Channel capacity: N.A. Channels available but not in use: N.A.
Basic Service
Subscribers: 15,512. Commercial subscribers: 4,371.
Programming (received off-air): KMCY (ABC) Minot; KMOT (FOX, NBC) Minot; KNDM (Heroes & Icons) Minot; KSRE (PBS) Minot; KXMC-TV (CBS) Minot; WGN-TV (IND) Chicago; 4 FMs.
Programming (via satellite): A&E; AMC; Animal Planet; BET; Bravo; Cartoon Network; CMT; CNBC; CNN; Comedy Central; C-SPAN; C-SPAN 2; CW PLUS; Discovery Channel; Discovery Life Channel; Disney Channel; E! HD; ESPN; ESPN2; EWTN Global Catholic Network; Food Network; Fox News Channel; Fox Sports 1; FOX Sports North; Freeform; FX; FXM; Great American Country; Hallmark Channel; HGTV; History; HLN; INSP; Lifetime; MSNBC; MTV; MTV2; NBCSN; Nickelodeon; OWN: Oprah Winfrey Network; Oxygen; Pop; QVC; Spike TV; Syfy; TBS; The Weather Channel; TLC; TNT; Travel Channel; Trinity Broadcasting Network (TBN); truTV; Turner Classic Movies; TV Land; Univision Studios; USA Network; VH1; WE tv.
Fee: $50.00 installation; $19.95 monthly.
Digital Basic Service
Subscribers: N.A.
Programming (via satellite): 3ABN; A&E HD; Animal Planet HD; AXS TV; BBC America; Bloomberg Television; Boomerang; BTN; Canal Sur; CBS Sports Network; Cine Mexicano; Cinelatino; CMT; CNN en Espanol; CNN HD; Cooking Channel; C-SPAN 3; Destination America; Discovery Kids Channel; Discovery Life Channel; Disney Channel HD; Disney XD; DIY Network; ESPN Classic; ESPN Deportes; ESPN HD; ESPNews; Food Network HD; Fox Business Network; FOX College Sports Central; FOX College Sports Pacific; Fox Deportes; Freeform HD; Fuse; FXM; FYI; Golf Channel; GolTV; Great American Country; GSN; HD Theater; HGTV HD; History en Espanol; History HD; History International; IFC; Investigation Discovery; ION Television; JUCE TV; LMN; MC; MTV Classic; MTV Hits; MTV Jams; MTV Live; MTV2; National Geographic Channel; National Geographic Channel HD; NBC Universo; NBCSN; NFL Network; NHL Network; Nick 2; Nick Jr.; Nicktoons; Outdoor Channel; OWN: Oprah Winfrey Network; Qubo; Reelz; RFD-TV; Science Channel; Sprout; Sundance TV; Syfy HD; TBS HD; TeenNick; Telemundo; Tennis Channel; TLC HD; TNT HD; Toon Disney en Espanol; Tr3s; Trinity Broadcasting Network (TBN); Turner Classic Movies; TV One; TVG Network; Universal HD; USA Network HD; Versus HD; VH1 Soul; WE tv.
Fee: $12.00 monthly.
Digital Pay Service 1
Pay Units: 5,180.
Programming (via satellite): Cinemax (multiplexed); Cinemax HD; Flix; HBO (multiplexed); HBO Latino; Showtime (multiplexed); Starz (multiplexed); Starz Encore (multiplexed); Starz HD; The Movie Channel (multiplexed); The Movie Channel HD.
Fee: $16.00 monthly (Cinemax, Showtime/TMC or Starz/Encore).
Video-On-Demand: No
Pay-Per-View
iN DEMAND (delivered digitally); Hot Choice (delivered digitally); Fresh (delivered digitally).
Internet Service
Operational: Yes.
Subscribers: 10,506.

Cable Systems—North Dakota

Broadband Service: MidcoNet.
Fee: $19.95 monthly.
Telephone Service
Digital: Operational
Fee: $18.00 monthly
Miles of Plant: 333.0 (coaxial); 81.0 (fiber optic). Homes passed: 31,500.
General Manager: Todd Jensen. Chief Technician: Brad Nixon. Programming Director: Wynne Haakenstad.
Ownership: Midcontinent Communications (MSO).; Comcast Cable Communications Inc. (MSO).

MINTO—Midcontinent Communications. Now served by GRAND FORKS, ND [ND0003]. ICA: ND0082.

MOTT—Midco, PO Box 5010, Sioux Falls, SD 57117. Phones: 605-229-1775; 800-888-1300. Fax: 605-229-0478. Web Site: http://www.midcocomm.com. ICA: ND0052.
TV Market Ranking: Outside TV Markets (MOTT). Franchise award date: March 2, 1992. Franchise expiration date: N.A. Began: June 15, 1980.
Channel capacity: N.A. Channels available but not in use: N.A.
Basic Service
Subscribers: 35. Commercial subscribers: 47.
Programming (received off-air): KBMY (ABC) Bismarck; KDSE (PBS) Dickinson; KFYR-TV (FOX, MeTV, NBC) Bismarck; KXMA-TV (CBS) Dickinson; KXMB-TV (CBS) Bismarck.
Programming (via satellite): A&E; AMC; Animal Planet; Cartoon Network; CMT; CNBC; CNN; C-SPAN; Discovery Channel; Disney Channel; ESPN; ESPN2; Fox News Channel; Freeform; HGTV; History; HLN; INSP; Lifetime; Nickelodeon; Outdoor Channel; QVC; Spike TV; Syfy; TBS; The Weather Channel; TLC; TNT; TV Land; USA Network; VH1; WE tv; WGN America.
Fee: $50.00 installation; $45.95 monthly.
Pay Service 1
Pay Units: N.A.
Programming (via satellite): HBO; Showtime; The Movie Channel.
Fee: $20.00 installation; $11.00 monthly (Showtime or TMC); $12.00 monthly (HBO).
Video-On-Demand: No
Internet Service
Operational: Yes.
Fee: $35.00 installation; $19.95 monthly.
Telephone Service
Digital: Operational
Fee: $18.00 monthly
Miles of Plant: 8.0 (coaxial); None (fiber optic). Homes passed: 545.
General Manager: Darrell Wrege. Programming Director: Wynne Haakenstad. Marketing Director: Fred Jamieson. Customer Service Manager: Kathy Fuhrmann.
Ownership: Midcontinent Communications (MSO).; Comcast Cable Communications Inc. (MSO).

MUNICH—United Communications. Formerly [ND0091]. This cable system has converted to IPTV, 411 7th Ave, PO Box 729, Langdon, ND 58249. Phones: 800-844-9708; 701-256-5156. Fax: 701-256-5150. E-mail: info@utma.com. Web Site: http://www.utma.com. Also serves Alsen, Bisbee, Bottineau, Calio, Calvin, Dunseith, Egeland, Kramer, Langdon, Milton, Osnabrock, Rock Lake, Rolette, Rolla, Sarles, Souris, St. John, Wales, Walhalla & Willow City. ICA: ND5154.

TV Market Ranking: Outside TV Markets (MUNICH, Rock Lake, Souris).
Channel capacity: N.A. Channels available but not in use: N.A.
Basic
Subscribers: 1,853.
Fee: $19.95 monthly.
Expanded Basic
Subscribers: 1,283.
Fee: $64.90 monthly.
Internet Service
Operational: Yes.
Telephone Service
Digital: Operational
General Manager: Perry Oyster. Assistant General Manager: Dannis Hansel. Facilities Manager: Ross Feil. Customer Service Manager: Kirsten Gendron.
Ownership: United Telephone Mutual Aid Corp.

MUNICH—United Communications. This cable system has converted to IPTV. See MUNICH, ND [ND5154]. ICA: ND0091.

NEW ENGLAND—Formerly served by New England Cablevision Inc. No longer in operation. ICA: ND0075.

NEW LEIPZIG—Formerly served by Northland Communications. No longer in operation. ICA: ND0113.

NEWBURG—SRT Communications. Now served by VELVA, ND [ND0059]. ICA: ND0175.

NORTHWOOD—MLGC. This cable system has converted to IPTV. Now served by ENDERLIN, ND [ND5000]. ICA: ND0224.

OAKES—DRN. Formerly [ND0226]. This cable system has converted to IPTV, 9628 Hwy 281, PO Box 69, Ellendale, ND 58436-0069. Phones: 877-559-4692; 701-344-5000. Fax: 701-344-4300. E-mail: customerservice@drtel.com. Web Site: http://www.drtel.net. Also serves Ashley, Cogswell, Crete, Dickey, Edgeley, Ellendale, Forbes, Forman, Fort Ransom, Fredonia, Fullerton, Guelph, Gwinner, Havana, Jud, Kathryn, Kulm, Lamoure, Lisbon, Litchville, Marion, Merricourt, Milnor, Rutland, Venturia & Verona. ICA: ND5032.
Channel capacity: N.A. Channels available but not in use: N.A.
Value Pak
Subscribers: 223.
Fee: $10.00 installation; $34.95 monthly. Includes 50+ channels.
Ultimate Family Pak
Subscribers: N.A.
Fee: $58.95 monthly. Includes 200 channels.
Spanish Pak
Subscribers: N.A.
Fee: $1.95 monthly. Includes 3 channels.
Sports Pak
Subscribers: N.A.
Fee: $3.95 monthly. Includes 13 channels.
Cinemax
Subscribers: N.A.
Fee: $12.95 monthly. Includes 8 channels.
HBO
Subscribers: N.A.
Fee: $15.95 monthly. Includes 6 channels.
Plex
Subscribers: N.A.
Fee: $4.95 monthly. Includes 3 channels.
Showtime
Subscribers: N.A.
Fee: $12.95 monthly. Includes 10 channels.

Starz/Encore
Subscribers: N.A.
Fee: $12.95 monthly. Includes 13 channels.
Internet Service
Operational: Yes.
Fee: $63.95-$179.95 monthly.
Telephone Service
Digital: Operational
Fee: $19.95 monthly
Chief Executive Officer & General Manager: Robert K. Johnson. Human Resources Manager: Sonja Bommersback. Marketing Manager: Janell Hauck. IS Applications Manager: Kari Nishek. Financial Manager: Troy Schilling. Plant Manager: Kent Schimke.
Ownership: Dickey Rural Services Inc.

OAKES—DRN. This cable system has converted to IPTV. Now served by OAKES, ND [ND5032]. ICA: ND0226.

OAKES—Formerly served by Cable Services Inc. No longer in operation. ICA: ND0038.

PARK RIVER—Polar Cablevision. Formerly [ND0026]. This cable system has converted to IPTV, 110 4th St East, PO Box 270, Park River, ND 58270. Phones: 800-284-7222; 701-284-7221. Fax: 701-284-7205. Web Site: http://www.polarcomm.com. Also serves Adams, Arthur, Brocket, Cavalier, Cavalier Air Force Station, Crystal, Edinburg, Fordville, Gilby, Hensel, Hoople, Hunter, Inkster, Lakota, Mayville, Michigan, Mountain, Neche, Niagara, Pembina, Petersburg, Pisek, Portland & St. Thomas. ICA: ND5106.
TV Market Ranking: 98 (Arthur, Hunter); Below 100 (Cavalier, Cavalier Air Force Station, Crystal, Gilby, Hensel, Lakota, Mountain, Neche, Pembina, St. Thomas); Outside TV Markets (Adams, Edinburg, Fordville, Hoople, Mayville, Michigan, Petersburg, Pisek, Portland).
Channel capacity: N.A. Channels available but not in use: N.A.
Digital Limited Basic
Subscribers: N.A.
Fee: $50.00 installation; $16.59 monthly. Includes 22 channels.
Digital Basic
Subscribers: 2,873.
Fee: $45.95 monthly. Includes 67 channels.
Digital Expanded Basic
Subscribers: N.A.
Fee: $54.95 monthly. Includes 111 channels & 50 music channels.
HD
Subscribers: N.A.
Fee: $12.95 monthly. Includes 61+ channels.
Sports Pak
Subscribers: N.A.
Fee: $9.95 monthly. Includes 15 channels.
Cinemax
Subscribers: N.A.
Fee: $7.95 monthly. Includes 8 channels.
Encore
Subscribers: N.A.
Fee: $5.95 monthly. Includes 10 channels.

HBO
Subscribers: N.A.
Fee: $14.95 monthly. Includes 6 channels.
Cinemax/HBO
Subscribers: N.A.
Fee: $19.95 monthly. Includes 14 channels.
Showtime/TMC/Flix
Subscribers: N.A.
Fee: $13.95 monthly. Includes 22 channels.
Starz/Encore
Subscribers: N.A.
Fee: $10.95 monthly. Includes 19 channels.
Internet Service
Operational: Yes.
Fee: $44.95-$54.95 monthly.
Telephone Service
Digital: Operational
Chief Executive Officer & General Manager: David L. Dunning.
Ownership: Polar Communications.

PARK RIVER—Polar Cablevision. This cable system has converted to IPTV. Now served by PARK RIVER, ND [ND5106]. ICA: ND0026.

PARSHALL (portions)—RTC, 24 Main St North, PO Box 68, Parshall, ND 58770-0068. Phones: 701-862-3115; 888-862-3115. Fax: 701-862-3008. E-mail: rtc@restel.com. Web Site: http://rtc.coop. Also serves Alexander (portions), Arnegard (portions), Douglas (portions), Garrison (portions), Keene (portions), Kenmare (portions), Makoti (portions), Mandaree (portions), Max (portions), New Town (portions), Plaza (portions), Ross (portions), Ryder (portions), Squaw Gap (portions), Watford City (portions), White Earth (portions) & White Shield (portions). ICA: ND0020.
TV Market Ranking: Below 100 (Alexander (portions), Arnegard (portions), Makoti (portions), Max (portions), Plaza (portions), Ryder (portions), Watford City (portions)); Outside TV Markets (Garrison (portions), Kenmare (portions), PARSHALL (PORTIONS), Squaw Gap (portions)). Franchise award date: N.A. Franchise expiration date: N.A. Began: November 1, 1981.
Channel capacity: N.A. Channels available but not in use: N.A.
Basic Service
Subscribers: 3,599 Includes IPTV subscribers. Commercial subscribers: 9.
Programming (received off-air): KMCY (ABC) Minot; KMOT (FOX, NBC) Minot; KNDM (Heroes & Icons) Minot; KSRE (PBS) Minot; KXMC-TV (CBS) Minot.
Programming (via satellite): EWTN Global Catholic Network; WGN America.
Fee: $30.00 installation; $17.95 monthly.
Digital Basic Service
Subscribers: N.A.
Programming (via satellite): A&E; Animal Planet; CMT; CNBC; CNN; Discovery Channel; Disney Channel; E! HD; ESPN; ESPN2; Food Network; Fox News Channel; FOX Sports Networks; Freeform; Great American Country; Hallmark Channel; HGTV; History; MSNBC; MTV; NBCSN; Nickelodeon; Spike TV; Syfy; TBS; The Weather Channel;

2017 Edition D-573

North Dakota—Cable Systems

TLC; TNT; Turner Classic Movies; TV Land; USA Network; VH1.
Fee: $59.95 monthly.
Digital Expanded Basic Service
Subscribers: N.A.
Fee: $75.95 monthly.
Pay Service 1
Pay Units: N.A.
Programming (via satellite): Cinemax (multiplexed); HBO; Starz (multiplexed); Starz Encore (multiplexed).
Fee: $15.95 monthly (Cinemax, Showtime/TMC or Starz/Encore), $18.95 monthly (HBO).
Video-On-Demand: Planned
Internet Service
Operational: Yes.
Fee: $25.00 installation; $54.95-$149.95 monthly.
Telephone Service
Analog: Operational
Fee: $15.00 monthly
Miles of Plant: 21.0 (coaxial); None (fiber optic).
Chief Executive Officer & General Manager: Shane Hart. Finance Manager: David Aamot. Outside Plant Manager, East: Chad Betz. Human Resources Manager: Gretchen Edwards. Operations Manager: Brooks Goodall. Marketing Manager: Kristin Jaeger. Construction Manager: Tim Jarski. Outside Plant Manager, West: Cory Johnson. Customer Service Manager: Lisa Schenfisch. Network Manager: Dan Schilla. Assistant Operations Manager: Jeff Symens.
Ownership: Reservation Telephone Cooperative.

PEMBINA—Polar Cablevision. This cable system has converted to IPTV. Now served by PARK RIVER, ND [ND5106]. ICA: ND0078.

RAY—Northwest Communications Coop, 111 Railroad Ave, PO Box 38, Ray, ND 58849. Phones: 701-568-3311; 800-245-5884; 701-568-3331. Fax: 701-568-7777. E-mail: ncc@nccray.com. Web Site: http://www.nccray.com. Also serves Bowbells, Columbus, Crosby, Flaxton, Grenora, Lignite, Noonan, Powers Lake, Round Prairie Twp., Tioga & Wildrose. ICA: ND0069.
TV Market Ranking: Below 100 (Grenora, RAY, Round Prairie Twp.); Outside TV Markets (Bowbells, Columbus, Crosby, Flaxton, Lignite, Noonan, Powers Lake, Tioga, Wildrose). Franchise award date: N.A. Franchise expiration date: N.A. Began: March 1, 1981.
Channel capacity: N.A. Channels available but not in use: N.A.
Basic Service
Subscribers: 2,026.
Programming (received off-air): KMCY (ABC) Minot; KMOT (FOX, NBC) Minot; KNDB (Heroes & Icons) Bismarck; KSRE (PBS) Minot; KUMV-TV (FOX, NBC) Williston; KXMC-TV (CBS) Minot; KXMD-TV (CBS) Williston; allband FM.
Programming (via satellite): A&E; AMC; Animal Planet; BTN; CNBC; CNN; Comedy Central; C-SPAN; CW PLUS; Discovery Channel; Disney Channel; Disney XD; DIY Network; ESPN; ESPN Classic; ESPN2; ESPNews; EWTN Global Catholic Network; FamilyNet; Food Network; Fox News Channel; FOX Sports North; Freeform; FX; Great American Country; Hallmark Channel; HGTV; History; HLN; INSP; Lifetime; MTV; National Geographic Channel; NBCSN; NFL Network; Nickelodeon; Outdoor Channel; QVC; RFD-TV; TBS; The Weather Channel;

TLC; TNT; Travel Channel; truTV; Turner Classic Movies; TV Land; USA Network; VH1; WGN America.
Fee: $25.00 installation; $61.50 monthly; $4.95 converter.
Digital Basic Service
Subscribers: N.A.
Programming (via satellite): A&E HD; AXS TV; BBC America; Bloomberg Television; Bravo; BTN HD; Cloo; Cooking Channel; Destination America; Discovery Channel HD; Discovery Kids Channel; Discovery Life Channel; DMX Music; ESPN HD; ESPN College Sports Central; FOX College Sports Pacific; Fox Sports 1; FSN HD; FXM; FYI; Golf Channel; GSN; History HD; History International; IFC; Investigation Discovery; LMN; MTV Classic; MTV Hits; MTV2; NFL Network HD; Nick Jr.; Nicktoons; OWN: Oprah Winfrey Network; Science Channel; TeenNick; TNT HD; VH1 Country; VH1 Soul; WE tv.
Digital Pay Service 1
Pay Units: N.A.
Programming (via satellite): Cinemax (multiplexed); Cinemax HD; Flix; HBO (multiplexed); HBO HD; Showtime (multiplexed); Showtime HD; Starz (multiplexed); Starz Encore (multiplexed); Starz HD; The Movie Channel (multiplexed).
Video-On-Demand: No
Internet Service
Operational: No, DSL.
Telephone Service
Analog: Operational
Miles of Plant: 41.0 (coaxial); None (fiber optic). Homes passed: 2,908.
Chief Executive Officer & General Manager: Dwight Schmitt. Operations Manager: Dean Rustad. Assistant Secretary & Treasurer: Todd Thompson.
Ownership: Northwest Communications Cooperative (MSO).

REGENT—Consolidated Cable Vision. Formerly [ND0201]. This cable system has converted to IPTV, 507 South Main, PO Box 1408, Dickinson, ND 58602. Phones: 888-225-5282; 701-483-4000. Fax: 701-483-0001. Web Site: http://www.ctctel.com. Also serves Belfield, Bowman, Dodge, Dunn Center, Halliday, Hettinger, Killdeer, Marmarth, Mott, New England, Reeder, Rhame, Richardton, Scranton, South Heart & Taylor. ICA: ND5109.
TV Market Ranking: Below 100 (Taylor). Channel capacity: N.A. Channels available but not in use: N.A.
Essential
Subscribers: 10,298.
Fee: $15.99 monthly.
Internet Service
Operational: Yes.
Fee: $48.00 installation; $29.95-$149.95 monthly.
Telephone Service
Digital: Operational
Fee: $20.00 monthly
Chief Operating Officer: Bryan Personne.
Ownership: Consolidated Telcom.

REGENT—Consolidated Cable Vision. This cable system has converted to IPTV. See REGENT, ND [ND5109]. ICA: ND0201.

ROLETTE—Midco. Now served by MINOT, ND [ND0004]. ICA: ND0094.

RUGBY—Midcontinent Communications. Now served by MINOT, ND [ND0004]. ICA: ND0018.

SANBORN—Formerly served by Cable Services Inc. No longer in operation. ICA: ND0204.

SAWYER—Formerly served by Sawyer CATV. No longer in operation. ICA: ND0134.

SELFRIDGE—Formerly served by West River Cable Television. No longer in operation. ICA: ND0056.

SHERWOOD—SRT Communications. Now served by VELVA, ND [ND0059]. ICA: ND0117.

SOLEN—Formerly served by Midcontinent Communications. No longer in operation. ICA: ND0055.

SOURIS—United Communications. This cable system has converted to IPTV. Now served by MUNICH, ND [ND5154]. ICA: ND0179.

SOUTH HEART—Midco, PO Box 5010, Sioux Falls, SD 57117. Phones: 800-888-1300; 605-229-1775. Fax: 605-229-0478. Web Site: http://www.midcocomm.com. Also serves Belfield & Dickinson. ICA: ND0013.
TV Market Ranking: Below 100 (Belfield, Dickinson, SOUTH HEART). Franchise award date: December 12, 1988. Franchise expiration date: N.A. Began: N.A.
Channel capacity: N.A. Channels available but not in use: N.A.
Basic Service
Subscribers: 686. Commercial subscribers: 2.
Programming (received off-air): KDSE (PBS) Dickinson; KQCD-TV (FOX, NBC) Dickinson; KXMA-TV (CBS) Dickinson.
Programming (via satellite): A&E; AMC; Animal Planet; Cartoon Network; CMT; CNBC; CNN; C-SPAN; Discovery Channel; Disney Channel; ESPN; ESPN2; Freeform; Hallmark Channel; HGTV; History; HLN; INSP; KMGH-TV (ABC, Azteca America) Denver; Lifetime; Nickelodeon; Outdoor Channel; QVC; Spike TV; Syfy; TBS; The Weather Channel; TLC; TNT; TV Land; USA Network; VH1; WE tv; WGN America.
Fee: $50.00 installation; $19.95 monthly.
Pay Service 1
Pay Units: N.A.
Programming (via satellite): HBO; Showtime; The Movie Channel.
Fee: $20.00 installation; $11.00 monthly (Showtime or TMC), $12.00 monthly (HBO).
Internet Service
Operational: No.
Telephone Service
None
Miles of Plant: 13.0 (coaxial); 3.0 (fiber optic).
General Manager: Darrell Wrege. Programming Director: Wynne Haakenstad. Marketing Director: Fred Jamieson. Customer Service Manager: Kathy Fuhrmann.
Ownership: Midcontinent Communications (MSO).; Comcast Cable Communications Inc. (MSO).

STANLEY—Midstate Telephone & Communications, 215 Main St South, PO Box 400, Stanley, ND 58784-0400. Phone: 701-628-2522. Fax: 701-628-3737. E-mail: servicedept@midstatetel.com. Web Site: http://www.midstatetel.com. Also serves Portal. ICA: ND0049.
TV Market Ranking: Outside TV Markets (Portal, STANLEY). Franchise award date:

N.A. Franchise expiration date: N.A. Began: February 1, 1979.
Channel capacity: N.A. Channels available but not in use: N.A.
Basic Service
Subscribers: N.A.
Programming (received off-air): KMCY (ABC) Minot; KMOT (FOX, NBC) Minot; KSRE (PBS) Minot; KXMC-TV (CBS) Minot.
Programming (via satellite): A&E; AMC; Animal Planet; Cartoon Network; CMT; CNBC; CNN; Comedy Central; C-SPAN 2; CW PLUS; Discovery Channel; E! HD; ESPN; ESPN Classic; ESPN2; EWTN Global Catholic Network; Food Network; Fox News Channel; FOX Sports Networks; Freeform; FX; FXM; Hallmark Channel; Hallmark Movies & Mysteries; HGTV; HLN; INSP; LMN; MTV; National Geographic Channel; Nickelodeon; Outdoor Channel; QVC; Radar Channel; RFD-TV; Spike TV; Starz Encore; Syfy; TBS; The Weather Channel; TLC; TNT; Travel Channel; Trinity Broadcasting Network (TBN); TV Land; USA Network; VH1; WGN America.
Fee: $20.00 installation.
Digital Basic Service
Subscribers: N.A.
Programming (via satellite): BBC America; Bloomberg Television; Destination America; Discovery Kids Channel; Discovery Life Channel; DMX Music; ESPN Classic; ESPNews; Fox Sports 1; FSN Digital Atlantic; FSN Digital Central; FSN Digital Pacific; FXM; FYI; Great American Country; GSN; History; INSP; Investigation Discovery; LMN; MTV Classic; MTV Hits; MTV Jams; MTV2; National Geographic Channel; Nick Jr.; Nicktoons; Outdoor Channel; OWN: Oprah Winfrey Network; Science Channel; Sundance TV; Syfy; TeenNick; Turner Classic Movies; VH1 Country; VH1 Soul; WE tv.
Pay Service 1
Pay Units: N.A.
Programming (via satellite): HBO.
Fee: $11.00 monthly.
Digital Pay Service 1
Pay Units: N.A.
Programming (via satellite): Cinemax (multiplexed); Flix; HBO (multiplexed); Showtime (multiplexed); Starz (multiplexed); Starz Encore (multiplexed); Sundance TV; The Movie Channel (multiplexed).
Fee: $9.00 monthly (Cinemax, Starz or Encore), $11.00 monthly (HBO), $12.00 monthly (Showtime/TMC/Flix/Sundance).
Internet Service
Operational: Yes.
Telephone Service
Analog: Operational
Miles of Plant: 12.0 (coaxial); None (fiber optic). Homes passed: 650.
General Manager: Mark Wilhelmi. Chief Technician & Marketing Director: Larry Fritel. Program Director: Deb Beehler.
Ownership: Midstate Telephone & Communications.

STEELE—Steele Cablevision, 200 East Broadway, PO Box 230, Steele, ND 58482. Phones: 888-475-2361; 701-475-2361. Fax: 701-475-2321. E-mail: bekcomm@bektel.com. Web Site: http://www.bektel.com. Also serves Linton, Wilton, Wing & Wishek. ICA: ND0227.
Channel capacity: N.A. Channels available but not in use: N.A.

Cable Systems—North Dakota

FULLY SEARCHABLE • CONTINUOUSLY UPDATED • DISCOUNT RATES FOR PRINT PURCHASERS

For more information call **800-771-9202** or visit **www.warren-news.com**

Basic Service
Subscribers: 132.
Programming (received off-air): KBME-TV (PBS) Bismarck; KBMY (ABC) Bismarck; KFYR-TV (FOX, MeTV, NBC) Bismarck; KNDB (Heroes & Icons) Bismarck; KXMB-TV (CBS) Bismarck.
Programming (via satellite): 3ABN; A&E; AMC; CNN; C-SPAN; C-SPAN 2; Disney Channel; ESPN; EWTN Global Catholic Network; Food Network; Fox News Channel; Fox Sports 1; Freeform; GSN; Hallmark Channel; HGTV; History; INSP; Lifetime; NASA TV; NBCSN; Outdoor Channel; RFD-TV; TBS; The Weather Channel; TNT; Trinity Broadcasting Network (TBN); truTV; Turner Classic Movies; WE tv; WGN America.
Fee: $24.00 monthly.
Video-On-Demand: No
Internet Service
Operational: Yes.
Fee: $41.95 monthly.
Telephone Service
Digital: Operational
Homes passed: 3,844.
Chief Executive Officer & General Manager: Derrick Bulawa. President: Brett Stroh. Vice President: Leo Meier. Customer Service Manager: Tammy Birrenkott.
Ownership: BEK Communications.

SYKESTON—DCT. This cable system has converted to IPTV. Now served by JAMESTOWN, ND [ND5005]. ICA: ND0152.

TAYLOR—Consolidated Cable Vision. This cable system has converted to IPTV. See REGENT, ND [ND5109]. ICA: ND0166.

TOWNER COUNTY (portions)—United Communications, 411 7th Ave, PO Box 729, Langdon, ND 58249. Phones: 800-844-9708; 701-256-5156. Fax: 701-256-5150. E-mail: info@utma.com. Web Site: http://www.utma.com. ICA: ND0229.
Channel capacity: N.A. Channels available but not in use: N.A.
Basic Service
Subscribers: 105.
Programming (received off-air): KNRR (FOX) Pembina; KRDK-TV (CBS, Decades, Movies!) Valley City; KVLY-TV (MeTV, NBC, This TV) Fargo; WDAZ-TV (ABC, CW) Devils Lake.
Programming (via satellite): WGN America.
Fee: $15.00 monthly.
Internet Service
Operational: Yes.
Telephone Service
Digital: Operational
General Manager: Perry Oyster. Assistant General Manager: Dennis Hansel. Customer Service Manager: Kirsten Gendron. Facilities Manager: Ross Feil.
Ownership: United Telephone Mutual Aid Corp.

UPHAM—Formerly served by RAE Cable. Now served by SRT Communications, VELVA, ND [ND0059]. ICA: ND0150.

VALLEY CITY—Cable Services Inc, PO Box 1995, Jamestown, ND 58402. Phones: 701-252-2225; 701-252-2225. Fax: 701-252-1105. E-mail: info@csicable.com. Web Site: http://csicable.com. ICA: ND0012.
TV Market Ranking: 98 (VALLEY CITY). Franchise award date: N.A. Franchise expiration date: N.A. Began: January 1, 1979.
Channel capacity: N.A. Channels available but not in use: N.A.

Basic Service
Subscribers: 1,090.
Programming (received off-air): KFME (PBS) Fargo; KJRR (FOX) Jamestown; KRDK-TV (CBS, Decades, Movies!) Valley City; KVLY-TV (MeTV, NBC, This TV) Fargo; WDAY-TV (ABC, CW) Fargo.
Programming (via satellite): 3ABN; A&E; Animal Planet; Bloomberg Television; Boomerang; BTN; Cartoon Network; CMT; CNBC; CNN; Comedy Central; C-SPAN; C-SPAN 2; C-SPAN 3; CW PLUS; Discovery Channel; Disney Channel; E! HD; ESPN; ESPN2; EWTN Global Catholic Network; Food Network; Fox News Channel; FOX Sports Networks; Freeform; FX; Great American Country; Hallmark Channel; Hallmark Movies & Mysteries; HGTV; History; HLN; INSP; Lifetime; MSNBC; MTV; NASA TV; NBCSN; Nickelodeon; Outdoor Channel; QVC; Spike TV; Syfy; TBS; The Weather Channel; TLC; TNT; Travel Channel; Trinity Broadcasting Network (TBN); Turner Classic Movies; TV Land; USA Network; various Canadian stations; VH1; WGN America.
Fee: $22.00 installation; $25.00 monthly.
Pay Service 1
Pay Units: N.A.
Programming (via satellite): Showtime; The Movie Channel.
Fee: $20.00 installation; $10.00 monthly.
Video-On-Demand: No
Internet Service
Operational: Yes. Began: December 31, 1999.
Broadband Service: In-house.
Fee: $30.00 installation; $29.99 monthly.
Telephone Service
Digital: Planned
Miles of Plant: 47.0 (coaxial); None (fiber optic). Homes passed: 2,500.
President & General Manager: Roy Sheppard. Chief Technician: Roger Nelson. Marketing Manager: Chris Sheppard.
Ownership: Cable Services Inc. (MSO).

VELVA—SRT Communications, 3615 North Broadway, PO Box 2027, Minot, ND 58702-2027. Phones: 800-737-9130; 701-858-1200. Fax: 701-858-1428. E-mail: email@srt.com. Web Site: http://www.srt.com. Also serves Antler, Berthold, Butte, Carpio, Deering, Des Lacs, Donnybrook, Granville, Karlsruhe, Maxbass, Metigoshe, Newburg, Sawyer, Sherwood, Tolley, Upham & Westhope. ICA: ND0059.
TV Market Ranking: Below 100 (Berthold, Carpio, Deering, Des Lacs, Granville, Karlsruhe, Maxbass, Sawyer, VELVA); Outside TV Markets (Antler, Butte, Donnybrook, Metigoshe, Newburg, Sherwood, Tolley, Upham, Westhope). Franchise award date: N.A. Franchise expiration date: N.A. Began: September 6, 1980.
Channel capacity: N.A. Channels available but not in use: N.A.
Basic Service
Subscribers: 1,324. Commercial subscribers: 125.
Programming (received off-air): KMCY (ABC) Minot; KMOT (FOX, NBC) Minot; KNDM (Heroes & Icons) Minot; KSRE (PBS) Minot; KXMC-TV (CBS) Minot.
Programming (via satellite): C-SPAN; TBS; The Weather Channel; WGN America.
Fee: $20.99 monthly.
Expanded Basic Service 1
Subscribers: 1,354.
Programming (via satellite): A&E; AMC; CMT; CNBC; CNN; Comedy Central; Discovery Channel; Disney Channel; Disney XD; ESPN; ESPN2; Fox News Channel; FOX Sports Networks; Freeform; FX; HGTV; History; HLN; Lifetime; MTV; NFL Network; Nickelodeon; Outdoor Channel; Spike TV; Syfy; TLC; TNT; Turner Classic Movies; TV Land; USA Network; VH1.
Fee: $48.99 monthly.
Digital Basic Service
Subscribers: N.A.
Digital Pay Service 1
Pay Units: N.A.
Programming (via satellite): Cinemax (multiplexed); HBO (multiplexed); Showtime (multiplexed); Starz (multiplexed); Starz Encore (multiplexed); The Movie Channel (multiplexed).
Fee: $16.00 monthly (each).
Video-On-Demand: No
Internet Service
Operational: Yes, DSL & dial-up.
Fee: $16.95-$99.95 monthly.
Telephone Service
Analog: Operational
Fee: $13.95-$20.95 monthly
Miles of Plant: 34.0 (coaxial); 595.0 (fiber optic). Homes passed: 3,744.
President: Tom Wentz Jr. Vice President: Stanley Vangsness. Chief Operating Officer: John Reiser.
Ownership: SRT Communications Inc.

WAHPETON—Midco, PO Box 5010, Sioux Falls, SD 57117. Phones: 701-642-5355; 800-888-1300 (Customer service); 605-229-1775 (Customer service). Web Site: http://www.midcocomm.com. Also serves Breckenridge, MN; Fairmount, Hankinson & Lidgerwood, ND. ICA: ND0007.
TV Market Ranking: Outside TV Markets (Breckenridge, Fairmount, Lidgerwood, WAHPETON, Hankinson). Franchise award date: N.A. Franchise expiration date: N.A. Began: July 1, 1969.
Channel capacity: N.A. Channels available but not in use: N.A.
Basic Service
Subscribers: 3,392.
Programming (received off-air): KCCO-TV (CBS) Alexandria; KFME (PBS) Fargo; KRDK-TV (CBS, Decades, Movies!) Valley City; KVLY-TV (MeTV, NBC, This TV) Fargo; KVRR (Antenna TV, FOX) Fargo; WDAY-TV (ABC, CW) Fargo; allband FM.
Programming (via satellite): A&E; AMC; Animal Planet; Bravo; Cartoon Network; CNBC; CNN; Comedy Central; C-SPAN; C-SPAN 2; CW PLUS; Discovery Channel; Discovery Life Channel; Disney Channel; E! HD; ESPN; ESPN2; EWTN Global Catholic Network; Food Network; Fox News Channel; Fox Sports 1; FOX Sports North; Freeform; FX; Hallmark Channel; HGTV; History; HLN; INSP; ION Television; Lifetime; MSNBC; MTV; Nickelodeon; Oxygen; Pop; QVC; Spike TV; Syfy; TBS; The Weather Channel; TLC; TNT; Travel Channel; truTV; TV Land; USA Network; VH1; WGN America.
Fee: $44.95 installation; $19.95 monthly; $3.00 converter.

Digital Basic Service
Subscribers: N.A.
Programming (via satellite): 3ABN; A&E HD; Animal Planet HD; AXS TV; BBC America; Bloomberg Television; Boomerang; BTN; Canal Sur; CBS Sports Network; Cine Mexicano; Cinelatino; CMT; CNN en Espanol; CNN HD; Cooking Channel; C-SPAN 3; Destination America; Discovery Channel HD; Discovery Kids Channel; Discovery Life Channel; Disney Channel HD; DIY Network; ESPN Classic; ESPN Deportes; ESPN HD; ESPN2 HD; ESPNews; EWTN Global Catholic Network; Food Network HD; Fox Business Network; FOX College Sports Central; FOX College Sports Pacific; Fox Deportes; Freeform HD; Fuse; FXM; FYI; Golf Channel; GolTV; Great American Country; GSN; HD Theater; HGTV HD; History en Espanol; History HD; History International; IFC; Investigation Discovery; ION Television; JUCE TV; LMN; MC; MTV Classic; MTV Hits; MTV Jams; MTV Live; MTV2; National Geographic Channel; National Geographic Channel HD; NBC Universo; NBCSN; NFL Network; Nick 2; Nick Jr.; Nicktoons; Outdoor Channel; OWN; Oprah Winfrey Network; Qubo; Reelz; RFD-TV; Sprout; Sundance TV; Syfy HD; TBS HD; TeenNick; Telemundo; Tennis Channel; TLC HD; TNT HD; Toon Disney en Espanol; Tr3s; Trinity Broadcasting Network (TBN); Turner Classic Movies; TV One; TVG Network; Universal HD; USA Network HD; Versus HD; VH1 Soul; WE tv.
Digital Pay Service 1
Pay Units: N.A.
Programming (via satellite): Cinemax; Cinemax HD; Flix; HBO (multiplexed); HBO Latino; Showtime (multiplexed); Showtime HD; Starz (multiplexed); Starz Encore (multiplexed); Starz HD; The Movie Channel (multiplexed); The Movie Channel HD.
Video-On-Demand: No
Pay-Per-View
iN DEMAND (delivered digitally); NHL Center Ice (delivered digitally); MLB Extra Innings (delivered digitally); ESPN (delivered digitally); NBA League Pass (delivered digitally); MLS Direct Kick (delivered digitally).
Internet Service
Operational: Yes.
Fee: $35.00 installation; $19.95 monthly.
Telephone Service
Digital: Operational
Fee: $18.00 monthly
Miles of Plant: 48.0 (coaxial); None (fiber optic). Homes passed: 5,842.
General Manager: Steve Schirber. Programming Director: Wynne Haakenstad. Chief Technician: Raymond Olson. Office Manager: Avis Althoff.
Ownership: Midcontinent Communications (MSO).; Comcast Cable Communications Inc. (MSO).

WATFORD CITY—RTC. Now served by PARHSALL, ND [ND0020]. ICA: ND0024.

WEST FARGO—Midco, PO Box 5010, Sioux Falls, SD 57117. Phone: 800-888-1300. Web Site: http://www.midcocomm.com. Also

North Dakota—Cable Systems

serves Dilworth, Moorhead, Oakport Twp. & Sabin, MN; Buffalo, Casselton, Fargo, Frontier, Harwood, Horace, Leonard, Mapleton, Oxbow & Reile's Acres, ND. ICA: ND0230.
TV Market Ranking: 98 (Buffalo, Casselton, Dilworth, Fargo, Frontier, Harwood, Horace, Leonard, Mapleton, Moorhead, Oakport Twp., Sabin, WEST FARGO).
Channel capacity: N.A. Channels available but not in use: N.A.
Basic Service
Subscribers: 14,622.
Fee: $19.95 monthly.
Programming Director: Wynne Haakenstad.
Ownership: Midcontinent Communications (MSO).

WESTHOPE—SRT Communications. Now served by VELVA, ND [ND0059]. ICA: ND0074.

WILLISTON—Midco, PO Box 5010, Sioux Falls, SD 57117. Phones: 800-888-1300; 605-229-1775. Fax: 605-229-0478; 701-572-9615. Web Site: http://www.midcocomm.com. Also serves Williston Twp. (portions). ICA: ND0006.
TV Market Ranking: Below 100 (WILLISTON, Williston Twp. (portions)). Franchise award date: N.A. Franchise expiration date: N.A. Began: June 1, 1967.
Channel capacity: N.A. Channels available but not in use: N.A.

Basic Service
Subscribers: 5,754.
Programming (received off-air): KUMV-TV (FOX, NBC) Williston; KWSE (PBS) Williston; KXMD-TV (CBS) Williston.
Programming (via satellite): A&E; AMC; Animal Planet; Cartoon Network; CMT; CNBC; CNN; Comedy Central; C-SPAN; C-SPAN 2; Discovery Channel; Disney Channel; E! HD; ESPN; ESPN2; EWTN Global Catholic Network; Food Network; Fox News Channel; FOX Sports North; Freeform; FX; Hallmark Channel; HGTV; History; HLN; INSP; ION Television; Lifetime; MSNBC; MTV; Nickelodeon; Pop; QVC; Spike TV; TBS; The Weather Channel; TLC; TNT; Travel Channel; Trinity Broadcasting Network (TBN); truTV; Turner Classic Movies; USA Network; VH1; WGN America.
Fee: $29.60 installation; $19.95 monthly.

Digital Basic Service
Subscribers: N.A.
Programming (via satellite): BBC America; Bravo; Discovery Digital Networks; Disney XD; DMX Music; ESPN Classic; ESPNews; Fox Sports 1; Fuse; FXM; FYI; Golf Channel; GSN; History International; IFC; LMN; MTV Classic; MTV Hits; MTV2; National Geographic Channel; NBCSN; Nick Jr.; Nicktoons; Outdoor Channel; Syfy; TeenNick; TV Land; VH1 Country; VH1 Soul; WE tv.

Digital Pay Service 1
Pay Units: N.A.
Programming (via satellite): Cinemax (multiplexed); HBO (multiplexed); Showtime (multiplexed); Starz Encore; The Movie Channel (multiplexed).
Video-On-Demand: No
Pay-Per-View
Hot Choice (delivered digitally); Playboy TV (delivered digitally); NBA TV (delivered digitally); Sports PPV (delivered digitally); iN DEMAND (delivered digitally).
Internet Service
Operational: Yes.
Fee: $35.00 installation; $19.95 monthly.

Telephone Service
Digital: Operational
Fee: $18.00 monthly
Miles of Plant: 82.0 (coaxial); None (fiber optic). Homes passed: 6,786.
General Manager: Todd Jensen. Chief Technician: Steve Peterson. Programming Director: Wynne Haakenstad.
Ownership: Midcontinent Communications (MSO).; Comcast Cable Communications Inc. (MSO).

WISHEK—Formerly served by Midcontinent Communications. No longer in operation. ICA: ND0044.

WOODWORTH—DCT. This cable system has converted to IPTV. Now served by JAMESTOWN, ND [ND5005]. ICA: ND0168.

WYNDMERE—Formerly served by Dickey Rural Networks. No longer in operation. ICA: ND0086.

YPSILANTI—DCT. This cable system has converted to IPTV. Now served by JAMESTOWN, ND [ND5005]. ICA: ND0169.

OHIO

Total Systems: 91
Total Communities Served: 2,102
Franchises Not Yet Operating: 0
Applications Pending: 0
Communities with Applications: 0
Number of Basic Subscribers: 2,178,861
Number of Expanded Basic Subscribers: 4,646
Number of Pay Units: 9,310

Top 100 Markets Represented: Pittsburgh, PA (10); Cincinnati, OH-Newport, KY (17); Columbus-Chillicothe (27); Charleston-Huntington, WV (36); Dayton-Kettering (41); Toledo (52); Youngstown (79); Fort Wayne-Roanoke, IN (82); Cleveland-Lorain-Akron (8); Wheeling, WV-Steubenville, OH (90).

For a list of cable communities in this section, see the Cable Community Index located in the back of Cable Volume 2.
For explanation of terms used in cable system listings, see p. D-11.

ADA—Time Warner Cable. Now served by COLUMBUS, OH [OH0002]. ICA: OH0313.

ADENA—Comcast Cable. Now served by WHEELING, WV [WV0004]. ICA: OH0181.

AKRON—Time Warner Cable. Now served by CLEVELAND (formerly Cleveland Heights), OH [OH0006]. ICA: OH0005.

ALBANY—Time Warner Cable. Now served by JACKSON, OH [OH0098]. ICA: OH0314.

AMBERLEY (village)—Time Warner Cable, 11252 Cornell Park Dr, Cincinnati, OH 45242. Phones: 937-294-6800; 513-489-5000. Fax: 513-489-5991. Web Site: http://www.timewarnercable.com. Also serves Union Twp, Wayne Twp. (Randolph County), West College Corner (town) & West Harrison (town), IN; Aberdeen (village), Adams Twp. (Champaign County), Adams Twp. (Clinton County), Adams Twp. (Darke County), Addyston (village), Allen Twp. (Darke County), Amelia (village), Anderson Twp. (Hamilton County), Anna (village), Ansonia (village), Arcanum (village), Arlington Heights (village), Batavia (village), Batavia Twp, Bath Twp. (Green County), Beavercreek, Beavercreek Twp., Bellbrook, Bethel (village), Bethel Twp. (Clark County), Bethel Twp. (Miami County), Blanchester (village), Blue Ash, Botkins (village), Bradford (village) (Darke County), Bradford (village) (Miami County), Brookville (village), Brown Twp. (Darke County), Brown Twp. (Miami County), Burketsville (village) (Darke County), Burketsville (village) (Mercer County), Butler County (portions), Butler Twp. (Darke County), Butler Twp. (Montgomery County), Butlerville (village), Camden (village), Carlisle, Casstown (village), Castine (village), Catawba (village), Cedarville (village), Cedarville Twp., Centerville, Cherry Fork (village), Cheviot, Chilo (village), Christiansburg (village), Cincinnati, Clark Twp. (Brown County), Clark Twp. (Clinton County), Clay Twp. (Montgomery County), Clayton (village), Clearcreek Twp. (Fairfield County), Cleves (village), Clifton (village) (Clark Champaign County), Clifton (village) (Greene County), Clinton Twp. (Shelby County), Colerain Twp. (Hamilton County), Colerain Twp. (Ross County), College Corner (village) (Butler County), College Corner (village) (Preble County), Columbia Twp. (Hamilton County), Concord Twp. (Champaign County), Corwin (village), Covington (village), Crosby Twp. (Hamilton County), Dayton, De Graff (village), Deer Park, Deerfield Twp. (Warren County), Delhi Twp., Dinsmore Twp., Dodson Twp., Donnelsville (village), Eaton (Preble County), Eldorado (village), Elizabeth Twp. (Miami County), Elmwood Place (village), Englewood, Enon (village), Evendale (village), Fairborn, Fairfax (village), Fairfield (Butler County), Fairfield Twp. (Butler County), Fairfield Twp. (Highland County), Farmersville (village), Fayetteville (village), Felicity (village), Fletcher (village), Forest Park, Franklin (Warren County), Franklin Twp. (Adams County), Franklin Twp. (Clermont County), Franklin Twp. (Shelby County), Franklin Twp. (Warren County), Gasper Twp., Georgetown (village), German Twp. (Clark County), German Twp. (Montgomery County), Germantown (town), Gettysburg (village), Glendale (village), Golf Manor (village), Gordon (village), Goshen Twp. (Clermont County), Gratis (village), Gratis Twp., Green Twp. (Brown County), Green Twp. (Clark County), Green Twp. (Clinton County), Green Twp. (Hamilton County), Green Twp. (Shelby County), Greenhills (village), Greenville (town), Hamer Twp., Hamersville (village), Hamilton, Harlan Twp., Harmony Twp. (Clark County), Harrison (village), Harrison Twp. (Champaign County), Harrison Twp. (Darke County), Harrison Twp. (Hamilton County), Harrison Twp. (Montgomery County), Harrison Twp. (Preble County), Higginsport (village), Highland, Hillsboro, Hollansburg (village), Huber Heights, Indian Hill (village), Israel Twp., Ithaca (village), Jackson Center (village), Jackson Twp. (Champaign County), Jackson Twp. (Clermont City), Jackson Twp. (Darke County), Jackson Twp. (Montgomery County), Jackson Twp. (Preble City), Jacksonburg (village), Jamestown (village), Jefferson Twp. (Clinton County), Jefferson Twp. (Montgomery County), Jefferson Twp. (Preble County), Johnson Twp. (Champaign County), Kettering, Lanier Twp., Laura (village), Lawrenceville (village), Lebanon, Leesburg (village), Lemon Twp., Lewis Twp., Lewisburg (village), Liberty Twp. (Adams County), Liberty Twp. (Butler County), Liberty Twp. (Darke County), Liberty Twp. (Highland County), Liberty Twp. (Logan County), Lincoln Heights (village), Lockington (village), Lockland, Logan County (portions), Lostcreek Twp., Loveland (Clermont County), Loveland (Hamilton County), Loveland (Warren County), Ludlow Falls (village), Lynchburg (village), Mad River Twp. (Champaign County), Mad River Twp. (Clark County), Madeira, Madison Twp. (Butler County), Madison Twp. (Clark County), Madison Twp. (Highland County), Madison Twp. (Montgomery County), Maineville (village), Manchester (village), Mariemont (village), Marion Twp. (Clinton County), Marshall Twp. (Clinton County), Martinsville (village), Mason, Mechanicsburg (village), Meigs Twp. (Adams County), Miami Twp. (Clermont County), Miami Twp. (Greene County), Miami Twp. (Hamilton County), Miami Twp. (Montgomery County), Miamisburg, Middletown (Butler County), Middletown (Warren County), Midland (village), Milford (Clermont County), Milford (Hamilton County), Millville (village), Monroe, Monroe Twp. (Clermont County), Monroe Twp. (Darke County), Monroe Twp. (Miami County), Monroe Twp. (Preble County), Montgomery, Moorefield Twp., Moraine, Morgan Twp. (Butler County), Morrow (village), Moscow (village), Mount Healthy, Mount Orab (village), Mutual (village), Naeve Twp., Neville (village), New Carlisle, New Jasper Twp., New Lebanon (village), New Madison (village), New Market Twp., New Miami (village), New Paris (village), New Richmond (village), New Vienna (village), New Weston (village), Newberry Twp., Newton Twp. (Miami County), Newtonsville (village), Newtown (village), North Bend (village), North College Hill, North Hampton (village), Norwood, Oakwood, Ohio Twp., Orange Twp., Owensville (village), Oxford, Oxford Twp. (Butler County), Palestine (village), Peebles (village), Penn Twp., Perry Twp. (Brown County), Perry Twp. (Fayette County), Perry Twp. (Montgomery County), Perry Twp. (Shelby County), Phillipsburg (village), Pierce Twp., Pike Twp. (Brown County), Pike Twp. (Clark County), Piqua, Pitsburg (village), Pleasant Hill (village), Pleasant Plain (village), Pleasant Twp. (Brown County), Pleasant Twp. (Clark County), Port Jefferson (village), Potsdam (village), Quincy (village), Randolph Twp. (Montgomery County), Reading, Reily Twp., Richland Twp. (Darke County), Ripley (village), Riverside, Rosewood (village), Ross Twp. (Butler County), Rossburg (village), Rush Twp. (Champaign County), Russellville (village), Salem Twp. (Champaign County), Salem Twp. (Highland County), Salem Twp. (Shelby County), Salem Twp. (Warren County), Scott Twp. (Brown County), Seaman (village), Seven Mile (village), Sharonville (Butler County), Sharonville (Hamilton County), Sidney, Silvercreek Twp., Silverton, Somers Twp., Somerville (village), South Charleston (village), South Lebanon (village), South Solon (village), South Vienna (village), Sprigg Twp., Spring Valley (village), Spring Valley Twp., Springboro, Springcreek Twp., Springdale, Springfield, Springfield Twp. (Clark County), Springfield Twp. (Hamilton County), St. Bernard, St. Clair Twp., St. Martin (village), St. Paris (village), Staunton Twp. (Brown County), Stonelick Twp., Sugar Creek Twp. (Greene County), Sycamore Twp. (Hamilton County), Symmes Twp. (Hamilton County), Tate Twp., Terrace Park (village), Tiffin Twp. (Adams County), Tipp City, Tremont City (village), Trenton, Trotwood, Troy, Turtle Creek Twp. (Warren County), Twin Twp. (Darke County), Twin Twp. (Preble County), Union, Union City (village), Union Twp. (Clermont County), Union Twp. (Clinton County), Union Twp. (Highland County), Union Twp. (Miami County), Union Twp. (Warren County), Urbana, Urbana Twp., Van Buren Twp. (Darke County), Vandalia, Verona (village) (Montgomery County), Verona (village) (Preble County), Washington Twp. (Clermont County), Washington Twp. (Clinton County), Washington Twp. (Darke County), Washington Twp. (Miami County), Washington Twp. (Montgomery County), Washington Twp. (Preble County), Washington Twp. (Shelby County), Wayne Lakes (village), Wayne Twp. (Clermont County), Wayne Twp. (Warren County), Waynesville (village), West Alexandria (village), West Carrollton, West Chester Twp. (Butler County), West Elkton (village), West Liberty (village), West Manchester (village), West Milton (village), West Union (village), Whitewater Twp., Williamsburg (village), Williamsburg Twp., Wilmington, Winchester (village), Winchester Twp., Woodington (village), Woodlawn (village), Woodstock (village), Wright-Patterson AFB, Wyoming, Xenia, Xenia Twp. & Yellow Springs (village), OH. ICA: OH0001.

TV Market Ranking: 17 (Adams Twp. (Clinton County), Addyston (village), AMBERLEY (VILLAGE), Amelia (village), Anderson Twp. (Hamilton County), Arlington Heights (village), Batavia (village), Batavia Twp., Bethel (village), Blanchester (village), Butlerville (village), Carlisle, Cheviot, Chilo (village), Cincinnati, Cleves (village), Colerain Twp. (Hamilton County), College Corner (village) (Butler County), College Corner (village) (Preble County), Columbia Twp. (Hamilton County), Deer Park, Delhi Twp., Elmwood Place (village), Fairfax (village), Fairfield (Butler County), Fairfield Twp. (Butler County), Fayetteville (village), Felicity (village), Franklin (Warren County), Franklin Twp. (Clermont County), Georgetown (village), Golf Manor (village), Green Twp. (Brown County), Green Twp. (Hamilton County), Greenhills (village), Hamersville (village), Hamilton, Harlan Twp., Harrison (village), Harrison Twp. (Hamilton County), Higginsport (village), Indian Hill (village), Jackson Twp. (Clermont City), Jacksonburg (village), Lemon Twp., Liberty Twp. (Butler County), Lincoln Heights (village), Lockland, Loveland (Clermont County), Loveland (Hamilton County), Madeira, Madison Twp. (Butler County), Mariemont (village), Marion Twp. (Clinton County), Martinsville (village), Miami Twp. (Clermont County), Miami Twp. (Hamilton County), Middletown (Butler County), Midland (village), Milford (Clermont County), Milford (Hamilton County), Millville (village), Monroe, Monroe Twp. (Clermont County), Morgan Twp. (Butler County), Morrow (village), Moscow (village), Mount Healthy, Mount Orab (village), Neville (village), New Miami (village), New Richmond (village), Newtonsville (village), Newtown (village), North Bend (village), North College Hill, Norwood, Ohio Twp., Owensville (village), Oxford, Oxford Twp. (Butler County), Perry Twp.

Ohio—Cable Systems

(Brown County), Pierce Twp., Pike Twp. (Brown County), Pleasant Plain (village), Reading, Reily Twp., Ross Twp. (Butler County), Seven Mile (village), Sharonville (Butler County), Silverton, Somerville (village), St. Bernard, St. Clair Twp., St. Martin (village), Sterling Twp. (Brown County), Stonelick Twp., Tate Twp., Terrace Park (village), Trenton, Turtle Creek Twp. (Warren County), Union Twp. (Clermont County), Washington Twp. (Clermont County), Wayne Twp. (Clermont County), West Chester Twp. (Butler County), West College Corner (town), West Harrison (town), Whitewater Twp., Williamsburg (village), Williamsburg Twp., Wyoming); 17,41 (Blue Ash, Butler County (portions), Crosby Twp. (Hamilton County), Deerfield Twp. (Warren County), Evendale (village), Forest Park, Glendale (village), Goshen Twp. (Clermont County), Lebanon, Loveland (Warren County), Maineville (village), Mason, Middletown (Warren County), Montgomery, Salem Twp. (Warren County), Sharonville (Hamilton County), South Lebanon (village), Springdale, Springfield Twp. (Hamilton County), Sycamore Twp. (Hamilton County), Symmes Twp. (Hamilton County), Union Twp. (Warren County), Woodlawn (village)); 27 (Catawba (village), Clearcreek Twp. (Fairfield County), Colerain Twp. (Ross County), Fairfield Twp. (Highland County), Franklin Twp. (Adams County), Harmony Twp. (Clark County), Highland, Hillsboro, Liberty Twp. (Highland County) (portions), Madison Twp. (Highland County), Meigs Twp. (Adams County) (portions), Peebles (village), Penn Twp. (portions), Perry Twp. (Fayette County), Pleasant Twp. (Clark County), Rush Twp. (Champaign County), South Solon (village), South Vienna (village), Springfield Twp. (Clark County), Woodstock (village)); 41 (Adams Twp. (Darke County), Allen Twp. (Darke County), Arcanum (village), Bath Twp. (Green County), Beavercreek, Beavercreek Twp., Bellbrook, Bethel Twp. (Clark County), Bethel Twp. (Miami County), Bradford (village) (Darke County), Bradford (village) (Miami County), Brookville (village), Brown Twp. (Miami County), Butler Twp. (Darke County), Butler Twp. (Montgomery County), Camden (village), Casstown (village), Castine (village), Cedarville (village), Cedarville Twp., Centerville, Clay Twp. (Montgomery County), Clayton (village), Clifton (village) (Clark County), Clifton (village) (Greene County), Clinton Twp. (Shelby County), Concord Twp. (Champaign County), Concord Twp. (Champaign County), Corwin (village), Covington (village), Dayton, Donnelsville (village), Eaton (Preble County), Eldorado (village), Elizabeth Twp. (Miami County), Englewood, Enon (village), Fairborn, Farmersville (village), Fletcher (village), Franklin Twp. (Warren County), Gasper Twp., German Twp. (Clark County), German Twp. (Montgomery County), Germantown (town), Gettysburg (village), Gordon (village), Gratis (village), Gratis Twp., Green Twp. (Clark County), Green Twp. (Clinton County), Green Twp. (Shelby County), Greenville (town), Harrison Twp. (Champaign County), Harrison Twp. (Darke County), Harrison Twp. (Montgomery County), Harrison Twp. (Preble County), Huber Heights, Israel Twp., Ithaca (village), Jackson Twp. (Champaign County), Jackson Twp. (Montgomery County), Jackson Twp. (Preble City), Jamestown (village), Jefferson Twp. (Clinton County), Jefferson Twp. (Montgomery County), Jefferson Twp. (Preble County), Johnson Twp. (Champaign County), Kettering, Lanier Twp., Laura (village), Lawrenceville (village), Lewisburg (village), Liberty Twp. (Darke County), Lostcreek Twp., Ludlow Falls (village), Mad River Twp. (Champaign County), Mad River Twp. (Clark County), Madison Twp. (Clark County), Madison Twp. (Montgomery County), Marshall Twp. (Clinton County), Mechanicsburg (village), Miami Twp. (Greene County), Miami Twp. (Montgomery County), Miamisburg, Monroe Twp. (Darke County), Monroe Twp. (Miami County), Monroe Twp. (Preble County), Moorefield Twp., Moraine, Mutual (village), Naeve Twp., New Carlisle, New Jasper Twp., New Lebanon (village), New Madison (village), New Paris (village), New Vienna (village), Newberry Twp., Newton Twp. (Miami County), North Hampton (village), Oakwood, Palestine (village), Perry Twp. (Montgomery County), Phillipsburg (village), Pike Twp. (Clark County), Piqua, Pitsburg (village), Pleasant Hill (village), Potsdam (village), Richland Twp. (Darke County), Riverside, Rosewood (village), Silvercreek Twp., Somers Twp., South Charleston (village), Spring Valley (village), Spring Valley Twp., Springboro, Springcreek Twp., Springfield, St. Paris (village), Staunton Twp., Sugar Creek Twp. (Greene County), Tipp City, Tremont City (village), Trotwood, Troy, Twin Twp. (Darke County), Twin Twp. (Preble County), Union, Union Twp. (Clinton County), Union Twp. (Miami County), Urbana, Urbana Twp., Van Buren Twp. (Darke County), Vandalia, Verona (village) (Montgomery County), Verona (village) (Preble County), Washington Twp. (Clinton County), Washington Twp. (Darke County), Washington Twp. (Miami County), Washington Twp. (Montgomery County), Washington Twp. (Preble County), Wayne Lakes (village), Wayne Twp. (Warren County), Waynesville (village), West Alexandria (village), West Carrollton, West Elkton (village), West Manchester (village), West Milton (village), Wilmington, Wright-Patterson AFB, Xenia, Xenia Twp., Yellow Springs (village)); Below 100 (Adams Twp. (Champaign County), Anna (village), Ansonia (village), Botkins (village), Brown Twp. (Darke County), Burketsville (village) (Darke County), Burketsville (village) (Mercer County), Christiansburg (village), De Graff (village), Dinsmore Twp., Franklin Twp. (Shelby County), Hollansburg (village), Jackson Center (village), Jackson Twp. (Darke County), Lockington (village), Logan County (portions), Orange Twp., Perry Twp. (Shelby County), Port Jefferson (village), Quincy (village), Rossburg (village), Rush Twp. (Champaign County), Salem Twp. (Champaign County), Salem Twp. (Shelby County), Scott Twp. (Brown County), Sidney, Sprigg Twp., Tiffin Twp. (Adams County), Union City, Union City (village), Washington Twp. (Shelby County), Wayne Twp. (Randolph County), West Liberty (village), West Union (village), Woodington (village), Liberty Twp. (Highland County) (portions), Meigs Twp. (Adams County) (portions)); Outside TV Markets (Aberdeen (village), Cherry Fork (village), Dodson Twp., Hamer Twp., Lewis Twp., Liberty Twp. (Adams County), Lynchburg (village), Manchester (village), New Market Twp., New Weston (village), Pleasant Twp. (Brown County), Ripley (village), Russellville (village), Salem Twp. (Highland County), Seaman (village), Union Twp. (Highland County), Winchester (village), Winchester Twp., Penn Twp. (portions)). Franchise award date: July 17, 1979. Franchise expiration date: N.A. Began: August 1, 1980.

Channel capacity: 62 (operating 2-way). Channels available but not in use: N.A.

Basic Service

Subscribers: 511,686.

Programming (received off-air): WCPO-TV (ABC, Escape) Cincinnati; WCVN-TV (PBS) Covington; WKRC-TV (CBS, CW) Cincinnati; WLWT (MeTV, NBC) Cincinnati; WPTD (PBS) Dayton; WPTO (PBS) Oxford; WSTR-TV (Antenna TV, MNT) Cincinnati; WXIX-TV (Bounce TV, FOX) Newport; allband FM.

Programming (via satellite): C-SPAN; C-SPAN 2; EWTN Global Catholic Network; ION Television; Pop; QVC; Trinity Broadcasting Network (TBN); WGN America.

Fee: $24.95-$61.55 installation; $24.50 monthly.

Expanded Basic Service 1

Subscribers: N.A.

Programming (via satellite): A&E; AMC; Animal Planet; BET; Cartoon Network; CNBC; CNN; Comedy Central; Discovery Channel; Disney Channel; E! HD; ESPN; ESPN Classic; ESPN2; Food Network; Fox News Channel; FOX Sports Ohio/Sports Time Ohio; Freeform; FX; Golf Channel; Great American Country; HGTV; History; HLN; Lifetime; LMN; MSNBC; MTV; National Geographic Channel; Nickelodeon; OWN: Oprah Winfrey Network; Oxygen; Spike TV; Syfy; TBS; The Weather Channel; TLC; TNT; Travel Channel; truTV; Turner Classic Movies; TV Land; USA Network; VH1; WE tv.

Digital Basic Service

Subscribers: N.A.

Programming (via satellite): BBC America; Bloomberg Television; Boomerang; CBS Sports Network; CMT; CNN International; Cooking Channel; C-SPAN 3; Discovery Life Channel; Disney XD; DIY Network; ESPNews; EVINE Live; EWTN Global Catholic Network; FOX College Sports Central; FOX College Sports Pacific; Fox Sports 1; Fox Sports 2; Fuse; FYI; GSN; Hallmark Channel; History International; HITS (Headend In The Sky); IFC; INSP; International Television (ITV); NBA TV; Nick Jr.; Nicktoons; Outdoor Channel; Ovation; TeenNick; Tennis Channel; The Word Network; Trinity Broadcasting Network (TBN).

Digital Pay Service 1

Pay Units: N.A.

Programming (via satellite): Cinemax (multiplexed); Deutsche Welle TV; FXM; HBO (multiplexed); Showtime (multiplexed); Starz (multiplexed); Starz Encore (multiplexed); Sundance TV; WAM! America's Kidz Network; Zee TV.

Fee: $12.99 monthly (each).

Video-On-Demand: Yes

Pay-Per-View

iN DEMAND.

Internet Service

Operational: Yes. Began: July 1, 1999.

Subscribers: 482,315.

Broadband Service: Road Runner.

Fee: $44.95 monthly.

Telephone Service

Digital: Operational

Subscribers: 241,375.

Miles of Plant: 27,794.0 (coaxial); 13,459.0 (fiber optic). Homes passed: 1,325,407.

President: Kevin G. Kidd. Vice President, Marketing: Rob Fordham. Vice President, Public Affairs & Government Relations: Pamela McDonald. Vice President, Operations: Vin Zachariah. Public Affairs Director: Karen Baxter.

Ownership: Time Warner Cable (MSO).

AMELIA—Formerly served by Adelphia Communications. No longer in operation. ICA: OH0041.

AMESVILLE—Formerly served by Riley Video Services. No longer in operation. ICA: OH0307.

AMSTERDAM—Crystal Broadband Networks, PO Box 180336, Chicago, IL 60618. Phones: 630-206-0447; 817-685-9588. E-mail: sales@crystalbn.com. Web Site: http://crystalbn.com. Also serves Bergholz, Loudon Twp. & Springfield Twp. (portions). ICA: OH0230.

TV Market Ranking: 90 (AMSTERDAM, Bergholz, Loudon Twp., Springfield Twp. (portions)). Franchise award date: N.A. Franchise expiration date: N.A. Began: February 1, 1969.

Channel capacity: N.A. Channels available but not in use: N.A.

Basic Service

Subscribers: 148.

Programming (received off-air): KDKA-TV (CBS, Decades) Pittsburgh; WNEO (PBS) Alliance; WPGH-TV (Antenna TV, FOX, The Country Network) Pittsburgh; WPXI (MeTV, NBC) Pittsburgh; WQED (PBS) Pittsburgh; WTAE-TV (ABC, This TV) Pittsburgh; WTOV-TV (MeTV, NBC) Steubenville; WTRF-TV (ABC, CBS, MNT) Wheeling; WYTV (ABC, MNT) Youngstown; allband FM.

Programming (via satellite): AMC; QVC; TBS.

Fee: $44.95 installation; $48.29 monthly.

Expanded Basic Service 1

Subscribers: N.A.

Programming (via satellite): A&E; Animal Planet; Cartoon Network; CNBC; CNN; Comedy Central; C-SPAN; C-SPAN 2; Discovery Channel; Disney Channel; ESPN; Fox News Channel; FOX Sports Ohio/Sports Time Ohio; Freeform; FX; Hallmark Channel; HGTV; ION Television; Lifetime; MoviePlex; MTV; Nickelodeon; Spike TV; TLC; TNT; Travel Channel; USA Network.

Fee: $28.64 monthly.

Digital Basic Service

Subscribers: N.A.

Programming (via satellite): BBC America; Bravo; Destination America; Discovery Kids Channel; ESPN Classic; ESPN2; ESPNews; Fox Sports 1; Golf Channel; GSN; History; IFC; Investigation Discovery; MC; National Geographic Channel; NBCSN; Nick Jr.; OWN: Oprah Winfrey Network; Science Channel; Turner Classic Movies; WE tv.

Fee: $11.00 monthly.

Digital Pay Service 1

Pay Units: N.A.

Programming (via satellite): Cinemax (multiplexed); HBO (multiplexed); Showtime (multiplexed); Starz (multiplexed); Starz Encore (multiplexed); The Movie Channel (multiplexed).

Fee: $12.00 monthly (each).

Video-On-Demand: No

Pay-Per-View

Playboy TV (delivered digitally); iN DEMAND (delivered digitally).

Internet Service

Operational: No.

Telephone Service

None

Miles of Plant: 16.0 (coaxial); None (fiber optic). Homes passed: 997.

General Manager: Ron Page. Program Manager: Shawn Smith.

Ownership: Crystal Broadband Networks (MSO).

ANDOVER—Formerly served by Cebridge Connections. Now served by Armstrong Cable Services, ZELIENOPLE, PA [PA0053]. ICA: OH0258.

ASHLAND—Armstrong Cable Services. Now served by ZELIENOPLE, PA [PA0053]. ICA: OH0079.

ASHLEY CORNER—Time Warner Cable, 7800 Crescent Executive Dr, Charlotte, NC 28217. Phones: 614-255-4997; 614-481-5000. Web Site: http://www.timewarnercable.com. Also serves South Webster (Scioto County). ICA: OH0377.
TV Market Ranking: 36 (South Webster (Scioto County)); Below 100 (ASHLEY CORNER).
Channel capacity: N.A. Channels available but not in use: N.A.
Basic Service
Subscribers: 103.
Programming (received off-air): WBNS-TV (Antenna TV, CBS, Decades) Columbus; WCHS-TV (ABC, Antenna TV) Charleston; WOWK-TV (CBS) Huntington; WPBO (PBS) Portsmouth; WQCW (CW) Portsmouth; WSAZ-TV (MNT, NBC, This TV) Huntington; WVAH-TV (FOX, The Country Network) Charleston.
Programming (via satellite): C-SPAN; QVC; The Weather Channel; Trinity Broadcasting Network (TBN); WGN America.
Fee: $49.99 installation; $24.50 monthly.
Expanded Basic Service 1
Subscribers: N.A.
Programming (via satellite): A&E; AMC; CMT; CNN; Discovery Channel; Disney Channel; ESPN; ESPN2; FOX Sports Ohio/Sports Time Ohio; Freeform; FX; HGTV; HLN; Lifetime; Nickelodeon; Spike TV; TBS; TLC; TNT; TV Land; USA Network.
Digital Basic Service
Subscribers: N.A.
Programming (via satellite): BBC America; Bravo; Discovery Kids Channel; ESPN Classic; ESPNews; Golf Channel; GSN; History; IFC; MC; NBCSN; Nick Jr.; OWN: Oprah Winfrey Network; Science Channel; Syfy; WE tv.
Fee: $52.40 monthly.
Digital Pay Service 1
Pay Units: N.A.
Programming (via satellite): Cinemax (multiplexed); HBO (multiplexed); Showtime (multiplexed); Starz (multiplexed); Starz Encore (multiplexed); The Movie Channel (multiplexed).
Video-On-Demand: No
Pay-Per-View
iN DEMAND (delivered digitally); Playboy TV (delivered digitally); Club Jenna (delivered digitally).
Internet Service
Operational: No.
Telephone Service
None
Miles of Plant: 44.0 (coaxial); None (fiber optic). Homes passed: 608.
President: Rhonda Fraas. Vice President & General Manager: David Kreiman. Vice President, Engineering: Randy Hall. Vice President, Government & Public Affairs: Mary Jo Green. Vice President, Marketing: Mark Psigoda. Senior Accounting Director: Karen Goodfellow. Technical Operations Director: Jim Cavender. Government Affairs Director: Steve Cuckler.
Ownership: Time Warner Cable (MSO).

ASHTABULA—Time Warner Cable. Now served by CLEVELAND (formerly Cleveland Heights), OH [OH0006]. ICA: OH0093.

ATHENS—Time Warner Cable, 7800 Crescent Executive Dr, Charlotte, NC 28217. Phones: 614-255-4997; 614-481-5000. Web Site: http://www.timewarnercable.com. Also serves Canaan Twp. (Athens County), Lee Twp. (Athens County), Nelsonville, New Marshfield & Waterloo Twp. ICA: OH0448.
TV Market Ranking: Below 100 (ATHENS (portions), Lee Twp. (Athens County)); Outside TV Markets (ATHENS (portions), Canaan Twp. (Athens County), Nelsonville, New Marshfield, Waterloo Twp.).
Channel capacity: N.A. Channels available but not in use: N.A.
Basic Service
Subscribers: 363.
Programming (received off-air): WBNS-TV (Antenna TV, CBS, Decades) Columbus; WCHS-TV (ABC, Antenna TV) Charleston; WCMH-TV (MeTV, NBC) Columbus; WOUB-TV (PBS) Athens; WOWK-TV (CBS) Huntington; WQCW (CW) Portsmouth; WSAZ-TV (MNT, NBC, This TV) Huntington; WSYX (ABC, Antenna TV, MNT, This TV) Columbus; WTTE (FOX) Columbus; WVPB-TV (PBS) Huntington.
Programming (via satellite): Animal Planet; C-SPAN; Disney Channel; Hallmark Channel; QVC; WGN America.
Fee: $49.99 installation; $24.50 monthly.
Expanded Basic Service 1
Subscribers: N.A.
Programming (via satellite): Cartoon Network; CMT; CNN; Discovery Channel; ESPN; ESPN2; Freeform; HLN; MTV; Nickelodeon; Spike TV; TBS; TNT; Turner Classic Movies; USA Network; VH1.
Digital Basic Service
Subscribers: N.A.
Programming (via satellite): BBC America; Bravo; Discovery Kids Channel; ESPN Classic; ESPNews; Golf Channel; GSN; HGTV; History; IFC; MC; NBCSN; Nick Jr.; OWN: Oprah Winfrey Network; Science Channel; Syfy; WE tv.
Digital Pay Service 1
Pay Units: N.A.
Programming (via satellite): Cinemax (multiplexed); HBO (multiplexed); Showtime (multiplexed); Starz (multiplexed); Starz Encore (multiplexed); The Movie Channel (multiplexed).
Fee: $12.00 monthly.
Video-On-Demand: No
Pay-Per-View
iN DEMAND (delivered digitally); Playboy TV (delivered digitally); Club Jenna (delivered digitally).
Internet Service
Operational: Yes.
Broadband Service: Road Runner.
Fee: $44.95 monthly.
Telephone Service
None
President: Rhonda Fraas. Vice President & General Manager: David Kreiman. Vice President, Marketing: Mark Psigoda. Vice President, Engineering: Randy Hall. Vice President, Government & Public Affairs: Mary Jo Green. Senior Accounting Director: Karen Goodfellow. Technical Operations Director: Jim Cavender. Government Affairs Director: Steve Cuckler.
Ownership: Time Warner Cable (MSO).

ATHENS—Time Warner Cable. Now served by COLUMBUS, OH [OH0002]. ICA: OH0074.

ATTICA (village)—Time Warner Cable. Now served by TIFFIN (formerly Fostoria), OH [OH0050]. ICA: OH0315.

FULLY SEARCHABLE • CONTINUOUSLY UPDATED • DISCOUNT RATES FOR PRINT PURCHASERS

For more information call **800-771-9202** or visit **www.warren-news.com**

ATWATER TWP.—Time Warner Cable. Now served by CLEVELAND (formerly Cleveland Heights), OH [OH0006]. ICA: OH0111.

AUBURN TWP.—Formerly served by Cebridge Connections. Now served by Suddenlink Communications, NELSON TWP., OH [OH0160]. ICA: OH0198.

AVA—Formerly served by Cebridge Connections. No longer in operation. ICA: OH0309.

BAINBRIDGE—Time Warner Cable, 7800 Crescent Executive Dr, Charlotte, NC 28217. Phones: 614-255-4997; 614-481-5000. Web Site: http://www.timewarnercable.com. Also serves Bourneville. ICA: OH0221.
TV Market Ranking: 27 (BAINBRIDGE, Bourneville). Franchise award date: June 3, 1974. Franchise expiration date: N.A. Began: February 15, 1974.
Channel capacity: N.A. Channels available but not in use: N.A.
Basic Service
Subscribers: 187.
Programming (received off-air): WBNS-TV (Antenna TV, CBS, Decades) Columbus; WCMH-TV (MeTV, NBC) Columbus; WCPO-TV (ABC, Escape) Cincinnati; WHIO-TV (CBS, MeTV) Dayton; WOSU-TV (PBS) Columbus; WSYX (ABC, Antenna TV, MNT, This TV) Columbus; WXIX-TV (Bounce TV, FOX) Newport; allband FM.
Programming (via satellite): A&E; AMC; Animal Planet; CMT; CNN; Discovery Channel; Disney Channel; ESPN; ESPN2; Freeform; Lifetime; MTV; Nickelodeon; QVC; Spike TV; TBS; The Weather Channel; TLC; TNT; USA Network; VH1; WGN America.
Fee: $49.99 installation; $24.50 monthly.
Pay Service 1
Pay Units: N.A.
Programming (via satellite): HBO; Showtime; Starz; Starz Encore; The Movie Channel.
Fee: $12.99 monthly (each).
Video-On-Demand: No
Internet Service
Operational: Yes.
Broadband Service: RoadRunner.
Fee: $24.95 monthly.
Telephone Service
Digital: Operational
Fee: $24.99 monthly
Miles of Plant: 45.0 (coaxial); None (fiber optic). Homes passed: 1,087.
President: Rhonda Fraas. Vice President & General Manager: David Kreiman. Vice President, Engineering: Randy Hall. Vice President, Government & Public Affairs: Mary Jo Green. Vice President, Marketing: Mark Psigoda. Senior Accounting Director: Karen Goodfellow. Technical Operations Director: Jim Cavender. Government Affairs Director: Steve Cuckler.
Ownership: Time Warner Cable (MSO).

BALTIMORE (village)—Time Warner Cable. Now served by COLUMBUS, OH [OH0002]. ICA: OH0159.

BARTON—Powhatan Point Cable Co, PO Box 67, Powhatan Point, OH 43942-0067. Phone: 740-795-5005. Also serves Crescent & Maynard. ICA: OH0212.
TV Market Ranking: 90 (BARTON, Crescent, Maynard). Franchise award date: N.A. Franchise expiration date: N.A. Began: December 1, 1965.
Channel capacity: 53 (not 2-way capable). Channels available but not in use: N.A.
Basic Service
Subscribers: 195.
Programming (received off-air): WFMJ-TV (CW, NBC) Youngstown; WKBN-TV (CBS) Youngstown; WOUC-TV (PBS) Cambridge; WPGH-TV (Antenna TV, FOX, The Country Network) Pittsburgh; WPNT (MNT) Pittsburgh; WQED (PBS) Pittsburgh; WTAE-TV (ABC, This TV) Pittsburgh; WTOV-TV (MeTV, NBC) Steubenville; WTRF-TV (ABC, CBS, MNT) Wheeling; allband FM.
Programming (via satellite): A&E; Animal Planet; Cartoon Network; CMT; CNN; Comedy Central; CW PLUS; Discovery Channel; ESPN; ESPN2; EWTN Global Catholic Network; Food Network; Fox News Channel; Fox Sports 1; FOX Sports Ohio/Sports Time Ohio; Freeform; FX; Golf Channel; Great American Country; Hallmark Channel; HGTV; History; Lifetime; Local Cable Weather; MTV; Nickelodeon; Outdoor Channel; QVC; Spike TV; Syfy; TBS; TLC; TNT; Travel Channel; truTV; Turner Classic Movies; TV Land; USA Network; VH1; WGN America.
Fee: $70.00 monthly.
Pay Service 1
Pay Units: N.A.
Programming (via satellite): HBO (multiplexed); Starz Encore.
Fee: $5.00 monthly (Encore), $12.00 monthly (HBO).
Video-On-Demand: No
Internet Service
Operational: Yes.
Fee: $40.00 monthly.
Telephone Service
None
Miles of Plant: 11.0 (coaxial); None (fiber optic). Homes passed: 1,166.
Vice President & General Manager: Kasmir Majewski.
Ownership: Powhatan Point Cable Co. (MSO).

BASCOM—BTC Multimedia, 5990 West Tiffin St, PO Box 316, Bascom, OH 44809-0316. Phone: 419-937-2222. Fax: 419-937-2299. E-mail: contact@bascomtelephone.com. Web Site: http://www.bascomtelephone.com. Also serves Fostoria, New Riegel & Tiffin. ICA: OH0457.
Channel capacity: N.A. Channels available but not in use: N.A.
Basic Service
Subscribers: 1,122.
Fee: $18.60 monthly.
Expanded Basic Service 1
Subscribers: 1,028.
Fee: $56.95 monthly.
Internet Service
Operational: Yes.
Fee: $29.90-$85.90 monthly.

Ohio—Cable Systems

Telephone Service
Digital: Operational
Assistant Manager: Donna J. Siebenaller.
Ownership: Bascom Mutual Telephone Co.

BAZETTA TWP.—Formerly served by Comcast Cable. Now served by Time Warner Cable, CLEVELAND, OH [OH0006]. ICA: OH0082.

BELLEFONTAINE—Time Warner Cable. Now served by TIFFIN, OH [OH0050]. ICA: OH0117.

BELLEVUE—Time Warner Cable. Now served by TIFFIN (formerly Fostoria), OH [OH0050]. ICA: OH0086.

BENTON RIDGE—Watch Communications, 3225 West Elm St., Lima, OH 45805. Phones: 419-859-2144; 800-589-3837; 419-999-2824. Fax: 419-999-2140. E-mail: info@watchtv.net. Web Site: http://www.watchtv.net. Also serves Blanchard Twp. (Hancock County), Liberty Twp. (Hancock County) & Union Twp. (Hancock County). ICA: OH0287.
TV Market Ranking: Below 100 (BENTON RIDGE, Blanchard Twp. (Hancock County), Liberty Twp. (Hancock County), Union Twp. (Hancock County)). Franchise award date: N.A. Franchise expiration date: N.A. Began: December 1, 1983.
Channel capacity: N.A. Channels available but not in use: N.A.
Digital Basic Service
Subscribers: 155.
Programming (received off-air): WBGU-TV (PBS) Bowling Green; WBNS-TV (Antenna TV, CBS, Decades) Columbus; WHIO-TV (CBS, MeTV) Dayton; WKEF (ABC, Antenna TV) Dayton; WLIO (CW, NBC) Lima; WOHL-CD (ABC, CBS) Lima; WPTA (ABC, MNT, NBC) Fort Wayne; WTLW (IND) Lima; WTVG (ABC, CW) Toledo.
Programming (via satellite): A&E; AMC; Animal Planet; BBC America; Cartoon Network; CMT; CNN; Comedy Central; C-SPAN; CW PLUS; Discovery Channel; Disney Channel; Disney XD; E!; ESPN; ESPN Classic; ESPN2; ESPNews; EWTN Global Catholic Network; Food Network; Fox News Channel; Fox Sports 1; FOX Sports Ohio/Sports Time Ohio; Freeform; FX; FYI; Golf Channel; Great American Country; GSN; HGTV; History; HLN; INSP; ION Television; Lifetime; MSNBC; MTV; Nickelodeon; Outdoor Channel; QVC; Spike TV; Syfy; TBS; The Weather Channel; TLC; TNT; Travel Channel; Trinity Broadcasting Network (TBN); truTV; Turner Classic Movies; TV Land; USA Network; VH1; WGN America.
Fee: $29.95 installation; $20.00 monthly.
Digital Pay Service 1
Pay Units: 6.
Programming (via satellite): Cinemax (multiplexed).
Fee: $25.00 installation; $7.99 monthly.
Digital Pay Service 2
Pay Units: 15.
Programming (via satellite): HBO (multiplexed).
Fee: $25.00 installation; $12.99 monthly.
Digital Pay Service 3
Pay Units: 8.
Programming (via satellite): Showtime (multiplexed); The Movie Channel (multiplexed).
Fee: $25.00 installation; $12.99 monthly.

Digital Pay Service 4
Pay Units: N.A.
Programming (via satellite): Starz (multiplexed); Starz Encore.
Video-On-Demand: No
Internet Service
Operational: Yes.
Telephone Service
Digital: Operational
Miles of Plant: 11.0 (coaxial); None (fiber optic). Homes passed: 290.
President & Chief Executive Officer: Ken Williams. Vice President & General Manager: Thomas Knippen. Installation Manager: Jim Hardin. Engineer: Mike Birkemeier.
Ownership: Benton Ridge Telephone Co.

BEREA—WOW! Internet, Cable & Phone, 7887 East Belleview Ave, Ste 1000, Englewood, CO 80111. Phones: 720-479-3500 (Corporate office); 866-496-9669 (Customer service). Fax: 720-479-3585. E-mail: wow_general@wideopenwest.com. Web Site: http://www.wowway.com. Also serves Avon Lake, Bay Village, Brecksville, Brook Park, Brooklyn, Cleveland, Cleveland Heights (portions), Cuyahoga Heights, Fairview Park, Garfield Heights, Independence, Linndale, Maple Heights, Middleburg Heights, North Olmsted, North Royalton, Shaker Heights, South Euclid, Strongsville, University Heights, Valley View & Westlake. ICA: OH0418. **Note:** This system is an overbuild.
TV Market Ranking: 8 (Avon Lake, Bay Village, BEREA, Brecksville, Brook Park, Brooklyn, Cleveland, Cleveland Heights (portions), Cuyahoga Heights, Fairview Park, Garfield Heights, Independence, Linndale, Maple Heights, Middleburg Heights, North Olmsted, North Royalton, Shaker Heights, South Euclid, Strongsville, University Heights, Valley View, Westlake). Franchise award date: April 1, 1996. Franchise expiration date: N.A. Began: N.A.
Channel capacity: N.A. Channels available but not in use: N.A.
Basic Service
Subscribers: 39,271.
Programming (received off-air): WBNX-TV (CW, Movies!, This TV) Akron; WEAO (PBS) Akron; WEWS-TV (ABC) Cleveland; WJW (Antenna TV, FOX) Cleveland; WKYC (NBC) Cleveland; WOIO (CBS, MeTV) Shaker Heights; WQHS-DT (getTV, UNV) Cleveland; WRLM (IND) Canton; WUAB (Bounce TV, MNT) Lorain; WVIZ (PBS) Cleveland; WVPX-TV (ION) Akron.
Programming (via satellite): EWTN Global Catholic Network; Fox News Channel; INSP; QVC; TBS; USA Network; WGN America.
Fee: $50.00 installation; $32.00 monthly.
Expanded Basic Service 1
Subscribers: N.A.
Programming (via satellite): A&E; AMC; Animal Planet; BET; Bravo; BTN; Cartoon Network; CMT; CNBC; CNN; Comedy Central; C-SPAN; C-SPAN 2; Discovery Channel; Disney Channel; Disney XD; E! HD; ESPN; ESPN Classic; ESPN2; EVINE Live; Food Network; Fox Sports 1; FOX Sports Ohio/Sports Time Ohio; Freeform; FX; Golf Channel; GSN; Hallmark Channel; HGTV; History; HLN; Lifetime; MSNBC; MTV; MTV2; National Geographic Channel; NBCSN; Nickelodeon; Nicktoons; OWN: Oprah Winfrey Network; Spike TV; Syfy; The Weather Channel; TLC; TNT; Travel Channel; truTV; Turner Classic Movies; TV Land; VH1.
Fee: $32.01 monthly.

Digital Basic Service
Subscribers: N.A.
Programming (via satellite): A&E HD; Animal Planet HD; AXS TV; BBC America; Bloomberg Television; BTN; BTN HD; CMT; Cooking Channel; Daystar TV Network; Destination America; Discovery Channel HD; Discovery Kids Channel; DIY Network; DMX Music; ESPN HD; ESPNews; Food Network HD; Fox Business Network; FOX College Sports Central; FOX College Sports Pacific; Fox HD; Fox News HD; FSN HD; FX HD; FXM; FYI; HD Theater; HGTV HD; History HD; History International; Investigation Discovery; Jewelry Television; LMN; MTV Classic; MTV Hits; Nat Geo WILD; National Geographic Channel HD; NFL Network; NFL Network HD; Nick 2; Nick Jr.; Outdoor Channel 2 HD; Oxygen; PBS HD; Science Channel; Sprout; Starz (multiplexed); Starz Encore (multiplexed); Sundance TV; TeenNick; Tennis Channel; TLC HD; TNT HD; Trinity Broadcasting Network (TBN).
Fee: $44.97 monthly.
Digital Pay Service 1
Pay Units: N.A.
Programming (via satellite): Cinemax (multiplexed); Cinemax HD; Cinemax On Demand; Flix; HBO (multiplexed); HBO HD; HBO on Demand; Showtime (multiplexed); Showtime HD; Showtime On Demand; Starz HD; The Movie Channel (multiplexed); The Movie Channel On Demand.
Fee: $15.00 monthly (Cinemax, HBO, Showtime/TMC/Flix or Starz).
Video-On-Demand: Yes
Pay-Per-View
Hot Choice (delivered digitally); iN DEMAND (delivered digitally); Special events (delivered digitally); Playboy TV (delivered digitally); ESPN (delivered digitally).
Internet Service
Operational: Yes.
Subscribers: 41,149.
Broadband Service: WOW! Internet.
Fee: $40.99-$72.99 monthly; $2.50 modem lease.
Telephone Service
Digital: Operational
Subscribers: 25,814.
Miles of Plant: 2,488.0 (coaxial); 581.0 (fiber optic). Homes passed: 150,191.
Chief Financial Officer: Rich Fish. Vice President & General Manager: Scott Neesley. Vice President, Sales & Marketing: Cathy Kuo. Regional General Manager: Scott Schup. Chief Technician: Cash Hagen.
Ownership: WideOpenWest LLC (MSO).

BERLIN TWP. (Mahoning County)—Armstrong Cable Services. Now served by ZELIENOPLE, PA [PA0053]. ICA: OH0161.

BETTSVILLE (village)—Time Warner Cable. Now served by TIFFIN (formerly Fostoria), OH [OH0050]. ICA: OH0179.

BEVERLY—Time Warner Cable, 1266 Dublin Rd, Columbus, OH 43215-1008. Phones: 614-255-4997; 614-481-5000. Fax: 614-481-5052. Web Site: http://www.timewarnercable.com. Also serves Barlow Twp., Belpre Twp. (Washington County), Chester Twp. (Meigs County), Coolville, Decatur Twp. (Washington County), Dunham Twp., Eagleport, Guysville, Hockingport, Malta, McConnelsville, Olive Twp. (Meigs County), Porterfield, Reedsville, Rome Twp. (Athens County), Stewart, Stockport, Tuppers Plains, Waterford Twp., Watertown & Windsor Twp. (Morgan County). ICA: OH0175.
TV Market Ranking: Below 100 (Barlow Twp., Belpre Twp. (Washington County), BEVERLY, Chester Twp. (Meigs County), Coolville, Decatur Twp. (Washington County), Dunham Twp., Eagleport, Guysville, Hockingport, Malta, McConnelsville, Olive Twp. (Meigs County), Porterfield, Reedsville, Rome Twp. (Athens County), Stewart, Stockport, Tuppers Plains, Waterford Twp., Watertown, Windsor Twp. (Morgan County)). Franchise award date: N.A. Franchise expiration date: N.A. Began: June 29, 1963.
Channel capacity: N.A. Channels available but not in use: N.A.
Basic Service
Subscribers: 4,407.
Programming (received off-air): WBNS-TV (Antenna TV, CBS, Decades) Columbus; WCHS-TV (ABC, Antenna TV) Charleston; WHIZ-TV (NBC) Zanesville; WOUB-TV (PBS) Athens; WSYX (ABC, Antenna TV, MNT, This TV) Columbus; WTAP-TV (FOX, MNT, NBC) Parkersburg; WVAH-TV (FOX, The Country Network) Charleston; allband FM.
Programming (via satellite): Pop; QVC; TBS; The Weather Channel; WGN America.
Fee: $29.95 installation; $21.25 monthly.
Expanded Basic Service 1
Subscribers: N.A.
Programming (via satellite): A&E; AMC; Animal Planet; BET; Bravo; Cartoon Network; CMT; CNBC; CNN; Comedy Central; C-SPAN; Discovery Channel; Disney Channel; Disney XD; E! HD; ESPN; ESPN2; Food Network; Fox News Channel; FOX Sports Ohio/Sports Time Ohio; Freeform; FX; Golf Channel; Hallmark Channel; HGTV; History; HLN; INSP; Lifetime; MSNBC; MTV; Nick Jr.; Nickelodeon; Spike TV; Syfy; TLC; TNT; Travel Channel; Trinity Broadcasting Network (TBN); truTV; TV Land; USA Network; VH1.
Fee: $15.60 monthly.
Digital Basic Service
Subscribers: N.A.
Programming (via satellite): BBC America; Bloomberg Television; CMT; Destination America; Discovery Kids Channel; Discovery Life Channel; DIY Network; ESPN Classic; ESPNews; ESPNU; Fox Business Network; Fox Sports 1; Fuse; FXM; Great American Country; GSN; INSP; Investigation Discovery; LMN; LOGO; MC; MTV Classic; MTV Hits; MTV Jams; MTV2; Nat Geo WILD; National Geographic Channel; Nick 2; Nicktoons; OWN: Oprah Winfrey Network; Science Channel; TeenNick; The Word Network; Turner Classic Movies; UP; WE tv.
Fee: $52.40 monthly.
Digital Expanded Basic Service
Subscribers: N.A.
Programming (via satellite): Flix; FOX College Sports Central; FOX College Sports Pacific; FYI; History International; IFC; NBCSN; Outdoor Channel; Sundance TV.
Digital Pay Service 1
Pay Units: N.A.
Programming (via satellite): Cinemax (multiplexed); HBO (multiplexed); Showtime (multiplexed); Starz (multiplexed); Starz Encore (multiplexed); The Movie Channel (multiplexed).
Fee: $12.99 monthly (each).
Video-On-Demand: Yes

Cable Systems—Ohio

FULLY SEARCHABLE • CONTINUOUSLY UPDATED • DISCOUNT RATES FOR PRINT PURCHASERS

For more information call **800-771-9202** or visit **www.warren-news.com**

Pay-Per-View
iN DEMAND (delivered digitally); Playboy TV (delivered digitally); Fresh (delivered digitally); Club Jenna (delivered digitally); Hot Choice (delivered digitally).

Internet Service
Operational: Yes.
Broadband Service: Road Runner.
Fee: $42.95 monthly.

Telephone Service
Digital: Operational
Fee: $44.95 monthly
Miles of Plant: 76.0 (coaxial); None (fiber optic).
President: Rhonda Fraas. Vice President & General Manager: David Kreiman. Vice President, Government & Public Affairs: Mary Jo Green. Vice President, Engineering: Randy Hall. Vice President, Marketing: Mark Psigoda. Technical Operations Director: David Bowen. Government Affairs Director: Steve Cuckler.
Ownership: Time Warner Cable (MSO).

BIG ISLAND TWP.—Time Warner Cable. Now served by COLUMBUS, OH [OH0002]. ICA: OH0317.

BLOOMINGDALE—Suddenlink Communications, 520 Maryville Centre Dr, Ste 300, St. Louis, MO 63141. Phone: 314-315-9400. Web Site: http://www.suddenlink.com. Also serves German (village), Ross Twp. (Jefferson County), Salem Twp. (Jefferson County), Springfield Twp. (Jefferson County) & Wayne Twp. (Jefferson County). ICA: OH0203.
TV Market Ranking: 10 (German (village)); 90 (BLOOMINGDALE, Ross Twp. (Jefferson County), Salem Twp. (Jefferson County), Springfield Twp. (Jefferson County), Wayne Twp. (Jefferson County)). Franchise award date: N.A. Franchise expiration date: N.A. Began: March 1, 1990.
Channel capacity: 62 (not 2-way capable). Channels available but not in use: N.A.

Basic Service
Subscribers: 283.
Programming (received off-air): KDKA-TV (CBS, Decades) Pittsburgh; WINP-TV (IND, ION) Pittsburgh; WPGH-TV (Antenna TV, FOX, The Country Network) Pittsburgh; WPNT (MNT) Pittsburgh; WPXI (MeTV, NBC) Pittsburgh; WQED (PBS) Pittsburgh; WTAE-TV (ABC, This TV) Pittsburgh; WTOV-TV (MeTV, NBC) Steubenville; WTRF-TV (ABC, CBS, MNT) Wheeling.
Programming (via satellite): QVC; TBS.
Fee: $59.95 installation; $22.99 monthly; $1.95 converter.

Expanded Basic Service 1
Subscribers: N.A.
Programming (via satellite): A&E; AMC; CNBC; CNN; C-SPAN; Discovery Channel; Disney Channel; ESPN; Freeform; History; HLN; Lifetime; MTV; Nickelodeon; Root Sports Pittsburgh; Spike TV; Syfy; The Weather Channel; TNT; TV Land; USA Network; VH1.
Fee: $22.00 monthly.

Pay Service 1
Pay Units: N.A.
Programming (via satellite): Cinemax; HBO; Showtime; The Movie Channel.
Fee: $11.00 monthly (Cinemax or HBO), $12.95 monthly (Showtime/TMC).

Internet Service
Operational: Yes.

Telephone Service
Digital: Operational
Miles of Plant: 56.0 (coaxial); None (fiber optic). Homes passed: 1,345.

Vice President, Corporate Finance: Michael Pflantz. General Manager: Peter Brown.
Ownership: Cequel Communications Holdings I LLC (MSO).

BLUFFTON (village)—Time Warner Cable. Now served by TIFFIN, OH [OH0050]. ICA: OH0214.

BOARDMAN TWP.—Armstrong Cable Services. Now served by ZELIENOPLE, PA [PA0053]. ICA: OH0024.

BOLIVAR (town)—Time Warner Cable. Now served by CLEVELAND (formerly Cleveland Heights), OH [OH0006]. ICA: OH0168.

BOWERSTON—Time Warner Cable, 7800 Crescent Executive Dr, Charlotte, NC 28217. Phones: 330-633-1874; 330-633-9203. Web Site: http://www.timewarnercable.com. Also serves Bowerston (rural portions) & Leesville. ICA: OH0404.
TV Market Ranking: 10 (BOWERSTON, Bowerston (rural portions), Leesville). Franchise award date: February 6, 1989. Franchise expiration date: N.A. Began: N.A.
Channel capacity: N.A. Channels available but not in use: N.A.

Basic Service
Subscribers: 86.
Programming (received off-air): WDLI-TV (TBN) Canton; WEWS-TV (ABC) Cleveland; WJW (Antenna TV, FOX) Cleveland; WKYC (NBC) Cleveland; WNEO (PBS) Alliance; WOIO (CBS, MeTV) Shaker Heights; WRLM (IND) Canton; WTOV-TV (MeTV, NBC) Steubenville; WTRF-TV (ABC, CBS, MNT) Wheeling; WUAB (Bounce TV, MNT) Lorain; WVPX-TV (ION) Akron.
Fee: $49.99 installation; $24.50 monthly.

Expanded Basic Service 1
Subscribers: N.A.
Programming (via satellite): A&E; Animal Planet; Cartoon Network; CNN; Disney Channel; ESPN; Freeform; HLN; MTV; Nickelodeon; Spike TV; TBS; TNT; USA Network.
Fee: $19.75 monthly.

Pay Service 1
Pay Units: N.A.
Programming (via satellite): HBO; Showtime; Starz; Starz Encore.
Fee: $4.00 monthly (Encore), $14.95 monthly (HBO, Showtime or Starz).

Video-On-Demand: No

Internet Service
Operational: Yes.

Telephone Service
Digital: Operational
Miles of Plant: 18.0 (coaxial); None (fiber optic). Homes passed: 420.
President: Stephen Fry. Area Vice President: Scott Miller. Vice President, Marketing: Patrick Burke. Vice President, Engineering: Al Costanzi. Vice President, Public Affairs: William Jasso. Senior Accounting Director: Karen Goodfellow. Government & Media Relations Director: Chris Thomas.
Ownership: Time Warner Cable (MSO).

BOWLING GREEN—Time Warner Cable. Now served by TIFFIN (formerly Fostoria), OH [OH0050]. ICA: OH0054.

BROOKFIELD TWP. (Trumbull County)—Formerly served by Northeast Cable TV. No longer in operation. ICA: OH0382.

BROUGHTON—Watch Communications, 3225 West Elm St, Lima, OH 45805. Phones: 800-589-3837; 419-999-2824. E-mail: info@watchtv.net. Web Site: http://www.watchtv.net. ICA: OH0449.
TV Market Ranking: 82 (BROUGHTON).
Channel capacity: N.A. Channels available but not in use: N.A.

Digital Basic Service
Subscribers: 271.
Fee: $29.95 installation; $9.99 monthly.

Internet Service
Operational: Yes.
Fee: $29.99-$139.99 monthly.

Telephone Service
Digital: Operational
Fee: $39.99 monthly
President & Chief Executive Officer: Ken Williams. Vice President & General Manager: Thomas Knippen.
Ownership: Benton Ridge Telephone Co. (MSO).

BRUNSWICK—Time Warner Cable. Now served by CLEVELAND (formerly Cleveland Heights), OH [OH0006]. ICA: OH0059.

BRYAN—Bryan Municipal Utilities, 841 East Edgerton St, Bryan, OH 43506-1413. Phones: 419-633-6100; 419-633-6130. Fax: 419-633-6105. E-mail: communications@cityofbryan.com. Web Site: http://www.cityofbryan.net. Also serves Pulaski Twp. ICA: OH0439. **Note:** This system is an overbuild.
TV Market Ranking: Below 100 (BRYAN, Pulaski Twp.).
Channel capacity: 116 (operating 2-way). Channels available but not in use: N.A.

Basic Service
Subscribers: 1,650.
Programming (received off-air): WANE-TV (Antenna TV, CBS) Fort Wayne; WBGU-TV (PBS) Bowling Green; WDFM-LP (IND) Defiance; WFFT-TV (FOX, MeTV) Fort Wayne; WFWA (PBS) Fort Wayne; WGTE-TV (PBS) Toledo; WINM (IND) Angola; WISE-TV (CW) Fort Wayne; WLMB (IND) Toledo; WNWO-TV (NBC, Retro TV) Toledo; WPTA (ABC, MNT, NBC) Fort Wayne; WTOL (CBS, MeTV) Toledo; WTVG (ABC, CW) Toledo; WUPW (FOX, TheCoolTV) Toledo.
Programming (via satellite): C-SPAN; C-SPAN 2; EWTN Global Catholic Network; INSP; QVC; The Weather Channel; Trinity Broadcasting Network (TBN); WGN America.
Fee: $21.65 monthly.

Expanded Basic Service 1
Subscribers: 1,535.
Programming (via satellite): A&E; AMC; Animal Planet; Cartoon Network; CMT; CNBC; CNN; Comedy Central; Discovery Channel; Discovery Life Channel; Disney Channel; Disney XD; E! HD; ESPN; ESPN Classic; ESPN2; ESPNews; Food Network; Fox News Channel; Fox Sports 1; FOX Sports Detroit; FOX Sports Ohio/Sports Time Ohio; Freeform; Fuse; FX; FYI; Golf Channel; GSN; Hallmark Channel; HGTV; History; HLN; Lifetime; LMN; MSNBC; MTV; MTV2; National Geographic Channel; NBCSN; Nickelodeon; Outdoor Channel; OWN: Oprah Winfrey Network; Spike TV; Syfy; TBS; TLC; TNT; Travel Channel; truTV; Turner Classic Movies; TV Land; Univision Studios; USA Network; VH1.
Fee: $53.20 monthly.

Digital Basic Service
Subscribers: N.A.
Programming (via satellite): A&E HD; AXS TV; BBC America; Bloomberg Television; Chiller; Cloo; CMT; Cooking Channel; Destination America; Destination America HD; Discovery Channel HD; Discovery Kids Channel; Disney Channel HD; DMX Music; ESPN HD; ESPN2 HD; ESPNU HD; Food Network HD; Fox Business Network; FOX College Sports Central; FOX College Sports Pacific; Fox News HD; FX HD; HD Theater; HGTV HD; History HD; History International; Investigation Discovery; MTV Classic; MTV Hits; National Geographic Channel; National Geographic Channel HD; Nicktoons; Noggin; Outdoor Channel 2 HD; RFD-TV; Science Channel; Science HD; Sprout; Syfy HD; TLC HD; Travel Channel HD; USA Network HD.
Fee: $10.00 monthly.

Digital Pay Service 1
Pay Units: N.A.
Programming (via satellite): Cinemax (multiplexed); Cinemax HD; HBO (multiplexed); HBO HD; Showtime (multiplexed); Showtime HD; Starz (multiplexed); Starz Encore (multiplexed); Starz HD; The Movie Channel.
Fee: $12.95 monthly (Cinemax), $14.25 monthly (Showtime/TMC or Starz/Encore), $14.95 monthly (HBO).

Pay-Per-View
iN DEMAND (delivered digitally).

Internet Service
Operational: Yes.
Broadband Service: In-house.
Fee: $28.00 monthly; $125.00 modem purchase.

Telephone Service
None
Utilities Director: Brian Carlin. Cable Communications Superintendent: Joe Ferrell. Chief Technician: Tracy Goodwin.
Ownership: Bryan Municipal Utilities.

BRYAN—Time Warner Cable. Now served by TIFFIN (formerly Fostoria), OH [OH0050]. ICA: OH0078.

BUCYRUS—Time Warner Cable. Now served by COLUMBUS, OH [OH0002]. ICA: OH0105.

CADIZ—Time Warner Cable, 7800 Crescent Executive Dr, Charlotte, NC 28217. Phones: 330-633-1874; 330-633-9203. Web Site: http://www.timewarnercable.com. ICA: OH0200.
TV Market Ranking: 90 (CADIZ). Franchise award date: N.A. Franchise expiration date: N.A. Began: June 1, 1970.
Channel capacity: N.A. Channels available but not in use: N.A.

2017 Edition D-581

Ohio—Cable Systems

Basic Service
Subscribers: 863.
Programming (received off-air): KDKA-TV (CBS, Decades) Pittsburgh; WDLI-TV (TBN) Canton; WNPB-TV (PBS) Morgantown; WOUC-TV (PBS) Cambridge; WPGH-TV (Antenna TV, FOX, The Country Network) Pittsburgh; WPXI (MeTV, NBC) Pittsburgh; WQED (PBS) Pittsburgh; WTAE-TV (ABC, This TV) Pittsburgh; WTOV-TV (MeTV, NBC) Steubenville; WTRF-TV (ABC, CBS, MNT) Wheeling.
Programming (via satellite): C-SPAN; CW PLUS; Discovery Channel; FOX Sports Ohio/Sports Time Ohio; QVC; TBS.
Fee: $49.99 installation; $24.50 monthly.

Expanded Basic Service 1
Subscribers: N.A.
Programming (via satellite): A&E; AMC; Animal Planet; BET; Cartoon Network; CMT; CNBC; CNN; Disney Channel; E! HD; ESPN; ESPN2; Fox News Channel; FOX Sports Ohio/Sports Time Ohio; Freeform; FX; Hallmark Channel; Lifetime; MoviePlex; MTV; Nickelodeon; Root Sports Pittsburgh; Spike TV; The Weather Channel; TNT; Travel Channel; truTV; TVG Network; USA Network.
Fee: $29.75 monthly.

Digital Basic Service
Subscribers: N.A.
Programming (via satellite): BBC America; Bravo; Destination America; Discovery Kids Channel; ESPN Classic; ESPNews; Fox Sports 1; Golf Channel; GSN; HGTV; History; IFC; Investigation Discovery; MC; National Geographic Channel; NBCSN; Nick Jr.; OWN; Oprah Winfrey Network; Science Channel; Turner Classic Movies; WE tv.
Fee: $10.50 monthly.

Digital Pay Service 1
Pay Units: N.A.
Programming (via satellite): Cinemax (multiplexed); HBO (multiplexed); Showtime (multiplexed); Starz (multiplexed); Starz Encore (multiplexed); The Movie Channel (multiplexed).
Fee: $12.99 monthly (each).

Video-On-Demand: No

Pay-Per-View
iN DEMAND (delivered digitally); Playboy TV (delivered digitally); Club Jenna (delivered digitally).

Internet Service
Operational: No.

Telephone Service
None
Miles of Plant: 26.0 (coaxial); None (fiber optic). Homes passed: 1,446.
President: Stephen Fry. Area Vice President: Scott Miller. Vice President, Marketing: Patrick Burke. Vice President, Engineering: Al Costanzi. Vice President, Public Affairs: William Jasso. Senior Accounting Director: Karen Goodfellow. Government & Media Relations Director: Chris Thomas.
Ownership: Time Warner Cable (MSO).

CALDWELL—Time Warner Cable, 7800 Crescent Executive Dr, Charlotte, NC 28217. Phones: 888-579-9959; 740-455-9705. Web Site: http://www.timewarnercable.com. Also serves Belle Valley & Caldwell (rural portions). ICA: OH0453.
TV Market Ranking: Below 100 (Belle Valley, Caldwell (rural portions), CALDWELL).
Channel capacity: N.A. Channels available but not in use: N.A.

Basic Service
Subscribers: 1,070. Commercial subscribers: 25.
Fee: $49.99 installation; $24.50 monthly

Senior Accounting Director: Karen Goodfellow.
Ownership: Time Warner Cable (MSO).

CALEDONIA—Time Warner Cable. Now served by MARION, OH [OH0040]. ICA: OH0257.

CAMBRIDGE—Time Warner Cable, 737 Howard St, Zanesville, OH 43701. Phones: 888-579-9959; 740-455-9705. Web Site: http://www.timewarnercable.com. Also serves Adams Twp. (Guernsey County), Cambridge Twp. (Guernsey County), Center Twp. (Guernsey County), Kimbolton, Liberty Twp. (Guernsey County), Monroe Twp. (Guernsey County) & Wheeling Twp. (Guernsey County). ICA: OH0088.
TV Market Ranking: Below 100 (Adams Twp. (Guernsey County), Cambridge Twp. (Guernsey County), Center Twp. (Guernsey County), Kimbolton, Liberty Twp. (Guernsey County), Monroe Twp. (Guernsey County), Wheeling Twp. (Guernsey County), CAMBRIDGE).
Channel capacity: N.A. Channels available but not in use: N.A.

Basic Service
Subscribers: 4,934. Commercial subscribers: 113.
Fee: $29.90 installation; $21.25 monthly.
Ownership: Time Warner Cable (MSO).

CAMERON—Formerly served by Cebridge Connections. No longer in operation. ICA: OH0310.

CANAAN TWP. (Madison County)—Time Warner Cable. Now served by SUBURBANS MOTOR HOME PARK, OH [OH0452]. ICA: OH0131.

CANTON—Time Warner Cable. Now served by CLEVELAND (formerly Cleveland Heights), OH [OH0006]. ICA: OH0008.

CAREY—Time Warner Cable. Now served by TIFFIN (formerly Fostoria), OH [OH0050]. ICA: OH0210.

CARROLLTON (village)—Time Warner Cable. Now served by CLEVELAND (formerly Cleveland Heights), OH [OH0006]. ICA: OH0201.

CELINA—Time Warner Cable. Now served by TIFFIN (formerly Fostoria), OH [OH0050]. ICA: OH0092.

CHANDLERSVILLE—Time Warner Cable. Now served by COLUMBUS, OH [OH0002]. ICA: OH0400.

CHILLICOTHE—Time Warner Cable, 1266 Dublin Rd, Columbus, OH 43215-1008. Phones: 614-255-4997; 614-481-5000 (Columbus office); 740-775-4288 (Chillicothe office). Fax: 614-481-5044. Web Site: http://www.timewarnercable.com. Also serves Adelphi, Benton Twp. (Pike County), Buckskin Twp., Coal Twp. (Jackson County), Concord Twp. (Ross County), Deerfield Twp. (Ross County), Elk Twp. (Vinton County), Frankfort, Franklin Twp. (Ross County), Green Twp., Hallsville, Harrison Twp. (Ross County), Huntington Twp. (Ross County), Jackson Twp. (Jackson County), Jasper (town), Jefferson Twp. (Ross County), Kingston, Laurelville, Liberty Twp. (Ross County), Mifflin Twp. (Pike County), Milledgeville, Newton Twp. (Pike County), Octa,

Paxton Twp., Pebble Twp., Pee Pee Twp. (Pike County), Piketon, Raccoon Twp., Richmond Dale, Rio Grande, Scioto Twp. (Ross County), Seal Twp., South Salem, Springfield Twp. (Ross County), Sunfish Twp., Twin Twp. (Ross County), Union Twp. (Ross County) & Waverly. ICA: OH0033.
TV Market Ranking: 27 (Adelphi, Benton Twp. (Pike County), Buckskin Twp., CHILLICOTHE, Coal Twp. (Jackson County), Concord Twp. (Ross County), Deerfield Twp. (Ross County), Elk Twp. (Vinton County), Frankfort, Franklin Twp. (Ross County), Green Twp., Hallsville, Harrison Twp. (Ross County), Huntington Twp. (Ross County), Jackson Twp. (Jackson County), Jasper (town), Jefferson Twp. (Ross County), Kingston, Laurelville, Liberty Twp. (Ross County), Mifflin Twp. (Pike County), Milledgeville, Newton Twp. (Pike County), Octa, Paxton Twp., Pebble Twp., Pee Pee Twp. (Pike County), Piketon, Richmond Dale, Scioto Twp. (Ross County), Seal Twp., South Salem, Springfield Twp. (Ross County), Sunfish Twp., Twin Twp. (Ross County), Union Twp. (Ross County), Waverly); 36 (Raccoon Twp., Rio Grande).
Franchise award date: N.A. Franchise expiration date: N.A. Began: September 11, 1964.
Channel capacity: N.A. Channels available but not in use: N.A.

Basic Service
Subscribers: 16,038.
Programming (received off-air): WBNS-TV (Antenna TV, CBS, Decades) Columbus; WCMH-TV (MeTV, NBC) Columbus; WHIO-TV (CBS, MeTV) Dayton; WOSU-TV (PBS) Columbus; WOUB-TV (PBS) Athens; WSYX (ABC, Antenna TV, MNT, This TV) Columbus; WTTE (FOX) Columbus; WWHO (CW) Chillicothe; 14 FMs.
Programming (via satellite): C-SPAN; C-SPAN 2; EWTN Global Catholic Network; Family Friendly Entertainment; Freeform; INSP; Pop; QVC; TBS; The Weather Channel; WGN America.
Fee: $29.95 installation; $21.25 monthly.

Expanded Basic Service 1
Subscribers: N.A.
Programming (via satellite): A&E; AMC; Animal Planet; BET; Bravo; Cartoon Network; CMT; CNBC; CNN; Comedy Central; Discovery Channel; Disney Channel; Disney XD; E! HD; ESPN; ESPN2; EVINE Live; Food Network; Fox News Channel; Fox Sports 1; FOX Sports Ohio/Sports Time Ohio; FX; FYI; Golf Channel; Great American Country; Hallmark Channel; HGTV; History; HLN; Lifetime; MSNBC; MTV; National Geographic Channel; Nickelodeon; Outdoor Channel; Oxygen; Spike TV; Syfy; TLC; TNT; Travel Channel; truTV; TV Land; USA Network; VH1; WE tv.

Digital Basic Service
Subscribers: N.A.
Programming (via satellite): BBC America; Bloomberg Television; Discovery Life Channel; DIY Network; ESPN Classic; ESPNews; Fuse; FXM; GSN; History International; NBCSN; Trinity Broadcasting Network (TBN); Turner Classic Movies.

Digital Expanded Basic Service
Subscribers: N.A.
Programming (via satellite): HITS (Headend In The Sky); MC; MTV Classic; Nick Jr.; Nicktoons; VH1 Country.

Digital Pay Service 1
Pay Units: N.A.
Programming (via satellite): ART America; Cinemax (multiplexed); Flix; HBO (multiplexed); RAI Italia; Showtime (multiplexed); Starz (multiplexed); Sundance TV; The Fil-

ipino Channel; The Movie Channel (multiplexed); TV Asia; TV5, La Television International; Zee TV.
Fee: $12.95 monthly (each).

Video-On-Demand: No

Pay-Per-View
HITS PPV 1-30 (delivered digitally).

Internet Service
Operational: Yes. Began: December 1, 2000.
Subscribers: 28,573.
Broadband Service: Road Runner.
Fee: $42.95 monthly.

Telephone Service
Digital: Operational
Subscribers: 18,133.
Miles of Plant: 3,199.0 (coaxial); 1,963.0 (fiber optic). Homes passed: 88,207.
President: Rhonda Fraas. Vice President & General Manager: David Kreiman. Vice President, Engineering: Randy Hall. Vice President, Sales & Marketing: Mark Psigoda. Plant Manager: Jim Cavender. Engineering Director: Bill Ricker. Marketing Director: Thomas Smith. Marketing Coordinator: Bonita Yeager.
Ownership: Time Warner Cable (MSO).

CHIPPEWA TWP.—Time Warner Cable. Now served by CLEVELAND (formerly Cleveland Heights), OH [OH0006]. ICA: OH0173.

CIRCLEVILLE—Time Warner Cable. Now served by COLUMBUS, OH [OH0002]. ICA: OH0087.

CIRCLEVILLE—Time Warner Cable. Now served by COLUMBUS, OH [OH0002]. ICA: OH0320.

CLAY CENTER/GIBSONBURG—Time Warner Cable. Now served by TIFFIN (formerly Fostoria), OH [OH0050]. ICA: OH0071.

CLEVELAND—Time Warner Cable, 3400 Lakeside Ave East, Cleveland, OH 44114-3754. Phones: 330-633-9203 (Akron regional office); 216-575-8016. Fax: 216-575-0212. Web Site: http://www.timewarnercable.com. Also serves Akron, Alliance, Amherst, Amherst Twp., Aquilla (village), Ashland, Ashtabula, Ashtabula Twp. (Ashtabula County), Atwater Twp., Auburn Twp., Aurora, Austinburg Twp., Avon, Avon Lake, Bailey Lakes, Bainbridge Twp., Baltic (village), Barberton, Barnhill (village), Bath Twp. (Summit County), Bay Village, Bazetta Twp., Beach City (village), Beachwood, Bedford, Bedford Heights, Bellville (village), Beloit (village), Bentleyville (village), Berea, Berlin Heights (village), Berlin Twp. (Erie County), Berlin Twp. (Holmes County), Bethlehem Twp. (Stark County), Big Prairie (village), Bolivar, Boston Heights (village), Boston Twp., Braceville Twp., Brady Lake (village), Bratenahl (village), Brecksville, Brewster, Briarwood Beach (village), Brimfield Twp., Bristol Twp. (Trumbull County), Bronson Twp., Brook Park, Brookfield Twp., Brooklyn, Brown Twp. (Carroll County), Brownhelm (town), Brunswick, Brunswick Hills, Burbank (village), Burton (village), Burton Twp., Butler Twp. (Columbiana County), Canaan Twp. (Wayne County), Canal Fulton, Canton, Canton Twp., Carlisle Twp., Carrollton (village), Cass Twp. (Muskingum County), Center Twp. (Columbiana County), Chagrin Falls (Twp.), Chagrin Falls (village), Champion Twp., Chardon, Chardon Twp., Charlestown Twp., Chatham Twp., Chester Twp. (Geauga County), Chippewa Lake Twp.,

Chippewa Twp., Claridon Twp. (Geauga County), Clarksfield Twp., Cleveland Heights, Clinton, Coitsville Twp., Columbia Twp. (Lorain County), Concord Twp. (Lake County), Congress Twp. (Wayne County), Conneaut, Copley Twp., Cortland (village), Coventry Twp., Craig Beach (village), Creston (village), Cuyahoga Falls, Cuyahoga Heights (village), Deerfield Twp. (Portage County), Dellroy (village), Dennison (village), Dover (Tuscarawas County), Dover Twp. (Tuscarawas County), Doylestown (village), East Canton (village), East Cleveland, East Sparta (village), Eastlake, Eaton Twp., Edinburg Twp., Elyria, Elyria Twp. (Lorain County), Euclid, Fairfield Twp. (Huron County), Fairlawn, Fairpoint Harbor (village), Farmington (village), Fitchville Twp., Florence Twp. (Erie County), Fowler Twp., Franklin Twp. (Coshocton County), Franklin Twp. (Portage County), Fredericksburg (village) (Wayne County), Garfield Heights, Garrettsville (village), Gates Mills (village), Geneva (Ashtabula County), Geneva Twp., Geneva-on-the-Lake (village), Girard, Glenmont (village), Glenwillow (village), Gloria Glens (village), Gnadenhutten (village), Goshen Twp., Grand River (village), Granger Twp., Green, Green Twp. (Mahoning County), Greenfield Estates, Greenfield Twp. (Huron County), Greenwich (village), Guilford Twp., Hambden Twp., Hanover Twp. (Columbiana County), Hanoverton (village), Hardy Twp., Harpersfield Twp., Harrison Twp. (Carroll County), Harrisville Twp., Hartford Twp. (Trumbull County), Hartland Twp., Hartville (village), Highland Heights, Hills & Dales (village), Hinckley Twp., Hiram (village), Hiram Twp., Holmesville (village), Howland Twp., Hubbard, Hubbard Twp., Hudson, Hunting Valley (village), Independence, Jackson Twp. (Stark County), Jefferson (village), Jefferson Twp. (Ashtabula County), Jefferson Twp. (Muskingum County), Jeromesville (village), Johnston Twp. (Trumbull County), Kent, Killbuck (village), Kingsville Twp., Kipton, Kirtland, Kirtland Hills (village), Knox Twp. (Columbiana County), Lafayette Twp. (Coshocton County), Lake Buckhorn, Lake Twp. (Stark County), Lakeline (village), Lakemore Twp., Lakeville (village), Lakewood, Lawrence Twp. (Stark County), Lawrence Twp. (Tuscarawas County), Lee Twp. (Carroll County), Lenox Twp., Leroy Twp. (Lake County), Lexington (village), Lexington Twp., Liberty Twp. (Trumbull County), Limaville (village), Linndale (village), Lisbon (village), Lodi (village), Lorain, Lordstown Twp., Loudon Twp. (Carroll County), Loudonville (Ashland County), Louisville, Lowellville (village), Lucas (village), Lyndhurst (village), Macedonia, Madison (village), Madison Twp. (Lake County), Madison Twp. (Muskingum County), Magnolia (village) (Carroll County), Magnolia (village) (Stark County), Malvern (village), Mansfield, Mantua (village), Mantua Twp., Maple Heights, Margaretta Twp., Marlboro Twp. (Stark County), Massillon, Mayfield Heights, Mayfield Village, Mecca Twp., Medina, Mentor, Mentor-on-the-Lake, Meyers Lake (village), Middleburg Heights, Middlefield (village), Middlefield Twp., Midvale (village), Mifflin (village), Mifflin Twp. (Ashland County), Mifflin Twp. (Richland County), Milan (village) (Erie County), Milan (village) (Huron County), Milan Twp., Mill Twp., Millersburg (village), Milton Twp. (Mahoning County), Mineral City (village), Minerva (village), Mogadore (village) (Portage County), Mogadore (village) (Summit County), Monroe Twp. (Ashtabula County), Monroeville (village), Montville Twp. (Medina County), Moreland Hills (village), Munroe Falls (village), Munson Twp., Nashville (village), Navarre, Nelson Ledges, Nelson Twp., New Franklin (village), New Garden, New Haven Twp., New London (village), New London Twp., New Philadelphia, New Russia Twp., Newburgh Heights (village), Newbury Twp., Newcomerstown (village), Newton Falls, Newton Twp. (Trumbull County), Niles, Nimishillen Twp., North Canton, North Fairfield (village), North Jackson (village), North Kingsville (village), North Olmsted, North Perry (village), North Randall (village), North Ridgeville, North Royalton, North Twp., Northfield (village), Northfield Center Twp., Norton, Norwalk, Norwalk Twp., Norwich Twp. (Huron County), Oakwood (village), Ontario, Orange (village), Orangeville (village), Osnaburg Twp., Oxford Twp. (Erie County), Painesville, Painesville Twp., Palmyra Twp., Paris Twp. (Stark County), Parma, Parral (village), Peninsula (village), Pepper Pike, Perry (village), Perry Twp. (Ashland County), Perry Twp. (Columbiana County), Perry Twp. (Lake County), Perry Twp. (Muskingum County), Perry Twp. (Richland County), Perrysville (village), Pike Twp. (Stark County), Plymouth (village) (Huron County), Plymouth (village) (Richland County), Plymouth Twp. (Ashtabula County), Plymouth Twp. (Richland County), Poland Twp., Polk (village), Port Washington (village), Put-in-Bay, Randolph Twp. (Portage County), Ravenna, Ravenna Twp., Reminderville (town), Rice Twp., Richfield (village), Richfield Twp. (Summit County), Richland Twp., Richmond Heights, Richmond Twp. (Huron County), Ridgefield Twp., Ripley Twp., Rittman (Medina County), Rittman (Wayne County), Rootstown Twp., Roswell (village), Rowsburg (village), Ruggles Twp., Russell Twp., Sagamore Hills Twp., Salem, Salem Twp. (Columbiana County), Sandusky Twp. (Richland County), Sandy Twp. (Stark County), Sandy Twp. (Tuscarawas County), Savannah (village), Saybrook Twp. (Ashtabula County), Sebring (village), Seven Hills, Seville (village), Shaker Heights, Shalersville Twp., Sharon Twp. (Medina County), Sheffield (village), Sheffield Lake, Sheffield Twp. (Ashtabula County), Sheffield Twp. (Lorain County), Shelby, Sherrodsville (village), Shiloh (village), Shreve (village), Silver Lake (village), Smith Twp. (Mahoning County), Solon, Somerset (village), South Amherst (village), South Euclid, South Russell (village), Southington Twp., Spencer (village), Spring Lakes Mobile Home Park, Springfield Twp. (Richland County), Springfield Twp. (Summit County), Sterling, Stone Creek Village, Stow, Strasburg (village), Streetsboro, Strongsville, Struthers, Suffield Twp., Sugar Bush Knolls (village), Sugarcreek (village), Tallmadge, Timberlake (village), Tiro, Townsend Twp. (Huron County), Troy Twp. (Richland County), Tuscarawas (village), Twinsburg, Twinsburg Twp., Uhrichsville, University Heights, Valley View (village), Vermilion, Vermilion Twp., Vienna Air Force Base, Vienna Twp., Wadsworth, Wadsworth Twp., Waite Hill (village), Wakeman (village), Wakerman Twp., Walnut Creek Twp., Walton Hills (village), Warren, Warren Twp. (Trumbull County), Warrensville Heights, Warrensville Twp., Warwick Twp., Washington Twp. (Richland County), Washington Twp. (Stark County), Wayne Twp. (Ashtabula County), Waynesburg (village), Weathersfield Twp., Weller Twp., West Farmington (village), West Salem (village), West Twp., Westfield Center, Westfield Twp., Westlake, Wickliffe, Willard, Willoughby (village), Willoughby Hills, Willowick, Willows Mobile Home Park, Wilmot (village), Windham (village), Windham Twp., Winona, Woodmere (village), Worthington Twp., Yankee Lake (village), Youngstown & Zoar (village), OH; Albion Borough, Clark Borough, Columbus Twp., Concord Twp. (Erie County), Conneaut Twp., Conneautville, Conneautville Borough, Corry, Cranesville Borough, Delaware Twp. (Mercer County), Elgin Borough, Elk Creek Twp., Fairview (Erie County), Farrell, Fredonia Borough, Girard Borough, Girard Twp. (Erie County), Greene Twp. (Erie County), Greenville Borough, Harborcreek Twp., Hempfield Twp. (Mercer County), Hermitage, Jefferson Twp., Lackawonnock Twp., Lake City Borough, Lawrence Park Twp., Lundys Lane, McKean Borough, McKean Twp. (Erie County), Mercer County (portions), Millcreek Twp. (Erie County), North East Borough, North East Twp., Platea Borough, Pymatuning Twp., Sharon, Sharpsville Borough, Shenango Twp., South Pymatuning Twp., Spring Twp. (Crawford County), Springboro Borough, Springfield Twp., Sugar Grove Twp., Summit Twp. (Erie County), Union City Borough, Union Twp. (Erie County), Waterford Borough (Erie County), Waterford Twp. (Erie County), Wesleyville Borough, West Middlesex Borough, West Salem Twp., Wheatland Borough & Wilmington Twp., PA. ICA: OH0006. **Note:** This system is an overbuild.

TV Market Ranking: 10 (North Twp.); 52 (Rice Twp.); 79 (Bazetta Twp., Bristol Twp. (Trumbull County), Brookfield Twp., Butler Twp. (Columbiana County), Center Twp. (Columbiana County), Champion Twp., Clark Borough, Coitsville Twp., Cortland (village), Delaware Twp. (Mercer County), Farmington (village), Farrell, Fowler Twp., Fredonia Borough, Girard, Goshen Twp., Green Twp. (Mahoning County), Greenville Borough, Hanover Twp. (Columbiana County), Hanoverton (village), Hartford Twp. (Trumbull County), Hempfield Twp. (Mercer County), Hermitage, Howland Twp., Hubbard, Hubbard Twp., Jefferson Twp., Johnston Twp. (Trumbull County), Lackawonnock Twp., Liberty Twp. (Trumbull County), Lisbon (village), Lowellville (village), Mercer County (portions), New Garden, Newton Twp. (Trumbull County), Niles, North Jackson (village), Orangeville (village), Poland Twp., Pymatuning Twp., Salem Twp. (Columbiana County), Sharon, Sharpsville Borough, Shenango Twp., Smith Twp. (Mahoning County), South Pymatuning Twp., Struthers, Sugar Grove Twp., Vienna Air Force Base, Vienna Twp., Warren, Wayne Twp. (Ashtabula County), Weathersfield Twp., West Farmington (village), West Middlesex Borough, West Salem Twp., Wheatland Borough, Wilmington Twp., Winona, Yankee Lake (village), Youngstown); 8 (Akron, Amherst, Amherst Twp., Aquilla (village), Auburn Twp., Aurora, Avon, Avon, Avon Lake, Bainbridge Twp., Barberton, Bath Twp. (Summit County), Bay Village, Beach City (village), Beachwood, Bedford, Bedford Heights, Beloit (village), Bentleyville (village), Berea, Berlin Heights (village), Berlin Twp. (Erie County), Bethlehem Twp. (Stark County), Bolivar, Boston Heights (village), Boston Twp., Braceville Twp., Bratenahl (village), Brecksville, Brewster, Briarwood Beach (village), Brimfield Twp., Bronson Twp., Brook Park, Brooklyn, Brown Twp. (Carroll County), Brownhelm (town), Brunswick, Brunswick, Brunswick Hills, Burbank (village), Burton (village), Burton Twp., Canaan Twp. (Wayne County), Canal Fulton, Canton, Canton Twp., Carlisle Twp., Chagrin Falls (Twp.), Chagrin Falls (village), Chardon, Chardon Twp., Chatham Twp., Chester Twp. (Geauga County), Chippewa Lake Twp., Chippewa Twp., Claridon Twp. (Geauga County), Clarksfield Twp., CLEVELAND, Cleveland Heights, Clinton, Columbia Twp. (Lorain County), Concord Twp. (Lake County), Congress Twp. (Wayne County), Copley Twp., Coventry Twp., Creston (village), Cuyahoga Falls, Cuyahoga Heights (village), Doylestown (village), East Canton (village), East Cleveland, East Sparta (village), Eastlake, Eaton Twp., Elyria, Elyria Twp. (Lorain County), Euclid, Fairfield Twp. (Huron County), Fairlawn, Fairpoint Harbor (village), Fitchville Twp., Florence Twp. (Erie County), Franklin Twp. (Portage County), Garfield Heights, Garrettsville (village), Gates Mills (village), Glenwillow (village), Gloria Glens (village), Grand River (village), Granger Twp., Green, Greenwich (village), Guilford Twp., Hambden Twp., Harrisville Twp., Hartland Twp., Hartville (village), Highland Heights, Hills & Dales (village), Hinckley Twp., Hiram (village), Hiram Twp., Hudson, Hunting Valley (village), Independence, Jackson Twp. (Stark County), Kent, Kipton, Kirtland, Kirtland Hills (village), Lafayette Twp. (Coshocton County), Lake Twp. (Stark County), Lakeline (village), Lakemore Twp., Lakewood, Lawrence Twp. (Stark County), Lawrence Twp. (Tuscarawas County), Lee Twp. (Carroll County), Leroy Twp. (Lake County), Limaville (village), Linndale (village), Lodi (village), Lorain, Lordstown Twp., Louisville, Lyndhurst (village), Macedonia, Magnolia (village) (Carroll County), Magnolia (village) (Stark County), Malvern (village), Mantua (village), Mantua Twp., Maple Heights, Margaretta Twp., Massillon, Mayfield Heights, Mayfield Village, Mecca Twp., Medina, Mentor, Mentor-on-the-Lake, Meyers Lake (village), Middleburg Heights, Middlefield (village), Middlefield Twp., Milan (village) (Erie County), Milan (village) (Huron County), Milan Twp., Mineral City (village), Mogadore (village) (Portage County), Mogadore (village) (Summit County), Monroeville (village), Montville Twp. (Medina County), Moreland Hills (village), Munroe Falls (village), Munson Twp., Nelson Ledges, Nelson Twp., New Franklin (village), New London (village), New London Twp., New Russia Twp., Newburgh Heights (village), Newbury Twp., Newton Falls, Nimishillen Twp., North Canton, North Fairfield (village), North Olmsted, North Randall (village), North Ridgeville, North Royalton, Northfield (village), Northfield Center Twp., Norton, Norwalk, Norwalk Twp., Oakwood (village), Orange (village), Osnaburg Twp., Oxford Twp. (Erie County), Painesville, Painesville Twp., Paris Twp. (Stark County), Parma, Peninsula (village), Pepper Pike, Perry (village), Perry Twp. (Ashland County) (portions), Perry Twp. (Columbiana County), Perry Twp. (Lake County), Pike Twp. (Stark County), Polk (village), Ravenna Twp., Reminderville (town), Richfield (village), Richfield Twp. (Summit County), Richmond Heights, Ridgefield Twp., Rittman (Medina County), Rittman (Wayne County), Russell Twp., Sagamore Hills Twp., Sandy Twp. (Stark County), Sandy Twp. (Tuscarawas County), Savannah (village), Sebring (village), Seven Hills, Seville (village), Shaker Heights, Shalersville Twp., Sharon Twp. (Medina County), Sheffield (village), Sheffield Lake, Sheffield Twp. (Lorain County), Silver Lake (village), Solon, South Amherst (village), South Euclid, South Russell (village), Southington Twp., Spencer (village), Springfield Twp. (Summit County), Sterling, Stow, Strasburg (village), Streetsboro, Strongsville,

Ohio—Cable Systems

Suffield Twp., Sugar Bush Knolls (village), Tallmadge, Timberlake (village), Townsend Twp. (Huron County), Twinsburg, Twinsburg Twp., University Heights, Valley View (village), Vermilion, Vermilion Twp., Wadsworth, Wadsworth Twp., Waite Hill (village), Wakeman (village), Wakerman Twp., Walton Hills (village), Warrensville Heights, Warrensville Twp., Waynesburg (village), West Salem (village), Westfield Center, Westfield Twp., Westlake, Wickliffe, Willoughby (village), Willoughby Hills, Willowick, Willows Mobile Home Park, Wilmot (village), Windham (village), Windham Twp., Woodmere (village), Zoar (village)); 8,79 (Alliance, Atwater Twp., Brady Lake (village), Charlestown Twp., Craig Beach (village), Deerfield Twp. (Portage County), Edinburg Twp., Knox Twp. (Columbiana County), Lexington Twp., Marlboro Twp. (Stark County), Milton Twp. (Mahoning County), Minerva (village), Navarre, Palmyra Twp., Randolph Twp. (Portage County), Ravenna, Rootstown Twp., Salem, Spring Lakes Mobile Home Park, Warren Twp. (Trumbull County), Washington Twp. (Stark County), West Twp.); 90 (Carrollton (village), Dellroy (village), Harrison Twp. (Carroll County), Loudon Twp. (Carroll County), Sherrodsville (village)); Below 100 (Albion Borough, Ashland, Bailey Lakes, Baltic (village), Barnhill (village), Bellville (village), Berlin Twp. (Holmes County), Big Prairie (village), Cass Twp. (Muskingum County), Columbus Twp., Concord Twp. (Erie County), Conneaut, Conneaut Twp., Conneautville, Conneautville Borough, Cranesville Borough, Dennison (village), Dover (Tuscarawas County), Dover Twp. (Tuscarawas County), Elgin Borough, Elk Creek Twp., Fairview (Erie County), Franklin Twp. (Coshocton County), Fredericksburg (village) (Wayne County), Girard Borough, Girard Twp. (Erie County), Glenmont (village), Gnadenhutten (village), Greene Twp. (Erie County), Greenfield Estates, Greenfield Twp. (Huron County), Hardy Twp., Holmesville (village), Jefferson Twp. (Muskingum County), Killbuck (village), Kingsville Twp., Lake Buckhorn, Lake City Borough, Lakeville (village), Lawrence Park Twp., Lexington (village), Loudonville (Ashland County), Lucas (village), Lundys Lane, Madison (village), Madison Twp. (Lake County), Madison Twp. (Muskingum County), McKean Borough, McKean Twp. (Erie County), Midvale (village), Mifflin (village), Mifflin Twp. (Ashland County), Mill Twp., Millcreek Twp. (Erie County), Millersburg (village), Nashville (village), New Haven Twp., Newcomerstown (village), North East Borough, North East Twp., North Kingsville (village), North Perry (village), Norwich Twp. (Huron County), Ontario, Parral (village), Perry Twp. (Muskingum County), Perry Twp. (Richland County), Perrysville (village), Platea Borough, Plymouth (village) (Huron County), Plymouth Twp. (Richland County), Port Washington (village), Richland Twp., Richmond Twp. (Huron County), Ripley Twp., Roswell (village), Rowsburg (village), Ruggles Twp., Sandusky Twp. (Richland County), Shiloh (village), Shreve (village), Somerset (village), Spring Twp. (Crawford County), Springboro Borough, Springfield Twp., Springfield Twp. (Richland County), Stone Creek Village, Sugarcreek (village), Summit Twp. (Erie County), Tiro, Troy Twp. (Richland County), Tuscarawas (village), Uhrichsville, Union City Borough, Union Twp. (Erie County), Walnut Creek Twp., Warwick Twp., Washington Twp. (Richland County), Waterford Borough (Erie County), Waterford Twp. (Erie County), Weller Twp., Wesleyville Borough, Worthington Twp., Corry, Harborcreek Twp., Jeromesville (village), Mansfield, New Philadelphia, Put-in-Bay, Shelby, Willard, Perry Twp. (Ashland County) (portions)); Outside TV Markets (Ashtabula Twp. (Ashtabula County), Austinburg Twp., Geneva (Ashtabula County), Geneva Twp., Geneva-on-the-Lake (village), Harpersfield Twp., Jefferson (village), Jefferson Twp. (Ashtabula County), Lenox Twp., Monroe Twp. (Ashtabula County), Plymouth Twp. (Ashtabula County), Saybrook Twp. (Ashtabula County), Sheffield Twp. (Ashtabula County), Ashtabula). Franchise award date: May 25, 1965. Franchise expiration date: N.A. Began: January 1, 1966.

Channel capacity: 65 (operating 2-way). Channels available but not in use: N.A.

Basic Service

Subscribers: 650,104.

Programming (received off-air): WBNX-TV (CW, Movies!, This TV) Akron; WEAO (PBS) Akron; WEWS-TV (ABC) Cleveland; WJW (Antenna TV, FOX) Cleveland; WKYC (NBC) Cleveland; WNEO (PBS) Alliance; WOIO (CBS, MeTV) Shaker Heights; WQHS-DT (getTV, UNV) Cleveland; WRLM (IND) Canton; WUAB (Bounce TV, MNT) Lorain; WVIZ (PBS) Cleveland; WVPX-TV (ION) Akron.

Programming (via satellite): EWTN Global Catholic Network; Pop; QVC; Scola; WGN America.

Fee: $29.95 installation; $21.50 monthly.

Expanded Basic Service 1

Subscribers: N.A.

Programming (via satellite): A&E; AMC; Animal Planet; BET; Bravo; Cartoon Network; CNBC; CNN; Comedy Central; C-SPAN; C-SPAN 2; Discovery Channel; Disney Channel; E! HD; ESPN; ESPN2; EVINE Live; Food Network; Fox News Channel; Fox Sports 1; FOX Sports Ohio/ Sports Time Ohio; Freeform; FX; Golf Channel; HGTV; History; HLN; Lifetime; MSNBC; MTV; MTV Classic; MTV2; Nickelodeon; Spike TV; Syfy; TBS; Telemundo; The Weather Channel; TLC; TNT; Travel Channel; truTV; TV Land; USA Network; VH1.

Fee: $46.50 monthly.

Digital Basic Service

Subscribers: N.A.

Programming (via satellite): 52MX; AXS TV; BBC America; Bloomberg Television; Cinelatino; CMT; CNN en Espanol; C-SPAN 3; Destination America; Discovery Kids Channel; Discovery Life Channel; Disney XD; DIY Network; ESPN Classic; ESPN Deportes; ESPN HD; ESPN2 HD; ESPNews; ESPNU; Fox Business Network; Fox Deportes; FOX Sports Ohio/Sports Time Ohio; Fuse; FXM; Great American Country; GSN; Hallmark Channel; HD Theater; History en Espanol; Investigation Discovery; LMN; LOGO; MC; MTV Hits; MTV Jams; Nat Geo WILD; National Geographic Channel; Nick 2; Nick Jr.; Nicktoons; OWN: Oprah Winfrey Network; Science Channel; TBS HD; TeenNick; The Word Network; TNT HD; Toon Disney en Espanol; Tr3s; Trinity Broadcasting Network (TBN); Turner Classic Movies; TV One; TVG Network; Universal HD; UP; VH1 Soul; WE tv.

Fee: $11.00 monthly.

Digital Expanded Basic Service

Subscribers: N.A.

Programming (via satellite): Cooking Channel; Flix; Fox Sports 2; FSN Digital Atlantic; FSN Digital Central; FSN Digital Pacific; FYI; History International; IFC; NBA TV; NBCSN; Outdoor Channel; Sundance TV; Tennis Channel.

Fee: $10.00 monthly.

Digital Pay Service 1

Pay Units: N.A.

Programming (via satellite): ART America; Cinemax (multiplexed); Cinemax HD; Cinemax On Demand; Flix; HBO (multiplexed); HBO HD; HBO on Demand; RAI Italia; RTN; Showtime (multiplexed); Showtime HD; Showtime On Demand; Starz (multiplexed); Starz Encore (multiplexed); Starz HD; Starz On Demand; The Filipino Channel; The Movie Channel (multiplexed); The Movie Channel On Demand; TV Asia; TV5, La Television International.

Fee: $12.99 monthly (each).

Video-On-Demand: Yes

Pay-Per-View

iN DEMAND; Sports PPV.

Internet Service

Operational: Yes. Began: February 14, 2001.

Subscribers: 619,780.

Broadband Service: Road Runner.

Fee: $45.95 monthly.

Telephone Service

Digital: Operational

Subscribers: 298,950.

Fee: $44.95 monthly

Miles of Plant: 35,659.0 (coaxial); 6,256.0 (fiber optic). Homes passed: 1,801,722.

President: Stephen Fry. Vice President & General Manager: Darrel Hegar. Government & Media Relations Director: Chris Thomas. Operations Manager: Derrick Moore. Marketing Manager: Dana Olden. Chief Technician: Jim Farone.

Ownership: Time Warner Cable (MSO).

CLEVELAND—Time Warner Cable. Now served by CLEVELAND (formerly Cleveland Heights), OH [OH0006]. ICA: OH0003.

COITSVILLE TWP.—Armstrong Cable Services. Now served by ZELIENOPLE, PA [PA0053]. ICA: OH0233.

COLLINSVILLE—Formerly served by Time Warner Cable. No longer in operation. ICA: OH0172.

COLUMBUS—Formerly served by Sprint Corp. No longer in operation. ICA: OH0390.

COLUMBUS—Time Warner Cable, 1266 Dublin Rd, Columbus, OH 43215-1008. Phones: 614-255-4997; 614-481-5000. Fax: 614-481-5052. Web Site: http://www.timewarnercable.com. Also serves Ada, Adamsville (village), Alexander Twp., Alexandria (village), Alger, Amanda Twp. (Fairfield County), Ashley (village), Ashville (village), Athens, Athens Twp. (Athens County), Baltimore (village), Bearfield Twp., Belle Center (village), Berkshire Twp., Berkshire Twp. (Delaware County), Berne Twp., Bexley, Big Island Twp., Blendon Twp. (Franklin County), Bloom Twp. (Fairfield County), Blue Rock, Bokes Creek Twp., Bowling Green Twp. (Licking County), Bowling Green Twp. (Muskingum County), Breman (village), Brice, Brown Twp. (Delaware County), Brown Twp. (Franklin County), Brush Creek Twp., Buck Twp. (Hardin County), Bucyrus, Bucyrus Twp., Burlington Twp., Bushcreek Twp. (Muskingum County), Canaan Twp. (Athens County), Canal Winchester, Cardington (village), Cardington Twp., Carroll (village), Cass Twp. (Muskingum County), Centerburg (village), Chandlersville, Chesterville (village), Circleville, Claiborne Twp., Clayton Twp., Clearcreek Twp., Clinton Twp. (Franklin County), Clinton Twp. (Knox County), College Twp., Concord Twp. (Delaware County), Crestline (village), Crooksville (village), Croton (village), Danville (village), Darby Twp. (Madison County), Darby Twp. (Pickaway County), Darby Twp. (Union County), Deer Creek Twp., Delaware, Delaware Twp. (Delaware County), Dover Twp. (Union County), Dresden (village), Dublin (Delaware County), Dublin (Franklin County), Duncan Falls, Dunkirk, East Liberty, Edison (village), Etna Twp., Etna Twp. (Licking County), Fairfield Beach (village), Falls Twp. (Hocking County), Forest (village), Franklin Twp. (Frankin County), Frazeyburg (village), Fredericktown (village), Fulton (village), Fultonham (village), Gahanna, Gahanna (Franklin County), Galena (village), Galion, Gambier (village), Genoa Twp. (Delaware County), Gilead Twp., Glenford, Grandview Heights, Granville (village), Gratiot (village), Green Camp (village), Greenfield Twp. (Fairfield County), Grove City, Groveport (village), Hale Twp., Hamilton Twp. (Franklin County), Harbor Hills (village), Harlem Twp. (Delaware County), Harrisburg, Harrisburg (village), Harrison Twp. (Licking County), Harrison Twp. (Pickaway County), Hartford (village), Hartford Twp. (Licking County), Hayden Heights MHP, Hide-A-Way Hills, Hilliar Twp. (Knox County), Hilliard, Holland, Holmes Twp., Homer Twp., Hopewell Twp. (Licking County), Hopewell Twp. (Muskingum County), Howard Twp., Jackson Twp. (Coschocton County), Jackson Twp. (Franklin County), Jackson Twp. (Knox County), Jackson Twp. (Muskingum County), Jackson Twp. (Perry County), Jefferson Twp. (Franklin County), Jefferson Twp. (Madison County), Jerome Twp., Jersey Twp., Johnstown (village), Junction City, Kenton, Kingston Twp., Kirkersville (village), La Rue (village), Lancaster, Leesburg Twp., Liberty Twp. (Delaware County), Liberty Twp. (Fairfield County), Liberty Twp. (Hardin County), Liberty Twp. (Knox County), Liberty Twp. (Union County), Licking Twp. (Licking County), Licking Twp. (Muskingum County), Linton Twp., Lithopolis, Lockbourne Village, Lykens Twp., Madison Twp. (Franklin County), Madison Twp. (Pickaway County), Magnetic Springs (village), Marble Cliff (village), Marengo (village), Marion Twp. (Hocking County), Martinsburg (village), Maumee, McGuffey, Middleburg, Middlebury Twp., Mifflin Twp. (Franklin County), Milford Center (village), Millersport (village), Minerva Park (village), Monroe Twp. (Logan County), Morris Twp., Mount Gilead (village), Mount Sterling (village), Mount Vernon, Mount Victory (village), Murray City, Muskingum Twp. (Muskingum County), New Albany, New Bloomington (village), New Concord (village), New Lexington (village), North Bloomfield Twp., North Lewisburg (village), North Robinson (village), Norwich (village), Norwich Twp. (Muskingum County), Oak Run Twp., Obetz (village), Orange Twp. (Delaware County), Orient (village), Ostrander (village), Ottawa Hills, Paris Twp. (Union County), Pataskala (village), Patterson (village), Perry County (portions), Perry Twp. (Franklin County), Perry Twp. (Logan County), Perry Twp. (Pickaway County), Peru Twp., Philo (village), Pickerington, Pike Twp. (Perry County), Plain City (village), Plain Twp. (Franklin County), Plainfield (village), Pleasant Twp. (Fairfield County), Pleasant Twp. (Franklin County), Pleasant Twp. (Knox County), Pleasant Twp. (Perry County), Pleasantville (village), Polk Twp., Porter Twp. (Delaware County), Powell Twp., Prairie Twp. (Franklin County), Prospect

Cable Systems—Ohio

(village), Prospect Twp., Radnor Twp., Reading Twp., Reynoldsburg, Rich Hill Twp., Richland Twp. (Fairfield County), Richland Twp. (Logan County), Richland Twp. (Wyandot County), Richwood (village), Ridgeway (village), Riverlea (village), Roseville (village) (Muskingum County), Roseville (village) (Perry County), Rush Creek Twp. (Fairfield County), Rushcreek Twp. (Logan County), Rushsylvania (village), Rushville (village), Salt Creek, Salt Creek Twp. (Muskingum County), Sandusky Twp. (Richland County), Sharon Twp. (Franklin County), Shawnee Hills (village), Somerford Twp., Sonora, South Bloomfield, South Bloomfield (village), South Zanesville, Sparta (village), Springfield Twp. (Muskingum County), St. Albans Twp., St. Albans Twp. (Licking County), Stoutsville (village), Sugar Grove (village), Sulphur Springs, Sunbury (village), Sylvania, Taylor Twp., The Plains (village), Thorn Twp., Thornville (village), Thurston (village), Trenton Twp., Trinway, Troy Twp. (Delaware County), Truro Twp., Union Twp. (Knox County), Union Twp. (Logan County), Union Twp. (Madison County), Union Twp. (Muskingum County), Union Twp. (Union County), Unionville Center (village), Upper Arlington, Urbancrest (village), Utica (village), Valley Hi (village), Valleyview (village), Vernon Twp. (Crawford County), Violet Twp., Waldo (village), Waldo Twp., Ward Twp., Washington Twp. (Franklin County), Washington Twp. (Licking County), Washington Twp. (Morrow County), Washington Twp. (Muskingum County), Wayne Twp. (Knox County), Wayne Twp. (Muskingum County), Wayne Twp. (Pickaway County), West Jefferson (village), West Lafayette Twp., West Mansfield (village), West Rushville (village), Westerville (Delaware County), Westerville (Franklin County), Wharton (village), Whetstone Twp., Whitehall, Worthington, Zane Twp. (Logan County) & Zanesville. ICA: OH0002.
TV Market Ranking: 27 (Alexandria (village), Amanda Twp. (Fairfield County), Ashley (village), Ashville (village), Baltimore (village), Berkshire Twp., Berkshire Twp. (Delaware County), Berne Twp., Bexley, Blendon Twp. (Franklin County), Bloom Twp. (Fairfield County), Brice, Brown Twp. (Delaware County), Brown Twp. (Franklin County), Burlington Twp., Canal Winchester, Carroll (village), Centerburg (village), Circleville, Clinton Twp. (Franklin County), COLUMBUS, Concord Twp. (Delaware County), Croton (village), Darby Twp. (Madison County), Darby Twp. (Pickaway County), Darby Twp. (Union County), Deer Creek Twp., Delaware, Delaware Twp. (Delaware County), Dover Twp. (Union County), Dublin (Delaware County), Dublin (Franklin County), Etna Twp., Etna Twp. (Licking County), Fairfield Beach (village), Falls Twp. (Hocking County) (portions), Franklin Twp. (Franklin County), Fulton (village), Gahanna, Gahanna (Franklin County), Galena (village), Genoa Twp. (Delaware County), Grandview Heights, Granville (village), Greenfield Twp. (Fairfield County), Grove City, Groveport (village), Hamilton Twp. (Franklin County), Harbor Hills (village), Harlem Twp. (Delaware County), Harrisburg, Harrisburg (village), Harrison Twp. (Licking County), Harrison Twp. (Pickaway County), Hartford (village), Hartford Twp. (Licking County), Hayden Heights MHP, Hide-A-Way Hills, Hilliard, Jackson Twp. (Franklin County), Jefferson Twp. (Franklin County), Jefferson Twp. (Madison County), Jerome Twp., Jersey Twp., Johnstown (village), Kingston Twp., Kirkersville (village), Lancaster, Leesburg Twp., Liberty Twp. (Delaware County), Liberty Twp. (Fairfield County), Liberty Twp. (Knox County) (portions), Liberty Twp. (Union County), Licking Twp. (Licking County), Lithopolis, Lockbourne Village, Madison Twp. (Franklin County), Madison Twp. (Pickaway County), Magnetic Springs (village), Marble Cliff (village), Marengo (village), Marion Twp. (Hocking County) (portions), Mifflin Twp. (Franklin County), Milford Center (village), Millersport (village), Minerva Park (village), Mount Sterling (village), Murray City, New Albany, North Lewisburg (village), Oak Run Twp., Obetz (village), Orange Twp. (Delaware County), Orient (village), Ostrander (village), Paris Twp. (Union County), Pataskala (village), Perry Twp. (Franklin County), Perry Twp. (Pickaway County), Peru Twp., Pickerington, Plain City (village), Plain Twp. (Franklin County), Pleasant Twp. (Fairfield County), Pleasant Twp. (Franklin County), Pleasantville (village), Porter Twp. (Delaware County), Powell Twp., Prairie Twp. (Franklin County), Prospect (village), Prospect Twp. (portions), Radnor Twp., Reading Twp. (portions), Reynoldsburg, Richland Twp. (Fairfield County), Richwood (village), Riverlea (village), Rushville (village), Sharon Twp. (Franklin County), Shawnee Hills (village), Somerford Twp., South Bloomfield, South Bloomfield (village), Sparta (village), St. Albans Twp. (Licking County), Stoutsville (village), Sugar Grove (village), Sunbury (village), Taylor Twp., Thorn Twp., Thornville (village), Thurston (village), Trenton Twp., Troy Twp. (Delaware County), Truro Twp., Union Twp. (Madison County), Union Twp. (Union County), Unionville Center (village), Upper Arlington, Urbancrest (village), Utica (village), Valleyview (village), Violet Twp., Waldo (village), Waldo Twp., Ward Twp., Washington Twp. (Franklin County), Washington Twp. (Licking County) (portions), Wayne Twp. (Pickaway County), West Jefferson (village), West Rushville (village), Westerville (Delaware County), Westerville (Franklin County), Whitehall, Worthington); 52 (Maumee, Ottawa Hills, Sylvania); 8 (Clearcreek Twp., Homer Twp.); Below 100 (Ada, Adamsville (village), Alexander Twp., Alger, Athens Twp. (Athens County), Bearfield Twp., Belle Center (village), Big Island Twp., Blue Rock, Bokes Creek Twp., Bowling Green Twp. (Licking County), Bowling Green Twp. (Muskingum County), Breman (village), Brush Creek Twp., Buck Twp. (Hardin County), Bucyrus Twp., Bushcreek Twp. (Muskingum County), Canaan Twp. (Athens County), Cardington (village), Cardington Twp., Cass Twp. (Muskingum County), Chandlersville, Chesterville (village), Claiborne Twp., Clayton Twp., Clinton Twp. (Knox County), College Twp., Crooksville (village), Danville (village), Dresden (village), Duncan Falls, Dunkirk, Edison (village), Forest (village), Frazeyburg (village), Fredericktown (village), Fultonham (village), Gambier (village), Gilead Twp., Glenford, Gratiot (village), Hale Twp. (portions), Holmes Twp., Hopewell Twp. (Licking County), Hopewell Twp. (Muskingum County), Howard Twp., Jackson Twp. (Coshocton County), Jackson Twp. (Knox County), Jackson Twp. (Muskingum County), Jackson Twp. (Perry County), Junction City, Liberty Twp. (Hardin County), Licking Twp. (Muskingum County), Linton Twp., Lykens Twp., Martinsburg (village), McGuffey, Middleburg, Middlebury Twp., Monroe Twp. (Logan County), Morris Twp., Mount Victory (village), Muskingum Twp. (Muskingum County), New Concord (village), New Lexington (village), North Bloomfield Twp., Norwich (village), Norwich Twp. (Muskingum County), Patterson (village), Perry County (portions), Perry Twp. (Logan County), Philo (village), Pike Twp. (Perry County), Plainfield (village), Pleasant Twp. (Perry County), Rich Hill Twp., Richland Twp. (Logan County), Richland Twp. (Wyandot County) (portions), Ridgeway (village), Roseville (village) (Muskingum County), Rush Creek Twp. (Fairfield County), Rushcreek Twp. (Logan County), Rushsylvania (village), Salt Creek, Salt Creek Twp. (Muskingum County), Sandusky Twp. (Richland County), Sonora, South Zanesville, Springfield Twp. (Muskingum County), St. Albans Twp., Sulphur Springs, The Plains (village), Trinway, Union Twp. (Knox County), Union Twp. (Logan County), Union Twp. (Muskingum County), Vernon Twp. (Crawford County), Washington Twp. (Morrow County), Washington Twp. (Muskingum County), Wayne Twp. (Knox County), Wayne Twp. (Muskingum County), West Lafayette Twp., Zane Twp. (Logan County), Athens, Bucyrus, Mount Gilead (village), Mount Vernon, Zanesville, Falls Twp. (Hocking County) (portions), Liberty Twp. (Knox County) (portions), Marion Twp. (Hocking County) (portions), Reading Twp. (portions), Washington Twp. (Licking County) (portions); Outside TV Markets (East Liberty, Green Camp (village), Hale Twp. (portions), La Rue (village), New Bloomington (village), Richland Twp. (Wyandot County) (portions), Valley Hi (village), Kenton, Prospect Twp. (portions)). Franchise award date: N.A. Franchise expiration date: N.A. Began: December 1, 1971.
Channel capacity: N.A. Channels available but not in use: N.A.

Basic Service
Subscribers: 346,044.
Programming (received off-air): WBNS-TV (Antenna TV, CBS, Decades) Columbus; WCMH-TV (MeTV, NBC) Columbus; WOSU-TV (PBS) Columbus; WSFJ-TV (TBN) Newark; WSYX (ABC, Antenna TV, MNT, This TV) Columbus; WTTE (FOX) Columbus; WUAB (Bounce TV, MNT) Lorain; WWHO (CW) Chillicothe.
Programming (via satellite): C-SPAN; C-SPAN 2; EVINE Live; Hallmark Channel; History; HLN; LWS Local Weather Station; Pop; QVC; TBS; TLC; WGN America.
Fee: $29.95 installation; $18.25 monthly.

Expanded Basic Service 1
Subscribers: N.A.
Programming (via satellite): A&E; AMC; Animal Planet; BBC America; BET; Bravo; Cartoon Network; CMT; CNBC; CNN; Comedy Central; Discovery Channel; Discovery Life Channel; Disney Channel; E! HD; ESPN; ESPN2; Food Network; Fox News Channel; FOX Sports Ohio/Sports Time Ohio; Freeform; FX; Golf Channel; HGTV; Jewelry Television; Lifetime; LMN; MTV; MTV2; National Geographic Channel; Nickelodeon; OWN: Oprah Winfrey Network; Oxygen; Spike TV; Syfy; The Weather Channel; TNT; Travel Channel; truTV; Turner Classic Movies; TV Land; Univision Studios; USA Network; VH1; WE tv.
Fee: $26.95 monthly.

Digital Basic Service
Subscribers: N.A.
Programming (via satellite): AXS TV; Bloomberg Television; Boomerang; CBS Sports Network; Cloo; CNN International; Cooking Channel; C-SPAN 3; Discovery Digital Networks; Disney Channel; Disney XD; DIY Network; ESPN Classic; ESPNews; EWTN Global Catholic Network; Food Network; FOX College Sports Central; FOX College Sports Pacific; Fox Sports 1; Fox Sports 2; Fuse; FXM; FYI; Great American Country; GSN; HD Theater; HGTV; History International; HITS (Headend In The Sky); IFC; INSP; La Familia Cosmovision; MC; MTV Classic; MTV Hits; NBA TV; Nick Jr.; Nicktoons; Outdoor Channel; Ovation; Starz Encore (multiplexed); Sundance TV; TeenNick; Tennis Channel; The Weather Channel; The Word Network; TNT HD; TV One; Universal HD.
Fee: $7.15 monthly.

Digital Pay Service 1
Pay Units: N.A.
Programming (via satellite): Cinemax (multiplexed); HBO (multiplexed); Showtime (multiplexed); Showtime HD; Starz; Starz Encore; The Movie Channel (multiplexed).
Fee: $12.95 monthly (each).

Video-On-Demand: Yes

Pay-Per-View
iN DEMAND (delivered digitally); NBA League Pass (delivered digitally); NHL Center Ice (delivered digitally); MLB Extra Innings (delivered digitally); MLS Direct Kick (delivered digitally).

Internet Service
Operational: Yes.
Subscribers: 337,305.
Broadband Service: Road Runner.
Fee: $69.95 installation; $44.95 monthly.

Telephone Service
Digital: Operational.
Subscribers: 153,038.
Fee: $44.95 monthly
Miles of Plant: 18,668.0 (coaxial); 6,274.0 (fiber optic). Homes passed: 917,703.
President: Rhonda Fraas. Vice President, Operations: Paul Schonewolf. Vice President, Engineering: Randy Hall. Vice President, Marketing: Mark Psigoda. Vice President, Public Affairs: Mary Jo Green. Vice President, Customer Service: Kathy Chamberlin. Government Affairs Director: Steve Cuckler.
Ownership: Time Warner Cable (MSO).

COLUMBUS—Time Warner Cable. Now served by COLUMBUS, OH [OH0002]. ICA: OH0007.

COLUMBUS—WOW! Internet, Cable & Phone, 7887 East Belleview Ave, Ste 1000, Englewood, CO 80111. Phones: 720-479-3500 (Corporate office); 866-496-9669 (Customer service). Fax: 720-479-3585.

2017 Edition D-585

Ohio—Cable Systems

E-mail: wow_general@wideopenwest.com. Web Site: http://www.wowway.com. Also serves Bexley, Blendon Twp., Brice, Canal Winchester, Clinton Twp., Dublin, Franklin Twp., Gahanna, Genoa Twp., Grandview Heights, Grove City, Hilliard, Jackson Twp., Madison Twp., Marble Cliff, Mifflin Twp., Minerva Park, New Rome, Norwich Twp., Obetz, Orange Twp. (Delaware County), Perry Twp., Pickerington, Prairie Twp., Reynoldsburg, Riverlea, Sharon Twp., Upper Arlington, Urbancrest, Valleyview, Violet Twp., Westerville, Whitehall & Worthington. ICA: OH0426.
Note: This system is an overbuild.
TV Market Ranking: 27 (Bexley, Blendon Twp., Brice, Canal Winchester, Clinton Twp., COLUMBUS, Dublin, Franklin Twp., Gahanna, Genoa Twp., Grandview Heights, Grove City, Hilliard, Jackson Twp., Madison Twp., Marble Cliff, Mifflin Twp., Minerva Park, New Rome, Norwich Twp., Obetz, Orange Twp. (Delaware County), Perry Twp., Pickerington, Prairie Twp., Reynoldsburg, Riverlea, Sharon Twp., Upper Arlington, Urbancrest, Valleyview, Violet Twp., Westerville, Whitehall, Worthington). Franchise award date: April 1, 1996. Franchise expiration date: N.A. Began: N.A.
Channel capacity: 21 (not 2-way capable). Channels available but not in use: N.A.

Basic Service
Subscribers: 64,306.
Programming (received off-air): WBNS-TV (Antenna TV, CBS, Decades) Columbus; WCMH-TV (MeTV, NBC) Columbus; WOSU-TV (PBS) Columbus; WSFJ-TV (TBN) Newark; WSYX (ABC, Antenna TV, MNT, This TV) Columbus; WTTE (FOX) Columbus; WWHO (CW) Chillicothe.
Programming (via satellite): C-SPAN; INSP; TBS; WGN America.
Fee: $50.00 installation; $32.00 monthly.

Expanded Basic Service 1
Subscribers: N.A.
Programming (via satellite): A&E; AMC; Animal Planet; BET; Bravo; BTN; Cartoon Network; CMT; CNBC; CNN; Comedy Central; C-SPAN 2; Discovery Channel; Disney Channel; Disney XD; E! HD; ESPN; ESPN Classic; ESPN2; EVINE Live; Food Network; Fox News Channel; Fox Sports 1; FOX Sports Ohio/Sports Time Ohio; Freeform; FX; Golf Channel; GSN; Hallmark Channel; HGTV; History; HLN; Lifetime; MSNBC; MTV; MTV2; National Geographic Channel; NBCSN; Nick Jr.; Nickelodeon; Nicktoons; OWN: Oprah Winfrey Network; QVC; Spike TV; Syfy; Telemundo; The Weather Channel; TLC; TNT; Travel Channel; truTV; Turner Classic Movies; TV Land; USA Network; VH1.
Fee: $33.01 monthly.

Digital Basic Service
Subscribers: N.A.
Programming (via satellite): A&E HD; Animal Planet HD; AXS TV; BBC America; Bloomberg Television; Bridges TV; BTN; BTN HD; CMT; Cooking Channel; Daystar TV Network; Destination America; Discovery Channel HD; Discovery Kids Channel; DIY Network; DMX Music; ESPN HD; ESPNews; EWTN Global Catholic Network; Food Network HD; Fox Business Network; FOX College Sports Central; FOX College Sports Pacific; Fox HD; Fox News HD; FSN HD; FX HD; FXM; FYI; HD Theater; here! On Demand; HGTV HD; History HD; History International; Investigation Discovery; Jewelry Television; LMN; MTV Classic; MTV Hits; Nat Geo WILD; National Geographic Channel HD; NFL Network; NFL Network HD; Nick 2; Oxygen; PBS HD; Science Channel; Sprout; Starz (multiplexed); Starz Encore (multiplexed); Sundance TV; TeenNick; The Word Network; TLC HD; TNT HD.
Fee: $26.98 monthly.

Digital Pay Service 1
Pay Units: N.A.
Programming (via satellite): Cinemax (multiplexed); Cinemax HD; Cinemax On Demand; Flix; HBO (multiplexed); HBO HD; HBO on Demand; Showtime (multiplexed); Showtime HD; Showtime On Demand; Starz HD; The Movie Channel (multiplexed); The Movie Channel On Demand.
Fee: $15.00 monthly (Cinemax, HBO, Showtime/TMC/Flix or Starz/Encore).

Video-On-Demand: Yes

Pay-Per-View
Hot Choice; iN DEMAND (delivered digitally); Special events (delivered digitally); Playboy TV (delivered digitally); ESPN.

Internet Service
Operational: Yes.
Subscribers: 71,059.
Broadband Service: WOW! Internet.
Fee: $40.99-$72.99 monthly; $2.50 modem lease.

Telephone Service
Digital: Operational
Subscribers: 33,105.
Miles of Plant: 5,052.0 (coaxial); 1,044.0 (fiber optic). Homes passed: 336,397.
Chief Financial Officer: Rich Fish. Vice President & General Manager: Scott Neesley. Vice President, Sales & Marketing: Cathy Kuo. Regional General Manager: Scott Schup. Chief Technician: Cash Hagen.
Ownership: WideOpenWest LLC (MSO).

COLUMBUS GROVE (village)—FairPoint Communications, 36 North Plum St, Germantown, OH 45327. Phones: 800-400-5588 (Customer Service); 419-659-2199 (Internet Technical Support). Web Site: http://www.fairpoint.com. ICA: OH0402. **Note:** This system is an overbuild.
TV Market Ranking: Below 100 (COLUMBUS GROVE (VILLAGE)). Franchise award date: September 9, 1996. Franchise expiration date: N.A. Began: May 1, 1997.
Channel capacity: N.A. Channels available but not in use: N.A.

Basic Service
Subscribers: 23.
Programming (received off-air): WBGU-TV (PBS) Bowling Green; WLIO (CW, NBC) Lima; WLMB (IND) Toledo; WNWO-TV (NBC, Retro TV) Toledo; WOHL-CD (ABC, CBS) Lima; WTLW (IND) Lima; WTOL (CBS, MeTV) Toledo; WTVG (ABC, CW) Toledo.
Programming (via satellite): Discovery Channel; Disney Channel; Fox News Channel; TBS; The Weather Channel; TLC; Univision Studios.
Fee: $21.25 monthly.

Expanded Basic Service 1
Subscribers: N.A.
Programming (via satellite): CMT; CNBC; Disney XD; ESPN; ESPN2; EWTN Global Catholic Network; Food Network; FOX Sports Ohio/Sports Time Ohio; Freeform; HGTV; Pop; Syfy; TV Land; USA Network.
Fee: $8.20 monthly.

Expanded Basic Service 2
Subscribers: N.A.
Programming (received off-air): WBNS-TV (Antenna TV, CBS, Decades) Columbus; WFFT-TV (FOX, MeTV) Fort Wayne; WISE-TV (CW) Fort Wayne; WLQP-LP (ABC) Lima; WPTA (ABC, MNT, NBC) Fort Wayne.
Programming (via satellite): 3ABN; A&E; AMC; Animal Planet; Cartoon Network; CNN; Comedy Central; C-SPAN; Fox Sports 1; FX; Golf Channel; GSN; Hallmark Channel; History; HLN; Lifetime; MTV; Nickelodeon; QVC; Spike TV; TNT; Travel Channel; truTV; Turner Classic Movies; VH1; WE tv; WGN America.
Fee: $14.55 monthly.

Pay Service 1
Pay Units: N.A.
Programming (via satellite): Cinemax; HBO; Playboy TV; Starz; Starz Encore.
Fee: $6.95 monthly (Starz/Encore), $7.95 monthly (Cinemax), $9.95 monthly (HBO), $12.95 monthly (Playboy).

Video-On-Demand: No

Pay-Per-View
iN DEMAND; Playboy TV.

Internet Service
Operational: Yes. Began: January 1, 1999.
Broadband Service: Qone.net.
Fee: $39.95 monthly.

Telephone Service
Digital: Operational
Miles of Plant: 25.0 (coaxial); 7.0 (fiber optic). Homes passed: 3,400.
Accounting Director: Angela Unruh.
Ownership: FairPoint Communications Inc.

COMMERCIAL POINT—Time Warner Cable, 7800 Crescent Executive Dr, Charlotte, NC 28217. Phones: 614-255-4997; 740-345-4329 (Newark office); 614-481-5000 (Columbus office). Web Site: http://www.timewarnercable.com. Also serves Darby Twp. (Pickaway County), Darbyville, Franklin County (portions), Jackson Twp. (Pickaway County), Muhlenberg Twp. & Scioto Twp. (Pickaway County). ICA: OH0213.
TV Market Ranking: 27 (COMMERCIAL POINT, Darby Twp. (Pickaway County), Darbyville, Jackson Twp. (Pickaway County), Muhlenberg Twp., Scioto Twp. (Pickaway County)). Franchise award date: July 14, 1988. Franchise expiration date: N.A. Began: October 1, 1989.
Channel capacity: N.A. Channels available but not in use: N.A.

Basic Service
Subscribers: 104.
Programming (received off-air): WBNS-TV (Antenna TV, CBS, Decades) Columbus; WCMH-TV (MeTV, NBC) Columbus; WOSU-TV (PBS) Columbus; WSYX (ABC, Antenna TV, MNT, This TV) Columbus; WTTE (FOX) Columbus; WWHO (CW) Chillicothe.
Programming (via satellite): TBS.
Fee: $49.99 installation; $24.50 monthly.

Expanded Basic Service 1
Subscribers: N.A.
Programming (via satellite): A&E; AMC; Animal Planet; Cartoon Network; CMT; CNN; Discovery Channel; Disney Channel; E! HD; ESPN; ESPN2; Fox News Channel; FOX Sports Ohio/Sports Time Ohio; Freeform; FX; HGTV; History; HLN; INSP; Lifetime; MSNBC; MTV; Nickelodeon; QVC; Spike TV; Syfy; The Weather Channel; TLC; TNT; Travel Channel; truTV; TV Land; USA Network; VH1; WGN America.

Digital Basic Service
Subscribers: N.A.
Programming (via satellite): BBC America; Bloomberg Television; Discovery Life Channel; ESPN Classic; ESPNews; FXM; Golf Channel; GSN; MC; NBCSN; Nicktoons; Outdoor Channel; Trinity Broadcasting Network (TBN); WE tv.
Fee: $52.40 monthly.

Digital Pay Service 1
Pay Units: N.A.
Programming (via satellite): Cinemax (multiplexed); HBO (multiplexed); Showtime (multiplexed); Starz (multiplexed); Starz Encore (multiplexed); The Movie Channel (multiplexed).
Fee: $12.99 monthly (each).

Video-On-Demand: No

Pay-Per-View
HITS PPV 1-14 (delivered digitally); Fresh (delivered digitally); Playboy TV (delivered digitally).

Internet Service
Operational: Yes.
Broadband Service: RoadRunner.
Fee: $24.95 monthly.

Telephone Service
Digital: Operational
Fee: $24.99 monthly
Miles of Plant: 101.0 (coaxial); None (fiber optic). Homes passed: 1,204.
President: Rhonda Fraas. Vice President & General Manager: David Kreiman. Vice President, Government & Public Affairs: Mary Jo Green. Vice President, Engineering: Randy Hall. Vice President, Marketing: Mark Psigoda. Senior Accounting Director: Karen Goodfellow. Technical Operations Director: Jim Cavender. Government Affairs Director: Steve Cuckler.
Ownership: Time Warner Cable (MSO).

CONCORD TWP. (Lake County)—Time Warner Cable. Now served by CLEVELAND (formerly Cleveland Heights), OH [OH0006]. ICA: OH0042.

CONGRESS TWP. (Wayne County)—Time Warner Cable. Now served by CLEVELAND (formerly Cleveland Heights), OH [OH0006]. ICA: OH0305.

CONVOY—NewWave Communications. Now served by MONROEVILLE, IN [IN0358]. ICA: OH0444.

CORNING—Zito Media, 102 S Main St, PO Box 665, Coudersport, PA 16915. Phones: 814-260-9055; 800-365-6988. E-mail: info@zitomedia.com. Web Site: http://www.zitomedia.com. Also serves Coal Twp. (Perry County), Hemlock, Hocking County, Monroe Twp. (Perry County), Moxahala, New Lexington (Perry County), New Straitsville, Oakfield, Pleasant Twp. (Perry County), Rendville, Salt Lick Twp. & Shawnee. ICA: OH0193.
TV Market Ranking: 27 (Hocking County (portions)); Below 100 (Coal Twp. (Perry County), CORNING, Hemlock, Monroe Twp. (Perry County), Moxahala, New Lexington (Perry County), New Straitsville, Oakfield, Pleasant Twp. (Perry County), Rendville, Salt Lick Twp., Shawnee, Hocking County (portions)); Outside TV Markets (Hocking County (portions)). Franchise award date: N.A. Franchise expiration date: N.A. Began: November 1, 1975.
Channel capacity: 37 (not 2-way capable). Channels available but not in use: N.A.

Basic Service
Subscribers: 70.
Programming (received off-air): WBNS-TV (Antenna TV, CBS, Decades) Columbus; WCMH-TV (MeTV, NBC) Columbus; WHIZ-TV (NBC) Zanesville; WOSU-TV (PBS) Columbus; WOUB-TV (PBS) Athens; WSFJ-TV (TBN) Newark; WSYX (ABC, Antenna TV, MNT, This TV) Columbus; WTTE (FOX) Columbus.
Programming (via satellite): C-SPAN; C-SPAN 2; INSP; The Weather Channel; Trinity Broadcasting Network (TBN); WGN America.
Fee: $29.95 installation; $19.73 monthly; $1.24 converter.

Cable Systems—Ohio

Expanded Basic Service 1
Subscribers: N.A.
Programming (via satellite): A&E; AMC; Animal Planet; Cartoon Network; CNN; Comedy Central; Discovery Channel; Disney Channel; DIY Network; E! HD; ESPN; ESPN2; EVINE Live; Food Network; Fox News Channel; Fox Sports 1; FOX Sports Ohio/Sports Time Ohio; Freeform; FX; Great American Country; GSN; Hallmark Channel; HGTV; History; HLN; Lifetime; LMN; MSNBC; MTV; Nickelodeon; Spike TV; Syfy; TBS; TLC; TNT; TV Land; USA Network; VH1.
Fee: $22.00 monthly.
Pay Service 1
Pay Units: N.A.
Fee: $17.50 installation; $3.99 monthly (Encore), $7.95 monthly (Cinemax), $11.95 monthly (HBO, Showtime or TMC).
Video-On-Demand: No
Pay-Per-View
iN DEMAND (delivered digitally); Playboy TV (delivered digitally); Fresh (delivered digitally).
Internet Service
Operational: No.
Telephone Service
None
Miles of Plant: 46.0 (coaxial); None (fiber optic). Homes passed: 1,572.
President: James Rigas.
Ownership: Zito Media (MSO).

COSHOCTON—Time Warner Cable, 737 Howard St, Zanesville, OH 43701. Phones: 888-579-9959; 740-455-9705. Web Site: http://www.timewarnercable.com. Also serves Conesville, Coshocton County (portions), Keene Twp. & Warsaw. ICA: OH0083.
TV Market Ranking: Below 100 (Conesville, COSHOCTON, Coshocton County (portions), Keene Twp., Warsaw).
Channel capacity: N.A. Channels available but not in use: N.A.
Basic Service
Subscribers: 5,225. Commercial subscribers: 101.
Fee: $29.95 installation; $21.25 monthly.
Ownership: Time Warner Cable (MSO).

CRAIG BEACH (village)—Time Warner Cable. Now served by CLEVELAND (formerly Cleveland Heights), OH [OH0006]. ICA: OH0231.

CRIDERSVILLE (village)—Time Warner Cable. Now served by TIFFIN, OH [OH0050]. ICA: OH0120.

CROOKSVILLE (village)—Time Warner Cable. Now served by COLUMBUS, OH [OH0002]. ICA: OH0153.

CROWN CITY—Formerly served by Vital Communications. Now served by Armstrong Cable Services, ZELIENOPLE, PA [PA0053]. ICA: OH0260.

CRYSTAL LAKE MOBILE HOME PARK—Formerly served by Time Warner Cable. No longer in operation. ICA: OH0435.

CUMBERLAND—Formerly served by Almega Cable. No longer in operation. ICA: OH0294.

DEFIANCE—Arthur Mutual Telephone. Formerly [OH0455]. This cable system has converted to IPTV, 21980 SR 637, Defiance, OH 43512. Phone: 419-393-2233. Web Site: http://www.artelco.net. ICA: OH5222.
TV Market Ranking: Outside TV Markets (DEFIANCE).
Channel capacity: N.A. Channels available but not in use: N.A.
Limited Basic
Subscribers: N.A.
Fee: $69.95 installation; $19.95 monthly. Includes 31 channels.
Expanded Basic
Subscribers: 66.
Fee: $54.91 monthly. Includes 112 channels.
Variety
Subscribers: N.A.
Fee: $62.95 monthly. Includes 137 channels plus 50 music channels.
Cinemax
Subscribers: 13.
Fee: $11.95 monthly. Includes 7 channels.
Encore
Subscribers: 2.
Fee: $6.95 monthly. Includes 6 channels.
HBO
Subscribers: 14.
Fee: $14.95 monthly. Includes 8 channels.
Showtime/TMC
Subscribers: 4.
Fee: $11.95 monthly. Includes 10 channels.
Starz/Encore
Subscribers: 13.
Fee: $12.95 monthly. Includes 10 channels.
Internet Service
Operational: Yes, DSL.
Fee: $24.95-$59.95 monthly.
Telephone Service
Digital: Operational
General Manager: Eric Roughton.
Ownership: Arthur Mutual Telephone Co.

DEFIANCE—Arthur Mutual Telephone. This cable system has converted to IPTV. See DEFIANCE, OH [OH5222]. ICA: OH0455.

DEFIANCE—Time Warner Cable, 310 Jefferson Ave, Defiance, OH 43512. Phones: 614-481-5000; 419-784-1992. Fax: 419-782-2640. Web Site: http://www.timewarnercable.com. Also serves Auglaize Twp., Defiance Twp., Highland Twp., Ney, Noble Twp., Richland Twp. (Defiance County), Tiffin Twp. (Defiance County) & Washington Twp. (Defiance County). ICA: OH0047.
TV Market Ranking: Below 100 (Auglaize Twp. (portions), Highland Twp., Ney, Noble Twp., Tiffin Twp. (Defiance County) (portions), Washington Twp. (Defiance County)); Outside TV Markets (Auglaize Twp. (portions), DEFIANCE, Defiance Twp., Richland Twp. (Defiance County), Tiffin Twp. (Defiance County) (portions)). Franchise award date: May 1, 1964. Franchise expiration date: N.A. Began: May 1, 1964.
Channel capacity: N.A. Channels available but not in use: N.A.
Basic Service
Subscribers: 5,526.
Programming (received off-air): WBGU-TV (PBS) Bowling Green; WDFM-LP (IND) Defiance; WGTE-TV (PBS) Toledo; WLIO (CW, NBC) Lima; WNWO-TV (NBC, Retro TV) Toledo; WPTA (ABC, MNT, NBC) Fort Wayne; WTOL (CBS, MeTV) Toledo; WTVG (ABC, CW) Toledo; WUPW (FOX, TheCoolTV) Toledo; 17 FMs.
Programming (via satellite): C-SPAN; QVC; truTV; TV5MONDE USA; WGN America.
Fee: $29.95 installation; $21.25 monthly.

Expanded Basic Service 1
Subscribers: N.A.
Programming (via satellite): A&E; Animal Planet; BET; CNBC; CNN; Comedy Central; Disney Channel; E! HD; ESPN; ESPN2; FOX Sports Networks; FOX Sports Ohio/Sports Time Ohio; Freeform; FX; Golf Channel; HGTV; History; HLN; Lifetime; MSNBC; MTV; Nickelodeon; Outdoor Channel; Pop; Syfy; TBS; The Weather Channel; TLC; Travel Channel; USA Network.
Fee: $16.30 monthly.
Expanded Basic Service 2
Subscribers: N.A.
Programming (via satellite): TNT.
Fee: $2.00 monthly.
Digital Basic Service
Subscribers: N.A.
Programming (via satellite): BBC America; Bloomberg Television; Discovery Life Channel; ESPN Classic; ESPNews; Fox Sports 1; GSN; IFC; INSP; MTV Classic; National Geographic Channel; Nick Jr.; Outdoor Channel; Trinity Broadcasting Network (TBN); VH1 Country; WE tv.
Fee: $11.95 monthly.
Digital Expanded Basic Service
Subscribers: N.A.
Programming (via satellite): HITS (Headend In The Sky).
Fee: $6.95 monthly.
Pay Service 1
Pay Units: N.A.
Programming (via satellite): HBO.
Fee: $15.49 monthly.
Digital Pay Service 1
Pay Units: N.A.
Programming (via satellite): Cinemax (multiplexed); HBO (multiplexed); Showtime (multiplexed); Starz (multiplexed); Starz Encore (multiplexed); The Movie Channel (multiplexed).
Fee: $12.99 monthly (each).
Video-On-Demand: No
Pay-Per-View
iN DEMAND (delivered digitally).
Internet Service
Operational: Yes.
Broadband Service: Road Runner.
Fee: $42.95 monthly.
Telephone Service
Digital: Operational
Miles of Plant: 169.0 (coaxial); None (fiber optic). Homes passed: 11,158.
President: Rhonda Fraas. Area Manager: Brad Wakely. General Manager: John Ellingson. Customer Service Manager: Cindy Sierra.
Ownership: Time Warner Cable (MSO).

DELHI TWP.—Formerly served by Adelphia Communications. No longer in operation. ICA: OH0053.

DELLROY—Time Warner Cable. Now served by CLEVELAND (formerly Cleveland Heights), OH [OH0006]. ICA: OH0238.

DELPHOS—Time Warner Cable. Now served by TIFFIN, OH [OH0050]. ICA: OH0143.

DENMARK TWP.—Zito Media, 102 S Main St, PO Box 665, Coudersport, PA 16915. Phones: 814-260-9055; 800-365-6988. E-mail: info@zitomedia.com. Web Site: http://www.zitomedia.com. Also serves Ashtabula County (eastern portion), Dorset Twp., Jefferson Twp. (Ashtabula County), Monroe Twp. (Ashtabula County), Pierpont Twp., Plymouth Twp. (Ashtabula County) & Sheffield Twp. (Ashtabula County). ICA: OH0228.
TV Market Ranking: 79 (Ashtabula County (eastern portion) (portions)); Below 100 (Monroe Twp. (Ashtabula County), Ashtabula County (eastern portion) (portions)); Outside TV Markets (DENMARK TWP., Dorset Twp., Jefferson Twp. (Ashtabula County), Pierpont Twp., Plymouth Twp. (Ashtabula County), Sheffield Twp. (Ashtabula County), Ashtabula County (eastern portion) (portions)). Franchise award date: N.A. Franchise expiration date: N.A. Began: January 24, 1992.
Channel capacity: 36 (not 2-way capable). Channels available but not in use: N.A.
Basic Service
Subscribers: 87.
Programming (received off-air): WEWS-TV (ABC) Cleveland; WICU-TV (NBC) Erie; WJET-TV (ABC) Erie; WJW (Antenna TV, FOX) Cleveland; WKYC (NBC) Cleveland; WOIO (CBS, MeTV) Shaker Heights; WQLN (PBS) Erie; WSEE-TV (CBS, CW) Erie; WUAB (Bounce TV, MNT) Lorain.
Programming (via satellite): A&E; AMC; CNN; Discovery Channel; Disney Channel; ESPN; FOX Sports Ohio/Sports Time Ohio; Freeform; Nickelodeon; QVC; Spike TV; TBS; The Weather Channel; TNT; Turner Classic Movies; USA Network; VH1.
Fee: $49.95 installation; $21.71 monthly; $3.00 converter.
Pay Service 1
Pay Units: N.A.
Programming (via satellite): Cinemax; HBO; Showtime; The Movie Channel.
Fee: $11.00 monthly (Cinemax), $11.50 monthly (HBO), $12.95 monthly (Showtime/TMC).
Video-On-Demand: No
Internet Service
Operational: No.
Telephone Service
None
Miles of Plant: 53.0 (coaxial); None (fiber optic). Homes passed: 1,014.
President: James Rigas.
Ownership: Zito Media (MSO).

DESHLER—Time Warner Cable, 7800 Crescent Executive Dr, Charlotte, NC 28217. Phone: 614-481-5000 (Columbus office). Web Site: http://www.timewarnercable.com. Also serves Bartlow Twp., Hamler, Holgate, Marion Twp. (Henry County) & Pleasant Twp. (Henry County). ICA: OH0191.
TV Market Ranking: Below 100 (Bartlow Twp., DESHLER, Hamler, Holgate, Marion Twp. (Henry County), Pleasant Twp. (Henry County)). Franchise award date:

Ohio—Cable Systems

N.A. Franchise expiration date: N.A. Began: June 1, 1983.
Channel capacity: N.A. Channels available but not in use: N.A.

Basic Service
Subscribers: 556.
Programming (received off-air): WBGU-TV (PBS) Bowling Green; WDFM-LP (IND) Defiance; WFFT-TV (FOX, MeTV) Fort Wayne; WGTE-TV (PBS) Toledo; WKBD-TV (CW) Detroit; WLIO (CW, NBC) Lima; WLMB (IND) Toledo; WMNT-CD (Antenna TV, MNT) Toledo; WNWO-TV (NBC, Retro TV) Toledo; WTOL (CBS, MeTV) Toledo; WTVG (ABC, CW) Toledo; WUPW (FOX, TheCoolTV) Toledo.
Programming (via satellite): Freeform; Pop; QVC; WGN America.
Fee: $49.99 installation; $24.50 monthly.

Expanded Basic Service 1
Subscribers: N.A.
Programming (via satellite): A&E; AMC; Animal Planet; BET; Bravo; Cartoon Network; CMT; CNBC; CNN; C-SPAN; C-SPAN 2; Discovery Channel; Disney Channel; E! HD; ESPN; ESPN2; EVINE Live; EWTN Global Catholic Network; Food Network; Fox News Channel; FOX Sports Detroit; FOX Sports Ohio/Sports Time Ohio; FX; Golf Channel; Great American Country; Hallmark Channel; HGTV; History; HLN; Lifetime; MSNBC; MTV; NBCSN; Nickelodeon; Oxygen; Spike TV; Syfy; TBS; The Weather Channel; TLC; TNT; Travel Channel; Trinity Broadcasting Network (TBN); truTV; TV Land; Univision Studios; USA Network; VH1.
Fee: $22.95 monthly.

Digital Basic Service
Subscribers: N.A.
Programming (via satellite): BBC America; Bloomberg Television; Discovery Life Channel; Disney XD; DIY Network; ESPN Classic; ESPNews; Fox Sports 1; FYI; GSN; History International; IFC; INSP; MC; National Geographic Channel; Nick 2; Nick Jr.; Outdoor Channel; Sundance TV; TeenNick; Turner Classic Movies; WE tv.
Fee: $11.95 monthly.

Digital Expanded Basic Service
Subscribers: N.A.
Programming (via satellite): ART America; Fox Deportes; HITS (Headend In The Sky); RAI Italia; RTN; Telemundo; The Filipino Channel; TV Asia; TV5, La Television International.
Fee: $6.95 monthly.

Digital Pay Service 1
Pay Units: N.A.
Programming (via satellite): Cinemax (multiplexed); Flix (multiplexed); HBO (multiplexed); Showtime (multiplexed); Starz (multiplexed); Starz Encore (multiplexed); The Movie Channel (multiplexed).
Fee: $12.99 monthly (each).

Video-On-Demand: No
Pay-Per-View
iN DEMAND (delivered digitally); ESPN (delivered digitally).

Internet Service
Operational: Yes.
Broadband Service: Road Runner.
Fee: $44.95 monthly.

Telephone Service
Digital: Operational
Fee: $44.95 monthly
Miles of Plant: 43.0 (coaxial); None (fiber optic). Homes passed: 1,769.
President: Rhonda Fraas. Vice President & General Manager: Brad Wakely. Vice President, Engineering: Randy Hall. Vice President, Marketing: Mark Psigoda. Senior Accounting Director: Karen Goodfellow. Technical Operations Director: John Ellingson.

Public Affairs Director: Brian Young. Public Affairs Manager: Patrick McCauley.
Ownership: Time Warner Cable (MSO).

DOYLESTOWN—Doylestown Communications, 81 North Portage St, Doylestown, OH 44230. Phone: 330-658-2121. Fax: 330-658-2272. E-mail: info@doylestowntelephone.com. Web Site: http://www.doylestowncommunications.com.
Also serves Chippewa Twp., Marshallville & Rittman. ICA: OH0447. **Note:** This system is an overbuild.
TV Market Ranking: 8 (Chippewa Twp., DOYLESTOWN, Rittman). Franchise award date: N.A. Franchise expiration date: N.A. Began: June 1, 1997.
Channel capacity: N.A. Channels available but not in use: N.A.

Basic Service
Subscribers: 283.
Programming (received off-air): WAOH-CD (Retro TV) Akron; WBNX-TV (CW, Movies!, This TV) Akron; WCPO-TV (ABC, Escape) Cincinnati; WEAO (PBS) Akron; WJW (Antenna TV, FOX) Cleveland; WKRC-TV (CBS, CW) Cincinnati; WKYC (NBC) Cleveland; WQHS-DT (getTV, UNV) Cleveland; WRLM (IND) Canton; WUAB (Bounce TV, MNT) Lorain; WVIZ (PBS) Cleveland; WVPX-TV (ION) Akron.
Programming (via satellite): Pop.
Fee: $23.83 monthly.

Expanded Basic Service 1
Subscribers: N.A.
Programming (via satellite): A&E; AMC; Animal Planet; Bravo; Cartoon Network; CMT; CNBC; CNN; Comedy Central; C-SPAN; C-SPAN 2; Discovery Channel; Discovery Life Channel; Disney Channel; Disney XD; E! HD; ESPN; ESPN Classic; ESPN2; EWTN Global Catholic Network; Food Network; Fox News Channel; Fox Sports 1; FOX Sports Ohio/Sports Time Ohio; Freeform; FX; Great American Country; GSN; HGTV; History; HLN; Lifetime; MSNBC; MTV; National Geographic Channel; Nickelodeon; QVC; Spike TV; Syfy; TBS; The Weather Channel; TLC; TNT; Travel Channel; Trinity Broadcasting Network (TBN); truTV; Turner Classic Movies; TV Land; USA Network; VH1; WE tv; WGN America.
Fee: $42.95 monthly.

Digital Basic Service
Subscribers: N.A.
Programming (via satellite): BBC America; Bloomberg Television; Cooking Channel; Discovery Digital Networks; DIY Network; DMX Music; ESPNews; FXM; FYI; Golf Channel; Hallmark Channel; History International; LMN; NFL Network; Nick Jr.; Nicktoons; Outdoor Channel; TeenNick.
Fee: $14.95 monthly.

Digital Pay Service 1
Pay Units: N.A.
Programming (via satellite): Cinemax (multiplexed); Flix; HBO (multiplexed); Showtime (multiplexed); Starz (multiplexed); Starz Encore (multiplexed); Sundance TV; The Movie Channel (multiplexed).
Fee: $10.95 monthly (Cinemax, HBO, Showtime/TMC/Flix/Sundance or Starz/Encore).

Video-On-Demand: No
Internet Service
Operational: Yes.
Fee: $24.95 monthly.

Telephone Service
Digital: Operational
Homes passed: 3,800.

President: Thomas Brockman. General Manager: Barb Webb. Technical Operations Manager: Dennis Hartman.
Ownership: Doylestown Communications Inc.

DRESDEN (village)—Time Warner Cable. Now served by COLUMBUS, OH [OH0002]. ICA: OH0218.

DUNKIRK—Time Warner Cable. Now served by COLUMBUS, OH [OH0002]. ICA: OH0276.

EAST CLEVELAND—East Cleveland Cable TV & Communications LLC, 1395 Hayden Ave, East Cleveland, OH 44112-1850. Phone: 216-851-2215. Fax: 216-851-0231. E-mail: info@ecctv.tv. Web Site: http://www.ecctv.tv. Also serves Bratenahl. ICA: OH0066.
TV Market Ranking: 8 (Bratenahl, EAST CLEVELAND). Franchise award date: January 1, 1981. Franchise expiration date: N.A. Began: November 20, 1981.
Channel capacity: N.A. Channels available but not in use: N.A.

Basic Service
Subscribers: 1,679.
Programming (received off-air): WBNX-TV (CW, Movies!, This TV) Akron; WEWS-TV (ABC) Cleveland; WJW (Antenna TV, FOX) Cleveland; WKYC (NBC) Cleveland; WOIO (CBS, MeTV) Shaker Heights; WQHS-DT (getTV, UNV) Cleveland; WUAB (Bounce TV, MNT) Lorain.
Programming (via satellite): A&E; Animal Planet; BET; Bravo; Cartoon Network; CNBC; CNN; Comedy Central; Discovery Channel; Disney Channel; E! HD; ESPN; FOX Sports Ohio/Sports Time Ohio; Freeform; History; HLN; Lifetime; MTV; Nickelodeon; Pop; Syfy; TBS; The Weather Channel; TLC; TNT; Trinity Broadcasting Network (TBN); truTV; USA Network; VH1; WGN America.
Fee: $25.00 installation; $20.45 monthly; $1.75 converter.

Pay Service 1
Pay Units: N.A.
Programming (via satellite): Cinemax; HBO; Showtime; The Movie Channel.
Fee: $7.95 monthly (Cinemax), $10.95 monthly (Showtime/TMC), $11.95 monthly (HBO).

Video-On-Demand: No
Pay-Per-View
iN DEMAND.
Internet Service
Operational: Yes.
Fee: $39.95-$64.95 monthly.
Telephone Service
None
Miles of Plant: 50.0 (coaxial); None (fiber optic). Homes passed: 10,500.
Vice President & General Manager: James Gruttadaurio. Chief Technician & Plant Manager: Ron Kessler. Customer Service Manager: Wayne Barnes.
Ownership: East Cleveland Cable TV LLC.

EAST LIVERPOOL—Comcast Cable. Now served by NEW MIDDLETOWN, OH [OH0145]. ICA: OH0062.

EAST PALESTINE—Comcast Cable. Now served by NEW MIDDLETOWN, OH [OH0145]. ICA: OH0099.

EATON—Time Warner Cable. Now served by AMBERLEY (village), OH [OH0001]. ICA: OH0045.

EDON—Formerly served by Vital Communications. No longer in operation. ICA: OH0240.

ELYRIA—Time Warner Cable. Now served by CLEVELAND (formerly Cleveland Heights), OH [OH0006]. ICA: OH0026.

EMPIRE—Jefferson County Cable Inc, 116 South 4th St, Toronto, OH 43964-1368. Phones: 800-931-9392; 740-537-2214. Fax: 740-537-2802. Web Site: http://www.voiceflight.biz. Also serves Jefferson County (portions) & Stratton. ICA: OH0456.
TV Market Ranking: 90 (EMPIRE, Jefferson County (portions), Stratton).
Channel capacity: N.A. Channels available but not in use: N.A.

Basic Service
Subscribers: 218.
Fee: $30.00 installation; $14.03 monthly.
Vice President: Joann Conner.
Ownership: Jefferson County Cable Inc. (MSO).

EUREKA—Formerly served by Vital Communications. No longer in operation. ICA: OH0378.

FAIRBORN—Time Warner Cable. Now served by AMBERLEY (village), OH [OH0001]. ICA: OH0432.

FAIRFIELD (Butler County)—Formerly served by Adelphia Communications. Now served by Time Warner Cable, AMBERLEY (village), OH [OH0001]. ICA: OH0376.

FAYETTE—Formerly served by Adelphia Communications. Now served by Time Warner Cable, TIFFIN, OH [OH0050]. ICA: OH0194.

FINDLAY—Time Warner Cable. Now served by TIFFIN (formerly Fostoria), OH [OH0050]. ICA: OH0036.

FLUSHING—Comcast Cable. Now served by WHEELING, WV [WV0004]. ICA: OH0243.

FOREST (village)—Time Warner Cable. Now served by COLUMBUS, OH [OH0002]. ICA: OH0222.

FORT JENNINGS—FJ Communications, 65 West Third St, PO Box 146, Fort Jennings, OH 45844-0146. Phones: 800-362-2764; 419-286-2181. Fax: 419-286-2193. E-mail: fjtc@bright.net. Web Site: http://www.fjtelephone.com. Also serves Jackson Twp., Jennings Twp., Marion Twp. & Sugar Creek Twp. ICA: OH0253.
TV Market Ranking: Below 100 (FORT JENNINGS). Franchise award date: N.A. Franchise expiration date: N.A. Began: September 1, 1987.
Channel capacity: 55 (not 2-way capable). Channels available but not in use: N.A.

Basic Service
Subscribers: 536.
Programming (received off-air): WANE-TV (Antenna TV, CBS) Fort Wayne; WBGU-TV (PBS) Bowling Green; WBNS-TV (Antenna TV, CBS, Decades) Columbus; WLIO (CW, NBC) Lima; WLQP-LP (ABC) Lima; WNWO-TV (NBC, Retro TV) Toledo; WOHL-CD (ABC, CBS) Lima; WPTA (ABC, MNT, NBC) Fort Wayne; WTLW (IND) Lima; WTOL (CBS, MeTV) Toledo; WTVG (ABC, CW) Toledo; WUPW (FOX, TheCoolTV) Toledo.
Programming (via satellite): A&E; BTN; Cartoon Network; CNN; CW PLUS; Discov-

ery Channel; Disney Channel; ESPN; ESPN Classic; ESPN2; EWTN Global Catholic Network; Food Network; Fox News Channel; FOX Sports Ohio/Sports Time Ohio; Freeform; FX; Hallmark Channel; Lifetime; MSNBC; MTV; National Geographic Channel; TBS; The Weather Channel; TLC; TNT; Travel Channel; Turner Classic Movies; TV Land; USA Network; VH1; WGN America.
Fee: $24.50 installation; $44.50 monthly.
Expanded Basic Service 1
Subscribers: N.A.
Programming (via satellite): CMT; Comedy Central; History; Nickelodeon; Spike TV.
Fee: $6.00 monthly.
Pay Service 1
Pay Units: N.A.
Programming (via satellite): HBO; Showtime; The Movie Channel.
Fee: $9.95 monthly (Showtime or TMC), $11.95 monthly (HBO).
Video-On-Demand: No
Internet Service
Operational: No, DSL.
Telephone Service
Digital: Operational
Miles of Plant: 93.0 (coaxial); 54.0 (fiber optic). Homes passed: 925.
General Manager: Michael Metzger. Chief Technician: David Will.
Ownership: Fort Jennings Telephone Co.

FORT RECOVERY—Comcast Cable. Now served by HENDRICKS COUNTY (portions), IN [IN0001]. ICA: OH0324.

FRANKFORT—Formerly served by Adelphia Communications. Now served by Time Warner Cable, CHILLICOTHE, OH [OH0033]. ICA: OH0227.

FRANKLIN FURNACE—Formerly served by Adelphia Communications. Now served by Time Warner Cable, ASHLAND, KY [KY0326]. ICA: OH0325.

FRAZEYBURG (village)—Time Warner Cable. Now served by COLUMBUS, OH [OH0002]. ICA: OH0271.

FREDERICKTOWN (village)—Time Warner Cable. Now served by COLUMBUS, OH [OH0002]. ICA: OH0326.

FREEPORT TWP.—Formerly served by Vital Communications. No longer in operation. ICA: OH0295.

FREMONT—Time Warner Cable. Now served by TIFFIN (formerly Fostoria), OH [OH0050]. ICA: OH0085.

FRIENDSHIP—Time Warner Cable. Now served by PORTSMOUTH, OH [OH0035]. ICA: OH0224.

FULTON TWP.—Formerly served by Adelphia Communications. Now served by Time Warner Cable, TIFFIN, OH [OH0050]. ICA: OH0327.

GALION—Time Warner Cable. Now served by COLUMBUS, OH [OH0002]. ICA: OH0077.

GALLIPOLIS—Zito Media, 102 S Main St, PO Box 665, Coudersport, PA 16915. Phones: 814-260-9055; 800-365-6988. E-mail: info@zitomedia.com. Web Site: http://www.zitomedia.com. Also serves Green Twp. (Gallia County), Springfield Twp. (Gallia County) & Vinton (village). ICA: OH0178.
TV Market Ranking: 36 (GALLIPOLIS, Green Twp. (Gallia County), Springfield Twp. (Gallia County), Vinton (village)). Franchise award date: N.A. Franchise expiration date: N.A. Began: January 1, 1984.
Channel capacity: N.A. Channels available but not in use: N.A.
Basic Service
Subscribers: 69.
Programming (received off-air): WCHS-TV (ABC, Antenna TV) Charleston; WLPX-TV (ION) Charleston; WOUB-TV (PBS) Athens; WOWK-TV (CBS) Huntington; WQCW (CW) Portsmouth; WSAZ-TV (MNT, NBC, This TV) Huntington; WVAH-TV (FOX, The Country Network) Charleston; WVPB-TV (PBS) Huntington.
Programming (via satellite): A&E; AMC; Cartoon Network; CMT; CNN; Discovery Channel; Disney Channel; ESPN; ESPN2; Freeform; FX; History; HLN; Lifetime; MTV; Nickelodeon; QVC; Spike TV; Syfy; TBS; The Weather Channel; TNT; Trinity Broadcasting Network (TBN); USA Network; VH1; WGN America.
Fee: $49.95 installation; $47.90 monthly.
Pay Service 1
Pay Units: N.A.
Programming (via satellite): Cinemax; HBO; Showtime.
Fee: $10.95 monthly (Cinemax or Showtime), $11.95 monthly (HBO).
Video-On-Demand: No
Internet Service
Operational: No.
Telephone Service
None
Miles of Plant: 43.0 (coaxial); None (fiber optic). Homes passed: 2,150.
President: James Rigas.
Ownership: Zito Media (MSO).

GERMANTOWN (town)—Time Warner Cable. Now served by AMBERLEY (village), OH [OH0001]. ICA: OH0158.

GLENCOE—Formerly served by Comcast Cable. No longer in operation. ICA: OH0298.

GLENMONT—Time Warner Cable. Now served by CLEVELAND (formerly Cleveland Heights), OH [OH0006]. ICA: OH0300.

GOSHEN TWP. (Clermont County)—Time Warner Cable. Now served by AMBERLEY (village), OH [OH0001]. ICA: OH0129.

GRAFTON—Formerly served by Grafton Cable Communications. Now served by GLW Broadband, WELLINGTON, OH [OH0189]. ICA: OH0133.

GREEN—Time Warner Cable. Now served by CLEVELAND (formerly Cleveland Heights), OH [OH0006]. ICA: OH0031.

GREEN MEADOWS—Formerly served by Time Warner Cable. No longer in operation. ICA: OH0286.

GREEN TWP. (Hamilton County)—Time Warner Cable. Now served by AMBERLEY (village), OH [OH0001]. ICA: OH0032.

GREENFIELD—Formerly served by Adelphia Communications. Now served by Time Warner Cable, COLUMBUS, OH [OH0002]. ICA: OH0157.

Cable Systems—Ohio

FULLY SEARCHABLE • CONTINUOUSLY UPDATED • DISCOUNT RATES FOR PRINT PURCHASERS
For more information call **800-771-9202** or visit **www.warren-news.com**

GREENFIELD ESTATES—Formerly served by World Cable. No longer in operation. ICA: OH0328.

GREENVILLE—Time Warner Cable. Now served by AMBERLEY (village), OH [OH0001]. ICA: OH0076.

GREENWOOD (village)—Formerly served by Adelphia Communications. No longer in operation. ICA: OH0329.

GUERNSEY COUNTY (portions)—Formerly served by Time Warner Cable. No longer in operation. ICA: OH0396.

GUILFORD LAKE—Formerly served by Time Warner Cable. No longer in operation. ICA: OH0220.

GUYSVILLE—Formerly served by Adelphia Communications. Now served by Time Warner Cable, BEVERLY, OH [OH0175]. ICA: OH0265.

HAMILTON—Time Warner Cable. Now served by AMBERLEY (village), OH [OH0001]. ICA: OH0022.

HANNIBAL—Crystal Broadband Networks, PO Box 180336, Chicago, IL 60618. Phones: 817-685-9588; 630-206-0447. E-mail: sales@crystalbn.com. Web Site: http://crystalbn.com. Also serves Clarington, Grandview Twp., Lee Twp. (Monroe County), Monroe County (eastern portion), New Matamoras, Ohio Twp. (Monroe County) & Sardis. ICA: OH0251.
TV Market Ranking: 90 (Clarington, HANNIBAL, Lee Twp. (Monroe County), Ohio Twp. (Monroe County), Sardis); Below 100 (New Matamoras). Franchise award date: N.A. Franchise expiration date: N.A. Began: September 1, 1959.
Channel capacity: N.A. Channels available but not in use: N.A.
Basic Service
Subscribers: 339.
Programming (received off-air): KDKA-TV (CBS, Decades) Pittsburgh; WBOY-TV (ABC, NBC) Clarksburg; WNPB-TV (PBS) Morgantown; WOUC-TV (PBS) Cambridge; WPNT (MNT) Pittsburgh; WPXI (MeTV, NBC) Pittsburgh; WTAE-TV (ABC, This TV) Pittsburgh; WTOV-TV (MeTV, NBC) Steubenville; WTRF-TV (ABC, CBS, MNT) Wheeling; WVFX (CW, FOX) Clarksburg; allband FM.
Programming (via satellite): QVC; TBS; WGN America.
Fee: $47.50 installation; $55.13 monthly; $.73 converter.
Expanded Basic Service 1
Subscribers: N.A.
Programming (via satellite): A&E; AMC; Animal Planet; CMT; CNN; Discovery Channel; Disney Channel; ESPN; ESPN2; Fox News Channel; Fox Sports 1; FOX Sports Ohio/Sports Time Ohio; Freeform; FX; HGTV; History; Lifetime; MSNBC; MTV; Nick Jr.; Nickelodeon; Root Sports Pittsburgh; Spike TV; The Weather Channel; TLC; TNT; TV Land; USA Network; VH1.
Fee: $8.56 monthly.
Digital Basic Service
Subscribers: N.A.
Programming (via satellite): BBC America; Bloomberg Television; CMT; Destination America; Discovery Kids Channel; Discovery Life Channel; Disney XD; ESPN Classic; ESPNews; Fuse; FXM; Golf Channel; Investigation Discovery; LMN; LOGO; MC; MTV Classic; MTV Hits; MTV Jams; MTV2; National Geographic Channel; Nick 2; Nicktoons; OWN: Oprah Winfrey Network; Science Channel; TeenNick; Tr3s; Trinity Broadcasting Network (TBN); Turner Classic Movies; VH1 Soul; WE tv.
Digital Expanded Basic Service
Subscribers: N.A.
Programming (via satellite): FYI; GSN; History International; IFC; NBCSN; Outdoor Channel.
Digital Pay Service 1
Pay Units: N.A.
Programming (via satellite): Cinemax (multiplexed); HBO (multiplexed); Showtime (multiplexed); Starz (multiplexed); Starz Encore (multiplexed); The Movie Channel (multiplexed).
Fee: $11.95 monthly (Cinemax, HBO, Showtime/TMC or Starz/Encore).
Video-On-Demand: No
Pay-Per-View
iN DEMAND (delivered digitally); Playboy TV (delivered digitally); Club Jenna (delivered digitally); Fresh (delivered digitally).
Internet Service
Operational: Yes.
Broadband Service: Road Runner.
Fee: $44.95 monthly.
Telephone Service
None
Miles of Plant: 39.0 (coaxial); 15.0 (fiber optic). Homes passed: 1,609.
General Manager: Ron Page. Program Manager: Shawn Smith.
Ownership: Crystal Broadband Networks (MSO).

HARRISON TWP. (Carroll County)—Time Warner Cable. Now served by CLEVELAND (formerly Cleveland Heights), OH [OH0006]. ICA: OH0249.

HAYDEN HEIGHTS—Formerly served by Time Warner Cable. No longer in operation. ICA: OH0301.

HICKSVILLE—Mediacom, 109 East 5th St, Ste A, Auburn, IN 46706. Phones: 845-695-2762; 260-927-3015. Fax: 260-347-4433. Web Site: http://www.mediacomcable.com. Also serves Antwerp. ICA: OH0169.
TV Market Ranking: 82 (Antwerp, HICKSVILLE). Franchise award date: N.A. Franchise expiration date: N.A. Began: March 4, 1981.
Channel capacity: N.A. Channels available but not in use: N.A.

2017 Edition

D-589

Ohio—Cable Systems

Basic Service
Subscribers: 498.
Programming (received off-air): WANE-TV (Antenna TV, CBS) Fort Wayne; WBGU-TV (PBS) Bowling Green; WFFT-TV (FOX, MeTV) Fort Wayne; WFWA (PBS) Fort Wayne; WINM (IND) Angola; WISE-TV (CW) Fort Wayne; WLIO (CW, NBC) Lima; WNWO-TV (NBC, Retro TV) Toledo; WPTA (ABC, MNT, NBC) Fort Wayne; WTVG (ABC, CW) Toledo.
Programming (via satellite): TBS.
Fee: $45.00 installation; $48.00 monthly.

Expanded Basic Service 1
Subscribers: N.A.
Programming (via satellite): A&E; AMC; Animal Planet; Bloomberg Television; Cartoon Network; CMT; CNBC; CNN; Comedy Central; C-SPAN; Discovery Channel; Disney Channel; E! HD; ESPN; ESPN2; Fox Sports 1; FOX Sports Midwest; Freeform; FX; FXM; FYI; Hallmark Channel; HGTV; History; HLN; Lifetime; LMN; MSNBC; MTV; Nickelodeon; Pop; QVC; Radar Channel; Spike TV; Syfy; The Weather Channel; TLC; TNT; Travel Channel; TV Land; USA Network; VH1; WGN America.
Fee: $34.00 monthly.

Digital Basic Service
Subscribers: N.A.
Programming (via satellite): BBC America; Discovery Digital Networks; DMX Music; ESPN Classic; Golf Channel; GSN; IFC; Turner Classic Movies.
Fee: $9.00 monthly.

Digital Pay Service 1
Pay Units: N.A.
Programming (via satellite): Cinemax (multiplexed); HBO (multiplexed); Showtime (multiplexed); Starz (multiplexed); Starz Encore (multiplexed); The Movie Channel (multiplexed).
Fee: $11.95 monthly (HBO, Cinemax, Showtime/TMC or Starz/Encore).

Video-On-Demand: Yes

Pay-Per-View
iN DEMAND (delivered digitally); Playboy TV (delivered digitally); Pleasure (delivered digitally); Fresh (delivered digitally); Shorteez (delivered digitally).

Internet Service
Operational: Yes.
Broadband Service: Mediacom High Speed Internet.
Fee: $59.95 installation; $40.95 monthly.

Telephone Service
Digital: Operational
Fee: $39.95 monthly
Miles of Plant: 40.0 (coaxial); 10.0 (fiber optic). Homes passed: 2,130.
Vice President, Financial Reporting: Kenneth J. Kohrs. Operations Director: Joe Poffenberger. Technical Operations Manager: Craig Grey.
Ownership: Mediacom LLC (MSO).

HIDE-A-WAY HILLS—Time Warner Cable. Now served by COLUMBUS, OH [OH0002]. ICA: OH0229.

HILLSBORO—Time Warner Cable. Now served by AMBERLEY (village), OH [OH0001]. ICA: OH0110.

HOPEDALE—Time Warner Cable, 7800 Crescent Executive Dr, Charlotte, NC 28217. Phones: 330-633-1874; 330-633-9203. Web Site: http://www.timewarnercable.com. ICA: OH0281.

TV Market Ranking: 90 (HOPEDALE). Franchise award date: N.A. Franchise expiration date: N.A. Began: April 1, 1975.
Channel capacity: N.A. Channels available but not in use: N.A.

Basic Service
Subscribers: 99.
Programming (received off-air): KDKA-TV (CBS, Decades) Pittsburgh; WOUC-TV (PBS) Cambridge; WPGH-TV (Antenna TV, FOX, The Country Network) Pittsburgh; WPXI (MeTV, NBC) Pittsburgh; WQED (PBS) Pittsburgh; WTAE-TV (ABC, This TV) Pittsburgh; WTOV-TV (MeTV, NBC) Steubenville; WTRF-TV (ABC, CBS, MNT) Wheeling; WVPX-TV (ION) Akron.
Programming (via satellite): Discovery Channel; Freeform; Hallmark Channel; TBS.
Fee: $49.99 installation; $24.50 monthly; $3.40 converter.

Expanded Basic Service 1
Subscribers: N.A.
Programming (via satellite): A&E; AMC; Animal Planet; Cartoon Network; CNBC; CNN; Disney Channel; ESPN; ESPN2; Fox News Channel; HLN; MoviePlex; Spike TV; TNT; USA Network.
Fee: $18.36 monthly.

Pay Service 1
Pay Units: N.A.
Programming (via satellite): HBO; Showtime; Starz; Starz Encore.
Fee: $4.00 monthly (Encore), $8.95 monthly (Starz), $14.95 monthly (HBO or Showtime).

Video-On-Demand: No

Internet Service
Operational: Yes.
Broadband Service: RoadRunner.

Telephone Service
None
Miles of Plant: 8.0 (coaxial); None (fiber optic). Homes passed: 419.
President: Stephen Fry. Area Vice President: Scot Miller. Vice President, Engineering: Al Costanzi. Vice President, Marketing: Patrick Burke. Vice President, Public Affairs: William Jasso. Government & Media Relations Director: Chris Thomas. Senior Accounting Director: Karen Goodfellow.
Ownership: Time Warner Cable (MSO).

HOWARD—Formerly served by Time Warner Cable. No longer in operation. ICA: OH0397.

HUBBARD TWP. (Trumbull County)—Formerly served by Northeast Cable TV. No longer in operation. ICA: OH0383.

HUNTINGTON TWP.—Formerly served by Adelphia Communications. Now served by Time Warner Cable, CHILLICOTHE, OH [OH0033]. ICA: OH0174.

IRONDALE—Comcast Cable. Now served by NEW MIDDLETOWN, OH [OH0145]. ICA: OH0285.

IRONTON—Formerly served by Comcast Cable. No longer in operation. ICA: OH0073.

JACKSON—Time Warner Cable, 1266 Dublin Rd, Columbus, OH 43215-1008. Phones: 614-255-4997; 614-481-5000. Fax: 614-481-5052. Web Site: http://www.timewarnercable.com. Also serves Albany, Beaver (village), Beaver Twp., Coalton, Dundas, Hamden, Liberty Twp. (Jackson County), Lick Twp. (Jackson County), Madison Twp. (Jackson County), Marion Twp. (Pike County), McArthur, Minford, Oak Hill, Union Twp. (Pike County), Wellston & Zaleski. ICA: OH0098.

TV Market Ranking: 27 (Beaver (village), Beaver Twp., Coalton, Dundas, Hamden, JACKSON, Liberty Twp. (Jackson County), Lick Twp. (Jackson County), Marion Twp. (Pike County), McArthur, Minford, Oak Hill, Union Twp. (Pike County), Wellston, Zaleski); 36 (Madison Twp. (Jackson County)); Outside TV Markets (Albany). Franchise award date: June 9, 1968. Franchise expiration date: N.A. Began: March 1, 1969.
Channel capacity: 65 (operating 2-way). Channels available but not in use: N.A.

Basic Service
Subscribers: 7,380.
Programming (received off-air): WBNS-TV (Antenna TV, CBS, Decades) Columbus; WCHS-TV (ABC, Antenna TV) Charleston; WCMH-TV (MeTV, NBC) Columbus; WOUB-TV (PBS) Athens; WOWK-TV (CBS) Huntington; WQCW (CW) Portsmouth; WSAZ-TV (MNT, NBC, This TV) Huntington; WVAH-TV (FOX, The Country Network) Charleston; WWHO (CW) Chillicothe; 16 FMs.
Programming (via satellite): C-SPAN; C-SPAN 2; EWTN Global Catholic Network; Freeform; INSP; Pop; TBS; WGN America.
Fee: $29.95 installation; $21.25 monthly.

Expanded Basic Service 1
Subscribers: N.A.
Programming (via satellite): A&E; AMC; Animal Planet; BET; Bravo; Cartoon Network; CMT; CNBC; CNN; Comedy Central; Discovery Channel; Disney Channel; Disney XD; E! HD; ESPN; ESPN2; EVINE Live; Food Network; Fox News Channel; Fox Sports 1; FOX Sports Ohio/Sports Time Ohio; FX; FYI; Golf Channel; Great American Country; Hallmark Channel; HGTV; History; HLN; Lifetime; MSNBC; MTV; National Geographic Channel; Nickelodeon; Outdoor Channel; Oxygen; QVC; Spike TV; Syfy; The Weather Channel; TLC; TNT; Travel Channel; truTV; TV Land; Univision Studios; USA Network; VH1; WE tv.

Digital Basic Service
Subscribers: N.A.
Programming (via satellite): BBC America; Bloomberg Television; CNBC; Discovery Life Channel; DIY Network; ESPN Classic; ESPNews; Fuse; FXM; GSN; History International; MC; NBCSN; Trinity Broadcasting Network (TBN); Turner Classic Movies.

Digital Expanded Basic Service
Subscribers: N.A.
Programming (via satellite): MTV Classic; Nick Jr.; Nicktoons; VH1 Country.

Digital Pay Service 1
Pay Units: N.A.
Programming (via satellite): ART America; Cinemax (multiplexed); Flix; HBO (multiplexed); HITS (Headend In The Sky); RAI Italia; Showtime (multiplexed); Starz (multiplexed); Starz Encore (multiplexed); Sundance TV; The Filipino Channel; The Movie Channel (multiplexed); TV Asia; TV5, La Television International; Zee TV.
Fee: $12.99 monthly (each).

Video-On-Demand: Yes

Pay-Per-View
Urban Xtra (delivered digitally); Hot Choice (delivered digitally); Fresh (delivered digitally); Playboy TV (delivered digitally).

Internet Service
Operational: Yes. Began: June 1, 2002.
Broadband Service: Road Runner.
Fee: $44.95 monthly.

Telephone Service
Digital: Operational
Fee: $44.95 monthly

Miles of Plant: 3,180.0 (coaxial); 1,496.0 (fiber optic). Homes passed: 87,407.
President: Rhonda Fraas. Vice President & General Manager: David Kreiman. Vice President, Public Affairs: Mary Jo Green. Vice President, Engineering: Randy Hall. Vice President, Marketing: Mark Psigoda. Technical Operations Director: Jim Cavender. Government Affairs Director: Steve Cuckler.
Ownership: Time Warner Cable (MSO).

JASPER (town)—Time Warner Cable. Now served by CHILLICOTHE, OH [OH0033]. ICA: OH0442.

JEROMESVILLE (village)—Time Warner Cable. Now served by CLEVELAND (formerly Cleveland Heights), OH [OH0006]. ICA: OH0266.

JEWETT—Time Warner Cable, 7800 Crescent Executive Dr, Charlotte, NC 28217. Phones: 330-633-1874; 330-633-9203. Web Site: http://www.timewarnercable.com. ICA: OH0283.
TV Market Ranking: 90 (JEWETT). Franchise award date: N.A. Franchise expiration date: N.A. Began: August 1, 1971.
Channel capacity: N.A. Channels available but not in use: N.A.

Basic Service
Subscribers: 58.
Programming (received off-air): KDKA-TV (CBS, Decades) Pittsburgh; WOUC-TV (PBS) Cambridge; WPGH-TV (Antenna TV, FOX, The Country Network) Pittsburgh; WPXI (MeTV, NBC) Pittsburgh; WQED (PBS) Pittsburgh; WTAE-TV (ABC, This TV) Pittsburgh; WTOV-TV (MeTV, NBC) Steubenville; WTRF-TV (ABC, CBS, MNT) Wheeling; WVPX-TV (ION) Akron; WYTV (ABC, MNT) Youngstown.
Programming (via satellite): Discovery Channel; QVC; TBS.
Fee: $49.99 installation; $24.50 monthly; $3.40 converter.

Expanded Basic Service 1
Subscribers: N.A.
Programming (via satellite): A&E; AMC; Animal Planet; Cartoon Network; CNBC; CNN; C-SPAN; E! HD; ESPN; ESPN2; Fox News Channel; Freeform; HGTV; ION Television; Lifetime; MoviePlex; MTV; Nickelodeon; Spike TV; TNT; Trinity Broadcasting Network (TBN); USA Network.
Fee: $22.46 monthly.

Pay Service 1
Pay Units: N.A.
Programming (via satellite): HBO; Showtime; Starz; Starz Encore.
Fee: $4.00 monthly (Encore), $14.95 monthly (HBO, Showtime or Starz).

Video-On-Demand: No

Internet Service
Operational: No.

Telephone Service
None
Miles of Plant: 5.0 (coaxial); None (fiber optic).
President: Stephen Fry. Area Vice President: Scott Miller. Vice President, Marketing: Patrick Burke. Vice President, Engineering: Al Costanzi. Vice President, Public Affairs: William Jasso. Senior Accounting Director: Karen Goodfellow. Government & Media Relations Director: Chris Thomas.
Ownership: Time Warner Cable (MSO).

KALIDA—Kalida Telephone Co, 121 East Main St, PO Box 267, Kalida, OH 45853. Phone: 419-532-3218. Fax: 419-532-3300.

E-mail: ktc@kalidatel.com. Web Site: http://www.kalidatel.com. Also serves Greensburg Twp., Jackson Twp. (Putnam County), Jennings Twp. (Putnam County), Perry Twp. (Putnam County), Sugar Creek Twp. (Putnam County) & Union Twp. (Putnam County). ICA: OH0277.

TV Market Ranking: Below 100 (Greensburg Twp., Jackson Twp. (Putnam County), Jennings Twp. (Putnam County), KALIDA, Perry Twp. (Putnam County), Sugar Creek Twp. (Putnam County), Union Twp. (Putnam County)). Franchise award date: December 7, 1981. Franchise expiration date: N.A. Began: May 1, 1985.

Channel capacity: 45 (operating 2-way). Channels available but not in use: N.A.

Basic Service
Subscribers: 783.
Programming (received off-air): WANE-TV (Antenna TV, CBS) Fort Wayne; WBGU-TV (PBS) Bowling Green; WBNS-TV (Antenna TV, CBS, Decades) Columbus; WLIO (CW, NBC) Lima; WNWO-TV (NBC, Retro TV) Toledo; WOHL-CD (ABC, CBS) Lima; WPTA (ABC, MNT, NBC) Fort Wayne; WTLW (IND) Lima; WTOL (CBS, MeTV) Toledo; WTVG (ABC, CW) Toledo; WUPW (FOX, TheCoolTV) Toledo; 1 FM.
Programming (via satellite): A&E; BTN; Cartoon Network; CNN; CW PLUS; Discovery Channel; Disney Channel; ESPN; ESPN Classic; ESPN2; EWTN Global Catholic Network; Food Network; Fox News Channel; FOX Sports Ohio/Sports Time Ohio; Freeform; FX; Hallmark Channel; Lifetime; MSNBC; MTV; National Geographic Channel; TBS; The Weather Channel; TLC; TNT; Travel Channel; Turner Classic Movies; TV Land; USA Network; VH1; WGN America.
Fee: $24.50 installation; $44.45 monthly.

Expanded Basic Service 1
Subscribers: N.A.
Programming (via satellite): CMT; Comedy Central; History; Nickelodeon; Spike TV.
Fee: $6.00 monthly.

Digital Basic Service
Subscribers: N.A.
Programming (via satellite): BBC America; Bloomberg Television; CMT; Destination America; Discovery Kids Channel; Disney XD; DMX Music; ESPN Classic; Fox Sports 1; Golf Channel; HGTV; IFC; Investigation Discovery; LMN; MTV Classic; MTV2; National Geographic Channel; NBCSN; Nick Jr.; Nicktoons; OWN; Oprah Winfrey Network; Science Channel; TeenNick; WE tv.
Fee: $13.50 monthly.

Digital Expanded Basic Service
Subscribers: N.A.
Programming (via satellite): Discovery Life Channel; ESPNews; Fuse; FXM; FYI; GSN; History International; Outdoor Channel.
Fee: $3.50 monthly.

Pay Service 1
Pay Units: N.A.
Programming (via satellite): HBO; Showtime; The Movie Channel.
Fee: $9.95 monthly (Showtime or TMC); $11.95 monthly (HBO).

Digital Pay Service 1
Pay Units: N.A.
Programming (via satellite): Cinemax (multiplexed); HBO (multiplexed); Showtime (multiplexed); Starz (multiplexed); Starz Encore (multiplexed); The Movie Channel (multiplexed).
Fee: $5.95 monthly (Encore), $8.95 monthly (Cinemax), $9.95 monthly (Showtime or TMC) and $11.95 monthly (HBO), $12.95 monthly (Starz/Encore), $13.95 monthly (Showtime/TMC).

Video-On-Demand: No

Internet Service
Operational: No, DSL & dial-up.

Telephone Service
Analog: Operational
Miles of Plant: 35.0 (coaxial); None (fiber optic). Homes passed: 1,005.
Treasurer & General Manager: Chris J. Phillips. Chief Technician: Chris Hoffman. Business Manager: Sue Gerdeman.
Ownership: Kalida Telephone Co.

KENT—Time Warner Cable. Now served by CLEVELAND (formerly Cleveland Heights), OH [OH0006]. ICA: OH0034.

KENTON—Time Warner Cable. Now served by COLUMBUS, OH [OH0002]. ICA: OH0128.

KETTERING—Time Warner Cable. Now served by AMBERLEY (village), OH [OH0001]. ICA: OH0010.

KEY—Formerly served by Comcast Cable. No longer in operation. ICA: OH0441.

KINGSTON—Formerly served by Adelphia Communications. Now served by Time Warner Cable, CHILLICOTHE, OH [OH0033]. ICA: OH0185.

KINSMAN—Formerly served by Cebridge Connections. Now served by Armstrong Cable Services, VERNON TWP., OH [OH0246]. ICA: OH0282.

KIRKERSVILLE (village)—Time Warner Cable. Now served by COLUMBUS, OH [OH0002]. ICA: OH0170.

KNOX TWP. (Jefferson County)—Suddenlink Communications, 520 Maryville Centre Dr, Ste 300, St. Louis, MO 63141. Phone: 314-315-9400. Web Site: http://www.suddenlink.com. Also serves Island Creek Twp. (Jefferson County) & Saline Twp. ICA: OH0239.

TV Market Ranking: 10,90 (Island Creek Twp. (Jefferson County), KNOX TWP. (JEFFERSON COUNTY), Saline Twp.). Franchise award date: N.A. Franchise expiration date: N.A. Began: March 1, 1990.

Channel capacity: 62 (not 2-way capable). Channels available but not in use: N.A.

Basic Service
Subscribers: 172.
Programming (received off-air): KDKA-TV (CBS, Decades) Pittsburgh; WPGH-TV (Antenna TV, FOX, The Country Network) Pittsburgh; WPNT (MNT) Pittsburgh; WPXI (MeTV, NBC) Pittsburgh; WQED (PBS) Pittsburgh; WTAE-TV (ABC, This TV) Pittsburgh; WTOV-TV (MeTV, NBC) Steubenville; WTRF-TV (ABC, CBS, MNT) Wheeling.
Programming (via satellite): QVC; TBS.
Fee: $59.95 installation; $22.99 monthly; $1.95 converter.

Expanded Basic Service 1
Subscribers: N.A.
Programming (via satellite): A&E; AMC; CNBC; CNN; C-SPAN; Discovery Channel; Disney Channel; ESPN; Freeform; History; HLN; Lifetime; MTV; Nickelodeon; Root Sports Pittsburgh; Spike TV; Syfy; The Weather Channel; TNT; TV Land; USA Network; VH1.
Fee: $20.00 monthly.

Pay Service 1
Pay Units: N.A.
Programming (via satellite): Cinemax; HBO; Showtime; The Movie Channel.
Fee: $11.00 monthly (Cinemax or HBO), $12.95 monthly (Showtime/TMC).

Internet Service
Operational: No.

Telephone Service
None
Miles of Plant: 33.0 (coaxial); None (fiber optic). Homes passed: 811.
Vice President, Corporate Finance: Michael Pflantz. General Manager: Terry Dickerhoof. Chief Technician: Tom Beat.
Ownership: Cequel Communications Holdings I LLC (MSO).

LA RUE (village)—Time Warner Cable. Now served by COLUMBUS, OH [OH0002]. ICA: OH0242.

LANCASTER—Time Warner Cable. Now served by COLUMBUS, OH [OH0002]. ICA: OH0039.

LEBANON—Cincinnati Bell Fioptics TV. This cable system has converted to IPTV, 221 East Fourth St, Cincinnati, OH 45202. Phones: 888-246-2355; 513-565-2210; 513-397-9900. Web Site: http://www.cincinnatibell.com/fioptics. Also serves Brookville, Cedar Grove, Guilford, Harrison, Kelso Twp., Lawrenceburg, Logan, Miller, New Trenton, Springfield Twp., West Harrison (Dearborn County), West Harrison (Franklin County) & Whitewater Twp., IN; Alexandria, Bellevue, California, Cold Spring, Covington, Crescent Springs, Crestview, Crestview Hills, Dayton, Edgewood, Elsmere, Erlanger, Florence, Fort Mitchell, Fort Thomas, Fort Wright, Highland Heights, Independence, Lakeside Park, Ludlow, Mason, Melbourne, Mentor, Newport, Park Hills, Silver Grove, Southgate, Taylor Mill, Union Twp., Villa Hills, Walton, Warsaw, Wilder & Woodlawn, KY; Addyston (village), Amberley (village), Amelia (village), Anderson Twp., Arlington Heights (village), Batavia (village), Batavia Twp., Bethel (village), Blue Ash, Butlerville (village), Carlisle (village) (Montgomery County), Carlisle (village) (Warren County), Cherry Grove, Cheviot, Cincinnati, Clark Twp., Clearcreek Twp., Cleves, Colerain Twp., Columbia Twp., Columbus, Corwin (village), Crosby Twp., Deer Park, Deerfield Twp., Delhi Twp., Elmwood Place (village), Evendale (village), Fairfax (village), Fairfield (Butler County), Fairfield (Hamilton County), Fairfield Twp., Forest Park, Franklin (village), Franklin Twp., Glendale, Glendale (village), Golf Manor (village), Goshen Twp., Green Twp., Greenhills (village), Hamilton, Hamilton Twp. (Butler County), Hamilton Twp. (Warren County), Hanover Twp., Harlan Twp., Harrison Twp., Indian Hill, Jackson Twp., Lemon Twp., Liberty Twp., Lincoln Heights (village), Lockland (village), Loveland (Clermont County), Loveland (Hamilton County), Loveland (Warren County), Madeira, Maineville (village), Mariemont (village), Mason, Miami Twp., Middletown (Butler County), Middletown (Warren County), Milford (Clermont County), Milford (Hamilton County), Milford Twp., Millville, Monroe (Butler County), Monroe (Warren County), Monroe Twp., Montgomery, Morgan, Morrow (village), Mount Healthy, New Miami (village), New Richmond (village), Newtonsville (village), Newtown (village), North Bend (village), North College Hill, Norwood, Ohio Twp., Owensville (village), Pierce Twp., Pike Twp., Pleasant Plain (village), Reading, Reily Twp., Ross Twp., Seven Mile, Sharonville (Butler County), Sharonville (Hamilton County), Silverton (village), Somerville (village), South Lebanon Twp., Springboro (Montgomery County), Springboro (Warren County), Springdale, Springfield Twp., St. Bernard (village), St. Clair Twp., Sterling Twp., Stonelick Twp., Sycamore Twp., Symmes Twp., Tate Twp., Terrace Park (village), Trenton, Turtlecreek Twp., Union Twp. (Clermont County), Union Twp. (Warren County), Washington Twp., Wayne Twp. (Butler County), Wayne Twp. (Warren County), Waynesville (village), West Chester Twp., Whitewater Twp., Williamsburg (village), Williamsburg Twp., Woodlawn (village) & Wyoming, OH. ICA: OH5053.

Channel capacity: N.A. Channels available but not in use: N.A.

Basic
Subscribers: 75,968.
Fee: $40.00 installation; $19.99 monthly. Includes 20+ channels.

Preferred
Subscribers: N.A.
Fee: $64.99 monthly. Includes 140+ channels - 80 in SD & 60 in HD.

Elite
Subscribers: N.A.
Fee: $74.99 monthly. Includes 285+ channels - 195 in SD & 90 in HD plus 46 music channels.

Max
Subscribers: N.A.

Max
Subscribers: N.A.

Internet Service
Operational: Yes.
Subscribers: 123,100.
Fee: $14.99-$69.99 monthly.

Telephone Service
Digital: Operational
Vice President & General Manager, Consumer Wireline: Darrick Zucco. Marketing Director: Jane Weiler.
Ownership: Cincinnati Bell Inc.

LEBANON—Cincinnati Bell. This cable system has converted to IPTV. See LEBANON, OH [OH5053]. ICA: OH0438.

LEBANON—Formerly served by Adelphia Communications. Now served by Time Warner Cable, AMBERLEY (village), OH [OH0001]. ICA: OH0171.

LEESBURG (village)—Time Warner Cable. Now served by AMBERLEY (village), OH [OH0001]. ICA: OH0205.

Ohio—Cable Systems

LEIPSIC—Orwell Communications, 70 South Maple St, Orwell, OH 44076. Phones: 800-400-5568; 419-596-3847. Web Site: http://www.fairpoint.com. Also serves Continental, Gilboa, Melrose, Miller City, Oakwood (Paulding County), Pandora & West Leipsic (village). ICA: OH0163.
TV Market Ranking: Below 100 (Continental, Gilboa, LEIPSIC, Melrose, Miller City, Oakwood (Paulding County), Pandora, West Leipsic (village)).
Channel capacity: N.A. Channels available but not in use: N.A.
Basic Service
Subscribers: 275.
Fee: $22.25 monthly.
Accounting Director: Angela Unruh.
Ownership: FairPoint Communications Inc. (MSO).

LIBERTY TWP. (Butler County)—Time Warner Cable. Now served by AMBERLEY (village), OH [OH0001]. ICA: OH0142.

LICKING COUNTY—Time Warner Cable. Now served by NEWARK, OH [OH0019]. ICA: OH0436.

LIMA—Time Warner Cable. Now served by TIFFIN (formerly Fostoria), OH [OH0050]. ICA: OH0020.

LINDSEY (village)—Time Warner Cable. Now served by TIFFIN (formerly Fostoria), OH [OH0050]. ICA: OH0333.

LISBON (village)—Time Warner Cable. Now served by CLEVELAND (formerly Cleveland Heights), OH [OH0006]. ICA: OH0182.

LODI (village)—Time Warner Cable. Now served by CLEVELAND (formerly Cleveland Heights), OH [OH0006]. ICA: OH0068.

LOGAN—Time Warner Cable, 1266 Dublin Rd, Columbus, OH 43215-1008. Phones: 614-255-4997; 614-481-5000. Fax: 614-481-5052. Web Site: http://www.timewarnercable.com. Also serves Enterprise, Good Hope Twp., Logan (rural portions) & Rockbridge. ICA: OH0232.
TV Market Ranking: 27 (Good Hope Twp., LOGAN, Logan (rural portions), Rockbridge); 41 (Enterprise). Franchise award date: N.A. Franchise expiration date: N.A. Began: October 1, 1989.
Channel capacity: N.A. Channels available but not in use: N.A.
Basic Service
Subscribers: 2,318.
Programming (received off-air): WBNS-TV (Antenna TV, CBS, Decades) Columbus; WCMH-TV (MeTV, NBC) Columbus; WOUB-TV (PBS) Athens; WSFJ-TV (TBN) Newark; WSYX (ABC, Antenna TV, MNT, This TV) Columbus; WTTE (FOX) Columbus.
Programming (via satellite): WGN America.
Fee: $29.95 installation; $21.25 monthly.
Expanded Basic Service 1
Subscribers: N.A.
Programming (via satellite): A&E; CMT; CNN; Discovery Channel; Disney Channel; ESPN; ESPN2; FOX Sports Ohio/Sports Time Ohio; Freeform; HGTV; History; Lifetime; MTV; Nickelodeon; Spike TV; TBS; The Weather Channel; TNT; Turner Classic Movies; USA Network.

Digital Basic Service
Subscribers: N.A.
Programming (via satellite): BBC America; Bravo; Discovery Digital Networks; ESPN Classic; ESPNews; Golf Channel; GSN; IFC; NBCSN; Nick Jr.; Syfy; WE tv.
Digital Pay Service 1
Pay Units: N.A.
Programming (via satellite): Cinemax (multiplexed); HBO (multiplexed); Showtime (multiplexed); Starz (multiplexed); Starz Encore (multiplexed); The Movie Channel (multiplexed).
Fee: $12.99 monthly (each).
Video-On-Demand: No
Pay-Per-View
Playboy TV (delivered digitally); Hits Movies & Events (delivered digitally).
Internet Service
Operational: Yes.
Broadband Service: Road Runner.
Fee: $44.95 monthly.
Telephone Service
Digital: Operational
President: Rhonda Fraas. Vice President & General Manager: David Kreiman. Vice President, Engineering: Randy Hall. Vice President, Marketing: Mark Psigoda. Vice President, Government & Public Affairs: Mary Jo Green. Technical Operations Director: Jim Cavender. Government Affairs Director: Steve Cuckler.
Ownership: Time Warner Cable (MSO).

LONDON—Time Warner Cable. Now served by SUBURBANS MOTOR HOME PARK, OH [OH0452]. ICA: OH0089.

LORAIN—Time Warner Cable. Now served by CLEVELAND (formerly Cleveland Heights), OH [OH0006]. ICA: OH0025.

LOUDONVILLE—Time Warner Cable. Now served by CLEVELAND (formerly Cleveland Heights), OH [OH0006]. ICA: OH0334.

LOWELL—Lowell Community TV Corp, 364 Water St, PO Box 364, Lowell, OH 45744. Phone: 740-896-2626. ICA: OH0335.
TV Market Ranking: Below 100 (LOWELL). Franchise award date: N.A. Franchise expiration date: N.A. Began: September 1, 1954.
Channel capacity: 12 (not 2-way capable). Channels available but not in use: N.A.
Basic Service
Subscribers: 50.
Programming (received off-air): WHIZ-TV (NBC) Zanesville; WKRN-TV (ABC) Nashville; WOUB-TV (PBS) Athens; WOWK-TV (CBS) Huntington; WTAP-TV (FOX, MNT, NBC) Parkersburg; WTRF-TV (ABC, CBS, MNT) Wheeling; allband FM.
Programming (via satellite): ESPN; TBS; TNT; WABC-TV (ABC, Live Well Network) New York; WGN America.
Fee: $45.00 installation; $66.50 monthly.
Internet Service
Operational: No.
Telephone Service
None
Miles of Plant: 5.0 (coaxial); None (fiber optic). Homes passed: 315.
Secretary & General Manager: Deborah A. Cline. Chief Technician: Steve Weckbacher.
Ownership: Lowell Community TV Corp.

LUCASVILLE—Time Warner Cable. Now served by PORTSMOUTH, OH [OH0035]. ICA: OH0113.

LUCKEY—Time Warner Cable. Now served by TIFFIN, OH [OH0050]. ICA: OH0216.

LYNCHBURG (village)—Time Warner Cable. Now served by AMBERLEY (village), OH [OH0001]. ICA: OH0268.

MACEDONIA—Time Warner Cable. Now served by CLEVELAND (formerly Cleveland Heights), OH [OH0006]. ICA: OH0043.

MALAGA TWP.—Formerly served by Richards TV Cable. No longer in operation. ICA: OH0270.

MANCHESTER—Formerly served by Adelphia Communications. Now served by Time Warner Cable, AMBERLEY (village), OH [OH0001]. ICA: OH0209.

MANSFIELD—Time Warner Cable. Now served by CLEVELAND (formerly Cleveland Heights), OH [OH0006]. ICA: OH0023.

MANTUA TWP.—Time Warner Cable. Now served by CLEVELAND (formerly Cleveland Heights), OH [OH0006]. ICA: OH0337.

MARGARETTA TWP.—Time Warner Cable. Now served by CLEVELAND (formerly Cleveland Heights), OH [OH0006]. ICA: OH0338.

MARIETTA—Formerly served by Charter Communications. Now served by Suddenlink Communications, PARKERSBURG, WV [WV0003]. ICA: OH0339.

MARION—Time Warner Cable, 160 North Greenwood St, Marion, OH 43302-3163. Phones: 740-387-2288; 740-387-3187; 419-784-1992 (Defiance office). Fax: 740-387-4891. Web Site: http://www.timewarnercable.com. Also serves Caledonia, Claridon Twp. (Marion County), Grand Prairie Twp., Marion Twp. (Marion County), Morral, Pleasant Twp. (Marion County), Prospect Twp. & Salt Rock Twp. ICA: OH0040.
TV Market Ranking: 27 (Prospect Twp.); Below 100 (Caledonia, Claridon Twp. (Marion County), Grand Prairie Twp., MARION, Marion Twp. (Marion County), Pleasant Twp. (Marion County), Salt Rock Twp.); Outside TV Markets (Morral). Franchise award date: N.A. Franchise expiration date: N.A. Began: September 19, 1966.
Channel capacity: N.A. Channels available but not in use: N.A.
Basic Service
Subscribers: 11,010.
Programming (received off-air): WBNS-TV (Antenna TV, CBS, Decades) Columbus; WCMH-TV (MeTV, NBC) Columbus; WOCB-CD (IND) Marion; WOSU-TV (PBS) Columbus; WSYX (ABC, Antenna TV, MNT, This TV) Columbus; WWHO (CW) Chillicothe.
Programming (via satellite): Pop; QVC; TLC; WGN America.
Fee: $29.95 installation; $21.25 monthly; $3.25 converter.
Expanded Basic Service 1
Subscribers: N.A.
Programming (via satellite): A&E; AMC; Animal Planet; BET; Bravo; Cartoon Network; CMT; CNBC; CNN; Comedy Central; C-SPAN; C-SPAN 2; Discovery Channel; Disney Channel; E! HD; ESPN; ESPN2; EVINE Live; EWTN Global Catholic Network; Food Network; Fox News Channel; Fox Sports 1; FOX Sports Ohio/Sports Time Ohio; FX; Hallmark Channel; HGTV; History; HLN; ION Television; Lifetime; MSNBC; MTV; Nick Jr.; Nickelodeon; Oxygen; Spike TV; Syfy; TBS; The Weather Channel; TNT; Travel Channel; truTV; TV Land; Univision Studios; USA Network; VH1; WPIX (Antenna TV, CW, This TV) New York.
Fee: $20.51 monthly.
Digital Basic Service
Subscribers: N.A.
Programming (via satellite): 52MX; BBC America; Bloomberg Television; Cinelatino; CMT; CNN en Espanol; Destination America; Discovery Kids Channel; Discovery Life Channel; Disney XD; DIY Network; DMX Music; ESPN Classic; ESPN Deportes; ESPNews; FOX College Sports Central; FOX College Sports Pacific; Fox Deportes; Fox Sports 2; Fuse; FXM; FYI; Golf Channel; Great American Country; GSN; History en Espanol; History International; IFC; Investigation Discovery; LMN; LOGO; MTV Classic; MTV Hits; MTV Jams; MTV2; Nat Geo WILD; National Geographic Channel; NBCSN; Nick 2; Nick Jr.; Nicktoons; Outdoor Channel; OWN: Oprah Winfrey Network; Science Channel; Sundance TV; TeenNick; The Word Network; Tr3s; Trinity Broadcasting Network (TBN); Turner Classic Movies; TVG Network; UP; VH1 Soul; WE tv.
Fee: $14.95 monthly.
Digital Pay Service 1
Pay Units: N.A.
Programming (via satellite): Cinemax (multiplexed); Flix; HBO (multiplexed); RAI Italia; RTN; Showtime (multiplexed); Starz (multiplexed); Starz Encore (multiplexed); TAC TV; The Filipino Channel; TV Asia; TV5, La Television International.
Fee: $12.99 monthly (each).
Video-On-Demand: No
Pay-Per-View
Playboy TV (delivered digitally); Fresh (delivered digitally); Shorteez; Hot Choice (delivered digitally); ESPN (delivered digitally); NHL Center Ice (delivered digitally); MLB Extra Innings (delivered digitally); iN DEMAND (delivered digitally).
Internet Service
Operational: Yes.
Subscribers: 9,194.
Broadband Service: Road Runner.
Fee: $42.95 monthly.
Telephone Service
Digital: Operational
Subscribers: 4,329.
Miles of Plant: 476.0 (coaxial); 274.0 (fiber optic). Homes passed: 25,906.
President: Rhonda Fraas. Vice President, Engineering: Randy Hall. Vice President, Sales & Marketing: Mark Psigoda. Area Manager: Brad Wakely. General Manager: John Ellingson.
Ownership: Time Warner Cable (MSO).

MARTINS FERRY—Comcast Cable. Now served by WHEELING, WV [WV0004]. ICA: OH0102.

MARTINSBURG (village)—Formerly served by National Cable Inc. No longer in operation. ICA: OH0341.

MARYSVILLE—Time Warner Cable. Now served by SUBURBANS MOTOR HOME PARK, OH [OH0452]. ICA: OH0097.

MASSILLON—MCTV, PO Box 1000, Massillon, OH 44648-1000. Phones: 330-345-8114; 330-833-4134. Fax: 330-833-9775. E-mail: rbgessner@massilloncabletv.com.

Web Site: http://www.mctvohio.com. Also serves Baughman Twp., Bethlehem Twp. (Stark County), Brewster, Canal Fulton, Green, Harmon, Jackson Twp. (Stark County), Lawrence Twp. (Stark County), Navarre, New Franklin, Paint Twp., Perry Twp. (Stark County), Salt Creek Twp., Sugar Creek Twp. (Stark County), Tuscarawas Twp. (Stark County) & Wayne County (eastern portion). ICA: OH0021.

TV Market Ranking: 8 (Baughman Twp., Bethlehem Twp. (Stark County), Brewster, Canal Fulton, Green, Harmon, Jackson Twp. (Stark County), Lawrence Twp. (Stark County), MASSILLON, Navarre, New Franklin, Paint Twp., Perry Twp. (Stark County), Salt Creek Twp., Sugar Creek Twp. (Stark County), Tuscarawas Twp. (Stark County), Wayne County (eastern portion)). Franchise award date: October 1, 1966. Franchise expiration date: N.A. Began: October 1, 1966.

Channel capacity: 116 (operating 2-way). Channels available but not in use: N.A.

Basic Service
Subscribers: 25,038.
Programming (received off-air): WBNX-TV (CW, Movies!, This TV) Akron; WDLI-TV (TBN) Canton; WEWS-TV (ABC) Cleveland; WJW (Antenna TV, FOX) Cleveland; WKYC (NBC) Cleveland; WNEO (PBS) Alliance; WOIO (CBS, MeTV) Shaker Heights; WQHS-DT (getTV, UNV) Cleveland; WRLM (IND) Canton; WUAB (Bounce TV, MNT) Lorain; WVIZ (PBS) Cleveland; WVPX-TV (ION) Akron.
Programming (via satellite): A&E; AMC; Animal Planet; BET; Boomerang; Bravo; BTN; Cartoon Network; CMT; CNBC; CNN; Comedy Central; C-SPAN; C-SPAN 2; Discovery Channel; Disney Channel; E! HD; ESPN; ESPN Classic; ESPN2; ESPNU; EWTN Global Catholic Network; Food Network; Fox News Channel; Fox Sports 1; FOX Sports Ohio/Sports Time Ohio; Freeform; FX; Golf Channel; Great American Country; GSN; Hallmark Channel; HGTV; History; HLN; INSP; ION Television; Lifetime; MSNBC; MTV; National Geographic Channel; Nickelodeon; OWN: Oprah Winfrey Network; Oxygen; Qubo; QVC; Reelz; Spike TV; Syfy; TBS; The Weather Channel; TLC; TNT; Travel Channel; truTV; Turner Classic Movies; TV Land; USA Network; VH1; Weatherscan; WGN America; zap2it Program Guide.
Fee: $30.00 installation; $29.95 monthly; $3.00 converter.

Digital Basic Service
Subscribers: N.A.
Programming (via satellite): A&E HD; AXS TV; BBC America; Bloomberg Television; Bravo HD; BTN HD; CBS Sports Network; Chiller; CMT; CNBC HD+; CNN HD; Cooking Channel; Destination America; Discovery Kids Channel; Discovery Life Channel; Disney XD; DIY Network; DMX Music; ESPN HD; ESPN2 HD; ESPNews; Fox Business Network; FOX Sports Ohio/Sports Time Ohio; FXM; FYI; HD Theater; History; History HD; History International; Investigation Discovery; LMN; MGM HD; MLB Network; MTV Classic; MTV Hits; MTV2; NBCSN; NHL Network; Nick Jr.; Nicktoons; Outdoor Channel; Science Channel; Sprout; Syfy HD; TBS HD; TeenNick; Tennis Channel; TNT HD; TV One; Universal HD; UP; USA Network HD; VH1 Soul; WE tv.
Fee: $7.50 monthly; $4.50 converter.

Digital Pay Service 1
Pay Units: 1,480.
Programming (via satellite): Cinemax (multiplexed).
Fee: $10.75 monthly.

Digital Pay Service 2
Pay Units: 4,121.
Programming (via satellite): HBO (multiplexed); HBO HD.
Fee: $10.00 installation; $14.25 monthly.

Digital Pay Service 3
Pay Units: 1,846.
Programming (via satellite): Flix; Showtime (multiplexed); Showtime HD; Sundance TV; The Movie Channel.
Fee: $14.00 monthly.

Digital Pay Service 4
Pay Units: 1,592.
Programming (via satellite): Starz (multiplexed); Starz Encore (multiplexed).
Fee: $11.50 monthly.

Video-On-Demand: Yes

Pay-Per-View
MLB Extra Innings (delivered digitally); NHL Center Ice (delivered digitally); iN DEMAND (delivered digitally).

Internet Service
Operational: Yes. Began: January 1, 1999.
Subscribers: 23,934.
Broadband Service: In-house.
Fee: $30.00 installation; $25.00-$40.00 monthly.

Telephone Service
Digital: Operational
Subscribers: 11,172.
Fee: $33.20-$47.95 monthly
Miles of Plant: 1,255.0 (coaxial); 304.0 (fiber optic). Homes passed: 46,772.
President: Robert Gessner. Chief Operating Officer: David Hoffer. Chief Technician: Tom Mogus. Marketing Director: Shannon Delaney. Ad Sales Manager: Elizabeth McAllister. Customer Service Manager: Brenda Murphy.
Ownership: MCTV (MSO).

McCONNELSVILLE—Formerly served by Adelphia Communications. Now served by Time Warner Cable, BEVERLY, OH [OH0175]. ICA: OH0177.

MEDINA—Armstrong Cable Services. Now served by ZELIENOPLE, PA [PA0053]. ICA: OH0067.

MENTOR—Time Warner Cable. Now served by CLEVELAND (formerly Cleveland Heights), OH [OH0006]. ICA: OH0015.

METAMORA—Formerly served by Adelphia Communications. Now served by Time Warner Cable, TIFFIN, OH [OH0050]. ICA: OH0255.

MIDDLEBURG (Noble County)—Formerly served by Cebridge Connections. No longer in operation. ICA: OH0312.

MIDDLETOWN—Time Warner Cable. Now served by AMBERLEY (village), OH [OH0001]. ICA: OH0018.

MIDWAY—Time Warner Cable, 7800 Crescent Executive Dr, Charlotte, NC 28217. Phone: 800-425-2255. Web Site: http://www.timewarnercable.com. Also serves Paint Twp. (Fayette County), Paint Twp. (Madison County), Plumwood & Range Twp. ICA: OH0451.

TV Market Ranking: 27 (MIDWAY, Paint Twp. (Fayette County), Paint Twp. (Madison County), Plumwood, Range Twp.).
Channel capacity: N.A. Channels available but not in use: N.A.

Basic Service
Subscribers: 105.
Fee: $49.99 installation; $24.50 monthly.
Senior Accounting Director: Karen Goodfellow.
Ownership: Time Warner Cable (MSO).

MILLERSBURG—Time Warner Cable. Now served by CLEVELAND (formerly Cleveland Heights), OH [OH0006]. ICA: OH0144.

MINERVA (village)—Time Warner Cable. Now served by CLEVELAND (formerly Cleveland Heights), OH [OH0006]. ICA: OH0132.

MINSTER—Time Warner Cable. Now served by TIFFIN (formerly Fostoria), OH [OH0050]. ICA: OH0164.

MORROW—Formerly served by Adelphia Communications. Now served by Time Warner Cable, AMBERLEY (village), OH [OH0001]. ICA: OH0115.

MOUNT EATON—MCTV. Now served by WOOSTER, OH [OH0061]. ICA: OH0344.

MOUNT GILEAD (village)—Time Warner Cable. Now served by COLUMBUS, OH [OH0002]. ICA: OH0166.

MOUNT ORAB—S. Bryer Cable TV Corp, PO Box 638, Cochranton, PA 16314. Phones: 330-876-0294 (Vernon office); 814-282-5223; 937-483-4403 (Mount Orab office). E-mail: bryer_scott@yahoo.com. Web Site: http://sbryercabletv.com. ICA: OH0345.
TV Market Ranking: 17 (MOUNT ORAB). Franchise award date: N.A. Franchise expiration date: N.A. Began: January 1, 1988.
Channel capacity: N.A. Channels available but not in use: N.A.

Basic Service
Subscribers: N.A.
Programming (received off-air): WCET (PBS) Cincinnati; WCPO-TV (ABC, Escape) Cincinnati; WHIO-TV (CBS, MeTV) Dayton; WKEF (ABC, Antenna TV) Dayton; WKRC-TV (CBS, CW) Cincinnati; WLWT (MeTV, NBC) Cincinnati; WPTD (PBS) Dayton; WSTR-TV (Antenna TV, MNT) Cincinnati; WXIX-TV (Bounce TV, FOX) Newport.
Programming (via satellite): Trinity Broadcasting Network (TBN); WGN America.
Fee: $37.45 installation.

Expanded Basic Service 1
Subscribers: N.A.
Programming (via satellite): A&E; AMC; Animal Planet; Bloomberg Television; Boomerang; Cartoon Network; Classic Arts Showcase; CMT; CNBC; CNN; Comedy Central; Cooking Channel; Crime & Investigation Network; C-SPAN; Discovery Channel; Disney Channel; Disney XD; DIY Network; E! HD; ESPN; ESPN2; EVINE Live; Food Network; Fox News Channel; Fox Sports 1; FOX Sports Ohio/Sports Time Ohio; Freeform; Great American Country; Hallmark Channel; Hallmark Movies & Mysteries; HGTV; History; HLN; Lifetime; LMN; MTV; Nick Jr.; Nickelodeon; OWN: Oprah Winfrey Network; Pop; QVC; RFD-TV; Spike TV; Syfy; TBS; The Weather Channel; TLC; TNT; Travel Channel; truTV; Turner Classic Movies; TV Land; USA Network; VH1; WE tv.
Fee: $17.00 monthly.

Pay Service 1
Pay Units: N.A.
Programming (via satellite): Cinemax; HBO; Showtime; The Movie Channel.
Fee: $12.95 monthly (each).

Video-On-Demand: No

Internet Service
Operational: Yes.
Fee: $34.80-$56.96 monthly.

Telephone Service
Digital: Operational
Fee: $32.80 monthly
Miles of Plant: 54.0 (coaxial); None (fiber optic). Homes passed: 2,372. Miles of plant (coax) includes miles of plant (fiber).
General Manager & Chief Technician: Scott Bryer. Customer Service Manager: Cathy Hyde.
Ownership: SBC-Tele (MSO).

MOUNT PLEASANT TWP.—Formerly served by Community TV Systems Cable Co. Now served by Comcast Cable, WHEELING, WV [WV0004]. ICA: OH0346.

MOUNT STERLING (village) (Muskingum County)—Time Warner Cable. Now served by COLUMBUS, OH [OH0002]. ICA: OH0237.

MOUNT VERNON—Time Warner Cable. Now served by COLUMBUS, OH [OH0002]. ICA: OH0095.

MURRAY CITY—Time Warner Cable. Now served by COLUMBUS, OH [OH0002]. ICA: OH0284.

NAPOLEON—Time Warner Cable. Now served by TIFFIN (formerly Fostoria), OH [OH0050]. ICA: OH0121.

NASHPORT—Formerly served by Time Warner Cable. No longer in operation. ICA: OH0247.

NELSON MOBILE HOME PARK—Formerly served by Time Warner Cable. No longer in operation. ICA: OH0306.

NELSON TWP.—Suddenlink Communications, 520 Maryville Centre Dr, Ste 300, St. Louis, MO 63141. Phones: 800-999-6845; 314-315-9400. Web Site: http://www.suddenlink.com. Also serves Auburn Twp., Bainbridge Twp., Blue Water Manor, Braceville Twp., Burton Twp., Farmington, Freedom Twp. (Portage County), Geauga County (portions), Middlefield Twp., Newberry Twp., Newbury

Ohio—Cable Systems

Twp., Newton Twp., Palmyra Twp., Paris Twp. (Portage County), Parkman, Parkman Twp., Shalersville Twp., Troy Twp. (Geauga County), Windham (Portage County) & Windham Twp. ICA: OH0160.

TV Market Ranking: 41 (Newberry Twp.); 79 (Farmington); 8 (Auburn Twp., Bainbridge Twp., Braceville Twp., Burton Twp., Geauga County (portions), Middlefield Twp., Newbury Twp., Shalersville Twp., Troy Twp. (Geauga County)); 8,79 (Blue Water Manor, Freedom Twp. (Portage County), NELSON TWP., Newton Twp., Palmyra Twp., Paris Twp. (Portage County), Parkman, Parkman Twp., Windham (Portage County), Windham Twp.). Franchise award date: June 25, 1988. Franchise expiration date: N.A. Began: November 1, 1989.

Channel capacity: 62 (operating 2-way). Channels available but not in use: N.A.

Basic Service
Subscribers: 1,288.
Programming (received off-air): WBNX-TV (CW, Movies!, This TV) Akron; WDLI-TV (TBN) Canton; WEWS-TV (ABC) Cleveland; WFMJ-TV (CW, NBC) Youngstown; WJW (Antenna TV, FOX) Cleveland; WKBN-TV (CBS) Youngstown; WKYC (NBC) Cleveland; WNEO (PBS) Alliance; WOIO (CBS, MeTV) Shaker Heights; WRLM (IND) Canton; WUAB (Bounce TV, MNT) Lorain; WVIZ (PBS) Cleveland; WVPX-TV (ION) Akron; WYTV (ABC, MNT) Youngstown.
Fee: $59.95 installation; $22.99 monthly; $1.95 converter.

Expanded Basic Service 1
Subscribers: N.A.
Programming (via satellite): A&E; AMC; Animal Planet; Cartoon Network; CNBC; CNN; Comedy Central; C-SPAN; Discovery Channel; Disney Channel; E! HD; ESPN; ESPN2; Food Network; Fox News Channel; FOX Sports Ohio/Sports Time Ohio; Freeform; FX; Great American Country; HGTV; History; HLN; Lifetime; MTV; Nickelodeon; QVC; Root Sports Pittsburgh; Spike TV; Syfy; TBS; The Weather Channel; TLC; TNT; Turner Classic Movies; TV Land; USA Network; VH1.
Fee: $25.00 monthly.

Digital Basic Service
Subscribers: N.A.
Programming (via satellite): BBC America; Bloomberg Television; Cloo; CMT; Discovery Digital Networks; Disney XD; DMX Music; ESPN Classic; ESPNews; Fox Sports 1; Fuse; FYI; Golf Channel; GSN; History International; IFC; LMN; NBCSN; Nick Jr.; Nicktoons; TeenNick; Trinity Broadcasting Network (TBN); WE tv.

Pay Service 1
Pay Units: N.A.
Programming (via satellite): Cinemax; HBO; Showtime; The Movie Channel.
Fee: $11.00 monthly (Cinemax or HBO), $12.95 monthly (Showtime/TMC).

Digital Pay Service 1
Pay Units: N.A.
Programming (via satellite): Cinemax (multiplexed); HBO (multiplexed); Showtime (multiplexed); Starz; Starz Encore (multiplexed); The Movie Channel (multiplexed).

Pay-Per-View
iN DEMAND (delivered digitally); Playboy TV (delivered digitally); Fresh (delivered digitally).

Internet Service
Operational: Yes. Began: October 4, 2004.
Broadband Service: Suddenlink High Speed Internet.
Fee: $20.00 installation; $20.95 monthly.

Telephone Service
None
Miles of Plant: 187.0 (coaxial); None (fiber optic). Homes passed: 4,564.
Senior Vice President, Corporate Finance: Michael Pflantz. General Manager: Peter Brown. Chief Technician: Tom Beat.
Ownership: Cequel Communications Holdings I LLC (MSO).

NELSONVILLE—Nelsonville TV Cable, 1 W Columbus St, Nelsonville, OH 45764. Phones: 740-767-2203; 740-594-2860; 740-753-2686. E-mail: oldcableman74@yahoo.com. Web Site: http://www.nelsonvilletv.com. Also serves Ames Twp., Athens County, Buchtel, Carbon Hill, Chauncey, Dover Twp., Glouster, Green Twp., Haydenville, Homer Twp., Jacksonville, Millfield, Starr Twp., The Plains, Trimble, Union Furnace, Ward Twp. & York Twp. ICA: OH0347.

TV Market Ranking: Below 100 (Athens County (portions), Buchtel, Carbon Hill, Chauncey, Glouster, Jacksonville, Millfield, The Plains, Trimble); Outside TV Markets (Athens County (portions), Haydenville, NELSONVILLE, Union Furnace). Franchise award date: N.A. Franchise expiration date: N.A. Began: December 8, 1952.

Channel capacity: 36 (not 2-way capable). Channels available but not in use: N.A.

Basic Service
Subscribers: 5,334.
Programming (received off-air): WBNS-TV (Antenna TV, CBS, Decades) Columbus; WCHS-TV (ABC, Antenna TV) Charleston; WCMH-TV (MeTV, NBC) Columbus; WHIZ-TV (NBC) Zanesville; WOUB-TV (PBS) Athens; WOWK-TV (CBS) Huntington; WQCW (CW) Portsmouth; WSAZ-TV (MNT, NBC, This TV) Huntington; WSFJ-TV (TBN) Newark; WTTE (FOX) Columbus; WVAH-TV (FOX, The Country Network) Charleston; allband FM.

Programming (via satellite): A&E; AMC; Animal Planet; BET; Cartoon Network; CNBC; CNN; Comedy Central; Discovery Channel; Disney Channel; E! HD; ESPN; ESPN Classic; ESPN2; Family Friendly Entertainment; Food Network; Fox News Channel; Fox Sports 1; FOX Sports Ohio/Sports Time Ohio; Freeform; FSN Digital Atlantic; FSN Digital Central; FSN Digital Pacific; FX; FXM; Great American Country; GSN; HGTV; History; HLN; Lifetime; MSNBC; MTV; MTV2; National Geographic Channel; Nickelodeon; Outdoor Channel; Spike TV; Syfy; TBS; The Weather Channel; TLC; TNT; Travel Channel; truTV; Turner Classic Movies; TV Land; VH1; WGN America.
Fee: $21.50 installation; $50.00 monthly.

Pay Service 1
Pay Units: N.A.
Programming (via satellite): Cinemax (multiplexed); Flix; HBO (multiplexed); Showtime (multiplexed); Starz (multiplexed); Starz Encore (multiplexed); Sundance TV; The Movie Channel.
Fee: $20.00 installation; $7.00 monthly (Showtime), $8.00 monthly (HBO).

Digital Pay Service 1
Pay Units: N.A.
Programming (via satellite): Cinemax (multiplexed); Flix; HBO (multiplexed); Showtime (multiplexed); Starz (multiplexed); Starz Encore (multiplexed); Sundance TV; The Movie Channel (multiplexed).

Video-On-Demand: No
Pay-Per-View
iN DEMAND.

Internet Service
Operational: Yes.
Subscribers: 2,631.
Fee: $12.00 installation; $39.95-$59.95 monthly.

Telephone Service
None
Miles of Plant: 724.0 (coaxial); 483.0 (fiber optic). Homes passed: 7,000.
President: Eugene R. Edwards. General Manager: Jim Edwards.
Ownership: Nelsonville TV Cable Inc.

NEW ATHENS—Formerly served by Richards TV Cable. No longer in operation. ICA: OH0348.

NEW CONCORD (village)—Time Warner Cable. Now served by COLUMBUS, OH [OH0002]. ICA: OH0226.

NEW HOLLAND—Time Warner Cable, 7800 Crescent Executive Dr, Charlotte, NC 28217. Phones: 614-255-4997; 614-481-5000. Web Site: http://www.timewarnercable.com. Also serves Clarksburg & Williamsport. ICA: OH0207.

TV Market Ranking: 27 (Clarksburg, NEW HOLLAND, Williamsport). Franchise award date: December 8, 1986. Franchise expiration date: N.A. Began: December 8, 1987.

Channel capacity: N.A. Channels available but not in use: N.A.

Basic Service
Subscribers: 49.
Programming (received off-air): WBNS-TV (Antenna TV, CBS, Decades) Columbus; WCMH-TV (MeTV, NBC) Columbus; WOSU-TV (PBS) Columbus; WSYX (ABC, Antenna TV, MNT, This TV) Columbus; WTTE (FOX) Columbus; WWHO (CW) Chillicothe.
Programming (via satellite): QVC; The Weather Channel; TLC; WGN America.
Fee: $49.99 installation; $24.50 monthly.

Expanded Basic Service 1
Subscribers: N.A.
Programming (via satellite): A&E; Animal Planet; CMT; CNN; Discovery Channel; Disney Channel; ESPN; ESPN2; Fox News Channel; Freeform; FX; HGTV; History; INSP; Lifetime; MSNBC; MTV; Nickelodeon; Spike TV; TBS; TNT; USA Network.

Digital Basic Service
Subscribers: N.A.
Programming (via satellite): BBC America; Bravo; Discovery Digital Networks; ESPN Classic; ESPNews; Golf Channel; GSN; IFC; NBCSN; Nick Jr.; Turner Classic Movies; WE tv.

Digital Pay Service 1
Pay Units: N.A.
Programming (via satellite): Cinemax (multiplexed); HBO (multiplexed); Showtime (multiplexed); Starz (multiplexed); Starz Encore (multiplexed); The Movie Channel (multiplexed).
Fee: $12.99 monthly (each).

Video-On-Demand: No
Pay-Per-View
Playboy TV (delivered digitally).

Internet Service
Operational: Yes.

Telephone Service
None
Miles of Plant: 38.0 (coaxial); None (fiber optic). Homes passed: 1,264.
President: Rhonda Fraas. Vice President & General Manager: David Kreiman. Vice President, Government & Public Affairs: Mary Jo Green. Vice President, Engineering: Randy Hall. Vice President, Marketing: Mark Psigoda. Senior Accounting Director: Karen Goodfellow. Technical Operations Director: Jim Cavender. Government Affairs Director: Steve Cuckler.
Ownership: Time Warner Cable (MSO).

NEW KNOXVILLE—NKTelco, 301 West South St, PO Box 219, New Knoxville, OH 45871. Phones: 888-658-3526; 419-629-1424; 419-753-5000; 419-753-2457. Fax: 419-753-2950. E-mail: info@nktelco.net. Web Site: http://www.nktelco.net. Also serves Anna, Botkins, Fort Loramie, Minster & New Bremen. ICA: OH0275. Note: This system is an overbuild.

TV Market Ranking: Below 100 (Anna, Botkins, Fort Loramie, Minster, New Bremen, NEW KNOXVILLE). Franchise award date: May 5, 1985. Franchise expiration date: N.A. Began: February 1, 1986.

Channel capacity: N.A. Channels available but not in use: N.A.

Basic Service
Subscribers: 4,029.
Programming (received off-air): WBGU-TV (PBS) Bowling Green; WBNS-TV (Antenna TV, CBS, Decades) Columbus; WDTN (Escape, Grit, NBC) Dayton; WHIO-TV (CBS, MeTV) Dayton; WKEF (ABC, Antenna TV) Dayton; WLIO (CW, NBC) Lima; WLMO-LP (CBS) Lima; WLQP-LP (ABC) Lima; WOHL-CD (ABC, CBS) Lima; WPTA (ABC, MNT, NBC) Fort Wayne; WPTD (PBS) Dayton; WRGT-TV (FOX, MNT, This TV) Dayton; WTLW (IND) Lima.
Programming (via satellite): CW PLUS; EVINE Live; QVC.
Fee: $24.95 installation; $58.99 monthly.

Expanded Basic Service 1
Subscribers: 2,017.
Programming (via satellite): A&E; Animal Planet; Boomerang; Bravo; Cartoon Network; CMT; CNBC; CNN; Comedy Central; C-SPAN; C-SPAN 2; Discovery Channel; Disney Channel; Disney XD; E! HD; ESPN; ESPN Classic; ESPNews; EWTN Global Catholic Network; Food Network; Fox News Channel; Fox Sports 1; FOX Sports Ohio/Sports Time Ohio; Freeform; FX; Golf Channel; GSN; Hallmark Channel; HGTV; History; HLN; HRTV; ION Television; Lifetime; MSNBC; MTV; National Geographic Channel; NBCSN; NFL Network; Nickelodeon; Pop; Spike TV; Syfy; TBS; The Weather Channel; TLC; TNT; Travel Channel; Trinity Broadcasting Network (TBN); truTV; Turner Classic Movies; TV Land; USA Network; VH1; WE tv; WGN America.
Fee: $30.00 monthly.

Digital Basic Service
Subscribers: N.A.
Programming (via satellite): BBC America; Bloomberg Television; Cloo; CMT; Discovery Digital Networks; DMX Music; ESPNews; FOX College Sports Central; FOX College Sports Pacific; FXM; FYI; Great American Country; History International; LMN; Nick Jr.; Nicktoons; Outdoor Channel; Ovation; TeenNick.
Fee: $39.00 monthly.

Digital Pay Service 1
Pay Units: N.A.
Programming (via satellite): Cinemax (multiplexed); Flix; HBO (multiplexed); Showtime (multiplexed); Starz (multiplexed); Starz Encore (multiplexed); Sundance TV; The Movie Channel (multiplexed).
Fee: $9.50 monthly (Cinemax), $9.95 monthly (HBO), $10.95 monthly (Showtime/Sundance/Flix/TMC), $13.50 monthly (Starz/Encore).

Video-On-Demand: No

Cable Systems—Ohio

Pay-Per-View
Playboy TV (delivered digitally); Fresh (delivered digitally); Shorteez (delivered digitally).

Internet Service
Operational: Yes, DSL.
Broadband Service: nktelco.net.
Fee: $59.95 installation; $19.95-$44.95 monthly; $10.00 modem lease; $200.00 modem purchase.

Telephone Service
Analog: Not Operational
Digital: Operational
Fee: $15.95 monthly

Miles of Plant: 40.0 (coaxial); 15.0 (fiber optic).
General Manager: Preston Meyer. Project Manager: Clint Conover. Sales & Marketing Director: Erin Brown. Controller: Susan Quellhorst.
Ownership: New Knoxville Telephone & Cable Co.

NEW LEXINGTON (village)—Time Warner Cable. Now served by COLUMBUS, OH [OH0002]. ICA: OH0148.

NEW LONDON (village)—Time Warner Cable. Now served by CLEVELAND (formerly Cleveland Heights), OH [OH0006]. ICA: OH0202.

NEW MATAMORAS—Formerly served by Adelphia Communications. Now served by Crystal Broadband Networks, HANNIBAL, OH [OH0251]. ICA: OH0245.

NEW MIDDLETOWN—Comcast Cable, 15 Summit Park Dr, Pittsburgh, PA 15275. Phones: 412-747-6400; 724-656-8230 (New Castle office). Fax: 412-747-6401. Web Site: http://www.comcast.com. Also serves Columbiana, East Liverpool, East Palestine, Fairfield, Hammondsville, Irondale, Leetonia, Liverpool Twp., Madison Twp. (Columbiana County), Middleton, New Waterford, Rogers (village), Salem, Springfield, St. Clair Twp. (Columbiana County), Unity, Washingtonville, Wellsville & Yellow Creek, OH; Bessemer, Mahoning Twp. (Lawrence County) & North Beaver Twp. (Lawrence County), PA. ICA: OH0145.
TV Market Ranking: 10,79 (East Liverpool, Fairfield, Liverpool Twp. (portions), Madison Twp. (Columbiana County), Unity); 79 (Bessemer, Columbiana, East Palestine, Leetonia, Mahoning Twp. (Lawrence County), Middleton, NEW MIDDLETOWN, New Waterford, North Beaver Twp. (Lawrence County), Springfield, Washingtonville); 79,90 (St. Clair Twp. (Columbiana County), Wellsville, Yellow Creek); 8,79 (Rogers (village), Salem); 90 (Hammondsville, Irondale). Franchise award date: N.A. Franchise expiration date: N.A. Began: March 1, 1983.
Channel capacity: N.A. Channels available but not in use: N.A.

Basic Service
Subscribers: 13,931.
Programming (received off-air): KDKA-TV (CBS, Decades) Pittsburgh; WFMJ-TV (CW, NBC) Youngstown; WKBN-TV (CBS) Youngstown; WNEO (PBS) Alliance; WPGH-TV (Antenna TV, FOX, The Country Network) Pittsburgh; WUAB (Bounce TV, MNT) Lorain; WYFX-LD (FOX, Laff) Youngstown; WYTV (ABC, MNT) Youngstown; allband FM.
Programming (via satellite): BET; CNBC; C-SPAN; Discovery Channel; Hallmark Channel; QVC; The Weather Channel.
Fee: $43.99 installation; $25.24 monthly.

Expanded Basic Service 1
Subscribers: N.A.
Programming (via satellite): A&E; AMC; Animal Planet; Cartoon Network; CMT; CNN; Comedy Central; C-SPAN; C-SPAN 2; Disney Channel; E! HD; ESPN; ESPN2; EWTN Global Catholic Network; Food Network; Fox News Channel; FOX Sports Networks; Freeform; FX; HGTV; History; HLN; Lifetime; MSNBC; MTV; NBCSN; Nickelodeon; Oxygen; Pennsylvania Cable Network; Root Sports Pittsburgh; Spike TV; TBS; TLC; TNT; Travel Channel; truTV; Turner Classic Movies; TV Land; USA Network; VH1.
Fee: $37.99 monthly.

Digital Basic Service
Subscribers: N.A.
Programming (via satellite): BBC America; Bloomberg Television; Bravo; Cooking Channel; C-SPAN 3; Discovery Kids Channel; Discovery Life Channel; Disney XD; DIY Network; DMX Music; ESPN Classic; ESPNews; EVINE Live; Fox Sports 1; FSN Digital Atlantic; FSN Digital Central; FSN Digital Pacific; Fuse; FXM; FYI; Golf Channel; Great American Country; GSN; History International; IFC; International Television (ITV); LMN; MC; MTV2; National Geographic Channel; Nick Jr.; Nicktoons; Outdoor Channel; Ovation; Sundance TV; Syfy; TeenNick; The Word Network; Trinity Broadcasting Network (TBN); WE tv; Weatherscan.
Fee: $10.95 monthly.

Digital Pay Service 1
Pay Units: N.A.
Programming (via satellite): Cinemax (multiplexed); Flix; HBO (multiplexed); RTN; Showtime (multiplexed); Starz (multiplexed); Starz Encore; The Movie Channel (multiplexed); TV Asia; Zee TV.

Video-On-Demand: Yes

Pay-Per-View
NBA TV (delivered digitally); NHL/MLB (delivered digitally); iN DEMAND (delivered digitally); Fresh (delivered digitally); Shorteez (delivered digitally); Playboy TV (delivered digitally); Hot Choice (delivered digitally); Sports PPV (delivered digitally).

Internet Service
Operational: Yes.
Subscribers: 11,402.
Broadband Service: Comcast High Speed Internet.
Fee: $42.95 monthly.

Telephone Service
Digital: Operational
Subscribers: 10,422.
Miles of Plant: 880.0 (coaxial); 441.0 (fiber optic). Homes passed: 32,056.
Regional Vice President: Linda Hossinger. Vice President, Technical Operations: Randy Bender. Vice President, Marketing: Donna Corning. Vice President, Public Affairs: Jody Doherty.
Ownership: Comcast Cable Communications Inc. (MSO).

NEW PHILADELPHIA—Time Warner Cable. Now served by CLEVELAND (formerly Cleveland Heights), OH [OH0006]. ICA: OH0030.

NEWARK—Time Warner Cable, 111 North 11th St, Newark, OH 43055. Phones: 614-481-5000 (Columbus office); 740-345-4329. Fax: 740-349-0823. Web Site: http://www.timewarnercable.com. Also serves Bennington, Buckeye Lake, Byesville, Cumberland, Eden Twp., Enoch Twp., Fallsbury Twp., Franklin Twp. (Licking County), Granville, Granville Twp. (Licking County), Hanover, Hanover Twp. (Licking County), Heath (Licking County), Hebron, Liberty Twp. (Licking County), Licking County (portions), Licking Twp. (Licking County), Madison Twp. (Licking County), Mary Ann Twp., McKean Twp., Nellie, Newton Twp. (Licking County), Perry Twp. (Licking County), St. Louisville, Union Twp. (Licking County), Virginia Twp., Walnut Twp. (Fairfield County) & Westland Twp. ICA: OH0019.
TV Market Ranking: 27 (Bennington, Buckeye Lake, Fallsbury Twp., Franklin Twp. (Licking County), Granville, Granville Twp. (Licking County), Heath (Licking County), Hebron, Liberty Twp. (Licking County), Licking Twp. (Licking County), Madison Twp. (Licking County), Mary Ann Twp. (portions), McKean Twp., NEWARK, Newton Twp. (Licking County), St. Louisville, Union Twp. (Licking County), Walnut Twp. (Fairfield County)); Below 100 (Byesville, Cumberland, Eden Twp., Enoch Twp., Hanover, Hanover Twp. (Licking County), Nellie, Perry Twp. (Licking County), Virginia Twp., Westland Twp., Mary Ann Twp. (portions)). Franchise award date: N.A. Franchise expiration date: N.A. Began: July 19, 1976.
Channel capacity: N.A. Channels available but not in use: N.A.

Basic Service
Subscribers: 21,451.
Programming (received off-air): WBNS-TV (Antenna TV, CBS, Decades) Columbus; WCMH-TV (MeTV, NBC) Columbus; WHIZ-TV (NBC) Zanesville; WOSU-TV (PBS) Columbus; WOUC-TV (PBS) Cambridge; WSFJ-TV (TBN) Newark; WSYX (ABC, Antenna TV, MNT, This TV) Columbus; WTTE (FOX) Columbus; WWHO (CW) Chillicothe; 19 FMs.
Programming (via satellite): C-SPAN; C-SPAN 2; EVINE Live; Pop; QVC; TBS; The Weather Channel; WGN America.
Fee: $29.95 installation; $24.50 monthly.

Expanded Basic Service 1
Subscribers: N.A.
Programming (via satellite): A&E; AMC; Animal Planet; BET; Bravo; Cartoon Network; CMT; CNBC; CNN; Comedy Central; Discovery Channel; Disney Channel; E! HD; ESPN; ESPN2; EWTN Global Catholic Network; Food Network; Fox News Channel; Fox Sports 1; FOX Sports Ohio/Sports Time Ohio; Freeform; FX; Hallmark Channel; HGTV; History; HLN; Lifetime; MSNBC; MTV; MTV2; Nickelodeon; Oxygen; Spike TV; Syfy; TLC; TNT; Travel Channel; truTV; Turner Classic Movies; TV Land; USA Network; VH1.
Fee: $22.32 monthly.

Digital Basic Service
Subscribers: N.A.
Programming (via satellite): BBC America; Bloomberg Television; C-SPAN 3; Discovery Life Channel; Disney XD; DIY Network; ESPN Classic; ESPNews; Fuse; FXM; Great American Country; GSN; LMN; MC; National Geographic Channel; Nick 2; Nick Jr.; Nicktoons; Outdoor Channel; TeenNick; The Word Network; Trinity Broadcasting Network (TBN); WE tv.
Fee: $14.95 monthly.

Digital Expanded Basic Service
Subscribers: N.A.
Programming (via satellite): CBS Sports Network; Fox Sports 2; FSN Digital Atlantic; FSN Digital Central; FSN Digital Pacific; FYI; Golf Channel; History International; IFC; NBCSN; Sundance TV; Tennis Channel.

Digital Pay Service 1
Pay Units: N.A.
Programming (via satellite): ART America; Cinemax (multiplexed); Flix (multiplexed); HBO (multiplexed); HITS (Headend In The Sky); RAI Italia; RTN; Showtime (multiplexed); Starz (multiplexed); Starz Encore; The Filipino Channel; The Movie Channel (multiplexed); TV Asia; TV5; La Television International.
Fee: $8.95 monthly (Cinemax, HBO, Showtime/TMC/Flix or Starz/Encore).

Video-On-Demand: Yes

Pay-Per-View
Hot Choice (delivered digitally); iN DEMAND (delivered digitally); Playboy TV (delivered digitally); Fresh (delivered digitally).

Internet Service
Operational: Yes. Began: August 1, 2001.
Subscribers: 24,883.
Broadband Service: Road Runner.
Fee: $44.95 monthly; $5.00 modem lease.

Telephone Service
Analog: Not Operational
Digital: Operational
Subscribers: 15,026.
Fee: $44.95 monthly
Miles of Plant: 1,854.0 (coaxial); 1,051.0 (fiber optic). Homes passed: 70,091.
President: Rhonda Fraas. Vice President & General Manager: David Kreiman. Vice President, Public Affairs: Mary Jo Green. Vice President, Engineering: Randy Hall. Vice President, Marketing: Mark Psigoda. Technical Operations Manager: David Bowen. Government Affairs Coordinator: Steve Cuckler. Marketing Coordinator: Sandra Tilton.
Ownership: Time Warner Cable (MSO).

NEWPORT—Formerly served by Vital Communications. No longer in operation. ICA: OH0264.

NEWTON FALLS—Time Warner Cable. Now served by CLEVELAND (formerly Cleveland Heights), OH [OH0006]. ICA: OH0114.

NORTH BALTIMORE (village)—Time Warner Cable. Now served by TIFFIN (formerly Fostoria), OH [OH0050]. ICA: OH0349.

NORTHWOOD—Time Warner Cable. Now served by TIFFIN, OH [OH0050]. ICA: OH0141.

NORWALK—Time Warner Cable. Now served by CLEVELAND (formerly Cleveland Heights), OH [OH0006]. ICA: OH0075.

NORWICH TWP. (Muskingum County)—Time Warner Cable. Now served by COLUMBUS, OH [OH0002]. ICA: OH0225.

Communications Daily
warren Communications News

Get the industry standard FREE —
For a no-obligation trial call 800-771-9202 or visit www.warren-news.com

2017 Edition
D-595

Ohio—Cable Systems

OAK HARBOR—Time Warner Cable. Now served by PORT CLINTON, OH [OH0060]. ICA: OH0351.

OAK HILL—Time Warner Cable. Now served by JACKSON, OH [OH0098]. ICA: OH0219.

OAKLAND—Time Warner Cable, 7800 Crescent Executive Dr, Charlotte, NC 28217. Phones: 614-255-4997; 614-481-5000. Web Site: http://www.timewarnercable.com. Also serves Amanda Twp. (Fairfield County), Circleville Twp., Clear Creek Twp. (Fairfield County), Hocking Twp., Pickaway Twp., Saltcreek Twp. (Pickaway County), Tarlton, Walnut Twp. (Pickaway County) & Washington Twp. (Pickaway County). ICA: OH0352.
TV Market Ranking: 27 (Amanda Twp. (Fairfield County), Circleville Twp., Clear Creek Twp. (Fairfield County), Hocking Twp., OAKLAND, Pickaway Twp., Saltcreek Twp. (Pickaway County), Saltcreek Twp. (Pickaway County), Tarlton, Walnut Twp. (Pickaway County), Washington Twp. (Pickaway County)).
Channel capacity: N.A. Channels available but not in use: N.A.

Basic Service
Subscribers: 384.
Programming (received off-air): WBNS-TV (Antenna TV, CBS, Decades) Columbus; WCMH-TV (MeTV, NBC) Columbus; WOSU-TV (PBS) Columbus; WOUB-TV (PBS) Athens; WSFJ-TV (TBN) Newark; WSYX (ABC, Antenna TV, MNT, This TV) Columbus; WTTE (FOX) Columbus; WWHO (CW) Chillicothe.
Programming (via satellite): AMC; Nickelodeon; QVC; TBS; WGN America.
Fee: $49.99 installation; $24.50 monthly.

Expanded Basic Service 1
Subscribers: N.A.
Programming (via satellite): A&E; CMT; CNN; Discovery Channel; Disney Channel; ESPN; ESPN2; Fox News Channel; Freeform; FX; HGTV; Lifetime; MSNBC; MTV; Spike TV; The Weather Channel; TLC; TNT; USA Network; WGN America.

Digital Basic Service
Subscribers: N.A.
Programming (via satellite): BBC America; Bloomberg Television; Bravo; Discovery Life Channel; ESPN Classic; ESPNews; FXM; Golf Channel; GSN; History International; IFC; MC; NBCSN; Nick Jr.; Nicktoons; Outdoor Channel; Syfy; Trinity Broadcasting Network (TBN); WE tv.

Digital Pay Service 1
Pay Units: N.A.
Programming (via satellite): Cinemax (multiplexed); HBO (multiplexed); Showtime (multiplexed); Starz (multiplexed); Starz Encore (multiplexed); The Movie Channel (multiplexed).
Fee: $12.99 monthly (each).

Video-On-Demand: No

Pay-Per-View
HITS PPV 1-6 (delivered digitally); Fresh (delivered digitally); Playboy TV (delivered digitally).

Internet Service
Operational: No.

Telephone Service
Digital: Operational
Miles of Plant: 175.0 (coaxial); None (fiber optic). Homes passed: 3,154.
President: Rhonda Fraas. Vice President & General Manager: David Kreiman. Vice President, Government & Public Affairs: Mary Jo Green. Vice President, Engineering: Randy Hall. Vice President, Marketing:

Mark Psigoda. Senior Accounting Director: Karen Goodfellow. Technical Operations Director: Jim Cavender. Government Affairs Director: Steve Cuckler.
Ownership: Time Warner Cable (MSO).

OBERLIN—Cable Co-op Inc, 27 East College St, Oberlin, OH 44074-1612. Phone: 440-775-4001. Fax: 440-775-1635. Web Site: http://www.oberlin.net. Also serves New Russia Twp. & Pittsfield Twp. ICA: OH0147.
TV Market Ranking: 8 (New Russia Twp., OBERLIN, Pittsfield Twp.). Franchise award date: June 27, 1986. Franchise expiration date: N.A. Began: January 25, 1988.
Channel capacity: 71 (operating 2-way). Channels available but not in use: N.A.

Basic Service
Subscribers: N.A.
Programming (received off-air): WBNX-TV (CW, Movies!, This TV) Akron; WEAO (PBS) Akron; WEWS-TV (ABC) Cleveland; WGGN-TV (IND) Sandusky; WJW (Antenna TV, FOX) Cleveland; WKYC (NBC) Cleveland; WOIO (CBS, MeTV) Shaker Heights; WQHS-DT (getTV, UNV) Cleveland; WUAB (Bounce TV, MNT) Lorain; WVIZ (PBS) Cleveland; WVPX-TV (ION) Akron; 20 FMs.
Programming (via satellite): A&E; AMC; Animal Planet; BET; Bravo; Cartoon Network; CMT; CNBC; CNN; Comedy Central; C-SPAN; C-SPAN 2; Discovery Channel; Discovery Life Channel; Disney Channel; DIY Network; E! HD; ESPN; ESPN Classic; ESPN2; Food Network; Fox News Channel; FOX Sports Ohio/Sports Time Ohio; Freeform; FX; Hallmark Channel; HGTV; History; HLN; Lifetime; MSNBC; MTV; National Geographic Channel; Nickelodeon; Ovation; Oxygen; Pop; QVC; Spike TV; Syfy; TBS; The Weather Channel; TLC; TNT; Travel Channel; truTV; Turner Classic Movies; TV Land; TV One; USA Network; VH1; WGN America.
Fee: $25.00 installation; $15.00 converter.

Digital Basic Service
Subscribers: N.A.
Programming (via satellite): BBC America; Bloomberg Television; Cloo; Cooking Channel; Disney XD; DMX Music; ESPN Classic; ESPNews; Fox Sports 1; FSN Digital Atlantic; FSN Digital Central; FSN Digital Pacific; Fuse; FXM; FYI; Golf Channel; Great American Country; History International; IFC; LMN; National Geographic Channel; NBCSN; Nick Jr.; Nicktoons; Outdoor Channel; OWN: Oprah Winfrey Network; TeenNick; Trinity Broadcasting Network (TBN); WE tv.

Pay Service 1
Pay Units: N.A.
Programming (via satellite): HBO.
Fee: $10.95 monthly.

Digital Pay Service 1
Pay Units: N.A.
Programming (via satellite): Cinemax (multiplexed); Flix; HBO (multiplexed); Showtime (multiplexed); Starz (multiplexed); Starz Encore (multiplexed); Sundance TV; The Movie Channel (multiplexed).

Video-On-Demand: No

Pay-Per-View
Movies & Events (delivered digitally); Playboy TV (delivered digitally); Fresh (delivered digitally); Shorteez (delivered digitally); Hot Choice (delivered digitally); NBA League Pass (delivered digitally); MLB Extra Innings (delivered digitally).

Internet Service
Operational: Yes.
Broadband Service: In-house.
Fee: $25.00 installation; $19.95-$71.45 monthly.

Telephone Service
None
Miles of Plant: 45.0 (coaxial); None (fiber optic). Homes passed: 2,900.
General Manager: Ralph L. Potts. Chief Technician: Engel Smit III. Customer Service Manager: Rita Casey.
Ownership: Cable Cooperative Inc.

OLMSTED TWP.—Formerly served by Olmsted Cable Co. Corp. Now served by Cox Communications, PARMA, OH [OH0009]. ICA: OH0223.

ORRVILLE—Armstrong Cable Services. Now served by ZELIENOPLE, PA [PA0053]. ICA: OH0109.

ORWELL—Orwell Communications, 70 South Maple St, Orwell, OH 44076. Phones: 419-596-3847; 800-400-5568. Web Site: http://www.fairpoint.com. Also serves Colebrook, North Bloomfield Twp., Rome Twp. & Windsor. ICA: OH0195.
TV Market Ranking: 79 (Colebrook, North Bloomfield Twp., ORWELL, Rome Twp., Windsor). Franchise award date: N.A. Franchise expiration date: N.A. Began: October 1, 1982.
Channel capacity: N.A. Channels available but not in use: N.A.

Basic Service
Subscribers: 547.
Programming (received off-air): WBNX-TV (CW, Movies!, This TV) Akron; WEWS-TV (ABC) Cleveland; WFMJ-TV (CW, NBC) Youngstown; WNEO (PBS) Alliance; WOIO (CBS, MeTV) Shaker Heights; WUAB (Bounce TV, MNT) Lorain; WVIZ (PBS) Cleveland; WYTV (ABC, MNT) Youngstown; allband FM.
Programming (via satellite): A&E; Animal Planet; Cartoon Network; CMT; CNN; Comedy Central; C-SPAN; Discovery Channel; Discovery Life Channel; Disney Channel; DIY Network; ESPN; ESPN Classic; ESPN2; Food Network; Fox News Channel; Fox Sports 1; FOX Sports Networks; Freeform; FX; Hallmark Channel; HGTV; History; HLN; Lifetime; MTV; National Geographic Channel; Nickelodeon; Outdoor Channel; QVC; Spike TV; Syfy; TBS; The Weather Channel; TLC; TNT; Trinity Broadcasting Network (TBN); Turner Classic Movies; TV Land; Univision Studios; USA Network; VH1.
Fee: $47.45 monthly.

Pay Service 1
Pay Units: N.A.
Programming (via satellite): HBO; Showtime.
Fee: $25.00 installation; $9.00 monthly (each).

Video-On-Demand: No

Internet Service
Operational: Yes.
Broadband Service: In-house.
Fee: $25.00 installation; $39.95 monthly; $10.00 modem lease; $200.00 modem purchase.

Telephone Service
Digital: Operational
Miles of Plant: 62.0 (coaxial); 14.0 (fiber optic). Homes passed: 1,600.
General Manager: John Campbell. Chief Technician: Paul Place. Accounting Director: Angela Unruh.
Ownership: FairPoint Communications Inc.

OTTAWA TWP.—Time Warner Cable. Now served by TIFFIN, OH [OH0050]. ICA: OH0137.

OTTOVILLE—OTEC Communication Co., 245 West 3rd St, PO Box 427, Ottoville, OH 45876-0427. Phone: 419-453-3324. Fax: 419-453-2468. E-mail: tomtc@bright.net. Web Site: http://ottovillemutual.com. Also serves Cloverdale, Dupont, Grover Hill, Hoaglin Twp., Jackson Twp. (Putnam County), Jackson Twp. (Van Wert County), Jennings Twp. (Putnam County), Latty Twp., Monterey Twp., Perry Twp. (Putnam County), Washington Twp. (Paulding County) & Washington Twp. (Van Wert County). ICA: OH0211.
TV Market Ranking: 82 (Grover Hill, Latty Twp.); Below 100 (Cloverdale, Hoaglin Twp., Jackson Twp. (Putnam County), Jackson Twp. (Van Wert County), Jennings Twp. (Putnam County), Monterey Twp., OTTOVILLE, Perry Twp. (Putnam County), Washington Twp. (Paulding County), Grover Hill). Franchise award date: April 7, 1980. Franchise expiration date: N.A. Began: October 1, 1983.
Channel capacity: N.A. Channels available but not in use: N.A.

Basic Service
Subscribers: 697.
Programming (received off-air): WANE-TV (Antenna TV, CBS) Fort Wayne; WBGU-TV (PBS) Bowling Green; WBNS-TV (Antenna TV, CBS, Decades) Columbus; WLIO (CW, NBC) Lima; WLQP-LP (ABC) Lima; WNWO-TV (NBC, Retro TV) Toledo; WOHL-CD (ABC, CBS) Lima; WPTA (ABC, MNT, NBC) Fort Wayne; WTLW (IND) Lima; WTOL (CBS, MeTV) Toledo; WTVG (ABC, CW) Toledo; WUPW (FOX, TheCoolTV) Toledo; allband FM.
Programming (via satellite): CW PLUS; EWTN Global Catholic Network; FOX Sports Ohio/Sports Time Ohio.
Fee: $35.00 installation; $18.95 monthly.

Expanded Basic Service 1
Subscribers: N.A.
Programming (via satellite): A&E; Cartoon Network; CMT; CNN; Comedy Central; Discovery Channel; Disney Channel; ESPN; ESPN Classic; ESPN2; Food Network; Fox News Channel; FOX Sports Ohio/Sports Time Ohio; Freeform; FX; Hallmark Channel; History; Lifetime; MSNBC; MTV; National Geographic Channel; Nickelodeon; Spike TV; TBS; The Weather Channel; TLC; TNT; Travel Channel; Turner Classic Movies; TV Land; USA Network; VH1; WGN America.
Fee: $12.05 monthly.

Pay Service 1
Pay Units: N.A.
Programming (via satellite): HBO; Showtime; The Movie Channel.
Fee: $12.45 monthly (Showtime or TMC), $16.95 monthly (HBO).

Pay-Per-View
Playboy TV (delivered digitally); Fresh (delivered digitally); Club Jenna (delivered digitally).

Internet Service
Operational: Yes.
Fee: $45.00 installation; $79.95-$174.95 monthly.

Telephone Service
Analog: Operational
Miles of Plant: 93.0 (coaxial); None (fiber optic). Homes passed: 1,175.
General Manager: William Honigford.
Ownership: OTEC Communication Co.

Cable Systems—Ohio

OWENSVILLE (village)—Time Warner Cable. Now served by AMBERLEY (village), OH [OH0001]. ICA: OH0368.

OXFORD—Time Warner Cable. Now served by AMBERLEY (village), OH [OH0001]. ICA: OH0101.

PARMA—Cox Communications, 6205 Peachtree Dunwoody Rd, 12th Floor, Atlanta, GA 30328. Phone: 404-269-6590. Web Site: http://www.cox.com. Also serves Berea, Broadview Heights, Brooklyn Heights, Fairview Park, Independence, Lakewood (Cuyahoga County), Olmsted Falls, Olmsted Twp., Parma Heights, Rocky River & Seven Hills. ICA: OH0009.
TV Market Ranking: 8 (Berea, Broadview Heights, Brooklyn Heights, Fairview Park, Independence, Lakewood (Cuyahoga County), Olmsted Falls, Olmsted Twp., PARMA, Parma Heights, Rocky River, Seven Hills). Franchise award date: March 12, 1973. Franchise expiration date: N.A. Began: May 1, 1980.
Channel capacity: 61 (operating 2-way). Channels available but not in use: N.A.
Basic Service
Subscribers: 43,867. Commercial subscribers: 892.
Programming (received off-air): WBNX-TV (CW, Movies!, This TV) Akron; WEAO (PBS) Akron; WEWS-TV (ABC) Cleveland; WJW (Antenna TV, FOX) Cleveland; WKYC (NBC) Cleveland; WOIO (CBS, MeTV) Shaker Heights; WQHS-DT (getTV, UNV) Cleveland; WRLM (IND) Canton; WUAB (Bounce TV, MNT) Lorain; WVIZ (PBS) Cleveland; WVPX-TV (ION) Akron; 3 FMs.
Programming (via satellite): FOX Sports Ohio/Sports Time Ohio; WGN America.
Fee: $23.85 installation; $24.99 monthly; $.50 converter.
Expanded Basic Service 1
Subscribers: N.A.
Programming (via satellite): A&E; AMC; Animal Planet; Cartoon Network; CMT; CNBC; CNN; Comedy Central; C-SPAN; C-SPAN 2; Discovery Channel; Disney Channel; E! HD; ESPN; ESPN2; EWTN Global Catholic Network; Food Network; Fox News Channel; Fox Sports 1; Freeform; FX; Hallmark Channel; HGTV; History; HLN; INSP; Lifetime; MSNBC; MTV; Nickelodeon; OWN: Oprah Winfrey Network; Oxygen; Pop; QVC; Scola; Spike TV; Syfy; TBS; The Weather Channel; TLC; TNT; Travel Channel; Trinity Broadcasting Network (TBN); truTV; Turner Classic Movies; TV Land; USA Network; VH1.
Fee: $37.65 monthly.
Digital Basic Service
Subscribers: N.A.
Programming (via satellite): BBC America; Bloomberg Television; Discovery Digital Networks; Disney XD; DIY Network; ESPN Classic; ESPNews; Flix; FYI; Golf Channel; History International; IFC; LMN; MC; Nick 2; Ovation; Sundance TV; Weatherscan.
Fee: $8.99 monthly.
Digital Pay Service 1
Pay Units: N.A.
Programming (via satellite): Cinemax (multiplexed); HBO (multiplexed); Showtime (multiplexed); Starz (multiplexed); Starz Encore (multiplexed); The Movie Channel (multiplexed).
Fee: $11.00 monthly (each).
Video-On-Demand: Yes
Pay-Per-View
ESPN Now (delivered digitally); Fresh (delivered digitally); Shorteez (delivered digitally); Hot Choice (delivered digitally); iN DEMAND (delivered digitally); Playboy TV (delivered digitally).
Internet Service
Operational: Yes.
Subscribers: 28,527.
Broadband Service: Cox High Speed Internet.
Fee: $9.99 installation; $26.95 monthly; $15.00 modem lease; $49.00 modem purchase.
Telephone Service
Digital: Operational
Subscribers: 25,296.
Fee: $8.00 monthly
Miles of Plant: 1,460.0 (coaxial); 366.0 (fiber optic). Homes passed: 117,774.
Vice President & General Manager: Kevin Haynes. Vice President, Tax: Mary Vickers. Public Relations & Government Affairs Director: Christy Bykowski. Marketing & Sales Director: Laura Morabito. Network Operations Director: Tim Yanda.
Ownership: Cox Communications Inc. (MSO).

PATASKALA (village)—Time Warner Cable. Now served by COLUMBUS, OH [OH0002]. ICA: OH0165.

PAULDING—Time Warner Cable, 7800 Crescent Executive Dr, Charlotte, NC 28217. Phones: 614-481-5000 (Columbus office); 419-429-7402. Web Site: http://www.timewarnercable.com. Also serves Cecil, Crane Twp. (Paulding County), Emerald Twp., Jackson Twp. (Paulding County), Latty & Paulding Twp. (Paulding County). ICA: OH0186.
TV Market Ranking: 82 (Cecil, Emerald Twp. (portions), Jackson Twp. (Paulding County), Latty, PAULDING, Paulding Twp. (Paulding County)); Below 100 (Crane Twp. (Paulding County)); Outside TV Markets (Emerald Twp. (portions)). Franchise award date: N.A. Franchise expiration date: N.A. Began: October 1, 1976.
Channel capacity: N.A. Channels available but not in use: N.A.
Basic Service
Subscribers: 710.
Programming (received off-air): WANE-TV (Antenna TV, CBS) Fort Wayne; WBGU-TV (PBS) Bowling Green; WDFM-LP (IND) Defiance; WFFT-TV (FOX, MeTV) Fort Wayne; WGTE-TV (PBS) Toledo; WINM (IND) Angola; WISE-TV (CW) Fort Wayne; WLIO (CW, NBC) Lima; WLMB (IND) Toledo; WNWO-TV (NBC, Retro TV) Toledo; WPTA (ABC, MNT, NBC) Fort Wayne; WTOL (CBS, MeTV) Toledo; WTVG (ABC, CW) Toledo; WUPW (FOX, TheCoolTV) Toledo; allband FM.
Programming (via satellite): Freeform; Pop; QVC; WGN America.
Fee: $49.99 installation; $24.50 monthly.
Expanded Basic Service 1
Subscribers: N.A.
Programming (via satellite): A&E; AMC; Animal Planet; BET; Bravo; Cartoon Network; CMT; CNBC; CNN; Comedy Central; C-SPAN; C-SPAN 2; Discovery Channel; Disney Channel; E! HD; ESPN; ESPN2; EVINE Live; EWTN Global Catholic Network; Food Network; Fox News Channel; FOX Sports Detroit; FOX Sports Ohio/Sports Time Ohio; FX; Hallmark Channel; HGTV; History; HLN; Lifetime; MSNBC; MTV; Nickelodeon; Oxygen; Spike TV; Syfy; TBS; The Weather Channel; TLC; TNT; Travel Channel; truTV; TV Land; Univision Studios; USA Network; VH1.
Fee: $17.84 monthly.
Digital Basic Service
Subscribers: N.A.
Programming (via satellite): BBC America; Bloomberg Television; Discovery Life Channel; Disney XD; DIY Network; DMX Music; Fox Sports 1; Fuse; FXM; Great American Country; GSN; HITS (Headend In The Sky); LMN; National Geographic Channel; Nick 2; Nick Jr.; Nicktoons; TeenNick; The Word Network; Trinity Broadcasting Network (TBN); Turner Classic Movies; WE tv.
Digital Expanded Basic Service
Subscribers: N.A.
Programming (via satellite): ESPN Classic; ESPNews; Flix; FSN Digital Atlantic; FSN Digital Central; FSN Digital Pacific; FYI; Golf Channel; History International; IFC; NBCSN; Outdoor Channel; RAI Italia; RTN; Sundance TV; TAC TV; The Filipino Channel; TV Asia; TV5, La Television International.
Digital Pay Service 1
Pay Units: N.A.
Programming (via satellite): Cinemax (multiplexed); HBO; Showtime (multiplexed); Starz (multiplexed); Starz Encore (multiplexed); The Movie Channel (multiplexed).
Fee: $12.99 monthly (each).
Video-On-Demand: No
Pay-Per-View
ESPN Now (delivered digitally); NHL Center Ice (delivered digitally); MLB Extra Innings (delivered digitally); Playboy TV (delivered digitally); Fresh (delivered digitally); Shorteez (delivered digitally); Hot Choice (delivered digitally); ESPN (delivered digitally).
Internet Service
Operational: Yes.
Broadband Service: Road Runner.
Fee: $44.95 monthly.
Telephone Service
Digital: Operational
Fee: $44.95 monthly.
Miles of Plant: 57.0 (coaxial); None (fiber optic). Homes passed: 2,558.
President: Rhonda Fraas. Vice President & General Manager: Brad Wakely. Vice President, Engineering: Randy Hall. Vice President, Marketing: Mark Psigoda. Senior Accounting Director: Karen Goodfellow. Technical Operations Director: John Ellingson. Government Affairs Director: Brian Young. Government Affairs Manager: Patrick McCauley.
Ownership: Time Warner Cable (MSO).

PAYNE—NewWave Communications. Now served by MONROEVILLE, IN [IN0358]. ICA: OH0445.

PEDRO—Formerly served by Windjammer Cable. No longer in operation. ICA: OH0244.

PEEBLES (village)—Time Warner Cable. Now served by AMBERLEY (village), OH [OH0001]. ICA: OH0197.

PHILO (village)—Time Warner Cable. Now served by COLUMBUS, OH [OH0002]. ICA: OH0354.

PIKETON—Time Warner Cable. Now served by CHILLICOTHE, OH [OH0033]. ICA: OH0199.

PINE LAKE TRAILER PARK—Formerly served by Marshall County Cable. No longer in operation. ICA: OH0355.

PIONEER—Formerly served by Windjammer Cable. No longer in operation. ICA: OH0273.

PIQUA—Formerly served by Time Warner Cable. No longer in operation. ICA: OH0065.

POLK (village)—Time Warner Cable. Now served by CLEVELAND (formerly Cleveland Heights), OH [OH0006]. ICA: OH0304.

PORT CLINTON—Time Warner Cable, 530 South Main St, Ste 1751, Akron, OH 44311-1090. Phones: 330-633-1874; 330-633-9203 (Regional office); 419-734-5905 (Port Clinton office). Fax: 330-633-7970. Web Site: http://www.timewarnercable.com. Also serves Bay Twp. (Ottawa County), Benton Twp. (Ottawa County), Carroll Twp. (Ottawa County), Catawba Island Twp. (Ottawa County), Danbury Twp. (Ottawa County), Erie Twp. (Ottawa County), Marblehead, Oak Harbor, Portage Twp. (Ottawa County), Rocky Ridge, Salem Twp. (Ottawa County) & Sandusky Twp. (Sandusky County). ICA: OH0060.
TV Market Ranking: 52 (Bay Twp. (Ottawa County), Benton Twp. (Ottawa County), Carroll Twp. (Ottawa County), Erie Twp. (Ottawa County), Marblehead, Oak Harbor, PORT CLINTON, Portage Twp. (Ottawa County), Rocky Ridge, Salem Twp. (Ottawa County), Sandusky Twp. (Sandusky County)); Below 100 (Catawba Island Twp. (Ottawa County), Danbury Twp. (Ottawa County)).
Channel capacity: N.A. Channels available but not in use: N.A.
Basic Service
Subscribers: 9,774.
Programming (received off-air): WBGU-TV (PBS) Bowling Green; WEWS-TV (ABC) Cleveland; WGGN-TV (IND) Sandusky; WGTE-TV (PBS) Toledo; WJW (Antenna TV, FOX) Cleveland; WKBD-TV (CW) Detroit; WLMB (IND) Toledo; WNWO-TV (NBC, Retro TV) Toledo; WTOL (CBS, MeTV) Toledo; WTVG (ABC, CW) Toledo; WUAB (Bounce TV, MNT) Lorain; WUPW (FOX, TheCoolTV) Toledo.
Programming (via satellite): FOX Sports Ohio/Sports Time Ohio; QVC; various Canadian stations; WGN America.
Fee: $29.95 installation; $24.50 monthly.
Expanded Basic Service 1
Subscribers: N.A.
Programming (via satellite): A&E; AMC; Animal Planet; Bravo; Cartoon Network; CMT; CNBC; CNN; Comedy Central; C-SPAN; C-SPAN 2; Discovery Channel; Disney Channel; E! HD; ESPN; ESPN2; EVINE Live; EWTN Global Catholic Network; Food Network; Fox News Channel; FOX Sports Detroit; FOX Sports Ohio/Sports Time Ohio; Freeform; FX; Golf Channel; Hallmark Channel; HGTV; History; HLN; ION Television; Lifetime; MSNBC; MTV; Nickelodeon; Oxygen; Pop; Spike TV; Syfy; TBS; The Weather Channel; TLC; TNT; Travel Channel; truTV; Turner Classic Movies; TV Land; Univision Studios; USA Network; VH1.
Fee: $37.25 monthly.
Digital Basic Service
Subscribers: N.A.
Programming (via satellite): 52MX; AXS TV; BBC America; Bloomberg Television; Cinelatino; CMT; CNN en Espanol; C-SPAN 3; Destination America; Discovery Kids Channel; Discovery Life Channel; Disney XD; DIY Network; ESPN Classic; ESPN Deportes; ESPN HD; ESPN2 HD; ESPNews; ESPNU; Fox Business Network; Fox Deportes; Fox Sports 1; FOX Sports Ohio/Sports Time Ohio; Fuse; FXM; Great American Country; GSN; HD Theater; History en Espanol; Investigation Discovery; LMN;

Ohio—Cable Systems

LOGO; MC; MTV Classic; MTV Hits; MTV Jams; MTV2; Nat Geo WILD; National Geographic Channel; Nick 2; Nick Jr.; Nicktoons; OWN: Oprah Winfrey Network; Pop; Science Channel; TBS HD; TeenNick; The Word Network; TNT HD; Toon Disney en Espanol; Tr3s; Trinity Broadcasting Network (TBN); TV One; Universal HD; UP; VH1 Soul; WE tv.
Fee: $11.00 monthly.

Digital Expanded Basic Service
Subscribers: N.A.
Programming (via satellite): CBS Sports Network; Cooking Channel; Flix; Fox Sports 2; FSN Digital Atlantic; FSN Digital Central; FSN Digital Pacific; FYI; History International; IFC; NBA TV; NBCSN; Outdoor Channel; Sundance TV; Tennis Channel.
Fee: $10.00 monthly.

Digital Pay Service 1
Pay Units: N.A.
Programming (via satellite): Cinemax (multiplexed); Cinemax HD; Flix; HBO (multiplexed); HBO HD; Showtime (multiplexed); Showtime HD; Starz (multiplexed); Starz Encore (multiplexed); Starz HD; The Movie Channel (multiplexed).
Fee: $12.99 monthly (each).

Video-On-Demand: No

Pay-Per-View
iN DEMAND (delivered digitally); Playboy TV (delivered digitally); Fresh (delivered digitally); Shorteez (delivered digitally); Hot Choice (delivered digitally); ESPN (delivered digitally); MLB Extra Innings (delivered digitally); NHL Network (delivered digitally).

Internet Service
Operational: Yes.
Subscribers: 7,161.
Broadband Service: Road Runner.
Fee: $45.95 monthly.

Telephone Service
Digital: Operational
Subscribers: 2,433.
Miles of Plant: 635.0 (coaxial); 190.0 (fiber optic). Homes passed: 21,745.
President: Stephen Fry. Area Vice President: Scott Miller. Area Manager: Carol Jagger. Vice President, Marketing: Patrick Burke. Vice President, Engineering: Al Costanzi. Vice President, Public Affairs: William Jasso. Government & Media Relations Director: Chris Thomas.
Ownership: Time Warner Cable (MSO).

PORT WILLIAM—Formerly served by Time Warner Cable. No longer in operation. ICA: OH0259.

PORTERFIELD—Formerly served by Adelphia Communications. No longer in operation. ICA: OH0372.

PORTSMOUTH—Time Warner Cable, 1266 Dublin Rd, Columbus, OH 43215-1008. Phones: 614-255-4997; 614-481-5000. Fax: 614-481-5052. Web Site: http://www.timewarnercable.com. Also serves Greenup County (portions), Lewis County (portions) & South Shore, KY; Bloom Twp. (Scioto County), Clay Twp. (Scioto County), Firebrick, Friendship, Harrison, Jefferson, Lucasville, Madison Twp. (Vinton County), Morgan Twp. (Scioto County), New Boston, Nile Twp., Porter Twp. (Scioto County), Rush Twp. (Scioto County), South Webster (village), Union Twp. (Scioto County), Valley Twp. (Scioto County), Vernon Twp. (Scioto County) & Washington Twp. (Scioto County), OH. ICA: OH0035.
TV Market Ranking: 17 (Harrison); 27 (Clay Twp. (Scioto County) (portions), Lucasville, Madison Twp. (Vinton County), Morgan Twp. (Scioto County), PORTSMOUTH (portions), Rush Twp. (Scioto County), Union Twp. (Scioto County) (portions), Valley Twp. (Scioto County)); 27,36 (Bloom Twp. (Scioto County) (portions)); 36 (Firebrick, Greenup County (portion), New Boston, Porter Twp. (Scioto County), South Shore, South Webster (village), Vernon Twp. (Scioto County)); Below 100 (Nile Twp., Washington Twp. (Scioto County), Friendship, Clay Twp. (Scioto County) (portions), PORTSMOUTH (portions), Union Twp. (Scioto County) (portions), Greenup County (portion)); Outside TV Markets (Jefferson). Franchise award date: N.A. Franchise expiration date: N.A. Began: December 18, 1962.
Channel capacity: N.A. Channels available but not in use: N.A.

Basic Service
Subscribers: 30,742.
Programming (received off-air): WBNS-TV (Antenna TV, CBS, Decades) Columbus; WCHS-TV (ABC, Antenna TV) Charleston; WKMR (PBS) Morehead; WLPX-TV (ION) Charleston; WLWT (MeTV, NBC) Cincinnati; WOWK-TV (CBS) Huntington; WPBO (PBS) Portsmouth; WQCW (CW) Portsmouth; WSAZ-TV (MNT, NBC, This TV) Huntington; WSYX (ABC, Antenna TV, MNT, This TV) Columbus; WTSF (Daystar TV) Ashland; WVAH-TV (FOX, The Country Network) Charleston; 12 FMs.
Programming (via satellite): C-SPAN; EWTN Global Catholic Network; Freeform; Pop; QVC; TBS; The Weather Channel; WGN America.
Fee: $29.95 installation; $15.50 monthly.

Expanded Basic Service 1
Subscribers: N.A.
Programming (via satellite): A&E; AMC; Animal Planet; BET; Bravo; Cartoon Network; CMT; CNBC; CNN; Comedy Central; Discovery Channel; Disney Channel; Disney XD; E! HD; ESPN; ESPN2; EVINE Live; Food Network; Fox News Channel; Fox Sports 1; FOX Sports Ohio/Sports Time Ohio; FX; FYI; Golf Channel; Great American Country; Hallmark Channel; HGTV; History; HLN; Lifetime; MSNBC; MTV; National Geographic Channel; Nick Jr.; Nickelodeon; Outdoor Channel; Oxygen; Spike TV; Syfy; TLC; TNT; Travel Channel; truTV; TV Land; Univision Studios; USA Network; VH1; WE tv.

Digital Basic Service
Subscribers: N.A.
Programming (via satellite): AXS TV; BBC America; Bloomberg Television; Cinelatino; CMT; CNN en Espanol; Destination America; Discovery Kids Channel; Discovery Life Channel; DIY Network; ESPN Classic; ESPN Deportes; ESPN HD; ESPN2 HD; ESPNews; ESPNU; Fox Business Network; Fox Deportes; FSN HD; Fuse; FXM; GSN; HD Theater; History en Espanol; History International; IFC; INSP; Investigation Discovery; LMN; LOGO; MC; MTV Classic; MTV Hits; MTV Jams; MTV2; Nat Geo WILD; NBCSN; Nick 2; Nicktoons; OWN: Oprah Winfrey Network; Science Channel; TBS HD; TeenNick; The Word Network; TNT HD; Tr3s; Trinity Broadcasting Network (TBN); Turner Classic Movies; TVG Network; Universal HD; UP; Versus HD; VH1 Soul.

Digital Expanded Basic Service
Subscribers: N.A.
Programming (via satellite): CBS Sports Network; FOX College Sports Central; FOX College Sports Pacific; Fox Sports 2; Tennis Channel.

Digital Pay Service 1
Pay Units: N.A.
Programming (via satellite): ART America; Cinemax (multiplexed); Cinemax HD; Flix; HBO (multiplexed); HBO HD; RAI Italia; Showtime (multiplexed); Showtime HD; Starz (multiplexed); Starz Encore (multiplexed); Starz HD; Sundance TV; The Filipino Channel; The Movie Channel (multiplexed); TV Asia; TV5, La Television International.
Fee: $12.99 monthly (each).

Video-On-Demand: Yes

Pay-Per-View
iN DEMAND (delivered digitally); Playboy TV (delivered digitally); Fresh (delivered digitally); Club Jenna (delivered digitally); Hot Choice (delivered digitally); ESPN (delivered digitally); NHL Center Ice (delivered digitally); MLB Extra Innings (delivered digitally); NBA League Pass (delivered digitally).

Internet Service
Operational: Yes.
Subscribers: 28,573.
Broadband Service: Road Runner.
Fee: $44.95 monthly.

Telephone Service
Digital: Operational
Subscribers: 18,133.
Fee: $44.95 monthly.
Miles of Plant: 3,199.0 (coaxial); 1,963.0 (fiber optic). Homes passed: 88,207.
President: Rhonda Fraas. Vice President & General Manager: David Kreiman. Vice President, Government & Public Affairs: Mary Jo Green. Vice President, Engineering: Randy Hall. Vice President, Marketing: Mark Psigoda. Technical Operations Director: Jim Cavender. Government Affairs Director: Steve Cuckler.
Ownership: Time Warner Cable (MSO).

POWHATAN POINT—Powhatan Point Cable Co, PO Box 67, Powhatan Point, OH 43942-0067. Phone: 740-795-5005. ICA: OH0356.
TV Market Ranking: 90 (POWHATAN POINT). Franchise award date: N.A. Franchise expiration date: N.A. Began: June 1, 1970.
Channel capacity: 54 (not 2-way capable). Channels available but not in use: N.A.

Basic Service
Subscribers: 333.
Programming (received off-air): KDKA-TV (CBS, Decades) Pittsburgh; WFMJ-TV (CW, NBC) Youngstown; WKBN-TV (CBS) Youngstown; WOUC-TV (PBS) Cambridge; WQED (PBS) Pittsburgh; WTAE-TV (ABC, This TV) Pittsburgh; WTOV-TV (MeTV, NBC) Steubenville; WTRF-TV (ABC, CBS, MNT) Wheeling.
Programming (via satellite): A&E; Animal Planet; Cartoon Network; CMT; CNN; Comedy Central; Discovery Channel; ESPN; ESPN2; Food Network; Fox News Channel; Fox Sports 1; Freeform; FX; Great American Country; Hallmark Channel; HGTV; Lifetime; MTV; Nickelodeon; Outdoor Channel; Root Sports Pittsburgh; Spike TV; Syfy; TBS; The Weather Channel; TLC; TNT; Travel Channel; Trinity Broadcasting Network (TBN); truTV; Turner Classic Movies; TV Land; USA Network; VH1; WABC-TV (ABC, Live Well Network) New York; WGN America.
Fee: $70.00 monthly.

Pay Service 1
Pay Units: N.A.
Programming (via satellite): HBO (multiplexed); Starz Encore.
Fee: $5.00 monthly (Encore), $12.00 monthly (HBO).

Video-On-Demand: No

Internet Service
Operational: Yes.
Fee: $35.00 monthly.

Telephone Service
None
Vice President & General Manager: Kasmir Majewski.
Ownership: Powhatan Point Cable Co. (MSO).

PROCTORVILLE—Formerly served by Lycom Communications. No longer in operation. ICA: OH0291.

PUT-IN-BAY—Time Warner Cable. Now served by CLEVELAND (formerly Cleveland Heights), OH [OH0006]. ICA: OH0357.

RAINSBORO—Formerly served by Adelphia Communications. Now served by Time Warner Cable, WASHINGTON COURT HOUSE, OH [OH0070]. ICA: OH0196.

RICHMOND DALE—Formerly served by Adelphia Communications. Now served by Time Warner Cable, CHILLICOTHE, OH [OH0033]. ICA: OH0262.

RIDGEVILLE CORNERS—RTEC Communications, 105 East Holland St, PO Box 408, Archbold, OH 43502. Phone: 419-267-8800. Fax: 419-267-8808. E-mail: info@rtecexpress.net. Web Site: http://www.rtecexpress.net. Also serves Adams Twp., Archbold, Freedom Twp., German Twp., Napoleon Twp., Richland Twp., Ridgeville Twp. & Springfield Twp. ICA: OH0358.
TV Market Ranking: Outside TV Markets (RIDGEVILLE CORNERS). Franchise award date: N.A. Franchise expiration date: N.A. Began: August 1, 1990.
Channel capacity: N.A. Channels available but not in use: N.A.

Basic Service
Subscribers: 1,000.
Programming (received off-air): WANE-TV (Antenna TV, CBS) Fort Wayne; WDFM-LP (IND) Defiance; WGTE-TV (PBS) Toledo; WISE-TV (CW) Fort Wayne; WKGB-TV (PBS) Bowling Green; WLIO (CW, NBC) Lima; WLMB (IND) Toledo; WNWO-TV (NBC, Retro TV) Toledo; WPTA (ABC, MNT, NBC) Fort Wayne; WTOL (CBS, MeTV) Toledo; WTVG (ABC, CW) Toledo; WUPW (FOX, TheCoolTV) Toledo.
Programming (via satellite): CNN; C-SPAN; C-SPAN 2; Fox News Channel; INSP; NASA TV; Pop; WGN America.
Fee: $19.95 installation; $62.50 monthly.

Expanded Basic Service 1
Subscribers: N.A.
Programming (received off-air): WBNS-TV (Antenna TV, CBS, Decades) Columbus.
Programming (via satellite): A&E; AMC; Animal Planet; Cartoon Network; CMT; CNBC; CNN International; Comedy Central; Discovery Channel; Disney Channel; Disney XD; DIY Network; E! HD; ESPN; ESPN Classic; ESPN2; ESPNews; Food Network; FOX Sports Detroit; FOX Sports Ohio/Sports Time Ohio; Freeform; FX; FXM; FYI; Golf Channel; Great American Country; GSN; Hallmark Channel; HGTV; History; HLN; Lifetime; LMN; MSNBC; MTV; National Geographic Channel; NBCSN; Nickelodeon; Outdoor Channel; QVC; Spike TV; Syfy; TBS; The Weather Channel; TLC; TNT; Travel Channel; Trinity Broadcasting Network (TBN); truTV; Turner Classic Movies; TV Land; Univision; Univision Studios; USA Network; VH1.
Fee: $43.00 monthly.

Cable Systems—Ohio

Expanded Basic Service 2
  Subscribers: N.A.
  Fee: $8.50 monthly.
Pay Service 1
  Pay Units: 21.
  Programming (via satellite): Cinemax.
  Fee: $11.50 monthly.
Pay Service 2
  Pay Units: 131.
  Programming (via satellite): HBO (multiplexed).
  Fee: $22.50 monthly.
Pay Service 3
  Pay Units: 26.
  Programming (via satellite): Showtime; The Movie Channel.
  Fee: $13.50 monthly.
Pay Service 4
  Pay Units: 33.
  Programming (via satellite): Starz (multiplexed); Starz Encore.
  Fee: $12.50 monthly.
Internet Service
  Operational: Yes.
  Fee: $29.95-$37.95 monthly.
Telephone Service
  Digital: Operational
  Fee: $9.00-$12.25 monthly
  General Manager: David Gobrogge. Assistant General Manager: Ken Miller. Outside Plant Manager: Brian Miller. Marketing Manager & Business Account Coordinator: Jayma Gobrogge.
  Ownership: RTEC Communications.

RIO GRANDE—Time Warner Cable. Now served by CHILLICOTHE, OH [OH0033]. ICA: OH0379.

RIPLEY—Formerly served by Adelphia Communications. Now served by Time Warner Cable, AMBERLEY (village), OH [OH0001]. ICA: OH0167.

RISING SUN (village)—Time Warner Cable. Now served by TIFFIN (formerly Fostoria), OH [OH0050]. ICA: OH0359.

RIVERSIDE—Time Warner Cable. Now served by AMBERLEY (village), OH [OH0001]. ICA: OH0011.

RIVERSIDE (Montgomery County)—Time Warner Cable. Now served by AMBERLEY (village), OH [OH0001]. ICA: OH0437.

ROBBINS MOBILE HOME PARK—Formerly served by Time Warner Cable. No longer in operation. ICA: OH0293.

ROCK CREEK—Zito Media, 102 S Main St, PO Box 665, Coudersport, PA 16915. Phones: 814-260-9055; 800-365-6988. E-mail: info@zitomedia.com. Web Site: http://www.zitomedia.com. Also serves Ashtabula County (portions), Austinburg Twp., Morgan Twp., Roaming Shores & Rome Twp. (Ashtabula County). ICA: OH0427.
  TV Market Ranking: 79 (Ashtabula County (portions)); Below 100 (Ashtabula County (portions)); Outside TV Markets (Austinburg Twp., Morgan Twp., Roaming Shores, ROCK CREEK, Rome Twp. (Ashtabula County), Ashtabula County (portions)). Channel capacity: N.A. Channels available but not in use: N.A.
Basic Service
  Subscribers: 177.
  Programming (received off-air): WBNX-TV (CW, Movies!, This TV) Akron; WEWS-TV (ABC) Cleveland; WJW (Antenna TV, FOX) Cleveland; WKYC (NBC) Cleveland; WOIO (CBS, MeTV) Shaker Heights; WQHS-DT (getTV, UNV) Cleveland; WRLM (IND) Canton; WUAB (Bounce TV, MNT) Lorain; WVIZ (PBS) Cleveland.
  Programming (via satellite): A&E; AMC; Animal Planet; BET; Cartoon Network; CNBC; CNN; Comedy Central; C-SPAN; Discovery Channel; Disney Channel; E! HD; ESPN; ESPN2; Food Network; Fox News Channel; FOX Sports Ohio/Sports Time Ohio; Freeform; FX; Great American Country; HGTV; History; HLN; ION Television; MSNBC; MTV; Nickelodeon; QVC; Spike TV; Syfy; TBS; The Weather Channel; TLC; TNT; Turner Classic Movies; TV Land; USA Network; VH1.
  Fee: $49.95 installation; $21.71 monthly; $1.95 converter.
Digital Basic Service
  Subscribers: N.A.
  Programming (via satellite): BBC America; Bloomberg Television; Cloo; Destination America; Discovery Kids Channel; Disney XD; ESPN Classic; ESPNews; EVINE Live; FOX College Sports Central; FOX College Sports Pacific; Fox Sports 1; Fuse; FYI; Golf Channel; GSN; History International; IFC; Investigation Discovery; NBCSN; Outdoor Channel; OWN; Oprah Winfrey Network; Science Channel; Sundance TV; Trinity Broadcasting Network (TBN); WE tv.
Pay Service 1
  Pay Units: N.A.
  Programming (via satellite): Cinemax; HBO; Showtime; The Movie Channel.
  Fee: $11.50 monthly (HBO), $12.95 monthly (Showtime).
Digital Pay Service 1
  Pay Units: N.A.
  Programming (via satellite): Cinemax (multiplexed); Flix; HBO (multiplexed); Showtime (multiplexed); Starz (multiplexed); Starz Encore (multiplexed); The Movie Channel (multiplexed).
Video-On-Demand: No
Pay-Per-View
  iN DEMAND (delivered digitally); Playboy TV (delivered digitally); Club Jenna (delivered digitally); Fresh (delivered digitally); Shorteez (delivered digitally).
Internet Service
  Operational: No.
Telephone Service
  None
  Miles of Plant: 50.0 (coaxial); None (fiber optic). Homes passed: 1,077.
  President: James Rigas.
  Ownership: Zito Media (MSO).

ROCKFORD (village)—Time Warner Cable. Now served by TIFFIN, OH [OH0050]. ICA: OH0204.

ROSS TWP. (Butler County)—Formerly served by Adelphia Communications. Now served by Time Warner Cable, AMBERLEY (village), OH [OH0001]. ICA: OH0127.

SALEM—Time Warner Cable. Now served by CLEVELAND (formerly Cleveland Heights), OH [OH0006]. ICA: OH0096.

SALINEVILLE—Crystal Broadband Networks, PO Box 180336, Chicago, IL 60618. Phones: 817-685-9588; 630-206-0447. Web Site: http://crystalbn.com. ICA: OH0254.
  TV Market Ranking: 79,90 (SALINEVILLE). Franchise award date: N.A. Franchise expiration date: N.A. Began: September 1, 1968.
  Channel capacity: N.A. Channels available but not in use: N.A.

FULLY SEARCHABLE • CONTINUOUSLY UPDATED • DISCOUNT RATES FOR PRINT PURCHASERS

For more information call **800-771-9202** or visit **www.warren-news.com**

Basic Service
  Subscribers: 71.
  Programming (received off-air): KDKA-TV (CBS, Decades) Pittsburgh; WFMJ-TV (CW, NBC) Youngstown; WKBN-TV (CBS) Youngstown; WNEO (PBS) Alliance; WPGH-TV (Antenna TV, FOX, The Country Network) Pittsburgh; WPNT (MNT) Pittsburgh; WPXI (MeTV, NBC) Pittsburgh; WQED (PBS) Pittsburgh; WTAE-TV (ABC, This TV) Pittsburgh; WTOV-TV (MeTV, NBC) Steubenville; WYTV (ABC, MNT) Youngstown.
  Programming (via satellite): Discovery Channel; TBS.
  Fee: $44.95 installation; $53.54 monthly.
Expanded Basic Service 1
  Subscribers: N.A.
  Programming (via satellite): A&E; AMC; Animal Planet; Cartoon Network; CNBC; CNN; C-SPAN; C-SPAN 2; Disney Channel; ESPN; ESPN2; Fox News Channel; FOX Sports Ohio/Sports Time Ohio; Freeform; Hallmark Channel; HGTV; ION Television; Lifetime; MTV; Nickelodeon; QVC; Spike TV; TLC; TNT; Travel Channel; USA Network.
  Fee: $21.75 monthly.
Digital Basic Service
  Subscribers: N.A.
  Programming (via satellite): BBC America; Bravo; Discovery Digital Networks; DMX Music; ESPN Classic; ESPNews; Fox Sports 1; Golf Channel; GSN; History; IFC; National Geographic Channel; Nick Jr.; Turner Classic Movies; WE tv.
  Fee: $9.00 monthly.
Digital Pay Service 1
  Pay Units: N.A.
  Programming (via satellite): Cinemax; HBO (multiplexed); Showtime (multiplexed); Starz Encore; The Movie Channel (multiplexed).
  Fee: $10.00 monthly (each).
Video-On-Demand: No
Pay-Per-View
  iN DEMAND (delivered digitally).
Internet Service
  Operational: No.
Telephone Service
  None
  Miles of Plant: 11.0 (coaxial); None (fiber optic). Homes passed: 648.
  General Manager: Ron Page. Program Manager: Shawn Smith.
  Ownership: Crystal Broadband Networks (MSO).

SANDUSKY—Buckeye Cable System Inc. Now served by TOLEDO, OH [OH0004]. ICA: OH0029.

SARAHSVILLE—Formerly served by Cebridge Connections. No longer in operation. ICA: OH0362.

SARDINIA—Formerly served by Crystal Broadband Networks. No longer in operation. ICA: OH0267.

SCIO—Time Warner Cable, 7800 Crescent Executive Dr, Charlotte, NC 28217. Phones: 330-633-1874; 330-633-9203; 330-868-5413 (Local office). Web Site: http://www.timewarnercable.com. ICA: OH0269.
  TV Market Ranking: 90 (SCIO). Franchise award date: N.A. Franchise expiration date: N.A. Began: December 1, 1976.
  Channel capacity: N.A. Channels available but not in use: N.A.
Basic Service
  Subscribers: 113.
  Programming (received off-air): KDKA-TV (CBS, Decades) Pittsburgh; WNEO (PBS) Alliance; WPGH-TV (Antenna TV, FOX, The Country Network) Pittsburgh; WPXI (MeTV, NBC) Pittsburgh; WTOV-TV (MeTV, NBC) Steubenville; WTRF-TV (ABC, CBS, MNT) Wheeling; WVPX-TV (ION) Akron; WYTV (ABC, MNT) Youngstown.
  Programming (via satellite): C-SPAN; QVC; TBS; TLC.
  Fee: $49.99 installation; $24.50 monthly; $3.40 converter.
Expanded Basic Service 1
  Subscribers: N.A.
  Programming (via satellite): A&E; AMC; Animal Planet; Cartoon Network; CNBC; CNN; Disney Channel; ESPN; Fox News Channel; FOX Sports Ohio/Sports Time Ohio; Freeform; Hallmark Channel; Lifetime; MoviePlex; Nickelodeon; Spike TV; The Weather Channel; TNT; truTV; USA Network.
  Fee: $24.96 monthly.
Pay Service 1
  Pay Units: N.A.
  Programming (via satellite): HBO; Showtime; Starz; Starz Encore.
  Fee: $4.00 monthly (Encore), $8.95 monthly (Starz), $14.95 monthly (HBO or Showtime).
Video-On-Demand: No
Internet Service
  Operational: Yes.
Telephone Service
  Digital: Operational
  Miles of Plant: 10.0 (coaxial); None (fiber optic). Homes passed: 539.
  President: Stephen Fry. Area Vice President: Rick Whaley. Vice President, Marketing: Patrick Burke. Vice President, Engineering: Al Costanzi. Vice President, Public Affairs: William Jasso. Senior Accounting Director: Karen Goodfellow. Government & Media Relations Director: Chris Thomas.
  Ownership: Time Warner Cable (MSO).

SCIPIO TWP. (Meigs County)—Time Warner Cable, 7800 Crescent Executive Dr, Charlotte, NC 28217. Phones: 614-255-4997; 614-481-5000. Web Site: http://www.timewarnercable.com. Also serves Alexander Twp., Bedford Twp., Rutland Twp. & Salisbury Twp. ICA: OH0274.
  TV Market Ranking: Below 100 (Alexander Twp., Bedford Twp., Rutland Twp., Salisbury Twp.). Franchise award date: March 4, 1989. Franchise expiration date: N.A. Began: January 1, 1990.
  Channel capacity: N.A. Channels available but not in use: N.A.

2017 Edition
D-599

Ohio—Cable Systems

Basic Service
Subscribers: 28.
Programming (received off-air): WCHS-TV (ABC, Antenna TV) Charleston; WOUB-TV (PBS) Athens; WOWK-TV (CBS) Huntington; WQCW (CW) Portsmouth; WSAZ-TV (MNT, NBC, This TV) Huntington; WVAH-TV (FOX, The Country Network) Charleston.
Programming (via satellite): WGN America.
Fee: $49.99 installation; $24.50 monthly.
Expanded Basic Service 1
Subscribers: N.A.
Programming (via satellite): A&E; CMT; CNN; Discovery Channel; ESPN; ESPN2; Freeform; History; MTV; Nickelodeon; Spike TV; TBS; The Weather Channel; TNT; Turner Classic Movies; USA Network.
Digital Basic Service
Subscribers: N.A.
Programming (via satellite): BBC America; Bloomberg Television; Bravo; Discovery Life Channel; ESPN Classic; ESPNews; FXM; Golf Channel; HGTV; IFC; NBCSN; Outdoor Channel; Syfy; Trinity Broadcasting Network (TBN); WE tv.
Digital Expanded Basic Service
Subscribers: N.A.
Programming (via satellite): MC; Nick Jr.; Nicktoons.
Digital Pay Service 1
Pay Units: N.A.
Programming (via satellite): Cinemax (multiplexed); HBO (multiplexed); Showtime (multiplexed); Starz (multiplexed); Starz Encore; The Movie Channel (multiplexed).
Fee: $12.99 monthly (each).
Video-On-Demand: No
Pay-Per-View
Hits Movies & Events (delivered digitally); Fresh (delivered digitally); Playboy TV (delivered digitally).
Internet Service
Operational: No.
Telephone Service
None
Miles of Plant: 53.0 (coaxial); None (fiber optic). Homes passed: 523.
President: Rhonda Fraas. Vice President & General Manager: David Kreiman. Vice President, Government & Public Affairs: Mary Jo Green. Vice President, Engineering: Randy Hall. Vice President, Marketing: Mark Psigoda. Senior Accounting Director: Karen Goodfellow. Technical Operations Director: Jim Cavender. Government Affairs Director: Steve Cuckler.
Ownership: Time Warner Cable (MSO).

SCOTT (village)—Formerly served by CableDirect. No longer in operation. ICA: OH0363.

SEAMAN (village)—Time Warner Cable. Now served by AMBERLEY (village), OH [OH0001]. ICA: OH0208.

SEBRING (village)—Time Warner Cable. Now served by CLEVELAND (formerly Cleveland Heights), OH [OH0006]. ICA: OH0126.

SENECAVILLE—Suddenlink Communications, 520 Maryville Centre Dr, Ste 300, St. Louis, MO 63141. Phones: 800-999-6845; 314-315-9400; 304-472-4193. Web Site: http://www.suddenlink.com. Also serves Buffalo, Byesville, Center Twp. (Guernsey County), Derwent, Jackson Twp. (Guernsey County), Lore City, Millwood Twp., Old Washington, Pleasant City, Quaker City, Richland Twp. (Guernsey County), Salesville, Valley Twp. (Guernsey County) & Wills Twp. ICA: OH0124.
TV Market Ranking: 90 (Millwood Twp., Quaker City, Salesville); Below 100 (Buffalo, Byesville, Center Twp. (Guernsey County), Derwent, Jackson Twp. (Guernsey County), Lore City, Old Washington, Pleasant City, Richland Twp. (Guernsey County), SENECAVILLE, Valley Twp. (Guernsey County), Wills Twp.).
Channel capacity: 36 (operating 2-way). Channels available but not in use: N.A.
Basic Service
Subscribers: 1,233. Commercial subscribers: 22.
Programming (received off-air): WBNS-TV (Antenna TV, CBS, Decades) Columbus; WHIZ-TV (NBC) Zanesville; WOUC-TV (PBS) Cambridge; WSYX (ABC, Antenna TV, MNT, This TV) Columbus; WTOV-TV (MeTV, NBC) Steubenville; WTRF-TV (ABC, CBS, MNT) Wheeling; WTTE (FOX) Columbus.
Programming (via satellite): C-SPAN; C-SPAN 2; INSP; The Weather Channel; Trinity Broadcasting Network (TBN); WABC-TV (ABC, Live Well Network) New York; WGN America.
Fee: $59.95 installation; $22.99 monthly; $1.24 converter.
Expanded Basic Service 1
Subscribers: N.A.
Programming (via satellite): A&E; AMC; Animal Planet; Cartoon Network; CNN; Comedy Central; Discovery Channel; Disney Channel; Disney XD; E! HD; ESPN; ESPN Classic; ESPN2; Fox News Channel; Fox Sports 1; FOX Sports Ohio/Sports Time Ohio; Freeform; FX; Great American Country; GSN; Hallmark Channel; HGTV; History; HLN; ION Television; Lifetime; MSNBC; MTV; National Geographic Channel; Nickelodeon; Outdoor Channel; Pop; Spike TV; Syfy; TBS; TLC; TNT; Travel Channel; TV Land; USA Network; VH1; WE tv.
Fee: $17.50 installation; $25.00 monthly.
Digital Basic Service
Subscribers: N.A.
Programming (via satellite): BBC America; Bloomberg Television; Cloo; Discovery Digital Networks; DMX Music; ESPNews; EVINE Live; FOX College Sports Central; FOX College Sports Pacific; Fuse; FXM; FYI; Golf Channel; History International; IFC; LMN; NBCSN; Turner Classic Movies.
Fee: $13.95 monthly.
Pay Service 1
Pay Units: N.A.
Programming (via satellite): Cinemax; HBO; Showtime; Starz Encore; The Movie Channel.
Fee: $3.99 monthly (Encore), $7.95 monthly (Cinemax).
Digital Pay Service 1
Pay Units: N.A.
Programming (via satellite): Cinemax (multiplexed); Flix; HBO (multiplexed); Showtime (multiplexed); Starz (multiplexed); Starz Encore (multiplexed); The Movie Channel (multiplexed).
Pay-Per-View
iN DEMAND (delivered digitally); Playboy TV (delivered digitally); Fresh (delivered digitally).
Internet Service
Operational: Yes. Began: August 15, 2004. Broadband Service: Suddenlink High Speed Internet.
Fee: $20.00 installation; $20.95 monthly.
Telephone Service
Digital: Operational
Miles of Plant: 109.0 (coaxial); None (fiber optic). Homes passed: 4,124.
Vice President, Corporate Finance: Michael Pflantz. General Manager: Peter Brown. Regional Engineer: Gene Wuchner.
Ownership: Cequel Communications Holdings I LLC (MSO).

SHELBY—Time Warner Cable. Now served by CLEVELAND (formerly Cleveland Heights), OH [OH0006]. ICA: OH0125.

SHERWOOD—Formerly [OH0365]. This cable system has converted to IPTV, 105 West Vine St, Sherwood, OH 43556. Phone: 419-899-2121. Fax: 419-899-4567. E-mail: phoneofc@saa.net; info@smta.cc. Web Site: http://smta.cc. ICA: OH5191.
Channel capacity: N.A. Channels available but not in use: N.A.
Local
Subscribers: 381.
Fee: $25.00 installation; $19.99 monthly. Includes 30+ channels; $4.95 converter.
Local Plus
Subscribers: N.A.
Fee: $29.99 monthly. Includes 45+ channels.
Basic
Subscribers: N.A.
Fee: $59.99 monthly. Includes 120+ channels.
Basic Plus
Subscribers: N.A.
Fee: $73.99 monthly. Includes 150+ channels.
Cinemax
Subscribers: N.A.
Fee: $12.99 monthly.
HBO
Subscribers: N.A.
Fee: $18.99 monthly.
Showtime/TMC/Flix
Subscribers: N.A.
Fee: $12.99 monthly.
Starz/Encore
Subscribers: N.A.
Fee: $11.99 monthly.
Internet Service
Operational: Yes.
Fee: $29.95-$69.95 monthly.
Telephone Service
Digital: Operational
Fee: $26.19 monthly
President: John Wirth. Vice President: Jim Timbrook. General Manager: Lynn Bergman.
Ownership: Sherwood Mutual Telephone Association Inc.

SHERWOOD—Shertel Cable. This cable system has converted to IPTV. See SHERWOOD, OH [OH5191]. ICA: OH0365.

SHREVE (village)—Time Warner Cable. Now served by CLEVELAND (formerly Cleveland Heights), OH [OH0006]. ICA: OH0366.

SIDNEY (town)—Time Warner Cable. Now served by AMBERLEY (village), OH [OH0001]. ICA: OH0080.

SMITHFIELD—Jefferson County Cable Inc, 116 South 4th St, Toronto, OH 43964-1368. Phones: 800-931-9392; 740-537-2214. Fax: 740-537-2802. Web Site: http://www.voiceflight.biz. Also serves Rush Run. ICA: OH0360.
TV Market Ranking: 10,90 (Rush Run); 90 (SMITHFIELD).
Channel capacity: 12 (not 2-way capable). Channels available but not in use: N.A.

Basic Service
Subscribers: 232.
Programming (received off-air): KDKA-TV (CBS, Decades) Pittsburgh; WPGH-TV (Antenna TV, FOX, The Country Network) Pittsburgh; WPXI (MeTV, NBC) Pittsburgh; WQED (PBS) Pittsburgh; WTAE-TV (ABC, This TV) Pittsburgh; WTOV-TV (MeTV, NBC) Steubenville; WTRF-TV (ABC, CBS, MNT) Wheeling.
Programming (via satellite): ESPN; Freeform; TBS; WGN America.
Fee: $25.00 installation; $14.03 monthly.
Pay Service 1
Pay Units: N.A.
Programming (via satellite): HBO.
Fee: $11.95 monthly.
Video-On-Demand: Planned
Internet Service
Operational: Yes.
Telephone Service
Digital: Operational
Fee: $36.00 monthly
Miles of Plant: 4.0 (coaxial); None (fiber optic).
Vice President: Joann Conner. General Manager: Bob Loveridge.
Ownership: Jefferson County Cable Inc. (MSO).

SOMERSET (village)—Time Warner Cable. Now served by CLEVELAND (formerly Cleveland Heights), OH [OH0006]. ICA: OH0290.

SOUTH POINT—Armstrong Cable Services. Now served by ZELIENOPLE, PA [PA0053]. ICA: WV0011.

SPRINGFIELD—Time Warner Cable. Now served by AMBERLEY (village), OH [OH0001]. ICA: OH0433.

ST. ANTHONY—Formerly served by Wabash Mutual Telephone. No longer in operation. ICA: OH5027.

ST. CLAIRSVILLE—Comcast Cable. Now served by WHEELING, WV [WV0004]. ICA: OH0454.

ST. HENRY—NKTelco, 301 West South St, PO Box 219, New Knoxville, OH 45871-0219. Phones: 888-658-3526; 419-629-1424; 419-753-5000. E-mail: info@nktelco.net. Web Site: http://www.nktelco.net. Also serves Coldwater & Montezuma. ICA: OH0461.
TV Market Ranking: Below 100 (Coldwater, Montezuma, ST. HENRY).
Channel capacity: N.A. Channels available but not in use: N.A.
Basic Service
Subscribers: 2,449.
Fee: $58.99 monthly.
Internet Service
Operational: Yes.
Fee: $59.95 installation; $19.95-$124.95 monthly.
Controller: Susan Quellhorst.
Ownership: New Knoxville Telephone & Cable Co. (MSO).

ST. MARY'S—Time Warner Cable. Now served by TIFFIN, OH [OH0050]. ICA: OH0123.

ST. MARYS TWP.—TSC Communications, 2 Willipie St, PO Box 408, Wapakoneta, OH 45895. Phones: 419-645-2100; 419-739-2200; 419-300-2300 (St. Marys Office). Fax: 419-739-2299. E-mail: marketing@telserco.com. Web Site: http://www.telserco.com.

Also serves Noble Twp. (Auglaize County). ICA: OH0459.

TV Market Ranking: Below 100 (Noble Twp. (Auglaize County), ST. MARYS TWP.).

Channel capacity: N.A. Channels available but not in use: N.A.

Basic Service

Subscribers: 2,351.

Fee: $26.85 installation; $13.99 monthly.

Chief Operating Officer: Lonnie C. Pedersen.

Ownership: TSC Communications Inc. (MSO).

ST. PARIS (village)—Time Warner Cable. Now served by AMBERLEY (village), OH [OH0001]. ICA: OH0176.

STEUBENVILLE—Comcast Cable. Now served by WHEELING, WV [WV0004]. ICA: OH0048.

STRUTHERS—Time Warner Cable. Now served by CLEVELAND (formerly Cleveland Heights), OH [OH0006]. ICA: OH0116.

SUBURBANS MOTOR HOME PARK—Time Warner Cable, 7800 Crescent Executive Dr, Charlotte, NC 28217. Phones: 877-455-6337 (Sales); 703-713-1723 (Herndon VA office). Web Site: http://www.timewarnercable.com. Also serves Brown Twp., Canaan Twp. (Madison County), Countryside Mobile Home Park, Darby, Dublin (Union County), Fairfield, Green Meadows Mobile Home Park, Jefferson Twp. (Madison County), Jerome, London, Marysville, Millcreek Twp., Monroe Twp. (Madison County), Norwich Twp. (Franklin County), Pike Twp. (Madison County), Pleasant Twp. (Madison County), Ponderosa Motor Home Park & Washington Twp. (Hardin County). ICA: OH0452.

TV Market Ranking: 17,27 (Fairfield); 27 (Brown Twp., Canaan Twp. (Madison County), Countryside Mobile Home Park, Darby, Dublin (Union County), Green Meadows Mobile Home Park, Jefferson Twp. (Madison County), Jerome, London, Marysville, Millcreek Twp., Monroe Twp. (Madison County), Norwich Twp. (Franklin County), Pike Twp. (Madison County), Pleasant Twp. (Madison County), Ponderosa Motor Home Park, SUBURBANS MOTOR HOME PARK); Below 100 (Washington Twp. (Hardin County)).

Channel capacity: N.A. Channels available but not in use: N.A.

Basic Service

Subscribers: 729. Commercial subscribers: 4.

Fee: $49.99 installation; $33.30 monthly.

Senior Accounting Director: Karen Goodfellow.

Ownership: Time Warner Cable (MSO).

SUMMERFIELD (village)—Formerly served by Almega Cable. No longer in operation. ICA: OH0303.

SUNBURY (village)—Time Warner Cable. Now served by COLUMBUS, OH [OH0002]. ICA: OH0370.

SYCAMORE TWP. (Wyandot County)—Time Warner Cable. Now served by TIFFIN (formerly Fostoria), OH [OH0050]. ICA: OH0215.

THOMPSON TWP. (Geauga County)—Zito Media, 102 S Main St, PO Box 665, Coudersport, PA 16915. Phones: 814-260-9055; 800-365-6988. E-mail: info@zitomedia.com. Web Site: http://www.zitomedia.com. Also serves Claridon, Hambden Twp. (Geauga County), Hartsgrove, Huntsburg Twp., Leroy Twp. (Lake County), Montville, Trumbull Twp. & Windsor. ICA: OH0162.

TV Market Ranking: 79 (Montville); 8 (Hambden Twp. (Geauga County), Huntsburg Twp., Leroy Twp. (Lake County), Trumbull Twp.); 8,79 (Claridon, Windsor); Outside TV Markets (Hartsgrove).

Channel capacity: 62 (not 2-way capable). Channels available but not in use: N.A.

Basic Service

Subscribers: 261.

Programming (received off-air): WBNX-TV (CW, Movies!, This TV) Akron; WEWS-TV (ABC) Cleveland; WJW (Antenna TV, FOX) Cleveland; WKYC (NBC) Cleveland; WOIO (CBS, MeTV) Shaker Heights; WQHS-DT (getTV, UNV) Cleveland; WRLM (IND) Canton; WUAB (Bounce TV, MNT) Lorain; WVIZ (PBS) Cleveland.

Programming (via satellite): ION Television; QVC.

Fee: $49.95 installation; $16.26 monthly; $1.95 converter.

Expanded Basic Service 1

Subscribers: N.A.

Programming (via satellite): A&E; AMC; Animal Planet; BET; Cartoon Network; CNBC; CNN; Comedy Central; C-SPAN; Discovery Channel; Disney Channel; E! HD; ESPN; ESPN2; Food Network; Fox News Channel; FOX Sports Ohio/Sports Time Ohio; Freeform; FX; Great American Country; HGTV; History; HLN; MSNBC; MTV; Nickelodeon; Spike TV; Syfy; TBS; The Weather Channel; TLC; TNT; Turner Classic Movies; TV Land; USA Network; VH1.

Fee: $20.00 monthly.

Digital Basic Service

Subscribers: N.A.

Programming (via satellite): BBC America; Bloomberg Television; Cloo; Destination America; Discovery Kids Channel; Disney XD; DMX Music; ESPN Classic; ESPNews; EVINE Live; FOX College Sports Central; FOX College Sports Pacific; Fox Sports 1; Fuse; FYI; Golf Channel; GSN; History International; IFC; Investigation Discovery; NBCSN; Outdoor Channel; OWN: Oprah Winfrey Network; Science Channel; Sundance TV; Trinity Broadcasting Network (TBN); WE tv.

Pay Service 1

Pay Units: N.A.

Programming (via satellite): Cinemax; HBO; Showtime; The Movie Channel.

Fee: $11.00 monthly (Cinemax or HBO), $12.95 monthly (Showtime/TMC).

Digital Pay Service 1

Pay Units: N.A.

Programming (via satellite): Cinemax (multiplexed); Flix; HBO (multiplexed); Showtime (multiplexed); Starz (multiplexed); Starz Encore (multiplexed); The Movie Channel (multiplexed).

Video-On-Demand: No

Pay-Per-View

iN DEMAND (delivered digitally); Playboy TV (delivered digitally); Club Jenna (delivered digitally); Fresh (delivered digitally); Shorteez (delivered digitally).

Internet Service

Operational: No.

Telephone Service

None

Miles of Plant: 137.0 (coaxial); None (fiber optic). Homes passed: 2,595.

President: James Rigas.

Ownership: Zito Media (MSO).

THORNVILLE (village)—Time Warner Cable. Now served by COLUMBUS, OH [OH0002]. ICA: OH0154.

TIFFIN—Time Warner Cable, 205 Crystal Ave, Findlay, OH 45840. Phones: 614-481-5000 (Columbus office); 419-429-7474. Fax: 419-429-7402. Web Site: http://www.timewarnercable.com. Also serves Adams Twp. (Seneca County), Allen Twp. (Hancock County), Allen Twp. (Ottawa County), Amanda Twp., Amanda Twp. (Hancock County), Amboy Twp., American Twp. (Allen County), Antrim Twp., Arcadia (village), Archbold, Arlington (village), Attica (village), Auglaize County (portions), Bairdstown (village), Ballville Twp., Bath Twp. (Allen County), Beaverdam (village), Bellefontaine, Bellevue, Bettsville (village), Big Spring Twp., Biglick Twp., Blakeslee, Blanchard Twp. (Hancock County), Blanchard Twp. (Putnam County), Bloom Twp. (Seneca County), Bloom Twp. (Wood County), Bloomdale (village), Bloomville (village), Bluffton (village), Bowling Green, Bradner (village), Brady Twp. (Williams County), Bryan, Buckland (village), Burgoon (village), Butler Twp. (Mercer County), Cairo (village), Carey, Cass Twp. (Hancock County), Celina, Center Twp. (Williams County), Center Twp. (Wood County), Chatfield Twp., Chickasaw, Clay Center (village), Clay Twp. (Auglaize County), Clay Twp. (Ottawa County), Clinton Twp. (Fulton County), Clinton Twp. (Seneca County), Clyde, Coldwater, Columbus Grove (village), Cranberry Prairie, Cranberry Twp., Crane Twp. (Wyandot County), Crawford Twp. (Wyandot County), Cridersville (village), Curtice (Lucas County), Curtice (Ottawa County), Custar (village), Cygnet (village), Cynthian Twp., Damascus Twp., Delaware Twp. (Hancock County), Delphos, Delta, Dover Twp. (Fulton County), Duchouquet Twp., Dunbridge, Eagle Twp. (Hancock County), Eden Twp. (Seneca County), Eden Twp. (Wyandot County), Edgerton (village), Edon, Elida (village), Elmore (village), Fayette, Findlay, Flatrock Twp., Florida, Fort Loramie, Fort Seneca, Fort Shawnee (village), Fostoria (Hancock County), Fostoria (Seneca County), Fostoria (Wood County), Franklin Twp. (Mercer County), Freedom Twp. (Wood County), Fremont, Fulton Twp., Genoa (village), German Twp. (Auglaize County), German Twp. (Fulton County), Gibsonburg (village), Glandorf (village), Gorham Twp., Goshen Twp. (Auglaize County), Grand Rapids, Grand Rapids Twp., Granville Twp. (Mercer County), Green Creek Twp. (Sandusky County), Green Springs (village) (Sandusky County), Green Springs (village) (Seneca County), Groton Twp., Harding Twp., Harpster (village), Harris Twp., Harrison Twp. (Henry County), Harrod (village), Haskins Twp., Haviland, Helena (village), Henry Twp. (Wood County), Hoaglin Twp., Hopewell Twp. (Mercer County), Hopewell Twp. (Seneca County), Huntsville (village), Jackson Twp. (Allen County), Jackson Twp. (Auglaize County), Jackson Twp. (Crawford County), Jackson Twp. (Hancock County), Jackson Twp. (Sandusky County), Jefferson Twp. (Mercer County), Jefferson Twp. (Williams County), Jenera (village), Jennings Twp., Jerry City (village), Jerusalem Twp., Kettlersville, Lafayette (village), Lake Twp. (Wood County), Liberty Center, Liberty Twp. (Hancock County), Liberty Twp. (Henry County), Liberty Twp. (Seneca County), Lima, Lindsey (village), Logan Twp., Loudon Twp. (Seneca County), Luckey, Lyme Twp., Lyons, Madison Twp. (Hancock County), Madison Twp. (Sandusky County), Malinta, Marion, Marion Twp. (Hancock County), Marion Twp. (Mercer County), Marion Twp. (Allen County), Marseilles (village), McClure (village), McComb (village), McLean (Shelby County), Mendon (village), Metamora, Middle Point (village), Middleton Twp, Middleton Twp. (Wood County), Millbury Twp., Milton Center (village), Minster, Monclova Twp., Monroe Twp. (Allen County), Monroe Twp. (Henry County), Montezuma, Montgomery Twp. (Wood County), Montpelier (village), Mount Blanchard (village), Mount Cory (village), Napoleon, Nevada (village), New Bremen, New Knoxville, New Riegel (village), New Washington (village), North Baltimore, Northwood, Old Fort, Orange Twp. (Hancock County), Orange Twp. (Shelby County), Oregon, Ottawa (village), Ottawa Twp., Pemberville, Perry Twp. (Logan County), Perry Twp. (Wood County), Perrysburg, Perrysburg Twp., Pettisville, Pike Twp. (Fulton County), Pioneer, Pitt Twp., Pleasant Twp. (Hancock County), Pleasant Twp. (Seneca County), Portage (village), Portage Twp. (Hancock County), Portage Twp. (Wood County), Providence Twp., Pulaski Twp. (Williams County), Pusheta Twp., Rawson (village), Reed Twp., Republic (village), Richland Twp. (Allen County), Riley Twp. (Sandusky County), Rising Sun (village), Rockford (village), Rossford, Roundhead Twp., Royalton Twp., Russells Point (village), Scipio Twp. (Seneca County), Scott (village), Scott Twp. (Sandusky County), Seneca Twp. (Seneca County), Shawnee Twp. (Allen County), Sherman Twp., Spencer Twp. (Allen County), Spencer Twp. (Lucas County), Spencerville (village), Springfield Twp. (Lucas County), St. Henry, St. Joseph (Williams County), St. Mary's, St. Mary's Twp., Stokes Twp. (Logan County), Stryker, Sugar Creek Twp. (Allen County), Sugar Creek Twp. (Putnam County), Superior Twp., Swan Creek Twp., Swanton, Swanton Twp., Sycamore Twp. (Wyandot County), Thompson Twp. (Seneca County), Tiffin Twp. (Defiance County), Toledo, Tontogany, Townsend Twp. (Sandusky County), Tymochtee Twp., Union Twp. (Hancock County), Uniopolis (village), Upper Sandusky, Van Buren (village), Van Buren Twp. (Shelby County), Van Buren Twp. (Hancock County), Vanlue (village), Venedocia (village), Venice Twp., Vickery, Walbridge, Wapakoneta, Washington, Washington Twp. (Auglaize County), Washington Twp. (Hancock County), Washington Twp. (Sandusky County), Washington Twp. (Van Wert County), Washington Twp. (Wood County), Waterville, Waterville Twp., Wauseon, Wayne (village), Wayne Twp. (Auglaize County), Waynesfield (village), Webster Twp., West Millgrove (village), West Unity, Weston (village), Weston Twp., Whitehouse, Williston, Willshire (village), Woodville Twp., Wren (village), York, York Twp. (Fulton County), York Twp. (Sandusky County) & Zanesfield (village). ICA: OH0050.

TV Market Ranking: 27 (Washington); 41 (Orange Twp. (Shelby County) (portions)); 52 (Allen Twp. (Ottawa County), Bairdstown (village), Bettsville (village), Bloom Twp. (Wood County), Bloomdale (village), Bowling Green, Bradner (village), Burgoon (village), Center Twp. (Wood County), Clay Center (village), Clay Twp. (Ottawa County), Clinton Twp. (Fulton County), Curtice (Lucas County), Curtice (Ottawa County), Custar (village), Cygnet (village), Delta, Dover Twp. (Fulton County), Dunbridge, Elmore (village), Fostoria (Wood County), Freedom Twp. (Wood County), Fremont, Fulton Twp., Genoa (village), Gibsonburg (village), Grand Rapids, Grand Rapids Twp., Harding Twp., Harris Twp., Harrison Twp. (Henry County), Haskins

Twp., Helena (village), Henry Twp. (Wood County), Jackson Twp. (Sandusky County), Jerry City (village), Jerusalem Twp., Lake Twp. (Wood County), Liberty Center, Liberty Twp. (Henry County), Liberty Twp. (Seneca County), Lindsey (village), Luckey, Lyons, Madison Twp. (Sandusky County), Malinta, McClure (village), Metamora, Middleton Twp, Middleton Twp. (Wood County), Millbury Twp., Milton Center (village), Monclova Twp., Monroe Twp. (Henry County) (portions), Montgomery Twp. (Wood County), Napoleon, North Baltimore, Oregon, Pemberville, Perry Twp. (Wood County), Perrysburg, Perrysburg Twp., Pettisville, Pike Twp. (Fulton County), Portage (village), Portage Twp. (Wood County), Rising Sun (village), Rossford, Spencer Twp. (Lucas County), Springfield Twp. (Lucas County), Swan Creek Twp., Swanton, Swanton Twp., Toledo, Tontogany, Vickery, Walbridge, Washington Twp. (Sandusky County), Washington Twp. (Wood County), Waterville, Waterville Twp., Wauseon, Wayne (village), Webster Twp., West Millgrove (village), Weston (village), Weston Twp., Whitehouse, Williston, Woodville Twp., York Twp. (Fulton County)); 8 (Groton Twp., Sherman Twp.); 82 (Edgerton (village), Haviland, Willshire (village), Wren (village)); 90 (York); Below 100 (Adams Twp. (Seneca County), Allen Twp. (Hancock County), Amanda Twp., Amanda Twp. (Hancock County), Amboy Twp., American Twp. (Allen County), Archbold, Arlington (village), Attica (village), Auglaize County (portions), Ballville Twp., Bath Twp. (Allen County), Beaverdam (village), Biglick Twp. (portions), Blakeslee, Blanchard Twp. (Hancock County), Blanchard Twp. (Putnam County), Bloom Twp. (Seneca County), Bloomville (village), Bluffton (village), Brady Twp. (Williams County), Buckland (village), Cairo (village), Cass Twp. (Hancock County), Center Twp. (Williams County), Chatfield Twp., Chickasaw, Clay Twp. (Auglaize County), Clinton Twp. (Seneca County), Clyde, Coldwater, Columbus Grove (village), Cranberry Twp., Crane Twp. (Wyandot County) (portions), Cynthian Twp., Delaware Twp. (Hancock County), Duchouquet Twp., Eagle Twp. (Hancock County), Eden Twp. (Wyandot County) (portions), Edon, Elida (village), Fayette, Fort Loramie, Fort Seneca, Fort Shawnee (village), Fostoria (Hancock County), Franklin Twp. (Mercer County), German Twp. (Auglaize County), German Twp. (Fulton County), Glandorf (village), Gorham Twp., Goshen Twp. (Auglaize County), Green Creek Twp. (Sandusky County), Green Springs (village) (Sandusky County), Green Springs (village) (Seneca County), Harrod (village), Hoaglin Twp., Hopewell Twp. (Mercer County), Huntsville (village), Jackson Twp. (Allen County), Jackson Twp. (Auglaize County), Jackson Twp. (Crawford County), Jackson Twp. (Hancock County), Jefferson Twp. (Mercer County), Jefferson Twp. (Williams County), Jenera (village), Jennings Twp., Kettlersville, Lafayette (village), Liberty Twp. (Hancock County), Logan Twp., Lyme Twp., Madison Twp. (Hancock County), Marion, Marion Twp. (Hancock County) (portions), Marion Twp. (Mercer County), Marion Twp. (Allen County), McComb (village), McLean (Shelby County), Mendon (village), Middle Point (village), Monroe Twp. (Allen County), Montezuma, Montpelier (village), Mount Blanchard (village), Mount Cory (village), Nevada (village), New Bremen, New Knoxville, New Washington (village), Old Fort, Orange Twp. (Hancock County), Ottawa (village), Perry Twp. (Logan County), Pioneer, Pleasant Twp. (Hancock County), Pleasant Twp. (Seneca County), Portage Twp. (Hancock County), Pusheta Twp., Rawson (village), Reed Twp., Republic (village), Richland Twp. (Allen County), Riley Twp. (Sandusky County), Roundhead Twp., Royalton Twp., Russells Point (village), Scipio Twp. (Seneca County), Scott (village), Scott (village), Scott Twp. (Sandusky County), Shawnee Twp. (Allen County), Spencer Twp. (Allen County), Spencerville (village), St. Joseph (Williams County), St. Mary's Twp., Stokes Twp. (Logan County), Stryker, Sugar Creek Twp. (Allen County), Sugar Creek Twp. (Putnam County), Superior Twp., Thompson Twp. (Seneca County), Tiffin Twp. (Defiance County) (portions), Townsend Twp. (Sandusky County), Union Twp. (Hancock County), Uniopolis (village), Van Buren Twp. (Shelby County), Venice Twp., Washington Twp. (Auglaize County), Washington Twp. (Van Wert County), Wayne Twp. (Auglaize County), West Unity, York Twp. (Sandusky County), Zanesfield (village), Bellefontaine, Bryan, Celina, Delphos, Findlay, Lima, Minster, Ottawa Twp., Rockford (village), St. Mary's, TIFFIN, Wapakoneta, Waynesfield (village), Orange Twp. (Shelby County) (portions)); Outside TV Markets (Amanda Twp. (Hancock County), Antrim Twp., Arcadia (village), Big Spring Twp., Biglick Twp. (portions), Butler Twp. (Mercer County), Carey, Cranberry Prairie, Crane Twp. (Wyandot County) (portions), Crawford Twp. (Wyandot County), Damascus Twp., Eden Twp. (Seneca County), Eden Twp. (Wyandot County) (portions), Flatrock Twp., Florida, Granville Twp. (Mercer County), Harpster (village), Hopewell Twp. (Seneca County), Loudon Twp. (Seneca County), Marion Twp. (Hancock County) (portions), Marseilles (village), New Riegel (village), Pitt Twp., Seneca Twp. (Seneca County), St. Henry, Tiffin Twp. (Defiance County) (portions), Tymochtee Twp., Van Buren (village), Van Buren Twp. (Hancock County), Vanlue (village), Washington Twp. (Hancock County), Fostoria (Seneca County), Sycamore Twp. (Wyandot County), Upper Sandusky, Monroe Twp. (Henry County) (portions)). Franchise award date: N.A. Franchise expiration date: N.A. Began: December 1, 1964.

Channel capacity: 65 (operating 2-way). Channels available but not in use: N.A.

Basic Service

Subscribers: 123,819.

Programming (received off-air): WBGU-TV (PBS) Bowling Green; WEWS-TV (ABC) Cleveland; WGGN-TV (IND) Sandusky; WGTE-TV (PBS) Toledo; WKBD-TV (CW) Detroit; WKYC (NBC) Cleveland; WLMB (IND) Toledo; WNWO-TV (NBC, Retro TV) Toledo; WTOL (CBS, MeTV) Toledo; WTVG (ABC, CW) Toledo; WUAB (Bounce TV, MNT) Lorain; WUPW (FOX, TheCoolTV) Toledo; allband FM.

Programming (via satellite): Pop; QVC.

Fee: $29.95 installation; $12.65 monthly; $2.95 converter.

Expanded Basic Service 1

Subscribers: N.A.

Programming (via satellite): A&E; AMC; Animal Planet; BET; Bravo; Cartoon Network; CMT; CNBC; CNN; Comedy Central; C-SPAN; C-SPAN 2; Discovery Channel; Disney Channel; E! HD; ESPN; ESPN Classic; ESPN2; EVINE Live; EWTN Global Catholic Network; Food Network; Fox News Channel; FOX Sports Ohio/Sports Time Ohio; Freeform; FX; Golf Channel; Hallmark Channel; HGTV; History; HLN; INSP; Lifetime; LMN; MSNBC; MTV; National Geographic Channel; NBCSN; Nickelodeon; Oxygen; Spike TV; Syfy; TBS; The Weather Channel; TLC; TNT; Travel Channel; truTV; Turner Classic Movies; TV Land; USA Network; VH1; WE tv.

Fee: $32.75 monthly.

Digital Basic Service

Subscribers: N.A.

Programming (via satellite): BBC America; Bloomberg Television; CNN International; Cooking Channel; C-SPAN 3; Discovery Life Channel; Disney XD; DIY Network; DMX Music; ESPNews; Fox Sports 1; FSN Digital Atlantic; FSN Digital Central; FSN Digital Pacific; Fuse; Great American Country; GSN; MTV Classic; MTV2; Nick Jr.; Outdoor Channel; Ovation; TeenNick.

Fee: $9.90 monthly.

Digital Pay Service 1

Pay Units: N.A.

Programming (via satellite): Cinemax (multiplexed); Flix; HBO (multiplexed); Showtime (multiplexed); Starz (multiplexed); Starz Encore (multiplexed); The Movie Channel (multiplexed).

Fee: $11.95 monthly (Cinemax, HBO, Showtime/Flix/TMC or Starz/Encore).

Video-On-Demand: Yes

Pay-Per-View

iN DEMAND (delivered digitally); Fresh (delivered digitally); Sports PPV (delivered digitally).

Internet Service

Operational: Yes.

Subscribers: 118,453.

Broadband Service: Road Runner.

Fee: $69.95 installation; $44.95 monthly.

Telephone Service

Digital: Operational

Subscribers: 59,164.

Fee: $44.95 monthly

Miles of Plant: 8,308.0 (coaxial); 4,155.0 (fiber optic). Homes passed: 318,593.

President: Rhonda Fraas. Vice President & General Manager: Brad Wakely. Vice President, Engineering: Randy Hall. Vice President, Marketing: Mark Psigoda. Technical Operations Director: John Ellingson. Government Affairs Director: Brian Young. Government Affairs Manager: Patrick McCauley.

Ownership: Time Warner Cable (MSO).

TOLEDO—Buckeye Broadband, 405 Madison Ave, Ste 2100, Toledo, OH 43604. Phones: 419-724-6212; 419-724-9800; 419-724-9802. Fax: 419-724-7074. E-mail: askus@cablesystem.com. Web Site: http://www.blockcommunications.com. Also serves Bedford Twp., Ida, Lost Peninsula, Riga Twp., Summerfield Twp. (Monroe County), Temperance, Whiteford & Whiteford Twp., MI; Allen Twp. (Ottawa County), Bay View, Berkey, Berlin Twp. (Erie County), Castalia, Groton Twp. (Erie County), Harbor View, Holland, Huron, Huron Twp. (Erie County), Margaretta Twp., Maumee, Middleton Twp., Milan Twp. (Erie County), Monclova Twp. (Lucas County), Northwood, Oregon, Ottawa Hills, Oxford Twp. (Erie County), Perkins Twp. (Erie County), Perrysburg Twp., Richfield Twp. (Lucas County), Rossford, Sandusky, Spencer Twp., Springfield Twp. (Lucas County), Sylvania, Sylvania Twp. (Lucas County), Townsend Twp., Washington Twp. (Lucas County), Waterville & Waterville Twp. (Lucas County), OH. ICA: OH0004.

Note: This system is an overbuild.

TV Market Ranking: 52 (Allen Twp. (Ottawa County), Bedford Twp., Bedford Twp., Berkey, Harbor View, Holland, Lost Peninsula, Maumee, Middleton Twp., Monclova Twp. (Lucas County), Northwood, Oregon, Ottawa Hills, Perrysburg Twp., Richfield Twp. (Lucas County), Riga Twp., Rossford, Spencer Twp., Springfield Twp. (Lucas County), Summerfield Twp. (Monroe County), Sylvania, Sylvania Twp. (Lucas County), TOLEDO, Townsend Twp., Washington Twp. (Lucas County), Waterville, Waterville Twp. (Lucas County), Whiteford, Whiteford Twp.); 8 (Bay View, Berlin Twp. (Erie County), Castalia, Groton Twp. (Erie County), Huron, Huron Twp. (Erie County), Margaretta Twp., Milan Twp. (Erie County), Oxford Twp. (Erie County), Perkins Twp. (Erie County), Sandusky). Franchise award date: May 17, 1965. Franchise expiration date: N.A. Began: March 15, 1966.

Channel capacity: 72 (operating 2-way). Channels available but not in use: N.A.

Basic Service

Subscribers: 96,295.

Programming (received off-air): WBGU-TV (PBS) Bowling Green; WCWG (Bounce TV, CW, Estrella TV, IND) Lexington; WDIV-TV (NBC, This TV) Detroit; WGTE-TV (PBS) Toledo; WJBK (Buzzr, FOX, Heroes & Icons, Movies!) Detroit; WKBD-TV (CW) Detroit; WLMB (IND) Toledo; WMNT-CD (Antenna TV, MNT) Toledo; WNWO-TV (NBC, Retro TV) Toledo; WTOL (CBS, MeTV) Toledo; WTVG (ABC, CW) Toledo; WUPW (FOX, TheCoolTV) Toledo; WXYZ-TV (ABC, Bounce TV) Detroit.

Programming (via satellite): C-SPAN; C-SPAN 2; EWTN Global Catholic Network; TLC.

Fee: $25.00 installation; $28.20 monthly; $2.02 converter.

Expanded Basic Service 1

Subscribers: N.A.

Programming (via satellite): A&E; AMC; Animal Planet; BET; Bravo; Cartoon Network; CNBC; CNN; Comedy Central; Discovery Channel; Disney Channel; E! HD; ESPN; ESPN Classic; ESPN2; EVINE Live; Fox News Channel; FOX Sports Detroit; FOX Sports Ohio/Sports Time Ohio; Freeform; FX; Golf Channel; Hallmark Channel; HGTV; History; History International; HLN; Lifetime; MTV; National Geographic Channel; Nickelodeon; QVC; Spike TV; Starz Encore; Syfy; TBS; Telemundo; The Weather Channel; TNT; Travel Channel; TV Land; USA Network; VH1; WGN America.

Fee: $28.34 monthly.

Digital Basic Service

Subscribers: N.A.

Programming (via satellite): BBC America; Bloomberg Television; Boomerang; Discovery Digital Networks; DIY Network; DMX Music; Food Network; Fox Sports 1; FSN Digital Atlantic; FSN Digital Central; FSN Digital Pacific; FYI; Great American Country; GSN; History International; MSNBC; NBCSN; Trinity Broadcasting Network (TBN); Turner Classic Movies; WE tv.

Fee: $6.95 monthly.

Pay Service 1

Pay Units: N.A.

Programming (via satellite): Cinemax; HBO (multiplexed); Showtime; The Movie Channel.

Fee: $5.00 installation; $9.95 monthly (Cinemax), $10.50 monthly (Showtime or TMC), $12.95 monthly (HBO).

Cable Systems—Ohio

Digital Pay Service 1
Pay Units: N.A.
Programming (via satellite): ART America; Cinemax (multiplexed); Flix; HBO (multiplexed); Playboy TV; Showtime (multiplexed); Starz (multiplexed); Starz Encore (multiplexed); The Movie Channel (multiplexed).
Fee: $9.95 monthly (Cinemax), $12.95 monthly (HBO, Showtime, TMC/Flix, Starz/Encore or ART).
Video-On-Demand: Yes
Pay-Per-View
ESPN Now (delivered digitally); Hot Choice (delivered digitally); iN DEMAND (delivered digitally); NBA League Pass (delivered digitally); Playboy TV (delivered digitally); Fresh (delivered digitally).
Internet Service
Operational: Yes.
Subscribers: 111,994.
Broadband Service: In-house.
Fee: $19.00 installation; $29.99 monthly.
Telephone Service
Digital: Operational
Subscribers: 25,430.
Fee: $13.75 monthly
Miles of Plant: 5,063.0 (coaxial); 2,800.0 (fiber optic). Homes passed: 241,634.
Vice President, Financial Operations: Patti Ankney. President & General Manager: Jeff Abbas. Treasurer: Rick Mlcek. Chief Technical Officer: Jim Wolsiffer. Marketing Director: Florence Buchanan. Government Affairs Director: Tom Dawson. Ad Sales Manager: Steve Piller.
Ownership: Block Communications Inc. (MSO).

TOLEDO—Formerly served by American Telecasting/WanTV. No longer in operation. ICA: OH0392.

TORONTO—Jefferson County Cable Inc, 116 South 4th St, Toronto, OH 43964-1368. Phones: 800-931-9392; 740-537-2214. Fax: 740-537-2802. Web Site: http://www.voiceflight.biz. Also serves Costonia, Jefferson County (portions), Pleasant Hill (Jefferson County), Pottery Addition & Taylortown. ICA: OH0371.
TV Market Ranking: 10,90 (Costonia, Jefferson County (portions), Pleasant Hill (Jefferson County), Pottery Addition, Taylortown, TORONTO). Franchise award date: N.A. Franchise expiration date: N.A. Began: December 1, 1984.
Channel capacity: 36 (not 2-way capable). Channels available but not in use: N.A.
Basic Service
Subscribers: 2,617.
Programming (received off-air): KDKA-TV (CBS, Decades) Pittsburgh; WKBN-TV (CBS) Youngstown; WPGH-TV (Antenna TV, FOX, The Country Network) Pittsburgh; WPXI (MeTV, NBC) Pittsburgh; WQED (PBS) Pittsburgh; WTAE-TV (ABC, This TV) Pittsburgh; WTOV-TV (MeTV, NBC) Steubenville; WTRF-TV (ABC, CBS, MNT) Wheeling; WYTV (ABC, MNT) Youngstown.
Programming (via satellite): ESPN.
Fee: $30.00 installation; $14.03 monthly.
Expanded Basic Service 1
Subscribers: N.A.
Programming (via satellite): CNBC; CNN; Disney Channel; Freeform; Lifetime; MTV; Nickelodeon; TBS; TNT; USA Network; WGN America.
Fee: $31.50 monthly.
Pay Service 1
Pay Units: N.A.
Programming (via satellite): Cinemax; HBO; The Movie Channel.

Fee: $8.60 monthly (Cinemax), $9.60 monthly (TMC), $11.00 monthly (HBO).
Video-On-Demand: Planned
Internet Service
Operational: Yes.
Fee: $25.00 installation; $41.95 monthly.
Telephone Service
Digital: Operational
Miles of Plant: 15.0 (coaxial); None (fiber optic).
Vice President: Joann Conner. General Manager: Bob Loveridge.
Ownership: Jefferson County Cable Inc. (MSO).

TROY—Time Warner Cable. Now served by AMBERLEY (village), OH [OH0001]. ICA: OH0069.

UPPER SANDUSKY—Time Warner Cable. Now served by TIFFIN (formerly Fostoria), OH [OH0050]. ICA: OH0138.

URBANA—Champaign Telephone Co. This cable system has converted to IPTV. See URBANA, OH [OH5029]. ICA: OH0443.

URBANA—CT Communications. Formerly [OH0443]. This cable system has converted to IPTV, 126 Scioto St, Urbana, OH 43078. Phones: 937-653-2227; 937-653-4000. Fax: 937-652-2777. E-mail: customerservice@ctcommunications.com. Web Site: http://www.ctcn.net. Also serves Bellefontaine & West Liberty. ICA: OH5029.
TV Market Ranking: 41 (URBANA); Below 100 (West Liberty).
Channel capacity: N.A. Channels available but not in use: N.A.
Basic
Subscribers: 957. Commercial subscribers: 35.
Fee: $35.00 installation; $20.27 monthly. Includes 19 channels plus 1 standard STB & 1 remote.
Plus Package
Subscribers: N.A.
Fee: $89.52 monthly. Includes 98 channels plus 45 music channels, 2 standard STB & 2 remotes.
HD
Subscribers: N.A.
Fee: $14.95 monthly.
Cinemax
Subscribers: N.A.
Fee: $11.95 monthly. Includes 4 channels.
HBO
Subscribers: N.A.
Fee: $11.99 monthly. Includes 11 channels.
Showtime/TMC
Subscribers: N.A.
Fee: $11.99 monthly. Includes 11 channels.
Starz/Encore
Subscribers: N.A.
Fee: $11.99 monthly. Includes 17 channels.
Internet Service
Operational: Yes.
Fee: $29.95-$74.95 monthly.
Telephone Service
Digital: Operational
President & Chief Executive Officer: Mike Conrad. Vice President & Chief Technical Officer: Tim Bolander.
Ownership: Champaign Telephone Co.

URBANA—Time Warner Cable. Now served by AMBERLEY (village), OH [OH0001]. ICA: OH0094.

VAN WERT—Time Warner Cable, 205 Crystal Ave, Findlay, OH 45840. Phone: 614-481-5000 (Columbus office). Fax: 419-429-7402. Web Site: http://www.timewarnercable.com. Also serves Liberty Twp. (Van Wert County), Ohio City, Pleasant Twp. (Putnam County), Pleasant Twp. (Van Wert County), Ridge Twp. (Van Wert County) & Union Twp. (Van Wert County). ICA: OH0104.
TV Market Ranking: 82 (Ohio City, Union Twp. (Van Wert County), VAN WERT); Below 100 (Liberty Twp. (Van Wert County), Pleasant Twp. (Putnam County), Pleasant Twp. (Van Wert County), Ridge Twp. (Van Wert County)). Franchise award date: N.A. Franchise expiration date: N.A. Began: October 1, 1974.
Channel capacity: N.A. Channels available but not in use: N.A.
Basic Service
Subscribers: 3,035.
Programming (received off-air): WANE-TV (Antenna TV, CBS) Fort Wayne; WBDT (Bounce TV, CW) Springfield; WBGU-TV (PBS) Bowling Green; WFFT-TV (FOX, MeTV) Fort Wayne; WFWA (PBS) Fort Wayne; WHIO-TV (CBS, MeTV) Dayton; WINM (IND) Angola; WISE-TV (CW) Fort Wayne; WLIO (CW, NBC) Lima; WOHL-CD (ABC, CBS) Lima; WPTA (ABC, MNT, NBC) Fort Wayne; WPTD (PBS) Dayton; WTLW (IND) Lima.
Programming (via satellite): Freeform; Pop; QVC; TBS; WGN America.
Fee: $29.95 installation; $21.25 monthly.
Expanded Basic Service 1
Subscribers: N.A.
Programming (via satellite): A&E; AMC; Animal Planet; BET; Bravo; Cartoon Network; CMT; CNBC; CNN; Comedy Central; C-SPAN; C-SPAN 2; Discovery Channel; Disney Channel; E! HD; ESPN; ESPN2; EVINE Live; EWTN Global Catholic Network; Fox News Channel; FOX Sports Detroit; FOX Sports Ohio/Sports Time Ohio; FX; Great American Country; Hallmark Channel; HGTV; History; HLN; Lifetime; MSNBC; MTV; Nickelodeon; Oxygen; Spike TV; Syfy; Telemundo; The Weather Channel; TLC; TNT; Travel Channel; Trinity Broadcasting Network (TBN); truTV; TV Land; USA Network; VH1.
Fee: $40.76 monthly.
Digital Basic Service
Subscribers: N.A.
Programming (via satellite): BBC America; Bloomberg Television; Discovery Life Channel; Disney XD; DIY Network; ESPN Classic; ESPNews; Fox Sports 1; Fuse; FYI; Golf Channel; GSN; History International; IFC; MC; National Geographic Channel; NBCSN; Outdoor Channel; Turner Classic Movies; WE tv.
Fee: $5.00 monthly (each tier).
Digital Expanded Basic Service
Subscribers: N.A.
Programming (via satellite): FSN Digital Atlantic; FSN Digital Central; FSN Digital Pacific; FXM; Nick 2; Nick Jr.; TeenNick.
Fee: $5.00 monthly.

Digital Pay Service 1
Pay Units: N.A.
Programming (via satellite): ART America; Cinemax (multiplexed); Flix; HBO (multiplexed); HITS (Headend In The Sky); RAI Italia; Showtime (multiplexed); Starz (multiplexed); Starz Encore (multiplexed); Sundance TV; The Filipino Channel; The Movie Channel (multiplexed); TV Asia; TV5; La Television International; Zee TV.
Fee: $11.95 monthly (Zhong Tian, TFC, ART, or SBTN), $14.95 monthly (TV Asia, TV5, RAI, MBC, or RTN), $15.00 monthly (Cinemax, HBO, Showtime/TMC or Starz), $24.95 monthly (TV Japan).
Video-On-Demand: No
Pay-Per-View
HITS PPV (delivered digitally); Hot Choice (delivered digitally); Playboy TV (delivered digitally); Fresh (delivered digitally); Shorteez (delivered digitally).
Internet Service
Operational: Yes.
Broadband Service: Road Runner.
Fee: $44.95 monthly.
Telephone Service
Digital: Operational
Fee: $44.95 monthly
Miles of Plant: 715.0 (coaxial); 547.0 (fiber optic). Homes passed: 26,218.
President: Rhonda Fraas. Vice President & General Manager: Brad Wakely. Vice President, Marketing: Randy Hall; Mark Psigoda. Technical Operations Director: John Ellingson. Government Affairs Director: Brian Young. Government Affairs Manager: Patrick McCauley.
Ownership: Time Warner Cable (MSO).

VANDALIA—Time Warner Cable. Now served by AMBERLEY (village), OH [OH0001]. ICA: OH0434.

VERNON TWP. (Trumbull County)—Armstrong Cable Services, One Armstrong Place, Butler, PA 16001. Phone: 877-277-5711. E-mail: info@zoominternet.net. Web Site: http://armstrongonewire.com/television. Also serves Andover Twp. (portions), Kinsman, Pymatuning State Park & Williamsfield. ICA: OH0246.
TV Market Ranking: 79 (Andover Twp. (portions), Kinsman, Pymatuning State Park, VERNON TWP. (TRUMBULL COUNTY), Williamsfield). Franchise award date: July 13, 1989. Franchise expiration date: N.A. Began: July 1, 1990.
Channel capacity: N.A. Channels available but not in use: N.A.
Basic Service
Subscribers: 378.
Programming (received off-air): WBNX-TV (CW, Movies!, This TV) Akron; WEWS-TV (ABC) Cleveland; WFMJ-TV (CW, NBC) Youngstown; WJW (Antenna TV, FOX) Cleveland; WKBN-TV (CBS) Youngstown; WKYC (NBC) Cleveland; WOIO (CBS, MeTV) Shaker Heights; WUAB (Bounce TV, MNT) Lorain; WVIZ (PBS) Cleveland; WYFX-LD (FOX, Laff) Youngstown; WYTV (ABC, MNT) Youngstown.

2017 Edition   D-603

Ohio—Cable Systems

Programming (via satellite): RFD-TV; TBS. Fee: $22.95 monthly; $1.95 converter.

Expanded Basic Service 1
Subscribers: N.A.
Programming (via satellite): A&E; AMC; Animal Planet; CMT; CNN; Comedy Central; Cooking Channel; C-SPAN; Discovery Channel; Disney Channel; ESPN; ESPN2; Food Network; Fox News Channel; Fox Sports 1; FOX Sports Ohio/Sports Time Ohio; Freeform; Great American Country; Hallmark Channel; Hallmark Movies & Mysteries; HGTV; HLN; INSP; Lifetime; LMN; MTV; National Geographic Channel; Nickelodeon; QVC; Spike TV; Syfy; The Weather Channel; TLC; TNT; Travel Channel; truTV; Turner Classic Movies; TV Land; USA Network; VH1.
Fee: $17.00 monthly.

Pay Service 1
Pay Units: N.A.
Programming (via satellite): Cinemax; HBO; Showtime; The Movie Channel.
Fee: $11.00 monthly (each).

Video-On-Demand: No

Internet Service
Operational: Yes.
Fee: $19.00-$44.80 monthly.

Telephone Service
Digital: Operational
Fee: $29.00 monthly

Miles of Plant: 45.0 (coaxial); None (fiber optic). Homes passed: 894.
Ownership: Armstrong Group of Companies (MSO).

VERSAILLES—Time Warner Cable, 7800 Crescent Executive Dr, Charlotte, NC 28217. Phones: 614-481-5000 (Columbus office); 419-784-1992. Web Site: http://www.timewarnercable.com. Also serves Adams Twp. (Darke County), Loramie Twp., North Star, Osgood, Patterson Twp., Russia, Wabash Twp., Wayne Twp. & Yorkshire. ICA: OH0190.
TV Market Ranking: 41 (Adams Twp. (Darke County), Loramie Twp., Russia, Wayne Twp. (portions)); Below 100 (Osgood, VERSAILLES); Outside TV Markets (North Star, Patterson Twp., Wabash Twp., Yorkshire, Wayne Twp. (portions)). Franchise award date: N.A. Franchise expiration date: N.A. Began: October 1, 1975.
Channel capacity: N.A. Channels available but not in use: N.A.

Basic Service
Subscribers: 1,110.
Programming (received off-air): WANE-TV (Antenna TV, CBS) Fort Wayne; WBDT (Bounce TV, CW) Springfield; WBGU-TV (PBS) Bowling Green; WBNS-TV (Antenna TV, CBS, Decades) Columbus; WDTN (Escape, Grit, NBC) Dayton; WFFT-TV (FOX, MeTV) Fort Wayne; WHIO-TV (CBS, MeTV) Dayton; WISE-TV (CW) Fort Wayne; WKEF (ABC, Antenna TV) Dayton; WKOI-TV (TBN) Richmond; WLIO (CW, NBC) Lima; WPTA (ABC, MNT, NBC) Fort Wayne; WPTD (PBS) Dayton; WRGT-TV (FOX, MNT, This TV) Dayton; WTLW (IND) Lima; allband FM.
Programming (via satellite): Freeform; QVC; TBS; WGN America.
Fee: $49.99 installation; $24.50 monthly.

Expanded Basic Service 1
Subscribers: N.A.
Programming (via satellite): A&E; AMC; Animal Planet; BET; Bravo; Cartoon Network; CMT; CNBC; CNN; C-SPAN; C-SPAN 2; Discovery Channel; Disney Channel; E! HD; ESPN; ESPN2; EVINE Live; EWTN Global Catholic Network; Food Network; Fox News Channel; FOX Sports Detroit; FOX Sports Ohio/Sports Time Ohio; FX; Great American Country; Hallmark Channel; HGTV; History; HLN; Lifetime; MSNBC; MTV; Nickelodeon; Oxygen; Pop; Telemundo; The Weather Channel; TLC; TNT; Travel Channel; Trinity Broadcasting Network (TBN); truTV; TV Land; USA Network; VH1.

Digital Basic Service
Subscribers: N.A.
Programming (via satellite): BBC America; Bloomberg Television; Discovery Life Channel; Disney XD; DIY Network; ESPN Classic; ESPNews; Fuse; FYI; Golf Channel; GSN; History International; IFC; MC; NBCSN; Outdoor Channel; truTV; Turner Classic Movies; WE tv.

Digital Expanded Basic Service
Subscribers: N.A.
Programming (via satellite): FSN Digital Atlantic; FSN Digital Central; FXM; HITS (Headend In The Sky); Nick Jr.; Nicktoons; Sundance TV; TeenNick.

Digital Pay Service 1
Pay Units: N.A.
Programming (via satellite): ART America; Cinemax (multiplexed); HBO (multiplexed); RAI Italia; RTN; Showtime (multiplexed); Starz (multiplexed); Starz Encore (multiplexed); The Filipino Channel; The Movie Channel (multiplexed); TV Asia; TV5, La Television International; Zee TV.
Fee: $12.99 monthly (each).

Video-On-Demand: No

Pay-Per-View
Playboy TV (delivered digitally); Hot Choice (delivered digitally); Fresh (delivered digitally); Shorteez (delivered digitally).

Internet Service
Operational: Yes.
Broadband Service: Road Runner.
Fee: $42.95 monthly.

Telephone Service
None

Miles of Plant: 58.0 (coaxial); None (fiber optic). Homes passed: 2,358.
President: Rhonda Fraas. Area Manager: Brad Wakely. General Manager: John Ellingson. Senior Accounting Director: Karen Goodfellow. Customer Service Manager: Cindy Sierra.
Ownership: Time Warner Cable (MSO).

WADSWORTH—Wadsworth Cable TV, 120 Maple St, Wadsworth, OH 44281-1825. Phones: 330-335-1521; 330-335-2888. Fax: 330-335-2822. E-mail: tvsupport@wadsnet.com. Web Site: http://www.wadsworthcitylink.com/city-link/citylink-cable-tv.html. ICA: OH0440. **Note:** This system is an overbuild.
TV Market Ranking: 8 (WADSWORTH).
Channel capacity: 75 (operating 2-way). Channels available but not in use: N.A.

Basic Service
Subscribers: 3,198.
Programming (received off-air): WAOH-CD (Retro TV) Akron; WBNX-TV (CW, Movies!, This TV) Akron; WDLI-TV (TBN) Canton; WEWS-TV (ABC) Cleveland; WJW (Antenna TV, FOX) Cleveland; WKYC (NBC) Cleveland; WNEO (PBS) Alliance; WOIO (CBS, MeTV) Shaker Heights; WQHS-DT (getTV, UNV) Cleveland; WUAB (Bounce TV, MNT) Lorain; WVIZ (PBS) Cleveland; WVPX-TV (ION) Akron.
Programming (via satellite): C-SPAN; C-SPAN 2; EWTN Global Catholic Network; INSP; Pop; QVC; The Weather Channel.
Fee: $55.80 monthly.

Expanded Basic Service 1
Subscribers: N.A.
Programming (via satellite): A&E; AMC; Animal Planet; Bravo; BTN; Cartoon Network; CMT; CNBC; CNN; Comedy Central; Discovery Channel; Discovery Life Channel; Disney Channel; E! HD; ESPN; ESPN Classic; ESPN2; Food Network; Fox News Channel; Fox Sports 1; FOX Sports Ohio/Sports Time Ohio; Freeform; FX; Golf Channel; Hallmark Channel; HGTV; History; HLN; Lifetime; MSNBC; MTV; National Geographic Channel; Nickelodeon; Spike TV; Syfy; TBS; TLC; TNT; Travel Channel; truTV; Turner Classic Movies; TV Land; USA Network; VH1; WE tv; WGN America.
Fee: $27.35 monthly.

Digital Basic Service
Subscribers: N.A.
Programming (via satellite): AXS TV; BBC America; Cooking Channel; Destination America; Discovery Channel HD; Disney XD; DIY Network; DMX Music; ESPN HD; ESPN2 HD; ESPNews; ESPNU; FOX College Sports Central; FOX College Sports Pacific; FYI; History International; IFC; Investigation Discovery; MTV Classic; MTV Hits; MTV2; National Geographic Channel; NBCSN; Nick Jr.; Nicktoons; Outdoor Channel; OWN: Oprah Winfrey Network; Oxygen; Science Channel; TeenNick; VH1 Country; VH1 Soul.
Fee: $9.00 monthly.

Pay Service 1
Pay Units: N.A.
Programming (via satellite): Cinemax; HBO; Starz; Starz Encore.
Fee: $12.75 monthly (Cinemax, HBO or Starz/Encore).

Digital Pay Service 1
Pay Units: N.A.
Programming (via satellite): Cinemax (multiplexed); Flix; HBO (multiplexed); Showtime (multiplexed); Starz (multiplexed); Starz Encore (multiplexed); The Movie Channel (multiplexed).
Fee: $10.75 monthly (Cinemax, HBO, Showtime/TMC/Flix or Starz/Encore).

Pay-Per-View
iN DEMAND (delivered digitally).

Internet Service
Operational: Yes.
Broadband Service: WadsNet.com.
Fee: $18.95-$45.95 monthly; $7.00 modem lease.

Telephone Service
None
Programming Manager: John Madding.
Ownership: Wadsworth Communications.

WAKEMAN—Time Warner Cable. Now served by CLEVELAND (formerly Cleveland Heights), OH [OH0006]. ICA: OH0373.

WAPAKONETA—Time Warner Cable. Now served by TIFFIN, OH [OH0050]. ICA: OH0119.

WAPAKONETA CITY—TSC Communications, 2 Willipie St, PO Box 408, Wapakoneta, OH 45895. Phones: 419-739-2200; 419-300-2300. Fax: 419-739-2299. E-mail: marketing@telserco.com. Web Site: http://www.telserco.com. Also serves Cridersville, Duchouquet Twp., Ft. Shawnee, Moulton Twp., Pusheta Twp., Shawnee Twp., St. Marys, St. Marys Twp., Union Twp. (Auglaize County) & Uniopolis. ICA: OH0460.
TV Market Ranking: Below 100 (Cridersville, Duchouquet Twp., Moulton Twp., Pusheta Twp., Shawnee Twp., Union Twp. (Auglaize County), Uniopolis, WAPAKONETA CITY).
Channel capacity: N.A. Channels available but not in use: N.A.

Basic Service
Subscribers: 3,573 Includes IPTV subscribers.
Fee: $26.85 installation; $13.99 monthly.

Internet Service
Operational: Yes.

Telephone Service
Digital: Operational
Chief Operating Officer: Lonnie C. Pedersen.
Ownership: TSC Communications Inc. (MSO).

WARNER—Zito Media, 102 S Main St, PO Box 665, Coudersport, PA 16915. Phones: 814-260-9055; 800-365-6988. E-mail: info@zitomedia.com. Web Site: http://www.zitomedia.com. Also serves Aurelius Twp., Dexter City, Dudley, Elba, Jackson Twp. (Noble County), Lower Salem, Macksburg, Salem Twp. (Washington County) & Whipple. ICA: OH0248.
TV Market Ranking: Below 100 (Aurelius Twp., Dexter City, Dudley, Elba, Jackson Twp. (Noble County), Lower Salem, Macksburg, Salem Twp. (Washington County), WARNER, Whipple). Franchise award date: April 3, 1985. Franchise expiration date: N.A. Began: N.A.
Channel capacity: 31 (not 2-way capable). Channels available but not in use: N.A.

Basic Service
Subscribers: 11.
Programming (received off-air): WCHS-TV (ABC, Antenna TV) Charleston; WDTV (CBS) Weston; WHIZ-TV (NBC) Zanesville; WKRN-TV (ABC) Nashville; WOUB-TV (PBS) Athens; WOWK-TV (CBS) Huntington; WSAZ-TV (MNT, NBC, This TV) Huntington; WTAP-TV (FOX, MNT, NBC) Parkersburg; WTOV-TV (MeTV, NBC) Steubenville; WTRF-TV (ABC, CBS, MNT) Wheeling.
Programming (via satellite): AMC; Animal Planet; CNN; Discovery Channel; Disney Channel; ESPN; Freeform; Great American Country; Lifetime; Nickelodeon; Spike TV; TBS; TNT; Trinity Broadcasting Network (TBN); USA Network; VH1; WGN America.
Fee: $49.95 installation; $48.85 monthly; $1.24 converter.

Pay Service 1
Pay Units: N.A.
Programming (via satellite): Cinemax; HBO; Showtime; The Movie Channel.
Fee: $17.50 installation; $7.95 monthly (Cinemax), $11.95 monthly (Showtime or TMC), $11.99 monthly (HBO).

Video-On-Demand: No

Internet Service
Operational: No.

Telephone Service
None

Miles of Plant: 29.0 (coaxial); None (fiber optic). Homes passed: 689.
President: James Rigas.
Ownership: Zito Media (MSO).

WARREN—Time Warner Cable. Now served by CLEVELAND (formerly Cleveland Heights), OH [OH0006]. ICA: OH0013.

WARREN TWP. (Trumbull County)—Formerly served by Northeast Cable TV. No longer in operation. ICA: OH0380.

WASHINGTON COURT HOUSE—Time Warner Cable, 1266 Dublin Rd, Columbus, OH 43215-1008. Phones: 614-255-4997;

Cable Systems—Ohio

614-481-5000. Fax: 614-481-5052. Web Site: http://www.timewarnercable.com. Also serves Bloomingburg, Concord Twp. (Fayette County), Greenfield, Jasper Twp., Jefferson Twp. (Fayette County), Jeffersonville, Madison Twp. (Highland County), Marion Twp. (Fayette County), New Holland (Fayette County), New Holland (Pickaway County), Paint Twp. (Fayette County), Paint Twp. (Highland County), Rainsboro Twp., Richland Twp. (Clinton County), Sabina & Wayne Twp. (Fayette County). ICA: OH0070.

TV Market Ranking: 27 (Bloomingburg, Greenfield, Madison Twp. (Highland County), Marion Twp. (Fayette County), New Holland (Fayette County), New Holland (Pickaway County), Paint Twp. (Fayette County), Paint Twp. (Highland County), Rainsboro Twp., WASHINGTON COURT HOUSE, Wayne Twp. (Fayette County)); 27,41 (Concord Twp. (Fayette County), Jasper Twp. (portions), Richland Twp. (Clinton County) (portions)); 41 (Jefferson Twp. (Fayette County), Jeffersonville, Sabina). Franchise award date: N.A. Franchise expiration date: N.A. Began: December 15, 1968.

Channel capacity: N.A. Channels available but not in use: N.A.

Basic Service
Subscribers: 7,416.
Programming (received off-air): WBNS-TV (Antenna TV, CBS, Decades) Columbus; WCMH-TV (MeTV, NBC) Columbus; WDTN (Escape, Grit, NBC) Dayton; WHIO-TV (CBS, MeTV) Dayton; WOSU-TV (PBS) Columbus; WPTD (PBS) Dayton; WSYX (ABC, Antenna TV, MNT, This TV) Columbus; WTTE (FOX) Columbus; WWHO (CW) Chillicothe; allband FM.
Programming (via satellite): C-SPAN; INSP; Pop; QVC; TBS; VH1; WGN America.
Fee: $29.95 installation; $21.25 monthly.

Expanded Basic Service 1
Subscribers: N.A.
Programming (via satellite): A&E; AMC; Animal Planet; Cartoon Network; CMT; CNN; Comedy Central; Discovery Channel; Disney Channel; Disney XD; E! HD; ESPN; ESPN2; Fox News Channel; FOX Sports Ohio/Sports Time Ohio; Freeform; FX; Great American Country; Hallmark Channel; HGTV; History; HLN; Lifetime; MSNBC; MTV; Nickelodeon; Spike TV; Syfy; The Weather Channel; TLC; TNT; Travel Channel; TV Land; USA Network.
Fee: $41.48 monthly.

Digital Basic Service
Subscribers: N.A.
Programming (via satellite): BBC America; Bloomberg Television; Discovery Digital Networks; DIY Network; ESPN Classic; ESPNews; Fox Sports 1; Fuse; FXM; FYI; Golf Channel; GSN; History International; MC; NBCSN; Outdoor Channel; Trinity Broadcasting Network (TBN); Turner Classic Movies; WE tv.
Fee: $12.49 monthly.

Digital Expanded Basic Service
Subscribers: N.A.
Programming (via satellite): IFC; MTV Classic; National Geographic Channel; Nick Jr.; Nicktoons; Sundance TV; VH1 Country.

Digital Pay Service 1
Pay Units: N.A.
Programming (via satellite): Cinemax (multiplexed); Flix; HBO (multiplexed); Showtime (multiplexed); Starz (multiplexed); Starz Encore (multiplexed); The Movie Channel (multiplexed).
Fee: $12.99 monthly (each).

Video-On-Demand: No

Pay-Per-View
HITS PPV (delivered digitally); Playboy TV (delivered digitally); Fresh (delivered digitally).

Internet Service
Operational: Yes.
Broadband Service: Road Runner.
Fee: $44.95 monthly.

Telephone Service
None
Miles of Plant: 226.0 (coaxial); 9.0 (fiber optic). Homes passed: 13,981.
President: Rhonda Fraas. Vice President & General Manager: David Kreiman. Vice President, Government & Public Affairs: Mary Jo Green. Vice President, Engineering: Randy Hall. Vice President, Marketing: Mark Psigoda. Technical Operations Director: Jim Cavender. Government Affairs Director: Steve Cuckler.
Ownership: Time Warner Cable (MSO).

WATERVILLE—Time Warner Cable. Now served by TIFFIN (formerly Fostoria), OH [OH0050]. ICA: OH0072.

WAUSEON—Time Warner Cable. Now served by TIFFIN, OH [OH0050]. ICA: OH0106.

WAVERLY—Formerly served by Adelphia Communications. Now served by Time Warner Cable, CHILLICOTHE, OH [OH0033]. ICA: OH0139.

WAYNESFIELD (village)—Time Warner Cable. Now served by TIFFIN, OH [OH0050]. ICA: OH0146.

WEATHERSFIELD TWP.—Formerly served by Northeast Cable TV. No longer in operation. ICA: OH0446.

WELLINGTON—GLW Broadband, 993 Commerce Dr, PO Box 67, Grafton, OH 44044. Phone: 440-926-3230. Fax: 440-926-2889. E-mail: support@glwb.net. Web Site: http://www.glwb.net. Also serves Brownhelm Twp., Camden Twp., Eaton Twp. (Lorain County), Grafton, Henrietta Twp., Kipton (village), Lagrange, Lagrange (village), Lagrange Twp., Penfield Twp., Pittsfield Twp., Rochester (village), Rochester Twp., Wellington (village) & Wellington Twp. ICA: OH0189.

TV Market Ranking: 8 (Brownhelm Twp., Camden Twp., Eaton Twp. (Lorain County), Grafton, Henrietta Twp., Kipton (village), Lagrange, Lagrange (village), Lagrange Twp., Penfield Twp., Pittsfield Twp., Rochester (village), Rochester Twp., WELLINGTON, Wellington (village), Wellington Twp.). Franchise award date: N.A. Franchise expiration date: N.A. Began: November 1, 1983.

Channel capacity: 52 (operating 2-way). Channels available but not in use: N.A.

Basic Service
Subscribers: N.A.
Programming (received off-air): WBNX-TV (CW, Movies!, This TV) Akron; WEWS-TV (ABC) Cleveland; WJW (Antenna TV, FOX) Cleveland; WKYC (NBC) Cleveland; WNEO (PBS) Alliance; WOIO (CBS, MeTV) Shaker Heights; WQHS-DT (getTV, UNV) Cleveland; WRLM (IND) Canton; WUAB (Bounce TV, MNT) Lorain; WVIZ (PBS) Cleveland; WVPX-TV (ION) Akron; allband FM.
Programming (via satellite): A&E; AMC; BTN; CMT; History; Lifetime; Nickelodeon; Pop; TBS; The Weather Channel; TLC; VH1.
Fee: $30.00 installation; $2.83 converter.

Expanded Basic Service 1
Subscribers: N.A.
Programming (via satellite): Animal Planet; Cartoon Network; CNBC; CNN; Comedy Central; C-SPAN; Discovery Channel; Disney Channel; Disney XD; E! HD; ESPN; ESPN Classic; ESPN2; Food Network; Fox News Channel; Fox Sports 1; FOX Sports Ohio/Sports Time Ohio; Freeform; FX; Hallmark Channel; HGTV; HLN; INSP; MSNBC; MTV; National Geographic Channel; NFL Network; OWN: Oprah Winfrey Network; QVC; Spike TV; Syfy; TNT; Travel Channel; truTV; TV Land; USA Network; WGN America.
Fee: $29.55 monthly.

Digital Basic Service
Subscribers: N.A.
Programming (via satellite): BBC America; Bloomberg Television; Bravo; Destination America; Discovery Kids Channel; Discovery Life Channel; DMX Music; ESPN; ESPN Classic; ESPN2; ESPNews; Fox Sports 1; Fuse; FXM; FYI; Golf Channel; GSN; HGTV; History International; IFC; Investigation Discovery; LMN; MTV Classic; MTV2; NBCSN; Nick Jr.; Outdoor Channel; OWN: Oprah Winfrey Network; Science Channel; Syfy; TeenNick; Trinity Broadcasting Network (TBN); Turner Classic Movies; VH1 Country; WE tv.
Fee: $14.30 monthly.

Pay Service 1
Pay Units: N.A.
Programming (via satellite): HBO.
Fee: $12.90 monthly.

Digital Pay Service 1
Pay Units: N.A.
Programming (via satellite): Cinemax (multiplexed); HBO (multiplexed); Showtime (multiplexed); Starz Encore (multiplexed); The Movie Channel (multiplexed).
Fee: $4.95 monthly (Encore), $12.90 monthly (Cinemax, HBO or Showtime/TMC).

Video-On-Demand: Planned

Internet Service
Operational: Yes.
Subscribers: 24,691.
Broadband Service: GLW Broadband.
Fee: $19.99 monthly.

Telephone Service
Digital: Operational
Subscribers: 11,755.
Miles of Plant: 23.0 (coaxial); None (fiber optic).
General Manager: Joel Large.
Ownership: GLW Broadband Inc.

WEST BELLAIRE—Bellaire Television Cable Co, PO Box 509, Bellaire, OH 43906. Phone: 740-767-6377. E-mail: cs@bellaire.tv. Web Site: http://www.bellaire.tv. Also serves Clarksburg, Glencoe, Gordon (village), Neffs, St. Clairsville, St. Joe & Stewartsville. ICA: OH0458.

Channel capacity: N.A. Channels available but not in use: N.A.

Basic Service
Subscribers: 482.
Fee: $30.00 installation; $79.95 monthly.
Miles of Plant: None (coaxial); 438.0 (fiber optic). Homes passed: 15,000.
President: Richard A. Nowak.
Ownership: Richard A Nowak.

WEST LAFAYETTE TWP.—Time Warner Cable. Now served by COLUMBUS, OH [OH0002]. ICA: OH0374.

WEST MANSFIELD (village)—Time Warner Cable. Now served by COLUMBUS, OH [OH0002]. ICA: OH0236.

WEST UNION—Time Warner Cable. Now served by AMBERLEY (village), OH [OH0001]. ICA: OH0152.

WILLARD—Time Warner Cable. Now served by CLEVELAND (formerly Cleveland Heights), OH [OH0006]. ICA: OH0108.

WILLOWS MOBILE HOME PARK—Time Warner Cable. Now served by CLEVELAND (formerly Cleveland Heights), OH [OH0006]. ICA: OH0302.

WILMINGTON—Time Warner Cable. Now served by AMBERLEY (village), OH [OH0001]. ICA: OH0112.

WINESBURG—Formerly served by National Cable Inc. No longer in operation. ICA: OH0375.

WOODSFIELD—City of Woodsfield, 221 South Main St, Woodsfield, OH 43793. Phone: 740-472-1865. Web Site: http://www.woodsfieldohio.org/woodsfield-cable-internet.html. Also serves Center Twp. (Monroe County), Lewisville & Summit Twp. ICA: OH0206.

TV Market Ranking: 90 (Center Twp. (Monroe County), Lewisville, Summit Twp., WOODSFIELD). Franchise award date: N.A. Franchise expiration date: N.A. Began: October 1, 1966.

Channel capacity: 43 (operating 2-way). Channels available but not in use: N.A.

Basic Service
Subscribers: N.A.
Programming (received off-air): KDKA-TV (CBS, Decades) Pittsburgh; WHIZ-TV (NBC) Zanesville; WOUC-TV (PBS) Cambridge; WTAE-TV (ABC, This TV) Pittsburgh; WTOV-TV (MeTV, NBC) Steubenville; WTRF-TV (ABC, CBS, MNT) Wheeling; allband FM.
Programming (via satellite): CNN; Discovery Channel; FOX Sports Networks; TBS; The Weather Channel; TLC; TNT; Trinity Broadcasting Network (TBN); USA Network; WABC-TV (ABC, Live Well Network) New York.
Fee: $61.25 installation; $47.99 monthly; $1.24 converter.

Expanded Basic Service 1
Subscribers: N.A.
Programming (via satellite): A&E; AMC; Cartoon Network; Comedy Central; C-SPAN; Disney Channel; Disney XD; ESPN; ESPN2; Fox Sports 1; Freeform; Great American Country; GSN; HGTV; History; HLN; INSP; Lifetime; MSNBC; MTV; National Geographic Channel; NBCSN; Nickelodeon; Spike TV; Syfy; TV Land; VH1; WE tv.
Fee: $23.00 monthly.

Digital Basic Service
Subscribers: N.A.
Programming (via satellite): BBC America; Bloomberg Television; Cloo; Discovery Digital Networks; ESPN Classic; ESPNews; EVINE Live; FOX College Sports Central; FOX College Sports Pacific; FXM; FYI; Golf Channel; History; History International; IFC; LMN; Outdoor Channel; Turner Classic Movies.
Fee: $13.95 monthly.

Pay Service 1
Pay Units: N.A.
Programming (via satellite): Cinemax; HBO; Showtime; Starz Encore; The Movie Channel.

2017 Edition

D-605

Ohio—Cable Systems

Fee: $3.99 monthly (Encore), $13.95 monthly (Cinemax), $13.95 monthly (Showtime or TMC), $11.99 monthly (HBO).
Digital Pay Service 1
Pay Units: N.A.
Programming (via satellite): Cinemax (multiplexed); Flix; HBO (multiplexed); Showtime (multiplexed); Starz (multiplexed); Starz Encore (multiplexed); The Movie Channel (multiplexed).
Pay-Per-View
iN DEMAND (delivered digitally); Playboy TV (delivered digitally); Fresh (delivered digitally).
Internet Service
Operational: Yes. Began: November 1, 2004.
Broadband Service: In-house.
Fee: $20.00 installation; $30.95 monthly.
Telephone Service
None
Miles of Plant: 23.0 (coaxial); None (fiber optic). Homes passed: 1,376.
General Manager: Sam McPeak. Office Manager: Krystal Boon.
Ownership: City of Woodsfield, OH (MSO).

WOOSTER—MCTV, PO Box 1000, Massillon, OH 44648-1000. Phones: 330-833-4134; 330-345-8114. Fax: 330-345-5265. Web Site: http://www.mctvohio.com. Also serves Apple Creek, Canaan Twp. (Wayne County), Chester Twp. (Wayne County), Clinton Twp. (Wayne County), Congress Twp., East Union Twp. (Wayne County), Franklin Twp. (Wayne County), Green Twp. (Wayne County), Mount Eaton, Paint Twp. (Wayne County), Perry Twp. (Ashland County), Plain Twp. (Wayne County), Salt Creek Twp., Smithville, Sugar Creek Twp. (Wayne County, southeastern portion), Wayne Twp. (Wayne County) & Wooster Twp. (Wayne County). ICA: OH0061.
TV Market Ranking: 8 (Apple Creek, Canaan Twp. (Wayne County), Chester Twp. (Wayne County), Clinton Twp. (Wayne County), Congress Twp., East Union Twp. (Wayne County), Franklin Twp. (Wayne County), Green Twp. (Wayne County), Mount Eaton, Paint Twp. (Wayne County), Plain Twp. (Wayne County), Salt Creek Twp., Smithville, Sugar Creek Twp. (Wayne County), Wayne Twp. (Wayne County), WOOSTER, Wooster Twp. (Wayne County)); Below 100 (Perry Twp. (Ashland County), Wayne County (southeastern portion)). Franchise award date: November 1, 1967. Franchise expiration date: N.A. Began: November 1, 1967.
Channel capacity: N.A. Channels available but not in use: N.A.
Basic Service
Subscribers: 12,435.
Programming (received off-air): WBNX-TV (CW, Movies!, This TV) Akron; WDLI-TV (TBN) Canton; WEWS-TV (ABC) Cleveland; WJW (Antenna TV, FOX) Cleveland; WKYC (NBC) Cleveland; WMFD-TV (IND) Mansfield; WNEO (PBS) Alliance; WOIO (CBS, MeTV) Shaker Heights; WQHS-DT (getTV, UNV) Cleveland; WRLM (IND) Canton; WUAB (Bounce TV, MNT) Lorain; WVIZ (PBS) Cleveland; WVPX-TV (ION) Akron.
Programming (via satellite): A&E; AMC; Animal Planet; BET; Boomerang; Bravo; BTN; Cartoon Network; CMT; CNBC; CNN; Comedy Central; C-SPAN; C-SPAN 2; Discovery Channel; Disney Channel; E! HD; ESPN; ESPN Classic; ESPN2; ESPNU; EWTN Global Catholic Network; Food Network; Fox News Channel; Fox Sports 1; FOX Sports Ohio/Sports Time Ohio; Freeform; FX; Golf Channel; Great American Country; GSN; Hallmark Channel; HGTV; History; HLN; INSP; ION Television; Lifetime; MLB Network; MSNBC; MTV; National Geographic Channel; Nickelodeon; OWN: Oprah Winfrey Network; Oxygen; Pop; Qubo; QVC; Reelz; Spike TV; Syfy; TBS; The Weather Channel; TLC; TNT; Travel Channel; truTV; Turner Classic Movies; TV Land; USA Network; VH1; Weatherscan; WGN America.
Fee: $29.95 monthly.

Digital Basic Service
Subscribers: N.A.
Programming (via satellite): A&E HD; AXS TV; BBC America; Bloomberg Television; Bravo HD; BTN HD; CBS Sports Network; Chiller; CMT; CNBC HD+; CNN HD; Cooking Channel; Destination America; Discovery Kids Channel; Discovery Life Channel; Disney XD; DIY Network; DMX Music; ESPN HD; ESPN2 HD; ESPNews; Fox Business Network; FOX Sports Ohio/Sports Time Ohio; FXM; FYI; HD Theater; History; History HD; History International; Investigation Discovery; LMN; MGM HD; MLB Network; MTV Classic; MTV Hits; MTV2; NBCSN; NHL Network; Nick Jr.; Nicktoons; Outdoor Channel; Science Channel; Sprout; Syfy HD; TBS HD; TeenNick; Tennis Channel; TNT HD; TV One; Universal HD; UP; USA Network HD; VH1 Soul; WE tv; Weatherscan.
Fee: $7.50 monthly.

Digital Pay Service 1
Pay Units: N.A.
Programming (via satellite): Cinemax (multiplexed); Flix; HBO (multiplexed); HBO HD; Showtime (multiplexed); Showtime HD; Starz (multiplexed); Starz Encore (multiplexed); Sundance TV; The Movie Channel (multiplexed).
Fee: $10.75 monthly (Cinemax), $11.50 monthly (Starz/Encore), $14.00 monthly (Showtime), $14.25 monthly (HBO).
Video-On-Demand: Yes

Pay-Per-View
iN DEMAND (delivered digitally); MLB Extra Innings (delivered digitally); NHL Center Ice (delivered digitally).
Internet Service
Operational: Yes. Began: May 1, 1999.
Subscribers: 11,654.
Broadband Service: Super Net.
Fee: $35.00 installation; $25.00-$59.95 monthly.
Telephone Service
Digital: Operational
Subscribers: 5,357.
Fee: $47.95 monthly
Miles of Plant: 925.0 (coaxial); 209.0 (fiber optic). Homes passed: 23,710.
President: Robert Gessner. Chief Operating Officer: David Hoffer. Chief Technician: Tom Mogus. Marketing Director: Shannon Delaney. Ad Sales Manager: Elizabeth McAllister. Customer Service Manager: Brenda Murphy.
Ownership: MCTV (MSO).

YELLOW SPRINGS—Time Warner Cable. Now served by AMBERLEY (village), OH [OH0001]. ICA: OH0103.

YOUNGSTOWN—Formerly served by Northeast Cable TV. No longer in operation. ICA: OH0384.

YOUNGSTOWN—Formerly served by Sprint Corp. No longer in operation. ICA: OH0389.

YOUNGSTOWN—Time Warner Cable. Now served by CLEVELAND (formerly Cleveland Heights), OH [OH0006]. ICA: OH0017.

ZANESVILLE—Time Warner Cable. Now served by COLUMBUS, OH [OH0002]. ICA: OH0037.

OKLAHOMA

Total Systems: 124	Communities with Applications: 0
Total Communities Served: 348	Number of Basic Subscribers: 459,000
Franchises Not Yet Operating: 0	Number of Expanded Basic Subscribers: 1,794
Applications Pending: 0	Number of Pay Units: 17,601

Top 100 Markets Represented: Oklahoma City (39); Tulsa (54).

For a list of cable communities in this section, see the Cable Community Index located in the back of Cable Volume 2.
For explanation of terms used in cable system listings, see p. D-11.

ACHILLE—Vyve Broadband, 1501 West Mississippi, Durant, OK 74701. Phone: 855-367-8983. Web Site: http://vyvebroadband.com. ICA: OK0342.
TV Market Ranking: Below 100 (ACHILLE).
Channel capacity: N.A. Channels available but not in use: N.A.
Basic Service
Subscribers: 33.
Fee: $59.99 installation; $25.00 monthly.
Chief Executive Officer: Bill Haggarty. Regional Vice President: Andrew Dearth. Senior Vice President, Financial Planning: Daniel J. White.
Ownership: Vyve Broadband LLC (MSO).

ADA—Cable One, 1610 Arlington St, Ada, OK 74820-2640. Phone: 580-332-8333. Fax: 580-332-4005. Web Site: http://www.cableone.net. Also serves Byng, Davis, Francis, Pontotoc County, Roff & Sulphur. ICA: OK0018.
TV Market Ranking: Below 100 (ADA, Byng, Davis, Francis, Pontotoc County, Roff, Sulphur). Franchise award date: N.A. Franchise expiration date: N.A. Began: June 1, 1965.
Channel capacity: N.A. Channels available but not in use: N.A.
Basic Service
Subscribers: 4,309. Commercial subscribers: 336.
Programming (received off-air): KAUT-TV (Escape, MNT) Oklahoma City; KETA-TV (PBS) Oklahoma City; KFOR-TV (Antenna TV, NBC) Oklahoma City; KOCO-TV (ABC, This TV) Oklahoma City; KOKH-TV (FOX, The Country Network, WeatherNation) Oklahoma City; KSBI (IND) Oklahoma City; KTEN (ABC, CW, NBC) Ada; KWTV-DT (CBS) Oklahoma City; KXII (CBS, FOX, MNT) Sherman; 10 FMs.
Programming (via satellite): CW PLUS; Pop; Trinity Broadcasting Network (TBN).
Fee: $90.00 installation; $35.00 monthly.
Expanded Basic Service 1
Subscribers: N.A.
Programming (via satellite): A&E; AMC; Animal Planet; BET; Cartoon Network; CMT; CNBC; CNN; C-SPAN; Discovery Channel; Disney Channel; E! HD; ESPN; ESPN2; Food Network; Fox News Channel; FOX Sports Southwest; Freeform; FX; HGTV; History; HLN; Lifetime; MSNBC; MTV; Nickelodeon; QVC; Spike TV; Syfy; TBS; The Weather Channel; TLC; TNT; Travel Channel; Turner Classic Movies; TV Land; USA Network; VH1.
Fee: $42.50 monthly.
Digital Basic Service
Subscribers: N.A.
Programming (via satellite): 3ABN; Boomerang; BYUtv; Discovery Digital Networks; Disney XD; DMX Music; ESPN Classic; ESPNews; FamilyNet; FOX College Sports Central; FOX College Sports Pacific; Fox HD; Fox Sports 1; Fox Sports 2; FXM; FYI; Golf Channel; Great American Country; Hallmark Channel; History International; HITS (Headend In The Sky); INSP; National Geographic Channel; Outdoor Channel; TNT HD; Trinity Broadcasting Network (TBN); truTV; TVG Network; Universal HD.
Digital Pay Service 1
Pay Units: N.A.
Programming (via satellite): Cinemax (multiplexed); Flix; HBO (multiplexed); Showtime (multiplexed); Showtime HD; Starz (multiplexed); Starz Encore (multiplexed); Sundance TV; The Movie Channel (multiplexed); The Movie Channel HD.
Fee: $15.00 monthly (each).
Video-On-Demand: No
Pay-Per-View
iN DEMAND (delivered digitally); Pleasure (delivered digitally); SexSee (delivered digitally); Juicy (delivered digitally); VaVoom (delivered digitally); ESPN (delivered digitally).
Internet Service
Operational: Yes. Began: April 1, 2000.
Subscribers: 6,046.
Broadband Service: CableONE.net.
Fee: $75.00 installation; $43.00 monthly; $5.00 modem lease.
Telephone Service
Digital: Operational
Subscribers: 2,091.
Fee: $39.95 monthly
Miles of Plant: 687.0 (coaxial); 136.0 (fiber optic). Homes passed: 17,336.
Vice President: Patrick A. Dolohanty. General Manager: Bill W. Dalton. Technical Operations Manager: Stanley Barnes. Chief Technician: Darren Flowers. Marketing Manager: David Cobb.
Ownership: Cable ONE Inc. (MSO).

ADAIR—Formerly served by Allegiance Communications. No longer in operation. ICA: OK0219.

AGRA—Formerly served by Allegiance Communications. No longer in operation. ICA: OK0260.

ALEX—Southern Plains Cable, PO Box 165, Medicine Park, OK 73557. Phones: 580-365-4235; 800-218-1856; 580-529-5000. Fax: 580-529-5556. E-mail: office@wichitaonline.net. Web Site: http://www.spcisp.net. ICA: OK0334.
TV Market Ranking: Below 100 (ALEX). Franchise award date: N.A. Franchise expiration date: N.A. Began: January 1, 1992.
Channel capacity: N.A. Channels available but not in use: N.A.
Basic Service
Subscribers: N.A.
Programming (received off-air): KAUT-TV (Escape, MNT) Oklahoma City; KETA-TV (PBS) Oklahoma City; KFOR-TV (Antenna TV, NBC) Oklahoma City; KOCB (CW) Oklahoma City; KOCO-TV (ABC, This TV) Oklahoma City; KOKH-TV (FOX, The Country Network, WeatherNation) Oklahoma City; KOPX-TV (ION) Oklahoma City; KTBO-TV (TBN) Oklahoma City; KWTV-DT (CBS) Oklahoma City.
Programming (via satellite): A&E; AMC; Animal Planet; CMT; CNN; Discovery Channel; ESPN; ESPN2; EVINE Live; Freeform; History; Lifetime; Local Cable Weather; Nickelodeon; Spike TV; Syfy; TBS; The Weather Channel; TLC; TNT; TV Land; USA Network; WGN America.
Fee: $45.00 installation.
Pay Service 1
Pay Units: N.A.
Programming (via satellite): Showtime; The Movie Channel.
Fee: $10.00 monthly (each).
Video-On-Demand: No
Internet Service
Operational: Yes.
Telephone Service
Analog: Not Operational
Digital: Planned
Miles of Plant: 6.0 (coaxial); None (fiber optic). Homes passed: 322.
President: Dustin Hilliary.
Ownership: Southern Plains Cable (MSO).

ALINE (town)—Formerly served by Blue Sky Cable LLC. No longer in operation. ICA: OK0387.

ALLEN (town)—Formerly served by Allegiance Communications. No longer in operation. ICA: OK0351.

ALTUS—Cable One, 618 North Main, Altus, OK 73521. Phone: 580-482-0523. Fax: 580-477-0911. E-mail: robin.graham@cableone.net. Web Site: http://www.cableone.net. Also serves Altus AFB, Blair, Frederick, Jackson County & Tipton. ICA: OK0017.
TV Market Ranking: Outside TV Markets (ALTUS, Altus AFB, Blair, Frederick, Jackson County, Tipton). Franchise award date: July 30, 1956. Franchise expiration date: N.A. Began: September 1, 1957.
Channel capacity: N.A. Channels available but not in use: N.A.
Basic Service
Subscribers: 2,801.
Programming (received off-air): KAUZ-TV (CBS, CW) Wichita Falls; KFDX-TV (NBC) Wichita Falls; KFOR-TV (Antenna TV, NBC) Oklahoma City; KJTL (Bounce TV, FOX) Wichita Falls; KOCB (CW) Oklahoma City; KOCO-TV (ABC, This TV) Oklahoma City; KOKH-TV (FOX, The Country Network, WeatherNation) Oklahoma City; KSWO-TV (ABC, TMO) Lawton; KWET (PBS) Cheyenne; KWTV-DT (CBS) Oklahoma City.
Programming (via satellite): 24/7 News Channel; A&E; AMC; Animal Planet; BET; Bravo; Cartoon Network; CMT; CNBC; CNN; C-SPAN; C-SPAN 2; Discovery Channel; Disney Channel; DMX Music; E! HD; ESPN; ESPN Classic; ESPN2; EVINE Live; Food Network; Fox News Channel; FOX Sports Southwest; Freeform; FX; HGTV; History; HLN; INSP; ION Television; Lifetime; MSNBC; MTV; Nickelodeon; Pop; QVC; Spike TV; Syfy; TBS; Telemundo; The Weather Channel; TLC; TNT; Trinity Broadcasting Network (TBN); Turner Classic Movies; TV Land; Univision Studios; USA Network; VH1; WGN America.
Fee: $35.00 monthly; $1.50 converter.
Digital Basic Service
Subscribers: N.A.
Programming (via satellite): 3ABN; Boomerang; BYUtv; Discovery Digital Networks; Disney XD; ESPN Classic; ESPNews; FamilyNet; FOX College Sports Central; FOX College Sports Pacific; Fox Sports 1; Fox Sports 2; FXM; FYI; Golf Channel; Great American Country; Hallmark Channel; History International; HITS (Headend In The Sky); INSP; National Geographic Channel; Outdoor Channel; TNT HD; Trinity Broadcasting Network (TBN); truTV; TVG Network; Universal HD.
Fee: $8.95 monthly.
Digital Pay Service 1
Pay Units: N.A.
Programming (via satellite): Cinemax (multiplexed); Flix; HBO (multiplexed); Showtime (multiplexed); Showtime HD; Starz (multiplexed); Starz Encore (multiplexed); Sundance TV; The Movie Channel (multiplexed); The Movie Channel HD.
Fee: $15.00 monthly.
Video-On-Demand: No
Pay-Per-View
Pleasure (delivered digitally); SexSee (delivered digitally); Juicy (delivered digitally); VaVoom (delivered digitally).
Internet Service
Operational: Yes. Began: January 1, 2003.
Subscribers: 3,929.
Broadband Service: CableONE.net.
Fee: $75.00 installation; $43.00 monthly.
Telephone Service
Digital: Operational
Subscribers: 1,314.
Fee: $39.95 monthly
Miles of Plant: 271.0 (coaxial); 32.0 (fiber optic). Homes passed: 13,853.
Vice President: Patrick A. Dolohanty. General Manager: George Wilburn. Technical Operations Manager: Ted Ramsey. Marketing Director: Robin Graham.
Ownership: Cable ONE Inc. (MSO).

ALVA—Suddenlink Communications, 131 East Main St, Enid, OK 73701. Phones: 314-315-9400; 580-327-1664. Web Site: http://www.

2017 Edition

D-607

Oklahoma—Cable Systems

suddenlink.com. Also serves Woods County (eastern portion). ICA: OK0063.
TV Market Ranking: Outside TV Markets (ALVA, Woods County (eastern portion)). Franchise award date: N.A. Franchise expiration date: N.A. Began: May 1, 1957.
Channel capacity: N.A. Channels available but not in use: N.A.
Basic Service
Subscribers: 689. Commercial subscribers: 145.
Programming (received off-air): KAUT-TV (Escape, MNT) Oklahoma City; KETA-TV (PBS) Oklahoma City; KFOR-TV (Antenna TV, NBC) Oklahoma City; KOCB (CW) Oklahoma City; KOCO-TV (ABC, This TV) Oklahoma City; KOKH-TV (FOX, The Country Network, WeatherNation) Oklahoma City; KSBI (IND) Oklahoma City; KTUZ-TV (TMO) Shawnee; KWTV-DT (CBS) Oklahoma City.
Programming (via satellite): A&E; AMC; Animal Planet; Cartoon Network; CMT; CNBC; CNN; Comedy Central; C-SPAN; Discovery Channel; Disney Channel; ESPN; ESPN2; Food Network; Fox News Channel; FOX Sports Southwest; Freeform; FX; Hallmark Channel; HGTV; History; Lifetime; MSNBC; MTV; Nickelodeon; Pop; Spike TV; Syfy; TBS; The Weather Channel; TLC; TNT; Travel Channel; Trinity Broadcasting Network (TBN); truTV; TV Land; USA Network; WGN America.
Fee: $54.95 installation; $31.70 monthly.
Digital Basic Service
Subscribers: N.A.
Programming (via satellite): BBC America; Bloomberg Television; Bravo; CMT; Destination America; Discovery Kids Channel; Disney XD; DMX Music; ESPNews; EVINE Live; FOX College Sports Central; FOX College Sports Pacific; Fox Sports 1; Fuse; FXM; Golf Channel; Great American Country; GSN; IFC; Investigation Discovery; LMN; MTV Hits; National Geographic Channel; NBCSN; Outdoor Channel; OWN; Oprah Winfrey Network; Sundance TV; Turner Classic Movies.
Digital Pay Service 1
Pay Units: N.A.
Programming (via satellite): Cinemax (multiplexed); HBO (multiplexed); Showtime (multiplexed); Starz (multiplexed); Starz Encore (multiplexed); The Movie Channel.
Pay-Per-View
iN DEMAND (delivered digitally); Fresh (delivered digitally); Spice: Xcess (delivered digitally).
Internet Service
Operational: Yes.
Broadband Service: Suddenlink High Speed Internet.
Fee: $45.95 installation; $24.95 monthly.
Telephone Service
Digital: Operational
Fee: $49.95 monthly
Miles of Plant: 43.0 (coaxial); 4.0 (fiber optic). Homes passed: 3,449.
Vice President, Accounting: Sabrina Warr. General Manager: Byron Mahaffey. Marketing Manager: Heather Eastwood. Chief Technician: Dave Lyon.
Ownership: Cequel Communications Holdings I LLC (MSO).

AMES—Pioneer Telephone Coop. This cable system has converted to IPTV. Now served by KINGFISHER, OK [OK5074]. ICA: OK0370.

ANADARKO—Suddenlink Communications, 520 Maryville Centre Dr, Ste 300, St. Louis, MO 63141. Phones: 800-999-6845 (Customer service); 314-909-9346; 314-315-9400. Web Site: http://www.suddenlink.com. ICA: OK0052.
TV Market Ranking: Below 100 (ANADARKO). Franchise award date: N.A. Franchise expiration date: N.A. Began: March 6, 1977.
Channel capacity: 41 (operating 2-way). Channels available but not in use: N.A.
Basic Service
Subscribers: 400. Commercial subscribers: 52.
Programming (received off-air): KAUT-TV (Escape, MNT) Oklahoma City; KETA-TV (PBS) Oklahoma City; KFOR-TV (Antenna TV, NBC) Oklahoma City; KOCB (CW) Oklahoma City; KOCM (Daystar TV) Norman; KOCO-TV (ABC, This TV) Oklahoma City; KOKH-TV (FOX, The Country Network, WeatherNation) Oklahoma City; KOPX-TV (ION) Oklahoma City; KSWO-TV (ABC, TMO) Lawton; KTBO-TV (TBN) Oklahoma City; KWTV-DT (CBS) Oklahoma City; allband FM.
Fee: $28.45 monthly.
Expanded Basic Service 1
Subscribers: N.A.
Programming (via satellite): A&E; AMC; Animal Planet; BET; Cartoon Network; CNBC; CNN; Comedy Central; C-SPAN; Discovery Channel; Disney Channel; E! HD; ESPN; ESPN2; Food Network; Fox News Channel; FOX Sports Southwest; Freeform; FX; Great American Country; HGTV; History; HLN; Lifetime; MTV; National Geographic Channel; Nickelodeon; QVC; Spike TV; Syfy; TBS; The Weather Channel; TLC; TNT; Turner Classic Movies; TV Land; Univision Studios; USA Network; VH1.
Fee: $24.00 monthly.
Digital Basic Service
Subscribers: N.A.
Programming (via satellite): BBC America; Bloomberg Television; Cloo; Discovery Digital Networks; Disney XD; ESPN Classic; ESPNews; EVINE Live; FOX College Sports Central; FOX College Sports Pacific; Fox Sports 1; Fuse; FYI; Golf Channel; GSN; History International; IFC; NBCSN; Outdoor Channel; WE tv.
Pay Service 1
Pay Units: N.A.
Programming (via satellite): HBO; Showtime; The Movie Channel.
Fee: $5.95 monthly (TMC), $9.95 monthly (Showtime), $10.95 monthly (HBO).
Digital Pay Service 1
Pay Units: N.A.
Programming (via satellite): Cinemax (multiplexed); Flix; HBO (multiplexed); Showtime (multiplexed); Starz (multiplexed); Starz Encore (multiplexed); The Movie Channel (multiplexed).
Video-On-Demand: No
Pay-Per-View
iN DEMAND (delivered digitally).
Internet Service
Operational: Yes. Began: December 17, 2002.
Broadband Service: Suddenlink High Speed Internet.
Fee: $45.95 installation; $24.95 monthly.
Telephone Service
Digital: Operational
Fee: $49.95 monthly
Miles of Plant: 65.0 (coaxial); None (fiber optic). Homes passed: 2,041.
Senior Vice President, Corporate Finance: Michael Pflantz. Regional Manager: Todd Cruthird. Marketing Director: Beverly Gambell. Chief Technician: Roger Campbell.
Ownership: Cequel Communications Holdings I LLC (MSO).

ANTLERS—Alliance Communications, PO Box 9090, Tyler, TX 75711. Phones: 903-561-4411; 800-842-8160; 501-679-6619 (Greenbrier, AR office). Web Site: http://www.alliancecable.net. ICA: OK0101.
TV Market Ranking: Outside TV Markets (ANTLERS). Franchise award date: N.A. Franchise expiration date: N.A. Began: November 1, 1963.
Channel capacity: 36 (not 2-way capable). Channels available but not in use: N.A.
Basic Service
Subscribers: 109.
Programming (received off-air): KHBS (ABC, CW) Fort Smith; KMSS-TV (FOX) Shreveport; KOET (PBS) Eufaula; KTEN (ABC, CW, NBC) Ada; KXII (CBS, FOX, MNT) Sherman; allband FM.
Programming (via satellite): A&E; AMC; CMT; CNN; Discovery Channel; Disney Channel; ESPN; ESPN2; Fox News Channel; FOX Sports Networks; Freeform; FYI; INSP; Lifetime; Nickelodeon; QVC; Spike TV; Syfy; TBS; The Weather Channel; TNT; Turner Classic Movies; USA Network; VH1; WGN America.
Fee: $45.00 installation; $22.45 monthly.
Pay Service 1
Pay Units: N.A.
Programming (via satellite): HBO; Showtime; Starz; Starz Encore; The Movie Channel.
Video-On-Demand: No
Internet Service
Operational: No.
Telephone Service
None
Miles of Plant: 15.0 (coaxial); None (fiber optic).
Chief Financial Officer: David Starrett. Vice President & General Manager: John Brinker. Vice President, Programming: Julie Newman.
Ownership: Buford Media Group LLC (MSO).

APACHE—Southern Plains Cable, PO Box 165, Medicine Park, OK 73557. Phones: 580-365-4235; 800-218-1856; 580-529-5000. Fax: 580-529-5556. E-mail: office@wichitaonline.net. Web Site: http://www.spcisp.net. ICA: OK0139.
TV Market Ranking: Below 100 (APACHE). Franchise award date: N.A. Franchise expiration date: N.A. Began: April 1, 1982.
Channel capacity: N.A. Channels available but not in use: N.A.
Basic Service
Subscribers: N.A.
Programming (received off-air): KAUT-TV (Escape, MNT) Oklahoma City; KETA-TV (PBS) Oklahoma City; KFOR-TV (Antenna TV, NBC) Oklahoma City; KJTL (Bounce TV, FOX) Wichita Falls; KOCO-TV (ABC, This TV) Oklahoma City; KOKH-TV (FOX, The Country Network, WeatherNation) Oklahoma City; KSWO-TV (ABC, TMO) Lawton; KWTV-DT (CBS) Oklahoma City.
Programming (via satellite): Trinity Broadcasting Network (TBN).
Fee: $45.00 installation.
Expanded Basic Service 1
Subscribers: N.A.
Programming (via satellite): A&E; AMC; Animal Planet; Cartoon Network; CMT; CNBC; CNN; Comedy Central; C-SPAN; C-SPAN 2; Discovery Channel; Disney Channel; E! HD; ESPN; ESPN Classic; ESPN2; ESPNews; EVINE Live; Fox News Channel; Freeform; FX; HGTV; History; HLN; INSP; Lifetime; Local Cable Weather; MTV; Nickelodeon; Outdoor Channel; QVC; RFD-TV; Spike TV; Syfy; TBS; Telemundo; The Weather Chan-

nel; TLC; TNT; Turner Classic Movies; TV Land; USA Network; WGN America.
Fee: $31.83 monthly.
Pay Service 1
Pay Units: N.A.
Programming (via satellite): Showtime; The Movie Channel.
Fee: $10.00 monthly (each).
Video-On-Demand: No
Internet Service
Operational: Yes.
Fee: $24.95 monthly.
Telephone Service
Digital: Planned
Miles of Plant: 12.0 (coaxial); None (fiber optic). Homes passed: 725.
President: Dustin Hilliary.
Ownership: Southern Plains Cable (MSO).

ARAPAHO—Formerly served by Full Circle Communications. No longer in operation. ICA: OK0187.

ARDMORE—Cable One, 811 West Broadway St, Ardmore, OK 73401-4526. Phones: 580-657-3312; 580-223-9600. Fax: 580-226-4472. E-mail: dwall@cableone.net. Web Site: http://www.cableone.net. Also serves Carter County, Dickson, Lone Grove, Madill, Marietta, Marshall County (northern portion) & Oakland. ICA: OK0012.
TV Market Ranking: Below 100 (Madill, Oakland, ARDMORE); Outside TV Markets (Carter County, Dickson, Marietta, Marshall County (northern portion), Lone Grove). Franchise award date: February 1, 1952. Franchise expiration date: N.A. Began: May 1, 1951.
Channel capacity: N.A. Channels available but not in use: N.A.
Basic Service
Subscribers: 4,772.
Programming (received off-air): KETA-TV (PBS) Oklahoma City; KTEN (ABC, CW, NBC) Ada; KXII (CBS, FOX, MNT) Sherman; 7 FMs.
Programming (via microwave): KFOR-TV (Antenna TV, NBC) Oklahoma City; KWTV-DT (CBS) Oklahoma City; WFAA (ABC) Dallas.
Programming (via satellite): A&E; AMC; Animal Planet; BET; Bravo; Cartoon Network; CMT; CNBC; CNN; Comedy Central; C-SPAN; C-SPAN 2; Discovery Channel; Disney Channel; E! HD; ESPN; ESPN Classic; ESPN2; EVINE Live; Food Network; Fox News Channel; FOX Sports Southwest; Freeform; FX; HGTV; History; HLN; Lifetime; MSNBC; MTV; Nickelodeon; Pop; QVC; Spike TV; Syfy; TBS; The Weather Channel; TLC; TNT; Trinity Broadcasting Network (TBN); Turner Classic Movies; TV Land; USA Network; VH1.
Fee: $90.00 installation; $35.00 monthly.
Digital Basic Service
Subscribers: N.A.
Programming (via satellite): 3ABN; Boomerang; BYUtv; Discovery Digital Networks; Disney XD; DMX Music; ESPN Classic; ESPNews; FamilyNet; FOX College Sports Central; FOX College Sports Pacific; Fox HD; Fox Sports 1; Fox Sports 2; FXM; FYI; Great American Country; Hallmark Channel; History International; HITS (Headend In The Sky); INSP; National Geographic Channel; Outdoor Channel; TNT HD; Trinity Broadcasting Network (TBN); truTV; Universal HD.
Fee: $8.95 monthly.
Digital Pay Service 1
Pay Units: N.A.
Programming (via satellite): Cinemax (multiplexed); Flix (multiplexed); HBO

Cable Systems—Oklahoma

FULLY SEARCHABLE • CONTINUOUSLY UPDATED • DISCOUNT RATES FOR PRINT PURCHASERS

For more information call **800-771-9202** or visit **www.warren-news.com**

(multiplexed); Showtime (multiplexed); Showtime HD; Starz (multiplexed); Starz Encore (multiplexed); Sundance TV; The Movie Channel (multiplexed); The Movie Channel HD.
Fee: $15.00 monthly (each).
Video-On-Demand: No
Pay-Per-View
iN DEMAND (delivered digitally); Pleasure (delivered digitally); SexSee (delivered digitally); Juicy (delivered digitally); VaVoom (delivered digitally); ESPN (delivered digitally).
Internet Service
Operational: Yes. Began: March 1, 2002.
Subscribers: 6,626.
Broadband Service: CableONE.net.
Fee: $75.00 installation; $43.00 monthly.
Telephone Service
Digital: Operational
Subscribers: 2,387.
Fee: $39.95 monthly
Miles of Plant: 744.0 (coaxial); 192.0 (fiber optic). Homes passed: 19,474.
Vice President: Patrick A. Dolohanty. General Manager: David H. Wall Jr. Chief Technician: Bill Reynolds.
Ownership: Cable ONE Inc. (MSO).

ARNETT—Pioneer Telephone Coop. This cable system has converted to IPTV. Now served by KINGFISHER, OK [OK5074]. ICA: OK0261.

ARPELAR—Vyve Broadband, 4 International Dr, Ste 330, Rye Brook, NY 10673. Phones: 800-937-1397; 405-395-1131; 405-275-6923. Web Site: http://vyvebroadband.com. Also serves Haywood & Stuart. ICA: OK0356.
TV Market Ranking: Below 100 (Stuart); Outside TV Markets (Haywood, ARPELAR).
Channel capacity: 36 (not 2-way capable). Channels available but not in use: N.A.
Basic Service
Subscribers: 15.
Programming (received off-air): KFOR-TV (Antenna TV, NBC) Oklahoma City; KOED-TV (PBS) Tulsa; KOKI-TV (FOX, MeTV) Tulsa; KOTV-DT (CBS, IND) Tulsa; KQCW-DT (CW, This TV) Muskogee; KTEN (ABC, CW, NBC) Ada; KTUL (ABC, Antenna TV, Retro TV) Tulsa.
Programming (via satellite): A&E; AMC; Animal Planet; CMT; CNN; Discovery Channel; Disney Channel; ESPN; FOX Sports Southwest; Freeform; History; Lifetime; Nickelodeon; Spike TV; Syfy; TBS; The Weather Channel; TNT; TV Land; USA Network; WGN America.
Fee: $64.95 installation; $25.00 monthly.
Pay Service 1
Pay Units: N.A.
Programming (via satellite): HBO; Showtime; Starz; Starz Encore.
Fee: $10.00 monthly (each).
Pay-Per-View
iN DEMAND (delivered digitally); Hot Choice (delivered digitally); Playboy TV (delivered digitally); Fresh (delivered digitally); Shorteez (delivered digitally).
Internet Service
Operational: No.
Telephone Service
None
Miles of Plant: 31.0 (coaxial); None (fiber optic). Homes passed: 436.
Chief Executive Officer: Bill Haggarty. Senior Vice President, Financial Planning: Daniel White. Regional Vice President: Andrew Dearth. Vice President, Marketing: Tracy Bass.
Ownership: Vyve Broadband LLC (MSO).

ASHER—Formerly served by CableDirect. No longer in operation. ICA: OK0230.

ATOKA—Formerly served by CommuniComm Services. Now served by Vyve Broadband, COALGATE, OK [OK0120]. ICA: OK0378.

AVANT—Community Cable & Broadband, 1550 West Rogers Blvd, PO Box 307, Skiatook, OK 74070-0307. Phones: 888-394-4772; 918-396-3019. Fax: 918-396-2081. E-mail: info@communitycablevision.com. Web Site: http://www.communitycablebroadband.com. ICA: OK0239.
TV Market Ranking: 54 (AVANT). Franchise award date: January 25, 1988. Franchise expiration date: N.A. Began: August 15, 1988.
Channel capacity: N.A. Channels available but not in use: N.A.
Basic Service
Subscribers: 57.
Programming (received off-air): KDOR-TV (TBN) Bartlesville; KJRH-TV (NBC) Tulsa; KOED-TV (PBS) Tulsa; KOKI-TV (FOX, MeTV) Tulsa; KOTV-DT (CBS, IND) Tulsa; KQCW-DT (CW, This TV) Muskogee; KRSU-TV (ETV) Claremore; KTUL (ABC, Antenna TV, Retro TV) Tulsa; KWHB (COZI TV, IND) Tulsa.
Programming (via microwave): KTFO-CD (UniMas) Austin.
Programming (via satellite): Cartoon Network; CMT; CNN; Discovery Channel; Disney Channel; ESPN; ESPN2; Freeform; HGTV; HLN; Nickelodeon; QVC; Spike TV; Syfy; TBS; TNT; Turner Classic Movies; USA Network; WGN America.
Fee: $29.95 installation; $32.95 monthly.
Pay Service 1
Pay Units: 7.
Programming (via satellite): HBO.
Fee: $11.50 monthly.
Pay Service 2
Pay Units: 6.
Programming (via satellite): Cinemax.
Fee: $11.50 monthly.
Video-On-Demand: No
Internet Service
Operational: Yes.
Fee: $44.95 installation.
Telephone Service
Digital: Operational
Fee: $39.95 monthly
Miles of Plant: 3.0 (coaxial); None (fiber optic). Homes passed: 178.
President & General Manager: Dennis Soule. Chief Technical Officer: Chris Tuttle.
Ownership: Community Cable & Broadband Inc. (MSO).

BARNSDALL—Community Cable & Broadband. Now served by SKIATOOK, OK [OK0065]. ICA: OK0118.

BARTLESVILLE—Cable One, 4127 Nowata Rd, Bartlesville, OK 74006-5120. Phone: 918-335-0123. Fax: 918-333-6757. Web Site: http://www.cableone.net. Also serves Dewey, Nowata & Nowata County. ICA: OK0010.
TV Market Ranking: Below 100 (BARTLESVILLE, Dewey, Nowata, Nowata County). Franchise award date: N.A. Franchise expiration date: N.A. Began: September 1, 1972.
Channel capacity: N.A. Channels available but not in use: N.A.
Basic Service
Subscribers: 7,417.
Programming (received off-air): KDOR-TV (TBN) Bartlesville; KJRH-TV (NBC) Tulsa; KMYT-TV (getTV, MNT, The Country Network) Tulsa; KOED-TV (PBS) Tulsa; KOKI-TV (FOX, MeTV) Tulsa; KOTV-DT (CBS, IND) Tulsa; KQCW-DT (CW, This TV) Muskogee; KRSU-TV (ETV) Claremore; KTPX-TV (ION) Okmulgee; KTUL (ABC, Antenna TV, Retro TV) Tulsa; KWHB (COZI TV, IND) Tulsa; 14 FMs.
Programming (via satellite): A&E; AMC; Animal Planet; BET; Cartoon Network; CMT; CNBC; CNN; Comedy Central; C-SPAN; C-SPAN 2; Discovery Channel; Disney Channel; ESPN; ESPN2; Food Network; Fox News Channel; FOX Sports Southwest; Freeform; FX; HGTV; History; HLN; Lifetime; MSNBC; MTV; Nickelodeon; Pop; QVC; Spike TV; Syfy; TBS; The Weather Channel; TLC; TNT; Turner Classic Movies; TV Land; USA Network; VH1; WGN America.
Fee: $90.00 installation; $35.00 monthly; $1.00 converter.
Digital Basic Service
Subscribers: N.A.
Programming (via satellite): 3ABN; Boomerang; BYUtv; Discovery Digital Networks; Disney XD; DMX Music; ESPN Classic; ESPNews; FamilyNet; FOX College Sports Central; FOX College Sports Pacific; Fox Sports 1; Fox Sports 2; FXM; FYI; Golf Channel; Hallmark Channel; History International; HITS (Headend In The Sky); INSP; National Geographic Channel; Outdoor Channel; TNT HD; Trinity Broadcasting Network (TBN); truTV.
Fee: $9.95 monthly.
Digital Pay Service 1
Pay Units: N.A.
Programming (via satellite): Cinemax (multiplexed); Flix; HBO (multiplexed); Showtime (multiplexed); Showtime HD; Starz (multiplexed); Starz Encore (multiplexed); Sundance TV; The Movie Channel (multiplexed); The Movie Channel HD.
Fee: $15.00 monthly (each).
Video-On-Demand: No
Pay-Per-View
iN DEMAND (delivered digitally); Pleasure (delivered digitally); SexSee (delivered digitally); Juicy (delivered digitally); VaVoom (delivered digitally).
Internet Service
Operational: Yes. Began: February 1, 2001.
Subscribers: 7,680.
Broadband Service: CableONE.net.
Fee: $75.00 installation; $43.00 monthly; $5.00 modem lease.
Telephone Service
Digital: Operational
Subscribers: 3,896.
Fee: $39.95 monthly
Miles of Plant: 703.0 (coaxial); 142.0 (fiber optic). Homes passed: 20,880.
Vice President: Patrick A. Dolohanty. General Manager: Dick Marnell. Chief Technician: Dennis Anderson. Marketing Director: Brett Dugan.
Ownership: Cable ONE Inc. (MSO).

BEAVER—PTCI. This cable system has converted to IPTV. Now served by GUYMON, OK [OK5005]. ICA: OK0114.

BEGGS—Formerly served by Allegiance Communications. No longer in operation. ICA: OK0154.

BENNINGTON—Formerly served by Allegiance Communications. No longer in operation. ICA: OK0352.

BESSIE—Formerly served by Cebridge Connections. No longer in operation. ICA: OK0380.

BILLINGS—Formerly served by Cebridge Connections. No longer in operation. ICA: OK0235.

BINGER—Formerly served by Cable West. No longer in operation. ICA: OK0262.

BLACKWELL—Get Real Cable, 412 West Blackwell Ave, Blackwell, OK 74631-2859. Phone: 580-363-5580. ICA: OK0036.
TV Market Ranking: Outside TV Markets (BLACKWELL). Franchise award date: October 1, 1964. Franchise expiration date: N.A. Began: October 1, 1964.
Channel capacity: N.A. Channels available but not in use: N.A.
Basic Service
Subscribers: N.A.
Programming (received off-air): KAUT-TV (Escape, MNT) Oklahoma City; KETA-TV (PBS) Oklahoma City; KFOR-TV (Antenna TV, NBC) Oklahoma City; KOCO-TV (ABC, This TV) Oklahoma City; KOKH-TV (FOX, The Country Network, WeatherNation) Oklahoma City; KSNW (NBC) Wichita; KWTV-DT (CBS) Oklahoma City.
Programming (via satellite): ION Television; LWS Local Weather Station; TBS; WGN America.
Fee: $38.00 installation; $6.88 monthly.
Expanded Basic Service 1
Subscribers: N.A.
Programming (via satellite): A&E; AMC; Animal Planet; Cartoon Network; CNN; Comedy Central; C-SPAN; Discovery Channel; Disney Channel; ESPN; ESPN2; Food Network; Fox News Channel; Fox Sports 1; FOX Sports Southwest; Freeform; FX; Golf Channel; Great American Country; GSN; HGTV; History; HLN; INSP; Lifetime; LMN; MoviePlex; MTV; Nickelodeon; Outdoor Channel; OWN: Oprah Winfrey Network; Pop; Spike TV; Syfy; The Weather Channel; TNT; Trinity Broadcasting Network (TBN); Turner Classic Movies; TV Land; Univision Studios; USA Network; VH1; WE tv.
Fee: $19.00 monthly.
Digital Basic Service
Subscribers: N.A.
Programming (via satellite): BBC America; Bloomberg Television; Bravo; Discovery Digital Networks; Disney XD; DMX Music; ESPN Classic; ESPN2; ESPNews; EVINE Live; Fuse; FXM; IFC; NBCSN; Sundance TV; The Word Network.
Pay Service 1
Pay Units: N.A.
Programming (via satellite): Cinemax; HBO; Showtime; Starz; Starz Encore; The Movie Channel.

2017 Edition D-609

Oklahoma—Cable Systems

Fee: $4.95 monthly (Starz/Encore), $7.95 monthly (Showtime), $10.95 monthly (Cinemax or HBO), $11.00 monthly (TMC).
Digital Pay Service 1
Pay Units: N.A.
Programming (via satellite): Cinemax (multiplexed); HBO (multiplexed); Showtime (multiplexed); Starz (multiplexed); Starz Encore (multiplexed); The Movie Channel (multiplexed).
Video-On-Demand: No
Pay-Per-View
ESPN Now (delivered digitally); Hot Choice (delivered digitally); iN DEMAND (delivered digitally).
Internet Service
Operational: Yes.
Telephone Service
Digital: Operational
Miles of Plant: 51.0 (coaxial); 6.0 (fiber optic). Homes passed: 3,817.
General Manager: Byron Mahaffey. Marketing Director: Heather Eastwood. Chief Technician: Richard Kindred.
Ownership: Get Real Cable.

BLAIR—Formerly served by LakeView Cable. No longer in operation. ICA: OK0181.

BLANCHARD—Pioneer Telephone Coop. This cable system has converted to IPTV. Now served by KINGFISHER, OK [OK5074]. ICA: OK0391.

BOISE CITY—PTCI. This cable system has converted to IPTV. Now served by GUYMON, OK [OK5005]. ICA: OK0119.

BOSHOKE—Formerly served by Cebridge Connections. No longer in operation. ICA: OK0263.

BOSWELL—Formerly served by Allegiance Communications. No longer in operation. ICA: OK0199.

BOYNTON—Formerly served by Allegiance Communications. No longer in operation. ICA: OK0245.

BRAGGS—Vyve Broadband, 4 International Dr, Ste 330, Rye Brook, NY 10573. Phones: 800-937-1397; 405-395-1131; 405-275-6923. Web Site: http://vyvebroadband.com. ICA: OK0264.
TV Market Ranking: Below 100 (BRAGGS). Franchise award date: N.A. Franchise expiration date: N.A. Began: May 15, 1990.
Channel capacity: 36 (not 2-way capable). Channels available but not in use: N.A.
Basic Service
Subscribers: 8.
Programming (received off-air): KGEB (IND) Tulsa; KHBS (ABC, CW) Fort Smith; KJRH-TV (NBC) Tulsa; KOED-TV (PBS) Tulsa; KOET (PBS) Eufaula; KOKI-TV (FOX, MeTV) Tulsa; KOTV-DT (CBS, IND) Tulsa; KTUL (ABC, Antenna TV, Retro TV) Tulsa.
Programming (via satellite): AMC; CMT; CNN; Discovery Channel; Disney Channel; ESPN; Freeform; HLN; MTV; Nickelodeon; Spike TV; TBS; The Weather Channel; TNT; USA Network; WGN America.
Fee: $64.95 installation; $62.59 monthly.
Pay Service 1
Pay Units: N.A.
Programming (via satellite): HBO.
Fee: $10.00 monthly.

Pay-Per-View
iN DEMAND (delivered digitally); Hot Choice (delivered digitally); Fresh (delivered digitally); Shorteez (delivered digitally); ESPN Now (delivered digitally).
Internet Service
Operational: No.
Telephone Service
None
Chief Executive Officer: Bill Haggarty. Senior Vice President, Financial Planning: Daniel White. Regional Vice President: Andrew Dearth. Vice President, Marketing: Tracy Bass.
Ownership: Vyve Broadband LLC (MSO).

BRECKINRIDGE—Formerly served by Cebridge Connections. No longer in operation. ICA: OK0265.

BRISTOW—Vyve Broadband, 4 International Dr, Ste 330, Rye Brook, NY 10573. Phones: 800-937-1397; 405-395-1131; 405-275-6923. Web Site: http://vyvebroadband.com. ICA: OK0394.
TV Market Ranking: 54 (BRISTOW).
Channel capacity: N.A. Channels available but not in use: N.A.
Basic Service
Subscribers: 229. Commercial subscribers: 43.
Programming (received off-air): KDOR-TV (TBN) Bartlesville; KJRH-TV (NBC) Tulsa; KMYT-TV (getTV, MNT, The Country Network) Tulsa; KOED-TV (PBS) Tulsa; KOKI-TV (FOX, MeTV) Tulsa; KOTV-DT (CBS, IND) Tulsa; KQCW-DT (CW, This TV) Muskogee; KTUL (ABC, Antenna TV, Retro TV) Tulsa; KWHB (COZI TV, IND) Tulsa.
Programming (via satellite): CNN; C-SPAN; Pop; QVC; The Weather Channel.
Fee: $64.95 installation; $25.00 monthly.
Expanded Basic Service 1
Subscribers: N.A.
Programming (via satellite): A&E; AMC; Animal Planet; BET; Bravo; Cartoon Network; CMT; CNBC; Discovery Channel; Disney Channel; ESPN; ESPN Classic; ESPN2; Fox News Channel; FOX Sports Southwest; Freeform; FX; Hallmark Channel; HGTV; History; HLN; Lifetime; MTV; NFL Network; Nickelodeon; Spike TV; Syfy; TBS; TLC; TNT; USA Network; VH1.
Fee: $34.91 monthly.
Digital Basic Service
Subscribers: N.A.
Programming (via satellite): BBC America; Bloomberg Television; Bravo; Church Channel; Discovery Life Channel; Disney XD; DMX Music; ESPN Classic; ESPN2; ESPNews; EVINE Live; Flix; Fox Sports 1; FSN Digital Atlantic; FSN Digital Central; FSN Digital Pacific; Fuse; FXM; FYI; Golf Channel; Great American Country; GSN; HGTV; History; History International; HITS (Headend In The Sky); IFC; JUCE TV; LMN; National Geographic Channel; NBCSN; Nick Jr.; Nicktoons; Outdoor Channel; Ovation; Starz Encore (multiplexed); Sundance TV; Syfy; TeenNick; The Word Network; Trinity Broadcasting Network (TBN); Turner Classic Movies; WE tv.
Pay Service 1
Pay Units: N.A.
Programming (via satellite): Cinemax; HBO; Showtime; Starz; Starz Encore.
Digital Pay Service 1
Pay Units: N.A.
Programming (via satellite): Cinemax (multiplexed); HBO (multiplexed); Showtime (multiplexed); Starz (multiplexed); The Movie Channel (multiplexed).

Pay-Per-View
iN DEMAND (delivered digitally); Hot Choice (delivered digitally); Playboy TV (delivered digitally); Fresh (delivered digitally); Shorteez (delivered digitally).
Internet Service
Operational: Yes.
Fee: $24.95 installation; $39.95 monthly.
Telephone Service
Digital: Operational
Chief Executive Officer: Bill Haggarty. Regional Vice President: Andrew Dearth. Vice President, Marketing: Tracy Bass. Vice President, Financial Planning: Daniel White.
Ownership: Vyve Broadband LLC (MSO).

BROKEN BOW—Broken Bow TV Cable Co. Inc, PO Box 548, Broken Bow, OK 74728. Phone: 580-584-3355. Fax: 580-584-3338. Web Site: http://www.pine-net.com. Also serves Eagletown, Hochatowa, Idabel (Shultz Community), Lukfata & McCurtain County (portions). ICA: OK0070.
TV Market Ranking: Outside TV Markets (BROKEN BOW, Eagletown, Hochatowa, Idabel (Shultz Community), Lukfata, McCurtain County (portions)). Franchise award date: N.A. Franchise expiration date: N.A. Began: February 15, 1964.
Channel capacity: N.A. Channels available but not in use: N.A.
Basic Service
Subscribers: 362.
Programming (received off-air): KETA-TV (PBS) Oklahoma City; KETG (PBS) Arkadelphia; KHBS (ABC, CW) Fort Smith; KSLA (Bounce TV, CBS, Grit, This TV) Shreveport; KTAL-TV (NBC) Texarkana; KTBS-TV (ABC) Shreveport; KTEN (ABC, CW, NBC) Ada.
Programming (via microwave): KTUL (ABC, Antenna TV, Retro TV) Tulsa; WFAA (ABC) Dallas.
Programming (via satellite): CNN; ESPN; Freeform; Lifetime; MTV; Nickelodeon; TBS; The Weather Channel; TNT; USA Network; WGN America; WPIX (Antenna TV, CW, This TV) New York.
Fee: $35.00 installation; $13.92 monthly; $3.00 converter.
Pay Service 1
Pay Units: N.A.
Programming (via satellite): Cinemax; HBO; Showtime; The Movie Channel.
Fee: $20.00 installation; $11.25 monthly (Cinemax or HBO), $11.95 monthly (Showtime or TMC).
Internet Service
Operational: Yes.
Subscribers: 780.
Telephone Service
None
Miles of Plant: 350.0 (coaxial); None (fiber optic). Homes passed: 4,500.
Vice President: Angela Whisenhunt. General Manager: Dale Fitzsimmons. Chief Technician: Jerry Whisenhunt.
Ownership: Broken Bow Television Co.

BUFFALO—Pioneer Telephone Coop. This cable system has converted to IPTV. Now served by KINGFISHER, OK [OK5074]. ICA: OK0151.

BURNS FLAT—Formerly served by Full Circle Communications. No longer in operation. ICA: OK0098.

BUTLER—Formerly served by Basic Cable Services Inc. No longer in operation. ICA: OK0240.

BYARS—Formerly served by Cebridge Connections. No longer in operation. ICA: OK0268.

CALUMET—Pioneer Telephone Coop. This cable system has converted to IPTV. Now served by KINGFISHER, OK [OK5074]. ICA: OK0238.

CALVIN—Formerly served by Allegiance Communications. No longer in operation. ICA: OK0254.

CAMARGO—Formerly served by Cebridge Connections. No longer in operation. ICA: OK0371.

CAMERON—Formerly served by Allegiance Communications. No longer in operation. ICA: OK0252.

CANADIAN—Lakeland Cable TV Inc, 194 Telephone Rd, PO Box 321, Crowder, OK 74430. Phone: 918-334-3700. Fax: 918-334-3202. E-mail: cvstaff@cvok.net. Web Site: http://cvok.net. Also serves Indianola. ICA: OK0269.
TV Market Ranking: Below 100 (Indianola); Outside TV Markets (CANADIAN). Franchise award date: N.A. Franchise expiration date: N.A. Began: April 1, 1982.
Channel capacity: N.A. Channels available but not in use: N.A.
Basic Service
Subscribers: 290.
Programming (received off-air): KGEB (IND) Tulsa; KJRH-TV (NBC) Tulsa; KMYT-TV (getTV, MNT, The Country Network) Tulsa; KOET (PBS) Eufaula; KOKI-TV (FOX, MeTV) Tulsa; KOTV-DT (CBS, IND) Tulsa; KQCW-DT (CW, This TV) Muskogee; KTPX-TV (ION) Okmulgee; KTUL (ABC, Antenna TV, Retro TV) Tulsa; KWHB (COZI TV, IND) Tulsa.
Programming (via satellite): C-SPAN; C-SPAN 2; Outdoor Channel; TBS; The Weather Channel; WGN America.
Fee: $60.00 installation; $19.99 monthly.
Expanded Basic Service 1
Subscribers: N.A.
Programming (via satellite): A&E; AMC; Animal Planet; CMT; CNN; Discovery Channel; Disney Channel; ESPN; ESPN Classic; ESPN2; Food Network; Fox News Channel; FOX Sports Southwest; Freeform; HGTV; History; Lifetime; NBCSN; Nickelodeon; Spike TV; Syfy; TLC; TNT; TV Land; USA Network.
Fee: $32.00 monthly.
Pay Service 1
Pay Units: N.A.
Programming (via satellite): Starz; Starz Encore; Starz Encore Westerns.
Fee: $3.06 monthly (Encore), $9.70 monthly (Starz/Encore).
Video-On-Demand: Yes
Internet Service
Operational: Yes.
Telephone Service
Digital: Operational
Miles of Plant: 33.0 (coaxial); 2.0 (fiber optic). Homes passed: 530.
General Manager: Charles O. Smith. Chief Technician: Gary Brooks. Secretary-Treasurer: Betty R. Smith.
Ownership: Lakeland Cable TV Inc.

CANEY—Formerly served by Allegiance Communications. No longer in operation. ICA: OK0353.

CANTON—Formerly served by Blue Sky Cable LLC. No longer in operation. ICA: OK0236.

Cable Systems—Oklahoma

CANUTE—Formerly served by Full Circle Communications. No longer in operation. ICA: OK0215.

CARMEN—Pioneer Telephone Coop. This cable system has converted to IPTV. Now served by KINGFISHER, OK [OK5074]. ICA: OK0234.

CARNEGIE—Carnegie Cable, 25 South Colorado St, PO Box 96, Carnegie, OK 73015-0096. Phone: 580-654-1002. Fax: 580-654-2699. E-mail: info@carnegiecable.com. Web Site: http://www.carnegietelephone.com. ICA: OK0107.
TV Market Ranking: Outside TV Markets (CARNEGIE). Franchise award date: N.A. Franchise expiration date: N.A. Began: July 1, 1974.
Channel capacity: N.A. Channels available but not in use: N.A.
Basic Service
Subscribers: 510.
Programming (received off-air): KAUT-TV (Escape, MNT) Oklahoma City; KETA-TV (PBS) Oklahoma City; KFOR-TV (Antenna TV, NBC) Oklahoma City; KOCB (CW) Oklahoma City; KOCM (Daystar TV) Norman; KOCO-TV (ABC, This TV) Oklahoma City; KOKH-TV (FOX, The Country Network, WeatherNation) Oklahoma City; KOPX-TV (ION) Oklahoma City; KSBI (IND) Oklahoma City; KSWO-TV (ABC, TMO) Lawton; KTBO-TV (TBN) Oklahoma City; KWTV-DT (CBS) Oklahoma City; allband FM.
Programming (via satellite): A&E; Animal Planet; Boomerang; Cartoon Network; CMT; Comedy Central; C-SPAN; C-SPAN 2; Discovery Channel; Disney Channel; DIY Network; ESPN; EVINE Live; Food Network; Fox News Channel; FOX Sports Southwest; Freeform; FX; Golf Channel; Great American Country; Hallmark Channel; HGTV; INSP; Lifetime; MSNBC; National Geographic Channel; QVC; Spike TV; TBS; TLC; TNT; truTV; Univision Studios; USA Network.
Fee: $20.00 installation; $46.95 monthly.
Digital Basic Service
Subscribers: N.A.
Programming (via satellite): BBC America; Bloomberg Television; Discovery Life Channel; Disney XD; DMX Music; ESPN Classic; ESPN2; ESPNews; Fox Sports 1; Fuse; FXM; FYI; Golf Channel; GSN; History; History International; IFC; LMN; National Geographic Channel; NBCSN; Outdoor Channel; Trinity Broadcasting Network (TBN); Turner Classic Movies; WE tv.
Fee: $15.95 monthly.
Pay Service 1
Pay Units: 150.
Programming (via satellite): Cinemax; HBO.
Fee: $9.00 monthly.
Digital Pay Service 1
Pay Units: 190.
Programming (via satellite): Cinemax (multiplexed); Flix; HBO; Showtime (multiplexed); Starz (multiplexed); Starz Encore (multiplexed); The Movie Channel (multiplexed).
Fee: $4.95 monthly (Encore), $5.95 monthly (Starz), $9.00 monthly (Cinemax), $11.00 monthly (HBO) $11.99 monthly (Showtime/TMC/Flix).
Internet Service
Operational: Yes, DSL & dial-up.
Telephone Service
Analog: Operational
Miles of Plant: 8.0 (coaxial); 6.0 (fiber optic). Homes passed: 748.
President: Lyn Johnson. Vice President & Chief Operating Officer: Gary Woodruff. Office Manager: Judy Patterson. Operations Manager: James Powers. Outside Plant Manager: Travis Ridgeway.
Ownership: Carnegie Cable.

CARNEY—Formerly served by Allegiance Communications. No longer in operation. ICA: OK0270.

CARTER—Formerly served by CableDirect. No longer in operation. ICA: OK0242.

CASHION—Formerly served by Cebridge Connections. No longer in operation. ICA: OK0233.

CATOOSA—Formerly served by Summit Digital. No longer in operation. ICA: OK0271.

CEMENT—Southern Plains Cable, PO Box 165, Medicine Park, OK 73557. Phones: 580-365-4235; 800-218-1856; 580-529-5000. Fax: 580-529-5556. E-mail: office@wichitaonline.net. Web Site: http://www.spcisp.net. Also serves Cyril, Elgin & Fletcher. ICA: OK0195.
TV Market Ranking: Below 100 (CEMENT, Cyril, Elgin, Fletcher). Franchise award date: N.A. Franchise expiration date: N.A. Began: December 1, 1981.
Channel capacity: N.A. Channels available but not in use: N.A.
Basic Service
Subscribers: N.A.
Programming (received off-air): KAUT-TV (Escape, MNT) Oklahoma City; KETA-TV (PBS) Oklahoma City; KFOR-TV (Antenna TV, NBC) Oklahoma City; KJTL (Bounce TV, FOX) Wichita Falls; KOCB (CW) Oklahoma City; KOCO-TV (ABC, This TV) Oklahoma City; KOKH-TV (FOX, The Country Network, WeatherNation) Oklahoma City; KSWO-TV (ABC, TMO) Lawton; KWTV-DT (CBS) Oklahoma City.
Programming (via satellite): A&E; AMC; Cartoon Network; CMT; CNN; Comedy Central; Discovery Channel; Disney Channel; E! HD; ESPN; ESPN2; EVINE Live; EWTN Global Catholic Network; Fox News Channel; Freeform; History; HLN; INSP; ION Television; Lifetime; Local Cable Weather; Nickelodeon; Spike TV; Syfy; TBS; The Weather Channel; TLC; TNT; Trinity Broadcasting Network (TBN); TV Land; USA Network; WGN America.
Fee: $45.00 installation.
Pay Service 1
Pay Units: N.A.
Programming (via satellite): The Movie Channel.
Fee: $10.00 monthly.
Video-On-Demand: No
Internet Service
Operational: Yes.
Telephone Service
Analog: Not Operational
Digital: Planned
Miles of Plant: 6.0 (coaxial); None (fiber optic). Homes passed: 384.
President: Dustin Hilliary.
Ownership: Southern Plains Cable (MSO).

CHANDLER—Vyve Broadband, 4 International Dr, Ste 330, Rye Brook, NY 10573. Phones: 800-937-1397; 405-395-1131; 405-275-6923. Web Site: http://vyvebroadband.com. ICA: OK0112.
TV Market Ranking: Outside TV Markets (CHANDLER). Franchise award date: N.A. Franchise expiration date: N.A. Began: May 1, 1981.
Channel capacity: N.A. Channels available but not in use: N.A.
Basic Service
Subscribers: 43. Commercial subscribers: 12.
Programming (received off-air): KAUT-TV (Escape, MNT) Oklahoma City; KETA-TV (PBS) Oklahoma City; KFOR-TV (Antenna TV, NBC) Oklahoma City; KOCB (CW) Oklahoma City; KOCO-TV (ABC, This TV) Oklahoma City; KOKH-TV (FOX, The Country Network, WeatherNation) Oklahoma City; KOPX-TV (ION) Oklahoma City; KTBO-TV (TBN) Oklahoma City; KWTV-DT (CBS) Oklahoma City.
Programming (via satellite): A&E; AMC; Animal Planet; Cartoon Network; CNBC; CNN; Discovery Channel; Disney Channel; ESPN; Fox News Channel; FOX Sports Southwest; Freeform; FX; HGTV; HLN; Lifetime; Nickelodeon; Spike TV; TBS; The Weather Channel; TLC; TNT; USA Network; WGN America.
Fee: $64.95 installation; $25.00 monthly; $3.30 converter.
Digital Basic Service
Subscribers: N.A.
Programming (via satellite): BBC America; Bloomberg Television; Bravo; Discovery Digital Networks; Disney XD; DMX Music; ESPN Classic; ESPN2; ESPNews; EVINE Live; Fox Sports 1; Fuse; FXM; Golf Channel; Great American Country; GSN; IFC; LMN; MBC America; NBCSN; Outdoor Channel; Sundance TV; Syfy; The Word Network; Turner Classic Movies.
Pay Service 1
Pay Units: N.A.
Programming (via satellite): HBO; Showtime; Starz; Starz Encore.
Fee: $10.00 installation; $14.19 monthly.
Digital Pay Service 1
Pay Units: N.A.
Programming (via satellite): Cinemax (multiplexed); HBO (multiplexed); Showtime (multiplexed); Starz (multiplexed); Starz Encore (multiplexed); The Movie Channel (multiplexed).
Video-On-Demand: No
Pay-Per-View
iN DEMAND (delivered digitally); Hot Choice (delivered digitally); Fresh (delivered digitally); Shorteez (delivered digitally); ESPN Now (delivered digitally).
Internet Service
Operational: Yes.
Fee: $24.95 installation; $39.95 monthly.
Telephone Service
Digital: Operational
Miles of Plant: 31.0 (coaxial); None (fiber optic). Homes passed: 1,592.
Chief Executive Officer: Bill Haggarty. Regional Vice President: Andrew Dearth. Vice President, Marketing: Tracy Bass. Senior Vice President, Financial Planning: Daniel White.
Ownership: Vyve Broadband LLC (MSO).

CHATTANOOGA—Formerly served by Southern Plains Cable. No longer in operation. ICA: OK0272.

CHELSEA—Formerly served by Charter Communications. Now served by Allegiance Communications, KETCHUM, OK [OK0179]. ICA: OK0127.

CHEROKEE—Formerly served by Alliance Communications Network. No longer in operation. ICA: OK0110.

CHEYENNE—James Mogg TV, PO Box 328, Cheyenne, OK 73628-0328. Phone: 580-497-2182. ICA: OK0147.
TV Market Ranking: Outside TV Markets (CHEYENNE).
Channel capacity: N.A. Channels available but not in use: N.A.
Basic Service
Subscribers: 98.
Programming (received off-air): KJTL (Bounce TV, FOX) Wichita Falls; KOCB (CW) Oklahoma City; KOCO-TV (ABC, This TV) Oklahoma City; KOKH-TV (FOX, The Country Network, WeatherNation) Oklahoma City; KOMI-CD Woodward; KWET (PBS) Cheyenne; 1 FM.
Programming (via microwave): KFOR-TV (Antenna TV, NBC) Oklahoma City; KWTV-DT (CBS) Oklahoma City.
Programming (via satellite): CNN; Discovery Channel; ESPN; Freeform; Spike TV; TBS; TNT; Trinity Broadcasting Network (TBN); USA Network; WGN America.
Fee: $26.00 monthly.
Internet Service
Operational: No.
Telephone Service
None
Miles of Plant: 6.0 (coaxial); None (fiber optic). Homes passed: 600.
Manager: James Mogg.
Ownership: James Mogg TV.

CHICKASHA—Suddenlink Communications, 916 South 4th St, Chickasha, OK 73018. Phones: 800-999-6845; 314-315-9400. Web Site: http://www.suddenlink.com. Also serves Grady County (portions). ICA: OK0023.
TV Market Ranking: 39 (Grady County (portions)); Below 100 (CHICKASHA, Grady County (portions)); Outside TV Markets (Grady County (portions)). Franchise award date: N.A. Franchise expiration date: N.A. Began: March 1, 1978.
Channel capacity: 81 (operating 2-way). Channels available but not in use: N.A.
Basic Service
Subscribers: 2,175. Commercial subscribers: 340.
Programming (received off-air): KAUT-TV (Escape, MNT) Oklahoma City; KETA-TV (PBS) Oklahoma City; KFOR-TV (Antenna TV, NBC) Oklahoma City; KOCB (CW) Oklahoma City; KOCM (Daystar TV) Norman; KOKH-TV (FOX, The Country Network, WeatherNation) Oklahoma City; KOPX-TV (ION) Oklahoma City; KSBI (IND) Oklahoma City; KTBO-TV (TBN) Oklahoma City; KWTV-DT (CBS) Oklahoma City; 18 FMs.
Programming (via satellite): C-SPAN; C-SPAN 2; Pop; QVC; Turner Classic Movies; WGN America.
Fee: $54.95 installation; $33.24 monthly.
Expanded Basic Service 1
Subscribers: N.A.
Programming (via satellite): A&E; AMC; Animal Planet; BET; Cartoon Network; CMT; CNBC; CNN; Comedy Central; Discovery Channel; Disney Channel; E! HD; ESPN; ESPN2; Food Network; Fox News Channel; FOX Sports Southwest; Freeform; FX; Golf Channel; HGTV; HLN; History; Lifetime; MSNBC; MTV; Nickelodeon; Spike TV; TBS; The Weather Channel; TLC; TNT; Travel Channel; truTV; Turner Classic Movies; TV Land; USA Network; VH1.
Fee: $4.95 monthly.
Digital Basic Service
Subscribers: N.A.
Programming (via satellite): AXS TV; BBC America; CMT; Cooking Channel; Discov-

Oklahoma—Cable Systems

ery Digital Networks; Disney XD; DIY Network; ESPN Classic; ESPN HD; ESPNews; EWTN Global Catholic Network; FYI; GSN; Hallmark Channel; HD Theater; History International; HITS (Headend In The Sky); LMN; MC; National Geographic Channel; Nick Jr.; Nicktoons; Outdoor Channel; Starz Encore (multiplexed); Sundance TV; TeenNick; Universal HD.

Digital Pay Service 1
Pay Units: N.A.
Programming (via satellite): Cinemax (multiplexed); HBO (multiplexed); HBO HD; Showtime (multiplexed); Showtime HD; Starz (multiplexed); The Movie Channel.

Video-On-Demand: No

Pay-Per-View
iN DEMAND (delivered digitally), Addressable: No; Playboy TV (delivered digitally).

Internet Service
Operational: Yes.
Broadband Service: Suddenlink High Speed Internet.
Fee: $45.95 installation; $24.95 monthly.

Telephone Service
Digital: Operational
Miles of Plant: 89.0 (coaxial); None (fiber optic). Homes passed: 7,608.
Senior Vice President, Corporate Finance: Michael Pflantz. Vice President, Accounting: Sabrina Warr. General Manager: R. C. Lewis. Marketing Director: Heather Eastwood.
Ownership: Cequel Communications Holdings I LLC (MSO).

CHICKEN CREEK—Formerly served by Eagle Media. No longer in operation. ICA: OK0368.

CHOUTEAU—Formerly served by BCI Broadband. Now served by Allegiance Communications, SALINA, OK [OK0071]. ICA: OK0358.

CLAREMORE—Formerly served by Zoom Media. No longer in operation. ICA: OK0451.

CLAYTON—Formerly served by Allegiance Communications. No longer in operation. ICA: OK0273.

CLAYTON—Oklahoma Western Telephone Co, 102 E Choctaw St, Clayton, OK 74536. Phone: 918-569-4111. E-mail: ljones. OWTC@yahoo.com. Web Site: http://www.oklahomawesterntelephone.com. ICA: OK0803.
TV Market Ranking: Outside TV Markets (CLAYTON).
Channel capacity: N.A. Channels available but not in use: N.A.

Basic Service
Subscribers: 74.
Fee: $20.00 monthly.
President: Kyle Wallace. Marketing Director: Linda Jones.
Ownership: Oklahoma Western Telephone Co.

CLEO SPRINGS—Formerly served by Blue Sky Cable LLC. No longer in operation. ICA: OK0227.

COALGATE—Vyve Broadband, 2804B FM 51 South, Decatur, TX 76234. Phone: 855-367-8983. Web Site: http://vyvebroadband.com. Also serves Atoka, Cottonwood, Stonewall, Tupelo & Tushka. ICA: OK0120.
TV Market Ranking: Below 100 (COALGATE, Cottonwood, Stonewall, Tupelo); Outside TV Markets (Atoka, Tushka). Franchise award date: N.A. Franchise expiration date: N.A. Began: February 1, 1974.
Channel capacity: N.A. Channels available but not in use: N.A.

Basic Service
Subscribers: 328.
Programming (received off-air): KETA-TV (PBS) Oklahoma City; KOCO-TV (ABC, This TV) Oklahoma City; KTEN (ABC, CW, NBC) Ada; KWTV-DT (CBS) Oklahoma City; KXII (CBS, FOX, MNT) Sherman; allband FM.
Programming (via satellite): C-SPAN; C-SPAN 2; CW PLUS; MyNetworkTV; Trinity Broadcasting Network (TBN); WXYZ-TV (ABC, Bounce TV) Detroit.
Fee: $59.95 installation; $25.00 monthly.

Expanded Basic Service
Subscribers: N.A.
Programming (via satellite): A&E; AMC; Animal Planet; BET; Bravo; Cartoon Network; CMT; CNBC; CNN; Comedy Central; Discovery Channel; Disney Channel; E! HD; ESPN; ESPN2; EVINE Live; Food Network; Fox News Channel; FOX Sports Southwest; Freeform; FX; Hallmark Channel; HGTV; History; HLN; Lifetime; Local Cable Weather; MSNBC; MTV; Nick Jr.; Nickelodeon; Pop; QVC; Spike TV; Syfy; TBS; The Weather Channel; TLC; TNT; Travel Channel; truTV; Turner Classic Movies; TV Land; USA Network; VH1; WE tv.
Fee: $49.95 installation; $20.25 monthly.

Digital Basic Service
Subscribers: N.A.
Programming (via satellite): BBC America; Bloomberg Television; Bravo; Church Channel; Cloo; CMT; Destination America; Discovery Kids Channel; Discovery Life Channel; Disney XD; DMX Music; ESPN Classic; ESPN2; ESPNews; EVINE Live; Fox Sports 1; Fuse; FXM; FYI; Golf Channel; Great American Country; GSN; HGTV; History; History International; IFC; Investigation Discovery; JUCE TV; LMN; LOGO; MTV Classic; MTV Hits; MTV Jams; MTV2; National Geographic Channel; NBCSN; Nick Jr.; Nicktoons; Outdoor Channel; Ovation; OWN: Oprah Winfrey Network; RFD-TV; Science Channel; TeenNick; The Word Network; Trinity Broadcasting Network (TBN); Turner Classic Movies; VH1 Soul; WE tv.

Pay Service 1
Pay Units: N.A.
Programming (via satellite): Cinemax; HBO (multiplexed); Starz; Starz Encore.
Fee: $20.00 installation; $9.95 monthly (Starz/Encore), $10.95 monthly (Cinemax), $12.95 monthly (HBO).

Digital Pay Service 1
Pay Units: N.A.
Programming (via satellite): Cinemax (multiplexed); Flix; HBO (multiplexed); Showtime (multiplexed); Starz (multiplexed); Starz Encore (multiplexed); Sundance TV; The Movie Channel (multiplexed).

Video-On-Demand: No

Pay-Per-View
iN DEMAND (delivered digitally); Hot Choice (delivered digitally); Playboy TV (delivered digitally); Fresh (delivered digitally); Spice Xcess (delivered digitally); Club Jenna (delivered digitally).

Internet Service
Operational: Yes.
Broadband Service: Net Commander.
Fee: $39.95 installation; $51.95 monthly.

Telephone Service
None
Miles of Plant: 139.0 (coaxial); None (fiber optic).
President & Chief Executive Officer: Jeffrey DeMond. Vice President, Residential Services: Vin Zachariah. Vice President, Marketing: Diane Quennoz. Vice President, Financial Planning: Daniel White.
Ownership: Vyve Broadband LLC (MSO).

COLBERT—Formerly served by Mediastream. No longer in operation. ICA: OK0068.

COLCORD—Formerly served by Allegiance Communications. No longer in operation. ICA: OK0204.

COLLINSVILLE—Community Cable & Broadband. Now served by SKIATOOK, OK [OK0065]. ICA: OK0069.

COMANCHE—Pioneer. This cable system has converted to IPTV. Now served by TEMPLE, OK [OK5051]. ICA: OK0177.

COMANCHE (eastern portions)—Formerly served by Vyve Broadband. No longer in operation. ICA: OK0396.

COOKSON—Formerly served by Eagle Media. No longer in operation. ICA: OK0367.

COPAN—Community Cable & Broadband, 1550 West Rogers Blvd, PO Box 307, Skiatook, OK 74070-0307. Phones: 888-394-4772; 918-396-3019. Fax: 918-396-2081. E-mail: info@communitycablevision.com. Web Site: http://www.communitycablebroadband.com. ICA: OK0168.
TV Market Ranking: Below 100 (COPAN).
Channel capacity: N.A. Channels available but not in use: N.A.

Basic Service
Subscribers: N.A.
Programming (received off-air): KDOR-TV (TBN) Bartlesville; KGEB (IND) Tulsa; KJRH-TV (NBC) Tulsa; KOED-TV (PBS) Tulsa; KOKI-TV (FOX, MeTV) Tulsa; KOTV-DT (CBS, IND) Tulsa; KQCW-DT (CW, This TV) Muskogee; KRSU-TV (ETV) Claremore; KTPX-TV (ION) Okmulgee; KTUL (ABC, Antenna TV, Retro TV) Tulsa; KWHB (COZI TV, IND) Tulsa.
Programming (via satellite): A&E; Cartoon Network; CMT; CNN; C-SPAN; Discovery Channel; Disney Channel; ESPN; ESPN2; Fox News Channel; FOX Sports Southwest; Freeform; HLN; Lifetime; MTV; Nickelodeon; QVC; Spike TV; Syfy; TBS; The Weather Channel; TLC; TNT; Turner Classic Movies; USA Network; WGN America.
Fee: $29.95 installation.

Video-On-Demand: No

Internet Service
Operational: Yes.
Fee: $44.95 monthly.

Telephone Service
None
Miles of Plant: 12.0 (coaxial); None (fiber optic). Homes passed: 446.
President & General Manager: Dennis Soule.
Ownership: Community Cable & Broadband Inc. (MSO).

CORN—Formerly served by Cable West. No longer in operation. ICA: OK0274.

COVINGTON—Pioneer Telephone Coop. This cable system has converted to IPTV. Now served by KINGFISHER, OK [OK5074]. ICA: OK0203.

CRESCENT—Formerly served by Suddenlink Communications. No longer in operation. ICA: OK0124.

CROMWELL—Vyve Broadband, 4 International Dr, Ste 330, Rye Brook, NY 10573. Phones: 800-937-1397; 405-395-1131; 405-275-6923. Web Site: http://vyvebroadband.com. ICA: OK0258.
TV Market Ranking: Below 100 (CROMWELL). Franchise award date: January 1, 1989. Franchise expiration date: N.A. Began: September 1, 1989.
Channel capacity: N.A. Channels available but not in use: N.A.

Basic Service
Subscribers: 4.
Programming (received off-air): KAUT-TV (Escape, MNT) Oklahoma City; KETA-TV (PBS) Oklahoma City; KFOR-TV (Antenna TV, NBC) Oklahoma City; KOCB (CW) Oklahoma City; KOCO-TV (ABC, This TV) Oklahoma City; KOKH-TV (FOX, The Country Network, WeatherNation) Oklahoma City; KOPX-TV (ION) Oklahoma City; KTBO-TV (TBN) Oklahoma City; KWTV-DT (CBS) Oklahoma City.
Programming (via satellite): A&E; AMC; Animal Planet; CMT; CNBC; CNN; Discovery Channel; Disney Channel; ESPN; ESPN2; Freeform; Lifetime; MTV; Nickelodeon; Spike TV; Syfy; TBS; TNT; Travel Channel; USA Network; WGN America.
Fee: $64.95 installation; $42.75 monthly.

Pay Service 1
Pay Units: N.A.
Programming (via satellite): HBO.
Fee: $10.00 monthly.

Video-On-Demand: No

Pay-Per-View
Hot Choice (delivered digitally); Playboy TV (delivered digitally); Fresh (delivered digitally); Shorteez (delivered digitally); iN DEMAND (delivered digitally).

Internet Service
Operational: No.

Telephone Service
None
Miles of Plant: 3.0 (coaxial); None (fiber optic). Homes passed: 110.
Chief Executive Officer: Bill Haggarty. Senior Vice President, Financial Planning: Daniel White. Regional Vice President: Andrew Dearth. Vice President, Marketing: Tracy Bass.
Ownership: Vyve Broadband LLC (MSO).

CROWDER—Lakeland Cable TV Inc, 194 Telephone Rd, PO Box 321, Crowder, OK 74430. Phone: 918-334-3700. Fax: 918-334-3202. E-mail: cvstaff@cvok.net. Web Site: http://cvok.net. ICA: OK0397.
TV Market Ranking: Outside TV Markets (CROWDER).
Channel capacity: N.A. Channels available but not in use: N.A.

Basic Service
Subscribers: 102.
Fee: $19.99 monthly.
Miles of Plant: 33.0 (coaxial); 2.0 (fiber optic). Homes passed: 530.
Secretary-Treasurer: Betty R. Smith.
Ownership: Lakeland Cable TV Inc. (MSO).

CUSHING—Suddenlink Communications, 520 Maryville Centre Dr, Ste 300, St. Louis, MO 63141. Phones: 800-999-6845; 314-315-9400; 918-225-0130. Web Site: http://www.suddenlink.com. ICA: OK0037.
TV Market Ranking: Outside TV Markets (CUSHING). Franchise award date: August 28, 1978. Franchise expiration date: N.A. Began: March 5, 1980.
Channel capacity: N.A. Channels available but not in use: N.A.

Cable Systems—Oklahoma

Basic Service
Subscribers: 1,348. Commercial subscribers: 80.
Programming (received off-air): KAUT-TV (Escape, MNT) Oklahoma City; KETA-TV (PBS) Oklahoma City; KFOR-TV (Antenna TV, NBC) Oklahoma City; KOCB (CW) Oklahoma City; KOCO-TV (ABC, This TV) Oklahoma City; KOKH-TV (FOX, The Country Network, WeatherNation) Oklahoma City; KOPX-TV (ION) Oklahoma City; KSBI (IND) Oklahoma City; KTBO-TV (TBN) Oklahoma City; KTUL (ABC, Antenna TV, Retro TV) Tulsa; KWTV-DT (CBS) Oklahoma City.
Programming (via satellite): C-SPAN; Jewelry Television; Pop; QVC; The Weather Channel; WGN America.
Fee: $54.95 installation; $34.24 monthly.

Expanded Basic Service 1
Subscribers: N.A.
Programming (via satellite): A&E; AMC; Animal Planet; BET; Bravo; Cartoon Network; CMT; CNBC; CNN; Comedy Central; C-SPAN 2; Discovery Channel; Disney Channel; E! HD; ESPN; ESPN Classic; ESPN2; EWTN Global Catholic Network; Food Network; Fox News Channel; FOX Sports Southwest; Freeform; FX; Hallmark Channel; HGTV; History; HLN; Lifetime; LMN; MSNBC; MTV; MTV2; Nickelodeon; OWN: Oprah Winfrey Network; Oxygen; Spike TV; Syfy; TBS; TLC; TNT; Travel Channel; truTV; TV Land; Univision Studios; USA Network; VH1.
Fee: $19.52 monthly.

Digital Basic Service
Subscribers: N.A.
Programming (via satellite): A&E HD; AXS TV; BBC America; Bloomberg Television; CBS Sports Network; CMT; Destination America; Discovery Kids Channel; Disney XD; DMX Music; ESPN HD; ESPNews; ESPNU; Food Network HD; Fox Sports 1; Fuse; FXM; FYI; Golf Channel; GSN; HD Theater; HGTV HD; History HD; History International; IFC; Investigation Discovery; LMN; MTV Classic; MTV Hits; National Geographic Channel; National Geographic Channel HD; NBCSN; Nick Jr.; Nicktoons; Science Channel; Starz Encore (multiplexed); TeenNick; TNT HD; Turner Classic Movies; VH1 Soul.
Fee: $20.00 installation; $17.00 monthly.

Pay Service 1
Pay Units: N.A.
Programming (via satellite): Cinemax; HBO; Showtime; Starz; Starz Encore.
Fee: $10.00 installation; $1.75 monthly (Showtime), $6.75 monthly (Encore), $12.95 monthly (Cinemax, HBO or Starz).

Digital Pay Service 1
Pay Units: N.A.
Programming (via satellite): Cinemax (multiplexed); HBO (multiplexed); HBO HD; Showtime (multiplexed); Showtime HD; Starz (multiplexed); The Movie Channel (multiplexed).

Video-On-Demand: No

Pay-Per-View
iN DEMAND (delivered digitally); Fresh (delivered digitally); Shorteez (delivered digitally); Playboy TV (delivered digitally); ESPN Now (delivered digitally).

Internet Service
Operational: Yes. Began: January 15, 2003.
Broadband Service: Suddenlink High Speed Internet.
Fee: $45.95 installation; $24.95 monthly; $10.00 modem lease; $99.95 modem purchase.

Telephone Service
Digital: Operational
Fee: $49.95 monthly
Miles of Plant: 63.0 (coaxial); 13.0 (fiber optic). Homes passed: 5,180.
Vice President, Accounting: Sabrina Warr. General Manager: Nicole Evans. Marketing Manager: Heather Eastwood. Chief Technician: Johnny Stanley.
Ownership: Cequel Communications Holdings I LLC (MSO).

CUSTER CITY—Pioneer Telephone Coop. This cable system has converted to IPTV. Now served by KINGFISHER, OK [OK5074]. ICA: OK0277.

CYRIL—Formerly served by Alliance Communications Network. No longer in operation. ICA: OK0372.

DACOMA—Pioneer Telephone Coop. This cable system has converted to IPTV. Now served by KINGFISHER, OK [OK5074]. ICA: OK0278.

DAVENPORT—Vi-Tel LLC, 223 Broadway, PO Box 789, Davenport, OK 74026-0789. Phones: 800-252-8854; 918-377-2241. Fax: 918-377-2506. E-mail: staff@cotc.net. Web Site: http://www2.cotc.net. ICA: OK0182.
TV Market Ranking: Below 100 (DAVENPORT). Franchise award date: N.A. Franchise expiration date: N.A. Began: April 1, 1983.
Channel capacity: N.A. Channels available but not in use: N.A.

Basic Service
Subscribers: 49.
Programming (received off-air): KAUT-TV (Escape, MNT) Oklahoma City; KETA-TV (PBS) Oklahoma City; KFOR-TV (Antenna TV, NBC) Oklahoma City; KJRH-TV (NBC) Tulsa; KOCB (CW) Oklahoma City; KOCO-TV (ABC, This TV) Oklahoma City; KOKH-TV (FOX, The Country Network, WeatherNation) Oklahoma City; KOPX-TV (ION) Oklahoma City; KSBI (IND) Oklahoma City; KTBO-TV (TBN) Oklahoma City; KWTV-DT (CBS) Oklahoma City.
Programming (via satellite): A&E; AMC; Animal Planet; Cartoon Network; CMT; CNN; Comedy Central; C-SPAN; Discovery Channel; Disney Channel; ESPN; ESPN2; FOX Sports Southwest; Freeform; HGTV; History; HLN; Lifetime; Nickelodeon; Spike TV; Syfy; TBS; The Weather Channel; TLC; TNT; truTV; Turner Classic Movies; TV Land; USA Network; WGN America.
Fee: $17.50 installation; $50.95 monthly.

Pay Service 1
Pay Units: 37.
Programming (via satellite): HBO.
Fee: $10.95 monthly.

Pay Service 2
Pay Units: 15.
Programming (via satellite): Showtime.
Fee: $10.95 monthly.

Internet Service
Operational: No, DSL & dial-up.

Telephone Service
Analog: Operational
Miles of Plant: 13.0 (coaxial); None (fiber optic). Homes passed: 485.
General Manager: Steve Guest.
Ownership: Vi-Tel LLC.

DAVIDSON—Formerly served by CableDirect. No longer in operation. ICA: OK0279.

DEER CREEK—Formerly served by CableDirect. No longer in operation. ICA: OK0280.

DELAWARE—Formerly served by Allegiance Communications. No longer in operation. ICA: OK0189.

DEPEW—Vyve Broadband, 4 International Dr, Ste 330, Rye Brook, NY 10573. Phones: 800-937-1397; 405-395-1131; 405-275-6923. Web Site: http://vyvebroadband.com. ICA: OK0212.
TV Market Ranking: Below 100 (DEPEW). Franchise award date: January 1, 1989. Franchise expiration date: N.A. Began: September 1, 1989.
Channel capacity: N.A. Channels available but not in use: N.A.

Basic Service
Subscribers: 5.
Programming (received off-air): KAUT-TV (Escape, MNT) Oklahoma City; KJRH-TV (NBC) Tulsa; KMYT-TV (getTV, MNT, The Country Network) Tulsa; KOED-TV (PBS) Tulsa; KOKH-TV (FOX, The Country Network, WeatherNation) Oklahoma City; KOTV-DT (CBS, IND) Tulsa; KQCW-DT (CW, This TV) Muskogee; KSBI (IND) Oklahoma City; KTPX-TV (ION) Okmulgee; KTUL (ABC, Antenna TV, Retro TV) Tulsa; KWHB (COZI TV, IND) Tulsa.
Programming (via satellite): A&E; CNBC; CNN; Discovery Channel; Disney Channel; ESPN; ESPN2; Freeform; HLN; Lifetime; MTV; Nickelodeon; Spike TV; Syfy; TBS; TNT; Travel Channel; USA Network; WGN America.
Fee: $64.95 installation; $25.00 monthly; $1.96 converter.

Pay Service 1
Pay Units: N.A.
Programming (via satellite): HBO.
Fee: $20.00 installation; $9.95 monthly.

Video-On-Demand: No

Pay-Per-View
iN DEMAND (delivered digitally); Hot Choice (delivered digitally); Playboy TV (delivered digitally); Fresh (delivered digitally); Shorteez (delivered digitally).

Internet Service
Operational: No.

Telephone Service
None
Miles of Plant: 4.0 (coaxial); None (fiber optic). Homes passed: 257.
Chief Executive Officer: Bill Haggarty. Senior Vice President, Financial Planning: Daniel White. Regional Vice President: Andrew Dearth. Vice President, Marketing: Tracy Bass.
Ownership: Vyve Broadband LLC (MSO).

DILL CITY—Formerly served by Cable West. No longer in operation. ICA: OK0188.

DISNEY—Omni III Cable TV Inc, 226 South 4th St, PO Box 308, Jay, OK 74346-0308. Phones: 888-400-5587; 918-253-4231. Fax: 918-253-3400. E-mail: brixey@brightok.net. Web Site: http://www.grand.net. Also serves Jay. ICA: OK0216.
TV Market Ranking: Outside TV Markets (DISNEY, Jay). Franchise award date: N.A. Franchise expiration date: N.A. Began: March 1, 1983.
Channel capacity: 34 (not 2-way capable). Channels available but not in use: N.A.

Basic Service
Subscribers: 518.
Programming (received off-air): KDOR-TV (TBN) Bartlesville; KJRH-TV (NBC) Tulsa; KOAM-TV (CBS) Pittsburg; KOKI-TV (FOX, MeTV) Tulsa; KOTV-DT (CBS, IND) Tulsa; KSNF (NBC) Joplin; KTUL (ABC, Antenna TV, Retro TV) Tulsa.
Programming (via satellite): A&E; AMC; Cartoon Network; CMT; CNN; C-SPAN; Discovery Channel; Disney Channel; ESPN; Freeform; History; HLN; Nickelodeon; QVC; Spike TV; TBS; The Weather Channel; TNT; Turner Classic Movies; USA Network; WGN America.
Fee: $20.00 installation; $26.50 monthly.

Pay Service 1
Pay Units: N.A.
Programming (via satellite): Cinemax; HBO; Showtime.
Fee: $10.00 installation; $13.00 monthly (each).

Video-On-Demand: No

Internet Service
Operational: No.

Telephone Service
None
Miles of Plant: 7.0 (coaxial); 15.0 (fiber optic).
General Manager: Rex Brixey.
Ownership: Omni III Cable TV Inc.

DOVER—Pioneer Telephone Coop. This cable system has converted to IPTV. Now served by KINGFISHER, OK [OK5074]. ICA: OK0250.

DRUMMOND—Pioneer Telephone Coop. This cable system has converted to IPTV. Now served by KINGFISHER, OK [OK5074]. ICA: OK0281.

DRUMRIGHT—Suddenlink Communications, 520 Maryville Centre Dr, Ste 300, St. Louis, MO 63141. Phones: 800-999-6845; 314-315-9400; 918-225-0130. Web Site: http://www.suddenlink.com. ICA: OK0393.
TV Market Ranking: Outside TV Markets (DRUMRIGHT).
Channel capacity: N.A. Channels available but not in use: N.A.

Basic Service
Subscribers: 390. Commercial subscribers: 57.
Programming (received off-air): KDOR-TV (TBN) Bartlesville; KFOR-TV (Antenna TV, NBC) Oklahoma City; KJRH-TV (NBC) Tulsa; KMYT-TV (getTV, MNT, The Country Network) Tulsa; KOCO-TV (ABC, This TV) Oklahoma City; KOED-TV (PBS) Tulsa; KOKI-TV (FOX, MeTV) Tulsa; KOTV-DT (CBS, IND) Tulsa; KQCW-DT (CW, This TV) Muskogee; KTPX-TV (ION) Okmulgee; KTUL (ABC, Antenna TV, Retro TV) Tulsa; KWHB (COZI TV, IND) Tulsa; KWTV-DT (CBS) Oklahoma City.
Programming (via satellite): C-SPAN; Pop; QVC; The Weather Channel; WGN America.
Fee: $54.95 installation; $34.24 monthly.

Expanded Basic Service 1
Subscribers: N.A.
Programming (via satellite): A&E; AMC; Animal Planet; BET; Bravo; Cartoon Network; CMT; CNBC; CNN; Comedy Central; C-SPAN 2; Discovery Channel; Disney Channel; E! HD; ESPN; ESPN Deportes; ESPN2; EWTN Global Catholic Network; Food Network; Fox News Channel; FOX Sports Southwest; Freeform; FX; HGTV; History; HLN; Lifetime; MSNBC; MTV; MTV2; Nickelodeon; OWN: Oprah Winfrey Network; Oxygen; Spike TV; Syfy; TBS; TLC; TNT; Travel Channel; truTV; TV Land; Univision Studios; USA Network; VH1.

Digital Basic Service
Subscribers: N.A.
Programming (via satellite): BBC America; Bloomberg Television; Discovery Life Channel; Disney XD; DMX Music; ESPN Classic; ESPNews; Fox Sports 1; Fuse; FXM; FYI; Golf Channel; GSN; HD Theater; History International; IFC; LMN; National Geographic

Oklahoma—Cable Systems

Channel; NBCSN; Nick Jr.; Nicktoons; Outdoor Channel; Starz Encore (multiplexed); TeenNick; Turner Classic Movies.

Digital Pay Service 1
Pay Units: N.A.
Programming (via satellite): Cinemax (multiplexed); HBO (multiplexed); Showtime (multiplexed); Showtime HD; Starz (multiplexed); The Movie Channel (multiplexed).

Video-On-Demand: No

Pay-Per-View
iN DEMAND (delivered digitally); Hot Choice (delivered digitally); Fresh (delivered digitally); Shorteez (delivered digitally); Playboy TV (delivered digitally).

Internet Service
Operational: Yes.
Broadband Service: Suddenlink High Speed Internet.
Fee: $45.95 installation; $24.95 monthly.

Telephone Service
Digital: Operational
Fee: $49.95 monthly

Miles of Plant: 31.0 (coaxial); 3.0 (fiber optic). Homes passed: 1,838.
Vice President, Accounting: Sabrina Warr. General Manager: Nicole Evans. Marketing Manager: Heather Eastwood. Chief Technician: Johnny Stanley.
Ownership: Cequel Communications Holdings I LLC (MSO).

DUKE—Formerly served by CableDirect. No longer in operation. ICA: OK0224.

DUNCAN—Cable One, 1206 North Hwy 81, Ste 30, Duncan, OK 73533-1795. Phone: 580-252-0992. Fax: 580-252-9488. E-mail: lthompson@cableone.net. Web Site: http://www.cableone.net. Also serves Marlow & Stephens County (portions). ICA: OK0013.

TV Market Ranking: Below 100 (DUNCAN, Marlow, Stephens County (portions)). Franchise award date: January 1, 1970. Franchise expiration date: N.A. Began: July 1, 1971.
Channel capacity: 51 (operating 2-way). Channels available but not in use: N.A.

Basic Service
Subscribers: 4,380.
Programming (received off-air): KAUZ-TV (CBS, CW) Wichita Falls; KETA-TV (PBS) Oklahoma City; KFDX-TV (NBC) Wichita Falls; KFOR-TV (Antenna TV, NBC) Oklahoma City; KJTL (Bounce TV, FOX) Wichita Falls; KOCO-TV (ABC, This TV) Oklahoma City; KOKH-TV (FOX, The Country Network, WeatherNation) Oklahoma City; KSWO-TV (ABC, TMO) Lawton; KWTV-DT (CBS) Oklahoma City; 6 FMs.
Programming (via satellite): C-SPAN; C-SPAN 2; CW PLUS; Pop; QVC; Telemundo.
Fee: $35.00 monthly; $1.60 converter.

Expanded Basic Service 1
Subscribers: N.A.
Programming (via satellite): A&E; AMC; Animal Planet; BET; Cartoon Network; CMT; CNBC; CNN; Discovery Channel; Disney Channel; ESPN; ESPN2; Food Network; Fox News Channel; FOX Sports Southwest; Freeform; FX; HGTV; History; HLN; INSP; Lifetime; MSNBC; MTV; Nickelodeon; Spike TV; Syfy; TBS; The Weather Channel; TLC; TNT; Travel Channel; Trinity Broadcasting Network (TBN); Turner Classic Movies; TV Land; USA Network; VH1.
Fee: $46.00 monthly.

Digital Basic Service
Subscribers: N.A.
Programming (via satellite): 3ABN; Boomerang; BYUtv; Discovery Digital Networks; Disney XD; DMX Music; ESPN Classic; ESPNews; FamilyNet; FOX College Sports Central; FOX College Sports Pacific; Fox HD; Fox Sports 1; Fox Sports 2; FXM; FYI; Golf Channel; Great American Country; Hallmark Channel; History International; HITS (Headend In The Sky); INSP; National Geographic Channel; Outdoor Channel; TNT HD; Trinity Broadcasting Network (TBN); truTV; TVG Network; Universal HD.

Digital Pay Service 1
Pay Units: 3,412.
Programming (via satellite): Cinemax (multiplexed); Flix; HBO (multiplexed); Showtime (multiplexed); Showtime HD; Starz (multiplexed); Starz Encore (multiplexed); Sundance TV; The Movie Channel (multiplexed); The Movie Channel HD.
Fee: $15.00 monthly (each).

Video-On-Demand: No

Pay-Per-View
iN DEMAND (delivered digitally); Pleasure (delivered digitally); SexSee (delivered digitally); Juicy (delivered digitally); VaVoom (delivered digitally).

Internet Service
Operational: Yes. Began: March 1, 2001.
Subscribers: 5,040.
Broadband Service: CableONE.net.
Fee: $75.00 installation; $43.00 monthly.

Telephone Service
Digital: Operational
Subscribers: 2,061.
Fee: $39.95 monthly

Miles of Plant: 418.0 (coaxial); 49.0 (fiber optic). Homes passed: 13,780.
Vice President: Patrick A. Dolohanty. General Manager: Deron Lindsay. Marketing Director: Steve Sutton. Chief Technician: Darrel Massie. Office Manager: Lita Thompson.
Ownership: Cable ONE Inc. (MSO).

DURANT—Vyve Broadband, 4 International Dr, Ste 330, Rye Brook, NY 10573. Phones: 800-937-1397; 580-924-2367; 800-752-4992. Web Site: http://vyvebroadband.com. Also serves Armstrong, Bokchito, Bryan County (portions), Buncombe Creek, Caddo, Calera, Cartwright, Colbert & Platter. ICA: OK0022.

TV Market Ranking: Below 100 (Armstrong, Bryan County (portions), Buncombe Creek, Caddo, Calera, Cartwright, Colbert, DURANT, Platter); Outside TV Markets (Bokchito). Franchise award date: November 10, 1980. Franchise expiration date: N.A. Began: September 1, 1958.
Channel capacity: N.A. Channels available but not in use: N.A.

Basic Service
Subscribers: 2,379.
Programming (received off-air): KETA-TV (PBS) Oklahoma City; KTEN (ABC, CW, NBC) Ada; KWTV-DT (CBS) Oklahoma City; KXII (CBS, FOX, MNT) Sherman; WFAA (ABC) Dallas; allband FM.
Programming (via satellite): CW PLUS; Fox Business Network.
Fee: $64.95 installation; $25.00 monthly.

Expanded Basic Service 1
Subscribers: N.A.
Programming (via satellite): A&E; AMC; Animal Planet; BET; Bravo; BYUtv; Cartoon Network; CMT; CNBC; CNN; Comedy Central; C-SPAN; C-SPAN 2; Discovery Channel; Disney Channel; E! HD; ESPN; ESPN Classic; ESPN2; ESPNews; EVINE Live; EWTN Global Catholic Network; Food Network; Fox News Channel; FOX Sports Southwest; Freeform; FX; Hallmark Channel; HGTV; History; HLN; ION Television; Lifetime; MSNBC; MTV; MyNetworkTV; Nickelodeon; Outdoor Channel; Pop; QVC; Spike TV; Syfy; TBS; The Weather Channel; TLC; TNT; Travel Channel; Trinity Broadcasting Network (TBN); truTV; TV Land; USA Network; VH1; WE tv.

Digital Basic Service
Subscribers: N.A.
Programming (via satellite): A&E HD; BBC America; Bloomberg Television; Bravo; Church Channel; CMT; Daystar TV Network; Destination America; Discovery Kids Channel; Discovery Life Channel; Disney XD; DMX Music; ESPN Classic; ESPN HD; ESPN2; ESPN2 HD; ESPNews; EVINE Live; Fox Sports 1; Fuse; FXM; FYI; Golf Channel; Great American Country; GSN; HD Theater; HGTV; History; History International; IFC; Investigation Discovery; JUCE TV; LMN; MTV Classic; MTV Hits; MTV Jams; MTV2; National Geographic Channel; NBCSN; Nick Jr.; Nicktoons; Outdoor Channel; Ovation; OWN; Oprah Winfrey Network; RFD-TV; Science Channel; TeenNick; The Word Network; TNT HD; Trinity Broadcasting Network (TBN); Turner Classic Movies; Universal HD; VH1 Soul; WE tv.

Pay Service 1
Pay Units: N.A.
Programming (via satellite): Cinemax (multiplexed); HBO (multiplexed); Starz (multiplexed); Starz Encore.
Fee: $9.95 monthly (Cinemax or Starz/Encore), $12.95 monthly (HBO).

Digital Pay Service 1
Pay Units: N.A.
Programming (via satellite): Cinemax (multiplexed); Flix; HBO (multiplexed); Showtime (multiplexed); Starz (multiplexed); Starz Encore (multiplexed); Starz HD; The Movie Channel (multiplexed).

Video-On-Demand: No

Pay-Per-View
iN DEMAND (delivered digitally); Hot Choice (delivered digitally); Playboy TV (delivered digitally); Fresh (delivered digitally); Spice Xcess (delivered digitally); Club Jenna (delivered digitally).

Internet Service
Operational: Yes. Began: December 1, 1997.
Broadband Service: Net Commander.
Fee: $39.95 installation; $51.95 monthly.

Telephone Service
Digital: Operational

Miles of Plant: 150.0 (coaxial); 30.0 (fiber optic).
President & Chief Executive Officer: Jeffrey DeMond. Senior Vice President, Financial Planning: Daniel White. Vice President, Marketing: Diane Quennoz. Vice President, Residential Services: Vin Zachariah.
Ownership: Vyve Broadband LLC (MSO).

DUSTIN—Formerly served by Allegiance Communications. No longer in operation. ICA: OK0237.

EAKLY—Hinton CATV Co. Now served by HINTON, OK [OK0140]. ICA: OK0282.

ELDORADO—Formerly served by Cable West. No longer in operation. ICA: OK0383.

ELK CITY—Cable One, PO Box 863, Elk City, OK 73648. Phone: 580-225-3244. Web Site: http://www.cableone.net. Also serves Beckham County (portions), Clinton, Cordell, Greer County (portions), Hobart, Kiowa County (portions), Mangum & Sayre. ICA: OK0032.

TV Market Ranking: Below 100 (Beckham County (portions), ELK CITY, Sayre, Kiowa County (portions)); Outside TV Markets (Clinton, Cordell, Greer County (portions), Mangum, Hobart, Kiowa County (portions)). Franchise award date: March 1, 1953. Franchise expiration date: N.A. Began: March 1, 1953.
Channel capacity: N.A. Channels available but not in use: N.A.

Basic Service
Subscribers: 3,574.
Programming (received off-air): KFOR-TV (Antenna TV, NBC) Oklahoma City; KOCB (CW) Oklahoma City; KOCO-TV (ABC, This TV) Oklahoma City; KOKH-TV (FOX, The Country Network, WeatherNation) Oklahoma City; KSBI (IND) Oklahoma City; KUOK (UNV) Woodward; KWET (PBS) Cheyenne; KWTV-DT (CBS) Oklahoma City.
Programming (via satellite): C-SPAN; ION Television; LWS Local Weather Station; Pop; QVC; TBS; WGN America.
Fee: $90.00 installation; $35.00 monthly; $3.25 converter.

Expanded Basic Service 1
Subscribers: N.A.
Programming (via satellite): A&E; AMC; Animal Planet; BET; Cartoon Network; CMT; CNBC; CNN; C-SPAN 2; Discovery Channel; Disney Channel; E! HD; ESPN; ESPN2; Food Network; Fox News Channel; FOX Sports Southwest; Freeform; FX; HGTV; History; HLN; Lifetime; MSNBC; MTV; Nickelodeon; Spike TV; Syfy; TBS; The Weather Channel; TLC; TNT; Trinity Broadcasting Network (TBN); Turner Classic Movies; TV Land; USA Network; VH1.
Fee: $35.00 installation; $46.00 monthly.

Digital Basic Service
Subscribers: N.A.
Programming (via satellite): 3ABN; Boomerang; BYUtv; Discovery Digital Networks; Disney XD; DMX Music; ESPN Classic; ESPNews; FamilyNet; FOX College Sports Central; FOX College Sports Pacific; Fox HD; Fox Sports 1; Fox Sports 2; FXM; FYI; Golf Channel; Great American Country; Hallmark Channel; History International; HITS (Headend In The Sky); INSP; National Geographic Channel; Outdoor Channel; TNT HD; Trinity Broadcasting Network (TBN); truTV; TVG Network; Universal HD.

Digital Pay Service 1
Pay Units: N.A.
Programming (via satellite): Cinemax (multiplexed); Flix; HBO (multiplexed); Showtime (multiplexed); Showtime HD; Starz (multiplexed); Starz Encore (multiplexed); Sundance TV; The Movie Channel (multiplexed); The Movie Channel HD.
Fee: $15.00 monthly (each package).

Video-On-Demand: No

Pay-Per-View
iN DEMAND (delivered digitally); Pleasure (delivered digitally); SexSee (delivered digitally); Juicy (delivered digitally); VaVoom (delivered digitally).

Internet Service
Operational: Yes. Began: October 1, 2001.
Broadband Service: CableONE.net.
Fee: $75.00 installation; $43.00 monthly.

Telephone Service
Digital: Operational
Fee: $39.95 monthly

Miles of Plant: 240.0 (coaxial); 32.0 (fiber optic). Homes passed: 15,080.
Vice President: Patrick A. Dolohanty. General Manager: Brook McDonald. Chief Technician: Tom Leistner. Office Manager: Melissa Briscoe.
Ownership: Cable ONE Inc. (MSO).

Cable Systems—Oklahoma

ELK CREEK—Formerly served by Eagle Media. No longer in operation. ICA: OK0364.

ENID—Suddenlink Communications, 131 East Main St, Enid, OK 73701. Phone: 314-315-9400. Web Site: http://www.suddenlink.com. Also serves Garfield County, North Enid & Vance AFB. ICA: OK0006.
TV Market Ranking: Outside TV Markets (ENID, Garfield County, North Enid, Vance AFB). Franchise award date: N.A. Franchise expiration date: N.A. Began: March 1, 1966.
Channel capacity: N.A. Channels available but not in use: N.A.
Basic Service
Subscribers: 9,684. Commercial subscribers: 852.
Programming (received off-air): KAUT-TV (Escape, MNT) Oklahoma City; KETA-TV (PBS) Oklahoma City; KFOR-TV (Antenna TV, NBC) Oklahoma City; KOCB (CW) Oklahoma City; KOCO-TV (ABC, This TV) Oklahoma City; KOKH-TV (FOX, The Country Network, WeatherNation) Oklahoma City; KOPX-TV (ION) Oklahoma City; KTBO-TV (TBN) Oklahoma City; KWTV-DT (CBS) Oklahoma City.
Programming (via satellite): Discovery Channel; FX; TBS.
Fee: $54.95 installation; $34.24 monthly; $1.50 converter.
Expanded Basic Service 1
Subscribers: N.A.
Programming (via satellite): A&E; AMC; Animal Planet; BET; Cartoon Network; CMT; CNBC; CNN; Comedy Central; C-SPAN; Disney Channel; ESPN; ESPN2; Fox News Channel; FOX Sports Southwest; Freeform; HGTV; History; HLN; INSP; Lifetime; MTV; Nickelodeon; QVC; Spike TV; Syfy; The Weather Channel; TLC; TNT; USA Network; VH1; WGN America.
Fee: $20.97 monthly.
Digital Basic Service
Subscribers: N.A.
Programming (via satellite): BBC America; Bravo; Discovery Digital Networks; ESPN Classic; Golf Channel; GSN; IFC; NBCSN; Turner Classic Movies; WE tv.
Fee: $9.00 monthly.
Pay Service 1
Pay Units: N.A.
Programming (via satellite): Cinemax; HBO; Showtime; Starz; Starz Encore.
Fee: $1.67 monthly (Encore), $6.75 monthly (Starz), $13.00 monthly (Cinemax), $13.51 monthly (HBO or Showtime).
Digital Pay Service 1
Pay Units: N.A.
Programming (via satellite): DMX Music; HBO (multiplexed); Showtime (multiplexed); Starz (multiplexed); Starz Encore (multiplexed); The Movie Channel.
Fee: $1.67 monthly (Encore), $6.75 monthly (Starz) $12.95 monthly (HBO or Showtime).
Video-On-Demand: No
Pay-Per-View
iN DEMAND (delivered digitally); Fresh (delivered digitally).
Internet Service
Operational: Yes.
Subscribers: 10,335.
Broadband Service: Suddenlink High Speed Internet.
Fee: $45.95 installation; $24.95 monthly.
Telephone Service
Digital: Operational
Subscribers: 4,834.
Fee: $49.95 monthly

Miles of Plant: 497.0 (coaxial); 93.0 (fiber optic). Homes passed: 25,749.
Senior Vice President, Corporate Finance: Michael Pflantz. Vice President, Accounting: Sabrina Warr. General Manager: Byron Mahaffey. Marketing Manager: Heather Eastwood. Chief Technician: Tom Richie.
Ownership: Cequel Communications Holdings I LLC (MSO).

ERICK—Reach Broadband, PO Box 507, Arp, TX 75750. Phones: 903-859-3789; 800-687-1258. E-mail: support@reachbroadband.net. Web Site: http://www.reachbroadband.net. ICA: OK0150.
TV Market Ranking: Below 100 (ERICK). Franchise award date: N.A. Franchise expiration date: N.A. Began: January 1, 1955.
Channel capacity: 41 (not 2-way capable). Channels available but not in use: N.A.
Basic Service
Subscribers: 426.
Programming (received off-air): KETA-TV (PBS) Oklahoma City; KOCO-TV (ABC, This TV) Oklahoma City; KOKH-TV (FOX, The Country Network, WeatherNation) Oklahoma City; KVII-TV (ABC, CW) Amarillo.
Programming (via microwave): KFOR-TV (Antenna TV, NBC) Oklahoma City; KWTV-DT (CBS) Oklahoma City.
Programming (via satellite): A&E; AMC; Animal Planet; Cartoon Network; CNN; C-SPAN; Discovery Channel; Disney Channel; E! HD; ESPN; ESPN2; FOX Sports Networks; Freeform; FX; Great American Country; HGTV; History; HLN; Lifetime; National Geographic Channel; Nickelodeon; Outdoor Channel; QVC; Spike TV; TBS; The Weather Channel; TLC; TNT; Travel Channel; Trinity Broadcasting Network (TBN); TV Land; USA Network.
Fee: $49.95 installation; $30.31 monthly.
Digital Basic Service
Subscribers: N.A.
Programming (via satellite): BBC America; Bloomberg Television; Cloo; Destination America; Discovery Kids Channel; Disney XD; DMX Music; ESPN Classic; ESPNews; EVINE Live; FOX College Sports Central; FOX College Sports Pacific; Fox Sports 1; Fuse; FYI; Golf Channel; GSN; History International; IFC; Investigation Discovery; NBCSN; Science Channel; Sundance TV; Turner Classic Movies; WE tv.
Pay Service 1
Pay Units: N.A.
Programming (via satellite): HBO; Showtime.
Fee: $20.00 installation; $9.95 monthly (Showtime), $10.95 monthly (HBO).
Digital Pay Service 1
Pay Units: N.A.
Programming (via satellite): Cinemax (multiplexed); Flix; HBO (multiplexed); Showtime (multiplexed); Starz (multiplexed); Starz Encore (multiplexed); The Movie Channel (multiplexed).
Video-On-Demand: No
Pay-Per-View
iN DEMAND; Playboy TV (delivered digitally).
Internet Service
Operational: No.
Telephone Service
None
Miles of Plant: 13.0 (coaxial); None (fiber optic). Homes passed: 614.
Controller: Jeffrey Lowe.
Ownership: RB3 LLC (MSO).

EUFAULA—Vyve Broadband, 4 International Dr, Ste 330, Rye Brook, NY 10573. Phone: 855-367-8983. Web Site: http://vyvebroadband.com. Also serves Checotah & McIntosh County (portions). ICA: OK0054.
TV Market Ranking: Below 100 (Checotah, EUFAULA); Outside TV Markets (McIntosh County (portions)). Franchise award date: N.A. Franchise expiration date: N.A. Began: July 1, 1973.
Channel capacity: 44 (2-way capable). Channels available but not in use: N.A.
Basic Service
Subscribers: 286.
Programming (received off-air): KGEB (IND) Tulsa; KJRH-TV (NBC) Tulsa; KMYT-TV (getTV, MNT, The Country Network) Tulsa; KOED-TV (PBS) Tulsa; KOKI-TV (FOX, MeTV) Tulsa; KOTV-DT (CBS, IND) Tulsa; KQCW-DT (CW, This TV) Muskogee; KTUL (ABC, Antenna TV, Retro TV) Tulsa; KWHB (COZI TV, IND) Tulsa.
Fee: $49.95 installation; $25.00 monthly.
Expanded Basic Service 1
Subscribers: N.A.
Programming (via satellite): A&E; AMC; BET; Cartoon Network; CNBC; CNN; C-SPAN; Discovery Channel; Disney Channel; E! HD; ESPN; ESPN2; Fox News Channel; FOX Sports Southwest; Freeform; FX; Great American Country; History; HLN; Lifetime; National Geographic Channel; Nickelodeon; Outdoor Channel; Pop; QVC; Spike TV; TBS; The Weather Channel; TLC; TNT; TV Land; USA Network.
Pay Service 1
Pay Units: N.A.
Programming (via satellite): HBO; Showtime; The Movie Channel.
Fee: $12.95 monthly (each).
Video-On-Demand: Yes
Pay-Per-View
iN DEMAND (delivered digitally); Playboy TV (delivered digitally); ESPN Now (delivered digitally); Sports PPV (delivered digitally).
Internet Service
Operational: No.
Telephone Service
None
Miles of Plant: 75.0 (coaxial); None (fiber optic). Homes passed: 3,482.
President & Chief Operating Officer: Jeffrey S. DeMond. Executive Vice President & Chief Financial Officer: Andrew C. Kober. Senior Vice President, General Counsel & Secretary: Marie Censoplano. Senior Vice President, Engineering & Chief Technology Officer: Dennis Davies. Senior Vice President, Financial Planning: Daniel J. White. Senior Vice President, Marketing & Customer Experience: Diane Quennoz. Senior Vice President, Residential Services: Vin Zachariah. Vice President, Network Planning: Alex Harris.
Ownership: Vyve Broadband LLC (MSO).

FAIRFAX—Cim Tel Cable Inc. Now served by MANNFORD, OK [OK0296]. ICA: OK0133.

FAIRVIEW—Suddenlink Communications, 520 Maryville Centre Dr, Ste 300, St. Louis, MO 63141. Phones: 800-999-6845; 314-315-9400; 314-315-9346. Web Site: http://www.suddenlink.com. ICA: OK0089.
TV Market Ranking: Outside TV Markets (FAIRVIEW). Franchise award date: N.A. Franchise expiration date: N.A. Began: July 1, 1967.
Channel capacity: N.A. Channels available but not in use: N.A.
Basic Service
Subscribers: 224.
Programming (received off-air): KAUT-TV (Escape, MNT) Oklahoma City; KETA-TV (PBS) Oklahoma City; KFOR-TV (Antenna TV, NBC) Oklahoma City; KOCB (CW) Oklahoma City; KOCO-TV (ABC, This TV) Oklahoma City; KOKH-TV (FOX, The Country Network, WeatherNation) Oklahoma City; KOMI-CD Woodward; KTBO-TV (TBN) Oklahoma City; KWTV-DT (CBS) Oklahoma City.
Programming (via satellite): A&E; AMC; CMT; CNN; C-SPAN; Discovery Channel; Disney Channel; E! HD; ESPN; Fox News Channel; FOX Sports Southwest; Freeform; HGTV; History; HLN; Lifetime; MTV; Nickelodeon; Outdoor Channel; QVC; Spike TV; Syfy; TBS; The Weather Channel; TLC; TNT; truTV; TV Land; USA Network; VH1; WGN America.
Fee: $28.45 monthly.
Pay Service 1
Pay Units: N.A.
Programming (via satellite): Cinemax; HBO; Showtime; The Movie Channel.
Fee: $9.95 monthly (Cinemax, Showtime or TMC), $10.95 monthly (HBO).
Video-On-Demand: No
Internet Service
Operational: Yes. Began: May 26, 2003.
Broadband Service: Suddenlink High Speed Internet.
Fee: $45.95 installation; $24.95 monthly.
Telephone Service
Digital: Operational
Fee: $49.95 monthly
Miles of Plant: 30.0 (coaxial); None (fiber optic). Homes passed: 1,234.
Senior Vice President, Corporate Finance: Michael Pflantz. Regional Manager: Todd Cruthird. Plant Manager: Roger Campbell. Regional Marketing Manager: Beverly Gambell.
Ownership: Cequel Communications Holdings I LLC (MSO).

FARGO—Pioneer Telephone Coop. This cable system has converted to IPTV. Now served by KINGFISHER, OK [OK5074]. ICA: OK0345.

FLETCHER—Formerly served by Reach Broadband. No longer in operation. ICA: OK0284.

FORT COBB—Cable West, 314 West Main St, PO Box 237, Mountain View, OK 73062. Phones: 800-960-7912; 580-347-3220. Fax: 580-347-2143. ICA: OK0285.

Oklahoma—Cable Systems

TV Market Ranking: Below 100 (FORT COBB). Franchise award date: June 2, 1980. Franchise expiration date: N.A. Began: N.A. Channel capacity: N.A. Channels available but not in use: N.A.

Basic Service
Subscribers: N.A.
Programming (received off-air): KAUT-TV (Escape, MNT) Oklahoma City; KETA-TV (PBS) Oklahoma City; KFOR-TV (Antenna TV, NBC) Oklahoma City; KOCB (CW) Oklahoma City; KOCO-TV (ABC, This TV) Oklahoma City; KOKH-TV (FOX, The Country Network, WeatherNation) Oklahoma City; KSWO-TV (ABC, TMO) Lawton; KWTV-DT (CBS) Oklahoma City.
Programming (via satellite): A&E; CMT; CNN; Discovery Channel; Disney Channel; ESPN; Freeform; HGTV; HLN; Lifetime; Nickelodeon; Syfy; TBS; The Weather Channel; TNT; Trinity Broadcasting Network (TBN); TV Land; USA Network; WGN America.
Fee: $29.95 installation; $2.95 converter.

Pay Service 1
Pay Units: N.A.
Programming (via satellite): Cinemax; HBO.
Fee: $9.00 monthly (Cinemax), $10.00 monthly (HBO).

Video-On-Demand: No

Internet Service
Operational: No.

Telephone Service
None
Miles of Plant: 6.0 (coaxial); None (fiber optic). Homes passed: 325.
General Manager & Chief Technician: Mickey Davis.
Ownership: Mickey Davis (MSO).

FORT GIBSON—Vyve Broadband, 4 International Dr, Ste 330, Rye Brook, NY 10573. Phones: 800-937-1397; 405-395-1131; 405-275-6923. Web Site: http://vyvebroadband.com. Also serves Okay. ICA: OK0090.
TV Market Ranking: Below 100 (FORT GIBSON, Okay). Franchise award date: November 1, 1971. Franchise expiration date: N.A. Began: April 1, 1977. Channel capacity: N.A. Channels available but not in use: N.A.

Basic Service
Subscribers: 307. Commercial subscribers: 11.
Programming (received off-air): KDOR-TV (TBN) Bartlesville; KGEB (IND) Tulsa; KJRH-TV (NBC) Tulsa; KMYT-TV (getTV, MNT, The Country Network) Tulsa; KOED-TV (PBS) Tulsa; KOKI-TV (FOX, MeTV) Tulsa; KOTV-DT (CBS, IND) Tulsa; KQCW-DT (CW, This TV) Muskogee; KRSU-TV (ETV) Claremore; KTPX-TV (ION) Okmulgee; KTUL (ABC, Antenna TV, Retro TV) Tulsa; KWHB (COZI TV, IND) Tulsa.
Programming (via satellite): C-SPAN; INSP; Pop; QVC; WGN America.
Fee: $64.95 installation; $25.00 monthly; $1.96 converter.

Expanded Basic Service 1
Subscribers: N.A.
Programming (via satellite): A&E; AMC; Animal Planet; Bravo; Cartoon Network; CMT; CNBC; CNN; Comedy Central; Discovery Channel; Disney Channel; E! HD; ESPN; ESPN2; Food Network; Fox News Channel; Fox Sports 1; FOX Sports Southwest; Freeform; FX; Golf Channel; Hallmark Channel; HGTV; History; HLN; Lifetime; MSNBC; MTV; National Geographic Channel; Nickelodeon; Outdoor Channel; Oxygen; Spike TV; Syfy; TBS; The Weather Channel; TLC; TNT; Travel Channel; truTV; Turner Classic Movies; TV Land; USA Network; VH1.
Fee: $41.00 monthly.

Digital Basic Service
Subscribers: N.A.
Programming (via satellite): BBC America; Discovery Digital Networks; Disney XD; ESPN Classic; MC; Sundance TV; WE tv.

Digital Pay Service 1
Pay Units: N.A.
Programming (via satellite): Cinemax (multiplexed); HBO (multiplexed); Showtime (multiplexed); Starz (multiplexed); Starz Encore (multiplexed); The Movie Channel (multiplexed).

Video-On-Demand: No

Pay-Per-View
iN DEMAND (delivered digitally); FOX Sports Networks (delivered digitally); Hot Choice (delivered digitally).

Internet Service
Operational: Yes. Began: December 31, 2005.
Subscribers: 435.
Fee: $24.95 installation; $39.95 monthly.

Telephone Service
Digital: Operational
Subscribers: 115.
Miles of Plant: 104.0 (coaxial); 24.0 (fiber optic). Homes passed: 2,033.
Chief Executive Officer: Bill Haggarty. Senior Vice President, Financial Planning: Daniel White. Regional Vice President: Andrew Dearth. Vice President, Marketing: Tracy Bass.
Ownership: Vyve Broadband LLC (MSO).

FORT SILL—Suddenlink Communications, 520 Maryville Centre Dr, Ste 300, St. Louis, MO 63141. Phones: 580-248-9954; 580-248-2060; 314-315-9400. Web Site: http://www.suddenlink.com. ICA: OK0031.
TV Market Ranking: Below 100 (FORT SILL). Franchise award date: January 1, 1980. Franchise expiration date: N.A. Began: September 1, 1980. Channel capacity: 38 (operating 2-way). Channels available but not in use: N.A.

Basic Service
Subscribers: 355.
Programming (received off-air): KAUZ-TV (CBS, CW) Wichita Falls; KETA-TV (PBS) Oklahoma City; KFDX-TV (NBC) Wichita Falls; KJTL (Bounce TV, FOX) Wichita Falls; KSWO-TV (ABC, TMO) Lawton; KWTV-DT (CBS) Oklahoma City.
Programming (via satellite): C-SPAN; Pop.
Fee: $28.45 monthly; $1.43 converter.

Expanded Basic Service 1
Subscribers: N.A.
Programming (via satellite): A&E; AMC; Animal Planet; BET; Bravo; Cartoon Network; CNBC; CNN; Comedy Central; Discovery Channel; Disney Channel; E! HD; ESPN; ESPN2; EWTN Global Catholic Network; Food Network; Fox News Channel; Fox Sports 1; FOX Sports Southwest; Freeform; FX; Great American Country; Hallmark Channel; HGTV; History; HLN; Lifetime; MSNBC; MTV; National Geographic Channel; Nickelodeon; Outdoor Channel; QVC; Spike TV; Syfy; TBS; The Weather Channel; TLC; TNT; truTV; Turner Classic Movies; TV Land; Univision Studios; USA Network; VH1.
Fee: $21.00 monthly.

Digital Basic Service
Subscribers: N.A.
Programming (via satellite): BBC America; Bloomberg Television; Cloo; Discovery Digital Networks; Disney XD; DMX Music; ESPN Classic; ESPNews; Fuse; FXM; FYI; Golf Channel; GSN; History International; IFC; NBCSN; Trinity Broadcasting Network (TBN); WE tv.
Fee: $3.99 monthly.

Pay Service 1
Pay Units: N.A.
Programming (via satellite): Cinemax; HBO; Showtime; The Movie Channel.

Digital Pay Service 1
Pay Units: N.A.
Programming (via satellite): Cinemax (multiplexed); HBO (multiplexed); Showtime (multiplexed); Starz (multiplexed); Starz Encore (multiplexed); The Movie Channel (multiplexed).

Video-On-Demand: No

Pay-Per-View
iN DEMAND (delivered digitally); Playboy TV (delivered digitally); Fresh (delivered digitally).

Internet Service
Operational: Yes. Began: November 29, 2004.
Broadband Service: Suddenlink High Speed Internet.
Fee: $45.95 installation; $24.95 monthly.

Telephone Service
Digital: Operational
Fee: $49.95 monthly
Miles of Plant: 60.0 (coaxial); None (fiber optic). Homes passed: 3,416.
Senior Vice President, Corporate Finance: Michael Pflantz. Regional Manager: Todd Cruthird. Marketing Director: Beverly Gambell.
Ownership: Cequel Communications Holdings I LLC (MSO).

FORT SUPPLY—Formerly served by CableDirect. No longer in operation. ICA: OK0376.

FREDERICK—Cable One. Now served by ALTUS, OK [OK0017]. ICA: OK0062.

FREEDOM—Formerly served by Pioneer Telephone Coop. No longer in operation. ICA: OK0247.

GANS—Formerly served by Allegiance Communications. No longer in operation. ICA: OK0172.

GARBER—Formerly served by Longview Communications. No longer in operation. ICA: OK0169.

GEARY—Formerly served by Cebridge Connections. No longer in operation. ICA: OK0145.

GERONIMO—Formerly served by CableDirect. No longer in operation. ICA: OK0197.

GERONIMO—Vyve Broadband, 1819 Airport Dr, Shawnee, OK 74804. Phone: 855-367-8983. Web Site: http://vyvebroadband.com. ICA: OK0395.
TV Market Ranking: Below 100 (GERONIMO). Channel capacity: N.A. Channels available but not in use: N.A.

Basic Service
Subscribers: 76.
Programming (received off-air): KAUZ-TV (CBS, CW) Wichita Falls; KETA-TV (PBS) Oklahoma City; KFDX-TV (NBC) Wichita Falls; KJTL (Bounce TV, FOX) Wichita Falls; KSWO-TV (ABC, TMO) Lawton.
Programming (via satellite): A&E; Animal Planet; CNN; C-SPAN; Discovery Channel; Disney Channel; ESPN; ESPN2; Fox Sports 1; Fuse; Great American Country; HGTV; History; LMN; National Geographic Channel; QVC; Syfy; TBS; The Weather Channel; TLC; TNT; Travel Channel; Trinity Broadcasting Network (TBN); Turner Classic Movies; WGN America.
Fee: $39.95 installation; $26.00 monthly.

Pay Service 1
Pay Units: N.A.
Programming (via satellite): HBO; Showtime (multiplexed).

Video-On-Demand: No

Internet Service
Operational: Yes.
Broadband Service: In-house.

Telephone Service
Digital: Operational
Homes passed: 125. Homes passed & miles of plant included in Pecan Valley.
President & Chief Operating Officer: Jeffrey DeMond. Executive Vice President & Chief Financial Officer: Andrew Kober. Senior Vice President, General Counsel & Secretary: Marie Censoplano. Senior Vice President, Engineering & Chief Technology Officer: Dennis Davies. Senior Vice President, Marketing & Customer Experience: Diane Quennoz. Senior Vice President, Residential Services: Vin Zachariah. Vice President, Network Planning: Alex Harris.
Ownership: Vyve Broadband LLC (MSO).

GLENCOE—Formerly served by Allegiance Communications. No longer in operation. ICA: OK0221.

GLENPOOL (southern portion)—Formerly served by Titan Broadband Services. No longer in operation. ICA: OK0388.

GOLTRY—Formerly served by Cebridge Connections. No longer in operation. ICA: OK0286.

GOODWELL—Vyve Broadband, 4 International Dr, Ste 330, Rye Brook, NY 10573. Phones: 800-937-1397; 405-275-6923; 405-395-1131. Web Site: http://vyvebroadband.com. ICA: OK0183.
TV Market Ranking: Outside TV Markets (GOODWELL). Franchise award date: N.A. Franchise expiration date: N.A. Began: May 1, 1983.
Channel capacity: N.A. Channels available but not in use: N.A.

Basic Service
Subscribers: 7.
Programming (received off-air): KCIT (FOX, This TV) Amarillo; KETA-TV (PBS) Oklahoma City; KPTF-DT (GLC) Farwell.
Programming (via microwave): KAMR-TV (IND, NBC) Amarillo; KFDA-TV (CBS, TMO) Amarillo; KVII-TV (ABC, CW) Amarillo.
Programming (via satellite): A&E; AMC; Animal Planet; Cartoon Network; CMT; CNN; Comedy Central; Discovery Channel; Disney Channel; ESPN; ESPN2; Food Network; Fox Sports 1; Freeform; Hallmark Channel; HGTV; History; HLN; Lifetime; MTV; Nickelodeon; Oxygen; QVC; Spike TV; Syfy; TBS; The Weather Channel; TLC; TNT; Travel Channel; TV Land; Univision Studios; USA Network; VH1.
Fee: $64.95 installation; $65.65 monthly.

Pay-Per-View
Hot Choice (delivered digitally); Playboy TV (delivered digitally); Fresh (delivered digitally); Shorteez (delivered digitally); iN DEMAND (delivered digitally).

Internet Service
Operational: No.

D-616

TV & Cable Factbook No. 85

Cable Systems—Oklahoma

Telephone Service
None
Miles of Plant: 6.0 (coaxial); None (fiber optic). Homes passed: 400.
Chief Executive Officer: Bill Haggarty. Senior Vice President, Financial Planning: Daniel White. Regional Vice President: Andrew Dearth. Vice President, Marketing: Tracy Bass.
Ownership: Vyve Broadband LLC (MSO).

GORE—Vyve Broadband, 4 International Dr, Ste 330, Rye Brook, OK 10573. Phones: 800-937-1397; 405-395-1131; 405-275-6923. Web Site: http://vyvebroadband.com. Also serves Webbers Falls. ICA: OK0164.
TV Market Ranking: Below 100 (GORE, Webbers Falls).
Channel capacity: N.A. Channels available but not in use: N.A.
Basic Service
Subscribers: 22. Commercial subscribers: 2.
Programming (received off-air): KFSM-TV (CBS, MNT) Fort Smith; KHBS (ABC, CW) Fort Smith; KJRH-TV (NBC) Tulsa; KOET (PBS) Eufaula; KOKI-TV (FOX, MeTV) Tulsa; KOTV-DT (CBS, IND) Tulsa; KTUL (ABC, Antenna TV, Retro TV) Tulsa.
Programming (via satellite): A&E; AMC; Animal Planet; Cartoon Network; CMT; CNBC; CNN; C-SPAN; Discovery Channel; Disney Channel; ESPN; ESPN2; Fox News Channel; FOX Sports Southwest; Freeform; HGTV; History; HLN; Lifetime; Nickelodeon; Outdoor Channel; QVC; Spike TV; Syfy; TBS; The Weather Channel; TLC; TNT; Travel Channel; Trinity Broadcasting Network (TBN); Turner Classic Movies; USA Network; WGN America.
Fee: $64.95 installation; $67.75 monthly.
Digital Basic Service
Subscribers: N.A.
Programming (via satellite): BBC America; Bloomberg Television; Bravo; Discovery Life Channel; Disney XD; DMX Music; ESPN Classic; ESPNews; EVINE Live; Fox Sports 1; Fuse; FXM; FYI; Golf Channel; GSN; History International; IFC; LMN; NBCSN; Nick Jr.; Pop; TeenNick; WE tv.
Pay Service 1
Pay Units: N.A.
Programming (via satellite): Cinemax; HBO; Showtime.
Fee: $9.50 monthly (Cinemax), $10.95 monthly (HBO).
Digital Pay Service 1
Pay Units: N.A.
Programming (via satellite): Cinemax (multiplexed); Flix; HBO (multiplexed); Showtime (multiplexed); Starz (multiplexed); Starz Encore (multiplexed); The Movie Channel (multiplexed).
Video-On-Demand: No
Pay-Per-View
iN DEMAND (delivered digitally); Hot Choice (delivered digitally); Playboy TV (delivered digitally); Fresh (delivered digitally); Shorteez (delivered digitally).
Internet Service
Operational: No.
Telephone Service
None
Miles of Plant: 17.0 (coaxial); None (fiber optic). Homes passed: 584.
Chief Executive Officer: Bill Haggarty. Regional Vice President: Andrew Dearth. Vice President, Marketing: Tracy Bass. Senior Vice President, Financial Planning: Daniel White.
Ownership: Vyve Broadband LLC (MSO).

GOTEBO—Formerly served by Basic Cable Services Inc. No longer in operation. ICA: OK0228.

GRACEMONT—Formerly served by Cable West. No longer in operation. ICA: OK0287.

GRANDFIELD—Southern Plains Cable, PO Box 165, Medicine Park, OK 73557. Phones: 580-365-4235; 800-218-1856; 580-529-5000. Fax: 580-529-5556. E-mail: office@wichitaonline.net. Web Site: http://www.spcisp.net. ICA: OK0143.
TV Market Ranking: Below 100 (GRANDFIELD). Franchise award date: N.A. Franchise expiration date: N.A. Began: October 1, 1982.
Channel capacity: N.A. Channels available but not in use: N.A.
Basic Service
Subscribers: N.A.
Programming (received off-air): KAUZ-TV (CBS, CW) Wichita Falls; KETA-TV (PBS) Oklahoma City; KFDX-TV (NBC) Wichita Falls; KJTL (Bounce TV, FOX) Wichita Falls; KSWO-TV (ABC, TMO) Lawton.
Programming (via satellite): Local Cable Weather; Telemundo; Trinity Broadcasting Network (TBN).
Fee: $45.00 installation.
Expanded Basic Service 1
Subscribers: N.A.
Programming (via satellite): A&E; AMC; Animal Planet; BET; CMT; CNBC; CNN; Comedy Central; Discovery Channel; Disney Channel; E! HD; ESPN; ESPN2; Fox News Channel; Fox Sports 1; FOX Sports Networks; Freeform; FX; HGTV; History; HLN; Lifetime; Nickelodeon; RFD-TV; Spike TV; Syfy; TBS; The Weather Channel; TLC; TNT; TV Land; USA Network.
Fee: $31.83 monthly.
Digital Basic Service
Subscribers: N.A.
Programming (via satellite): Alterna'TV; AZ TV; BBC America; Bloomberg Television; Bravo; Church Channel; Cloo; CMT; Cooking Channel; Daystar TV Network; Destination America; Discovery Kids Channel; Disney XD; FOX College Sports Central; FOX College Sports Pacific; Fuse; FXM; FYI; Golf Channel; Great American Country; GSN; History International; IFC; INSP; Investigation Discovery; JUCE TV; LMN; MTV Classic; MTV Hits; MTV Jams; Nat Geo WILD; National Geographic Channel; NBCSN; Nick Jr.; Nicktoons; Ovation; OWN; Oprah Winfrey Network; Science Channel; Sprout; Sundance TV; TeenNick; The Word Network; TVG Network; VH1 Soul; WE tv.
Fee: $23.95 monthly.
Digital Expanded Basic Service
Subscribers: N.A.
Programming (via satellite): 52MX; Cine Mexicano; Cinelatino; CNN en Espanol; ESPN Deportes; Fox Deportes; HBO Latino; History en Espanol; Tr3s; ViendoMovies.
Pay Service 1
Pay Units: N.A.
Programming (via satellite): Showtime; The Movie Channel.
Fee: $7.00 monthly (each).
Digital Pay Service 1
Pay Units: N.A.
Programming (via satellite): Cinemax (multiplexed); Flix (multiplexed); HBO (multiplexed); Showtime (multiplexed); Starz (multiplexed); Starz Encore (multiplexed); The Movie Channel (multiplexed).
Fee: $12.00 monthly (each).
Video-On-Demand: No

Pay-Per-View
iN DEMAND (delivered digitally); Hot Choice (delivered digitally); Playboy TV (delivered digitally); Fresh (delivered digitally); Spice: Xcess (delivered digitally).
Internet Service
Operational: No.
Telephone Service
Analog: Not Operational
Digital: Planned
Miles of Plant: 13.0 (coaxial); None (fiber optic). Homes passed: 650.
President: Dustin Hilliary.
Ownership: Southern Plains Cable (MSO).

GRANITE—Formerly served by Cable West. No longer in operation. ICA: OK0134.

GROVE—Suddenlink Communications, 3643 US Hwy 59, Grove, OK 74344. Phones: 314-315-9400; 800-999-6845 (Customer service); 918-786-5131. Web Site: http://www.suddenlink.com. Also serves Delaware County (northern portion). ICA: OK0039.
TV Market Ranking: Below 100 (Delaware County (northern portion) (portions)); Outside TV Markets (Delaware County (northern portion) (portions), GROVE). Franchise award date: November 1, 1972. Franchise expiration date: N.A. Began: July 1, 1973.
Channel capacity: 42 (not 2-way capable). Channels available but not in use: N.A.
Basic Service
Subscribers: 1,414. Commercial subscribers: 226.
Programming (received off-air): KDOR-TV (TBN) Bartlesville; KJRH-TV (NBC) Tulsa; KOED-TV (PBS) Tulsa; KOKI-TV (FOX, MeTV) Tulsa; KOTV-DT (CBS, IND) Tulsa; KQCW-DT (CW, This TV) Muskogee; KTPX-TV (ION) Okmulgee; KTUL (ABC, Antenna TV, Retro TV) Tulsa; allband FM.
Programming (via satellite): A&E; AMC; Animal Planet; Cartoon Network; CMT; CNN; Discovery Channel; Disney Channel; ESPN; ESPN2; Food Network; Fox News Channel; FOX Sports Southwest; Freeform; FX; HGTV; HLN; MoviePlex; Nickelodeon; Pop; QVC; Spike TV; TBS; The Weather Channel; TLC; TNT; USA Network; WGN America.
Fee: $54.95 installation; $31.08 monthly; $1.50 converter.
Digital Basic Service
Subscribers: N.A.
Programming (via satellite): BBC America; Discovery Digital Networks; Disney XD; DMX Music; ESPN Classic; ESPNews; Fox Sports 1; Fuse; FYI; Golf Channel; GSN; History; History International; IFC; LMN; NBCSN; Starz Encore.
Digital Pay Service 1
Pay Units: N.A.
Programming (via satellite): Cinemax (multiplexed); HBO (multiplexed); Showtime (multiplexed); Starz (multiplexed); The Movie Channel (multiplexed).
Video-On-Demand: No
Pay-Per-View
iN DEMAND (delivered digitally); Playboy TV (delivered digitally).

Internet Service
Operational: Yes.
Broadband Service: Suddenlink High Speed Internet.
Telephone Service
Digital: Operational
Miles of Plant: 172.0 (coaxial); 19.0 (fiber optic). Homes passed: 5,770.
Senior Vice President, Corporate Finance: Michael Pflantz. Vice President, Accounting: Sabrina Warr. General Manager: Billy Jowell. Chief Technician: Allan Popp. Marketing Manager: Heather Eastwood. Office Manager: Bondy Sager.
Ownership: Cequel Communications Holdings I LLC (MSO).

GUYMON—PTCI, 2222 Northwest Hwy 64, Guymon, OK 73942. Phones: 580-338-2556; 800-562-2556. Fax: 580-338-8260. E-mail: support@ptsi.net. Web Site: http://www.ptsi.net. Also serves Adams, Balko, Beaver, Boise City, Bryan's Corner, Felt, Floris, Forgan, Gate, Goodwell, Hardesty, Hooker, Keyes, Laverne, Optima, Texhoma, Turpin & Tyrone, OK; Booker, Perryton, Spearman & Texhoma, TX. ICA: OK5005.
TV Market Ranking: Outside TV Markets (Gate, Adams, Beaver, Boise City, Booker, Felt, Hardesty, Hooker, Laverne, Spearman, Texhoma).
Channel capacity: N.A. Channels available but not in use: N.A.
Basic
Subscribers: 2,839.
Fee: $45.00 installation; $25.00 monthly. Includes 22 channels & 2 receivers.
Expanded
Subscribers: N.A.
Fee: $70.00 monthly. Includes 84 channels.
Basic HD
Subscribers: N.A.
Fee: $5.00 monthly. Includes 7 channels.
Expanded HD
Subscribers: N.A.
Fee: $9.99 monthly. Includes 54 channels.
Cinemax
Subscribers: N.A.
Fee: $16.00 monthly. Includes 8 channels.
HBO
Subscribers: N.A.
Fee: $16.85 monthly. Includes 7 channels.
Showtime/TMC
Subscribers: N.A.
Fee: $14.90 monthly. Includes 2 channels.
Starz/Encore
Subscribers: N.A.
Fee: $14.75 monthly. Includes 12 channels.
Internet Service
Operational: Yes.
Fee: $44.99-$99.99 monthly.
Telephone Service
Digital: Operational
Chief Executive Officer & General Manager: Shawn Hanson.
Ownership: Panhandle Telephone Cooperative Inc.

GUYMON—Vyve Broadband, 4 International Dr, Ste 330, Rye Brook, NY 10573. Phones: 800-937-1397; 405-275-6923; 405-395-

Oklahoma—Cable Systems

1131. Web Site: http://vyvebroadband.com. ICA: OK0053.
TV Market Ranking: Outside TV Markets (GUYMON). Franchise award date: N.A. Franchise expiration date: N.A. Began: July 15, 1955.
Channel capacity: N.A. Channels available but not in use: N.A.

Basic Service
Subscribers: 202. Commercial subscribers: 43.
Programming (received off-air): KCIT (FOX, This TV) Amarillo; KPTF-DT (GLC) Farwell; 5 FMs.
Programming (via microwave): KAMR-TV (IND, NBC) Amarillo; KETA-TV (PBS) Oklahoma City; KFDA-TV (CBS, TMO) Amarillo; KVII-TV (ABC, CW) Amarillo.
Programming (via satellite): C-SPAN; C-SPAN 2; CW PLUS; Telemundo; The Weather Channel; UniMas; Univision; Univision Studios; WGN America.
Fee: $64.95 installation; $25.00 monthly.

Expanded Basic Service 1
Subscribers: N.A.
Programming (via satellite): A&E; AMC; Animal Planet; Cartoon Network; CMT; CNN; Discovery Channel; Disney Channel; ESPN; ESPN2; Fox News Channel; FOX Sports Southwest; Freeform; HLN; Lifetime; MTV; Nickelodeon; Spike TV; Syfy; TBS; TLC; TNT; TV Land; USA Network; VH1.
Fee: $35.76 monthly.

Digital Basic Service
Subscribers: N.A.
Programming (via satellite): BBC America; Bloomberg Television; Bravo; Cinemax; Destination America; Discovery Kids Channel; Disney XD; ESPN Classic; ESPNews; EVINE Live; Fox Sports 1; Fuse; FXM; FYI; Golf Channel; Great American Country; GSN; HBO; HGTV; History; History International; IFC; Investigation Discovery; LMN; MBC America; NBCSN; Outdoor Channel; OWN; Oprah Winfrey Network; Showtime; Starz; Sundance TV; The Movie Channel; Trinity Broadcasting Network (TBN); Turner Classic Movies.

Pay Service 1
Pay Units: N.A.
Programming (via satellite): HBO.

Digital Pay Service 1
Pay Units: N.A.
Programming (via satellite): Starz Encore (multiplexed).
Fee: $9.95 monthly (Cinemax), $10.95 monthly (HBO, Showtime, Starz or TMC).

Video-On-Demand: No
Internet Service
Operational: Yes.
Fee: $24.95 installation; $39.95 monthly.

Telephone Service
Digital: Operational
Miles of Plant: 40.0 (coaxial); None (fiber optic). Homes passed: 3,050.
Chief Executive Officer: Bill Haggarty. Senior Vice President, Financial Planning: Daniel White. Regional Vice President: Andrew Dearth. Vice President, Marketing: Tracy Bass.
Ownership: Vyve Broadband LLC (MSO).

HAILEYVILLE—Vyve Broadband, 4 International Dr, Ste 330, Rye Brook, NY 10573. Phones: 800-937-1397; 405-395-1131; 405-275-6923. Web Site: http://vyvebroadband.com. Also serves Hartshorne. ICA: OK0083.
TV Market Ranking: Outside TV Markets (HAILEYVILLE, Hartshorne). Franchise award date: N.A. Franchise expiration date: N.A. Began: July 1, 1965.
Channel capacity: N.A. Channels available but not in use: N.A.

Basic Service
Subscribers: 134. Commercial subscribers: 11.
Programming (received off-air): KJRH-TV (NBC) Tulsa; KMYT-TV (getTV, MNT, The Country Network) Tulsa; KOET (PBS) Eufaula; KOKI-TV (FOX, MeTV) Tulsa; KOTV-DT (CBS, IND) Tulsa; KQCW-DT (CBS, This TV) Muskogee; KTEN (ABC, CW, NBC) Ada; KTUL (ABC, Antenna TV, Retro TV) Tulsa; KWHB (COZI TV, IND) Tulsa; allband FM.
Programming (via satellite): C-SPAN; QVC; Trinity Broadcasting Network (TBN); WGN America.
Fee: $64.95 installation; $25.00 monthly; $1.96 converter.

Expanded Basic Service 1
Subscribers: 107.
Programming (via satellite): A&E; AMC; Animal Planet; Cartoon Network; CMT; CNBC; CNN; Comedy Central; Discovery Channel; Disney Channel; E! HD; ESPN; ESPN2; Food Network; Fox News Channel; Fox Sports 1; FOX Sports Southwest; Freeform; FX; HGTV; History; HLN; Lifetime; MTV; Nickelodeon; Outdoor Channel; Oxygen; Spike TV; Syfy; TBS; The Weather Channel; TLC; TNT; Travel Channel; truTV; Turner Classic Movies; TV Land; USA Network; VH1.
Fee: $35.76 monthly.

Digital Basic Service
Subscribers: N.A.
Programming (via satellite): BBC America; Bloomberg Television; Discovery Life Channel; Disney XD; DIY Network; DMX Music; ESPN Classic; ESPNews; FYI; GSN; History International; IFC; LMN; Nick 2; Nick Jr.; Nicktoons; Sundance TV; TeenNick; TV Guide Interactive Inc.; WE tv.

Digital Pay Service 1
Pay Units: N.A.
Programming (via satellite): Cinemax (multiplexed); Flix; HBO (multiplexed); Showtime (multiplexed); Starz (multiplexed); Starz Encore (multiplexed); The Movie Channel (multiplexed).

Video-On-Demand: No
Pay-Per-View
iN DEMAND (delivered digitally); Hot Choice (delivered digitally); Playboy TV (delivered digitally); Fresh (delivered digitally); Shorteez (delivered digitally).

Internet Service
Operational: No.
Telephone Service
None
Miles of Plant: 45.0 (coaxial); None (fiber optic). Homes passed: 1,619.
Chief Executive Officer: Bill Haggarty. Senior Vice President, Financial Planning: Daniel White. Regional Vice President: Andrew Dearth. Vice President, Marketing: Tracy Bass.
Ownership: Vyve Broadband LLC (MSO).

HAMMON—Formerly served by Rapid Cable. No longer in operation. ICA: OK0220.

HARDESTY—PTCI. This cable system has converted to IPTV. Now served by GUYMON, OK [OK5005]. ICA: OK5032.

HARDESTY—PTCI. This cable system has converted to IPTV. Now served by GUYMON, OK [OK5005]. ICA: OK0373.

HASKELL—Formerly served by Allegiance Communications. No longer in operation. ICA: OK0096.

HEALDTON—Suddenlink Communications, 520 Maryville Centre Dr, Ste 300, St. Louis, MO 63141. Phones: 800-999-6845 (Customer service); 314-315-9400; 314-315-9346. Web Site: http://www.suddenlink.com. Also serves Cornish, Ringling & Wilson. ICA: OK0055.
TV Market Ranking: Outside TV Markets (Cornish, HEALDTON, Ringling, Wilson). Franchise award date: N.A. Franchise expiration date: N.A. Began: September 1, 1974.
Channel capacity: 41 (2-way capable). Channels available but not in use: N.A.

Basic Service
Subscribers: 490.
Programming (received off-air): KAUZ-TV (CBS, CW) Wichita Falls; KETA-TV (PBS) Oklahoma City; KFDX-TV (NBC) Wichita Falls; KFOR-TV (Antenna TV, NBC) Oklahoma City; KJTL (Bounce TV, FOX) Wichita Falls; KOCO-TV (ABC, This TV) Oklahoma City; KOKH-TV (FOX, The Country Network, WeatherNation) Oklahoma City; KTEN (ABC, CW, NBC) Ada; KWTV-DT (CBS) Oklahoma City; KXII (CBS, FOX, MNT) Sherman.
Programming (via satellite): A&E; CMT; CNN; Discovery Channel; Disney Channel; ESPN; FOX Sports Southwest; Freeform; History; HLN; Lifetime; Nickelodeon; QVC; Spike TV; TBS; The Weather Channel; TNT; Trinity Broadcasting Network (TBN); Turner Classic Movies; TV Land; USA Network; WGN America.
Fee: $39.95 installation; $28.45 monthly.

Pay Service 1
Pay Units: N.A.
Programming (via satellite): HBO; Showtime; The Movie Channel.
Fee: $7.95 monthly (TMC), $9.95 monthly (Showtime), $10.95 monthly (HBO).

Video-On-Demand: No
Internet Service
Operational: Yes.
Subscribers: 361.
Broadband Service: Suddenlink High Speed Internet.

Telephone Service
None
Miles of Plant: 68.0 (coaxial); None (fiber optic). Homes passed: 3,683.
Senior Vice President, Corporate Finance: Michael Pflantz. Regional Manager: Todd Cruthird. Regional Marketing Manager: Beverly Gambell. Plant Manager: Kriss Miller.
Ownership: Cequel Communications Holdings I LLC (MSO).

HEAVENER—Suddenlink Communications, 520 Maryville Centre Dr, Ste 300, St. Louis, MO 63141. Phones: 800-999-6845; 314-315-9400; 314-315-9346. Web Site: http://www.suddenlink.com. Also serves Le Flore County (portions). ICA: OK0103.
TV Market Ranking: Outside TV Markets (HEAVENER, Le Flore County (portions)). Franchise award date: N.A. Franchise expiration date: N.A. Began: March 1, 1965.
Channel capacity: N.A. Channels available but not in use: N.A.

Basic Service
Subscribers: 149.
Programming (received off-air): KAFT (PBS) Fayetteville; KFSM-TV (CBS, MNT) Fort Smith; KFTA-TV (FOX, NBC) Fort Smith; KHBS (ABC, CW) Fort Smith; KOKI-TV (FOX, MeTV) Tulsa; KOTV-DT (CBS, IND) Tulsa; KTUL (ABC, Antenna TV, Retro TV) Tulsa; allband FM.
Programming (via microwave): KETA-TV (PBS) Oklahoma City.
Programming (via satellite): A&E; CMT; CNN; C-SPAN; Discovery Channel; Disney Channel; ESPN; FOX Sports Southwest; Freeform; HGTV; History; HLN; Lifetime; Nickelodeon; QVC; Spike TV; TBS; The Weather Channel; TNT; Turner Classic Movies; TV Land; USA Network; WGN America.
Fee: $39.95 installation; $28.45 monthly.

Pay Service 1
Pay Units: N.A.
Programming (via satellite): HBO; Showtime; The Movie Channel.
Fee: $35.00 installation; $7.95 monthly (TMC), $9.95 monthly (Showtime), $10.95 monthly (HBO).

Video-On-Demand: No
Internet Service
Operational: Yes. Began: March 24, 2004.
Broadband Service: Suddenlink High Speed Internet.
Fee: $45.95 installation; $24.95 monthly.

Telephone Service
Digital: Operational
Fee: $49.95 monthly
Miles of Plant: 25.0 (coaxial); None (fiber optic). Homes passed: 1,130.
Senior Vice President, Corporate Finance: Michael Pflantz. Regional Manager: Todd Cruthird. Regional Marketing Manager: Beverly Gambell. Plant Manager: Danny Keith.
Ownership: Cequel Communications Holdings I LLC (MSO).

HECTORVILLE—Formerly served by Quality Cablevision of Oklahoma Inc. No longer in operation. ICA: OK0336.

HELENA—Pioneer Telephone Coop. This cable system has converted to IPTV. Now served by KINGFISHER, OK [OK5074]. ICA: OK0153.

HENNESSEY—Pioneer Telephone Coop. This cable system has converted to IPTV. Now served by KINGFISHER, OK [OK5074]. ICA: OK0113.

HENRYETTA—Suddenlink Communications, 2510 Elliott St, Muskogee, OK 74403. Phones: 314-315-9400; 877-694-9474. Web Site: http://www.suddenlink.com. Also serves Dewar & Okmulgee County (portions). ICA: OK0049.
TV Market Ranking: Below 100 (Dewar, HENRYETTA, Okmulgee County (portions)).
Channel capacity: N.A. Channels available but not in use: N.A.

Basic Service
Subscribers: 782. Commercial subscribers: 77.
Fee: $54.95 installation; $33.24 monthly.
Senior Vice President, Corporate Finance: Michael Pflantz. Vice President, Accounting: Sabrina Warr.
Ownership: Cequel Communications Holdings I LLC (MSO).

HINTON—Hinton CATV Co, 126 West Main St, Hinton, OK 73047. Phone: 405-542-3211. Fax: 405-542-3131. E-mail: hintoncatv@hintonet.net. Web Site: http://www.hintontelephone.com. Also serves Cedar Lake, Colony, Eakly, Hydro & Lookeba. ICA: OK0140.
TV Market Ranking: Outside TV Markets (Cedar Lake, Colony, Eakly, HINTON, Hydro, Lookeba). Franchise award date:

Cable Systems—Oklahoma

N.A. Franchise expiration date: N.A. Began: July 1, 1983.
Channel capacity: N.A. Channels available but not in use: N.A.
Basic Service
  Subscribers: 417.
  Programming (received off-air): KAUT-TV (Escape, MNT) Oklahoma City; KETA-TV (PBS) Oklahoma City; KFOR-TV (Antenna TV, NBC) Oklahoma City; KOCB (CW) Oklahoma City; KOCO-TV (ABC, This TV) Oklahoma City; KOKH-TV (FOX, The Country Network, WeatherNation) Oklahoma City; KTBO-TV (TBN) Oklahoma City; KWTV-DT (CBS) Oklahoma City.
  Programming (via satellite): CNN; Disney Channel; ESPN; Hallmark Channel; TBS; TNT; WGN America.
  Fee: $25.00 installation; $59.50 monthly.
Pay Service 1
  Pay Units: N.A.
  Programming (via satellite): Cinemax; HBO; Showtime.
  Fee: $10.99 monthly (Cinemax or Showtime), $13.99 monthly (HBO).
Video-On-Demand: No
Internet Service
  Operational: Yes, DSL.
  Broadband Service: Hinton Net.
  Fee: $27.95-$64.95 monthly.
Telephone Service
  Analog: Operational
  Miles of Plant: 27.0 (coaxial); None (fiber optic).
  General Manager & Chief Technician: Kenneth Doughty. Secretary-Treasurer: Jason Doughty.
  Ownership: Hinton CATV Co.

HOBART—Cable One. Now served by ELK CITY, OK [OK0032]. ICA: OK0067.

HOLDENVILLE—Vyve Broadband, 4 International Dr, Ste 330, Rye Brook, NY 10573. Phones: 800-937-1397; 405-395-1131; 405-275-6923. Web Site: http://vyvebroadband.com. ICA: OK0061.
  TV Market Ranking: Below 100 (HOLDENVILLE). Franchise award date: N.A. Franchise expiration date: N.A. Began: September 1, 1967.
  Channel capacity: 36 (not 2-way capable). Channels available but not in use: N.A.
Basic Service
  Subscribers: 159. Commercial subscribers: 23.
  Programming (received off-air): KETA-TV (PBS) Oklahoma City; KFOR-TV (Antenna TV, NBC) Oklahoma City; KOCO-TV (ABC, This TV) Oklahoma City; KOKI-TV (FOX, MeTV) Tulsa; KOPX-TV (ION) Oklahoma City; KOTV-DT (CBS, IND) Tulsa; KTBO-TV (TBN) Oklahoma City; KTEN (ABC, CW, NBC) Ada; KWTV-DT (CBS) Oklahoma City; allband FM.
  Programming (via satellite): A&E; AMC; Animal Planet; Cartoon Network; CMT; CNBC; CNN; Comedy Central; Discovery Channel; Disney Channel; ESPN; ESPN Classic; ESPN2; Food Network; Fox News Channel; FOX Sports Southwest; Freeform; FX; Hallmark Channel; HGTV; History; Lifetime; MTV; NFL Network; QVC; Spike TV; Syfy; TBS; The Weather Channel; TLC; TNT; TV Land; USA Network; VH1.
  Fee: $64.95 installation; $25.00 monthly.
Digital Basic Service
  Subscribers: N.A.
  Programming (via satellite): 52MX; BBC America; Bloomberg Television; Bravo; Cine Mexicano; Cinelatino; Cloo; CMT; CNN en Espanol; Destination America; Discovery Kids Channel; Discovery Life Channel; Disney XD; DMX Music; ESPN Classic; ESPN2; ESPNews; EVINE Live; Flix; FOX College Sports Central; FOX College Sports Pacific; Fox Deportes; Fox Sports 1; Fuse; FXM; FYI; Golf Channel; Great American Country; GSN; HGTV; History; History en Espanol; History International; IFC; Investigation Discovery; LMN; MTV Classic; MTV Hits; MTV2; National Geographic Channel; NBCSN; Nick Jr.; Nicktoons; Outdoor Channel; Ovation; OWN: Oprah Winfrey Network; Science Channel; Starz Encore (multiplexed); Sundance TV; Syfy; TeenNick; The Word Network; Tr3s; Trinity Broadcasting Network (TBN); Turner Classic Movies; VH1 Soul; WE tv.
Pay Service 1
  Pay Units: N.A.
  Programming (via satellite): HBO; Showtime; Starz; Starz Encore.
  Fee: $1.75 monthly (Encore), $6.75 monthly (Starz), $12.95 monthly (HBO or Showtime).
Digital Pay Service 1
  Pay Units: N.A.
  Programming (via satellite): Cinemax (multiplexed); HBO (multiplexed); HBO Latino; Showtime (multiplexed); Starz (multiplexed); The Movie Channel (multiplexed).
Video-On-Demand: No
Pay-Per-View
  iN DEMAND (delivered digitally); Hot Choice (delivered digitally); Playboy TV (delivered digitally); Fresh (delivered digitally); Shorteez (delivered digitally).
Internet Service
  Operational: Yes.
  Fee: $24.95 installation; $39.95 monthly.
Telephone Service
  Digital: Operational
  Miles of Plant: 24.0 (coaxial); None (fiber optic). Homes passed: 2,373.
  Chief Executive Officer: Bill Haggarty. Senior Vice President, Financial Planning: Daniel White. Regional Vice President: Andrew Dearth. Vice President, Marketing: Tracy Bass.
  Ownership: Vyve Broadband LLC (MSO).

HOLLIS—Pioneer Telephone Coop. This cable system has converted to IPTV. Now served by KINGFISHER, OK [OK5074]. ICA: OK0087.

HOMINY—Community Cable & Broadband, 1550 West Rogers Blvd, PO Box 307, Skiatook, OK 74070-0307. Phones: 888-394-4772; 918-396-3019. Fax: 918-396-2081. E-mail: info@communitycablevision.com. Web Site: http://www.communitycablebroadband.com. ICA: OK0085.
  TV Market Ranking: 54 (HOMINY). Franchise award date: June 20, 1979. Franchise expiration date: N.A. Began: January 1, 1980.
  Channel capacity: N.A. Channels available but not in use: N.A.
Basic Service
  Subscribers: N.A.
  Programming (received off-air): KDOR-TV (TBN) Bartlesville; KGEB (IND) Tulsa; KJRH-TV (NBC) Tulsa; KOED-TV (PBS) Tulsa; KOKI-TV (FOX, MeTV) Tulsa; KOTV-DT (CBS, IND) Tulsa; KTPX-TV (ION) Okmulgee; KTUL (ABC, Antenna TV, Retro TV) Tulsa; KWHB (COZI TV, IND) Tulsa; allband FM.
  Programming (via microwave): KTFO-CD (UniMas) Austin.
  Programming (via satellite): A&E; AMC; Animal Planet; BET; Cartoon Network; CMT; CNN; Comedy Central; C-SPAN; CW PLUS; Discovery Channel; Disney Channel; ESPN; ESPN Classic; ESPN2; Food Network; Fox News Channel; FOX Sports Southwest; Freeform; FX; Hallmark Channel; HGTV; History; Lifetime; MoviePlex; MTV; National Geographic Channel; Nickelodeon; Outdoor Channel; OWN: Oprah Winfrey Network; Oxygen; QVC; Spike TV; Syfy; TBS; The Weather Channel; TLC; TNT; Travel Channel; truTV; Turner Classic Movies; TV Land; USA Network; VH1; WE tv; WGN America.
  Fee: $29.95 installation.
Digital Basic Service
  Subscribers: N.A.
  Programming (via satellite): BBC America; Bloomberg Television; Bravo; Church Channel; Destination America; Discovery Kids Channel; Discovery Life Channel; Disney XD; DMX Music; ESPN Classic; ESPN2; ESPNews; EVINE Live; FOX College Sports Central; FOX College Sports Pacific; Fox Sports 1; Fuse; FXM; FYI; Golf Channel; Great American Country; GSN; HGTV; History; History International; IFC; Investigation Discovery; JUCE TV; LMN; MBC America; MTV Classic; MTV Hits; MTV Jams; MTV2; National Geographic Channel; NBCSN; Nick Jr.; Nicktoons; Outdoor Channel; Ovation; OWN: Oprah Winfrey Network; Science Channel; Syfy; TeenNick; The Word Network; Trinity Broadcasting Network (TBN); Turner Classic Movies; VH1 Country; VH1 Soul; WE tv.
  Fee: $21.00 monthly.
Digital Pay Service 1
  Pay Units: N.A.
  Programming (via satellite): Cinemax (multiplexed); Flix; HBO (multiplexed); Showtime (multiplexed); Starz (multiplexed); Starz Encore (multiplexed); Sundance TV; The Movie Channel (multiplexed).
  Fee: $11.50 monthly (Cinemax, HBO, Showtime/TMC/Flix/Sundance or Starz/Encore).
Internet Service
  Operational: Yes.
  Broadband Service: In-house.
  Fee: $44.95 monthly.
Telephone Service
  Digital: Operational
  Miles of Plant: 12.0 (coaxial); None (fiber optic). Homes passed: 1,547.
  President & General Manager: Dennis Soule. Chief Technical Officer: Chris Tuttle.
  Ownership: Community Cable & Broadband Inc. (MSO).

HOOKER—PTCI. This cable system has converted to IPTV. Now served by GUYMON, OK [OK5005]. ICA: OK0125.

HOWE—Formerly served by Allegiance Communications. No longer in operation. ICA: OK0243.

HUGO—Suddenlink Communications, 520 Maryville Centre Dr, Ste 300, St. Louis, MO 63141. Phone: 314-315-9400. Web Site: http://www.suddenlink.com. Also serves Choctaw County (portions). ICA: OK0050.
  TV Market Ranking: Outside TV Markets (Choctaw County (portions), HUGO). Franchise award date: June 1, 1976. Franchise expiration date: N.A. Began: August 1, 1976.
  Channel capacity: N.A. Channels available but not in use: N.A.
Basic Service
  Subscribers: 708.
  Programming (received off-air): KETA-TV (PBS) Oklahoma City; KTEN (ABC, CW, NBC) Ada; KXII (CBS, FOX, MNT) Sherman; allband FM.
  Programming (via satellite): AMC; BET; Cartoon Network; CMT; CNBC; CNN; Discovery Channel; Disney Channel; ESPN; Fox News Channel; FOX Sports Southwest; Freeform; FX; Hallmark Channel; HLN; Lifetime; MTV; Nickelodeon; QVC; Spike TV; TBS; The Weather Channel; TNT; Trinity Broadcasting Network (TBN); truTV; Turner Classic Movies; USA Network; WGN America.
  Programming (via translator): KDFW (FOX) Dallas; KTVT (CBS, Decades) Fort Worth; KXAS-TV (COZI TV, NBC) Fort Worth; WFAA (ABC) Dallas.
  Fee: $35.23 installation; $28.45 monthly; $1.24 converter.
Pay Service 1
  Pay Units: N.A.
  Programming (via satellite): Cinemax; HBO; Showtime.
Pay-Per-View
  Special events.
Internet Service
  Operational: Yes. Began: December 22, 2003.
  Broadband Service: Suddenlink High Speed Internet.
  Fee: $45.95 installation; $24.95 monthly.
Telephone Service
  Digital: Operational
  Fee: $49.95 monthly
  Miles of Plant: 59.0 (coaxial); None (fiber optic). Homes passed: 3,300.
  Senior Vice President, Corporate Finance: Michael Pflantz. Regional Manager: Todd Cruthird. General Manager & Chief Technician: Lindy Loftin. Marketing Director: Beverly Gambell.
  Ownership: Cequel Communications Holdings I LLC (MSO).

HULBERT—Vyve Broadband, 4 International Dr, Ste 330, Rye Brook, NY 10573. Phones: 800-937-1397; 405-395-1131; 405-275-6923. Web Site: http://vyvebroadband.com. ICA: OK0202.
  TV Market Ranking: Below 100 (HULBERT). Franchise award date: January 1, 1989. Franchise expiration date: N.A. Began: September 1, 1989.
  Channel capacity: N.A. Channels available but not in use: N.A.
Basic Service
  Subscribers: 11. Commercial subscribers: 1.
  Programming (received off-air): KJRH-TV (NBC) Tulsa; KMYT-TV (getTV, MNT, The Country Network) Tulsa; KOED-TV (PBS) Tulsa; KOKI-TV (FOX, MeTV) Tulsa; KOTV-DT (CBS, IND) Tulsa; KRSU-TV (ETV) Claremore; KTUL (ABC, Antenna TV, Retro TV) Tulsa; KWHB (COZI TV, IND) Tulsa.
  Programming (via satellite): A&E; CMT; CNN; Discovery Channel; ESPN; Freeform; Lifetime; Nickelodeon; Spike TV; TBS; TNT; USA Network; WGN America.
  Fee: $64.95 installation; $45.75 monthly; $1.96 converter.
Pay Service 1
  Pay Units: N.A.
  Programming (via satellite): HBO.
  Fee: $9.95 monthly.
Video-On-Demand: No
Internet Service
  Operational: No.
Telephone Service
  None
  Miles of Plant: 5.0 (coaxial); None (fiber optic). Homes passed: 293.
  Chief Executive Officer: Bill Haggarty. Senior Vice President, Financial Planning: Daniel

Oklahoma—Cable Systems

White. Vice President, Marketing: Tracy Bass. General Manager: Andrew Dearth. Ownership: Vyve Broadband LLC (MSO).

HUNTER (town)—Formerly served by Pioneer Telephone Coop. No longer in operation. ICA: OK0288.

IDABEL—Suddenlink Communications, 520 Maryville Centre Dr, Ste 300, St. Louis, MO 63141. Phones: 800-999-6845; 314-315-9400. Web Site: http://www.suddenlink.com. Also serves McCurtain County (portions). ICA: OK0056.
TV Market Ranking: Outside TV Markets (IDABEL). Franchise award date: January 17, 1961. Franchise expiration date: N.A. Began: October 10, 1961.
Channel capacity: 40 (operating 2-way). Channels available but not in use: N.A.
Basic Service
Subscribers: 287.
Programming (received off-air): KOET (PBS) Eufaula; KTAL-TV (NBC) Texarkana; KTEN (ABC, CW, NBC) Ada.
Programming (via satellite): C-SPAN; Pop; Trinity Broadcasting Network (TBN).
Programming (via translator): KDFW (FOX) Dallas; KSLA (Bounce TV, CBS, Grit, This TV) Shreveport; KTBS-TV (ABC) Shreveport; KTVT (CBS, Decades) Fort Worth.
Fee: $15.31 installation; $27.45 monthly; $2.22 converter.
Expanded Basic Service 1
Subscribers: N.A.
Programming (via satellite): A&E; AMC; Animal Planet; BET; Cartoon Network; CNBC; CNN; Comedy Central; Discovery Channel; Disney Channel; E! HD; ESPN; ESPN2; Food Network; Fox News Channel; FOX Sports Southwest; Freeform; FX; Great American Country; HGTV; History; HLN; Lifetime; MSNBC; MTV; National Geographic Channel; Nickelodeon; Outdoor Channel; Spike TV; Syfy; TBS; The Weather Channel; TLC; TNT; Turner Classic Movies; TV Land; Univision Studios; USA Network; VH1.
Fee: $15.31 installation; $18.00 monthly.
Digital Basic Service
Subscribers: N.A.
Programming (via satellite): BBC America; Bloomberg Television; Cloo; Discovery Digital Networks; Disney XD; DMX Music; ESPN Classic; ESPNews; EVINE Live; FOX College Sports Central; FOX College Sports Pacific; Fox Sports 1; Fuse; FYI; Golf Channel; GSN; History; History International; IFC; NBCSN; WE tv.
Pay Service 1
Pay Units: N.A.
Programming (via satellite): Cinemax; HBO (multiplexed); Showtime; The Movie Channel.
Fee: $15.31 installation; $13.95 monthly (each).
Pay-Per-View
iN DEMAND (delivered digitally); Playboy TV (delivered digitally); Fresh (delivered digitally).
Internet Service
Operational: Yes. Began: May 19, 2003. Broadband Service: Suddenlink High Speed Internet.
Fee: $45.95 installation; $24.95 monthly.
Telephone Service
Digital: Operational
Fee: $49.95 monthly
Miles of Plant: 49.0 (coaxial); None (fiber optic). Homes passed: 2,864.
Senior Vice President, Corporate Finance: Michael Pflantz. General Manager: Marianne Bogy. Regional Manager: Todd Cruthird. Chief Technician: Sonny Myers. Customer Service Manager: Jeanie Acker. Ownership: Cequel Communications Holdings I LLC (MSO).

INOLA—BCI Broadband. Now served by SALINA, OK [OK0071]. ICA: OK0129.

JET—Formerly served by Cebridge Connections. No longer in operation. ICA: OK0290.

JONES—Formerly served by Almega Cable. No longer in operation. ICA: OK0291.

KANSAS—Formerly served by Allegiance Communications. No longer in operation. ICA: OK0292.

KAW CITY—Formerly served by Community Cablevision Co. No longer in operation. ICA: OK0231.

KELLYVILLE—Vyve Broadband, 4 International Dr, Ste 330, Rye Brook, NY 10573. Phones: 800-937-1397; 405-395-1131; 405-275-6923. Web Site: http://vyvebroadband.com. ICA: OK0171.
TV Market Ranking: 54 (KELLYVILLE). Franchise award date: June 13, 1983. Franchise expiration date: N.A. Began: April 1, 1985.
Channel capacity: N.A. Channels available but not in use: N.A.
Basic Service
Subscribers: 12. Commercial subscribers: 2.
Programming (received off-air): KDOR-TV (TBN) Bartlesville; KJRH-TV (NBC) Tulsa; KMYT-TV (getTV, MNT, The Country Network) Tulsa; KOED-TV (PBS) Tulsa; KOKI-TV (FOX, MeTV) Tulsa; KOTV-DT (CBS, IND) Tulsa; KQCW-DT (CW, This TV) Muskogee; KTPX-TV (ION) Okmulgee; KTUL (ABC, Antenna TV, Retro TV) Tulsa; KWHB (COZI TV, IND) Tulsa.
Programming (via satellite): A&E; AMC; Animal Planet; CMT; CNBC; CNN; Discovery Channel; Disney Channel; E! HD; ESPN; ESPN2; Fox Sports 1; Freeform; History; Lifetime; MTV; Nickelodeon; Oxygen; Spike TV; Syfy; TBS; The Weather Channel; TNT; Travel Channel; USA Network; WGN America.
Fee: $64.95 installation; $25.00 monthly.
Digital Basic Service
Subscribers: N.A.
Programming (via satellite): BBC America; Bloomberg Television; Bravo; Discovery Life Channel; Disney XD; DMX Music; ESPN Classic; EVINE Live; Fuse; FXM; FYI; Golf Channel; GSN; HGTV; History International; IFC; LMN; NBCSN; Nick Jr.; Outdoor Channel; Pop; TeenNick; TLC; Turner Classic Movies; WE tv.
Pay Service 1
Pay Units: N.A.
Programming (via satellite): Cinemax; HBO; Showtime.
Fee: $10.95 monthly (Showtime), $11.95 monthly (HBO).
Digital Pay Service 1
Pay Units: N.A.
Programming (via satellite): Cinemax (multiplexed); Flix; HBO (multiplexed); Showtime (multiplexed); Starz (multiplexed); Starz Encore (multiplexed); The Movie Channel (multiplexed).
Video-On-Demand: No

Pay-Per-View
iN DEMAND (delivered digitally); Hot Choice (delivered digitally); Playboy TV (delivered digitally); Fresh (delivered digitally); Shorteez (delivered digitally).
Internet Service
Operational: No.
Telephone Service
None
Miles of Plant: 7.0 (coaxial); None (fiber optic). Homes passed: 453.
Chief Executive Officer: Bill Haggarty. Senior Vice President, Financial Planning: Daniel White. Regional Vice President: Andrew Dearth. Vice President, Marketing: Tracy Bass.
Ownership: Vyve Broadband LLC (MSO).

KEOTA—Vyve Broadband, 4 International Dr, Ste 330, Rye Brook, NY 10573. Phones: 800-937-1397; 405-395-1131; 405-275-6923. Web Site: http://vyvebroadband.com. ICA: OK0218.
TV Market Ranking: Below 100 (KEOTA). Franchise award date: April 1, 1982. Franchise expiration date: N.A. Began: April 15, 1982.
Channel capacity: N.A. Channels available but not in use: N.A.
Basic Service
Subscribers: 18.
Programming (received off-air): KFSM-TV (CBS, MNT) Fort Smith; KHBS (ABC, CW) Fort Smith; KOET (PBS) Eufaula; KOKI-TV (FOX, MeTV) Tulsa; KQCW-DT (CW, This TV) Muskogee; KTUL (ABC, Antenna TV, Retro TV) Tulsa; KWHB (COZI TV, IND) Tulsa.
Programming (via satellite): A&E; Animal Planet; CMT; CNBC; CNN; Discovery Channel; Disney Channel; E! HD; ESPN; ESPN2; Freeform; History; Lifetime; MSNBC; MTV; Nickelodeon; QVC; Spike TV; Syfy; TBS; TNT; Travel Channel; Trinity Broadcasting Network (TBN); Turner Classic Movies; USA Network; WGN America.
Fee: $64.95 installation; $45.75 monthly; $1.00 converter.
Pay Service 1
Pay Units: N.A.
Programming (via satellite): Cinemax; HBO.
Fee: $9.00 monthly (HBO).
Video-On-Demand: No; No
Pay-Per-View
iN DEMAND (delivered digitally); Hot Choice (delivered digitally); Playboy TV (delivered digitally); Fresh (delivered digitally); Shorteez (delivered digitally).
Internet Service
Operational: No.
Telephone Service
None
Miles of Plant: 7.0 (coaxial); None (fiber optic). Homes passed: 238.
Chief Executive Officer: Bill Haggarty. Senior Vice President, Financial Planning: Daniel White. Regional Vice President: Andrew Dearth. Vice President, Marketing: Tracy Bass.
Ownership: Vyve Broadband LLC (MSO).

KETCHUM—Vyve Broadband, 4 International Dr, Ste 330, Rye Brook, NY 10573. Phones: 800-937-1397; 405-395-1131; 405-275-6923. Web Site: http://vyvebroadband.com. Also serves Afton, Bernice, Chelsea, Fairland, Grand Lake, Grove, Langley, Monkey Island, Spavinaw & Strang. ICA: OK0179.
TV Market Ranking: Below 100 (Afton, Chelsea, Fairland); Outside TV Markets (Bernice, Grand Lake, Grove, KETCHUM, Langley, Monkey Island, Spavinaw, Strang). Franchise award date: October 4, 1979. Franchise expiration date: N.A. Began: January 1, 1983.
Channel capacity: N.A. Channels available but not in use: N.A.
Basic Service
Subscribers: 1,276. Commercial subscribers: 380.
Programming (received off-air): KDOR-TV (TBN) Bartlesville; KJRH-TV (NBC) Tulsa; KMYT-TV (getTV, MNT, The Country Network) Tulsa; KOAM-TV (CBS) Pittsburg; KODE-TV (ABC) Joplin; KOED-TV (PBS) Tulsa; KOKI-TV (FOX, MeTV) Tulsa; KOTV-DT (CBS, IND) Tulsa; KQCW-DT (CW, This TV) Muskogee; KRSU-TV (ETV) Claremore; KSNF (NBC) Joplin; KTPX-TV (ION) Okmulgee; KTUL (ABC, Antenna TV, Retro TV) Tulsa; KWHB (COZI TV, IND) Tulsa.
Programming (via satellite): C-SPAN; QVC; WGN America.
Fee: $64.95 installation; $25.00 monthly; $1.96 converter.
Expanded Basic Service 1
Subscribers: 1,373.
Programming (via satellite): A&E; AMC; Animal Planet; Bravo; Cartoon Network; CMT; CNBC; CNN; Comedy Central; Discovery Channel; Disney Channel; E! HD; ESPN; ESPN2; Food Network; Fox News Channel; FOX Sports Southwest; Freeform; FX; Hallmark Channel; HGTV; History; HLN; Lifetime; LMN; MSNBC; MTV; Nickelodeon; Outdoor Channel; Oxygen; RFD-TV; Spike TV; Syfy; TBS; The Weather Channel; TLC; TNT; Travel Channel; TV Land; USA Network; VH1.
Fee: $41.00 monthly.
Digital Basic Service
Subscribers: N.A.
Programming (via satellite): A&E HD; AXS TV; BBC America; Bloomberg Television; Chiller; Cloo; CMT; Destination America; Discovery Kids Channel; Discovery Life Channel; Disney XD; ESPN Classic; ESPN HD; ESPN2 HD; ESPNews; ESPNU; EVINE Live; Flix; Food Network HD; FOX College Sports Central; FOX College Sports Pacific; Fox Sports 1; Fuse; FXM; FYI; Golf Channel; Great American Country; GSN; HD Theater; HGTV HD; History International; IFC; Investigation Discovery; MC; MTV Classic; MTV Hits; MTV2; National Geographic Channel; National Geographic Channel HD; NBCSN; Nick Jr.; Nicktoons; Outdoor Channel 2 HD; OWN: Oprah Winfrey Network; Science Channel; Starz Encore (multiplexed); Sundance TV; TeenNick; The Word Network; Turner Classic Movies; Universal HD; VH1 Soul; WE tv.
Digital Pay Service 1
Pay Units: N.A.
Programming (via satellite): Cinemax (multiplexed); Flix; HBO (multiplexed); HBO HD; Showtime (multiplexed); Showtime HD; Starz (multiplexed); Starz Encore (multiplexed); Starz HD; The Movie Channel (multiplexed).
Fee: $20.00 installation; $9.95 monthly (each).
Video-On-Demand: Yes
Pay-Per-View
iN DEMAND (delivered digitally); Club Jenna (delivered digitally); Spice: Xcess (delivered digitally); Playboy TV (delivered digitally); Fresh (delivered digitally).
Internet Service
Operational: Yes.
Subscribers: 1,073.
Fee: $24.95 installation; $39.95 monthly.
Telephone Service
Digital: Operational
Subscribers: 135.

Cable Systems—Oklahoma

Miles of Plant: 649.0 (coaxial); 140.0 (fiber optic). Homes passed: 6,238.
Chief Executive Officer: Bill Haggarty. Senior Vice President, Financial Planning: Daniel White. Regional Vice President: Andrew Dearth. Vice President, Marketing: Tracy Bass.
Ownership: Vyve Broadband LLC (MSO).

KINGFISHER—Pioneer Telephone Coop. Formerly [OK0800]. This cable system has converted to IPTV, 202 West Broadway, Kingfisher, OK 73750. Phones: 405-375-0404; 888-782-2667. E-mail: website@pldi.net. Web Site: http://www.ptci.com. Also serves Aline, Ames, Apache, Arnett, Blanchard, Bradley, Buffalo, Calumet, Canton, Carmen, Carter, Chester, Cleo Springs, Covington, Crescent, Custer City, Dacoma, Deer Creek, Dibble, Douglas, Dover, Drummond, Fargo, Fay, Fort Supply, Freedom, Gage, Garber, Geary, Gould, Harmon, Helena, Hennessey, Hollis, Hopeston, Hunter, Lahoma, Lamont, Longdale, Loyal, Marshall, May, Meno, Mooreland, Mutual, Nash, Newcastle, Oakwood, Okarche, Okeene, Orlando, Pond Creek, Putnam, Quinlan, Ringwood, Seiling, Sentinel, Sharon, Shattuck, Thomas, Wakita, Watonga & Waynoka. ICA: OK5074.
TV Market Ranking: 39 (Blanchard, Newcastle); Outside TV Markets (Arnett, Buffalo, Gould, Helena, Hennessey, Hollis, KINGFISHER, Mooreland, Okeene, Pond Creek, Seiling, Shattuck, Thomas, Wakita, Watonga, Gage).
Channel capacity: N.A. Channels available but not in use: N.A.
Limited Basic
Subscribers: 8,680.
Fee: $245.00 installation; $62.85 monthly. Includes 70+ channels.
Complete Basic
Subscribers: 7,583.
Fee: $68.95 monthly. Includes 160+ channels.
HD
Subscribers: N.A.
Fee: $11.95 monthly. Includes 65 channels.
Disney Family Movies
Subscribers: N.A.
Fee: $4.99 monthly.
Cinemax
Subscribers: N.A.
Fee: $12.95 monthly. Includes 4 channels.
HBO
Subscribers: N.A.
Fee: $15.95 monthly. Includes 5 channels.
Showtime
Subscribers: N.A.
Fee: $12.95 monthly. Includes 4 channels.
Starz/Encore
Subscribers: N.A.
Fee: $12.95 monthly. Includes 8 channels.
Video-On-Demand: Yes
Internet Service
Operational: Yes.
Fee: $24.95-$99.95 monthly.
Telephone Service
Digital: Operational
Fee: $6.95-$9.95 monthly
General Manager: Richard Ruhl. Vice President, Finance & Administration: Jim Eaton. Vice President, Network Operations: Jerry Kadavy. Vice President, Sales & Service: Jeff Martin.
Ownership: Pioneer Telephone Cooperative Inc.

KINGFISHER—Pioneer Telephone Coop. This cable system has converted to IPTV. Now served by KINGFISHER, OK [OK5074]. ICA: OK0800.

KINGSTON—Formerly served by Allegiance Communications. Now served by Vyve Broadband, KINGSTON (formerly Tishomingo), OK [OK0064]. ICA: OK0343.

KINGSTON—Vyve Broadband, 2804B FM 51 South, Decatur, TX 76234. Phones: 800-937-1397; 580-924-2367; 800-752-4992. Web Site: http://vyvebroadband.com. Also serves Johnston County (portions), Ravia & Tishomingo. ICA: OK0064.
TV Market Ranking: Below 100 (KINGSTON); Outside TV Markets (Ravia, Tishomingo). Franchise award date: N.A. Franchise expiration date: N.A. Began: March 15, 1972.
Channel capacity: N.A. Channels available but not in use: N.A.
Basic Service
Subscribers: 169.
Programming (received off-air): KETA-TV (PBS) Oklahoma City; KTEN (ABC, CW, NBC) Ada; KWTV-DT (CBS) Oklahoma City; KXII (CBS, FOX, MNT) Sherman; WFAA (ABC) Dallas; allband FM.
Programming (via satellite): CW PLUS; Local Cable Weather; QVC; Telemundo.
Fee: $59.99 installation; $25.00 monthly.
Expanded Basic Service 1
Subscribers: N.A.
Programming (via satellite): A&E; AMC; Animal Planet; BET; Bravo; Cartoon Network; CMT; CNBC; CNN; Comedy Central; C-SPAN; Discovery Channel; Disney Channel; E! HD; ESPN; ESPN Classic; ESPN2; ESPNews; EVINE Live; Food Network; Fox News Channel; FOX Sports Southwest; Freeform; FX; Hallmark Channel; HGTV; History; HLN; ION Television; Lifetime; MSNBC; MTV; MyNetworkTV; Nick Jr.; Nickelodeon; Outdoor Channel; Pop; Spike TV; Syfy; TBS; The Weather Channel; TLC; TNT; Travel Channel; Trinity Broadcasting Network (TBN); truTV; TV Land; USA Network; VH1; WE tv.
Digital Basic Service
Subscribers: N.A.
Programming (via satellite): BBC America; Bloomberg Television; Bravo; Church Channel; CMT; Daystar TV Network; Destination America; Discovery Kids Channel; Discovery Life Channel; Disney XD; DMX Music; ESPN Classic; EVINE Live; Fox Sports 1; Fuse; FXM; FYI; Golf Channel; Great American Country; GSN; HGTV; History; History International; IFC; Investigation Discovery; JUCE TV; LMN; MTV Classic; MTV Hits; MTV Jams; MTV2; National Geographic Channel; NBCSN; Nick Jr.; Nicktoons; Outdoor Channel; Ovation; OWN: Oprah Winfrey Network; RFD-TV; Science Channel; TeenNick; The Word Network; Trinity Broadcasting Network (TBN); Turner Classic Movies; VH1 Soul; WE tv.
Digital Pay Service 1
Pay Units: N.A.
Programming (via satellite): Cinemax (multiplexed); Flix; HBO (multiplexed); Showtime (multiplexed); Starz (multiplexed); Starz Encore (multiplexed); The Movie Channel (multiplexed).
Video-On-Demand: No
Pay-Per-View
iN DEMAND (delivered digitally); Hot Choice (delivered digitally); Playboy TV (delivered digitally); Fresh (delivered digitally); Spice; Xcess (delivered digitally); Club Jenna (delivered digitally).
Internet Service
Operational: Yes.
Broadband Service: Net Commander.
Fee: $39.95 installation; $51.95 monthly.

Access the most current data instantly
FREE TRIAL @
www.warren-news.com/factbook.htm

Telephone Service
None
Miles of Plant: 60.0 (coaxial); 10.0 (fiber optic). Homes passed: 1,866.
President & Chief Executive Officer: Jeffrey DeMond. Senior Vice President, Financial Planning: Daniel White. Vice President, Residential Services: Vin Zachariah. Vice President, Marketing: Diane Quennoz.
Ownership: Vyve Broadband LLC (MSO).

KONAWA—Formerly served by Allegiance Communications. No longer in operation. ICA: OK0131.

KREMLIN—Formerly served by Cebridge Connections. No longer in operation. ICA: OK0293.

LAHOMA—Pioneer Telephone Coop. This cable system has converted to IPTV. Now served by KINGFISHER, OK [OK5074]. ICA: OK0382.

LAKE ELLSWORTH—Formerly served by LakeView Cable. No longer in operation. ICA: OK0385.

LAKE LAWTONKA—Southern Plains Cable, PO Box 165, Medicine Park, OK 73557. Phones: 800-218-1856; 580-529-5000. Fax: 580-529-5556. E-mail: office@spcisp.net. Web Site: http://www.spcisp.net. ICA: OK0386.
TV Market Ranking: Below 100 (LAKE LAWTONKA).
Channel capacity: N.A. Channels available but not in use: N.A.
Basic Service
Subscribers: N.A.
Programming (received off-air): KAUT-TV (Escape, MNT) Oklahoma City; KAUZ-TV (CBS, CW) Wichita Falls; KETA-TV (PBS) Oklahoma City; KFDX-TV (NBC) Wichita Falls; KFOR-TV (Antenna TV, NBC) Oklahoma City; KJTL (Bounce TV, FOX) Wichita Falls; KOCB (CW) Oklahoma City; KOCO-TV (ABC, This TV) Oklahoma City; KOKH-TV (FOX, The Country Network, WeatherNation) Oklahoma City; KSWO-TV (ABC, TMO) Lawton; KWTV-DT (CBS) Oklahoma City.
Programming (via satellite): A&E; Cartoon Network; CMT; CNN; C-SPAN; Discovery Channel; Disney Channel; ESPN; Freeform; History; HLN; Spike TV; Syfy; TBS; The Weather Channel; TLC; TNT; Travel Channel; Trinity Broadcasting Network (TBN); Turner Classic Movies; TV Land; USA Network; WGN America.
Fee: $35.00 installation.
Pay Service 1
Pay Units: N.A.
Programming (via satellite): HBO; Showtime (multiplexed).
Fee: $8.50 monthly (Showtime), $10.00 monthly (HBO).
Video-On-Demand: No
Internet Service
Operational: Yes.

Telephone Service
None
President: Dustin Hilliary. Chief Financial Officer: Dean Pennello.
Ownership: Southern Plains Cable (MSO).

LAKE TENKILLER—Formerly served by Cox Communications. No longer in operation. ICA: OK0328.

LAMONT—Formerly served by Blue Sky Cable LLC. No longer in operation. ICA: OK0211.

LANGSTON—Vyve Broadband, 4 International Dr, Ste 330, Rye Brook, NY 10573. Phones: 800-937-1397; 405-275-6923; 405-395-1131. Web Site: http://vyvebroadband.com. Also serves Coyle. ICA: OK0275.
TV Market Ranking: Outside TV Markets (Coyle, LANGSTON). Franchise award date: December 27, 1988. Franchise expiration date: N.A. Began: March 1, 1989.
Channel capacity: N.A. Channels available but not in use: N.A.
Basic Service
Subscribers: N.A. Commercial subscribers: 203.
Programming (received off-air): KAUT-TV (Escape, MNT) Oklahoma City; KETA-TV (PBS) Oklahoma City; KFOR-TV (Antenna TV, NBC) Oklahoma City; KOCB (CW) Oklahoma City; KOCO-TV (ABC, This TV) Oklahoma City; KOKH-TV (FOX, The Country Network, WeatherNation) Oklahoma City; KTBO-TV (TBN) Oklahoma City; KWTV-DT (CBS) Oklahoma City.
Programming (via microwave): KOPX-TV (ION) Oklahoma City.
Programming (via satellite): A&E; AMC; BET; CMT; CNBC; CNN; Comedy Central; C-SPAN; Discovery Channel; Disney Channel; E! HD; ESPN; ESPN2; Fox Sports 1; Freeform; History; Lifetime; MTV; Nickelodeon; Oxygen; QVC; Spike TV; Syfy; TBS; The Weather Channel; TLC; TNT; Travel Channel; USA Network; WGN America.
Fee: $64.95 installation; $54.25 monthly; $1.96 converter.
Video-On-Demand: No
Pay-Per-View
Hot Choice (delivered digitally); Playboy TV (delivered digitally); Fresh (delivered digitally); Shorteez (delivered digitally); iN DEMAND (delivered digitally).
Internet Service
Operational: No.
Telephone Service
None
Miles of Plant: 9.0 (coaxial); None (fiber optic). Homes passed: 349.
Chief Executive Officer: Bill Haggarty. Regional Vice President: Andrew Dearth. Vice President, Marketing: Tracy Bass. Senior Vice President, Financial Planning: Daniel White.
Ownership: Vyve Broadband LLC (MSO).

2017 Edition   D-621

Oklahoma—Cable Systems

LAVERNE—PTCI. This cable system has converted to IPTV. Now served by GUYMON, OK [OK5005]. ICA: OK0132.

LAWTON (village)—Fidelity Communications, 64 North Clark St, Sullivan, MO 63080. Phones: 800-392-8070; 573-468-8081. Fax: 573-468-5440. E-mail: custserv@fidelitycommunications.com. Web Site: http://www.fidelitycommunications.com. Also serves Comanche County. ICA: OK0004.
TV Market Ranking: Below 100 (Comanche County, LAWTON (VILLAGE)). Franchise award date: N.A. Franchise expiration date: N.A. Began: March 20, 1968.
Channel capacity: N.A. Channels available but not in use: N.A.
Basic Service
Subscribers: 12,907.
Programming (received off-air): KAUZ-TV (CBS, CW) Wichita Falls; KETA-TV (PBS) Oklahoma City; KFDX-TV (NBC) Wichita Falls; KFOR-TV (Antenna TV, NBC) Oklahoma City; KJTL (Bounce TV, FOX) Wichita Falls; KSWO-TV (ABC, TMO) Lawton; KWTV-DT (CBS) Oklahoma City.
Programming (via satellite): TBS; The Weather Channel; WGN America.
Fee: $25.00 installation; $28.99 monthly.
Expanded Basic Service 1
Subscribers: N.A.
Programming (via satellite): A&E; AMC; Animal Planet; BET; Boomerang; Cartoon Network; Classic Arts Showcase; CMT; CNBC; CNN; Comedy Central; C-SPAN; C-SPAN 2; Discovery Channel; Disney Channel; Disney XD; DIY Network; E! HD; ESPN; ESPN2; Fox News Channel; Fox Sports 1; FOX Sports Southwest; Freeform; FX; FXM; Golf Channel; GSN; HGTV; History; HLN; INSP; Lifetime; LMN; MTV; MTV2; National Geographic Channel; Nickelodeon; Outdoor Channel; OWN; Oprah Winfrey Network; Pop; QVC; Spike TV; Syfy; Telemundo; TLC; TNT; Travel Channel; Trinity Broadcasting Network (TBN); truTV; TV Land; USA Network; VH1.
Fee: $11.00 installation; $36.05 monthly.
Digital Basic Service
Subscribers: N.A.
Programming (via satellite): AXS TV; DMX Music; ESPN HD; ESPN2 HD; Food Network HD; HD Theater; HGTV HD; National Geographic Channel HD; Universal HD.
Fee: $13.95 monthly.
Digital Pay Service 1
Pay Units: N.A.
Programming (via satellite): Cinemax (multiplexed); Flix; HBO (multiplexed); Playboy TV; Showtime (multiplexed); Starz (multiplexed); Starz Encore (multiplexed); Sundance TV; The Movie Channel (multiplexed).
Fee: $20.00 installation; $10.00 monthly (Cinemax or Starz/Encore), $12.00 monthly (Showtime/TMC), $13.50 monthly (HBO), $14.95 monthly (Playboy).
Video-On-Demand: No
Internet Service
Operational: Yes.
Subscribers: 11,868.
Broadband Service: Lawton Cablevision.
Fee: $35.00 installation; $21.95 monthly.
Telephone Service
Digital: Operational
Subscribers: 7,080.
Miles of Plant: 630.0 (coaxial); 165.0 (fiber optic). Homes passed: 49,915.
President: John T. Davis. Senior Vice President: John Colbert. Marketing Director:

Robert Trottmann. Public Relations Manager: Craig Montgomery.
Ownership: Fidelity Communications Co. (MSO).

LEEDEY—Formerly served by Rapid Cable. No longer in operation. ICA: OK0381.

LINDSAY—Suddenlink Communications, 916 South 4th St, Chickasha, OK 73018. Phones: 800-999-6845; 314-315-9400. Fax: 405-224-3760. Web Site: http://www.suddenlink.com. Also serves Erin Springs. ICA: OK0073.
TV Market Ranking: Below 100 (Erin Springs, LINDSAY). Franchise award date: September 1, 1977. Franchise expiration date: N.A. Began: March 15, 1979.
Channel capacity: 81 (not 2-way capable). Channels available but not in use: N.A.
Basic Service
Subscribers: 293. Commercial subscribers: 42.
Programming (received off-air): KAUT-TV (Escape, MNT) Oklahoma City; KETA-TV (PBS) Oklahoma City; KFOR-TV (Antenna TV, NBC) Oklahoma City; KOCB (CW) Oklahoma City; KOCO-TV (ABC, This TV) Oklahoma City; KOKH-TV (FOX, The Country Network, WeatherNation) Oklahoma City; KOPX-TV (ION) Oklahoma City; KSBI (IND) Oklahoma City; KTBO-TV (TBN) Oklahoma City; KWTV-DT (CBS) Oklahoma City.
Programming (via satellite): A&E; AMC; Animal Planet; Cartoon Network; CMT; CNN; C-SPAN; Discovery Channel; Disney Channel; E! HD; ESPN; ESPN2; Food Network; Fox News Channel; FOX Sports Southwest; Freeform; HGTV; History; HLN; Lifetime; MSNBC; MTV; Nickelodeon; QVC; Spike TV; Syfy; TBS; The Weather Channel; TLC; TNT; Travel Channel; truTV; TV Land; Univision Studios; USA Network; VH1; WGN America.
Fee: $54.95 installation; $33.24 monthly.
Digital Basic Service
Subscribers: N.A.
Programming (via satellite): BBC America; Bloomberg Television; Bravo; Discovery Life Channel; Disney XD; ESPN Classic; ESPNews; EVINE Live; Fox Sports 1; Fuse; FXM; Golf Channel; Great American Country; GSN; IFC; LMN; MC; National Geographic Channel HD; NBCSN; Outdoor Channel; Sundance TV; The Word Network; Turner Classic Movies.
Pay Service 1
Pay Units: N.A.
Programming (via satellite): HBO.
Fee: $12.95 monthly.
Digital Pay Service 1
Pay Units: N.A.
Programming (via satellite): Cinemax (multiplexed); HBO (multiplexed); Showtime (multiplexed); Starz (multiplexed); Starz Encore (multiplexed); The Movie Channel (multiplexed).
Video-On-Demand: No
Pay-Per-View
Shorteez (delivered digitally); Fresh (delivered digitally); Playboy TV (delivered digitally); Hot Choice (delivered digitally); iN DEMAND (delivered digitally).
Internet Service
Operational: Yes.
Broadband Service: Suddenlink High Speed Internet.
Telephone Service
Digital: Operational
Miles of Plant: 29.0 (coaxial); None (fiber optic). Homes passed: 1,849.

Senior Vice President, Corporate Finance: Michael Pflantz. Vice President, Accounting: Sabrina Warr. General Manager: R. C. Lewis. Marketing Manager: Heather Eastwood.
Ownership: Cequel Communications Holdings I LLC (MSO).

LONE WOLF—Formerly served by Cable West. No longer in operation. ICA: OK0377.

LONGDALE—Formerly served by LongView Communications. No longer in operation. ICA: OK0257.

LONGTOWN—Formerly served by Allegiance Communications. No longer in operation. ICA: OK0294.

LUTHER—Formerly served by Allegiance Communications. No longer in operation. ICA: OK0225.

MANGUM—Cable One. Now served by ELK CITY, OK [OK0032]. ICA: OK0079.

MANNFORD—Cim Tel Cable Inc, 103-D Cimarron St, PO Box 160, Mannford, OK 74044. Phones: 918-865-3311; 918-865-3314. Fax: 918-865-7786. E-mail: staff@cimtel.net. Web Site: http://cimtel.net. Also serves Cleveland, Fairfax, Jennings, Osage, Pawnee, Prue & Westport. ICA: OK0296.
TV Market Ranking: 54 (Cleveland, MANNFORD, Osage, Prue, Westport); Outside TV Markets (Fairfax, Jennings, Pawnee). Franchise award date: N.A. Franchise expiration date: N.A. Began: January 1, 1982.
Channel capacity: N.A. Channels available but not in use: N.A.
Basic Service
Subscribers: 2,096.
Programming (received off-air): KDOR-TV (TBN) Bartlesville; KGEB (IND) Tulsa; KJRH-TV (NBC) Tulsa; KMYT-TV (getTV, MNT, The Country Network) Tulsa; KOED-TV (PBS) Tulsa; KOKI-TV (FOX, MeTV) Tulsa; KOTV-DT (CBS, IND) Tulsa; KQCW-DT (CW, This TV) Muskogee; KRSU-TV (ETV) Claremore; KTPX-TV (ION) Okmulgee; KTUL (ABC, Antenna TV, Retro TV) Tulsa; KWHB (COZI TV, IND) Tulsa.
Programming (via satellite): A&E; AMC; CMT; CNN; C-SPAN; Discovery Channel; Disney Channel; ESPN; ESPN2; Fox News Channel; FOX Sports Networks; Freeform; FX; History; HLN; Lifetime; Nickelodeon; Pop; QVC; Spike TV; Syfy; TBS; The Weather Channel; TLC; TNT; Travel Channel; USA Network; VH1; WGN America.
Fee: $30.00 installation; $27.99 monthly.
Digital Basic Service
Subscribers: N.A.
Programming (via satellite): Animal Planet; Bravo; Cartoon Network; CNBC; Comedy Central; C-SPAN 2; DMX Music; E! HD; ESPN Classic; ESPNews; Food Network; Fox Sports 1; Golf Channel; Great American Country; GSN; Hallmark Channel; HGTV; MSNBC; MTV; National Geographic Channel; Outdoor Channel; Oxygen; Turner Classic Movies; TV Land; WE tv.
Fee: $39.99 monthly.
Pay Service 1
Pay Units: 385.
Programming (via satellite): HBO.
Fee: $10.99 monthly.
Pay Service 2
Pay Units: 112.
Programming (via satellite): Cinemax.
Fee: $10.99 monthly.

Digital Pay Service 1
Pay Units: N.A.
Programming (via satellite): Cinemax (multiplexed); Flix; HBO (multiplexed); Showtime (multiplexed); Starz (multiplexed); Starz Encore (multiplexed); Sundance TV; The Movie Channel (multiplexed).
Fee: $10.99 monthly (Cinemax, Encore or HBO), $17.99 (Showtime/Starz/Flix/Sundance/TMC).
Video-On-Demand: No
Internet Service
Operational: Yes, DSL.
Telephone Service
Analog: Operational
General Manager & Chief Technician: Robert Berryman.
Ownership: Cim Tel Cable Inc. (MSO).

MARLAND—Formerly served by Allegiance Communications. No longer in operation. ICA: OK0297.

MARSHALL—Pioneer Telephone Coop. This cable system has converted to IPTV. Now served by KINGFISHER, OK [OK5074]. ICA: OK0298.

MARTHA—Formerly served by CableDirect. No longer in operation. ICA: OK0299.

MAUD—Formerly served by Allegiance Communications. No longer in operation. ICA: OK0178.

McALESTER—Vyve Broadband, 4 International Dr, Ste 330, Rye Brook, NY 10573. Phones: 800-937-1397; 405-395-1131; 405-275-6923. Web Site: http://vyvebroadband.com. Also serves Alderson & Krebs. ICA: OK0019.
TV Market Ranking: Outside TV Markets (Alderson, Krebs, MCALESTER). Franchise award date: August 26, 1961. Franchise expiration date: N.A. Began: February 1, 1963.
Channel capacity: 70 (operating 2-way). Channels available but not in use: N.A.
Basic Service
Subscribers: 2,151.
Programming (received off-air): KJRH-TV (NBC) Tulsa; KMYT-TV (getTV, MNT, The Country Network) Tulsa; KOED-TV (PBS) Tulsa; KOKI-TV (FOX, MeTV) Tulsa; KOTV-DT (CBS, IND) Tulsa; KQCW-DT (CW, This TV) Muskogee; KTEN (ABC, CW, NBC) Ada; KTPX-TV (ION) Okmulgee; KTUL (ABC, Antenna TV, Retro TV) Tulsa; KWHB (COZI TV, IND) Tulsa; 12 FMs.
Programming (via microwave): KFOR-TV (Antenna TV, NBC) Oklahoma City; KWTV-DT (CBS) Oklahoma City.
Programming (via satellite): C-SPAN; C-SPAN 2; Pop; QVC; The Weather Channel; WGN America.
Fee: $64.95 installation; $25.00 monthly; $2.00 converter.
Expanded Basic Service 1
Subscribers: N.A.
Programming (via satellite): A&E; AMC; Animal Planet; BET; Bravo; Cartoon Network; CMT; CNBC; CNN; Comedy Central; Discovery Channel; Disney Channel; E! HD; ESPN; ESPN Classic; ESPN2; ESPNU; EVINE Live; EWTN Global Catholic Network; Food Network; Fox News Channel; FOX Sports Southwest; Freeform; FX; Hallmark Channel; HGTV; History; HLN; Lifetime; LMN; MoviePlex; MSNBC; MTV; National Geographic Channel; NFL Network; Nickelodeon; RFD-TV; Spike TV; Syfy; TBS; TLC; TNT; Travel Channel; Trinity Broad-

Cable Systems—Oklahoma

casting Network (TBN); truTV; TV Land; Univision Studios; USA Network; VH1. Fee: $33.91 monthly.

Digital Basic Service
Subscribers: N.A.
Programming (via satellite): 3ABN; A&E HD; AXS TV; BBC America; Bloomberg Television; Bravo; BYUtv; Church Channel; Cine Mexicano; Cinelatino; Cloo; CMT; CNN en Espanol; Colours; Daystar TV Network; Destination America; Discovery Kids Channel; Discovery Life Channel; Disney XD; DMX Music; ESPN Classic; ESPN Deportes; ESPN HD; ESPN2 HD; ESPNews; EVINE Live; FamilyNet; Flix; Food Network HD; FOX College Sports Central; FOX College Sports Pacific; Fox Deportes; Fox Sports 1; Fuse; FXM; FYI; GEB America; Golf Channel; Great American Country; GSN; HD Theater; HGTV HD; History; History en Espanol; History International; IFC; Investigation Discovery; JUCE TV; La Familia Cosmovision; LMN; MTV Classic; MTV Hits; MTV2; National Geographic Channel; National Geographic Channel HD; NBC Universo; NBCSN; Nick Jr.; Nicktoons; Outdoor Channel; Outdoor Channel 2 HD; OWN: Oprah Winfrey Network; Science Channel; Starz Encore (multiplexed); Sundance TV; Syfy; TeenNick; The Word Network; Tr3s; Trinity Broadcasting Network (TBN); Turner Classic Movies; ULTRA HDPlex; Universal HD; UP; WE tv; World Harvest Television.

Pay Service 1
Pay Units: N.A.
Programming (via satellite): Cinemax; HBO; Showtime; Starz; Starz Encore.
Fee: $6.75 monthly.

Digital Pay Service 1
Pay Units: N.A.
Programming (via satellite): Cinemax (multiplexed); HBO (multiplexed); HBO HD; HBO Latino; Showtime (multiplexed); Showtime HD; Starz (multiplexed); Starz HD; The Movie Channel (multiplexed).

Video-On-Demand: No
Pay-Per-View
Hot Choice (delivered digitally); iN DEMAND (delivered digitally); Fresh (delivered digitally); Playboy TV (delivered digitally); Spice: Xcess (delivered digitally); Club Jenna (delivered digitally).

Internet Service
Operational: Yes. Began: December 31, 2002.
Subscribers: 2,053.
Broadband Service: Cox High Speed Internet.
Fee: $24.95 installation; $39.95 monthly.

Telephone Service
Digital: Operational
Subscribers: 373.
Miles of Plant: 346.0 (coaxial); 72.0 (fiber optic). Homes passed: 12,491.
Chief Executive Officer: Bill Haggarty. Senior Vice President, Financial Planning: Daniel White. Regional Vice President: Andrew Dearth. Vice President, Marketing: Tracy Bass.
Ownership: Vyve Broadband LLC (MSO).

McCURTAIN—Formerly served by Allegiance Communications. No longer in operation. ICA: OK0244.

MEDICINE PARK—Southern Plains Cable, PO Box 165, Medicine Park, OK 73557. Phones: 800-218-1856; 580-529-5000. Fax: 580-529-5556. E-mail: office@spcisp.net. Web Site: http://www.spcisp.net. ICA: OK0116.
TV Market Ranking: Below 100 (MEDICINE PARK). Franchise award date: N.A. Franchise expiration date: N.A. Began: September 1, 1977.
Channel capacity: N.A. Channels available but not in use: N.A.

Basic Service
Subscribers: N.A.
Programming (received off-air): KAUT-TV (Escape, MNT) Oklahoma City; KAUZ-TV (CBS, CW) Wichita Falls; KETA-TV (PBS) Oklahoma City; KFDX-TV (NBC) Wichita Falls; KFOR-TV (Antenna TV, NBC) Oklahoma City; KJTL (Bounce TV, FOX) Wichita Falls; KOCB (CW) Oklahoma City; KOKH-TV (FOX, The Country Network, WeatherNation) Oklahoma City; KSWO-TV (ABC, TMO) Lawton; KWTV-DT (CBS) Oklahoma City; allband FM.
Programming (via satellite): A&E; CMT; CNN; C-SPAN; Discovery Channel; Disney Channel; ESPN; Freeform; History; HLN; Nickelodeon; Spike TV; Syfy; TBS; The Weather Channel; TLC; TNT; Travel Channel; Trinity Broadcasting Network (TBN); Turner Classic Movies; TV Land; USA Network; WGN America.
Fee: $35.00 installation.

Pay Service 1
Pay Units: N.A.
Programming (via satellite): HBO; Showtime (multiplexed).
Fee: $9.95 monthly (Showtime), $10.95 monthly (HBO).

Video-On-Demand: No
Internet Service
Operational: No.
Telephone Service
None
Miles of Plant: 15.0 (coaxial); None (fiber optic). Homes passed: 850.
President: Dustin Hilliary. Chief Financial Officer: Dean Pennello.
Ownership: Southern Plains Cable (MSO).

MENO—Formerly served by CableDirect. No longer in operation. ICA: OK0255.

MIAMI—Cable One, 2600 Davis Blvd, Joplin, MO 64804. Phones: 918-542-1811 (Customer service); 918-542-1568. E-mail: mslyman@cableone.net. Web Site: http://www.cableone.net. Also serves Commerce, North Miami & Ottawa County. ICA: OK0021.
TV Market Ranking: Below 100 (Commerce, MIAMI, North Miami, Ottawa County (portions)); Outside TV Markets (Ottawa County (portions)). Franchise award date: March 15, 1965. Franchise expiration date: N.A. Began: July 5, 1968.
Channel capacity: N.A. Channels available but not in use: N.A.

Basic Service
Subscribers: 2,325.
Programming (received off-air): KFJX (FOX) Pittsburg; KJRH-TV (NBC) Tulsa; KODE-TV (ABC) Joplin; KOED-TV (PBS) Tulsa; KOTV-DT (CBS, IND) Tulsa; KOZJ (PBS) Joplin; KSNF (NBC) Joplin; KTUL (ABC, Antenna TV, Retro TV) Tulsa; 10 FMs.
Programming (via satellite): C-SPAN; C-SPAN 2; CW PLUS; EWTN Global Catholic Network; Pop; QVC; TBS; Trinity Broadcasting Network (TBN); WGN America.
Fee: $90.00 installation; $35.00 monthly.

Expanded Basic Service 1
Subscribers: N.A.
Programming (via satellite): A&E; AMC; Animal Planet; Cartoon Network; CMT; CNBC; CNN; Comedy Central; Discovery Channel; Disney Channel; ESPN; ESPN2; Food Network; Fox News Channel; FOX Sports Southwest; Freeform; FX; HGTV; History;
HLN; Lifetime; MSNBC; MTV; Nickelodeon; Spike TV; Syfy; The Weather Channel; TLC; TNT; Turner Classic Movies; TV Land; USA Network; VH1.
Fee: $42.50 monthly.

Digital Basic Service
Subscribers: N.A.
Programming (via satellite): 3ABN; Boomerang; BYUtv; Discovery Digital Networks; Disney XD; DMX Music; ESPN Classic; ESPNews; FamilyNet; FOX College Sports Central; FOX College Sports Pacific; Fox Sports 1; Fox Sports 2; FXM; FYI; Golf Channel; Great American Country; Hallmark Channel; History International; HITS (Headend In The Sky); INSP; National Geographic Channel; Outdoor Channel; TNT HD; Trinity Broadcasting Network (TBN); truTV; TVG Network; Universal HD.

Digital Pay Service 1
Pay Units: N.A.
Programming (via satellite): Cinemax (multiplexed); Flix; HBO (multiplexed); Showtime (multiplexed); Showtime HD; Starz (multiplexed); Starz Encore (multiplexed); Sundance TV; The Movie Channel (multiplexed); The Movie Channel HD.
Fee: $15.00 monthly (each).

Video-On-Demand: No
Pay-Per-View
iN DEMAND (delivered digitally); Pleasure (delivered digitally); SexSee (delivered digitally); Juicy (delivered digitally); VaVoom (delivered digitally).

Internet Service
Operational: Yes. Began: November 1, 2001.
Broadband Service: CableONE.net.
Fee: $75.00 installation; $43.00 monthly; $5.00 modem lease.

Telephone Service
Digital: Operational
Fee: $39.95 monthly
Miles of Plant: 156.0 (coaxial); None (fiber optic). Homes passed: 8,265.
Vice President: Patrick A. Dolohanty. General Manager: Mike Slyman. Chief Technician: Danny Douthit.
Ownership: Cable ONE Inc. (MSO).

MILBURN—Formerly served by Allegiance Communications. No longer in operation. ICA: OK0253.

MOORELAND—Pioneer Telephone Coop. This cable system has converted to IPTV. Now served by KINGFISHER, OK [OK5074]. ICA: OK0392.

MORRIS (town)—Formerly served by Allegiance Communications. No longer in operation. ICA: OK0152.

MORRISON—Formerly served by Allegiance Communications. No longer in operation. ICA: OK0357.

MOUNDS—Vyve Broadband, 4 International Dr, Ste 330, Rye Brook, NY 10573. Phones: 800-937-1397; 405-395-1131; 405-275-6923. Web Site: http://vyvebroadband.com. ICA: OK0175.
TV Market Ranking: 54 (MOUNDS). Franchise award date: February 1, 1980. Franchise expiration date: N.A. Began: January 1, 1983.
Channel capacity: N.A. Channels available but not in use: N.A.

Basic Service
Subscribers: 29.
Programming (received off-air): KGEB (IND) Tulsa; KJRH-TV (NBC) Tulsa; KMYT-TV (getTV, MNT, The Country Network) Tulsa; KOED-TV (PBS) Tulsa; KOKI-TV (FOX, MeTV) Tulsa; KOTV-DT (CBS, IND) Tulsa; KQCW-DT (CW, This TV) Muskogee; KTPX-TV (ION) Okmulgee; KTUL (ABC, Antenna TV, Retro TV) Tulsa; KWHB (COZI TV, IND) Tulsa.
Programming (via satellite): A&E; AMC; Animal Planet; BET; Cartoon Network; CMT; CNBC; CNN; C-SPAN; Discovery Channel; Disney Channel; E! HD; ESPN; ESPN2; Food Network; Fox News Channel; Fox Sports 1; Freeform; FX; History; HLN; Lifetime; MTV; Nickelodeon; Oxygen; QVC; Spike TV; Syfy; TBS; The Weather Channel; TLC; TNT; Travel Channel; USA Network; VH1; WGN America.
Fee: $64.95 installation; $64.75 monthly.

Digital Basic Service
Subscribers: N.A.
Programming (via satellite): BBC America; Bloomberg Television; Bravo; Chiller; Cloo; CMT; Destination America; Discovery Kids Channel; Discovery Life Channel; Disney XD; DMX Music; ESPN Classic; EVINE Live; Flix; FOX College Sports Central; FOX College Sports Pacific; Fuse; FXM; FYI; Golf Channel; Great American Country; GSN; HGTV; History International; IFC; Investigation Discovery; LMN; MTV Classic; MTV Hits; MTV2; National Geographic Channel; NBCSN; Nick Jr.; Nicktoons; Outdoor Channel; OWN: Oprah Winfrey Network; RFD-TV; Science Channel; Starz Encore (multiplexed); Sundance TV; TeenNick; Trinity Broadcasting Network (TBN); Turner Classic Movies; VH1 Soul; WE tv.

Pay Service 1
Pay Units: N.A.
Programming (via satellite): Cinemax; HBO.
Fee: $20.00 installation; $10.00 monthly (each).

Digital Pay Service 1
Pay Units: N.A.
Programming (via satellite): Cinemax (multiplexed); HBO (multiplexed); Showtime (multiplexed); Starz (multiplexed); The Movie Channel (multiplexed).

Video-On-Demand: No
Pay-Per-View
iN DEMAND (delivered digitally); Spice: Xcess (delivered digitally); Playboy TV (delivered digitally); Fresh (delivered digitally); Club Jenna (delivered digitally).

Internet Service
Operational: No.
Telephone Service
None
Miles of Plant: 7.0 (coaxial); None (fiber optic). Homes passed: 444.
Chief Executive Officer: Bill Haggarty. Senior Vice President, Financial Planning: Daniel

Oklahoma—Cable Systems

White. Regional Vice President: Andrew Dearth. Vice President, Marketing: Tracy Bass.
Ownership: Vyve Broadband LLC (MSO).

MOUNTAIN PARK—Vyve Broadband, 1819 Airport Dr, Shawnee, OK 74804. Phone: 855-367-8983. Web Site: http://vyvebroadband.com. Also serves Snyder. ICA: OK0300.
TV Market Ranking: Below 100 (MOUNTAIN PARK, Snyder).
Channel capacity: N.A. Channels available but not in use: N.A.
Basic Service
Subscribers: N.A.
Programming (received off-air): KAUZ-TV (CBS, CW) Wichita Falls; KETA-TV (PBS) Oklahoma City; KFDX-TV (NBC) Wichita Falls; KFOR-TV (Antenna TV, NBC) Oklahoma City; KJBO-LP (MNT) Wichita Falls; KJTL (Bounce TV, FOX) Wichita Falls; KOCO-TV (ABC, This TV) Oklahoma City; KSWO-TV (ABC, TMO) Lawton.
Programming (via satellite): INSP; QVC; Trinity Broadcasting Network (TBN).
Fee: $50.00 installation.
Expanded Basic Service 1
Subscribers: N.A.
Programming (via satellite): A&E; AMC; Animal Planet; BET; Cartoon Network; CNN; Comedy Central; C-SPAN; Discovery Channel; Disney Channel; Disney XD; E! HD; ESPN; ESPN2; FamilyNet; Food Network; Fox News Channel; Freeform; Great American Country; HGTV; History; HLN; Lifetime; MSNBC; Outdoor Channel; Syfy; TBS; Telemundo; The Weather Channel; TLC; TNT; Travel Channel; USA Network; WGN America.
Fee: $21.97 monthly.
Digital Basic Service
Subscribers: N.A.
Programming (via satellite): BBC America; Bloomberg Television; Discovery Life Channel; Disney XD; DMX Music; ESPN Classic; ESPNews; Fox Sports 1; FXM; FYI; Golf Channel; GSN; History International; LMN; Starz Encore (multiplexed); Turner Classic Movies.
Fee: $17.00 monthly.
Pay Service 1
Pay Units: N.A.
Programming (via satellite): Cinemax; HBO; Showtime; The Movie Channel.
Fee: $8.95 monthly (TMC), $10.95 monthly (Showtime), $12.95 monthly (HBO).
Digital Pay Service 1
Pay Units: N.A.
Programming (via satellite): Cinemax (multiplexed); Flix; HBO (multiplexed); Showtime (multiplexed); Starz (multiplexed); The Movie Channel (multiplexed).
Fee: $8.95 monthly (TMC), $10.95 monthly (Cinemax or Showtime), $12.95 monthly (HBO).
Video-On-Demand: No
Pay-Per-View
iN DEMAND (delivered digitally); Hot Choice (delivered digitally); Playboy TV (delivered digitally); Fresh (delivered digitally); Shorteez (delivered digitally).
Internet Service
Operational: Yes.
Broadband Service: In-house.
Fee: $29.95 monthly.
Telephone Service
Digital: Planned

Miles of Plant: 22.0 (coaxial); None (fiber optic). Homes passed: 951.
President & Chief Operating Officer: Jeffrey DeMond. Executive Vice President & Chief Financial Officer: Andrew Kober. Senior Vice President, General Counsel & Secretary: Marie Censoplano. Senior Vice President, Engineering & Chief Technology Officer: Dennis Davies. Senior Vice President, Marketing & Customer Experience: Diane Quennoz. Senior Vice President, Residential Services: Vin Zachariah. Vice President, Network Planning: Alex Harris.
Ownership: Vyve Broadband LLC (MSO).

MOUNTAIN VIEW—Mountain View Cable TV, 314 West Main St, PO Box 237, Mountain View, OK 73062. Phone: 800-980-7912. Fax: 580-347-2143. ICA: OK0166.
TV Market Ranking: Outside TV Markets (MOUNTAIN VIEW). Franchise award date: March 19, 1969. Franchise expiration date: N.A. Began: May 1, 1969.
Channel capacity: N.A. Channels available but not in use: N.A.
Basic Service
Subscribers: N.A.
Programming (received off-air): KAUT-TV (Escape, MNT) Oklahoma City; KETA-TV (PBS) Oklahoma City; KFOR-TV (Antenna TV, NBC) Oklahoma City; KOCB (CW) Oklahoma City; KOCO-TV (ABC, This TV) Oklahoma City; KOKH-TV (FOX, The Country Network, WeatherNation) Oklahoma City; KSWO-TV (ABC, TMO) Lawton; KWTV-DT (CBS) Oklahoma City; 20 FMs.
Programming (via satellite): ESPN; TBS.
Fee: $20.00 installation.
Pay Service 1
Pay Units: N.A.
Programming (via satellite): Cinemax; HBO.
Fee: $15.00 installation; $9.00 monthly (each).
Video-On-Demand: No
Internet Service
Operational: No.
Telephone Service
None
Miles of Plant: 9.0 (coaxial); None (fiber optic). Homes passed: 448.
General Manager & Chief Technician: Mickey Davis.
Ownership: Mickey Davis.

MUSKOGEE—Suddenlink Communications, 2510 Elliott St, Muskogee, OK 74403. Phones: 314-315-9400; 918-687-7511 (Customer service). Fax: 918-687-3291. Web Site: http://www.suddenlink.com. Also serves Muskogee County, Wagoner & Wagoner County (eastern portion). ICA: OK0009.
TV Market Ranking: 54 (Muskogee County (portions), Wagoner, Wagoner County (eastern portion)); Below 100 (MUSKOGEE, Muskogee County (portions), Wagoner County (eastern portion)). Franchise award date: January 1, 1969. Franchise expiration date: N.A. Began: July 1, 1971.
Channel capacity: N.A. Channels available but not in use: N.A.
Basic Service
Subscribers: 7,649. Commercial subscribers: 660.
Programming (received off-air): KDOR-TV (TBN) Bartlesville; KJRH-TV (NBC) Tulsa; KMYT-TV (getTV, MNT, The Country Network) Tulsa; KOED-TV (PBS) Tulsa; KOKI-TV (FOX, MeTV) Tulsa; KOTV-DT (CBS, IND) Tulsa; KQCW-DT (CW, This TV) Muskogee; KRSU-TV (ETV) Claremore; KTPX-TV (ION) Okmulgee; KTUL (ABC, Antenna TV, Retro TV) Tulsa; KWHB (COZI TV, IND) Tulsa.
Programming (via satellite): C-SPAN 2; Discovery Channel; FX; Pop; TBS; WGN America.
Fee: $49.95 installation; $34.24 monthly; $.74 converter.
Expanded Basic Service 1
Subscribers: N.A.
Programming (via satellite): A&E; AMC; Animal Planet; BET; Bravo; Cartoon Network; CMT; CNBC; CNN; Comedy Central; C-SPAN; Disney Channel; E! HD; ESPN; ESPN2; EWTN Global Catholic Network; Food Network; Fox News Channel; FOX Sports Southwest; Freeform; HGTV; History; HLN; Lifetime; MoviePlex; MSNBC; MTV; MTV2; Nickelodeon; QVC; Spike TV; Syfy; The Weather Channel; TLC; TNT; Travel Channel; truTV; TV Land; Univision Studios; USA Network; VH1.
Digital Basic Service
Subscribers: N.A.
Programming (via satellite): BBC America; Bloomberg Television; Discovery Digital Networks; Disney XD; ESPN Classic; ESPNews; Fox Sports 1; Fuse; FYI; Golf Channel; GSN; History International; IFC; LMN; MC; NBCSN; Nick Jr.; Nicktoons; TeenNick; Turner Classic Movies.
Pay Service 1
Pay Units: N.A.
Programming (via satellite): Cinemax (multiplexed); HBO; Showtime; Starz; Starz Encore.
Fee: $12.59 monthly (Cinemax, HBO or Showtime).
Digital Pay Service 1
Pay Units: N.A.
Programming (via satellite): Cinemax (multiplexed); HBO (multiplexed); Showtime (multiplexed); Starz (multiplexed); The Movie Channel (multiplexed).
Video-On-Demand: No
Pay-Per-View
ESPN Now (delivered digitally); Playboy TV (delivered digitally); Shorteez (delivered digitally); Fresh (delivered digitally); Hot Choice (delivered digitally); iN DEMAND (delivered digitally).
Internet Service
Operational: Yes. Began: December 1, 2002.
Subscribers: 7,870.
Broadband Service: Suddenlink High Speed Internet.
Fee: $45.95 installation; $24.95 monthly.
Telephone Service
Digital: Operational
Subscribers: 3,838.
Fee: $49.95 monthly
Miles of Plant: 670.0 (coaxial); 113.0 (fiber optic). Homes passed: 36,739.
Senior Vice President, Corporate Finance: Michael Pflantz. Vice President, Accounting: Sabrina Warr. General Manager: Billy Jewell. Marketing Manager: Heather Eastwood.
Ownership: Cequel Communications Holdings I LLC (MSO).

NASH—Pioneer Telephone Coop. This cable system has converted to IPTV. Now served by KINGFISHER, OK [OK5074]. ICA: OK0301.

NEWCASTLE—Pioneer Telephone Coop. This cable system has converted to IPTV. Now served by KINGFISHER, OK [OK5074]. ICA: OK0302.

NEWKIRK—Vyve Broadband, 4 International Dr, Ste 330, Rye Brook, NY 10573. Phones: 800-937-1397; 405-395-1131; 405-275-6923. Web Site: http://vyvebroadband.com. ICA: OK0303.
TV Market Ranking: Outside TV Markets (NEWKIRK).
Channel capacity: N.A. Channels available but not in use: N.A.
Basic Service
Subscribers: 69. Commercial subscribers: 17.
Programming (received off-air): KETA-TV (PBS) Oklahoma City; KFOR-TV (Antenna TV, NBC) Oklahoma City; KOCO-TV (ABC, This TV) Oklahoma City; KOTV-DT (CBS, IND) Tulsa; KSAS-TV (Antenna TV, FOX) Wichita; KSNW (NBC) Wichita; KWTV-DT (CBS) Oklahoma City.
Programming (via satellite): CNN; C-SPAN; C-SPAN 2; CW PLUS; EVINE Live; Pop; QVC; The Weather Channel; Trinity Broadcasting Network (TBN); WGN America.
Fee: $64.95 installation; $25.00 monthly.
Digital Basic Service
Subscribers: N.A.
Programming (via satellite): 52MX; BBC America; Bloomberg Television; Bravo; Cine Mexicano; Cinelatino; Cloo; CMT; CNN en Espanol; Destination America; Discovery Kids Channel; Discovery Life Channel; Disney XD; DMX Music; ESPN Classic; ESPN2; ESPNews; EVINE Live; Flix; FOX College Sports Central; FOX College Sports Pacific; Fox Deportes; Fox Sports 1; Fuse; FXM; FYI; Golf Channel; Great American Country; GSN; HGTV; History; History en Espanol; History International; IFC; Investigation Discovery; LMN; MTV Classic; MTV Hits; MTV2; National Geographic Channel; NBCSN; Nick Jr.; Nicktoons; Outdoor Channel; Ovation; OWN: Oprah Winfrey Network; Science Channel; Starz Encore (multiplexed); Sundance TV; Syfy; TeenNick; The Word Network; Toon Disney en Espanol; Tr3s; Trinity Broadcasting Network (TBN); Turner Classic Movies; VH1 Soul; WE tv.
Pay Service 1
Pay Units: N.A.
Programming (via satellite): HBO; Showtime; Starz Encore.
Fee: $1.70 monthly.
Digital Pay Service 1
Pay Units: N.A.
Programming (via satellite): Cinemax (multiplexed); HBO (multiplexed); HBO Latino; Showtime (multiplexed); Starz (multiplexed); The Movie Channel (multiplexed).
Pay-Per-View
iN DEMAND (delivered digitally); Hot Choice (delivered digitally); Playboy TV (delivered digitally); Fresh (delivered digitally); Shorteez (delivered digitally).
Internet Service
Operational: Yes.
Fee: $24.95 installation; $39.95 monthly.
Telephone Service
Digital: Operational
Miles of Plant: 19.0 (coaxial); None (fiber optic).
Chief Executive Officer: Bill Haggarty. Senior Vice President, Financial Planning: Daniel White. Regional Vice President: Andrew Dearth. Vice President, Marketing: Tracy Bass.
Ownership: Vyve Broadband LLC (MSO).

NINNEKAH—Formerly served by Cable West. No longer in operation. ICA: OK0163.

NOBLE—Formerly served by Cebridge Connections. Now served by Suddenlink Communications, PURCELL, OK [OK0048]. ICA: OK0084.

Cable Systems—Oklahoma

NOWATA—Cable One. Now served by BARTLESVILLE, OK [OK0010]. ICA: OK0075.

OCHELATA—Community Cable & Broadband, 1550 West Rogers Blvd, PO Box 307, Skiatook, OK 74070-0307. Phones: 888-394-4772; 918-396-3019. Fax: 918-396-2081. E-mail: info@communitycablevision.com. Web Site: http://www.communitycablebroadband.com. ICA: OK0148.
TV Market Ranking: 54 (OCHELATA). Franchise award date: October 1, 1983. Franchise expiration date: N.A. Began: December 31, 1983.
Channel capacity: N.A. Channels available but not in use: N.A.
Basic Service
Subscribers: N.A.
Programming (received off-air): KDOR-TV (TBN) Bartlesville; KJRH-TV (NBC) Tulsa; KOED-TV (PBS) Tulsa; KOKI-TV (FOX, MeTV) Tulsa; KOTV-DT (CBS, IND) Tulsa; KQCW-DT (CW, This TV) Muskogee; KRSU-TV (ETV) Claremore; KTPX-TV (ION) Okmulgee; KTUL (ABC, Antenna TV, Retro TV) Tulsa; KWHB (COZI TV, IND) Tulsa.
Programming (via satellite): A&E; Cartoon Network; CMT; CNN; C-SPAN; Discovery Channel; Disney Channel; ESPN; ESPN2; Freeform; HGTV; History; HLN; MTV; Nickelodeon; QVC; Spike TV; Syfy; TBS; The Weather Channel; TLC; TNT; Turner Classic Movies; USA Network; WGN America.
Programming (via translator): KTFO-CD (UniMas) Austin.
Fee: $29.95 installation.
Video-On-Demand: No
Internet Service
Operational: Yes.
Fee: $44.95 monthly.
Telephone Service
None
Miles of Plant: 21.0 (coaxial); None (fiber optic). Homes passed: 531.
President & General Manager: Dennis Soule. Chief Technical Officer: Chris Tuttle.
Ownership: Community Cable & Broadband Inc. (MSO).

OILTON—Community Cable & Broadband. Now served by YALE, OK [OK0141]. Phone: 888-394-4772. ICA: OK0162.

OKARCHE—Pioneer Telephone Coop. This cable system has converted to IPTV. Now served by KINGFISHER, OK [OK5074]. ICA: OK0176.

OKAY—BCI Broadband. Now served by FORT GIBSON, OK [OK0090]. ICA: OK0161.

OKEENE—Pioneer Telephone Coop. This cable system has converted to IPTV. Now served by KINGFISHER, OK [OK5074]. ICA: OK0146.

OKEMAH—Vyve Broadband, 4 International Dr, Ste 330, Rye Brook, NY 10573. Phones: 800-937-1397; 405-275-6923; 405-395-1131. Web Site: http://vyvebroadband.com. ICA: OK0111.
TV Market Ranking: Below 100 (OKEMAH). Franchise award date: N.A. Franchise expiration date: N.A. Began: February 11, 1979.
Channel capacity: N.A. Channels available but not in use: N.A.
Basic Service
Subscribers: 98. Commercial subscribers: 28.
Programming (received off-air): KETA-TV (PBS) Oklahoma City; KFOR-TV (Antenna TV, NBC) Oklahoma City; KJRH-TV (NBC) Tulsa; KMYT-TV (getTV, MNT, The Country Network) Tulsa; KOCB (CW) Oklahoma City; KOKI-TV (FOX, MeTV) Tulsa; KOTV-DT (CBS, IND) Tulsa; KTBO-TV (TBN) Oklahoma City; KTPX-TV (ION) Okmulgee; KTUL (ABC, Antenna TV, Retro TV) Tulsa; KWTV-DT (CBS) Oklahoma City.
Programming (via satellite): CNBC; CNN; C-SPAN; Fox News Channel; FOX Sports Southwest; QVC; The Weather Channel; TLC.
Fee: $64.95 installation; $25.00 monthly.
Expanded Basic Service 1
Subscribers: 94.
Programming (via satellite): A&E; AMC; Animal Planet; Cartoon Network; CMT; Comedy Central; Discovery Channel; Disney Channel; ESPN; ESPN2; Food Network; Freeform; FX; Hallmark Channel; History; Lifetime; MTV; NFL Network; Nickelodeon; Spike TV; TBS; TNT; TV Land; USA Network.
Fee: $35.76 monthly.
Digital Basic Service
Subscribers: N.A.
Programming (via satellite): BBC America; Bloomberg Television; Bravo; Cine Mexicano; Cinelatino; Cloo; CMT; CNN en Espanol; Destination America; Discovery Kids Channel; Discovery Life Channel; Disney XD; DMX Music; ESPN Classic; ESPN Deportes; ESPN2; ESPNews; EVINE Live; Flix; FOX College Sports Central; FOX College Sports Pacific; Fox Deportes; Fox Sports 1; Fuse; FXM; FYI; Golf Channel; Great American Country; GSN; HGTV; History; History en Espanol; History International; IFC; Investigation Discovery; LMN; MTV Classic; MTV Hits; MTV2; National Geographic Channel; NBC Universo; NBCSN; Nick Jr.; Nicktoons; Outdoor Channel; OWN; Oprah Winfrey Network; Science Channel; Starz Encore (multiplexed); Sundance TV; Syfy; TeenNick; The Word Network; Tr3s; Trinity Broadcasting Network (TBN); Turner Classic Movies; UP; VH1 Soul; ViendoMovies; WE tv.
Pay Service 1
Pay Units: N.A.
Programming (via satellite): Showtime; Starz; Starz Encore.
Digital Pay Service 1
Pay Units: N.A.
Programming (via satellite): Cinemax (multiplexed); HBO (multiplexed); HBO Latino; Showtime (multiplexed); Starz (multiplexed); The Movie Channel (multiplexed).
Pay-Per-View
iN DEMAND (delivered digitally); Hot Choice (delivered digitally); Fresh (delivered digitally); Playboy TV (delivered digitally); Spice: Xcess (delivered digitally); Club Jenna (delivered digitally).
Internet Service
Operational: Yes.
Fee: $24.95 installation; $39.95 monthly.
Telephone Service
Digital: Operational
Miles of Plant: 22.0 (coaxial); None (fiber optic). Homes passed: 910.
Chief Executive Officer: Bill Haggarty. Regional Vice President: Andrew Dearth. Vice President, Marketing: Tracy Bass. Senior Vice President, Financial Planning: Daniel White.
Ownership: Vyve Broadband LLC (MSO).

OKLAHOMA CITY—Cox Communications, 6205 Peachtree Dunwoody Rd, 12th Floor, Atlanta, GA 30328. Phone: 404-269-6590. Web Site: http://www.cox.com. Also serves Bethany, Canadian County (portions), Choctaw, Cleveland County (portions), Del City, Edmond, El Reno, Forest Park, Guthrie, Harrah, Lake Aluma, Logan County (portions), Midwest City, Moore, Mustang, Nichols Hills, Norman, Spencer, The Village, Valley Brook, Warr Acres & Yukon. ICA: OK0002.
TV Market Ranking: 32 (Logan County (portions)); 39 (Bethany, Canadian County (portions), Choctaw, Cleveland County (portions), Del City, Edmond, El Reno, Forest Park, Guthrie, Harrah, Lake Aluma, Midwest City, Moore, Mustang, Nichols Hills, Norman, OKLAHOMA CITY, Spencer, The Village, Valley Brook, Warr Acres, Yukon). Franchise award date: May 4, 1980. Franchise expiration date: N.A. Began: May 4, 1980.
Channel capacity: 60 (operating 2-way). Channels available but not in use: N.A.
Basic Service
Subscribers: 196,231.
Programming (received off-air): KAUT-TV (Escape, MNT) Oklahoma City; KETA-TV (PBS) Oklahoma City; KFOR-TV (Antenna TV, NBC) Oklahoma City; KOCB (CW) Oklahoma City; KOCO-TV (ABC, This TV) Oklahoma City; KOKH-TV (FOX, The Country Network, WeatherNation) Oklahoma City; KOPX-TV (ION) Oklahoma City; KSBI (IND) Oklahoma City; KTBO-TV (TBN) Oklahoma City; KWTV-DT (CBS) Oklahoma City.
Programming (via satellite): C-SPAN; Pop; TBS; WGN America.
Fee: $21.60 installation; $21.99 monthly.
Expanded Basic Service 1
Subscribers: N.A.
Programming (via satellite): A&E; AMC; Animal Planet; BET; Bravo; Cartoon Network; CMT; CNBC; CNN; Comedy Central; Discovery Channel; Disney Channel; E! HD; ESPN; ESPN2; Food Network; Fox News Channel; Fox Sports 1; FOX Sports Southwest; Freeform; FX; Golf Channel; HGTV; History; HLN; INSP; Lifetime; MSNBC; MTV; NBCSN; Nickelodeon; QVC; Spike TV; Syfy; The Weather Channel; TLC; TNT; Travel Channel; truTV; Turner Classic Movies; TV Land; USA Network; VH1.
Fee: $21.60 installation; $25.79 monthly.
Digital Basic Service
Subscribers: N.A.
Programming (via satellite): BBC America; Bloomberg Television; Discovery Digital Networks; Disney XD; ESPN Classic; EWTN Global Catholic Network; GSN; IFC; Nick Jr.; Starz Encore; Sundance TV; Weatherscan.
Fee: $16.00 monthly.
Pay Service 1
Pay Units: N.A.
Programming (via satellite): Cinemax; HBO (multiplexed); Showtime (multiplexed); The Movie Channel.
Fee: $11.00 monthly (each).
Digital Pay Service 1
Pay Units: N.A.
Programming (via satellite): Cinemax (multiplexed); HBO (multiplexed); HITS (Headend In The Sky); Showtime (multiplexed); Starz (multiplexed); The Movie Channel (multiplexed).
Fee: $6.95 monthly (Canales N), $12.00 monthly (Cinemax/HBO), $16.00 monthly (Showtime/Starz/TMC).
Video-On-Demand: Yes
Pay-Per-View
ESPN Now (delivered digitally); Hot Choice; iN DEMAND; iN DEMAND (delivered digitally).
Internet Service
Operational: Yes.
Subscribers: 210,698.
Broadband Service: Cox High Speed Internet.
Fee: $149.00 installation; $54.95 monthly; $199.95 modem purchase.
Telephone Service
Digital: Operational
Subscribers: 148,764.
Fee: $29.95 monthly
Miles of Plant: 9,370.0 (coaxial); 2,429.0 (fiber optic). Homes passed: 503,411.
President & General Manager: David Bialis. Vice President, Operations: John Bowen. Vice President, Marketing: Mollie Andrews. Vice President, Tax: Mary Vickers.
Ownership: Cox Communications Inc. (MSO).

OKLAHOMA CITY—Formerly served by WANTV of OKC. No longer in operation. ICA: OK0333.

OKMULGEE—Suddenlink Communications, 2510 Elliott St, Muskogee, OK 74403. Phone: 314-315-9400. Fax: 918-687-3291. Web Site: http://www.suddenlink.com. Also serves Okmulgee County (central portion). ICA: OK0026.
TV Market Ranking: 54 (OKMULGEE, Okmulgee County (central portion) (portions)); Below 100 (Okmulgee County (central portion) (portions)). Franchise award date: January 1, 1977. Franchise expiration date: N.A. Began: January 1, 1974.
Channel capacity: N.A. Channels available but not in use: N.A.
Basic Service
Subscribers: 1,398. Commercial subscribers: 309.
Programming (received off-air): KDOR-TV (TBN) Bartlesville; KGEB (IND) Tulsa; KJRH-TV (NBC) Tulsa; KMYT-TV (getTV, MNT, The Country Network) Tulsa; KOED-TV (PBS) Tulsa; KOKI-TV (FOX, MeTV) Tulsa; KOTV-DT (CBS, IND) Tulsa; KQCW-DT (CW, This TV) Muskogee; KTPX-TV (ION) Okmulgee; KTUL (ABC, Antenna TV, Retro TV) Tulsa; KWHB (COZI TV, IND) Tulsa; allband FM.
Programming (via satellite): C-SPAN; C-SPAN 2; EWTN Global Catholic Network; Pop; QVC; The Weather Channel; WGN America.
Fee: $40.00 installation; $33.24 monthly; $.98 converter.
Expanded Basic Service 1
Subscribers: N.A.
Programming (via satellite): A&E; AMC; Animal Planet; BET; Bravo; Cartoon Network; CMT; CNBC; CNN; Comedy Central; Discovery Channel; Disney Channel; E! HD; ESPN; ESPN2; Food Network; Fox News Channel; FOX Sports Southwest; Freeform; FX; HGTV; History; HLN; Lifetime; MSNBC; MTV; MTV2; Nickelodeon; Spike TV; Syfy; TBS; TLC; TNT; Travel Channel; truTV; TV Land; USA Network; VH1.
Fee: $25.04 monthly.
Digital Basic Service
Subscribers: N.A.
Programming (via satellite): BBC America; Bloomberg Television; Discovery Life Channel; Disney XD; ESPN Classic; ESPNews; Fox Sports 1; Fuse; FYI; Golf Channel; GSN; History International; IFC; LMN; MC; National Geographic Channel; NBCSN; Nick Jr.; Nicktoons; Outdoor Channel; TeenNick; Turner Classic Movies.
Digital Pay Service 1
Pay Units: N.A.
Programming (via satellite): Cinemax (multiplexed); HBO (multiplexed); Showtime

2017 Edition   D-625

Oklahoma—Cable Systems

(multiplexed); Starz (multiplexed); Starz Encore; The Movie Channel (multiplexed).
Video-On-Demand: No
Pay-Per-View
Playboy TV (delivered digitally); Shorteez (delivered digitally); Fresh (delivered digitally); Hot Choice (delivered digitally); iN DEMAND (delivered digitally).
Internet Service
Operational: Yes.
Fee: $45.95 installation; $24.95 monthly.
Telephone Service
Digital: Operational
Fee: $49.95 monthly
Miles of Plant: 170.0 (coaxial); 29.0 (fiber optic). Homes passed: 10,493.
Senior Vice President, Corporate Finance: Michael Pflantz. General Manager: Billy Jewell. Marketing Manager: Heather Eastwood.
Ownership: Cequel Communications Holdings I LLC (MSO).

OLUSTEE—Formerly served by Basic Cable Services Inc. No longer in operation. ICA: OK0223.

OOLOGAH—Formerly served by Allegiance Communications. No longer in operation. ICA: OK0144.

ORLANDO—Formerly served by CableDirect. No longer in operation. ICA: OK0256.

PANAMA—Vyve Broadband, 4 International Dr, Ste 330, Rye Brook, NY 10573. Phones: 800-937-1397; 405-395-1131; 405-275-6923. Web Site: http://vyvebroadband.com. Also serves Le Flore County (unincorporated areas) & Shady Point. ICA: OK0109.
TV Market Ranking: Below 100 (Le Flore County (unincorporated areas) (portions), PANAMA, Shady Point); Outside TV Markets (Le Flore County (unincorporated areas) (portions)). Franchise award date: N.A. Franchise expiration date: N.A. Began: November 1, 1979.
Channel capacity: 36 (operating 2-way). Channels available but not in use: N.A.
Basic Service
Subscribers: 73.
Programming (received off-air): KFSM-TV (CBS, MNT) Fort Smith; KFTA-TV (FOX, NBC) Fort Smith; KHBS (ABC, CW) Fort Smith; KNWA-TV (FOX, NBC) Rogers; KOET (PBS) Eufaula; KTUL (ABC, Antenna TV, Retro TV) Tulsa.
Programming (via satellite): A&E; AMC; Animal Planet; Cartoon Network; CMT; CNN; Comedy Central; Discovery Channel; Disney Channel; ESPN; ESPN2; Food Network; Fox News Channel; FOX Sports Southwest; Freeform; FX; Hallmark Channel; HGTV; History; HLN; MTV; NFL Network; Nickelodeon; QVC; Spike TV; Syfy; TBS; The Weather Channel; TNT; Trinity Broadcasting Network (TBN); TV Land; USA Network; WGN America.
Fee: $64.95 installation; $67.75 monthly.
Digital Basic Service
Subscribers: N.A.
Programming (via satellite): 52MX; BBC America; Bloomberg Television; Bravo; Cine Mexicano; Cinelatino; Cloo; CMT; CNN en Espanol; Destination America; Discovery Kids Channel; Discovery Life Channel; Disney XD; DMX Music; ESPN Classic; ESPN2; ESPNews; EVINE Live; Flix; FOX College Sports Central; FOX College Sports Pacific; Fox Deportes; Fox Sports 1; Fuse; FXM; FYI; Golf Channel; Great American Country; GSN; HGTV; History; History en Espanol; History International; IFC; Investigation Discovery; LMN; MTV Classic; MTV Hits; MTV2; National Geographic Channel; NBCSN; Nick Jr.; Nicktoons; Outdoor Channel; Ovation; OWN: Oprah Winfrey Network; Science Channel; Starz Encore (multiplexed); Sundance TV; Syfy; TeenNick; The Word Network; Toon Disney en Espanol; Tr3s; Trinity Broadcasting Network (TBN); Turner Classic Movies; UP; VH1 Soul; WE tv.
Pay Service 1
Pay Units: N.A.
Programming (via satellite): HBO; Showtime; Starz; Starz Encore; The Movie Channel.
Fee: $10.00 monthly (each).
Digital Pay Service 1
Pay Units: N.A.
Programming (via satellite): Cinemax (multiplexed); HBO (multiplexed); HBO Latino; Showtime (multiplexed); Starz (multiplexed); The Movie Channel (multiplexed).
Pay-Per-View
iN DEMAND (delivered digitally); Hot Choice (delivered digitally); Playboy TV (delivered digitally); Fresh (delivered digitally); Shorteez (delivered digitally).
Internet Service
Operational: Yes.
Fee: $24.95 installation; $39.95 monthly.
Telephone Service
None
Miles of Plant: 25.0 (coaxial); None (fiber optic). Homes passed: 947.
Chief Executive Officer: Bill Haggarty. Senior Vice President, Financial Planning: Daniel White. Regional Vice President: Andrew Dearth. Vice President, Marketing: Tracy Bass.
Ownership: Vyve Broadband LLC (MSO).

PAOLI—Formerly served by Cebridge Connections. No longer in operation. ICA: OK0210.

PARADISE HILL—Formerly served by Eagle Media. No longer in operation. ICA: OK0366.

PARK HILL—Formerly served by Eagle Media. No longer in operation. ICA: OK0350.

PAULS VALLEY—Suddenlink Communications, 916 South 4th St, Chickasha, OK 73018. Phones: 800-999-6845; 314-315-9400. Web Site: http://www.suddenlink.com. Also serves Garvin County (unincorporated areas) & Wynnewood. ICA: OK0033.
TV Market Ranking: Below 100 (Garvin County (unincorporated areas) (portions), PAULS VALLEY, Wynnewood); Outside TV Markets (Garvin County (unincorporated areas) (portions)). Franchise award date: N.A. Franchise expiration date: N.A. Began: October 20, 1969.
Channel capacity: N.A. Channels available but not in use: N.A.
Basic Service
Subscribers: 1,270. Commercial subscribers: 196.
Programming (received off-air): KAUT-TV (Escape, MNT) Oklahoma City; KETA-TV (PBS) Oklahoma City; KFOR-TV (Antenna TV, NBC) Oklahoma City; KOCB (CW) Oklahoma City; KOCO-TV (ABC, This TV) Oklahoma City; KOKH-TV (FOX, The Country Network, WeatherNation) Oklahoma City; KOPX-TV (ION) Oklahoma City; KTEN (ABC, CW, NBC) Ada; KWTV-DT (CBS) Oklahoma City; KXII (CBS, FOX, MNT) Sherman; 20 FMs.
Programming (via satellite): C-SPAN; C-SPAN 2; Pop; WGN America.
Fee: $54.95 installation; $33.24 monthly.
Expanded Basic Service 1
Subscribers: N.A.
Programming (received off-air): KSBI (IND) Oklahoma City; KTBO-TV (TBN) Oklahoma City.
Programming (via satellite): A&E; AMC; Animal Planet; BET; Cartoon Network; CMT; CNBC; CNN; Comedy Central; Discovery Channel; Disney Channel; E! HD; ESPN; ESPN2; Food Network; Fox News Channel; FOX Sports Networks; Freeform; FX; Golf Channel; HGTV; History; HLN; Lifetime; MSNBC; MTV; MTV2; Nickelodeon; Oxygen; QVC; Spike TV; Syfy; TBS; The Weather Channel; TLC; TNT; Travel Channel; truTV; Turner Classic Movies; TV Land; Univision Studios; USA Network; VH1.
Fee: $39.96 monthly.
Digital Basic Service
Subscribers: N.A.
Programming (via satellite): BBC America; Bloomberg Television; Cooking Channel; Discovery Life Channel; Disney XD; DIY Network; ESPN Classic; ESPNews; EWTN Global Catholic Network; FYI; GSN; Hallmark Channel; History International; HITS (Headend In The Sky); IFC; LMN; MC; National Geographic Channel; Nick 2; Nick Jr.; Nicktoons; Outdoor Channel; Sundance TV; TeenNick; WAM! America's Kidz Network.
Pay Service 1
Pay Units: N.A.
Programming (via satellite): HBO.
Fee: $13.95 monthly.
Digital Pay Service 1
Pay Units: N.A.
Programming (via satellite): Cinemax (multiplexed); HBO (multiplexed); Showtime (multiplexed); Starz; Starz Encore (multiplexed); The Movie Channel (multiplexed).
Video-On-Demand: No
Pay-Per-View
iN DEMAND (delivered digitally); Playboy TV (delivered digitally); Fresh (delivered digitally); Shorteez (delivered digitally); Hot Choice (delivered digitally); ESPN (delivered digitally); NBA League Pass (delivered digitally); NHL Center Ice (delivered digitally); MLB Extra Innings (delivered digitally).
Internet Service
Operational: Yes.
Broadband Service: Suddenlink High Speed Internet.
Fee: $45.95 installation; $24.95 monthly.
Telephone Service
Digital: Operational
Miles of Plant: 85.0 (coaxial); None (fiber optic). Homes passed: 4,933.
Senior Vice President, Corporate Finance: Michael Pflantz. General Manager: Eugene Biller. Marketing Manager: Heather Eastwood. Chief Technician: Gene Reed.
Ownership: Cequel Communications Holdings I LLC (MSO).

PAWHUSKA—Vyve Broadband, 4 International Dr, Ste 330, Rye Brook, NY 10573. Phones: 800-937-1397; 405-395-1131; 405-275-6923. Web Site: http://vyvebroadband.com. Also serves Osage County (portions). ICA: OK0060.
TV Market Ranking: Below 100 (Osage County (portions), PAWHUSKA). Franchise award date: N.A. Franchise expiration date: N.A. Began: September 1, 1974.
Channel capacity: N.A. Channels available but not in use: N.A.
Basic Service
Subscribers: 145.
Programming (received off-air): KDOR-TV (TBN) Bartlesville; KGEB (IND) Tulsa; KJRH-TV (NBC) Tulsa; KMYT-TV (getTV, MNT, The Country Network) Tulsa; KOED-TV (PBS) Tulsa; KOKI-TV (FOX, MeTV) Tulsa; KOTV-DT (CBS, IND) Tulsa; KQCW-DT (CW, This TV) Muskogee; KRSU-TV (ETV) Claremore; KTPX-TV (ION) Okmulgee; KTUL (ABC, Antenna TV, Retro TV) Tulsa; KWHB (COZI TV, IND) Tulsa; allband FM.
Programming (via satellite): A&E; AMC; Animal Planet; Cartoon Network; CMT; CNBC; CNN; C-SPAN; Discovery Channel; Disney Channel; ESPN; ESPN Classic; ESPN2; Food Network; Fox News Channel; FOX Sports Southwest; Freeform; FX; Hallmark Channel; HGTV; History; Lifetime; MoviePlex; MSNBC; MTV; Nickelodeon; Outdoor Channel; QVC; Spike TV; Syfy; TBS; The Weather Channel; TLC; TNT; truTV; USA Network; VH1; WGN America.
Fee: $64.95 installation; $65.55 monthly.
Digital Basic Service
Subscribers: N.A.
Programming (via satellite): 52MX; BBC America; Bloomberg Television; Bravo; Cine Mexicano; Cinelatino; Cloo; CMT; CNN en Espanol; Destination America; Discovery Kids Channel; Discovery Life Channel; Disney XD; DMX Music; ESPN Classic; ESPN2; ESPNews; EVINE Live; Flix; FOX College Sports Central; FOX College Sports Pacific; Fox Deportes; Fox Sports 1; Fuse; FXM; FYI; Golf Channel; Great American Country; GSN; HGTV; History; History en Espanol; History International; IFC; Investigation Discovery; LMN; MTV Classic; MTV Hits; MTV2; National Geographic Channel; NBCSN; Nick Jr.; Nicktoons; Outdoor Channel; Ovation; OWN: Oprah Winfrey Network; Science Channel; Starz Encore (multiplexed); Sundance TV; Syfy; TeenNick; The Word Network; Toon Disney en Espanol; Tr3s; Trinity Broadcasting Network (TBN); Turner Classic Movies; VH1 Soul; WE tv.
Pay Service 1
Pay Units: N.A.
Programming (via satellite): HBO; Showtime; Starz; Starz Encore.
Fee: $11.50 monthly (each).
Digital Pay Service 1
Pay Units: N.A.
Programming (via satellite): Cinemax (multiplexed); HBO (multiplexed); Showtime (multiplexed); Starz (multiplexed); The Movie Channel (multiplexed).
Video-On-Demand: No
Pay-Per-View
iN DEMAND (delivered digitally); Hot Choice (delivered digitally); Playboy TV (delivered digitally); Fresh (delivered digitally); Shorteez (delivered digitally).
Internet Service
Operational: Yes.
Fee: $24.95 installation; $39.95 monthly.
Telephone Service
Digital: Operational
Miles of Plant: 37.0 (coaxial); None (fiber optic). Homes passed: 2,462.
Chief Executive Officer: Bill Haggarty. Senior Vice President, Financial Planning: Daniel White. Regional Vice President: Andrew Dearth. Vice President, Marketing: Tracy Bass.
Ownership: Vyve Broadband LLC (MSO).

PAWNEE—Cim Tel Cable Inc. Now served by MANNFORD, OK [OK0296]. ICA: OK0117.

Cable Systems—Oklahoma

PECAN VALLEY—Vyve Broadband, 1819 Airport Dr, Shawnee, OK 74804. Phone: 855-367-8983. Web Site: http://vyvebroadband.com. Also serves Cache & Indiahoma. ICA: OK0105.

TV Market Ranking: Below 100 (Indiahoma, PECAN VALLEY). Franchise award date: N.A. Franchise expiration date: N.A. Began: January 1, 1987.

Channel capacity: N.A. Channels available but not in use: N.A.

Basic Service
Subscribers: 574.
Programming (received off-air): KAUT-TV (Escape, MNT) Oklahoma City; KAUZ-TV (CBS, CW) Wichita Falls; KETA-TV (PBS) Oklahoma City; KFDX-TV (NBC) Wichita Falls; KFOR-TV (Antenna TV, NBC) Oklahoma City; KJTL-TV (Bounce TV, FOX) Wichita Falls; KSWO-TV (ABC, TMO) Lawton; KWTV-DT (CBS) Oklahoma City.
Programming (via satellite): A&E; AMC; CMT; CNN; C-SPAN; Discovery Channel; Disney Channel; E! HD; ESPN; Fox News Channel; FOX Sports Southwest; Freeform; History; HLN; Lifetime; Nickelodeon; QVC; Spike TV; Syfy; TBS; The Weather Channel; TLC; TNT; Trinity Broadcasting Network (TBN); TV Land; USA Network; WGN America.
Fee: $39.95 installation; $26.00 monthly.

Pay Service 1
Pay Units: N.A.
Programming (via satellite): HBO; Showtime; The Movie Channel.
Fee: $7.95 monthly (TMC), $9.95 monthly (Showtime), $10.95 monthly (HBO).

Internet Service
Operational: Yes.
Broadband Service: In-house.

Telephone Service
Digital: Operational
Miles of Plant: 63.0 (coaxial); None (fiber optic). Homes passed: 1,424. Homes passed & miles of plant includes Geronimo
President & Chief Operating Officer: Jeffrey DeMond. Executive Vice President & Chief Financial Officer: Andrew Kober. Senior Vice President, General Counsel & Secretary: Marie Censoplano. Senior Vice President, Engineering & Chief Technology Officer: Dennis Davies. Senior Vice President, Marketing & Customer Experience: Diane Quennoz. Senior Vice President, Residential Services: Vin Zachariah. Vice President, Network Planning: Alex Harris.
Ownership: Vyve Broadband LLC (MSO).

PERRY—Suddenlink Communications, 617 1/2 Delaware St, Perry, OK 73077. Phones: 800-999-6845; 314-315-9400; 405-377-7785. Web Site: http://www.suddenlink.com. Also serves Noble County (portions). ICA: OK0057.

TV Market Ranking: Outside TV Markets (Noble County (portions), PERRY). Franchise award date: September 1, 1977. Franchise expiration date: N.A. Began: January 1, 1979.

Channel capacity: N.A. Channels available but not in use: N.A.

Basic Service
Subscribers: 664.
Programming (received off-air): KAUT-TV (Escape, MNT) Oklahoma City; KETA-TV (PBS) Oklahoma City; KFOR-TV (Antenna TV, NBC) Oklahoma City; KOCB (CW) Oklahoma City; KOCO-TV (ABC, This TV) Oklahoma City; KOKH-TV (FOX, The Country Network, WeatherNation) Oklahoma City; KOPX-TV (ION) Oklahoma City; KSBI (IND) Oklahoma City; KTBO-TV (TBN) Oklahoma City; KWTV-DT (CBS) Oklahoma City; 10 FMs.
Programming (via satellite): Daystar TV Network; TBS; The Weather Channel; WGN America.
Fee: $54.95 installation; $34.24 monthly; $3.30 converter.

Expanded Basic Service 1
Subscribers: N.A.
Programming (via satellite): A&E; AMC; Animal Planet; Cartoon Network; CMT; CNBC; CNN; Comedy Central; C-SPAN; Discovery Channel; Disney Channel; ESPN; ESPN2; Fox News Channel; FOX Sports Southwest; Freeform; HGTV; History; HLN; Lifetime; MoviePlex; Nickelodeon; QVC; Spike TV; Syfy; TLC; TNT; TV Land; USA Network; VH1.
Fee: $17.85 monthly.

Digital Basic Service
Subscribers: N.A.
Programming (via satellite): BBC America; Bloomberg Television; Discovery Life Channel; Disney XD; ESPN Classic; ESPN2; ESPNews; EVINE Live; Fox Sports 1; Fuse; FXM; Golf Channel; Great American Country; GSN; IFC; MC; National Geographic Channel; NBCSN; Outdoor Channel; Sundance TV; The Word Network.
Fee: $13.95 monthly.

Pay Service 1
Pay Units: N.A.
Programming (via satellite): Cinemax; HBO; Starz Encore.
Fee: $10.00 installation; $1.75 monthly (Starz), $6.75 monthly (Encore), $10.68 monthly (Cinemax or HBO).

Digital Pay Service 1
Pay Units: N.A.
Programming (via satellite): Cinemax (multiplexed); HBO (multiplexed); Showtime (multiplexed); Starz (multiplexed); Starz Encore (multiplexed); The Movie Channel (multiplexed).

Video-On-Demand: No

Pay-Per-View
iN DEMAND (delivered digitally); Hot Choice (delivered digitally); Adult PPV (delivered digitally); ESPN Now (delivered digitally); ESPN (delivered digitally).

Internet Service
Operational: Yes.
Broadband Service: Suddenlink High Speed Internet.

Telephone Service
Digital: Operational
Miles of Plant: 49.0 (coaxial); 5.0 (fiber optic). Homes passed: 3,037.
Senior Vice President, Corporate Finance: Michael Pflantz. General Manager: Nicole Evans. Marketing Manager: Heather Eastwood. Chief Technician: Johnny Stanley.
Ownership: Cequel Communications Holdings I LLC (MSO).

PICHER—Formerly served by Mediacom. No longer in operation. ICA: OK0093.

PIEDMONT—Formerly served by Almega Cable. No longer in operation. ICA: OK0374.

POCASSET—Formerly served by CableDirect. No longer in operation. ICA: OK0305.

POCOLA—Cox Communications. Now served by FORT SMITH, AR [AR0003]. ICA: OK0099.

PONCA CITY—Cable One, 303 North 4th St, PO Box 2149, Ponca City, OK 74602-2149. Phone: 580-762-6684. Fax: 580-762-0312. Web Site: http://www.cableone.net. Also serves Kay County (portions), Osage County (portions) & Tonkawa. ICA: OK0014.

TV Market Ranking: 54 (Osage County (portions); Below 100 (Osage County (portions)); Outside TV Markets (Kay County (portions), PONCA CITY, Tonkawa, Osage County (portions)). Franchise award date: N.A. Franchise expiration date: N.A. Began: March 1, 1967.

Channel capacity: N.A. Channels available but not in use: N.A.

Basic Service
Subscribers: 4,257.
Programming (received off-air): KAUT-TV (Escape, MNT) Oklahoma City; KETA-TV (PBS) Oklahoma City; KFOR-TV (Antenna TV, NBC) Oklahoma City; KJRH-TV (NBC) Tulsa; KOCB (CW) Oklahoma City; KOCO-TV (ABC, This TV) Oklahoma City; KOKH-TV (FOX, The Country Network, WeatherNation) Oklahoma City; KOKI-TV (FOX, MeTV) Tulsa; KOTV-DT (CBS, IND) Tulsa; KSBI (IND) Oklahoma City; KSNW (NBC) Wichita; KTEW-LD Ponca City; KTUL (ABC, Antenna TV, Retro TV) Tulsa; KWTV-DT (CBS) Oklahoma City.
Programming (via satellite): A&E; AMC; BET; Cartoon Network; CMT; CNBC; CNN; C-SPAN; C-SPAN 2; Discovery Channel; Disney Channel; ESPN; ESPN2; Fox News Channel; FOX Sports Southwest; Freeform; FX; HGTV; History; HLN; Lifetime; MSNBC; MTV; Nickelodeon; Pop; QVC; Spike TV; Syfy; TBS; The Weather Channel; TLC; TNT; Travel Channel; Trinity Broadcasting Network (TBN); TV Land; Univision Studios; USA Network; VH1.
Fee: $90.00 installation; $35.00 monthly.

Digital Basic Service
Subscribers: N.A.
Programming (via satellite): 3ABN; Boomerang; BYUtv; Discovery Digital Networks; Disney XD; DMX Music; ESPN Classic; ESPNews; FamilyNet; FOX College Sports Central; FOX College Sports Pacific; Fox Sports 1; Fox Sports 2; FXM; FYI; Golf Channel; Hallmark Channel; History International; HITS (Headend In The Sky); INSP; National Geographic Channel; Outdoor Channel; TNT HD; Trinity Broadcasting Network (TBN); truTV; Universal HD.
Fee: $48.95 monthly.

Digital Pay Service 1
Pay Units: N.A.
Programming (via satellite): Cinemax (multiplexed); Flix; HBO (multiplexed); Showtime (multiplexed); Showtime HD; Starz (multiplexed); Starz Encore (multiplexed); Sundance TV; The Movie Channel (multiplexed); The Movie Channel HD.
Fee: $15.00 monthly (each).

Video-On-Demand: No

Pay-Per-View
iN DEMAND (delivered digitally); Pleasure (delivered digitally); SexSee (delivered digitally); Juicy (delivered digitally); VaVoom (delivered digitally).

Internet Service
Operational: Yes. Began: December 1, 2000.
Subscribers: 3,941.
Broadband Service: CableONE.net.
Fee: $75.00 installation; $43.00 monthly; $5.00 modem lease.

Telephone Service
Digital: Operational
Subscribers: 1,270.
Fee: $39.95 monthly
Miles of Plant: 496.0 (coaxial); 185.0 (fiber optic). Homes passed: 16,753.
Vice President: Patrick A. Dolohanty. General Manager: Danny Thompson. Plant Manager: Ray Snider. Marketing Director: Terry Bush. Office Manager: Vicki Hardesty.
Ownership: Cable ONE Inc. (MSO).

POND CREEK—Pioneer Telephone Coop. This cable system has converted to IPTV. Now served by KINGFISHER, OK [OK5074]. ICA: OK0185.

PORTER—Formerly served by Allegiance Communications. No longer in operation. ICA: OK0306.

PORUM—Vyve Broadband, 4 International Dr, Ste 330, Rye Brook, NY 10573. Phones: 800-937-1397; 405-395-1131; 405-275-6923. Web Site: http://vyvebroadband.com. ICA: OK0196.

TV Market Ranking: Below 100 (PORUM). Franchise award date: July 1, 1981. Franchise expiration date: N.A. Began: January 1, 1982.

Channel capacity: N.A. Channels available but not in use: N.A.

Basic Service
Subscribers: N.A.
Programming (received off-air): KJRH-TV (NBC) Tulsa; KMYT-TV (getTV, MNT, The Country Network) Tulsa; KOET (PBS) Eufaula; KOKI-TV (FOX, MeTV) Tulsa; KOTV-DT (CBS, IND) Tulsa; KQCW-DT (CW, This TV) Muskogee; KTUL (ABC, Antenna TV, Retro TV) Tulsa; KWHB (COZI TV, IND) Tulsa.
Programming (via satellite): A&E; AMC; Animal Planet; CMT; CNBC; CNN; Discovery Channel; Disney Channel; E! HD; ESPN; ESPN2; Freeform; History; HLN; Lifetime; MSNBC; Nickelodeon; QVC; Spike TV; Syfy; TBS; TLC; TNT; Travel Channel; USA Network; WGN America.
Fee: $64.95 installation; $54.25 monthly.

Pay Service 1
Pay Units: N.A.
Programming (via satellite): Cinemax; HBO.
Fee: $9.00 monthly (HBO).

Video-On-Demand: No

Pay-Per-View
iN DEMAND (delivered digitally); Hot Choice (delivered digitally); Playboy TV (delivered digitally); Fresh (delivered digitally); Shorteez (delivered digitally).

Internet Service
Operational: No.

Telephone Service
None
Miles of Plant: 6.0 (coaxial); None (fiber optic). Homes passed: 309.
Chief Executive Officer: Bill Haggarty. Senior Vice President, Financial Planning: Daniel White. Regional Vice President: Andrew Dearth. Vice President, Marketing: Tracy Bass.
Ownership: Vyve Broadband LLC (MSO).

PORUM LANDING—Vyve Broadband, 4 International Dr, Ste 330, Rye Brook, NY 10573. Phones: 800-937-1397; 405-395-1131; 405-275-6923. Web Site: http://vyvebroadband.com. ICA: OK0307.

TV Market Ranking: Outside TV Markets (PORUM LANDING). Franchise award date: N.A. Franchise expiration date: N.A. Began: June 1, 1990.

Channel capacity: 36 (not 2-way capable). Channels available but not in use: N.A.

Basic Service
Subscribers: 2.
Programming (received off-air): KJRH-TV (NBC) Tulsa; KMYT-TV (getTV, MNT, The Country Network) Tulsa; KOED-TV (PBS) Tulsa; KOKI-TV (FOX, MeTV) Tulsa; KOTV-DT (CBS, IND) Tulsa; KQCW-DT (CW, This

Oklahoma—Cable Systems

TV) Muskogee; KTUL (ABC, Antenna TV, Retro TV) Tulsa.
Programming (via satellite): A&E; AMC; CMT; CNN; Discovery Channel; Disney Channel; ESPN; Freeform; History; Lifetime; Nickelodeon; QVC; Spike TV; TBS; The Weather Channel; TNT; USA Network; WGN America.
Fee: $64.95 installation; $51.49 monthly.

Pay Service 1
Pay Units: N.A.
Programming (via satellite): HBO; Showtime.
Fee: $10.00 monthly (each).

Pay-Per-View
iN DEMAND (delivered digitally); Hot Choice (delivered digitally); Playboy TV (delivered digitally); Fresh (delivered digitally); Shorteez (delivered digitally).

Internet Service
Operational: No.

Telephone Service
None
Miles of Plant: 25.0 (coaxial); None (fiber optic). Homes passed: 771.
Chief Executive Officer: Bill Haggarty. Senior Vice President, Financial Planning: Daniel White. Regional Vice President: Andrew Dearth. Vice President, Marketing: Tracy Bass.
Ownership: Vyve Broadband LLC (MSO).

POTEAU—Suddenlink Communications, 520 Maryville Centre Dr, Ste 300, St. Louis, MO 63141. Phones: 314-315-9400; 800-999-8876. Web Site: http://www.suddenlink.com. Also serves Le Flore County (portions). ICA: OK0308.
TV Market Ranking: Below 100 (Le Flore County (portions), POTEAU). Franchise award date: July 1, 1962. Franchise expiration date: N.A. Began: July 1, 1962.
Channel capacity: 41 (operating 2-way). Channels available but not in use: N.A.

Basic Service
Subscribers: 836.
Programming (received off-air): KAFT (PBS) Fayetteville; KFSM-TV (CBS, MNT) Fort Smith; KHBS (ABC, CW) Fort Smith; KMYT-TV (getTV, MNT, The Country Network) Tulsa; KNWA-TV (FOX, NBC) Rogers; KOET (PBS) Eufaula; KTUL (ABC, Antenna TV, Retro TV) Tulsa; allband FM.
Programming (via satellite): INSP; QVC; Trinity Broadcasting Network (TBN).
Fee: $28.45 monthly.

Expanded Basic Service 1
Subscribers: N.A.
Programming (via satellite): A&E; AMC; Animal Planet; Cartoon Network; CNBC; CNN; Comedy Central; C-SPAN; Discovery Channel; Disney Channel; E! HD; ESPN; ESPN2; Food Network; Fox News Channel; FOX Sports Southwest; Freeform; FX; Great American Country; Hallmark Channel; HGTV; History; HLN; Lifetime; MSNBC; MTV; National Geographic Channel; Nickelodeon; Outdoor Channel; Spike TV; Syfy; TBS; The Weather Channel; TLC; TNT; Travel Channel; Turner Classic Movies; TV Land; USA Network; VH1.
Fee: $23.00 monthly.

Digital Basic Service
Subscribers: N.A.
Programming (via satellite): BBC America; Bloomberg Television; Bravo; Cloo; Discovery Digital Networks; Disney XD; DMX Music; ESPN Classic; ESPNews; Fox Sports 1; Fuse; FYI; Golf Channel; GSN; History International; IFC; NBCSN; WE tv.
Fee: $3.99 monthly.

Pay Service 1
Pay Units: N.A.
Programming (via satellite): HBO; Showtime; The Movie Channel.
Fee: $7.95 monthly (TMC), $9.95 monthly (Showtime), $10.95 monthly (HBO).

Digital Pay Service 1
Pay Units: N.A.
Programming (via satellite): Cinemax (multiplexed); HBO (multiplexed); Showtime (multiplexed); Starz (multiplexed); Starz Encore (multiplexed); The Movie Channel (multiplexed).

Video-On-Demand: No

Pay-Per-View
iN DEMAND (delivered digitally); Playboy TV (delivered digitally); Fresh (delivered digitally).

Internet Service
Operational: Yes. Began: June 23, 2002.
Broadband Service: Suddenlink High Speed Internet.
Fee: $45.95 installation; $24.95 monthly.

Telephone Service
Digital: Operational
Fee: $49.95 monthly
Miles of Plant: 125.0 (coaxial); None (fiber optic). Homes passed: 3,108.
Senior Vice President, Corporate Finance: Michael Pflantz. Regional Manager: Todd Cruthird. Area Manager: Carl Miller. Regional Marketing Manager: Beverly Gambell. Plant Manager: Danny Keith.
Ownership: Cequel Communications Holdings I LLC (MSO).

PRESTON—Formerly served by Quality Cablevision of Oklahoma Inc. No longer in operation. ICA: OK0338.

PRYOR—Vyve Broadband, 1819 Airport Dr, Shawnee, OK 74804. Phone: 855-367-8983. E-mail: support@vyvebb.com. Web Site: http://vyvebroadband.com. Also serves Mayes County (portions). ICA: OK0046.
TV Market Ranking: 54 (Mayes County (portions)); Outside TV Markets (PRYOR, Mayes County (portions)). Franchise award date: August 5, 1972. Franchise expiration date: N.A. Began: November 22, 1974.
Channel capacity: N.A. Channels available but not in use: N.A.

Basic Service
Subscribers: 550.
Programming (received off-air): KDOR-TV (TBN) Bartlesville; KGEB (IND) Tulsa; KJRH-TV (NBC) Tulsa; KMYT-TV (getTV, MNT, The Country Network) Tulsa; KOED-TV (PBS) Tulsa; KOKI-TV (FOX, MeTV) Tulsa; KOTV-DT (CBS, IND) Tulsa; KQCW-DT (CW, This TV) Muskogee; KRSU-TV (ETV) Claremore; KTPX-TV (ION) Okmulgee; KTUL (ABC, Antenna TV, Retro TV) Tulsa; KWHB (COZI TV, IND) Tulsa; allband FM.
Programming (via satellite): Freeform.
Fee: $35.00 installation; $38.59 monthly.

Expanded Basic Service 1
Subscribers: N.A.
Programming (via satellite): A&E; AMC; Animal Planet; Cartoon Network; CMT; CNN; Comedy Central; C-SPAN; Discovery Channel; Discovery Life Channel; Disney Channel; ESPN; ESPN Classic; ESPN2; EVINE Live; Food Network; Fox News Channel; FOX Sports Southwest; FX; HGTV; History; HLN; INSP; Lifetime; MSNBC; MTV; National Geographic Channel; Nickelodeon; OWN: Oprah Winfrey Network; Oxygen; Pop; Spike TV; Syfy; TBS; The Weather Channel; TLC; TNT; Travel Channel; TV Land; USA Network; WE tv; WGN America.
Fee: $28.16 monthly.

Digital Basic Service
Subscribers: N.A.
Programming (via satellite): BBC America; Bloomberg Television; Discovery Digital Networks; Disney XD; ESPNews; Fox Sports 1; FYI; Golf Channel; GSN; History International; LMN; MC; MTV Classic; MTV Hits; MTV2; NBCSN; Nick Jr.; Nicktoons; Outdoor Channel; Ovation; TeenNick; Turner Classic Movies.
Fee: $25.49 monthly.

Digital Pay Service 1
Pay Units: N.A.
Programming (via satellite): Cinemax (multiplexed); FXM; HBO; IFC; Showtime; Starz; Starz Encore (multiplexed); Sundance TV; The Movie Channel (multiplexed).
Fee: $13.00 monthly (each).

Video-On-Demand: No

Pay-Per-View
Fresh (delivered digitally); Shorteez (delivered digitally); Hot Choice (delivered digitally).

Internet Service
Operational: No.

Telephone Service
None
Miles of Plant: None (coaxial); 36.0 (fiber optic).
Senior Vice President, Financial Planning: Daniel J. White.
Ownership: Vyve Broadband LLC (MSO).

PRYOR (outside areas)—Formerly served by Time Warner Cable. No longer in operation. ICA: OK0354.

PURCELL—Suddenlink Communications, 520 Maryville Centre Dr, Ste 300, St. Louis, MO 63141. Phones: 314-315-9400; 800-999-6845. Web Site: http://www.suddenlink.com. Also serves Blanchard, Cleveland County (portions), Lexington, Maysville, McClain County (portions), Noble & Wayne. ICA: OK0048.
TV Market Ranking: 39 (Blanchard, Cleveland County (portions), Lexington, McClain County (portions) (portions), Noble, PURCELL; Below 100 (Maysville, Wayne, McClain County (portions) (portions)); Outside TV Markets (McClain County (portions) (portions)). Franchise award date: N.A. Franchise expiration date: N.A. Began: November 1, 1976.
Channel capacity: 40 (operating 2-way). Channels available but not in use: N.A.

Basic Service
Subscribers: 1,050.
Programming (received off-air): KAUT-TV (Escape, MNT) Oklahoma City; KETA-TV (PBS) Oklahoma City; KFOR-TV (Antenna TV, NBC) Oklahoma City; KOCB (CW) Oklahoma City; KOCM (Daystar TV) Norman; KOCO-TV (ABC, This TV) Oklahoma City; KOKH-TV (FOX, The Country Network, WeatherNation) Oklahoma City; KOPX-TV (ION) Oklahoma City; KSBI (IND) Oklahoma City; KTBO-TV (TBN) Oklahoma City; KWTV-DT (CBS) Oklahoma City; allband FM.
Fee: $28.45 monthly.

Expanded Basic Service 1
Subscribers: N.A.
Programming (via satellite): A&E; AMC; Animal Planet; Cartoon Network; CMT; CNN; Comedy Central; C-SPAN; Discovery Channel; Disney Channel; E! HD; ESPN; ESPN2; Food Network; Fox News Channel; FOX Sports Southwest; Freeform; FX; Great American Country; Hallmark Channel; HGTV; History; HLN; Lifetime; MTV; Nickelodeon; Outdoor Channel; QVC; Spike TV; Syfy; TBS; The Weather Channel; TLC; TNT; Turner Classic Movies; TV Land; Univision Studios; USA Network; VH1.

Digital Basic Service
Subscribers: N.A.
Programming (via satellite): BBC America; Bloomberg Television; Cloo; Discovery Digital Networks; Disney XD; DMX Music; ESPN Classic; ESPNews; EVINE Live; FOX College Sports Central; FOX College Sports Pacific; Fox Sports 1; Fuse; FYI; Golf Channel; GSN; History International; IFC; NBCSN; WE tv.

Pay Service 1
Pay Units: N.A.
Programming (via satellite): Cinemax; HBO; Showtime; The Movie Channel.

Digital Pay Service 1
Pay Units: N.A.
Programming (via satellite): Cinemax (multiplexed); HBO (multiplexed); Showtime (multiplexed); Starz (multiplexed); Starz Encore (multiplexed); The Movie Channel (multiplexed).

Video-On-Demand: No

Pay-Per-View
iN DEMAND (delivered digitally); Playboy TV (delivered digitally); Fresh (delivered digitally).

Internet Service
Operational: Yes. Began: January 21, 2003.
Broadband Service: Suddenlink High Speed Internet.
Fee: $45.95 installation; $24.95 monthly.

Telephone Service
Digital: Operational
Fee: $49.95 monthly
Miles of Plant: 85.0 (coaxial); None (fiber optic). Homes passed: 5,320.
Senior Vice President, Corporate Finance: Michael Pflantz. General Manager: Charles Hembree. Regional Manager: Todd Cruthird. Chief Technician: Kurt Widmer.
Ownership: Cequel Communications Holdings I LLC (MSO).

QUINTON—Vyve Broadband, 4 International Dr, Ste 330, Rye Brook, NY 10573. Phones: 800-937-1397; 405-395-1131; 405-275-6923. Web Site: http://vyvebroadband.com. Also serves Kinta. ICA: OK0156.
TV Market Ranking: Outside TV Markets (QUINTON). Franchise award date: N.A. Franchise expiration date: N.A. Began: January 1, 1977.
Channel capacity: N.A. Channels available but not in use: N.A.

Basic Service
Subscribers: 35.
Programming (received off-air): KJRH-TV (NBC) Tulsa; KMYT-TV (getTV, MNT, The Country Network) Tulsa; KOET (PBS) Eufaula; KOKI-TV (FOX, MeTV) Tulsa; KOTV-DT (CBS, IND) Tulsa; KQCW-DT (CW, This TV) Muskogee; KTUL (ABC, Antenna TV, Retro TV) Tulsa; KWHB (COZI TV, IND) Tulsa.
Programming (via satellite): A&E; AMC; Animal Planet; Cartoon Network; CMT; CNN; C-SPAN; Discovery Channel; Disney Channel; E! HD; ESPN; ESPN2; Fox News Channel; FOX Sports Southwest; Freeform; HGTV; History; HLN; Lifetime; Nickelodeon; Outdoor Channel; Spike TV; Syfy; TBS; The Weather Channel; TLC; TNT; Travel Channel; Turner Classic Movies; USA Network; WGN America.
Fee: $64.95 installation; $64.75 monthly.

Cable Systems—Oklahoma

Digital Basic Service
Subscribers: N.A.
Programming (via satellite): BBC America; Bloomberg Television; Bravo; Chiller; Cloo; CMT; Destination America; Discovery Kids Channel; Discovery Life Channel; Disney XD; DMX Music; ESPN Classic; ESPNews; Flix; Fuse; FXM; FYI; Golf Channel; GSN; History International; IFC; Investigation Discovery; LMN; MTV Classic; MTV Hits; MTV2; National Geographic Channel; NBCSN; Nick Jr.; Nicktoons; OWN; Oprah Winfrey Network; RFD-TV; Science Channel; Starz Encore (multiplexed); TeenNick; Trinity Broadcasting Network (TBN); VH1 Soul; WE tv.

Pay Service 1
Pay Units: N.A.
Programming (via satellite): Cinemax; HBO; Showtime.
Fee: $9.00 monthly (HBO).

Digital Pay Service 1
Pay Units: N.A.
Programming (via satellite): Cinemax (multiplexed); HBO (multiplexed); Showtime (multiplexed); Starz (multiplexed); The Movie Channel (multiplexed).

Video-On-Demand: No

Pay-Per-View
iN DEMAND (delivered digitally); Club Jenna (delivered digitally); Spice: Xcess (delivered digitally); Playboy TV (delivered digitally); Fresh (delivered digitally).

Internet Service
Operational: No.

Telephone Service
None

Miles of Plant: 22.0 (coaxial); None (fiber optic). Homes passed: 643.
Chief Executive Officer: Bill Haggarty. Senior Vice President, Financial Planning: Daniel White. Regional Vice President: Andrew Dearth. Vice President, Marketing: Tracy Bass.
Ownership: Vyve Broadband LLC (MSO).

RALSTON—Formerly served by Allegiance Communications. No longer in operation. ICA: OK0241.

RAMONA—Community Cable & Broadband, 1550 West Rogers Blvd, PO Box 307, Skiatook, OK 74070-0307. Phones: 888-394-4772; 918-396-3019. Fax: 918-396-2081. E-mail: info@communitycablevision.com. Web Site: http://www.communitycablebroadband.com. ICA: OK0206.
TV Market Ranking: 54 (RAMONA). Franchise award date: N.A. Franchise expiration date: N.A. Began: January 1, 1984.
Channel capacity: N.A. Channels available but not in use: N.A.

Basic Service
Subscribers: N.A.
Programming (received off-air): KDOR-TV (TBN) Bartlesville; KGEB (IND) Tulsa; KJRH-TV (NBC) Tulsa; KOED-TV (PBS) Tulsa; KOKI-TV (FOX, MeTV) Tulsa; KOTV-DT (CBS, IND) Tulsa; KQCW-DT (CW, This TV) Muskogee; KRSU-TV (ETV) Claremore; KTPX-TV (ION) Okmulgee; KTUL (ABC, Antenna TV, Retro TV) Tulsa; KWHB (COZI TV, IND) Tulsa.
Programming (via microwave): KTFO-CD (UniMas) Austin.
Programming (via satellite): A&E; Cartoon Network; CMT; CNN; C-SPAN; Discovery Channel; Disney Channel; ESPN; ESPN2; Fox News Channel; FOX Sports Southwest; Freeform; HLN; Lifetime; MTV; Nickelodeon; QVC; Spike TV; Syfy; TBS; The Weather Channel; TLC; TNT; Turner Classic Movies; USA Network; WGN America.
Fee: $29.95 installation.

Video-On-Demand: No

Internet Service
Operational: Yes.
Fee: $44.95 monthly.

Telephone Service
None

Miles of Plant: 8.0 (coaxial); None (fiber optic). Homes passed: 276.
President & General Manager: Dennis Soule. Chief Technical Officer: Chris Tuttle.
Ownership: Community Cable & Broadband Inc. (MSO).

RANDLETT—Formerly served by Cable Television Inc. No longer in operation. ICA: OK0335.

RATTAN—Formerly served by Allegiance Communications. No longer in operation. ICA: OK0355.

RED ROCK—Formerly served by Blue Sky Cable LLC. No longer in operation.. ICA: OK0251.

RINGWOOD—Pioneer Telephone Coop. This cable system has converted to IPTV. Now served by KINGFISHER, OK [OK5074]. ICA: OK0375.

RIPLEY—Formerly served by CableDirect. No longer in operation. ICA: OK0232.

ROCKY—Formerly served by CableDirect. No longer in operation. ICA: OK0249.

ROGERS COUNTY (northern portion)—Time Warner Cable, 16021 South Highway 66, Claremore, OK 74017. Phone: 918-342-9482. Fax: 918-341-8443. Web Site: http://www.timewarnercable.com. Also serves Mayes County (western portion) & Tulsa (northwestern portion). ICA: OK0104.
TV Market Ranking: 54 (Mayes County (western portion) (portions), ROGERS COUNTY (NORTHERN PORTION) (portions), Tulsa (northwestern portion)); Below 100 (ROGERS COUNTY (NORTHERN PORTION) (portions)); Outside TV Markets (Mayes County (western portion) (portions), ROGERS COUNTY (NORTHERN PORTION) (portions)). Franchise award date: N.A. Franchise expiration date: N.A. Began: July 6, 1992.
Channel capacity: N.A. Channels available but not in use: N.A.

Basic Service
Subscribers: 482.
Programming (received off-air): KDOR-TV (TBN) Bartlesville; KGEB (IND) Tulsa; KJRH-TV (NBC) Tulsa; KOET (PBS) Eufaula; KOKI-TV (FOX, MeTV) Tulsa; KOTV-DT (CBS, IND) Tulsa; KQCW-DT (CW, This TV) Muskogee; KTFO-CD (UniMas) Austin; KTPX-TV (ION) Okmulgee; KTUL (ABC, Antenna TV, Retro TV) Tulsa; KWHB (COZI TV, IND) Tulsa.
Programming (via satellite): CNN; C-SPAN; Pop; QVC; The Weather Channel; WGN America.
Fee: $35.95 installation; $24.25 monthly.

Digital Basic Service
Subscribers: N.A.
Programming (via satellite): A&E; AMC; Animal Planet; Cartoon Network; CMT; CNBC; Comedy Central; C-SPAN 2; Discovery Channel; Discovery Life Channel; Disney Channel; Disney XD; E! HD; ESPN; ESPN2; Food Network; Fox News Channel; Fox Sports 1; FOX Sports Southwest; Freeform; FX; FYI; Great American Country; Hallmark Channel; HGTV; History; History International; HLN; Lifetime; MSNBC; National Geographic Channel; Nick Jr.; Nickelodeon; Spike TV; Syfy; TBS; TLC; TNT; Travel Channel; Trinity Broadcasting Network (TBN); truTV; Turner Classic Movies; TV Land; USA Network.
Fee: $21.74 monthly.

Digital Expanded Basic Service
Subscribers: N.A.
Programming (via satellite): BBC America; Bloomberg Television; Bravo; Destination America; Discovery Kids Channel; DMX Music; ESPN Classic; ESPNews; Fuse; FXM; Golf Channel; GSN; IFC; Investigation Discovery; LMN; MTV Classic; MTV2; NBCSN; Nicktoons; Outdoor Channel; Ovation; OWN; Oprah Winfrey Network; Science Channel; Sundance TV; TeenNick; WE tv.
Fee: $15.95 monthly.

Digital Pay Service 1
Pay Units: N.A.
Programming (via satellite): Cinemax (multiplexed); HBO (multiplexed); HD Theater; Showtime (multiplexed); Starz (multiplexed); Starz Encore (multiplexed); The Movie Channel (multiplexed).
Fee: $15.95 monthly (each).

Video-On-Demand: No

Pay-Per-View
iN DEMAND (delivered digitally); Playboy TV (delivered digitally).

Internet Service
Operational: Yes.

Telephone Service
Digital: Operational
General Manager: Mike Miller. Chief Technician: Paul Stanley.
Ownership: Time Warner Cable (MSO).

ROOSEVELT—Formerly served by Cable West. No longer in operation. ICA: OK0246.

RUSH SPRINGS—Formerly served by Reach Broadband. No longer in operation. ICA: OK0121.

RUSH SPRINGS—Southern Plains Cable, PO Box 165, Medicine Park, OK 73557. Phones: 800-218-1856; 580-529-5000. Fax: 580-529-5556. E-mail: office@spcisp.net. Web Site: http://www.spcisp.net. ICA: OK0802.
TV Market Ranking: Below 100 (RUSH SPRINGS).
Channel capacity: N.A. Channels available but not in use: N.A.
Manager: Mike Rowell.
Ownership: Southern Plains Cable (MSO).

RYAN—Formerly served by Almega Cable. No longer in operation. ICA: OK0184.

SALINA—Vyve Broadband, 4 International Dr, Ste 330, Rye Brook, NY 10573. Phones: 800-937-1397; 405-395-1131. Web Site: http://vyvebroadband.com. Also serves Chouteau, Inola & Locust Grove. ICA: OK0071.
TV Market Ranking: 54 (Inola); Below 100 (Chouteau, Locust Grove); Outside TV Markets (SALINA). Franchise award date: April 1, 1980. Franchise expiration date: N.A. Began: May 1, 1983.
Channel capacity: N.A. Channels available but not in use: N.A.

Basic Service
Subscribers: 210.
Programming (received off-air): KDOR-TV (TBN) Bartlesville; KJRH-TV (NBC) Tulsa; KMYT-TV (getTV, MNT, The Country Network) Tulsa; KOAM-TV (CBS) Pittsburg; KODE-TV (ABC) Joplin; KOED-TV (PBS) Tulsa; KOKI-TV (FOX, MeTV) Tulsa; KOTV-DT (CBS, IND) Tulsa; KQCW-DT (CW, This TV) Muskogee; KRSU-TV (ETV) Claremore; KSNF (NBC) Joplin; KTPX-TV (ION) Okmulgee; KTUL (ABC, Antenna TV, Retro TV) Tulsa; KWHB (COZI TV, IND) Tulsa.
Programming (via satellite): C-SPAN; QVC; WGN America.
Fee: $64.95 installation; $25.00 monthly.

Expanded Basic Service 1
Subscribers: N.A.
Programming (via satellite): A&E; AMC; Animal Planet; Bravo; Cartoon Network; CMT; CNBC; CNN; Comedy Central; Discovery Channel; Disney Channel; E! HD; ESPN; ESPN2; Food Network; Fox News Channel; FOX Sports Southwest; Freeform; FX; Hallmark Channel; HGTV; History; HLN; Lifetime; LMN; MSNBC; MTV; Nickelodeon; Outdoor Channel; Oxygen; RFD-TV; Spike TV; Syfy; TBS; The Weather Channel; TLC; TNT; Travel Channel; TV Land; USA Network; VH1.
Fee: $41.00 monthly.

Digital Basic Service
Subscribers: N.A.
Programming (via satellite): A&E HD; AXS TV; BBC America; Bloomberg Television; Chiller; Cloo; CMT; Destination America; Discovery Kids Channel; Discovery Life Channel; Disney XD; DMX Music; ESPN Classic; ESPN HD; ESPN2 HD; ESPNews; ESPNU; EVINE Live; Flix; Food Network HD; FOX College Sports Central; FOX College Sports Pacific; Fox Sports 1; Fuse; FXM; FYI; Golf Channel; Great American Country; GSN; HD Theater; HGTV HD; History International; IFC; Investigation Discovery; MTV Classic; MTV Hits; MTV2; National Geographic Channel; National Geographic Channel HD; NBCSN; Nick Jr.; Nicktoons; Outdoor Channel 2 HD; OWN; Oprah Winfrey Network; Science Channel; Starz Encore (multiplexed); Sundance TV; TeenNick; The Word Network; Turner Classic Movies; Universal HD; VH1 Soul; WE tv.

Digital Pay Service 1
Pay Units: N.A.
Programming (via satellite): Cinemax (multiplexed); Flix; HBO (multiplexed); HBO HD; Showtime (multiplexed); Showtime HD; Starz (multiplexed); Starz Encore (multiplexed); Starz HD; The Movie Channel (multiplexed).

Video-On-Demand: No

Pay-Per-View
iN DEMAND (delivered digitally); Club Jenna (delivered digitally); Spice: Xcess (delivered digitally); Playboy TV (delivered digitally); Fresh (delivered digitally).

Internet Service
Operational: Yes.
Fee: $24.95 installation; $39.95 monthly.

Telephone Service
Digital: Operational
Miles of Plant: 43.0 (coaxial); None (fiber optic). Homes passed: 1,967.
Chief Executive Officer: Bill Haggarty. Regional Vice President: Andrew Dearth. Vice President, Marketing: Tracy Bass. Senior Vice President, Financial Planning: Daniel White.
Ownership: Vyve Broadband LLC (MSO).

SALLISAW—Suddenlink Communications, 520 Maryville Centre Dr, Ste 300, St. Louis, MO 63141. Phones: 918-775-3211; 314-315-9400; 314-315-9346. Web Site: http://www.suddenlink.com. ICA: OK0043.

2017 Edition

D-629

Oklahoma—Cable Systems

TV Market Ranking: Below 100 (SALLISAW). Franchise award date: N.A. Franchise expiration date: N.A. Began: June 1, 1966.
Channel capacity: 40 (operating 2-way). Channels available but not in use: N.A.

Basic Service
Subscribers: 512. Commercial subscribers: 67.
Programming (received off-air): KETA-TV (PBS) Oklahoma City; KFSM-TV (CBS, MNT) Fort Smith; KHBS (ABC, CW) Fort Smith; KJRH-TV (NBC) Tulsa; KNWA-TV (FOX, NBC) Rogers; KOKI-TV (FOX, MeTV) Tulsa; KOTV-DT (CBS, IND) Tulsa; KTUL (ABC, Antenna TV, Retro TV) Tulsa.
Programming (via satellite): C-SPAN; Pop; QVC; The Weather Channel; WGN America.
Fee: $28.45 monthly; $1.34 converter.

Expanded Basic Service 1
Subscribers: N.A.
Programming (via satellite): A&E; AMC; Animal Planet; Cartoon Network; CNBC; CNN; Comedy Central; Discovery Channel; Disney Channel; E!; ESPN; ESPN2; Food Network; Fox News Channel; FOX Sports Southwest; Freeform; FX; Great American Country; HGTV; History; HLN; INSP; Lifetime; MSNBC; MTV; National Geographic Channel; Nickelodeon; Outdoor Channel; Spike TV; Syfy; TBS; TLC; TNT; TV Land; Univision Studios; USA Network; VH1.
Fee: $16.54 installation; $19.95 monthly.

Digital Basic Service
Subscribers: N.A.
Programming (via satellite): BBC America; Cloo; Discovery Digital Networks; Disney XD; DMX Music; ESPN Classic; ESPNews; Fox Sports 1; Fuse; FYI; Golf Channel; GSN; History International; IFC; NBCSN; Turner Classic Movies; WE tv.
Fee: $3.99 monthly.

Pay Service 1
Pay Units: N.A.
Programming (via satellite): Cinemax; HBO; Showtime; Starz; Starz Encore.
Fee: $1.75 monthly (Encore), $4.75 monthly (Starz), $12.39 monthly (Cinemax), $12.82 monthly (Showtime), $12.83 monthly (HBO).

Digital Pay Service 1
Pay Units: N.A.
Programming (via satellite): Cinemax (multiplexed); HBO (multiplexed); Showtime (multiplexed); Starz (multiplexed); Starz Encore (multiplexed); The Movie Channel (multiplexed).

Video-On-Demand: No

Pay-Per-View
iN DEMAND (delivered digitally); Playboy TV (delivered digitally).

Internet Service
Operational: Yes. Began: November 24, 2003.
Broadband Service: Suddenlink High Speed Internet.
Fee: $45.95 installation; $24.95 monthly.

Telephone Service
Digital: Operational
Fee: $49.95 monthly
Miles of Plant: 90.0 (coaxial); None (fiber optic). Homes passed: 3,740.
Vice President, Corporate Finance: Michael Pflantz. Regional Manager: Todd Cruthird. General Manager & Chief Technician: Danny Keith. Marketing Director: Beverly Gambell.
Ownership: Cequel Communications Holdings I LLC (MSO).

SAND POINT—Formerly served by Allegiance Communications. No longer in operation. ICA: OK0344.

SAVANNA—Vyve Broadband, 4 International Dr, Ste 330, Rye Brook, NY 10573. Phones: 800-937-1397; 405-395-1131; 405-275-6923. Web Site: http://vyvebroadband.com. Also serves Kiowa, McAlester Army Ammunition Plant & Pittsburg. ICA: OK0310.
TV Market Ranking: Outside TV Markets (Kiowa, McAlester Army Ammunition Plant, Pittsburg, SAVANNA). Franchise award date: N.A. Franchise expiration date: N.A. Began: January 1, 1988.
Channel capacity: N.A. Channels available but not in use: N.A.

Basic Service
Subscribers: 27.
Programming (received off-air): KJRH-TV (NBC) Tulsa; KOET (PBS) Eufaula; KOTV-DT (CBS, IND) Tulsa; KTEN (ABC, CW, NBC) Ada; KTUL (ABC, Antenna TV, Retro TV) Tulsa; KXII (CBS, FOX, MNT) Sherman.
Programming (via satellite): A&E; AMC; Animal Planet; Cartoon Network; CMT; CNN; C-SPAN; Discovery Channel; Disney Channel; ESPN; ESPN2; Fox News Channel; FOX Sports Networks; FOX Sports Southwest; Freeform; HGTV; History; HLN; INSP; Lifetime; Nickelodeon; Outdoor Channel; QVC; Spike TV; Syfy; TBS; The Weather Channel; TLC; TNT; Travel Channel; Turner Classic Movies; USA Network; WGN America.
Fee: $64.95 installation; $65.65 monthly.

Pay Service 1
Pay Units: N.A.
Programming (via satellite): Cinemax; HBO; Showtime.
Fee: $9.00 monthly (HBO).

Video-On-Demand: No

Pay-Per-View
iN DEMAND (delivered digitally); Hot Choice; Playboy TV (delivered digitally); Fresh (delivered digitally); Shorteez (delivered digitally).

Internet Service
Operational: No.

Telephone Service
None
Miles of Plant: 36.0 (coaxial); None (fiber optic). Homes passed: 755.
Chief Executive Officer: Bill Haggarty. Senior Vice President, Financial Planning: Daniel White. Regional Vice President: Andrew Dearth. Vice President, Marketing: Tracy Bass.
Ownership: Vyve Broadband LLC (MSO).

SCHULTER—Formerly served by Allegiance Communications. No longer in operation. ICA: OK0311.

SEILING—Pioneer Telephone Coop. This cable system has converted to IPTV. Now served by KINGFISHER, OK [OK5074]. ICA: OK0122.

SEMINOLE—Suddenlink Communications, 1010 East Strothers, Seminole, OK 74868. Phones: 800-999-6845; 314-315-9400. Web Site: http://www.suddenlink.com. ICA: OK0042.
TV Market Ranking: Below 100 (SEMINOLE). Franchise award date: N.A. Franchise expiration date: N.A. Began: November 17, 1975.
Channel capacity: N.A. Channels available but not in use: N.A.

Basic Service
Subscribers: 1,080. Commercial subscribers: 222.
Programming (received off-air): KAUT-TV (Escape, MNT) Oklahoma City; KETA-TV (PBS) Oklahoma City; KFOR-TV (Antenna TV, NBC) Oklahoma City; KOCB (CW) Oklahoma City; KOCO-TV (ABC, This TV) Oklahoma City; KOKH-TV (FOX, The Country Network, WeatherNation) Oklahoma City; KOPX-TV (ION) Oklahoma City; KTBO-TV (TBN) Oklahoma City; KTEN (ABC, CW, NBC) Ada; KWTV-DT (CBS) Oklahoma City; allband FM.
Programming (via satellite): A&E; Animal Planet; Cartoon Network; CMT; CNBC; CNN; C-SPAN; C-SPAN 2; Discovery Channel; Disney Channel; Fox News Channel; Freeform; FX; HGTV; HLN; Lifetime; MTV; Nickelodeon; Pop; QVC; Syfy; TBS; The Weather Channel; TLC; TNT; truTV; TV Land; Univision Studios; WGN America.
Fee: $54.95 installation; $33.24 monthly.

Expanded Basic Service 1
Subscribers: N.A.
Programming (via satellite): AMC; BET; Bravo; Comedy Central; E! HD; ESPN; EWTN Global Catholic Network; Food Network; FOX Sports Southwest; History; MSNBC; Spike TV; Travel Channel; USA Network; VH1.
Fee: $21.99 monthly.

Digital Basic Service
Subscribers: N.A.
Programming (via satellite): BBC America; Bloomberg Television; Discovery Digital Networks; Disney XD; DMX Music; ESPN Classic; ESPNews; Fox Sports 1; Fuse; FYI; Golf Channel; GSN; History International; IFC; LMN; NBCSN; Turner Classic Movies.

Pay Service 1
Pay Units: N.A.
Programming (via satellite): Cinemax; HBO; Showtime; Starz.
Fee: $20.00 installation; $10.00 monthly (Cinemax or HBO).

Digital Pay Service 1
Pay Units: N.A.
Programming (via satellite): Cinemax (multiplexed); HBO (multiplexed); Showtime (multiplexed); Starz (multiplexed); The Movie Channel (multiplexed).

Video-On-Demand: No

Pay-Per-View
ESPN Now (delivered digitally); Playboy TV (delivered digitally); Shorteez (delivered digitally); Fresh (delivered digitally); Hot Choice (delivered digitally); iN DEMAND.

Internet Service
Operational: Yes.
Broadband Service: Suddenlink High Speed Internet.
Fee: $45.95 installation; $24.95 monthly.

Telephone Service
Digital: Operational
Fee: $49.95 monthly
Miles of Plant: 105.0 (coaxial); 31.0 (fiber optic). Homes passed: 6,401.
Senior Vice President, Corporate Finance: Michael Pflantz. General Manager: Eugene Biller. Marketing Manager: Heather Eastwood. Chief Technician: Gene Reed.
Ownership: Cequel Communications Holdings I LLC (MSO).

SENTINEL—Formerly served by Cable West. No longer in operation. ICA: OK0157.

SHATTUCK—Pioneer Telephone Coop. This cable system has converted to IPTV. Now served by KINGFISHER, OK [OK5074]. ICA: OK0135.

SHAWNEE—Vyve Broadband, 4 International Dr, Ste 330, Rye Brook, NY 10573. Phones: 800-937-1397; 405-275-6923; 405-395-1131. Web Site: http://vyvebroadband.com. Also serves Bethel Acres, Dale, Earlsboro, McLoud, Meeker, Pottawatomie County (portions), Prague & Tecumseh. ICA: OK0016.
TV Market Ranking: 39 (Bethel Acres, Dale, McLoud, Meeker, Pottawatomie County (portions) (portions), SHAWNEE, Tecumseh); Below 100 (Earlsboro, Prague, Pottawatomie County (portions) (portions)). Franchise award date: October 1, 1978. Franchise expiration date: N.A. Began: October 1, 1979.
Channel capacity: N.A. Channels available but not in use: N.A.

Basic Service
Subscribers: 3,401.
Programming (received off-air): KAUT-TV (Escape, MNT) Oklahoma City; KETA-TV (PBS) Oklahoma City; KFOR-TV (Antenna TV, NBC) Oklahoma City; KOCB (CW) Oklahoma City; KOCO-TV (ABC, This TV) Oklahoma City; KOKH-TV (FOX, The Country Network, WeatherNation) Oklahoma City; KOPX-TV (ION) Oklahoma City; KSBI (IND) Oklahoma City; KTBO-TV (TBN) Oklahoma City; KTUZ-TV (TMO) Shawnee; KUOK (UNV) Woodward; KWTV-DT (CBS) Oklahoma City; 14 FMs.
Programming (via satellite): A&E; AMC; CMT; CNBC; CNN; C-SPAN; Daystar TV Network; Discovery Channel; E! HD; Fox News Channel; HLN; INSP; Lifetime; MTV; Nickelodeon; QVC; Syfy; The Weather Channel; TV Land; USA Network; WGN America.
Fee: $64.95 installation; $25.00 monthly.

Expanded Basic Service 1
Subscribers: N.A.
Programming (via satellite): Animal Planet; BET; Bravo; Cartoon Network; Comedy Central; C-SPAN 2; Disney Channel; ESPN; ESPN2; ESPNU; Food Network; Fox Sports 1; FOX Sports Southwest; Freeform; FX; FXM; Golf Channel; GSN; Hallmark Channel; HGTV; History; MSNBC; National Geographic Channel; NBCSN; Outdoor Channel; Oxygen; RFD-TV; Spike TV; TBS; TLC; TNT; Travel Channel; truTV; Turner Classic Movies; VH1; WE tv.
Fee: $31.91 monthly.

Digital Basic Service
Subscribers: N.A.
Programming (via satellite): A&E HD; AXS TV; BBC America; Bloomberg Television; CMT; Destination America; Discovery Kids Channel; Disney XD; DIY Network; ESPN Classic; ESPN Deportes; ESPN HD; ESPN2 HD; ESPNews; Flix; Food Network HD; FOX College Sports Central; FOX College Sports Pacific; Fox Deportes; Fox Sports 2; FYI; Great American Country; HD Theater; HGTV HD; History International; IFC; Investigation Discovery; LMN; MC; MTV Classic; MTV Hits; MTV Jams; MTV2; mtvU; National Geographic Channel HD; Nick Jr.; Nicktoons; Outdoor Channel 2 HD; OWN: Oprah Winfrey Network; Science Channel; Starz Encore (multiplexed); Sundance TV; TeenNick; Tr3s; Universal HD; VH1 Soul.

Digital Pay Service 1
Pay Units: N.A.
Programming (via satellite): Cinemax (multiplexed); HBO (multiplexed); HBO HD; Showtime (multiplexed); Showtime HD; Starz (multiplexed); Starz Encore (multiplexed); Starz HD; The Movie Channel (multiplexed).
Fee: $20.00 installation; $10.45 monthly (HBO, Showtime, TMC or Cinemax/HBO HD/Showtime HD/Starz HDTV).

Video-On-Demand: No

Pay-Per-View
Hot Choice (delivered digitally); Special events (delivered digitally); Club Jenna (delivered digitally); iN DEMAND (deliv-

Cable Systems—Oklahoma

ered digitally); Fresh (delivered digitally); Shorteez (delivered digitally); Spice: Xcess (delivered digitally).
Internet Service
Operational: Yes.
Subscribers: 4,730.
Broadband Service: ISP Alliance.
Fee: $24.95 installation; $39.95 monthly.
Telephone Service
Digital: Operational
Subscribers: 1,121.
Miles of Plant: 847.0 (coaxial); 166.0 (fiber optic). Homes passed: 24,047. Miles of plant (coax) includes miles of plant (fiber).
Chief Executive Officer: Bill Haggarty. Senior Vice President, Financial Planning: Daniel White. Regional Vice President: Andrew Dearth. Vice President, Marketing: Tracy Bass.
Ownership: Vyve Broadband LLC (MSO).

SHIDLER—Formerly served by Community Cablevision Co. No longer in operation. ICA: OK0390.

SKIATOOK—Community Cable & Broadband, 1550 West Rogers Blvd, PO Box 307, Skiatook, OK 74070-0307. Phones: 888-394-4772; 918-396-3019. Fax: 918-396-2081. E-mail: info@communitycablevision.com. Web Site: http://www.communitycablebroadband.com. Also serves Barnsdall & Sperry. ICA: OK0065.
TV Market Ranking: 54 (Barnsdall, SKIATOOK, Sperry). Franchise award date: September 6, 1979. Franchise expiration date: N.A. Began: January 1, 1980.
Channel capacity: N.A. Channels available but not in use: N.A.
Basic Service
Subscribers: N.A.
Programming (received off-air): KDOR-TV (TBN) Bartlesville; KGEB (IND) Tulsa; KJRH-TV (NBC) Tulsa; KOED-TV (PBS) Tulsa; KOKI-TV (FOX, MeTV) Tulsa; KOTV-DT (CBS, IND) Tulsa; KRSU-TV (ETV) Claremore; KTPX-TV (ION) Okmulgee; KTUL (ABC, Antenna TV, Retro TV) Tulsa; KWHB (COZI TV, IND) Tulsa; allband FM.
Programming (via microwave): KTFO-CD (UniMas) Austin.
Programming (via satellite): A&E; AMC; Animal Planet; BET; Cartoon Network; CMT; CNN; Comedy Central; C-SPAN; Discovery Channel; Disney Channel; ESPN; ESPN Classic; ESPN2; Food Network; Fox News Channel; FOX Sports Southwest; Freeform; FX; Hallmark Channel; HGTV; History; Lifetime; MoviePlex; MTV; National Geographic Channel; Nickelodeon; Outdoor Channel; OWN: Oprah Winfrey Network; Oxygen; QVC; Spike TV; Syfy; TBS; The Weather Channel; TLC; TNT; Travel Channel; truTV; Turner Classic Movies; TV Land; USA Network; VH1; WGN America.
Fee: $29.95 installation.
Digital Basic Service
Subscribers: N.A.
Programming (via satellite): BBC America; Bloomberg Television; Church Channel; Cloo; Destination America; Discovery Kids Channel; Discovery Life Channel; Disney XD; DMX Music; ESPN Classic; ESPN2; ESPNews; EVINE Live; Flix; FOX College Sports Central; FOX College Sports Pacific; Fox Sports 1; Fuse; FXM; FYI; Golf Channel; Great American Country; GSN; HGTV; History; History International; IFC; International Television (ITV); Investigation Discovery; JUCE TV; LMN; MBC America; MTV Classic; MTV Hits; MTV Jams; MTV2; National Geographic Channel; NBCSN; Nick Jr.; Nicktoons; Outdoor Channel; Ovation; OWN: Oprah Winfrey Network; Sundance TV; Syfy; TeenNick; The Word Network; Trinity Broadcasting Network (TBN); Turner Classic Movies; VH1 Country; VH1 Soul; WE tv.
Fee: $24.00 monthly.
Digital Pay Service 1
Pay Units: N.A.
Programming (via satellite): Cinemax (multiplexed); HBO (multiplexed); Showtime (multiplexed); Starz (multiplexed); Starz Encore (multiplexed); The Movie Channel (multiplexed).
Fee: $11.50 monthly (Cinemax, HBO, Showtime/TMC/Flix/Sundance or Starz/Encore).
Video-On-Demand: No
Pay-Per-View
iN DEMAND (delivered digitally).
Internet Service
Operational: Yes.
Broadband Service: In-house.
Fee: $29.95 installation; $44.95 monthly.
Telephone Service
Digital: Operational
Fee: $39.95 monthly
Miles of Plant: 24.0 (coaxial); None (fiber optic). Homes passed: 2,536.
President & General Manager: Dennis Soule. Chief Technical Officer: Chris Tuttle.
Ownership: Community Cable & Broadband Inc. (MSO).

SNYDER—Formerly served by LongView Communications. Now served by Vyve Broadband, MOUNTAIN PARK, OK [OK0300]. ICA: OK0158.

SOPER—Formerly served by Soper Cable TV. No longer in operation. ICA: OK0312.

SPIRO—Suddenlink Communications, 520 Maryville Centre Dr, Ste 300, St. Louis, MO 63141. Phones: 800-999-6845; 314-315-9400; 314-315-9346. Web Site: http://www.suddenlink.com. Also serves Le Flore County (portions). ICA: OK0313.
TV Market Ranking: Below 100 (Le Flore County (portions), SPIRO). Franchise award date: August 1, 1969. Franchise expiration date: N.A. Began: August 1, 1969.
Channel capacity: N.A. Channels available but not in use: N.A.
Basic Service
Subscribers: 327. Commercial subscribers: 12.
Programming (received off-air): KAFT (PBS) Fayetteville; KETA-TV (PBS) Oklahoma City; KFSM-TV (CBS, MNT) Fort Smith; KFTA-TV (FOX, NBC) Fort Smith; KHBS (ABC, CW) Fort Smith; KJRH-TV (NBC) Tulsa; KOKI-TV (FOX, MeTV) Tulsa; KTUL (ABC, Antenna TV, Retro TV) Tulsa; allband FM.
Programming (via satellite): A&E; CMT; CNN; Discovery Channel; Disney Channel; ESPN; Freeform; History; HLN; Nickelodeon; Spike TV; TBS; The Weather Channel; TNT; Turner Classic Movies; TV Land; USA Network; WGN America.
Fee: $28.45 monthly.
Pay Service 1
Pay Units: N.A.
Programming (via satellite): HBO; Showtime; The Movie Channel.
Fee: $6.95 monthly (Showtime), $11.00 monthly (HBO or TMC).
Video-On-Demand: No

Internet Service
Operational: Yes. Began: October 6, 2003.
Broadband Service: Suddenlink High Speed Internet.
Fee: $45.95 installation; $24.95 monthly.
Telephone Service
Digital: Operational
Fee: $49.95 monthly
Miles of Plant: 38.0 (coaxial); None (fiber optic). Homes passed: 1,460.
Vice President, Corporate Finance: Michael Pflantz. Regional Manager: Todd Cruthird. General Manager: Dave Walker. Marketing Director: Beverly Gambell. Chief Technician: Carl Miller.
Ownership: Cequel Communications Holdings I LLC (MSO).

STERLING—Southern Plains Cable, PO Box 165, Medicine Park, OK 73557. Phones: 800-218-1856; 580-529-5000. Fax: 580-365-4126. E-mail: office@wichitaonline.net. Web Site: http://www.spcisp.net. ICA: OK0208.
TV Market Ranking: Below 100 (STERLING). Franchise award date: N.A. Franchise expiration date: N.A. Began: October 1, 1982.
Channel capacity: N.A. Channels available but not in use: N.A.
Basic Service
Subscribers: N.A.
Programming (received off-air): KAUT-TV (Escape, MNT) Oklahoma City; KAUZ-TV (CBS, CW) Wichita Falls; KETA-TV (PBS) Oklahoma City; KFDX-TV (NBC) Wichita Falls; KFOR-TV (Antenna TV, NBC) Oklahoma City; KJTL (Bounce TV, FOX) Wichita Falls; KOCB (CW) Oklahoma City; KOCO-TV (ABC, This TV) Oklahoma City; KOKH-TV (FOX, The Country Network, WeatherNation) Oklahoma City; KSWO-TV (ABC, TMO) Lawton; KTBO-TV (TBN) Oklahoma City; KWTV-DT (CBS) Oklahoma City.
Programming (via satellite): A&E; AMC; Animal Planet; Cartoon Network; CMT; CNN; C-SPAN; Discovery Channel; ESPN; ESPN2; EVINE Live; EWTN Global Catholic Network; Fox News Channel; Freeform; HGTV; History; Lifetime; Local Cable Weather; Nickelodeon; Outdoor Channel; Spike TV; Syfy; TBS; The Weather Channel; TLC; TNT; Turner Classic Movies; TV Land; USA Network; WGN America.
Fee: $45.00 installation.
Pay Service 1
Pay Units: N.A.
Programming (via satellite): Cinemax; HBO; Showtime; The Movie Channel.
Fee: $10.00 monthly (each).
Video-On-Demand: No
Internet Service
Operational: Yes.
Telephone Service
Analog: Not Operational
Digital: Planned
Miles of Plant: 6.0 (coaxial); None (fiber optic). Homes passed: 300.
President: Dustin Hilliary.
Ownership: Southern Plains Cable (MSO).

STIGLER—Vyve Broadband, 4 International Dr, Ste 330, Rye Brook, NY 10573. Phones: 800-937-1397; 405-395-1131; 405-275-6923. Web Site: http://vyvebroadband.com. Also serves Haskell County & Whitefield. ICA: OK0081.
TV Market Ranking: Below 100 (Haskell County (portions)); Outside TV Markets (Haskell County (portions), STIGLER, Whitefield). Franchise award date: November 18, 1968. Franchise expiration date: N.A. Began: August 1, 1970.
Channel capacity: N.A. Channels available but not in use: N.A.
Basic Service
Subscribers: 132.
Programming (received off-air): KFSM-TV (CBS, MNT) Fort Smith; KJRH-TV (NBC) Tulsa; KMYT-TV (getTV, MNT, The Country Network) Tulsa; KOET (PBS) Eufaula; KOKI-TV (FOX, MeTV) Tulsa; KOTV-DT (CBS, IND) Tulsa; KQCW-DT (CW, This TV) Muskogee; KTUL (ABC, Antenna TV, Retro TV) Tulsa; allband FM.
Programming (via satellite): A&E; AMC; Cartoon Network; CMT; CNBC; CNN; C-SPAN; Discovery Channel; Disney Channel; ESPN; ESPN Classic; ESPN2; Food Network; Fox News Channel; FOX Sports Southwest; Freeform; FX; Hallmark Channel; HGTV; History; Lifetime; NFL Network; Nickelodeon; QVC; Spike TV; TBS; The Weather Channel; TNT; truTV; TV Land; USA Network; VH1.
Fee: $64.95 installation; $67.75 monthly.
Digital Basic Service
Subscribers: N.A.
Programming (via satellite): 52MX; Animal Planet; BBC America; Bloomberg Television; Bravo; Cine Mexicano; Cinelatino; Cloo; CMT; CNN en Espanol; Destination America; Discovery Kids Channel; Discovery Life Channel; Disney XD; DMX Music; ESPN Classic; ESPN2; ESPNews; EVINE Live; Flix; FOX College Sports Central; FOX College Sports Pacific; Fox Deportes; Fox Sports 1; Fuse; FXM; FYI; Golf Channel; Great American Country; GSN; HGTV; History; History en Espanol; History International; IFC; Investigation Discovery; LMN; MTV Classic; MTV Hits; MTV2; National Geographic Channel; NBCSN; Nick Jr.; Nicktoons; Outdoor Channel; Ovation; OWN: Oprah Winfrey Network; Science Channel; Starz Encore (multiplexed); Sundance TV; Syfy; TeenNick; The Word Network; Toon Disney en Espanol; Tr3s; Trinity Broadcasting Network (TBN); Turner Classic Movies; VH1 Soul; WE tv.
Pay Service 1
Pay Units: N.A.
Programming (via satellite): Cinemax; HBO; Showtime; Starz; Starz Encore.
Fee: $7.95 monthly (Cinemax), $9.95 monthly (Showtime), $10.50 monthly (HBO).
Digital Pay Service 1
Pay Units: N.A.
Programming (via satellite): Cinemax (multiplexed); HBO (multiplexed); Showtime (multiplexed); Starz (multiplexed); The Movie Channel (multiplexed).
Video-On-Demand: No
Pay-Per-View
iN DEMAND (delivered digitally); Hot Choice (delivered digitally); Playboy TV (delivered digitally); Fresh (delivered digitally); Shorteez (delivered digitally).
Internet Service
Operational: Yes.
Fee: $24.95 installation; $39.95 monthly.
Telephone Service
Digital: Operational
Miles of Plant: 39.0 (coaxial); None (fiber optic). Homes passed: 1,645.
Chief Executive Officer: Bill Haggarty. Senior Vice President, Financial Planning: Daniel White. Regional Vice President: Andrew Dearth. Vice President, Marketing: Tracy Bass.
Ownership: Vyve Broadband LLC (MSO).

Oklahoma—Cable Systems

STILLWATER—Suddenlink Communications, 802 East 6th Ave, Stillwater, OK 74074. Phones: 800-999-6845; 314-315-9400. Web Site: http://www.suddenlink.com. Also serves Payne County (portions) & Perkins. ICA: OK0008.
TV Market Ranking: Outside TV Markets (Perkins, STILLWATER). Franchise award date: January 27, 2000. Franchise expiration date: N.A. Began: November 1, 1971.
Channel capacity: N.A. Channels available but not in use: N.A.

Basic Service
Subscribers: 6,924. Commercial subscribers: 1,988.
Programming (received off-air): KAUT-TV (Escape, MNT) Oklahoma City; KETA-TV (PBS) Oklahoma City; KFOR-TV (Antenna TV, NBC) Oklahoma City; KOCB (CW) Oklahoma City; KOCO-TV (ABC, This TV) Oklahoma City; KOKH-TV (FOX, The Country Network, WeatherNation) Oklahoma City; KOPX-TV (ION) Oklahoma City; KOTV-DT (CBS, IND) Tulsa; KSBI (IND) Oklahoma City; KTBO-TV (TBN) Oklahoma City; KTUL (ABC, Antenna TV, Retro TV) Tulsa; KWTV-DT (CBS) Oklahoma City; 39 FMs.
Programming (via satellite): C-SPAN; Daystar TV Network; NASA TV; Pop; QVC; The Weather Channel; WGN America.
Fee: $74.99 installation; $21.09 monthly; $.78 converter.

Expanded Basic Service 1
Subscribers: N.A.
Programming (via satellite): A&E; AMC; Animal Planet; BET; Bravo; Cartoon Network; CMT; CNBC; CNN; Comedy Central; C-SPAN 2; Discovery Channel; Disney Channel; E! HD; ESPN; ESPN2; EWTN Global Catholic Network; Food Network; Fox News Channel; FOX Sports Southwest; Freeform; FX; HGTV; History; HLN; Lifetime; MoviePlex; MSNBC; MTV; MTV2; Nickelodeon; OWN: Oprah Winfrey Network; Oxygen; Spike TV; Syfy; TBS; TLC; TNT; Travel Channel; truTV; TV Land; Univision Studios; USA Network; VH1.
Fee: $36.00 monthly.

Digital Basic Service
Subscribers: N.A.
Programming (via satellite): BBC America; Bloomberg Television; Discovery Digital Networks; Disney XD; DMX Music; ESPN; ESPN Classic; ESPNews; Fox Sports 1; Fuse; FXM; FYI; Golf Channel; GSN; HD Theater; History International; IFC; LMN; NBCSN; Nick Jr.; Nicktoons; TeenNick; Turner Classic Movies.
Fee: $20.00 installation; $16.00 monthly.

Pay Service 1
Pay Units: 3,585.
Programming (via satellite): Cinemax.
Fee: $10.00 installation; $12.95 monthly.

Pay Service 2
Pay Units: 1,148.
Programming (via satellite): HBO.
Fee: $10.00 installation; $12.95 monthly.

Pay Service 3
Pay Units: 1,164.
Programming (via satellite): Showtime.
Fee: $10.00 installation; $12.95 monthly.

Pay Service 4
Pay Units: 3,644.
Programming (via satellite): Starz.
Fee: $10.00 installation; $6.75 monthly.

Pay Service 5
Pay Units: 3,696.
Programming (via satellite): Starz Encore.
Fee: $10.00 installation; $1.75 monthly.

Digital Pay Service 1
Pay Units: N.A.
Programming (via satellite): HBO; Showtime; Starz (multiplexed); Starz Encore (multiplexed); The Movie Channel.

Video-On-Demand: No

Pay-Per-View
iN DEMAND (delivered digitally); Hot Choice (delivered digitally); Fresh (delivered digitally); Shorteez (delivered digitally); Playboy TV (delivered digitally).

Internet Service
Operational: Yes. Began: August 31, 2001. Subscribers: 10,789.
Broadband Service: Suddenlink High Speed Internet.
Fee: $45.95 installation; $24.95 monthly.

Telephone Service
Digital: Operational
Subscribers: 2,868.
Fee: $49.95 monthly
Miles of Plant: 658.0 (coaxial); 130.0 (fiber optic). Homes passed: 40,024.
Senior Vice President, Corporate Finance: Michael Pflantz. General Manager: Nicole Evans. Marketing Manager: Heather Eastwood. Chief Technician: Johnny Stanley.
Ownership: Cequel Communications Holdings I LLC (MSO).

STILWELL—Vyve Broadband, 4 International Dr, Ste 330, Rye Brook, NY 10573. Phones: 800-937-1397; 405-395-1131; 405-275-6923. Web Site: http://vyvebroadband.com. ICA: OK0314.
TV Market Ranking: Below 100 (STILWELL). Franchise award date: N.A. Franchise expiration date: N.A. Began: July 1, 1982.
Channel capacity: N.A. Channels available but not in use: N.A.

Basic Service
Subscribers: 71.
Programming (received off-air): KFSM-TV (CBS, MNT) Fort Smith; KJRH-TV (NBC) Tulsa; KMYT-TV (getTV, MNT, The Country Network) Tulsa; KOED-TV (PBS) Tulsa; KOKI-TV (FOX, MeTV) Tulsa; KOTV-DT (CBS, IND) Tulsa; KQCW-DT (CW, This TV) Muskogee; KTUL (ABC, Antenna TV, Retro TV) Tulsa.
Programming (via satellite): A&E; AMC; Animal Planet; Cartoon Network; CMT; CNBC; CNN; Comedy Central; C-SPAN; Discovery Channel; Disney Channel; E! HD; ESPN; ESPN2; Fox News Channel; Fox Sports 1; FOX Sports Southwest; Freeform; FX; HGTV; History; HLN; Lifetime; MTV; Nickelodeon; Oxygen; Pop; QVC; Spike TV; Syfy; TBS; The Weather Channel; TLC; TNT; Travel Channel; Trinity Broadcasting Network (TBN); truTV; Turner Classic Movies; TV Land; USA Network; VH1; WGN America.
Fee: $64.95 installation; $70.95 monthly.

Digital Basic Service
Subscribers: N.A.
Programming (via satellite): BBC America; Bloomberg Television; Bravo; Chiller; Cloo; CMT; Destination America; Discovery Kids Channel; Discovery Life Channel; Disney XD; DMX Music; ESPN Classic; ESPNews; Flix; Fuse; FXM; FYI; Investigation Discovery; LMN; MTV Classic; MTV Hits; MTV2; National Geographic Channel; NBCSN; Nick Jr.; Nicktoons; Outdoor Channel; OWN: Oprah Winfrey Network; RFD-TV; Science Channel; Starz Encore (multiplexed); Sundance TV; TeenNick; Trinity Broadcasting Network (TBN); VH1 Soul; WE tv.

Digital Pay Service 1
Pay Units: N.A.
Programming (via satellite): Cinemax (multiplexed); HBO (multiplexed); Showtime (multiplexed); Starz (multiplexed); The Movie Channel.

Video-On-Demand: No

Pay-Per-View
iN DEMAND (delivered digitally); Club Jenna (delivered digitally); Playboy TV (delivered digitally); Fresh (delivered digitally); Spice: Xcess (delivered digitally).

Internet Service
Operational: No.

Telephone Service
None
Miles of Plant: 36.0 (coaxial); None (fiber optic).
Chief Executive Officer: Bill Haggarty. Regional Vice President: Andrew Dearth. Vice President, Marketing: Tracy Bass. Senior Vice President, Financial Planning: Daniel White.
Ownership: Vyve Broadband LLC (MSO).

STONEWALL—Formerly served by CommuniComm Services. Now served by Vyve Broadband, COALGATE, OK [OK0120]. ICA: OK0379.

STRANG—Formerly served by Allegiance Communications. Now served by Vyve Broadband, KETCHUM, OK [OK0179]. ICA: OK0259.

STRATFORD—Vyve Broadband, 4 International Dr, Ste 330, Rye Brook, NY 10573. Phones: 800-937-1397; 405-395-1131; 405-275-6923. Web Site: http://vyvebroadband.com. ICA: OK0315.
TV Market Ranking: Below 100 (STRATFORD). Franchise award date: June 3, 1980. Franchise expiration date: N.A. Began: June 1, 1981.
Channel capacity: N.A. Channels available but not in use: N.A.

Basic Service
Subscribers: 24.
Programming (received off-air): KAUT-TV (Escape, MNT) Oklahoma City; KETA-TV (PBS) Oklahoma City; KFOR-TV (Antenna TV, NBC) Oklahoma City; KOCB (CW) Oklahoma City; KOCO-TV (ABC, This TV) Oklahoma City; KOKH-TV (FOX, The Country Network, WeatherNation) Oklahoma City; KTEN (ABC, CW, NBC) Ada; KWTV-DT (CBS) Oklahoma City.
Programming (via satellite): C-SPAN; QVC; Trinity Broadcasting Network (TBN); WGN America.
Fee: $64.95 installation; $25.00 monthly.

Expanded Basic Service 1
Subscribers: 20.
Programming (via satellite): A&E; AMC; Animal Planet; CMT; CNBC; CNN; Comedy Central; C-SPAN 2; Discovery Channel; Disney Channel; E! HD; ESPN; Fox News Channel; FOX Sports Southwest; Freeform; History; HLN; Lifetime; MTV; Nickelodeon; Spike TV; Syfy; TBS; The Weather Channel; TLC; TNT; Travel Channel; TV Land; USA Network; WE tv.
Fee: $38.91 monthly.

Digital Basic Service
Subscribers: N.A.
Programming (via satellite): BBC America; Bloomberg Television; Bravo; Chiller; Cloo; CMT; Destination America; Discovery Kids Channel; Discovery Life Channel; Disney XD; DMX Music; ESPN Classic; ESPNews; EVINE Live; Flix; FOX College Sports Central; FOX College Sports Pacific; Fox Sports 1; Fuse; FXM; FYI; Golf Channel; Great American Country; GSN; HGTV; History International; IFC; Investigation Discovery; LMN; MTV Classic; MTV Hits; MTV2; National Geographic Channel; NBCSN; Nick Jr.; Nicktoons; OWN: Oprah Winfrey Network; RFD-TV; Science Channel; Starz Encore (multiplexed); Sundance TV; TeenNick; Turner Classic Movies; VH1 Soul.

Digital Pay Service 1
Pay Units: N.A.
Programming (via satellite): Cinemax (multiplexed); HBO (multiplexed); Showtime (multiplexed); Starz (multiplexed); The Movie Channel (multiplexed).

Video-On-Demand: No

Pay-Per-View
iN DEMAND (delivered digitally); Spice: Xcess (delivered digitally); Fresh (delivered digitally); Playboy TV (delivered digitally); Club Jenna (delivered digitally).

Internet Service
Operational: No.
Fee: $24.95 installation; $39.95 monthly.

Telephone Service
None
Miles of Plant: 13.0 (coaxial); None (fiber optic). Homes passed: 805.
Chief Executive Officer: Bill Haggarty. Senior Vice President, Financial Planning: Daniel White. Regional Vice President: Andrew Dearth. Vice President, Marketing: Tracy Bass.
Ownership: Vyve Broadband LLC (MSO).

STRINGTOWN—Formerly served by Allegiance Communications. No longer in operation. ICA: OK0339.

STROUD—Vyve Broadband, 4 International Dr, Ste 330, Rye Brook, NY 10573. Phones: 800-937-1397; 405-395-1131; 405-275-6923. Web Site: http://vyvebroadband.com. ICA: OK0100.
TV Market Ranking: Outside TV Markets (STROUD). Franchise award date: July 12, 1994. Franchise expiration date: N.A. Began: May 1, 1981.
Channel capacity: N.A. Channels available but not in use: N.A.

Basic Service
Subscribers: 42.
Programming (received off-air): KAUT-TV (Escape, MNT) Oklahoma City; KETA-TV (PBS) Oklahoma City; KFOR-TV (Antenna TV, NBC) Oklahoma City; KOCB (CW) Oklahoma City; KOCO-TV (ABC, This TV) Oklahoma City; KOKH-TV (FOX, The Country Network, WeatherNation) Oklahoma City; KOTV-DT (CBS, IND) Tulsa; KTBO-TV (TBN) Oklahoma City; KWTV-DT (CBS) Oklahoma City.
Programming (via satellite): A&E; AMC; Animal Planet; Bravo; Cartoon Network; CMT; CNBC; CNN; C-SPAN; C-SPAN 2; Discovery Channel; Disney Channel; ESPN; ESPN Classic; ESPN2; Food Network; Fox News Channel; FOX Sports Southwest; Freeform; FX; Hallmark Channel; HGTV; History; HLN; Lifetime; MTV; NFL Network; Nickelodeon; QVC; Spike TV; Syfy; TBS; The Weather Channel; TLC; TNT; USA Network; WGN America.
Fee: $64.95 installation; $25.00 monthly; $3.30 converter.

Digital Basic Service
Subscribers: N.A.
Programming (via satellite): 52MX; BBC America; Bloomberg Television; Cine Mexicano; Cinelatino; CMT; CNN en Espanol; Destination America; Discovery Life Channel; Disney XD; DMX Music; ESPN Clas-

Cable Systems—Oklahoma

sic; ESPN2; ESPNews; EVINE Live; Flix; FOX College Sports Central; FOX College Sports Pacific; Fox Deportes; Fox Sports 1; Fuse; FXM; FYI; Golf Channel; Great American Country; GSN; HGTV; History; History en Espanol; History International; IFC; Investigation Discovery; LMN; MTV Classic; MTV2; mtvU; National Geographic Channel; NBCSN; Nick Jr.; Nicktoons; Outdoor Channel; Ovation; OWN: Oprah Winfrey Network; Science Channel; Starz Encore (multiplexed); Sundance TV; Syfy; TeenNick; The Word Network; Toon Disney en Espanol; Tr3s; Trinity Broadcasting Network (TBN); Turner Classic Movies; TV Land; VH1 Soul; WE tv.
Fee: $13.95 monthly.

Pay Service 1
Pay Units: N.A.
Programming (via satellite): HBO; Showtime; Starz; Starz Encore.
Fee: $10.00 installation; $14.19 monthly.

Digital Pay Service 1
Pay Units: N.A.
Programming (via satellite): Cinemax (multiplexed); HBO (multiplexed); Showtime (multiplexed); Starz (multiplexed); The Movie Channel (multiplexed).

Pay-Per-View
iN DEMAND (delivered digitally); Hot Choice (delivered digitally); Fresh (delivered digitally); Spice: Xcess (delivered digitally); Club Jenna (delivered digitally); Playboy TV (delivered digitally).

Internet Service
Operational: No.

Telephone Service
None
Miles of Plant: 26.0 (coaxial); None (fiber optic). Homes passed: 1,716.
Chief Executive Officer: Bill Haggarty. Senior Vice President, Financial Planning: Daniel White. Regional Vice President: Andrew Dearth. Vice President, Marketing: Tracy Bass.
Ownership: Vyve Broadband LLC (MSO).

TAHLEQUAH—Tahlequah Cable TV Inc, 110 East Keetoowah St, PO Box 1689, Tahlequah, OK 74465-1689. Phone: 918-456-1102. Fax: 918-456-1172. E-mail: tahlequahcabletvcs@cablelynx.com. Web Site: http://www.tahlequahcabletv.com. ICA: OK0034.
TV Market Ranking: Below 100 (TAHLEQUAH). Franchise award date: May 7, 2002. Franchise expiration date: N.A. Began: July 1, 1980.
Channel capacity: N.A. Channels available but not in use: N.A.

Basic Service
Subscribers: 1,781. Commercial subscribers: 11.
Programming (received off-air): KDOR-TV (TBN) Bartlesville; KGEB (IND) Tulsa; KJRH-TV (NBC) Tulsa; KMYT-TV (getTV, MNT, The Country Network) Tulsa; KOED-TV (PBS) Tulsa; KOKI-TV (FOX, MeTV) Tulsa; KOTV-DT (CBS, IND) Tulsa; KRSU-TV (ETV) Claremore; KTPX-TV (ION) Okmulgee; KTUL (ABC, Antenna TV, Retro TV) Tulsa; KWHB (COZI TV, IND) Tulsa; allband FM.
Programming (via satellite): A&E; AMC; Animal Planet; Cartoon Network; CMT; CNN; Comedy Central; C-SPAN; C-SPAN 2; Discovery Channel; Disney Channel; DIY Network; ESPN; ESPN2; EVINE Live; Food Network; Fox News Channel; FOX Sports Southwest; Freeform; FX; Hallmark Channel; HGTV; History; HLN; Lifetime; MTV; Nickelodeon; Pop; Spike TV; Syfy; TBS; The Weather Channel; TLC; TNT; Travel Channel; Turner Classic Movies; TV Land; Univision; Univision Studios; USA Network; VH1; WGN America.
Fee: $69.95 installation; $31.90 monthly.

Digital Basic Service
Subscribers: N.A.
Programming (via satellite): BBC America; CMT; Destination America; Discovery Kids Channel; Discovery Life Channel; Disney XD; DMX Music; ESPNews; Fox Sports 1; FSN Digital Atlantic; FSN Digital Central; FSN Digital Pacific; FYI; Golf Channel; Great American Country; GSN; History International; Investigation Discovery; LMN; MTV Classic; MTV Hits; MTV Jams; MTV2; National Geographic Channel; Nick 2; Nick Jr.; Nicktoons; Outdoor Channel; OWN: Oprah Winfrey Network; Science Channel; TeenNick; Tr3s; VH1 Soul; WE tv.
Fee: $10.00 monthly.

Digital Pay Service 1
Pay Units: N.A.
Programming (via satellite): Cinemax (multiplexed); HBO (multiplexed); Showtime (multiplexed); Starz (multiplexed); Starz Encore (multiplexed).
Fee: $12.95 monthly (Cinemax), $14.95 monthly (HBO or Starz/Encore).

Video-On-Demand: No

Pay-Per-View
iN DEMAND (delivered digitally); special events.

Internet Service
Operational: Yes. Began: January 1, 2000.
Broadband Service: Cablelynx.
Fee: $24.95 monthly.

Telephone Service
Analog: Not Operational
Digital: Operational
Fee: $45.70 monthly
Miles of Plant: 186.0 (coaxial); None (fiber optic). Homes passed: 8,650.
Vice President, Administration: Charlotte A. Dial. General Manager: Robert Sluptick. Chief Technician: Steve Crone. Office Manager: Shirley Little.
Ownership: WEHCO Video Inc. (MSO).

TALALA—Formerly served by Quality Cablevision of Oklahoma Inc. No longer in operation. ICA: OK0340.

TALIHINA—Formerly served by Allegiance Communications. No longer in operation. ICA: OK0136.

TALOGA—Taloga Cable TV, 114A South Broadway, PO Box 218, Taloga, OK 73667-0218. Phone: 580-328-5262. Fax: 580-328-5262. E-mail: support@talogatv.com. ICA: OK0222.
TV Market Ranking: Outside TV Markets (TALOGA). Franchise award date: March 1, 1980. Franchise expiration date: N.A. Began: March 1, 1980.
Channel capacity: N.A. Channels available but not in use: N.A.

Basic Service
Subscribers: 65.
Programming (received off-air): KAUT-TV (Escape, MNT) Oklahoma City; KFOR-TV (Antenna TV, NBC) Oklahoma City; KOCB (CW) Oklahoma City; KOCO-TV (ABC, This TV) Oklahoma City; KOKH-TV (FOX, The Country Network, WeatherNation) Oklahoma City; KWET (PBS) Cheyenne; KWTV-DT (CBS) Oklahoma City.
Programming (via satellite): A&E; CMT; Comedy Central; C-SPAN; C-SPAN 2; Discovery Channel; ESPN; Food Network; Fox News Channel; FOX Sports Southwest; Hallmark Channel; History; ION Television; Lifetime; Nickelodeon; QVC; Spike TV; Syfy; TBS; The Weather Channel; TLC; TNT; Travel Channel; Trinity Broadcasting Network (TBN); Turner Classic Movies; USA Network.
Fee: $30.00 installation; $6.00 monthly; $3.00 converter.

Pay Service 1
Pay Units: 50.
Programming (via satellite): Cinemax; HBO; Showtime; Starz; The Movie Channel.
Fee: $12.00 monthly (each).

Video-On-Demand: No

Internet Service
Operational: Yes. Began: January 1, 2000.
Subscribers: 60.
Broadband Service: InterTECH.
Fee: $150.00 installation; $35.00 monthly.

Telephone Service
None
Miles of Plant: 9.0 (coaxial); None (fiber optic). Homes passed: 170.
President & General Manager: Glenn Gore.
Ownership: Taloga Cable TV.

TERRAL—Formerly served by Almega Cable. No longer in operation. ICA: OK0229.

THOMAS—Pioneer Telephone Coop. This cable system has converted to IPTV. Now served by KINGFISHER, OK [OK5074]. ICA: OK0155.

TIPTON—Formerly served by LakeView Cable. No longer in operation. ICA: OK0191.

TRYON—Formerly served by Allegiance Communications. No longer in operation. ICA: OK0316.

TULSA—Cox Communications, 6205 Peachtree Dunwoody Rd, 12th Floor, Atlanta, GA 30328. Phone: 404-269-6590. Web Site: http://www.cox.com. Also serves Bixby, Broken Arrow, Catoosa, Claremore, Coweta, Creek County (portions), Glenpool, Jenks, Kiefer, Osage County (portions), Owasso, Rogers County (portions), Sand Springs, Sapulpa, Tulsa County (portions) & Wagoner County (portions). ICA: OK0001.
TV Market Ranking: 54 (Bixby, Broken Arrow, Catoosa, Claremore, Coweta, Creek County (portions), Glenpool, Jenks, Kiefer, Osage County (portions), Owasso, Rogers County (portions), Sand Springs, Sapulpa, TULSA, Tulsa County (portions), Wagoner County (portions)); Below 100 (Osage County (portions), Rogers County (portions)); Outside TV Markets (Creek County (portions), Osage County (portions), Rogers County (portions), Wagoner County (portions)). Franchise award date: June 1, 1971. Franchise expiration date: N.A. Began: January 18, 1974.
Channel capacity: N.A. Channels available but not in use: N.A.

Basic Service
Subscribers: 131,062. Commercial subscribers: 4,773.
Programming (received off-air): KDOR-TV (TBN) Bartlesville; KGEB (IND) Tulsa; KJRH-TV (NBC) Tulsa; KMYT-TV (getTV, MNT, The Country Network) Tulsa; KOED-TV (PBS) Tulsa; KOKI-TV (FOX, MeTV) Tulsa; KOTV-DT (CBS, IND) Tulsa; KQCW-DT (CW, This TV) Muskogee; KRSU-TV (ETV) Claremore; KTUL (ABC, Antenna TV, Retro TV) Tulsa; KWHB (COZI TV, IND) Tulsa.
Programming (via satellite): ION Television; Pop; QVC; Univision Studios; WGN America.
Fee: $30.00 installation; $21.99 monthly.

Expanded Basic Service 1
Subscribers: N.A.
Programming (via satellite): A&E; AMC; Animal Planet; BET; Bravo; Cartoon Network; CMT; CNBC; CNN; Comedy Central; C-SPAN; C-SPAN 2; Discovery Channel; Disney Channel; E! HD; ESPN; ESPN2; Food Network; Fox News Channel; FOX Sports Southwest; Freeform; FX; HGTV; History; HLN; Lifetime; MSNBC; MTV; Nickelodeon; OWN: Oprah Winfrey Network; Spike TV; TBS; The Weather Channel; TLC; TNT; Travel Channel; truTV; TV Land; USA Network; VH1.
Fee: $32.24 monthly.

Digital Basic Service
Subscribers: N.A.
Programming (via satellite): BBC America; Bloomberg Television; Cooking Channel; Discovery Life Channel; Disney XD; DIY Network; ESPN; ESPN Classic; ESPNews; EWTN Global Catholic Network; FamilyNet; Fox Sports 1; FYI; Golf Channel; Great American Country; GSN; Hallmark Channel; HD Theater; History International; HITS (Headend In The Sky); IFC; LMN; MC; National Geographic Channel; NBA TV; NBCSN; NFL Network; Nick 2; Nick Jr.; Nicktoons; Outdoor Channel; Oxygen; Sprout; Starz Encore (multiplexed); Starz Encore Family; Sundance TV; Syfy; TeenNick; Turner Classic Movies; TV One; Universal HD; WE tv.
Fee: $13.50 monthly.

Digital Pay Service 1
Pay Units: N.A.
Programming (via satellite): Cinemax (multiplexed); HBO; Showtime; Starz (multiplexed); Starz HD; The Movie Channel.
Fee: $12.00 monthly (each package).

Video-On-Demand: No

Pay-Per-View
Hot Choice (delivered digitally); iN DEMAND (delivered digitally); Playboy TV (delivered digitally); Fresh (delivered digitally); Shorteez (delivered digitally); NBA League Pass (delivered digitally); NHL Center Ice (delivered digitally); MLB Extra Innings (delivered digitally).

Internet Service
Operational: Yes.
Subscribers: 141,288.
Broadband Service: Cox High Speed Internet.
Fee: $99.95 installation; $34.95 monthly; $10.00 modem lease.

Telephone Service
Digital: Operational
Subscribers: 92,633.
Fee: $12.36 monthly
Miles of Plant: 6,988.0 (coaxial); 1,637.0 (fiber optic). Homes passed: 343,805.
President & General Manager: Dave Bialis. Vice President, Operations: John Bowen. Vice President, Marketing: Mollie Andrews. Vice President, Tax: Mary Vickers. Communications Director: Cristine Martin.
Ownership: Cox Communications Inc. (MSO).

TULSA COUNTY (western portion)—Formerly served by Summit Digital. No longer in operation. ICA: OK0341.

TURPIN—Formerly served by Allegiance Communications. No longer in operation. ICA: OK0317.

TUTTLE—Formerly served by Vidia Communications. No longer in operation. ICA: OK0137.

Oklahoma—Cable Systems

TYRONE—Formerly served by Allegiance Communications. No longer in operation. ICA: OK0318.

UNION CITY—Formerly served by Vidia Communications. No longer in operation. ICA: OK0319.

VALLIANT—Formerly served by Allegiance Communications. No longer in operation. ICA: OK0167.

VELMA—Formerly served by Reach Broadband. No longer in operation. ICA: OK0320.

VERDEN—Formerly served by Cable West. No longer in operation. ICA: OK0321.

VERDIGRIS—Formerly served by Allegiance Communications. No longer in operation. ICA: OK0094.

VIAN—Vyve Broadband, 4 International Dr, Ste 330, Rye Brook, NY 10573. Phones: 800-937-1397; 405-395-1131; 405-275-6923. Web Site: http://vyvebroadband.com. ICA: OK0130.
TV Market Ranking: Below 100 (VIAN). Franchise award date: January 28, 1980. Franchise expiration date: N.A. Began: N.A.
Channel capacity: N.A. Channels available but not in use: N.A.
Basic Service
Subscribers: 54.
Programming (received off-air): KFSM-TV (CBS, MNT) Fort Smith; KGEB (IND) Tulsa; KHBS (ABC, CW) Fort Smith; KJRH-TV (NBC) Tulsa; KOET (PBS) Eufaula; KOKI-TV (FOX, MeTV) Tulsa; KQCW-DT (CW, This TV) Muskogee; KTUL (ABC, Antenna TV, Retro TV) Tulsa; KWHB (COZI TV, IND) Tulsa.
Programming (via satellite): A&E; AMC; Animal Planet; Cartoon Network; CMT; CNBC; CNN; Comedy Central; C-SPAN; Discovery Channel; Disney Channel; E! HD; ESPN; ESPN2; Food Network; Fox News Channel; Fox Sports 1; FOX Sports Southwest; Freeform; FX; Hallmark Channel; HGTV; History; HLN; INSP; Lifetime; MSNBC; Nickelodeon; Outdoor Channel; Oxygen; QVC; Spike TV; Syfy; TBS; The Weather Channel; TLC; TNT; Travel Channel; truTV; Turner Classic Movies; USA Network; WGN America.
Fee: $64.95 installation; $67.75 monthly.
Digital Basic Service
Subscribers: N.A.
Programming (via satellite): BBC America; Bloomberg Television; Bravo; Chiller; Cloo; CMT; Destination America; Discovery Kids Channel; Discovery Life Channel; Disney XD; DMX Music; ESPN Classic; ESPNews; EVINE Live; Flix; FOX College Sports Central; FOX College Sports Pacific; Fuse; FXM; FYI; Golf Channel; GSN; History International; IFC; Investigation Discovery; LMN; MTV Classic; MTV Hits; MTV2; National Geographic Channel; NBCSN; Nick Jr.; Nicktoons; OWN: Oprah Winfrey Network; RFD-TV; Science Channel; Starz Encore (multiplexed); Sundance TV; TeenNick; Trinity Broadcasting Network (TBN); VH1 Soul; WE tv.
Pay Service 1
Pay Units: N.A.
Programming (via satellite): Cinemax; HBO; Showtime.
Fee: $9.00 monthly (HBO).
Digital Pay Service 1
Pay Units: N.A.
Programming (via satellite): Cinemax (multiplexed); HBO (multiplexed); Showtime (multiplexed); Starz (multiplexed); The Movie Channel (multiplexed).
Video-On-Demand: No
Pay-Per-View
iN DEMAND (delivered digitally); Club Jenna (delivered digitally); Playboy TV (delivered digitally); Fresh (delivered digitally); Spice: Xcess (delivered digitally).
Internet Service
Operational: No.
Telephone Service
None
Miles of Plant: 16.0 (coaxial); None (fiber optic). Homes passed: 750.
Chief Executive Officer: Bill Haggarty. Senior Vice President, Financial Planning: Daniel White. Regional Vice President: Andrew Dearth. Vice President, Marketing: Tracy Bass.
Ownership: Vyve Broadband LLC (MSO).

VICI—Formerly served by Rapid Cable. No longer in operation. ICA: OK0174.

VINITA—Cable One, 2600 Davis Blvd, Joplin, MO 64804. Phone: 918-256-7871. E-mail: mslyman@cableone.net. Web Site: http://www.cableone.net. Also serves Craig County. ICA: OK0322.
TV Market Ranking: Below 100 (Craig County (portions)); Outside TV Markets (Craig County (portions), VINITA). Franchise award date: November 18, 1975. Franchise expiration date: N.A. Began: July 1, 1979.
Channel capacity: N.A. Channels available but not in use: N.A.
Basic Service
Subscribers: 696.
Programming (received off-air): KGEB (IND) Tulsa; KJRH-TV (NBC) Tulsa; KOAM-TV (CBS) Pittsburg; KODE-TV (ABC) Joplin; KOED-TV (PBS) Tulsa; KOKI-TV (FOX, MeTV) Tulsa; KOTV-DT (CBS, IND) Tulsa; KQCW-DT (CW, This TV) Muskogee; KRSU-TV (ETV) Claremore; KSNF (NBC) Joplin; KTPX-TV (ION) Okmulgee; KTUL (ABC, Antenna TV, Retro TV) Tulsa; KWHB (COZI TV, IND) Tulsa; 2 FMs.
Programming (via satellite): A&E; AMC; Animal Planet; Cartoon Network; CMT; CNN; C-SPAN; Discovery Channel; Disney Channel; ESPN; ESPN2; Food Network; Fox News Channel; FOX Sports Southwest; Freeform; FX; HGTV; History; HLN; ION Television; Lifetime; MSNBC; MTV; Nickelodeon; Pop; QVC; Spike TV; Syfy; TBS; The Weather Channel; TLC; TNT; Turner Classic Movies; TV Land; USA Network; VH1.
Fee: $90.00 installation; $35.00 monthly; $1.56 converter.
Digital Basic Service
Subscribers: N.A.
Programming (via satellite): Boomerang; BYUtv; Discovery Digital Networks; Disney XD; DMX Music; ESPN Classic; ESPNews; FamilyNet; Fox Sports 1; Fox Sports 2; FSN Digital Atlantic; FSN Digital Central; FSN Digital Pacific; FXM; FYI; Golf Channel; Great American Country; Hallmark Channel; History; History International; HITS (Head-end In The Sky); INSP; National Geographic Channel; Outdoor Channel; truTV; TVG Network.
Fee: $46.00 monthly.
Digital Pay Service 1
Pay Units: N.A.
Programming (via satellite): Cinemax (multiplexed); Flix; HBO (multiplexed); Showtime (multiplexed); Starz (multiplexed); Starz Encore (multiplexed); Sundance TV; The Movie Channel (multiplexed).
Fee: $7.00 monthly (each).
Video-On-Demand: No
Pay-Per-View
Hot Choice; iN DEMAND; Fresh; iN DEMAND (delivered digitally); Pleasure (delivered digitally); Sports PPV (delivered digitally).
Internet Service
Operational: Yes. Began: December 1, 2001.
Broadband Service: CableONE.net.
Fee: $75.00 installation; $43.00 monthly; $5.00 modem lease.
Telephone Service
Digital: Operational
Fee: $39.95 monthly
Miles of Plant: 61.0 (coaxial); None (fiber optic). Homes passed: 3,172.
Vice President: Patrick A. Dolohanty. General Manager: Mike Slyman. Chief Technician: Bob Young. Marketing & Office Director: Sandy Shultz.
Ownership: Cable ONE Inc. (MSO).

WAGONER—Vyve Broadband, 4 International Dr, Ste 330, Rye Brook, NY 10573. Phone: 800-937-1397. Web Site: http://vyvebroadband.com. ICA: OK0801.
TV Market Ranking: 54 (WAGONER).
Channel capacity: N.A. Channels available but not in use: N.A.
Basic Service
Subscribers: 43.
Fee: $64.95 installation; $25.00 monthly.
Expanded Basic Service 1
Subscribers: 42.
Fee: $39.96 monthly.
Senior Vice President, Financial Planning: Daniel White.
Ownership: Vyve Broadband LLC (MSO).

WAKITA—Pioneer Telephone Coop. This cable system has converted to IPTV. Now served by KINGFISHER, OK [OK5074]. ICA: OK0226.

WALTERS—Alliance Communications, PO Box 9090, Tyler, TX 75711. Phones: 903-561-4411; 800-842-8160; 501-679-6619 (Greenbrier, AR office). Web Site: http://www.alliancecable.net. Also serves Temple. ICA: OK0108.
TV Market Ranking: Below 100 (Temple, WALTERS). Franchise award date: N.A. Franchise expiration date: N.A. Began: January 1, 1978.
Channel capacity: 46 (not 2-way capable). Channels available but not in use: N.A.
Basic Service
Subscribers: 92.
Programming (received off-air): KAUZ-TV (CBS, CW) Wichita Falls; KETA-TV (PBS) Oklahoma City; KFDX-TV (NBC) Wichita Falls; KFOR-TV (Antenna TV, NBC) Oklahoma City; KJTL (Bounce TV, FOX) Wichita Falls; KSWO-TV (ABC, TMO) Lawton; KWTV-DT (CBS) Oklahoma City.
Programming (via satellite): A&E; Animal Planet; Cartoon Network; CNBC; CNN; C-SPAN; Discovery Channel; Disney Channel; E! HD; ESPN; ESPN2; Fox News Channel; FOX Sports Southwest; Freeform; Great American Country; HGTV; History; HLN; Lifetime; MSNBC; MTV; National Geographic Channel; Nickelodeon; QVC; Spike TV; Syfy; TBS; The Weather Channel; TLC; TNT; Trinity Broadcasting Network (TBN); truTV; TV Land; USA Network.
Fee: $45.00 installation; $22.45 monthly.

Pay Service 1
Pay Units: N.A.
Programming (via satellite): HBO; Showtime; The Movie Channel.
Fee: $10.95 monthly.
Video-On-Demand: No
Pay-Per-View
iN DEMAND (delivered digitally); Playboy TV (delivered digitally); Shorteez (delivered digitally).
Internet Service
Operational: No.
Telephone Service
None
Miles of Plant: 35.0 (coaxial); None (fiber optic). Homes passed: 1,710.
Chief Financial Officer: David Starrett. Vice President & General Manager: John Brinker. Vice President, Programming: Julie Newman.
Ownership: Buford Media Group LLC (MSO).

WANETTE—Formerly served by Cebridge Connections. No longer in operation. ICA: OK0323.

WAPANUCKA—Formerly served by Allegiance Communications. No longer in operation. ICA: OK0337.

WARNER—Cross Telephone Co, 704 3rd Ave, PO Box 9, Warner, OK 74469. Phones: 800-828-6567; 918-463-2921. Fax: 918-463-2551. E-mail: staff@crosstel.net. Web Site: http://www.crosstel. ICA: OK0160.
TV Market Ranking: Below 100 (WARNER). Franchise award date: January 1, 1984. Franchise expiration date: N.A. Began: January 1, 1984.
Channel capacity: N.A. Channels available but not in use: N.A.
Digital Basic Service
Subscribers: N.A.
Programming (received off-air): KDOR-TV (TBN) Bartlesville; KGEB (IND) Tulsa; KJRH-TV (NBC) Tulsa; KMYT-TV (getTV, MNT, The Country Network) Tulsa; KOED-TV (PBS) Tulsa; KOKI-TV (FOX, MeTV) Tulsa; KOTV-DT (CBS, IND) Tulsa; KTPX-TV (ION) Okmulgee; KTUL (ABC, Antenna TV, Retro TV) Tulsa; KWHB (COZI TV, IND) Tulsa.
Programming (via satellite): A&E; AMC; Animal Planet; BBC America; BET; Bloomberg Television; BYUtv; CMT; CNN; C-SPAN; C-SPAN 2; CW PLUS; Destination America; Discovery Channel; Discovery Kids Channel; Disney Channel; Disney XD; DIY Network; DMX Music; ESPN; ESPN Classic; ESPN2; ESPNews; EWTN Global Catholic Network; Fox News Channel; FOX Sports Southwest; Freeform; FX; FYI; Hallmark Channel; HGTV; History; History International; HLN; IFC; INSP; Investigation Discovery; Lifetime; LMN; MSNBC; MTV; MTV Classic; MTV Hits; MTV2; National Geographic Channel; Nick Jr.; Nickelodeon; Nicktoons; OWN: Oprah Winfrey Network; Oxygen; QVC; RFD-TV; Science Channel; Spike TV; Syfy; TBS; TeenNick; The Weather Channel; TLC; TNT; Travel Channel; truTV; Turner Classic Movies; TV Land; USA Network; VH1; WE tv; WGN America.
Digital Expanded Basic Service
Subscribers: N.A.
Programming (via satellite): Bravo; Cartoon Network; CNBC; Comedy Central; Cooking Channel; E! HD; Food Network; Fox Sports 1; FXM; Golf Channel; Great American Country; GSN; NBCSN; Outdoor Channel.

Cable Systems—Oklahoma

Digital Pay Service 1
Pay Units: N.A.
Programming (via satellite): Cinemax (multiplexed); HBO (multiplexed); Starz (multiplexed); Starz Encore (multiplexed).
Video-On-Demand: Planned
Internet Service
Operational: Yes, DSL.
Telephone Service
Digital: Operational
Miles of Plant: 30.0 (coaxial); None (fiber optic). Homes passed: 650.
General Manager: R. David Right. Chief Technician & Program Director: Troy Duncan. Marketing Director: Ashley Thompson. Customer Service Manager: Dale Wiggins.
Ownership: V. David & Billie Lynn Miller.

WASHINGTON (portions)—Formerly served by Cebridge Connections. No longer in operation. ICA: OK0248.

WATONGA—Pioneer Telephone Coop. This cable system has converted to IPTV. Now served by KINGFISHER, OK [OK5074]. ICA: OK0082.

WAUKOMIS—Formerly served by Adelphia Cable. No longer in operation. ICA: OK0369.

WAURIKA—Alliance Communications, PO Box 9090, Tyler, TX 75711. Phones: 903-561-4411; 800-842-8160; 501-679-6619 (Greenbrier, AR office). Web Site: http://www.alliancecable.net. ICA: OK0106.
TV Market Ranking: Below 100 (WAURIKA). Franchise award date: June 5, 1978. Franchise expiration date: N.A. Began: September 1, 1981.
Channel capacity: 41 (not 2-way capable). Channels available but not in use: N.A.
Basic Service
Subscribers: 67.
Programming (received off-air): KAUZ-TV (CBS, CW) Wichita Falls; KETA-TV (PBS) Oklahoma City; KFDX-TV (NBC) Wichita Falls; KFOR-TV (Antenna TV, NBC) Oklahoma City; KJTL (Bounce TV, FOX) Wichita Falls; KOCO-TV (ABC, This TV) Oklahoma City; KOKH-TV (FOX, The Country Network, WeatherNation) Oklahoma City; KSWO-TV (ABC, TMO) Lawton; KWTV-DT (CBS) Oklahoma City.
Programming (via satellite): A&E; CNBC; CNN; C-SPAN; Discovery Channel; Disney Channel; ESPN; ESPN2; Fox News Channel; FOX Sports Networks; Freeform; FX; Great American Country; HGTV; History; HLN; INSP; Lifetime; National Geographic Channel; Nickelodeon; QVC; Spike TV; The Weather Channel; TLC; TNT; Trinity Broadcasting Network (TBN); Turner Classic Movies; USA Network.
Fee: $45.00 installation; $22.45 monthly.
Pay Service 1
Pay Units: N.A.
Programming (via satellite): HBO; Showtime; The Movie Channel.
Fee: $10.95 monthly.
Video-On-Demand: No
Internet Service
Operational: No.
Telephone Service
None
Miles of Plant: 16.0 (coaxial); None (fiber optic). Homes passed: 1,030.
Chief Financial Officer: David Starrett. Vice President & General Manager: John Brinker. Vice President, Programming: Julie Newman.
Ownership: Buford Media Group LLC (MSO).

WAYNOKA—Formerly served by Waynoka Community TV. No longer in operation. ICA: OK0149.

WEATHERFORD—Suddenlink Communications, 520 Maryville Centre Dr, Ste 300, St. Louis, MO 63141. Phones: 580-774-2288; 877-423-2743 (Customer service); 314-315-9400. Web Site: http://www.suddenlink.com. Also serves Hydro. ICA: OK0045.
TV Market Ranking: Outside TV Markets (Hydro, WEATHERFORD). Franchise award date: July 1, 1967. Franchise expiration date: N.A. Began: July 1, 1967.
Channel capacity: 45 (operating 2-way). Channels available but not in use: N.A.
Basic Service
Subscribers: 1,269. Commercial subscribers: 264.
Programming (received off-air): KAUT-TV (Escape, MNT) Oklahoma City; KETA-TV (PBS) Oklahoma City; KFOR-TV (Antenna TV, NBC) Oklahoma City; KOCB (CW) Oklahoma City; KOCO-TV (ABC, This TV) Oklahoma City; KOKH-TV (FOX, The Country Network, WeatherNation) Oklahoma City; KOPX-TV (ION) Oklahoma City; KSBI (IND) Oklahoma City; KWTV-DT (CBS) Oklahoma City; allband FM.
Fee: $28.45 monthly.
Expanded Basic Service 1
Subscribers: N.A.
Programming (via satellite): A&E; AMC; Animal Planet; BET; Bravo; Cartoon Network; CNBC; CNN; Comedy Central; C-SPAN; Discovery Channel; Disney Channel; E! HD; ESPN; ESPN2; EWTN Global Catholic Network; Food Network; Fox News Channel; Fox Sports 1; FOX Sports Southwest; Freeform; FX; Golf Channel; Great American Country; Hallmark Channel; HGTV; History; HLN; INSP; Lifetime; MSNBC; MTV; National Geographic Channel; Nickelodeon; Outdoor Channel; Pop; QVC; Spike TV; Syfy; TBS; The Weather Channel; TLC; TNT; Travel Channel; Trinity Broadcasting Network (TBN); Turner Classic Movies; TV Land; Univision Studios; USA Network; VH1.
Fee: $24.00 monthly.
Digital Basic Service
Subscribers: N.A.
Programming (via satellite): BBC America; Bloomberg Television; Cloo; Discovery Digital Networks; Disney XD; ESPN Classic; ESPNews; Fuse; FYI; GSN; History International; IFC; NBCSN; Sundance TV; WE tv.
Fee: $3.99 monthly.
Pay Service 1
Pay Units: N.A.
Programming (via satellite): HBO; Showtime; The Movie Channel.
Fee: $35.00 installation; $5.95 monthly (TMC), $9.95 monthly (Showtime), $10.95 monthly (HBO).
Digital Pay Service 1
Pay Units: N.A.
Programming (via satellite): Cinemax (multiplexed); HBO (multiplexed); Showtime (multiplexed); Starz (multiplexed); Starz Encore (multiplexed); The Movie Channel (multiplexed).
Video-On-Demand: No
Pay-Per-View
iN DEMAND (delivered digitally); Playboy TV (delivered digitally).
Internet Service
Operational: Yes. Began: June 23, 2002. Broadband Service: Suddenlink High Speed Internet.
Fee: $45.95 installation; $24.95 monthly.

Telephone Service
Digital: Operational
Fee: $49.95 monthly
Miles of Plant: 89.0 (coaxial); None (fiber optic). Homes passed: 4,900.
Vice President, Corporate Finance: Michael Pflantz. Regional Manager: Todd Cruthird. General Manager: Dave Walker. Marketing Director: Beverly Gambell. Chief Technician: Roger Campbell.
Ownership: Cequel Communications Holdings I LLC (MSO).

WELCH—Formerly served by Allegiance Communications. No longer in operation. ICA: OK0190.

WELEETKA—Formerly served by Allegiance Communications. No longer in operation. ICA: OK0165.

WELLSTON—Formerly served by Allegiance Communications. No longer in operation. ICA: OK0192.

WESTVILLE—Formerly served by Vyve Broadband. No longer in operation. ICA: OK0138.

WETUMKA—Formerly served by Vyve Broadband. No longer in operation. ICA: OK0325.

WEWOKA—Suddenlink Communications, 1010 East Strothers, Seminole, OK 74868. Phones: 314-315-9400; 877-694-9474. Web Site: http://www.suddenlink.com. ICA: OK0077.
TV Market Ranking: Below 100 (WEWOKA). Channel capacity: N.A. Channels available but not in use: N.A.
Basic Service
Subscribers: 479. Commercial subscribers: 93.
Fee: $54.95 installation; $33.24 monthly.
Senior Vice President, Corporate Finance: Michael Pflantz.
Ownership: Cequel Communications Holdings I LLC (MSO).

WHITE HORN COVE—Formerly served by Lake Area TV Cable. No longer in operation. ICA: OK0095.

WILBURTON—Vyve Broadband, 4 International Dr, Ste 330, Rye Brook, NY 10573. Phones: 800-937-1397; 405-395-1131; 405-275-6923. Web Site: http://vyvebroadband.com. Also serves Red Oak. ICA: OK0088.
TV Market Ranking: Outside TV Markets (Red Oak, WILBURTON). Franchise award date: N.A. Franchise expiration date: N.A. Began: October 1, 1962.
Channel capacity: N.A. Channels available but not in use: N.A.
Basic Service
Subscribers: 221.
Programming (received off-air): KJRH-TV (NBC) Tulsa; KMYT-TV (getTV, MNT, The Country Network) Tulsa; KOET (PBS) Eufaula; KOKI-TV (FOX, MeTV) Tulsa; KOTV-DT (CBS, IND) Tulsa; KQCW-DT (CW, This TV) Muskogee; KTEN (ABC, CW, NBC) Ada; KTPX-TV (ION) Okmulgee; KTUL (ABC, Antenna TV, Retro TV) Tulsa; KWHB (COZI TV, IND) Tulsa; allband FM.
Programming (via satellite): C-SPAN; QVC; Trinity Broadcasting Network (TBN); WGN America.
Fee: $64.95 installation; $25.00 monthly; $1.96 converter.

Expanded Basic Service 1
Subscribers: 158.
Programming (via satellite): A&E; AMC; Animal Planet; Cartoon Network; CMT; CNBC; CNN; Comedy Central; Discovery Channel; Disney Channel; E! HD; ESPN; ESPN2; Food Network; Fox News Channel; Fox Sports 1; FOX Sports Southwest; Freeform; FX; HGTV; History; HLN; Lifetime; MTV; Nickelodeon; Outdoor Channel; Oxygen; Spike TV; Syfy; TBS; The Weather Channel; TLC; TNT; Travel Channel; truTV; Turner Classic Movies; TV Land; USA Network; VH1.
Fee: $37.86 monthly.
Digital Basic Service
Subscribers: N.A.
Programming (via satellite): BBC America; Bloomberg Television; CMT; Destination America; Discovery Kids Channel; Disney XD; DIY Network; ESPN Classic; ESPNU; Flix; FYI; GSN; History International; IFC; Investigation Discovery; LOGO; MC; MTV Classic; MTV Hits; MTV Jams; MTV2; Nick 2; Nick Jr.; Nicktoons; OWN: Oprah Winfrey Network; Science Channel; Starz Encore (multiplexed); Sundance TV; TeenNick; Tr3s; Turner Classic Movies; VH1 Soul; WE tv.
Digital Pay Service 1
Pay Units: N.A.
Programming (via satellite): Cinemax (multiplexed); HBO (multiplexed); Showtime (multiplexed); Starz (multiplexed); Starz Encore (multiplexed); The Movie Channel (multiplexed).
Video-On-Demand: No
Pay-Per-View
iN DEMAND (delivered digitally); Spice Xcess (delivered digitally); Club Jenna (delivered digitally); Playboy TV (delivered digitally); Fresh (delivered digitally); Shorteez (delivered digitally).
Internet Service
Operational: No.
Telephone Service
None
Miles of Plant: 80.0 (coaxial); None (fiber optic). Homes passed: 1,950.
Chief Executive Officer: Bill Haggarty. Regional Vice President: Andrew Dearth. Vice President, Marketing: Tracy Bass. Senior Vice President, Financial Planning: Daniel White.
Ownership: Vyve Broadband LLC (MSO).

WISTER—Formerly served by Allegiance Communications. No longer in operation. ICA: OK0193.

WOODALL—Formerly served by Eagle Media. No longer in operation. ICA: OK0365.

WOODWARD—Suddenlink Communications, 520 Maryville Centre Dr, Ste 300, St. Louis, MO 63141. Phones: 580-254-5944; 800-999-6845; 314-315-9400; 314-315-9346. Web Site: http://www.suddenlink.com. Also serves Mooreland. ICA: OK0029.
TV Market Ranking: Outside TV Markets (Mooreland, WOODWARD). Franchise award date: March 18, 1956. Franchise expiration date: N.A. Began: April 1, 1956.
Channel capacity: N.A. Channels available but not in use: N.A.
Basic Service
Subscribers: 1,052. Commercial subscribers: 286.
Programming (received off-air): KETA-TV (PBS) Oklahoma City; KOCB (CW) Oklahoma City; KOMI-CD Woodward; KUOK (UNV) Woodward.

Oklahoma—Cable Systems

Programming (via microwave): KFOR-TV (Antenna TV, NBC) Oklahoma City; KOCO-TV (ABC, This TV) Oklahoma City; KOKH-TV (FOX, The Country Network, WeatherNation) Oklahoma City; KWTV-DT (CBS) Oklahoma City.
Programming (via satellite): QVC; The Weather Channel.
Fee: $28.45 monthly.

Expanded Basic Service 1
Subscribers: N.A.
Programming (via microwave): KVDA (TMO) San Antonio.
Programming (via satellite): A&E; AMC; Animal Planet; Cartoon Network; CNBC; CNN; Comedy Central; C-SPAN; Discovery Channel; Disney Channel; Disney XD; E! HD; ESPN; ESPN2; Food Network; Fox News Channel; FOX Sports Southwest; Freeform; FX; Great American Country; Hallmark Channel; HGTV; History; HLN; IFC; Lifetime; MSNBC; MTV; National Geographic Channel; Nickelodeon; Outdoor Channel; Spike TV; Syfy; TBS; TLC; TNT; Travel Channel; Trinity Broadcasting Network (TBN); Turner Classic Movies; TV Land; USA Network; VH1.
Fee: $24.00 monthly.

Digital Basic Service
Subscribers: N.A.
Programming (via satellite): BBC America; Cloo; Discovery Digital Networks; DMX Music; ESPN Classic; ESPNews; Fox Sports 1; Fuse; FYI; Golf Channel; GSN; History International; NBCSN; WE tv.
Fee: $3.99 monthly.

Pay Service 1
Pay Units: N.A.
Programming (via satellite): Cinemax; HBO; Showtime; The Movie Channel.
Fee: $10.00 installation; $5.95 monthly (TMC), $9.95 monthly (Cinemax or Showtime), $10.95 monthly (HBO).

Digital Pay Service 1
Pay Units: N.A.
Programming (via satellite): Cinemax (multiplexed); HBO (multiplexed); Showtime (multiplexed); Starz; Starz Encore (multiplexed); The Movie Channel (multiplexed).
Video-On-Demand: No
Pay-Per-View
iN DEMAND (delivered digitally); Playboy TV (delivered digitally); Fresh (delivered digitally).
Internet Service
Operational: Yes. Began: October 1, 2002.
Broadband Service: Suddenlink High Speed Internet.
Fee: $45.95 installation; $24.95 monthly.
Telephone Service
Digital: Operational
Fee: $49.95 monthly
Miles of Plant: 130.0 (coaxial); None (fiber optic). Homes passed: 6,026.
Vice President, Corporate Finance: Michael Pflantz. General Manager: Dave Walker. Marketing Director: Beverly Gambell. Chief Technician: Jeff Smith.
Ownership: Cequel Communications Holdings I LLC (MSO).

WRIGHT CITY—Formerly served by Allegiance Communications. No longer in operation. ICA: OK0198.

WYANDOTTE—Formerly served by Allegiance Communications. No longer in operation. ICA: OK0327.

WYNONA—Community Cable & Broadband, 1550 West Rogers Blvd, PO Box 307, Skiatook, OK 74070-0307. Phones: 888-394-4772; 918-396-3019. Fax: 918-396-2081. E-mail: info@communitycablevision.com. Web Site: http://www.communitycablebroadband.com. ICA: OK0214.
TV Market Ranking: Below 100 (WYNONA). Franchise award date: October 15, 1986. Franchise expiration date: N.A. Began: February 1, 1987.
Channel capacity: N.A. Channels available but not in use: N.A.

Basic Service
Subscribers: N.A.
Programming (received off-air): KDOR-TV (TBN) Bartlesville; KJRH-TV (NBC) Tulsa; KOED-TV (PBS) Tulsa; KOKI-TV (FOX, MeTV) Tulsa; KOTV-DT (CBS, IND) Tulsa; KQCW-DT (CW, This TV) Muskogee; KRSU-TV (ETV) Claremore; KTFO-CD (UniMas) Austin; KTPX-TV (ION) Okmulgee; KTUL (ABC, Antenna TV, Retro TV) Tulsa; KWHB (COZI TV, IND) Tulsa.
Programming (via satellite): Cartoon Network; CMT; CNN; Discovery Channel; Disney Channel; ESPN; ESPN2; FOX Sports Southwest; Freeform; HGTV; HLN; QVC; Spike TV; Syfy; TBS; TNT; Turner Classic Movies; USA Network; WGN America.
Fee: $29.95 installation.
Video-On-Demand: No
Internet Service
Operational: Yes.
Fee: $44.95 monthly.
Telephone Service
None
Miles of Plant: 4.0 (coaxial); None (fiber optic). Homes passed: 254.
President & General Manager: Dennis Soule. Chief Technical Officer: Chris Tuttle.
Ownership: Community Cable & Broadband Inc. (MSO).

YALE—Community Cable & Broadband, 1550 West Rogers Blvd, PO Box 307, Skiatook, OK 74070-0307. Phones: 888-394-4772; 918-396-3019. Fax: 918-396-2081. E-mail: info@communitycablevision.com. Web Site: http://www.communitycablebroadband.com. Also serves Oilton. ICA: OK0141.
TV Market Ranking: Outside TV Markets (YALE, Oilton). Franchise award date: March 24, 1987. Franchise expiration date: N.A. Began: April 20, 1983.
Channel capacity: N.A. Channels available but not in use: N.A.

Basic Service
Subscribers: N.A.
Programming (received off-air): KFOR-TV (Antenna TV, NBC) Oklahoma City; KJRH-TV (NBC) Tulsa; KOCB (CW) Oklahoma City; KOCO-TV (ABC, This TV) Oklahoma City; KOED-TV (PBS) Tulsa; KOKH-TV (FOX, The Country Network, WeatherNation) Oklahoma City; KQCW-DT (CW, This TV) Muskogee; KTBO-TV (TBN) Oklahoma City; KTFO-CD (UniMas) Austin; KTPX-TV (ION) Okmulgee; KTUL (ABC, Antenna TV, Retro TV) Tulsa; KWHB (COZI TV, IND) Tulsa; KWTV-DT (CBS) Oklahoma City.
Programming (via satellite): A&E; Cartoon Network; CMT; CNN; C-SPAN; Discovery Channel; Disney Channel; ESPN; ESPN2; FOX Sports Southwest; Freeform; HLN; MTV; Nickelodeon; QVC; Spike TV; Syfy; TBS; The Weather Channel; TLC; TNT; Turner Classic Movies; USA Network; VH1; WGN America.
Fee: $29.95 installation.
Video-On-Demand: No
Internet Service
Operational: Yes.
Fee: $44.95 monthly.
Telephone Service
None
Miles of Plant: 10.0 (coaxial); None (fiber optic). Homes passed: 704.
President & General Manager: Dennis Soule. Chief Technical Officer: Chris Tuttle.
Ownership: Community Cable & Broadband Inc. (MSO).

OREGON

Total Systems: 47
Total Communities Served: 261
Franchises Not Yet Operating: 0
Applications Pending: 0
Communities with Applications: 0
Number of Basic Subscribers: 601,063
Number of Expanded Basic Subscribers: 176,250
Number of Pay Units: 197

Top 100 Markets Represented: Portland (29).

For a list of cable communities in this section, see the Cable Community Index located in the back of Cable Volume 2.
For explanation of terms used in cable system listings, see p. D-11.

ARLINGTON—Formerly served by Arlington TV Cooperative Inc. No longer in operation. ICA: OR0106.

ASHLAND—Ashland TV. Formerly [OR0174]. This cable system has converted to IPTV, 485 E Main St, Ashland, OR 97520. Phone: 541-488-9207. E-mail: info@ashlandhome.net; customercare@ashlandhome.net. Web Site: http://www.ashlandhome.net. ICA: OR5023.
TV Market Ranking: Franchise award date: N.A. Franchise expiration date: N.A. Began: March 1, 2007.
Channel capacity: 109 (not 2-way capable). Channels available but not in use: N.A.
Community Lifeline
Subscribers: N.A.
Fee: $42.05 installation; $24.99 monthly. Includes 38 channels - 33 in SD & 5 in HD.
Expanded Basic
Subscribers: N.A.
Fee: $60.99 monthly. Includes 108 channels - 95 in SD & 13 in HD.
Expanded Plus
Subscribers: N.A.
Fee: $69.99 monthly. Includes 117 channels - 100 in SD & 17 in HD.
HBO
Subscribers: N.A.
Fee: $17.32 monthly. Includes 4 channels.
Video-On-Demand: No
Internet Service
Operational: Yes.
Fee: $38.99-$79.99 monthly.
Telephone Service
None
President: Gary Nelson.
Ownership: Ashland Home Net.

ASHLAND—Ashland TV. This cable system has converted to IPTV. See ASHLAND, OR [OR5023]. ICA: OR0174.

ASTORIA—Charter Communications, 12405 Powerscourt Dr, St. Louis, MO 63131. Phones: 636-207-5100 (Corporate office); 360-828-6700; 360-828-6600. Fax: 360-828-6795. Web Site: http://www.charter.com. Also serves Cannon Beach, Clatskanie, Clatsop County, Columbia County (northern portion), Gearhart, Hammond, Seaside & Warrenton, OR; Ilwaco, Long Beach, Nahcotta, Naselle, Ocean Park, Oysterville, Pacific County & Seaview, WA. ICA: OR0012.
TV Market Ranking: Outside TV Markets (ASTORIA, Cannon Beach, Clatskanie, Clatsop County, Columbia County (northern portion), Gearhart, Hammond, Ilwaco, Long Beach, Nahcotta, Naselle, Ocean Park, Oysterville, Pacific County, Seaside, Seaview, Warrenton). Franchise award date: January 1, 1971. Franchise expiration date: N.A. Began: November 25, 1948.
Channel capacity: N.A. Channels available but not in use: N.A.

Digital Basic Service
Subscribers: 9,887.
Programming (via satellite): BBC America; Discovery Digital Networks; DIY Network; FYI; History International; IFC; LMN; MC; Nick Jr.; Sundance TV; TeenNick.
Fee: $26.99 monthly.
Digital Expanded Basic Service
Subscribers: N.A.
Programming (via satellite): AMC; Animal Planet; Bravo; Cartoon Network; CMT; CNBC; Comedy Central; C-SPAN 2; Discovery Channel; Disney Channel; Disney XD; E! HD; ESPN; ESPN2; Food Network; Fox Sports 1; Freeform; Golf Channel; Hallmark Channel; History; HLN; Lifetime; MSNBC; National Geographic Channel; NBCSN; Northwest Cable News; Oxygen; Spike TV; Syfy; The Weather Channel; TNT; Travel Channel; truTV; Turner Classic Movies; TV Land; VH1.
Fee: $42.99 monthly.
Digital Pay Service 1
Pay Units: N.A.
Programming (via satellite): Cinemax (multiplexed); Flix; HBO (multiplexed); Showtime (multiplexed); Starz (multiplexed); Starz Encore (multiplexed); The Movie Channel (multiplexed).
Fee: $10.00 installation; $10.95 monthly (Cinemax, Showtime/Flix or TMC), $11.95 monthly (HBO).
Video-On-Demand: Yes
Pay-Per-View
Hot Choice (delivered digitally); iN DEMAND (delivered digitally); Playboy TV (delivered digitally); Fresh (delivered digitally); Shorteez (delivered digitally).
Internet Service
Operational: Yes. Began: November 30, 2001.
Subscribers: 8,187.
Broadband Service: Charter Internet.
Fee: $29.99 monthly.
Telephone Service
Digital: Operational
Subscribers: 2,212.
Miles of Plant: 1,076.0 (coaxial); 327.0 (fiber optic). Homes passed: 33,774.
Vice President: Frank Antonovich. General Manager: Linda Kimberly. Technical Operations Director: Brian Lindholme. Marketing Director: Diane Long. Accounting Director: David Sovanski.
Ownership: Charter Communications Inc. (MSO).

BEAVERCREEK—BCT. Formerly [OR0167]. This cable system has converted to IPTV, 15223 South Henrici Rd, Oregon City, OR 97045. Phone: 503-632-3113. Fax: 503-632-4159. E-mail: support@bctonline.com. Web Site: http://www.bctelco.com. Also serves Mulino & Oregon City. ICA: OR5024.
TV Market Ranking: 29 (Oregon City).
Channel capacity: N.A. Channels available but not in use: N.A.
Limited
Subscribers: N.A.
Fee: $25.00 monthly. Includes 26 channels.
Standard
Subscribers: N.A.
Fee: $62.00 monthly. Includes 57 channels.
Classic
Subscribers: N.A.
Fee: $75.00 monthly. Includes 150 channels, Encore Movie Pak, one STB & one remote.
Choice
Subscribers: N.A.
Fee: $91.00 monthly. Includes 150 channels, Encore Movie Pak, one premium multiplex (Cinemax, HBO, Starz or Showtime), one STB & one remote.
Plus Choice
Subscribers: N.A.
Fee: $107.00 monthly. Includes 150 channels, Encore Movie Pak, two premium multiplexes (Cinemax, HBO, Showtime or Starz), one STB & one remote.
Premium Choice Plus
Subscribers: N.A.
Fee: $123.00 monthly. Includes 150 channels, Encore Movie Pak, three premium multiplexes (Cinemax, HBO, Showtime or Starz), one STB & one remote.
Ultra Choice
Subscribers: N.A.
Fee: $131.00 monthly. Includes 150 channels, Encore Movie Pak, all premium multiplexes (Cinemax, HBO, Showtime & Starz), one STB & one remote.
HDTV
Subscribers: N.A.
Fee: $29.95 installation; $10.00 monthly. Includes 25 channels.
Video-On-Demand: No
Internet Service
Operational: Yes.
Fee: $31.95 monthly.
Telephone Service
Digital: Operational
Fee: $24.00 monthly
President: Paul Hauer. Vice President, Operations: Mark Beaudry. IT & Engineering Director: David Warner. Marketing & Member Services Director: Tangee Summerhill-Bishop.
Ownership: Beaver Creek Cooperative Telephone Co.

BEAVERCREEK—BCT. This cable system has converted to IPTV. See BEAVERCREEK, OR [OR5024]. ICA: OR0167.

BEAVERTON—Comcast Cable. Now served by PORTLAND, OR [OR0001]. ICA: OR0002.

BEND—BendBroadband, 63090 Sherman Rd, Bend, OR 97701-5750. Phones: 541-388-5820 (Administrative office); 541-382-5551; 541-549-1911. Fax: 541-385-3271. Web Site: http://www.bendbroadband.com. Also serves Black Butte Ranch, Deschutes County (unincorporated areas), Redmond, Sisters & Terrebonne. ICA: OR0013.
TV Market Ranking: Below 100 (BEND, Black Butte Ranch, Deschutes County (unincorporated areas), Redmond, Sisters, Terrebonne). Franchise award date: January 1, 1955. Franchise expiration date: N.A. Began: September 1, 1955.
Channel capacity: N.A. Channels available but not in use: N.A.

Digital Basic Service
Subscribers: 31,936.
Programming (received off-air): KBNZ-LD (CBS) Bend; KFXO-LD (FOX) Bend; KOHD (ABC) Bend; KOPB-TV (PBS) Portland; KTVZ (CW, NBC) Bend; KVAL-TV (CBS, This TV) Eugene.
Programming (via satellite): A&E; A&E HD; AMC; Animal Planet; Animal Planet HD; Bio HD; Bloomberg Television; BlueHighways TV; Boomerang; Bravo; Bravo HD; BTN; BTN HD; BYUtv; Cartoon Network; Cartoon Network HD; CBS Sports Network; CMT; CNBC; CNBC HD+; CNN; CNN HD; Comcast SportsNet California; Comedy Central; C-SPAN; C-SPAN 2; CW PLUS; Discovery Channel HD; Discovery Kids Channel; Disney Channel; Disney Channel HD; Disney XD; DIY Network; E! HD; ESPN; ESPN Classic; ESPN HD; ESPN2; ESPN2 HD; ESPNU; EWTN Global Catholic Network; Food Network; Food Network HD; Fox Business Network; Fox Business Network HD; Fox News Channel; Fox News HD; Freeform; Freeform HD; FSN HD; FX; FX HD; FYI; Golf Channel; Hallmark Channel; here! TV; HGTV; HGTV HD; History; History HD; HLN; Investigation Discovery; Lifetime; Lifetime HD; MC; MSNBC; MTV; NASA TV; National Geographic Channel; National Geographic Channel HD; NBCSN; Nick Jr.; Nickelodeon; Nicktoons; Outdoor Channel; Outdoor Channel 2 HD; Oxygen; QVC; Reelz; RLTV; Science Channel; Spike TV; Sprout; Syfy; Syfy HD; TBS; TBS HD; TeenNick; Telemundo; The Weather Channel; The Weather Channel HD; TLC; TLC HD; TNT; TNT HD; Toon Disney HD; Travel Channel; Travel Channel HD; Trinity Broadcasting Network (TBN); truTV; Turner Classic Movies; TV Land; USA Network; USA Network HD; Versus HD; VH1.
Fee: $39.50 installation; $19.99 monthly.
Digital Expanded Basic Service
Subscribers: N.A.
Programming (via satellite): AXS TV; BBC America; CBS Sports Network HD; Chiller; Cloo; CMT; Cooking Channel; Crime & Investigation Network; Destination America; Discovery Life Channel; ESPNews; ESPNews HD; FOX College Sports Central; FOX College Sports Pacific; Fox Sports 1; Fox Sports 2; Fuse; FXM; GSN; Hallmark Movie

2017 Edition   D-637

Oregon—Cable Systems

Channel HD; Hallmark Movies & Mysteries; HD Theater; History; History International; IFC; MGM HD; MTV Classic; MTV Hits; MTV Live; MTV2; OWN: Oprah Winfrey Network; RFD-TV; Science HD; Smithsonian Channel HD; Starz Encore (multiplexed); Tennis Channel; Tennis Channel HD; The Africa Channel; Universal HD; WE tv.

Digital Pay Service 1
Pay Units: N.A.
Programming (via satellite): Cinemax (multiplexed); Cinemax HD; HBO (multiplexed); HBO HD; Showtime (multiplexed); Showtime HD; Starz (multiplexed); Starz HD; The Movie Channel (multiplexed); The Movie Channel HD.
Fee: $15.25 monthly (Cinemax, HBO, Showtime/TMC or Starz).

Video-On-Demand: Yes

Pay-Per-View
Playboy TV (delivered digitally); Fresh (delivered digitally).

Internet Service
Operational: Yes. Began: April 1, 1998.
Subscribers: 36,053.
Broadband Service: InstaNet.
Fee: $39.50 installation; $26.95-$89.99 monthly; $10.00 modem lease; $99.00 modem purchase.

Telephone Service
Analog: Not Operational
Digital: Operational
Subscribers: 11,979.
Fee: $14.95-$29.95 monthly
Miles of Plant: 1,984.0 (coaxial); 480.0 (fiber optic). Homes passed: 74,945.
President & Chief Executive Officer: Amy C. Tykeson. Vice President, Business Operations: John Farwell. Treasurer: Thomas H. Palmer. Chief Technology Officer: Frank Miller.
Ownership: Telephone and Data Systems.

BEND—Formerly served by WANTV. No longer in operation. ICA: OR0164.

BLY—Formerly served by Bly Cable Co. No longer in operation. ICA: OR0110.

BOARDMAN—Formerly served by Rapid Cable. No longer in operation. ICA: OR0070.

BONANZA—Formerly served by Almega Cable. No longer in operation. ICA: OR0109.

BORING—Formerly served by Community Cable Inc. No longer in operation. ICA: OR0125.

BROOKINGS—Charter Communications. Now served by CRESCENT CITY, CA [CA0155]. ICA: OR0173.

BROOKS—Formerly served by Country Cablevision Ltd. No longer in operation. ICA: OR0088.

BROWNSVILLE—Formerly served by Rapid Cable. No longer in operation. ICA: OR0079.

BURNS—Charter Communications, 12405 Powerscourt Dr, St. Louis, MO 63131. Phones: 636-207-5100 (Corporate office); 509-396-0613; 509-783-0132; 509-222-2500. Fax: 509-735-3795. Web Site: http://www.charter.com. Also serves Harney County (portions) & Hines. ICA: OR0045.
TV Market Ranking: Outside TV Markets (BURNS, Harney County (portions), Hines). Franchise award date: N.A. Franchise expiration date: N.A. Began: June 1, 1956.
Channel capacity: N.A. Channels available but not in use: N.A.

Digital Basic Service
Subscribers: 539.
Programming (via satellite): BBC America; Bloomberg Television; Discovery Life Channel; DMX Music; ESPN Classic; ESPNews; Fox Sports 1; FXM; Golf Channel; IFC; MTV Classic; National Geographic Channel; NBCSN; Nick Jr.; Turner Classic Movies; TV Guide Interactive Inc.; VH1 Country.
Fee: $26.99 monthly.

Digital Expanded Basic Service
Subscribers: N.A.
Programming (via satellite): A&E; AMC; Animal Planet; Bravo; Cartoon Network; CMT; CNBC; CNN; Comedy Central; Discovery Channel; Disney Channel; DIY Network; E! HD; ESPN; ESPN2; Food Network; Fox News Channel; Freeform; FX; GSN; Hallmark Channel; HGTV; History; HLN; Lifetime; MSNBC; MTV; Nickelodeon; Northwest Cable News; Outdoor Channel; Oxygen; Spike TV; Syfy; TBS; The Weather Channel; TLC; TNT; Travel Channel; truTV; Univision Studios; USA Network; VH1; WE tv.
Fee: $50.99 monthly.

Digital Pay Service 1
Pay Units: N.A.
Programming (via satellite): Cinemax (multiplexed); HBO (multiplexed); Showtime (multiplexed); Starz (multiplexed); Starz Encore (multiplexed); The Movie Channel (multiplexed).
Fee: $20.00 installation; $7.95 monthly (Cinemax, Encore & HBO).

Video-On-Demand: No

Pay-Per-View
iN DEMAND (delivered digitally); Playboy TV (delivered digitally); Fresh (delivered digitally).

Internet Service
Operational: No.

Telephone Service
None
Homes passed: 2,493. Miles of plant included in Kennewick, WA.
General Manager: Linda Kimberly. Technical Operations Manager: Jeff Hopkins. Marketing Director: Diane Long. Program Director: Lloyd Swain. Accounting Director: David Sovanski.
Ownership: Charter Communications Inc. (MSO).

BUTTE FALLS—Formerly served by Almega Cable. No longer in operation. ICA: OR0127.

CANBY—Wave Broadband. Now served by SILVERTON, OR [OR0047]. ICA: OR0017.

CASCADE LOCKS—City of Cascade Locks Cable TV, 140 Southwest WaNaPa, PO Box 308, Cascade Locks, OR 97014. Phone: 541-374-8484. Fax: 541-374-8752. E-mail: thupp@cascade-locks.or.us. Web Site: http://www.cascade-locks.or.us. ICA: OR0087.
TV Market Ranking: Below 100 (CASCADE LOCKS). Franchise award date: N.A. Franchise expiration date: N.A. Began: January 1, 1971.
Channel capacity: N.A. Channels available but not in use: N.A.

Basic Service
Subscribers: 164.
Programming (received off-air): KATU (ABC, MeTV) Portland; KGW (Estrella TV, NBC) Portland; KOIN (CBS) Portland; KOPB-TV (PBS) Portland; KPDX (Escape, MNT) Vancouver; KPTV (COZI TV, FOX, Laff) Portland.
Programming (via satellite): A&E; CNN; Discovery Channel; Disney Channel; ESPN; HGTV; History; Lifetime; Nickelodeon; Spike TV; Syfy; TBS; TNT; TV Land; USA Network; WGN America.
Fee: $35.00 installation; $30.00 monthly.

Pay Service 1
Pay Units: 87.
Programming (via satellite): HBO.
Fee: $8.75 monthly.

Video-On-Demand: No

Internet Service
Operational: Yes. Began: March 21, 2002.
Broadband Service: In-house.
Fee: $25.00 installation; $25.00 monthly.

Telephone Service
None
Miles of Plant: 15.0 (coaxial); None (fiber optic). Homes passed: 438.
General Manager: Tracy Hupp. Finance Officer: Marianne Bump. Chief Technician: Ed Winnett.
Ownership: City of Cascade Locks Cable TV.

CAVE JUNCTION—Formerly served by Almega Cable. No longer in operation. ICA: OR0054.

CHILOQUIN—Formerly served by Almega Cable. No longer in operation. ICA: OR0090.

COLTON—ColtonTel, PO Box 68, Colton, OR 97017. Phone: 503-824-3211. Fax: 503-824-9944. E-mail: customercare@coltontel.com. Web Site: http://www.coltontel.com. ICA: OR0176.
TV Market Ranking: 29 (COLTON).
Channel capacity: 48 (not 2-way capable). Channels available but not in use: N.A.

Basic Service
Subscribers: 345.
Programming (received off-air): KATU (ABC, MeTV) Portland; KGW (Estrella TV, NBC) Portland; KNMT (TBN) Portland; KOIN (CBS) Portland; KOPB-TV (PBS) Portland; KPDX (Escape, MNT) Vancouver; KPTV (COZI TV, FOX, Laff) Portland; KPXG-TV (ION) Salem; KRCW-TV (Antenna TV, CW, This TV) Salem.
Programming (via satellite): C-SPAN; Northwest Cable News; Pop; QVC; The Weather Channel.
Fee: $35.00 installation; $26.95 monthly.

Expanded Basic Service 1
Subscribers: 250.
Programming (via satellite): A&E; AMC; Animal Planet; Cartoon Network; CMT; CNBC; CNN; Comedy Central; Discovery Channel; Disney Channel; E! HD; ESPN; ESPN2; Food Network; Fox News Channel; Fox Sports 1; FOX Sports Networks; Freeform; FX; Hallmark Channel; HGTV; History; HLN; Lifetime; MTV; NBCSN; Nickelodeon; Outdoor Channel; RFD-TV; Spike TV; Syfy; TBS; TLC; TNT; Travel Channel; truTV; Turner Classic Movies; TV Land; Univision; USA Network; VH1; WGN America.
Fee: $18.20 monthly.

Digital Basic Service
Subscribers: 123.
Programming (via satellite): 3ABN; BBC America; BYUtv; Chiller; CMT; Cooking Channel; Destination America; Discovery Kids Channel; Discovery Life Channel; Disney XD; DIY Network; ESPN Classic; ESPNU; Estrella TV; FYI; Golf Channel; Great American Country; GSN; Hallmark Channel; Hallmark Movies & Mysteries; History International; Investigation Discovery; LMN; MC; MTV Classic; MTV Hits; MTV Jams; MTV2; National Geographic Channel; Nick 2; Nick Jr.; Nicktoons; OWN: Oprah Winfrey Network; Oxygen; Science Channel; Sundance TV; TeenNick; Tr3s; VH1 Soul; WE tv.
Fee: $14.00 monthly.

Digital Pay Service 1
Pay Units: 110.
Programming (via satellite): Cinemax (multiplexed); Flix; HBO (multiplexed); Showtime (multiplexed); Starz (multiplexed); Starz Encore (multiplexed); The Movie Channel (multiplexed).

Video-On-Demand: No

Pay-Per-View
Vubiquity Inc. (delivered digitally).

Internet Service
Operational: Yes.

Telephone Service
Analog: Operational
Miles of Plant: 64.0 (coaxial); None (fiber optic). Homes passed: 968.
General Manager: Steven Krogue. Assistant Manager: Marlene Muhs. Plant Manager: Dave Conditt. Financial Officer & Accountant: Stephanie Sauvageau.
Ownership: ColtonTel.

CONDON—J & N Cable, 614 South Columbus Ave, Goldendale, WA 98620-9006. Phones: 800-752-9809; 509-773-5359. Fax: 509-773-7090. E-mail: customersupport@jncable.net. Web Site: http://www.jncable.com. ICA: OR0093.
TV Market Ranking: Outside TV Markets (CONDON). Franchise award date: N.A. Franchise expiration date: N.A. Began: January 1, 1955.
Channel capacity: N.A. Channels available but not in use: N.A.

Basic Service
Subscribers: N.A.
Programming (received off-air): KATU (ABC, MeTV) Portland; KGW (Estrella TV, NBC) Portland; KOIN (CBS) Portland; KOPB-TV (PBS) Portland; KPDX (Escape, MNT) Vancouver; KPTV (COZI TV, FOX, Laff) Portland; KRCW-TV (Antenna TV, CW, This TV) Salem; allband FM.
Programming (via satellite): 3ABN; A&E; AMC; Animal Planet; Cartoon Network; CNBC; CNN; C-SPAN; C-SPAN 2; Discovery Channel; Disney Channel; DIY Network; ESPN; ESPN Classic; ESPN2; ESPNews; EVINE Live; EWTN Global Catholic Network; Food Network; Fox News Channel; Fox Sports 1; FOX Sports Networks; Freeform; Golf Channel; Great American Country; Hallmark Channel; HGTV; History; HLN; ION Television; Lifetime; MSNBC; NBCSN; Northwest Cable News; Outdoor Channel; QVC; Syfy; TBS; The Weather Channel; TLC; TNT; Travel Channel; Trinity Broadcasting Network (TBN); truTV; Turner Classic Movies; USA Network.
Fee: $20.00 installation.

Pay Service 1
Pay Units: N.A.
Programming (via satellite): Cinemax (multiplexed); HBO (multiplexed); Showtime (multiplexed); The Movie Channel.
Fee: $12.95 monthly (each).

Video-On-Demand: No

Internet Service
Operational: Yes. Began: December 31, 2001.
Broadband Service: InterTECH.
Fee: $39.95 monthly.

Telephone Service
Digital: Operational
Miles of Plant: 14.0 (coaxial); None (fiber optic). Homes passed: 320.

Cable Systems—Oregon

President & General Manager: John Kusky. Vice President & Marketing Manager: Nancy Kusky.
Ownership: J & N Cable Systems Inc. (MSO).

COOS BAY—Charter Communications, 12405 Powerscourt Dr, St. Louis, MO 63131. Phones: 636-207-5100 (Corporate office); 360-828-6700; 360-828-6600. Fax: 360-828-6795. Web Site: http://www.charter.com. Also serves Bandon, Coos County (northern portion), Coquille, Douglas County (portions), Gardiner, Hauser, Lakeside, Myrtle Point, North Bend, Port Orford, Reedsport & Winchester Bay. ICA: OR0015.
TV Market Ranking: Below 100 (Bandon, COOS BAY, Coos County (northern portion), Coquille, Douglas County (portions), Gardiner, Hauser, Lakeside, Myrtle Point, North Bend, Reedsport, Winchester Bay); Outside TV Markets (Port Orford). Franchise award date: N.A. Franchise expiration date: N.A. Began: October 1, 1954.
Channel capacity: 78 (operating 2-way). Channels available but not in use: N.A.

Digital Basic Service
Subscribers: 10,005.
Programming (via satellite): BBC America; Bloomberg Television; Boomerang; CNN en Espanol; Discovery Digital Networks; DIY Network; ESPN Classic; FYI; History International; IFC; LMN; MC; Nick 2; Nick Jr.; Sundance TV; TeenNick.
Fee: $26.99 monthly.

Digital Expanded Basic Service
Subscribers: N.A.
Programming (via satellite): A&E; AMC; Animal Planet; Bravo; Cartoon Network; CMT; CNBC; CNN; Comedy Central; Discovery Channel; Disney Channel; Disney XD; E! HD; ESPN; ESPN2; Food Network; Fox News Channel; Fox Sports 1; Freeform; FX; FXM; Golf Channel; Great American Country; GSN; Hallmark Channel; HGTV; History; HLN; Lifetime; MSNBC; National Geographic Channel; NBCSN; Nickelodeon; Northwest Cable News; Outdoor Channel; Oxygen; Spike TV; Syfy; TBS; Telemundo; The Weather Channel; TLC; TNT; Travel Channel; truTV; Turner Classic Movies; TV Land; USA Network; VH1; WE tv.
Fee: $42.99 monthly.

Digital Pay Service 1
Pay Units: N.A.
Programming (via satellite): Cinemax (multiplexed); Flix; HBO (multiplexed); Showtime (multiplexed); Starz; Starz Encore (multiplexed); The Movie Channel (multiplexed).
Fee: $10.00 monthly (Cinemax, HBO, Showtime/Flix, Starz/Encore or TMC).
Video-On-Demand: Yes

Pay-Per-View
Hot Choice (delivered digitally); Fresh (delivered digitally); Playboy TV (delivered digitally); iN DEMAND (delivered digitally).

Internet Service
Operational: Yes. Began: November 1, 2001.
Subscribers: 10,777.
Broadband Service: Charter Internet.
Fee: $29.99 monthly; $4.95 modem lease.

Telephone Service
Digital: Operational
Subscribers: 3,101.
Miles of Plant: 996.0 (coaxial); 340.0 (fiber optic). Homes passed: 35,151.
Vice President: Frank Antonovich. General Manager: Linda Kimberly. Technical Operations Director: Brian Lindholme. Marketing Director: Diane Long. Accounting Director: David Sovanski.
Ownership: Charter Communications Inc. (MSO).

CORVALLIS—Comcast Cable. Now served by PORTLAND, OR [OR0001]. ICA: OR0008.

COTTAGE GROVE—Charter Communications, 12405 Powerscourt Dr, St. Louis, MO 63131. Phones: 636-207-5100 (Corporate office); 360-828-6700; 360-828-6600. Fax: 360-828-6795. Web Site: http://www.charter.com. Also serves Coburg, Creswell, Douglas County (northern portion), Drain, Lane County (portions), Lowell, Oakridge, Veneta & Westfir. ICA: OR0073.
TV Market Ranking: Below 100 (Coburg, COTTAGE GROVE, Creswell, Drain, Lane County (Portions), Lowell, Veneta); Outside TV Markets (Oakridge, Westfir). Franchise award date: N.A. Franchise expiration date: N.A. Began: July 1, 1983.
Channel capacity: N.A. Channels available but not in use: N.A.

Digital Basic Service
Subscribers: 3,450.
Programming (via satellite): BBC America; Bloomberg Television; DIY Network; FYI; LMN; MC; Nick Jr.
Fee: $26.99 monthly.

Digital Expanded Basic Service
Subscribers: N.A.
Programming (via satellite): Animal Planet; Bravo; Cartoon Network; CMT; CNN; Discovery Channel; E! HD; ESPN; Food Network; Fox News Channel; Fox Sports 1; Freeform; FX; HGTV; History; HLN; Lifetime; MSNBC; Nickelodeon; Spike TV; Syfy; TLC; TNT; Travel Channel; truTV; Turner Classic Movies; TV Land.
Fee: $42.99 monthly.

Digital Pay Service 1
Pay Units: N.A.
Programming (via satellite): Cinemax (multiplexed); Flix; HBO (multiplexed); Showtime (multiplexed); Starz; Starz Encore (multiplexed); The Movie Channel (multiplexed).
Fee: $10.00 monthly (Cinemax, HBO, Showtime/Flix or TMC).
Video-On-Demand: No

Pay-Per-View
Shorteez (delivered digitally); Fresh (delivered digitally); Playboy TV (delivered digitally); iN DEMAND (delivered digitally).

Internet Service
Operational: No.

Telephone Service
None
Miles of Plant: 531.0 (coaxial); None (fiber optic). Homes passed: 19,768.
Vice President: Frank Antonovich. General Manager: Linda Kimberly. Technical Operations Director: Brian Lindholme. Marketing Director: Diane Long. Accounting Director: David Sovanski.
Ownership: Charter Communications Inc. (MSO).

COVE—Formerly served by Almega Cable. No longer in operation. ICA: OR0099.

DALLAS—Charter Communications, 12405 Powerscourt Dr, St. Louis, MO 63131. Phones: 636-207-5100 (Corporate office); 360-828-6700; 360-828-6600. Fax: 360-828-6795. Web Site: http://www.charter.com. Also serves Falls City, Independence, Jefferson, Marion County (southwestern portion), Monmouth & Polk County (portions). ICA: OR0039.
TV Market Ranking: Below 100 (DALLAS, Falls City, Independence, Jefferson, Marion County (southwestern portion), Monmouth, Polk County (portions)). Franchise award date: N.A. Franchise expiration date: N.A. Began: April 1, 1966.
Channel capacity: N.A. Channels available but not in use: N.A.

Digital Basic Service
Subscribers: 1,693.
Programming (via satellite): BBC America; Bloomberg Television; Bravo; Discovery Digital Networks; DIY Network; ESPN Classic; ESPNews; FOX College Sports Central; FOX College Sports Pacific; Fox Sports 2; Fuse; FXM; FYI; GSN; History International; IFC; LMN; MC; NFL Network; Nick Jr.; Nicktoons; Outdoor Channel; TeenNick; TV Guide Interactive Inc.
Fee: $26.99 monthly.

Digital Expanded Basic Service
Subscribers: N.A.
Programming (via satellite): AMC; Animal Planet; CNN; Comedy Central; Discovery Channel; Discovery Life Channel; Disney Channel; Disney XD; E! HD; ESPN; ESPN2; Food Network; Fox News Channel; Fox Sports 1; Freeform; FX; History; HLN; Lifetime; MSNBC; NBCSN; Nickelodeon; Northwest Cable News; Spike TV; Syfy; The Weather Channel; TLC; TNT; Travel Channel; TV Land; Univision Studios; WE tv.
Fee: $42.99 monthly.

Digital Pay Service 1
Pay Units: N.A.
Programming (via satellite): Cinemax (multiplexed); Flix; HBO (multiplexed); Showtime (multiplexed); Starz (multiplexed); Starz Encore (multiplexed); The Movie Channel (multiplexed).
Fee: $25.00 installation; $5.95 monthly (Encore), $11.95 monthly (Cinemax, HBO, Showtime, Starz/Flix or TMC).
Video-On-Demand: Yes

Pay-Per-View
iN DEMAND (delivered digitally); Hot Choice (delivered digitally); Playboy TV (delivered digitally); Fresh (delivered digitally); Shorteez (delivered digitally).

Internet Service
Operational: Yes. Began: October 1, 2007.
Broadband Service: Charter Internet.
Fee: $29.99 monthly.

Telephone Service
Digital: Operational
Miles of Plant: 180.0 (coaxial); 8.0 (fiber optic). Homes passed: 10,061.
Vice President: Frank Antonovich. General Manager: Linda Kimberly. Technical Operations Director: Brian Lindholme. Marketing Director: Diane Long. Accounting Director: David Sovanski.
Ownership: Charter Communications Inc. (MSO).

DAYVILLE—Formerly served by Blue Mountain TV Cable Co. No longer in operation. ICA: OR0120.

DEPOE BAY—Wave Broadband, 401 Parkplace Center, Ste 500, Kirkland, WA 98033. Phones: 425-576-8200; 866-928-3123; 866-496-9669. E-mail: jpenney@wavebroadband.com. Web Site: http://www.wavebroadband.com. Also serves Lincoln Beach, Lincoln County (portions), Salmon River, Siletz, Siletz River & South Beach. ICA: OR0134.
TV Market Ranking: Outside TV Markets (DEPOE BAY, Lincoln Beach, Lincoln County (portions), Salmon River, Siletz, Siletz River, South Beach). Franchise award date: N.A. Franchise expiration date: N.A. Began: June 1, 1956.
Channel capacity: N.A. Channels available but not in use: N.A.

Basic Service
Subscribers: 1,500.
Programming (received off-air): KATU (ABC, MeTV) Portland; KGW (Estrella TV, NBC) Portland; KOIN (CBS) Portland; KOPB-TV (PBS) Portland; KPDX (Escape, MNT) Vancouver; KPTV (COZI TV, FOX, Laff) Portland; allband FM.
Programming (via satellite): A&E; AMC; Animal Planet; Bravo; CNBC; CNN; Comedy Central; C-SPAN; Discovery Channel; Disney Channel; E! HD; ESPN; ESPN2; Food Network; Fox News Channel; Freeform; FX; HGTV; History; HLN; Lifetime; National Geographic Channel; Nickelodeon; Northwest Cable News; Pop; QVC; Spike TV; Syfy; TBS; The Weather Channel; TLC; TNT; Travel Channel; Trinity Broadcasting Network (TBN); TV Land; USA Network; WGN America.
Fee: $29.95 installation; $25.95 monthly.

Digital Basic Service
Subscribers: N.A.
Programming (via satellite): BBC America; Discovery Kids Channel; DMX Music; ESPNews; Fox Sports 1; FYI; Golf Channel; GSN; History International; IFC; LMN; NBCSN.
Fee: $17.40 monthly.

Digital Pay Service 1
Pay Units: N.A.
Programming (via satellite): Cinemax (multiplexed); HBO (multiplexed); Showtime (multiplexed); Starz (multiplexed); Starz Encore (multiplexed); The Movie Channel (multiplexed).
Fee: $10.00 monthly (each).
Video-On-Demand: No

Pay-Per-View
Playboy TV (delivered digitally); iN DEMAND (delivered digitally).

Internet Service
Operational: Yes.
Broadband Service: Millennium Cable-Speed.
Fee: $49.95 installation; $37.95 monthly.

Telephone Service
Digital: Operational
Miles of Plant: 122.0 (coaxial); None (fiber optic). Homes passed: 5,800.
President & Chief Operating Officer: Steve Friedman. Chief Financial Officer: Wayne Schattenkerk.
Ownership: WaveDivision Holdings LLC (MSO).

DUFUR—Northstate Cablevision, 180 Northeast 2nd St, PO Box 297, Dufur, OR 97021. Phone: 541-467-2409. E-mail: support@ortelco.net. Web Site: http://www.ortelco.net. ICA: OR0097.
TV Market Ranking: Outside TV Markets (DUFUR). Franchise award date: April 16, 1984. Franchise expiration date: N.A. Began: June 1, 1955.
Channel capacity: N.A. Channels available but not in use: N.A.

Basic Service
Subscribers: 43.
Programming (received off-air): KATU (ABC, MeTV) Portland; KGW (Estrella TV, NBC) Portland; KOIN (CBS) Portland; KOPB-TV (PBS) Portland; KPDX (Escape, MNT) Vancouver; KPTV (COZI TV, FOX, Laff) Portland; KRHP-CD (IND) The Dalles; allband FM.

Oregon—Cable Systems

CABLE & TV STATION COVERAGE
Atlas 2017
The perfect companion to the Television & Cable Factbook
To order call 800-771-9202 or visit www.warren-news.com

Programming (via satellite): Discovery Channel; Disney Channel; Freeform; Spike TV; TBS.
Fee: $30.00 installation; $13.50 monthly.
Pay Service 1
Pay Units: N.A.
Programming (via satellite): HBO.
Fee: $10.00 installation; $9.95 monthly.
Internet Service
Operational: No, DSL.
Telephone Service
Analog: Operational
Fee: $12.45 monthly
Miles of Plant: 5.0 (coaxial); None (fiber optic).
General Manager: Gary E. Miller. Network Technician: Herb Watts.
Ownership: Northstate Cablevision Co.

ELGIN—Elgin TV Assn. Inc, 830 Alder St, PO Box 246, Elgin, OR 97827-0246. Phone: 541-437-4575. E-mail: cs@elgintv.com. Web Site: http://www.elgintv.com. ICA: OR0076.
TV Market Ranking: Outside TV Markets (ELGIN). Franchise award date: N.A. Franchise expiration date: N.A. Began: October 1, 1955.
Channel capacity: N.A. Channels available but not in use: N.A.
Basic Service
Subscribers: N.A.
Programming (received off-air): KATU (ABC, MeTV) Portland; KGW (Estrella TV, NBC) Portland; KHQ-TV (NBC) Spokane; KOIN (CBS) Portland; KPDX (Escape, MNT) Vancouver; KPTV (COZI TV, FOX, Laff) Portland; KREM (CBS, TheCoolTV) Spokane; KTVB (NBC) Boise; KTVR (PBS) La Grande; KXLY-TV (ABC, MeTV) Spokane.
Programming (via satellite): A&E; AMC; CMT; CNN; C-SPAN; Discovery Channel; Disney Channel; ESPN; Freeform; HGTV; Northwest Cable News; Outdoor Channel; Spike TV; Syfy; TBS; TLC; TNT; TV Land; USA Network; WGN America.
Pay Service 1
Pay Units: N.A.
Programming (via satellite): HBO; Showtime.
Fee: $10.00 installation; $10.00 monthly (each).
Internet Service
Operational: Yes.
Broadband Service: ParaSun Technologies (ISP & Tech support) and SBC to Net.
Fee: $50.00 installation; $43.95 monthly.
Telephone Service
None
Miles of Plant: 20.0 (coaxial); None (fiber optic). Homes passed: 750.
Chief Technician: Michael McCants. Office Manager: Coral Rose.
Ownership: Elgin TV Assn. Inc.

ENTERPRISE—Crystal Broadband Networks, PO Box 180336, Chicago, IL 60618. Phones: 877-319-0328; 630-206-0447. E-mail: njohnson@crystalbn.com. Web Site: http://crystalbn.com. Also serves Joseph, Lostine, Wallowa & Wallowa Lake. ICA: OR0048.

TV Market Ranking: Outside TV Markets (ENTERPRISE, Joseph, Lostine, Wallowa, Wallowa Lake). Franchise award date: N.A. Franchise expiration date: N.A. Began: June 1, 1955.
Channel capacity: N.A. Channels available but not in use: N.A.
Basic Service
Subscribers: N.A.
Programming (received off-air): KATU (ABC, MeTV) Portland; KEZI (ABC, MeTV) Eugene; KFXO-LD (FOX) Bend; KOAB-TV (PBS) Bend; KOIN (CBS) Portland; KPDX (Escape, MNT) Vancouver; KTVZ (CW, NBC) Bend; 14 FMs.
Programming (via satellite): C-SPAN.
Fee: $30.50 installation; $1.00 converter.
Expanded Basic Service 1
Subscribers: N.A.
Programming (via satellite): A&E; CMT; CNBC; CNN; Discovery Channel; Disney Channel; ESPN; ESPN2; Fox News Channel; Freeform; Hallmark Channel; HGTV; History; HLN; Lifetime; Nickelodeon; QVC; Spike TV; Syfy; TBS; TLC; TNT; Turner Classic Movies; USA Network; VH1.
Fee: $12.95 monthly.
Pay Service 1
Pay Units: N.A.
Programming (via satellite): Cinemax; HBO.
Fee: $10.00 installation; $10.00 monthly (each).
Video-On-Demand: No
Internet Service
Operational: No, DSL.
Telephone Service
None
Miles of Plant: 100.0 (coaxial); None (fiber optic). Homes passed: 2,000.
General Manager: Nidhin Johnson.
Ownership: Crystal Broadband Networks (MSO).

ESTACADA—Reliance Connects, 301 South Broadway St, PO Box 357, Estacada, OR 97023. Phones: 503-630-4213; 503-630-3545. Fax: 503-630-8944. E-mail: info@rconnects.com. Web Site: http://relianceconnects.com. Also serves Clackamas County, Corbett & Eagle Creek. ICA: OR0068.
TV Market Ranking: 29 (Clackamas County, ESTACADA). Franchise award date: February 1, 1983. Franchise expiration date: N.A. Began: March 10, 1983.
Channel capacity: 60 (not 2-way capable). Channels available but not in use: N.A.
Basic Service
Subscribers: 777.
Programming (received off-air): KATU (ABC, MeTV) Portland; KGW (Estrella TV, NBC) Portland; KNMT (TBN) Portland; KOIN (CBS) Portland; KOPB-TV (PBS) Portland; KPDX (Escape, MNT) Vancouver; KPTV (COZI TV, FOX, Laff) Portland; KPXG-TV (ION) Salem; KRCW-TV (Antenna TV, CW, This TV) Salem; KUNP-LD (MundoMax, UNV) Portland.
Programming (via satellite): A&E; AMC; Animal Planet; Cartoon Network; CMT; CNBC; CNN; Comedy Central; C-SPAN; Discovery Channel; Disney Channel; E! HD; ESPN; ESPN2; Food Network; Fox News Channel; Fox Sports 1; Freeform; FX; Hallmark Channel; HGTV; History; HLN; Lifetime; MTV; Nickelodeon; Northwest Cable News; Outdoor Channel; Pop; QVC; RFD-TV; Spike TV; Syfy; TBS; The Weather Channel; TLC; TNT; Travel Channel; truTV; Turner Classic Movies; TV Land; Univision; USA Network; VH1; WGN America.
Fee: $7.50 installation; $26.95 monthly.
Digital Basic Service
Subscribers: N.A.
Programming (via satellite): BBC America; Cooking Channel; Discovery Digital Networks; DMX Music; Nick 2; Nick Jr.; Nicktoons; TeenNick.
Fee: $6.95 monthly.
Digital Pay Service 1
Pay Units: N.A.
Programming (via satellite): Cinemax (multiplexed); Flix; HBO (multiplexed); Showtime (multiplexed); Starz (multiplexed); Starz Encore (multiplexed); Sundance TV; The Movie Channel (multiplexed).
Fee: $13.99 monthly (Cinemax, HBO, Showtime/TMC/Flix or Starz/Encore).
Pay-Per-View
iN DEMAND; Vubiquity Inc. (delivered digitally); ETC (delivered digitally); Pleasure (delivered digitally); Playboy TV.
Internet Service
Operational: No, DSL.
Telephone Service
Analog: Operational
Miles of Plant: 77.0 (coaxial); None (fiber optic). Homes passed: 2,500.
General Manager: Dennis S. Anderson. Engineering Manager: Dennis Anderson. Chief Technician: Steve Valiant.
Ownership: Reliance Connects.

EUGENE—Comcast Cable. Now served by PORTLAND, OR [OR0001]. ICA: OR0004.

FLORENCE—Charter Communications, 12405 Powerscourt Dr, St. Louis, MO 63131. Phones: 636-207-5100 (Corporate office); 360-828-6700; 360-828-6600. Fax: 360-828-6795. Web Site: http://www.charter.com. Also serves Dunes City & Lane County (portions). ICA: OR0030.
TV Market Ranking: Below 100 (Lane County (portions) (portions)); Outside TV Markets (Dunes City, FLORENCE, Lane County (portions) (portions)). Franchise award date: May 1, 1965. Franchise expiration date: N.A. Began: July 1, 1965.
Channel capacity: N.A. Channels available but not in use: N.A.
Digital Basic Service
Subscribers: 2,169.
Programming (via satellite): BBC America; Bloomberg Television; Boomerang; CNN en Espanol; CNN International; Discovery Digital Networks; ESPN Classic; ESPNews; FOX College Sports Central; FOX College Sports Pacific; Fox Sports 2; FYI; History International; IFC; LMN; MC; NFL Network; Nick Jr.; Nicktoons; Sundance TV; TeenNick.
Fee: $26.99 monthly.
Digital Expanded Basic Service
Subscribers: N.A.
Programming (via satellite): A&E; AMC; Animal Planet; Bravo; Cartoon Network; CMT; CNBC; CNN; Comedy Central; Discovery Channel; Disney Channel; Disney XD; DIY Network; E! HD; ESPN; ESPN2; Food Network; Fox News Channel; Fox Sports 1; Freeform; FX; FXM; Golf Channel; Great American Country; GSN; Hallmark Channel; HGTV; History; HLN; Lifetime; MSNBC; MTV; MTV2; National Geographic Channel; NBCSN; Nickelodeon; Northwest Cable News; Outdoor Channel; Oxygen; Spike TV; Syfy; TBS; Telemundo; TLC; TNT; Travel Channel; truTV; Turner Classic Movies; TV Land; USA Network; VH1; WE tv.
Fee: $42.99 monthly.
Digital Pay Service 1
Pay Units: N.A.
Programming (via satellite): Cinemax (multiplexed); Flix; HBO (multiplexed); Showtime (multiplexed); Starz (multiplexed); Starz Encore (multiplexed); The Movie Channel (multiplexed).
Video-On-Demand: Yes
Pay-Per-View
iN DEMAND; Spice; Spice2.
Internet Service
Operational: Yes.
Broadband Service: Charter Internet.
Fee: $29.99 monthly.
Telephone Service
Digital: Operational
Miles of Plant: 130.0 (coaxial); None (fiber optic). Homes passed: 7,521.
Vice President: Frank Antonovich. General Manager: Linda Kimberly. Technical Operations Director: Brian Lindholme. Marketing Director: Diane Long. Accounting Director: David Sovanski.
Ownership: Charter Communications Inc. (MSO).

FOSSIL—Fossil Community TV Inc., PO Box 209, Fossil, OR 97830-0209. Phone: 541-763-2698. ICA: OR0104.
TV Market Ranking: Outside TV Markets (FOSSIL). Franchise award date: N.A. Franchise expiration date: N.A. Began: May 1, 1955.
Channel capacity: 12 (not 2-way capable). Channels available but not in use: N.A.
Basic Service
Subscribers: N.A.
Programming (received off-air): KATU (ABC, MeTV) Portland; KEPR-TV (CBS, CW) Pasco; KGW (Estrella TV, NBC) Portland; KNDU (NBC) Richland; KOIN (CBS) Portland; KOPB-TV (PBS) Portland; KPTV (COZI TV, FOX, Laff) Portland; KVEW (ABC, MeTV, MNT) Kennewick; allband FM.
Programming (via satellite): A&E; AMC; CNN; Discovery Channel; Disney Channel; Freeform; History; TBS; TNT.
Fee: $25.00 installation.
Pay Service 1
Pay Units: N.A.
Programming (via satellite): Showtime.
Fee: $10.00 monthly.
Video-On-Demand: No
Internet Service
Operational: No.
Telephone Service
None
Miles of Plant: 9.0 (coaxial); None (fiber optic). Homes passed: 240.
General Manager: Ron Deluca. Chief Technician: Steve Conlee.
Ownership: Fossil Community TV Inc.

GILCHRIST—Formerly served by Country Cablevision Ltd. No longer in operation. ICA: OR0137.

GLENDALE—Formerly served by Almega Cable. No longer in operation. ICA: OR0138.

GLIDE—Formerly served by Glide Cablevision. No longer in operation. ICA: OR0139.

GOLD BEACH—Charter Communications. Now served by CRESCENT CITY, CA [CA0155]. ICA: OR0044.

Cable Systems—Oregon

GOVERNMENT CAMP—CharlieVision, PO Box 10, Government Camp, OR 97028-0010. Phone: 503-272-3333. Fax: 503-272-3800. E-mail: charliesmountain@gmail.com. ICA: OR0168.
TV Market Ranking: Outside TV Markets (GOVERNMENT CAMP).
Channel capacity: N.A. Channels available but not in use: N.A.
Basic Service
Subscribers: 90.
Programming (received off-air): KATU (ABC, MeTV) Portland; KGW (Estrella TV, NBC) Portland; KOIN (CBS) Portland; KOPB-TV (PBS) Portland; KPTV (COZI TV, FOX, Laff) Portland.
Programming (via satellite): A&E; Cartoon Network; CNN; Discovery Channel; ESPN; ESPN2; Spike TV; TBS; TNT; WGN America.
Fee: $25.00 monthly.
Pay Service 1
Pay Units: N.A.
Programming (via satellite): HBO.
Fee: $2.50 monthly.
Video-On-Demand: No
Internet Service
Operational: No.
Telephone Service
None
Miles of Plant: 7.0 (coaxial); None (fiber optic). Homes passed: 300.
Chief Technician: Mike Beckman.
Ownership: Government Camp Cable.

GRANTS PASS—Charter Communications. Now served by MEDFORD, OR [OR0006]. ICA: OR0010.

GREEN ACRES—Greenacres TV Cable, 93688 Cordell Ln, Coos Bay, OR 97420. Phone: 541-267-4788. ICA: OR0163.
TV Market Ranking: Below 100 (GREEN ACRES). Franchise award date: N.A. Franchise expiration date: N.A. Began: August 1, 1993.
Channel capacity: 13 (2-way capable). Channels available but not in use: N.A.
Basic Service
Subscribers: 35.
Programming (received off-air): KCBY-TV (CBS, This TV) Coos Bay; KEZI (ABC, MeTV) Eugene; KLSR-TV (FOX) Eugene; KMCB (NBC) Coos Bay; KOAC-TV (PBS) Corvallis; KOBI (NBC) Medford.
Fee: $100.00 installation; $27.50 monthly.
Expanded Basic Service 1
Subscribers: N.A.
Programming (via satellite): CNN; Discovery Channel; ESPN; TBS; TNT; Trinity Broadcasting Network (TBN); WGN America.
Fee: $8.50 monthly.
Internet Service
Operational: No.
Miles of Plant: 5.0 (coaxial); None (fiber optic). Homes passed: 140.
General Manager: Wayne Morgan.
Ownership: Wayne E. Morgan.

HAINES—Formerly served by Almega Cable. No longer in operation. ICA: OR0108.

HALFWAY—Formerly served by Charter Communications. No longer in operation. ICA: OR0140.

HALSEY—Roome Telecommunications Inc. No longer in operation. ICA: OR0100.

HELIX—Formerly served by Helix Communications. No longer in operation. ICA: OR0119.

HEPPNER—Heppner TV Inc, 162 North Main St, PO Box 815, Heppner, OR 97836-0587. Phone: 800-862-8508. Fax: 541-676-9655. E-mail: windtech@windwave.org. Web Site: http://www.windwave.org. Also serves Ione & Lexington. ICA: OR0077.
TV Market Ranking: Outside TV Markets (HEPPNER, Ione, Lexington). Franchise award date: March 1, 1955. Franchise expiration date: N.A. Began: June 1, 1955.
Channel capacity: N.A. Channels available but not in use: N.A.
Basic Service
Subscribers: N.A.
Programming (received off-air): KEPR-TV (CBS, CW) Pasco; KNDU (NBC) Richland; KOPB-TV (PBS) Portland; KPDX (Escape, MNT) Vancouver; KVEW (ABC, MeTV, MNT) Kennewick; allband FM.
Programming (via microwave): KATU (ABC, MeTV) Portland; KGW (Estrella TV, NBC) Portland; KOIN (CBS) Portland; KPTV (COZI TV, FOX, Laff) Portland.
Programming (via satellite): A&E; CNN; Discovery Channel; Disney Channel; ESPN; Freeform; Spike TV; Syfy; TBS; TLC; TNT; USA Network; VH1; WGN America.
Fee: $20.00 installation.
Pay Service 1
Pay Units: N.A.
Programming (via satellite): HBO.
Fee: $12.50 installation; $11.00 monthly.
Video-On-Demand: No
Internet Service
Operational: No, Wireless.
Fee: $75.00 installation.
Telephone Service
None
Miles of Plant: 17.0 (coaxial); 4.0 (fiber optic). Homes passed: 700.
President: Nate Arbogast. Vice President: Don Russel. Office Manager: Sandy Matthews. Chief Technician: Thomas Rawlins.
Ownership: WindWave Communications.

IDANHA—Formerly served by Wave Broadband. No longer in operation. ICA: OR0101.

IMBLER—Formerly served by Almega Cable. No longer in operation. ICA: OR0116.

IONE—Formerly served by Ione TV Co-op. Now served by Heppner TV Inc., HEPPNER, OR [OR0077]. ICA: OR0114.

KLAMATH FALLS—Charter Communications, 12405 Powerscourt Dr, St. Louis, MO 63131. Phones: 636-207-5100 (Corporate office); 360-828-6700; 360-828-6600. Fax: 360-828-6795. Web Site: http://www.charter.com. Also serves Klamath County (unincorporated areas). ICA: OR0011.
TV Market Ranking: Below 100 (Klamath County (unincorporated areas), KLAMATH FALLS). Franchise award date: N.A. Franchise expiration date: N.A. Began: January 1, 1953.
Channel capacity: N.A. Channels available but not in use: N.A.
Digital Basic Service
Subscribers: 7,867.
Programming (via satellite): BBC America; Bloomberg Television; CNN en Espanol; CNN International; Discovery Life Channel; ESPN Classic; ESPNews; FOX College Sports Central; FOX College Sports Pacific; Fox Deportes; Fox Sports 2; Fuse; FXM; FYI; History International; IFC; LMN; MC; NFL Network; Nick Jr.; Nicktoons; Sundance TV; TeenNick; TV Guide Interactive Inc.
Fee: $26.99 monthly.

Digital Expanded Basic Service
Subscribers: N.A.
Programming (via satellite): A&E; AMC; Animal Planet; Bravo; Cartoon Network; CMT; CNBC; CNN; Comedy Central; Discovery Channel; Disney Channel; Disney XD; DIY Network; E! HD; ESPN; ESPN2; Food Network; Fox News Channel; Fox Sports 1; Freeform; FX; Golf Channel; GSN; Hallmark Channel; HGTV; History; HLN; Lifetime; MSNBC; MTV; MTV2; National Geographic Channel; NBCSN; Nickelodeon; Northwest Cable News; Outdoor Channel; Oxygen; Spike TV; Syfy; TBS; The Weather Channel; TLC; TNT; Travel Channel; truTV; Turner Classic Movies; TV Land; Univision; Univision Studios; USA Network; VH1; WE tv.
Fee: $50.99 monthly.
Digital Pay Service 1
Pay Units: N.A.
Programming (via satellite): Cinemax (multiplexed); Flix; HBO (multiplexed); Showtime (multiplexed); Starz (multiplexed); Starz Encore; The Movie Channel (multiplexed).
Video-On-Demand: Yes
Pay-Per-View
iN DEMAND (delivered digitally); Hot Choice (delivered digitally); Playboy TV (delivered digitally); Fresh (delivered digitally); Shorteez (delivered digitally).
Internet Service
Operational: Yes.
Subscribers: 10,297.
Broadband Service: Charter Internet.
Fee: $29.99 monthly.
Telephone Service
Digital: Operational
Subscribers: 2,943.
Fee: $29.99 monthly
Miles of Plant: 601.0 (coaxial); 162.0 (fiber optic). Homes passed: 26,062.
Vice President: Frank Antonovich. General Manager: Linda Kimberly. Technical Operations Director: Greg Lemming. Marketing Manager: Dolly Brock. Office Manager: Kelly Williams. Accounting Director: David Sovanski.
Ownership: Charter Communications Inc. (MSO).

KNAPPA—Formerly served by Rapid Cable. No longer in operation. ICA: OR0071.

LA GRANDE—Charter Communications, 12405 Powerscourt Dr, St. Louis, MO 63131. Phones: 636-207-5100 (Corporate office); 509-396-0613; 509-783-0132; 509-222-2500. Fax: 509-735-3795. Web Site: http://www.charter.com. Also serves Island City, Union & Union County. ICA: OR0028.
TV Market Ranking: Outside TV Markets (Island City, LA GRANDE, Union, Union County). Franchise award date: January 1, 1954. Franchise expiration date: N.A. Began: September 29, 1954.
Channel capacity: N.A. Channels available but not in use: N.A.
Basic Service
Subscribers: 1,728.
Programming (received off-air): KTVB (NBC) Boise; KTVR (PBS) La Grande; KUNP-LD (MundoMax, UNV) Portland.
Programming (via microwave): KATU (ABC, MeTV) Portland; KGW (Estrella TV, NBC) Portland; KOIN (CBS) Portland; KPDX (Escape, MNT) Vancouver; KPTV (COZI TV, FOX, Laff) Portland.
Programming (via satellite): A&E; AMC; Animal Planet; CNBC; CNN; C-SPAN; Discovery Channel; Disney Channel; Disney XD; E! HD; ESPN; Fox News Channel; Freeform; FX; Hallmark Channel; HLN; Lifetime; MTV; Nickelodeon; Northwest Cable News; QVC; Spike TV; TBS; The Weather Channel; TLC; TNT; Travel Channel; truTV; USA Network; VH1.
Fee: $29.99 installation; $26.99 monthly.
Digital Basic Service
Subscribers: N.A.
Programming (via satellite): BBC America; Bloomberg Television; Bravo; Discovery Life Channel; DMX Music; ESPN Classic; ESPN2; ESPNews; Fox Sports 1; FXM; Golf Channel; GSN; HGTV; History; IFC; MTV Classic; National Geographic Channel; NBCSN; Nick Jr.; Outdoor Channel; Syfy; Trinity Broadcasting Network (TBN); Turner Classic Movies; TV Guide Interactive Inc.; VH1 Country; WE tv.
Digital Pay Service 1
Pay Units: N.A.
Programming (via satellite): Cinemax (multiplexed); HBO (multiplexed); Showtime (multiplexed); Starz (multiplexed); Starz Encore (multiplexed); The Movie Channel (multiplexed).
Video-On-Demand: No
Pay-Per-View
iN DEMAND (delivered digitally); Fresh (delivered digitally); Playboy TV (delivered digitally).
Internet Service
Operational: Yes.
Broadband Service: Charter Internet.
Fee: $19.99 monthly.
Telephone Service
Digital: Operational
Fee: $14.99 monthly
Homes passed: 12,085. Miles of plant included in Kennewick, WA
General Manager: Linda Kimberly. Technical Operations Manager: Jeff Hopkins. Marketing Director: Diane Long. Program Director: Lloyd Swain. Accounting Director: David Sovanski.
Ownership: Charter Communications Inc. (MSO).

LA PINE—Crestview Cable TV, 350 NE Dunham St., Prineville, OR 97754. Phones: 541-447-4342; 800-285-2330. E-mail: customerservice@crestviewcable.com. Web Site: http://www.crestviewcable.com. ICA: OR0142.
TV Market Ranking: Below 100 (LA PINE). Franchise award date: N.A. Franchise expiration date: N.A. Began: October 1, 1988.
Channel capacity: N.A. Channels available but not in use: N.A.
Basic Service
Subscribers: 1,330.
Programming (received off-air): KATU (ABC, MeTV) Portland; KBNZ-LD (CBS) Bend; KEZI (ABC, MeTV) Eugene; KFXO-LD (FOX) Bend; KOAB-TV (PBS) Bend; KOHD (ABC) Bend; KOIN (CBS) Portland; KPDX (Escape, MNT) Vancouver; KTVZ (CW, NBC) Bend.
Programming (via satellite): C-SPAN.
Fee: $30.50 installation; $23.59 monthly.
Expanded Basic Service 1
Subscribers: N.A.
Programming (via satellite): A&E; CMT; CNBC; CNN; Discovery Channel; Disney Channel; ESPN; ESPN2; Fox News Channel; Freeform; Hallmark Channel; HGTV; History; HLN; Lifetime; Nickelodeon; QVC; Spike TV; Syfy; TBS; TLC; TNT; Turner Classic Movies; USA Network; VH1.
Fee: $20.94 monthly.

2017 Edition D-641

Oregon—Cable Systems

CABLE & TV STATION COVERAGE
The perfect companion to the Television & Cable Factbook
To order call 800-771-9202 or visit www.warren-news.com

Digital Basic Service
Subscribers: N.A.
Programming (via satellite): A&E HD; BBC America; Bloomberg Television; Chiller; Cloo; CMT; CNN HD; Destination America; Discovery Family; Discovery Life Channel; Disney Channel HD; Disney XD; DMX Music; ESPN HD; ESPN2 HD; ESPNews; ESPNU; Food Network HD; Fox Business Network; FOX College Sports Central; FOX College Sports Pacific; Fox Sports 1; Freeform HD; FSN HD; Fuse; FXM; FYI; Golf Channel; History HD; History International; Investigation Discovery; LMN; MTV Classic; MTV2; NBCSN; Nick Jr.; Nicktoons; Northwest Cable News; Outdoor Channel; OWN: Oprah Winfrey Network; QVC HD; Science Channel; TBS HD; TeenNick; TNT HD; Travel Channel HD; USA Network HD; WE tv.
Fee: $17.82 monthly.

Digital Pay Service 1
Pay Units: N.A.
Programming (via satellite): Cinemax (multiplexed); HBO (multiplexed); Starz (multiplexed); Starz Encore (multiplexed).
Fee: $10.00 monthly (Cinemax), $12.00 monthly (Starz/Encore), $12.99 monthly (HBO).

Video-On-Demand: No
Internet Service
Operational: Yes.
Fee: $19.20 installation; $44.95 monthly.
Telephone Service
Digital: Operational
Miles of Plant: 100.0 (coaxial); None (fiber optic).
President: Patricia C. Smullin. General Manager: Mike O Herron. Chief Technical Officer: Joe Smalling. Marketing Director: Ann Brown.
Ownership: California-Oregon Broadcasting Inc. (MSO).

LACOMB—Formerly served by Wave Broadband. No longer in operation. ICA: OR0078.

LAKEVIEW—Charter Communications, 12405 Powerscourt Dr, St. Louis, MO 63131. Phones: 636-207-5100 (Corporate office); 360-828-6700; 360-828-6600. Fax: 360-828-6795. Web Site: http://www.charter.com. Also serves Lake County (portions). ICA: OR0051.
TV Market Ranking: Outside TV Markets (Lake County (portions), LAKEVIEW). Franchise award date: N.A. Franchise expiration date: N.A. Began: August 1, 1956.
Channel capacity: N.A. Channels available but not in use: N.A.
Digital Basic Service
Subscribers: 302.
Programming (via satellite): BBC America; Bloomberg Television; Bravo; Discovery Digital Networks; Disney XD; DMX Music; Fox Sports 1; Fuse; FXM; FYI; Golf Channel; GSN; History International; IFC; LMN; Nick Jr.; Outdoor Channel; Pop; TeenNick; Trinity Broadcasting Network (TBN); Turner Classic Movies; WAM! America's Kidz Network; WE tv.
Fee: $26.99 monthly.

Digital Expanded Basic Service
Subscribers: N.A.
Programming (via satellite): A&E; AMC; Animal Planet; Bravo; Cartoon Network; CMT; CNN; Discovery Life Channel; Disney Channel; E! HD; ESPN; ESPN2; Food Network; Fox News Channel; Freeform; FX; HGTV; History; HLN; Lifetime; MTV; NBCSN; Nickelodeon; Spike TV; Syfy; TBS; The Weather Channel; TLC; TNT; truTV; Univision Studios; USA Network.
Fee: $47.99 monthly.

Digital Pay Service 1
Pay Units: N.A.
Programming (via satellite): Cinemax (multiplexed); Flix; HBO (multiplexed); Showtime (multiplexed); Starz (multiplexed); Starz Encore (multiplexed); The Movie Channel (multiplexed).
Video-On-Demand: No
Pay-Per-View
iN DEMAND (delivered digitally).
Internet Service
Operational: Yes.
Broadband Service: Charter Internet.
Fee: $19.99 monthly.
Telephone Service
None
Miles of Plant: 48.0 (coaxial); 6.0 (fiber optic). Homes passed: 2,109.
Vice President: Frank Antonovich. General Manager: Linda Kimberly. Technical Operations Director: Greg Lemming. Marketing Manager: Dolly Brock. Office Manager: Kelly Williams. Accounting Director: David Sovanski.
Ownership: Charter Communications Inc. (MSO).

LEBANON—Comcast Cable. Now served by PORTLAND, OR [OR0001]. ICA: OR0024.

LINCOLN CITY—Charter Communications, 12405 Powerscourt Dr, St. Louis, MO 63131. Phones: 636-207-5100 (Corporate office); 360-828-6700; 360-828-6600. Fax: 360-828-6795. Web Site: http://www.charter.com. Also serves Bay City, Cloverdale, Garibaldi, Lincoln County (portions), Manzanita, Nehalem, Netarts, Newport, Rockaway Beach, Tillamook, Tillamook County (portions), Toledo, Waldport, Wheeler & Yachats. ICA: OR0020.
TV Market Ranking: Below 100 (Lincoln County (portions) (portions), Tillamook (portions)); Outside TV Markets (Bay City, Cloverdale, Garibaldi, LINCOLN CITY, Lincoln County (portions) (portions), Manzanita, Nehalem, Netarts, Newport, Rockaway Beach, Tillamook (portions), Tillamook, Toledo, Waldport, Wheeler, Yachats). Franchise award date: January 1, 1955. Franchise expiration date: N.A. Began: October 22, 1954.
Channel capacity: N.A. Channels available but not in use: N.A.
Digital Basic Service
Subscribers: 13,661.
Programming (via satellite): BBC America; Bloomberg Television; Boomerang; CMT; CNN en Espanol; CNN International; Discovery Digital Networks; ESPN Classic; ES-PNews; FOX College Sports Central; FOX College Sports Pacific; Fox Sports 2; FYI; GSN; History International; IFC; LMN; MC; NFL Network; Nick 2; Nick Jr.; Sundance TV; TeenNick; WE tv.
Fee: $26.99 monthly.

Digital Expanded Basic Service
Subscribers: N.A.
Programming (via satellite): A&E; AMC; Animal Planet; Bravo; Cartoon Network; CMT; CNBC; CNN; Comedy Central; Discovery Channel; Discovery Life Channel; Disney Channel; Disney XD; DIY Network; E! HD; ESPN; ESPN2; EVINE Live; Food Network; Fox Sports 1; Freeform; FX; FXM; Golf Channel; GSN; Hallmark Channel; HGTV; HLN; ION Television; Lifetime; MSNBC; MTV; National Geographic Channel; NBCSN; Nickelodeon; Northwest Cable News; Outdoor Channel; Oxygen; Spike TV; Syfy; TBS; The Weather Channel; TLC; TNT; Travel Channel; truTV; Turner Classic Movies; TV Land; Univision Studios; USA Network; VH1.
Fee: $42.99 monthly.

Digital Pay Service 1
Pay Units: N.A.
Programming (via satellite): Cinemax (multiplexed); Flix; HBO (multiplexed); Showtime (multiplexed); Starz (multiplexed); Starz Encore (multiplexed); The Movie Channel (multiplexed).
Fee: $11.95 monthly (Cinemax, HBO, Showtime/Flix, Starz/Encore or TMC).
Video-On-Demand: Yes
Pay-Per-View
Hot Choice (delivered digitally); iN DEMAND (delivered digitally); Playboy TV (delivered digitally); Fresh (delivered digitally); Shorteez (delivered digitally).
Internet Service
Operational: Yes. Began: March 1, 2001.
Subscribers: 10,613.
Broadband Service: Charter Internet.
Fee: $29.99 monthly.
Telephone Service
Digital: Operational
Subscribers: 2,611.
Miles of Plant: 1,412.0 (coaxial); 466.0 (fiber optic). Homes passed: 39,508.
Vice President: Frank Antonovich. General Manager: Linda Kimberly. Technical Operations Director: Brian Lindholme. Marketing Director: Diane Long. Accounting Director: David Sovanski.
Ownership: Charter Communications Inc. (MSO).

MACLEAY—Formerly served by Country Cablevision Ltd. No longer in operation. ICA: OR0064.

MADRAS—Crestview Cable TV, 350 NE Dunham St., Prineville, OR 97754. Phones: 541-475-2969; 541-447-4342. E-mail: customerservice@crestviewcable.com. Web Site: http://www.crestviewcable.com. Also serves Culver & Metolius. ICA: OR0146.
TV Market Ranking: Below 100 (Culver); Outside TV Markets (MADRAS, Metolius). Franchise award date: January 1, 1955. Franchise expiration date: N.A. Began: June 1, 1955.
Channel capacity: N.A. Channels available but not in use: N.A.
Basic Service
Subscribers: 1,251.
Programming (received off-air): KATU (ABC, MeTV) Portland; KFXO-LD (FOX) Bend; KGW (Estrella TV, NBC) Portland; KOAB-TV (PBS) Bend; KOIN (CBS) Portland; KPDX (Escape, MNT) Vancouver; KTVZ (CW, NBC) Bend; 14 FMs.
Programming (via satellite): C-SPAN; Pop; QVC; Univision Studios.
Fee: $32.00 installation; $27.77 monthly; $.86 converter.

Expanded Basic Service 1
Subscribers: N.A.
Programming (via satellite): A&E; AMC; Animal Planet; CMT; CNBC; CNN; Comedy Central; C-SPAN 2; Discovery Channel; Disney Channel; Disney XD; ESPN; ESPN2; ES-PNews; Food Network; Fox News Channel; Freeform; Hallmark Channel; HGTV; History; HLN; Lifetime; MSNBC; MTV; NBCSN; Nickelodeon; Northwest Cable News; Spike TV; Syfy; TBS; TLC; TNT; Travel Channel; Trinity Broadcasting Network (TBN); Turner Classic Movies; TV Land; USA Network; VH1; WE tv.
Fee: $23.05 monthly.

Digital Basic Service
Subscribers: N.A.
Programming (via satellite): BBC America; Bloomberg Television; Cloo; Discovery Life Channel; DMX Music; FOX College Sports Central; FOX College Sports Pacific; Fox Sports 1; Fuse; FXM; FYI; Golf Channel; History International; HITS (Headend In The Sky); Outdoor Channel.
Fee: $4.55 monthly.

Digital Pay Service 1
Pay Units: N.A.
Programming (via satellite): Cinemax (multiplexed); HBO (multiplexed); Starz (multiplexed); Starz Encore (multiplexed).
Fee: $10.00 monthly (Cinemax), $12.00 monthly (HBO or Starz/Encore).

Video-On-Demand: No
Pay-Per-View
iN DEMAND (delivered digitally); Playboy TV (delivered digitally); Fresh (delivered digitally).
Internet Service
Operational: Yes. Began: December 1, 2000.
Broadband Service: In-house.
Fee: $69.95 installation; $44.95 monthly; $10.00 modem lease.
Telephone Service
Analog: Not Operational
Digital: Operational
Fee: $34.95 monthly
Miles of Plant: 59.0 (coaxial); None (fiber optic).
President: Patricia C. Smullin. General Manager: Mike OHerron. Chief Technical Officer: Joe Smalling. Marketing Director: Ann Brown.
Ownership: California-Oregon Broadcasting Inc. (MSO).

MALIN—Formerly served by Almega Cable. No longer in operation. ICA: OR0092.

MAPLETON—Formerly served by Rapid Communications. No longer in operation. ICA: OR0161.

MEDFORD—Charter Communications, 12405 Powerscourt Dr, St. Louis, MO 63131. Phones: 636-207-5100 (Corporate office); 360-828-6700; 360-828-6600. Fax: 360-828-6795. Web Site: http://www.charter.com. Also serves Ashland, Central Point, Eagle Point, Gold Hill, Grants Pass, Jackson County, Jacksonville, Josephine County (portions), Phoenix, Rogue River & Talent. ICA: OR0006.
TV Market Ranking: Below 100 (Ashland, Central Point, Eagle Point, Gold Hill, Jackson County, Jacksonville, Josephine

Cable Systems—Oregon

County (portions), MEDFORD, Phoenix, Rogue River, Talent, Grants Pass). Franchise award date: N.A. Franchise expiration date: N.A. Began: January 1, 1958.
Channel capacity: 62 (operating 2-way). Channels available but not in use: N.A.

Digital Basic Service
Subscribers: 34,023.
Programming (via satellite): BBC America; Bloomberg Television; Discovery Digital Networks; DIY Network; ESPN Classic; ESPNews; FXM; FYI; GSN; History International; IFC; LMN; MC; MSNBC; Nick Jr.; Nicktoons; Outdoor Channel; TeenNick; Turner Classic Movies.
Fee: $26.99 monthly.

Digital Expanded Basic Service
Subscribers: N.A.
Programming (via satellite): A&E; AMC; Animal Planet; Bravo; Cartoon Network; CMT; CNBC; CNN; Comedy Central; Discovery Life Channel; Disney Channel; Disney XD; E! HD; ESPN; ESPN2; EWTN Global Catholic Network; Food Network; Fox Sports 1; Freeform; FX; Golf Channel; HGTV; History; HLN; Lifetime; National Geographic Channel; NBCSN; Nickelodeon; Oxygen; Spike TV; Syfy; The Weather Channel; TNT; Travel Channel; truTV; TV Land; USA Network; VH1; WE tv.
Fee: $50.99 monthly.

Digital Pay Service 1
Pay Units: N.A.
Programming (via satellite): Cinemax (multiplexed); DMX Music; Flix; HBO (multiplexed); Showtime (multiplexed); Sundance TV; The Movie Channel (multiplexed).
Fee: $12.95 monthly (Cinemax, DMX, HBO or Showtime/Flix/Sundance/TMC).

Video-On-Demand: Yes

Pay-Per-View
iN DEMAND (delivered digitally); Fresh (delivered digitally); Shorteez (delivered digitally).

Internet Service
Operational: Yes. Began: December 1, 2000.
Subscribers: 45,144.
Broadband Service: Charter Internet.
Fee: $29.99 monthly.

Telephone Service
Digital: Operational
Subscribers: 12,341.
Fee: $29.99 monthly.
Miles of Plant: 2,899.0 (coaxial); 991.0 (fiber optic). Homes passed: 118,096.
Vice President: Frank Antonovich. General Manager: Linda Kimberly. Technical Operations Director: Greg Lemming. Marketing Manager: Dolly Brock. Office Manager: Kelly Williams. Accounting Director: David Sovanski.
Ownership: Charter Communications Inc. (MSO).

MERRILL—Formerly served by Almega Cable. No longer in operation. ICA: OR0081.

MILTON-FREEWATER—Charter Communications. Now served by KENNEWICK, WA [WA0008]. ICA: OR0043.

MILWAUKIE—Comcast Cable. Now served by PORTLAND, OR [OR0001]. ICA: OR0018.

MONROE—Monroe Telephone Co. This cable system has converted to IPTV. See MONROE, OR [OR5001]. ICA: OR0105.

MONROE—Monroe Telephone. Formerly [OR0105]. This cable system has converted to IPTV, 575 Commercial St, PO Box 130, Monroe, OR 97456-0130. Phone: 541-847-5135. Fax: 541-847-9997. E-mail: telco@monroetel.com. Web Site: http://www.monroetel.com. ICA: OR5001.
TV Market Ranking: Below 100 (MONROE).
Channel capacity: N.A. Channels available but not in use: N.A.

Bronze
Subscribers: 257.
Fee: $34.95 monthly; $4.95 converter.

Internet Service
Operational: Yes.

Telephone Service
Digital: Operational
Ownership: Monroe Telephone Co.

MORO—J & N Cable, 614 South Columbus Ave, Goldendale, WA 98620-9006. Phones: 800-752-9809; 509-773-5359. Fax: 509-773-7090. E-mail: customersupport@jncable.net. Web Site: http://www.jncable.com. ICA: OR0111.
TV Market Ranking: Outside TV Markets (MORO). Franchise award date: November 3, 1954. Franchise expiration date: N.A. Began: January 1, 1955.
Channel capacity: N.A. Channels available but not in use: N.A.

Basic Service
Subscribers: N.A.
Programming (received off-air): KEPR-TV (CBS, CW) Pasco; KNDU (NBC) Richland; KRCW-TV (Antenna TV, CW, This TV) Salem; KVEW (ABC, MeTV, MNT) Kennewick.
Programming (via microwave): KATU (ABC, MeTV) Portland; KGW (Estrella TV, NBC) Portland; KOIN (CBS) Portland; KOPB-TV (PBS) Portland; KPDX (Escape, MNT) Vancouver; KPTV (COZI TV, FOX, Laff) Portland.
Programming (via satellite): A&E; AMC; Cartoon Network; CNN; C-SPAN; C-SPAN 2; Discovery Channel; Disney Channel; ESPN; ESPN2; Fox News Channel; FOX Sports Networks; Freeform; Hallmark Channel; HGTV; History; HLN; Northwest Cable News; QVC; Syfy; TBS; TLC; TNT; Trinity Broadcasting Network (TBN); Turner Classic Movies; USA Network; WGN America.
Fee: $25.00 installation; $24.95 monthly; $15.00 converter.

Pay Service 1
Pay Units: N.A.
Programming (via satellite): HBO.

Video-On-Demand: No

Internet Service
Operational: No.

Telephone Service
None
Miles of Plant: 9.0 (coaxial); None (fiber optic). Homes passed: 150.
President & General Manager: John Kusky. Vice President & Marketing Manager: Nancy Kusky.
Ownership: J & N Cable Systems Inc.

MOUNT VERNON—Blue Mountain TV Cable Co, 300 Highland Terrace, PO Box 267, Mount Vernon, OR 97865-0267. Phone: 541-932-4613. Fax: 541-932-4613. E-mail: bmtv@bluemountaindigital.com. Web Site: http://www.bmtvcable.com. Also serves Canyon City, John Day, Prairie City & Seneca. ICA: OR0061.
TV Market Ranking: Outside TV Markets (Canyon City, John Day, MOUNT VERNON, Seneca, Prairie City). Franchise award date: N.A. Franchise expiration date: N.A. Began: October 1, 1954.
Channel capacity: N.A. Channels available but not in use: N.A.

Basic Service
Subscribers: 363.
Programming (received off-air): KATU (ABC, MeTV) Portland; KGW (Estrella TV, NBC) Portland; KOIN (CBS) Portland; KOPB-TV (PBS) Portland; KPDX (Escape, MNT) Vancouver; KPTV (COZI TV, FOX, Laff) Portland; 4 FMs.
Programming (via satellite): 3ABN; CW PLUS; Discovery Channel; Disney Channel; ESPN; ESPN2; Fox News Channel; Freeform; HGTV; Outdoor Channel; QVC; Syfy; TBS; WGN America.
Fee: $20.00 installation; $28.50 monthly.

Video-On-Demand: No

Internet Service
Operational: Yes.
Subscribers: 60.
Fee: $24.95-$54.95 monthly.

Telephone Service
None
Miles of Plant: 30.0 (coaxial); None (fiber optic). Homes passed: 1,445.
General Manager: Chuck McKenna.
Ownership: Blue Mountain TV Cable Co. (MSO).

MYRTLE CREEK—Charter Communications. Now served by ROSEBURG, OR [OR0016]. ICA: OR0021.

NEWBERG—Comcast Cable. Now served by PORTLAND, OR [OR0001]. ICA: OR0014.

NORTH POWDER—Formerly served by Almega Cable. No longer in operation. ICA: OR0107.

ODELL—Valley TV Co-op Inc, 614 South Columbus Ave, Goldendale, WA 98620-9006. Phones: 509-773-5359; 541-352-7278. Fax: 541-352-7277. ICA: OR0102.
TV Market Ranking: Outside TV Markets (ODELL). Franchise award date: N.A. Franchise expiration date: N.A. Began: April 1, 1955.
Channel capacity: N.A. Channels available but not in use: N.A.

Basic Service
Subscribers: N.A.
Programming (received off-air): KATU (ABC, MeTV) Portland; KGW (Estrella TV, NBC) Portland; KOIN (CBS) Portland; KOPB-TV (PBS) Portland; KPTV (COZI TV, FOX, Laff) Portland.
Programming (via satellite): A&E; Discovery Channel; Disney Channel; ESPN; Freeform; Great American Country; National Geographic Channel; Outdoor Channel; Spike TV; Syfy; TBS; TLC; TNT; Univision Studios; WGN America.
Fee: $25.00 installation; $27.50 monthly.

Pay Service 1
Pay Units: N.A.
Programming (via satellite): HBO; The Movie Channel.
Fee: $10.00 monthly.

Internet Service
Operational: No.
Homes passed & miles of plant included in Parkdale
Chief Technician: John Kusky.
Ownership: Valley TV Co-op Inc. (MSO).

OREGON CITY (unincorporated areas)—Clear Creek Telephone & TeleVision, 18238 South Fischers Mill Rd, Oregon City, OR 97045-9612. Phone: 503-631-2101. Fax: 503-631-2098. E-mail: info@clearcreek.coop. Web Site: http://www.ccmtc.com. Also serves Redland. ICA: OR0180.
TV Market Ranking: 29 (Redland).
Channel capacity: N.A. Channels available but not in use: N.A.

Basic Service
Subscribers: 1,117.
Programming (received off-air): KATU (ABC, MeTV) Portland; KGW (Estrella TV, NBC) Portland; KNMT (TBN) Portland; KOIN (CBS) Portland; KOPB-TV (PBS) Portland; KPDX (Escape, MNT) Vancouver; KPTV (COZI TV, FOX, Laff) Portland; KPXG-TV (ION) Salem; KRCW-TV (Antenna TV, CW, This TV) Salem.
Programming (via satellite): CNN; C-SPAN; C-SPAN 2; Freeform; Lifetime; Pop; QVC.
Fee: $26.00 monthly.

Expanded Basic Service 1
Subscribers: N.A.
Programming (via satellite): A&E; AMC; Animal Planet; Cartoon Network; CMT; CNBC; Comedy Central; Discovery Channel; Discovery Life Channel; Disney Channel; ESPN; ESPN2; Food Network; Fox News Channel; HGTV; History; HLN; INSP; MTV; Nickelodeon; Northwest Cable News; OWN; Oprah Winfrey Network; Spike TV; Syfy; TBS; The Weather Channel; TLC; TNT; Travel Channel; Turner Classic Movies; TV Land; Univision Studios; USA Network; VH1; WGN America.
Fee: $19.95 monthly.

Digital Basic Service
Subscribers: N.A.
Programming (via satellite): BBC America; Discovery Digital Networks; ESPNews; Fox Sports 1; Golf Channel; GSN; IFC; MC.
Fee: $55.00 monthly.

Pay Service 1
Pay Units: N.A.
Programming (via satellite): Cinemax; HBO (multiplexed); Showtime (multiplexed); The Movie Channel.
Fee: $10.50 monthly (Cinemax or TMC), $12 monthly (HBO or Showtime).

Digital Pay Service 1
Pay Units: N.A.
Programming (via satellite): Cinemax (multiplexed); Flix; HBO (multiplexed); Showtime (multiplexed); Sundance TV; The Movie Channel (multiplexed).
Fee: $10.50 monthly (Cinemax or Flix/Sundance/TMC), $11.75 monthly (HBO or Showtime).

Video-On-Demand: No

Pay-Per-View
iN DEMAND (delivered digitally); Playboy TV (delivered digitally); Fresh (delivered digitally).

Internet Service
Operational: Yes.
Broadband Service: ccwebster.net.
Fee: $50.00 installation; $32.99-$117.95 monthly.

Telephone Service
Analog: Operational
President: Mitchell Moore. IT Manager: Rick Lundh. Sales Director: Erin Grewe.
Ownership: Clear Creek Telephone & Television.

OTIS—Formerly served by Wave Broadband. No longer in operation. ICA: OR0175.

PARKDALE—Valley TV Co-op Inc, 614 South Columbus Ave, Goldendale, WA 98620-9006. Phones: 509-773-5359; 541-352-7278. Fax: 541-352-7277. Also serves Mount Hood. ICA: OR0147.
TV Market Ranking: Outside TV Markets (Mount Hood, PARKDALE). Franchise

2017 Edition   D-643

Oregon—Cable Systems

award date: N.A. Franchise expiration date: N.A. Began: January 1, 1955.
Channel capacity: N.A. Channels available but not in use: N.A.
Basic Service
Subscribers: N.A.
Programming (received off-air): KATU (ABC, MeTV) Portland; KGW (Estrella TV, NBC) Portland; KOIN (CBS) Portland; KOPB-TV (PBS) Portland; KPTV (COZI TV, FOX, Laff) Portland.
Programming (via satellite): A&E; Discovery Channel; Disney Channel; ESPN; Freeform; Great American Country; National Geographic Channel; Outdoor Channel; Spike TV; Syfy; TBS; TLC; TNT; Univision Studios; WGN America.
Pay Service 1
Pay Units: N.A.
Programming (via satellite): HBO; The Movie Channel.
Fee: $10.00 monthly.
Internet Service
Operational: No.
Miles of Plant: 130.0 (coaxial); None (fiber optic). Homes passed: 4,000. Homes passed & miles of plant include Odell.
Chief Technician: John Kusky.
Ownership: Valley TV Co-op Inc. (MSO).

PENDLETON—Charter Communications. Now served by KENNEWICK, WA [WA0008]. ICA: OR0019.

PORTLAND—Comcast Cable, 9605 Southwest Nimbus Ave, Beaverton, OR 97008-7198. Phone: 503-605-6000. Fax: 503-605-6226. Web Site: http://www.comcast.com. Also serves Adair Village, Albany, Aloha, Amity, Banks, Beaverton, Benton County (portions), Carlton, Clackamas County (portions), Columbia City, Cornelius, Corvallis, Dayton, Deer Island, Dundee, Durham, Eugene, Fairview, Forest Grove, Gaston, Gladstone, Gresham, Happy Valley, Harrisburg, Hayden Island, Hillsboro, Johnson City, Junction City, Keizer, King City, Lafayette, Lake Oswego, Lane County (portions), Lebanon, Linn County (western portion), Marion County (portions), Maywood Park, McMinnville, Millersburg, Milwaukie, Multnomah County (portions), Newberg, North Plains, Oregon City, Philomath, Polk County (portions), Rivergrove, Salem, Scappoose, Sherwood, Sodaville, Springfield, St. Helens, Sweet Home, Tangent, Tigard, Troutdale, Tualatin, Warren, Washington County (portions), Waterloo, West Linn, Wilsonville, Wood Village & Yamhill. ICA: OR0001.
TV Market Ranking: 29 (Aloha, Banks, Beaverton, Carlton, Clackamas County (portions), Columbia City, Cornelius, Dayton, Deer Island, Dundee, Durham, Fairview, Forest Grove, Gaston, Gladstone, Gresham, Happy Valley, Hayden Island, Hillsboro, Johnson City, King City, Lafayette, Lake Oswego, Maywood Park, McMinnville, Milwaukie, Multnomah County (portions), Newberg, North Plains, Oregon City, PORTLAND, Rivergrove, Scappoose, Sherwood, St. Helens, Tigard, Troutdale, Tualatin, Tualatin, Warren, Washington County (portions), West Linn, Wilsonville, Wood Village, Yamhill); Below 100 (Adair Village, Albany, Amity, Benton County (portions), Harrisburg, Junction City, Keizer, Lane County (portions) (portions), Lebanon, Linn County (western portion), Millersburg, Philomath, Sodaville, Springfield, Sweet Home, Tangent, Waterloo, Corvallis, Eugene, Salem); Outside TV Markets (Lane County (portions) (portions)). Franchise

award date: May 1, 1981. Franchise expiration date: N.A. Began: February 1, 1982.
Channel capacity: 30 (operating 2-way). Channels available but not in use: N.A.
Basic Service
Subscribers: 441,379.
Programming (received off-air): KATU (ABC, MeTV) Portland; KGW (Estrella TV, NBC) Portland; KNMT (TBN) Portland; KOIN (CBS) Portland; KOPB-TV (PBS) Portland; KPDX (Escape, MNT) Vancouver; KPTV (COZI TV, FOX, Laff) Portland; KPXG-TV (ION) Salem; KRCW-TV (Antenna TV, CW, This TV) Salem.
Programming (via satellite): C-SPAN; C-SPAN 2; Discovery Channel; EVINE Live; Hallmark Channel; Pop; QVC; Univision Studios; WGN America.
Fee: $40.00 installation; $19.82 monthly.
Expanded Basic Service 1
Subscribers: 176,000.
Programming (via satellite): A&E; AMC; Animal Planet; BET; Cartoon Network; CMT; CNBC; CNN; Comedy Central; Disney Channel; E! HD; ESPN; ESPN2; Food Network; Fox News Channel; Freeform; FX; Golf Channel; HGTV; History; HLN; Lifetime; MSNBC; MTV; Nickelodeon; Northwest Cable News; Oxygen; Spike TV; Syfy; TBS; The Weather Channel; TLC; TNT; Travel Channel; truTV; TV Land; USA Network; VH1.
Fee: 40.73-$47.90 monthly.
Digital Basic Service
Subscribers: N.A.
Programming (via satellite): BBC America; Bloomberg Television; Bravo; Discovery Life Channel; Disney XD; DMX Music; ESPN Classic; ESPNews; EWTN Global Catholic Network; Fox Sports 1; FSN Digital Atlantic; FSN Digital Central; FSN Digital Pacific; Fuse; FXM; FYI; Great American Country; GSN; History International; HITS (Headend In The Sky); IFC; LMN; National Geographic Channel; NBCSN; Nick Jr.; Nicktoons; Outdoor Channel; Ovation; Sundance TV; TeenNick; The Word Network; Turner Classic Movies; WE tv; Weatherscan.
Fee: $10.95 monthly.
Digital Pay Service 1
Pay Units: N.A.
Programming (via satellite): Cinemax; Flix; HBO (multiplexed); RTN; Showtime (multiplexed); Starz (multiplexed); The Filipino Channel; The Movie Channel (multiplexed).
Fee: $14.99 monthly (CCTV4, Filipino Channel, Russian TV Network or Starz); $18.15 monthly (Cinemax, HBO, Showtime or TMC).
Video-On-Demand: Yes
Pay-Per-View
iN DEMAND (delivered digitally); Sports PPV (delivered digitally); Urban Xtra (delivered digitally); Fresh (delivered digitally); Shorteez (delivered digitally); Playboy TV (delivered digitally).
Internet Service
Operational: Yes.
Subscribers: 520,655.
Broadband Service: Comcast High Speed Internet.
Fee: $99.95 installation; $52.95 monthly; $3.00 modem lease.
Telephone Service
Digital: Operational
Subscribers: 247,139.
Fee: $44.95 monthly
Miles of Plant: 17,931.0 (coaxial); 4,083.0 (fiber optic). Homes passed: 1,097,225.
Vice President, Technical Operations: Mike Mason. Vice President, Marketing: Lars Lo-

fas. General Manager: Hank Fore. Ad Sales Manager: Tim Corken. Marketing Director: Brad Nosler. Public Relations Director: Theressa Davis.
Ownership: Comcast Cable Communications Inc. (MSO).

PORTLAND (western portion)—Comcast Cable. Now served by PORTLAND, OR [OR0001]. ICA: OR0009.

POWERS—Formerly served by Charter Communications. No longer in operation. ICA: OR0094.

PRAIRIE CITY—Blue Mountain TV Cable Co. Now served by MOUNT VERNON, OR [OR0061]. ICA: OR0084.

PRINEVILLE—Crestview Cable TV, 350 NE Dunham St., Prineville, OR 97754. Phones: 800-285-2330; 541-447-4342. E-mail: customerservice@crestviewcable.com. Web Site: http://www.crestviewcable.com. ICA: OR0038.
TV Market Ranking: Below 100 (PRINEVILLE). Franchise award date: N.A. Franchise expiration date: N.A. Began: June 1, 1971.
Channel capacity: N.A. Channels available but not in use: N.A.
Basic Service
Subscribers: 1,625.
Programming (received off-air): KATU (ABC, MeTV) Portland; KFXO-LD (FOX) Bend; KGW (Estrella TV, NBC) Portland; KOAB-TV (PBS) Bend; KOIN (CBS) Portland; KPDX (Escape, MNT) Vancouver; KTVZ (CW, NBC) Bend; 14 FMs.
Programming (via satellite): C-SPAN; Pop; QVC; Univision Studios.
Fee: $32.00 installation; $27.77 monthly; $.86 converter.
Expanded Basic Service 1
Subscribers: N.A.
Programming (via satellite): A&E; AMC; Animal Planet; CMT; CNBC; CNN; Comedy Central; C-SPAN 2; Discovery Channel; Disney Channel; Disney XD; ESPN; ESPN2; ESPNews; Food Network; Fox News Channel; Freeform; Hallmark Channel; HGTV; History; HLN; Lifetime; MSNBC; MTV; NBCSN; Nickelodeon; Northwest Cable News; Spike TV; Syfy; TBS; TLC; TNT; Travel Channel; Trinity Broadcasting Network (TBN); Turner Classic Movies; TV Land; USA Network; VH1; WE tv.
Fee: $26.31 monthly.
Digital Basic Service
Subscribers: N.A.
Programming (via satellite): BBC America; Bloomberg Television; Cloo; Discovery Life Channel; DMX Music; FOX College Sports Central; FOX College Sports Pacific; Fox Sports 1; Fuse; FXM; FYI; Golf Channel; History International; HITS (Headend In The Sky); Outdoor Channel.
Fee: $20.17 monthly.
Digital Pay Service 1
Pay Units: N.A.
Programming (via satellite): Cinemax (multiplexed); HBO (multiplexed); Starz (multiplexed); Starz Encore (multiplexed).
Fee: $10.00 monthly (Cinemax), $12.00 monthly (Starz/Encore), $12.99 monthly (HBO).
Video-On-Demand: No
Pay-Per-View
iN DEMAND (delivered digitally); Playboy TV (delivered digitally); Fresh (delivered digitally).

Internet Service
Operational: Yes. Began: December 1, 2000.
Broadband Service: In-house.
Fee: $19.20 installation; $44.95 monthly; $10.00 modem lease.
Telephone Service
Analog: Not Operational
Digital: Operational
Miles of Plant: 80.0 (coaxial); None (fiber optic).
President: Patricia C. Smullin. General Manager: Mike OHerron. Chief Technical Officer: Joe Smalling. Marketing Director: Ann Brown.
Ownership: California-Oregon Broadcasting Inc. (MSO).

PRINEVILLE—Formerly served by Central Vision. No longer in operation. ICA: OR0169.

PROSPECT—Formerly served by Almega Cable. No longer in operation. ICA: OR0096.

RAINIER—J & N Cable, 614 South Columbus Ave, Goldendale, WA 98620-9006. Phones: 800-752-9809; 509-773-5359. Fax: 509-773-7090. E-mail: customersupport@jncable.net. Web Site: http://www.jncable.com. ICA: OR0058.
TV Market Ranking: Below 100 (RAINIER). Franchise award date: January 1, 1958. Franchise expiration date: N.A. Began: January 1, 1958.
Channel capacity: N.A. Channels available but not in use: N.A.
Basic Service
Subscribers: 235.
Programming (received off-air): KATU (ABC, MeTV) Portland; KGPX-TV (ION) Spokane; KGW (Estrella TV, NBC) Portland; KOIN (CBS) Portland; KOPB-TV (PBS) Portland; KPDX (Escape, MNT) Vancouver; KPTV (COZI TV, FOX, Laff) Portland; allband FM.
Programming (via satellite): A&E; AMC; Animal Planet; Cartoon Network; CNBC; CNN; Comedy Central; Discovery Channel; Disney Channel; Disney XD; E! HD; ESPN; ESPN2; EVINE Live; Fox News Channel; FOX Sports Networks; Freeform; FX; Great American Country; Hallmark Channel; HGTV; History; HLN; Lifetime; MSNBC; MTV; Nickelodeon; QVC; Spike TV; Syfy; TBS; TLC; TNT; Trinity Broadcasting Network (TBN); TV Land; USA Network; VH1; WGN America.
Fee: $25.00 installation; $14.95 monthly.
Digital Basic Service
Subscribers: N.A.
Programming (via satellite): BBC America; Bravo; CMT; Destination America; Discovery Kids Channel; DMX Music; EVINE Live; Fuse; FYI; GSN; History International; Investigation Discovery; MTV Classic; MTV2; National Geographic Channel; Nick Jr.; OWN: Oprah Winfrey Network; Science Channel; TeenNick; Trinity Broadcasting Network (TBN); WE tv.
Fee: $15.95 monthly.
Digital Expanded Basic Service
Subscribers: N.A.
Programming (via satellite): ESPN Classic; ESPNews; FOX College Sports Central; FOX College Sports Pacific; Fox Sports 1; Golf Channel; IFC; LMN; NBCSN.
Fee: $15.95 monthly.
Pay Service 1
Pay Units: N.A.
Programming (via satellite): HBO.
Fee: $10.00 installation; $9.95 monthly.

Cable Systems—Oregon

FULLY SEARCHABLE • CONTINUOUSLY UPDATED • DISCOUNT RATES FOR PRINT PURCHASERS

For more information call **800-771-9202** or visit **www.warren-news.com**

Digital Pay Service 1
Pay Units: N.A.
Programming (via satellite): Cinemax (multiplexed); HBO (multiplexed); Showtime (multiplexed); Starz (multiplexed); Starz Encore; The Movie Channel.
Fee: $10.95 monthly (Cinemax), $12.00 monthly (Showtime/TMC), $12.95 monthly (HBO).
Video-On-Demand: Planned
Pay-Per-View
special events (delivered digitally); Playboy TV (delivered digitally).
Internet Service
Operational: No.
Telephone Service
None
Miles of Plant: 36.0 (coaxial); None (fiber optic). Homes passed: 1,800.
President & General Manager: John Kusky. Vice President: Nancy Kusky.
Ownership: J & N Cable Systems Inc. (MSO).

REDMOND—Formerly served by Central Vision. No longer in operation. ICA: OR0166.

RICHLAND—Eagle Valley Communications, 349 1st St, PO Box 180, Richland, OR 97870. Phones: 800-366-0795; 541-893-6116. Fax: 541-893-6903. Web Site: http://www.eagletelephone.com. Also serves New Bridge. ICA: OR0113.
TV Market Ranking: Outside TV Markets (New Bridge, RICHLAND).
Channel capacity: N.A. Channels available but not in use: N.A.
Basic Service
Subscribers: N.A.
Programming (received off-air): KBOI-TV (CBS, CW) Boise; KIVI-TV (ABC, Escape, FOX) Nampa; KTRV-TV (MeTV, MNT, Movies!, This TV) Nampa; KTVB (NBC) Boise; WKRN-TV (ABC) Nashville; WSEE-TV (CBS, CW) Erie.
Programming (via satellite): A&E; AMC; Animal Planet; CMT; CNBC; CNN; C-SPAN; Discovery Channel; Disney Channel; ESPN; ESPN2; Fox News Channel; Freeform; History; HLN; Lifetime; MTV; Nickelodeon; Northwest Cable News; Spike TV; Starz Encore; Syfy; TBS; The Weather Channel; TLC; TNT; USA Network; WNBC (COZI TV, NBC) New York.
Fee: $25.00 installation.
Pay Service 1
Pay Units: N.A.
Programming (via satellite): Cinemax; HBO.
Fee: $15.00 installation; $4.50 - $10.00 monthly (each).
Video-On-Demand: No
Internet Service
Operational: No, DSL.
Telephone Service
Analog: Operational
Chief Technician & Program Director: Gary Fehrenbach. Plant Manager: Mike Lattin. Marketing Director: Marcia Lincoln.
Ownership: Eagle Valley Communications (MSO).

ROSE LODGE—Formerly served by Wave Broadband. No longer in operation. ICA: OR0150.

ROSEBURG—Charter Communications, 12405 Powerscourt Dr, St. Louis, MO 63131. Phones: 636-207-5100 (Corporate office); 360-828-6700; 360-828-6600. Fax: 360-828-6795. Web Site: http://www.charter.com. Also serves Canyonville, Dillard, Douglas County (portions), Myrtle Creek, Oakland, Riddle, Sutherlin, Tri-City & Winston. ICA: OR0016.
TV Market Ranking: Below 100 (Canyonville, Dillard, Douglas County (portions), Myrtle Creek, Oakland, Riddle, ROSEBURG, Sutherlin, Tri-City, Winston). Franchise award date: November 1, 1973. Franchise expiration date: N.A. Began: January 1, 1954.
Channel capacity: N.A. Channels available but not in use: N.A.
Digital Basic Service
Subscribers: 8,721.
Programming (via satellite): BBC America; Bloomberg Television; Boomerang; DIY Network; FYI; LMN; MC; Nick Jr.
Fee: $26.99 monthly.
Digital Expanded Basic Service
Subscribers: N.A.
Programming (via satellite): A&E; AMC; Animal Planet; Bravo; Cartoon Network; CMT; CNBC; CNN; Comedy Central; Discovery Channel; Disney Channel; Disney XD; E! HD; ESPN; ESPN2; Food Network; Fox News Channel; Fox Sports 1; Freeform; FX; FXM; Golf Channel; GSN; Hallmark Channel; HGTV; History; HLN; Lifetime; MSNBC; MTV; National Geographic Channel; NBCSN; Nickelodeon; Northwest Cable News; Spike TV; Syfy; TBS; The Weather Channel; TLC; TNT; Travel Channel; truTV; Turner Classic Movies; TV Land; USA Network; VH1; WE tv.
Fee: $50.99 monthly.
Digital Pay Service 1
Pay Units: N.A.
Programming (via satellite): Cinemax (multiplexed); Flix; HBO (multiplexed); Showtime (multiplexed); Starz; Starz Encore; The Movie Channel (multiplexed).
Fee: $25.00 installation; $5.00 monthly (Cinemax, HBO, Showtime/Flix, Starz/Encore or TMC).
Video-On-Demand: Yes
Pay-Per-View
Hot Choice (delivered digitally); Shorteez (delivered digitally); Fresh (delivered digitally); Playboy TV (delivered digitally); iN DEMAND (delivered digitally).
Internet Service
Operational: Yes.
Subscribers: 9,754.
Broadband Service: Charter Internet.
Fee: $29.99 monthly.
Telephone Service
Digital: Operational
Subscribers: 4,322.
Miles of Plant: 884.0 (coaxial); 279.0 (fiber optic). Homes passed: 36,249.
Vice President: Frank Antonovich. General Manager: Mike O'Herron. Technical Operations Director: Greg Lemming. Marketing Manager: Dolly Brock. Office Manager: Kelly Williams. Accounting Director: David Sovanski.
Ownership: Charter Communications Inc. (MSO).

SALEM—Comcast Cable. Now served by PORTLAND, OR [OR0001]. ICA: OR0005.

SALEM (southeastern portion)—Formerly served by Mill Creek Cable TV Inc. No longer in operation. ICA: OR0086.

SANDY—Wave Broadband, 401 Parkplace Center, Ste 500, Kirkland, WA 98033. Phones: 866-928-3123; 425-576-8200. Fax: 425-576-8221. Web Site: http://www.wavebroadband.com. Also serves Clackamas County (portions) & Wemme. ICA: OR0063.
TV Market Ranking: 29 (Clackamas County (portions) (portions), SANDY); Below 100 (Clackamas County (portions) (portions)); Outside TV Markets (Wemme, Clackamas County (portions) (portions)). Franchise award date: N.A. Franchise expiration date: N.A. Began: December 1, 1980.
Channel capacity: N.A. Channels available but not in use: N.A.
Basic Service
Subscribers: 2,676.
Programming (received off-air): KATU (ABC, MeTV) Portland; KGW (Estrella TV, NBC) Portland; KNMT (TBN) Portland; KOIN (CBS) Portland; KOPB-TV (PBS) Portland; KPDX (Escape, MNT) Vancouver; KPTV (COZI TV, FOX, Laff) Portland; KRCW-TV (Antenna TV, CW, This TV) Salem; KUNP (MundoMax, UNV) La Grande; 15 FMs.
Programming (via satellite): A&E; Comedy Central; C-SPAN; ESPN; ESPN2; Freeform; HGTV; MTV; MyNetworkTV; Nickelodeon; Pop; QVC; TBS; USA Network; VH1; WGN America.
Fee: $29.95 installation; $25.95 monthly.
Expanded Basic Service 1
Subscribers: N.A.
Programming (via satellite): AMC; Animal Planet; Bravo; Cartoon Network; CMT; CNBC; CNN; C-SPAN 2; Discovery Channel; Discovery Life Channel; Disney Channel; E! HD; Food Network; Fox News Channel; Fox Sports 1; FX; FXM; Golf Channel; History; HLN; Lifetime; MSNBC; National Geographic Channel; NBCSN; Northwest Cable News; Oxygen; Spike TV; Syfy; The Weather Channel; TLC; TNT; Travel Channel; truTV; Turner Classic Movies; TV Land.
Fee: $4.39 monthly.
Digital Basic Service
Subscribers: N.A.
Programming (via satellite): BBC America; Destination America; Discovery Kids Channel; FYI; History International; IFC; Investigation Discovery; MC; OWN: Oprah Winfrey Network; Science Channel; TV Guide Interactive Inc.
Digital Expanded Basic Service
Subscribers: N.A.
Programming (via satellite): CMT; DIY Network; LMN; MTV Classic; MTV Jams; MTV2; Nick Jr.; Nicktoons; TeenNick; Tr3s; VH1 Soul.
Digital Expanded Basic Service 2
Subscribers: N.A.
Programming (via satellite): ESPN Classic; ESPNews; FOX College Sports Central; FOX College Sports Pacific; Fox Sports 2.
Digital Pay Service 1
Pay Units: N.A.
Programming (via satellite): Cinemax (multiplexed); Flix; HBO (multiplexed); Showtime (multiplexed); The Movie Channel (multiplexed).
Fee: $29.95 installation.
Video-On-Demand: No
Pay-Per-View
iN DEMAND; Hot Choice (delivered digitally); Playboy TV (delivered digitally); iN DEMAND (delivered digitally); Fresh (delivered digitally); Shorteez (delivered digitally).
Internet Service
Operational: Yes.
Subscribers: 2,688.
Fee: $29.95-$74.95 monthly.
Telephone Service
Digital: Operational
Subscribers: 1,133.
Fee: $29.95 monthly
Miles of Plant: 428.0 (coaxial); 117.0 (fiber optic). Homes passed: 11,992.
Chief Financial Officer: Wayne Schattenkerk. General Manager: Tim Peters. Marketing Director: Adam Lazara.
Ownership: WaveDivision Holdings LLC (MSO).

SCIO—Scio Cablevision Inc, 38982 Southeast 2nd Ave, PO Box 1100, Scio, OR 97374-1100. Phone: 503-394-3366. Fax: 503-394-3999. E-mail: smt@smt-net.com. Web Site: http://www.smt-net.com. ICA: OR0151.
TV Market Ranking: Below 100 (SCIO). Franchise award date: January 1, 1982. Franchise expiration date: N.A. Began: December 1, 1982.
Channel capacity: N.A. Channels available but not in use: N.A.
Basic Service
Subscribers: 727.
Programming (received off-air): KATU (ABC, MeTV) Portland; KGW (Estrella TV, NBC) Portland; KOIN (CBS) Portland; KOPB-TV (PBS) Portland; KPDX (Escape, MNT) Vancouver; KPTV (COZI TV, FOX, Laff) Portland; KPXG-TV (ION) Salem; KRCW-TV (Antenna TV, CW, This TV) Salem.
Programming (via satellite): A&E; AMC; Animal Planet; Cartoon Network; CMT; CNBC; CNN; Comedy Central; C-SPAN; Discovery Channel; Disney Channel; ESPN; ESPN2; Food Network; Fox News Channel; Freeform; FX; Hallmark Channel; HGTV; History; HLN; Lifetime; MSNBC; MTV; National Geographic Channel; Nickelodeon; Northwest Cable News; Outdoor Channel; RFD-TV; Spike TV; Syfy; TBS; The Weather Channel; TLC; TNT; Travel Channel; Trinity Broadcasting Network (TBN); truTV; TV Land; USA Network; VH1; WE tv; WGN America.
Fee: $53.00 monthly.
Digital Basic Service
Subscribers: N.A.
Programming (via satellite): BBC America; Bloomberg Television; Bravo; Cloo; CMT; Daystar TV Network; Destination America; Discovery Kids Channel; Discovery Life Channel; Disney XD; DMX Music; ESPN Classic; ESPN2; ESPNews; FOX College Sports Central; FOX College Sports Pacific; Fox Sports 1; Fuse; FXM; FYI; Golf Channel; Great American Country; GSN; HGTV; History; History International; IFC; Investigation Discovery; LMN; MTV Classic; MTV2; National Geographic Channel; NBCSN; Nick Jr.; Nicktoons; Outdoor Channel; OWN: Oprah Winfrey Network; Science Channel; Syfy; TeenNick; The Word Net-

2017 Edition   D-645

Oregon—Cable Systems

work; Trinity Broadcasting Network (TBN); Turner Classic Movies; UP; WE tv.
Fee: $17.00 monthly.
Digital Pay Service 1
Pay Units: N.A.
Programming (via satellite): Cinemax (multiplexed); Flix; HBO (multiplexed); Showtime (multiplexed); Starz (multiplexed); Starz Encore (multiplexed); The Movie Channel (multiplexed).
Video-On-Demand: No
Internet Service
Operational: Yes.
Telephone Service
Analog: Operational
Miles of Plant: 60.0 (coaxial); 30.0 (fiber optic). Homes passed: 900.
General Manager: Tom Barth.
Ownership: Scio Cablevision Inc.

SENECA—Blue Mountain TV Cable Co. Now served by MOUNT VERNON, OR [OR0061]. ICA: OR0122.

SHADY COVE—Formerly served by Almega Cable. No longer in operation. ICA: OR0152.

SHERIDAN—Wave Broadband. Now served by SILVERTON, OR [OR0047]. ICA: OR0052.

SILETZ—Formerly served by Millennium Digital Media. Now served by Wave Broadband, DEPOE BAY, OR [OR0134]. ICA: OR0080.

SILVERTON—Wave Broadband, 401 Parkplace Center, Ste 500, Kirkland, WA 98033. Phones: 503-981-1891; 866-928-3123; 503-982-4085. Web Site: http://www.wavebroadband.com. Also serves Aurora, Barlow, Canby, Clackamas, Clackamas County (portions), Donald, Gervais, Grand Ronde, Hubbard, Marion County (portions), Molalla, Mount Angel, Sheridan, Sublimity, Willamina & Woodburn. ICA: OR0047.
TV Market Ranking: 29 (Aurora, Barlow, Canby, Clackamas, Clackamas County (portions) (portions), Donald, Gervais, Hubbard, Molalla, Molalla, Mount Angel, Woodburn); Below 100 (Grand Ronde, SILVERTON, Sublimity, Willamina, Sheridan, Clackamas County (portions) (portions)); Outside TV Markets (Clackamas County (portions) (portions)). Franchise award date: March 3, 1980. Franchise expiration date: N.A. Began: September 1, 1980.
Channel capacity: N.A. Channels available but not in use: N.A.
Basic Service
Subscribers: 13,010.
Programming (received off-air): KATU (ABC, MeTV) Portland; KGW (Estrella TV, NBC) Portland; KNMT (TBN) Portland; KOIN (CBS) Portland; KOPB-TV (PBS) Portland; KPDX (Escape, Laff) Vancouver; KPTV (COZI TV, FOX, Laff) Portland; KPXG-TV (ION) Salem; KRCW-TV (Antenna TV, CW, This TV) Salem.
Programming (via satellite): C-SPAN; C-SPAN 2; EWTN Global Catholic Network; INSP; Jewelry Television; Pop; QVC; Univision Studios.
Fee: $29.95 installation; $25.95 monthly; $1.61 converter.
Expanded Basic Service 1
Subscribers: N.A.
Programming (via satellite): A&E; AMC; Animal Planet; Bravo; Cartoon Network; CNN; Comedy Central; Discovery Life Channel; Disney XD; DIY Network; E! HD; ESPN; ESPN2; Food Network; Fox News Channel; Fox Sports 1; Freeform; FX; Golf Channel; Hallmark Channel; HGTV; History;

HLN; Lifetime; MSNBC; MTV; National Geographic Channel; NBCSN; Nickelodeon; Northwest Cable News; Oxygen; Syfy; TBS; Telemundo; The Weather Channel; TLC; Travel Channel; TV Land; Univision; VH1; WE tv.
Fee: $5.37 monthly.
Expanded Basic Service 2
Subscribers: N.A.
Programming (via satellite): CMT; Discovery Channel; Disney Channel; Spike TV; TNT; USA Network.
Fee: $8.80 monthly.
Digital Basic Service
Subscribers: N.A.
Programming (via satellite): BBC America; Bloomberg Television; Discovery Digital Networks; ESPN Classic; ESPNews; FOX College Sports Central; FOX College Sports Pacific; Fox Deportes; Fox Sports 2; Fuse; FXM; FYI; GSN; History International; IFC; LMN; MC; NFL Network; Nick Jr.; Nicktoons; Outdoor Channel; Sundance TV; TeenNick; truTV; Turner Classic Movies; TV Guide Interactive Inc.
Digital Pay Service 1
Pay Units: N.A.
Programming (via satellite): Cinemax (multiplexed); Flix; HBO (multiplexed); Showtime (multiplexed); Starz (multiplexed); Starz Encore (multiplexed); The Movie Channel (multiplexed).
Fee: $25.00 installation; $11.95 monthly (Cinemax, HBO, Showtime or TMC).
Video-On-Demand: No
Pay-Per-View
iN DEMAND (delivered digitally); Hot Choice (delivered digitally); Playboy TV (delivered digitally); Fresh (delivered digitally); Shorteez (delivered digitally).
Internet Service
Operational: Yes.
Subscribers: 20,391.
Telephone Service
Digital: Operational
Subscribers: 6,850.
Miles of Plant: 1,847.0 (coaxial); 507.0 (fiber optic). Homes passed: 65,445.
Chief Financial Officer: Wayne Schattenkerk. General Manager: Ross Waggoner. Technical Operations Manager: Lynn Tussing.
Ownership: WaveDivision Holdings LLC (MSO).

SOUTH BEACH—Formerly served by Millennium Digital Media. Now served by Wave Broadband, DEPOE BAY, OR [OR0134]. ICA: OR0153.

SOUTH SALEM—Formerly served by Country Cablevision Ltd. No longer in operation. ICA: OR0160.

ST. HELENS—Comcast Cable. Now served by PORTLAND, OR [OR0001]. ICA: OR0027.

ST. PAUL (town)—Formerly served by St. Paul Cooperative Telephone Assoc. No longer in operation. ICA: OR0154.

SUMPTER—Formerly served by Almega Cable. No longer in operation. ICA: OR0112.

SUNRIVER—BendBroadband, 63090 Sherman Rd, Bend, OR 97701-5750. Phone: 541-388-5820. Web Site: http://www.bendbroadband.com. Also serves Curry County (portions) & Spring River. ICA: OR0155.
TV Market Ranking: Below 100 (Spring River, SUNRIVER); Outside TV Markets (Curry County (portions)). Franchise award date:

N.A. Franchise expiration date: N.A. Began: October 1, 1969.
Channel capacity: 59 (operating 2-way). Channels available but not in use: N.A.
Basic Service
Subscribers: 3,669.
Programming (received off-air): KBNZ-LD (CBS) Bend; KEZI (ABC, MeTV) Eugene; KFXO-LD (FOX) Bend; KOAB-TV (PBS) Bend; KOHD (ABC) Bend; KOIN (CBS) Portland; KOPB-TV (PBS) Portland; KPTV (COZI TV, FOX, Laff) Portland; KTVZ (CW, NBC) Bend; 30 DMX.
Programming (via satellite): A&E; Cartoon Network; CMT; CNBC; CNN; C-SPAN; Discovery Channel; Discovery Life Channel; Disney Channel; E! HD; ESPN; ESPN2; EVINE Live; EWTN Global Catholic Network; Food Network; Fox News Channel; Freeform; Golf Channel; HGTV; History; HLN; Lifetime; NBCSN; Nickelodeon; Outdoor Channel; OWN: Oprah Winfrey Network; Pop; Spike TV; Syfy; TBS; The Weather Channel; TLC; TNT; Travel Channel; Trinity Broadcasting Network (TBN); Turner Classic Movies; USA Network; VH1.
Fee: $27.50 monthly; $4.95 converter.
Digital Basic Service
Subscribers: N.A.
Programming (via satellite): BBC America; Bloomberg Television; Chiller; Cloo; CMT; Comedy Central; Cooking Channel; Destination America; Discovery Life Channel; Disney XD; DMX Music; ESPN Classic; ESPNews; ESPNU; Fox Business Network; Fox Sports 1; Fuse; FXM; FYI; Hallmark Channel; Hallmark Movies & Mysteries; History International; IFC; Investigation Discovery; MSNBC; MTV Classic; MTV2; National Geographic Channel; Nick Jr.; Nicktoons; Science Channel; Syfy; TeenNick; Telemundo; Trinity Broadcasting Network (TBN); Turner Classic Movies; WE tv.
Fee: $14.95 monthly.
Digital Expanded Basic Service
Subscribers: N.A.
Programming (via satellite): A&E HD; ESPN HD; ESPN2 HD; Food Network HD; HD Theater; HGTV HD; National Geographic Channel HD; Syfy HD; Universal HD; USA Network HD.
Fee: $10.95 monthly.
Digital Pay Service 1
Pay Units: N.A.
Programming (via satellite): HBO (multiplexed); Showtime (multiplexed); Starz (multiplexed); Starz Encore (multiplexed); Starz HD; The Movie Channel (multiplexed).
Fee: $11.95 monthly (Starz/Encore), $14.95 monthly (Showtime/TMC), $15.25 monthly (HBO).
Video-On-Demand: No
Pay-Per-View
Playboy TV; iN DEMAND (delivered digitally).
Internet Service
Operational: Yes, Dial-up.
Fee: $50.00 installation; $39.95 monthly.
Telephone Service
None
Miles of Plant: 82.0 (coaxial); None (fiber optic).
Chief Executive Officer: Amy Tykeson.
Ownership: Telephone and Data Systems.

THE DALLES—Charter Communications, 12405 Powerscourt Dr, St. Louis, MO 63131. Phones: 636-207-5100 (Corporate office); 360-828-6700; 360-828-6600. Fax: 360-828-6795. Web Site: http://www.charter.com. Also serves Hood River, Hood River County & Wasco County, OR; Bin-

gen, Dallesport, Klickitat, Klickitat County (portions) & White Salmon, WA. ICA: OR0025.
TV Market Ranking: Outside TV Markets (Bingen, Dallesport, Hood River, Hood River County, Klickitat, Klickitat County (portions), THE DALLES, Wasco County, White Salmon). Franchise award date: January 1, 1954. Franchise expiration date: N.A. Began: June 1, 1954.
Channel capacity: N.A. Channels available but not in use: N.A.
Digital Basic Service
Subscribers: 4,007.
Programming (via satellite): BBC America; Discovery Digital Networks; DIY Network; FYI; History International; IFC; LMN; MC; Nick 2; Nick Jr.; TeenNick.
Fee: $26.99 monthly.
Digital Expanded Basic Service
Subscribers: N.A.
Programming (via satellite): A&E; AMC; Bravo; Cartoon Network; CMT; CNBC; CNN; Comedy Central; Discovery Channel; Disney Channel; Disney XD; E! HD; Food Network; Fox Sports 1; FXM; Golf Channel; GSN; Hallmark Channel; History; HLN; Lifetime; MSNBC; National Geographic Channel; NBCSN; Nickelodeon; Northwest Cable News; OWN: Oprah Winfrey Network; Spike TV; Syfy; The Weather Channel; TLC; TNT; Trinity Broadcasting Network (TBN); truTV; Turner Classic Movies; TV Land; Univision; WE tv; WGN America.
Fee: $42.99 monthly.
Digital Pay Service 1
Pay Units: N.A.
Programming (via satellite): Cinemax (multiplexed); Flix; HBO (multiplexed); Showtime (multiplexed); Starz (multiplexed); Starz Encore (multiplexed); The Movie Channel (multiplexed).
Fee: $10.00 installation; $10.95 monthly (Cinemax, Showtime/Flix, Starz/Encore or TMC), $11.95 monthly (HBO).
Video-On-Demand: Yes
Pay-Per-View
iN DEMAND; Fresh; Hot Choice (delivered digitally); iN DEMAND (delivered digitally); Playboy TV (delivered digitally); Fresh (delivered digitally); Shorteez (delivered digitally).
Internet Service
Operational: Yes.
Broadband Service: Charter Internet.
Fee: $29.99 monthly.
Telephone Service
Digital: Operational
Miles of Plant: 253.0 (coaxial); 80.0 (fiber optic). Homes passed: 16,812.
Vice President: Frank Antonovich. General Manager: Linda Kimberly. Technical Operations Director: Brian Lindholme. Marketing Director: Diane Long. Accounting Director: David Sovanski.
Ownership: Charter Communications Inc. (MSO).

TURNER—Wave Broadband, 401 Parkplace Center, Ste 500, Kirkland, WA 98033. Phones: 866-928-3123; 503-981-1891 (Woodburn administrative office); 888-222-5314. Web Site: http://www.wavebroadband.com. Also serves Aumsville, Gates, Lyons, Mehama, Mill City & Stayton. ICA: OR0065.
TV Market Ranking: Below 100 (Aumsville, Gates, Lyons, Mehama, Mill City, TURNER, Stayton). Franchise award date: October 1, 1981. Franchise expiration date: N.A. Began: February 2, 1982.
Channel capacity: N.A. Channels available but not in use: N.A.

Cable Systems—Oregon

Basic Service
Subscribers: N.A.
Programming (received off-air): KATU (ABC, MeTV) Portland; KGW (Estrella TV, NBC) Portland; KNMT (TBN) Portland; KOAC-TV (PBS) Corvallis; KOIN (CBS) Portland; KOPB-TV (PBS) Portland; KPDX (Escape, MNT) Vancouver; KPTV (COZI TV, FOX, Laff) Portland; KPXG-TV (ION) Salem; KRCW-TV (Antenna TV, CW, This TV) Salem.
Programming (via satellite): EVINE Live; Northwest Cable News; Pop; QVC; Univision Studios; WGN America.
Fee: $60.00 installation; $3.75 converter.

Expanded Basic Service 1
Subscribers: N.A.
Programming (via satellite): A&E; AMC; Animal Planet; Bravo; Cartoon Network; CMT; CNBC; CNN; Comedy Central; Cooking Channel; C-SPAN; Discovery Channel; Disney Channel; DIY Network; ESPN; ESPN Classic; ESPN2; EWTN Global Catholic Network; Food Network; Fox News Channel; Fox Sports 1; Freeform; FX; Great American Country; Hallmark Channel; HGTV; History; HLN; INSP; Jewelry Television; Lifetime; MSNBC; MTV; National Geographic Channel; NBCSN; Nickelodeon; Outdoor Channel; OWN; Oprah Winfrey Network; Spike TV; Syfy; TBS; The Weather Channel; TLC; TNT; Travel Channel; truTV; TV Land; USA Network; VH1.
Fee: $51.95 monthly.

Digital Basic Service
Subscribers: N.A.
Programming (via satellite): BBC America; Bravo; Cloo; CMT; Destination America; Discovery Kids Channel; Disney XD; DMX Music; ESPN2; ESPNews; Fuse; FYI; Golf Channel; GSN; History International; IFC; Investigation Discovery; MTV Classic; MTV2; Nick Jr.; Science Channel; TeenNick; Turner Classic Movies; WE tv.
Fee: $33.95 monthly.

Digital Pay Service 1
Pay Units: N.A.
Programming (via satellite): Cinemax (multiplexed); Flix; HBO (multiplexed); Showtime (multiplexed); Starz (multiplexed); Starz Encore (multiplexed); The Movie Channel (multiplexed).
Fee: $16.00 monthly (HBO, Cinemax, Showtime/TMC/Flix, or Starz/Encore).
Video-On-Demand: No
Pay-Per-View
iN DEMAND (delivered digitally); Playboy TV (delivered digitally).
Internet Service
Operational: Yes. Began: October 1, 2002.
Subscribers: 20,391.
Broadband Service: Cable Rocket.
Fee: $24.95-$74.95 monthly; $6.00 modem lease.
Telephone Service
Digital: Operational
Subscribers: 6,850.
Miles of Plant: 180.0 (coaxial); 6.0 (fiber optic). Homes passed: 7,643.
Chief Financial Officer: Wayne Schattenkerk. General Manager: Ross Waggoner. Technical Operations Manager: Lynn Tussing. Marketing Manager: Elizabeth Regan.
Ownership: WaveDivision Holdings LLC (MSO).

TYGH VALLEY—Formerly served by J & N Cable. No longer in operation. ICA: OR0117.

UMATILLA—Formerly served by Rapid Cable. No longer in operation. ICA: OR0053.

VERNONIA—Vernonia CATV Inc., 536 1st Ave, Vernonia, OR 97064-1115. Phone: 503-429-5103. ICA: OR0083.
TV Market Ranking: 29 (VERNONIA). Franchise award date: N.A. Franchise expiration date: N.A. Began: March 1, 1969.
Channel capacity: N.A. Channels available but not in use: N.A.
Basic Service
Subscribers: 100.
Programming (received off-air): KATU (ABC, MeTV) Portland; KGW (Estrella TV, NBC) Portland; KOIN (CBS) Portland; KOPB-TV (PBS) Portland; KPDX (Escape, MNT) Vancouver; KPTV (COZI TV, FOX, Laff) Portland.
Programming (via satellite): A&E; Animal Planet; Cartoon Network; CMT; CNBC; CNN; C-SPAN; Discovery Channel; Food Network; Fox Sports 1; Great American Country; HGTV; History; ION Television; Lifetime; MSNBC; MTV; National Geographic Channel; NBCSN; Nickelodeon; Spike TV; Syfy; TBS; The Weather Channel; TLC; TNT; Turner Classic Movies; TV Land; USA Network; VH1; WGN America.
Fee: $40.00 installation; $36.00 monthly.
Pay Service 1
Pay Units: N.A.
Programming (via satellite): Cinemax; HBO.
Fee: $9.45 - $12.55 monthly (each).
Internet Service
Operational: No.
Telephone Service
None
Miles of Plant: 7.0 (coaxial); None (fiber optic).
Owner: Mike Seager.
Ownership: Vernonia CATV Inc.

WALDPORT—Alsea River Cable Co, PO Box 1238, Waldport, OR 97394. Phone: 541-563-4807. Fax: 541-563-7341. Also serves Lincoln County (portions), Little Albany, Tidewater & Westwood Village. ICA: OR0069.
TV Market Ranking: Outside TV Markets (Lincoln County (portions), Little Albany, Tidewater, WALDPORT, Westwood Village). Franchise award date: January 1, 1996. Franchise expiration date: N.A. Began: January 1, 1969.
Channel capacity: N.A. Channels available but not in use: N.A.
Basic Service
Subscribers: 516. Commercial subscribers: 2.
Programming (received off-air): KATU (ABC, MeTV) Portland; KEZI (ABC, MeTV) Eugene; KGW (Estrella TV, NBC) Portland; KOAC-TV (PBS) Corvallis; KOIN (CBS) Portland; KPDX (Escape, MNT) Vancouver; KPTV (COZI TV, FOX, Laff) Portland; KVAL-TV (CBS, This TV) Eugene.
Programming (via satellite): A&E; CNBC; CNN; C-SPAN 2; Discovery Channel; Disney Channel; ESPN; Freeform; Lifetime; MTV; Nickelodeon; QVC; Spike TV; TBS; TLC; TNT; Turner Classic Movies; USA Network; WGN America.
Fee: $25.00 installation; $34.00 monthly.
Pay Service 1
Pay Units: N.A.
Programming (via satellite): Cinemax; HBO.
Fee: $9.50 monthly (each).
Video-On-Demand: No
Internet Service
Operational: No.
Telephone Service
None
Miles of Plant: 15.0 (coaxial); None (fiber optic). Homes passed: 1,010.
General Manager & Chief Technician: James Dale Haslett.
Ownership: James Dale Haslett.

WARM SPRINGS—Formerly served by American Telecasting of America Inc. No longer in operation. ICA: OR0085.

WASCO—Formerly served by J & N Cable. No longer in operation. ICA: OR0159.

WESTON—Formerly served by Rapid Cable. No longer in operation. ICA: OR0075.

WESTPORT—Formerly served by Almega Cable. No longer in operation. ICA: OR0170.

WOODBURN—Wave Broadband. Now served by SILVERTON, OR [OR0047]. ICA: OR0023.

PENNSYLVANIA

Total Systems: 107	Communities with Applications: 0
Total Communities Served: 2,593	Number of Basic Subscribers: 2,364,881
Franchises Not Yet Operating: 0	Number of Expanded Basic Subscribers: 85,716
Applications Pending: 0	Number of Pay Units: 42,583

Top 100 Markets Represented: Pittsburgh (10); Baltimore, MD (14); Wilkes Barre-Scranton (49); Philadelphia, PA-Burlington, NJ (4); Harrisburg-Lancaster-York (57); Johnstown-Altoona (74); Youngstown, OH (79); Wheeling, WV-Steubenville, OH (90).

For a list of cable communities in this section, see the Cable Community Index located in the back of Cable Volume 2.
For explanation of terms used in cable system listings, see p. D-11.

ADAMS TWP. (Cambria County)—Comcast Cable. Now served by BLAIRSVILLE, PA [PA0320]. ICA: PA0133.

ADDISON TWP. (southern portion)—Somerfield Cable TV Co, 6511 National Pike, Addison, PA 15411-2153. Phones: 800-344-3084; 814-395-3084. Fax: 814-395-5037. E-mail: sc-tv@sctv.net. Web Site: http://www.somerfield.biz. Also serves Accident (unincorporated areas), Friendsville (unincorporated areas), Garrett County (portions) & Grantsville (unincorporated areas), MD; Addison, PA. ICA: PA0307.

TV Market Ranking: Outside TV Markets (Accident (unincorporated areas), Addison, Garrett County (portions), ADDISON TWP. (SOUTHERN PORTION)). Franchise award date: N.A. Franchise expiration date: N.A. Began: April 1, 1989.

Channel capacity: N.A. Channels available but not in use: N.A.

Basic Service
Subscribers: N.A.
Programming (received off-air): KDKA-TV (CBS, Decades) Pittsburgh; WGPT (PBS) Oakland; WJAC-TV (MeTV, NBC) Johnstown; WPCW (CW) Jeannette; WPNT (MNT) Pittsburgh; WPXI (MeTV, NBC) Pittsburgh; WQED (PBS) Pittsburgh; WTAE-TV (ABC, This TV) Pittsburgh; WWCP-TV (FOX) Johnstown.
Programming (via satellite): Cornerstone Television; Hallmark Channel; ION Television; Local Cable Weather; Outdoor Channel; Pop; QVC; TBS; The Weather Channel; Trinity Broadcasting Network (TBN); WGN America.
Fee: $25.00 installation; $3.00 converter.

Digital Basic Service
Subscribers: N.A.
Programming (via satellite): 3ABN; A&E; A&E HD; AMC; Animal Planet; Animal Planet HD; AWE; AXS TV; BBC America; BET; BET Gospel; Boomerang; Bravo; Bravo HD; BTN; Cartoon Network; Church Channel; Cloo; CMT; CNBC; CNN; Comedy Central; Cooking Channel; C-SPAN; C-SPAN 2; C-SPAN 3; Daystar TV Network; Destination America; Discovery Channel; Discovery Channel HD; Discovery Kids Channel; Discovery Life Channel; Disney Channel; Disney Channel HD; Disney XD; DIY Network; DMX Music; E! HD; ESPN; ESPN Classic; ESPN HD; ESPN2; ESPN2 HD; ESPNews; ESPNU; EWTN Global Catholic Network; Family Friendly Entertainment; FamilyNet; Food Network; Food Network HD; Fox Business Network; Fox Business Network HD; FOX College Sports Central; FOX College Sports Pacific; Fox News Channel; Fox Sports 1; Freeform; Freeform HD; FX; FX HD; FXM; FYI; GEB America; Golf Channel; Great American Country; GSN; Hallmark Movies & Mysteries; HGTV; HGTV HD; History; History HD; History International; HLN; IFC; iN DEMAND; INSP; Investigation Discovery; JUCE TV; Lifetime; Lifetime Movie Network HD; LMN; MSNBC; MTV; MTV Classic; MTV Hits; MTV Jams; MTV2; National Geographic Channel; NBCSN; NFL Network; Nick 2; Nick Jr.; Nickelodeon; Nicktoons; Outdoor Channel 2 HD; OWN: Oprah Winfrey Network; RFD HD; RFD-TV; Root Sports Pittsburgh; Science Channel; Science HD; Smile of a Child TV; Spike TV; Syfy; Syfy HD; TeenNick; TLC; TNT; TNT HD; Toon Disney HD; Travel Channel; truTV; Turner Classic Movies; TV Land; Universal HD; Univision; Univision Studios; USA Network; USA Network HD; VH1; Vme TV; WE tv.
Fee: $55.00 monthly.

Digital Pay Service 1
Pay Units: N.A.
Programming (via satellite): Cinemax (multiplexed); Flix; HBO (multiplexed); Showtime (multiplexed); Starz (multiplexed); Starz Encore (multiplexed); The Movie Channel (multiplexed).
Fee: $7.25 monthly (Encore), $8.00 monthly (Cinemax, Showtime, Starz or TMC/Flix), $12.00 monthly (HBO).

Video-On-Demand: No

Pay-Per-View
iN DEMAND (delivered digitally); ESPN (delivered digitally); Adult (delivered digitally).

Internet Service
Operational: No.

Telephone Service
None

Miles of Plant: 85.0 (coaxial); 30.0 (fiber optic). Homes passed: 900.
General Manager & Chief Technician: Michael J. Diehl.
Ownership: Somerfield Cable TV Co.

ALDAN—Comcast Cable. Now served by PHILADELPHIA, PA [PA0005]. ICA: PA0002.

ALLENSVILLE—Formerly served by Valley Cable Systems. No longer in operation. ICA: PA0285.

ALLENTOWN—RCN. Formerly served by NORTHAMPTON BOROUGH, PA [PA0008]. This cable system has converted to IPTV, 196 Van Buren St, Ste 300, Herndon, VA 20170. Phones: 800-746-4726; 609-681-2281. Web Site: http://www.rcn.com. Also serves Alburtis, Allen Twp., Bangor Borough, Bath, Belfast, Bethlehem, Bethlehem Twp., Breinigsville, Catasauqua, Cementon, Center City, Center Valley, Cetronia, Cherryville, College Hill, Collingdale, Colwyn, Coopersburg, Coplay, Danielsville, Dorneyville, East Allen Twp., East Bangor, East Texas, Easton, Egypt, Emmaus, Foglesville, Forks Twp., Fountain Hill Borough, Freemansburg Borough, Germansville, Glendon, Greenawalds, Hanover Twp. (Lehigh County), Hanover Twp. (Northampton County), Hellertown, Hokendauqua, Jacobsburg, Jordan Creek, Klecknersville, Kuhnsville, Laurys Station, Lehigh Twp., Lehigh Valley, Lower Macungie Twp., Lower Nazareth Twp., Lower Saucon Twp., Lowhill Twp., Macungie, Mountainville, Nazareth, New Tripoli, North Catasauqua Borough, North Whitehall Twp., Northampton, Orefield, Palmer Twp., Pen Argyl, Philadelphia (suburbs), Plainfield Twp., Rieglesville, Roseto, Salisbury Twp., Saucon Valley, Schnecksville, Slatington, South Mountain, South Whitehall Twp., Stockertown, Tatamy, Treichlers, Trexlertown, Upper Macungie Twp., Upper Nazareth Twp., Upper Saucon Twp., Walnutport, Washington Twp., Wescosville, West Easton Borough, Westbrook Park, Whitehall, Williams Twp., Wilson, Wind Gap & Yeadon. ICA: PA5201.

TV Market Ranking: Below 100 (ALLENTOWN, ALLENTOWN, PEN ARGYL, Allen Twp., Bangor Borough, Bath, Bethlehem, Bethlehem Twp., Catasauqua, Coplay, East Allen Twp., Easton, Forks Twp., Fountain Hill Borough, Freemansburg Borough, Hanover Twp. (Lehigh County), Hanover Twp. (Northampton County), Hellertown, Lehigh Twp., Lower Macungie Twp., Lower Nazareth Twp., Lower Saucon Twp., Lowhill Twp., Nazareth, North Catasauqua Borough, North Whitehall Twp., Northampton, Palmer Twp., Plainfield Twp., Roseto, Salisbury Twp., South Whitehall Twp., Stockertown, Tatamy, Upper Macungie Twp., Upper Saucon Twp., Washington Twp., West Easton Borough, Whitehall, Wilson, Wind Gap).

Channel capacity: N.A. Channels available but not in use: N.A.

Limited Basic
Subscribers: 80,319. Commercial subscribers: 2,523.
Fee: $30.74 monthly. Includes 46 channels - 39 in SD & 17 in HD. Additional $9.95 HD equipment fee for HD channels.

Signature Digital Cable
Subscribers: N.A.
Fee: $59.99 monthly. Includes 298 channels - 227 in SD & 71 in HD. Additional $9.95 HD equipment fee for HD channels.

HD Expanded Pack
Subscribers: N.A.
Fee: $8.99 monthly. Includes 6 additional HD channels. Additional $9.95 HD equipment fee for HD channels.

Premiere Movies & Entertainment
Subscribers: N.A.
Fee: $10.99 monthly. Includes 31 channels - 27 in SD & 4 in HD. Additional $9.95 HD equipment fee for HD channels.

Premiere Family & Children
Subscribers: N.A.
Fee: $5.99 monthly. Includes 19 channels - 17 in SD & 2 in HD. Additional $9.95 HD equipment fee for HD channels.

Premiere News & Information
Subscribers: N.A.
Fee: $5.99 monthly. Includes 21 channels - 16 in SD & 5 in HD. Additional $9.95 HD equipment fee for HD channels.

Premiere Sports
Subscribers: N.A.
Fee: $9.99 monthly. Includes 36 channels - 28 in SD & 8 in HD. Additional $9.95 HD equipment fee for HD channels.

Premiere Total Pack
Subscribers: N.A.
Fee: $16.95 monthly. Includes 109 channels - 88 in SD & 21 in HD. Additional $9.95 HD equipment fee for HD channels.

MiVision Lite
Subscribers: N.A.
Fee: $12.00 monthly. Includes 40 channels in Spanish.

MiVision Plus
Subscribers: N.A.
Fee: $22.95 monthly. 44 channels in Spanish.

Cinemax
Subscribers: N.A.
Fee: $9.99 monthly. Includes 16 channels - 8 in SD & 8 in HD plus Cinemax on Demand & MAXGo. Additional $9.95 HD equipment fee for HD channels.

HBO
Subscribers: N.A.
Fee: $15.95 monthly. Includes 14 channels - 7 in SD & 7 in HD plus HBO on Demand & HBO Go. Additional $9.95 HD equipment fee for HD channels.

Cinemax/HBO
Subscribers: N.A.
Fee: $19.95 monthly. Includes 16 channels of Cinemax - 8 in SD & 8 in HD & 14 channels of HBO - 7 in SD & 7 in HD plus Cinemax on Demand, HBO on Demand, MAXGo & HB Go. Additional $9.95 HD equipment fee for HD channels.

Showtime/TMC
Subscribers: N.A.
Fee: $4.95 monthly. Includes 20 channels - 9 in SD & 11 in HD plus Showtime on Demand & The Movie Channel on Demand. Additional $9.95 HD equipment fee for HD channels.

Starz
Subscribers: N.A.
Fee: $5.00 monthly. Includes 13 channels - 9 in SD & 4 in HD plus Starz on Demand. Additional $9.95 HD equipment fee for HD channels.

Video-On-Demand: Yes

Cable Systems—Pennsylvania

Internet Service
Operational: Yes.
Fee: $39.99-$74.99 monthly.
Telephone Service
Digital: Operational
Fee: $29.99 monthly
Vice President & General Manager: Jamie Hill.
Ownership: RCN Corp.

ALLENTOWN—Service Electric Cable TV & Communications, 2260 Ave A, Bethlehem, PA 18017-2170. Phones: 610-841-4100 (Customer service for phone services); 610-865-9100; 800-232-9100. Fax: 610-865-5031. E-mail: office@secv.com. Web Site: http://www.sectv.com. Also serves Alburtis, Allen Twp., Bangor Boro, Bath Boro, Bethlehem, Bethlehem Twp., Bridgeton Twp., Bushkill Twp., Catasauqua Boro, Chapman Boro, Coopersburg Boro, Coplay Boro, Durham Twp., East Allen Twp., East Bangor Boro, Easton, Emmaus, Forks Twp., Fountain Hill Boro, Freemansburg Boro, Glendon, Greenwich Twp., Hanover Twp., Haycock Twp., Hellertown Boro, Hereford Twp. (Berks County), Lehigh Valley, Longswamp Twp. (portions), Lower Macungie Twp., Lower Milford Twp., Lower Mount Bethel Twp., Lower Nazareth Twp., Lower Saucon Twp., Lowhill Twp., Lynn Twp., Macungie, Milford Twp., Moore Twp., Nazareth Boro, Nockamixon Twp., North Catasauqua Boro, North Whitehall Twp., Northampton County (portions), Palmer Twp., Pen Argyl Boro, Plainfield Twp., Portland Boro, Richland Twp., Riegelsville Boro, Roseto Boro, Salisbury Twp., South Whitehall Twp., Springfield Twp., Stockertown, Tatamy Boro, Tinicum Twp., Upper Macungie Twp., Upper Milford Twp., Upper Mount Bethel Twp., Upper Nazareth Twp., Upper Saucon Twp., Washington Twp., Weisenberg Twp., West Easton, Whitehall Twp., Williams Twp., Wilson & Wind Gap Boro. ICA: PA0006.

TV Market Ranking: 4 (Haycock Twp., Upper Mount Bethel Twp.); Below 100 (Alburtis, Allen Twp., ALLENTOWN, Bangor Boro, Bath Boro, Bethlehem, Bridgeton Twp., Bushkill Twp., Catasauqua Boro, Chapman Boro, Coopersburg Boro, Coplay Boro, East Allen Twp., East Bangor Boro, Easton, Emmaus, Forks Twp., Fountain Hill Boro, Freemansburg Boro, Glendon, Greenwich Twp., Hanover Twp., Hellertown Boro, Hereford Twp. (Berks County), Longswamp Twp. (portions), Lower Macungie Twp., Lower Milford Twp., Lower Mount Bethel Twp., Lower Nazareth Twp., Lower Saucon Twp., Lowhill Twp., Lynn Twp., Macungie, Milford Twp., Moore Twp., Nazareth Boro, Nockamixon Twp., North Catasauqua Boro, North Whitehall Twp., Northampton County (portions), Palmer Twp., Palmer Twp., Pen Argyl Boro, Plainfield Twp., Portland Boro, Richland Twp., Roseto Boro, South Whitehall Twp., Springfield Twp., Stockertown, Tatamy Boro, Upper Macungie Twp., Upper Milford Twp., Upper Nazareth Twp., Upper Saucon Twp., Washington Twp., Weisenberg Twp., West Easton, Whitehall Twp., Williams Twp., Wilson, Wind Gap Boro, Lehigh Valley); Outside TV Markets (Durham Twp., Riegelsville Boro). Franchise award date: January 1, 1955. Franchise expiration date: N.A. Began: January 1, 1951.
Channel capacity: 80 (not 2-way capable). Channels available but not in use: N.A.

Basic Service
Subscribers: 81,438.
Programming (received off-air): KYW-TV (CBS, Decades) Philadelphia; WBPH-TV (IND) Bethlehem; WCAU (COZI TV, NBC) Philadelphia; WFMZ-TV (Retro TV) Allentown; WGTW-TV (TBN) Burlington; WLVT-TV (PBS) Allentown; WNBC (COZI TV, NBC) New York; WNEP-TV (ABC, Antenna TV) Scranton; WNYW (FOX, Movies!) New York; WPHL-TV (Antenna TV, MNT, This TV) Philadelphia; WPIX (Antenna TV, CW, This TV) New York; WPPX-TV (ION) Wilmington; WPSG (CW) Philadelphia; WPVI-TV (ABC, Live Well Network) Philadelphia; WTVE (IND) Reading; WTXF-TV (Buzzr, FOX, Movies!) Philadelphia; WWOR-TV (Buzzr, Heroes & Icons, MNT) Secaucus; allband FM.
Programming (via satellite): C-SPAN; EVINE Live; EWTN Global Catholic Network; INSP; Pennsylvania Cable Network; Pop; QVC.
Fee: $49.95 installation; $19.99 monthly; $4.95 converter.

Expanded Basic Service 1
Subscribers: 8,235.
Programming (via satellite): A&E; AMC; Animal Planet; BBC America; BET; Cartoon Network; CMT; CNBC; CNN; Comcast SportsNet Philadelphia; Comedy Central; C-SPAN 2; Discovery Channel; Disney Channel; Disney XD; E! HD; ESPN; ESPN Classic; ESPN2; ESPNews; Food Network; Fox News Channel; Fox Sports 1; Freeform; FX; Golf Channel; GSN; Hallmark Channel; HGTV; History; HLN; Lifetime; Local Cable Weather; MSNBC; MTV; NBCSN; Nickelodeon; Outdoor Channel; Oxygen; Portuguese Channel; Spike TV; Syfy; TBS; The Weather Channel; TLC; TNT; Travel Channel; truTV; Turner Classic Movies; TV Land; USA Network; VH1; WE tv.
Fee: $46.24 monthly; $4.95 converter.

Digital Basic Service
Subscribers: N.A.
Fee: $8.99 monthly.

Digital Pay Service 1
Pay Units: 11,268.
Programming (via satellite): Cinemax (multiplexed); Flix; HBO (multiplexed) Playboy TV; RAI Italia; Showtime (multiplexed); Starz (multiplexed); Starz Encore (multiplexed); The Movie Channel (multiplexed); Zee TV.
Fee: $10.95 monthly (Cinemax or Starz), $11.05 monthly (Filipino or Playboy), $12.95 monthly (HBO or Showtime/TMC) & $14.99 monthly (Zee TV).

Video-On-Demand: Yes

Pay-Per-View
Sports PPV (delivered digitally); Movies, Special Events (delivered digitally).

Internet Service
Operational: Yes. Began: January 1, 1995.
Subscribers: 57,997.
Broadband Service: ProLog Express.
Fee: $39.95 installation; $24.95-$49.95 monthly.

Telephone Service
Analog: Not Operational
Digital: Operational
Subscribers: 34,045.
Fee: $29.95 monthly
Miles of Plant: 6,003.0 (coaxial); 1,454.0 (fiber optic). Homes passed: 241,249.
General Manager: John J. Capparell. Marketing Director: Steve Salash. Program Director: Andy Himmelwright. Chief Technician: Jeffrey Kelly. Regulatory Affairs Director: Arlean Lilly. Customer Service Manager: John Ritter.
Ownership: Service Electric Cable TV Inc. (MSO).

ALTOONA—Atlantic Broadband, 120 Southmont Blvd, Johnstown, PA 15905. Phones: 888-536-9600 (Customer service); 814-535-3506. Fax: 814-535-7749. E-mail: info@atlanticbb.com. Web Site: http://atlanticbb.com. Also serves Allegheny Twp. (Blair County), Antis Twp., Bellwood, Birmingham Borough, Blair Twp. (Blair County), Bloomfield Twp., Canoe Creek, Cass Twp. (Huntingdon County), Cassville, Catherine Twp., Clay Twp. (Huntingdon County), Claysburg, Duncansville, Frankstown, Frankstown Twp., Frankstown Twp. (Blair County), Freedom Twp. (Blair County), Gallitzin, Greenfield Twp. (Blair County), Hollidaysburg, Huston, Huston Twp. (Blair County), Juniata Twp. (Blair County), Kimmell Twp., Logan Twp. (Blair County), Mapleton, Martinsburg, Newry, North Woodbury Twp., Pavia Twp., Roaring Spring, Saltillo, Snyder, Spruce Creek Twp., Taylor Twp. (Blair County), Three Springs, Todd Twp. (Huntingdon County), Tyrone, Tyrone Twp. (Blair County), Warriors Mark, Woodbury, Woodbury Twp. (Bedford County) & Woodbury Twp. (Blair County). ICA: PA0018.

TV Market Ranking: 74 (Allegheny Twp. (Blair County), ALTOONA, Antis Twp., Bellwood, Birmingham Borough, Blair Twp. (Blair County), Bloomfield Twp., Canoe Creek, Cass Twp. (Huntingdon County), Cassville, Catherine Twp., Clay Twp. (Huntingdon County), Claysburg, Duncansville, Frankstown, Frankstown Twp., Frankstown Twp. (Blair County), Freedom Twp. (Blair County), Gallitzin, Greenfield Twp. (Blair County), Hollidaysburg, Huston, Huston Twp. (Blair County), Juniata Twp. (Blair County), Kimmell Twp., Logan Twp. (Blair County), Mapleton, Martinsburg, Newry, North Woodbury Twp., Pavia Twp., Roaring Spring, Saltillo, Snyder, Spruce Creek Twp., Taylor Twp. (Blair County), Three Springs, Todd Twp. (Huntingdon County), Todd Twp. (Huntingdon County), Tyrone, Tyrone Twp. (Blair County), Warriors Mark, Woodbury Twp. (Bedford County), Woodbury Twp. (Blair County)). Franchise award date: April 1, 1962. Franchise expiration date: N.A. Began: April 21, 1962.
Channel capacity: 77 (operating 2-way). Channels available but not in use: N.A.

Basic Service
Subscribers: 25,127.
Programming (received off-air): KDKA-TV (CBS, Decades) Pittsburgh; WATM-TV (ABC, This TV) Altoona; WHVL-LP (MNT) State College, etc.; WJAC-TV (MeTV, NBC) Johnstown; WKBS-TV (IND) Altoona; WPCW (CW) Jeannette; WPSU-TV (PBS) Clearfield; WTAE-TV (ABC, This TV) Pittsburgh; WTAJ-TV (CBS) Altoona; WWCP-TV (FOX) Johnstown; allband FM.
Programming (via satellite): C-SPAN; C-SPAN 2; EVINE Live; EWTN Global Catholic Network; HRTV; ION Television; Jewelry Television; MyNetworkTV; Pennsylvania Cable Network; Pop; QVC; World.
Fee: $40.00 installation; $32.83 monthly; $.67 converter.

Expanded Basic Service 1
Subscribers: N.A.
Programming (via satellite): A&E; AMC; Animal Planet; BET; Bravo; Cartoon Network; CMT; CNBC; CNN; Comedy Central; Discovery Channel; Disney Channel; Disney XD; E! HD; ESPN; ESPN Classic; ESPN2; Food Network; Fox News Channel; Fox Sports 1; Freeform; FX; Golf Channel; GSN; Hallmark Channel; HGTV; History; HLN; INSP; Lifetime; MSNBC; MTV; National Geographic Channel; NBCSN; Nickelodeon; Nicktoons; Outdoor Channel; Oxygen; Root Sports Pittsburgh; Spike TV; Syfy; TBS; The Weather Channel; TLC; TNT; Travel Channel; truTV; Turner Classic Movies; TV Land; USA Network; VH1.
Fee: $39.04 monthly.

Digital Basic Service
Subscribers: N.A.
Programming (via satellite): A&E HD; Animal Planet HD; BBC America; Bloomberg Television; Boomerang; Chiller; CMT; Destination America; Discovery Channel HD; Discovery Kids Channel; Disney Channel HD; DIY Network; DMX Music; ESPN HD; ESPN2 HD; ESPNews; ESPNU; Fox News HD; Fox Sports 2; Fuse; FYI; Great American Country; HD Theater; History HD; History International; IFC; Investigation Discovery; LMN; MTV Classic; MTV Hits; MTV Jams; MTV2; NFL Network; Nick 2; Nick Jr.; Outdoor Channel 2 HD; OWN: Oprah Winfrey Network; Root Sports Pittsburgh; RTV; Science Channel; Science HD; Starz; Starz Encore; Starz HD; Syfy HD; TBS HD; TeenNick; TLC HD; TNT HD; Tr3s; TVG Network; USA Network HD; VH1 Soul; WE tv.
Fee: $18.95 monthly.

Digital Pay Service 1
Pay Units: N.A.
Programming (via satellite): Cinemax (multiplexed); Cinemax HD; Flix; HBO (multiplexed); HBO HD; Showtime (multiplexed); Showtime HD; The Movie Channel (multiplexed).
Fee: $15.95 monthly (Cinemax/Cinemax HD, HBO/HBO HD or Showtime/Showtime HD/TMC/Flix).

Video-On-Demand: Yes

Pay-Per-View
Hot Choice (delivered digitally); iN DEMAND (delivered digitally).

Internet Service
Operational: Yes.
Subscribers: 30,689.
Broadband Service: Atlantic Broadband High-Speed Internet.
Fee: $24.95-$57.95 monthly.

Telephone Service
Digital: Operational
Subscribers: 15,912.
Fee: $44.95 monthly
Miles of Plant: 1,758.0 (coaxial); 562.0 (fiber optic). Homes passed: 46,320.
Senior Vice President & General Counsel: Bartlett Leber. Vice President: David Dane. General Manager: Mike Papasergi. Technical Operations Director: Charles Sorchilla. Marketing & Customer Service Director: Dara Leslie. Marketing Director: Natalie Kurchak.
Ownership: Atlantic Broadband (MSO).

ARMAGH—Comcast Cable. Now served by BLAIRSVILLE, PA [PA0320]. ICA: PA0153.

ARNOT—Blue Ridge Communications. Now served by MANSFIELD, PA [PA0421]. ICA: PA0308.

AUBURN—Comcast Cable. Now served by HARRISBURG, PA [PA0009]. ICA: PA0448.

AULTMAN—Formerly served by Adelphia Communications. No longer in operation. ICA: PA0309.

AVELLA—Blue Devil Cable TV Inc. Now served by BURGETTSTOWN, PA [PA0323]. ICA: PA0310.

BASTRESS TWP.—Formerly served by Bastress TV Cable Association. No longer in operation. ICA: PA0313.

2017 Edition
D-649

Pennsylvania—Cable Systems

BEACH LAKE—Blue Ridge Communications, 613 3rd St, PO Box 215, Palmerton, PA 18071-0215. Phone: 610-826-2551. Web Site: http://www.brctv.com. ICA: PA0314.
TV Market Ranking: 49 (BEACH LAKE). Franchise award date: N.A. Franchise expiration date: N.A. Began: January 1, 1971.
Channel capacity: 42 (operating 2-way). Channels available but not in use: N.A.

Basic Service
Subscribers: N.A.
Programming (received off-air): WABC-TV (ABC, Live Well Network) New York; WCBS-TV (CBS, Decades) New York; WNBC (COZI TV, NBC) New York; WNEP-TV (ABC, Antenna TV) Scranton; WNET (PBS) Newark; WNYW (FOX, Movies!) New York; WOLF-TV (CW, FOX, MNT) Hazleton; WPIX (Antenna TV, CW, This TV) New York; WPVI-TV (ABC, Live Well Network) Philadelphia; WQPX-TV (ION) Scranton; WSKG-TV (PBS) Binghamton; WSWB (CW, MeTV) Scranton; WVIA-TV (PBS) Scranton; WWOR-TV (Bounce TV, Buzzr, Heroes & Icons, MNT) Secaucus; WYOU (CBS) Scranton.
Programming (via satellite): HLN; WGN America.
Fee: $22.50 installation; $14.68 monthly.

Expanded Basic Service 1
Subscribers: N.A.
Programming (via satellite): A&E; AMC; Animal Planet; CMT; CNBC; CNN; Comedy Central; C-SPAN; Discovery Channel; Disney Channel; E! HD; ESPN; ESPN2; EWTN Global Catholic Network; Food Network; Fox News Channel; Fox Sports 1; Freeform; FX; Golf Channel; HGTV; History; HSN2; Lifetime; LMN; MSG; MSNBC; MTV; NBCSN; Nickelodeon; OWN: Oprah Winfrey Network; Pennsylvania Cable Network; Pop; QVC; Spike TV; Syfy; TBS; The Weather Channel; TLC; TNT; Travel Channel; Trinity Broadcasting Network (TBN); truTV; Turner Classic Movies; TV Land; USA Network; VH1; WE tv; YES Network.
Fee: $25.66 monthly.

Digital Basic Service
Subscribers: N.A.
Programming (via satellite): Concert TV; Discovery Digital Networks; Disney XD; FSN Digital Atlantic; FSN Digital Central; FSN Digital Pacific; FXM; HRTV; MC; National Geographic Channel; NBA TV; Nick 2; Nick Jr.; Nicktoons; Outdoor Channel; TeenNick.
Fee: $35.00 installation; $9.95 monthly.

Digital Expanded Basic Service
Subscribers: N.A.
Programming (via satellite): BBC America; Bloomberg Television; Boomerang; Cooking Channel; DIY Network; FYI; Hallmark Channel; History International; LWS Local Weather Station.
Fee: $5.00 monthly.

Pay Service 1
Pay Units: N.A.
Programming (via satellite): Cinemax; HBO; Showtime.
Fee: $11.50 monthly (Cinemax or Showtime), $12.50 monthly (HBO).

Digital Pay Service 1
Pay Units: N.A.
Programming (via satellite): Cinemax (multiplexed); Flix; HBO (multiplexed); Showtime (multiplexed); Starz (multiplexed); Starz Encore (multiplexed); Sundance TV; The Movie Channel (multiplexed).
Fee: $12.50 monthly (Cinemax, Showtime or TMC), $12.95 monthly (Starz), $13.50 monthly (HBO).

Video-On-Demand: No

Pay-Per-View
iN DEMAND; iN DEMAND (delivered digitally); Adult PPV (delivered digitally).

Internet Service
Operational: No.

Telephone Service
None
Vice President, Operations: Richard Semmel. General Manager: Mark Masonheimer. Fiber Manager: Randy Semmel. Chief Technician: Garry Woods.
Ownership: Pencor Services Inc. (MSO).

BEAVER FALLS—Comcast Cable. Now served by PITTSBURGH, PA [PA0001]. ICA: PA0065.

BEAVER SPRINGS—Formerly served by Service Electric Cable TV & Communications. No longer in operation. ICA: PA0259.

BEAVER VALLEY—Formerly served by Comcast Cable. No longer in operation. ICA: PA0157.

BEAVERTOWN—Formerly served by Nittany Media Inc. No longer in operation. ICA: PA0315.

BEDFORD—Comcast Cable. Now served by BLAIRSVILLE, PA [PA0320]. ICA: PA0082.

BELLEVILLE—Zampelli Electronics, PO Box 830, Lewistown, PA 17044-0830. Phone: 717-248-1544. ICA: PA0316.
TV Market Ranking: Outside TV Markets (BELLEVILLE).
Channel capacity: 14 (not 2-way capable). Channels available but not in use: N.A.

Basic Service
Subscribers: N.A.
Programming (received off-air): WGAL (NBC, This TV) Lancaster; WHP-TV (CBS, MNT) Harrisburg; WHTM-TV (ABC, Retro TV) Harrisburg; WJAC-TV (MeTV, NBC) Johnstown; WNEP-TV (ABC, Antenna TV) Scranton; WPSU-TV (PBS) Clearfield; WTAJ-TV (CBS) Altoona; WVIA-TV (PBS) Scranton; WXBU (CW) Lancaster; 1 FM.
Programming (via satellite): Disney Channel; ESPN; TBS; WGN America.
Fee: $25.00 installation; $10.75 monthly.

Pay Service 1
Pay Units: N.A.
Programming (via satellite): The Movie Channel.
Fee: $10.95 monthly.

Video-On-Demand: No

Internet Service
Operational: No.

Telephone Service
None
General Manager & Chief Technician: Joe Zampelli.
Ownership: Zampelli TV (MSO).

BENSALEM—Comcast Cable. Now served by EATONTOWN BOROUGH, NJ [NJ0009]. ICA: PA0027.

BENTLEY CREEK—Blue Ridge Communications, 613 3rd St, PO Box 215, Palmerton, PA 18071-0215. Phone: 610-826-2551. Web Site: http://www.brctv.com. Also serves Bradford County, Centerville (Bradford County) & Fassett. ICA: PA0317.
TV Market Ranking: Below 100 (BENTLEY CREEK, Bradford County, Centerville (Bradford County), Fassett). Franchise award date: N.A. Franchise expiration date: N.A. Began: January 1, 1975.
Channel capacity: 12 (not 2-way capable). Channels available but not in use: N.A.

Basic Service
Subscribers: N.A.
Programming (received off-air): WBNG-TV (CBS, CW) Binghamton; WENY-TV (ABC, CW) Elmira; WETM-TV (IND, NBC) Elmira; WICZ-TV (FOX) Binghamton; WSKG-TV (PBS) Binghamton; WSWB (CW, MeTV) Scranton; WVIA-TV (PBS) Scranton; WYOU (CBS) Scranton; allband FM.
Programming (via satellite): A&E; Disney Channel; Fox Sports 1; Freeform; Lifetime; Pennsylvania Cable Network; QVC; Syfy; The Weather Channel; TLC.
Fee: $22.50 installation; $15.30 monthly.

Expanded Basic Service 1
Subscribers: N.A.
Programming (via satellite): AMC; Animal Planet; CNN; Discovery Channel; ESPN; ESPN2; FX; HGTV; History; MTV; NBCSN; Nickelodeon; Spike TV; TBS; TNT; Trinity Broadcasting Network (TBN); USA Network; VH1; WPIX (Antenna TV, CW, This TV) New York.
Fee: $24.91 monthly.

Digital Basic Service
Subscribers: N.A.
Programming (via satellite): BBC America; Bloomberg Television; Discovery Kids Channel; Disney XD; ESPN Classic; ESPNews; Fox Sports 1; FYI; Golf Channel; GSN; History International; LMN; MC; National Geographic Channel; NBCSN; Nick Jr.; Outdoor Channel; Sundance TV; TeenNick; The Word Network; Turner Classic Movies.
Fee: $35.00 installation; $18.90 monthly.

Pay Service 1
Pay Units: N.A.
Programming (via satellite): HBO; The Movie Channel.
Fee: $15.00 installation; $9.00 monthly (each).

Digital Pay Service 1
Pay Units: N.A.
Programming (via satellite): Cinemax (multiplexed); HBO (multiplexed); Showtime (multiplexed); Starz (multiplexed); Starz Encore (multiplexed); The Movie Channel (multiplexed).
Fee: $12.50 monthly (Cinemax, Showtime or TMC), $12.95 monthly (Starz), $13.50 monthly (HBO).

Video-On-Demand: No

Pay-Per-View
Sports PPV (delivered digitally); ESPN Now (delivered digitally); iN DEMAND (delivered digitally).

Internet Service
Operational: No.

Telephone Service
None
Miles of Plant: 14.0 (coaxial); None (fiber optic).
Vice President, Operations: Richard Semmel. General Manager: Mark Masonheimer. Fiber Manager: Randy Semmel. Chief Technician: Garry Woods.
Ownership: Pencor Services Inc. (MSO).

BERWICK—MetroCast Communications, 70 East Lancaster Ave, Frazer, PA 19355. Phones: 800-952-1001; 570-802-5679. Fax: 570-802-5640. Web Site: http://www.metrocast.com. Also serves Beach Haven, Benton, Black Creek Twp., Briar Creek, Conyngham, Dorrance, Greenwood Twp., Hunlock Creek, Jackson Twp. (Columbia County), Larksville, Mifflin Twp., Millville, Nescopeck, Newport Twp., North Centre Twp., North Union Twp. (Schuylkill County), Nuangola, Orange Twp., Orangeville, Plymouth Twp. (Luzerne County), Rice Twp., Salem Twp. (Luzerne County), Shickshinny, Slocum Twp., South Centre Twp., Stillwater, Sugarloaf, Sugarloaf Twp., Union Twp. (Luzerne County), Wapwallopen & West Nanticoke. ICA: PA0094.
TV Market Ranking: 49 (Beach Haven, Benton, BERWICK, Black Creek Twp., Briar Creek, Conyngham, Dorrance, Greenwood Twp., Hunlock Creek, Jackson Twp. (Columbia County), Larksville, Mifflin Twp., Millville, Nescopeck, Newport Twp., Nuangola, Orange Twp., Orangeville, Plymouth Twp. (Luzerne County), Rice Twp., Salem Twp. (Luzerne County), Shickshinny, South Centre Twp., Stillwater, Sugarloaf, Sugarloaf Twp., Union Twp. (Luzerne County), Wapwallopen, West Nanticoke); 94 (North Centre Twp.); Below 100 (North Union Twp. (Schuylkill County)). Franchise award date: January 1, 1947. Franchise expiration date: N.A. Began: December 1, 1950.
Channel capacity: 78 (operating 2-way). Channels available but not in use: N.A.

Basic Service
Subscribers: 8,352.
Programming (received off-air): WBRE-TV (NBC) Wilkes-Barre; WNEP-TV (ABC, Antenna TV) Scranton; WOLF-TV (CW, FOX, MNT) Hazleton; WQMY (MNT) Williamsport; WQPX-TV (ION) Scranton; WSWB (CW, MeTV) Scranton; WVIA-TV (PBS) Scranton; WYLN-LP (America One) Hazleton; WYOU (CBS) Scranton; allband FM.
Programming (via microwave): WWOR-TV (Bounce TV, Buzzr, Heroes & Icons, MNT) Secaucus.
Programming (via satellite): Pop; QVC; WPIX (Antenna TV, CW, This TV) New York.
Fee: $49.95 installation; $31.95 monthly; $1.35 converter.

Expanded Basic Service 1
Subscribers: N.A.
Programming (via satellite): A&E; AMC; Animal Planet; Bravo; Cartoon Network; CMT; CNBC; CNN; Comcast SportsNet Philadelphia; Comedy Central; C-SPAN; Discovery Channel; Disney Channel; E! HD; ESPN; ESPN2; Food Network; Fox News Channel; Fox Sports 1; Freeform; FX; FXM; Hallmark Channel; Hallmark Movies & Mysteries; HGTV; History; HLN; Lifetime; MSNBC; MTV; National Geographic Channel; NBCSN; Nickelodeon; Outdoor Channel; Pennsylvania Cable Network; Root Sports Pittsburgh; Spike TV; Syfy; TBS; The Weather Channel; TLC; TNT; Travel Channel; Trinity Broadcasting Network (TBN); truTV; TV Land; USA Network; VH1; WE tv.
Fee: $25.92 installation; $28.74 monthly.

Digital Basic Service
Subscribers: N.A.
Programming (via satellite): AWE; AXS TV; BBC America; Bloomberg Television; Boomerang; CMT; Discovery Digital Networks; Disney XD; DMX Music; ESPN HD; ESPN2 HD; ESPNU; Fuse; FYI; GSN; HD Theater; History International; LMN; MTV Classic; MTV2; National Geographic Channel HD; NFL Network; NFL Network HD; Nick Jr.; Nicktoons; Outdoor Channel 2 HD; TeenNick; TNT HD; Universal HD; UP.
Fee: $7.95 monthly.

Digital Expanded Basic Service
Subscribers: N.A.
Programming (via satellite): ESPN Classic; ESPNews; FOX College Sports Central; FOX College Sports Pacific; Fox Sports 2;

Cable Systems—Pennsylvania

Golf Channel; IFC; Starz HD; Turner Classic Movies.
Fee: $9.95 monthly.
Digital Pay Service 1
Pay Units: N.A.
Programming (via satellite): Cinemax (multiplexed); Cinemax HD; Flix; HBO (multiplexed); HBO HD; Showtime (multiplexed); Showtime HD; The Movie Channel (multiplexed).
Fee: $9.95 monthly (Cinemax), $10.95 monthly (HBO or Showtime/TMC).
Video-On-Demand: No
Pay-Per-View
ESPN Now (delivered digitally); iN DEMAND (delivered digitally); Sports PPV (delivered digitally).
Internet Service
Operational: Yes.
Subscribers: 5,969.
Broadband Service: MetroCast Internet.
Fee: $41.95 monthly; $9.95 modem lease; $199.95 modem purchase.
Telephone Service
Digital: Operational
Subscribers: 2,447.
Miles of Plant: 919.0 (coaxial); 356.0 (fiber optic). Homes passed: 25,376.
Chief Financial Officer: Shawn P. Flannery. General Manager: Tom Carey. Mid-Atlantic Regional Engineer: Jeff Shearer. Marketing Manager: Chrissy Carey.
Ownership: Harron Communications LP (MSO).

BETHEL—Comcast Cable. Now served by PITTSBURGH, PA [PA0001]. ICA: PA0318.

BIG POND—Formerly served by Barrett's TV Cable System. No longer in operation. ICA: PA0319.

BIGLER TWP.—Comcast Cable. Now served by HARRISBURG, PA [PA0009]. ICA: PA0159.

BIRDSBORO—Service Electric Cablevision, 6400 Perkiomen Ave, PO Box 8, Birdsboro, PA 19508. Phones: 800-344-0347; 610-582-5317. Fax: 610-582-3094. E-mail: corporateoffice@secv.com. Web Site: http://www.sectv.com. Also serves Amity Twp. (Berks County), Brecknock Twp. (Berks County), Caernarvon Twp. (Berks County), Caernarvon Twp. (Lancaster County), Cumru, District Twp., Earl Twp. (Lancaster County), East Nantmeal Twp., Elverson Borough, Exeter Twp. (Berks County), Fleetwood, Honey Brook Borough, Honeybrook Twp. (Chester County), Kutztown, Longswamp Twp. (portions), Lyon Station, Maidencreek, Maidencreek Twp., Maxatawny Twp., Oley, Pike Twp., Richmond Twp., Robeson Twp., Rockland Twp., Ruscombmanor Twp., St. Lawrence, Topton, Union Twp. (Berks County), Warwick, Warwick Twp. (Berks County) & Warwick Twp. (Chester County). ICA: PA0070.
TV Market Ranking: 4 (Maidencreek, Oley, Warwick); 4,57 (Warwick Twp. (Chester County)); 57 (Amity Twp. (Berks County), BIRDSBORO, Brecknock Twp. (Berks County), Caernarvon Twp. (Berks County), Caernarvon Twp. (Lancaster County), Cumru, Earl Twp. (Lancaster County), East Nantmeal Twp., Elverson Borough, Exeter Twp. (Berks County), Honey Brook Borough, Honeybrook Twp. (Chester County), Robeson Twp., St. Lawrence, Union Twp. (Berks County), Warwick Twp. (Berks County)); Below 100 (District Twp., Fleetwood, Kutztown, Longswamp Twp. (portions), Lyon Station, Maidencreek Twp., Maxatawny Twp., Pike Twp., Richmond Twp., Rockland Twp., Ruscombmanor Twp., Topton). Franchise award date: N.A. Franchise expiration date: N.A. Began: January 1, 1956.
Channel capacity: N.A. Channels available but not in use: N.A.
Basic Service
Subscribers: 27,017.
Programming (received off-air): KYW-TV (CBS, Decades) Philadelphia; WCAU (COZI TV, NBC) Philadelphia; WFMZ-TV (Retro TV) Allentown; WGAL (NBC, This TV) Lancaster; WGTW-TV (TBN) Burlington; WHYY-TV (PBS) Wilmington; WLVT-TV (PBS) Allentown; WPHL-TV (Antenna TV, MNT, This TV) Philadelphia; WPMT (Antenna TV, FOX) York; WPPX-TV (ION) Wilmington; WPSG (CW) Philadelphia; WPVI-TV (ABC, Live Well Network) Philadelphia; WTVE (IND) Reading; WTXF-TV (Buzzr, FOX, Movies!) Philadelphia; WUVP-DT (getTV, UNV) Vineland; WXBU (CW) Lancaster; allband FM.
Programming (via satellite): C-SPAN; EVINE Live; EWTN Global Catholic Network; HLN; Pennsylvania Cable Network; QVC; The Weather Channel; Travel Channel.
Fee: $61.00 installation; $19.95 monthly.
Expanded Basic Service 1
Subscribers: N.A.
Programming (via satellite): A&E; AMC; Animal Planet; BET; Bravo; Cartoon Network; CMT; CNBC; CNN; Comcast SportsNet Philadelphia; Comedy Central; Discovery Channel; Discovery Life Channel; Disney Channel; Disney XD; E! HD; ESPN; ESPN Classic; ESPN2; Food Network; Fox News Channel; Fox Sports 1; Freeform; FX; HGTV; History; Lifetime; MSNBC; MTV; National Geographic Channel; NFL Network; Nickelodeon; Outdoor Channel; Spike TV; Syfy; TBS; TLC; TNT; truTV; TV Land; USA Network; VH1; WE tv.
Fee: $26.95 monthly.
Digital Basic Service
Subscribers: N.A.
Programming (via satellite): 3ABN; AXS TV; BBC America; Bloomberg Television; Boomerang; BYUtv; CBS Sports Network; Church Channel; CMT; Colours; Cooking Channel; Daystar TV Network; Destination America; Discovery Kids Channel; DIY Network; ESPN HD; ESPN2 HD; ESPNews; ESPNU; FamilyNet; Food Network HD; FOX College Sports Central; FOX College Sports Pacific; Fox Sports 2; Fuse; FXM; FYI; GEB America; Golf Channel; Great American Country; Hallmark Channel; Hallmark Movies & Mysteries; HD Theater; HGTV HD; History International; IFC; INSP; Investigation Discovery; JUCE TV; LMN; MC; MTV Classic; MTV Hits; MTV Jams; MTV Live; MTV2; Nat Geo WILD; National Geographic Channel HD; NBCSN; NFL Network HD; NHL Network; Nick 2; Nick Jr.; Nicktoons; Outdoor Channel 2 HD; Ovation; OWN: Oprah Winfrey Network; Penn National Racing Alive; Science Channel; Smile of a Child TV; Sprout; TBS HD; TeenNick; Tennis Channel; TNT HD; Tr3s; Trinity Broadcasting Network (TBN); Turner Classic Movies; Universal HD; VH1 Soul.
Fee: $25.05 monthly.
Digital Pay Service 1
Pay Units: 21,648.
Programming (via satellite): Cinemax (multiplexed); Cinemax HD; Flix; HBO (multiplexed); HBO HD; Showtime (multiplexed); Showtime HD; Starz (multiplexed); Starz Encore (multiplexed); Starz HD; The Movie Channel (multiplexed); The Movie Channel HD.
Fee: $31.00 installation; $11.50 monthly (Cinemax), $12.45 monthly (Starz/Encore), $14.45 monthly (HBO or Showtime/TMC/Flix).
Video-On-Demand: No
Pay-Per-View
Sports PPV (delivered digitally); iN DEMAND (delivered digitally).
Internet Service
Operational: Yes. Began: August 1, 2001.
Subscribers: 20,189.
Broadband Service: ProLog Express.
Fee: $61.00 installation; $22.95-$52.95 monthly; $4.95 modem lease; $99.95 modem purchase.
Telephone Service
Analog: Not Operational
Digital: Operational
Subscribers: 5,276.
Fee: $44.95 monthly
Miles of Plant: 2,530.0 (coaxial); 918.0 (fiber optic). Homes passed: 50,922.
General Manager: Karl Kowatch. Engineering Director: Jim Dorsa. Regulatory Affairs Director: Arlean Lilly. Customer Service Manager: Barb Fazekas.
Ownership: Service Electric Cable TV Inc. (MSO).

BLAIRSVILLE—Comcast Cable, 15 Summit Park Dr, Pittsburgh, PA 15275. Phones: 412-747-6400; 724-459-9042 (Blairsville office). Fax: 412-747-6401. Web Site: http://www.comcast.com. Also serves Accident, Friendsville, Grantsville & McHenry, MD; Adams Twp. (Cambria County), Allegheny Twp. (Cambria County), Allegheny Twp. (Somerset County), Allegheny Twp. (Westmoreland County), Alum Bank, Applewold, Armagh, Armstrong Twp. (Indiana County), Ashville Borough, Banks Twp. & Barr Twp., Beccaria Twp., Bedford, Bedford Twp., Bell Twp. (Westmoreland County), Berlin Borough, Bethel Twp. (Armstrong County), Black Lick Twp., Black Twp., Blacklick Twp., Boggs Twp. (Armstrong County), Bolivar Borough, Boswell Borough, Brothersvalley Twp., Buffington Twp., Burnside Twp. (Clearfield County), Burrell Twp. (Armstrong County), Burrell Twp. (Indiana County), Cadogan, Cambria Twp., Carrolltown Borough, Cassandra Borough, Center Twp. (Indiana County), Central City Borough, Cherry Tree Borough, Cherryhill Twp., Clarksburg, Clearfield Twp., Clymer Borough, Coalport, Colerain Twp. (Bedford County), Commodore (Indiana County), Conemaugh, Conemaugh Twp. (Indiana County), Cowanshannock Twp., Creekside, Cresson, Cresson Twp., Croyle Twp., Dayton Borough, Dean Twp. (Cambria County), Delmont Borough, Derry, Derry Borough, Derry Twp. (Westmoreland County), Dixonville (Indiana County), East Carroll Twp., East Conemaugh, East Conemaugh Borough, East Franklin Twp., East Providence Twp., East St. Clair Twp. (Bedford County), East Wheatfield Twp., Ebensburg, Ebensburg Borough, Ehrenfeld Borough, Elder Twp., Elderton Borough, Ernest Borough, Everett Borough, Export Borough, Fairfield Twp. (Westmoreland County), Ford City, Ford Cliff, Freeport, Gallitzin Borough, Gallitzin Twp., Garrett, Gilpin, Gilpin Twp., Glen Campbell, Glen Hope Borough, Glendale (Clearfield County), Green Twp. (Indiana County), Harrison Twp. (Bedford County), Hastings Borough, Homer City, Hooversville Borough, Hopewell Twp. (Bedford County), Hyndman Borough, Indian Lake Borough, Indiana Twp., Irvona Borough, Jackson Twp. (Cambria County), Jenner Twp., Jennerstown Borough, Juniata Twp. (portions, Huntingdon County), Kiskiminetas Twp., Kittanning Borough, Kittanning Twp., Latrobe, Laurel Mountain Park, Ligonier Borough, Ligonier Twp., Lilly Borough, Lincoln Twp., Londonderry Twp. (Bedford County), Loretto Borough, Loyalhanna, Loyalhanna Twp., Madison Twp. (Armstrong County), Mahoning Twp. (Armstrong County), Manns Choice Borough, Manor (portions, Westmoreland County), Manor Twp. (Armstrong County), Manorville, Marion Center, Meyersdale, Milford Twp. (Somerset County), Montgomery Twp. (Indiana County), Murrysville (Municipality), Nanty Glo, Napier Twp. (Bedford County), New Baltimore Borough (Somerset County), New Florence Borough, New Paris Borough, North Apollo, North Buffalo, Northern Cambria, Ogle Twp., Paint Borough, Paint Twp. (Somerset County), Parks Twp., Patton Borough, Penn Twp. (Westmoreland County), Pine Twp. (Armstrong County), Pine Twp. (Indiana County), Plum Borough, Plumcreek Twp., Plumville Borough, Portage Borough, Portage Twp. (Cambria County), Quemahoning Twp. (Somerset County), Rainsburg Borough, Rayburn Twp., Rayne Twp., Reade Twp. (Cambria County), Rockwood, Rural Valley Borough, Salem Twp. (Westmoreland County), Sankertown Borough, Scalp Level Borough, Schellsburg Borough, Seward Borough, Shade Twp. (Somerset County), Shanksville Borough, Shelocta Borough, Snake Spring Valley Twp., Somerset Borough, Somerset Twp. (Somerset County), South Bend Twp., South Buffalo Twp., South Fork Borough, South Mahoning Twp., St. Clair Twp., Stonycreek Twp. (Somerset County), Stoystown Borough, Sugarcreek Twp., Summerhill Borough, Summerhill Twp., Susquehanna Twp. (Cambria County), Tunnelhill Borough, Unity Twp., Upper Burrell Twp., Valley Twp. (Armstrong County), Vintondale Borough, Washington, Washington Twp. (Armstrong County), Washington Twp. (Cambria County), Washington Twp. (Westmoreland County), West Carroll Twp., West Franklin Twp., West Kittanning, West Providence Twp., West St. Clair Twp., West Wheatfield Twp., White Twp. (Cambria County), White Twp. (Indiana County), Wilmore Borough, Windber Borough, Worthington, Young Twp. (Indiana County), Young Twp. (Jefferson County) & Youngstown, PA. ICA: PA0320.
TV Market Ranking: 10 (Allegheny Twp. (Westmoreland County), Applewold, Bell Twp. (Westmoreland County), Bethel Twp. (Armstrong County), Burrell Twp. (Armstrong County), Cadogan, Derry Twp. (Westmoreland County), Export Borough, Ford Cliff, Freeport, Gilpin, Gilpin Twp., Indiana Twp., Kiskiminetas Twp., Latrobe, Loyalhanna, Manor (portions, Westmoreland County), Manor Twp. (Armstrong County), Manorville, Murrysville (Municipality), North Apollo, North Buffalo, Parks Twp., Penn Twp. (Westmoreland County), Plum Borough, Salem Twp. (Westmoreland County), South Buffalo Twp., Upper Burrell Twp., Washington, Washington Twp. (Westmoreland County), West Franklin Twp.); 10,74 (Delmont Borough, Derry Borough, Loyalhanna Twp., Unity Twp.); 74 (Adams Twp. (Cambria County), Allegheny Twp. (Cambria County), Allegheny Twp. (Somerset County), Alum Bank, Armagh, Armstrong Twp. (Indiana County), Ashville Borough, Banks Twp., Barr Twp., Beccaria Twp., Bedford, Bedford Twp., Berlin Borough, Black Lick Twp., Black Twp., BLAIRSVILLE, Bolivar Borough, Boswell Borough, Brothersval-

Pennsylvania—Cable Systems

ley Twp., Buffington Twp., Burnside Twp. (Clearfield County), Burrell Twp. (Indiana County), Cambria Twp., Carrolltown Borough, Cassandra Borough, Center Twp. (Indiana County), Central City Borough, Cherry Tree Borough, Cherryhill Twp., Clarksburg, Clearfield Twp., Clymer Borough, Coalport, Colerain Twp. (Bedford County), Commodore (Indiana County), Conemaugh, Conemaugh Twp. (Indiana County), Creekside, Cresson, Cresson Twp., Croyle Twp., Dean Twp. (Cambria County), Derry, Dixonville (Indiana County), East Carroll Twp., East Conemaugh, East Conemaugh Borough, East Providence Twp., East St. Clair Twp. (Bedford County), East Wheatfield Twp., Ebensburg, Ebensburg Borough, Ehrenfeld Borough, Elder Twp., Ernest Borough, Everett Borough, Fairfield Twp. (Westmoreland County), Gallitzin Borough, Gallitzin Twp., Garrett, Glen Campbell, Glen Hope Borough, Green Twp. (Indiana County), Harrison Twp. (Bedford County), Hastings Borough, Homer City, Hooversville Borough, Hopewell Twp. (Bedford County), Indian Lake Borough, Irvona Borough, Jackson Twp. (Cambria County), Jenner Twp., Jennerstown Borough, Juniata Twp. (portions, Huntingdon County), Laurel Mountain Park, Ligonier Borough, Ligonier Twp., Lilly Borough, Lincoln Twp., Loretto Borough, Manns Choice Borough, Marion Center, Milford Twp. (Somerset County), Montgomery Twp. (Indiana County), Nanty Glo, Napier Twp. (Bedford County), New Baltimore Borough (Somerset County), New Florence Borough, New Paris Borough, Northern Cambria, Ogle Twp., Paint Borough, Paint Twp. (Somerset County), Patton Borough, Pine Twp. (Indiana County), Plumville Borough, Portage Borough, Portage Twp. (Cambria County), Quemahoning Twp. (Somerset County), Rayne Twp., Reade Twp. (Cambria County), Rockwood, Sankertown Borough, Scalp Level Borough, Schellsburg Borough, Seward Borough, Shade Twp. (Somerset County), Shanksville Borough, Shelocta Borough, Snake Spring Valley Twp., Somerset Borough, Somerset Twp. (Somerset County), South Bend Twp., South Fork Borough, St. Clair Twp., Stonycreek Twp. (Somerset County), Stoystown Borough, Summerhill Borough, Summerhill Twp., Susquehanna Twp. (Cambria County), Tunnelhill Borough, Vintondale Borough, Washington Twp. (Cambria County), West Carroll Twp., West Providence Twp., West St. Clair Twp., West Wheatfield Twp., White Twp. (Cambria County), White Twp. (Indiana County), Wilmore Borough, Windber Borough, Young Twp. (Indiana County), Youngstown); Below 100 (Ford City, Kittanning Borough, West Kittanning, Worthington); Outside TV Markets (Accident, Boggs Twp. (Armstrong County), Cowanshannock Twp., Dayton Borough, East Franklin Twp., Friendsville, Glendale (Clearfield County), Hyndman Borough, Kittanning Twp., Londonderry Twp. (Bedford County), Madison Twp. (Armstrong County), Mahoning Twp. (Armstrong County), McHenry, Pine Twp. (Armstrong County), Rainsburg Borough, Rayburn Twp., Rural Valley Borough, Sugarcreek Twp., Valley Twp. (Armstrong County), Washington Twp. (Armstrong County), Young Twp. (Jefferson County), Meyersdale). Franchise award date: N.A.

Franchise expiration date: N.A. Began: March 1, 1965.
Channel capacity: 5 (operating 2-way). Channels available but not in use: N.A.

Basic Service
Subscribers: 76,724. Commercial subscribers: 1,329.
Programming (received off-air): KDKA-TV (CBS, Decades) Pittsburgh; WEPA-CD (COZI TV, IND, Movies!, Retro TV) Pittsburgh; WINP-TV (IND, ION) Pittsburgh; WJAC-TV (MeTV, NBC) Johnstown; WPCB-TV (IND) Greensburg; WPCW (CW) Jeannette; WPGH-TV (Antenna TV, FOX, The Country Network) Pittsburgh; WPNT (MNT) Pittsburgh; WPSU-TV (PBS) Clearfield; WPXI (MeTV, NBC) Pittsburgh; WQED (PBS) Pittsburgh; WTAE-TV (ABC, This TV) Pittsburgh; WTAJ-TV (CBS) Altoona; allband FM.
Programming (via satellite): Fuse; QVC; TBS; WGN America.
Fee: $29.50-$42.75 installation; $44.76 monthly.

Expanded Basic Service 1
Subscribers: N.A.
Programming (via microwave): Pittsburgh Cable News Channel.
Programming (via satellite): A&E; AMC; Animal Planet; BET; Bravo; Cartoon Network; CMT; CNBC; CNN; Comedy Central; C-SPAN; C-SPAN 2; Discovery Channel; Disney Channel; E! HD; ESPN; ESPN2; EWTN Global Catholic Network; Food Network; Fox News Channel; Freeform; FX; Golf Channel; HGTV; History; HLN; HRTV; ION Television; Lifetime; MSNBC; MTV; Nickelodeon; Oxygen; Pennsylvania Cable Network; Pop; Root Sports Pittsburgh; Spike TV; Syfy; The Weather Channel; TLC; TNT; Travel Channel; truTV; TV Land; USA Network; VH1.
Fee: $38.50 monthly.

Digital Basic Service
Subscribers: N.A.
Programming (via satellite): BBC America; Bloomberg Television; Destination America; Discovery Kids Channel; Discovery Life Channel; Disney XD; DIY Network; Fox Sports 1; FXM; Great American Country; GSN; INSP; Investigation Discovery; LMN; National Geographic Channel; Nick 2; Nick Jr.; Nicktoons; OWN: Oprah Winfrey Network; Science Channel; TeenNick; The Word Network; Trinity Broadcasting Network (TBN); Turner Classic Movies; WE tv.
Fee: $15.95 monthly.

Digital Pay Service 1
Pay Units: N.A.
Programming (via satellite): Cinemax (multiplexed); HBO (multiplexed); MC; Showtime (multiplexed); Starz (multiplexed); Starz Encore (multiplexed); The Movie Channel (multiplexed).
Fee: $15.95 monthly (each).

Video-On-Demand: Yes

Pay-Per-View
HITS (Headend In The Sky) (delivered digitally); Hot Choice (delivered digitally); iN DEMAND; iN DEMAND (delivered digitally); Playboy TV (delivered digitally); Fresh (delivered digitally).

Internet Service
Operational: Yes.
Subscribers: 73,063.
Broadband Service: Comcast High Speed Internet.
Fee: $42.95 monthly.

Telephone Service
Digital: Operational
Subscribers: 37,207.
Fee: $44.95 monthly

Miles of Plant: 5,571.0 (coaxial); 2,502.0 (fiber optic). Homes passed: 205,633.
Regional Vice President: Linda Hossinger. Vice President, Technical Operations: Randy Bender. Vice President, Marketing: Donna Corning. Vice President, Public Affairs: Jody Doherty.
Ownership: Comcast Cable Communications Inc. (MSO).

BLOOMSBURG—Service Electric Cable TV & Communications. Now served by SUNBURY (village), PA [PA0029]. ICA: PA0088.

BLOSERVILLE—Kuhn Communications, 301 West Main St, Walnut Bottom, PA 17266. Phones: 800-771-7072; 717-532-8857. Fax: 717-532-5563. Web Site: http://www.kuhncom.net. ICA: PA0474.
TV Market Ranking: 57 (BLOSERVILLE).
Channel capacity: N.A. Channels available but not in use: N.A.

Basic Service
Subscribers: 414.
Fee: $30.00 installation; $15.45 monthly.
President & General Manager: Earl W. Kuhn.
Ownership: Kuhn Communications (MSO).

BLOSSBURG—Formerly served by Williamson Road TV Co. Inc. No longer in operation. ICA: PA0321.

BOYERS—Formerly served by Cebridge Connections. Now served by Armstrong Cable Services, ZELIENOPLE, PA [PA0053]. ICA: PA0276.

BRADFORD—Atlantic Broadband, 24 Main St, Bradford, PA 16701. Phones: 888-536-9600; 814-368-8590. Fax: 814-362-2190. E-mail: info@atlanticbb.com. Web Site: http://atlanticbb.com. Also serves Carrollton (town) & Limestone, NY; Bradford Twp. (McKean County), Foster Twp. (McKean County), Lafayette Twp. & Lewis Run, PA. ICA: PA0085.
TV Market Ranking: Below 100 (BRADFORD, Bradford Twp. (McKean County), Carrollton (town), Foster Twp. (McKean County), Lewis Run, Limestone). Franchise award date: April 16, 1954. Franchise expiration date: N.A. Began: April 16, 1954.
Channel capacity: 79 (operating 2-way). Channels available but not in use: N.A.

Basic Service
Subscribers: 3,144.
Programming (received off-air): WGRZ (Antenna TV, NBC, WeatherNation) Buffalo; WICU-TV (NBC) Erie; WIVB-TV (CBS) Buffalo; WKBW-TV (ABC, Escape) Buffalo; WNYB (IND) Jamestown; WPSU-TV (PBS) Clearfield; WSEE-TV (CBS, CW) Erie; WUTV (FOX, The Country Network) Buffalo; allband FM.
Programming (via satellite): C-SPAN; EWTN Global Catholic Network; INSP; Jewelry Television; Pennsylvania Cable Network; Pop; QVC; WGN America; World.
Fee: $40.00 installation; $34.19 monthly; $1.60 converter.

Expanded Basic Service 1
Subscribers: N.A.
Programming (via satellite): A&E; AMC; Animal Planet; Bravo; Cartoon Network; CMT; CNBC; CNN; Comedy Central; Discovery Channel; Disney Channel; E! HD; ESPN; ESPN Classic; ESPN2; Food Network; Fox News Channel; Fox Sports 1; Freeform; FX; Golf Channel; Hallmark Channel; HGTV; History; HLN; Lifetime; LMN; MSG; MSNBC; MTV; National Geographic Channel; Nickelodeon; Outdoor Channel; OWN: Oprah Winfrey Network; Oxygen; Root Sports Pittsburgh; Spike TV; Syfy; TBS; The Weather Channel; TLC; TNT; Travel Channel; truTV; Turner Classic Movies; TV Land; USA Network; VH1.
Fee: $37.47 monthly.

Digital Basic Service
Subscribers: N.A.
Programming (via satellite): A&E HD; Animal Planet HD; BBC America; Bloomberg Television; Boomerang; Chiller; CMT; Destination America; Discovery Channel HD; Discovery Kids Channel; Disney Channel HD; Disney XD; DIY Network; ESPN HD; ESPN2 HD; ESPNews; ESPNU; Fox Sports 2; FYI; HD Theater; History International; IFC; Investigation Discovery; MC; MTV Classic; MTV Hits; MTV Jams; MTV2; NFL Network; NFL Network HD; Nick 2; Nick Jr.; Nicktoons; Root Sports Pittsburgh; Science Channel; Starz (multiplexed); Starz Encore (multiplexed); Syfy HD; TBS HD; TeenNick; TLC HD; TNT HD; Tr3s; USA Network HD; VH1 Soul; WE tv; Weatherscan.
Fee: $18.95 monthly.

Digital Pay Service 1
Pay Units: 400.
Programming (via satellite): HBO (multiplexed).
Fee: $15.95 monthly.

Digital Pay Service 2
Pay Units: 215.
Programming (via satellite): Cinemax (multiplexed).
Fee: $15.95 monthly.

Digital Pay Service 3
Pay Units: N.A.
Programming (via satellite): Flix; Showtime (multiplexed); The Movie Channel (multiplexed).
Fee: $15.95 monthly.

Video-On-Demand: No

Pay-Per-View
iN DEMAND (delivered digitally); Hot Choice (delivered digitally); Spice: Xcess (delivered digitally); Club Jenna (delivered digitally); Fresh (delivered digitally); Shorteez (delivered digitally); Playboy TV (delivered digitally).

Internet Service
Operational: Yes.
Broadband Service: Atlantic Broadband High-Speed Internet.
Fee: $24.95-$57.95 monthly.

Telephone Service
Digital: Operational
Fee: $44.95 monthly
Miles of Plant: 232.0 (coaxial); 63.0 (fiber optic). Homes passed: 61,233.
Senior Vice President & General Counsel: Leslie Brown. Vice President: David Dane. General Manager: Mike Papasergi. Technical Operations Director: Charles Sorchilla. Chief Technician: Richard C. Himes. Marketing & Customer Service Director: Dara Leslie. Marketing Manager: Natalie Kurchak.
Ownership: Atlantic Broadband (MSO).

BRAVE—Zito Media, 102 S Main St, PO Box 665, Coudersport, PA 16915. Phones: 814-260-9055; 800-365-6988. E-mail: info@zitomedia.com. Web Site: http://www.zitomedia.com. Also serves Spraggs (Greene County) & Wayne Twp., PA; Blacksville, Daybrook, Fairfield, Mooresville, Pentress, Wadestown & Wana, WV. ICA: PA0201.
TV Market Ranking: 90 (BRAVE, Spraggs (Greene County), Wadestown, Wana,

Cable Systems—Pennsylvania

Wayne Twp.); Below 100 (Blacksville, Daybrook, Fairfield, Mooresville, Pentress).
Channel capacity: 39 (not 2-way capable).
Channels available but not in use: N.A.
Basic Service
Subscribers: 159.
Programming (received off-air): KDKA-TV (CBS, Decades) Pittsburgh; WBOY-TV (ABC, NBC) Clarksburg; WDTV (CBS) Weston; WNPB-TV (PBS) Morgantown; WPGH-TV (Antenna TV, FOX, The Country Network) Pittsburgh; WPNT (MNT) Pittsburgh; WPXI (MeTV, NBC) Pittsburgh; WQED (PBS) Pittsburgh; WTAE-TV (ABC, This TV) Pittsburgh; WTRF-TV (ABC, CBS, MNT) Wheeling.
Programming (via satellite): WGN America.
Fee: $49.95 installation; $22.41 monthly; $1.24 converter.
Expanded Basic Service 1
Subscribers: N.A.
Programming (via satellite): AMC; Animal Planet; Cartoon Network; CNN; C-SPAN; Discovery Channel; Disney Channel; E! HD; ESPN; ESPN2; Fox News Channel; Fox Sports 1; Freeform; FX; Golf Channel; Great American Country; GSN; HGTV; History; Lifetime; Nickelodeon; Outdoor Channel; Root Sports Pittsburgh; Spike TV; Syfy; TBS; The Weather Channel; TLC; TNT; Trinity Broadcasting Network (TBN); USA Network; WE tv.
Fee: $16.93 monthly.
Digital Basic Service
Subscribers: N.A.
Programming (via satellite): Bloomberg Television; Cloo; Discovery Digital Networks; DMX Music; ESPN Classic; ESPNews; EVINE Live; FOX College Sports Central; FOX College Sports Pacific; Fuse; FXM; FYI; History International; IFC; LMN; National Geographic Channel; NBCSN; Turner Classic Movies.
Pay Service 1
Pay Units: N.A.
Programming (via satellite): Cinemax; HBO; Showtime; Starz Encore; The Movie Channel.
Digital Pay Service 1
Pay Units: N.A.
Programming (via satellite): Cinemax (multiplexed); Flix; HBO (multiplexed); Showtime (multiplexed); Starz (multiplexed); Starz Encore (multiplexed); The Movie Channel (multiplexed).
Video-On-Demand: No
Pay-Per-View
iN DEMAND (delivered digitally); Playboy TV (delivered digitally); Fresh (delivered digitally).
Internet Service
Operational: Yes.
Subscribers: 14.
Telephone Service
None
Miles of Plant: 34.0 (coaxial); 5.0 (fiber optic). Homes passed: 400.
President: James Rigas.
Ownership: Zito Media (MSO).

BROAD TOP CITY—Formerly served by Adelphia Communications. Now served by Comcast Cable, HARRISBURG, PA [PA0009]. ICA: PA0224.

BROCKWAY—Brockway TV Inc, 501 Main St, Brockway, PA 15824-1326. Phone: 814-268-6565. Fax: 814-265-1300. Also serves Horton Twp. (Elk County), Sandy Twp., Snyder Twp. (Jefferson County) & Washington Twp. (Jefferson County). ICA: PA0182.

TV Market Ranking: Outside TV Markets (BROCKWAY, Horton Twp. (Elk County), Sandy Twp., Snyder Twp. (Jefferson County), Washington Twp. (Jefferson County)). Franchise award date: N.A. Franchise expiration date: N.A. Began: April 1, 1952.
Channel capacity: N.A. Channels available but not in use: N.A.
Basic Service
Subscribers: 63.
Programming (received off-air): KDKA-TV (CBS, Decades) Pittsburgh; WATM-TV (ABC, This TV) Altoona; WJAC-TV (MeTV, NBC) Johnstown; WKBS-TV (IND) Altoona; WPCW (CW) Jeannette; WPGH-TV (Antenna TV, FOX, The Country Network) Pittsburgh; WPNT (MNT) Pittsburgh; WPSU-TV (PBS) Clearfield; WPXI (MeTV, NBC) Pittsburgh; WQED (PBS) Pittsburgh; WTAE-TV (ABC, This TV) Pittsburgh; WTAJ-TV (CBS) Altoona; WWCP-TV (FOX) Johnstown; 18 FMs.
Programming (via satellite): A&E; AMC; Cartoon Network; CMT; CNN; Discovery Channel; ESPN; ESPN2; EWTN Global Catholic Network; Freeform; FX; FXM; History; HLN; Lifetime; National Geographic Channel; Nickelodeon; Outdoor Channel; Pennsylvania Cable Network; QVC; Root Sports Pittsburgh; Spike TV; TBS; The Weather Channel; TLC; TNT; Turner Classic Movies; USA Network; VH1; WGN America.
Fee: $100.00 installation; $25.00 monthly.
Digital Basic Service
Subscribers: N.A.
Programming (via satellite): BBC America; Bloomberg Television; Cloo; Discovery Life Channel; DMX Music; Fuse; FXM; FYI; Great American Country; GSN; HGTV; History; History International; LMN; National Geographic Channel; Nick Jr.; Nicktoons; Ovation; Sundance TV; Syfy; TeenNick; The Word Network; Trinity Broadcasting Network (TBN); Turner Classic Movies; WE tv.
Fee: $12.95 monthly; $6.25 converter.
Digital Expanded Basic Service
Subscribers: N.A.
Programming (via satellite): ESPN Classic; ESPN2; ESPNews; Fox Sports 1; FSN Digital Atlantic; FSN Digital Central; FSN Digital Pacific; Golf Channel; NBCSN; Outdoor Channel.
Fee: $4.95 monthly.
Digital Pay Service 1
Pay Units: N.A.
Programming (via satellite): Cinemax (multiplexed); Flix; HBO (multiplexed); Showtime (multiplexed); Starz (multiplexed); Starz Encore (multiplexed); Sundance TV; The Movie Channel (multiplexed).
Fee: $11.50 monthly (Cinemax, Showtime or Starz/Encore); $14.00 monthly (HBO).
Video-On-Demand: No
Internet Service
Operational: Yes.
Broadband Service: In-house.
Fee: $20.00 installation; $24.95 monthly.
Telephone Service
None
Miles of Plant: 55.0 (coaxial); None (fiber optic). Homes passed: 1,930.
General Manager: Laurie Wayne. Chief Technician: Howard Olay. Chairman: Michael S. Arnold.
Ownership: Brockway TV Inc.

BROTHERSVALLEY TWP.—Comcast Cable. Now served by BLAIRSVILLE, PA [PA0320]. ICA: PA0132.

BRUSH VALLEY TWP.—Formerly served by Brush Valley Cablevision. No longer in operation. ICA: PA0322.

BUFFALO TWP.—Formerly served by D&E Communications/Windstream. IPTV service no longer in operation. ICA: PA5198.

BURGETTSTOWN—Blue Devil Cable TV Inc, 116 South 4th St, Toronto, OH 43964-1368. Phones: 740-537-2030; 800-931-9392. Fax: 740-537-2802. Web Site: http://bluedevilcabletv.com. Also serves Avella & Smith Twp. ICA: PA0323.
TV Market Ranking: 10,90 (Avella, BURGETTSTOWN, Smith Twp.). Franchise award date: N.A. Franchise expiration date: N.A. Began: October 1, 1974.
Channel capacity: N.A. Channels available but not in use: N.A.
Basic Service
Subscribers: 867.
Programming (received off-air): KDKA-TV (CBS, Decades) Pittsburgh; WPGH-TV (Antenna TV, FOX, The Country Network) Pittsburgh; WPNT (MNT) Pittsburgh; WPXI (MeTV, NBC) Pittsburgh; WQED (PBS) Pittsburgh; WTAE-TV (ABC, This TV) Pittsburgh; WTOV-TV (MeTV, NBC) Steubenville; WTRF-TV (ABC, CBS, MNT) Wheeling.
Programming (via satellite): CNN; ESPN; Freeform; Lifetime; MTV; Nickelodeon; TBS; TNT; USA Network; WGN America.
Fee: $35.00 installation; $14.03 monthly.
Pay Service 1
Pay Units: 221.
Programming (via satellite): HBO; The Movie Channel.
Fee: $10.60 monthly (TMC), $11.66 monthly (HBO).
Video-On-Demand: No
Internet Service
Operational: No.
Telephone Service
None
Miles of Plant: 23.0 (coaxial); None (fiber optic).
Vice President: Joanne Conner. General Manager: David Bates.
Ownership: Blue Devil Cable TV Inc. (MSO).

BUTLER—Armstrong Cable Services. Now served by ZELIENOPLE, PA [PA0053]. ICA: PA0044.

CALIFORNIA—Armstrong Cable Services. Now served by ZELIENOPLE, PA [PA0053]. ICA: PA0099.

CALLENSBURG—Formerly served by Cebridge Connections. Now served by Armstrong Cable Services, BUTLER, PA [PA0044]. ICA: PA0258.

CAMP HILL CORRECTIONAL INSTITUTE—Formerly served by Suddenlink Communications. No longer in operation. ICA: PA0324.

CANADOHTA LAKE—Master Vision, PO Box 203, PO Box 203, Cambridge Springs, PA 16403. Phones: 888-827-2259; 814-398-1946. E-mail: mastervision@mvbloomfield.net. Web Site: http://www.canlakecable.net. Also serves Bloomfield Twp. ICA: PA0446.
TV Market Ranking: Below 100 (Bloomfield Twp., CANADOHTA LAKE).
Channel capacity: N.A. Channels available but not in use: N.A.

Basic Service
Subscribers: N.A.
Programming (received off-air): WFMJ-TV (CW, NBC) Youngstown; WFPX (FOX) Erie; WICU-TV (NBC) Erie; WJET-TV (ABC) Erie; WKBN-TV (CBS) Youngstown; WQLN (PBS) Erie; WSEE-TV (CBS, CW) Erie.
Programming (via satellite): A&E; CNN; Discovery Channel; ESPN; ESPN2; Freeform; Great American Country; History; HLN; Lifetime; MTV; Nickelodeon; QVC; Root Sports Pittsburgh; Spike TV; Syfy; TBS; The Weather Channel; TLC; TNT; Turner Classic Movies; TV Land; USA Network; WGN America.
Fee: $50.00 installation; $67.98 monthly.
Pay Service 1
Pay Units: N.A.
Programming (via satellite): HBO.
Fee: $15.00 monthly.
Internet Service
Operational: Yes.
Fee: $36.00 monthly.
Telephone Service
None
General Manager: Chris Caldwell.
Ownership: Master Vision Cable (MSO).

CANOE CREEK—Atlantic Broadband. Now served by ALTOONA, PA [PA0018]. ICA: PA0439.

CANONSBURG—Comcast Cable. Now served by PITTSBURGH, PA [PA0001]. ICA: PA0057.

CANTON—Zito Media, 102 S Main St, PO Box 665, Coudersport, PA 16915. Phones: 814-260-9055; 800-365-6988. E-mail: info@zitomedia.com. Web Site: http://www.zitomedia.com. Also serves Alba, Canton Twp. (Bradford County), East Canton, Grover & Ward Twp. ICA: PA0184.
TV Market Ranking: Below 100 (Alba, CANTON, Canton Twp. (Bradford County), East Canton, Grover, Ward Twp.). Franchise award date: N.A. Franchise expiration date: N.A. Began: May 1, 1956.
Channel capacity: N.A. Channels available but not in use: N.A.
Basic Service
Subscribers: 363.
Programming (received off-air): WBRE-TV (NBC) Wilkes-Barre; WETM-TV (IND, NBC) Elmira; WNEP-TV (ABC, Antenna TV) Scranton; WOLF-TV (CW, FOX, MNT) Hazleton; WQMY (MNT) Williamsport; WSKG-TV (PBS) Binghamton; WSWB (CW, MeTV) Scranton; WVIA-TV (PBS) Scranton; WYOU (CBS) Scranton; allband FM.
Programming (via satellite): Discovery Channel; ESPN; Hallmark Channel; Lifetime.
Fee: $49.95 installation; $25.23 monthly.
Expanded Basic Service 1
Subscribers: N.A.
Programming (via satellite): CNBC; Disney Channel; Freeform; HGTV; MTV; Nickelodeon; TBS; TNT; USA Network.
Fee: $14.00 monthly.
Expanded Basic Service 2
Subscribers: N.A.
Programming (via satellite): A&E; Animal Planet; CNN; Comedy Central; ESPN2; Food Network; Fox News Channel; Fox Sports 1; FX; Great American Country; History; HLN; Outdoor Channel; QVC; Spike TV; Syfy; The Weather Channel; TLC; Trinity Broadcasting Network (TBN); Turner Classic Movies; TV Land; VH1; WGN America.
Fee: $11.00 monthly.

Pennsylvania—Cable Systems

Pay Service 1
Pay Units: 200.
Programming (via satellite): HBO.
Fee: $11.00 monthly.
Video-On-Demand: No
Internet Service
Operational: No.
Telephone Service
None
Miles of Plant: 41.0 (coaxial); 70.0 (fiber optic). Homes passed: 1,450.
President: James Rigas.
Ownership: Zito Media (MSO).

CARBONDALE TWP. (Lackawanna County)—Adams Cable Service, 19 North Main St, Carbondale, PA 18407-2303. Phones: 570-282-6121; 888-222-0077. Fax: 570-282-3787. E-mail: frontdesk@echoes.net. Web Site: http://www.adamscable.com. Also serves Browndale, Canaan Twp. (Wayne County), Carbondale, Clifford, Clifford Twp. (Susquehanna County), Clinton Twp. (Wayne County), Fell Twp., Forest City, Greenfield Twp. (Lackawanna County), Jefferson Twp. (Lackawanna County), Jermyn, Lake Twp. (Wayne County), Madison Twp. (Lackawanna County), Mayfield, Mount Pleasant Twp. (Wayne County), Paupack Twp. (Wayne County), Prompton, Richmondale Village, Salem Twp. (Wayne County), Scott Twp. (Wayne County), South Canaan Twp., Sterling, Texas Twp., Uniondale, Vandling Borough & Waymart. ICA: PA0067.
TV Market Ranking: 49 (Browndale, Canaan Twp. (Wayne County), Carbondale, CARBONDALE TWP. (LACKAWANNA COUNTY), Clifford, Clifford Twp. (Susquehanna County), Clinton Twp. (Wayne County), Fell Twp., Forest City, Greenfield Twp. (Lackawanna County), Jefferson Twp. (Lackawanna County), Jermyn, Lake Twp. (Wayne County), Madison Twp. (Lackawanna County), Mayfield, Mount Pleasant Twp. (Wayne County), Paupack Twp. (Wayne County), Prompton, Richmondale Village, Salem Twp. (Wayne County), Scott Twp. (Wayne County), South Canaan Twp., Sterling, Texas Twp., Uniondale, Vandling Borough, Waymart). Franchise award date: February 1, 1965. Franchise expiration date: N.A. Began: July 1, 1962.
Channel capacity: 78 (operating 2-way). Channels available but not in use: N.A.
Basic Service
Subscribers: 14,813.
Programming (received off-air): WBRE-TV (NBC) Wilkes-Barre; WNEP-TV (ABC, Antenna TV) Scranton; WOLF-TV (CW, FOX, MNT) Hazleton; WQMY (MNT) Williamsport; WQPX-TV (ION) Scranton; WSWB (CW, MeTV) Scranton; WVIA-TV (PBS) Scranton; WYOU (CBS) Scranton.
Programming (via satellite): C-SPAN; EWTN Global Catholic Network; Pennsylvania Cable Network; Pop; QVC; The Weather Channel.
Fee: $40.00 installation; $22.99 monthly.
Expanded Basic Service 1
Subscribers: N.A.
Programming (via satellite): A&E; AMC; Animal Planet; Bravo; Cartoon Network; CMT; CNBC; CNN; Comcast SportsNet Philadelphia; Comedy Central; Discovery Channel; Disney Channel; E! HD; ESPN; ESPN Classic; ESPN2; Food Network; Fox News Channel; Fox Sports 1; Freeform; FX; Golf Channel; GSN; Hallmark Channel; HGTV; History; HLN; Lifetime; LMN; MSNBC; MTV; National Geographic Channel; NBCSN; NFL Network; Nickelodeon; Spike TV; Syfy; TBS; TLC; TNT; Travel Channel; truTV; Turner Classic Movies; TV Land; USA Network; VH1; WE tv; YES Network.
Fee: $30.00 monthly.
Digital Basic Service
Subscribers: N.A.
Programming (via satellite): Boomerang; Cloo; CNN International; Destination America; Discovery Kids Channel; Disney XD; DIY Network; Fuse; FXM; FYI; Great American Country; History International; Investigation Discovery; ION Television; MTV2; NASA TV; Nick 2; Nick Jr.; Nicktoons; Outdoor Channel; Ovation; OWN: Oprah Winfrey Network; Oxygen; Qubo; RFD-TV; Science Channel; Sprout; TeenNick; Telemundo; Worship Network.
Fee: $10.00 monthly.
Digital Expanded Basic Service
Subscribers: N.A.
Programming (via satellite): AWE; BBC America; Bloomberg Television; CBS Sports Network; CMT; CNBC World; Cooking Channel; Crime & Investigation Network; Discovery Life Channel; ESPNews; ESPNU; FOX College Sports Central; FOX College Sports Pacific; Fox Sports 2; Hallmark Channel; Hallmark Movies & Mysteries; History; HRTV; LMN; LOGO; MTV Classic; MTV Hits; MTV Jams; NBA TV; Tennis Channel; VH1 Soul; WGN America.
Fee: $8.00 monthly.
Pay Service 1
Pay Units: N.A.
Programming (via satellite): HBO (multiplexed).
Fee: $15.00 installation; $12.00 monthly.
Digital Pay Service 1
Pay Units: N.A.
Programming (via satellite): Cinemax (multiplexed); Flix; HBO (multiplexed); Showtime (multiplexed); Starz (multiplexed); Starz Encore (multiplexed); The Movie Channel (multiplexed).
Fee: $14.99 monthly (Starz/Encore), $16.99 monthly (Showtime/TMC/Flix), $19.99 monthly (HBO/Showtime).
Video-On-Demand: No
Pay-Per-View
iN DEMAND (delivered digitally); Playboy TV (delivered digitally); Club Jenna (delivered digitally); Spice: Xcess (delivered digitally); Shorteez (delivered digitally); Hustler TV (delivered digitally); Hot Choice (delivered digitally).
Internet Service
Operational: Yes. Began: June 1, 1998.
Subscribers: 14,534.
Broadband Service: Adams CATV.
Fee: $40.00 installation; $24.99-$59.99 monthly.
Telephone Service
Digital: Operational
Subscribers: 5,701.
Fee: $29.99 monthly
Miles of Plant: 1,600.0 (coaxial); 532.0 (fiber optic). Homes passed: 30,000.
President: Douglas V.R. Adams. General Manager: Wendy Hartman. Chief Technician: John Wallis. Technical Supervisor: Gary Rixner. Collections Manager: Ed Burell. Office Manager: Becky Oakley.
Ownership: Adams CATV Inc. (MSO).

CARLISLE—Comcast Cable. Now served by HARRISBURG, PA [PA0009]. ICA: PA0047.

CARNEGIE—Comcast Cable. Now served by PITTSBURGH, PA [PA0001]. ICA: PA0045.

CARROLLTOWN—Formerly served by Adelphia Communications. Now served by Comcast Cable, BLAIRSVILLE, PA [PA0320]. ICA: PA0461.

CARROLLTOWN BOROUGH—Formerly served by Adelphia Communications. Now served by Comcast Cable, BLAIRSVILLE, PA [PA0320]. ICA: PA0078.

CASS TWP. (Schuylkill County)—J. B. Cable, PO Box 268, Minersville, PA 17954-0268. Phone: 570-544-5582. Also serves Branch Twp., Foster Twp. (Schuylkill County), Primrose & Reilly Twp. ICA: PA0395.
TV Market Ranking: Below 100 (Branch Twp., CASS TWP. (SCHUYLKILL COUNTY), Foster Twp. (Schuylkill County), Reilly Twp., Primrose). Franchise award date: N.A. Franchise expiration date: N.A. Began: January 1, 1950.
Channel capacity: 36 (not 2-way capable). Channels available but not in use: N.A.
Basic Service
Subscribers: N.A.
Programming (received off-air): KYW-TV (CBS, Decades) Philadelphia; WCAU (COZI TV, NBC) Philadelphia; WFMZ-TV (Retro TV) Allentown; WGAL (NBC, This TV) Lancaster; WNEP-TV (ABC, Antenna TV) Scranton; WOLF-TV (CW, FOX, MNT) Hazleton; WPHL-TV (Antenna TV, MNT, This TV) Philadelphia; WPMT (Antenna TV, FOX) York; WPVI-TV (ABC, Live Well Network) Philadelphia; WTXF-TV (Buzzr, FOX, Movies!) Philadelphia; WVIA-TV (PBS) Scranton; WYOU (CBS) Scranton.
Programming (via satellite): CMT; CNN; Discovery Channel; ESPN; TBS; TNT; USA Network.
Fee: $40.00 installation.
Video-On-Demand: No
Internet Service
Operational: No.
Telephone Service
None
Miles of Plant: 34.0 (coaxial); None (fiber optic).
General Manager: Thomas O'Brien. Chief Technician: Edward Goodman.
Ownership: J. B. Cable.

CASTLE SHANNON—Comcast Cable. Now served by PITTSBURGH, PA [PA0001]. ICA: PA0457.

CHICORA—Armstrong Cable Services. Now served by ZELIENOPLE, PA [PA0053]. ICA: PA0206.

CLARENDON—Clarendon TV Association, PO Box 315, Clarendon, PA 16313-0315. Phones: 814-723-6011; 814-726-3972 (Administrative office). Also serves Clarendon Heights & Stoneham. ICA: PA0240.
TV Market Ranking: Below 100 (CLARENDON, Clarendon Heights, Stoneham). Franchise award date: N.A. Franchise expiration date: N.A. Began: January 1, 1955.
Channel capacity: N.A. Channels available but not in use: N.A.
Basic Service
Subscribers: N.A.
Programming (received off-air): WFXP (FOX) Erie; WICU-TV (NBC) Erie; WIVB-TV (CBS) Buffalo; WJET-TV (ABC) Erie; WPSU-TV (PBS) Clearfield; allband FM.
Programming (via satellite): Discovery Channel; ESPN; Nickelodeon; Spike TV; TBS; TNT; USA Network; WGN America.
Fee: $22.50 installation.
Video-On-Demand: No
Internet Service
Operational: No.
Telephone Service
None
Miles of Plant: 10.0 (coaxial); None (fiber optic). Homes passed: 450.
President: Brian Mealy.
Ownership: Clarendon TV Association.

CLARION BOROUGH—Comcast Cable. Now served by OIL CITY, PA [PA0086]. ICA: PA0137.

CLAYSVILLE—Formerly served by Blue Devil Cable TV Inc. No longer in operation. ICA: PA0265.

CLEARFIELD—Atlantic Broadband, 313 1/2 Cherry St, Clearfield, PA 16803. Phones: 888-536-9600 (Customer service), 814-535-3506. Fax: 814-535-7749. E-mail: info@atlanticbb.com. Web site: http://atlanticbb.com. Also serves Bloom Twp., Boggs Twp. (Clearfield County), Bradford Twp. (Clearfield County), Curwensville (Clearfield County), Grampian, Greenwood Twp. (Clearfield County), Knox Twp. (Clearfield County), Lawrence Twp. (Clearfield County), Penn Twp. & Pike Twp. (Clearfield County). ICA: PA0084.
TV Market Ranking: 74 (Boggs Twp. (Clearfield County), Curwensville (Clearfield County), Grampian); Outside TV Markets (Bloom Twp., Bradford Twp. (Clearfield County), CLEARFIELD, Greenwood Twp. (Clearfield County), Knox Twp., Lawrence Twp. (Clearfield County), Penn Twp., Pike Twp. (Clearfield County)). Franchise award date: N.A. Franchise expiration date: N.A. Began: February 1, 1952.
Channel capacity: 67 (operating 2-way). Channels available but not in use: N.A.
Basic Service
Subscribers: 3,277.
Programming (received off-air): KDKA-TV (CBS, Decades) Pittsburgh; WATM-TV (ABC, This TV) Altoona; WJAC-TV (MeTV, NBC) Johnstown; WKBS-TV (IND) Altoona; WPSU-TV (PBS) Clearfield; WTAE-TV (ABC, This TV) Pittsburgh; WTAJ-TV (CBS) Altoona; WWCP-TV (FOX) Johnstown; 11 FMs.
Programming (via satellite): C-SPAN; C-SPAN 2; EVINE Live; EWTN Global Catholic Network; Pennsylvania Cable Network; Pop; QVC; WPIX (Antenna TV, CW, This TV) New York.
Fee: $40.00 installation; $28.33 monthly; $1.60 converter.
Expanded Basic Service 1
Subscribers: N.A.
Programming (via satellite): A&E; AMC; Animal Planet; Bravo; Cartoon Network; CMT; CNBC; CNN; Comedy Central; Discovery Channel; Disney Channel; E! HD; ESPN; ESPN2; Food Network; Fox News Channel; Fox Sports 1; Freeform; FX; Golf Channel; Hallmark Channel; HGTV; History; HLN; ION Television; Lifetime; MSNBC; MTV; National Geographic Channel; NBCSN; Nickelodeon; Nicktoons; OWN: Oprah Winfrey Network; Oxygen; Root Sports Pittsburgh; Spike TV; Syfy; TBS; The Weather Channel; TLC; TNT; Travel Channel; truTV; Turner Classic Movies; TV Land; USA Network; VH1.
Fee: $43.56 monthly.
Digital Basic Service
Subscribers: 658.
Programming (via satellite): A&E HD; Animal Planet HD; BBC America; Bloomberg Television; Boomerang; CMT; Destination

Cable Systems—Pennsylvania

America; Discovery Channel HD; Discovery Kids Channel; Disney XD; DIY Network; DMX Music; ESPN Classic; ESPN HD; ESPN2 HD; ESPNews; Fox Sports 2; FYI; HD Theater; History International; IFC; INSP; Investigation Discovery; LMN; MTV Classic; MTV Hits; MTV Jams; MTV2; NFL Network; Nick 2; Nick Jr.; Root Sports Pittsburgh; Science Channel; Starz; Starz Encore; TBS HD; TeenNick; TNT HD; Tr3s; VH1 Soul; WE tv.

Digital Pay Service 1
Pay Units: 310.
Programming (via satellite): HBO (multiplexed).
Fee: $15.95 monthly.

Digital Pay Service 2
Pay Units: 150.
Programming (via satellite): Cinemax (multiplexed).
Fee: $15.95 monthly.

Digital Pay Service 3
Pay Units: N.A.
Programming (via satellite): Flix; Showtime (multiplexed); The Movie Channel (multiplexed).
Fee: $15.95 monthly.

Video-On-Demand: No

Pay-Per-View
iN DEMAND (delivered digitally); Hot Choice (delivered digitally); Spice: Xcess (delivered digitally); Club Jenna (delivered digitally); Fresh (delivered digitally); Shorteez (delivered digitally); Playboy TV (delivered digitally).

Internet Service
Operational: Yes.
Broadband Service: Atlantic Broadband High-Speed Internet.
Fee: $24.95 monthly.

Telephone Service
Digital: Operational
Fee: $44.95-$57.95 monthly
Miles of Plant: 31,461.0 (coaxial); 8,575.0 (fiber optic). Homes passed: 11,187.
Senior Vice President & General Counsel: Leslie Brown. Vice President: David Dane. General Manager: Mike Papasergi. Technical Operations Director: Charles Serchilla. Marketing & Customer Service Director: Dara Leslie. Marketing Manager: Natalie Kurchak.
Ownership: Atlantic Broadband (MSO).

CLINTONVILLE—Armstrong Cable Services. Now served by ZELIENOPLE, PA [PA0053]. ICA: PA0325.

COALPORT—Comcast Cable. Now served by BLAIRSVILLE, PA [PA0320]. ICA: PA0158.

COATESVILLE—Comcast Cable. Now served by PHILADELPHIA, PA [PA0005]. ICA: PA0014.

COGAN STATION—Zito Media, 102 S Main St, PO Box 665, Coudersport, PA 16915. Phones: 814-260-9055; 800-365-6988. E-mail: info@zitomedia.com. Web Site: http://www.zitomedia.com. Also serves Hepburnville, Perryville, Quiggleville & Trout Run. ICA: PA0207.
TV Market Ranking: Below 100 (COGAN STATION, Hepburnville, Perryville, Quiggleville, Trout Run). Franchise award date: N.A. Franchise expiration date: N.A. Began: June 1, 1953.
Channel capacity: N.A. Channels available but not in use: N.A.

Basic Service
Subscribers: 534.
Programming (received off-air): WBRE-TV (NBC) Wilkes-Barre; WNEP-TV (ABC, Antenna TV) Scranton; WSWB (CW, MeTV) Scranton; WVIA-TV (PBS) Scranton; WYOU (CBS) Scranton; allband FM.
Programming (via satellite): A&E; Animal Planet; CNBC; CNN; Comedy Central; CTV Inc.; Discovery Channel; ESPN; ESPN2; Fox News Channel; Fox Sports 1; Freeform; FX; Hallmark Channel; History; HLN; Lifetime; MTV; Nickelodeon; Outdoor Channel; QVC; Spike TV; Syfy; TBS; The Weather Channel; TLC; TNT; Trinity Broadcasting Network (TBN); TV Land; USA Network; VH1; WGN America.
Fee: $50.00 installation; $25.23 monthly.

Pay Service 1
Pay Units: 300.
Programming (via satellite): Showtime.
Fee: $15.00 installation; $11.00 monthly.

Video-On-Demand: No

Internet Service
Operational: No.

Telephone Service
None
Miles of Plant: 35.0 (coaxial); 70.0 (fiber optic).
President: James Rigas.
Ownership: Zito Media (MSO).

CONNELLSVILLE—Armstrong Cable Services. Now served by ZELIENOPLE, PA [PA0053]. ICA: PA0046.

COOPERSTOWN—Formerly served by Cebridge Connections. Now served by Armstrong Cable Services, ZELIENOPLE, PA [PA0053]. ICA: PA0214.

CORAOPOLIS—Comcast Cable. Now served by PITTSBURGH, PA [PA0001]. ICA: PA0061.

CORRY—Time Warner Cable. Now served by CLEVELAND (formerly Cleveland Heights), OH [OH0006]. ICA: PA0113.

COUDERSPORT—Zito Media, 102 S Main St, PO Box 665, Coudersport, PA 16915. Phones: 814-260-9055; 800-365-6988. Fax: 814-260-9580. E-mail: info@zitomedia.com. Web Site: http://www.zitomedia.com. Also serves Annin Twp., Austin Borough, Emporium, Eulalia Twp., Genesee Twp., Gibson Twp., Hebron Twp., Liberty Twp. (McKean County), Lumber Twp. (Cameron County), Port Allegany, Portage Twp. (Potter Twp.), Roulette Twp., Shippen, Shippen Twp. (Cameron County) & Sweden Valley. ICA: PA0121.
TV Market Ranking: Outside TV Markets (Annin Twp., Austin Borough, COUDERSPORT, Emporium, Eulalia Twp., Genesee Twp., Gibson Twp., Hebron Twp., Liberty Twp. (McKean County), Lumber Twp. (Cameron County), Port Allegany, Portage Twp. (Potter Twp.), Roulette Twp., Shippen, Shippen Twp. (Cameron County)). Franchise award date: January 1, 1952. Franchise expiration date: N.A. Began: March 1, 1953.
Channel capacity: 70 (operating 2-way). Channels available but not in use: N.A.

Basic Service
Subscribers: 3,356.
Programming (received off-air): WGRZ (Antenna TV, NBC, WeatherNation) Buffalo; WIVB-TV (CBS) Buffalo; WJAC-TV (MeTV, NBC) Johnstown; WKBW-TV (ABC, Escape) Buffalo; WNED-TV (PBS) Buffalo; WPSU-TV (PBS) Clearfield; WTAJ-TV (CBS) Altoona; WWCP-TV (FOX) Johnstown.
Programming (via satellite): Pop; WGN America; WPIX (Antenna TV, CW, This TV) New York.
Fee: $49.95 installation; $20.55 monthly; $4.50 converter.

Expanded Basic Service 1
Subscribers: N.A.
Programming (via satellite): A&E; AMC; Animal Planet; Cartoon Network; CMT; CNBC; CNN; Comedy Central; C-SPAN; C-SPAN 2; Discovery Channel; Disney Channel; E! HD; ESPN; ESPN Classic; ESPN2; EWTN Global Catholic Network; Food Network; Fox News Channel; Fox Sports 1; Freeform; FX; Hallmark Channel; HGTV; History; HLN; INSP; Lifetime; MSG; MSNBC; MTV; NFL Network; Nickelodeon; Outdoor Channel; Oxygen; Pennsylvania Cable Network; QVC; Root Sports Pittsburgh; Spike TV; Syfy; TBS; The Weather Channel; TLC; TNT; Travel Channel; Trinity Broadcasting Network (TBN); truTV; Turner Classic Movies; TV Land; USA Network; VH1.
Fee: $31.90 monthly.

Digital Basic Service
Subscribers: N.A.
Programming (via satellite): A&E HD; BBC America; Bio HD; Bloomberg Television; Boomerang; Cartoon Network HD; CNN HD; Destination America; Discovery Channel HD; Discovery Kids Channel; Discovery Life Channel; Disney Channel HD; Disney XD; ESPN HD; ESPN2 HD; ESPNews; ESPNews HD; Food Network HD; Fox Sports 1; Freeform HD; FSN HD; FX HD; FXM; Golf Channel; Great American Country; GSN; HD Theater; HGTV HD; HRTV; INSP; Investigation Discovery; Lifetime HD; Lifetime Movie Network HD; LMN; MC; MTV Classic; MTV Hits; MTV Jams; MTV2; NFL Network HD; NHL Network; NHL Network HD; Nick 2; Nick Jr.; Nicktoons; Outdoor Channel 2 HD; OWN: Oprah Winfrey Network; RFD-TV; Science Channel; Science HD; TBS HD; TeenNick; The Word Network; TLC HD; TNT HD; Trinity Broadcasting Network (TBN); VH1 Country; VH1 Soul; WAM! America's Kidz Network; WE tv.
Fee: $11.95 monthly.

Digital Expanded Basic Service
Subscribers: N.A.
Programming (via satellite): DIY Network; Flix; FSN Digital Atlantic; FSN Digital Central; FSN Digital Pacific; FYI; History International; IFC; NBCSN; Outdoor Channel; Sundance TV.
Fee: $10.00 monthly.

Digital Pay Service 1
Pay Units: N.A.
Programming (via satellite): Cinemax (multiplexed); Cinemax HD; Flix; HBO (multiplexed); HBO HD; Showtime (multiplexed); Showtime HD; Starz (multiplexed); Starz Encore (multiplexed); Starz HD; The Movie Channel (multiplexed).
Fee: $8.00 monthly (Cinemax or Starz/Encore), $10.00 monthly (HBO or Showtime/TMC/Flix).

Video-On-Demand: Yes

Pay-Per-View
iN DEMAND (delivered digitally); NHL Center Ice (delivered digitally); MLB Extra Innings (delivered digitally).

Internet Service
Operational: Yes.
Subscribers: 3,638.
Fee: $42.95 monthly.

Telephone Service
Digital: Operational
Subscribers: 1,924.
Fee: $35.00 monthly

Miles of Plant: 100.0 (coaxial); 20.0 (fiber optic). Homes passed: 8,000.
President: James Rigas.
Ownership: Zito Media.

CRESSON—Comcast Cable. Now served by BLAIRSVILLE, PA [PA0320]. ICA: PA0118.

CROSBY—Formerly served by GMP-County Cable. No longer in operation. ICA: PA0301.

CURTIN TWP.—Formerly served by Adelphia Communications. Now served by Comcast Cable, HARRISBURG, PA [PA0009]. ICA: PA0215.

DALLAS—Comcast Cable. Now served by HARRISBURG, PA [PA0009]. ICA: PA0087.

DALLAS CORRECTIONAL INSTITUTE—Formerly served by Suddenlink Communications. No longer in operation. ICA: PA0200.

DANVILLE—CATV Service Inc, 115 Mill St, PO Box 198, Danville, PA 17821-0198. Phones: 570-275-3101 (Customer service); 570-275-8410. Fax: 570-275-3888. E-mail: catvserv@ptd.net. Also serves East Buffalo Twp., Kelly Twp. (Union County), Lewisburg, Liberty Twp. (Montour County), Limestone Twp. (Montour County), Mahoning Twp. (Montour County), Mayberry Twp. (Montour County), McEwensville, Milton, Montour County, Riverside (Northumberland County), Turbot Twp., Turbotville, Valley Twp. (Montour County), Washingtonville, Watsontown, West Chillisquaque Twp. (portions), West Hemlock Twp. & White Deer Twp. ICA: PA0054.
TV Market Ranking: Below 100 (DANVILLE, East Buffalo Twp., Kelly Twp. (Union County), Lewisburg, Liberty Twp. (Montour County), Limestone Twp. (Montour County), Mahoning Twp. (Montour County), Mayberry Twp. (Montour County), McEwensville, Milton, Montour County, Riverside (Northumberland County), Turbot Twp., Turbotville, Valley Twp. (Montour County), Washingtonville, Watsontown, West Chillisquaque Twp. (portions), West Hemlock Twp., White Deer Twp.). Franchise award date: N.A. Franchise expiration date: N.A. Began: May 1, 1953.
Channel capacity: 24 (operating 2-way). Channels available but not in use: N.A.

Basic Service
Subscribers: 12,492.
Programming (received off-air): WHTM-TV (ABC, Retro TV) Harrisburg; WITF-TV (PBS) Harrisburg; WNEP-TV (ABC, Antenna TV) Scranton; WSWB (CW, MeTV) Scranton; WVIA-TV (PBS) Scranton; WYOU (CBS) Scranton; allband FM.
Programming (via microwave): WPHL-TV (Antenna TV, MNT, This TV) Philadelphia; WPIX (Antenna TV, CW, This TV) New York; WTXF-TV (Buzzr, FOX, Movies!) Philadelphia.
Programming (via satellite): CNBC; EWTN Global Catholic Network; Freeform; TBS.
Fee: $50.00 installation; $19.95 monthly.

Expanded Basic Service 1
Subscribers: N.A.
Programming (via satellite): A&E; AMC; CNN; C-SPAN; Discovery Channel; ESPN; Food Network; FX; HLN; Lifetime; MTV; Nickelodeon; QVC; Spike TV; The Weather Channel; TNT; USA Network; VH1.
Fee: $41.50 monthly.

Digital Basic Service
Subscribers: N.A.
Fee: $11.95 monthly.

2017 Edition D-655

Pennsylvania—Cable Systems

CABLE & TV STATION COVERAGE
Atlas 2017
The perfect companion to the Television & Cable Factbook
To order call 800-771-9202 or visit www.warren-news.com

Pay Service 1
Pay Units: N.A.
Programming (via satellite): Cinemax (multiplexed); HBO (multiplexed).
Fee: $35.00 installation; $10.00 monthly (Cinemax), $11.00 monthly (HBO).
Video-On-Demand: No
Pay-Per-View
iN DEMAND (delivered digitally), Addressable: No.
Internet Service
Operational: Yes. Began: December 31, 2001.
Subscribers: 8,035.
Broadband Service: ProLog Express.
Fee: $31.95-$59.95 monthly; $9.95 modem lease.
Telephone Service
Digital: Operational
Subscribers: 2,618.
Fee: $44.95 monthly
Miles of Plant: 710.0 (coaxial); 293.0 (fiber optic). Homes passed: 25,648.
General Manager: Sam Haulman. Chief Technician: Matt Kujat. Marketing & Program Director: Dave Skelton.
Ownership: CATV Service Inc.

DARLINGTON TWP. (Beaver County)—Comcast Cable. Now served by PITTSBURGH, PA [PA0001]. ICA: PA0144.

DERRY/DECATUR—Atlantic Broadband, 120 Southmont Blvd, Johnstown, PA 15905. Phones: 888-536-9600 (Customer service); 814-535-3506. Fax: 814-535-7749. E-mail: info@atlanticbb.com. Web Site: http://atlanticbb.com. Also serves Decatur & Lewistown. ICA: PA0175.
TV Market Ranking: Outside TV Markets (Lewistown). Franchise award date: January 1, 1972. Franchise expiration date: N.A. Began: January 1, 1956.
Channel capacity: N.A. Channels available but not in use: N.A.
Basic Service
Subscribers: 271.
Programming (received off-air): WGAL (NBC, This TV) Lancaster; WHP-TV (CBS, MNT) Harrisburg; WHTM-TV (ABC, Retro TV) Harrisburg; WITF-TV (PBS) Harrisburg; WPIX (Antenna TV, CW, This TV) New York; WPMT (Antenna TV, FOX) York; WTAJ-TV (CBS) Altoona; WVIA-TV (PBS) Scranton; WXBU (CW) Lancaster; allband FM.
Programming (via satellite): C-SPAN; QVC.
Fee: $40.00 installation; $33.84 monthly.
Expanded Basic Service 1
Subscribers: N.A.
Programming (via satellite): A&E; AMC; Animal Planet; Bravo; Cartoon Network; CMT; CNN; Comedy Central; Discovery Channel; Disney Channel; E! HD; ESPN; ESPN2; Food Network; Fox News Channel; Fox Sports 1; Freeform; FX; Hallmark Channel; HGTV; History; HLN; INSP; Lifetime; MSNBC; MTV; National Geographic Channel; Nickelodeon; OWN: Oprah Winfrey Network; Oxygen; Root Sports Pittsburgh; Spike TV; Syfy; TBS; The Weather Channel; TLC; TNT; Travel Channel; truTV; TV Land; USA Network; VH1.
Fee: $58.60 installation; $38.50 monthly.
Digital Basic Service
Subscribers: N.A.
Programming (via satellite): BBC America; Bloomberg Television; CMT; Cooking Channel; Destination America; Discovery Kids Channel; Discovery Life Channel; Disney XD; DMX Music; ESPN Classic; ESPNews; Fox Sports 1; Fuse; FYI; Golf Channel; GSN; History International; IFC; Investigation Discovery; LMN; MTV Classic; MTV2; Nick Jr.; Nicktoons; Outdoor Channel; Science Channel; Starz (multiplexed); Starz Encore (multiplexed); TeenNick; Trinity Broadcasting Network (TBN).
Fee: $21.90 monthly.
Digital Pay Service 1
Pay Units: N.A.
Programming (via satellite): Cinemax (multiplexed); HBO (multiplexed); Showtime (multiplexed); The Movie Channel (multiplexed).
Video-On-Demand: No
Pay-Per-View
iN DEMAND (delivered digitally).
Internet Service
Operational: No.
Telephone Service
None
Miles of Plant: 50.0 (coaxial); None (fiber optic). Homes passed: 1,610.
Chief Financial Officer: Patrick Bratton. Senior Vice President & General Counsel: Leslie Brown. Vice President: David Dane. General Manager: Mike Papasergi. Technical Operations Director: Charles Sorchilla. Marketing & Customer Service Director: Dara Leslie. Marketing Manager: Natalie Kurchak.
Ownership: Atlantic Broadband (MSO).

DILLSBURG—Formerly served by Adelphia Communications. Now served by Comcast Cable, HARRISBURG, PA [PA0009]. ICA: PA0326.

DOYLESBURG—Valley Cable Systems, 21700 Path Valley Rd, PO Box 1078, Doylesburg, PA 17219. Phone: 717-349-7717. Also serves Blairs Mills, Fannett Twp. (Franklin County) & Tell Twp. ICA: PA0286.
TV Market Ranking: 74 (Fannett Twp. (Franklin County), Tell Twp.); Outside TV Markets (Blairs Mills, DOYLESBURG, Fannett Twp. (Franklin County)). Franchise award date: January 1, 1982. Franchise expiration date: N.A. Began: February 1, 1981.
Channel capacity: N.A. Channels available but not in use: N.A.
Basic Service
Subscribers: N.A.
Programming (received off-air): WATM-TV (ABC, This TV) Altoona; WGAL (NBC, This TV) Lancaster; WHAG-TV (IND) Hagerstown; WJAC-TV (MeTV, NBC) Johnstown; WJAL (IND) Hagerstown; WJZ-TV (CBS, Decades) Baltimore; WMPB (PBS) Baltimore; WPMT (Antenna TV, FOX) York; WTAJ-TV (CBS) Altoona; WTTG (Buzzr, FOX) Washington.
Programming (via satellite): CMT; C-SPAN; Discovery Channel; ESPN; Freeform; QVC; Syfy; TBS; TNT; Trinity Broadcasting Network (TBN).
Fee: $40.00 installation.
Internet Service
Operational: No.
Miles of Plant: 20.0 (coaxial); None (fiber optic). Homes passed: 125.
General Manager & Chief Technician: Barry L. Kepner.
Ownership: Valley Cable Systems (MSO).

DU BOIS—Formerly served by Adelphia Communications. Now served by Comcast Cable, PUNXSUTAWNEY, PA [PA0397]. ICA: PA0093.

DUNCANNON—Blue Ridge Communications. Now served by NEWBERRY TWP., PA [PA0105]. ICA: PA0117.

DUNMORE BOROUGH—Comcast Cable. Now served by HARRISBURG, PA [PA0009]. ICA: PA0022.

DUSHORE—Blue Ridge Communications. Now served by TUNKHANNOCK, PA [PA0367]. ICA: PA0327.

EAST BUFFALO TWP.—Formerly served by D&E Communications/Windstream. IPTV service no longer in operation. ICA: PA5291.

EAST CONEMAUGH—Formerly served by Adelphia Communications. Now served by Comcast Cable, BLAIRSVILLE, PA [PA0320]. ICA: PA0217.

EAST SMITHFIELD—North Penn Video, 4145 Rt 549, Mansfield, PA 16933-9238. Phones: 570-596-6737; 570-549-6737. Fax: 570-549-2500. E-mail: nptinfo@npacc.net. Web Site: http://www.northpenntelephone.com. Also serves Columbia Twp. (Bradford Count), Jackson Twp. (Butler County), Roseville, Rutland Twp., South Creek Twp., Sullivan Twp., Troy Twp., Ulster Twp. & Wells Twp. ICA: PA0280.
TV Market Ranking: 10 (Jackson Twp. (Butler County)); Below 100 (Columbia Twp. (Bradford Count), EAST SMITHFIELD, Roseville, Rutland Twp., South Creek Twp., Sullivan Twp., Troy Twp., Ulster Twp., Wells Twp.). Franchise award date: N.A. Franchise expiration date: N.A. Began: October 15, 1965.
Channel capacity: N.A. Channels available but not in use: N.A.
Basic Service
Subscribers: 100.
Programming (received off-air): WBNG-TV (CBS, CW) Binghamton; WBRE-TV (NBC) Wilkes-Barre; WENY-TV (ABC, CW) Elmira; WETM-TV (IND, NBC) Elmira; WICZ-TV (FOX) Binghamton; WNEP-TV (ABC, Antenna TV) Scranton; WSKG-TV (PBS) Binghamton; WSWB (CW, MeTV) Scranton; WVIA-TV (PBS) Scranton.
Programming (via satellite): C-SPAN; ION Television; Pennsylvania Cable Network; QVC.
Fee: $25.00 installation; $14.95 monthly.
Expanded Basic Service 1
Subscribers: N.A.
Programming (via satellite): A&E; AMC; Animal Planet; BTN; Cartoon Network; CMT; CNBC; CNN; Comedy Central; Discovery Channel; Disney Channel; E! HD; ESPN; ESPN2; EWTN Global Catholic Network; Food Network; Fox News Channel; Fox Sports 1; Freeform; FX; Great American Country; GSN; Hallmark Channel; HGTV; History; HLN; Lifetime; MSNBC; MTV; National Geographic Channel; Nickelodeon; Outdoor Channel; RFD-TV; Root Sports Pittsburgh; Science Channel; Spike TV; Syfy; TBS; The Weather Channel; TLC; TNT; Travel Channel; Trinity Broadcasting Network (TBN); truTV; Turner Classic Movies; TV Land; USA Network; VH1; WGN America; YES Network.
Fee: $23.00 monthly.
Internet Service
Operational: No, DSL.
Telephone Service
Analog: Operational
Miles of Plant: 8.0 (coaxial); None (fiber optic).
President: Robert Wagner. Vice President & General Manager: Marshall L. McClure. Vice President: Pete McClure. Engineer: Frank Pilling.
Ownership: Community Cable Corp. of Pennsylvania.

EAST WATERFORD—Formerly served by Valley Cable Systems. No longer in operation. ICA: PA0290.

EASTON—Service Electric Cable TV & Communications. Now served by ALLENTOWN, PA [PA0006]. ICA: PA0035.

EASTVILLE—Formerly served by Eastville TV Cable. No longer in operation. ICA: PA0306.

EAU CLAIRE—Formerly served by Cebridge Connections. Now served by Armstrong Cable Services. ZELIENOPLE, PA [PA0053]. ICA: PA0269.

EDINBORO—Coaxial Cable TV Corp, 105 Walker Dr, Edinboro, PA 16412-2237. Phones: 814-734-1424; 800-684-1681. Fax: 814-734-8898. E-mail: info@coaxpa.com. Web Site: http://www.coaxialcabletv.com. Also serves Cambridge Springs, Cambridge Twp. (Crawford County), Franklin Twp. (Erie County), Leboeuf Twp., Richmond Twp. (Crawford County), Rockdale Twp. (Crawford County), Townville, Venango, Venango Twp. (Crawford County), Washington Twp. (Erie County) & Woodcock Borough. ICA: PA0115.
TV Market Ranking: Below 100 (Cambridge Springs, Cambridge Twp. (Crawford County), EDINBORO, Franklin Twp. (Erie County), Leboeuf Twp., Richmond Twp. (Crawford County), Rockdale Twp. (Crawford County), Townville, Venango, Venango Twp. (Crawford County), Washington Twp. (Erie County), Woodcock Borough). Franchise award date: July 1, 1967. Franchise expiration date: N.A. Began: July 1, 1967.
Channel capacity: N.A. Channels available but not in use: N.A.
Digital Basic Service
Subscribers: 136.
Programming (via satellite): Bloomberg Television; Bravo; Discovery Digital Networks; DMX Music; ESPN Classic; Fox Sports 1; FYI; History International; LMN; MTV Classic; MTV2; National Geographic Channel; TeenNick; VH1 Country; WE tv.
Fee: $39.95 monthly.
Digital Pay Service 1
Pay Units: N.A.
Programming (via satellite): Cinemax (multiplexed); Flix; FXM; HBO (multiplexed); Showtime (multiplexed); Starz (multiplexed); Starz Encore (multiplexed); The Movie Channel (multiplexed).

Fee: $11.95 monthly (each).
Video-On-Demand: No
Pay-Per-View
iN DEMAND (delivered digitally); Fresh (delivered digitally).
Internet Service
Operational: Yes.
Subscribers: 300.
Fee: free installation; $25.95-$45.95 monthly.
Telephone Service
Digital: Operational
Fee: $34.95 monthly
Miles of Plant: 200.0 (coaxial); 60.0 (fiber optic). Homes passed: 5,400.
Chief Administrative Officer: Aaron Phillips. General Manager: Chris Lovell.
Ownership: Coaxial Cable TV Corp.

ELDERTON BOROUGH—Comcast Cable. Now served by BLAIRSVILLE, PA [PA0320]. ICA: PA0229.

ELDRED TWP.—Herr Cable Co, RR 4, Box 108, Montoursville, PA 17754. Phone: 570-435-2780. Also serves Barbours, Fairfield Twp. (Lycoming County), Hillsgrove, Plunketts Creek Twp. & Warrensville. ICA: PA0389.
TV Market Ranking: Below 100 (Barbours, ELDRED TWP., Fairfield Twp. (Lycoming County), Hillsgrove).
Channel capacity: N.A. Channels available but not in use: N.A.
Basic Service
Subscribers: 637.
Programming (received off-air): WBRE-TV (NBC) Wilkes-Barre; WNEP-TV (ABC, Antenna TV) Scranton; WOLF-TV (CW, FOX, MNT) Hazleton; WQMY (MNT) Williamsport; WSWB (CW, MeTV) Scranton; WVIA-TV (PBS) Scranton; WYOU (CBS) Scranton.
Programming (via satellite): A&E; AMC; Animal Planet; Bravo; CNBC; CNN; C-SPAN; Discovery Channel; Discovery Life Channel; Disney Channel; ESPN; ESPN2; EVINE Live; EWTN Global Catholic Network; Food Network; Fox News Channel; Fox Sports 1; Freeform; FX; Great American Country; Hallmark Channel; HGTV; History; HLN; INSP; Lifetime; National Geographic Channel; Outdoor Channel; QVC; RFD-TV; Syfy; TBS; The Weather Channel; TLC; TNT; Turner Classic Movies; TV Land; USA Network.
Fee: $30.00 monthly.
Pay Service 1
Pay Units: N.A.
Programming (via satellite): HBO (multiplexed).
Internet Service
Operational: No.
Telephone Service
None
Miles of Plant: 100.0 (coaxial); None (fiber optic). Homes passed: 1,750.
General Manager & Chief Technician: Al Herr.
Ownership: Herr Cable Co.

ELIZABETHTOWN—Comcast Cable. Now served by HARRISBURG, PA [PA0009]. ICA: PA0068.

ELKLAND—Time Warner Cable. Now served by DEWITT, NY [NY0013]. ICA: PA0160.

EMMAUS—Service Electric Cable TV & Communications. Now served by ALLENTOWN, PA [PA0006]. ICA: PA0081.

EPHRATA—Blue Ridge Communications, 613 3rd St, PO Box 215, Palmerton, PA 18071-0215. Phones: 800-222-5377; 610-826-2552; 610-826-2551; 717-733-4111; 717-484-2266 (Customer service). Web Site: http://www.brctv.com. Also serves Adamstown, Akron, Brecknock Twp. (Lancaster County), Caernarvon Twp. (Lancaster County), Clay Twp. (Lancaster County), Denver, Earl Twp. (Lancaster County), East Cocalico Twp., East Earl Twp. (portions), Elizabeth Twp. (Lancaster County), Ephrata Twp. (Lancaster County), Lititz, Manheim, Penn Twp. (Lancaster County), Rapho Twp. (Lancaster County), South Heidelberg Twp. (Berks County), Spring Twp. (Berks County), Terre Hill, Warwick Twp. (Lancaster County), West Cocalico Twp. & West Earl Twp. (northern portion). ICA: PA0031.
TV Market Ranking: 57 (Adamstown, Akron, Brecknock Twp. (Lancaster County), Caernarvon Twp. (Lancaster County), Clay Twp. (Lancaster County), Denver, Earl Twp. (Lancaster County), East Cocalico Twp., East Earl Twp. (portions), Elizabeth Twp. (Lancaster County), EPHRATA, Ephrata Twp. (Lancaster County), Lititz, Manheim, Penn Twp. (Lancaster County), Rapho Twp. (Lancaster County), South Heidelberg Twp. (Berks County), Spring Twp. (Berks County), Terre Hill, Warwick Twp. (Lancaster County), West Cocalico Twp., West Earl Twp. (northern portion). Franchise award date: N.A. Franchise expiration date: N.A. Began: November 11, 1965.
Channel capacity: 80 (operating 2-way). Channels available but not in use: N.A.
Basic Service
Subscribers: 27,702. Commercial subscribers: 674.
Programming (received off-air): KYW-TV (CBS, Decades) Philadelphia; WCAU (COZI TV, NBC) Philadelphia; WGAL (NBC, This TV) Lancaster; WGCB-TV (MeTV) Red Lion; WHP-TV (CBS, MNT) Harrisburg; WHTM-TV (ABC, Retro TV) Harrisburg; WITF-TV (PBS) Harrisburg; WPHL-TV (Antenna TV, MNT, This TV) Philadelphia; WPMT (Antenna TV, FOX) York; WPSG (CW) Philadelphia; WPVI-TV (ABC, Live Well Network) Philadelphia; WTXF-TV (Buzzr, FOX, Movies!) Philadelphia; WXBU (CW) Lancaster; allband FM.
Programming (via satellite): C-SPAN; C-SPAN 2; WGN America.
Fee: $49.95 installation; $27.09 monthly.
Expanded Basic Service 1
Subscribers: N.A.
Programming (via satellite): A&E; AMC; Animal Planet; Bravo; Cartoon Network; CMT; CNBC; CNN; Comcast SportsNet Mid-Atlantic; Comcast SportsNet Philadelphia; Comedy Central; Discovery Channel; Disney Channel; E! HD; ESPN; ESPN Classic; ESPN2; EWTN Global Catholic Network; Food Network; Fox News Channel; Fox Sports 1; Freeform; FX; Golf Channel; GSN; Hallmark Channel; HGTV; History; HLN; INSP; ION Television; Lifetime; LMN; MSNBC; MTV; NBCSN; Nickelodeon; OWN: Oprah Winfrey Network; Pennsylvania Cable Network; Praise Television; QVC; Spike TV; Syfy; TBS; The Weather Channel; TLC; TNT; Travel Channel; Trinity Broadcasting Network (TBN); truTV; Turner Classic Movies; TV Land; USA Network; VH1; WE tv.
Fee: $31.24 monthly.
Digital Basic Service
Subscribers: N.A.
Programming (via satellite): Discovery Digital Networks; Disney XD; FSN Digital Atlantic; FSN Digital Central; FSN Digital Pacific; FXM; HRTV; MC; National Geographic Channel; Nick 2; Nick Jr.; Nicktoons; Outdoor Channel; TeenNick.
Fee: $35.00 installation; $9.95 monthly.
Digital Expanded Basic Service
Subscribers: N.A.
Programming (via satellite): BBC America; Bloomberg Television; Boomerang; Cooking Channel; DIY Network; FYI; History International; LWS Local Weather Station.
Fee: $5.00 monthly.
Digital Pay Service 1
Pay Units: N.A.
Programming (via satellite): Cinemax (multiplexed); Flix; HBO (multiplexed); Showtime (multiplexed); Starz (multiplexed); Starz Encore (multiplexed); Sundance TV; The Movie Channel (multiplexed).
Fee: $12.50 monthly (Cinemax or Showtime/Flix/Sundance/TMC), $12.95 monthly (Starz/Encore), $13.50 monthly (HBO).
Video-On-Demand: Yes
Pay-Per-View
iN DEMAND; iN DEMAND (delivered digitally); Sports PPV (delivered digitally); adult PPV (delivered digitally).
Internet Service
Operational: Yes.
Subscribers: 19,528.
Broadband Service: ProLog Express.
Fee: $50.00 installation; $36.95 monthly; $10.00 modem lease; $59.95 modem purchase.
Telephone Service
Digital: Operational
Subscribers: 3,685.
Miles of Plant: 1,570.0 (coaxial); 594.0 (fiber optic). Homes passed: 42,697.
President: David Masenheimer. Vice President, Operations: Richard Semmel. General Manager: Mark Masonheimer. Chief Technician: Randy Semmel.
Ownership: Pencor Services Inc. (MSO).

ERIE—Time Warner Cable, 3627 Zimmerman Rd, Erie, PA 16510-2642. Phones: 330-633-9203 (Akron office); 814-898-1656. Fax: 814-456-5162. Web Site: http://www.timewarnercable.com. ICA: PA0019.
TV Market Ranking: Below 100 (ERIE). Franchise award date: N.A. Franchise expiration date: N.A. Began: December 14, 1981.
Channel capacity: N.A. Channels available but not in use: N.A.
Basic Service
Subscribers: 18,857.
Programming (received off-air): WFXP (FOX) Erie; WICU-TV (NBC) Erie; WJET-TV (ABC) Erie; WQLN (PBS) Erie; WSEE-TV (CBS, CW) Erie; allband FM.
Programming (via satellite): C-SPAN; C-SPAN 2; EVINE Live; QVC; WGN America.
Fee: $29.95 installation; $21.25 monthly; $.57 converter.
Expanded Basic Service 1
Subscribers: N.A.
Programming (via satellite): A&E; AMC; Animal Planet; BET; Bravo; Cartoon Network; CMT; CNBC; CNN; Comedy Central; Discovery Channel; Discovery Life Channel; Disney Channel; E! HD; ESPN; ESPN Classic; ESPN2; EWTN Global Catholic Network; Food Network; Fox News Channel; FOX Sports Ohio/Sports Time Ohio; Freeform; FX; Golf Channel; Great American Country; Hallmark Channel; HGTV; History; HLN; INSP; ION Television; Lifetime; LMN; MSNBC; MTV; MTV2; NBCSN; Nickelodeon; OWN: Oprah Winfrey Network; Oxygen; Pop; Root Sports Pittsburgh; Spike TV; Syfy; TBS; The Weather Channel; TLC; TNT; Travel Channel; Trinity Broadcasting Network (TBN); truTV; Turner Classic Movies; TV Land; Univision Studios; USA Network; VH1; WE tv.
Fee: $35.89 monthly.
Digital Basic Service
Subscribers: N.A.
Programming (via satellite): AXS TV; BBC America; Bloomberg Television; Boomerang; CBS Sports Network; CMT; CNN International; Cooking Channel; C-SPAN 3; Daystar TV Network; Discovery Kids Channel; Disney Channel; Disney XD; DIY Network; ESPN; ESPNews; FOX College Sports Central; FOX College Sports Pacific; Fox Sports 1; Fox Sports 2; Fuse; FXM; FYI; GSN; HD Theater; History International; HITS (Headend In The Sky); IFC; MC; MTV2; National Geographic Channel; NBA TV; Nick Jr.; Nicktoons; Outdoor Channel; TeenNick; Tennis Channel; The Word Network; TNT; TVG Network; VH1.
Fee: $15.51 monthly.
Digital Pay Service 1
Pay Units: N.A.
Programming (via satellite): ART America; Cinemax (multiplexed); Deutsche Welle TV; HBO (multiplexed); RAI Italia; Showtime (multiplexed); Starz (multiplexed); Starz Encore (multiplexed); Sundance TV; The Movie Channel (multiplexed); TV Asia; Zee TV.
Fee: $12.99 monthly (each).
Video-On-Demand: Yes
Pay-Per-View
Hot Choice; iN DEMAND; Playboy TV; Spice.
Internet Service
Operational: Yes. Began: September 1, 2002.
Broadband Service: Road Runner.
Fee: $99.00 installation; $44.95 monthly.
Telephone Service
Digital: Operational
Fee: $44.95 monthly
Miles of Plant: 269.0 (coaxial); None (fiber optic). Homes passed: 49,000.
President: Stephen Fry. Area Vice President: Rick Whaley. Vice President, Engineering: Al Costanzi. Vice President, Marketing: Patrick Burke. Vice President, Public Affairs: William Jasso. General Manager: Brian Frederick. Office Manager: Dana Bachman.
Ownership: Time Warner Cable (MSO).

FANNETTSBURG—Formerly served by Fannettsburg Cable TV Co. No longer in operation. ICA: PA0331.

Pennsylvania—Cable Systems

FAWN GROVE—Formerly served by Armstrong Cable Services. No longer in operation. ICA: PA0152.

FOREST CITY—Adams Cable Service. Now served by CARBONDALE TWP. (Lackawanna County), PA [PA0067]. ICA: PA0179.

FORT INDIANTOWN GAP—Gap Cable TV Inc, 1 Washington Rd, Annville, PA 17003. Phones: 218-687-2400; 717-865-0511. Also serves East Hanover Twp. (Lebanon County) & Union Twp. (Lebanon County). ICA: PA0332.

TV Market Ranking: 57 (East Hanover Twp. (Lebanon County), FORT INDIANTOWN GAP, Union Twp. (Lebanon County)). Franchise award date: December 5, 1991. Franchise expiration date: N.A. Began: August 15, 1992.

Channel capacity: N.A. Channels available but not in use: N.A.

Basic Service
Subscribers: N.A.
Programming (received off-air): WGAL (NBC, This TV) Lancaster; WGCB-TV (MeTV) Red Lion; WHP-TV (CBS, MNT) Harrisburg; WHTM-TV (ABC, Retro TV) Harrisburg; WITF-TV (PBS) Harrisburg; WPMT (Antenna TV, FOX) York; WXBU (CW) Lancaster.
Programming (via satellite): A&E; AMC; BET; Cartoon Network; CNBC; CNN; Comedy Central; C-SPAN; C-SPAN 2; Discovery Channel; Disney Channel; ESPN; ESPN2; Freeform; HLN; Lifetime; MTV; Nickelodeon; Spike TV; Syfy; TBS; The Weather Channel; TLC; TNT; USA Network; VH1; WGN America; WPIX (Antenna TV, CW, This TV) New York.
Fee: $30.00 installation; $3.40 converter.

Pay Service 1
Pay Units: N.A.
Programming (via satellite): Cinemax; HBO; Showtime; The Movie Channel.
Fee: $11.00 monthly (each).

Video-On-Demand: No

Internet Service
Operational: Yes, DSL.
Broadband Service: In-house.
Fee: $35.00 installation; $46.40 monthly.

Telephone Service
None

Miles of Plant: 18.0 (coaxial); None (fiber optic).
General Manager & Chief Technician: George Bryce.
Ownership: Gap Cable TV Inc. (MSO).

FORT LOUDON—Comcast Cable. Now served by HARRISBURG, PA [PA0009]. ICA: PA0333.

FRANKLIN (Venango County)—Time Warner Cable, 7800 Crescent Executive Dr, Charlotte, NC 28217. Phones: 330-633-9203; 814-898-1656. Web Site: http://www.timewarnercable.com. Also serves Cranberry (Venango County), Frenchcreek Twp. (Venango County), Jackson Twp. (Venango County), Mineral Twp., Oakland Twp. (Venango County), Polk Borough, Reno, Sandy Creek Twp. (Venango County) & Sugarcreek (Venango County). ICA: PA0100.

TV Market Ranking: Outside TV Markets (Cranberry (Venango County), FRANKLIN (VENANGO COUNTY), Frenchcreek Twp. (Venango County), Jackson Twp. (Venango County), Mineral Twp., Oakland Twp. (Venango County), Polk Borough, Reno, Sandy Creek Twp. (Venango County), Sugarcreek (Venango County)). Franchise award date: N.A. Franchise expiration date: N.A. Began: October 1, 1954.

Channel capacity: 83 (not 2-way capable). Channels available but not in use: N.A.

Basic Service
Subscribers: 3,567.
Programming (received off-air): KDKA-TV (CBS, Decades) Pittsburgh; WICU-TV (NBC) Erie; WJET-TV (ABC) Erie; WPCB-TV (IND) Greensburg; WPGH-TV (Antenna TV, FOX, The Country Network) Pittsburgh; WPNT (MNT) Pittsburgh; WPXI (MeTV, NBC) Pittsburgh; WQED (PBS) Pittsburgh; WQLN (PBS) Erie; WSEE-TV (CBS, CW) Erie; WTAE-TV (ABC, This TV) Pittsburgh; allband FM.
Programming (via satellite): BET; C-SPAN; Disney Channel; ESPN; Freeform; Lifetime; Pop; QVC; TBS; The Weather Channel; TLC; TNT; USA Network.
Fee: $49.99 installation; $24.50 monthly.

Expanded Basic Service 1
Subscribers: N.A.
Programming (via satellite): A&E; AMC; Animal Planet; Bravo; Cartoon Network; CMT; CNBC; CNN; Comedy Central; Discovery Channel; E! HD; ESPN Classic; ESPN2; EVINE Live; EWTN Global Catholic Network; Food Network; Fox News Channel; FX; Great American Country; Hallmark Channel; HGTV; History; HLN; MSNBC; MTV; NBCSN; Nickelodeon; OWN: Oprah Winfrey Network; Oxygen; Pennsylvania Cable Network; Root Sports Pittsburgh; Spike TV; Syfy; Travel Channel; truTV; TV Land; VH1; WE tv.
Fee: $27.12 monthly.

Digital Basic Service
Subscribers: N.A.
Programming (via satellite): BBC America; Bloomberg Television; Discovery Digital Networks; Disney XD; ESPNews; Fox Sports 1; Fuse; Golf Channel; GSN; LMN; MC; MTV Classic; MTV2; National Geographic Channel; Nick Jr.; Outdoor Channel; Ovation; TeenNick; Turner Classic Movies.
Fee: $16.62 monthly.

Digital Expanded Basic Service
Subscribers: N.A.
Programming (via satellite): FXM; IFC; Starz Encore; Sundance TV.
Fee: $4.95 monthly.

Digital Pay Service 1
Pay Units: N.A.
Programming (via satellite): Cinemax; HBO; Showtime (multiplexed); Starz (multiplexed); The Movie Channel (multiplexed).
Fee: $12.99 monthly (each).

Video-On-Demand: No

Pay-Per-View
iN DEMAND (delivered digitally); Fresh (delivered digitally); Shorteez (delivered digitally); Hot Choice (delivered digitally).

Internet Service
Operational: Yes.
Broadband Service: Road Runner.

Telephone Service
Digital: Operational

Miles of Plant: 307.0 (coaxial); 86.0 (fiber optic). Homes passed: 7,921.
President: Stephen Fry. Area Vice President: Rick Whaley. Vice President, Engineering: Al Costanzi. Vice President, Marketing: Patrick Burke. Vice President, Government & Media Relations: Bill Jasso. Senior Accounting Director: Karen Goodfellow. General Manager: Brian Frederick. Office Manager: Dana Bachman.
Ownership: Time Warner Cable (MSO).

FREEPORT—Formerly served by Adelphia Communications. Now served by Comcast Cable, BLAIRSVILLE, PA [PA0320]. ICA: PA0334.

GAINES—Formerly served by Gaines-Watrous TV Inc. No longer in operation. ICA: PA0266.

GALETON—Blue Ridge Communications. Now served by MANSFIELD, PA [PA0421]. ICA: PA0222.

GARLAND—Formerly served by Cebridge Connections. No longer in operation. ICA: PA0291.

GETTYSBURG—Comcast Cable. Now served by HARRISBURG, PA [PA0009]. ICA: PA0106.

GLEN ROCK—Formerly served by Adelphia Communications. Now served by Comcast Cable, HARRISBURG, PA [PA0009]. ICA: PA0336.

GRAHAM TWP.—Tele-Media. Now served by SNOW SHOE, PA [PA0188]. ICA: PA0251.

GRAMPIAN—Atlantic Broadband. Now served by CLEARFIELD, PA [PA0084]. ICA: PA0236.

GRANVILLE TWP.—Nittany Media Inc. Now served by MIFFLINTOWN, PA [PA0365]. ICA: PA0337.

GREEN TWP. (Indiana County)—Formerly served by Adelphia Communications. Now served by Comcast Cable, BLAIRSVILLE, PA [PA0320]. ICA: PA0338.

GREENBURR—Formerly served by Greenburr TV Cable. No longer in operation. ICA: PA0339.

GREENE COUNTY—Formerly served by DuCom Cable TV. No longer in operation. ICA: PA0437.

GREENSBURG—Comcast Cable, 15 Summit Park Dr, Pittsburgh, PA 15275. Phones: 412-747-6400; 724-845-1338; 412-875-1100; 412-771-8100. Fax: 412-747-6401. Web Site: http://www.comcast.com. Also serves Adamsburg, Arona, Confluence, Derry, East Huntingdon Twp., Hempfield Twp. (Westmoreland County), Henry Clay Twp., Hunker, Irwin, Lower Turkeyfoot Twp., Madison, Manor, Markleysburg, New Alexandria, New Stanton, North Huntingdon Twp. (portions), North Irwin, Ohiopyle, Penn Borough, Penn Twp. (Westmoreland County), Salem Twp. (Westmoreland County), Sewickley (portions), South Greensburg, South Huntingdon Twp., South Versailles, South Versailles Twp. (portions), Southwest Greensburg, Unity Twp. (Westmoreland County), Ursina Borough, White Oak (portions) & Youngwood, PA; Bruceton Mills & Preston County (portions), WV. ICA: PA0015.

TV Market Ranking: 10 (Adamsburg, Arona, East Huntingdon Twp., Hempfield Twp. (Westmoreland County), Hunker, Irwin, Madison, Manor, New Alexandria, New Stanton, North Huntingdon Twp. (portions), North Irwin, Penn Borough, Penn Twp. (Westmoreland County), Salem Twp. (Westmoreland County), Sewickley (portions), South Huntingdon Twp., South Versailles Twp. (portions), Southwest Greensburg, White Oak (portions)); 10,74 (GREENSBURG, South Greensburg, Youngwood); 74 (Derry, Unity Twp. (Westmoreland County)); Below 100 (Lower Turkeyfoot Twp., Ursina Borough, Preston County (portions) (portions)); Outside TV Markets (Bruceton Mills, Confluence, Henry Clay Twp., Ohiopyle, Markleysburg, Preston County (portions) (portions)). Franchise award date: January 1, 1966. Franchise expiration date: N.A. Began: March 1, 1966.

Channel capacity: N.A. Channels available but not in use: N.A.

Basic Service
Subscribers: 45,259. Commercial subscribers: 1,027.
Programming (received off-air): KDKA-TV (CBS, Decades) Pittsburgh; WINP-TV (IND, ION) Pittsburgh; WJAC-TV (MeTV, NBC) Johnstown; WPCB-TV (IND) Greensburg; WPCW (CW) Jeannette; WPGH-TV (Antenna TV, FOX, The Country Network) Pittsburgh; WPNT (MNT) Pittsburgh; WPXI (MeTV, NBC) Pittsburgh; WQED (PBS) Pittsburgh; WTAE-TV (ABC, This TV) Pittsburgh; 19 FMs.
Programming (via satellite): C-SPAN; Discovery Channel; QVC; TBS.
Fee: $29.50-$42.75 installation; $24.24 monthly; $1.85 converter.

Expanded Basic Service 1
Subscribers: N.A.
Programming (via satellite): A&E; AMC; Animal Planet; BET; Cartoon Network; CMT; CNBC; CNN; Comedy Central; C-SPAN 2; Disney Channel; E! HD; ESPN; ESPN2; EVINE Live; EWTN Global Catholic Network; Food Network; Fox News Channel; Freeform; FX; Golf Channel; Hallmark Channel; HGTV; History; HLN; ION Television; Lifetime; MSNBC; MTV; Nickelodeon; Oxygen; Pennsylvania Cable Network; Pittsburgh Cable News Channel; Pop; Root Sports Pittsburgh; Spike TV; Syfy; The Weather Channel; TLC; TNT; Travel Channel; truTV; TV Land; USA Network; VH1; WGN America.
Fee: $39.85 monthly.

Digital Basic Service
Subscribers: N.A.
Programming (via satellite): BBC America; Bravo; Discovery Digital Networks; Disney XD; DMX Music; ESPN Classic; ESPNews; Fox Sports 1; FSN Digital Atlantic; FSN Digital Central; FSN Digital Pacific; Fuse; FXM; FYI; Great American Country; GSN; History International; IFC; LMN; MC; National Geographic Channel; NBCSN; Nick Jr.; Nicktoons; Outdoor Channel; Ovation; Sundance TV; TeenNick; The Word Network; Trinity Broadcasting Network (TBN); Turner Classic Movies; WE tv; Weatherscan.
Fee: $10.95 monthly; $4.60 converter.

Digital Pay Service 1
Pay Units: N.A.
Programming (via satellite): Cinemax (multiplexed); Flix; HBO (multiplexed); Showtime (multiplexed); Starz (multiplexed); Starz Encore (multiplexed); The Movie Channel (multiplexed).
Fee: $8.00 monthly (each).

Video-On-Demand: Yes

Pay-Per-View
ESPN Now (delivered digitally); Sports PPV (delivered digitally); Hot Choice (delivered digitally); NBA TV (delivered digitally); iN DEMAND (delivered digitally); Urban Xtra (delivered digitally); Fresh (delivered digitally); Shorteez (delivered digitally); Playboy TV (delivered digitally).

Cable Systems—Pennsylvania

Internet Service
Operational: Yes.
Subscribers: 41,223.
Broadband Service: Comcast High Speed Internet.
Fee: $42.95 monthly.
Telephone Service
Digital: Operational
Subscribers: 25,555.
Fee: $44.95 monthly
Miles of Plant: 3,278.0 (coaxial); 1,768.0 (fiber optic). Homes passed: 121,030.
Regional Vice President: Linda Hossinger. Vice President, Technical Operations: Randy Bender. Vice President, Marketing: Donna Corning. Vice President, Public Affairs: Jody Doherty.
Ownership: Comcast Cable Communications Inc. (MSO).

GREENTOWN—Formerly served by Blue Ridge Communications. No longer in operation. ICA: PA0177.

GREENVILLE BOROUGH—Time Warner Cable. Now served by CLEVELAND (formerly Cleveland Heights), OH [OH0006]. ICA: PA0116.

GROVE CITY—Armstrong Cable Services. Now served by ZELIENOPLE, PA [PA0053]. ICA: PA0089.

HAMBURG—Comcast Cable. Now served by HARRISBURG, PA [PA0009]. ICA: PA0102.

HAMPTON TWP.—Comcast Cable. Now served by PITTSBURGH, PA [PA0001]. ICA: PA0455.

HARBORCREEK TWP.—Time Warner Cable. Now served by CLEVELAND (formerly Cleveland Heights), OH [OH0006]. ICA: PA0025.

HARRISBURG—Comcast Cable, 1311 South Duke St, Lancaster, PA 17603. Phones: 484-288-6500; 717-960-3100 (Harrisburg office). Web Site: http://www.comcast.com. Also serves Cascade, Frederick County (portions) & Washington County (portions), MD; Abbottstown, Abington Twp. (Montgomery County), Adams County (portions), Alexandria Borough, Allison Twp., Alsace Twp., Annville, Anthony Twp., Antrim Twp., Archbald Borough, Arendtsville, Armagh, Armstrong Twp. (Lycoming County), Asylum Twp., Auburn, Avis, Avoca, Ayr Twp., Bald Eagle Twp. (Clinton County), Bart Twp., Bastress Twp., Beech Creek Borough, Beech Creek Twp., Bellefonte Borough, Bendersville, Benner Twp., Benton Twp. (Lackawanna County), Bern Twp., Bern Twp. (Berks County), Bernville, Berrysburg, Berwick Twp. (Adams County), Bethel (Berks County), Bethel Twp. (Lebanon County), Bigler Twp., Biglerville, Blakely Borough, Blue Ball, Boggs Twp. (Centre County), Boggs Twp. (Clearfield County), Bonneauville, Brady Twp. (Huntingdon County), Brady Twp. (Lycoming County), Branch Twp., Brecknock Twp. (Lancaster County), Brisbin Borough, Broad Top City, Broad Top Twp., Brown Twp. (Mifflin County), Buffalo Twp. (Perry County), Burnham Borough, Butler Twp. (Adams County), Caernarvon Twp. (Lancaster County), Camp Hill, Carbon Twp., Carlisle, Carlisle Barracks, Carroll Twp. (Perry County), Carroll Twp. (York County), Carroll Valley, Cass Twp. (Schuylkill County), Castanea, Catherine Twp., Center Twp. (Snyder County), Centerport, Centre Hall Borough, Centre Twp., Chambersburg, Chanceford, Chapman Twp. (Clinton County), Chester Hill Borough, Chinchilla, Christiana, Clarks Green Borough, Clarks Summit Borough, Clay (Lancaster County), Cleona, Clinton Twp. (Lycoming County), Coaldale Borough (Schuylkill County), Coalmont Borough, Colebrook, College Twp. (Centre County), Columbia, Conestoga (Lancaster County), Conewago Twp. (Adams County), Conewago Twp. (Dauphin County), Conoy Twp., Cornwall, Covington Twp. (Clearfield County), Crawford Twp., Cressona, Cumberland Twp. (Adams County), Cummings Twp., Cumru Twp., Curtin Twp., Dallas, Dallas Twp., Dallastown, Dalmatia, Dalton Borough, Dauphin Borough, Decatur Twp. (Mifflin County), Deer Lake Borough (Schuylkill County), Delaware Twp. (Northumberland County), Derry Twp. (Dauphin County), Derry Twp. (Mifflin County), Dickinson Twp. (Cumberland County), Dickson City, Dillsburg, Dover Borough, Dover Twp., Drumore Twp., Dublin Twp. (Huntingdon County), Duboistown Borough, Dudley Borough, Dunmore Borough, Dunnstable Twp., Dupont Borough, Duryea Borough, Eagles Mere Borough, Earl Twp. (Lancaster County), East Berlin (Adams County), East Donegal Twp., East Drumore Twp., East Earl Twp., East Hanover Twp. (Dauphin County), East Hanover Twp. (Lebanon County), East Hempfield Twp., East Lampeter Twp., East Manchester Twp., East Norwegian Twp., East Pennsboro Twp., East Petersburg, East Prospect, Eden, Edwardsville, Elizabeth Twp. (Lancaster County), Elizabethtown, Elizabethville, Elmhurst Twp., Exeter Borough, Exeter Twp., Exeter Twp. (Luzerne County), Exeter Twp. (Wyoming County), Factoryville Borough, Fairfield, Fairfield Twp. (Lycoming County), Fairivew Twp. (York County), Felton, Ferguson Twp., Flemington, Fort Loudon, Forty Fort, Franklin Twp. (Adams County), Franklin Twp. (Huntingdon County), Franklin Twp. (Luzerne County), Franklintown, Freedom Twp. (Adams County), Friedensburg, Fulton Twp., Gap, Germany Twp., Gettysburg, Glen Rock Borough, Glenburn Twp., Goldsboro, Granville, Gratz, Greencastle Borough, Greene Twp. (Clinton County), Greene Twp. (Franklin County), Greenwich Twp., Greenwood Twp. (Perry County), Gregg Twp. (Union County), Guilford Twp., Gulich Twp., Halfmoon Twp., Halifax Borough, Halifax Twp., Hallam Borough, Hamburg, Hamilton Twp. (Adams County), Hamilton Twp. (Franklin County), Hamiltonban Twp., Hampden Twp. (Cumberland County), Hanover Borough, Harris Twp. (Centre County), Harveys Lake Borough, Hegins Twp., Heidelberg Twp. (Berks County), Heidelberg Twp. (Lebanon County), Heidelberg Twp. (York County), Hellam, Hellam Twp. (York County), Henderson Twp. (Huntingdon County), Hepburn Twp., Hershey, Hickory Twp. (Lawrence County), Highland Twp. (Adams County), Highspire Borough, Hopewell Borough, Hopewell Twp. (Bedford County), Houtzdale, Howard Borough, Howard Twp., Howe Twp., Hubley Twp., Hughestown Borough, Hughesville Borough, Hummelstown Borough, Huntingdon Twp. (Adams County), Jackson Twp. (Dauphin County), Jackson Twp. (Lebanon County), Jackson Twp. (York County), Jacobus, Jefferson Twp. (Berks County), Jefferson Twp. (Dauphin County), Jefferson Twp. (Lackawanna County), Jenkins Borough, Jersey Shore, Jessup Borough, Jonestown (Lebanon County), Juniata Terrace, Juniata Twp. (Perry County), Juniata Twp. (portions, Huntingdon County), Kenhorst, Kingston, Kinzers, Kistler Borough, La Plume Twp., La Porte Borough, Laflin Borough, Lamar Twp. (Clinton County), Lancaster (Lancaster County), Landingville, Laporte Twp. (Sullivan County), Latimore Twp., Laureldale, Leacock Twp., Lebanon, Leesport, Lehman Twp. (Luzerne County), Lemoyne Borough, Lenhartsville, Leola, Letterkenny Twp. (Franklin County), Lewis Twp., Lewistown, Liberty Twp. (Adams County), Liberty Twp. (Bedford County), Liberty Twp. (Centre County), Limestone Twp. (Lycoming County), Limestone Twp. (Montour County), Lincoln Twp. (Bedford County), Little Britain, Littlestown, Liverpool Twp., Llewellyn, Lock Haven, Logan Twp. (Huntingdon County), Loganton Borough, Loganville, Lower Allen Twp., Lower Alsace Twp., Lower Frankford Twp., Lower Heidelberg Twp., Lower Mahanoy Twp., Lower Mifflin Twp., Lower Paxton Twp., Lower Swatara Twp., Lower Windsor Twp., Loyalsock Twp., Luzerne, Lycoming Twp., Lykens Borough, Lykens Twp., Madison Twp. (Columbia County), Madison Twp. (Lackawanna County), Mahoning Twp. (Lawrence County), Maidencreek Twp., Manchester Borough, Manchester Twp. (York County), Manheim, Manheim Twp. (York County), Manor (portions, Westmoreland County), Marietta, Marion Twp. (Berks County), Marion Twp. (Centre County), Marklesburg Borough, Martic Twp., Marysville, Maytown, McConnellsburg Borough, McSherrystown, Mechanicsburg, Mechanicsville (Schuylkill County), Menallen Twp., Mercersburg Borough, Metal Twp., Middle Paxton, Middlecreek Twp. (Lebanon County), Middlesex, Middlesex Twp. (Cumberland County), Middleton Twp., Middletown (Dauphin County), Mifflin Twp. (Dauphin County), Mifflin Twp. (Lycoming County), Milesburg, Mill Creek Borough, Mill Hall Borough, Miller Twp. (Huntingdon County), Millersburg Borough, Millerstown, Millersville, Milroy, Minersville, Mohnton, Monroe Twp. (Bradford County), Monroe Twp. (Cumberland County), Monroeton, Mont Alto Borough, Montgomery Twp. (Franklin County), Montgomery Twp. (Lycoming County), Montoursville Borough, Moosic, Morris Twp., Moscow Borough, Mount Carbon, Mount Gretna, Mount Holly Springs, Mount Joy Borough, Mount Joy Twp. (Adams County), Mount Joy Twp. (Lancaster County), Mount Penn, Mount Pleasant (Adams County), Mount Union Borough, Mount Wolf, Mountville, Muhlenberg (Berks County), Muncy Borough, Muncy Creek Twp., Muncy Twp., Myerstown, Nanticoke, Narvon, Neshannock Twp., New Castle, New Castle Twp. (Schuylkill County), New Cumberland, New Freedom, New Holland, New Oxford, Newberry Twp., Newport Borough, Newton Hamilton, Newton Twp. (Lackawanna County), Newville Borough, Nicholson Borough, Nicholson Twp., Nippenose Twp., North Abington Twp., North Annville Twp., North Bend, North Codorus Twp., North Cornwall, North Heidelberg, North Lebanon Twp., North Londonderry Twp., North Manheim Twp., North Middleton Twp., North Towanda, North York, Northmoreland Twp., Norwegian Twp., Noyes Twp., Old Forge, Old Lycoming Twp., Oliver Twp. (Perry County), Olyphant Borough, Oneida Twp., Ontelaunee, Orwigsburg, Osceola Mills Borough, Oxford Twp., Palmyra Borough, Paradise Twp. (Lancaster County), Paradise Twp. (York County), Patton Twp., Paxtang, Peckville, Penbrook Borough, Penn Twp. (Berks County), Penn Twp. (Cumberland County), Penn Twp. (Huntingdon County), Penn Twp. (Lycoming County), Penn Twp. (York County), Pequea (Lancaster County), Perry (Berks County), Peters Twp. (Franklin County), Petersburg Borough, Philipsburg Borough, Piatt Twp., Picture Rocks Borough, Pillow, Pine Creek Twp., Pine Grove Borough, Pine Grove Twp. (Schuylkill County), Pittston, Pittston Borough, Plain Grove Twp., Plains, Plymouth, Port Clinton, Port Matilda, Porter Twp. (Clinton County), Porter Twp. (Huntingdon County), Porter Twp. (Lycoming County), Porter Twp. (Schuylkill County), Potter Twp. (Centre County), Pottsville, Providence Twp., Pulaski Twp. (Lawrence County), Quarryville, Quincy Twp., Railroad, Ramey Borough, Ransom Twp., Rapho Twp. (Lancaster County), Reading, Reading Twp., Red Lion Borough, Reed Twp., Reedsville, Renovo Borough, Richland (Lebanon County), Roaring Brook Twp., Robesonia, Rouzerville, Royalton Borough, Ruscombmanor Twp., Rush Twp. (Centre County), Rush Twp. (Schuylkill County), Rye Twp., Sadsbury Twp. (Lancaster County), Salisbury Twp. (Lancaster County), Salladasburg Borough, Saxton Borough, Schuylkill Haven, Scott Twp. (Lackawanna County), Scott Twp. (Lawrence County), Scranton, Seltzer, Seven Valleys, Shady Grove, Shartlesville, Shenango Twp. (Lawrence County), Shermans Dale, Shillington, Shippensburg, Shippensburg Twp., Shiremanstown, Shirley Twp., Shirleysburg Borough, Shoemakersville, Shrewsbury, Shrewsbury Twp. (Lycoming County), Shrewsbury Twp. (Sullivan County), Silver Spring Twp., Sinking Spring, Smithfield Twp. (Huntingdon County), Snyder Twp. (Blair County), South Abington Twp., South Annville Twp., South Hanover Twp., South Heidelberg Twp., South Lebanon, South Londonderry Twp., South Manheim Twp., South Middleton Twp., South New Castle Borough, South Philipsburg Borough, South Renovo, South Williamsport, Southampton Twp., Southampton Twp. (Franklin County), Spring Garden Twp., Spring Grove, Spring Twp. (Berks County), Spring Twp. (Centre County), Spring Twp. (Perry County), Springbrook Twp. (Lackawanna County), Springettsbury Twp., Springfield Twp., St. Thomas Twp., State College, State Line, Steelton, Straban Twp., Strasburg Borough, Strasburg Twp., Strausstown, Susquehanna Twp. (Dauphin County), Susquehanna Twp. (Juniata County), Susquehanna Twp. (Lycoming County), Swatara, Swatara Twp. (Dauphin County), Swatara Twp. (Lebanon County), Swoyersville, Taylor, Taylor Twp. (Centre County), Temple, Throop, Tilden Twp., Todd Twp. (Fulton County), Todd Twp. (Huntingdon County), Towanda Borough, Towanda Twp., Tower City, Tremont Twp., Tulpehocken Twp., Turbot Twp. (Northumberland County), Tuscarora Twp. (Perry County), Tyrone Borough, Tyrone Twp., Union Twp.

ADVANCED TVFactbook
FULLY SEARCHABLE • CONTINUOUSLY UPDATED • DISCOUNT RATES FOR PRINT PURCHASERS
For more information call **800-771-9202** or visit **www.warren-news.com**

Pennsylvania—Cable Systems

(Adams County), Union Twp. (Huntington County), Union Twp. (Lawrence County), Union Twp. (Lebanon County), Upper Allen Twp., Upper Bern Twp., Upper Leacock Twp., Upper Mahantango Twp., Upper Paxton Twp. (Dauphin County), Upper Tulpehocken Twp., Walker Twp. (Centre County), Walker Twp. (Huntingdon County), Walnut Grove (York County), Warrington Twp., Washington Twp. (Butler County), Washington Twp. (Dauphin County), Washington Twp. (Franklin County), Washington Twp. (Lycoming County), Washington Twp. (Schuylkill County), Washington Twp. (York County), Watson Twp., Wayne Twp. (Clinton County), Wayne Twp. (Dauphin County), Wayne Twp. (Lawrence County), Wayne Twp. (Mifflin County), Wayne Twp. (Schuylkill County), Waynesboro, Wells Twp., Wernersville, West Brunswick Twp., West Cocalico Twp., West Cornwall Twp., West Donegal Twp., West Earl Twp., West Fairview, West Hanover Twp. (Dauphin County), West Hempfield Twp. (Lancaster County), West Lampeter Twp., West Lawn, West Lebanon, West Manchester Twp., West Manheim, West Pennsboro Twp. (Cumberland County), West Pittston Borough, West Reading, West Wyoming Borough, West York, Wiconisco, Williams Twp. (Dauphin County), Williamsburg Borough, Williamsport Borough, Williamstown (Dauphin County), Wilmington Twp. (Lawrence County), Windsor, Windsor Borough, Windsor Twp., Wolf Twp., Womelsdorf, Wood Twp., Woodbury Twp., Woodward Twp. (Lycoming County), Wormleysburg Borough, Worth Twp., Wrightsville, Wyoming, Wyomissing, Wyomissing Hills, Wysox Twp., Yatesville Borough, Yoe Borough, York, York Haven Borough, York Springs Borough, Yorkana Borough & Zulinger, PA. ICA: PA0009.

TV Market Ranking: 10 (Manor (portions, Westmoreland County)); 10,79 (Wayne Twp. (Lawrence County)); 4 (Abington Twp. (Montgomery County)); 49 (Archbald Borough, Avoca, Benton Twp. (Lackawanna County), Blakely Borough, Chinchilla, Clarks Green Borough, Clarks Summit Borough, Coaldale Borough (Schuylkill County), Dallas, Dallas Twp., Dalton Borough, Dickson City, Dunmore Borough, Dupont Borough, Duryea Borough, Edwardsville, Elmhurst Twp., Exeter Borough, Exeter Twp. (Luzerne County), Exeter Twp. (Wyoming County), Factoryville Borough, Forty Fort, Franklin Twp. (Luzerne County), Glenburn Twp., Harveys Lake Borough, Hughestown Borough, Jefferson Twp. (Lackawanna County), Jenkins Borough, Jessup Borough, Kingston, La Plume Twp., La Porte Borough, Laflin Borough, Laporte Twp. (Sullivan County), Lehman Twp. (Luzerne County), Luzerne, Madison Twp. (Lackawanna County), Moosic, Moscow Borough, Nanticoke, Newton Twp. (Lackawanna County), Nicholson Borough, Nicholson Twp., North Abington Twp., Northmoreland Twp., Old Forge, Olyphant Borough, Peckville, Pittston, Pittston Borough, Plains, Plymouth, Ransom Twp., Roaring Brook Twp., Rush Twp. (Schuylkill County), Scott Twp. (Lackawanna County), Scranton, South Abington Twp., Springbrook Twp. (Lackawanna County), Swoyersville, Taylor, Throop, West Pittston Borough, West Wyoming Borough, Wyoming, Yatesville Borough); 57 (Abbottstown, Adams County (portions), Alsace Twp., Annville, Arendtsville, Bart Twp., Bendersville, Bern Twp., Bern Twp. (Berks County), Bernville, Berrysburg, Berwick Twp. (Adams County), Bethel (Berks County), Bethel Twp. (Lebanon County), Biglerville, Blue Ball, Bonneauville, Brecknock Twp. (Lancaster County), Buffalo Twp. (Perry County), Butler Twp. (Adams County), Caernarvon Twp. (Lancaster County), Camp Hill, Carlisle, Carlisle Barracks, Carroll Twp. (Perry County), Carroll Twp. (York County), Carroll Valley, Centerport, Chanceford, Christiana, Clay (Lancaster County), Cleona, Colebrook, Columbia, Conestoga (Lancaster County), Conewago Twp. (Adams County), Conewago Twp. (Dauphin County), Conoy Twp., Cornwall, Cumru Twp., Dallastown, Dalmatia, Dauphin Borough, Derry Twp. (Dauphin County), Dickinson Twp. (Cumberland County), Dillsburg, Dover Borough, Dover Twp., Drumore Twp., Earl Twp. (Lancaster County), East Berlin (Adams County), East Donegal Twp., East Drumore Twp., East Earl Twp., East Hanover Twp. (Dauphin County), East Hanover Twp. (Lebanon County), East Hempfield Twp., East Lampeter Twp., East Manchester Twp., East Pennsboro Twp., East Petersburg, East Prospect, Eden, Elizabeth Twp. (Lancaster County), Elizabethtown, Elizabethville, Exeter Twp., Fairfield, Felton, Franklin Twp. (Adams County), Franklintown, Freedom Twp. (Adams County), Fulton Twp., Gap, Germany Twp., Gettysburg, Glen Rock Borough, Goldsboro, Gratz, Greenwood Twp. (Perry County), Halifax Borough, Halifax Twp., Hallam Borough, Hamilton Twp. (Adams County), Hamiltonban Twp., Hampden Twp. (Cumberland County), Hanover Borough, HARRISBURG, Hegins Twp., Heidelberg Twp. (Berks County), Heidelberg Twp. (Lebanon County), Heidelberg Twp. (York County), Hellam, Hellam Twp. (York County), Highland Twp. (Adams County), Highspire Borough, Howe Twp., Hubley Twp., Hummelstown Borough, Jackson Twp. (Dauphin County), Jackson Twp. (Lebanon County), Jackson Twp. (York County), Jacobus, Jefferson Twp. (Berks County), Jefferson Twp. (Dauphin County), Jonestown (Lebanon County), Juniata Twp. (Perry County), Kenhorst, Kinzers, Lancaster (Lancaster County), Laureldale, Leacock Twp., Lebanon, Leesport, Lemoyne Borough, Leola, Liberty Twp. (Adams County), Little Britain, Littlestown, Liverpool Twp., Loganville, Lower Allen Twp., Lower Alsace Twp., Lower Frankford Twp., Lower Heidelberg Twp., Lower Mahanoy Twp., Lower Mifflin Twp., Lower Paxton Twp., Lower Swatara Twp., Lower Windsor Twp., Lykens Borough, Lykens Twp., Maidencreek Twp., Manchester Borough, Manchester Twp. (York County), Manheim, Manheim Twp. (York County), Marietta, Marion Twp. (Berks County), Martic Twp., Marysville, Maytown, McSherrystown, Mechanicsburg, Menallen Twp., Middle Paxton, Middlecreek Twp. (Lebanon County), Middlesex, Middlesex Twp. (Cumberland County), Middleton Twp., Middletown (Dauphin County), Mifflin Twp. (Dauphin County), Millersburg Borough, Millerstown, Millersville, Mohnton, Monroe Twp. (Cumberland County), Mount Carbon, Mount Gretna, Mount Holly Springs, Mount Joy Borough, Mount Joy Twp. (Adams County), Mount Joy Twp. (Lancaster County), Mount Penn, Mount Pleasant (Adams County), Mount Wolf, Mountville, Muhlenberg (Berks County), Myerstown, Narvon, New Cumberland, New Freedom, New Holland, New Oxford, Newberry Twp., Newport Borough, Newville Borough, North Annville Twp., North Codorus Twp., North Cornwall, North Heidelberg, North Lebanon Twp., North Londonderry Twp., North Middleton Twp., North York, Oliver Twp. (Perry County), Oxford Twp., Palmyra Borough, Paradise Twp. (Lancaster County), Paradise Twp. (York County), Paxtang, Penbrook Borough, Penn Twp. (Berks County), Penn Twp. (Cumberland County), Penn Twp. (York County), Pequea (Lancaster County), Pillow, Pine Grove Borough, Pine Grove Twp. (Schuylkill County), Porter Twp. (Schuylkill County), Providence Twp., Quarryville, Railroad, Rapho Twp. (Lancaster County), Reading, Reading Twp., Red Lion Borough, Reed Twp., Richland (Lebanon County), Robesonia, Royalton Borough, Ruscombmanor Twp., Rye Twp., Sadsbury Twp. (Lancaster County), Salisbury Twp. (Lancaster County), Seven Valleys, Shartlesville, Shermans Dale, Shillington, Shiremanstown, Shrewsbury, Silver Spring Twp., Sinking Spring, South Annville Twp., South Hanover Twp., South Heidelberg Twp., South Lebanon, South Londonderry Twp., South Middleton Twp., Spring Garden Twp., Spring Grove, Spring Twp. (Berks County), Spring Twp. (Perry County), Springettsbury Twp., Springfield Twp., Steelton, Straban Twp., Strasburg Borough, Strasburg Twp., Strausstown, Susquehanna Twp. (Dauphin County), Susquehanna Twp. (Juniata County), Swatara, Swatara Twp. (Dauphin County), Swatara Twp. (Lebanon County), Temple, Tilden Twp., Tower City, Tremont Twp., Tulpehocken Twp., Tuscarora Twp. (Perry County), Tyrone Twp., Union Twp. (Adams County), Union Twp. (Lebanon County), Upper Allen Twp., Upper Bern Twp., Upper Leacock Twp., Upper Mahantango Twp., Upper Paxton Twp. (Dauphin County), Upper Tulpehocken Twp., Walnut Grove (York County), Warrington Twp., Washington Twp. (Dauphin County), Washington Twp. (York County), Wayne Twp. (Dauphin County), Wernersville, West Cocalico Twp., West Cornwall Twp., West Donegal Twp., West Earl Twp., West Fairview, West Hanover Twp. (Dauphin County), West Hempfield Twp. (Lancaster County), West Lampeter Twp., West Lawn, West Lebanon, West Manchester Twp., West Manheim, West Pennsboro Twp. (Cumberland County), West Reading, West York, Wiconisco, Williams Twp. (Dauphin County), Williamstown (Dauphin County), Windsor, Windsor Borough, Womelsdorf, Wormleysburg Borough, Wrightsville, Wyomissing, Wyomissing Hills, Yoe Borough, York, York Haven Borough, York Springs Borough, Yorkana Borough); 74 (Alexandria Borough, Bigler Twp., Boggs Twp. (Clearfield County), Brady Twp. (Huntingdon County), Brisbin Borough, Broad Top City, Broad Top Twp., Carbon Twp., Catherine Twp., Chester Hill Borough, Coalmont Borough, College Twp. (Centre County), Dudley Borough, Ferguson Twp., Franklin Twp. (Huntingdon County), Halfmoon Twp., Harris Twp. (Centre County) (portions), Henderson Twp. (Huntingdon County), Hopewell Borough, Hopewell Twp. (Bedford County), Houtzdale, Huntingdon Twp. (Adams County), Juniata Twp. (portions, Huntingdon County), Kistler Borough, Liberty Twp. (Bedford County), Lincoln Twp. (Bedford County), Logan Twp. (Huntingdon County), Marklesburg Borough, Mill Creek Borough, Miller Twp. (Huntingdon County), Morris Twp., Mount Union Borough, Newton Hamilton, Oneida Twp., Osceola Mills Borough, Patton Twp., Penn Twp. (Huntingdon County), Petersburg Borough, Philipsburg Borough, Port Matilda, Porter Twp. (Huntingdon County), Ramey Borough, Rush Twp. (Centre County), Saxton Borough, Shirley Twp., Shirleysburg Borough, Smithfield Twp. (Huntingdon County), Snyder Twp. (Blair County), South Philipsburg Borough, State College, Taylor Twp. (Centre County), Todd Twp. (Huntingdon County), Tyrone Borough, Union Twp. (Huntington County), Walker Twp. (Huntingdon County), Wayne Twp. (Mifflin County), Wells Twp., Williamsburg Borough, Woodbury Twp., Worth Twp.); 79 (Hickory Twp. (Lawrence County), Mahoning Twp. (Lawrence County), Neshannock Twp., New Castle, Plain Grove Twp., Pulaski Twp. (Lawrence County), Scott Twp. (Lawrence County), Shenango Twp. (Lawrence County), South New Castle Borough, Union Twp. (Lawrence County), Wilmington Twp. (Lawrence County)); 9,14 (Frederick County (portions) (portions)); Below 100 (Allison Twp., Anthony Twp., Antrim Twp., Armstrong Twp. (Lycoming County), Asylum Twp., Avis, Ayr Twp., Bald Eagle Twp. (Clinton County), Beech Creek Borough, Brady Twp. (Lycoming County), Branch Twp., Cascade, Cass Twp. (Schuylkill County), Castanea, Center Twp. (Snyder County), Chambersburg, Clinton Twp. (Lycoming County), Crawford Twp., Cressona, Cumberland Twp. (Adams County), Cummings Twp., Deer Lake Borough (Schuylkill County), Duboistown Borough, Dunnstable Twp., Eagles Mere Borough, East Norwegian Twp., Fairfield Twp. (Lycoming County), Flemington, Fort Loudon, Friedensburg, Greencastle Borough, Greene Twp. (Clinton County), Greene Twp. (Franklin County), Gregg Twp. (Union County), Guilford Twp., Hamburg, Hamilton Twp. (Franklin County), Hepburn Twp., Hughesville Borough, Jersey Shore, Lamar Twp. (Clinton County), Landingville, Lenhartsville, Letterkenny Twp. (Franklin County), Liberty Twp. (Centre County), Limestone Twp. (Lycoming County), Limestone Twp. (Montour County), Llewellyn, Loganton Borough, Loyalsock Twp., Lycoming Twp., Madison Twp. (Columbia County), Marion Twp. (Centre County), McConnellsburg Borough, Mechanicsville (Schuylkill County), Mercersburg Borough, Metal Twp., Mifflin Twp. (Lycoming County), Mill Hall Borough, Minersville, Monroe Twp. (Bradford County), Monroeton, Mont Alto Borough, Montgomery Twp. (Franklin County), Montgomery Twp. (Lycoming County), Montoursville Borough, Muncy Borough, Muncy Creek Twp., Muncy Twp., New Castle Twp. (Schuylkill County), Nippenose Twp., North Bend, North Manheim Twp., North Towanda, Norwegian Twp., Old Lycoming Twp., Orwigsburg, Penn Twp. (Lycoming County), Peters Twp. (Franklin County), Piatt Twp., Picture Rocks Borough, Pine Creek Twp., Porter Twp. (Clinton County), Porter Twp. (Lycoming County), Quincy Twp., Rouzerville, Salladasburg Borough, Schuylkill Haven, Seltzer, Shady Grove, Shippensburg Twp., Shoemakersville, Shrewsbury Twp. (Lycoming County), Shrewsbury Twp. (Sullivan County), South Manheim Twp., South Williamsport, Southampton Twp., Southampton Twp. (Franklin County), St. Thomas Twp., State Line, Susquehanna Twp. (Lycoming County), Todd Twp. (Fulton County), Towanda Twp., Turbot Twp. (Northumberland County), Walker Twp. (Centre County), Washington County (por-

Cable Systems—Pennsylvania

tions), Washington Twp. (Franklin County), Washington Twp. (Lycoming County), Watson Twp., Wayne Twp. (Clinton County), Wayne Twp. (Schuylkill County), Waynesboro, West Brunswick Twp., Windsor Twp., Wolf Twp., Woodward Twp. (Lycoming County), Wysox Twp., Zulinger, Auburn, Beech Creek Twp. (portions), Chapman Twp. (Clinton County) (portions), Howard Twp. (portions), Lock Haven, Pottsville, Shippensburg, Towanda Borough, Williamsport Borough, Frederick County (portions) (portions)); Outside TV Markets (Armagh, Bastress Twp., Bellefonte Borough, Benner Twp. (portions), Boggs Twp. (Centre County), Brown Twp. (Mifflin County), Burnham Borough, Centre Hall Borough, Covington Twp. (Clearfield County), Curtin Twp., Decatur Twp. (Mifflin County), Delaware Twp. (Northumberland County), Derry Twp. (Mifflin County), Dublin Twp. (Huntingdon County), Granville, Howard Borough, Juniata Terrace, Milesburg, Milroy, Noyes Twp., Potter Twp. (Centre County), Renovo Borough, South Renovo, Spring Twp. (Centre County), Washington Twp. (Butler County), Beech Creek Twp. (portions), Chapman Twp. (Clinton County) (portions), Howard Twp. (portions), Lewis Twp., Lewistown, Reedsville, Harris Twp. (Centre County) (portions)). Franchise award date: December 1, 1965. Franchise expiration date: N.A. Began: December 1, 1965.
Channel capacity: 20 (operating 2-way). Channels available but not in use: N.A.

Basic Service
Subscribers: 572,273. Commercial subscribers: 35,813.
Programming (received off-air): WGAL (NBC, This TV) Lancaster; WGCB-TV (MeTV) Red Lion; WHP-TV (CBS, MNT) Harrisburg; WHTM-TV (ABC, Retro TV) Harrisburg; WITF-TV (PBS) Harrisburg; WPHL-TV (Antenna TV, MNT, This TV) Philadelphia; WPMT (Antenna TV, FOX) York; WXBU (CW) Lancaster.
Programming (via satellite): Comcast Network Philadelphia; C-SPAN; Pop; QVC; WPIX (Antenna TV, CW, This TV) New York.
Fee: $42.75 installation; $25.24 monthly; $1.02 converter.

Expanded Basic Service 1
Subscribers: N.A.
Programming (via satellite): A&E; AMC; Animal Planet; BET; Box; Bravo; Cartoon Network; CMT; CNBC; CNN; Comcast SportsNet Mid-Atlantic; Comcast SportsNet Philadelphia; Comedy Central; C-SPAN 2; Discovery Channel; Disney Channel; E! HD; ESPN; ESPN Classic; ESPN2; Food Network; Fox News Channel; Fox Sports 1; Freeform; FX; Golf Channel; GSN; HGTV; History; HLN; INSP; ION Television; Lifetime; MSNBC; MTV; MTV2; NBCSN; Nickelodeon; OWN: Oprah Winfrey Network; Pennsylvania Cable Network; Spike TV; Syfy; TBS; The Weather Channel; TLC; TNT; truTV; Turner Classic Movies; TV Land; Univision Studios; USA Network; VH1.
Fee: $33.90 monthly.

Digital Basic Service
Subscribers: N.A.
Programming (via satellite): BBC America; C-SPAN 3; Discovery Digital Networks; Disney XD; DMX Music; ESPNews; EVINE Live; Flix; IFC; National Geographic Channel; Nick 2; Nick Jr.; Starz Encore; Sundance TV; TeenNick; Weatherscan.
Fee: $14.95 monthly.

Digital Pay Service 1
Pay Units: N.A.
Programming (via satellite): Cinemax (multiplexed); HBO (multiplexed); Showtime (multiplexed); Starz (multiplexed); The Movie Channel (multiplexed).
Video-On-Demand: Yes
Pay-Per-View
iN DEMAND; iN DEMAND (delivered digitally); NBA TV (delivered digitally); Hot Choice (delivered digitally); Playboy TV (delivered digitally); Fresh (delivered digitally); Shorteez (delivered digitally); Pleasure (delivered digitally); ESPN Now (delivered digitally); Sports PPV (delivered digitally).
Internet Service
Operational: Yes. Began: December 6, 1999.
Subscribers: 534,412.
Broadband Service: Comcast High Speed Internet.
Fee: $42.95 monthly; $3.00 modem lease; $299.00 modem purchase.
Telephone Service
Digital: Operational
Subscribers: 278,845.
Miles of Plant: 38,051.0 (coaxial); 10,861.0 (fiber optic). Homes passed: 1,533,702.
Regional Vice President: Jim Samaha. Vice President, Marketing: Larry Goldman. Technical Operations Director: William Mays. Marketing Manager: Jason Wicht. Public Relations Director: Gabe Weissman.
Ownership: Comcast Cable Communications Inc. (MSO).

HARRISBURG—Formerly served by Gap Cable TV. No longer in operation. ICA: PA0406.

HARRISON VALLEY—Zito Media, 102 S Main St, PO Box 665, Coudersport, PA 16915. Phones: 814-260-9055; 800-365-6988. E-mail: info@zitomedia.com. Web Site: http://www.zitomedia.net. Also serves Ulysses & Westfield. ICA: PA0479.
TV Market Ranking: Outside TV Markets (HARRISON VALLEY, Ulysses, Westfield).
Channel capacity: 70 (not 2-way capable). Channels available but not in use: N.A.
Basic Service
Subscribers: 59.
Fee: $49.95 installation; $19.00 monthly.
President: James Rigas.
Ownership: Zito Media (MSO).

HARTLEY TWP.—Formerly served by D&E Communications/Windstream. IPTV service no longer in operation. ICA: PA5305.

HARTSLOG—Formerly served by Milestone Communications LP. No longer in operation. ICA: PA0440.

HAWLEY—Blue Ridge Communications. Now served by MILFORD, PA [PA0369]. ICA: PA0342.

HAZEN—Zito Media, 102 S Main St, PO Box 665, Coudersport, PA 16915. Phones: 814-260-9055; 800-365-6988. Fax: 814-260-9580. E-mail: info@zitomedia.com. Web Site: http://www.zitomedia.com. Also serves Pinecreek, Polk Twp. (Jefferson County), Snyder Twp., Warsaw Twp. & Washington Twp. (Jefferson County). ICA: PA0223.
TV Market Ranking: Outside TV Markets (HAZEN, Pinecreek, Polk Twp. (Jefferson County), Snyder Twp., Warsaw Twp., Washington Twp. (Jefferson County)).
Franchise award date: November 12, 1989. Franchise expiration date: N.A. Began: August 1, 1990.
Channel capacity: N.A. Channels available but not in use: N.A.
Basic Service
Subscribers: 3,700.
Programming (received off-air): WATM-TV (ABC, This TV) Altoona; WJAC-TV (MeTV, NBC) Johnstown; WKBS-TV (IND) Altoona; WPNT (MNT) Pittsburgh; WPSU-TV (PBS) Clearfield; WTAE-TV (ABC, This TV) Pittsburgh; WTAJ-TV (CBS) Altoona; WWCP-TV (FOX) Johnstown.
Programming (via satellite): A&E; Cartoon Network; CMT; CNN; Comedy Central; C-SPAN; CW PLUS; Discovery Channel; Disney Channel; ESPN; ESPN2; EWTN Global Catholic Network; Fox News Channel; Fox Sports 1; Freeform; FX; HGTV; History; HLN; Lifetime; MSNBC; MTV; Nickelodeon; QVC; Root Sports Pittsburgh; Spike TV; Syfy; TBS; The Weather Channel; TLC; TNT; Trinity Broadcasting Network (TBN); Turner Classic Movies; TV Land; USA Network; VH1; WGN America.
Fee: $39.95 installation.
Pay Service 1
Pay Units: N.A.
Programming (via satellite): Cinemax; HBO; Showtime.
Fee: $9.00 - $11.95 monthly (each).
Internet Service
Operational: Yes.
Subscribers: 3,638.
Telephone Service
Digital: Operational
Subscribers: 1,924.
Miles of Plant: 105.0 (coaxial); 20.0 (fiber optic). Homes passed: 8,000.
President: James Rigas.
Ownership: Zito Media (MSO).

HAZLETON—Service Electric Cablevision, 16 Maplewood Dr, PO Box R, Hazleton, PA 18201. Phones: 570-454-3841; 610-432-2210 (Corporate office). Fax: 570-454-3652. E-mail: corporateoffice@secv.com. Web Site: http://www.sectv.com. Also serves Ashland, Banks Twp. (Carbon County), Barry Twp., Beaver Meadows, Blythe Twp., Butler Twp. (Luzerne County), Centralia, Conyngham Borough, Delano, Dorrance Twp., East Brunswick Twp., East Norwegian Twp., East Union Twp., Foster Twp. (Luzerne County), Frackville, Freeland, Gilberton, Girardville, Gordon, Hazle Twp., Jeddo Borough, Kline Twp., Mahanoy City, Mahanoy Twp., McAdoo Borough, New Castle Twp., New Ringgold, Norwegian Twp., Ringtown, Rush Twp. (Schuylkill County), Ryan Twp., Schuylkill County (portions), Shenandoah, St. Clair (Schuylkill County), Sugarloaf Twp., Tamaqua, Union Twp. (Schuylkill County), Walker Twp. (Northumberland County), West Hazleton Borough, West Mahanoy, West Mahanoy Twp. & West Penn Twp. (northwestern portion). ICA: PA0050.
TV Market Ranking: 49 (Banks Twp. (Carbon County), Beaver Meadows, Blythe Twp., Butler Twp. (Luzerne County), Centralia, Conyngham Borough, Delano, Dorrance Twp., East Union Twp., Foster Twp. (Luzerne County), Freeland, Hazle Twp., HAZLETON, Jeddo Borough, Kline Twp., Mahanoy City, Mahanoy Twp., McAdoo Borough, Rush Twp. (Schuylkill County), Shenandoah, Sugarloaf Twp., Tamaqua, Union Twp. (Schuylkill County), West Hazleton Borough, West Mahanoy Twp.); Below 100 (Ashland, Barry Twp., East Brunswick Twp., East Norwegian Twp., Frackville, Gilberton, Girardville, Gordon, New Castle Twp., New Ringgold, Norwegian Twp., Ringtown, Ryan Twp., Schuylkill County (portions), St. Clair (Schuylkill County), Walker Twp. (Northumberland County), West Mahanoy, West Penn Twp. (northwestern portion)). Franchise award date: January 1, 1952. Franchise expiration date: N.A. Began: January 1, 1952.
Channel capacity: N.A. Channels available but not in use: N.A.
Basic Service
Subscribers: 26,321.
Programming (received off-air): KYW-TV (CBS, Decades) Philadelphia; WBRE-TV (NBC) Wilkes-Barre; WNEP-TV (ABC, Antenna TV) Scranton; WOLF-TV (CW, FOX, MNT) Hazleton; WPVI-TV (ABC, Live Well Network) Philadelphia; WQMY (MNT) Williamsport; WQPX-TV (ION) Scranton; WSWB (CW, MeTV) Scranton; WVIA-TV (PBS) Scranton; WYLN-LP (America One) Hazleton; WYOU (CBS) Scranton; allband FM.
Programming (via microwave): WPIX (Antenna TV, CW, This TV) New York; WWOR-TV (Bounce TV, Buzzr, Heroes & Icons, MNT) Secaucus.
Programming (via satellite): C-SPAN; Disney Channel; EVINE Live; EWTN Global Catholic Network; Pennsylvania Cable Network; QVC; Univision Studios.
Fee: $61.00 installation; $19.95 monthly; $2.56 converter.

Expanded Basic Service 1
Subscribers: 17,400.
Programming (via satellite): A&E; AMC; Animal Planet; Bravo; Cartoon Network; CMT; CNBC; CNN; Comcast SportsNet Philadelphia; Comedy Central; Discovery Channel; Discovery Life Channel; Disney XD; E! HD; ESPN; ESPN Classic; ESPN2; Food Network; Fox News Channel; Fox Sports 1; Freeform; FX; HGTV; HLN; Lifetime; MSNBC; MTV; National Geographic Channel; NFL Network; Nickelodeon; Outdoor Channel; Root Sports Pittsburgh; Spike TV; Syfy; TBS; The Weather Channel; TLC; TNT; Travel Channel; truTV; TV Land; USA Network; VH1; WE tv; YES Network.
Fee: $54.95 monthly.

Digital Basic Service
Subscribers: N.A.
Programming (via satellite): 3ABN; 52MX; AXS TV; BBC America; Bloomberg Television; Boomerang; BYUtv; CBS Sports Network; Church Channel; Cine Mexicano; CMT; CNN en Espanol; Colours; Cooking Channel; Daystar TV Network; Destination America; Discovery Kids Channel; Enlace USA; ESPN Deportes; ESPN HD; ESPN2 HD; ESPNews; FamilyNet; Food Network HD; FOX College Sports Central; FOX Col-

Pennsylvania—Cable Systems

lege Sports Pacific; Fox Deportes; Fox Sports 2; Fuse; FXM; FYI; GEB America; Golf Channel; Great American Country; GSN; Hallmark Channel; Hallmark Movies & Mysteries; HD Theater; HGTV HD; History International; HRTV; IFC; INSP; Investigation Discovery; JUCE TV; La Familia Cosmovision; LMN; MC; MTV Classic; MTV Hits; MTV Jams; MTV Live; MTV2; Nat Geo WILD; National Geographic Channel HD; NBC Universo; NBCSN; NFL Network HD; NHL Network; Nick 2; Nick Jr.; Nicktoons; Outdoor Channel 2 HD; Ovation; OWN: Oprah Winfrey Network; Science Channel; Smile of a Child TV; Sprout; TBS HD; TeenNick; Telemundo; Tennis Channel; TNT HD; Tr3s; Trinity Broadcasting Network (TBN); Turner Classic Movies; ULTRA HDPlex; UniMas; Universal HD; Univision; VH1 Soul; YES HD.
Fee: $19.00 monthly.

Digital Pay Service 1
Pay Units: N.A.
Programming (via satellite): Cinemax (multiplexed); Flix; HBO (multiplexed); HBO HD; Showtime (multiplexed); Showtime HD; Starz (multiplexed); Starz Encore (multiplexed); Starz HD; The Movie Channel (multiplexed); The Movie Channel HD.
Fee: $35.00 installation; $11.50 monthly (Cinemax), $12.45 monthly (Starz/Encore), $14.45 monthly (HBO or Showtime/TMC/Flix).

Video-On-Demand: No

Pay-Per-View
iN DEMAND (delivered digitally); MLB Extra Innings (delivered digitally); NHL Center Ice (delivered digitally); NBA League Pass (delivered digitally); ESPN (delivered digitally).

Internet Service
Operational: Yes.
Subscribers: 9,218.
Broadband Service: ProLog Express.
Fee: $61.00 installation; $22.95-$52.95 monthly; $4.95 modem lease; $99.95 modem purchase.

Telephone Service
Analog: Not Operational
Digital: Operational
Subscribers: 3,056.
Fee: $44.95 monthly
Miles of Plant: 531.0 (coaxial); 410.0 (fiber optic). Homes passed: 31,372.
General Manager: Timothy M. Trently. Regulatory Affairs Director: Arlean Lilly. Customer Service & Office Manager: Suzanne Matuella.
Ownership: Service Electric Cable TV Inc. (MSO).

HEMLOCK FARMS DEVELOPMENT—Blue Ridge Communications. Now served by MILFORD, PA [PA0369]. ICA: PA0343.

HERNDON—Formerly served by Pike's Peak TV Association. No longer in operation. ICA: PA0344.

HERSHEY—Comcast Cable. Now served by HARRISBURG, PA [PA0009]. ICA: PA0052.

HOLLAND—Formerly served by Comcast Cable. No longer in operation. ICA: PA0345.

HONESDALE—Blue Ridge Communications. Now served by MILFORD, PA [PA0369]. ICA: PA0346.

HONEY GROVE—Formerly served by Nittany Media. No longer in operation. ICA: PA0347.

HUNTINGDON—Comcast Cable. Now served by HARRISBURG, PA [PA0009]. ICA: PA0107.

HUNTINGTON TWP. (Luzerne County)—Formerly served by Comcast Cable. No longer in operation. ICA: PA0300.

HYNDMAN BOROUGH—Formerly served by Adelphia Communications. Now served by Comcast Cable, BLAIRSVILLE, PA [PA0320]. ICA: PA0227.

ICKESBURG—Nittany Media Inc. Now served by MIFFLINTOWN, PA [PA0365]. ICA: PA0275.

INDIANA TWP.—Formerly served by Adelphia Communications. Now served by Comcast Cable, BLAIRSVILLE, PA [PA0320]. ICA: PA0463.

JACKSON TWP. (Tioga County)—Blue Ridge Communications, 613 3rd St, PO Box 215, Palmerton, PA 18071-0215. Phone: 800-222-5377. Web Site: http://www.brctv.com. Also serves Roseville, Rutland Twp. & Wells Twp. (Bradford County). ICA: PA0480.
TV Market Ranking: Below 100 (JACKSON TWP. (TIOGA COUNTY), Roseville, Wells Twp. (Bradford County)).
Channel capacity: N.A. Channels available but not in use: N.A.

Basic Service
Subscribers: 169.
Fee: $49.95 installation; $43.89 monthly.
Miles of Plant: None (coaxial); 66.0 (fiber optic). Homes passed: 776.
President: David Masenheimer.
Ownership: Pencor Services Inc. (MSO).

JAMESTOWN—Formerly served by Cebridge Connections. Now served by Armstrong Cable Services, ZELIENOPLE, PA [PA0053]. ICA: PA0202.

JAMISON—Formerly served by Comcast Cable. No longer in operation. ICA: PA0033.

JOHNSONBURG—Johnsonburg Community TV Co, 424 Center St, PO Box 248, Johnsonburg, PA 15845. Phone: 814-965-4888. Fax: 814-965-4040. ICA: PA0174.
TV Market Ranking: Outside TV Markets (JOHNSONBURG). Franchise award date: October 1, 1953. Franchise expiration date: N.A. Began: October 1, 1953.
Channel capacity: N.A. Channels available but not in use: N.A.

Basic Service
Subscribers: 648.
Programming (received off-air): KDKA-TV (CBS, Decades) Pittsburgh; WICU-TV (NBC) Erie; WJAC-TV (MeTV, NBC) Johnstown; WKBW-TV (ABC, Escape) Buffalo; WPSU-TV (PBS) Clearfield; WTAJ-TV (CBS) Altoona; WWCP-TV (FOX) Johnstown; allband FM.
Programming (via satellite): A&E; AMC; CNN; Discovery Channel; ESPN; EWTN Global Catholic Network; Freeform; HLN; Lifetime; Nickelodeon; Spike TV; TBS; The Weather Channel; TNT; USA Network; WGN America.
Fee: $56.89 monthly.

Pay Service 1
Pay Units: N.A.
Programming (via satellite): Cinemax; HBO; Showtime.
Fee: $25.00 installation; $7.00 monthly (Cinemax), $12.25 monthly (Showtime), $13.90 monthly (HBO).

Video-On-Demand: Planned

Internet Service
Operational: No.

Telephone Service
None
Miles of Plant: 30.0 (coaxial); None (fiber optic). Homes passed: 1,620.
Manager & Board Secretary: Harry Horne. Chief Technician: Jerry Muroski.
Ownership: Johnsonburg Community TV Co. Inc.

JOHNSONBURG—Zito Media, 102 S Main St, PO Box 665, Coudersport, PA 16915. Phones: 814-260-9055; 800-365-6988. Fax: 814-260-9580. E-mail: info@zitomedia.com. Web Site: http://www.zitomedia.com. ICA: PA0472.
TV Market Ranking: Outside TV Markets (JOHNSONBURG).
Channel capacity: N.A. Channels available but not in use: N.A.

Basic Service
Subscribers: N.A.
Programming (received off-air): WATM-TV (ABC, This TV) Altoona; WGRZ (Antenna TV, NBC, WeatherNation) Buffalo; WIVB-TV (CBS) Buffalo; WJAC-TV (MeTV, NBC) Johnstown; WKBW-TV (ABC, Escape) Buffalo; WNED-TV (PBS) Buffalo; WPSU-TV (PBS) Clearfield; WTAE-TV (ABC, This TV) Pittsburgh; WTAJ-TV (CBS) Altoona; WWCP-TV (FOX) Johnstown.
Programming (via satellite): A&E; AMC; Animal Planet; Bravo; Cartoon Network; CMT; CNBC; CNN; Comedy Central; C-SPAN; Discovery Channel; Disney Channel; E! HD; ESPN; ESPN Classic; ESPN2; ESPNews; EWTN Global Catholic Network; Food Network; Fox News Channel; Fox Sports 1; Freeform; FX; Hallmark Channel; HGTV; History; HLN; INSP; Lifetime; MSNBC; MTV; NFL Network; Nickelodeon; Outdoor Channel; Pennsylvania Cable Network; QVC; Root Sports Pittsburgh; Spike TV; Syfy; TBS; The Weather Channel; TLC; TNT; Travel Channel; Trinity Broadcasting Network (TBN); truTV; Turner Classic Movies; TV Guide; TV Land; USA Network; VH1; WGN America; WPIX (Antenna TV, CW, This TV) New York.
Fee: $39.95 installation; $42.64 monthly.

Digital Basic Service
Subscribers: N.A.
Programming (via satellite): A&E HD; AMC; Bio HD; Cartoon Network HD; CNN HD; C-SPAN 2; Destination America; Discovery Channel HD; Disney Channel HD; ESPN HD; ESPN2 HD; ESPNews HD; Food Network HD; Freeform HD; FX HD; HD Theater; HGTV HD; IFC; Lifetime HD; Lifetime Movie Network HD; LMN; National Geographic Channel HD; NFL Network HD; NHL Network HD; Outdoor Channel 2 HD; Root Sports Pittsburgh; Science HD; TBS HD; TLC HD; TNT HD; WE tv.

Digital Pay Service 1
Pay Units: N.A.
Programming (via satellite): Cinemax HD; HBO HD; Showtime HD; Starz HD.

Video-On-Demand: Yes

Pay-Per-View
NHL Center Ice (delivered digitally); MLB Extra Innings (delivered digitally).

Internet Service
Operational: Yes.
Fee: $30.51 monthly.

Telephone Service
Digital: Operational
Fee: $20.00-$35.00 monthly

President: James Rigas.
Ownership: Zito Media.

JOHNSTOWN—Atlantic Broadband, 120 Southmont Blvd, Johnstown, PA 15905. Phones: 814-535-3506; 888-536-9600 (Customer service). Fax: 814-535-7749. E-mail: info@atlanticbb.com. Web Site: http://atlanticbb.com. Also serves Benson, Brownstown (Cambria County), Conemaugh Twp. (Cambria County), Conemaugh Twp. (Somerset County), Daisytown (Cambria County), Dale (Cambria County), East Taylor Twp., Ferndale (Cambria County), Franklin (Cambria County), Geistown, Jackson Twp. (Cambria County), Jenner Twp. (Somerset County), Jerome, Lorain, Lower Yoder Twp., Middle Taylor Twp., Paint Twp. (Somerset County), Quemahoning Twp. (Somerset County), Richland Twp. (Cambria County), Southmont, Stonycreek Twp. (Cambria County), Upper Yoder Twp., West Taylor Twp. & Westmont (Cambria County). ICA: PA0026.
TV Market Ranking: 74 (Benson, Brownstown (Cambria County), Conemaugh Twp. (Cambria County), Conemaugh Twp. (Somerset County), Daisytown (Cambria County), Dale (Cambria County), East Taylor Twp., Ferndale (Cambria County), Franklin (Cambria County), Geistown, Jackson Twp. (Cambria County), Jenner Twp. (Somerset County), Jerome, JOHNSTOWN, Lorain, Lower Yoder Twp., Middle Taylor Twp., Nanty-Glo (portions), Paint Twp. (Somerset County), Quemahoning Twp. (Somerset County), Richland Twp. (Cambria County), Southmont, Stonycreek Twp. (Cambria County), Summerhill (portions), Upper Yoder Twp., West Taylor Twp., Westmont (Cambria County)). Franchise award date: February 23, 1983. Franchise expiration date: N.A. Began: August 1, 1960.
Channel capacity: N.A. Channels available but not in use: N.A.

Basic Service
Subscribers: 18,291.
Programming (received off-air): KDKA-TV (CBS, Decades) Pittsburgh; WATM-TV (ABC, This TV) Altoona; WHVL-LP (MNT) State College, etc.; WJAC-TV (MeTV, NBC) Johnstown; WKBS-TV (IND) Altoona; WPCW (CW) Jeannette; WPSU-TV (PBS) Clearfield; WQED (PBS) Pittsburgh; WTAE-TV (ABC, This TV) Pittsburgh; WTAJ-TV (CBS) Altoona; WWCP-TV (FOX) Johnstown.
Programming (via satellite): C-SPAN; C-SPAN 2; EVINE Live; EWTN Global Catholic Network; HRTV; ION Television; Jewelry Television; Pennsylvania Cable Network; Pop; QVC; World.
Fee: $40.00 installation; $33.39 monthly.

Expanded Basic Service 1
Subscribers: 18,174.
Programming (via satellite): A&E; AMC; Animal Planet; BET; Bravo; Cartoon Network; CMT; CNBC; CNN; Comedy Central; Discovery Channel; Disney Channel; Disney XD; E! HD; ESPN; ESPN Classic; ESPN2; Food Network; Fox News Channel; Fox Sports 1; Freeform; FX; Golf Channel; GSN; Hallmark Channel; HGTV; History; HLN; INSP; Lifetime; MSNBC; MTV; National Geographic Channel; NBCSN; Nickelodeon; Nicktoons; Outdoor Channel; Oxygen; Root Sports Pittsburgh; Spike TV; Syfy; TBS; The Weather Channel; TLC; TNT; Travel Channel; truTV; Turner Classic Movies; TV Land; USA Network; VH1.
Fee: $25.00 installation; $45.59 monthly.

D-662　　TV & Cable Factbook No. 85

Cable Systems—Pennsylvania

Digital Basic Service
Subscribers: N.A.
Programming (via satellite): A&E HD; Animal Planet HD; BBC America; Bloomberg Television; Boomerang; Chiller; Cinemax HD; CMT; Destination America; Discovery Kids Channel; Disney Channel HD; DIY Network; ESPN HD; ESPN2 HD; ESPNews; ESPNU; Fox News HD; Fox Sports 2; Fuse; FYI; Great American Country; HBO HD; HD Theater; History HD; History International; IFC; Investigation Discovery; LMN; MC; MTV Classic; MTV Hits; MTV Jams; MTV2; NFL Network; NFL Network HD; Nick 2; Nick Jr.; Outdoor Channel 2 HD; OWN: Oprah Winfrey Network; Root Sports Pittsburgh; RTV; Science Channel; Science HD; Showtime HD; Starz (multiplexed); Starz Encore; Starz HD; Syfy HD; TBS HD; TeenNick; TLC HD; TNT HD; Tr3s; TVG Network; USA Network HD; VH1 Soul; WE tv.
Fee: $18.95 monthly.
Digital Pay Service 1
Pay Units: N.A.
Programming (via satellite): Cinemax (multiplexed); Flix; HBO (multiplexed); Showtime (multiplexed); The Movie Channel (multiplexed).
Fee: $15.95 monthly (Cinemax, HBO or Showtime/TMC/Flix).
Video-On-Demand: No
Pay-Per-View
iN DEMAND (delivered digitally); Hot Choice (delivered digitally).
Internet Service
Operational: Yes.
Subscribers: 16,546.
Broadband Service: Atlantic Broadband High-Speed Internet.
Fee: $24.95-$57.95 monthly.
Telephone Service
Digital: Operational
Subscribers: 8,374.
Fee: $44.95 monthly
Miles of Plant: 929.0 (coaxial); 257.0 (fiber optic). Homes passed: 20,978.
Senior Vice President & General Counsel: Bartlett Leber. Vice President: David Dane. General Manager: Dan Feiertag. Technical Operations Director: Charles Sorchilla. Marketing & Customer Service Director: Dara Leslie. Program Director: Natalie Kurchak.
Ownership: Atlantic Broadband (MSO).

KANE—Comcast Cable. Now served by PUNXSUTAWNEY, PA [PA0397]. ICA: PA0125.

KELLETTVILLE—Formerly served by Cebridge Connections. No longer in operation. ICA: PA0270.

KELLY TWP.—Formerly served by D&E Communications/Windstream. IPTV service no longer in operation. ICA: PA5307.

KENNETT SQUARE BOROUGH—Comcast Cable. Now served by PHILADELPHIA, PA [PA0005]. ICA: PA0071.

KING OF PRUSSIA—Comcast Cable. Now served by EATONTOWN BOROUGH, NJ [NJ0009]. ICA: PA0059.

KISKIMINETAS TWP.—Comcast Cable. Now served by BLAIRSVILLE, PA [PA0320]. ICA: PA0074.

KITTANNING—Comcast Cable. Now served by BLAIRSVILLE, PA [PA0320]. ICA: PA0351.

KUTZTOWN—Home Net. Formerly [PA0452]. This cable system has converted to IPTV, 45 Railroad St, Kutztown, PA 19530-1112. Phone: 610-683-5722. Fax: 610-683-6729. E-mail: huservices@kutztownboro.org. Web Site: http://www.huhomenet.com. ICA: PA5144.
Channel capacity: N.A. Channels available but not in use: N.A.
Internet Service
Operational: Yes.
Miles of Plant: None (coaxial); 27.0 (fiber optic).
General Manager: Frank Caruso. Chief Technician: Mark Arnold. Marketing Director: Gina Wiand.
Ownership: Borough of Kutztown.

KUTZTOWN—Hometown Utilicom. This cable system has converted to IPTV. See KUTZTOWN, PA [PA5144]. ICA: PA0452.

KYLERTOWN—Formerly served by TeleMedia. No longer in operation. ICA: PA0449.

LAIRDSVILLE—Formerly served by Ralph Herr TV. No longer in operation. ICA: PA0305.

LAKEWOOD—Hancock Video. Now served by HANCOCK, NY [NY0147]. ICA: PA0282.

LANCASTER—Comcast Cable. Now served by HARRISBURG, PA [PA0009]. ICA: PA0010.

LANDISBURG—Kuhn Communications, 301 West Main St, Walnut Bottom, PA 17266. Phones: 800-771-7072; 717-532-8857. Fax: 717-532-5563. E-mail: kuhncom1@kuhncom.net. Web Site: http://www.kuhncom.net. Also serves Perry County (portions). ICA: PA0393.
TV Market Ranking: 57 (LANDISBURG, Perry County (portions)).
Channel capacity: N.A. Channels available but not in use: N.A.
Basic Service
Subscribers: 410.
Programming (received off-air): WGAL (NBC, This TV) Lancaster; WHP-TV (CBS, MNT) Harrisburg; WHTM-TV (ABC, Retro TV) Harrisburg; WITF-TV (PBS) Harrisburg; WPIX (Antenna TV, CW, This TV) New York; WPMT (Antenna TV, FOX) York; WXBU (CW) Lancaster.
Programming (via satellite): Animal Planet; ESPN; Spike TV.
Fee: $30.00 installation; $15.45 monthly.
Expanded Basic Service 1
Subscribers: N.A.
Programming (via satellite): CMT; CNN; Freeform; MTV; TBS; TNT; USA Network; WGN America.
Expanded Basic Service 2
Subscribers: N.A.
Programming (via satellite): A&E; Bravo; Cartoon Network; Comcast SportsNet Philadelphia; Discovery Channel; Disney Channel; ESPN2; Fox News Channel; Fox Sports 1; FOX Sports Networks; FX; HGTV; History; HLN; Nickelodeon; Outdoor Channel; Syfy; The Weather Channel; TLC; Trinity Broadcasting Network (TBN); Turner Classic Movies; TV Land; VH1.
Digital Basic Service
Subscribers: N.A.
Programming (via satellite): AXS TV; BBC America; Bloomberg Television; Bravo; Cloo; Daystar TV Network; Discovery Digital Networks; DMX Music; ESPN Classic; ESPNews; EVINE Live; Fox Sports 1; FSN Digital Atlantic; FSN Digital Central; FSN Digital Pacific; Fuse; FXM; FYI; Golf Channel; Great American Country; GSN; HGTV; History; History International; IFC; LMN; National Geographic Channel; NBCSN; Nick Jr.; Nicktoons; Outdoor Channel; Syfy; TeenNick; The Word Network; Trinity Broadcasting Network (TBN); Turner Classic Movies; WE tv.
Pay Service 1
Pay Units: N.A.
Programming (via satellite): HBO; The Movie Channel.
Digital Pay Service 1
Pay Units: N.A.
Programming (via satellite): Cinemax (multiplexed); HBO (multiplexed); Showtime (multiplexed); Starz (multiplexed); Starz Encore (multiplexed); The Movie Channel (multiplexed).
Video-On-Demand: No
Pay-Per-View
iN DEMAND (delivered digitally); Playboy TV (delivered digitally); Fresh (delivered digitally).
Internet Service
Operational: Yes.
Broadband Service: kuhncom.net.
Fee: $50.00 installation; $24.95 monthly.
Telephone Service
Digital: Operational
President & General Manager: Earl Kuhn. Office Manager: Tracy Reath.
Ownership: Kuhn Communications (MSO).

LANSDALE—Comcast Cable. Now served by EATONTOWN BOROUGH, NJ [NJ0009]. ICA: PA0352.

LAPORTE TWP.—Comcast Cable. Now served by HARRISBURG, PA [PA0009]. ICA: PA0413.

LATROBE—Comcast Cable. Now served by BLAIRSVILLE, PA [PA0320]. ICA: PA0470.

LAURELTON—Formerly served by D&E Communications. No longer in operation. ICA: PA5282.

LAWRENCEVILLE—Formerly served by Time Warner Cable. No longer in operation. ICA: PA0354.

LEBANON—Comcast Cable. Now served by HARRISBURG, PA [PA0009]. ICA: PA0024.

LEHIGHTON—Blue Ridge Communications, 613 3rd St, PO Box 215, Palmerton, PA 18071-0215. Phone: 610-826-2551 (Administrative office). Fax: 610-826-7626. Web Site: http://www.brctv.com. Also serves Albrightsville, Allen Twp., Bowmanstown, Coaldale, East Penn Twp., Eldred Twp. (Monroe County), Franklin Twp. (Carbon County), Heidelberg Twp. (Lehigh County), Jim Thorpe, Kidder Twp. (Carbon County), Lansford, Lehigh Twp. (Northampton County), Lower Towamensing Twp., Lynn Twp. (Lehigh County), Mahoning Twp. (Carbon County), Nesquehoning, North Whitehall Twp., Palmerton, Parryville, Penn Forest Twp., Reynolds, Rush Twp., Slatington, Summit Hill, Towamensing Twp., Walker Twp. (Schuylkill County), Walnutport, Washington Twp. (Carbon County), Weissport & West Penn Twp. (southeastern portion). ICA: PA0042.
TV Market Ranking: 49 (Albrightsville, Bowmanstown, Coaldale, East Penn Twp., Franklin Twp. (Carbon County), Jim Thorpe, Kidder Twp. (Carbon County), Lansford, LEHIGHTON, Lower Towamensing Twp., Mahoning Twp. (Carbon County), Nesquehoning, Palmerton, Parryville, Penn Forest Twp., Rush Twp., Summit Hill, Towamensing Twp., Washington Twp. (Carbon County), Weissport; Below 100 (Allen Twp., Eldred Twp. (Monroe County), Heidelberg Twp. (Lehigh County), Lehigh Twp. (Northampton County), Lynn Twp. (Lehigh County), North Whitehall Twp., Reynolds, Slatington, Walker Twp. (Schuylkill County), Walnutport, West Penn Twp. (southeastern portion)). Franchise award date: N.A. Franchise expiration date: N.A. Began: September 14, 1951.
Channel capacity: 79 (operating 2-way). Channels available but not in use: N.A.
Basic Service
Subscribers: 30,415. Commercial subscribers: 931.
Programming (received off-air): KYW-TV (CBS, Decades) Philadelphia; WCAU (COZI TV, NBC) Philadelphia; WFMZ-TV (Retro TV) Allentown; WLVT-TV (PBS) Allentown; WNEP-TV (ABC, Antenna TV) Scranton; WNYW (FOX, Movies!) New York; WOLF-TV (CW, FOX, MNT) Hazleton; WPIX (Antenna TV, CW, This TV) New York; WPSG (CW) Philadelphia; WPVI-TV (ABC, Live Well Network) Philadelphia; WQPX-TV (ION) Scranton; WSWB (CW, MeTV) Scranton; WTXF-TV (Buzzr, FOX, Movies!) Philadelphia; WVIA-TV (PBS) Scranton; WWOR-TV (Bounce TV, Buzzr, Heroes & Icons, MNT) Secaucus; WYOU (CBS) Scranton; allband FM.
Programming (via satellite): HLN.
Fee: $49.95 installation; $27.80 monthly.
Expanded Basic Service 1
Subscribers: N.A.
Programming (via satellite): A&E; AMC; Animal Planet; Bravo; Cartoon Network; CMT; CNBC; CNN; Comcast SportsNet Philadelphia; Comedy Central; C-SPAN; Discovery Channel; Discovery Life Channel; Disney Channel; E! HD; ESPN; ESPN Classic; ESPN2; ESPNews; EVINE Live; EWTN Global Catholic Network; Food Network; Fox News Channel; Fox Sports 1; Freeform; FX; Golf Channel; GSN; Hallmark Channel; HGTV; History; INSP; Lifetime; LMN; MSG; MSNBC; MTV; NBCSN; Nickelodeon; Pennsylvania Cable Network; QVC; Spike TV; Syfy; TBS; The Weather Channel; TLC; TNT; Travel Channel; truTV; Turner Classic Movies; TV Land; Univision Studios; USA Network; VH1; WE tv; YES Network.
Fee: $31.69 monthly.
Digital Basic Service
Subscribers: N.A.
Programming (via satellite): Discovery Digital Networks; Disney XD; FSN Digital Atlantic; FSN Digital Central; FSN Digital Pacific; FXM; HRTV; MC; National Geographic Channel; Nick 2; Nick Jr.; Nicktoons; Outdoor Channel; TeenNick.
Fee: $9.95 monthly.
Digital Expanded Basic Service
Subscribers: N.A.
Programming (via satellite): BBC America; Bloomberg Television; Boomerang; Cooking Channel; DIY Network; FYI; History International; LWS Local Weather Station.
Fee: $5.00 monthly.
Digital Pay Service 1
Pay Units: N.A.
Programming (via satellite): Cinemax (multiplexed); Flix; HBO (multiplexed); Showtime (multiplexed); Starz (multiplexed); Starz Encore (multiplexed); Sundance TV; The Movie Channel (multiplexed).
Fee: $12.50 monthly (Cinemax or Showtime/Flix/Sundance/TMC), $12.95

Pennsylvania—Cable Systems

monthly (Starz/Encore), $13.50 monthly (HBO).
Video-On-Demand: Yes
Pay-Per-View
iN DEMAND; iN DEMAND (delivered digitally); adult PPV (delivered digitally).
Internet Service
Operational: Yes.
Subscribers: 25,763.
Broadband Service: ProLog Express.
Fee: $36.95 monthly; $10.00 modem lease; $59.95 modem purchase.
Telephone Service
Digital: Operational
Subscribers: 11,538.
Miles of Plant: 2,503.0 (coaxial); 698.0 (fiber optic). Homes passed: 47,330.
President: David Masenheimer. Vice President, Operations: Richard Semmel. General Manager: Mark Masonheimer. Chief Technician: Randy Semmel.
Ownership: Pencor Services Inc. (MSO).

LEROY TWP.—Blue Ridge Communications. Now served by TROY, PA [PA0165]. ICA: PA0302.

LEVITTOWN—Formerly served by Comcast Cable. No longer in operation. ICA: PA0016.

LEWIS TWP.—Comcast Cable. Now served by HARRISBURG, PA [PA0009]. ICA: PA0375.

LEWIS TWP.—Formerly served by D&E Communications/Windstream. IPTV service no longer in operation. ICA: PA5308.

LEWISBURG—Formerly served by Lewisburg CATV. Now served by CATV Service Inc., DANVILLE, PA [PA0054]. ICA: PA0356.

LEWISBURG—Windstream (formerly D&E Communications.) This cable system has converted to IPTV. Now served by STATE COLLEGE, PA [PA5280]. ICA: PA0390.

LEWISTOWN—Comcast Cable. Now served by HARRISBURG, PA [PA0009]. ICA: PA0092.

LIBERTY—Blue Ridge Communications. Now served by MANSFIELD, PA [PA0421]. ICA: PA0478.

LIGONIER—Formerly served by Adelphia Communications. Now served by Comcast Cable, BLAIRSVILLE, PA [PA0320]. ICA: PA0462.

LIMESTONE—Atlantic Broadband. Now served by MIFFLINBURG, PA [PA0131]. ICA: PA0197.

LIMESTONE TWP.—Formerly served by D&E Communications/Windstream. IPTV service no longer in operation. ICA: PA5309.

LIMESTONE TWP. (Lycoming County)—Comcast Cable. Now served by HARRISBURG, PA [PA0009]. ICA: PA0247.

LINESVILLE—Formerly served by Cebridge Connections. No longer in operation. ICA: PA0196.

LIVERPOOL—Zampelli Electronics, PO Box 830, Lewistown, PA 17044-0830. Phone: 717-248-1544. ICA: PA0359.
TV Market Ranking: 57 (LIVERPOOL).
Channel capacity: N.A. Channels available but not in use: N.A.
Basic Service
Subscribers: N.A.
Programming (received off-air): WGAL (NBC, This TV) Lancaster; WHP-TV (CBS, MNT) Harrisburg; WHTM-TV (ABC, Retro TV) Harrisburg; WPMT (Antenna TV, FOX) York.
Video-On-Demand: No
Internet Service
Operational: No.
Telephone Service
None
General Manager & Chief Technician: Joe Zampelli.
Ownership: Zampelli TV (MSO).

LOCK HAVEN—Comcast Cable. Now served by HARRISBURG, PA [PA0009]. ICA: PA0111.

LOGANTON—Formerly served by TV Cable Associates Inc. No longer in operation. ICA: PA0271.

LONDONDERRY TWP. (Bedford County)—Leap Cable TV, PO Box 703, Hyndman, PA 15545-0703. Phone: 814-842-3370. Also serves Harrison Twp. (Bedford County). ICA: PA0360.
TV Market Ranking: 74 (Harrison Twp. (Bedford County)). Franchise award date: N.A. Franchise expiration date: N.A. Began: July 1, 1981.
Channel capacity: 30 (not 2-way capable). Channels available but not in use: N.A.
Basic Service
Subscribers: 3.
Programming (received off-air): KDKA-TV (CBS, Decades) Pittsburgh; WJAC-TV (MeTV, NBC) Johnstown; WPSU-TV (PBS) Clearfield; WTAE-TV (ABC, This TV) Pittsburgh; WTAJ-TV (CBS) Altoona.
Programming (via satellite): Freeform; TBS; TNT.
Fee: $33.00 monthly.
Pay Service 1
Pay Units: N.A.
Programming (via satellite): HBO.
Fee: $10.99 monthly.
Video-On-Demand: No
Internet Service
Operational: No.
Telephone Service
None
Miles of Plant: 22.0 (coaxial); None (fiber optic). Homes passed: 150.
General Manager: Don T. Leap.
Ownership: Don T. Leap.

LOOMIS LAKE—Formerly served by Adams Cable Service. No longer in operation. ICA: PA0361.

LOWER MERION TWP.—Comcast Cable. Now served by PHILADELPHIA, PA [PA0005]. ICA: PA0048.

LOWER OXFORD TWP.—Armstrong Cable Services. Now served by ABINGDON, MD [MD0019]. ICA: PA0098.

LYKENS BOROUGH—Comcast Cable. Now served by HARRISBURG, PA [PA0009]. ICA: PA0096.

MAHAFFEY—Formerly served by Adelphia Communications. Now served by Comcast Cable, PUNXSUTAWNEY, PA [PA0397]. ICA: PA0363.

MAHANOY CITY—Service Electric Cable Company. Now served by HAZLETON, PA [PA0050]. ICA: PA0055.

MALVERN—Comcast Cable. Now served by PHILADELPHIA, PA [PA0005]. ICA: PA0034.

MAMMOTH—Citizens Cable Communications. This cable system has converted to IPTV. See MAMMOTH, PA [PA5000]. ICA: PA0400.

MAMMOTH—Citizens Telecom. Formerly [PA0400]. This cable system has converted to IPTV, 2748 Rt. 982, PO Box 156, Mammoth, PA 15664. Phones: 724-423-5555; 724-423-3000. Fax: 724-423-3003. E-mail: marketing@wpa.net. Web Site: http://www.wpa.net. Also serves Acme, Baggaley, Hecla, Hostetter, Humphreys, Kecksburg, Laurelville, Lawson Heights, Marguerite, Mutual, Norvelt, Pleasant Unity, United, Whitney & Youngstown. ICA: PA5000.
TV Market Ranking: 10 (MAMMOTH).
Channel capacity: N.A. Channels available but not in use: N.A.
Essentials
Subscribers: N.A.
Fee: $10.00 monthly. Includes 36 channels - 26 in SD & 10 in HD.
Classic
Subscribers: N.A.
Fee: $55.00 monthly. Includes 136 channels - 75 in SD & 61 in HD.
Deluxe
Subscribers: N.A.
Fee: $65.00 monthly. Includes 213 channels - 132 in SD & 81 in HD.
Digital Extra Tier
Subscribers: N.A.
Fee: $5.99 monthly. Includes 11 channels.
Cinemax
Subscribers: N.A.
Fee: $15.50 monthly. Includes 9 channels - 8 in SD & 1 in HD.
HBO
Subscribers: N.A.
Fee: $17.00 monthly. Includes 7 channels - 6 in SD & 1 in HD.
Showtime/TMC
Subscribers: N.A.
Fee: $15.50 monthly. Includes 12 channels - 11 in SD & 1 in HD.
Starz/Encore
Subscribers: N.A.
Fee: $15.50 monthly. Includes 14 channels - 13 in SD & 1 in HD.
Internet Service
Operational: Yes.
Fee: $24.99-$59.99 monthly.
Telephone Service
Digital: Operational
Fee: $34.99 monthly

President: Dennis Cutrell. General Manager: Arnold Cutrell. Marketing & Ad Sales Manager: Sharalyn DeFlorio.
Ownership: Citizens Cable Communications.

MANSFIELD—Blue Ridge Communications, 613 3rd St, PO Box 215, Palmerton, PA 18071-0215. Phone: 610-826-2551. Web Site: http://www.brctv.com. Also serves Arnot, Bloss, Blossburg, Catlin Hollow, Charleston Twp., Covington Twp., Delmar Twp., Duncan Twp., Gaines Twp., Galeton, Kennedyville, Lambs Creek, Liberty, Mainesburg, Middlebury, Pike Twp. (Potter County), Putnam Twp., Richmond Twp., Shippen Twp. (Tioga County), Sullivan Twp., Wellsboro & West Branch Twp. (Potter County). ICA: PA0421.
TV Market Ranking: Below 100 (Bloss, Blossburg, Charleston Twp., Covington Twp., Delmar Twp., Duncan Twp., Gaines Twp., Lambs Creek, Mainesburg, Putnam Twp., Richmond Twp., Sullivan Twp., Arnot, Liberty, MANSFIELD); Outside TV Markets (Catlin Hollow, Galeton, Kennedyville, Middlebury, Pike Twp. (Potter County), Shippen Twp. (Tioga County), West Branch Twp. (Potter County), Wellsboro). Franchise award date: N.A. Franchise expiration date: N.A. Began: October 1, 1951.
Channel capacity: N.A. Channels available but not in use: N.A.
Basic Service
Subscribers: 5,104. Commercial subscribers: 236.
Programming (received off-air): WBNG-TV (CBS, CW) Binghamton; WENY-TV (ABC, CW) Elmira; WETM-TV (IND, NBC) Elmira; WSKG-TV (PBS) Binghamton; WVIA-TV (PBS) Scranton; WYDC (FOX, MNT) Corning; WYOU (CBS) Scranton; 2 FMs.
Programming (via microwave): WPIX (Antenna TV, CW, This TV) New York.
Programming (via satellite): C-SPAN; C-SPAN 2; WGN America.
Fee: $49.95 installation; $27.08 monthly.
Expanded Basic Service 1
Subscribers: N.A.
Programming (via satellite): A&E; AMC; Animal Planet; BET; Cartoon Network; CMT; CNBC; CNN; Comedy Central; Discovery Channel; Disney Channel; E! HD; ESPN; ESPN2; EWTN Global Catholic Network; Food Network; Fox News Channel; Fox Sports 1; Freeform; FX; Hallmark Channel; HGTV; History; HLN; Lifetime; LMN; MSNBC; MTV; NBCSN; Nickelodeon; Pennsylvania Cable Network; QVC; Root Sports Pittsburgh; Spike TV; Syfy; TBS; The Weather Channel; TLC; TNT; Travel Channel; Trinity Broadcasting Network (TBN); truTV; Turner Classic Movies; TV Land; USA Network; VH1.
Fee: $27.99 monthly.
Digital Basic Service
Subscribers: N.A.
Programming (via satellite): Discovery Digital Networks; Disney XD; ESPN Classic; ESPNews; FXM; GSN; MC; National Geographic Channel; Nick Jr.; Outdoor Channel; TeenNick.
Fee: $35.00 installation; $9.95 monthly.
Digital Expanded Basic Service
Subscribers: N.A.
Programming (via satellite): BBC America; Bloomberg Television; FYI; Golf Channel; History International.
Fee: $5.00 monthly.
Digital Pay Service 1
Pay Units: N.A.
Programming (via satellite): Cinemax (multiplexed); Flix; HBO (multiplexed); Showtime (multiplexed); Starz (mul-

Cable Systems—Pennsylvania

tiplexed); Starz Encore (multiplexed); Sundance TV; The Movie Channel (multiplexed).
Fee: $12.50 monthly (Cinemax or Showtime/Flix/Sundance/TMC), $12.95 monthly (Starz/Encore), $13.50 monthly (HBO).
Video-On-Demand: No
Pay-Per-View
iN DEMAND; iN DEMAND (delivered digitally); Adult PPV (delivered digitally); Sports PPV (delivered digitally).
Internet Service
Operational: Yes.
Broadband Service: ProLog Express.
Fee: $36.95 monthly; $10.00 modem lease; $59.95 modem purchase.
Telephone Service
None
Miles of Plant: 154.0 (coaxial); None (fiber optic).
President: David Masenheimer. Vice President, Operations: Richard Semmel. General Manager: Mark Masonheimer. Fiber Manager: Randy Semmel. Chief Technician: Garry Wood.
Ownership: Pencor Services Inc. (MSO).

MARIENVILLE—Formerly served by Armstrong Cable Services. No longer in operation. ICA: PA0221.

MARKLEYSBURG—Comcast Cable. Now served by GREENSBURG, PA [PA0015]. ICA: PA0129.

MATAMORAS—Cablevision. Now served by WARWICK, NY [NY0045]. ICA: PA0168.

McALEVYS FORT—Atlantic Broadband, 120 Southmont Blvd, Johnstown, PA 15905. Phones: 888-536-9600 (Customer service); 814-535-3506. Fax: 814-535-7749. E-mail: info@atlanticbb.com. Web Site: http://atlanticbb.com. Also serves Barree Twp., Jackson Twp. (Huntingdon County) & West Twp. ICA: PA0441.
TV Market Ranking: 74 (Barree Twp., Jackson Twp. (Huntingdon County), MCALEVYS FORT, West Twp.). Franchise award date: N.A. Franchise expiration date: N.A. Began: N.A.
Channel capacity: N.A. Channels available but not in use: N.A.
Basic Service
Subscribers: 53.
Programming (received off-air): WATM-TV (ABC, This TV) Altoona; WJAC-TV (MeTV, NBC) Johnstown; WKBS-TV (IND) Altoona; WPSU-TV (PBS) Clearfield; WTAJ-TV (CBS) Altoona; WWCP-TV (FOX) Johnstown.
Programming (via satellite): A&E; AMC; Animal Planet; CMT; CNN; Comedy Central; Discovery Channel; ESPN; ESPN2; Fox News Channel; Freeform; FX; History; HLN; Lifetime; Nickelodeon; QVC; Root Sports Pittsburgh; Spike TV; Syfy; TBS; The Weather Channel; TLC; TNT; Trinity Broadcasting Network (TBN); TV Land; USA Network; WGN America.
Fee: $40.00 installation; $52.48 monthly; $2.50 converter.
Pay Service 1
Pay Units: N.A.
Programming (via satellite): Showtime; The Movie Channel.
Fee: $13.95 monthly (each).
Internet Service
Operational: Yes.
Telephone Service
None
Miles of Plant: 39.0 (coaxial); 16.0 (fiber optic). Homes passed: 4,241.

Chief Financial Officer: Patrick Bratton. Senior Vice President & General Counsel: Leslie Brown. Vice President: David Dane. General Manager: Mike Papasergi. Technical Operations Director: Charles Sorchilla. Marketing & Customer Service Director: Dara Leslie. Marketing Manager: Natalie Kurchak.
Ownership: Atlantic Broadband (MSO).

McCLURE—Nittany Media Inc., 18 Juniata St, PO Box 111, Lewistown, PA 17044. Phones: 800-692-7401; 717-248-3733. Fax: 717-248-3732. E-mail: info@nittanymedia.com. Web Site: http://www.nittanymedia.com. Also serves West Beaver Twp. ICA: PA0255.
TV Market Ranking: Outside TV Markets (MCCLURE, West Beaver Twp.). Franchise award date: N.A. Franchise expiration date: N.A. Began: May 1, 1953.
Channel capacity: N.A. Channels available but not in use: N.A.
Basic Service
Subscribers: N.A.
Programming (received off-air): WGAL (NBC, This TV) Lancaster; WHP-TV (CBS, MNT) Harrisburg; WHTM-TV (ABC, Retro TV) Harrisburg; WHVL-LP (MNT) State College, etc.; WITF-TV (PBS) Harrisburg; WNEP-TV (ABC, Antenna TV) Scranton; WOLF-TV (CW, FOX, MNT) Hazleton; WPMT (Antenna TV, FOX) York; WPSU-TV (PBS) Clearfield; WTAJ-TV (CBS) Altoona; WVIA-TV (PBS) Scranton; WXBU (CW) Lancaster; allband FM.
Programming (via satellite): Bloomberg Television; C-SPAN; La Familia Cosmovision; Pennsylvania Cable Network; QVC.
Fee: $25.00 installation; $17.40 monthly.
Expanded Basic Service 1
Subscribers: N.A.
Programming (via satellite): A&E; AMC; Animal Planet; Boomerang; Bravo; Cartoon Network; CMT; CNBC; CNN; Comedy Central; Cornerstone Television; C-SPAN 2; Discovery Channel; Discovery Life Channel; Disney Channel; ESPN; ESPN2; Food Network; Fox News Channel; Fox Sports 1; FOX Sports Networks; Freeform; FX; Great American Country; Hallmark Channel; HGTV; History; HLN; INSP; ION Television; Lifetime; MSNBC; MTV; Nickelodeon; Outdoor Channel; Spike TV; Syfy; TBS; The Weather Channel; TLC; TNT; Travel Channel; Trinity Broadcasting Network (TBN); TV Land; USA Network; VH1; WGN America.
Fee: $27.10 monthly.
Digital Basic Service
Subscribers: N.A.
Programming (via satellite): AXS TV; BBC America; Bloomberg Television; Bravo; Cloo; CMT; Cooking Channel; Discovery Digital Networks; Disney XD; DMX Music; ESPN HD; ESPN2; Fox Sports 1; Fuse; FXM; FYI; GSN; HD Theater; HGTV; History; History International; LMN; Nick Jr.; Nicktoons; Outdoor Channel; Syfy; TeenNick; Trinity Broadcasting Network (TBN); TV Land; WE tv.
Fee: $15.99 monthly.
Digital Expanded Basic Service
Subscribers: N.A.
Programming (via satellite): ESPN Classic; ESPN2; Golf Channel; NBCSN.
Fee: $3.99 monthly.
Digital Expanded Basic Service 2
Subscribers: N.A.
Programming (via satellite): IFC; Turner Classic Movies.
Fee: $1.99 monthly.

Digital Pay Service 1
Pay Units: N.A.
Programming (via satellite): Cinemax (multiplexed); Flix; HBO (multiplexed); Showtime (multiplexed); Starz (multiplexed); Starz Encore (multiplexed); The Movie Channel (multiplexed).
Fee: $12.99 monthly (each).
Video-On-Demand: No
Pay-Per-View
iN DEMAND.
Internet Service
Operational: Yes.
Fee: $39.95 monthly.
Telephone Service
Analog: Operational
Miles of Plant: 3.0 (coaxial); None (fiber optic).
General Manager: Anna H. Hain. Chief Technician: Michael Hain.
Ownership: Nittany Media Inc. (MSO).

McCONNELLSBURG BOROUGH—Comcast Cable. Now served by HARRISBURG, PA [PA0009]. ICA: PA0148.

McVEYTOWN—Zampelli Electronics, PO Box 830, Lewistown, PA 17044-0830. Phone: 717-248-1544. Also serves Mattawana. ICA: PA0366.
TV Market Ranking: 74 (Mattawana, MCVEYTOWN).
Channel capacity: 5 (not 2-way capable). Channels available but not in use: N.A.
Basic Service
Subscribers: N.A.
Programming (received off-air): WGAL (NBC, This TV) Lancaster; WHP-TV (CBS, MNT) Harrisburg; WHTM-TV (ABC, Retro TV) Harrisburg; WTAJ-TV (CBS) Altoona.
Video-On-Demand: No
Internet Service
Operational: No.
Telephone Service
None
General Manager & Chief Technician: Joe Zampelli.
Ownership: Zampelli TV (MSO).

MEADVILLE—Armstrong Cable Services. Now served by ZELIENOPLE, PA [PA0053]. ICA: PA0062.

MERCER COUNTY (portions)—Time Warner Cable. Now served by CLEVELAND (formerly Cleveland Heights), OH [OH0006]. ICA: PA0471.

METAL TWP.—Valley Cable Systems, 21700 Path Valley Rd, PO Box 1078, Doylesburg, PA 17219. Phone: 717-349-7717. ICA: PA0330.
TV Market Ranking: Below 100 (METAL TWP.). Franchise award date: January 1, 1987. Franchise expiration date: N.A. Began: January 1, 1987.
Channel capacity: N.A. Channels available but not in use: N.A.
Basic Service
Subscribers: N.A.
Programming (received off-air): WDCA (Heroes & Icons, MNT, Movies!, Mundo-

Max) Washington; WGAL (NBC, This TV) Lancaster; WHAG-TV (IND) Hagerstown; WHP-TV (CBS, MNT) Harrisburg; WHTM-TV (ABC, Retro TV) Harrisburg; WITF-TV (PBS) Harrisburg; WJAC-TV (MeTV, NBC) Johnstown; WJAL (IND) Hagerstown; WJLA-TV (ABC, MeTV, Retro TV) Washington; WMPT (PBS) Annapolis; WPMT (Antenna TV, FOX) York; WTAJ-TV (CBS) Altoona; WTTG (Buzzr, FOX) Washington; WXBU (CW) Lancaster.
Programming (via satellite): CMT; CNBC; CNN; Discovery Channel; Disney Channel; ESPN; ESPN2; Freeform; MTV; Nickelodeon; QVC; Spike TV; TBS; The Weather Channel; TNT; USA Network; VH1; WGN America.
Fee: $40.00 installation.
Pay Service 1
Pay Units: N.A.
Programming (via satellite): The Movie Channel.
Fee: $9.54 monthly.
Internet Service
Operational: No.
Miles of Plant: 10.0 (coaxial); None (fiber optic).
General Manager & Chief Technician: Barry L. Kepner.
Ownership: Valley Cable Systems (MSO).

MEYERSDALE—Comcast Cable. Now served by BLAIRSVILLE, PA [PA0320]. ICA: PA0192.

MIDLAND—Comcast Cable. Now served by PITTSBURGH, PA [PA0001]. ICA: PA0456.

MIDWAY BOROUGH—Formerly served by Adelphia Communications. Now served by Comcast Cable, PITTSBURGH, PA [PA0001]. ICA: PA0187.

MIFFLINBURG—Atlantic Broadband, 120 Southmont Blvd, Johnstown, PA 15905. Phones: 888-536-9600 (Customer service); 814-535-3506. Fax: 814-539-7749. E-mail: info@atlanticbb.com. Web Site: http://atlanticbb.com. Also serves Buffalo Twp. (Union County), Glen Iron, Hartleton, Hartley Twp., Laurelton, Lewis Twp. (Union County), Limestone, Limestone Twp. (Union County), Swengel, Union County (portions), Weikert & West Buffalo Twp. (portions). ICA: PA0131.
TV Market Ranking: Below 100 (Buffalo Twp. (Union County), Glen Iron, Hartleton, Hartley Twp., Laurelton, Lewis Twp. (Union County), Limestone Twp. (Union County), MIFFLINBURG, Swengel, Union County (portions), Weikert, West Buffalo Twp. (portions)); Outside TV Markets (Lewis Twp. (Union County), Limestone). Franchise award date: N.A. Franchise expiration date: N.A. Began: October 17, 1962.
Channel capacity: N.A. Channels available but not in use: N.A.
Basic Service
Subscribers: 502. Commercial subscribers: 19.
Programming (received off-air): WBRE-TV (NBC) Wilkes-Barre; WGAL (NBC, This TV)

Pennsylvania—Cable Systems

Lancaster; WHTM-TV (ABC, Retro TV) Harrisburg; WITF-TV (PBS) Harrisburg; WNEP-TV (ABC, Antenna TV) Scranton; WOLF-TV (CW, FOX, MNT) Hazleton; WVIA-TV (PBS) Scranton; WXBU (CW) Lancaster; WYOU (CBS) Scranton; allband FM.
Programming (via satellite): QVC; WPIX (Antenna TV, CW, This TV) New York.
Fee: $40.00 installation; $35.03 monthly.

Expanded Basic Service 1
Subscribers: 441.
Fee: $38.01 monthly.

Digital Basic Service
Subscribers: N.A.
Programming (via satellite): BBC America; CMT; Destination America; Discovery Kids Channel; Disney XD; DMX Music; ESPNews; Fuse; FYI; History International; IFC; Investigation Discovery; MTV Classic; MTV2; Nick Jr.; Science Channel; Starz; Starz Encore (multiplexed); TeenNick; WE tv.
Fee: $18.95 monthly.

Digital Pay Service 1
Pay Units: N.A.
Programming (via satellite): Cinemax (multiplexed); HBO (multiplexed); Showtime (multiplexed); The Movie Channel (multiplexed).
Fee: $14.95 monthly (Cinemax, HBO or Showtime/TMC).

Video-On-Demand: No
Pay-Per-View
iN DEMAND (delivered digitally); Club Jenna (delivered digitally); Playboy TV (delivered digitally).

Internet Service
Operational: Yes.
Broadband Service: Atlantic Broadband High-Speed Internet.
Fee: $23.95-$30.95 monthly.

Telephone Service
Analog: Operational
Miles of Plant: 137.0 (coaxial); None (fiber optic). Homes passed: 3,315.
Chief Financial Officer: Patrick Bratton. Senior Vice President & General Counsel: Leslie Brown. Vice President: David Dane. General Manager: Mike Papasergi. Technical Operations Director: Charles Sorchilla. Marketing & Customer Service Director: Dara Leslie. Marketing Manager: Natalie Kurchak.
Ownership: Atlantic Broadband (MSO).

MIFFLINTOWN—Nittany Media Inc., 18 Juniata St, PO Box 111, Lewistown, PA 17044. Phones: 800-692-7401; 717-248-3733. Fax: 717-248-3732. E-mail: info@nittanymedia.com. Web Site: http://www.nittanymedia.com. Also serves Bratton Twp., Center Twp. (Perry County), Delaware Twp. (Juniata County), Fayette Twp., Fermanagh Twp., Granville Twp., Greenwood Twp. (Juniata County), Ickesburg, Lewistown, McAlisterville, Mifflin, Milford Twp., Monroe Twp. (Juniata County), New Bloomfield, Old Port, Oliver Twp., Port Royal, Richfield, Saville Twp., Thompsontown, Turbett Twp. & West Perry Twp. ICA: PA0365.
TV Market Ranking: 57 (Center Twp. (Perry County), Ickesburg, New Bloomfield, Old Port, Port Royal, Richfield, Saville Twp., Thompsontown); Outside TV Markets (Bratton Twp., Delaware Twp. (Juniata County), Fayette Twp., Fermanagh Twp., Granville Twp., Greenwood Twp. (Juniata County), McAlisterville, Mifflin, MIFFLINTOWN, Milford Twp., Monroe Twp. (Juniata County), Oliver Twp., Turbett Twp., West Perry Twp., Lewistown).
Channel capacity: N.A. Channels available but not in use: N.A.

Basic Service
Subscribers: 2,541.
Programming (received off-air): WGAL (NBC, This TV) Lancaster; WHP-TV (CBS, MNT) Harrisburg; WHTM-TV (ABC, Retro TV) Harrisburg; WHVL-LP (MNT) State College, etc.; WITF-TV (PBS) Harrisburg; WNEP-TV (ABC, Antenna TV) Scranton; WOLF-TV (CW, FOX, MNT) Hazleton; WPMT (Antenna TV, FOX) York; WPSU-TV (PBS) Clearfield; WTAJ-TV (CBS) Altoona; WVIA-TV (PBS) Scranton; WXBU (CW) Lancaster.
Programming (via satellite): Bloomberg Television; C-SPAN; La Familia Cosmovision; Pennsylvania Cable Network; QVC.
Fee: $17.40 monthly.

Expanded Basic Service 1
Subscribers: N.A.
Programming (via satellite): A&E; AMC; Animal Planet; Boomerang; Bravo; Cartoon Network; CMT; CNBC; CNN; Comedy Central; Cornerstone Television; C-SPAN 2; Discovery Channel; Discovery Life Channel; Disney Channel; ESPN; ESPN2; Food Network; Fox News Channel; Fox Sports 1; FOX Sports Networks; Freeform; FX; Great American Country; Hallmark Channel; HGTV; History; HLN; INSP; ION Television; Lifetime; MSNBC; MTV; Nickelodeon; Outdoor Channel; Spike TV; Syfy; TBS; The Weather Channel; TLC; TNT; Travel Channel; Trinity Broadcasting Network (TBN); TV Land; USA Network; VH1; WGN America.
Fee: $27.10 monthly.

Digital Basic Service
Subscribers: N.A.
Programming (via satellite): AXS TV; BBC America; Bloomberg Television; Bravo; Cloo; CMT; Cooking Channel; Discovery Digital Networks; Disney XD; DMX Music; ESPN HD; ESPN2; Fox Sports 1; Fuse; FXM; FYI; GSN; HD Theater; HGTV; History; History International; LMN; Nick Jr.; Nicktoons; Outdoor Channel; Syfy; TeenNick; Trinity Broadcasting Network (TBN); TV Land; WE tv.
Fee: $15.99 monthly.

Digital Expanded Basic Service
Subscribers: N.A.
Programming (via satellite): ESPN Classic; ESPN2; Golf Channel; NBCSN.
Fee: $3.99 monthly.

Digital Expanded Basic Service 2
Subscribers: N.A.
Programming (via satellite): IFC; Turner Classic Movies.
Fee: $1.99 monthly.

Digital Pay Service 1
Pay Units: N.A.
Programming (via satellite): Cinemax (multiplexed); Flix; HBO (multiplexed); Showtime (multiplexed); Starz (multiplexed); Starz Encore (multiplexed); The Movie Channel (multiplexed).
Fee: $12.99 monthly (each).

Video-On-Demand: No
Pay-Per-View
iN DEMAND (delivered digitally).

Internet Service
Operational: Yes. Began: January 1, 2001.
Subscribers: 1,290.
Broadband Service: NMAX.
Fee: $40.00 installation; $34.99 monthly.

Telephone Service
Analog: Operational
Miles of Plant: 425.0 (coaxial); 135.0 (fiber optic). Homes passed: 8,000.
General Manager: Anna H. Hain. Chief Technician: Michael Hain.
Ownership: Nittany Media Inc. (MSO).

MIFFLINTOWN—Nittany Media Inc. Now served by MIFFLINTOWN (formerly Lewistown), PA [PA0365]. ICA: PA0368.

MILFORD—Blue Ridge Communications, 613 3rd St, PO Box 215, Palmerton, PA 18071-0215. Phones: 610-826-2551; 570-296-8200. Web Site: http://www.brctv.com. Also serves Berlin Twp. (Wayne County), Bethany, Bohemia, Cherry Ridge Twp. (Wayne County), Clifton Twp., Coolbaugh Twp., Damascus Twp., Dingman Twp., Dreher Twp., Dyberry Twp., Gouldsboro, Greene Twp. (Pike County), Hawley, Hemlock Farms Development, Honesdale, Lackawaxen Twp., Milford Twp. (Pike County), Palmyra Twp. (Pike County), Palmyra Twp. (Wayne County), Paupack Twp. (Wayne County), Porter Twp. (Pike County), Shohola Twp. & Texas Twp. (Wayne County). ICA: PA0369.
TV Market Ranking: 49 (Berlin Twp. (Wayne County), Bethany, Cherry Ridge Twp. (Wayne County), Coolbaugh Twp., Damascus Twp., Dreher Twp., Dyberry Twp., Hawley, Honesdale, Lackawaxen Twp., Palmyra Twp. (Pike County), Palmyra Twp. (Wayne County), Paupack Twp. (Wayne County), Shohola Twp., Texas Twp. (Wayne County)); Below 100 (Bohemia, Clifton Twp., Dingman Twp., Gouldsboro, Greene Twp. (Pike County), MILFORD, Milford Twp. (Pike County), Porter Twp. (Pike County), Hemlock Farms Development). Franchise award date: N.A. Franchise expiration date: N.A. Began: December 1, 1965.
Channel capacity: 42 (operating 2-way). Channels available but not in use: N.A.

Basic Service
Subscribers: 23,785. Commercial subscribers: 723.
Programming (received off-air): WABC-TV (ABC, Live Well Network) New York; WCBS-TV (CBS, Decades) New York; WMBC-TV (Azteca America) Newton; WNBC (COZI TV, NBC) New York; WNEP-TV (ABC, Antenna TV) Scranton; WNET (PBS) Newark; WNYW (FOX, Movies!) New York; WOLF-TV (CW, FOX, MNT) Hazleton; WPHL-TV (Antenna TV, MNT, This TV) Philadelphia; WPIX (Antenna TV, CW, This TV) New York; WSKG-TV (PBS) Binghamton; WTBY-TV (TBN) Poughkeepsie; WVIA-TV (PBS) Scranton; WWOR-TV (Bounce TV, Buzzr, Heroes & Icons, MNT) Secaucus; WYOU (CBS) Scranton; allband FM.
Programming (via satellite): Pennsylvania Cable Network.
Fee: $49.95 installation; $27.74 monthly.

Expanded Basic Service 1
Subscribers: N.A.
Programming (via satellite): A&E; AMC; Animal Planet; Cartoon Network; CMT; CNBC; CNN; Comedy Central; C-SPAN; Discovery Channel; Disney Channel; E! HD; ESPN; ESPN2; EWTN Global Catholic Network; Food Network; Fox News Channel; Fox Sports 1; Freeform; FX; Golf Channel; HGTV; History; HLN; Lifetime; LMN; MSG; MSNBC; MTV; NBCSN; Nickelodeon; OWN: Oprah Winfrey Network; Pop; QVC; Spike TV; Syfy; TBS; The Weather Channel; TLC; TNT; Travel Channel; truTV; Turner Classic Movies; TV Land; USA Network; VH1; WE tv; YES Network.
Fee: $28.09 monthly.

Digital Basic Service
Subscribers: N.A.
Programming (via satellite): Concert TV; Discovery Digital Networks; Disney XD; FSN Digital Atlantic; FSN Digital Central; FSN Digital Pacific; FXM; HRTV; MC; National Geographic Channel; Nick 2; Nick Jr.; Nicktoons; Outdoor Channel; TeenNick.
Fee: $35.00 installation; $9.95 monthly.

Digital Expanded Basic Service
Subscribers: N.A.
Programming (via satellite): BBC America; Bloomberg Television; Boomerang; Cooking Channel; DIY Network; FYI; Hallmark Channel; History International.
Fee: $5.00 monthly.

Pay Service 1
Pay Units: N.A.
Programming (via satellite): Cinemax; HBO; Showtime.
Fee: $11.50 monthly (Cinemax or Showtime), $12.50 monthly (HBO).

Digital Pay Service 1
Pay Units: N.A.
Programming (via satellite): Cinemax (multiplexed); Flix; HBO (multiplexed); Showtime (multiplexed); Starz (multiplexed); Starz Encore (multiplexed); Sundance TV; The Movie Channel (multiplexed).
Fee: $12.50 monthly (Cinemax or Showtime/Flix/Sundance/TMC), $12.95 monthly (Starz/Encore), $13.50 monthly (HBO).

Video-On-Demand: Yes
Pay-Per-View
iN DEMAND; iN DEMAND (delivered digitally); adult (delivered digitally).

Internet Service
Operational: Yes.
Broadband Service: ProLog Express.
Fee: $34.95 monthly; $10.00 modem lease; $59.95 modem purchase.

Telephone Service
None
President: David Masenheimer. Vice President, Operations: Richard Semmel. General Manager: Mark Masonheimer. Fiber Manager: Randy Semmel. Chief Technician: Garry Woods.
Ownership: Pencor Services Inc. (MSO).

MILL VILLAGE—Formerly served by Cebridge Connections. Now served by Armstrong Cable Services, ZELIENOPLE, PA [PA0053]. ICA: PA0277.

MILLERSBURG BOROUGH—Comcast Cable. Now served by HARRISBURG, PA [PA0009]. ICA: PA0373.

MILLHEIM—Millheim TV Transmission Co., 160 West Alley, PO Box 365, Millheim, PA 16854. Phone: 814-349-4837. Fax: 814-349-5857. Also serves Aaronsburg, Coburn & Spring Mills. ICA: PA0216.
TV Market Ranking: Below 100 (Aaronsburg, Coburn, MILLHEIM, Spring Mills). Franchise award date: January 1, 1996. Franchise expiration date: N.A. Began: January 1, 1962.
Channel capacity: N.A. Channels available but not in use: N.A.

Basic Service
Subscribers: N.A.
Programming (received off-air): WBRE-TV (NBC) Wilkes-Barre; WHTM-TV (ABC, Retro TV) Harrisburg; WJAC-TV (MeTV, NBC) Johnstown; WKBS-TV (IND) Altoona; WNEP-TV (ABC, Antenna TV) Scranton; WOLF-TV (CW, FOX, MNT) Hazleton; WSWB (CW, MeTV) Scranton; WTAJ-TV (CBS) Altoona; WVIA-TV (PBS) Scranton; allband FM.
Programming (via satellite): A&E; AMC; Animal Planet; CMT; CNN; Discovery Channel; Disney Channel; ESPN; ESPN2; Fox News Channel; Freeform; FX; History;

Cable Systems—Pennsylvania

FULLY SEARCHABLE • CONTINUOUSLY UPDATED • DISCOUNT RATES FOR PRINT PURCHASERS

For more information call **800-771-9202** or visit **www.warren-news.com**

Nickelodeon; Outdoor Channel; QVC; Root Sports Pittsburgh; Spike TV; TBS; TLC; TNT; TV Land; USA Network; WGN America; WPIX (Antenna TV, CW, This TV) New York.
Pay Service 1
Pay Units: N.A.
Programming (via satellite): HBO.
Fee: $10.00 installation; $10.00 monthly.
Video-On-Demand: No
Internet Service
Operational: No.
Telephone Service
None
Miles of Plant: 55.0 (coaxial); None (fiber optic). Homes passed: 800.
General Manager: Wayne Rishel. Technical Engineer: David McClintick. Office Manager: Vickie Saserman.
Ownership: Millheim TV Transmission Co.

MILLMONT—Formerly served by D&E Communications. No longer in operation. ICA: PA5283.

MONROEVILLE—Comcast Cable. Now served by PITTSBURGH, PA [PA0001]. ICA: PA0023.

MONTGOMERY TWP. (Lycoming County)—Comcast Cable. Now served by HARRISBURG, PA [PA0009]. ICA: PA0056.

MONTROSE BOROUGH—Time Warner Cable. Now served by DEWITT, NY [NY0013]. ICA: PA0171.

MONUMENT—Formerly served by Monument TV. No longer in operation. ICA: PA0376.

MOUNT MORRIS—Comcast Cable. Now served by PITTSBURGH, PA [PA0001]. ICA: PA0254.

MOUNT OLIVER—Formerly served by Mount Oliver TV Cable/Adelphia Cable. Now served by Comcast Cable, PITTSBURGH, PA [PA0001]. ICA: PA0162.

MOUNT PLEASANT MILLS—Zampelli Electronics, PO Box 830, Lewistown, PA 17044-0830. Phone: 717-248-1544. Also serves Monroe, Port Trevorton & West Perry Twp. ICA: PA0377.
TV Market Ranking: 57 (MOUNT PLEASANT MILLS, West Perry Twp.); Outside TV Markets (Port Trevorton). Franchise award date: N.A. Franchise expiration date: N.A. Began: January 1, 1965.
Channel capacity: 18 (not 2-way capable). Channels available but not in use: N.A.
Basic Service
Subscribers: N.A.
Programming (received off-air): WBRE-TV (NBC) Wilkes-Barre; WGAL (NBC, This TV) Lancaster; WGCB-TV (MeTV) Red Lion; WHP-TV (CBS, MNT) Harrisburg; WHTM-TV (ABC, Retro TV) Harrisburg; WITF-TV (PBS) Harrisburg; WNEP-TV (ABC, Antenna TV) Scranton; WOLF-TV (CW, FOX, MNT) Hazleton; WPHL-TV (Antenna TV, MNT, This TV) Philadelphia; WPMT (Antenna TV, FOX) York; WTXF-TV (Buzzr, FOX, Movies!) Philadelphia; WVIA-TV (PBS) Scranton; WXBU (CW) Lancaster.
Programming (via satellite): Discovery Channel; ESPN; Spike TV; TBS; USA Network; WGN America.
Video-On-Demand: No
Internet Service
Operational: No.
Telephone Service
None
Miles of Plant: 25.0 (coaxial); None (fiber optic).
General Manager & Chief Technician: Joe Zampelli.
Ownership: Zampelli TV (MSO).

MUNCY VALLEY—Blue Ridge Communications, 613 3rd St, PO Box 215, Palmerton, PA 18071-0215. Phone: 800-222-5377. Web Site: http://www.brctv.com. Also serves Davidson Twp. ICA: PA0476.
TV Market Ranking: Below 100 (Davidson Twp., MUNCY VALLEY).
Channel capacity: N.A. Channels available but not in use: N.A.
Basic Service
Subscribers: 34. Commercial subscribers: 7.
Fee: $40.00 installation; $16.83 monthly.
President: David Masenheimer.
Ownership: Pencor Services Inc. (MSO).

MURRYSVILLE—Formerly served by Adelphia Communications. No longer in operation. ICA: PA0378.

NANTY GLO—Formerly served by Adelphia Communications. Now served by Comcast Cable, BLAIRSVILLE, PA [PA0320]. ICA: PA0145.

NEELYTON—Formerly served by Valley Cable Systems. No longer in operation. ICA: PA0298.

NEW BALTIMORE—Comcast Cable. Now served by BLAIRSVILLE, PA [PA0320]. ICA: PA0292.

NEW BERLIN—Formerly served by D&E Communications/Windstream. IPTV service no longer in operation. ICA: PA5284.

NEW BETHLEHEM—Formerly served by Adelphia Communications. Now served by Comcast Cable, PUNXSUTAWNEY, PA [PA0397]. ICA: PA0167.

NEW BLOOMFIELD—Nittany Media Inc. Now served by MIFFLINTOWN, PA [PA0365]. ICA: PA0380.

NEW CASTLE—Comcast Cable. Now served by HARRISBURG, PA [PA0009]. ICA: PA0041.

NEW COLUMBIA—Formerly served by D&E Communications. No longer in operation. ICA: PA5285.

NEW ENTERPRISE—Atlantic Broadband, 120 Southmont Blvd, Johnstown, PA 15905. Phone: 800-400-5568. Web Site: http://atlanticbb.com. Also serves East St. Clair Twp. (Bedford County), King Twp., South Woodbury Twp. & St. Clairsville. ICA: PA0477.
TV Market Ranking: 74 (East St. Clair Twp. (Bedford County), King Twp., NEW ENTERPRISE, South Woodbury Twp., St. Clairsville).
Channel capacity: N.A. Channels available but not in use: N.A.
Basic Service
Subscribers: 848.
Fee: $45.40 monthly.
Senior Vice President & General Manager: Bartlett F. Leber.
Ownership: Atlantic Broadband (MSO).

NEW MILFORD TWP.—Adams Cable Service. Now served by THOMPSON TWP, PA [PA0414]. ICA: PA0381.

NEW WILMINGTON—Armstrong Cable Services. Now served by ZELIENOPLE, PA [PA0053]. ICA: PA0382.

NEWBERRY TWP.—Blue Ridge Communications, 613 3rd St, PO Box 215, Palmerton, PA 18071-0215. Phones: 610-826-2551; 800-232-2273 (Customer service); 717-938-6501. Web Site: http://www.brctv.com. Also serves Carroll Twp. (Perry County), Duncannon, Fairview Twp. (York County), Lewisberry, Miller Twp. (Perry County), New Buffalo, Penn Twp. (Perry County), Reed Twp. (Perry County), Rye Twp., Warrington Twp. (York County), Watts Twp., Wellsville & Wheatfield Twp. ICA: PA0105.
TV Market Ranking: 57 (Carroll Twp. (Perry County), Duncannon, Fairview Twp. (York County), Lewisberry, Miller Twp. (Perry County), New Buffalo, NEWBERRY TWP., Penn Twp. (Perry County), Reed Twp. (Perry County), Rye Twp., Warrington Twp. (York County), Watts Twp., Wellsville, Wheatfield Twp.). Franchise award date: N.A. Franchise expiration date: N.A. Began: May 1, 1982.
Channel capacity: 63 (operating 2-way). Channels available but not in use: N.A.
Basic Service
Subscribers: 7,183. Commercial subscribers: 108.
Programming (received off-air): WGAL (NBC, This TV) Lancaster; WGCB-TV (MeTV) Red Lion; WHP-TV (CBS, MNT) Harrisburg; WHTM-TV (ABC, Retro TV) Harrisburg; WITF-TV (PBS) Harrisburg; WPHL-TV (Antenna TV, MNT, This TV) Philadelphia; WPMT (Antenna TV, FOX) York; WTXF-TV (Buzzr, FOX, Movies!) Philadelphia; WXBU (CW) Lancaster.
Fee: $49.95 installation; $20.49 monthly.
Expanded Basic Service 1
Subscribers: N.A.
Programming (via satellite): A&E; AMC; Animal Planet; Bravo; Cartoon Network; CMT; CNBC; CNN; Comcast SportsNet Mid-Atlantic; Comcast SportsNet Philadelphia; Comedy Central; C-SPAN; Discovery Channel; Disney Channel; E! HD; ESPN; ESPN2; EWTN Global Catholic Network; Food Network; Fox News Channel; Fox Sports 1; Freeform; FX; Golf Channel; GSN; Hallmark Channel; HGTV; History; HLN; INSP; Lifetime; LMN; MSNBC; MTV; National Geographic Channel; NBCSN; Nickelodeon; OWN: Oprah Winfrey Network; QVC; Root Sports Pittsburgh; Spike TV; Syfy; TBS; The Weather Channel; TLC; TNT; Travel Channel; Trinity Broadcasting Network (TBN); truTV; Turner Classic Movies; TV Land; USA Network; VH1; WE tv.
Fee: $32.14 monthly.
Digital Basic Service
Subscribers: N.A.
Programming (via satellite): AXS TV; Boomerang; Comcast SportsNet Philadelphia; Cooking Channel; Discovery Life Channel; Disney XD; DIY Network; ESPN; EVINE Live; FOX College Sports Central; FOX College Sports Pacific; FXM; FYI; Great American Country; History International; HRTV; IFC; MTV Classic; MTV2; NBA TV; NFL Network; Nick 2; Nick Jr.; Nicktoons; Outdoor Channel; Oxygen; TeenNick; Tennis Channel.
Fee: $14.95 monthly.
Digital Pay Service 1
Pay Units: N.A.
Programming (via satellite): Cinemax (multiplexed); Flix; HBO (multiplexed); HBO HD; Showtime (multiplexed); Showtime HD; Starz; Starz Encore (multiplexed); Sundance TV; The Movie Channel (multiplexed).
Fee: $12.50 monthly (Cinemax, Showtime or TMC), $12.95 monthly (Starz), $13.50 monthly (HBO).
Video-On-Demand: Yes
Pay-Per-View
iN DEMAND.
Internet Service
Operational: Yes.
Subscribers: 4,553.
Broadband Service: ProLog Express.
Fee: $36.95 monthly.
Telephone Service
Digital: Operational
Subscribers: 723.
Miles of Plant: 385.0 (coaxial); 111.0 (fiber optic). Homes passed: 7,520.
President: David Masenheimer. Vice President, Operations: Richard Semmel. General Manager: Mark Masonheimer. Chief Technician: Randy Semmel.
Ownership: Pencor Services Inc. (MSO).

NEWBURG—Kuhn Communications, 301 West Main St, Walnut Bottom, PA 17266. Phones: 800-771-7072; 717-532-8857. Web Site: http://www.kuhncom.net. Also serves Hopewell Twp. ICA: PA0272.
TV Market Ranking: Outside TV Markets (Hopewell Twp., NEWBURG).
Channel capacity: N.A. Channels available but not in use: N.A.
Basic Service
Subscribers: 420.
Fee: $30.00 installation; $15.45 monthly.
President & General Manager: Earl W. Kuhn.
Ownership: Kuhn Communications (MSO).

NEWPORT BOROUGH—Comcast Cable. Now served by HARRISBURG, PA [PA0009]. ICA: PA0454.

NEWTOWN BOROUGH—Comcast Cable. Now served by EATONTOWN BOROUGH, NJ [NJ0009]. ICA: PA0083.

NORRISTOWN—Comcast Cable. Now served by EATONTOWN BOROUGH, NJ [NJ0009]. ICA: PA0028.

NORTH BETHLEHEM TWP.—Bentleyville Communications, 908 W Frontview St, Dodge City, KS 67801. Phones: 800-400-5568; 724-267-3333; 724-239-2501. Web Site: http://www.fairpoint.com. Also serves Amwell Twp., Bentleyville, Ellsworth, Fal-

2017 Edition
D-667

Pennsylvania—Cable Systems

lowfield Twp., Somerset Twp. (Washington County) & South Strabane Twp. ICA: PA0442.
Note: This system is an overbuild.
TV Market Ranking: 10 (Bentleyville, Ellsworth, Fallowfield Twp., Somerset Twp. (Washington County), South Strabane Twp.); 10,90 (Amwell Twp., NORTH BETHLEHEM TWP.). Franchise award date: January 1, 1992. Franchise expiration date: N.A. Began: N.A.
Channel capacity: N.A. Channels available but not in use: N.A.

Basic Service
Subscribers: 901.
Programming (received off-air): KDKA-TV (CBS, Decades) Pittsburgh; WINP-TV (IND, ION) Pittsburgh; WPCB-TV (IND) Greensburg; WPCW (CW) Jeannette; WPGH-TV (Antenna TV, FOX, The Country Network) Pittsburgh; WPNT (MNT) Pittsburgh; WPXI (MeTV, NBC) Pittsburgh; WQED (PBS) Pittsburgh; WTAE-TV (ABC, This TV) Pittsburgh.
Programming (via satellite): A&E; AMC; Animal Planet; Cartoon Network; CMT; CNBC; CNN; Comedy Central; C-SPAN; Discovery Channel; Disney Channel; Disney XD; E! HD; ESPN; ESPN2; EWTN Global Catholic Network; Food Network; Fox News Channel; Fox Sports 1; Freeform; FX; Golf Channel; Hallmark Channel; HGTV; History; HLN; ION Television; Lifetime; LMN; MSNBC; MTV; Nickelodeon; Outdoor Channel; Pennsylvania Cable Network; QVC; Root Sports Pittsburgh; Spike TV; Syfy; TBS; The Weather Channel; TLC; TNT; Trinity Broadcasting Network (TBN); Turner Classic Movies; TV Land; USA Network; VH1; Vubiquity Inc.; WE tv; WGN America.
Fee: $42.00 installation; $58.00 monthly; $3.00 converter.

Pay Service 1
Pay Units: 40.
Programming (via satellite): Cinemax.
Fee: $12.50 monthly.

Pay Service 2
Pay Units: 59.
Programming (via satellite): The Movie Channel.
Fee: $11.00 monthly.

Pay Service 3
Pay Units: 100.
Programming (via satellite): HBO.
Fee: $14.25 monthly.

Pay Service 4
Pay Units: 18.
Programming (via satellite): Playboy TV.
Fee: $12.00 monthly.

Pay Service 5
Pay Units: 72.
Programming (via satellite): Showtime.
Fee: $11.75 monthly.

Video-On-Demand: No
Pay-Per-View
iN DEMAND; Playboy TV.

Internet Service
Operational: Yes. Began: March 1, 1995.
Broadband Service: Nauticaus.
Fee: $40.50 installation; $44.95 monthly; $80.00 modem purchase.

Telephone Service
Digital: Operational
Fee: $39.95 monthly
Miles of Plant: 93.0 (coaxial); 15.0 (fiber optic). Homes passed: 2,894.
Senior Vice President, Governmental Affairs: Pat Morse. Plant Manager: Walter R. Ziemba. Chief Technician: John B. Conkle. Marketing Director: Pam Joy. Accounting Director: Angela Unruh.
Ownership: FairPoint Communications Inc.

NORTH CLARION—Armstrong Cable Services. Now served by ZELIENOPLE, PA [PA0053]. ICA: PA0142.

NORTHAMPTON—RCN Corp. This cable system has converted to IPTV. See ALLENTOWN, PA [PA5201]. ICA: PA0008.

OIL CITY—Comcast Cable, 219 North Findley St, Punxsutawney, PA 15767-2020. Phone: 814-938-6130. Fax: 514-938-7622. Web Site: http://www.comcast.com. Also serves Clarion Borough, Clarion Twp., Cornplanter Twp. (Venango County), Cranberry Twp. (Venango County), Emlenton Borough, Foxburg Borough, Hovey Twp., Madison Twp., Monroe Twp. (Clarion County), Oakland Twp., Parker, Parker Twp., Perry Twp. (Clarion County), Piney Twp., Richland Twp. (Clarion County), Richland Twp. (Venango County), Rimersburg, Rouseville Borough, Sligo, St. Petersburg Borough, Strattanville Borough, Sugarcreek Borough & Toby Twp. ICA: PA0086.
TV Market Ranking: Outside TV Markets (Clarion Twp., Cornplanter Twp. (Venango County), Cranberry Twp. (Venango County), Emlenton Borough, Foxburg Borough, Hovey Twp., Madison Twp., Monroe Twp. (Clarion County), Oakland Twp., OIL CITY, Parker, Parker Twp., Perry Twp. (Clarion County), Piney Twp., Richland Twp. (Clarion County), Richland Twp. (Venango County), Rimersburg, Rouseville Borough, Sligo, St. Petersburg Borough, Strattanville Borough, Sugarcreek Borough, Toby Twp., Clarion Borough). Franchise award date: October 1, 1951. Franchise expiration date: N.A. Began: October 1, 1951.
Channel capacity: N.A. Channels available but not in use: N.A.

Basic Service
Subscribers: 6,885. Commercial subscribers: 173.
Programming (received off-air): KDKA-TV (CBS, Decades) Pittsburgh; WICU-TV (NBC) Erie; WJET-TV (ABC) Erie; WPCB-TV (IND) Greensburg; WPGH-TV (Antenna TV, FOX, The Country Network) Pittsburgh; WPXI (MeTV, NBC) Pittsburgh; WQED (PBS) Pittsburgh; WQLN (PBS) Erie; WSEE-TV (CBS, CW) Erie; WTAE-TV (ABC, This TV) Pittsburgh; allband FM.
Programming (via satellite): C-SPAN; C-SPAN 2; ESPN; Freeform; Hallmark Channel; Pop; TBS.
Fee: $29.50-$42.75 installation; $25.24 monthly; $3.00 converter.

Expanded Basic Service 1
Subscribers: N.A.
Programming (via satellite): A&E; AMC; Animal Planet; Cartoon Network; CNN; Discovery Channel; Disney Channel; Fox News Channel; FX; HGTV; HLN; Lifetime; MSNBC; MTV; Nickelodeon; Pennsylvania Cable Network; QVC; Root Sports Pittsburgh; Spike TV; The Weather Channel; TLC; TNT; truTV; TV Land; USA Network; VH1.
Fee: $20.00 installation; $3.00 monthly.

Digital Basic Service
Subscribers: N.A.
Programming (via satellite): BBC America; Bravo; Destination America; Discovery Kids Channel; ESPN Classic; ESPN2; ESPNews; Golf Channel; GSN; History; IFC; Investigation Discovery; NBCSN; Outdoor Channel; OWN: Oprah Winfrey Network; Science Channel; Syfy; Turner Classic Movies; WE tv.
Fee: $15.95 monthly.

Digital Expanded Basic Service
Subscribers: N.A.
Programming (via satellite): National Geographic Channel; Nick Jr.; VH1 Country.

Pay Service 1
Pay Units: N.A.
Programming (via satellite): Cinemax; HBO; Starz.
Fee: $20.00 installation; $10.20 monthly (Cinemax), $11.40 monthly (Showtime), $11.80 monthly (HBO).

Digital Pay Service 1
Pay Units: N.A.
Programming (via satellite): Cinemax; HBO; Showtime; Starz; The Movie Channel.

Video-On-Demand: No
Pay-Per-View
Hot Choice (delivered digitally); Fresh (delivered digitally); Playboy TV (delivered digitally).

Internet Service
Operational: Yes.
Subscribers: 5,320.
Broadband Service: Comcast High Speed Internet.
Fee: $42.95 monthly.

Telephone Service
Digital: Operational
Subscribers: 2,830.
Miles of Plant: 514.0 (coaxial); 156.0 (fiber optic). Homes passed: 19,818.
General Manager: Scott Brush. Technical Operations Manager: Bob Brush. Marketing Manager: David Smith. Office Manager: Suzanne Smith.
Ownership: Comcast Cable Communications Inc. (MSO).

OLD PORT—Nittany Media Inc. Now served by MIFFLINTOWN, PA [PA0365]. ICA: PA0287.

ORRSTOWN—Kuhn Communications, 301 West Main St, Walnut Bottom, PA 17266. Phones: 800-771-7072; 717-532-8857. Fax: 717-532-5563. Web Site: http://www.kuhncom.net. ICA: PA0218.
TV Market Ranking: Below 100 (ORRSTOWN).
Channel capacity: N.A. Channels available but not in use: N.A.

Basic Service
Subscribers: 493.
Fee: $30.00 installation; $15.45 monthly.
President & General Manager: Earl W. Kuhn.
Ownership: Kuhn Communications (MSO).

ORVISTON—Formerly served by Orviston TV. No longer in operation. ICA: PA0385.

OSWAYO—Zito Media, 102 S Main St, PO Box 665, Coudersport, PA 16915. Phones: 814-260-9055; 800-365-6988. Fax: 814-260-9580. E-mail: info@zitomedia.com. Web Site: http://www.zitomedia.com. Also serves Genesee. ICA: PA0386.
TV Market Ranking: Outside TV Markets (Genesee, OSWAYO). Franchise award date: January 1, 1989. Franchise expiration date: N.A. Began: January 1, 1989.
Channel capacity: N.A. Channels available but not in use: N.A.

Basic Service
Subscribers: 3,700.
Programming (received off-air): WGRZ (Antenna TV, NBC, WeatherNation) Buffalo; WIVB-TV (CBS) Buffalo; WJAC-TV (MeTV, NBC) Johnstown; WKBW-TV (ABC, Escape) Buffalo; WNED-TV (PBS) Buffalo; WPSU-TV (PBS) Clearfield; WTAJ-TV (CBS) Altoona; WWCP-TV (FOX) Johnstown.
Programming (via satellite): WGN America; WPIX (Antenna TV, CW, This TV) New York.
Fee: $29.95 installation.

Expanded Basic Service 1
Subscribers: N.A.
Programming (via satellite): A&E; AMC; Animal Planet; Cartoon Network; CMT; CNBC; CNN; C-SPAN; C-SPAN 2; Discovery Channel; Disney Channel; E! HD; ESPN; ESPN Classic; ESPN2; EWTN Global Catholic Network; Food Network; Fox News Channel; Freeform; FX; Hallmark Channel; HGTV; History; HLN; INSP; Lifetime; MSG; MSNBC; MTV; NFL Network; Nickelodeon; QVC; Root Sports Pittsburgh; Spike TV; Syfy; TBS; The Weather Channel; TLC; TNT; Trinity Broadcasting Network (TBN); Turner Classic Movies; TV Land; USA Network; VH1.
Fee: $18.05 monthly.

Digital Basic Service
Subscribers: N.A.
Programming (via satellite): BBC America; Bloomberg Television; Boomerang; C-SPAN 3; Destination America; Discovery Kids Channel; Discovery Life Channel; Disney XD; ESPN HD; ESPN2 HD; ESPNews; Fox Sports 1; FXM; Golf Channel; Great American Country; GSN; HRTV; INSP; Investigation Discovery; LMN; MC; MTV Classic; MTV Hits; MTV Jams; MTV2; Nick 2; Nicktoons; OWN: Oprah Winfrey Network; RFD-TV; Science Channel; TeenNick; The Word Network; Trinity Broadcasting Network (TBN); VH1 Country; VH1 Soul; WE tv.
Fee: $15.95 monthly.

Digital Expanded Basic Service
Subscribers: N.A.
Programming (via satellite): DIY Network; Flix; FSN Digital Atlantic; FSN Digital Central; FSN Digital Pacific; FYI; History International; IFC; NBCSN; Outdoor Channel; Sundance TV.
Fee: $10.00 monthly.

Digital Pay Service 1
Pay Units: N.A.
Programming (via satellite): Cinemax (multiplexed); Cinemax HD; Flix; HBO (multiplexed); HBO HD; Showtime (multiplexed); Showtime HD; Starz (multiplexed); Starz Encore (multiplexed); Starz HD; The Movie Channel (multiplexed).
Fee: $8.00 monthly (Cinemax or Starz/Encore), $10.00 monthly (HBO or Showtime/TMC/Flix).

Video-On-Demand: Planned
Pay-Per-View
iN DEMAND (delivered digitally); NHL Center Ice (delivered digitally); MLB Extra Innings (delivered digitally).

Internet Service
Operational: Yes.
Subscribers: 3,638.
Fee: $42.95 monthly.

Telephone Service
Digital: Operational
Subscribers: 1,924.
Fee: $35.00 monthly
Miles of Plant: 100.0 (coaxial); 20.0 (fiber optic). Homes passed: 8,000.
President: James Rigas.
Ownership: Zito Media (MSO).

PARKS TWP.—Comcast Cable. Now served by BLAIRSVILLE, PA [PA0320]. ICA: PA0388.

PENN HILLS—Comcast Cable. Now served by PITTSBURGH, PA [PA0001]. ICA: PA0458.

Cable Systems—Pennsylvania

PHILADELPHIA—Comcast Cable, 200 Cresson Blvd, PO Box 0989, Oaks, PA 19456-0989. Phone: 215-286-1700. Fax: 215-286-7790. Web Site: http://www.comcast.com. Also serves Arden, Ardencroft, Ardentown, Bellefonte, Elsmere, New Castle, New Castle County (portions), Newark, Newport & Wilmington, DE; Aldan, Aston Twp., Atglen, Avondale Borough, Bethel Twp. (Delaware County), Birmingham Twp., Brookhaven, Caln Twp., Chadds Ford Twp., Chester, Chester Heights, Chester Twp., Clifton Heights, Coatesville, Collingdale, Colwyn, Concord Twp. (Delaware County), Concordville, Darby Borough, Darby Twp., Downingtown Borough, East Bradford Twp., East Brandywine Twp., East Caln Twp., East Fallowfield Twp. (Chester County), East Goshen Twp., East Lansdowne, East Marlborough Twp., East Whiteland Twp., Easttown Twp., Eddystone (Delaware County), Edgemont Twp., Folcroft, Franklin Twp. (Chester County), Glenolden, Haverford Twp., Honey Brook, Kennett Square Borough, Kennett Twp., Lansdowne, London Britain Twp., London Grove Twp., Lower Chichester Twp., Lower Merion Twp., Lower Moreland Twp., Malvern, Marcus Hook, Marple Twp., Media Borough, Middletown Twp., Millbourne, Modena Borough, Morton (Delaware County), Narberth Borough, Nether Providence Twp., New Garden Twp., New London Twp., Newtown Twp., Norwood, Parkesburg Borough, Parkside, Penn Twp. (Chester County), Pennsbury Twp., Pocopson Twp., Prospect Park, Radnor, Ridley Park (Delaware County), Ridley Twp., Rose Valley, Rutledge, Sadsbury Twp. (Chester County), Sharon Hill, South Coatesville Borough, Springfield, Swarthmore, Thornbury Twp. (Chester County), Thornbury Twp. (Delaware County), Tinicum Twp., Trainer, Tredyffrin Twp., Upland, Upper Chichester Twp., Upper Darby, Upper Moreland Twp., Upper Oxford Twp., Upper Providence, Upper Uwchlan Twp., Uwchlan Twp., Valley Twp. (Chester County), Wallace Twp., West Bradford Twp., West Brandywine Twp., West Caln Twp., West Chester Borough, West Goshen Twp., West Grove Borough, West Nantmeal Twp., West Pikeland Twp., West Sadsbury Twp., West Vincent Twp., West Whiteland Twp., Westtown Twp., Willistown Twp. & Yeadon, PA. ICA: PA0005.
TV Market Ranking: 4 (Aldan, Arden, Ardencroft, Ardentown, Aston Twp., Bellefonte, Bethel Twp. (Delaware County), Birmingham Twp., Brookhaven, Chadds Ford Twp., Chester, Chester Heights, Chester Twp., Clifton Heights, Collingdale, Colwyn, Concord Twp. (Delaware County), Concordville, Darby Borough, Darby Twp., East Goshen Twp., East Lansdowne, East Whiteland Twp., Eddystone (Delaware County), Edgemont Twp., Elsmere, Folcroft, Glenolden, Haverford Twp., Lansdowne, Lower Chichester Twp., Lower Merion Twp., Lower Moreland Twp., Malvern, Marcus Hook, Marple Twp., Media Borough, Middletown Twp., Millbourne, Narberth Borough, Nether Providence Twp., New Castle, New Castle County (portions) (portions), Newport, Newtown Twp., Norwood, Parkside, Pennsbury Twp., PHILADELPHIA, Prospect Park, Radnor, Ridley Park (Delaware County), Ridley Twp., Rose Valley, Rutledge, Sharon Hill, Springfield, Swarthmore, Thornbury Twp. (Chester County), Thornbury Twp. (Delaware County), Tinicum Twp., Trainer, Tredyffrin Twp., Upland, Upper Chichester Twp., Upper Darby, Upper Moreland Twp., Upper Providence, West Vincent Twp., West Whiteland Twp., Willistown Twp.,

Wilmington, Yeadon); 4,57 (Avondale Borough, Caln Twp., Coatesville, Downingtown Borough, East Bradford Twp., East Brandywine Twp., East Caln Twp., East Fallowfield Twp. (Chester County), East Marlborough Twp., Kennett Square Borough, London Britain Twp., London Grove Twp., New Garden Twp., Upper Oxford Twp., Wallace Twp.); 57 (Atglen, Franklin Twp. (Chester County), Honey Brook, Kennett Twp., Modena Borough, New London Twp., Parkesburg Borough, Penn Twp. (Chester County), Pocopson Twp., Sadsbury Twp. (Chester County), South Coatesville Borough, Upper Uwchlan Twp., Uwchlan Twp., Valley Twp. (Chester County), West Bradford Twp., West Brandywine Twp., West Caln Twp., West Chester Borough, West Goshen Twp., West Grove Borough, West Nantmeal Twp., West Pikeland Twp., West Sadsbury Twp., Westtown Twp.); Below 100 (Newark, New Castle County (portions) (portions)). Franchise award date: November 1, 1984. Franchise expiration date: N.A. Began: September 1, 1986.
Channel capacity: N.A. Channels available but not in use: N.A.

Basic Service
Subscribers: 505,915.
Programming (received off-air): KYW-TV (CBS, Decades) Philadelphia; WBPH-TV (IND) Bethlehem; WCAU (COZI TV, NBC) Philadelphia; WFMZ-TV (Retro TV) Allentown; WFPA-CD (UniMas) Philadelphia; WGTW-TV (TBN) Burlington; WHYY-TV (PBS) Wilmington; WLVT-TV (PBS) Allentown; WMCN-TV (Bounce TV, Tuff TV) Atlantic City; WNJS (PBS) Camden; WPHL-TV (Antenna TV, MNT, This TV) Philadelphia; WPPX-TV (ION) Wilmington; WPSG (CW) Philadelphia; WPVI-TV (ABC, Live Well Network) Philadelphia; WTVE (IND) Reading; WTXF-TV (Buzzr, FOX, Movies!) Philadelphia; WUVP-DT (getTV, UNV) Vineland; WYBE (ETV, IND) Philadelphia.
Programming (via satellite): A&E; AMC; Animal Planet; BET; Bravo; Cartoon Network; CNBC; CNN; Comcast Network Philadelphia; Comcast SportsNet Philadelphia; Comedy Central; C-SPAN; C-SPAN 2; Discovery Channel; Disney Channel; E! HD; ESPN; ESPN2; EWTN Global Catholic Network; Food Network; Fox News Channel; Fox Sports 1; Freeform; FX; Golf Channel; GSN; Hallmark Channel; HGTV; History; HLN; Lifetime; MSNBC; MTV; NBCSN; Nickelodeon; Pennsylvania Cable Network; Pop; QVC; Spike TV; Syfy; TBS; The Weather Channel; TLC; TNT; truTV; Turner Classic Movies; TV Land; TV One; USA Network; VH1.
Fee: $23.00 monthly.

Digital Basic Service
Subscribers: N.A.
Programming (via satellite): BBC America; Comcast SportsNet Philadelphia; Discovery Digital Networks; DMX Music; ESPN HD; ESPN2 HD; Flix; HD Theater; Mid-Atlantic Sports Network (MASN); MTV Live; NBA TV; Nick Jr.; Starz Encore; Sundance TV; TeenNick; TNT HD; Universal HD; Versus HD; Weatherscan; WeatherVision.
Fee: $6.15 monthly.

Digital Pay Service 1
Pay Units: N.A.
Programming (via satellite): Cinemax (multiplexed); Cinemax HD; HBO (multiplexed); HBO HD; Showtime (multiplexed); Showtime HD; Starz (multiplexed); Starz HD; The Movie Channel (multiplexed).
Fee: $15.35 monthly (each).
Video-On-Demand: Yes

Pay-Per-View
iN DEMAND (delivered digitally); Fresh; Shorteez; Sports PPV (delivered digitally).
Internet Service
Operational: Yes. Began: March 1, 2002.
Subscribers: 456,007.
Broadband Service: Comcast High Speed Internet.
Fee: $42.95 monthly.
Telephone Service
Digital: Operational
Subscribers: 289,784.
Fee: $44.95 monthly
Miles of Plant: 24,173.0 (coaxial); 3,762.0 (fiber optic). Homes passed: 1,366,330.
Senior Regional Vice President: Amy Smith. Vice President, Technical Operations: Rich Massi. Vice President, Marketing: Chip Goodman.
Ownership: Comcast Cable Communications Inc. (MSO).

PHILADELPHIA (Area 1)—Comcast Cable. Now served by PHILADELPHIA, PA [PA0005]. ICA: PA0003.

PHILADELPHIA (Area 2)—Comcast Cable. Now served by PHILADELPHIA, PA [PA0005]. ICA: PA0004.

PHILADELPHIA (suburbs)—RCN Corp. This cable system has converted to IPTV. See ALLENTOWN, PA [PA5201]. ICA: PA0447.

PHILIPSBURG BOROUGH—Comcast Cable. Now served by HARRISBURG, PA [PA0009]. ICA: PA0109.

PINOAK—Formerly served by Armstrong Cable Services. No longer in operation. ICA: PA0284.

PITCAIRN—Pitcairn Community Cable System, 582 6th St, Pitcairn, PA 15140-1200. Phone: 412-372-6500. Fax: 412-373-1464. E-mail: PCC@PitcairnBorough.us. ICA: PA0166.
TV Market Ranking: 10 (PITCAIRN). Franchise award date: N.A. Franchise expiration date: N.A. Began: November 1, 1952.
Channel capacity: 40 (not 2-way capable). Channels available but not in use: N.A.

Basic Service
Subscribers: N.A.
Programming (received off-air): KDKA-TV (CBS, Decades) Pittsburgh; WINP-TV (IND, ION) Pittsburgh; WPCB-TV (IND) Greensburg; WPGH-TV (Antenna TV, FOX, The Country Network) Pittsburgh; WPNT (MNT) Pittsburgh; WPXI (MeTV, NBC) Pittsburgh; WQED (PBS) Pittsburgh; WTAE-TV (ABC, This TV) Pittsburgh.
Programming (via satellite): A&E; AMC; CMT; CNN; Discovery Channel; Disney Channel; ESPN; ESPN2; EWTN Global Catholic Network; Freeform; Lifetime; MTV; Nickelodeon; QVC; Root Sports Pittsburgh; Spike TV; TBS; TNT; USA Network; WGN America.
Fee: $35.00 installation; $55.50 monthly.

Pay Service 1
Pay Units: N.A.
Programming (via satellite): HBO; Showtime.
Fee: $14.98 monthly (each).
Video-On-Demand: No
Internet Service
Operational: Yes.
Fee: $57.90 monthly.
Telephone Service
None
Miles of Plant: 10.0 (coaxial); None (fiber optic). Homes passed: 1,750.
Borough Manager: Gary Parks.
Ownership: Pitcairn Community Antenna System.

PITTSBURGH—Comcast Cable, 15 Summit Park Dr, Pittsburgh, PA 15275. Phone: 412-747-6400. Fax: 412-747-6401. Web Site: http://www.comcast.com. Also serves Aliquippa, Ambridge, Amwell Twp., Apollo Borough, Arnold, Aspinwall, Avalon, Avonmore, Baden, Baldwin, Beaver, Beaver Falls, Bell Acres, Belle Vernon, Bellevue, Ben Avon, Ben Avon Heights, Bethel, Big Beaver Twp., Blawnox Borough, Brackenridge Borough, Braddock Borough, Braddock Hills, Brentwood, Bridgeville, Bridgewater, Brighton Twp., Buffalo Twp. (Butler County), Buffalo Twp. (Washington County), Canonsburg, Carnegie, Carroll Twp. (Washington County), Castle Shannon, Cecil, Center Twp. (Beaver County), Chalfant, Charleroi, Chartiers Twp., Chestnut Ridge, Cheswick Borough, Chippewa Twp., Churchill Borough, Clairton, Claysville Borough, Clinton Twp., Collier Twp., Conway, Coraopolis, Crafton, Crescent Twp., Cuddy, Darlington Borough, Darlington Twp. (Beaver County), Daugherty Twp., Donegal Twp. (Washington County), Donora, Dormont, Dravosburg, Duquesne, East Deer Twp., East McKeesport Borough, East Pittsburgh Borough, East Rochester, East Vandergrift Borough, East Washington, Eastvale, Eastvale Borough, Economy, Edgewood, Edgeworth, Elizabeth Borough, Elizabeth Twp., Emsworth, Enon Valley Borough, Etna, Fallowfield Twp., Fallston, Fallston Borough, Fawn Twp. (Allegheny County), Findlay Twp. (Allegheny County), Finleyville, Florence, Forest Hills, Forward Twp. (Allegheny County), Fox Chapel, Franklin Park, Franklin Twp., Frazer Twp., Freedom, Georgetown Borough, Glasgow, Glassport, Glenfield, Gratztown, Green Tree, Greene Twp. (Beaver County), Hampton Twp., Hanover Twp. (Beaver County), Hanover Twp. (Washington County), Harmar Twp., Harmony Twp., Harrison Twp. (Allegheny County), Haysville, Heidelberg, Homestead, Hookstown Borough, Hopewell Twp. (Beaver County), Houston, Hyde Park Borough, Independence Twp., Industry, Ingram, Jefferson, Kennedy, Kilbuck, Leechburg Borough, Leet Twp., Leetsdale, Liberty, Lincoln, Lowber, Lower Burrell, McCandless, McDonald, McKees Rocks, McKeesport, Midland, Midway Borough, Millvale, Monaca, Monessen, Monongahela, Monroeville, Moon, Morris, Mount Lebanon, Mount Morris, Mount Oliver, Mount Pleasant, Mount Pleasant Twp.,

2017 Edition

D-669

Pennsylvania—Cable Systems

Munhall, Neville Twp., New Beaver Borough, New Brighton, New Brighton Borough, New Eagle, New Galilee Borough, New Kensington, New Sewickley Twp., North Belle Vernon, North Braddock Borough, North Charleroi, North Fayette Twp., North Franklin Twp., North Huntingdon Twp., North Stabane, North Versailles Twp., Nottingham, Nottingham Twp., Oakdale, Oakmont Borough, O'Hara Twp., Ohio Twp., Ohioville, Oklahoma Borough, Osborne, Patterson, Patterson Heights, Patterson Heights Borough, Patterson Twp., Penn Hills, Pennsbury Village, Perry Twp. (Lawrence County), Peters Twp., Pleasant Hills Borough, Port Vue, Potter Twp. (Beaver County), Presto, Pulaski, Pulaski Twp., Raccoon Twp., Rankin Borough, Reserve Twp. (Allegheny County), Richland Twp. (Allegheny County), Robinson, Robinson Twp. (Washington County), Rochester, Rochester Twp., Ross Twp. (Allegheny County), Rosslyn Farms, Rostraver, Rostraver Twp., Saltsburg, Scott Twp. (Allegheny Twp.), Sewickley (portions), Sewickley Heights Borough, Sewickley Hills, Shaler, Shaler Twp., Sharpsburg, Shippingport Borough, Smith Twp. (Washington County), Somerset, South Beaver Twp., South Fayette Twp., South Franklin Twp., South Heights, South Park, South Strabane Twp., Speers, Springdale Borough, Springdale Twp. (Allegheny County), Sutersville, Swissvale Borough, Tarentum Borough, Thornburg, Trafford Borough, Turtle Creek Borough, Twilight, Union Twp. (Washington County), Upper St. Clair Twp., Vandergrift Borough, Vanport, Verona Borough, Versailles, Wall, Washington, Waynesburg Borough, West Alexander, West Deer Twp., West Elizabeth, West Homestead, West Leechburg Borough, West Mayfield, West Mayfield Borough, West Mifflin, West Newton, West View, Whitaker, White Oak (portions), White Twp. (Beaver County), Whitehall, Wilkins Twp., Wilkinsburg & Wilmerding. ICA: PA0001.

TV Market Ranking: 10 (Aliquippa, Ambridge, Amwell Twp., Apollo Borough, Arnold, Aspinwall, Avalon, Baden, Baldwin, Bell Acres, Belle Vernon, Bellevue, Ben Avon, Ben Avon Heights, Bethel, Blawnox Borough, Brackenridge Borough, Braddock Borough, Braddock Hills, Brentwood, Bridgeville, Bridgewater, Brighton Twp., Buffalo Twp. (Butler County), Buffalo Twp. (Washington County), Canonsburg, Carnegie, Carroll Twp. (Washington County), Castle Shannon, Center Twp. (Beaver County), Chalfant, Charleroi, Chartiers Twp., Cheswick Borough, Churchill Borough, Clairton, Clinton Twp., Collier Twp., Conway, Coraopolis, Crafton, Crescent Twp., Cuddy, Darlington Twp. (Beaver County), Donora, Dormont, Dravosburg, Duquesne, East Deer Twp., East McKeesport Borough, East Pittsburgh Borough, East Vandergrift Borough, East Washington, Eastvale Borough, Economy, Edgewood, Edgeworth, Elizabeth Borough, Elizabeth Twp., Emsworth, Etna, Fallowfield Twp., Fallston Borough, Fawn Twp. (Allegheny County), Findlay Twp. (Allegheny County), Forest Hills, Forward Twp. (Allegheny County), Fox Chapel, Franklin Park, Franklin Twp., Frazer Twp., Georgetown Borough, Glasgow, Glassport, Glenfield, Gratztown, Green Tree, Hampton Twp., Hanover Twp. (Beaver County), Harmar Twp., Harmony Twp., Harrison Twp. (Allegheny County), Haysville, Heidelberg, Homestead, Hopewell Twp. (Beaver County), Hyde Park Borough, Independence Twp., Ingram, Kennedy, Kilbuck, Leechburg Borough, Leet Twp., Leetsdale, Liberty, Lincoln, Lowber, Lower Burrell, McCandless, McDonald, McKees Rocks, McKeesport, Midway Borough, Millvale, Monessen, Monongahela, Monroeville, Moon, Mount Oliver, Mount Pleasant Twp., Munhall, Neville Twp., New Brighton Borough, New Eagle, New Kensington, New Sewickley Twp., North Belle Vernon, North Braddock Borough, North Charleroi, North Fayette Twp., North Franklin Twp., North Huntingdon Twp., North Versailles Twp., Oakdale, Oakmont Borough, O'Hara Twp., Ohio Twp., Ohioville, Oklahoma Borough, Osborne, Patterson, Patterson Heights Borough, Penn Hills, Pennsbury Village, PITTSBURGH, Pleasant Hills Borough, Port Vue, Potter Twp. (Beaver County), Presto, Rankin Borough, Reserve Twp. (Allegheny County), Richland Twp. (Allegheny County), Robinson Twp. (Washington County), Rosslyn Farms, Rostraver, Rostraver Twp., Sewickley (portions), Sewickley Heights Borough, Sewickley Hills, Shaler, Shaler Twp., Sharpsburg, South Franklin Twp., South Heights, South Park, South Strabane Twp., Speers, Springdale Borough, Springdale Twp. (Allegheny County), Stowe Twp. (Allegheny County), Sutersville, Swissvale Borough, Tarentum Borough, Thornburg, Trafford Borough, Turtle Creek Borough, Twilight, Vandergrift Borough, Verona Borough, Versailles, Wall, Washington, West Deer Twp., West Elizabeth, West Homestead, West Leechburg Borough, West Mayfield Borough, West Mifflin, West Newton, West View, Whitaker, White Oak (portions), White Twp. (Beaver County), Whitehall, Wilkins Twp., Wilkinsburg, Wilmerding); 10,74 (Avonmore); 10,79 (Beaver, Beaver Falls, Chippewa Twp., Daugherty Twp., East Rochester, Eastvale, Fallston, Freedom, Monaca, New Brighton, Patterson Heights, Patterson Twp., Perry Twp. (Lawrence County), Rochester, Rochester Twp., Vanport, West Mayfield); 10,90 (Cecil, Claysville Borough, Donegal Twp. (Washington County), Finleyville, Florence, Greene Twp. (Beaver County), Hanover Twp. (Washington County), Hookstown Borough, Houston, Jefferson, Morris, Mount Lebanon, Mount Pleasant, North Stabane, Nottingham, Nottingham Twp., Raccoon Twp., Robinson, Smith Twp. (Washington County), Somerset, Union Twp. (Washington County), Upper St. Clair Twp., West Alexander); 74,10 (Saltsburg); 79 (Pulaski, Pulaski Twp.); 90 (Waynesburg Borough); Below 100 (Mount Morris). Franchise award date: N.A. Franchise expiration date: N.A. Began: December 1, 1980.

Channel capacity: 19 (operating 2-way). Channels available but not in use: N.A.

Basic Service
Subscribers: 343,933. Commercial subscribers: 16,175.
Programming (received off-air): KDKA-TV (CBS, Decades) Pittsburgh; WINP-TV (IND, ION) Pittsburgh; WPCB-TV (IND) Greensburg; WPCW (CW) Jeannette; WPGH-TV (Antenna TV, FOX, The Country Network) Pittsburgh; WPNT (MNT) Pittsburgh; WPXI (MeTV, NBC) Pittsburgh; WQED (PBS) Pittsburgh; WTAE-TV (ABC, This TV) Pittsburgh.
Programming (via satellite): C-SPAN; C-SPAN 2; EWTN Global Catholic Network; Pop; QVC; Radar Channel; The Weather Channel; WGN America.
Fee: $29.50-$42.75 installation; $25.24 monthly.

Expanded Basic Service 1
Subscribers: N.A.
Programming (via satellite): A&E; AMC; Animal Planet; BET; Cartoon Network; CMT; CNBC; CNN; Comedy Central; Discovery Channel; Disney Channel; E! HD; ESPN; ESPN2; Food Network; Fox News Channel; Freeform; FX; Golf Channel; GSN; Hallmark Channel; HGTV; History; HLN; ION Television; Lifetime; MSNBC; MTV; NBCSN; Nickelodeon; Oxygen; Pennsylvania Cable Network; Pittsburgh Cable News Channel; Root Sports Pittsburgh; Spike TV; TBS; TLC; TNT; Travel Channel; truTV; Turner Classic Movies; TV Land; USA Network; VH1.
Fee: $39.84 monthly.

Digital Basic Service
Subscribers: N.A.
Programming (via satellite): BBC America; Bloomberg Television; Bravo; CBS Sports Network; CMT; Comcast Network Philadelphia; Cooking Channel; C-SPAN 3; Daystar TV Network; Discovery Digital Networks; Disney XD; DIY Network; ESPN Classic; ESPN HD; ESPN2 HD; ESPNews; EVINE Live; Flix; FOX College Sports Central; FOX College Sports Pacific; Fox Sports 1; Fuse; FXM; FYI; GolTV; Great American Country; HD Theater; History International; HRTV; IFC; Jewelry Television; LMN; LOGO; MC; MoviePlex; MTV Live; Nat Geo WILD; National Geographic Channel; NBA TV; NFL Network; Nick 2; Nick Jr.; Nicktoons; Outdoor Channel; Sprout; Starz Encore (multiplexed); Sundance TV; Syfy; TeenNick; Tennis Channel; The Word Network; TNT HD; Trinity Broadcasting Network (TBN); TV One; TVG Network; Universal HD; WE tv; Weatherscan.
Fee: $10.95 monthly.

Digital Pay Service 1
Pay Units: N.A.
Programming (via satellite): Cinemax (multiplexed); Cinemax HD; HBO (multiplexed); HBO HD; Playboy TV; RAI Italia; RTN; Showtime (multiplexed); Showtime HD; Starz (multiplexed); Starz HD; The Movie Channel (multiplexed); TV Asia; Zee TV.
Fee: $8.00 monthly (each).

Video-On-Demand: Yes

Pay-Per-View
iN DEMAND (delivered digitally); Playboy TV (delivered digitally); Fresh (delivered digitally); Hot Choice (delivered digitally); NBA League Pass (delivered digitally); NHL Center Ice (delivered digitally); MLB Extra Innings (delivered digitally).

Internet Service
Operational: Yes.
Subscribers: 299,331.
Broadband Service: Comcast High Speed Internet.
Fee: $42.95 monthly.

Telephone Service
Digital: Operational
Subscribers: 230,540.
Fee: $44.95 monthly
Miles of Plant: 14,932.0 (coaxial); 3,959.0 (fiber optic). Homes passed: 850,202.
Regional Vice President: Linda Hossinger. Vice President, Technical Operations: Randy Bender. Vice President, Marketing: Donna Coming. Vice President, Public Affairs: Jody Doherty.
Ownership: Comcast Cable Communications Inc. (MSO).

PLUM—Comcast Cable. Now served by BLAIRSVILLE, PA [PA0320]. ICA: PA0465.

PLUMER—Formerly served by Cebridge Connections. No longer in operation. ICA: PA0238.

PORT ROYAL—Nittany Media Inc. Now served by MIFFLINTOWN, PA [PA0365]. ICA: PA0392.

PORTAGE—Formerly served by Adelphia Communications. Now served by Comcast Cable, BLAIRSVILLE, PA [PA0320]. ICA: PA0146.

POTTSTOWN—Comcast Cable. Now served by EATONTOWN BOROUGH, NJ [NJ0009]. ICA: PA0394.

POTTSVILLE—Comcast Cable. Now served by HARRISBURG, PA [PA0009]. ICA: PA0060.

POTTSVILLE—Wire Television Corp, 603 East Market St, Pottsville, PA 17901-2718. Phone: 570-622-4501. Fax: 570-622-8340. E-mail: customerserv@wtvaccess.com. Web Site: http://www.wtvaccess.com. Also serves Palo Alto & Port Carbon. ICA: PA0123.
TV Market Ranking: Below 100 (Palo Alto, Port Carbon, POTTSVILLE). Franchise award date: N.A. Franchise expiration date: N.A. Began: June 11, 1951.
Channel capacity: N.A. Channels available but not in use: N.A.

Basic Service
Subscribers: 649.
Programming (received off-air): KYW-TV (CBS, Decades) Philadelphia; WCAU (COZI TV, NBC) Philadelphia; WFMZ-TV (Retro TV) Allentown; WGAL (NBC, This TV) Lancaster; WHP-TV (CBS, MNT) Harrisburg; WHTM-TV (ABC, Retro TV) Harrisburg; WITF-TV (PBS) Harrisburg; WNEP-TV (ABC, Antenna TV) Scranton; WOLF-TV (CW, FOX, MNT) Hazleton; WPIX (Antenna TV, CW, This TV) New York; WPSG (CW) Philadelphia; WSWB (CW, MeTV) Scranton; WTXF-TV (Buzzr, FOX, Movies!) Philadelphia; WVIA-TV (PBS) Scranton; allband FM.
Programming (via satellite): A&E; AMC; Animal Planet; Bloomberg Television; Cartoon Network; CMT; CNN; Comcast SportsNet Philadelphia; Comedy Central; C-SPAN 2; Discovery Channel; Disney Channel; ESPN; ESPN2; EWTN Global Catholic Network; Food Network; Fox News Channel; Freeform; FX; Hallmark Channel; HGTV; History; INSP; ION Television; Lifetime; LMN; MTV; National Geographic Channel; Nickelodeon; Pennsylvania Cable Network; QVC; Spike TV; Syfy; TBS; The Weather Channel; TLC; TNT; Travel Channel; truTV; TV Land; USA Network; VH1; WGN America.
Fee: $37.50 installation; $82.62 monthly.

Digital Basic Service
Subscribers: N.A.
Programming (via satellite): BBC America; Bravo; Daystar TV Network; Destination America; Discovery Kids Channel; Discovery Life Channel; DMX Music; ESPN Classic; ESPNews; EVINE Live; FOX College Sports Central; FOX College Sports Pacific; Fox Sports 1; FXM; Golf Channel; Great American Country; GSN; HGTV; History; IFC; Investigation Discovery; MTV Classic; National Geographic Channel; NBCSN; Nick Jr.; Nicktoons; Outdoor Channel; OWN: Oprah Winfrey Network; Science Channel; The Word Network; Trinity Broadcasting Network (TBN); Turner Classic Movies; UP; VH1 Country; WE tv.
Fee: $21.95 monthly.

Cable Systems—Pennsylvania

Pay Service 1
Pay Units: N.A.
Programming (via satellite): Cinemax; HBO.
Fee: $15.00 installation; $15.95 monthly (each).

Digital Pay Service 1
Pay Units: N.A.
Programming (via satellite): Cinemax (multiplexed); Flix; HBO (multiplexed); Playboy TV; Showtime (multiplexed); Starz (multiplexed); Starz Encore (multiplexed); The Movie Channel.
Fee: $15.95 monthly (Cinemax, HBO, Showtime/TMC/Flix or Starz/Encore).

Pay-Per-View
iN DEMAND (delivered digitally); Fresh (delivered digitally); Club Jenna (delivered digitally).

Internet Service
Operational: Yes. Began: March 1, 2001.
Broadband Service: Wtvaccess.
Fee: $49.95 installation; $24.95-$59.95 monthly; $10.00 modem lease; $150.00 modem purchase.

Telephone Service
None
Miles of Plant: 33.0 (coaxial); None (fiber optic).
Channel capacity: N.A. Channels available but not in use: N.A.
General Manager: Margaret Davenport. Chief Technician: Brian Brennan.
Ownership: Wire Tele-View Corp. (MSO).

PULASKI—Comcast Cable. Now served by PITTSBURGH, PA [PA0001]. ICA: PA0396.

PUNXSUTAWNEY—Comcast Cable, 15 Summit Park Dr, Pittsburgh, PA 15275. Phones: 814-938-6130 (Punxsutawny office); 412-747-6400. Fax: 412-747-6401. Web Site: http://www.comcast.com. Also serves Beaver Twp. (Jefferson County), Bell Twp. (Clearfield County), Bell Twp. (Jefferson County), Big Run, Brady Twp. (Clearfield County), Brookville, Brookville Borough, Burnside, Canoe Twp., Clover Twp., Corsica Borough, Du Bois, Duke Center, Eldred Twp. (Jefferson County), Eldred Twp. (McKean County), Fairmount City, Falls Creek Borough, Foster Twp. (McKean County), Gaskill Twp., Hamlin Twp., Hawthorn, Henderson Twp. (Jefferson County), Highland Twp. (Elk County), Horton Twp. (Elk County), James City, Kane, Keating Twp. (McKean County), Knox Twp. (Clarion County), Knox Twp. (Jefferson County), Limestone Twp. (Clarion County), Mahaffey, McCalmont Twp., Mount Jewett Borough, New Bethlehem, Oak Ridge, Oliver Twp. (Jefferson County), Otto Twp., Perry Twp. (Jefferson County), Pine Creek Twp. (Jefferson County), Porter, Redbank Twp. (Clarion County), Reynoldsville, Ridgway Borough, Ridgway Twp., Ringgold Twp., Rixford, Rose Twp., Rossiter, Sandy Twp., Smethport, Snyder Twp. (Jefferson County), South Bethlehem, Summerville Borough, Sykesville, Timblin, Troutville Borough, Union Twp. (Clearfield County), Union Twp. (Jefferson County), Washington Twp. (Jefferson County), Westover, Wetmore Twp., Winslow Twp., Worthville & Young Twp. (Jefferson County). ICA: PA0397.
TV Market Ranking: 74 (Westover); Below 100 (Knox Twp. (Clarion County) (portions)); Outside TV Markets (Beaver Twp. (Jefferson County), Bell Twp. (Clearfield County), Bell Twp. (Jefferson County), Big Run, Brady Twp. (Clearfield County), Brookville, Brookville Borough, Burnside, Canoe Twp., Clover Twp., Corsica Borough, Du Bois, Duke Center, Eldred Twp. (Jefferson County), Eldred Twp. (McKean County), Fairmount City, Falls Creek Borough, Foster Twp. (McKean County), Gaskill Twp., Hamlin Twp., Hawthorn, Henderson Twp. (Jefferson County), Highland Twp. (Elk County), Horton Twp. (Elk County), James City, Keating Twp. (McKean County), Knox Twp. (Clarion County) (portions), Knox Twp. (Jefferson County), Mahaffey, McCalmont Twp., Mount Jewett Borough, New Bethlehem, Oak Ridge, Oliver Twp. (Jefferson County), Otto Twp., Perry Twp. (Jefferson County), Pine Creek Twp. (Jefferson County), Porter, PUNXSUTAWNEY, Redbank Twp. (Clarion County), Reynoldsville, Ridgway Borough, Ridgway Twp., Ringgold Twp., Rixford, Rose Twp., Rossiter, Sandy Twp., Snyder Twp. (Jefferson County), South Bethlehem, Summerville Borough, Sykesville, Timblin, Troutville Borough, Union Twp. (Clearfield County), Union Twp. (Jefferson County), Washington Twp. (Jefferson County), Wetmore Twp., Winslow Twp., Worthville, Young Twp. (Jefferson County), Kane, Limestone Twp. (Clarion County), Smethport). Franchise award date: N.A. Franchise expiration date: N.A. Began: December 1, 1964.
Channel capacity: N.A. Channels available but not in use: N.A.

Basic Service
Subscribers: 15,576. Commercial subscribers: 410.
Programming (received off-air): KDKA-TV (CBS, Decades) Pittsburgh; WATM-TV (ABC, This TV) Altoona; WJAC-TV (MeTV, NBC) Johnstown; WPCB-TV (IND) Greensburg; WPCW (CW) Jeannette; WPNT (MNT) Pittsburgh; WPSU-TV (PBS) Clearfield; WPXI (MeTV, NBC) Pittsburgh; WQED (PBS) Pittsburgh; WTAE-TV (ABC, This TV) Pittsburgh; WTAJ-TV (CBS) Altoona; WWCP-TV (FOX) Johnstown; 20 FMs.
Programming (via satellite): EVINE Live; Pop; QVC; WGN America.
Fee: $29.50-$42.75 installation; $26.20 monthly; $2.00 converter.

Expanded Basic Service 1
Subscribers: N.A.
Programming (via satellite): A&E; AMC; Animal Planet; Bravo; Cartoon Network; CMT; CNBC; CNN; Comedy Central; C-SPAN; C-SPAN 2; Discovery Channel; Disney Channel; E! HD; ESPN; ESPN2; EWTN Global Catholic Network; Food Network; Fox News Channel; Freeform; FX; Hallmark Channel; HGTV; History; HLN; HRTV; Lifetime; MSNBC; MTV; Nickelodeon; Oxygen; Pennsylvania Cable Network; Root Sports Pittsburgh; Spike TV; Syfy; TBS; The Weather Channel; TLC; TNT; Travel Channel; truTV; Turner Classic Movies; TV Land; USA Network; VH1.
Fee: $34.60 monthly.

Digital Basic Service
Subscribers: N.A.
Programming (via satellite): BBC America; Bloomberg Television; Discovery Life Channel; ESPNews; Fox Sports 1; FXM; Golf Channel; GSN; NBCSN; Outdoor Channel; Trinity Broadcasting Network (TBN).
Fee: $10.95 monthly.

Digital Expanded Basic Service
Subscribers: N.A.
Programming (via satellite): MC; National Geographic Channel; Nick 2; Nick Jr.; Nicktoons; TeenNick.
Fee: $5.00 monthly.

Digital Pay Service 1
Pay Units: 6,662.
Programming (via satellite): Cinemax (multiplexed); HBO (multiplexed); Showtime (multiplexed); Starz (multiplexed); Starz Encore (multiplexed); The Movie Channel (multiplexed).

Video-On-Demand: Yes

Pay-Per-View
HITS PPV 1-30 (delivered digitally); Hot Choice (delivered digitally); Fresh (delivered digitally); Playboy TV (delivered digitally).

Internet Service
Operational: Yes.
Subscribers: 7,553.
Broadband Service: Comcast High Speed Internet.
Fee: $42.95 monthly.

Telephone Service
Digital: Operational
Subscribers: 4,214.
Miles of Plant: 990.0 (coaxial); 639.0 (fiber optic). Homes passed: 26,182.
Regional Vice President: Linda Hossinger. Vice President, Technical Operations: Randy Bender. Vice President, Public Affairs: Jody Doherty. Marketing Manager: Donna Corning.
Ownership: Comcast Cable Communications Inc. (MSO).

RALSTON—Zito Media, 102 S Main St, PO Box 665, Coudersport, PA 16915. Phones: 814-260-9055; 800-365-6988. E-mail: info@zitomedia.com. Web Site: http://www.zitomedia.com. Also serves Roaring Branch. ICA: PA0253.
TV Market Ranking: Below 100 (RALSTON, Roaring Branch). Franchise award date: N.A. Franchise expiration date: N.A. Began: January 1, 1952.
Channel capacity: N.A. Channels available but not in use: N.A.

Basic Service
Subscribers: 73.
Programming (received off-air): WBRE-TV (NBC) Wilkes-Barre; WNEP-TV (ABC, Antenna TV) Scranton; WSWB (CW, MeTV) Scranton; WVIA-TV (PBS) Scranton; WYOU (CBS) Scranton; allband FM.
Programming (via satellite): A&E; Animal Planet; CNBC; CNN; Comedy Central; CTV Inc.; Discovery Channel; ESPN; ESPN2; Fox News Channel; Fox Sports 1; Freeform; FX; Hallmark Channel; History; HLN; Lifetime; MTV; Nickelodeon; Outdoor Channel; QVC; Spike TV; Syfy; TBS; The Weather Channel; TLC; TNT; Trinity Broadcasting Network (TBN); TV Land; USA Network; VH1; WGN America.
Fee: $49.95 installation; $18.23 monthly.

Pay Service 1
Pay Units: N.A.
Programming (via satellite): Showtime.
Fee: $11.00 monthly.

Video-On-Demand: No

Internet Service
Operational: No.

Telephone Service
None
Miles of Plant: 15.0 (coaxial); None (fiber optic). Homes passed: 230.
President: James Rigas.
Ownership: Zito Media (MSO).

RAYNE TWP.—Formerly served by Satterlee Leasing Inc. No longer in operation. ICA: PA0399.

READING—Comcast Cable. Now served by HARRISBURG, PA [PA0009]. ICA: PA0012.

READING—Formerly served by Digital Wireless Systems. No longer in operation. ICA: PA0430.

REEDSVILLE—Comcast Cable. Now served by HARRISBURG, PA [PA0009]. ICA: PA0150.

RENO—Time Warner Cable. Now served by FRANKLIN (Venango County), PA [PA0100]. ICA: PA0273.

RETREAT CORRECTIONAL INSTITUTION—Formerly served by Suddenlink Communications. No longer in operation. ICA: PA0445.

RICHFIELD—Formerly served by Zampelli Electronics. No longer in operation. ICA: PA0225.

RIDGWAY BOROUGH—Formerly served by Adelphia Communications. Now served by Comcast Cable, PUNXSUTAWNEY, PA [PA0397]. ICA: PA0124.

RIDLEY PARK—RCN. Formerly served by PHILADELPHIA (suburbs), PA [PA0447]. This cable system has converted to IPTV, 196 Van Buren St, Ste 300, Herndon, VA 20170. Phones: 800-746-4726; 609-681-2281. Web Site: http://www.rcn.com. Also serves Beverly Hills, Clifton Heights, Cobbs Creek, Crum Lynne, Darby, Darby Twp., Drexel Hill, East Lansdowne, Eddystone, Essington, Folcroft, Folsom, Glenolden, Havertown, Holmes, Lansdowne, Mertztown, Millbourne, Moore Twp., Morton, Norwood, Primos, Prospect Park, Ridley Twp., Rutledge, Secane, Sharon Hill, Springfield, Swarthmore, Tinicum, Upper Darby & Woodlyn. ICA: PA5261.
TV Market Ranking: Below 100 (MOORE TWP.).
Channel capacity: N.A. Channels available but not in use: N.A.

Limited Basic
Subscribers: 13,917. Commercial subscribers: 308.
Fee: $28.00 monthly. Includes 42 channels - 32 in SD & 10 in HD. Additional $9.95 HD equipment fee for HD channels.

Signature Digital Cable
Subscribers: N.A.
Fee: $59.99 monthly. Includes 285 channels - 219 in SD & 66 in HD. Additional $9.95 HD equipment fee for HD channels.

HD Expanded Pack
Subscribers: N.A.
Fee: $8.99 monthly. Includes 6 additional HD channels. Additional $9.95 HD equipment fee for HD channels.

Premiere Movies & Entertainment
Subscribers: N.A.
Fee: $10.99 monthly. Includes 30 channels - 26 in SD & 4 in HD. Additional $9.95 HD equipment fee for HD channels.

Premiere Family & Children
Subscribers: N.A.
Fee: $5.99 monthly. Includes 19 channels - 17 in SD & 2 in HD. Additional $9.95 HD equipment fee for HD channels.

Premiere News & Information
Subscribers: N.A.
Fee: $5.99 monthly. Includes 19 channels - 14 in SD & 5 in HD. Additional $9.95 HD equipment fee for HD channels.

Premiere Sports
Subscribers: N.A.
Fee: $9.99 monthly. Includes 32 channels - 24 in SD & 8 in HD. Additional $9.95 HD equipment fee for HD channels.

Pennsylvania—Cable Systems

Premiere Total Pack
 Subscribers: N.A.
 Fee: $20.95 monthly. Includes 109 channels - 88 in SD & 21 in HD. Additional $9.95 HD equipment fee for HD channels.

MiVision Lite
 Subscribers: N.A.
 Fee: $12.00 monthly. Includes 40 channels in Spanish.

MiVision Plus
 Subscribers: N.A.
 Fee: $22.95 monthly. Includes 44 channels in Spanish.

Cinemax
 Subscribers: N.A.
 Fee: $9.95 monthly. Includes 16 channels - 8 in SD & 8 in HD plus Cinemax on Demand & MAXGo. Additional $9.95 HD equipment fee for HD channels.

HBO
 Subscribers: N.A.
 Fee: $15.95 monthly. Includes 14 channels - 7 in SD & 7 in HD plus HBO on Demand & HBO Go. Additional $9.95 HD equipment fee for HD channels.

Cinemax/HBO
 Subscribers: N.A.
 Fee: $19.95 monthly. Includes 16 channels of Cinemax - 8 in SD & 8 in HD & 14 channels of HBO - 7 in SD & 7 in HD plus Cinemax on Demand, HBO on Demand, MAXGo & HBO Go. Additional $9.95 HD equipment fee for HD channels.

Showtime/TMC
 Subscribers: N.A.
 Fee: $4.95 monthly. Includes 20 channels - 9 in SD & 11 in HD plus Showtime on Demand & The Movie Channel on Demand. Additional $9.95 HD equipment fee for HD channels.

Starz
 Subscribers: N.A.
 Fee: $5.00 monthly. Includes 13 channels - 9 in SD & 4 in HD plus Starz on Demand. Additional $9.95 HD equipment fee for HD channels.

Video-On-Demand: Yes
Internet Service
 Operational: Yes.
 Fee: $39.99-$49.99 monthly.
Telephone Service
 Digital: Operational
 Fee: $29.99 monthly
Vice President & General Manager: Jamie Hill.
Ownership: RCN Corp.

ROBINSON TWP. (Allegheny County)—Formerly served by Comcast Cable. No longer in operation. ICA: PA0401.

ROCHESTER TWP.—Comcast Cable. Now served by PITTSBURGH, PA [PA0001]. ICA: PA0076.

ROCKMERE—Formerly served by Cebridge Connections. Now served by Armstrong Cable Services, ZELIENOPLE, PA [PA0053]. ICA: PA0237.

ROCKWOOD—Formerly served by Adelphia Communications. Now served by Comcast Cable, BLAIRSVILLE, PA [PA0320]. ICA: PA0402.

ROME—Beaver Valley Cable Co, 36150 Rte 187, Rome, PA 18837-9802. Phones: 800-391-9615; 570-247-2512. Fax: 570-247-2494. E-mail: bvc@cableracer.com. Web Site: http://www.beavervalleycable.com. Also serves Allis Hollow, Hornbrook, Le Raysville, Le Raysville Borough, Little Meadows, Little Meadows Borough, North Orwell, North Rome, Potterville, Rome Borough, Sheshequin Twp., Ulster & Warren Center Twp. ICA: PA0403.
TV Market Ranking: 49 (Little Meadows); Below 100 (Allis Hollow, Le Raysville, Le Raysville Borough, Little Meadows Borough, North Orwell, North Rome, Potterville, ROME, Rome Borough, Sheshequin Twp., Ulster, Warren Center Twp.).
Channel capacity: 70 (operating 2-way). Channels available but not in use: N.A.
Basic Service
 Subscribers: 640.
 Programming (received off-air): WBNG-TV (CBS, CW) Binghamton; WBRE-TV (NBC) Wilkes-Barre; WENY-TV (ABC, CW) Elmira; WETM-TV (IND, NBC) Elmira; WNEP-TV (ABC, Antenna TV) Scranton; WOLF-TV (CW, FOX, MNT) Hazleton; WQPX-TV (ION) Scranton; WSKG-TV (PBS) Binghamton; WSWB (CW, MeTV) Scranton; WVIA-TV (PBS) Scranton; WYOU (CBS) Scranton.
 Programming (via satellite): 3ABN; A&E; AMC; Animal Planet; Bravo; Cartoon Network; CMT; CNBC; CNN; Comedy Central; Discovery Channel; Disney Channel; Disney XD; ESPN; ESPN Classic; ESPN2; EWTN Global Catholic Network; Fox News Channel; Fox Sports 1; Freeform; FX; Great American Country; Lifetime; MTV; National Geographic Channel; NBCSN; Nickelodeon; Outdoor Channel; Pop; Root Sports Pittsburgh; Spike TV; Syfy; TBS; The Weather Channel; TLC; TNT; Trinity Broadcasting Network (TBN); truTV; TV Land; USA Network; VH1; WGN America.
 Fee: $58.00 installation; $57.00 monthly.
Expanded Basic Service 1
 Subscribers: 193.
 Fee: $54.00 monthly.
Digital Basic Service
 Subscribers: N.A.
 Programming (via satellite): BBC America; Discovery Digital Networks; ESPNews; FOX College Sports Central; FOX College Sports Pacific; Golf Channel; GSN; HGTV; History; IFC; Nick Jr.; Turner Classic Movies.
 Fee: $30.00 installation; $14.95 monthly.
Digital Pay Service 1
 Pay Units: 60.
 Programming (via satellite): HBO (multiplexed).
 Fee: $12.19 monthly.
Digital Pay Service 2
 Pay Units: N.A.
 Programming (via satellite): Cinemax (multiplexed); Showtime (multiplexed); Starz Encore; The Movie Channel (multiplexed).
 Fee: $10.60 monthly (Cinemax or Starz/Encore), $12.19 monthly (Showtime/TMC).
Video-On-Demand: No
Pay-Per-View
 iN DEMAND (delivered digitally); Hot Choice (delivered digitally); Pleasure (delivered digitally).
Internet Service
 Operational: Yes. Began: November 1, 2002.
 Subscribers: 550.
 Broadband Service: Cableracer.
 Fee: $50.00 installation; $41.00 monthly.
Telephone Service
 None
Miles of Plant: 110.0 (coaxial); 33.0 (fiber optic). Homes passed: 2,000.
President & General Manager: Doug Soden. Chief Technician: Gary Powers. IT Technician & Office Manager: Bonnie Gray.
Ownership: Beaver Valley Cable Inc.

ROSE TWP.—Formerly served by Adelphia Communications. Now served by Comcast Cable, PUNXSUTAWNEY, PA [PA0397]. ICA: PA0135.

ROSS TWP. (Allegheny County)—Comcast Cable. Now served by PITTSBURGH, PA [PA0001]. ICA: PA0032.

RURAL VALLEY—Comcast Cable. Now served by BLAIRSVILLE, PA [PA0320]. ICA: PA0199.

SABULA—Zito Media, 102 S Main St, PO Box 665, Coudersport, PA 16915. Phones: 814-260-9055; 800-365-6988. Fax: 814-260-9580. E-mail: info@zitomedia.com. Web Site: http://www.zitomedia.com. ICA: PA0249.
TV Market Ranking: Outside TV Markets (SABULA). Franchise award date: August 1, 1989. Franchise expiration date: N.A. Began: August 1, 1990.
Channel capacity: N.A. Channels available but not in use: N.A.
Basic Service
 Subscribers: N.A.
 Programming (received off-air): WATM-TV (ABC, This TV) Altoona; WJAC-TV (MeTV, NBC) Johnstown; WKBS-TV (IND) Altoona; WPNT (MNT) Pittsburgh; WPSU-TV (PBS) Clearfield; WTAE-TV (ABC, This TV) Pittsburgh; WTAJ-TV (CBS) Altoona; WWCP-TV (FOX) Johnstown.
 Programming (via satellite): A&E; AMC; Animal Planet; Cartoon Network; CMT; CNBC; CNN; C-SPAN; CW PLUS; Discovery Channel; Disney Channel; ESPN; ESPN Classic; ESPN2; EWTN Global Catholic Network; Fox News Channel; Freeform; FX; HGTV; History; HLN; INSP; Lifetime; MSNBC; MTV; Nickelodeon; QVC; Root Sports Pittsburgh; Spike TV; TBS; The Weather Channel; TLC; TNT; Trinity Broadcasting Network (TBN); Turner Classic Movies; TV Land; USA Network; VH1; WGN America.
 Fee: $29.95 installation; $44.50 monthly; $7.95 converter.
Digital Basic Service
 Subscribers: N.A.
 Programming (via satellite): BBC America; Bloomberg Television; Boomerang; C-SPAN 3; Destination America; Discovery Kids Channel; Discovery Life Channel; Disney XD; ESPN HD; ESPN2 HD; ESPNews; Fox Sports 1; FXM; Golf Channel; Great American Country; GSN; HRTV; INSP; Investigation Discovery; LMN; MC; MTV Classic; MTV Hits; MTV Jams; MTV2; Nick 2; Nick Jr.; Nicktoons; OWN: Oprah Winfrey Network; RFD-TV; Science Channel; TeenNick; The Word Network; Trinity Broadcasting Network (TBN); VH1 Country; VH1 Soul; WAM! America's Kidz Network; WE tv.
 Fee: $15.95 monthly.
Digital Expanded Basic Service
 Subscribers: N.A.
 Programming (via satellite): DIY Network; Flix; FSN Digital Atlantic; FSN Digital Central; FSN Digital Pacific; FYI; History International; IFC; NBCSN; Outdoor Channel; Sundance TV.
 Fee: $10.00 monthly.
Digital Pay Service 1
 Pay Units: N.A.
 Programming (via satellite): Cinemax (multiplexed); Cinemax HD; HBO (multiplexed); HBO HD; Showtime (multiplexed); Showtime HD; Starz (multiplexed); Starz Encore (multiplexed); Starz HD; The Movie Channel (multiplexed).
 Fee: $8.00 monthly (Cinemax or Starz/Encore), $10.00 monthly (HBO or Showtime/TMC/Flix).
Video-On-Demand: Yes
Pay-Per-View
 iN DEMAND (delivered digitally); NHL Center Ice (delivered digitally); MLB Extra Innings (delivered digitally).
Internet Service
 Operational: Yes.
 Fee: $49.95 monthly.
Telephone Service
 Digital: Operational
 Fee: $35.00 monthly
President: James Rigas.
Ownership: Zito Media (MSO).

SALTILLO—Saltillo TV Cable Corp, PO Box 89, Saltillo, PA 17253-0089. Phone: 814-448-2443. Fax: 814-448-9182. ICA: PA0404.
TV Market Ranking: 74 (SALTILLO). Franchise award date: N.A. Franchise expiration date: N.A. Began: January 1, 1964.
Channel capacity: 47 (not 2-way capable). Channels available but not in use: N.A.
Basic Service
 Subscribers: N.A.
 Programming (received off-air): WBAL-TV (NBC) Baltimore; WGAL (NBC, This TV) Lancaster; WHTM-TV (ABC, Retro TV) Harrisburg; WJAC-TV (MeTV, NBC) Johnstown; WJZ-TV (CBS, Decades) Baltimore; WMAR-TV (ABC, Bounce TV) Baltimore; WPMT (Antenna TV, FOX) York; WPSU-TV (PBS) Clearfield; WTAJ-TV (CBS) Altoona; WTTG (Buzzr, FOX) Washington.
 Programming (via satellite): Cartoon Network; CMT; CNN; Discovery Channel; Disney Channel; ESPN; ESPN2; Freeform; Hallmark Channel; History; QVC; Spike TV; TBS; TNT; Trinity Broadcasting Network (TBN); Turner Classic Movies; TV Land; USA Network; VH1; WGN America.
 Fee: $100.00 installation.
Pay Service 1
 Pay Units: N.A.
 Programming (via satellite): HBO.
 Fee: $13.00 monthly.
Video-On-Demand: No
Internet Service
 Operational: No.
Telephone Service
 None
Ownership: Saltillo TV Cable Corp.

SALTLICK TWP.—Laurel Highland Total Communications, 4157 Main St, PO Box 168, Stahlstown, PA 15687. Phones: 724-593-0011; 724-593-2411. Fax: 724-593-2423.

Cable Systems—Pennsylvania

E-mail: jstough@lhtot.com. Web Site: http://www.lhtc.co. Also serves Acme, Champion, Connellsville, Cook Twp., Donegal, Donegal Twp. (Westmoreland County), Hunker, Indian Creek, Indian Head, Jones Mills, Ligonier Borough, Melcroft, Mill Run, New Stanton, Normalville, Rector, Ruffsdale, Stahlstown, West Newton, White, Wyano & Yukon. ICA: PA0348.
TV Market Ranking: 10 (Hunker, Jones Mills, New Stanton, Ruffsdale, West Newton); 74 (Champion, Cook Twp., Donegal, Donegal Twp. (Westmoreland County), Indian Creek, Indian Head, Ligonier Borough, Melcroft, Mill Run, Normalville, Rector, SALTLICK TWP., Stahlstown, White); 74,10 (Wyano, Yukon); Below 100 (Acme, Connellsville). Franchise award date: N.A. Franchise expiration date: N.A. Began: January 1, 1967.
Channel capacity: 37 (not 2-way capable). Channels available but not in use: N.A.

Basic Service
Subscribers: 3,122.
Programming (received off-air): KDKA-TV (CBS, Decades) Pittsburgh; WJAC-TV (MeTV, NBC) Johnstown; WPCB-TV (IND) Greensburg; WPGH-TV (Antenna TV, FOX, The Country Network) Pittsburgh; WPNT (MNT) Pittsburgh; WPXI (MeTV, NBC) Pittsburgh; WQED (PBS) Pittsburgh; WTAE-TV (ABC, This TV) Pittsburgh.
Programming (via satellite): A&E; AMC; Animal Planet; Bloomberg Television; Boomerang; Bravo; Cartoon Network; CMT; CNN; Comedy Central; C-SPAN; Discovery Channel; Disney Channel; E! HD; ESPN; ESPN Classic; ESPN2; EWTN Global Catholic Network; FamilyNet; Food Network; Fox News Channel; Fox Sports 1; Freeform; FX; FXM; Golf Channel; Great American Country; Hallmark Channel; Hallmark Movies & Mysteries; HGTV; History; HLN; Lifetime; LMN; MSNBC; National Geographic Channel; Nickelodeon; Outdoor Channel; Paramount Network (UPN); Pennsylvania Cable Network; QVC; Root Sports Pittsburgh; Spike TV; Syfy; TBS; The Weather Channel; TLC; TNT; Travel Channel; Trinity Broadcasting Network (TBN); truTV; TV Land; USA Network; VH1.
Fee: $13.95 monthly.

Pay Service 1
Pay Units: N.A.
Programming (via satellite): Cinemax; HBO; Showtime; The Movie Channel.
Fee: $8.00 monthly (Cinemax), $15.00 monthly (HBO), $15.95 monthly (Showtime/TMC).

Internet Service
Operational: Yes.

Telephone Service
Digital: Operational
Miles of Plant: 322.0 (coaxial); 60.0 (fiber optic). Homes passed: 5,400.
President & Chief Executive Officer: James J. Kail. Plant Manager: Jeffrey A. Stough.
Ownership: Laurel Highland Total Communications.

SANDY LAKE—Formerly served by Cebridge Connections. Now served by Armstrong Cable Services, ZELIENOPLE, PA [PA0053]. ICA: PA0176.

SANDY TWP. (Clearfield County)—Formerly served by Satterlee Leasing Inc. No longer in operation. ICA: PA0405.

SAYRE BOROUGH—Time Warner Cable. Now served by DEWITT, NY [NY0013]. ICA: PA0079.

SCHUYLKILL TWP.—Formerly served by MetroCast Communications. No longer in operation. ICA: PA0450.

SCRANTON—Comcast Cable. Now served by HARRISBURG, PA [PA0009]. ICA: PA0011.

SELLERSVILLE—Comcast Cable. Now served by EATONTOWN BOROUGH, NJ [NJ0009]. ICA: PA0017.

SHADE GAP—Shade Gap TV Assn, HC 83 Box 398, Shade Gap, PA 17255-9317. Phone: 814-259-3415. Also serves Dublin Twp. (Huntingdon County). ICA: PA0283.
TV Market Ranking: Outside TV Markets (Dublin Twp. (Huntingdon County), SHADE GAP). Franchise award date: N.A. Franchise expiration date: N.A. Began: January 1, 1953.
Channel capacity: 19 (not 2-way capable). Channels available but not in use: N.A.

Basic Service
Subscribers: N.A.
Programming (received off-air): WGAL (NBC, This TV) Lancaster; WHAG-TV (IND) Hagerstown; WHTM-TV (ABC, Retro TV) Harrisburg; WJAC-TV (MeTV, NBC) Johnstown; WPMT (Antenna TV, FOX) York; WPSU-TV (PBS) Clearfield; WTAJ-TV (CBS) Altoona; allband FM.
Programming (via satellite): AMC; CMT; Discovery Channel; Disney Channel; ESPN; Food Network; Freeform; Hallmark Channel; Nickelodeon; Spike TV; TBS; TNT; Trinity Broadcasting Network (TBN); USA Network; WGN America.

Pay Service 1
Pay Units: N.A.
Programming (via satellite): Cinemax.
Fee: $6.00 monthly.

Video-On-Demand: No

Internet Service
Operational: No.

Telephone Service
None
Miles of Plant: 4.0 (coaxial); None (fiber optic). Homes passed: 133.
General Manager: Donald E. Naugle. Secretary-Treasurer: Mary McMullen.
Ownership: Shade Gap TV Assn.

SHARON—Time Warner Cable. Now served by CLEVELAND (formerly Cleveland Heights), OH [OH0006]. ICA: PA0038.

SHEFFIELD—WestPA.net Inc, 216 Pennsylvania Ave W, PO Box 703, Warren, PA 16365. Phones: 877-726-9462; 814-726-9462. Fax: 814-723-9585. E-mail: info@westpa.net. Web Site: http://www.westpa.net. Also serves Barnes, Ludlow, Saybrook, Tiona & Weldbank. ICA: PA0473.
TV Market Ranking: Below 100 (Barnes, Ludlow, Saybrook, SHEFFIELD, Tiona, Weldbank).
Channel capacity: N.A. Channels available but not in use: N.A.

Internet Service
Operational: Yes.
Fee: $24.95 monthly.

Telephone Service
Digital: Operational
Fee: $29.95 monthly
General Manager: Elaine Bailey.
Ownership: WestPA.net Inc.

SHEFFIELD—WestPA.net Inc. Now served by SHEFFIELD, PA [PA0473]. ICA: PA0246.

SHENANDOAH—Service Electric Cablevision. Now served by HAZLETON, PA [PA0050]. ICA: PA0114.

SHIPPENSBURG—Comcast Cable. Now served by HARRISBURG, PA [PA0009]. ICA: PA0066.

SHIPPENVILLE—Atlantic Broadband, 24 Main St, Bradford, PA 16701. Phones: 888-536-9600 (Customer service); 814-535-3506. Fax: 814-535-7749. E-mail: info@atlanticbb.com. Web Site: http://atlanticbb.com. Also serves Ashland Twp., Beaver Twp. (Clarion County), Clarion County (portions), Elk Twp. (Clarion County), Knox, Knox Twp. (Clarion County), Limestone Twp. (Clarion County), Monroe Twp. (Clarion County), Ninevah, Paint Twp. (Clarion County), Piney, Porter Twp. (Clarion County), Redbank Twp. (Clarion County) & Salem Twp. (Clarion County). ICA: PA0387.
TV Market Ranking: Below 100 (Knox Twp. (Clarion County) (portions)); Outside TV Markets (Ashland Twp., Beaver Twp. (Clarion County), Clarion County (portions), Elk Twp. (Clarion County), Knox, Knox Twp. (Clarion County) (portions), Limestone Twp. (Clarion County), Limestone Twp. (Clarion County), Monroe Twp. (Clarion County), Ninevah, Paint Twp. (Clarion County), Piney, Porter Twp. (Clarion County), Redbank Twp. (Clarion County), Salem Twp. (Clarion County), SHIPPENVILLE). Franchise award date: N.A. Franchise expiration date: N.A. Began: April 1, 1973.
Channel capacity: 67 (operating 2-way). Channels available but not in use: N.A.

Basic Service
Subscribers: 915. Commercial subscribers: 54.
Programming (received off-air): KDKA-TV (CBS, Decades) Pittsburgh; WJAC-TV (MeTV, NBC) Johnstown; WKBN-TV (CBS) Youngstown; WPCB-TV (IND) Greensburg; WPCW (CW) Jeannette; WPGH-TV (Antenna TV, FOX, The Country Network) Pittsburgh; WPNT (MNT) Pittsburgh; WPSU-TV (PBS) Clearfield; WPXI (MeTV, NBC) Pittsburgh; WQED (PBS) Pittsburgh; WTAE-TV (ABC, This TV) Pittsburgh; WYTV (ABC, MNT) Youngstown.
Programming (via satellite): C-SPAN; HRTV; Pennsylvania Cable Network; QVC; Trinity Broadcasting Network (TBN).
Fee: $40.00 installation; $34.79 monthly.

Expanded Basic Service 1
Subscribers: 774.
Programming (via satellite): A&E; AMC; Animal Planet; Bravo; Cartoon Network; CMT; CNBC; CNN; Comedy Central; Discovery Channel; Disney Channel; E! HD; ESPN; ESPN2; Food Network; Fox News Channel; Fox Sports 1; Freeform; FX; Hallmark Channel; HGTV; History; HLN; Lifetime; LMN; MSNBC; MTV; Nickelodeon; Outdoor Channel; OWN: Oprah Winfrey Network; Root Sports Pittsburgh; Spike TV; Syfy; TBS; The Weather Channel; TLC; TNT; Travel Channel; truTV; Turner Classic Movies; TV Land; USA Network; VH1.
Fee: $45.75 monthly.

Digital Basic Service
Subscribers: N.A.
Programming (via satellite): BBC America; Bloomberg Television; CMT; Destination America; Discovery Kids Channel; Disney XD; ESPN Classic; ESPNews; Fox Sports 2; FYI; GSN; History International; Investigation Discovery; MC; MTV Classic; MTV Hits; MTV2; NFL Network; Nick Jr.; Nicktoons; Science Channel; Starz (multiplexed); Starz Encore (multiplexed); TeenNick; VH1 Soul; WE tv; WeatherVision.
Fee: $18.95 monthly.

Digital Pay Service 1
Pay Units: N.A.
Programming (via satellite): Cinemax (multiplexed); Flix; HBO (multiplexed); Showtime (multiplexed); The Movie Channel (multiplexed).
Fee: $15.95 monthly (HBO, Cinemax or Showime/TMC/Flix).

Video-On-Demand: No

Pay-Per-View
iN DEMAND (delivered digitally); Hot Choice (delivered digitally); Fresh (delivered digitally); Playboy TV (delivered digitally); Club Jenna (delivered digitally); Spice: Xcess (delivered digitally).

Internet Service
Operational: Yes.
Broadband Service: Atlantic Broadband High-Speed Internet.
Fee: $24.95-$57.95 monthly.

Telephone Service
None
Miles of Plant: 7,723.0 (coaxial); 2,735.0 (fiber optic). Homes passed: 1,981.
Chief Financial Officer: Patrick Bratton. Senior Vice President & General Counsel: Leslie Brown. Vice President: David Dane. General Manager: Mike Papasergi. Technical Operations Director: Charles Sorchilla. Marketing & Customer Service Director: Dara Leslie. Marketing Manager: Natalie Kurchak.
Ownership: Atlantic Broadband (MSO).

SHIPPENVILLE—Atlantic Broadband. Now served by SHIPPENVILLE, PA [PA0387]. ICA: PA0198.

SHIPPINGPORT BOROUGH—Comcast Cable. Now served by PITTSBURGH, PA [PA0001]. ICA: PA0296.

SHIRLEY TWP.—Formerly served by Adelphia Communications. Now served by Comcast Cable, HARRISBURG, PA [PA0009]. ICA: PA0139.

SIX MILE RUN—Six Mile Run TV Assn., 1171 Six Mile Run Rd, Six Mile Run, PA 16679-9260. Phone: 814-928-4093. ICA: PA0295.
TV Market Ranking: 74 (SIX MILE RUN). Franchise award date: January 1, 1950. Franchise expiration date: N.A. Began: April 20, 1951.
Channel capacity: 14 (not 2-way capable). Channels available but not in use: N.A.

2017 Edition
D-673

Pennsylvania—Cable Systems

Basic Service
Subscribers: N.A.
Programming (received off-air): WATM-TV (ABC, This TV) Altoona; WJAC-TV (MeTV, NBC) Johnstown; WPSU-TV (PBS) Clearfield; WTAJ-TV (CBS) Altoona; WWCP-TV (FOX) Johnstown; allband FM.
Programming (via satellite): BET; Cartoon Network; CNN; ESPN; TBS; Turner Classic Movies; USA Network; WGN America.
Fee: $40.00 installation.

Pay Service 1
Pay Units: N.A.
Programming (via satellite): HBO.
Fee: $8.50 monthly.

Video-On-Demand: No

Internet Service
Operational: No.

Telephone Service
None

Miles of Plant: 3.0 (coaxial); None (fiber optic). Homes passed: 144.
General Manager: Richard W. White. Chief Technician: Harold Colbert.
Ownership: Six Mile Run TV Association.

SMETHPORT—Comcast Cable. Now served by PUNXSUTAWNEY, PA [PA0397]. ICA: PA0147.

SNOW SHOE—Tele-Media, 804 Jacksonville Rd, PO Box 39, Bellefonte, PA 16823-0039. Phones: 800-704-4254; 814-353-2025. Fax: 814-353-2072. Web Site: http://www.tele-media.com. Also serves Boggs Twp. (Clearfield County), Burnside (Clearfield County), Cooper Twp., Cooper Twp. (Clearfield County), Covington Twp. (Clearfield County), Girard Twp., Graham Twp., Karthaus Twp., Morrisdale, Walker & Wallaceton. ICA: PA0188.
TV Market Ranking: 74 (Boggs Twp. (Clearfield County), Cooper Twp. (portions), Morrisdale, Wallaceton); Outside TV Markets (Cooper Twp. (Clearfield County), Covington Twp. (Clearfield County), Covington Twp. (Clearfield County), Girard Twp., Graham Twp., SNOW SHOE, Cooper Twp. (portions)). Franchise award date: N.A. Franchise expiration date: N.A. Began: May 1, 1957.
Channel capacity: N.A. Channels available but not in use: N.A.

Basic Service
Subscribers: 1,449.
Programming (received off-air): WATM-TV (ABC, This TV) Altoona; WHVL-LP (MNT) State College, etc.; WJAC-TV (MeTV, NBC) Johnstown; WKBS-TV (IND) Altoona; WPSU-TV (PBS) Clearfield; WTAJ-TV (CBS) Altoona; WWCP-TV (FOX) Johnstown; allband FM.
Programming (via satellite): C-SPAN; C-SPAN 2; QVC; The Weather Channel; WGN America.
Fee: $65.00 installation; $26.55 monthly; $1.24 converter.

Expanded Basic Service 1
Subscribers: N.A.
Programming (via satellite): A&E; Animal Planet; Celebrity Shopping Network; CNN; Comedy Central; Discovery Channel; Disney Channel; Disney XD; ESPN; ESPN2; EWTN Global Catholic Network; Food Network; Fox News Channel; Fox Sports 1; Freeform; FX; Great American Country; GSN; Hallmark Channel; HGTV; History; HLN; Lifetime; MSNBC; MTV; National Geographic Channel; NBCSN; Nickelodeon; Outdoor Channel; Root Sports Pittsburgh; Spike TV; Syfy; TBS; TLC; TNT; Turner Classic Movies; TV Land; USA Network; VH1; WE tv.
Fee: $31.40 monthly.

Digital Basic Service
Subscribers: N.A.
Programming (via satellite): BBC America; Bloomberg Television; Cloo; Destination America; Discovery Kids Channel; DMX Music; ESPN Classic; ESPNews; EVINE Live; FOX College Sports Central; FOX College Sports Pacific; FXM; FYI; Golf Channel; Great American Country; History International; IFC; Investigation Discovery; LMN; OWN: Oprah Winfrey Network; Science Channel; Trinity Broadcasting Network (TBN).
Fee: $20.45 monthly.

Digital Pay Service 1
Pay Units: N.A.
Programming (via satellite): Cinemax (multiplexed); Flix; HBO (multiplexed); Showtime (multiplexed); Starz (multiplexed); Starz Encore (multiplexed); The Movie Channel (multiplexed).
Fee: $9.45 monthly (Cinemax), $11.00 monthly (Starz/Encore), $12.50 monthly (HBO or Showtime/TMC/Flix).

Video-On-Demand: No

Internet Service
Operational: Yes.
Subscribers: 823.
Broadband Service: In-house.
Fee: $27.95 monthly.

Telephone Service
Digital: Operational
Subscribers: 342.

Miles of Plant: 274.0 (coaxial); 77.0 (fiber optic). Homes passed: 3,953. Homes passed & miles of plant included in Zion.
President: Robert D. Stemler. General Manager & Chief Technician: John Hockenberry.
Ownership: Tele-Media Corp. (MSO).

SOMERSET—Formerly served by Cebridge Connections. Now served by Armstrong Cable Services, ZELIENOPLE, PA [PA0053]. ICA: PA0128.

SOMERSET TWP.—Formerly served by Adelphia Communications. Now served by Comcast Cable, BLAIRSVILLE, PA [PA0320]. ICA: PA0091.

SOUTH BUFFALO TWP.—Formerly served by South Buffalo Cablevision. Now served by Comcast Cable, BLAIRSVILLE, PA [PA0320]. ICA: PA0257.

SOUTH CREEK TWP.—Blue Ridge Communications, 613 3rd St, PO Box 215, Palmerton, PA 18071-0215. Phone: 800-222-5377. Web Site: http://www.brctv.com. Also serves Ashland & Chemung, NY; Ridgebury Twp., PA. ICA: PA0481.
Channel capacity: N.A. Channels available but not in use: N.A.

Basic Service
Subscribers: 175.
Fee: $49.95 installation; $16.86 monthly.
President: David Masenheimer.
Ownership: Pencor Services Inc. (MSO).

SOUTH FORK—Formerly served by Adelphia Communications. Now served by Comcast Cable, BLAIRSVILLE, PA [PA0320]. ICA: PA0189.

SPARTANSBURG—Zito Media, 102 S Main St, PO Box 665, Coudersport, PA 16915. Phones: 814-260-9055; 800-365-6988. Fax: 814-260-9580. E-mail: info@zitomedia.com. Web Site: http://www.zitomedia.com. Also serves Sparta Twp. (Crawford County).
ICA: PA0438.
TV Market Ranking: Below 100 (Sparta Twp. (Crawford County), SPARTANSBURG).
Channel capacity: N.A. Channels available but not in use: N.A.

Basic Service
Subscribers: 2.
Programming (received off-air): WFXP (FOX) Erie; WICU-TV (NBC) Erie; WJET-TV (ABC) Erie; WQLN (PBS) Erie; WSEE-TV (CBS, CW) Erie.
Programming (via satellite): Animal Planet; Cartoon Network; CNN; C-SPAN 2; Discovery Channel; Disney Channel; ESPN; ESPN2; Freeform; HLN; Lifetime; MTV; Nickelodeon; QVC; Syfy; TBS; TNT; Travel Channel; Trinity Broadcasting Network (TBN); USA Network; VH1; WGN America.
Fee: $49.95 installation; $33.70 monthly; $2.50 converter.

Pay Service 1
Pay Units: N.A.
Programming (via satellite): HBO.
Fee: $12.95 monthly.

Internet Service
Operational: No.

Telephone Service
None

Miles of Plant: 5.0 (coaxial); None (fiber optic). Homes passed: 150.
President: James Rigas.
Ownership: Zito Media (MSO).

SPRING MILLS—Formerly served by Spring Mills TV Co. Now served by Millheim TV Transmission Co., MILLHEIM, PA [PA0216]. ICA: PA0268.

SPRING TWP. (Crawford County)—Formerly served by Adelphia Communications. Now served by Time Warner Cable, CLEVELAND, OH [OH0006]. ICA: PA0230.

SPRUCE CREEK TWP.—Atlantic Broadband. Now served by ALTOONA, PA [PA0018]. ICA: PA0274.

ST. MARY'S—Zito Media, 102 S Main St, PO Box 665, Coudersport, PA 16915. Phones: 814-260-9055; 800-365-6988. Fax: 814-260-9580. E-mail: info@zitomedia.com. Web Site: http://www.zitomedia.com. Also serves Benzinger Twp., Daguscahonda, Fox Twp. (Elk County), Jay Twp., Kersey & Ridgeway Twp. ICA: PA0101.
TV Market Ranking: Outside TV Markets (Benzinger Twp., Daguscahonda, Fox Twp. (Elk County), Jay Twp., Kersey, Ridgeway Twp., ST. MARY'S). Franchise award date: N.A. Franchise expiration date: N.A. Began: May 1, 1953.
Channel capacity: N.A. Channels available but not in use: N.A.

Basic Service
Subscribers: 2,627.
Programming (received off-air): WATM-TV (ABC, This TV) Altoona; WJAC-TV (MeTV, NBC) Johnstown; WPCB-TV (IND) Greensburg; WPSU-TV (PBS) Clearfield; WTAE-TV (ABC, This TV) Pittsburgh; WTAJ-TV (CBS) Altoona; WWCP-TV (FOX) Johnstown.
Programming (via satellite): C-SPAN; C-SPAN 2; EWTN Global Catholic Network; INSP; Pennsylvania Cable Network; Pop; QVC; Trinity Broadcasting Network (TBN); WGN America; WPIX (Antenna TV, CW, This TV) New York.
Fee: $49.95 installation; $18.48 monthly; $1.75 converter.

Expanded Basic Service 1
Subscribers: N.A.
Programming (via satellite): A&E; AMC; Animal Planet; Bravo; Cartoon Network; CMT; CNBC; CNN; Comedy Central; Discovery Channel; Disney Channel; E! HD; ESPN; ESPN Classic; ESPN2; ESPNews; Food Network; Fox News Channel; Fox Sports 1; Freeform; FX; Hallmark Channel; HGTV; History; HLN; Lifetime; LMN; MSNBC; MTV; NFL Network; Nickelodeon; Outdoor Channel; Root Sports Pittsburgh; Spike TV; Syfy; TBS; The Weather Channel; TLC; TNT; Travel Channel; truTV; Turner Classic Movies; TV Land; USA Network; VH1.
Fee: $43.48 monthly.

Digital Basic Service
Subscribers: N.A.
Programming (via satellite): A&E HD; BBC America; Bio HD; Bloomberg Television; Cartoon Network HD; CNN HD; Destination America; Discovery Channel HD; Discovery Kids Channel; Discovery Life Channel; Disney Channel HD; DMX Music; ESPN HD; ESPN2 HD; ESPNews HD; Food Network HD; FOX College Sports Central; FOX College Sports Pacific; Fox Sports 1; Fox Sports 2; Freeform HD; FSN HD; Fuse; FX HD; FYI; GSN; HD Theater; HGTV HD; History International; IFC; Investigation Discovery; Lifetime HD; Lifetime Movie Network HD; LMN; MTV Classic; MTV Hits; MTV2; NFL Network HD; NHL Network HD; Nick Jr.; Nicktoons; Outdoor Channel 2 HD; OWN: Oprah Winfrey Network; Science Channel; Science HD; TBS HD; TeenNick; TLC HD; TNT HD; VH1 Country; WE tv.
Fee: $5.60 monthly.

Digital Pay Service 1
Pay Units: N.A.
Programming (via satellite): Cinemax (multiplexed); Cinemax HD; Flix; HBO (multiplexed); HBO HD; Showtime (multiplexed); Showtime HD; Starz (multiplexed); Starz Encore (multiplexed); Starz HD; Sundance TV; The Movie Channel (multiplexed).
Fee: $6.54 monthly (Cinemax), $10.25 monthly (Starz/Encore), $11.45 monthly (Showtime/TMC/Flix/Sundance), $16.66 monthly (HBO).

Video-On-Demand: No

Pay-Per-View
iN DEMAND (delivered digitally); Playboy TV (delivered digitally).

Internet Service
Operational: Yes.
Subscribers: 3,638.
Fee: $30.51 monthly.

Telephone Service
Digital: Operational
Subscribers: 1,924.
Fee: $20.00 monthly

Miles of Plant: 100.0 (coaxial); 20.0 (fiber optic). Homes passed: 8,000.
President: James Rigas.
Ownership: Zito Media (MSO).

STATE COLLEGE—Comcast Cable. Now served by HARRISBURG, PA [PA0009]. ICA: PA0037.

STATE COLLEGE—Windstream (formerly D&E Communications). New IPTV service no longer available, 4001 Rodney Parham Rd, Little Rock, AR 72212. Phones: 877-759-9020; 866-971-9463; 501-748-7000. Fax: 501-748-6392. E-mail: support@windstream.net. Web Site: http://www.windstream.com. Also serves Hartleton,

Cable Systems—Pennsylvania

Lewisburg, Mifflinburg & Milton. ICA: PA5280.
Channel capacity: N.A. Channels available but not in use: N.A.
Basic
Subscribers: 467.
Fee: $25.00 monthly.
Internet Service
Operational: Yes.
Fee: $36.99 monthly.
Telephone Service
Digital: Operational
Fee: $44.99 monthly
President & Chief Operating Officer: Tony Thomas. Chief Financial Officer: Bob Gunderman. Executive Vice President, Operations: Mark Faris. Executive Vice President, Engineering & Chief Technology Officer: Randy Nicklas.
Ownership: Windstream Communications Inc.

STATE COLLEGE—Windstream (formerly D&E Communications.) This cable system has converted to IPTV. Now served by STATE COLLEGE, PA [PA5280]. ICA: PA0391.

STROUDSBURG—Blue Ridge Communications, 613 3rd St, PO Box 215, Palmerton, PA 18071-0215. Phones: 610-826-2551; 800-622-8925 (Customer service); 570-421-0780. Web Site: http://www.brctv.com. Also serves Barrett Twp., Buck Hill Falls, Chestnuthill Twp., Delaware Water Gap, East Stroudsburg, Hamilton Twp. (Monroe County), Jackson Twp. (Monroe County), Lehman Twp. (Pike County), Middle Smithfield, Middle Smithfield Twp., Mount Pocono, Paradise Twp. (Monroe County), Pocono Lake, Pocono Twp., Polk Twp. (Monroe County), Price Twp. (Monroe County), Ross Twp. (Monroe County), Smithfield Twp. (Monroe County), Stroud Twp. (Monroe County) & Tobyhanna Twp. (Monroe County). ICA: PA0411.
TV Market Ranking: 49 (Barrett Twp., Buck Hill Falls, Chestnuthill Twp., Jackson Twp. (Monroe County), Middle Smithfield, Mount Pocono, Paradise Twp. (Monroe County), Pocono Lake, Pocono Twp., Polk Twp. (Monroe County), Price Twp. (Monroe County), Smithfield Twp. (Monroe County), Stroud Twp. (Monroe County), STROUDSBURG, Tobyhanna Twp. (Monroe County)); Below 100 (Delaware Water Gap, East Stroudsburg, Hamilton Twp. (Monroe County), Ross Twp. (Monroe County)); Outside TV Markets (Lehman Twp. (Pike County), Middle Smithfield Twp.). Franchise award date: N.A. Franchise expiration date: N.A. Began: March 31, 1952.
Channel capacity: 79 (operating 2-way). Channels available but not in use: N.A.
Basic Service
Subscribers: 43,018. Commercial subscribers: 1,838.
Programming (received off-air): KYW-TV (CBS, Decades) Philadelphia; WCAU (COZI TV, NBC) Philadelphia; WCBS-TV (CBS, Decades) New York; WFMZ-TV (Retro TV) Allentown; WLVT-TV (PBS) Allentown; WNBC (COZI TV, NBC) New York; WNEP-TV (ABC, Antenna TV) Scranton; WNYW (FOX, Movies!) New York; WOLF-TV (CW, FOX, MNT) Hazleton; WPIX (Antenna TV, CW, This TV) New York; WPSG (CW) Philadelphia; WPVI-TV (ABC, Live Well Network) Philadelphia; WQPX-TV (ION) Scranton; WSWB (CW, MeTV) Scranton; WVIA-TV (PBS) Scranton; WWOR-TV (Bounce TV, Buzzr, Heroes & Icons, MNT) Secaucus; WYOU (CBS) Scranton; allband FM.

Programming (via satellite): HLN.
Fee: $49.95 installation; $27.80 monthly.
Expanded Basic Service 1
Subscribers: N.A.
Programming (via satellite): A&E; AMC; Animal Planet; BET; Bravo; Cartoon Network; CMT; CNBC; CNN; Comcast SportsNet Philadelphia; Comedy Central; C-SPAN; Discovery Channel; Disney Channel; E! HD; ESPN; ESPN Classic; ESPN2; ESPNews; EVINE Live; EWTN Global Catholic Network; Food Network; Fox News Channel; Fox Sports 1; Freeform; FX; Golf Channel; HGTV; History; Lifetime; LMN; MSG; MSNBC; MTV; NBCSN; Nickelodeon; OWN: Oprah Winfrey Network; Pennsylvania Cable Network; QVC; Spike TV; Syfy; TBS; The Weather Channel; TLC; TNT; Travel Channel; Trinity Broadcasting Network (TBN); truTV; Turner Classic Movies; TV Land; Univision Studios; USA Network; VH1; WE tv; YES Network.
Fee: $31.69 monthly.
Digital Basic Service
Subscribers: N.A.
Programming (via satellite): Discovery Digital Networks; Disney XD; FSN Digital Atlantic; FSN Digital Central; FSN Digital Pacific; FXM; FYI; HRTV; MC; National Geographic Channel; Nick 2; Nick Jr.; Nicktoons; Outdoor Channel; TeenNick.
Fee: $35.00 installation; $9.95 monthly.
Digital Expanded Basic Service
Subscribers: N.A.
Programming (via satellite): BBC America; Bloomberg Television; Boomerang; Cooking Channel; DIY Network; Hallmark Channel; History International; LWS Local Weather Station.
Fee: $5.00 monthly.
Digital Pay Service 1
Pay Units: N.A.
Programming (via satellite): Cinemax (multiplexed); Flix; HBO (multiplexed); Showtime (multiplexed); Starz (multiplexed); Starz Encore (multiplexed); Sundance TV; The Movie Channel (multiplexed).
Fee: $12.50 monthly (Cinemax or Showtime/Flix/Sundance/TMC), $12.95 monthly (Starz/Encore), $13.50 monthly (HBO).
Video-On-Demand: Yes
Pay-Per-View
iN DEMAND; iN DEMAND (delivered digitally); adult PPV (delivered digitally).
Internet Service
Operational: Yes.
Subscribers: 26,789.
Broadband Service: ProLog Express.
Fee: $34.95 monthly; $10.00 modem lease; $59.95 modem purchase.
Telephone Service
Digital: Operational
Subscribers: 13,045.
Miles of Plant: 3,719.0 (coaxial); 703.0 (fiber optic). Homes passed: 68,581.
President: David Masenheimer. Vice President, Operations: Richard Semmel. General Manager: Mark Masonheimer. Fiber Manager: Randy Semmel. Chief Technician: Garry Woods.
Ownership: Pencor Services Inc. (MSO)

SUGAR GROVE—Formerly served by Atlantic Broadband. Now served by WARREN, PA [PA0090]. ICA: PA0412.

SUGARLOAF TWP.—MetroCast Communications. Now served by BERWICK, PA [PA0094]. ICA: PA0256.

SUMMERVILLE—Formerly served by Adelphia Communications. Now served by Comcast Cable, PUNXSUTAWNEY, PA [PA0397]. ICA: PA0232.

SUNBURY (village)—Service Electric Cablevision, 500 Grant St, Sunbury, PA 17801-2500. Phone: 570-286-5951. Fax: 570-286-9710. E-mail: sunburyoffice@secv.com. Web Site: http://www.sectv.com. Also serves Aristes, Beaver Twp. (Snyder County), Beavertown Borough, Bloomsburg, Buffalo Twp. (Union County), Catawissa Borough, Catawissa Twp., Center Twp. (Snyder County), Centre Twp. (Snyder County), Cleveland Twp., Coal, Coal Twp. (Northumberland County), Cooper Twp. (Montour County), Delaware Twp. (Northumberland County), Derry Twp. (Montour County), East Buffalo Twp., East Cameron Twp., East Chillisquaque Twp., Elysburg, Franklin Twp. (Columbia County), Franklin Twp. (Northumberland County), Franklin Twp. (Snyder County), Freeburg, Gregg Twp. (Union County), Hemlock Twp., Herndon, Jackson Twp. (Northumberland County), Jackson Twp. (Snyder County), Jordan Twp., Kelly Twp., Kreamer, Kulpmont (Northumberland County), Lewis Twp. (Northumberland County), Lewisburg, Liberty Twp. (Montour County), Limestone Twp. (Union County), Locust Twp., Lower Mahanoy Twp., Mahoning Twp. (Montour County), Main Twp., Marion Heights, McEwensville, Middleburg, Middleburg Borough, Middlecreek Twp., Milton, Monroe Twp. (Snyder County), Montour Twp. (Columbia County), Mount Carmel Borough, Mount Carmel Twp. (Northumberland County), Mount Pleasant Twp. (Columbia County), New Berlin, North Centre (portions), Northumberland, Orange Twp. (Columbia County), Paxinos, Paxtonville, Penn Twp. (Snyder County), Penns Creek, Point Twp. (Northumberland County), Ralpho Twp., Riverside, Roaring Creek Twp., Rockefeller Twp., Scott Twp. (Columbia County), Selinsgrove, Shamokin, Shamokin Dam, Shamokin Twp., Snydertown (Northumberland County), South Centre Twp. (Columbia County), Spring Twp. (Snyder County), Strong, Turbot Twp., Turbotville, Union Twp. (Union County), Upper Augusta Twp., Upper Mahanoy Twp., Washington Twp. (Northumberland County), Washington Twp. (Snyder County), Washingtonville, Watsontown, West Cameron Twp., West Chillisquaque Twp., West Hemlock Twp. & Zerbe Twp. ICA: PA0029.
TV Market Ranking: 49 (Bloomsburg, Hemlock Twp., Main Twp., Montour Twp. (Columbia County), Mount Pleasant Twp. (Columbia County), North Centre (portions), Orange Twp. (Columbia County), Scott Twp. (Columbia County), South Centre Twp. (Columbia County); 57 (Lower Mahanoy Twp.); Below 100 (Aristes, Beavertown Borough, Buffalo Twp. (Union County), Catawissa Borough, Catawissa Twp. (portions), Center Twp. (Snyder County), Centre Twp. (Snyder County), Cleveland Twp., Coal, Coal Twp. (Northumberland County), Cooper Twp. (Montour County), Derry Twp. (Montour County),

FULLY SEARCHABLE • CONTINUOUSLY UPDATED • DISCOUNT RATES FOR PRINT PURCHASERS
For more information call **800-771-9202** or visit **www.warren-news.com**

East Buffalo Twp., East Cameron Twp., East Chillisquaque Twp., Elysburg, Franklin Twp. (Columbia County), Franklin Twp. (Northumberland County), Franklin Twp. (Snyder County), Freeburg, Gregg Twp. (Union County), Herndon, Jackson Twp. (Northumberland County), Jackson Twp. (Snyder County), Jordan Twp., Kelly Twp., Kreamer, Kulpmont (Northumberland County), Lewis Twp. (Northumberland County), Lewisburg, Liberty Twp. (Montour County), Limestone Twp. (Union County), Locust Twp., Mahoning Twp. (Montour County), Marion Heights, McEwensville, Middleburg, Middleburg Borough, Middlecreek Twp., Milton, Monroe Twp. (Snyder County), Mount Carmel Borough, Mount Carmel Twp. (Northumberland County), New Berlin, Northumberland, Penn Twp. (Snyder County), Penns Creek, Point Twp. (Northumberland County), Ralpho Twp., Riverside, Roaring Creek Twp., Rockefeller Twp., Selinsgrove, Shamokin, Shamokin Dam, Shamokin Twp., Snydertown (Northumberland County), Spring Twp. (Snyder County), Strong, SUNBURY (VILLAGE), Turbot Twp., Turbotville, Upper Mahanoy Twp., Washington Twp. (Northumberland County), Washington Twp. (Snyder County), Washingtonville, Watsontown, West Cameron Twp., West Chillisquaque Twp., West Hemlock Twp., Zerbe Twp.); Outside TV Markets (Beaver Twp. (Snyder County), Catawissa Twp. (portions), Delaware Twp. (Northumberland County), Little Mahanoy Twp., Paxinos, Paxtonville, SUNBURY (VILLAGE), Union Twp. (Union County), Upper Augusta Twp.). Franchise award date: N.A. Franchise expiration date: N.A. Began: May 1, 1953.
Channel capacity: 24 (operating 2-way). Channels available but not in use: N.A.
Basic Service
Subscribers: 38,056.
Programming (received off-air): WBRE-TV (NBC) Wilkes-Barre; WGAL (NBC, This TV) Lancaster; WHP-TV (CBS, MNT) Harrisburg; WHTM-TV (ABC, Retro TV) Harrisburg; WITF-TV (PBS) Harrisburg; WNEP-TV (ABC, Antenna TV) Scranton; WOLF-TV (CW, FOX, MNT) Hazleton; WPIX (Antenna TV, CW, This TV) New York; WPVI-TV (ABC, Live Well Network) Philadelphia; WQMY (MNT) Williamsport; WQPX-TV (ION) Scranton; WSWB (CW, MeTV) Scranton; WVIA-TV (PBS) Scranton; WWOR-TV (Bounce TV, Buzzr, Heroes & Icons, MNT) Secaucus; WXBU (CW) Lancaster; WYOU (CBS) Scranton; allband FM.
Programming (via satellite): C-SPAN; EWTN Global Catholic Network; INSP; Pennsylvania Cable Network; QVC; The Weather Channel.
Fee: $61.00 installation; $19.95 monthly.
Expanded Basic Service 1
Subscribers: 32,844.
Programming (via satellite): A&E; AMC; Animal Planet; BBC America; BET; Bravo; Cartoon Network; CMT; CNBC; CNN; Comcast SportsNet Philadelphia; Comedy Central;

2017 Edition   D-675

Pennsylvania—Cable Systems

Discovery Channel; Discovery Life Channel; Disney Channel; Disney XD; E! HD; ESPN; ESPN Classic; ESPN2; Food Network; Fox News Channel; Fox Sports 1; Freeform; FX; Hallmark Channel; HGTV; History; HLN; Lifetime; MSNBC; MTV; National Geographic Channel; NFL Network; Nickelodeon; Outdoor Channel; Root Sports Pittsburgh; Spike TV; Syfy; TBS; TLC; TNT; Travel Channel; truTV; TV Land; Univision Studios; USA Network; VH1.
Fee: $54.95 monthly.

Digital Basic Service
Subscribers: N.A.
Programming (via satellite): 3ABN; Bloomberg Television; Boomerang; BYUtv; CBS Sports Network; Church Channel; CMT; Colours; Cooking Channel; Daystar TV Network; Destination America; Discovery Kids Channel; DIY Network; ESPNews; ESPNU; FamilyNet; FOX College Sports Central; FOX College Sports Pacific; Fox Sports 2; Fuse; FXM; FYI; GEB America; Golf Channel; Great American Country; GSN; Hallmark Movies & Mysteries; History International; HRTV; IFC; Investigation Discovery; JUCE TV; LMN; MC; MTV Classic; MTV Hits; MTV Jams; MTV2; Nat Geo WILD; NBCSN; NHL Network; Nick 2; Nick Jr.; Nicktoons; Ovation; OWN; Oprah Winfrey Network; Science Channel; Smile of a Child TV; Sprout; Tennis Channel; Trinity Broadcasting Network (TBN); Turner Classic Movies; VH1 Soul; WE tv.
Fee: $54.45 monthly; $2.95 converter.

Digital Expanded Basic Service
Subscribers: N.A.
Programming (via satellite): Cine Mexicano; CNN en Espanol; Discovery Familia; Enlace USA; ESPN Deportes; Fox Deportes; La Familia Cosmovision; NBC Universo; Telemundo; Tr3s; ULTRA HDPlex; UniMas; Univision.
Fee: $3.95 monthly.

Digital Expanded Basic Service 2
Subscribers: N.A.
Programming (via satellite): A&E HD; Animal Planet HD; AXS TV; CNN HD; Discovery Channel HD; Disney Channel HD; ESPN HD; ESPN2 HD; Food Network HD; Fox News HD; Freeform HD; FX HD; Hallmark Movie Channel HD; HD Theater; HGTV HD; History HD; MTV Live; National Geographic Channel HD; NFL Network HD; NHL Network HD; Outdoor Channel 2 HD; Science HD; TBS HD; The Weather Channel HD; TLC HD; TNT HD; Universal HD; Versus HD.
Fee: $11.00 monthly.

Digital Pay Service 1
Pay Units: N.A.
Programming (via satellite): Cinemax (multiplexed); Cinemax HD; Flix; HBO (multiplexed); HBO HD; Showtime (multiplexed); Showtime HD; Starz (multiplexed); Starz Encore (multiplexed); Starz HD; The Movie Channel (multiplexed); The Movie Channel HD.
Fee: $61.00 installation; $11.50 monthly (Cinemax), $12.45 monthly (Starz/Encore), $14.45 monthly (HBO or Showtime/TMC/Flix); $2.95 converter.

Video-On-Demand: No

Pay-Per-View
iN DEMAND (delivered digitally); Sports PPV (delivered digitally).

Internet Service
Operational: Yes. Began: January 1, 2001. Broadband Service: ProLog Express.
Fee: $61.00 installation; $22.95-$52.95 monthly; $4.95 modem lease; $59.95 modem purchase

Telephone Service
Analog: Not Operational
Digital: Operational
Subscribers: 2,618.
Fee: $44.95 monthly
Miles of Plant: 710.0 (coaxial); 293.0 (fiber optic).
General Manager: Dwight Walter. Regulatory Affairs Director: Arlean Lilly. Field Manager: John Kurtz. Office Manager: Lindy Mannello.
Ownership: Service Electric Cable TV Inc. (MSO).

SWENGEL—Formerly served by D&E Communications. No longer in operation. ICA: PA5286.

TARENTUM BOROUGH—Comcast Cable. Now served by PITTSBURGH, PA [PA0001]. ICA: PA0424.

THOMPSON TWP.—Adams Cable Service, 19 North Main St, Carbondale, PA 18407. Phones: 570-282-6121; 888-222-0077. E-mail: frontdesk@echoes.net. Web Site: http://www.adamscable.com. Also serves Ararat Twp., Brooklyn Twp., Great Bend, Great Bend Borough, Great Bend Twp., Hallstead Borough, Harford, Harmony Twp., Hop Bottom, Jackson Twp., Lanesboro, Lathrop Twp., New Milford Borough, New Milford Twp., Oakland Borough, Oakland Twp., Preston Twp., Starrucca Borough, Susquehanna Depot Borough & Thompson Borough. ICA: PA0414.
TV Market Ranking: 49 (Brooklyn Twp., Hallstead Borough, Harford, Hop Bottom, Jackson Twp., Lathrop Twp., New Milford Borough, New Milford Twp., Preston Twp., Susquehanna Depot Borough, Thompson Borough, THOMPSON TWP.); Below 100 (Ararat Twp., Great Bend, Great Bend Borough, Great Bend Twp., Harmony Twp., Lanesboro, Oakland Borough, Oakland Twp., Starrucca Borough).
Channel capacity: N.A. Channels available but not in use: N.A.

Basic Service
Subscribers: 2,596.
Fee: $40.00 installation; $22.99 monthly.
President: Douglas V.R. Adams.
Ownership: Adams CATV Inc. (MSO).

THOMPSONTOWN—Nittany Media Inc. Now served by MIFFLINTOWN, PA [PA0365]. ICA: PA0415.

THREE SPRINGS—Atlantic Broadband. Now served by ALTOONA, PA [PA0018]. ICA: PA0233.

TIDIOUTE—Formerly served by Cebridge Connections. No longer in operation. ICA: PA0183.

TIMBLIN—Formerly served by Adelphia Communications. Now served by Comcast Cable, PUNXSUTAWNEY, PA [PA0397]. ICA: PA0349.

TITUSVILLE—Armstrong Cable Services. Now served by ZELIENOPLE, PA [PA0053]. ICA: PA0475.

TITUSVILLE—Formerly served by Cebridge Connections. Now served by Armstrong Cable Services, ZELIENOPLE, PA [PA0053]. ICA: PA0416.

TOBY TWP.—Formerly served by Adelphia Communications. Now served by Comcast Cable, OIL CITY, PA [PA0086]. ICA: PA0186.

TOWANDA BOROUGH—Comcast Cable. Now served by HARRISBURG, PA [PA0009]. ICA: PA0138.

TOWNVILLE—Formerly served by Cebridge Connections. Now served by Armstrong Cable Services, ZELIENOPLE, PA [PA0053]. ICA: PA0278.

TRAPPE—Comcast Cable. Now served by EATONTOWN BOROUGH, NJ [NJ0009]. ICA: PA0453.

TREASURE LAKE—Zito Media, 102 S Main St, PO Box 665, Coudersport, PA 16915. Phones: 814-260-9055; 800-365-6988. Fax: 814-260-9580. E-mail: info@zitomedia.com. Web Site: http://www.zitomedia.com. Also serves Huston Twp. (Clearfield County), Penfield & Sandy. ICA: PA0451.
TV Market Ranking: Outside TV Markets (Huston Twp. (Clearfield County), Penfield, Sandy, TREASURE LAKE). Franchise award date: January 1, 1986. Franchise expiration date: N.A. Began: N.A.
Channel capacity: N.A. Channels available but not in use: N.A.

Basic Service
Subscribers: 994.
Programming (received off-air): WATM-TV (ABC, This TV) Altoona; WJAC-TV (MeTV, NBC) Johnstown; WKBS-TV (IND) Altoona; WPNT (MNT) Pittsburgh; WPSU-TV (PBS) Clearfield; WTAE-TV (ABC, This TV) Pittsburgh; WTAJ-TV (CBS) Altoona; WWCP-TV (FOX) Johnstown.
Programming (via satellite): CW PLUS.
Fee: $49.95 installation; $17.00 monthly.

Expanded Basic Service 1
Subscribers: N.A.
Programming (via satellite): A&E; AMC; Animal Planet; Bravo; Cartoon Network; CMT; CNBC; CNN; Comedy Central; C-SPAN; C-SPAN 2; Discovery Channel; Disney Channel; E! HD; ESPN; ESPN Classic; ESPN2; EWTN Global Catholic Network; Food Network; Fox News Channel; Fox Sports 1; Freeform; FX; Golf Channel; Hallmark Channel; HGTV; History; HLN; INSP; Lifetime; MSNBC; MTV; NFL Network; Nickelodeon; Outdoor Channel; Pennsylvania Cable Network; QVC; Root Sports Pittsburgh; Spike TV; Syfy; TBS; The Weather Channel; TLC; TNT; Travel Channel; Trinity Broadcasting Network (TBN); truTV; Turner Classic Movies; TV Land; USA Network; VH1; WGN America.
Fee: $32.00 monthly.

Digital Basic Service
Subscribers: N.A.
Programming (via satellite): BBC America; Bloomberg Television; Boomerang; C-SPAN 3; Destination America; Discovery Kids Channel; Discovery Life Channel; Disney XD; ESPN HD; ESPN2 HD; ESPNews; Fox HD; Fox Sports 1; FXM; Golf Channel; Great American Country; GSN; HRTV; INSP; Investigation Discovery; LMN; MC; MTV Classic; MTV Hits; MTV Jams; MTV2; Nick 2; Nick Jr.; Nicktoons; OWN; Oprah Winfrey Network; RFD-TV; Science Channel; TeenNick; The Word Network; Trinity Broadcasting Network (TBN); VH1 Country; VH1 Soul; WE tv.
Fee: $11.95 monthly.

Digital Expanded Basic Service
Subscribers: N.A.
Programming (via satellite): DIY Network; Flix; FSN Digital Atlantic; FSN Digital Central; FSN Digital Pacific; FYI; History International; IFC; NBCSN; Outdoor Channel; Sundance TV.
Fee: $10.00 monthly.

Digital Pay Service 1
Pay Units: N.A.
Programming (via satellite): Cinemax (multiplexed); Cinemax HD; Flix; HBO (multiplexed); HBO HD; Showtime (multiplexed); Showtime HD; Starz (multiplexed); Starz Encore (multiplexed); Starz HD; The Movie Channel (multiplexed).
Fee: $8.00 monthly (Cinemax or Starz/Encore), $10.00 monthly (HBO or Showtime/TMC).

Video-On-Demand: Yes

Pay-Per-View
iN DEMAND (delivered digitally); NHL Center Ice (delivered digitally); MLB Extra Innings (delivered digitally).

Internet Service
Operational: Yes.
Broadband Service: In-house.
Fee: $49.95 monthly.

Telephone Service
Digital: Operational
Fee: $35.00 monthly
Miles of Plant: 140.0 (coaxial); None (fiber optic). Homes passed: 5,000. Homes passed & miles of plant (coax) include Weedville.
President: James Rigas.
Ownership: Zito Media (MSO).

TREMONT—Wire Television Corp, 603 East Market St, Pottsville, PA 17901-2718. Phone: 570-622-4501. Fax: 570-622-8340. E-mail: customerserv@wtvaccess.com. Web Site: http://www.wtvaccess.com. Also serves Frailey Twp. & Zerbe. ICA: PA0204.
TV Market Ranking: Below 100 (Frailey Twp., TREMONT, Zerbe). Franchise award date: N.A. Franchise expiration date: N.A. Began: June 18, 1952.
Channel capacity: N.A. Channels available but not in use: N.A.

Basic Service
Subscribers: 309.
Programming (received off-air): KYW-TV (CBS, Decades) Philadelphia; WGAL (NBC, This TV) Lancaster; WHP-TV (CBS, MNT) Harrisburg; WHTM-TV (ABC, Retro TV) Harrisburg; WHYY-TV (PBS) Wilmington; WITF-TV (PBS) Harrisburg; WNEP-TV (ABC, Antenna TV) Scranton; WPMT (Antenna TV, FOX) York; WPSG (CW) Philadelphia; WSWB (CW, MeTV) Scranton; WTXF-TV (Buzzr, FOX, Movies!) Philadelphia; WXBU (CW) Lancaster; allband FM.
Programming (via satellite): A&E; AMC; Animal Planet; Bloomberg Television; Cartoon Network; CMT; CNN; Comcast SportsNet Philadelphia; Comedy Central; C-SPAN 2; Discovery Channel; Disney Channel; ESPN; ESPN Classic; ESPN2; EWTN Global Catholic Network; Food Network; Fox News Channel; Freeform; FX; Hallmark Channel; HGTV; History; INSP; ION Television; Lifetime; LMN; MTV; National Geographic Channel; Nickelodeon; Pennsylvania Cable Network; QVC; Spike TV; Syfy; TBS; The Weather Channel; TLC; TNT; Travel Channel; truTV; TV Land; USA Network; VH1; WGN America; WPIX (Antenna TV, CW, This TV) New York.
Fee: $37.50 installation; $82.62 monthly.

Digital Basic Service
Subscribers: N.A.
Programming (via satellite): BBC America; Bravo; Daystar TV Network; Destination America; Discovery Kids Channel; Discovery Life Channel; DMX Music; ESPN Clas-

Cable Systems—Pennsylvania

sic; ESPNews; EVINE Live; FOX College Sports Central; FOX College Sports Pacific; Fox Sports 1; FXM; Golf Channel; Great American Country; GSN; HGTV; History; IFC; Investigation Discovery; MTV Classic; National Geographic Channel; NBCSN; Nick Jr.; Nicktoons; Outdoor Channel; OWN: Oprah Winfrey Network; Science Channel; The Word Network; Trinity Broadcasting Network (TBN); Turner Classic Movies; UP; VH1 Country; WE tv.
Fee: $21.95 monthly.

Pay Service 1
Pay Units: N.A.
Programming (via satellite): Cinemax; HBO.
Fee: $15.00 installation; $15.95 monthly (each).

Digital Pay Service 1
Pay Units: N.A.
Programming (via satellite): Cinemax (multiplexed); Flix; HBO (multiplexed); Playboy TV; Showtime (multiplexed); Starz (multiplexed); Starz Encore (multiplexed); The Movie Channel.
Fee: $15.95 monthly (Cinemax, HBO, Playboy, Showtime/TMC/Flix or Starz/Encore).

Pay-Per-View
iN DEMAND (delivered digitally); Fresh (delivered digitally); Club Jenna (delivered digitally); Sports PPV (delivered digitally).

Internet Service
Operational: Yes. Began: November 1, 2001.
Subscribers: 13.
Broadband Service: Wtvaccess.
Fee: $49.95 installation; $24.95-$59.95 monthly; $10.00 modem lease; $150.00 modem purchase.

Telephone Service
None
Miles of Plant: 14.0 (coaxial); None (fiber optic). Homes passed: 1,800.
General Manager: Darlene Mills. Chief Technician: Brian Brennan.
Ownership: Wire Tele-View Corp. (MSO).

TROY—Blue Ridge Communications, 613 3rd St, PO Box 215, Palmerton, PA 18071-0215. Phone: 610-826-2551. Web Site: http://www.brctv.com. Also serves Austinville, Burlington, Burlington Borough, Columbia Crossroads, Columbia Twp. (Bradford County), East Troy, Franklindale Twp., Granville Twp. (Bradford County), Leroy Twp., Monroe Twp. (Bradford County), Powell, Powell Twp., Ridgebury Twp., South Creek Twp., Springfield Twp. (Bradford County), Sylvania, Sylvania Borough, Troy Twp. & West Burlington Twp. ICA: PA0165.
TV Market Ranking: Below 100 (Austinville, Burlington, Burlington Borough, Columbia Crossroads, Columbia Twp. (Bradford County), East Troy, Franklindale Twp., Granville Twp. (Bradford County), Monroe Twp. (Bradford County), Powell Twp., Ridgebury Twp., Ridgebury Twp., Springfield Twp. (Bradford County), Sylvania, Sylvania Borough, TROY, Troy Twp., West Burlington Twp., Leroy Twp.); Outside TV Markets (Powell). Franchise award date: N.A. Franchise expiration date: N.A. Began: June 1, 1958.
Channel capacity: 35 (operating 2-way). Channels available but not in use: N.A.

Basic Service
Subscribers: 911.
Programming (received off-air): WBNG-TV (CBS, CW) Binghamton; WENY-TV (ABC, CW) Elmira; WETM-TV (IND, NBC) Elmira; WSKG-TV (PBS) Binghamton; WVIA-TV (PBS) Scranton; WYDC (FOX, MNT)

Corning; WYOU (CBS) Scranton; allband FM.
Programming (via satellite): C-SPAN; C-SPAN 2; WGN America; WPIX (Antenna TV, CW, This TV) New York.
Fee: $49.95 installation; $27.08 monthly.

Expanded Basic Service 1
Subscribers: N.A.
Programming (via satellite): A&E; AMC; Animal Planet; BET; Cartoon Network; CMT; CNBC; CNN; Comedy Central; Discovery Channel; Disney Channel; E! HD; ESPN; ESPN2; EWTN Global Catholic Network; Food Network; Fox News Channel; Fox Sports 1; Freeform; FX; Hallmark Channel; HGTV; History; HLN; Lifetime; LMN; MSNBC; MTV; NBCSN; Nickelodeon; Pennsylvania Cable Network; QVC; Root Sports Pittsburgh; Spike TV; Syfy; TBS; The Weather Channel; TLC; TNT; Travel Channel; Trinity Broadcasting Network (TBN); truTV; Turner Classic Movies; TV Land; USA Network; VH1.
Fee: $27.99 monthly.

Digital Basic Service
Subscribers: N.A.
Programming (via satellite): Disney XD; DMX Music; ESPN Classic; ESPNews; Fox Sports 1; FXM; GSN; National Geographic Channel; NBCSN; Nick Jr.; Outdoor Channel; TeenNick.
Fee: $13.95 monthly.

Digital Expanded Basic Service
Subscribers: N.A.
Programming (via satellite): BBC America; Bloomberg Television; Discovery Digital Networks; FYI; Golf Channel; History International.
Fee: $5.00 monthly.

Pay Service 1
Pay Units: N.A.
Programming (via satellite): Cinemax; HBO; Showtime.
Fee: $11.50 monthly (Cinemax or Showtime), $12.50 monthly (HBO).

Digital Pay Service 1
Pay Units: N.A.
Programming (via satellite): Cinemax (multiplexed); Flix; HBO (multiplexed); Showtime (multiplexed); Starz (multiplexed); Starz Encore (multiplexed); Sundance TV; The Movie Channel (multiplexed).
Fee: $12.50 monthly (Cinemax, Showtime or TMC), $12.95 monthly (Starz), $13.50 monthly (HBO).

Video-On-Demand: No

Pay-Per-View
iN DEMAND; Sports PPV (delivered digitally); iN DEMAND (delivered digitally).

Internet Service
Operational: No.

Telephone Service
None
Miles of Plant: 25.0 (coaxial); None (fiber optic). Homes passed: 1,800.
President: David Masenheimer. Vice President, Operations: Richard Semmel. General Manager: Mark Masenheimer. Fiber Manager: Randy Semmel. Chief Technician: Garry Woods.
Ownership: Pencor Services Inc. (MSO).

TUNKHANNOCK—Blue Ridge Communications, 613 3rd St, PO Box 215, Palmerton, PA 18071-0215. Phones: 610-826-2551; 800-275-0724 (Customer service); 570-836-5422. Web Site: http://www.brctv.com. Also serves Albany Twp., Braintrim Twp., Camptown, Cherry Twp. (Sullivan County), Colley Twp. (Sullivan County), Dallas, Dallas Twp., Dushore, Eaton Twp., Eatonville,

Falls Twp. (Wyoming County), Forkston Twp., Hunlock Creek, Huntington Twp. (Luzerne County), Kunkle, Laceyville, Lake Carey, Lake Twp. (Luzerne County), Lake Winola, Lemon Twp., Mehoopany, Meshoppen, Meshoppen Borough, Meshoppen Twp., Monroe Twp., New Albany, Newton Twp. (Lackawanna County), Noxen, Overfield Twp., Sweet Valley, Terry Twp., Tunkhannock Twp. (Wyoming County), Tuscarora Twp. (Bradford County), Union Twp., Washington Twp. (Wyoming County), Wilmot Twp., Windham Twp., Wyalusing Borough, Wyalusing Twp. & Wyoming County. ICA: PA0367.
TV Market Ranking: 49 (Braintrim Twp., Cherry Twp. (Sullivan County), Colley Twp. (Sullivan County), Dallas, Dallas Twp., Dushore, Eaton Twp., Eatonville, Falls Twp. (Wyoming County), Forkston Twp., Hunlock Creek, Huntington Twp. (Luzerne County), Kunkle, Laceyville, Lake Carey, Lake Twp. (Luzerne County), Lake Winola, Lemon Twp., Mehoopany, Meshoppen, Meshoppen Borough, Meshoppen Twp., Monroe Twp., Newton Twp. (Lackawanna County), Noxen, Overfield Twp., Sweet Valley, Terry Twp., TUNKHANNOCK, Tunkhannock Twp. (Wyoming County), Tuscarora Twp. (Bradford County), Union Twp., Washington Twp. (Wyoming County), Wilmot Twp., Windham Twp., Wyoming County); Below 100 (Camptown, Wyalusing Borough, Wyalusing Twp.); Outside TV Markets (Albany Twp., New Albany). Franchise award date: N.A. Franchise expiration date: N.A. Began: September 1, 1966.
Channel capacity: 42 (operating 2-way). Channels available but not in use: N.A.

Basic Service
Subscribers: 6,891. Commercial subscribers: 202.
Programming (received off-air): WBNG-TV (CBS, CW) Binghamton; WBRE-TV (NBC) Wilkes-Barre; WICZ-TV (FOX) Binghamton; WNEP-TV (ABC, Antenna TV) Scranton; WOLF-TV (CW, FOX, MNT) Hazleton; WPIX (Antenna TV, CW, This TV) New York; WQMY (MNT) Williamsport; WQPX-TV (ION) Scranton; WSKG-TV (PBS) Binghamton; WSWB (CW, MeTV) Scranton; WVIA-TV (PBS) Scranton; WYOU (CBS) Scranton.
Programming (via satellite): WGN America.
Fee: $49.95 installation; $27.89 monthly.

Expanded Basic Service 1
Subscribers: N.A.
Programming (via satellite): A&E; AMC; Animal Planet; Bravo; Cartoon Network; CMT; CNBC; CNN; Comedy Central; C-SPAN; Discovery Channel; Disney Channel; E! HD; ESPN; ESPN2; EWTN Global Catholic Network; Food Network; Fox News Channel; Fox Sports 1; Freeform; FX; GSN; Hallmark Channel; HGTV; History; HLN; INSP; Lifetime; LMN; MSG; MSNBC; MTV; National Geographic Channel; NBCSN; NFL Network; Nickelodeon; OWN: Oprah Winfrey Network; Pennsylvania Cable Network; QVC; Root Sports Pittsburgh; Spike TV; SportsNet New York; Syfy; TBS; The Weather Channel; TLC; TNT; Travel Chan-

nel; truTV; Turner Classic Movies; TV Land; USA Network; VH1; WE tv; YES Network.
Fee: $31.95 monthly.

Digital Basic Service
Subscribers: N.A.
Programming (via satellite): BBC America; Bloomberg Television; CMT; Destination America; Discovery Kids Channel; Discovery Life Channel; Disney XD; ESPN Classic; ESPNews; EVINE Live; FOX College Sports Central; FOX College Sports Pacific; FXM; FYI; Golf Channel; Great American Country; History International; IFC; Investigation Discovery; MC; MTV Classic; MTV Hits; MTV2; Nick Jr.; Outdoor Channel; RFD-TV; Science Channel; Sprout; TeenNick; Trinity Broadcasting Network (TBN); VH1 Soul.
Fee: $35.00 installation; $14.95 monthly.

Digital Pay Service 1
Pay Units: N.A.
Programming (via satellite): Cinemax (multiplexed); Flix; HBO (multiplexed); Showtime (multiplexed); Starz (multiplexed); Starz Encore (multiplexed); Sundance TV; The Movie Channel (multiplexed).
Fee: $12.50 monthly (Cinemax, Showtime/Flix/Sundance or TMC), $12.95 monthly (Starz/Encore), $13.50 monthly (HBO).

Video-On-Demand: No

Pay-Per-View
iN DEMAND; iN DEMAND (delivered digitally); Sports PPV (delivered digitally); Adult PPV (delivered digitally).

Internet Service
Operational: Yes.
Broadband Service: ProLog Express.
Fee: $50.00 installation; $36.95 monthly; $10.00 modem lease; $59.95 modem purchase.

Telephone Service
None
Miles of Plant: 178.0 (coaxial); None (fiber optic).
President: David Masenheimer. Vice President, Operations: Richard Semmel. General Manager: Mark Masonheimer. Chief Technician: Randy Semmel.
Ownership: Pencor Services Inc. (MSO).

TYLERSVILLE—Tylersville Community TV Cable Assoc, 1133 Summer Mountain Rd, Loganton, PA 17747. Phone: 570-725-3865. ICA: PA0417.
TV Market Ranking: Below 100 (TYLERSVILLE). Franchise award date: N.A. Franchise expiration date: N.A. Began: January 1, 1972.
Channel capacity: N.A. Channels available but not in use: N.A.

Basic Service
Subscribers: 115.
Programming (received off-air): WBRE-TV (NBC) Wilkes-Barre; WNEP-TV (ABC, Antenna TV) Scranton; WOLF-TV (CW, FOX, MNT) Hazleton; WPSU-TV (PBS) Clearfield; WSWB (CW, MeTV) Scranton; WTAJ-TV (CBS) Altoona; WVIA-TV (PBS) Scranton; WYOU (CBS) Scranton.
Programming (via satellite): A&E; CNN; ESPN; Freeform; Hallmark Channel; His-

Pennsylvania—Cable Systems

tory; RFD-TV; Spike TV; Starz; TBS; TNT; TV Land.
Fee: $17.00 monthly.
Pay Service 1
Pay Units: N.A.
Programming (via satellite): Starz; Starz Encore.
Internet Service
Operational: No.
Telephone Service
None
Miles of Plant: 6.0 (coaxial); None (fiber optic).
President & Chief Technician: Jim Breon.
Ownership: Tylersville Community TV Association Inc.

TYRONE—Formerly served by Adelphia Communications. Now served by Comcast Cable, HARRISBURG, PA [PA0009]. ICA: PA0418.

ULYSSES BOROUGH—Time Warner Cable. Now served by BUFFALO, NY [NY0216]. ICA: PA0419.

UNION TWP. (Centre County)—Country Cable, 196 South Main St, Pleasant Gap, PA 16823-3221. Phone: 814-359-3161. Fax: 814-359-2145. Also serves Fleming Borough & Huston Twp. (Centre County). ICA: PA0209.
TV Market Ranking: Outside TV Markets (Fleming Borough, Huston Twp. (Centre County)). Franchise award date: N.A. Franchise expiration date: N.A. Began: June 1, 1974.
Channel capacity: N.A. Channels available but not in use: N.A.
Basic Service
Subscribers: 421.
Programming (received off-air): WATM-TV (ABC, This TV) Altoona; WJAC-TV (MeTV, NBC) Johnstown; WKBS-TV (IND) Altoona; WNEP-TV (ABC, Antenna TV) Scranton; WPSU-TV (PBS) Clearfield; WTAJ-TV (CBS) Altoona; WVIA-TV (PBS) Scranton; WWCP-TV (FOX) Johnstown.
Programming (via satellite): A&E; Animal Planet; Cartoon Network; CNN; Discovery Channel; Disney Channel; ESPN; ESPN2; Freeform; Nickelodeon; Outdoor Channel; Pop; Root Sports Pittsburgh; Spike TV; TBS; TNT; Turner Classic Movies; TV Land; USA Network; WGN America.
Fee: $50.00 installation; $52.00 monthly.
Pay Service 1
Pay Units: N.A.
Programming (via satellite): HBO.
Fee: $20.00 installation; $13.86 monthly.
Video-On-Demand: No
Internet Service
Operational: No.
Telephone Service
None
Miles of Plant: 70.0 (coaxial); None (fiber optic). Homes passed: 925.
General Manager & Chief Technician: Lee Dorman.
Ownership: Country Cable TV.

UNION TWP. (Huntingdon County)—Formerly served by Atlantic Broadband. No longer in operation. ICA: PA0208.

UNION TWP. (Union County)—Formerly served by D&E Communications/Windstream. IPTV service no longer in operation. ICA: PA5310.

UNIONTOWN—Atlantic Broadband, 320 Bailey Ave, Uniontown, PA 15401. Phones: 888-536-9600 (Customer service); 814-535-3506. Fax: 814-535-7749. E-mail: info@atlanticbb.com. Web Site: http://atlanticbb.com. Also serves Beallsville, Bentleyville, Bobtown, Brownsville, Carmichaels, Centerville, Clarksville, Cokeburg, Crucible, Cumberland Twp. (Greene County), Dawson, Deemston, Dunkard Twp., East Bethlehem Twp. (Washington County), Ellsworth, Fairchance, Fayette City (Fayette County), Georges Twp. (Fayette County), German Twp. (Fayette County), Glassworks, Greene County (portions), Greene Twp. (Greene County), Greensboro, Hopwood, Isabella, Jefferson (Greene County), Keisterville, La Belle, Lower Tyrone Twp., Luzerne Twp., Mapletown, Marianna, Masontown, Menallen Twp. (Fayette County), Monongahela Twp., Morgan Twp., Nemacolin, Nicholson Twp. (Fayette County), North Bethlehem Twp. (portions), North Union Twp., Perry Twp. (Fayette County), Perryopolis, Point Marion, Redstone Twp. (Fayette County), Rices Landing, Rostraver (Westmoreland County), Smithfield, Smithton, Smock (portions), Somerset Twp. (Washington County), South Huntingdon Twp., South Union Twp., Springhill Twp. (Fayette County), Springhill Twp. (Greene County), Washington Twp. (Fayette County), West Bethlehem Twp. & West Pike Run Twp., PA; Monongalia County (portions), WV. ICA: PA0020.
TV Market Ranking: 10 (Beallsville, Bentleyville, Brownsville, Centerville, Crucible, Dawson, Deemston, East Bethlehem Twp. (Washington County), Ellsworth, Fairchance, Fayette City (Fayette County), Georges Twp. (Fayette County), German Twp. (Fayette County), Hopwood, Hopwood, Isabella, Keisterville, La Belle, Lower Tyrone Twp., Marianna, Masontown, Menallen Twp. (Fayette County), Morgan Twp., Nicholson Twp. (Fayette County), North Bethlehem Twp. (portions), North Union Twp., Perryopolis, Point Marion, Redstone Twp. (Fayette County), Rices Landing, Rostraver (Westmoreland County), Smithton, Smock (portions), Somerset Twp. (Washington County), South Huntingdon Twp., Washington Twp. (Fayette County), West Bethlehem Twp., West Pike Run Twp.); 10,90 (Cokeburg); 90 (Clarksville, Greene County (portions) (portions), Jefferson (Greene County)); Below 100 (Bobtown, Dunkard Twp., Monongalia County (portions) (portions), South Union Twp., Greene County (portions) (portions)); Outside TV Markets (Carmichaels, Cumberland Twp. (Greene County), Glassworks, Greensboro, Mapletown, Monongahela Twp., Monongalia County (portions) (portions), Nemacolin, Smithfield, Springhill Twp. (Fayette County), Springhill Twp. (Greene County), Greene County (portions) (portions)).
Franchise award date: January 1, 1966. Franchise expiration date: N.A. Began: January 1, 1966.
Channel capacity: 20 (operating 2-way). Channels available but not in use: N.A.
Basic Service
Subscribers: 18,030. Commercial subscribers: 628.
Programming (received off-air): KDKA-TV (CBS, Decades) Pittsburgh; WNPB-TV (PBS) Morgantown; WPCB-TV (IND) Greensburg; WPCW (CW) Jeannette; WPGH-TV (Antenna TV, FOX, The Country Network) Pittsburgh; WPNT (MNT) Pittsburgh; WPXI (MeTV, NBC) Pittsburgh; WQED (PBS) Pittsburgh; WTAE-TV (ABC, This TV) Pittsburgh.
Planned programming (received off-air): WWCP-TV (FOX) Johnstown.
Programming (via satellite): C-SPAN; C-SPAN 2; EWTN Global Catholic Network; Pennsylvania Cable Network; Pop; QVC; Trinity Broadcasting Network (TBN).
Fee: $40.00 installation; $34.56 monthly.
Expanded Basic Service 1
Subscribers: N.A.
Programming (via satellite): A&E; AMC; Animal Planet; BET; Bravo; Cartoon Network; CMT; CNBC; CNN; Comedy Central; Discovery Channel; Discovery Life Channel; Disney Channel; Disney XD; E! HD; ESPN; ESPN2; ESPNews; Food Network; Fox News Channel; Fox Sports 1; Freeform; FX; Golf Channel; Hallmark Channel; HGTV; History; HLN; HRTV; Lifetime; MSNBC; MTV; National Geographic Channel; NBCSN; Nickelodeon; Oxygen; Pittsburgh Cable News Channel; Root Sports Pittsburgh; Spike TV; Syfy; TBS; The Weather Channel; TLC; TNT; Travel Channel; truTV; TV Land; USA Network; VH1.
Fee: $38.61 monthly.
Digital Basic Service
Subscribers: N.A.
Programming (via satellite): A&E HD; BBC America; Bloomberg Television; Boomerang; CMT; Destination America; Discovery Kids Channel; DIY Network; ESPN Classic; ESPN HD; Fox Sports 2; FYI; Great American Country; HD Theater; History International; IFC; Investigation Discovery; LMN; MC; MTV Classic; MTV Hits; MTV Jams; MTV2; NFL Network; Nick 2; Nick Jr.; Nicktoons; OWN: Oprah Winfrey Network; Root Sports Pittsburgh; RTV; Science Channel; Starz; Starz HD; TeenNick; TNT HD; Tr3s; VH1 Soul; WE tv; WeatherVision.
Fee: $18.95 monthly.
Digital Pay Service 1
Pay Units: N.A.
Programming (via satellite): Cinemax (multiplexed); Cinemax HD; Flix; HBO (multiplexed); HBO HD; Showtime (multiplexed); The Movie Channel (multiplexed).
Fee: $20.00 installation; $15.95 monthly (Cinemax/Cinemax HD, HBO/HBO HD or Showtime/TMC/Flix).
Video-On-Demand: No
Pay-Per-View
iN DEMAND (delivered digitally); Fresh (delivered digitally); Club Jenna (delivered digitally); Playboy TV (delivered digitally); Hot Choice (delivered digitally).
Internet Service
Operational: Yes.
Subscribers: 19,923.
Broadband Service: Atlantic Broadband High-Speed Internet.
Fee: $24.95-$57.95 monthly.
Telephone Service
Digital: Operational
Subscribers: 9,044.
Fee: $44.95 monthly
Miles of Plant: 1,707.0 (coaxial); 404.0 (fiber optic). Homes passed: 21,819.
Senior Vice President & General Counsel: Bartlett Leber. Vice President: David Dane. General Manager: Mike Papasergi. Technical Operations Director: Charles Sorchilla. Marketing & Customer Service Director: Dara Leslie. Marketing Manager: Natalie Kurchak.
Ownership: Atlantic Broadband (MSO).

VICKSBURG—Formerly served by D&E Communications. No longer in operation. ICA: PA5287.

WALNUT—Formerly served by Penn CATV of Walnut. No longer in operation. ICA: PA0281.

WALNUT BOTTOM—Kuhn Communications, 301 West Main St, Walnut Bottom, PA 17266. Phones: 800-771-7072; 717-532-8857. Fax: 717-532-5563. E-mail: kuhncom1@kuhncom.net. Web Site: http://www.kuhncom.net. ICA: PA0220.
TV Market Ranking: 57 (WALNUT BOTTOM). Franchise award date: N.A. Franchise expiration date: N.A. Began: January 1, 1978.
Channel capacity: N.A. Channels available but not in use: N.A.
Basic Service
Subscribers: 968.
Programming (received off-air): WGAL (NBC, This TV) Lancaster; WHAG-TV (IND) Hagerstown; WHP-TV (CBS, MNT) Harrisburg; WHTM-TV (ABC, Retro TV) Harrisburg; WITF-TV (PBS) Harrisburg; WPIX (Antenna TV, CW, This TV) New York; WPMT (Antenna TV, FOX) York; WXBU (CW) Lancaster.
Programming (via satellite): ESPN; HLN; Spike TV.
Fee: $30.00 installation; $15.45 monthly.
Expanded Basic Service 1
Subscribers: N.A.
Programming (via satellite): A&E; Animal Planet; CNN; C-SPAN; Discovery Channel; Disney Channel; ESPN2; Food Network; Freeform; Outdoor Channel; Pennsylvania Cable Network; QVC; TBS; The Weather Channel; Travel Channel; TV Land; USA Network.
Expanded Basic Service 2
Subscribers: N.A.
Programming (via satellite): AMC; Cartoon Network; CMT; CNBC; Comcast SportsNet Philadelphia; Comedy Central; E! HD; Fox News Channel; FOX Sports Networks; FX; Hallmark Channel; HGTV; History; Lifetime; MSNBC; MTV; Nickelodeon; TLC; TNT; Trinity Broadcasting Network (TBN); Turner Classic Movies; VH1; WGN America.
Digital Basic Service
Subscribers: N.A.
Programming (via satellite): BBC America; Bloomberg Television; Bravo; Daystar TV Network; Discovery Life Channel; Disney XD; DMX Music; ESPN Classic; ESPNews; EVINE Live; FOX College Sports Central; FOX College Sports Pacific; Fox Sports 1; Fuse; FXM; FYI; Golf Channel; Great American Country; GSN; HGTV; History; History International; IFC; LMN; MTV Classic; MTV2; National Geographic Channel; NBCSN; Nick Jr.; Nicktoons; Outdoor Channel; Syfy; TeenNick; The Word Network; Trinity Broadcasting Network (TBN); Turner Classic Movies; TV Land; VH1 Country; WE tv.
Pay Service 1
Pay Units: N.A.
Programming (via satellite): Cinemax; HBO; Starz; The Movie Channel.
Fee: $9.60 monthly (each).
Digital Pay Service 1
Pay Units: N.A.
Programming (via satellite): Cinemax (multiplexed); HBO (multiplexed); Showtime (multiplexed); Starz (multiplexed); Starz Encore (multiplexed); The Movie Channel (multiplexed).
Video-On-Demand: No
Internet Service
Operational: Yes. Began: January 1, 2001.
Broadband Service: kuhncom.net.
Fee: $50.00 installation; $29.95 monthly.
Telephone Service
Digital: Operational
Miles of Plant: 37.0 (coaxial); None (fiber optic). Homes passed: 1,640.

Cable Systems—Pennsylvania

President & General Manager: Earl W. Kuhn. Office Manager: Tracy Reath.
Ownership: Kuhn Communications (MSO).

WARREN—Atlantic Broadband, 14 Biddle St, Warren, PA 16365. Phones: 888-536-9600 (Customer service); 814-535-3506. Fax: 814-535-7749. E-mail: info@atlanticbb.com. Web Site: http://atlanticbb.com. Also serves Conewango Twp. (Warren County), Glade Twp. (Warren County), Mead Twp. (Warren County), Pine Grove Twp. (Warren County), Pleasant Twp. (Warren County), Sugar Grove & Warren County. ICA: PA0090.
TV Market Ranking: Below 100 (Conewango Twp. (Warren County), Glade Twp. (Warren County), Mead Twp. (Warren County), Pine Grove Twp. (Warren County), Pleasant Twp. (Warren County), Sugar Grove, WARREN, Warren County). Franchise award date: March 1, 1952. Franchise expiration date: N.A. Began: February 1, 1953.
Channel capacity: 68 (operating 2-way). Channels available but not in use: N.A.
Basic Service
Subscribers: 3,951. Commercial subscribers: 164.
Programming (received off-air): WFXP (FOX) Erie; WGRZ (Antenna TV, NBC, WeatherNation) Buffalo; WICU-TV (NBC) Erie; WJET-TV (ABC) Erie; WKBW-TV (ABC, Escape) Buffalo; WPSU-TV (PBS) Clearfield; WSEE-TV (CBS, CW) Erie; allband FM.
Programming (via satellite): C-SPAN; C-SPAN 2; EWTN Global Catholic Network; INSP; Jewelry Television; Pennsylvania Cable Network; Pop; QVC; Trinity Broadcasting Network (TBN); World.
Fee: $40.00 installation; $25.51 monthly; $1.77 converter.
Expanded Basic Service 1
Subscribers: 3,300.
Programming (via satellite): A&E; AMC; Animal Planet; Bravo; Cartoon Network; CMT; CNBC; CNN; Comedy Central; Discovery Channel; Disney Channel; E! HD; ESPN; ESPN Classic; ESPN2; Food Network; Fox News Channel; Fox Sports 1; Freeform; FX; Golf Channel; Hallmark Channel; HGTV; History; HLN; Lifetime; MSNBC; MTV; National Geographic Channel; Nickelodeon; Outdoor Channel; OWN: Oprah Winfrey Network; Oxygen; Root Sports Pittsburgh; Spike TV; Syfy; TBS; The Weather Channel; TLC; TNT; Travel Channel; truTV; Turner Classic Movies; TV Land; USA Network; VH1.
Fee: $55.03 monthly.
Digital Basic Service
Subscribers: N.A.
Programming (via satellite): A&E HD; Animal Planet HD; BBC America; Bloomberg Television; Boomerang; Chiller; CMT; Destination America; Discovery Channel HD; Discovery Kids Channel; Disney Channel HD; Disney XD; DIY Network; DMX Music; ESPN HD; ESPN2 HD; ESPNews; ESPNU; Fox Sports 2; FYI; HD Theater; History International; IFC; Investigation Discovery; LMN; MTV Classic; MTV Hits; MTV Jams; MTV2; NFL Network; NFL Network HD; Nick 2; Nick Jr.; Nicktoons; Root Sports Pittsburgh; Science Channel; Starz (multiplexed); Starz Encore (multiplexed); Syfy HD; TBS HD; TeenNick; TLC HD; TNT HD; Tr3s; USA Network HD; VH1 Soul; WE tv.
Fee: $18.95 monthly.
Digital Pay Service 1
Pay Units: 400.
Programming (via satellite): HBO (multiplexed).
Fee: $15.95 monthly.
Digital Pay Service 2
Pay Units: 210.
Programming (via satellite): Cinemax (multiplexed).
Fee: $15.95 monthly.
Digital Pay Service 3
Pay Units: N.A.
Programming (via satellite): Flix; Showtime (multiplexed); The Movie Channel (multiplexed).
Fee: $15.95 monthly.
Video-On-Demand: No
Pay-Per-View
iN DEMAND (delivered digitally); Playboy TV (delivered digitally); Fresh (delivered digitally); Shorteez (delivered digitally); Club Jenna (delivered digitally); Spice Hot (delivered digitally); Hot Choice (delivered digitally).
Internet Service
Operational: Yes. Began: February 1, 2002.
Subscribers: 3,456.
Broadband Service: Atlantic Broadband High-Speed Internet.
Fee: $24.95-$57.95 monthly.
Telephone Service
Digital: Operational
Subscribers: 1,090.
Fee: $44.95 monthly
Miles of Plant: 220.0 (coaxial); 70.0 (fiber optic). Homes passed: 9,710.
Chief Financial Officer: Patrick Bratton. Senior Vice President & General Counsel: Leslie Brown. Vice President: David Dane. General Manager: Mike Papasergi. Technical Operations Director: Charles Sorchilla. Marketing & Customer Service Director: Dara Leslie. Marketing Manager: Natalie Kurchak.
Ownership: Atlantic Broadband (MSO).

WARRIORS MARK—Atlantic Broadband. Now served by ALTOONA, PA [PA0018]. ICA: PA0434.

WASHINGTON—Comcast Cable. Now served by PITTSBURGH, PA [PA0001]. ICA: PA0058.

WATERFALL—Waterfall Community TV, PO Box 3, Waterfall, PA 16689-0003. Phone: 814-685-3464. Fax: 814-685-3447. Also serves New Grenada & Wells Tannery. ICA: PA0260.
TV Market Ranking: 74 (New Grenada, WATERFALL, Wells Tannery). Franchise award date: N.A. Franchise expiration date: N.A. Began: January 1, 1973.
Channel capacity: 21 (not 2-way capable). Channels available but not in use: N.A.
Basic Service
Subscribers: N.A.
Programming (received off-air): WDCA (Heroes & Icons, MNT, Movies!, Mundo-Max) Washington; WGAL (NBC, This TV) Lancaster; WPMT (Antenna TV, FOX) York; WPSU-TV (PBS) Clearfield; WTTG (Buzzr, FOX) Washington; WXBU (CW) Lancaster.
Programming (via satellite): Cartoon Network; CMT; CNN; Discovery Channel; ESPN; Freeform; TBS; TNT; Turner Classic Movies.
Fee: $50.00 installation.
Pay Service 1
Pay Units: N.A.
Programming (via satellite): Cinemax; HBO.
Fee: $10.00 monthly (each).
Video-On-Demand: No
Internet Service
Operational: No.
Telephone Service
None
Miles of Plant: 15.0 (coaxial); None (fiber optic).
General Manager: Tom Newman.
Ownership: Tom Newman.

WATTSBURG—Formerly served by Cebridge Connections. Now served by Armstrong Cable Services, ZELIENOPLE, PA [PA0053]. ICA: PA0248.

WAYNESBURG BOROUGH—Comcast Cable. Now served by PITTSBURGH, PA [PA0001]. ICA: PA0134.

WEATHERLY—MetroCast Communications, 70 East Lancaster Ave, Frazier, PA 19355. Phones: 800-952-1001; 800-633-8578; 570-802-5679. Web Site: http://www.metrocast.com. Also serves Bear Creek Twp., Blakeslee, Blythe Twp., Brockton, Chestnuthill Twp., Cumbola, Dennison Twp., East Side, Foster Twp. (Luzerne County), Kaska, Kidder Twp., Lake Harmony, Lausanne Twp, Lehigh Twp. (Carbon County), Mary D, Middleport, Monroe County (portions), New Philadelphia, Packer Twp., Penn Lake Park (borough), Schuylkill County (portions), Tamaqua, Tobyhanna Twp., Tunkhannock Twp., Tuscarora & White Haven. ICA: PA0141.
TV Market Ranking: 49 (Bear Creek Twp., Blakeslee, Blythe Twp., Chestnuthill Twp., Dennison Twp., East Side, Foster Twp. (Luzerne County), Kidder Twp., Lake Harmony, Lausanne Twp, Lehigh Twp. (Carbon County), Monroe County (portions), Packer Twp., Penn Lake Park (borough), Schuylkill County (portions) (portions), Tobyhanna Twp., Tunkhannock Twp., WEATHERLY, White Haven); Below 100 (Brockton, Cumbola, Kaska, Mary D, Middleport, New Philadelphia, Tamaqua, Tuscarora, Schuylkill County (portions) (portions)). Franchise award date: January 1, 1972. Franchise expiration date: N.A. Began: March 22, 1973.
Channel capacity: N.A. Channels available but not in use: N.A.
Basic Service
Subscribers: 4,519.
Programming (received off-air): KYW-TV (CBS, Decades) Philadelphia; WBRE-TV (NBC) Wilkes-Barre; WCAU (COZI TV, NBC) Philadelphia; WLVT-TV (PBS) Allentown; WNEP-TV (ABC, Antenna TV) Scranton; WOLF-TV (CW, FOX, MNT) Hazleton; WPHL-TV (Antenna TV, MNT, This TV) Philadelphia; WPIX (Antenna TV, CW, This TV) New York; WSWB (CW, MeTV) Scranton; WVIA-TV (PBS) Scranton; WYLN-LP (America One) Hazleton; WYOU (CBS) Scranton; allband FM.
Programming (via microwave): WWOR-TV (Bounce TV, Buzzr, Heroes & Icons, MNT) Secaucus.
Programming (via satellite): EWTN Global Catholic Network; Pop; QVC.
Fee: $49.95 installation; $31.95 monthly; $1.35 converter.
Expanded Basic Service 1
Subscribers: 4,355.
Programming (via satellite): A&E; AMC; Animal Planet; Bloomberg Television; Bravo; Cartoon Network; CMT; CNBC; CNN; Comcast SportsNet Philadelphia; Comedy Central; C-SPAN; Discovery Channel; Disney Channel; E! HD; ESPN; ESPN2; Food Network; Fox News Channel; Freeform; FX; FXM; HGTV; History; HLN; Lifetime; MSNBC; MTV; National Geographic Channel; NBCSN; Nickelodeon; Outdoor Channel; Pennsylvania Cable Network; Spike TV; Syfy; TBS; The Weather Channel; TLC; TNT; Travel Channel; Trinity Broadcasting Network (TBN); truTV; TV Land; USA Network; VH1; WE tv.
Fee: $24.38 monthly.
Digital Basic Service
Subscribers: N.A.
Programming (via satellite): AWE; AXS TV; BBC America; CMT; Discovery Digital Networks; Disney XD; DMX Music; Fox Sports 1; Fuse; FYI; GSN; HD Theater; LMN; MTV Classic; MTV2; NFL Network; Nick Jr.; Nicktoons; Outdoor Channel 2 HD; TeenNick; TNT HD; Universal HD.
Fee: $25.92 installation; $7.95 monthly.
Digital Expanded Basic Service
Subscribers: N.A.
Programming (via satellite): ESPN Classic; ESPNews; Golf Channel; History International; IFC; Starz (multiplexed); Starz Encore (multiplexed); Turner Classic Movies.
Fee: $9.95 monthly.
Digital Pay Service 1
Pay Units: N.A.
Programming (via satellite): Cinemax (multiplexed); HBO (multiplexed); Showtime (multiplexed); Showtime HD; Starz HD; The Movie Channel (multiplexed).
Fee: $12.95 monthly (Cinemax, HBO or Showtime/TMC).
Video-On-Demand: No
Pay-Per-View
iN DEMAND.
Internet Service
Operational: Yes. Began: April 1, 2002.
Broadband Service: MetroCast Internet.
Fee: $39.95 monthly.
Telephone Service
None
Miles of Plant: 112.0 (coaxial); 6.0 (fiber optic).
Chief Financial Officer: Shawn P. Flannery. General Manager: Tom Carey. Mid-Atlantic Regional Engineer: Jeff Shearer. Marketing Manager: Chrissy Carey.
Ownership: Harron Communications LP (MSO).

WEEDVILLE—Zito Media, 102 S Main St, PO Box 665, Coudersport, PA 16915. Phones: 814-260-9055; 800-365-6988. Fax: 814-260-9580. E-mail: info@zitomedia.com. Web Site: http://www.zitomedia.com. Also serves Caledonia. ICA: PA0234.
TV Market Ranking: Outside TV Markets (Caledonia, WEEDVILLE). Franchise award date: N.A. Franchise expiration date: N.A. Began: January 1, 1959.
Channel capacity: N.A. Channels available but not in use: N.A.
Basic Service
Subscribers: N.A.
Programming (received off-air): WATM-TV (ABC, This TV) Altoona; WJAC-TV (MeTV, NBC) Johnstown; WKBS-TV (IND) Altoona; WPNT (MNT) Pittsburgh; WPSU-TV (PBS) Clearfield; WTAE-TV (ABC, This TV) Pittsburgh; WTAJ-TV (CBS) Altoona; WWCP-TV (FOX) Johnstown.
Programming (via satellite): CW PLUS; WGN America.
Fee: $29.95 installation; $16.95 monthly.
Expanded Basic Service 1
Subscribers: N.A.
Programming (via satellite): A&E; AMC; Animal Planet; Cartoon Network; CMT; CNBC; CNN; Comedy Central; C-SPAN; Discovery Channel; Disney Channel; E! HD; ESPN; ESPN Classic; ESPN2; EWTN Global Catholic Network; Food Network; Fox News Channel; Freeform; FX; Hallmark Channel; HGTV; History; HLN; INSP; Lifetime; MSNBC; MTV; NFL Network; Nickelodeon; QVC; Root Sports Pittsburgh;

2017 Edition

D-679

Pennsylvania—Cable Systems

Spike TV; Syfy; TBS; The Weather Channel; TLC; TNT; Trinity Broadcasting Network (TBN); Turner Classic Movies; TV Land; USA Network; VH1.
Fee: $21.55 monthly.
Digital Basic Service
Subscribers: N.A.
Programming (via satellite): BBC America; Bloomberg Television; Boomerang; C-SPAN 3; Destination America; Discovery Kids Channel; Discovery Life Channel; Disney XD; ESPN HD; ESPN2 HD; ESPNews; Fox Sports 1; Golf Channel; Great American Country; GSN; HRTV; INSP; Investigation Discovery; LMN; MC; MTV Classic; MTV Hits; MTV Jams; MTV2; Nick 2; Nick Jr.; Nicktoons; OWN; Oprah Winfrey Network; RFD-TV; Science Channel; TeenNick; The Word Network; Trinity Broadcasting Network (TBN); VH1 Country; VH1 Soul; WAM! America's Kidz Network; WE tv.
Fee: $15.95 monthly.
Digital Expanded Basic Service
Subscribers: N.A.
Programming (via satellite): DIY Network; Flix; FSN Digital Atlantic; FSN Digital Central; FSN Digital Pacific; FYI; History International; IFC; NBCSN; Outdoor Channel; Sundance TV.
Fee: $10.00 monthly.
Digital Pay Service 1
Pay Units: N.A.
Programming (via satellite): Cinemax (multiplexed); Cinemax HD; Flix; HBO (multiplexed); HBO HD; Showtime (multiplexed); Showtime HD; Starz (multiplexed); Starz Encore (multiplexed); Starz HD; The Movie Channel (multiplexed).
Fee: $8.00 monthly (Cinemax or Starz/Encore), $10.00 monthly (HBO or Showtime/TMC/Flix).
Video-On-Demand: Planned
Pay-Per-View
iN DEMAND (delivered digitally).
Internet Service
Operational: Yes.
Fee: $49.95 monthly.
Telephone Service
Digital: Operational
Fee: $35.00 monthly
Homes passed & miles of plant (coax) included in Treasure Lake.
President: James Rigas.
Ownership: Zito Media (MSO).

WEST ALEXANDER—Comcast Cable. Now served by PITTSBURGH, PA [PA0001]. ICA: PA0235.

WEST BUFFALO TWP.—Formerly served by D&E Communications/Windstream. IPTV service no longer in operation. ICA: PA5293.

WEST BURLINGTON TWP.—Formerly served by Barrett's TV Cable System. No longer in operation. ICA: PA0303.

WEST CHILLISQUAQUE TWP.—Formerly served by D&E Communications/Windstream. IPTV service no longer in operation. ICA: PA5311.

WEST DEER TWP.—Comcast Cable. Now served by PITTSBURGH, PA [PA0001]. ICA: PA0459.

WEST MIFFLIN—Formerly served by Adelphia Communications. Now served by Comcast Cable, PITTSBURGH, PA [PA0001]. ICA: PA0422.

WEST NEWTON—Formerly served by Adelphia Communications. Now served by Comcast Cable, PITTSBURGH, PA [PA0001]. ICA: PA0423.

WESTFIELD—Westfield Community Antenna, 121 Strang St, Westfield, PA 16950-1313. Phone: 814-367-5190. Fax: 814-367-5586. Also serves Westfield Twp. ICA: PA0185.
TV Market Ranking: Outside TV Markets (WESTFIELD, Westfield Twp.). Franchise award date: N.A. Franchise expiration date: N.A. Began: September 1, 1952.
Channel capacity: N.A. Channels available but not in use: N.A.
Basic Service
Subscribers: 667.
Programming (received off-air): WENY-TV (ABC, CW) Elmira; WETM-TV (IND, NBC) Elmira; WIVB-TV (CBS) Buffalo; WKBW-TV (ABC, Escape) Buffalo; WPSU-TV (PBS) Clearfield; WSKG-TV (PBS) Binghamton; allband FM.
Programming (via satellite): 3ABN; A&E; Cartoon Network; CMT; CNN; C-SPAN 2; Discovery Channel; ESPN; ESPN2; Fox Sports 1; Freeform; FX; Great American Country; Hallmark Channel; HGTV; History; HLN; KTLA (Antenna TV, CW, This TV) Los Angeles; Lifetime; Nickelodeon; Outdoor Channel; QVC; RFD-TV; Root Sports Pittsburgh; Spike TV; Syfy; TBS; The Weather Channel; TNT; Trinity Broadcasting Network (TBN); Turner Classic Movies; TV Land; USA Network; WGN America; WPIX (Antenna TV, CW, This TV) New York.
Fee: Free installation; $52.00 monthly.
Pay Service 1
Pay Units: 54.
Programming (via satellite): HBO.
Fee: $13.00 monthly.
Video-On-Demand: No
Internet Service
Operational: No.
Telephone Service
None
Miles of Plant: 23.0 (coaxial); None (fiber optic). Homes passed: 1,450.
President: Ronald H. MacKnight. General Manager: Marlo Kroeck. Chief Technician: Stan Taft.
Ownership: Westfield Community Antenna Assn. Inc.

WESTLINE—Formerly served by Keystone Wilcox Cable TV Inc. No longer in operation. ICA: PA0427.

WHITE DEER TWP.—Formerly served by D&E Communications/Windstream. IPTV service no longer in operation. ICA: PA5289.

WILCOX—Zito Media, 102 S Main St, PO Box 665, Coudersport, PA 16915. Phones: 814-260-9055; 800-365-6988. Fax: 814-260-9580. E-mail: info@zitomedia.com. Web Site: http://www.zitomedia.com. Also serves Jones Twp. ICA: PA0241.
TV Market Ranking: Outside TV Markets (Jones Twp., WILCOX). Franchise award date: October 1, 1978. Franchise expiration date: N.A. Began: October 1, 1978.
Channel capacity: 36 (operating 2-way). Channels available but not in use: N.A.
Basic Service
Subscribers: 134.
Programming (received off-air): WATM-TV (ABC, This TV) Altoona; WGRZ (Antenna TV, NBC, WeatherNation) Buffalo; WIVB-TV (CBS) Buffalo; WJAC-TV (MeTV, NBC) Johnstown; WKBW-TV (ABC, Escape) Buffalo; WNED-TV (PBS) Buffalo; WPSU-TV (PBS) Clearfield; WTAJ-TV (CBS) Altoona; WWCP-TV (FOX) Johnstown; allband FM.
Programming (via satellite): WGN America.
Fee: $49.95 installation; $17.06 monthly.
Expanded Basic Service 1
Subscribers: N.A.
Programming (via satellite): A&E; AMC; Animal Planet; Cartoon Network; CMT; CNBC; CNN; C-SPAN 2; Discovery Channel; Disney Channel; E! HD; ESPN; ESPN2; EWTN Global Catholic Network; Food Network; Fox News Channel; Fox Sports 1; Freeform; FX; Hallmark Channel; HGTV; History; HLN; INSP; Lifetime; MSNBC; MTV; NFL Network; Nickelodeon; Outdoor Channel; Oxygen; QVC; Root Sports Pittsburgh; Spike TV; Syfy; TBS; The Weather Channel; TLC; TNT; Trinity Broadcasting Network (TBN); truTV; Turner Classic Movies; TV Land; USA Network; VH1.
Fee: $30.00 monthly.
Digital Basic Service
Subscribers: N.A.
Programming (via satellite): A&E HD; Animal Planet HD; BBC America; Bio HD; Bloomberg Television; Boomerang; Cartoon Network HD; CMT; CNN HD; C-SPAN 3; Destination America; Discovery Channel HD; Discovery Kids Channel; Discovery Life Channel; Disney Channel HD; Disney XD; ESPN HD; ESPN2 HD; ESPNews; ESPNews HD; ESPNU HD; Food Network HD; Fox HD; Fox Sports 1; Freeform HD; FSN HD; FX HD; FXM; Golf Channel; Great American Country; GSN; HD Theater; HGTV HD; History HD; HRTV; INSP; Investigation Discovery; Lifetime HD; Lifetime Movie Network HD; LMN; MC; MTV Classic; MTV Hits; MTV Jams; MTV2; NFL Network HD; NHL Network; NHL Network HD; Nick 2; Nick Jr.; Nickelodeon; Outdoor Channel 2 HD; OWN; Oprah Winfrey Network; RFD-TV; Science Channel; Science HD; TBS HD; TeenNick; The Word Network; TLC HD; TNT HD; Trinity Broadcasting Network (TBN); VH1 Soul; WE tv.
Fee: $31.90 monthly.
Digital Expanded Basic Service
Subscribers: N.A.
Programming (via satellite): DIY Network; Flix; FOX College Sports Central; FOX College Sports Pacific; FYI; History International; IFC; NBCSN; Outdoor Channel; Sundance TV.
Fee: $10.00 monthly.
Digital Pay Service 1
Pay Units: N.A.
Programming (via satellite): Cinemax (multiplexed); Cinemax HD; Flix; HBO (multiplexed); HBO HD; Showtime (multiplexed); Showtime HD; Starz (multiplexed); Starz Encore (multiplexed); The Movie Channel (multiplexed).

Fee: $8.00 monthly (Cinemax or Starz/Encore), $10.00 monthly (HBO or Showtime/TMC/Flix).
Video-On-Demand: Yes
Internet Service
Operational: Yes.
Fee: $42.95 monthly.
Telephone Service
Analog: Not Operational
Digital: Operational
Fee: $35.00 monthly
Miles of Plant: 30.0 (coaxial); None (fiber optic). Homes passed: 500.
President: James Rigas.
Ownership: Zito Media (MSO).

WILKES-BARRE—Service Electric Cable Company, 15 J Campbell Collins Dr, Wilkes-Barre, PA 18702. Phone: 570-825-8508. Fax: 570-822-2601. E-mail: corporateoffice@secv.com. Web Site: http://www.sectv.com. Also serves Ashley, Bear Creek Twp., Buck Twp., Courtdale, Fairview Twp. (Luzerne County), Hanover Twp. (Luzerne County), Kingston (Luzerne County), Laurel Run, Mountain Top, Pringle, Rice Twp., Sugar Notch, Warrior Run Borough, Wilkes-Barre Twp. & Wright Twp. ICA: PA0036.
TV Market Ranking: 49 (Ashley, Bear Creek Twp., Buck Twp., Courtdale, Fairview Twp. (Luzerne County), Hanover Twp. (Luzerne County), Kingston (Luzerne County), Laurel Run, Mountain Top, Pringle, Rice Twp., Sugar Notch, Warrior Run Borough, WILKES-BARRE, Wilkes-Barre Twp., Wright Twp.). Franchise award date: N.A. Franchise expiration date: N.A. Began: January 1, 1951.
Channel capacity: N.A. Channels available but not in use: N.A.
Basic Service
Subscribers: 16,607.
Programming (received off-air): KYW-TV (CBS, Decades) Philadelphia; WBRE-TV (NBC) Wilkes-Barre; WCAU (COZI TV, NBC) Philadelphia; WNEP-TV (ABC, Antenna TV) Scranton; WQPX-TV (ION) Scranton; WSWB (CW, MeTV) Scranton; WTXF-TV (Buzzr, FOX, Movies!) Philadelphia; WVIA-TV (PBS) Scranton; WWOR-TV (Bounce TV, Buzzr, Heroes & Icons, MNT) Secaucus; WYOU (CBS) Scranton; allband FM.
Programming (via satellite): C-SPAN; EVINE Live; EWTN Global Catholic Network; Food Network; Ovation; Pennsylvania Cable Network; Pop; QVC; WPIX (Antenna TV, CW, This TV) New York.
Fee: $36.00 installation; $19.99 monthly.
Expanded Basic Service 1
Subscribers: N.A.
Programming (via satellite): A&E; AMC; Animal Planet; Bravo; Cartoon Network; CNBC; CNN; Comcast SportsNet Philadelphia; Comedy Central; Discovery Channel; Discovery Life Channel; E! HD; ESPN; ESPN Classic; ESPN2; ESPNews; Fox News Channel; Fox Sports 1; Freeform; FX; FXM; Hallmark Channel; HGTV; History; HLN; Lifetime; LMN; MTV; National Geographic Channel; NBCSN; Nickelodeon; Outdoor Channel; OWN; Oprah Winfrey Network; Penn National Racing Alive; Spike TV; Syfy; TBS; The Weather Channel; TLC; TNT; Travel Channel; truTV; Turner Classic Movies; TV Land; USA Network; VH1; WE tv.
Fee: $29.96 monthly.
Digital Basic Service
Subscribers: N.A.
Programming (via satellite): AXS TV; Boomerang; CMT; C-SPAN 2; Discovery Digital Networks; DIY Network; Fox Sports

Cable Systems—Pennsylvania

2; FSN Digital Atlantic; FSN Digital Central; FSN Digital Pacific; FYI; Golf Channel; HD Theater; History International; IFC; LMN; MC; MTV; Nick 2; Nick Jr.; Outdoor Channel; TeenNick; TNT HD; TVG Network; WALN Cable Radio.
Fee: $5.99 monthly.
Digital Pay Service 1
Pay Units: N.A.
Programming (via satellite): Cinemax (multiplexed); HBO (multiplexed); Showtime (multiplexed); Showtime HD; Starz (multiplexed); Starz Encore (multiplexed); Starz HD; The Movie Channel (multiplexed).
Fee: $13.00 monthly (HBO), $11.00 monthly (Cinemax), $5.99 monthly (Showtime), $10.00 monthly (Starz/Encore).
Video-On-Demand: Planned
Internet Service
Operational: Yes. Began: December 31, 1996.
Subscribers: 13,102.
Broadband Service: ProLog Express.
Fee: $50.00 installation; $32.95 monthly; $100.00 modem purchase.
Telephone Service
Digital: Operational
Subscribers: 3,732.
Miles of Plant: 587.0 (coaxial); 317.0 (fiber optic). Homes passed: 45,685.
General Manager: William Brayford. Chief Technician: Robert Jais. Regulatory Affairs Director: Arlean Lilly.
Ownership: Service Electric Cable TV Inc. (MSO).

WILLIAMS TWP.—Formerly served by NORTHAMPTON BOROUGH, PA [PA0008]. RCN. This cable system has converted to IPTV. Now served by ALLENTOWN, PA [PA5201]. ICA: PA5243.

WILLIAMSBURG (Blair County)—Formerly served by Adelphia Communications. No longer in operation. ICA: PA0205.

WILLIAMSPORT—Comcast Cable. Now served by HARRISBURG, PA [PA0009]. ICA: PA0040.

WILLOW GROVE—Formerly served by Comcast Cable. No longer in operation. ICA: PA0425.

WINFIELD—Formerly served by D&E Communications. No longer in operation. ICA: PA5290.

WOODBURY—Atlantic Broadband. Now served by ALTOONA, PA [PA0018]. ICA: PA0426.

YORK—Comcast Cable. Now served by HARRISBURG, PA [PA0009]. ICA: PA0013.

YOUNGSVILLE—Youngsville TV Corp, 3 West Main St, Youngsville, PA 16371-1420. Phone: 814-563-3336. Fax: 814-563-7299. E-mail: ytv@eaglezip.net. Web Site: http://youngsvilletv.com. Also serves Brokenstraw Twp., Irvine & Pittsfield. ICA: PA0190.
TV Market Ranking: Below 100 (Brokenstraw Twp., Irvine, Pittsfield, YOUNGSVILLE).
Channel capacity: N.A. Channels available but not in use: N.A.
Basic Service
Subscribers: 992.
Programming (received off-air): KDKA-TV (CBS, Decades) Pittsburgh; WFPX-TV (ION) Fayetteville; WGRZ (Antenna TV, NBC, WeatherNation) Buffalo; WICU-TV (NBC) Erie; WJET-TV (ABC) Erie; WKBW-TV (ABC, Escape) Buffalo; WPSU-TV (PBS) Clearfield; WQLN (PBS) Erie; WSEE-TV (CBS, CW) Erie; allband FM.
Programming (via satellite): A&E; AMC; Animal Planet; Bloomberg Television; CMT; CNN; C-SPAN; C-SPAN 2; CW PLUS; Discovery Channel; Disney Channel; DIY Network; ESPN; ESPN Classic; ESPN2; EWTN Global Catholic Network; Food Network; Fox News Channel; Fox Sports 1; Freeform; FX; Golf Channel; Great American Country; Hallmark Channel; HGTV; History; HLN; Lifetime; MTV; NASA TV; National Geographic Channel; Nickelodeon; Outdoor Channel; Pennsylvania Cable Network; Root Sports Pittsburgh; RTV; Spike TV; Syfy; TBS; TLC; TNT; Travel Channel; Trinity Broadcasting Network (TBN); TV Land; USA Network; VH1; WGN America.
Fee: $150.00 installation; $37.00 monthly.
Pay Service 1
Pay Units: 196.
Programming (via satellite): HBO.
Fee: $12.00 monthly.
Video-On-Demand: No
Internet Service
Operational: No.
Telephone Service
None
Miles of Plant: 28.0 (coaxial); 28.0 (fiber optic). Homes passed: 1,230.
President: Rick Hutley. General Manager: Scott D. Barber Sr.
Ownership: Youngsville TV Corp.

ZELIENOPLE—Armstrong Cable Services, One Armstrong Place, Butler, PA 16001. Phone: 877-277-5711. E-mail: info@zoominternet.net. Web Site: http://armstrongonewire.com/television. Also serves Boyd County (portions), Catlettsburg, Flatwoods, Greenup, Greenup County (eastern portion) & Wurtland, KY; Andover, Andover Village, Ashland, Athalia, Austintown Twp., Baughman Twp., Beaver Twp., Berlin Twp. (Mahoning County), Blooming Grove Twp. (Richland County), Boardman Twp., Brighton Twp., Brunswick Hills Twp., Butler Twp. (Richland County), Campbell, Canfield, Canfield Twp., Chesapeake, Clear Creek Twp., Coitsville Twp., Crown City, Dalton, East Union Twp., Ellsworth Twp., Fayette Twp., Goshen, Grafton Twp., Granger Twp., Green Twp. (Mahoning County), Green Twp. (Wayne County), Guyan Twp., Hayesville, Hubbard Twp. (Trumbull County), Jackson Twp. (Mahoning County), Lafayette Twp. (portions), Litchfield Twp. (portions), Liverpool Twp., Mahoning County (portions), Marshallville, McDonald (village), Medina, Medina Twp., Mifflin Twp. (Ashland County), Milton Twp. (Ashland County), Milton Twp. (Mahoning County), Minton Twp. (Wayne County), Montgomery Twp. (Ashland County), Montville Twp., Orange Twp. (Ashland County), Orrville, Perry Twp. (Lawrence County), Poland, Poland Twp., Proctorville, Rome Twp. (Lawrence County), Smith Twp. (Mahoning County), South Point, Springfield Twp. (Mahoning County), Sugar Creek Twp. (Wayne County), Sullivan Twp., Troy Twp. (Ashland County), Union Twp. (Lawrence County), Weathersfield Twp. (Trumbull County), Weller Twp. (Richland County), Windsor Twp. (Lawrence County) & York Twp., OH; Adams Twp. (Butler County), Allegheny Twp. (Venango County), Allenport, Barkeyville, Big Beaver, Blooming Valley, Boyers, Bradford Woods, Brady Twp., Brady Twp. (Butler County), Bradys Bend Twp., Brokenstraw Twp., Bruin, Buffalo Twp. (Butler County), Bullskin Twp., Butler, Butler Twp. (Butler County), California, Callensburg, Callery, Center Twp. (Butler County), Centerville, Cherry Twp., Chicora, Clay Twp. (Lancaster County), Clearfield Twp., Clinton Twp. (Butler County), Clinton Twp. (Venango County), Clintonville, Coal Center, Cochranton, Concord Twp. (Butler County), Conneaut Lake, Connellsville, Connellsville Twp. (Fayette County), Connoquenessing Borough, Connoquenessing Twp. (Butler County), Coolspring Twp. (portions), Cooperstown, Cornplanter Twp. (Venango County), Cranberry Twp. (Butler County), Daugherty Twp., Deer Creek Twp. (Mercer County), Deerfield Twp. (Warren County), Donegal Twp. (Butler County), Donegal Twp. (Westmoreland County), Dunbar, Dunbar Twp., Dunlevy, East Brady, East Butler, East Huntingdon Twp., East Lackawannock Twp. (portions), Eau Claire, Elco, Ellport, Ellwood City, Evans City, Everson, Fairview Borough, Fairview Twp. (Butler County), Farmington Twp. (Clarion County), Findley Twp. (Mercer County), Forward, Forward Twp., Franklin (Venango County), Franklin Twp. (Beaver County), Franklin Twp. (Butler County), Franklin Twp. (Fayette County), Grove City, Guys Mills, Hampton Twp. (Allegheny County), Harmony, Harrisville, Homewood, Hydetown, Irwin Twp. (Venango County), Jackson Center, Jackson Twp. (Butler County), Jamestown, Jefferson Twp. (Fayette County), Karns City, Koppel, Lancaster Twp. (Butler County), Lawrence County (southern portion), Leeper, Liberty Twp. (Mercer County), Limestone Twp. (Warren County), Long Branch, Marion Twp. (Butler County), Mars, Marshall Twp., Meadville, Mercer, Mercer Twp. (portions), Middlesex Twp., Mill Village, Mount Pleasant, Mount Pleasant Twp. (Westmoreland County), Muddycreek Twp., New Beaver, New Sewickley Twp., New Vernon Twp., New Wilmington, Newell, North Beaver Twp. (Lawrence County), North Clarion, North Sewickley Twp., North Union Twp., Oakland Twp. (Butler County), Parker Twp., Penn Twp. (Butler County), Perry Twp. (Lawrence County), Perry Twp. (Mercer County), Petrolia, Pine Twp. (Allegheny County), Pine Twp. (Butler County), Pine Twp. (Mercer County), Plain Grove Twp., Pleasant Twp., Pleasantville, Portersville, Prospect, Richland Twp. (Allegheny County), Rockland Twp. (Venango County), Rockmere, Roscoe, Saegertown, Sandy Creek Twp. (Mercer County), Sandy Lake, Sandy Lake Twp., Saxonburg, Scottdale, Seven Fields, Sheakleyville, Sheakleyville Twp., Slippery Rock (Butler County), Slippery Rock Twp. (Butler County), Slippery Rock Twp. (Lawrence County), Somerset, Somerset County (portions), Somerset Twp. (Somerset County), South Huntingdon Twp., South Shenango Twp., Southwest Twp., Springfield Twp. (Mercer County), Stockdale, Stoneboro, Sugarcreek (Venango County), Sugarcreek Twp. (Armstrong County), Summit Twp. (Butler County), Taylor Twp. (Lawrence County), Tidioute, Tionesta, Tionesta Twp., Titusville, Townville, Treesdale, Triumph Twp., Utica, Valencia, Vanderbilt, Venango Twp. (Butler County), Volant Borough, Wampum, Washington Twp. (Butler County), Washington Twp. (Clarion County), Washington Twp. (Lawrence County), Watson Twp., Wattsburg, Wayne Twp. (Lawrence County), West Brownsville, West Deer Twp. (portions), West Franklin Twp., West Liberty, West Mead Twp., West Pike Run Twp., West Sunbury, Winfield Twp., Wolf Creek Twp. & Worth Twp., PA; Boone County (portions), Ceredo, Kenova, Pennsboro, Wayne County (northern portion) & West Union, WV. ICA: PA0053. **Note:** This system is an overbuild.
TV Market Ranking: 10 (Adams Twp. (Butler County), Allenport, Boyers, Bradford Woods, Buffalo Twp. (Butler County), Butler, Butler Twp. (Butler County), California, Callery, Center Twp. (Butler County), Clearfield Twp., Clinton Twp. (Butler County), Coal Center, Connoquenessing Borough, Connoquenessing Twp. (Butler County), Cranberry Twp. (Butler County), Daugherty Twp. (Butler County), Donegal Twp. (Butler County) (portions), Dunlevy, East Butler, East Huntingdon Twp., Elco, Ellwood City, Evans City, Everson, Forward, Forward Twp., Franklin Twp. (Butler County), Franklin Twp. (Fayette County), Hampton Twp. (Allegheny County), Harmony, Jackson Twp. (Butler County), Jefferson Twp. (Fayette County), Lancaster Twp. (Butler County), Long Branch, Marion Twp. (Butler County), Mars, Marshall Twp., Middlesex Twp., Mount Pleasant Twp. (Westmoreland County), Muddycreek Twp., Newell, Penn Twp. (Butler County), Pine Twp. (Allegheny County), Pine Twp. (Butler County), Portersville, Prospect, Richland Twp. (Allegheny County), Roscoe, Saxonburg, Scottdale, Seven Fields, Slippery Rock Twp. (Lawrence County), South Huntingdon Twp., Stockdale, Summit Twp. (Butler County), Treesdale, Valencia, Vanderbilt, West Brownsville, West Deer Twp. (portions), West Franklin Twp., West Pike Run Twp., Winfield Twp., ZELIENOPLE); 10,74 (Mount Pleasant); 10,79 (Big Beaver, Ellport, Franklin Twp. (Beaver County), Homewood, Koppel, New Beaver, North Beaver Twp. (Lawrence County), North Sewickley Twp., Perry Twp. (Lawrence County), Taylor Twp. (Lawrence County), Wampum, Wayne Twp. (Lawrence County)); 36 (Boone County (portions) (portions), Boyd County (portions), Catlettsburg, Ceredo, Chesapeake, Crown City, Fayette Twp., Flatwoods, Greenup, Greenup County (eastern portion), Guyan Twp., Kenova, Perry Twp. (Lawrence County), Proctorville, Rome Twp. (Lawrence County), South Point, Union Twp. (Lawrence County), Wayne County (northern portion), Windsor Twp. (Lawrence County), Wurtland); 57 (Clay Twp. (Lancaster County)); 74 (Donegal Twp. (Westmoreland County), Somerset, Somerset County (portions) (portions), Somerset Twp. (Somerset County)); 79 (Andover Village, Austintown Twp., Beaver Twp., Berlin Twp. (Mahoning County), Boardman Twp., Campbell, Canfield, Canfield Twp., Coitsville Twp., Coolspring Twp. (portions), Deer Creek Twp. (Mer-

Pennsylvania—Cable Systems

cer County), East Lackawannock Twp. (portions), Ellsworth Twp., Findley Twp. (Mercer County), Goshen, Green Twp. (Mahoning County), Grove City, Hubbard Twp. (Trumbull County), Jackson Center, Jackson Twp. (Mahoning County), Jamestown, Liberty Twp. (Mercer County), McDonald (village), Mercer, Mercer Twp. (portions), Milton Twp. (Mahoning County), New Sewickley Twp., New Vernon Twp., New Wilmington, Perry Twp. (Mercer County), Pine Twp. (Mercer County) (portions), Plain Grove Twp., Poland, Poland Twp., Sandy Creek Twp. (Mercer County), Sandy Lake Twp. (portions), Sheakleyville, Slippery Rock (Butler County), Slippery Rock Twp. (Butler County), Smith Twp. (Mahoning County), South Shenango Twp., Springfield Twp. (Mahoning County), Springfield Twp. (Mercer County), Stoneboro, Volant Borough, Washington Twp. (Lawrence County), Weathersfield Twp. (Trumbull County), West Liberty, Wolf Creek Twp. (portions), Worth Twp.); 8 (Baughman Twp., Brighton Twp., Brunswick Hills Twp., Dalton, East Union Twp., Grafton Twp., Granger Twp., Green Twp. (Wayne County), Lafayette Twp. (portions), Litchfield Twp. (portions), Liverpool Twp., Marshallville, Medina, Medina Twp., Minton Twp. (Wayne County), Montville Twp., Orrville, Sugar Creek Twp. (Wayne County), Sullivan Twp., York Twp.); 89 (Brady Twp. (Butler County)); Below 100 (Blooming Grove Twp. (Richland County), Blooming Valley, Brady Twp., Brokenstraw Twp., Butler Twp. (Richland County), Cherry Twp., Concord Twp. (Butler County), Connellsville Twp. (Fayette County), Deerfield Twp. (Warren County), Dunbar, Dunbar Twp., Guys Mills, Hayesville, Mifflin Twp. (Ashland County), Mill Village, Milton Twp. (Ashland County), Montgomery Twp. (Ashland County), North Union Twp., Orange Twp. (Ashland County), Pleasant Twp., Saegertown, Sheakleyville Twp., Southwest Twp., Townville, Troy Twp. (Ashland County), Watson Twp., Wattsburg, Weller Twp. (Richland County), West Mead Twp., West Sunbury, Ashland, Connellsville, Meadville, Pennsboro, West Union, Boone County (portions) (portions), Somerset County (portions) (portions)); Outside TV Markets (Allegheny Twp. (Venango County), Athalia, Barkeyville, Bradys Bend Twp., Bruin, Callensburg, Centerville, Chicora, Clinton Twp. (Venango County), Clintonville, Cochranton, Conneaut Lake, Cooperstown, Cornplanter Twp. (Venango County), East Brady, Eau Claire, Fairview Borough, Fairview Twp. (Butler County), Farmington Twp. (Clarion County), Franklin (Venango County), Harrisville, Hydetown, Irwin Twp. (Venango County), Karns City, Leeper, Oakland Twp. (Butler County), Parker Twp., Petrolia, Pleasantville, Rockland Twp. (Venango County), Rockmere, Sandy Lake, Sugarcreek (Venango County), Sugarcreek Twp. (Armstrong County), Tionesta, Tionesta Twp., Utica, Venango Twp. (Butler County), Washington Twp. (Butler County), Washington Twp. (Clarion County), North Clarion, Titusville, Donegal Twp. (Butler County) (portions), Somerset County (portions) (portions), Pine Twp. (Mercer County) (portions), Sandy Lake Twp. (portions)). Franchise award date: February 1, 1983. Franchise expiration date: N.A. Began: January 1, 1969.

Channel capacity: 63 (operating 2-way). Channels available but not in use: N.A.

Digital Basic Service
Subscribers: 195,202.

Programming (via satellite): A&E; AMC; Animal Planet; Bravo; Cartoon Network; CMT; CNBC; CNN; Comedy Central; C-SPAN; Discovery Channel; Disney Channel; E! HD; ESPN; ESPN2; EVINE Live; EWTN Global Catholic Network; Food Network; Fox News Channel; Freeform; FX; HGTV; History; HLN; Lifetime; MC; MSNBC; MTV; Nickelodeon; Nicktoons; Pennsylvania Cable Network; Pittsburgh Cable News Channel; Pop; QVC; Root Sports Pittsburgh; Spike TV; Syfy; TBS; The Weather Channel; TLC; TNT; Travel Channel; truTV; Turner Classic Movies; TV Land; USA Network; VH1.

Fee: $35.00 installation; $24.95 monthly.

Digital Expanded Basic Service
Subscribers: N.A.

Programming (via satellite): BBC America; Bloomberg Television; Boomerang; Chiller; Cloo; CMT; Cooking Channel; Destination America; Discovery Kids Channel; Discovery Life Channel; Disney XD; DIY Network; ESPN Classic; ESPNews; ESPNU; Fox Sports 1; FYI; Golf Channel; Great American Country; GSN; Hallmark Channel; Hallmark Movies & Mysteries; History International; HRTV; Investigation Discovery; Jewelry Television; LMN; MTV Classic; MTV Hits; MTV Jams; MTV2; National Geographic Channel; NBC Universo; NBCSN; NFL Network; NHL Network; Nick 2; Nick Jr.; Outdoor Channel; OWN: Oprah Winfrey Network; Oxygen; RFD-TV; RTV; Science Channel; Sprout; TeenNick; Tennis Channel; Tr3s; VH1 Soul; WE tv.

Fee: $12.00 monthly.

Digital Expanded Basic Service 2
Subscribers: N.A.

Programming (via satellite): A&E HD; Animal Planet HD; AXS TV; Bravo HD; CNN HD; Discovery Channel HD; Disney Channel HD; ESPN HD; ESPN2 HD; Food Network HD; Fox News HD; FSN HD; FX HD; Golf Channel HD; Hallmark Movie Channel HD; HD Theater; HGTV HD; History HD; MGM HD; MTV Live; National Geographic Channel HD; NFL Network HD; NHL Network HD; Outdoor Channel 2 HD; QVC HD; Science HD; Syfy HD; TBS HD; The Weather Channel HD; TLC HD; TNT HD; Universal HD; USA Network HD; Versus HD.

Fee: $9.00 monthly.

Digital Pay Service 1
Pay Units: N.A.

Programming (via satellite): Cinemax (multiplexed); Cinemax HD; Flix; HBO (multiplexed); HBO HD; Showtime (multiplexed); Showtime HD; Starz (multiplexed); Starz Encore (multiplexed); Starz HD; The Movie Channel (multiplexed); TV5MONDE USA.

Fee: $13.95 monthly (Cinemax, HBO, Showtime/TMC/Flix or Starz/Encore).

Video-On-Demand: Yes

Pay-Per-View
ESPN Now (delivered digitally); Hot Choice (delivered digitally); iN DEMAND (delivered digitally); Sports PPV (delivered digitally).

Internet Service
Operational: Yes. Began: April 1, 1998.
Subscribers: 163,339.
Broadband Service: Armstrong Zoom.
Fee: $39.95 monthly.

Telephone Service
Digital: Operational
Subscribers: 97,533.
Fee: $34.95 monthly
Miles of Plant: 10,462.0 (coaxial); 6,111.0 (fiber optic). Homes passed: 290,650.
Vice President, Marketing: Jud Stewart. Vice President, Financial Reporting: Mark Rankin. General Manager: Joe Taylor. Chief Engineer: Barry Osche. Program Director: Matt Lutz. Marketing Manager: Andrea Lucas. Customer Service Manager: Connie Swartfegger.
Ownership: Armstrong Group of Companies (MSO).

ZION—Tele-Media, 804 Jacksonville Rd, PO Box 39, Bellefonte, PA 16823-0039. Phones: 800-704-4254; 814-353-2025. Fax: 814-353-2072. Web Site: http://www.tele-media.com. Also serves Hublersburg, Marion Twp. (Centre County), Mingoville, Spring Twp. (Centre County) & Walker Twp. (Centre County). ICA: PA0193.

TV Market Ranking: Outside TV Markets (Hublersburg, Mingoville, Spring Twp. (Centre County), Walker Twp. (Centre County), ZION). Franchise award date: N.A. Franchise expiration date: N.A. Began: January 1, 1974.

Channel capacity: N.A. Channels available but not in use: N.A.

Basic Service
Subscribers: 656.

Programming (received off-air): WATM-TV (ABC, This TV) Altoona; WJAC-TV (MeTV, NBC) Johnstown; WKBS-TV (IND) Altoona; WPMT (Antenna TV, FOX) York; WPSU-TV (PBS) Clearfield; WTAJ-TV (CBS) Altoona; allband FM.

Programming (via satellite): CNN; History; HLN; QVC; TBS; The Weather Channel; TV Land; WGN America.

Fee: $48.40 installation; $24.40 monthly.

Expanded Basic Service 1
Subscribers: N.A.

Programming (via satellite): A&E; AMC; Cartoon Network; CMT; Comedy Central; Discovery Channel; Disney Channel; ESPN; Food Network; Fox News Channel; FOX Sports Networks; Freeform; FX; HGTV; Lifetime; MTV; Nickelodeon; Outdoor Channel; Spike TV; TLC; TNT; USA Network; VH1.

Fee: $31.93 monthly.

Digital Basic Service
Subscribers: N.A.

Programming (via satellite): BBC America; Bloomberg Television; DMX Music; FYI; Golf Channel; GSN; History; INSP; NBCSN; Outdoor Channel; Syfy; Trinity Broadcasting Network (TBN); Turner Classic Movies.

Fee: $19.45 monthly.

Digital Pay Service 1
Pay Units: N.A.

Programming (via satellite): Cinemax (multiplexed); HBO (multiplexed); Showtime (multiplexed); Starz (multiplexed); Starz Encore (multiplexed); The Movie Channel.

Fee: $7.00 monthly (Cinemax), $9.00 monthly (Starz/Encore), $12.00 monthly (HBO), $12.50 monthly (Showtime/TMC).

Video-On-Demand: No

Pay-Per-View
special events (delivered digitally).

Internet Service
Operational: Yes.
Subscribers: 540.
Broadband Service: In-house.
Fee: $99.95 installation; $27.95 monthly; $9.95 modem lease.

Telephone Service
Digital: Operational
Miles of Plant: 251.0 (coaxial); None (fiber optic). Homes passed: 5,926. Homes passed & miles of plant include Snow Shoe
President: Robert D. Stemler. General Manager & Chief Technician: John Hockenberry.
Ownership: Tele-Media Corp. (MSO).

RHODE ISLAND

Total Systems:	2	Communities with Applications:	0
Total Communities Served:	42	Number of Basic Subscribers:	203,540
Franchises Not Yet Operating:	0	Number of Expanded Basic Subscribers:	0
Applications Pending:	0	Number of Pay Units:	0

Top 100 Markets Represented: Hartford-New Haven-New Britain-Waterbury-New London, CT (19); Providence, RI-New Bedford, MA (33); Boston-Cambridge-Worcester-Lawrence, MA (6).

For a list of cable communities in this section, see the Cable Community Index located in the back of Cable Volume 2.
For explanation of terms used in cable system listings, see p. D-11.

BURRILLVILLE (town)—Cox Communications. Now served by WEST WARWICK, RI [RI0001]. ICA: RI0016.

CRANSTON—Cox Communications. Now served by WEST WARWICK, RI [RI0001]. ICA: RI0004.

NEW SHOREHAM—Formerly served by Block Island Cable TV. No longer in operation. ICA: RI0013.

NEWPORT—Cox Communications. Now served by WEST WARWICK, RI [RI0001]. ICA: RI0011.

NEWPORT & LINCOLN—Cox Communications. Now served by WEST WARWICK, RI [RI0001]. ICA: RI0002.

WARREN—Full Channel Inc, 57 Everett St, Warren, RI 02885-1909. Phones: 401-247-2250; 401-247-1250. Fax: 401-247-0191. Web Site: http://www.fullchannel.com. Also serves Barrington & Bristol County (portions). ICA: RI0009.
TV Market Ranking: 33 (Barrington, Bristol County (portions), WARREN). Franchise award date: November 1, 1974. Franchise expiration date: N.A. Began: February 2, 1984.
Channel capacity: N.A. Channels available but not in use: N.A.
Basic Service
Subscribers: 5,126.
Programming (received off-air): WFXT (FOX, Movies!) Boston; WGBH-TV (PBS) Boston; WGBX-TV (PBS) Boston; WHDH (NBC, This TV) Boston; WJAR (MeTV, NBC) Providence; WLNE-TV (ABC) New Bedford; WLWC (CW, LATV, Movies!) New Bedford; WNAC-TV (FOX, Laff, MNT) Providence; WPRI-TV (CBS, TheCoolTV) Providence; WPXQ-TV (ION) Block Island; WSBE-TV (PBS) Providence; WSBK-TV (MNT) Boston; WUNI (Bounce TV, LATV, UNV) Worcester; allband FM.
Programming (via satellite): A&E; AMC; Animal Planet; Bloomberg Television; Boomerang; Cartoon Network; CNBC; CNN; Comcast SportsNet New England; Comedy Central; C-SPAN; C-SPAN 2; Discovery Channel; DIY Network; E! HD; ESPN; ESPN2; EVINE Live; EWTN Global Catholic Network; Food Network; Fox News Channel; Fox Sports 1; Freeform; Golf Channel; Hallmark Channel; HGTV; History; HLN; Lifetime; MSNBC; MTV; MTV2; NASA TV; National Geographic Channel; NBCSN; New England Sports Network; Nickelodeon; OWN: Oprah Winfrey Network; Pop; Portuguese Channel; QVC; Spike TV; Syfy; TBS; The Weather Channel; TLC; TNT; Travel Channel; Trinity Broadcasting Network (TBN); truTV; TV Land; USA Network; VH1.
Fee: $55.99 installation; $15.45 monthly; $3.00 converter.
Digital Basic Service
Subscribers: N.A.
Programming (via satellite): BBC America; Bravo; Discovery Digital Networks; ESPN Classic; ESPNews; FXM; FYI; GSN; History International; IFC; LMN; MC; Nick Jr.; Outdoor Channel; TeenNick; Turner Classic Movies; WE tv.
Fee: $4.95 monthly.
Pay Service 1
Pay Units: N.A.
Programming (via satellite): Cinemax; HBO (multiplexed); Showtime; The Movie Channel.
Fee: $10.00 installation; $12.95 monthly (Cinemax, HBO or Showtime/TMC).
Digital Pay Service 1
Pay Units: N.A.
Programming (via satellite): Cinemax (multiplexed); Flix; HBO (multiplexed); Showtime (multiplexed); Starz (multiplexed); Starz Encore (multiplexed); Sundance TV; The Movie Channel (multiplexed).
Fee: $12.95 monthly (Cinemax, HBO, Showtime/TMC/Flix or Starz/Encore).
Video-On-Demand: No
Pay-Per-View
iN DEMAND; ESPN Now (delivered digitally); Hot Choice (delivered digitally); iN DEMAND (delivered digitally); Playboy TV (delivered digitally); Fresh (delivered digitally); Shorteez (delivered digitally).
Internet Service
Operational: Yes.
Subscribers: 3,642.
Broadband Service: In-house.
Fee: $59.95 installation; $25.99-$33.99 monthly; $9.95 modem lease; $79.95 modem purchase.
Telephone Service
Digital: Operational
Subscribers: 976.
Fee: $25.99-$34.99 monthly
Miles of Plant: 419.0 (coaxial); 285.0 (fiber optic). Homes passed: 20,485.
President & Chief Executive Officer: Linda Jones Maaia. Vice President: Levi C. Maaia. Chief Technician: Richard Adams.
Ownership: Full Channel Inc.

WEST WARWICK—Cox Communications, 6205 Peachtree Dunwoody Rd, 12th Floor, Atlanta, GA 30328. Phones: 401-383-1919 (Administrative office); 404-269-6590. Web Site: http://www.cox.com. Also serves Barrington, Bradford, Bristol, Bristol County, Burrillville (town), Central Falls, Charlestown, Coventry, Cranston, Cumberland, East Greenwich, East Providence, Exeter (town), Foster, Glocester (town), Hopkinton, Jamestown, Johnston, Lincoln, Little Compton, Middletown, Narragansett, Newport, Newport County, Newport Naval Base, North Kingstown, North Providence, North Smithfield, Pawtucket, Providence, Providence County, Richmond, Scituate (town), Smithfield, South Kingstown, Tiverton, Warwick, West Greenwich, Westerly & Woonsocket. ICA: RI0001.
TV Market Ranking: 19 (Bradford, Charlestown, Hopkinton, West Greenwich, Westerly); 19,33 (Exeter (town)), Narragansett, Richmond, South Kingstown); 33 (Barrington, Bristol, Bristol County, Coventry, Cranston, East Greenwich, East Providence, Foster, Glocester (town), Jamestown, Johnston, Lincoln, Little Compton, Middletown, Newport, Newport Naval Base, North Kingstown, Providence, Scituate (town), Tiverton, Warwick, WEST WARWICK, Woonsocket); 6 (Central Falls, Cumberland, Providence County); 6,33 (North Providence, North Smithfield, Pawtucket, Smithfield). Franchise award date: November 1, 1974. Franchise expiration date: N.A. Began: August 18, 1982.
Channel capacity: 61 (operating 2-way). Channels available but not in use: N.A.
Basic Service
Subscribers: 198,414. Commercial subscribers: 8,886.
Programming (received off-air): WGBH-TV (PBS) Boston; WGBX-TV (PBS) Boston; WJAR (MeTV, NBC) Providence; WLNE-TV (ABC) New Bedford; WLWC (CW, LATV, Movies!) New Bedford; WNAC-TV (FOX, Laff, MNT) Providence; WPRI-TV (CBS, TheCoolTV) Providence; WSBE-TV (PBS) Providence; WUNI (Bounce TV, LATV, UNV) Worcester.
Programming (via satellite): Cox Sports Television; EWTN Global Catholic Network; ION Television; Pop; QVC; Rhode Island News Channel.
Fee: $29.99 installation; $24.99 monthly.
Expanded Basic Service 1
Subscribers: N.A.
Programming (via satellite): A&E; AMC; Animal Planet; BET; Bravo; Cartoon Network; CMT; CNBC; CNN; Comcast SportsNet New England; Comedy Central; C-SPAN; C-SPAN 2; Discovery Channel; Disney Channel; E! HD; ESPN; ESPN2; EVINE Live; Food Network; Fox News Channel; Freeform; FX; HGTV; History; HLN; Lifetime; MSNBC; MTV; MTV2; New England Sports Network; Nickelodeon; OWN: Oprah Winfrey Network; Portuguese Channel; Spike TV; Syfy; TBS; Telemundo; The Weather Channel; TLC; TNT; Travel Channel; truTV; TV Land; USA Network; VH1.
Fee: $50.11 installation; $33.45 monthly.
Digital Basic Service
Subscribers: N.A.
Programming (via satellite): BBC America; Bloomberg Television; Boomerang; CMT; CNN International; Cooking Channel; Discovery Life Channel; Disney XD; DIY Network; ESPN Classic; ESPNews; Fox Sports 1; Fox Sports 2; FYI; Golf Channel; GolTV; GSN; Hallmark Channel; HD Theater; History International; HITS (Headend In The Sky); IFC; INSP; LMN; MC; MTV Live; National Geographic Channel; NBA TV; NBCSN; NFL Network; Nick Jr.; Nicktoons; Oxygen; RAI Italia; Sprout; TeenNick; TNT HD; Trinity Broadcasting Network (TBN); Turner Classic Movies; TV One; TV5, La Television International; Universal HD.
Fee: $12.95 monthly.
Digital Pay Service 1
Pay Units: N.A.
Programming (via satellite): Cinemax (multiplexed); HBO (multiplexed); Showtime (multiplexed); Showtime HD; Starz (multiplexed); Starz Encore (multiplexed); Sundance TV; The Movie Channel (multiplexed).
Fee: $10.95 monthly.
Video-On-Demand: Yes
Pay-Per-View
iN DEMAND (delivered digitally); Playboy TV (delivered digitally); Shorteez (delivered digitally).
Internet Service
Operational: Yes. Began: February 1, 1998.
Subscribers: 185,688.
Broadband Service: Cox High Speed Internet.
Fee: $99.95 installation; $39.95 monthly; $15.00 modem lease; $299.00 modem purchase.
Telephone Service
Digital: Operational
Subscribers: 144,283.
Fee: $11.95 monthly
Miles of Plant: 9,305.0 (coaxial); 3,491.0 (fiber optic). Homes passed: 512,800.
Vice President & Regional Manager: Paul Cronin. Vice President, Network Services: Allan Gardiner. Vice President, Marketing: Doreen Studley. Vice President, Tax: Mary Vickers. Vice President, Government & Public Affairs: John Wolfe. Marketing Director: Mark Cameron. Public Relations Director: Leigh Ann Woisard.
Ownership: Cox Communications Inc. (MSO).

WESTERLY—Cox Communications. Now served by WEST WARWICK, RI [RI0001]. ICA: RI0008.

2017 Edition

SOUTH CAROLINA

Total Systems: 30	Communities with Applications: 0
Total Communities Served: 332	Number of Basic Subscribers: 722,075
Franchises Not Yet Operating: 0	Number of Expanded Basic Subscribers: 2,800
Applications Pending: 0	Number of Pay Units: 98,767

Top 100 Markets Represented: Columbia (100); Charlotte, NC (42); Greenville-Spartanburg-Anderson, SC-Asheville, NC (46).

For a list of cable communities in this section, see the Cable Community Index located in the back of Cable Volume 2.
For explanation of terms used in cable system listings, see p. D-11.

ABBEVILLE—Charter Communications. Now served by SPARTANBURG, SC [SC0003]. ICA: SC0041.

AIKEN—Atlantic Broadband, 520 Pine Log Rd, Aiken, SC 29803. Phones: 888-301-8649; 803-648-8362. Fax: 803-642-9241. E-mail: info@atlanticbb.com. Web Site: http://atlanticbb.com. Also serves Burnettown, Gloverville, Jackson, Langley & New Ellenton. ICA: SC0106.
TV Market Ranking: Below 100 (AIKEN, Burnettown, Gloverville, Jackson, Langley, New Ellenton). Franchise award date: June 7, 1977. Franchise expiration date: N.A. Began: December 1, 1968.
Channel capacity: N.A. Channels available but not in use: N.A.
Basic Service
Subscribers: 12,135. Commercial subscribers: 272.
Programming (received off-air): WAGT (CW, NBC) Augusta; WCES-TV (PBS) Wrens; WEBA-TV (PBS) Allendale; WFXG (Bounce TV, FOX, This TV) Augusta; WIS (Bounce TV, NBC, This TV) Columbia; WJBF (ABC, MeTV) Augusta; WOLO-TV (ABC, MeTV) Columbia; WRDW-TV (CBS, MNT, The Country Network) Augusta.
Programming (via satellite): C-SPAN; C-SPAN 2; CW PLUS; MyNetworkTV; Pop; QVC; The Weather Channel.
Fee: $40.00 installation; $31.99 monthly.
Expanded Basic Service 1
Subscribers: N.A.
Programming (via satellite): A&E; AMC; Animal Planet; BET; Bravo; Cartoon Network; CMT; CNBC; CNN; Comedy Central; Discovery Channel; Disney Channel; E! HD; ESPN; ESPN Classic; ESPN2; Food Network; Fox News Channel; Fox Sports 1; FOX Sports South/SportSouth; Freeform; FX; FXM; Golf Channel; Great American Country; GSN; Hallmark Channel; HGTV; History; HLN; INSP; Lifetime; MSNBC; MTV; National Geographic Channel; Nickelodeon; Spike TV; Syfy; TBS; TLC; TNT; Travel Channel; Trinity Broadcasting Network (TBN); truTV; Turner Classic Movies; TV Land; USA Network; VH1.
Fee: $29.96 monthly.
Digital Basic Service
Subscribers: N.A.
Programming (via satellite): 3ABN; A&E HD; Animal Planet HD; AXS TV; BBC America; Bloomberg Television; Boomerang; BYUtv; Chiller; Church Channel; Cloo; CMT; Cooking Channel; Daystar TV Network; Destination America; Discovery Channel HD; Discovery Kids Channel; Discovery Life Channel; Disney Channel HD; Disney XD; DIY Network; ESPN HD; ESPN2 HD; ESPNews; ESPNU; EWTN Global Catholic Network; FOX College Sports Central; FOX College Sports Pacific; Fox Sports 2; Fuse; FYI; GEB America; HD Theater; History International; IFC; Investigation Discovery; ION Television; JUCE TV; LMN; MC; MTV Classic; MTV Hits; MTV Jams; MTV2; Nat Geo WILD; NBCSN; NFL Network; NFL Network HD; Nick Jr.; Nicktoons; Outdoor Channel; Oxygen; RLTV; Science Channel; Starz (multiplexed); Starz Encore (multiplexed); Starz HD; Syfy HD; TBS HD; TeenNick; Tennis Channel; TLC HD; TNT HD; TVG Network; UP; USA Network HD; VH1 Soul; WE tv; Weatherscan.
Fee: $17.95 monthly.
Digital Pay Service 1
Pay Units: N.A.
Programming (via satellite): Cinemax (multiplexed); Cinemax HD; Flix; HBO (multiplexed); HBO HD; Showtime (multiplexed); Showtime HD; The Movie Channel (multiplexed).
Fee: $14.95 monthly (Cinemax/Cinemax HD, HBO/HBO HD or Showtime/Showtime HD/TMC/Flix).
Video-On-Demand: Yes
Pay-Per-View
iN DEMAND (delivered digitally); Playboy TV (delivered digitally); Fresh (delivered digitally); Club Jenna (delivered digitally); Shorteez (delivered digitally); Spice: Xcess (delivered digitally).
Internet Service
Operational: Yes. Began: January 18, 2004.
Subscribers: 11,507.
Broadband Service: Atlantic Broadband High-Speed Internet.
Fee: $21.95-$55.95 monthly; $5.00 modem lease.
Telephone Service
Digital: Operational
Subscribers: 5,957.
Fee: $44.95 monthly.
Miles of Plant: 1,538.0 (coaxial); 536.0 (fiber optic). Homes passed: 27,465. Homes passed includes Allendale, Bamburg & Barnwell.
Vice President & General Manager: Sam McGill. Senior Vice President & General Counsel: Bartlett Leber. Technical Supervisor: Jim Walker.
Ownership: Atlantic Broadband (MSO).

ALLENDALE—Atlantic Broadband, 520 Pine Log Rd, Aiken, SC 29803. Phone: 888-301-8649 (Customer service). Fax: 803-642-9241. E-mail: info@atlanticbb.com. Web Site: http://atlanticbb.com. Also serves Allendale County & Fairfax. ICA: SC0166.
TV Market Ranking: Below 100 (Allendale County); Outside TV Markets (ALLENDALE, Allendale County, Fairfax).
Channel capacity: N.A. Channels available but not in use: N.A.
Basic Service
Subscribers: 435.
Programming (received off-air): WAGT (CW, NBC) Augusta; WCES-TV (PBS) Wrens; WEBA-TV (PBS) Allendale; WFXG (Bounce TV, FOX, This TV) Augusta; WIS (Bounce TV, NBC, This TV) Columbia; WJBF (ABC, MeTV) Augusta; WOLO-TV (ABC, MeTV) Columbia; WRDW-TV (CBS, MNT, The Country Network) Augusta.
Programming (via satellite): C-SPAN; C-SPAN 2; CW PLUS; MyNetworkTV; Pop; QVC; The Weather Channel.
Fee: $40.00 installation; $31.99 monthly.
Expanded Basic Service 1
Subscribers: N.A.
Programming (via satellite): A&E; AMC; Animal Planet; BET; Bravo; Cartoon Network; CMT; CNBC; CNN; Comedy Central; Discovery Channel; Disney Channel; E! HD; ESPN; ESPN Classic; ESPN2; Food Network; Fox News Channel; Fox Sports 1; FOX Sports South/SportSouth; Freeform; FX; FXM; Golf Channel; Great American Country; GSN; Hallmark Channel; HGTV; History; HLN; INSP; Lifetime; MSNBC; MTV; National Geographic Channel; Nickelodeon; Spike TV; Syfy; TBS; TLC; TNT; Travel Channel; Trinity Broadcasting Network (TBN); truTV; Turner Classic Movies; TV Land; USA Network; VH1.
Fee: $29.96 monthly.
Digital Basic Service
Subscribers: 210.
Programming (via satellite): 3ABN; A&E HD; Animal Planet HD; AXS TV; BBC America; Bloomberg Television; Boomerang; BYUtv; Chiller; Church Channel; Cloo; CMT; Cooking Channel; Daystar TV Network; Destination America; Discovery Channel HD; Discovery Kids Channel; Discovery Life Channel; Disney Channel HD; Disney XD; DIY Network; ESPN HD; ESPN2 HD; ESPNews; ESPNU; EWTN Global Catholic Network; Fuse; FYI; GEB America; HD Theater; History International; IFC; Investigation Discovery; ION Television; JUCE TV; LMN; MC; MTV Classic; MTV Hits; MTV Jams; MTV2; Nat Geo WILD; NBCSN; NFL Network; NFL Network HD; Nick Jr.; Nicktoons; Outdoor Channel; Oxygen; RLTV; Science Channel; Starz (multiplexed); Starz Encore (multiplexed); Starz HD; TBS HD; TeenNick; TLC HD; TNT HD; TVG Network; UP; VH1 Soul; WE tv; Weatherscan.
Fee: $75.99 monthly.
Digital Pay Service 1
Pay Units: N.A.
Programming (via satellite): Cinemax (multiplexed); Cinemax HD; Flix; HBO (multiplexed); HBO HD; Showtime (multiplexed); Showtime HD; The Movie Channel (multiplexed).
Fee: $14.95 monthly (Cinemax, HBO or Showtime/TMC/Flix).
Video-On-Demand: Planned
Pay-Per-View
iN DEMAND (delivered digitally); Playboy TV (delivered digitally); Fresh (delivered digitally); Shorteez (delivered digitally); Spice: Xcess (delivered digitally); Club Jenna (delivered digitally).
Internet Service
Operational: Yes.
Broadband Service: Atlantic Broadband High-Speed Internet.
Fee: $21.95-$55.95 monthly.
Telephone Service
Digital: Operational
Fee: $49.95 monthly
Homes passed included in Aiken.
Vice President & General Manager: Sam McGill. Senior Vice President & General Counsel: Bartlett Leber. Chief Financial Officer: Patrick Bratton. Technical Supervisor: Jim Walker.
Ownership: Atlantic Broadband.

ANCHOR POINT—Formerly served by Charter Communications. No longer in operation. ICA: SC0107.

ANDERSON—Charter Communications. Now served by SPARTANBURG, SC [SC0003]. ICA: SC0011.

AWENDAW—Formerly served by US Cable of Coastal Texas LP. Now served by Comcast Cable, NORTH CHARLESTON, SC [SC0001]. ICA: SC0094.

BAMBERG—Atlantic Broadband, 520 Pine Log Rd, Aiken, SC 29803. Phone: 888-301-8649 (Customer service). Fax: 803-642-9241. E-mail: info@atlanticbb.com. Web Site: http://atlanticbb.com. Also serves Bamberg County & Denmark. ICA: SC0167.
TV Market Ranking: Outside TV Markets (BAMBERG, Bamberg County, Denmark).
Channel capacity: N.A. Channels available but not in use: N.A.
Basic Service
Subscribers: 631.
Programming (received off-air): WAGT (CW, NBC) Augusta; WCES-TV (PBS) Wrens; WEBA-TV (PBS) Allendale; WFXG (Bounce TV, FOX, This TV) Augusta; WIS (Bounce TV, NBC, This TV) Columbia; WJBF (ABC, MeTV) Augusta; WOLO-TV (ABC, MeTV) Columbia; WRDW-TV (CBS, MNT, The Country Network) Augusta.
Programming (via satellite): C-SPAN; C-SPAN 2; CW PLUS; MyNetworkTV; Pop; QVC; The Weather Channel.
Fee: $40.00 installation; $31.99 monthly.
Expanded Basic Service 1
Subscribers: N.A.
Programming (via satellite): A&E; AMC; Animal Planet; BET; Bravo; Cartoon Network; CMT; CNBC; CNN; Comedy Central; Discovery Channel; Disney Channel; E! HD; ESPN; ESPN Classic; ESPN2; Food Network; Fox News Channel; Fox Sports 1; FOX Sports South/SportSouth; Freeform;

Cable Systems—South Carolina

FX; FXM; Golf Channel; Great American Country; GSN; Hallmark Channel; HGTV; History; HLN; INSP; Lifetime; MSNBC; MTV; National Geographic Channel; Nickelodeon; Spike TV; Syfy; TBS; TLC; TNT; Travel Channel; Trinity Broadcasting Network (TBN); truTV; Turner Classic Movies; TV Land; USA Network; VH1.
Fee: $29.96 monthly.

Digital Basic Service
Subscribers: 333.
Programming (via satellite): 3ABN; A&E HD; Animal Planet HD; AXS TV; BBC America; Bloomberg Television; Boomerang; BYUtv; Chiller; Church Channel; Cloo; CMT; Cooking Channel; Daystar TV Network; Destination America; Discovery Channel HD; Discovery Kids Channel; Discovery Life Channel; Disney Channel HD; Disney XD; DIY Network; ESPN HD; ESPN2 HD; ESPNews; ESPNU; EWTN Global Catholic Network; Family Friendly Entertainment; Fuse; FYI; GEB America; HD Theater; History International; IFC; Investigation Discovery; ION Television; JUCE TV; LMN; MC; MTV Classic; MTV Hits; MTV Jams; MTV2; Nat Geo WILD; NBCSN; NFL Network; NFL Network HD; Nick Jr.; Nicktoons; Outdoor Channel; Oxygen; RLTV; Science Channel; Starz (multiplexed); Starz Encore (multiplexed); Starz HD; TBS HD; TeenNick; TLC HD; TNT HD; TVG Network; VH1 Soul; WE tv; Weatherscan.
Fee: $75.99 monthly.

Digital Pay Service 1
Pay Units: N.A.
Programming (via satellite): Cinemax (multiplexed); Cinemax HD; Flix; HBO (multiplexed); HBO HD; Showtime (multiplexed); Showtime HD; The Movie Channel (multiplexed).
Fee: $14.95 monthly (Cinemax, HBO or Showtime/TMC/Flix).

Video-On-Demand: Planned

Pay-Per-View
iN DEMAND (delivered digitally); Fresh (delivered digitally); Spice: Xcess (delivered digitally); Shorteez (delivered digitally); Club Jenna (delivered digitally); Playboy TV (delivered digitally).

Internet Service
Operational: Yes.
Broadband Service: Atlantic Broadband High-Speed Internet.
Fee: $21.95-$55.95 monthly.

Telephone Service
Digital: Operational
Fee: $49.95 monthly
Homes passed included in Aiken.
Vice President & General Manager: Sam McGill. Senior Vice President & General Counsel: Bartlett Leber. Chief Financial Officer: Patrick Bratton. Technical Supervisor: Jim Walker.
Ownership: Atlantic Broadband (MSO).

BARNWELL—Atlantic Broadband, 520 Pine Log Rd, Aiken, SC 29803. Phone: 888-301-8649 (Customer service). Fax: 803-642-9241. E-mail: info@atlanticbb.com. Web Site: http://atlanticbb.com. Also serves Barnwell County, Blackville, Elko, Snelling & Williston. ICA: SC0018.
TV Market Ranking: Below 100 (Barnwell County (portions), Snelling, Williston); Outside TV Markets (BARNWELL, Barnwell County (portions), Blackville, Elko). Franchise award date: December 14, 1965. Franchise expiration date: N.A. Began: December 1, 1966.
Channel capacity: N.A. Channels available but not in use: N.A.

Basic Service
Subscribers: 971.
Programming (received off-air): WAGT (CW, NBC) Augusta; WCES-TV (PBS) Wrens; WEBA-TV (PBS) Allendale; WFXG (Bounce TV, FOX, This TV) Augusta; WIS (Bounce TV, NBC, This TV) Columbia; WJBF (ABC, MeTV) Augusta; WOLO-TV (ABC, MeTV) Columbia; WRDW-TV (CBS, MNT, The Country Network) Augusta; allband FM.
Programming (via satellite): C-SPAN; C-SPAN 2; CW PLUS; MyNetworkTV; Pop; QVC; The Weather Channel.
Fee: $40.00 installation; $31.99 monthly.

Expanded Basic Service 1
Subscribers: N.A.
Programming (via satellite): A&E; AMC; Animal Planet; BET; Bravo; Cartoon Network; CMT; CNBC; CNN; Comedy Central; Discovery Channel; Disney Channel; E! HD; ESPN; ESPN Classic; ESPN2; Food Network; Fox News Channel; Fox Sports 1; FOX Sports South/SportSouth; Freeform; FX; FXM; Golf Channel; Great American Country; GSN; Hallmark Channel; HGTV; History; HLN; INSP; Lifetime; MSNBC; MTV; National Geographic Channel; Nickelodeon; Spike TV; Syfy; TBS; TLC; TNT; Travel Channel; Trinity Broadcasting Network (TBN); truTV; Turner Classic Movies; TV Land; USA Network; VH1.
Fee: $29.96 monthly.

Digital Basic Service
Subscribers: 547.
Programming (via satellite): 3ABN; A&E HD; Animal Planet HD; AXS TV; BBC America; Bloomberg Television; Boomerang; BYUtv; Chiller; Church Channel; Cloo; CMT; Cooking Channel; Daystar TV Network; Destination America; Discovery Channel HD; Discovery Kids Channel; Discovery Life Channel; Disney Channel HD; Disney XD; DIY Network; ESPN HD; ESPN2 HD; ESPNews; ESPNU; EWTN Global Catholic Network; Family Friendly Entertainment; Fuse; FYI; GEB America; HD Theater; History International; IFC; Investigation Discovery; ION Television; JUCE TV; LMN; MC; MTV Classic; MTV Hits; MTV Jams; MTV2; Nat Geo WILD; NBCSN; NFL Network; NFL Network HD; Nick Jr.; Nicktoons; Outdoor Channel; Oxygen; RLTV; Science Channel; Starz (multiplexed); Starz Encore (multiplexed); Starz HD; TBS HD; TeenNick; TLC HD; TNT HD; TVG Network; VH1 Soul; WE tv; Weatherscan.
Fee: $75.99 monthly.

Digital Pay Service 1
Pay Units: N.A.
Programming (via satellite): Cinemax (multiplexed); Cinemax HD; Flix; HBO (multiplexed); HBO HD; Showtime (multiplexed); Showtime HD; The Movie Channel (multiplexed).
Fee: $14.95 monthly (Cinemax, HBO or Showtime/TMC/Flix).

Video-On-Demand: Planned

Pay-Per-View
iN DEMAND (delivered digitally); Playboy TV (delivered digitally); Fresh (delivered digitally); Spice: Xcess (delivered digitally); Shorteez (delivered digitally); Club Jenna (delivered digitally).

Internet Service
Operational: Yes.
Broadband Service: Atlantic Broadband High-Speed Internet.
Fee: $21.95-$55.95 monthly.

Telephone Service
Digital: Operational
Fee: $49.95 monthly
Miles of Plant: 338.0 (coaxial); None (fiber optic). Homes passed included in Aiken.
Vice President & General Manager: Sam McGill. Senior Vice President & General Counsel: Bartlett Leber. Chief Financial Officer: Patrick Bratton. Technical Supervisor: Jim Walker.
Ownership: Atlantic Broadband (MSO).

BEAUFORT USMC AIR STATION—Comcast Cable, One Comcast Center, Philadelphia, PA 19103. Phones: 843-554-4100; 843-747-1403. Web Site: http://www.comcast.com. ICA: SC0168.
TV Market Ranking: Below 100 (BEAUFORT USMC AIR STATION).
Channel capacity: N.A. Channels available but not in use: N.A.

Basic Service
Subscribers: 117. Commercial subscribers: 147.
Programming (received off-air): WCSC-TV (Bounce TV, CBS) Charleston; WGWG (The Country Network) Charleston; WJCL (ABC) Savannah; WJWJ-TV (PBS) Beaufort; WSAV-TV (MeTV, MNT, NBC) Savannah; WTGS (Antenna TV, FOX) Hardeeville; WTOC-TV (Bounce TV, CBS, This TV) Savannah.
Programming (via satellite): CW PLUS; QVC; TBS.
Fee: $20.00 installation; $15.56 monthly.

Expanded Basic Service 1
Subscribers: N.A.
Programming (via satellite): A&E; AMC; Animal Planet; BET; Bravo; Cartoon Network; CMT; CNBC; CNN; Comcast/Charter Sports Southeast (CSS); Comedy Central; C-SPAN; C-SPAN 2; Discovery Channel; Disney Channel; E! HD; ESPN; ESPN2; Food Network; Fox News Channel; Fox Sports 1; Freeform; FX; Golf Channel; Great American Country; GSN; HGTV; History; HLN; Lifetime; MSNBC; MTV; NBCSN; Nickelodeon; Spike TV; Syfy; The Weather Channel; TLC; TNT; truTV; TV Land; USA Network; VH1; WGN America.
Fee: $21.95 monthly.

Digital Basic Service
Subscribers: 74.
Programming (via satellite): Flix; MC; Starz Encore (multiplexed); Sundance TV.
Fee: $9.95 monthly; $2.50 converter.

Digital Pay Service 1
Pay Units: N.A.
Programming (via satellite): Cinemax (multiplexed); HBO (multiplexed); Showtime (multiplexed); The Movie Channel (multiplexed).
Fee: $13.95 monthly (each).

Video-On-Demand: No

Pay-Per-View
iN DEMAND (delivered digitally); Playboy TV (delivered digitally); Fresh (delivered digitally); Shorteez (delivered digitally).

Internet Service
Operational: Yes.
Broadband Service: Comcast High Speed Internet.
Fee: $42.95 monthly.

Telephone Service
None
Vice President, Accounting: Joan Ritchie. General Manager: Bill Watson. Technical Operations Director: Anthony Douglas. Chief Technician: Bob Bradshaw. Marketing Director: Sean O'Connell. Marketing Manager: Audrey Jones.
Ownership: Comcast Cable Communications Inc. (MSO).

BELTON—Charter Communications. Now served by SPARTANBURG, SC [SC0003]. ICA: SC0028.

BENNETTSVILLE—MetroCast Communications, 70 East Lancaster Ave, Frazer, PA 19355. Phones: 800-952-1001; 843-479-4063. Web Site: http://www.metrocast.com. Also serves Clio, Marlboro County, McColl & Tatum. ICA: SC0037.
TV Market Ranking: Below 100 (BENNETTSVILLE, Clio, Marlboro County (portions), Tatum); Outside TV Markets (Marlboro County (portions), McColl). Franchise award date: September 1, 1990. Franchise expiration date: N.A. Began: May 15, 1991.
Channel capacity: N.A. Channels available but not in use: N.A.

Basic Service
Subscribers: 1,899.
Programming (received off-air): WBTW (Antenna TV, CBS, MNT) Florence; WECT (Bounce TV, NBC) Wilmington; WFXB (FOX, MeTV) Myrtle Beach; WIS (Bounce TV, NBC, This TV) Columbia; WJPM-TV (PBS) Florence; WPDE-TV (ABC) Florence; WSOC-TV (ABC) Charlotte; WWMB (CW) Florence.
Programming (via satellite): A&E; Animal Planet; BET; Cartoon Network; CMT; CNBC; CNN; C-SPAN; CW PLUS; Discovery Channel; Disney Channel; E! HD; ESPN; ESPN2; Family Friendly Entertainment; Food Network; Fox News Channel; Fox Sports 1; FOX Sports South/SportSouth; Freeform; FX; Great American Country; Hallmark Channel; HGTV; History; HLN; INSP; Lifetime; MTV; National Geographic Channel; Nickelodeon; Outdoor Channel; QVC; Spike TV; Syfy; TBS; The Weather Channel; TLC; TNT; Travel Channel; Trinity Broadcasting Network (TBN); truTV; Turner Classic Movies; TV Land; USA Network; VH1.
Fee: $49.95 installation; $35.95 monthly; $47.99 converter.

Digital Basic Service
Subscribers: N.A.
Programming (via satellite): BBC America; Bloomberg Television; Bravo; CMT; Destination America; Discovery Kids Channel; Discovery Life Channel; DMX Music; ESPNews; Golf Channel; IFC; Investigation Discovery; LMN; MTV Classic; MTV2; Nick Jr.; Nicktoons; OWN: Oprah Winfrey Network; Science Channel; WE tv.
Fee: $5.00 monthly.

Digital Pay Service 1
Pay Units: N.A.
Programming (via satellite): Cinemax (multiplexed); Flix; HBO (multiplexed); Showtime (multiplexed); Starz (multiplexed); Starz Encore (multiplexed); The Movie Channel (multiplexed).

Video-On-Demand: No

Pay-Per-View
iN DEMAND (delivered digitally); Playboy TV (delivered digitally); Fresh (delivered digitally).

Internet Service
Operational: Yes.
Broadband Service: MetroCast Internet.
Fee: $42.99 monthly.

Telephone Service
None
Miles of Plant: 138.0 (coaxial); 25.0 (fiber optic). Homes passed: 8,400.
Vice President & Corporate Controller: Brian W. Earnshaw. Acting General Manager: Bernard Hazelwood. Technical Operations Manager: Leroy Hendricks.
Ownership: Harron Communications LP (MSO).

South Carolina—Cable Systems

BETHUNE—Formerly served by Pine Tree Cablevision. No longer in operation. ICA: SC0110.

BETHUNE—Sandhill Telephone Cooperative, 122 S Main St, Jefferson, SC 29718. Phone: 843-658-3434. Fax: 843-658-7700. E-mail: yourshtc@shtc.net. Web Site: http://shtc.net. Also serves Chesterfield, Jefferson, McBee, Pageland, Patrick & Ruby. ICA: SC5035.
TV Market Ranking: Outside TV Markets (BETHUNE, Chesterfield). Franchise award date: N.A. Franchise expiration date: N.A. Began: July 1, 1983.
Channel capacity: N.A. Channels available but not in use: N.A.
Local Choice
Subscribers: 2,375.
Programming (received off-air): WAXN-TV (getTV, IND) Kannapolis; WBTV (Bounce TV, CBS) Charlotte; WCCB (CW, MeTV) Charlotte; WCNC-TV (NBC) Charlotte; WIS (Bounce TV, NBC, This TV) Columbia; WJPM-TV (PBS) Florence; WJZY (Antenna TV, FOX, Heroes & Icons, Movies!, The Country Network) Belmont; WMYT-TV (Buzzr, IND, MNT) Rock Hill; WPDE-TV (ABC) Florence; WSOC-TV (ABC) Charlotte; WUNG-TV (PBS) Concord.
Programming (via satellite): QVC; WGN America.
Fee: $40.00 installation; $29.95 monthly. Includes 26 channels.
Total Choice
Subscribers: N.A.
Programming (via satellite): A&E; AMC; Animal Planet; Bravo; Cartoon Network; CMT; CNBC; CNN; Comedy Central; C-SPAN; Discovery Channel; Disney Channel; E! HD; ESPN; ESPN Classic; ESPN2; Food Network; Fox News Channel; Fox Sports 1; Freeform; FX; GSN; Hallmark Channel; HGTV; History; HLN; INSP; Lifetime; MTV; Nickelodeon; Outdoor Channel; Spike TV; Syfy; TBS; The Weather Channel; TLC; TNT; TV Land; USA Network; VH1.
Fee: $59.95 monthly. Includes 105 channels.
EPIX
Subscribers: N.A.
Programming (via satellite): EPIX; EPIX 2; EPIX 3; EPIX Drive-In.
Fee: $2.95 monthly. Includes 4 channels.
Starz/Encore
Subscribers: N.A.
Programming (via satellite): Starz.
Fee: $12.00 monthly. Includes 13 channels.
Video-On-Demand: No
Pay-Per-View
iN DEMAND (delivered digitally); Hot Choice (delivered digitally); Playboy TV (delivered digitally); Fresh (delivered digitally); Shorteez (delivered digitally).
Internet Service
Operational: Yes.
Fee: $39.99-$99.99 monthly.
Telephone Service
Digital: Operational
Chief Executive Officer & General Manager: Lee Chambers.
Ownership: Sandhill Telephone Cooperative (MSO).

BISHOPVILLE—Time Warner Cable. Now served by COLUMBIA, SC [SC0002]. ICA: SC0111.

BLUFFTON (village)—Hargray, 856 William Hilton Pkwy, PO Box 5976, Hilton Head, SC 29938. Phones: 877-427-4729; 843-341-1501. Fax: 843-815-1974. E-mail: customercare@htc.hargray.com. Web Site: http://www.hargray.com. Also serves Georgia State Prison, Pooler, Reidsville, Savannah & Tattnall County (portions), GA; Beaufort County (southern portion), Callawassie Island, Estill, Hardeeville, Hilton Head Island, Okatie & Ridgeland, SC. ICA: SC0020.
TV Market Ranking: Below 100 (Beaufort County southern portion), BLUFFTON (VILLAGE), Georgia State Prison, Okatie, Reidsville, Tattnall County (portions), Estill, Hardeeville, Pooler, Ridgeland); Outside TV Markets (Tattnall County (portions)). Franchise award date: March 1, 1984. Franchise expiration date: N.A. Began: August 1, 1984.
Channel capacity: N.A. Channels available but not in use: N.A.
Basic Service
Subscribers: 31,959.
Programming (received off-air): WCSC-TV (Bounce TV, CBS) Charleston; WJCL (ABC) Savannah; WJWJ-TV (PBS) Beaufort; WSAV-TV (MeTV, MNT, NBC) Savannah; WTOC-TV (Bounce TV, CBS, This TV) Savannah.
Programming (via satellite): C-SPAN; EWTN Global Catholic Network; QVC; The Weather Channel; Trinity Broadcasting Network (TBN); WGN America.
Fee: $50.00 installation; $17.38 monthly.
Video-On-Demand: Yes
Pay-Per-View
iN DEMAND (delivered digitally).
Internet Service
Operational: Yes.
Subscribers: 28,068.
Telephone Service
Digital: Operational
Miles of Plant: 2,073.0 (coaxial); 2,562.0 (fiber optic). Homes passed: 59,157.
Chairman & Chief Executive Officer: Michael Gottdenker. Chief Financial Officer: Andrew J. Rein. Senior Vice President, Sales & Business Development: Chris McCorkendale. Vice President, Sales & Marketing: Gerrit Albert. Vice President, Network & Information Technology: Tom Walsh.
Ownership: Hargray Communications Group Inc. (MSO).

BLUFFTON (village)—Hargray. Now served by BLUFFTON (village), SC [SC0020]. ICA: SC0042.

BOWMAN—Formerly served by Almega Cable. No longer in operation. ICA: SC0112.

BRIARCLIFF ACRES—Formerly served by Cablevision Industries Inc. Now served by Time Warner Cable, COLUMBIA, SC [SC0002]. ICA: SC0027.

BRISSEY ROCK—Formerly served by KLiP Interactive. No longer in operation. ICA: SC0165.

BROWNS FERRY—Time Warner Cable. Now served by COLUMBIA, SC [SC0002]. ICA: SC0089.

CALHOUN FALLS—Comcast Cable. Now served by ELBERTON, GA [GA0192]. ICA: SC0075.

CAMDEN—TruVista Communications, 112 York St, PO Box 160, Chester, SC 29706. Phones: 800-768-1212; 803-385-2191. Fax: 803-581-2226. Web Site: http://truvista.net. Also serves Cassatt, Kershaw County & Lugoff. ICA: SC0113
TV Market Ranking: 100 (CAMDEN, Cassatt, Kershaw County (portions), Lugoff); Below 100 (Kershaw County (portions)); Outside TV Markets (Kershaw County (portions)). Franchise award date: N.A. Franchise expiration date: N.A. Began: December 15, 1978.
Channel capacity: 49 (operating 2-way). Channels available but not in use: N.A.
Basic Service
Subscribers: 2,805.
Programming (received off-air): WACH (FOX) Columbia; WIS (Bounce TV, NBC, This TV) Columbia; WKTC (Antenna TV, CW, MNT, Retro TV, TMO) Sumter; WLTX (Antenna TV, CBS) Columbia; WOLO-TV (ABC, MeTV) Columbia; WRJA-TV (PBS) Sumter.
Programming (via satellite): INSP; Pop; QVC; Trinity Broadcasting Network (TBN); WGN America.
Fee: $39.99 installation; $20.99 monthly; $1.45 converter.
Expanded Basic Service 1
Subscribers: N.A.
Programming (via satellite): A&E; AMC; Animal Planet; BET; Bravo; Cartoon Network; CMT; CNBC; CNN; Comcast/Charter Sports Southeast (CSS); Comedy Central; C-SPAN; Discovery Channel; Disney Channel; Disney XD; DIY Network; E! HD; ESPN; ESPN Classic; ESPN2; EVINE Live; Food Network; Fox News Channel; Fox Sports 1; FOX Sports South/SportSouth; Freeform; FX; Golf Channel; GSN; Hallmark Channel; HGTV; History; HLN; Lifetime; MTV; National Geographic Channel; Nickelodeon; Outdoor Channel; Oxygen; Spike TV; Syfy; TBS; The Weather Channel; TLC; TNT; Travel Channel; truTV; Turner Classic Movies; TV Land; UP; USA Network; VH1; WE tv; WGN America.
Fee: $15.00 installation; $31.30 monthly.
Digital Basic Service
Subscribers: N.A.
Programming (via satellite): A&E HD; AXS TV; BBC America; Bloomberg Television; Boomerang; CBS Sports Network; Church Channel; Cloo; CMT; CNN en Espanol; CNN International; Cooking Channel; Discovery Channel HD; Discovery Kids Channel; ESPN HD; ESPN2 HD; ESPNews; ESPNU; Fox Deportes; Fox Sports 2; FSN Digital Atlantic; FSN Digital Central; FSN Digital Pacific; Fuse; FXM; FYI; Hallmark Movies & Mysteries; HD Theater; History International; IFC; INSP; Investigation Discovery; ION Television; Lifetime Movie Network HD; LMN; MC; MSNBC; MTV Classic; MTV Hits; MTV Jams; MTV2; NBCSN; Nick 2; Nick Jr.; Nicktoons; Ovation; OWN: Oprah Winfrey Network; PBS HD; Science Channel; Sundance TV; Syfy HD; TBS HD; TeenNick; TLC HD; TNT HD; Tr3s; TV Guide Interactive Inc.; Universal HD; USA Network HD; VH1 Soul.
Digital Pay Service 1
Pay Units: N.A.
Programming (via satellite): Cinemax (multiplexed); Cinemax HD; Flix; HBO (multiplexed); HBO HD; Showtime (multiplexed); Showtime HD; Starz (multiplexed); Starz Encore (multiplexed); Starz HD; The Movie Channel (multiplexed).
Fee: $11.45 monthly (Cinemax, HBO or Showtime/TMC/Flix).
Video-On-Demand: No
Pay-Per-View
iN DEMAND (delivered digitally); XTSY (delivered digitally); Playboy TV (delivered digitally); Fresh (delivered digitally); Shorteez (delivered digitally); Club Jenna (delivered digitally); Spice: Xcess (delivered digitally); Playboy en Espanol (delivered digitally).
Internet Service
Operational: Yes.
Subscribers: 3,152.
Broadband Service: In-house.
Telephone Service
Digital: Operational
Subscribers: 1,833.
Miles of Plant: 648.0 (coaxial); 224.0 (fiber optic). Homes passed: 7,808. Homes passed included in Chester.
President & Chief Executive Officer: Brian Singleton. Senior Vice President, Sales & Marketing: Allison Jakubecy. Video Services Manager: Tony Helms.
Ownership: TruVista Communications (MSO).

CAMERON—Formerly served by Almega Cable. No longer in operation. ICA: SC0159.

CHARLESTON—WOW! Internet, Cable & Phone, 7887 East Belleview Ave, Ste 1000, Englewood, CO 80111. Phones: 720-479-3500; 843-225-6100; 706-645-8553 (Corporate office); 843-225-1000 (Customer service). Fax: 720-479-3585. E-mail: wow_general@wideopenwest.com. Web Site: http://www.wowway.com. Also serves Berkeley County (portions), Hanahan, Ladson, Lincolnville, Mount Pleasant, North Charleston & Summerville. ICA: SC0158.
Note: This system is an overbuild.
TV Market Ranking: Below 100 (Berkeley County (portions), CHARLESTON, Hanahan, Ladson, Lincolnville, Mount Pleasant, North Charleston, Summerville). Franchise award date: April 28, 1998. Franchise expiration date: N.A. Began: January 1, 1991.
Channel capacity: N.A. Channels available but not in use: N.A.
Basic Service
Subscribers: 10,020.
Programming (received off-air): WCBD-TV (CW, NBC) Charleston; WCIV (ABC, MeTV, MNT) Charleston; WCSC-TV (Bounce TV, CBS) Charleston; WGWG (The Country Network) Charleston; WITV (PBS) Charleston; WLCN-CD (Christian TV Network) Charleston; WTAT-TV (FOX) Charleston.
Programming (via satellite): A&E; AMC; Animal Planet; BET; Bloomberg Television; Bravo; Cartoon Network; CMT; CNBC; CNN; Comedy Central; C-SPAN; C-SPAN 2; CW PLUS; Discovery Channel; Disney Channel; Disney XD; E! HD; ESPN; ESPN2; EVINE Live; Food Network; Fox News Channel; Fox Sports 1; FOX Sports South/SportSouth; Freeform; FX; Golf Channel; Great American Country; GSN; Hallmark Channel; HGTV; History; HLN; INSP; Lifetime; LMN; MSNBC; MTV; MTV2; Nick At Nite; Nickelodeon; Outdoor Channel; OWN: Oprah Winfrey Network; Oxygen; Pop; QVC; Spike TV; Syfy; TBS; The Weather Channel; TLC; TNT; Travel Channel; Trinity Broadcasting Network (TBN); truTV; Turner Classic Movies; TV Land; Univision Studios; USA Network; VH1; WE tv; WGN America.
Fee: $50.00 installation; $33.00 monthly.
Digital Basic Service
Subscribers: N.A. Included in Valley Twp., AL
Programming (via satellite): AXS TV; BBC America; Boomerang; CBS Sports Network; Church Channel; CMT; C-SPAN 3; Destination America; Discovery Kids Channel; Discovery Life Channel; DIY Network; ESPN HD; ESPN2 HD; ESPNews; ESPNU; EWTN Global Catholic Network; FOX College Sports Central; FOX College Sports Pacific; Fox Sports 2; Hallmark Movies & Mysteries; HD Theater; IFC; Investigation

Cable Systems—South Carolina

FULLY SEARCHABLE • CONTINUOUSLY UPDATED • DISCOUNT RATES FOR PRINT PURCHASERS

For more information call **800-771-9202** or visit **www.warren-news.com**

Discovery; Jewelry Television; JUCE TV; MC; MTV Classic; MTV Hits; MTV Jams; NBCSN; NFL Network; Nick 2; Nick Jr.; Nicktoons; Ovation; OWN: Oprah Winfrey Network; Science Channel; TeenNick; Tennis Channel; TNT HD; Tr3s; Universal HD; UP; VH1 Soul.

Pay Service 1
Pay Units: N.A.
Programming (via satellite): HBO; Showtime.

Digital Pay Service 1
Pay Units: N.A.
Programming (via satellite): Cinemax (multiplexed); Flix; HBO (multiplexed); HBO HD; Showtime (multiplexed); Starz (multiplexed); Starz Encore (multiplexed); Starz HD; The Movie Channel (multiplexed).

Video-On-Demand: Yes

Pay-Per-View
iN DEMAND (delivered digitally); Spice: Xcess (delivered digitally); Club Jenna (delivered digitally); Playboy TV (delivered digitally); Fresh (delivered digitally); Shorteez (delivered digitally); Hot Choice (delivered digitally); ESPN Now (delivered digitally).

Internet Service
Operational: Yes.
Fee: $29.95 installation; $59.95 monthly; $9.00 modem lease; $249.00 modem purchase.

Telephone Service
Analog: Not Operational
Digital: Operational
Homes passed: 69,100.
Chief Executive Officer: Colleen Abdoulah.
President: Steven Cochran. Chief Financial Officer: Rich Fish.
Ownership: WideOpenWest LLC (MSO).

CHERAW—Time Warner Cable. Now served by COLUMBIA, SC [SC0002]. ICA: SC0038.

CHESTER—TruVista Communications, 112 York St, PO Box 160, Chester, SC 29706. Phones: 803-581-9160; 800-768-1212; 803-385-2191. Fax: 803-581-2226. Web Site: http://truvista.net. Also serves Chester County (unincorporated areas), Great Falls & Richburg. ICA: SC0034.
TV Market Ranking: Below 100 (CHESTER, Chester County (unincorporated areas), Great Falls, Richburg). Franchise award date: December 4, 1978. Franchise expiration date: N.A. Began: October 1, 1978.
Channel capacity: N.A. Channels available but not in use: N.A.

Basic Service
Subscribers: 2,281.
Programming (received off-air): WAXN-TV (getTV, IND) Kannapolis; WBTV (Bounce TV, CBS) Charlotte; WCCB (CW, MeTV) Charlotte; WCNC-TV (NBC) Charlotte; WIS (Bounce TV, NBC, This TV) Columbia; WJZY (Antenna TV, FOX, Heroes & Icons, Movies!, The Country Network) Belmont; WMYT-TV (Buzzr, IND, MNT) Rock Hill; WNSC-TV (PBS) Rock Hill; WSOC-TV (ABC) Charlotte; WSPA-TV (CBS, MeTV) Spartanburg.
Programming (via satellite): Pop; QVC; Trinity Broadcasting Network (TBN).
Fee: $39.99 installation; $20.99 monthly; $3.50 converter.

Expanded Basic Service 1
Subscribers: N.A.
Programming (via satellite): A&E; AMC; Animal Planet; BET; Bravo; Cartoon Network; CMT; CNBC; CNN; Comcast/Charter Sports Southeast (CSS); Comedy Central; C-SPAN; C-SPAN 2; Discovery Channel; Disney Channel; Disney XD; DIY Network; E! HD; ESPN; ESPN Classic; ESPN2; EVINE Live; Food Network; Fox News Channel; Fox Sports 1; FOX Sports South/SportSouth; Freeform; FX; Golf Channel; GSN; Hallmark Channel; HGTV; History; HLN; Lifetime; MTV; National Geographic Channel; Nickelodeon; Outdoor Channel; Oxygen; Spike TV; Syfy; TBS; The Weather Channel; TLC; TNT; Travel Channel; truTV; Turner Classic Movies; TV Land; UP; USA Network; VH1; WE tv; WGN America.
Fee: $9.00 monthly.

Digital Basic Service
Subscribers: N.A.
Programming (via satellite): A&E HD; AXS TV; BBC America; Bloomberg Television; Boomerang; CBS Sports Network; Church Channel; Cloo; CMT; CNN en Espanol; CNN International; Destination America; Discovery Channel HD; Discovery Kids Channel; ESPN HD; ESPN2 HD; ESPNews; ESPNU; Fox Deportes; Fox Sports 2; FSN Digital Atlantic; FSN Digital Central; FSN Digital Pacific; Fuse; FXM; FYI; Hallmark Movies & Mysteries; HD Theater; History International; IFC; INSP; Investigation Discovery; ION Television; Lifetime Movie Network HD; LMN; MC; MSNBC; MTV Classic; MTV Hits; MTV Jams; MTV2; NBCSN; Nick 2; Nick Jr.; Nicktoons; Ovation; OWN: Oprah Winfrey Network; PBS HD; Science Channel; Sundance TV; Syfy HD; TBS HD; TeenNick; TLC HD; TNT HD; Tr3s; Universal HD; USA Network HD; VH1 Soul.

Digital Pay Service 1
Pay Units: N.A.
Programming (via satellite): Cinemax (multiplexed); Cinemax HD; Flix; HBO (multiplexed); HBO HD; Showtime (multiplexed); Showtime HD; Starz (multiplexed); Starz Encore (multiplexed); Starz HD; The Movie Channel (multiplexed).
Fee: $15.69 installation; $9.95 monthly (Cinemax/Cinemax HD); $11.95 monthly (HBO/HBO HD or Showtime/Showtime HD/TMC/Flix).

Video-On-Demand: No

Pay-Per-View
XTSY (delivered digitally); Club Jenna (delivered digitally); iN DEMAND (delivered digitally); Spice: Xcess (delivered digitally); Playboy en Espanol (delivered digitally); Fresh (delivered digitally); Playboy TV (delivered digitally); Shorteez (delivered digitally).

Internet Service
Operational: Yes.
Broadband Service: In-house.

Telephone Service
Analog: Operational
Miles of Plant: 95.0 (coaxial); None (fiber optic). Homes passed: 20,000.
President & Chief Executive Officer: Brian Singleton. Senior Vice President, Sales & Marketing: Allison Jakubecy. Video Services Manager: Tony Helms.
Ownership: TruVista Communications (MSO).

CHESTERFIELD (town)—Formerly served by NewWave Communications. This cable system has converted to IPTV. Now served by Sandhill Telephone Coop., BETHUNE, SC [SC5035]. ICA: SC0087.

COLUMBIA—Time Warner Cable, 3347 Platt Springs Rd, West Columbia, SC 29170. Phones: 803-791-5061; 803-251-5300. Fax: 803-251-5345. Web Site: http://www.timewarnercable.com. Also serves East Laurinburg, Gibson, Laurinburg, Maxton, Robeson County (portions), Rowland & Scotland County, NC; Andrews, Arcadia Lakes, Atlantic Beach, Batesburg, Berkeley County (portions), Bishopville, Blythewood, Briarcliff Acres, Browns Ferry, Calhoun County (portions), Cayce, Chapin, Charleston, Cheraw, Chesterfield County, Clarendon County, Conway, Cordova, Darlington, Darlington County, Dillon, Dillon County, Dorchester County (portions), Eastover, Elgin, Florence, Florence County, Forest Acres, Fort Jackson, Georgetown, Georgetown County, Goose Creek, Greeleyville, Harbison, Hartsville, Hemingway, Horry County, Irmo, Johnsonville, Kershaw County (portions), Kingstree, Lake City, Lake Murray, Lake View, Lane, Latta, Lee County, Leesville, Lexington, Lexington County, Lincolnville, Little Mountain, Manning, Marion, Marion County, Mayesville, Moncks Corner, Mullins, Myrtle Beach, Newberry County (portions), Nichols, North Charleston, North Myrtle Beach, North Stone, Orangeburg, Orangeburg County (portions), Pamplico, Pawley's Island, Paxville, Pelion, Pineridge, Pinewood, Quinby, Ravenwood, Richland County, Ridgeville, Saluda County (portions), Sampit, Scranton, Shaw AFB, Society Hill, South Congaree, Springdale, St. Matthews, Summerton, Summerville, Sumter, Sumter County, Surfside Beach, Timmonsville, West Columbia & Williamsburg County, SC. ICA: SC0002.
TV Market Ranking: 100 (Arcadia Lakes, Blythewood, Calhoun County (portions), Cayce, Chapin, COLUMBIA, Eastover, Forest Acres, Fort Jackson, Harbison, Irmo, Kershaw County (portions), Lake Murray, Lexington, Lexington County (portions), Little Mountain, Newberry County (portions), Orangeburg County (portions), Pelion, Pineridge, Pinewood, Ravenwood, Richland County, Saluda County (portions), Shaw AFB, South Congaree, Springdale, St. Matthews, Sumter, Sumter County (portions), West Columbia); 73 (Maxton, Robeson County (portions), Scotland County (portions)); Below 100 (Atlantic Beach, Bishopville, Briarcliff Acres, Browns Ferry, Charleston, Chesterfield County (portions), Clarendon County, Conway, Darlington, Darlington County, Dillon, Dillon County, Elgin, Florence, Georgetown (portions), Georgetown County, Goose Creek, Greeleyville, Hartsville, Hemingway, Horry County, Johnsonville, Lake City, Lake View, Latta, Lee County, Lincolnville, Manning, Marion, Mayesville, Moncks Corner, Mullins, Myrtle Beach, Nichols, North Charleston, North Myrtle Beach, North Stone, Pawley's Island, Paxville, Quinby, Ridgeville, Sampit, Scranton, Society Hill, Summerton, Summerville, Surfside Beach, Timmonsville, Williamsburg County, Williamsburg County (portions), Berkeley County (portions), Dorchester County (portions), Calhoun County (portions), Kershaw County (portions), Orangeburg County (portions), Sumter County (portions), Robeson County (portions), Scotland County (portions)); Outside TV Markets (Andrews, Batesburg, Cheraw, Chesterfield County (portions), Cordova, East Laurinburg, Georgetown (portions), Georgetown County, Gibson, Kingstree, Laurinburg, Leesville, Orangeburg, Rowland, Williamsburg County, Williamsburg County (portions), Berkeley County (portions), Dorchester County (portions), Kershaw County (portions), Lexington County (portions), Newberry County (portions), Saluda County (portions), Robeson County (portions), Scotland County (portions)). Franchise award date: November 2, 1977. Franchise expiration date: N.A. Began: December 1, 1977.
Channel capacity: 66 (operating 2-way). Channels available but not in use: N.A.

Basic Service
Subscribers: 270,436.
Programming (received off-air): WACH (FOX) Columbia; WIS (Bounce TV, NBC, This TV) Columbia; WKTC (Antenna TV, CW, MNT, Retro TV, TMO) Sumter; WLTX (Antenna TV, CBS) Columbia; WOLO-TV (ABC, MeTV) Columbia; WRLK-TV (PBS) Columbia.
Programming (via satellite): C-SPAN; Pop; QVC; WGN America.
Fee: $42.50 installation; $19.99 monthly; $2.63 converter.

Expanded Basic Service 1
Subscribers: N.A.
Programming (via satellite): A&E; AMC; Animal Planet; BET; Bravo; Cartoon Network; CMT; CNBC; CNN; Comedy Central; C-SPAN 2; Discovery Channel; Discovery Life Channel; Disney Channel; E! HD; ESPN; ESPN Classic; ESPN2; Food Network; Fox News Channel; FOX Sports South/SportSouth; Freeform; Golf Channel; Hallmark Channel; HGTV; History; HLN; INSP; ION Television; Lifetime; LMN; MSNBC; MTV; National Geographic Channel; NBCSN; Nickelodeon; OWN: Oprah Winfrey Network; Oxygen; Spike TV; Syfy; TBS; The Weather Channel; TLC; TNT; Travel Channel; truTV; Turner Classic Movies; TV Land; USA Network; VH1; WE tv.
Fee: $27.01 monthly.

Digital Basic Service
Subscribers: N.A.
Programming (via satellite): BBC America; Bloomberg Television; Boomerang; Cooking Channel; C-SPAN 3; Discovery Digital Networks; Disney XD; DIY Network; ESPNews; FamilyNet; Fox Sports 1; Fox Sports 2; FSN Digital Atlantic; FSN Digital Central; FSN Digital Pacific; Fuse; FXM; FYI; Great American Country; GSN; History International; HITS (Headend In The Sky); Jewelry Television; MC; NBA TV; Nick Jr.; Nicktoons; Outdoor Channel; Ovation; TeenNick; Tennis Channel; Trinity Broadcasting Network (TBN).
Fee: $4.95 monthly (movie, sports or Canales N), $5.95 monthly (variety).

Digital Pay Service 1
Pay Units: 79,000.
Programming (via satellite): Cinemax (multiplexed); Flix (multiplexed); HBO (multiplexed); IFC; Showtime (multiplexed); Starz Encore (multiplexed); Sundance TV (multiplexed); The Movie Channel (multiplexed).

2017 Edition   **D-687**

South Carolina—Cable Systems

Fee: $10.95 monthly (each).
Video-On-Demand: Yes
Pay-Per-View
NBA League Pass (delivered digitally); NHL Center Ice (delivered digitally); MLB Extra Innings (delivered digitally).
Internet Service
Operational: Yes.
Subscribers: 274,458.
Broadband Service: AOL for Broadband; EarthLink; Road Runner.
Fee: $49.95 monthly; $7.00 modem lease.
Telephone Service
Digital: Operational
Subscribers: 134,156.
Fee: $44.95 monthly
Miles of Plant: 19,488.0 (coaxial); 3,388.0 (fiber optic). Homes passed: 775,848.
President, Network Operations & Engineering: Mike Munley. Vice President & General Manager: Chris Whitaker. Vice President, Public Affairs: Dan E. Jones. Vice President, Operations & Voice: Charlene Keyes. Vice President, Marketing: Dan Santelle. Regional Vice President, Communications: Susan Leepson. Technical Operations Director: David Sykes.
Ownership: Time Warner Cable (MSO).; Advance/Newhouse Partnership (MSO).

COTTAGEVILLE—Formerly served by Pine Tree Cablevision. No longer in operation. ICA: SC0114.

CROSS—Formerly served by Pine Tree Cablevision. No longer in operation. ICA: SC0115.

CROSS HILL—Formerly served by KLiP Interactive. No longer in operation. ICA: SC0040.

DANIEL ISLAND—Home Telecom, 579 Stoney Landing Rd, PO Box 1194, Moncks Corner, SC 29461. Phones: 888-746-4482; 843-471-2200; 843-761-9101. Fax: 843-761-9199. Web Site: http://www.homesc.com. Also serves Berkeley County (unincorporated areas), Bonneau, Cross, Goose Creek, Harleyville, Macedonia, Moncks Corner, North Charleston (portions), Pimlico, Pinopolis, Santee Circle, St. Stephen, Summerville & Whitesville. ICA: SC0132.
TV Market Ranking: Below 100 (Cross, DANIEL ISLAND, Moncks Corner); Outside TV Markets (Bonneau, Harleyville). Franchise award date: N.A. Franchise expiration date: N.A. Began: October 1, 1980.
Channel capacity: N.A. Channels available but not in use: N.A.
Digital Basic Service
Subscribers: 9,577.
Programming (received off-air): WCBD-TV (CW, NBC) Charleston; WCSC-TV (Bounce TV, CBS) Charleston; WGWG (The Country Network) Charleston; WITV (PBS) Charleston; WTAT-TV (FOX) Charleston.
Programming (via satellite): C-SPAN; The Weather Channel; WGN America.
Fee: $47.00 installation; $12.95 monthly.
Digital Expanded Basic Service
Subscribers: N.A.
Programming (received off-air): WCIV (ABC, MeTV, MNT) Charleston

Programming (via satellite): A&E; AMC; Animal Planet; BET; Bloomberg Television; Bravo; Cartoon Network; CMT; CNBC; CNN; Comedy Central; Discovery Channel; Disney Channel; E! HD; ESPN; ESPN Classic; ESPN2; Food Network; Fox News Channel; FOX Sports South/SportSouth; Freeform; FX; Great American Country; HGTV; History; HLN; Lifetime; MTV; National Geographic Channel; Nickelodeon; Pop; QVC; Syfy; TBS; TLC; Travel Channel; Trinity Broadcasting Network (TBN); truTV; Turner Classic Movies; TV Land; USA Network; VH1.
Fee: $35.00 installation; $27.00 monthly; $2.25 converter.
Digital Expanded Basic Service 2
Subscribers: 1,800.
Programming (via satellite): AXS TV; BBC America; Cloo; C-SPAN 2; Discovery Digital Networks; DMX Music; ESPNews; Fox Sports 1; FYI; Golf Channel; GSN; Hallmark Channel; HD Theater; History International; IFC; INSP; LMN; MSNBC; NBCSN; Nick Jr.; Nicktoons; Outdoor Channel; PBS HD; TeenNick; WE tv.
Fee: $42.00 monthly.
Digital Pay Service 1
Pay Units: 580.
Programming (via satellite): Cinemax (multiplexed); Flix; HBO (multiplexed); Showtime (multiplexed); Showtime HD; Starz (multiplexed); Starz Encore (multiplexed); The Movie Channel; The Movie Channel HD.
Fee: $12.95 monthly (Cinemax, Showtime or Starz/Encore), $15.95 monthly (HBO).
Video-On-Demand: No
Pay-Per-View
iN DEMAND (delivered digitally).
Internet Service
Operational: Yes.
Subscribers: 1,117.
Broadband Service: HomeExpress.
Fee: $99.00 installation; $44.95-$119.95 monthly.
Telephone Service
Digital: Operational
Fee: $15.62-$18.34 monthly
Miles of Plant: 296.0 (coaxial); 250.0 (fiber optic). Homes passed: 12,000.
Chief Executive Officer & Vice Chair: Robert L. Helmly. President & Chief Operating Officer: William S. Helmly. Senior Vice President, Corporate Operations: H. Keith Oliver. Controller: Alan Smoak Jr. Engineering Director: Robert P. Abbott Jr. Sales & Business Development Director: Judy S. Cronin. Customer Operations Director: Julie Forte. Support Operations Director: Robert Hemly Jr. Program Director: Caoimhe Higgins. Plant Operations Director: Eddie G. McGriff Jr. Marketing Director: Gina Shuler. Administrative Services Director: Denny Thompson. Information Services Manager: Patrick Archibald. Switching & Networking Manager: William Dangerfield. Regional Stores Manager: Debra Ford. Installation & Repairs Manager: Thomas Higgins. Business Development Manager: Luke Lapierre. Plant Support Manager: Bernard Motte. Installation & Repair Manager: Victor Smith.
Ownership: Home Telecom (MSO).

DAUFUSKIE ISLAND—Resorts Cable TV, 2190 South Hwy 27, Somerset, KY 42501. Phone: 606-679-3427. Fax: 606-678-4178. ICA: SC0116.
TV Market Ranking: Below 100 (DAUFUSKIE ISLAND). Franchise award date: N.A. Franchise expiration date: N.A. Began: September 1, 1989.
Channel capacity: N.A. Channels available but not in use: N.A.
Basic Service
Subscribers: 120.
Programming (received off-air): WJCL (ABC) Savannah; WSAV-TV (MeTV, MNT, NBC) Savannah; WTGS (Antenna TV, FOX) Hardeeville; WTOC-TV (Bounce TV, CBS, This TV) Savannah; WVAN-TV (PBS) Savannah.
Programming (via satellite): A&E; AMC; Animal Planet; Bravo; CNBC; CNN; C-SPAN; Discovery Channel; Disney Channel; ESPN; ESPN2; Fox News Channel; Freeform; Golf Channel; History; HLN; Lifetime; Syfy; TBS; The Weather Channel; TLC; TNT; Travel Channel; USA Network; WE tv; WGN America.
Fee: $35.00 monthly.
Pay Service 1
Pay Units: 21.
Programming (via satellite): Showtime.
Fee: $10.00 monthly.
Pay Service 2
Pay Units: 50.
Programming (via satellite): HBO.
Fee: $12.00 monthly.
Video-On-Demand: No
Internet Service
Operational: No.
Telephone Service
None
Chief Technician: George Lawson. Office Manager: Beth Wright.
Ownership: Resorts Cable TV.

DEBORDIEU COLONY—Formerly served by Time Warner Cable. No longer in operation. ICA: SC0047.

DILLON—Formerly served by Adelphia Communications. Now served by Time Warner Cable, COLUMBIA, SC [SC0002]. ICA: SC0036.

EDGEFIELD—Northland Communications, 235 North Creek Blvd, Greenwood, SC 29649. Phones: 888-667-8452; 864-229-5421. Fax: 864-229-6609. Web Site: http://www.yournorthland.com. Also serves Edgefield County (portions) & Johnston. ICA: SC0171.
TV Market Ranking: Below 100 (EDGEFIELD, Edgefield County (portions), Johnston).
Channel capacity: N.A. Channels available but not in use: N.A.
Basic Service
Subscribers: 377.
Fee: $75.00 installation; $47.64 monthly.
Executive Vice President: Richard I. Clark.
Ownership: Northland Communications Corp. (MSO).

EHRHARDT—Formerly served by Almega Cable. No longer in operation. ICA: SC0160.

ELLOREE—Formerly served by Pine Tree Cablevision. No longer in operation. ICA: SC0099.

ESTILL—Hargray. Now served by BLUFFTON (village), SC [SC0020]. ICA: SC0118.

FIVE POINTS—Northland Cable Television. Now served by SENECA, SC [SC0019]. ICA: SC0081.

FLORENCE—Time Warner Cable. Now served by COLUMBIA, SC [SC0002]. ICA: SC0005.

FOLLY BEACH—Formerly served by US Cable of Coastal Texas L.P. Now served by Comcast Cable, NORTH CHARLESTON, SC [SC0001]. ICA: SC0052.

FORT MILL—Comporium Communications. Now served by ROCK HILL, SC [SC0138]. ICA: SC0120.

GAFFNEY—Charter Communications. Now served by SPARTANBURG, SC [SC0003]. ICA: SC0021.

GASTON—Formerly served by Pine Tree Cablevision. No longer in operation. ICA: SC0080.

GEORGETOWN—Southern Coastal Cable, 2101 South Fraser St, Georgetown, SC 29440. Phone: 843-546-2200. E-mail: support@sccctv.net. Web Site: http://www.southerncoastalcable.com. Also serves Georgetown County (portions). ICA: SC0172.
TV Market Ranking: Below 100 (GEORGETOWN, Georgetown County (portions) (portions)); Outside TV Markets (Georgetown County (portions) (portions)).
Channel capacity: N.A. Channels available but not in use: N.A.
Basic Service
Subscribers: N.A.
Fee: $18.00 monthly.
Internet Service
Operational: Yes.
Fee: $24.95-$49.95 monthly.
Plant Manager: John Sumner.
Ownership: Southern Coastal Cable.

GILBERT—Comporium Cable, 1660 Juniper Springs Rd, Gilbert, SC 29054. Phones: 803-685-3121; 803-894-3121. Fax: 803-892-2123. E-mail: cabletv@comporium.net. Web Site: http://www.comporium.com. Also serves Aiken County (portions), Lake Murray, Lexington County (northwestern portion), Monetta, Ridge Spring, Saluda County (eastern portion), Summit & Swansea. ICA: SC0148.
TV Market Ranking: 100 (Aiken County (portions), GILBERT, Lake Murray, Lexington County (northwestern portion), Saluda County (eastern portion), Summit, Swansea; Below 100 (Monetta, Ridge Spring, Aiken County (portions)). Franchise award date: N.A. Franchise expiration date: N.A. Began: November 29, 1991.
Channel capacity: N.A. Channels available but not in use: N.A.
Basic Service
Subscribers: 3,309.
Programming (received off-air): WACH (FOX) Columbia; WIS (Bounce TV, NBC, This TV) Columbia; WKTC (Antenna TV, CW, MNT, Retro TV, TMO) Sumter; WLTX (Antenna TV, CBS) Columbia; WOLO-TV (ABC, MeTV) Columbia; WRLK-TV (PBS) Columbia.
Programming (via satellite): Pop; TBS.
Fee: $50.00 installation; $13.45 monthly.
Expanded Basic Service 1
Subscribers: 1,000.
Programming (via satellite): A&E; Cartoon Network; CMT; CNN; Discovery Channel;

Cable Systems—South Carolina

FULLY SEARCHABLE • CONTINUOUSLY UPDATED • DISCOUNT RATES FOR PRINT PURCHASERS
For more information call **800-771-9202** or visit **www.warren-news.com**

ESPN; ESPN2; Freeform; Hallmark Channel; Lifetime; Nickelodeon; Spike TV; SportSouth; The Weather Channel; TLC; TNT.
Digital Basic Service
Subscribers: N.A.
Programming (via satellite): AMC; Animal Planet; BBC America; BET; Bloomberg Television; CMT; CNBC; CNN; Comedy Central; C-SPAN; C-SPAN 2; Discovery Digital Networks; Disney Channel; DMX Music; ESPN Classic; ESPN HD; ESPN2 HD; ESPNews; ESPNU; Food Network; Fox News Channel; FOX Sports Networks; FX; FYI; GSN; HD Theater; HGTV; History; HLN; ION Television; MSNBC; National Geographic Channel; National Geographic Channel HD; NBCSN; Nicktoons; QVC; RFD-TV; Syfy; Travel Channel; truTV; Turner Classic Movies; TV Land; USA Network.
Fee: $26.50 monthly.
Digital Expanded Basic Service
Subscribers: N.A.
Programming (via satellite): Bravo; Cloo; Cooking Channel; Disney XD; DIY Network; Fox Sports 1; Fuse; FXM; Golf Channel; History International; IFC; LMN; Nick Jr.; Outdoor Channel; Oxygen; TeenNick; WE tv.
Fee: $5.00 monthly.
Digital Pay Service 1
Pay Units: 300.
Programming (via satellite): Cinemax (multiplexed).
Fee: $10.99 monthly.
Digital Pay Service 2
Pay Units: 300.
Programming (via satellite): HBO (multiplexed).
Fee: $10.99 monthly.
Digital Pay Service 3
Pay Units: N.A.
Programming (via satellite): Flix; Starz (multiplexed); Starz Encore (multiplexed).
Fee: $9.95 monthly.
Digital Pay Service 4
Pay Units: 134.
Programming (via satellite): Showtime (multiplexed); The Movie Channel (multiplexed).
Fee: $10.99 monthly.
Video-On-Demand: No
Pay-Per-View
iN DEMAND (delivered digitally).
Internet Service
Operational: Yes.
Telephone Service
Analog: Operational
Miles of Plant: 40.0 (coaxial); None (fiber optic).
Executive Vice President, Marketing: John Barnes Jr. Executive Vice President, Cable TV & Affiliate Relations: William C. Beaty Jr. Vice President: L.B. Spearman. Chief Technician: Gary Butler. Broadband Engineering Manager: Brian Bendt. Customer Service Manager: Lorretta Sanders.
Ownership: Comporium Communications.

GRAY COURT—Charter Communications. Now served by SPARTANBURG, SC [SC0003]. ICA: SC0013.

GREENVILLE COUNTY—Formerly served by KLiP Interactive. No longer in operation. ICA: SC0164.

GREENWOOD—Northland Cable Television, 235 North Creek Blvd, Greenwood, SC 29649. Phones: 800-248-5421; 864-229-5421. Fax: 864-229-6609. Web Site: http://www.yournorthland.com. Also serves Abbeville County (unincorporated areas), Greenwood County, Hodges, Laurens County

(portions), Ninety-Six & Ware Shoals. ICA: SC0014.
TV Market Ranking: 46 (Abbeville County (unincorporated areas), Greenwood County (portions), Hodges, Ware Shoals); Outside TV Markets (GREENWOOD, Ninety-Six, Greenwood County (portions)). Franchise award date: N.A. Franchise expiration date: N.A. Began: March 1, 1968.
Channel capacity: N.A. Channels available but not in use: N.A.
Basic Service
Subscribers: 6,190.
Programming (received off-air): WGGS-TV (IND) Greenville; WHNS (COZI TV, Escape, FOX) Greenville; WIS (Bounce TV, NBC, This TV) Columbia; WLOS (ABC, Antenna TV) Asheville; WMYA-TV (MNT, The Country Network) Anderson; WNEH (PBS) Greenwood; WSPA-TV (CBS, MeTV) Spartanburg; WYCW (CW) Asheville; WYFF (NBC, Movies!) Greenville; allband FM.
Programming (via satellite): A&E; Animal Planet; BET; Cartoon Network; CNBC; CNN; Comedy Central; C-SPAN; C-SPAN 2; Discovery Channel; Disney Channel; ESPN; ESPN2; Food Network; Fox News Channel; FOX Sports South/SportSouth; FX; FXM; Golf Channel; Great American Country; Hallmark Channel; HGTV; History; HLN; INSP; Lifetime; MTV; National Geographic Channel; NFL Network; Nickelodeon; QVC; Spike TV; Syfy; TBS; The Weather Channel; TLC; TNT; truTV; Turner Classic Movies; TV Land; USA Network; VH1; WGN America.
Fee: $75.00 installation; $47.64 monthly; $1.03 converter.
Digital Basic Service
Subscribers: N.A.
Programming (via satellite): BBC America; Bloomberg Television; Bravo; Cine Mexicano; CNN en Espanol; Destination America; Discovery Kids Channel; Discovery Life Channel; DMX Music; ESPN Deportes; ESPN2 HD; ESPNews; Food Network HD; Fox Deportes; Fox Sports 1; HGTV HD; History en Espanol; IFC; Investigation Discovery; NBC Universo; Science Channel; TNT HD; Tr3s; Trinity Broadcasting Network (TBN); Versus HD; ViendoMovies; WE tv.
Fee: $1.00 monthly.
Digital Expanded Basic Service
Subscribers: N.A.
Programming (via satellite): AXS TV; ESPN HD; HD Theater; National Geographic Channel HD; Universal HD.
Fee: $5.99 monthly.
Pay Service 1
Pay Units: 1,200.
Programming (via satellite): HBO (multiplexed).
Fee: $14.95 installation; $13.00 monthly.
Digital Pay Service 1
Pay Units: 4,000.
Programming (via satellite): Cinemax (multiplexed); Flix; HBO (multiplexed); Showtime (multiplexed); Starz (multiplexed); Starz Encore (multiplexed); The Movie Channel (multiplexed).
Fee: $14.75 monthly (Cinemax, HBO, Starz/Encore or Showtime/TMC/Flix).
Video-On-Demand: Planned
Pay-Per-View
iN DEMAND (delivered digitally); Playboy TV (delivered digitally); Fresh (delivered digitally); Hot Choice (delivered digitally).
Internet Service
Operational: Yes.
Subscribers: 4,674.
Broadband Service: Northland Express.
Fee: $42.99 monthly.

Telephone Service
Digital: Operational
Subscribers: 1,963.
Fee: $29.99 monthly
Miles of Plant: 925.0 (coaxial); 348.0 (fiber optic). Homes passed: 33,713.
Executive Vice President: Richard L. Clark. General Manager: Bill Staley. Plant Manager: Cliff Jackson. Marketing Coordinator: Derquis Mitchell.
Ownership: Northland Communications Corp. (MSO).

GREER—Charter Communications. Now served by SPARTANBURG, SC [SC0003]. ICA: SC0030.

HAMPTON—Comcast Cable. Now served by NORTH CHARLESTON, SC [SC0001]. ICA: SC0154.

HARDEEVILLE—Hargray. Now served by BLUFFTON (village), SC [SC0020]. ICA: SC0122.

HARTSVILLE—Time Warner Cable. Now served by COLUMBIA, SC [SC0002]. ICA: SC0025.

HARTWELL VILLAS—Formerly served by Charter Communications. No longer in operation. ICA: SC0123.

HILDA—Formerly served by Pine Tree Cablevision. No longer in operation. ICA: SC0091.

HILTON HEAD ISLAND—Hargray, 856 William Hilton Pkwy, PO Box 5976, Hilton Head, SC 29938. Phones: 877-427-4729; 843-341-1501. Fax: 843-815-1974. E-mail: customercare@htc.hargray.com. Web Site: http://www.hargray.com. Also serves Sun City. ICA: SC5000.
Channel capacity: N.A. Channels available but not in use: N.A.
Internet Service
Operational: Yes.
Telephone Service
Digital: Operational
Chairman & Chief Executive Officer: Michael Gottdenker. Chief Financial Officer: Andrew J. Rein. Senior Vice President, Sales & Business Development: Chris McCorkendale. Vice President, Sales & Marketing: Gerrit Albert. Vice President, Network & Information Technology: Tom Walsh.
Ownership: Hargray Communications Group Inc.

HILTON HEAD ISLAND—Time Warner Cable, 3347 Platt Springs Rd, West Columbia, SC 29170. Phones: 803-791-5061; 843-251-5300; 843-913-7940 (Myrtle Beach office). Fax: 843-251-5345. Web Site: http://www.timewarnercable.com. Also serves Beaufort County, Bluffton, Hardeeville, Jasper County (portions) & Sun City. ICA: SC0010.
Note: This system is an overbuild.
TV Market Ranking: Below 100 (Beaufort County, Bluffton, Hardeeville, Hardeeville, HILTON HEAD ISLAND). Franchise award

date: January 1, 1961. Franchise expiration date: N.A. Began: September 17, 1962.
Channel capacity: N.A. Channels available but not in use: N.A.
Basic Service
Subscribers: 19,604.
Programming (received off-air): WBTW (Antenna TV, CBS, MNT) Florence; WECT (Bounce TV, NBC) Wilmington; WFXB (FOX, MeTV) Myrtle Beach; WHMC (PBS) Conway; WIS (Bounce TV, NBC, This TV) Columbia; WPDE-TV (ABC) Florence; WTAT-TV (FOX) Charleston; WUNJ-TV (PBS) Wilmington; WWMB (CW) Florence.
Programming (via satellite): C-SPAN; ION Television; LWS Local Weather Station; TBS; WGN America.
Fee: $42.50 installation; $19.99 monthly.
Expanded Basic Service 1
Subscribers: N.A.
Programming (via satellite): A&E; AMC; Animal Planet; BET; Bravo; Cartoon Network; CMT; CNBC; CNN; Comedy Central; Discovery Channel; Disney Channel; E! HD; ESPN; ESPN2; EWTN Global Catholic Network; Food Network; Fox News Channel; Fox Sports 1; Freeform; FX; Golf Channel; Hallmark Channel; HGTV; History; HLN; Lifetime; LMN; MSNBC; MTV; National Geographic Channel; NBCSN; Nickelodeon; Oxygen; Pop; QVC; Spike TV; Syfy; The Weather Channel; TLC; TNT; Travel Channel; Trinity Broadcasting Network (TBN); truTV; Turner Classic Movies; TV Land; USA Network; VH1; WE tv.
Fee: $28.00 installation; $21.45 monthly.
Digital Basic Service
Subscribers: N.A.
Programming (via satellite): BBC America; Bloomberg Television; Cooking Channel; C-SPAN 3; Discovery Digital Networks; Disney XD; DIY Network; ESPN Classic; ESPNews; Flix; FSN Digital Atlantic; FSN Digital Central; FSN Digital Pacific; Fuse; FXM; FYI; Great American Country; GSN; History International; HITS (Headend In The Sky); IFC; Jewelry Television; MC; Nick Jr.; Outdoor Channel; Ovation; Starz Encore (multiplexed); Sundance TV.
Fee: $4.95 monthly (movie, sports or Canales N), $5.95 monthly (variety).
Pay Service 1
Pay Units: N.A.
Programming (via satellite): Cinemax (multiplexed); HBO (multiplexed); Showtime (multiplexed).
Fee: $9.95 monthly.
Digital Pay Service 1
Pay Units: N.A.
Programming (via satellite): Cinemax (multiplexed); HBO (multiplexed); Showtime (multiplexed); Starz (multiplexed); The Movie Channel.
Fee: $10.95 monthly (each).
Video-On-Demand: Yes
Pay-Per-View
Fresh; Hot Choice (delivered digitally); iN DEMAND (delivered digitally); Playboy TV (delivered digitally); Fresh (delivered digitally); Sports PPV (delivered digitally).

2017 Edition   D-689

South Carolina—Cable Systems

Internet Service
Operational: Yes. Began: January 1, 1999.
Subscribers: 15,849.
Broadband Service: Road Runner.
Fee: $99.00 installation; $39.95 monthly.

Telephone Service
Digital: Operational
Subscribers: 8,175.
Fee: $44.95 monthly
Miles of Plant: 1,010.0 (coaxial); 114.0 (fiber optic). Homes passed: 41,742.
Vice President & General Manager: Chris Whitaker. Regional Vice President, Communications: Susan Leepson. Vice President, Public Affairs: Dan E. Jones. Vice President, Network Operations & Engineering: Mike Munley. Vice President, Marketing: Dan Santelle. Vice President, Operations: Michael Smith.
Ownership: Time Warner Cable (MSO).; Advance/Newhouse Partnership (MSO).

HOLLY HILL—Formerly served by Almega Cable. No longer in operation. ICA: SC0088.

HOLLYWOOD—Formerly served by US Cable of Coastal Texas LP. Now served by Comcast Cable, NORTH CHARLESTON, SC [SC0001]. ICA: SC0061.

HOMEWOOD—Horry Telephone Coop, 3480 Hwy 701 North, PO Box 1820, Conway, SC 29528-1820. Phones: 800-824-6779; 843-365-2151; 843-365-2154. Fax: 843-365-1111. E-mail: customerservice@htcinc.net. Web Site: http://www.htcinc.net. Also serves Aynor, Bucksport, Conway, Georgetown County (portions), Horry County (portions), Little River, Longs, Loris, Murrells Inlet, Myrtle Beach, North Myrtle Beach (portions), Socastee & Wampee. ICA: SC0016.
TV Market Ranking: Below 100 (Aynor, Bucksport, Conway, Georgetown County (portions), HOMEWOOD, Little River, Longs, Loris, Murrells Inlet, Myrtle Beach, North Myrtle Beach (portions), Socastee, Wampee). Franchise award date: January 1, 1980. Franchise expiration date: N.A. Began: October 11, 1983.
Channel capacity: N.A. Channels available but not in use: N.A.

Basic Service
Subscribers: 45,830.
Programming (received off-air): WBTW (Antenna TV, CBS, MNT) Florence; WCSC-TV (Bounce TV, CBS) Charleston; WECT (Bounce TV, NBC) Wilmington; WFXB (FOX, MeTV) Myrtle Beach; WHMC (PBS) Conway; WIS (Bounce TV, NBC, This TV) Columbia; WPDE-TV (ABC) Florence; WWMB (CW) Florence.
Programming (via satellite): Freeform; HLN; Pop; QVC; TBS; WGN America.
Fee: $35.00 installation; $23.05 monthly; $2.50 converter.

Expanded Basic Service 1
Subscribers: N.A.
Programming (via satellite): A&E; AMC; Animal Planet; BET; Cartoon Network; CMT; CNBC; CNN; Comedy Central; C-SPAN; Discovery Channel; Disney Channel; E! HD; ESPN; ESPN2; Fox News Channel; Fox Sports 1; FX; Golf Channel; HGTV; History; Lifetime; MTV; Nickelodeon; OWN: Oprah Winfrey Network; Spike TV; Syfy; The Weather Channel; TLC; TNT; Travel Channel; Trinity Broadcasting Network (TBN); truTV; Turner Classic Movies; TV Land; USA Network; VH1.
Fee: $23.50 monthly.

Digital Basic Service
Subscribers: N.A.
Programming (via satellite): BBC America; Bloomberg Television; Discovery Digital Networks; DIY Network; FYI; History International; IFC; ION Television; MTV Classic; MTV2; National Geographic Channel; Nick Jr.; Outdoor Channel; TeenNick; VH1 Country.
Fee: $8.49 monthly; $6.95 converter.

Digital Pay Service 1
Pay Units: N.A.
Programming (via satellite): Cinemax; Flix; HBO; Showtime (multiplexed); Sundance TV; The Movie Channel.
Fee: $12.95 monthly (each).

Video-On-Demand: Yes
Pay-Per-View
Hot Choice; iN DEMAND; movies; special events.

Internet Service
Operational: Yes, DSL & dial-up.
Subscribers: 26,975.
Broadband Service: In-house.
Fee: $24.95 monthly; $10.00 modem lease.

Telephone Service
Analog: Operational
Miles of Plant: 3,379.0 (coaxial); 236,924.0 (fiber optic). Homes passed: 78,214.
President: Ken Summerall. Chief Executive Officer: Mike Hagg. Chief Technician: Jim Morgan. Marketing Director: Tom Vitt.
Ownership: Horry Telephone Cooperative Inc.

HOPKINS—Formerly served by Pine Tree Cablevision. No longer in operation. ICA: SC0156.

IVA—Charter Communications. Now served by SPARTANBURG, SC [SC0003]. ICA: SC0125.

JEFFERSON—Formerly served by Pine Tree Cablevision. No longer in operation. ICA: SC0126.

JOHNS ISLAND—Formerly served by US Cable of Coastal Texas LP. Now served by Comcast Cable, NORTH CHARLESTON, SC [SC0001]. ICA: SC0054.

JOHNSONVILLE—Time Warner Cable. Now served by COLUMBIA, SC [SC0002]. ICA: SC0057.

LADY'S ISLAND—Comcast Cable, 4400 Belle Oaks Dr, North Charleston, SC 29405. Phones: 843-554-4100; 843-747-1403. Fax: 843-266-3272. Web Site: http://www.comcast.com. Also serves Beaufort, Dataw Island, Fripp Island & St. Helena Island. ICA: SC0056.
TV Market Ranking: Below 100 (Beaufort, Dataw Island, Fripp Island, LADY'S ISLAND, St. Helena Island).
Channel capacity: N.A. Channels available but not in use: N.A.

Basic Service
Subscribers: 3,125. Commercial subscribers: 277.
Programming (received off-air): WCBD-TV (CW, NBC) Charleston; WCIV (ABC, MeTV, MNT) Charleston; WCSC-TV (Bounce TV, CBS) Charleston; WGWG (The Country Network) Charleston; WITV (PBS) Charleston; WTAT-TV (FOX) Charleston.
Programming (via satellite): AMC; Discovery Channel; FX; ION Television; TBS; TNT; WGN America.
Fee: $52.95-$67.00 installation; $23.20 monthly.

Expanded Basic Service 1
Subscribers: N.A.
Programming (via satellite): A&E; Animal Planet; BET; Bravo; Cartoon Network; CNBC; CNN; Comcast/Charter Sports Southeast (CSS); Comedy Central; C-SPAN; C-SPAN 2; Disney Channel; E! HD; ESPN; ESPN Classic; ESPN2; Food Network; Fox News Channel; Fox Sports 1; Freeform; Golf Channel; Great American Country; GSN; Hallmark Channel; HGTV; History; HLN; INSP; Lifetime; MSNBC; MTV; NBCSN; Nickelodeon; OWN: Oprah Winfrey Network; Pop; QVC; Spike TV; SportSouth; Syfy; The Weather Channel; TLC; Travel Channel; Trinity Broadcasting Network (TBN); truTV; Turner Classic Movies; TV Land; Univision Studios; USA Network; VH1.
Fee: $21.52 monthly.

Digital Basic Service
Subscribers: N.A.
Programming (via satellite): BBC America; CMT; Cooking Channel; C-SPAN 3; Discovery Digital Networks; Disney XD; DIY Network; ESPN HD; ESPNews; EVINE Live; EWTN Global Catholic Network; Flix (multiplexed); FYI; HD Theater; History International; Jewelry Television; LMN; LOGO; MC; MoviePlex; National Geographic Channel; NFL Network; Nick 2; Nick Jr.; Sprout; Starz Encore (multiplexed); Sundance TV (multiplexed); TeenNick; TNT HD; TV One; Weatherscan.
Fee: $9.95 monthly.

Digital Pay Service 1
Pay Units: N.A.
Programming (via satellite): Cinemax (multiplexed); Cinemax HD; HBO (multiplexed); HBO HD; Playboy TV; Showtime (multiplexed); Showtime HD; Starz (multiplexed); Starz HD; The Movie Channel (multiplexed).
Fee: $13.95 monthly (Cinemax/Cinemax HD, HBO/HBO HD, Showtime/Showtime HD, Starz/Starz HDTV or TMC).

Video-On-Demand: No
Pay-Per-View
iN DEMAND (delivered digitally); iN DEMAND; Playboy TV (delivered digitally); Hot Choice (delivered digitally); Fresh (delivered digitally); Pleasure (delivered digitally); Shorteez (delivered digitally); ESPN (delivered digitally); NBA League Pass (delivered digitally); NHL Center Ice (delivered digitally); MLB Extra Innings (delivered digitally).

Internet Service
Operational: Yes.
Broadband Service: Comcast High Speed Internet.
Fee: $42.95 monthly.

Telephone Service
None
Miles of Plant: 311.0 (coaxial); None (fiber optic). Homes passed: 9,515.
General Manager: Bill Watson. Technical Operations Director: Anthony Douglas. Chief Technician: Bob Bradshaw. Marketing Director: Sean O'Connell. Marketing Manager: Audrey Jones.
Ownership: Comcast Cable Communications Inc. (MSO).

LAKE CITY—Time Warner Cable. Now served by COLUMBIA, SC [SC0002]. ICA: SC0128.

LAKE VIEW—Time Warner Cable. Now served by COLUMBIA, SC [SC0002]. ICA: SC0066.

LAMAR—Formerly served by Pine Tree Cablevision. No longer in operation. ICA: SC0129.

LANCASTER—Comporium Communications. Now served by ROCK HILL, SC [SC0138]. ICA: SC0023.

LANE—Time Warner Cable. Now served by COLUMBIA, SC [SC0002]. ICA: SC0155.

LAURENS—Charter Communications. Now served by SPARTANBURG, SC [SC0003]. ICA: SC0022.

LITTLE RIVER—Formerly served by Time Warner Cable. No longer in operation. ICA: SC0130.

LOCKHART—Charter Communications. Now served by SPARTANBURG, SC [SC0003]. ICA: SC0098.

LUGOFF—Formerly served by Pine Tree Cablevision. No longer in operation. ICA: SC0076.

McCLELLANVILLE—Formerly served by Allegiance Communications. No longer in operation. ICA: SC0101.

McCORMICK—Formerly served by McCormick Cable. No longer in operation. ICA: SC0079.

McCORMICK COUNTY—Formerly served by KLiP Interactive. No longer in operation. ICA: SC0100.

MOUNT PLEASANT—Comcast Cable. Now served by NORTH CHARLESTON, SC [SC0001]. ICA: SC0149.

MULLINS—Time Warner Cable. Now served by COLUMBIA, SC [SC0002]. ICA: SC0032.

MYRTLE BEACH—Time Warner Cable. Now served by COLUMBIA, SC [SC0002]. ICA: SC0007.

NEWBERRY—Comcast Cable, 2060 Bear Village Ct, PO Box 674, Newberry, SC 29108. Phones: 706-733-7712; 706-738-0091. Fax: 706-739-1871. Web Site: http://www.comcast.com. Also serves Newberry County (portions) & Prosperity. ICA: SC0035.
TV Market Ranking: 100 (Newberry County (portions)); Outside TV Markets (NEWBERRY, Prosperity, Newberry County (portions)). Franchise award date: March 9, 1968. Franchise expiration date: N.A. Began: June 1, 1968.
Channel capacity: N.A. Channels available but not in use: N.A.

Basic Service
Subscribers: 2,258. Commercial subscribers: 213.
Programming (received off-air): WACH (FOX) Columbia; WIS (Bounce TV, NBC, This TV) Columbia; WJZY (Antenna TV, FOX, Heroes & Icons, Movies!, The Country Network) Belmont; WLOS (ABC, Antenna TV) Asheville; WLTX (Antenna TV, CBS) Columbia; WOLO-TV (ABC, MeTV) Columbia; WRLK-TV (PBS) Columbia; WSPA-TV (CBS, MeTV) Spartanburg; WYFF (NBC, Movies!) Greenville; 17 FMs.
Programming (via satellite): QVC; WGN America.
Fee: $32.00-$43.00 installation; $15.34 monthly; $2.00 converter.

Expanded Basic Service 1
Subscribers: N.A.
Programming (via satellite): A&E; AMC; Animal Planet; BET; Cartoon Network; CMT; CNBC; CNN; Comcast/Charter

Cable Systems—South Carolina

Sports Southeast (CSS); Comedy Central; C-SPAN; C-SPAN 2; Disney Channel; E! HD; ESPN; ESPN2; Food Network; Fox News Channel; Fox Sports 1; FOX Sports South/SportSouth; Freeform; FX; Golf Channel; GSN; HGTV; History; HLN; ION Television; Lifetime; MTV; NBCSN; Nickelodeon; Pop; Syfy; The Weather Channel; TLC; Travel Channel; Trinity Broadcasting Network (TBN); truTV; Turner Classic Movies; TV Land; USA Network.
Fee: $30.04 monthly.
Digital Basic Service
Subscribers: N.A.
Programming (via satellite): BBC America; Discovery Digital Networks; Flix (multiplexed); MC; Nick 2; Nick Jr.; Starz Encore (multiplexed); Sundance TV (multiplexed); TeenNick; WAM! America's Kidz Network.
Fee: $12.95 monthly.
Pay Service 1
Pay Units: N.A.
Programming (via satellite): HBO.
Fee: $10.00 installation; $12.95 monthly.
Digital Pay Service 1
Pay Units: N.A.
Programming (via satellite): Cinemax (multiplexed); HBO (multiplexed); Showtime (multiplexed); The Movie Channel (multiplexed).
Video-On-Demand: No
Pay-Per-View
iN DEMAND (delivered digitally); Hot Choice (delivered digitally).
Internet Service
Operational: Yes.
Broadband Service: Comcast High Speed Internet.
Fee: $42.95 monthly.
Telephone Service
Digital: Operational
Miles of Plant: 181.0 (coaxial); None (fiber optic). Homes passed: 4,999.
Engineering Director: Harry Hess. Technical Operations Director: Butch Jernigan. Area Marketing Director: Joey Fortier.
Ownership: Comcast Cable Communications Inc. (MSO).

NORTH—Formerly served by Pine Tree Cablevision. No longer in operation. ICA: SC0092.

NORTH CHARLESTON—Comcast Cable, 4400 Belle Oaks Dr, North Charleston, SC 29405. Phones: 843-554-4100; 843-747-1403. Fax: 843-266-3272. Web Site: http://www.comcast.com. Also serves Adams Run, Awendaw, Beaufort County (portions), Berkeley County (portions), Brunson, Charleston Air Force Base, Charleston County (northern portion), Charleston Naval Base, Edisto Beach, Folly Beach, Goose Creek, Hampton, Hampton County (portions), Hanahan, Hollywood, Hunley Park, Isle of Palms, James Island, Jasper County (portions), Johns Island, Kiawah Island, Meggett, Mount Pleasant, Ravenel, Rockville, Seabrook Island, Sullivan's Island, Summerville, Varnville, Wadmalaw Island, Walterboro, Wild Dunes & Yemassee. ICA: SC0001.
TV Market Ranking: Below 100 (Adams Run, Awendaw, Beaufort County (portions), Charleston Air Force Base, Charleston County (northern portion), Charleston Naval Base, Edisto Beach, Folly Beach, Goose Creek, Hanahan, Hollywood, Hunley Park, Isle of Palms, James Island, Jasper County (portions), Johns Island, Kiawah Island, Meggett, Mount Pleasant, Ravenel, Rockville, Seabrook Island, Sullivan's Island, Summerville, Wadmalaw Island, Wild Dunes, Yemassee, Berkeley County (portions)); Outside TV Markets (Brunson, Hampton County (portions), Varnville, Berkeley County (portions), Hampton, Walterboro). Franchise award date: N.A. Franchise expiration date: N.A. Began: January 1, 1973.
Channel capacity: 58 (operating 2-way). Channels available but not in use: N.A.
Basic Service
Subscribers: 89,736. Commercial subscribers: 4,983.
Programming (received off-air): WCBD-TV (CW, NBC) Charleston; WCIV (ABC, MeTV, MNT) Charleston; WCSC-TV (Bounce TV, CBS) Charleston; WGWG (The Country Network) Charleston; WIS (Bounce TV, NBC, This TV) Columbia; WITV (PBS) Charleston; WJWJ-TV (PBS) Beaufort; WTAT-TV (FOX) Charleston.
Fee: $42.91-$67.95 installation; $23.20 monthly; $.74 converter.
Expanded Basic Service 1
Subscribers: N.A.
Programming (via satellite): A&E; Animal Planet; BET; Cartoon Network; CMT; CNN; Comcast SportsNet Philadelphia; Comedy Central; C-SPAN; Disney Channel; E! HD; ESPN; ESPN2; Food Network; Fox News Channel; Fox Sports 1; Freeform; FX; Golf Channel; Hallmark Channel; HGTV; History; HLN; INSP; Lifetime; NBCSN; Nickelodeon; QVC; Syfy; The Weather Channel; TLC; TNT; truTV; TV Land; VH1.
Fee: $42.90 monthly.
Expanded Basic Service 2
Subscribers: N.A.
Programming (via satellite): AMC; Discovery Channel; Spike TV; TBS.
Fee: $2.48 monthly.
Digital Basic Service
Subscribers: N.A.
Programming (via satellite): BBC America; Cinemax; Destination America; Discovery Kids Channel; Disney XD; ESPNews; Flix; HBO; Investigation Discovery; MC; Nick 2; Nick Jr.; Showtime; Starz Encore; TeenNick; The Movie Channel.
Fee: $14.95 monthly.
Video-On-Demand: Yes
Pay-Per-View
Hot Choice; iN DEMAND; Shorteez; Playboy TV; Pleasure; special events; Fresh.
Internet Service
Operational: Yes.
Subscribers: 75,245.
Broadband Service: Comcast High Speed Internet.
Fee: $42.95 monthly; $7.00 modem lease; $199.00 modem purchase.
Telephone Service
Digital: Operational
Subscribers: 30,051.
Miles of Plant: 5,411.0 (coaxial); 1,232.0 (fiber optic). Homes passed: 226,088.
General Manager: Bill Watson. Technical Operations Director: Anthony Douglas. Chief Technician: Bob Bradshaw. Marketing Director: Sean O'Connell. Marketing Manager: Audrey Jones.
Ownership: Comcast Cable Communications Inc. (MSO).

NORWAY—Formerly served by Almega Cable. No longer in operation. ICA: SC0161.

PAGELAND—Formerly served by NewWave Communications. This cable system has converted to IPTV. Now served by Sandhill Telephone Coop., BETHUNE, SC [SC5035]. ICA: SC0082.

PICKENS—Charter Communications. Now served by SPARTANBURG, SC [SC0003]. ICA: SC0135.

REGENT PARK—Formerly served by Comporium Communications. No longer in operation. ICA: SC0150.

RIDGELAND—Hargray. Now served by BLUFFTON (village), SC [SC0020]. ICA: SC0137.

RIDGEVILLE—Time Warner Cable. Now served by COLUMBIA, SC [SC0002]. ICA: SC0151.

RIDGEWAY—TruVista Communications. Now served by WINNSBORO, SC [SC0048]. ICA: SC0169.

ROCK HILL—Comporium Communications, 330 East Black St, Rock Hill, SC 29730. Phones: 803-283-1000 (Customer service); 803-326-6011 (Business service); 803-324-9011 (Residence service). Fax: 803-326-5708. Web Site: http://www.comporium.com. Also serves Chester County (unincorporated areas), Fairfield County (northern portion), Fort Lawn, Fort Mill, Great Falls, Heath Springs, Hickory Grove, Kershaw, Lake Wylie Woods, Lancaster, Lancaster County (portions), Richburg, River Hills, Sharon, Tega Cay, York & York County. ICA: SC0138.
TV Market Ranking: 42 (Fort Lawn, Fort Mill, Lake Wylie Woods, Lancaster, Lancaster County (portions), Richburg, River Hills, ROCK HILL, Tega Cay, York); 42,46 (Chester County (unincorporated areas) (portions), York County (portions)); 46 (Hickory Grove, Sharon); Below 100 (Fairfield County (northern portion), Great Falls, Heath Springs, Richburg, Chester County (unincorporated areas) (portions), York County (portions)); Outside TV Markets (Kershaw). Franchise award date: January 1, 1965. Franchise expiration date: N.A. Began: January 1, 1967.
Channel capacity: 25 (operating 2-way). Channels available but not in use: N.A.
Basic Service
Subscribers: 45,981.
Programming (received off-air): WAXN-TV (getTV, IND) Kannapolis; WBTV (Bounce TV, CBS) Charlotte; WCCB (CW, MeTV) Charlotte; WCNC-TV (NBC) Charlotte; WJZY (Antenna TV, FOX, Heroes & Icons, Movies!, The Country Network) Belmont; WNSC-TV (PBS) Rock Hill; WSOC-TV (ABC) Charlotte; WTVI (PBS) Charlotte; allband FM.
Programming (via satellite): C-SPAN; C-SPAN 2; Pop; QVC; Trinity Broadcasting Network (TBN).
Fee: $35.00 installation; $15.95 monthly; $2.10 converter.
Expanded Basic Service 1
Subscribers: N.A.
Programming (via satellite): A&E; AMC; Animal Planet; BET; Cartoon Network; CMT; CNBC; CNN; Comedy Central; Discovery Channel; Disney Channel; ESPN; ESPN Classic; ESPN2; Food Network; Fox News Channel; Freeform; FX; Golf Channel; HGTV; History; HLN; Lifetime; MSNBC; MTV; Nickelodeon; Spike TV; Syfy; TBS; The Weather Channel; TLC; TNT; Turner Classic Movies; TV Land; USA Network; VH1.
Fee: $32.35 monthly.
Digital Basic Service
Subscribers: N.A.
Programming (via satellite): BBC America; CNN en Espanol; Discovery Digital Networks; Disney XD; DIY Network; DMX Music; Fox Sports 1; FYI; GSN; History International; ION Television; LMN; National Geographic Channel; Nick 2; Nick Jr.; Outdoor Channel; Ovation; The Weather Channel.
Fee: $12.95 monthly.
Pay Service 1
Pay Units: 13,182.
Programming (via satellite): Cinemax; HBO; Showtime; Starz; The Movie Channel.
Fee: $12.95 monthly (Cinemax, HBO, Showtime/TMC or Starz/Encore).
Digital Pay Service 1
Pay Units: N.A.
Programming (via satellite): HBO (multiplexed); Showtime (multiplexed); Starz (multiplexed); Starz Encore (multiplexed).
Fee: $12.95 monthly (Cinemax, HBO, Showtime/TMC or Starz/Encore).
Video-On-Demand: No
Pay-Per-View
iN DEMAND (delivered digitally).
Internet Service
Operational: Yes.
Subscribers: 55,317.
Broadband Service: InfoAve.net.
Fee: $49.95 installation; $44.95 monthly; $7.00 modem lease.
Telephone Service
Analog: Operational
Miles of Plant: 4,955.0 (coaxial); 214.0 (fiber optic). Homes passed: 124,343.
Executive Vice President, Cable TV & Affiliate Relations: William C. Beaty Jr. Executive Vice President, Marketing: John Barnes Jr. Vice President, Media Content: Karl Skroban. Broadband Engineering Manager: Brian Bendt.
Ownership: Comporium Communications.

ROWESVILLE—Formerly served by Almega Cable. No longer in operation. ICA: SC0162.

SALEM—Charter Communications. Now served by SPARTANBURG, SC [SC0003]. ICA: SC0139.

SALUDA—Northland Communications, 235 North Creek Blvd, Greenwood, SC 29649. Phones: 888-667-8452; 864-229-5421. Fax: 864-229-6609. Web Site: http://www.yournorthland.com. Also serves Saluda County (portions). ICA: SC0170.
TV Market Ranking: Outside TV Markets (SALUDA, Saluda County (portions)).
Channel capacity: N.A. Channels available but not in use: N.A.
Basic Service
Subscribers: 188.
Fee: $75.00 installation; $47.64 monthly.

2017 Edition   D-691

South Carolina—Cable Systems

CABLE & TV STATION COVERAGE
Atlas 2017
The perfect companion to the Television & Cable Factbook
To order call 800-771-9202 or visit www.warren-news.com

Internet Service
Operational: Yes.
Subscribers: 60.
Telephone Service
Digital: Operational
Subscribers: 29.
Miles of Plant: 45.0 (coaxial); 34.0 (fiber optic). Homes passed: 1,855.
Executive Vice President: Richard I. Clark.
Ownership: Northland Communications Corp. (MSO).

SAMPIT—Time Warner Cable. Now served by COLUMBIA, SC [SC0002]. ICA: SC0090.

SANTEE—Formerly served by Almega Cable. No longer in operation. ICA: SC0140.

SENECA—Northland Cable Television, 9A Boardwalk Place, Seneca, SC 29678. Phones: 888-667-8452; 864-882-0002. Fax: 864-873-9094. E-mail: seneca@northlandcabletv.com. Web Site: http://www.yournorthland.com. Also serves Central, Clemson, Five Points, Liberty, Norris, Oconee County (portions), Pendleton, Pickens, Pickens County, Six Mile, Walhalla, West Union & Westminster. ICA: SC0019.
TV Market Ranking: 46 (Central, Clemson, Five Points, Liberty, Norris, Oconee County (portions), Pendleton, Pickens, Pickens County, SENECA, Six Mile, Walhalla, West Union, Westminster). Franchise award date: April 11, 1977. Franchise expiration date: N.A. Began: June 1, 1979.
Channel capacity: N.A. Channels available but not in use: N.A.
Basic Service
Subscribers: 4,438.
Programming (received off-air): WGGS-TV (IND) Greenville; WGTA (Decades, Heroes & Icons, Movies!) Toccoa; WHNS (COZI TV, Escape, FOX) Greenville; WLOS (ABC, Antenna TV) Asheville; WMYA-TV (MNT, The Country Network) Anderson; WNTV (PBS) Greenville; WSPA-TV (CBS, MeTV) Spartanburg; WYCW (CW) Asheville; WYFF (NBC, Movies!) Greenville.
Programming (via satellite): A&E; Animal Planet; BET; CNBC; CNN; C-SPAN; Discovery Channel; ESPN; Food Network; Fox News Channel; FOX Sports South/SportSouth; Great American Country; Pop; QVC; TBS; The Weather Channel; TLC; TNT; WGN America.
Fee: $75.00 installation; $47.64 monthly.
Expanded Basic Service 1
Subscribers: N.A.
Programming (via satellite): Cartoon Network; Comedy Central; ESPN2; FX; FXM; Golf Channel; HGTV; History; HLN; Lifetime; MTV; National Geographic Channel; Nickelodeon; Spike TV; Syfy; Travel Channel; Turner Classic Movies; TV Land; USA Network; VH1.
Fee: $11.30 monthly.
Digital Basic Service
Subscribers: N.A.
Programming (via satellite): BBC America; Bloomberg Television; Bravo; Discovery Digital Networks; DMX Music; Fox Sports 1; FXM; Golf Channel; GSN; IFC; NBCSN;
Outdoor Channel; Trinity Broadcasting Network (TBN); WE tv.
Fee: $8.70 monthly.
Pay Service 1
Pay Units: N.A.
Programming (via satellite): Cinemax; HBO.
Fee: $10.00 monthly (each).
Digital Pay Service 1
Pay Units: N.A.
Programming (via satellite): Cinemax (multiplexed); Flix; HBO (multiplexed); Showtime (multiplexed); Starz (multiplexed); Starz Encore (multiplexed); The Movie Channel (multiplexed).
Fee: $10.00 monthly (Cinemax, HBO, Showtime/TMC/Flix or Starz/Encore).
Video-On-Demand: No
Pay-Per-View
iN DEMAND (delivered digitally); Playboy TV (delivered digitally); Fresh (delivered digitally).
Internet Service
Operational: Yes.
Subscribers: 6,026.
Broadband Service: Northland Express.
Fee: $42.99 monthly.
Telephone Service
Digital: Operational
Subscribers: 1,722.
Miles of Plant: 1,091.0 (coaxial); 135.0 (fiber optic). Homes passed: 31,869.
Executive Vice President: Richard I. Clark. Regional Manager: Bill Staley. Technical Manager: Travis Blakely. Plant Manager: Alan Boggs. Marketing Manager: Melinda Harbin. Office Manager: Sharon Martin.
Ownership: Northland Communications Corp. (MSO).

SPARTANBURG—Charter Communications, 725 Union St, Burnsville, NC 28714. Phones: 314-543-2236; 636-207-5100 (Corporate office); 864-254-7260. Web Site: http://www.charter.com. Also serves Columbus, Landran, Saluda & Tryon, NC; Abbeville, Abbeville County (portions), Anderson, Anderson County (portions), Belton, Blacksburg, Buffalo, Campobello, Central Pacolet, Cherokee County (unincorporated areas), Chesnee, Chester County (unincorporated areas), Clinton, Cowpens, Donalds, Due West, Duncan, Easley, Ebenezer, Enoree, Fountain Inn, Gaffney, Gray Court, Greenville County, Greer, Hornea Path, Inman, Iva, Jonesville, Keowee Key, Landrum, Laurens, Laurens County (portions), Lockhart, Lyman, Mauldin, Newberry, Newberry County (portions), Oconee County (unincorporated areas), Pacolet, Pacolet Mills, Pickens, Pickens County (portions), Reidville, Salem, Simpsonville, Spartanburg County, Starr, Travelers Rest, Union, Union County (portions), Wellford, West Pelzer, Whitmire, Williamston & Woodruff, SC. ICA: SC0003.
TV Market Ranking: 100,46 (Newberry County (portions)); 46 (Abbeville, Abbeville County (portions), Anderson, Anderson County (portions), Blacksburg, Buffalo, Campobello, Central Pacolet, Cherokee County (unincorporated areas), Chesnee, Chester County (unincorporated areas) (portions), Clinton, Columbus, Cowpens, Donalds,
Due West, Duncan, Easley, Ebenezer, Enoree, Fountain Inn, Gaffney, Gray Court, Greenville County, Greer, Hornea Path, Inman, Iva, Jonesville, Keowee Key, Landran, Landrum, Laurens, Laurens County (portions), Lockhart, Lyman, Mauldin, Oconee County (unincorporated areas) (portions), Pacolet, Pacolet Mills, Pickens, Pickens County (portions), Reidville, Salem, Saluda, Simpsonville, SPARTANBURG, Spartanburg County, Starr, Travelers Rest, Tryon, Union, Union County (portions), Wellford, West Pelzer, Williamston, Woodruff); Below 100 (Chester County (unincorporated areas) (portions), Oconee County (unincorporated areas) (portions), Union County (portions)); Outside TV Markets (Newberry, Whitmire, Newberry County (portions), Laurens County (portions), Oconee County (unincorporated areas) (portions), Union County (portions)). Franchise award date: March 1, 1968. Franchise expiration date: N.A. Began: March 23, 1972.
Channel capacity: 60 (operating 2-way). Channels available but not in use: N.A.
Digital Basic Service
Subscribers: 155,214.
Programming (via satellite): AXS TV; BBC America; Bloomberg Television; Boomerang; CNN International; Cooking Channel; Discovery Life Channel; ESPN; ESPN Classic; ESPNews; EWTN Global Catholic Network; FOX College Sports Central; FOX College Sports Pacific; Fox Sports 2; Fuse; FYI; Great American Country; HD Theater; History International; HITS (Headend In The Sky); IFC; LMN; MC; NFL Network; Nick 2; Nick Jr.; Nicktoons; Sundance TV; TeenNick; TV One; Univision; Weatherscan.
Fee: $49.99 installation; $26.99 monthly.
Digital Expanded Basic Service
Subscribers: N.A.
Programming (via satellite): A&E; Animal Planet; Bravo; Cartoon Network; CMT; CNBC; CNN; Comcast/Charter Sports Southeast (CSS); Comedy Central; Discovery Channel; Disney Channel; Disney XD; DIY Network; E! HD; ESPN; ESPN2; Food Network; Fox News Channel; Fox Sports 1; FOX Sports South/SportSouth; Freeform; FX; Golf Channel; GSN; Hallmark Channel; HGTV; History; HLN; Lifetime; MSNBC; MTV; MTV2; National Geographic Channel; NBCSN; Nickelodeon; Oxygen; Spike TV; Syfy; TBS; TLC; TNT; Travel Channel; truTV; Turner Classic Movies; TV Land; USA Network; VH1; WE tv.
Fee: $31.36 installation; $44.50 monthly.
Digital Pay Service 1
Pay Units: N.A.
Programming (via satellite): Cinemax (multiplexed); Flix; HBO (multiplexed); HBO HD; Playboy TV; Showtime (multiplexed); Showtime HD; Starz (multiplexed); Starz Encore (multiplexed); The Movie Channel (multiplexed).
Fee: $15.95 monthly.
Video-On-Demand: Yes
Pay-Per-View
iN DEMAND (delivered digitally); Playboy TV (delivered digitally); Fresh (delivered digitally); Shorteez (delivered digitally); NHL Center Ice (delivered digitally); MLB Extra Innings (delivered digitally).
Internet Service
Operational: Yes.
Subscribers: 156,095.
Broadband Service: Charter Internet.
Fee: $29.99 monthly.
Telephone Service
Digital: Operational
Subscribers: 88,021.
Miles of Plant: 15,445.0 (coaxial); 4,006.0 (fiber optic). Homes passed: 485,037.
Vice President & General Manager: Anthony Pope. Operations Manager: Pat Hayes. Marketing Director: Brooke Sinclair. Accounting Director: David Sovanski.
Ownership: Charter Communications Inc. (MSO).

SPARTANBURG—Charter Communications. Now served by SPARTANBURG, SC [SC0003]. ICA: SC0004.

SPRINGFIELD—Formerly served by Almega Cable. No longer in operation. ICA: SC0163.

ST. GEORGE—Formerly served by Almega Cable. No longer in operation. ICA: SC0078.

ST. STEPHEN—Formerly served by Pine Tree Cablevision. No longer in operation. ICA: SC0141.

SUMMERTON—Time Warner Cable. Now served by COLUMBIA, SC [SC0002]. ICA: SC0077.

SUMMERVILLE—Time Warner Cable. Now served by COLUMBIA, SC [SC0002]. ICA: SC0012.

SUN CITY—Hargray. This system has converted to IPTV. Now served by HILTON HEAD ISLAND, SC [SC5000]. ICA: SC5001.

SURFSIDE BEACH—Time Warner Cable. Now served by COLUMBIA, SC [SC0002]. ICA: SC0006.

SWANSEA—Formerly served by Pine Tree Cablevision. No longer in operation. ICA: SC0097.

THE SUMMIT—Formerly served by Adelphia Communications. No longer in operation. ICA: SC0142.

TRAVELERS REST—Charter Communications. Now served by SPARTANBURG, SC [SC0003]. ICA: SC0143.

TURBEVILLE—FTC. Formerly [SC0085]. This cable system has converted to IPTV, 1101 East Main St, Kingstree, SC 29556. Phones: 843-382-2333; 888-218-5050; 843-382-1387. Web Site: http://www.ftci.net. Also serves Andrews, Bishopville, Clarendon County (portions), Coward, Florence County (portions), Georgetown County (portions), Greeleyville, Kingstree, Lake City, Lane, Lee County (portions), Lynchburg, Manning, Mayesville, Olanta, Paxville, Pinewood, Scranton, Summerton, Sumter, Sumter County (portions) & Williamsburg County (portions). ICA: SC5026.
Channel capacity: N.A. Channels available but not in use: N.A.
Vision Plus
Subscribers: 14,923. Commercial subscribers: 28.
Fee: $53.95 monthly. Includes 200+ channels.
Vision Xtra
Subscribers: N.A.
Fee: $63.90 monthly. Includes 240+ channels.

Cable Systems—South Carolina

Premium Pass
Subscribers: N.A.
Fee: $15.95 monthly/one movie package, $28.95/two movie packages, $38.95/three movie packages, $49.95/four movie packages. Movie packages include Cinemax, HBO, Showtime & Starz/Encore.
Internet Service
Operational: Yes.
Fee: $34.95-$104.95 monthly.
Telephone Service
Digital: Operational
Chief Executive Officer: Brad Erwin. Marketing Manager: Guy Dent Adams.
Ownership: Farmers Telephone Cooperative Inc.

TURBEVILLE—FTC. This cable system has converted to IPTV. See TURBEVILLE, SC [SC5026]. ICA: SC0085.

UNION—Charter Communications. Now served by SPARTANBURG, SC [SC0003]. ICA: SC0033.

WAGENER—Formerly served by Pine Tree Cablevision. No longer in operation. ICA: SC0102.

WALTERBORO—Comcast Cable. Now served by NORTH CHARLESTON, SC [SC0001]. ICA: SC0145.

WEST PELZER—Charter Communications. Now served by SPARTANBURG, SC [SC0003]. ICA: SC0009.

WHITMIRE—Charter Communications. Now served by SPARTANBURG, SC [SC0003]. ICA: SC0065.

WILD DUNES—Comcast Cable. Now served by NORTH CHARLESTON, SC [SC0001]. ICA: SC0064.

WILLIAMSTON—Charter Communications. Now served by SPARTANBURG, SC [SC0003]. ICA: SC0062.

WINNSBORO—Fairfield Communications, 112 York St, PO Box 160, Chester, SC 29706. Phones: 800-768-1212; 803-635-6459; 803-385-2191. Fax: 803-581-2226. Web Site: http://truvista.net. Also serves Fairfield County (portions) & Ridgeway. ICA: SC0048.
TV Market Ranking: 100 (Fairfield County (portions), Ridgeway, WINNSBORO). Franchise award date: N.A. Franchise expiration date: N.A. Began: October 15, 1980.
Channel capacity: N.A. Channels available but not in use: N.A.
Basic Service
Subscribers: 1,275.
Programming (received off-air): WACH (FOX) Columbia; WIS (Bounce TV, NBC, This TV) Columbia; WLTX (Antenna TV, CBS) Columbia; WOLO-TV (ABC, MeTV) Columbia; WRLK-TV (PBS) Columbia.
Programming (via satellite): C-SPAN 2; Pop; QVC; Trinity Broadcasting Network (TBN).
Fee: $39.99 installation; $20.99 monthly.

Digital Basic Service
Subscribers: N.A.
Programming (via satellite): A&E HD; AXS TV; BBC America; Bloomberg Television; Boomerang; CBS Sports Network; Church Channel; Cloo; CMT; CNN en Espanol; CNN International; Cooking Channel; Destination America; Discovery Channel HD; Discovery Kids Channel; ESPN HD; ESPN2 HD; ESPNews; ESPNU; Fox Deportes; Fox Sports 2; FSN Digital Atlantic; FSN Digital Central; FSN Digital Pacific; Fuse; FXM; FYI; Hallmark Movies & Mysteries; HD Theater; History International; IFC; INSP; Investigation Discovery; ION Television; Lifetime Movie Network HD; LMN; MC; MSNBC; MTV Classic; MTV Hits; MTV Jams; MTV2; NBCSN; Nick 2; Nick Jr.; Ovation; OWN: Oprah Winfrey Network; PBS HD; Science Channel; Sundance TV; Syfy HD; TBS HD; TeenNick; TLC HD; TNT HD; Tr3s; Universal HD; USA Network HD; VH1 Soul.
Digital Pay Service 1
Pay Units: N.A.
Programming (via satellite): Cinemax (multiplexed); Cinemax HD; Flix; HBO (multiplexed); HBO HD; Showtime (multiplexed); Showtime HD; Starz (multiplexed); Starz Encore (multiplexed); Starz HD; The Movie Channel (multiplexed).
Video-On-Demand: No
Pay-Per-View
iN DEMAND (delivered digitally); Special events (delivered digitally); XTSY (delivered digitally); Club Jenna (delivered digitally); Spice: Xcess (delivered digitally); Playboy en Espanol (delivered digitally); Playboy TV (delivered digitally); Fresh (delivered digitally); Shorteez (delivered digitally).
Internet Service
Operational: Yes.
Broadband Service: In-house.
Telephone Service
Analog: Operational
Miles of Plant: 48.0 (coaxial); None (fiber optic).
President & Chief Executive Officer: Brian Singleton. Senior Vice President, Sales & Marketing: Allison Jakubecy. Video Service Manager: Tony Helms.
Ownership: TruVista Communications (MSO).

2017 Edition

SOUTH DAKOTA

Total Systems: 43	Communities with Applications: 0
Total Communities Served: 229	Number of Basic Subscribers: 150,158
Franchises Not Yet Operating: 0	Number of Expanded Basic Subscribers: 469
Applications Pending: 0	Number of Pay Units: 2,293

Top 100 Markets Represented: Sioux Falls-Mitchell (85).

For a list of cable communities in this section, see the Cable Community Index located in the back of Cable Volume 2.
For explanation of terms used in cable system listings, see p. D-11.

ABERDEEN—Midco, PO Box 5010, Sioux Falls, SD 57117. Phones: 605-229-1775; 800-888-1300. Fax: 605-229-0572. Web Site: http://www.midcocomm.com. Also serves Bath, Bowdle, Bristol, Brown County, Doland, Frederick, Ipswich, Java, Mina, Mobridge, Prairiewood (village), Redfield, Roscoe, Roslyn, Selby, Walworth County (portions), Warner, Waubay & Webster. ICA: SD0003.
TV Market Ranking: Below 100 (ABERDEEN, Bath, Bristol, Brown County (portions), Frederick, Ipswich, Mina, Roslyn, Warner, Waubay, Webster, Prairiewood (village)); Outside TV Markets (Bowdle, Brown County (portions), Doland, Java, Redfield, Roscoe, Selby, Walworth County (portions), Mobridge). Franchise award date: August 16, 1968. Franchise expiration date: N.A. Began: July 1, 1970.
Channel capacity: N.A. Channels available but not in use: N.A.

Basic Service
Subscribers: 9,890.
Programming (received off-air): KABY-TV (ABC) Aberdeen; KDLO-TV (CBS, MNT) Florence; KDLT-TV (Antenna TV, NBC) Sioux Falls; KDSD-TV (PBS) Aberdeen; KTTM (FOX, This TV) Huron; KWSD (MeTV, Retro TV) Sioux Falls; 5 FMs.
Programming (via satellite): A&E; AMC; Animal Planet; BET; Bravo; Cartoon Network; CMT; CNBC; CNN; Comedy Central; C-SPAN; C-SPAN 2; Discovery Channel; Discovery Life Channel; Disney Channel; E! HD; ESPN; ESPN Classic; ESPN2; ESPNews; EWTN Global Catholic Network; Food Network; Fox News Channel; Fox Sports 1; FOX Sports North; Freeform; FX; FXM; HGTV; History; HLN; INSP; Lifetime; MSNBC; MTV; NBCSN; Nickelodeon; Outdoor Channel; OWN: Oprah Winfrey Network; Pop; QVC; Spike TV; Syfy; TBS; The Weather Channel; TLC; TNT; Travel Channel; truTV; Turner Classic Movies; TV Land; USA Network; VH1; WE tv; WGN America.
Fee: $50.00 installation; $19.95 monthly.

Digital Basic Service
Subscribers: N.A.
Programming (via satellite): BBC America; Bloomberg Television; Discovery Digital Networks; Disney XD; DMX Music; ESPNews; Fuse; FYI; Golf Channel; GSN; History; IFC; LMN; MTV Classic; Nick Jr.; Sundance TV; TeenNick; VH1 Country; VH1 Soul.

Digital Pay Service 1
Pay Units: N.A.
Programming (via satellite): Cinemax (multiplexed); HBO (multiplexed); Showtime (multiplexed); Starz (multiplexed); Starz Encore (multiplexed); The Movie Channel (multiplexed).
Fee: $11.00 monthly (each).
Video-On-Demand: No

Pay-Per-View
Hot Choice (delivered digitally); iN DEMAND; Sports PPV (delivered digitally).
Internet Service
Operational: Yes. Began: June 1, 1998.
Subscribers: 8,680.
Broadband Service: MidcoNet.
Fee: $35.00 installation; $19.95 monthly; $10.00 modem lease.
Telephone Service
Digital: Operational
Subscribers: 4,134.
Fee: $18.00 monthly
Miles of Plant: 248.0 (coaxial); 95.0 (fiber optic). Homes passed: 24,976.
General Manager: Clay Stevens. Marketing Director: Mark Powell. Programming Director: Wynne Haakenstad. Customer Service Manager: Chris VanDover.
Ownership: Midcontinent Communications (MSO).; Comcast Cable Communications Inc. (MSO).

ABERDEEN TWP.—Formerly served by ITC. No longer in operation. ICA: SD5061.

ALEXANDRIA—TrioTel Communications Inc. This cable system has converted to IPTV. Now served by SALEM, SD [SD5106]. ICA: SD0097.

ARMOUR—Golden West Telecommunications. Now served by FREEMAN, SD [SD0038]. ICA: SD0149.

ASHTON—Formerly served by Midcontinent Communications. No longer in operation. ICA: SD0150.

ASTORIA—Formerly served by Satellite Cable Services Inc. This cable system has converted to IPTV. Now served by ITC, CLEAR LAKE, SD [SD5042]. ICA: SD0151.

AVON—Golden West Telecommunications. Now served by FREEMAN, SD [SD0038]. ICA: SD0079.

BERESFORD—Beresford Cablevision Inc, 120 East Main St., Beresford, SD 57004. Phones: 605-763-2008; 605-763-2500. Fax: 605-763-7112. E-mail: phone@bmtc.net. Web Site: http://www.bmtc.net. ICA: SD0032.
TV Market Ranking: 85 (BERESFORD). Franchise award date: N.A. Franchise expiration date: N.A. Began: January 1, 1983.
Channel capacity: N.A. Channels available but not in use: N.A.

Basic Service
Subscribers: 506.
Programming (received off-air): KCAU-TV (ABC) Sioux City; KDLT-TV (Antenna TV, NBC) Sioux Falls; KELO-TV (CBS, MNT) Sioux Falls; KMEG (Azteca America, CBS, Decades) Sioux City; KPTH (FOX, MNT, This TV) Sioux City; KSFY-TV (ABC, CW) Sioux Falls; KTIV (CW, MeTV, NBC) Sioux City; KTTW (FOX, This TV) Sioux Falls; KUSD-TV (PBS) Vermillion; KWSD (MeTV, Retro TV) Sioux Falls.
Fee: $25.00 installation; $25.00 monthly; $1.00 converter.

Expanded Basic Service 1
Subscribers: 469.
Programming (via satellite): A&E; AMC; Animal Planet; Boomerang; Bravo; Cartoon Network; CMT; CNN; Comedy Central; C-SPAN; Discovery Channel; Disney Channel; DIY Network; ESPN; ESPN Classic; ESPN2; Food Network; Fox News Channel; Fox Sports 1; FOX Sports Networks; Freeform; FX; HGTV; History; Lifetime; MTV; National Geographic Channel; Nickelodeon; Outdoor Channel; Spike TV; Syfy; TBS; The Weather Channel; TLC; TNT; Turner Classic Movies; TV Land; USA Network; VH1; WGN America.
Fee: $15.85 monthly.

Digital Basic Service
Subscribers: 115.
Programming (via satellite): BBC America; Bloomberg Television; Bravo; CMT; Destination America; Discovery Kids Channel; Discovery Life Channel; Disney XD; DMX Music; ESPN Classic; ESPN2; ESPNews; FOX College Sports Central; FOX College Sports Pacific; Fox Sports 1; Fuse; FXM; FYI; Golf Channel; Great American Country; GSN; History International; IFC; Investigation Discovery; MTV Classic; MTV Jams; MTV2; NBCSN; Nick Jr.; Nicktoons; Outdoor Channel; Ovation; OWN: Oprah Winfrey Network; Science Channel; Sundance TV; TeenNick; truTV; VH1 Soul; WE tv.
Fee: $34.00 monthly.

Pay Service 1
Pay Units: N.A.
Programming (via satellite): HBO; Showtime.
Fee: $25.00 installation; $12.92 monthly (each).

Digital Pay Service 1
Pay Units: N.A.
Programming (via satellite): Cinemax (multiplexed); Flix; HBO (multiplexed); Showtime (multiplexed); Starz (multiplexed); Starz Encore; The Movie Channel (multiplexed).
Fee: $8.50 monthly (Starz), $11.00 monthly (Cinemax), $13.50 monthly (HBO or Showtime/TMC/Flix).
Video-On-Demand: No
Internet Service
Operational: No, DSL.
Telephone Service
None
Miles of Plant: 47.0 (coaxial); None (fiber optic). Homes passed: 870.
General Manager: Todd Hansen. Marketing Director & Lead Technologist: Dean Jacob-
son. Cable Technician: Ted Lyle. Finance Officer: Kathy Moller.
Ownership: Beresford Cablevision Inc.

BISON—West River Cable Television, 801 Coleman Ave, PO Box 39, Bison, SD 57620. Phones: 605-244-5213; 605-244-5236; 888-411-5651. Fax: 605-244-7288. E-mail: westriver@sdplains.com. Web Site: http://www.westrivercatv.com. Also serves Buffalo, Lemmon, McIntosh & Newell. ICA: SD0103.
TV Market Ranking: Below 100 (Newell); Outside TV Markets (BISON, Buffalo, Lemmon, McIntosh). Franchise award date: May 12, 1982. Franchise expiration date: N.A. Began: December 1, 1982.
Channel capacity: N.A. Channels available but not in use: N.A.

Basic Service
Subscribers: 611.
Programming (received off-air): KHME (MeTV, This TV) Rapid City; KOTA-TV (ABC, FOX) Rapid City; KPSD-TV (PBS) Eagle Butte.
Programming (via microwave): KFYR-TV (FOX, MeTV, NBC) Bismarck.
Programming (via satellite): A&E; AMC; Animal Planet; Cartoon Network; CMT; CNBC; CNN; Comedy Central; C-SPAN; C-SPAN 2; Discovery Channel; Disney Channel; ESPN; ESPN2; EWTN Global Catholic Network; Food Network; Freeform; FX; Great American Country; Hallmark Channel; Hallmark Movies & Mysteries; HGTV; History; HLN; INSP; KCNC-TV (CBS, Decades) Denver; Lifetime; LMN; MTV; MTV2; National Geographic Channel; NBCSN; Nick Jr.; Nickelodeon; Outdoor Channel; OWN: Oprah Winfrey Network; Pop; QVC; Spike TV; Syfy; TBS; The Weather Channel; TLC; TNT; Travel Channel; truTV; Turner Classic Movies; TV Land; USA Network; VH1; WE tv; WGN America.
Fee: $35.00 installation; $55.95 monthly.
Video-On-Demand: No
Internet Service
Operational: No.
Telephone Service
None
Miles of Plant: 28.0 (coaxial); None (fiber optic). Homes passed: 1,713.
General Manager: Jerry Reisenauer. Assistant Manager: Colgan Huber. Telecommunications Manager: Colle Nash.
Ownership: West River Cooperative Telephone Co.

BOULDER CANYON—Midco. Now served by RAPID CITY, SD [SD0002]. ICA: SD0132.

BRITTON—Venture Communications. This cable system has converted to IPTV, 218 Commercial Ave SE, PO Box 157, Highmore, SD 57345-0157. Phones: 800-824-7282; 605-852-2224. Fax: 605-852-2404.

Cable Systems—South Dakota

E-mail: venture@venturecomm.net. Web Site: http://www.venturecomm.net. Also serves Amherst, Eden, Lake City, Langford & Pierpont. ICA: SD5099.
TV Market Ranking: Below 100 (Langford, Pierpont); Outside TV Markets (BRITTON, Eden). Franchise award date: N.A. Franchise expiration date: N.A. Began: May 1, 1979.
Channel capacity: N.A. Channels available but not in use: N.A.
Core
Subscribers: N.A.
Programming (received off-air): KABY-TV (ABC) Aberdeen; KDLO-TV (CBS, MNT) Florence; KDLT-TV (Antenna TV, NBC) Sioux Falls; KTTW (FOX, This TV) Sioux Falls; KUSD-TV (PBS) Vermillion.
Programming (via satellite): C-SPAN; CW PLUS; ESPN; EWTN Global Catholic Network; ION Television; Local Cable Weather; MyNetworkTV; QVC; The Weather Channel; Trinity Broadcasting Network (TBN); WGN America.
Fee: $49.95 installation; $19.95 monthly.
Basic
Subscribers: 999.
Programming (via satellite): A&E; AMC; Animal Planet; BBC America; Bloomberg Television; Bravo; Cartoon Network; CMT; CNBC; CNN; Comedy Central; C-SPAN 2; Destination America; Discovery Channel; Discovery Kids Channel; Disney Channel; Disney XD; DIY Network; DMX Music; E! HD; ESPN Classic; ESPN2; ESPNews; Food Network; Fox News Channel; Fox Sports 1; FOX Sports North; FX; FXM; Golf Channel; Great American Country; GSN; Hallmark Channel; Hallmark Movies & Mysteries; HGTV; History; HLN; Investigation Discovery; Lifetime; LMN; MSNBC; MTV; MTV Classic; MTV Hits; MTV2; National Geographic Channel; NBCSN; NFL Network; Nick Jr.; Nickelodeon; Nicktoons; Outdoor Channel; OWN: Oprah Winfrey Network; Oxygen; RFD-TV; Science Channel; Spike TV; Syfy; TBS; TeenNick; TLC; TNT; Travel Channel; truTV; Turner Classic Movies; TV Land; USA Network; VH1; WE tv.
Fee: $60.99 monthly.
Video-On-Demand: No
Pay-Per-View
Playboy TV (delivered digitally); Fresh (delivered digitally).
Internet Service
Operational: Yes.
Fee: $40.95-$150.95 monthly.
Telephone Service
Digital: Operational
General Manager: Randy Houdek. Assistant General Manager: Randy Olson. Chief Technician: Brad Ryan.
Ownership: Venture Communications Cooperative (MSO).

BRITTON—Venture Communications. This cable system has converted to IPTV. See BRITTON, SD [SD5099]. ICA: SD0041.

BROOKINGS—Mediacom, 1504 2nd St SE, PO Box 110, Waseca, MN 56093. Phones: 845-695-2762; 507-835-2356. Fax: 507-835-4567. Web Site: http://www.mediacomcable.com. Also serves Arlington, Aurora, Bruce, Castlewood, Colman, De Smet, Egan, Elkton, Estelline, Flandreau, Hayti, Lake Norden, Lake Preston, Volga & White. ICA: SD0005.
TV Market Ranking: 85 (Colman, Egan); Below 100 (De Smet, Estelline, Hayti, Lake Norden); Outside TV Markets (Arlington, Aurora, BROOKINGS, Bruce, Elkton, Flandreau, Lake Preston, Volga, White). Franchise award date: June 1, 1989. Franchise expiration date: N.A. Began: July 1, 1970.
Channel capacity: N.A. Channels available but not in use: N.A.
Basic Service
Subscribers: 3,852.
Programming (received off-air): KDLT-TV (Antenna TV, NBC) Sioux Falls; KELO-TV (CBS, MNT) Sioux Falls; KESD-TV (PBS) Brookings; KSFY-TV (ABC, CW) Sioux Falls; KTTW (FOX, This TV) Sioux Falls; allband FM.
Programming (via satellite): C-SPAN; C-SPAN 2; ION Television; Pop; QVC; WGN America.
Fee: $44.30 installation; $42.00 monthly.
Expanded Basic Service 1
Subscribers: N.A.
Programming (via satellite): A&E; AMC; Animal Planet; Bravo; Cartoon Network; CNBC; CNN; Comedy Central; Discovery Channel; Disney Channel; E! HD; ESPN; ESPN2; EWTN Global Catholic Network; Food Network; Fox News Channel; Fox Sports 1; FOX Sports North; Freeform; FX; Great American Country; Hallmark Channel; HGTV; History; HLN; INSP; Lifetime; MSNBC; MTV; Nickelodeon; RFD-TV; Spike TV; Syfy; TBS; The Weather Channel; TLC; TNT; Travel Channel; Trinity Broadcasting Network (TBN); truTV; TV Land; Univision; USA Network; VH1; WE tv.
Digital Basic Service
Subscribers: N.A.
Programming (via satellite): AXS TV; BBC America; Bloomberg Television; Discovery Life Channel; DMX Music; ESPN; ESPN2; ESPNews; Fuse; FXM; FYI; Golf Channel; GSN; HD Theater; History International; HITS (Headend In The Sky); IFC; LMN; National Geographic Channel; Nick Jr.; Nicktoons; Outdoor Channel; TeenNick; Turner Classic Movies; Universal HD.
Digital Pay Service 1
Pay Units: 906.
Programming (via satellite): Cinemax (multiplexed); Flix (multiplexed); HBO (multiplexed); HBO HD; Showtime (multiplexed); Showtime HD; Starz (multiplexed); Starz Encore (multiplexed); Starz HD; Sundance TV (multiplexed); The Movie Channel (multiplexed); The Movie Channel HD.
Fee: $6.75 monthly (Starz), $10.95 monthly (Cinemax, HBO or Showtime).
Video-On-Demand: No
Pay-Per-View
Mediacom PPV (delivered digitally); ESPN (delivered digitally); Fresh (delivered digitally); Shorteez (delivered digitally); Playboy TV (delivered digitally); Pleasure (delivered digitally).
Internet Service
Operational: Yes.
Broadband Service: Mediacom High Speed Internet.
Fee: $29.95 monthly; $10.00 modem lease.
Telephone Service
Digital: Operational
Miles of Plant: 644.0 (coaxial); 5.0 (fiber optic). Homes passed: 8,842.
Vice President: Bill Jenson. Vice President, Financial Reporting: Kenneth J. Kohrs. Sales & Marketing Director: Lori Huberty. Engineering Manager: Kraig Kaiser.
Ownership: Mediacom LLC (MSO).

BRUCE—Mediacom. Now served by BROOKINGS, SD [SD0005]. ICA: SD0153.

BRYANT—Formerly served by Satellite Cable Services Inc. This cable system has converted to IPTV. Now served by ITC, CLEAR LAKE, SD [SD5042]. ICA: SD0100.

BUFFALO—Formerly served by West River Cable Television. No longer in operation. ICA: SD0106.

BURKE—Golden West Telecommunications. Now served by WINNER, SD [SD0021]. ICA: SD0062.

CARTHAGE—Alliance Communications. This cable system has converted to IPTV. Now served by HOWARD, SD [SD5082]. ICA: SD0244.

CASTLEWOOD—Mediacom. Now served by BROOKINGS, SD [SD0005]. ICA: SD0098.

CAVOUR—Formerly served by Midcontinent Communications. No longer in operation. ICA: SD0155.

CHERRY CREEK—Formerly served by Cheyenne River Sioux Tribe Telephone Authority. No longer in operation. ICA: SD0157.

CHESTER—Formerly served by Satellite Cable Services Inc. This cable system has converted to IPTV. Now served by ITC, CLEAR LAKE, SD [SD5042]. ICA: SD0158.

CLARK—Formerly served by Satellite Cable Services Inc. This cable system has converted to IPTV. Now served by ITC, CLEAR LAKE, SD [SD5042]. ICA: SD0160.

CLEAR LAKE—Formerly served by HD Electric Cooperative. No longer in operation. ICA: SD0227.

CLEAR LAKE—ITC. Formerly [SD0047]. This cable system has converted to IPTV, 312 Fourth St West, PO Box 920, Clear Lake, SD 57226. Phones: 800-417-8667; 605-874-2181. Fax: 605-874-2014. E-mail: info@itctel.com. Web Site: http://itc-web.com. Also serves Elkton & Hendricks, MN; Altamont, Astoria, Aurora, Bradley, Brandt, Brookings, Bryant, Bushnell, Castlewood, Chester, Clark, Crocker, Elkton, Estelline, Florence, Gary, Goodwin, Hayti, Henry, La Bolt, Lake Benton, Lake Norden, Milbank, Nunda, Raymond, Revillo, Rutland, Sinai, South Shore, Standburg, Stockholm, Toronto, Ward, Waubay, Webster, Wentworth, White & Willow Lake, SD. ICA: SD5042.
Channel capacity: N.A. Channels available but not in use: N.A.
Broadcast Basic
Subscribers: 5,423.
Fee: $42.95 monthly.
Best Seat Video
Subscribers: N.A.
Fee: $62.95 monthly.
Best Seat Premium
Subscribers: N.A.
Fee: $73.95 monthly.
HD
Subscribers: N.A.
Fee: $9.95 monthly.
Cinemax
Subscribers: N.A.
Fee: $13.95 monthly.
HBO
Subscribers: N.A.
Fee: $17.95 monthly.
NFL RedZone
Subscribers: N.A.
Fee: $49.95 per season.
Showtime/TMC
Subscribers: N.A.
Fee: $14.95 monthly.
Starz/Encore
Subscribers: N.A.
Fee: $12.95 monthly.
Internet Service
Operational: Yes.
Fee: $22.95-$124.95 monthly.
Telephone Service
Digital: Operational
Fee: $17.50 monthly
President: Penny Krause. General Manager: Jerry Heiberger.
Ownership: Interstate Telecommunications Cooperative Inc.

CLEAR LAKE—ITC. This cable system has converted to IPTV. See CLEAR LAKE, SD [SD5042]. ICA: SD0047.

COLMAN—Clarity Telecom. Now served by VIBORG, SD [SD0071]. ICA: SD0249.

COLMAN—Mediacom. Now served by BROOKINGS, SD [SD0005]. ICA: SD0093.

CONDE—Formerly served by Satellite Cable Services Inc. This cable system has converted to IPTV. Now served by James Valley Telecommunications, GROTON, SD [SD5005]. ICA: SD0163.

CORSICA—Golden West Telecommunications. Now served by FREEMAN, SD [SD0038]. ICA: SD0094.

CRESBARD—Venture Communications. Formerly [SD0245]. This cable system has converted to IPTV, 218 Commercial Ave SE, PO Box 157, Highmore, SD 57345-0157. Phones: 605-852-2224; 800-824-7282. Fax: 605-852-2404. E-mail: venture@venturecomm.net. Web Site: http://www.venturecomm.net. ICA: SD5104.
TV Market Ranking: Below 100 (CRESBARD). Channel capacity: N.A. Channels available but not in use: N.A.
Core
Subscribers: N.A.
Fee: $19.95 monthly.
Basic
Subscribers: 80.
Fee: $60.99 monthly.
Internet Service
Operational: Yes.
Fee: $40.95-$150.95 monthly.
General Manager: Randy Houdek. Assistant General Manager: Randy Olson. Chief Technician: Brad Ryan.
Ownership: Venture Communications Cooperative (MSO).

CRESBARD—Venture Communications. This cable system has converted to IPTV. See CRESBARD, SD [SD5104]. ICA: SD0245.

CUSTER—Golden West Telecommunications, 415 Crown St, PO Box 411, Wall, SD 57790-0411. Phones: 855-888-7777; 605-528-3211; 605-279-1020; 605-279-2161. Fax: 605-279-2727. E-mail: info@goldenwest.com. Web Site: http://www.goldenwest.com. Also serves Buffalo Gap, Custer County (unincorporated areas), Edgemont, Fall River County, Hill City, Hot Springs & Oelrichs. ICA: SD0034.

South Dakota—Cable Systems

TV Market Ranking: Below 100 (CUSTER, Custer County (unincorporated areas) (portions), Hill City); Outside TV Markets (Buffalo Gap, Custer County (unincorporated areas) (portions), Edgemont, Fall River County, Hot Springs, Oelrichs). Franchise award date: N.A. Franchise expiration date: N.A. Began: September 1, 1980.
Channel capacity: N.A. Channels available but not in use: N.A.

Basic Service
Subscribers: 2,403.
Programming (received off-air): KBHE-TV (PBS) Rapid City; KCLO-TV (CBS) Rapid City; KHME (MeTV, This TV) Rapid City; KKRA-LP (ION) Rapid City; KNBN (MNT, NBC) Rapid City; KOTA-TV (ABC, FOX) Rapid City; KWBH-LP (NBC) Rapid City; allband FM.
Programming (via satellite): A&E; AMC; Animal Planet; Cartoon Network; CMT; CNBC; CNN; Comedy Central; C-SPAN; Discovery Channel; Disney Channel; ESPN; ESPN2; EWTN Global Catholic Network; Fox News Channel; Fox Sports 1; Freeform; FX; HGTV; History; HLN; KWGN-TV (CW, This TV) Denver; Lifetime; MTV; Nickelodeon; Outdoor Channel; Pop; QVC; Root Sports Rocky Mountain; Spike TV; Syfy; TBS; The Weather Channel; TLC; TNT; Trinity Broadcasting Network (TBN); Turner Classic Movies; TV Land; USA Network; VH1; WE tv.
Fee: $29.95 installation; $23.57 monthly.

Digital Basic Service
Subscribers: N.A.
Programming (via satellite): BBC America; CMT; Destination America; Discovery Kids Channel; Fuse; History International; Investigation Discovery; LMN; MTV Classic; MTV Hits; MTV2; NFL Network; Nick Jr.; Nicktoons; OWN: Oprah Winfrey Network; Science Channel; Sundance TV; VH1 Soul.
Fee: $10.00 installation; $12.00 monthly.

Digital Pay Service 1
Pay Units: N.A.
Programming (via satellite): Cinemax (multiplexed); HBO (multiplexed); Showtime (multiplexed); Starz (multiplexed); Starz Encore (multiplexed); The Movie Channel (multiplexed).
Fee: $12.00 monthly (Cinemax, HBO, Showtime/TMC or Starz/Encore).

Video-On-Demand: No

Internet Service
Operational: Yes.
Broadband Service: In-house.
Fee: $19.95 monthly.

Telephone Service
Digital: Operational
Miles of Plant: 85.0 (coaxial); None (fiber optic). Homes passed: 3,928.
General Manager: George Strandell. Chief Technician: Randy Shepard. Marketing Director: Greg Oleson. Customer Service Manager: Jody Bielmaier. Cable Television Manager: Rick Reed.
Ownership: Golden West Cablevision (MSO).

DAKOTA DUNES—Long Lines. Now served by SALIX, IA [IA0510]. ICA: SD0253.

DELL RAPIDS—Golden West Telecommunications, 415 Crown St, PO Box 411, Wall, SD 57790-0411. Phones: 855-888-7777; 605-528-3211; 605-279-1020; 605-279-2161. Fax: 605-279-2727. E-mail: info@goldenwest.com. Web Site: http://www.goldenwest.com. Also serves Hartford, Humboldt, Minnehaha County, Montrose & Trent. ICA: SD0028.
TV Market Ranking: 85 (DELL RAPIDS, Hartford, Humboldt, Minnehaha County, Montrose, Trent). Franchise award date: August 1, 1982. Franchise expiration date: N.A. Began: August 1, 1982.
Channel capacity: N.A. Channels available but not in use: N.A.

Basic Service
Subscribers: 1,550.
Programming (received off-air): KDLT-TV (Antenna TV, NBC) Sioux Falls; KPLO-TV (CBS, MNT) Reliance; KPRY-TV (ABC) Pierre; KTTM (FOX, This TV) Huron; KUSD-TV (PBS) Vermillion.
Programming (via satellite): A&E; AMC; Animal Planet; Cartoon Network; CMT; CNBC; CNN; Comedy Central; C-SPAN; C-SPAN 2; Discovery Channel; Disney Channel; DIY Network; E! HD; ESPN; ESPN2; EWTN Global Catholic Network; Fox News Channel; Freeform; Great American Country; Hallmark Channel; HGTV; History; HLN; INSP; ION Television; Lifetime; MTV; National Geographic Channel; Nickelodeon; Outdoor Channel; OWN: Oprah Winfrey Network; QVC; Spike TV; Syfy; TBS; The Weather Channel; TLC; TNT; Travel Channel; TV Land; USA Network; VH1; WGN America.
Fee: $29.95 installation; $24.46 monthly.

Pay Service 1
Pay Units: N.A.
Programming (via satellite): HBO; Showtime; Starz Encore.
Fee: $2.30 monthly (Encore), $11.95 monthly (HBO or Showtime).

Video-On-Demand: No

Internet Service
Operational: No, DSL & dial-up.

Telephone Service
Digital: Operational
Miles of Plant: 106.0 (coaxial); 75.0 (fiber optic). Homes passed: 2,770.
General Manager: George Strandell. Chief Technician: Randy Shepard. Marketing Director: Greg Oleson. Customer Service Manager: Jody Bielmaier. Cable Television Manager: Rick Reed.
Ownership: Golden West Cablevision (MSO).

DELMONT—Midstate Communications. Now served by WHITE LAKE, SD [SD0026]. ICA: SD0141.

EAGLE BUTTE—Cheyenne River Sioux Tribe Telephone. This cable system has converted to IPTV. See EAGLE BUTTE, SD [SD5048]. ICA: SD0164.

EAGLE BUTTE—CRST Telephone Authority. Formerly [SD0164]. This cable system has converted to IPTV, 100 Main St, PO Box 39, Eagle Butte, SD 57625. Phones: 605-964-3307; 605-964-2600. Fax: 605-964-1000. E-mail: info@crstta.com. Web Site: http://www.crstta.com. Also serves Dupree. ICA: SD5048.
Channel capacity: N.A. Channels available but not in use: N.A.

Limited Basic
Subscribers: N.A.
Fee: $20.00 installation; $46.00 monthly. Includes 15 channels.

Expanded Basic
Subscribers: N.A.
Fee: $89.00 monthly. Includes 93 channels.

Variety
Subscribers: N.A.
Fee: $3.19 monthly. Includes 10 channels.

Hispanic
Subscribers: N.A.
Fee: $4.99 monthly. Includes 8 channels.

HD
Subscribers: N.A.
Fee: $4.75 monthly. Includes 13 channels.

Showtime/TMC
Subscribers: N.A.
Fee: $15.89 monthly. Includes 20 channels.

Starz/Encore
Subscribers: N.A.
Fee: $14.85 monthly. Includes 22 channels.

Internet Service
Operational: Yes.

Telephone Service
Digital: Operational
General Manager: J. D. Williams. Assistant General Manager: Mona Thompson.
Ownership: Cheyenne River Sioux Tribe Telephone Authority.

EDEN—Venture Communications Cooperative. This cable system has converted to IPTV. Now served by BRITTON, SD [SD5099]. ICA: SD0165.

EDGEMONT—Golden West Telecommunications. Now served by CUSTER, SD [SD0034]. ICA: SD0043.

EMERY—TrioTel Communications Inc. This system has converted to IPTV. Now served by SALEM, SD [SD5106]. ICA: SD0107.

ESTELLINE—Mediacom. Now served by BROOKINGS, SD [SD0005]. ICA: SD0076.

ETHAN—Santel Communications. Now served by WOONSOCKET, SD [SD5020]. ICA: SD5016.

ETHAN—Santel Communications. This cable system has converted to IPTV. Now served by WOONSOCKET, SD [SD5020]. ICA: SD0167.

EUREKA—Valley Telecommunications Coop. Assn. This cable system has converted to IPTV. Now served by HERREID, SD [SD5032]. ICA: SD0040.

EUREKA—Valley Telecommunications Coop. Assn. This cable system has converted to IPTV. Now served by HERREID, SD [SD5032]. ICA: SD5030.

FAIRFAX—Golden West Telecommunications. Now served by WINNER, SD [SD0021]. ICA: SD0169.

FAITH—West River Cable Television, 801 Coleman Ave, PO Box 39, Bison, SD 57620. Phones: 605-244-5213; 888-411-5651; 605-244-5236. Fax: 605-244-7288. E-mail: westriver@sdplains.com. Web Site: http://www.westrivercatv.com. ICA: SD0102.
TV Market Ranking: Outside TV Markets (FAITH). Franchise award date: April 1, 1986. Franchise expiration date: N.A. Began: March 1, 1983.
Channel capacity: N.A. Channels available but not in use: N.A.

Basic Service
Subscribers: 20.
Programming (received off-air): KCLO-TV (CBS) Rapid City; KHME (MeTV, This TV) Rapid City; KOTA-TV (ABC, FOX) Rapid City; KPSD-TV (PBS) Eagle Butte.
Programming (via microwave): KARE (NBC, WeatherNation) Minneapolis.
Programming (via satellite): A&E; AMC; Animal Planet; CMT; CNN; C-SPAN; Discovery Channel; Disney Channel; ESPN; ESPN2; Freeform; HGTV; Lifetime; Nickelodeon; Spike TV; TBS; The Weather Channel; TLC; TNT; USA Network; WGN America.
Fee: $50.00 installation; $55.95 monthly.

Pay Service 1
Pay Units: 9.
Programming (via satellite): HBO.
Fee: $10.00 monthly.

Internet Service
Operational: No.

Telephone Service
None
Miles of Plant: 6.0 (coaxial); 6.0 (fiber optic). Homes passed: 234.
General Manager: Jerry Reisonauer. Assistant Manager: Colgan Huber. Telecommunications Manager: Colle Nash.
Ownership: West River Cooperative Telephone Co. (MSO).

FAULKTON—Venture Communications. Formerly [SD0170]. This cable system has converted to IPTV, 218 Commercial Ave SE, PO Box 157, Highmore, SD 57345-0157. Phones: 800-824-7282; 605-852-2224. Fax: 605-598-4100. E-mail: venture@venturecomm.net. Web Site: http://www.venturecomm.net. Also serves Orient. ICA: SD5103.
TV Market Ranking: Outside TV Markets (FAULKTON, Orient). Franchise award date: N.A. Franchise expiration date: N.A. Began: February 1, 1981.
Channel capacity: N.A. Channels available but not in use: N.A.

Core
Subscribers: N.A.
Programming (received off-air): KABY-TV (ABC) Aberdeen; KDLO-TV (CBS, MNT) Florence; KDLT-TV (Antenna TV, NBC) Sioux Falls; KQSD-TV (PBS) Lowry; KTTM (FOX, This TV) Huron.
Programming (via satellite): C-SPAN; C-SPAN 2; EWTN Global Catholic Network; The Weather Channel; Trinity Broadcasting Network (TBN); WGN America.
Fee: $19.95 monthly.

Basic
Subscribers: 373.
Programming (via satellite): A&E; AMC; Animal Planet; Cartoon Network; CMT; CNN; Comedy Central; Discovery Channel; Disney Channel; E! HD; ESPN; ESPN2; Food Network; Fox News Channel; Fox Sports 1; FOX Sports Networks; Freeform; FX; Golf Channel; Hallmark Channel; HGTV; History; HLN; Lifetime; MTV; NBCSN; Nickelodeon; Spike TV; Syfy; TBS; TLC; TNT; Travel Channel; truTV; Turner Classic Movies; TV Land; USA Network; VH1.
Fee: $49.95 installation; $60.99 monthly.

Video-On-Demand: No

Internet Service
Operational: Yes.
Fee: $40.95-$150.95 monthly.

Telephone Service
Digital: Operational
General Manager: Randy Houdek. Assistant General Manager: Randy Olson. Chief Technician: Brad Ryan.
Ownership: Venture Communications Cooperative (MSO).

FAULKTON—Venture Communications. This cable system has converted to IPTV. See FAULKTON, SD [SD5103]. ICA: SD0170.

FLORENCE—Formerly served by Satellite Cable Services Inc. This cable system has converted to IPTV. Now served by ITC, CLEAR LAKE, SD [SD5042]. ICA: SD0171.

Cable Systems—South Dakota

FORT PIERRE—Midco, PO Box 5010, Sioux Falls, SD 57117. Phones: 800-456-0564; 605-223-9036 (Local office); 800-888-1300 (Customer service). Fax: 605-229-0478. Web Site: http://www.midcocomm.com. Also serves Pierre. ICA: SD0172.
TV Market Ranking: Below 100 (FORT PIERRE, Pierre). Franchise award date: June 17, 1985. Franchise expiration date: N.A. Began: N.A.
Channel capacity: N.A. Channels available but not in use: N.A.
Basic Service
Subscribers: 4,178.
Programming (received off-air): KDLT-TV (Antenna TV, NBC) Sioux Falls; KPLO-TV (CBS, MNT) Reliance; KPRY-TV (ABC) Pierre; KTSD-TV (PBS) Pierre; KTTW (FOX, This TV) Sioux Falls; 5 FMs.
Programming (via satellite): A&E; AMC; Animal Planet; Cartoon Network; CMT; CNBC; CNN; Comedy Central; C-SPAN; C-SPAN 2; Discovery Channel; Discovery Life Channel; Disney Channel; ESPN; ESPN Classic; ESPN2; ESPNews; EWTN Global Catholic Network; Food Network; Fox News Channel; Fox Sports 1; FOX Sports North; Freeform; FX; Hallmark Channel; HGTV; History; HLN; INSP; ION Television; Lifetime; MSNBC; MTV; NBCSN; Nickelodeon; Outdoor Channel; Pop; QVC; Spike TV; Syfy; TBS; The Weather Channel; TLC; TNT; Travel Channel; truTV; Turner Classic Movies; TV Land; USA Network; VH1; WE tv; WGN America.
Fee: $25.00 installation; $19.95 monthly.
Digital Basic Service
Subscribers: N.A.
Programming (via satellite): AXS TV; BBC America; Bloomberg Television; Discovery Digital Networks; Disney XD; DMX Music; ESPN; Fuse; FYI; Golf Channel; GSN; HD Theater; History International; IFC; LMN; Nick Jr.; Nicktoons; Sundance TV; TeenNick.
Fee: $9.00 monthly.
Digital Pay Service 1
Pay Units: N.A.
Programming (via satellite): Cinemax (multiplexed); HBO (multiplexed); Showtime (multiplexed); Showtime HD; Starz (multiplexed); Starz Encore (multiplexed); Starz HD (multiplexed); The Movie Channel (multiplexed).
Video-On-Demand: No
Pay-Per-View
Hot Choice (delivered digitally); iN DEMAND (delivered digitally); Sports PPV (delivered digitally).
Internet Service
Operational: Yes.
Subscribers: 4,088.
Broadband Service: MidcoNet.
Fee: $35.00 installation; $19.95 monthly; $10.00 modem lease; $39.00 modem purchase.
Telephone Service
Digital: Operational
Subscribers: 2,030.
Fee: $18.00 monthly
Miles of Plant: 130.0 (coaxial); 39.0 (fiber optic). Homes passed: 9,090.
General Manager: Lonnie Schumacher. Marketing Director: Fred Jamieson. Programming Director: Wynne Haakenstad. Customer Service Manager: Kathy Fuhrmann.
Ownership: Midcontinent Communications (MSO).; Comcast Cable Communications Inc. (MSO).

FRANKFORT—James Valley Telecommunications. This cable system has converted to IPTV. Now served by GROTON, SD [SD5005]. ICA: SD0173.

FREEMAN—Golden West Telecommunications, 415 Crown St, PO Box 411, Wall, SD 57790-0411. Phones: 855-888-7777; 605-528-3211; 605-279-1020; 605-279-2161. Fax: 605-279-2727. E-mail: info@goldenwest.com. Web Site: http://www.goldenwest.com. Also serves Armour, Avon, Bridgewater, Canistota, Corsica, Marion, Menno, Plankinton, Scotland & Springfield. ICA: SD0038.
TV Market Ranking: 85 (Armour, Bridgewater, Canistota, Corsica, Marion, Plankinton); Outside TV Markets (FREEMAN, Menno, Scotland, Avon, Springfield). Franchise award date: N.A. Franchise expiration date: N.A. Began: December 9, 1981.
Channel capacity: N.A. Channels available but not in use: N.A.
Basic Service
Subscribers: 2,304.
Programming (received off-air): KDLT-TV (Antenna TV, NBC) Sioux Falls; KELO-TV (CBS, MNT) Sioux Falls; KSFY-TV (ABC, CW) Sioux Falls; KTTW (FOX, This TV) Sioux Falls; KUSD-TV (PBS) Vermillion; KWSD (MeTV, Retro TV) Sioux Falls.
Programming (via satellite): CNN; C-SPAN; Freeform; ION Television; Pop; QVC; WGN America.
Fee: $29.95 installation; $24.46 monthly.
Expanded Basic Service 1
Subscribers: N.A.
Programming (via satellite): A&E; AMC; Animal Planet; Bravo; Cartoon Network; CMT; CNBC; Comedy Central; C-SPAN 2; Discovery Channel; Discovery Life Channel; Disney Channel; Disney XD; E! HD; Enlace USA; ESPN; ESPN2; Food Network; Fox News Channel; Fox Sports 1; FX; Hallmark Channel; HGTV; History; HLN; INSP; Lifetime; MSNBC; MTV; Nickelodeon; RFD-TV; Spike TV; Syfy; TBS; The Weather Channel; TLC; TNT; Travel Channel; truTV; Turner Classic Movies; TV Land; Univision Studios; USA Network; VH1; WE tv.
Fee: $32.45 monthly.
Digital Basic Service
Subscribers: N.A.
Programming (received off-air): KSFY-TV (ABC, CW) Sioux Falls.
Programming (via satellite): BBC America; Destination America; Discovery Kids Channel; DMX Music; ESPNews; Fuse; FXM; FYI; Golf Channel; GSN; History International; IFC; INSP; Investigation Discovery; LMN; MTV Classic; MTV Hits; MTV2; National Geographic Channel; Nick Jr.; Nicktoons; Outdoor Channel; OWN: Oprah Winfrey Network; TeenNick.
Fee: $12.00 monthly.
Digital Pay Service 1
Pay Units: N.A.
Programming (via satellite): Cinemax (multiplexed); HBO (multiplexed); HITS (Head-end In The Sky); Showtime (multiplexed); Starz (multiplexed); Starz Encore (multiplexed); The Movie Channel (multiplexed).
Video-On-Demand: No
Pay-Per-View
ESPN; Fresh (delivered digitally); Shorteez (delivered digitally); Playboy TV (delivered digitally); Pleasure (delivered digitally).
Internet Service
Operational: Yes.
Broadband Service: Mediacom High Speed Internet.
Fee: $29.95 monthly; $10.00 modem lease.
Telephone Service
Analog: Not Operational
Digital: Operational
Miles of Plant: 129.0 (coaxial); 368.0 (fiber optic). Homes passed: 4,366.

Vice President: Bill Jensen. Vice President, Financial Reporting: Kenneth J. Kohrs. General Manager: Ron Albritton. Cable TV Director: Rick Reed.
Ownership: Golden West Cablevision (MSO).

GARRETSON—Alliance Communications, 612 3rd St, PO Box 349, Garretson, SD 57030-0349. Phones: 800-701-4980; 800-842-8160. Fax: 605-594-6776. E-mail: email@alliancecom.net. Web Site: http://www.alliancecable.net. Also serves Inwood & Larchwood, IA; Hills, MN; Alcester, Baltic, Brandon, Corson, Crooks, Hudson, Sherman & Valley Springs, SD. ICA: SD0016.
TV Market Ranking: 85 (Brandon, Corson). Franchise award date: N.A. Franchise expiration date: N.A. Began: December 10, 1981.
Channel capacity: 41 (not 2-way capable). Channels available but not in use: N.A.
Basic Service
Subscribers: 7,924 Includes IPTV subscribers.
Programming (received off-air): KDLT-TV (Antenna TV, NBC) Sioux Falls; KELO-TV (CBS, MNT) Sioux Falls; KSFY-TV (ABC, CW) Sioux Falls; KTTW (FOX, This TV) Sioux Falls; KUSD-TV (PBS) Vermillion.
Programming (via satellite): A&E; AMC; Animal Planet; Bloomberg Television; Bravo; BTN; Cartoon Network; CMT; CNN; Comedy Central; C-SPAN; Discovery Channel; Disney Channel; ESPN; ESPN Classic; ESPN2; EWTN Global Catholic Network; Food Network; Fox News Channel; Fox Sports 1; FOX Sports Networks; Freeform; FX; Golf Channel; Great American Country; Hallmark Channel; HGTV; History; HLN; ION Television; Lifetime; LWS Local Weather Station; MTV; MyNetworkTV; National Geographic Channel; NFL Network; Nickelodeon; Outdoor Channel; QVC; Spike TV; Syfy; TBS; The Weather Channel; TLC; TNT; Travel Channel; truTV; Turner Classic Movies; TV Land; USA Network; VH1; WGN America.
Fee: $51.00 installation; $37.95 monthly.
Video-On-Demand: No
Internet Service
Operational: Yes.
Telephone Service
Digital: Operational
Subscribers: 4,908.
Fee: $14.00 monthly
Miles of Plant: None (coaxial); 1,960.0 (fiber optic).
General Manager: Don Snyders.
Ownership: Alliance Communications.

GARY—Formerly served by Satellite Cable Services Inc. Now served by ITC, CLEAR LAKE, SD [SD5042]. ICA: SD0174.

GEDDES—Midstate Communications. Now served by WHITE LAKE, SD [SD0026]. ICA: SD0175.

GETTYSBURG—Venture Communications. Formerly [SD0036]. This cable system has converted to IPTV, 218 Commercial Ave SE, PO Box 157, Highmore, SD 57345-0157. Phones: 800-824-7282; 605-852-2224. Fax: 605-852-2404. E-mail: venture@venturecomm.net. Web Site: http://www.venturecomm.net. Also serves Agar, Akaska, Bowdle (rural), Java (rural), Lebanon, Roscoe (rural) & Selby (rural). ICA: SD5023.
Channel capacity: N.A. Channels available but not in use: N.A.
Core
Subscribers: N.A.
Fee: $19.95 monthly.
Basic
Subscribers: 653.
Fee: $60.99 monthly.
Internet Service
Operational: Yes.
Fee: $40.95-$150.95 monthly.
Telephone Service
Digital: Operational
General Manager: Randy Houdek. Assistant General Manager: Randy Olson. Chief Technician: Brad Ryan.
Ownership: Venture Communications Cooperative.

GETTYSBURG—Venture Communications. This cable system has converted to IPTV. See GETTYSBURG, SD [SD5023]. ICA: SD0036.

GLENHAM—Valley Telecommunications Coop. Assn. This cable system has converted to IPTV. Now served by HERREID, SD [SD5032]. ICA: SD5031.

GLENHAM—Valley Telecommunications Coop. Assn. This cable system has converted to IPTV. Now served by HERREID, SD [SD5032]. ICA: SD0143.

GREGORY—Golden West Telecommunications. Now served by WINNER, SD [SD0021]. ICA: SD0042.

GROTON—James Valley Telecommunications. Formerly [SD0030]. This cable system has converted to IPTV, 235 East 1st Ave, PO Box 260, Groton, SD 57445. Phones: 800-556-6525; 605-397-2323. Fax: 605-397-2350. E-mail: jvinfo@jamesvalley.com. Web Site: http://www.jamesvalley.com. Also serves Andover, Brentford, Chelsea, Claremont, Columbia, Conde, Ferney, Frankfort, Hecla, Houghton, Mansfield, Mellette, Northville, Redfield, Stratford & Turton. ICA: SD5005.
TV Market Ranking: Below 100 (GROTON). Channel capacity: N.A. Channels available but not in use: N.A.
Local TV
Subscribers: 2,652.
Fee: $4.95 monthly.
Family View
Subscribers: N.A.
Fee: $60.95 monthly.
Expanded View
Subscribers: N.A.
Fee: $67.95 monthly.
Cinemax
Subscribers: N.A.
Fee: $16.95 monthly.

ADVANCED TVFactbook

FULLY SEARCHABLE • CONTINUOUSLY UPDATED • DISCOUNT RATES FOR PRINT PURCHASERS

For more information call **800-771-9202** or visit **www.warren-news.com**

South Dakota—Cable Systems

HBO
  Subscribers: N.A.
  Fee: $16.95 monthly.
NFL RedZone
  Subscribers: N.A.
  Fee: $39.95 per season.
Playboy
  Subscribers: N.A.
  Fee: $13.95 monthly.
Showtime/TMC/Flix
  Subscribers: N.A.
  Fee: $16.95 monthly.
Starz/Encore
  Subscribers: N.A.
  Fee: $16.95 monthly.
Internet Service
  Operational: Yes.
  Fee: $43.95-$53.95 monthly.
Telephone Service
  Digital: Operational
  Fee: $17.00-$21.45 monthly
Chief Executive Officer: James Groft. Chief Financial Officer: Tanya Berndt. Officer & Customer Service Manager: Nancy Larsen. IT Manager: Jason Hill. Assistant Plant Operations Manager: Pat Schumacher.
Ownership: James Valley Telecommunications.

GROTON—James Valley Telecommunications. This cable system has converted to IPTV. Now served by GROTON, SD [SD5005]. ICA: SD0030.

HART RANCH—Midco. Now served by RAPID CITY, SD [SD0002]. ICA: SD0251.

HARTFORD—Golden West Telecommunications. Now served by DELL RAPIDS, SD [SD0028]. ICA: SD0057.

HAYTI—Mediacom. Now served by BROOKINGS, SD [SD0005]. ICA: SD0120.

HENRY—Formerly served by Satellite Cable Services Inc. Now served by ITC, CLEAR LAKE, SD [SD5042]. ICA: SD0176.

HERREID—Valley Telecommunications Coop. Assn. Formerly [SD0091]. This cable system has converted to IPTV, 102 Main St S, PO Box 7, Herreid, SD 57632-0007. Phones: 800-437-2615; 605-437-2615. Fax: 605-437-2200. E-mail: valley@valleytel.net. Web Site: http://www.valleytel.net. Also serves Eureka, Glenham, Hosmer, Leola, Mound City & Pollock. ICA: SD5032.
Channel capacity: N.A. Channels available but not in use: N.A.
Economy
  Subscribers: N.A.
  Fee: $32.99 monthly. Includes 16 channels.
Basic
  Subscribers: 1,344.
  Fee: $70.00 installation; $46.99 monthly. Includes 91 channels.
Expanded Basic
  Subscribers: N.A.
  Fee: $50.99 monthly. Includes 140 channels plus 50 music channels.
HD
  Subscribers: N.A.
  Fee: $14.99 monthly. Includes 74 channels.
Cinemax
  Subscribers: N.A.
  Fee: $12.99 monthly. Includes 4 channels.
HBO
  Subscribers: N.A.
  Fee: $15.99 monthly. Includes 5 channels.
NFL RedZone
  Subscribers: N.A.
  Fee: $5.95 monthly per season.

Playboy
  Subscribers: N.A.
  Fee: $16.99 monthly.
Showtime/TMC/Flix
  Subscribers: N.A.
  Fee: $12.99 monthly. Includes 10 channels.
Starz/Encore
  Subscribers: N.A.
  Fee: $12.99 monthly. Includes 11 channels.
Internet Service
  Operational: Yes.
  Fee: $42.50-$84.99 monthly.
Telephone Service
  Digital: Operational
  Fee: $16.00 monthly
Chief Executive Officer & General Manager: Darin T. LaCoursiere.
Ownership: Valley Telecommunications Cooperative Association.

HERREID—Valley Telecommunications Coop. Assn. This cable system has converted to IPTV. Now served by HERREID, SD [SD5032]. ICA: SD0091.

HIGHMORE—Venture Communications. This cable system has converted to IPTV., 218 Commercial Ave SE, PO Box 157, Highmore, SD 57345-0157. Phones: 800-824-7282; 605-852-2224. Fax: 605-852-2404. E-mail: venture@venturecomm.net. Web Site: http://www.venturecomm.net. Also serves Blunt, Harrold, Hitchcock, Holabird, Hoven, Onaka, Ree Heights, Seneca, Stephan, Tolstoy, Tulare & Wessington. ICA: SD5022.
Channel capacity: N.A. Channels available but not in use: N.A.
Core
  Subscribers: N.A.
  Fee: $19.95 monthly.
Basic
  Subscribers: 1,496.
  Fee: $60.99 monthly.
Internet Service
  Operational: Yes.
  Fee: $40.95-$150.95 monthly.
Telephone Service
  Digital: Operational
General Manager: Randy Houdek. Assistant General Manager: Randy Olson. Chief Technician: Brad Ryan.
Ownership: Venture Communications Cooperative.

HILL CITY—Golden West Telecommunications. Now served by CUSTER, SD [SD0034]. ICA: SD0088.

HOSMER—Valley Telecommunications Coop. Assn. This cable system has converted to IPTV. Now served by HERREID, SD [SD5032]. ICA: SD0117.

HOT SPRINGS—Golden West Telecommunications. Now served by CUSTER, SD [SD0034]. ICA: SD0018.

HOVEN—Venture Communications Cooperative. This cable system has converted to IPTV. Now served by HIGHMORE, SD [SD5022]. ICA: SD0082.

HOWARD—Alliance Communications. Formerly [SD0052]. This cable system has converted to IPTV, 290 Broadview, Greenbriar, AR 72058. Phones: 800-842-8160; 605-594-3411. Fax: 605-594-6776. E-mail: email@alliancecom.net. Web Site: http://www.alliancecable.net. Also serves Carthage, Oldham & Ramona. ICA: SD5082.
Channel capacity: N.A. Channels available but not in use: N.A.
Basic Choice
  Subscribers: 880.
  Fee: $51.00 installation; $33.95 monthly. Includes 77 channels.
Elite Choice
  Subscribers: 335.
  Fee: $46.95 monthly. Includes 126 channels plus music channels.
HD
  Subscribers: N.A.
  Fee: $8.00 monthly. Includes 74 channels.
Cinemax
  Subscribers: N.A.
  Fee: $9.95 monthly. Includes 4 channels.
HBO
  Subscribers: N.A.
  Fee: $16.95 monthly. Includes 5 channels.
Showtime
  Subscribers: N.A.
  Fee: $13.95 monthly. Includes 10 channels.
Starz/Encore
  Subscribers: N.A.
  Fee: $9.95 monthly. Includes 12 channels.
Internet Service
  Operational: Yes.
  Fee: $14.95-$199.95 monthly.
Telephone Service
  Digital: Operational
  Fee: $14.00 monthly
General Manager: Don Snyder.
Ownership: Alliance Communications.

HOWARD—Alliance Communications. This cable system has converted to IPTV. See HOWARD, SD [SD5082]. ICA: SD0052.

HUDSON—Alliance Communications. Now served by GARRETSON, SD [SD0016]. ICA: SD0254.

HUDSON—Formerly served by Sioux Valley Wireless. Now served by Alliance Communications, GARRETSON, SD [SD0016]. ICA: SD0142.

HURON—Midco, PO Box 5010, Sioux Falls, SD 57117. Phones: 800-888-1300; 605-352-4302. Fax: 605-352-2413. Web Site: http://www.midcocomm.com. Also serves Beadle County (portions), Miller, St. Lawrence & Wolsey. ICA: SD0006.
TV Market Ranking: Below 100 (HURON, Wolsey); Outside TV Markets (Beadle County (portions), Miller, St. Lawrence). Franchise award date: December 1, 1984. Franchise expiration date: N.A. Began: December 1, 1968.
Channel capacity: N.A. Channels available but not in use: N.A.
Basic Service
  Subscribers: 3,793.
  Programming (received off-air): KABY-TV (ABC) Aberdeen; KDLO-TV (CBS, MNT) Florence; KDLT-TV (Antenna TV, NBC) Sioux Falls; KELO-TV (CBS, MNT) Sioux Falls; KESD-TV (PBS) Brookings; KTTM (FOX, This TV) Huron; KWSD (MeTV, Retro TV) Sioux Falls; 5 FMs.
  Programming (via satellite): A&E; AMC; Animal Planet; BET; Bravo; Cartoon Network; CMT; CNBC; CNN; Comedy Central; C-SPAN; C-SPAN 2; Discovery Channel; Discovery Life Channel; Disney Channel; E! HD; ESPN; ESPN Classic; ESPN2; ESPNews; EWTN Global Catholic Network; Food Network; Fox News Channel; Fox Sports 1; FOX Sports North; Freeform; FX; FXM; Hallmark Channel; HGTV; History; HLN; INSP; ION Television; Lifetime; MSNBC; MTV; NBCSN; Nickelodeon; Outdoor Channel; OWN: Oprah Winfrey Network; Pop; QVC; Spike TV; Syfy; TBS; The Weather Channel; TLC; TNT; Travel Channel; Trinity Broadcasting Network (TBN); truTV; Turner Classic Movies; TV Land; USA Network; VH1; WE tv; WGN America.
  Fee: $50.00 installation; $19.95 monthly.
Digital Basic Service
  Subscribers: N.A.
  Programming (via satellite): AXS TV; BBC America; Bloomberg Television; Discovery Digital Networks; Disney XD; DMX Music; ESPN; Fuse; FYI; Golf Channel; GSN; HD Theater; History International; IFC; LMN; Nick Jr.; Nicktoons; Sundance TV; Teen-Nick.
Digital Pay Service 1
  Pay Units: N.A.
  Programming (via satellite): Cinemax (multiplexed); Cinemax HD; HBO (multiplexed); HBO HD; Showtime (multiplexed); Showtime HD; Starz (multiplexed); Starz Encore (multiplexed); Starz HD; The Movie Channel (multiplexed).
Video-On-Demand: No
Pay-Per-View
  iN DEMAND (delivered digitally); NFL Network (delivered digitally); ESPN Sports PPV (delivered digitally); NBA TV (delivered digitally); MLS Direct Kick (delivered digitally); NHL Center Ice (delivered digitally); MLB Extra Innings (delivered digitally).
Internet Service
  Operational: Yes. Began: June 1, 1998.
  Broadband Service: MidcoNet.
  Fee: $35.00 installation; $19.95 monthly.
Telephone Service
  Digital: Operational
  Fee: $18.00 monthly
Miles of Plant: 114.0 (coaxial); None (fiber optic). Homes passed: 8,362.
General Manager: Lonnie Schumacher. Programming Director: Wynne Haakenstad. Marketing Director: Fred Jamieson. Customer Service Manager: Kathy Fuhrmann.
Ownership: Midcontinent Communications (MSO).; Comcast Cable Communications Inc. (MSO).

IROQUOIS—Formerly served by Midcontinent Communications. No longer in operation. ICA: SD0128.

JEFFERSON—Formerly served by Jefferson Satellite Telecommunications Inc. Now served by Long Lines, SALIX, IA [IA0510]. ICA: SD0179.

KENNEBEC—Kennebec Telephone Co. Inc, 220 South Main St, PO Box 158, Kennebec, SD 57544-0158. Phones: 888-868-3390; 605-869-2220. Fax: 605-869-2221. E-mail: knbctel@kennebectelephone.com. Web Site: http://www.kennebectelephone.com. Also serves Presho. ICA: SD0130.
TV Market Ranking: Below 100 (KENNEBEC, Presho). Franchise award date: April 1, 1980. Franchise expiration date: N.A. Began: November 1, 1982.
Channel capacity: N.A. Channels available but not in use: N.A.
Basic Service
  Subscribers: 169. Commercial subscribers: 12.
  Programming (received off-air): KDLT-TV (Antenna TV, NBC) Sioux Falls; KOTA-TV (ABC, FOX) Rapid City; KPLO-TV (CBS, MNT) Reliance; KPRY-TV (ABC) Pierre; KTSD-TV (PBS) Pierre.

Cable Systems—South Dakota

Programming (via microwave): KARE (NBC, WeatherNation) Minneapolis.
Programming (via satellite): A&E; AMC; Animal Planet; Cartoon Network; CMT; CNBC; CNN; Comedy Central; C-SPAN; C-SPAN 2; CW PLUS; Discovery Channel; Disney Channel; ESPN; ESPN2; ESPNews; EWTN Global Catholic Network; Food Network; Fox News Channel; Freeform; FX; Great American Country; Hallmark Channel; HGTV; History; HLN; INSP; ION Television; Lifetime; Local Cable Weather; MTV; Nickelodeon; QVC; RFD-TV; Spike TV; TBS; The Weather Channel; TLC; TNT; Trinity Broadcasting Network (TBN); Turner Classic Movies; TV Land; USA Network; VH1; WGN America.
Fee: $45.00 installation; $45.95 monthly.
Pay Service 1
Pay Units: N.A.
Programming (via satellite): Cinemax; HBO; Showtime; The Movie Channel.
Fee: $9.95 monthly (Cinemax, Showtime or TMC), $13.95 monthly (HBO).
Video-On-Demand: No
Internet Service
Operational: No, DSL & dial-up.
Telephone Service
Analog: Operational
Miles of Plant: 17.0 (coaxial); None (fiber optic). Homes passed: 444.
President & General Manager: Rod Bowar. Plant Manager: Matt Collins. Office Manager: Trusty Mertens. Marketing Manager: Jason Thiry.
Ownership: Kennebec Telephone Co. Inc.

KIMBALL—Midstate Communications. Now served by WHITE LAKE, SD [SD0026]. ICA: SD0077.

LAKE ANDES—Formerly served by Satellite Cable Services Inc. Now served by Fort Randall Cable, TRIPP, SD [SD0087]. ICA: SD0072.

LAKE NORDEN—Mediacom. Now served by BROOKINGS, SD [SD0005]. ICA: SD0114.

LANGFORD—Venture Communications Cooperative. This cable system has converted to IPTV. Now served by BRITTON, SD [SD5099]. ICA: SD0095.

LEMMON—West River Cable Television. Now served by BISON, SD [SD0103]. ICA: SD0033.

LEOLA—Valley Telecommunications Coop. Assn. This cable system has converted to IPTV. Now served by HERREID, SD [SD5032]. ICA: SD5034.

LEOLA—Valley Telecommunications Coop. Assn. This cable system has converted to IPTV. Now served by HERREID, SD [SD5032]. ICA: SD0065.

LETCHER—Santel Communications. Now served by WOONSOCKET, SD [SD5020]. ICA: SD5017.

LOWER BRULE—Golden West Telecommunications. Now served by WINNER, SD [SD0021]. ICA: SD0247.

McINTOSH—West River Cable Television. Now served by BISON, SD [SD0103]. ICA: SD0138.

MCLAUGHLIN—Formerly served by West River Cable Television. No longer in operation. ICA: SD0185.

MELLETTE—Formerly served by Satellite Cable Services Inc. This cable system has converted to IPTV. Now served by James Valley Telecommunications, GROTON, SD [SD5005]. ICA: SD0086.

MISSION TWP.—Golden West Telecommunications. Now served by WINNER, SD [SD0021]. ICA: SD0048.

MITCHELL—Midco, PO Box 5010, Sioux Falls, SD 57117. Phones: 800-456-0564; 605-229-1775; 800-888-1300. Fax: 605-996-6821. Web Site: http://www.midcocomm.com. ICA: SD0007.
TV Market Ranking: 85 (MITCHELL). Franchise award date: N.A. Franchise expiration date: N.A. Began: January 1, 1952.
Channel capacity: N.A. Channels available but not in use: N.A.
Basic Service
Subscribers: 2,448.
Programming (received off-air): KDLT-TV (Antenna TV, NBC) Sioux Falls; KELO-TV (CBS, MNT) Sioux Falls; KESD-TV (PBS) Brookings; KSFY-TV (ABC, CW) Sioux Falls; KTTM (FOX, This TV) Huron; KWSD (MeTV, Retro TV) Sioux Falls.
Programming (via satellite): A&E; AMC; Animal Planet; BET; Bravo; Cartoon Network; CMT; CNBC; CNN; Comedy Central; C-SPAN; C-SPAN 2; Discovery Channel; Disney Channel; E! HD; ESPN; ESPN Classic; ESPN2; ESPNews; EWTN Global Catholic Network; Food Network; Fox News Channel; Fox Sports 1; FOX Sports Networks; Freeform; FX; HGTV; History; HLN; INSP; Lifetime; MSNBC; MTV; NBCSN; Nickelodeon; Outdoor Channel; OWN: Oprah Winfrey Network; Pop; QVC; Spike TV; Syfy; TBS; The Weather Channel; TLC; TNT; Travel Channel; truTV; Turner Classic Movies; TV Land; USA Network; VH1; WE tv; WGN America.
Fee: $30.00 installation; $19.95 monthly.
Digital Basic Service
Subscribers: N.A.
Programming (via satellite): BBC America; Bloomberg Television; Discovery Digital Networks; Disney XD; DMX Music; ESPNews; FYI; Golf Channel; GSN; History; IFC; LMN; Nick Jr.; Sundance TV; TeenNick.
Digital Pay Service 1
Pay Units: N.A.
Programming (via satellite): Cinemax; HBO (multiplexed); Showtime; Starz; Starz Encore; The Movie Channel.
Video-On-Demand: No
Pay-Per-View
iN DEMAND (delivered digitally); Sports PPV (delivered digitally).
Internet Service
Operational: Yes.
Broadband Service: MidcoNet.
Fee: $35.00 installation; $19.95 monthly; $10.00 modem lease.
Telephone Service
Digital: Operational
Fee: $18.00 monthly
Miles of Plant: 81.0 (coaxial); 14.0 (fiber optic). Homes passed: 8,013.
General Manager & Chief Technician: George Bosak. Programming Director: Wynne Haakenstad. Marketing Director: Mark Powell.
Ownership: Midcontinent Communications (MSO).; Comcast Cable Communications Inc. (MSO).

MITCHELL—Mitchell Telecom. Formerly [SD0256]. This cable system has converted to IPTV, 1801 North Main St, Mitchell, SD 57301. Phone: 605-990-1000. Fax: 605-990-1010. E-mail: info@mitchelltelecom.com. Web Site: http://www.mitchelltelecom.com. ICA: SD5105.
TV Market Ranking: 85 (MITCHELL).
Channel capacity: N.A. Channels available but not in use: N.A.
Basic TV
Subscribers: 1,737.
Fee: $54.95 monthly.
Digital TV
Subscribers: N.A.
Fee: $64.95 monthly.
Cinemax
Subscribers: N.A.
Fee: $16.95 monthly.
HBO
Subscribers: N.A.
Fee: $16.95 monthly.
Showtime/TMC
Subscribers: N.A.
Fee: $16.95 monthly.
Starz/Encore
Subscribers: N.A.
Fee: $16.95 monthly.
Internet Service
Operational: Yes.
Fee: $19.95-$42.95 monthly.
Telephone Service
Digital: Operational
Fee: $24.95 monthly
Chief Executive Officer & General Manager: Ryan Thompsn.
Ownership: Mitchell Telecom.

MITCHELL—Mitchell Telecom. This cable system has converted to IPTV. See MITCHELL, SD [SD5105]. ICA: SD0256.

MOBRIDGE—Midcontinent Communications. Now served by ABERDEEN, SD [SD0003]. ICA: SD0186.

MONROE—Formerly served by Sioux Valley Wireless. No longer in operation. ICA: SD0187.

MONTROSE—Golden West Telecommunications. Now served by DELL RAPIDS, SD [SD0028]. ICA: SD0224.

MOUND CITY—Valley Telecommunications Coop. Assn. This cable system has converted to IPTV. Now served by HERREID, SD [SD5032]. ICA: SD5035.

MOUNT VERNON—Santel Communications. This cable system has converted to IPTV. Now served by WOONSOCKET, SD [SD5020]. ICA: SD0188.

MOUNT VERNON—Santel Communications. This cable system has converted to IPTV. Now served by WOONSOCKET, SD [SD5020]. ICA: SD5013.

NEW EFFINGTON—RC Technologies. Formerly [SD018]. This cable system has converted to IPTV, 1018 6th St SE, Watertown, SD 57201. Phones: 800-256-6854; 605-637-5211. Fax: 605-637-5302.
E-mail: rctv@tnics.com. Web Site: http://www.tnics.com. Also serves Claire City, Veblen & Wilmot. ICA: SD5067.
TV Market Ranking: Outside TV Markets (NEW EFFINGTON, Veblen).
Channel capacity: N.A. Channels available but not in use: N.A.
Local
Subscribers: 249.
Programming (received off-air): KDLT-TV (Antenna TV, NBC) Sioux Falls; KDSD-TV (PBS) Aberdeen; KELO-TV (CBS, MNT) Sioux Falls; KSFY-TV (ABC, CW) Sioux Falls; KTTW (FOX, This TV) Sioux Falls; KVRR (Antenna TV, FOX) Fargo.
Programming (via satellite): The Weather Channel; WGN America.
Fee: $29.95 installation; $29.95 monthly. Includes 28 channels.
Basic
Subscribers: 195.
Programming (via satellite): A&E; Animal Planet; Bloomberg Television; Bravo; Cartoon Network; CNBC; CNN; Comedy Central; C-SPAN; C-SPAN 2; Discovery Channel; Disney XD; DIY Network; DMX Music; E! HD; ESPN; ESPN Classic; ESPN2; ESPNews; EWTN Global Catholic Network; Food Network; Fox News Channel; Fox Sports 1; FOX Sports North; Freeform; FX; FXM; Great American Country; GSN; Hallmark Channel; HGTV; History; HLN; Lifetime; LMN; MSNBC; MTV; National Geographic Channel; Nickelodeon; Outdoor Channel; Oxygen; RFD-TV; Spike TV; Syfy; TBS; TLC; TNT; truTV; Turner Classic Movies; TV Land; USA Network; VH1.
Fee: $75.00 monthly. Includes 87 channels plus music channels.
Expanded
Subscribers: N.A.
Programming (via satellite): Nick Jr.; Teen-Nick.
Fee: $14.95 monthly. Includes 41 channels.
HD
Subscribers: N.A.
Fee: $9.95 monthly. Includes 77 channels.
Bang U
Subscribers: N.A.
Fee: $12.95 monthly. Includes 1 channel.
Cinemax
Subscribers: N.A.
Fee: $14.95 monthly. Includes 4 channels.
HBO
Subscribers: N.A.
Programming (via satellite): HBO (multiplexed).
Fee: $18.95 monthly. Includes 5 channels.
NFL RedZone
Subscribers: N.A.
Fee: $59.95 per season.
Playboy
Subscribers: N.A.
Fee: $12.95 monthly. Includes 1 channel.
Showtime/TMC
Subscribers: N.A.
Fee: $16.95 monthly. Includes 10 channels.
Starz/Starz Encore
Subscribers: N.A.
Programming (via satellite): Starz (multiplexed); Starz Encore (multiplexed).

2017 Edition
D-699

South Dakota—Cable Systems

Fee: $14.95 monthly. Includes 10 channels.
Video-On-Demand: No
Internet Service
  Operational: Yes.
Telephone Service
  Digital: Operational
General Manager: Scott Bostrom. Operations Manager: Colin Bronson. Sales & Marketing Manager: Sara Broz. IT Manager: Paul Gravdahl. Billing & Customer Care Manager: Wanda Heesch.
Ownership: RC Technologies Corp. (MSO).

NEW EFFINGTON—RC Technologies. This cable system has converted to IPTV. See NEW EFFINGTON, SD [SD5064]. ICA: SD0189.

NEWELL—Formerly served by West River Cable Television. No longer in operation. ICA: SD0078.

OACOMA—Midstate Communications. Now served by WHITE LAKE, SD [SD0026]. ICA: SD0135.

OELRICHS—Golden West Telecommunications. Now served by CUSTER, SD [SD0034]. ICA: SD0190.

OLDHAM—Alliance Communications. This cable system has converted to IPTV. Now served by HOWARD, SD [SD5082]. ICA: SD0191.

ONIDA—Venture Communications. Formerly [SD0092]. This cable system has converted to IPTV, 218 Commercial Ave SE, PO Box 157, Highmore, SD 57345-0157. Phones: 800-824-7282; 605-852-2224. Fax: 605-852-2404. E-mail: venture@venturecomm.net. Web Site: http://www.venturecomm.net. ICA: SD5024.
Channel capacity: N.A. Channels available but not in use: N.A.
Core
  Subscribers: N.A.
  Fee: $19.95 monthly.
Basic
  Subscribers: 426.
  Fee: $60.99 monthly.
Internet Service
  Operational: Yes.
  Fee: $40.95-$150.95 monthly.
Telephone Service
  Digital: Operational
General Manager: Randy Houdek. Assistant General Manager: Randy Olson. Chief Technician: Brad Ryan.
Ownership: Venture Communications Cooperative.

ONIDA—Venture Communications. This cable system has converted to IPTV. See ONIDA, SD [SD5024]. ICA: SD0092.

PARKSTON—Santel Communications. This cable system has converted to IPTV. Now served by WOONSOCKET, SD [SD5020]. ICA: SD5018.

PICKSTOWN—Formerly served by Satellite Cable Services Inc. Now served by Fort Randall Cable, TRIPP, SD [SD0087]. ICA: SD0193.

PIERPONT—Venture Communications Cooperative. This cable system has converted to IPTV. Now served by BRITTON, SD [SD5099]. ICA: SD0194.

PINE RIDGE—Golden West Telecommunications, 415 Crown St, PO Box 411, Wall, SD 57790-0411. Phones: 855-888-7777; 605-528-3211; 605-867-1166. Fax: 605-279-2727. E-mail: info@goldenwest.com. Web Site: http://www.goldenwest.com. Also serves Evergreen Housing, Horse Creek, Kyle, Manderson, Martin & Wanblee. ICA: SD0037.
TV Market Ranking: Below 100 (Evergreen Housing); Outside TV Markets (Kyle, Manderson, Martin, PINE RIDGE, Wanblee).
Channel capacity: 52 (2-way capable). Channels available but not in use: N.A.
Basic Service
  Subscribers: 1,219.
  Programming (received off-air): KBHE-TV (PBS) Rapid City; KELO-TV (CBS, MNT) Sioux Falls; KHME (MeTV, This TV) Rapid City; KNBN (MNT, NBC) Rapid City; KOTA-TV (ABC, FOX) Rapid City.
  Programming (via satellite): A&E; Animal Planet; Cartoon Network; CNN; Discovery Channel; ESPN; ESPN2; ESPNews; Freeform; FX; Great American Country; History; HLN; Lifetime; MTV; Nickelodeon; QVC; Spike TV; Sundance TV; Syfy; TBS; TLC; TNT; Trinity Broadcasting Network (TBN); TV Land; USA Network; VH1; WGN America.
  Fee: $29.95 installation; $23.57 monthly.
Pay Service 1
  Pay Units: N.A.
  Programming (via satellite): Cinemax; HBO; Showtime (multiplexed); The Movie Channel.
  Fee: $10.00 monthly.
Video-On-Demand: No
Internet Service
  Operational: No.
Telephone Service
  Digital: Operational
Miles of Plant: 8.0 (coaxial); None (fiber optic).
General Manager: George Strandell. Cable TV Director: Rick Reed.
Ownership: Golden West Cablevision (MSO).

PLANKINTON—Golden West Telecommunications. Now served by FREEMAN, SD [SD0038]. ICA: SD0248.

PLATTE—Midstate Communications. Now served by WHITE LAKE, SD [SD0026]. ICA: SD0049.

POLLOCK—Formerly served by Valley Cable & Satellite Communications Inc. This cable system has converted to IPTV. Now served by Valley Telecommunications Coop. Assn., HERREID, SD [SD5032]. ICA: SD0195.

POLLOCK—Valley Telecommunications Coop. Assn. This cable system has converted to IPTV. Now served by HERREID, SD [SD5032]. ICA: SD5036.

PRAIRIE ACRES ESTATES—Formerly served by Midcontinent Communications. No longer in operation. ICA: SD0222.

PRAIRIEWOOD (village)—Midcontinent Communications. Now served by ABERDEEN, SD [SD0003]. ICA: SD0196.

RAMONA—Alliance Communications. This cable system has converted to IPTV. See HOWARD, SD [SD5082]. ICA: SD0198.

RAPID CITY—Clarity Telecom, 4850 Sugarloaf Pkwy, Ste 209-356, Lawrenceville, GA 30044. Phones: 720-479-3500; 866-399-8647. E-mail: sales@claritytel.com. Web Site: http://www.claritycomm.net. Also serves Belle Fourche, Black Hawk, Box Elder, Deadwood, Lawrence County (portions), Lead, Meade County (portions), Pennington County (portions), Piedmont, Spearfish, Sturgis, Summerset & Whitewood. ICA: SD0252.
Note: This system is an overbuild.
TV Market Ranking: Below 100 (Belle Fourche, Black Hawk, Box Elder, Box Elder, Deadwood, Lawrence County (portions), Lead, Meade County (portions), Pennington County (portions), Piedmont, RAPID CITY, Spearfish, Sturgis, Summerset, Whitewood).
Channel capacity: N.A. Channels available but not in use: N.A.
Basic Service
  Subscribers: 13,063.
  Programming (received off-air): KBHE-TV (PBS) Rapid City; KCLO-TV (CBS) Rapid City; KHME (MeTV, This TV) Rapid City; KKRA-LP (ION) Rapid City; KNBN (MNT, NBC) Rapid City; KOTA-TV (ABC, FOX) Rapid City; KWBH-LP (NBC) Rapid City.
  Programming (via satellite): A&E; AMC; Animal Planet; BET; Bravo; Cartoon Network; CMT; CNBC; CNN; Comedy Central; C-SPAN; C-SPAN 2; Discovery Channel; Discovery Life Channel; Disney Channel; Disney XD; DIY Network; E! HD; ESPN; ESPN Classic; ESPN2; ESPNews; EWTN Global Catholic Network; Food Network; Fox News Channel; Fox Sports 1; FOX Sports Networks; Freeform; FX; Golf Channel; Great American Country; GSN; Hallmark Channel; HGTV; History; HLN; INSP; Lifetime; MoviePlex; MSNBC; MTV; National Geographic Channel; NBCSN; Nickelodeon; Outdoor Channel; Ovation; Pop; QVC; Spike TV; Syfy; TBS; The Weather Channel; TLC; TNT; Travel Channel; Trinity Broadcasting Network (TBN); truTV; Turner Classic Movies; TV Land; USA Network; VH1; WE tv; WGN America.
  Fee: $25.00 installation; $33.00 monthly.
Digital Basic Service
  Subscribers: N.A.
  Programming (via satellite): AXS TV; BBC America; Cinemax; Cooking Channel; Destination America; Discovery Channel; Discovery Kids Channel; DIY Network; DMX Music; ESPN; Fuse; FYI; HBO; History International; IFC; Investigation Discovery; LMN; Nick 2; Nick Jr.; OWN: Oprah Winfrey Network; Science Channel; Showtime; TeenNick; The Movie Channel.
  Fee: $6.95 converter.
Digital Pay Service 1
  Pay Units: N.A.
  Programming (via satellite): Cinemax (multiplexed); Flix; HBO (multiplexed); Showtime; Starz (multiplexed); Starz Encore (multiplexed); Sundance TV; The Movie Channel (multiplexed).
Video-On-Demand: Yes
Pay-Per-View
  Sports PPV (delivered digitally).
Internet Service
  Operational: Yes.
  Fee: $29.95 installation; $39.95 monthly.
Telephone Service
  Analog: Not Operational
  Digital: Operational
Miles of Plant: 840.0 (coaxial); 245.0 (fiber optic). Homes passed included in Viborg.
Chief Executive Officer: Jim Gleason.
Ownership: Clarity Telecom (MSO).

RAPID CITY—Formerly served by USA Digital TV. No longer in operation. ICA: SD0233.

RAPID CITY—Midco, PO Box 5010, Sioux Falls, SD 57117. Phones: 800-888-1300; 605-342-1870; 605-343-0595. Fax: 605-388-9166. Web Site: http://www.midcocomm.com. Also serves Belle Fourche, Black Hawk, Boulder Canyon, Box Elder, Central City, Countryside Mobile Home Park, Deadwood, Ellsworth AFB, Hart Ranch, Lawrence County (northern portion), Lead, Meade County (western portion), Pennington County (portions), Piedmont, Spearfish, Sturgis, Summerset & Whitewood. ICA: SD0002.
TV Market Ranking: Below 100 (Belle Fourche, Black Hawk, Box Elder, Central City, Countryside Mobile Home Park, Deadwood, Ellsworth AFB, Lawrence County (northern portion), Lead, Meade County (western portion), Pennington County (portions), Piedmont, RAPID CITY, Sturgis, Summerset, Boulder Canyon, Hart Ranch, Spearfish, Whitewood). Franchise award date: N.A. Franchise expiration date: N.A. Began: October 6, 1958.
Channel capacity: N.A. Channels available but not in use: N.A.
Basic Service
  Subscribers: 16,763.
  Programming (received off-air): KBHE-TV (PBS) Rapid City; KCLO-TV (CBS) Rapid City; KHME (MeTV, This TV) Rapid City; KKRA-LP (ION) Rapid City; KOTA-TV (ABC, FOX) Rapid City.
  Programming (via satellite): A&E; AMC; Animal Planet; BET; Bloomberg Television; Bravo; Cartoon Network; CMT; CNBC; CNN; Comedy Central; C-SPAN; C-SPAN 2; CW PLUS; Discovery Channel; Disney Channel; Disney XD; E! HD; ESPN; ESPN Classic; ESPN2; ESPNews; EWTN Global Catholic Network; Food Network; Fox News Channel; Fox Sports 1; FOX Sports North; Freeform; FX; Golf Channel; Great American Country; GSN; Hallmark Channel; HGTV; History; HLN; INSP; KNBC (COZI TV, NBC) Los Angeles; Lifetime; MSNBC; MTV; NBCSN; Nickelodeon; Outdoor Channel; Oxygen; Pop; QVC; Root Sports Rocky Mountain; Spike TV; Syfy; TBS; The Weather Channel; TLC; TNT; Travel Channel; Trinity Broadcasting Network (TBN); truTV; Turner Classic Movies; TV Land; USA Network; VH1; WE tv; WGN America.
  Fee: $43.50 installation; $19.95 monthly; $3.25 converter.
Digital Basic Service
  Subscribers: N.A.
  Programming (via satellite): 3ABN; A&E HD; Animal Planet HD; AXS TV; BBC America; Bloomberg Television; Boomerang; BTN; Canal Sur; CBS Sports Network; Cine Mexicano; Cinelatino; CMT; CNN en Espanol; CNN HD; Cooking Channel; C-SPAN 3; Destination America; Discovery Channel HD; Discovery Kids Channel; Disney Channel HD; Disney XD; DIY Network; ESPN Deportes; ESPN HD; ESPN2 HD; Food Network HD; Fox Business Network; FOX College Sports Central; FOX College Sports Pacific; Fox Deportes; Freeform HD; FSN HD; Fuse; FYI; Golf Channel; GolTV; Great American Country; HD Theater; HGTV HD; History en Espanol; History HD; History International; IFC; Investigation Discovery; ION Television; JUCE TV; LMN; MC; MTV Classic; MTV Hits; MTV Jams; MTV Live; MTV2; National Geographic Channel; National Geographic Channel HD; NBC Universo; NFL Network; NHL Network; Nick 2; Nick Jr.; Nicktoons; OWN: Oprah Winfrey Network; Qubo; Reelz; RFD-TV; Science Channel; Sprout; Sundance TV; Syfy HD;

Cable Systems—South Dakota

TBS HD; TeenNick; Telemundo; Tennis Channel; TLC HD; TNT HD; Tr3s; Trinity Broadcasting Network (TBN); TV One; TVG Network; Universal HD; USA Network HD; Versus HD; VH1 Soul; ViendoMovies.
Fee: $13.50 monthly.
Digital Pay Service 1
Pay Units: N.A.
Programming (via satellite): Cinemax (multiplexed); Cinemax HD; HBO (multiplexed); HBO HD; HBO Latino; Showtime (multiplexed); Showtime HD; Starz (multiplexed); Starz Encore (multiplexed); Starz HD; The Movie Channel (multiplexed); The Movie Channel HD.
Video-On-Demand: Yes
Pay-Per-View
iN DEMAND (delivered digitally); Hot Choice (delivered digitally); Playboy TV (delivered digitally).
Internet Service
Operational: Yes.
Broadband Service: MidcoNet.
Fee: $35.00 installation; $18.00 monthly.
Telephone Service
Digital: Operational
Fee: $18.00 monthly
Miles of Plant: 491.0 (coaxial); None (fiber optic). Homes passed: 42,092.
General Manager: Jerry Steever. Chief Technician: Dave Gorsuch. Programming Director: Wynne Haakenstad.
Ownership: Midcontinent Communications (MSO).

RAYMOND—Formerly served by Satellite Cable Services Inc. Now served by ITC, CLEAR LAKE, SD [SD5042]. ICA: SD0199.

REDFIELD—Formerly served by Spink Electric. No longer in operation. ICA: SD0234.

RELIANCE—Golden West Telecommunications. Now served by WINNER, SD [SD0021]. ICA: SD0200.

RIMROCK—Formerly served by Midco. No longer in operation. ICA: SD0221.

ROSEBUD—Golden West Telecommunications. Now served by WINNER, SD [SD0021]. ICA: SD0203.

ROSHOLT—Venture Communications. Formerly [SD0115]. This cable system has converted to IPTV, 218 Commercial Ave SE, PO Box 157, Highmore, SD 57345-0157. Phones: 800-824-7282; 605-852-2224. Fax: 605-852-2404. E-mail: venture@venturecomm.net. Web Site: http://www.venturecomm.net. ICA: SD5100.
TV Market Ranking: Outside TV Markets (ROSHOLT). Franchise award date: N.A. Franchise expiration date: N.A. Began: December 1, 1979.
Channel capacity: N.A. Channels available but not in use: N.A.
Core
Subscribers: N.A.
Programming (received off-air): KABY-TV (ABC) Aberdeen; KDLO-TV (CBS, MNT) Florence; KDLT-TV (Antenna TV, NBC) Sioux Falls; KTTW (FOX, This TV) Sioux Falls; KUSD-TV (PBS) Vermillion; KVLY-TV (MeTV, NBC, This TV) Fargo; KVRR (Antenna TV, FOX) Fargo; KWCM-TV (PBS) Appleton; WDAY-TV (ABC, CW) Fargo.
Programming (via satellite): C-SPAN; CW PLUS; EWTN Global Catholic Network; ION Television; MyNetworkTV; QVC; The Weather Channel; Trinity Broadcasting Network (TBN); Weatherscan; WGN America.
Fee: $49.95 installation; $19.95 monthly.
Basic
Subscribers: 239.
Programming (via satellite): A&E; AMC; Animal Planet; BBC America; Bloomberg Television; Bravo; Cartoon Network; CMT; CNBC; CNN; Comedy Central; C-SPAN 2; Destination America; Discovery Channel; Discovery Kids Channel; Disney Channel; Disney XD; DIY Network; DMX Music; E! HD; ESPN; ESPN Classic; ESPN2; ESPNews; Food Network; Fox News Channel; Fox Sports 1; FOX Sports North; Freeform; FX; FXM; Golf Channel; Great American Country; GSN; Hallmark Channel; Hallmark Movies & Mysteries; HGTV; History; HLN; Investigation Discovery; Lifetime; LMN; MSNBC; MTV; MTV Classic; MTV Hits; MTV2; National Geographic Channel; NBCSN; NFL Network; Nick Jr.; Nickelodeon; Nicktoons; Outdoor Channel; OWN: Oprah Winfrey Network; Oxygen; RFD-TV; Science Channel; Spike TV; Syfy; TBS; TeenNick; TLC; TNT; Travel Channel; truTV; Turner Classic Movies; TV Land; USA Network; VH1; WE tv.
Fee: $60.99 monthly.
Video-On-Demand: No
Pay-Per-View
Playboy TV (delivered digitally); Fresh (delivered digitally).
Internet Service
Operational: Yes.
Fee: $40.95-$150.95 monthly.
Telephone Service
Digital: Operational
General Manager: Randy Houdek. Assistant General Manager: Randy Olson. Chief Technician: Brad Ryan.
Ownership: Venture Communications Cooperative (MSO).

ROSHOLT—Venture Communications. This cable system has converted to IPTV. See ROSHOLT, SD [SD5100]. ICA: SD0115.

SALEM—TrioTel Communications Inc, 330 South Nebraska St, PO Box 630, Salem, SD 57058-0630. Phones: 800-242-1925; 605-425-2238. Fax: 605-425-2712. E-mail: customerservice@triotel.net. Web Site: http://www.triotel.net. Also serves Alexandria, Canova, Emery, Spencer & Winfred. ICA: SD5106.
TV Market Ranking: 85 (Canova, Emery, SALEM, Spencer). Franchise award date: N.A. Franchise expiration date: N.A. Began: November 1, 1983.
Channel capacity: N.A. Channels available but not in use: N.A.
Simply Right
Subscribers: 1,378.
Programming (received off-air): KAUN-LP (Retro TV) Sioux Falls; KDLT-TV (Antenna TV, NBC) Sioux Falls; KELO-TV (CBS, MNT) Sioux Falls; KSFY-TV (ABC, CW) Sioux Falls; KTTM (FOX, This TV) Huron; KUSD-TV (PBS) Vermillion.
Programming (via satellite): CW PLUS; EWTN Global Catholic Network; LWS Local Weather Station; QVC; Trinity Broadcasting Network (TBN); WGN America.
Fee: $20.00 installation; $20.95 monthly.
Preferred Choice
Subscribers: N.A.
Programming (via satellite): A&E; AMC; Animal Planet; Bloomberg Television; Bravo; Cartoon Network; CMT; CNBC; CNN; Comedy Central; C-SPAN; Discovery Channel; Disney Channel; Disney XD; DIY Network; DMX Music; E!; ESPN; ESPN Classic; ESPN2; ESPNews; Food Network; Fox News Channel; Fox Sports 1; Freeform; FX; FXM; Golf Channel; Great American Country; GSN; Hallmark Channel; HGTV; History; HLN; Lifetime; MSNBC; MTV; MTV Classic; MTV Hits; MTV2; National Geographic Channel; NBCSN; Nick Jr.; Nickelodeon; Nicktoons; Outdoor Channel; OWN: Oprah Winfrey Network; Oxygen; RFD-TV; Spike TV; Syfy; TBS; TeenNick; The Weather Channel; TLC; TNT; Travel Channel; truTV; Turner Classic Movies; TV Land; USA Network; VH1; WE tv.
Fee: $35.00 monthly.
HD
Subscribers: N.A.
Fee: $10.95 monthly.
Cinemax
Subscribers: N.A.
Programming (via satellite): Cinemax (multiplexed).
Fee: $10.95 monthly.
HBO
Subscribers: N.A.
Programming (via satellite): HBO (multiplexed).
Fee: $11.95 monthly.
NFL RedZone
Subscribers: N.A.
Fee: $49.95 per season.
Playboy
Subscribers: N.A.
Programming (via satellite): Playboy TV.
Fee: $7.95 monthly.
Showtime
Subscribers: N.A.
Programming (via satellite): Showtime (multiplexed).
Fee: $10.95 monthly.
Starz/Starz Encore
Subscribers: N.A.
Programming (via satellite): Starz (multiplexed); Starz Encore (multiplexed).
Fee: $10.95 monthly.
Video-On-Demand: No
Pay-Per-View
iN DEMAND (delivered digitally); Spice (delivered digitally); Playboy TV (delivered digitally).
Internet Service
Operational: Yes.
Fee: $99.00-$125.00 installation; $39.95-$125.00 monthly.
Telephone Service
Digital: Operational
Fee: $18.00 monthly
Miles of Plant: None (coaxial); 900.0 (fiber optic).
General Manager & Chief Executive Officer: Bryan K. Roth. Chief Technician: Tim Wenande. Marketing Director: Jan Larson. Customer Service Manager: Heather Kranz.
Ownership: TrioTel Communications Inc.

SIOUX FALLS—Midco, PO Box 5010, Sioux Falls, SD 57117. Phones: 800-456-0564; 605-339-3339 (Local office); 605-229-1775; 800-888-1300. Fax: 605-229-0572. Web Site: http://www.midcocomm.com. Also serves Baltic, Brandon, Canton, Colton, Crooks, Harrisburg, Humboldt, Lennox, Madison, Renner, Shindler & Tea. ICA: SD0001.
TV Market Ranking: 85 (Baltic, Brandon, Canton, Colton, Crooks, Harrisburg, Humboldt, Lennox, Renner, Shindler, SIOUX FALLS, Tea); Outside TV Markets (Madison). Franchise award date: May 30, 1969. Franchise expiration date: N.A. Began: December 29, 1969.
Channel capacity: 22 (operating 2-way). Channels available but not in use: N.A.
Basic Service
Subscribers: 38,158.
Programming (received off-air): KAUN-LP (Retro TV) Sioux Falls; KDLT-TV (Antenna TV, NBC) Sioux Falls; KELO-TV (CBS, MNT) Sioux Falls; KSFY-TV (ABC, CW) Sioux Falls; KSMN (PBS) Worthington; KTTW (FOX, This TV) Sioux Falls; KUSD-TV (PBS) Vermillion; KWSD (MeTV, Retro TV) Sioux Falls.
Programming (via satellite): A&E; AMC; Animal Planet; BET; Bravo; Cartoon Network; Celebrity Shopping Network; CMT; CNBC; CNN; Comedy Central; C-SPAN; C-SPAN 2; Discovery Channel; Discovery Life Channel; Disney Channel; E! HD; ESPN; ESPN2; EWTN Global Catholic Network; Food Network; Fox News Channel; Fox Sports 1; FOX Sports North; Freeform; FX; Hallmark Channel; HGTV; History; HLN; INSP; Lifetime; MSNBC; MTV; MyNetworkTV; NBCSN; Nickelodeon; Outdoor Channel; OWN: Oprah Winfrey Network; Pop; QVC; Spike TV; Syfy; TBS; The Weather Channel; TLC; TNT; Travel Channel; truTV; Turner Classic Movies; TV Land; Univision Studios; USA Network; VH1; WE tv; WGN America.
Fee: $25.00 installation; $19.95 monthly; $2.00 converter.
Digital Basic Service
Subscribers: N.A.
Programming (via satellite): 3ABN; AXS TV; BBC America; Bloomberg Television; Boomerang; CBS Sports Network; Cine Mexicano; CMT; CNN en Espanol; Cooking Channel; C-SPAN 3; Destination America; Discovery Kids Channel; Discovery Life Channel; Disney XD; DIY Network; ESPN Classic; ESPN Deportes; ESPN HD; ESPN2 HD; ESPNews; Fox Business Network; FOX College Sports Central; FOX College Sports Pacific; Fox Deportes; Fuse; FYI; Golf Channel; GolTV; Great American Country; GSN; HD Theater; Historia en Espanol; History International; IFC; Investigation Discovery; JUCE TV; LMN; MC; MTV Classic; MTV Hits; MTV Jams; MTV Live; MTV2; National Geographic Channel; National Geographic Channel HD; NBC Universo; NHL Network; Nick 2; Nick Jr.; Nicktoons; Outdoor Channel; OWN: Oprah Winfrey Network; Science Channel; Sprout; Sundance TV; TeenNick; Telemundo; Tennis Channel; TNT HD; Tr3s; Trinity Broadcasting Network (TBN); Turner Classic Movies; TV One; TVG Network; Universal HD; Versus HD; VH1 Soul; WE tv.
Digital Pay Service 1
Pay Units: N.A.
Programming (via satellite): Cinemax (multiplexed); Cinemax HD; HBO (multiplexed); HBO HD; Showtime (multiplexed); Starz (multiplexed); Starz Encore (multiplexed); Starz HD; The Movie Channel (multiplexed); The Movie Channel HD.
Fee: $25.00 installation; $11.35 monthly (each).
Video-On-Demand: No
Pay-Per-View
iN DEMAND (delivered digitally); MLS Direct Kick (delivered digitally); NBA League Pass (delivered digitally); Hot Choice (delivered digitally).
Internet Service
Operational: Yes. Began: June 1, 1998.
Subscribers: 43,567.
Broadband Service: MidcoNet.
Fee: $35.00 installation; $19.95 monthly; $10.00 modem lease.

2017 Edition   D-701

South Dakota—Cable Systems

Telephone Service
Digital: Operational
Subscribers: 16,637.
Fee: $18.00 monthly
Miles of Plant: 1,322.0 (coaxial); 399.0 (fiber optic). Homes passed: 93,685.
General Manager: Todd Curtis. Program Director: Wynne Haakenstad. Engineering Director: Tom Heier. Marketing Director: Trish McCann. Chief Technician: Dana Storm. Installation Manager: Mike Drummond.
Ownership: Midcontinent Communications (MSO).; Comcast Cable Communications Inc. (MSO).

SISSETON—Venture Communications. Formerly [SD0023]. This cable system has converted to IPTV, 218 Commercial Ave SE, PO Box 157, Highmore, SD 57345-0157. Phones: 605-852-2224; 800-824-7282. Fax: 605-852-2404. E-mail: venture@venturecomm.net. Web Site: http://www.venturecomm.net. Also serves Grenville & Roslyn (rural). ICA: SD5101.
TV Market Ranking: Outside TV Markets (SISSETON). Franchise award date: N.A. Franchise expiration date: N.A. Began: February 1, 1977.
Channel capacity: N.A. Channels available but not in use: N.A.
Core
Subscribers: 924.
Programming (received off-air): KABY-TV (ABC) Aberdeen; KDLO-TV (CBS, MNT) Florence; KDLT-TV (Antenna TV, NBC) Sioux Falls; KTTW (FOX, This TV) Sioux Falls; KUSD-TV (PBS) Vermillion; KVLY-TV (MeTV, NBC, This TV) Fargo; KVRR (Antenna TV, FOX) Fargo; KWCM-TV (PBS) Appleton; WDAY-TV (ABC, CW) Fargo.
Programming (via satellite): C-SPAN; CW PLUS; EWTN Global Catholic Network; ION Television; LWS Local Weather Station; MyNetworkTV; QVC; The Weather Channel; Trinity Broadcasting Network (TBN); WGN America.
Fee: $49.95 installation; $19.95 monthly.
Basic
Subscribers: 905.
Programming (via satellite): A&E; AMC; Animal Planet; BBC America; Bloomberg Television; Bravo; Cartoon Network; CMT; CNBC; CNN; Comedy Central; C-SPAN 2; Destination America; Discovery Channel; Discovery Kids Channel; Disney Channel; Disney XD; DIY Network; DMX Music; E! HD; ESPN; ESPN Classic; ESPN2; ESPNews; Food Network; Fox News Channel; Fox Sports 1; FOX Sports North; Freeform; FX; FXM; Golf Channel; Great American Country; GSN; Hallmark Channel; Hallmark Movies & Mysteries; HGTV; History; HLN; Investigation Discovery; Lifetime; LMN; MSNBC; MTV Classic; MTV Hits; MTV2; National Geographic Channel; NBCSN; NFL Network; Nick Jr.; Nickelodeon; Nicktoons; Outdoor Channel; OWN; Oprah Winfrey Network; Oxygen; RFD-TV; Science Channel; Spike TV; Syfy; TBS; TeenNick; TLC; TNT; Travel Channel; truTV; Turner Classic Movies; TV Land; USA Network; VH1; WE tv.
Fee: $60.99 monthly.
Video-On-Demand: No
Pay-Per-View
iN DEMAND (delivered digitally); Playboy TV (delivered digitally); Fresh (delivered digitally).
Internet Service
Operational: Yes.
Fee: $40.95-$150.95 monthly.

Telephone Service
Analog: Operational
General Manager: Randy Houdek. Assistant General Manager: Randy Olson. Chief Technician: Brad Ryan.
Ownership: Venture Communications Cooperative (MSO).

SISSETON—Venture Communications. This cable system has converted to IPTV. See SISSETON, SD [SD5101]. ICA: SD0023.

SPEARFISH—Midco. Now served by RAPID CITY, SD [SD0002]. ICA: SD0010.

SPRINGFIELD—Golden West Telecommunications. Now served by FREEMAN, SD [SD0038]. ICA: SD0070.

ST. FRANCIS—Golden West Telecommunications. Now served by WINNER, SD [SD0021]. ICA: SD0050.

SUMMIT—Formerly served by Satellite Cable Services Inc. This cable system has converted to IPV. Now served by RC Technologies, SUMMIT, SD [SD5073]. ICA: SD0207.

SUMMIT—RC Technologies. Formerly [SD0207]. This cable system has converted to IPTV, 1018 6th St SE, Watertown, SD 57201. Phones: 800-256-6854; 605-637-5211. Fax: 605-637-5302. E-mail: rctv@tnics.com. Web Site: http://www.tnics.com. ICA: SD5073.
Channel capacity: N.A. Channels available but not in use: N.A.
Local
Subscribers: 54.
Fee: $29.95 monthly. Includes 28 channels.
Basic
Subscribers: 52.
Fee: $75.00 monthly. Includes 87 channels plus music channels.
Expanded
Subscribers: N.A.
Fee: $14.95 monthly. Includes 41 channels.
HD
Subscribers: N.A.
Fee: $9.95 monthly. Includes 77 channels.
Bang U
Subscribers: N.A.
Fee: $12.95 monthly. Includes 1 channels.
Cinemax
Subscribers: N.A.
Fee: $14.95 monthly. Includes 4 channels.
HBO
Subscribers: N.A.
Fee: $18.95 monthly. Includes 5 channels.
NFL RedZone
Subscribers: N.A.
Fee: $59.95 per season.
Playboy
Subscribers: N.A.
Fee: $12.95 monthly. Includes 1 channel.
Showtime/TMC
Subscribers: N.A.
Fee: $16.95 monthly. Includes 10 channels.
Starz/Starz Encore
Subscribers: N.A.
Fee: $14.95 monthly. Includes 10 channels.
Internet Service
Operational: Yes.
Telephone Service
Digital: Operational
General Manager: Scott Bostrom. Operations Manager: Colin Bronson. Sales & Marketing Manager: Sara Broz. IT Manager: Paul Gravdahl. Billing & Customer Care Manager: Wanda Heesch.
Ownership: RC Technologies Corp.

TABOR—Formerly served by Satellite Cable Services Inc. Now served by Fort Randall Cable, TRIPP, SD [SD0087]. ICA: SD0208.

TAKINI—Formerly served by Cheyenne River Sioux Tribe Telephone Authority. No longer in operation. ICA: SD0209.

TIMBER LAKE—Formerly served by West River Cable Television. No longer in operation. ICA: SD0085.

TORONTO—Formerly served by Satellite Cable Services Inc. Now served by ITC, CLEAR LAKE, SD [SD5042]. ICA: SD0210.

TRENT—Golden West Telecommunications. Now served by DELL RAPIDS, SD [SD0028]. ICA: SD0211.

TRIPP—Fort Randall Cable, 1605 Laurel St, PO Box 608, Tyndall, SD 57066. Phones: 888-283-7667; 605-589-3366. Fax: 605-589-3695. E-mail: bruce@hcinet.net. Web Site: http://www.hcinet.net. Also serves Lake Andes, Parkston, Pickstown, Tabor, Tyndall & Wagner. ICA: SD0087.
TV Market Ranking: Outside TV Markets (Lake Andes, Parkston, Pickstown, Tabor, TRIPP, Tyndall, Wagner). Franchise award date: N.A. Franchise expiration date: N.A. Began: September 1, 1983.
Channel capacity: N.A. Channels available but not in use: N.A.
Basic Service
Subscribers: N.A.
Programming (received off-air): KDLV-TV (NBC) Mitchell; KELO-TV (CBS, MNT) Sioux Falls; KSFY-TV (ABC, CW) Sioux Falls; KUSD-TV (PBS) Vermillion.
Programming (via satellite): CNN; ESPN; Freeform; TBS; USA Network; WGN America.
Fee: $29.95 installation.
Digital Basic Service
Subscribers: N.A.
Programming (via satellite): Bloomberg Television; Bravo; Discovery Life Channel; Disney XD; DMX Music; ESPN Classic; ESPN2; ESPNews; Fox Sports 1; Fuse; FXM; FYI; Golf Channel; GSN; HGTV; History; History International; IFC; LMN; National Geographic Channel; NBCSN; Outdoor Channel; Syfy; Trinity Broadcasting Network (TBN); Turner Classic Movies; WE tv.
Fee: $10.95 monthly.
Pay Service 1
Pay Units: N.A.
Programming (via satellite): Cinemax; HBO; Showtime.
Fee: $9.95 installation; $11.95 monthly (each).
Digital Pay Service 1
Pay Units: N.A.
Programming (via satellite): Cinemax (multiplexed); HBO (multiplexed); Showtime (multiplexed); Starz (multiplexed); Starz Encore (multiplexed); The Movie Channel (multiplexed).
Fee: $11.95 monthly (Cinemax, HBO, Showtime/TMC or Starz/Encore).
Video-On-Demand: No
Pay-Per-View
Sports PPV (delivered digitally); ESPN Now (delivered digitally); Fresh (delivered digitally); Playboy TV (delivered digitally); Hot Choice (delivered digitally).
Internet Service
Operational: Yes.
Fee: $39.99 monthly.

Telephone Service
None
Treasurer & General Manager: Bruce Hanson. Office Manager: Deb Wagner.
Ownership: Hanson Communications Inc. (MSO).

TRIPP—Santel Communications. This cable system has converted to IPTV. Now served by WOONSOCKET, SD [SD5020]. ICA: SD5019.

TYNDALL—Formerly served by Satellite Cable Services Inc. Now served by Fort Randall Cable, TRIPP, SD [SD0087]. ICA: SD0045.

VALLEY SPRINGS—Alliance Communications. Now served by GARRETSON, SD [SD0016]. ICA: SD0084.

VERMILLION—Formerly served by Mediacom. Now served by Midco, YANKTON, SD [SD0009]. ICA: SD0012.

VIBORG—Clarity Telcom, 4850 Sugarloaf Pkwy, Ste 209-356, Lawrenceville, GA 30044. Phones: 720-479-3500; 866-399-8647. E-mail: sales@claritytel.com. Web Site: http://www.claritycomm.net. Also serves Lakeside, Sioux City (northern portion) & Storm Lake, IA; Alcester, Canton (portions), Centerville, Chancellor, Colman, Elk Point, Flandreau, Gayville, Harrisburg, Hurley, Irene, Lennox, Madison, Parker, Tea, Wakonda, Watertown, Worthing & Yankton, SD. ICA: SD0071. **Note:** This system is an overbuild.
TV Market Ranking: 85 (Canton (portions), Centerville, Chancellor, Colman, Flandreau, Harrisburg, Hurley, Lennox, Madison, Parker, Tea, VIBORG, Worthing); Below 100 (Elk Point, Gayville, Sioux City (northern portion), Watertown); Outside TV Markets (Alcester, Irene, Lakeside, Wakonda, Yankton, Storm Lake). Franchise award date: February 7, 1983. Franchise expiration date: N.A. Began: July 1, 1983.
Channel capacity: N.A. Channels available but not in use: N.A.
Basic Service
Subscribers: 10,663.
Programming (received off-air): KCAU-TV (ABC) Sioux City; KDLT-TV (Antenna TV, NBC) Sioux Falls; KELO-TV (CBS, MNT) Sioux Falls; KSFY-TV (ABC, CW) Sioux Falls; KSIN-TV (PBS) Sioux City; KTIV (CW, MeTV, NBC) Sioux City; KTTW (FOX, This TV) Sioux Falls; KUSD-TV (PBS) Vermillion; KXNE-TV (PBS) Norfolk.
Programming (via satellite): A&E; AMC; Animal Planet; Bravo; Cartoon Network; CMT; CNBC; CNN; Comedy Central; C-SPAN; Discovery Channel; Disney Channel; Disney XD; E! HD; ESPN; ESPN2; EWTN Global Catholic Network; Food Network; Fox News Channel; Fox Sports 1; FOX Sports North; Freeform; FX; FXM; Golf Channel; HGTV; History; HLN; INSP; ION Television; Lifetime; LMN; MSNBC; MTV; Nickelodeon; Outdoor Channel; Pop; QVC; Spike TV; Syfy; TBS; The Weather Channel; TLC; TNT; Travel Channel; truTV; Turner Classic Movies; TV Land; USA Network; VH1; WGN America.
Fee: $25.00 installation; $33.00 monthly.
Digital Basic Service
Subscribers: N.A.
Programming (via satellite): AXS TV; BBC America; Bloomberg Television; Cooking Channel; Discovery Life Channel; DIY Network; ESPN; ESPNews; Flix; FOX College Sports Central; FOX College Sports Pacific;

Cable Systems—South Dakota

Fuse; FYI; GSN; Hallmark Channel; HD Theater; History International; IFC; MC; National Geographic Channel; Nick Jr.; Nicktoons; Starz Encore Family; Sundance TV; TeenNick; WE tv.

Pay Service 1
Pay Units: N.A.
Programming (via satellite): HBO; Showtime.
Fee: $10.00 installation; $9.85 monthly (each).

Digital Pay Service 1
Pay Units: N.A.
Programming (via satellite): Cinemax (multiplexed); Cinemax HD; HBO (multiplexed); HBO HD; HITS (Headend In The Sky); Showtime (multiplexed); Showtime HD; Starz (multiplexed); Starz Encore (multiplexed); The Movie Channel (multiplexed).

Video-On-Demand: Yes

Pay-Per-View
iN DEMAND (delivered digitally); Hot Choice (delivered digitally).

Internet Service
Operational: Yes.
Fee: $29.95 installation; $39.95 monthly.

Telephone Service
Analog: Not Operational
Digital: Operational
Homes passed: 113,000. Homes passed includes Rapid City, Adrian MN & Marshall MN

Chief Executive Officer: Jim Gleason.
Ownership: Clarity Telecom (MSO).

WAGNER—Formerly served by Satellite Cable Services Inc. Now served by Fort Randall Cable, TRIPP, SD [SD0087]. ICA: SD0039.

WALL—Golden West Telecommunications, 415 Crown St, PO Box 411, Wall, SD 57790-0411. Phones: 855-888-7777; 605-528-3211; 605-279-1020; 605-279-2161. Fax: 605-279-2727. E-mail: info@goldenwest.com. Web Site: http://www.goldenwest.com. Also serves Kadoka, Midland, New Underwood & Philip. ICA: SD0068.

TV Market Ranking: Below 100 (New Underwood); Outside TV Markets (Kadoka, Midland, Wall, WALL). Franchise award date: October 15, 1982. Franchise expiration date: N.A. Began: October 15, 1982.
Channel capacity: N.A. Channels available but not in use: N.A.

Basic Service
Subscribers: 1,095.
Programming (received off-air): KBHE-TV (PBS) Rapid City; KCLO-TV (CBS) Rapid City; KHME (MeTV, This TV) Rapid City; KKRA-LP (ION) Rapid City; KNBN (MNT, NBC) Rapid City; KOTA-TV (ABC, FOX) Rapid City.
Programming (via satellite): A&E; AMC; Animal Planet; Cartoon Network; CMT; CNBC; CNN; C-SPAN; C-SPAN 2; CW PLUS; Discovery Channel; Disney Channel; ESPN; ESPN Classic; ESPN2; EWTN Global Catholic Network; Food Network; Fox News Channel; Freeform; FX; Hallmark Channel; HGTV; History; HLN; INSP; Lifetime; MTV; National Geographic Channel; NFL Network; Nickelodeon; Outdoor Channel; Pop; QVC; Spike TV; TBS; The Weather Channel; TLC; TNT; Turner Classic Movies; TV Land; USA Network; VH1; WGN America.
Fee: $29.95 installation; $23.57 monthly.

Digital Basic Service
Subscribers: N.A.
Programming (via satellite): A&E; BBC America; Bloomberg Television; Discovery Digital Networks; Disney XD; DMX Music; ESPN; ESPN Classic; EVINE Live; Fox Sports 1; Fuse; FXM; Golf Channel; GSN; HGTV; History; History International; IFC; LMN; National Geographic Channel; NBCSN; Nick Jr.; Nicktoons; Ovation; TeenNick; The Word Network; Trinity Broadcasting Network (TBN); WE tv.
Fee: $14.95 monthly.

Pay Service 1
Pay Units: N.A.
Programming (via satellite): HBO; Showtime; The Movie Channel.
Fee: $9.95 monthly (TMC), $10.95 monthly (Showtime), $11.95 monthly (HBO).

Digital Pay Service 1
Pay Units: N.A.
Programming (via satellite): Cinemax (multiplexed); Flix; HBO (multiplexed); Showtime (multiplexed); Starz (multiplexed); Starz Encore (multiplexed); The Movie Channel (multiplexed).
Fee: $6.95 monthly (Encore), $11.95 monthly (Cinemax, Showtime or TMC), $12.95 monthly (HBO), $13.95 monthly (Starz/Encore).

Video-On-Demand: No

Pay-Per-View
iN DEMAND (delivered digitally); Hot Choice (delivered digitally); Playboy TV (delivered digitally); Fresh (delivered digitally); Shorteez (delivered digitally).

Internet Service
Operational: No, DSL & dial-up.

Telephone Service
Digital: Operational
Miles of Plant: 175.0 (coaxial); None (fiber optic). Homes passed: 3,500.
General Manager: George Strandell. Cable Television Manager: Rick Reed. Chief Technician: Randy Shepard. Marketing Director: Greg Oleson. Customer Service Manager: Jody Bielmaier.
Ownership: Golden West Cablevision (MSO).

WATERTOWN—Clarity Telcom. Now served by VIBORG, SD [SD0071]. ICA: SD0250.

WATERTOWN—Midco, PO Box 5010, Sioux Falls, SD 57117. Phones: 605-882-9140 (Local office), 605-229-1775; 800-888-1300. Fax: 605-229-0478. Web Site: http://www.midcocomm.com. Also serves Big Stone City, Big Stone Twp., Ortonville & Ortonville Twp., MN; Codington County (portions), Grant County (portions) & Milbank, SD. ICA: SD0004.

TV Market Ranking: Below 100 (Codington County (portions), Grant County (portions), WATERTOWN); Outside TV Markets (Big Stone City, Big Stone Twp., Milbank, Ortonville, Ortonville Twp.). Franchise award date: N.A. Franchise expiration date: N.A. Began: June 29, 1973.
Channel capacity: N.A. Channels available but not in use: N.A.

Basic Service
Subscribers: 5,930.
Programming (received off-air): KABY-TV (ABC) Aberdeen; KDLO-TV (CBS, MNT) Florence; KDLT-TV (Antenna TV, NBC) Sioux Falls; KESD-TV (PBS) Brookings; KTTW (FOX, This TV) Sioux Falls; KWSD (MeTV, Retro TV) Sioux Falls; allband FM.
Programming (via satellite): A&E; AMC; Animal Planet; Bravo; Cartoon Network; CMT; CNBC; CNN; Comedy Central; C-SPAN; C-SPAN 2; Discovery Channel; Disney Channel; E! HD; ESPN; ESPN Classic; ESPN2; ESPNews; EWTN Global Catholic Network; Food Network; Fox News Channel; Fox Sports 1; FOX Sports Networks; Freeform; FX; Great American Country; Hallmark Channel; HGTV; History; HLN; INSP; Lifetime; MSNBC; MTV; NBCSN; Nickelodeon; Outdoor Channel; OWN; Oprah Winfrey Network; Pop; QVC; Spike TV; Starz; Starz Encore; Syfy; TBS; The Weather Channel; TLC; TNT; Travel Channel; truTV; Turner Classic Movies; TV Land; USA Network; VH1; WE tv; WGN America.
Fee: $29.95 installation; $19.95 monthly; $.43 converter.

Digital Basic Service
Subscribers: N.A.
Programming (via satellite): BBC America; Bloomberg Television; Discovery Digital Networks; Disney XD; DMX Music; FYI; Golf Channel; GSN; History; IFC; LMN; MTV2; Nick Jr.; Sundance TV; TeenNick.

Pay Service 1
Pay Units: N.A.
Programming (via satellite): Cinemax; HBO.
Fee: $15.00 installation; $9.95 monthly (each).

Digital Pay Service 1
Pay Units: N.A.
Programming (via satellite): Cinemax (multiplexed); HBO (multiplexed); Showtime (multiplexed); Starz (multiplexed); Starz Encore (multiplexed); The Movie Channel (multiplexed).

Video-On-Demand: No

Pay-Per-View
iN DEMAND (delivered digitally); Hot Choice (delivered digitally); Fresh (delivered digitally).

Internet Service
Operational: Yes. Began: January 1, 1996.
Subscribers: 6,158.
Broadband Service: MidcoNet.
Fee: $35.00 installation; $19.95 monthly; $10.00 modem lease; $149.00 modem purchase.

Telephone Service
Digital: Operational
Subscribers: 4,380.
Fee: $18.00 monthly
Miles of Plant: 257.0 (coaxial); 103.0 (fiber optic). Homes passed: 16,638.
General Manager: Paul Foust. Chief Technician: Bob Spilde. Programming Director: Wynne Haakenstad.
Ownership: Midcontinent Communications (MSO).

WENTWORTH—Formerly served by Satellite Cable Services Inc. Now served by ITC, CLEAR LAKE, SD [SD5042]. ICA: SD0215.

WESSINGTON—Venture Communications. This cable system has converted to IPTV. Now served by HIGHMORE, SD [SD5022]. ICA: SD0060.

WESSINGTON—Venture Communications. This cable system has converted to IPTV. Now served by HIGHMORE, SD [SD5022]. ICA: SD0109.

WESSINGTON SPRINGS—Venture Communications. Formerly [SD0051]. This cable system has converted to IPTV, 218 Commercial Ave SE, PO Box 157, Highmore, SD 57345-0157. Phones: 800-824-7282; 605-852-2224. Fax: 605-852-2404. E-mail: venture@venturecomm.net. Web Site: http://www.venturecomm.net. Also serves Lane. ICA: SD5102.

TV Market Ranking: Below 100 (WESSINGTON SPRINGS). Franchise award date: N.A. Franchise expiration date: N.A. Began: December 15, 1980.
Channel capacity: N.A. Channels available but not in use: N.A.

Core
Subscribers: 508.
Programming (received off-air): KABY-TV (ABC) Aberdeen; KDLO-TV (CBS, MNT) Florence; KDLT-TV (Antenna TV, NBC) Sioux Falls; KTTW (FOX, This TV) Sioux Falls; KUSD-TV (PBS) Vermillion.
Programming (via satellite): C-SPAN; C-SPAN 2; CW PLUS; EWTN Global Catholic Network; ION Television; Local Cable Weather; MyNetworkTV; QVC; The Weather Channel; Trinity Broadcasting Network (TBN); WGN America.
Fee: $49.95 installation; $19.95 monthly.

Basic
Subscribers: 487.
Programming (via satellite): A&E; AMC; Animal Planet; BBC America; Bloomberg Television; Bravo; Cartoon Network; CMT; CNBC; CNN; Comedy Central; Destination America; Discovery Channel; Discovery Kids Channel; Disney Channel; Disney XD; DIY Network; DMX Music; E! HD; ESPN; ESPN Classic; ESPN2; ESPNews; Food Network; Fox News Channel; Fox Sports 1; FOX Sports North; Freeform; FX; FXM; Golf Channel; Great American Country; GSN; Hallmark Channel; HGTV; History; HLN; Investigation Discovery; Lifetime; LMN; MSNBC; MTV; MTV Classic; MTV Hits; MTV2; National Geographic Channel; NBCSN; NFL Network; Nick Jr.; Nickelodeon; Nicktoons; Outdoor Channel; OWN; Oprah Winfrey Network; Oxygen; RFD-TV; Science Channel; Spike TV; Syfy; TBS; TeenNick; TLC; TNT; Travel Channel; truTV; Turner Classic Movies; TV Land; USA Network; VH1; WE tv.
Fee: $60.99 monthly.

Video-On-Demand: No

Pay-Per-View
Playboy TV (delivered digitally); Fresh (delivered digitally).

Internet Service
Operational: Yes.
Fee: $40.95-$150.95 monthly.

Telephone Service
Digital: Operational
General Manager: Randy Houdek. Assistant General Manager: Randy Olson. Chief Technician: Brad Ryan.
Ownership: Venture Communications Cooperative (MSO).

WESSINGTON SPRINGS—Venture Communications. This cable system has converted to IPTV. See WESSINGTON SPRINGS, SD [SD5102]. ICA: SD0051.

WEST WHITLOCK—Formerly served by Western Telephone Company. No longer in operation. ICA: SD0216.

WHITE—Mediacom. Now served by BROOKINGS, SD [SD0005]. ICA: SD0105.

WHITE LAKE—Midstate Communications, 215 Main St South, PO Box 400, Stanley, ND 58784-0400. Phone: 701-628-2522. Fax: 605-778-8080. E-mail: midstate@midstatesd.net. Web Site: http://www.midstatetel.com. Also serves Chamberlain, Delmont, Geddes, Kimball, Oacoma, Platte, Pukwana & Stickney. ICA: SD0026.

TV Market Ranking: 85 (Delmont, Stickney, WHITE LAKE); Below 100 (Chamberlain, Kimball, Oacoma, Pukwana); Outside TV Markets (Geddes, Platte). Franchise award date: December 7, 1988. Franchise expiration date: N.A. Began: N.A.
Channel capacity: N.A. Channels available but not in use: N.A.

South Dakota—Cable Systems

Basic Service
Subscribers: 607.
Programming (received off-air): KCSD-TV (PBS) Sioux Falls; KDLT-TV (Antenna TV, NBC) Sioux Falls; KPLO-TV (CBS, MNT) Reliance; KPRY-TV (ABC) Pierre; KTTW (FOX, This TV) Sioux Falls.
Programming (via satellite): A&E; CMT; CNBC; CNN; Comedy Central; CW PLUS; Discovery Channel; Disney Channel; E! HD; ESPN; ESPN2; EWTN Global Catholic Network; Fox News Channel; FOX Sports North; Freeform; FX; Hallmark Channel; History; HLN; INSP; ION Television; Lifetime; Local Cable Weather; MTV; National Geographic Channel; NFL Network; Nickelodeon; QVC; RFD-TV; Spike TV; TBS; The Weather Channel; TLC; TNT; Travel Channel; Trinity Broadcasting Network (TBN); TV Land; USA Network; VH1; WGN America.
Fee: $57.00 installation; $34.95 monthly.

Digital Basic Service
Subscribers: N.A.
Programming (via satellite): A&E; AMC; Animal Planet; Bravo; Cartoon Network; CMT; CNBC; CNN; Comedy Central; Crime & Investigation Network; C-SPAN; C-SPAN 2; CW PLUS; Discovery Channel; Disney Channel; Disney XD; DIY Network; E! HD; ESPN; ESPN Classic; ESPN2; ESPNews; EWTN Global Catholic Network; FamilyNet; Food Network; FOX College Sports Central; FOX College Sports Pacific; Fox News Channel; Fox Sports 1; FOX Sports North; Freeform; FX; FXM; FYI; Golf Channel; Great American Country; GSN; Hallmark Channel; HGTV; History; History International; HLN; INSP; ION Television; Lifetime; MSNBC; MTV; MTV Classic; MTV2; NBCSN; NFL Network; Nick Jr.; Nickelodeon; Nicktoons; Outdoor Channel; OWN: Oprah Winfrey Network; QVC; RFD-TV; Spike TV; Syfy; TBS; TeenNick; The Weather Channel; TLC; TNT; Travel Channel; Trinity Broadcasting Network (TBN); truTV; Turner Classic Movies; TV Land; USA Network; VH1; WE tv; WGN America.
Fee: $45.00 monthly.

Digital Pay Service 1
Pay Units: N.A.
Programming (via satellite): Cinemax (multiplexed); Flix; HBO (multiplexed); Showtime (multiplexed); Starz (multiplexed); Starz Encore (multiplexed); The Movie Channel (multiplexed).
Fee: $8.45 monthly (Cinemax or Starz/Encore), $13.95 monthly (HBO or Showtime/TMC/Flix).

Video-On-Demand: No

Internet Service
Operational: Yes.

Telephone Service
Analog: Operational
General Manager: Mark Benton. Plant Manager: Fay Jandreau. Marketing Manager: Chad Mutziger. Office Manager: Peg Reinesch.
Ownership: Midstate Communications.

WHITEWOOD—Midcontinent Communications. Now served by RAPID CITY, SD [SD0002]. ICA: SD0219.

WILLOW LAKE—Formerly served by Satellite Cable Services Inc. Now served by ITC, CLEAR LAKE, SD [SD5042]. ICA: SD0112.

WILMOT—RC Technologies. This cable system has converted to IPTV. Now served by NEW EFFINGTON, SD [SD5067]. ICA: SD5074.

WILMOT—RC Technologies. This cable system has converted to IPTV. See NEW EFFINGTON, SD [SD5067]. ICA: SD0089.

WINNER—Golden West Telecommunications, 415 Crown St, PO Box 411, Wall, SD 57790-0411. Phones: 855-888-7777; 605-528-3211; 605-279-1020; 605-279-2161. Fax: 605-279-2727. E-mail: info@goldenwest.com. Web Site: http://www.goldenwest.com. Also serves Antelope, Bonesteel, Burke, Colome, Fairfax, Gregory, Lower Brule, Mission Twp., Murdo, Reliance, Rosebud, St. Francis & White River. ICA: SD0021.
TV Market Ranking: Below 100 (Lower Brule, Reliance); Outside TV Markets (Antelope, Bonesteel, Colome, Murdo, White River, WINNER, Burke, Fairfax, Gregory, Mission Twp., Rosebud, St. Francis). Franchise award date: October 19, 1987. Franchise expiration date: N.A. Began: November 1, 1968.
Channel capacity: 69 (operating 2-way). Channels available but not in use: N.A.

Basic Service
Subscribers: 2,913.
Programming (received off-air): KPLO-TV (CBS, MNT) Reliance; KPRY-TV (ABC) Pierre; KTSD-TV (PBS) Pierre; KTTM (FOX, This TV) Huron; allband FM.
Programming (via microwave): KDLT-TV (Antenna TV, NBC) Sioux Falls.
Programming (via satellite): A&E; AMC; Animal Planet; Cartoon Network; CMT; CNBC; CNN; Comedy Central; C-SPAN; C-SPAN 2; CW PLUS; Discovery Channel; Disney Channel; ESPN; ESPN2; EWTN Global Catholic Network; Food Network; Fox News Channel; Fox Sports 1; FOX Sports North; Freeform; FX; Hallmark Channel; HGTV; History; HLN; INSP; KWGN-TV (CW, This TV) Denver; Lifetime; MTV; NBCSN; Nickelodeon; Outdoor Channel; Pop; QVC; Spike TV; Syfy; TBS; The Weather Channel; TLC; TNT; Trinity Broadcasting Network (TBN); truTV; Turner Classic Movies; TV Land; USA Network; VH1; WE tv; WGN America.
Fee: $29.95 installation; $24.46 monthly.

Pay Service 1
Pay Units: N.A.
Programming (via satellite): Cinemax; HBO; Showtime; The Movie Channel.
Fee: $10.00 monthly (each).

Video-On-Demand: No

Internet Service
Operational: Yes.
Fee: $22.95-$49.95 monthly.

Telephone Service
Digital: Operational
Miles of Plant: 182.0 (coaxial); 397.0 (fiber optic). Homes passed: 4,627.
General Manager: George Strandell. Chief Technician: Randy Shepard. Marketing Director: Greg Oleson. Customer Service Manager: Jody Bielmaier. Cable Television Manager: Rick Reed.
Ownership: Golden West Cablevision (MSO).

WOLSEY—Santel Communications. This cable system has converted to IPTV. Now served by WOONSOCKET, SD [SD5020]. ICA: SD5021.

WOONSOCKET—Santel Communications. Formerly [SD0096]. This cable system has converted to IPTV, 308 South Dumont Ave, PO Box 67, Woonsocket, SD 57385-0067. Phones: 888-978-7777; 605-796-4411. Fax: 605-796-4419. E-mail: info@santel.net. Web Site: http://www.santel.net. Also serves Alpena (town), Artesian, Ethan, Letcher, Mount Vernon, Parkston, Tripp & Wolsey. ICA: SD5020.
TV Market Ranking: 85 (Artesian, Ethan, Letcher, Mount Vernon, Parkston, Tripp, WOONSOCKET); Below 100 (Alpena (town), Wolsey).
Channel capacity: N.A. Channels available but not in use: N.A.

Limited
Subscribers: 20.
Fee: $75.00 installation; $25.00 monthly.

Basic Value
Subscribers: N.A.
Fee: $43.95 monthly.

Premier
Subscribers: N.A.
Fee: $56.95 monthly.

Internet Service
Operational: Yes.
Fee: $25.00 installation; $39.95-$99.95 monthly; $10.00 modem lease.

Telephone Service
Analog: Operational
Fee: $14.50 monthly
General Manager: Ryan Thompson. Customer Service Manager: Pam Kopfmann. Marketing Manager: Greg McCurry. Network Operations Manager: Mark Wilson.
Ownership: Santel Communications.

WOONSOCKET—Santel Communications. This cable system has converted to IPTV. Now served by WOONSOCKET, SD [SD5020]. ICA: SD0096.

YALE—Formerly served by Midcontinent Communications. No longer in operation. ICA: SD0220.

YANKTON—Midco, PO Box 5010, Sioux Falls, SD 57117. Phones: 800-888-1300; 605-223-9036. Web Site: http://www.midcocomm.com. Also serves Gayville, Meckling & Vermillion. ICA: SD0009.
TV Market Ranking: Below 100 (Meckling, Vermillion); Outside TV Markets (YANKTON, Gayville). Franchise award date: N.A. Franchise expiration date: N.A. Began: April 1, 1980.
Channel capacity: N.A. Channels available but not in use: N.A.

Basic Service
Subscribers: 4,695.
Programming (received off-air): KAUN-LP (Retro TV) Sioux Falls; KCAU-TV (ABC) Sioux City; KDLT-TV (Antenna TV, NBC) Sioux Falls; KELO-TV (CBS, MNT) Sioux Falls; KSFY-TV (ABC, CW) Sioux Falls; KSIN-TV (PBS) Sioux City; KTIV (CW, MeTV, NBC) Sioux City; KTTW (FOX, This TV) Sioux Falls; KUSD-TV (PBS) Vermillion; KXNE-TV (PBS) Norfolk.
Programming (via satellite): A&E; AMC; Animal Planet; Bravo; Cartoon Network; CMT; CNBC; CNN; Comedy Central; C-SPAN; Discovery Channel; Disney Channel; E! HD; ESPN; ESPN2; EWTN Global Catholic Network; Food Network; Fox News Channel; Fox Sports 1; FOX Sports North; Freeform; FX; Hallmark Channel; HGTV; History; HLN; HSN; INSP; Lifetime; MSNBC; MTV; Nickelodeon; Pop; QVC; Spike TV; Syfy; TBS; The Weather Channel; This TV; TLC; TNT; Travel Channel; Trinity Broadcasting Network (TBN); truTV; Turner Classic Movies; TV Land; Univision; USA Network; VH1; WE tv; WGN America.
Fee: $19.95 monthly.

Digital Basic Service
Subscribers: N.A.
Programming (via satellite): A&E HD; AMC HD; Animal Planet HD; BBC America; Boomerang; BTN; BTN HD; Canal Sur; CBS Sports Network; Centric; Cine Mexicano; Cinelatino; Cloo; CMT; CNN en Espanol; CNN HD; Cooking Channel; C-SPAN 2; C-SPAN 3; Destination America; Discovery Channel HD; Discovery Family; Discovery Life Channel; Disney Channel HD; Disney XD; DIY Network; ESPN Classic; ESPN Deportes; ESPN HD; ESPN2 HD; ESPNews; ESPNU; Food Network HD; FOX College Sports Central; FOX College Sports Pacific; Fox News HD; Freeform HD; FSN HD; Fuse; FX HD; FXM; FYI; Golf Channel; Golf Channel HD; GolTV; GSN; HD Theater; HGTV HD; History en Espanol; History HD; History International; IFC; iN DEMAND; Investigation Discovery; ION Television; LMN; MC; MLB Network; MLB Network HD; MTV Jams; MTV Live; National Geographic Channel; National Geographic Channel HD; NBC Universo; NBCSN; NFL Network; NFL Network HD; NFL RedZone; NHL Network; Nick 2; Nick Jr.; Nicktoons; Outdoor Channel; OWN: Oprah Winfrey Network; Qubo; Reelz; RFD-TV; Science Channel; Science HD; Spike TV HD; Sprout; Syfy HD; TBS HD; TeenNick; Telemundo; Tennis Channel; The Sportsman Channel; The Weather Channel HD; TLC HD; TNT HD; Tr3s; TV One; TVG Network; Universal HD; USA Network HD; Versus HD; ViendoMovies; WE tv.
Fee: $24.95 monthly.

Digital Pay Service 1
Pay Units: N.A.
Programming (via satellite): Cinemax (multiplexed); Cinemax HD; Flix (multiplexed); HBO (multiplexed); HBO HD; Showtime (multiplexed); Showtime HD; Starz (multiplexed); Starz Encore (multiplexed); Starz HD; Sundance TV (multiplexed); The Movie Channel (multiplexed); The Movie Channel HD.

Video-On-Demand: No

Pay-Per-View
ESPN (delivered digitally); Fresh (delivered digitally); Shorteez (delivered digitally); Playboy TV (delivered digitally); Pleasure (delivered digitally); Mediacom PPV (delivered digitally).

Internet Service
Operational: Yes.
Subscribers: 5,162.
Broadband Service: MidcoNet.
Fee: $35.00 installation; $19.95 monthly.

Telephone Service
Digital: Operational
Subscribers: 2,139.
Fee: $18.00 monthly
Miles of Plant: 211.0 (coaxial); 47.0 (fiber optic). Homes passed: 13,882.
Programming Director: Wynne Haakenstad.
Ownership: Midcontinent Communications (MSO).

TENNESSEE

Total Systems: 51	Communities with Applications: 0
Total Communities Served: 565	Number of Basic Subscribers: 1,082,149
Franchises Not Yet Operating: 0	Number of Expanded Basic Subscribers: 590
Applications Pending: 0	Number of Pay Units: 1,965

Top 100 Markets Represented: Memphis (26); Nashville (30); Greenville-Spartanburg-Anderson, SC-Asheville, NC (46); Knoxville (71); Chattanooga (78); Huntsville-Decatur, AL (96).

For a list of cable communities in this section, see the Cable Community Index located in the back of Cable Volume 2.
For explanation of terms used in cable system listings, see p. D-11.

ALCOA—Charter Communications, 1774 Henry G Lane St, Maryville, TN 37801. Phones: 636-207-5100 (Corporate office); 865-983-8200; 865-984-1400. Web Site: http://www.charter.com. Also serves Blount County (portions), Farragut, Gatlinburg, Knox County (portions), Lenoir City, Loudon, Loudon County (portions), Louisville, Madisonville, Maryville, Monroe County (portions), Philadelphia, Pigeon Forge, Sevier County (portions), Sevierville, Seymour, Sweetwater & Telco Village. ICA: TN0151.
TV Market Ranking: 71 (ALCOA, Blount County (portions), Farragut, Gatlinburg, Knox County (portions), Loudon, Loudon County (portions), Louisville, Maryville, Pigeon Forge, Sevierville, Seymour); Below 100 (Monroe County (portions), Loudon County (portions)); Outside TV Markets (Sweetwater, Madisonville, Monroe County (portions)). Franchise award date: January 1, 1979. Franchise expiration date: N.A. Began: January 1, 1979.
Channel capacity: 70 (operating 2-way). Channels available but not in use: N.A.
Digital Basic Service
Subscribers: 50,502.
Programming (via satellite): AXS TV; BBC America; Bloomberg Television; CNN International; Cooking Channel; Discovery Digital Networks; DIY Network; ESPN Classic; ESPN HD; ESPNews; FOX College Sports Central; FOX College Sports Pacific; Fox Sports 2; FXM; FYI; Great American Country; HD Theater; History International; IFC; Jewelry Television; LMN; MC; NFL Network; Nick 2; Nick Jr.; Nicktoons; Sundance TV; TeenNick; TV Guide Interactive Inc.
Fee: $49.99 installation; $26.99 monthly.
Digital Expanded Basic Service
Subscribers: N.A.
Programming (via satellite): A&E; AMC; Animal Planet; BET; Bravo; Cartoon Network; CMT; CNBC; CNN; Comcast/Charter Sports Southeast (CSS); Comedy Central; C-SPAN; C-SPAN 2; Discovery Channel; Disney Channel; Disney XD; E! HD; ESPN; ESPN2; Food Network; Fox News Channel; Fox Sports 1; FOX Sports South/SportSouth; Freeform; FX; Golf Channel; GSN; Hallmark Channel; HGTV; History; HLN; INSP; Lifetime; MSNBC; MTV; National Geographic Channel; NBCSN; Nickelodeon; Oxygen; Pop; QVC; Spike TV; Syfy; TBS; Telemundo; The Weather Channel; TLC; TNT; Travel Channel; Trinity Broadcasting Network (TBN); truTV; Turner Classic Movies; TV Land; USA Network; VH1; WE tv.
Fee: $50.99 monthly.
Digital Pay Service 1
Pay Units: N.A.
Programming (via satellite): Cinemax (multiplexed); Flix; HBO (multiplexed); HBO HD; Showtime (multiplexed); Showtime HD; Starz (multiplexed); Starz Encore (multiplexed); The Movie Channel (multiplexed).
Video-On-Demand: Yes
Pay-Per-View
Special events.
Internet Service
Operational: Yes. Began: April 1, 1999.
Subscribers: 48,682.
Broadband Service: Charter Internet.
Fee: $29.99 monthly; $9.95 modem lease; $200.00 modem purchase.
Telephone Service
Digital: Operational
Subscribers: 10,756.
Fee: $29.99 monthly
Miles of Plant: 4,226.0 (coaxial); 1,404.0 (fiber optic). Homes passed: 121,797.
Technical Operations Director: Grant Evans. Marketing Director: Pat Hollenbeck. Government Relations Director: Nick Pavlis. Accounting Director: David Sovanski. Assistant Controller: Brent Trask. Chief Technician: Mark Haley. Marketing Manager: Angie Lee.
Ownership: Charter Communications Inc. (MSO).

ALTAMONT—Charter Communications. Now served by MANCHESTER, TN [TN0032]. ICA: TN0126.

ASHLAND CITY—Comcast Cable. Now served by NASHVILLE, TN [TN0002]. ICA: TN0052.

ATHENS—Comcast Cable. Now served by KNOXVILLE, TN [TN0004]. ICA: TN0024.

BENTON—Comcast Cable. Now served by KNOXVILLE, TN [TN0004]. ICA: TN0127.

BENTON COUNTY (portions)—Benton County Cable, PO Box 430, Camden, TN 38320. Phones: 855-556-8423; 931-535-2521; 731-584-7100. Fax: 731-584-0913. E-mail: bcc_info@bentoncountycable.net; info@bentoncable.com. Web Site: http://www.bentoncable.com. Also serves Big Sandy & Eva. ICA: TN0210.
TV Market Ranking: Outside TV Markets (BENTON COUNTY (PORTIONS), Big Sandy, Eva).
Channel capacity: N.A. Channels available but not in use: N.A.
Internet Service
Operational: Yes.
Fee: $19.95-$64.95 monthly.
Telephone Service
None
Ownership: Benton County Cable.

BOLIVAR (town)—Time Warner Cable, 7800 Crescent Executive Dr, Charlotte, NC 28217. Phones: 800-686-2200; 212-364-8200. Web Site: http://www.timewarnercable.com. Also serves Hardeman County (portions). ICA: TN0051.
TV Market Ranking: Below 100 (BOLIVAR (TOWN), Hardeman County (portions)). Franchise award date: April 8, 1980. Franchise expiration date: N.A. Began: August 1, 1981.
Channel capacity: N.A. Channels available but not in use: N.A.
Basic Service
Subscribers: 784. Commercial subscribers: 120.
Programming (received off-air): WATN-TV (ABC) Memphis; WBBJ-TV (ABC, CBS, MeTV) Jackson; WHBQ-TV (Decades, FOX, Movies!) Memphis; WKNO (PBS) Memphis; WLJT-DT (PBS) Lexington; WLMT (CW, MeTV, MNT) Memphis; WMC-TV (Bounce TV, NBC, This TV) Memphis; WPXX-TV (ION, MNT) Memphis; WREG-TV (Antenna TV, CBS) Memphis.
Programming (via satellite): C-SPAN; C-SPAN 2; EVINE Live; INSP; QVC; Trinity Broadcasting Network (TBN); WGN America.
Fee: $49.99 installation; $23.99 monthly.
Expanded Basic Service 1
Subscribers: N.A.
Programming (via satellite): A&E; AMC; Animal Planet; BET; Bravo; Cartoon Network; CMT; CNBC; CNN; Comedy Central; Discovery Channel; Disney Channel; E! HD; ESPN; ESPN Classic; ESPN2; Food Network; Fox News Channel; Fox Sports 1; Freeform; FX; Golf Channel; Hallmark Channel; HGTV; History; HLN; Lifetime; MSNBC; MTV; Nickelodeon; Outdoor Channel; Spike TV; Syfy; TBS; The Weather Channel; TLC; TNT; Travel Channel; truTV; TV Land; USA Network; VH1.
Fee: $42.95 monthly.
Digital Basic Service
Subscribers: N.A.
Programming (via satellite): BBC America; Bloomberg Television; Cloo; Discovery Digital Networks; Disney XD; DMX Music; ESPNews; FXM; FYI; Great American Country; History International; IFC; LMN; NBCSN; Nick Jr.; Nicktoons; TeenNick; The Word Network; Turner Classic Movies.
Digital Pay Service 1
Pay Units: 264.
Programming (via satellite): Cinemax (multiplexed); Flix; HBO (multiplexed); Showtime (multiplexed); Starz (multiplexed); Starz Encore (multiplexed); The Movie Channel (multiplexed).
Video-On-Demand: No
Pay-Per-View
iN DEMAND (delivered digitally); Hot Choice (delivered digitally); Playboy TV (delivered digitally); Fresh (delivered digitally); Shorteez (delivered digitally).

Internet Service
Operational: Yes.
Subscribers: 362.
Broadband Service: SpeedNet.
Fee: $40.00 installation; $31.99 monthly.
Telephone Service
Digital: Operational
Subscribers: 215.
Fee: $34.99 monthly
Miles of Plant: 101.0 (coaxial); 27.0 (fiber optic). Homes passed: 3,595.
Chairman & Chief Executive Officer: Glenn A. Britt. President & Chief Operations Officer: Robert D. Marcus. Senior Accounting Director: Karen Goodfellow.
Ownership: Time Warner Cable (MSO).

BRADFORD—Formerly served by NewWave Communications. Now served by Time Warner Cable, MAYFIELD, KY [KY0037]. ICA: TN0178.

BRISTOL—BTES, PO Box 549, Bristol, TN 37621. Phone: 423-968-1526. Fax: 423-793-5520. E-mail: customerservice@btes.net. Web Site: http://www.btes.net. ICA: TN0211.
Channel capacity: N.A. Channels available but not in use: N.A.
Basic Service
Subscribers: 12,725. Commercial subscribers: 180.
Programming (received off-air): WCYB-TV (CW, Decades, NBC) Bristol; WEMT (FOX, Movies!, This TV) Greeneville; WETP-TV (PBS) Sneedville; WJHL-TV (ABC, MeTV) Johnson City; WKPT-TV (COZI TV, Escape, MeTV, MNT) Kingsport; WLFG (IND, PBJ, Retro TV) Grundy; WSBN-TV (PBS) Norton.
Programming (via satellite): HSN; QVC; WGN America.
Fee: $11.95 monthly.
Expanded Basic Service 1
Subscribers: N.A.
Fee: $49.95 monthly.
Internet Service
Operational: Yes.
Fee: $16.95-$69.95 monthly.
Telephone Service
Digital: Operational
Fee: $22.90 monthly
Chief Executive Officer: Dr. Michael Browder. Business Development Manager: April Eads.
Ownership: Bristol Tennessee Essential Services.

BRISTOL—BTES, PO Box 549, Bristol, TN 37621. Phone: 423-968-1526. Fax: 423-793-5520. E-mail: customerservice@btes.net. Web Site: http://www.btes.net. ICA: TN5020.
Channel capacity: N.A. Channels available but not in use: N.A.

2017 Edition D-705

Tennessee—Cable Systems

Digital Basic
Subscribers: N.A.
Fee: $65.20 monthly plus $9.95 STB fee.
Spanish
Subscribers: N.A.
Fee: $4.95 monthly.
Sports
Subscribers: N.A.
Fee: $4.00 monthly.
Cinemax
Subscribers: N.A.
Fee: $15.95 monthly.
HBO
Subscribers: N.A.
Fee: $17.95 monthly.
Showtime/TMC
Subscribers: N.A.
Fee: $15.95 monthly.
Starz/Encore
Subscribers: N.A.
Fee: $13.95 monthly.
Internet Service
Operational: Yes.
Fee: $16.95-$69.95 monthly.
Telephone Service
Digital: Operational
Fee: $22.90 monthly
Chief Executive Officer: Dr. Michael Browder. Business Development Manager: April L. Eads.
Ownership: Bristol Tennessee Essential Services.

BRISTOL—Charter Communications. Now served by KINGSPORT, TN [TN0007]. ICA: TN0198.

BROWNSVILLE—Time Warner Cable, 7800 Crescent Executive Dr, Charlotte, NC 28217. Phones: 800-686-2200; 212-364-8200. Web Site: http://www.timewarnercable.com. Also serves Gates, Halls, Haywood County (portions), Henning, Lauderdale County (unincorporated areas) & Ripley. ICA: TN0054.
TV Market Ranking: Below 100 (BROWNSVILLE, Haywood County (portions)); Outside TV Markets (Gates, Halls, Henning, Lauderdale County (unincorporated areas), Ripley). Franchise award date: N.A. Franchise expiration date: N.A. Began: March 1, 1981.
Channel capacity: N.A. Channels available but not in use: N.A.
Basic Service
Subscribers: 3,012. Commercial subscribers: 180.
Programming (received off-air): WATN-TV (ABC) Memphis; WBBJ-TV (ABC, CBS, MeTV) Jackson; WHBQ-TV (Decades, FOX, Movies!) Memphis; WKNO (PBS) Memphis; WLMT (CW, MeTV, MNT) Memphis; WMC-TV (Bounce TV, NBC, This TV) Memphis; WPXX-TV (ION, MNT) Memphis; WREG-TV (Antenna TV, CBS) Memphis.
Programming (via satellite): C-SPAN; C-SPAN 2; EVINE Live; INSP; QVC; Trinity Broadcasting Network (TBN); WGN America.
Fee: $49.95 installation; $23.99 monthly.
Expanded Basic Service 1
Subscribers: N.A.
Programming (via satellite): A&E; AMC; Animal Planet; BET; Bravo; Cartoon Network; CMT; CNBC; CNN; Comedy Central; Discovery Channel; Disney Channel; E! HD; ESPN; ESPN Classic; ESPN2; Food Network; Fox News Channel; Fox Sports 1; Freeform; FX; Golf Channel; GSN; Hallmark Channel; HGTV; History; HLN; Lifetime; MSNBC; MTV; Nickelodeon; Outdoor Channel; Spike TV; Syfy; TBS; The Weather Channel; TLC; TNT; Travel Channel; truTV; TV Land; USA Network; VH1.
Fee: $54.99 monthly.
Digital Basic Service
Subscribers: N.A.
Programming (via satellite): BBC America; Bloomberg Television; Cloo; Discovery Digital Networks; Disney XD; DMX Music; ESPNews; FXM; FYI; Great American Country; History International; IFC; LMN; NBCSN; Nick Jr.; Nicktoons; TeenNick; The Word Network; Turner Classic Movies.
Digital Pay Service 1
Pay Units: 1,411.
Programming (via satellite): Cinemax (multiplexed); Flix; HBO (multiplexed); Showtime (multiplexed); Starz (multiplexed); Starz Encore (multiplexed); The Movie Channel (multiplexed).
Video-On-Demand: No
Pay-Per-View
Hot Choice (delivered digitally); Playboy TV (delivered digitally); Fresh (delivered digitally); Shorteez (delivered digitally); iN DEMAND (delivered digitally).
Internet Service
Operational: Yes.
Subscribers: 1,455.
Broadband Service: SpeedNet.
Fee: $40.00 installation; $31.99 monthly.
Telephone Service
Digital: Operational
Subscribers: 971.
Fee: $34.99 monthly
Miles of Plant: 264.0 (coaxial); None (fiber optic). Homes passed: 12,536.
Chairman & Chief Executive Officer: Glenn A. Britt. President & Chief Operations Officer: Robert D. Marcus. Senior Accounting Director: Karen Goodfellow.
Ownership: Time Warner Cable (MSO).

BYRDSTOWN—Celina Cable, 17525 Highland Dr, McKenzie, TN 38201. Phone: 731-352-2980. Fax: 731-352-3533. Also serves Pickett County. ICA: TN0109.
TV Market Ranking: Below 100 (Pickett County (portions)); Outside TV Markets (BYRDSTOWN, Pickett County (portions)). Franchise award date: N.A. Franchise expiration date: N.A. Began: January 1, 1968.
Channel capacity: N.A. Channels available but not in use: N.A.
Basic Service
Subscribers: N.A.
Programming (received off-air): WBKO (ABC, CW, FOX) Bowling Green; WCTE (PBS) Cookeville; WKRN-TV (ABC) Nashville; WNPT (PBS) Nashville; WSMV-TV (COZI TV, NBC, TNN) Nashville; WTVF (CBS, Laff, This TV) Nashville; WZTV (Antenna TV, FOX, WeatherNation) Nashville.
Programming (via satellite): A&E; CMT; CNBC; CNN; C-SPAN; C-SPAN 2; Discovery Channel; Disney Channel; ESPN; Freeform; HGTV; HLN; Lifetime; Nickelodeon; Outdoor Channel; QVC; Spike TV; TBS; The Weather Channel; TNT; USA Network; WGN America.
Fee: $32.95 installation; $35.00 monthly.
Pay Service 1
Pay Units: N.A.
Programming (via satellite): Cinemax; HBO; Starz; Starz Encore.
Fee: $8.95 monthly (Encore/Starz), $10.95 monthly (Cinemax), $12.95 monthly (HBO).
Internet Service
Operational: Yes.
Telephone Service
None
Miles of Plant: 25.0 (coaxial); None (fiber optic). Homes passed: 606.
General Manager: Gary Blount.
Ownership: Celina Cable Communications (MSO).

CALHOUN—Charter Communications. Now served by CLEVELAND, TN [TN0013]. ICA: TN0129.

CARTER COUNTY (portions)—Zito Media, 102 S Main St, PO Box 665, Coudersport, PA 16915. Phones: 814-260-9055; 800-365-6988. E-mail: info@zitomedia.com. Web Site: http://www.zitomedia.com. Also serves Simerly Creek, Unicoi & Unicoi County (portions). ICA: TN0105.
TV Market Ranking: Below 100 (CARTER COUNTY (PORTIONS), Unicoi County (portions), Simerly Creek, Unicoi). Franchise award date: N.A. Franchise expiration date: N.A. Began: June 1, 1990.
Channel capacity: N.A. Channels available but not in use: N.A.
Basic Service
Subscribers: 37.
Programming (received off-air): WCYB-TV (CW, Decades, NBC) Bristol; WEMT (FOX, Movies!, This TV) Greeneville; WETP-TV (PBS) Sneedville; WJHL-TV (ABC, CBS, MeTV) Johnson City; WKPT-TV (COZI TV, Escape, MeTV, MNT) Kingsport.
Programming (via satellite): A&E; Animal Planet; CMT; CNN; Discovery Channel; Disney Channel; ESPN; ESPN2; Freeform; HGTV; MTV; Nickelodeon; Spike TV; TBS; TNT; Trinity Broadcasting Network (TBN); Turner Classic Movies; USA Network; WGN America.
Fee: $49.95 installation; $42.35 monthly.
Pay Service 1
Pay Units: N.A.
Programming (via satellite): HBO.
Fee: $9.95 monthly.
Video-On-Demand: No
Pay-Per-View
iN DEMAND (delivered digitally); Hot Choice (delivered digitally); Playboy TV (delivered digitally); Fresh (delivered digitally); Shorteez (delivered digitally).
Internet Service
Operational: No.
Telephone Service
None
Miles of Plant: 32.0 (coaxial); None (fiber optic). Homes passed: 620.
President: James Rigas.
Ownership: Zito Media (MSO).

CARTHAGE—Comcast Cable. Now served by NASHVILLE, TN [TN0002]. ICA: TN0131.

CELINA—Celina Cable, 17525 Highland Dr, McKenzie, TN 38201. Phone: 731-352-2980. Fax: 731-352-3533. Also serves Clay County (unincorporated areas) & Livingston. ICA: TN0096.
TV Market Ranking: Below 100 (CELINA, Livingston); Outside TV Markets (Clay County (unincorporated areas)). Franchise award date: N.A. Franchise expiration date: N.A. Began: July 1, 1988.
Channel capacity: 36 (not 2-way capable). Channels available but not in use: N.A.
Basic Service
Subscribers: N.A.
Programming (received off-air): WBKO (ABC, CW, FOX) Bowling Green; WCTE (PBS) Cookeville; WKRN-TV (ABC) Nashville; WNAB (CW, The Country Network) Nashville; WNPX-TV (ION) Cookeville; WSMV-TV (COZI TV, NBC, TNN) Nashville; WTVF (CBS, Laff, This TV) Nashville; WZTV (Antenna TV, FOX, WeatherNation) Nashville.
Programming (via satellite): A&E; Comedy Central; C-SPAN; Freeform; Lifetime; Nickelodeon; QVC.
Fee: $30.25 installation; $17.25 monthly.
Expanded Basic Service 1
Subscribers: N.A.
Programming (via satellite): AMC; Animal Planet; Boomerang; Cartoon Network; CMT; CNBC; CNN; Discovery Channel; Disney Channel; ESPN; ESPN2; Fox News Channel; FX; HGTV; History; HLN; MTV; Outdoor Channel; Syfy; TBS; The Weather Channel; TLC; TNT; Travel Channel; Trinity Broadcasting Network (TBN); TV Land; USA Network; VH1; WGN America.
Fee: $33.75 monthly.
Pay Service 1
Pay Units: N.A.
Programming (via satellite): Cinemax; HBO; The Movie Channel.
Fee: $11.18 monthly (each).
Video-On-Demand: No
Internet Service
Operational: Yes.
Telephone Service
None
Miles of Plant: 35.0 (coaxial); None (fiber optic). Homes passed: 1,050.
General Manager: Gary Blount.
Ownership: Celina Cable Communications (MSO).

CENTERVILLE—Charter Communications. Now served by COLUMBIA, TN [TN0017]. ICA: TN0204.

CHAPEL HILL—Formerly served by Small Town Cable. No longer in operation. ICA: TN0089.

CHATTANOOGA—Comcast Cable. Now served by KNOXVILLE, TN [TN0004]. ICA: TN0003.

CHATTANOOGA—EPB, 10 West Martin Luther King Blvd, Chattanooga, TN 37402-1813. Phone: 423-648-1372. Web Site: http://www.epb.net. Also serves Catoosa County (portions), Dade County (portions), Flintstone, Lookout Mountain, Marion County (portions), Rossville, Walker County (portions) & Wildwood, GA; Apison, Bakewell, Collegedale, East Ridge, Graysville, Guild, Hamilton County (portions), Harrison, Hixson, Lakesite, Lookout Mountain, Lupton City, McDonald, Ooltewah, Red Bank, Ridgeside, Sale Creek, Signal Mountain, Soddy Daisy, Walden & Whiteside, TN. ICA: TN0214.
Channel capacity: N.A. Channels available but not in use: N.A.
Basic Service
Subscribers: 54,271.
Fee: $14.99 monthly.
Expanded Basic Service 1
Subscribers: N.A.
Fee: $67.99 monthly.
Internet Service
Operational: Yes.
Fee: $57.99-$69.99 monthly.
Telephone Service
Digital: Operational
Subscribers: 23,171.
Fee: $22.99 monthly
Miles of Plant: None (coaxial); 4,060.0 (fiber optic). Homes passed: 177,969.
Chief Executive Officer: Harold E. DePriest. Chief Operating Officer: Dave Wade. Exec-

Cable Systems—Tennessee

utive Vice President & Chief Financial Officer: Greg Eaves. Vice President, Corporate Communications: Danna Bailey. Vice President, Economic Growth & Government Relations: Diana Bullock. Vice President, Customer Service: Kathy Burns. Vice President, New Products: Kathy Espeth. Vice President, IT: David Johnson. Vice President, Technical Operations: Ryan Keel. Vice President, Marketing: J. Ed Marston.
Ownership: EPB.

CLARKSVILLE—Charter Communications, PO Box 908, Clarksville, TN 37041. Phones: 314-543-2236; 636-207-5100 (Corporate office); 865-983-8200; 865-984-1400. Web Site: http://www.charter.com. Also serves Ashland City, Cheatham County (portions), Coopertown, Montgomery County (portions), Pleasant View & Robertson County (portions). ICA: TN0009.
TV Market Ranking: 30 (Ashland City, Cheatham County (portions), Coopertown, Pleasant View, Robertson County (portions)); Outside TV Markets (CLARKSVILLE, Montgomery County (portions)). Franchise award date: January 1, 1978. Franchise expiration date: N.A. Began: October 2, 1978.
Channel capacity: 67 (operating 2-way). Channels available but not in use: N.A.
Digital Basic Service
Subscribers: 25,056.
Programming (via satellite): BBC America; Bloomberg Television; CNN en Espanol; CNN International; Discovery Digital Networks; DIY Network; ESPN; ESPN Classic; ESPNews; FOX College Sports Central; FOX College Sports Pacific; Fox Sports 2; Fuse; FXM; FYI; Great American Country; GSN; HD Theater; History International; IFC; International Television (ITV); LMN; MC; NFL Network; Nick 2; Nick Jr.; Nicktoons; Sundance TV; TeenNick; TV Guide Interactive Inc.; WE tv.
Fee: $49.99 installation; $26.99 monthly.
Digital Expanded Basic Service
Subscribers: N.A.
Programming (via satellite): A&E; AMC; Animal Planet; BET; Bravo; Cartoon Network; CMT; CNBC; CNN; Comcast/Charter Sports Southeast (CSS); Comedy Central; Discovery Channel; Disney Channel; Disney XD; E! HD; ESPN; ESPN2; Food Network; Fox News Channel; Fox Sports 1; FOX Sports South/SportSouth; Freeform; FX; Golf Channel; Hallmark Channel; HGTV; History; HLN; Lifetime; MSNBC; MTV; National Geographic Channel; NBCSN; Nickelodeon; Oxygen; Spike TV; Syfy; TBS; The Weather Channel; TLC; TNT; Travel Channel; truTV; Turner Classic Movies; TV Land; USA Network; VH1.
Fee: $45.00 monthly.
Digital Pay Service 1
Pay Units: N.A.
Programming (via satellite): Cinemax (multiplexed); Flix; HBO (multiplexed); HBO HD; Showtime (multiplexed); Showtime HD; Starz; Starz Encore; The Movie Channel (multiplexed).
Video-On-Demand: Yes
Pay-Per-View
iN DEMAND (delivered digitally); NHL Center Ice (delivered digitally); MLB Extra Innings (delivered digitally); Playboy TV (delivered digitally); Fresh (delivered digitally); Shorteez (delivered digitally).
Internet Service
Operational: Yes. Began: January 1, 2001.
Subscribers: 26,510.
Broadband Service: Charter Internet.
Fee: $29.99 monthly; $9.95 modem lease.

Telephone Service
Digital: Operational
Subscribers: 4,901.
Miles of Plant: 2,909.0 (coaxial); 708.0 (fiber optic). Homes passed: 88,099.
Operations Manager: Tony Fox. Technical Operations Director: Ron Janson. Marketing Director: Pat Hollenbeck. Accounting Director: David Sovanski. Marketing Manager: Wiley Bird.
Ownership: Charter Communications Inc. (MSO).

CLARKSVILLE—Formerly served by Virginia Communications Inc. No longer in operation. ICA: TN0182.

CLEVELAND—Charter Communications, 12405 Powerscourt Dr, St. Louis, MO 63131. Phones: 636-207-5100 (Corporate office); 877-581-3485. Fax: 423-476-1621. Web Site: http://www.charter.com. Also serves Bradley County, Calhoun, Charleston, Dayton, Decatur, Graysville, McMinn County & Rhea County (portions). ICA: TN0013.
TV Market Ranking: 78 (Bradley County, Calhoun, Charleston, CLEVELAND, Dayton, Graysville, McMinn County, Rhea County (portions)); Below 100 (Decatur). Franchise award date: N.A. Franchise expiration date: N.A. Began: October 1, 1976.
Channel capacity: 70 (operating 2-way). Channels available but not in use: N.A.
Digital Basic Service
Subscribers: 19,952.
Programming (via satellite): BBC America; Discovery Digital Networks; DIY Network; ESPN Classic; ESPNews; FOX College Sports Central; FOX College Sports Pacific; Fox Sports 2; FXM; FYI; Great American Country; History International; HITS (Headend In The Sky); IFC; Jewelry Television; LMN; MC; MTV Classic; MTV2; NFL Network; Nick 2; Nick Jr.; Nicktoons; Sundance TV; TeenNick; TV Guide Interactive Inc.
Fee: $26.99 monthly.
Digital Expanded Basic Service
Subscribers: N.A.
Programming (via satellite): A&E; AMC; Animal Planet; BET; Bravo; Cartoon Network; CMT; CNBC; CNN; Comcast/Charter Sports Southeast (CSS); Comedy Central; Discovery Channel; Disney Channel; Disney XD; E! HD; ESPN; Food Network; Fox News Channel; Fox Sports 1; FOX Sports South/SportSouth; Freeform; FX; Golf Channel; GSN; Hallmark Channel; HGTV; History; HLN; Lifetime; MSNBC; MTV; National Geographic Channel; NBCSN; Nickelodeon; Oxygen; Pop; Spike TV; Syfy; TBS; Telemundo; The Weather Channel; TLC; TNT; Travel Channel; truTV; Turner Classic Movies; TV Land; Univision; USA Network; VH1; WE tv.
Fee: $50.99 monthly.
Digital Pay Service 1
Pay Units: N.A.
Programming (via satellite): Flix; HBO (multiplexed); Showtime (multiplexed); Starz (multiplexed); Starz Encore (multiplexed); The Movie Channel (multiplexed).
Fee: $15.00 installation; $10.95 monthly (each).
Video-On-Demand: Yes
Pay-Per-View
iN DEMAND (delivered digitally); Playboy TV (delivered digitally); Fresh (delivered digitally); Shorteez (delivered digitally); NHL Center Ice (delivered digitally); MLB Extra Innings (delivered digitally).
Internet Service
Operational: Yes.
Subscribers: 18,192.

Broadband Service: Charter Internet.
Fee: $29.99 monthly.
Telephone Service
Digital: Operational
Subscribers: 4,236.
Fee: $29.99 monthly
Miles of Plant: 2,355.0 (coaxial); 634.0 (fiber optic). Homes passed: 56,809.
Operations Manager: Mike Burns. Technical Operations Director: Grant Evans. Marketing Director: Pat Hollenbeck. Accounting Director: David Sovanski. Technical Operations Manager: David Ogle. Office Manager: Connie Wilson.
Ownership: Charter Communications Inc. (MSO).

CLIFTON—Charter Communications. Now served by JACKSON CITY, TN [TN0008]. ICA: TN0120.

COBBLY NOB—Comcast Cable. Now served by KNOXVILLE, TN [TN0004]. ICA: TN0193.

COLUMBIA—Charter Communications, 12405 Powerscourt Dr, St. Louis, MO 63131. Phones: 636-207-5100 (Corporate office); 865-983-8200; 865-984-1400. Fax: 865-983-0383. Web Site: http://www.charter.com. Also serves Lauderdale County (portions), AL; Bedford County (portions), Belfast, Centerville, Giles County (portions), Hohenwald, Iron City, Lawrence County (portions), Lawrenceburg, Lewis County (portions), Lewisburg, Loretto, Marshall County (portions), Maury County (portions), Mount Pleasant, Pulaski, Shelbyville (portions), Spring Hill, St. Joseph, Thompson's Station, Westpoint & Williamson County (portions), TN. ICA: TN0017.
TV Market Ranking: 30 (Spring Hill, Thompson's Station, Williamson County (portions)); 96 (Giles County (portions), Lawrence County (portions), Pulaski); Below 100 (Bedford County (portions), Belfast, Iron City, Lauderdale County (portions), St. Joseph, Westpoint, Lawrenceburg, Loretto, Marshall County (portions), Lawrence County (portions)); Outside TV Markets (COLUMBIA, Hohenwald, Lewis County (portions), Mount Pleasant, Centerville, Lewisburg, Marshall County (portions), Lawrence County (portions)). Franchise award date: N.A. Franchise expiration date: N.A. Began: October 15, 1967.
Channel capacity: 67 (operating 2-way). Channels available but not in use: N.A.
Digital Basic Service
Subscribers: 22,402.
Programming (via satellite): BBC America; Boomerang; CNN International; Destination America; Discovery Kids Channel; DIY Network; DMX Music; ESPN Classic; ESPNews; FOX College Sports Central; FOX College Sports Pacific; Fox Sports 2; FYI; Great American Country; History International; IFC; Investigation Discovery; LMN; NFL Network; Nick 2; Nick Jr.; Nicktoons; Outdoor Channel; OWN: Oprah Winfrey Network; Sundance TV; TeenNick.
Fee: $26.99 monthly.
Digital Expanded Basic Service
Subscribers: N.A.
Programming (via satellite): A&E; AMC; Animal Planet; BET; Cartoon Network; CMT; CNBC; CNN; Comedy Central; Discovery Channel; Discovery Life Channel; Disney Channel; Disney XD; E! HD; ESPN; ESPN2; Food Network; Fox News Channel; Fox Sports 1; FOX Sports South/SportSouth; Freeform; FX; Golf Channel; GSN;

Hallmark Channel; HGTV; History; HLN; Lifetime; MSNBC; MTV; National Geographic Channel; NBCSN; Nickelodeon; Oxygen; Spike TV; Syfy; TBS; Telemundo; The Weather Channel; TLC; TNT; Travel Channel; truTV; Turner Classic Movies; TV Land; Univision; Univision Studios; USA Network; VH1; WE tv.
Fee: $45.00 monthly.
Digital Pay Service 1
Pay Units: N.A.
Programming (via satellite): Cinemax (multiplexed); HBO (multiplexed); Starz (multiplexed).
Video-On-Demand: Yes
Pay-Per-View
Playboy TV (delivered digitally); Fresh (delivered digitally); Shorteez (delivered digitally).
Internet Service
Operational: Yes.
Subscribers: 20,702.
Broadband Service: Charter Internet.
Fee: $29.99 monthly.
Telephone Service
Digital: Operational
Subscribers: 4,344.
Fee: $29.99 monthly
Miles of Plant: 3,254.0 (coaxial); 1,030.0 (fiber optic). Homes passed: 80,235.
Operations Manager: Sean Hendrix. Marketing Director: Pat Hollenbeck. Sales & Marketing Manager: Jo Ann Placke. Accounting Director: David Sovanski.
Ownership: Charter Communications Inc. (MSO).

COLUMBIA—CPWS Broadband, 201 Pickens Ln, PO Box 379, Columbia, TN 38401. Phone: 931-388-4833. Fax: 931-388-5287. E-mail: jim.clark@cpws.com. Web Site: http://www.cpws.com. ICA: TN0191. **Note:** This system is an overbuild.
TV Market Ranking: Outside TV Markets (COLUMBIA).
Channel capacity: N.A. Channels available but not in use: N.A.
Basic Service
Subscribers: 4,412.
Programming (received off-air): WHTN (Christian TV Network) Murfreesboro; WKRN-TV (ABC) Nashville; WNAB (CW, The Country Network) Nashville; WNPT (PBS) Nashville; WSMV-TV (COZI TV, NBC, TNN) Nashville; WTVF (CBS, Laff, This TV) Nashville; WUXP-TV (MNT) Nashville; WZTV (Antenna TV, FOX, WeatherNation) Nashville.
Programming (via satellite): INSP; Pop; QVC; TBS; The Weather Channel; Trinity Broadcasting Network (TBN); WGN America.
Fee: $23.50 monthly.
Expanded Basic Service 1
Subscribers: N.A.
Programming (via satellite): A&E; AMC; Animal Planet; BET; Bravo; Cartoon Network; CMT; CNBC; CNN; Comcast/Charter Sports Southeast (CSS); Comedy Central; C-SPAN; C-SPAN 2; Discovery Channel; Disney Channel; Disney XD; E! HD; ESPN; ESPN Classic; ESPN2; EWTN Global Catholic Network; Food Network; Fox News Channel; Fox Sports 1; FOX Sports South/SportSouth; Freeform; FX; Golf Channel; Great American Country; GSN; Hallmark Channel; HGTV; History; HLN; ION Television; Lifetime; MSNBC; MTV; National Geographic Channel; NBCSN; Nickelodeon; Outdoor Channel; Oxygen; RFD-TV; Spike TV; Syfy; TLC; TNT; Travel Channel; truTV; Turner Classic Movies; TV Land; Univision

2017 Edition D-707

Tennessee—Cable Systems

Studios; USA Network; VH1; WE tv; World Harvest Television.
Fee: $36.00 monthly.

Digital Basic Service
Subscribers: N.A.
Programming (via satellite): 3ABN; BBC America; Bloomberg Television; Boomerang; CMT; CNN International; Cooking Channel; Destination America; Discovery Kids Channel; DIY Network; ESPNews; FamilyNet; FOX College Sports Central; FOX College Sports Pacific; Fuse; FXM; FYI; History International; IFC; Investigation Discovery; JUCE TV; LMN; MC; MTV Classic; MTV Jams; MTV2; Nick Jr.; Nicktoons; OWN: Oprah Winfrey Network; Science Channel; TeenNick; VH1 Soul; WAM! America's Kidz Network.
Fee: $4.00 monthly.

Digital Expanded Basic Service
Subscribers: N.A.
Programming (via satellite): A&E HD; Animal Planet HD; Cine Mexicano; CNN en Espanol; Discovery Channel HD; Discovery Familia; Enlace USA; ESPN Deportes; ESPN HD; Food Network HD; Fox Deportes; HD Theater; HGTV HD; History HD; La Familia Cosmovision; NBC Universo; Outdoor Channel 2 HD; Science HD; TLC HD; TNT HD; Toon Disney en Espanol; Tr3s; ULTRA HDPlex; Universal HD; VideoRola.
Fee: $6.00 monthly (Canales), $12.95 monthly (HD Pak).

Pay Service 1
Pay Units: N.A.
Programming (via satellite): HBO (multiplexed).
Fee: $12.80 monthly.

Digital Pay Service 1
Pay Units: N.A.
Programming (via satellite): Cinemax (multiplexed); Cinemax HD; Flix; HBO (multiplexed); HBO HD; Showtime (multiplexed); Showtime HD; Starz (multiplexed); Starz Encore (multiplexed); Starz HD; Sundance TV; The Movie Channel (multiplexed); The Movie Channel HD.
Fee: $13.75 monthly (Cinemax), $15.85 monthly (Starz/Encore), $16.75 monthly (HBO), $17.76 monthly (Showtime/TMC).

Video-On-Demand: No

Pay-Per-View
iN DEMAND (delivered digitally).

Internet Service
Operational: Yes.
Subscribers: 2,808.
Broadband Service: XpressNet.
Fee: $24.95-$76.95 monthly.

Telephone Service
None
Miles of Plant: 312.0 (coaxial); 85.0 (fiber optic). Homes passed: 18,775.
General Manager: Jim Clark. Office Manager: Martha Mayberry. Chief Technician: Marty Helms. Marketing Director: Johnna Watson. Broadband Manager: Glenn Jernigan.
Ownership: Columbia Power & Water Systems.

COOKEVILLE—Charter Communications, 12405 Powerscourt Dr, St. Louis, MO 63131. Phones: 636-207-5100 (Corporate office); 865-983-8200; 865-984-1400. Fax: 865-983-0383. Web Site: http://www.charter.com. Also serves Algood, Baxter, Doyle, Monterey, Putnam County (portions), Sparta & White County (portions). ICA: TN0020.
TV Market Ranking: Below 100 (Algood, Baxter, Doyle, Monterey, Putnam County (portions), Sparta, White County (portions)).

Franchise award date: N.A. Franchise expiration date: N.A. Began: January 1, 1968.
Channel capacity: 67 (operating 2-way). Channels available but not in use: N.A.

Digital Basic Service
Subscribers: 12,190.
Programming (via satellite): BBC America; Bloomberg Television; Boomerang; CNN International; Discovery Digital Networks; DIY Network; DMX Music; ESPN Classic; ESPNews; FOX College Sports Central; FOX College Sports Pacific; Fox Sports 2; FXM; FYI; Great American Country; History International; IFC; LMN; NFL Network; Nick 2; Nick Jr.; Nicktoons; Outdoor Channel; Sundance TV; TeenNick.
Fee: $26.99 monthly.

Digital Expanded Basic Service
Subscribers: N.A.
Programming (via satellite): A&E; AMC; Animal Planet; BET; Bravo; Cartoon Network; CMT; CNBC; CNN; Comedy Central; Discovery Channel; Discovery Life Channel; Disney Channel; Disney XD; E! HD; ESPN; ESPN2; Food Network; Fox News Channel; Fox Sports 1; FOX Sports South/SportSouth; FX; Golf Channel; GSN; Hallmark Channel; HGTV; History; HLN; Lifetime; MSNBC; MTV; National Geographic Channel; NBCSN; Nickelodeon; Oxygen; Spike TV; Syfy; TBS; Telemundo; The Weather Channel; TLC; TNT; Travel Channel; truTV; Turner Classic Movies; TV Land; Univision; Univision Studios; USA Network; VH1; WE tv.
Fee: $45.00 monthly.

Digital Pay Service 1
Pay Units: N.A.
Programming (via satellite): Cinemax; HBO; Starz (multiplexed).

Video-On-Demand: No

Pay-Per-View
Playboy TV (delivered digitally); Fresh (delivered digitally); Shorteez (delivered digitally).

Internet Service
Operational: Yes.
Subscribers: 14,895.
Broadband Service: Charter Internet.
Fee: $29.99 monthly; $5.00 modem lease.

Telephone Service
Digital: Operational
Subscribers: 1,898.
Fee: $29.99 monthly
Miles of Plant: 2,149.0 (coaxial); 509.0 (fiber optic). Homes passed: 49,380.
Operations Director: Sean Hendrix. Marketing Director: Pat Hollenbeck. Accounting Director: David Sovanski. Sales & Marketing Manager: Jo Ann Placke.
Ownership: Charter Communications Inc. (MSO).

CORNERSVILLE—Formerly served by Small Town Cable. No longer in operation. ICA: TN0133.

COUNCE—Pickwick Cablevision, PO Box 12, Counce, TN 38365. Phone: 731-689-5722. Fax: 731-689-3632. Web Site: http://www.pickwickcable.net. Also serves Hardin County (portions) & Pickwick Dam. ICA: TN0100.
TV Market Ranking: Below 100 (Pickwick Dam, Hardin County (portions)); Outside TV Markets (COUNCE, Hardin County (portions)). Franchise award date: N.A. Franchise expiration date: N.A. Began: July 1, 1978.
Channel capacity: N.A. Channels available but not in use: N.A.

Basic Service
Subscribers: N.A.
Programming (received off-air): WBBJ-TV (ABC, CBS, MeTV) Jackson; WHBQ-TV (Decades, FOX, Movies!) Memphis; WJKT (FOX) Jackson; WKNO (PBS) Memphis; WMC-TV (Bounce TV, NBC, This TV) Memphis; WREG-TV (Antenna TV, CBS) Memphis.
Programming (via satellite): A&E; Cartoon Network; CMT; CNBC; CNN; Comcast/Charter Sports Southeast (CSS); C-SPAN; Discovery Channel; ESPN; ESPN2; Food Network; Fox News Channel; Freeform; FX; Hallmark Channel; HGTV; History; HLN; Lifetime; National Geographic Channel; Nickelodeon; QVC; Spike TV; TBS; The Weather Channel; TNT; Turner Classic Movies; TV Land; USA Network; WGN America.
Fee: $25.00 installation.

Digital Basic Service
Subscribers: N.A.
Programming (via satellite): BBC America; Bloomberg Television; Bravo; Cloo; CMT; Discovery Digital Networks; DMX Music; Fuse; FXM; FYI; Great American Country; GSN; History International; IFC; LMN; National Geographic Channel; Nick Jr.; Nicktoons; Ovation; Sundance TV; TeenNick; The Word Network; UP; WE tv.
Fee: $14.65 monthly.

Digital Expanded Basic Service
Subscribers: N.A.
Programming (via satellite): ESPN Classic; ESPNews; FOX College Sports Central; FOX College Sports Pacific; Fox Sports 1; Golf Channel; NBCSN; Outdoor Channel.
Fee: $11.80 monthly.

Digital Expanded Basic Service 2
Subscribers: N.A.
Programming (via satellite): ESPN Classic; ESPNews; FOX College Sports Central; FOX College Sports Pacific; Fox Sports 1; Golf Channel; NBCSN; Outdoor Channel.
Fee: $7.30 monthly.

Pay Service 1
Pay Units: N.A.
Programming (via satellite): Cinemax; HBO.
Fee: $15.00 installation; $8.60 monthly (Cinemax), $11.20 monthly (HBO).

Digital Pay Service 1
Pay Units: N.A.
Programming (via satellite): Cinemax (multiplexed); HBO (multiplexed); Showtime (multiplexed); Starz (multiplexed); Starz Encore (multiplexed); The Movie Channel (multiplexed).
Fee: $9.00 monthly (Cinemax or TMC), $11.25 monthly (HBO), $13.50 monthly (Showtime).

Video-On-Demand: No

Internet Service
Operational: Yes.
Broadband Service: In-house.
Fee: $29.95-$59.95 monthly.

Telephone Service
None
Miles of Plant: 60.0 (coaxial); None (fiber optic). Homes passed: 1,200.
General Manager: Robert Campbell Sr.
Ownership: Pickwick Cablevision.

COVINGTON—Comcast Cable. Now served by MEMPHIS, TN [TN0001]. ICA: TN0066.

CROSSVILLE—Charter Communications, 848 Livingston Rd, Ste 103, Crossville, TN 38555. Phones: 636-207-5100 (Corporate office); 314-543-2236; 865-984-1400. Web Site: http://www.charter.com. Also serves Cumberland County & Lake Tansi. ICA: TN0134.
TV Market Ranking: Below 100 (CROSSVILLE, Cumberland County, Lake Tansi). Franchise award date: N.A. Franchise expiration date: N.A. Began: July 21, 1979.
Channel capacity: N.A. Channels available but not in use: N.A.

Digital Basic Service
Subscribers: 3,183.
Programming (via satellite): BBC America; Bloomberg Television; Boomerang; CNN International; Discovery Digital Networks; DIY Network; ESPN Classic; ESPNews; FOX College Sports Central; FOX College Sports Pacific; Fox Sports 2; Fuse; FXM; FYI; Great American Country; History International; IFC; LMN; NFL Network; Nick 2; Nick Jr.; Nicktoons; Outdoor Channel; Sundance TV; TeenNick.
Fee: $26.99 monthly.

Digital Expanded Basic Service
Subscribers: N.A.
Programming (via satellite): A&E; AMC; Animal Planet; BET; Bravo; Cartoon Network; CMT; CNBC; CNN; Comedy Central; Discovery Channel; Discovery Life Channel; Disney Channel; Disney XD; E! HD; ESPN; ESPN2; Food Network; Fox News Channel; Fox Sports 1; FOX Sports South/SportSouth; Freeform; FX; Golf Channel; GSN; Hallmark Channel; HGTV; History; HLN; Lifetime; MSNBC; MTV; National Geographic Channel; NBCSN; Nickelodeon; Oxygen; Spike TV; Syfy; TBS; Telemundo; The Weather Channel; TLC; TNT; Travel Channel; truTV; Turner Classic Movies; TV Land; Univision; Univision Studios; USA Network; VH1; WE tv.
Fee: $45.00 monthly.

Digital Pay Service 1
Pay Units: N.A.
Programming (via satellite): Cinemax; HBO; Starz (multiplexed).

Video-On-Demand: No

Pay-Per-View
Playboy TV (delivered digitally); Fresh (delivered digitally); Shorteez (delivered digitally).

Internet Service
Operational: Yes.
Broadband Service: Charter Internet.
Fee: $29.99 monthly.

Telephone Service
None
Operations Manager: Sean Hendrix. Assistant Controller: Brent Trask. Marketing Director: Pat Hollenbeck. Accounting Director: David Sovanski. Sales & Marketing Manager: Jo Ann Placke.
Ownership: Charter Communications Inc. (MSO).

CUMBERLAND COUNTY—Spirit Broadband, 302 Woodlawn Road, Crossville, TN 38555. Phones: 877-368-2110; 615-368-2115. Web Site: http://www.spiritbb.com. Also serves Crab Orchard, Crossville & Pleasant Hill. ICA: TN0159.
TV Market Ranking: Below 100 (Crab Orchard, Crossville, CUMBERLAND COUNTY, Pleasant Hill). Franchise award date: N.A. Franchise expiration date: N.A. Began: July 1, 1988.
Channel capacity: N.A. Channels available but not in use: N.A.

Basic Service
Subscribers: N.A.
Programming (received off-air): WATE-TV (ABC, Laff) Knoxville; WBIR-TV (MeTV, NBC) Knoxville; WCTE (PBS) Cookeville; WTNZ (FOX, This TV) Knoxville; WTVF (CBS, Laff, This TV) Nashville.

Cable Systems—Tennessee

Programming (via satellite): A&E; AMC; Animal Planet; Cartoon Network; CNBC; CNN; Comedy Central; C-SPAN; C-SPAN 2; Discovery Central; Disney Channel; Disney XD; ESPN; ESPN Classic; ESPN2; ESPNews; FamilyNet; Fox News Channel; Fox Sports 1; FX; Golf Channel; HGTV; History; HLN; Lifetime; LMN; MSNBC; MTV; MTV2; National Geographic Channel; NBCSN; Nick Jr.; Nickelodeon; Nicktoons; QVC; Spike TV; Syfy; TBS; The Weather Channel; TLC; TNT; Travel Channel; TV Land; USA Network; VH1; WGN America.
Fee: $40.00 installation.
Digital Basic Service
Subscribers: N.A.
Fee: $15.00 monthly.
Pay Service 1
Pay Units: N.A.
Programming (via satellite): Cinemax; HBO.
Fee: $12.00 monthly (each).
Video-On-Demand: Yes
Internet Service
Operational: Yes.
Fee: $29.95-$34.95 monthly.
Telephone Service
Digital: Operational
Fee: $29.95 monthly
Miles of Plant: 287.0 (coaxial); 120.0 (fiber optic). Homes passed: 7,000.
President & General Manager: Vince King. Chief Technician: Brian Langham.
Ownership: Spirit Broadband.

DANDRIDGE—Haywood Cablevision, 4930 Jonathan Creek Rd, Waynesville, NC 28785. Phones: 866-571-8671; 828-926-2288. Fax: 678-682-9727. Web Site: http://www.cbvnol.com. ICA: TN0201.
TV Market Ranking: 71 (DANDRIDGE).
Channel capacity: N.A. Channels available but not in use: N.A.
Basic Service
Subscribers: N.A.
Programming (received off-air): WATE-TV (ABC, Laff) Knoxville; WBIR-TV (MeTV, NBC) Knoxville; WBXX-TV (CW, Escape) Crossville; WETP-TV (PBS) Sneedville; WKNX-TV (Retro TV) Knoxville; WKOP-TV (PBS) Knoxville; WPXK-TV (ION) Jellico; WTNZ (FOX, This TV) Knoxville; WVLT-TV (CBS, MNT) Knoxville.
Programming (via satellite): C-SPAN; C-SPAN 2; EVINE Live; EWTN Global Catholic Network; INSP; QVC; Trinity Broadcasting Network (TBN).
Expanded Basic Service 1
Subscribers: N.A.
Programming (via satellite): A&E; AMC; CMT; CNN; Discovery Channel; Disney Channel; Disney XD; DIY Network; ESPN; ESPN Classic; ESPN2; Fox News Channel; Freeform; FX; HGTV; History; HLN; Lifetime; MTV; Nickelodeon; Spike TV; TBS; The Weather Channel; TLC; TNT; Travel Channel; TV Land; USA Network; VH1.
Digital Basic Service
Subscribers: N.A.
Programming (via satellite): Bloomberg Television; Discovery Life Channel; Disney XD; ESPN Classic; ESPNews; FOX College Sports Central; FOX College Sports Pacific; Fox Sports 1; FXM; FYI; Golf Channel; Great American Country; GSN; IFC; MC; National Geographic Channel; NBCSN; Nick Jr.; Nicktoons; Outdoor Channel; Ovation; Sundance TV; TeenNick; Turner Classic Movies; WE tv.
Digital Pay Service 1
Pay Units: N.A.
Programming (via satellite): Cinemax (multiplexed); HBO (multiplexed); Showtime (multiplexed); Starz Encore (multiplexed); The Movie Channel (multiplexed).
Video-On-Demand: No
Internet Service
Operational: Yes.
Broadband Service: In-house.
Fee: $43.95 monthly.
Telephone Service
Digital: Operational
General Manager: Bryan Hyder. Chief Technician: Terry Sersland.
Ownership: Carolina Mountain Cablevision Inc. (MSO).

DAYTON—Charter Communications. Now served by CLEVELAND, TN [TN0013]. ICA: TN0064.

DECATUR—Charter Communications. Now served by CLEVELAND, TN [TN0013]. ICA: TN0117.

DOVER—Mediacom. Now served by TRENTON, KY [KY0101]. ICA: TN0092.

DRESDEN (village)—Formerly served by Dresden Cable Inc. No longer in operation. ICA: TN0102.

DUNLAP—Bledsoe Telephone Coop. Now served by PIKEVILLE, TN [TN0158]. ICA: TN0040.

DYER—Time Warner Cable. Now served by MAYFIELD, KY [KY0037]. ICA: TN0057.

DYERSBURG—Cable One, 1930 Brewer Rd, Dyersburg, TN 38025-0888. Phone: 731-285-4174. Web Site: http://www.cableone.net. Also serves Dyer County. ICA: TN0025.
TV Market Ranking: Below 100 (Dyer County (portions), DYERSBURG (portions)); Outside TV Markets (Dyer County (portions), DYERSBURG (portions)). Franchise award date: May 24, 1966. Franchise expiration date: N.A. Began: April 1, 1967.
Channel capacity: N.A. Channels available but not in use: N.A.
Basic Service
Subscribers: 3,328.
Programming (received off-air): KFVS-TV (CBS, CW, MeTV) Cape Girardeau; WATN-TV (ABC) Memphis; WBBJ-TV (ABC, CBS, MeTV) Jackson; WHBQ-TV (Decades, FOX, Movies!) Memphis; WKNO (PBS) Memphis; WLJT-DT (PBS) Lexington; WLMT (CW, MeTV, MNT) Memphis; WMC-TV (Bounce TV, NBC, This TV) Memphis; WPSD-TV (Antenna TV, NBC) Paducah; WREG-TV (Antenna TV, CBS) Memphis.
Programming (via satellite): A&E; AMC; Animal Planet; BET; Cartoon Network; CMT; CNBC; CNN; C-SPAN; C-SPAN 2; Discovery Channel; Disney Channel; ESPN; ESPN2; Fox News Channel; Freeform; FX; HGTV; History; HLN; ION Television; Lifetime; MSNBC; MTV; Nickelodeon; Pop; QVC; Spike TV; Syfy; TBS; The Weather Channel; TLC; TNT; Travel Channel; Trinity Broadcasting Network (TBN); Turner Classic Movies; TV Land; USA Network; VH1; WGN America.
Fee: $75.00 installation; $29.00 monthly.
Digital Basic Service
Subscribers: N.A.
Programming (via satellite): 3ABN; Boomerang; BYUtv; Discovery Digital Networks; Disney XD; DMX Music; ESPN Classic; ESPNews; FamilyNet; FOX College Sports Central; FOX College Sports Pacific; Fox Sports 1; Fox Sports 2; FXM; FYI; Golf Channel; Great American Country; Hallmark Channel; History International; HITS (Headend In The Sky); INSP; National Geographic Channel; TNT HD; Trinity Broadcasting Network (TBN); truTV; TVG Network; Universal HD.
Fee: $46.00 monthly.
Digital Pay Service 1
Pay Units: N.A.
Programming (via satellite): Cinemax (multiplexed); Flix (multiplexed); HBO (multiplexed); Showtime (multiplexed); Showtime HD; Starz (multiplexed); Starz Encore (multiplexed); Sundance TV (multiplexed); The Movie Channel (multiplexed); The Movie Channel HD.
Fee: $15.00 monthly.
Video-On-Demand: No
Pay-Per-View
Pleasure (delivered digitally); SexSee (delivered digitally); Juicy (delivered digitally); VaVoom (delivered digitally).
Internet Service
Operational: Yes. Began: June 1, 2001.
Subscribers: 4,005.
Broadband Service: CableONE.net.
Fee: $75.00 installation; $43.00 monthly.
Telephone Service
Digital: Operational
Subscribers: 1,543.
Fee: $39.95 monthly
Miles of Plant: 533.0 (coaxial); 82.0 (fiber optic). Homes passed: 11,150.
Vice President: Patrick A. Dolohanty. General Manager: Jim Duck. Chief Technician: George Downs.
Ownership: Cable ONE Inc. (MSO).

EAGLEVILLE—Formerly served by Small Town Cable. No longer in operation. ICA: TN0136.

ELIZABETHTON—Charter Communications. Now served by KINGSPORT, TN [TN0007]. ICA: TN0199.

ERIN—Peoples CATV Inc, 236 East Capitol St, Jackson, MS 39201. Phones: 800-832-2515; 931-289-4221. Fax: 931-289-4220. Web Site: http://tec.com. Also serves Henry & Tennessee Ridge. ICA: TN0083.
TV Market Ranking: Outside TV Markets (Henry, ERIN, Tennessee Ridge). Franchise award date: March 1, 1983. Franchise expiration date: N.A. Began: March 1, 1984.
Channel capacity: N.A. Channels available but not in use: N.A.
Basic Service
Subscribers: 766.
Programming (received off-air): WKRN-TV (ABC) Nashville; WNAB (CW, The Country Network) Nashville; WNPT (PBS) Nashville; WSMV-TV (COZI TV, NBC, TNN) Nashville; WTVF (CBS, Laff, This TV) Nashville; WZTV (Antenna TV, FOX, WeatherNation) Nashville.
Programming (via satellite): C-SPAN; QVC; The Weather Channel; Trinity Broadcasting Network (TBN).
Fee: $25.00 installation; $17.95 monthly.
Expanded Basic Service 1
Subscribers: N.A.
Programming (via satellite): A&E; Animal Planet; Cartoon Network; CMT; CNN; Comedy Central; Discovery Channel; Disney Channel; E! HD; ESPN; ESPN2; Fox News Channel; Freeform; FX; Golf Channel; Hallmark Channel; HGTV; History; MTV; Nickelodeon; Oxygen; RFD-TV; Spike TV; Syfy; TBS; TLC; TNT; Travel Channel; Turner Classic Movies; TV Land; USA Network; VH1; WGN America.
Fee: $24.00 monthly.

Digital Basic Service
Subscribers: 60.
Programming (via satellite): BBC America; Bravo; Cloo; Discovery Digital Networks; Disney XD; DMX Music; ESPN Classic; ESPNews; Fox Sports 1; FXM; FYI; GSN; History International; IFC; NBCSN; Nick Jr.; Nicktoons; Outdoor Channel; TeenNick; WE tv.
Fee: $19.95 monthly.
Pay Service 1
Pay Units: 139.
Programming (via satellite): Cinemax.
Fee: $25.00 installation; $11.95 monthly.
Pay Service 2
Pay Units: 151.
Programming (via satellite): HBO.
Fee: $11.95 monthly.
Digital Pay Service 1
Pay Units: N.A.
Programming (via satellite): Cinemax (multiplexed); HBO (multiplexed); Showtime (multiplexed); Starz (multiplexed); Starz Encore (multiplexed); The Movie Channel (multiplexed).
Fee: $10.00 monthly (each).
Video-On-Demand: No
Internet Service
Operational: Yes, DSL.
Telephone Service
Analog: Operational
Miles of Plant: 108.0 (coaxial); None (fiber optic).
Vice President: James Garner. General Manager: James H. Coakley. Chief Technician: Steve Hall. Marketing Director: Fay Lair. Program Director: Irene Wilbanks.
Ownership: Telephone Electronics Corp. (TEC) (MSO).

FAIRFIELD GLADE—Comcast Cable. Now served by KNOXVILLE, TN [TN0004]. ICA: TN0081.

FAYETTEVILLE—Charter Communications. Now served by MANCHESTER, TN [TN0032]. ICA: TN0185.

FAYETTEVILLE—Fayette Public Utilities, 408 West College St, PO Box 120, Fayetteville, TN 37334-0120. Phones: 800-379-2534; 931-433-1522. Fax: 931-433-0646. E-mail: customerservice@fpu-tn.com. Web Site: http://www.fpu-tn.com. Also serves Lincoln County (portions). ICA: TN0192. **Note:** This system is an overbuild.
TV Market Ranking: 96 (FAYETTEVILLE, Lincoln County (portions)). Franchise award date: N.A. Franchise expiration date: N.A. Began: March 21, 2001.
Channel capacity: 72 (operating 2-way). Channels available but not in use: N.A.
Basic Service
Subscribers: 2,694.
Programming (received off-air): WAAY-TV (ABC) Huntsville; WAFF (Bounce TV, NBC, This TV) Huntsville; WHDF (CW) Florence; WHNT-TV (Antenna TV, CBS) Huntsville; WKRN-TV (ABC) Nashville; WNPT (PBS) Nashville; WSMV-TV (COZI TV, NBC, TNN) Nashville; WTVF (CBS, Laff, This TV) Nashville; WZDX (FOX, MeTV, MNT) Huntsville.
Programming (via satellite): C-SPAN; C-SPAN 2; ESPNews; Food Network; QVC; TBS; The Weather Channel; WGN America.
Fee: $59.04 monthly.
Expanded Basic Service 1
Subscribers: N.A.
Programming (via satellite): A&E; AMC; Animal Planet; BET; Bravo; Cartoon Network; CMT; CNBC; CNN; Comedy Central; Discovery Channel; Disney Channel; Disney XD; E! HD; ESPN; ESPN Classic;

2017 Edition   D-709

Tennessee—Cable Systems

ESPN2; Fox News Channel; Fox Sports 1; FOX Sports South/SportSouth; Freeform; FX; Golf Channel; Great American Country; GSN; Hallmark Channel; HGTV; History; HLN; ION Television; Lifetime; MSNBC; MTV; National Geographic Channel; Nickelodeon; Outdoor Channel; Spike TV; Syfy; TLC; TNT; Travel Channel; Trinity Broadcasting Network (TBN); Turner Classic Movies; TV Land; USA Network; VH1; WE tv.
Fee: $41.00 monthly.
Digital Basic Service
Subscribers: N.A.
Programming (via satellite): BBC America; Discovery Digital Networks; DIY Network; DMX Music; Fuse; FYI; History International; IFC; LMN.
Fee: $14.45 monthly.
Pay Service 1
Pay Units: N.A.
Programming (via satellite): HBO (multiplexed).
Fee: $10.95 monthly.
Digital Pay Service 1
Pay Units: N.A.
Programming (via satellite): Cinemax (multiplexed); Flix; HBO (multiplexed); Showtime (multiplexed); Starz (multiplexed); Starz Encore (multiplexed); Sundance TV; The Movie Channel (multiplexed).
Fee: $8.95 monthly (Cinemax), $9.95 monthly (Starz/Encore), $12.95 monthly (HBO), & $12.95 monthly (Showtime/TMC/Flix/Sundance).
Video-On-Demand: Planned
Pay-Per-View
Hot Choice (delivered digitally); iN DEMAND (delivered digitally).
Internet Service
Operational: Yes.
Broadband Service: In-house.
Fee: $39.45-$71.28 monthly; $10.00 modem lease.
Telephone Service
Digital: Operational
Miles of Plant: 30.0 (coaxial); None (fiber optic).
Chief Executive Officer & General Manager: Britt Dye.
Ownership: Fayetteville Public Utilities.

FLINTVILLE—Charter Communications. Now served by MANCHESTER, TN [TN0032]. ICA: TN0189.

FRIENDSHIP—Cable One, 1930 Brewer Rd, Dyersburg, TN 83024. Phone: 731-285-4174. Web Site: http://www.cableone.net. ICA: TN0212.
TV Market Ranking: Below 100 (FRIENDSHIP).
Channel capacity: N.A. Channels available but not in use: N.A.
Basic Service
Subscribers: 54.
Fee: $90.00 installation; $29.00 monthly.
Vice President: Patrick A. Dolohanty.
Ownership: Cable ONE Inc. (MSO).

FRIENDSVILLE (town)—Comcast Cable. Now served by KNOXVILLE, TN [TN0004]. ICA: TN0062.

GAINESBORO—Gainesboro CATV Inc., 302 Minor St, 513, Gainesboro, TN 38562. Phone: 931-268-9612. Also serves Jackson County (portions). ICA: TN0213.
TV Market Ranking: Below 100 (GAINESBORO, Jackson County portions).
Channel capacity: N.A. Channels available but not in use: N.A.
Basic Service
Subscribers: N.A.
Fee: $50.00 installation; $46.00 monthly.
Internet Service
Operational: Yes.
Fee: $50.00 installation; $30.00-$55.00 monthly.
President: Jeff Spivey.
Ownership: Gainesboro CATV Inc.

GATLINBURG—Charter Communications. Now served by ALCOA, TN [TN0151]. ICA: TN0140.

GRAY—Comcast Cable. Now served by KNOXVILLE, TN [TN0004]. ICA: TN0142.

GREENVILLE—Comcast Cable. Now served by KNOXVILLE, TN [TN0004]. ICA: TN0022.

GRIMSLEY—Comcast Cable. Now served by KNOXVILLE, TN [TN0004]. ICA: TN0197.

HARRIMAN—Comcast Cable. Now served by KNOXVILLE, TN [TN0004]. ICA: TN0021.

HARTSVILLE—Comcast Cable. Now served by NASHVILLE, TN [TN0002]. ICA: TN0099.

HENDERSON—Charter Communications. Now served by JACKSON CITY, TN [TN0008]. ICA: TN0074.

HENRY—Peoples CATV Inc. Now served by ERIN, TN [TN0083]. ICA: TN0144.

HOHENWALD—Charter Communications. Now served by COLUMBIA, TN [TN0017]. ICA: TN0055.

HUMBOLDT—Click1.Net, 314 North 22nd Ave, PO Box 408, Humboldt, TN 38343. Phone: 731-784-5000. Fax: 731-784-7474. E-mail: support@click1.net. Web Site: http://www.click1.net. Also serves Medina. ICA: TN0046.
TV Market Ranking: Below 100 (HUMBOLDT, Medina). Franchise award date: N.A. Franchise expiration date: N.A. Began: January 1, 1970.
Channel capacity: N.A. Channels available but not in use: N.A.
Basic Service
Subscribers: 2,907.
Programming (received off-air): WATN-TV (ABC) Memphis; WBBJ-TV (ABC, CBS, MeTV) Jackson; WHBQ-TV (Decades, FOX, Movies!) Memphis; WJKT (FOX) Jackson; WKNO (PBS) Memphis; WLFT-CD (MeTV, Soul of the South, The Country Network) Baton Rouge; WLJT-DT (PBS) Lexington; WLMT (CW, MeTV, MNT) Memphis; WMC-TV (Bounce TV, NBC, This TV) Memphis; WPXX-TV (ION, MNT) Memphis; WREG-TV (Antenna TV, CBS) Memphis.
Programming (via satellite): C-SPAN; C-SPAN 2; Family Friendly Entertainment; Pop; QVC; WGN America.
Fee: $25.00 installation; $26.00 monthly; $1.25 converter.
Expanded Basic Service 1
Subscribers: N.A.
Programming (via satellite): A&E; AMC; Animal Planet; BET; Bravo; Cartoon Network; CMT; CNBC; CNN; Comcast/Charter Sports Southeast (CSS); Comedy Central; Discovery Channel; Disney Channel; DIY Network; E! HD; ESPN; ESPN Classic; ESPN2; EWTN Global Catholic Network; Food Network; Fox News Channel; Fox Sports 1; FOX Sports Midwest; FOX Sports South/Sport-South; Freeform; FX; Great American Country; Hallmark Channel; HGTV; History; HLN; INSP; Lifetime; MSNBC; MTV; National Geographic Channel; NBCSN; Nickelodeon; Oxygen; RFD-TV; Spike TV; Syfy; TBS; The Weather Channel; TLC; TNT; Travel Channel; Trinity Broadcasting Network (TBN); truTV; Turner Classic Movies; TV Land; USA Network; VH1; Weatherscan.
Fee: $37.00 monthly.
Digital Basic Service
Subscribers: N.A.
Programming (via satellite): A&E HD; BBC America; Bloomberg Television; CBS Sports Network; CMT; Destination America; Discovery Kids Channel; Disney XD; DMX Music; ESPN HD; ESPN2 HD; ESPNews; ESPNU; Fox Business Network; FOX College Sports Central; FOX College Sports Pacific; Fuse; FXM; FYI; Golf Channel; GSN; HD Theater; History International; Investigation Discovery; JUCE TV; LMN; MTV Classic; MTV Hits; MTV Jams; MTV2; National Geographic Channel HD; Nick Jr.; Nicktoons; Outdoor Channel; OWN; Oprah Winfrey Network; Science Channel; Starz Encore; TeenNick; VH1 Soul; WAM! America's Kidz Network; WE tv.
Fee: $13.00 monthly.
Digital Pay Service 1
Pay Units: N.A.
Programming (via satellite): Cinemax (multiplexed); Flix; HBO (multiplexed); Showtime (multiplexed); Starz (multiplexed); Starz HD (multiplexed); Sundance TV; The Movie Channel (multiplexed).
Fee: $14.00 monthly (Cinemax, HBO, Showtime/TMC/Flix or Starz/Encore).
Video-On-Demand: Yes
Pay-Per-View
Fresh (delivered digitally); Spice: Xcess (delivered digitally); Playboy TV (delivered digitally); Hot Choice (delivered digitally); iN DEMAND (delivered digitally).
Internet Service
Operational: Yes.
Fee: $29.95-$49.95 monthly.
Telephone Service
None
Miles of Plant: 105.0 (coaxial); None (fiber optic).
President: Frank Warmath. General Manager: Mark Love. Office Manager: Brandy Kemp.
Ownership: InfoStructure Inc.

HUNTLAND—Mediacom, 123 Ware Dr NE, Huntsville, AL 35811-1061. Phones: 845-695-2762; 850-934-7700 (Gulf Breeze regional office); 256-852-7427. Fax: 256-851-7708. Web Site: http://www.mediacomcable.com. ICA: TN0116.
TV Market Ranking: 96 (HUNTLAND). Franchise award date: April 26, 1982. Franchise expiration date: N.A. Began: January 1, 1984.
Channel capacity: N.A. Channels available but not in use: N.A.
Basic Service
Subscribers: 38.
Programming (received off-air): WAAY-TV (ABC) Huntsville; WAFF (Bounce TV, NBC, This TV) Huntsville; WHIQ (PBS) Huntsville; WHNT-TV (Antenna TV, CBS) Huntsville; WKRN-TV (ABC) Nashville; WSMV-TV (COZI TV, NBC, TNN) Nashville; WZDX (FOX, MeTV) Huntsville.
Fee: $38.00 monthly; $1.00 converter.
Expanded Basic Service 1
Subscribers: N.A.
Programming (via satellite): AMC; CNN; Discovery Channel; ESPN; Freeform; Lifetime; MTV; Nickelodeon; QVC; Spike TV; TBS; TNT; USA Network; WGN America.
Fee: $15.68 monthly.
Pay Service 1
Pay Units: N.A.
Programming (via satellite): Cinemax; Flix; HBO; Showtime.
Fee: $2.95 monthly (Flix), $9.95 monthly (Cinemax, HBO or Showtime).
Video-On-Demand: No
Internet Service
Operational: No.
Telephone Service
None
Homes passed: 423. Miles of plant included in Madison County, AL
Vice President: David Servies. Vice President, Financial Reporting: Kenneth J. Kohrs. General Manager: Tommy Hill. Technical Operations Supervisor: Mark Darwin. Sales & Marketing Manager: Joey Nagem. Customer Service Supervisor: Sandy Acklin.
Ownership: Mediacom LLC (MSO).

HUNTSVILLE—Comcast Cable. Now served by KNOXVILLE, TN [TN0004]. ICA: TN0195.

JACKSON CITY—Charter Communications, 12405 Powerscourt Dr, St. Louis, MO 63131. Phones: 636-207-5100 (Corporate office); 865-983-8200; 865-984-1400 (Maryville office); 731-424-3290 (Local office). Fax: 865-983-0383. Web Site: http://www.charter.com. Also serves Adamsville, Alamo, Atwood, Bells, Bethel Springs, Bruceton, Camden, Chester County (portions), Clarksburg, Clifton, Collinwood, Crockett County (portions), Crump, Decatur County (portions), Decaturville, Gadsden, Gibson, Gibson County (portions), Gleason, Greenfield, Hardin County (portions), Henderson, Henderson County, Henry County (unincorporated areas), Hollow Rock, Huntingdon, Lexington, Madison County (portions), Martin, Maury City, McKenzie, McLemoresville, McNairy, McNairy County (portions), Milan, Milledgeville, Newbern, Obion, Obion County (unincorporated areas), Paris, Parsons, Rives, Saltillo, Savannah, Selmer, Sharon, Trezevant, Trimble, Troy, Union City, Wayne County (portions), Waynesboro & Woodland Mills. ICA: TN0008.
TV Market Ranking: Below 100 (Alamo, Atwood, Bells, Bethel Springs, Chester County (portions), Clarksburg, Collinwood, Crockett County (portions), Gadsden, Gibson, Henderson, Henderson County, Huntingdon, JACKSON CITY, Madison County (portions), Maury City, McLemoresville, McNairy, Milan, Trezevant, Decatur County (portions), Gibson County (portions), Hardin County (portions), Lexington, McNairy County (portions), Selmer, Wayne County (portions), Waynesboro); Outside TV Markets (Adamsville, Bruceton, Camden, Crump, Decaturville, Gleason, Greenfield, Henry County (unincorporated areas), Hollow Rock, Milledgeville, Obion, Obion County (unincorporated areas), Parsons, Rives, Saltillo, Savannah, Sharon, Trimble, Troy, Union City, Woodland Mills, Clifton, Decatur County (portions), Gibson County (portions), Hardin County (portions), JACKSON CITY, Martin, McKenzie, McNairy County (portions), Newbern, Paris, Wayne County (portions)).
Channel capacity: N.A. Channels available but not in use: N.A.
Digital Basic Service
Subscribers: 43,419.
Programming (via satellite): AXS TV; BBC America; Bloomberg Television;

Boomerang; CNN en Espanol; Discovery Digital Networks; DIY Network; ESPN; ESPN Classic; ESPNews; FOX College Sports Central; FOX College Sports Pacific; Fox Sports 2; Fuse; FXM; FYI; Great American Country; HD Theater; History International; IFC; LMN; MC; NFL Network; Nick 2; Nick Jr.; Nicktoons; Outdoor Channel; Sundance TV; TeenNick; TV Guide Interactive Inc.
Fee: $26.99 monthly.

Digital Expanded Basic Service
Subscribers: N.A.
Programming (via satellite): A&E; AMC; Animal Planet; BET; Bravo; Cartoon Network; CMT; CNBC; CNN; Comcast/Charter Sports Southeast (CSS); Comedy Central; C-SPAN; C-SPAN 2; Discovery Channel; Disney Channel; Disney XD; E! HD; ESPN; ESPN2; Food Network; Fox News Channel; Fox Sports 1; FOX Sports South/SportSouth; Freeform; FX; Golf Channel; GSN; Hallmark Channel; HGTV; History; HLN; INSP; Lifetime; MSNBC; MTV; National Geographic Channel; Nickelodeon; Oxygen; Pop; QVC; Spike TV; Syfy; TBS; The Weather Channel; TLC; TNT; Travel Channel; Trinity Broadcasting Network (TBN); truTV; Turner Classic Movies; TV Land; USA Network; VH1; WE tv.
Fee: $45.00 monthly.

Digital Pay Service 1
Pay Units: N.A.
Programming (via satellite): Cinemax (multiplexed); HBO (multiplexed); HBO HD; Showtime (multiplexed); Showtime HD; Starz (multiplexed); Starz Encore (multiplexed); The Movie Channel (multiplexed).
Video-On-Demand: Yes

Pay-Per-View
iN DEMAND (delivered digitally); NHL Center Ice (delivered digitally); MLB Extra Innings (delivered digitally); Playboy TV (delivered digitally); Fresh (delivered digitally); Shorteez (delivered digitally).

Internet Service
Operational: Yes.
Subscribers: 37,978.
Broadband Service: Charter Internet.
Fee: $29.99 monthly.

Telephone Service
Digital: Operational
Subscribers: 8,383.
Fee: $29.99 monthly
Miles of Plant: 6,129.0 (coaxial); 1,803.0 (fiber optic). Homes passed: 155,937.
Technical Operations Director: Ron Janson. Marketing Director: Pat Hollenbeck. Accounting Director: David Sovanski. Marketing Manager: Wiley Bird. Operations Manager: Tony Fox.
Ownership: Charter Communications Inc. (MSO).

JAMESTOWN—Comcast Cable. Now served by KNOXVILLE, TN [TN0004]. ICA: TN0196.

JASPER—Charter Communications, 12405 Powerscourt Dr, St. Louis, MO 63131. Phones: 636-207-5100 (Corporate office); 423-728-4087; 865-984-1400 (Maryville office); 423-478-1934. Fax: 423-476-1621. Web Site: http://www.charter.com. Also serves Bridgeport & Stevenson, AL; Trenton, GA; Kimball, Marion County, New Hope, South Pittsburg & Whitwell, TN. ICA: TN0070.
TV Market Ranking: 78 (Bridgeport, JASPER, Kimball, Marion County, New Hope, South Pittsburg, Stevenson, Trenton, Whitwell). Franchise award date: March 1, 1983. Franchise expiration date: N.A. Began: July 1, 1983.
Channel capacity: N.A. Channels available but not in use: N.A.

Digital Basic Service
Subscribers: 6,929.
Programming (via satellite): BBC America; Discovery Life Channel; DIY Network; ESPN Classic; ESPNews; FOX College Sports Central; FOX College Sports Pacific; Fox Sports 2; FXM; FYI; Great American Country; History International; HITS (Headend In The Sky); IFC; Jewelry Television; LMN; MC; MTV Classic; MTV2; NFL Network; Nick 2; Nick Jr.; Nicktoons; Sundance TV; TeenNick; TV Guide Interactive Inc.
Fee: $26.99 monthly.

Digital Expanded Basic Service
Subscribers: N.A.
Programming (via satellite): A&E; AMC; Animal Planet; BET; Bravo; Cartoon Network; CMT; CNBC; CNN; Comcast/Charter Sports Southeast (CSS); Comedy Central; Discovery Channel; Disney XD; E! HD; ESPN; ESPN2; Food Network; Fox News Channel; Fox Sports 1; FOX Sports South/SportSouth; Freeform; FX; Golf Channel; GSN; Hallmark Channel; HGTV; History; HLN; Lifetime; MSNBC; MTV; National Geographic Channel; NBCSN; Nickelodeon; Oxygen; Pop; Spike TV; Syfy; TBS; The Weather Channel; TLC; TNT; Travel Channel; truTV; Turner Classic Movies; TV Land; USA Network; VH1; WE tv.
Fee: $3.50 monthly.

Digital Pay Service 1
Pay Units: N.A.
Programming (via satellite): Cinemax (multiplexed); HBO (multiplexed); Showtime (multiplexed); Starz (multiplexed); Starz Encore (multiplexed); The Movie Channel (multiplexed).
Video-On-Demand: Yes

Internet Service
Operational: Yes.
Subscribers: 4,937.
Broadband Service: Charter Internet.
Fee: $29.99 monthly.

Telephone Service
Digital: Operational
Subscribers: 1,069.
Miles of Plant: 1,010.0 (coaxial); 271.0 (fiber optic). Homes passed: 19,204.
Operations Manager: Mike Burns. Technical Operations Manager: David Ogle. Marketing Director: Pat Hollenbeck. Accounting Director: David Sovanski.
Ownership: Charter Communications Inc. (MSO).

JELLICO—Access Cable Television Inc, 302 Enterprise Dr, Somerset, KY 42501. Phone: 606-677-2444. Fax: 606-677-2443. E-mail: cable@accesshsd.net. Web Site: http://www.accesshsd.com. Also serves Whitley County (southern portion), KY; Campbell County (portions), TN. ICA: TN0056.
TV Market Ranking: Below 100 (Campbell County (portions), JELLICO, Whitley County (southern portion)). Franchise award date: N.A. Franchise expiration date: N.A. Began: April 1, 1979.
Channel capacity: N.A. Channels available but not in use: N.A.

Basic Service
Subscribers: 819.
Programming (received off-air): WAGV (IND) Harlan; WATE-TV (ABC, Laff) Knoxville; WBXX-TV (CW, Escape) Crossville; WETP-TV (PBS) Sneedville; WKSO-TV (PBS) Somerset; WKYT-TV (CBS, CW) Lexington; WLEX-TV (MeTV, NBC) Lexington; WTNZ (FOX, This TV) Knoxville; WVLT-TV (CBS, MNT) Knoxville; WYMT-TV (CBS, CW) Hazard.
Programming (via satellite): AMC; CMT; CNN; Discovery Channel; E! HD; ESPN; HLN; ION Television; MTV; Nickelodeon; QVC; Syfy; TLC; Trinity Broadcasting Network (TBN); VH1; WGN America.
Fee: $25.00 installation; $28.50 monthly; $3.00 converter.

Expanded Basic Service 1
Subscribers: 590.
Programming (via satellite): A&E; Cartoon Network; Disney Channel; ESPN2; Fox News Channel; Freeform; FX; Hallmark Channel; HGTV; History; Lifetime; Outdoor Channel; Spike TV; TBS; The Weather Channel; TNT; TV Land; USA Network.
Fee: $10.80 monthly.

Pay Service 1
Pay Units: N.A.
Programming (via satellite): Cinemax; HBO.
Fee: $11.95 monthly (each).
Video-On-Demand: No

Internet Service
Operational: Yes.

Telephone Service
Digital: Operational
Fee: $24.95 monthly
Miles of Plant: 90.0 (coaxial); None (fiber optic). Homes passed: 2,938.
President & Manager: Roy Baker.
Ownership: Access Cable Television Inc. (MSO).

JOHNSON CITY—Charter Communications. Now served by KINGSPORT, TN [TN0007]. ICA: TN0010.

KINGSPORT—Charter Communications, 105 Jack White Dr, Kingsport, TN 37664. Phones: 314-543-2236; 636-207-5100 (Corporate office); 423-247-7631. Web Site: http://www.charter.com. Also serves Bluff City, Bristol, Carter County (portions), Church Hill, Elizabethton, Hawkins County, Johnson City, Mount Carmel, Piney Flats, Reddy Creek, Rogersville, Stoney Creek, Sullivan County & Wautauga, TN; Bristol, Scott County (portions) & Washington County (portions), VA. ICA: TN0007.
TV Market Ranking: Below 100 (Bluff City, Bristol, Carter County (portions), Church Hill, Elizabethton, Hawkins County, Johnson City, KINGSPORT, Mount Carmel, Scott County (portions), Sullivan County, Washington County (portions), Wautauga, Stoney Creek). Franchise award date: May 17, 1966. Franchise expiration date: N.A. Began: December 1, 1980.
Channel capacity: 67 (operating 2-way). Channels available but not in use: N.A.

Digital Basic Service
Subscribers: 54,003.
Programming (via satellite): AXS TV; BBC America; Boomerang; CNN en Espanol; CNN International; Discovery Digital Networks; DIY Network; ESPN; ESPN Classic; ESPNews; FOX College Sports Central; FOX College Sports Pacific; Fox Sports 2; FXM; FYI; Great American Country; HD Theater; History International; IFC; Jewelry Television; LMN; MC; NFL Network; Nick 2; Nick Jr.; Nicktoons; Outdoor Channel; Sundance TV; TeenNick; TV Guide Interactive Inc.
Fee: $49.99 installation; $26.99 monthly.

Digital Expanded Basic Service
Subscribers: N.A.
Programming (via satellite): A&E; AMC; Animal Planet; BET; Bravo; Cartoon Network; CMT; CNBC; CNN; Comedy Central; Discovery Channel; Discovery Life Channel; Disney Channel; Disney XD; E! HD; ESPN; ESPN2; Food Network; Fox News Channel; Fox Sports 1; FOX Sports South/SportSouth; Freeform; FX; Golf Channel; GSN; Hallmark Channel; HGTV; History; HLN; Lifetime; MSNBC; MTV; National Geographic Channel; NBCSN; Nickelodeon; Oxygen; Spike TV; Syfy; TBS; TLC; TNT; Travel Channel; Trinity Broadcasting Network (TBN); truTV; Turner Classic Movies; TV Land; USA Network; VH1; WE tv.
Fee: $45.00 monthly.

Digital Pay Service 1
Pay Units: N.A.
Programming (via satellite): Cinemax (multiplexed); Flix; HBO (multiplexed); HBO HD; Showtime (multiplexed); Showtime HD; Starz (multiplexed); Starz Encore (multiplexed); The Movie Channel (multiplexed).
Video-On-Demand: Yes

Pay-Per-View
Pleasure (delivered digitally); Playboy TV (delivered digitally); Fresh (delivered digitally); Shorteez (delivered digitally); iN DEMAND (delivered digitally); NHL Center Ice (delivered digitally); MLB Extra Innings (delivered digitally).

Internet Service
Operational: Yes.
Subscribers: 47,032.
Broadband Service: Charter Internet.
Fee: $29.99 monthly; $10.00 modem lease; $199.00 modem purchase.

Telephone Service
Digital: Operational
Subscribers: 10,635.
Fee: $29.99 monthly
Miles of Plant: 4,705.0 (coaxial); 1,385.0 (fiber optic). Homes passed: 152,410.
Operations Manager: Tony Falin. Technical Operations Manager: Bruce Cocke. Marketing Director: Pat Hollenbeck. Accounting Director: David Sovanski. Sales & Marketing Manager: Kevin Kick.
Ownership: Charter Communications Inc. (MSO).

KNOXVILLE—Comcast Cable, 5720 Asheville Hwy, Knoxville, TN 37924-2701. Phones: 865-637-5411; 865-971-1544. Fax: 865-862-5092. Web Site: http://www.comcast.com. Also serves Catoosa County (portions), Chickamauga, Dade County (portions), Fort Oglethorpe, Lafayette, Lookout Mountain, Rossville, Walker & Walker County (portions), GA; Allardt, Anderson County (portions), Athens, Baileyton, Benton, Blaine, Blount County (portions), Bristol, Bulls Gap, Bybee, Campbell County (portions), Carter County (portions), Caryville, Chattanooga,

Tennessee—Cable Systems

Chuckey, Clarkrange, Claxton, Clinton, Coalfield, Cobbly Nob, Cocke County (portions), Collegedale, Cosby, Crossville, Cumberland County (portions), Deer Lodge, Delano, East Ridge, Embreeville, Englewood, Erwin, Etowah, Fairfield Glade, Fall Branch, Fentress County (portions), Friendsville (town), Gatlinburg, Gray, Greenback (town), Greene County (portions), Greenville, Grimsley, Hamblen County (portions), Hamilton County (portions), Hampton, Harriman, Hawkins County (portions), Helenwood, Huntsville, Jacksboro, Jamestown, Jefferson County (portions), Johnson City, Jonesborough, Kingston, Knox County (portions), Kodak, La Follette, Lake City, Lakesite, Lancing, Lookout Mountain, Loudon County (portions), Louisville, Luttrell, Marion County (portions), Maynardville, McMinn County (portions), Meadowview, Midtown, Midway, Monroe, Morgan County (portions), Mosheim, Newport, Niota, Norris, Oak Ridge, Oakdale, Ocoee, Oldfort, Oliver Springs, Oneida, Parrottsville, Petros, Pigeon Forge, Pittman Center, Polk County (portions), Powell, Red Bank, Riceville, Ridgeside, Roane County (portions), Rockford, Rockwood, Russellville, Scott County (portions), Sequatchie County (portions), Sevier County (portions), Sevierville, Signal Mountain, Soddy Daisy, Sullivan County (portions), Sunbright, Tellico Plains, Townsend, Tusculum, Unicoi, Union County (portions), Vonore, Walden, Walden Creek, Wartburg, Washington County (portions), Wears Valley, Whitesburg & Winfield, TN; Abingdon, Appalachia (town), Atkins, Ben Hur, Big Stone Gap (town), Burson Place, Carroll County (portions), Chilhowie, Clintwood (town), Coeburn (town), Dickenson County (portions), Duffield (town), Fries (town), Galax, Glade Spring, Grayson County (portions), Hillsville (town), Independence (town), Jonesville (town), Lee County (portions), Marion (town), Norton, Pennington Gap (town), Saltville, Seven Mile Ford, Smyth County (portions), Sugar Grove, Wise (town) & Wise County (town), VA. ICA: TN0004.

TV Market Ranking: 18 (Rossville (portions)); 18,78 (Lafayette, Walker County (portions)); 46 (Greene County (portions)); 71 (Anderson County (portions), Blaine, Blount County (portions), Campbell County (portions), Caryville, Claxton, Clinton, Cobbly Nob, Friendsville (town), Gatlinburg, Greenback (town), Harriman, Jacksboro, Jefferson County (portions), Kingston, Knox County (portions), KNOXVILLE, Kodak, La Follette, Lake City, Louisville, Luttrell, Maynardville, Midtown, Morgan County (portions), Newport, Norris, Oak Ridge, Oakdale, Oliver Springs, Petros, Pigeon Forge, Pittman Center, Powell, Roane County (portions), Rockford, Sevier County (portions), Sevierville, Townsend, Union County (portions), Vonore, Walden Creek, Wears Valley); 78 (Benton, Catoosa County (portions), Chattanooga, Chickamauga, Collegedale, Dade County (portions), East Ridge, Fort Oglethorpe, Hamilton County (portions), Lakesite, Lookout Mountain, Lookout Mountain, Marion County (portions), McMinn County (portions), Ocoee, Oldfort, Polk County (portions), Red Bank, Ridgeside, Sequatchie County (portions), Signal Mountain, Soddy Daisy, Walden, Walker); 96 (Coalfield); Below 100 (Abingdon, Allardt, Appalachia (town), Atkins, Baileyton, Ben Hur, Big Stone Gap (town), Bristol, Bulls Gap, Burson Place, Bybee, Carter County (portions), Chilhowie, Chuckey, Clarkrange, Clintwood (town), Cocke County (portions), Coeburn (town), Cosby, Crossville, Cumberland County (portions), Deer Lodge, Delano, Dickenson County (portions), Duffield (town), Embreeville, Englewood, Erwin, Etowah, Fall Branch, Fentress County (portions), Hamblen County (portions), Hampton, Hawkins County (portions), Helenwood, Johnson City, Jonesborough, Jonesville (town), Lancing, Meadowview, Midway, Monroe, Mosheim, Niota, Oneida, Parrottsville, Pennington Gap (town), Riceville, Rockwood, Russellville, Saltville, Scott County (portions), Seven Mile Ford, Smyth County (portions), Sugar Grove, Sullivan County (portions), Sunbright, Tellico Plains, Tusculum, Unicoi, Washington County (portions), Whitesburg, Winfield, Wise (town) (portions), Wise County (town) (portions), Athens, Fairfield Glade, Glade Spring, Gray, Greenville, Grimsley, Huntsville, Jamestown, Lee County (portions), Marion (town), Norton, Wartburg, Greene County (portions), Campbell County (portions), Jefferson County (portions), Morgan County (portions), Roane County (portions), McMinn County (portions), Polk County (portions)); Outside TV Markets (Carroll County (portions), Fries (town), Grayson County (portions), Hillsville (town), Independence (town), Wise County (town) (portions), Galax, Lee County (portions), Sequatchie County (portions)). Franchise award date: June 17, 1973. Franchise expiration date: N.A. Began: March 1, 1975.

Channel capacity: 47 (operating 2-way). Channels available but not in use: N.A.

Basic Service
Subscribers: 259,232. Commercial subscribers: 23,478.
Programming (received off-air): WATE-TV (ABC, Laff) Knoxville; WBIR-TV (MeTV, NBC) Knoxville; WBXX-TV (CW, Escape) Crossville; WKOP-TV (PBS) Knoxville; WPXK-TV (ION) Jellico; WTNZ (FOX, This TV) Knoxville; WVLR (Christian TV Network) Tazewell; WVLT-TV (CBS, MNT) Knoxville; 2 FMs.
Programming (via satellite): QVC; WGN America.
Fee: $49.99-$79.99 installation; $26.10 monthly.

Expanded Basic Service 1
Subscribers: N.A.
Programming (via satellite): A&E; AMC; Animal Planet; BET; Bravo; Cartoon Network; CMT; CNBC; CNN; Comcast/Charter Sports Southeast (CSS); Comedy Central; C-SPAN; C-SPAN 2; Discovery Channel; Disney Channel; DIY Network; E! HD; ESPN; ESPN Classic; ESPN2; Food Network; Fox News Channel; Fox Sports 1; FOX Sports Networks; Freeform; FX; Golf Channel; Great American Country; GSN; Hallmark Channel; HGTV; HLN; HSN2; INSP; Lifetime; MSNBC; MTV; NBCSN; Nickelodeon; OWN: Oprah Winfrey Network; Pop; Spike TV; Syfy; TBS; The Weather Channel; TLC; TNT; Trinity Broadcasting Network (TBN); truTV; Turner Classic Movies; TV Land; USA Network; VH1.
Fee: $38.24 monthly.

Digital Basic Service
Subscribers: N.A.
Programming (via satellite): BBC America; Cooking Channel; C-SPAN 3; Discovery Digital Networks; Disney XD; DMX Music; ESPNews; Flix; FYI; History International; National Geographic Channel; Nick 2; Nick Jr.; Sundance TV; TeenNick; WAM! America's Kidz Network; Weatherscan.
Fee: $14.95 monthly.

Digital Pay Service 1
Pay Units: N.A.
Programming (via satellite): Cinemax (multiplexed); HBO (multiplexed); Showtime (multiplexed); Starz (multiplexed); The Movie Channel (multiplexed).
Fee: $13.99 monthly (each).
Video-On-Demand: Yes
Pay-Per-View
iN DEMAND (delivered digitally); Playboy TV (delivered digitally); Fresh (delivered digitally); Shorteez (delivered digitally); Pleasure (delivered digitally); ESPN Now (delivered digitally); Sports PPV (delivered digitally).
Internet Service
Operational: Yes. Began: January 1, 2001.
Subscribers: 201,669.
Broadband Service: Comcast High Speed Internet.
Fee: $42.95 monthly; $7.00 modem lease.
Telephone Service
Digital: Operational
Subscribers: 97,973.
Fee: $44.95 monthly
Miles of Plant: 21,634.0 (coaxial); 4,917.0 (fiber optic). Homes passed: 675,083.
Vice President & General Manager: Kirk Dale. Technical Operations Director: Charlie Goodreau. Engineering Manager: Hank Swindle. Marketing Director: Kristopher Workman. Government & Community Affairs Director: Russell Byrd.
Ownership: Comcast Cable Communications Inc. (MSO).

KNOXVILLE—Formerly served by Tennessee Wireless Inc. No longer in operation. ICA: TN0180.

KNOXVILLE—WOW! Internet, Cable & Phone, 7887 East Belleview Ave, Ste 1000, Englewood, CO 80111. Phones: 720-479-3500; 706-645-8553 (Corporate office); 865-357-1000 (Customer service). Fax: 720-479-3585. E-mail: wow_general@ wideopenwest.com. Web Site: http:// www.wowway.com. ICA: TN0208. **Note:** This system is an overbuild.
TV Market Ranking: 71 (KNOXVILLE).
Channel capacity: N.A. Channels available but not in use: N.A.
Basic Service
Subscribers: 5,698.
Programming (received off-air): WATE-TV (ABC, Laff) Knoxville; WBIR-TV (MeTV, NBC) Knoxville; WBXX-TV (CW, Escape) Crossville; WKNX-TV (Retro TV) Knoxville; WKOP-TV (PBS) Knoxville; WTNZ (FOX, This TV) Knoxville; WVLR (Christian TV Network) Tazewell; WVLT-TV (CBS, MNT) Knoxville.
Programming (via satellite): MyNetworkTV; QVC.
Fee: $50.00 installation; $33.00 monthly.
Expanded Basic Service 1
Subscribers: N.A.
Programming (via satellite): A&E; AMC; Animal Planet; BET; Bravo; Cartoon Network; CMT; CNBC; CNN; Comcast/Charter Sports Southeast (CSS); Comedy Central; C-SPAN; C-SPAN 2; Discovery Channel; Disney Channel; Disney XD; E! HD; ESPN; ESPN2; EVINE Live; Food Network; Fox News Channel; Fox Sports 1; FOX Sports South/SportSouth; Freeform; FX; Golf Channel; Great American Country; Hallmark Channel; HGTV; History; HLN; ION Television; Lifetime; LMN; MSNBC; MTV; Nickelodeon; Outdoor Channel; OWN: Oprah Winfrey Network; Oxygen; Pop; Spike TV; Syfy; TBS; The Weather Channel; TLC; TNT; Travel Channel; Trinity Broadcasting Network (TBN); truTV; Turner Classic Movies; TV Land; Univision Studios; UP; USA Network; VH1; WGN America.
Digital Basic Service
Subscribers: N.A.
Programming (via satellite): Animal Planet HD; AXS TV; BBC America; Bloomberg Television; Church Channel; CMT; Cooking Channel; C-SPAN 3; Destination America; Discovery Kids Channel; Discovery Life Channel; DIY Network; DMX Music; ESPN HD; ESPN2 HD; ESPNU; EWTN Global Catholic Network; Fuse; FXM; FYI; Golf Channel; Hallmark Movies & Mysteries; HD Theater; History International; IFC; INSP; Investigation Discovery; Jewelry Television; JUCE TV; MTV Classic; MTV Hits; MTV Jams; MTV2; mtvU; NBCSN; NFL Network; Nick 2; Nick Jr.; Nicktoons; QVC HD; Science Channel; Science HD; TBS HD; TeenNick; TLC; TNT HD; Tr3s; Universal HD; Versus HD; VH1 Soul; WE tv; Weatherscan.
Digital Pay Service 1
Pay Units: N.A.
Programming (via satellite): Cinemax (multiplexed); Cinemax HD; Discovery Channel HD; Flix; HBO (multiplexed); HBO HD; Showtime (multiplexed); Showtime HD; Starz (multiplexed); Starz Encore (multiplexed); Starz HD; Sundance TV; The Movie Channel (multiplexed).
Video-On-Demand: Yes
Pay-Per-View
iN DEMAND (delivered digitally); ESPN (delivered digitally); Fresh (delivered digitally); Playboy TV (delivered digitally); Shorteez (delivered digitally); Hot Choice (delivered digitally); Spice; Xcess (delivered digitally); Club Jenna (delivered digitally).
Internet Service
Operational: Yes.
Fee: $54.95 monthly.
Telephone Service
Digital: Operational
Fee: $19.80 monthly
Homes passed: 39,700.
Chief Executive Officer: Colleen Abdoulah. President: Steven Cochran. Chief Financial Officer: Rich Fish.
Ownership: WideOpenWest LLC (MSO).

KODAK—Comcast Cable. Now served by KNOXVILLE, TN [TN0004]. ICA: TN0194.

LA FOLLETTE—Comcast Cable. Now served by KNOXVILLE, TN [TN0004]. ICA: TN0035.

LAFAYETTE—Comcast Cable. Now served by NASHVILLE, TN [TN0002]. ICA: TN0085.

LAUREL BLOOMERY—Formerly served by Charter Communications. No longer in operation. ICA: TN0146.

LAWRENCEBURG—Charter Communications. Now served by COLUMBIA, TN [TN0017]. ICA: TN0147.

LEBANON—Charter Communications, 12405 Powerscourt Dr, St. Louis, MO 63131. Phones: 636-207-5100 (Corporate office); 865-983-8200; 865-984-1400. Fax: 865-983-0383. Web Site: http://www.charter.com. Also serves Alexandria, DeKalb County (portions), Dowelltown, Gordonsville, Liberty, Smith County (unincorporated areas), Watertown & Wilson County (portions). ICA: TN0029.
TV Market Ranking: 30 (LEBANON, Wilson County (portions)); Below 100 (Alexan-

Cable Systems—Tennessee

dria, Dowelltown, Gordonsville, Liberty, Smith County (unincorporated areas), Watertown, Wilson County (portions)). Franchise award date: N.A. Franchise expiration date: N.A. Began: April 6, 1981.
Channel capacity: 71 (operating 2-way). Channels available but not in use: N.A.

Digital Basic Service
Subscribers: 8,081.
Programming (via satellite): BBC America; Bloomberg Television; Boomerang; CNN International; Discovery Digital Networks; DIY Network; ESPN Classic; ESPNews; FOX College Sports Central; FOX College Sports Pacific; Fox Sports 2; FXM; FYI; Great American Country; History International; IFC; LMN; MC; NFL Network; Nick 2; Nick Jr.; Nicktoons; Outdoor Channel; Sundance TV; TeenNick.
Fee: $26.99 monthly.

Digital Expanded Basic Service
Subscribers: N.A.
Programming (via satellite): A&E; AMC; Animal Planet; BET; Bravo; Cartoon Network; CMT; CNBC; CNN; Comedy Central; Discovery Channel; Discovery Life Channel; Disney Channel; Disney XD; E! HD; ESPN; ESPN2; Food Network; Fox News Channel; Fox Sports 1; FOX Sports South/SportSouth; Freeform; FX; Golf Channel; GSN; Hallmark Channel; HGTV; History; HLN; Lifetime; MSNBC; MTV; National Geographic Channel; NBCSN; Nickelodeon; Oxygen; Spike TV; Syfy; TBS; Telemundo; The Weather Channel; TLC; TNT; Travel Channel; truTV; Turner Classic Movies; TV Land; Univision; Univision Studios; USA Network; VH1; WE tv.
Fee: $45.00 monthly.

Digital Pay Service 1
Pay Units: N.A.
Programming (via satellite): Cinemax; HBO (multiplexed); Starz.

Video-On-Demand: No

Pay-Per-View
Playboy TV (delivered digitally); Fresh (delivered digitally); Shorteez (delivered digitally).

Internet Service
Operational: Yes.
Subscribers: 7,835.
Broadband Service: Charter Internet.
Fee: $29.99 monthly.

Telephone Service
Digital: Operational
Subscribers: 1,605.
Miles of Plant: 923.0 (coaxial); 372.0 (fiber optic). Homes passed: 23,400.
Operations Manager: Sean Hendrix. Marketing Director: Patt Hollenbeck. Sales & Marketing Manager: Jo Ann Placke. Accounting Director: David Sovanski.
Ownership: Charter Communications Inc. (MSO).

LEWISBURG—Charter Communications. Now served by COLUMBIA, TN [TN0017]. ICA: TN0049.

LEXINGTON—Charter Communications. Now served by JACKSON CITY, TN [TN0008]. ICA: TN0047.

LINDEN—Formerly served by Two Rivers Media. No longer in operation. ICA: TN0098.

LIVINGSTON—Comcast Cable, 2919 Ring Rd, Elizabethtown, KY 42701. Phones: 270-605-7719; 270-765-2731. Fax: 270-737-2731. Web Site: http://www.comcast.com. ICA: TN0078.

TV Market Ranking: Below 100 (LIVINGSTON). Franchise award date: November 4, 1963. Franchise expiration date: N.A. Began: May 1, 1966.
Channel capacity: N.A. Channels available but not in use: N.A.

Basic Service
Subscribers: 552. Commercial subscribers: 72.
Programming (received off-air): WCTE (PBS) Cookeville; WKRN-TV (ABC) Nashville; WNPT (PBS) Nashville; WSMV-TV (COZI TV, NBC, TNN) Nashville; WTVF (CBS, Laff, This TV) Nashville; WZTV (Antenna TV, FOX, WeatherNation) Nashville; 1 FM.
Programming (via satellite): CMT; CNN; Discovery Channel; Disney Channel; ESPN; Freeform; HLN; Lifetime; MTV; Nickelodeon; Spike TV; TBS; The Weather Channel; TNT; USA Network; WGN America.
Fee: $67.95 installation; $53.70 monthly.

Digital Basic Service
Subscribers: N.A.
Programming (via satellite): BBC America; CMT; C-SPAN 3; Discovery Digital Networks; Disney XD; ESPNews; Flix; FYI; History International; LMN; MC; MoviePlex; National Geographic Channel; NFL Network; Nick 2; Nick Jr.; Nicktoons; Sprout; Starz Encore (multiplexed); Sundance TV; TeenNick; TV One.
Fee: $14.95 monthly.

Digital Pay Service 1
Pay Units: N.A.
Programming (via satellite): Cinemax (multiplexed); HBO (multiplexed); Showtime (multiplexed); Starz (multiplexed); The Movie Channel (multiplexed).
Fee: $13.05 monthly (each).

Video-On-Demand: No

Pay-Per-View
iN DEMAND (delivered digitally); Hot Choice (delivered digitally).

Internet Service
Operational: Yes. Began: May 4, 2004.
Subscribers: 409.
Broadband Service: Comcast High Speed Internet.
Fee: $42.95 monthly.

Telephone Service
None
Miles of Plant: 76.0 (coaxial); 17.0 (fiber optic). Homes passed: 2,290.
General Manager: Tim Hagan. Technical Operations Director: Bob Tarp. Marketing Director: Laurie Nicholson.
Ownership: Comcast Cable Communications Inc. (MSO).

LOBELVILLE—Formerly served by Two Rivers Media. No longer in operation. ICA: TN0149.

LORETTO—Charter Communications. Now served by COLUMBIA, TN [TN0017]. ICA: TN0068.

LOUDON—Charter Communications. Now served by ALCOA, TN [TN0151]. ICA: TN0148.

LYNCHBURG—Comcast Cable. Now served by NASHVILLE, TN [TN0002]. ICA: TN0119.

LYNNVILLE—Formerly served by Small Town Cable. No longer in operation. ICA: TN0123.

MADISONVILLE—Charter Communications. Now served by ALCOA, TN [TN0151]. ICA: TN0176.

Access the most current data instantly
FREE TRIAL @ ADVANCED TVFactbook
TELCO/IPTV • CABLE TV • TV STATIONS
www.warren-news.com/factbook.htm

MANCHESTER—Charter Communications, 12405 Powerscourt Dr, St. Louis, MO 63131. Phones: 636-207-5100 (Corporate office); 865-983-8200; 865-984-1400. Fax: 865-983-0383. Web Site: http://www.charter.com. Also serves Altamont, Bedford County (portions), Beersheba Springs, Bell Buckle, Centertown, Coalmont, Coffee County (portions), Fayetteville, Flintville, Franklin County (portions), Gruetli-Laager, Grundy County (portions), Lincoln County (portions), McMinnville, Monteagle, Moore County (portions), Morrison, Palmer, Sewanee, Shelbyville (portions), Spencer, Tracy City, Tullahoma, Van Buren County (portions), Viola, Warren County (portions) & Wartrace. ICA: TN0032.
TV Market Ranking: 78 (Gruetli-Laager, Grundy County (portions), Palmer, Tracy City); 96 (Fayetteville, Flintville, Franklin County (portions), Lincoln County (portions)); Below 100 (Bedford County (portions), Bell Buckle, Centertown, Morrison, Shelbyville (portions), Spencer, Van Buren County (portions), Warren County (portions), Wartrace, Coffee County (portions), MANCHESTER, Moore County (portions), Tullahoma); Outside TV Markets (Altamont, Beersheba Springs, Coalmont, McMinnville, Sewanee, Viola, Coffee County (portions), Monteagle, Moore County (portions), Grundy County (portions), Franklin County (portions)). Franchise award date: N.A. Franchise expiration date: N.A. Began: May 1, 1969.
Channel capacity: N.A. Channels available but not in use: N.A.

Digital Basic Service
Subscribers: 17,548.
Programming (via satellite): BBC America; Bloomberg Television; Boomerang; CNN International; Discovery Digital Networks; DIY Network; DMX Music; ESPN Classic; ESPNews; FOX College Sports Central; FOX College Sports Pacific; Fox Sports 2; FXM; FYI; Great American Country; History International; IFC; LMN; NBCSN; NFL Network; Nick 2; Nick Jr.; Nicktoons; Outdoor Channel; Sundance TV; TeenNick.
Fee: $26.99 monthly.

Digital Expanded Basic Service
Subscribers: N.A.
Programming (via satellite): A&E; AMC; Animal Planet; BET; Bravo; Cartoon Network; CMT; CNBC; CNN; Comedy Central; Discovery Channel; Discovery Life Channel; Disney Channel; Disney XD; E! HD; ESPN; ESPN2; Food Network; Fox News Channel; Fox Sports 1; FOX Sports South/SportSouth; Freeform; FX; Golf Channel; GSN; Hallmark Channel; HGTV; History; HLN; Lifetime; MSNBC; MTV; National Geographic Channel; Nickelodeon; Oxygen; Spike TV; Syfy; TBS; Telemundo; The Weather Channel; TLC; TNT; Travel Channel; truTV; Turner Classic Movies; TV Land; Univision; Univision Studios; USA Network; VH1; WE tv.
Fee: $45.00 monthly.

Digital Pay Service 1
Pay Units: N.A.
Programming (via satellite): Cinemax (multiplexed); HBO (multiplexed); Starz (multiplexed).

Video-On-Demand: No

Pay-Per-View
Playboy TV (delivered digitally); Fresh (delivered digitally); Shorteez (delivered digitally).

Internet Service
Operational: Yes. Began: February 1, 2001.
Subscribers: 13,359.
Broadband Service: Charter Internet.
Fee: $29.99 monthly.

Telephone Service
Digital: Operational
Subscribers: 2,036.
Fee: $29.99 monthly
Miles of Plant: 2,617.0 (coaxial); 1,048.0 (fiber optic). Homes passed: 63,544.
Operations Manager: Sean Hendrix. Marketing Director: Pat Hollenbeck. Sales & Marketing Manager: Jo Ann Placke. Accounting Director: David Sovanski.
Ownership: Charter Communications Inc. (MSO).

MARTIN—Charter Communications. Now served by JACKSON CITY, TN [TN0008]. ICA: TN0205.

MAYNARDVILLE—Comcast. Now served by KNOXVILLE, TN [TN0004]. ICA: TN0077.

MCEWEN—Charter Communications, 24 Circle Dr, McKenzie, TN 38201. Phones: 314-543-2236; 636-207-5100 (Corporate office); 865-983-8200; 865-984-1400. Web Site: http://www.charter.com. ICA: TN0107.
TV Market Ranking: Outside TV Markets (MCEWEN). Franchise award date: February 10, 1983. Franchise expiration date: N.A. Began: December 1, 1984.
Channel capacity: N.A. Channels available but not in use: N.A.

Digital Basic Service
Subscribers: 62.
Programming (via satellite): BBC America; Bloomberg Television; Discovery Life Channel; Disney XD; ESPN Classic; ESPNews; Fuse; FXM; FYI; GSN; History International; IFC; LMN; MC; Nick 2; Nick Jr.; Nicktoons; Sundance TV; TeenNick; TV Guide Interactive Inc.; WE tv.
Fee: $49.99 installation; $26.99 monthly.

Digital Expanded Basic Service
Subscribers: N.A.
Programming (via satellite): A&E; AMC; Bravo; Cartoon Network; CMT; CNBC; CNN; Comedy Central; Discovery Channel; Disney Channel; E! HD; ESPN; ESPN2; Fox News Channel; Fox Sports 1; Freeform; FX; Golf Channel; HGTV; History; HLN; Lifetime; MTV; Nickelodeon; Oxygen; Spike TV; Syfy; TBS; The Weather Channel; TLC; TNT; Turner Classic Movies; TV Land; USA Network; VH1.
Fee: $45.00 monthly.

2017 Edition D-713

Tennessee—Cable Systems

Digital Pay Service 1
Pay Units: N.A.
Programming (via satellite): Cinemax (multiplexed); Flix; HBO (multiplexed); Showtime (multiplexed); Starz (multiplexed); Starz Encore; The Movie Channel (multiplexed).
Video-On-Demand: No
Pay-Per-View
iN DEMAND (delivered digitally); Playboy TV (delivered digitally); Fresh (delivered digitally).
Internet Service
Operational: No.
Telephone Service
None
Miles of Plant: 31.0 (coaxial); None (fiber optic). Homes passed: 916.
Operations Manager: Tony Fox. Technical Operations Manager: Ron Janson. Marketing Director: Pat Hollenbeck. Marketing Manager: Wiley Bird. Accounting Director: David Sovanski.
Ownership: Charter Communications Inc. (MSO).

McKENZIE—Charter Communications. Now served by JACKSON CITY, TN [TN0008]. ICA: TN0063.

MEMPHIS—Comcast Cable, 3251 Players Club Pkwy, Memphis, TN 38125. Phones: 901-259-2225; 901-365-1770. Fax: 901-369-4515. Web Site: http://www.comcast.com. Also serves Crittenden County (portions), Earle, Marion, Parkin, Sunset & West Memphis, AR; Alcorn, Byhalia, Coldwater, Como, Crenshaw, DeSoto County (portions), Hernando, Horn Lake, Marshall County (portions), Olive Branch, Robinsonville, Sardis, Senatobia, Sledge, Southaven, Tate County (portions), Tippah County (portions), Tunica, Tunica County (portions), Walls & Walnut, MS; Arlington, Bartlett, Braden, Brighton, Burlison, Collierville, Covington, Fayette County (portions), Gallaway, Garland, Germantown, Gilt Edge, Grand Junction, Hardeman County (portions), Haywood County (portions), La Grange, Lakeland, Mason, Middleton, Moscow, Oakland, Piperton, Rossville, Saulsbury, Shelby County (portions), Somerville, Stanton, Tipton County (portions), Whiteville & Williston, TN. ICA: TN0001.
TV Market Ranking: 26 (Arlington, Bartlett, Braden, Brighton, Burlison, Byhalia, Coldwater, Collierville, Covington, Crittenden County (portions), DeSoto County (portions), Earle, Fayette County (portions), Gallaway, Germantown, Gilt Edge, Hernando, Horn Lake, Lakeland, Marion, Marshall County (portions), Mason, MEMPHIS, Moscow, Oakland, Olive Branch, Parkin, Piperton, Robinsonville, Rossville, Senatobia, Shelby County (portions), Southaven, Sunset, Tate County (portions), Tipton County (portions), Tunica County (portions), Walls, West Memphis, Williston); Below 100 (Alcorn, Como, Grand Junction, Hardeman County (portions), Haywood County (portions), La Grange, Saulsbury, Somerville, Stanton, Tippah County (portions), Walnut, Whiteville); Outside TV Markets (Crenshaw, Garland, Middleton, Sardis, Sledge, Tunica). Franchise award date: N.A. Franchise expiration date: N.A. Began: February 1, 1976.
Channel capacity: N.A. Channels available but not in use: N.A.

Basic Service
Subscribers: 160,090. Commercial subscribers: 17,054.
Programming (received off-air): WATN-TV (ABC) Memphis; WBUY-TV (TBN) Holly Springs; WHBQ-TV (Decades, FOX, Movies!) Memphis; WKNO (PBS) Memphis; WLMT (CW, MeTV, MNT) Memphis; WMC-TV (Bounce TV, NBC, This TV) Memphis; WPXX-TV (ION, MNT) Memphis; WREG-TV (Antenna TV, CBS) Memphis.
Programming (via satellite): C-SPAN; C-SPAN 2; EWTN Global Catholic Network; Pop; QVC.
Fee: $29.95-$67.95 installation; $30.75 monthly.

Expanded Basic Service 1
Subscribers: N.A.
Programming (via satellite): A&E; AMC; Animal Planet; BET; Cartoon Network; CNBC; CNN; Comedy Central; Discovery Channel; Disney Channel; E! HD; ESPN; EVINE Live; Food Network; FOX Sports South/SportSouth; Freeform; FX; FXM; Hallmark Channel; HLN; Lifetime; MSNBC; MTV; MTV2; Nickelodeon; Spike TV; Starz Encore; TBS; The Weather Channel; TLC; TNT; Travel Channel; truTV; TV Land; USA Network; VH1; WGN America.
Fee: $44.69 monthly.

Digital Basic Service
Subscribers: N.A.
Programming (via satellite): BBC America; Discovery Digital Networks; Disney XD; ESPN Classic; Fox Sports 1; Golf Channel; GSN; History; LMN; MC; NBC Universo; Nick Jr.; Outdoor Channel; Sundance TV.
Fee: $15.76 monthly.

Digital Pay Service 1
Pay Units: N.A.
Programming (via satellite): Cinemax (multiplexed); HBO (multiplexed); Showtime (multiplexed); Starz (multiplexed); The Movie Channel (multiplexed).
Fee: $10.00 monthly (each).

Video-On-Demand: Yes
Pay-Per-View
iN DEMAND; Playboy TV; Pleasure; Spice.
Internet Service
Operational: Yes. Began: October 1, 1997.
Subscribers: 143,702.
Broadband Service: Comcast High Speed Internet.
Fee: $42.95 monthly.
Telephone Service
Digital: Operational
Subscribers: 63,416.
Miles of Plant: 11,328.0 (coaxial); 1,273.0 (fiber optic). Homes passed: 454,235.
Vice President & General Manager: Terry Kennedy. Technical Operations Director: Jim Davies. Government Affairs Director: Otha Brandon. Marketing & Sales Director: Linda Brashear. Plant Manager: Keith Bell.
Ownership: Comcast Cable Communications Inc. (MSO).

MILLINGTON—Millington CATV, 4880 Navy Rd, Millington, TN 38053. Phone: 901-872-7000. Also serves Atoka, Munford, Northaven, Shelby County (portions) & Tipton County (portions). ICA: TN0027.
TV Market Ranking: 26 (Atoka, MILLINGTON, Munford, Northaven, Shelby County (portions), Tipton County (portions)). Franchise award date: June 1, 1982. Franchise expiration date: N.A. Began: May 1, 1982.
Channel capacity: N.A. Channels available but not in use: N.A.

Basic Service
Subscribers: 3,778.
Programming (received off-air): WATN-TV (ABC) Memphis; WBUY-TV (TBN) Holly Springs; WHBQ-TV (Decades, FOX, Movies!) Memphis; WKNO (PBS) Memphis; WLMT (CW, MeTV, MNT) Memphis; WMC-TV (Bounce TV, NBC, This TV) Memphis; WPXX-TV (ION, MNT) Memphis; WREG-TV (Antenna TV, CBS) Memphis.
Programming (via satellite): A&E; AMC; Animal Planet; BET; Cartoon Network; CMT; CNN; Comedy Central; C-SPAN; Discovery Channel; Disney Channel; E! HD; ESPN; ESPN Classic; ESPN2; Food Network; Fox News Channel; Fox Sports 1; Freeform; FX; Hallmark Channel; HGTV; History; HLN; Hot Choice; Lifetime; MTV; Nickelodeon; Outdoor Channel; Pop; Spike TV; Syfy; TBS; The Weather Channel; TLC; TNT; Travel Channel; TV Land; USA Network; VH1; WGN America.
Fee: $52.01 monthly.

Digital Basic Service
Subscribers: N.A.
Programming (via satellite): A&E HD; AXS TV; Bloomberg Television; Boomerang; Cloo; CMT; Cooking Channel; Crime & Investigation Network; C-SPAN 3; Disney XD; DIY Network; ESPN HD; Fuse; FYI; GSN; HD Theater; History; History International; MC; NASA TV; NBCSN; Nick 2; Nick Jr.; Nicktoons; RFD-TV; TeenNick; Turner Classic Movies; WE tv.
Fee: $16.00 monthly.

Digital Expanded Basic Service
Subscribers: N.A.
Programming (via satellite): ESPNews; Flix; FOX College Sports Central; FOX College Sports Pacific; Fox Sports 2; FXM; Golf Channel; HITS (Headend In The Sky); IFC; Sundance TV.
Fee: $2.99 monthly (sports, movies or Canales).

Pay Service 1
Pay Units: N.A.
Programming (via satellite): Cinemax; HBO.

Digital Pay Service 1
Pay Units: N.A.
Programming (via satellite): Cinemax (multiplexed); Cinemax HD; HBO (multiplexed); HBO HD; Showtime (multiplexed); Showtime HD; Starz (multiplexed); Starz Encore (multiplexed); The Movie Channel (multiplexed); The Movie Channel HD.
Fee: $12.00 monthly (each).

Video-On-Demand: No
Pay-Per-View
iN DEMAND; iN DEMAND (delivered digitally); SexSee (delivered digitally); XTSY (delivered digitally); VaVoom (delivered digitally); Juicy (delivered digitally).
Internet Service
Operational: Yes.
Fee: $44.95 monthly.
Telephone Service
None
Miles of Plant: 400.0 (coaxial); 17.0 (fiber optic).
Vice President, External Affairs: John D. Strode.
Ownership: Ritter Communications.

MINOR HILL—Formerly served by Small Town Cable. No longer in operation. ICA: TN0111.

MONTEAGLE—Charter Communications. Now served by MANCHESTER, TN [TN0032]. ICA: TN0016.

MONTGOMERY COUNTY (portions)—Charter Communications. Now served by CLARKSVILLE, TN [TN0009]. ICA: TN0152.

MORRISTOWN—Charter Communications, PO Box 1620, Morristown, TN 37816. Phones: 314-543-2236; 636-207-5100 (Corporate office); 423-247-7631. Web Site: http://www.charter.com. Also serves Baneberry, Bean Station, Cocke County, Dandridge, Grainger County (northeastern portion), Hamblen County, Jefferson City, Jefferson County, New Market, Newport, Rutledge & White Pine. ICA: TN0154.
TV Market Ranking: 71 (Dandridge, Hamblen County (portions), Jefferson City, Jefferson County (portions), New Market, Rutledge); Below 100 (Baneberry, Bean Station, Cocke County, Grainger County (northeastern portion), MORRISTOWN, Newport, White Pine, Hamblen County (portions), Jefferson County (portions)). Franchise award date: N.A. Franchise expiration date: N.A. Began: February 23, 1964.
Channel capacity: 66 (operating 2-way). Channels available but not in use: N.A.

Digital Basic Service
Subscribers: 16,306.
Programming (via satellite): AXS TV; BBC America; Cooking Channel; Discovery Digital Networks; DIY Network; ESPN; ESPN Classic; ESPNews; FOX College Sports Central; FOX College Sports Pacific; Fox Sports 2; FXM; FYI; Great American Country; History International; IFC; Jewelry Television; LMN; MC; NFL Network; Nick 2; Nick Jr.; Nicktoons; Outdoor Channel; Sundance TV; TeenNick.
Fee: $49.99 installation; $26.99 monthly.

Digital Expanded Basic Service
Subscribers: N.A.
Programming (via satellite): A&E; AMC; Animal Planet; BET; Bravo; Cartoon Network; CMT; CNBC; CNN; Comcast/Charter Sports Southeast (CSS); Comedy Central; Discovery Channel; Discovery Life Channel; Disney Channel; Disney XD; E! HD; ESPN; ESPN2; Food Network; Fox News Channel; Fox Sports 1; FOX Sports South/SportSouth; Freeform; FX; Golf Channel; GSN; Hallmark Channel; HGTV; History; HLN; Lifetime; MSNBC; MTV; National Geographic Channel; NBCSN; Nickelodeon; Oxygen; Spike TV; Syfy; TBS; TLC; TNT; Travel Channel; Trinity Broadcasting Network (TBN); truTV; Turner Classic Movies; TV Land; USA Network; VH1; WE tv.
Fee: $45.00 monthly.

Digital Pay Service 1
Pay Units: N.A.
Programming (via satellite): Cinemax (multiplexed); Flix (multiplexed); HBO (multiplexed); HBO HD; Showtime (multiplexed); Showtime HD; Starz (multiplexed); Starz Encore (multiplexed); The Movie Channel (multiplexed).

Video-On-Demand: Yes
Pay-Per-View
Hot Choice; iN DEMAND; Fresh; Fresh (delivered digitally); special events.
Internet Service
Operational: Yes.
Subscribers: 14,127.
Broadband Service: Charter Internet.
Fee: $29.99 monthly.
Telephone Service
Digital: Operational
Subscribers: 3,445.
Fee: $29.99 monthly.
Miles of Plant: 1,551.0 (coaxial); 443.0 (fiber optic). Homes passed: 48,513.
Operations Manager: Tony Falin. Marketing Director: Pat Hollenbeck. Sales & Marketing

Cable Systems—Tennessee

Manager: Kevin Kick. Accounting Director: David Sovanski.
Ownership: Charter Communications Inc. (MSO).

MOUNTAIN CITY—Charter Communications. Now served by HICKORY, NC [NC0009]. ICA: TN0067.

NASHVILLE—Comcast Cable, 660 Mainstream Dr, PO Box 280570, Nashville, TN 37228-0570. Phones: 615-244-2122; 615-244-7462. Fax: 615-255-6528. Web Site: http://www.comcast.com. Also serves Fort Campbell, Franklin & Simpson County (portions), KY; Adams, Arrington, Ashland City, Bon Aqua, Brentwood, Brush Creek, Burns, Cannon County (portions), Carthage, Cedar Hill, Charlotte Hall, Cheatham County (portions), Cottontown, Cowan, Cross Plains, Cumberland Furnace, Davidson County (portions), Decherd, DeKalb County (portions), Dickson, Dickson County (portions), Dowelltown, Elmwood, Estill Springs, Fairview, Franklin, Franklin County (portions), Gallatin, Goodlettsville, Greenbrier, Hartsville, Hendersonville, Hermitage, Hickman County (portions), Humphreys County (portions), Joelton, Kingston Springs, La Vergne, Lafayette, Lebanon, Lyles, Lynchburg, Macon County (portions), Millersville, Mitchellville, Mount Juliet, Murfreesboro, New Deal, Nolensville, Old Hickory, Orlinda, Pegram, Portland, Readyville, Ridgetop, Robertson County (portions), Rutherford County (portions), Slayden, Smithville, Smyrna, South Carthage, Springfield, Sumner County (portions), Temple Hills, Tennessee City, Vanleer, Waverly, Westmoreland, White Bluff, White House, Whites Creek, Williamsburg, Williamson County (portions), Wilson County (portions), Winchester, Woodbury & Wrigley, TN. ICA: TN0002.
TV Market Ranking: 30 (Adams, Arrington, Ashland City, Bon Aqua, Brentwood, Brush Creek, Burns, Cedar Hill, Charlotte Hall, Cheatham County (portions), Cottontown, Cross Plains, Cumberland Furnace, Davidson County (portions), Dickson, Fairview, Franklin, Gallatin, Goodlettsville, Greenbrier, Hartsville, Hendersonville, Hermitage, Hickman County (portions), Joelton, Kingston Springs, La Vergne, Lebanon, Lyles, Millersville, Mitchellville, Mount Juliet, Murfreesboro, NASHVILLE, New Deal, Nolensville, Old Hickory, Orlinda, Pegram, Portland, Readyville, Ridgetop, Robertson County (portions), Rutherford County (portions), Simpson County (portions), Smyrna, Springfield, Sumner County (portions), Temple Hills, Tennessee City, White Bluff, White House, Whites Creek, Williamsburg, Williamson County (portions), Wilson County (portions), Wrigley); 96 (Franklin County (portions)); Below 100 (Cannon County (portions), Carthage, DeKalb County (portions), Dowelltown, Elmwood, Lafayette, Macon County (portions), South Carthage, Westmoreland, Smithville, Woodbury, Hickman County (portions), Simpson County (portions), Wilson County (portions)); Outside TV Markets (Cowan, Decherd, Estill Springs, Humphreys County (portions), Slayden, Vanleer, Waverly, Winchester, Fort Campbell, Lynchburg, Franklin County (portions)). Franchise award date: February 1, 1979. Franchise expiration date: N.A. Began: February 1, 1979.
Channel capacity: N.A. Channels available but not in use: N.A.

Basic Service
Subscribers: 279,210. Commercial subscribers: 21,239.
Programming (received off-air): WHTN (Christian TV Network) Murfreesboro; WKRN-TV (ABC) Nashville; WNPT (PBS) Nashville; WPGD-TV (TBN) Hendersonville; WSMV-TV (COZI TV, NBC, TNN) Nashville; WTVF (CBS, Laff, This TV) Nashville; WUXP-TV (MNT) Nashville; WZTV (Antenna TV, FOX, WeatherNation) Nashville.
Programming (via satellite): Pop; TBS; The Weather Channel; WGN America.
Fee: $52.95-$67.95 installation; $26.14 monthly.

Expanded Basic Service 1
Subscribers: N.A.
Programming (via satellite): A&E; AMC; BET; Bravo; Cartoon Network; CMT; CNBC; CNN; Comedy Central; C-SPAN; C-SPAN 2; Discovery Channel; Disney Channel; E! HD; ESPN; EVINE Live; Freeform; FX; FXM; Hallmark Channel; History; HLN; Lifetime; MTV; Nickelodeon; Pop; QVC; Spike TV; Syfy; TLC; TNT; truTV; USA Network; VH1.
Fee: $31.26 monthly.

Digital Basic Service
Subscribers: N.A.
Programming (via satellite): BBC America; C-SPAN 3; Discovery Digital Networks; Disney XD; DMX Music; ESPN Classic; Flix; Fox Sports 1; FYI; Golf Channel; GSN; History International; IFC; INSP; LMN; Nick Jr.; Sundance TV; TeenNick; Turner Classic Movies; Weatherscan.
Fee: $10.00 monthly.

Pay Service 1
Pay Units: N.A.
Programming (via satellite): Cinemax; HBO; Showtime; The Movie Channel.
Fee: $8.00 monthly (each).

Digital Pay Service 1
Pay Units: N.A.
Programming (via satellite): Cinemax (multiplexed); HBO (multiplexed); Showtime (multiplexed); Starz (multiplexed); Starz Encore (multiplexed); The Movie Channel (multiplexed).

Video-On-Demand: Yes

Pay-Per-View
Hot Choice; Hot Choice (delivered digitally); iN DEMAND; iN DEMAND (delivered digitally); Playboy TV; Playboy TV (delivered digitally); Pleasure (delivered digitally); Fresh (delivered digitally); Shorteez (delivered digitally); Sports PPV (delivered digitally).

Internet Service
Operational: Yes.
Subscribers: 283,326.
Broadband Service: Comcast High Speed Internet.
Fee: $42.95 monthly; $15.00 modem lease; $240.00 modem purchase.

Telephone Service
Digital: Operational
Subscribers: 131,101.
Fee: $44.95 monthly
Miles of Plant: 17,658.0 (coaxial); 4,150.0 (fiber optic). Homes passed: 795,034.
Area Vice President & General Manager: John Gauder. Technical Operations Director: Joe Pell. Marketing Director: Martine Mahoney. Marketing Manager: Will Jefferson.
Ownership: Comcast Cable Communications Inc. (MSO).

NEW TAZEWELL—Vyve Broadband, 4 International Dr, Ste 330, Rye Brook, NY 10573. Phones: 800-937-1397; 423-626-9107. Web Site: http://vyvebroadband.com. Also serves Arthur, Claiborne County (portions), Cumberland Gap, Harrogate, Lone Mountain, Shawanee, Speedwell & Tazewell. ICA: TN0038.
TV Market Ranking: 71 (Lone Mountain); Below 100 (Arthur, Claiborne County (portions), Cumberland Gap, Harrogate, NEW TAZEWELL, Shawanee, Speedwell, Tazewell). Franchise award date: January 1, 1977. Franchise expiration date: N.A. Began: August 1, 1978.
Channel capacity: N.A. Channels available but not in use: N.A.

Basic Service
Subscribers: 3,155.
Programming (received off-air): WATE-TV (ABC, Laff) Knoxville; WBIR-TV (MeTV, NBC) Knoxville; WBXX-TV (CW, Escape) Crossville; WETP-TV (PBS) Sneedville; WKNX-TV (Retro TV) Knoxville; WLFG (IND, PBJ, Retro TV) Grundy; WPXK-TV (ION) Jellico; WTNZ (FOX, This TV) Knoxville; WVLR (Christian TV Network) Tazewell; WVLT-TV (CBS, MNT) Knoxville; WYMT-TV (CBS, CW) Hazard.
Programming (via satellite): C-SPAN; Discovery Channel; Pop; QVC; WGN America.
Fee: $25.00 monthly.

Expanded Basic Service 1
Subscribers: N.A.
Programming (via satellite): A&E; AMC; Animal Planet; Boomerang; Bravo; Cartoon Network; CMT; CNBC; CNN; Comcast/Charter Sports Southeast (CSS); Comedy Central; Cooking Channel; C-SPAN 2; Disney Channel; DIY Network; E! HD; ESPN; ESPN Classic; ESPN2; ESPNews; EVINE Live; Food Network; Fox News Channel; Fox Sports 1; FOX Sports South/SportSouth; Freeform; FX; FXM; Great American Country; Hallmark Channel; HGTV; History; HLN; Lifetime; MSNBC; MTV; National Geographic Channel; Nick Jr.; Nickelodeon; Outdoor Channel; Spike TV; Syfy; TBS; The Weather Channel; TLC; TNT; Travel Channel; Trinity Broadcasting Network (TBN); truTV; TV Land; UP; USA Network; VH1; WE tv.
Fee: $19.96 monthly.

Digital Basic Service
Subscribers: N.A.
Programming (via satellite): BBC America; Bloomberg Television; Bravo; Cloo; CMT; Daystar TV Network; Destination America; Discovery Kids Channel; Discovery Life Channel; Disney XD; DMX Music; ESPN Classic; ESPN2; ESPNews; Fox Sports 1; Fuse; FXM; FYI; Golf Channel; Great American Country; GSN; HGTV; History International; IFC; Investigation Discovery; LMN; MTV Classic; MTV Hits; MTV Jams; MTV2; National Geographic Channel; NBCSN; Nicktoons; Outdoor Channel; Ovation; OWN; Oprah Winfrey Network; RFD-TV; Science Channel; Starz Encore (multiplexed); Syfy; TeenNick; The Word Network; Trinity Broadcasting Network (TBN); Turner Classic Movies; TV One; VH1 Soul; WE tv.
Fee: $17.00 monthly.

Digital Pay Service 1
Pay Units: N.A.
Programming (via satellite): Cinemax (multiplexed); Flix; HBO (multiplexed); Showtime (multiplexed); Starz (multiplexed); The Movie Channel (multiplexed).
Fee: $13.95 monthly (each).

Video-On-Demand: No

Pay-Per-View
iN DEMAND (delivered digitally); ESPN (delivered digitally); Playboy TV (delivered digitally); Fresh (delivered digitally); Club Jenna (delivered digitally); Spice: Xcess (delivered digitally); Hot Choice (delivered digitally).

Internet Service
Operational: Yes.
Broadband Service: Net Commander.
Fee: $39.95 installation; $51.95 monthly.

Telephone Service
Digital: Operational
Miles of Plant: 200.0 (coaxial); None (fiber optic). Homes passed: 12,000.
President & Chief Executive Officer: Jeffrey DeMond. Senior Vice President, Financial Planning: Daniel White. Vice President, Residential Services: Vin Zachariah. Vice President, Marketing: Diane Quennoz.
Ownership: Vyve Broadband LLC (MSO).

NEWBERN—Charter Communications. Now served by JACKSON CITY, TN [TN0008]. ICA: TN0072.

NEWBERN—Charter Communications. Now served by JACKSON CITY, TN [TN0008]. ICA: TN0206.

NEWPORT—Haywood Cablevision, 4930 Jonathan Creek Rd, Waynesville, NC 28785. Phones: 866-571-8671; 828-926-2288. Fax: 678-682-9727. Web Site: http://www.cbvnol.com. ICA: TN0203.
TV Market Ranking: 71 (NEWPORT).
Channel capacity: N.A. Channels available but not in use: N.A.

Basic Service
Subscribers: N.A.
Programming (received off-air): WATE-TV (ABC, Laff) Knoxville; WBIR-TV (MeTV, NBC) Knoxville; WEMT (FOX, Movies!, This TV) Greeneville; WETP-TV (PBS) Sneedville; WVLT-TV (CBS, MNT) Knoxville.
Programming (via satellite): CMT; CNN; Discovery Channel; Nickelodeon; Spike TV; The Weather Channel.

Expanded Basic Service 1
Subscribers: N.A.
Programming (via satellite): Disney Channel; ESPN; ESPN2; Fox News Channel; Freeform; HGTV; HLN; Lifetime; MTV; TBS; TNT; Trinity Broadcasting Network (TBN); Turner Classic Movies; USA Network; VH1.

Pay Service 1
Pay Units: N.A.
Programming (via satellite): HBO; Showtime.

Internet Service
Operational: Yes.
Fee: $43.95 monthly.

Telephone Service
Digital: Operational
General Manager: Bryan Hyder. Chief Technician: Terry Sersland.
Ownership: Carolina Mountain Cablevision Inc. (MSO).

Tennessee—Cable Systems

NORRIS—Comcast Cable. Now served by KNOXVILLE, TN [TN0004]. ICA: TN0156.

OAK RIDGE—Comcast Cable. Now served by KNOXVILLE, TN [TN0004]. ICA: TN0012.

ORME—BlueBridge Media, 231 South Cedar Ave, South Pittsburg, TN 37380. Phone: 423-837-2000. Web Site: http://www.bluebridgemedia.com. Also serves Dunlap, Jasper, Kimball, Sequatchie County (portions), South Pittsburg & Whitwell. ICA: TN0215.
TV Market Ranking: 78 (Dunlap, Jasper, Kimball, ORME, Sequatchie County (portions), South Pittsburg, Whitwell); Outside TV Markets (Sequatchie County (portions)).
Channel capacity: N.A. Channels available but not in use: N.A.
Basic Service
 Subscribers: 599.
 Fee: $14.95 monthly.
 Ownership: BlueBridge Media.

OVERTON COUNTY (portions)—Overton County Cable, 17525 Highland Dr, McKenzie, TN 38201. Phones: 207-824-9911; 731-352-2980; 931-823-1114. Fax: 731-352-3533. ICA: TN0184.
TV Market Ranking: Below 100 (OVERTON COUNTY (PORTIONS)).
Channel capacity: 40 (not 2-way capable). Channels available but not in use: N.A.
Basic Service
 Subscribers: N.A.
 Programming (received off-air): WCTE (PBS) Cookeville; WKRN-TV (ABC) Nashville; WNAB (CW, The Country Network) Nashville; WSMV-TV (COZI TV, NBC, TNN) Nashville; WTVF (CBS, Laff, This TV) Nashville; WUXP-TV (MNT) Nashville; WZTV (Antenna TV, FOX, WeatherNation) Nashville.
 Programming (via satellite): A&E; AMC; Animal Planet; Cartoon Network; CMT; CNBC; CNN; C-SPAN; Discovery Channel; Disney Channel; ESPN; FOX Sports South/SportSouth; Freeform; HGTV; History; Lifetime; MTV; Nickelodeon; Spike TV; Syfy; TBS; TLC; TNT; truTV; Turner Classic Movies; USA Network; VH1; WGN America.
 Fee: $10.78 installation; $12.50 monthly.
Pay Service 1
 Pay Units: N.A.
 Programming (via satellite): Cinemax; HBO; Showtime.
 Fee: $10.31 monthly (each).
Video-On-Demand: No
Internet Service
 Operational: Yes.
Telephone Service
 None
Miles of Plant: 187.0 (coaxial); None (fiber optic).
General Manager: Gary Blount.
Ownership: Celina Cable Communications (MSO).

PARIS—Charter Communications. Now served by JACKSON CITY, TN [TN0008]. ICA: TN0030.

PARSONS—Charter Communications. Now served by JACKSON CITY, TN [TN0008]. ICA: TN0084.

PIKEVILLE—Bledsoe Telephone Coop, 338 Cumberland Ave, PO Box 609, Pikeville, TN 37367-0609. Phone: 423-447-2121. E-mail: bledsoe@bledsoe.net. Web Site: http://www.bledsoe.net. Also serves Bledsoe County (portions), Cumberland County (portions), Dunlap, Hamilton County (portions), Sequatchie County (portions) & Van Buren County (portions). ICA: TN0158.
Channel capacity: N.A. Channels available but not in use: N.A.
Basic Service
 Subscribers: 2,993. Commercial subscribers: 4.
 Programming (received off-air): WDEF-TV (Bounce TV, CBS, Escape) Chattanooga; WDSI-TV (FOX, MNT) Chattanooga; WFLI-TV (CW, MeTV) Cleveland; WRCB (Antenna TV, NBC) Chattanooga; WTCI (PBS) Chattanooga; WTVC (ABC, This TV, WeatherNation) Chattanooga.
 Programming (via satellite): A&E; CMT; CNN; Discovery Channel; ESPN; FOX Sports South/SportSouth; HLN; HSN; Spike TV; TBS; The Weather Channel; TLC; TNT; Trinity Broadcasting Network (TBN); TV Land; USA Network; WGN America.
 Fee: $40.00 installation; $17.95 monthly.
Pay Service 1
 Pay Units: N.A.
 Programming (via satellite): The Movie Channel.
 Fee: $10.50 monthly.
Internet Service
 Operational: Yes.
 Fee: $99.00 installation; $29.95-$89.95 monthly.
Telephone Service
 Digital: Operational
General Manager: Greg Anderson.
Ownership: Bledsoe Telephone Cooperative.

PORTLAND—Comcast Cable. Now served by NASHVILLE, TN [TN0002]. ICA: TN0080.

PULASKI—Charter Communications. Now served by COLUMBIA, TN [TN0017]. ICA: TN0018.

RED BOILING SPRINGS—Formerly served by Celina Cable. This cable system has converted to IPTV. Now served by NCTC, SCOTTSVILLE, KY [KY5016]. ICA: TN0114.

RIPLEY—Formerly served by NewWave Communications. Now served by Time Warner Cable, BROWNSVILLE, TN [TN0054]. ICA: TN0160.

ROGERSVILLE—Charter Communications. Now served by KINGSPORT, TN [TN0007]. ICA: TN0190.

ROGERSVILLE—Middle Tennessee Broadband, 8279 Horton Highway, College Grove, TN 37046. Phones: 877-368-2110; 615-815-1600. Web Site: http://www.midtnbb.com. Also serves Hawkins County (central portion) & Surgoinsville. ICA: TN0087.
TV Market Ranking: Below 100 (Hawkins County (central portion), ROGERSVILLE, Surgoinsville). Franchise award date: N.A. Franchise expiration date: N.A. Began: December 1, 1988.
Channel capacity: N.A. Channels available but not in use: N.A.
Basic Service
 Subscribers: N.A.
 Programming (received off-air): WBIR-TV (MeTV, NBC) Knoxville; WCYB-TV (CW, Decades, NBC) Bristol; WETP-TV (PBS) Sneedville; WJHL-TV (ABC, CBS, MeTV) Johnson City; WKPT-TV (COZI TV, Escape, MeTV, MNT) Kingsport; WLOS (ABC, Antenna TV) Asheville.
 Programming (via satellite): A&E; CMT; CNN; Comedy Central; Discovery Channel; Disney Channel; ESPN; Freeform; HLN; Lifetime; MTV; QVC; Spike TV; TBS; The Weather Channel; TNT; USA Network; WGN America.
 Fee: $30.00 installation; $27.50 monthly.
Pay Service 1
 Pay Units: N.A.
 Programming (via satellite): HBO; Showtime.
 Fee: $30.00 installation; $9.95 monthly (each).
Video-On-Demand: Yes
Internet Service
 Operational: Yes.
Telephone Service
 Analog: Not Operational
 Digital: Operational
General Manager: Vince King.
Ownership: Middle Tennessee Broadband (MSO).

SAVANNAH—Charter Communications. Now served by JACKSON CITY, TN [TN0008]. ICA: TN0041.

SELMER—Charter Communications. Now served by JACKSON CITY, TN [TN0008]. ICA: TN0060.

SMITHVILLE—Comcast Cable. Now served by NASHVILLE, TN [TN0002]. ICA: TN0076.

SNEEDVILLE—Zito Media, 102 S Main St, PO Box 665, Coudersport, PA 16915. Phones: 814-260-9055; 800-365-6988. E-mail: info@zitomedia.com. Web Site: http://www.zitomedia.com. ICA: TN0113.
TV Market Ranking: Below 100 (SNEEDVILLE). Franchise award date: N.A. Franchise expiration date: N.A. Began: January 1, 1966.
Channel capacity: N.A. Channels available but not in use: N.A.
Basic Service
 Subscribers: 182.
 Programming (received off-air): WATE-TV (ABC, Laff) Knoxville; WBIR-TV (MeTV, NBC) Knoxville; WEMT (FOX, Movies!, This TV) Greeneville; WETP-TV (PBS) Sneedville; WVLT-TV (CBS, MNT) Knoxville.
 Programming (via satellite): C-SPAN; INSP; ION Television; QVC; Trinity Broadcasting Network (TBN); WGN America.
 Fee: $49.95 installation; $17.95 monthly; $2.00 converter.
Expanded Basic Service 1
 Subscribers: N.A.
 Programming (via satellite): A&E; AMC; Bravo; Cartoon Network; CMT; CNBC; CNN; Comedy Central; Discovery Channel; Disney Channel; E! HD; ESPN; ESPN2; Food Network; Fox News Channel; Fox Sports 1; FOX Sports South/SportSouth; Freeform; FX; Golf Channel; Hallmark Channel; HGTV; History; HLN; Lifetime; MSNBC; MTV; National Geographic Channel; Nickelodeon; Oxygen; Spike TV; Syfy; TBS; The Weather Channel; TLC; TNT; Turner Classic Movies; TV Land; USA Network; VH1.
Digital Basic Service
 Subscribers: N.A.
 Programming (via satellite): BBC America; Bloomberg Television; Discovery Life Channel; Disney XD; ESPN Classic; ESPNews; Fuse; FXM; FYI; GSN; History International; IFC; LMN; MC; Nick 2; Nick Jr.; Nicktoons; Sundance TV; TeenNick; WE tv.
Digital Pay Service 1
 Pay Units: N.A.
 Programming (via satellite): Cinemax (multiplexed); Flix; HBO (multiplexed); Showtime (multiplexed); Starz (multiplexed); Starz Encore; The Movie Channel (multiplexed).
Video-On-Demand: No
Pay-Per-View
 Hot Choice; iN DEMAND; special events.
Internet Service
 Operational: Yes.
Telephone Service
 Digital: Operational
Miles of Plant: 26.0 (coaxial); None (fiber optic). Homes passed: 500.
President: James Rigas.
Ownership: Zito Media (MSO).

SOUTH FULTON—Time Warner Cable. Now served by MAYFIELD, KY [KY0037]. ICA: TN0209.

SPRING CITY—Spring City Cable TV Inc, 140 Ellis St, PO Box 729, Spring City, TN 37381-0729. Phone: 423-365-7288. Fax: 423-365-4800. Also serves Rhea County. ICA: TN0086.
TV Market Ranking: 78 (Rhea County (portions)); Below 100 (SPRING CITY, Rhea County (portions)). Franchise award date: N.A. Franchise expiration date: N.A. Began: October 1, 1982.
Channel capacity: N.A. Channels available but not in use: N.A.
Basic Service
 Subscribers: N.A.
 Programming (received off-air): WATE-TV (ABC, Laff) Knoxville; WBIR-TV (MeTV, NBC) Knoxville; WBXX-TV (CW, Escape) Crossville; WDEF-TV (Bounce TV, CBS, Escape) Chattanooga; WDSI-TV (FOX, MNT) Chattanooga; WELF-TV (TBN) Dalton; WFLI-TV (CW, MeTV) Cleveland; WPXK-TV (ION) Jellico; WTCI (PBS) Chattanooga; WTNZ (FOX, This TV) Knoxville; WTVC (ABC, This TV, WeatherNation) Chattanooga; WVLT-TV (CBS, MNT) Knoxville.
 Programming (via satellite): TBS; WGN America.
 Fee: $31.50 installation.
Expanded Basic Service 1
 Subscribers: N.A.
 Programming (via satellite): A&E; Animal Planet; Cartoon Network; CBS Sports Network; CMT; CNBC; CNN; Comedy Central; C-SPAN; C-SPAN 2; Discovery Channel; ESPN; ESPN2; Food Network; Fox News Channel; Fox Sports 1; FOX Sports South/SportSouth; Freeform; FX; FXM; Hallmark Channel; HGTV; History; HLN; Lifetime; MTV; Nickelodeon; Outdoor Channel; QVC; Spike TV; Syfy; The Weather Channel; TLC; TNT; Travel Channel; Turner Classic Movies; TV Land; USA Network; VH1.
 Fee: $42.95 monthly.
Pay Service 1
 Pay Units: N.A.
 Programming (via satellite): Cinemax; HBO.
 Fee: $11.50 monthly (each).
Video-On-Demand: No
Internet Service
 Operational: Yes.
Telephone Service
 None
Miles of Plant: 32.0 (coaxial); None (fiber optic).
General Manager: Walter Hooper. Chief Technician: John Beasley.
Ownership: Spring City Cable TV Inc.

STONEY CREEK—Charter Communications. Now served by KINGSPORT, TN [TN0007]. ICA: TN0200.

Cable Systems—Tennessee

SUMMERTOWN—Formerly served by Small Town Cable. No longer in operation. ICA: TN0171.

TALBOTT—Haywood Cablevision, 4930 Jonathan Creek Rd, Waynesville, NC 28785. Phones: 866-571-8671; 828-926-2288. Fax: 678-682-9727. Web Site: http://www.cbvnol.com. ICA: TN0202.
TV Market Ranking: Below 100 (TALBOTT).
Channel capacity: N.A. Channels available but not in use: N.A.
Basic Service
Subscribers: N.A.
Programming (received off-air): WATE-TV (ABC, Laff) Knoxville; WBIR-TV (MeTV, NBC) Knoxville; WEMT (FOX, Movies!, This TV) Greeneville; WETP-TV (PBS) Sneedville; WJHL-TV (ABC, CBS, MeTV) Johnson City; WKPT-TV (COZI TV, Escape, MeTV, MNT) Kingsport; WVIR-TV (CW, NBC, WeatherNation) Charlottesville; WVLT-TV (CBS, MNT) Knoxville.
Expanded Basic Service 1
Subscribers: N.A.
Programming (via satellite): CMT; CNN; Discovery Channel; Disney Channel; ESPN; ESPN2; Fox News Channel; Freeform; HGTV; HLN; Lifetime; MTV; Nickelodeon; Spike TV; TBS; The Weather Channel; TNT; Trinity Broadcasting Network (TBN); Turner Classic Movies; USA Network; VH1.
Pay Service 1
Pay Units: N.A.
Programming (via satellite): HBO; Showtime.
Internet Service
Operational: Yes.
Fee: $43.95 monthly.
Telephone Service
Digital: Operational
General Manager: Bryan Hyder. Chief Technician: Terry Sersland.
Ownership: Carolina Mountain Cablevision Inc. (MSO).

TEN MILE—Charter Communications, 12405 Powerscourt Dr, St. Louis, MO 63131. Phones: 636-207-5100 (Corporate office); 423-728-4087; 423-478-1934; 865-984-1400 (Maryville office). Fax: 423-476-1621. Web Site: http://www.charter.com. Also serves Kingston. ICA: TN0073.
TV Market Ranking: 71 (Kingston); Below 100 (TEN MILE). Franchise award date: N.A. Franchise expiration date: N.A. Began: October 1, 1989.
Channel capacity: N.A. Channels available but not in use: N.A.
Digital Basic Service
Subscribers: 224.
Programming (via satellite): BBC America; Bloomberg Television; Discovery Life Channel; Disney Channel; E! HD; ESPN; ESPN2; ESPN Classic; FYI; History International; IFC; LMN; MC; Nick 2; Nick Jr.; Nicktoons; Sundance TV; TeenNick; TV Guide Interactive Inc.; WE tv.
Fee: $26.99 monthly.
Digital Expanded Basic Service
Subscribers: N.A.
Programming (via satellite): A&E; AMC; Bravo; Cartoon Network; CMT; CNBC; CNN; Comedy Central; C-SPAN; Discovery Channel; Disney Channel; E! HD; ESPN; ESPN2; Fox News Channel; Fox Sports 1; Freeform; FX; Golf Channel; HGTV; History; HLN; Lifetime; MTV; Nickelodeon; Oxygen; Spike TV; Syfy; TBS; The Weather Channel; TLC; TNT; Travel Channel; Trinity Broadcasting Network (TBN); TV Land; USA Network; VH1.
Fee: $50.99 monthly.
Digital Pay Service 1
Pay Units: N.A.
Programming (via satellite): Cinemax (multiplexed); Flix; HBO (multiplexed); Showtime (multiplexed); Starz (multiplexed); Starz Encore; The Movie Channel (multiplexed).
Video-On-Demand: No
Internet Service
Operational: No.
Telephone Service
None
Miles of Plant: 100.0 (coaxial); None (fiber optic). Homes passed: 2,084.
Operations Manager: Mike Burns. Technical Operations Director: Grant Evans. Technical Operations Manager: David Ogle. Marketing Director: Pat Hollenbeck. Office Manager: Connie Wilson. Accounting Director: David Sovanski.
Ownership: Charter Communications Inc. (MSO).

TIPTONVILLE—Time Warner Cable. Now served by MAYFIELD, KY [KY0037]. ICA: TN0059.

TRENTON—Trenton TV Cable Co, 45 Howell Ln, PO Box 345, Trenton, TN 38382-0345. Phone: 731-855-2808. Fax: 731-855-9512. ICA: TN0071.
TV Market Ranking: Below 100 (TRENTON). Franchise award date: N.A. Franchise expiration date: N.A. Began: May 1, 1968.
Channel capacity: N.A. Channels available but not in use: N.A.
Basic Service
Subscribers: 896.
Programming (received off-air): KFVS-TV (CBS, CW, MeTV) Cape Girardeau; WATN-TV (ABC) Memphis; WBBJ-TV (ABC, CBS, MeTV) Jackson; WHBQ-TV (Decades, FOX, Movies!) Memphis; WJKT (FOX) Jackson; WKNO (PBS) Memphis; WLJT-DT (PBS) Lexington; WMC-TV (Bounce TV, NBC, This TV) Memphis; WPSD-TV (Antenna TV, NBC) Paducah; WREG-TV (Antenna TV, CBS) Memphis.
Fee: $40.00 installation; $22.45 monthly.
Expanded Basic Service 1
Subscribers: N.A.
Programming (via satellite): A&E; BET; CMT; CNN; C-SPAN; Discovery Channel; ESPN; ESPN2; Freeform; HGTV; HLN; Lifetime; Spike TV; Syfy; TBS; The Weather Channel; TNT; Trinity Broadcasting Network (TBN); Turner Classic Movies; USA Network; VH1; WGN America.
Fee: $27.25 monthly.
Pay Service 1
Pay Units: N.A.
Programming (via satellite): Cinemax; HBO; Showtime; Starz.
Fee: $12.00 monthly (each).
Internet Service
Operational: Yes.
Subscribers: 461.
Broadband Service: In-house.
Fee: $25.95 monthly.
Telephone Service
None
Miles of Plant: 127.0 (coaxial); 23.0 (fiber optic). Homes passed: 2,650.
President & General Manager: Stephen Nowell.
Ownership: Stephen Nowell.

TURTLETOWN—Ellijay Telephone Co. No longer in operation. ICA: TN0065.

UNICOI—Zito Media. Now served by CARTER COUNTY (portions), TN [TN0105]. ICA: TN0207.

UNION CITY—Formerly served by MetroVision. No longer in operation. ICA: TN0181.

VONORE—Comcast Cable. Now served by KNOXVILLE, TN [TN0004]. ICA: TN0115.

WALDEN CREEK—Comcast Cable. Now served by KNOXVILLE, TN [TN0004]. ICA: TN0031.

WARTBURG—Comcast Cable. Now served by KNOXVILLE, TN [TN0004]. ICA: TN0019.

WAVERLY—Comcast Cable. Now served by NASHVILLE, TN [TN0002]. ICA: TN0075.

WAYNESBORO—Charter Communications. Now served by JACKSON CITY, TN [TN0008]. ICA: TN0093.

WESTMORELAND—Comcast Cable. Now served by NASHVILLE, TN [TN0002]. ICA: TN0104.

WESTPOINT—Charter Communications. Now served by COLUMBIA, TN [TN0017]. ICA: TN0124.

WHITE HOUSE—Comcast Cable. Now served by NASHVILLE, TN [TN0002]. ICA: TN0050.

WHITESBURG—Formerly served by Adelphia Communications. Now served by Comcast Cable, KNOXVILLE, TN [TN0004]. ICA: TN0079.

WINCHESTER—Comcast Cable. Now served by NASHVILLE, TN [TN0002]. ICA: TN0045.

WOODBURY—Comcast Cable. Now served by NASHVILLE, TN [TN0002]. ICA: TN0101.

TEXAS

Total Systems: 289	Communities with Applications: 0
Total Communities Served: 1,185	Number of Basic Subscribers: 2,454,291
Franchises Not Yet Operating: 0	Number of Expanded Basic Subscribers: 255,371
Applications Pending: 0	Number of Pay Units: 136,503

Top 100 Markets Represented: Dallas-Fort Worth (12); Houston (15); San Antonio (45); Texarkana, TX-Shreveport, LA (58); Beaumont-Port Arthur (88); Amarillo (95).

For a list of cable communities in this section, see the Cable Community Index located in the back of Cable Volume 2.
For explanation of terms used in cable system listings, see p. D-11.

ABERNATHY—NTS Communications. Formerly [TX0388]. This cable system has converted to IPTV, 1220 Broadway, Lubbock, TX 79401. Phones: 800-658-2150; 806-797-0687. Fax: 806-788-3381. E-mail: info@ntscom.com. Web Site: http://www.ntscom.com. ICA: TX5542.
TV Market Ranking: Below 100 (ABERNATHY). Franchise award date: August 14, 1978. Franchise expiration date: N.A. Began: November 1, 1979.
Channel capacity: N.A. Channels available but not in use: N.A.
Gold
Subscribers: N.A.
Programming (received off-air): KAMC (ABC, Bounce TV) Lubbock; KBZO-LD (UNV) Lubbock; KCBD (NBC, This TV) Lubbock; KJTV-TV (FOX) Lubbock; KLBK-TV (CBS) Lubbock; KLCW-TV (CW) Wolfforth; KPTB-DT (GLC) Lubbock; KRPV-DT (GLC) Roswell; KTTZ-TV (PBS) Lubbock; KXTQ-CD (TMO) Lubbock.
Programming (via satellite): A&E; AMC; CNN; Discovery Channel; Disney Channel; E! HD; ESPN; ESPN2; Fox News Channel; FOX Sports Southwest; Freeform; FX; Great American Country; HGTV; History; HLN; INSP; Lifetime; MSNBC; MTV; National Geographic Channel; Nickelodeon; QVC; Spike TV; TBS; The Weather Channel; TLC; TNT; TV Land; USA Network; VH1.
Fee: $29.95 installation; $65.00 monthly. Includes 150+ channels plus music & 1 digital receiver.
Platinum
Subscribers: N.A.
Fee: $85.00 monthly. Includes 230+ channels plus music, 1 whole home DVR & 1 digital receiver.
HBO
Subscribers: N.A.
Programming (via satellite): HBO.
Fee: $9.95 monthly.
Showtime
Subscribers: N.A.
Programming (via satellite): Showtime.
Fee: $9.95 monthly.
Video-On-Demand: No
Internet Service
Operational: Yes.
Fee: $44.99-$134.99 monthly.
Telephone Service
Digital: Operational
Fee: $19.99 monthly
President & Chief Executive Officer: Cyrus Driver. Executive Vice President & Chief Operating Officer: Deborah Crawford. Executive Vice President & Chief Financial Officer: Don Pittman. Senior Vice President, Product Management: Angel Kandahari. Vice President & General Counsel: Daniel Wheeler. Vice President, Products & Marketing: Roberto Chang. Vice President, Human Resources: Wendy J. Lee. Vice President, Service Delivery & IT Strategy: Michael McDaniel. Vice President, RUS Projects: Aaron Peters.
Ownership: NTS Communications Inc. (MSO).

ABERNATHY—NTS Communications. This cable system has converted to IPTV. See ABERNATHY, TX [TX5542]. ICA: TX0388.

ABILENE—Suddenlink Communications, 902 South Clark Ave, Abilene, TX 79605. Phones: 314-315-9400; 915-698-3585. Web Site: http://www.suddenlink.com. Also serves Dyess AFB, Taylor County (northern portion) & Tye. ICA: TX0019.
TV Market Ranking: Below 100 (ABILENE, Dyess AFB, Taylor County (northern portion), Tye). Franchise award date: January 1, 1964. Franchise expiration date: N.A. Began: April 1, 1965.
Channel capacity: 92 (operating 2-way). Channels available but not in use: 12.
Basic Service
Subscribers: 19,129. Commercial subscribers: 3,278.
Programming (received off-air): KIDZ-LD Abilene; KPCB-DT (GLC) Snyder; KRBC-TV (Bounce TV, NBC) Abilene; KTAB-TV (CBS) Abilene; KTES-LP (CW, This TV) Abilene; KTXS-TV (ABC, CW, This TV, TMO) Sweetwater; KXVA (FOX, MNT) Abilene; allband FM.
Programming (via microwave): KERA-TV (PBS) Dallas.
Programming (via satellite): C-SPAN; C-SPAN 2; Pop; QVC; The Weather Channel; Univision.
Fee: $40.00 installation; $34.57 monthly.
Expanded Basic Service 1
Subscribers: N.A.
Programming (via satellite): A&E; AMC; Animal Planet; BET; Bravo; Cartoon Network; CMT; CNBC; CNN; Comedy Central; CW PLUS; Discovery Channel; Disney Channel; E! HD; ESPN; ESPN2; Food Network; Fox News Channel; Fox Sports 1; FOX Sports Southwest; Freeform; FX; HGTV; History; HLN; INSP; Lifetime; LMN; MSNBC; MTV; MTV2; NBCSN; Nickelodeon; Oxygen; Spike TV; Syfy; TBS; TLC; TNT; Travel Channel; TV Land; USA Network; VH1.
Fee: $41.99 monthly.
Digital Basic Service
Subscribers: N.A.
Programming (via satellite): A&E HD; AXS TV; Bandamax; BBC America; Bloomberg Television; Boomerang; CBS Sports Network; Cine Mexicano; Cinelatino; CMT; CNN en Espanol; Cooking Channel; De Pelicula; De Pelicula Clasico; Destination America; Discovery Kids Channel; Disney XD; DIY Network; ESPN Classic; ESPN Deportes; ESPN HD; ESPN2 HD; ESPNews; ESPNU; EVINE Live; EWTN Global Catholic Network; Food Network HD; FOX College Sports Central; FOX College Sports Pacific; Fox Deportes; Fox Sports 2; FSN HD; Fuse; FYI; Golf Channel; Great American Country; GSN; Hallmark Channel; HD Theater; HGTV HD; History en Espanol; History International; IFC; Investigation Discovery; Jewelry Television; MC; MTV Classic; MTV Hits; mtvU; National Geographic Channel; National Geographic Channel HD; NBC Universo; Nick Jr.; Nicktoons; NickToons en Espanol; Outdoor Channel; OWN; Oprah Winfrey Network; Science Channel; Starz Encore (multiplexed); Sundance TV; Sur; TeenNick; Telehit; Tennis Channel; TNT HD; Toon Disney en Espanol; Tr3s; truTV; Turner Classic Movies; UniMas; Universal HD; Univision; UP; VideoRola; WE tv.
Fee: $14.95 monthly.
Pay Service 1
Pay Units: 2,671.
Programming (via satellite): Cinemax.
Fee: $2.00 installation; $11.38 monthly.
Pay Service 2
Pay Units: 9,368.
Programming (via satellite): Starz Encore.
Fee: $8.81 installation; $1.75 monthly.
Pay Service 3
Pay Units: 3,986.
Programming (via satellite): HBO.
Fee: $2.00 installation; $11.38 monthly.
Pay Service 4
Pay Units: 1,273.
Programming (via satellite): Showtime.
Fee: $2.00 installation; $11.38 monthly.
Pay Service 5
Pay Units: 6,290.
Programming (via satellite): Starz.
Fee: $8.81 installation; $4.75 monthly.
Digital Pay Service 1
Pay Units: 7,596.
Programming (via satellite): Cinemax (multiplexed); HBO (multiplexed); HBO HD; HBO Latino; Showtime (multiplexed); Showtime HD; Starz (multiplexed); Starz Encore; Starz HD; The Movie Channel (multiplexed).
Video-On-Demand: No
Pay-Per-View
iN DEMAND (delivered digitally); Playboy TV (delivered digitally); Fresh (delivered digitally); Shorteez (delivered digitally); Spice: Xcess (delivered digitally); Club Jenna (delivered digitally).
Internet Service
Operational: Yes. Began: December 1, 2000.
Subscribers: 25,144.
Broadband Service: Suddenlink High Speed Internet.
Fee: $49.95 installation; $24.95 monthly; $15.00 modem lease; $249.99 modem purchase.
Telephone Service
Analog: Not Operational
Digital: Operational
Subscribers: 11,557.
Fee: $48.95 monthly
Miles of Plant: 1,149.0 (coaxial); 362.0 (fiber optic). Homes passed: 69,433.
Senior Vice President, Corporate Finance: Michael Pflantz. Vice President, Accounting: Sabrina Warr. Regional Manager: Bill Flowers. Area Manager: Chris Christiansen.
Ownership: Cequel Communications Holdings I LLC (MSO).

ACE—Formerly served by Jones Broadcasting. No longer in operation. ICA: TX0995.

ACKERLY—Formerly served by National Cable Inc. No longer in operation. ICA: TX0681.

ADKINS—Formerly served by Almega Cable. No longer in operation. ICA: TX0346.

ADRIAN—Formerly served by Sunset Cablevision. No longer in operation. ICA: TX0706.

ALBA—Formerly served by Almega Cable. No longer in operation. ICA: TX0603.

ALBANY—Suddenlink Communications, 520 Maryville Centre Dr, Ste 300, St. Louis, MO 63141. Phones: 800-999-6845 (Customer service); 314-315-9400. Web Site: http://www.suddenlink.com. ICA: TX0337.
TV Market Ranking: Below 100 (ALBANY). Franchise award date: N.A. Franchise expiration date: N.A. Began: January 1, 1960.
Channel capacity: N.A. Channels available but not in use: N.A.
Basic Service
Subscribers: 194. Commercial subscribers: 34.
Programming (received off-air): KRBC-TV (Bounce TV, NBC) Abilene; KTAB-TV (CBS) Abilene; KTXS-TV (ABC, CW, This TV, TMO) Sweetwater; 8 FMs.
Programming (via microwave): KERA-TV (PBS) Dallas; KTVT (CBS, Decades) Fort Worth; WFAA (ABC) Dallas.
Programming (via satellite): Discovery Channel; QVC; TBS; The Weather Channel; Trinity Broadcasting Network (TBN).
Fee: $28.45 monthly.
Expanded Basic Service 1
Subscribers: 168.
Programming (via satellite): AMC; Animal Planet; Cartoon Network; CNN; Disney Channel; ESPN; Fox News Channel; Freeform; FX; HGTV; HLN; Lifetime; MTV; Spike TV; TLC; TNT; USA Network.
Fee: $39.95 installation; $39.50 monthly.

D-718   TV & Cable Factbook No. 85

Cable Systems—Texas

Pay Service 1
Pay Units: N.A.
Programming (via satellite): Cinemax; HBO; Starz; Starz Encore.
Fee: $1.75 monthly (Encore), $6.75 monthly (Starz), $10.95 monthly (Cinemax), $13.65 monthly (HBO).
Video-On-Demand: No
Internet Service
Operational: Yes. Began: November 12, 2003.
Broadband Service: Suddenlink High Speed Internet.
Fee: $49.95 installation; $38.95 monthly.
Telephone Service
None
Miles of Plant: 26.0 (coaxial); None (fiber optic). Homes passed: 1,110.
Senior Vice President, Corporate Finance: Michael Pflantz. Regional Manager: Todd Cruthird. Plant Manager: Bobby Smith.
Ownership: Cequel Communications Holdings I LLC (MSO).

ALGOA—Formerly served by Almega Cable. No longer in operation. ICA: TX0335.

ALICE—Time Warner Cable. Now served by CORPUS CHRISTI, TX [TX0010]. ICA: TX0102.

ALLEN—Time Warner Cable. Now served by DALLAS, TX [TX0003]. ICA: TX0100.

ALLENDALE—Formerly served by Cebridge Connections. No longer in operation. ICA: TX0707.

ALPINE—Baja Broadband, 525 Junction Rd, Madison, WI 53717. Phones: 575-437-3101; 877-422-5282; 800-996-8788. Fax: 608-830-5519. E-mail: comments@tdstelecom.com. Web Site: http://www.bajabroadband.com. Also serves Brewster County (portions). ICA: TX0875.
TV Market Ranking: Outside TV Markets (ALPINE, Brewster County (portions)). Franchise award date: July 5, 1985. Franchise expiration date: N.A. Began: July 1, 1985.
Channel capacity: 36 (not 2-way capable). Channels available but not in use: N.A.
Basic Service
Subscribers: 454.
Programming (received off-air): KASA-TV (COZI TV, FOX) Santa Fe; KMLM-DT (GLC) Odessa; KOAT-TV (ABC, Estrella TV) Albuquerque; KOSA-TV (CBS, MNT) Odessa; KPBT-TV (PBS) Odessa; KPEJ-TV (FOX) Odessa; KTLE-LP (TMO) Odessa; KUPB (UNV) Midland; KWES-TV (CW, NBC, TMO) Odessa; allband FM.
Programming (via satellite): A&E; Animal Planet; Cartoon Network; CMT; CNBC; CNN; Comedy Central; C-SPAN; Discovery Channel; Discovery Life Channel; Disney Channel; E! HD; ESPN; ESPN2; EVINE Live; EWTN Global Catholic Network; Fox News Channel; Fox Sports 1; FOX Sports Southwest; Freeform; FX; Great American Country; Hallmark Channel; HGTV; History; HLN; Lifetime; MTV; National Geographic Channel; Nickelodeon; Outdoor Channel; Oxygen; Pop; Spike TV; Syfy; TBS; The Weather Channel; TLC; TNT; Trinity Broadcasting Network (TBN); Turner Classic Movies; TV Land; UniMas; USA Network; VH1; WGN America.
Fee: $35.00 installation; $62.10 monthly; $.86 converter.

Digital Basic Service
Subscribers: N.A.
Programming (via satellite): BBC America; Bloomberg Television; Bravo; Cloo; CMT; Destination America; Discovery Kids Channel; Disney XD; DMX Music; ESPN Classic; ESPNews; Fox Sports 1; Fuse; FXM; FYI; Golf Channel; GSN; History International; IFC; Investigation Discovery; LMN; MTV Classic; MTV2; NBCSN; Nick Jr.; Outdoor Channel; OWN: Oprah Winfrey Network; Science Channel; Starz Encore (multiplexed); TeenNick; WE tv.
Fee: $21.39 monthly.
Digital Expanded Basic Service
Subscribers: N.A.
Programming (via satellite): Cine Mexicano; Cinelatino; CNN en Espanol; ESPN Deportes; Fox Deportes; History en Espanol; NBC Universo; Tr3s; ViendoMovies.
Fee: $4.95 monthly.
Pay Service 1
Pay Units: N.A.
Programming (via satellite): Cinemax; HBO; Showtime.
Fee: $12.95 monthly (each).
Digital Pay Service 1
Pay Units: N.A.
Programming (via satellite): Cinemax (multiplexed); HBO (multiplexed); Showtime (multiplexed); Starz (multiplexed); The Movie Channel.
Fee: $8.95 monthly (Starz), $11.95 monthly (Cinemax, HBO, Showtime or TMC).
Video-On-Demand: No
Pay-Per-View
iN DEMAND (delivered digitally); Fresh (delivered digitally); Playboy TV (delivered digitally).
Internet Service
Operational: No.
Telephone Service
None
Homes passed & miles of plant included in Seminole.
Vice President, Corporate Finance: Carl Shapiro. Assistant Treasurer: Noel Hutton.
Ownership: TDS Telecom (MSO).

ALTO—Formerly served by Almega Cable. No longer in operation. ICA: TX0435.

ALTON—Time Warner Cable. Now served by PHARR, TX [TX0017]. ICA: TX0066.

ALUM CREEK—Formerly served by Time Warner Cable. No longer in operation. ICA: TX0615.

ALVARADO—Formerly served by Almega Cable. No longer in operation. ICA: TX0270.

AMARILLO—Suddenlink Communications, 5800 West 45th Ave, Amarillo, TX 79109-5206. Phones: 314-315-9400; 806-358-4801. Fax: 806-354-7419. Web Site: http://www.suddenlink.com. Also serves Canyon, Lake Tanglewood, Rolling Hills & Tulia. ICA: TX0014.
TV Market Ranking: 95 (AMARILLO, Canyon, Lake Tanglewood, Rolling Hills); Outside TV Markets (Tulia). Franchise award date: July 1, 1980. Franchise expiration date: N.A. Began: January 1, 1970.
Channel capacity: 78 (operating 2-way). Channels available but not in use: N.A.
Basic Service
Subscribers: 41,619. Commercial subscribers: 3,574.
Programming (received off-air): KACV-TV (PBS) Amarillo; KAMR-TV (IND, NBC) Amarillo; KCIT (FOX, This TV) Amarillo; KCPN-LP (MNT) Amarillo; KFDA-TV (CBS, TMO) Amarillo; KPTF-DT (GLC) Farwell; KVII-TV (ABC, CW) Amarillo; 10 FMs.
Programming (via satellite): C-SPAN; CW PLUS; EWTN Global Catholic Network; INSP; Pop; QVC; The Weather Channel; Trinity Broadcasting Network (TBN); Univision Studios; WGN America.
Fee: $40.00 installation; $31.77 monthly.
Expanded Basic Service 1
Subscribers: 31,077.
Programming (via satellite): A&E; AMC; Animal Planet; BET; Bravo; Cartoon Network; CMT; CNBC; CNN; Comedy Central; C-SPAN 2; Discovery Channel; Disney Channel; E! HD; ESPN; ESPN2; Food Network; Fox News Channel; Fox Sports 1; FOX Sports Southwest; Freeform; FX; HGTV; History; HLN; Lifetime; LMN; MSNBC; MTV; MTV2; NBCSN; Nickelodeon; Spike TV; Syfy; TBS; TLC; TNT; Travel Channel; truTV; Turner Classic Movies; TV Land; Univision; USA Network; VH1.
Fee: $7.51 monthly.
Digital Basic Service
Subscribers: N.A.
Programming (via satellite): A&E HD; AXS TV; Bandamax; BBC America; Bloomberg Television; CBS Sports Network; Cine Mexicano; Cinelatino; CMT; CNN en Espanol; Cooking Channel; De Pelicula; De Pelicula Clasico; Destination America; Discovery Kids Channel; Disney XD; DIY Network; ESPN Classic; ESPN Deportes; ESPN HD; ESPN2 HD; ESPNews; ESPNU; EVINE Live; Food Network HD; FOX College Sports Central; FOX College Sports Pacific; Fox Deportes; Fox Sports 2; FSN HD; Fuse; FYI; Golf Channel; Great American Country; GSN; Hallmark Channel; HD Theater; HGTV HD; History en Espanol; History International; IFC; Investigation Discovery; Jewelry Television; MTV Classic; MTV Hits; mtvU; National Geographic Channel; National Geographic Channel HD; NBC Universo; Nick Jr.; Nicktoons; NickToons en Espanol; Outdoor Channel; OWN: Oprah Winfrey Network; Oxygen; Science Channel; Starz Encore (multiplexed); Sundance TV; Sur; TeenNick; Telehit; Tennis Channel; TNT HD; Toon Disney en Espanol; Tr3s; Universal HD; Univision; UP; VideoRola; WE tv.
Pay Service 1
Pay Units: 5,645.
Programming (via satellite): Cinemax.
Fee: $10.95 monthly.
Pay Service 2
Pay Units: 7,596.
Programming (via satellite): Starz Encore.
Pay Service 3
Pay Units: 6,609.
Programming (via satellite): HBO.
Fee: $12.95 monthly.
Pay Service 4
Pay Units: 5,277.
Programming (via satellite): Showtime.
Pay Service 5
Pay Units: 309.
Programming (via satellite): Starz.
Digital Pay Service 1
Pay Units: 14,477.
Programming (via satellite): Cinemax (multiplexed); HBO (multiplexed); HBO HD; HBO Latino; Showtime (multiplexed); Showtime HD; Starz (multiplexed); Starz HD; The Movie Channel (multiplexed).
Video-On-Demand: No
Pay-Per-View
iN DEMAND (delivered digitally); Playboy TV (delivered digitally); Fresh (delivered digitally); Shorteez (delivered digitally); Spice: Xcess (delivered digitally); Club Jenna (delivered digitally).
Internet Service
Operational: Yes.
Subscribers: 40,191.
Broadband Service: Suddenlink High Speed Internet.
Fee: $49.95 installation; $24.95 monthly.
Telephone Service
Digital: Operational
Subscribers: 18,377.
Fee: $48.95 monthly
Miles of Plant: 1,899.0 (coaxial); 825.0 (fiber optic). Homes passed: 103,550.
Vice President & Manager: Connie Wharton. Senior Vice President, Corporate Finance: Michael Pflantz. Vice President, Accounting: Sabrina Warr. Marketing Director: Alisa Mathies. Chief Technician: Charlie Johnson.
Ownership: Cequel Communications Holdings I LLC (MSO).

ANAHUAC—Formerly served by Carrell Communications. No longer in operation. ICA: TX0376.

ANDERSON—Formerly served by National Cable Inc. No longer in operation. ICA: TX0666.

ANDREWS—Suddenlink Communications, 412 West Broadway St, Andrews, TX 79714-6222. Phones: 314-315-9400; 800-235-4233. Fax: 915-523-3325. Web Site: http://www.suddenlink.com. Also serves Andrews County. ICA: TX0141.
TV Market Ranking: Below 100 (ANDREWS, Andrews County (portions)); Outside TV Markets (Andrews County (portions)). Franchise award date: N.A. Franchise expiration date: N.A. Began: March 1, 1972.
Channel capacity: N.A. Channels available but not in use: N.A.
Basic Service
Subscribers: 2,580. Commercial subscribers: 151.
Programming (received off-air): KMID (ABC) Midland; KMLM-DT (GLC) Odessa; KOSA-TV (CBS, MNT) Odessa; KPBT-TV (PBS) Odessa; KPEJ-TV (FOX) Odessa; KTLE-LP (TMO) Odessa; KUPB (UNV) Midland; KWES-TV (CW, NBC, TMO) Odessa; KWWT (Antenna TV, MeTV, Movies!, Retro TV, This TV) Odessa.
Programming (via satellite): C-SPAN; MyNetworkTV; Pop; QVC; TBS; The Weather Channel; WGN America.
Fee: $28.11 monthly; $3.85 converter.
Expanded Basic Service 1
Subscribers: N.A.
Programming (via satellite): A&E; AMC; Animal Planet; BET; Bravo; Cartoon Network; CMT; CNBC; CNN; Comedy Central; Discovery Channel; Disney Channel; E! HD; ESPN; ESPN2; EWTN Global Catholic Network; Food Network; Fox News Channel; Fox Sports 1; FOX Sports Southwest; Freeform; FX; Hallmark Channel; HGTV; History; HLN; Lifetime; LMN; MSNBC; MTV; MTV2; NBC Universo; NBCSN; Nickelodeon; Spike TV; Syfy; TLC; TNT; Travel Channel; Turner Classic Movies; TV Land; UniMas; USA Network; VH1.
Fee: $38.00 installation; $24.93 monthly.
Digital Basic Service
Subscribers: N.A.
Programming (via satellite): A&E HD; AXS TV; Bandamax; BBC America; Bloomberg Television; Boomerang; CBS Sports Net-

2017 Edition

D-719

Texas—Cable Systems

work; Cine Mexicano; Cinelatino; CMT; CNN en Espanol; Cooking Channel; De Pelicula; De Pelicula Clasico; Destination America; Discovery Kids Channel; Disney XD; DIY Network; ESPN Classic; ESPN Deportes; ESPN HD; ESPN2 HD; ESPNews; ESPNU; EVINE Live; Food Network HD; FOX College Sports Central; FOX College Sports Pacific; Fox Deportes; Fox Sports 2; FSN HD; Fuse; FYI; Golf Channel; Great American Country; GSN; HD Theater; HGTV HD; History en Espanol; History International; IFC; INSP; Investigation Discovery; Jewelry Television; MC; MTV Classic; MTV Hits; mtvU; National Geographic Channel; National Geographic Channel HD; NBC Universo; Nick Jr.; Nicktoons; NickToons en Espanol; Outdoor Channel; OWN: Oprah Winfrey Network; Oxygen; Science Channel; Sundance TV; Sur; TeenNick; Telehit; Tennis Channel; TNT HD; Tr3s; Trinity Broadcasting Network (TBN); truTV; UniMas; Universal HD; Univision; UP; VideoRola; WE tv.

Pay Service 1
Pay Units: N.A.
Programming (via satellite): Cinemax; HBO; Showtime; Starz.
Fee: $9.95 monthly (Cinemax, Showtime or Starz), $13.00 monthly (HBO).

Digital Pay Service 1
Pay Units: N.A.
Programming (via satellite): Cinemax (multiplexed); HBO (multiplexed); HBO HD; HBO Latino; Showtime (multiplexed); Showtime HD; Starz (multiplexed); Starz Encore (multiplexed); Starz HD; The Movie Channel (multiplexed).
Video-On-Demand: No

Pay-Per-View
iN DEMAND (delivered digitally); Playboy TV (delivered digitally); Fresh (delivered digitally); Shorteez (delivered digitally); Spice: Xcess (delivered digitally); Club Jenna (delivered digitally).

Internet Service
Operational: Yes. Began: January 1, 2003.
Broadband Service: Suddenlink High Speed Internet.
Fee: $45.95 installation; $29.95 monthly.

Telephone Service
Digital: Operational
Fee: $44.95 monthly
Miles of Plant: 95.0 (coaxial); None (fiber optic). Homes passed: 3,974.
Senior Vice President, Corporate Finance: Michael Pflantz. Vice President, Accounting: Sabrina Warr. General Manager: Archie Kountz. Marketing Director: Diane Bower. Chief Technician: Harold Vilas.
Ownership: Cequel Communications Holdings I LLC (MSO).

ANGLETON—NewWave Communications, One Montgomery Plaza, 4th Floor, Sikeston, MO 63801. Phones: 573-472-9500; 888-863-9928. Fax: 573-472-9518. E-mail: info@newwave.com. Web Site: http://www.newwavecom.com. Also serves Bailey's Prairie & Danbury. ICA: TX0091.
TV Market Ranking: Below 100 (ANGLETON, Bailey's Prairie, Danbury). Franchise award date: December 1, 1979. Franchise expiration date: N.A. Began: April 18, 1979.
Channel capacity: N.A. Channels available but not in use: N.A.

Basic Service
Subscribers: 1,883.
Programming (received off-air): KETH-TV (TBN) Houston; KFTH-DT (getTV, UniMas) Alvin; KHOU (Bounce TV, CBS) Houston; KIAH (Antenna TV, CW) Houston; KLTJ (Daystar TV, ETV) Galveston; KPRC-TV (NBC, This TV) Houston; KPXB-TV (ION) Conroe; KRIV (FOX) Houston; KTMD (TMO) Galveston; KTRK-TV (ABC, Live Well Network) Houston; KTXH (Buzzr, MNT, Movies!) Houston; KUBE-TV (COZI TV, MeTV) Baytown; KUHT (PBS) Houston; KXLN-DT (UNV) Rosenberg; KYAZ (Azteca America, IND) Katy; KZJL (Estrella TV) Houston.
Programming (via satellite): C-SPAN; QVC; TBS; WGN America.
Fee: $35.00 installation; $31.94 monthly.

Expanded Basic Service 1
Subscribers: N.A.
Programming (via satellite): A&E; AMC; Animal Planet; BET; Bravo; Cartoon Network; CMT; CNBC; CNN; Discovery Channel; ESPN; ESPN Classic; ESPN2; Food Network; Fox Deportes; Fox News Channel; FOX Sports Southwest; Freeform; FX; HGTV; History; HLN; INSP; Lifetime; MSNBC; MTV; National Geographic Channel; Nickelodeon; Pop; Spike TV; Syfy; The Weather Channel; TLC; TNT; Travel Channel; truTV; Turner Classic Movies; TV Land; USA Network; VH1.
Fee: $54.70 monthly.

Digital Basic Service
Subscribers: N.A.
Programming (via satellite): BBC America; Bloomberg Television; Discovery Digital Networks; DMX Music; ESPN; ESPNews; Fox Sports 1; FXM; FYI; Golf Channel; GSN; HD Theater; History International; IFC; LMN; Nick Jr.; Nicktoons; Outdoor Channel; TeenNick; Universal HD; WE tv.
Fee: $12.95 monthly.

Pay Service 1
Pay Units: N.A.
Programming (via satellite): HBO.
Fee: $13.45 monthly.

Digital Pay Service 1
Pay Units: 364.
Programming (via satellite): Cinemax (multiplexed); Cinemax HD; Flix; HBO (multiplexed); HBO HD; Showtime (multiplexed); Showtime HD; Starz (multiplexed); Starz Encore (multiplexed); The Movie Channel (multiplexed).
Fee: $8.00 monthly (Starz), $9.00 monthly (Cinemax), $15.00 monthly (Showtime/TMC), $17.00 monthly (HBO) or $26.00 monthly (HBO/Cinemax).

Video-On-Demand: No

Pay-Per-View
iN DEMAND (delivered digitally); Playboy TV (delivered digitally); Fresh (delivered digitally); Shorteez (delivered digitally).

Internet Service
Operational: Yes.
Fee: $39.95 installation; $39.99-$79.99 monthly; $6.00 modem lease; $39.95 modem purchase.

Telephone Service
Digital: Operational
Fee: $39.95 monthly
Miles of Plant: 165.0 (coaxial); None (fiber optic). Homes passed: 8,071.
General Manager: Mark Bookout.
Ownership: NewWave Communications LLC (MSO).

ANNA—Suddenlink Communications. Now served by PILOT POINT, TX [TX0286]. ICA: TX0709.

ANSON—Suddenlink Communications, 520 Maryville Centre Dr, Ste 300, St. Louis, MO 63141. Phones: 800-999-6845 (Customer service); 314-315-9400; 314-315-9346. Web Site: http://www.suddenlink.com. Also serves Jones County (portions). ICA: TX0323.
TV Market Ranking: Below 100 (ANSON, Jones County (portions)). Franchise award date: July 1, 1962. Franchise expiration date: N.A. Began: August 1, 1968.
Channel capacity: N.A. Channels available but not in use: N.A.

Basic Service
Subscribers: 180. Commercial subscribers: 15.
Programming (received off-air): KRBC-TV (Bounce TV, NBC) Abilene; KTAB-TV (CBS) Abilene; KTXS-TV (ABC, CW, This TV, TMO) Sweetwater; 4 FMs.
Programming (via satellite): BET; C-SPAN; Lifetime; QVC; TBS; The Weather Channel.
Fee: $28.45 monthly.

Expanded Basic Service 1
Subscribers: N.A.
Programming (via satellite): A&E; AMC; Animal Planet; Cartoon Network; CMT; CNN; Discovery Channel; ESPN; Fox News Channel; FOX Sports Southwest; Freeform; FX; HGTV; MTV; Nickelodeon; Spike TV; TLC; TNT; USA Network.
Fee: $39.95 installation; $23.00 monthly.

Pay Service 1
Pay Units: N.A.
Programming (via satellite): Cinemax; HBO; Starz; Starz Encore.
Fee: $1.71 monthly (Encore), $6.75 monthly (Starz), $12.50 monthly (Cinemax), $13.00 monthly (HBO).

Video-On-Demand: No

Internet Service
Operational: Yes. Began: November 12, 2003.
Broadband Service: Suddenlink High Speed Internet.
Fee: $49.95 installation; $29.95 monthly.

Telephone Service
Digital: Operational
Fee: $44.95 monthly
Miles of Plant: 25.0 (coaxial); None (fiber optic). Homes passed: 1,205.
Senior Vice President, Corporate Finance: Michael Pflantz. Regional Manager: Todd Cruthird. Plant Manager: Bobby Smith.
Ownership: Cequel Communications Holdings I LLC (MSO).

ANTON—Formerly served by NTS Communications. No longer in operation.. ICA: TX0506.

AQUA VISTA—Formerly served by Cebridge Connections. No longer in operation. ICA: TX0912.

ARANSAS PASS—Cable One, 1045 South Commercial St, PO Box 1570, Aransas Pass, TX 78336-5305. Phone: 361-758-7621. Fax: 361-758-7096. E-mail: mschooley@cableone.net. Web Site: http://www.cableone.net. Also serves Aransas County (portions), City by the Sea, Gregory, Ingleside, Ingleside on the Bay, Palm Harbor RV Park, San Patricio County & Taft. ICA: TX0097.
TV Market Ranking: Below 100 (Aransas County (portions), ARANSAS PASS, ARANSAS PASS, City by the Sea, Gregory, Ingleside, Ingleside on the Bay, Palm Harbor RV Park, San Patricio County, Taft). Franchise award date: April 27, 1979. Franchise expiration date: N.A. Began: June 1, 1981.
Channel capacity: 53 (operating 2-way). Channels available but not in use: N.A.

Basic Service
Subscribers: 4,368.
Programming (received off-air): KEDT (PBS) Corpus Christi; KIII (ABC, MeTV) Corpus Christi; KRIS-TV (CW, Grit, NBC) Corpus Christi; KTOV-LP Corpus Christi; KZTV (CBS) Corpus Christi.
Programming (via satellite): A&E; AMC; Animal Planet; BET; Cartoon Network; CMT; CNBC; CNN; Comedy Central; C-SPAN; C-SPAN 2; CW PLUS; Discovery Channel; Disney Channel; ESPN; ESPN2; Food Network; Fox Deportes; Fox News Channel; FOX Sports Southwest; Freeform; FX; HGTV; History; HLN; ION Television; Lifetime; MSNBC; MTV; Nickelodeon; Pop; QVC; Syfy; TBS; Telemundo; The Weather Channel; TLC; Turner Classic Movies; TV Land; Univision Studios; USA Network; VH1.
Fee: $30.00 installation; $35.00 monthly; $1.68 converter.

Digital Basic Service
Subscribers: N.A.
Programming (via satellite): DMX Music.
Fee: $4.95 installation; $11.15 monthly.

Digital Expanded Basic Service
Subscribers: 2,100.
Programming (via satellite): 3ABN; Boomerang; BYUtv; Discovery Digital Networks; Disney XD; ESPN Classic; ESPNews; FamilyNet; FOX College Sports Central; FOX College Sports Pacific; Fox Sports 1; Fox Sports 2; FXM; FYI; Golf Channel; Great American Country; Hallmark Channel; History International; HITS (Headend In The Sky); INSP; National Geographic Channel; Outdoor Channel; TNT HD; Trinity Broadcasting Network (TBN); truTV; Universal HD.
Fee: $4.00 monthly.

Digital Pay Service 1
Pay Units: N.A.
Programming (via satellite): Cinemax (multiplexed); Flix; HBO (multiplexed); Showtime (multiplexed); Showtime HD; The Movie Channel (multiplexed); The Movie Channel HD.
Fee: $20.00 installation; $15.00 monthly (each package).

Video-On-Demand: No

Pay-Per-View
Pleasure (delivered digitally); Shorteez (delivered digitally); Shorteez (delivered digitally); ETC (delivered digitally); Playboy TV (delivered digitally); Playboy TV (delivered digitally); Fresh (delivered digitally); Fresh (delivered digitally).

Internet Service
Operational: Yes. Began: October 1, 2001.
Subscribers: 5,462.
Broadband Service: CableONE.net.
Fee: $75.00 installation; $43.00 monthly; $5.00 modem lease.

Telephone Service
Digital: Operational
Subscribers: 2,986.
Fee: $39.95 monthly
Miles of Plant: 331.0 (coaxial); 107.0 (fiber optic). Homes passed: 17,741.
Vice President: Patrick A. Dolohanty. General Manager: David King. Chief Technician: Martin Schooley.
Ownership: Cable ONE Inc. (MSO).

ARCHER CITY—Time Warner Cable. Now served by WICHITA FALLS, TX [TX0026]. ICA: TX0710.

ARCOLA—Formerly served by Almega Cable. No longer in operation. ICA: TX0243.

D-720   TV & Cable Factbook No. 85

Cable Systems—Texas

ARGYLE—Formerly served by SouthTel Communications LP. No longer in operation. ICA: TX0533.

ARLINGTON—Time Warner Cable. Now served by DALLAS, TX [TX0003]. ICA: TX0011.

ARP—Formerly served by Zoom Media. No longer in operation. ICA: TX0374.

ASHERTON—Time Warner Cable. Now served by CRYSTAL CITY, TX [TX0147]. ICA: TX0536.

ASPERMONT—Formerly served by Alliance Communications Network. No longer in operation. ICA: TX0461.

ATASCOSA—Formerly served by Almega Cable. No longer in operation. ICA: TX0309.

ATHENS—Suddenlink Communications, 109 North High St, Henderson, TX 75652. Phones: 314-315-9400; 800-999-6845 (Customer service); 903-675-5917. Web Site: http://www.suddenlink.com. Also serves Caney City, Enchanted Oaks, Gun Barrel City, Henderson County (portions), Log Cabin, Mabank, Malakoff, Payne Springs, Seven Points (southern portion), Star Harbor, Tool & Trinidad. ICA: TX0711.
TV Market Ranking: Below 100 (ATHENS, Henderson County (portions) (portions)); Outside TV Markets (Caney City, Enchanted Oaks, Henderson County (portions) (portions), Log Cabin, Payne Springs, Seven Points (southern portion), Star Harbor, Tool, Trinidad, Gun Barrel City). Franchise award date: N.A. Franchise expiration date: N.A. Began: October 15, 1968.
Channel capacity: N.A. Channels available but not in use: N.A.
Basic Service
Subscribers: 4,555. Commercial subscribers: 317.
Programming (received off-air): KDAF (Antenna TV, CW, This TV) Dallas; KDFI (Bounce TV, Buzzr, Heroes & Icons, MNT, Movies!) Dallas; KDFW (FOX) Dallas; KERA-TV (PBS) Dallas; KETK-TV (Estrella TV, NBC) Jacksonville; KLTV (ABC, Bounce TV, TMO) Tyler; KNHL (IND) Hastings; KPXD-TV (ION) Arlington; KSTR-DT (getTV, UniMas) Irving; KTVT (CBS, Decades) Fort Worth; KTXA (IND, MeTV) Fort Worth; KUVN-DT (UNV) Garland; KXAS-TV (COZI TV, NBC) Fort Worth; KXTX-TV (TMO) Dallas; KYTX (CBS, COZI TV, CW) Nacogdoches; WFAA (ABC) Dallas; allband FM.
Programming (via satellite): C-SPAN; Jewelry Television; QVC; TBS; The Weather Channel; Trinity Broadcasting Network (TBN).
Fee: $54.95 installation; $34.24 monthly.
Expanded Basic Service 1
Subscribers: N.A.
Programming (via satellite): A&E; AMC; Animal Planet; BET; Bravo; Cartoon Network; CMT; CNBC; CNN; Comedy Central; Discovery Channel; Disney Channel; Disney XD; E! HD; ESPN; ESPN Classic; ESPN2; Food Network; Fox News Channel; Fox Sports 1; FOX Sports Southwest; Freeform; FX; Great American Country; HGTV; History; HLN; Lifetime; LMN; MSNBC; MTV; NBCSN; Nickelodeon; Outdoor Channel; OWN: Oprah Winfrey Network; Oxygen; Pop; Spike TV; Syfy; TLC; TNT; Travel Channel; truTV; Turner Classic Movies; TV Land; Univision; USA Network; VH1; WE tv.
Fee: $14.17 monthly.
Digital Basic Service
Subscribers: N.A.
Programming (via satellite): A&E HD; AXS TV; Bandamax; BBC America; Bloomberg Television; Boomerang; CBS Sports Network; Cine Mexicano; Cinelatino; CMT; CNN en Espanol; Cooking Channel; Cox Sports Television; De Pelicula; De Pelicula Clasico; Destination America; Discovery Kids Channel; DIY Network; Enlace USA; ESPN Deportes; ESPN HD; ESPN2 HD; ESPNews; ESPNU; FamilyNet; Food Network HD; Fox Deportes; Fox Sports 2; Fuse; FXM; FYI; Golf Channel; GSN; Hallmark Channel; HD Theater; HGTV HD; History en Espanol; History International; IFC; Investigation Discovery; MC; MTV Classic; MTV Hits; MTV2; Nat Geo WILD; National Geographic Channel; National Geographic Channel HD; NBC Universo; Nick Jr.; Nicktoons; Ritmoson; Science Channel; Starz Encore (multiplexed); Sundance TV; Sur; TeenNick; Telehit; Tennis Channel; TNT HD; Toon Disney en Espanol; Tr3s; TV One; ULTRA HDPlex; Universal HD; Univision; UP; VideoRola; Weatherscan.
Digital Pay Service 1
Pay Units: N.A.
Programming (via satellite): Cinemax (multiplexed); HBO (multiplexed); HBO HD; HBO Latino; Showtime (multiplexed); Showtime HD; Starz (multiplexed); Starz HD; The Movie Channel (multiplexed).
Fee: $26.95 monthly.
Video-On-Demand: No
Pay-Per-View
iN DEMAND (delivered digitally); Fresh (delivered digitally); Shorteez (delivered digitally); Playboy TV (delivered digitally); Playboy en Espanol (delivered digitally).
Internet Service
Operational: Yes.
Subscribers: 1,408.
Broadband Service: Suddenlink High Speed Internet.
Fee: $49.95 installation; $38.95 monthly.
Telephone Service
Digital: Operational
Subscribers: 522.
Miles of Plant: 410.0 (coaxial); 85.0 (fiber optic). Homes passed: 10,337.
Senior Vice President, Corporate Finance: Michael Pflantz. Vice President, Accounting: Sabrina Warr. General Manager: Nathan Geick. Chief Technician: Ronnie Babcock.
Ownership: Cequel Communications Holdings I LLC (MSO).

ATLANTA—Fidelity Communications, 64 North Clark St, Sullivan, MO 63080. Phones: 800-392-8070; 903-938-1302 (Marshall office); 855-262-7434. E-mail: fidelityinfo@fidelitycommunications.com. Web Site: http://www.fidelitycommunications.com. Also serves Cass County (portions) & Queen City. ICA: TX0188.
TV Market Ranking: 58 (ATLANTA, Cass County (portions), Queen City); Below 100 (Cass County (portions)); Outside TV Markets (Cass County (portions)). Franchise award date: September 1, 1978. Franchise expiration date: N.A. Began: April 1, 1980.
Channel capacity: N.A. Channels available but not in use: N.A.
Basic Service
Subscribers: N.A. Commercial subscribers: 84.
Programming (received off-air): KLTS-TV (PBS) Shreveport; KMSS-TV (FOX) Shreveport; KPXJ (Antenna TV, CW, MeTV, Movies!) Minden; KSHV-TV (MNT) Shreveport; KSLA (Bounce TV, CBS, Grit, This TV) Shreveport; KTAL-TV (NBC) Texarkana; KTBS-TV (ABC) Shreveport; allband FM.
Programming (via satellite): A&E; AMC; BET; CMT; CNBC; CNN; Comedy Central; Discovery Channel; ESPN; FOX Sports Southwest; Freeform; HLN; Lifetime; MTV; Nickelodeon; Pop; QVC; Spike TV; TNT; Trinity Broadcasting Network (TBN).
Fee: $29.99 installation; $36.46 monthly; $2.61 converter.
Expanded Basic Service 1
Subscribers: N.A.
Programming (via satellite): Disney Channel; E! HD; TBS; The Weather Channel; USA Network; WGN America.
Fee: $6.73 monthly.
Pay Service 1
Pay Units: N.A.
Programming (via satellite): Cinemax; HBO; Showtime; The Movie Channel.
Fee: $12.95 monthly (each).
Video-On-Demand: No
Pay-Per-View
iN DEMAND.
Internet Service
Operational: No.
Telephone Service
None
Miles of Plant: 74.0 (coaxial); None (fiber optic). Homes passed: 3,680.
General Manager, AR/MO/LA/TX: Andy Davis. Ownership: Fidelity Communications Co. (MSO).

AUSTIN—Grande Communications, 1923 East 7th St, Ste 100, Austin, TX 78702. Phones: 512-878-4010; 512-220-4600 (Customer service); 512-878-4000 (Corporate office). E-mail: info@grandecom.com. Web Site: http://mygrande.com. Also serves Cedar Park, Leander, Pflugerville, Round Rock, Sunset Valley & Westlake Hills. ICA: TX0989. **Note:** This system is an overbuild.
TV Market Ranking: Below 100 (AUSTIN, Cedar Park, Leander, Leander). Franchise award date: April 20, 2000. Franchise expiration date: N.A. Began: February 1, 2001.
Channel capacity: N.A. Channels available but not in use: N.A.
Basic Service
Subscribers: 9,654.
Programming (received off-air): KBVO-CD (UniMas) Austin; KCWX (MNT, This TV) Fredericksburg; KEYE-TV (CBS, TMO) Austin; KLRU (PBS) Austin; KNVA (CW, Grit, TheCoolTV) Austin; KTBC (Buzzr, FOX, Movies!) Austin; KTFO-CD (UniMas) Austin; KVUE (ABC, Estrella TV) Austin; KXAN-TV (COZI TV, NBC) Austin.
Programming (via satellite): C-SPAN; C-SPAN 2; LWS Local Weather Station; Pop; QVC; WGN America.
Fee: $27.49 monthly.
Expanded Basic Service 1
Subscribers: N.A.
Programming (via satellite): A&E; AMC; Animal Planet; BET; Bravo; Cartoon Network; CNBC; CNN; Comedy Central; Discovery Channel; Disney Channel; Disney XD; E! HD; ESPN; ESPN Classic; ESPN2; EWTN Global Catholic Network; Food Network; Fox Deportes; Fox News Channel; Fox Sports 1; FOX Sports Southwest; Freeform; FX; Golf Channel; Great American Country; GSN; Hallmark Channel; HGTV; History; HLN; Lifetime; MSNBC; MTV; NBC Universo; Nickelodeon; OWN: Oprah Winfrey Network; Oxygen; Pop; Spike TV; Syfy; TBS; Telemundo; The Weather Channel; TLC; TNT; Travel Channel; Trinity Broadcasting Network (TBN); truTV; TV Land; Univision; USA Network; VH1.
Fee: $32.00 monthly.
Digital Basic Service
Subscribers: N.A.
Programming (via satellite): BBC America; Bloomberg Television; Boomerang; CBS Sports Network; Cooking Channel; Discovery Digital Networks; DIY Network; ESPN; ESPNews; FOX College Sports Central; FOX College Sports Pacific; Fox Sports 2; Fuse; FXM; FYI; GolTV; HD Theater; History International; HITS (Headend In The Sky); IFC; LMN; MC; National Geographic Channel; NBA TV; NBCSN; NFL Network; Nick Jr.; Nicktoons; Outdoor Channel; TeenNick; Tennis Channel; The Word Network; TNT; Turner Classic Movies; TVG Network; Universal HD; WE tv.
Fee: $27.45 monthly.
Digital Pay Service 1
Pay Units: N.A.
Programming (via satellite): Cinemax (multiplexed); Cinemax HD; Flix (multiplexed); HBO (multiplexed); HBO HD; Showtime (multiplexed); Showtime HD; Starz (multiplexed); Starz Encore (multiplexed); Starz HD; Sundance TV (multiplexed); The Movie Channel (multiplexed).
Fee: $12.00 monthly (Cinemax, HBO, Showtime/Sundance/TMC/Flix or Starz/Encore).
Video-On-Demand: No
Pay-Per-View
special events (delivered digitally); sports (delivered digitally); Hot Choice (delivered digitally); Playboy TV (delivered digitally); Fresh (delivered digitally); Shorteez (delivered digitally).
Internet Service
Operational: Yes.
Fee: $29.99-$44.99 monthly.
Telephone Service
Digital: Operational
Fee: $19.99 monthly
Vice President, Marketing: Pete Drozdoff. Vice President, Network Operations & Engineering: Lamar Horton. Vice President, Customer Care: Dawn Blydenburgh. General Manager: Matt Rohre.
Ownership: Grande Communications Networks Inc. (MSO).

AUSTIN—Time Warner Cable, 12012 North Mo Pac Expy, Austin, TX 78758-2904. Phones: 512-485-6000; 512-485-6100. Fax: 512-485-6105. Web Site: http://www.timewarnercable.com. Also serves Bastrop, Bastrop County (portions), Bee Cave, Bell County (portions), Bellmead, Belton, Bertram, Beverly Hills, Briarcliff, Bruceville-Eddy, Buda, Burnet, Caldwell County (portions), Cedar Park, Cedar Valley, China Spring, Copperas Cove, Coryell County (portions), Driftwood, Dripping Springs, Elgin, Elm Mott, Fort Hood, Fredericksburg, Gillespie County (portions), Granada Hills (portions), Harker Heights, Hays, Hewitt, Holland, Horseshoe Bay, Hutto, Jonestown, Kempner, Killeen, Kyle, Lacy-Lakeview, Lago Vista, Lakeway, Lampasas County (portions), Leander, Liberty Hill, Lorena, Manor, Marble Falls, McDade, McGregor, McLennan County (portions), Mountain City, Mustang Ridge, Niederwald, Nolanville, Pflugerville (Travis County), Pflugerville (Williamson County), Point Venture, Robinson, Rollingwood, Round Rock, San Leanna, Smithville, Spicewood, Sunset Valley, Taylor, Temple, The Hills, Thorndale, Thrall, Travis County (portions), Uhland (Caldwell County), Uhland (Hays County),

2017 Edition   D-721

Texas—Cable Systems

Volente, Waco, West Lake Hills, Williamson County (portions) & Woodway. ICA: TX0005.
Note: This system is an overbuild.
TV Market Ranking: Below 100 (AUSTIN, Bastrop, Bee Cave, Bell County (portions), Bellmead, Belton, Bertram, Beverly Hills, Briarcliff, Bruceville-Eddy, Buda, Burnet, Caldwell County (portions) (portions), Cedar Park, Cedar Valley, China Spring, Copperas Cove, Coryell County (portions), Driftwood, Dripping Springs, Elgin, Elm Mott, Fort Hood, Fredericksburg, Gillespie County (portions), Granada Hills (portions), Harker Heights, Hays, Hewitt, Holland, Horseshoe Bay, Horseshoe Bay, Hutto, Jonestown, Kempner, Kyle, Lacy-Lakeview, Lago Vista, Lakeway, Lampasas County (portions), Leander, Liberty Hill, Lorena, Manor, Marble Falls, McDade, McGregor, McLennan County (portions), Mountain City, Mustang Ridge, Niederwald, Nolanville, Pflugerville (Travis County), Pflugerville (Williamson County), Point Venture, Robinson, Rollingwood, Round Rock, San Leanna, Spicewood, Sunset Valley, Taylor, Temple, The Hills, Thorndale, Thrall, Travis County (portions), Uhland (Caldwell County), Uhland (Hays County), Volente, West Lake Hills, Williamson County (portions), Woodway, Killeen, Waco); Outside TV Markets (Smithville). Franchise award date: December 1, 1963. Franchise expiration date: N.A. Began: September 1, 1963.
Channel capacity: 80 (operating 2-way). Channels available but not in use: N.A.
Basic Service
Subscribers: 270,549.
Programming (received off-air): KCWX (MNT, This TV) Fredericksburg; KEYE-TV (CBS, TMO) Austin; KLRU (PBS) Austin; KNVA (CW, Grit, TheCoolTV) Austin; KTBC (Buzzr, FOX, Movies!) Austin; KVUE (ABC, Estrella TV) Austin; KXAN-TV (COZI TV, NBC) Austin; allband FM.
Programming (via satellite): C-SPAN; Pop; WGN America.
Fee: $39.99 installation; $28.00 monthly; $5.95 converter.
Expanded Basic Service 1
Subscribers: 194,000.
Programming (via satellite): A&E; AMC; Animal Planet; BET; Bravo; Cartoon Network; CMT; CNBC; CNN; Comedy Central; Discovery Channel; Disney Channel; E! HD; ESPN; ESPN2; Food Network; Fox News Channel; FOX Sports Southwest; Freeform; FX; Golf Channel; Hallmark Channel; HGTV; History; HLN; ION Television; Lifetime; MSNBC; MTV; National Geographic Channel; Nickelodeon; Oxygen; QVC; Spike TV; Syfy; TBS; Telemundo; The Weather Channel; TLC; TNT; Travel Channel; truTV; Turner Classic Movies; TV Land; Univision; USA Network; VH1; WE tv.
Fee: $33.40 monthly.
Digital Basic Service
Subscribers: N.A.
Programming (via satellite): A&E; A&E HD; AMC; Animal Planet; BBC America; Bloomberg Television; Bravo; Celebrity Shopping Network; Cloo; CMT; CNN; CNN HD; Comedy Central; Cooking Channel; C-SPAN; C-SPAN 2; C-SPAN 3; Destination America; Discovery Channel; Discovery Life Channel; DIY Network; E! HD; ESPN; ESPN Classic; ESPN HD; ESPN2; ESPN2 HD; ESPNews; ESPNU; EVINE Live; EWTN Global Catholic Network; Food Network; Fox Business Network; Fox News Channel; FOX Sports Southwest; Fuse; FX; FYI; GemsTV; Great American Country; GSN; HD Theater; HGTV; History; History International; HLN; INSP; Investigation Discovery; Jewelry Television; Lifetime; LMN; LOGO; MSNBC; MTV; MTV Classic; MTV Live; MTV2; Nat Geo WILD; National Geographic Channel; Outdoor Channel; Ovation; OWN: Oprah Winfrey Network; Oxygen; QVC; Science Channel; Spike TV; Syfy; TBS; TBS HD; TLC; TNT; TNT HD; Travel Channel; Trinity Broadcasting Network (TBN); truTV; Turner Classic Movies; TV Land; Universal HD; UP; USA Network; VH1; WE tv.
Fee: $9.95 monthly.
Digital Expanded Basic Service
Subscribers: N.A.
Programming (via satellite): Boomerang; Canal Sur; Cartoon Network; Cartoon Network en Espanol; CBS Sports Network; Cinelatino; CNN en Espanol; Discovery Kids Channel; Disney Channel; Disney XD; Docu TVE; ESPN Deportes; FOX College Sports Central; FOX College Sports Pacific; Fox Deportes; Fox Sports 1; Fox Sports 2; Freeform; FXM; Golf Channel; Hallmark Channel; HTV; IFC; Infinito; ION Television; La Familia Cosmovision; NBA TV; NBC Universo; NBCSN; Nick 2; Nick Jr.; Nickelodeon; Nicktoons; Starz Encore (multiplexed); Sundance TV; TeenNick; Telemundo; Tennis Channel; Toon Disney en Espanol; Tr3s; Univision; VideoRola.
Digital Pay Service 1
Pay Units: 15,936.
Programming (via satellite): Cinemax (multiplexed); HBO (multiplexed); Showtime (multiplexed); Starz (multiplexed); The Movie Channel (multiplexed).
Fee: $14.99 monthly (each).
Video-On-Demand: Yes
Pay-Per-View
iN DEMAND (delivered digitally); NBA TV (delivered digitally); Playboy TV (delivered digitally).
Internet Service
Operational: Yes.
Subscribers: 299,351.
Broadband Service: Road Runner; EarthLink; AOL; Stick.net.
Fee: $99.95 installation; $44.95 monthly.
Telephone Service
Digital: Operational
Subscribers: 166,246.
Fee: $44.95 monthly
Miles of Plant: 16,954.0 (coaxial); 5,180.0 (fiber optic). Homes passed: 924,757.
Division President: Katherine Brabson. Vice President, Human Resources: Beth Bayes. Vice President, Marketing & Sales: Terri Weber Cumbie. Vice President, Public Affairs: Stacy Schmitt. Vice President, Technical Operations: Ed Tagg. Vice President, Engineering: Lew Suders. Public Affairs Director: Roger Heaney. Program Director: George Warmingham.
Ownership: Time Warner Cable (MSO).; Advance/Newhouse Partnership (MSO).

AUSTIN (portions)—Grande Communications. Now served by AUSTIN, TX [TX0989]. ICA: TX5533.

AVINGER—Formerly served by Almega Cable. No longer in operation. ICA: TX0597.

AZTEC—Formerly served by Cebridge Connections. No longer in operation. ICA: TX0492.

BAIRD—Formerly served by Brownwood TV Cable Service Inc. No longer in operation. ICA: TX0212.

BALLINGER—Vyve Broadband, 4 International Dr, Ste 330, Rye Brook, NY 10573. Phones: 800-937-1397; 405-275-6923; 405-395-1131. Web Site: http://vyvebroadband.com. ICA: TX0964.
TV Market Ranking: Outside TV Markets (BALLINGER).
Channel capacity: 36 (2-way capable). Channels available but not in use: N.A.
Basic Service
Subscribers: 185. Commercial subscribers: 44.
Programming (received off-air): KERA-TV (PBS) Dallas; KLST (CBS) San Angelo; KPCB-DT (GLC) Snyder; KRBC-TV (Bounce TV, NBC) Abilene; KTAB-TV (CBS) Abilene; KTXA (IND, MeTV) Fort Worth; KXVA (FOX, MNT) Abilene; WFAA (ABC) Dallas.
Programming (via satellite): CNN; C-SPAN; HLN; INSP; QVC; Telemundo; The Weather Channel; Trinity Broadcasting Network (TBN); UniMas; Univision Studios.
Fee: $64.95 installation; $25.00 monthly; $.25 converter.
Expanded Basic Service 1
Subscribers: N.A.
Programming (via satellite): A&E; AMC; Cartoon Network; CMT; Discovery Channel; Disney Channel; ESPN; ESPN2; Fox News Channel; FOX Sports Southwest; Freeform; FX; Hallmark Channel; HGTV; Lifetime; MTV; NFL Network; Nickelodeon; Spike TV; TBS; TLC; TNT; TV Land; USA Network.
Fee: $38.00 installation; $24.50 monthly.
Digital Basic Service
Subscribers: N.A.
Programming (via satellite): 52MX; BBC America; Bloomberg Television; Bravo; Cine Mexicano; Cinelatino; Cloo; CNN en Espanol; Destination America; Discovery Kids Channel; Discovery Life Channel; Disney XD; DMX Music; ESPN Classic; ESPN2; ESPNews; EVINE Live; Flix; FOX College Sports Central; FOX College Sports Pacific; Fox Deportes; Fox Sports 1; Fuse; FXM; FYI; Golf Channel; Great American Country; GSN; HGTV; History; History en Espanol; History International; IFC; Investigation Discovery; LMN; MTV Classic; MTV Hits; MTV2; National Geographic Channel; NBCSN; Nick Jr.; Nicktoons; Outdoor Channel; Ovation; OWN: Oprah Winfrey Network; Science Channel; Starz Encore (multiplexed); Sundance TV; Syfy; TeenNick; The Word Network; Toon Disney en Espanol; Tr3s; Trinity Broadcasting Network (TBN); Turner Classic Movies; VH1 Country; VH1 Soul; WE tv.
Digital Pay Service 1
Pay Units: N.A.
Programming (via satellite): Cinemax (multiplexed); HBO (multiplexed); HBO Latino; Showtime (multiplexed); Starz (multiplexed); The Movie Channel (multiplexed).
Video-On-Demand: No
Pay-Per-View
iN DEMAND (delivered digitally); Hot Choice (delivered digitally); Playboy TV (delivered digitally); Fresh (delivered digitally); Shorteez (delivered digitally).
Internet Service
Operational: Yes.
Fee: $24.95 installation; $39.95 monthly.
Telephone Service
Digital: Operational
Miles of Plant: 33.0 (coaxial); None (fiber optic).
Chief Executive Officer: Bill Haggarty. Senior Vice President, Financial Planning: Daniel White. Regional Vice President: Andrew Dearth. Vice President, Marketing: Tracy Bass.
Ownership: Vyve Broadband LLC (MSO).

BALMORHEA—Mountain Zone TV, 307 E Ave East, Alpine, TX 79830. Phones: 800-446-5661; 432-837-2300. Fax: 432-837-5423. E-mail: mtnzone@sbcglobal.net. Web Site: http://www.mountainzonetv.net. ICA: TX0714.
TV Market Ranking: Outside TV Markets (BALMORHEA). Franchise award date: N.A. Franchise expiration date: N.A. Began: January 1, 1967.
Channel capacity: N.A. Channels available but not in use: N.A.
Basic Service
Subscribers: N.A.
Programming (received off-air): KLRN (PBS) San Antonio; KMID (ABC) Midland; KMLM-DT (GLC) Odessa; KOSA-TV (CBS, MNT) Odessa; KPEJ-TV (FOX) Odessa; KWES-TV (CW, NBC, TMO) Odessa; allband FM.
Programming (via satellite): A&E; Animal Planet; Cartoon Network; CNN; C-SPAN; Discovery Channel; Disney Channel; ESPN; ESPN2; EWTN Global Catholic Network; Food Network; Fox News Channel; Freeform; Great American Country; HGTV; History; Lifetime; MTV; NFL Network; Nickelodeon; TBS; Telemundo; The Weather Channel; TLC; TNT; Turner Classic Movies; TV Land; UniMas; Univision; Univision Studios; USA Network; VH1; WGN America.
Fee: $25.00 installation.
Pay Service 1
Pay Units: N.A.
Programming (via satellite): Cinemax; HBO; Showtime.
Fee: $10.00 installation; $6.00 - $10.00 monthly (each).
Video-On-Demand: No
Internet Service
Operational: Yes.
Fee: $150.00 installation; $60.00 monthly.
Telephone Service
None
Miles of Plant: 5.0 (coaxial); None (fiber optic).
General Manager: Steve Neu. Office Manager: Lawrence Neu.
Ownership: Mountain Zone TV Systems (MSO).

BANDERA—CommZoom, 2438 Boardwalk, San Antonio, TX 78217. Phone: 844-858-8500. Web Site: http://www.commzoom.com. ICA: TX0445.
TV Market Ranking: Outside TV Markets (BANDERA).
Channel capacity: N.A. Channels available but not in use: N.A.
Basic Service
Subscribers: 65.
Fee: $52.01 monthly.
Chief Executive Officer: Bob Cohen.
Ownership: CommZoom Communications LLC (MSO).

BARSTOW—Formerly served by Almega Cable. No longer in operation. ICA: TX0616.

BARTLETT—Reveille Broadband, 1008 Giddings St, PO Box 39, Lexington, TX 78947. Phones: 979-773-4700; 866-489-4739. Fax: 979-773-4733. E-mail: mariesullivan@reveillebroadband.com. Web Site: http://www.reveillebroadband.com. Also serves Granger. ICA: TX0287.

Cable Systems—Texas

TV Market Ranking: Below 100 (BARTLETT, Granger).
Channel capacity: N.A. Channels available but not in use: N.A.
Basic Service
Subscribers: 168.
Fee: $42.86 monthly.
Ownership: Reveille Broadband (MSO).

BATESVILLE—Formerly served by Almega Cable. No longer in operation. ICA: TX0886.

BAY CITY—NewWave Communications. Now served by WHARTON, TX [TX0171]. ICA: TX0104.

BEACH CITY—Formerly served by Carrell Communications. No longer in operation. ICA: TX0373.

BEAUMONT COLONY—Formerly served by Carrell Communications. No longer in operation. ICA: TX0564.

BEDFORD—Time Warner Cable. Now served by DALLAS, TX [TX0003]. ICA: TX0028.

BEDIAS—Formerly served by Almega Cable. No longer in operation. ICA: TX0669.

BEEVILLE—Time Warner Cable. Now served by CORPUS CHRISTI, TX [TX0010]. ICA: TX0113.

BELLEVUE—Formerly served by Cebridge Connections. No longer in operation. ICA: TX0716.

BEN BOLT—Formerly served by National Cable Inc. Now served by Time Warner Cable, CORPUS CHRISTI, TX [TX0010]. ICA: TX0717.

BEN WHEELER—Formerly served by Zoom Media. No longer in operation. ICA: TX0487.

BENAVIDES—Time Warner Cable. Now served by CORPUS CHRISTI, TX [TX0010]. ICA: TX0477.

BENJAMIN—Formerly served by Jayroc Cablevision. No longer in operation. ICA: TX0718.

BENTSEN GROVE—Formerly served by CableDirect. No longer in operation. ICA: TX0235.

BIG LAKE—Suddenlink Communications, 520 Maryville Centre Dr, Ste 300, St. Louis, MO 63141. Phones: 800-999-6845; 314-315-9400. Web Site: http://www.suddenlink.com. ICA: TX0720.
TV Market Ranking: Outside TV Markets (BIG LAKE). Franchise award date: N.A. Franchise expiration date: N.A. Began: June 1, 1958.
Channel capacity: 22 (operating 2-way). Channels available but not in use: N.A.
Basic Service
Subscribers: 180. Commercial subscribers: 36.
Programming (received off-air): KLST (CBS) San Angelo; KMID (ABC) Midland; KMLM-DT (GLC) Odessa; KOSA-TV (CBS, MNT) Odessa; KPEJ-TV (FOX) Odessa; KRMA-TV (PBS) Denver; KUPB (UNV) Midland; KWES-TV (CW, NBC, TMO) Odessa; 12 FMs.

Programming (via satellite): QVC; Univision.
Fee: $28.45 monthly.
Expanded Basic Service 1
Subscribers: N.A.
Programming (via satellite): A&E; AMC; Animal Planet; Cartoon Network; CNBC; CNN; Comedy Central; C-SPAN; Discovery Channel; Disney Channel; E! HD; ESPN; ESPN2; Food Network; Fox News Channel; FOX Sports Southwest; Freeform; FX; Great American Country; Hallmark Channel; HGTV; History; HLN; Lifetime; MSNBC; MTV; National Geographic Channel; Nickelodeon; Outdoor Channel; Spike TV; Syfy; TBS; The Weather Channel; TLC; TNT; Turner Classic Movies; TV Land; USA Network; VH1.
Fee: $19.95 monthly.
Digital Basic Service
Subscribers: N.A.
Programming (via satellite): BBC America; Bloomberg Television; Cloo; Discovery Digital Networks; Disney XD; DMX Music; ESPN Classic; ESPNews; EVINE Live; FOX College Sports Central; FOX College Sports Pacific; Fox Sports 1; Fuse; FYI; Golf Channel; GSN; History International; IFC; NBCSN; Sundance TV; Trinity Broadcasting Network (TBN); WE tv.
Fee: $3.99 monthly.
Pay Service 1
Pay Units: N.A.
Programming (via satellite): Cinemax; HBO; Showtime; Starz Encore.
Fee: $11.00 monthly (HBO).
Digital Pay Service 1
Pay Units: N.A.
Programming (via satellite): Cinemax (multiplexed); Flix; HBO (multiplexed); Showtime (multiplexed); Starz (multiplexed); Starz Encore (multiplexed); The Movie Channel (multiplexed).
Pay-Per-View
iN DEMAND (delivered digitally); Playboy TV (delivered digitally); Fresh (delivered digitally); Shorteez (delivered digitally).
Internet Service
Operational: Yes. Began: January 28, 2004.
Broadband Service: Suddenlink High Speed Internet.
Fee: $49.95 installation; $38.95 monthly.
Telephone Service
None
Miles of Plant: 16.0 (coaxial); None (fiber optic).
Senior Vice President, Corporate Finance: Michael Pflantz. General Manager: Daniel Anderson. Chief Technician: Phil Pool.
Ownership: Cequel Communications Holdings I LLC.

BIG SPRING—Suddenlink Communications, 2006 Birdwell Ln, Big Spring, TX 79702-6012. Phones: 314-315-9400; 915-267-3821. Fax: 915-264-0779. Web Site: http://www.suddenlink.com. Also serves Coahoma & Howard County. ICA: TX0063.
TV Market Ranking: Below 100 (BIG SPRING, Coahoma, Howard County). Franchise award date: January 1, 1961. Franchise expiration date: N.A. Began: September 1, 1961.
Channel capacity: N.A. Channels available but not in use: N.A.
Basic Service
Subscribers: 4,718. Commercial subscribers: 693.
Programming (received off-air): KERA-TV (PBS) Dallas; KMID (ABC) Midland; KMLM-DT (GLC) Odessa; KOSA-TV (CBS, MNT) Odessa; KPEJ-TV (FOX) Odessa; KWAB-TV (NBC) Big Spring; WFAA (ABC) Dallas; all-band FM.
Programming (via satellite): CNN; C-SPAN; C-SPAN 2; Freeform; HLN; TBS; The Weather Channel; TLC; TV Land.
Fee: $40.00 installation; $36.19 monthly.
Expanded Basic Service 1
Subscribers: N.A.
Programming (via satellite): A&E; AMC; BET; CNBC; Discovery Channel; Disney Channel; ESPN; FOX Sports Southwest; Great American Country; HGTV; History; Lifetime; Nickelodeon; Spike TV; Syfy; TNT; USA Network; VH1.
Fee: $11.12 monthly.
Digital Basic Service
Subscribers: N.A.
Programming (via satellite): Discovery Digital Networks; DMX Music; ESPN Classic; ESPN2; Fox Sports 1; MTV Classic; NBCSN; VH1 Country; WE tv.
Pay Service 1
Pay Units: N.A.
Programming (via satellite): HBO; Showtime; The Movie Channel.
Fee: $35.00 installation; $9.88 monthly (each).
Digital Pay Service 1
Pay Units: N.A.
Programming (via satellite): Cinemax (multiplexed); HBO (multiplexed); Showtime (multiplexed); Starz (multiplexed); The Movie Channel (multiplexed).
Video-On-Demand: No
Pay-Per-View
iN DEMAND.
Internet Service
Operational: Yes.
Broadband Service: Suddenlink High Speed Internet.
Fee: $49.95 installation; $24.95 monthly.
Telephone Service
Digital: Operational
Fee: $48.95 monthly
Miles of Plant: 189.0 (coaxial); None (fiber optic). Homes passed: 12,500.
Vice President, Accounting: Sabrina Warr. Senior Vice President, Corporate Finance: Michael Pflantz. General Manager: Archie Kountz. Chief Technician: Vern Bloodworth.
Ownership: Cequel Communications Holdings I LLC (MSO).

BIG WELLS—Formerly served by Almega Cable. No longer in operation. ICA: TX0887.

BIRCH CREEK—Reveille Broadband, 1008 Giddings St, PO Box 39, Lexington, TX 78947. Phones: 979-773-3215; 979-773-4700. Fax: 979-773-4733. E-mail: mariesullivan@reveillebroadband.com. Web Site: http://www.reveillebroadband.com. ICA: TX0885.
TV Market Ranking: Below 100 (BIRCH CREEK).
Channel capacity: N.A. Channels available but not in use: N.A.
Basic Service
Subscribers: N.A.
Programming (received off-air): KEYE-TV (CBS, TMO) Austin; KLRU (PBS) Austin; KNVA (CW, Grit, TheCoolTV) Austin; KTBC (Buzzr, FOX, Movies!) Austin; KVUE (ABC, Estrella TV) Austin; KXAN-TV (COZI TV, NBC) Austin.
Programming (via satellite): A&E; AMC; Animal Planet; BET; Boomerang; Cartoon Network; CMT; CNN; Comedy Central; C-SPAN; C-SPAN 2; Discovery Channel; Disney Channel; E! HD; ESPN; ESPN2; Food Network; Fox News Channel; Fox Sports 1; FOX Sports Southwest; Freeform; FX; Great American Country; GSN; Hallmark Channel; Hallmark Movies & Mysteries; HGTV; History; HLN; Lifetime; National Geographic Channel; Nick Jr.; Nickelodeon; QVC; Spike TV; Syfy; TBS; The Weather Channel; TLC; TNT; Travel Channel; Trinity Broadcasting Network (TBN); truTV; Turner Classic Movies; TV Land; Univision Studios; USA Network; VH1; WGN America.
Fee: $35.00 installation.
Pay Service 1
Pay Units: N.A.
Programming (via satellite): HBO; The Movie Channel.
Fee: $10.95 monthly.
Internet Service
Operational: Yes.
Telephone Service
Analog: Not Operational
Digital: Operational
Miles of Plant: 13.0 (coaxial); None (fiber optic). Homes passed: 350.
Chief Executive Officer: Marie Sullivan. President: Jeff Sullivan. Vice President: Cory Savage. Chief Technology Officer: Jason Sembera. Office Manager: Laura Tillery.
Ownership: Reveille Broadband (MSO).

BISHOP—Time Warner Cable. Now served by CORPUS CHRISTI, TX [TX0010]. ICA: TX0332.

BLACKWELL—NewWave Communications, One Montgomery Plaza, 4th Floor, Sikeston, MO 63801. Phones: 573-472-9500; 888-863-9928. Fax: 573-472-9518. E-mail: info@newwave.com. Web Site: http://www.newwavecom.com. ICA: TX0472.
TV Market Ranking: Below 100 (BLACKWELL). Franchise award date: N.A. Franchise expiration date: N.A. Began: December 1, 1987.
Channel capacity: N.A. Channels available but not in use: N.A.
Basic Service
Subscribers: 21.
Programming (received off-air): KLST (CBS) San Angelo; KPCB-DT (GLC) Snyder; KRBC-TV (Bounce TV, NBC) Abilene; KTAB-TV (CBS) Abilene; KTXS-TV (ABC, CW, This TV, TMO) Sweetwater; KXVA (FOX, MNT) Abilene.
Programming (via satellite): AMC; Animal Planet; CMT; CNN; Discovery Channel; ESPN; History; Lifetime; QVC; Spike TV; Syfy; TBS; The Weather Channel; TLC; TNT; Turner Classic Movies; USA Network; WGN America.
Fee: $35.00 installation; $48.38 monthly.
Pay Service 1
Pay Units: N.A.
Programming (via satellite): HBO.
Fee: $14.95 installation; $13.95 monthly.
Internet Service
Operational: No.
Telephone Service
None
Miles of Plant: 18.0 (coaxial); None (fiber optic). Homes passed included in Merkel
General Manager: Mark Bookout.
Ownership: NewWave Communications LLC (MSO).

BLANCO—Formerly served by Zoom Media. No longer in operation. ICA: TX1022.

BLANKET—Formerly served by National Cable Inc. No longer in operation. ICA: TX0643.

2017 Edition
D-723

Texas—Cable Systems

BLESSING—Formerly served by Bay City Cablevision. Now served by NewWave Communications, WHARTON, TX [TX0171]. ICA: TX0490.

BLOOMING GROVE—Formerly served by Almega Cable. No longer in operation. ICA: TX0424.

BLOOMINGTON—Formerly served by Almega Cable. No longer in operation. ICA: TX0469.

BOERNE—GVTC Communications. Formerly [TX0315]. This cable system has converted to IPTV, 36101 FM3159, New Braunfels, TX 78132-5900. Phones: 800-367-4882; 830-885-4411. Fax: 830-885-2400. Web Site: http://gvtc.com. Also serves Blanco, Bulverde, Canyon Lake, Fair Oaks Ranch, Gonzales, Indian Hills & Tapatio Springs. ICA: TX5465.
Channel capacity: 67 (not 2-way capable). Channels available but not in use: N.A.
Limited Basic
Subscribers: 16,253.
Fee: $27.45 monthly.
Internet Service
Operational: Yes.
President & Chief Executive Officer: Ritchie Sorrells. Chief Financial Officer: Mark Gitter. Vice President, Regulatory Affairs & Business Operations: Robert Hunt. Vice President, Sales & Marketing: Jeff Mnick. Vice President, Network Services: George O'Neal. Vice President, Product, Business Development & Strategic Planning: Josh Pettiette.
Ownership: GVTC Communications.

BOERNE (portions)—GVTC Communications. Formerly [TX0315]. This cable system has converted to IPTV. See BOERNE (portions) [TX5465]. ICA: TX0315.

BOLING—Formerly served by Cebridge Connections. No longer in operation. ICA: TX0485.

BOOKER—PTCI. This cable system has converted to IPTV. Now served by GUYMON, OK [OK5005]. ICA: TX0456.

BORGER—Cable One, 1059 Coronado Circle, Borger, TX 79007. Phones: 806-274-4447; 806-273-3744. Web Site: http://www.cableone.net. Also serves Dumas, Fritch, Pampa, Panhandle, Stinnett, Sunray & White Deer. ICA: TX0068.
TV Market Ranking: 95 (Fritch, Panhandle); Below 100 (BORGER, Dumas, Stinnett, Sunray, White Deer); Outside TV Markets (Pampa). Franchise award date: N.A. Franchise expiration date: N.A. Began: February 1, 1978.
Channel capacity: N.A. Channels available but not in use: N.A.
Basic Service
Subscribers: 4,679.
Programming (received off-air): KACV-TV (PBS) Amarillo; KAMR-TV (IND, NBC) Amarillo; KCIT (FOX, This TV) Amarillo; KFDA-TV (CBS, TMO) Amarillo; KPTF-DT (GLC) Farwell; KVII-TV (ABC, CW) Amarillo; 7 FMs.
Programming (via satellite): C-SPAN; C-SPAN 2; CW PLUS; Pop; QVC; TBS; Telemundo; WGN America.
Fee: $90.00 installation; $35.00 monthly.

Expanded Basic Service 1
Subscribers: N.A.
Programming (via satellite): A&E; AMC; Animal Planet; BET; Cartoon Network; CNBC; CNN; Discovery Channel; Disney Channel; ESPN; ESPN2; Food Network; Fox Deportes; Fox News Channel; FOX Sports Southwest; Freeform; FX; HGTV; History; HLN; Lifetime; MSNBC; MTV; Nickelodeon; Spike TV; Syfy; The Weather Channel; TLC; TNT; Trinity Broadcasting Network (TBN); Turner Classic Movies; TV Land; USA Network; VH1.
Fee: $46.00 monthly.
Digital Basic Service
Subscribers: N.A.
Programming (via satellite): 3ABN; Boomerang; BYUtv; Discovery Digital Networks; Disney XD; DMX Music; ESPN Classic; ESPNews; FamilyNet; FOX College Sports Central; FOX College Sports Pacific; Fox Sports 1; Fox Sports 2; FXM; FYI; Golf Channel; Great American Country; Hallmark Channel; History International; HITS (Headend In The Sky); INSP; National Geographic Channel; Outdoor Channel; TNT HD; Trinity Broadcasting Network (TBN); truTV; Universal HD.
Digital Pay Service 1
Pay Units: N.A.
Programming (via satellite): Cinemax (multiplexed); Flix; HBO (multiplexed); Showtime (multiplexed); Showtime HD; Starz (multiplexed); Sundance TV; The Movie Channel.
Fee: $15.00 installation; $15.00 monthly (each).
Video-On-Demand: No
Pay-Per-View
iN DEMAND (delivered digitally); Pleasure (delivered digitally); SexSee (delivered digitally); Juicy (delivered digitally); VaVoom (delivered digitally).
Internet Service
Operational: Yes. Began: December 1, 2002.
Subscribers: 6,291.
Broadband Service: CableONE.net.
Fee: $75.00 installation; $43.00 monthly; $5.00 modem lease.
Telephone Service
Digital: Operational
Subscribers: 2,021.
Fee: $39.95 monthly
Miles of Plant: 663.0 (coaxial); 238.0 (fiber optic). Homes passed: 28,102.
Vice President: Patrick A. Dolohanty. General Manager: Terry Harris. Chief Technician: Rodger Hooks. Marketing Manager: Donna Litterell. Office Manager: Dawn Rowell.
Ownership: Cable ONE Inc. (MSO).

BOWIE—Vyve Broadband, 2804B FM 51 South, Decatur, TX 76234. Phone: 855-367-8983. Web Site: http://vyvebroadband.com. ICA: TX0191.
TV Market Ranking: Below 100 (BOWIE). Franchise award date: October 1, 1984. Franchise expiration date: N.A. Began: October 1, 1969.
Channel capacity: N.A. Channels available but not in use: N.A.
Basic Service
Subscribers: 286.
Programming (received off-air): KAUZ-TV (CBS, CW) Wichita Falls; KDAF (Antenna TV, CW, This TV) Dallas; KDFI (Bounce TV, Buzzr, Heroes & Icons, MNT, Movies!) Dallas; KDFW (FOX) Dallas; KDTN (Daystar TV, ETV) Denton; KERA-TV (PBS) Dallas; KFDX-TV (NBC) Wichita Falls; KJTL (Bounce TV, FOX) Wichita Falls; KMPX (Estrella TV) Decatur; KSWO-TV (ABC, TMO) Lawton; KTVT (CBS, Decades) Fort Worth; KXTX-TV (TMO) Dallas; 2 FMs.
Fee: $59.99 installation; $25.00 monthly.
Expanded Basic Service 1
Subscribers: N.A.
Programming (received off-air): KPXD-TV (ION) Arlington.
Programming (via satellite): A&E; AMC; Animal Planet; BET; Bravo; Cartoon Network; CMT; CNBC; CNN; Comedy Central; C-SPAN; Discovery Channel; Disney Channel; ESPN; ESPN2; EVINE Live; Food Network; Fox News Channel; FOX Sports Southwest; Freeform; FX; HGTV; History; HLN; Lifetime; MTV; Nick Jr.; Nickelodeon; Pop; QVC; Radar Channel; Spike TV; Syfy; TBS; The Weather Channel; TLC; TNT; Travel Channel; Trinity Broadcasting Network (TBN); TV Land; USA Network; VH1; WE tv.
Fee: $43.95 monthly.
Digital Basic Service
Subscribers: N.A.
Programming (via satellite): BBC America; Bloomberg Television; Bravo; CMT; Destination America; Discovery Kids Channel; Discovery Life Channel; DMX Music; ESPN Classic; ESPN2; ESPNews; Fox Sports 1; Golf Channel; GSN; HGTV; History; IFC; Investigation Discovery; MTV Classic; National Geographic Channel; NBCSN; Nick Jr.; Nicktoons; Outdoor Channel; OWN; Oprah Winfrey Network; Science Channel; Syfy; Trinity Broadcasting Network (TBN); Turner Classic Movies; TV Land; WE tv.
Pay Service 1
Pay Units: N.A.
Programming (via satellite): Cinemax; HBO (multiplexed); Starz; Starz Encore.
Digital Pay Service 1
Pay Units: N.A.
Programming (via satellite): Cinemax (multiplexed); Flix; HBO (multiplexed); Showtime (multiplexed); Starz (multiplexed); Starz Encore (multiplexed); The Movie Channel (multiplexed).
Fee: $5.00 monthly (Encore), $11.00 monthly (Starz), $11.95 monthly (Cinemax), $13.95 monthly (HBO or Showtime/TMC/Flix).
Video-On-Demand: No
Pay-Per-View
iN DEMAND (delivered digitally); Playboy TV (delivered digitally); Fresh (delivered digitally); Club Jenna (delivered digitally).
Internet Service
Operational: Yes, DSL & dial-up.
Broadband Service: Net Commander.
Fee: $39.95 installation; $51.95 monthly.
Telephone Service
None
Miles of Plant: 42.0 (coaxial); None (fiber optic). Homes passed included in Decatur.
President & Chief Executive Officer: Jeffrey DeMond. Vice President, Residential Services: Vin Zachariah. Vice President, Marketing: Diane Quennoz. Senior Vice President, Financial Planning: Daniel White.
Ownership: Vyve Broadband LLC (MSO).

BOYD—Formerly served by SouthTel Communications LP. No longer in operation. ICA: TX0279.

BRACKETTVILLE—Formerly served by Almega Cable. No longer in operation. ICA: TX0356.

BRADY—Formerly served by Central Texas Communications. No longer in operation. ICA: TX1036.

BRADY—Suddenlink Communications, 520 Maryville Centre Dr, Ste 300, St. Louis, MO 63141. Phones: 877-423-2743; 314-315-9400. Web Site: http://www.suddenlink.com. Also serves McCulloch County (portions). ICA: TX0180.
TV Market Ranking: Outside TV Markets (BRADY, McCulloch County (portions)). Franchise award date: N.A. Franchise expiration date: N.A. Began: September 1, 1965.
Channel capacity: 41 (operating 2-way). Channels available but not in use: N.A.
Basic Service
Subscribers: 558. Commercial subscribers: 89.
Programming (received off-air): KBVO (Laff, MNT) Llano; KIDY (FOX, MNT) San Angelo; KLST (CBS) San Angelo; KTXS-TV (ABC, CW, This TV, TMO) Sweetwater; 4 FMs.
Programming (via satellite): KRMA-TV (PBS) Denver; Pop.
Fee: $28.45 monthly.
Expanded Basic Service 1
Subscribers: N.A.
Programming (via satellite): A&E; AMC; Animal Planet; BET; Bravo; Cartoon Network; CNBC; CNN; Comedy Central; C-SPAN; CW PLUS; Discovery Channel; Disney Channel; E! HD; ESPN; ESPN Classic; ESPN2; EWTN Global Catholic Network; Food Network; Fox News Channel; Fox Sports 1; FOX Sports Southwest; Freeform; FX; Golf Channel; Great American Country; Hallmark Channel; HGTV; History; HLN; INSP; Lifetime; MSNBC; MTV; National Geographic Channel; Nickelodeon; Outdoor Channel; QVC; Spike TV; Syfy; TBS; Telemundo; The Weather Channel; TLC; TNT; Travel Channel; Trinity Broadcasting Network (TBN); Turner Classic Movies; TV Land; Univision; Univision Studios; USA Network; VH1.
Fee: $25.00 monthly.
Digital Basic Service
Subscribers: N.A.
Programming (via satellite): BBC America; Bloomberg Television; Cloo; Discovery Digital Networks; Disney XD; DMX Music; ESPNews; Fuse; FXM; FYI; GSN; History International; HITS (Headend In The Sky); IFC; NBCSN; Sundance TV; WE tv.
Fee: $3.99 monthly.
Pay Service 1
Pay Units: N.A.
Programming (via satellite): HBO; Showtime; The Movie Channel.
Fee: $35.00 installation; $7.95 monthly (TMC), $9.95 monthly (Showtime), $10.95 monthly (HBO).
Digital Pay Service 1
Pay Units: N.A.
Programming (via satellite): Cinemax (multiplexed); HBO (multiplexed); Showtime (multiplexed); Starz (multiplexed); Starz Encore (multiplexed); The Movie Channel (multiplexed).
Video-On-Demand: No
Pay-Per-View
iN DEMAND (delivered digitally); Playboy TV (delivered digitally); Fresh (delivered digitally); Shorteez (delivered digitally).
Internet Service
Operational: Yes. Began: June 23, 2002.
Broadband Service: Suddenlink High Speed Internet.
Fee: $45.95 installation; $29.95 monthly.
Telephone Service
Digital: Operational
Fee: $44.95 monthly
Miles of Plant: 46.0 (coaxial); None (fiber optic). Homes passed: 2,932.

Cable Systems—Texas

Senior Vice President, Corporate Finance: Michael Pflantz. Regional Manager: Todd Cruthird. Marketing Director: Beverly Gambell. Chief Technician: Walt VanLue.
Ownership: Cequel Communications Holdings I LLC (MSO).

BRAZORIA—Coastal Link Communications, 314 West Texas St, PO Box 2008, Brazoria, TX 77422. Phone: 979-798-2121. E-mail: customercare@btel.com. Web Site: http://www.btel.com. Also serves Jones Creek. ICA: TX1034.
TV Market Ranking: Below 100 (BRAZORIA, Jones Creek).
Channel capacity: N.A. Channels available but not in use: N.A.
Basic Service
Subscribers: 1,072.
Fee: $29.49 monthly.
Vice President, Network Operations: Charlie Greenberg.
Ownership: Coastal Link Communications LLC.

BRAZORIA—Formerly served by Suddenlink Communications. No longer in operation. ICA: TX0128.

BRECKENRIDGE—Suddenlink Communications, 520 Maryville Centre Dr, Ste 300, St. Louis, MO 63141. Phones: 254-559-8962; 877-423-2743 (Customer service); 314-315-9400. Web Site: http://www.suddenlink.com. ICA: TX0184.
TV Market Ranking: Outside TV Markets (BRECKENRIDGE). Franchise award date: N.A. Franchise expiration date: N.A. Began: January 1, 1952.
Channel capacity: 38 (operating 2-way). Channels available but not in use: N.A.
Basic Service
Subscribers: 937. Commercial subscribers: 103.
Programming (received off-air): KIDZ-LD Abilene; KPCB-DT (GLC) Snyder; KRBC-TV (Bounce TV, NBC) Abilene; KTAB-TV (CBS) Abilene; KTXS-TV (ABC, CW, This TV, TMO) Sweetwater; KXVA (FOX, MNT) Abilene; allband FM.
Programming (via microwave): KERA-TV (PBS) Dallas; KXTX-TV (TMO) Dallas; WFAA (ABC) Dallas.
Programming (via satellite): C-SPAN; QVC; The Weather Channel; Trinity Broadcasting Network (TBN); Univision Studios.
Fee: $28.45 monthly.
Expanded Basic Service 1
Subscribers: N.A.
Programming (via satellite): A&E; AMC; Animal Planet; Cartoon Network; CNBC; CNN; Discovery Channel; Disney Channel; ESPN; ESPN2; Food Network; Fox News Channel; FOX Sports Southwest; Freeform; FX; Great American Country; Hallmark Channel; HGTV; History; HLN; INSP; Lifetime; MTV; National Geographic Channel; Nickelodeon; Outdoor Channel; Spike TV; Syfy; TBS; TLC; TNT; Travel Channel; TV Land; USA Network.
Fee: $39.95 installation; $25.00 monthly.
Digital Basic Service
Subscribers: N.A.
Programming (via satellite): BBC America; Bloomberg Television; Cloo; Discovery Digital Networks; Disney XD; DMX Music; ESPN Classic; ESPNews; Fox Sports 1; Fuse; FYI; Golf Channel; GSN; History International; HITS (Headend In The Sky); IFC; NBCSN; Turner Classic Movies; WE tv.
Fee: $3.99 monthly.

Pay Service 1
Pay Units: N.A.
Programming (via satellite): Cinemax; HBO; Showtime; Starz; Starz Encore.
Fee: $1.75 monthly (Encore), $6.75 monthly (Starz), $13.02 monthly (Cinemax), $14.01 monthly (HBO or Showtime).
Digital Pay Service 1
Pay Units: N.A.
Programming (via satellite): Cinemax (multiplexed); HBO (multiplexed); Showtime (multiplexed); Starz (multiplexed); Starz Encore (multiplexed); The Movie Channel (multiplexed).
Video-On-Demand: No
Pay-Per-View
iN DEMAND (delivered digitally); Playboy TV (delivered digitally); Fresh (delivered digitally).
Internet Service
Operational: Yes. Began: March 1, 2002.
Subscribers: 1,060.
Broadband Service: Suddenlink High Speed Internet.
Fee: $45.95 installation; $29.95 monthly.
Telephone Service
Digital: Operational
Fee: $44.95 monthly
Miles of Plant: 161.0 (coaxial); 14.0 (fiber optic). Homes passed: 4,370.
Vice President, Corporate Finance: Michael Pflantz. Regional Manager: Todd Cruthird. Plant Manager: Bobby Smith.
Ownership: Cequel Communications Holdings I LLC (MSO).

BREMOND—Zito Media, 102 S Main St, PO Box 665, Coudersport, PA 16915. Phones: 814-260-9055; 800-365-6988. E-mail: info@zitomedia.com. Web Site: http://www.zitomedia.com. ICA: TX0723.
TV Market Ranking: Outside TV Markets (BREMOND).
Channel capacity: N.A. Channels available but not in use: N.A.
Basic Service
Subscribers: 63.
Programming (received off-air): KAKW-DT (getTV, UNV) Killeen; KCEN-TV (Antenna TV, MeTV, MundoMax, NBC) Temple; KNCT (PBS) Belton; KWKT-TV (Estrella TV, FOX, MNT) Waco; KWTX-TV (CBS, CW) Waco; KXXV (ABC, TMO) Waco.
Programming (via satellite): A&E; AMC; Animal Planet; BET; Cartoon Network; CNN; C-SPAN; Discovery Channel; Disney Channel; ESPN; ESPN2; Fox News Channel; Freeform; Fuse; FX; Great American Country; HGTV; HLN; INSP; Lifetime; Outdoor Channel; QVC; TBS; The Weather Channel; TLC; TNT; USA Network; WGN America.
Fee: $49.95 installation; $45.34 monthly.
Pay Service 1
Pay Units: N.A.
Programming (via satellite): HBO; Showtime; Starz Encore.
Internet Service
Operational: No.
Telephone Service
None
Miles of Plant: 12.0 (coaxial); None (fiber optic). Homes passed: 634.
President: James Rigas.
Ownership: Zito Media (MSO).

BRENHAM—Suddenlink Communications, 520 Maryville Centre Dr, Ste 300, St. Louis, MO 63141. Phones: 979-836-6901; 800-999-6845 (Customer service); 314-315-9400. Web Site: http://www.suddenlink.com. Also serves Grimes County

ADVANCED TVFactbook

FULLY SEARCHABLE • CONTINUOUSLY UPDATED • DISCOUNT RATES FOR PRINT PURCHASERS
For more information call **800-771-9202** or visit **www.warren-news.com**

(portions), Navasota & Washington County (portions). ICA: TX0124.
TV Market Ranking: Below 100 (BRENHAM, Grimes County (portions), Washington County (portions), Navasota). Franchise award date: September 1, 1964. Franchise expiration date: N.A. Began: September 1, 1971.
Channel capacity: N.A. Channels available but not in use: N.A.
Basic Service
Subscribers: 1,932. Commercial subscribers: 527.
Programming (received off-air): KAMU-TV (PBS) College Station; KBTX-TV (CBS, CW) Bryan; KHOU (Bounce TV, CBS) Houston; KIAH (Antenna TV, CW) Houston; KPRC-TV (NBC, This TV) Houston; KPXB-TV (ION) Conroe; KRIV (FOX) Houston; KTRK-TV (ABC, Live Well Network) Houston; KTXH (Buzzr, MNT, Movies!) Houston; KUHT (PBS) Houston; KVUE (ABC, Estrella TV) Austin; KYAZ (Azteca America, IND) Katy; allband FM.
Programming (via satellite): A&E; BET; Cartoon Network; CNN; Discovery Channel; ESPN; Food Network; Fox Deportes; Fox News Channel; FOX Sports Southwest; FX; HGTV; HLN; National Geographic Channel; Pop; QVC; TBS; Telemundo; The Weather Channel; TLC; TNT; Trinity Broadcasting Network (TBN); Univision Studios; USA Network.
Fee: $28.45 monthly.
Expanded Basic Service 1
Subscribers: N.A.
Programming (via satellite): Animal Planet; CMT; CNBC; Comedy Central; C-SPAN; E! HD; ESPN2; FXM; Great American Country; Hallmark Channel; History; Lifetime; MTV; Nickelodeon; Spike TV; Syfy; Turner Classic Movies; TV Land.
Fee: $50.00 installation; $23.00 monthly.
Digital Basic Service
Subscribers: N.A.
Programming (via satellite): BBC America; Bloomberg Television; Bravo; Discovery Life Channel; DMX Music; Fox Sports 1; Golf Channel; GSN; IFC; NBCSN; Outdoor Channel; TV Guide Interactive Inc.; WE tv.
Fee: $51.99 monthly.
Pay Service 1
Pay Units: 79.
Programming (via satellite): HBO.
Fee: $10.00 installation; $10.00 monthly.
Digital Pay Service 1
Pay Units: N.A.
Programming (via satellite): Cinemax; HBO (multiplexed); Showtime; Starz (multiplexed); Starz Encore (multiplexed); The Movie Channel.
Video-On-Demand: No
Pay-Per-View
Sports PPV (delivered digitally); Playboy TV (delivered digitally); Fresh (delivered digitally).
Internet Service
Operational: Yes. Began: January 1, 2006.
Broadband Service: Suddenlink High Speed Internet.
Fee: $45.95 installation; $29.95 monthly.

Telephone Service
Digital: Operational
Fee: $44.95 monthly
Miles of Plant: 118.0 (coaxial); 17.0 (fiber optic).
Vice President, Corporate Finance: Michael Pflantz. General Manager: Ken Holle.
Ownership: Cequel Communications Holdings I LLC (MSO).

BRIDGE CITY—Time Warner Cable. Now served by PORT ARTHUR (formerly Beaumont), TX [TX0022]. ICA: TX0145.

BROOKELAND—Formerly served by Cebridge Connections. No longer in operation. ICA: TX0513.

BROOKSHIRE—Formerly served by Northland Cable Television. No longer in operation. ICA: TX0353.

BROWNFIELD—NTS Communications. This cable system has converted to IPTV. Now served by WOLFFORTH, TX [TX5540]. ICA: TX0151.

BROWNSVILLE—Time Warner Cable. Now served by PHARR, TX [TX0017]. ICA: TX0726.

BROWNWOOD—Formerly served by Brownwood TV Cable Service Inc. No longer in operation. ICA: TX0059.

BRUNI—Formerly served by Windjammer Cable. No longer in operation. ICA: TX0680.

BRYAN—Suddenlink Communications, 4114 East 29th St, Bryan, TX 77802-4302. Phones: 888-822-5151; 314-315-9400. Fax: 979-268-0139. Web Site: http://www.suddenlink.com. Also serves Brazos County (unincorporated areas) & College Station. ICA: TX0020.
TV Market Ranking: Below 100 (Brazos County (unincorporated areas), BRYAN, College Station). Franchise award date: July 1, 1953. Franchise expiration date: N.A. Began: January 1, 1954.
Channel capacity: N.A. Channels available but not in use: N.A.
Basic Service
Subscribers: 23,864. Commercial subscribers: 5,775.
Programming (received off-air): KAGS-LD (MundoMax, NBC) Bryan; KAMU-TV (PBS) College Station; KBTX-TV (CBS, CW) Bryan; KCEN-TV (Antenna TV, MeTV, MundoMax, NBC) Temple; KRHD-CD (ABC) Bryan; KTRK-TV (ABC, Live Well Network) Houston; KUHT (PBS) Houston; KXXV (ABC, TMO) Waco; KYLE-TV (FOX) Bryan; 21 FMs.
Programming (via satellite): C-SPAN; CW PLUS; Pop; QVC; TBS; WGN America.
Fee: $54.95 installation; $35.24 monthly.
Expanded Basic Service 1
Subscribers: N.A.
Programming (via satellite): A&E; AMC; Animal Planet; BET; Bravo; Cartoon Net-

2017 Edition

D-725

Texas—Cable Systems

CABLE & TV STATION COVERAGE
Atlas 2017
The perfect companion to the Television & Cable Factbook
To order call 800-771-9202 or visit www.warren-news.com

work; CMT; CNBC; CNN; Comedy Central; C-SPAN 2; Discovery Channel; Disney Channel; E! HD; ESPN; ESPN2; EWTN Global Catholic Network; Food Network; Fox News Channel; Fox Sports 1; FOX Sports Southwest; Freeform; FX; Great American Country; HGTV; History; HLN; INSP; Jewelry Television; Lifetime; LMN; MSNBC; MTV; MTV2; NBCSN; Nickelodeon; Outdoor Channel; Spike TV; Syfy; The Weather Channel; TLC; TNT; Travel Channel; Trinity Broadcasting Network (TBN); truTV; Turner Classic Movies; TV Land; Univision; USA Network; VH1.
Fee: $20.31 monthly.

Digital Basic Service
Subscribers: N.A.
Programming (via satellite): A&E HD; AXS TV; Bandamax; BBC America; Bloomberg Television; Boomerang; CBS Sports Network; Cine Mexicano; Cinelatino; CMT; CNN en Espanol; Cooking Channel; Cox Sports Television; De Pelicula; De Pelicula Clasico; Destination America; Discovery Kids Channel; Disney XD; DIY Network; Enlace USA; ESPN Classic; ESPN Deportes; ESPN HD; ESPN2 HD; ESPNews; ESPNU; FamilyNet; Food Network HD; Fox Deportes; Fox Sports 2; FSN HD; Fuse; FYI; Golf Channel; GSN; Hallmark Channel; HD Theater; HGTV HD; History en Espanol; History International; IFC; Investigation Discovery; MC; MTV Classic; MTV Hits; MTV Live; mtvU; Nat Geo WILD; National Geographic Channel; National Geographic Channel HD; NBC Universo; Nick Jr.; Nicktoons; NickToons en Espanol; OWN: Oprah Winfrey Network; Oxygen; Ritmoson; Science Channel; Starz Encore (multiplexed); Sundance TV; Sur; TeenNick; Telehit; Tennis Channel; TNT HD; Toon Disney en Espanol; Tr3s; TV One; ULTRA HDPlex; UniMas; Universal HD; Univision; UP; VideoRola; WE tv; Weatherscan.
Fee: $10.00 monthly.

Digital Pay Service 1
Pay Units: N.A.
Programming (via satellite): Cinemax (multiplexed); HBO (multiplexed); HBO HD; HBO Latino; Showtime (multiplexed); Showtime HD; Starz (multiplexed); Starz HD; The Movie Channel (multiplexed).
Fee: $21.95 monthly.
Video-On-Demand: No
Pay-Per-View
iN DEMAND (delivered digitally); Fresh (delivered digitally); Shorteez (delivered digitally); Playboy TV (delivered digitally); Club Jenna (delivered digitally); Hot Choice (delivered digitally); Spice: Xcess (delivered digitally); Playboy en Espanol (delivered digitally).
Internet Service
Operational: Yes.
Broadband Service: Suddenlink High Speed Internet.
Fee: $49.95 installation; $24.95 monthly.
Telephone Service
Digital: Operational
Subscribers: 11,212.
Fee: $48.95 monthly
Miles of Plant: 1,253.0 (coaxial); 604.0 (fiber optic). Homes passed: 83,717.

Senior Vice President, Corporate Finance: Michael Pflantz. Regional Vice President: Jim Ruel. Vice President, Accounting: Sabrina Warr. General Manager: Tom Way. Chief Technician: Mike Lavender. Customer Service Manager: Mike Kehere.
Ownership: Cequel Communications Holdings I LLC (MSO).

BRYSON—Vyve Broadband, 2804B FM 51 South, Decatur, TX 76234. Phone: 855-367-8983. Web Site: http://vyvebroadband.com. ICA: TX0144.
TV Market Ranking: Outside TV Markets (BRYSON).
Channel capacity: N.A. Channels available but not in use: N.A.
Basic Service
Subscribers: 25.
Fee: $59.99 installation; $25.00 monthly.
Senior Vice President, Financial Planning: Daniel White.
Ownership: Vyve Broadband LLC (MSO).

BUCKHOLTS—Formerly served by National Cable Inc. No longer in operation. ICA: TX0903.

BUDA (portions)—Grande Communications. Now served by AUSTIN, TX [TX0989]. ICA: TX5535.

BUFFALO—Formerly served by Northland Cable Television. No longer in operation. ICA: TX0426.

BUFFALO SPRINGS LAKE—Formerly served by Almega Cable. No longer in operation. ICA: TX0574.

BUNA—Formerly served by Cable Plus Inc. No longer in operation. ICA: TX0983.

BURKBURNETT—Suddenlink Communications, 520 Maryville Centre Dr, Ste 300, St. Louis, MO 63141. Phones: 800-999-6845; 877-423-2743 (Customer service); 314-315-9400; 314-315-9346. Web Site: http://www.suddenlink.com. Also serves Iowa Park. ICA: TX0154.
TV Market Ranking: Below 100 (BURKBURNETT, Iowa Park). Franchise award date: N.A. Franchise expiration date: N.A. Began: January 1, 1980.
Channel capacity: 37 (operating 2-way). Channels available but not in use: N.A.
Basic Service
Subscribers: 1,166. Commercial subscribers: 65.
Programming (received off-air): KAUZ-TV (CBS, CW) Wichita Falls; KFDX-TV (NBC) Wichita Falls; KJBO-LP (MNT) Wichita Falls; KJTL (Bounce TV, FOX) Wichita Falls; KSWO-TV (ABC, TMO) Lawton; 2 FMs.
Programming (via satellite): INSP; QVC.
Programming (via translator): K44GS-D Wichita Falls.
Fee: $28.45 monthly.
Expanded Basic Service 1
Subscribers: N.A.
Programming (via satellite): A&E; AMC; Animal Planet; Bravo; Cartoon Network;

Celebrity Shopping Network; CNBC; CNN; Comedy Central; C-SPAN; Discovery Channel; Disney Channel; E! HD; ESPN; ESPN2; Food Network; Fox News Channel; Fox Sports 1; FOX Sports Southwest; Freeform; FX; Golf Channel; Great American Country; Hallmark Channel; HGTV; History; HLN; Lifetime; MSNBC; MTV; National Geographic Channel; Nickelodeon; Outdoor Channel; Pop; Spike TV; Syfy; TBS; The Weather Channel; TLC; TNT; Travel Channel; truTV; Turner Classic Movies; TV Land; Univision; Univision Studios; USA Network; VH1.
Fee: $39.95 installation; $25.00 monthly.

Digital Basic Service
Subscribers: N.A.
Programming (via satellite): BBC America; Bloomberg Television; Cloo; CMT; Discovery Digital Networks; Disney XD; DMX Music; ESPN Classic; ESPNews; Fuse; FYI; GSN; History International; IFC; LMN; NBCSN; Nick Jr.; Nicktoons; TeenNick; Trinity Broadcasting Network (TBN); WE tv.

Pay Service 1
Pay Units: N.A.
Programming (via satellite): Cinemax; HBO; Showtime; Starz; Starz Encore.
Fee: $1.75 monthly (Encore), $6.75 monthly (Starz), $12.84 monthly (Cinemax), $13.83 monthly (HBO).

Digital Pay Service 1
Pay Units: N.A.
Programming (via satellite): Cinemax (multiplexed); HBO (multiplexed); Showtime (multiplexed); Starz; Starz Encore (multiplexed); The Movie Channel (multiplexed).
Video-On-Demand: No
Pay-Per-View
iN DEMAND (delivered digitally); Playboy TV (delivered digitally); Fresh (delivered digitally).
Internet Service
Operational: Yes. Began: April 1, 2002.
Broadband Service: Suddenlink High Speed Internet.
Fee: $45.95 installation; $29.95 monthly.
Telephone Service
Digital: Operational
Fee: $44.95 monthly
Miles of Plant: 102.0 (coaxial); None (fiber optic). Homes passed: 5,993.
Senior Vice President, Corporate Finance: Michael Pflantz. Regional Manager: Todd Cruthird. Area Manager: Larry Bryant. Plant Manager: Ron Johnson.
Ownership: Cequel Communications Holdings I LLC (MSO).

BURLESON—Pathway. Formerly [TX0103]. This cable system has converted to IPTV, 427 North Broadway Blvd, Joshua, TX 76058. Phone: 817-484-2222. Fax: 817-447-0169. Web Site: http://www.usapathway.com. Also serves Joshua. ICA: TX5530.
TV Market Ranking: 12 (Joshua).
Channel capacity: N.A. Channels available but not in use: N.A.
Basic
Subscribers: 84.
Fee: $44.95 monthly. Includes 70+ channels.
Internet Service
Operational: Yes.
Fee: $29.95-$79.95 monthly.
Telephone Service
Digital: Operational
Fee: $15.95 monthly
President: Steve Allen.
Ownership: Pathway ComTel.

BURLESON—Pathway. This cable system has converted to IPTV. Now served by BURLESON, TX [TX5530]. ICA: TX0103.

BURTON—Formerly served by Reveille Broadband. No longer in operation. ICA: TX0409.

BYERS—Formerly served by Byers-Petrolia Cable TV/North Texas Telephone Co. No longer in operation. ICA: TX0448.

CACTUS—Formerly served by Elk River TV Cable Co. No longer in operation. ICA: TX0730.

CADDO PEAK—North Texas Broadband, PO Box 676, Aubery, TX 76227. Phones: 888-365-2930; 940-365-2930. E-mail: customerservice@northtxbroadband.com. Web Site: http://northtxbroadband.com. Also serves Johnson County (portions) & Tarrant County (portions). ICA: TX0259.
TV Market Ranking: 12 (CADDO PEAK, Johnson County (portions), Tarrant County (portions)).
Channel capacity: 36 (not 2-way capable). Channels available but not in use: N.A.
Basic Service
Subscribers: 12.
Programming (received off-air): KDAF (Antenna TV, CW, This TV) Dallas; KDFI (Bounce TV, Buzzr, Heroes & Icons, MNT, Movies!) Dallas; KDFW (FOX) Dallas; KERA-TV (PBS) Dallas; KTVT (CBS, Decades) Fort Worth; KTXA (IND, MeTV) Fort Worth; KXAS-TV (COZI TV, NBC) Fort Worth; KXTX-TV (TMO) Dallas; WFAA (ABC) Dallas.
Programming (via satellite): A&E; CMT; CNN; Discovery Channel; Disney Channel; ESPN; FOX Sports Southwest; Freeform; HLN; Lifetime; Nickelodeon; Spike TV; TBS; TNT; USA Network; WGN America.
Fee: $40.00 installation; $41.95 monthly.
Pay Service 1
Pay Units: N.A.
Programming (via satellite): Cinemax; HBO; Showtime.
Video-On-Demand: No
Internet Service
Operational: Yes.
Fee: $50.00 installation; $24.95 monthly; $5.00 modem lease; $55.00 modem purchase.
Telephone Service
Digital: Operational
Miles of Plant: 161.0 (coaxial); 32.0 (fiber optic). Homes passed: 3,200.
General Manager: Curtis Davis.
Ownership: North Texas Broadband.

CALDWELL—Suddenlink Communications, 520 Maryville Centre Dr, Ste 300, St. Louis, MO 63141. Phones: 877-423-2743; 314-315-9400. Web Site: http://www.suddenlink.com. ICA: TX0206.
TV Market Ranking: Below 100 (CALDWELL). Franchise award date: October 13, 1970. Franchise expiration date: N.A. Began: October 1, 1971.
Channel capacity: N.A. Channels available but not in use: N.A.
Basic Service
Subscribers: 296. Commercial subscribers: 66.
Programming (received off-air): KAMU-TV (PBS) College Station; KBTX-TV (CBS, CW) Bryan; KCEN-TV (Antenna TV, MeTV, MundoMax, NBC) Temple; KIAH (Antenna TV, CW) Houston; KTBC (Buzzr, FOX, Movies!) Austin; KTXH (Buzzr, MNT,

Cable Systems—Texas

Movies!) Houston; KVUE (ABC, Estrella TV) Austin; KWKT-TV (Estrella TV, FOX, MNT) Waco; KXAN-TV (COZI TV, NBC) Austin; KYLE-TV (FOX) Bryan; allband FM.
Programming (via satellite): A&E; Cartoon Network; CMT; CNN; Discovery Channel; Disney Channel; ESPN; Fox News Channel; FOX Sports Southwest; Freeform; HGTV; History; HLN; Lifetime; Nickelodeon; QVC; Spike TV; TBS; The Weather Channel; TLC; TNT; Trinity Broadcasting Network (TBN); TV Land; USA Network; WGN America.
Fee: $28.45 monthly.

Pay Service 1
Pay Units: N.A.
Programming (via satellite): HBO; Showtime; The Movie Channel.
Fee: $7.95 monthly (TMC), $9.95 monthly (Showtime), $10.95 monthly (HBO).

Internet Service
Operational: Yes. Began: May 5, 2003.
Broadband Service: Suddenlink High Speed Internet.
Fee: $45.95 installation; $29.95 monthly.

Telephone Service
Digital: Operational
Fee: $44.95 monthly
Miles of Plant: 32.0 (coaxial); None (fiber optic). Homes passed: 1,523.
Senior Vice President, Corporate Finance: Michael Pflantz. Regional Manager: Todd Cruthird. Regional Marketing Manager: Beverly Gambell. Plant Manager: Carl Gillit.
Ownership: Cequel Communications Holdings I LLC (MSO).

CALVERT—Zito Media, 102 S Main St, PO Box 665, Coudersport, PA 16915. Phones: 814-260-9055; 800-365-6988. E-mail: info@zitomedia.com. Web Site: http://www.zitomedia.com. ICA: TX0731.
TV Market Ranking: Below 100 (CALVERT). Franchise award date: N.A. Franchise expiration date: N.A. Began: N.A.
Channel capacity: N.A. Channels available but not in use: N.A.

Basic Service
Subscribers: 57.
Programming (received off-air): KBTX-TV (CBS, CW) Bryan; KCEN-TV (Antenna TV, MeTV, MundoMax, NBC) Temple; KNCT (PBS) Belton; KWKT-TV (Estrella TV, FOX, MNT) Waco; KWTX-TV (CBS, CW) Waco; KXXV (ABC, TMO) Waco.
Programming (via satellite): A&E; Animal Planet; BET; Cartoon Network; CNN; C-SPAN; Discovery Channel; Disney Channel; ESPN; ESPN2; Fox News Channel; Freeform; Fuse; FX; Great American Country; HGTV; History; HLN; INSP; Lifetime; Outdoor Channel; QVC; TBS; The Weather Channel; TLC; TNT; Turner Classic Movies; USA Network; WGN America.
Fee: $49.95 installation; $45.34 monthly.

Pay Service 1
Pay Units: N.A.
Programming (via satellite): HBO; Showtime; Starz Encore.

Internet Service
Operational: No.

Telephone Service
None
Miles of Plant: 9.0 (coaxial); None (fiber optic). Homes passed: 700.
President: James Rigas.
Ownership: Zito Media (MSO).

CAMERON—Zito Media, 102 S Main St, PO Box 665, Coudersport, PA 16915. Phones: 814-260-9055; 800-365-6988. E-mail: info@zitomedia.com. Web Site: http://www.zitomedia.com. Also serves Milam County (portions). ICA: TX0160.
TV Market Ranking: Below 100 (CAMERON); Outside TV Markets (Milam County (portions)). Franchise award date: N.A. Franchise expiration date: N.A. Began: January 1, 1973.
Channel capacity: N.A. Channels available but not in use: N.A.

Basic Service
Subscribers: 472.
Programming (received off-air): KCEN-TV (Antenna TV, MeTV, MundoMax, NBC) Temple; KEYE-TV (CBS, TMO) Austin; KLRU (PBS) Austin; KNCT (PBS) Belton; KVUE (ABC, Estrella TV) Austin; KWKT-TV (Estrella TV, FOX, MNT) Waco; KWTX-TV (CBS, CW) Waco; KXXV (ABC, TMO) Waco; allband FM.
Programming (via satellite): A&E; AMC; Animal Planet; BET; Cartoon Network; CNBC; CNN; Comedy Central; C-SPAN; Discovery Channel; Disney Channel; Disney XD; E! HD; ESPN; Food Network; Fox News Channel; Fox Sports 1; FOX Sports Southwest; Freeform; Fuse; FX; Great American Country; Hallmark Channel; HGTV; History; HLN; INSP; Lifetime; QVC; TBS; The Weather Channel; TLC; TNT; Travel Channel; Turner Classic Movies; USA Network; WGN America.
Fee: $49.95 installation; $20.40 monthly.

Digital Basic Service
Subscribers: N.A.
Programming (via satellite): BBC America; Bloomberg Television; Discovery Life Channel; DMX Music; ESPN Classic; ESPNews; FSN Digital Atlantic; FSN Digital Central; FSN Digital Pacific; FYI; Golf Channel; GSN; History International; National Geographic Channel; Outdoor Channel; Syfy; WE tv.
Fee: $13.95 monthly.

Digital Expanded Basic Service
Subscribers: N.A.
Programming (via satellite): DMX Music; FXM; LMN; Starz Encore.
Fee: $13.95 monthly.

Pay Service 1
Pay Units: N.A.
Programming (via satellite): Cinemax; HBO; Showtime; The Movie Channel.
Fee: $12.00 monthly (each).

Digital Pay Service 1
Pay Units: N.A.
Programming (via satellite): Cinemax (multiplexed); Flix; HBO (multiplexed); Showtime (multiplexed); The Movie Channel (multiplexed).
Fee: $13.90 monthly.

Video-On-Demand: No

Pay-Per-View
ESPN Now (delivered digitally); Hot Choice (delivered digitally); Playboy TV (delivered digitally); Fresh (delivered digitally); Shorteez (delivered digitally); Urban Xtra (delivered digitally).

Internet Service
Operational: Yes.
Fee: $49.95 installation; $44.95 monthly.

Telephone Service
Digital: Operational
Miles of Plant: 41.0 (coaxial); None (fiber optic). Homes passed: 2,845.
President: James Rigas.
Ownership: Zito Media (MSO).

CAMERON COUNTY (southern portion)—Formerly served by Ridgewood Cablevision. No longer in operation. ICA: TX1018.

CAMP WOODS—Formerly served by Cebridge Connections. No longer in operation. ICA: TX0559.

CAMPBELL—Formerly served by CableSouth Inc. No longer in operation. ICA: TX0581.

CANADIAN—Suddenlink Communications, 520 Maryville Centre Dr, Ste 300, St. Louis, MO 63141. Phones: 800-999-6845 (Customer service); 314-315-9400. Web Site: http://www.suddenlink.com. Also serves Hemphill County (portions). ICA: TX0334.
TV Market Ranking: Outside TV Markets (CANADIAN, Hemphill County (portions)). Franchise award date: N.A. Franchise expiration date: N.A. Began: September 1, 1958.
Channel capacity: N.A. Channels available but not in use: N.A.

Basic Service
Subscribers: 238. Commercial subscribers: 60.
Programming (via microwave): KAMR-TV (IND, NBC) Amarillo; KCIT (FOX, This TV) Amarillo; KETA-TV (PBS) Oklahoma City; KFDA-TV (CBS, TMO) Amarillo; KVII-TV (ABC, CW) Amarillo.
Programming (via satellite): A&E; AMC; Animal Planet; CMT; CNN; C-SPAN; Discovery Channel; Disney Channel; E! HD; ESPN; Fox News Channel; FOX Sports Southwest; Freeform; History; HLN; Lifetime; Nickelodeon; QVC; Spike TV; TBS; The Weather Channel; TLC; TNT; Trinity Broadcasting Network (TBN); TV Land; USA Network; WGN America.
Fee: $28.45 monthly.

Pay Service 1
Pay Units: N.A.
Programming (via satellite): Cinemax; HBO; Showtime; The Movie Channel.
Fee: $7.95 monthly (TMC), $9.95 monthly (Cinemax or Showtime), $10.95 monthly (HBO).

Video-On-Demand: No

Internet Service
Operational: Yes. Began: June 23, 2003.
Broadband Service: Suddenlink High Speed Internet.
Fee: $49.95 installation; $38.95 monthly.

Telephone Service
None
Miles of Plant: 23.0 (coaxial); None (fiber optic). Homes passed: 1,122.
Vice President, Corporate Finance: Michael Pflantz. Marketing Director: Beverly Gambell. Chief Technician: Rick Rattan.
Ownership: Cequel Communications Holdings I LLC (MSO).

CANTON—East Texas Cable Co, 24285 State Hwy 64 East, Canton, TX 75103-6187. Phone: 903-567-2260. Fax: 903-567-4048. E-mail: info@etcable.net. Web Site: http://www.etcable.net. ICA: TX0280.
TV Market Ranking: Outside TV Markets (CANTON). Franchise award date: N.A. Franchise expiration date: N.A. Began: July 1, 1983.
Channel capacity: 35 (operating 2-way). Channels available but not in use: N.A.

Basic Service
Subscribers: 1,201.
Programming (received off-air): KDAF (Antenna TV, CW, This TV) Dallas; KDFI (Bounce TV, Buzzr, Heroes & Icons, MNT, Movies!) Dallas; KDFW (FOX) Dallas; KDTX-TV (TBN) Dallas; KERA-TV (PBS) Dallas; KETK-TV (Estrella TV, NBC) Jacksonville; KLTV (ABC, Bounce TV, TMO) Tyler; KPDX (Escape, MNT) Vancouver; KSTR-DT (getTV, UniMas) Irving; KTVT (CBS, Decades) Fort Worth; KTXA (IND, MeTV) Fort Worth; KXAS-TV (COZI TV, NBC) Fort Worth; WFAA (ABC) Dallas.
Programming (via satellite): The Weather Channel; Univision Studios; WGN America.
Fee: $39.00 installation; $14.25 monthly.

Expanded Basic Service 1
Subscribers: N.A.
Programming (via satellite): A&E; AMC; Animal Planet; Bloomberg Television; Cartoon Network; CMT; CNBC; CNN; C-SPAN; C-SPAN 2; Discovery Channel; Disney XD; Fox News Channel; Fox Sports 1; Freeform; Great American Country; History; HLN; Lifetime; MTV; National Geographic Channel; Spike TV; Syfy; TBS; TLC; Travel Channel; Turner Classic Movies; TV Land; VH1; WE tv.
Fee: $11.75 monthly.

Expanded Basic Service 2
Subscribers: N.A.
Programming (via satellite): Disney Channel; ESPN; ESPN2; FOX Sports Southwest; FX; HGTV; Nickelodeon; TNT; USA Network.
Fee: $11.50 monthly.

Digital Basic Service
Subscribers: N.A.
Programming (via satellite): New Urban Entertainment; BBC America; Bloomberg Television; Cloo; Discovery Digital Networks; DMX Music; ESPN Classic; ESPN2; ESPNews; EVINE Live; Fox Sports 1; FSN Digital Atlantic; FSN Digital Central; FSN Digital Pacific; FXM; FYI; Golf Channel; Great American Country; GSN; HGTV; History; History International; MBC America; National Geographic Channel; Nick Jr.; Nicktoons; Outdoor Channel; Syfy; TeenNick; The Word Network; Trinity Broadcasting Network (TBN); Turner Classic Movies; WE tv.
Fee: $20.99 monthly.

Pay Service 1
Pay Units: N.A.
Programming (via satellite): Cinemax; HBO; Showtime.
Fee: $8.95 monthly (Cinemax), $9.95 monthly (Showtime), $10.95 monthly (HBO).

Digital Pay Service 1
Pay Units: N.A.
Programming (via satellite): Cinemax (multiplexed); Flix; HBO (multiplexed); Showtime (multiplexed); Starz (multiplexed); Starz Encore (multiplexed); Sundance TV; The Movie Channel (multiplexed).
Fee: $7.95 monthly (Cinemax), $9.95 monthly (HBO), $10.95 monthly (Showtime/TMC or Starz/Encore).

Video-On-Demand: Yes

Pay-Per-View
iN DEMAND (delivered digitally); Hot Choice (delivered digitally); Playboy TV (delivered digitally); Fresh (delivered digitally); Shorteez (delivered digitally); Sports PPV (delivered digitally).

Internet Service
Operational: Yes.
Broadband Service: In-house.
Fee: $25.95-$50.95 monthly; $70.00 modem purchase.

Telephone Service
Digital: Operational
Fee: $30.99 monthly
Miles of Plant: 54.0 (coaxial); None (fiber optic). Homes passed: 1,450.
Manager: Staci McGinnes.
Ownership: Jim Roby.

2017 Edition
D-727

Texas—Cable Systems

CANYON LAKE—GVTC. This cable system has converted to IPTV. Now served by BOERNE, TX [TX5465]. ICA: TX0199.

CARLSBAD—Formerly served by Cebridge Connections. No longer in operation. ICA: TX0733.

CARMINE—Formerly served by Reveille Broadband. No longer in operation. ICA: TX0653.

CAROLINA COVE—Formerly served by Cablevision of Walker County. No longer in operation. ICA: TX0568.

CARROLLTON—Charter Communications, 5227 FM 813, Waxahachie, TX 75165. Phones: 636-207-5100 (Corporate office); 817-810-9171; 940-898-0583 (Denton office); 817-298-3600 (Fort Worth office). Web Site: http://www.charter.com. Also serves Addison. ICA: TX0734.
TV Market Ranking: 12 (Addison, CARROLLTON). Franchise award date: January 1, 1987. Franchise expiration date: N.A. Began: June 1, 1987.
Channel capacity: N.A. Channels available but not in use: N.A.
Digital Basic Service
Subscribers: 33. Commercial subscribers: 30.
Programming (via satellite): BBC America; Bloomberg Television; Discovery Digital Networks; DIY Network; ESPN Classic; FYI; History International; LMN; MC; National Geographic Channel; Nick Jr.; Sundance TV; TeenNick; WE tv.
Fee: $26.99 monthly.
Digital Expanded Basic Service
Subscribers: N.A.
Programming (via satellite): A&E; AMC; Animal Planet; BET; Bravo; CMT; CNBC; CNN; Comedy Central; Discovery Channel; Disney Channel; Disney XD; E! HD; ESPN; ESPN2; Fox News Channel; FOX Sports Southwest; Freeform; HGTV; History; HLN; Lifetime; MTV; Nickelodeon; Spike TV; The Weather Channel; TLC; TNT; TV Land; USA Network; VH1.
Fee: $48.99 monthly.
Digital Expanded Basic Service 2
Subscribers: N.A.
Programming (via satellite): Fox Sports 2; FSN Digital Atlantic; FSN Digital Central; FSN Digital Pacific; NBCSN; NFL Network.
Digital Pay Service 1
Pay Units: N.A.
Programming (via satellite): Cinemax (multiplexed); Flix; HBO (multiplexed); Showtime (multiplexed); The Movie Channel (multiplexed).
Video-On-Demand: No
Pay-Per-View
Hot Choice (delivered digitally); Playboy TV (delivered digitally); Fresh (delivered digitally); Shorteez (delivered digitally); iN DEMAND (delivered digitally).
Internet Service
Operational: No.
Telephone Service
None
Miles of Plant: 181.0 (coaxial); 11.0 (fiber optic). Homes passed: 3,866.
Marketing Director: Kathleen Griffin. Assistant Controller: Brent Trask. Accounting Director: David Sovanski.
Ownership: Charter Communications Inc. (MSO).

CARTHAGE—Fidelity Communications, 64 North Clark St, Sullivan, MO 63080. Phones: 800-392-8070; 903-938-1302 (Marshall office); 855-262-7434. E-mail: fidelityinfo@fidelitycommunications.com. Web Site: http://www.fidelitycommunications.com. ICA: TX0193.
TV Market Ranking: Outside TV Markets (CARTHAGE). Franchise award date: January 1, 1972. Franchise expiration date: N.A. Began: April 1, 1973.
Channel capacity: N.A. Channels available but not in use: N.A.
Basic Service
Subscribers: 495. Commercial subscribers: 85.
Programming (received off-air): KETK-TV (Estrella TV, NBC) Jacksonville; KLTS-TV (PBS) Shreveport; KMSS-TV (FOX) Shreveport; KPXJ (Antenna TV, CW, MeTV, Movies!) Minden; KSHV-TV (MNT) Shreveport; KSLA (Bounce TV, CBS, Grit, This TV) Shreveport; KTAL-TV (NBC) Texarkana; KTBS-TV (ABC) Shreveport; allband FM.
Programming (via satellite): A&E; Animal Planet; BET; CNBC; C-SPAN; E! HD; ESPN2; Freeform; FX; Lifetime; MTV; Nickelodeon; QVC; Syfy; TBS; The Weather Channel; TLC; Trinity Broadcasting Network (TBN); TV Land; Univision; WGN America.
Fee: $29.99 installation; $39.63 monthly; $2.61 converter.
Expanded Basic Service 1
Subscribers: N.A.
Programming (via satellite): AMC; Cartoon Network; CMT; CNN; Discovery Channel; Discovery Life Channel; Disney Channel; ESPN; Food Network; Fox News Channel; FOX Sports Southwest; FXM; HGTV; History; HLN; NBCSN; Spike TV; TNT; USA Network.
Fee: $17.63 monthly.
Pay Service 1
Pay Units: N.A.
Programming (via satellite): Cinemax; HBO; Showtime; The Movie Channel.
Fee: $12.95 monthly (each).
Video-On-Demand: No
Pay-Per-View
Urban Xtra; iN DEMAND; Fresh.
Internet Service
Operational: No.
Telephone Service
None
Miles of Plant: 86.0 (coaxial); None (fiber optic). Homes passed: 4,963.
General Manager, AR/MO/LA/TX: Andy Davis.
Ownership: Fidelity Communications Co. (MSO).

CASTROVILLE—Formerly served by Charter Communications. Now served by CommZoom, HONDO, TX [TX0218]. ICA: TX0427.

CEDAR CREEK—Formerly served by Trust Cable. No longer in operation. ICA: TX0901.

CEDAR SPRINGS—Formerly served by Cebridge Connections. No longer in operation. ICA: TX0628.

CENTER—Suddenlink Communications, 520 Maryville Centre Dr, Ste 300, St. Louis, MO 63141. Phones: 877-423-2743 (Customer service); 314-315-9346; 314-315-9400. Web Site: http://www.suddenlink.com. Also serves San Augustine. ICA: TX0192.
TV Market Ranking: Below 100 (CENTER, San Augustine). Franchise award date: N.A. Franchise expiration date: N.A. Began: July 1, 1970.
Channel capacity: 105 (operating 2-way). Channels available but not in use: N.A.
Basic Service
Subscribers: 504. Commercial subscribers: 250.
Programming (received off-air): KLTS-TV (PBS) Shreveport; KMSS-TV (FOX) Shreveport; KPXJ (Antenna TV, CW, MeTV, Movies!) Minden; KTAL-TV (NBC) Texarkana; KTBS-TV (ABC) Shreveport; KTRE (ABC, TMO) Lufkin; KYTX (CBS, COZI TV, CW) Nacogdoches; allband FM.
Programming (via satellite): C-SPAN; Trinity Broadcasting Network (TBN).
Fee: $39.95 installation; $28.45 monthly.
Expanded Basic Service 1
Subscribers: N.A.
Programming (via satellite): A&E; Animal Planet; BET; Bravo; Cartoon Network; Celebrity Shopping Network; CNBC; CNN; Comedy Central; Discovery Channel; Disney Channel; E! HD; ESPN; ESPN2; Food Network; Fox News Channel; Fox Sports 1; FOX Sports Southwest; Freeform; FX; Golf Channel; Great American Country; Hallmark Channel; HGTV; History; HLN; Lifetime; MSNBC; MTV; National Geographic Channel; Nickelodeon; Outdoor Channel; Pop; QVC; Spike TV; Syfy; TBS; The Weather Channel; TLC; TNT; Travel Channel; Turner Classic Movies; TV Land; Univision; Univision Studios; USA Network; VH1.
Digital Basic Service
Subscribers: N.A.
Programming (via satellite): BBC America; Bloomberg Television; Cloo; CMT; Discovery Digital Networks; Disney XD; DMX Music; ESPN Classic; ESPNews; Fuse; FYI; GSN; History International; HITS (Headend In The Sky); IFC; LMN; NBCSN; Nick Jr.; Nicktoons; TeenNick; WE tv.
Pay Service 1
Pay Units: N.A.
Programming (via satellite): Cinemax; HBO; Showtime; The Movie Channel.
Fee: $5.95 monthly (Showtime), $10.00 monthly (Cinemax, HBO or TMC).
Digital Pay Service 1
Pay Units: N.A.
Programming (via satellite): Cinemax (multiplexed); HBO (multiplexed); Showtime (multiplexed); Starz; Starz Encore (multiplexed); The Movie Channel (multiplexed).
Video-On-Demand: No
Pay-Per-View
iN DEMAND (delivered digitally); Playboy TV (delivered digitally); Fresh (delivered digitally).
Internet Service
Operational: Yes. Began: May 12, 2003.
Broadband Service: Suddenlink High Speed Internet.
Fee: $45.95 installation; $29.95 monthly.
Telephone Service
Digital: Operational
Fee: $44.95 monthly
Miles of Plant: 65.0 (coaxial); None (fiber optic). Homes passed: 3,800.
Senior Vice President, Corporate Finance: Michael Pflantz. Regional Manager: Todd Cruthird. Area Manager: Marianne Bogy. Plant Manager: Henry Harris.
Ownership: Cequel Communications Holdings I LLC (MSO).

CENTER POINT—Formerly served by Almega Cable. No longer in operation. ICA: TX0913.

CENTERVILLE—Formerly served by Almega Cable. No longer in operation. ICA: TX0463.

CENTRAL—Formerly served by Almega Cable. No longer in operation. ICA: TX0339.

CHANNING—Formerly served by Sunset Cablevision. No longer in operation. ICA: TX0737.

CHAPPELL HILL—Formerly served by Reveille Broadband. No longer in operation. ICA: TX0888.

CHARLOTTE—Formerly served by Zoom Media. No longer in operation. ICA: TX0508.

CHEEK—Formerly served by Cebridge Connections. No longer in operation. ICA: TX0576.

CHEROKEE COUNTY (northern portions)—Formerly served by Reach Broadband. No longer in operation. ICA: TX0988.

CHESTER—Formerly served by Cebridge Connections. No longer in operation. ICA: TX0671.

CHILDRESS—Formerly served by Cebridge Connections. Now served by Suddenlink Communications, WELLINGTON, TX [TX0313]. ICA: TX0195.

CHILLICOTHE—Formerly served by Almega Cable. No longer in operation. ICA: TX0530.

CHILTON—Formerly served by Galaxy Cablevision. No longer in operation. ICA: TX0598.

CHINA—Formerly served by CMA Cablevision. No longer in operation. ICA: TX0738.

CHRISTOVAL—Formerly served by Almega Cable. No longer in operation. ICA: TX0589.

CLARENDON—Suddenlink Communications, 520 Maryville Centre Dr, Ste 300, St. Louis, MO 63141. Phones: 800-999-6845; 314-315-9400. Web Site: http://www.suddenlink.com. ICA: TX0398.
TV Market Ranking: Outside TV Markets (CLARENDON). Franchise award date: N.A. Franchise expiration date: N.A. Began: June 15, 1962.
Channel capacity: N.A. Channels available but not in use: N.A.
Basic Service
Subscribers: 146. Commercial subscribers: 58.
Programming (received off-air): KACV-TV (PBS) Amarillo; KAMR-TV (IND, NBC) Amarillo; KCIT (FOX, This TV) Amarillo; KFDA-TV (CBS, TMO) Amarillo; KVII-TV (ABC, CW) Amarillo; allband FM.
Programming (via satellite): AMC; Animal Planet; CMT; CNN; C-SPAN; Discovery Channel; Disney Channel; E! HD; ESPN; Fox News Channel; FOX Sports Southwest; Freeform; HGTV; History; HLN; Lifetime; Nickelodeon; QVC; Spike TV; Syfy; TBS; The Weather Channel; TLC; TNT; TV Land; USA Network; WGN America.
Fee: $28.45 monthly.
Pay Service 1
Pay Units: N.A.
Programming (via satellite): HBO; Showtime; The Movie Channel.
Fee: $20.00 installation; $7.95 monthly (TMC), $9.95 monthly (Showtime), $10.95 monthly (HBO).
Video-On-Demand: No
Internet Service
Operational: Yes. Began: June 11, 2004.
Broadband Service: Suddenlink High Speed Internet.
Fee: $49.95 installation; $38.95 monthly.

Cable Systems—Texas

Telephone Service
None
Miles of Plant: 24.0 (coaxial); None (fiber optic). Homes passed: 812.
Senior Vice President, Corporate Finance: Michael Pflantz. Regional Manager: Todd Cruthird. Regional Marketing Manager: Beverly Gambell. Plant Manager: Rick Rattan.
Ownership: Cequel Communications Holdings I LLC (MSO).

CLARKSVILLE—Suddenlink Communications, 520 Maryville Centre Dr, Ste 300, St. Louis, MO 63141. Phones: 877-423-2743 (Customer service); 314-315-9400. Web Site: http://www.suddenlink.com. Also serves Annona, Avery, Blossom, Bogata, Deport, Detroit, Lamar County (portions) & Talco. ICA: TX0200.
TV Market Ranking: Outside TV Markets (Annona, Avery, Blossom, Bogata, CLARKSVILLE, Deport, Detroit, Lamar County (portions), Talco). Franchise award date: N.A. Franchise expiration date: N.A. Began: March 1, 1963.
Channel capacity: 21 (operating 2-way). Channels available but not in use: N.A.

Basic Service
Subscribers: 1,276. Commercial subscribers: 58.
Programming (received off-air): KMSS-TV (FOX) Shreveport; KPXJ (Antenna TV, CW, MeTV, Movies!) Minden; KTAL-TV (NBC) Texarkana; KTBS-TV (ABC) Shreveport; all-band FM.
Programming (via microwave): KDFW (FOX) Dallas; KERA-TV (PBS) Dallas; KTVT (CBS, Decades) Fort Worth; KXAS-TV (COZI TV, NBC) Fort Worth; WFAA (ABC) Dallas.
Programming (via satellite): QVC; The Weather Channel.
Fee: $54.95 installation; $38.24 monthly.

Expanded Basic Service 1
Subscribers: N.A.
Programming (via microwave): KDTX-TV (TBN) Dallas.
Programming (via satellite): A&E; AMC; Animal Planet; BET; Cartoon Network; CNBC; CNN; Comedy Central; Discovery Channel; Disney Channel; E! HD; ESPN; ESPN2; Food Network; Fox News Channel; FOX Sports Southwest; Freeform; FX; Great American Country; HGTV; History; HLN; Lifetime; MSNBC; MTV; National Geographic Channel; Nickelodeon; Outdoor Channel; Spike TV; Syfy; TBS; TLC; TNT; Travel Channel; Turner Classic Movies; TV Land; Univision Studios; USA Network; VH1.
Fee: $23.00 monthly.

Digital Basic Service
Subscribers: N.A.
Programming (via satellite): BBC America; Bloomberg Television; Cloo; Discovery Digital Networks; Disney XD; DMX Music; ESPN Classic; ESPNews; Fox Sports 1; Fuse; FYI; Golf Channel; GSN; History International; IFC; NBCSN; Trinity Broadcasting Network (TBN); WE tv.
Fee: $3.99 monthly.

Pay Service 1
Pay Units: N.A.
Programming (via satellite): Cinemax; HBO; Showtime; The Movie Channel.
Fee: $5.95 monthly (Showtime), $10 monthly (Cinemax, HBO or TMC).

Digital Pay Service 1
Pay Units: N.A.
Programming (via satellite): Cinemax (multiplexed); HBO (multiplexed); Showtime (multiplexed); Starz; Starz Encore (multiplexed); The Movie Channel (multiplexed).

Video-On-Demand: No

Pay-Per-View
iN DEMAND (delivered digitally); Playboy TV (delivered digitally); Fresh (delivered digitally).

Internet Service
Operational: Yes. Began: June 1, 2003.
Broadband Service: Suddenlink High Speed Internet.
Fee: $45.95 installation; $29.95 monthly.

Telephone Service
Digital: Operational
Fee: $44.95 monthly
Miles of Plant: 126.0 (coaxial); None (fiber optic). Homes passed: 6,299.
Senior Vice President, Corporate Finance: Michael Pflantz. Vice President, Accounting: Sabrina Warr. Regional Manager: Todd Cruthird. Area Manager: Marianne Bogy. Plant Manager: Sonny Myers.
Ownership: Cequel Communications Holdings I LLC (MSO).

CLAUDE—Formerly served by Almega Cable. No longer in operation. ICA: TX0516.

CLEBURNE—Charter Communications. Now served by FORT WORTH (northern portions), TX [TX0008]. ICA: TX1003.

CLEVELAND—NewWave Communications, One Montgomery Plaza, 4th Floor, Sikeston, MO 63801. Phones: 573-472-9500; 888-863-9928. Fax: 573-472-9518. E-mail: info@newwave.com. Web Site: http://www.newwavecom.com. Also serves North Cleveland. ICA: TX0170.
TV Market Ranking: Below 100 (CLEVELAND, North Cleveland). Franchise award date: May 10, 1977. Franchise expiration date: N.A. Began: November 1, 1978.
Channel capacity: N.A. Channels available but not in use: N.A.

Basic Service
Subscribers: 428.
Programming (received off-air): KETH-TV (TBN) Houston; KFTH-DT (getTV, UniMas) Alvin; KHOU (Bounce TV, CBS) Houston; KIAH (Antenna TV, CW) Houston; KLTJ (Daystar TV, ETV) Galveston; KPRC-TV (NBC, This TV) Houston; KPXB-TV (ION) Conroe; KRIV (FOX) Houston; KTMD (TMO) Galveston; KTRK-TV (ABC, Live Well Network) Houston; KTXH (Buzzr, MNT, Movies!) Houston; KUHT (PBS) Houston; KXLN-DT (UNV) Rosenberg; KYAZ (Azteca America, IND) Katy.
Programming (via satellite): C-SPAN; QVC; WGN America.
Fee: $35.00 installation; $34.93 monthly.

Expanded Basic Service 1
Subscribers: N.A.
Programming (via satellite): A&E; AMC; Animal Planet; BET; Bravo; Cartoon Network; CMT; CNBC; CNN; Comedy Central; Discovery Channel; ESPN; ESPN Classic; ESPN2; Food Network; Fox News Channel; FOX Sports Southwest; Freeform; FX; History; HLN; Lifetime; MTV; National Geographic Channel; Nickelodeon; Outdoor Channel; Spike TV; Syfy; TBS; The Weather Channel; TLC; TNT; truTV; TV Land; Univision; USA Network; VH1.
Fee: $53.65 monthly.

Digital Basic Service
Subscribers: N.A.
Programming (via satellite): BBC America; Discovery Digital Networks; DMX Music; ESPNews; Fox Sports 1; FYI; Golf Channel; GSN; HGTV; History International; IFC; LMN; Nick Jr.; Nicktoons; Starz Encore; TeenNick; Turner Classic Movies; WE tv.
Fee: $10.00 monthly.

Pay Service 1
Pay Units: N.A.
Programming (via satellite): HBO.
Fee: $14.95 installation; $13.95 monthly.

Digital Pay Service 1
Pay Units: N.A.
Programming (via satellite): Cinemax (multiplexed); HBO (multiplexed); Showtime (multiplexed); Starz (multiplexed); Starz Encore (multiplexed).
Fee: $7.00 monthly (Starz), $9.00 monthly (Cinemax), $11.00 monthly (Starz/Encore), $15.00 monthly (Showtime/TMC) or $25.00 monthly (HBO/Cinemax).

Video-On-Demand: No

Pay-Per-View
iN DEMAND (delivered digitally); Playboy TV (delivered digitally).

Internet Service
Operational: Yes.
Fee: $39.95 installation; $19.99-$29.99 monthly; $6.00 modem lease; $39.95 modem purchase.

Telephone Service
Digital: Operational
Miles of Plant: 84.0 (coaxial); None (fiber optic). Homes passed: 3,000.
Regional General Manager: Jerry Smith.
Ownership: NewWave Communications LLC (MSO).

CLIFTON—LynnStar Communications, 4500 Mercantile Plz, Ste 300, Fort Worth, TX 76137. Phones: 888-575-9230; 682-730-0900. Fax: 682-730-6400. Web Site: http://lynnstar.net; http://www.lynnstarcomm.com. ICA: TX0288.
TV Market Ranking: Below 100 (CLIFTON). Franchise award date: N.A. Franchise expiration date: N.A. Began: February 1, 1982.
Channel capacity: N.A. Channels available but not in use: N.A.

Basic Service
Subscribers: 174.
Programming (received off-air): KCEN-TV (Antenna TV, MeTV, MundoMax, NBC) Temple; KDAF (Antenna TV, CW, This TV) Dallas; KDFI (Bounce TV, Buzzr, Heroes & Icons, MNT, Movies!) Dallas; KDFW (FOX) Dallas; KERA-TV (PBS) Dallas; KSTR-DT (getTV, UniMas) Irving; KTVT (CBS, Decades) Fort Worth; KWKT-TV (Estrella TV, FOX, MNT) Waco; KWTX-TV (CBS, CW) Waco; KXAS-TV (COZI TV, NBC) Fort Worth; KXTX-TV (TMO) Dallas; KXXV (ABC, TMO) Waco; WFAA (ABC) Dallas.
Fee: $49.95 installation; $27.41 monthly.

Expanded Basic Service 1
Subscribers: N.A.
Programming (via satellite): A&E; AMC; Animal Planet; Cartoon Network; CNBC; CNN; Comedy Central; C-SPAN; Discovery Channel; Disney Channel; E! HD; ESPN; ESPN2; Food Network; Fox News Channel; Fox Sports 1; FOX Sports Southwest; Freeform; FX; Great American Country; Hallmark Channel; HGTV; History; HLN; INSP; Lifetime; MSNBC; MTV; Nickelodeon; Outdoor Channel; QVC; Spike TV; Syfy; TBS; The Weather Channel; TLC; TNT; Travel Channel; Turner Classic Movies; TV Land; USA Network; VH1.
Fee: $23.10 monthly.

Pay Service 1
Pay Units: N.A.
Programming (via satellite): Cinemax; HBO; Showtime; Starz; Starz Encore.
Fee: $12.95 monthly (Cinemax, Encore, HBO or Starz).

Video-On-Demand: No

Internet Service
Operational: Yes.
Broadband Service: Rapid High Speed Internet.
Fee: $100.00 installation; $29.95 monthly.

Telephone Service
None
Miles of Plant: 24.0 (coaxial); None (fiber optic). Homes passed: 1,410.
Chairman of the Board & Government Relations Director: S. Gene Yarbrough. Chief Executive Officer, Executive Vice President & Board Member: Chris Romine. Chief Operations Officer, Executive Vice President & Board Member: Steve Sizemore. Vice President & Business Development & Countertrade Director: Gary Majors. Vice President & Programming & Vendor Relations Director: Gus Salvino. Vice President & Investor Relations Manager: Daniel J. Sweeney. Accounting Manager: Sheila Magness.
Ownership: Lynnstar Communications (MSO).

COLEMAN—LynnStar Communications, 4500 Mercantile Plz, Ste 300, Fort Worth, TX 76137. Phones: 888-575-9230; 682-730-0900. Fax: 682-730-6400. Web Site: http://lynnstar.net; http://www.lynnstarcomm.com. ICA: TX0178.
TV Market Ranking: Outside TV Markets (COLEMAN). Franchise award date: August 1, 1958. Franchise expiration date: N.A. Began: April 1, 1959.
Channel capacity: N.A. Channels available but not in use: N.A.

Basic Service
Subscribers: 107.
Programming (received off-air): KLST (CBS) San Angelo; KPCB-DT (GLC) Snyder; KRBC-TV (Bounce TV, NBC) Abilene; KRPV-DT (GLC) Roswell; KTAB (CBS) Abilene; KTXS-TV (ABC, CW, This TV, TMO) Sweetwater; KXVA (FOX, MNT) Abilene.
Programming (via microwave): KDFW (FOX) Dallas; KERA-TV (PBS) Dallas; WFAA (ABC) Dallas.
Programming (via satellite): C-SPAN.
Fee: $49.95 installation; $21.93 monthly.

Expanded Basic Service 1
Subscribers: N.A.
Programming (via satellite): A&E; AMC; Animal Planet; Bravo; Cartoon Network; CMT; CNBC; CNN; Comedy Central; Disney Channel; E! HD; ESPN; ESPN2; Fox News Channel; Fox Sports 1; FOX Sports Southwest; Freeform; FX; FXM; Golf Channel; HGTV; History; HLN; Lifetime; MTV; Nickelodeon; Outdoor Channel; Oxygen; Spike TV; Syfy; TBS; The Weather Channel; TLC; TNT; Turner Classic Movies; TV Land; Univision Studios; USA Network; VH1.
Fee: $18.00 monthly.

Digital Basic Service
Subscribers: N.A.
Programming (via satellite): BBC America; Bloomberg Television; CMT; Destination America; Discovery Kids Channel; Discovery Life Channel; Disney XD; DIY Network; ESPN Classic; FYI; GSN; History International; IFC; Investigation Discovery; LMN; MC; MTV Classic; Nick 2; Nick Jr.; Nicktoons; OWN: Oprah Winfrey Network; Science Channel; Sundance TV; TeenNick; VH1 Soul; WE tv.

Digital Pay Service 1
Pay Units: N.A.
Programming (via satellite): Cinemax (multiplexed); Flix; HBO (multiplexed); Showtime (multiplexed); Starz (multiplexed); Starz Encore (multiplexed); The Movie Channel (multiplexed).

2017 Edition

D-729

Texas—Cable Systems

Fee: $20.00 installation; $9.95 monthly.
Video-On-Demand: No
Pay-Per-View
iN DEMAND (delivered digitally); Pleasure (delivered digitally); SexSee (delivered digitally).
Internet Service
Operational: Yes.
Telephone Service
None
Miles of Plant: 47.0 (coaxial); None (fiber optic). Homes passed: 2,990.
Chairman of the Board & Government Relations Director: S. Gene Yarbrough. Chief Executive Officer, Executive Vice President & Board Member: Chris Romine. Chief Operations Officer, Executive Vice President & Board Member: Steve Sizemore. Vice President & Business Development & Countertrade Director: Gary Majors. Vice President & Programming & Vendor Relations Director: Gus Salvino. Vice President & Investor Relations Manager: Daniel J. Sweeney. Accounting Manager: Sheila Magness.
Ownership: Lynnstar Communications (MSO).

COLEMAN COUNTY—Formerly served by Coleman County Telecommunications. No longer in operation. ICA: TX1035.

COLETO CREEK—Formerly served by National Cable Inc. No longer in operation. ICA: TX0626.

COLMESNEIL—Formerly served by Carrell Communications. No longer in operation. ICA: TX0475.

COLORADO CITY—NTS Communications. Formerly [TX0172]. This cable system has converted to IPTV, 1220 Broadway, Lubbock, TX 79401. Phones: 800-658-2150; 806-797-0687. Fax: 806-788-3381. E-mail: info@ntscom.com. Web Site: http://www.ntscom.com. ICA: TX5543.
TV Market Ranking: Below 100 (COLORADO CITY).
Channel capacity: N.A. Channels available but not in use: N.A.
Gold
Subscribers: 517.
Fee: $65.00 monthly. Includes 150+ channels plus music & 1 digital receiver.
Platinum
Subscribers: N.A.
Fee: $85.00 monthly. Includes 230+ channels plus music, 1 whole home DVR & 1 digital receiver.
Internet Service
Operational: Yes.
Fee: $44.99-$134.99 monthly.
Telephone Service
Digital: Operational
Fee: $19.99 monthly
President & Chief Executive Officer: Cyrus Driver. Executive Vice President & Chief Operating Officer: Deborah Crawford. Executive Vice President & Chief Financial Officer: Don Pittman. Senior Vice President, Product Management: Angel Kandahari. Vice President & General Counsel: Daniel Wheeler. Vice President, Products & Marketing: Roberto Chang. Vice President, Human Resources: Wendy J. Lee. Vice President, Service Delivery & IT Strategy: Michael McDaniel. Vice President, RUS Projects: Aaron Peters.
Ownership: NTS Communications Inc.

COLORADO CITY—NTS Communications. This cable system has converted to IPTV. See COLORADO CITY, TX [TX5543]. ICA: TX0172.

COLUMBUS—Time Warner Cable, 7800 Crescent Executive Dr, Charlotte, NC 28217. Phones: 972-899-7300 (Flower Mound division office); 830-257-4709. Web Site: http://www.timewarnercable.com. Also serves Colorado County (portions) & Eagle Lake. ICA: TX0257.
TV Market Ranking: Below 100 (Colorado County (portions), Eagle Lake); Outside TV Markets (Colorado County (portions), COLUMBUS). Franchise award date: N.A. Franchise expiration date: N.A. Began: June 1, 1974.
Channel capacity: N.A. Channels available but not in use: N.A.
Basic Service
Subscribers: 799.
Programming (received off-air): KETH-TV (TBN) Houston; KFTH-DT (getTV, UniMas) Alvin; KHOU (Bounce TV, CBS) Houston; KIAH (Antenna TV, CW) Houston; KLTJ (Daystar TV, ETV) Galveston; KPRC-TV (NBC, This TV) Houston; KPXB-TV (ION) Conroe; KRIV (FOX) Houston; KTMD (TMO) Galveston; KTRK-TV (ABC, Live Well Network) Houston; KTXH (Buzzr, MNT, Movies!) Houston; KUBE-TV (COZI TV, MeTV) Baytown; KUHT (PBS) Houston; KXLN-DT (UNV) Rosenberg; KYAZ (Azteca America, IND) Katy; KZJL (Estrella TV) Houston; 1 FM.
Programming (via satellite): Cartoon Network; CNBC; CNN; C-SPAN; C-SPAN 2; Discovery Channel; Freeform; TBS; The Weather Channel; TNT; WGN America.
Fee: $49.99 installation; $28.00 monthly.
Expanded Basic Service 1
Subscribers: N.A.
Programming (via satellite): A&E; AMC; Animal Planet; BET; Bravo; CMT; Disney Channel; E! HD; ESPN; ESPN2; EVINE Live; Food Network; Fox News Channel; FOX Sports Southwest; FX; Golf Channel; GSN; Hallmark Channel; HGTV; History; HLN; Lifetime; MoviePlex; MSNBC; MTV; National Geographic Channel; NBC Universo; Nickelodeon; Oxygen; Spike TV; Syfy; TLC; Travel Channel; truTV; Turner Classic Movies; TV Land; USA Network; VH1; WE tv.
Fee: $31.30 monthly.
Digital Basic Service
Subscribers: N.A.
Programming (via satellite): BBC America; Bloomberg Television; Cloo; Cooking Channel; Discovery Life Channel; Disney XD; DIY Network; DMX Music; ESPN Classic; ESPNews; FOX College Sports Central; FOX College Sports Pacific; Fox Deportes; Fox Sports 1; Fuse; FXM; Great American Country; IFC; LMN; NBA TV; NBCSN; Nick Jr.; Nicktoons; Outdoor Channel; Starz Encore (multiplexed); Sundance TV (multiplexed); TeenNick; Tennis Channel.
Fee: $5.00 monthly, $8.95 monthly (Value Tier, Sports Tier or Movie Tier).
Digital Pay Service 1
Pay Units: N.A.
Programming (via satellite): Cinemax (multiplexed); HBO (multiplexed); Showtime (multiplexed); Starz (multiplexed); The Movie Channel.
Fee: $14.99 monthly (each).
Video-On-Demand: No
Internet Service
Operational: Yes.
Subscribers: 416.
Telephone Service
Digital: Operational
Subscribers: 184.
Miles of Plant: 139.0 (coaxial); 184.0 (fiber optic). Homes passed: 4,868. Homes passed included in Gonzales.

President: Connie Wharton. Vice President & General Manager: Mike McKee. Senior Accounting Director: Karen Goodfellow. Engineering Director: Charlotte Strong. Chief Technician: Bill Wilcox.
Ownership: Time Warner Cable (MSO).; Advance/Newhouse Partnership (MSO).

COMANCHE—LynnStar Communications, 4500 Mercantile Plz, Ste 300, Fort Worth, TX 76137. Phones: 888-575-9230; 682-730-0900. Fax: 682-730-6400. Web Site: http://lynnstar.net; http://www.lynnstarcomm.com. ICA: TX0227.
TV Market Ranking: Outside TV Markets (COMANCHE). Franchise award date: N.A. Franchise expiration date: N.A. Began: September 1, 1958.
Channel capacity: N.A. Channels available but not in use: N.A.
Basic Service
Subscribers: 49.
Programming (received off-air): KRBC-TV (Bounce TV, NBC) Abilene; KTAB-TV (CBS) Abilene; allband FM.
Programming (via microwave): KDAF (Antenna TV, CW, This TV) Dallas; KDFW (FOX) Dallas; KERA-TV (PBS) Dallas; KXAS-TV (COZI TV, NBC) Fort Worth; WFAA (ABC) Dallas.
Programming (via satellite): Disney Channel; QVC; TLC; Trinity Broadcasting Network (TBN).
Fee: $49.95 installation; $23.59 monthly; $3.51 converter.
Expanded Basic Service 1
Subscribers: N.A.
Programming (via satellite): A&E; AMC; Bravo; Cartoon Network; CMT; CNBC; CNN; Comedy Central; Discovery Channel; E! HD; ESPN; ESPN2; Fox News Channel; Fox Sports 1; Freeform; FX; HGTV; History; HLN; Lifetime; MTV; Nickelodeon; Oxygen; Spike TV; Syfy; TBS; The Weather Channel; TNT; Turner Classic Movies; TV Land; Univision; USA Network; VH1.
Fee: $18.00 monthly.
Digital Basic Service
Subscribers: N.A.
Programming (via satellite): BBC America; Bloomberg Television; CMT; Destination America; Discovery Kids Channel; Discovery Life Channel; Disney XD; DIY Network; ESPN Classic; FYI; GSN; History International; Investigation Discovery; LMN; MC; MTV Classic; MTV Hits; MTV2; Nick 2; Nick Jr.; Nicktoons; OWN: Oprah Winfrey Network; Sundance TV; TeenNick; Tr3s; VH1 Soul.
Digital Pay Service 1
Pay Units: N.A.
Programming (via satellite): Cinemax (multiplexed); Flix; HBO (multiplexed); Showtime (multiplexed); Starz (multiplexed); Starz Encore; The Movie Channel (multiplexed).
Video-On-Demand: No
Pay-Per-View
iN DEMAND (delivered digitally).
Internet Service
Operational: No.
Telephone Service
None
Miles of Plant: 50.0 (coaxial); None (fiber optic). Homes passed: 2,000.
Chairman of the Board & Government Relations Director: S. Gene Yarbrough. Chief Executive Officer, Executive Vice President & Board Member: Chris Romine. Chief Operations Officer, Executive Vice President & Board Member: Steve Sizemore. Vice President & Business Development & Counter-

trade Director: Gary Majors. Vice President & Programming & Vendor Relations Director: Gus Salvino. Vice President & Investor Relations Manager: Daniel J. Sweeney. Accounting Manager: Sheila Magness.
Ownership: Lynnstar Communications (MSO).

COMBINE—Formerly served by Charter Communications. No longer in operation. ICA: TX0917.

COMFORT—CommZoom, 2438 Boardwalk, San Antonio, TX 78217. Phones: 844-858-8500; 830-995-2813. Web Site: http://www.commzoom.com. ICA: TX1015.
TV Market Ranking: Below 100 (COMFORT). Franchise award date: N.A. Franchise expiration date: N.A. Began: January 1, 1980.
Channel capacity: N.A. Channels available but not in use: N.A.
Basic Service
Subscribers: 167.
Programming (received off-air): KABB (FOX, The Country Network) San Antonio; KCWX (MNT, This TV) Fredericksburg; KENS (CBS, Estrella TV) San Antonio; KLRN (PBS) San Antonio; KPXL-TV (ION) Uvalde; KSAT-TV (ABC, MeTV) San Antonio; KVDA (TMO) San Antonio; KWEX-DT (getTV, UNV) San Antonio; WOAI-TV (IND, NBC) San Antonio.
Programming (via satellite): A&E; AMC; CMT; CNN; Discovery Channel; ESPN; ESPN2; Fox News Channel; FOX Sports Southwest; Freeform; Hallmark Channel; HGTV; History; HLN; Lifetime; Nickelodeon; QVC; RFD-TV; Spike TV; TBS; The Movie Channel; The Weather Channel; TLC; TNT; Turner Classic Movies; TV Land; UniMas; Univision; USA Network; VH1; WGN America.
Fee: $44.99 monthly.
Pay Service 1
Pay Units: N.A.
Programming (via satellite): Showtime.
Internet Service
Operational: No.
Telephone Service
None
Miles of Plant: 23.0 (coaxial); None (fiber optic). Homes passed: 660. Homes passed & miles of plant include La Vernia.
Chief Executive Officer: Bob Cohen.
Ownership: CommZoom Communications LLC (MSO).

COMFORT—Formerly served by Cebridge Connections. No longer in operation. ICA: TX0400.

CONROE—Suddenlink Communications, PO Box 696, Conroe, TX 77305. Phones: 314-315-9400; 903-595-4321. Web Site: http://www.suddenlink.com. Also serves Montgomery County, Panorama Village & Willis. ICA: TX0741.
TV Market Ranking: 15 (Montgomery County (portions)); Below 100 (CONROE, Panorama Village, Willis, Montgomery County (portions)). Franchise award date: N.A. Franchise expiration date: N.A. Began: September 1, 1969.
Channel capacity: N.A. Channels available but not in use: N.A.
Basic Service
Subscribers: 9,505. Commercial subscribers: 790.
Programming (received off-air): KETH-TV (TBN) Houston; KFTH-DT (getTV, UniMas) Alvin; KHOU (Bounce TV, CBS) Houston;

Cable Systems—Texas

KIAH (Antenna TV, CW) Houston; KLTJ (Daystar TV, ETV) Galveston; KPRC-TV (NBC, This TV) Houston; KPXB-TV (ION) Conroe; KRIV (FOX) Houston; KTBU (IND) Conroe; KTMD (TMO) Galveston; KTRK-TV (ABC, Live Well Network) Houston; KTXH (Buzzr, MNT, Movies!) Houston; KUBE-TV (COZI TV, MeTV) Baytown; KUHT (PBS) Houston; KXLN-DT (UNV) Rosenberg; KYAZ (Azteca America, IND) Katy; KZJL (Estrella TV) Houston; 1 FM.
Programming (via satellite): Pop; TBS; Univision.
Fee: $54.95 installation; $35.24 monthly.

Expanded Basic Service 1
Subscribers: N.A.
Programming (via satellite): A&E; AMC; Animal Planet; BET; Bravo; Cartoon Network; CMT; CNBC; CNN; Comedy Central; C-SPAN; C-SPAN 2; Discovery Channel; Disney Channel; E! HD; ESPN; ESPN2; Food Network; Fox News Channel; FOX Sports Southwest; Freeform; FX; Great American Country; HGTV; History; HLN; Lifetime; MTV; NBCSN; Nickelodeon; Spike TV; Syfy; The Weather Channel; TLC; TNT; Travel Channel; truTV; USA Network; VH1.

Digital Basic Service
Subscribers: N.A.
Programming (via satellite): A&E HD; AXS TV; Bandamax; BBC America; Bloomberg Television; Cine Mexicano; Cinelatino; CMT; CNN en Espanol; Cooking Channel; De Pelicula; De Pelicula Clasico; Destination America; Discovery Kids Channel; Disney XD; DIY Network; Enlace USA; ESPN Classic; ESPN Deportes; ESPN HD; ESPN2 HD; ESPNews; ESPNU; Food Network HD; Fox Deportes; Fox Sports 1; Fuse; FYI; Golf Channel; GSN; Hallmark Channel; HD Theater; HGTV HD; History en Espanol; History International; IFC; Investigation Discovery; LMN; MC; MTV Classic; MTV Hits; MTV2; National Geographic Channel; National Geographic Channel HD; NBC Universo; Nick Jr.; Nicktoons; Outdoor Channel; OWN: Oprah Winfrey Network; Ritmoson; Science Channel; Starz Encore (multiplexed); Sundance TV; Sur; TeenNick; Telehit; Tennis Channel; TNT HD; Toon Disney en Espanol; Tr3s; Turner Classic Movies; ULTRA HDPlex; Universal HD; VideoRola.

Digital Pay Service 1
Pay Units: N.A.
Programming (via satellite): Cinemax (multiplexed); HBO (multiplexed); HBO HD; HBO Latino; Showtime (multiplexed); Showtime HD; Starz (multiplexed); Starz HD; The Movie Channel (multiplexed).
Video-On-Demand: Yes
Pay-Per-View
iN DEMAND (delivered digitally); Fresh (delivered digitally); Playboy TV (delivered digitally).
Internet Service
Operational: Yes.
Broadband Service: Suddenlink High Speed Internet.
Fee: $49.95 installation; $29.95 monthly.
Telephone Service
Digital: Operational
Miles of Plant: 169.0 (coaxial); None (fiber optic).
Senior Vice President, Corporate Finance: Michael Pflantz. Vice President, Accounting: Sabrina Warr. General Manager: Nathan Geick.
Ownership: Cequel Communications Holdings I LLC (MSO).

CONROE WEST—Formerly served by Suddenlink Communications. No longer in operation. ICA: TX0742.

COOLIDGE—Formerly served by Northland Cable Television. No longer in operation. ICA: TX0569.

COOPER—Alliance Communications, PO Box 9090, Tyler, TX 75711. Phones: 903-561-4411; 501-679-6619 (Greenbrier, AR office); 800-842-8160. Web Site: http://www.alliancecable.net. Also serves Delta County (portions). ICA: TX0099.
TV Market Ranking: Below 100 (COOPER, Delta County (portions)). Franchise award date: N.A. Franchise expiration date: N.A. Began: April 1, 1963.
Channel capacity: N.A. Channels available but not in use: N.A.

Basic Service
Subscribers: 55.
Programming (received off-air): KDAF (Antenna TV, CW, This TV) Dallas; KDFI (Bounce TV, Buzzr, Heroes & Icons, MNT, Movies!) Dallas; KDFW (FOX) Dallas; KERA-TV (PBS) Dallas; KPXD-TV (ION) Arlington; KSTR-DT (getTV, UniMas) Irving; KTVT (CBS, Decades) Fort Worth; KTXA (IND, MeTV) Fort Worth; KTXD-TV (IND) Greenville; KUVN-DT (UNV) Garland; KXAS-TV (COZI TV, NBC) Fort Worth; KXTX-TV (TMO) Dallas; WFAA (ABC) Dallas; allband FM.
Programming (via satellite): C-SPAN; C-SPAN 2; QVC; Trinity Broadcasting Network (TBN); WGN America.
Fee: $22.45 monthly; $2.00 converter.

Expanded Basic Service 1
Subscribers: N.A.
Programming (via satellite): A&E; AMC; Animal Planet; BET; CMT; CNBC; CNN; Comedy Central; Discovery Channel; Disney Channel; E! HD; ESPN; ESPN2; Food Network; Fox News Channel; FOX Sports Southwest; Freeform; FX; Golf Channel; Hallmark Channel; History; HLN; Lifetime; MSNBC; MTV; NBCSN; Nickelodeon; Spike TV; TBS; The Weather Channel; TLC; TNT; truTV; Turner Classic Movies; TV Land; USA Network; VH1.
Fee: $13.51 installation; $28.25 monthly.

Digital Basic Service
Subscribers: N.A.
Programming (via satellite): BBC America; Bravo; Cartoon Network; CMT; Destination America; Discovery Kids Channel; Discovery Life Channel; Disney XD; ESPN Classic; ESPNews; Fox Sports 1; FYI; GSN; HGTV; History International; IFC; Investigation Discovery; LMN; MC; MTV Classic; MTV Jams; MTV2; National Geographic Channel; Nick 2; Nick Jr.; Outdoor Channel; OWN: Oprah Winfrey Network; Science Channel; Starz Encore (multiplexed); Syfy; TeenNick; Travel Channel; WE tv.

Digital Pay Service 1
Pay Units: N.A.
Programming (via satellite): Cinemax (multiplexed); HBO (multiplexed); Showtime (multiplexed); Starz (multiplexed); The Movie Channel (multiplexed).
Video-On-Demand: No
Pay-Per-View
iN DEMAND (delivered digitally); Playboy TV (delivered digitally); Fresh (delivered digitally); ESPN (delivered digitally).
Internet Service
Operational: No.
Broadband Service: In-house.
Telephone Service
None
Miles of Plant: 18.0 (coaxial); 5.0 (fiber optic). Homes passed: 1,542.
Chief Financial Officer: David Starrett. Vice President & General Manager: John Brinker.

Vice President, Programming: Julie Newman.
Ownership: Buford Media Group LLC (MSO).

CORPUS CHRISTI—Grande Communications, 6441 Saratoga Blvd, Corpus Christi, TX 78414. Phones: 512-878-4010; 512-878-4000; 361-334-4600 (Customer service). Web Site: http://mygrande.com. ICA: TX0979.
Note: This system is an overbuild.
TV Market Ranking: Below 100 (CORPUS CHRISTI). Franchise award date: November 10, 1999. Franchise expiration date: N.A. Began: July 1, 2000.
Channel capacity: N.A. Channels available but not in use: N.A.

Basic Service
Subscribers: 17,833.
Programming (received off-air): KCBO-LP (IND) Corpus Christi; KCRP-CD (UniMas) Corpus Christi; KDFW (FOX) Dallas; KEDT (PBS) Corpus Christi; KIII (ABC, MeTV) Corpus Christi; KORO (LATV, UNV) Corpus Christi; KRIS-TV (CW, Grit, NBC) Corpus Christi; KTMV-LP (IND) Corpus Christi; KTOV-LP Corpus Christi; KXPX-LP (MundoMax) Corpus Christi; KZTV (CBS) Corpus Christi.
Programming (via satellite): Azteca; C-SPAN 2; LWS Local Weather Station; Pop; QVC; Telemundo; WGN America.
Fee: $27.49 monthly.

Expanded Basic Service 1
Subscribers: N.A.
Programming (via satellite): A&E; AMC; Animal Planet; BET; Bravo; Cartoon Network; CMT; CNBC; CNN; Comedy Central; C-SPAN; Discovery Channel; Disney Channel; Disney XD; E! HD; ESPN; ESPN Classic; ESPN2; EWTN Global Catholic Network; Food Network; Fox Deportes; Fox News Channel; Fox Sports 1; FOX Sports Southwest; Freeform; FX; Golf Channel; Great American Country; GSN; Hallmark Channel; HGTV; History; HLN; Lifetime; MSNBC; MTV; National Geographic Channel; NBC Universo; NBCSN; Nickelodeon; OWN: Oprah Winfrey Network; Oxygen; Spike TV; Syfy; TBS; The Weather Channel; TLC; TNT; Travel Channel; Trinity Broadcasting Network (TBN); truTV; Turner Classic Movies; TV Land; Univision; USA Network; VH1.
Fee: $29.00 monthly.

Digital Basic Service
Subscribers: N.A.
Programming (via satellite): BBC America; Boomerang; CBS Sports Network; Colours; Cooking Channel; Discovery Life Channel; DIY Network; ESPN; ESPNews; FamilyNet; FOX College Sports Central; FOX College Sports Pacific; Fox Sports 2; Fuse; FXM; FYI; GolTV; HD Theater; History International; HITS (Headend In The Sky); LMN; MC; NBA TV; NFL Network; Nick 2; Nick Jr.; Nicktoons; Radar Channel; TeenNick; Tennis Channel; TNT; TVG Network; Univision Studios.
Fee: $14.00 monthly.

Digital Pay Service 1
Pay Units: N.A.
Programming (via satellite): Cinemax (multiplexed); Cinemax HD; Flix (multiplexed); HBO (multiplexed); HBO HD; Showtime (multiplexed); Showtime HD; Starz (multiplexed); Starz Encore (multiplexed); Sundance TV (multiplexed); The Movie Channel (multiplexed).
Fee: $12.99 monthly (Cinemax, HBO, Starz/Encore or Showtime/FlixSundance/TMC).
Video-On-Demand: No

Pay-Per-View
Playboy TV (delivered digitally); Fresh (delivered digitally); ESPN Now (delivered digitally); Hot Choice (delivered digitally); iN DEMAND (delivered digitally); Pleasure (delivered digitally); Shorteez (delivered digitally); Sports PPV (delivered digitally).

Internet Service
Operational: Yes.
Subscribers: 20,808.
Fee: $34.99-$64.99 monthly.

Telephone Service
Digital: Operational
Subscribers: 10,730.
Fee: $19.99 monthly
Miles of Plant: 1,540.0 (coaxial); 243.0 (fiber optic). Homes passed: 71,948.
Vice President, Customer Care: Dawn Blydenburgh. Vice President, Marketing: Pete Drozdoff. Vice President, Network Operations & Engineering: Lamar Horton. Vice President, Technical Operations: Shane Schilling. General Manager: Matt Rohre.
Ownership: Grande Communications Networks Inc. (MSO).

CORPUS CHRISTI—Time Warner Cable, 4060 South Padre Island Dr, Corpus Christi, TX 78411-4402. Phones: 972-899-7300 (Flower Mound office); 361-698-6259. Fax: 361-857-5038. Web Site: http://www.timewarnercable.com. Also serves Alice, Aqua Dulce, Banquete, Bee County (portions), Beevilla, Ben Bolt, Benavides, Bishop, Brooks County (portions), Corpus Christi Naval Air Station, Driscoll, Duval County (portions), Falfurrias, Jim Wells County (portions), Lake City, Lakeside, Mathis, Nueces County, Odem, Orange Grove, Premont, Refugio, Robstown, San Diego (Duval County), San Diego (Jim Wells County), San Patricio, San Patricio County, Skidmore, Tynan & Woodsboro. ICA: TX0010.
TV Market Ranking: Below 100 (Banquete, Bishop, CORPUS CHRISTI, Corpus Christi Naval Air Station, Driscoll, Nueces County, Odem, Robstown, San Patricio County, Orange Grove); Outside TV Markets (Aqua Dulce, Bee County (portions), Ben Bolt, Benavides, Brooks County (portions), Duval County (portions), Falfurrias, Jim Wells County (portions), Jim Wells County (portions), Lake City, Premont, Refugio, San Diego (Duval County), San Patricio, Skidmore, Tynan, Woodsboro, Alice, Beeville, Mathis). Franchise award date: N.A. Fran-

2017 Edition

D-731

Texas—Cable Systems

chise expiration date: N.A. Began: February 1, 1972.
Channel capacity: 80 (operating 2-way). Channels available but not in use: N.A.
Basic Service
Subscribers: 53,170.
Programming (received off-air): KDFW (FOX) Dallas; KEDT (PBS) Corpus Christi; KIII (ABC, MeTV) Corpus Christi; KORO (LATV, UNV) Corpus Christi; KRIS-TV (CW, Grit, NBC) Corpus Christi; KTMV-LP (IND) Corpus Christi; KTOV-LP Corpus Christi; KZTV (CBS) Corpus Christi; 14 FMs.
Programming (via satellite): Discovery Channel; Weatherscan; WGN America.
Fee: $39.99 installation; $28.00 monthly.
Expanded Basic Service 1
Subscribers: N.A.
Programming (via satellite): A&E; AMC; Animal Planet; BET; Bravo; Cartoon Network; CMT; CNBC; CNN; Comedy Central; C-SPAN; C-SPAN 2; Disney Channel; E! HD; ESPN; ESPN Classic; ESPN2; ESPNews; EWTN Global Catholic Network; Food Network; Fox News Channel; Fox Sports 1; FOX Sports Southwest; Freeform; FX; Golf Channel; Great American Country; Hallmark Channel; HGTV; History; HLN; Lifetime; LMN; MSNBC; MTV; National Geographic Channel; NBC Universo; NBCSN; Nickelodeon; Oxygen; QVC; Spike TV; Syfy; TBS; The Weather Channel; TLC; TNT; Travel Channel; truTV; Turner Classic Movies; TV Land; Univision; USA Network; VH1; WE tv.
Fee: $28.60 monthly.
Digital Basic Service
Subscribers: N.A.
Programming (via satellite): AXS TV; BBC America; Bloomberg Television; Cooking Channel; Discovery Digital Networks; Disney XD; DIY Network; ESPN HD; FamilyNet; Fuse; FYI; GSN; HD Theater; History International; HITS (Headend In The Sky); IFC; MC; MLB Network; NBA League Pass; NBA TV; NHL Center Ice; Nick 2; Nick Jr.; Nicktoons; Ovation; TeenNick; TNT HD; Trinity Broadcasting Network (TBN).
Fee: $8.04 monthly.
Digital Expanded Basic Service
Subscribers: N.A.
Programming (via satellite): FOX College Sports Central; FOX College Sports Pacific; Fox Sports 2; Outdoor Channel; Tennis Channel.
Fee: $8.95 monthly.
Digital Expanded Basic Service 2
Subscribers: N.A.
Programming (via satellite): FXM; Starz Encore; Sundance TV.
Fee: $8.95 monthly.
Digital Pay Service 1
Pay Units: N.A.
Programming (via satellite): Cinemax (multiplexed); Flix; HBO (multiplexed); HBO HD; Showtime (multiplexed); Showtime HD; Starz (multiplexed); Starz Encore (multiplexed); The Movie Channel (multiplexed).
Fee: $14.99 monthly (each).
Video-On-Demand: Yes
Pay-Per-View
iN DEMAND; Hot Choice (delivered digitally); Fresh (delivered digitally); Shorteez (delivered digitally); Playboy TV (delivered digitally); Spice Live (delivered digitally).
Internet Service
Operational: Yes.
Subscribers: 53,988.
Broadband Service: Road Runner.
Fee: $44.99 installation; $44.95 monthly.
Telephone Service
Digital: Operational
Subscribers: 21,631.

Fee: $44.95 monthly.
Miles of Plant: 4,144.0 (coaxial); 661.0 (fiber optic). Homes passed: 210,913.
President: Connie Wharton. Vice President & General Manager: Mike McKee. Engineering Director: Charlotte Strong. Public Affairs Manager: Vicki Triplett.
Ownership: Time Warner Cable (MSO).; Advance/Newhouse Partnership (MSO).

CORRIGAN—Telecom Cable, 1321 Louetta Rd, Ste 1020, Cypress, TX 77429. Phone: 888-240-4589. E-mail: information@telecomcable.net. Web Site: http://telecomcable.net. ICA: TX1039.
TV Market Ranking: Below 100 (CORRIGAN).
Channel capacity: N.A. Channels available but not in use: N.A.
Basic Service
Subscribers: 64.
Fee: $5.86 monthly.
Manager: Anthony Luna.
Ownership: Telecom Cable LLC (MSO).

CORSICANA—Northland Cable Television, 1500 North Beaton St, Corsicana, TX 75110. Phones: 903-872-3131; 800-872-3905. Fax: 903-872-6623. E-mail: corsicana@northlandcabletv.com. Web Site: http://www.yournorthland.com. Also serves Navarro County (portions). ICA: TX0082.
TV Market Ranking: Outside TV Markets (CORSICANA, Navarro County (portions)).
Franchise award date: N.A. Franchise expiration date: N.A. Began: May 1, 1971.
Channel capacity: 58 (operating 2-way). Channels available but not in use: N.A.
Basic Service
Subscribers: 1,545.
Programming (received off-air): KDAF (Antenna TV, CW, This TV) Dallas; KDFI (Bounce TV, Buzzr, Heroes & Icons, MNT, Movies!) Dallas; KDFW (FOX) Dallas; KDTN (Daystar TV, ETV) Denton; KERA-TV (PBS) Dallas; KETK-TV (Estrella TV, NBC) Jacksonville; KFWD (MundoMax) Fort Worth; KSTR-DT (getTV, UniMas) Irving; KTVT (CBS, Decades) Fort Worth; KTXA (IND, MeTV) Fort Worth; KWTX-TV (CBS, CW) Waco; KXAS-TV (COZI TV, NBC) Fort Worth; KXTX-TV (TMO) Dallas; KXXV (ABC, TMO) Waco; WFAA (ABC) Dallas; 16 FMs.
Programming (via satellite): A&E; Animal Planet; BET; Cartoon Network; CNBC; CNN; C-SPAN; Discovery Channel; ESPN; ESPN2; Fox News Channel; FOX Sports Southwest; Great American Country; Hallmark Channel; HGTV; HLN; National Geographic Channel; Pop; QVC; Spike TV; Starz; TBS; The Weather Channel; TLC; TNT; Travel Channel; Trinity Broadcasting Network (TBN); Univision; Univision Studios; USA Network; WGN America.
Fee: $60.00 installation; $47.64 monthly.
Expanded Basic Service 1
Subscribers: N.A.
Programming (via satellite): Comedy Central; E! HD; Food Network; Freeform; FX; Golf Channel; History; Lifetime; MTV; Nickelodeon; Outdoor Channel; QVC; Syfy; Telemundo; Trinity Broadcasting Network (TBN); Turner Classic Movies; VH1.
Fee: $42.29 monthly.
Digital Basic Service
Subscribers: N.A.
Programming (via satellite): BBC America; Bloomberg Television; Discovery Digital Networks; DMX Music; Fox Sports 1.
Fee: $51.99 monthly.

Digital Expanded Basic Service
Subscribers: N.A.
Programming (via satellite): Bravo; Discovery Life Channel; GSN; HITS (Headend In The Sky); IFC; NBCSN; WE tv.
Pay Service 1
Pay Units: N.A.
Programming (via satellite): HBO.
Fee: $10.00 installation.
Digital Pay Service 1
Pay Units: N.A.
Programming (via satellite): Cinemax (multiplexed); Flix; HBO (multiplexed); Showtime (multiplexed); Starz (multiplexed); Starz Encore (multiplexed); The Movie Channel (multiplexed).
Fee: $14.75 monthly (each).
Video-On-Demand: No
Internet Service
Operational: Yes.
Broadband Service: Northland Express.
Fee: $42.99 monthly.
Telephone Service
Digital: Operational
Miles of Plant: 130.0 (coaxial); None (fiber optic). Homes passed: 8,977.
Executive Vice President: Richard I. Clark. Regional Manager: Richard Gammon. Plant Manager: Terry Granger. Chief Technician: Bobby Brady. Office Manager: Diane Ball.
Ownership: Northland Communications Corp.

COTULLA—Time Warner Cable. Now served by DILLEY (formerly Pearsall), TX [TX0196]. ICA: TX0266.

COUNTRY CLUB SHORES—Formerly served by CableSouth Inc. No longer in operation. ICA: TX0743.

COUNTRY HAVEN—Formerly served by Cebridge Connections. No longer in operation. ICA: TX0961.

CRANDALL—Formerly served by Almega Cable. No longer in operation. ICA: TX0554.

CRANE—Suddenlink Communications, 520 Maryville Centre Dr, Ste 300, St. Louis, MO 63141. Phones: 877-423-2743; 314-315-9400. Web Site: http://www.suddenlink.com. Also serves Crane County (portions). ICA: TX0228.
TV Market Ranking: Below 100 (CRANE, Crane County (portions)). Franchise award date: April 30, 1987. Franchise expiration date: N.A. Began: April 1, 1978.
Channel capacity: N.A. Channels available but not in use: N.A.
Basic Service
Subscribers: 194.
Programming (received off-air): KMID (ABC) Midland; KMLM-DT (GLC) Odessa; KOSA-TV (CBS, MNT) Odessa; KPBT-TV (PBS) Odessa; KPEJ-TV (FOX) Odessa; KWES-TV (CW, NBC, TMO) Odessa; allband FM.
Programming (via satellite): A&E; CMT; CNN; C-SPAN; Discovery Channel; Disney Channel; ESPN; FOX Sports Southwest; Freeform; HLN; Lifetime; Nickelodeon; QVC; Spike TV; TBS; The Weather Channel; TLC; TNT; TV Land; Univision; USA Network; WGN America.
Fee: $28.45 monthly.
Pay Service 1
Pay Units: N.A.
Programming (via satellite): HBO; Showtime; The Movie Channel.
Fee: $7.95 monthly (TMC), $9.95 monthly (Showtime), $10.95 monthly (HBO).

Internet Service
Operational: Yes. Began: May 19, 2003.
Broadband Service: Suddenlink High Speed Internet.
Fee: $45.95 installation; $29.95 monthly.
Telephone Service
None
Miles of Plant: 28.0 (coaxial); None (fiber optic). Homes passed: 1,974.
Senior Vice President, Corporate Finance: Michael Pflantz. Regional Manager: Todd Cruthird. Regional Marketing Manager: Beverly Gambell. Plant Manager: Manuel Gonzales.
Ownership: Cequel Communications Holdings I LLC (MSO).

CRANFILLS GAP—Formerly served by National Cable Inc. No longer in operation. ICA: TX0904.

CRAWFORD—Zito Media, 102 S Main St, PO Box 665, Coudersport, PA 16915. Phones: 814-260-9055; 800-365-6988. E-mail: info@zitomedia.com. Web Site: http://www.zitomedia.com. ICA: TX0584.
TV Market Ranking: Below 100 (CRAWFORD). Franchise award date: N.A. Franchise expiration date: N.A. Began: January 1, 1984.
Channel capacity: N.A. Channels available but not in use: N.A.
Basic Service
Subscribers: 16.
Programming (received off-air): KCEN-TV (Antenna TV, MeTV, MundoMax, NBC) Temple; KNCT (PBS) Belton; KTVT (CBS, Decades) Fort Worth; KWKT-TV (Estrella TV, FOX, MNT) Waco; KWTX-TV (CBS, CW) Waco; KXXV (ABC, TMO) Waco; WFAA (ABC) Dallas.
Programming (via satellite): A&E; AMC; Animal Planet; Cartoon Network; CNN; Discovery Channel; Disney Channel; ESPN; ESPN2; Fox News Channel; Freeform; Fuse; Great American Country; HGTV; HLN; INSP; Lifetime; Outdoor Channel; QVC; TBS; TLC; TNT; USA Network; WGN America.
Fee: $49.95 installation; $45.85 monthly.
Pay Service 1
Pay Units: N.A.
Programming (via satellite): Cinemax; HBO; Showtime.
Fee: $12.00 monthly (each).
Internet Service
Operational: No.
Telephone Service
None
Miles of Plant: 8.0 (coaxial); None (fiber optic). Homes passed: 261.
President: James Rigas.
Ownership: Zito Media (MSO).

CROCKETT—Northland Cable Television, 1202 East Houston Ave, PO Box 1228, Crockett, TX 75835-1228. Phones: 888-667-8452; 800-615-1110; 936-544-2031. Fax: 409-544-9660. Web Site: http://www.yournorthland.com. Also serves Houston County (portions). ICA: TX0159.
TV Market Ranking: Outside TV Markets (CROCKETT, Houston County (portions)). Franchise award date: N.A. Franchise expiration date: N.A. Began: August 1, 1963.
Channel capacity: N.A. Channels available but not in use: N.A.
Basic Service
Subscribers: 562.
Programming (received off-air): KBTX-TV (CBS, CW) Bryan; KETK-TV (Estrella TV, NBC) Jacksonville; KFXL-LD Lufkin; KTRE

Cable Systems—Texas

(ABC, TMO) Lufkin; KYTX (CBS, COZI TV, CW) Nacogdoches; 5 FMs.
Programming (via microwave): KHOU (Bounce TV, CBS) Houston; KIAH (Antenna TV, CW) Houston; KRIV (FOX) Houston; KTRK-TV (ABC, Live Well Network) Houston; KUHT (PBS) Houston.
Programming (via satellite): A&E; BET; Cartoon Network; CNBC; CNN; C-SPAN; Discovery Channel; ESPN; Fox News Channel; FOX Sports Southwest; Great American Country; Hallmark Channel; HGTV; HLN; Outdoor Channel; Pop; QVC; TBS; Telemundo; The Weather Channel; TLC; TNT; Travel Channel; Trinity Broadcasting Network (TBN); Univision Studios; USA Network; WGN America.
Fee: $75.00 installation; $47.64 monthly.

Expanded Basic Service 1
Subscribers: N.A.
Programming (via satellite): Animal Planet; E! HD; ESPN2; Food Network; FXM; History; Lifetime; Nickelodeon; Spike TV; Syfy; Turner Classic Movies.
Fee: $49.99 monthly.

Digital Basic Service
Subscribers: N.A.
Programming (via satellite): Bloomberg Television; Bravo; Discovery Life Channel; DMX Music; Fox Sports 1; Golf Channel; GSN; IFC; WE tv.
Fee: $54.99 monthly.

Pay Service 1
Pay Units: 200.
Programming (via satellite): HBO.
Fee: $14.00 monthly.

Digital Pay Service 1
Pay Units: 25.
Programming (via satellite): Cinemax (multiplexed).
Fee: $14.75 monthly.

Digital Pay Service 2
Pay Units: N.A.
Programming (via satellite): HBO (multiplexed).
Fee: $14.75 monthly.

Digital Pay Service 3
Pay Units: 30.
Programming (via satellite): Showtime (multiplexed); The Movie Channel (multiplexed).
Fee: $14.75 monthly.

Digital Pay Service 4
Pay Units: 100.
Programming (via satellite): Starz (multiplexed); Starz Encore (multiplexed).
Fee: $14.75 monthly.

Video-On-Demand: No

Pay-Per-View
Sports PPV (delivered digitally); iN DEMAND (delivered digitally).

Internet Service
Operational: Yes.
Fee: $42.99 monthly.

Telephone Service
Digital: Operational
Miles of Plant: 69.0 (coaxial); None (fiber optic). Homes passed: 3,541.
Executive Vice President: Richard I. Clark. Regional Manager: Brent Richey. Office Manager: Linda Richie. Chief Technician: John Guys.
Ownership: Northland Communications Corp. (MSO).

CROSBYTON—Reach Broadband, PO Box 507, Arp, TX 75750. Phones: 903-859-3789; 800-687-1258. Web Site: http://www.reachbroadband.net. ICA: TX0384.
TV Market Ranking: Below 100 (CROSBYTON). Franchise award date: October 1, 1978. Franchise expiration date: N.A. Began: October 1, 1978.
Channel capacity: 61 (not 2-way capable). Channels available but not in use: N.A.

Basic Service
Subscribers: 58.
Programming (received off-air): KAMC (ABC, Bounce TV) Lubbock; KBZO-LD (UNV) Lubbock; KJTV-TV (FOX) Lubbock; KLBK-TV (CBS) Lubbock; KLCW-TV (CW) Wolfforth; KRPV-DT (GLC) Roswell; KTTZ-TV (PBS) Lubbock; allband FM.
Programming (via satellite): AMC; Animal Planet; Cartoon Network; CNN; Discovery Channel; Disney Channel; E! HD; ESPN; ESPN2; Fox News Channel; FOX Sports Southwest; Freeform; FX; Great American Country; HGTV; History; HLN; Lifetime; National Geographic Channel; Nickelodeon; QVC; Spike TV; TBS; The Weather Channel; TLC; TNT; Trinity Broadcasting Network (TBN); TV Land; USA Network; VH1.
Fee: $49.95 installation; $27.43 monthly.

Pay Service 1
Pay Units: N.A.
Programming (via satellite): Cinemax; HBO.
Fee: $9.95 monthly (each).

Video-On-Demand: No

Internet Service
Operational: Yes.

Telephone Service
None
Miles of Plant: 12.0 (coaxial); None (fiber optic). Homes passed: 869.
Regional Manager: Ronnie Stafford. Office Manager: Jan Gibson. Controller: Jeffrey Lowe.
Ownership: RB3 LLC (MSO).

CROWELL—Formerly served by Alliance Communications. No longer in operation. ICA: TX0509.

CRYSTAL BEACH—Formerly served by Rapid Cable. No longer in operation. ICA: TX0132.

CRYSTAL CITY—Time Warner Cable, 1313 West Carlton Rd, Laredo, TX 78041. Phones: 956-721-0600; 972-899-7300 (Flower Mound office); 956-721-0607. Fax: 956-721-0612. Web Site: http://www.timewarnercable.com. Also serves Asherton, Carrizo Springs, Dimmit County (portions) & Zavala County (portions). ICA: TX0147.
TV Market Ranking: Below 100 (Dimmit County (portions), Zavala County (portions)); Outside TV Markets (Asherton, Carrizo Springs, CRYSTAL CITY, Dimmit County (portions), Zavala County (portions)). Franchise award date: N.A. Franchise expiration date: N.A. Began: September 1, 1968.
Channel capacity: N.A. Channels available but not in use: N.A.

Basic Service
Subscribers: 1,155.
Programming (received off-air): KABB (FOX, The Country Network) San Antonio; KGNS-TV (ABC, CW, NBC, TMO) Laredo; KPXL-TV (ION) Uvalde; allband FM.
Programming (via microwave): KENS (CBS, Estrella TV) San Antonio; KLRN (PBS) San Antonio; KSAT-TV (ABC, MeTV) San Antonio; KWEX-DT (getTV, UNV) San Antonio; WOAI-TV (IND, NBC) San Antonio.
Programming (via satellite): AMC; Animal Planet; BET; Bravo; Cartoon Network; CNN; Comedy Central; C-SPAN; C-SPAN 2; Discovery Channel; Disney Channel; E! HD; ESPN; ESPN Classic; ESPN2; EVINE Live; EWTN Global Catholic Network; Food Network; Fox Deportes; Fox News Channel; FOX Sports Southwest; FX; Golf Channel; Great American Country; Hallmark Channel; HGTV; History; HLN; Lifetime; MoviePlex; MSNBC; MTV; National Geographic Channel; NBC Universo; Nickelodeon; OWN: Oprah Winfrey Network; Oxygen; Pop; QVC; Spike TV; Syfy; TBS; Telemundo; The Weather Channel; TNT; Travel Channel; Trinity Broadcasting Network (TBN); truTV; Turner Classic Movies; TV Land; Univision; USA Network; VH1; WE tv.
Fee: $39.99 installation; $56.00 monthly; $2.00 converter.

Digital Basic Service
Subscribers: N.A.
Programming (via satellite): BBC America; Bloomberg Television; Discovery Digital Networks; Disney XD; ESPN Classic; ESPNews; FOX College Sports Central; FOX College Sports Pacific; Fox Sports 1; Fuse; FXM; FYI; GSN; History International; IFC; LMN; MC; NBA TV; NBCSN; Nick Jr.; Nicktoons; Outdoor Channel; Starz Encore; Sundance TV (multiplexed); TeenNick; Tennis Channel.
Fee: $7.00 monthy (value tier), $8.95 monthly (each additional tier).

Digital Pay Service 1
Pay Units: 173.
Programming (via satellite): Cinemax (multiplexed); HBO (multiplexed); Showtime (multiplexed); Starz (multiplexed); The Movie Channel.
Fee: $14.99 monthly (each).

Video-On-Demand: No

Pay-Per-View
iN DEMAND (delivered digitally); Fresh (delivered digitally); Shorteez (delivered digitally); Playboy TV (delivered digitally); MLB Extra Innings (delivered digitally); NHL Center Ice (delivered digitally); NBA League Pass (delivered digitally).

Internet Service
Operational: Yes.

Telephone Service
Digital: Operational
Miles of Plant: 163.0 (coaxial); 36.0 (fiber optic). Homes passed: 7,037.
President: Connie Wharton. Vice President & General Manager: Michael Carrosquiola. Operations Director: Marco Reyes. Public Affairs Manager: Celinda Gonzalez. Technical Operations Manager: Eduardo Ruiz.
Ownership: Time Warner Cable (MSO).; Advance/Newhouse Partnership (MSO).

CUERO—Time Warner Cable. Now served by GONZALES, TX [TX0209]. ICA: TX0202.

CUMBY—Formerly served by Cebridge Connections. No longer in operation. ICA: TX0567.

CUSHING—Formerly served by Almega Cable. No longer in operation. ICA: TX0604.

CUT AND SHOOT—Formerly served by Northland Cable Television. No longer in operation. ICA: TX0746.

FULLY SEARCHABLE • CONTINUOUSLY UPDATED • DISCOUNT RATES FOR PRINT PURCHASERS
For more information call **800-771-9202** or visit **www.warren-news.com**

CYPRESS—Formerly served by Almega Cable. No longer in operation. ICA: TX0284.

DAINGERFIELD—Suddenlink Communications, 520 Maryville Centre Dr, Ste 300, St. Louis, MO 63141. Phones: 800-999-6845; 314-315-9400. Web Site: http://www.suddenlink.com. Also serves Cason, Cass County (portions), Hughes Springs, Lone Star & Morris County. ICA: TX0152.
TV Market Ranking: Below 100 (Cass County (portions), Hughes Springs, Lone Star, Morris County (portions)); Outside TV Markets (Cason, DAINGERFIELD, Morris County (portions)). Franchise award date: N.A. Franchise expiration date: N.A. Began: July 31, 1979.
Channel capacity: 62 (operating 2-way). Channels available but not in use: N.A.

Basic Service
Subscribers: 933.
Programming (received off-air): KLTS-TV (PBS) Shreveport; KLTV (ABC, Bounce TV, TMO) Tyler; KMSS-TV (FOX) Shreveport; KSHV-TV (MNT) Shreveport; KSLA (Bounce TV, CBS, Grit, This TV) Shreveport; KTAL-TV (NBC) Texarkana; KTBS-TV (ABC) Shreveport.
Programming (via satellite): QVC; The Weather Channel.
Fee: $28.45 monthly; $1.50 converter.

Expanded Basic Service 1
Subscribers: N.A.
Programming (via satellite): A&E; AMC; Animal Planet; BET; Cartoon Network; CNBC; CNN; Comedy Central; Discovery Channel; Disney Channel; E! HD; ESPN; ESPN2; Food Network; Fox News Channel; FOX Sports Southwest; Freeform; FX; Great American Country; Hallmark Channel; HGTV; History; HLN; Lifetime; MSNBC; MTV; National Geographic Channel; Nickelodeon; Spike TV; Syfy; TBS; TLC; TNT; Trinity Broadcasting Network (TBN); truTV; Turner Classic Movies; TV Land; USA Network; VH1.
Fee: $25.00 monthly.

Digital Basic Service
Subscribers: N.A.
Programming (via satellite): BBC America; Bloomberg Television; Cloo; Discovery Digital Networks; Disney XD; DMX Music; ESPN Classic; ESPNews; Fox Sports 1; Fuse; FYI; Golf Channel; GSN; History; History International; IFC; NBCSN; Outdoor Channel; WE tv.
Fee: $3.99 monthly.

Pay Service 1
Pay Units: N.A.
Programming (via satellite): Cinemax; HBO; Showtime; The Movie Channel.
Fee: $7.95 monthly (Cinemax), $10.95 monthly (HBO), $12.95 monthly (Showtime or TMC).

Digital Pay Service 1
Pay Units: N.A.
Programming (via satellite): Cinemax (multiplexed); HBO (multiplexed); Showtime (multiplexed); Starz (multiplexed); Starz Encore (multiplexed); The Movie Channel (multiplexed).

2017 Edition   D-733

Texas—Cable Systems

CABLE & TV STATION COVERAGE
Atlas 2017
The perfect companion to the Television & Cable Factbook
To order call 800-771-9202 or visit www.warren-news.com

Pay-Per-View
iN DEMAND (delivered digitally); Fresh (delivered digitally); Playboy TV (delivered digitally).

Internet Service
Operational: Yes. Began: August 1, 2003.
Broadband Service: Suddenlink High Speed Internet.
Fee: $49.95 installation; $29.95 monthly.

Telephone Service
Digital: Operational
Fee: $44.95 monthly
Miles of Plant: 110.0 (coaxial); None (fiber optic). Homes passed: 3,929.
Vice President, Corporate Finance: Michael Pflantz. General Manager: Mike Burns.
Ownership: Cequel Communications Holdings I LLC (MSO).

DALHART—Vyve Broadband, 4 International Dr, Ste 330, Rye Brook, NY 10573. Phones: 800-937-1397; 806-249-4820 (Customer service); 405-275-6923. Web Site: http://vyvebroadband.com. Also serves Dallam County. ICA: TX0182.
TV Market Ranking: Outside TV Markets (DALHART, Dallam County). Franchise award date: N.A. Franchise expiration date: N.A. Began: August 1, 1962.
Channel capacity: 46 (not 2-way capable). Channels available but not in use: N.A.

Basic Service
Subscribers: 165. Commercial subscribers: 14.
Programming (received off-air): KACV-TV (PBS) Amarillo; KAMR-TV (IND, NBC) Amarillo; KCIT (FOX, This TV) Amarillo; KFDA-TV (CBS, TMO) Amarillo; KPTF-DT (GLC) Farwell; KVII-TV (ABC, CW) Amarillo; 6 FMs.
Programming (via satellite): C-SPAN; C-SPAN 2; CW PLUS; Pop; QVC; Telemundo; The Weather Channel; UniMas; Univision Studios; WGN America.
Fee: $64.95 installation; $25.00 monthly.

Expanded Basic Service 1
Subscribers: N.A.
Programming (via satellite): A&E; AMC; Animal Planet; Bravo; CMT; CNBC; CNN; Comedy Central; Discovery Channel; Disney Channel; ESPN; ESPN2; Food Network; Fox News Channel; FOX Sports Southwest; Freeform; FX; FXM; Hallmark Channel; HGTV; HLN; INSP; Lifetime; MTV; NFL Network; Nickelodeon; RFD-TV; Spike TV; Syfy; TBS; TLC; TNT; Travel Channel; TV Land; USA Network; VH1.
Fee: $32.76 monthly.

Digital Basic Service
Subscribers: N.A.
Programming (via satellite): BBC America; Bloomberg Television; Bravo; Cine Mexicano; Cinelatino; Cloo; CMT; CNN en Espanol; Destination America; Discovery Kids Channel; Discovery Life Channel; Disney XD; DMX Music; ESPN Classic; ESPN Deportes; ESPN2; ESPNews; EVINE Live; Flix; FOX College Sports Central; FOX College Sports Pacific; Fox Deportes; Fox Sports 1; Fuse; FXM; FYI; Golf Channel; Great American Country; GSN; HGTV; History; History en Espanol; History International; IFC; Investigation Discovery; LMN; MTV Classic; MTV Hits; MTV2; National Geographic Channel; NBC Universo; NBCSN; Nick Jr.; Nicktoons; Outdoor Channel; OWN: Oprah Winfrey Network; Science Channel; Starz Encore (multiplexed); Sundance TV; Syfy; TeenNick; The Word Network; Tr3s; Trinity Broadcasting Network (TBN); Turner Classic Movies; UP; VH1 Soul; ViendoMovies; WE tv.

Pay Service 1
Pay Units: N.A.
Programming (via satellite): HBO.

Digital Pay Service 1
Pay Units: N.A.
Programming (via satellite): Cinemax (multiplexed); HBO (multiplexed); Showtime (multiplexed); Starz (multiplexed); The Movie Channel (multiplexed).

Video-On-Demand: No

Pay-Per-View
iN DEMAND (delivered digitally); Hot Choice (delivered digitally); Playboy TV (delivered digitally); Fresh (delivered digitally); Spice: Xcess (delivered digitally); Club Jenna (delivered digitally).

Internet Service
Operational: Yes.

Telephone Service
Digital: Operational
Miles of Plant: 60.0 (coaxial); None (fiber optic). Homes passed: 2,898.
Chief Executive Officer: Bill Haggarty. Regional Vice President: Andrew Dearth. Vice President, Marketing: Tracy Bass. Senior Vice President, Financial Planning: Daniel White.
Ownership: Vyve Broadband LLC (MSO).

DALHART—XIT Communications. Formerly [TX1023]. This cable system has converted to IPTV, 12324 US Hwy 87, PO Box 71, Dalhart, TX 79022. Phones: 806-244-3355; 800-232-3312; 806-384-3311. Fax: 806-384-3311. E-mail: xitcom@xit.net. Web Site: http://www.xit.net. Also serves Boys Ranch, Channing, Hartley, Stratford & Texline. ICA: TX5049.
TV Market Ranking: Outside TV Markets (DALHART).
Channel capacity: N.A. Channels available but not in use: N.A.

Limited Basic
Subscribers: 1,449.
Programming (received off-air): KACV-TV (PBS) Amarillo; KAMR-TV (IND, NBC) Amarillo; KCIT (FOX, This TV) Amarillo; KFDA-TV (CBS, TMO) Amarillo; KVII-TV (ABC, CW) Amarillo.
Programming (via satellite): C-SPAN; C-SPAN 2; EWTN Global Catholic Network; INSP; ION Television; QVC; The Weather Channel; Trinity Broadcasting Network (TBN); WGN America; WPIX (Antenna TV, CW, This TV) New York.
Fee: $65.00 installation; $23.75 monthly.

Xpanded Pak
Subscribers: N.A.
Programming (via satellite): A&E; AMC; Animal Planet; BBC America; BET; Cartoon Network; CMT; CNBC; CNN; Comedy Central; Cooking Channel; Destination America; Discovery Channel; Discovery Kids Channel; Disney Channel; Disney XD; DIY Network; E! HD; ESPN; ESPN Classic; ESPN2; Food Network; Fox Deportes; Fox News Channel; Fox Sports 1; FOX Sports Southwest; Freeform; FX; FXM; Golf Channel; Great American Country; GSN; Hallmark Channel; HGTV; History; HLN; Investigation Discovery; Lifetime; LMN; MSNBC; MTV; NBCSN; NFL Network; Nick Jr.; Nickelodeon; Outdoor Channel; OWN: Oprah Winfrey Network; Oxygen; RFD-TV; Science Channel; Spike TV; Starz Encore (multiplexed); Syfy; TBS; TLC; TNT; Travel Channel; Turner Classic Movies; TV Land; Univision Studios; USA Network; VH1; WE tv.
Fee: $51.00 monthly.

HD
Subscribers: N.A.
Fee: $10.95 monthly.

Internet Service
Operational: Yes.
Fee: $39.00-$89.00 monthly.

Telephone Service
Digital: Operational
General Manager: Darrell Dennis.
Ownership: XIT Communications (MSO).

DALHART—XIT Communications. This cable system has converted to IPTV. See DALHART, TX [TX5049]. ICA: TX1023.

DALLAS—Time Warner Cable, 1565 Chenault St, Dallas, TX 75228. Phones: 214-370-6200; 972-830-3800; 214-328-2882 (Administrative office). Fax: 214-320-7484, 972-830-3921. Web Site: http://www.timewarnercable.com. Also serves Addison (town), Allen, Arlington, Bedford, Carrollton, Cedar Hill, Cockrell Hill, Colleyville, Collin County (portions), Coppell, Dallas County, Dalworthington Gardens (town), De Soto, Denton County (portions), Double Oak (town), Euless (village), Fairview (town), Farmers Branch, Farmersville, Flower Mound (town), Frisco (town) (Collin County), Frisco (town) (Denton County), Garland, Grand Prairie, Grapevine, Hebron, Highland Village, Hunt County (portions), Hutchins, Irving, Lancaster, Lewisville, McKinney, Mesquite, Murphy, Pantego (village), Parker, Plano, Princeton, Richardson, Rowlett, Sachse, St. Paul, Sunnyvale (town), The Colony & Wylie. ICA: TX0003.
TV Market Ranking: 12 (Addison (town), Allen, Arlington, Bedford, Carrollton, Cedar Hill, Cockrell Hill, Colleyville, Collin County (portions), Coppell, DALLAS, Dallas County, Dalworthington Gardens (town), De Soto, Denton County (portions), Double Oak (town), Euless (village), Fairview (town), Farmers Branch, Farmersville, Flower Mound (town), Frisco (town) (Collin County), Garland, Grand Prairie, Grapevine, Hebron, Highland Village, Hunt County (portions), Hutchins, Irving, Lancaster, Lewisville, McKinney, Mesquite, Murphy, Pantego (village), Parker, Plano, Princeton, Richardson, Rowlett, Rowlett, Sachse, St. Paul, Sunnyvale (town), Wylie); Below 100 (Collin County (portions), Hunt County (portions)). Franchise award date: April 4, 1981. Franchise expiration date: N.A. Began: January 1, 1982.
Channel capacity: N.A. Channels available but not in use: N.A.

Basic Service
Subscribers: 304,828.
Programming (received off-air): KAZD (Azteca America, IND) Lake Dallas; KDAF (Antenna TV, CW, This TV) Dallas; KDFI (Bounce TV, Buzzr, Heroes & Icons, MNT, Movies!) Dallas; KDFW (FOX) Dallas; KDTN (Daystar TV, ETV) Denton; KDTX-TV (TBN) Dallas; KERA-TV (PBS) Dallas; KFWD (MundoMax) Fort Worth; KMPX (Estrella TV) Decatur; KODF-LD (IND) Britton; KPXD-TV (ION) Arlington; KSTR-DT (getTV, UniMas) Irving; KTVT (CBS, Decades) Fort Worth; KTXA (IND, MeTV) Fort Worth; KTXD-TV (IND) Greenville; KUVN-DT (UNV) Garland; KXAS-TV (COZI TV, NBC) Fort Worth; KXTX-TV (TMO) Dallas; WFAA (ABC) Dallas; 22 FMs.
Programming (via satellite): C-SPAN 2; Discovery Channel; QVC; TBS; WGN America.
Fee: $39.99 installation; $28.00 monthly; $1.90 converter.

Expanded Basic Service 1
Subscribers: N.A.
Programming (via satellite): A&E; Animal Planet; BET; Cartoon Network; CMT; CNBC; CNN; Comedy Central; C-SPAN; Disney Channel; E! HD; ESPN; ESPN Classic; ESPN2; EWTN Global Catholic Network; Food Network; Fox News Channel; FOX Sports Southwest; Freeform; FX; Golf Channel; GSN; HGTV; History; HLN; Lifetime; MSNBC; MTV; MTV2; NBCSN; Nickelodeon; Oxygen; Spike TV; Syfy; The Weather Channel; TLC; TNT; Travel Channel; truTV; Turner Classic Movies; TV One; Univision; USA Network; VH1.
Fee: $33.15 monthly.

Digital Basic Service
Subscribers: N.A.
Programming (via satellite): AMC; BBC America; Bloomberg Television; Boomerang; Bravo; CMT; CNBC; CNN International; Cooking Channel; C-SPAN 3; Discovery Digital Networks; Disney XD; DIY Network; ESPN Classic; ESPNews; EWTN Global Catholic Network; FamilyNet; FOX College Sports Central; FOX College Sports Pacific; Fox Sports 1; Fuse; FXM; FYI; Great American Country; Hallmark Channel; HD Theater; History International; HITS (Headend In The Sky); IFC; LMN; MC; Mnet; MSNBC; National Geographic Channel; NBA TV; Nick 2; Nick Jr.; Nicktoons; Outdoor Channel; Sundance TV; TeenNick; Tennis Channel; TNT HD; TV Asia; TV Land; WE tv; Zee TV.
Fee: $9.95 monthly.

Digital Pay Service 1
Pay Units: N.A.
Programming (via satellite): Cinemax (multiplexed); Flix; HBO (multiplexed); Showtime (multiplexed); Showtime HD; Starz; Starz Encore; Starz HD; The Movie Channel (multiplexed).
Fee: $14.99 monthly (each).

Video-On-Demand: Yes

Pay-Per-View
iN DEMAND; MLB Extra Innings (delivered digitally); Hot Choice (delivered digitally); Playboy TV (delivered digitally); Fresh (delivered digitally); Shorteez (delivered digitally); NBA League Pass (delivered digitally); NHL Center Ice (delivered digitally).

Internet Service
Operational: Yes.
Subscribers: 399,904.
Broadband Service: Road Runner.
Fee: $29.95 installation; $42.95 monthly; $3.00 modem lease.

Telephone Service
Digital: Operational
Subscribers: 137,977.
Fee: $44.95 monthly
Miles of Plant: 28,445.0 (coaxial); 11,192.0 (fiber optic). Homes passed: 1,611,659.
President & General Manager: Robert Moel. Vice President, Government & Public Affairs: Dick Kirby. Vice President, Technical

Cable Systems—Texas

Operations: Michael McDonald. Vice President, Marketing: Robert Shurtleff. Public Affairs Director: Gary Underwood.
Ownership: Time Warner Cable (MSO).

DALLAS (northwest suburbs)—Grande Communications, 500 Tittle Rd, Ste 400, Lewisville, TX 75056. Phones: 512-878-4000 (Corporate office); 877-238-6891. Web Site: http://mygrande.com. Also serves Allen, Argyle, Arlington, Carrollton, Corinth, Denton, Fairview, Flower Mound, Frisco, Lake Dallas, Lantanna, Lewisville, Little Elm, Lucas, McKinney, Plano & Roanoke. ICA: TX1006. **Note:** This system is an overbuild.
TV Market Ranking: 12 (Allen, Argyle, Arlington, Carrollton, DALLAS (NORTHWEST SUBURBS), Denton, Frisco, Lake Dallas, Lewisville, McKinney, Plano, Roanoke).
Channel capacity: N.A. Channels available but not in use: N.A.
Basic Service
Subscribers: 10,726.
Programming (received off-air): KAZD (Azteca America, IND) Lake Dallas; KDAF (Antenna TV, CW, This TV) Dallas; KDFI (Bounce TV, Buzzr, Heroes & Icons, MNT, Movies!) Dallas; KDFW (FOX) Dallas; KDTN (Daystar TV, ETV) Denton; KDTX-TV (TBN) Dallas; KERA-TV (PBS) Dallas; KFWD (MundoMax) Fort Worth; KMPX (Estrella TV) Decatur; KSTR-DT (getTV, UniMas) Irving; KTVT (CBS, Decades) Fort Worth; KTXA (IND, MeTV) Fort Worth; KUVN-DT (UNV) Garland; KXAS-TV (COZI TV, NBC) Fort Worth; KXTX-TV (TMO) Dallas; WFAA (ABC) Dallas.
Programming (via satellite): C-SPAN.
Fee: $27.49 monthly.
Expanded Basic Service 1
Subscribers: N.A.
Programming (via satellite): A&E; AMC; Animal Planet; BET; Bravo; Cartoon Network; CMT; CNBC; CNN; Comedy Central; C-SPAN 2; Discovery Channel; Disney Channel; Disney XD; E! HD; ESPN; ESPN Classic; ESPN2; Food Network; Fox News Channel; FOX Sports Networks; Freeform; FX; Golf Channel; HGTV; History; HLN; Lifetime; MSNBC; MTV; Nickelodeon; OWN: Oprah Winfrey Network; Pop; QVC; Spike TV; Starz Encore; Syfy; TBS; The Weather Channel; TLC; TNT; Travel Channel; truTV; Turner Classic Movies; TV Land; USA Network; VH1.
Fee: $28.95 monthly.
Digital Basic Service
Subscribers: N.A.
Programming (via satellite): BBC America; Boomerang; CBS Sports Network; Cooking Channel; C-SPAN 3; Destination America; Discovery Kids Channel; DIY Network; ESPNews; Fox Deportes; Fox Sports 1; Fox Sports 2; Fuse; FXM; FYI; History International; Investigation Discovery; LMN; National Geographic Channel; NBA TV; NBCSN; NFL Network; Nick 2; Nick Jr.; Nicktoons; TeenNick; Tennis Channel; WE tv.
Fee: $35.98 monthly.
Pay Service 1
Pay Units: N.A.
Programming (via satellite): Cinemax; HBO (multiplexed); Showtime; Starz; The Movie Channel.
Digital Pay Service 1
Pay Units: N.A.
Programming (via satellite): Cinemax (multiplexed); Flix; HBO (multiplexed); Showtime; Starz (multiplexed); Starz Encore (multiplexed); Sundance TV; The Movie Channel.
Video-On-Demand: No

Internet Service
Operational: Yes, DSL & dial-up.
Broadband Service: Grande High Speed Internet.
Fee: $19.95 monthly.
Telephone Service
Analog: Not Operational
Digital: Operational
Fee: $9.00 monthly
General Manager: J. Lyn Findley. Video Services Director: Diane Wigington.
Ownership: Grande Communications Networks Inc. (MSO).

DARROUZETT—Formerly served by Panhandle Telephone Coop. Inc. No longer in operation. ICA: TX0662.

DE KALB—Formerly served by BCI Broadband. Now served by Vyve Broadband, NEW BOSTON, TX [TX0204]. ICA: TX0324.

DE LEON—Reach Broadband, PO Box 507, Arp, TX 75750. Phones: 903-859-3789; 800-687-1258. Web Site: http://www.reachbroadband.net. ICA: TX0310.
TV Market Ranking: Outside TV Markets (DE LEON). Franchise award date: N.A. Franchise expiration date: N.A. Began: February 1, 1962.
Channel capacity: N.A. Channels available but not in use: N.A.
Basic Service
Subscribers: 172.
Programming (received off-air): KRBC-TV (Bounce TV, NBC) Abilene; KTAB-TV (CBS) Abilene; allband FM.
Programming (via microwave): KDFW (FOX) Dallas; KERA-TV (PBS) Dallas; KTVT (CBS, Decades) Fort Worth; KXAS-TV (COZI TV, NBC) Fort Worth; WFAA (ABC) Dallas.
Programming (via satellite): C-SPAN; Discovery Channel; QVC; TBS; The Weather Channel.
Fee: $49.95 installation; $28.72 monthly.
Expanded Basic Service 1
Subscribers: N.A.
Programming (via satellite): AMC; Animal Planet; Cartoon Network; CNBC; CNN; ESPN; Fox News Channel; FOX Sports Southwest; Freeform; FX; Hallmark Channel; HGTV; HLN; Lifetime; Spike TV; TLC; TNT; USA Network.
Fee: $20.00 monthly.
Pay Service 1
Pay Units: N.A.
Programming (via satellite): Cinemax; HBO; Starz; Starz Encore.
Fee: $1.75 monthly (Encore), $6.75 monthly (Starz), $12.90 monthly (Cinemax or HBO).
Video-On-Demand: No
Internet Service
Operational: Yes.
Subscribers: 187.
Broadband Service: Rapid High Speed Internet.
Fee: $100.00 installation; $29.95 monthly.
Telephone Service
None
Miles of Plant: 45.0 (coaxial); None (fiber optic). Homes passed: 1,223.
Regional Manager: Ronnie Stafford. Office Manager: Jan Gibson. Controller: Jeffrey Lowe.
Ownership: RB3 LLC (MSO).

DE SOTO—Time Warner Cable. Now served by DALLAS, TX [TX0003]. ICA: TX0053.

DECATUR—Vyve Broadband, 2804B FM 51 South, Decatur, TX 76234. Phone: 855-367-8983. Web Site: http://vyvebroadband.com. Also serves Alvord, Bridgeport, Chico, Lake Bridgeport & Runaway Bay. ICA: TX0168.
TV Market Ranking: Below 100 (Alvord, Bridgeport, Chico, Lake Bridgeport, Runaway Bay, DECATUR). Franchise award date: September 1, 1979. Franchise expiration date: N.A. Began: June 1, 1980.
Channel capacity: N.A. Channels available but not in use: N.A.
Basic Service
Subscribers: 517.
Programming (received off-air): KAUZ-TV (CBS, CW) Wichita Falls; KDAF (Antenna TV, CW, This TV) Dallas; KDFI (Bounce TV, Buzzr, Heroes & Icons, MNT, Movies!) Dallas; KDFW (FOX) Dallas; KDTN (Daystar TV, ETV) Denton; KERA-TV (PBS) Dallas; KSTR-DT (getTV, UniMas) Irving; KTVT (CBS, Decades) Fort Worth; KTXA (IND, MeTV) Fort Worth; KXAS-TV (COZI TV, NBC) Fort Worth; KXTX-TV (TMO) Dallas; WFAA (ABC) Dallas.
Fee: $59.99 installation; $25.00 monthly.
Expanded Basic Service 1
Subscribers: N.A.
Programming (received off-air): KMPX (Estrella TV) Decatur; KPXD-TV (ION) Arlington; KUVN-DT (UNV) Garland.
Programming (via satellite): A&E; AMC; Animal Planet; BET; Bravo; Cartoon Network; CMT; CNBC; CNN; Comedy Central; C-SPAN; Discovery Channel; Disney Channel; ESPN; ESPN2; EVINE Live; Food Network; Fox News Channel; FOX Sports Southwest; Freeform; FX; HGTV; History; HLN; Lifetime; Local Cable Weather; MTV; Nick Jr.; Nickelodeon; Pop; QVC; Spike TV; Syfy; TBS; The Weather Channel; TLC; TNT; Travel Channel; Trinity Broadcasting Network (TBN); TV Land; USA Network; VH1; WE tv.
Fee: $43.95 monthly.
Digital Basic Service
Subscribers: N.A.
Programming (via satellite): BBC America; Bloomberg Television; Bravo; CMT; Destination America; Discovery Kids Channel; Discovery Life Channel; DMX Music; ESPN Classic; ESPN2; ESPNews; Fox Sports 1; Golf Channel; GSN; HGTV; History; IFC; Investigation Discovery; MTV Classic; National Geographic Channel; NBCSN; Nick Jr.; Nicktoons; Outdoor Channel; OWN: Oprah Winfrey Network; Science Channel; Syfy; Trinity Broadcasting Network (TBN); Turner Classic Movies; TV Land; WE tv.
Fee: $17.04 monthly.
Pay Service 1
Pay Units: N.A.
Programming (via satellite): Cinemax; HBO (multiplexed); Starz; Starz Encore.
Digital Pay Service 1
Pay Units: N.A.
Programming (via satellite): Cinemax (multiplexed); Flix; HBO (multiplexed); Showtime (multiplexed); Starz (multiplexed); Starz Encore (multiplexed); The Movie Channel (multiplexed).
Video-On-Demand: No
Pay-Per-View
iN DEMAND (delivered digitally); Playboy TV (delivered digitally); Spice (delivered digitally).
Internet Service
Operational: Yes.
Subscribers: 398.
Broadband Service: Net Commander.
Fee: $39.95 installation; $51.95 monthly.

Telephone Service
None
Miles of Plant: 42.0 (coaxial); 67.0 (fiber optic). Homes passed: 2,345. Homes passed includes Bowie, Jacksboro & Springtown
President & Chief Executive Officer: Jeffrey DeMond. Vice President, Marketing: Diane Quennoz. Vice President, Financial Planning: Daniel White. Vice President, Residential Services: Vin Zachariah.
Ownership: Vyve Broadband LLC (MSO).

DEL RIO—Time Warner Cable, 1313 West Carlton Rd, Laredo, TX 78041. Phones: 956-721-0600; 956-721-0607; 972-899-7300 (Flower Mound office). Fax: 956-721-0612. Web Site: http://www.timewarnercable.com. Also serves Laughlin AFB & Val Verde County (portions). ICA: TX0056.
TV Market Ranking: Below 100 (DEL RIO, Laughlin AFB, Val Verde County (portions) (portions)); Outside TV Markets (Val Verde County (portions) (portions)). Franchise award date: N.A. Franchise expiration date: N.A. Began: September 1, 1955.
Channel capacity: N.A. Channels available but not in use: N.A.
Basic Service
Subscribers: 6,273.
Programming (received off-air): KABB (FOX, The Country Network) San Antonio; KMYS (CW) Kerrville; KNIC-DT (Laff, UniMas) Blanco; KPXL-TV (ION) Uvalde; KVDA (TMO) San Antonio; 3 FMs.
Programming (via microwave): KENS (CBS, Estrella TV) San Antonio; KLRN (PBS) San Antonio; KSAT-TV (ABC, MeTV) San Antonio; KWEX-DT (getTV, UNV) San Antonio; WOAI-TV (IND, NBC) San Antonio.
Programming (via satellite): A&E; AMC; Animal Planet; Azteca; BET; Bravo; Cartoon Network; CMT; CNN; Comedy Central; C-SPAN; C-SPAN 2; Discovery Channel; Disney Channel; E! HD; ESPN; ESPN2; EWTN Global Catholic Network; Food Network; Fox Deportes; Fox News Channel; FOX Sports Southwest; Freeform; FX; Golf Channel; Great American Country; Hallmark Channel; HGTV; History; HLN; Lifetime; MoviePlex; MSNBC; MTV; National Geographic Channel; Nickelodeon; OWN: Oprah Winfrey Network; Oxygen; Pop; QVC; Spike TV; Syfy; TBS; Telemundo; The Weather Channel; TLC; TNT; Travel Channel; Trinity Broadcasting Network (TBN); Turner Classic Movies; TV Land; Univision; USA Network; various Mexican stations; VH1; WE tv.
Fee: $39.99 installation; $64.00 monthly.
Digital Basic Service
Subscribers: N.A.
Programming (via satellite): A&E; AMC; Animal Planet; AXS TV; BBC America; BET; Bloomberg Television; Boomerang; Bravo; Cartoon Network; Cloo; CMT; CNN; Comedy Central; C-SPAN; C-SPAN 2; C-SPAN 3; Destination America; Discovery Channel; Discovery Kids Channel; Discovery Life Channel; Disney Channel; Disney XD; DIY Network; E! HD; ESPN; ESPN Classic; ESPN HD; ESPN2; ESPN2 HD; ESPNews; ESPNU; EWTN Global Catholic Network; Food Network; Fox News Channel; Fox Sports 1; Freeform; Fuse; FX; FYI; Golf Channel; Great American Country; GSN; Hallmark Channel; HD Theater; HGTV; History; History International; HLN; Investigation Discovery; La Familia Cosmovision; Lifetime; LMN; MC; MoviePlex; MSNBC; MTV; MTV Classic; MTV Hits; MTV2; Nat Geo WILD; National Geographic Channel; NBC Universo; NBCSN; Nick Jr.; Nickelodeon; Nicktoons; OWN: Oprah Winfrey Network; Oxy-

2017 Edition D-735

Texas—Cable Systems

gen; Pop; QVC; Spike TV; Syfy; TBS; TeenNick; The Weather Channel; TLC; TNT; TNT HD; Tr3s; Travel Channel; Trinity Broadcasting Network (TBN); Turner Classic Movies; TV Land; Univision; USA Network; VH1; VH1 Country; WE tv.
Fee: $4.99 monthly.

Digital Expanded Basic Service
Subscribers: N.A.
Programming (via satellite): Canal Sur; Cinelatino; CNN en Espanol; ESPN Deportes; FOX College Sports Central; FOX College Sports Pacific; Fox Sports 1; FOX Sports Southwest; FXM; IFC; NBA TV; NBCSN; Starz Encore (multiplexed); Sundance TV; Tennis Channel; VideoRola.

Digital Pay Service 1
Pay Units: N.A.
Programming (via satellite): Cinemax (multiplexed); HBO (multiplexed); Showtime (multiplexed); Starz (multiplexed); The Movie Channel (multiplexed).
Fee: $14.99 monthly (each).

Video-On-Demand: No

Pay-Per-View
iN DEMAND (delivered digitally); Hot Choice (delivered digitally); Fresh (delivered digitally); Shorteez (delivered digitally); NBA League Pass (delivered digitally); MLB Extra Innings (delivered digitally); NHL Center Ice (delivered digitally).

Internet Service
Operational: Yes.
Subscribers: 7,774.
Broadband Service: Road Runner.
Fee: $49.99 installation; $44.95 monthly.

Telephone Service
Digital: Operational
Subscribers: 2,264.
Fee: $44.95 monthly
Miles of Plant: 502.0 (coaxial); 214.0 (fiber optic). Homes passed: 21,680.
President: Connie Wharton. Vice President & General Manager: Michael Carrosquiola. Public Affairs Manager: Celinda Gonzalez. Operations Director: Marco Reyes. Technical Operations Manager: Eduardo Ruiz.
Ownership: Time Warner Cable (MSO).; Advance/Newhouse Partnership (MSO).

DENTON—Charter Communications, 12405 Powerscourt Dr, St. Louis, MO 63131. Phones: 636-207-5100 (Corporate office); 817-810-9171; 817-298-3600; 940-898-0583 (Denton office). Web Site: http://www.charter.com. Also serves Corinth, Hickory Creek, Lake Dallas & Shady Shores. ICA: TX0040.
TV Market Ranking: 12 (Corinth, DENTON, Hickory Creek, Lake Dallas, Shady Shores). Franchise award date: January 20, 1979. Franchise expiration date: N.A. Began: November 1, 1979.
Channel capacity: N.A. Channels available but not in use: N.A.

Digital Basic Service
Subscribers: 9,023.
Programming (via satellite): BBC America; Discovery Digital Networks; Disney XD; FYI; GSN; History International; IFC; LMN; MC; National Geographic Channel; Nick 2; Nick Jr.; Nicktoons; Sundance TV; TeenNick; WE tv.
Fee: $26.99 monthly.

Digital Expanded Basic Service
Subscribers: N.A.
Programming (via satellite): A&E; AMC; Animal Planet; BET; Bravo; Cartoon Network; CMT; CNBC; CNN; Comedy Central; Discovery Channel; Disney Channel; E! HD; ESPN; ESPN2; EVINE Live; Food Network; Fox News Channel; Fox Sports 1;

FOX Sports Southwest; Freeform; FX; Hallmark Channel; HGTV; History; HLN; Lifetime; MSNBC; MTV; NBCSN; Nickelodeon; Spike TV; Syfy; TBS; The Weather Channel; TLC; TNT; Travel Channel; Turner Classic Movies; TV Land; Univision; USA Network; VH1; Weatherscan.
Fee: $48.99 monthly.

Digital Expanded Basic Service 2
Subscribers: N.A.
Programming (via satellite): ESPNews; Fox Sports 2; FSN Digital Atlantic; FSN Digital Central; FSN Digital Pacific; Golf Channel; HITS (Headend In The Sky); NFL Network.

Digital Pay Service 1
Pay Units: N.A.
Programming (via satellite): Cinemax (multiplexed); Flix; HBO (multiplexed); Showtime (multiplexed); Starz (multiplexed); Starz Encore (multiplexed); The Movie Channel (multiplexed).

Video-On-Demand: No

Pay-Per-View
Playboy TV (delivered digitally); Fresh (delivered digitally); Shorteez (delivered digitally); iN DEMAND (delivered digitally).

Internet Service
Operational: Yes.
Subscribers: 9,913.
Broadband Service: Charter Internet.
Fee: $9.99 installation; $29.99 monthly.

Telephone Service
Digital: Operational
Subscribers: 197.
Fee: $29.95 monthly
Miles of Plant: 1,414.0 (coaxial); 126.0 (fiber optic). Homes passed: 60,904.
Vice President & General Manager: Wayne Cramp. Technical Operations Director: John Linton. Marketing Director: Kathleen Griffin. Accounting Director: David Sovanski.
Ownership: Charter Communications Inc. (MSO).

DEVINE—CommZoom, 2438 Boardwalk, San Antonio, TX 78217. Phone: 844-858-8500. Web Site: http://www.commzoom.com. Also serves Lytle, Medina County (portions) & Natalia. ICA: TX0747.
TV Market Ranking: 45 (DEVINE, Lytle, Medina County (portions), Natalia) Below 100 (Medina County (portions)). Franchise award date: N.A. Franchise expiration date: N.A. Began: November 1, 1981.
Channel capacity: N.A. Channels available but not in use: N.A.

Basic Service
Subscribers: 70.
Programming (received off-air): KABB (FOX, The Country Network) San Antonio; KENS (CBS, Estrella TV) San Antonio; KHCE-TV (TBN) San Antonio; KLRN (PBS) San Antonio; KMOL-LD (Movies!, NBC) Victoria; KMYS (CW) Kerrville; KPXL-TV (ION) Uvalde; KSAT-TV (ABC, MeTV) San Antonio; KVDA (TMO) San Antonio; KWEX-DT (getTV, UNV) San Antonio.
Programming (via satellite): C-SPAN; ESPN; QVC.
Fee: $49.95 installation; $62.36 monthly.

Expanded Basic Service 1
Subscribers: N.A.
Programming (via satellite): A&E; AMC; Bravo; Cartoon Network; CMT; CNBC; CNN; Comedy Central; Discovery Channel; Disney Channel; E! HD; ESPN2; Fox News Channel; Fox Sports 1; FOX Sports Southwest; Freeform; FX; HGTV; History; HLN; Lifetime; MTV; Nickelodeon; Oxygen; Spike TV; Syfy; TBS; The Weather Channel; TLC; TNT; Travel Channel; Turner Classic Movies; TV Land; USA Network; VH1.
Fee: $20.00 monthly.

Digital Basic Service
Subscribers: N.A.
Programming (via satellite): BBC America; Bloomberg Television; Discovery Life Channel; Disney XD; DIY Network; ESPN Classic; ESPNews; FYI; GSN; History International; IFC; LMN; MC; Nick 2; Nick Jr.; Nicktoons; Sundance TV; TeenNick; TV Guide Interactive Inc.; WE tv.

Digital Pay Service 1
Pay Units: N.A.
Programming (via satellite): Cinemax (multiplexed); Flix; HBO (multiplexed); Showtime (multiplexed); Starz (multiplexed); Starz Encore (multiplexed); The Movie Channel (multiplexed).
Fee: $11.95 monthly (Cinemax, HBO, Showtime or TMC).

Video-On-Demand: No

Pay-Per-View
iN DEMAND (delivered digitally).

Internet Service
Operational: Yes.

Telephone Service
None
Miles of Plant: 92.0 (coaxial); None (fiber optic). Homes passed: 2,786.
Chief Executive Officer: Bob Cohen.
Ownership: CommZoom Communications LLC (MSO).

DIANA—Formerly served by Almega Cable. No longer in operation. ICA: TX0566.

DICKENS—Formerly served by Almega Cable. No longer in operation. ICA: TX0748.

DILLEY—Time Warner Cable, 1313 West Carlton Rd, Laredo, TX 78041. Phones: 956-721-0600; 972-899-7300 (Flower Mound office); 956-721-0607. Fax: 956-721-0612. Web Site: http://www.timewarnercable.com. Also serves Cotulla, Frio County (portions), La Salle County (portions) & Pearsall. ICA: TX0196.
TV Market Ranking: 45 (Frio County (portions); Outside TV Markets (Cotulla, La Salle County (portions), DILLEY, Pearsall, Frio County (portions)). Franchise award date: N.A. Franchise expiration date: N.A. Began: May 1, 1975.
Channel capacity: N.A. Channels available but not in use: N.A.

Basic Service
Subscribers: 1,930.
Programming (received off-air): KABB (FOX, The Country Network) San Antonio; KENS (CBS, Estrella TV) San Antonio; KLRN (PBS) San Antonio; KMYS (CW) Kerrville; KPXL-TV (ION) Uvalde; KSAT-TV (ABC, MeTV) San Antonio; KVDA (TMO) San Antonio; KWEX-DT (getTV, UNV) San Antonio; WOAI-TV (IND, NBC) San Antonio.
Programming (via satellite): A&E; AMC; Animal Planet; BET; Bravo; Cartoon Network; CMT; CNBC; CNN; Comedy Central; C-SPAN; C-SPAN 2; Discovery Channel; Disney Channel; E! HD; ESPN; ESPN2; EVINE Live; EWTN Global Catholic Network; Food Network; Fox Deportes; Fox News Channel; FOX Sports Southwest; Freeform; FX; Golf Channel; Great American Country; Hallmark Channel; HGTV; History; HLN; Lifetime; MoviePlex; MSNBC; MTV; National Geographic Channel; NBC Universo; Nickelodeon; Outdoor Channel; OWN: Oprah Winfrey Network; Oxygen; Pop; QVC; Spike TV; Syfy; TBS; The Weather Channel; TLC; TNT; Travel Channel; Trinity Broadcasting Network (TBN); truTV; Turner Classic Movies; TV Land; Univision; USA Network; VH1; WE tv.
Fee: $39.99 installation; $56.00 monthly.

Digital Basic Service
Subscribers: N.A.
Programming (via satellite): BBC America; Bloomberg Television; Discovery Life Channel; Disney XD; ESPN Classic; ESPNews; FOX College Sports Central; FOX College Sports Pacific; Fox Sports 1; Fuse; FXM; FYI; GSN; History International; IFC; LMN; MC; MTV2; NBA TV; NBCSN; Nick Jr.; Nicktoons; Outdoor Channel; Starz Encore; Sundance TV (multiplexed); TeenNick; Tennis Channel; VH1 Country.
Fee: $7.00 monthly (value tier), $8.95 monthly (each additional tier).

Digital Pay Service 1
Pay Units: N.A.
Programming (via satellite): Cinemax (multiplexed); HBO (multiplexed); Showtime (multiplexed); Starz (multiplexed); The Movie Channel (multiplexed).
Fee: $14.99 monthly (each).

Pay-Per-View
iN DEMAND (delivered digitally); Fresh (delivered digitally); Playboy TV (delivered digitally); Hot Choice (delivered digitally); NBA League Pass (delivered digitally); NHL Center Ice (delivered digitally); MLB Extra Innings (delivered digitally).

Internet Service
Operational: Yes.

Telephone Service
Digital: Operational
Homes passed: 5,086.
President: Connie Wharton. Vice President & General Manager: Michael Carrosquiola. Operations Director: Marcos Reyes. Public Affairs Manager: Celinda Gonzalez. Technical Operations Manager: Eduardo Ruiz.
Ownership: Time Warner Cable (MSO).; Advance/Newhouse Partnership (MSO).

DILLEY—Time Warner Cable. Now served by DILLEY (formerly Pearsall), TX [TX0196]. ICA: TX0344.

DIME BOX—Formerly served by Reveille Broadband. No longer in operation. ICA: TX0601.

DIMMITT—Suddenlink Communications, 520 Maryville Centre Dr, Ste 300, St. Louis, MO 63141. Phones: 800-999-6845; 314-315-9400. Web Site: http://www.suddenlink.com. ICA: TX0255.
TV Market Ranking: Outside TV Markets (DIMMITT). Franchise award date: N.A. Franchise expiration date: N.A. Began: February 1, 1964.
Channel capacity: N.A. Channels available but not in use: N.A.

Basic Service
Subscribers: 182.
Programming (received off-air): KACV-TV (PBS) Amarillo; KAMR-TV (IND, NBC) Amarillo; KCIT (FOX, This TV) Amarillo; KFDA-TV (CBS, TMO) Amarillo; KJTV-TV (FOX) Lubbock; KLBK-TV (CBS) Lubbock; KVII-TV (ABC, CW) Amarillo; allband FM.
Programming (via satellite): A&E; Animal Planet; CMT; CNN; C-SPAN; Discovery Channel; Disney Channel; E! HD; ESPN; Fox News Channel; FOX Sports Southwest; Freeform; History; HLN; Nickelodeon; Spike TV; TBS; Telemundo; The Weather Channel; TNT; Turner Classic Movies; TV Land; USA Network; WGN America.
Fee: $28.45 monthly.

Pay Service 1
Pay Units: N.A.
Programming (via satellite): HBO; Showtime; The Movie Channel.

Cable Systems—Texas

Fee: $15.00 installation; $7.95 monthly (TMC), $9.95 monthly (Showtime), $10.95 monthly (HBO).
Video-On-Demand: No
Internet Service
Operational: Yes. Began: June 19, 2003.
Broadband Service: Cebridge High Speed Cable Internet.
Fee: $49.95 installation; $25.95 monthly.
Telephone Service
None
Miles of Plant: 25.0 (coaxial); None (fiber optic). Homes passed: 1,680.
Vice President, Corporate Finance: Michael Pflantz. Regional Manager: Todd Cruthird. Regional Marketing Manager: Beverly Gambell.
Ownership: Cequel Communications Holdings I LLC (MSO).

DIXIE—Formerly served by Northland Communications. No longer in operation. ICA: TX0911.

DRISCOLL—Time Warner Cable. Now served by CORPUS CHRISTI, TX [TX0010]. ICA: TX1007.

DUBLIN—Northland Cable Television. Now served by STEPHENVILLE, TX [TX0098]. ICA: TX0749.

DUNCANVILLE—Charter Communications, 206 E Center St, Duncanville, TX 75116. Phones: 636-207-5100 (Corporate office); 817-810-9171; 817-298-3600. Web Site: http://www.charter.com. ICA: TX0080.
TV Market Ranking: 12 (DUNCANVILLE). Franchise award date: June 8, 1979. Franchise expiration date: N.A. Began: April 6, 1980.
Channel capacity: N.A. Channels available but not in use: N.A.
Digital Basic Service
Subscribers: 1,677. Commercial subscribers: 49.
Programming (via satellite): BBC America; Bloomberg Television; Discovery Life Channel; Disney XD; DIY Network; FYI; History International; IFC; LMN; MC; Sundance TV.
Fee: $26.99 monthly.
Digital Expanded Basic Service
Subscribers: N.A.
Programming (via satellite): A&E; AMC; Animal Planet; BET; Bravo; Cartoon Network; CMT; CNBC; CNN; Comedy Central; C-SPAN 2; Discovery Channel; Disney Channel; E! HD; ESPN; ESPN Classic; ESPN2; Food Network; Fox News Channel; Fox Sports 1; FOX Sports Southwest; Freeform; FX; Golf Channel; Great American Country; GSN; Hallmark Channel; HGTV; History; HLN; Lifetime; MSNBC; MTV; National Geographic Channel; NBCSN; Nickelodeon; Oxygen; QVC; Spike TV; Syfy; TBS; The Weather Channel; TLC; TNT; Travel Channel; truTV; Turner Classic Movies; TV Land; Univision; USA Network; VH1; WE tv.
Fee: $48.99 monthly.
Digital Expanded Basic Service 2
Subscribers: N.A.
Programming (via satellite): Fox Deportes; Fox Sports 2; FSN Digital Atlantic; FSN Digital Central; FSN Digital Pacific; NFL Network.
Digital Pay Service 1
Pay Units: N.A.
Programming (via satellite): Cinemax (multiplexed); Flix; HBO (multiplexed); Showtime (multiplexed); Starz (multiplexed); Starz Encore (multiplexed); The Movie Channel (multiplexed).
Video-On-Demand: No
Pay-Per-View
Hot Choice (delivered digitally); Fresh (delivered digitally); Shorteez (delivered digitally); iN DEMAND (delivered digitally).
Internet Service
Operational: Yes.
Broadband Service: Charter Internet.
Fee: $29.99 monthly.
Telephone Service
None
Miles of Plant: 114.0 (coaxial); 54.0 (fiber optic). Homes passed: 13,384.
Vice President & General Manager: Wayne Cramp. Assistant Controller: Brent Trask. Technical Operations Director: John Linton. Marketing Director: Kathleen Griffin. Accounting Director: David Sovanski.
Ownership: Charter Communications Inc. (MSO).

EAGLE LAKE—Time Warner Cable. Now served by COLUMBUS, TX [TX0257]. ICA: TX0278.

EAGLE PASS—Time Warner Cable, 1313 West Carlton Rd, Laredo, TX 78041. Phones: 956-721-0600; 972-899-7300 (Flower Mound office); 956-721-0607. Fax: 956-721-0612. Web Site: http://www.timewarnercable.com. Also serves Maverick County (portions) & Quemado. ICA: TX0067.
TV Market Ranking: Below 100 (EAGLE PASS, Maverick County, Quemado). Franchise award date: N.A. Franchise expiration date: N.A. Began: September 1, 1959.
Channel capacity: N.A. Channels available but not in use: N.A.
Basic Service
Subscribers: 6,752.
Programming (received off-air): KMYS (CW) Kerrville; KPXL-TV (ION) Uvalde; 4 FMs.
Programming (via microwave): KABB (FOX, The Country Network) San Antonio; KENS (CBS, Estrella TV) San Antonio; KLRN (PBS) San Antonio; KSAT-TV (ABC, MeTV) San Antonio; KWEX-DT (getTV, UNV) San Antonio; WOAI-TV (IND, NBC) San Antonio.
Programming (via satellite): C-SPAN; C-SPAN 2; Disney Channel; QVC; various Mexican stations.
Fee: $39.99 installation; $28.00 monthly; $2.00 converter.
Expanded Basic Service 1
Subscribers: N.A.
Programming (via satellite): A&E; AMC; Animal Planet; Bravo; Cartoon Network; CNN; Comedy Central; Discovery Channel; E! HD; ESPN; ESPN2; EVINE Live; EWTN Global Catholic Network; Food Network; Fox Deportes; Fox News Channel; FOX Sports Southwest; FX; Golf Channel; HGTV; History; HLN; Lifetime; MSNBC; MTV; Nickelodeon; OWN: Oprah Winfrey Network; Oxygen; Spike TV; Syfy; TBS; Telemundo; The Weather Channel; TLC; TNT; Travel Channel; Turner Classic Movies; TV Land; Univision; USA Network; WE tv.
Fee: $27.50 monthly.
Digital Basic Service
Subscribers: N.A.
Programming (via satellite): BBC America; Bloomberg Television; Destination America; Discovery Kids Channel; Discovery Life Channel; Disney XD; ESPN Classic; ESPNews; FYI; GSN; History International; LMN; MTV Classic; MTV Hits; MTV2; NBA TV; NBCSN; Nick Jr.; Nicktoons; TeenNick; VH1 Country.
Fee: $5.00 monthly.
Digital Expanded Basic Service
Subscribers: N.A.
Programming (via satellite): CNN en Espanol; DMX Music; FOX College Sports Central; FOX College Sports Pacific; Fox Deportes; Fox Sports 1; FXM; HTV; IFC; Infinito; La Familia Cosmovision; NBA TV; NBCSN; Starz Encore (multiplexed); Sundance TV; Tennis Channel; various Mexican stations; VideoRola.
Digital Pay Service 1
Pay Units: N.A.
Programming (via satellite): Cinemax (multiplexed); HBO (multiplexed); Showtime (multiplexed); Starz (multiplexed); The Movie Channel (multiplexed).
Fee: $14.99 monthly (each).
Video-On-Demand: No
Pay-Per-View
Hot Choice (delivered digitally); Hot Choice (delivered digitally); iN DEMAND (delivered digitally); adult (delivered digitally); adult (delivered digitally); adult (delivered digitally); adult (delivered digitally); director's cut- adult (delivered digitally); MLB Extra Innings (delivered digitally); NBA League Pass (delivered digitally).
Internet Service
Operational: Yes.
Broadband Service: Road Runner.
Fee: $49.99 installation; $44.95 monthly.
Telephone Service
Digital: Operational
Fee: $44.95 monthly
Miles of Plant: 159.0 (coaxial); None (fiber optic).
President: Connie Wharton. Vice President & General Manager: Michael Carrosquiola. Operations Director: Marco Reyes. Public Affairs Manager: Celinda Gonzalez. Technical Operations Manager: Eduardo Ruiz.
Ownership: Time Warner Cable (MSO).; Advance/Newhouse Partnership (MSO).

EAST MOUNTAIN—Formerly served by Gilmer Cable. No longer in operation. ICA: TX0750.

EASTLAND—Suddenlink Communications, 520 Maryville Centre Dr, Ste 300, St. Louis, MO 63141. Phones: 432-943-4335; 877-423-2743 (Customer service); 314-315-9400. Web Site: http://www.suddenlink.com. Also serves Cisco, Eastland County, Olden & Ranger. ICA: TX0131.
TV Market Ranking: Outside TV Markets (Cisco, EASTLAND, Eastland County, Olden, Ranger). Franchise award date: N.A. Franchise expiration date: N.A. Began: August 1, 1958.
Channel capacity: N.A. Channels available but not in use: N.A.
Basic Service
Subscribers: 1,221. Commercial subscribers: 237.
Programming (received off-air): KIDZ-LD Abilene; KPCB-DT (GLC) Snyder; KRBC-TV (Bounce TV, NBC) Abilene; KTAB-TV (CBS) Abilene; KTXS-TV (ABC, CW, This TV, TMO) Sweetwater; KXVA (FOX, MNT) Abilene; all-band FM.
Programming (via microwave): KERA-TV (PBS) Dallas; WFAA (ABC) Dallas.
Programming (via satellite): C-SPAN; CW PLUS; Pop; QVC; Univision Studios.
Fee: $28.45 monthly.
Expanded Basic Service 1
Subscribers: N.A.
Programming (via satellite): A&E; AMC; Animal Planet; BET; Bravo; Cartoon Network; Celebrity Shopping Network; CNBC; CNN; Comedy Central; Discovery Channel; Disney Channel; E! HD; ESPN; ESPN2; Food Network; Fox News Channel; Fox Sports 1; FOX Sports Southwest; Freeform; FX; Golf Channel; Great American Country; Hallmark Channel; HGTV; History; HLN; Jewelry Television; Lifetime; MSNBC; MTV; National Geographic Channel; Nickelodeon; Outdoor Channel; Spike TV; Syfy; TBS; The Weather Channel; TLC; TNT; Travel Channel; Turner Classic Movies; TV Land; Univision; USA Network; VH1.
Fee: $39.95 installation; $25.00 monthly.
Digital Basic Service
Subscribers: N.A.
Programming (via satellite): BBC America; Bloomberg Television; Cloo; CMT; Destination America; Discovery Kids Channel; Disney XD; DMX Music; ESPN Classic; ESPNews; Fuse; FYI; GSN; History International; IFC; Investigation Discovery; LMN; MTV Classic; MTV2; NBCSN; Nick Jr.; Nicktoons; OWN: Oprah Winfrey Network; Science Channel; TeenNick; Trinity Broadcasting Network (TBN); WE tv.
Fee: $3.99 monthly.
Pay Service 1
Pay Units: N.A.
Programming (via satellite): Cinemax; HBO; Showtime; Starz; Starz Encore.
Fee: $1.75 monthly (Encore), $6.75 monthly (Starz), $12.90 monthly (Cinemax, HBO or Showtime).
Digital Pay Service 1
Pay Units: N.A.
Programming (via satellite): Cinemax (multiplexed); HBO (multiplexed); Showtime (multiplexed); Starz; Starz Encore (multiplexed); The Movie Channel (multiplexed).
Video-On-Demand: No
Pay-Per-View
iN DEMAND (delivered digitally); Playboy TV (delivered digitally); Club Jenna (delivered digitally); Fresh (delivered digitally).
Internet Service
Operational: Yes. Began: March 2, 2002.
Broadband Service: Suddenlink High Speed Internet.
Fee: $45.95 installation; $29.95 monthly.
Telephone Service
Digital: Operational
Fee: $44.95 monthly
Miles of Plant: 124.0 (coaxial); None (fiber optic). Homes passed: 4,824.
Senior Vice President, Corporate Finance: Michael Pflantz. Regional Manager: Todd Cruthird.
Ownership: Cequel Communications Holdings I LLC (MSO).

ECTOR—TV Cable of Grayson County, 501 Spur 316 Hwy, Ste. 106, PO Box 2084, Pottsboro, TX 75076. Phones: 888-815-0636; 903-786-7477. E-mail: tvcable@graysoncable.com. Web Site: http://www.graysoncable.com. ICA: TX0585.
TV Market Ranking: Below 100 (ECTOR). Franchise award date: N.A. Franchise expiration date: N.A. Began: April 1, 1985.
Channel capacity: 54 (not 2-way capable). Channels available but not in use: N.A.
Basic Service
Subscribers: 36.
Programming (received off-air): KDFW (FOX) Dallas; KERA-TV (PBS) Dallas; KPXD-TV (ION) Arlington; KTVT (CBS, Decades) Fort Worth; KXAS-TV (COZI TV, NBC) Fort Worth; KXII (CBS, FOX, MNT) Sherman; WFAA (ABC) Dallas.
Programming (via satellite): TBS.
Fee: $45.95 installation; $46.95 monthly.

Texas—Cable Systems

Pay Service 1
Pay Units: N.A.
Programming (via satellite): Cinemax; HBO; Showtime.
Fee: $3.20 monthly (Showtime), $7.00 monthly (Cinemax), $12.00 monthly (HBO).
Internet Service
Operational: Yes.
Fee: $35.00 installation; $24.99-$149.95 monthly.
Telephone Service
None
Miles of Plant: 10.0 (coaxial); None (fiber optic). Homes passed: 278.
General Manager: Chuck Davis.
Ownership: Chuck Davis (MSO).

ECTOR COUNTY (portions)—Ridgewood Cablevision, 3700 South County Rd 1316, Odessa, TX 79765. Phone: 432-563-4330. Fax: 432-563-0104. E-mail: rwc@ridgewoodcable.com. Web Site: http://www.ridgewoodcable.com. ICA: TX1016.
TV Market Ranking: Below 100 (ECTOR COUNTY (PORTIONS)).
Channel capacity: N.A. Channels available but not in use: N.A.
Basic Service
Subscribers: N.A.
Programming (received off-air): KMID (ABC) Midland; KMLM-DT (GLC) Odessa; KOSA-TV (CBS, MNT) Odessa; KPBT-TV (PBS) Odessa; KPEJ-TV (FOX) Odessa; KUPB (UNV) Midland; KWES-TV (CW, NBC, TMO) Odessa.
Programming (via satellite): A&E; AMC; Animal Planet; Cartoon Network; CMT; CNN; C-SPAN; C-SPAN 2; Discovery Channel; Disney Channel; Disney XD; ESPN; ESPN2; Food Network; Fox News Channel; FOX Sports Networks; Freeform; Hallmark Channel; HGTV; History; HLN; Lifetime; MoviePlex; MTV; National Geographic Channel; Nickelodeon; QVC; Spike TV; Syfy; TBS; Telemundo; The Weather Channel; TLC; TNT; Travel Channel; Turner Classic Movies; TV Land; USA Network; VH1; WGN America.
Pay Service 1
Pay Units: N.A.
Programming (via satellite): Cinemax (multiplexed); HBO (multiplexed); Showtime (multiplexed); The Movie Channel.
Fee: $6.95 monthly (Showtime/TMC), $7.95 montlhy (HBO/Cinemax).
Internet Service
Operational: Yes.
General Manager & Chief Technician: Bob Randolph.
Ownership: Ridgewood Cable (MSO).

EDCOUCH—Time Warner Cable. Now served by PHARR, TX [TX0017]. ICA: TX0185.

EDEN—LynnStar Communications, 4500 Mercantile Plz, Ste 300, Fort Worth, TX 76137. Phones: 888-575-9230; 682-730-0900. Fax: 682-730-6400. Web Site: http://lynnstar.net; http://www.lynnstarcomm.com. Also serves Concho County (portions). ICA: TX0434.
TV Market Ranking: Below 100 (Concho County (portions)); Outside TV Markets (EDEN). Franchise award date: N.A. Franchise expiration date: N.A. Began: January 1, 1973.
Channel capacity: 41 (not 2-way capable). Channels available but not in use: N.A.
Basic Service
Subscribers: 92.
Programming (received off-air): KIDY (FOX, MNT) San Angelo; KLST (CBS) San Angelo; KRBC-TV (Bounce TV, NBC) Abilene; KTXS-TV (ABC, CW, This TV, TMO) Sweetwater; 2 FMs.
Programming (via satellite): A&E; Animal Planet; Cartoon Network; CMT; CNN; Discovery Channel; Disney Channel; ESPN; Fox News Channel; FOX Sports Southwest; Freeform; HLN; KRMA-TV (PBS) Denver; Lifetime; Nickelodeon; QVC; Spike TV; TBS; The Weather Channel; TLC; TNT; Trinity Broadcasting Network (TBN); Turner Classic Movies; TV Land; USA Network; WGN America.
Fee: $49.95 installation; $25.83 monthly.
Pay Service 1
Pay Units: N.A.
Programming (via satellite): HBO; Showtime; The Movie Channel.
Fee: $35.00 installation; $7.95 monthly (TMC), $9.95 monthly (Showtime), $10.95 monthly (HBO).
Video-On-Demand: No
Internet Service
Operational: No.
Telephone Service
None
Miles of Plant: 24.0 (coaxial); None (fiber optic). Homes passed: 687.
Chairman of the Board & Government Relations Director: S. Gene Yarbrough. Chief Executive Officer, Executive Vice President & Board Member: Chris Romine. Chief Operations Officer, Executive Vice President & Board Member: Steve Sizemore. Vice President & Business Development & Countertrade Director: Gary Majors. Vice President & Programming & Vendor Relations Director: Gus Salvino. Vice President & Investor Relations Manager: Daniel J. Sweeney. Accounting Manager: Sheila Magness.
Ownership: Lynnstar Communications (MSO).

EDNA—NewWave Communications. Now served by WHARTON, TX [TX0171]. ICA: TX0207.

EGAN—North Texas Broadband, PO Box 676, Aubery, TX 76227. Phones: 888-365-2930; 940-365-2930. E-mail: customerservice@northtxbroadband.com. Web Site: http://northtxbroadband.com. Also serves Egan County (portions). ICA: TX0366.
TV Market Ranking: 12 (EGAN, Egan County (portions)); Outside TV Markets (Egan County (portions)).
Channel capacity: 36 (not 2-way capable). Channels available but not in use: N.A.
Basic Service
Subscribers: 20.
Programming (received off-air): KDAF (Antenna TV, CW, This TV) Dallas; KDFI (Bounce TV, Buzzr, Heroes & Icons, MNT, Movies!) Dallas; KDFW (FOX) Dallas; KERA-TV (PBS) Dallas; KPXD-TV (ION) Arlington; KTVT (CBS, Decades) Fort Worth; KTXA (IND, MeTV) Fort Worth; KXAS-TV (COZI TV, NBC) Fort Worth; KXTX-TV (TMO) Dallas; WFAA (ABC) Dallas.
Programming (via satellite): A&E; AMC; CMT; CNN; Discovery Channel; Disney Channel; ESPN; FOX Sports Southwest; Freeform; HLN; Nickelodeon; Spike TV; TBS; TNT; Trinity Broadcasting Network (TBN); USA Network; WGN America.
Fee: $39.95 installation; $41.95 monthly.
Pay Service 1
Pay Units: N.A.
Programming (via satellite): Cinemax; HBO; Showtime.
Fee: $5.95 monthly (Showtime), $10.95 monthly (Cinemax or HBO).
Internet Service
Operational: Yes.
Telephone Service
None
Miles of Plant: 49.0 (coaxial); None (fiber optic). Homes passed: 959.
General Manager: Curtis Davis.
Ownership: North Texas Broadband (MSO).

EL CAMPO—NewWave Communications. Now served by WHARTON, TX [TX0171]. ICA: TX0133.

EL PASO—Time Warner Cable, 7010 Airport Rd, El Paso, TX 79906. Phones: 915-772-8777; 972-899-7300 (Flower Mound division office); 915-772-1123. Fax: 915-772-4605. Web Site: http://www.timewarnercable.com. Also serves Anthony, Dona Ana County (portions), La Union, Santa Sunland Park & Vado, NM; Anthony, Biggs Airfield, Borderland, Canutillo, Clint, El Paso County, Fabens, Fort Bliss, Homestead Homes, Horizon City, San Elizario, Socorro, Vinton & Westway, TX. ICA: TX0009.
TV Market Ranking: Below 100 (Anthony, Anthony, Biggs Airfield, Borderland, Canutillo, Clint, Dona Ana County (portions), EL PASO, El Paso County, Fabens, Fort Bliss, Homestead Homes, Horizon City, La Union, San Elizario, Santa Teresa, Socorro, Sunland Park, Vado, Vinton, Westway). Franchise award date: January 1, 1968. Franchise expiration date: N.A. Began: February 1, 1972.
Channel capacity: N.A. Channels available but not in use: N.A.
Basic Service
Subscribers: 62,820.
Programming (received off-air): KCOS (PBS) El Paso; KDBC-TV (CBS, MNT, This TV) El Paso; KFOX-TV (FOX, Retro TV) El Paso; KINT-TV (LATV, UNV) El Paso; KRWG-TV (PBS) Las Cruces; KSCE (ETV, Punch TV) Las Cruces; KTDO (TMO) Las Cruces; KTFN (MundoMax, UniMas) El Paso; KTSM-TV (Estrella TV, NBC) El Paso; KVIA-TV (ABC, Azteca America, CW) El Paso; 16 FMs.
Programming (via satellite): KTLA (Antenna TV, CW, This TV) Los Angeles.
Fee: $39.99 installation; $23.00 monthly.
Expanded Basic Service 1
Subscribers: N.A.
Programming (via satellite): A&E; AMC; Animal Planet; BET; Bravo; Cartoon Network; CMT; CNBC; CNN; Comedy Central; C-SPAN; C-SPAN 2; Discovery Channel; Disney Channel; E! HD; ESPN; ESPN Classic; ESPN2; EVINE Live; EWTN Global Catholic Network; Food Network; Fox Deportes; Fox News Channel; FOX Sports Southwest; Freeform; FX; Golf Channel; Great American Country; HGTV; History; HLN; ION Television; Lifetime; LMN; MSNBC; MTV; National Geographic Channel; Nickelodeon; OWN: Oprah Winfrey Network; Oxygen; QVC; Spike TV; Syfy; TBS; The Weather Channel; Time Warner Cable SportsChannel (Kansas City); TLC; TNT; Travel Channel; truTV; Turner Classic Movies; TV Land; Univision; USA Network; VH1; WE tv.
Fee: $38.29 monthly.
Digital Basic Service
Subscribers: N.A.
Programming (via satellite): BBC America; Boomerang; Cloo; Cooking Channel; Discovery Life Channel; Disney XD; DIY Network; ESPNews; Flix (multiplexed); FOX College Sports Central; FOX College Sports Pacific; Fox Sports 1; Fox Sports 2; FXM; FYI; GSN; Hallmark Channel; History International; HITS (Headend In The Sky); IFC; NBA TV; NBC Universo; NBCSN; Nick Jr.; Nicktoons; Outdoor Channel; Ovation; Sundance TV; TeenNick; Tennis Channel.
Fee: $5.00 monthly, $8.94 monthly (Encore, Sports or Canales N tiers).
Digital Pay Service 1
Pay Units: N.A.
Programming (via satellite): Cinemax (multiplexed); HBO (multiplexed); Showtime (multiplexed); Starz (multiplexed); Starz Encore (multiplexed); The Movie Channel (multiplexed).
Fee: $14.99 monthly (each).
Video-On-Demand: Yes
Pay-Per-View
iN DEMAND (delivered digitally); Hot Choice (delivered digitally); Playboy TV (delivered digitally); Fresh (delivered digitally); Shorteez (delivered digitally); NBA League Pass (delivered digitally); ESPN (delivered digitally); MLB Extra Innings (delivered digitally).
Internet Service
Operational: Yes. Began: September 1, 1997.
Subscribers: 93,527.
Broadband Service: Road Runner.
Fee: $49.99 installation; $44.95 monthly.
Telephone Service
Digital: Operational
Subscribers: 27,493.
Fee: $44.95 monthly
Miles of Plant: 4,383.0 (coaxial); 2,468.0 (fiber optic). Homes passed: 314,161.
President: Connie Wharton. Vice President & General Manager: Michael G. Carrosquiola. Public Affairs Director: Rene Hurtado. Technical Operations Director: Ismael Molina.
Ownership: Time Warner Cable (MSO).; Advance/Newhouse Partnership (MSO).

ELDORADO—Formerly served by Reach Broadband. No longer in operation. ICA: TX0342.

ELECTRA—Suddenlink Communications, 520 Maryville Centre Dr, Ste 300, St. Louis, MO 63141. Phones: 800-999-6845; 314-315-9400. Web Site: http://www.suddenlink.com. ICA: TX0285.
TV Market Ranking: Below 100 (ELECTRA). Franchise award date: N.A. Franchise expiration date: N.A. Began: April 1, 1978.
Channel capacity: N.A. Channels available but not in use: N.A.
Basic Service
Subscribers: 157.
Programming (received off-air): KAUZ-TV (CBS, CW) Wichita Falls; KFDX-TV (NBC) Wichita Falls; KJTL (Bounce TV, FOX) Wichita Falls; KSWO-TV (ABC, TMO) Lawton; allband FM.
Programming (via satellite): Discovery Channel; QVC; TBS; The Weather Channel; truTV.
Programming (via translator): KERA-TV (PBS) Dallas.
Fee: $28.45 monthly.
Expanded Basic Service 1
Subscribers: N.A.
Programming (via satellite): AMC; Animal Planet; Cartoon Network; CNBC; CNN; C-SPAN; ESPN; Fox News Channel; Freeform; FX; HGTV; HLN; Lifetime; MTV; Spike TV; TLC; TNT; USA Network.
Fee: $39.95 installation; $23.00 monthly.
Pay Service 1
Pay Units: N.A.
Programming (via satellite): Cinemax; HBO; Starz; Starz Encore.

Cable Systems—Texas

Fee: $1.75 monthly (Encore), $6.75 monthly (Starz), $13.59 monthly (Cinemax or HBO).
Video-On-Demand: No
Internet Service
Operational: Yes. Began: November 12, 2003.
Broadband Service: Suddenlink High Speed Internet.
Fee: $49.95 installation; $43.95 monthly.
Telephone Service
None
Miles of Plant: 22.0 (coaxial); None (fiber optic). Homes passed: 1,208.
Senior Vice President, Corporate Finance: Michael Pflantz. Regional Manager: Todd Cruthird. Plant Manager: Ron Johnson.
Ownership: Cequel Communications Holdings I LLC (MSO).

ELLINGER—Formerly served by National Cable Inc. No longer in operation. ICA: TX0751.

ELMO—Formerly served by Almega Cable. No longer in operation. ICA: TX0489.

EMORY—Formerly served by Alliance Communications Network. No longer in operation. ICA: TX0375.

ENCINAL—Formerly served by Telecom Cable. No longer in operation. ICA: TX0565.

ENNIS—Charter Communications. Now served by MIDLOTHIAN, TX [TX0122]. ICA: TX0123.

EVANT—Formerly served by Almega Cable. No longer in operation. ICA: TX0631.

FAIRFIELD—Northland Cable Television, 515 West Tyler St, Mexia, TX 76667. Phones: 800-792-3087; 254-562-2872. Fax: 254-562-6454. Web Site: http://www.yournorthland.com. Also serves Teague. ICA: TX0150.
TV Market Ranking: Outside TV Markets (FAIRFIELD, Teague). Franchise award date: February 1, 1965. Franchise expiration date: N.A. Began: November 1, 1968.
Channel capacity: N.A. Channels available but not in use: N.A.
Basic Service
Subscribers: 384.
Programming (received off-air): KCEN-TV (Antenna TV, MeTV, MundoMax, NBC) Temple; KDAF (Antenna TV, CW, This TV) Dallas; KDFI (Bounce TV, Buzzr, Heroes & Icons, MNT, Movies!) Dallas; KDFW (FOX) Dallas; KERA-TV (PBS) Dallas; KFWD (MundoMax) Fort Worth; KPXD-TV (ION) Arlington; KTVT (CBS, Decades) Fort Worth; KTXA (IND, MeTV) Fort Worth; KWKT-TV (Estrella TV, FOX, MNT) Waco; KWTX-TV (CBS, CW) Waco; KXAS-TV (COZI TV, NBC) Fort Worth; KXTX-TV (TMO) Dallas; KXXV (ABC, TMO) Waco; WFAA (ABC) Dallas; allband FM.
Programming (via satellite): A&E; Animal Planet; BET; Cartoon Network; CNBC; CNN; C-SPAN; Discovery Channel; ESPN; Food Network; Fox News Channel; FOX Sports Southwest; Great American Country; Hallmark Channel; HGTV; History; HLN; Pop; QVC; TBS; The Weather Channel; TLC; TNT; Trinity Broadcasting Network (TBN); Univision Studios; USA Network.
Fee: $75.00 installation; $47.64 monthly.
Expanded Basic Service 1
Subscribers: N.A.
Programming (via satellite): Comedy Central; E! HD; ESPN2; FXM; Lifetime; MTV; Nickelodeon; Spike TV; Syfy; Turner Classic Movies.
Fee: $49.99 monthly.
Digital Basic Service
Subscribers: N.A.
Programming (via satellite): BBC America; Bloomberg Television; Bravo; Discovery Life Channel; DMX Music; Fox Sports 1; Golf Channel; GSN; IFC; NBCSN; Outdoor Channel; WE tv.
Fee: $34.99 monthly.
Pay Service 1
Pay Units: 200.
Programming (via satellite): HBO.
Fee: $35.00 installation; $14.00 monthly.
Pay Service 2
Pay Units: 30.
Programming (via satellite): Showtime.
Fee: $35.00 installation; $10.00 monthly.
Pay Service 3
Pay Units: 100.
Programming (via satellite): Starz; Starz Encore.
Fee: $35.00 installation; $10.00 monthly.
Digital Pay Service 1
Pay Units: 30.
Programming (via satellite): Cinemax (multiplexed); HBO (multiplexed); Showtime (multiplexed); Starz (multiplexed); Starz Encore (multiplexed); The Movie Channel (multiplexed).
Fee: $14.75 monthly (Cinemax, HBO, Showtime/TMC or Starz/Encore).
Video-On-Demand: No
Pay-Per-View
Sports PPV (delivered digitally); iN DEMAND (delivered digitally).
Internet Service
Operational: Yes.
Fee: $42.99 monthly.
Telephone Service
Digital: Operational
Miles of Plant: 92.0 (coaxial); None (fiber optic). Homes passed: 3,835.
Executive Vice President: Richard I. Clark. General Manager: Brent Richey. Chief Technician: Joe Lopez. Office Manager: Pamela Elliott.
Ownership: Northland Communications Corp. (MSO).

FALFURRIAS—Time Warner Cable. Now served by CORPUS CHRISTI, TX [TX0010]. ICA: TX0269.

FANNETT—Formerly served by Almega Cable. No longer in operation. ICA: TX0319.

FARMERSVILLE—Time Warner Cable. Now served by DALLAS, TX [TX0003]. ICA: TX1000.

FAYETTEVILLE—Formerly served by Grisham TV Cable Co. No longer in operation. ICA: TX0985.

FENTRESS—Formerly served by National Cable Inc. No longer in operation. ICA: TX0611.

FLAT—Formerly served by National Cable Inc. No longer in operation. ICA: TX0699.

FLATONIA—Formerly served by Almega Cable. No longer in operation. ICA: TX0755.

FLORENCE—Formerly served by Windjammer Cable. No longer in operation. ICA: TX0539.

FLORESVILLE—Formerly served by Clear Vu Cable. No longer in operation. ICA: TX0236.

FLOWER MOUND—Time Warner Cable. Now served by DALLAS, TX [TX0003]. ICA: TX0107.

FLOYDADA—Suddenlink Communications. Now served by PLAINVIEW, TX [TX0076]. ICA: TX0237.

FOLLETT—Formerly served by Panhandle Telephone Coop. Inc. No longer in operation. ICA: TX0610.

FORSAN—Formerly served by National Cable Inc. No longer in operation. ICA: TX0695.

FORT BEND COUNTY (portions)—Formerly served by Rapid Cable. Now served by Comcast Cable, HOUSTON, TX [TX0001]. ICA: TX1010.

FORT DAVIS—Mountain Zone TV, 307 E Ave East, Alpine, TX 79830. Phones: 800-446-5661; 432-729-4347; 432-837-2300. Fax: 432-837-5423. E-mail: mtnzone@sbcglobal.net. Web Site: http://www.mountainzonetv.net. ICA: TX0531.
TV Market Ranking: Outside TV Markets (FORT DAVIS). Franchise award date: September 10, 1965. Franchise expiration date: N.A. Began: December 1, 1965.
Channel capacity: 61 (operating 2-way). Channels available but not in use: N.A.
Basic Service
Subscribers: N.A.
Programming (received off-air): KMID (ABC) Midland; KOSA-TV (CBS, MNT) Odessa; KWES-TV (CW, NBC, TMO) Odessa; allband FM.
Programming (via satellite): A&E; CMT; CNN; Discovery Channel; ESPN; Freeform; KMGH-TV (ABC, Azteca America) Denver; KRMA-TV (PBS) Denver; Nickelodeon; Spike TV; TBS; The Weather Channel; TLC; TNT; Trinity Broadcasting Network (TBN); Turner Classic Movies; Univision; WGN America.
Fee: $35.00 installation; $48.00 monthly.
Pay Service 1
Pay Units: N.A.
Programming (via satellite): Cinemax; HBO; Showtime.
Fee: $10.00 installation; $7.50 monthly.
Video-On-Demand: No
Internet Service
Operational: Yes. Began: April 1, 2006.
Fee: $150.00 installation; $60.00 monthly.
Telephone Service
None
Miles of Plant: 21.0 (coaxial); None (fiber optic). Homes passed: 450.
General Manager: Steve Neu. Office Manager: Lawrence Neu.
Ownership: Mountain Zone TV Systems (MSO).

FORT STOCKTON—Baja Broadband, 525 Junction Rd, Madison, WI 53717. Phones: 575-437-3101; 877-422-5282; 800-996-8788. Fax: 608-830-5519. E-mail: comments@tdstelecom.com. Web Site: http://www.bajabroadband.com. ICA: TX1029.

FULLY SEARCHABLE • CONTINUOUSLY UPDATED • DISCOUNT RATES FOR PRINT PURCHASERS
For more information call **800-771-9202** or visit **www.warren-news.com**

TV Market Ranking: Outside TV Markets (FORT STOCKTON).
Channel capacity: N.A. Channels available but not in use: N.A.
Basic Service
Subscribers: 1,101.
Programming (received off-air): KMID (ABC) Midland; KMLM-DT (GLC) Odessa; KOSA-TV (CBS, MNT) Odessa; KPBT-TV (PBS) Odessa; KPEJ-TV (FOX) Odessa; KTLE-LP (TMO) Odessa; KUPB (UNV) Midland; KWES-TV (CW, NBC, TMO) Odessa; KWWT (Antenna TV, MeTV, Movies!, Retro TV, This TV) Odessa.
Programming (via satellite): ESPN Deportes; EVINE Live; EWTN Global Catholic Network; Fox News Channel; HLN; HSN; Lifetime; Pop; TBS; Trinity Broadcasting Network (TBN); UniMas; WGN America.
Fee: $29.95-$39.96 installation; $24.26 monthly.
Expanded Basic Service 1
Subscribers: N.A.
Programming (via satellite): A&E; AMC; Animal Planet; Cartoon Network; CMT; CNBC; CNN; Comedy Central; C-SPAN; Discovery Channel; Discovery Life Channel; Disney Channel; FOX Sports Networks; Freeform; FX; HGTV; History; MoviePlex; MTV; Nick At Nite; Nickelodeon; Spike TV; Syfy; The Weather Channel; TLC; TNT; USA Network; VH1.
Fee: $29.83 monthly.
Digital Basic Service
Subscribers: N.A.
Programming (via satellite): BBC America; Bloomberg Television; Bravo; Cloo; CMT; Destination America; Discovery Kids Channel; Disney XD; DMX Music; ESPNews; Fox Sports 1; Fuse; FXM; FYI; Golf Channel; GSN; History International; IFC; Investigation Discovery; LMN; MTV Classic; MTV2; NBC Universo; NBCSN; NFL Network; Nick Jr.; OWN: Oprah Winfrey Network; Science Channel; Starz Encore (multiplexed); TeenNick; Turner Classic Movies; WE tv.
Fee: $23.39 monthly.
Digital Expanded Basic Service
Subscribers: N.A.
Programming (via satellite): ESPN Classic; ESPNews; Fox Sports 1; NFL Network; NFL RedZone; Outdoor Channel.
Fee: $3.95 monthly.
Digital Expanded Basic Service 2
Subscribers: N.A.
Programming (via satellite): Cine Mexicano; Cinelatino; CNN en Espanol; ESPN Deportes; History en Espanol; NBC Universo; Tr3s; ViendoMovies.
Fee: $4.95 monthly.
Pay Service 1
Pay Units: N.A.
Programming (via satellite): Cinemax; HBO.
Fee: $13.95 monthly (each).
Digital Pay Service 1
Pay Units: N.A.
Programming (via satellite): Cinemax (multiplexed); HBO (multiplexed); Showtime (multiplexed); Starz (multiplexed); The Movie Channel (multiplexed).

2017 Edition D-739

Texas—Cable Systems

Fee: $9.95 monthly (Starz), $12.95 monthly Cinemax, HBO, Showtime or TMC).
Video-On-Demand: No
Pay-Per-View
Playboy TV (delivered digitally); Fresh (delivered digitally).
Internet Service
Operational: Yes.
Telephone Service
Digital: Operational
Vice President, Corporate Finance: Carl Shapiro. Assistant Treasurer: Noel Hutton.
Ownership: TDS Telecom (MSO).

FORT WORTH (northern portions)—Charter Communications, 12405 Powerscourt Dr, St. Louis, MO 63131. Phones: 636-207-5100 (Corporate office); 817-810-9171; 817-298-3600. Web Site: http://www.charter.com. Also serves Azle, Benbrook, Blue Mound, Burleson, Cleburne, Crowley, Edgecliff Village, Everman, Forest Hill, Fort Worth Naval Air Station, Glen Rose, Granbury, Haltom City, Haslet, Hood County (portions), Hurst, Keller, Kennedale, Lake Worth, Lakeside, Mansfield, North Richland Hills, Northlake, Oak Trail Shores, Parker County (portions), Richland Hills, River Oaks, Roanoke, Saginaw, Sanctuary, Sansom Park, Somervell County (portions), Southlake, Trophy Club, Watauga, Weatherford, Westlake, Westover Hills, Westworth Village & White Settlement. ICA: TX0008.
TV Market Ranking: 12 (Azle, Benbrook, Blue Mound, Burleson, Cleburne, Crowley, Edgecliff Village, Everman, Forest Hill, FORT WORTH (NORTHERN PORTIONS), Fort Worth Naval Air Station, Granbury, Haltom City, Haslet, Hood County (portions), Hurst, Keller, Kennedale, Lake Worth, Lakeside, Mansfield, North Richland Hills, Northlake, Parker County (portions), Richland Hills, River Oaks, Roanoke, Saginaw, Sanctuary, Sansom Park, Southlake, Southlake, Trophy Club, Watauga, Weatherford, Westlake, Westover Hills, Westworth Village, White Settlement, Willow Park); Outside TV Markets (Glen Rose, Somervell County (portions), Hood County (portions)). Franchise award date: March 1, 1980. Franchise expiration date: N.A. Began: January 1, 1982.
Channel capacity: 71 (operating 2-way). Channels available but not in use: N.A.
Digital Basic Service
Subscribers: 84,992.
Programming (via satellite): BBC America; Bloomberg Television; Discovery Digital Networks; DIY Network; FXM; FYI; Great American Country; History International; IFC; LMN; MC; Sundance TV; Weatherscan.
Fee: $26.99 monthly.
Digital Expanded Basic Service
Subscribers: N.A.
Programming (via satellite): A&E; AMC; Animal Planet; BET; Bravo; Cartoon Network; CMT; CNBC; CNN; Comedy Central; Discovery Channel; Disney Channel; Disney XD; E! HD; ESPN; ESPN Classic; ESPN2; Food Network; Fox Deportes; Fox News Channel; Fox Sports 1; FOX Sports Southwest; Freeform; FX; Golf Channel; GSN; Hallmark Channel; HGTV; History; HLN; Lifetime; MSNBC; MTV; National Geographic Channel; NBC Universo; NBCSN; Nickelodeon; Oxygen; Spike TV; Syfy; TBS; The Weather Channel; TLC; TNT; Travel Channel; truTV; Turner Classic Movies; TV Land; Univision; USA Network; VH1; WE tv.
Fee: $48.99 monthly.

Digital Pay Service 1
Pay Units: N.A.
Programming (via satellite): Cinemax (multiplexed); Flix; HBO (multiplexed); Showtime (multiplexed); Starz (multiplexed); Starz Encore (multiplexed); The Movie Channel (multiplexed).
Fee: $7.95 monthly (Cinemax), $9.95 monthly (HBO, Showtime/Flix or TMC).
Video-On-Demand: Yes
Pay-Per-View
ETC (delivered digitally); iN DEMAND (delivered digitally); Pleasure (delivered digitally).
Internet Service
Operational: Yes.
Subscribers: 47,905.
Broadband Service: Charter Internet.
Fee: $29.99 monthly; $15.00 modem lease; $259.00 modem purchase.
Telephone Service
Digital: Operational
Subscribers: 19,224.
Fee: $29.99 monthly
Miles of Plant: 9,031.0 (coaxial); 2,511.0 (fiber optic). Homes passed: 514,417.
Vice President & General Manager: Wayne Cramp. Technical Operations Director: John Linton. Marketing Director: Kathleen Griffin. Accounting Director: David Sovanski. Marketing Manager: Sherry Matlock.
Ownership: Charter Communications Inc. (MSO).

FRANKLIN—Zito Media, 102 S Main St, PO Box 665, Coudersport, PA 16915. Phones: 814-260-9055; 800-365-6988. E-mail: info@zitomedia.com. Web Site: http://www.zitomedia.com. ICA: TX0758.
TV Market Ranking: Below 100 (FRANKLIN).
Channel capacity: N.A. Channels available but not in use: N.A.
Basic Service
Subscribers: 130.
Programming (received off-air): KBTX-TV (CBS, CW) Bryan; KCEN-TV (Antenna TV, MeTV, MundoMax, NBC) Temple; KNCT (PBS) Belton; KWTX-TV (CBS, CW) Waco; KXXV (ABC, TMO) Waco.
Programming (via satellite): A&E; AMC; Animal Planet; BET; Cartoon Network; CNN; C-SPAN; Discovery Channel; Disney Channel; E! HD; ESPN; ESPN2; Fox News Channel; FOX Sports Southwest; Freeform; Fuse; FX; Great American Country; Hallmark Channel; HGTV; History; HLN; INSP; Lifetime; Outdoor Channel; QVC; TBS; The Weather Channel; TLC; TNT; USA Network; WGN America.
Fee: $49.95 installation; $49.85 monthly.
Pay Service 1
Pay Units: N.A.
Programming (via satellite): HBO; Showtime; Starz Encore.
Internet Service
Operational: No.
Telephone Service
None
Miles of Plant: 11.0 (coaxial); None (fiber optic). Homes passed: 750.
President: James Rigas.
Ownership: Zito Media (MSO).

FREDERICKSBURG—Time Warner Cable. Now served by AUSTIN, TX [TX0005]. ICA: TX0149.

FREER—Alliance Communications, PO Box 9090, Tyler, TX 75711. Phones: 405-395-1131 (Greenbrier, AR office); 800-842-8160. E-mail: email@alliancecom.net. Web Site: http://www.alliancecable.net. Also serves

Duval County (northern portion). ICA: TX0225.
TV Market Ranking: Outside TV Markets (Duval County (northern portion), FREER). Franchise award date: N.A. Franchise expiration date: N.A. Began: January 1, 1968.
Channel capacity: N.A. Channels available but not in use: N.A.
Basic Service
Subscribers: 144.
Programming (received off-air): KDFW (FOX) Dallas; KEDT (PBS) Corpus Christi; KIII (ABC, MeTV) Corpus Christi; KORO (LATV, UNV) Corpus Christi; KRIS-TV (CW, Grit, NBC) Corpus Christi; KUQI (FOX, IND) Corpus Christi; KZTV (CBS) Corpus Christi.
Programming (via satellite): A&E; AMC; Animal Planet; Bravo; Cartoon Network; CMT; CNBC; CNN; Comedy Central; C-SPAN; CW PLUS; Discovery Channel; Disney Channel; ESPN; ESPN2; EWTN Global Catholic Network; Food Network; Fox News Channel; Fox Sports 1; FOX Sports Southwest; Freeform; FX; Hallmark Channel; HGTV; History; HLN; Lifetime; MSNBC; MTV; National Geographic Channel; NBC Universo; NBCSN; Nickelodeon; Oxygen; QVC; Spike TV; Syfy; TBS; Telemundo; The Weather Channel; TLC; TNT; Travel Channel; Trinity Broadcasting Network (TBN); truTV; Turner Classic Movies; TV Land; UniMas; Univision; USA Network; VH1; WE tv.
Fee: $34.99 installation; $22.45 monthly.
Pay Service 1
Pay Units: N.A.
Programming (via satellite): HBO; Showtime; Starz; Starz Encore; The Movie Channel.
Fee: $12.95 monthly (each).
Internet Service
Operational: No.
Telephone Service
None
Miles of Plant: 18.0 (coaxial); None (fiber optic). Homes passed: 1,980.
Chief Financial Officer: David Starrett. Vice President & General Manager: John Brinker. Vice President, Programming: Julie Newman.
Ownership: Buford Media Group LLC (MSO).

FRIONA—Formerly served by Reach Broadband. No longer in operation. ICA: TX0277.

FRUITVALE—Formerly served by Almega Cable. No longer in operation. ICA: TX0580.

GAINESVILLE—Suddenlink Communications, 104 North Morris St, Gainesville, TX 76240-4242. Phones: 800-999-6845; 314-315-9400. Web Site: http://www.suddenlink.com. Also serves Cooke County & Oak Ridge. ICA: TX0117.
TV Market Ranking: Below 100 (Cooke County (portions), GAINESVILLE); Outside TV Markets (Cooke County (portions), Oak Ridge). Franchise award date: N.A. Franchise expiration date: N.A. Began: March 2, 1967.
Channel capacity: N.A. Channels available but not in use: N.A.
Basic Service
Subscribers: 2,870. Commercial subscribers: 278.
Programming (received off-air): KDAF (Antenna TV, CW, This TV) Dallas; KDFW (FOX) Dallas; KDTN (Daystar TV, ETV) Denton; KERA-TV (PBS) Dallas; KMPX (Estrella TV) Decatur; KPXD-TV (ION) Arlington; KTVT (CBS, Decades) Fort Worth; KTXA (IND, MeTV) Fort Worth; KUVN-DT (UNV) Garland; KXAS-TV (COZI TV, NBC) Fort Worth;

KXII (CBS, FOX, MNT) Sherman; KXTX-TV (TMO) Dallas; WFAA (ABC) Dallas.
Programming (via satellite): Discovery Channel; Great American Country; QVC; TBS.
Fee: $54.95 installation; $33.24 monthly; $2.00 converter.
Expanded Basic Service 1
Subscribers: N.A.
Programming (via satellite): A&E; AMC; BET; CMT; CNBC; CNN; C-SPAN; Disney Channel; ESPN; Fox News Channel; FOX Sports Southwest; Freeform; FX; HLN; Lifetime; MTV; Nickelodeon; Spike TV; The Weather Channel; TNT; USA Network.
Fee: $11.68 monthly.
Digital Basic Service
Subscribers: N.A.
Programming (via satellite): BBC America; Discovery Digital Networks; DMX Music; ESPN Classic; ESPN2; Fox Sports 1; Golf Channel; GSN; HGTV; History; NBCSN; Starz Encore; Syfy; Turner Classic Movies; TV Land; WE tv.
Pay Service 1
Pay Units: N.A.
Programming (via satellite): Cinemax; HBO; Showtime; Starz Encore.
Video-On-Demand: No
Pay-Per-View
Movies; special events.
Internet Service
Operational: Yes.
Broadband Service: Suddenlink High Speed Internet.
Fee: $45.95 installation; $29.95 monthly.
Telephone Service
Digital: Operational
Fee: $44.95 monthly
Miles of Plant: 288.0 (coaxial); 93.0 (fiber optic). Homes passed: 11,005.
Senior Vice President, Corporate Finance: Michael Pflantz. Vice President, Accounting: Sabrina Warr.
Ownership: Cequel Communications Holdings I LLC (MSO).

GANADO—NewWave Communications. Now served by WHARTON, TX [TX0171]. ICA: TX0428.

GARDEN CITY—Formerly served by National Cable Inc. No longer in operation. ICA: TX0760.

GARDENDALE—Formerly served by Cebridge Connections. No longer in operation. ICA: TX0575.

GARLAND—Time Warner Cable. Now served by DALLAS, TX [TX0003]. ICA: TX0013.

GARRISON—Formerly served by Almega Cable. No longer in operation. ICA: TX0528.

GARWOOD—Formerly served by National Cable Inc. No longer in operation. ICA: TX0573.

GARY—Formerly served by Almega Cable. No longer in operation. ICA: TX0399.

GATESVILLE—Suddenlink Communications, PO Box 739, Gatesville, TX 76528. Phones: 888-822-5151 (Customer service); 314-315-9400. Web Site: http://www.suddenlink.com. Also serves Fort Gates & South Mountain. ICA: TX0167.
TV Market Ranking: Below 100 (Fort Gates, GATESVILLE, South Mountain). Franchise

Cable Systems—Texas

award date: N.A. Franchise expiration date: N.A. Began: January 1, 1952.
Channel capacity: N.A. Channels available but not in use: N.A.

Basic Service
Subscribers: 225. Commercial subscribers: 193.
Programming (received off-air): KAKW-DT (getTV, UNV) Killeen; KCEN-TV (Antenna TV, MeTV, MundoMax, NBC) Temple; KNCT (PBS) Belton; KTBC (Buzzr, FOX, Movies!) Austin; KWKT-TV (Estrella TV, FOX, MNT) Waco; KWTX-TV (CBS, CW) Waco; KXXV (ABC, TMO) Waco; WFAA (ABC) Dallas; 4 FMs.
Programming (via satellite): CNBC; C-SPAN; HLN; INSP; TBS; The Weather Channel; TLC; WGN America.
Fee: $54.95 installation; $33.24 monthly.

Expanded Basic Service 1
Subscribers: N.A.
Programming (via satellite): A&E; AMC; CNN; Discovery Channel; Disney Channel; ESPN; ESPN2; Fox News Channel; FOX Sports Southwest; Freeform; Great American Country; Independent Music Network; Lifetime; Nickelodeon; Spike TV; TNT; USA Network; VH1.

Digital Basic Service
Subscribers: N.A.
Programming (via satellite): BBC America; Bloomberg Television; Discovery Digital Networks; Disney XD; DMX Music; ESPN Classic; ESPNews; Fox Sports 1; Fuse; FYI; Golf Channel; GSN; HGTV; History; History International; LMN; MBC America; NBCSN; Outdoor Channel; Starz Encore; Sundance TV; Syfy; The Word Network; Trinity Broadcasting Network (TBN).

Digital Pay Service 1
Pay Units: N.A.
Programming (via satellite): Cinemax (multiplexed); HBO (multiplexed); Showtime (multiplexed); Starz (multiplexed); The Movie Channel (multiplexed).
Fee: $10.00 monthly (HBO, Showtime, Starz or TMC).

Video-On-Demand: No
Pay-Per-View
iN DEMAND (delivered digitally); Playboy TV (delivered digitally); Fresh (delivered digitally); Shorteez (delivered digitally).

Internet Service
Operational: No.
Telephone Service
Digital: Operational
Miles of Plant: 66.0 (coaxial); None (fiber optic). Homes passed: 3,380.
Senior Vice President, Corporate Finance: Michael Pflantz. Vice President, Accounting: Sabrina Warr. General Manager: Gail Ussery.
Ownership: Cequel Communications Holdings I LLC (MSO).

GAUSE—Formerly served by National Cable Inc. No longer in operation. ICA: TX0660.

GEORGE WEST—Time Warner Cable, 7800 Crescent Executive Dr, Charlotte, NC 28217. Phones: 972-899-7300 (Flower Mound office); 361-698-6259. Web Site: http://www.timewarnercable.com. ICA: TX0343.
TV Market Ranking: Outside TV Markets (GEORGE WEST). Franchise award date: N.A. Franchise expiration date: N.A. Began: December 1, 1981.
Channel capacity: N.A. Channels available but not in use: N.A.

Basic Service
Subscribers: 110.
Programming (received off-air): KDFW (FOX) Dallas; KEDT (PBS) Corpus Christi; KIII (ABC, MeTV) Corpus Christi; KORO (LATV, UNV) Corpus Christi; KRIS-TV (CW, Grit, NBC) Corpus Christi; KSAT-TV (ABC, MeTV) San Antonio; KVDA (TMO) San Antonio; KZTV (CBS) Corpus Christi.
Programming (via satellite): Cartoon Network; QVC.
Fee: $49.99 installation; $28.00 monthly.

Expanded Basic Service 1
Subscribers: N.A.
Programming (via satellite): A&E; AMC; Animal Planet; Bravo; CMT; CNBC; CNN; Comedy Central; C-SPAN; Discovery Channel; Disney Channel; E! HD; ESPN; ESPN2; EWTN Global Catholic Network; Food Network; Fox News Channel; Fox Sports 1; FOX Sports Southwest; Freeform; FX; Golf Channel; Great American Country; HGTV; History; HLN; Lifetime; MSNBC; MTV; National Geographic Channel; NBCSN; Nickelodeon; Oxygen; Spike TV; Syfy; TBS; The Weather Channel; TLC; TNT; Travel Channel; truTV; Turner Classic Movies; TV Land; Univision; USA Network; VH1.
Fee: $28.60 monthly.

Pay Service 1
Pay Units: N.A.
Programming (via satellite): HBO; Showtime; Starz; Starz Encore.
Fee: $3.75 monthly (Encore), $12.95 monthly (HBO, Showtime or Starz).

Internet Service
Operational: Yes.
Telephone Service
Digital: Operational
Miles of Plant: 43.0 (coaxial); 4.0 (fiber optic). Homes passed: 1,131.
President: Connie Wharton. Vice President & General Manager: Mike McKee. Senior Accounting Director: Karen Goodfellow. Engineering Director: Charlotte Strong. Public Affairs Manager: Vicki Triplett.
Ownership: Time Warner Cable (MSO).; Advance/Newhouse Partnership (MSO).

GEORGETOWN—Suddenlink Communications, 111 North College St, Georgetown, TX 78626-4101. Phones: 314-315-9400; 512-930-3085. Fax: 512-869-2962. Web Site: http://www.suddenlink.com. ICA: TX0081.
TV Market Ranking: Below 100 (GEORGETOWN). Franchise award date: January 1, 1972. Franchise expiration date: N.A. Began: January 1, 1972.
Channel capacity: 80 (operating 2-way). Channels available but not in use: N.A.

Basic Service
Subscribers: 15,223. Commercial subscribers: 466.
Programming (received off-air): KAKW-DT (getTV, UNV) Killeen; KCEN-TV (Antenna TV, MeTV, MundoMax, NBC) Temple; KEYE-TV (CBS, TMO) Austin; KLRU (PBS) Austin; KNVA (CW, Grit, TheCoolTV) Austin; KTBC (Buzzr, FOX, Movies!) Austin; KVUE (ABC, Estrella TV) Austin.
Programming (via satellite): C-SPAN; INSP; Pop; QVC; UniMas; WGN America.
Fee: $54.95 installation; $33.24 monthly; $1.50 converter.

Expanded Basic Service 1
Subscribers: N.A.
Programming (via satellite): A&E; AMC; Animal Planet; BET; Bravo; Cartoon Network; CMT; CNBC; CNN; Comedy Central; C-SPAN 2; Discovery Channel; Disney Channel; E! HD; ESPN; ESPN2; EVINE Live; EWTN Global Catholic Network; Food Network; Fox News Channel; Fox Sports 1; FOX Sports Southwest; Freeform; FX; Golf Channel; Great American Country; HGTV; History; HLN; Jewelry Television; Lifetime; LMN; MSNBC; MTV; NBCSN; Nickelodeon; Spike TV; Syfy; TBS; Telemundo; The Weather Channel; TLC; TNT; Travel Channel; Trinity Broadcasting Network (TBN); truTV; Turner Classic Movies; TV Land; Univision; USA Network; VH1.
Fee: $12.49 monthly.

Digital Basic Service
Subscribers: N.A.
Programming (via satellite): A&E HD; AXS TV; Bandamax; BBC America; Bloomberg Television; Boomerang; BYUtv; CBS Sports Network; Cine Mexicano; Cinelatino; CMT; CNN en Espanol; Cooking Channel; Cox Sports Television; De Pelicula; De Pelicula Clasico; Destination America; Discovery Kids Channel; Disney XD; DIY Network; Enlace USA; ESPN Classic; ESPN Deportes; ESPN HD; ESPN2 HD; ESPNews; ESPNU; FamilyNet; Food Network HD; Fox Deportes; Fox Sports 2; Fuse; FYI; GSN; Hallmark Channel; HD Theater; HGTV HD; History en Espanol; History International; IFC; Investigation Discovery; MC; MTV Classic; MTV Hits; MTV2; Nat Geo WILD; National Geographic Channel; National Geographic Channel HD; NBC Universo; Nick Jr.; Nicktoons; Outdoor Channel; OWN; Oprah Winfrey Network; Oxygen; Ritmoson; Science Channel; Starz Encore (multiplexed); Sundance TV; Sur; TeenNick; Telehit; Telemundo; Tennis Channel; TNT HD; Toon Disney en Espanol; Tr3s; TV One; ULTRA HDPlex; Universal HD; Univision; UP; VideoRola; WE tv; Weatherscan.

Digital Pay Service 1
Pay Units: N.A.
Programming (via satellite): Cinemax (multiplexed); HBO (multiplexed); HBO HD; HBO Latino; Showtime (multiplexed); Showtime HD; Starz (multiplexed); Starz HD; The Movie Channel (multiplexed).

Video-On-Demand: No
Pay-Per-View
iN DEMAND (delivered digitally); Fresh (delivered digitally); Shorteez (delivered digitally); Playboy TV (delivered digitally); Playboy en Espanol (delivered digitally); Playboy en Espanol (delivered digitally).

Internet Service
Operational: Yes.
Subscribers: 27,246.
Broadband Service: Suddenlink High Speed Internet.

Telephone Service
Digital: Operational
Subscribers: 14,033.
Miles of Plant: 228.0 (coaxial); 29.0 (fiber optic).
Senior Vice President, Corporate Finance: Michael Pflantz. Vice President, Accounting: Sabrina Warr. General Manager: Dale Hoffman. Chief Technician & Marketing Director: Wesley Houghteling.
Ownership: Cequel Communications Holdings I LLC (MSO).

GILMER—Formerly served by Gilmer Cable. No longer in operation. ICA: TX0229.

GLADEWATER—Suddenlink Communications, 507 Northeast Loop 485, Gladewater, TX 75647-2545. Phones: 314-315-9400; 903-845-4036. Fax: 903-845-4038. Web Site: http://www.suddenlink.com. Also serves Clarksville City, Liberty City, Union Grove, Warren City & White Oak. ICA: TX0558.
TV Market Ranking: Below 100 (Clarksville City, GLADEWATER, Liberty City, Union Grove, Warren City, White Oak). Franchise award date: N.A. Franchise expiration date: N.A. Began: March 1, 1974.
Channel capacity: 26 (operating 2-way). Channels available but not in use: N.A.

Basic Service
Subscribers: 2,920. Commercial subscribers: 159.
Programming (received off-air): KCEB (CW, MundoMax) Longview; KERA-TV (PBS) Dallas; KETK-TV (Estrella TV, NBC) Jacksonville; KFXK-TV (FOX) Longview; KLPN-LD (MNT) Longview; KLTV (ABC, Bounce TV, TMO) Tyler; KSLA (Bounce TV, CBS, Grit, This TV) Shreveport; KXAS-TV (COZI TV, NBC) Fort Worth; KYTX (CBS, COZI TV, CW) Nacogdoches; WFAA (ABC) Dallas.
Programming (via satellite): Trinity Broadcasting Network (TBN).
Fee: $54.95 installation; $35.24 monthly.

Expanded Basic Service 1
Subscribers: N.A.
Programming (via satellite): A&E; AMC; Animal Planet; BET; Bravo; Cartoon Network; CNBC; CNN; Comedy Central; C-SPAN; Discovery Channel; Disney Channel; E! HD; ESPN; ESPN2; Food Network; Fox News Channel; FOX Sports Southwest; Freeform; FX; Great American Country; HGTV; History; HLN; Jewelry Television; Lifetime; MSNBC; MTV; National Geographic Channel; Nickelodeon; Outdoor Channel; Spike TV; Syfy; TBS; The Weather Channel; TLC; TNT; Travel Channel; Turner Classic Movies; TV Land; Univision Studios; USA Network; VH1.
Fee: $15.53 monthly.

Digital Basic Service
Subscribers: N.A.
Programming (via satellite): BBC America; Bloomberg Television; Cloo; Discovery Digital Networks; Disney XD; DMX Music; ESPN Classic; ESPNews; EVINE Live; FOX College Sports Central; FOX College Sports Pacific; Fox Sports 1; Fuse; Golf Channel; GSN; History International; IFC; NBCSN; Sundance TV; WE tv.

Pay Service 1
Pay Units: N.A.
Programming (via satellite): Cinemax; Flix; HBO; Showtime.

Digital Pay Service 1
Pay Units: N.A.
Programming (via satellite): Cinemax (multiplexed); Flix; HBO (multiplexed); Showtime (multiplexed); Starz (multiplexed); Starz Encore (multiplexed); The Movie Channel (multiplexed).

Video-On-Demand: No
Pay-Per-View
iN DEMAND (delivered digitally); Playboy TV (delivered digitally); Fresh (delivered digitally); NBA TV (delivered digitally); ESPN Now (delivered digitally).

Internet Service
Operational: Yes.
Broadband Service: Suddenlink High Speed Internet.
Fee: $49.95 installation; $38.95 monthly.

Telephone Service
None
Miles of Plant: 130.0 (coaxial); None (fiber optic). Homes passed: 6,600.
Senior Vice President, Corporate Finance: Michael Pflantz. Vice President, Accounting: Sabrina Warr. General Manager: Chris Downing. Chief Technician: Tim Moran.
Ownership: Cequel Communications Holdings I LLC (MSO).

GLEN ROSE—Formerly served by Glen Rose CATV. No longer in operation. ICA: TX0362.

2017 Edition
D-741

Texas—Cable Systems

CABLE & TV STATION COVERAGE

Atlas 2017

The perfect companion to the Television & Cable Factbook
To order call 800-771-9202 or visit www.warren-news.com

GODLEY—Formerly served by Almega Cable. No longer in operation. ICA: TX0562.

GOLDEN—Formerly served by Almega Cable. No longer in operation. ICA: TX0538.

GOLDSMITH—Formerly served by Cebridge Connections. No longer in operation. ICA: TX0670.

GOLDTHWAITE—Formerly served by Almega Cable. No longer in operation. ICA: TX0761.

GOLDTHWAITE—Formerly served by Central Texas Communications. No longer in operation. ICA: TX1037.

GOLIAD—CommZoom, 2438 Boardwalk, San Antonio, TX 78217. Phone: 844-858-8500. Web Site: http://www.commzoom.com. ICA: TX0395.
TV Market Ranking: Below 100 (GOLIAD). Franchise award date: N.A. Franchise expiration date: N.A. Began: April 1, 1969.
Channel capacity: N.A. Channels available but not in use: N.A.
Basic Service
Subscribers: 71.
Programming (received off-air): KABB (FOX, The Country Network) San Antonio; KAVU-TV (ABC) Victoria; KENS (CBS, Estrella TV) San Antonio; KLRN (PBS) San Antonio; KMOL-LD (Movies!, NBC) Victoria; KSAT-TV (ABC, MeTV) San Antonio; KVCT (FOX, This TV, TMO) Victoria; KZTV (CBS) Corpus Christi; allband FM.
Programming (via satellite): Bravo; Cartoon Network; CMT; CNN; Discovery Life Channel; E! HD; ESPN; Freeform; HLN; Nickelodeon; Oxygen; QVC; Syfy; The Weather Channel; TLC; Travel Channel; Univision Studios; USA Network.
Fee: $49.95 installation; $60.63 monthly.
Expanded Basic Service 1
Subscribers: N.A.
Programming (via satellite): A&E; AMC; Animal Planet; CNBC; Discovery Channel; Disney Channel; Food Network; Fox News Channel; FOX Sports Southwest; FX; History; Lifetime; MSNBC; MTV; Spike TV; TBS; TNT; TV Land; VH1.
Fee: $20.00 monthly.
Pay Service 1
Pay Units: N.A.
Programming (via satellite): HBO; Showtime; The Movie Channel.
Fee: $11.95 monthly (each).
Video-On-Demand: No
Pay-Per-View
iN DEMAND (delivered digitally); Hot Choice (delivered digitally); Playboy TV (delivered digitally); Fresh (delivered digitally); Shorteez (delivered digitally).
Internet Service
Operational: No.
Telephone Service
None
Miles of Plant: 22.0 (coaxial); None (fiber optic). Homes passed: 952.

Chief Executive Officer: Bob Cohen.
Ownership: CommZoom Communications LLC (MSO).

GOLINDA—Formerly served by National Cable Inc. No longer in operation. ICA: TX0905.

GONZALES—Time Warner Cable, 7800 Crescent Executive Dr, Charlotte, NC 28217. Phones: 830-257-4709; 972-899-7300 (Flower Mound division office). Web Site: http://www.timewarnercable.com. Also serves Cuero, DeWitt County (portions), Gonzales County (portions), Lavaca County (portions) & Yoakum. ICA: TX0209.
TV Market Ranking: Below 100 (Cuero, Yoakum, DeWitt County (portions), Lavaca County (portions)); Outside TV Markets (GONZALES, Gonzales County (portions), DeWitt County (portions), Lavaca County (portions)). Franchise award date: N.A. Franchise expiration date: N.A. Began: November 15, 1973.
Channel capacity: N.A. Channels available but not in use: N.A.
Basic Service
Subscribers: 2,779. Commercial subscribers: 115.
Programming (received off-air): KABB (FOX, The Country Network) San Antonio; KAVU-TV (ABC) Victoria; KENS (CBS, Estrella TV) San Antonio; KEYE-TV (CBS, TMO) Austin; KLRN (PBS) San Antonio; KMYS (CW) Kerrville; KSAT-TV (ABC, MeTV) San Antonio; KTBC (Buzzr, FOX, Movies!) Austin; KVDA (TMO) San Antonio; KWEX-DT (getTV, UNV) San Antonio; WOAI-TV (IND, NBC) San Antonio; allband FM.
Programming (via satellite): C-SPAN.
Fee: $49.99 installation; $28.00 monthly; $16.69 converter.
Expanded Basic Service 1
Subscribers: 1,912.
Programming (via satellite): A&E; AMC; Animal Planet; BET; Cartoon Network; CMT; CNBC; CNN; Comedy Central; C-SPAN 2; Discovery Channel; Disney Channel; E! HD; ESPN; ESPN2; EWTN Global Catholic Network; Food Network; Fox News Channel; FOX Sports Southwest; Freeform; FX; Golf Channel; Hallmark Channel; HD Theater; HGTV; History; HLN; Lifetime; MSNBC; MTV; National Geographic Channel; NBC Universo; Nickelodeon; Oxygen; QVC; Spike TV; Starz Encore; Syfy; TBS; The Weather Channel; TLC; TNT; TNT HD; Travel Channel; Trinity Broadcasting Network (TBN); truTV; Turner Classic Movies; TV Land; Univision Studios; USA Network; VH1; WE tv.
Fee: $31.30 monthly.
Digital Basic Service
Subscribers: N.A.
Programming (via satellite): AXS TV; BBC America; Bloomberg Television; Cooking Channel; Discovery Digital Networks; Disney XD; DIY Network; DMX Music; ESPN Classic; ESPN HD; ESPNews; FOX College Sports Central; FOX College Sports Pacific; Fox Deportes; Fox Sports 1; Fuse; FXM; Great American Country; GSN; IFC; LMN;

NBA TV; NBCSN; Nick Jr.; Nicktoons; Outdoor Channel; Starz Encore (multiplexed); Sundance TV; TeenNick; Tennis Channel.
Fee: $5.00 monthly, $8.95 monthly (each tier).
Digital Pay Service 1
Pay Units: 94.
Programming (via satellite): Cinemax; HBO; Showtime; Starz; The Movie Channel.
Fee: $12.95 monthly (each).
Video-On-Demand: No
Pay-Per-View
iN DEMAND Previews (delivered digitally); MLB Extra Innings (delivered digitally); iN DEMAND (delivered digitally); Fresh (delivered digitally); Shorteez (delivered digitally); Hot Choice (delivered digitally); Playboy TV (delivered digitally); Spice Hot (delivered digitally); NBA League Pass (delivered digitally).
Internet Service
Operational: Yes.
Subscribers: 2,197.
Broadband Service: RoadRunner.
Fee: $44.95 monthly.
Telephone Service
Digital: Operational
Subscribers: 986.
Fee: $44.95 monthly
Miles of Plant: 336.0 (coaxial); 370.0 (fiber optic). Homes passed: 10,382. Homes passed includes Columbus.
President: Connie Wharton. Vice President & General Manager: Mike McKee. Senior Accounting Director: Karen Goodfellow. Engineering Director: Charlotte Strong. Chief Technician: Bill Wilcox.
Ownership: Time Warner Cable (MSO).; Advance/Newhouse Partnership (MSO).

GOODRICH—Livingston Communications (formerly Versalink). This cable system has converted to IPTV, 701 West Church St, Livingston, TX 77351. Phones: 936-327-3201; 936-327-4309. E-mail: support@livcom.us. Web Site: http://www.livcom.us. ICA: TX5565.
TV Market Ranking: Outside TV Markets (GOODRICH).
Channel capacity: N.A. Channels available but not in use: N.A.
Basic Service
Subscribers: N.A.
Programming (received off-air): KBTX-TV (CBS, CW) Bryan; KCTL-LD Livingston; KETX-LP (IND) Livingston; KHOU (Bounce TV, CBS) Houston; KIAH (Antenna TV, CW) Houston; KPRC-TV (NBC, This TV) Houston; KPXB-TV (ION) Conroe; KRIV (FOX) Houston; KTRE (ABC, TMO) Lufkin; KTRK-TV (ABC, Live Well Network) Houston; KTXH (Buzzr, MNT, Movies!) Houston; KUHT (PBS) Houston.
Programming (via satellite): CNN; Freeform; TBS.
Video-On-Demand: No
Internet Service
Operational: Yes.
Fee: $59.95-$119.95 monthly.
Telephone Service
Digital: Operational
Fee: $11.73 monthly
President: Curt Walzel. Vice President & Business Manager: Gene Ainsworth.
Ownership: Livingston Communications (MSO).

GOODRICH—Livingston Communications (formerly Versalink). This cable system has converted to IPTV. See GOODRICH, TX [TX5565]. ICA: TX0174.

GORDON—Formerly served by Mallard Cablevision. No longer in operation. ICA: TX0593.

GORDONVILLE—TV Cable of Grayson County, 501 Spur 316 Hwy, Ste. 106, PO Box 2084, Pottsboro, TX 75076. Phones: 888-815-0636; 903-786-7477. E-mail: tvcable@graysoncable.com. Web Site: http://www.graysoncable.com. Also serves Sherwood Shores. ICA: TX0413.
TV Market Ranking: Below 100 (GORDONVILLE, Sherwood Shores).
Channel capacity: 36 (not 2-way capable). Channels available but not in use: N.A.
Basic Service
Subscribers: 122.
Programming (received off-air): KDAF (Antenna TV, CW, This TV) Dallas; KDFI (Bounce TV, Buzzr, Heroes & Icons, MNT, Movies!) Dallas; KERA-TV (PBS) Dallas; KTEN (ABC, CW, NBC) Ada; KTXA (IND, MeTV) Fort Worth; KXAS-TV (COZI TV, NBC) Fort Worth; KXII (CBS, FOX, MNT) Sherman; KXTX-TV (TMO) Dallas; WFAA (ABC) Dallas.
Programming (via satellite): A&E; AMC; Animal Planet; CNN; C-SPAN; C-SPAN 2; Discovery Channel; Disney Channel; ESPN; ESPN2; Fox News Channel; Fox Sports 1; FOX Sports Southwest; Freeform; FX; FXM; Golf Channel; Great American Country; Hallmark Channel; HGTV; History; HLN; Lifetime; MSNBC; MTV; National Geographic Channel; Nickelodeon; Outdoor Channel; QVC; Radar Channel; Spike TV; Syfy; TBS; The Weather Channel; TLC; TNT; Trinity Broadcasting Network (TBN); truTV; Turner Classic Movies; TV Land; USA Network; WGN America.
Fee: $46.95 monthly.
Pay Service 1
Pay Units: N.A.
Programming (via satellite): HBO; Showtime; The Movie Channel.
Fee: $9.50 monthly (Showtime/TMC) or $11.95 monthly (HBO).
Internet Service
Operational: Yes.
Fee: $24.99-$149.95 monthly.
Telephone Service
Digital: Operational
Miles of Plant: 20.0 (coaxial); None (fiber optic). Homes passed: 750.
General Manager: Chuck Davis.
Ownership: Chuck Davis (MSO).

GOREE—Formerly served by Jayroc Cablevision. No longer in operation. ICA: TX0762.

GORMAN—Reach Broadband, PO Box 507, Arp, TX 75750. Phones: 903-859-3789; 800-687-1258. Web Site: http://www.reachbroadband.net. ICA: TX0464.
TV Market Ranking: Outside TV Markets (GORMAN). Franchise award date: N.A. Franchise expiration date: N.A. Began: October 1, 1968.
Channel capacity: 35 (not 2-way capable). Channels available but not in use: N.A.
Basic Service
Subscribers: 54.
Programming (received off-air): KRBC-TV (Bounce TV, NBC) Abilene; KTAB-TV (CBS) Abilene; allband FM.
Programming (via microwave): KDFW (FOX) Dallas; KERA-TV (PBS) Dallas; KTVT (CBS, Decades) Fort Worth; KXAS-TV (COZI TV, NBC) Fort Worth; KXTX-TV (TMO) Dallas; WFAA (ABC) Dallas.
Programming (via satellite): Discovery Channel; FX; QVC; TBS; The Weather Channel.
Fee: $49.95 installation; $28.20 monthly.

Cable Systems—Texas

Expanded Basic Service 1
Subscribers: N.A.
Programming (via satellite): AMC; Animal Planet; Cartoon Network; CNBC; CNN; ESPN; Fox News Channel; FOX Sports Southwest; Freeform; HGTV; HLN; Spike TV; TLC; TNT; USA Network.
Fee: $18.00 monthly.
Pay Service 1
Pay Units: N.A.
Programming (via satellite): Cinemax; HBO; Showtime; Starz; Starz Encore.
Fee: $6.75 monthly (Starz), $12.90 monthly (Cinemax or HBO).
Video-On-Demand: No
Internet Service
Operational: Yes.
Telephone Service
None
Miles of Plant: 16.0 (coaxial); None (fiber optic). Homes passed: 579.
Regional Manager: Ronnie Stafford. Office Manager: Jan Gibson. Controller: Jeffrey Lowe.
Ownership: RB3 LLC (MSO).

GRAFORD—Vyve Broadband, 2804B FM 51 South, Decatur, TX 76234. Phone: 855-367-8983. Web Site: http://vyvebroadband.com. ICA: TX1045.
TV Market Ranking: Outside TV Markets (GRAFORD).
Channel capacity: N.A. Channels available but not in use: N.A.
Basic Service
Subscribers: 15.
Fee: $59.99 installation; $25.00 monthly.
Vice President, Financial Planning: Daniel White.
Ownership: Vyve Broadband LLC (MSO).

GRAHAM—Zito Media, 102 S Main St, PO Box 665, Coudersport, PA 16915. Phones: 814-260-9055; 800-365-6988. E-mail: info@zitomedia.com. Web Site: http://www.zitomedia.com. Also serves Young County. ICA: TX0142.
TV Market Ranking: Outside TV Markets (GRAHAM, Young County). Franchise award date: May 15, 1952. Franchise expiration date: N.A. Began: June 1, 1952.
Channel capacity: N.A. Channels available but not in use: N.A.
Basic Service
Subscribers: 841.
Programming (received off-air): KDTN (Daystar TV, ETV) Denton; KMPX (Estrella TV) Decatur; KPXD-TV (ION) Arlington; KSTR-DT (getTV, UniMas) Irving; KTXD-TV (IND) Greenville; 18 FMs.
Programming (via microwave): KAZD (Azteca America, IND) Lake Dallas; KDAF (Antenna TV, CW, This TV) Dallas; KDFI (Bounce TV, Buzzr, Heroes & Icons, MNT, Movies!) Dallas; KDFW (FOX) Dallas; KDTX-TV (TBN) Dallas; KERA-TV (PBS) Dallas; KFWD (MundoMax) Fort Worth; KTVT (CBS, Decades) Fort Worth; KTXA (IND, MeTV) Fort Worth; KXAS-TV (COZI TV, NBC) Fort Worth; KXTX-TV (TMO) Dallas; WFAA (ABC) Dallas.
Programming (via satellite): Azteca; C-SPAN; C-SPAN 2; Discovery Channel; QVC; TBS; WGN America.
Fee: $49.95 installation; $21.75 monthly.
Expanded Basic Service 1
Subscribers: N.A.
Programming (via satellite): A&E; Animal Planet; BET; Cartoon Network; CMT; CNBC; CNN; Comedy Central; Disney Channel; E! HD; ESPN; ESPN Classic; ESPN2; EWTN Global Catholic Network; Food Network; Fox News Channel; FOX Sports Southwest; Freeform; FX; Golf Channel; GSN; HGTV; History; HLN; Lifetime; MSNBC; MTV; MTV2; NBCSN; Nickelodeon; Oxygen; Pop; Spike TV; Syfy; The Weather Channel; TLC; TNT; Travel Channel; truTV; Turner Classic Movies; TV Land; TV One; Univision; Univision Studios; USA Network; VH1.
Digital Basic Service
Subscribers: N.A.
Programming (via satellite): AMC; AXS TV; BBC America; Bloomberg Television; Boomerang; Bravo; Canal Sur; Cartoon Network en Espanol; Cinelatino; CMT; CNN en Espanol; CNN International; Cooking Channel; C-SPAN 3; Destination America; Discovery Kids Channel; Discovery Life Channel; Disney XD; DIY Network; Enlace USA; ESPN HD; ESPNews; ESPNU; EVINE Live; FamilyNet; FOX College Sports Central; FOX College Sports Pacific; Fox Deportes; Fox Sports 1; Fox Sports 2; Fuse; FXM; FYI; Great American Country; Hallmark Channel; HD Theater; History en Espanol; History International; IFC; Infinito; Investigation Discovery; La Familia Cosmovision; LMN; MC; Mnet; MTV Classic; MTV Hits; MTV Jams; MTV2; National Geographic Channel; NBA TV; NBC Universo; Nick 2; Nick Jr.; Nicktoons; Outdoor Channel; OWN; Oprah Winfrey Network; Science Channel; Starz Encore (multiplexed); Sundance TV; TeenNick; Tennis Channel; The Word Network; TNT HD; Toon Disney en Espanol; Tr3s; TV Land; Universal HD; UP; VH1 Soul; VideoRola; WE tv.
Digital Pay Service 1
Pay Units: N.A.
Programming (via satellite): Cinemax (multiplexed); Cinemax HD; Flix; HBO (multiplexed); HBO HD; Showtime (multiplexed); Showtime HD; Starz (multiplexed); Starz HD; The Movie Channel (multiplexed); TV Asia; Zee TV.
Video-On-Demand: No
Pay-Per-View
iN DEMAND (delivered digitally); Fresh (delivered digitally); Playboy TV (delivered digitally); Hot Choice (delivered digitally); Shorteez (delivered digitally); Playboy en Espanol (delivered digitally); ESPN (delivered digitally); NBA League Pass (delivered digitally); NHL Center Ice (delivered digitally); MLB Extra Innings (delivered digitally).
Internet Service
Operational: Yes.
Telephone Service
Digital: Operational
Miles of Plant: 137.0 (coaxial); 61.0 (fiber optic). Homes passed: 4,973.
President: James Rigas.
Ownership: Zito Media (MSO).

GRANADA HILLS—Time Warner Cable. Now served by AUSTIN, TX [TX0005]. ICA: TX0763.

GRANBURY—Charter Communications. Now served by FORT WORTH (northern portions), TX [TX0008]. ICA: TX0764.

GRAND PRAIRIE—Time Warner Cable. Now served by DALLAS, TX [TX0003]. ICA: TX0030.

GRANDFALLS—Formerly served by Almega Cable. No longer in operation. ICA: TX0765.

GRAPE CREEK—NewWave Communications, One Montgomery Plaza, 4th Floor, Sikeston, MO 63801. Phones: 573-472-9500; 888-863-9928. Fax: 573-472-9518. E-mail: info@newwave.com. Web Site: http://www.newwavecom.com. ICA: TX0326.
TV Market Ranking: Below 100 (GRAPE CREEK). Franchise award date: October 1, 1980. Franchise expiration date: N.A. Began: July 1, 1982.
Channel capacity: N.A. Channels available but not in use: N.A.
Basic Service
Subscribers: 37.
Programming (received off-air): KIDY (FOX, MNT) San Angelo; KLST (CBS) San Angelo; KSAN-TV (NBC) San Angelo; KTXS-TV (ABC, CW, This TV, TMO) Sweetwater.
Programming (via satellite): A&E; AMC; Cartoon Network; CMT; CNN; Disney Channel; ESPN; Freeform; Lifetime; Spike TV; Syfy; TBS; The Weather Channel; TLC; TNT; TV Land; Univision Studios; USA Network; WGN America.
Fee: $35.00 installation; $37.75 monthly.
Pay Service 1
Pay Units: N.A.
Programming (via satellite): HBO.
Fee: $14.95 installation; $13.95 monthly.
Video-On-Demand: No
Internet Service
Operational: No.
Telephone Service
None
Miles of Plant: 45.0 (coaxial); None (fiber optic). Homes passed included in Merkel.
Regional General Manager: Jerry Smith.
Ownership: NewWave Communications LLC (MSO).

GRAPELAND—Suddenlink Communications, 520 Maryville Centre Dr, Ste 300, St. Louis, MO 63141. Phones: 800-999-6845 (Customer service); 314-315-9400. Fax: 903-561-5485. Web Site: http://www.suddenlink.com. Also serves Latexo. ICA: TX0382.
TV Market Ranking: Outside TV Markets (GRAPELAND, Latexo). Franchise award date: N.A. Franchise expiration date: N.A. Began: April 1, 1974.
Channel capacity: 57 (operating 2-way). Channels available but not in use: N.A.
Basic Service
Subscribers: 123.
Programming (received off-air): KFXK-TV (FOX) Longview; KLTV (ABC, Bounce TV, TMO) Tyler; KTRE (ABC, TMO) Lufkin; KTVT (CBS, Decades) Fort Worth; allband FM.
Programming (via microwave): KXAS-TV (COZI TV, NBC) Fort Worth; WFAA (ABC) Dallas.
Programming (via satellite): CNN; Discovery Channel; ESPN; Nickelodeon; Spike TV; TBS; TNT; USA Network; WGN America.
Fee: $39.95 installation; $28.45 monthly.
Pay Service 1
Pay Units: N.A.
Programming (via satellite): Cinemax; HBO; Showtime.
Fee: $10.95 monthly (Cinemax or HBO); $11.00 monthly (Showtime).
Video-On-Demand: No

Internet Service
Operational: Yes. Began: July 24, 2004.
Subscribers: 64.
Broadband Service: Suddenlink High Speed Internet.
Fee: $49.95 installation; $38.95 monthly.
Telephone Service
None
Miles of Plant: 69.0 (coaxial); 11.0 (fiber optic). Homes passed: 1,071.
Senior Vice President, Corporate Finance: Michael Pflantz. Regional Manager: Todd Cruthird. Plant Manager: David Burrell.
Ownership: Cequel Communications Holdings I LLC (MSO).

GRAYSON COUNTY—TV Cable of Grayson County, 501 Spur 316 Hwy, Ste. 106, PO Box 2084, Pottsboro, TX 75076. Phones: 888-815-0636; 903-786-7477. E-mail: tvcable@graysoncable.com. Web Site: http://www.graysoncable.com. ICA: TX1014.
TV Market Ranking: Below 100 (GRAYSON COUNTY).
Channel capacity: N.A. Channels available but not in use: N.A.
Basic Service
Subscribers: 137.
Programming (received off-air): KDAF (Antenna TV, CW, This TV) Dallas; KDFI (Bounce TV, Buzzr, Heroes & Icons, MNT, Movies!) Dallas; KDFW (FOX) Dallas; KERA-TV (PBS) Dallas; KTEN (ABC, CW, NBC) Ada; KTVT (CBS, Decades) Fort Worth; KXAS-TV (COZI TV, NBC) Fort Worth; KXII (CBS, FOX, MNT) Sherman; WFAA (ABC) Dallas.
Programming (via satellite): A&E; AMC; Animal Planet; Bloomberg Television; Boomerang; Cartoon Network; CMT; CNBC; CNN; C-SPAN; C-SPAN 2; Discovery Channel; ESPN; ESPN2; Fox News Channel; Fox Sports 1; FOX Sports Southwest; Freeform; FX; FXM; Golf Channel; Great American Country; HGTV; History; HLN; Lifetime; MTV; National Geographic Channel; Nickelodeon; Outdoor Channel; QVC; Radar Channel; Spike TV; Syfy; TBS; The Weather Channel; TLC; TNT; Travel Channel; Trinity Broadcasting Network (TBN); truTV; TV Land; USA Network; VH1; WGN America.
Fee: $35.00 installation; $46.95 monthly.
Pay Service 1
Pay Units: N.A.
Programming (via satellite): HBO (multiplexed).
Video-On-Demand: No
Internet Service
Operational: Yes.
Broadband Service: Cable Rocket.
Fee: $35.00 installation; $24.99-$149.95 monthly; $55.00 modem purchase.
Telephone Service
Digital: Operational
General Manager: Chuck Davis.
Ownership: Chuck Davis (MSO).

GREENVILLE—GEUS, 2810 Wesley St, Greenville, TX 75401. Phone: 903-457-2800. Fax: 903-454-9249. E-mail: jtyler@

Texas—Cable Systems

geus.org; administration@geus.org. Web Site: http://www.geus.org. ICA: TX0998.
Note: This system is an overbuild.
TV Market Ranking: Below 100 (GREENVILLE). Franchise award date: N.A. Franchise expiration date: N.A. Began: June 29, 2001.
Channel capacity: N.A. Channels available but not in use: N.A.

Basic Service
Subscribers: 3,832.
Programming (received off-air): KDAF (Antenna TV, CW, This TV) Dallas; KDFI (Bounce TV, Buzzr, Heroes & Icons, MNT, Movies!) Dallas; KDFW (FOX) Dallas; KDTX-TV (TBN) Dallas; KERA-TV (PBS) Dallas; KPXD-TV (ION) Arlington; KSTR-DT (getTV, UniMas) Irving; KTVT (CBS, Decades) Fort Worth; KTXA (IND, MeTV) Fort Worth; KTXD-TV (IND) Greenville; KUVN-DT (UNV) Garland; KXAS-TV (COZI TV, NBC) Fort Worth; KXTX-TV (TMO) Dallas; WFAA (ABC) Dallas.
Programming (via satellite): Daystar TV Network; The Weather Channel; WGN America.
Fee: $28.50 installation; $21.95 monthly.

Expanded Basic Service 1
Subscribers: N.A.
Programming (via satellite): A&E; AMC; Animal Planet; BET; Bravo; Cartoon Network; CMT; CNBC; CNN; Comedy Central; C-SPAN; C-SPAN 2; Discovery Channel; Disney Channel; DIY Network; E! HD; ESPN; ESPN2; EWTN Global Catholic Network; FamilyNet; Food Network; Fox News Channel; FOX Sports Southwest; Freeform; FX; Great American Country; Hallmark Channel; HGTV; History; HLN; Lifetime; MSNBC; MTV; National Geographic Channel; Nickelodeon; OWN: Oprah Winfrey Network; Oxygen; QVC; Spike TV; Syfy; TBS; TLC; TNT; Travel Channel; truTV; Turner Classic Movies; TV Land; Univision; USA Network; VH1.
Fee: $35.95 monthly.

Digital Basic Service
Subscribers: N.A.
Programming (via satellite): AXS TV; BBC America; Bloomberg Television; Discovery Life Channel; Disney XD; DMX Music; ESPN; ESPN Classic; ESPNews; Fox Sports 1; Fox Sports 2; FSN Digital Atlantic; FSN Digital Central; FSN Digital Pacific; FXM; FYI; Golf Channel; GSN; HD Theater; History International; IFC; LMN; NBCSN; NFL Network; Nick Jr.; Nicktoons; Outdoor Channel; TeenNick; WE tv.
Fee: $44.95 monthly.

Digital Pay Service 1
Pay Units: N.A.
Programming (via satellite): Cinemax (multiplexed); Flix (multiplexed); HBO (multiplexed); HITS (Headend In The Sky); Showtime (multiplexed); Starz (multiplexed); Starz Encore (multiplexed); Sundance TV (multiplexed); The Movie Channel (multiplexed).
Fee: $6.95 monthly (Canales N), $7.95 monthly (Cinemax), $10.95 monthly (Starz/Encore), $12.95 monthly (HBO or Showtime/Flix/Sundance/TMC).

Video-On-Demand: Yes

Pay-Per-View
special events (delivered digitally).

Internet Service
Operational: Yes.
Subscribers: 3,262.
Broadband Service: In-house.
Fee: $41.95 monthly.

Telephone Service
None
Miles of Plant: 402.0 (coaxial); 118.0 (fiber optic). Homes passed: 10,000.
General Manager: David McCalla. Customer Service Manager: Jimmy Dickey. Engineering & Operations Manager: Mark Stapp. Cable & Internet Manager: Jim Tyler. Marketing & Public Relations Supervisor: Cory Hogan. Cable & Internet Customer Services Supervisor: Brenda Shelby.
Ownership: GEUS.

GREENVILLE—Time Warner Cable, 1565 Chenault St, Dallas, TX 75228. Phones: 214-370-6200; 214-328-2882; 903-455-0012 (Greenville office). Fax: 204-320-7484. Web Site: http://www.timewarnercable.com. Also serves Commerce & Greenville (rural areas). ICA: TX0078.
TV Market Ranking: Below 100 (Commerce, GREENVILLE, Greenville (rural areas)). Franchise award date: November 1, 1966. Franchise expiration date: N.A. Began: June 1, 1967.
Channel capacity: N.A. Channels available but not in use: N.A.

Basic Service
Subscribers: 3,667.
Programming (received off-air): KDAF (Antenna TV, CW, This TV) Dallas; KDFI (Bounce TV, Buzzr, Heroes & Icons, MNT, Movies!) Dallas; KDFW (FOX) Dallas; KDTN (Daystar TV, ETV) Denton; KDTX-TV (TBN) Dallas; KERA-TV (PBS) Dallas; KPXD-TV (ION) Arlington; KSTR-DT (getTV, UniMas) Irving; KTVT (CBS, Decades) Fort Worth; KTXA (IND, MeTV) Fort Worth; KTXD-TV (IND) Greenville; KUVN-DT (UNV) Garland; KXAS-TV (COZI TV, NBC) Fort Worth; KXTX-TV (TMO) Dallas; WFAA (ABC) Dallas.
Programming (via satellite): Pop; QVC; WGN America.
Fee: $39.99 installation; $24.99 monthly.

Expanded Basic Service 1
Subscribers: N.A.
Programming (via satellite): A&E; AMC; Animal Planet; BET; Cartoon Network; CMT; CNBC; CNN; Comedy Central; C-SPAN; C-SPAN 2; Discovery Channel; Disney Channel; E! HD; ESPN; ESPN2; EWTN Global Catholic Network; Food Network; Fox News Channel; FOX Sports Southwest; Freeform; FX; Golf Channel; Great American Country; Hallmark Channel; History; HLN; Lifetime; MSNBC; MTV; NBC Universo; NBCSN; Nickelodeon; Oxygen; Spike TV; TBS; The Weather Channel; TLC; TNT; Travel Channel; truTV; Turner Classic Movies; TV Land; Univision; USA Network; VH1.
Fee: $36.75 monthly.

Digital Basic Service
Subscribers: N.A.
Programming (via satellite): AXS TV; BBC America; Bravo; CMT; Destination America; Discovery Kids Channel; Discovery Life Channel; ESPN Classic; ESPN HD; ESPNews; GSN; HD Theater; HGTV; IFC; Investigation Discovery; LMN; MC; MTV Classic; MTV2; National Geographic Channel; Nick Jr.; OWN: Oprah Winfrey Network; Science Channel; Starz Encore (multiplexed); Syfy; TeenNick; TNT HD; Trinity Broadcasting Network (TBN); Universal HD; WE tv.
Fee: $15.00 monthly.

Digital Expanded Basic Service
Subscribers: N.A.
Programming (via satellite): Bloomberg Television; Canal Sur; Cinelatino; CNN en Espanol; Disney XD; Enlace USA; Fox Deportes; Fox Sports 1; Fuse; FXM; FYI; History en Espanol; History International; Infinito; MTV Jams; Nick 2; Outdoor Channel; Toon Disney en Espanol; Tr3s; VideoRola.

Digital Pay Service 1
Pay Units: N.A.
Programming (via satellite): Cinemax (multiplexed); Cinemax HD; HBO (multiplexed); HBO HD; Showtime (multiplexed); Showtime HD; Starz (multiplexed); Starz HD; The Movie Channel.
Fee: $14.99 monthly (each).

Video-On-Demand: No

Pay-Per-View
iN DEMAND (delivered digitally); Fresh (delivered digitally); Playboy TV (delivered digitally); ESPN (delivered digitally).

Internet Service
Operational: Yes.
Broadband Service: Road Runner.

Telephone Service
Digital: Operational
Miles of Plant: 147.0 (coaxial); None (fiber optic). Homes passed: 8,573.
President: Robert Moel. Vice President, Government & Public Affairs: Dick Kirby. Vice President, Technical Operations: Michael McDonald. Vice President, Marketing: Robert Shurtleff. Public Affairs Director: Gary Underwood. Office Manager: LaTonya Smiley-Rizby.
Ownership: Time Warner Cable (MSO).

GREENWOOD—Ridgewood Cablevision, 3700 South County Rd 1316, Odessa, TX 79765. Phone: 432-563-4330. Fax: 432-563-0104. E-mail: rwc@ridgewoodcable.com. Web Site: http://www.ridgewoodcable.com. ICA: TX1017.
TV Market Ranking: Below 100 (GREENWOOD).
Channel capacity: N.A. Channels available but not in use: N.A.

Basic Service
Subscribers: N.A.
Programming (received off-air): KERA-TV (PBS) Dallas; KMLM-DT (GLC) Odessa; KPEJ-TV (FOX) Odessa; KTVT (CBS, Decades) Fort Worth; KXAS-TV (COZI TV, NBC) Fort Worth; WFAA (ABC) Dallas.
Programming (via satellite): A&E; AMC; Animal Planet; Cartoon Network; CMT; CNN; C-SPAN; C-SPAN 2; Discovery Channel; Disney Channel; Disney XD; ESPN; ESPN2; Food Network; Fox News Channel; Fox Sports 1; FOX Sports Southwest; Freeform; Golf Channel; HGTV; History; HLN; Lifetime; MTV; National Geographic Channel; NBCSN; Nickelodeon; Outdoor Channel; QVC; Spike TV; Syfy; TBS; Telemundo; The Weather Channel; TLC; TNT; Turner Classic Movies; TV Land; Univision Studios; USA Network; VH1; WGN America.
Fee: $37.95 monthly.

Pay Service 1
Pay Units: N.A.
Programming (via satellite): Cinemax (multiplexed); HBO (multiplexed); Showtime (multiplexed); The Movie Channel.
Fee: $6.95 monthly (Showtime/TMC), $7.95 monthly (HBO/Cinemax).

Internet Service
Operational: Yes.
General Manager & Chief Technician: Bob Randolph.
Ownership: Ridgewood Cable (MSO).

GROOM—Formerly served by Almega Cable. No longer in operation. ICA: TX0458.

GROVETON—Formerly served by Almega Cable. No longer in operation. ICA: TX0486.

GRUVER—Formerly served by Elk River TV Cable Co. No longer in operation. ICA: TX0768.

GUN BARREL CITY—Suddenlink Communications. Now served by ATHENS, TX [TX0711]. ICA: TX0084.

GUSTINE—Formerly served by Cable Unlimited. No longer in operation. ICA: TX0605.

GUY—Formerly served by Cebridge Connections. No longer in operation. ICA: TX0439.

HALE CENTER—NTS Communications. Formerly [TX0402]. This cable system has converted to IPTV, 1220 Broadway, Lubbock, TX 79401. Phones: 800-658-2150; 806-797-0687. Fax: 806-788-3381. E-mail: info@ntscom.com. Web Site: http://www.ntscom.com. ICA: TX5544.
TV Market Ranking: Below 100 (HALE CENTER). Franchise award date: August 7, 1978. Franchise expiration date: N.A. Began: August 1, 1981.
Channel capacity: N.A. Channels available but not in use: N.A.

Gold
Subscribers: N.A.
Programming (received off-air): KAMC (ABC, Bounce TV) Lubbock; KCBD (NBC, This TV) Lubbock; KJTV-TV (FOX) Lubbock; KLBK-TV (CBS) Lubbock; KTTZ-TV (PBS) Lubbock; KVDA (TMO) San Antonio.
Programming (via satellite): A&E; AMC; Cartoon Network; CMT; CNN; Discovery Channel; Disney Channel; E! HD; ESPN; FOX Sports Southwest; Freeform; HGTV; History; HLN; Lifetime; Nickelodeon; QVC; Spike TV; Syfy; TBS; The Weather Channel; TLC; TNT; Trinity Broadcasting Network (TBN); TV Land; USA Network; WGN America.
Fee: $29.95 installation; $65.00 monthly. Includes 150+ channels plus music & 1 digital receiver.

Platinum
Subscribers: N.A.
Fee: $85.00 monthly. Includes 230+ channels plus music, 1 whole home DVR & 1 digital receiver.

HBO
Subscribers: N.A.
Programming (via satellite): HBO.
Fee: $9.95 monthly.

Showtime
Subscribers: N.A.
Programming (via satellite): Showtime.
Fee: $9.95 monthly.

The Movie Channel
Subscribers: N.A.
Programming (via satellite): The Movie Channel.
Fee: $7.95 monthly.

Video-On-Demand: No

Internet Service
Operational: Yes.
Fee: $44.99-$134.99 monthly.

Telephone Service
Digital: Operational
Fee: $19.99 monthly
President & Chief Executive Officer: Cyrus Driver. Executive Vice President & Chief Operating Officer: Deborah Crawford. Executive Vice President & Chief Financial Officer: Don Pittman. Senior Vice President, Product Management: Angel Kandahari. Vice President & General Counsel: Daniel Wheeler. Vice President, Products & Marketing: Roberto Chang. Vice President, Human Resources: Wendy J. Lee. Vice President, Service Delivery & IT

Cable Systems—Texas

FULLY SEARCHABLE • CONTINUOUSLY UPDATED • DISCOUNT RATES FOR PRINT PURCHASERS

For more information call **800-771-9202** or visit **www.warren-news.com**

Strategy: Michael McDaniel. Vice President, RUS Projects: Aaron Peters.
Ownership: NTS Communications Inc. (MSO).

HALE CENTER—NTS Communications. This cable system has converted to IPTV. See HALE CENTER, TX [TX5544]. ICA: TX0402.

HAMILTON—Northland Cable Television, 975 North Lillian St, PO Box 70, Stephenville, TX 76401-0070. Phones: 888-667-8452; 254-968-4189. Fax: 254-968-8350. E-mail: brent_richey@northlandcabletv.com. Web Site: http://www.yournorthland.com. ICA: TX0267.
TV Market Ranking: Outside TV Markets (HAMILTON). Franchise award date: January 1, 1963. Franchise expiration date: N.A. Began: June 1, 1963.
Channel capacity: N.A. Channels available but not in use: N.A.
Basic Service
Subscribers: 127.
Programming (received off-air): KCEN-TV (Antenna TV, MeTV, MundoMax, NBC) Temple; KDAF (Antenna TV, CW, This TV) Dallas; KDFW (FOX) Dallas; KERA-TV (PBS) Dallas; KSTR-DT (getTV, UniMas) Irving; KTVT (CBS, Decades) Fort Worth; KWTX-TV (CBS, CW) Waco; KXAS-TV (COZI TV, NBC) Fort Worth; KXXV (ABC, TMO) Waco; WFAA (ABC) Dallas; allband FM.
Programming (via satellite): C-SPAN; ESPN; Great American Country; Hallmark Channel; Pop; TBS; Telemundo; The Weather Channel; TLC; Travel Channel; Trinity Broadcasting Network (TBN); Univision Studios; WGN America.
Fee: $17.00 installation; $47.64 monthly; $1.00 converter.
Expanded Basic Service 1
Subscribers: N.A.
Programming (via satellite): A&E; AMC; Cartoon Network; CNN; Discovery Channel; ESPN2; FOX Sports Southwest; FX; HGTV; HLN; Lifetime; Nickelodeon; QVC; Spike TV; TNT; Turner Classic Movies; USA Network.
Fee: $46.99 monthly.
Pay Service 1
Pay Units: N.A.
Programming (via satellite): HBO.
Fee: $17.00 installation; $13.50 monthly.
Internet Service
Operational: No.
Telephone Service
None
Miles of Plant: 46.0 (coaxial); None (fiber optic). Homes passed: 1,549.
Executive Vice President: Richard I. Clark. Regional Manager: Brent Richey. Chief Engineer: Greg Perry. Office Manager: Linda Smith.
Ownership: Northland Communications Corp. (MSO).

HAMLIN—Suddenlink Communications, 520 Maryville Centre Dr, Ste 300, St. Louis, MO 63141. Phones: 800-999-6845 (Customer service); 314-315-9400. Web Site: http://www.suddenlink.com. Also serves Jones County (portions). ICA: TX0294.
TV Market Ranking: Below 100 (HAMLIN, Jones County (portions)). Franchise award date: June 16, 1966. Franchise expiration date: N.A. Began: August 1, 1968.
Channel capacity: N.A. Channels available but not in use: N.A.
Basic Service
Subscribers: 177.
Programming (received off-air): KRBC-TV (Bounce TV, NBC) Abilene; KTAB-TV (CBS)

Abilene; KTXS-TV (ABC, CW, This TV, TMO) Sweetwater; 4 FMs.
Programming (via satellite): BET; C-SPAN; Lifetime; QVC; TBS; The Weather Channel.
Fee: $39.95 installation; $28.45 monthly.
Expanded Basic Service 1
Subscribers: N.A.
Programming (via satellite): A&E; AMC; Animal Planet; Cartoon Network; CMT; CNN; Discovery Channel; ESPN; Fox News Channel; FOX Sports Southwest; Freeform; FX; HGTV; MTV; Nickelodeon; Spike TV; TLC; TNT; USA Network.
Fee: $39.95 installation; $23.00 monthly.
Pay Service 1
Pay Units: N.A.
Programming (via satellite): Cinemax; HBO; Starz; Starz Encore.
Fee: $1.71 monthly (Encore), $6.75 monthly (Starz), $12.50 monthly (Cinemax), $13.00 monthly (HBO).
Video-On-Demand: No
Internet Service
Operational: Yes. Began: October 6, 2003.
Broadband Service: Suddenlink High Speed Internet.
Fee: $49.95 installation; $25.95 monthly.
Telephone Service
None
Miles of Plant: 22.0 (coaxial); None (fiber optic). Homes passed: 1,363.
Senior Vice President, Corporate Finance: Michael Pflantz. Regional Manager: Todd Cruthird. Plant Manager: Bobby Smith.
Ownership: Cequel Communications Holdings I LLC (MSO).

HAPPY—Formerly served by Almega Cable. No longer in operation. ICA: TX0583.

HARBOR POINT—Formerly served by CableSouth Inc. No longer in operation. ICA: TX0769.

HARLINGEN—Time Warner Cable. Now served by PHARR, TX [TX0017]. ICA: TX0036.

HARPER—Formerly served by Cable Comm Ltd. No longer in operation. ICA: TX0622.

HARRIS COUNTY (northern portion)—Charter Communications. Now served by MONTGOMERY COUNTY (portions), TX [TX0044]. ICA: TX0213.

HARRIS COUNTY (portions)—Comcast Cable. Now served by HOUSTON, TX [TX0001]. ICA: TX1030.

HART—Reach Broadband, PO Box 507, Arp, TX 75750. Phones: 903-859-3789; 800-687-1258. Web Site: http://www.reachbroadband.net. ICA: TX0534.
TV Market Ranking: Outside TV Markets (HART). Franchise award date: N.A. Franchise expiration date: N.A. Began: April 1, 1982.
Channel capacity: 36 (not 2-way capable). Channels available but not in use: N.A.
Basic Service
Subscribers: 16.
Programming (received off-air): KACV-TV (PBS) Amarillo; KAMC (ABC, Bounce TV) Lubbock; KAMR-TV (IND, NBC) Amarillo; KCBD (NBC, This TV) Lubbock; KCIT (FOX, This TV) Amarillo; KFDA-TV (CBS, TMO) Amarillo; KJTV-TV (FOX) Lubbock; KVII-TV (ABC, CW) Amarillo; allband FM.
Programming (via satellite): A&E; CMT; CNN; Discovery Channel; Disney Channel; ESPN; Freeform; History; Nickelodeon;

Spike TV; TBS; Telemundo; The Weather Channel; TLC; TNT; Trinity Broadcasting Network (TBN); TV Land; USA Network; WGN America.
Fee: $49.95 installation; $56.33 monthly.
Pay Service 1
Pay Units: N.A.
Programming (via satellite): HBO; Showtime.
Fee: $15.00 installation; $9.95 monthly (Showtime), $10.95 monthly (HBO).
Video-On-Demand: No
Internet Service
Operational: Yes.
Telephone Service
None
Miles of Plant: 8.0 (coaxial); None (fiber optic). Homes passed: 373.
Regional Manager: Ronnie Stafford. Office Manager: Jan Gibson. Controller: Jeffrey Lowe.
Ownership: RB3 LLC (MSO).

HASKELL—Formerly served by Alliance Communications. Now served by WesTex Telephone Cooperative, 1500 West Business 20, Stanton, TX 79782. Phones: 432-263-0091 (Big Spring office); 432-756-3826. Web Site: http://www.westex.coop. ICA: TX0321.
TV Market Ranking: Outside TV Markets (HASKELL). Franchise award date: N.A. Franchise expiration date: N.A. Began: January 1, 1962.
Channel capacity: N.A. Channels available but not in use: N.A.
Basic Service
Subscribers: 92.
Programming (received off-air): KIDZ-LD Abilene; KRBC-TV (Bounce TV, NBC) Abilene; KTAB-TV (CBS) Abilene; KTXS-TV (ABC, CW, This TV, TMO) Sweetwater; KXVA (FOX, MNT) Abilene; 2 FMs.
Programming (via satellite): C-SPAN; KRMA-TV (PBS) Denver; QVC; Trinity Broadcasting Network (TBN).
Fee: $45.00 installation; $22.45 monthly.
Expanded Basic Service 1
Subscribers: 64.
Programming (via satellite): A&E; AMC; Animal Planet; Bravo; Cartoon Network; CMT; CNBC; CNN; Comedy Central; Discovery Channel; Disney Channel; E! HD; ESPN; ESPN2; Fox News Channel; Fox Sports 1; FOX Sports Southwest; Freeform; FX; FXM; Golf Channel; HGTV; History; HLN; Lifetime; MSNBC; MTV; NBCSN; Nickelodeon; Oxygen; Spike TV; Syfy; TBS; The Weather Channel; TLC; TNT; Travel Channel; Turner Classic Movies; TV Land; Univision Studios; USA Network; VH1.
Fee: $18.00 monthly.
Digital Basic Service
Subscribers: N.A.
Programming (via satellite): BBC America; Bloomberg Television; Destination America; Discovery Kids Channel; Discovery Life Channel; Disney XD; DIY Network; ESPN Classic; FYI; GSN; History International; IFC; Investigation Discovery; LMN; MC; Nick 2; Nick Jr.; Nicktoons; OWN: Oprah

Winfrey Network; Sundance TV; TeenNick; WE tv.
Fee: $12.95 monthly.
Pay Service 1
Pay Units: N.A.
Programming (via satellite): Cinemax; Flix; HBO; Showtime (multiplexed); Starz Encore; The Movie Channel.
Fee: $35.00 installation; $3.95 monthly (Encore), $9.95 monthly (Cinemax, HBO or Showtime).
Digital Pay Service 1
Pay Units: N.A.
Programming (via satellite): Cinemax (multiplexed); HBO (multiplexed); Starz (multiplexed).
Video-On-Demand: No
Pay-Per-View
ETC (delivered digitally); Pleasure (delivered digitally).
Internet Service
Operational: No.
Telephone Service
None
Miles of Plant: 28.0 (coaxial); None (fiber optic). Homes passed: 1,186.
Ownership: WesTex Telecommunications (MSO).

HASSE—Formerly served by Cable Unlimited. No longer in operation. ICA: TX0550.

HAWKINS—Suddenlink Communications, 520 Maryville Centre Dr, Ste 300, St. Louis, MO 63141. Phones: 800-999-6845; 314-315-9400. Web Site: http://www.suddenlink.com. Also serves Big Sandy, Gladewater (portions), Gregg County (portions), Owentown, Smith County (portions), Winona & Wood County (portions). ICA: TX0289.
TV Market Ranking: Below 100 (Big Sandy, Gladewater (portions), Gregg County (portions), HAWKINS, Owentown, Smith County (portions), Winona, Wood County (portions)). Franchise award date: N.A. Franchise expiration date: N.A. Began: February 1, 1983.
Channel capacity: N.A. Channels available but not in use: N.A.
Basic Service
Subscribers: 244.
Programming (received off-air): KDFW (FOX) Dallas; KERA-TV (PBS) Dallas; KFXK-TV (FOX) Longview; KLTV (ABC, Bounce TV, TMO) Tyler; KTVT (CBS, Decades) Fort Worth; KXAS-TV (COZI TV, NBC) Fort Worth; WFAA (ABC) Dallas.
Programming (via satellite): ESPN; Freeform; TBS.
Fee: $39.95 installation; $28.45 monthly.
Pay Service 1
Pay Units: N.A.
Programming (via satellite): Cinemax; Flix; HBO; Showtime.
Fee: $1.95 monthly (Flix), $7.00 monthly (Cinemax or Showtime), $12.00 monthly (HBO).
Video-On-Demand: No

2017 Edition
D-745

Texas—Cable Systems

Internet Service
Operational: Yes. Began: August 1, 2003.
Broadband Service: Suddenlink High Speed Internet.
Fee: $49.95 installation; $25.95 monthly.

Telephone Service
Digital: Operational
Fee: $44.95 monthly
Miles of Plant: 89.0 (coaxial); None (fiber optic). Homes passed: 2,156.
Senior Vice President, Corporate Finance: Michael Pflantz. Regional Manager: Todd Cruthird. Plant Manager: Sonny Myers.
Ownership: Cequel Communications Holdings I LLC (MSO).

HAWLEY—Formerly served by Jayroc Cablevision. No longer in operation. ICA: TX0974.

HEARNE—Suddenlink Communications, 4114 East 29th St, Bryan, TX 77802-4302. Phones: 314-315-9400; 888-822-5151. Fax: 979-268-0139. Web Site: http://www.suddenlink.com. Also serves Robertson County (portions). ICA: TX0231.
TV Market Ranking: Below 100 (HEARNE, Robertson County (portions)). Franchise award date: November 1, 1968. Franchise expiration date: N.A. Began: November 1, 1968.
Channel capacity: 36 (2-way capable). Channels available but not in use: N.A.

Basic Service
Subscribers: 267. Commercial subscribers: 57.
Programming (received off-air): KAKW-DT (getTV, UNV) Killeen; KAMU-TV (PBS) College Station; KBTX-TV (CBS, CW) Bryan; KCEN-TV (Antenna TV, MeTV, MundoMax, NBC) Temple; KXXV (ABC, TMO) Waco; KYLE-TV (FOX) Bryan; allband FM.
Programming (via satellite): A&E; AMC; BET; CMT; CNN; C-SPAN; Discovery Channel; Disney Channel; ESPN; ESPN2; FOX Sports Southwest; Freeform; Great American Country; GSN; HGTV; History; HLN; ION Television; Lifetime; Nickelodeon; QVC; Spike TV; TBS; The Weather Channel; TNT; Trinity Broadcasting Network (TBN); TV Land; USA Network; WGN America.
Fee: $54.95 installation; $45.64 monthly.

Pay Service 1
Pay Units: N.A.
Programming (via satellite): Cinemax; HBO.
Fee: $10.00 monthly (Cinemax), $11.00 monthly (HBO).
Video-On-Demand: No

Internet Service
Operational: Yes.
Broadband Service: Suddenlink High Speed Internet.

Telephone Service
Digital: Operational
Miles of Plant: 30.0 (coaxial); None (fiber optic). Homes passed: 1,830.
Senior Vice President, Corporate Finance: Michael Pflantz. Vice President, Accounting: Sabrina Warr. General Manager: Randy Rodgers. Marketing Director: Jennie Kipp. Chief Technician: Jim Davis.
Ownership: Cequel Communications Holdings I LLC (MSO).

HEBBRONVILLE—Alliance Communications, PO Box 9090, Tyler, TX 75711. Phones: 903-561-4411; 800-842-8160; 501-679-6619 (Greenbrier, AR office). Web Site: http://www.alliancecable.net. ICA: TX0260.
TV Market Ranking: Outside TV Markets (HEBBRONVILLE). Franchise award date: N.A. Franchise expiration date: N.A. Began: January 1, 1968.
Channel capacity: N.A. Channels available but not in use: N.A.

Basic Service
Subscribers: 284.
Programming (via microwave): KDFW (FOX) Dallas; KEDT (PBS) Corpus Christi; KIII (ABC, MeTV) Corpus Christi; KRIS-TV (CW, Grit, NBC) Corpus Christi; KZTV (CBS) Corpus Christi.
Programming (via satellite): A&E; AMC; Animal Planet; Bravo; Cartoon Network; CMT; CNBC; CNN; Comedy Central; C-SPAN; CW PLUS; Discovery Channel; Disney Channel; ESPN; ESPN2; EWTN Global Catholic Network; Fox News Channel; FOX Sports Southwest; Freeform; FX; Hallmark Channel; HGTV; History; HLN; Lifetime; MSNBC; MTV; NBC Universo; Nickelodeon; Oxygen; Spike TV; TBS; Telemundo; The Weather Channel; TLC; TNT; Travel Channel; Trinity Broadcasting Network (TBN); truTV; Turner Classic Movies; UniMas; Univision; Univision Studios; USA Network; VH1; WE tv.
Fee: $50.51 installation; $22.45 monthly.

Digital Basic Service
Subscribers: N.A.
Programming (via satellite): A&E; AMC; Animal Planet; BBC America; Bravo; Cartoon Network; CMT; CNBC; CNN; Comedy Central; C-SPAN; C-SPAN 3; Destination America; Discovery Kids Channel; Discovery Life Channel; Disney Channel; Disney XD; DIY Network; ESPN; ESPN Classic; ESPN2; ESPNews; EWTN Global Catholic Network; Food Network; Fox Business Network; Fox News Channel; FOX Sports Southwest; Freeform; FX; Golf Channel; GSN; Hallmark Channel; HGTV; History; HLN; IFC; Investigation Discovery; La Familia Cosmovision; Lifetime; MC; MSNBC; MTV; MTV Classic; Nat Geo WILD; National Geographic Channel; NBC Universo; NBCSN; Nick Jr.; Nickelodeon; Oxygen; Science Channel; Spike TV; Syfy; TBS; TeenNick; The Weather Channel; TLC; TNT; Travel Channel; Trinity Broadcasting Network (TBN); truTV; Turner Classic Movies; TV Land; Univision; USA Network; VH1; WE tv.
Fee: $7.00 monthly.

Digital Expanded Basic Service
Subscribers: N.A.
Programming (via satellite): Starz Encore (multiplexed).
Fee: $8.95 monthly.

Digital Pay Service 1
Pay Units: N.A.
Programming (via satellite): Cinemax (multiplexed); HBO (multiplexed); Showtime (multiplexed); Starz (multiplexed); The Movie Channel (multiplexed).
Fee: $12.95 monthly (each).
Video-On-Demand: No
Pay-Per-View
iN DEMAND (delivered digitally); Hot Choice (delivered digitally); Fresh (delivered digitally).

Internet Service
Operational: No.
Telephone Service
None
Miles of Plant: 35.0 (coaxial); None (fiber optic). Homes passed: 1,629.
Chief Financial Officer: David Starrett. Vice President & General Manager: John Brinker. Vice President, Programming: Julie Newman.
Ownership: Buford Media Group LLC (MSO).

HEDLEY—Formerly served by Almega Cable. No longer in operation. ICA: TX0772.

HEIGHTS (unincorporated areas)—Formerly served by Almega Cable. No longer in operation. ICA: TX0143.

HEMPHILL—Formerly served by Almega Cable. No longer in operation. ICA: TX1019.

HEMPSTEAD—NewWave Communications, One Montgomery Plaza, 4th Floor, Sikeston, MO 63801. Phones: 573-472-9500; 888-863-9928. Fax: 573-472-9518. E-mail: info@newwave.com. Web Site: http://www.newwavecom.com. ICA: TX0305.
TV Market Ranking: Below 100 (HEMPSTEAD). Franchise award date: N.A. Franchise expiration date: N.A. Began: May 1, 1982.
Channel capacity: N.A. Channels available but not in use: N.A.

Basic Service
Subscribers: 79.
Programming (received off-air): KETH-TV (TBN) Houston; KFTH-DT (getTV, UniMas) Alvin; KHOU (Bounce TV, CBS) Houston; KIAH (Antenna TV, CW) Houston; KLTJ (Daystar TV, ETV) Galveston; KPRC-TV (NBC, This TV) Houston; KRIV (FOX) Houston; KTMD (TMO) Galveston; KTRK-TV (ABC, Live Well Network) Houston; KTXH (Buzzr, MNT, Movies!) Houston; KUHT (PBS) Houston; KXLN-DT (UNV) Rosenberg; KYAZ (Azteca America, IND) Katy; allband FM.
Programming (via satellite): C-SPAN.
Fee: $35.00 installation; $34.44 monthly.

Expanded Basic Service 1
Subscribers: N.A.
Programming (via satellite): A&E; AMC; BET; Cartoon Network; CMT; CNN; Discovery Channel; Disney Channel; ESPN; Fox News Channel; Freeform; History; Lifetime; MTV; Nickelodeon; Spike TV; TBS; The Weather Channel; TNT; TV Land; USA Network.
Fee: $21.50 monthly.

Digital Basic Service
Subscribers: N.A.
Programming (via satellite): BBC America; Bloomberg Television; Bravo; Discovery Digital Networks; DMX Music; ESPN Classic; ESPN2; ESPNews; Fox Sports 1; Fuse; FXM; FYI; Golf Channel; GSN; HGTV; History International; IFC; LMN; National Geographic Channel; NBCSN; Outdoor Channel; Sundance TV; Syfy; Trinity Broadcasting Network (TBN); Turner Classic Movies; WE tv.
Fee: $11.00 monthly.

Pay Service 1
Pay Units: N.A.
Programming (via satellite): Cinemax; HBO; Showtime.
Fee: $14.95 installation; $10.95 monthly (Cinemax), $13.95 monthly (HBO or Showtime).

Digital Pay Service 1
Pay Units: N.A.
Programming (via satellite): Cinemax (multiplexed); Flix; HBO (multiplexed); Showtime (multiplexed); Starz (multiplexed); Starz Encore (multiplexed); The Movie Channel (multiplexed).
Fee: $8.00 monthly (Starz), $9.00 monthly (Cinemax), $11.00 monthly (Starz/Encore), $15.00 monthly (Showtime/TMC), $16.00 monthly (HBO) or $26.00 monthly (HBO/Cinemax).
Video-On-Demand: No
Pay-Per-View
iN DEMAND (delivered digitally); Hot Choice (delivered digitally); Playboy TV (delivered digitally); Fresh (delivered digitally); Club Jenna (delivered digitally); Spice: Xcess (delivered digitally).

Internet Service
Operational: Yes.
Fee: $39.99-$79.99 monthly; $6.00 modem lease.

Telephone Service
Digital: Operational
Miles of Plant: 31.0 (coaxial); None (fiber optic). Homes passed: 1,542.
Regional General Manager: Jerry Smith.
Ownership: NewWave Communications LLC (MSO).

HENDERSON—Suddenlink Communications, 109 North High St, Henderson, TX 75652. Phones: 888-722-5151 (Customer service); 314-315-9400. Fax: 903-657-7766. Web Site: http://www.suddenlink.com. Also serves Rusk County. ICA: TX0140.
TV Market Ranking: Below 100 (HENDERSON, Rusk County). Franchise award date: January 1, 1968. Franchise expiration date: N.A. Began: September 5, 1968.
Channel capacity: N.A. Channels available but not in use: N.A.

Basic Service
Subscribers: 2,465.
Programming (received off-air): KETK-TV (Estrella TV, NBC) Jacksonville; KFXK-TV (FOX) Longview; KLPN-LD (MNT) Longview; KLTV (ABC, Bounce TV, TMO) Tyler; KYTX (CBS, COZI TV, CW) Nacogdoches; 6 FMs.
Programming (via microwave): KERA-TV (PBS) Dallas; KXTX-TV (TMO) Dallas.
Programming (via satellite): C-SPAN; Pop; QVC; Univision Studios; WGN America.
Fee: $54.95 installation; $33.24 monthly.

Expanded Basic Service 1
Subscribers: N.A.
Programming (via satellite): A&E; AMC; Animal Planet; BET; Bravo; Cartoon Network; CMT; CNBC; CNN; Comedy Central; C-SPAN 2; Discovery Channel; Disney Channel; E! HD; ESPN; ESPN2; EWTN Global Catholic Network; Food Network; Fox News Channel; Fox Sports 1; FOX Sports Southwest; Freeform; FX; Great American Country; HGTV; History; HLN; INSP; Jewelry Television; Lifetime; LMN; MSNBC; MTV; NBCSN; Nickelodeon; Outdoor Channel; Spike TV; Syfy; TBS; The Weather Channel; TLC; TNT; Travel Channel; Trinity Broadcasting Network (TBN); truTV; Turner Classic Movies; TV Land; Univision; USA Network; VH1.
Fee: $18.99 monthly.

Digital Basic Service
Subscribers: N.A.
Programming (via satellite): A&E HD; AXS TV; Bandamax; BBC America; Bloomberg Television; Boomerang; CBS Sports Network; Cine Mexicano; Cinelatino; CMT; CNN en Espanol; Cooking Channel; Cox Sports Television; De Pelicula; De Pelicula Clasico; Destination America; Discovery Kids Channel; Disney XD; DIY Network; Enlace USA; ESPN Classic; ESPN Deportes; ESPN HD; ESPN2 HD; ESPNews; ESPNU; FamilyNet; Food Network HD; Fox Deportes; Fox Sports 2; Fuse; FYI; Golf Channel; GSN; Hallmark Channel; HD Theater; HGTV HD; History en Espanol; History International; IFC; Investigation Discovery; MC; MTV Classic; MTV Hits; MTV2; Nat Geo WILD; National Geographic Channel; National Geographic Channel HD; NBC Universo; Nick Jr.; Nicktoons; OWN: Oprah Winfrey Network; Oxygen; Ritmoson; Science Channel; Starz Encore (multiplexed); Sundance TV; Sur; TeenNick; Telehit; Tennis

Cable Systems—Texas

Channel; TNT HD; Toon Disney en Espanol; Tr3s; TV One; ULTRA HDPlex; UniMas; Universal HD; Univision; UP; VideoRola; WE tv; Weatherscan.

Digital Pay Service 1
Pay Units: N.A.
Programming (via satellite): Cinemax (multiplexed); HBO (multiplexed); HBO HD; HBO Latino; Showtime (multiplexed); Showtime HD; Starz (multiplexed); Starz HD; The Movie Channel (multiplexed).

Video-On-Demand: No

Pay-Per-View
iN DEMAND (delivered digitally); Fresh (delivered digitally); Shorteez (delivered digitally); Playboy TV (delivered digitally); Playboy en Espanol (delivered digitally).

Internet Service
Operational: Yes.
Broadband Service: Suddenlink High Speed Internet.
Fee: $45.95 installation; $29.95 monthly.

Telephone Service
Digital: Operational
Fee: $44.95 monthly
Miles of Plant: 98.0 (coaxial); None (fiber optic). Homes passed: 4,500.
Vice President, Accounting: Sabrina Warr. General Manager: Ronnie Powell. Chief Technician: James McCain.
Ownership: Cequel Communications Holdings I LLC (MSO).

HENRIETTA—Suddenlink Communications, 520 Maryville Centre Dr, Ste 300, St. Louis, MO 63141. Phones: 800-999-6845 (Customer service); 314-315-9400. Fax: 903-561-5485. Web Site: http://www.suddenlink.com. ICA: TX0314.
TV Market Ranking: Below 100 (HENRIETTA). Franchise award date: N.A. Franchise expiration date: N.A. Began: September 1, 1978.
Channel capacity: N.A. Channels available but not in use: N.A.

Basic Service
Subscribers: 141.
Programming (received off-air): KAUZ-TV (CBS, CW) Wichita Falls; KFDX-TV (NBC) Wichita Falls; KJTL (Bounce TV, FOX) Wichita Falls; KSWO-TV (ABC, TMO) Lawton; allband FM.
Programming (via satellite): Discovery Channel; Hallmark Channel; QVC; TBS; The Weather Channel.
Programming (via translator): KERA-TV (PBS) Dallas.
Fee: $39.95 installation; $28.45 monthly.

Expanded Basic Service 1
Subscribers: N.A.
Programming (via satellite): AMC; Animal Planet; Cartoon Network; CNBC; CNN; C-SPAN; Disney Channel; ESPN; Fox News Channel; Freeform; FX; HGTV; HLN; Lifetime; MTV; Spike TV; TLC; TNT; truTV; USA Network.
Fee: $39.95 installation; $23.00 monthly.

Pay Service 1
Pay Units: N.A.
Programming (via satellite): Cinemax; HBO; Starz; Starz Encore.
Fee: $1.75 monthly (Encore), $6.75 monthly (Starz), $13.59 monthly (Cinemax or HBO).

Video-On-Demand: No

Internet Service
Operational: Yes. Began: May 1, 2003.
Broadband Service: Suddenlink High Speed Internet.
Fee: $49.95 installation; $25.95 monthly.

Telephone Service
None
Miles of Plant: 24.0 (coaxial); None (fiber optic). Homes passed: 1,205.
Senior Vice President, Corporate Finance: Michael Pflantz. Regional Manager: Todd Cruthird. Plant Manager: Ron Johnson.
Ownership: Cequel Communications Holdings I LLC (MSO).

HEREFORD—WT Services (formerly XIT), 119 E Fourth St, Hereford, TX 79045. Phone: 806-360-9000. E-mail: CustomerCare@wtrt.net. Web Site: http://wtservices.net. ICA: TX0125.
Channel capacity: N.A. Channels available but not in use: N.A.

Basic Service
Subscribers: 2,160.
Fee: $26.00 monthly.

Internet Service
Operational: Yes.

Telephone Service
Digital: Operational
Chief Executive Officer & General Manager: Amy Linzey.
Ownership: West Texas Rural Telephone Cooperative.

HICO—Formerly served by Northland Cable Television. No longer in operation. ICA: TX0774.

HIDALGO—Time Warner Cable. Now served by PHARR, TX [TX0017]. ICA: TX0244.

HIGGINS—Formerly served by Almega Cable. No longer in operation. ICA: TX0590.

HIGHLAND RANGE—Formerly served by Highland Cable. No longer in operation. ICA: TX0676.

HILLSBORO—Northland Cable Television, 1500 North Beaton St, Corsicana, TX 75110. Phones: 888-667-8452; 254-582-9793. E-mail: hillsboro@northlandcabletv.com. Web Site: http://www.yournorthland.com. Also serves Hill County (portions). ICA: TX0175.
TV Market Ranking: Below 100 (Hill County (portions), HILLSBORO). Franchise award date: June 19, 1990. Franchise expiration date: N.A. Began: December 1, 1979.
Channel capacity: N.A. Channels available but not in use: N.A.

Basic Service
Subscribers: 158.
Programming (received off-air): KCEN-TV (Antenna TV, MeTV, MundoMax, NBC) Temple; KDAF (Antenna TV, CW, This TV) Dallas; KDFI (Bounce TV, Buzzr, Heroes & Icons, MNT, Movies!) Dallas; KDFW (FOX) Dallas; KDTN (Daystar TV, ETV) Denton; KDTX-TV (TBN) Dallas; KERA-TV (PBS) Dallas; KFWD (MundoMax) Fort Worth; KTVT (CBS, Decades) Fort Worth; KTXA (IND, MeTV) Fort Worth; KWKT-TV (Estrella TV, FOX, MNT) Waco; KWTX-TV (CBS, CW) Waco; KXAS-TV (COZI TV, NBC) Fort Worth; KXTX-TV (TMO) Dallas; KXXV (ABC, TMO) Waco; WFAA (ABC) Dallas.
Programming (via satellite): A&E; Animal Planet; BET; Cartoon Network; CNBC; CNN; C-SPAN; Discovery Channel; ESPN; ESPN2; Food Network; Fox News Channel; FOX Sports Southwest; FX; FXM; Golf Channel; Great American Country; HGTV; History; HLN; Lifetime; MTV; National Geographic Channel; Nickelodeon; QVC; Spike TV; TBS; The Weather Channel; TLC; TNT; Turner Classic Movies; TV Land; Univision Studios; USA Network; WGN America.
Fee: $60.00 installation; $47.64 monthly.

Digital Basic Service
Subscribers: N.A.
Programming (via satellite): Discovery Kids Channel; DMX Music; ESPNews; Golf Channel; LMN; Outdoor Channel; OWN: Oprah Winfrey Network; Science Channel; Trinity Broadcasting Network (TBN); WE tv.
Fee: $44.99 monthly.

Pay Service 1
Pay Units: N.A.
Programming (via satellite): HBO.

Digital Pay Service 1
Pay Units: N.A.
Programming (via satellite): Cinemax (multiplexed); Flix; HBO (multiplexed); Showtime (multiplexed); Starz (multiplexed); Starz Encore (multiplexed); The Movie Channel (multiplexed).
Fee: $10.00 monthly (each).

Video-On-Demand: No

Pay-Per-View
iN DEMAND (delivered digitally); Playboy TV (delivered digitally); Fresh (delivered digitally).

Internet Service
Operational: Yes.
Broadband Service: Northland Express.
Fee: $39.99 monthly.

Telephone Service
None
Miles of Plant: 48.0 (coaxial); None (fiber optic). Homes passed: 3,006.
Regional Manager: Mike Taylor. Chief Technician: Bobby Brady. Marketing Director: Joanne Williams.
Ownership: Northland Communications Corp. (MSO).

HOLIDAY LAKES—Formerly served by Cebridge Connections. No longer in operation. ICA: TX0514.

HOLLIDAY—Time Warner Cable. Now served by WICHITA FALLS, TX [TX0026]. ICA: TX0422.

HOMER—Formerly served by Almega Cable. No longer in operation. ICA: TX0300.

HONDO—CommZoom, 2438 Boardwalk, San Antonio, TX 78217. Phone: 844-858-8500. Web Site: http://www.commzoom.com. Also serves Castroville & Medina County (portions). ICA: TX0218.
TV Market Ranking: 45 (Castroville, Medina County (portions)); Outside TV Markets (HONDO, Medina County (portions)). Franchise award date: January 1, 1980. Franchise expiration date: N.A. Began: January 1, 1981.
Channel capacity: N.A. Channels available but not in use: N.A.

Basic Service
Subscribers: 399.
Programming (received off-air): KABB (FOX, The Country Network) San Antonio; KENS (CBS, Estrella TV) San Antonio; KHCE-TV (TBN) San Antonio; KLRN (PBS) San Antonio; KMOL-LD (Movies!, NBC) Victoria; KMYS (CW) Kerrville; KPXL-TV (ION) Uvalde; KSAT-TV (ABC, MeTV) San Antonio; KVDA (TMO) San Antonio; KWEX-DT (getTV, UNV) San Antonio.
Programming (via satellite): QVC; Univision.
Fee: $49.95 installation; $62.56 monthly; $1.71 converter.

Expanded Basic Service 1
Subscribers: N.A.
Programming (via satellite): A&E; AMC; Animal Planet; Bravo; Cartoon Network; CMT; CNN; Comedy Central; C-SPAN; Discovery Channel; Disney Channel; E! HD; ESPN; ESPN Classic; ESPN2; Food Network; Fox Deportes; Fox News Channel; Fox Sports I; FOX Sports Southwest; Freeform; Golf Channel; HGTV; History; HLN; Lifetime; MSNBC; MTV; Nickelodeon; Outdoor Channel; Spike TV; Syfy; TBS; The Weather Channel; TLC; TNT; Travel Channel; Turner Classic Movies; TV Land; USA Network; WGN America.
Fee: $18.00 monthly.

Digital Basic Service
Subscribers: N.A.
Programming (via satellite): BBC America; Bloomberg Television; CMT; Discovery Digital Networks; Disney XD; DIY Network; FYI; History; History International; IFC; LMN; MC; Nick 2; Nick Jr.; Science Channel; TeenNick.

Digital Pay Service 1
Pay Units: N.A.
Programming (via satellite): Cinemax (multiplexed); HBO (multiplexed); Showtime (multiplexed); The Movie Channel (multiplexed).

Video-On-Demand: No

Pay-Per-View
iN DEMAND (delivered digitally); Spice 2 (delivered digitally); Playboy TV (delivered digitally).

Internet Service
Operational: Yes.
Broadband Service: Rapid High Speed Internet.
Fee: $29.95 monthly.

Telephone Service
None
Miles of Plant: 31.0 (coaxial); None (fiber optic). Homes passed: 1,375.
Chief Executive Officer: Bob Cohen.
Ownership: CommZoom Communications LLC (MSO).

HONEY GROVE—Formerly served by Suddenlink Communications. No longer in operation. ICA: TX0776.

HOOKS—Allegiance Communications. Now served by NEW BOSTON, TX [TX0204]. ICA: TX0272.

HOUSTON—Comcast Cable, 8590 West Tidwell Rd, Houston, TX 77040. Phones: 713-895-2484; 713-462-1900. Fax: 713-895-1239. Web Site: http://www.comcast.com. Also serves Alvin, Bacliff, Bayou Vista, Baytown, Bear Creek, Bellaire, Brazoria County (portions), Brookside Village, Bunker Hill (village), Chambers County (portions), Channelview, Clear Lake Shores, Clute, Conroe, Crosby, Cypress Trails, Dayton, Deer Park, Dickinson, El Lago, Enclave at Pavillion, Fleetwood, Fleetwood Oaks, Forest Bend, Fort Bend County (portions), Freeport, Friendswood, Fulshear, Galena Park, Galveston, Galveston County (portions), Harris County, Harris County (portions), Hedwig village, Highlands, Hillcrest Village, Hillshire Village, Hitchcock, Humble, Hunter Creek Village, Jacinto City, Jamaica Beach (village), Jersey Village, Katy, Kemah, La Marque, La Porte, Lake Jackson, League City, Liberty, Liberty County (portions), Magnolia, Meadows Place, Meyerland, Missouri City, Montgomery County (portions), Morgans Point, Nassau Bay, Needville, Pasadena, Pearland, Piney Point, Richmond, Richwood,

2017 Edition

D-747

Texas—Cable Systems

Rosenberg, Santa Fe, Seabrook, Shenandoah (unincorporated areas), Shoreacres, South Houston, Southside Place, Spring, Spring Valley, Stafford, Sugar Land, Taylor Lake Village, Texas City, The Woodlands, Tiki Island (village), Tomball, Webster & West University Place. ICA: TX0001.

TV Market Ranking: 15 (Alvin, Bacliff, Baytown, Bear Creek, Bellaire, Brazoria County (portions), Brookside Village, Bunker Hill (village), Chambers County (portions), Channelview, Clear Lake Shores, Crosby, Cypress Trails, Deer Park, Dickinson, El Lago, Enclave at Pavillion, Fleetwood, Fleetwood Oaks, Forest Bend, Fort Bend County (portions), Friendswood, Fulshear, Galena Park, Galveston (portions), Harris County, Harris County (portions), Hedwig village, Highlands, Hillcrest Village, Hillshire Village, HOUSTON, Humble, Hunter Creek Village, Jacinto City, Jersey Village, Katy, Kemah, La Porte, League City, Magnolia, Meadows Place, Meyerland, Missouri City, Montgomery County (portions), Morgans Point, Nassau Bay, Pasadena, Pearland, Piney Point, Richmond, Rosenberg, Santa Fe, Seabrook, Shenandoah (unincorporated areas), Shoreacres, South Houston, Southside Place, Spring, Spring Valley, Stafford, Sugar Land, Taylor Lake Village, The Woodlands, Tomball, Webster, West University Place); 88 (Liberty County (portions)); Below 100 (Bayou Vista, Clute, Conroe, Dayton, Freeport, Galveston, Hitchcock, Jamaica Beach (village), La Marque, Lake Jackson, Liberty, Needville, Richwood, Texas City, Tiki Island (village), Brazoria County (portions), Fort Bend County (portions), Galveston (portions), Harris County (portions), Montgomery County (portions)). Franchise award date: N.A. Franchise expiration date: N.A. Began: August 1, 1979.

Channel capacity: N.A. Channels available but not in use: N.A.

Basic Service
Subscribers: 568,447.
Programming (received off-air): KETH-TV (TBN) Houston; KFTH-DT (getTV, UniMas) Alvin; KHOU (Bounce TV, CBS) Houston; KIAH (Antenna TV, CW) Houston; KLTJ (Daystar TV, ETV) Galveston; KPRC-TV (NBC, This TV) Houston; KPXB-TV (ION) Conroe; KRIV (FOX) Houston; KTBU (IND) Conroe; KTMD (TMO) Galveston; KTRK-TV (ABC, Live Well Network) Houston; KTXH (Buzzr, MNT, Movies!) Houston; KUBE-TV (COZI TV, MeTV) Baytown; KUHT (PBS) Houston; KXLN-DT (UNV) Rosenberg; KYAZ (Azteca America, IND) Katy; KZJL (Estrella TV) Houston; 4 FMs.
Programming (via satellite): ActiveVideo; CNN International; Pop; WGN America.
Fee: $67.95 installation; $33.70 monthly; $2.76 converter.

Expanded Basic Service 1
Subscribers: N.A.
Programming (via satellite): A&E; AMC; Animal Planet; BET; Bravo; Cartoon Network; CNBC; CNN; Comedy Central; C-SPAN; C-SPAN 2; Discovery Channel; Disney Channel; E! HD; ESPN; ESPN2; EVINE Live; Food Network; Fox News Channel; FOX Sports Southwest; Freeform; FX; Golf Channel; Hallmark Channel; HGTV; History; HLN; Lifetime; LMN; MSNBC; MTV; National Geographic Channel; NBC Universo; NBCSN; Nickelodeon; QVC; Spike TV; Syfy; TBS; The Weather Channel; TLC; TNT; Travel Channel; truTV; Turner Classic Movies; Univision; USA Network; VH1; WE tv.
Fee: $25.39 installation; $28.79 monthly.

Digital Basic Service
Subscribers: N.A.
Programming (via satellite): BBC America; Bloomberg Television; CMT; C-SPAN 3; Discovery Life Channel; Disney XD; ESPN Classic; ESPNews; EWTN Global Catholic Network; Fuse; Great American Country; INSP; LWS Local Weather Station; MC; MTV Classic; MTV2; NASA TV; Nick Jr.; Oxygen; Tennis Channel; TV Land.
Fee: $3.00 monthly.

Digital Expanded Basic Service
Subscribers: N.A.
Programming (via satellite): Cooking Channel; DIY Network; FamilyNet; FYI; GSN; History International; Investigation Discovery; Ovation.
Fee: $5.00 monthly.

Digital Expanded Basic Service 2
Subscribers: N.A.
Programming (via satellite): Fox Sports 1; FSN Digital Atlantic; FSN Digital Central; FSN Digital Pacific; Outdoor Channel.
Fee: $2.00 monthly.

Digital Pay Service 1
Pay Units: N.A.
Programming (via satellite): ART America; Cinemax (multiplexed); FXM; HBO (multiplexed); HITS (Headend In The Sky); IFC; Korean Channel; RTN; Saigon Broadcasting Television Network (SBTN); Showtime (multiplexed); Starz; Sundance TV; The Movie Channel (multiplexed); TV Asia; Zee TV.
Fee: $4.95 installation; $3.00 monthly (Canales N or FMC/IFC/Encore/Sundance), $8.00 monthly (Starz), $9.95 monthly (RAI or TV5), $10.00 monthly (Cinemax, HBO, Showtime or TMC), $11.95 monthly (CTN), $12.95 monthly ART or Korean), $14.95 monthly (RTN, SPN, TV Asia or Zee TV).

Video-On-Demand: Yes

Pay-Per-View
Playboy TV; movies.

Internet Service
Operational: Yes. Began: October 1, 1999.
Subscribers: 598,736.
Broadband Service: Comcast High Speed Internet.
Fee: $99.99 installation; $44.95 monthly.

Telephone Service
Digital: Operational
Subscribers: 249,716.
Fee: $44.95 monthly
Miles of Plant: 34,844.0 (coaxial); 9,194.0 (fiber optic). Homes passed: 2,129,851. Miles of plant (fiber) included in miles of plant (coax).
Vice President & General Manager: Tony Speller. Vice President, Operations: Keith Coogan. Vice President, Customer Care: Marie Grumbles. Vice President, Public Affairs: Ray Purser.
Ownership: Comcast Cable Communications Inc. (MSO).

HOUSTON—En-Touch Systems Inc, 11011 Richmond Ave, Ste 425, Houston, TX 77042. Phones: 281-225-0539; 832-590-5500; 281-225-1000 (Customer service). Fax: 281-225-0539. E-mail: marketing@entouch.net. Web Site: http://www.entouch.net. Also serves Cypress, Harris County (portions), Katy, Missouri City, Richmond, Rosharon, Spring & Sugar Land. ICA: TX0982. **Note:** This system is an overbuild.

TV Market Ranking: 15 (Cypress, Harris County (portions), HOUSTON, Katy, Missouri City, Richmond, Spring, Sugar Land). Franchise award date: N.A. Franchise expiration date: N.A. Began: January 1, 1996.

Channel capacity: N.A. Channels available but not in use: N.A.

Basic Service
Subscribers: 9,616.
Programming (received off-air): KETH-TV (TBN) Houston; KFTH-DT (getTV, UniMas) Alvin; KHOU (Bounce TV, CBS) Houston; KIAH (Antenna TV, CW) Houston; KLTJ (Daystar TV, ETV) Galveston; KPRC-TV (NBC, This TV) Houston; KPXB-TV (ION) Conroe; KRIV (FOX) Houston; KTBU (IND) Conroe; KTMD (TMO) Galveston; KTRK-TV (ABC, Live Well Network) Houston; KTXH (Buzzr, MNT, Movies!) Houston; KUBE-TV (COZI TV, MeTV) Baytown; KUHT (PBS) Houston; KXLN-DT (UNV) Rosenberg; KYAZ (Azteca America, IND) Katy; KZJL (Estrella TV) Houston.
Programming (via satellite): Animal Planet; BET; Cartoon Network; CMT; CNBC; CNN; Discovery Channel; Disney XD; Fox News Channel; Freeform; Hallmark Channel; HLN; Lifetime; MSNBC; MTV; Nickelodeon; QVC; TBS; The Weather Channel; TLC; TNT; Travel Channel; TV Land; VH1.
Fee: $14.99 monthly.

Expanded Basic Service 1
Subscribers: N.A.
Programming (via satellite): A&E; AMC; Bravo; Comedy Central; C-SPAN; C-SPAN 2; Discovery Life Channel; Disney Channel; E! HD; ESPN; ESPN2; Food Network; FOX Sports Southwest; FX; HGTV; History; Syfy; truTV; Turner Classic Movies; USA Network.
Fee: $24.00 monthly.

Digital Basic Service
Subscribers: N.A.
Programming (via satellite): AXS TV; BBC America; Bloomberg Television; Discovery Digital Networks; DMX Music; ESPN Classic; ESPN HD; Fuse; FYI; Golf Channel; GSN; HD Theater; History International; LMN; National Geographic Channel; Nick Jr.; Nicktoons; Outdoor Channel; TeenNick; TNT HD; WE tv.
Fee: $46.50 monthly.

Digital Expanded Basic Service
Subscribers: N.A.
Programming (via satellite): ESPNews; Flix; FOX College Sports Central; FOX College Sports Pacific; Fox Sports 1; FXM; HITS (Headend In The Sky); IFC; NBCSN; Starz Encore (multiplexed); Sundance TV.
Fee: $3.50 monthly (sports tier), $4.50 monthly (movie tier or Americas tier).

Digital Pay Service 1
Pay Units: N.A.
Programming (via satellite): ART America; CCTV-Documentary; Cinemax (multiplexed); HBO (multiplexed); HBO HD; MBC America; RAI Italia; Saigon Broadcasting Television Network (SBTN); Showtime (multiplexed); Showtime HD; Starz (multiplexed); The Movie Channel (multiplexed); TV Asia; TV5MONDE USA.
Fee: $7.95 monthly (Starz), $9.95 monthly (Cinemax), $15.95 (Showtime, TMC or HBO).

Video-On-Demand: Planned

Pay-Per-View
iN DEMAND (delivered digitally); Shorteez (delivered digitally); Playboy TV (delivered digitally); Hot Choice (delivered digitally); Fresh (delivered digitally); NBA League Pass (delivered digitally); NHL Center Ice (delivered digitally); MLB Extra Innings (delivered digitally).

Internet Service
Operational: Yes.
Broadband Service: BroadbandNOW!.
Fee: $11.95 monthly; $14.95 modem lease.

Telephone Service
Digital: Operational
Fee: $48.50 monthly
Miles of Plant: 1,500.0 (coaxial); None (fiber optic). Homes passed: 15,000.
Manager: Matt Friesen. Operations Director: Wesley Pennix. Marketing Manager: Arlene Thomas.
Ownership: En-Touch Systems Inc.

HOUSTON—Formerly served by Sprint Corp. No longer in operation. ICA: TX0893.

HOUSTON—Formerly served by Wavevision/TVMAX. No longer in operation. ICA: TX1009.

HOUSTON—Phonoscope Ltd, 6105 Westline Dr, Houston, TX 77036-3515. Phone: 832-436-4000. Fax: 713-271-4334. E-mail: contact@phonoscopeglobal.com. Web Site: http://www.phonoscope.com. Also serves Fort Bend County (portions), Richmond & Rosenberg. ICA: TX0777.

TV Market Ranking: 15 (Fort Bend County (portions), HOUSTON, Richmond, Rosenberg); Below 100 (Fort Bend County (portions)). Franchise award date: September 1, 1986. Franchise expiration date: N.A. Began: January 1, 1987.

Channel capacity: N.A. Channels available but not in use: N.A.

Basic Service
Subscribers: 246.
Programming (received off-air): KETH-TV (TBN) Houston; KFTH-DT (getTV, UniMas) Alvin; KHOU (Bounce TV, CBS) Houston; KIAH (Antenna TV, CW) Houston; KLTJ (Daystar TV, ETV) Galveston; KPRC-TV (NBC, This TV) Houston; KPXB-TV (ION) Conroe; KRIV (FOX) Houston; KTBU (IND) Conroe; KTMD (TMO) Galveston; KTRK-TV (ABC, Live Well Network) Houston; KTXH (Buzzr, MNT, Movies!) Houston; KUBE-TV (COZI TV, MeTV) Baytown; KUHT (PBS) Houston; KXLN-DT (UNV) Rosenberg; KYAZ (Azteca America, IND) Katy; KZJL (Estrella TV) Houston.
Programming (via satellite): A&E; AMC; Animal Planet; BET; Bloomberg Television; Cartoon Network; CMT; CNBC; CNN; CNN International; Comedy Central; C-SPAN; C-SPAN 2; C-SPAN 3; Discovery Channel; Discovery Life Channel; Disney Channel; E! HD; ESPN; ESPN Classic; ESPN2; Food Network; Fox News Channel; FOX Sports Southwest; Freeform; FX; Hallmark Channel; HGTV; History; HLN; Lifetime; MSNBC; MTV; NASA TV; Nickelodeon; Oxygen; Pop; QVC; Spike TV; Syfy; TBS; The Weather Channel; TLC; TNT; Travel Channel; truTV; Turner Classic Movies; TV Land; USA Network; VH1; WGN America.
Fee: $25.00 installation; $36.95 monthly.

Digital Basic Service
Subscribers: N.A.
Programming (via satellite): AWE; BBC America; CBS Sports Network; Cloo; Colours; Cooking Channel; Discovery Digital Networks; Disney XD; DIY Network; DMX Music; ESPNews; EWTN Global Catholic Network; Flix; Food Network HD; Fox Sports 1; FSN Digital Atlantic; FSN Digital Central; FSN Digital Pacific; Fuse; FXM; FYI; Golf Channel; Great American Country; GSN; HD Theater; HGTV HD; History International; HITS (Headend In The Sky); IFC; JUCE TV; LMN; National Geographic

Channel; National Geographic Channel HD; NBCSN; NFL Network; Nick Jr.; Nicktoons; Outdoor Channel; Ovation; Soundtrack Channel; Sundance TV; TeenNick; Tennis Channel; The Word Network; Trinity Broadcasting Network (TBN); Universal HD; WE tv.
Fee: $12.00 monthly.
Digital Pay Service 1
Pay Units: N.A.
Programming (via satellite): Cinemax (multiplexed); HBO (multiplexed); Showtime (multiplexed); Starz (multiplexed); Starz Encore (multiplexed); The Movie Channel (multiplexed).
Fee: $9.95 monthly (Starz/Encore), $12.95 monthly (Showtime/TMC), $18.95 monthly (HBO/Cinemax).
Video-On-Demand: Planned
Pay-Per-View
iN DEMAND (delivered digitally); Fresh (delivered digitally); Shorteez (delivered digitally); Playboy TV (delivered digitally); Hustler TV (delivered digitally); Hot Choice (delivered digitally); ESPN (delivered digitally).
Internet Service
Operational: Yes.
Broadband Service: In-house.
Fee: $25.00 installation; $19.95 monthly.
Telephone Service
Digital: Operational
Fee: $29.95 monthly
Homes passed: 10,000.
President: Rhonda Druke. Program Director: Otis Dyson. Accounting Manager: Jamie Chatari. Technical Operations Manager: Ron Cruz. Marketing Manager: Tracy Garrett.
Ownership: Phonoscope Ltd.

HOWARDWICK—Formerly served by Almega Cable. No longer in operation. ICA: TX0602.

HUBBARD—Formerly served by Almega Cable. No longer in operation. ICA: TX0393.

HUDSON—Suddenlink Communications. Now served by LUFKIN, TX [TX0051]. ICA: TX0357.

HULL—Formerly served by Carrell Communications. No longer in operation. ICA: TX0299.

HUNTINGTON—Vyve Broadband, 2504 Westwood Dr, Westlake, LA 70669. Phone: 855-367-8983. Web Site: http://vyvebroadband.com. ICA: TX0417.
TV Market Ranking: Below 100 (HUNTINGTON).
Channel capacity: N.A. Channels available but not in use: N.A.
Basic Service
Subscribers: 44.
Fee: $59.99 installation; $51.99 monthly.
Senior Vice President, Financial Planning: Daniel J. White.
Ownership: Vyve Broadband LLC (MSO).

HUNTSVILLE—Suddenlink Communications, 1620 Normal Park, Huntsville, TX 77340-4235. Phones: 314-315-9400; 888-822-5151. Fax: 409-295-5851. Web Site: http://www.suddenlink.com. Also serves Elkins Lake & Walker County. ICA: TX0094.
TV Market Ranking: Below 100 (Elkins Lake, HUNTSVILLE, Walker County (portions)); Outside TV Markets (Walker County (portions)). Franchise award date: N.A. Franchise expiration date: N.A. Began: August 9, 1962.
Channel capacity: N.A. Channels available but not in use: N.A.
Basic Service
Subscribers: 3,610. Commercial subscribers: 1,769.
Programming (received off-air): KBTX-TV (CBS, CW) Bryan; KFTH-DT (getTV, UniMas) Alvin; KHOU (Bounce TV, CBS) Houston; KHTX-LP (IND) Huntsville; KIAH (Antenna TV, CW) Houston; KPRC-TV (NBC, This TV) Houston; KPXB-TV (ION) Conroe; KRIV (FOX) Houston; KTBU (IND) Conroe; KTMD (TMO) Galveston; KTRK-TV (ABC, Live Well Network) Houston; KTXH (Buzzr, MNT, Movies!) Houston; KUBE-TV (COZI TV, MeTV) Baytown; KUHT (PBS) Houston; KXLN-DT (UNV) Rosenberg; KYAZ (Azteca America, IND) Katy; allband FM.
Programming (via satellite): EWTN Global Catholic Network; FOX Sports Southwest; Jewelry Television; TBS; The Weather Channel.
Fee: $54.95 installation; $33.24 monthly; $2.25 converter.
Expanded Basic Service 1
Subscribers: N.A.
Programming (via satellite): A&E; AMC; Animal Planet; BET; Bravo; Cartoon Network; CMT; CNBC; CNN; Comedy Central; C-SPAN; C-SPAN 2; Discovery Channel; Disney Channel; E! HD; ESPN; ESPN2; Food Network; Fox News Channel; Fox Sports 1; Freeform; FX; Great American Country; HGTV; History; HLN; Lifetime; LMN; MSNBC; MTV; NBCSN; Nickelodeon; OWN: Oprah Winfrey Network; Oxygen; QVC; Spike TV; TLC; TNT; Travel Channel; truTV; TV Land; Univision; USA Network; VH1.
Digital Basic Service
Subscribers: N.A.
Programming (via satellite): A&E HD; AXS TV; Bandamax; BBC America; Bloomberg Television; CBS Sports Network; Cine Mexicano; Cinelatino; CMT; CNN en Espanol; Cooking Channel; De Pelicula; De Pelicula Clasico; Destination America; Discovery Kids Channel; Disney XD; DIY Network; Enlace USA; ESPN Classic; ESPN Deportes; ESPN HD; ESPN2 HD; ESPNews; ESPNU; Food Network HD; Fox Deportes; Fox Sports 2; FSN HD; Fuse; FYI; Golf Channel; GSN; Hallmark Channel; HD Theater; HGTV HD; History en Espanol; History International; IFC; Investigation Discovery; MC; MTV Classic; MTV Hits; MTV Live; MTV2; mtvU; Nat Geo WILD; National Geographic Channel; National Geographic Channel HD; NBC Universo; Nick Jr.; Nicktoons; NickToons en Espanol; Outdoor Channel; Ritmoson; Science Channel; Starz Encore (multiplexed); Sundance TV; Sur; Syfy; TeenNick; Telehit; TNT HD; Toon Disney en Espanol; Tr3s; Turner Classic Movies; ULTRA HDPlex; Universal HD; Univision; VideoRola.
Digital Pay Service 1
Pay Units: N.A.
Programming (via satellite): Cinemax (multiplexed); HBO (multiplexed); HBO HD; HBO Latino; Showtime (multiplexed); Showtime HD; Starz (multiplexed); Starz HD; The Movie Channel (multiplexed).
Video-On-Demand: No
Pay-Per-View
Playboy TV (delivered digitally); Fresh (delivered digitally); iN DEMAND (delivered digitally); NBA TV (delivered digitally); ESPN Now (delivered digitally).
Internet Service
Operational: Yes.
Subscribers: 8,582.
Broadband Service: Suddenlink High Speed Internet.
Telephone Service
Digital: Operational
Subscribers: 1,804.
Miles of Plant: 372.0 (coaxial); 46.0 (fiber optic). Homes passed: 15,250.
Senior Vice President, Corporate Finance: Michael Pflantz. Vice President, Accounting: Sabrina Warr. General Manager: Johnnie D. Schmidt. Chief Technician: Mark Schmidt.
Ownership: Cequel Communications Holdings I LLC (MSO).

IDALOU—NTS Communications. Formerly [TX0406]. This cable system has converted to IPTV, 1220 Broadway, Lubbock, TX 79401. Phones: 800-658-2150; 806-797-0687. Fax: 806-788-3381. E-mail: info@ntscom.com. Web Site: http://www.ntscom.com. ICA: TX5554.
TV Market Ranking: Below 100 (IDALOU). Franchise award date: December 13, 1988. Franchise expiration date: N.A. Began: May 1, 1980.
Channel capacity: 61 (not 2-way capable). Channels available but not in use: N.A.
Gold
Subscribers: N.A.
Programming (received off-air): KAMC (ABC, Bounce TV) Lubbock; KCBD (NBC, This TV) Lubbock; KJTV-TV (FOX) Lubbock; KLBK-TV (CBS) Lubbock; KPTB-DT (GLC) Lubbock; KTTZ-TV (PBS) Lubbock.
Programming (via satellite): AMC; Cartoon Network; CMT; CNN; Discovery Channel; Disney Channel; E! HD; ESPN; Fox News Channel; FOX Sports Southwest; Freeform; HGTV; History; HLN; Lifetime; Nickelodeon; QVC; Spike TV; TBS; The Weather Channel; TLC; TNT; Travel Channel; Trinity Broadcasting Network (TBN); TV Land; USA Network; WGN America.
Programming (via translator): KVDA (TMO) San Antonio.
Fee: $65.00 monthly. Includes 150+ channels plus music channels & 1 digital receiver.
Platinum
Subscribers: N.A.
Fee: $85.00 monthly. Includes 230+ channels plus music channels, HD channels, 1 whole home DVR & 1 digital receiver.
Cinemax
Subscribers: N.A.
Programming (via satellite): Cinemax.
Fee: $9.95 monthly.
HBO
Subscribers: N.A.
Programming (via satellite): HBO.
Fee: $9.95 monthly.
Video-On-Demand: No
Internet Service
Operational: Yes.
Fee: $44.99-$134.99 monthly.
Telephone Service
Digital: Operational
President & Chief Executive Officer: Cyrus Driver. Executive Vice President & Chief Operating Officer: Deborah Crawford. Executive Vice President & Chief Financial Officer: Don Pittman. Senior Vice President, Product Management: Angel Kandahari. Vice President & General Counsel: Daniel Wheeler. Vice President, Products & Marketing: Roberto Chang. Vice President, Human Resources: Wendy J. Lee. Vice President, Service Delivery & IT Strategy: Michael McDaniel. Vice President, RUS Projects: Aaron Peters.
Ownership: NTS Communications Inc. (MSO).

IDALOU—NTS Communications. This cable system has converted to IPTV. See IDALOU, TX [TX5554]. ICA: TX0406.

IMPERIAL—Formerly served by Cebridge Connections. No longer in operation. ICA: TX0968.

INDIAN SPRINGS—Formerly served by Cebridge Connections. No longer in operation. ICA: TX0385.

INGRAM—Suddenlink Communications, 520 Maryville Centre Dr, Ste 300, St. Louis, MO 63141. Phones: 877-423-2743; 314-315-9400. Web Site: http://www.suddenlink.com. Also serves Hunt & Kerr County (portions). ICA: TX0232.
TV Market Ranking: Below 100 (Hunt, INGRAM, Kerr County (portions)). Franchise award date: N.A. Franchise expiration date: N.A. Began: November 1, 1966.
Channel capacity: 41 (operating 2-way). Channels available but not in use: N.A.
Basic Service
Subscribers: 506.
Programming (received off-air): KABB (FOX, The Country Network) San Antonio; KENS (CBS, Estrella TV) San Antonio; KLRN (PBS) San Antonio; KMOL-LD (Movies!, NBC) Victoria; KMYS (CW) Kerrville; KPXL-TV (ION) Uvalde; KSAT-TV (ABC, MeTV) San Antonio; allband FM.
Fee: $28.45 monthly.
Expanded Basic Service 1
Subscribers: N.A.
Programming (via satellite): A&E; AMC; Animal Planet; Bravo; Cartoon Network; CNBC; CNN; Comedy Central; C-SPAN; Discovery Channel; Disney Channel; E! HD; ESPN; ESPN2; Food Network; Fox News Channel; Fox Sports 1; FOX Sports Southwest; Freeform; FX; Golf Channel; Great American Country; Hallmark Channel; HGTV; History; HLN; Lifetime; MSNBC; MTV; National Geographic Channel; Nickelodeon; Outdoor Channel; QVC; Spike TV; Syfy; TBS; The Weather Channel; TLC; TNT; Travel Channel; Trinity Broadcasting Network (TBN); Turner Classic Movies; TV Land; Univision; Univision Studios; USA Network; VH1.
Fee: $26.00 monthly.

Texas—Cable Systems

Digital Basic Service
Subscribers: N.A.
Programming (via satellite): BBC America; Bloomberg Television; Cloo; Discovery Digital Networks; Disney XD; DMX Music; ESPN Classic; ESPNews; Fuse; FYI; GSN; History; History International; IFC; NBCSN; Sundance TV; WE tv.
Fee: $3.99 monthly.

Pay Service 1
Pay Units: N.A.
Programming (via satellite): Cinemax; HBO; Showtime; The Movie Channel.
Fee: $7.95 monthly (TMC), $9.95 monthly (Cinemax or Showtime), $10.95 monthly (HBO).

Digital Pay Service 1
Pay Units: N.A.
Programming (via satellite): Cinemax (multiplexed); HBO (multiplexed); Showtime (multiplexed); Starz (multiplexed); Starz Encore (multiplexed); The Movie Channel (multiplexed).

Pay-Per-View
iN DEMAND (delivered digitally); Playboy TV (delivered digitally); Fresh (delivered digitally); Shorteez (delivered digitally).

Internet Service
Operational: Yes. Began: July 1, 2002.
Broadband Service: Suddenlink High Speed Internet.
Fee: $45.95 installation; $29.95 monthly.

Telephone Service
Digital: Operational
Fee: $44.95 monthly
Miles of Plant: 112.0 (coaxial); None (fiber optic). Homes passed: 2,274.
Senior Vice President, Corporate Finance: Michael Pflantz. Regional Manager: Todd Cruthird. Regional Marketing Manager: Beverly Gambell. Plant Manager: Jimmy Welch.
Ownership: Cequel Communications Holdings I LLC (MSO).

IOLA—Formerly served by National Cable Inc. No longer in operation. ICA: TX0677.

IOWA PARK—Formerly served by Cebridge Connections. Now served by Suddenlink Communications, BURKBURNETT, TX [TX0154]. ICA: TX0211.

IRAAN—LynnStar Communications, 4500 Mercantile Plz, Ste 300, Fort Worth, TX 76137. Phones: 575-437-3101; 888-575-9230; 682-730-0900. Fax: 682-730-6400. Web Site: http://lynnstar.net; http://www.lynnstarcomm.com. ICA: TX1028.
TV Market Ranking: Outside TV Markets (IRAAN).
Channel capacity: N.A. Channels available but not in use: N.A.

Basic Service
Subscribers: 58.
Programming (received off-air): KMID (ABC) Midland; KMLM-DT (GLC) Odessa; KOSA-TV (CBS, MNT) Odessa; KPBT-TV (PBS) Odessa; KPEJ-TV (FOX) Odessa; KTLE-LP (TMO) Odessa; KUPB (UNV) Midland; KWES-TV (CW, NBC, TMO) Odessa; KWWT (Antenna TV, MeTV, Movies!, Retro TV, This TV) Odessa.
Programming (via satellite): A&E; C-SPAN; Freeform; Hallmark Channel; HSN; Lifetime; TBS; The Weather Channel; Trinity Broadcasting Network (TBN); WGN America.
Fee: $49.95 installation; $23.72 monthly.

Expanded Basic Service 1
Subscribers: N.A.
Programming (via satellite): AMC; Animal Planet; Cartoon Network; CMT; CNN; Discovery Channel; Disney Channel; ESPN; ESPN2; Fox News Channel; FOX Sports Networks; History; MoviePlex; MTV; National Geographic Channel; Nick At Nite; Nickelodeon; Spike TV; Syfy; TLC; TNT; Travel Channel; UniMas; USA Network; VH1.
Fee: $28.35 monthly.

Digital Basic Service
Subscribers: N.A.
Programming (via satellite): BBC America; Bloomberg Television; Bravo; Centric; Cloo; CMT; Destination America; Discovery Kids Channel; Discovery Life Channel; Disney XD; DMX Music; ESPN Classic; ESPNews; FOX College Sports Central; FOX College Sports Pacific; Fox Sports 1; Fuse; FXM; FYI; Golf Channel; Great American Country; GSN; HGTV; History International; IFC; Investigation Discovery; LMN; MTV Classic; MTV Hits; MTV2; NBCSN; Nick Jr.; Outdoor Channel; OWN; Oprah Winfrey Network; Science Channel; Starz Encore (multiplexed); TeenNick; The Word Network; Turner Classic Movies; VH1 Soul; WE tv.
Fee: $20.90 monthly.

Pay Service 1
Pay Units: N.A.
Programming (via satellite): HBO.
Fee: $13.95 monthly.

Digital Pay Service 1
Pay Units: N.A.
Programming (via satellite): Cinemax (multiplexed); HBO (multiplexed); Showtime (multiplexed); Starz (multiplexed); The Movie Channel (multiplexed).
Fee: $9.95 monthly (Starz), $12.95 monthly (Cinemax, HBO, Showtime or TMC).

Video-On-Demand: No

Pay-Per-View
Playboy TV (delivered digitally); Fresh (delivered digitally).

Internet Service
Operational: No.

Telephone Service
None
Chairman of the Board & Government Relations Director: S. Gene Yarbrough. Chief Executive Officer, Executive Vice President & Board Member: Chris Romine. Chief Operations Officer, Executive Vice President & Board Member: Steve Sizemore. Vice President & Business Development & Countertrade Director: Gary Majors. Vice President & Programming & Vendor Relations Director: Gus Salvino. Vice President & Investor Relations Manager: Daniel J. Sweeney. Accounting Manager: Sheila Magness.
Ownership: Lynnstar Communications (MSO).

IRVING—Time Warner Cable. Now served by DALLAS, TX [TX0003]. ICA: TX0016.

ITALY—Formerly served by Almega Cable. No longer in operation. ICA: TX1001.

JACKSBORO—Vyve Broadband, 2804B FM 51 South, Decatur, TX 76234. Phones: 800-937-1397; 940-627-3099. Web Site: http://vyvebroadband.com. ICA: TX0781.
TV Market Ranking: Below 100 (JACKSBORO). Franchise award date: March 1, 1977. Franchise expiration date: N.A. Began: June 14, 1977.
Channel capacity: N.A. Channels available but not in use: N.A.

Basic Service
Subscribers: 354.
Programming (received off-air): KAUZ-TV (CBS, CW) Wichita Falls; KDAF (Antenna TV, CW, This TV) Dallas; KDFI (Bounce TV, Buzzr, Heroes & Icons, MNT, Movies!) Dallas; KDFW (FOX) Dallas; KERA-TV (PBS) Dallas; KFDX-TV (NBC) Wichita Falls; KJTL (Bounce TV, FOX) Wichita Falls; KTVT (CBS, Decades) Fort Worth; KTXA (IND, MeTV) Fort Worth; KXAS-TV (COZI TV, NBC) Fort Worth; KXTX-TV (TMO) Dallas; WFAA (ABC) Dallas; allband FM.
Fee: $55.95 installation; $25.00 monthly.

Expanded Basic Service 1
Subscribers: N.A.
Programming (via satellite): A&E; AMC; Animal Planet; BET; Bravo; Cartoon Network; CMT; CNBC; CNN; Comedy Central; C-SPAN; Discovery Channel; Disney Channel; E! HD; ESPN; ESPN2; EVINE Live; EWTN Global Catholic Network; Food Network; Fox News Channel; FOX Sports Southwest; Freeform; FX; HGTV; History; HLN; Lifetime; MTV; Nick Jr.; Nickelodeon; Pop; QVC; Radar Channel; Spike TV; Syfy; TBS; The Weather Channel; TLC; TNT; Travel Channel; Trinity Broadcasting Network (TBN); truTV; Turner Classic Movies; TV Land; Univision Studios; USA Network; VH1; WE tv.
Fee: $43.95 monthly.

Digital Basic Service
Subscribers: N.A.
Programming (via satellite): BBC America; Bloomberg Television; Bravo; Church Channel; Cloo; CMT; Destination America; Discovery Kids Channel; Discovery Life Channel; Disney XD; DMX Music; ESPN Classic; ESPN2; ESPNews; EVINE Live; Fox Sports 1; Fuse; FXM; FYI; Golf Channel; Great American Country; GSN; HGTV; History; History International; IFC; Investigation Discovery; JUCE TV; LMN; MTV Classic; MTV Hits; MTV Jams; MTV2; National Geographic Channel; NBCSN; Nick Jr.; Nicktoons; Outdoor Channel; Ovation; OWN: Oprah Winfrey Network; Science Channel; Sundance TV; Syfy; TeenNick; The Word Network; Trinity Broadcasting Network (TBN); Turner Classic Movies; UP; VH1 Soul; WE tv.
Fee: $9.99 monthly.

Pay Service 1
Pay Units: N.A.
Programming (via satellite): Cinemax; HBO (multiplexed); Starz; Starz Encore.
Fee: $20.00 installation.

Digital Pay Service 1
Pay Units: N.A.
Programming (via satellite): Cinemax (multiplexed); Flix; HBO (multiplexed); Showtime (multiplexed); Starz (multiplexed); Starz Encore (multiplexed); The Movie Channel (multiplexed).
Fee: $20.00 installation; $5.00 monthly (Encore), $11.00 monthly (Starz), $11.95 monthly (Cinemax), $13.95 monthly (HBO or Showtime/TMC/Flix).

Video-On-Demand: No

Pay-Per-View
iN DEMAND (delivered digitally); Hot Choice (delivered digitally); Playboy TV (delivered digitally); Fresh (delivered digitally); Spice; Xcess (delivered digitally); Club Jenna (delivered digitally).

Internet Service
Operational: Yes.
Broadband Service: Net Commander.
Fee: $39.95 installation; $51.95 monthly.

Telephone Service
None
Miles of Plant: 33.0 (coaxial); None (fiber optic). Homes passed included in Decatur.
President & Chief Executive Officer: Jeffrey DeMond. Senior Vice President, Financial Planning: Daniel White. Vice President, Residential Services: Vin Zachariah. Vice President, Marketing: Diane Quennoz.
Ownership: Vyve Broadband LLC (MSO).

JACKSONVILLE—Suddenlink Communications, 316 South Main St, Jacksonville, TX 75766. Phones: 314-315-9400; 903-586-8122. Web Site: http://www.suddenlink.com. Also serves Cherokee County. ICA: TX0110.
TV Market Ranking: Below 100 (Cherokee County, JACKSONVILLE). Franchise award date: January 1, 1969. Franchise expiration date: N.A. Began: July 3, 1953.
Channel capacity: N.A. Channels available but not in use: N.A.

Basic Service
Subscribers: 2,395. Commercial subscribers: 259.
Programming (received off-air): KDFW (FOX) Dallas; KERA-TV (PBS) Dallas; KETK-TV (Estrella TV, NBC) Jacksonville; KFXK-TV (FOX) Longview; KLPN-LD (MNT) Longview; KLTV (ABC, Bounce TV, TMO) Tyler; KTVT (CBS, Decades) Fort Worth; KXAS-TV (COZI TV, NBC) Fort Worth; KXTX-TV (TMO) Dallas; WFAA (ABC) Dallas; 6 FMs.
Programming (via satellite): Comedy Central; FOX Sports Southwest; ION Television; Lifetime; Pop; QVC; TBS; truTV; VH1.
Fee: $40.00 installation; $32.24 monthly.

Expanded Basic Service 1
Subscribers: N.A.
Programming (via satellite): A&E; Animal Planet; BET; Cartoon Network; CNBC; CNN; C-SPAN; C-SPAN 2; Discovery Channel; ESPN; Food Network; Fox News Channel; FOX Sports Southwest; Freeform; FX; Great American Country; HGTV; HLN; INSP; MoviePlex; MSNBC; MTV; Nickelodeon; Spike TV; The Weather Channel; TLC; TNT; Univision; USA Network.
Fee: $19.25 monthly.

Digital Basic Service
Subscribers: N.A.
Programming (via satellite): Discovery Digital Networks; ESPN Classic; ESPN2; Fox Sports 1; Golf Channel; GSN; History; NBCSN; Starz Encore; Syfy; Turner Classic Movies; TV Land; WE tv.

Pay Service 1
Pay Units: N.A.
Programming (via satellite): Cinemax; HBO; Showtime; Starz; Starz Encore.
Fee: $1.75 monthly (Encore), $6.75 monthly (Starz), $9.00 monthly (Cinemax), $10.95 monthly (HBO).

Digital Pay Service 1
Pay Units: N.A.
Programming (via satellite): Cinemax (multiplexed); HBO (multiplexed); Showtime (multiplexed); Starz (multiplexed); The Movie Channel (multiplexed).

Video-On-Demand: No

Pay-Per-View
iN DEMAND; iN DEMAND (delivered digitally).

Internet Service
Operational: Yes.
Broadband Service: Suddenlink High Speed Internet.
Fee: $45.95 installation; $29.95 monthly; $10.00 modem lease; $75.00 modem purchase.

Telephone Service
Digital: Operational
Fee: $44.95 monthly
Miles of Plant: 96.0 (coaxial); None (fiber optic). Homes passed: 6,114.
Senior Vice President, Corporate Finance: Michael Pflantz. Vice President, Accounting: Sabrina Warr. General Manager:

Cable Systems—Texas

Ronnie Powell. Chief Technician: Brad Casey.
Ownership: Cequel Communications Holdings I LLC (MSO).

JARRELL—Suddenlink Communications, 111 North College St, Georgetown, TX 78626-4101. Phones: 314-315-9400; 512-930-3085. Fax: 512-869-2962. Web Site: http://www.suddenlink.com. ICA: TX0972.
TV Market Ranking: Below 100 (JARRELL).
Channel capacity: N.A. Channels available but not in use: N.A.
Basic Service
Subscribers: 61.
Programming (received off-air): KCEN-TV (Antenna TV, MeTV, MundoMax, NBC) Temple; KEYE-TV (CBS, TMO) Austin; KLRU (PBS) Austin; KNVA (CW, Grit, TheCoolTV) Austin; KTBC (Buzzr, FOX, Movies!) Austin; KVUE (ABC, Estrella TV) Austin; KWTX-TV (CBS, CW) Waco; KXXV (ABC, TMO) Waco.
Programming (via satellite): C-SPAN; QVC; TBS; TV Land; WGN America.
Fee: $40.00 installation; $33.24 monthly; $1.50 converter.
Expanded Basic Service 1
Subscribers: N.A.
Programming (via satellite): A&E; AMC; Animal Planet; CMT; CNBC; CNN; Discovery Channel; Disney Channel; ESPN; Freeform; HGTV; History; HLN; Lifetime; MTV; Nickelodeon; Spike TV; Syfy; The Weather Channel; TLC; TNT; Trinity Broadcasting Network (TBN); Turner Classic Movies; Univision Studios; USA Network; VH1.
Fee: $15.50 monthly.
Digital Basic Service
Subscribers: N.A.
Programming (via satellite): BBC America; Bloomberg Television; Destination America; Discovery Kids Channel; Disney XD; DMX Music; ESPN Classic; ESPNews; Fox Sports 1; Fuse; FYI; Golf Channel; GSN; History International; Investigation Discovery; LMN; NBCSN; OWN; Oprah Winfrey Network; Science Channel; Starz Encore (multiplexed); Sundance TV.
Pay Service 1
Pay Units: N.A.
Programming (via satellite): Cinemax (multiplexed); HBO; Showtime; Starz Encore.
Fee: $8.99 monthly (Showtime), $9.99 monthly (Cinemax or Encore), $11.49 monthly (HBO).
Digital Pay Service 1
Pay Units: N.A.
Programming (via satellite): Cinemax (multiplexed); HBO (multiplexed); Showtime (multiplexed); Starz (multiplexed); Starz Encore; The Movie Channel (multiplexed).
Video-On-Demand: No
Pay-Per-View
iN DEMAND (delivered digitally); Playboy TV (delivered digitally); Fresh (delivered digitally).
Internet Service
Operational: Yes.
Broadband Service: Suddenlink High Speed Internet.
Telephone Service
Digital: Operational
Senior Vice President, Corporate Finance: Michael Pflantz. Vice President, Accounting: Sabrina Warr. General Manager: Dale E. Hoffman. Chief Technician & Marketing Director: Wesley Houghteling.
Ownership: Cequel Communications Holdings I LLC (MSO).

JASPER—NewWave Communications, One Montgomery Plaza, 4th Floor, Sikeston, MO 63801. Phones: 573-472-9500; 888-863-9928. Fax: 573-472-9518. E-mail: info@newwave.com. Web Site: http://www.newwavecom.com. ICA: TX0157.
TV Market Ranking: Outside TV Markets (JASPER). Franchise award date: November 14, 1977. Franchise expiration date: N.A. Began: August 1, 1967.
Channel capacity: N.A. Channels available but not in use: N.A.
Basic Service
Subscribers: 1,060.
Programming (received off-air): KBMT (ABC) Beaumont; KBTV-TV (Bounce TV, FOX) Port Arthur; KFDM (CBS, CW) Beaumont; KVHP (FOX) Lake Charles; allband FM.
Programming (via microwave): KUHT (PBS) Houston.
Programming (via satellite): C-SPAN; ION Television; QVC; The Weather Channel; Trinity Broadcasting Network (TBN).
Fee: $35.00 installation; $33.93 monthly.
Expanded Basic Service 1
Subscribers: N.A.
Programming (via satellite): A&E; AMC; Animal Planet; BET; Cartoon Network; CMT; CNBC; CNN; Comedy Central; Discovery Channel; ESPN; ESPN2; Food Network; Fox News Channel; FOX Sports Southwest; Freeform; FX; Hallmark Channel; HGTV; History; HLN; INSP; Lifetime; MTV; Nickelodeon; Outdoor Channel; Pop; Spike TV; Syfy; TBS; TLC; TNT; Travel Channel; Turner Classic Movies; TV Land; USA Network; VH1; WGN America.
Fee: $53.70 monthly.
Digital Basic Service
Subscribers: N.A.
Programming (via satellite): BBC America; Discovery Digital Networks; DMX Music; ESPN Classic; ESPNews; Fox Sports 1; FYI; Golf Channel; GSN; History International; IFC; LMN; NBCSN; TeenNick; WE tv.
Fee: $10.00 monthly.
Digital Pay Service 1
Pay Units: N.A.
Programming (via satellite): Cinemax (multiplexed); HBO (multiplexed); Showtime (multiplexed); Starz (multiplexed); Starz Encore (multiplexed); The Movie Channel (multiplexed).
Fee: $7.00 monthly (Starz), $9.00 monthly (Cinemax), $15.00 monthly (Showtime/TMC), $16.00 monthly (HBO) or $26.00 monthly (HBO/Cinemax).
Video-On-Demand: No
Pay-Per-View
iN DEMAND (delivered digitally); Club Jenna (delivered digitally); Playboy TV (delivered digitally).
Internet Service
Operational: Yes.
Fee: $39.95 installation; $36.99-$46.99 monthly; $6.00 modem lease; $39.95 modem purchase.
Telephone Service
Digital: Operational
Fee: $39.95 monthly
Miles of Plant: 139.0 (coaxial); None (fiber optic). Homes passed: 3,900.
Regional General Manager: Jerry Smith.
Ownership: NewWave Communications LLC (MSO).

JAYTON—Formerly served by Jayroc Cablevision. No longer in operation. ICA: TX0557.

JEWETT—Formerly served by Northland Cable Television. No longer in operation. ICA: TX0541.

JOAQUIN—NewWave Communications. Now served by LOGANSPORT, LA [LA0096]. ICA: TX1032.

JOHNSON CITY—Formerly served by Almega Cable. No longer in operation. ICA: TX0560.

JOSEPHINE—Formerly served by Almega Cable. No longer in operation. ICA: TX0784.

JOSHUA—Pathway. This cable system has converted to IPTV. Now served by BURLESON, TX [TX5530]. ICA: TX5531.

JOSHUA—Pathway. This cable system has converted to IPTV. Now served by BURLESON, TX [TX5530]. ICA: TX0785.

JOURDANTON—Alliance Communications, PO Box 9090, Tyler, TX 75711. Phones: 903-561-4411; 800-842-8160; 501-679-6619 (Greenbrier, AR office). Web Site: http://www.alliancecable.net. Also serves Atascosa County & Poteet. ICA: TX0238.
TV Market Ranking: 45 (Atascosa County (portions), JOURDANTON, Poteet); Outside TV Markets (Atascosa County (portions)). Franchise award date: N.A. Franchise expiration date: N.A. Began: April 12, 1982.
Channel capacity: N.A. Channels available but not in use: N.A.
Basic Service
Subscribers: 137.
Programming (received off-air): KABB (FOX, The Country Network) San Antonio; KENS (CBS, Estrella TV) San Antonio; KLRN (PBS) San Antonio; KMYS (CW) Kerrville; KPXL-TV (ION) Uvalde; KSAT-TV (ABC, MeTV) San Antonio; KVDA (TMO) San Antonio; KWEX-DT (getTV, UNV) San Antonio; WOAI-TV (IND, NBC) San Antonio.
Programming (via satellite): TNT.
Fee: $50.51 installation; $22.45 monthly.
Pay Service 1
Pay Units: N.A.
Programming (via satellite): HBO; Showtime; Starz Encore; The Movie Channel.
Fee: $2.75 monthly (Encore), $12.95 monthly (HBO, Showtime or TMC).
Internet Service
Operational: No.
Telephone Service
None
Miles of Plant: 33.0 (coaxial); None (fiber optic). Homes passed: 1,839.
Vice President & General Manager: John Brinker. Vice President, Programming: Julie Newman.
Ownership: Buford Media Group LLC (MSO).

JUNCTION—Suddenlink Communications, 520 Maryville Centre Dr, Ste 300, St. Louis, MO 63141. Phones: 800-999-6845 (Customer service); 314-315-9400. Web Site: http://www.suddenlink.com. Also serves Kimble County (portions). ICA: TX0320.
TV Market Ranking: Outside TV Markets (JUNCTION, Kimble County (portions)). Franchise award date: N.A. Franchise expiration date: N.A. Began: June 1, 1957.
Channel capacity: N.A. Channels available but not in use: N.A.
Basic Service
Subscribers: 169.
Programming (received off-air): KIDY (FOX, MNT) San Angelo; KLST (CBS) San Angelo; KTXS-TV (ABC, CW, This TV, TMO) Sweetwater; KXAN-TV (COZI TV, NBC) Austin; 4 FMs.
Programming (via microwave): KBVO (Laff, MNT) Llano; WFAA (ABC) Dallas.

Programming (via satellite): A&E; Animal Planet; CMT; CNN; Discovery Channel; Disney Channel; ESPN; Fox News Channel; FOX Sports Southwest; Freeform; History; HLN; KRMA-TV (PBS) Denver; Lifetime; Nickelodeon; QVC; Spike TV; TBS; Telemundo; The Weather Channel; TLC; TNT; Trinity Broadcasting Network (TBN); TV Land; USA Network; WGN America.
Fee: $28.45 monthly.
Pay Service 1
Pay Units: N.A.
Programming (via satellite): HBO; Showtime; The Movie Channel.
Fee: $10.00 installation; $7.95 monthly (TMC), $9.95 monthly (Showtime), $10.95 monthly (HBO).
Video-On-Demand: No
Internet Service
Operational: Yes. Began: January 26, 2004.
Subscribers: 127.
Broadband Service: Suddenlink High Speed Internet.
Fee: $49.95 installation; $25.95 monthly.
Telephone Service
Digital: Operational
Fee: $44.95 monthly
Miles of Plant: 32.0 (coaxial); None (fiber optic). Homes passed: 1,100.
Senior Vice President, Corporate Finance: Michael Pflantz. Regional Manager: Todd Cruthird. Regional Marketing Manager: Beverly Gambell. Plant Manager: Jimmy Welch.
Ownership: Cequel Communications Holdings I LLC (MSO).

KATY (southern portion)—Formerly served by Cebridge Connections. No longer in operation. ICA: TX0786.

KAUFMAN—Suddenlink Communications, 520 Maryville Centre Dr, Ste 300, St. Louis, MO 63141. Phones: 314-315-9400; 877-794-2724. Web Site: http://www.suddenlink.com. Also serves Oak Grove. ICA: TX0262.
TV Market Ranking: 12 (KAUFMAN, Oak Grove). Franchise award date: N.A. Franchise expiration date: N.A. Began: March 23, 1981.
Channel capacity: N.A. Channels available but not in use: N.A.
Basic Service
Subscribers: 89.
Programming (received off-air): KDAF (Antenna TV, CW, This TV) Dallas; KDFI (Bounce TV, Buzzr, Heroes & Icons, MNT, Movies!) Dallas; KDFW (FOX) Dallas; KDTX-TV (TBN) Dallas; KERA-TV (PBS) Dallas; KFWD (MundoMax) Fort Worth; KMPX (Estrella TV) Decatur; KPXD-TV (ION) Arlington; KSTR-DT (getTV, UniMas) Irving; KTVT (CBS, Decades) Fort Worth; KTXA (IND, MeTV) Fort Worth; KUVN-DT (UNV) Garland; KXAS-TV (COZI TV, NBC) Fort Worth; KXTX-TV (TMO) Dallas; WFAA (ABC) Dallas.
Programming (via satellite): A&E; Animal Planet; BET; CNN; C-SPAN; Discovery Channel; ESPN; Fox News Channel; FOX Sports Southwest; Great American Country; HGTV; HLN; Pop; QVC; Spike TV; TBS; The Weather Channel; TNT; Univision.
Fee: $40.00 installation; $38.24 monthly.
Expanded Basic Service 1
Subscribers: N.A.
Programming (via satellite): AMC; Cartoon Network; CNBC; Comedy Central; ESPN2; Fox Deportes; FX; FXM; Hallmark Channel; History; Lifetime; MTV; Nickelodeon; Syfy; Turner Classic Movies; USA Network.
Fee: $41.29 monthly.

2017 Edition

D-751

Texas—Cable Systems

Digital Basic Service
Subscribers: N.A.
Programming (via satellite): Bloomberg Television; Discovery Digital Networks; DMX Music; Fox Sports 1; Golf Channel; GSN; Outdoor Channel; Starz Encore; Sundance TV; Trinity Broadcasting Network (TBN); WE tv.
Fee: $10.70 monthly.
Pay Service 1
Pay Units: N.A.
Programming (via satellite): Cinemax; HBO; Showtime.
Fee: $11.00 monthly (Cinemax or Showtime), $13.50 monthly (HBO).
Digital Pay Service 1
Pay Units: N.A.
Programming (via satellite): Cinemax (multiplexed); Flix; HBO (multiplexed); Showtime (multiplexed); The Movie Channel (multiplexed).
Fee: $10.00 monthly (each).
Pay-Per-View
iN DEMAND (delivered digitally); Hot Choice (delivered digitally); Playboy TV (delivered digitally); Fresh (delivered digitally); ESPN Now (delivered digitally); Sports PPV (delivered digitally).
Internet Service
Operational: Yes.
Fee: $42.99 monthly.
Telephone Service
Digital: Operational
Miles of Plant: 61.0 (coaxial); None (fiber optic). Homes passed: 2,120.
Senior Vice President, Corporate Finance: Michael Pflantz. Vice President, Accounting: Sabrina Warr.
Ownership: Cequel Communications Holdings I LLC (MSO).

KELLER—Millennium Telcom, 4800 Keller Hicks Rd, Forth Worth, TX 76244. Phone: 817-745-2000. Fax: 817-745-2029. Also serves Fort Worth, Haslet, Southlake, Tarrant County (portions), Wautaga & Westlake. ICA: TX1049.
TV Market Ranking: 12 (Fort Worth, Haslet, KELLER, Southlake, Tarrant County (portions), Wautaga).
Channel capacity: N.A. Channels available but not in use: N.A.
Basic Service
Subscribers: 4,187.
Fee: $17.95 monthly.
Executive Vice President: A. Craig Knight. Secretary, Board of Managers: Don Lee. Chief Technician: Billy Golden.
Ownership: Millennium Telcom LLC.

KEMPNER—Formerly served by National Cable Inc. No longer in operation. ICA: TX0674.

KENEDY—CommZoom, 2438 Boardwalk, San Antonio, IA 78217. Phone: 844-858-8500. Web Site: http://www.commzoom.com. Also serves Karnes City. ICA: TX0281.
TV Market Ranking: Outside TV Markets (Karnes City, KENEDY). Franchise award date: N.A. Franchise expiration date: N.A. Began: July 1, 1977.
Channel capacity: 41 (2-way capable). Channels available but not in use: N.A.
Basic Service
Subscribers: 299.
Programming (received off-air): KABB (FOX, The Country Network) San Antonio; KENS (CBS, Estrella TV) San Antonio; KLRN (PBS) San Antonio; KMYS (CW) Kerrville; KSAT-TV (ABC, MeTV) San Antonio; KVDA (TMO) San Antonio; KWEX-DT (getTV, UNV) San Antonio; WOAI-TV (IND, NBC) San Antonio; 1 FM.
Programming (via satellite): A&E; Animal Planet; CMT; CNN; Discovery Channel; Disney Channel; ESPN; EWTN Global Catholic Network; Fox News Channel; FOX Sports Southwest; Freeform; HLN; Nickelodeon; QVC; Spike TV; TBS; The Weather Channel; TLC; TNT; Trinity Broadcasting Network (TBN); Turner Classic Movies; TV Land; USA Network; WGN America.
Fee: $49.95 installation; $55.72 monthly.
Pay Service 1
Pay Units: N.A.
Programming (via satellite): HBO; Showtime; The Movie Channel.
Fee: $25.00 installation; $7.95 monthly (TMC), $9.95 monthly (Showtime), $10.95 monthly (HBO).
Video-On-Demand: No
Internet Service
Operational: No.
Telephone Service
None
Miles of Plant: 65.0 (coaxial); None (fiber optic). Homes passed: 2,412.
Chief Executive Officer: Bob Cohen.
Ownership: CommZoom Communications LLC (MSO).

KENEFICK—Formerly served by Carrell Communications. No longer in operation. ICA: TX0438.

KERENS—Formerly served by Northland Cable Television. No longer in operation. ICA: TX0443.

KERMIT—Suddenlink Communications, 520 Maryville Centre Dr, Ste 300, St. Louis, MO 63141. Phones: 877-423-2743; 314-315-9400. Web Site: http://www.suddenlink.com. Also serves Winkler County (portions). ICA: TX0161.
TV Market Ranking: Below 100 (Winkler County (portions)); Outside TV Markets (KERMIT). Franchise award date: March 26, 1991. Franchise expiration date: N.A. Began: August 1, 1972.
Channel capacity: 70 (operating 2-way). Channels available but not in use: N.A.
Basic Service
Subscribers: 405.
Programming (received off-air): KMID (ABC) Midland; KMLM-DT (GLC) Odessa; KOSA-TV (CBS, MNT) Odessa; KPEJ-TV (FOX) Odessa; KUPB (UNV) Midland; KWES-TV (CW, NBC, TMO) Odessa.
Programming (via satellite): KMGH-TV (ABC, Azteca America) Denver; KRMA-TV (PBS) Denver; QVC.
Fee: $28.45 monthly.
Expanded Basic Service 1
Subscribers: N.A.
Programming (via satellite): A&E; AMC; Animal Planet; BET; Bravo; Cartoon Network; CNN; Comedy Central; C-SPAN; Discovery Channel; Disney Channel; E! HD; ESPN; ESPN2; EWTN Global Catholic Network; Food Network; Fox Deportes; Fox News Channel; FOX Sports Southwest; Freeform; FX; Golf Channel; Great American Country; Hallmark Channel; HGTV; History; HLN; Lifetime; MSNBC; MTV; National Geographic Channel; Nickelodeon; Outdoor Channel; Pop; Spike TV; Syfy; TBS; Telemundo; The Weather Channel; TLC; TNT; Trinity Broadcasting Network (TBN); Turner Classic Movies; TV Land; Univision; USA Network; VH1.
Fee: $26.00 monthly.

Digital Basic Service
Subscribers: N.A.
Programming (via satellite): BBC America; Bloomberg Television; Cloo; Discovery Digital Networks; Disney XD; DMX Music; ESPN Classic; ESPNews; Fox Sports 1; Fuse; FYI; GSN; History; History International; HITS (Headend In The Sky); IFC; NBCSN; WE tv.
Fee: $3.99 monthly.
Pay Service 1
Pay Units: N.A.
Programming (via satellite): HBO; Showtime; Starz; Starz Encore; The Movie Channel.
Fee: $6.95 monthly (Starz/Encore), $7.95 monthly (TMC), $9.95 monthly (Showtime), $10.95 monthly (HBO).
Digital Pay Service 1
Pay Units: N.A.
Programming (via satellite): Cinemax (multiplexed); HBO (multiplexed); Showtime (multiplexed); Starz (multiplexed); Starz Encore (multiplexed); The Movie Channel (multiplexed).
Pay-Per-View
iN DEMAND (delivered digitally); Playboy TV (delivered digitally); Fresh (delivered digitally).
Internet Service
Operational: Yes. Began: June 23, 2002.
Broadband Service: Suddenlink High Speed Internet.
Fee: $45.95 installation; $29.95 monthly.
Telephone Service
Digital: Operational
Fee: $44.95 monthly
Miles of Plant: 33.0 (coaxial); None (fiber optic). Homes passed: 3,528.
Senior Vice President, Corporate Finance: Michael Pflantz. Regional Manager: Todd Cruthird. Area Manager: Chris Christiansen. Regional Marketing Manager: Beverly Gambell. Plant Manager: Manuel Gonzales.
Ownership: Cequel Communications Holdings I LLC (MSO).

KERRVILLE—Time Warner Cable, 900 Sidney Baker St, Kerrville, TX 78028-3353. Phones: 972-899-7300 (Flower Mound division office); 830-257-4709. Fax: 830-257-6776. Web Site: http://www.timewarnercable.com. Also serves Kerr County (portions). ICA: TX0061.
TV Market Ranking: Below 100 (Kerr County (portions), KERRVILLE). Franchise award date: N.A. Franchise expiration date: N.A. Began: January 1, 1957.
Channel capacity: N.A. Channels available but not in use: N.A.
Basic Service
Subscribers: 5,369.
Programming (received off-air): KABB (FOX, The Country Network) San Antonio; KCWX (MNT, This TV) Fredericksburg; KENS (CBS, Estrella TV) San Antonio; KLRN (PBS) San Antonio; KMYS (CW) Kerrville; KNIC-DT (Laff, UniMas) Blanco; KPXL-TV (ION) Uvalde; KSAT-TV (ABC, MeTV) San Antonio; KVDA (TMO) San Antonio; KVDF-CD (Azteca America) San Antonio; WOAI-TV (IND, NBC) San Antonio.
Programming (via satellite): KMEX-DT (UNV) Los Angeles; Pop.
Fee: $39.99 installation; $28.00 monthly.
Expanded Basic Service 1
Subscribers: N.A.
Programming (via satellite): A&E; AMC; Animal Planet; BET; Bravo; Cartoon Network; CMT; CNBC; CNN; Comedy Central; C-SPAN; C-SPAN 2; Discovery Channel; Disney Channel; E! HD; ESPN; ESPN2; EVINE Live; EWTN Global Catholic Network; Food Network; Fox News Channel; FOX Sports Southwest; Freeform; FX; Golf Channel; Great American Country; Hallmark Channel; HGTV; History; HLN; Lifetime; LMN; MoviePlex; MSNBC; MTV; National Geographic Channel; NBCSN; Nickelodeon; OWN: Oprah Winfrey Network; Oxygen; QVC; Spike TV; Syfy; TBS; The Weather Channel; TLC; TNT; Travel Channel; Trinity Broadcasting Network (TBN); truTV; Turner Classic Movies; TV Land; Univision; USA Network; VH1; WE tv.
Fee: $31.00 monthly.
Digital Basic Service
Subscribers: N.A.
Programming (via satellite): A&E; AMC; Animal Planet; AXS TV; BBC America; BET; Bloomberg Television; Boomerang; Bravo; Cartoon Network; Cloo; CMT; CNBC; CNN; Comedy Central; Cooking Channel; C-SPAN; C-SPAN 2; C-SPAN 3; Daystar TV Network; Destination America; Discovery Channel; Discovery Kids Channel; Discovery Life Channel; Disney Channel; Disney XD; DIY Network; E! HD; ESPN; ESPN Classic; ESPN HD; ESPN2; ESPN2 HD; ESPNews; ESPNU; EVINE Live; EWTN Global Catholic Network; Food Network; Fox Business Network; Fox News Channel; Fox Sports 1; FOX Sports Southwest; Freeform; Fuse; FX; FYI; Golf Channel; Great American Country; GSN; Hallmark Channel; HD Theater; HGTV; History; History International; HLN; Investigation Discovery; La Familia Cosmovision; Lifetime; LMN; MC; MoviePlex; MSNBC; MTV; MTV Classic; MTV Hits; MTV2; Nat Geo WILD; National Geographic Channel; NBA TV; Nick Jr.; Nickelodeon; Nicktoons; Outdoor Channel; OWN: Oprah Winfrey Network; Oxygen; QVC; Spike TV; Syfy; TBS; TeenNick; The Weather Channel; TLC; TNT; TNT HD; Travel Channel; Trinity Broadcasting Network (TBN); truTV; Turner Classic Movies; TV Land; Universal HD; Univision; USA Network; VH1; VH1 Country; WE tv.
Fee: $5.00 monthly.
Digital Expanded Basic Service
Subscribers: N.A.
Programming (via satellite): FOX College Sports Central; FOX College Sports Pacific; Fox Deportes; FXM; IFC; NBA TV; NBCSN; Starz Encore (multiplexed); Sundance TV; Tennis Channel.
Fee: $8.95 monthly (Sports Tier or Movie Tier).
Digital Pay Service 1
Pay Units: N.A.
Programming (via satellite): Cinemax (multiplexed); HBO (multiplexed); HBO HD; Showtime (multiplexed); Showtime HD; Starz (multiplexed); The Movie Channel (multiplexed).
Fee: $14.99 monthly (each).
Video-On-Demand: No
Pay-Per-View
iN DEMAND (delivered digitally); Hot Choice (delivered digitally); Shorteez (delivered digitally); Fresh (delivered digitally); Playboy TV (delivered digitally); MLB Extra Innings (delivered digitally); NBA League Pass (delivered digitally); NHL Center Ice (delivered digitally).
Internet Service
Operational: Yes.
Subscribers: 4,763.
Broadband Service: RoadRunner.
Fee: $49.99 installation; $44.95 monthly.
Telephone Service
Digital: Operational
Subscribers: 1,888.

D-752

TV & Cable Factbook No. 85

Cable Systems—Texas

Miles of Plant: 390.0 (coaxial); 90.0 (fiber optic). Homes passed: 16,733.
President: Connie Wharton. Vice President & General Manager: Mike McKee. Engineering Director: Charlotte Strong. Chief Technician: Jay Burton.
Ownership: Time Warner Cable (MSO).; Advance/Newhouse Partnership (MSO).

KILGORE—Formerly served by Almega Cable. Now served by LONGVIEW, TX [TX0033]. ICA: TX0505.

KILGORE—Kilgore Cable TV Co. Now served by LONGVIEW, TX [TX0033]. ICA: TX0130.

KILLEEN—Time Warner Cable. Now served by AUSTIN, TX [TX0005]. ICA: TX0023.

KINGSVILLE—NewWave Communications, One Montgomery Plaza, 4th Floor, Sikeston, MO 63801. Phones: 573-472-9500; 888-863-9928. Fax: 573-472-9518. E-mail: info@newwave.com. Web Site: http://www.newwavecom.com. Also serves Naval Air Station Kingsville. ICA: TX0926.
TV Market Ranking: Outside TV Markets (KINGSVILLE, Naval Air Station Kingsville). Franchise award date: October 1, 1980. Franchise expiration date: N.A. Began: October 1, 1980.
Channel capacity: N.A. Channels available but not in use: N.A.
Basic Service
Subscribers: 1,764.
Programming (received off-air): KEDT (PBS) Corpus Christi; KIII (ABC, MeTV) Corpus Christi; KORO (LATV, UNV) Corpus Christi; KRIS-TV (CW, Grit, NBC) Corpus Christi; KTOV-LP Corpus Christi; KZTV (CBS) Corpus Christi.
Programming (via satellite): C-SPAN; CW PLUS; ESPN Classic; EWTN Global Catholic Network; Food Network; Fox Deportes; National Geographic Channel; Pop; QVC; TBS; Telemundo; Trinity Broadcasting Network (TBN); TV Land; Univision; WGN America.
Fee: $35.00 installation; $34.78 monthly.
Expanded Basic Service 1
Subscribers: N.A.
Programming (via satellite): A&E; AMC; Animal Planet; BET; Cartoon Network; CMT; CNN; Comedy Central; Discovery Channel; E! HD; ESPN; ESPN2; Fox News Channel; Freeform; FX; GSN; HGTV; History; HLN; Lifetime; LMN; MTV; Nickelodeon; Spike TV; Syfy; The Weather Channel; TLC; TNT; USA Network; VH1.
Fee: $29.00 monthly.
Digital Basic Service
Subscribers: N.A.
Programming (via satellite): BBC America; Bloomberg Television; Discovery Digital Networks; DMX Music; ESPNews; Fox Sports 1; FXM; FYI; Golf Channel; HD Theater; History International; IFC; Nick Jr.; Nicktoons; Outdoor Channel; TeenNick; Turner Classic Movies; Universal HD; WE tv.
Fee: $11.00 monthly.
Pay Service 1
Pay Units: N.A.
Programming (via satellite): HBO.
Fee: $14.95 installation; $13.95 monthly.
Digital Pay Service 1
Pay Units: N.A.
Programming (via satellite): Cinemax (multiplexed); Flix (multiplexed); Showtime (multiplexed); Showtime HD; Starz (multiplexed); Starz Encore (multiplexed); The Movie Channel (multiplexed).
Fee: $8.00 monthly (Starz), $9.00 monthly (Cinemax), $11.00 monthly (Starz/Encore), $15.00 monthly (Showtime/TMC), $17.00 monthly (HBO) or $26.00 monthly (HBO/Cinemax).
Video-On-Demand: No
Pay-Per-View
iN DEMAND (delivered digitally); Playboy TV (delivered digitally); Fresh (delivered digitally).
Internet Service
Operational: Yes. Began: December 2, 2001.
Subscribers: 1,500.
Fee: $39.95 installation; $39.99-$79.99 monthly; $6.00 modem lease; $39.95 modem purchase.
Telephone Service
Digital: Operational
Fee: $39.95 monthly
Miles of Plant: 114.0 (coaxial); 14.0 (fiber optic).
General Manager: Mark Bookout.
Ownership: NewWave Communications LLC (MSO).

KINGWOOD—Suddenlink Communications, 520 Maryville Centre Dr, Ste 300, St. Louis, MO 63141. Phones: 281-360-2576; 800-999-6845; 314-315-9400; 281-360-7500. Web Site: http://www.suddenlink.com. Also serves April Sound Subdivision, Huffman, Indian Shore, Lake Conroe East, Montgomery, Montgomery County, Montgomery County (portions), Oklahoma, Patton Village, Porter, Porter (portions), Porter Heights (unincorporated areas), Roman Forest, Splendora, Walden (village) & Woodbranch Village. ICA: TX0052.
TV Market Ranking: 15 (Huffman, Indian Shore, KINGWOOD, Montgomery County (portions), Montgomery County (portions), Patton Village, Porter, Porter (portions), Porter Heights (unincorporated areas), Roman Forest, Splendora, Woodbranch Village; Below 100 (April Sound Subdivision, Lake Conroe East, Montgomery, Walden (village), Montgomery County (portions)). Franchise award date: January 1, 1972. Franchise expiration date: N.A. Began: September 1, 1974.
Channel capacity: N.A. Channels available but not in use: N.A.
Basic Service
Subscribers: 23,631. Commercial subscribers: 502.
Programming (received off-air): KETH-TV (TBN) Houston; KFTH-DT (getTV, UniMas) Alvin; KHOU (Bounce TV, CBS) Houston; KIAH (Antenna TV, CW) Houston; KLTJ (Daystar TV, ETV) Galveston; KPRC-TV (NBC, This TV) Houston; KPXB-TV (ION) Conroe; KRIV (FOX) Houston; KTBU (IND) Conroe; KTMD (TMO) Galveston; KTRK-TV (ABC, Live Well Network) Houston; KTXH (Buzzr, MNT, Movies!) Houston; KUBE-TV (COZI TV, MeTV) Baytown; KUHT (PBS) Houston; KXLN-DT (UNV) Rosenberg; KYAZ (Azteca America, IND) Katy; KZJL (Estrella TV) Houston; 14 FMs.
Programming (via satellite): Pop; WGN America.
Fee: $49.95 installation; $37.99 monthly; $5.00 converter.
Expanded Basic Service 1
Subscribers: N.A.
Programming (via satellite): A&E; AMC; Animal Planet; BET; Bravo; Cartoon Network; CMT; CNBC; CNN; Comedy Central; C-SPAN; C-SPAN 2; Discovery Channel; Disney Channel; E! HD; ESPN; ESPN2; EWTN Global Catholic Network; Food Network; Fox News Channel; Fox Sports 1; FOX Sports Southwest; Freeform; FX; Golf Channel; Hallmark Channel; HGTV; History; HLN; Lifetime; LMN; MSNBC; MTV; Nickelodeon; Outdoor Channel; Oxygen; Spike TV; Syfy; TBS; The Weather Channel; TLC; TNT; Travel Channel; truTV; Turner Classic Movies; TV Land; USA Network; VH1.
Fee: $27.00 monthly.
Digital Basic Service
Subscribers: N.A.
Programming (via satellite): BBC America; Bloomberg Television; C-SPAN 3; Discovery Digital Networks; Disney XD; DIY Network; DMX Music; ESPN Classic; ESPNews; FSN Digital Atlantic; FSN Digital Central; FSN Digital Pacific; Fuse; FXM; FYI; GSN; History International; IFC; National Geographic Channel; NBCSN; Nick Jr.; Nicktoons; Sundance TV; TeenNick; WE tv.
Fee: $3.99 monthly.
Digital Pay Service 1
Pay Units: N.A.
Programming (via satellite): Cinemax (multiplexed); Flix; HBO (multiplexed); Showtime (multiplexed); Starz (multiplexed); Starz Encore (multiplexed); The Movie Channel (multiplexed).
Fee: $8.95 monthly (Starz/Encore), $9.95 monthly (Cinemax), $11.95 monthly (Showtime/TMC), $12.95 monthly (HBO).
Video-On-Demand: No
Pay-Per-View
iN DEMAND (delivered digitally); Playboy TV (delivered digitally); Fresh (delivered digitally).
Internet Service
Operational: Yes. Began: June 3, 2004.
Subscribers: 16,355.
Broadband Service: Suddenlink High Speed Internet.
Fee: $49.95 installation; $24.95 monthly.
Telephone Service
Digital: Operational
Subscribers: 7,041.
Fee: $48.95 monthly
Miles of Plant: 685.0 (coaxial); 220.0 (fiber optic). Homes passed: 31,297.
Senior Vice President, Corporate Finance: Michael Pflantz. Regional Manager: Todd Cruthird. Marketing Director: Beverly Gambell. Plant Manager: Kyle Spell.
Ownership: Cequel Communications Holdings I LLC (MSO).

KIRBYVILLE—Formerly served by CommuniComm Services. No longer in operation. ICA: TX0345.

KNOX CITY—Formerly served by Alliance Communications. No longer in operation. ICA: TX0429.

KOSSE—Formerly served by Almega Cable. No longer in operation. ICA: TX0577.

KOUNTZE—Time Warner Cable. Now served by PORT ARTHUR (formerly Beaumont), TX [TX0022]. ICA: TX0386.

KRESS—Formerly served by Almega Cable. No longer in operation. ICA: TX0588.

KRUM—Suddenlink Communications, 520 Maryville Centre Dr, Ste 300, St. Louis, MO 63141. Phones: 800-999-6845 (Customer service); 314-315-9400. Web Site: http://www.suddenlink.com. ICA: TX0517.
TV Market Ranking: Below 100 (KRUM). Franchise award date: N.A. Franchise expiration date: N.A. Began: August 1, 1984.
Channel capacity: 54 (operating 2-way). Channels available but not in use: N.A.
Basic Service
Subscribers: 362. Commercial subscribers: 3.
Programming (received off-air): KAZD (Azteca America, IND) Lake Dallas; KDFI (Bounce TV, Buzzr, Heroes & Icons, MNT, Movies!) Dallas; KDFW (FOX) Dallas; KDTN (Daystar TV, ETV) Denton; KERA-TV (PBS) Dallas; KMPX (Estrella TV) Decatur; KPXD-TV (ION) Arlington; KSTR-DT (getTV, UniMas) Irving; KTVT (CBS, Decades) Fort Worth; KTXA (IND, MeTV) Fort Worth; KUVN-DT (UNV) Garland; KXAS-TV (COZI TV, NBC) Fort Worth; KXII (CBS, FOX, MNT) Sherman; KXTX-TV (TMO) Dallas; WFAA (ABC) Dallas.
Programming (via satellite): C-SPAN; QVC; TBS; Trinity Broadcasting Network (TBN); Univision; WGN America.
Fee: $54.95 installation; $38.24 monthly.
Expanded Basic Service 1
Subscribers: N.A.
Programming (via satellite): A&E; AMC; Animal Planet; BET; Bravo; Cartoon Network; CNBC; CNN; Comedy Central; Discovery Channel; Disney Channel; E! HD; ESPN; ESPN2; Food Network; Fox News Channel; Fox Sports 1; FOX Sports Southwest; Freeform; FX; Golf Channel; Great American Country; Hallmark Channel; HGTV; History; HLN; Lifetime; MSNBC; MTV; National Geographic Channel; Nickelodeon; Outdoor Channel; Pop; Spike TV; Syfy; TBS; The Weather Channel; TLC; TNT; Travel Channel; truTV; Turner Classic Movies; TV Land; USA Network; VH1.
Fee: $24.95 monthly.
Digital Basic Service
Subscribers: N.A.
Programming (via satellite): AXS TV; BBC America; Bloomberg Television; Cloo; C-SPAN 3; Discovery Digital Networks; Disney XD; ESPN; ESPN Classic; ESPNews; FOX College Sports Central; FOX College Sports Pacific; Fox Sports 2; Fuse; FXM; FYI; GSN; HD Theater; History; History International; HITS (Headend In The Sky); IFC; MC; NBCSN; Sundance TV; WE tv.
Fee: $3.99 monthly.
Digital Pay Service 1
Pay Units: N.A.
Programming (via satellite): Cinemax (multiplexed); Flix; HBO (multiplexed); HBO HD; Showtime (multiplexed); Showtime HD; Starz (multiplexed); Starz Encore (multiplexed); The Movie Channel (multiplexed).
Video-On-Demand: No
Pay-Per-View
iN DEMAND (delivered digitally); Playboy TV (delivered digitally).
Internet Service
Operational: Yes. Began: December 22, 2003.
Broadband Service: Suddenlink High Speed Internet.
Fee: $49.95 installation; $38.95 monthly.
Telephone Service
Digital: Operational
Miles of Plant: 10.0 (coaxial); None (fiber optic). Homes passed: 415.
Senior Vice President, Corporate Finance: Michael Pflantz. Vice President, Accounting: Sabrina Warr. Regional Manager: Todd Cruthird. Area Manager: Rodney Fletcher. Plant Manager: Judy Cheney.
Ownership: Cequel Communications Holdings I LLC (MSO).

Texas—Cable Systems

LA GRANGE—NewWave Communications, One Montgomery Plaza, 4th Floor, Sikeston, MO 63801. Phones: 573-472-9500; 888-863-9928. Fax: 573-472-9518. E-mail: info@newwave.com. Web Site: http://www.newwavecom.com. Also serves Giddings, Hallettsville, Schulenburg & Weimar. ICA: TX0073.
TV Market Ranking: Outside TV Markets (Giddings, Hallettsville, LA GRANGE, Schulenburg, Weimar). Franchise award date: January 11, 1978. Franchise expiration date: N.A. Began: December 1, 1962.
Channel capacity: N.A. Channels available but not in use: N.A.
Basic Service
Subscribers: 2,135.
Programming (received off-air): KEYE-TV (CBS, TMO) Austin; KHOU (Bounce TV, CBS) Houston; KLRU (PBS) Austin; KNVA (CW, Grit, TheCoolTV) Austin; KSAT-TV (ABC, MeTV) San Antonio; KTBC (Buzzr, FOX, Movies!) Austin; KTRK-TV (ABC, Live Well Network) Houston; KTXH (Buzzr, MNT, Movies!) Houston; KVUE (ABC, Estrella TV) Austin; KXAN-TV (COZI TV, NBC) Austin; KXLN-DT (UNV) Rosenberg; KYAZ (Azteca America, IND) Katy; allband FM.
Programming (via satellite): A&E; AMC; BET; Cartoon Network; CMT; CNBC; CNN; C-SPAN; Discovery Channel; E! HD; ESPN; ESPN2; Fox News Channel; FOX Sports Southwest; Freeform; Hallmark Channel; HGTV; History; HLN; Lifetime; MTV; Nickelodeon; QVC; Spike TV; Syfy; TBS; The Weather Channel; TLC; TNT; Trinity Broadcasting Network (TBN); TV Land; Univision; USA Network; VH1; WGN America.
Fee: $35.00 installation; $32.98 monthly; $1.31 converter.
Digital Basic Service
Subscribers: N.A.
Programming (via satellite): BBC America; Discovery Digital Networks; DMX Music; ESPN Classic; ESPNews; Fox Sports 1; FYI; Golf Channel; GSN; History International; IFC; LMN; National Geographic Channel; Nick Jr.; Nicktoons; Outdoor Channel; TeenNick; Turner Classic Movies; WE tv.
Fee: $10.00 monthly.
Pay Service 1
Pay Units: N.A.
Programming (via satellite): HBO; Showtime.
Fee: $14.95 installation; $13.95 monthly (each).
Digital Pay Service 1
Pay Units: N.A.
Programming (via satellite): Cinemax (multiplexed); HBO (multiplexed); Showtime (multiplexed); Starz (multiplexed); Starz Encore (multiplexed); The Movie Channel (multiplexed).
Fee: $8.00 monthly (Starz), $9.00 monthly (Cinemax), $15.00 monthly (Showtime/TMC), $17.00 monthly (HBO) or $26.00 monthly (HBO/Cinemax).
Video-On-Demand: No
Pay-Per-View
iN DEMAND (delivered digitally); Playboy TV (delivered digitally).
Internet Service
Operational: Yes.
Fee: $36.95 installation; $39.99-$79.99 monthly; $6.00 modem lease; $39.95 modem purchase.
Telephone Service
Digital: Operational
Miles of Plant: 170.0 (coaxial); 56.0 (fiber optic). Homes passed: 9,820.
Regional General Manager: Jerry Smith.
Ownership: NewWave Communications LLC (MSO).

LA GRULLA—Time Warner Cable. Now served by PHARR, TX [TX0017]. ICA: TX0788.

LA PRYOR—Formerly served by Almega Cable. No longer in operation. ICA: TX0789.

LA VERNIA—CommZoom, 2438 Boardwalk, San Antonio, TX 78217. Phones: 844-858-8500; 830-995-2813. Web Site: http://www.commzoom.com. ICA: TX0441.
TV Market Ranking: 45 (LA VERNIA). Franchise award date: November 5, 1985. Franchise expiration date: N.A. Began: March 1, 1986.
Channel capacity: N.A. Channels available but not in use: N.A.
Basic Service
Subscribers: 4.
Programming (received off-air): KENS (CBS, Estrella TV) San Antonio; KLRN (PBS) San Antonio; KSAT-TV (ABC, MeTV) San Antonio; KWEX-DT (getTV, UNV) San Antonio; WOAI-TV (IND, NBC) San Antonio.
Programming (via satellite): ESPN; Freeform; HLN; Nickelodeon; TBS; The Movie Channel; TNT.
Fee: $44.99 monthly.
Video-On-Demand: No
Internet Service
Operational: No.
Telephone Service
None
Miles of plant & homes passed included in Comfort.
Chief Executive Officer: Bob Cohen.
Ownership: CommZoom Communications LLC (MSO).

LAKE ARROWHEAD—Formerly served by Buford Media Group. No longer in operation. ICA: TX0923.

LAKE BROWNWOOD—Formerly served by National Cable Inc. No longer in operation. ICA: TX0419.

LAKE BUCHANAN—Formerly served by Northland Cable Television. No longer in operation. ICA: TX0800.

LAKE CHEROKEE—Alliance Communications, PO Box 9090, Tyler, TX 75711. Phones: 903-561-4411; 800-842-8160; 501-679-6619 (Greenbrier, AR office). Web Site: http://www.alliancecable.net. Also serves Beckville, Easton, Gregg County (unincorporated areas), Lakeport, Panola County (unincorporated areas), Rusk County (unincorporated areas) & Tatum. ICA: TX0795.
TV Market Ranking: Below 100 (Beckville, LAKE CHEROKEE, Lakeport, Tatum). Franchise award date: N.A. Franchise expiration date: N.A. Began: October 1, 1984.
Channel capacity: N.A. Channels available but not in use: N.A.
Basic Service
Subscribers: 418.
Programming (received off-air): KETK-TV (Estrella TV, NBC) Jacksonville; KFXK-TV (FOX) Longview; KLTS-TV (PBS) Shreveport; KLTV (ABC, Bounce TV, TMO) Tyler; KSLA (Bounce TV, CBS, Grit, This TV) Shreveport; KTAL-TV (NBC) Texarkana; KTBS-TV (ABC) Shreveport; KYTX (CBS, COZI TV, CW) Nacogdoches.
Programming (via satellite): CW PLUS; QVC; Univision Studios.
Fee: $41.95 installation; $22.45 monthly.

Expanded Basic Service 1
Subscribers: N.A.
Programming (via satellite): A&E; AMC; Animal Planet; BET; Cartoon Network; CNBC; CNN; Comedy Central; C-SPAN; Discovery Channel; Disney Channel; E! HD; ESPN; ESPN2; Food Network; Fox News Channel; FOX Sports Southwest; Freeform; FX; FYI; Great American Country; HGTV; History; HLN; Lifetime; MSNBC; MTV; National Geographic Channel; Nickelodeon; Outdoor Channel; Spike TV; Syfy; TBS; The Weather Channel; TLC; TNT; Travel Channel; Trinity Broadcasting Network (TBN); Turner Classic Movies; TV Land; USA Network; VH1.
Fee: $26.00 monthly.
Pay Service 1
Pay Units: N.A.
Programming (via satellite): Cinemax; Flix; HBO; Showtime; The Movie Channel.
Fee: $12.95 monthly (Cinemax, Flix, HBO or Showtime/TMC).
Video-On-Demand: No
Internet Service
Operational: Yes.
Fee: $100.00 installation; $29.95 monthly.
Telephone Service
None
Miles of Plant: 104.0 (coaxial); None (fiber optic). Homes passed: 3,239.
Chief Financial Officer: David Starrett. Vice President & General Manager: John Brinker. Vice President, Programming: Julie Newman.
Ownership: Buford Media Group LLC (MSO).

LAKE GRAHAM—Westlake Cable, 12902 FM 2178, Olney, TX 76374. Phones: 800-687-7311; 940-873-4563. Fax: 940-873-4563. ICA: TX1012.
TV Market Ranking: Outside TV Markets (LAKE GRAHAM).
Channel capacity: N.A. Channels available but not in use: N.A.
Basic Service
Subscribers: 66.
Programming (received off-air): KAUZ-TV (CBS, CW) Wichita Falls; KFDX-TV (NBC) Wichita Falls; KJTL (Bounce TV, FOX) Wichita Falls; KSWO-TV (ABC, TMO) Lawton.
Programming (via satellite): CNBC; CNN; C-SPAN; Discovery Channel; Disney XD; Freeform; HLN; TBS; The Weather Channel; TLC; Trinity Broadcasting Network (TBN); TV Land; WGN America.
Fee: $35.00 installation; $26.00 monthly.
Expanded Basic Service 1
Subscribers: N.A.
Programming (via satellite): A&E; AMC; Animal Planet; Cartoon Network; CMT; Disney Channel; ESPN; ESPN2; Food Network; Fox News Channel; Fox Sports 1; FOX Sports Southwest; FX; Hallmark Channel; HGTV; History; Lifetime; MTV; Nickelodeon; Outdoor Channel; Shepherd's Chapel Network; Syfy; TNT; Travel Channel; Turner Classic Movies; USA Network; VH1.
Fee: $16.91 monthly.
Digital Basic Service
Subscribers: N.A.
Programming (via satellite): BBC America; Bravo; Cloo; Discovery Digital Networks; EVINE Live; FOX College Sports Central; FOX College Sports Pacific; Fuse; FXM; FYI; Golf Channel; Great American Country; GSN; History; History International; IFC; LMN; National Geographic Channel; NBCSN; Nick Jr.; Nicktoons; Ovation; Sundance TV; TeenNick; Turner Classic Movies; WE tv.
Fee: $20.95 monthly.

Pay Service 1
Pay Units: N.A.
Programming (via satellite): Cinemax; HBO.
Fee: $13.47 monthly.
Digital Pay Service 1
Pay Units: N.A.
Programming (via satellite): Cinemax (multiplexed); Flix; HBO (multiplexed); Showtime (multiplexed); Starz (multiplexed); Starz Encore (multiplexed); The Movie Channel (multiplexed).
Fee: $13.47 monthly (HBO/Cinemax), $7.01 monthly (Showtime/TMC or Starz/Encore).
Video-On-Demand: No
Internet Service
Operational: Yes.
Broadband Service: In-house.
Fee: $24.95 monthly; $5.00 modem lease; $59.95 modem purchase.
Telephone Service
None
Miles of Plant: 5.0 (coaxial); None (fiber optic).
General Manager & Chief Technician: Bill Tyler. Marketing & Program Director: Jan Tyler.
Ownership: Bill Tyler (MSO).

LAKE HILLS—Formerly served by Zoom Media. No longer in operation. ICA: TX1021.

LAKE PALESTINE EAST—Suddenlink Communications. Now served by TYLER, TX [TX0027]. ICA: TX0220.

LAKE PALESTINE WEST—Suddenlink Communications. Now served by TYLER, TX [TX0027]. ICA: TX0368.

LAMESA—Northland Cable Television, 1012 South 1st St, Lamesa, TX 79331-6147. Phone: 806-872-8561. Fax: 806-872-8825. E-mail: brent_richey@northlandcabletv.com. Web Site: http://www.yournorthland.com. Also serves Dawson County (unincorporated areas). ICA: TX0148.
TV Market Ranking: Below 100 (Dawson County (unincorporated areas) (portions); Outside TV Markets (Dawson County (unincorporated areas) (portions), LAMESA). Franchise award date: January 1, 1966. Franchise expiration date: N.A. Began: April 1, 1966.
Channel capacity: N.A. Channels available but not in use: N.A.
Basic Service
Subscribers: 370.
Programming (received off-air): KAMC (ABC, Bounce TV) Lubbock; KCBD (NBC, This TV) Lubbock; KJTV-TV (FOX) Lubbock; KLBK-TV (CBS) Lubbock; KMID (ABC) Midland; KMLM-DT (GLC) Odessa; KPEJ-TV (FOX) Odessa; KPTB-DT (GLC) Lubbock; KTTZ-TV (PBS) Lubbock; KUPB (UNV) Midland; allband FM.
Programming (via satellite): A&E; Animal Planet; Cartoon Network; CNBC; CNN; Comedy Central; C-SPAN; Discovery Channel; ESPN; ESPN2; Food Network; Fox News Channel; FOX Sports Southwest; FX; FXM; Great American Country; Hallmark Channel; HGTV; History; HITS (Headend In The Sky); HLN; Lifetime; MTV; National Geographic Channel; Nickelodeon; Pop; QVC; Spike TV; Syfy; TBS; Telemundo; The Weather Channel; TLC; TNT; Travel Channel; Trinity Broadcasting Network (TBN); Turner Classic Movies; Univision; USA Network; VH1.
Fee: $60.00 installation; $47.64 monthly.

Cable Systems—Texas

Digital Basic Service
Subscribers: N.A.
Programming (via satellite): BBC America; Discovery Digital Networks; Fox Sports 1; Golf Channel; GSN; Outdoor Channel.
Fee: $52.69 monthly.

Digital Expanded Basic Service
Subscribers: N.A.
Programming (via satellite): Bloomberg Television; DMX Music; Outdoor Channel; WE tv.

Digital Pay Service 1
Pay Units: N.A.
Programming (via satellite): Cinemax (multiplexed); Flix; HBO (multiplexed); Showtime (multiplexed); Starz (multiplexed); Starz Encore (multiplexed); The Movie Channel (multiplexed).

Video-On-Demand: No

Internet Service
Operational: Yes.
Broadband Service: Northland Express.
Fee: $42.99 monthly.

Telephone Service
Digital: Operational
Miles of Plant: 57.0 (coaxial); None (fiber optic). Homes passed: 4,100.
Regional Manager: Brent Richey. General Manager & Chief Technician: Mickey Flanagan. Office Manager: Beverlee Kinnison.
Ownership: Northland Communications Corp. (MSO).

LAMPASAS—Suddenlink Communications, 520 Maryville Centre Dr, Ste 300, St. Louis, MO 63141. Phones: 314-315-9400; 512-556-8244. Web site: http://www.suddenlink.com. Also serves Lampasas County. ICA: TX0183.
TV Market Ranking: Below 100 (LAMPASAS, Lampasas County (portions)); Outside TV Markets (Lampasas County (portions)). Franchise award date: March 29, 1962. Franchise expiration date: N.A. Began: January 1, 1964.
Channel capacity: 53 (operating 2-way). Channels available but not in use: N.A.

Basic Service
Subscribers: 596.
Programming (received off-air): KAKW-DT (getTV, UNV) Killeen; KCEN-TV (Antenna TV, MeTV, MundoMax, NBC) Temple; KNCT (PBS) Belton; KNVA (CW, Grit, TheCoolTV) Austin; KTBC (Buzzr, FOX, Movies!) Austin; KVUE (ABC, Estrella TV) Austin; KWKT-TV (Estrella TV, FOX, MNT) Waco; KWTX-TV (CBS, CW) Waco; KXXV (ABC, TMO) Waco.
Programming (via satellite): Pop; The Weather Channel.
Fee: $28.45 monthly; $1.02 converter.

Expanded Basic Service 1
Subscribers: N.A.
Programming (via satellite): A&E; AMC; Animal Planet; Cartoon Network; CNBC; CNN; Comedy Central; C-SPAN; C-SPAN 2; Discovery Channel; Disney Channel; E! HD; ESPN; ESPN2; Food Network; Fox News Channel; FOX Sports Southwest; Freeform; FX; Great American Country; HGTV; History; HLN; INSP; Lifetime; MSNBC; MTV; National Geographic Channel; Nickelodeon; Outdoor Channel; QVC; Spike TV; Syfy; TBS; TLC; TNT; Turner Classic Movies; TV Land; Univision; USA Network.
Fee: $25.00 monthly.

Digital Basic Service
Subscribers: N.A.
Programming (via satellite): BBC America; Cloo; Discovery Digital Networks; Disney XD; DMX Music; ESPN Classic; ESPNews;
Fox Sports 1; Fuse; FYI; Golf Channel; GSN; History International; IFC; NBCSN; WE tv.
Fee: $3.99 monthly.

Pay Service 1
Pay Units: N.A.
Programming (via satellite): Cinemax; HBO; Showtime; The Movie Channel.
Fee: $15.70 installation; $12.95 monthly (Showtime or TMC), $15.95 monthly (Cinemax or HBO).

Digital Pay Service 1
Pay Units: N.A.
Programming (via satellite): Cinemax (multiplexed); HBO (multiplexed); Showtime (multiplexed); Starz (multiplexed); Starz Encore (multiplexed); The Movie Channel (multiplexed).

Video-On-Demand: No

Pay-Per-View
iN DEMAND (delivered digitally); Playboy TV (delivered digitally).

Internet Service
Operational: Yes. Began: November 12, 2003.
Broadband Service: Suddenlink High Speed Internet.
Fee: $45.95 installation; $29.95 monthly; $9.95 modem lease.

Telephone Service
Digital: Operational
Fee: $44.95 monthly
Miles of Plant: 52.0 (coaxial); 3.0 (fiber optic). Homes passed: 2,852.
Senior Vice President, Corporate Finance: Michael Pflantz. Regional Manager: Todd Cruthird. Marketing Director: Beverly Gambell.
Ownership: Cequel Communications Holdings I LLC (MSO).

LANEVILLE—Formerly served by Cebridge Connections. No longer in operation. ICA: TX0796.

LANSING—Formerly served by Zoom Media. No longer in operation. ICA: TX0336.

LAREDO—Time Warner Cable, 1313 West Carlton Rd, Laredo, TX 78041. Phones: 956-721-0600; 956-721-0607; 972-899-7300 (Flower Mound division office). Fax: 956-721-0612. Web Site: http://www.timewarnercable.com. Also serves El Cenizo, Rio Bravo, San Ygnacio, Webb County (portions) & Zapata. ICA: TX0029.
TV Market Ranking: Below 100 (El Cenizo, LAREDO, Rio Bravo, Webb County (portions) (portions), San Ygnacio); Outside TV Markets (Webb County (portions) (portions), Zapata). Franchise award date: N.A. Franchise expiration date: N.A. Began: November 1, 1961.
Channel capacity: N.A. Channels available but not in use: N.A.

Basic Service
Subscribers: 32,910.
Programming (received off-air): KGNS-TV (ABC, CW, TMO) Laredo; KLDO-TV (FOX, LATV, UNV) Laredo; KVTV Laredo [LICENSED & SILENT]; KXOF-CD (FOX, MundoMax) Laredo.
Programming (via microwave): KABB (FOX, The Country Network) San Antonio; KENS (CBS, Estrella TV) San Antonio; KLRN (PBS) San Antonio; KSAT-TV (ABC, MeTV) San Antonio.
Programming (via satellite): Azteca; C-SPAN; C-SPAN 2; EVINE Live; EWTN Global Catholic Network; QVC; various Mexican stations (multiplexed); WGN America.
Fee: $39.99 installation; $25.50 monthly.

Expanded Basic Service 1
Subscribers: N.A.
Programming (via satellite): A&E; AMC; Animal Planet; Bravo; Cartoon Network; CMT; CNBC; CNN; Comedy Central; Discovery Channel; Disney Channel; E! HD; ESPN; ESPN2; EVINE Live; Food Network; Fox News Channel; FOX Sports Southwest; Freeform; Fuse; FX; Golf Channel; HGTV; History; HLN; ION Television; Lifetime; LMN; MSNBC; MTV; National Geographic Channel; NBC Universo; Nickelodeon; OWN: Oprah Winfrey Network; Oxygen; Pop; Spike TV; Syfy; TBS; Telemundo; The Weather Channel; TLC; TNT; Tr3s; Travel Channel; truTV; TV Land; UniMas; Univision; USA Network; VH1; WE tv.
Fee: $36.71 monthly.

Digital Basic Service
Subscribers: N.A.
Programming (via satellite): A&E; AMC; Animal Planet; AXS TV; BBC America; Bloomberg Television; Boomerang; Bravo; Cartoon Network; Cloo; CMT; CNBC; CNN; Comedy Central; Cooking Channel; C-SPAN; C-SPAN 2; C-SPAN 3; Daystar TV Network; Destination America; Discovery Channel; Discovery Kids Channel; Discovery Life Channel; Disney Channel; Disney XD; DIY Network; E! HD; ESPN; ESPN Classic; ESPN HD; ESPN2; ESPN2 HD; ESPNews; ESPNU; EWTN Global Catholic Network; Food Network; Food Network On Demand; Fox Business Network; Fox News Channel; Fox Sports 1; FOX Sports Southwest; Freeform; Fuse; FX; FYI; Golf Channel; Great American Country; GSN; Hallmark Channel; HD Theater; HGTV; HGTV On Demand; History; History International; HLN; Investigation Discovery; ION Television; La Familia Cosmovision; Lifetime; LMN; MC; MSNBC; MTV; MTV Classic; MTV Hits; MTV2; Nat Geo WILD; National Geographic Channel; NBCSN; Nick Jr.; Nickelodeon; Nicktoons; Outdoor Channel; Ovation; OWN: Oprah Winfrey Network; Oxygen; Pop; QVC; Science Channel; Spike TV; Syfy; TBS; TeenNick; The Weather Channel; TLC; TNT; TNT HD; Tr3s; Travel Channel; Trinity Broadcasting Network (TBN); truTV; Turner Classic Movies; TV Guide Network; Universal HD; USA Network; VH1; WE tv.
Fee: $5.04 monthly.

Digital Expanded Basic Service
Subscribers: N.A.
Programming (via satellite): Canal Sur; Cinelatino; CNN en Espanol; ESPN Deportes; Flix; FOX College Sports Central; FOX College Sports Pacific; Fox Deportes; Fox Life; Fox Sports 2; FOX Sports Southwest; FXM; HTV; Infinito; La Familia Cosmovision; NBA TV; NBC Universo; Starz Encore; Sundance TV; Tennis Channel; Toon Disney en Espanol; Tr3s; Univision; VideoRola.

Digital Pay Service 1
Pay Units: N.A.
Programming (via satellite): Cinemax (multiplexed); Cinemax On Demand; HBO (multiplexed); HBO GO; HBO HD; Showtime
(multiplexed); Showtime HD; Showtime On Demand; Starz (multiplexed); The Movie Channel (multiplexed); The Movie Channel On Demand.
Fee: $14.99 monthly (each).

Video-On-Demand: Yes

Pay-Per-View
Hot Choice (delivered digitally); NBA (delivered digitally); ESPN Now (delivered digitally); iN DEMAND (delivered digitally); Shorteez (delivered digitally); Fresh (delivered digitally); Variety; iN DEMAND (delivered digitally); Playboy TV (delivered digitally); Spice.

Internet Service
Operational: Yes. Began: April 1, 2001.
Subscribers: 28,482.
Broadband Service: Road Runner.
Fee: $49.99 installation; $44.95 monthly.

Telephone Service
Digital: Operational
Subscribers: 11,625.
Fee: $44.95 monthly
Miles of Plant: 1,496.0 (coaxial); 339.0 (fiber optic). Homes passed: 85,644.
President: Connie Wharton. Vice President & General Manager: Michael Carrosquiola. Operations Director: Marco Reyes. Public Affairs Manager: Celinda Gonzalez. Technical Operations Manager: Eduardo Ruiz.
Ownership: Time Warner Cable (MSO).; Advance/Newhouse Partnership (MSO).

LAS GALLINAS—Formerly served by Almega Cable. No longer in operation. ICA: TX0239.

LEANDER—Suddenlink Communications, 111 North College St, Georgetown, TX 78626-4101. Phones: 314-315-9400; 512-930-3085. Fax: 512-869-2962. Web Site: http://www.suddenlink.com. ICA: TX0251.
TV Market Ranking: Below 100 (LEANDER). Franchise award date: January 1, 1980. Franchise expiration date: N.A. Began: December 1, 1981.
Channel capacity: 78 (operating 2-way). Channels available but not in use: N.A.

Basic Service
Subscribers: 2,071. Commercial subscribers: 20.
Programming (received off-air): KAKW-DT (getTV, UNV) Killeen; KCEN-TV (Antenna TV, MeTV, MundoMax, NBC) Temple; KEYE-TV (CBS, TMO) Austin; KLRU (PBS) Austin; KNVA (CW, Grit, TheCoolTV) Austin; KTBC (Buzzr, FOX, Movies!) Austin; KVUE (ABC, Estrella TV) Austin.
Programming (via satellite): C-SPAN; INSP; Pop; QVC; UniMas; WGN America.
Fee: $54.95 installation; $33.24 monthly; $1.50 converter.

Expanded Basic Service 1
Subscribers: N.A.
Programming (via satellite): A&E; AMC; Animal Planet; BET; Bravo; Cartoon Network; CMT; CNBC; CNN; Comedy Central; C-SPAN 2; Discovery Channel; Disney Channel; E! HD; ESPN; ESPN2; EVINE Live; EWTN Global Catholic Network; Food Network; Fox News Channel; Fox Sports 1; FOX Sports Southwest; Freeform; FX; Golf

2017 Edition

D-755

Texas—Cable Systems

Channel; Great American Country; HGTV; History; HLN; Jewelry Television; Lifetime; LMN; MSNBC; MTV; NBCSN; Nickelodeon; Spike TV; Syfy; TBS; Telemundo; The Weather Channel; TLC; TNT; Travel Channel; Trinity Broadcasting Network (TBN); truTV; Turner Classic Movies; TV Land; Univision; USA Network; VH1.
Fee: $15.50 monthly.

Digital Basic Service
Subscribers: N.A.
Programming (via satellite): A&E HD; AXS TV; Bandamax; BBC America; Bloomberg Television; Boomerang; BYUtv; Cine Mexicano; Cinelatino; CMT; CNN en Espanol; Cooking Channel; Cox Sports Television; De Pelicula; De Pelicula Clasico; Destination America; Discovery Kids Channel; Disney XD; DIY Network; Enlace USA; ESPN Classic; ESPN Deportes; ESPN HD; ESPN2 HD; ESPNews; ESPNU; FamilyNet; Food Network HD; Fox Deportes; Fox Sports 2; Fuse; FYI; GSN; Hallmark Channel; HD Theater; HGTV HD; History en Espanol; History International; IFC; Investigation Discovery; MC; MTV Classic; MTV Hits; MTV2; Nat Geo WILD; National Geographic Channel; National Geographic Channel HD; NBC Universo; Nick Jr.; Nicktoons; Outdoor Channel; OWN: Oprah Winfrey Network; Oxygen; Ritmoson; Science Channel; Starz Encore (multiplexed); Sundance TV; Sur; TeenNick; Telehit; Telemundo; Tennis Channel; TNT HD; Toon Disney en Espanol; Tr3s; TV One; ULTRA HDPlex; Universal HD; Univision; UP; VideoRola; WE tv; Weatherscan.

Digital Pay Service 1
Pay Units: N.A.
Programming (via satellite): Cinemax (multiplexed); HBO (multiplexed); HBO HD; HBO Latino; Showtime (multiplexed); Showtime HD; Starz (multiplexed); Starz HD; The Movie Channel (multiplexed).

Video-On-Demand: No

Pay-Per-View
iN DEMAND (delivered digitally); Fresh (delivered digitally); Shorteez (delivered digitally); Playboy TV (delivered digitally); Playboy en Espanol (delivered digitally).

Internet Service
Operational: Yes.
Broadband Service: Suddenlink High Speed Internet.
Fee: $99.95 installation; $25.95 monthly; $10.00 modem lease.

Telephone Service
Digital: Operational
Fee: $44.95 monthly
Miles of Plant: 60.0 (coaxial); 9.0 (fiber optic). Homes passed: 4,311.
Senior Vice President, Corporate Finance: Michael Pflantz. Vice President, Accounting: Sabrina Warr. General Manager: Dale Hoffman. Chief Technician & Marketing Director: Wesley Houghteling.
Ownership: Cequel Communications Holdings I LLC (MSO).

LEFORS—Formerly served by Almega Cable. No longer in operation. ICA: TX0563.

LEONA—Formerly served by Charter Communications. No longer in operation. ICA: TX0702.

LEONARD—Formerly served by Zoom Media. No longer in operation. ICA: TX0367.

LEVELLAND—NTS Communications. This cable system has converted to IPTV. Now served by WOLFFORTH, TX [TX5540]. ICA: TX0112.

LEXINGTON—Reveille Broadband, 1008 Giddings St, PO Box 39, Lexington, TX 78947. Phones: 979-773-3215; 979-773-4700. Fax: 979-773-4733. E-mail: mariesullivan@reveillebroadband.com. Web Site: http://www.reveillebroadband.com. ICA: TX0522.
TV Market Ranking: Outside TV Markets (LEXINGTON). Franchise award date: January 1, 1983. Franchise expiration date: N.A. Began: January 1, 1983.
Channel capacity: N.A. Channels available but not in use: N.A.

Basic Service
Subscribers: N.A.
Programming (received off-air): KEYE-TV (CBS, TMO) Austin; KLRU (PBS) Austin; KNVA (CW, Grit, TheCoolTV) Austin; KTBC (Buzzr, FOX, Movies!) Austin; KVUE (ABC, Estrella TV) Austin; KXAN-TV (COZI TV, NBC) Austin.
Programming (via satellite): AMC; Animal Planet; BET; Boomerang; Cartoon Network; CMT; CNN; Comedy Central; C-SPAN; C-SPAN 2; Discovery Channel; Disney Channel; E! HD; ESPN; ESPN2; Food Network; Fox News Channel; Fox Sports 1; FOX Sports Southwest; Freeform; FX; Great American Country; GSN; Hallmark Channel; Hallmark Movies & Mysteries; HGTV; History; HLN; Lifetime; National Geographic Channel; Nick Jr.; Nickelodeon; QVC; Spike TV; Syfy; TBS; The Weather Channel; TLC; TNT; Travel Channel; Trinity Broadcasting Network (TBN); truTV; Turner Classic Movies; TV Land; Univision Studios; USA Network; VH1; WGN America.
Fee: $35.00 installation.

Pay Service 1
Pay Units: N.A.
Programming (via satellite): HBO; The Movie Channel.
Fee: $10.95 monthly.

Internet Service
Operational: Yes.
Fee: $50.00 installation; $39.95 monthly.

Telephone Service
Digital: Operational
Subscribers: 140.
Miles of Plant: 9.0 (coaxial); None (fiber optic). Homes passed: 400.
Chief Executive Officer: Marie Sullivan. President: Jeff Sullivan. Vice President: Cory Savage. Chief Technology Officer: Jason Sembera. Office Manager: Laura Tillery.
Ownership: Reveille Broadband (MSO).

LIBERTY—Formerly served by Time Warner Cable. Now served by Comcast Cable, HOUSTON, TX [TX0001]. ICA: TX0129.

LINDEN—Formerly served by Reach Broadband. No longer in operation. ICA: TX0381.

LIPAN—Formerly served by Almega Cable. No longer in operation. ICA: TX0987.

LITTLE RIVER-ACADEMY—Grande Communications, 401 Carlson Circle, San Marcos, TX 78666. Phones: 855-286-6666; 512-878-4600. Web Site: http://mygrande.com. ICA: TX0499.
TV Market Ranking: Below 100 (LITTLE RIVER-ACADEMY). Franchise award date: N.A. Franchise expiration date: N.A. Began: August 1, 1982.
Channel capacity: N.A. Channels available but not in use: N.A.

Basic Service
Subscribers: 155.
Programming (received off-air): KCEN-TV (Antenna TV, MeTV, MundoMax, NBC) Temple; KEYE-TV (CBS, TMO) Austin; KNCT (PBS) Belton; KNVA (CW, Grit, TheCoolTV) Austin; KTBC (Buzzr, FOX, Movies!) Austin; KWKT-TV (Estrella TV, FOX, MNT) Waco; KWTX-TV (CBS, CW) Waco; KXAN-TV (COZI TV, NBC) Austin; KXXV (ABC, TMO) Waco; WFAA (ABC) Dallas.
Programming (via satellite): Univision Studios; WGN America.
Fee: $25.00 installation; $10.95 monthly.

Expanded Basic Service 1
Subscribers: N.A.
Programming (via satellite): A&E; AMC; Animal Planet; BET; Cartoon Network; CMT; CNBC; CNN; Comedy Central; C-SPAN; C-SPAN 2; Discovery Channel; Disney Channel; E! HD; ESPN; ESPN2; Food Network; Fox News Channel; FOX Sports Southwest; Freeform; FX; Hallmark Channel; HGTV; History; HLN; ION Television; Lifetime; MSNBC; MTV; MTV Classic; National Geographic Channel; Nickelodeon; QVC; Spike TV; Syfy; TBS; The Weather Channel; TLC; TNT; Travel Channel; Trinity Broadcasting Network (TBN); Turner Classic Movies; TV Land; USA Network.
Fee: $17.00 monthly.

Digital Basic Service
Subscribers: N.A.
Programming (via satellite): BBC America; Bloomberg Television; Bravo; Daystar TV Network; Discovery Digital Networks; Disney XD; DMX Music; ESPN Classic; ESPNews; EVINE Live; Fox Sports 1; FSN Digital Atlantic; FSN Digital Central; FSN Digital Pacific; FXM; FYI; Golf Channel; Great American Country; GSN; HGTV; History; History International; IFC; International Television (ITV); LMN; National Geographic Channel; NBCSN; Outdoor Channel; Ovation; Syfy; The Word Network; Trinity Broadcasting Network (TBN); Turner Classic Movies; WE tv.
Fee: $15.00 installation; $49.00 monthly.

Digital Expanded Basic Service
Subscribers: N.A.
Programming (via satellite): Nick Jr.; Nicktoons; TeenNick.

Pay Service 1
Pay Units: N.A.
Programming (via satellite): Showtime.
Fee: $11.00 monthly.

Digital Pay Service 1
Pay Units: N.A.
Programming (via satellite): Cinemax (multiplexed); HBO (multiplexed); Showtime (multiplexed); Starz (multiplexed); Starz Encore (multiplexed).
Fee: $7.00 monthly (Cinemax), $11.00 monthly (HBO, Showtime, or Starz/Encore).

Video-On-Demand: No

Internet Service
Operational: Yes. Began: December 31, 2004.
Subscribers: 298.
Broadband Service: VVM Internet Services.
Fee: $20.00 installation; $40.00 monthly.

Telephone Service
Digital: Planned
Miles of Plant: 9.0 (coaxial); None (fiber optic). Homes passed: 450.
Senior Vice President, Operations & General Manager: Matthew Rohre. Vice President, Technical Operations: Shane Schilling. Vice President, Marketing: Pete Drozdoff.
Ownership: Grande Communications Networks Inc. (MSO).

LIVERPOOL—Formerly served by Almega Cable. No longer in operation. ICA: TX0333.

LIVINGSTON—Formerly served by Suddenlink Communications. No longer in operation. ICA: TX0208.

LLANO—Northland Cable Television, 1101 Mission Hill Dr, PO Box 366, Marble Falls, TX 78654-0366. Phones: 888-667-8452; 830-693-0487; 830-693-7500. Fax: 830-693-6056. E-mail: marblefalls@northlandcabletv.com. Web Site: http://www.yournorthland.com. ICA: TX0996.
TV Market Ranking: Below 100 (LLANO).
Channel capacity: 38 (not 2-way capable). Channels available but not in use: N.A.

Basic Service
Subscribers: 144.
Programming (received off-air): KBVO (Laff, MNT) Llano; KCWX (MNT, This TV) Fredericksburg; KEYE-TV (CBS, TMO) Austin; KLRU (PBS) Austin; KNVA (CW, Grit, TheCoolTV) Austin; KTBC (Buzzr, FOX, Movies!) Austin; KVUE (ABC, Estrella TV) Austin.
Programming (via satellite): A&E; Animal Planet; Cartoon Network; CNN; C-SPAN; Discovery Channel; ESPN; Fox News Channel; FOX Sports Southwest; Great American Country; Hallmark Channel; HGTV; History; HLN; Lifetime; National Geographic Channel; QVC; Spike TV; Syfy; TBS; The Weather Channel; TLC; TNT; Trinity Broadcasting Network (TBN); Turner Classic Movies; TV Land; USA Network.
Fee: $75.00 installation; $47.64 monthly.

Pay Service 1
Pay Units: N.A.
Programming (via satellite): Cinemax; HBO.
Fee: $11.50 Cinemax (monthly) 13.50 monthly (HBO).

Internet Service
Operational: Yes.

Telephone Service
Digital: Operational
Executive Vice President: Richard I. Clark. Regional Manager: Larson Lloyd. Marketing Director: Gaye Tharett. Plant Manager: Ron Gardner.
Ownership: Northland Communications Corp. (MSO).

LOCKHART—Time Warner Cable. Now served by SAN MARCOS, TX [TX0849]. ICA: TX0163.

LOCKNEY—Reach Broadband, PO Box 507, Arp, TX 75750. Phones: 903-859-3789; 800-687-1258. Web Site: http://www.reachbroadband.net. ICA: TX0414.
TV Market Ranking: Outside TV Markets (LOCKNEY). Franchise award date: December 10, 1980. Franchise expiration date: N.A. Began: May 15, 1981.
Channel capacity: 41 (2-way capable). Channels available but not in use: N.A.

Basic Service
Subscribers: 74.
Programming (received off-air): KAMC (ABC, Bounce TV) Lubbock; KCBD (NBC, This TV) Lubbock; KJTV-TV (FOX) Lubbock; KLBK-TV (CBS) Lubbock; KTTZ-TV (PBS) Lubbock; KVII-TV (ABC, CW) Amarillo.
Programming (via satellite): A&E; AMC; Cartoon Network; CMT; CNN; Discovery Channel; Disney Channel; E! HD; ESPN; Freeform; History; HLN; Lifetime; Nickelodeon; QVC; Spike TV; Syfy; TBS; The Weather Channel; TLC; TNT; TV Land; USA Network; WGN America.
Fee: $49.95 installation; $26.30 monthly.

Cable Systems—Texas

Pay Service 1
Pay Units: N.A.
Programming (via satellite): Cinemax; HBO.
Fee: $9.95 monthly (each).
Video-On-Demand: No
Internet Service
Operational: Yes.
Telephone Service
None
Miles of Plant: 12.0 (coaxial); None (fiber optic). Homes passed: 778.
Regional Manager: Ronnie Stafford. Office Manager: Jan Gibson. Controller: Jeffrey Lowe.
Ownership: RB3 LLC (MSO).

LOLITA—Formerly served by Clearview Cable. No longer in operation. ICA: TX0637.

LOMETA—Formerly served by Almega Cable. No longer in operation. ICA: TX0599.

LONGVIEW—Longview Cable Television, 711 North High St, PO Box 151, Longview, TX 75601. Phones: 903-758-3052; 903-758-9991. Fax: 903-758-3083. E-mail: longviewcs@cablelynx.com. Web Site: http://www.longviewcabletv.com. Also serves Kilgore. ICA: TX0033.
TV Market Ranking: Below 100 (LONGVIEW, Kilgore). Franchise award date: June 1, 1965. Franchise expiration date: N.A. Began: August 1, 1972.
Channel capacity: 77 (operating 2-way). Channels available but not in use: N.A.

Basic Service
Subscribers: 11,019. Commercial subscribers: 16.
Programming (received off-air): KDFW (FOX) Dallas; KERA-TV (PBS) Dallas; KETK-TV (Estrella TV, NBC) Jacksonville; KFXK-TV (FOX) Longview; KLPN-LD (MNT) Longview; KLTS-TV (PBS) Shreveport; KLTV (ABC, Bounce TV, TMO) Tyler; KSLA (Bounce TV, CBS, Grit, This TV) Shreveport; KTAL-TV (NBC) Texarkana; KTBS-TV (ABC) Shreveport; KXAS-TV (COZI TV, NBC) Fort Worth; KYTX (CBS, COZI TV, CW) Nacogdoches.
Programming (via satellite): A&E; AMC; Animal Planet; BET; Cartoon Network; CMT; CNBC; CNN; Comedy Central; C-SPAN; C-SPAN 2; Discovery Channel; Disney Channel; ESPN; ESPN Classic; ESPN2; EVINE Live; EWTN Global Catholic Network; Food Network; Fox News Channel; FOX Sports Southwest; Freeform; FX; Hallmark Channel; HGTV; History; HLN; ION Television; Lifetime; MTV; NASA TV; National Geographic Channel; Nickelodeon; Pop; QVC; Spike TV; Syfy; TBS; Telemundo; The Weather Channel; TLC; TNT; Travel Channel; Trinity Broadcasting Network (TBN); Turner Classic Movies; TV Land; Univision; Univision Studios; USA Network; VH1.
Fee: $49.95 installation; $31.90 monthly; $3.65 converter.

Digital Basic Service
Subscribers: N.A.
Programming (via satellite): BBC America; CMT; Destination America; Discovery Kids Channel; Discovery Life Channel; Disney XD; DMX Music; ESPNews; Fox Sports 1; FSN Digital Atlantic; FSN Digital Central; FSN Digital Pacific; FYI; Golf Channel; Great American Country; GSN; History International; Investigation Discovery; LMN; MTV Classic; MTV Hits; MTV Jams; MTV2; National Geographic Channel; Nick 2; Nick Jr.; Nicktoons; Outdoor Channel; OWN: Oprah Winfrey Network; Science Channel; TeenNick; Tr3s; VH1 Soul; WE tv.
Fee: $10.00 monthly.

Digital Expanded Basic Service
Subscribers: N.A.
Programming (via satellite): AXS TV; Discovery Channel HD; ESPN HD; Outdoor Channel.
Fee: $5.00 monthly.

Digital Pay Service 1
Pay Units: N.A.
Programming (via satellite): Cinemax (multiplexed); Cinemax HD; HBO (multiplexed); HBO HD; Starz (multiplexed); Starz Encore (multiplexed); Starz HD.
Fee: $12.95 monthly (Cinemax, HBO or Starz/Encore).
Video-On-Demand: No
Pay-Per-View
Sports PPV (delivered digitally); iN DEMAND (delivered digitally).
Internet Service
Operational: Yes. Began: March 1, 2001.
Subscribers: 12,619.
Broadband Service: Cablelynx.
Fee: $24.95-$44.95 monthly; $10.00 modem lease.
Telephone Service
Digital: Operational
Subscribers: 2,059.
Fee: $45.70 monthly
Miles of Plant: 1,255.0 (coaxial); 327.0 (fiber optic). Homes passed: 54,784.
Vice President & Regional Manager: Don Deem. Vice President, Marketing & Programming: Lori Haight. Vice President, Administration: Charlotta A. Dial. General Manager: Brandi Turner. Plant Manager: George Doss. Business Manager: Cynthia Walters.
Ownership: WEHCO Video Inc. (MSO).

LOOP—Formerly served by National Cable Inc. No longer in operation. ICA: TX0686.

LORAINE (town)—Formerly served by Almega Cable. No longer in operation. ICA: TX0529.

LORENA—Time Warner Cable. Now served by AUSTIN, TX [TX0005]. ICA: TX0801.

LORENZO—Formerly served by Almega Cable. No longer in operation. ICA: TX0484.

LOS FRESNOS—Time Warner Cable. Now served by PHARR, TX [TX0017]. ICA: TX0264.

LOST PINES—Suddenlink Communications, 520 Maryville Centre Dr, Ste 300, St. Louis, MO 63141. Phones: 800-999-6845; 314-315-9400. Web Site: http://www.suddenlink.com. Also serves Bastrop County (portions). ICA: TX0950.
TV Market Ranking: Below 100 (Bastrop County (portions), LOST PINES).
Channel capacity: N.A. Channels available but not in use: N.A.

Basic Service
Subscribers: 132.
Programming (received off-air): KEYE-TV (CBS, TMO) Austin; KLRU (PBS) Austin; KTBC (Buzzr, FOX, Movies!) Austin; KVUE (ABC, Estrella TV) Austin; KXAN-TV (COZI TV, NBC) Austin.
Programming (via satellite): A&E; BET; CMT; CNN; Discovery Channel; E! HD; ESPN; Freeform; HLN; Lifetime; Nickelodeon; Spike TV; Syfy; TBS; The Weather Channel; TNT; Trinity Broadcasting Network (TBN); USA Network; WGN America.
Fee: $28.45 monthly.

Pay Service 1
Pay Units: N.A.
Programming (via satellite): Cinemax; HBO; Showtime.
Fee: $10.95 monthly (each).
Video-On-Demand: No
Internet Service
Operational: Yes. Began: June 10, 2004.
Broadband Service: Suddenlink High Speed Internet.
Fee: $49.95 installation; $38.95 monthly.
Telephone Service
None
Miles of Plant: 86.0 (coaxial); None (fiber optic). Homes passed: 1,870.
Vice President, Corporate Finance: Michael Pflantz. Regional Manager: Todd Cruthird. Plant Manager: Carl Gillit.
Ownership: Cequel Communications Holdings I LLC (MSO).

LOTT—Zito Media, 102 S Main St, PO Box 665, Coudersport, PA 16915. Phones: 814-260-9055; 800-365-6988. E-mail: info@zitomedia.com. Web Site: http://www.zitomedia.com. ICA: TX0515.
TV Market Ranking: Below 100 (LOTT). Franchise award date: N.A. Franchise expiration date: N.A. Began: May 1, 1984.
Channel capacity: N.A. Channels available but not in use: N.A.

Basic Service
Subscribers: 25.
Programming (received off-air): KCEN-TV (Antenna TV, MeTV, MundoMax, NBC) Temple; KNCT (PBS) Belton; KWKT-TV (Estrella TV, FOX, MNT) Waco; KWTX-TV (CBS, CW) Waco; KXXV (ABC, TMO) Waco.
Programming (via satellite): A&E; Animal Planet; BET; Cartoon Network; CNN; C-SPAN; Discovery Channel; Disney Channel; ESPN; ESPN2; Fox News Channel; Freeform; Fuse; Great American Country; HLN; INSP; Lifetime; Outdoor Channel; TBS; The Weather Channel; TLC; TNT; Turner Classic Movies; Univision; USA Network; WGN America.
Fee: $49.95 installation; $40.41 monthly.

Pay Service 1
Pay Units: N.A.
Programming (via satellite): Cinemax; HBO; Showtime.
Fee: $9.00 monthly (each).
Internet Service
Operational: No.
Telephone Service
None
Miles of Plant: 9.0 (coaxial); None (fiber optic). Homes passed: 359.
President: James Rigas.
Ownership: Zito Media (MSO).

LOUISE—NewWave Communications. Now served by WHARTON, TX [TX0171]. ICA: TX0579.

LOVELADY—Formerly served by Almega Cable. No longer in operation. ICA: TX0956.

LOWRY CROSSING—Suddenlink Communications. Now served by TERRELL, TX [TX0920]. ICA: TX0256.

LUBBOCK—NTS Communications. This cable system has converted to IPTV. Now served by WOLFFORTH, TX [TX5540]. ICA: TX0802.

LUBBOCK—Suddenlink Communications, 6710 Hartford Ave, Lubbock, TX 79413. Phones: 314-315-9400; 806-793-2222 (Customer service). Web Site: http://www.suddenlink.com. Also serves Post, Shallowater, Wolfforth & Woodrow. ICA: TX0012.
TV Market Ranking: Below 100 (LUBBOCK, Shallowater, Wolfforth, Woodrow); Outside TV Markets (Post). Franchise award date: February 25, 1965. Franchise expiration date: N.A. Began: March 1, 1965.
Channel capacity: N.A. Channels available but not in use: N.A.

Basic Service
Subscribers: 29,951. Commercial subscribers: 4,076.
Programming (received off-air): KAMC (ABC, Bounce TV) Lubbock; KBZO-LD (UNV) Lubbock; KCBD (NBC, This TV) Lubbock; KJTV-TV (FOX) Lubbock; KLBK-TV (CBS) Lubbock; KLCW-TV (CW) Wolfforth; KPTB-DT (GLC) Lubbock; KTTZ-TV (PBS) Lubbock; KXTQ-CD (TMO) Lubbock; 10 FMs.
Programming (via satellite): C-SPAN; C-SPAN 2; Jewelry Television; Pop; QVC; Trinity Broadcasting Network (TBN); WGN America.
Fee: $40.00 installation; $33.94 monthly.

Expanded Basic Service 1
Subscribers: N.A.
Programming (via satellite): A&E; AMC; Animal Planet; BET; Bravo; Cartoon Network; CMT; CNBC; CNN; Comedy Central; Discovery Channel; Disney Channel; E! HD; ESPN; ESPN2; Food Network; Fox News Channel; Fox Sports 1; FOX Sports Southwest; Freeform; FX; Hallmark Channel; HGTV; History; HLN; Lifetime; LMN; MSNBC; MTV; MTV2; NBC Universo; NBCSN; Nickelodeon; Spike TV; Syfy; TBS; The Weather Channel; TLC; TNT; Travel Channel; Turner Classic Movies; TV Land; UniMas; USA Network; VH1.
Fee: $41.99 monthly.

Digital Basic Service
Subscribers: N.A.
Programming (via satellite): A&E HD; AXS TV; Bandamax; BBC America; Bloomberg Television; Boomerang; CBS Sports Network; Cine Mexicano; Cinelatino; CMT; CNN en Espanol; Cooking Channel; De Pelicula; De Pelicula Clasico; Destination America; Discovery Kids Channel; Disney XD; DIY Network; ESPN Classic; ESPN Deportes; ESPN HD; ESPN2 HD; ESPNews; ESPNU; EVINE Live; EWTN Global Catholic Network; Food Network HD; FOX College Sports Central; FOX College Sports Pacific; Fox Deportes; Fox Sports 2; FSN HD; Fuse; FYI; Golf Channel; Great American Country; GSN; HD Theater; HGTV HD; History en Espanol; History International; IFC; INSP; Investigation Discovery; MC; MTV Classic; MTV Hits; mtvU; National Geographic Channel; National Geographic Channel HD; NBC Universo; Nick Jr.; Nicktoons; NickToons en Espanol; Outdoor Channel; OWN: Oprah Winfrey Network; Oxygen; Science Channel; Starz Encore (multiplexed); Sundance TV; Sur; TeenNick; Telehit; Tennis Channel; TNT HD; Toon Disney en Espanol; Tr3s; truTV; UniMas; Universal HD; Univision; UP; VideoRola; WE tv.
Fee: $14.95 monthly.

Pay Service 1
Pay Units: N.A.
Programming (via satellite): Cinemax; HBO; Showtime; Starz.
Fee: $11.00 monthly (Cinemax, HBO, Starz or Showtime).

2017 Edition   D-757

Texas—Cable Systems

Digital Pay Service 1
Pay Units: 21,282.
Programming (via satellite): Cinemax (multiplexed); HBO (multiplexed); HBO HD; Showtime (multiplexed); Showtime HD; Starz (multiplexed); Starz HD; The Movie Channel (multiplexed).
Fee: $10.00 monthly (Cinemax, HBO, Starz or Showtime/TMC).
Video-On-Demand: No
Pay-Per-View
iN DEMAND (delivered digitally); Playboy TV (delivered digitally); Fresh (delivered digitally); Shorteez (delivered digitally); Spice: Xcess (delivered digitally); Club Jenna (delivered digitally).
Internet Service
Operational: Yes. Began: December 1, 2000.
Subscribers: 32,818.
Broadband Service: Suddenlink High Speed Internet.
Fee: $49.95 installation; $24.95 monthly; $15.00 modem lease; $249.00 modem purchase.
Telephone Service
Digital: Operational
Subscribers: 13,583.
Fee: $48.95 monthly
Miles of Plant: 1,629.0 (coaxial); 777.0 (fiber optic). Homes passed: 118,054.
Senior Vice President, Corporate Finance: Michael Pflantz. Vice President & Manager: Connie Wharton. Vice President, Accounting: Sabrina Warr. Marketing Director: Wayde Klein. Chief Technician: John Linton.
Ownership: Cequel Communications Holdings I LLC (MSO).

LUBBOCK COUNTY (southeastern portion)—Formerly served by Almega Cable. No longer in operation. ICA: TX0348.

LUCAS—Suddenlink Communications. Now served by TERRELL, TX [TX0920]. ICA: TX0329.

LUEDERS—Formerly served by Jayroc Cablevision. No longer in operation. ICA: TX0803.

LUFKIN—Suddenlink Communications, 1415 South 1st St, Lufkin, TX 75901-4499. Phones: 800-584-5610; 314-315-9400. Fax: 936-634-6889. Web Site: http://www.suddenlink.com. Also serves Angelina County, Burke, Diboll, Fuller Springs, Hudson & Polk County (portions). ICA: TX0051.
TV Market Ranking: Below 100 (Angelina County, Burke, Diboll, Fuller Springs, LUFKIN, Polk County (portions), Hudson); Outside TV Markets (Polk County (portions)). Franchise award date: June 17, 1958. Franchise expiration date: N.A. Began: February 27, 1960.
Channel capacity: N.A. Channels available but not in use: N.A.
Basic Service
Subscribers: 5,912. Commercial subscribers: 573.
Programming (received off-air): KCEB (CW, MundoMax) Longview; KFXK-TV (FOX) Longview; KFXL-LD Lufkin; KHOU (Bounce TV, CBS) Houston; KIBN-LD Lufkin; KLUF-LP Lufkin; KPRC-TV (NBC, This TV) Houston; KTRE (ABC, TMO) Lufkin; KTRK-TV (ABC, Live Well Network) Houston; KUHT (PBS) Houston; KXTX-TV (TMO) Dallas; KYTX (CBS, COZI TV, CW) Nacogdoches; 7 FMs.

Programming (via satellite): QVC; TBS; Univision Studios.
Fee: $49.95 installation; $32.24 monthly.
Expanded Basic Service 1
Subscribers: N.A.
Programming (via satellite): A&E; Animal Planet; BET; Bravo; Cartoon Network; CMT; CNBC; CNN; Comedy Central; C-SPAN; C-SPAN 2; Discovery Channel; Disney Channel; E! HD; ESPN; ESPN2; EWTN Global Catholic Network; Food Network; Fox News Channel; FOX Sports Southwest; Freeform; FX; Great American Country; HGTV; History; HLN; INSP; Jewelry Television; Lifetime; LMN; MTV; MTV2; NBCSN; Nickelodeon; OWN: Oprah Winfrey Network; Pop; Spike TV; Syfy; The Weather Channel; TLC; TNT; Travel Channel; truTV; Turner Classic Movies; TV Land; USA Network; VH1.
Fee: $10.95 monthly.
Digital Basic Service
Subscribers: N.A.
Programming (via satellite): A&E HD; AXS TV; Bandamax; BBC America; Bloomberg Television; Boomerang; CBS Sports Network; Cine Mexicano; Cinelatino; CMT; CNN en Espanol; Cooking Channel; De Pelicula; De Pelicula Clasico; Destination America; Discovery Kids Channel; Disney XD; DIY Network; Enlace USA; ESPN Classic; ESPN Deportes; ESPN HD; ESPNews; ESPNU; FamilyNet; Food Network HD; Fox Deportes; Fox Sports 1; Fox Sports 2; FSN HD; Fuse; FYI; Golf Channel; GSN; Hallmark Channel; HD Theater; HGTV HD; History en Espanol; History International; IFC; Investigation Discovery; MC; MTV Classic; MTV Hits; Nat Geo WILD; National Geographic Channel; National Geographic Channel HD; NBC Universo; Nick Jr.; Nicktoons; NickToons en Espanol; Outdoor Channel; Ritmoson; Science Channel; Starz Encore (multiplexed); Sundance TV; Sur; TeenNick; Telehit; Tennis Channel; TNT HD; Tr3s; Trinity Broadcasting Network (TBN); Turner Classic Movies; ULTRA HDPlex; UniMas; Universal HD; Univision; VideoRola; Weatherscan.
Digital Pay Service 1
Pay Units: N.A.
Programming (via satellite): Cinemax (multiplexed); HBO (multiplexed); HBO HD; HBO Latino; Showtime (multiplexed); Showtime HD; Starz (multiplexed); Starz HD; The Movie Channel (multiplexed).
Video-On-Demand: No
Pay-Per-View
iN DEMAND (delivered digitally); Fresh (delivered digitally); Shorteez (delivered digitally); Playboy TV (delivered digitally); Club Jenna (delivered digitally); Spice: Xcess (delivered digitally).
Internet Service
Operational: Yes.
Subscribers: 5,594.
Broadband Service: Suddenlink High Speed Internet.
Fee: $49.95 installation; $24.95 monthly.
Telephone Service
Digital: Operational
Subscribers: 3,076.
Fee: $48.95 monthly
Miles of Plant: 668.0 (coaxial); 100.0 (fiber optic). Homes passed: 30,022.
Senior Vice President, Corporate Finance: Michael Pflantz. Vice President, Accounting: Sabrina Warr. General Manager: Glenn Parker. Chief Technician: Jerry Teer. Marketing Director: Mike Evans.
Ownership: Cequel Communications Holdings I LLC (MSO).

LULING—Time Warner Cable. Now served by SAN MARCOS, TX [TX0849]. ICA: TX0221.

LYONS—Reveille Broadband, 1008 Giddings St, PO Box 39, Lexington, TX 78947. Phones: 979-773-3215; 979-773-4700. Fax: 979-773-4733. E-mail: mariesullivan@reveillebroadband.com. Web Site: http://www.reveillebroadband.com. Also serves Burleson County (portions) & Somerville. ICA: TX0331.
TV Market Ranking: Below 100 (Burleson County (portions), LYONS, Somerville). Franchise award date: November 20, 1985. Franchise expiration date: N.A. Began: February 1, 1986.
Channel capacity: N.A. Channels available but not in use: N.A.
Basic Service
Subscribers: N.A.
Programming (received off-air): KAMU-TV (PBS) College Station; KBTX-TV (CBS, CW) Bryan; KTBC (Buzzr, FOX, Movies!) Austin; KVUE (ABC, Estrella TV) Austin; KWKT-TV (Estrella TV, FOX, MNT) Waco; KXAN-TV (COZI TV, NBC) Austin.
Programming (via microwave): KHOU (Bounce TV, CBS) Houston; KTXH (Buzzr, MNT, Movies!) Houston.
Programming (via satellite): A&E; AMC; BET; Cartoon Network; CMT; CNN; Discovery Channel; Disney Channel; ESPN; FOX Sports Southwest; Freeform; HGTV; History; MTV; Nickelodeon; QVC; Spike TV; TBS; The Weather Channel; TLC; TNT; Trinity Broadcasting Network (TBN); USA Network; WGN America.
Fee: $54.95 installation.
Pay Service 1
Pay Units: N.A.
Programming (via satellite): HBO; Showtime; The Movie Channel.
Fee: $12.95 monthly (each).
Video-On-Demand: No
Internet Service
Operational: Yes.
Telephone Service
None
Miles of Plant: 15.0 (coaxial); None (fiber optic). Homes passed: 847.
Chief Executive Officer: Marie Sullivan. President: Jeff Sullivan. Vice President: Cory Savage. Chief Technology Officer: Jason Sembera. Office Manager: Laura Tillery.
Ownership: Reveille Broadband (MSO).

MADISONVILLE—Northland Cable Television, 1202 East Houston Ave, PO Box 1228, Crockett, TX 75835-1228. Phones: 888-667-8452; 936-544-2031; 800-615-1110. Fax: 409-544-9660. Web Site: http://www.yournorthland.com. Also serves Madison County. ICA: TX0242.
TV Market Ranking: Below 100 (Madison County (portions), MADISONVILLE); Outside TV Markets (Madison County (portions)). Franchise award date: N.A. Franchise expiration date: N.A. Began: August 1, 1955.
Channel capacity: N.A. Channels available but not in use: N.A.
Basic Service
Subscribers: 209.
Programming (received off-air): KAMU-TV (PBS) College Station; KBTX-TV (CBS, CW) Bryan; KCEN-TV (Antenna TV, MeTV, MundoMax, NBC) Temple; KETK-TV (Estrella TV, NBC) Jacksonville; KHOU (Bounce TV, CBS) Houston; KIAH (Antenna TV, CW) Houston; KRHD-CD (ABC) Bryan; KRIV (FOX) Houston; KTRK-TV (ABC, Live Well Network) Houston; KTXH (Buzzr, MNT,

Movies!) Houston; KYLE-TV (FOX) Bryan; allband FM.
Programming (via satellite): BET; Cartoon Network; CNBC; C-SPAN; Discovery Channel; ESPN; Fox News Channel; Hallmark Channel; INSP; National Geographic Channel; Pop; QVC; TBS; Telemundo; The Weather Channel; TLC; TNT; Trinity Broadcasting Network (TBN); Univision Studios.
Fee: $75.00 installation; $47.64 monthly.
Expanded Basic Service 1
Subscribers: N.A.
Programming (via satellite): A&E; Animal Planet; CNN; ESPN2; Food Network; FOX Sports Southwest; FXM; HGTV; History; HLN; Lifetime; Nickelodeon; Outdoor Channel; Spike TV; Syfy; TNT; Turner Classic Movies; USA Network.
Fee: $49.99 monthly.
Digital Basic Service
Subscribers: N.A.
Programming (via satellite): Discovery Digital Networks; DMX Music; Fox Sports 1; Golf Channel; GSN.
Fee: $54.99 monthly.
Digital Expanded Basic Service
Subscribers: N.A.
Programming (via satellite): Bloomberg Television; Bravo; Discovery Life Channel; IFC; WE tv.
Pay Service 1
Pay Units: 100.
Programming (via satellite): HBO.
Fee: $14.00 monthly.
Pay Service 2
Pay Units: 45.
Programming (via satellite): Cinemax.
Pay Service 3
Pay Units: 45.
Programming (via satellite): Showtime.
Pay Service 4
Pay Units: 65.
Programming (via satellite): Starz; Starz Encore.
Digital Pay Service 1
Pay Units: N.A.
Programming (via satellite): Cinemax (multiplexed); Flix; HBO (multiplexed); Showtime (multiplexed); Starz (multiplexed); Starz Encore (multiplexed); Sundance TV.
Fee: $10.00 monthly (each).
Video-On-Demand: No
Internet Service
Operational: Yes.
Telephone Service
Digital: Operational
Miles of Plant: 49.0 (coaxial); None (fiber optic). Homes passed: 1,800.
Executive Vice President: Richard I. Clark. General Manager: Brent Richey. Chief Technician: John Guys. Office Manager: Linda Richie.
Ownership: Northland Communications Corp. (MSO).

MAGNOLIA—Formerly served by Versalink Media. No longer in operation. ICA: TX0301.

MALAKOFF—Formerly served by Northland Cable Television. Now served by Suddenlink Communications, ATHENS, TX [TX0711]. ICA: TX0806.

MANOR—Formerly served by Almega Cable. No longer in operation. ICA: TX0470.

MANVEL—NewWave Communications. Now served by WHARTON, TX [TX0171]. ICA: TX0986.

Cable Systems—Texas

MARATHON—Mountain Zone TV, 307 E Ave East, Alpine, TX 79830. Phones: 800-446-5661; 432-729-4347; 432-837-2300. Fax: 432-837-5423. E-mail: mtnzone@sbcglobal.net. Web Site: http://www.mountainzonetv.net. ICA: TX0613.
TV Market Ranking: Outside TV Markets (MARATHON). Franchise award date: N.A. Franchise expiration date: N.A. Began: October 1, 1968.
Channel capacity: N.A. Channels available but not in use: N.A.

Basic Service
Subscribers: N.A.
Programming (received off-air): KMID (ABC) Midland; KOSA-TV (CBS, MNT) Odessa; KPEJ-TV (FOX) Odessa; KWES-TV (CW, NBC, TMO) Odessa; allband FM.
Programming (via satellite): A&E; CMT; CNN; Discovery Channel; ESPN; Freeform; KMGH-TV (ABC, Azteca America) Denver; KRMA-TV (PBS) Denver; Nickelodeon; Spike TV; TBS; The Weather Channel; TLC; TNT; Turner Classic Movies; Univision; WGN America.
Fee: $25.00 installation; $48.00 monthly.

Pay Service 1
Pay Units: N.A.
Programming (via satellite): HBO; Showtime.
Fee: $10.00 installation.

Video-On-Demand: No

Internet Service
Operational: Yes.
Fee: $150.00 installation; $60.00 monthly.

Telephone Service
None
Miles of Plant: 8.0 (coaxial); None (fiber optic). Homes passed: 225.
General Manager: Steve Neu. Office Manager: Lawrence Neu.
Ownership: Mountain Zone TV Systems (MSO).

MARBLE FALLS—Northland Cable Television, 1101 Mission Hill Dr, Marble Falls, TX 78654. Phones: 888-667-8452; 830-693-0487; 830-693-7500. Fax: 830-693-6056. E-mail: marblefalls@northlandcabletv.com. Web Site: http://www.yournorthland.com. Also serves Burnet, Cottonwood Shores, Granite Shoals, Highland Haven, Horseshoe Bay, Kingsland, Lake L.B. Johnson, Meadowlakes & Sunrise Beach. ICA: TX0807.
TV Market Ranking: Below 100 (Burnet, Cottonwood Shores, Granite Shoals, Highland Haven, Horseshoe Bay, Kingsland, Lake L.B. Johnson, MARBLE FALLS, Meadowlakes, Sunrise Beach).
Channel capacity: N.A. Channels available but not in use: N.A.

Basic Service
Subscribers: 2,614.
Programming (received off-air): KBVO (Laff, MNT) Llano; KCWX (MNT, This TV) Fredericksburg; KEYE-TV (CBS, TMO) Austin; KLRU (PBS) Austin; KNVA (CW, Grit, TheCoolTV) Austin; KTBC (Buzzr, FOX, Movies!) Austin; KVUE (ABC, Estrella TV) Austin.
Programming (via satellite): A&E; AMC; Cartoon Network; CNBC; CNN; C-SPAN; Discovery Channel; ESPN; Food Network; Fox News Channel; FOX Sports Southwest; Great American Country; Hallmark Channel; HGTV; History; HLN; National Geographic Channel; Pop; QVC; TBS; Telemundo; The Weather Channel; TLC; TNT; Trinity Broadcasting Network (TBN); Univision Studios; USA Network.
Fee: $75.00 installation; $47.64 monthly.

Expanded Basic Service 1
Subscribers: N.A.
Programming (via satellite): Animal Planet; Comedy Central; ESPN2; FX; FXM; Lifetime; MTV; Nickelodeon; Outdoor Channel; Spike TV; Syfy; Turner Classic Movies; VH1.
Fee: $43.29 monthly.

Digital Basic Service
Subscribers: N.A.
Programming (via satellite): BBC America; Discovery Digital Networks; DMX Music; Fox Sports 1; Golf Channel; GSN; Outdoor Channel.
Fee: $51.99 monthly.

Digital Expanded Basic Service
Subscribers: N.A.
Programming (via satellite): Bloomberg Television; Bravo; Discovery Life Channel; IFC; WE tv.

Pay Service 1
Pay Units: N.A.
Programming (via satellite): Cinemax; HBO.
Fee: $11.95 monthly (Cinemax), $13.50 monthly (HBO).

Digital Pay Service 1
Pay Units: N.A.
Programming (via satellite): Cinemax (multiplexed); Flix; HBO (multiplexed); Showtime (multiplexed); Starz (multiplexed); Starz Encore (multiplexed); The Movie Channel (multiplexed).

Video-On-Demand: No

Internet Service
Operational: Yes.
Broadband Service: Northland Express.
Fee: $42.99 monthly.

Telephone Service
Analog: Not Operational
Digital: Operational
Fee: $29.99 monthly
Miles of Plant: 213.0 (coaxial); 1.0 (fiber optic). Homes passed: 10,775.
Executive Vice President: Richard I. Clark. Regional Manager: Larson Lloyd. Marketing Director: Bonnie Moran. Plant Manager: Ron Gardner.
Ownership: Northland Communications Corp. (MSO).

MARFA—Marfa TV Cable Co. Inc, 307 E Ave East, Alpine, TX 79830. Phones: 432-729-4347; 800-446-5661; 432-837-2300. Fax: 432-837-5423. E-mail: mtnzone@sbcglobal.net. Web Site: http://www.mountainzonetv.net. ICA: TX0360.
TV Market Ranking: Outside TV Markets (MARFA). Franchise award date: February 18, 1957. Franchise expiration date: N.A. Began: September 1, 1958.
Channel capacity: N.A. Channels available but not in use: N.A.

Basic Service
Subscribers: N.A.
Programming (via microwave): KMLM-DT (GLC) Odessa.
Programming (via satellite): A&E; Animal Planet; Cartoon Network; CNN; Comedy Central; C-SPAN; Discovery Channel; Disney Channel; ESPN; ESPN2; EWTN Global Catholic Network; Food Network; Fox News Channel; FOX Sports Southwest; Great American Country; HGTV; History; HLN; Lifetime; MTV; NFL Network; Nickelodeon; QVC; Syfy; TBS; Telemundo; The Weather Channel; TLC; TNT; Trinity Broadcasting Network (TBN); Turner Classic Movies; TV Land; UniMas; Univision; Univision Studios; USA Network; VH1; WGN America.
Programming (via translator): KABB (FOX, The Country Network) San Antonio; KLRN (PBS) San Antonio; KMID (ABC) Midland; KOSA-TV (CBS, MNT) Odessa; KTSM-TV (Estrella TV, NBC) El Paso; KVIA-TV (ABC, Azteca America, CW) El Paso; KWES-TV (CW, NBC, TMO) Odessa.
Fee: $25.00 installation; $48.00 monthly.

Digital Basic Service
Subscribers: N.A.
Programming (via satellite): DMX Music; ESPN Classic; FYI; History International; LMN; NBCSN; WE tv.

Pay Service 1
Pay Units: N.A.
Programming (via satellite): Cinemax; HBO; Showtime.

Digital Pay Service 1
Pay Units: N.A.
Programming (via satellite): Cinemax (multiplexed); HBO (multiplexed); Showtime (multiplexed); Starz (multiplexed); Starz Encore (multiplexed).

Video-On-Demand: No

Internet Service
Operational: Yes. Began: June 1, 2005.
Fee: $150.00 installation; $60.00 monthly.

Telephone Service
None
Miles of Plant: 16.0 (coaxial); None (fiber optic). Homes passed: 1,012.
General Manager: Steve Neu. Office Manager: Lawrence Neu.
Ownership: Mountain Zone TV Systems (MSO).

MARLIN—Northland Cable Television, 515 West Tyler St, Mexia, TX 76667. Phones: 254-562-2872; 800-792-3087. Fax: 254-562-6454. E-mail: mexia@northlandcabletv.com. Web Site: http://www.yournorthland.com. ICA: TX0203.
TV Market Ranking: Below 100 (MARLIN). Franchise award date: January 1, 1964. Franchise expiration date: N.A. Began: March 1, 1965.
Channel capacity: N.A. Channels available but not in use: N.A.

Basic Service
Subscribers: 130.
Programming (received off-air): KCEN-TV (Antenna TV, MeTV, MundoMax, NBC) Temple; KERA-TV (PBS) Dallas; KTVT (CBS, Decades) Fort Worth; KTXA (IND, MeTV) Fort Worth; KWKT-TV (Estrella TV, FOX, MNT) Waco; KWTX-TV (CBS, CW) Waco; KXXV (ABC, TMO) Waco; WFAA (ABC) Dallas.
Programming (via satellite): INSP; QVC; Telemundo; Univision Studios.
Fee: $35.00 installation; $47.64 monthly.

Expanded Basic Service 1
Subscribers: N.A.
Programming (via satellite): A&E; Animal Planet; BET; Cartoon Network; CNBC; Comedy Central; C-SPAN; Discovery Channel; E! HD; ESPN; ESPN2; Food Network; Fox News Channel; FOX Sports Southwest; FX; FXM; Great American Country; Hallmark Channel; HGTV; History; Lifetime; Nickelodeon; Outdoor Channel; Spike TV; Syfy; TBS; The Weather Channel; TLC; TNT; Turner Classic Movies; TV Land; USA Network.
Fee: $35.00 installation; $47.99 monthly.

Digital Basic Service
Subscribers: N.A.
Programming (via satellite): Bravo; Destination America; Discovery Life Channel; DMX Music; ESPNews; EVINE Live; Fox Sports 1; Golf Channel; IFC; Investigation Discovery; LMN; OWN: Oprah Winfrey Network; RFD-TV; Science Channel; WE tv.
Fee: $8.00 monthly.

Pay Service 1
Pay Units: 40.
Programming (via satellite): HBO.
Fee: $11.50 monthly (Cinemax), $13.50 monthly (HBO).

Digital Pay Service 1
Pay Units: 35.
Programming (via satellite): Cinemax (multiplexed).
Fee: $14.00 monthly.

Digital Pay Service 2
Pay Units: 20.
Programming (via satellite): Starz (multiplexed); Starz Encore (multiplexed).
Fee: $14.00 monthly.

Digital Pay Service 3
Pay Units: N.A.
Programming (via satellite): Flix; HBO (multiplexed).
Fee: $14.00 monthly.

Digital Pay Service 4
Pay Units: 15.
Programming (via satellite): Showtime (multiplexed); The Movie Channel (multiplexed).
Fee: $14.00 monthly.

Pay-Per-View
Sports PPV (delivered digitally); iN DEMAND (delivered digitally).

Internet Service
Operational: No.

Telephone Service
None
Miles of Plant: 41.0 (coaxial); None (fiber optic). Homes passed: 2,800.
Executive Vice President: Richard I. Clark. General Manager: Brent Richey. Chief Technician: James Feverston.
Ownership: Northland Communications Corp. (MSO).

MARSHALL—Fidelity Communications, 64 North Clark St, Sullivan, MO 63080. Phones: 800-392-8070; 903-938-1302 (Marshall office); 855-262-7434. E-mail: fidelityinfo@fidelitycommunications.com. Web Site: http://www.fidelitycommunications.com. Also serves Hallsville, Harrison County (portions), Jefferson & Marion County (portions). ICA: TX0083.
TV Market Ranking: 58 (Harrison County (portions), Marion County (portions), MARSHALL; Below 100 (Hallsville, Jefferson, Harrison County (portions), Marion County (portions)). Franchise award date: November 15, 1965. Franchise expiration date: N.A. Began: February 1, 1974.
Channel capacity: N.A. Channels available but not in use: N.A.

Basic Service
Subscribers: 3,053. Commercial subscribers: 427.
Programming (received off-air): KETK-TV (Estrella TV, NBC) Jacksonville; KLTS-TV (PBS) Shreveport; KMSS-TV (FOX) Shreveport; KPXJ (Antenna TV, CW, MeTV, Movies!) Minden; KSHV-TV (MNT) Shreveport; KSLA (Bounce TV, CBS, Grit, This TV) Shreveport; KTAL-TV (NBC) Texarkana; KTBS-TV (ABC) Shreveport; allband FM.
Programming (via satellite): C-SPAN; INSP; QVC; The Weather Channel; Trinity Broadcasting Network (TBN); Univision.
Fee: $29.99 installation; $28.99 monthly.

Expanded Basic Service 1
Subscribers: N.A.
Programming (via satellite): A&E; AMC; BET; CMT; CNBC; Comedy Central; E! HD; ESPN2; Fox News Channel; Fox Sports 1; Freeform; FX; HLN; Lifetime; MTV; Nickelodeon; Syfy; TLC; TV Land.

2017 Edition D-759

Texas—Cable Systems

Digital Basic Service
Subscribers: N.A.
Programming (via satellite): BBC America; Discovery Digital Networks; Disney XD; DIY Network; ESPN Classic; FYI; History International; IFC; MC; Nick Jr.; TeenNick; TV Guide Interactive Inc.; WE tv.

Digital Pay Service 1
Pay Units: N.A.
Programming (via satellite): Cinemax (multiplexed); Flix; HBO (multiplexed); Showtime (multiplexed); Starz (multiplexed); The Movie Channel (multiplexed).
Fee: $8.99 -$14.99 monthly.

Video-On-Demand: No

Pay-Per-View
Hot Choice (delivered digitally); iN DEMAND (delivered digitally); Playboy TV (delivered digitally); Fresh (delivered digitally); Shorteez (delivered digitally).

Internet Service
Operational: Yes.
Fee: $29.99 monthly.

Telephone Service
Digital: Operational
Miles of Plant: 274.0 (coaxial); None (fiber optic). Homes passed: 14,172.
General Manager, AR/MO/LA/TX: Andy Davis.
Ownership: Fidelity Communications Co. (MSO).

MART—LynnStar Communications, 4500 Mercantile Plz, Ste 300, Fort Worth, TX 76137. Phones: 888-575-9230; 682-730-0900. Fax: 682-730-6400. Web Site: http://lynnstar.net; http://www.lynnstarcomm.com. ICA: TX0359.
TV Market Ranking: Below 100 (MART). Franchise award date: N.A. Franchise expiration date: N.A. Began: January 1, 1983.
Channel capacity: N.A. Channels available but not in use: N.A.

Basic Service
Subscribers: 92.
Programming (received off-air): KCEN-TV (Antenna TV, MeTV, MundoMax, NBC) Temple; KDFW (FOX) Dallas; KERA-TV (PBS) Dallas; KTVT (CBS, Decades) Fort Worth; KWKT-TV (Estrella TV, FOX, MNT) Waco; KWTX-TV (CBS, CW) Waco; KXAS-TV (COZI TV, NBC) Fort Worth; KXTX-TV (TMO) Dallas; KXXV (ABC, TMO) Waco; WFAA (ABC) Dallas.
Programming (via satellite): Discovery Channel; TBS; TLC.
Fee: $49.95 installation; $28.28 monthly.

Expanded Basic Service 1
Subscribers: N.A.
Programming (via satellite): AMC; Animal Planet; Cartoon Network; CNBC; CNN; C-SPAN; Disney Channel; ESPN; Fox News Channel; Freeform; FX; HGTV; HLN; Lifetime; Nickelodeon; QVC; Spike TV; The Weather Channel; TNT; USA Network.
Fee: $23.10 monthly.

Pay Service 1
Pay Units: N.A.
Programming (via satellite): Cinemax; HBO; Starz; Starz Encore.
Fee: $6.75 monthly (Starz), $12.95 monthly (Cinemax, Encore or HBO).

Video-On-Demand: No

Internet Service
Operational: Yes.
Subscribers: 23.
Broadband Service: Rapid High Speed Internet.
Fee: $100.00 installation; $29.95 monthly.

Telephone Service
None
Miles of Plant: 24.0 (coaxial); None (fiber optic). Homes passed: 1,019.

Chairman of the Board & Government Relations Director: S. Gene Yarbrough. Chief Executive Officer, Executive Vice President & Board Member: Chris Romine. Chief Operations Officer, Executive Vice President & Board Member: Steve Sizemore. Vice President & Business Development & Countertrade Director: Gary Majors. Vice President & Programming & Vendor Relations Director: Gus Salvino. Vice President & Investor Relations Manager: Daniel J. Sweeney. Accounting Manager: Sheila Magness.
Ownership: Lynnstar Communications (MSO).

MASON—LynnStar Communications, 4500 Mercantile Plz, Ste 300, Fort Worth, TX 76137. Phones: 888-575-9230; 682-730-0900. Fax: 682-730-6400. Web Site: http://lynnstar.net; http://www.lynnstarcomm.com. Also serves Mason County (portions). ICA: TX0363.
TV Market Ranking: Below 100 (MASON). Franchise award date: N.A. Franchise expiration date: N.A. Began: January 1, 1967.
Channel capacity: N.A. Channels available but not in use: N.A.

Basic Service
Subscribers: 134.
Programming (received off-air): KEYE-TV (CBS, TMO) Austin; KLRU (PBS) Austin; KLST (CBS) San Angelo; KTBC (Buzzr, FOX, Movies!) Austin; KVUE (ABC, Estrella TV) Austin; KXAN-TV (COZI TV, NBC) Austin; 8 FMs.
Programming (via satellite): A&E; CMT; CNN; Discovery Channel; ESPN; Fox News Channel; FOX Sports Southwest; Freeform; FX; HGTV; Spike TV; TBS; The Weather Channel; TNT; Trinity Broadcasting Network (TBN); TV Land; USA Network.
Fee: $49.95 installation; $27.70 monthly.

Pay Service 1
Pay Units: N.A.
Programming (via satellite): Cinemax; HBO; Starz; Starz Encore.
Fee: $6.95 monthly (Starz/Encore), $10.63 monthly (HBO), $10.95 monthly (Cinemax).

Video-On-Demand: No

Internet Service
Operational: Yes.
Subscribers: 34.
Broadband Service: Rapid High Speed Internet.
Fee: $100.00 installation; $29.95 monthly.

Telephone Service
None
Miles of Plant: 39.0 (coaxial); None (fiber optic). Homes passed: 1,051.
Chairman of the Board & Government Relations Director: S. Gene Yarbrough. Chief Executive Officer, Executive Vice President & Board Member: Chris Romine. Chief Operations Officer, Executive Vice President & Board Member: Steve Sizemore. Vice President & Business Development & Countertrade Director: Gary Majors. Vice President & Programming & Vendor Relations Director: Gus Salvino. Vice President & investor Relations Manager: Daniel J. Sweeney. Accounting Manager: Sheila Magness.
Ownership: Lynnstar Communications (MSO).

MATADOR (town)—Reach Broadband, PO Box 507, Arp, TX 75750. Phones: 903-859-3789; 800-687-1258. Web Site: http://www.reachbroadband.net. ICA: TX0500.
TV Market Ranking: Outside TV Markets (MATADOR (TOWN)). Franchise award date: N.A. Franchise expiration date: N.A. Began: November 1, 1957.
Channel capacity: 61 (not 2-way capable). Channels available but not in use: N.A.

Basic Service
Subscribers: 21.
Programming (received off-air): KAMC (ABC, Bounce TV) Lubbock; KCBD (NBC, This TV) Lubbock; KJTV-TV (FOX) Lubbock; KLBK-TV (CBS) Lubbock.
Programming (via satellite): AMC; Animal Planet; Cartoon Network; CMT; CNN; Discovery Channel; Disney Channel; E! HD; ESPN; FOX Sports Southwest; Freeform; History; HLN; KRMA-TV (PBS) Denver; Lifetime; QVC; Spike TV; TBS; The Weather Channel; TLC; TNT; Travel Channel; Trinity Broadcasting Network (TBN); TV Land; USA Network; WGN America.
Fee: $29.95 installation; $29.38 monthly.

Pay Service 1
Pay Units: N.A.
Programming (via satellite): Cinemax; HBO.
Fee: $9.95 monthly (each).

Video-On-Demand: No

Internet Service
Operational: Yes.

Telephone Service
None
Miles of Plant: 11.0 (coaxial); None (fiber optic). Homes passed: 394.
Regional Manager: Ronnie Stafford. Office Manager: Jan Gibson.
Ownership: RB3 LLC (MSO).

MATHIS—Time Warner Cable. Now served by CORPUS CHRISTI, TX [TX0010]. ICA: TX0216.

MAUD—BCI Broadband. Now served by NEW BOSTON, TX [TX0204]. ICA: TX0482.

MAURICEVILLE—Formerly served by Cebridge Connections. No longer in operation. ICA: TX0808.

MAY—Formerly served by Cable Unlimited. No longer in operation. ICA: TX0683.

McCAMEY—Reach Broadband, PO Box 507, Arp, TX 75750. Phones: 575-437-3101; 800-687-1258; 903-859-3789. E-mail: support@reachbroadband.net. Web Site: http://www.reachbroadband.net. ICA: TX1027.
TV Market Ranking: Outside TV Markets (MC-CAMEY).
Channel capacity: N.A. Channels available but not in use: N.A.

Basic Service
Subscribers: 102.
Programming (received off-air): KMID (ABC) Midland; KMLM-DT (GLC) Odessa; KOSA-TV (CBS, MNT) Odessa; KPBT-TV (PBS) Odessa; KPEJ-TV (FOX) Odessa; KUPB (UNV) Midland; KWES-TV (CW, NBC, TMO) Odessa; KWWT (Antenna TV, MeTV, Movies!, Retro TV, This TV) Odessa.
Programming (via satellite): Animal Planet; C-SPAN; Fox News Channel; HSN; Lifetime; MSNBC; TBS; TNT; Trinity Broadcasting Network (TBN); UniMas; WGN America.
Fee: $49.96 installation; $24.84 monthly.

Expanded Basic Service 1
Subscribers: N.A.
Programming (via satellite): A&E; AMC; Cartoon Network; CMT; CNN; Discovery Channel; Discovery Life Channel; Disney Channel; ESPN; ESPN2; FOX Sports Networks; Freeform; FX; Hallmark Channel; History; MoviePlex; MTV; National Geographic Channel; Nick At Nite; Nickelodeon; Spike TV; Syfy; TLC; USA Network; VH1.
Fee: $28.35 monthly.

Digital Basic Service
Subscribers: N.A.
Programming (via satellite): BBC America; Bloomberg Television; Bravo; Centric; Cloo; CMT; Destination America; Discovery Kids Channel; Discovery Life Channel; Disney XD; DMX Music; ESPN Classic; ESPNews; FOX College Sports Central; FOX College Sports Pacific; Fox Sports 1; Fuse; FXM; FYI; Golf Channel; Great American Country; GSN; HGTV; History International; IFC; Investigation Discovery; LMN; MTV Classic; MTV Hits; MTV2; NBCSN; Nick Jr.; Outdoor Channel; OWN; Oprah Winfrey Network; Science Channel; Starz Encore (multiplexed); TeenNick; The Word Network; Turner Classic Movies; VH1 Soul; WE tv.
Fee: $20.90 monthly.

Pay Service 1
Pay Units: N.A.
Programming (via satellite): Cinemax; HBO.
Fee: $13.95 monthly (each).

Digital Pay Service 1
Pay Units: N.A.
Programming (via satellite): Cinemax (multiplexed); HBO (multiplexed); Showtime (multiplexed); Starz (multiplexed); The Movie Channel (multiplexed).
Fee: $9.95 monthly (Starz), $12.95 monthly (Cinemax, HBO, Showtime or TMC).

Video-On-Demand: No

Pay-Per-View
Playboy TV (delivered digitally); Fresh (delivered digitally).

Internet Service
Operational: No.

Telephone Service
None
Controller: Jeffrey Lowe.
Ownership: RB3 LLC (MSO).

MEDINA—Formerly served by Medina Cable Ltd. No longer in operation. ICA: TX0684.

MEMPHIS—Reach Broadband, PO Box 507, Arp, TX 75750. Phone: 800-687-1258. Web Site: http://www.reachbroadband.net. Also serves Hall County (portions). ICA: TX0302.
TV Market Ranking: Outside TV Markets (Hall County (portions), MEMPHIS). Franchise award date: N.A. Franchise expiration date: N.A. Began: July 1, 1958.
Channel capacity: 29 (not 2-way capable). Channels available but not in use: N.A.

Basic Service
Subscribers: 56.
Programming (via microwave): KAMR-TV (IND, NBC) Amarillo; KETA-TV (PBS) Oklahoma City; KFDA-TV (CBS, TMO) Amarillo; KVII-TV (ABC, CW) Amarillo.
Programming (via satellite): CMT; C-SPAN; Discovery Channel; Disney Channel; ESPN; Freeform; INSP; Lifetime; MTV; Nickelodeon; Spike TV; TBS; The Weather Channel; TNT; Turner Classic Movies; USA Network; WGN America.
Fee: $49.95 installation; $26.63 monthly.

Pay Service 1
Pay Units: N.A.
Programming (via satellite): Cinemax; HBO.
Fee: $20.00 installation; $11.65 monthly (each).

Internet Service
Operational: Yes.

Telephone Service
None
Miles of Plant: 23.0 (coaxial); None (fiber optic). Homes passed: 1,275.

Cable Systems—Texas

Regional Manager: Ronnie Stafford. Office Manager: Jan Gibson. Controller: Jeffrey Lowe.
Ownership: RB3 LLC (MSO).

MENARD—LynnStar Communications, 4500 Mercantile Plz, Ste 300, Fort Worth, TX 74145. Phones: 888-575-9230; 682-730-0900. Fax: 682-730-6400. Web Site: http://lynnstar.net; http://www.lynnstarcomm.com. Also serves Menard County (portions). ICA: TX0392.
TV Market Ranking: Outside TV Markets (MENARD, Menard County (portions)). Franchise award date: N.A. Franchise expiration date: N.A. Began: November 1, 1958.
Channel capacity: 41 (not 2-way capable). Channels available but not in use: N.A.

Basic Service
Subscribers: 100.
Programming (received off-air): KIDY (FOX, MNT) San Angelo; KLST (CBS) San Angelo; KTXS-TV (ABC, CW, This TV, TMO) Sweetwater; 5 FMs.
Programming (via microwave): KDTX-TV (TBN) Dallas; KRBC-TV (Bounce TV, NBC) Abilene.
Programming (via satellite): A&E; Animal Planet; CMT; CNN; Discovery Channel; Disney Channel; ESPN; Fox News Channel; FOX Sports Southwest; Freeform; HLN; KRMA-TV (PBS) Denver; Lifetime; Nickelodeon; QVC; Spike TV; TBS; Telemundo; The Weather Channel; TLC; TNT; Trinity Broadcasting Network (TBN); Turner Classic Movies; TV Land; USA Network; WGN America.
Fee: $49.95 installation; $26.24 monthly.

Pay Service 1
Pay Units: N.A.
Programming (via satellite): HBO; Showtime; The Movie Channel.
Fee: $7.95 monthly (TMC), $9.95 monthly (Showtime), $10.95 monthly (HBO).

Video-On-Demand: No

Internet Service
Operational: No.

Telephone Service
None
Miles of Plant: 20.0 (coaxial); None (fiber optic). Homes passed: 844.
Chairman of the Board & Government Relations Director: S. Gene Yarbrough. Chief Executive Officer, Executive Vice President & Board Member: Chris Romine. Chief Operations Officer, Executive Vice President & Board Member: Steve Sizemore. Vice President & Business Development & Countertrade Director: Gary Majors. Vice President & Programming & Vendor Relations Director: Gus Salvino. Vice President & Investor Relations Manager: Daniel J. Sweeney. Accounting Manager: Sheila Magness.
Ownership: Lynnstar Communications (MSO).

MERIDIAN—Formerly served by Almega Cable. No longer in operation. ICA: TX0446.

MERKEL—NewWave Communications, One Montgomery Plaza, 4th Floor, Sikeston, MO 63801. Phones: 573-472-9500; 888-863-9928. Fax: 573-472-9518. E-mail: info@newwave.com. Web Site: http://www.newwavecom.com. ICA: TX0355.
TV Market Ranking: Below 100 (MERKEL). Franchise award date: September 20, 1971. Franchise expiration date: N.A. Began: July 1, 1972.
Channel capacity: N.A. Channels available but not in use: N.A.

Basic Service
Subscribers: 116.
Programming (received off-air): KRBC-TV (Bounce TV, NBC) Abilene; KTAB-TV (CBS) Abilene; KTXS-TV (ABC, CW, This TV, TMO) Sweetwater; allband FM.
Programming (via satellite): A&E; CMT; CNN; Discovery Channel; Disney Channel; ESPN; Freeform; Lifetime; MTV; Nickelodeon; Spike TV; TBS; The Weather Channel; TNT; USA Network; WGN America.
Fee: $35.00 installation; $34.78 monthly.

Expanded Basic Service 1
Subscribers: N.A.
Programming (via satellite): AMC; Animal Planet; Cartoon Network; ESPN2; Fox News Channel; FOX Sports Southwest; HGTV; History; HLN; INSP; QVC; Syfy; TLC; Turner Classic Movies; TV Land; VH1.
Fee: $24.00 monthly.

Pay Service 1
Pay Units: N.A.
Programming (via satellite): HBO.
Fee: $9.95 installation; $11.95 monthly.

Video-On-Demand: No

Internet Service
Operational: Yes.
Broadband Service: CMA.
Fee: $39.95 installation; $40.95 monthly; $6.95 modem lease; $149.95 modem purchase.

Telephone Service
None
Miles of Plant: 18.0 (coaxial); None (fiber optic). Homes passed: 5,341. Homes passed includes Blackwell, Grape Creek, Robert Lee, Roscoe & Tuscola
Regional General Manager: Jerry Smith.
Ownership: NewWave Communications LLC (MSO).

MERTZON—Formerly served by Reach Broadband. No longer in operation. ICA: TX0810.

MEXIA—Northland Cable Television, 515 West Tyler St, Mexia, TX 76667. Phones: 254-562-2872; 800-792-3087. Fax: 254-562-6454. Web Site: http://www.yournorthland.com. Also serves Groesbeck, Lake Mexia & Tehuacana. ICA: TX0166.
TV Market Ranking: Outside TV Markets (Groesbeck, Lake Mexia, MEXIA, Tehuacana). Franchise award date: April 15, 1965. Franchise expiration date: N.A. Began: December 7, 1966.
Channel capacity: N.A. Channels available but not in use: N.A.

Basic Service
Subscribers: 1,026.
Programming (received off-air): KCEN-TV (Antenna TV, MeTV, MundoMax, NBC) Temple; KDFI (Bounce TV, Buzzr, Heroes & Icons, MNT, Movies!) Dallas; KDFW (FOX) Dallas; KERA-TV (PBS) Dallas; KTVT (CBS, Decades) Fort Worth; KTXA (IND, MeTV) Fort Worth; KWKT-TV (Estrella TV, FOX, MNT) Waco; KWTX-TV (CBS, CW) Waco; KXAS-TV (COZI TV, NBC) Fort Worth; KXXV (ABC, TMO) Waco; WFAA (ABC) Dallas; allband FM.
Programming (via satellite): A&E; Animal Planet; BET; Cartoon Network; CNBC; CNN; C-SPAN; Discovery Channel; ESPN; Food Network; Fox Deportes; Fox News Channel; FOX Sports Southwest; Great American Country; Hallmark Channel; HGTV; History; HLN; National Geographic Channel; Outdoor Channel; Pop; QVC; TBS; Telemundo; The Weather Channel; TLC; TNT; Travel Channel; Trinity Broadcasting Network (TBN); Univision Studios; USA Network.
Fee: $75.00 installation; $47.64 monthly.

Expanded Basic Service 1
Subscribers: N.A.
Programming (via satellite): Comedy Central; E! HD; ESPN2; FXM; Lifetime; MTV; Nickelodeon; Spike TV; Syfy; Turner Classic Movies.
Fee: $49.99 monthly.

Digital Basic Service
Subscribers: N.A.
Programming (via satellite): BBC America; Bloomberg Television; Bravo; Discovery Life Channel; DMX Music; Fox Sports 1; Golf Channel; GSN; IFC; NBCSN; WE tv.
Fee: $54.99 monthly.

Pay Service 1
Pay Units: 300.
Programming (via satellite): HBO.
Fee: $35.00 installation; $14.00 monthly.

Pay Service 2
Pay Units: 90.
Programming (via satellite): Showtime.
Fee: $35.00 installation; $10.00 monthly.

Pay Service 3
Pay Units: 250.
Programming (via satellite): Starz; Starz Encore.
Fee: $35.00 installation; $10.00 monthly.

Digital Pay Service 1
Pay Units: 70.
Programming (via satellite): Cinemax (multiplexed); HBO (multiplexed); Showtime (multiplexed); Starz (multiplexed); Starz Encore (multiplexed); Sundance TV.
Fee: $10.00 monthly (each).

Video-On-Demand: No

Pay-Per-View
iN DEMAND (delivered digitally); Sports PPV (delivered digitally).

Internet Service
Operational: Yes.
Fee: $42.99 monthly.

Telephone Service
Analog: Not Operational
Digital: Operational
Fee: $29.99 monthly
Miles of Plant: 115.0 (coaxial); 19.0 (fiber optic). Homes passed: 6,800.
Executive Vice President: Richard I. Clark. General Manager: Brent Richey. Chief Technician: Joe Lopez. Office Manager: Pamela Elliott.
Ownership: Northland Communications Corp. (MSO).

MIAMI—Formerly served by Elk River TV Cable Co. No longer in operation. ICA: TX0459.

MIDLAND—Suddenlink Communications, 2530 South Midkiff Rd, Midland, TX 79701. Phone: 314-315-9400. Web Site: http://www.suddenlink.com. Also serves Midland County (portions). ICA: TX0024.
TV Market Ranking: Below 100 (MIDLAND, Midland County (portions)). Franchise award date: N.A. Franchise expiration date: N.A. Began: October 19, 1968.
Channel capacity: 54 (operating 2-way). Channels available but not in use: N.A.

Basic Service
Subscribers: 15,298. Commercial subscribers: 1,610.
Programming (received off-air): KMID (ABC) Midland; KMLM-DT (GLC) Odessa; KOSA-TV (CBS, MNT) Odessa; KPBT-TV (PBS) Odessa; KPEJ-TV (FOX) Odessa; KTLE-LP (TMO) Odessa; KUPB (UNV) Midland; KWES-TV (CW, NBC, TMO) Odessa; 9 FMs.
Programming (via satellite): C-SPAN; C-SPAN 2; ION Television; Pop; QVC; TBS; The Weather Channel; WGN America.
Fee: $40.00 installation; $33.94 monthly.

Expanded Basic Service 1
Subscribers: 14,254.
Programming (via satellite): A&E; AMC; Animal Planet; BET; Bravo; Cartoon Network; CMT; CNBC; CNN; Comedy Central; Discovery Channel; Disney Channel; E! HD; ESPN; ESPN2; EWTN Global Catholic Network; Food Network; Fox News Channel; FOX Sports Southwest; Freeform; FX; GSN; Hallmark Channel; HGTV; History; HLN; Lifetime; MoviePlex; MSNBC; MTV; MTV2; NBC Universo; NBCSN; Nickelodeon; Spike TV; Syfy; TLC; TNT; Travel Channel; Turner Classic Movies; TV Land; USA Network; VH1.
Fee: $15.00 installation; $39.99 monthly.

Digital Basic Service
Subscribers: N.A.
Programming (via satellite): BBC America; Bloomberg Television; Cooking Channel; Discovery Channel; Disney XD; DIY Network; ESPN; ESPN Classic; ESPNews; EVINE Live; EWTN Global Catholic Network; Fox Sports 2; FSN Digital Atlantic; FSN Digital Central; FSN Digital Pacific; Fuse; FYI; Golf Channel; Great American Country; History International; HITS (Headend In The Sky); IFC; iN DEMAND; LMN; National Geographic Channel; NBA TV; Nick Jr.; Nicktoons; Outdoor Channel; Oxygen; Starz Encore; Sundance TV; TeenNick; Tennis Channel; Trinity Broadcasting Network (TBN); truTV; Universal HD; UP; WAM! America's Kidz Network.
Fee: $14.95 monthly.

Pay Service 1
Pay Units: N.A.
Programming (via satellite): Cinemax; HBO; Showtime; Starz.
Fee: $15.00 installation; $8.95 monthly (Cinemax), $9.95 monthly (Showtime), $10.95 monthly (TMC), $11.95 monthly (HBO).

Digital Pay Service 1
Pay Units: 14,563.
Programming (via satellite): Cinemax (multiplexed); Flix; HBO; MC; Showtime (multiplexed); Starz; The Movie Channel (multiplexed).
Fee: $10.00 monthly (each).

Video-On-Demand: No

Pay-Per-View
iN DEMAND (delivered digitally); NBA TV (delivered digitally); Sports PPV (delivered digitally); Adult (delivered digitally).

Internet Service
Operational: Yes.
Subscribers: 24,210.
Broadband Service: Suddenlink High Speed Internet.
Fee: $49.95 installation; $24.95 monthly; $15.00 modem lease; $249.95 modem purchase.

Telephone Service
Digital: Operational
Subscribers: 10,528.
Fee: $48.95 monthly
Miles of Plant: 1,651.0 (coaxial); 309.0 (fiber optic). Homes passed: 72,174.
Senior Vice President, Corporate Finance: Michael Pflantz. Vice President, Accounting: Sabrina Warr. Regional Manager: Bill Flowers. Area Manager: Chris Christiansen.
Ownership: Cequel Communications Holdings I LLC (MSO).

2017 Edition   D-761

Texas—Cable Systems

MIDLOTHIAN—Charter Communications, 5227 FM 813, Waxahachie, TX 75165. Phones: 636-207-5100 (Corporate office); 972-938-9288. Web Site: http://www.charter.com. Also serves Alma, Ellis County (portions), Ennis, Garrett, Glenn Heights, Oak Leaf, Ovilla, Palmer, Pecan Hill, Red Oak & Waxahachie. ICA: TX0122.
TV Market Ranking: 12 (Ellis County (portions), Ennis, Garrett, Glenn Heights, MIDLOTHIAN, Oak Leaf, Ovilla, Ovilla, Palmer, Pecan Hill, Red Oak, Waxahachie); Outside TV Markets (Alma). Franchise award date: N.A. Franchise expiration date: N.A. Began: February 1, 1982.
Channel capacity: 71 (operating 2-way). Channels available but not in use: N.A.
Digital Basic Service
Subscribers: 2,448. Commercial subscribers: 90.
Programming (via satellite): BBC America; Bloomberg Television; Discovery Digital Networks; DIY Network; ESPN Classic; Fuse; FXM; FYI; Great American Country; History International; IFC; LMN; MC; Nick 2; Nick Jr.; Nicktoons; Sundance TV; TeenNick; WE tv.
Fee: $26.99 monthly.
Digital Expanded Basic Service
Subscribers: N.A.
Programming (via satellite): A&E; AMC; BET; CMT; CNN; Discovery Channel; Disney Channel; Disney XD; E! HD; ESPN; ESPN2; Fox News Channel; FOX Sports Southwest; Freeform; HLN; Lifetime; MTV; Nickelodeon; Spike TV; TLC.
Fee: $48.99 monthly.
Digital Expanded Basic Service 2
Subscribers: N.A.
Programming (via satellite): ESPNews; Fox Sports 2; FSN Digital Atlantic; FSN Digital Central; FSN Digital Pacific; HITS (Headend In The Sky); NFL Network.
Digital Pay Service 1
Pay Units: N.A.
Programming (via satellite): Cinemax (multiplexed); HBO (multiplexed); Showtime (multiplexed); Starz (multiplexed); Starz Encore (multiplexed); The Movie Channel (multiplexed).
Video-On-Demand: No
Pay-Per-View
iN DEMAND (delivered digitally); ETC (delivered digitally); The Erotic Network (delivered digitally); Pleasure (delivered digitally); Playboy TV (delivered digitally); Fresh (delivered digitally); Shorteez (delivered digitally).
Internet Service
Operational: Yes.
Broadband Service: Charter Internet.
Fee: $29.99 monthly.
Telephone Service
None
Miles of Plant: 8,962.0 (coaxial); 2,479.0 (fiber optic). Homes passed: 513,990.
Vice President & General Manager: Wayne Cramp. Marketing Director: Kathleen Griffin. Technical Operations Director: John Linton. Accounting Director: David Sovanski. Assistant Controller: Brent Trask. Technical Supervisor: Daryl Gross.
Ownership: Charter Communications Inc. (MSO).

MIDWAY—Formerly served by Almega Cable. No longer in operation. ICA: TX0675.

MILES—Formerly served by Allegiance Communications. No longer in operation. ICA: TX0963.

MILLSAP—Formerly served by Mallard Cablevision. No longer in operation. ICA: TX0523.

MINEOLA—Suddenlink Communications, 403 West Broad St, Mineola, TX 75773-2066. Phone: 314-315-9400. Fax: 903-569-2662. Web Site: http://www.suddenlink.com. Also serves Grand Saline, Hideaway, Lindale, Quitman, Smith County, Van Zandt County & Wood County. ICA: TX0812.
TV Market Ranking: Below 100 (Grand Saline, Hideaway, Lindale, MINEOLA, Quitman, Smith County (portions), Van Zandt County (portions), Wood County (portions)); Outside TV Markets (Smith County (portions), Van Zandt County (portions), Wood County (portions)). Franchise award date: N.A. Franchise expiration date: N.A. Began: January 1, 1963.
Channel capacity: 22 (operating 2-way). Channels available but not in use: N.A.
Basic Service
Subscribers: 5,302. Commercial subscribers: 388.
Programming (received off-air): KCEB (CW, MundoMax) Longview; KDFW (FOX) Dallas; KERA-TV (PBS) Dallas; KETK-TV (Estrella TV, NBC) Jacksonville; KFXK-TV (FOX) Longview; KLPN-LD (MNT) Longview; KLTV (ABC, Bounce TV, TMO) Tyler; KTXA (IND, MeTV) Fort Worth; KXAS-TV (COZI TV, NBC) Fort Worth; KXTX-TV (TMO) Dallas; KYTX (CBS, COZI TV, CW) Nacogdoches; WFAA (ABC) Dallas; allband FM.
Programming (via satellite): C-SPAN; C-SPAN 2; Pop; QVC; TBS; The Weather Channel; WGN America.
Fee: $49.95 installation; $32.24 monthly.
Expanded Basic Service 1
Subscribers: 5,000.
Programming (via satellite): A&E; AMC; Animal Planet; BET; Cartoon Network; CNBC; CNN; Comedy Central; Discovery Channel; Disney Channel; ESPN; ESPN2; Food Network; Fox News Channel; FOX Sports Southwest; Freeform; FX; Golf Channel; Great American Country; HGTV; History; HLN; INSP; Lifetime; MTV; Nickelodeon; Spike TV; Syfy; TLC; TNT; Trinity Broadcasting Network (TBN); Turner Classic Movies; TV Land; Univision Studios; USA Network; VH1.
Fee: $10.00 installation; $11.50 monthly.
Digital Basic Service
Subscribers: N.A.
Programming (via satellite): A&E HD; AXS TV; BBC America; Bloomberg Television; Boomerang; CBS Sports Network; CMT; Cooking Channel; Destination America; Discovery Kids Channel; Disney XD; DIY Network; ESPN Classic; ESPN HD; ESPNews; ESPNU; FamilyNet; Food Network HD; Fox Sports 1; Fox Sports 2; Fuse; FYI; GSN; Hallmark Channel; HD Theater; HGTV HD; History International; Investigation Discovery; LMN; MC; MTV Classic; MTV Hits; MTV2; National Geographic Channel; National Geographic Channel HD; NBCSN; Nick Jr.; Nicktoons; Outdoor Channel; OWN: Oprah Winfrey Network; Oxygen; Science Channel; Starz Encore (multiplexed); Sundance TV; TeenNick; Tennis Channel; TNT HD; truTV; Universal HD; UP; WE tv; Weatherscan.
Digital Pay Service 1
Pay Units: N.A.
Programming (via satellite): Cinemax (multiplexed); HBO (multiplexed); HBO HD; Showtime (multiplexed); Showtime HD; Starz (multiplexed); Starz HD; The Movie Channel.
Video-On-Demand: No
Pay-Per-View
iN DEMAND (delivered digitally); Playboy TV (delivered digitally); Fresh (delivered digitally).
Internet Service
Operational: Yes.
Subscribers: 5,426.
Broadband Service: Suddenlink High Speed Internet.
Fee: $49.95 installation; $38.95 monthly.
Telephone Service
Digital: Operational
Subscribers: 3,418.
Miles of Plant: 267.0 (coaxial); 103.0 (fiber optic). Homes passed: 13,116.
Senior Vice President, Corporate Finance: Michael Pflantz. Vice President, Accounting: Sabrina Warr. General Manager: Clyde Bowling. Chief Technician: Glen Lovette.
Ownership: Cequel Communications Holdings I LLC (MSO).

MINERAL WELLS—Suddenlink Communications, 103 Southeast 9th Ave, Mineral Wells, TX 76067. Phones: 888-822-5151 (Customer service); 940-325-9586 (Administrative office); 314-315-9400. Web Site: http://www.suddenlink.com. Also serves Palo Pinto County (portions). ICA: TX0106.
TV Market Ranking: Below 100 (Palo Pinto County (portions)); Outside TV Markets (MINERAL WELLS, Palo Pinto County (portions)). Franchise award date: N.A. Franchise expiration date: N.A. Began: June 1, 1951.
Channel capacity: N.A. Channels available but not in use: N.A.
Basic Service
Subscribers: 2,467. Commercial subscribers: 198.
Programming (received off-air): KDAF (Antenna TV, CW, This TV) Dallas; KDFI (Bounce TV, Buzzr, Heroes & Icons, MNT, Movies!) Dallas; KDFW (FOX) Dallas; KDTN (Daystar TV, ETV) Denton; KDTX-TV (TBN) Dallas; KERA-TV (PBS) Dallas; KNHL (IND) Hastings; KPXD-TV (ION) Arlington; KSTR-DT (getTV, UniMas) Irving; KTVT (CBS, Decades) Fort Worth; KTXA (IND, MeTV) Fort Worth; KUVN-DT (UNV) Garland; KXAS-TV (COZI TV, NBC) Fort Worth; KXTX-TV (TMO) Dallas; WFAA (ABC) Dallas; 13 FMs.
Programming (via satellite): C-SPAN; Jewelry Television; TBS; The Weather Channel; WGN America.
Fee: $38.24 installation; $34.24 monthly; $2.00 converter.
Expanded Basic Service 1
Subscribers: N.A.
Programming (via satellite): A&E; AMC; Animal Planet; BET; Bravo; Cartoon Network; CMT; CNBC; CNN; Comedy Central; C-SPAN 2; Discovery Channel; Disney Channel; E! HD; ESPN; ESPN Classic; ESPN2; EWTN Global Catholic Network; Food Network; Fox News Channel; Fox Sports 1; FOX Sports Southwest; Freeform; FX; Great American Country; HGTV; History; HLN; INSP; Lifetime; LMN; MSNBC; MTV; NBCSN; Nickelodeon; Outdoor Channel; OWN: Oprah Winfrey Network; Oxygen; Pop; QVC; Spike TV; TLC; TNT; Travel Channel; truTV; TV Land; Univision; USA Network; VH1.
Fee: $13.28 monthly.
Digital Basic Service
Subscribers: N.A.
Programming (via satellite): A&E HD; AXS TV; Bandamax; BBC America; Bloomberg Television; CBS Sports Network; Cine Mexicano; Cinelatino; CMT; CNN en Espanol; Cooking Channel; De Pelicula; De Pelicula Clasico; Destination America; Discovery Kids Channel; Disney XD; DIY Network; Enlace USA; ESPN Deportes; ESPN HD; ESPN2 HD; ESPNews; ESPNU; Food Network HD; Fox Deportes; Fox Sports 2; Fuse; FYI; Golf Channel; GSN; Hallmark Channel; HD Theater; HGTV HD; History en Espanol; History HD; History International; IFC; Investigation Discovery; MC; MTV Classic; MTV Hits; MTV2; Nat Geo WILD; National Geographic Channel; National Geographic Channel HD; NBC Universo; Nick Jr.; Nicktoons; NickToons en Espanol; Ritmoson; Science Channel; Starz Encore (multiplexed); Sundance TV; Sur; Syfy; TeenNick; Telehit; TNT HD; Toon Disney en Espanol; Tr3s; Trinity Broadcasting Network (TBN); Turner Classic Movies; ULTRA HDPlex; Universal HD; Univision; VideoRola; WE tv.
Pay Service 1
Pay Units: N.A.
Programming (via satellite): Starz.
Fee: $10.00 installation; $10.95 monthly.
Digital Pay Service 1
Pay Units: N.A.
Programming (via satellite): Cinemax (multiplexed); HBO (multiplexed); HBO HD; Showtime (multiplexed); Showtime HD; Starz (multiplexed); Starz HD; The Movie Channel (multiplexed).
Video-On-Demand: No
Pay-Per-View
iN DEMAND (delivered digitally); Fresh (delivered digitally); Playboy TV (delivered digitally).
Internet Service
Operational: Yes.
Broadband Service: Suddenlink High Speed Internet.
Fee: $49.95 installation; $24.95 monthly.
Telephone Service
Digital: Operational
Fee: $48.95 monthly
Miles of Plant: 120.0 (coaxial); None (fiber optic). Homes passed: 6,270.
Senior Vice President, Corporate Finance: Michael Pflantz. Vice President, Accounting: Sabrina Warr. General Manager: Raymond Greenwood. Chief Technician: Scott Wilber.
Ownership: Cequel Communications Holdings I LLC (MSO).

MONAHANS—Suddenlink Communications, 520 Maryville Centre Dr, Ste 300, St. Louis, MO 63141. Phones: 432-943-4335; 877-423-2743 (Customer service); 314-315-9400. Web Site: http://www.suddenlink.com. Also serves Thorntonville & Ward County. ICA: TX0134.
TV Market Ranking: Below 100 (Ward County (portions)); Outside TV Markets (MONAHANS, Thorntonville, Ward County (portions)). Franchise award date: July 24, 1990. Franchise expiration date: N.A. Began: December 1, 1972.
Channel capacity: N.A. Channels available but not in use: N.A.
Basic Service
Subscribers: 591.
Programming (received off-air): KMID (ABC) Midland; KMLM-DT (GLC) Odessa; KOSA-TV (CBS, MNT) Odessa; KPBT-TV (PBS) Odessa; KPEJ-TV (FOX) Odessa; KTLE-LP (TMO) Odessa; KUPB (UNV) Midland; KWES-TV (CW, NBC, TMO) Odessa; 6 FMs.
Fee: $28.45 monthly.

Cable Systems—Texas

Expanded Basic Service 1
Subscribers: N.A.
Programming (via satellite): A&E; AMC; Animal Planet; BET; Cartoon Network; CNBC; CNN; Comedy Central; C-SPAN; CW PLUS; Discovery Channel; Disney Channel; E! HD; ESPN; ESPN2; EWTN Global Catholic Network; Food Network; Fox News Channel; FOX Sports Southwest; Freeform; FX; Great American Country; HGTV; History; HLN; Lifetime; MSNBC; MTV; National Geographic Channel; Nickelodeon; Pop; QVC; Spike TV; Syfy; TBS; The Weather Channel; TLC; TNT; Travel Channel; Turner Classic Movies; TV Land; Univision; USA Network; VH1.
Fee: $24.00 monthly.

Digital Basic Service
Subscribers: N.A.
Programming (via satellite): 52MX; BBC America; Cine Mexicano; Cinelatino; Cloo; CMT; CNN en Espanol; Destination America; Discovery Kids Channel; Disney XD; DMX Music; ESPN Classic; ESPN Deportes; ESPNews; Fox Deportes; Fox Sports 1; Fuse; FYI; Golf Channel; GSN; History en Espanol; History International; IFC; Investigation Discovery; LMN; MTV Classic; MTV2; NBCSN; Nick Jr.; OWN: Oprah Winfrey Network; Science Channel; TeenNick; Tr3s; ViendoMovies; WE tv.
Fee: $3.99 monthly.

Pay Service 1
Pay Units: N.A.
Programming (via satellite): Cinemax; HBO; Showtime; The Movie Channel.
Fee: $15.00 installation; $5.95 monthly (TMC), $9.95 monthly (Cinemax or Showtime), $10.95 monthly (HBO).

Digital Pay Service 1
Pay Units: N.A.
Programming (via satellite): Cinemax (multiplexed); HBO (multiplexed); Showtime (multiplexed); Starz; Starz Encore (multiplexed); The Movie Channel (multiplexed).

Video-On-Demand: No

Pay-Per-View
iN DEMAND (delivered digitally); Playboy TV (delivered digitally); Club Jenna (delivered digitally).

Internet Service
Operational: Yes. Began: June 1, 2003.
Broadband Service: Suddenlink High Speed Internet.
Fee: $45.95 installation; $29.95 monthly.

Telephone Service
Digital: Operational
Fee: $44.95 monthly
Miles of Plant: 68.0 (coaxial); None (fiber optic). Homes passed: 4,682.
Vice President, Corporate Finance: Michael Pflantz. Regional Manager: Todd Cruthird. Marketing Director: Beverly Gambell.
Ownership: Cequel Communications Holdings I LLC (MSO).

MONT BELVIEU—Suddenlink Communications, 520 Maryville Centre Dr, Ste 300, St. Louis, MO 63141. Phones: 877-423-2743 (Customer service); 314-315-9400. Web Site: http://www.suddenlink.com. Also serves Baytown, Chambers County (western portion), Harris County (southeastern portion), Liberty County (southeastern portion) & Old River-Winfree. ICA: TX0156.
TV Market Ranking: 15 (Baytown, Harris County (southeastern portion), MONT BELVIEU, Old River-Winfree); 15,88 (Chambers County (western portion) (portions), Liberty County (southeastern portion) (portions)); Below 100 (Liberty County (southeastern portion) (portions)).
Channel capacity: 62 (operating 2-way). Channels available but not in use: N.A.

Basic Service
Subscribers: 658.
Programming (received off-air): KETH-TV (TBN) Houston; KFTH-DT (getTV, Uni-Mas) Alvin; KHOU (Bounce TV, CBS) Houston; KIAH (Antenna TV, CW) Houston; KLTJ (Daystar TV, ETV) Galveston; KPRC-TV (NBC, This TV) Houston; KRIV (FOX) Houston; KTBU (IND) Conroe; KTMD (TMO) Galveston; KTRK-TV (ABC, Live Well Network) Houston; KTXH (Buzzr, MNT, Movies!) Houston; KUBE-TV (COZI TV, MeTV) Baytown; KUHT (PBS) Houston; KXLN-DT (UNV) Rosenberg; KYAZ (Azteca America, IND) Katy; KZJL (Estrella TV) Houston.
Programming (via satellite): C-SPAN; Jewelry Television.
Fee: $28.45 monthly; $2.15 converter.

Expanded Basic Service 1
Subscribers: N.A.
Programming (via satellite): A&E; Animal Planet; BET; Cartoon Network; CNBC; CNN; Discovery Channel; Disney Channel; E! HD; ESPN; ESPN2; Fox News Channel; Fox Sports 1; FOX Sports Southwest; Freeform; FX; Great American Country; HGTV; HLN; Lifetime; MTV; National Geographic Channel; Nickelodeon; QVC; Spike TV; Syfy; TBS; The Weather Channel; TLC; TNT; Turner Classic Movies; TV Land; USA Network; VH1.
Fee: $23.00 monthly.

Digital Basic Service
Subscribers: N.A.
Programming (via satellite): BBC America; Bloomberg Television; Cloo; Discovery Kids Channel; Disney XD; DMX Music; Fuse; FYI; History; History International; IFC; LMN; MTV2; Nick Jr.; Nicktoons; OWN: Oprah Winfrey Network; Science Channel; TeenNick; WE tv.
Fee: $3.99 monthly.

Digital Expanded Basic Service
Subscribers: N.A.
Programming (via satellite): ESPN Classic; ESPNews; Golf Channel; GSN; NBCSN; Outdoor Channel.

Pay Service 1
Pay Units: N.A.
Programming (via satellite): Cinemax; HBO; Showtime; The Movie Channel.
Fee: $12.00 monthly (Cinemax or HBO), $12.95 monthly (Showtime/TMC).

Digital Pay Service 1
Pay Units: N.A.
Programming (via satellite): Cinemax (multiplexed); HBO (multiplexed); Showtime (multiplexed); Starz; Starz Encore (multiplexed); The Movie Channel (multiplexed).

Video-On-Demand: No

Pay-Per-View
iN DEMAND (delivered digitally); Playboy TV (delivered digitally); Fresh (delivered digitally).

Internet Service
Operational: Yes. Began: July 14, 2003.
Broadband Service: Suddenlink High Speed Internet.
Fee: $45.95 installation; $29.95 monthly.

Telephone Service
Digital: Operational
Fee: $44.95 monthly
Miles of Plant: 139.0 (coaxial); None (fiber optic). Homes passed: 3,932.
Vice President, Corporate Finance: Michael Pflantz. General Manager: Mike Burns. Chief Technician: Mayla Zubeck.
Ownership: Cequel Communications Holdings I LLC (MSO).

MONTAGUE—Formerly served by Cebridge Connections. No longer in operation. ICA: TX0700.

MONTGOMERY COUNTY (portions)—Charter Communications, 2455 FM 2920, Spring, TX 77388. Phones: 314-543-2236; 636-207-5100 (Corporate office); 817-810-9171; 817-298-3600. Web Site: http://www.charter.com. Also serves Harris County (northern portion), Oak Ridge North, Rayford Forest, Shenandoah, Spring & Woodloch. ICA: TX0044.
TV Market Ranking: 15 (Harris County (northern portion), MONTGOMERY COUNTY (PORTIONS), Oak Ridge North, Rayford Forest, Shenandoah, Spring, Woodloch). Franchise award date: N.A. Franchise expiration date: N.A. Began: January 1, 1979.
Channel capacity: 73 (operating 2-way). Channels available but not in use: N.A.

Digital Basic Service
Subscribers: 3,961.
Programming (via satellite): BBC America; Bloomberg Television; Destination America; Discovery Kids Channel; DIY Network; ESPNews; Fox Sports 2; FXM; FYI; Golf Channel; History International; IFC; Investigation Discovery; LMN; MC; Nick Jr.; OWN: Oprah Winfrey Network; Sundance TV; Turner Classic Movies.
Fee: $49.99 installation; $26.99 monthly.

Digital Expanded Basic Service
Subscribers: N.A.
Programming (via satellite): A&E; AMC; Animal Planet; BET; Bravo; Cartoon Network; CNBC; CNN; Comedy Central; C-SPAN; C-SPAN 2; Discovery Channel; Discovery Life Channel; Disney Channel; Disney XD; E! HD; ESPN Classic; ESPN2; Food Network; Fox News Channel; Fox Sports 1; FOX Sports Southwest; Freeform; FX; Great American Country; GSN; Hallmark Channel; HGTV; History; HLN; Lifetime; MSNBC; MTV; National Geographic Channel; NBCSN; Nickelodeon; Oxygen; Spike TV; Syfy; The Weather Channel; TLC; TNT; Travel Channel; truTV; TV Land; Univision; USA Network; VH1; WE tv.
Fee: $20.97 installation; $15.65 monthly.

Pay Service 1
Pay Units: N.A.
Programming (via satellite): Flix; Showtime (multiplexed); Starz Encore (multiplexed); The Movie Channel (multiplexed).
Fee: $8.00 monthly.

Digital Pay Service 1
Pay Units: N.A.
Programming (via satellite): Cinemax; HBO; Starz (multiplexed).

Video-On-Demand: No

Internet Service
Operational: Yes. Began: January 1, 2002.
Subscribers: 2,681.
Broadband Service: Charter Internet.
Fee: $29.99 monthly.

Telephone Service
None
Miles of Plant: 1,093.0 (coaxial); 194.0 (fiber optic). Homes passed: 44,040.
Vice President & General Manager: Wayne Cramp. Marketing Director: Kathleen Griffin. Technical Operations Director: John Linton. Accounting Director: David Sovanski. Technical Operations Manager: Robert Hurd.
Ownership: Charter Communications Inc. (MSO).

MONTGOMERY COUNTY (unincorporated areas)—Formerly served by Versalink Media. No longer in operation. ICA: TX0967.

MOODY—Grande Communications, 401 Carlson Circle, San Marcos, TX 78666. Phones: 855-286-6666; 512-878-4600. Web Site: http://mygrande.com. ICA: TX0501.
TV Market Ranking: Below 100 (MOODY). Franchise award date: N.A. Franchise expiration date: N.A. Began: April 1, 1981.
Channel capacity: N.A. Channels available but not in use: N.A.

Basic Service
Subscribers: 99.
Programming (received off-air): KCEN-TV (Antenna TV, MeTV, MundoMax, NBC) Temple; KEYE-TV (CBS, TMO) Austin; KNCT (PBS) Belton; KNVA (CW, Grit, TheCoolTV) Austin; KTBC (Buzzr, FOX, Movies!) Austin; KWKT-TV (Estrella TV, FOX, MNT) Waco; KWTX-TV (CBS, CW) Waco; KXAN-TV (COZI TV, NBC) Austin; KXXV (ABC, TMO) Waco; WFAA (ABC) Dallas.
Programming (via satellite): Univision Studios; WGN America.
Fee: $25.00 installation; $10.95 monthly.

Expanded Basic Service 1
Subscribers: N.A.
Programming (via satellite): A&E; AMC; Animal Planet; BET; Cartoon Network; CMT; CNBC; CNN; Comedy Central; C-SPAN; C-SPAN 2; Discovery Channel; Disney Channel; E! HD; ESPN; ESPN2; Food Network; Fox News Channel; FOX Sports Southwest; Freeform; FX; Hallmark Channel; HGTV; History; HLN; ION Television; Lifetime; MSNBC; MTV; National Geographic Channel; Nickelodeon; QVC; Spike TV; Syfy; TBS; The Weather Channel; TLC; TNT; Travel Channel; Trinity Broadcasting Network (TBN); Turner Classic Movies; TV Land; USA Network; VH1.
Fee: $17.00 monthly.

Digital Basic Service
Subscribers: N.A.
Programming (via satellite): BBC America; Bloomberg Television; Bravo; Daystar TV Network; Discovery Digital Networks; Disney XD; DMX Music; ESPN Classic; ESPNews; EVINE Live; Fox Sports 1; FSN Digital Atlantic; FSN Digital Central; FSN Digital Pacific; Fuse; FXM; FYI; Golf Channel; Great American Country; GSN; HGTV; History; History International; IFC; International Television (ITV); LMN; National Geographic Channel; NBCSN; Outdoor Channel; Ovation; Syfy; The Word Network; Trinity Broadcasting Network (TBN); Turner Classic Movies; WE tv.
Fee: $15.00 installation; $49.00 monthly.

Pay Service 1
Pay Units: N.A.
Programming (via satellite): HBO; Showtime; The Movie Channel.
Fee: $11.00 monthly (HBO, Showtime or TMC), $13.50 monthly (Showtime/TMC), $19.50 monthly (HBO/TMC), $21.00 monthly (HBO/Showtime), $23.00 monthly (HBO/Showtime/TMC).

Digital Pay Service 1
Pay Units: N.A.
Programming (via satellite): Cinemax (multiplexed); HBO; Showtime (multiplexed); Starz (multiplexed); Starz Encore (multiplexed).

2017 Edition

D-763

Texas—Cable Systems

Fee: $7.00 monthly (Cinemax), $11.00 monthly (HBO, Showtime or Starz/Encore).
Video-On-Demand: No
Pay-Per-View
Hot Choice (delivered digitally); iN DEMAND (delivered digitally).
Internet Service
Operational: Yes. Began: December 31, 2004.
Broadband Service: VVM Internet Services.
Fee: $20.00 installation; $40.00 monthly.
Telephone Service
Digital: Planned
Miles of Plant: 10.0 (coaxial); None (fiber optic). Homes passed: 450.
Senior Vice President, Operations & General Manager: Matthew Rohre. Vice President, Marketing: Pete Drozdoff. Vice President, Technical Operations: Shane Schilling.
Ownership: Grande Communications Networks Inc. (MSO).

MORAN—Formerly served by Jayroc Cablevision. No longer in operation. ICA: TX0975.

MORGAN'S POINT RESORT—Grande Communications, 401 Carlson Circle, San Marcos, TX 78666. Phones: 855-286-6666; 512-878-4600. Web Site: http://mygrande.com. ICA: TX0814.
TV Market Ranking: Below 100 (MORGAN'S POINT RESORT).
Channel capacity: N.A. Channels available but not in use: N.A.
Basic Service
Subscribers: 992.
Programming (received off-air): KCEN-TV (Antenna TV, MeTV, MundoMax, NBC) Temple; KEYE-TV (CBS, TMO) Austin; KNCT (PBS) Belton; KNVA (CW, Grit, TheCoolTV) Austin; KTBC (Buzzr, FOX, Movies!) Austin; KWKT-TV (Estrella TV, FOX, MNT) Waco; KWTX-TV (CBS, CW) Waco; KXAN-TV (COZI TV, NBC) Austin; KXXV (ABC, TMO) Waco; WFAA (ABC) Dallas.
Programming (via satellite): Univision Studios; WGN America.
Fee: $25.00 installation; $10.95 monthly.
Expanded Basic Service 1
Subscribers: N.A.
Programming (via satellite): A&E; AMC; Animal Planet; BET; Cartoon Network; CMT; CNBC; CNN; Comedy Central; C-SPAN; C-SPAN 2; Discovery Channel; Disney Channel; E! HD; ESPN; ESPN2; Food Network; Fox News Channel; FOX Sports Southwest; Freeform; FX; Hallmark Channel; HGTV; History; HLN; ION Television; Lifetime; MSNBC; MTV; National Geographic Channel; Nickelodeon; QVC; Spike TV; Syfy; TBS; The Weather Channel; TLC; TNT; Travel Channel; Trinity Broadcasting Network (TBN); Turner Classic Movies; TV Land; USA Network; VH1.
Fee: $17.00 monthly.
Digital Basic Service
Subscribers: N.A.
Programming (via satellite): BBC America; Bloomberg Television; Bravo; Daystar TV Network; Discovery Digital Networks; Disney XD; DMX Music; ESPN Classic; ESPNews; EVINE Live; Fox Sports 1; FSN Digital Atlantic; FSN Digital Central; FSN Digital Pacific; Fuse; FXM; FYI; Golf Channel; Great American Country; GSN; HGTV; History; History International; IFC; International Television (ITV); LMN; National Geographic Channel; NBCSN; Outdoor Channel; Ovation; Syfy; The Word Network; Trinity Broadcasting Network (TBN); Turner Classic Movies; WE tv.
Fee: $15.00 installation; $49.00 monthly.
Pay Service 1
Pay Units: N.A.
Programming (via satellite): HBO; Showtime; The Movie Channel.
Fee: $11.00 monthly (HBO, Showtime or TMC), $13.50 monthly (Showtime/TMC), $19.50 monthly (HBO/TMC), $21.00 monthly (HBO/Showtime), $23.00 monthly (HBO/Showtime/TMC).
Digital Pay Service 1
Pay Units: N.A.
Programming (via satellite): Cinemax (multiplexed); HBO (multiplexed); Showtime (multiplexed); Starz (multiplexed); Starz Encore (multiplexed).
Fee: $7.00 monthly (Cinemax), $11.00 monthly (HBO, Showtime or Starz/Encore).
Video-On-Demand: No
Pay-Per-View
Hot Choice (delivered digitally); iN DEMAND (delivered digitally).
Internet Service
Operational: Yes. Began: December 31, 2004.
Subscribers: 298.
Broadband Service: VVM Internet Services.
Fee: $20.00 installation; $40.00 monthly.
Telephone Service
Digital: Planned
Miles of Plant: 10.0 (coaxial); None (fiber optic).
Senior Vice President, Operations & General Manager: Matthew Rohre. Vice President, Technical Operations: Shane Schilling. Vice President, Marketing: Pete Drozdoff.
Ownership: Grande Communications Networks Inc. (MSO).

MOSS BLUFF—Formerly served by Carrell Communications. No longer in operation. ICA: TX0474.

MOULTON—Formerly served by National Cable Inc. No longer in operation. ICA: TX0497.

MOUND—Formerly served by National Cable Inc. No longer in operation. ICA: TX0701.

MOUNT ENTERPRISE—Formerly served by Cebridge Connections. No longer in operation. ICA: TX0973.

MOUNT PLEASANT—Suddenlink Communications, PO Box 1236, Mount Pleasant, TX 75456. Phone: 314-315-9400. Fax: 903-572-5669. Web Site: http://www.suddenlink.com. Also serves Titus County (portions) & Winfield. ICA: TX0089.
TV Market Ranking: Outside TV Markets (MOUNT PLEASANT, Titus County (portions), Winfield). Franchise award date: N.A. Franchise expiration date: N.A. Began: October 1, 1968.
Channel capacity: N.A. Channels available but not in use: N.A.
Basic Service
Subscribers: 2,122. Commercial subscribers: 381.
Programming (received off-air): KCEB (CW, MundoMax) Longview; KLTS-TV (PBS) Shreveport; KLTV (ABC, Bounce TV, TMO) Tyler; KMSS-TV (FOX) Shreveport; KSHV-TV (MNT) Shreveport; KSLA (Bounce TV, CBS, Grit, This TV) Shreveport; KTAL-TV (NBC) Texarkana; KTBS-TV (ABC) Shreveport; KYTX (CBS, COZI TV, CW) Nacogdoches; 9 FMs.
Programming (via microwave): KERA-TV (PBS) Dallas; KXAS-TV (COZI TV, NBC) Fort Worth; WFAA (ABC) Dallas.
Programming (via satellite): C-SPAN; Discovery Channel; QVC; TBS; The Weather Channel; WGN America.
Fee: $40.00 installation; $35.24 monthly; $2.00 converter.
Expanded Basic Service 1
Subscribers: N.A.
Programming (via satellite): A&E; AMC; Animal Planet; BET; Bravo; Cartoon Network; CMT; CNBC; CNN; Comedy Central; C-SPAN 2; Disney Channel; E! HD; ESPN; ESPN2; EWTN Global Catholic Network; Food Network; Fox News Channel; Fox Sports 1; FOX Sports Southwest; Freeform; FX; Great American Country; HGTV; History; HLN; INSP; Jewelry Television; Lifetime; LMN; MSNBC; MTV; NBCSN; Nickelodeon; Outdoor Channel; Spike TV; Telemundo; TLC; TNT; Travel Channel; Trinity Broadcasting Network (TBN); truTV; Turner Classic Movies; TV Land; Univision; Univision Studios; USA Network; VH1.
Fee: $11.15 monthly.
Digital Basic Service
Subscribers: N.A.
Programming (via satellite): A&E HD; AXS TV; Bandamax; BBC America; Bloomberg Television; Boomerang; Cine Mexicano; Cinelatino; CMT; CNN en Espanol; Cooking Channel; Cox Sports Television; De Pelicula; De Pelicula Clasico; Destination America; Discovery Kids Channel; Disney XD; DIY Network; Enlace USA; ESPN Classic; ESPN Deportes; ESPN HD; ESPN2 HD; ESPNews; ESPNU; FamilyNet; Food Network HD; Fox Deportes; Fox Sports 2; Fuse; FYI; Golf Channel; GSN; Hallmark Channel; HD Theater; HGTV HD; History en Espanol; History International; IFC; Investigation Discovery; MC; MTV Classic; MTV Hits; MTV2; Nat Geo WILD; National Geographic Channel; National Geographic Channel HD; NBC Universo; Nick Jr.; Nicktoons; OWN: Oprah Winfrey Network; Oxygen; Ritmoson; Science Channel; Starz Encore (multiplexed); Sundance TV; Sur; TeenNick; Telehit; Telemundo; Tennis Channel; Tr3s; TV One; ULTRA HDPlex; UniMas; Universal HD; Univision; Univision Studios; UP; VideoRola; WE tv; Weatherscan.
Digital Pay Service 1
Pay Units: N.A.
Programming (via satellite): Cinemax (multiplexed); HBO (multiplexed); HBO HD; Showtime (multiplexed); Showtime HD; Starz (multiplexed); Starz HD; The Movie Channel (multiplexed).
Video-On-Demand: No
Pay-Per-View
iN DEMAND (delivered digitally); Fresh (delivered digitally); Shorteez (delivered digitally); Playboy TV (delivered digitally); Playboy en Espanol (delivered digitally).
Internet Service
Operational: Yes.
Broadband Service: Suddenlink High Speed Internet.
Fee: $49.95 installation; $24.95 monthly.
Telephone Service
Digital: Operational
Fee: $48.95 monthly
Miles of Plant: 89.0 (coaxial); None (fiber optic). Homes passed: 8,218.
Senior Vice President, Corporate Finance: Michael Pflantz. Vice President, Accounting: Sabrina Warr. General Manager & Chief Technician: Ron Eubanks.
Ownership: Cequel Communications Holdings I LLC (MSO).

MOUNT VERNON—Suddenlink Communications, 1506 Shadywood Ln, PO Box 1236, Mount Pleasant, TX 75455. Phone: 314-315-9400. Fax: 903-572-5669. Web Site: http://www.suddenlink.com. Also serves Franklin County (portions). ICA: TX0311.
TV Market Ranking: Outside TV Markets (Franklin County (portions), MOUNT VERNON). Franchise award date: N.A. Franchise expiration date: N.A. Began: August 1, 1968.
Channel capacity: 35 (operating 2-way). Channels available but not in use: N.A.
Basic Service
Subscribers: 577. Commercial subscribers: 76.
Programming (received off-air): KCEB (CW, MundoMax) Longview; KETK-TV (Estrella TV, NBC) Jacksonville; KFXK-TV (FOX) Longview; KLTV (ABC, Bounce TV, TMO) Tyler; KSHV-TV (MNT) Shreveport; KSLA (Bounce TV, CBS, Grit, This TV) Shreveport; KTBS-TV (ABC) Shreveport; KYTX (CBS, COZI TV, CW) Nacogdoches.
Programming (via microwave): KERA-TV (PBS) Dallas; KXAS-TV (COZI TV, NBC) Fort Worth; WFAA (ABC) Dallas.
Programming (via satellite): C-SPAN; HLN; QVC; TBS; The Weather Channel; WGN America.
Fee: $40.00 installation; $35.24 monthly.
Expanded Basic Service 1
Subscribers: N.A.
Programming (via satellite): A&E; AMC; Animal Planet; BET; Bravo; Cartoon Network; CMT; CNBC; CNN; Comedy Central; C-SPAN 2; Discovery Channel; Disney Channel; E! HD; ESPN; ESPN2; EWTN Global Catholic Network; Food Network; Fox News Channel; Fox Sports 1; FOX Sports Southwest; Freeform; FX; Great American Country; HGTV; History; INSP; Jewelry Television; Lifetime; LMN; MSNBC; MTV; NBCSN; Nickelodeon; Outdoor Channel; Spike TV; Syfy; Telemundo; TLC; TNT; Travel Channel; Trinity Broadcasting Network (TBN); truTV; Turner Classic Movies; TV Land; Univision; Univision Studios; USA Network; VH1.
Fee: $11.63 monthly.
Digital Basic Service
Subscribers: N.A.
Programming (via satellite): A&E HD; AXS TV; Bandamax; BBC America; Bloomberg Television; CBS Sports Network; Cine Mexicano; Cinelatino; CMT; CNN en Espanol; Cooking Channel; Cox Sports Television; De Pelicula; De Pelicula Clasico; Destination America; Discovery Kids Channel; Disney XD; DIY Network; Enlace USA; ESPN Classic; ESPN Deportes; ESPN HD; ESPN2 HD; ESPNews; ESPNU; FamilyNet; Food Network HD; Fox Deportes; Fox Sports 2; Fuse; FYI; Golf Channel; GSN; Hallmark Channel; HD Theater; HGTV HD; History en Espanol; History International; IFC; Investigation Discovery; MC; MTV Classic; MTV Hits; MTV2; Nat Geo WILD; National Geographic Channel; National Geographic Channel HD; NBC Universo; Nick Jr.; Nicktoons; OWN: Oprah Winfrey Network; Oxygen; Ritmoson; Science Channel; Starz Encore (multiplexed); Sundance TV; Sur; TeenNick; Telehit; Telemundo; Tennis Channel; TNT HD; Toon Disney en Espanol; Tr3s; TV One; ULTRA HDPlex; UniMas; Universal HD; Univision; Univision Studios; UP; VideoRola; WE tv; Weatherscan.
Digital Pay Service 1
Pay Units: N.A.
Programming (via satellite): Cinemax (multiplexed); HBO (multiplexed); HBO HD; HBO Latino; Showtime (multiplexed); Showtime

Cable Systems—Texas

HD; Starz (multiplexed); Starz HD; The Movie Channel (multiplexed).
Video-On-Demand: No
Pay-Per-View
iN DEMAND (delivered digitally); Fresh (delivered digitally); Shorteez (delivered digitally); Playboy TV (delivered digitally); Playboy en Espanol (delivered digitally).
Internet Service
Operational: Yes.
Broadband Service: Suddenlink High Speed Internet.
Fee: $49.95 installation; $29.95 monthly.
Telephone Service
None
Miles of Plant: 19.0 (coaxial); None (fiber optic). Homes passed: 1,215.
Senior Vice President, Corporate Finance: Michael Pflantz. Vice President, Accounting: Sabrina Warr. General Manager & Chief Technician: Ron Eubanks.
Ownership: Cequel Communications Holdings I LLC (MSO).

MULESHOE—Reach Broadband, PO Box 507, Arp, TX 75750. Phones: 903-859-3789; 800-687-1258. Web Site: http://www.reachbroadband.net. Also serves Amherst, Earth & Sudan. ICA: TX0164.
TV Market Ranking: Below 100 (MULESHOE); Outside TV Markets (Amherst, Earth, Sudan). Franchise award date: January 1, 1959. Franchise expiration date: N.A. Began: February 1, 1959.
Channel capacity: N.A. Channels available but not in use: N.A.
Basic Service
Subscribers: 265.
Programming (received off-air): KAMC (ABC, Bounce TV) Lubbock; KCBD (NBC, This TV) Lubbock; KENW (PBS) Portales; KJTV-TV (FOX) Lubbock; KLBK-TV (CBS) Lubbock; KPTB-DT (GLC) Lubbock; KVII-TV (ABC, CW) Amarillo; allband FM.
Programming (via satellite): A&E; AMC; Animal Planet; AMC; CMT; CNN; Comedy Central; C-SPAN; Discovery Channel; Disney Channel; E! HD; ESPN; FOX Sports Southwest; Freeform; History; HLN; Lifetime; Nickelodeon; QVC; Spike TV; TBS; The Weather Channel; TLC; TNT; Trinity Broadcasting Network (TBN); TV Land; USA Network; WGN America.
Programming (via translator): KVDA (TMO) San Antonio.
Fee: $49.95 installation; $26.30 monthly.
Pay Service 1
Pay Units: N.A.
Programming (via satellite): HBO; Showtime; The Movie Channel.
Fee: $20.00 installation; $7.95 monthly (TMC), $9.95 monthly (Showtime), $10.95 monthly (HBO).
Video-On-Demand: No
Internet Service
Operational: Yes.
Telephone Service
None
Miles of Plant: 81.0 (coaxial); None (fiber optic). Homes passed: 3,116.
Regional Manager: Ronnie Stafford. Office Manager: Jan Gibson. Controller: Jeffrey Lowe.
Ownership: RB3 LLC (MSO).

MUNDAY—Formerly served by Alliance Communications. Now served by WesTex Telephone Cooperative, 1500 West Business 20, Stanton, TX 79782. Phones: 432-263-0091 (Big Spring office); 432-756-3826. Web Site: http://www.westex.coop. ICA: TX0415.

TV Market Ranking: Outside TV Markets (MUNDAY). Franchise award date: N.A. Franchise expiration date: N.A. Began: January 1, 1963.
Channel capacity: N.A. Channels available but not in use: N.A.
Basic Service
Subscribers: 41.
Programming (received off-air): KAUZ-TV (CBS, CW) Wichita Falls; KFDX-TV (NBC) Wichita Falls; KJTL (Bounce TV, FOX) Wichita Falls; KRBC-TV (Bounce TV, NBC) Abilene; KSWO-TV (ABC, TMO) Lawton; KTAB-TV (CBS) Abilene; KTXS-TV (ABC, CW, This TV, TMO) Sweetwater; allband FM.
Programming (via satellite): KRMA-TV (PBS) Denver; QVC; WGN America.
Fee: $45.00 installation; $22.45 monthly.
Expanded Basic Service 1
Subscribers: N.A.
Programming (via satellite): AMC; Animal Planet; CMT; CNN; Comedy Central; C-SPAN; Discovery Channel; Disney Channel; E! HD; ESPN; ESPN2; FOX Sports Southwest; Freeform; HGTV; History; Lifetime; MSNBC; MTV; Nickelodeon; Oxygen; Spike TV; Syfy; TBS; The Weather Channel; TLC; TNT; Trinity Broadcasting Network (TBN); Turner Classic Movies; TV Land; Univision Studios; USA Network; VH1.
Fee: $18.00 monthly.
Pay Service 1
Pay Units: N.A.
Programming (via satellite): Cinemax; HBO; Showtime.
Fee: $30.00 installation; $9.95 monthly (each).
Video-On-Demand: No
Pay-Per-View
iN DEMAND (delivered digitally); Hot Choice (delivered digitally); Playboy TV (delivered digitally); Fresh (delivered digitally); Shorteez (delivered digitally).
Internet Service
Operational: No.
Telephone Service
None
Miles of Plant: 26.0 (coaxial); 2.0 (fiber optic). Homes passed: 772.
Ownership: WesTex Telecommunications (MSO).

MUSTANG RIDGE—Formerly served by Almega Cable. No longer in operation. ICA: TX0467.

MYRTLE SPRINGS—Formerly served by Cebridge Connections. No longer in operation. ICA: TX0625.

NACOGDOCHES—Suddenlink Communications, 409 North Fredonia St, Nacogdoches, TX 75961-5010. Phones: 314-315-9400; 888-822-5151. Web Site: http://www.suddenlink.com. Also serves Appleby & Nacogdoches County. ICA: TX0065.
TV Market Ranking: Below 100 (Appleby, NACOGDOCHES, Nacogdoches County). Franchise award date: N.A. Franchise expiration date: N.A. Began: September 1, 1960.
Channel capacity: N.A. Channels available but not in use: N.A.
Basic Service
Subscribers: 6,465. Commercial subscribers: 1,212.
Programming (received off-air): KFXK-TV (FOX) Longview; KPRC-TV (NBC, This TV) Houston; KSLA (Bounce TV, CBS, Grit, This TV) Shreveport; KTRE (ABC, TMO) Lufkin; KYTX (CBS, COZI TV, CW) Nacogdoches; 6 FMs.

Programming (via microwave): KERA-TV (PBS) Dallas; KTVT (CBS, Decades) Fort Worth; KXTX-TV (TMO) Dallas.
Programming (via satellite): CNN; C-SPAN; ESPN; FOX Sports Southwest; HLN; INSP; ION Television; TBS; The Weather Channel; TLC; Univision Studios.
Fee: $35.00 installation; $35.24 monthly.
Expanded Basic Service 1
Subscribers: N.A.
Programming (via satellite): A&E; AMC; Animal Planet; BET; Bravo; Cartoon Network; CMT; CNBC; Comedy Central; C-SPAN 2; Discovery Channel; Disney Channel; E! HD; ESPN2; Food Network; Fox News Channel; Fox Sports 1; Freeform; FX; Great American Country; HGTV; History; Lifetime; MSNBC; MTV; NBCSN; Nickelodeon; Outdoor Channel; Oxygen; Pop; Spike TV; Syfy; TNT; Travel Channel; Trinity Broadcasting Network (TBN); TV Land; Univision; USA Network; VH1; VideoRola; Weatherscan.
Digital Basic Service
Subscribers: N.A.
Programming (via satellite): BBC America; Bloomberg Television; Discovery Digital Networks; Disney XD; ESPN Classic; ESPNews; Fuse; FYI; Golf Channel; GSN; Hallmark Channel; History International; IFC; LMN; MC; Sundance TV; Turner Classic Movies.
Pay Service 1
Pay Units: N.A.
Programming (via satellite): Cinemax; HBO; Showtime; The Movie Channel.
Fee: $10.00 monthly (Showtime).
Digital Pay Service 1
Pay Units: N.A.
Programming (via satellite): Cinemax (multiplexed); Flix; HBO (multiplexed); Showtime (multiplexed); Starz (multiplexed); The Movie Channel (multiplexed).
Video-On-Demand: No
Pay-Per-View
iN DEMAND (delivered digitally); Playboy TV (delivered digitally); Hot Choice (delivered digitally); Fresh (delivered digitally); NBA TV (delivered digitally); ESPN Now (delivered digitally).
Internet Service
Operational: Yes.
Subscribers: 7,138.
Broadband Service: Suddenlink High Speed Internet.
Fee: $49.95 installation; $24.95 monthly.
Telephone Service
Digital: Operational
Subscribers: 2,642.
Fee: $48.95 monthly
Miles of Plant: 544.0 (coaxial); 76.0 (fiber optic). Homes passed: 23,287.
Senior Vice President, Corporate Finance: Michael Pflantz. Vice President, Accounting: Sabrina Warr. General Manager: Brad Haile.
Ownership: Cequel Communications Holdings I LLC (MSO).

NAPLES (town)—Formerly served by Alliance Communications Network. No longer in operation. ICA: TX0295.

NAVASOTA—Suddenlink Communications. Now served by BRENHAM, TX [TX0124]. ICA: TX0210.

NAZARETH—Formerly served by Elk River TV Cable Co. No longer in operation. ICA: TX0817.

NEW BOSTON—Vyve Broadband, 4 International Dr, Ste 330, Rye Brook, NY 10573. Phones: 800-937-1397; 405-395-

1131; 405-275-6923. Web Site: http://vyvebroadband.com. Also serves Bowie County (portions), De Kalb, Hooks, Maud & Red River Army Depot. ICA: TX0204.
TV Market Ranking: 58 (Bowie County (portions) (portions), De Kalb, Hooks, Maud, NEW BOSTON, Red River Army Depot); Outside TV Markets (Bowie County (portions) (portions)). Franchise award date: N.A. Franchise expiration date: N.A. Began: January 1, 1979.
Channel capacity: 35 (operating 2-way). Channels available but not in use: N.A.
Basic Service
Subscribers: 688. Commercial subscribers: 57.
Programming (received off-air): KLTS-TV (PBS) Shreveport; KMSS-TV (FOX) Shreveport; KPXJ (Antenna TV, CW, MeTV, Movies!) Minden; KSHV-TV (MNT) Shreveport; KSLA (Bounce TV, CBS, Grit, This TV) Shreveport; KTAL-TV (NBC) Texarkana; KTBS-TV (ABC) Shreveport.
Programming (via satellite): CNBC; CNN; C-SPAN; HLN; Pop; QVC; The Weather Channel; Trinity Broadcasting Network (TBN); WGN America.
Fee: $64.95 installation; $25.00 monthly.
Expanded Basic Service 1
Subscribers: N.A.
Programming (via satellite): A&E; AMC; Animal Planet; BET; Cartoon Network; CMT; Comedy Central; Discovery Channel; Disney Channel; ESPN; ESPN Classic; ESPN2; Fox News Channel; FOX Sports Southwest; Freeform; FX; Hallmark Channel; HGTV; History; Lifetime; MoviePlex; MTV; NFL Network; Nickelodeon; Spike TV; Syfy; TBS; TLC; TNT; TV Land; USA Network; VH1.
Fee: $34.66 monthly.
Digital Basic Service
Subscribers: N.A.
Programming (via satellite): 3ABN; A&E; BBC America; Bloomberg Television; Bravo; BYUtv; Church Channel; Cine Mexicano; Cinelatino; Cloo; CMT; CNN en Espanol; Daystar TV Network; Destination America; Discovery Kids Channel; Discovery Life Channel; Disney XD; DMX Music; ESPN Classic; ESPNews; EVINE Live; FamilyNet; Flix; FOX College Sports Central; FOX College Sports Pacific; Fox Deportes; Fox Sports 1; Fuse; FXM; GEB America; Golf Channel; Great American Country; GSN; History; History en Espanol; History International; IFC; Investigation Discovery; JUCE TV; La Familia Cosmovision; LMN; MTV Classic; MTV Hits; MTV2; National Geographic Channel; NBCSN; Nick Jr.; Nicktoons; Outdoor Channel; OWN: Oprah Winfrey Network; Science Channel; Starz Encore (multiplexed); Sundance TV; Syfy; TeenNick; The Word Network; Toon Disney en Espanol; Tr3s; Trinity Broadcasting Network (TBN); Turner Classic Movies; ULTRA HDPlex; UP; WE tv.
Pay Service 1
Pay Units: N.A.
Programming (via satellite): HBO; Showtime; Starz; Starz Encore.
Fee: $11.95 monthly (each).
Digital Pay Service 1
Pay Units: N.A.
Programming (via satellite): Cinemax (multiplexed); HBO (multiplexed); Showtime (multiplexed); Starz (multiplexed); The Movie Channel (multiplexed).
Video-On-Demand: No
Pay-Per-View
iN DEMAND (delivered digitally); Hot Choice (delivered digitally); Playboy TV (delivered digitally); Fresh (delivered digitally); Shorteez (delivered digitally)

Texas—Cable Systems

Internet Service
Operational: Yes.
Fee: $24.95 installation; $39.95 monthly.
Telephone Service
Digital: Operational
Miles of Plant: 34.0 (coaxial); None (fiber optic). Homes passed: 2,323.
Chief Executive Officer: Bill Haggarty. Senior Vice President, Financial Planning: Daniel White. Regional Vice President: Andrew Dearth. Vice President, Marketing: Tracy Bass.
Ownership: Vyve Broadband LLC (MSO).

NEW CANEY—Formerly served by Suddenlink Communications. No longer in operation. ICA: TX0105.

NEW SUMMERFIELD—Formerly served by Almega Cable. No longer in operation. ICA: TX0818.

NEW ULM—Formerly served by National Cable Inc. No longer in operation. ICA: TX0819.

NEW WAVERLY—Cablevision of Walker County, 1304 10th St, Huntsville, TX 77320-3804. Phone: 936-291-2288. ICA: TX0999.
TV Market Ranking: Below 100 (NEW WAVERLY).
Channel capacity: 36 (not 2-way capable). Channels available but not in use: N.A.
Basic Service
Subscribers: N.A.
Programming (received off-air): KBTX-TV (CBS, CW) Bryan; KHOU (Bounce TV, CBS) Houston; KIAH (Antenna TV, CW) Houston; KPRC-TV (NBC, This TV) Houston; KRIV (FOX) Houston; KTBU (IND) Conroe; KTRK-TV (ABC, Live Well Network) Houston; KTXH (Buzzr, MNT, Movies!) Houston; KUHT (PBS) Houston; KXLN-DT (UNV) Rosenberg; KYAZ (Azteca America, IND) Katy.
Programming (via satellite): A&E; AMC; BET; C-SPAN; Discovery Channel; ESPN2; HLN; ION Television; Lifetime; MTV; Nickelodeon; Syfy; TBS; Trinity Broadcasting Network (TBN); VH1; WGN America.
Fee: $29.95 installation; $32.79 monthly.
Pay Service 1
Pay Units: N.A.
Programming (via satellite): Cinemax; HBO.
Fee: $13.99 monthly.
Video-On-Demand: No
Internet Service
Operational: No.
Telephone Service
Analog: Operational
General Manager: Caroline Walker. Chief Technician: Kenny Hanson.
Ownership: Cablevision of Walker County (MSO).

NEWCASTLE—Zito Media, 102 S Main St, Coudersport, PA 16915. Phones: 800-687-7311; 940-873-4563. Web Site: http://www.zitomedia.net. ICA: TX1011.
TV Market Ranking: Outside TV Markets (NEWCASTLE).
Channel capacity: N.A. Channels available but not in use: N.A.
Basic Service
Subscribers: 75.
Programming (received off-air): KAUZ-TV (CBS, CW) Wichita Falls; KFDX-TV (NBC) Wichita Falls; KJTL (Bounce TV, FOX) Wichita Falls; KSWO-TV (ABC, TMO) Lawton.
Programming (via satellite): CNBC; CNN; C-SPAN; Discovery Channel; Disney XD; Freeform; HLN; TBS; The Weather Channel; TLC; Trinity Broadcasting Network (TBN); TV Land; WGN America.
Fee: $35.00 installation; $25.00 monthly.
Expanded Basic Service 1
Subscribers: N.A.
Programming (via satellite): A&E; AMC; Animal Planet; Cartoon Network; CMT; Disney Channel; ESPN; ESPN2; Food Network; Fox News Channel; Fox Sports 1; FOX Sports Southwest; FX; Hallmark Channel; HGTV; History; Lifetime; MTV; Nickelodeon; Outdoor Channel; Shepherd's Chapel Network; Spike TV; Syfy; TNT; Travel Channel; Turner Classic Movies; USA Network; VH1.
Fee: $16.91 monthly.
Digital Basic Service
Subscribers: N.A.
Programming (via satellite): BBC America; Bravo; Cloo; Discovery Digital Networks; DMX Music; EVINE Live; FOX College Sports Central; FOX College Sports Pacific; Fuse; FXM; FYI; Golf Channel; Great American Country; GSN; History; History International; IFC; LMN; National Geographic Channel; NBCSN; Nick Jr.; Nicktoons; Ovation; TeenNick; Turner Classic Movies; WE tv.
Fee: $20.95 monthly.
Pay Service 1
Pay Units: N.A.
Programming (via satellite): Cinemax; HBO.
Fee: $13.47 monthly.
Digital Pay Service 1
Pay Units: N.A.
Programming (via satellite): Cinemax (multiplexed); HBO; Showtime (multiplexed); Starz (multiplexed); Starz Encore (multiplexed); The Movie Channel (multiplexed).
Fee: $13.47 monthly (HBO & Cinemax), $7.01 montlhly (Showtime/TMC or Starz/Encore).
Video-On-Demand: No
Internet Service
Operational: Yes.
Broadband Service: In-house.
Fee: $24.95 monthly; $5.00 modem lease; $59.95 modem purchase.
Telephone Service
None
Vice President, Engineering & Operations: Steven Pawlik.
Ownership: Zito Media (MSO).

NIXON—Formerly served by Almega Cable. No longer in operation. ICA: TX0431.

NOCONA—Suddenlink Communications, 520 Maryville Centre Dr, Ste 300, St. Louis, MO 63141. Phones: 800-999-6845; 314-315-9400. Web Site: http://www.suddenlink.com. ICA: TX0282.
TV Market Ranking: Outside TV Markets (NOCONA). Franchise award date: N.A. Franchise expiration date: N.A. Began: December 25, 1971.
Channel capacity: N.A. Channels available but not in use: N.A.
Basic Service
Subscribers: 211.
Programming (received off-air): KAUZ-TV (CBS, CW) Wichita Falls; KERA-TV (PBS) Dallas; KFDX-TV (NBC) Wichita Falls; KJTL (Bounce TV, FOX) Wichita Falls; KSWO-TV (ABC, TMO) Lawton; KXAS-TV (COZI TV, NBC) Fort Worth; KXII (CBS, FOX, MNT) Sherman; WFAA (ABC) Dallas.
Programming (via satellite): C-SPAN; CW PLUS.
Fee: $28.45 monthly.
Expanded Basic Service 1
Subscribers: N.A.
Programming (via satellite): A&E; AMC; Animal Planet; Bravo; Cartoon Network; Celebrity Shopping Network; CNBC; CNN; Comedy Central; Discovery Channel; Disney Channel; E! HD; ESPN; ESPN2; Food Network; Fox News Channel; Fox Sports 1; FOX Sports Southwest; Freeform; FX; Great American Country; Hallmark Channel; HGTV; History; HLN; INSP; Jewelry Television; Lifetime; MSNBC; MTV; National Geographic Channel; Nickelodeon; Outdoor Channel; Spike TV; Syfy; TBS; The Weather Channel; TLC; TNT; Travel Channel; Turner Classic Movies; TV Land; Univision Studios; USA Network; VH1.
Fee: $23.00 monthly.
Digital Basic Service
Subscribers: N.A.
Programming (via satellite): BBC America; Bloomberg Television; Cloo; Destination America; Discovery Kids Channel; Disney XD; DMX Music; ESPN Classic; ESPNews; EVINE Live; FOX College Sports Central; FOX College Sports Pacific; Fuse; FYI; Golf Channel; GSN; History International; IFC; Investigation Discovery; NBCSN; OWN; Oprah Winfrey Network; Science Channel; Sundance TV; Trinity Broadcasting Network (TBN); WE tv.
Pay Service 1
Pay Units: N.A.
Programming (via satellite): HBO; Showtime; Starz; Starz Encore; The Movie Channel.
Digital Pay Service 1
Pay Units: N.A.
Programming (via satellite): Cinemax (multiplexed); Flix; HBO (multiplexed); Showtime (multiplexed); Starz (multiplexed); Starz Encore (multiplexed); The Movie Channel (multiplexed).
Video-On-Demand: No
Pay-Per-View
iN DEMAND (delivered digitally); Playboy TV (delivered digitally); Club Jenna (delivered digitally); Fresh (delivered digitally); Spice: Xcess (delivered digitally).
Internet Service
Operational: Yes. Began: June 1, 2003.
Broadband Service: Suddenlink High Speed Internet.
Fee: $49.95 installation; $29.95 monthly.
Telephone Service
None
Miles of Plant: 25.0 (coaxial); None (fiber optic). Homes passed: 1,400.
Senior Vice President, Corporate Finance: Michael Pflantz. Regional Manager: Tod Cruthird. Chief Technician: Scott Wilber.
Ownership: Cequel Communications Holdings I LLC (MSO).

NOME—Formerly served by Carrell Communications. No longer in operation. ICA: TX0644.

NORDHEIM—Formerly served by National Cable Inc. No longer in operation. ICA: TX0661.

NORMANGEE—Formerly served by Almega Cable. No longer in operation. ICA: TX0494.

NORTH SILSBEE—Formerly served by Carrell Communications. No longer in operation. ICA: TX0380.

NORTH ZULCH—Formerly served by Almega Cable. No longer in operation. ICA: TX0678.

NURSERY—Formerly served by National Cable Inc. No longer in operation. ICA: TX0555.

OAKWOOD—Formerly served by Charter Communications. No longer in operation. ICA: TX0526.

ODESSA—Cable One, 4701 East 52nd St, PO Box 14350, Odessa, TX 79768-4350. Phones: 432-363-7200; 877-692-2253. Fax: 432-363-2007. E-mail: jmorris@cableone.net. Web Site: http://www.cableone.net. Also serves Ector County. ICA: TX0025.
TV Market Ranking: Below 100 (Ector County, ODESSA). Franchise award date: November 10, 1970. Franchise expiration date: N.A. Began: December 10, 1968.
Channel capacity: N.A. Channels available but not in use: N.A.
Basic Service
Subscribers: 10,671.
Programming (received off-air): KMID (ABC) Midland; KOSA-TV (CBS, MNT) Odessa; KPBT-TV (PBS) Odessa; KPEJ-TV (FOX) Odessa; KPTB-DT (GLC) Lubbock; KTLE-LP (TMO) Odessa; KUPB (UNV) Midland; KWES-TV (CW, NBC, TMO) Odessa; KWWT (Antenna TV, MeTV, Movies!, Retro TV, This TV) Odessa.
Programming (via satellite): LATV; UniMas; Univision.
Fee: $90.00 installation; $29.00 monthly.
Expanded Basic Service 1
Subscribers: N.A.
Programming (via satellite): A&E; AMC; Animal Planet; BET; Bravo; Cartoon Network; CMT; CNBC; CNN; Comedy Central; C-SPAN; C-SPAN 2; Discovery Channel; Disney Channel; E! HD; ESPN; ESPN Classic; ESPN2; EVINE Live; EWTN Global Catholic Network; Food Network; Fox News Channel; FOX Sports Southwest; Freeform; FX; Golf Channel; Great American Country; HGTV; History; HLN; Lifetime; MSNBC; MTV; Nickelodeon; Pop; QVC; Spike TV; Syfy; TBS; The Weather Channel; TLC; TNT; Travel Channel; Trinity Broadcasting Network (TBN); Turner Classic Movies; TV Land; USA Network; VH1.
Digital Basic Service
Subscribers: N.A.
Programming (via satellite): 3ABN; A&E HD; Boomerang; BYUtv; Cine Mexicano; CNN HD; Discovery Channel HD; Discovery Kids Channel; Disney Channel HD; Disney XD; ESPN Classic; ESPN Deportes; ESPN HD; ESPN2 HD; ESPNews; ESPNU; FamilyNet; Food Network HD; FOX College Sports Central; FOX College Sports Pacific; Fox Deportes; Fox Sports 1; Fox Sports 2; Freeform HD; FX HD; FXM; FYI; Golf Channel; Great American Country; GSN; Hallmark Channel; HD Theater; HGTV HD; History HD; History International; HITS (Headend In The Sky); INSP; La Familia Cosmovision; MC; National Geographic Channel; National Geographic Channel HD; NBC Universo; Outdoor Channel; OWN; Oprah Winfrey Network; Science Channel; TBS HD; The Movie Channel HD; TLC HD; TNT HD; Toon Disney en Espanol; Trinity Broadcasting Network (TBN); TVG Network; Universal HD; WE tv.
Fee: $12.95 monthly.
Pay Service 1
Pay Units: N.A.
Programming (via satellite): HBO.
Digital Pay Service 1
Pay Units: N.A.
Programming (via satellite): Cinemax (multiplexed); Flix; HBO (multiplexed); HBO HD; HBO Latino; Showtime (multiplexed); Showtime HD; Starz (multiplexed); Starz Encore (multiplexed); Sundance TV; The Movie Channel (multiplexed).

Fee: $10.00 installation; $15.00 monthly (each package).
Video-On-Demand: No
Pay-Per-View
iN DEMAND (delivered digitally); special events (delivered digitally); ESPN (delivered digitally); SexSee (delivered digitally); Juicy (delivered digitally); VaVoom (delivered digitally).
Internet Service
Operational: Yes. Began: September 19, 2002.
Subscribers: 10,828.
Broadband Service: CableONE.net.
Fee: $75.00 installation; $39.93 monthly; $5.00 modem lease.
Telephone Service
Digital: Operational
Subscribers: 5,205.
Fee: $39.95 monthly
Miles of Plant: 818.0 (coaxial); 130.0 (fiber optic). Homes passed: 47,544.
Vice President: Patrick A. Dolohanty. General Manager: Terri Hale. Chief Technician: Jerry Morris. Marketing Director: Joni Holdridge.
Ownership: Cable ONE Inc. (MSO).

ODESSA—Grande Communications, 3001 West Cuthbert Ave, Midland, TX 79701. Phones: 512-878-4600 (Corporate office); 432-272-4600. Web Site: http://mygrande.com. Also serves Midland. ICA: TX0984.
Note: This system is an overbuild.
TV Market Ranking: Below 100 (Midland, ODESSA). Franchise award date: February 10, 2000. Franchise expiration date: N.A. Began: November 30, 2000.
Channel capacity: N.A. Channels available but not in use: N.A.
Basic Service
Subscribers: 19,210.
Programming (received off-air): KMID (ABC) Midland; KMLM-DT (GLC) Odessa; KOSA-TV (CBS, MNT) Odessa; KPBT-TV (PBS) Odessa; KPEJ-TV (FOX) Odessa; KTOV-LP Corpus Christi; KUPB (UNV) Midland; KWES-TV (CW, NBC, TMO) Odessa.
Programming (via satellite): C-SPAN; C-SPAN 2; LWS Local Weather Station; Pop; QVC; Telemundo; UniMas; WGN America.
Fee: $27.49 monthly.
Expanded Basic Service 1
Subscribers: N.A.
Programming (via satellite): A&E; AMC; Animal Planet; BET; Bravo; Cartoon Network; CMT; CNBC; CNN; Comedy Central; Discovery Channel; Disney Channel; Disney XD; E! HD; ESPN; ESPN Classic; ESPN2; EWTN Global Catholic Network; Food Network; Fox Deportes; Fox News Channel; Fox Sports 1; FOX Sports Southwest; Freeform; FX; Golf Channel; Great American Country; GSN; Hallmark Channel; HGTV; History; HLN; Lifetime; MSNBC; MTV; National Geographic Channel; NBC Universo; NBCSN; Nickelodeon; OWN; Oprah Winfrey Network; Oxygen; Special events; Spike TV; Syfy; TBS; The Weather Channel; TLC; TNT; Travel Channel; Trinity Broadcasting Network (TBN); truTV; Turner Classic Movies; TV Land; Univision; USA Network; VH1.
Fee: $30.00 monthly.
Digital Basic Service
Subscribers: N.A.
Programming (via satellite): BBC America; Boomerang; CBS Sports Network; Cooking Channel; Discovery Digital Networks; DIY Network; ESPN; ESPNews; FamilyNet; FOX College Sports Central; FOX College Sports Pacific; Fox Sports 2; Fuse; FXM; FYI; Golf Channel; HD Theater; History International;
HITS (Headend In The Sky); LMN; MC; NBA TV; NFL Network; Nick Jr.; Nicktoons; TeenNick; Tennis Channel; TNT; TVG Network; Universal HD.
Fee: $24.00 monthly and $9.95 monthly HDTV tier.
Digital Pay Service 1
Pay Units: N.A.
Programming (via satellite): Cinemax; Flix (multiplexed); HBO; Showtime; Starz (multiplexed); Starz Encore (multiplexed); Starz HD; Sundance TV (multiplexed); The Movie Channel (multiplexed).
Fee: $12.99 monthly (Cinemax, HBO, Starz/Encore or Showtime/TMC/Flix/Sundance).
Video-On-Demand: No
Pay-Per-View
Playboy TV (delivered digitally); Fresh (delivered digitally); Hot Choice (delivered digitally); iN DEMAND (delivered digitally); Pleasure (delivered digitally); Shorteez (delivered digitally); Sports PPV (delivered digitally).
Internet Service
Operational: Yes. Began: November 30, 2000.
Fee: $34.99-$34.99 monthly.
Telephone Service
Digital: Operational
Fee: $19.99 monthly
Vice President, Marketing: Pete Drozdoff. Vice President, Network Operations & Engineering: Lamar Horton. Vice President, Technical Operations: Shane Schilling. Vice President, Customer Care: Dawn Blydenburgh. General Manager: Matt Rohre.
Ownership: Grande Communications Networks Inc. (MSO).

O'DONNELL—NTS Communications. Formerly [TX0496]. This cable system has converted to IPTV, 1220 Broadway, Lubbock, TX 79401. Phones: 800-658-2150; 806-797-0687. Fax: 806-788-3381. E-mail: info@ntscom.com. Web Site: http://www.ntscom.com. ICA: TX5556.
TV Market Ranking: Outside TV Markets (O'DONNELL). Franchise award date: July 1, 1980. Franchise expiration date: N.A. Began: March 9, 1976.
Channel capacity: N.A. Channels available but not in use: N.A.
Gold
Subscribers: N.A.
Programming (received off-air): KAMC (ABC, Bounce TV) Lubbock; KCBD (NBC, This TV) Lubbock; KJTV-TV (FOX) Lubbock; KLBK-TV (CBS) Lubbock; KLCW-TV (CW) Wolfforth; KPTB-DT (GLC) Lubbock; KTTZ-TV (PBS) Lubbock; KXTQ-CD (TMO) Lubbock.
Programming (via satellite): A&E; Animal Planet; Cartoon Network; CMT; CNN; Comedy Central; Discovery Channel; ESPN; ESPN2; FOX Sports Southwest; Freeform; HGTV; History; Lifetime; Nickelodeon; QVC; Spike TV; TBS; The Weather Channel; TLC; TNT; Turner Classic Movies; TV Land; Univision Studios; USA Network; WGN America.
Fee: $65.00 monthly. Includes 150+ channels plus music & 1 digital receiver.
Platinum
Subscribers: N.A.
Fee: $85.00 monthly. Includes 230+ channels plus music channels, HD channels, 1 whole home DVR & 1 digital receiver.
Video-On-Demand: No
Internet Service
Operational: Yes.
Fee: $44.99-$134.99 monthly.
Telephone Service
Digital: Operational
Fee: $19.99 monthly
President & Chief Executive Officer: Cyrus Driver. Executive Vice President & Chief Operating Officer: Deborah Crawford. Executive Vice President & Chief Financial Officer: Don Pittman. Senior Vice President, Product Management: Angel Kandahari. Vice President & General Counsel: Daniel Wheeler. Vice President, Products & Marketing: Roberto Chang. Vice President, Human Resources: Wendy J. Lee. Vice President, Service Delivery & IT Strategy: Michael McDaniel. Vice President, RUS Projects: Aaron Peters.
Ownership: NTS Communications Inc. (MSO).

O'DONNELL—NTS Communications. This cable system has converted to IPTV. See O'DONNELL, TZ [TX5556]. ICA: TX0496.

OILTON—Formerly served by Windjammer Cable. No longer in operation. ICA: TX0825.

OKLAHOMA—Suddenlink Communications. Now served by KINGWOOD, TX [TX0052]. ICA: TX0308.

OLNEY—Suddenlink Communications, 520 Maryville Centre Dr, Ste 300, St. Louis, MO 63141. Phones: 877-423-2743; 314-315-9400. Web Site: http://www.suddenlink.com. Also serves Young County (portions). ICA: TX0215.
TV Market Ranking: Outside TV Markets (OLNEY, Young County (portions)). Franchise award date: N.A. Franchise expiration date: N.A. Began: October 1, 1971.
Channel capacity: N.A. Channels available but not in use: N.A.
Basic Service
Subscribers: 281. Commercial subscribers: 106.
Programming (via satellite): C-SPAN; Discovery Channel; Hallmark Channel; QVC; TBS; The Weather Channel; TLC.
Programming (via translator): KAUZ-TV (CBS, CW) Wichita Falls; KERA-TV (PBS) Dallas; KFDX-TV (NBC) Wichita Falls; KJTL (Bounce TV, FOX) Wichita Falls; KSWO-TV (ABC, TMO) Lawton; KTVT (CBS, Decades) Fort Worth; KXAS-TV (COZI TV, NBC) Fort Worth; WFAA (ABC) Dallas.
Fee: $27.45 monthly.
Expanded Basic Service 1
Subscribers: N.A.
Programming (via satellite): AMC; Animal Planet; Cartoon Network; CNBC; CNN; Disney Channel; ESPN; Fox News Channel; Freeform; FX; HGTV; HLN; Lifetime; MTV; Spike TV; TNT; truTV; USA Network.
Fee: $39.95 installation; $25.00 monthly.
Pay Service 1
Pay Units: N.A.
Programming (via satellite): Cinemax; HBO; Showtime; Starz; Starz Encore.
Fee: $1.75 monthly (Encore), $6.75 monthly (Starz), $12.84 monthly (Cinemax), $13.83 monthly (HBO or Showtime).
Internet Service
Operational: Yes. Began: June 5, 2003.
Broadband Service: Suddenlink High Speed Internet.
Fee: $49.95 installation; $25.95 monthly.
Telephone Service
None
Miles of Plant: 31.0 (coaxial); None (fiber optic). Homes passed: 2,085.
Senior Vice President, Corporate Finance: Michael Pflantz. Regional Manager: Todd Cruthird. Regional Marketing Manager: Beverly Gambell. Plant Manager: Ron Johnson.
Ownership: Cequel Communications Holdings I LLC (MSO).

OLTON—NTS Communications. Formerly [TX0387]. This cable system has converted to IPTV, 1220 Broadway, Lubbock, TX 79401. Phones: 800-658-2150; 806-797-0687. Fax: 806-788-3381. E-mail: info@ntscom.com. Web Site: http://www.ntscom.com. ICA: TX5557.
TV Market Ranking: Outside TV Markets (OLTON). Franchise award date: December 4, 1978. Franchise expiration date: N.A. Began: July 1, 1981.
Channel capacity: N.A. Channels available but not in use: N.A.
Gold
Subscribers: N.A.
Programming (received off-air): KAMC (ABC, Bounce TV) Lubbock; KCBD (NBC, This TV) Lubbock; KJTV-TV (FOX) Lubbock; KLBK-TV (CBS) Lubbock; KPTB-DT (GLC) Lubbock; KTTZ-TV (PBS) Lubbock.
Programming (via satellite): A&E; AMC; Animal Planet; Cartoon Network; CMT; CNN; Discovery Channel; Disney Channel; ESPN; Fox News Channel; FOX Sports Southwest; Freeform; History; Lifetime; Nickelodeon; QVC; Spike TV; Syfy; TBS; The Weather Channel; TLC; TNT; Trinity Broadcasting Network (TBN); TV Land; USA Network; WGN America.
Programming (via translator): KVDA (TMO) San Antonio.
Fee: $65.00 monthly. Includes 150+ channels plus music channels & 1 digital receiver.
Platinum
Subscribers: N.A.
Fee: $85.00 monthly. Includes 230+ channels plus music channels, HD channels, 1 whole home DVR & 1 digital receiver.
Video-On-Demand: No
Internet Service
Operational: Yes.
Fee: $44.99-$134.99 monthly.
Telephone Service
Digital: Operational
Fee: $19.99 monthly
President & Chief Executive Officer: Cyrus Driver. Executive Vice President & Chief Operating Officer: Deborah Crawford. Executive Vice President & Chief Financial Officer: Don Pittman. Senior Vice President, Product Management: Angel Kandahari. Vice President & General Counsel: Daniel Wheeler. Vice President, Products & Marketing: Roberto Chang. Vice President, Human Resources: Wendy J. Lee. Vice President, Service Delivery & IT Strategy: Michael McDaniel. Vice President, RUS Projects: Aaron Peters.
Ownership: NTS Communications Inc. (MSO).

OLTON—NTS Communications. This cable system has converted to IPTV. See OLTON, TX [TX5557]. ICA: TX0387.

ONALASKA—Suddenlink Communications, 520 Maryville Centre Dr, Ste 300, St. Louis, MO 63141. Phones: 800-999-6845 (Customer service); 314-315-9400. Web Site: http://www.suddenlink.com. Also serves Coldspring, Point Blank, Shepherd & Trinity. ICA: TX0851.

Texas—Cable Systems

TV Market Ranking: Outside TV Markets (Coldspring, ONALASKA, Point Blank, Shepherd, Trinity). Franchise award date: N.A. Franchise expiration date: N.A. Began: January 31, 1972.
Channel capacity: 35 (operating 2-way). Channels available but not in use: N.A.

Basic Service
Subscribers: 2,271.
Programming (received off-air): KBTX-TV (CBS, CW) Bryan; KETK-TV (Estrella TV, NBC) Jacksonville; KIAH (Antenna TV, CW) Houston; KPRC-TV (NBC, This TV) Houston; KRIV (FOX) Houston; KTRE (ABC, TMO) Lufkin; KTRK-TV (ABC, Live Well Network) Houston; KTXH (Buzzr, MNT, Movies!) Houston; KUHT (PBS) Houston; KYTX (CBS, COZI TV, CW) Nacogdoches; 9 FMs.
Fee: $28.45 monthly.

Expanded Basic Service 1
Subscribers: N.A.
Programming (via satellite): A&E; AMC; Animal Planet; BET; Cartoon Network; CNBC; CNN; Comedy Central; Discovery Channel; Disney Channel; E! HD; ESPN; ESPN2; Food Network; Fox News Channel; FOX Sports Southwest; Freeform; FX; Great American Country; HGTV; History; HLN; Lifetime; MSNBC; MTV; National Geographic Channel; Nickelodeon; Outdoor Channel; Spike TV; Syfy; TBS; The Weather Channel; TLC; TNT; Trinity Broadcasting Network (TBN); Turner Classic Movies; USA Network.

Digital Basic Service
Subscribers: N.A.
Programming (via satellite): BBC America; Bloomberg Television; Cloo; Discovery Digital Networks; Disney XD; DMX Music; ESPN Classic; ESPNews; EVINE Live; FOX College Sports Central; FOX College Sports Pacific; Fox Sports 1; Fuse; FYI; Golf Channel; GSN; History International; IFC; NBCSN; Sundance TV; WE tv.

Pay Service 1
Pay Units: N.A.
Programming (via satellite): Cinemax; HBO; Showtime.
Fee: $9.95 monthly (Cinemax or Showtime), $12.00 monthly (HBO).

Digital Pay Service 1
Pay Units: N.A.
Programming (via satellite): Cinemax (multiplexed); Flix; HBO (multiplexed); Showtime (multiplexed); Starz (multiplexed); Starz Encore (multiplexed); The Movie Channel (multiplexed).

Video-On-Demand: No

Pay-Per-View
iN DEMAND (delivered digitally); Playboy TV (delivered digitally); Fresh (delivered digitally); Shorteez (delivered digitally).

Internet Service
Operational: Yes. Began: June 3, 2004.
Subscribers: 140.
Broadband Service: Suddenlink High Speed Internet.
Fee: $49.95 installation; $38.95 monthly.

Telephone Service
None
Miles of Plant: 200.0 (coaxial); 12.0 (fiber optic).
Vice President, Corporate Finance: Michael Pflantz. General Manager: Jim Cox. Office Manager: Timmie Adams. Marketing Manager: Beverly Gambell.
Ownership: Cequel Communications Holdings I LLC (MSO).

ORANGE—Time Warner Cable. Now served by PORT ARTHUR (formerly Beaumont), TX [TX0022]. ICA: TX0058.

ORANGE GROVE—Time Warner Cable. Now served by CORPUS CHRISTI, TX [TX0010]. ICA: TX0510.

ORE CITY—Formerly served by Rapid Communications. No longer in operation. ICA: TX0542.

OYSTER CREEK—Formerly served by Almega Cable. No longer in operation. ICA: TX0283.

OYSTER CREEK—Telecom Cable, 1321 Louetta Rd, Ste 1020, Cypress, TX 77429. Phone: 888-240-4589. E-mail: information@telecomcable.net. Web Site: http://telecomcable.net. ICA: TX1040.
TV Market Ranking: Below 100 (OYSTER CREEK).
Channel capacity: N.A. Channels available but not in use: N.A.

Basic Service
Subscribers: 2.
Fee: $13.00 monthly.
Manager: Anthony Luna.
Ownership: Telecom Cable LLC (MSO).

OZONA—Circle Bar Cable TV Inc, 906 11th St, PO Box 777, Ozona, TX 76943. Phone: 325-392-3323. Fax: 325-392-5878. ICA: TX0252.
TV Market Ranking: Outside TV Markets (OZONA). Franchise award date: N.A. Franchise expiration date: N.A. Began: February 9, 1955.
Channel capacity: N.A. Channels available but not in use: N.A.

Basic Service
Subscribers: N.A.
Programming (received off-air): KLST (CBS) San Angelo; KSAN-TV (NBC) San Angelo; 9 FMs.
Programming (via microwave): KMID (ABC) Midland; KPEJ-TV (FOX) Odessa.
Programming (via satellite): A&E; CNN; Discovery Channel; Disney Channel; ESPN; Freeform; History; KRMA-TV (PBS) Denver; Lifetime; Nickelodeon; Spike TV; TBS; Telemundo; The Weather Channel; TLC; TNT; Trinity Broadcasting Network (TBN); Turner Classic Movies; VH1; WGN America.
Fee: $30.00 installation.

Pay Service 1
Pay Units: N.A.
Programming (via satellite): HBO.
Fee: $10.00 installation; $10.00 monthly.

Video-On-Demand: No

Internet Service
Operational: No.

Telephone Service
None
Miles of Plant: 50.0 (coaxial); None (fiber optic). Homes passed: 1,700.
General Manager: Tony Shields.
Ownership: UNEV Communications Inc. (MSO).

PADUCAH (town)—Suddenlink Communications, 520 Maryville Centre Dr, Ste 300, St. Louis, MO 63141. Phones: 800-999-6845 (Customer service); 314-315-9400. Web Site: http://www.suddenlink.com. ICA: TX0405.
TV Market Ranking: Outside TV Markets (PADUCAH (TOWN). Franchise award date: N.A. Franchise expiration date: N.A. Began: August 1, 1954.
Channel capacity: N.A. Channels available but not in use: N.A.

Basic Service
Subscribers: 148.
Programming (received off-air): KJTV-TV (FOX) Lubbock; allband FM.
Programming (via microwave): KACV-TV (PBS) Amarillo; KAMR-TV (IND, NBC) Amarillo; KCIT (FOX, This TV) Amarillo; KFDA-TV (CBS, TMO) Amarillo; KTVT (CBS, Decades) Fort Worth; KVII-TV (ABC, CW) Amarillo.
Programming (via satellite): A&E; AMC; Animal Planet; Cartoon Network; CMT; CNN; Discovery Channel; Disney Channel; E! HD; ESPN; Fox News Channel; FOX Sports Southwest; Freeform; History; HLN; Lifetime; QVC; Spike TV; Syfy; TBS; The Weather Channel; TLC; TNT; Travel Channel; Trinity Broadcasting Network (TBN); TV Land; USA Network; WGN America.
Fee: $28.45 monthly.

Pay Service 1
Pay Units: N.A.
Programming (via satellite): Cinemax; HBO; Showtime.
Fee: $9.95 monthly (each).

Video-On-Demand: No

Internet Service
Operational: Yes. Began: December 22, 2003.
Broadband Service: Suddenlink High Speed Internet.
Fee: $49.95 installation; $38.95 monthly.

Telephone Service
None
Miles of Plant: 16.0 (coaxial); None (fiber optic). Homes passed: 923.
Senior Vice President, Corporate Finance: Michael Pflantz. Regional Manager: Todd Cruthird. Regional Marketing Manager: Beverly Gambell. Plant Manager: Rick Rattan.
Ownership: Cequel Communications Holdings I LLC (MSO).

PALACIOS—NewWave Communications. Now served by WHARTON, TX [TX0171]. ICA: TX0223.

PALESTINE—Zito Media, 102 S Main St, PO Box 665, Coudersport, PA 16915. Phones: 814-260-9055; 800-365-6988. Fax: 913-563-5454. E-mail: info@zitomedia.com. Web Site: http://www.zitomedia.com. Also serves Anderson County & Elkhart. ICA: TX0070.
TV Market Ranking: Below 100 (Anderson County (portions), Elkhart, PALESTINE); Outside TV Markets (Anderson County (portions)). Franchise award date: N.A. Franchise expiration date: N.A. Began: January 1, 1955.
Channel capacity: N.A. Channels available but not in use: N.A.

Basic Service
Subscribers: 1,967.
Programming (received off-air): KDTN (Daystar TV, ETV) Denton; KETK-TV (Estrella TV, NBC) Jacksonville; KFXK-TV (FOX) Longview; 18 FMs.
Programming (via microwave): KDFW (FOX) Dallas; KERA-TV (PBS) Dallas; KTVT (CBS, Decades) Fort Worth; KXAS-TV (COZI TV, NBC) Fort Worth; KXTX-TV (TMO) Dallas; WFAA (ABC) Dallas.
Programming (via satellite): BET; CNN; C-SPAN; Freeform; Lifetime; QVC; TBS; The Weather Channel; Trinity Broadcasting Network (TBN); WGN America.
Fee: $49.95 installation; $18.28 monthly.

Expanded Basic Service 1
Subscribers: N.A.
Programming (via satellite): A&E; AMC; Animal Planet; Cartoon Network; CMT; CNBC; Comedy Central; Discovery Channel; Disney Channel; E! HD; ESPN; ESPN2; EWTN Global Catholic Network; Food Network; Fox News Channel; Golf Channel; Hallmark Channel; HGTV; History; HLN; INSP; MSNBC; MTV; Nickelodeon; Oxygen; Spike TV; TLC; TNT; Travel Channel; Turner Classic Movies; Univision Studios; USA Network; VH1.
Fee: $10.05 monthly.

Digital Basic Service
Subscribers: N.A.
Programming (via satellite): BBC America; Bloomberg Television; Bravo; Destination America; Discovery Kids Channel; Discovery Life Channel; Disney XD; ESPN Classic; ESPNews; Fox Sports 1; Fuse; FXM; FYI; GSN; History International; IFC; International Television (ITV); Investigation Discovery; MC; MTV Jams; MTV2; NBA TV; NBCSN; Nick Jr.; Nicktoons; Outdoor Channel; Ovation; Science Channel; Sundance TV; Syfy; TeenNick; TV Land; WE tv.
Fee: $9.95 monthly.

Digital Pay Service 1
Pay Units: N.A.
Programming (via satellite): Cinemax (multiplexed); Flix; HBO (multiplexed); Showtime (multiplexed); Starz (multiplexed); Starz Encore (multiplexed); The Movie Channel (multiplexed).
Fee: $16.99 monthly (Cinemax, Encore, Flix, HBO, Showtime, Starz or TMC).

Video-On-Demand: No

Pay-Per-View
iN DEMAND (delivered digitally); Fresh (delivered digitally); Shorteez (delivered digitally); Playboy TV (delivered digitally).

Internet Service
Operational: Yes.

Telephone Service
Digital: Operational
Miles of Plant: 187.0 (coaxial); None (fiber optic). Homes passed: 10,247.
President: James Rigas.
Ownership: Zito Media (MSO).

PALO PINTO—Formerly served by Mallard Cablevision. No longer in operation. ICA: TX0639.

PARADISE—Formerly served by CableSouth Inc. No longer in operation. ICA: TX0679.

PARIS—Suddenlink Communications, 25 19th St SE, Paris, TX 75460-6101. Phone: 314-315-9400. Fax: 903-595-1929. Web Site: http://www.suddenlink.com. Also serves Hopewell, Lamar County (unincorporated areas), Reno (Lamar County), Roxton & Toco. ICA: TX0060.
TV Market Ranking: Outside TV Markets (Hopewell, Lamar County (unincorporated areas), PARIS, Reno (Lamar County), Roxton, Toco). Franchise award date: June 11, 1984. Franchise expiration date: N.A. Began: April 1, 1956.
Channel capacity: 78 (operating 2-way). Channels available but not in use: N.A.

Basic Service
Subscribers: 5,354. Commercial subscribers: 645.
Programming (received off-air): KTEN (ABC, CW, NBC) Ada; KXII (CBS, FOX, MNT) Sherman; 14 FMs.
Programming (via microwave): KDFW (FOX) Dallas; KERA-TV (PBS) Dallas; KTVT (CBS, Decades) Fort Worth; KXAS-TV (COZI TV, NBC) Fort Worth; WFAA (ABC) Dallas.
Programming (via satellite): C-SPAN; Trinity Broadcasting Network (TBN).
Fee: $38.00 installation; $32.24 monthly; $2.00 converter.

Cable Systems—Texas

Expanded Basic Service 1
Subscribers: N.A.
Programming (via satellite): A&E; AMC; Animal Planet; BET; Cartoon Network; CNN; Comedy Central; C-SPAN 2; Discovery Channel; Disney Channel; E! HD; ESPN; ESPN2; Food Network; Fox News Channel; FOX Sports Southwest; Freeform; FX; Great American Country; HGTV; History; HLN; Independent Music Network; Lifetime; MSNBC; MTV; Nickelodeon; Outdoor Channel; Spike TV; Syfy; The Weather Channel; TLC; TNT; Travel Channel; truTV; Turner Classic Movies; TV Land; Univision; USA Network; VH1.
Fee: $4.19 installation; $17.59 monthly.
Digital Basic Service
Subscribers: N.A.
Programming (via satellite): BBC America; Bloomberg Television; Boomerang; Cooking Channel; Cox Sports Television; Discovery Life Channel; Disney XD; DIY Network; ESPN Classic; ESPNews; FamilyNet; Fox Sports 1; Fox Sports 2; Fuse; FXM; FYI; Golf Channel; GSN; Hallmark Channel; History International; IFC; LMN; MC; National Geographic Channel; NBCSN; Oxygen; Starz Encore; Sundance TV; Tennis Channel; TV One; UP; WE tv.
Digital Pay Service 1
Pay Units: N.A.
Programming (via satellite): Cinemax (multiplexed); HBO (multiplexed); Showtime (multiplexed); Starz (multiplexed); The Movie Channel (multiplexed).
Video-On-Demand: Yes
Pay-Per-View
iN DEMAND (delivered digitally); Fresh (delivered digitally); Playboy TV (delivered digitally); Hot Choice (delivered digitally); Shorteez (delivered digitally).
Internet Service
Operational: Yes.
Subscribers: 5,684.
Telephone Service
Digital: Operational
Subscribers: 3,422.
Miles of Plant: 399.0 (coaxial); 108.0 (fiber optic). Homes passed: 16,623.
Senior Vice President, Corporate Finance: Michael Pflantz. General Manager: Tim Masters. Chief Technician: Bob Holmon.
Ownership: Cequel Communications Holdings I LLC (MSO).

PARKWAY VILLAGE—Formerly served by Time Warner Cable. No longer in operation. ICA: TX0668.

PECOS—Suddenlink Communications, 520 Maryville Centre Dr, Ste 300, St. Louis, MO 63141. Phones: 800-999-6845; 314-315-9400. Web Site: http://www.suddenlink.com. Also serves Reeves County (portions). ICA: TX0138.
TV Market Ranking: Outside TV Markets (PECOS, Reeves County (portions)). Franchise award date: July 12, 1979. Franchise expiration date: N.A. Began: March 17, 1955.
Channel capacity: 61 (operating 2-way). Channels available but not in use: N.A.
Basic Service
Subscribers: 822.
Programming (via microwave): KMID (ABC) Midland; KMLM-DT (GLC) Odessa; KOSA-TV (CBS, MNT) Odessa; KPEJ-TV (FOX) Odessa; KWES-TV (CW, NBC, TMO) Odessa.
Programming (via satellite): KMGH-TV (ABC, Azteca America) Denver; KRMA-TV (PBS) Denver; QVC; WGN America.
Fee: $28.45 monthly.

Expanded Basic Service 1
Subscribers: N.A.
Programming (via microwave): KUPB (UNV) Midland.
Programming (via satellite): A&E; AMC; Animal Planet; BET; Bravo; Cartoon Network; CNBC; CNN; Comedy Central; C-SPAN; Discovery Channel; Disney Channel; E! HD; ESPN; ESPN2; EWTN Global Catholic Network; Food Network; Fox News Channel; Fox Sports 1; FOX Sports Southwest; Freeform; FX; Golf Channel; Great American Country; Hallmark Channel; HGTV; History; HLN; Lifetime; MSNBC; MTV; National Geographic Channel; Nickelodeon; Outdoor Channel; Pop; Spike TV; Syfy; TBS; Telemundo; The Weather Channel; TLC; TNT; Travel Channel; Trinity Broadcasting Network (TBN); truTV; Turner Classic Movies; TV Land; Univision; USA Network; VH1.
Fee: $26.00 monthly.
Digital Basic Service
Subscribers: N.A.
Programming (via satellite): BBC America; Bloomberg Television; Cloo; Discovery Digital Networks; Disney XD; DMX Music; ESPN Classic; ESPNews; FOX College Sports Central; FOX College Sports Pacific; Fuse; FXM; FYI; GSN; History; History International; HITS (Headend In The Sky); IFC; NBCSN; Sundance TV; WE tv.
Fee: $3.99 monthly.
Pay Service 1
Pay Units: N.A.
Programming (via satellite): Cinemax; HBO; Showtime; The Movie Channel.
Fee: $5.95 monthly (TMC), $9.95 monthly (Cinemax or Showtime), $10.95 monthly (HBO).
Digital Pay Service 1
Pay Units: N.A.
Programming (via satellite): Cinemax (multiplexed); HBO (multiplexed); Showtime (multiplexed); Starz (multiplexed); Starz Encore (multiplexed); The Movie Channel (multiplexed).
Video-On-Demand: No
Pay-Per-View
iN DEMAND (delivered digitally); Playboy TV (delivered digitally); Fresh (delivered digitally); Shorteez (delivered digitally).
Internet Service
Operational: Yes. Began: March 1, 2002. Broadband Service: Suddenlink High Speed Internet.
Fee: $45.95 installation; $29.95 monthly.
Telephone Service
Digital: Operational
Fee: $44.95 monthly
Miles of Plant: 64.0 (coaxial); None (fiber optic). Homes passed: 4,586.
Senior Vice President, Corporate Finance: Michael Pflantz. Regional Manager: Todd Cruthird. Marketing Director: Beverly Gambell.
Ownership: Cequel Communications Holdings I LLC (MSO).

PELICAN BAY—Formerly served by SouthTel Communications LP. No longer in operation. ICA: TX0832.

PERRIN—Formerly served by Mallard Cablevision. No longer in operation. ICA: TX0640.

PERRYTON—Vyve Broadband, 4 International Dr, Ste 330, Rye Brook, NY 10573. Phones: 800-937-1397; 405-395-1131; 405-275-6923. Web Site: http://vyvebroadband.com. ICA: TX0165.
TV Market Ranking: Outside TV Markets (PERRYTON). Franchise award date: July 17,

FULLY SEARCHABLE • CONTINUOUSLY UPDATED • DISCOUNT RATES FOR PRINT PURCHASERS
For more information call **800-771-9202** or visit **www.warren-news.com**

1957. Franchise expiration date: N.A. Began: January 1, 1957.
Channel capacity: 42 (operating 2-way). Channels available but not in use: N.A.
Basic Service
Subscribers: 369.
Programming (received off-air): KACV-TV (PBS) Amarillo; KAMR-TV (IND, NBC) Amarillo; KCIT (FOX, This TV) Amarillo; KFDA-TV (CBS, TMO) Amarillo; KPTF-DT (GLC) Farwell; KVII-TV (ABC, CW) Amarillo.
Programming (via satellite): C-SPAN; C-SPAN 2; CW PLUS; EVINE Live; Pop; QVC; Telemundo; The Weather Channel; UniMas; Univision; Univision Studios; WGN America.
Fee: $64.95 installation; $25.00 monthly; $2.25 converter.
Expanded Basic Service 1
Subscribers: N.A.
Programming (via satellite): A&E; AMC; Animal Planet; Bravo; Cartoon Network; CMT; CNBC; CNN; Comedy Central; Discovery Channel; Disney Channel; ESPN; ESPN2; Food Network; Fox News Channel; FOX Sports Southwest; Freeform; FX; Hallmark Channel; HGTV; History; HLN; Lifetime; MoviePlex; MTV; NFL Network; Nickelodeon; Spike TV; TBS; TLC; TNT; TV Land; USA Network; VH1.
Fee: $34.66 monthly.
Digital Basic Service
Subscribers: N.A.
Programming (via satellite): BBC America; Bloomberg Television; Bravo; Cine Mexicano; Cinelatino; Cloo; CMT; CNN en Espanol; Destination America; Discovery Kids Channel; Discovery Life Channel; Disney XD; DMX Music; ESPN Classic; ESPN Deportes; ESPNews; EVINE Live; Flix; FOX College Sports Central; FOX College Sports Pacific; Fox Deportes; Fox Sports 1; Fuse; FXM; FYI; Golf Channel; Great American Country; GSN; HGTV; History; History en Espanol; History International; IFC; Investigation Discovery; LMN; MTV Classic; MTV Hits; MTV2; National Geographic Channel; NBC Universo; NBCSN; Nick Jr.; Nicktoons; Outdoor Channel; OWN; Oprah Winfrey Network; Science Channel; Starz Encore (multiplexed); Sundance TV; Syfy; TeenNick; The Word Network; Tr3s; Trinity Broadcasting Network (TBN); Turner Classic Movies; UP; VH1 Soul; ViendoMovies; WE tv.
Pay Service 1
Pay Units: N.A.
Programming (via satellite): HBO.
Digital Pay Service 1
Pay Units: N.A.
Programming (via satellite): Cinemax (multiplexed); HBO (multiplexed); HBO Latino; Showtime (multiplexed); Starz (multiplexed); The Movie Channel (multiplexed).
Video-On-Demand: No
Pay-Per-View
iN DEMAND (delivered digitally); Hot Choice (delivered digitally); Playboy TV (delivered digitally); Fresh (delivered digitally); Spice; Xcess (delivered digitally); Club Jenna (delivered digitally).

Internet Service
Operational: Yes.
Subscribers: 292.
Fee: $24.95 installation; $39.95 monthly.
Telephone Service
Digital: Operational
Subscribers: 42.
Miles of Plant: 70.0 (coaxial); 8.0 (fiber optic). Homes passed: 4,242.
Chief Executive Officer: Bill Haggarty. Regional Vice President: Andrew Dearth. Vice President, Marketing: Tracy Bass. Senior Vice President, Financial Planning: Daniel White.
Ownership: Vyve Broadband LLC (MSO).

PETERSBURG—Formerly served by Almega Cable. No longer in operation. ICA: TX0483.

PETTUS—Formerly served by National Cable Inc. No longer in operation. ICA: TX0561.

PFLUGERVILLE—Suddenlink Communications, 111 North College St, Georgetown, TX 78626-4101. Phones: 903-595-4321 (Tyler office); 800-999-6845 (Customer service); 314-315-9400. Web Site: http://www.suddenlink.com. Also serves Travis County (portions). ICA: TX0127.
TV Market Ranking: Below 100 (PFLUGERVILLE, Travis County (portions)). Franchise award date: N.A. Franchise expiration date: N.A. Began: January 18, 1980.
Channel capacity: 78 (operating 2-way). Channels available but not in use: N.A.
Basic Service
Subscribers: 4,310. Commercial subscribers: 79.
Programming (received off-air): KEYE-TV (CBS, TMO) Austin; KLRU (PBS) Austin; KNVA (CW, Grit, TheCoolTV) Austin; KTBC (Buzzr, FOX, Movies!) Austin; KVUE (ABC, Estrella TV) Austin; KXAN-TV (COZI TV, NBC) Austin.
Programming (via satellite): C-SPAN; Pop; QVC; Trinity Broadcasting Network (TBN); WGN America.
Fee: $49.95 installation; $33.24 monthly; $1.50 converter.
Expanded Basic Service 1
Subscribers: N.A.
Programming (via satellite): A&E; AMC; Animal Planet; BET; Cartoon Network; CMT; CNBC; CNN; Comedy Central; C-SPAN 2; Discovery Channel; Disney Channel; E! HD; ESPN; ESPN2; Food Network; Fox News Channel; Fox Sports 1; FOX Sports Southwest; Freeform; FX; Golf Channel; HGTV; History; HLN; Lifetime; MSNBC; MTV; NBCSN; Nickelodeon; Spike TV; Syfy; TBS; The Weather Channel; TLC; TNT; Travel Channel; truTV; Turner Classic Movies; TV Land; Univision Studios; USA Network; VH1.
Fee: $27.99 monthly.
Digital Basic Service
Subscribers: N.A.
Programming (via satellite): BBC America; Bloomberg Television; Cooking Channel; Discovery Digital Networks; Disney XD; DIY Network; ESPN Classic; ESPNews; Fuse;

2017 Edition

D-769

Texas—Cable Systems

FYI; GSN; History International; LMN; MC; Outdoor Channel; Starz Encore; Sundance TV.

Pay Service 1
Pay Units: N.A.
Programming (via satellite): Cinemax (multiplexed); HBO (multiplexed); Showtime; Starz; Starz Encore.
Fee: $8.99 monthly (Showtime), $9.99 monthly (Cinemax or Starz/Encore), $11.99 monthly (HBO).

Digital Pay Service 1
Pay Units: N.A.
Programming (via satellite): Cinemax (multiplexed); HBO (multiplexed); Showtime (multiplexed); Starz (multiplexed); The Movie Channel (multiplexed).
Video-On-Demand: No

Pay-Per-View
ESPN Now (delivered digitally); Playboy TV (delivered digitally); Hot Choice (delivered digitally); Fresh (delivered digitally); iN DEMAND.

Internet Service
Operational: Yes.
Broadband Service: Suddenlink High Speed Internet.
Fee: $45.95 installation; $29.95 monthly.

Telephone Service
Digital: Operational
Fee: $44.95 monthly
Miles of Plant: 190.0 (coaxial); 18.0 (fiber optic). Homes passed: 12,211.
Senior Vice President, Corporate Finance: Michael Pflantz. General Manager: Dale Hoffman. Chief Technician & Marketing Director: Wesley Houghteling.
Ownership: Cequel Communications Holdings I LLC (MSO).

PHARR—Time Warner Cable, 2921 South Expwy 83, PO Box 2327, Harlingen, TX 78551-2327. Phones: 956-230-0465; 972-899-7300 (Flower Mound office); 956-425-7880. Fax: 956-412-0959. Web Site: http://www.timewarnercable.com. Also serves Alamo, Alton, Brownsville, Cameron County (portions), Combes, Donna, Edcouch, Edinburg, Elsa, Escobares, Fronton, Garceno, Garciasville, Harlingen, Hidalgo, Hidalgo County (portions), Indian Lake, La Feria, La Grulla, La Joya, La Rosita, La Villa, Laguna Heights, Laguna Vista, Las Milpas, Lopezville, Los Barreras, Los Fresnos, Los Saenz, Lyford, McAllen, Mercedes, Mission, Olmito, Palm Valley, Palmhurst, Palmview, Penitas, Port Isabel, Primera, Rancho Viejo, Raymondville, Rio Del Sol, Rio Grande City, Rio Hondo, Roma, San Benito, San Juan (Hidalgo County), Santa Cruz, Santa Rosa, South Padre Island, Starr County (portions), Sullivan City, Weslaco & Willacy County (portions). ICA: TX0017.
TV Market Ranking: Below 100 (Alamo, Alton, Brownsville, Cameron County (portions), Combes, Donna, Edcouch, Edinburg, Elsa, Escobares, Fronton, Garceno, Garciasville, Hidalgo, Hidalgo County (portions), Indian Lake, La Feria, La Grulla, La Joya, La Rosita, La Villa, Laguna Heights, Laguna Vista, Las Milpas, Lopezville, Los Barreras, Los Fresnos, Los Saenz, Lyford, McAllen, Mercedes, Mission, Olmito, Palm Valley, Palmhurst, Palmview, Penitas, Port Isabel, Primera, Rancho Viejo, Raymondville, Rio Del Sol, Rio Grande City, Rio Hondo, Roma, San Benito, San Juan (Hidalgo County), Santa Cruz, Santa Rosa, South Padre Island, Starr County (portions), Sullivan City, Weslaco, Willacy County (portions), Harlingen, PHARR). Franchise award date: N.A. Franchise expiration date: N.A. Began: January 1, 1966.
Channel capacity: N.A. Channels available but not in use: N.A.

Basic Service
Subscribers: 113,851.
Programming (received off-air): KAZH-LP (Azteca America) McAllen; KFXV-LD (CW) McAllen; KGBT-TV (CBS, IND) Harlingen; KLUJ-TV (TBN) Harlingen; KMBH (COZI TV, PBS) Harlingen; KNVO (UNV) McAllen; KRGV-TV (ABC, MeTV, This TV) Weslaco; KTLM (TMO) Rio Grande City; KVEO-TV (Estrella TV, NBC) Brownsville; KXFX-CD (UniMas) Brownsville.
Programming (via satellite): Bravo; C-SPAN; QVC; various Mexican stations.
Fee: $39.99 installation; $28.00 monthly.

Expanded Basic Service 1
Subscribers: N.A.
Programming (via satellite): A&E; AMC; Animal Planet; Cartoon Network; CMT; CNBC; CNN; Comedy Central; C-SPAN 2; Discovery Channel; Disney Channel; E! HD; ESPN; ESPN2; EWTN Global Catholic Network; Food Network; Fox Deportes; Fox News Channel; FOX Sports Southwest; Freeform; FX; Golf Channel; Great American Country; Hallmark Channel; HGTV; History; HLN; INSP; Jewelry Television; Lifetime; LMN; MSNBC; MTV; National Geographic Channel; NBC Universo; Nickelodeon; Oxygen; Spike TV; Syfy; TBS; The Weather Channel; TLC; TNT; Travel Channel; truTV; Turner Classic Movies; TV Land; Univision; USA Network; VH1; WE tv.
Fee: $27.15 monthly.

Digital Basic Service
Subscribers: N.A.
Programming (via satellite): A&E; AMC; Animal Planet; AXS TV; BBC America; BBC America On Demand; Bloomberg Television; Boomerang; Bravo; Cartoon Network; Cloo; CMT; CNN; Comedy Central; Cooking Channel; C-SPAN; C-SPAN 2; C-SPAN 3; Daystar TV Network; Destination America; Discovery Channel; Discovery Kids Channel; Discovery Life Channel; Disney Channel; Disney XD; DIY Network; E! HD; ESPN; ESPN Classic; ESPN HD; ESPN2; ESPN2 HD; ESPNews; ESPNU; EWTN Global Catholic Network; Food Network; Food Network On Demand; Fox Business Network; Fox Deportes; Fox News Channel; FOX Sports Southwest; Freeform; Fuse; FX; FYI; Golf Channel; Great American Country; GSN; Hallmark Channel; HD Theater; HGTV; HGTV On Demand; History; History International; HLN; IFC; INSP; Investigation Discovery; Jewelry Television; Lifetime; LMN; MC; MSNBC; MTV; MTV Classic; MTV Hits; MTV2; Nat Geo WILD; National Geographic Channel; National Geographic Channel On Demand; NBA TV; NBCSN; Nick Jr.; Nickelodeon; Nicktoons; OWN: Oprah Winfrey Network; Oxygen; Oxygen On Demand; QVC; Science Channel; Spike TV; Syfy; TBS; TeenNick; The Weather Channel; TLC; TNT; TNT HD; Travel Channel; truTV; Turner Classic Movies; TV Guide Network; TV Land; UniMas; Universal HD; Univision; USA Network; VH1; WE tv.
Fee: $5.00 monthly.

Digital Expanded Basic Service
Subscribers: N.A.
Programming (via satellite): Canal Sur; Cinelatino; CNN en Espanol; ESPN Deportes; FOX College Sports Central; FOX College Sports Pacific; Fox Life; Fox Sports 1; Fox Sports 2; FXM; HTV; Infinito; La Familia Cosmovision; NBA TV; NBC Universo; Starz Encore; Sundance TV; Tennis Channel; Toon Disney en Espanol; Tr3s; VideoRola.

Digital Pay Service 1
Pay Units: N.A.
Programming (via satellite): Cinemax (multiplexed); Cinemax On Demand; HBO (multiplexed); HBO GO; HBO HD; Showtime (multiplexed); Showtime HD; Showtime On Demand; Starz (multiplexed); The Movie Channel (multiplexed); The Movie Channel On Demand.
Fee: $14.99 monthly (each).
Video-On-Demand: Yes

Pay-Per-View
NBA League Pass (delivered digitally); NHL Center Ice (delivered digitally); MLB Extra Innings (delivered digitally); Hot Choice (delivered digitally); iN DEMAND (delivered digitally); Playboy TV (delivered digitally); Fresh (delivered digitally); Shorteez (delivered digitally).

Internet Service
Operational: Yes. Began: November 30, 2001.
Subscribers: 119,432.
Broadband Service: Road Runner.
Fee: $49.99 installation; $44.95 monthly.

Telephone Service
Digital: Operational
Subscribers: 42,773.
Fee: $44.95 monthly
Miles of Plant: 6,718.0 (coaxial); 1,531.0 (fiber optic). Homes passed: 413,897.
President: Gordon Harp. Vice President: Brad Wackley. Engineering Director: John Linton. Technical Operations Manager: Ana Rodriguez.
Ownership: Time Warner Cable (MSO).; Advance/Newhouse Partnership (MSO).

PILOT POINT—Suddenlink Communications, 520 Maryville Centre Dr, Ste 300, St. Louis, MO 63141. Phones: 314-315-9400; 972-347-9779. Web Site: http://www.suddenlink.com. Also serves Anna, Aubrey, Celina, Gunter, Krugerville, Lakewood Village, Little Elm, Melissa, Oak Point, Prosper, Sanger & Tioga. ICA: TX0286.
TV Market Ranking: 12 (Lakewood Village, Little Elm, Oak Point, Prosper); Below 100 (Anna, Aubrey, Celina, Gunter, Krugerville, Melissa, PILOT POINT, Sanger, Tioga). Franchise award date: N.A. Franchise expiration date: N.A. Began: June 1, 1982.
Channel capacity: 54 (operating 2-way). Channels available but not in use: N.A.

Basic Service
Subscribers: 5,795. Commercial subscribers: 58.
Programming (received off-air): KAZD (Azteca America, IND) Lake Dallas; KDAF (Antenna TV, CW, This TV) Dallas; KDFI (Bounce TV, Buzzr, Heroes & Icons, MNT, Movies!) Dallas; KDFW (FOX) Dallas; KDTN (Daystar TV, ETV) Denton; KERA-TV (PBS) Dallas; KMPX (Estrella TV) Decatur; KPXD-TV (ION) Arlington; KSTR-DT (getTV, UniMas) Irving; KTVT (CBS, Decades) Fort Worth; KTXA (IND, MeTV) Fort Worth; KUVN-DT (UNV) Garland; KXAS-TV (COZI TV, NBC) Fort Worth; KXII (CBS, FOX, MNT) Sherman; KXTX-TV (TMO) Dallas; WFAA (ABC) Dallas.
Programming (via satellite): C-SPAN; QVC; Trinity Broadcasting Network (TBN); Univision; WGN America.
Fee: $49.95 installation; $38.24 monthly.

Expanded Basic Service 1
Subscribers: N.A.
Programming (via satellite): A&E; AMC; Animal Planet; BET; Bravo; Cartoon Network; CNBC; CNN; Comedy Central; Discovery Channel; Disney Channel; E! HD; ESPN; ESPN2; Food Network; Fox News Channel; Fox Sports 1; FOX Sports Southwest; Freeform; FX; Golf Channel; Great American Country; Hallmark Channel; HGTV; History; HLN; Lifetime; MSNBC; MTV; National Geographic Channel; Nickelodeon; Outdoor Channel; Pop; Spike TV; Syfy; TBS; The Weather Channel; TLC; TNT; Travel Channel; truTV; Turner Classic Movies; TV Land; USA Network; VH1.

Digital Basic Service
Subscribers: N.A.
Programming (via satellite): AXS TV; BBC America; Bloomberg Television; Cloo; C-SPAN 3; Discovery Digital Networks; Disney XD; ESPN Classic; ESPNews; FOX College Sports Central; FOX College Sports Pacific; Fox Sports 2; Fuse; FXM; FYI; GSN; HD Theater; History International; HITS (Head-end In The Sky); IFC; MC; NBCSN; Sundance TV; WE tv.

Digital Pay Service 1
Pay Units: N.A.
Programming (via satellite): Cinemax (multiplexed); Flix; HBO (multiplexed); Showtime (multiplexed); Showtime HD; Starz (multiplexed); Starz Encore (multiplexed); The Movie Channel (multiplexed).
Video-On-Demand: No

Pay-Per-View
iN DEMAND (delivered digitally); Playboy TV (delivered digitally).

Internet Service
Operational: Yes.
Subscribers: 9,882.
Broadband Service: Suddenlink High Speed Internet.
Fee: $49.95 installation; $25.95 monthly.

Telephone Service
Digital: Operational
Subscribers: 3,185.
Fee: $44.95 monthly
Miles of Plant: 802.0 (coaxial); 112.0 (fiber optic). Homes passed: 37,664.
Senior Vice President, Corporate Finance: Michael Pflantz. Regional Manager: Todd Cruthird.
Ownership: Cequel Communications Holdings I LLC (MSO).

PITTSBURG—Suddenlink Communications, 1506 Shadywood Ln, PO Box 1236, Mount Pleasant, TX 75455. Phone: 314-315-9400. Fax: 903-572-5669. Web Site: http://www.suddenlink.com. Also serves Camp County (portions). ICA: TX0219.
TV Market Ranking: Outside TV Markets (PITTSBURG). Franchise award date: N.A. Franchise expiration date: N.A. Began: November 1, 1969.
Channel capacity: 36 (operating 2-way). Channels available but not in use: N.A.

Basic Service
Subscribers: 654. Commercial subscribers: 79.
Programming (received off-air): KETK-TV (Estrella TV, NBC) Jacksonville; KFXK-TV (FOX) Longview; KLTV (ABC, Bounce TV, TMO) Tyler; KSHV-TV (MNT) Shreveport; KSLA (Bounce TV, CBS, Grit, This TV) Shreveport.
Programming (via microwave): KERA-TV (PBS) Dallas; KXAS-TV (COZI TV, NBC) Fort Worth; WFAA (ABC) Dallas.
Programming (via satellite): C-SPAN; Discovery Channel; HLN; TBS; The Weather Channel.
Fee: $54.95 installation; $35.24 monthly.

Expanded Basic Service 1
Subscribers: N.A.
Programming (via satellite): A&E; AMC; BET; Cartoon Network; CNN; Disney Channel; ESPN; ESPN2; Fox News Channel; FOX Sports Southwest; Freeform; FX; ION Television; Lifetime; MoviePlex; MTV; Nickelodeon; OWN: Oprah Winfrey Network; QVC; Spike TV; TLC; TNT; Univision; Univision Studios; USA Network.
Fee: $10.97 monthly.

Digital Basic Service
Subscribers: N.A.
Programming (via satellite): BBC America; Bloomberg Television; Discovery Digital Networks; Disney XD; ESPN Classic; ESPNews; Fox Sports 1; Fuse; Golf Channel; GSN; LMN; MC; Starz Encore; truTV.

Pay Service 1
Pay Units: N.A.
Programming (via satellite): Cinemax; HBO; Showtime; Starz; Starz Encore.
Fee: $25.00 installation; $11.00 monthly (Cinemax, HBO or Showtime).

Digital Pay Service 1
Pay Units: N.A.
Programming (via satellite): Cinemax (multiplexed); HBO (multiplexed); Showtime (multiplexed); Starz (multiplexed); The Movie Channel (multiplexed).

Video-On-Demand: No

Pay-Per-View
ESPN Now (delivered digitally); Fresh (delivered digitally); Hot Choice (delivered digitally); iN DEMAND (delivered digitally).

Internet Service
Operational: Yes.
Broadband Service: Suddenlink High Speed Internet.
Fee: $49.95 installation; $25.95 monthly.

Telephone Service
Digital: Operational
Miles of Plant: 33.0 (coaxial); None (fiber optic). Homes passed: 2,016.
Senior Vice President, Corporate Finance: Michael Pflantz. General Manager & Chief Technician: Ron Eubanks.
Ownership: Cequel Communications Holdings I LLC (MSO).

PLACEDO—Formerly served by National Cable Inc. No longer in operation. ICA: TX0641.

PLAINS—Formerly served by Almega Cable. No longer in operation. ICA: TX0457.

PLAINVIEW—Suddenlink Communications, 2301 West 5th St, PO Box 428, Plainview, TX 79073. Phone: 314-315-9400. Fax: 806-293-1152. Web Site: http://www.suddenlink.com. Also serves Floydada & Hale County. ICA: TX0076.
TV Market Ranking: Below 100 (Hale County (portions)); Outside TV Markets (Hale County (portions), PLAINVIEW, Floydada). Franchise award date: N.A. Franchise expiration date: N.A. Began: March 15, 1965.
Channel capacity: 116 (operating 2-way). Channels available but not in use: N.A.

Basic Service
Subscribers: 4,264.
Programming (received off-air): KAMC (ABC, Bounce TV) Lubbock; KAMR-TV (IND, NBC) Amarillo; KCBD (NBC, This TV) Lubbock; KJTV-TV (FOX) Lubbock; KLBK-TV (CBS) Lubbock; KPTB-DT (GLC) Lubbock; KTTZ-TV (PBS) Lubbock; KVII-TV (ABC, CW) Amarillo; allband FM.
Programming (via satellite): C-SPAN; Hallmark Channel; Pop; Telemundo; The Weather Channel; Trinity Broadcasting Network (TBN); WGN America.
Fee: $36.05 installation; $33.42 monthly.

Expanded Basic Service 1
Subscribers: N.A.
Programming (via satellite): A&E; AMC; Animal Planet; BET; Cartoon Network; CNBC; CNN; Comedy Central; Discovery Channel; Disney Channel; E! HD; ESPN; ESPN2; Food Network; Fox News Channel; Fox Sports 1; FOX Sports Southwest; Freeform; FX; Great American Country; HGTV; History; HLN; ION Television; Lifetime; MSNBC; MTV; NBC Universo; NBCSN; Nickelodeon; Outdoor Channel; Spike TV; Syfy; TBS; TLC; TNT; Travel Channel; Turner Classic Movies; TV Land; Univision; USA Network; VH1.

Digital Basic Service
Subscribers: N.A.
Programming (via satellite): BBC America; Bloomberg Television; Boomerang; Discovery Digital Networks; Disney XD; Golf Channel; GSN; HITS (Headend In The Sky); IFC; LMN; Sundance TV; truTV.

Pay Service 1
Pay Units: N.A.
Programming (via satellite): Cinemax; HBO (multiplexed); Showtime; Starz; Starz Encore; The Movie Channel.
Fee: $35.00 installation.

Digital Pay Service 1
Pay Units: N.A.
Programming (via satellite): Cinemax (multiplexed); HBO (multiplexed); Showtime (multiplexed); Starz (multiplexed); Starz Encore; The Movie Channel (multiplexed).
Fee: $10.00 monthly (each).

Video-On-Demand: No

Pay-Per-View
iN DEMAND; iN DEMAND (delivered digitally); Sports PPV (delivered digitally).

Internet Service
Operational: Yes.
Subscribers: 3,884.
Broadband Service: Suddenlink High Speed Internet.
Fee: $49.95 installation; $24.95 monthly.

Telephone Service
Digital: Operational
Subscribers: 1,764.
Fee: $48.95 monthly
Miles of Plant: 184.0 (coaxial); 71.0 (fiber optic). Homes passed: 13,772.
Senior Vice President, Corporate Finance: Michael Pflantz. General Manager: Pete Strom. Chief Technician: Roger Jones.
Ownership: Cequel Communications Holdings I LLC (MSO).

PLANO—Time Warner Cable. Now served by DALLAS, TX [TX0003]. ICA: TX0833.

PLEAK—Formerly served by Almega Cable. No longer in operation. ICA: TX0265.

PLEASANT VALLEY—Formerly served by CableDirect. No longer in operation. ICA: TX0466.

PLEASANTON—CommZoom, 2438 Boardwalk, San Antonio, TX 78217. Phone: 844-858-8500. Web Site: http://www.commzoom.com. Also serves Atascosa County (portions). ICA: TX0194.
TV Market Ranking: 45 (Atascosa County (portions) (portions), PLEASANTON); Outside TV Markets (Atascosa County (portions) (portions), PLEASANTON). Franchise award date: October 2, 1979. Franchise expiration date: N.A. Began: October 31, 1980.
Channel capacity: N.A. Channels available but not in use: N.A.

Basic Service
Subscribers: 112.
Programming (received off-air): KABB (FOX, The Country Network) San Antonio; KENS (CBS, Estrella TV) San Antonio; KLRN (PBS) San Antonio; KMOL-LD (Movies!, NBC) Victoria; KMYS (CW) Kerrville; KPXL-TV (ION) Uvalde; KSAT-TV (ABC, MeTV) San Antonio; KVDA (TMO) San Antonio; KWEX-DT (getTV, UNV) San Antonio; 15 FMs.
Programming (via satellite): A&E; AMC; CMT; CNBC; C-SPAN; ESPN; FOX Sports Southwest; Freeform; HLN; Lifetime; Nickelodeon; QVC; Spike TV; Syfy; Univision.
Fee: $49.95 installation; $62.70 monthly.

Expanded Basic Service 1
Subscribers: N.A.
Programming (via satellite): CNN; Discovery Channel; Disney Channel; E! HD; MSNBC; MTV; TBS; TNT; USA Network; WGN America.
Fee: $18.00 monthly.

Pay Service 1
Pay Units: N.A.
Programming (via satellite): Cinemax; HBO; Showtime; The Movie Channel.
Fee: $11.95 monthly (each).

Video-On-Demand: No

Internet Service
Operational: Yes.

Telephone Service
None
Miles of Plant: 56.0 (coaxial); None (fiber optic). Homes passed: 2,138.
Chief Executive Officer: Bob Cohen.
Ownership: CommZoom Communications LLC (MSO).

PLUM GROVE—Formerly served by Carrell Communications. No longer in operation. ICA: TX0437.

PONDER—Formerly served by SouthTel Communications LP. No longer in operation. ICA: TX0512.

PORT ARANSAS—Formerly served by Charter Communications. Now served by Time Warner Cable, ROCKPORT, TX [TX0116]. ICA: TX0835.

PORT ARTHUR—Time Warner Cable, 602 North Hwy 69, Nederland, TX 77627. Phones: 409-727-5867; 409-720-5500; 972-899-7300 (Flower Mound office). Fax: 409-727-5050. Web Site: http://www.timewarnercable.com. Also serves Beaumont, Bridge City, Chambers County (portions), Groves, Hardin County (portions), Kountze, Lumberton, Nederland, Orange, Orange County (portions), Pine Forest, Pinehurst, Port Acres, Port Neches, Rose Hill Acres, Sabine Pass, Silsbee, South Port Arthur, Vidor & West Orange. ICA: TX0022.
TV Market Ranking: 15,88 (Chambers County (portions)); 88 (Beaumont, Bridge City, Groves, Hardin County (portions), Kountze, Lumberton, Nederland, Orange, Orange County (portions), Pine Forest, Pinehurst, Port Acres, PORT ARTHUR, Port Neches, Rose Hill Acres, Sabine Pass, Silsbee, South Port Arthur, Vidor, West Orange); Outside TV Markets (Hardin County (portions). Franchise award date: June 1, 1973. Franchise expiration date: N.A. Began: June 1, 1973.
Channel capacity: N.A. Channels available but not in use: N.A.

Basic Service
Subscribers: 56,894.
Programming (received off-air): KBMT (ABC) Beaumont; KBTV-TV (Bounce TV, FOX) Port Arthur; KFDM (CBS, CW) Beaumont; KITU-TV (TBN) Beaumont; KUHT (PBS) Houston; 17 FMs.
Programming (via satellite): C-SPAN; C-SPAN 2; Pop; WGN America.
Fee: $39.99 installation; $28.00 monthly; $1.50 converter.

Expanded Basic Service 1
Subscribers: N.A.
Programming (via satellite): A&E; AMC; Animal Planet; BET; Bravo; Cartoon Network; CMT; CNBC; CNN; Comedy Central; Discovery Channel; Discovery Life Channel; Disney Channel; E! HD; ESPN; ESPN2; EVINE Live; EWTN Global Catholic Network; Food Network; Fox News Channel; FOX Sports Southwest; Freeform; FX; Golf Channel; Great American Country; Hallmark Channel; HGTV; History; HLN; ION Television; Lifetime; LMN; MoviePlex; MSNBC; MTV; National Geographic Channel; NBCSN; Nickelodeon; OWN: Oprah Winfrey Network; Oxygen; QVC; Spike TV; Syfy; TBS; The Weather Channel; TLC; TNT; Travel Channel; truTV; Turner Classic Movies; TV Land; Univision; Univision Studios; USA Network; VH1; WE tv.
Fee: $30.80 monthly.

Digital Basic Service
Subscribers: N.A.
Programming (via satellite): A&E; AMC; Animal Planet; AXS TV; BBC America; Bloomberg Television; Boomerang; Bravo; Cartoon Network; Cloo; CMT; CNBC; CNN; Comedy Central; Cooking Channel; C-SPAN; C-SPAN 2; C-SPAN 3; Daystar TV Network; Destination America; Discovery Channel; Discovery Kids Channel; Discovery Life Channel; Disney Channel; Disney XD; DIY Network; E! HD; ESPN; ESPN Classic; ESPN HD; ESPN2; ESPN2 HD; ESPNews; ESPNU; EVINE Live; EWTN Global Catholic Network; FamilyNet; Food Network; Food Network On Demand; Fox Business Network; Fox News Channel; Fox Sports 1; FOX Sports Southwest; Freeform; Fuse; FX; FYI; Golf Channel; Great American Country; Hallmark Channel; HD Theater; HGTV; HGTV On Demand; History; History International; HLN; IFC; Investigation Discovery; ION Television; La Familia Cosmovision; Lifetime; LMN; MC; MoviePlex; MSNBC; MTV; MTV Classic; MTV Hits; MTV2; Nat Geo WILD; National Geographic Channel; NBCSN; Nick Jr.; Nickelodeon; Nicktoons; OWN: Oprah Winfrey Network; Oxygen; Pop; QVC; Science Channel; Spike TV; Syfy; TBS; TBS HD; TeenNick; The Weather Channel; TLC; TNT; TNT HD; Tr3s; Travel Channel; truTV; Turner Classic Movies; TV Guide Network; TV Land; Universal HD; USA Network; VH1; WE tv.
Fee: $5.00 monthly.

Digital Expanded Basic Service
Subscribers: N.A.
Programming (via satellite): Canal Sur; Cinelatino; CNN en Espanol; ESPN Deportes; FOX College Sports Central; FOX College Sports Pacific; Fox Deportes; Fox Life; Fox Sports 1; Fox Sports 2; FXM; HTV; Infinito; La Familia Cosmovision; NBA TV; Starz Encore (multiplexed); Sundance TV; Tennis Channel; Toon Disney en Espanol; Tr3s; UniMas; Univision; Univision Studios; VideoRola.

Texas—Cable Systems

Digital Pay Service 1
Pay Units: N.A.
Programming (via satellite): Cinemax (multiplexed); Cinemax On Demand; HBO (multiplexed); HBO GO; HBO HD; Showtime (multiplexed); Showtime HD; Showtime On Demand; Starz (multiplexed); The Movie Channel (multiplexed); The Movie Channel On Demand.
Fee: $14.99 monthly (each).
Video-On-Demand: Yes
Pay-Per-View
iN DEMAND (delivered digitally); Playboy TV (delivered digitally); NHL Center Ice (delivered digitally); Fresh (delivered digitally); Shorteez (delivered digitally); Hot Choice (delivered digitally); NBA League Pass (delivered digitally); MLB Extra Innings (delivered digitally).
Internet Service
Operational: Yes. Began: July 1, 2001.
Subscribers: 54,443.
Broadband Service: Road Runner.
Fee: $49.99 installation; $44.95 monthly.
Telephone Service
Digital: Operational
Subscribers: 24,020.
Fee: $44.95 monthly
Miles of Plant: 4,147.0 (coaxial); 1,436.0 (fiber optic). Homes passed: 172,376.
President: Connie Wharton. Vice President & General Manager: Roy Rudd. Engineering Director: Herscel Stracner. Public Affairs Manager: George Perrett.
Ownership: Time Warner Cable (MSO).; Advance/Newhouse Partnership (MSO).

PORT ARTHUR—Time Warner Cable. Now served by PORT ARTHUR (formerly Beaumont), TX [TX0022]. ICA: TX0018.

PORT ISABEL—Time Warner Cable. Now served by PHARR, TX [TX0017]. ICA: TX0197.

PORT LAVACA—Cable One, 501 North Virginia St, Port Lavaca, TX 77979-3019. Phone: 361-552-9621. Fax: 361-552-7074. E-mail: dking@cableone.net. Web Site: http://www.cableone.net. Also serves Calhoun County & Point Comfort. ICA: TX0146.
TV Market Ranking: Below 100 (Calhoun County, Point Comfort, PORT LAVACA). Franchise award date: January 1, 1958. Franchise expiration date: N.A. Began: July 1, 1958.
Channel capacity: N.A. Channels available but not in use: N.A.
Basic Service
Subscribers: 1,958.
Programming (received off-air): KAVU-TV (ABC) Victoria; KEDT (PBS) Corpus Christi; KVCT (FOX, This TV, TMO) Victoria; 12 FMs.
Programming (via microwave): KHOU (Bounce TV, CBS) Houston; KHTV-CD Los Angeles; KPRC-TV (NBC, This TV) Houston; KTRK-TV (ABC, Live Well Network) Houston.
Programming (via satellite): A&E; AMC; Animal Planet; BET; Cartoon Network; CMT; CNBC; CNN; Comedy Central; C-SPAN; C-SPAN 2; Discovery Channel; Disney Channel; ESPN; ESPN2; Food Network; Fox Deportes; Fox News Channel; FOX Sports Southwest; Freeform; FX; HGTV; History; HLN; Lifetime; MSNBC; MTV; Nickelodeon; Pop; Spike TV; Syfy; TBS; Telemundo; The Weather Channel; TLC; TNT; Turner Classic Movies; TV Land; USA Network; VH1.
Fee: $30.00 installation; $35.00 monthly.

Digital Basic Service
Subscribers: N.A.
Programming (via satellite): Boomerang; Discovery Digital Networks; Disney XD; DMX Music; ESPN Classic; ESPNews; Fox Sports 1; FYI; History International; National Geographic Channel; truTV.
Digital Pay Service 1
Pay Units: N.A.
Programming (via satellite): Cinemax (multiplexed); Flix; HBO (multiplexed); Showtime (multiplexed); Sundance TV; The Movie Channel (multiplexed).
Fee: $15.00 monthly (each).
Video-On-Demand: No
Pay-Per-View
iN DEMAND (delivered digitally); Pleasure (delivered digitally); SexSee (delivered digitally); Juicy (delivered digitally); VaVoom (delivered digitally); ESPN (delivered digitally).
Internet Service
Operational: Yes. Began: May 1, 2002.
Broadband Service: CableONE.net.
Fee: $75.00 installation; $43.00 monthly; $5.00 modem lease.
Telephone Service
Digital: Operational
Fee: $39.95 monthly
Miles of Plant: 82.0 (coaxial); None (fiber optic). Homes passed: 4,964.
Vice President: Patrick A. Dolohanty. General Manager: David King. Chief Technician: Martin Schooley. Office Manager: Jamie Mosmeyer.
Ownership: Cable ONE Inc. (MSO).

PORT O'CONNOR—Time Warner Cable. Now served by SEADRIFT, TX [TX0433]. ICA: TX0369.

PORTER—Suddenklink Communications. Now served by KINGWOOD, TX [TX0052]. ICA: TX0312.

PORTLAND—Formerly served by Charter Communications. Now served by Time Warner Cable, ROCKPORT, TX [TX0116]. ICA: TX0136.

POSSUM KINGDOM LAKE—Vyve Broadband, 2804B FM 51 South, Decatur, TX 76234. Phone: 800-937-1397. Web Site: http://vyvebroadband.com. ICA: TX1046.
TV Market Ranking: Outside TV Markets (POSSUM KINGDOM LAKE).
Channel capacity: N.A. Channels available but not in use: N.A.
Basic Service
Subscribers: 198.
Fee: $59.99 installation; $25.00 monthly.
Senior Vice President, Financial Planning: Daniel White.
Ownership: Vyve Broadband LLC (MSO).

POST—Suddenlink Communications. Now served by LUBBOCK, TX [TX0012]. ICA: TX0241.

POTOSI—Formerly served by Jayroc Cablevision. No longer in operation. ICA: TX0837.

POTTSBORO—TV Cable of Grayson County, 501 Spur 316 Hwy, Ste. 106, PO Box 2084, Pottsboro, TX 75076. Phones: 888-815-0636; 903-786-7477. E-mail: tvcable@graysoncable.com. Web Site: http://www.graysoncable.com. Also serves Southmayd. ICA: TX0502.
TV Market Ranking: Below 100 (POTTSBORO, Southmayd). Franchise award date: N.A.

Franchise expiration date: N.A. Began: June 1, 1983.
Channel capacity: 42 (not 2-way capable). Channels available but not in use: N.A.
Basic Service
Subscribers: 535.
Programming (received off-air): KDAF (Antenna TV, CW, This TV) Dallas; KDFI (Bounce TV, Buzzr, Heroes & Icons, MNT, Movies!) Dallas; KERA-TV (PBS) Dallas; KTEN (ABC, CW, NBC) Ada; KTVT (CBS, Decades) Fort Worth; KTXA (IND, MeTV) Fort Worth; KXAS-TV (COZI TV, NBC) Fort Worth; KXII (CBS, FOX, MNT) Sherman; KXTX-TV (TMO) Dallas; WFAA (ABC) Dallas.
Programming (via satellite): CMT; CNN; Discovery Channel; Disney Channel; ESPN; Freeform; MTV; Nickelodeon; TBS; TNT; WGN America.
Fee: $35.00 installation; $21.13 monthly.
Pay Service 1
Pay Units: N.A.
Programming (via satellite): HBO; Starz; Starz Encore.
Fee: $9.50 monthly (Starz/Encore), $11.95 monthly (HBO).
Internet Service
Operational: Yes.
Fee: $24.99-$149.95 monthly.
Telephone Service
Digital: Operational
Fee: $29.95 monthly
Miles of Plant: 9.0 (coaxial); None (fiber optic).
General Manager: Chuck Davis.
Ownership: Chuck Davis (MSO).

POWDERLY—Formerly served by Almega Cable. No longer in operation. ICA: TX0361.

PRAIRIE VIEW—Suddenlink Communications, 520 Maryville Centre Dr, Ste 300, St. Louis, MO 63141. Phones: 800-999-6845 (Customer service); 314-315-9400. Web Site: http://www.suddenlink.com. Also serves Waller. ICA: TX0304.
TV Market Ranking: Below 100 (Waller, PRAIRIE VIEW). Franchise award date: N.A. Franchise expiration date: N.A. Began: July 1, 1983.
Channel capacity: N.A. Channels available but not in use: N.A.
Basic Service
Subscribers: 325.
Programming (received off-air): KHOU (Bounce TV, CBS) Houston; KIAH (Antenna TV, CW) Houston; KPRC-TV (NBC, This TV) Houston; KRIV (FOX) Houston; KTRK-TV (ABC, Live Well Network) Houston; KTXH (Buzzr, MNT, Movies!) Houston; KUHT (PBS) Houston; KYAZ (Azteca America, IND) Katy; KZJL (Estrella TV) Houston.
Programming (via satellite): A&E; AMC; Animal Planet; BET; Cartoon Network; CMT; CNBC; CNN; Comedy Central; C-SPAN; Discovery Channel; E! HD; ESPN; ESPN2; Fox News Channel; Freeform; Hallmark Channel; HGTV; History; HLN; Lifetime; MTV; Nickelodeon; Pop; Syfy; TBS; The Weather Channel; TLC; TNT; Turner Classic Movies; USA Network; VH1.
Fee: $55.82 monthly.
Pay Service 1
Pay Units: N.A.
Programming (via satellite): Cinemax; HBO; Showtime.
Fee: $9.00 monthly (each).
Video-On-Demand: No
Internet Service
Operational: No.

Telephone Service
None
Miles of Plant: 44.0 (coaxial); None (fiber optic). Homes passed: 1,266.
Senior Vice President, Corporate Finance: Michael Pflantz. Regional Manager: Todd Cruthird.
Ownership: Cequel Communications Holdings I LLC (MSO).

PREMONT—Time Warner Cable. Now served by CORPUS CHRISTI, TX [TX0010]. ICA: TX0352.

PRESIDIO—Presidio TV Cable, 307 E Ave East, Alpine, TX 79830. Phones: 432-729-4347; 800-446-5661; 432-837-2300. Fax: 432-837-5423. E-mail: mtnzone@sbcglobal.net. Web Site: http://www.mountainzonetv.net. ICA: TX0432.
TV Market Ranking: Outside TV Markets (PRESIDIO). Franchise award date: April 2, 1982. Franchise expiration date: N.A. Began: May 1, 1973.
Channel capacity: N.A. Channels available but not in use: N.A.
Basic Service
Subscribers: N.A.
Programming (via satellite): A&E; Animal Planet; Azteca; Cartoon Network; CNN; Comedy Central; C-SPAN; Discovery Channel; Disney Channel; ESPN; ESPN2; EWTN Global Catholic Network; Fox News Channel; FOX Sports Southwest; Great American Country; HGTV; History; HLN; Lifetime; MTV; NFL Network; Nickelodeon; Syfy; TBS; Telemundo; The Weather Channel; TLC; TNT; Turner Classic Movies; TV Land; UniMas; Univision; Univision Studios; USA Network; various Mexican stations; VH1; WGN America.
Programming (via translator): KABB (FOX, The Country Network) San Antonio; KLRN (PBS) San Antonio; KMID (ABC) Midland; KMLM-DT (GLC) Odessa; KOSA-TV (CBS, MNT) Odessa; KTSM-TV (Estrella TV, NBC) El Paso; KVIA-TV (ABC, Azteca America, CW) El Paso; KWES-TV (CW, NBC, TMO) Odessa.
Fee: $25.00 installation; $48.00 monthly.
Pay Service 1
Pay Units: N.A.
Programming (via satellite): Cinemax; HBO; Showtime.
Fee: $10.00 installation.
Video-On-Demand: No
Internet Service
Operational: Yes. Began: June 1, 2004.
Broadband Service: In-house.
Fee: $150.00 installation; $60.00 monthly.
Telephone Service
None
Miles of Plant: 25.0 (coaxial); None (fiber optic). Homes passed: 700.
General Manager: Steve Neu. Office Manager: Lawrence Neu.
Ownership: Mountain Zone TV Systems (MSO).

PRESTON PENINSULA—Vyve Broadband, 4 International Dr, Ste 330, Rye Brook, NY 10573. Phones: 800-937-1397; 405-275-6923; 405-395-1131. Web Site: http://vyvebroadband.com. Also serves Pottsboro. ICA: TX0838.
TV Market Ranking: Below 100 (Pottsboro, PRESTON PENINSULA). Franchise award date: January 17, 1989. Franchise expiration date: N.A. Began: August 1, 1983.
Channel capacity: N.A. Channels available but not in use: N.A.

Cable Systems—Texas

Basic Service
Subscribers: 118.
Programming (received off-air): KDAF (Antenna TV, CW, This TV) Dallas; KDFI (Bounce TV, Buzzr, Heroes & Icons, MNT, Movies!) Dallas; KDFW (FOX) Dallas; KERA-TV (PBS) Dallas; KTEN (ABC, CW, NBC) Ada; KTVT (CBS, Decades) Fort Worth; KTXA (IND, MeTV) Fort Worth; KXAS-TV (COZI TV, NBC) Fort Worth; KXII (CBS, FOX, MNT) Sherman; KXTX-TV (TMO) Dallas; WFAA (ABC) Dallas.
Programming (via satellite): A&E; AMC; Animal Planet; Bravo; Cartoon Network; CMT; CNBC; CNN; Comedy Central; C-SPAN; Discovery Channel; Disney Channel; E! HD; ESPN; ESPN2; Food Network; Fox News Channel; FOX Sports Southwest; Freeform; FX; GSN; Hallmark Channel; HGTV; History; HLN; Lifetime; MSNBC; MTV; National Geographic Channel; Nickelodeon; Oxygen; QVC; Spike TV; Syfy; TBS; The Weather Channel; TLC; TNT; Travel Channel; Trinity Broadcasting Network (TBN); truTV; TV Land; USA Network; VH1.
Fee: $64.95 installation; $70.95 monthly.

Digital Basic Service
Subscribers: N.A.
Programming (via satellite): BBC America; BET; Bloomberg Television; Bravo; Discovery Life Channel; Disney XD; DMX Music; EVINE Live; Fox Sports 1; Fuse; FXM; FYI; Golf Channel; GSN; HGTV; History International; IFC; LMN; NBCSN; Nick Jr.; Outdoor Channel; TeenNick; Trinity Broadcasting Network (TBN); Turner Classic Movies; WE tv.

Pay Service 1
Pay Units: N.A.
Programming (via satellite): Cinemax; HBO; Showtime.
Fee: $9.00 monthly (each).

Digital Pay Service 1
Pay Units: N.A.
Programming (via satellite): Cinemax (multiplexed); Flix; HBO (multiplexed); Showtime (multiplexed); Starz (multiplexed); Starz Encore (multiplexed); The Movie Channel (multiplexed).

Video-On-Demand: No

Pay-Per-View
Hot Choice (delivered digitally); Playboy TV (delivered digitally); Fresh (delivered digitally); Shorteez (delivered digitally); iN DEMAND (delivered digitally).

Internet Service
Operational: No.

Telephone Service
None

Miles of Plant: 90.0 (coaxial); 14.0 (fiber optic). Homes passed: 6,690.
Chief Executive Officer: Bill Haggarty. Senior Vice President, Financial Planning: Daniel White. Regional Vice President: Andrew Dearth. Vice President, Marketing: Tracy Bass.
Ownership: Vyve Broadband LLC (MSO).

PRICE—Formerly served by Almega Cable. No longer in operation. ICA: TX0648.

PROGRESO—Formerly served by CableDirect. No longer in operation. ICA: TX0630.

QUANAH—Suddenlink Communications, 520 Maryville Centre Dr, Ste 300, St. Louis, MO 63141. Phones: 800-999-6845 (Customer service); 314-315-9400. Web Site: http://www.suddenlink.com. ICA: TX0839.
TV Market Ranking: Outside TV Markets (QUANAH). Franchise award date: N.A. Franchise expiration date: N.A. Began: April 1, 1963.
Channel capacity: N.A. Channels available but not in use: N.A.

Basic Service
Subscribers: 205.
Programming (received off-air): KAMR-TV (IND, NBC) Amarillo; KAUZ-TV (CBS, CW) Wichita Falls; KFDA-TV (CBS, TMO) Amarillo; KFDX-TV (NBC) Wichita Falls; KJTL (Bounce TV, FOX) Wichita Falls; KSWO-TV (ABC, TMO) Lawton; KWET (PBS) Cheyenne.
Programming (via satellite): A&E; AMC; Animal Planet; CMT; CNN; C-SPAN; Discovery Channel; Disney Channel; E! HD; ESPN; FOX Sports Southwest; Freeform; Hallmark Channel; HLN; Lifetime; Nickelodeon; QVC; Spike TV; Syfy; TBS; The Weather Channel; TLC; TNT; TV Land; USA Network; WGN America.
Fee: $28.45 monthly.

Pay Service 1
Pay Units: N.A.
Programming (via satellite): HBO; Showtime; The Movie Channel.
Fee: $7.95 monthly (TMC), $9.95 monthly (Showtime), $10.95 monthly (HBO).

Video-On-Demand: No

Internet Service
Operational: Yes. Began: December 29, 2003.
Broadband Service: Suddenlink High Speed Internet.
Fee: $49.95 installation; $38.95 monthly.

Telephone Service
None

Miles of Plant: 33.0 (coaxial); None (fiber optic). Homes passed: 1,634.
Senior Vice President, Corporate Finance: Michael Pflantz. Regional Manager: Todd Cruthird. Regional Marketing Manager: Beverly Gambell. Plant Manager: Ron Johnson.
Ownership: Cequel Communications Holdings I LLC (MSO).

QUEMADO—Time Warner Cable. Now served by EAGLE PASS, TX [TX0067]. ICA: TX1008.

QUINLAN—Formerly served by Zoom Media. No longer in operation. ICA: TX0793.

QUITAQUE—Formerly served by Almega Cable. No longer in operation. ICA: TX0840.

RALLS—Reach Broadband, PO Box 507, Arp, TX 75750. Phones: 903-859-3789; 800-687-1258. E-mail: support@reachbroadband.net. Web Site: http://www.reachbroadband.net. ICA: TX0377.
TV Market Ranking: Outside TV Markets (RALLS). Franchise award date: October 14, 1977. Franchise expiration date: N.A. Began: October 1, 1978.
Channel capacity: 61 (not 2-way capable). Channels available but not in use: N.A.

Basic Service
Subscribers: 42.
Programming (received off-air): KAMC (ABC, Bounce TV) Lubbock; KCBD (NBC, This TV) Lubbock; KJTV-TV (FOX) Lubbock; KLBK-TV (CBS) Lubbock; KPTB-DT (GLC) Lubbock; KTTZ-TV (PBS) Lubbock.
Programming (via satellite): AMC; CMT; CNN; Discovery Channel; Disney Channel; E! HD; ESPN; FOX Sports Southwest; Freeform; History; Lifetime; Nickelodeon; QVC; Spike TV; Syfy; TBS; The Weather Channel; TLC; TNT; Trinity Broadcasting Network (TBN); TV Land; USA Network; WGN America.
Programming (via translator): KVDA (TMO) San Antonio.
Fee: $49.95 installation; $26.30 monthly.

Pay Service 1
Pay Units: N.A.
Programming (via satellite): Cinemax; HBO.
Fee: $9.95 monthly (each).

Video-On-Demand: No

Internet Service
Operational: Yes.

Telephone Service
None

Miles of Plant: 13.0 (coaxial); None (fiber optic). Homes passed: 833.
Regional Manager: Ronnie Stafford. Office Manager: Jan Gibson. Controller: Jeffrey Lowe.
Ownership: RB3 LLC (MSO).

RANKIN—LynnStar Communications, 4500 Mercantile Plz, Ste 300, Fort Worth, TX 76137. Phones: 575-437-3101; 888-575-9230; 682-730-0900. Fax: 682-730-6400. Web Site: http://lynnstar.net; http://www.lynnstarcomm.com. ICA: TX1026.
TV Market Ranking: Outside TV Markets (RANKIN).
Channel capacity: N.A. Channels available but not in use: N.A.

Basic Service
Subscribers: 61.
Programming (received off-air): KMID (ABC) Midland; KMLM-DT (GLC) Odessa; KOSA-TV (CBS, MNT) Odessa; KPBT-TV (PBS) Odessa; KPEJ-TV (FOX) Odessa; KUPB (UNV) Midland; KWES-TV (CW, NBC, TMO) Odessa.
Programming (via satellite): Animal Planet; C-SPAN; HSN; Lifetime; TBS; Trinity Broadcasting Network (TBN); WGN America.
Fee: $49.95 installation; $23.72 monthly.

Expanded Basic Service 1
Subscribers: N.A.
Programming (via satellite): A&E; AMC; Cartoon Network; CMT; CNN; Discovery Channel; Discovery Life Channel; Disney Channel; ESPN; ESPN2; Food Network; Fox News Channel; FOX Sports Networks; Freeform; Hallmark Channel; HGTV; History; MoviePlex; MTV; National Geographic Channel; Nick At Nite; Nickelodeon; Spike TV; Syfy; The Weather Channel; TLC; TNT; UniMas; USA Network; VH1.
Fee: $28.35 monthly.

Digital Basic Service
Subscribers: N.A.
Programming (via satellite): BBC America; Bloomberg Television; Bravo; Centric; Cloo; CMT; Destination America; Discovery Kids Channel; Disney XD; DMX Music; ESPN Classic; ESPNews; FOX College Sports Central; FOX College Sports Pacific; Fox Sports 1; Fuse; FXM; FYI; Golf Channel; Great American Country; GSN; HGTV; History International; IFC; Investigation Discovery; LMN; MTV Classic; MTV Hits; MTV2; NBCSN; Nick Jr.; Outdoor Channel; OWN; Oprah Winfrey Network; Science Channel; Starz Encore (multiplexed); TeenNick; The Word Network; Turner Classic Movies; VH1 Soul; WE tv.
Fee: $20.90 monthly.

Pay Service 1
Pay Units: N.A.
Programming (via satellite): Cinemax; HBO.
Fee: $13.95 monthly (each).

Digital Pay Service 1
Pay Units: N.A.
Programming (via satellite): Cinemax (multiplexed); HBO (multiplexed); Showtime (multiplexed); Starz (multiplexed); The Movie Channel (multiplexed).
Fee: $9.95 monthly (Starz), $12.95 monthly (Cinemax, HBO, Showtime or TMC).

Video-On-Demand: No

Pay-Per-View
Playboy TV (delivered digitally); Fresh (delivered digitally).

Internet Service
Operational: No.

Telephone Service
None

Chairman of the Board & Government Relations Director: S. Gene Yarbrough. Chief Executive Officer, Executive Vice President & Board Member: Chris Romine. Chief Operations Officer, Executive Vice President & Board Member: Steve Sizemore. Vice President & Business Development & Countertrade Director: Gary Majors. Vice President & Programming & Vendor Relations Director: Gus Salvino. Vice President & Investor Relations Manager: Daniel J. Sweeney. Accounting Manager: Sheila Magness.
Ownership: Lynnstar Communications (MSO).

RAYMONDVILLE—Time Warner Cable. Now served by PHARR, TX [TX0017]. ICA: TX0173.

RAYWOOD—Formerly served by Cebridge Connections. No longer in operation. ICA: TX0340.

REALITOS—Formerly served by National Cable Inc. No longer in operation. ICA: TX0841.

REDWATER—Cable One. Now served by TEXARKANA, TX [TX0031]. ICA: TX0436.

REFUGIO—Time Warner Cable. Now served by CORPUS CHRISTI, TX [TX0010]. ICA: TX0214.

REKLAW—Formerly served by Almega Cable. No longer in operation. ICA: TX0698.

RENO (Parker County)—Formerly served by Almega Cable. No longer in operation. ICA: TX0261.

RICARDO—Formerly served by Riviera Cable TV. No longer in operation. ICA: TX0664.

RICHLAND SPRINGS—Formerly served by Almega Cable. No longer in operation. ICA: TX0632.

RIESEL—Formerly served by Cabletex Systems Inc. No longer in operation. ICA: TX0556.

RIO GRANDE CITY—Time Warner Cable. Now served by PHARR, TX [TX0017]. ICA: TX0181.

RIO VISTA—Formerly served by National Cable Inc. No longer in operation. ICA: TX0535.

RISING STAR—Formerly served by Brownwood TV Cable Service Inc. No longer in operation. ICA: TX0354.

RIVER OAKS—Charter Communications. Now served by FORT WORTH (northern portions), TX [TX0008]. ICA: TX0884.

RIVERSIDE—Formerly served by Almega Cable. No longer in operation. ICA: TX0527.

RIVIERA—Formerly served by Riviera Cable TV. No longer in operation. ICA: TX0657.

2017 Edition
D-773

Texas—Cable Systems

ROARING SPRINGS (town)—Formerly served by Almega Cable. No longer in operation. ICA: TX0960.

ROBERT LEE—NewWave Communications, One Montgomery Plaza, 4th Floor, Sikeston, MO 63801. Phones: 573-472-9500; 888-863-9928. Fax: 573-472-9518. E-mail: info@newwave.com. Web Site: http://www.newwavecom.com. Also serves Bronte, Coke County (portions) & Tom Green County (portions). ICA: TX0327.
TV Market Ranking: Below 100 (Bronte, ROBERT LEE, Tom Green County (portions)). Franchise award date: February 23, 1979. Franchise expiration date: N.A. Began: August 1, 1980.
Channel capacity: N.A. Channels available but not in use: N.A.
Basic Service
Subscribers: 122.
Programming (received off-air): KIDY (FOX, MNT) San Angelo; KLST (CBS) San Angelo; KSAN-TV (NBC) San Angelo; KTAB-TV (CBS) Abilene; KTXS-TV (ABC, CW, This TV, TMO) Sweetwater; allband FM.
Programming (via satellite): Animal Planet; ESPN2; Fox News Channel; FX; HLN; ION Television; Nickelodeon; QVC; TBS; The Weather Channel; Trinity Broadcasting Network (TBN); Turner Classic Movies; WGN America.
Fee: $35.00 installation; $36.78 monthly.
Expanded Basic Service 1
Subscribers: N.A.
Programming (via satellite): A&E; AMC; Cartoon Network; CMT; CNN; Discovery Channel; ESPN; Freeform; HGTV; History; Lifetime; Spike TV; TLC; TNT; TV Land; USA Network.
Fee: $48.70 monthly.
Pay Service 1
Pay Units: N.A.
Programming (via satellite): HBO.
Fee: $14.95 installation; $17.00 monthly.
Video-On-Demand: No
Internet Service
Operational: No.
Telephone Service
None
Miles of Plant: 41.0 (coaxial); None (fiber optic). Homes passed included in Merkel.
Regional General Manager: Jerry Smith.
Ownership: NewWave Communications LLC (MSO).

ROBY—Formerly served by Almega Cable. No longer in operation. ICA: TX0844.

ROCHESTER—Formerly served by Jayroc Cablevision. No longer in operation. ICA: TX0845.

ROCKDALE—Suddenlink Communications, 520 Maryville Centre Dr, Ste 300, St. Louis, MO 63141. Phones: 877-423-2743 (Customer service); 314-315-9400. Web Site: http://www.suddenlink.com. ICA: TX0158.
TV Market Ranking: Outside TV Markets (ROCKDALE). Franchise award date: June 8, 1971. Franchise expiration date: N.A. Began: August 1, 1972.
Channel capacity: 58 (operating 2-way). Channels available but not in use: N.A.
Basic Service
Subscribers: 471. Commercial subscribers: 96.
Programming (received off-air): KCEN-TV (Antenna TV, MeTV, MundoMax, NBC) Temple; KEYE-TV (CBS, TMO) Austin; KLRU (PBS) Austin; KTBC (Buzzr, FOX, Movies!) Austin; KVUE (ABC, Estrella TV) Austin; KWKT-TV (Estrella TV, FOX, MNT) Waco; KWTX-TV (CBS, CW) Waco; KXAN-TV (COZI TV, NBC) Austin; allband FM.
Programming (via satellite): QVC; Univision Studios.
Fee: $28.45 monthly.
Expanded Basic Service 1
Subscribers: N.A.
Programming (via satellite): A&E; AMC; Animal Planet; BET; Cartoon Network; CNBC; CNN; Comedy Central; C-SPAN; Discovery Channel; Disney Channel; E! HD; ESPN; ESPN2; Fox News Channel; FOX Sports Southwest; Freeform; FX; Great American Country; HGTV; History; HLN; Lifetime; MSNBC; MTV; National Geographic Channel; Nickelodeon; Outdoor Channel; Spike TV; Syfy; TBS; The Weather Channel; TLC; TNT; Travel Channel; Trinity Broadcasting Network (TBN); Turner Classic Movies; TV Land; USA Network; VH1.
Fee: $24.00 monthly.
Digital Basic Service
Subscribers: N.A.
Programming (via satellite): BBC America; Cloo; Discovery Digital Networks; Disney XD; DMX Music; ESPN Classic; ESPNews; Fox Sports 1; Fuse; FYI; Golf Channel; GSN; History; History International; HITS (Head-end In The Sky); IFC; NBCSN; WE tv.
Fee: $3.99 monthly.
Pay Service 1
Pay Units: N.A.
Programming (via satellite): Cinemax; HBO; Showtime; The Movie Channel.
Fee: $5.95 monthly (TMC), $9.95 monthly (Cinemax, HBO or Showtime).
Digital Pay Service 1
Pay Units: N.A.
Programming (via satellite): Cinemax (multiplexed); HBO (multiplexed); Showtime (multiplexed); Starz (multiplexed); Starz Encore (multiplexed); The Movie Channel (multiplexed).
Video-On-Demand: No
Pay-Per-View
iN DEMAND (delivered digitally); Playboy TV (delivered digitally).
Internet Service
Operational: Yes. Began: November 2, 2002.
Subscribers: 434.
Broadband Service: Suddenlink High Speed Internet.
Fee: $45.95 installation; $29.95 monthly.
Telephone Service
Digital: Operational
Fee: $44.95 monthly
Miles of Plant: 79.0 (coaxial); 7.0 (fiber optic). Homes passed: 3,298.
Vice President, Corporate Finance: Michael Pflantz. Regional Manager: Todd Cruthird. Marketing Director: Beverly Gambell. Chief Technician: Walt VanLue.
Ownership: Cequel Communications Holdings I LLC (MSO).

ROCKPORT—Time Warner Cable, 821 Market St, Portland, TX 78374. Phone: 361-643-5313. Web Site: http://www.timewarnercable.com. Also serves Aransas County (portions), Fulton, Port Aransas, Portland & Sinton. ICA: TX0116.
TV Market Ranking: Below 100 (Aransas County (portions), Fulton, Port Aransas, Portland, ROCKPORT, Sinton). Franchise award date: N.A. Franchise expiration date: N.A. Began: December 1, 1979.
Channel capacity: N.A. Channels available but not in use: N.A.
Basic Service
Subscribers: 6,999. Commercial subscribers: 169.
Programming (received off-air): KCBO-LP (IND) Corpus Christi; KEDT (PBS) Corpus Christi; KIII (ABC, MeTV) Corpus Christi; KORO (LATV, UNV) Corpus Christi; KRIS-TV (CW, Grit, NBC) Corpus Christi; KTOV-LP Corpus Christi; KXPX-LP (MundoMax) Corpus Christi; KZTV (CBS) Corpus Christi; 5 FMs.
Programming (via satellite): C-SPAN; Pop; QVC; The Weather Channel; Trinity Broadcasting Network (TBN); Univision; WGN America.
Fee: $29.99 installation; $31.45 monthly.
Expanded Basic Service 1
Subscribers: 6,700.
Programming (via satellite): A&E; AMC; Animal Planet; BET; Cartoon Network; CMT; CNBC; CNN; Comedy Central; Discovery Channel; Disney Channel; Disney XD; E! HD; ESPN; ESPN Classic; ESPN2; Food Network; Fox News Channel; FOX Sports Southwest; Freeform; FX; FXM; HGTV; History; HLN; Lifetime; MSNBC; MTV; NBCSN; Nickelodeon; Oxygen; Spike TV; Syfy; TBS; TLC; TNT; Travel Channel; Turner Classic Movies; TV Land; USA Network; VH1; WE tv.
Fee: $4.57 monthly.
Digital Basic Service
Subscribers: N.A.
Programming (via satellite): BBC America; Bloomberg Television; Destination America; Discovery Kids Channel; Discovery Life Channel; DIY Network; FOX College Sports Central; FOX College Sports Pacific; Fox Deportes; Fox Sports 2; FYI; History International; IFC; Investigation Discovery; MC; OWN: Oprah Winfrey Network; Sundance TV.
Digital Pay Service 1
Pay Units: N.A.
Programming (via satellite): Cinemax (multiplexed); HBO (multiplexed); Starz (multiplexed); Starz Encore (multiplexed).
Video-On-Demand: No
Pay-Per-View
Hot Choice (delivered digitally).
Internet Service
Operational: Yes. Began: January 1, 2003.
Fee: $29.99 monthly; $10.00 modem lease.
Telephone Service
Digital: Operational
Miles of Plant: 404.0 (coaxial); None (fiber optic). Homes passed: 22,259.
Ownership: Time Warner Cable (MSO).

ROCKSPRINGS—Formerly served by Almega Cable. No longer in operation. ICA: TX0480.

ROCKWALL—Charter Communications, 920 Whitmore Dr, Rockwall, TX 63131. Phones: 314-543-2236; 636-207-5100 (Corporate office); 817-810-9171; 817-298-3600. Web Site: http://www.charter.com. ICA: TX0155.
TV Market Ranking: 12 (ROCKWALL). Franchise award date: January 17, 1989. Franchise expiration date: N.A. Began: January 1, 1983.
Channel capacity: N.A. Channels available but not in use: N.A.
Digital Basic Service
Subscribers: 1,994.
Programming (via satellite): BBC America; Discovery Digital Networks; DMX Music; Fuse; FYI; History International; IFC; LMN; Nick Jr.; Sundance TV; TeenNick; Turner Classic Movies.
Fee: $49.99 installation; $26.99 monthly.
Digital Expanded Basic Service
Subscribers: N.A.
Programming (via satellite): ESPN Classic; ESPNews; Fox Sports 2; NBCSN; NFL Network.
Digital Pay Service 1
Pay Units: N.A.
Programming (via satellite): Cinemax (multiplexed); HBO (multiplexed); Showtime (multiplexed); Starz Encore (multiplexed); The Movie Channel (multiplexed).
Video-On-Demand: No
Pay-Per-View
Fresh (delivered digitally); ETC (delivered digitally); The Erotic Network (delivered digitally); iN DEMAND (delivered digitally).
Internet Service
Operational: Yes.
Broadband Service: Charter Internet.
Fee: $29.99 monthly.
Telephone Service
None
Miles of Plant: 655.0 (coaxial); 41.0 (fiber optic). Homes passed: 7,951.
Vice President & General Manager: Wayne Cramp. Technical Operations Director: John Linton. Marketing Director: Kathleen Griffin. Accounting Director: David Sovanski.
Ownership: Charter Communications Inc. (MSO).

ROGERS—Grande Communications, 401 Carlson Circle, San Marcos, TX 78666. Phones: 855-286-6666; 512-878-4600. Web Site: http://mygrande.com. ICA: TX0548.
TV Market Ranking: Below 100 (ROGERS). Franchise award date: N.A. Franchise expiration date: N.A. Began: June 1, 1983.
Channel capacity: N.A. Channels available but not in use: N.A.
Basic Service
Subscribers: 128.
Programming (received off-air): KAKW-DT (getTV, UNV) Killeen; KBTX-TV (CBS, CW) Bryan; KCEN-TV (Antenna TV, MeTV, MundoMax, NBC) Temple; KNCT (PBS) Belton; KWKT-TV (Estrella TV, FOX, MNT) Waco; KWTX-TV (CBS, CW) Waco; KXXV (ABC, TMO) Waco.
Programming (via satellite): EWTN Global Catholic Network; Local Cable Weather; QVC; Telemundo; Trinity Broadcasting Network (TBN); WGN America.
Fee: $25.00 installation; $10.95 monthly.
Expanded Basic Service 1
Subscribers: N.A.
Programming (received off-air): KEYE-TV (CBS, TMO) Austin; KNVA (CW, Grit, TheCoolTV) Austin; KTBC (Buzzr, FOX, Movies!) Austin; KXAN-TV (COZI TV, NBC) Austin; WFAA (ABC) Dallas.
Programming (via satellite): A&E; AMC; Animal Planet; BET; Cartoon Network; CMT; CNBC; CNN; Comedy Central; C-SPAN; C-SPAN 2; Discovery Channel; Disney Channel; DIY Network; E! HD; ESPN; ESPN2; Food Network; Fox News Channel; Fox Sports 1; FOX Sports Networks; FX; Golf Channel; Hallmark Channel; HGTV; History; HLN; ION Television; Lifetime; MSNBC; MTV; National Geographic Channel; Nickelodeon; RFD-TV; Spike TV; Syfy; TBS; The Weather Channel; TLC; TNT; Travel Channel; truTV; Turner Classic Movies; TV Land; USA Network; VH1.
Fee: $14.00 monthly.
Digital Basic Service
Subscribers: N.A.
Programming (via satellite): BBC America; Bloomberg Television; Bravo; Cloo; CMT; Daystar TV Network; Discovery Life Chan-

D-774   TV & Cable Factbook No. 85

Cable Systems—Texas

nel; Disney XD; ESPN Classic; ESPNews; EVINE Live; FOX College Sports Central; FOX College Sports Pacific; FXM; FYI; Great American Country; GSN; History; History International; IFC; LMN; NBCSN; Nick Jr.; Nicktoons; Outdoor Channel; Ovation; Sundance TV; TeenNick; The Word Network; WE tv.

Pay Service 1
Pay Units: N.A.
Programming (via satellite): HBO; Showtime; The Movie Channel.

Digital Pay Service 1
Pay Units: N.A.
Programming (via satellite): Cinemax (multiplexed); Flix; HBO (multiplexed); Showtime (multiplexed); Starz (multiplexed); Starz Encore (multiplexed); The Movie Channel (multiplexed).

Video-On-Demand: No

Internet Service
Operational: Yes. Began: May 1, 2006.
Broadband Service: VVM Internet Services.
Fee: $20.00 installation; $40.00 monthly.

Telephone Service
Digital: Planned
Miles of Plant: 8.0 (coaxial); None (fiber optic). Homes passed: 350.
Senior Vice President, Operations & General Manager: Matthew Rohre. Vice President, Marketing: Pete Drozdoff. Vice President, Technical Operations: Shane Schilling.
Ownership: Grande Communications Networks Inc. (MSO).

ROMA—Time Warner Cable. Now served by PHARR, TX [TX0017]. ICA: TX0118.

ROSCOE—NewWave Communications, One Montgomery Plaza, 4th Floor, Sikeston, MO 63801. Phones: 573-472-9500; 888-863-9928. Fax: 573-472-9518. E-mail: info@newwave.com. Web Site: http://www.newwavecom.com. ICA: TX0471.
TV Market Ranking: Below 100 (ROSCOE). Franchise award date: November 20, 1968. Franchise expiration date: N.A. Began: August 1, 1971.
Channel capacity: N.A. Channels available but not in use: N.A.

Basic Service
Subscribers: 57.
Programming (received off-air): KPCB-DT (GLC) Snyder; KRBC-TV (Bounce TV, NBC) Abilene; KTAB-TV (CBS) Abilene; KTES-LP (CW, This TV) Abilene; KTXS-TV (ABC, CW, This TV, TMO) Sweetwater; KXVA (FOX, MNT) Abilene; allband FM.
Programming (via satellite): Freeform; QVC; The Weather Channel; Univision Studios.
Fee: $35.00 installation; $29.85 monthly.

Expanded Basic Service 1
Subscribers: N.A.
Programming (via satellite): A&E; AMC; Animal Planet; Cartoon Network; CMT; CNN; Discovery Channel; ESPN; ESPN2; FOX Sports Southwest; FX; HGTV; Lifetime; MTV; Nickelodeon; Spike TV; Syfy; TBS; TLC; TNT; Turner Classic Movies; TV Land; USA Network; VH1; WGN America.
Fee: $47.70 monthly.

Pay Service 1
Pay Units: 55.
Programming (via satellite): HBO.
Fee: $14.95 installation; $13.95 monthly.

Video-On-Demand: No

Internet Service
Operational: No.

Telephone Service
None
Miles of Plant: 13.0 (coaxial); None (fiber optic). Homes passed included in Merkel.

Regional General Manager: Jerry Smith.
Ownership: NewWave Communications LLC (MSO).

ROSE CITY—Formerly served by Cebridge Connections. No longer in operation. ICA: TX0606.

ROSEBUD—Formerly served by DMS Cable. No longer in operation. ICA: TX0389.

ROTAN—Suddenlink Communications, 520 Maryville Centre Dr, Ste 300, St. Louis, MO 63141. Phones: 800-999-6845 (Customer service); 314-315-9400. Web Site: http://www.suddenlink.com. ICA: TX0365.
TV Market Ranking: Below 100 (ROTAN). Franchise award date: January 1, 1966. Franchise expiration date: N.A. Began: August 1, 1968.
Channel capacity: N.A. Channels available but not in use: N.A.

Basic Service
Subscribers: 130.
Programming (received off-air): KRBC-TV (Bounce TV, NBC) Abilene; KTAB-TV (CBS) Abilene; KTXS-TV (ABC, CW, This TV, TMO) Sweetwater; 4 FMs.
Programming (via satellite): BET; C-SPAN; Lifetime; QVC; TBS; The Weather Channel.
Fee: $28.45 monthly.

Expanded Basic Service 1
Subscribers: N.A.
Programming (via satellite): A&E; AMC; Animal Planet; Cartoon Network; CMT; CNN; Discovery Channel; ESPN; Fox News Channel; FOX Sports Southwest; Freeform; FX; HGTV; MTV; Nickelodeon; Spike TV; TLC; TNT; USA Network.
Fee: $39.95 installation; $23.00 monthly.

Pay Service 1
Pay Units: N.A.
Programming (via satellite): Cinemax; HBO; Starz; Starz Encore.
Fee: $1.71 monthly (Encore), $6.75 monthly (Starz),$12.50 monthly (Cinemax), $13.00 monthly (HBO).

Video-On-Demand: No

Internet Service
Operational: Yes. Began: November 12, 2003.
Broadband Service: Suddenlink High Speed Internet.
Fee: $49.95 installation; $38.95 monthly.

Telephone Service
None
Miles of Plant: 15.0 (coaxial); None (fiber optic). Homes passed: 926.
Senior Vice President, Corporate Finance: Michael Pflantz. Regional Manager: Todd Cruthird. Plant Manager: Bobby Smith.
Ownership: Cequel Communications Holdings I LLC (MSO).

ROUND ROCK (portions)—Grande Communications. Now served by AUSTIN, TX [TX0989]. ICA: TX5536.

ROYSE CITY—Suddenlink Communications. Now served by TERRELL, TX [TX0920]. ICA: TX0325.

RULE—Formerly served by Alliance Communications. No longer in operation. ICA: TX1005.

RUNGE—Formerly served by Almega Cable. No longer in operation. ICA: TX0959.

RUSK—Suddenlink Communications, 520 Maryville Centre Dr, Ste 300, St. Louis, MO 63141. Phones: 800-999-6845; 314-315-9400. Web Site: http://www.suddenlink.com. Also serves Cherokee County (portions). ICA: TX0253.
TV Market Ranking: Below 100 (Cherokee County (portions), RUSK). Franchise award date: N.A. Franchise expiration date: N.A. Began: January 1, 1963.
Channel capacity: N.A. Channels available but not in use: N.A.

Basic Service
Subscribers: 422. Commercial subscribers: 72.
Programming (received off-air): KETK-TV (Estrella TV, NBC) Jacksonville; KFXK-TV (FOX) Longview; KLTV (ABC, Bounce TV, TMO) Tyler; KSLA (Bounce TV, CBS, Grit, This TV) Shreveport.
Programming (via microwave): KDFW (FOX) Dallas; KERA-TV (PBS) Dallas; KTVT (CBS, Decades) Fort Worth; KXAS-TV (COZI TV, NBC) Fort Worth; WFAA (ABC) Dallas.
Programming (via satellite): A&E; CMT; CNN; C-SPAN; Discovery Channel; ESPN; FOX Sports Southwest; Freeform; HLN; Lifetime; MTV; Nickelodeon; Spike TV; TBS; The Weather Channel; TNT.
Fee: $28.45 monthly.

Pay Service 1
Pay Units: N.A.
Programming (via satellite): Cinemax; Flix; HBO; Showtime; The Movie Channel.
Fee: $1.95 monthly (Flix), $7.00 monthly (Cinemax or Showtime), $9.00 monthly (TMC), $12.00 monthly (HBO).

Video-On-Demand: No

Internet Service
Operational: Yes. Began: March 10, 2004.
Broadband Service: Suddenlink High Speed Internet.
Fee: $45.95 installation; $29.95 monthly.

Telephone Service
Digital: Operational
Fee: $44.95 monthly
Miles of Plant: 35.0 (coaxial); None (fiber optic). Homes passed: 1,912.
Vice President, Corporate Finance: Michael Pflantz. Regional Manager: Todd Cruthird. Plant Manager: Henry Harris.
Ownership: Cequel Communications Holdings I LLC (MSO).

SABINAL—Formerly served by Almega Cable. No longer in operation. ICA: TX0442.

SALADO—Grande Communications, 401 Carlson Circle, San Marcos, TX 78666. Phones: 855-286-6666; 512-878-4600. Web Site: http://mygrande.com. ICA: TX0504.
TV Market Ranking: Below 100 (SALADO). Franchise award date: N.A. Franchise expiration date: N.A. Began: February 1, 1982.
Channel capacity: N.A. Channels available but not in use: N.A.

Basic Service
Subscribers: 293.
Programming (received off-air): KCEN-TV (Antenna TV, MeTV, MundoMax, NBC) Temple; KEYE-TV (CBS, TMO) Austin; KNCT (PBS) Belton; KNVA (CW, Grit, TheCoolTV) Austin; KTBC (Buzzr, FOX, Movies!) Austin; KWKT-TV (Estrella TV, FOX, MNT) Waco; KWTX-TV (CBS, CW) Waco; KXAN-TV (COZI TV, NBC) Austin; KXXV (ABC, TMO) Waco; WFAA (ABC) Dallas.
Programming (via satellite): Univision Studios; WGN America.
Fee: $25.00 installation; $10.95 monthly.

Expanded Basic Service 1
Subscribers: N.A.
Programming (via satellite): A&E; AMC; Animal Planet; BET; Cartoon Network; CMT; CNBC; CNN; Comedy Central; C-SPAN; C-SPAN 2; Discovery Channel; Disney Channel; E! HD; ESPN; ESPN2; Food Network; Fox News Channel; FOX Sports Southwest; Freeform; FX; Hallmark Channel; HGTV; History; HLN; ION Television; Lifetime; MSNBC; MTV; National Geographic Channel; Nickelodeon; QVC; Spike TV; Syfy; TBS; The Weather Channel; TLC; TNT; Travel Channel; Trinity Broadcasting Network (TBN); Turner Classic Movies; TV Land; USA Network; VH1.
Fee: $18.00 monthly.

Digital Basic Service
Subscribers: N.A.
Programming (via satellite): BBC America; Bloomberg Television; Bravo; Daystar TV Network; Discovery Digital Networks; Disney XD; DMX Music; ESPN Classic; ESPNews; EVINE Live; Fox Sports 1; FSN Digital Atlantic; FSN Digital Central; FSN Digital Pacific; Fuse; FXM; FYI; Golf Channel; Great American Country; GSN; HGTV; History; History International; IFC; International Television (ITV); LMN; National Geographic Channel; NBCSN; Outdoor Channel; Ovation; Syfy; The Word Network; Trinity Broadcasting Network (TBN); Turner Classic Movies; WE tv.
Fee: $15.00 installation; $49.00 monthly.

Pay Service 1
Pay Units: N.A.
Programming (via satellite): HBO; Showtime; The Movie Channel.
Fee: $11.00 monthly (HBO, Showtime or TMC), $13.50 monthly (Showtime/TMC), $19.50 monthly (HBO/TMC), $21.00 monthly (HBO/Showtime), $23.00 monthly (HBO/Showtime/TMC).

Digital Pay Service 1
Pay Units: N.A.
Programming (via satellite): Cinemax (multiplexed); HBO (multiplexed); Showtime (multiplexed); Starz (multiplexed); Starz Encore (multiplexed).
Fee: $7.00 monthly (Cinemax), $11.00 monthly (HBO, Showtime or Starz/Encore).

Video-On-Demand: No

Pay-Per-View
Hot Choice (delivered digitally); iN DEMAND (delivered digitally).

Internet Service
Operational: Yes. Began: December 31, 2004.
Subscribers: 298.
Broadband Service: VVM Internet Services.
Fee: $20.00 installation; $40.00 monthly.

Telephone Service
Digital: Planned
Miles of Plant: 12.0 (coaxial); None (fiber optic). Homes passed: 450.
Senior Vice President, Operations & General Manager: Matthew Rohre. Vice President, Marketing: Pete Drozdoff. Vice President, Technical Operations: Shane Schilling.
Ownership: Grande Communications Networks Inc. (MSO).

SAN ANGELO—Formerly served by C & W Enterprises Inc. No longer in operation. ICA: TX1033.

SAN ANGELO—Suddenlink Communications, 4272 West Houston Harte Expy, San Angelo, TX 76901. Phones: 314-315-9400. Fax: 915-486-4182. Web Site: http://www.suddenlink.com. Also serves Goodfellow AFB. ICA: TX0021.

Texas—Cable Systems

TV Market Ranking: Below 100 (Goodfellow AFB, SAN ANGELO). Franchise award date: October 1, 1957. Franchise expiration date: N.A. Began: October 1, 1958.
Channel capacity: N.A. Channels available but not in use: N.A.

Basic Service
Subscribers: 20,656. Commercial subscribers: 3,446.
Programming (received off-air): KANG-LP (UNV) San Angelo; KERA-TV (PBS) Dallas; KEUS-CD (UniMas) San Angelo; KIDY (FOX, MNT) San Angelo; KLST (CBS) San Angelo; KSAN-TV (NBC) San Angelo; KTXE-LD (ABC) San Angelo; WFAA (ABC) Dallas.
Programming (via satellite): C-SPAN; C-SPAN 2; CW PLUS; INSP; Pop; QVC; TBS; Telemundo; Trinity Broadcasting Network (TBN).
Fee: $40.00 installation; $26.08 monthly; $3.36 converter.

Expanded Basic Service 1
Subscribers: N.A.
Programming (via satellite): A&E; AMC; Animal Planet; BET; Bravo; Cartoon Network; CMT; CNBC; CNN; Comedy Central; Discovery Channel; Disney Channel; E!; HD; ESPN; ESPN2; Food Network; Fox News Channel; Fox Sports 1; FOX Sports Southwest; Freeform; FX; HGTV; History; HLN; Lifetime; LMN; MSNBC; MTV; MTV2; NBCSN; Nickelodeon; Spike TV; Syfy; The Weather Channel; TLC; TNT; Travel Channel; truTV; Turner Classic Movies; TV Land; Univision; USA Network; VH1.
Fee: $38.00 installation; $20.54 monthly.

Digital Basic Service
Subscribers: N.A.
Programming (via satellite): A&E HD; AXS TV; Bandamax; BBC America; Bloomberg Television; Boomerang; CBS Sports Network; Cine Mexicano; Cinelatino; CMT; CNN en Espanol; Cooking Channel; De Pelicula; De Pelicula Clasico; Destination America; Discovery Kids Channel; Disney XD; DIY Network; ESPN Classic; ESPN Deportes; ESPN HD; ESPN2 HD; ESPNews; ESPNU; EVINE Live; EWTN Global Catholic Network; Food Network HD; FOX College Sports Central; FOX College Sports Pacific; Fox Deportes; Fox Sports 2; FSN HD; Fuse; FYI; Golf Channel; Great American Country; GSN; Hallmark Channel; HD Theater; HGTV HD; History en Espanol; History International; IFC; Investigation Discovery; Jewelry Television; MC; MTV Classic; MTV Hits; mtvU; National Geographic Channel; National Geographic Channel HD; NBC Universo; Nick Jr.; Nicktoons; NickToons en Espanol; Outdoor Channel; OWN: Oprah Winfrey Network; Oxygen; Science Channel; Starz Encore (multiplexed); Sundance TV; Sur; TeenNick; Telehit; Tennis Channel; TNT HD; Toon Disney en Espanol; Tr3s; Universal HD; Univision; UP; VideoRola; WE tv.
Fee: $8.65 monthly.

Pay Service 1
Pay Units: 919.
Programming (via satellite): Cinemax.
Fee: $10.00 monthly.

Pay Service 2
Pay Units: 2,505.
Programming (via satellite): HBO (multiplexed).
Fee: $10.95 monthly.

Pay Service 3
Pay Units: 139.
Programming (via satellite): Showtime; Starz; Starz Encore.
Fee: $3.97 monthly (Encore), $3.98 monthly (Starz), $6.75 monthly (Showtime).

Digital Pay Service 1
Pay Units: 6,544.
Programming (via satellite): Cinemax (multiplexed); HBO (multiplexed); HBO HD; HBO Latino; Showtime (multiplexed); Showtime HD; Starz (multiplexed); Starz HD; The Movie Channel (multiplexed).
Fee: $6.75 monthly (Showtime or TMC), $7.95 monthly (Starz), $12.95 monthly (HBO).
Video-On-Demand: No

Pay-Per-View
iN DEMAND (delivered digitally); Playgirl TV (delivered digitally); Fresh (delivered digitally); Shorteez (delivered digitally); Spice: Xcess (delivered digitally); Club Jenna (delivered digitally).

Internet Service
Operational: Yes. Began: October 1, 1999.
Subscribers: 23,158.
Broadband Service: Suddenlink High Speed Internet.
Fee: $49.95 installation; $24.95 monthly; $15.00 modem lease; $249.95 modem purchase.

Telephone Service
Digital: Operational
Subscribers: 10,636.
Fee: $48.95 monthly

Miles of Plant: 1,058.0 (coaxial); 258.0 (fiber optic). Homes passed: 50,576.
Vice President & Manager: Connie Wharton. Vice President, Accounting: Sabrina Warr. Technical Operations Manager: Robert E. Amo. Customer Service Manager: Naomi Gonzales. Marketing Manager: Mike Johnson. Marketing Coordinator: Eric Wiemers.
Ownership: Cequel Communications Holdings I LLC (MSO).

SAN ANTONIO—Grande Communications, 6480 North New Braunfels Ave, San Antonio, TX 78209. Phones: 512-878-4000 (Corporate office); 210-320-4600. Fax: 210-320-4010. Web Site: http://mygrande.com. Also serves Alamo Heights, Balcones Heights, Castle Hills, Kirby, Olmos Park, Terrell Hills, Universal City & Windcrest (portions). ICA: TX0990. **Note:** This system is an overbuild.
TV Market Ranking: 45 (Alamo Heights, Balcones Heights, Castle Hills, SAN ANTONIO, Terrell Hills, Universal City). Franchise award date: May 18, 2000. Franchise expiration date: N.A. Began: February 1, 2001.
Channel capacity: N.A. Channels available but not in use: N.A.

Basic Service
Subscribers: 9,515.
Programming (received off-air): KABB (FOX, The Country Network) San Antonio; KCWX (MNT, This TV) Fredericksburg; KENS (CBS, Estrella TV) San Antonio; KHCE-TV (TBN) San Antonio; KLRN (PBS) San Antonio; KMYS (CW) Kerrville; KNIC-CD (UniMas) San Antonio; KPXL-TV (ION) Uvalde; KSAT-TV (ABC, MeTV) San Antonio; KVDA (TMO) San Antonio; KWEX-DT (getTV, UNV) San Antonio; WOAI-TV (IND, NBC) San Antonio.
Programming (via satellite): Azteca; C-SPAN; C-SPAN 2; LWS Local Weather Station; Pop; QVC; WGN America.
Fee: $27.49 monthly.

Expanded Basic Service 1
Subscribers: N.A.
Programming (via satellite): A&E; AMC; Animal Planet; BET; Bravo; Cartoon Network; CMT; CNBC; CNN; Comedy Central; Discovery Channel; Disney Channel; Disney XD; E! HD; ESPN; ESPN Classic; ESPN2; EWTN Global Catholic Network; Food Network; Fox Deportes; Fox News Channel; Fox Sports 1; FOX Sports Southwest; Freeform; FX; Golf Channel; Great American Country; GSN; Hallmark Channel; HGTV; History; HLN; INSP; Lifetime; MSNBC; MTV; NBC Universo; Nickelodeon; OWN: Oprah Winfrey Network; Oxygen; Spike TV; Syfy; TBS; The Weather Channel; TLC; TNT; Travel Channel; truTV; TV Land; Univision; USA Network; VH1.
Fee: $38.00 monthly.

Digital Basic Service
Subscribers: N.A.
Programming (via satellite): BBC America; Bloomberg Television; Boomerang; CBS Sports Network; Cooking Channel; Discovery Kids Channel; DIY Network; ESPN; ESPNews; FOX College Sports Central; FOX College Sports Pacific; Fox Sports 2; Fuse; FXM; FYI; GolTV; HD Theater; History International; HITS (Headend In The Sky); IFC; LMN; MC; National Geographic Channel; NBA TV; NBCSN; NFL Network; Nick Jr.; Nicktoons; Outdoor Channel; Teen-Nick; Tennis Channel; The Word Network; TNT; Turner Classic Movies; TVG Network; Universal HD; WE tv.
Fee: $17.00 monthly; $5.00 converter.

Digital Pay Service 1
Pay Units: N.A.
Programming (via satellite): Cinemax (multiplexed); Cinemax HD; Flix (multiplexed); HBO (multiplexed); HBO HD; Showtime (multiplexed); Showtime HD; Starz (multiplexed); Starz Encore (multiplexed); Starz HD; Sundance TV (multiplexed); The Movie Channel (multiplexed).
Fee: $12.00 monthly (Cinemax, HBO, Showtime/Flix Sundance/TMC or Starz/Encore).
Video-On-Demand: No

Pay-Per-View
Sports PPV (delivered digitally); iN DEMAND (delivered digitally); Hot Choice (delivered digitally); Playboy TV (delivered digitally); Fresh (delivered digitally); Shorteez (delivered digitally).

Internet Service
Operational: Yes, DSL & dial-up.
Fee: $34.99-$64.99 monthly.

Telephone Service
Digital: Operational
Fee: $19.99 monthly
Vice President, Marketing: Pete Drozdoff. Vice President, Network Operations & Engineering: Lamar Horton. Vice President, Technical Operations: Shane Schilling. Vice President, Customer Care: Dawn Blydenburgh. General Manager: Matt Rohre.
Ownership: Grande Communications Networks Inc. (MSO).

SAN ANTONIO—Time Warner Cable, 1900 Blue Crest Ln, San Antonio, TX 78247. Phones: 210-244-0500; 210-352-4600. Fax: 210-352-4278. Web Site: http://www.timewarnercable.com. Also serves Alamo Heights, Atascosa County (portions), Balcones Heights, Bexar County (portions), Boerne, Brooks AFB, Bulverde, Canyon Lake, Castle Hills, China Grove, Cibolo, Cibolo Creek (Bexar), Comal County (portions), Converse, Elmendorf, Fair Oaks Ranch (Bexar County), Fair Oaks Ranch (Comal County), Fair Oaks Ranch (Kendall County), Floresville, Fort Sam Houston, Garden Ridge, Geronimo, Grey Forest, Guadalupe County, Helotes, Hill Country Village, Hollywood Park, Kelly AFB, Kendall County (portions), Kirby, La Coste, Lackland AFB, Leon Springs, Leon Valley, Live Oak, Marion, Medina County, New Braunfels, Northcliff, Olmos Park, Palm Park, Randolph AFB, Scenic Oaks, Schertz, Seguin, Selma, Shavano Park, Somerset, Terrell Hills, Universal City, Wilson County (portions) & Windcrest. ICA: TX0002.
TV Market Ranking: 45 (Alamo Heights, Atascosa County (portions), Balcones Heights, Bexar County (portions), Brooks AFB, Bulverde, Canyon Lake, Castle Hills, China Grove, Cibolo, Comal County (portions), Converse, Elmendorf, Fair Oaks Ranch (Bexar County), Fair Oaks Ranch (Comal County), Fair Oaks Ranch (Kendall County), Floresville, Fort Sam Houston, Garden Ridge, Geronimo, Grey Forest, Guadalupe County (portions), Helotes, Hill Country Village, Hollywood Park, Kelly AFB, Kendall County (portions), Kirby, La Coste, Lackland AFB, Leon Springs, Leon Valley, Live Oak, Marion, Medina County (portions), New Braunfels, Olmos Park, Palm Park, Randolph AFB, SAN ANTONIO, Scenic Oaks, Schertz, Selma, Shavano Park, Somerset, Terrell Hills, Universal City, Wilson County (portions), Windcrest); Outside TV Markets (Seguin, Atascosa County (portions), Comal County (portions), Guadalupe County (portions)). Franchise award date: September 1, 1978. Franchise expiration date: N.A. Began: September 1, 1979.
Channel capacity: N.A. Channels available but not in use: N.A.

Basic Service
Subscribers: 238,706.
Programming (received off-air): KABB (FOX, The Country Network) San Antonio; KCWX (MNT, This TV) Fredericksburg; KENS (CBS, Estrella TV) San Antonio; KHCE-TV (TBN) San Antonio; KLRN (PBS) San Antonio; KMYS (CW) Kerrville; KNIC-DT (Laff, UniMas) Blanco; KPXL-TV (ION) Uvalde; KSAT-TV (ABC, MeTV) San Antonio; KVDA (TMO) San Antonio; KWEX-DT (getTV, UNV) San Antonio; WOAI-TV (IND, NBC) San Antonio; 28 FMs.
Programming (via satellite): Azteca; Nickelodeon; Univision.
Fee: $39.99 installation; $28.00 monthly; $.17 converter.

Expanded Basic Service 1
Subscribers: N.A.
Programming (via satellite): A&E; AMC; Animal Planet; BET; Bravo; Cartoon Network; CMT; CNBC; CNN; Comedy Central; C-SPAN; C-SPAN 2; Discovery Channel; Disney Channel; E! HD; ESPN; ESPN2; EVINE Live; Food Network; Fox News Channel; FOX Sports Southwest; Freeform; FX; Golf Channel; Hallmark Channel; HGTV; History; HLN; Lifetime; LMN; MSNBC; MTV; National Geographic Channel; NBC Universo; NBCSN; OWN: Oprah Winfrey Network; Oxygen; Pop; QVC; Spike TV; Syfy; The Weather Channel; TLC; TNT; Travel Channel; truTV; Turner Classic Movies; TV Land; USA Network; VH1; WE tv.
Fee: $36.10 monthly.

Expanded Basic Service 2
Subscribers: N.A.
Programming (via satellite): TBS; WGN America.
Fee: $2.50 monthly.

Digital Basic Service
Subscribers: N.A.
Programming (via satellite): A&E HD; AXS TV; BBC America; BBC America On Demand; Bloomberg Television; Boomerang; Canal Sur; Cartoon Network en Espanol; CBS Sports Network; Celebrity Shopping Network; Cinelatino; Cloo; CNN en Espanol; CNN HD; CNN International; Cooking Channel; C-SPAN 3; Destination America; Discovery Kids Channel; Discovery Life Channel; Disney XD; DIY Network; ESPN Classic; ESPN Deportes; ESPN HD; ESPN2 HD;

Cable Systems—Texas

ESPNews; ESPNU; Flix; Food Network HD; Fox Business Network; FOX College Sports Central; FOX College Sports Pacific; Fox Deportes; Fox Sports 1; Fox Sports 2; Fuse; FXM; FYI; Great American Country; GSN; HD Theater; HGTV HD; History HD; History International; HITN; HTV; IFC; Infinito; Investigation Discovery; Jewelry Television; La Familia Cosmovision; Lifetime Movie Network HD; LOGO; MC; MTV Classic; MTV Live; MTV2; Nat Geo WILD; National Geographic Channel HD; National Geographic Channel On Demand; NBA TV; NHL Network; NHL Network HD; Nick 2; Nick Jr.; Nicktoons; Outdoor Channel; Ovation; Oxygen On Demand; Science Channel; Starz Encore (multiplexed); Sundance TV; TBS HD; TeenNick; Tennis Channel; TNT HD; Toon Disney en Espanol; Tr3s; TV Guide Network; Universal HD; Versus HD; Video-Rola; Vme TV.
Fee: $22.20 monthly; $3.07 converter.

Digital Pay Service 1
Pay Units: N.A.
Programming (via satellite): Cinemax HD; Cinemax On Demand; Deutsche Welle TV; HBO (multiplexed); HBO HD; HBO on Demand; Saigon Broadcasting Television Network (SBTN); Showtime (multiplexed); Showtime HD; Showtime On Demand; Starz (multiplexed); Starz HD; The Filipino Channel; The Movie Channel (multiplexed); The Movie Channel HD; The Movie Channel On Demand; TV Asia; Zee TV.
Fee: $14.99 monthly (each).

Video-On-Demand: Yes

Pay-Per-View
Playboy TV (delivered digitally); Playboy en Espanol (delivered digitally); NBA League Pass (delivered digitally); MLB Extra Innings (delivered digitally); NHL Center Ice (delivered digitally); MLS Direct Kick (delivered digitally).

Internet Service
Operational: Yes. Began: May 1, 2000.
Subscribers: 289,989.
Broadband Service: Road Runner.
Fee: $39.95 installation; $39.95 monthly.

Telephone Service
Digital: Operational
Subscribers: 145,921.
Miles of Plant: 14,054.0 (coaxial); 2,528.0 (fiber optic). Homes passed: 828,521.
President: John Owen. Vice President, Engineering: Norrie Bush. Vice President, Field Operations: Keith Coogan. Vice President, Marketing & New Product Development: Corky Roth. Vice President, Government & Public Affairs: Jon Gary Herrera. Public Affairs Manager: Melissa Sorola.
Ownership: Time Warner Cable (MSO).

SAN ANTONIO (portions)—Grande Communications. Now served by SAN ANTONIO, TX [TX0990]. ICA: TX5534.

SAN AUGUSTINE—Formerly served by Cebridge Connections. Now served by Suddenlink Communications, CENTER, TX [TX0192]. ICA: TX0317.

SAN CARLOS—Formerly served by CableDirect. No longer in operation. ICA: TX0624.

SAN LEON—Formerly served by Almega Cable. No longer in operation. ICA: TX0240.

SAN MARCOS—Grande Communications, 341 Carlson Circle, San Marcos, TX 78666. Phones: 512-220-4600; 512-878-4000 (Corporate office). Web Site: http:// mygrande.com. Also serves New Braunfels & Windcrest (portions). ICA: TX0991.
TV Market Ranking: Below 100 (SAN MARCOS).
Channel capacity: N.A. Channels available but not in use: N.A.

Basic Service
Subscribers: 3,173. Commercial subscribers: 1,099.
Fee: $44.95 installation; $27.49 monthly.

Internet Service
Operational: Yes.
Fee: $29.99-$44.99 monthly.

Telephone Service
Digital: Operational
Fee: $19.99 monthly
Vice President, Marketing: Pete Drozdoff. Vice President, Network Operations & Engineering: Lamar Horton. Vice President, Technical Operations: Shane Schilling. Vice President, Customer Care: Dawn Blydenburgh. General Manager: Matt Rohre.
Ownership: Grande Communications Networks Inc. (MSO).

SAN MARCOS—Time Warner Cable, 7820 Crescent Executive Dr, Charlotte, NC 28217. Phones: 877-455-6337 (Sales); 703-713-1723 (Herndon VA office). Web Site: http://www.timewarnercable.com. Also serves Hays County (northeastern portion), Lockhart, Luling, Martindale, Maxwell, Staples, Wimberley & Woodcreek. ICA: TX0849.
TV Market Ranking: Below 100 (Hays County (northeastern portion), Lockhart, Martindale, Maxwell, SAN MARCOS, Wimberley, Woodcreek); Outside TV Markets (Luling, Staples).
Channel capacity: N.A. Channels available but not in use: N.A.

Basic Service
Subscribers: 11,939. Commercial subscribers: 255.
Fee: $39.99 installation; $24.99 monthly.

Internet Service
Operational: Yes.
Subscribers: 18,990.

Telephone Service
Digital: Operational
Subscribers: 7,092.
Miles of Plant: 1,986.0 (coaxial); 706.0 (fiber optic). Homes passed: 43,874.
Ownership: Time Warner Cable (MSO).

SAN PATRICIO COUNTY—Time Warner Cable. Now served by CORPUS CHRISTI, TX [TX0010]. ICA: TX0473.

SAN SABA—Central Texas Communications, 1012 Reilley St, PO Box 627, Goldthwaite, TX 76844. Phones: 800-535-8904; 325-648-2237. Web Site: http://www.centex.net. ICA: TX1038.
TV Market Ranking: Below 100 (SAN SABA).
Channel capacity: N.A. Channels available but not in use: N.A.

Basic Service
Subscribers: 21.
Fee: $14.45 monthly.
Chief Operating Officer: Jamey Wigley.
Ownership: Central Texas Communicatons Inc. (MSO).

SAN SABA—Suddenlink Communications, 520 Maryville Centre Dr, Ste 300, St. Louis, MO 63141. Phones: 800-999-6845; 314-315-9400. Web Site: http://www.suddenlink.com. ICA: TX0291.
TV Market Ranking: Below 100 (SAN SABA). Franchise award date: N.A. Franchise expiration date: N.A. Began: August 1, 1957.
Channel capacity: N.A. Channels available but not in use: N.A.

Communications Daily
Warren Communications News

Get the industry standard FREE —
For a no-obligation trial call 800-771-9202 or visit www.warren-news.com

Basic Service
Subscribers: 154. Commercial subscribers: 33.
Programming (received off-air): KCEN-TV (Antenna TV, MeTV, MundoMax, NBC) Temple; KNCT (PBS) Belton; KWKT-TV (Estrella TV, FOX, MNT) Waco; KWTX-TV (CBS, CW) Waco; KXXV (ABC, TMO) Waco; 4 FMs.
Programming (via satellite): C-SPAN; Univision Studios.
Fee: $28.45 monthly.

Expanded Basic Service 1
Subscribers: N.A.
Programming (via satellite): A&E; AMC; Animal Planet; Cartoon Network; CNBC; CNN; Comedy Central; Discovery Channel; Disney Channel; E! HD; ESPN; ESPN2; Food Network; Fox News Channel; FOX Sports Southwest; Freeform; FX; Great American Country; Hallmark Channel; HGTV; History; HLN; Jewelry Television; Lifetime; MSNBC; MTV; National Geographic Channel; Nickelodeon; Outdoor Channel; QVC; Spike TV; Syfy; TBS; The Weather Channel; TLC; TNT; Trinity Broadcasting Network (TBN); Turner Classic Movies; TV Land; Univision; USA Network; VH1.
Fee: $23.00 monthly.

Digital Basic Service
Subscribers: N.A.
Programming (via satellite): BBC America; Bloomberg Television; Cloo; Destination America; Discovery Kids Channel; Disney XD; DMX Music; ESPN Classic; ESPNews; EVINE Live; FOX College Sports Central; FOX College Sports Pacific; Fox Sports 1; Fuse; FYI; Golf Channel; GSN; History International; IFC; Investigation Discovery; NBCSN; OWN: Oprah Winfrey Network; Science Channel; Sundance TV; WE tv.

Pay Service 1
Pay Units: N.A.
Programming (via satellite): HBO; Showtime; The Movie Channel.
Fee: $5.95 monthly (TMC), $9.95 monthly (Showtime), $10.95 monthly (HBO).

Digital Pay Service 1
Pay Units: N.A.
Programming (via satellite): Cinemax (multiplexed); Flix; HBO (multiplexed); Showtime (multiplexed); Starz (multiplexed); Starz Encore (multiplexed); The Movie Channel (multiplexed).

Video-On-Demand: No

Pay-Per-View
iN DEMAND (delivered digitally); Playboy TV (delivered digitally); Club Jenna (delivered digitally); Fresh (delivered digitally); Spice (delivered digitally).

Internet Service
Operational: Yes. Began: August 19, 2004.
Broadband Service: Suddenlink High Speed Internet.
Fee: $49.95 installation; $25.95 monthly.

Telephone Service
None
Miles of Plant: 36.0 (coaxial); None (fiber optic). Homes passed: 1,354.

Vice President, Corporate Finance: Michael Pflantz. Marketing Director: Beverly Gambell.
Ownership: Cequel Communications Holdings I LLC (MSO).

SAN YGNACIO—Time Warner Cable. Now served by LAREDO, TX [TX0029]. ICA: TX0647.

SANDERSON—Mountain Zone TV, 307 E Ave East, Alpine, TX 79830. Phones: 800-446-5661; 432-837-2300. E-mail: mtnzone@sbcglobal.net. Web Site: http://www.mountainzonetv.net. ICA: TX1025.
TV Market Ranking: Outside TV Markets (SANDERSON).
Channel capacity: N.A. Channels available but not in use: N.A.
General Manager: Steve Neu.
Ownership: Mountain Zone TV Systems.

SANDIA—Formerly served by National Cable Inc. No longer in operation. ICA: TX0667.

SANTA ANNA—Formerly served by Brownwood TV Cable Service Inc. No longer in operation. ICA: TX0425.

SANTA FE (unincorporated areas)—Formerly served by Almega Cable. No longer in operation. ICA: TX0411.

SARGENT—Formerly served by Almega Cable. No longer in operation. ICA: TX0248.

SEADRIFT—Time Warner Cable, 7800 Crescent Executive Dr, Charlotte, NC 28217. Phones: 972-899-7300 (Flower Mound office); 361-698-6259. Web Site: http://www.timewarnercable.com. Also serves Port O'Connor. ICA: TX0433.
TV Market Ranking: Below 100 (SEADRIFT); Outside TV Markets (Port O'Connor). Franchise award date: N.A. Franchise expiration date: N.A. Began: December 1, 1981.
Channel capacity: N.A. Channels available but not in use: N.A.

Basic Service
Subscribers: 218.
Programming (received off-air): KAVU-TV (ABC) Victoria; KEDT (PBS) Corpus Christi; KIII (ABC, MeTV) Corpus Christi; KRIS-TV (CW, Grit, NBC) Corpus Christi; KVCT (FOX, This TV, TMO) Victoria; KZTV (CBS) Corpus Christi.
Programming (via satellite): QVC; WGN America.
Fee: $49.99 installation; $28.00 monthly.

Expanded Basic Service 1
Subscribers: N.A.
Programming (via satellite): A&E; Animal Planet; Cartoon Network; CNBC; CNN; Comedy Central; Discovery Channel; Disney Channel; E! HD; ESPN; ESPN2; Food Network; Fox News Channel; Fox Sports 1; FOX Sports Southwest; Freeform; FX; HGTV; History; HLN; Lifetime; MTV; National Geographic Channel; NBCSN; Nickelodeon; Spike TV; TBS; The Weather

2017 Edition

D-777

Texas—Cable Systems

Channel; TLC; TNT; truTV; Turner Classic Movies; USA Network.
Fee: $28.60 monthly.

Pay Service 1
Pay Units: N.A.
Programming (via satellite): HBO; Showtime; Starz; Starz Encore.
Fee: $14.99 monthly (each).

Internet Service
Operational: Yes.

Telephone Service
Digital: Operational
Miles of Plant: 9.0 (coaxial); None (fiber optic). Homes passed: 690.
President: Connie Wharton. Vice President & General Manager: Mike McKee. Engineering Director: Charlotte Strong. Senior Accounting Director: Karen Goodfellow. Public Affairs Manager: Vicki Triplett.
Ownership: Time Warner Cable (MSO).; Advance/Newhouse Partnership (MSO).

SEALY—NewWave Communications, One Montgomery Plaza, 4th Floor, Sikeston, MO 63801. Phones: 573-472-9500; 888-863-9928. Fax: 573-472-9518. E-mail: info@newwave.com. Web Site: http://www.newwavecom.com. Also serves Bellville. ICA: TX0292.
TV Market Ranking: Below 100 (Bellville, SEALY). Franchise award date: January 1, 1980. Franchise expiration date: N.A. Began: June 1, 1981.
Channel capacity: N.A. Channels available but not in use: N.A.

Basic Service
Subscribers: 453.
Programming (received off-air): KETH-TV (TBN) Houston; KFTH-DT (getTV, UniMas) Alvin; KHOU (Bounce TV, CBS) Houston; KIAH (Antenna TV, CW) Houston; KLTJ (Daystar TV, ETV) Galveston; KPRC-TV (NBC, This TV) Houston; KRIV (FOX) Houston; KTMD (TMO) Galveston; KTRK-TV (ABC, Live Well Network) Houston; KTXH (Buzzr, MNT, Movies!) Houston; KUHT (PBS) Houston; KXLN-DT (UNV) Rosenberg; KYAZ (Azteca America, IND) Katy; allband FM.
Programming (via satellite): C-SPAN.
Fee: $35.00 installation; $30.98 monthly.

Expanded Basic Service 1
Subscribers: N.A.
Programming (via satellite): A&E; AMC; BET; Cartoon Network; CMT; CNN; Discovery Channel; ESPN; Fox News Channel; FOX Sports Southwest; Freeform; History; Lifetime; MTV; Nickelodeon; Spike TV; TBS; The Weather Channel; TNT; TV Land; USA Network.
Fee: $50.70 monthly.

Digital Basic Service
Subscribers: N.A.
Programming (via satellite): BBC America; Bloomberg Television; Bravo; Discovery Digital Networks; DMX Music; ESPN Classic; ESPN2; ESPNews; Fox Sports 1; FXM; FYI; Golf Channel; GSN; HGTV; History International; IFC; LMN; National Geographic Channel; Nick Jr.; Nicktoons; Outdoor Channel; Syfy; TeenNick; Trinity Broadcasting Network (TBN); Turner Classic Movies; WE tv.
Fee: $11.00 monthly.

Pay Service 1
Pay Units: N.A.
Programming (via satellite): Cinemax; HBO; Showtime.
Fee: $14.95 installation; $10.95 monthly (Cinemax), $13.95 monthly (HBO or Showtime).

Digital Pay Service 1
Pay Units: N.A.
Programming (via satellite): Cinemax (multiplexed); Flix; HBO (multiplexed); Showtime (multiplexed); Starz (multiplexed); Starz Encore (multiplexed); Sundance TV; The Movie Channel (multiplexed).
Fee: $8.00 monthly (Starz), $9.00 monthly (Cinemax), $11.00 monthly (Starz/Encore), $17.00 monthly (HBO) or $26.00 monthly (HBO/Cinemax).

Video-On-Demand: No

Pay-Per-View
Hot Choice (delivered digitally); iN DEMAND (delivered digitally); Playboy TV (delivered digitally); Fresh (delivered digitally); Shorteez (delivered digitally).

Internet Service
Operational: Yes.
Fee: $39.95 installation; $39.95-$79.99 monthly; $6.00-$8.99 modem lease; $39.95 modem purchase.

Telephone Service
Digital: Operational
Miles of Plant: 130.0 (coaxial); None (fiber optic).
Regional General Manager: Jerry Smith.
Ownership: NewWave Communications LLC (MSO).

SEALY—NewWave Communications. Now served by SEALY (formerly Bellville), TX [TX0292]. ICA: TX0994.

SEBASTIAN—Formerly served by Fiesta Cable. No longer in operation. ICA: TX0481.

SEMINOLE—Baja Broadband, 525 Junction Rd, Madison, WI 53717. Phones: 575-437-3101; 877-422-5282; 800-996-8788. Fax: 608-830-5519. E-mail: comments@tdstelecom.com. Web Site: http://www.bajabroadband.com. Also serves Denver City, Gaines County (portions), Seagraves & Yoakum County (portions). ICA: TX0074.
TV Market Ranking: Below 100 (Gaines County (portions), SEMINOLE); Outside TV Markets (Denver City, Gaines County (portions), Seagraves, Yoakum County (portions)). Franchise award date: N.A. Franchise expiration date: N.A. Began: July 1, 1953.
Channel capacity: N.A. Channels available but not in use: N.A.

Basic Service
Subscribers: 1,178.
Programming (received off-air): KAMC (ABC, Bounce TV) Lubbock; KBIM-TV (CBS, The Country Network) Roswell; KCBD (NBC, This TV) Lubbock; KJTV-TV (FOX) Lubbock; KMID (ABC) Midland; KMLM-DT (GLC) Odessa; KOSA-TV (CBS, MNT) Odessa; KPEJ-TV (FOX) Odessa; KTTZ-TV (PBS) Lubbock; KUPB (UNV) Midland; KUPT (MNT) Hobbs [Licensed & silent]; KWES-TV (CW, NBC, TMO) Odessa; KXTQ-CD (TMO) Lubbock; 1 FM.
Programming (via satellite): Fox News Channel; INSP; Lifetime; Pop; TNT; WGN America.
Fee: $36.95 monthly; $.90 converter.

Expanded Basic Service 1
Subscribers: N.A.
Programming (via satellite): A&E; AMC; Animal Planet; Cartoon Network; CMT; CNBC; CNN; C-SPAN; Discovery Channel; Discovery Life Channel; Disney Channel; DIY Network; E! HD; ESPN; ESPN2; EVINE Live; Food Network; FOX Sports Southwest; Freeform; FX; HGTV; History; HLN; MovieFlex; MTV; National Geographic Channel; Nickelodeon; OWN; Oprah Winfrey Network; Spike TV; Syfy; TBS; Telemundo; The Weather Channel; TLC; TV Land; USA Network; VH1.
Fee: $28.11 monthly.

Digital Basic Service
Subscribers: N.A.
Programming (via satellite): BBC America; Bloomberg Television; Bravo; Disney XD; DMX Music; ESPN Classic; ESPNews; FOX College Sports Central; FOX College Sports Pacific; Fox Sports 1; Fuse; FXM; FYI; Golf Channel; Great American Country; GSN; History International; IFC; LMN; NBCSN; Nick Jr.; Outdoor Channel; Starz Encore (multiplexed); TeenNick; The Word Network; Trinity Broadcasting Network (TBN); Turner Classic Movies; WE tv.
Fee: $20.90 monthly.

Pay Service 1
Pay Units: N.A.
Programming (via satellite): Cinemax; HBO.
Fee: $12.95 monthly (each).

Digital Pay Service 1
Pay Units: N.A.
Programming (via satellite): Cinemax (multiplexed); HBO (multiplexed); Showtime (multiplexed); Starz (multiplexed); The Movie Channel (multiplexed).
Fee: $8.95 monthly (Starz), $11.95 monthly (Cinemax, HBO, Showtime, or TMC).

Video-On-Demand: No

Pay-Per-View
Fresh (delivered digitally); Playboy TV (delivered digitally); iN DEMAND.

Internet Service
Operational: Yes.
Broadband Service: Warp Drive Online.
Fee: $27.95-$54.95 monthly.

Telephone Service
Digital: Operational
Miles of Plant: 1,292.0 (coaxial); None (fiber optic). Homes passed: 65,091. Miles of plant & homes passed include Alpine, West Odessa, Carlsbad NM, Chama NM, Jal NM, & Lea County NM
Vice President, Corporate Finance: Carl Shapiro. Assistant Treasurer: Noel Hutton.
Ownership: TDS Telecom (MSO).

SEVEN POINTS (northern portion)—Formerly served by Trust Cable. No longer in operation. ICA: TX0423.

SEYMOUR—Suddenlink Communications, 520 Maryville Centre Dr, Ste 300, St. Louis, MO 63141. Phones: 800-999-6845; 314-315-9400. Web Site: http://www.suddenlink.com. ICA: TX0254.
TV Market Ranking: Outside TV Markets (SEYMOUR). Franchise award date: N.A. Franchise expiration date: N.A. Began: February 1, 1977.
Channel capacity: N.A. Channels available but not in use: N.A.

Basic Service
Subscribers: 146. Commercial subscribers: 26.
Programming (received off-air): KAUZ-TV (CBS, CW) Wichita Falls; KFDX-TV (NBC) Wichita Falls; KJTL (Bounce TV, FOX) Wichita Falls; KSWO-TV (ABC, TMO) Lawton; allband FM.
Programming (via satellite): C-SPAN; Discovery Channel; Hallmark Channel; Lifetime; QVC; TBS; The Weather Channel; TLC.
Fee: $28.45 monthly.

Expanded Basic Service 1
Subscribers: N.A.
Programming (via satellite): AMC; Animal Planet; Cartoon Network; CNN; Disney Channel; ESPN; Fox News Channel; Freeform; FX; HGTV; HLN; MTV; Nickelodeon; Spike TV; TNT; USA Network.
Fee: $39.95 installation; $25.00 monthly.

Pay Service 1
Pay Units: N.A.
Programming (via satellite): Cinemax; HBO; Starz; Starz Encore.
Fee: $1.75 monthly (Encore), $6.75 monthly (Starz), $12.84 monthly (Cinemax), $13.83 monthly (HBO).

Video-On-Demand: No

Internet Service
Operational: Yes. Began: October 6, 2003.
Broadband Service: Suddenlink High Speed Internet.
Fee: $49.95 installation; $43.95 monthly.

Telephone Service
None
Miles of Plant: 29.0 (coaxial); None (fiber optic). Homes passed: 1,700.
Vice President, Corporate Finance: Michael Pflantz. Regional Manager: Todd Cruthird. Plant Manager: Ron Johnson.
Ownership: Cequel Communications Holdings I LLC (MSO).

SHAMROCK—Suddenlink Communications, 520 Maryville Centre Dr, Ste 300, St. Louis, MO 63141. Phones: 800-999-6845 (Customer service); 314-315-9400; 806-256-3944. Web Site: http://www.suddenlink.com. ICA: TX0318.
TV Market Ranking: Outside TV Markets (SHAMROCK). Franchise award date: N.A. Franchise expiration date: N.A. Began: August 1, 1957.
Channel capacity: N.A. Channels available but not in use: N.A.

Basic Service
Subscribers: 185. Commercial subscribers: 68.
Programming (received off-air): KWET (PBS) Cheyenne.
Programming (via microwave): KAMR-TV (IND, NBC) Amarillo; KCIT (FOX, This TV) Amarillo; KETA-TV (PBS) Oklahoma City; KFDA-TV (CBS, TMO) Amarillo; KVII-TV (ABC, CW) Amarillo.
Programming (via satellite): AMC; Animal Planet; Cartoon Network; CMT; CNN; Discovery Channel; Disney Channel; E! HD; ESPN; Fox News Channel; FOX Sports Southwest; Freeform; HGTV; History; HLN; INSP; Lifetime; Nickelodeon; QVC; Spike TV; Syfy; TBS; The Weather Channel; TLC; TNT; truTV; TV Land; USA Network; WGN America.
Fee: $28.45 monthly.

Pay Service 1
Pay Units: N.A.
Programming (via satellite): Cinemax; HBO; Showtime; The Movie Channel.
Fee: $5.95 monthly (TMC), $9.95 monthly (Cinemax or Showtime), $10.95 monthly (HBO).

Video-On-Demand: No

Internet Service
Operational: Yes. Began: February 11, 2004.
Broadband Service: Suddenlink High Speed Internet.
Fee: $49.95 installation; $25.95 monthly.

Telephone Service
Digital: Operational
Fee: $44.95 monthly
Miles of Plant: 25.0 (coaxial); None (fiber optic). Homes passed: 1,313.
Senior Vice President, Corporate Finance: Michael Pflantz. Marketing Director: Bev-

Cable Systems—Texas

erly Gambell. Chief Technician: Rick Rattan.
Ownership: Cequel Communications Holdings I LLC (MSO).

SHEFFIELD—Formerly served by Ector Cable. No longer in operation. ICA: TX0691.

SHERIDAN—Formerly served by National Cable Inc. No longer in operation. ICA: TX0645.

SHERMAN—Cable One, 3720 Texoma Pkwy, PO Box 1223, Sherman, TX 75091-1223. Phone: 903-893-6548. Fax: 903-868-2754. E-mail: webmaster@cableone.net. Web Site: http://www.cableone.net. Also serves Bells, Bonham, Denison, Fannin County (portions), Grayson County (northern portion), Howe, Knollwood, Ravenna, Savoy, Tom Bean, Van Alstyne & Whitewright. ICA: TX0042.
TV Market Ranking: Below 100 (Bells, Bonham, Denison, Fannin County (portions), Grayson County (northern portion), Howe, Knollwood, Ravenna, Savoy, SHERMAN, Tom Bean, Van Alstyne, Whitewright). Franchise award date: March 7, 1966. Franchise expiration date: N.A. Began: August 1, 1957.
Channel capacity: 58 (operating 2-way). Channels available but not in use: N.A.
Basic Service
Subscribers: 10,709.
Programming (received off-air): KDAF (Antenna TV, CW, This TV) Dallas; KDFI (Bounce TV, Buzzr, Heroes & Icons, MNT, Movies!) Dallas; KDFW (FOX) Dallas; KDTX-TV (TBN) Dallas; KERA-TV (PBS) Dallas; KSTR-DT (getTV, UniMas) Irving; KTEN (ABC, CW, NBC) Ada; KTVT (CBS, Decades) Fort Worth; KTXA (IND, MeTV) Fort Worth; KTXD-TV (IND) Greenville; KUVN-DT (UNV) Garland; KXAS-TV (COZI TV, NBC) Fort Worth; KXII (CBS, FOX, MNT) Sherman; KXTX-TV (TMO) Dallas; WFAA (ABC) Dallas.
Programming (via satellite): Animal Planet; C-SPAN; C-SPAN 2; Daystar TV Network; EWTN Global Catholic Network; Pop; QVC.
Fee: $90.00 installation; $35.00 monthly; $.45 converter.
Expanded Basic Service 1
Subscribers: N.A.
Programming (via satellite): A&E; AMC; BET; Bravo; Cartoon Network; CMT; CNBC; CNN; Comedy Central; Discovery Channel; Disney Channel; ESPN; ESPN2; Fox News Channel; FOX Sports Southwest; Freeform; FX; HGTV; History; HLN; Lifetime; MSNBC; MTV; Nickelodeon; Spike TV; Syfy; TBS; The Weather Channel; TLC; TNT; Turner Classic Movies; TV Land; USA Network; VH1.
Fee: $46.00 monthly.
Digital Basic Service
Subscribers: N.A.
Programming (via satellite): 3ABN; Boomerang; BYUtv; Discovery Digital Networks; Disney XD; DMX Music; ESPN Classic; ESPNews; FamilyNet; FOX College Sports Central; FOX College Sports Pacific; Fox HD; Fox Sports 1; Fox Sports 2; FXM; FYI; Golf Channel; Great American Country; Hallmark Channel; History International; HITS (Headend In The Sky); INSP; National Geographic Channel; Outdoor Channel; TNT HD; Trinity Broadcasting Network (TBN); truTV; TVG Network; Universal HD.
Fee: $18.95 monthly.
Digital Pay Service 1
Pay Units: N.A.
Programming (via satellite): Cinemax (multiplexed); Flix; HBO (multiplexed); Showtime (multiplexed); Showtime HD; Starz (multiplexed); Starz Encore (multiplexed); Sundance TV; The Movie Channel (multiplexed); The Movie Channel HD.
Fee: $15.00 monthly (each).
Video-On-Demand: No
Pay-Per-View
iN DEMAND (delivered digitally); Pleasure (delivered digitally); SexSee (delivered digitally); Juicy (delivered digitally); VaVoom (delivered digitally).
Internet Service
Operational: Yes. Began: October 1, 2001.
Subscribers: 14,218.
Broadband Service: CableONE.net.
Fee: $75.00 installation; $43.00 monthly; $5.00 modem lease.
Telephone Service
Digital: Operational
Subscribers: 5,502.
Fee: $39.95 monthly
Miles of Plant: 1,225.0 (coaxial); 88.0 (fiber optic). Homes passed: 46,371.
Vice President: Patrick A. Dolohanty. General Manager: Claude H. Edwards. Chief Technician: Rod Ralls. Program Director: Darla Hutcherson. Marketing Director: Donna Perry. Customer Service Manager: Donna Webb.
Ownership: Cable ONE Inc. (MSO).

SHINER—Formerly served by Almega Cable. No longer in operation. ICA: TX0383.

SIERRA BLANCA—Formerly served by Sierra Cable TV. No longer in operation. ICA: TX0853.

SILSBEE—Time Warner Cable. Now served by PORT ARTHUR (formerly Beaumont), TX [TX0022]. ICA: TX0079.

SILVERTON—Formerly served by Reach Broadband. No longer in operation. ICA: TX0525.

SINTON—Formerly served by Charter Communications. Now served by Time Warner Cable, ROCKPORT, TX [TX0116]. ICA: TX0224.

SKELLYTOWN—Formerly served by Almega Cable. No longer in operation. ICA: TX0586.

SLATON—Formerly served by NTS Communications. This cable system has converted to IPTV. Now served by WOLFFORTH, TX [TX5540]. ICA: TX0201.

SMILEY—Formerly served by National Cable Inc. No longer in operation. ICA: TX0652.

SMITH COUNTY (portions)—East Texas Cable Co., 24285 State Hwy 64 East, Canton, TX 75103-6187. Phone: 903-567-2260. Fax: 903-567-4048. Web Site: http://www.etcable.net. ICA: TX1048.
TV Market Ranking: Below 100 (SMITH COUNTY (PORTIONS)); Outside TV Markets (SMITH COUNTY (PORTIONS)).
Channel capacity: N.A. Channels available but not in use: N.A.
President & Chief Executive Officer: Jim Roby.
Ownership: Jim Roby (MSO).

SMITHVILLE—Reveille Broadband, 1008 Giddings St, PO Box 39, Lexington, TX 78947. Phones: 979-773-3215; 979-773-4700. Fax: 979-773-4733. E-mail: mariesullivan@reveillebroadband.com. Web Site: http://www.reveillebroadband.com. Also serves Lake Thunderbird Estates. ICA: TX0951.
TV Market Ranking: Below 100 (Lake Thunderbird Estates); Outside TV Markets (SMITHVILLE). Franchise award date: June 1, 2003. Franchise expiration date: N.A. Began: N.A.
Channel capacity: N.A. Channels available but not in use: N.A.
Basic Service
Subscribers: N.A.
Programming (received off-air): KEYE-TV (CBS, TMO) Austin; KLRU (PBS) Austin; KNVA (CW, Grit, TheCoolTV) Austin; KTBC (Buzzr, FOX, Movies!) Austin; KVUE (ABC, Estrella TV) Austin; KXAN-TV (COZI TV, NBC) Austin.
Programming (via satellite): A&E; AMC; Animal Planet; BET; Boomerang; Cartoon Network; CMT; CNN; Comedy Central; C-SPAN; C-SPAN 2; Discovery Channel; Disney Channel; E! HD; ESPN; ESPN2; Food Network; Fox News Channel; Fox Sports 1; FOX Sports Southwest; Freeform; FX; Great American Country; GSN; Hallmark Channel; Hallmark Movies & Mysteries; HGTV; History; HLN; Lifetime; National Geographic Channel; Nick Jr.; Nickelodeon; QVC; Spike TV; Syfy; TBS; The Weather Channel; TLC; TNT; Travel Channel; Trinity Broadcasting Network (TBN); truTV; Turner Classic Movies; TV Land; Univision Studios; USA Network; VH1; WGN America.
Fee: $35.00 installation.
Pay Service 1
Pay Units: N.A.
Programming (via satellite): HBO; The Movie Channel.
Fee: $10.95 monthly (each).
Internet Service
Operational: Yes.
Telephone Service
Analog: Not Operational
Digital: Operational
Miles of Plant: 12.0 (coaxial); None (fiber optic).
Chief Executive Officer: Marie Sullivan. President: Jeff Sullivan. Vice President: Corey Savage. Chief Technology Officer: Jason Sembera. Office Manager: Laura Tillery.
Ownership: Reveille Broadband (MSO).

SNOOK—Formerly served by National Cable Inc. No longer in operation. ICA: TX0854.

SNYDER—Formerly served by Snyder Microwave Communications LC. No longer in operation. ICA: TX0897.

SNYDER—Suddenlink Communications, 2211 Avenue R, Snyder, TX 79549. Phones: 888-822-5151 (Customer service); 314-315-9400. Fax: 915-573-6360. Web Site: http://www.suddenlink.com. Also serves Hermleigh & Scurry County (portions). ICA: TX0120.
TV Market Ranking: Below 100 (Hermleigh, Scurry County (portions), SNYDER). Franchise award date: N.A. Franchise expiration date: N.A. Began: December 1, 1958.
Channel capacity: 30 (operating 2-way). Channels available but not in use: N.A.
Basic Service
Subscribers: 2,608. Commercial subscribers: 354.
Programming (received off-air): KCBD (NBC, This TV) Lubbock; KERA-TV (PBS) Dallas; KJTV-TV (FOX) Lubbock; KLBK-TV (CBS) Lubbock; KPCB-DT (GLC) Snyder; KRBC-TV (Bounce TV, NBC) Abilene; KTAB-TV (CBS) Abilene; KTES-LP (CW, This TV) Abilene; KTXS-TV (ABC, CW, This TV, TMO) Sweetwater; KXVA (FOX, MNT) Abilene; WFAA (ABC) Dallas; allband FM.
Programming (via satellite): C-SPAN; C-SPAN 2; Pop; QVC; Univision Studios.
Fee: $40.00 installation; $32.10 monthly.
Expanded Basic Service 1
Subscribers: N.A.
Programming (via satellite): A&E; AMC; Animal Planet; BET; Bravo; Cartoon Network; CMT; CNBC; CNN; Comedy Central; CW PLUS; Discovery Channel; Disney Channel; E! HD; ESPN; ESPN2; Food Network; Fox News Channel; Fox Sports 1; FOX Sports Southwest; Freeform; FX; HGTV; History; HLN; Lifetime; LMN; MSNBC; MTV; MTV2; NBCSN; Nickelodeon; Oxygen; Spike TV; Syfy; TBS; The Weather Channel; TLC; TNT; Travel Channel; truTV; TV Land; USA Network; VH1.
Fee: $13.52 monthly.
Digital Basic Service
Subscribers: N.A.
Programming (via satellite): A&E HD; AXS TV; Bandamax; BBC America; Bloomberg Television; Boomerang; CBS Sports Network; Cine Mexicano; Cinelatino; CMT; CNN en Espanol; Cooking Channel; De Pelicula; De Pelicula Clasico; Destination America; Discovery Kids Channel; Disney XD; DIY Network; DMX Music; ESPN Classic; ESPN Deportes; ESPN HD; ESPN2 HD; ESPNews; ESPNU; EVINE Live; EWTN Global Catholic Network; Food Network HD; FOX College Sports Central; FOX College Sports Pacific; Fox Deportes; Fox Sports 2; Fuse; FYI; Golf Channel; Great American Country; GSN; Hallmark Channel; HD Theater; HGTV HD; History en Espanol; History International; IFC; Investigation Discovery; Jewelry Television; MTV Classic; MTV Hits; National Geographic Channel; National Geographic Channel HD; NBC Universo; Nick Jr.; Nicktoons; Outdoor Channel; OWN: Oprah Winfrey Network; Science Channel; Starz Encore (multiplexed); Sundance TV; Teen Nick; Telehit; Tennis Channel; TNT HD; Toon Disney en Espanol; Tr3s; Turner Classic Movies; UniMas; Universal HD; Univision; UP; VideoRola; WE tv.
Pay Service 1
Pay Units: N.A.
Programming (via satellite): Cinemax; HBO; Showtime; Starz.
Fee: $40.00 installation; $10.50 monthly (each).
Digital Pay Service 1
Pay Units: N.A.
Programming (via satellite): Cinemax (multiplexed); HBO (multiplexed); HBO HD; HBO Latino; Showtime (multiplexed); Showtime HD; Starz (multiplexed); Starz Encore; Starz HD; The Movie Channel.
Video-On-Demand: No
Pay-Per-View
iN DEMAND (delivered digitally); Fresh (delivered digitally); Shorteez (delivered digitally); Playboy TV (delivered digitally).
Internet Service
Operational: Yes.
Broadband Service: Suddenlink High Speed Internet.
Fee: $45.95 installation; $29.95 monthly.
Telephone Service
Digital: Operational
Fee: $44.95 monthly
Miles of Plant: 108.0 (coaxial); None (fiber optic). Homes passed: 5,620.
Senior Vice President, Corporate Finance: Michael Pflantz. General Manager: Victor Means. Chief Technician: Peter Pena.
Ownership: Cequel Communications Holdings I LLC (MSO).

Texas—Cable Systems

SONORA—Suddenlink Communications, 520 Maryville Centre Dr, Ste 300, St. Louis, MO 63141. Phones: 877-423-2743 (Customer service); 314-315-9400. Web Site: http://www.suddenlink.com. Also serves Sutton County (portions). ICA: TX0245.
TV Market Ranking: Outside TV Markets (SONORA). Franchise award date: N.A. Franchise expiration date: N.A. Began: April 1, 1955.
Channel capacity: N.A. Channels available but not in use: N.A.
Basic Service
Subscribers: 245. Commercial subscribers: 36.
Programming (received off-air): KIDY (FOX, MNT) San Angelo; KLST (CBS) San Angelo; KSAN-TV (NBC) San Angelo; KTXS-TV (ABC, CW, This TV, TMO) Sweetwater; 4 FMs.
Programming (via satellite): A&E; Animal Planet; CMT; CNN; C-SPAN; Discovery Channel; Disney Channel; ESPN; Fox News Channel; FOX Sports Southwest; Freeform; History; HLN; KRMA-TV (PBS) Denver; Lifetime; Nickelodeon; QVC; Spike TV; TBS; The Weather Channel; TLC; TNT; Trinity Broadcasting Network (TBN); Turner Classic Movies; TV Land; USA Network; WGN America.
Programming (via translator): KVDA (TMO) San Antonio.
Fee: $28.45 monthly.
Pay Service 1
Pay Units: N.A.
Programming (via satellite): HBO; Showtime; The Movie Channel.
Fee: $5.95 monthly (TMC), $9.95 monthly (Showtime), $10.95 monthly (HBO).
Video-On-Demand: No
Internet Service
Operational: Yes. Began: October 5, 2004.
Subscribers: 105.
Broadband Service: Suddenlink High Speed Internet.
Fee: $45.95 installation; $29.95 monthly.
Telephone Service
Digital: Operational
Fee: $44.95 monthly
Miles of Plant: 58.0 (coaxial); None (fiber optic). Homes passed: 1,360.
Vice President, Corporate Finance: Michael Pflantz. Regional Manager: Todd Cruthird. Marketing Director: Beverly Gambell.
Ownership: Cequel Communications Holdings I LLC (MSO).

SOUR LAKE—NewWave Communications, One Montgomery Plaza, 4th Floor, Sikeston, MO 63801. Phones: 573-472-9500; 888-863-9928. Fax: 573-472-9518. E-mail: info@newwave.com. Web Site: http://www.newwavecom.com. Also serves Bevil Oaks & China. ICA: TX0162.
TV Market Ranking: 88 (Bevil Oaks, China, SOUR LAKE). Franchise award date: February 1, 1983. Franchise expiration date: N.A. Began: N.A.
Channel capacity: N.A. Channels available but not in use: N.A.
Basic Service
Subscribers: 946.
Programming (received off-air): KWBB; KBMT (ABC) Beaumont; KBTV-TV (Bounce TV, FOX) Port Arthur; KFDM (CBS, CW) Beaumont; KIAH (Antenna TV, CW) Houston; KITU-TV (TBN) Beaumont; KRIV (FOX) Houston; KTRK-TV (ABC, Live Well Network) Houston; KTXH (Buzzr, MNT, Movies!) Houston; KUHT (PBS) Houston; KVHP (FOX) Lake Charles; KYAZ (Azteca America, IND) Katy.

Programming (via satellite): The Weather Channel.
Fee: $35.00 installation; $33.89 monthly.
Expanded Basic Service 1
Subscribers: N.A.
Programming (via satellite): A&E; AMC; Animal Planet; BET; Bravo; CMT; CNBC; CNN; Comedy Central; C-SPAN; Discovery Channel; Disney XD; ESPN; ESPN2; Food Network; Fox News Channel; FOX Sports Networks; Freeform; FX; Hallmark Channel; History; HLN; Lifetime; MTV; Nickelodeon; Outdoor Channel; QVC; Spike TV; Syfy; TBS; TLC; TNT; Travel Channel; truTV; TV Land; USA Network; VH1; WGN America.
Fee: $54.20 monthly.
Digital Basic Service
Subscribers: N.A.
Programming (via satellite): BBC America; Bloomberg Television; Discovery Digital Networks; ESPN Classic; ESPNews; Fox Sports 1; FXM; FYI; Golf Channel; GSN; HGTV; History International; IFC; LMN; National Geographic Channel; NBCSN; Nick Jr.; TeenNick; Trinity Broadcasting Network (TBN); Turner Classic Movies; WE tv.
Fee: $11.00 monthly.
Digital Pay Service 1
Pay Units: N.A.
Programming (via satellite): DMX Music; HBO (multiplexed); Showtime (multiplexed); Starz; Starz Encore (multiplexed); The Movie Channel (multiplexed).
Fee: $9.95 installation; $8.00 monthly (Starz), $9.00 (Cinemax), $11.00 monthly (Starz/Encore), $15.00 monthly (Showtime/TMC), $17.00 monthly (HBO) or $26.00 monthly (HBO/Cinemax).
Video-On-Demand: No
Pay-Per-View
iN DEMAND (delivered digitally); Club Jenna (delivered digitally); Fresh (delivered digitally); Playboy TV (delivered digitally).
Internet Service
Operational: Yes.
Fee: $39.95 installation; $39.99–$79.99 monthly; $6.00-$8.99 modem lease; $39.95 modem purchase.
Telephone Service
Digital: Operational
Fee: $39.95 monthly
Miles of Plant: 120.0 (coaxial); None (fiber optic). Homes passed: 3,500.
Regional General Manager: Jerry Smith.
Ownership: NewWave Communications LLC (MSO).

SOUTH SHORES—Formerly served by Cable Unlimited. No longer in operation. ICA: TX0966.

SOUTH SILSBEE—Formerly served by Cebridge Connections. No longer in operation. ICA: TX0614.

SPEARMAN—PTCI. This cable system has converted to IPTV. Now served by GUYMON, OK [OK5005]. ICA: TX0298.

SPICEWOOD BEACH—Formerly served by Charter Communications. No longer in operation. ICA: TX0633.

SPLENDORA—Formerly served by Almega Cable. No longer in operation. ICA: TX0372.

SPRINGTOWN—Vyve Broadband, 2804B FM 51 South, Decatur, TX 76234. Phone: 855-367-8983. Web Site: http://vyvebroadband.com. ICA: TX0390.

TV Market Ranking: 12 (SPRINGTOWN). Franchise award date: September 1, 1983. Franchise expiration date: N.A. Began: September 1, 1983.
Channel capacity: N.A. Channels available but not in use: N.A.
Basic Service
Subscribers: 46.
Programming (received off-air): KDAF (Antenna TV, CW, This TV) Dallas; KDFI (Bounce TV, Buzzr, Heroes & Icons, MNT, Movies!) Dallas; KDFW (FOX) Dallas; KDTN (Daystar TV, ETV) Denton; KDTX-TV (TBN) Dallas; KERA-TV (PBS) Dallas; KTVT (CBS, Decades) Fort Worth; KTXA (IND, MeTV) Fort Worth; KXAS-TV (COZI TV, NBC) Fort Worth; KXTX-TV (TMO) Dallas; WFAA (ABC) Dallas.
Fee: $59.99 installation; $56.99 monthly.
Expanded Basic Service 1
Subscribers: N.A.
Programming (via satellite): A&E; AMC; CMT; CNBC; CNN; C-SPAN; Discovery Channel; Disney Channel; ESPN; FOX Sports Southwest; Freeform; HLN; MTV; Nickelodeon; QVC; Spike TV; TBS; TeenNick; The Weather Channel; TNT; USA Network; WGN America.
Fee: $41.95 monthly.
Digital Basic Service
Subscribers: N.A.
Programming (via satellite): BBC America; Bloomberg Television; Bravo; Cloo; Destination America; Discovery Kids Channel; Discovery Life Channel; DMX Music; ESPN Classic; ESPNews; Fox Sports 1; Fuse; FYI; Golf Channel; Great American Country; GSN; HGTV; History; History International; IFC; Investigation Discovery; LMN; MTV Hits; MTV2; National Geographic Channel; NBCSN; Nicktoons; Outdoor Channel; OWN; Oprah Winfrey Network; Science Channel; Sundance TV; Turner Classic Movies; WE tv.
Fee: $7.00 monthly.
Pay Service 1
Pay Units: N.A.
Programming (via satellite): Cinemax; HBO (multiplexed); Starz.
Digital Pay Service 1
Pay Units: N.A.
Programming (via satellite): Cinemax (multiplexed); Flix; HBO (multiplexed); Showtime (multiplexed); Starz (multiplexed); Starz Encore (multiplexed); The Movie Channel (multiplexed).
Fee: $5.00 monthly (Encore), $11.00 monthly (Starz), $11.95 monthly (Cinemax), $13.95 monthly (HBO or Showtime/TMC/Flix).
Video-On-Demand: No
Pay-Per-View
iN DEMAND (delivered digitally); Hot Choice (delivered digitally); Playboy TV (delivered digitally); Spice (delivered digitally); Spice 2 (delivered digitally).
Internet Service
Operational: No.
Telephone Service
None
Miles of Plant: 44.0 (coaxial); None (fiber optic). Included in Decatur.
President & Chief Executive Officer: Jeffrey DeMond. Vice President, Residential Services: Vin Zachariah. Vice President, Marketing: Diane Quennoz. Vice President, Financial Planning: Daniel White.
Ownership: Vyve Broadband LLC (MSO).

SPUR—Formerly served by Almega Cable. No longer in operation. ICA: TX0358.

SPURGER—Formerly served by Carrell Communications. No longer in operation. ICA: TX0882.

ST. FRANCIS VILLAGE—Formerly served by National Cable Inc. No longer in operation. ICA: TX0544.

ST. JO—Formerly served by Rapid Cable. Now served by Nortex Communications, VALLEY VIEW, TX [TX0792]. ICA: TX0571.

STAMFORD—Formerly served by Alliance Communications. Now served by WesTex Telephone Cooperative, 1500 West Business 20, Stanton, TX 79782. Phones: 432-263-0091 (Big Spring office); 432-756-3826. Web Site: http://www.westex.coop. ICA: TX0247.
TV Market Ranking: Below 100 (STAMFORD). Franchise award date: N.A. Franchise expiration date: N.A. Began: April 1, 1961.
Channel capacity: N.A. Channels available but not in use: N.A.
Basic Service
Subscribers: 180.
Programming (received off-air): KIDZ-LD Abilene; KRBC-TV (Bounce TV, NBC) Abilene; KRMA-TV (PBS) Denver; KTAB-TV (CBS) Abilene; KTXS-TV (ABC, CW, This TV, TMO) Sweetwater; KXVA (FOX, MNT) Abilene.
Programming (via satellite): C-SPAN; ESPN; ESPN2; FOX Sports Southwest; MTV; QVC; TBS; TNT; WGN America.
Fee: $45.00 installation; $22.45 monthly.
Expanded Basic Service 1
Subscribers: N.A.
Programming (received off-air): KDTX-TV (TBN) Dallas.
Programming (via satellite): A&E; AMC; Animal Planet; CMT; CNN; Comedy Central; Discovery Channel; Disney Channel; E! HD; Freeform; HGTV; History; HLN; Lifetime; MSNBC; NBCSN; Nickelodeon; Oxygen; Spike TV; Syfy; The Weather Channel; TLC; Trinity Broadcasting Network (TBN); Turner Classic Movies; TV Land; Univision Studios; USA Network; VH1.
Fee: $27.55 monthly.
Digital Basic Service
Subscribers: N.A.
Programming (via satellite): BBC America; Bloomberg Television; Discovery Digital Networks; Disney XD; DIY Network; ESPN Classic; ESPNews; Flix; FYI; History International; IFC; MC.
Fee: $12.95 monthly.
Pay Service 1
Pay Units: N.A.
Programming (via satellite): Showtime.
Fee: $9.95 monthly.
Digital Pay Service 1
Pay Units: N.A.
Programming (via satellite): Cinemax (multiplexed); HBO (multiplexed); Showtime; Starz Encore (multiplexed); The Movie Channel (multiplexed).
Video-On-Demand: No
Internet Service
Operational: No.
Telephone Service
None
Miles of Plant: 28.0 (coaxial); None (fiber optic). Homes passed: 1,747.
Ownership: WesTex Telecommunications (MSO).

STANTON—Formerly served by Almega Cable. No longer in operation. ICA: TX0350.

Cable Systems—Texas

STANTON—WesTex Telecom. This cable system has converted to IPTV. See STANTON, TX [TX5564]. ICA: TX1031.

STANTON—WesTex. Formerly [TX1031]. This cable system has converted to IPTV, 1500 West Business 20, Stanton, TX 79782. Phone: 432-756-3826. Web Site: http://www.westex.coop. Also serves Coahoma. ICA: TX5564.
TV Market Ranking: Below 100 (STANTON). Channel capacity: N.A. Channels available but not in use: N.A.
Good TVee
Subscribers: 373.
Fee: $45.95 monthly. Includes 78 channels.
Better TVee
Subscribers: N.A.
Fee: $54.95 monthly. Includes 190 channels.
Best TVee
Subscribers: N.A.
Fee: $94.95 monthly.
HBO
Subscribers: N.A.
Fee: $23.28 monthly.
NFL RedZone
Subscribers: N.A.
Fee: $54.50 per season.
Showtime/TMC
Subscribers: N.A.
Fee: $17.50 monthly.
Starz/Encore
Subscribers: N.A.
Fee: $17.50 monthly.
The Movie Channel
Subscribers: N.A.
Fee: $17.50 monthly.
Internet Service
Operational: Yes.
Fee: $19.95-$49.95 monthly.
President: Joe D. Schwartz.
Ownership: WesTex Telecommunications.

STEPHENVILLE—Northland Cable Television, 975 North Lillian St, PO Box 70, Stephenville, TX 76401-0070. Phone: 254-968-4189. Fax: 254-968-8350. Web Site: http://www.yournorthland.com. Also serves Dublin. ICA: TX0098.
TV Market Ranking: Outside TV Markets (STEPHENVILLE, Dublin). Franchise award date: N.A. Franchise expiration date: N.A. Began: July 15, 1967.
Channel capacity: N.A. Channels available but not in use: N.A.
Basic Service
Subscribers: 1,287.
Programming (received off-air): KDAF (Antenna TV, CW, This TV) Dallas; KDFI (Bounce TV, Buzzr, Heroes & Icons, MNT, Movies!) Dallas; KDFW (FOX) Dallas; KERA-TV (PBS) Dallas; KPXD-TV (ION) Arlington; KSTR-DT (getTV, UniMas) Irving; KTVT (CBS, Decades) Fort Worth; KTXA (IND, MeTV) Fort Worth; KWTX-TV (CBS, CW) Waco; KXAS-TV (COZI TV, NBC) Fort Worth; KXTX-TV (TMO) Dallas; WFAA (ABC) Dallas; allband FM.
Programming (via satellite): A&E; Animal Planet; Cartoon Network; CNBC; CNN; Comedy Central; C-SPAN; Discovery Channel; Disney Channel; ESPN; ESPN2; Food Network; Fox News Channel; FOX Sports Southwest; FX; FXM; Golf Channel; Great American Country; Hallmark Channel; HGTV; History; HLN; Lifetime; MTV; NBCSN; Nickelodeon; Outdoor Channel; QVC; Spike TV; Syfy; TBS; The Weather Channel; TLC; TNT; Travel Channel; Trinity Broadcasting Network (TBN); Turner Classic Movies; TV Land; Univision Studios; USA Network; VH1.
Fee: $75.00 installation; $47.64 monthly.
Digital Basic Service
Subscribers: N.A.
Programming (via satellite): BBC America; Bloomberg Television; Bravo; Destination America; Discovery Kids Channel; Discovery Life Channel; DMX Music; ESPNews; Fox Sports 1; IFC; Investigation Discovery; National Geographic Channel; OWN: Oprah Winfrey Network; Science Channel; WE tv.
Fee: $8.70 monthly.
Digital Expanded Basic Service
Subscribers: N.A.
Programming (via satellite): ESPN HD; HD Theater; TNT HD; Universal HD.
Fee: $5.99 monthly.
Pay Service 1
Pay Units: N.A.
Programming (via satellite): HBO.
Fee: $13.50 monthly.
Digital Pay Service 1
Pay Units: N.A.
Programming (via satellite): Cinemax (multiplexed); Flix; HBO (multiplexed); Showtime (multiplexed); Starz (multiplexed); Starz Encore (multiplexed); The Movie Channel (multiplexed).
Fee: $14.75 monthly (Cinemax, HBO, Starz/Encore, or Showtime/TMC/Flix).
Video-On-Demand: No
Pay-Per-View
iN DEMAND (delivered digitally); Hot Choice (delivered digitally); Playboy TV (delivered digitally); Fresh (delivered digitally).
Internet Service
Operational: Yes.
Fee: $42.99 monthly.
Telephone Service
Digital: Operational
Miles of Plant: 96.0 (coaxial); None (fiber optic). Homes passed: 7,300.
Executive Vice President: Richard I. Clark. General Manager: Melissa Gonzalez. Chief Technician: Bobby Smith.
Ownership: Northland Communications Corp. (MSO).

STERLING CITY—Formerly served by Reach Broadband. No longer in operation. ICA: TX0856.

STOCKDALE—Formerly served by Windjammer Cable. No longer in operation. ICA: TX1020.

STONY POINT—Formerly served by Almega Cable. No longer in operation. ICA: TX0303.

STRATFORD—Formerly served by Almega Cable. No longer in operation. ICA: TX0404.

STRAWN—Formerly served by Strawn TV Cable Inc. No longer in operation. ICA: TX0596.

SULLIVAN CITY—Time Warner Cable. Now served by PHARR, TX [TX0017]. ICA: TX0328.

SULPHUR SPRINGS—Suddenlink Communications, 520 Maryville Centre Dr, Ste 300, St. Louis, MO 63141. Phone: 314-315-9400. Web Site: http://www.suddenlink.com. Also serves Como & Hopkins County (portions). ICA: TX0859.
TV Market Ranking: Below 100 (Como, SULPHUR SPRINGS, Hopkins County (portions) (portions)); Outside TV Markets (Hopkins County (portions) (portions)). Franchise award date: N.A. Franchise expiration date: N.A. Began: June 1, 1954.
Channel capacity: 42 (not 2-way capable). Channels available but not in use: N.A.
Basic Service
Subscribers: 3,319. Commercial subscribers: 308.
Programming (received off-air): KDFW (FOX) Dallas; KERA-TV (PBS) Dallas; KETK-TV (Estrella TV, NBC) Jacksonville; KLTV (ABC, Bounce TV, TMO) Tyler; KTVT (CBS, Decades) Fort Worth; KTXD-TV (IND) Greenville; KXAS-TV (COZI TV, NBC) Fort Worth; KXTX-TV (TMO) Dallas; WFAA (ABC) Dallas; allband FM.
Programming (via satellite): C-SPAN; ESPN; HLN; TBS; The Weather Channel; TLC; Trinity Broadcasting Network (TBN); TV Land.
Fee: $49.95 installation; $35.24 monthly.
Expanded Basic Service 1
Subscribers: N.A.
Programming (via satellite): AMC; BET; Cartoon Network; CNN; Discovery Channel; Disney Channel; FOX Sports Southwest; Freeform; Great American Country; Lifetime; Nickelodeon; Spike TV; Syfy; TNT; USA Network; VH1.
Fee: $13.43 monthly.
A la Carte 1
Subscribers: N.A.
Programming (via satellite): TBS.
Fee: $.69 monthly.
Pay Service 1
Pay Units: N.A.
Programming (via satellite): Cinemax; HBO; Showtime; Starz; The Movie Channel.
Fee: $21.95 monthly.
Video-On-Demand: No
Internet Service
Operational: Yes.
Subscribers: 3,172.
Broadband Service: Suddenlink High Speed Internet.
Telephone Service
Digital: Operational
Subscribers: 2,334.
Miles of Plant: 333.0 (coaxial); 74.0 (fiber optic). Homes passed: 10,237.
Senior Vice President, Corporate Finance: Michael Pflantz. General Manager: Joe Suggs. Chief Technician: Tim Gaunder.
Ownership: Cequel Communications Holdings I LLC (MSO).

SUNDOWN—Formerly served by Almega Cable. No longer in operation. ICA: TX0410.

SWEENY—NewWave Communications. Now served by WHARTON, TX [TX0171]. ICA: TX0246.

SWEETWATER—Suddenlink Communications, 1118 East Broadway, PO Box 688, Sweetwater, TX 79556. Phone: 314-315-9400. Fax: 915-235-3164. Web Site: http://www.suddenlink.com. Also serves Nolan County (northern portion). ICA: TX0108.
TV Market Ranking: Below 100 (Nolan County (northern portion), SWEETWATER). Franchise award date: April 24, 1962. Franchise expiration date: N.A. Began: July 1, 1966. Channel capacity: N.A. Channels available but not in use: N.A.
Basic Service
Subscribers: 2,059. Commercial subscribers: 276.
Programming (received off-air): KERA-TV (PBS) Dallas; KIDZ-LD Abilene; KPCB-DT (GLC) Snyder; KRBC-TV (Bounce TV, NBC) Abilene; KTAB-TV (CBS) Abilene; KTXS-TV (ABC, CW, This TV, TMO) Sweetwater; KXVA (FOX, MNT) Abilene; WFAA (ABC) Dallas.
Programming (via satellite): C-SPAN; C-SPAN 2; Pop; QVC; The Weather Channel; Trinity Broadcasting Network (TBN); Univision Studios.
Fee: $40.00 installation; $34.57 monthly; $3.00 converter.
Expanded Basic Service 1
Subscribers: N.A.
Programming (via satellite): A&E; AMC; Animal Planet; BET; Bravo; Cartoon Network; CMT; CNBC; CNN; Comedy Central; CW PLUS; Discovery Channel; Disney Channel; E! HD; ESPN; ESPN2; Food Network; Fox News Channel; FOX Sports Southwest; Freeform; FX; HGTV; History; HLN; INSP; Lifetime; LMN; MSNBC; MTV; MTV2; NBCSN; Nickelodeon; Oxygen; Spike TV; Syfy; TBS; TLC; TNT; Travel Channel; TV Land; USA Network; VH1.
Fee: $12.59 monthly.
Digital Basic Service
Subscribers: N.A.
Programming (via satellite): A&E HD; AXS TV; Bandamax; BBC America; Bloomberg Television; Boomerang; CBS Sports Network; Cine Mexicano; Cinelatino; CMT; CNN en Espanol; Cooking Channel; De Pelicula; De Pelicula Clasico; Destination America; Discovery Kids Channel; Disney XD; DIY Network; ESPN Classic; ESPN Deportes; ESPN HD; ESPN2 HD; ESPNews; ESPNU; EVINE Live; EWTN Global Catholic Network; Food Network HD; FOX College Sports Central; FOX College Sports Pacific; Fox Deportes; Fox Sports 1; Fox Sports 2; FSN HD; Fuse; FYI; Golf Channel; Great American Country; GSN; Hallmark Channel; HD Theater; HGTV HD; History en Espanol; History International; IFC; Investigation Discovery; Jewelry Television; MC; MTV Classic; MTV Hits; mtvU; National Geographic Channel; National Geographic Channel HD; NBC Universo; Nick Jr.; Nicktoons; NickToons en Espanol; Outdoor Channel; OWN: Oprah Winfrey Network; Science Channel; Starz Encore (multiplexed); Sundance TV; Sur; TeenNick; Telehit; Tennis Channel; TNT HD; Toon Disney en Espanol; Tr3s; truTV; Turner Classic Movies; UniMas; Universal HD; Univision; UP; VideoRola; WE tv.
Pay Service 1
Pay Units: N.A.
Programming (via satellite): Cinemax; HBO; Showtime; Starz; Starz Encore.
Fee: $10.00 installation; $1.75 monthly (Encore), $10.95 monthly (Cinemax, HBO or Showtime).
Digital Pay Service 1
Pay Units: N.A.
Programming (via satellite): Cinemax (multiplexed); HBO (multiplexed); HBO HD; HBO Latino; Showtime (multiplexed); Showtime HD; Starz (multiplexed); Starz Encore; Starz HD; The Movie Channel.
Video-On-Demand: No
Pay-Per-View
iN DEMAND (delivered digitally); Playboy TV (delivered digitally); Fresh (delivered digitally); Shorteez (delivered digitally); Spice: Xcess (delivered digitally); Club Jenna (delivered digitally).
Internet Service
Operational: Yes.
Broadband Service: Suddenlink High Speed Internet.
Fee: $49.95 installation; $24.95 monthly.
Telephone Service
Digital: Operational
Fee: $48.95 monthly
Miles of Plant: 87.0 (coaxial); None (fiber optic). Homes passed: 6,226.

2017 Edition

D-781

Texas—Cable Systems

Senior Vice President, Corporate Finance: Michael Pflantz. General Manager: Victor Means. Chief Technician: Bill Neely. Ownership: Cequel Communications Holdings I LLC (MSO).

TAHOKA—NTS Communications. Formerly [TX0322]. This cable system has converted to IPTV, 1220 Broadway, Lubbock, TX 79401. Phones: 800-658-2150; 806-797-0687. Fax: 806-788-3381. E-mail: info@ntscom.com. Web Site: http://www.ntscom.com. ICA: TX5558.

TV Market Ranking: Below 100 (TAHOKA). Franchise award date: April 9, 1979. Franchise expiration date: N.A. Began: April 9, 1979.

Channel capacity: N.A. Channels available but not in use: N.A.

Gold
Subscribers: N.A.
Programming (received off-air): KAMC (ABC, Bounce TV) Lubbock; KCBD (NBC, This TV) Lubbock; KJTV-TV (FOX) Lubbock; KLBK-TV (CBS) Lubbock; KLCW-TV (CW) Wolfforth; KPTB-DT (GLC) Lubbock; KTTZ-TV (PBS) Lubbock; KXTQ-CD (TMO) Lubbock.
Programming (via satellite): A&E; Animal Planet; Cartoon Network; CMT; CNN; Discovery Channel; Disney Channel; ESPN; ESPN2; FOX Sports Southwest; Freeform; HGTV; Lifetime; MTV; Nickelodeon; Outdoor Channel; QVC; Spike TV; TBS; The Weather Channel; TLC; TNT; Turner Classic Movies; TV Land; Univision Studios; USA Network; WGN America.
Fee: $65.00 monthly. Includes 150+ channels plus music channels & 1 digital receiver.

Platinum
Subscribers: N.A.
Fee: $85.00 monthly. Includes 230+ channels plus music channels, HD channels, 1 whole home DVR & 1 digital receiver.

Video-On-Demand: No

Internet Service
Operational: Yes.
Fee: $44.99-$134.99 monthly.

Telephone Service
Digital: Operational
Fee: $19.99 monthly

President & Chief Executive Officer: Cyrus Driver. Executive Vice President & Chief Operating Officer: Deborah Crawford. Executive Vice President & Chief Financial Officer: Don Pittman. Senior Vice President, Product Management: Angel Kandahari. Vice President & General Counsel: Daniel Wheeler. Vice President, Products & Marketing: Roberto Chang. Vice President, Human Resources: Wendy J. Lee. Vice President, Sales & Marketing: Nathan Hasse. Vice President, Service Delivery & IT Strategy: Michael McDaniel. Vice President, RUS Projects: Aaron Peters. Ownership: NTS Communications Inc. (MSO).

TAHOKA—NTS Communications. This cable system has converted to IPTV. See TAHOKA, TX [TX5558]. ICA: TX0322.

TARKINGTON PRAIRIE—Formerly served by Jones Broadcasting. No longer in operation. ICA: TX0997.

TEMPLE—Grande Communications, 401 Carlson Circle, San Marcos, TX 78666. Phones: 855-286-6666; 512-878-4600. Web Site: http://mygrande.com. ICA: TX0861.

TV Market Ranking: Below 100 (TEMPLE). Channel capacity: N.A. Channels available but not in use: N.A.

Basic Service
Subscribers: 247.
Programming (received off-air): KAKW-DT (getTV, UNV) Killeen; KCEN-TV (Antenna TV, MeTV, MundoMax, NBC) Temple; KEYE-TV (CBS, TMO) Austin; KNCT (PBS) Belton; KNVA (CW, Grit, TheCoolTV) Austin; KTBC (Buzzr, FOX, Movies!) Austin; KWKT-TV (Estrella TV, FOX, MNT) Waco; KWTX-TV (CBS, CW) Waco; KXAN-TV (COZI TV, NBC) Austin; KXXV (ABC, TMO) Waco; WFAA (ABC) Dallas.
Programming (via satellite): A&E; AMC; Animal Planet; BET; Cartoon Network; CMT; CNBC; CNN; Comedy Central; C-SPAN; C-SPAN 2; CW PLUS; Discovery Channel; Disney Channel; DIY Network; E! HD; ESPN; ESPN2; EWTN Global Catholic Network; Food Network; Fox News Channel; Fox Sports 1; FOX Sports Networks; Freeform; FX; Golf Channel; Hallmark Channel; HGTV; History; HLN; ION Television; Lifetime; Local Cable Weather; MSNBC; MTV; National Geographic Channel; Nickelodeon; QVC; RFD-TV; Spike TV; Syfy; TBS; Telemundo; The Weather Channel; TLC; TNT; Travel Channel; Trinity Broadcasting Network (TBN); truTV; Turner Classic Movies; TV Land; USA Network; VH1; WGN America.
Fee: $25.00 installation; $10.95 monthly.

Digital Basic Service
Subscribers: N.A.
Programming (via satellite): BBC America; Bloomberg Television; Bravo; Cloo; CMT; Daystar TV Network; Destination America; Discovery Kids Channel; Discovery Life Channel; Disney XD; ESPN Classic; ESPNews; EVINE Live; FOX College Sports Central; FOX College Sports Pacific; Fox Sports 1; Fuse; FXM; FYI; Golf Channel; Great American Country; GSN; HGTV; History; History International; IFC; Investigation Discovery; LMN; MC; MTV Classic; MTV Hits; MTV2; National Geographic Channel; NBCSN; Nick Jr.; Nicktoons; Outdoor Channel; Ovation; OWN: Oprah Winfrey Network; Science Channel; Syfy; TeenNick; The Word Network; Trinity Broadcasting Network (TBN); Turner Classic Movies; VH1 Soul; WE tv.

Pay Service 1
Pay Units: N.A.
Programming (via satellite): HBO; Showtime; The Movie Channel.

Digital Pay Service 1
Pay Units: N.A.
Programming (via satellite): Cinemax (multiplexed); Flix; HBO (multiplexed); Showtime (multiplexed); Starz (multiplexed); Starz Encore (multiplexed); Sundance TV; The Movie Channel (multiplexed).

Video-On-Demand: No

Internet Service
Operational: Yes. Began: December 31, 2004.
Subscribers: 298.
Broadband Service: VVM Internet Services.
Fee: $20.00 installation; $40.00 monthly.

Telephone Service
Digital: Planned

Senior Vice President, Operations & General Manager: Matthew Rohre. Vice President, Technical Operations: Shane Schilling. Vice President, Marketing: Pete Drozdoff. Ownership: Grande Communications Networks Inc. (MSO).

TENAHA—Formerly served by Almega Cable. No longer in operation. ICA: TX0507.

TERRELL—Suddenlink Communications, 520 Maryville Centre Dr, Ste 300, St. Louis, MO 63141. Phones: 800-999-6845; 314-315-9400; 314-315-9346. Fax: 903-561-5485. Web Site: http://www.suddenlink.com. Also serves Balch Springs, Collin County (portions), Dallas County (portions), Fairview, Fate, Forest Grove, Forney, Happy Country Homes, Heath, Kaufman County, Lowry Crossing, Lucas, McClendon-Chisolm, Mobile City, New Hope, Oak Ridge, Rockwall County (portions), Royse City, Seagoville & Talty. ICA: TX0920.

TV Market Ranking: 12 (Balch Springs, Collin County (portions), Dallas County (portions), Fairview, Fate, Forest Grove, Forney, Happy Country Homes, Heath, Kaufman County (portions), Lowry Crossing, Lucas, McClendon-Chisolm, Mobile City, New Hope, Oak Ridge, Rockwall County (portions), Royse City, Seagoville, Talty, TERRELL); Outside TV Markets (Kaufman County (portions)).

Channel capacity: 42 (operating 2-way). Channels available but not in use: N.A.

Basic Service
Subscribers: 6,735. Commercial subscribers: 292.
Programming (received off-air): KDAF (Antenna TV, CW, This TV) Dallas; KDFI (Bounce TV, Buzzr, Heroes & Icons, MNT, Movies!) Dallas; KDFW (FOX) Dallas; KDTN (Daystar TV, ETV) Denton; KDTX-TV (TBN) Dallas; KERA-TV (PBS) Dallas; KFWD (MundoMax) Fort Worth; KMPX (Estrella TV) Decatur; KNHL (IND) Hastings; KPXD-TV (ION) Arlington; KSTR-DT (getTV, UniMas) Irving; KTVT (CBS, Decades) Fort Worth; KTXA (IND, MeTV) Fort Worth; KTXD-TV (IND) Greenville; KUVN-DT (UNV) Garland; KXAS-TV (COZI TV, NBC) Fort Worth; KXTX-TV (TMO) Dallas; WFAA (ABC) Dallas.
Programming (via satellite): C-SPAN.
Fee: $49.95 installation; $38.24 monthly.

Expanded Basic Service 1
Subscribers: N.A.
Programming (via satellite): A&E; AMC; Animal Planet; BET; Bravo; Cartoon Network; Celebrity Shopping Network; CNBC; CNN; Comedy Central; Discovery Channel; Disney Channel; E! HD; ESPN; ESPN Classic; ESPN2; Food Network; Fox News Channel; Fox Sports 1; FOX Sports Southwest; Freeform; FX; Golf Channel; Great American Country; Hallmark Channel; HGTV; History; HLN; Lifetime; LMN; MSNBC; MTV; National Geographic Channel; Nickelodeon; Outdoor Channel; Pop; Spike TV; Syfy; TBS; The Weather Channel; TLC; TNT; Travel Channel; truTV; Turner Classic Movies; TV Land; Univision; USA Network; VH1.

Digital Basic Service
Subscribers: N.A.
Programming (via satellite): AXS TV; BBC America; Bloomberg Television; Cloo; CMT; C-SPAN 3; Discovery Digital Networks; Disney XD; ESPNews; FOX College Sports Central; FOX College Sports Pacific; Fox Sports 2; Fuse; FXM; FYI; GSN; HD Theater; History International; HITS (Headend In The Sky); IFC; LOGO; MC; NBCSN; Nick 2; Nick Jr.; Nicktoons; Sundance TV; TeenNick; WE tv.

Pay Service 1
Pay Units: N.A.
Programming (via satellite): Cinemax; HBO; Showtime; The Movie Channel.
Fee: $10.95 monthly (TMC), $11.00 monthly (Cinemax, HBO or Showtime).

Digital Pay Service 1
Pay Units: N.A.
Programming (via satellite): Cinemax (multiplexed); Flix; HBO (multiplexed); Showtime (multiplexed); Showtime HD; Starz (multiplexed); Starz Encore (multiplexed); The Movie Channel (multiplexed).

Video-On-Demand: No

Pay-Per-View
iN DEMAND (delivered digitally); Playboy TV (delivered digitally).

Internet Service
Operational: Yes. Began: August 1, 2002.
Subscribers: 10,124.
Broadband Service: Suddenlink High Speed Internet.
Fee: $49.95 installation; $38.95 monthly.

Telephone Service
Digital: Operational
Subscribers: 4,232.

Miles of Plant: 1,162.0 (coaxial); 278.0 (fiber optic). Homes passed: 42,665.
Senior Vice President, Corporate Finance: Michael Pflantz. Regional Manager: Todd Cruthird. Area Manager: Rodney Fletcher. Plant Manager: Steven Williams. Ownership: Cequel Communications Holdings I LLC (MSO).

TEXARKANA—Cable One, 401 Baylor St, Texarkana, TX 75501-3270. Phone: 903-838-2225. Fax: 903-792-3919. E-mail: jbutler@cableone.net. Web Site: http://www.cableone.net. Also serves Fouke, Miller County (portions) & Texarkana, AR; Bowie County, Bowie County (portions), Leary, Nash, Red Lick, Redwater & Wake Village, TX. ICA: TX0031.

TV Market Ranking: 58 (Bowie County, Bowie County (portions), Fouke, Leary, Miller County (portions), Nash, Red Lick, Redwater, Texarkana, TEXARKANA, Wake Village). Franchise award date: June 1, 1973. Franchise expiration date: N.A. Began: April 1, 1974.

Channel capacity: N.A. Channels available but not in use: N.A.

Basic Service
Subscribers: 9,842.
Programming (received off-air): KETG (PBS) Arkadelphia; KLFI-CD (My Family TV) Texarkana; KMSS-TV (FOX) Shreveport; KPXJ (Antenna TV, CW, MeTV, Movies!) Minden; KSHV-TV (MNT) Shreveport; KSLA (Bounce TV, CBS, Grit, This TV) Shreveport; KTAL-TV (NBC) Texarkana; KTBS-TV (ABC) Shreveport.
Programming (via microwave): KATV (ABC, Retro TV) Little Rock.
Programming (via satellite): A&E; AMC; Animal Planet; BET; Bravo; Cartoon Network; CMT; CNBC; CNN; Comedy Central; C-SPAN; C-SPAN 2; Discovery Channel; Disney Channel; ESPN; ESPN2; Food Network; Fox News Channel; FOX Sports Southwest; Freeform; FX; HGTV; History; HLN; ION Television; Lifetime; MSNBC; MTV; Nickelodeon; Pop; QVC; Spike TV; Syfy; TBS; The Weather Channel; TLC; TNT; Trinity Broadcasting Network (TBN); Turner Classic Movies; TV Land; USA Network; VH1; WGN America.
Fee: $90.00 installation; $35.00 monthly; $2.50 converter.

Digital Basic Service
Subscribers: N.A.
Programming (via satellite): 24/7 News Channel; 3ABN; Boomerang; BYUtv; Discovery Digital Networks; Disney XD; DMX Music; ESPN Classic; ESPNews; FamilyNet; FOX College Sports Central; FOX College Sports Pacific; Fox Sports 1; Fox Sports 2; FXM; FYI; Golf Channel; Hall-

mark Channel; History International; HITS (Headend In The Sky); INSP; LWS Local Weather Station; National Geographic Channel; Outdoor Channel; TNT HD; Trinity Broadcasting Network (TBN); truTV; TVG Network; Universal HD.
Fee: $9.95 installation; $46.00 monthly.
Digital Pay Service 1
Pay Units: N.A.
Programming (via satellite): Cinemax (multiplexed); Flix (multiplexed); HBO (multiplexed); Showtime (multiplexed); Showtime HD; Starz (multiplexed); Starz Encore (multiplexed); Sundance TV (multiplexed); The Movie Channel (multiplexed); The Movie Channel HD.
Fee: $9.95 installation; $15.00 monthly (each package).
Video-On-Demand: No
Pay-Per-View
iN DEMAND (delivered digitally); Pleasure (delivered digitally); SexSee (delivered digitally); Juicy (delivered digitally); VaVoom (delivered digitally).
Internet Service
Operational: Yes. Began: November 1, 2000.
Subscribers: 12,413.
Broadband Service: CableONE.net.
Fee: $75.00 installation; $43.00 monthly; $5.00 modem lease.
Telephone Service
Digital: Operational
Subscribers: 4,807.
Fee: $39.95 monthly
Miles of Plant: 1,593.0 (coaxial); 216.0 (fiber optic). Homes passed: 42,565.
Vice President: Patrick A. Dolohanty. General Manager: Jay Butler. Chief Technician: John Lanier. Marketing Director: Donna Chatman. Program Director: Jeannie Mitchell.
Ownership: Cable ONE Inc. (MSO).

TEXHOMA—PTCI. This cable system has converted to IPTV. Now served by GUYMON, OK [OK5005]. ICA: TX0476.

TEXLINE—Formerly served by Baja Broadband. No longer in operation. ICA: TX0642.

THORNTON—Formerly served by National Cable Inc. No longer in operation. ICA: TX0592.

THREE RIVERS—CommZoom, 2438 Boardwalk, San Antonio, TX 78217. Phone: 844-858-8500. Web Site: http://www.commzoom.com. ICA: TX0401.
TV Market Ranking: Outside TV Markets (THREE RIVERS). Franchise award date: January 1, 1978. Franchise expiration date: N.A. Began: October 1, 1978.
Channel capacity: N.A. Channels available but not in use: N.A.
Basic Service
Subscribers: 42.
Programming (received off-air): KABB (FOX, The Country Network) San Antonio; KEDT (PBS) Corpus Christi; KENS (CBS, Estrella TV) San Antonio; KIII (ABC, MeTV) Corpus Christi; KMOL-LD (Movies!, NBC) Victoria; KMYS (CW) Kerrville; KPXL-TV (ION) Uvalde; KRIS-TV (CW, Grit, NBC) Corpus Christi; KSAT-TV (ABC, MeTV) San Antonio; KWEX-DT (getTV, UNV) San Antonio; KZTV (CBS) Corpus Christi; allband FM.
Programming (via satellite): ESPN; FOX Sports Southwest; Freeform; TBS; TNT.
Fee: $49.95 installation; $57.91 monthly.

Expanded Basic Service 1
Subscribers: N.A.
Programming (via satellite): CMT; CNN; Discovery Channel; Disney Channel; Spike TV.
Fee: $20.00 monthly.
Pay Service 1
Pay Units: N.A.
Programming (via satellite): Cinemax; HBO; Showtime.
Fee: $11.95 monthly (each).
Video-On-Demand: No
Pay-Per-View
iN DEMAND (delivered digitally); Hot Choice (delivered digitally); Playboy TV (delivered digitally); Fresh (delivered digitally); Shorteez (delivered digitally).
Internet Service
Operational: No.
Telephone Service
None
Miles of Plant: 15.0 (coaxial); None (fiber optic). Homes passed: 892.
Chief Executive Officer: Bob Cohen.
Ownership: CommZoom Communications LLC (MSO).

THROCKMORTON—Throckmorton Cablevision, 12902 FM 2178, Olney, TX 76374. Phones: 800-687-7311; 940-873-4563. ICA: TX0511.
TV Market Ranking: Outside TV Markets (THROCKMORTON). Franchise award date: N.A. Franchise expiration date: N.A. Began: January 1, 1982.
Channel capacity: N.A. Channels available but not in use: N.A.
Basic Service
Subscribers: 130.
Programming (received off-air): KAUZ-TV (CBS, CW) Wichita Falls; KFDX-TV (NBC) Wichita Falls; KIDZ-LD Abilene; KJTL (Bounce TV, FOX) Wichita Falls; KRBC-TV (Bounce TV, NBC) Abilene; KSWO-TV (ABC, TMO) Lawton; 2 FMs.
Programming (via satellite): CNBC; CNN; C-SPAN; Discovery Channel; Disney Channel; Freeform; Spike TV; TBS; The Weather Channel; TLC; Trinity Broadcasting Network (TBN); TV Land; Univision Studios; WGN America.
Fee: $30.00 installation; $25.00 monthly.
Expanded Basic Service 1
Subscribers: N.A.
Programming (via satellite): A&E; AMC; Animal Planet; Cartoon Network; CMT; Disney XD; ESPN; ESPN Classic; ESPN2; Food Network; Fox News Channel; Fox Sports 1; FOX Sports Southwest; FX; Hallmark Channel; HGTV; History; HLN; Lifetime; MTV; NBCSN; Nickelodeon; Outdoor Channel; Syfy; TNT; Travel Channel; USA Network; VH1.
Fee: $10.83 monthly.
Digital Basic Service
Subscribers: N.A.
Programming (via satellite): BBC America; Bravo; Cloo; Discovery Digital Networks; DMX Music; EVINE Live; FOX College Sports Central; FOX College Sports Pacific; Fuse; FXM; FYI; Golf Channel; Great American Country; GSN; History; History International; IFC; National Geographic Channel; NBCSN; Nick Jr.; Nicktoons; Ovation; TeenNick; Turner Classic Movies; WE tv.
Fee: $21.05 monthly.
Pay Service 1
Pay Units: N.A.
Programming (via satellite): Cinemax; HBO.
Fee: $13.55 monthly.

Digital Pay Service 1
Pay Units: N.A.
Programming (via satellite): Cinemax (multiplexed); Flix; HBO (multiplexed); Showtime (multiplexed); Starz; Starz Encore (multiplexed); Sundance TV; The Movie Channel (multiplexed).
Fee: $13.55 monthly (HBO/Cinemax), $7.01 monthly (Starz/Encore & Showtime/TMC).
Video-On-Demand: No
Internet Service
Operational: Yes.
Broadband Service: In-house.
Fee: $24.95 monthly; $5.00 modem lease; $59.95 modem purchase.
Telephone Service
None
Miles of Plant: 14.0 (coaxial); None (fiber optic).
General Manager & Chief Technician: Bill Tyler. Marketing & Program Director: Jan Tyler.
Ownership: Bill Tyler (MSO).

THUNDERBIRD BAY—Formerly served by Cable Unlimited. No longer in operation. ICA: TX0408.

TILDEN—Formerly served by Almega Cable. No longer in operation. ICA: TX0663.

TIMPSON—Formerly served by Almega Cable. No longer in operation. ICA: TX0572.

TOLAR—Formerly served by Charter Communications. No longer in operation. ICA: TX1002.

TOLEDO VILLAGE—Formerly served by Carrell Communications. No longer in operation. ICA: TX0864.

TRENT—Formerly served by Jayroc Cablevision. No longer in operation. ICA: TX0976.

TRINITY—Formerly served by Cebridge Connections. Now served by Suddenlink Communications, ONALASKA, TX [TX0851]. ICA: TX0205.

TROY—Grande Communications, 401 Carlson Circle, San Marcos, TX 78666. Phones: 855-286-6666; 512-878-4600. Web Site: http://mygrande.com. ICA: TX0532.
TV Market Ranking: Below 100 (TROY). Franchise award date: N.A. Franchise expiration date: N.A. Began: October 1, 1981.
Channel capacity: N.A. Channels available but not in use: N.A.
Basic Service
Subscribers: 245.
Programming (received off-air): KCEN-TV (Antenna TV, MeTV, MundoMax, NBC) Temple; KEYE-TV (CBS, TMO) Austin; KNCT (PBS) Belton; KNVA (CW, Grit, TheCoolTV) Austin; KTBC (Buzzr, FOX, Movies!) Austin; KWKT-TV (Estrella TV, FOX, MNT) Waco; KWTX-TV (CBS, CW) Waco; KXAN-TV (COZI TV, NBC) Austin; KXXV (ABC, TMO) Waco; WFAA (ABC) Dallas.
Programming (via satellite): Univision Studios; WGN America.
Fee: $25.00 installation; $10.95 monthly.
Expanded Basic Service 1
Subscribers: N.A.
Programming (via satellite): A&E; AMC; Animal Planet; BET; Cartoon Network; CMT; CNBC; CNN; Comedy Central; C-SPAN; C-SPAN 2; Discovery Channel; Disney Channel; E! HD; ESPN; ESPN2;

Food Network; Fox News Channel; FOX Sports Southwest; Freeform; FX; Hallmark Channel; HGTV; History; HLN; ION Television; Lifetime; MSNBC; MTV; National Geographic Channel; Nickelodeon; QVC; Spike TV; Syfy; TBS; The Weather Channel; TLC; TNT; Travel Channel; Trinity Broadcasting Network (TBN); Turner Classic Movies; TV Land; USA Network; VH1.
Fee: $18.00 monthly.
Digital Basic Service
Subscribers: N.A.
Programming (via satellite): BBC America; Bloomberg Television; Bravo; Daystar TV Network; Discovery Digital Networks; Disney XD; DMX Music; ESPN Classic; ESPNews; EVINE Live; Fox Sports 1; FSN Digital Atlantic; FSN Digital Central; FSN Digital Pacific; Fuse; FXM; FYI; Golf Channel; Great American Country; GSN; HGTV; History; History International; IFC; LMN; National Geographic Channel; NBCSN; Outdoor Channel; Ovation; Syfy; The Word Network; Trinity Broadcasting Network (TBN); Turner Classic Movies; WE tv.
Fee: $15.00 installation; $49.00 monthly.
Pay Service 1
Pay Units: N.A.
Programming (via satellite): HBO; Showtime; The Movie Channel.
Fee: $11.00 monthly (HBO, Showtime or TMC), $13.50 monthly (Showtime/TMC), $19.50 monthly (HBO/TMC), $21.00 monthly (HBO/Showtime), $23.00 monthly (HBO/Showtime/TMC).
Digital Pay Service 1
Pay Units: N.A.
Programming (via satellite): Cinemax (multiplexed); HBO (multiplexed); Showtime (multiplexed); Starz (multiplexed); Starz Encore (multiplexed).
Fee: $7.00 monthly (Cinemax), $11.00 monthly (HBO, Showtime or Starz/Encore).
Video-On-Demand: No
Internet Service
Operational: Yes. Began: December 31, 2004.
Subscribers: 298.
Broadband Service: VVM Internet Services.
Fee: $20.00 installation; $40.00 monthly.
Telephone Service
Digital: Planned
Miles of Plant: 8.0 (coaxial); None (fiber optic). Homes passed: 375.
Senior Vice President, Operations & General Manager: Matthew Rohre. Vice President, Technical Operations: Shane Schilling. Vice President, Marketing: Pete Drozdoff.
Ownership: Grande Communications Networks Inc. (MSO).

TULETA—Formerly served by National Cable Inc. No longer in operation. ICA: TX0907.

TULIA—Suddenlink Communications. Now served by AMARILLO, TX [TX0014]. ICA: TX0226.

TURKEY—Formerly served by Elk River TV Cable Co. No longer in operation. ICA: TX0900.

TUSCOLA—NewWave Communications, One Montgomery Plaza, 4th Floor, Sikeston, MO 63801. Phones: 573-472-9500; 888-863-9928. Fax: 573-472-9518. E-mail: info@newwave.com. Web Site: http://www.newwavecom.com. Also serves Buffalo Gap. ICA: TX0176.
TV Market Ranking: Below 100 (Buffalo Gap, TUSCOLA). Franchise award date: Febru-

Texas—Cable Systems

ary 15, 1983. Franchise expiration date: N.A. Began: December 30, 1983.
Channel capacity: N.A. Channels available but not in use: N.A.

Basic Service
Subscribers: 34.
Programming (received off-air): KRBC-TV (Bounce TV, NBC) Abilene; KTAB-TV (CBS) Abilene; KTXS-TV (ABC, CW, This TV, TMO) Sweetwater; KXVA (FOX, MNT) Abilene.
Programming (via satellite): Food Network; QVC; Syfy; TBS; The Weather Channel; Trinity Broadcasting Network (TBN); VH1; WGN America.
Fee: $35.00 installation; $53.30 monthly.

Expanded Basic Service 1
Subscribers: N.A.
Programming (via satellite): A&E; AMC; Animal Planet; CMT; CNN; Discovery Channel; ESPN; ESPN2; Freeform; HGTV; Lifetime; MTV; Nickelodeon; Spike TV; TLC; TNT; TV Land; USA Network.
Fee: $23.55 monthly.

Pay Service 1
Pay Units: N.A.
Programming (via satellite): HBO.
Fee: $14.95 installation; $13.95 monthly.

Video-On-Demand: No

Internet Service
Operational: No.

Telephone Service
None

Miles of Plant: 71.0 (coaxial); None (fiber optic). Homes passed included in Merkel
Regional General Manager: Jerry Smith.
Ownership: NewWave Communications LLC (MSO).

TYLER—Suddenlink Communications, 322 North Glenwood Blvd, Tyler, TX 75702. Phones: 314-315-9400; 903-595-4321. Fax: 903-593-6189. Web Site: http://www.suddenlink.com. Also serves Anderson County (unincorporated areas), Berryville, Bullard, Chandler, Flint (unincorporated areas), Frankston, Gresham (unincorporated areas), Jackson's Landing (unincorporated aresas), Lake Palestine East, Lake Palestine West, Lake Tyler, New Chapel Hill, Noonday, Red Ackers, Smith (unincorporated areas), Smith County & Whitehouse. ICA: TX0027.
TV Market Ranking: Below 100 (Anderson County (unincorporated areas), Berryville, Bullard, Chandler, Flint (unincorporated areas), Frankston, Gresham (unincorporated areas), Jackson's Landing (unincorporated aresas), Lake Tyler, New Chapel Hill, Noonday, Red Ackers, Smith (unincorporated areas), Smith County, TYLER, Whitehouse, Lake Palestine East, Lake Palestine West). Franchise award date: January 1, 1970. Franchise expiration date: N.A. Began: March 1, 1951.
Channel capacity: N.A. Channels available but not in use: N.A.

Basic Service
Subscribers: 26,786.
Programming (received off-air): KCEB (CW, MundoMax) Longview; KDFW (FOX) Dallas; KERA-TV (PBS) Dallas; KETK-TV (Estrella TV, NBC) Jacksonville; KFXK-TV (FOX) Longview; KLPN-LD (MNT) Longview; KLTV (ABC, Bounce TV, TMO) Tyler; KXTX-TV (TMO) Dallas; KYTX (CBS, COZI TV, CW) Nacogdoches; WFAA (ABC) Dallas; 18 FMs.
Programming (via satellite): C-SPAN; Pop; QVC; TBS; Univision Studios.
Fee: $38.00 installation; $35.24 monthly.

Expanded Basic Service 1
Subscribers: N.A.
Programming (via satellite): A&E; AMC; Animal Planet; BET; Bravo; Cartoon Network; CMT; CNBC; CNN; Comedy Central; C-SPAN 2; Discovery Channel; Disney Channel; E! HD; ESPN; ESPN2; EVINE Live; EWTN Global Catholic Network; Food Network; Fox News Channel; Fox Sports 1; FOX Sports Southwest; Freeform; FX; Great American Country; HGTV; History; HLN; INSP; Jewelry Television; Lifetime; LMN; MSNBC; MTV; NBCSN; Nickelodeon; Outdoor Channel; Spike TV; Syfy; The Weather Channel; TLC; TNT; Travel Channel; Trinity Broadcasting Network (TBN); truTV; Turner Classic Movies; TV Land; Univision; USA Network; VH1.
Fee: $14.26 monthly.

Digital Basic Service
Subscribers: N.A.
Programming (via satellite): A&E HD; AXS TV; Bandamax; BBC America; Bloomberg Television; Boomerang; CBS Sports Network; Cine Mexicano; Cinelatino; CMT; CNN en Espanol; Cooking Channel; Cox Sports Television; De Pelicula; De Pelicula Clasico; Destination America; Discovery Kids Channel; Disney XD; DIY Network; Enlace USA; ESPN Classic; ESPN Deportes; ESPN HD; ESPN2 HD; ESPNews; ESPNU; FamilyNet; Food Network HD; Fox Deportes; Fox Sports 2; FSN HD; Fuse; FYI; Golf Channel; GSN; Hallmark Channel; HD Theater; HGTV HD; History en Espanol; History International; IFC; Investigation Discovery; MC; MTV Classic; MTV Hits; MTV2; Nat Geo WILD; National Geographic Channel; National Geographic Channel HD; NBC Universo; Nick Jr.; Nicktoons; NickToons en Espanol; OWN: Oprah Winfrey Network; Oxygen; Ritmoson; Science Channel; Starz Encore (multiplexed); Sundance TV; Sur; TeenNick; Telehit; Tennis Channel; TNT HD; Toon Disney en Espanol; Tr3s; TV One; ULTRA HDPlex; UniMas; Universal HD; Univision; UP; VideoRola; WE tv; Weatherscan.
Fee: $10.00 monthly.

Digital Pay Service 1
Pay Units: N.A.
Programming (via satellite): Cinemax (multiplexed); HBO (multiplexed); HBO HD; HBO Latino; Showtime (multiplexed); Showtime HD; Starz (multiplexed); Starz HD; The Movie Channel (multiplexed).
Fee: $6.75 monthly (Starz), $10.95 monthly (HBO), $11.50 monthly (Showtime or TMC).

Video-On-Demand: No

Pay-Per-View
iN DEMAND (delivered digitally); Fresh (delivered digitally); Shorteez (delivered digitally); Playboy TV (delivered digitally); Club Jenna (delivered digitally); Hot Choice (delivered digitally); Spice; Xcess (delivered digitally); Playboy en Espanol (delivered digitally).

Internet Service
Operational: Yes.
Subscribers: 25,509.
Broadband Service: Suddenlink High Speed Internet.
Fee: $49.95 installation; $24.95 monthly.

Telephone Service
Digital: Operational
Subscribers: 13,401.
Fee: $48.95 monthly
Miles of Plant: 1,255.0 (coaxial); 576.0 (fiber optic). Homes passed: 62,570.
Senior Vice President, Corporate Finance: Michael Pflantz. General Manager: Vince Thomas.
Ownership: Cequel Communications Holdings I LLC (MSO).

UNIVERSITY PARK—Charter Communications, 3403 Kings Rd, Dallas, TX 75209. Phones: 636-207-5100 (Corporate office); 817-810-9171; 817-298-3600. Web Site: http://www.charter.com. Also serves Highland Park. ICA: TX0062.
TV Market Ranking: 12 (Highland Park, UNIVERSITY PARK). Franchise award date: April 1, 1979. Franchise expiration date: N.A. Began: January 1, 1980.
Channel capacity: N.A. Channels available but not in use: N.A.

Digital Basic Service
Subscribers: 1,710. Commercial subscribers: 147.
Programming (via satellite): BBC America; Bloomberg Television; Discovery Digital Networks; DIY Network; FYI; History International; IFC; LMN; MC; Nick 2; Nick Jr.; Nicktoons; Sundance TV; TeenNick.
Fee: $26.99 monthly.

Digital Expanded Basic Service
Subscribers: N.A.
Programming (via satellite): A&E; AMC; Animal Planet; Bravo; Cartoon Network; CMT; CNBC; CNN; Comedy Central; Discovery Channel; Disney Channel; Disney XD; E! HD; ESPN; ESPN Classic; ESPN2; Food Network; Fox News Channel; Fox Sports 1; FOX Sports Southwest; Freeform; FX; Golf Channel; GSN; Hallmark Channel; HGTV; History; HLN; Lifetime; MSNBC; MTV; National Geographic Channel; NBCSN; Nickelodeon; Oxygen; Spike TV; Syfy; TBS; The Weather Channel; TLC; TNT; Travel Channel; truTV; Turner Classic Movies; TV Land; USA Network; VH1; WE tv.
Fee: $48.99 monthly.

Digital Expanded Basic Service 2
Subscribers: N.A.
Programming (via satellite): Fox Deportes; Fox Sports 2; FSN Digital Atlantic; FSN Digital Central; FSN Digital Pacific; NFL Network.

Digital Expanded Basic Service 3
Subscribers: N.A.
Programming (via satellite): AXS TV; Discovery Channel; ESPN; HBO; Showtime.

Digital Pay Service 1
Pay Units: N.A.
Programming (via satellite): Cinemax (multiplexed); Flix (multiplexed); HBO (multiplexed); Showtime (multiplexed); Starz (multiplexed); Starz Encore; The Movie Channel (multiplexed).

Video-On-Demand: No

Pay-Per-View
Hot Choice (delivered digitally); ETC (delivered digitally); The Erotic Network (delivered digitally); Pleasure (delivered digitally); iN DEMAND (delivered digitally); FOX Sports Networks (delivered digitally).

Internet Service
Operational: Yes.
Broadband Service: Charter Internet.
Fee: $29.99 monthly.

Telephone Service
None
Miles of Plant: 82.0 (coaxial); 5.0 (fiber optic). Homes passed: 12,868.
Vice President & General Manager: Wayne Cramp. Technical Operations Director: John Linton. Assistant Controller: Brent Trask. Marketing Director: Kathleen Griffin. Accounting Director: David Sovanski.
Ownership: Charter Communications Inc. (MSO).

UVALDE—Time Warner Cable, 7800 Crescent Executive Dr, Charlotte, NC 28217. Phones: 956-721-0600; 972-899-7300 (Flower Mound office); 956-721-0607. Web Site: http://www.timewarnercable.com. Also serves Knippa & Uvalde County (portions). ICA: TX0095.
TV Market Ranking: Below 100 (Knippa, UVALDE, Uvalde County (portions)). Franchise award date: N.A. Franchise expiration date: N.A. Began: June 25, 1955.
Channel capacity: N.A. Channels available but not in use: N.A.

Basic Service
Subscribers: 2,984.
Programming (received off-air): KABB (FOX, The Country Network) San Antonio; KENS (CBS, Estrella TV) San Antonio; KLRN (PBS) San Antonio; KMYS (CW) Kerrville; KNIC-CD (UniMas) San Antonio; KPXL-TV (ION) Uvalde; KSAT-TV (ABC, MeTV) San Antonio; KVDA (TMO) San Antonio; KWEX-DT (getTV, UNV) San Antonio; WOAI-TV (IND, NBC) San Antonio; allband FM.
Programming (via satellite): Azteca; C-SPAN 2; The Weather Channel; WGN America.
Fee: $49.99 installation; $28.00 monthly; $.92 converter.

Expanded Basic Service 1
Subscribers: N.A.
Programming (via satellite): A&E; AMC; Animal Planet; BET; Cartoon Network; CMT; CNBC; CNN; Comedy Central; C-SPAN; Discovery Channel; Disney Channel; E! HD; ESPN; ESPN2; EVINE Live; EWTN Global Catholic Network; Food Network; Fox News Channel; FOX Sports Southwest; Freeform; FX; Golf Channel; Great American Country; Hallmark Channel; HGTV; History; HLN; Lifetime; MoviePlex; MSNBC; MTV; National Geographic Channel; NBC Universo; Nickelodeon; OWN: Oprah Winfrey Network; Oxygen; Pop; QVC; Spike TV; Syfy; TBS; TLC; TNT; Travel Channel; Trinity Broadcasting Network (TBN); truTV; Turner Classic Movies; TV Land; USA Network; VH1; WE tv.
Fee: $33.45 monthly.

Digital Basic Service
Subscribers: N.A.
Programming (via satellite): A&E; AMC; Animal Planet; AXS TV; BBC America; BET; Bloomberg Television; Boomerang; Bravo; Cartoon Network; Cloo; CMT; CNBC; CNN; Comedy Central; C-SPAN; C-SPAN 2; C-SPAN 3; Destination America; Discovery Channel; Discovery Kids Channel; Discovery Life Channel; Disney Channel; Disney XD; DIY Network; E! HD; ESPN Classic; ESPN HD; ESPN2; ESPN2 HD; ESPNews; ESPNU; EVINE Live; EWTN Global Catholic Network; Food Network; Fox Business Network; FOX College Sports Central; FOX College Sports Pacific; Fox Deportes; Fox News Channel; Fox Sports 1; FOX Sports Southwest; Freeform; Fuse; FX; FYI; Golf Channel; Great American Country; GSN; Hallmark Channel; HD Theater; HGTV; History; History International; HLN; Investigation Discovery; La Familia Cosmovision; Lifetime; LMN; MC; MoviePlex; MSNBC; MTV; MTV Classic; MTV Hits; MTV2; Nat Geo WILD; National Geographic Channel; NBC Universo; Nick Jr.; Nickelodeon; Nicktoons; OWN: Oprah Winfrey Network; Oxygen; Pop; QVC; Science Channel; Spike TV; Syfy; TBS; TeenNick; The Weather Channel; TLC; TNT; TNT HD; Tr3s; Travel Channel; Trinity Broadcasting Network (TBN); truTV; Turner Classic Movies; TV Land; USA Network; VH1; VH1 Country; WE tv.
Fee: $5.00 monthly.

Cable Systems—Texas

Digital Expanded Basic Service
Subscribers: N.A.
Programming (via satellite): Boomerang; Canal Sur; Cinelatino; CNN en Espanol; ESPN Deportes; Fox Sports 1; FXM; IFC; NBA TV; NBCSN; Starz Encore (multiplexed); Sundance TV; Tennis Channel; Tr3s; VideoRola.
Digital Pay Service 1
Pay Units: N.A.
Programming (via satellite): Cinemax (multiplexed); HBO (multiplexed); HBO HD; Showtime (multiplexed); Showtime HD; Starz (multiplexed); The Movie Channel.
Fee: $14.99 monthly (each).
Video-On-Demand: No
Pay-Per-View
iN DEMAND (delivered digitally); Fresh (delivered digitally); Playboy TV (delivered digitally); Hot Choice (delivered digitally); NBA League Pass (delivered digitally); MLS Direct Kick (delivered digitally); NHL Center Ice (delivered digitally); MLB Extra Innings (delivered digitally).
Internet Service
Operational: Yes.
Broadband Service: RoadRunner.
Fee: $49.99 installation; $44.95 monthly.
Telephone Service
Digital: Operational
Fee: $44.95 monthly
Miles of Plant: 104.0 (coaxial); None (fiber optic). Homes passed: 7,425.
President: Connie Wharton. Vice President & General Manager: Michael Carrosquiola. Senior Accounting Director: Karen Goodfellow. Operations Director: Marco Reyes. Public Affairs Manager: Celinda Gonzales. Technical Operations Manager: Eduardo Ruiz.
Ownership: Time Warner Cable (MSO).; Advance/Newhouse Partnership (MSO).

VALENTINE—Formerly served by Valentine TV Cable. No longer in operation. ICA: TX0692.

VALLEY MILLS—LynnStar Communications, 4500 Mercantile Plz, Ste 300, Fort Worth, TX 76137. Phones: 888-575-9230; 682-730-0900. Fax: 682-730-6400. Web Site: http://lynnstar.net; http://www.lynnstarcomm.com. ICA: TX0444.
TV Market Ranking: Below 100 (VALLEY MILLS). Franchise award date: July 15, 1989. Franchise expiration date: N.A. Began: December 28, 1983.
Channel capacity: N.A. Channels available but not in use: N.A.
Basic Service
Subscribers: 49.
Programming (received off-air): KCEN-TV (Antenna TV, MeTV, MundoMax, NBC) Temple; KDFI (Bounce TV, Buzzr, Heroes & Icons, MNT, Movies!) Dallas; KERA-TV (PBS) Dallas; KSTR-DT (getTV, UniMas) Irving; KTVT (CBS, Decades) Fort Worth; KUVN-DT (UNV) Garland; KWKT-TV (Estrella TV, FOX, MNT) Waco; KWTX-TV (CBS, CW) Waco; KXAS-TV (COZI TV, NBC) Fort Worth; KXTX-TV (TMO) Dallas; KXXV (ABC, TMO) Waco; WFAA (ABC) Dallas.
Programming (via satellite): A&E; AMC; Animal Planet; Cartoon Network; CMT; CNN; C-SPAN; Discovery Channel; Disney Channel; ESPN; ESPN2; Fox Sports 1; FOX Sports Southwest; Freeform; HGTV; History; HLN; INSP; Lifetime; Nickelodeon; Spike TV; Syfy; TBS; The Weather Channel; TLC; TNT; TV Land; USA Network; VH1; WGN America.
Fee: $49.95 installation; $51.38 monthly.

Pay Service 1
Pay Units: N.A.
Programming (via satellite): Cinemax; HBO.
Fee: $12.95 monthly (each).
Video-On-Demand: No
Internet Service
Operational: Yes.
Telephone Service
None
Miles of Plant: 9.0 (coaxial); None (fiber optic). Homes passed: 414.
Chairman of the Board & Government Relations Director: S. Gene Yarbrough. Chief Executive Officer, Executive Vice President & Board Member: Chris Romine. Chief Operations Officer, Executive Vice President & Board Member: Steve Sizemore. Vice President & Business Development & Countertrade Director: Gary Majors. Vice President & Programming & Vendor Relations Director: Gus Salvino. Vice President & Investor Relations Manager: Daniel J. Sweeney. Accounting Manager: Sheila Magness.
Ownership: Lynnstar Communications (MSO).

VALLEY VIEW—Nortex Communications, 205 North Walnut St, PO Box 587, Muenster, TX 76252-2780. Phone: 940-759-2251. Fax: 940-759-5557. E-mail: info@nortex.net. Web Site: http://www.nortex.com. Also serves Collinsville, Lake Kiowa, Lindsay, Muenster & St. Jo. ICA: TX0792.
TV Market Ranking: Below 100 (Collinsville, LAKE KIOWA, Muenster, St. Jo, VALLEY VIEW); Outside TV Markets (Lindsay). Franchise award date: N.A. Franchise expiration date: N.A. Began: August 1, 1996.
Channel capacity: N.A. Channels available but not in use: N.A.
Basic Service
Subscribers: 1,853.
Programming (received off-air): KDAF (Antenna TV, CW, This TV) Dallas; KDFI (Bounce TV, Buzzr, Heroes & Icons, MNT, Movies!) Dallas; KFWD (MundoMax) Fort Worth; KMPX (Estrella TV) Decatur; KTXA (IND, MeTV) Fort Worth; KXTX-TV (TMO) Dallas.
Programming (via satellite): A&E; CMT; CNBC; CNN; C-SPAN; Discovery Channel; Disney Channel; E! HD; ESPN; ESPN2; EVINE Live; EWTN Global Catholic Network; Fox News Channel; FOX Sports Southwest; Freeform; Golf Channel; HGTV; History; HLN; ION Television; Lifetime; MSNBC; Nickelodeon; QVC; Spike TV; TBS; The Weather Channel; TLC; TNT; Travel Channel; Trinity Broadcasting Network (TBN); Turner Classic Movies; TV Land; UniMas; USA Network; WGN America.
Fee: $40.00 installation; $16.00 monthly; $4.95 converter.
Digital Basic Service
Subscribers: N.A.
Programming (via satellite): Bloomberg Television; Discovery Life Channel; Disney XD; DMX Music; ESPN Classic; Fox Sports 1; FSN Digital Atlantic; FSN Digital Central; FSN Digital Pacific; Fuse; FXM; FYI; Great American Country; History International; LMN; National Geographic Channel; NBCSN; Outdoor Channel; Syfy; WE tv.
Fee: $10.00 monthly; $4.95 converter.
Pay Service 1
Pay Units: N.A.
Programming (via satellite): Cinemax; HBO; Showtime.
Digital Pay Service 1
Pay Units: N.A.
Programming (via satellite): Cinemax (multiplexed); Flix; HBO (multiplexed);

Showtime (multiplexed); Starz (multiplexed); Starz Encore (multiplexed); The Movie Channel (multiplexed).
Fee: $10.00 monthly (each).
Video-On-Demand: No
Internet Service
Operational: Yes.
Fee: $29.95-$59.95 monthly.
Telephone Service
Digital: Operational
Miles of Plant: 111.0 (coaxial); 15.0 (fiber optic). Homes passed: 3,521.
President & Chief Executive Officer: Alvin M. Fuhrman. General Manager: Joey Anderson. Network Engineer: Mack Isaacs. Marketing Director: Tara Swirczynski.
Ownership: Nortex Communications (MSO).

VAN HORN—Reach Broadband, PO Box 507, Arp, TX 75750. Phones: 575-437-3101; 800-687-1258; 903-859-3789. E-mail: support@reachbroadband.net. Web Site: http://www.reachbroadband.net. ICA: TX1024.
TV Market Ranking: Outside TV Markets (VAN HORN).
Channel capacity: N.A. Channels available but not in use: N.A.
Basic Service
Subscribers: 151.
Programming (received off-air): KDBC-TV (CBS, MNT, This TV) El Paso; KFOX-TV (FOX, Retro TV) El Paso; KPBT-TV (PBS) Odessa; KTSM-TV (Estrella TV, NBC) El Paso; KVIA-TV (ABC, Azteca America, CW) El Paso; KWES-TV (CW, NBC, TMO) Odessa.
Programming (via satellite): A&E; Animal Planet; Cartoon Network; CMT; CNN; C-SPAN; Discovery Channel; Discovery Life Channel; Disney Channel; ESPN; ESPN2; EVINE Live; EWTN Global Catholic Network; FOX Sports Networks; Freeform; FX; Hallmark Channel; HLN; HSN; Lifetime; MTV; National Geographic Channel; Nick At Nite; Nickelodeon; Spike TV; Syfy; TBS; Telemundo; The Weather Channel; TLC; TNT; Trinity Broadcasting Network (TBN); Turner Classic Movies; Univision; USA Network; VH1; WGN America.
Fee: $49.95 installation; $51.18 monthly.
Digital Basic Service
Subscribers: N.A.
Programming (via satellite): BBC America; Bloomberg Television; Bravo; Centric; Cloo; CMT; Destination America; Discovery Kids Channel; Disney XD; DMX Music; ESPN Classic; ESPNews; Fox Sports 1; FSN Digital Atlantic; FSN Digital Central; FSN Digital Pacific; Fuse; FXM; FYI; Golf Channel; Great American Country; GSN; HGTV; History International; IFC; Investigation Discovery; LMN; MTV Classic; MTV Hits; MTV2; NBCSN; Nick Jr.; Outdoor Channel; OWN; Oprah Winfrey Network; Science Channel; Starz Encore (multiplexed); TeenNick; The Word Network; VH1 Soul; WE tv.
Fee: $20.90 monthly.
Pay Service 1
Pay Units: N.A.
Programming (via satellite): HBO.
Fee: $13.95 monthly.
Digital Pay Service 1
Pay Units: N.A.
Programming (via satellite): Cinemax (multiplexed); HBO (multiplexed); Showtime (multiplexed); Starz (multiplexed); The Movie Channel (multiplexed).
Fee: $9.95 monthly (Starz), $12.95 monthly (HBO, Cinemax, Showtime or TMC).
Video-On-Demand: No

Pay-Per-View
Playboy TV (delivered digitally); Fresh (delivered digitally).
Internet Service
Operational: No.
Telephone Service
None
Controller: Jeffrey Lowe.
Ownership: RB3 LLC (MSO).

VEGA—XIT Communications. Formerly [TX0868]. This cable system has converted to IPTV, 12324 US Hwy 87, PO Box 71, Dalhart, TX 79022. Phones: 806-244-3355; 800-232-3312; 806-384-3311. Fax: 806-384-3311. E-mail: xitcom@xit.net. Web Site: http://www.xit.net. ICA: TX5081.
Channel capacity: N.A. Channels available but not in use: N.A.
Lifeline
Subscribers: 73.
Fee: $65.00 installation; $17.95 monthly.
Internet Service
Operational: Yes.
Fee: $39.00-$89.00 monthly.
Telephone Service
Digital: Operational
General Manager: Darrell Dennis.
Ownership: XIT Communications.

VEGA—XIT Communications. This cable system has converted to IPTV. See VEGA, TX [TX5081]. ICA: TX0868.

VERNON—Suddenlink Communications, 520 Maryville Centre Dr, Ste 300, St. Louis, MO 63141. Phones: 940-552-2217; 800-999-6845 (Customer service); 314-315-9400. Web Site: http://www.suddenlink.com. ICA: TX0119.
TV Market Ranking: Outside TV Markets (VERNON). Franchise award date: N.A. Franchise expiration date: N.A. Began: November 1, 1976.
Channel capacity: 37 (operating 2-way). Channels available but not in use: N.A.
Basic Service
Subscribers: 1,114. Commercial subscribers: 202.
Programming (received off-air): KAUZ-TV (CBS, CW) Wichita Falls; KFDX-TV (NBC) Wichita Falls; KJTL (Bounce TV, FOX) Wichita Falls; KSWO-TV (ABC, TMO) Lawton; allband FM.
Programming (via satellite): C-SPAN; KRMA-TV (PBS) Denver; Pop; QVC; The Weather Channel; Univision; Univision Studios.
Fee: $28.45 monthly.
Expanded Basic Service 1
Subscribers: N.A.
Programming (via satellite): A&E; AMC; Animal Planet; BET; Bravo; Cartoon Network; CNBC; CNN; Comedy Central; Discovery Channel; Disney Channel; E! HD; ESPN; ESPN2; EWTN Global Catholic Network; Food Network; Fox News Channel; Fox Sports 1; FOX Sports Southwest; Freeform; FX; Golf Channel; Great American Country; Hallmark Channel; HGTV; History; HLN; Lifetime; MSNBC; MTV; National Geographic Channel; Nickelodeon; Outdoor Channel; Spike TV; Syfy; TBS; Telemundo; TLC; TNT; Travel Channel; truTV; Turner Classic Movies; TV Land; USA Network; VH1.
Fee: $39.95 installation; $24.00 monthly.
Digital Basic Service
Subscribers: N.A.
Programming (via satellite): BBC America; Bloomberg Television; Cloo; Discovery Digital Networks; Disney XD; DMX Music; ESPN Classic; ESPNews; EVINE Live; FOX

2017 Edition

D-785

Texas—Cable Systems

College Sports Central; FOX College Sports Pacific; Fuse; FXM; FYI; GSN; History; History International; IFC; NBCSN; Sundance TV; Trinity Broadcasting Network (TBN); WE tv.

Pay Service 1
Pay Units: N.A.
Programming (via satellite): Cinemax; HBO; Showtime; Starz; Starz Encore.
Fee: $1.75 monthly (Encore), $6.75 monthly (Starz), $12.62 monthly (Cinemax), $13.59 monthly (HBO).

Digital Pay Service 1
Pay Units: N.A.
Programming (via satellite): Cinemax (multiplexed); Flix; HBO (multiplexed); Showtime (multiplexed); Starz (multiplexed); Starz Encore (multiplexed); The Movie Channel (multiplexed).

Video-On-Demand: No

Pay-Per-View
iN DEMAND (delivered digitally); Playboy TV (delivered digitally); Fresh (delivered digitally); Shorteez (delivered digitally).

Internet Service
Operational: Yes. Began: March 1, 2002.
Broadband Service: Suddenlink High Speed Internet.
Fee: $45.95 installation; $29.95 monthly.

Telephone Service
Digital: Operational
Fee: $44.95 monthly
Miles of Plant: 81.0 (coaxial); None (fiber optic). Homes passed: 5,783.
Vice President, Corporate Finance: Michael Pflantz. Regional Manager: Todd Cruthird. Plant Manager: Ron Johnson.
Ownership: Cequel Communications Holdings I LLC (MSO).

VICTORIA—Suddenlink Communications, 105 East Industrial Dr, Victoria, TX 77901-3344. Phone: 314-315-9400. Fax: 361-576-5295. Web Site: http://www.suddenlink.com. Also serves Victoria County (unincorporated areas). ICA: TX0043.
TV Market Ranking: Below 100 (VICTORIA, Victoria County (unincorporated areas)). Franchise award date: January 1, 1955. Franchise expiration date: N.A. Began: January 12, 1954.
Channel capacity: N.A. Channels available but not in use: N.A.

Basic Service
Subscribers: 13,747.
Programming (received off-air): KAVU-TV (ABC) Victoria; KMOL-LD (Movies!, NBC) Victoria; KUNU-LD (CBS) Victoria; KVCT (FOX, This TV, TMO) Victoria; 21 FMs.
Programming (via microwave): KENS (CBS, Estrella TV) San Antonio; KLRN (PBS) San Antonio; KUHT (PBS) Houston; KVTX-LP (TMO) Victoria.
Programming (via satellite): C-SPAN; C-SPAN 2; CW PLUS; EWTN Global Catholic Network; INSP; Pop; QVC; The Weather Channel; Trinity Broadcasting Network (TBN); WGN America.
Fee: $35.00 installation; $35.24 monthly.

Expanded Basic Service 1
Subscribers: N.A.
Programming (via satellite): A&E; AMC; Animal Planet; BET; Bravo; Cartoon Network; CMT; CNBC; CNN; Comedy Central; Discovery Channel; Disney Channel; E! HD; ESPN; ESPN2; Food Network; Fox Deportes; Fox News Channel; Fox Sports 1; FOX Sports Southwest; Freeform; FX; Golf Channel; Great American Country; HGTV; History; HLN; Jewelry Television; Lifetime; LMN; MSNBC; MTV; NBCSN; Nickelodeon; Outdoor Channel; Oxygen; Spike TV; Syfy; TBS; TLC; TNT; Travel Channel; truTV; Turner Classic Movies; TV Land; Univision; USA Network; VH1; WE tv; Weatherscan.
Fee: $20.63 monthly.

Digital Basic Service
Subscribers: N.A.
Programming (via satellite): A&E HD; AXS TV; Bandamax; BBC America; Bloomberg Television; Boomerang; CBS Sports Network; Cine Mexicano; Cinelatino; CMT; CNN en Espanol; Cooking Channel; De Pelicula; De Pelicula Clasico; Destination America; Discovery Kids Channel; Disney XD; DIY Network; Enlace USA; ESPN Classic; ESPN Deportes; ESPN HD; ESPN2 HD; ESPNews; ESPNU; Food Network HD; Fox Deportes; Fox Sports 2; FSN HD; Fuse; FYI; GSN; Hallmark Channel; HD Theater; HGTV HD; History en Espanol; History International; IFC; Investigation Discovery; MC; MTV Classic; MTV Hits; MTV Jams; MTV Live; MTV2; Nat Geo WILD; National Geographic Channel; National Geographic Channel HD; NBC Universo; Nick Jr.; Nicktoons; NickToons en Espanol; OWN: Oprah Winfrey Network; Ritmoson; Science Channel; Starz Encore (multiplexed); Sundance TV; Sur; TeenNick; Telehit; Tennis Channel; TNT HD; Toon Disney en Espanol; Tr3s; ULTRA HDPlex; UniMas; Universal HD; Univision; VH1 Soul; VideoRola.
Fee: $8.65 monthly.

Digital Pay Service 1
Pay Units: N.A.
Programming (via satellite): Cinemax (multiplexed); HBO (multiplexed); HBO HD; HBO Latino; Showtime (multiplexed); Showtime HD; Starz (multiplexed); Starz HD; The Movie Channel (multiplexed).
Fee: $7.95 monthly (Starz/Encore), $10.00 monthly (Cinemax), $11.00 monthly (HBO).

Video-On-Demand: No

Pay-Per-View
iN DEMAND (delivered digitally); Fresh (delivered digitally); Shorteez (delivered digitally); Playboy TV (delivered digitally); Club Jenna (delivered digitally); Spice: Xcess (delivered digitally); Playboy en Espanol (delivered digitally).

Internet Service
Operational: Yes.
Subscribers: 12,697.
Broadband Service: Suddenlink High Speed Internet.
Fee: $49.95 installation; $24.95 monthly.

Telephone Service
Digital: Operational
Subscribers: 5,932.
Fee: $48.95 monthly
Miles of Plant: 740.0 (coaxial); 49.0 (fiber optic). Homes passed: 30,354.
Senior Vice President, Corporate Finance: Michael Pflantz. General Manager: Ray Griffith. Chief Technician: James Farrow.
Ownership: Cequel Communications Holdings I LLC (MSO).

VIDOR—Time Warner Cable. Now served by PORT ARTHUR (formerly Beaumont), TX [TX0022]. ICA: TX0093.

VIDOR (southern portion)—Formerly served by Cebridge Connections. No longer in operation. ICA: TX0551.

WACO—Grande Communications, 7200 Imperial Dr, Waco, TX 76712-6623. Phone: 254-235-4600. Fax: 254-235-2099. Web Site: http://mygrande.com. Also serves Bellmead, Beverly Hills, Hewitt, Lacy Lakeview, Robinson & Woodway. ICA: TX0980. **Note:** This system is an overbuild.
TV Market Ranking: Below 100 (Hewitt, Lacy Lakeview, WACO, Woodway). Franchise award date: January 6, 1999. Franchise expiration date: N.A. Began: November 1, 1999.
Channel capacity: N.A. Channels available but not in use: N.A.

Basic Service
Subscribers: 15,107.
Programming (received off-air): KAKW-DT (getTV, UNV) Killeen; KCEN-TV (Antenna TV, MeTV, MundoMax, NBC) Temple; KWKT-TV (Estrella TV, FOX, MNT) Waco; KWTX-TV (CBS, CW) Waco; KXXV (ABC, TMO) Waco; WFAA (ABC) Dallas.
Programming (via satellite): C-SPAN; LWS Local Weather Station; QVC; Telemundo; WGN America.
Fee: $27.49 monthly.

Expanded Basic Service 1
Subscribers: N.A.
Programming (via satellite): A&E; AMC; Animal Planet; BET; Bravo; Cartoon Network; CMT; CNBC; CNN; Comedy Central; C-SPAN 2; Discovery Channel; Disney Channel; Disney XD; E! HD; ESPN; ESPN Classic; ESPN2; EWTN Global Catholic Network; Food Network; Fox Deportes; Fox News Channel; Fox Sports 1; FOX Sports Southwest; Freeform; FX; FXM; Golf Channel; Great American Country; GSN; Hallmark Channel; HGTV; History; HLN; Lifetime; LMN; MSNBC; MTV; NBC Universo; NBCSN; Nickelodeon; OWN: Oprah Winfrey Network; Oxygen; special events; Spike TV; Syfy; TBS; The Weather Channel; TLC; TNT; Travel Channel; Trinity Broadcasting Network (TBN); truTV; Turner Classic Movies; TV Land; Univision; USA Network; VH1.
Fee: $28.00 monthly.

Digital Basic Service
Subscribers: N.A.
Programming (via satellite): BBC America; Boomerang; CBS Sports Network; Colours; Cooking Channel; Discovery Life Channel; DIY Network; ESPN; ESPNews; FamilyNet; FOX College Sports Central; FOX College Sports Pacific; Fox Sports 2; Fuse; FYI; GolTV; HD Theater; History International; HITS (Headend In The Sky); MC; National Geographic Channel; NBA TV; NFL Network; Nick 2; Nick Jr.; Nicktoons; TeenNick; Tennis Channel; TNT; TVG Network; Universal HD.
Fee: $16.00 monthly (Basic), $4.00 monthly (Canales N), $9.95 monthly (HDTV Tier).

Digital Pay Service 1
Pay Units: N.A.
Programming (via satellite): Cinemax (multiplexed); Cinemax HD; Flix (multiplexed); HBO (multiplexed); HBO HD; Showtime (multiplexed); Showtime HD; Starz (multiplexed); Starz Encore (multiplexed); Starz HD; Sundance TV (multiplexed); The Movie Channel (multiplexed).
Fee: $9.99 monthly (Cinemax, HBO, Starz/Encore or Showtime/TMC/Flix/Sundance).

Pay-Per-View
Playboy TV; Spice (delivered digitally); Shorteez (delivered digitally); Pleasure (delivered digitally); Hot Choice (delivered digitally); iN DEMAND (delivered digitally); Sports PPV (delivered digitally).

Internet Service
Operational: Yes. Began: January 1, 1999.
Subscribers: 14,756.
Fee: $34.99-$64.99 monthly.

Telephone Service
Digital: Operational
Subscribers: 9,374.
Fee: $19.99 monthly
Miles of Plant: 1,341.0 (coaxial); 256.0 (fiber optic). Homes passed: 54,443.
General Manager: Matt Rohre. Vice President, Customer Care: Dawn Blydenburgh. Vice President, Marketing: Pete Drozdoff. Vice President, Network Operations & Engineering: Lamar Horton. Vice President, Technical Operations: Shane Schilling.
Ownership: Grande Communications Networks Inc. (MSO).

WACO—Time Warner Cable. Now served by AUSTIN, TX [TX0005]. ICA: TX0015.

WAELDER—Formerly served by National Cable Inc. No longer in operation. ICA: TX0518.

WALDEN (village)—Suddenlink Communications. Now served by KINGWOOD, TX [TX0052]. ICA: TX0869.

WALLIS—Formerly served by Rapid Cable. No longer in operation. ICA: TX0275.

WALNUT SPRINGS—Formerly served by National Cable Inc. No longer in operation. ICA: TX0871.

WATERWOOD—Cablevision of Walker County, 1304 10th St, Huntsville, TX 77320-3804. Phone: 936-291-2288. Fax: 936-291-0890. Also serves San Jacinto County (portions). ICA: TX0872.
TV Market Ranking: Below 100 (WATERWOOD). Franchise award date: N.A. Franchise expiration date: N.A. Began: January 1, 1976.
Channel capacity: N.A. Channels available but not in use: N.A.

Basic Service
Subscribers: N.A.
Programming (received off-air): KBTX-TV (CBS, CW) Bryan; KHOU (Bounce TV, CBS) Houston; KPRC-TV (NBC, This TV) Houston; KPXB-TV (ION) Conroe; KRIV (FOX) Houston; KTBU (IND) Conroe; KTRK-TV (ABC, Live Well Network) Houston; KTXH (Buzzr, MNT, Movies!) Houston; KUHT (PBS) Houston.
Programming (via satellite): A&E; AMC; CMT; CNBC; CNN; C-SPAN; Discovery Channel; ESPN; Food Network; Fox News Channel; FOX Sports Southwest; Freeform; Golf Channel; HGTV; History; HLN; Lifetime; Nickelodeon; Spike TV; TBS; The Weather Channel; TNT; USA Network; VH1; WGN America.
Fee: $39.95 installation; $32.79 monthly.

Digital Basic Service
Subscribers: N.A.
Programming (via satellite): BBC America; Bloomberg Television; Destination America; Discovery Kids Channel; Discovery Life Channel; Disney XD; DMX Music; ESPN Classic; ESPN2; ESPNews; Fox Sports 1; Fuse; FXM; FYI; Golf Channel; GSN; HGTV; History; History International; LMN; MTV Classic; MTV Hits; MTV2; National Geographic Channel; NBCSN; Nick Jr.; Outdoor Channel; Ovation; OWN: Oprah Winfrey Network; Sundance TV; Syfy; TeenNick; Trinity Broadcasting Network (TBN); Turner Classic Movies; VH1 Country; VH1 Soul; WE tv.
Fee: $12.07 monthly.

Digital Pay Service 1
Pay Units: N.A.
Programming (via satellite): Cinemax (multiplexed); HBO (multiplexed); Showtime

Cable Systems—Texas

(multiplexed); Starz (multiplexed); Starz Encore (multiplexed); The Movie Channel (multiplexed).
Fee: $11.99 monthly (Showtime/TMC or Starz/Encore), $13.99 monthly (Cinemax/HBO).

Video-On-Demand: No

Pay-Per-View
iN DEMAND (delivered digitally); ESPN Now (delivered digitally); Sports PPV (delivered digitally).

Internet Service
Operational: No.

Telephone Service
Analog: Operational

Miles of Plant: 26.0 (coaxial); None (fiber optic).
General Manager: Caroline Walker. Chief Technician: Kenny Hanson.
Ownership: Cablevision of Walker County (MSO).

WEATHERFORD—Charter Communications. Now served by FORT WORTH (northern portions), TX [TX0008]. ICA: TX1004.

WEINERT—Formerly served by Jayroc Cablevision. No longer in operation. ICA: TX0873.

WELCH—Formerly served by National Cable Inc. No longer in operation. ICA: TX0910.

WELLINGTON—Suddenlink Communications, 520 Maryville Centre Dr, Ste 300, St. Louis, MO 63141. Phones: 806-447-2061; 314-315-9400. Web Site: http://www.suddenlink.com. Also serves Childress & Collingsworth County. ICA: TX0313.
TV Market Ranking: Below 100 (Collingsworth County (portions)); Outside TV Markets (Collingsworth County (portions), WELLINGTON). Franchise award date: May 2, 1955. Franchise expiration date: N.A. Began: May 1, 1955.
Channel capacity: N.A. Channels available but not in use: N.A.

Basic Service
Subscribers: 778. Commercial subscribers: 94.
Programming (via microwave): KAMR-TV (IND, NBC) Amarillo; KCIT (FOX, This TV) Amarillo; KFDA-TV (CBS, TMO) Amarillo; KVII-TV (ABC, CW) Amarillo.
Programming (via satellite): CMT; CNN; C-SPAN; Discovery Channel; Disney Channel; ESPN; Freeform; Hallmark Channel; HLN; Lifetime; MTV; Nickelodeon; Spike TV; The Weather Channel; TNT; Turner Classic Movies; USA Network.
Fee: $28.45 monthly.

Pay Service 1
Pay Units: N.A.
Programming (via satellite): Cinemax; HBO.
Fee: $20.00 installation; $12.00 monthly (each).

Video-On-Demand: No

Internet Service
Operational: Yes. Began: September 16, 2004.
Subscribers: 742.
Broadband Service: Suddenlink High Speed Internet.
Fee: $49.95 installation; $29.95 monthly.

Telephone Service
Digital: Operational
Fee: $49.95 monthly
Miles of Plant: 116.0 (coaxial); 48.0 (fiber optic). Homes passed: 4,344.
Vice President, Corporate Finance: Michael Pflantz. General Manager: Genarah Manuel. Chief Technician: Tim Cummings.
Ownership: Cequel Communications Holdings I LLC (MSO).

WELLMAN—Formerly served by National Cable Inc. No longer in operation. ICA: TX0874.

WELLS—Formerly served by Cebridge Connections. No longer in operation. ICA: TX0546.

WESLACO—Time Warner Cable. Now served by PHARR, TX [TX0017]. ICA: TX0048.

WEST—LynnStar Communications, 4500 Mercantile Plz, Ste 300, Fort Worth, TX 76137. Phones: 888-575-9230; 682-730-0900. Fax: 682-730-6400. Web Site: http://lynnstar.net; http://www.lynnstarcomm.com. ICA: TX0371.
TV Market Ranking: Below 100 (WEST). Franchise award date: N.A. Franchise expiration date: N.A. Began: May 1, 1982.
Channel capacity: N.A. Channels available but not in use: N.A.

Basic Service
Subscribers: 150.
Programming (received off-air): KCEN-TV (Antenna TV, MeTV, MundoMax, NBC) Temple; KDFW (FOX) Dallas; KERA-TV (PBS) Dallas; KTVT (CBS, Decades) Fort Worth; KWKT-TV (Estrella TV, FOX, MNT) Waco; KWTX-TV (CBS, CW) Waco; KXAS-TV (COZI TV, NBC) Fort Worth; KXTX-TV (TMO) Dallas; KXXV (ABC, TMO) Waco; WFAA (ABC) Dallas.
Programming (via satellite): Discovery Channel; TBS; TLC.
Fee: $49.95 installation; $25.64 monthly.

Expanded Basic Service 1
Subscribers: N.A.
Programming (via satellite): AMC; Animal Planet; Cartoon Network; CNBC; CNN; C-SPAN; Disney Channel; ESPN; Fox News Channel; Freeform; FX; HGTV; HLN; Lifetime; Nickelodeon; QVC; Spike TV; The Weather Channel; TNT; USA Network.
Fee: $23.10 monthly.

Pay Service 1
Pay Units: N.A.
Programming (via satellite): Cinemax; HBO; Starz; Starz Encore.
Fee: $12.95 monthly (each).

Video-On-Demand: No

Internet Service
Operational: Yes.

Telephone Service
None

Miles of Plant: 19.0 (coaxial); None (fiber optic). Homes passed: 935.
Chairman of the Board & Government Relations Director: S. Gene Yarbrough. Chief Executive Officer, Executive Vice President & Board Member: Chris Romine. Chief Operations Officer, Executive Vice President & Board Member: Steve Sizemore. Vice President & Business Development & Countertrade Director: Gary Majors. Vice President & Programming & Vendor Relations Director: Gus Salvino. Vice President & Investor Relations Manager: Daniel J. Sweeney. Accounting Manager: Sheila Magness.
Ownership: Lynnstar Communications (MSO).

WEST COLUMBIA—NewWave Communications. Now served by WHARTON, TX [TX0171]. ICA: TX0233.

WEST GRAYSON COUNTY—TV Cable of Grayson County. Now served by GRAYSON COUNTY, TX [TX1014]. ICA: TX1013.

WEST ODESSA—Reach Broadband, PO Box 507, Arp, TX 75750. Phones: 575-437-3101; 903-859-3789; 800-687-1258. E-mail: support@reachbroadband.net. Web Site: http://www.reachbroadband.net. ICA: TX0969.
TV Market Ranking: Below 100 (WEST ODESSA).
Channel capacity: N.A. Channels available but not in use: N.A.

Basic Service
Subscribers: 461.
Programming (received off-air): KMID (ABC) Midland; KOSA-TV (CBS, MNT) Odessa; KPEJ-TV (FOX) Odessa; KRPV-DT (GLC) Roswell; KUPB (UNV) Midland; KWES-TV (CW, NBC, TMO) Odessa.
Programming (via satellite): CMT; C-SPAN; Discovery Channel; Disney Channel; Fox News Channel; FX; Lifetime; Nickelodeon; Pop; Spike TV; TBS; Telemundo; The Weather Channel; TNT; Trinity Broadcasting Network (TBN); WGN America.
Fee: $49.95 installation; $28.47 monthly; $.90 converter.

Expanded Basic Service 1
Subscribers: N.A.
Programming (via satellite): A&E; AMC; Animal Planet; Cartoon Network; CNN; Discovery Life Channel; ESPN; ESPN2; FOX Sports Southwest; Freeform; Hallmark Channel; HGTV; HLN; MoviePlex; MTV; Outdoor Channel; Syfy; TLC; USA Network; VH1.
Fee: $16.86 monthly.

Pay Service 1
Pay Units: N.A.
Programming (via satellite): HBO.
Programming (via translator): Showtime.
Fee: $12.95 monthly (each).

Video-On-Demand: No

Pay-Per-View
iN DEMAND (delivered digitally); Playboy TV (delivered digitally); Fresh (delivered digitally).

Internet Service
Operational: Yes.

Telephone Service
None
Homes passed & miles of plant included in Seminole
Controller: Jeffrey Lowe.
Ownership: RB3 LLC (MSO).

WESTBROOK—Formerly served by National Cable Inc. No longer in operation. ICA: TX0877.

WESTHOFF—Formerly served by National Cable Inc. No longer in operation. ICA: TX0909.

WESTON LAKES—Telecom Cable, 1321 Louetta Rd, Ste 1020, Cypress, TX 77429. Phone: 888-240-4589. E-mail: information@telecomcable.net. Web Site: http://telecomcable.net. ICA: TX1041.
TV Market Ranking: 15 (WESTON LAKES).
Channel capacity: N.A. Channels available but not in use: N.A.

Basic Service
Subscribers: 20.
Fee: $13.00 monthly.
Chief Financial Officer: Bradley C. Veis.
Ownership: Telecom Cable LLC (MSO).

WHARTON—NewWave Communications, One Montgomery Plaza, 4th Floor, Sikeston, MO 63801. Phones: 573-472-9500; 888-863-9928. Fax: 573-472-9518. E-mail: info@newwavecom.com. Web Site: http://www.newwavecom.com. Also serves Bay City, Blessing, Brazoria County (unincorporated areas), Columbia Lakes, Edna, El Campo, Ganado, Jackson County (unincorporated areas), Louise, Manvel, Markham, Matagorda County (unincorporated areas), Palacios, Pearland, Sweeny, Van Vleck, West Columbia & Wharton County (unincorporated areas). ICA: TX0171.
TV Market Ranking: 15 (Manvel, Pearland); Below 100 (Columbia Lakes, WHARTON, Edna, Ganado, West Columbia); Outside TV Markets (Markham, Matagorda County (unincorporated areas), Van Vleck, Bay City, Blessing, El Campo, Louise, Palacios, Sweeny). Franchise award date: N.A. Franchise expiration date: N.A. Began: November 1, 1973.
Channel capacity: 79 (operating 2-way). Channels available but not in use: N.A.

Basic Service
Subscribers: 11,539.
Programming (received off-air): KETH-TV (TBN) Houston; KFTH-DT (getTV, UniMas) Alvin; KHOU (Bounce TV, CBS) Houston; KIAH (Antenna TV, CW) Houston; KLTJ (Daystar TV, ETV) Galveston; KPRC-TV (NBC, This TV) Houston; KRIV (FOX) Houston; KTBU (IND) Conroe; KTMD (TMO) Galveston; KTRK-TV (ABC, Live Well Network) Houston; KTXH (Buzzr, MNT, Movies!) Houston; KUBE-TV (COZI TV, MeTV) Baytown; KUHT (PBS) Houston; KXLN-DT (UNV) Rosenberg; KYAZ (Azteca America, IND) Katy; KZJL (Estrella TV) Houston; allband FM.
Programming (via satellite): A&E; AMC; Animal Planet; BET; Bravo; Cartoon Network; CMT; CNN; C-SPAN; C-SPAN 2; Discovery Channel; Disney Channel; E! HD; ESPN; ESPN Classic; ESPN2; EWTN Global Catholic Network; Food Network; Fox News Channel; Fox Sports 1; Freeform; FX; HGTV; History; HLN; ION Television; Lifetime; MSNBC; MTV; Nickelodeon; Oxygen; Pop; QVC; Spike TV; Syfy; TBS; The Weather Channel; TLC; TNT; Travel Channel; TV Land; USA Network; VH1; WGN America.
Fee: $30.00 installation; $30.93 monthly; $2.00 converter.

Digital Basic Service
Subscribers: N.A.
Programming (via satellite): 52MX; BBC America; Bloomberg Television; Cine Mexicano; Cinelatino; CMT; CNN en Espanol; Destination America; Discovery Kids Channel; Disney XD; DIY Network; ESPN Deportes; ESPN HD; ESPNews; Fox Deportes; FYI; Golf Channel; GSN; HD Theater; History en Espanol; History International; IFC; Investigation Discovery; MTV Classic; NBCSN; Nick Jr.; Nicktoons; Outdoor Channel 2 HD; OWN: Oprah Winfrey Network; RFD-TV; Science Channel; Tr3s; Turner Classic Movies; ViendoMovies; WE tv.
Fee: $10.00 monthly.

Digital Pay Service 1
Pay Units: N.A.
Programming (via satellite): Cinemax (multiplexed); Flix; HBO (multiplexed); HBO Latino; Showtime (multiplexed); Showtime HD; Starz (multiplexed); Starz Encore (multiplexed); Starz HD; The Movie Channel (multiplexed); The Movie Channel HD.
Fee: $8.00 monthly (Starz), $9.00 monthly (Cinemax), $11.00 monthly (Starz/Encore), $15.00 monthly (Showtime/TMC), $17.00 monthly (HBO) or $26.00 monthly (HBO/Cinemax).

Video-On-Demand: No

Texas—Cable Systems

Pay-Per-View
iN DEMAND (delivered digitally); Fresh (delivered digitally); Playboy TV (delivered digitally).
Internet Service
Operational: Yes, DSL & dial-up. Began: January 1, 2002.
Fee: $17.05 installation; $39.99-$79.99 monthly; $6.00-$8.99 modem lease.
Telephone Service
Digital: Operational
Miles of Plant: 295.0 (coaxial); 116.0 (fiber optic). Homes passed: 10,509.
General Manager: Mark Bookout.
Ownership: NewWave Communications LLC (MSO).

WHEELER—Formerly served by Elk River TV Cable Co. No longer in operation. ICA: TX0460.

WHITEFACE—Formerly served by Cebridge Connections. No longer in operation. ICA: TX0879.

WHITESBORO—Suddenlink Communications, 104 North Morris St, Gainesville, TX 76240-4242. Phone: 314-315-9400. Web Site: http://www.suddenlink.com. Also serves Grayson County (portions) & Sadler. ICA: TX0271.
TV Market Ranking: Below 100 (Sadler, WHITESBORO, Grayson County (portions)). Franchise award date: N.A. Franchise expiration date: N.A. Began: July 1, 1967.
Channel capacity: N.A. Channels available but not in use: N.A.
Basic Service
Subscribers: 763. Commercial subscribers: 57.
Programming (received off-air): KDAF (Antenna TV, CW, This TV) Dallas; KDFW (FOX) Dallas; KDTN (Daystar TV, ETV) Denton; KERA-TV (PBS) Dallas; KMPX (Estrella TV) Decatur; KTEN (ABC, CW, NBC) Ada; KTVT (CBS, Decades) Fort Worth; KTXA (IND, MeTV) Fort Worth; KXAS-TV (COZI TV, NBC) Fort Worth; KXII (CBS, FOX, MNT) Sherman; KXTX-TV (TMO) Dallas; WFAA (ABC) Dallas.
Programming (via satellite): C-SPAN; Discovery Channel; QVC; TBS; The Weather Channel.
Fee: $54.95 installation; $35.24 monthly.
Expanded Basic Service 1
Subscribers: N.A.
Programming (via satellite): AMC; Animal Planet; Cartoon Network; CNBC; CNN; Disney Channel; ESPN; ESPN2; Fox News Channel; FOX Sports Southwest; Freeform; FX; Great American Country; HLN; Lifetime; MoviePlex; NBCSN; Nickelodeon; Spike TV; TLC; TNT; truTV; USA Network.
Fee: $11.63 monthly.
Pay Service 1
Pay Units: N.A.
Programming (via satellite): HBO; Showtime; Starz; Starz Encore.
Fee: $7.50 installation; $10.95 monthly (HBO or Showtime).
Video-On-Demand: No
Internet Service
Operational: Yes.
Broadband Service: Suddenlink High Speed Internet.
Fee: $49.95 installation; $25.95 monthly.
Telephone Service
Digital: Operational
Miles of Plant: 27.0 (coaxial); None (fiber optic). Homes passed: 1,530.

Senior Vice President, Corporate Finance: Michael Pflantz. General Manager: Ricky Allen. Chief Technician: Gary Hinkle.
Ownership: Cequel Communications Holdings I LLC (MSO).

WHITNEY—LynnStar Communications, 4500 Mercantile Plz, Ste 300, Fort Worth, TX 76137. Phones: 888-575-9230; 682-730-0900. Fax: 682-730-6400. Web Site: http://lynnstar.net; http://www.lynnstarcomm.com. Also serves Lake Whitney. ICA: TX0403.
TV Market Ranking: Below 100 (Lake Whitney, WHITNEY). Franchise award date: N.A. Franchise expiration date: N.A. Began: October 1, 1982.
Channel capacity: N.A. Channels available but not in use: N.A.
Basic Service
Subscribers: 37.
Programming (received off-air): KDAF (Antenna TV, CW, This TV) Dallas; KDFI (Bounce TV, Buzzr, Heroes & Icons, MNT, Movies!) Dallas; KDFW (FOX) Dallas; KDTX-TV (TBN) Dallas; KERA-TV (PBS) Dallas; KSTR-DT (getTV, UniMas) Irving; KTVT (CBS, Decades) Fort Worth; KTXA (IND, MeTV) Fort Worth; KUVN-DT (UNV) Garland; KWTX-TV (CBS, CW) Waco; KXAS-TV (COZI TV, NBC) Fort Worth; KXTX-TV (TMO) Dallas; WFAA (ABC) Dallas.
Programming (via satellite): A&E; C-SPAN; WGN America.
Fee: $49.95 installation; $61.98 monthly.
Expanded Basic Service 1
Subscribers: N.A.
Programming (via satellite): AMC; Animal Planet; CMT; CNN; Discovery Channel; Disney Channel; Disney XD; E! HD; ESPN; ESPN2; ESPNews; Fox News Channel; FOX Sports Southwest; Freeform; HGTV; History; HLN; Lifetime; MTV; National Geographic Channel; Nickelodeon; Spike TV; TBS; The Weather Channel; TLC; TNT; Travel Channel; TV Land; USA Network.
Fee: $23.10 monthly.
Video-On-Demand: No
Pay-Per-View
Hot Choice (delivered digitally); Playboy TV (delivered digitally); Fresh (delivered digitally); Shorteez (delivered digitally); iN DEMAND (delivered digitally).
Internet Service
Operational: Yes.
Telephone Service
None
Miles of Plant: 62.0 (coaxial); None (fiber optic). Homes passed: 2,514.
Chairman of the Board & Government Relations Director: S. Gene Yarbrough. Chief Executive Officer, Executive Vice President & Board Member: Chris Romine. Chief Operations Officer, Executive Vice President & Board Member: Steve Sizemore. Vice President & Business Development & Countertrade Director: Gary Magness. Vice President & Programming & Vendor Relations Director: Gus Salvino. Vice President & Investor Relations Manager: Daniel J. Sweeney. Accounting Manager: Sheila Magness.
Ownership: Lynnstar Communications (MSO).

WICHITA FALLS—Time Warner Cable, 3225 Maurine St, Wichita Falls, TX 76306-6828. Phones: 940-855-5701; 940-855-4321; 972-899-7300 (Flower Mound office). Fax: 940-855-0465. Web Site: http://www.timewarnercable.com. Also serves Archer City, Holliday, Lakeside City, Sheppard AFB & Wichita County (portions). ICA: TX0026.

TV Market Ranking: Below 100 (Archer City, Holliday, Lakeside City, Sheppard AFB, Wichita County (portions), WICHITA FALLS). Franchise award date: N.A. Franchise expiration date: N.A. Began: November 1, 1979.
Channel capacity: N.A. Channels available but not in use: N.A.
Basic Service
Subscribers: 12,932.
Programming (received off-air): KAUZ-TV (CBS, CW) Wichita Falls; KFDX-TV (NBC) Wichita Falls; KJBO-LP (MNT) Wichita Falls; KJTL (Bounce TV, FOX) Wichita Falls; KKTM-LP Altus; KSWO-TV (ABC, TMO) Lawton; WFTV (ABC, Escape) Orlando; 24 FMs.
Programming (via microwave): KERA-TV (PBS) Dallas.
Programming (via satellite): Christian Television Network; CW PLUS; Radar Channel; WGN America.
Fee: $39.99 installation; $28.00 monthly.
Expanded Basic Service 1
Subscribers: N.A.
Programming (via satellite): A&E; AMC; Animal Planet; BET; Bravo; Cartoon Network; CMT; CNBC; CNN; Comedy Central; C-SPAN; C-SPAN 2; Discovery Channel; Disney Channel; E! HD; ESPN; ESPN2; EVINE Live; Food Network; Fox News Channel; FOX Sports Southwest; Freeform; FX; FXM; Golf Channel; Hallmark Channel; HGTV; History; HLN; ION Television; Lifetime; LMN; MSNBC; MTV; National Geographic Channel; Nickelodeon; OWN; Oprah Winfrey Network; Oxygen; Pop; QVC; Spike TV; Sundance TV; Syfy; TBS; The Weather Channel; TLC; TNT; Travel Channel; Trinity Broadcasting Network (TBN); truTV; TV Land; Univision; USA Network; VH1; WE tv.
Fee: $32.10 monthly.
Digital Basic Service
Subscribers: N.A.
Programming (via satellite): A&E; AMC; Animal Planet; AXS TV; BBC America; BBC America On Demand; BET; Bloomberg Television; Boomerang; Bravo; Cartoon Network; Cloo; CMT; CNBC; CNN; Comedy Central; Cooking Channel; C-SPAN; C-SPAN 2; C-SPAN 3; Daystar TV Network; Destination America; Discovery Channel; Discovery Kids Channel; Discovery Life Channel; Disney Channel; Disney XD; DIY Network; E! HD; ESPN; ESPN Classic; ESPN HD; ESPN2; ESPN2 HD; ESPNews; ESPNU; EVINE Live; EWTN Global Catholic Network; FamilyNet; Food Network; Food Network On Demand; Fox Business Network; Fox News Channel; Fox Sports 1; FOX Sports Southwest; Freeform; Fuse; FX; FXM; Golf Channel; Great American Country; Hallmark Channel; HD Theater; HGTV; HGTV On Demand; History; HLN; IFC; Investigation Discovery; ION Television; La Familia Cosmovision; Lifetime; LMN; MC; MSNBC; MTV; MTV Classic; MTV Hits; MTV2; Nat Geo WILD; National Geographic Channel; National Geographic Channel On Demand; NBA TV; NBCSN; Nick Jr.; Nickelodeon; Nicktoons; Ovation; OWN; Oprah Winfrey Network; Oxygen; Oxygen On Demand; Pop; QVC; Science Channel; Spike TV; Syfy; TBS; TeenNick; The Weather Channel; TLC; TNT; TNT HD; Travel Channel; Trinity Broadcasting Network (TBN); truTV; Turner Classic Movies; TV Land; Universal HD; Univision; USA Network; VH1; WE tv.
Fee: $5.00 monthly.

Digital Expanded Basic Service
Subscribers: N.A.
Programming (via satellite): FOX College Sports Central; FOX College Sports Pacific; Fox Sports 1; Fox Sports 2; IFC; NBA TV; Starz Encore (multiplexed); Tennis Channel.
Digital Pay Service 1
Pay Units: N.A.
Programming (via satellite): Cinemax (multiplexed); Cinemax On Demand; HBO (multiplexed); HBO GO; HBO HD; Showtime (multiplexed); Showtime HD; Showtime On Demand; Starz (multiplexed); The Movie Channel (multiplexed); The Movie Channel On Demand.
Fee: $14.99 monthly (each).
Video-On-Demand: Yes
Pay-Per-View
iN DEMAND (delivered digitally); Fresh (delivered digitally); Shorteez (delivered digitally); Hot Choice (delivered digitally); NBA League Pass (delivered digitally); MLB Extra Innings (delivered digitally); NHL Center Ice (delivered digitally).
Internet Service
Operational: Yes. Began: December 31, 2001.
Subscribers: 15,064.
Broadband Service: Road Runner.
Fee: $49.99 installation; $44.95 monthly.
Telephone Service
Digital: Operational
Subscribers: 5,641.
Fee: $44.95 monthly
Miles of Plant: 918.0 (coaxial); 330.0 (fiber optic). Homes passed: 54,886.
President: Connie Wharton. Vice President & General Manager: Mike McKee. Public Affairs Manager: Vicki McCann.
Ownership: Time Warner Cable (MSO).; Advance/Newhouse Partnership (MSO).

WICKETT—Formerly served by Almega Cable. No longer in operation. ICA: TX0880.

WILDWOOD—Formerly served by Daybreak Communications. No longer in operation. ICA: TX0537.

WILLOW PARK—Formerly served by Mallard Cablevision. No longer in operation. ICA: TX0177.

WILLS POINT—Formerly served by Zoom Media. No longer in operation. ICA: TX0338.

WILMER—Formerly served by Metro Cable. No longer in operation. ICA: TX0307.

WILSON—Formerly served by Charter Communications. No longer in operation. ICA: TX0650.

WINK—Formerly served by Almega Cable. No longer in operation. ICA: TX0478.

WINNIE—Time Warner Cable, 7820 Crescent Executive Dr, Charlotte, NC 28217. Phones: 877-455-6337 (Sales); 703-713-1723 (Herndon VA office). Web Site: http://www.timewarnercable.com. Also serves Stowell. ICA: TX0258.
TV Market Ranking: 88 (Stowell, WINNIE).
Channel capacity: N.A. Channels available but not in use: N.A.
Basic Service
Subscribers: 639. Commercial subscribers: 11.
Fee: $19.95 installation; $24.99 monthly.
Ownership: Time Warner Cable (MSO).

Cable Systems—Texas

WINNSBORO—Suddenlink Communications, 220 Linda Dr, Sulphur Springs, TX 75482-4355. Phone: 314-315-9400. Web Site: http://www.suddenlink.com. Also serves Wood County (portions). ICA: TX0978.
TV Market Ranking: Outside TV Markets (WINNSBORO, Wood County (portions)).
Channel capacity: 42 (not 2-way capable). Channels available but not in use: N.A.
Basic Service
Subscribers: 766. Commercial subscribers: 90.
Programming (received off-air): KDFW (FOX) Dallas; KERA-TV (PBS) Dallas; KETK-TV (Estrella TV, NBC) Jacksonville; KFXK-TV (FOX) Longview; KLTV (ABC, Bounce TV, TMO) Tyler; KSLA (Bounce TV, CBS, Grit, This TV) Shreveport; KTVT (CBS, Decades) Fort Worth; KXAS-TV (COZI TV, NBC) Fort Worth; KXTX-TV (TMO) Dallas; WFAA (ABC) Dallas.
Programming (via satellite): HLN; ION Television; TBS; The Weather Channel; Trinity Broadcasting Network (TBN); WGN America.
Fee: $54.95 installation; $35.24 monthly.
Expanded Basic Service 1
Subscribers: N.A.
Programming (via satellite): A&E; AMC; CNBC; CNN; Discovery Channel; ESPN; FOX Sports Southwest; Freeform; Great American Country; Lifetime; Nickelodeon; Spike TV; Syfy; TLC; TNT; TV Land; USA Network.
Fee: $13.90 monthly.
Pay Service 1
Pay Units: N.A.
Programming (via satellite): HBO; Showtime; Starz; The Movie Channel.
Fee: $5.00 monthly (HBO), $6.00 monthly (Showtime/TMC), $7.95 monthly (Starz).
Video-On-Demand: No
Internet Service
Operational: Yes.
Broadband Service: Suddenlink High Speed Internet.
Telephone Service
Digital: Operational
Miles of Plant: 36.0 (coaxial); None (fiber optic). Homes passed: 1,850.
Senior Vice President, Corporate Finance: Michael Pflantz. General Manager: Joe Suggs.
Ownership: Cequel Communications Holdings I LLC (MSO).

WINTERS—Vyve Broadband, 4 International Dr, Ste 330, Rye Brook, NY 10573. Phones: 800-937-1397; 405-395-1131; 405-275-6923. Web Site: http://vyvebroadband.com. ICA: TX0965.
TV Market Ranking: Outside TV Markets (WINTERS).
Channel capacity: N.A. Channels available but not in use: N.A.
Basic Service
Subscribers: 105.
Programming (received off-air): KERA-TV (PBS) Dallas; KLST (CBS) San Angelo; KPCB-DT (GLC) Snyder; KRBC-TV (Bounce TV, NBC) Abilene; KTAB-TV (CBS) Abilene; KTXA (IND, MeTV) Fort Worth; KTXS-TV (ABC, CW, This TV, TMO) Sweetwater; KXVA (FOX, MNT) Abilene; WFAA (ABC) Dallas.
Programming (via satellite): CNN; C-SPAN; HLN; INSP; ION Television; QVC; Telemundo; The Weather Channel; Trinity Broadcasting Network (TBN); UniMas; Univision Studios.
Fee: $64.95 installation; $25.00 monthly; $.25 converter.
Expanded Basic Service 1
Subscribers: 96.
Programming (via satellite): A&E; AMC; Animal Planet; CMT; Discovery Channel; Disney Channel; ESPN; ESPN2; Fox News Channel; FOX Sports Southwest; Freeform; FX; Hallmark Channel; HGTV; Lifetime; MTV; NFL Network; Nickelodeon; Spike TV; TBS; TLC; TNT; USA Network.
Fee: $34.66 monthly.
Digital Basic Service
Subscribers: N.A.
Programming (via satellite): 52MX; BBC America; Bloomberg Television; Bravo; Cine Mexicano; Cinelatino; Cloo; CMT; CNN en Espanol; Destination America; Discovery Kids Channel; Discovery Life Channel; Disney XD; DMX Music; ESPN Classic; ESPN2; ESPNews; EVINE Live; Flix; FOX College Sports Central; FOX College Sports Pacific; Fox Deportes; Fox Sports 1; Fuse; FXM; FYI; Golf Channel; Great American Country; GSN; HGTV; History; History en Espanol; History International; IFC; Investigation Discovery; LMN; MTV Classic; MTV Hits; MTV2; National Geographic Channel; NBCSN; Nick Jr.; Nicktoons; Outdoor Channel; Ovation; OWN; Oprah Winfrey Network; Science Channel; Starz Encore (multiplexed); Sundance TV; Syfy; TeenNick; The Word Network; Toon Disney en Espanol; Tr3s; Trinity Broadcasting Network (TBN); Turner Classic Movies; UP; VH1 Soul; WE tv.
Digital Pay Service 1
Pay Units: N.A.
Programming (via satellite): Cinemax (multiplexed); HBO (multiplexed); Showtime (multiplexed); Starz (multiplexed); The Movie Channel (multiplexed).
Pay-Per-View
iN DEMAND (delivered digitally); Playboy TV (delivered digitally); Fresh (delivered digitally); Shorteez (delivered digitally).
Internet Service
Operational: Yes.
Fee: $24.95 installation; $39.95 monthly.
Telephone Service
Digital: Operational
Miles of Plant: 19.0 (coaxial); None (fiber optic). Homes passed: 792.
Chief Executive Officer: Bill Haggarty. Regional Vice President: Andrew Dearth. Vice President, Marketing: Tracy Bass. Senior Vice President, Financial Planning: Daniel White.
Ownership: Vyve Broadband LLC (MSO).

WODEN—Formerly served by Almega Cable. No longer in operation. ICA: TX0553.

WOLFE CITY—Formerly served by Zoom Media. No longer in operation. ICA: TX0449.

WOLFFORTH—NTS Communications, 1220 Broadway, Lubbock, TX 79401. Phones: 800-658-2150; 806-797-0687. Fax: 806-788-3381. E-mail: info@ntscom.com. Web Site: http://www.ntscom.com. Also serves Brownfield, Cochran County (portions), Friendship, Lamesa, Levelland, Littlefield, Lubbock, Meadow, Morton, New Deal, Reese AFB, Ropesville, Shallowater, Slaton, Smyer & Whitharral. ICA: TX5540.
TV Market Ranking: Below 100 (Lubbock, Meadow, New Deal, Reese AFB, Ropesville, Shallowater, Slaton, Smyer).
Channel capacity: N.A. Channels available but not in use: N.A.
Gold
Subscribers: 7,514.
Fee: $65.00 monthly. Includes 150+ channels plus music channels & 1 digital receiver.
Platinum
Subscribers: N.A.
Fee: $85.00 monthly. Includes 230+ channels plus music channels, HD channels, 1 whole home DVR & 1 digital receiver.
Internet Service
Operational: Yes.
Fee: $34.99 monthly.
Telephone Service
Digital: Operational
Fee: $19.99 monthly
President & Chief Executive Officer: Cyrus Driver. Executive Vice President & Chief Operating Officer: Deborah Crawford. Executive Vice President & Chief Financial Officer: Don Pittman. Senior Vice President, Product Management: Angel Kandahari. Vice President & General Counsel: Daniel Wheeler. Vice President, Products & Marketing: Roberto Chang. Vice President, Human Resources: Wendy J. Lee. Vice President, Service Delivery & IT Strategy: Michael McDaniel. Vice President, RUS Projects: Aaron Peters.
Ownership: NTS Communications Inc.

WOODROW—South Plains Telephone Cooperative, 2425 Marshall St, Lubbock, TX 79415. Phone: 806-763-2301. E-mail: support@sptc.net. Web Site: http://www.sptc.net. Also serves Arnett, Cone, Cotton Center, Edmondson, Fieldton, McAdoo & Pettit. ICA: TX1047.
TV Market Ranking: Below 100 (Arnett, WOODROW); Outside TV Markets (Cotton Center, COTTON CENTER, Edmondson, Fieldton, McAdoo, Pettit).
Channel capacity: N.A. Channels available but not in use: N.A.
Basic Service
Subscribers: 221.
Fee: $70.00 monthly.
Chief Executive Officer & General Manager: Scotty Hart.
Ownership: Southern Plains Telephone Cooperative.

WOODROW—Suddenlink Communications. Now served by LUBBOCK, TX [TX0012]. ICA: TX0330.

WOODVILLE—NewWave Communications, One Montgomery Plaza, 4th Floor, Sikeston, MO 63801. Phones: 573-472-9500; 888-863-9928. Fax: 573-472-9518. E-mail: info@newwave.com. Web Site: http://www.newwavecom.com. ICA: TX0981.
TV Market Ranking: Outside TV Markets (WOODVILLE).
Channel capacity: N.A. Channels available but not in use: N.A.
Basic Service
Subscribers: 163.
Programming (received off-air): KBMT (ABC) Beaumont; KFDM (CBS, CW) Beaumont; KHOU (Bounce TV, CBS) Houston; KIAH (Antenna TV, CW) Houston; KRIV (FOX) Houston; KTRK-TV (ABC, Live Well Network) Houston; KTXH (Buzzr, MNT, Movies!) Houston; KUHT (PBS) Houston; KYTX (CBS, COZI TV, CW) Nacogdoches.
Programming (via satellite): Trinity Broadcasting Network (TBN).
Fee: $35.00 installation; $33.93 monthly.
Expanded Basic Service 1
Subscribers: N.A.
Programming (via satellite): A&E; AMC; Animal Planet; BET; CMT; CNN; Discovery Channel; ESPN; Food Network; Fox News Channel; FOX Sports Southwest; Freeform; FX; HGTV; History; Lifetime; MTV; Nickelodeon; QVC; Spike TV; Syfy; TBS; The Weather Channel; TLC; TNT; TV Land; USA Network; VH1; WGN America.
Fee: $27.50 monthly.
Digital Basic Service
Subscribers: N.A.
Programming (via satellite): Discovery Digital Networks; DMX Music; ESPN Classic; ESPNews; Fox Sports 1; FYI; Golf Channel; GSN; History; LMN; NBCSN; Nick Jr.; TeenNick.
Fee: $10.00 monthly.
Digital Pay Service 1
Pay Units: N.A.
Programming (via satellite): Cinemax (multiplexed); Flix; HBO (multiplexed); Showtime (multiplexed); Starz (multiplexed); Starz Encore (multiplexed); The Movie Channel (multiplexed).
Fee: $7.00 monthly (Starz), $9.00 monthly (Cinemax), $15.00 monthly (Showtime/TMC), $16.00 monthly (HBO) or $25.00 monthly (HBO/Cinemax).
Video-On-Demand: No
Pay-Per-View
iN DEMAND (delivered digitally); Playboy TV (delivered digitally).
Internet Service
Operational: Yes.
Fee: $39.95 installation; $36.99-$46.99 monthly; $6.00 modem lease; $39.95 modem purchase.
Telephone Service
Digital: Operational
Miles of Plant: 124.0 (coaxial); None (fiber optic). Homes passed: 6,234.
Regional General Manager: Jerry Smith.
Ownership: NewWave Communications LLC (MSO).

WORTHAM—Formerly served by Northland Cable Television. No longer in operation. ICA: TX0549.

WYLIE—Time Warner Cable. Now served by DALLAS, TX [TX0003]. ICA: TX0109.

YOAKUM—Time Warner Cable. Now served by GONZALES, TX [TX0209]. ICA: TX0883.

YORKTOWN—Formerly served by Almega Cable. No longer in operation. ICA: TX0349.

ZAPATA—Time Warner Cable. Now served by LAREDO, TX [TX0029]. ICA: TX0198.

ZAVALLA—Formerly served by Almega Cable. No longer in operation. ICA: TX0379.

ZION HILL—Formerly served by National Cable Inc. No longer in operation. ICA: TX0766.

UTAH

Total Systems: 27	Communities with Applications: 0
Total Communities Served: 202	Number of Basic Subscribers: 257,483
Franchises Not Yet Operating: 0	Number of Expanded Basic Subscribers: 2,950
Applications Pending: 0	Number of Pay Units: 284

Top 100 Markets Represented: Salt Lake City (48).

For a list of cable communities in this section, see the Cable Community Index located in the back of Cable Volume 2.
For explanation of terms used in cable system listings, see p. D-11.

BEAVER—South Central Communications. Now served by ENOCH, UT [UT0071]. ICA: UT0035.

BLANDING—Emery Telcom. Now served by EMERY, UT [UT0098]. ICA: UT0032.

BRIAN HEAD—South Central Communications. Now served by ENOCH, UT [UT0071]. ICA: UT0069.

BRIGHAM CITY—Comcast Cable. Now served by SALT LAKE CITY, UT [UT0001]. ICA: UT0013.

BRIGHAM CITY—Formerly served by Connected Lyfe. No longer in operation. ICA: UT5072.

CASTLE DALE—Emery Telcom. Now served by EMERY, UT [UT0098]. ICA: UT0017.

CEDAR CITY—Baja Broadband, 525 Junction Rd, Madison, WI 53717. Phones: 636-207-5100 (Corporate office); 516-803-2300 (Corporate office); 877-273-7626; 435-586-8334. Fax: 608-830-5519. E-mail: customersupport@tdstelecom.com. Web Site: http://www.hellotds.com. Also serves Iron County (portions). ICA: UT0015.
TV Market Ranking: Below 100 (CEDAR CITY, Iron County (portions)). Franchise award date: September 18, 1975. Franchise expiration date: N.A. Began: December 10, 1979.
Channel capacity: N.A. Channels available but not in use: N.A.
Digital Basic Service
Subscribers: 1,327.
Programming (via satellite): A&E HD; Altitude Sports & Entertainment; AXS TV; Bandamax; BBC America; Bloomberg Television; Bravo; CBS Sports Network; Cine Mexicano; Cinelatino; CMT; CNN en Espanol; Cooking Channel; De Pelicula; De Pelicula Clasico; Destination America; Discovery Kids Channel; Discovery Life Channel; Disney XD; DIY Network; DMX Music; ESPN Classic; ESPN Deportes; ESPN HD; ESPN2 HD; ESPNews; Food Network HD; FOX College Sports Central; FOX College Sports Pacific; Fox Deportes; Fox Sports 1; Fuse; FXM; FYI; Golf Channel; GolTV; GSN; HD Theater; HGTV HD; History en Espanol; History HD; History International; IFC; Investigation Discovery; Lifetime Movie Network HD; LMN; MTV Classic; MTV Hits; MTV Jams; MTV2; Nat Geo WILD; National Geographic Channel; National Geographic Channel HD; NBC Universo; NBCSN; Nick 2; Nick Jr.; Nicktoons; Outdoor Channel; OWN: Oprah Winfrey Network; RFD-TV; Science Channel; Sprout; Syfy HD; TBS HD; Teen-Nick; Telehit; TNT HD; Tr3s; Trinity Broadcasting Network (TBN); Universal HD; UP;
USA Network HD; Versus HD; VH1 Soul; ViendoMovies.
Fee: $36.50 monthly.
Digital Expanded Basic Service
Subscribers: N.A.
Programming (via satellite): A&E; Altitude Sports & Entertainment; AMC; Animal Planet; BYUtv; Cartoon Network; CMT; CNBC; CNN; Comedy Central; C-SPAN 2; Discovery Channel; Disney Channel; E! HD; ESPN; ESPN2; Food Network; Fox News Channel; Freeform; FX; Hallmark Channel; HGTV; History; HLN; INSP; Lifetime; MSNBC; MTV; Nickelodeon; Oxygen; Pop; QVC; Root Sports Rocky Mountain; Spike TV; Syfy; TBS; The Weather Channel; TLC; TNT; Travel Channel; truTV; Turner Classic Movies; TV Land; USA Network; VH1.
Fee: $58.98 monthly.
Digital Pay Service 1
Pay Units: N.A.
Programming (via satellite): Cinemax (multiplexed); Flix; HBO (multiplexed); HBO HD; Showtime (multiplexed); Showtime HD; Starz (multiplexed); Starz Encore (multiplexed); Starz HD; The Movie Channel (multiplexed); The Movie Channel HD.
Fee: $1.75 monthly (Encore), $6.75 monthly (Starz), $13.15 monthly (HBO, Showtime or TMC).
Video-On-Demand: No
Pay-Per-View
ESPN (delivered digitally); iN DEMAND (delivered digitally).
Internet Service
Operational: Yes.
Broadband Service: Charter Internet.
Fee: $55.95 monthly.
Telephone Service
Digital: Operational
Fee: $49.99 monthly
Miles of Plant: 78.0 (coaxial); None (fiber optic). Homes passed: 9,300.
Assistant Treasurer: Noel Hutton.
Ownership: TDS Telecom (MSO).

CEDAR CITY—Formerly served by Connected Lyfe. No longer in operation. ICA: UT5073.

CEDAR HILLS—Formerly served by Connected Lyfe. No longer in operation. ICA: UT5074.

CENTERFIELD—CentraCom, 35 South State St, PO Box 7, Fairview, UT 84629-0007. Phones: 800-427-8449; 435-427-3331. Fax: 435-427-3200. Web Site: http://centracom.com. Also serves Axtell & Gunnison. ICA: UT0037.
TV Market Ranking: Outside TV Markets (Axtell, CENTERFIELD, Gunnison). Franchise award date: N.A. Franchise expiration date: N.A. Began: January 1, 1984.
Channel capacity: N.A. Channels available but not in use: N.A.
Basic Service
Subscribers: 213. Commercial subscribers: 21.
Programming (received off-air): KUEN (ETV) Ogden.
Programming (via satellite): BYUtv.
Programming (via translator): KBYU-TV (PBS) Provo; KJZZ-TV (IND) Salt Lake City; KSL-TV (NBC) Salt Lake City; KSTU (Antenna TV, FOX) Salt Lake City; KTVX (ABC, MeTV) Salt Lake City; KUED (PBS) Salt Lake City; KUPX-TV (ION) Provo; KUTV (CBS, This TV) Salt Lake City.
Fee: $49.95 installation; $19.95 monthly; $1.50 converter.
Expanded Basic Service 1
Subscribers: 166.
Programming (via satellite): A&E; AMC; Animal Planet; Cartoon Network; CBS Sports Network; CMT; CNN; Comedy Central; Discovery Channel; Disney Channel; ESPN; ESPN2; Fox News Channel; FOX Sports Networks; Freeform; FX; Hallmark Channel; Lifetime; MTV; Nickelodeon; Outdoor Channel; QVC; Spike TV; TBS; The Weather Channel; TLC; TNT; TV Land; USA Network; VH1; WGN America.
Fee: $40.50 monthly.
Digital Basic Service
Subscribers: N.A.
Programming (via satellite): BBC America; Bravo; Cloo; Discovery Digital Networks; Disney XD; DMX Music; ESPN Classic; ESPN2; ESPNews; EVINE Live; Fox Sports 1; FSN Digital Atlantic; FSN Digital Central; FSN Digital Pacific; Fuse; FYI; Golf Channel; Great American Country; GSN; HGTV; History; History International; IFC; LMN; MBC America; National Geographic Channel; NBCSN; Nick Jr.; Syfy; TeenNick; The Word Network; Turner Classic Movies; WE tv.
Fee: $56.95 monthly.
Digital Pay Service 1
Pay Units: N.A.
Programming (via satellite): Cinemax (multiplexed); Flix; HBO (multiplexed); Showtime (multiplexed); Starz (multiplexed); Starz Encore (multiplexed); The Movie Channel (multiplexed).
Fee: $11.95 monthly (Cinemax, Showtime/TMC, or Starz/Encore), $12.95 monthly (HBO).
Video-On-Demand: No
Pay-Per-View
Special events (delivered digitally).
Internet Service
Operational: Yes.
Broadband Service: Precis Internet.
Fee: $39.95 monthly.
Telephone Service
Digital: Operational
Fee: $35.00 monthly
Miles of Plant: 350.0 (coaxial); 100.0 (fiber optic). Homes passed: 12,000.
President & General Manager: Eddie L. Cox. CATV Manager: George Lee. Chief Engineer: Kenny Roberts.
Ownership: Central Telcom Services LLC (MSO).

CENTERVILLE—Formerly served by Connected Lyfe. No longer in operation. ICA: UT5075.

CENTRAL—CentraCom, 35 South State St, PO Box 7, Fairview, UT 84629-0007. Phone: 800-427-8449. Web Site: http://centracom.com. Also serves Annabella, Austin, Elsinore, Glenwood, Mayfield & Monroe. ICA: UT0070.
TV Market Ranking: Outside TV Markets (Annabella, Austin, CENTRAL, Elsinore, Monroe, Glenwood, Mayfield).
Channel capacity: N.A. Channels available but not in use: N.A.
Basic Service
Subscribers: 281.
Fee: $40.95 installation; $19.95 monthly.
Expanded Basic Service 1
Subscribers: 242.
Fee: $40.50 monthly.
President & General Manager: Eddie L. Cox.
Ownership: Central Telcom Services LLC (MSO).

CLEVELAND—Emery Telcom. Now served by EMERY, UT [UT0098]. ICA: UT0055.

COALVILLE—Formerly served by Comcast Cable. No longer in operation. ICA: UT0049.

DELTA—CentraCom, 35 South State St, PO Box 7, Fairview, UT 84629-0007. Phones: 800-427-8449; 775-826-3544; 775-333-6626. Web Site: http://centracom.com. Also serves Hinckley & Lynndyl. ICA: UT0024.
TV Market Ranking: Outside TV Markets (DELTA). Franchise award date: September 9, 1981. Franchise expiration date: N.A. Began: June 1, 1983.
Channel capacity: N.A. Channels available but not in use: N.A.
Basic Service
Subscribers: 61.
Programming (via satellite): TBS; WGN America.
Programming (via translator): KBYU-TV (PBS) Provo; KJZZ-TV (IND) Salt Lake City; KSL-TV (NBC) Salt Lake City; KSTU (Antenna TV, FOX) Salt Lake City; KTVX (ABC, MeTV) Salt Lake City; KUCW (CW, Movies!, The Country Network) Ogden; KUED (PBS) Salt Lake City; KUEN (ETV) Ogden; KUTV (CBS, This TV) Salt Lake City.
Fee: $49.95 installation; $19.95 monthly; $1.50 converter.
Expanded Basic Service 1
Subscribers: 43.
Programming (via satellite): AMC; Animal Planet; Cartoon Network; CMT; CNN; Comedy Central; C-SPAN; C-SPAN 2; Dis-

Cable Systems—Utah

covery Channel; Disney Channel; ESPN; ESPN2; Freeform; Great American Country; Hallmark Channel; History; HLN; Lifetime; MTV; Nickelodeon; QVC; Root Sports Rocky Mountain; Spike TV; Syfy; The Weather Channel; TLC; TNT; Travel Channel; TV Land; USA Network; VH1.
Fee: $40.50 monthly.

Digital Basic Service
Subscribers: N.A.
Programming (via satellite): BBC America; Bloomberg Television; Bravo; CMT; Destination America; Discovery Kids Channel; Discovery Life Channel; Disney XD; DMX Music; ESPN Classic; ESPNews; Fox Sports 1; Fuse; FXM; FYI; Golf Channel; GSN; History International; IFC; Investigation Discovery; LMN; MTV Classic; MTV2; National Geographic Channel; NBCSN; Nick Jr.; Nicktoons; Outdoor Channel; OWN: Oprah Winfrey Network; Science Channel; TeenNick; Trinity Broadcasting Network (TBN).
Fee: $72.95 monthly.

Digital Pay Service 1
Pay Units: N.A.
Programming (via satellite): Cinemax (multiplexed); HBO (multiplexed); Showtime (multiplexed); Starz (multiplexed); Starz Encore (multiplexed); The Movie Channel (multiplexed).

Video-On-Demand: No
Internet Service
Operational: No.
Telephone Service
None
Miles of Plant: 25.0 (coaxial); None (fiber optic). Homes passed: 1,200.
President & General Manager: Eddie L. Cox.
Ownership: Central Telcom Services LLC (MSO).

DUCHESNE—Strata Networks, 211 East 200 North, PO Box 398, Roosevelt, UT 84066-0398. Phone: 435-622-5007. Fax: 435-646-2000. E-mail: company@stratanetworks.com. Web Site: http://www.stratanetworks.com. Also serves Maeser, Naples, Roosevelt, Uintah County & Vernal. ICA: UT0052.
TV Market Ranking: Outside TV Markets (DUCHESNE, Maeser, Roosevelt). Franchise award date: N.A. Franchise expiration date: N.A. Began: October 1, 1981.
Channel capacity: N.A. Channels available but not in use: N.A.

Digital Basic Service
Subscribers: 1,690.
Programming (via satellite): A&E; A&E HD; Altitude Sports & Entertainment; AMC; Animal Planet; Animal Planet HD; Antenna TV; BYUtv; Cartoon Network; CMT; CNBC; CNN; Comedy Central; Comedy Central HD; C-SPAN; C-SPAN 2; Discovery Channel; Discovery Channel HD; Disney Channel HD; E! HD; ESPN; ESPN HD; ESPN2; ESPN2 HD; Food Network; Food Network HD; Fox News Channel; Fox News HD; Freeform; Freeform HD; FX; FX HD; Hallmark Channel; HGTV; HGTV HD; History; History HD; HLN; HSN; INSP; Lifetime; Lifetime HD; MC; MSNBC; MTV; Nickelodeon; Oxygen; Oxygen HD; Pop; QVC; Root Sports Rocky Mountain; Spike TV; Spike TV HD; Syfy; Syfy HD; TBS; The Country Network; The Weather Channel; The Weather Channel HD; TheCoolTV; TLC; TLC HD; TNT; TNT HD; Travel Channel; Travel Channel HD; truTV; Turner Classic Movies; TV Land; USA Network; USA Network HD; VH1; Vme TV; WGN America; WGN America HD.
Programming (via translator): KBYU-TV (PBS) Provo; KJZZ-TV (IND) Salt Lake City;

KSL-TV (NBC) Salt Lake City; KSTU (Antenna TV, FOX) Salt Lake City; KTVX (ABC, MeTV) Salt Lake City; KUCW (CW, Movies!, The Country Network) Ogden; KUED (PBS) Salt Lake City; KUEN (ETV) Ogden; KUPX-TV (ION) Provo; KUTV (CBS, This TV) Salt Lake City.
Fee: $40.00 installation; $24.99 monthly.

Digital Expanded Basic Service
Subscribers: N.A.
Programming (via satellite): American Heroes Channel; BBC America; Bloomberg Television; Bravo; Bravo HD; CBS Sports Network; Centric; Chiller; CMT; Cooking Channel; Destination America; Destination America HD; Discovery Kids Channel; Discovery Life Channel; Disney XD; DIY Network; ESPNews; ESPNU; ESPNU HD; Fox Business Network; Fox Business Network HD; Fox Sports 1; Fuse; FXM; FYI; Golf Channel; Golf Channel HD; GSN; HD Theater; History International; Investigation Discovery; Lifetime Movie Network HD; LMN; MTV Classic; MTV Hits; MTV Jams; MTV2; Nat Geo WILD; Nat Geo WILD HD; National Geographic Channel; National Geographic Channel HD; NBCSN; NFL Network; NFL Network HD; Nick 2; Nick Jr.; Nicktoons; Outdoor Channel; Outdoor Channel HD; OWN: Oprah Winfrey Network; RFD-TV; Science Channel; Science HD; Sprout; Starz Encore (multiplexed); TeenNick; The Sportsman Channel; Tr3s; Trinity Broadcasting Network (TBN); Universal HD; Versus HD; VH1 Soul; Youtoo America.
Fee: $33.21 monthly.

Digital Expanded Basic Service 2
Subscribers: N.A.
Programming (via satellite): ESPN Classic; ESPNU; FOX College Sports Central; FOX College Sports Pacific; Fox Sports 2; NFL Network; NFL RedZone.
Fee: $4.99 monthly.

Digital Pay Service 1
Pay Units: N.A.
Programming (via satellite): Cinemax (multiplexed); HBO (multiplexed); Showtime (multiplexed); Starz (multiplexed); Starz Encore (multiplexed); The Movie Channel (multiplexed).
Fee: $9.99 monthly (Starz/Encore), $12.99 monthly (HBO, Cinemax or Showtime/TMC).

Video-On-Demand: No
Pay-Per-View
iN DEMAND (delivered digitally); Playboy TV (delivered digitally).
Internet Service
Operational: No, DSL.
Telephone Service
Analog: Operational
Miles of Plant: 18.0 (coaxial); None (fiber optic).
Chief Executive Officer & General Manager: Bruce Todd. Chief Operating Officer: Jeff Goodrich. Marketing Manager: Tyler Rasmussen.
Ownership: Strata Networks (MSO).

DUGWAY AFB—CentraCom, 35 South State St, PO Box 7, Fairview, UT 84629-0007. Phones: 800-427-8449; 877-427-2888; 435-831-4404. Fax: 435-427-3200. Web Site: http://centracom.com. ICA: UT0046.
TV Market Ranking: Outside TV Markets (DUGWAY AFB). Franchise award date: N.A. Franchise expiration date: N.A. Began: October 15, 1980.
Channel capacity: N.A. Channels available but not in use: N.A.

Communications Daily

Warren Communications News

Get the industry standard FREE —
For a no-obligation trial call 800-771-9202 or visit www.warren-news.com

Basic Service
Subscribers: 85.
Programming (received off-air): KBYU-TV (PBS) Provo; KJZZ-TV (IND) Salt Lake City; KPNZ (Estrella TV) Ogden; KSL-TV (NBC) Salt Lake City; KSTU (Antenna TV, FOX) Salt Lake City; KTVX (ABC, MeTV) Salt Lake City; KUED (PBS) Salt Lake City; KUPX-TV (ION) Provo; KUTV (CBS, This TV) Salt Lake City.
Programming (via satellite): C-SPAN; Hallmark Channel; INSP; NASA TV; QVC; The Weather Channel; WGN America.
Fee: $29.95 installation; $19.95 monthly.

Expanded Basic Service 1
Subscribers: 74.
Programming (via satellite): A&E; AMC; Animal Planet; BET; Cartoon Network; CMT; CNN; Comedy Central; Discovery Channel; DIY Network; E! HD; ESPN; ESPN2; Food Network; Fox News Channel; FOX Sports Networks; Freeform; FX; FXM; GSN; HGTV; History; HLN; Lifetime; MTV; Nickelodeon; Outdoor Channel; Oxygen; Spike TV; Syfy; TBS; TLC; TNT; truTV; Turner Classic Movies; TV Land; USA Network; VH1.
Fee: $40.50 monthly.

Pay Service 1
Pay Units: N.A.
Programming (via satellite): Cinemax; HBO (multiplexed); Showtime; Starz; Starz Encore; The Movie Channel.
Video-On-Demand: No
Internet Service
Operational: Yes.
Broadband Service: In-house.
Fee: $19.95 installation; $35.95 monthly.
Telephone Service
None
Miles of Plant: 7.0 (coaxial); None (fiber optic). Homes passed: 555.
President & General Manager: Eddie L. Cox. CATV Manager: George Lee. Chief Engineer: Kenny Roberts.
Ownership: Central Telcom Services LLC (MSO).

EAST CARBON—Emery Telcom. Now served by EMERY, UT [UT0098]. ICA: UT0050.

EMERY—Emery Telecom, 445 East Hwy 29, PO Box 629, Orangeville, UT 84537. Phones: 435-748-2223; 888-749-1090. Web Site: http://www.emerytelcom.com. Also serves Blanding, Castle Dale, Clawson, Cleveland, East Carbon, Elmo, Ferron, Green River, Helper, Huntington, Kenilworth, Moab, Monticello, Orangeville, Price, Sunnyside & Wellington. ICA: UT0098.
TV Market Ranking: Outside TV Markets (Castle Dale, Cleveland, East Carbon, Elmo, EMERY, Ferron, Green River, Helper, Huntington, Kenilworth, Moab, Monticello, Orangeville, Price, Sunnyside, Wellington). Franchise award date: N.A. Franchise expiration date: N.A. Began: November 1, 1981.
Channel capacity: 40 (operating 2-way). Channels available but not in use: N.A.

Basic Service
Subscribers: 3,534. Commercial subscribers: 940.
Programming (received off-air): KJZZ-TV (IND) Salt Lake City; KPNZ (Estrella TV) Ogden; KUEN (ETV) Ogden; KUPX-TV (ION) Provo; KUWB-LD Bloomington.
Programming (via translator): KBYU-TV (PBS) Provo; KSL-TV (NBC) Salt Lake City; KSTU (Antenna TV, FOX) Salt Lake City; KTVX (ABC, MeTV) Salt Lake City; KUED (PBS) Salt Lake City; KUTV (CBS, This TV) Salt Lake City.
Fee: $29.95 installation; $14.95 monthly.

Expanded Basic Service 1
Subscribers: N.A.
Programming (via satellite): A&E; AMC; Animal Planet; Cartoon Network; CMT; CNBC; CNN; Comedy Central; Discovery Channel; Disney Channel; ESPN; Fox News Channel; Freeform; FX; Hallmark Channel; Lifetime; Nickelodeon; QVC; Root Sports Rocky Mountain; Spike TV; TBS; The Weather Channel; TLC; TNT; USA Network; WGN America.
Fee: $28.25 monthly.

Digital Basic Service
Subscribers: N.A.
Programming (via satellite): BBC America; Bravo; Discovery Digital Networks; Disney XD; DMX Music; ESPN Classic; ESPN2; ESPNews; EVINE Live; Fox Sports 1; FSN Digital Atlantic; FSN Digital Central; FSN Digital Pacific; Fuse; FYI; Golf Channel; Great American Country; GSN; HGTV; History; History International; IFC; LMN; MBC America; National Geographic Channel; NBCSN; Syfy; The Word Network; Turner Classic Movies; WE tv.
Fee: $5.55 monthly.

Digital Pay Service 1
Pay Units: N.A.
Programming (via satellite): Cinemax (multiplexed); Flix; HBO (multiplexed); Showtime (multiplexed); Starz (multiplexed); Starz Encore (multiplexed); The Movie Channel (multiplexed).
Fee: $12.95 monthly (each).

Video-On-Demand: No
Pay-Per-View
iN DEMAND (delivered digitally); Playboy TV (delivered digitally).
Internet Service
Operational: No.
Telephone Service
None
Miles of Plant: 11.0 (coaxial); None (fiber optic).
General Manager: Brock Johansen. Assistant General Manager: Jared Anderson. Chief Financial Officer: Darren Woolsey.
Ownership: Emery Telcom (MSO).

ENOCH—South Central Communications, 45 North 100 West, PO Box 555, Escalante, UT 84726-0555. Phones: 888-826-4211; 435-826-4211. Fax: 435-826-4900. Web Site: http://www.socen.com. Also serves Beaver, Brian Head, Minersville, Paragonah & Parowan. ICA: UT0071.
TV Market Ranking: Below 100 (ENOCH, Paragonah, Brian Head, Parowan); Out-

2017 Edition
D-791

Utah—Cable Systems

side TV Markets (Beaver, Minersville). Franchise award date: March 1, 1988. Franchise expiration date: N.A. Began: September 15, 1988.
Channel capacity: N.A. Channels available but not in use: N.A.

Basic Service
Subscribers: 412. Commercial subscribers: 184.
Programming (received off-air): KCSG (MeTV, My Family TV) Cedar City.
Programming (via satellite): C-SPAN; C-SPAN 2; Pop; QVC.
Programming (via translator): KBYU-TV (PBS) Provo; KJZZ-TV (IND) Salt Lake City; KSL-TV (NBC) Salt Lake City; KSTU (Antenna TV, FOX) Salt Lake City; KTVX (ABC, MeTV) Salt Lake City; KUCW (CW, Movies!, The Country Network) Ogden; KUED (PBS) Salt Lake City; KUTV (CBS, This TV) Salt Lake City.
Fee: $45.00 installation; $52.95 monthly.

Expanded Basic Service 1
Subscribers: N.A.
Programming (via satellite): A&E; AMC; Animal Planet; Cartoon Network; CMT; CNBC; CNN; Comedy Central; Discovery Channel; Disney Channel; E! HD; ESPN; ESPN2; Food Network; Fox News Channel; Fox Sports 1; Freeform; FX; Great American Country; Hallmark Channel; HGTV; History; HLN; INSP; Lifetime; MSNBC; MTV; NBCSN; Nickelodeon; Outdoor Channel; Root Sports Rocky Mountain; Spike TV; Syfy; TBS; The Weather Channel; TLC; TNT; Travel Channel; Turner Classic Movies; TV Land; USA Network; VH1; WGN America.
Fee: $36.45 monthly.

Pay Service 1
Pay Units: N.A.
Programming (via satellite): Cinemax; HBO.
Fee: $11.00 monthly (each).

Video-On-Demand: No

Pay-Per-View
iN DEMAND (delivered digitally); Playboy TV (delivered digitally); ESPN Now (delivered digitally); Fresh (delivered digitally).

Internet Service
Operational: Yes, DSL.
Fee: $29.95 monthly.

Telephone Service
Analog: Operational
Miles of Plant: 74.0 (coaxial); None (fiber optic). Homes passed: 1,000.
Chief Executive Officer: Michael R. East. General Manager & Chief Technician: Greg Barton.
Ownership: South Central Communications (MSO).

ENTERPRISE—South Central Communications, 45 North 100 West, PO Box 555, Escalante, UT 84726-0555. Phones: 888-826-4211; 435-826-4211. Fax: 435-826-4900. Web Site: http://www.socen.com. ICA: UT0056.
TV Market Ranking: Below 100 (ENTERPRISE). Franchise award date: November 13, 1986. Franchise expiration date: N.A. Began: September 21, 1987.
Channel capacity: N.A. Channels available but not in use: N.A.

Basic Service
Subscribers: 41.
Programming (via satellite): A&E; AMC; Animal Planet; CMT; CNN; C-SPAN; Discovery Channel; Disney Channel; E! HD; ESPN; ESPN2; Freeform; HGTV; History; HLN; KTLA (Antenna TV, CW, This TV) Los Angeles; Nickelodeon; Outdoor Channel; QVC; Root Sports Rocky Mountain; Spike TV; Syfy; TBS; The Weather Channel; TLC; TNT; Turner Classic Movies; TV Land; USA Network; VH1; WGN America.
Programming (via translator): KBYU-TV (PBS) Provo; KJZZ-TV (IND) Salt Lake City; KSL-TV (NBC) Salt Lake City; KSTU (Antenna TV, FOX) Salt Lake City; KTVX (ABC, MeTV) Salt Lake City; KUCW (CW, Movies!, The Country Network) Ogden; KUED (PBS) Salt Lake City; KUEN (ETV) Ogden; KUTV (CBS, This TV) Salt Lake City.
Fee: $45.00 installation; $44.95 monthly.

Pay Service 1
Pay Units: N.A.
Programming (via satellite): HBO; Showtime.
Fee: $21.50 installation; $11.00 monthly (each).

Video-On-Demand: No

Internet Service
Operational: No, DSL & dial-up.

Telephone Service
Analog: Operational
Miles of Plant: 8.0 (coaxial); None (fiber optic). Homes passed: 375.
Chief Executive Officer: Michael R. East. General Manager & Chief Technician: Greg Barton.
Ownership: South Central Communications (MSO).

EPHRAIM—CentraCom, 35 South State St, PO Box 7, Fairview, UT 84629-0007. Phone: 800-427-8449. Web Site: http://centracom.com. Also serves Manti. ICA: UT0022.
TV Market Ranking: Outside TV Markets (EPHRAIM, Manti).
Channel capacity: N.A. Channels available but not in use: N.A.

Basic Service
Subscribers: 370.
Fee: $49.95 installation; $19.95 monthly.

Expanded Basic Service 1
Subscribers: 293.
Fee: $40.50 monthly.
President & General Manager: Eddie L. Cox.
Ownership: Central Telcom Services LLC (MSO).

ESCALANTE—South Central Communications. Now served by PANGUITCH, UT [UT0043]. ICA: UT0083.

EUREKA—CentraCom. Now served by SANTAQUIN, UT [UT0041]. ICA: UT0057.

FARMINGTON—Comcast Cable. Now served by SALT LAKE CITY, UT [UT0001]. ICA: UT0004.

FERRON—Emery Telcom. Now served by EMERY, UT [UT0098]. ICA: UT0054.

FIELDING—Comcast Cable. Now served by TREMONTON, UT [UT0096]. ICA: UT0051.

FILLMORE—CentraCom, 35 South State St, PO Box 7, Fairview, UT 84629-0007. Phone: 800-427-8449. Web Site: http://centracom.com. Also serves Holden & Scipio. ICA: UT0036.
TV Market Ranking: Outside TV Markets (FILLMORE, Holden). Franchise award date: N.A. Franchise expiration date: N.A. Began: March 1, 1985.
Channel capacity: 40 (operating 2-way). Channels available but not in use: N.A.

Basic Service
Subscribers: 92.
Programming (received off-air): KBYU-TV (PBS) Provo; KPNZ (Estrella TV) Ogden; KUCW (CW, Movies!, The Country Network) Ogden; KUEN (ETV) Ogden; KUPX-TV (ION) Provo.
Programming (via translator): KJZZ-TV (IND) Salt Lake City; KSL-TV (NBC) Salt Lake City; KSTU (Antenna TV, FOX) Salt Lake City; KTVX (ABC, MeTV) Salt Lake City; KUED (PBS) Salt Lake City; KUTV (CBS, This TV) Salt Lake City.
Fee: $49.95 installation; $19.95 monthly; $1.50 converter.

Expanded Basic Service 1
Subscribers: 69.
Programming (via satellite): A&E; AMC; Animal Planet; CMT; CNN; Comedy Central; Discovery Channel; Disney Channel; ESPN; Fox News Channel; Freeform; FX; Lifetime; Nickelodeon; QVC; Root Sports Rocky Mountain; Spike TV; TBS; The Weather Channel; TLC; TNT; USA Network; WGN America.
Fee: $40.50 monthly.

Digital Basic Service
Subscribers: N.A.
Programming (via satellite): BBC America; Bravo; Discovery Digital Networks; Disney XD; DMX Music; ESPN Classic; ESPN2; ESPNews; EVINE Live; FOX College Sports Central; FOX College Sports Pacific; Fox Sports 1; Fuse; FYI; Golf Channel; Great American Country; GSN; HGTV; History; History International; IFC; LMN; National Geographic Channel; NBCSN; The Word Network; Turner Classic Movies; WE tv.
Fee: $15.95 monthly.

Digital Pay Service 1
Pay Units: N.A.
Programming (via satellite): Cinemax (multiplexed); Flix; HBO (multiplexed); Showtime (multiplexed); Starz (multiplexed); Starz Encore; The Movie Channel (multiplexed).
Fee: $12.95 monthly (HBO, Cinemax, Showtime/TMC/Flix, or Starz/Encore).

Video-On-Demand: No

Pay-Per-View
iN DEMAND (delivered digitally); Playboy TV (delivered digitally).

Internet Service
Operational: Yes.
Fee: $29.95 monthly.

Telephone Service
None
Miles of Plant: 10.0 (coaxial); None (fiber optic). Homes passed: 795.
President & General Manager: Eddie L. Cox.
Ownership: Central Telcom Services LLC (MSO).

GLENWOOD—CentraCom. Now served by CENTRAL, UT [UT0070]. ICA: UT0084.

GOSHEN—CentraCom. Now served by SANTAQUIN, UT [UT0041]. ICA: UT0063.

GREEN RIVER—Emery Telcom. Now served by EMERY, UT [UT0098]. ICA: UT0059.

HEBER CITY—Comcast Cable. Now served by SALT LAKE CITY, UT [UT0001]. ICA: UT0018.

HUNTSVILLE—HLS Communications, 5500 West 10400 North, Ellwood, UT 84337. Phone: 435-257-5280. Also serves Eden. ICA: UT0064.
TV Market Ranking: 48 (Eden, HUNTSVILLE). Franchise award date: N.A. Franchise expiration date: N.A. Began: October 1, 1986.
Channel capacity: N.A. Channels available but not in use: N.A.

Basic Service
Subscribers: 39.
Programming (received off-air): KBYU-TV (PBS) Provo; KJZZ-TV (IND) Salt Lake City; KSL-TV (NBC) Salt Lake City; KSTU (Antenna TV, FOX) Salt Lake City; KTVX (ABC, MeTV) Salt Lake City; KUCW (CW, Movies!, The Country Network) Ogden; KUED (PBS) Salt Lake City; KUTV (CBS, This TV) Salt Lake City.
Programming (via satellite): A&E; AMC; Animal Planet; CNBC; CNN; Cooking Channel; C-SPAN; Discovery Channel; Disney Channel; DIY Network; ESPN; ESPN2; EVINE Live; Freeform; Great American Country; HGTV; History; HLN; Outdoor Channel; RFD-TV; Spike TV; Syfy; TBS; TLC; TNT; Travel Channel; WGN America.
Fee: $25.00 installation; $26.95 monthly.

Pay Service 1
Pay Units: N.A.
Programming (via satellite): HBO.
Fee: $14.00 monthly.

Internet Service
Operational: No.

Telephone Service
None
Miles of Plant: 3.0 (coaxial); None (fiber optic).
General Manager: Steve Haramoto. Chief Technician: Jeekenan Haramoto.
Ownership: Steven Haramoto.

HURRICANE—Formerly served by Charter Communications. Now served by Baja Broadband, ST. GEORGE, UT [UT0007]. ICA: UT0027.

KAMAS—All West Communications. This cable system has converted to IPTV. See OAKLEY, UT [UT5034]. ICA: UT0053.

KANAB—South Central Communications. Now served by PANGUITCH, UT [UT0043]. ICA: UT0033.

KANARRAVILLE—Formerly served by South Central Communications. No longer in operation. ICA: UT0067.

LAYTON—Formerly served by Connected Lyfe. No longer in operation. ICA: UT5076.

LINDON—Formerly served by Connected Lyfe. No longer in operation. ICA: UT5077.

LINDON—Formerly served by Nuvont Communications. IPTV service no longer in operation. ICA: UT5028.

LOGAN—Comcast Cable. Now served by SALT LAKE CITY, UT [UT0001]. ICA: UT0006.

LYMAN—South Central Communications, 45 North 100 West, PO Box 555, Escalante, UT 84726-0555. Phones: 888-826-4211; 435-826-4211. Fax: 435-826-4900. Web Site: http://www.socen.com. Also serves Bicknell & Loa. ICA: UT0073.
TV Market Ranking: Outside TV Markets (Bicknell, Loa, LYMAN). Franchise award date: N.A. Franchise expiration date: N.A. Began: May 1, 1984.
Channel capacity: N.A. Channels available but not in use: N.A.

Basic Service
Subscribers: 43.
Programming (via satellite): A&E; AMC; Animal Planet; Cartoon Network; CMT; CNBC; CNN; CW PLUS; Discovery Channel; Disney

Cable Systems—Utah

FULLY SEARCHABLE • CONTINUOUSLY UPDATED • DISCOUNT RATES FOR PRINT PURCHASERS

For more information call **800-771-9202** or visit **www.warren-news.com**

Channel; E! HD; ESPN; ESPN2; Fox News Channel; Freeform; History; HLN; INSP; Lifetime; Nickelodeon; Outdoor Channel; QVC; RFD-TV; Root Sports Rocky Mountain; Spike TV; TBS; TLC; TNT; Travel Channel; TV Land; USA Network; WGN America. Programming (via translator): KBYU-TV (PBS) Provo; KJZZ-TV (IND) Salt Lake City; KSL-TV (NBC) Salt Lake City; KSTU (Antenna TV, FOX) Salt Lake City; KTVX (ABC, MeTV) Salt Lake City; KUED (PBS) Salt Lake City; KUEN (ETV) Ogden; KUTV (CBS, This TV) Salt Lake City.
Fee: $45.00 installation; $52.95 monthly.
Pay Service 1
Pay Units: N.A.
Programming (via satellite): Cinemax; HBO.
Fee: $11.00 monthly (each).
Video-On-Demand: No
Internet Service
Operational: No, DSL & dial-up.
Telephone Service
Analog: Operational
Miles of Plant: 24.0 (coaxial); None (fiber optic). Homes passed: 480.
Chief Executive Officer: Michael R. East. General Manager & Chief Technician: Greg Barton.
Ownership: South Central Communications (MSO).

MANILA—Formerly served by Myvocom. No longer in operation. ICA: UT0058.

MAYFIELD—CentraCom. Now served by CENTRAL, UT [UT0070]. ICA: UT0088.

MIDVALE—Formerly served by Connected Lyfe. No longer in operation. ICA: UT5078.

MIDVALE—Formerly served by Nuvont Communications. IPTV service no longer in operation. ICA: UT5023.

MILFORD—South Central Communications, 45 North 100 West, PO Box 555, Escalante, UT 84726-0555. Phones: 888-826-4211; 435-826-4211. Fax: 435-826-4900. Web Site: http://www.socen.com. ICA: UT0074.
TV Market Ranking: Outside TV Markets (MILFORD). Franchise award date: N.A. Franchise expiration date: N.A. Began: March 1, 1983.
Channel capacity: 40 (operating 2-way). Channels available but not in use: N.A.
Basic Service
Subscribers: 22.
Programming (received off-air): KBYU-TV (PBS) Provo; KPNZ (Estrella TV) Ogden; KUCW (CW, Movies!, The Country Network) Ogden; KUEN (ETV) Ogden; KUPX-TV (ION) Provo.
Programming (via translator): KJZZ-TV (IND) Salt Lake City; KSL-TV (NBC) Salt Lake City; KSTU (Antenna TV, FOX) Salt Lake City; KTVX (ABC, MeTV) Salt Lake City; KUED (PBS) Salt Lake City; KUTV (CBS, This TV) Salt Lake City.
Fee: $49.95 installation; $44.95 monthly.
Expanded Basic Service 1
Subscribers: N.A.
Programming (via satellite): A&E; AMC; Animal Planet; CMT; CNN; Comedy Central; Discovery Channel; Disney Channel; ESPN; Fox News Channel; Freeform; FX; Lifetime; Nickelodeon; QVC; Root Sports Rocky Mountain; Spike TV; TBS; The Weather Channel; TLC; TNT; USA Network; WGN America.
Fee: $25.00 monthly.

Digital Basic Service
Subscribers: N.A.
Programming (via satellite): BBC America; Bravo; Discovery Digital Networks; Disney XD; DMX Music; ESPN Classic; ESPN2; ESPNews; EVINE Live; FOX College Sports Central; FOX College Sports Pacific; Fox Sports 1; Fuse; FYI; Golf Channel; Great American Country; GSN; HGTV; History; History International; IFC; LMN; National Geographic Channel; NBCSN; The Word Network; Turner Classic Movies; WE tv.
Fee: $15.95 monthly.
Digital Pay Service 1
Pay Units: N.A.
Programming (via satellite): Cinemax (multiplexed); Flix; HBO (multiplexed); Showtime (multiplexed); Starz (multiplexed); Starz Encore (multiplexed); The Movie Channel (multiplexed).
Fee: $12.95 monthly (HBO, Cinemax, Showtime/TMC/Flix, or Starz/Encore).
Video-On-Demand: No
Pay-Per-View
iN DEMAND (delivered digitally); Playboy TV (delivered digitally).
Internet Service
Operational: Yes.
Fee: $29.95 monthly.
Telephone Service
Analog: Operational
Miles of Plant: 7.0 (coaxial); None (fiber optic). Homes passed: 394.
Chief Executive Officer: Michael R. East. Operations Director: Kerry Alvey. General Manager: Jeff Bushnell.
Ownership: South Central Communications (MSO).

MINERSVILLE—South Central Communications. Now served by ENOCH, UT [UT0071]. ICA: UT0062.

MOAB—Emery Telcom. Now served by EMERY, UT [UT0098], UT. ICA: UT0016.

MONA—CentraCom. Now served by SANTAQUIN, UT [UT0041]. ICA: UT0065.

MONTICELLO—Emery Telcom. Now served by EMERY, UT [UT0098]. ICA: UT0044.

MORGAN CITY—Formerly served by Comcast Cable. No longer in operation. ICA: UT0048.

MORGAN COUNTY (portions)—Formerly served by Comcast Cable. No longer in operation. ICA: UT0094.

MORONI—CentraCom, 35 South State St, PO Box 7, Fairview, UT 84629-0007. Phone: 800-427-8449. Web Site: http://centracom.com. Also serves Fountain Green. ICA: UT0042.
TV Market Ranking: Outside TV Markets (Fountain Green, MORONI).
Channel capacity: N.A. Channels available but not in use: N.A.
Basic Service
Subscribers: 164.
Fee: $49.95 installation; $19.95 monthly.
Expanded Basic Service 1
Subscribers: 144.
Fee: $47.00 monthly.
Miles of Plant: 31.0 (coaxial); 32.0 (fiber optic). Homes passed: 878.
President & General Manager: Eddie L. Cox.
Ownership: Central Telcom Services LLC (MSO).

MOUNT PLEASANT—CentraCom, 35 South State St, PO Box 7, Fairview, UT 84629-0007. Phone: 800-427-8449. Web Site: http://centracom.com. Also serves Fairview, Sanpete County (portions) & Spring City. ICA: UT0023.
TV Market Ranking: Below 100 (Sanpete County (portions)); Outside TV Markets (Fairview, MOUNT PLEASANT, Spring City).
Channel capacity: N.A. Channels available but not in use: N.A.
Basic Service
Subscribers: 438.
Fee: $49.95 installation; $19.95 monthly.
Expanded Basic Service 1
Subscribers: 334.
Fee: $40.50 monthly.
President & General Manager: Eddie L. Cox.
Ownership: Central Telcom Services LLC (MSO).

MURRAY—Formerly served by Connected Lyfe. No longer in operation. ICA: UT5079.

MURRAY—Formerly served by Nuvont Communications. IPTV service no longer in operation. ICA: UT5024.

NEPHI—CentraCom, 35 South State St, PO Box 7, Fairview, UT 84629-0007. Phone: 800-427-8449. Web Site: http://centracom.com. ICA: UT0028.
TV Market Ranking: Outside TV Markets (NEPHI). Franchise award date: N.A. Franchise expiration date: N.A. Began: January 1, 1981.
Channel capacity: N.A. Channels available but not in use: N.A.
Basic Service
Subscribers: 232.
Programming (received off-air): KBYU-TV (PBS) Provo; KJZZ-TV (IND) Salt Lake City; KPNZ (Estrella TV) Ogden; KSL-TV (NBC) Salt Lake City; KSTU (Antenna TV, FOX) Salt Lake City; KTMW (Grit, IND, Laff, Retro TV) Salt Lake City; KTVX (ABC, MeTV) Salt Lake City; KUCW (CW, Movies!, The Country Network) Ogden; KUED (PBS) Salt Lake City; KUEN (ETV) Ogden; KUPX-TV (ION) Provo; KUTH-DT (getTV, UNV) Provo; KUTV (CBS, This TV) Salt Lake City.
Programming (via satellite): BYUtv; C-SPAN; C-SPAN 2; Discovery Channel; FX; Lifetime; QVC; TBS.
Fee: $50.00 installation; $19.95 monthly.
Expanded Basic Service 1
Subscribers: 222.
Programming (via satellite): A&E; AMC; Animal Planet; BET; Cartoon Network; CMT; CNBC; CNN; Comedy Central; Disney Channel; E! HD; ESPN; ESPN2; Food Network; Fox News Channel; FOX Sports Networks; Freeform; Golf Channel; Great American Country; GSN; Hallmark Channel; HGTV; History; HLN; INSP; MSNBC; MTV; NBCSN; Nickelodeon; Oxygen; Spike TV; Telemundo; The Weather Channel; TLC; TNT; Travel Channel; truTV; TV Land; Univision; USA Network; VH1.
Fee: $40.50 monthly.

Digital Basic Service
Subscribers: N.A.
Programming (via satellite): BBC America; Bravo; Cooking Channel; Discovery Digital Networks; DIY Network; DMX Music; ESPN; ESPN Classic; ESPN2; ESPNews; EVINE Live; HITS (Headend In The Sky); IFC; International Television (ITV); MC; National Geographic Channel; NBA TV; Nick Jr.; Syfy; The Word Network; Trinity Broadcasting Network (TBN); Turner Classic Movies; TV Land; WE tv; Weatherscan.
Fee: $14.95 monthly.
Digital Expanded Basic Service
Subscribers: N.A.
Programming (via satellite): Bloomberg Television; Discovery Life Channel; Disney XD; Fox Sports 1; FSN Digital Atlantic; FSN Digital Central; FSN Digital Pacific; Fuse; FXM; FYI; History International; LMN; Nicktoons; Outdoor Channel; Ovation; Sundance TV; TeenNick.
Fee: $5.00 monthly.
Pay Service 1
Pay Units: N.A.
Programming (via satellite): HBO; Showtime.
Fee: $13.99 monthly (Showtime), $14.99 monthly (HBO).
Digital Pay Service 1
Pay Units: N.A.
Programming (via satellite): Cinemax (multiplexed); Flix; HBO (multiplexed); Showtime (multiplexed); Starz (multiplexed); The Movie Channel (multiplexed).
Fee: $16.95 monthly (HBO, Cinemax, Starz, Showtime, or TMC).
Video-On-Demand: No
Pay-Per-View
iN DEMAND (delivered digitally); Fresh (delivered digitally); Shorteez (delivered digitally); Playboy TV (delivered digitally); ESPN Now (delivered digitally); Sports PPV (delivered digitally); NBA League Pass (delivered digitally); Urban Xtra (delivered digitally).
Internet Service
Operational: Yes.
Telephone Service
None
President & General Manager: Eddie L. Cox.
Ownership: Central Telcom Services LLC (MSO).

NEW HARMONY—Formerly served by South Central Communications. No longer in operation. ICA: UT0068.

OAKLEY—All West Communications. Formerly served by Kamas, UT [UT0053]. This cable system has converted to IPTV, 50 West 100 North, Kamas, UT 84036. Phones: 866-255-9378; 435-783-4361. Fax: 435-783-4928. E-mail: questions@allwest.net. Web Site: http://www.allwest.net. Also serves Coalville, Deer Mountain, Echo, Evanston, Francis, Heber (portions), Henefer, Hoytsville, Kamas, Marion, Peoa, Promontory, Randolph Twp., Timber Lakes, Tuhaye, Wanship, Woodland & Woodruff, UT; Cokeville & Uinta County (portions), WY. ICA: UT5034.

Utah—Cable Systems

TV Market Ranking: 48 (MARION, OAKLEY, PEOA); Below 100 (FRANCIS, KAMAS); Outside TV Markets (COKEVILLE).
Channel capacity: N.A. Channels available but not in use: N.A.
Local Choice
Subscribers: 2,214.
Fee: $27.95 monthly. 34 channels - 26 in SD & 8 in HD. $10.95 HD equipment fee for HD channels.
Basic Choice
Subscribers: N.A.
Fee: $57.95 monthly. 143 channels - 95 in SD & 48 in HD plus 47 music channels. $10.95 HD equipment fee for HD channels.
Expanded Choice
Subscribers: N.A.
Fee: $63.85 monthly. 172 channels - 117 in SD & 55 in HD plus 47 music channels. $10.95 HD equipment fee for HD channels.
Total Choice
Subscribers: N.A.
Fee: $105.95 monthly. Includes all 172 channels, 47 music channels & all Cinemax, Showtime, Encore, Starz & HBO channels. $10.95 HD equipment fee for HD channels.
Cinemax Choice
Subscribers: N.A.
Fee: $12.95 monthly. 8 channels.
Showtime Choice
Subscribers: N.A.
Fee: $12.95 monthly. 9 channels including Showtime, TMC & Flix. $10.95 HD equipment fee for HD channels.
Starz/Encore Choice
Subscribers: N.A.
Fee: $14.95 monthly. 14 channels. $10.95 HD equipment fee for HD channels.
HBO Choice
Subscribers: N.A.
Fee: $14.95 monthly. 7 channels.
Video-On-Demand: Yes
Internet Service
Operational: Yes.
Fee: $39.95-$109.95 monthly.
Telephone Service
Digital: Operational
Fee: $16.50-$22.00 monthly
President: Matthew Weller.
Ownership: All West Communications.

Ogden—Comcast Cable. Now served by SALT LAKE CITY, UT [UT0001]. ICA: UT0008.

OREM—Formerly served by Connected Lyfe. No longer in operation. ICA: UT5080.

OREM—Formerly served by Nuvont Communications. IPTV service no longer in operation. ICA: UT5025.

PANGUITCH—South Central Communications, 45 North 100 West, PO Box 555, Escalante, UT 84726-0555. Phones: 888-826-4211; 435-826-4211. Fax: 435-826-4900. Web Site: http://www.socen.com. Also serves Fredonia, AZ; Bryce, Circleville, Escalante, Kanab & Tropic, UT. ICA: UT0043.
TV Market Ranking: Outside TV Markets (Bryce, Circleville, Fredonia, PANGUITCH, Tropic, Escalante, Kanab). Franchise award date: N.A. Franchise expiration date: N.A. Began: February 22, 1982.
Channel capacity: N.A. Channels available but not in use: N.A.
Basic Service
Subscribers: 457.
Programming (via satellite): A&E; AMC; Animal Planet; Cartoon Network; CMT; CNN; Comedy Central; Discovery Channel; Disney Channel; E! HD; ESPN; ESPN2; Fox News Channel; Freeform; Hallmark Channel; HGTV; History; Lifetime; MTV; Nickelodeon; Outdoor Channel; QVC; Root Sports Rocky Mountain; Spike TV; Syfy; TBS; TLC; TNT; Turner Classic Movies; TV Land; USA Network; VH1; WGN America.
Programming (via translator): KBYU-TV (PBS) Provo; KJZZ-TV (IND) Salt Lake City; KSL-TV (NBC) Salt Lake City; KSTU (Antenna TV, FOX) Salt Lake City; KTVX (ABC, MeTV) Salt Lake City; KUCW (CW, Movies!, The Country Network) Ogden; KUED (PBS) Salt Lake City; KUTV (CBS, This TV) Salt Lake City.
Fee: $45.00 installation; $52.95 monthly.
Pay Service 1
Pay Units: N.A.
Programming (via satellite): Cinemax; HBO.
Fee: $11.00 monthly (each).
Video-On-Demand: No
Internet Service
Operational: No, DSL & dial-up.
Telephone Service
Analog: Operational
Miles of Plant: 16.0 (coaxial); None (fiber optic). Homes passed: 1,300.
Chief Executive Officer: Michael R. East. General Manager & Chief Technician: Greg Barton.
Ownership: South Central Communications (MSO).

PANGUITCH (portions)—South Central Communications. Now served by PANGUITCH, UT [UT0043]. ICA: UT0089.

PARAGONAH—South Central Communications. Now served by ENOCH, UT [UT0071]. ICA: UT0085.

PARK CITY—Comcast Cable. Now served by SALT LAKE CITY, UT [UT0001]. ICA: UT0010.

PAROWAN—South Central Communications. Now served by ENOCH, UT [UT0071]. ICA: UT0034.

PAYSON—Formerly served by Connected Lyfe. No longer in operation. ICA: UT5081.

PAYSON (town)—Formerly served by Nuvont Communications. IPTV service no longer in operation. ICA: UT5026.

PERRY—Formerly served by Connected Lyfe. No longer in operation. ICA: UT5082.

PLEASANT GROVE—Comcast Cable. Now served by SALT LAKE CITY, UT [UT0001]. ICA: UT0097.

PRICE—Emery Telcom. Now served by EMERY, UT [UT0098]. ICA: UT0011.

PROVO—Comcast Cable. Now served by SALT LAKE CITY, UT [UT0001]. ICA: UT0005.

PROVO—Formerly served by Nuvont Communications. IPTV service no longer in operation. ICA: UT5027.

PROVO—Formerly served by Provo Cable. No longer in operation. ICA: UT0086.

RANDOLPH TWP.—All West Communications. This cable system has converted to IPTV. See OAKLEY, UT [UT5034]. ICA: UT0066.

RICHFIELD—CentraCom, 35 South State St, Po Box 7, Fairview, UT 84629-0007. Phone: 800-427-8449. Web Site: http://centracom.com. ICA: UT0020.
TV Market Ranking: Outside TV Markets (RICHFIELD).
Channel capacity: N.A. Channels available but not in use: N.A.
Basic Service
Subscribers: 469.
Fee: $49.95 installation; $19.95 monthly.
Expanded Basic Service 1
Subscribers: 388.
Fee: $40.50 monthly.
President & General Manager: Eddie L. Cox.
Ownership: Central Telcom Services LLC (MSO).

RICHMOND—Comcast Cable. Now served by SALT LAKE CITY, UT [UT0001]. ICA: UT0021.

RIVERDALE—Comcast Cable. Now served by SALT LAKE CITY, UT [UT0001]. ICA: UT0075.

RIVERTON—Formerly served by Connected Lyfe. No longer in operation. ICA: UT5083.

ROCKVILLE—Formerly served by Baja Broadband. No longer in operation. ICA: UT0077.

ROOSEVELT—Strata Networks. Now served by DUCHESNE, UT [UT0052]. ICA: UT0030.

SALEM—Comcast Cable. Now served by PROVO, UT [UT0005]. ICA: UT0009.

SALINA—CentraCom, 35 South State St, PO Box 7, Fairview, UT 84629-0007. Phone: 800-427-8449. Web Site: http://centracom. com. Also serves Aurora, Redmond, Sevier County & Sigurd. ICA: UT0029.
TV Market Ranking: Outside TV Markets (Aurora, Redmond, SALINA, Sevier County, Sigurd, Sigurd).
Channel capacity: N.A. Channels available but not in use: N.A.
Basic Service
Subscribers: 273.
Fee: $49.95 installation; $19.95 monthly.
Expanded Basic Service 1
Subscribers: 224.
Fee: $40.50 monthly.
President & General Manager: Eddie L. Cox.
Ownership: Central Telcom Services LLC (MSO).

SALT LAKE CITY—Comcast Cable, 9602 South 300 West, Sandy, UT 84070. Phones: 855-782-1061; 801-401-2500. Fax: 801-401-3397. Web Site: http://www.comcast.com. Also serves Franklin & Franklin County (portions), ID; Alpine, American Fork, Bear River City, Bluffdale, Bountiful, Box Elder County (portions), Brigham City, Cache County (portions), Cedar Hills, Centerville, Clarkston, Clearfield, Clinton, Corinne, Cornish, Davis, Davis County (portions), Deweyville, Draper, Elk Ridge, Farmington, Farr West, Fielding, Fruit Heights, Garland, Grantsville, Harrisville, Heber City, Herriman, Highland, Hill AFB, Holladay, Honeyville, Hooper, Hyde Park, Hyrum, Kaysville, Layton, Lehi, Lewiston, Lindon, Logan, Mapleton, Mendon, Midvale, Midway, Millville, Murray, Newton, Nibley, North Logan, North Ogden, North Salt Lake, Ogden, Orem, Paradise, Park City, Payson, Perry, Plain City, Pleasant Grove, Pleasant View, Plymouth, Providence, Provo, Richmond, River Heights, Riverdale, Riverton, Roy, Salem, Salt Lake County (portions), Sandy, Saratoga Springs, Smithfield, South Jordan, South Ogden, South Salt Lake City, South Weber, Spanish Fork City, Spring Lake, Springville, Stansbury Park, Summit County (portions), Sunset, Syracuse, Taylorsville, Tooele, Tremonton, Uintah City, Utah County (portions), Wasatch County (portions), Washington Terrace, Weber County (portions), Wellsville, West Bountiful, West Haven, West Jordan, West Point, West Valley City, Willard & Woods Cross, UT. ICA: UT0001.
TV Market Ranking: 48 (Alpine, American Fork, Bluffdale, Bountiful, Cedar Hills, Centerville, Clearfield, Clinton, Davis, Davis County (portions), Draper, Farmington, Fruit Heights, Grantsville, Harrisville, Heber City, Herriman, Highland, Hill AFB, Holladay, Hooper, Kaysville, Layton, Lehi, Lindon, Midvale, Midway, Murray, North Salt Lake, Ogden, Orem, Park City, Pleasant Grove, Riverdale, Riverton, Roy, SALT LAKE CITY, Salt Lake County (portions), Sandy, Saratoga Springs, South Jordan, South Ogden, South Salt Lake City, South Weber, South Weber, Stansbury Park, Summit County (portions), Sunset, Syracuse, Taylorsville, Tooele, Uintah City, Utah County (portions) (portions), Wasatch County (portions) (portions), Washington Terrace, Weber County (portions), Weber County (portions), West Bountiful, West Haven, West Jordan, West Point, West Valley City, Woods Cross); Below 100 (Bear River City, Cache County (portions), Corinne, Deweyville, Elk Ridge, Farr West, Fielding, Garland, Honeyville, Hyrum, Lewiston, Mapleton, Mendon, Millville, Nibley, North Ogden, Paradise, Payson, Perry, Plain City, Pleasant View, Plymouth, Providence, River Heights, Salem, Smithfield, Spanish Fork City, Spring Lake, Wellsville, Willard, Box Elder County (portions), Brigham City, Logan, Provo, Richmond, Springville, Tremonton, Utah County (portions) (portions), Wasatch County (portions) (portions), Weber County (portions)); Outside TV Markets (Cache County (portions), Clarkston, Cornish, Franklin, Franklin County (portions), Hyde Park, Newton, North Logan, Summit County (portions)). Franchise award date: January 1, 1966. Franchise expiration date: N.A. Began: March 1, 1970.
Channel capacity: N.A. Channels available but not in use: N.A.
Basic Service
Subscribers: 226,660.
Programming (received off-air): KBYU-TV (PBS) Provo; KJZZ-TV (IND) Salt Lake City; KPNZ (Estrella TV) Ogden; KSL-TV (NBC) Salt Lake City; KSTU (Antenna TV, FOX) Salt Lake City; KTMW (Grit, IND, Laff, Retro TV) Salt Lake City; KTVX (ABC, MeTV) Salt Lake City; KUED (PBS) Salt Lake City; KUEN (ETV) Ogden; KUPX-TV (ION) Provo; KUTV (CBS, This TV) Salt Lake City.
Programming (via satellite): C-SPAN; C-SPAN 2; Discovery Channel; FX; Hallmark Channel; INSP; Lifetime; QVC; TBS; Telemundo; Travel Channel; TV Land.
Programming (via translator): KUCW (CW, Movies!, The Country Network) Ogden.
Fee: $40.00 installation; $28.11 monthly; $1.90 converter.
Expanded Basic Service 1
Subscribers: N.A.
Programming (via satellite): A&E; AMC; Animal Planet; BET; Cartoon Network; CMT; CNBC; CNN; Comedy Central; Disney Chan-

D-794

TV & Cable Factbook No. 85

Cable Systems—Utah

nel; E! HD; ESPN; ESPN2; Food Network; Fox News Channel; Freeform; Great American Country; GSN; History; HLN; MSNBC; MTV; NBCSN; Nickelodeon; Oxygen; Root Sports Rocky Mountain; Spike TV; The Weather Channel; TLC; TNT; truTV; Univision; USA Network; VH1.
Fee: $31.13 installation; $40.29 monthly.

Digital Basic Service
Subscribers: N.A.
Programming (via satellite): BBC America; Bravo; Discovery Digital Networks; DMX Music; ESPN Classic; ESPN2; ESPNews; EVINE Live; Golf Channel; GSN; HGTV; IFC; National Geographic Channel; NBA TV; NBCSN; Nick Jr.; Syfy; The Word Network; Trinity Broadcasting Network (TBN); Turner Classic Movies; TV Land; WE tv.
Fee: $14.95 monthly.

Digital Expanded Basic Service
Subscribers: N.A.
Programming (via satellite): Bloomberg Television; Disney XD; Fox Sports 1; FSN Digital Atlantic; FSN Digital Central; FSN Digital Pacific; Fuse; FXM; FYI; History International; LMN; Nicktoons; Outdoor Channel; Ovation; Sundance TV; TeenNick.
Fee: $5.00 monthly.

Digital Pay Service 1
Pay Units: N.A.
Programming (via satellite): Cinemax (multiplexed); HBO (multiplexed); Showtime (multiplexed); Starz (multiplexed); The Movie Channel (multiplexed).
Fee: $16.95 monthly (each).

Video-On-Demand: Yes

Pay-Per-View
iN DEMAND (delivered digitally); Playboy TV (delivered digitally); Fresh (delivered digitally); Shorteez (delivered digitally).

Internet Service
Operational: Yes.
Subscribers: 302,791.
Broadband Service: Comcast High Speed Internet.
Fee: $42.95 monthly; $3.00 modem lease.

Telephone Service
Digital: Operational
Subscribers: 132,692.
Fee: $44.95 monthly
Miles of Plant: 16,351.0 (coaxial); 2,754.0 (fiber optic). Homes passed: 829,996.
Area Vice President: Scott Tenney. Technical Operations Director: Mike Spaulding. Chief Technician: Everett Preece. Marketing Director: Dan Williams. Marketing Manager: Lisa Jenkins. Community & Government Affairs Director: Steve Proper.
Ownership: Comcast Cable Communications Inc. (MSO).

SALT LAKE CITY—Formerly served by TechnoVision Inc. No longer in operation. ICA: UT0082.

SANDY—Comcast Cable. Now served by SALT LAKE CITY, UT [UT0001]. ICA: UT0002.

SANTAQUIN—CentraCom, 35 South State St, PO Box 7, Fairview, UT 84629-0007. Phone: 800-427-8449. Web Site: http://centracom.com. Also serves Eureka, Goshen, Mona & Utah County (portions). ICA: UT0041.
TV Market Ranking: Below 100 (SANTAQUIN, Utah County (portions), Eureka, Goshen, Mona).
Channel capacity: N.A. Channels available but not in use: N.A.

Basic Service
Subscribers: 493.
Fee: $40.95 installation; $19.95 monthly.

Expanded Basic Service 1
Subscribers: 305.
Fee: $40.50 monthly.
President & General Manager: Eddie L. Cox.
Ownership: Central Telcom Services LLC (MSO).

SOUTH JORDAN—CenturyLink Prism (formerly Qwest). This cable system has converted to IPTV, 250 East 200 South, 1604, Salt Lake City, UT 84111. Phone: 800-475-7526. E-mail: prismtveverywhere@centurylink.net. Web Site: http://www.centurylink.com/prismtv. Also serves Salt Lake City. ICA: UT5021.
Channel capacity: N.A. Channels available but not in use: N.A.

Prism Essential
Subscribers: N.A.
Fee: $34.99 monthly. Includes 140+ channels including music channels.

Prism Complete
Subscribers: N.A.
Fee: $39.99 monthly. Includes 190+ channels including music channels.

Prism Preferred
Subscribers: N.A.
Fee: $49.99 monthly. Includes 290+ channels including Showtime/TMC & Starz/Encore.

Prism Premium
Subscribers: N.A.
Fee: $79.99 monthly. Includes 320+ channels including all premium movie channels.

Prism Paquette Latino
Subscribers: N.A.
Fee: $8.49 monthly.

Cinemax
Subscribers: N.A.
Fee: $12.99 monthly.

HBO
Subscribers: N.A.
Fee: $14.99 monthly.

Showtime/TMC
Subscribers: N.A.
Fee: $14.99 monthly.

Starz/Encore
Subscribers: N.A.
Fee: $12.99 monthly.

Video-On-Demand: Yes

Internet Service
Operational: Yes.
Fee: $29.95 monthly.

Telephone Service
Digital: Operational
Vice President, Operations: Jeremy Ferkin.
Ownership: CenturyLink.

SOUTH JORDAN—Formerly served by Qwest Choice TV. This cable system has converted to IPTV. Now served by Centurylink, SOUTH JORDAN, UT [UT5021]. ICA: UT0091.

SPANISH FORK—Spanish Fork Community Network, 65 South 630 West, Spanish Fork, UT 84660-2077. Phones: 801-804-4410; 801-798-2877 (Customer service); 801-804-4500. Fax: 801-798-5025. E-mail: info@sfcn.org. Web Site: http://www.sfcn.org. ICA: UT0090. **Note:** This system is an overbuild.
TV Market Ranking: Below 100 (SPANISH FORK).
Channel capacity: N.A. Channels available but not in use: N.A.

Basic Service
Subscribers: 14,305.
Programming (received off-air): KBYU-TV (PBS) Provo; KJZZ-TV (IND) Salt Lake City; KPNZ (Estrella TV) Ogden; KSL-TV (NBC) Salt Lake City; KSTU (Antenna TV, FOX) Salt Lake City; KTMW (Grit, IND, Laff, Retro TV) Salt Lake City; KTVX (ABC, MeTV) Salt Lake City; KUCW (CW, Movies!, The Country Network) Ogden; KUEN (ETV) Ogden; KUPX-TV (ION) Provo; KUTV (CBS, This TV) Salt Lake City.
Programming (via satellite): BYUtv; C-SPAN; TBS; The Weather Channel.
Fee: $17.54 monthly.

Expanded Basic Service 1
Subscribers: N.A.
Programming (via satellite): A&E; AMC; Animal Planet; Cartoon Network; CBS Sports Network; CMT; CNBC; CNN; Comedy Central; C-SPAN 2; Discovery Channel; Discovery Life Channel; Disney Channel; Disney XD; DIY Network; E! HD; ESPN; ESPN Classic; ESPN2; ESPNews; Food Network; Fox News Channel; Fox Sports 1; Freeform; FX; FXM; Golf Channel; Great American Country; Hallmark Channel; HGTV; History; HLN; INSP; Lifetime; MoviePlex; MSNBC; MTV; National Geographic Channel; NBCSN; Nickelodeon; Outdoor Channel; Ovation; OWN: Oprah Winfrey Network; QVC; Root Sports Rocky Mountain; Spike TV; Syfy; TLC; TNT; Travel Channel; truTV; Turner Classic Movies; TV Land; USA Network; VH1.
Fee: $48.54 monthly.

Digital Basic Service
Subscribers: N.A.
Programming (via satellite): AXS TV; BBC America; Cloo; Destination America; Discovery Channel HD; Discovery Kids Channel; DMX Music; ESPN HD; FYI; GSN; History International; IFC; Investigation Discovery; MTV Classic; MTV2; Nick Jr.; Science Channel; TeenNick; VH1 Country; VH1 Soul; WE tv.
Fee: $57.67 monthly.

Digital Pay Service 1
Pay Units: N.A.
Programming (via satellite): Cinemax (multiplexed); Flix; HBO (multiplexed); Showtime (multiplexed); Starz (multiplexed); Starz Encore (multiplexed); Sundance TV; The Movie Channel (multiplexed).
Fee: $11.00 monthly (Starz/Encore), $12.00 monthly (Flix, Showtime, Sundance & TMC), $16.00 monthly (Cinemax & HBO).

Video-On-Demand: No

Internet Service
Operational: Yes.
Subscribers: 6,887.
Broadband Service: In-house.
Fee: $28.00-$68.00 monthly.

Telephone Service
Digital: Operational
Subscribers: 2,316.
Miles of Plant: 55.0 (coaxial); None (fiber optic).
General Manager: John Bowcut. Chief Technician: Dan Henderson.
Ownership: Spanish Fork Community Network.

SPRINGVILLE—Comcast Cable. Now served by SALT LAKE CITY, UT [UT0001]. ICA: UT0095.

ST. GEORGE—Baja Broadband, 525 Junction Rd, Madison, WI 53717. Phones: 702-346-5205 (Mesquite, NV office); 877-422-5282; 435-628-3681. Fax: 608-830-5519. E-mail: customersupportut@bajabb.tv. Web Site: http://www.bajabroadband.com. Also serves Mohave, AZ; Bunkerville & Mesquite, NV; Hurricane, Ivins, La Verkin, Leeds, Santa Clara, Toquerville, Washington & Washington County (portions), UT. ICA: UT0007.
TV Market Ranking: Below 100 (Hurricane, Ivins, La Verkin, Leeds, Mesquite, Santa Clara, ST. GEORGE, Toquerville, Washington, Washington County (portions)). Franchise award date: October 1, 1977. Franchise expiration date: N.A. Began: December 15, 1978.
Channel capacity: 78 (operating 2-way). Channels available but not in use: N.A.

Basic Service
Subscribers: 5,249.
Programming (received off-air): KCSG (MeTV, My Family TV) Cedar City; KMYU (MNT, This TV) St. George.
Programming (via satellite): BYUtv; Pop; QVC; WGN America.
Programming (via translator): KBYU-TV (PBS) Provo; KHSV (Antenna TV, MNT) Las Vegas; KJZZ-TV (IND) Salt Lake City; KPNZ (Estrella TV) Ogden; KSL-TV (NBC) Salt Lake City; KSTU (Antenna TV, FOX) Salt Lake City; KTVX (ABC, MeTV) Salt Lake City; KUCW (CW, Movies!, The Country Network) Ogden; KUED (PBS) Salt Lake City; KUTH-DT (getTV, UNV) Provo; KUTV (CBS, This TV) Salt Lake City.
Fee: $53.00 installation; $36.50 monthly.

Expanded Basic Service 1
Subscribers: N.A.
Programming (via satellite): A&E; AMC; Animal Planet; Bravo; Cartoon Network; CMT; CNBC; CNN; Comedy Central; C-SPAN; C-SPAN 2; Discovery Channel; Discovery Life Channel; Disney Channel; Disney XD; E! HD; ESPN; ESPN Classic; ESPN2; EWTN Global Catholic Network; Food Network; Fox News Channel; Fox Sports 1; Freeform; FX; FXM; Golf Channel; GSN; Hallmark Channel; HGTV; History; HLN; INSP; Lifetime; LMN; MSNBC; MTV; National Geographic Channel; NBCSN; Nickelodeon; Root Sports Rocky Mountain; Spike TV; Syfy; TBS; The Weather Channel; TLC; TNT; Travel Channel; truTV; Turner Classic Movies; TV Land; Univision; USA Network; VH1; WE tv.
Fee: $26.70 monthly.

Digital Basic Service
Subscribers: N.A.
Programming (via satellite): BBC America; Bloomberg Television; CMT; Destination America; Discovery Kids Channel; DIY Network; Fox Business Network; Fox Sports 2; FYI; History International; IFC; Investigation Discovery; MC; MTV Classic; MTV Hits; MTV Jams; MTV2; Nat Geo WILD; Nick 2; Nick Jr.; OWN: Oprah Winfrey Network;

2017 Edition

Utah—Cable Systems

Science Channel; Sundance TV; TeenNick; Tr3s; VH1 Soul.
Fee: $11.95 monthly.

Digital Expanded Basic Service
Subscribers: N.A.
Programming (via satellite): CBS Sports Network; ESPNews; FOX College Sports Central; FOX College Sports Pacific; Fox Sports 2; MavTV; Outdoor Channel.

Digital Expanded Basic Service 2
Subscribers: N.A.
Programming (via satellite): A&E HD; ESPN HD; Food Network HD; FSN HD; FX HD; Golf Channel HD; HGTV HD; History HD; National Geographic Channel HD; TBS HD; TNT HD; Versus HD.

Digital Expanded Basic Service 3
Subscribers: N.A.
Programming (via satellite): AXS TV; Universal HD.

Digital Pay Service 1
Pay Units: N.A.
Programming (via satellite): Cinemax (multiplexed); Cinemax HD; Flix; HBO (multiplexed); HBO HD; Showtime (multiplexed); Showtime HD; Starz (multiplexed); Starz Encore (multiplexed); Starz HD; The Movie Channel (multiplexed); The Movie Channel HD.
Fee: $10.50 monthly (Cinemax/Cinemax HD, Encore, HBO/HBO HD, Showtime/Showtime HD/TMC HD/Flix or Starz/Starz HDTV).

Video-On-Demand: No

Pay-Per-View
iN DEMAND (delivered digitally); Playboy TV (delivered digitally); Fresh (delivered digitally); Spice: Xcess (delivered digitally).

Internet Service
Operational: Yes. Began: September 1, 2000.
Subscribers: 18,384.

Broadband Service: In-house.
Fee: $49.99 installation; $34.99 monthly; $5.00 modem lease; $69.95 modem purchase.

Telephone Service
Digital: Operational
Subscribers: 6,344.
Miles of Plant: 1,492.0 (coaxial); 267.0 (fiber optic). Homes passed: 59,254.
Chief Executive Officer: William A. Schuler. Chief Operating Officer: Phillip Klein. Vice President, Corporate Finance: Carl Shapiro. Assistant Treasurer: Noel Hutton. Technical Operations Manager: Ed Farnum. Office Manager: Misty Snow.
Ownership: TDS Telecom (MSO).

ST. GEORGE—Formerly served by Prime Time Communications. No longer in operation. ICA: UT5022.

STANSBURY PARK—Comcast Cable. Now served by SALT LAKE CITY, UT [UT0001]. ICA: UT0093.

TOOELE—Comcast Cable. Now served by STANSBURY PARK, UT [UT0093]. ICA: UT0012.

TREMENTON—Formerly served by Connected Lyfe. No longer in operation. ICA: UT5084.

TREMONTON—Comcast Cable. Now served by SALT LAKE CITY, UT [UT0001]. ICA: UT0096.

VERNAL—Formerly served by Bresnan Communications. No longer in operation. ICA: UT0014.

VINEYARD—Formerly served by Connected Lyfe. No longer in operation. ICA: UT5085.

WASHINGTON—Formerly served by Connected Lyfe. No longer in operation. ICA: UT5086.

WENDOVER—CentraCom, 35 South State St, PO Box 7, Fairview, UT 84629-0007. Phones: 800-427-8449; 435-427-3331. Fax: 435-427-3200. Web Site: http://centracom.com. Also serves West Wendover. ICA: NV0054.
TV Market Ranking: Outside TV Markets (WENDOVER, West Wendover).
Channel capacity: N.A. Channels available but not in use: N.A.

Basic Service
Subscribers: 533. Commercial subscribers: 27.
Programming (received off-air): KJZZ-TV (IND) Salt Lake City; KSL-TV (NBC) Salt Lake City; KSTU (Antenna TV, FOX) Salt Lake City; KTVX (ABC, MeTV) Salt Lake City; KUED (PBS) Salt Lake City; KUTV (CBS, This TV) Salt Lake City.
Programming (via satellite): A&E; AMC; Animal Planet; CMT; CNBC; CNN; C-SPAN; Discovery Channel; Disney Channel; ESPN; ESPN2; FOX Sports Networks; Freeform; HGTV; Lifetime; MTV; Nickelodeon; Pop; QVC; Spike TV; Syfy; TBS; The Weather Channel; TNT; Turner Classic Movies; TV Land; Univision; USA Network; WGN America.
Fee: $49.95 installation; $19.95 monthly.

Expanded Basic Service 1
Subscribers: 446.
Fee: $40.50 monthly.

Digital Basic Service
Subscribers: N.A.

Pay Service 1
Pay Units: 45.
Programming (via satellite): Cinemax.
Fee: $12.95 monthly.

Pay Service 2
Pay Units: 101.
Programming (via satellite): HBO.
Fee: $12.95 monthly.

Pay Service 3
Pay Units: 49.
Programming (via satellite): Showtime.
Fee: $12.95 monthly.

Pay Service 4
Pay Units: 89.
Programming (via satellite): Starz; Starz Encore.
Fee: $12.95 monthly (Starz).

Video-On-Demand: No

Internet Service
Operational: Yes.
Subscribers: 274.

Telephone Service
Digital: Operational
Subscribers: 25.
Miles of Plant: 49.0 (coaxial); 3.0 (fiber optic). Homes passed: 2,229.
President & General Manager: Eddie L. Cox.
Ownership: Central Telcom Services LLC (MSO).

WENDOVER—Formerly served by Precis Communications. Now served by CentraCom, WENDOVER, NV [NV0054]. ICA: UT0025.

WEST VALLEY CITY—Formerly served by Connected Lyfe. No longer in operation. ICA: UT5087.

WEST VALLEY CITY—Formerly served by Nuvont Communications. IPTV service no longer in operation. ICA: UT5029.

WINCHESTER—Formerly served by South Central Communications. No longer in operation. ICA: UT0087.

VERMONT

Total Systems: 10	Communities with Applications: 0
Total Communities Served: 271	Number of Basic Subscribers: 283,972
Franchises Not Yet Operating: 0	Number of Expanded Basic Subscribers: 826
Applications Pending: 0	Number of Pay Units: 0

Top 100 Markets Represented: Albany-Schenectady-Troy, NY (34).

For a list of cable communities in this section, see the Cable Community Index located in the back of Cable Volume 2.
For explanation of terms used in cable system listings, see p. D-11.

BARRE—Charter Communications. Now served by DANVILLE (town) (formerly St. Johnsbury), VT [VT0009]. ICA: VT0005.

BENNINGTON—Comcast Cable. Now served by BURLINGTON, VT [VT0001]. ICA: VT0004.

BERLIN—Comcast Cable. Now served by BURLINGTON, VT [VT0001]. ICA: VT0061.

BLOOMFIELD TWP.—Formerly served by Adelphia Communications. No longer in operation. ICA: VT0038.

BRADFORD—Charter Communications. Now served by DANVILLE (town) (formerly St. Johnsbury), VT [VT0009]. ICA: VT0021.

BRAINTREE—Formerly served by Adelphia Cable-Berlin. Now served by BURLINGTON, VT [VT0001]. ICA: VT0039.

BRATTLEBORO—Comcast Cable. Now served by BURLINGTON, VT [VT0001]. ICA: VT0010.

BURLINGTON—Comcast Cable, 43 Comcast Way, South Burlington, VT 05403-6056. Phones: 800-266-2278; 802-419-6629. Fax: 802-658-5488. Web Site: http://www.comcast.com. Also serves Agawam, Amherst, Bernardston, Buckland, Chester, Conway, Deerfield, Erving, Gill, Granby, Granville, Greenfield, Hardwick, Hatfield, Holyoke, Huntington, Longmeadow, Monson, Montague, Northampton, Northfield, Palmer, Pelham, Shelburne, South Hadley, Southwick, Springfield, Sunderland, Ware, Warren, West Springfield, Westfield, Westhampton, Whately & Williamsburg, MA; Alstead, Andover, Canaan, Charlestown, Claremont, Cornish (town), Cornish Flat, Danbury (town), Drewsville, Enfield, Gilsum, Grantham, Hanover, Hill, Hinsdale, Langdon, Lebanon, New London, Newport, North Walpole, Plainfield (town), Salisbury (town), South Charlestown, Sunapee, Walpole, West Chesterfield, West Lebanon, Wilmot & Winchester, NH; Arlington, Ascutney, Athens, Bakersfield, Barton, Bellows Falls, Bennington, Berkshire, Berlin, Bethel, Bomoseen, Bondville, Braintree, Brandon, Brattleboro, Bridgewater, Brighton, Bristol, Bromley, Brookfield, Brownington, Calais, Cambridgeport, Castleton, Cavendish, Center Rutland, Charleston, Charlotte, Chester, Chester Depot, Chittenden, Clarendon, Colchester, Coventry, Danby, Derby, Derby Line, Dorset, Duxbury, East Fairfield, East Montpelier, Enosburg, Enosburg Falls, Essex Center, Essex Junction, Fair Haven, Fairfax, Fairfield, Ferrisburg, Forest Dale, Georgia, Glover, Grafton, Grand Isle, Greensboro, Guilford, Hardwick, Hartford, Hartland, Highgate Center, Hinesburg, Holland, Hubbardton, Huntington, Hyde Park, Ira, Irasburg, Island Pond, Jamaica, Jay, Jericho, Johnson, Killington, Leicester, Lincoln, Londonderry, Ludlow, Manchester, Manchester Center, Mendon, Middlebury, Middlesex, Middletown Springs, Milton, Monkton Boro, Montgomery, Montpelier, Moretown, Morgan, Morrisville, Morrisville, Mount Holly, Mount Tabor, New Haven, Newport, Newport Center, North Bennington, North Ferrisburg, North Hartland, North Hero, North Troy, Norwich, Old Bennington, Orleans, Pawlet, Perkinsville, Pittsford, Plainfield, Plymouth, Poultney, Pownal, Proctor, Proctorsville, Randolph, Reading, Richford, Richmond, Rochester, Rockingham, Rupert, Rutland, Saxtons River, Shaftsbury, Shelburne, Sheldon, Shrewsbury, South Burlington, South Hero, Springfield, St. Albans, St. Albans (town), St. George (town), Starksboro Twp., Stratton, Sunderland, Swanton, Swanton (village), Taftsville, Tinmouth, Troy, Tyson, Underhill (town), Vergennes, Vernon, Walden, Wallingford, Waltham (town), Waterbury, Weathersfield (town), Wells, West Pawlet, West Rutland, Westfield, Westford, Westminster, Weston, Weybridge, White River Junction, Wilder, Williston, Windsor, Winhall, Winooski, Woodbury, Woodford, Woodstock & Worcester, VT. ICA: VT0001.

TV Market Ranking: 19 (Agawam, Granville, Holyoke, Huntington, Longmeadow, Southwick, West Springfield, Westfield); 19,6 (Springfield); 34 (Bennington, North Bennington, Old Bennington, Pownal, Shaftsbury, Woodford); 6 (Hardwick, Monson, Palmer, Pelham, Ware, Warren); Below 100 (Alstead, Amherst, Andover, Arlington, Ascutney, Bakersfield, Bernardston, Bethel, Braintree, Bridgewater, Bristol, Buckland, BURLINGTON, Canaan, Cavendish, Center Rutland, Chester, Chester, Chester Depot, Chittenden, Clarendon, Colchester, Conway, Cornish (town), Cornish Flat, Danbury (town), Deerfield, Drewsville, Duxbury, East Fairfield, Enfield, Erving, Essex Center, Essex Junction, Ferrisburg, Georgia, Gill, Granby, Grantham, Greenfield, Guilford, Hanover, Hartford, Hartland, Hatfield, Hill, Hinesburg, Hinsdale, Huntington, Hyde Park, Jericho, Johnson, Killington, Langdon, Lebanon, Londonderry, Ludlow, Mendon, Middlebury, Middlesex, Milton, Montague, Moretown, Morrisville, Morrisville, Mount Holly, New London, Newport, North Hartland, Northfield, Norwich, Perkinsville, Plainfield (town), Plymouth, Proctorsville, Randolph, Reading, Richmond, Rochester, Rockingham, Salisbury (town), Shelburne, Shrewsbury, South Burlington, South Charlestown, South Hadley, Springfield, St. Albans, St. George (town), Starksboro Twp., Stratton, Sunapee, Sunderland, Swanton (village), Taftsville, Underhill (town), Vergennes, Wallingford, Waterbury, Weathersfield (town), West Chesterfield, West Lebanon, Westhampton, Weston, Weybridge, Whately, White River Junction, Wilder, Williamsburg, Williston, Wilmot, Windsor, Winooski, Woodstock, Brattleboro, Claremont, Montpelier, Northampton, Rutland); Outside TV Markets (Athens, Barton, Bellows Falls, Berlin, Bomoseen, Bondville, Brandon, Bromley, Brookfield, Calais, Cambridgeport, Castleton, Charleston, Charlotte, Chester Depot, Coventry, Danby, Derby, Derby Line, Dorset, East Montpelier, Enosburg, ENOSBURG FALLS, Fair Haven, Forest Dale, Gilsum, Glover, Grafton, Greensboro, Hardwick, Hubbardton, Ira, Irasburg, Jamaica, Leicester, Manchester, Manchester Center, Middletown Springs, Montgomery, Mount Tabor, Newport, Newport Center, North Troy, North Walpole, Orleans, Pawlet, Pittsford, Plainfield, Poultney, Proctor, Richford, Rupert, Saxtons River, Sunderland, Tinmouth, Troy, Tyson, Vernon, Walden, Walpole, Wells, West Pawlet, West Rutland, Westminster, Winchester, Winhall, Woodbury, Worcester). Franchise award date: January 1, 1952. Franchise expiration date: N.A. Began: May 1, 1952.

Channel capacity: 55 (operating 2-way). Channels available but not in use: N.A.

Basic Service
Subscribers: 267,429. Commercial subscribers: 1,648.
Programming (received off-air): WCAX-TV (CBS, Movies!) Burlington; WCFE-TV (PBS) Plattsburgh; WETK (PBS) Burlington; WFFF-TV (FOX, IND) Burlington; WPTZ (MeTV, NBC, This TV) Plattsburgh; WVNY (ABC) Burlington; 26 FMs.
Programming (via satellite): Pop; TBS; TLC; WPIX (Antenna TV, CW, This TV) New York.
Fee: $31.95-$46.00 installation; $29.75 monthly.

Expanded Basic Service 1
Subscribers: N.A.
Programming (via satellite): A&E; Animal Planet; Cartoon Network; CMT; CNBC; CNN; Comedy Central; C-SPAN; C-SPAN 2; Discovery Channel; Disney Channel; E! HD; ESPN; ESPN2; EVINE Live; EWTN Global Catholic Network; Food Network; Fox News Channel; Freeform; FX; Hallmark Channel; HGTV; History; HLN; INSP; ION Television; Lifetime; MSNBC; New England Cable News; Nickelodeon; Oxygen; QVC; Spike TV; Syfy; The Weather Channel; TNT; Travel Channel; truTV; TV Land; WSBK-TV (MNT) Boston.
Fee: $36.75 monthly.

Digital Basic Service
Subscribers: N.A.
Programming (via satellite): BBC America; Bloomberg Television; Discovery Life Channel; Disney XD; DIY Network; ESPN Classic; ESPNews; Fox Sports 1; Fuse; FXM; FYI; Golf Channel; Great American Country; GSN; History International; MC; NBCSN; Nick Jr.; Nicktoons; Outdoor Channel; TeenNick; The Word Network; Trinity Broadcasting Network (TBN); WE tv.

Digital Expanded Basic Service
Subscribers: N.A.
Programming (via satellite): HITS (Headend In The Sky); IFC; National Geographic Channel; Sundance TV; Turner Classic Movies.

Digital Pay Service 1
Pay Units: N.A.
Programming (via satellite): ART America; Cinemax (multiplexed); Flix; HBO (multiplexed); RAI Italia; RTN; Showtime (multiplexed); Starz (multiplexed); Starz Encore (multiplexed); The Filipino Channel; The Movie Channel (multiplexed); TV Asia; TV5; La Television International; Zee TV.
Fee: $11.50 monthly (each).

Video-On-Demand: Yes

Pay-Per-View
Urban Xtra (delivered digitally); Hot Choice (delivered digitally); Shorteez (delivered digitally); Fresh (delivered digitally); HITS (delivered digitally); Playboy TV (delivered digitally); iN DEMAND.

Internet Service
Operational: Yes. Began: August 1, 1999.
Subscribers: 225,751.
Broadband Service: Comcast High Speed Internet.
Fee: $42.95 monthly.

Telephone Service
Digital: Operational.
Subscribers: 151,974.

Miles of Plant: 16,039.0 (coaxial); 4,322.0 (fiber optic). Homes passed: 521,028.
Area Vice President: Dan Blakeman. Regional Vice President: Steve Hackley. Vice President, Technical Operations: Raymond Kowalinski. Vice President, Sales & Marketing: Mark Adamy. Public Relations Manager: Marc Goodman.
Ownership: Comcast Cable Communications Inc. (MSO).

CHARLESTON—Comcast Cable. Now served by BURLINGTON, VT [VT0001]. ICA: VT0043.

CHELSEA—Charter Communications. Now served by DANVILLE (town) (formerly St. Johnsbury), VT [VT0009]. ICA: VT0027.

COVENTRY TWP.—Formerly served by Adelphia Communications. No longer in operation. ICA: VT0044.

DERBY—Comcast Cable. Now served by BURLINGTON, VT [VT0001]. ICA: VT0013.

EAST CORINTH—Formerly served by Olsen TV. No longer in operation. ICA: VT0030.

2017 Edition — D-797

Vermont—Cable Systems

ENOSBURG FALLS—Comcast Cable. Now served by BURLINGTON, VT [VT0001]. ICA: VT0024.

IRASBURG TWP.—Formerly served by Adelphia Communications. No longer in operation. ICA: VT0054.

JACKSONVILLE—Formerly served by Area Telecable. No longer in operation. ICA: VT0088.

JAMAICA TWP.—Southern Vermont Cable Co. Now served by PUTNEY, VT [VT0067]. ICA: VT0055.

JEFFERSONVILLE—Jeffersonville Cable TV Corp, 172 Thomas Ln, PO Box 453, Stowe, VT 05672. Phone: 802-253-9282. Fax: 802-253-7812. E-mail: stoweaccess@stoweaccess.com. Web Site: http://www.stoweaccess.com. Also serves Cambridge, Cambridge Junction & Smugglers Notch. ICA: VT0056.
  TV Market Ranking: Below 100 (Cambridge, Cambridge Junction, JEFFERSONVILLE, Smugglers Notch). Franchise award date: N.A. Franchise expiration date: N.A. Began: July 1, 1988.
  Channel capacity: N.A. Channels available but not in use: N.A.
Basic Service
  Subscribers: N.A.
  Programming (received off-air): WCAX-TV (CBS, Movies!) Burlington; WETK (PBS) Burlington; WPTZ (MeTV, NBC, This TV) Plattsburgh; WVNY (ABC) Burlington.
  Programming (via satellite): A&E; CNN; Comedy Central; C-SPAN; Discovery Channel; Disney Channel; ESPN; Freeform; History; HLN; New England Sports Network; Spike TV; Syfy; TBS; The Weather Channel; TLC; TNT; USA Network.
  Fee: $60.00 installation.
Expanded Basic Service 1
  Subscribers: N.A.
  Programming (via satellite): AMC; Animal Planet; CMT; CNBC; ESPN2; Food Network; Fox News Channel; Great American Country; Lifetime; MTV; Nickelodeon; TV Land; VH1.
Digital Basic Service
  Subscribers: N.A.
  Programming (via satellite): Bravo; Discovery Digital Networks; Disney XD; ESPN Classic; ESPN2; ESPNews; Fox Sports 1; FXM; FYI; Golf Channel; GSN; HGTV; History International; IFC; MC; NBCSN; Nick Jr.; Nicktoons; Outdoor Channel; TeenNick; Turner Classic Movies.
  Fee: $25.00 installation; $20.00 monthly.
Pay Service 1
  Pay Units: N.A.
  Programming (via satellite): HBO.
  Fee: $10.00 monthly.
Digital Pay Service 1
  Pay Units: N.A.
  Programming (via satellite): Cinemax; Flix; HBO (multiplexed); Showtime (multiplexed); Starz; Starz Encore (multiplexed); The Movie Channel (multiplexed).
  Fee: $14.28 monthly (Showtime & TMC), $14.95 monthly (Starz & Encore), $17.00 monthly (HBO & Cinemax).
Video-On-Demand: No
Internet Service
  Operational: Yes.
  Broadband Service: In-house.
  Fee: $75.00 installation; $40.00-$69.95 monthly; $20.00 modem lease; $110.00 modem purchase.
Telephone Service
  Digital: Operational
  Fee: $31.95 monthly
  Miles of Plant: 26.0 (coaxial); 36.0 (fiber optic).
  General Manager: Rick Rothammer.
  Ownership: Stowe Cablevision Inc. (MSO).

MANCHESTER—Formerly served by Adelphia Communications. Now served by Comcast, BURLINGTON, VT [VT0001]. ICA: VT0008.

MONTPELIER—Comcast Cable. Now served by BURLINGTON, VT [VT0001]. ICA: VT0092.

MOUNT ASCUTNEY—Formerly served by New England Wireless Inc. No longer in operation. ICA: VT0091.

NEWFANE—Southern Vermont Cable Co, PO Box 166, Bondville, VT 05340-0166. Phones: 802-297-2179; 800-544-5931. Fax: 802-297-3714. E-mail: escialabba@svcable.net. Web Site: http://www.svcable.net. ICA: VT0023.
  TV Market Ranking: Below 100 (NEWFANE).
  Channel capacity: N.A. Channels available but not in use: N.A.
Basic Service
  Subscribers: 1,241.
  Fee: $18.95 monthly.
Internet Service
  Operational: Yes.
  Subscribers: 971.
Telephone Service
  Digital: Operational
  Subscribers: 487.
  Miles of Plant: 87.0 (coaxial); 49.0 (fiber optic). Homes passed: 1,597.
  President: Ernest Scialabba.
  Ownership: Southern Vermont Cable Co. (MSO).

NORTHFIELD (village)—Trans-Video Inc, 56 Depot Sq, Unit 1, Northfield, VT 05663-6723. Phone: 802-485-3811. Fax: 802-485-8451. E-mail: info@trans-video.net. Web Site: http://www.trans-video.net. Also serves Berlin, Northfield (town) & Riverton. ICA: VT0018.
  TV Market Ranking: Outside TV Markets (Berlin, Northfield (town), NORTHFIELD (VILLAGE), Riverton). Franchise award date: N.A. Franchise expiration date: N.A. Began: December 21, 1951.
  Channel capacity: N.A. Channels available but not in use: N.A.
Basic Service
  Subscribers: 1,231. Commercial subscribers: 4.
  Programming (received off-air): WCAX-TV (CBS, Movies!) Burlington; WETK (PBS) Burlington; WFFF-TV (FOX, IND) Burlington; WPTZ (MeTV, NBC, This TV) Plattsburgh; WVNY (ABC) Burlington; allband FM.
  Programming (via satellite): Animal Planet; Discovery Channel; HGTV; TBS; TLC; Travel Channel.
  Fee: $40.00 installation; $29.95 monthly; $3.73 converter.
Expanded Basic Service 1
  Subscribers: 826.
  Programming (via satellite): A&E; AMC; Bravo; Cartoon Network; CMT; CNBC; CNN; Comcast SportsNet Mid-Atlantic; Comedy Central; Disney Channel; E! HD; ESPN; ESPN Classic; ESPN2; Food Network; Fox News Channel; Fox Sports 1; Freeform; FX; Hallmark Channel; History; Lifetime; LMN; MTV; National Geographic Channel; NBCSN; New England Sports Network; Nickelodeon; Outdoor Channel; OWN: Oprah Winfrey Network; Pop; Spike TV; Syfy; The Weather Channel; truTV; Turner Classic Movies; TV Land; USA Network; VH1; WE tv; WGN America; WPIX (Antenna TV, CW, This TV) New York; WSBK-TV (MNT) Boston.
  Fee: $20.00 installation; $8.26 monthly.
Digital Basic Service
  Subscribers: 202.
  Programming (via satellite): A&E HD; BBC America; Chiller; CMT; Cooking Channel; C-SPAN; C-SPAN 2; Destination America; Discovery Kids Channel; Discovery Life Channel; Disney XD; DIY Network; DMX Music; ESPN HD; ESPN2 HD; ESPNews; ESPNU; Food Network HD; Fuse; FXM; FYI; Golf Channel; GSN; HD Theater; HGTV HD; History HD; History International; IFC; Investigation Discovery; MSNBC; MTV Classic; MTV Hits; MTV Jams; MTV2; Nat Geo WILD; National Geographic Channel HD; New England Sports Network; Nick Jr.; Oxygen; RFD-TV; Science Channel; Sprout; Sundance TV; TeenNick; Trinity Broadcasting Network (TBN); Universal HD; VH1 Soul.
  Fee: $15.00 monthly.
Digital Pay Service 1
  Pay Units: N.A.
  Programming (via satellite): Cinemax (multiplexed); Flix; HBO (multiplexed); Showtime (multiplexed); Starz (multiplexed); Starz Encore; Starz HD; The Movie Channel (multiplexed).
  Fee: $11.73 monthly (each).
Video-On-Demand: No
Pay-Per-View
  iN DEMAND (delivered digitally); Fresh (delivered digitally); Playboy TV (delivered digitally).
Internet Service
  Operational: Yes. Began: August 1, 2000.
  Broadband Service: Trans-video.net.
  Fee: $32.95-$44.95 monthly.
Telephone Service
  Digital: Operational
  Fee: $34.95 monthly
  Miles of Plant: 40.0 (coaxial); 6.0 (fiber optic). Homes passed: 1,900.
  President & General Manager: George L. Goodrich III. Office Manager: Jill Goodrich.
  Ownership: Trans-Video Inc.

PUTNEY—Southern Vermont Cable Co, PO Box 166, Bondville, VT 05340-0166. Phones: 802-297-2179; 800-544-5931. Fax: 802-297-3714. E-mail: escialabba@svcable.net. Web Site: http://www.svcable.net. ICA: VT0067.
  TV Market Ranking: Below 100 (PUTNEY). Franchise award date: October 1, 1988. Franchise expiration date: N.A. Began: January 1, 1978.
  Channel capacity: N.A. Channels available but not in use: N.A.
Basic Service
  Subscribers: 834.
  Programming (received off-air): WBIN-TV (Antenna TV, IND, WeatherNation) Derry; WCDC-TV (ABC) Adams; WEKW-TV (PBS) Keene; WMUR-TV (ABC, MeTV) Manchester; WNNE (NBC) Hartford; WVTA (PBS) Windsor; allband FM.
  Programming (via satellite): CatholicTV; C-SPAN; ION Television; Pop; QVC.
  Programming (via translator): WBZ-TV (CBS, Decades) Boston; WCAX-TV (CBS, Movies!) Burlington; WCVB-TV (ABC, MeTV) Boston; WFXT (FOX, Movies!) Boston; WHDH (NBC, This TV) Boston; WPIX (Antenna TV, CW, This TV) New York; WSBK-TV (MNT) Boston.
  Fee: $45.00 installation; $18.95 monthly.
Expanded Basic Service 1
  Subscribers: N.A.
  Programming (via satellite): A&E; AMC; Animal Planet; BBC America; Cartoon Network; CMT; CNBC; CNN; Comcast SportsNet New England; Comedy Central; C-SPAN 2; Discovery Channel; Disney Channel; E! HD; ESPN; ESPN2; EVINE Live; EWTN Global Catholic Network; FamilyNet; Food Network; Fox News Channel; Fox Sports 1; FX; Hallmark Channel; HGTV; History; HLN; Lifetime; MSNBC; MTV; NBCSN; New England Cable News; Nickelodeon; Oxygen; Spike TV; Syfy; TBS; The Weather Channel; TLC; TNT; Travel Channel; truTV; Turner Classic Movies; TV Land; USA Network; VH1; WGN America.
  Fee: $17.00 monthly.
Pay Service 1
  Pay Units: N.A.
  Programming (via satellite): HBO; Showtime; The Movie Channel.
  Fee: $27.50 installation; $9.95 monthly (HBO), $10.95 monthly (Showtime & TMC).
Video-On-Demand: No
Internet Service
  Operational: Yes.
  Fee: $55.00 installation; $19.95 monthly.
Telephone Service
  Digital: Operational
  Fee: $34.95 monthly
  Miles of Plant: 97.0 (coaxial); None (fiber optic). Homes passed: 2,100. Homes passed & miles of plant include Townshend
  General Manager & Chief Technician: Ernest Scialabba.
  Ownership: Southern Vermont Cable Co. (MSO).

RICHMOND—Formerly served by Adelphia Communications. Now served by Comcast Cable, BURLINGTON, VT [VT0001]. ICA: VT0068.

ROCHESTER—Formerly served by Adelphia Communications. Now served by Comcast Cable, BURLINGTON, VT [VT0001]. ICA: VT0069.

RUTLAND—Comcast Cable. Now served by BURLINGTON, VT [VT0001]. ICA: VT0003.

RUTLAND—Formerly served by Satellite Signals of New England. No longer in operation. ICA: VT0086.

SPRINGFIELD—Comcast Cable. Now served by BURLINGTON, VT [VT0001]. ICA: VT0002.

ST. JOHNSBURY—Charter Communications, 12405 Powerscourt Dr, St. Louis, MO 63131. Phones: 636-207-5100 (Corporate office); 508-853-1515. Fax: 508-854-5042. Web Site: http://www.charter.com. Also serves Bath, Haverhill, North Haverhill, Piermont, Pike & Woodsville, NH; Barnet, Barre, Berlin, Bradford, Chelsea, Concord, Danville (town), East Barre, East Burke, East Montpelier, East Ryegate, East St. Johnsbury, Graniteville, Groton, Lyndon, Lyndon Center, Lyndon Corners, Lyndonville, Marshfield, McIndoe Falls, Newbury, Passumpsic, Peacham, Plainfield, Sheffield, South Barre, South Royalton, South Ryegate, St. Johnsbury Center, Sutton, Washington (town), Waterford, Wells River, West Burke & Williamstown, VT. ICA: VT0009.

Cable Systems—Vermont

TV Market Ranking: Below 100 (Bradford, Chelsea, East Barre, Graniteville, Haverhill, Newbury, North Haverhill, Piermont, Pike, South Royalton, Williamstown); Outside TV Markets (Barnet, Barre, Bath, Berlin, Concord, East Burke, East Montpelier, East Ryegate, East St. Johnsbury, Groton, Lyndon, Lyndon Center, Lyndon Corners, Lyndonville, Marshfield, McIndoe Falls, Passumpsic, Peacham, Plainfield, Sheffield, South Barre, South Ryegate, ST. JOHNSBURY, St. Johnsbury Center, Sutton, Waterford, Wells River, West Burke, Woodsville, Danville (town)). Franchise award date: January 1, 1954. Franchise expiration date: N.A. Began: March 1, 1954.
Channel capacity: 75 (operating 2-way). Channels available but not in use: N.A.

Digital Basic Service
Subscribers: 9,674.
Programming (via satellite): BBC America; Bloomberg Television; CBS Sports Network; Discovery Life Channel; DIY Network; ESPN Classic; ESPNews; FOX College Sports Central; FOX College Sports Pacific; Fox Sports 2; Fuse; FYI; History International; IFC; Jewelry Television; LMN; MC; Nick 2; Nick Jr.; Nicktoons; Sundance TV; TeenNick; WE tv.
Fee: $26.99 monthly.

Digital Expanded Basic Service
Subscribers: N.A.
Programming (via satellite): A&E; AMC; Animal Planet; Bravo; Cartoon Network; CMT; CNBC; CNN; Comcast SportsNet New England; Comedy Central; Discovery Channel; Disney Channel; Disney XD; E! HD; ESPN; ESPN2; Food Network; Fox News Channel; Fox Sports 1; Freeform; FX; Golf Channel; GSN; Hallmark Channel; HGTV; History; HLN; Lifetime; MSNBC; MTV; MTV2; National Geographic Channel; NBCSN; New England Cable News; New England Sports Network; Nickelodeon; Oxygen; Spike TV; Syfy; TBS; The Weather Channel; TLC; TNT; Travel Channel; truTV; Turner Classic Movies; TV Land; USA Network; VH1.
Fee: $55.00 monthly.

Digital Pay Service 1
Pay Units: N.A.
Programming (via satellite): Cinemax (multiplexed); HBO (multiplexed); Showtime (multiplexed); Starz (multiplexed); Starz Encore (multiplexed); The Movie Channel (multiplexed).
Video-On-Demand: No
Pay-Per-View
Shorteez (delivered digitally); Playboy en Espanol (delivered digitally); Playboy TV (delivered digitally); Fresh (delivered digitally); NHL Center Ice (delivered digitally); MLB Extra Innings (delivered digitally); iN DEMAND (delivered digitally).

Internet Service
Operational: Yes.
Subscribers: 9,196.
Broadband Service: Charter Internet.
Fee: $29.99 monthly; $5.00 modem lease.

Telephone Service
Digital: Operational
Subscribers: 3,325.
Miles of Plant: 1,031.0 (coaxial); 418.0 (fiber optic). Homes passed: 25,104.
Vice President & General Manager: Greg Garabedian. Technical Operations Director: George Duffy. Technical Operations Manager: Rick Smith. Marketing Director: Dennis Jerome. Accounting Director: David Sovanski.
Ownership: Charter Communications Inc. (MSO).

STOWE—Stowe Cablevision Inc, 172 Thomas Ln, PO Box 453, Stowe, VT 05672. Phone: 802-253-9282. Fax: 802-253-7812. E-mail: stoweaccess@stoweaccess.com. Web Site: http://www.stoweaccess.com. ICA: VT0074.
TV Market Ranking: Below 100 (STOWE). Franchise award date: N.A. Franchise expiration date: N.A. Began: January 1, 1985.
Channel capacity: N.A. Channels available but not in use: N.A.

Basic Service
Subscribers: 781.
Programming (received off-air): WCAX-TV (CBS, Movies!) Burlington; WETK (PBS) Burlington; WFFF-TV (FOX, IND) Burlington; WPTZ (MeTV, NBC, This TV) Plattsburgh; WVNY (ABC) Burlington.
Programming (via satellite): A&E; AMC; Animal Planet; CMT; CNBC; CNN; Comedy Central; C-SPAN; Discovery Channel; Disney Channel; ESPN; ESPN2; Food Network; Fox News Channel; Freeform; Great American Country; History; HLN; Lifetime; MTV; New England Sports Network; Nickelodeon; Spike TV; Syfy; TBS; The Weather Channel; TLC; TNT; TV Land; USA Network; VH1.
Fee: $45.00 monthly.

Digital Basic Service
Subscribers: 183.
Programming (via satellite): Bravo; Discovery Digital Networks; Disney XD; ESPN Classic; ESPN2; ESPNews; Fox Sports 1; Fuse; FXM; FYI; Golf Channel; GSN; HGTV; History International; IFC; LMN; NBCSN; Nick Jr.; Nicktoons; Outdoor Channel; TeenNick; Turner Classic Movies; WE tv.
Fee: $20.00 monthly.

Pay Service 1
Pay Units: N.A.
Programming (via satellite): HBO.
Fee: $10.00 monthly.

Digital Pay Service 1
Pay Units: N.A.
Programming (via satellite): Cinemax (multiplexed); Flix; HBO (multiplexed); Showtime (multiplexed); Starz (multiplexed); Starz Encore; The Movie Channel (multiplexed).
Fee: $14.28 monthly (Showtime, TMC, & Flix), $14.95 monthly (Starz & Encore), $17.00 monthly (HBO & Cinemax).
Video-On-Demand: No
Pay-Per-View
Playboy TV (delivered digitally).

Internet Service
Operational: Yes. Began: January 1, 2001.
Subscribers: 200.
Broadband Service: Green Mountain Access.
Fee: $75.00 installation; $40.00-$69.95 monthly; $20.00 modem lease; $110.00 modem purchase.

Telephone Service
Digital: Operational
Fee: $31.95 monthly
Miles of Plant: 84.0 (coaxial); 31.0 (fiber optic). Homes passed: 1,860.
President: Richard Landy. General Manager: Rick Rothammer.
Ownership: Stowe Cablevision Inc. (MSO).

TOWNSHEND—Southern Vermont Cable Co, PO Box 166, Bondville, VT 05340-0166. Phones: 802-297-2179; 800-544-5931. Fax: 802-297-3714. E-mail: escialabba@svcable.net. Web Site: http://www.svcable.net. Also serves West Townshend. ICA: VT0076.
TV Market Ranking: Outside TV Markets (TOWNSHEND, West Townshend).
Channel capacity: N.A. Channels available but not in use: N.A.

Basic Service
Subscribers: N.A.
Programming (received off-air): WBIN-TV (Antenna TV, IND, WeatherNation) Derry; WCAX-TV (CBS, Movies!) Burlington; WCDC-TV (ABC) Adams; WEKW-TV (PBS) Keene; WMUR-TV (ABC, MeTV) Manchester; WNNE (NBC) Hartford; WVTA (PBS) Windsor.
Programming (via satellite): CatholicTV; C-SPAN; ION Television; Pop; QVC.
Programming (via translator): WBPX-TV (ION) Boston; WBZ-TV (CBS, Decades) Boston; WCVB-TV (ABC, MeTV) Boston; WFXT (FOX, Movies!) Boston; WHDH (NBC, This TV) Boston; WPIX (Antenna TV, CW, This TV) New York; WSBK-TV (MNT) Boston.
Fee: $30.00 installation; $16.95 monthly.

Expanded Basic Service 1
Subscribers: N.A.
Programming (via satellite): A&E; AMC; Animal Planet; BBC America; Bravo; Cartoon Network; CMT; CNBC; CNN; Comcast SportsNet New England; Comedy Central; C-SPAN 2; Discovery Channel; Disney Channel; E! HD; ESPN; ESPN2; EVINE Live; EWTN Global Catholic Network; FamilyNet; Food Network; Fox News Channel; Fox Sports 1; FX; Hallmark Channel; HGTV; History; HLN; Lifetime; MSNBC; MTV; NBCSN; New England Cable News; New England Sports Network; Nickelodeon; Oxygen; Spike TV; Syfy; TBS; The Weather Channel; TLC; TNT; Travel Channel; truTV; Turner Classic Movies; TV Land; USA Network; VH1; WGN America.
Fee: $17.00 monthly.

Pay Service 1
Pay Units: N.A.
Programming (via satellite): HBO; Showtime; The Movie Channel.
Fee: $9.95 monthly (HBO), $10.95 monthly each (Showtime & TMC).
Video-On-Demand: No

Internet Service
Operational: Yes.
Fee: $55.00 installation; $19.95 monthly.

Telephone Service
Digital: Operational
Fee: $34.95 monthly
Homes passed & miles of plant included in Putney
General Manager & Chief Technician: Ernest Scialabba.
Ownership: Southern Vermont Cable Co. (MSO).

WAITSFIELD—Waitsfield Cable Co, 3898 Main St, PO Box 9, Waitsfield, VT 05673-0009. Phone: 802-496-5800. Fax: 802-496-7040. E-mail: csdept@waitsfieldcable.com. Web Site: http://www.waitsfieldcable.com. Also serves Bolton, Duxbury, Fayston, Moretown, Warren & Washington County (portions). ICA: VT0014.
TV Market Ranking: Below 100 (Bolton, Duxbury, Fayston, Moretown, WAITSFIELD, Warren). Franchise award date:

FULLY SEARCHABLE • CONTINUOUSLY UPDATED • DISCOUNT RATES FOR PRINT PURCHASERS

For more information call **800-771-9202** or visit **www.warren-news.com**

N.A. Franchise expiration date: N.A. Began: October 1, 1982.
Channel capacity: N.A. Channels available but not in use: N.A.

Digital Basic Service
Subscribers: 2,397.
Programming (received off-air): WCAX-TV (CBS, Movies!) Burlington; WETK (PBS) Burlington; WFFF-TV (FOX, IND) Burlington; WPTZ (MeTV, NBC, This TV) Plattsburgh; WVNY (ABC) Burlington; WVPT (PBS) Staunton; 2 FMs.
Programming (via satellite): C-SPAN; C-SPAN 2; C-SPAN 3; HD Theater; various Canadian stations; WGN America.
Programming (via translator): WPIX (Antenna TV, CW, This TV) New York; WSBK-TV (MNT) Boston.
Fee: $25.00 installation; $27.95 monthly.

Digital Expanded Basic Service
Subscribers: N.A.
Programming (via satellite): A&E; A&E HD; AMC; Animal Planet; Cartoon Network; CMT; CNBC; CNN; CNN HD; Comedy Central; Discovery Channel; Disney Channel; Disney Channel HD; Disney XD; E! HD; ESPN; ESPN HD; ESPN2; ESPN2 HD; Food Network; Food Network HD; Fox News Channel; Freeform; Freeform HD; FX; History; History HD; HLN; Lifetime; MSNBC; MTV; National Geographic Channel; National Geographic Channel HD; NBCSN; New England Sports Network; NFL Network; NFL Network HD; Nickelodeon; Oxygen; Spike TV; TBS; TBS HD; The Weather Channel; TLC; TNT; TNT HD; Travel Channel; Travel Channel HD; truTV; TV Land; USA Network; VH1.
Fee: $32.00 monthly.

Digital Expanded Basic Service 2
Subscribers: N.A.
Programming (via satellite): BBC America; Bio HD; Bloomberg Television; Bravo; Cloo; CMT; Destination America; Discovery Kids Channel; Discovery Life Channel; DIY Network; DMX Music; ESPN Classic; ESPNews; ESPNU; Fox Sports 1; Fuse; FYI; Golf Channel; GSN; Hallmark Channel; HGTV; HGTV HD; History International; HRTV; IFC; Investigation Discovery; LMN; MTV Classic; MTV Hits; MTV2; Nick Jr.; Outdoor Channel; Outdoor Channel 2 HD; OWN: Oprah Winfrey Network; Science Channel; Sundance TV; Syfy; TeenNick; Tennis Channel; Trinity Broadcasting Network (TBN); Turner Classic Movies; Versus HD; VH1 Soul; WE tv.
Fee: $17.00 monthly.

Digital Pay Service 1
Pay Units: N.A.
Programming (via satellite): Cinemax (multiplexed); Cinemax HD; HBO (multiplexed); HBO HD; Showtime (multiplexed); Showtime HD; Starz (multiplexed); Starz Encore (multiplexed); Starz HD; The Movie Channel (multiplexed).
Fee: $12.95 monthly (HBO, Cinemax, Showtime/TMC, or Starz/Encore).
Video-On-Demand: No

Vermont—Cable Systems

Pay-Per-View
iN DEMAND (delivered digitally); MLB Extra Innings; NBA League Pass (delivered digitally).

Internet Service
Operational: No, DSL & dial-up.

Telephone Service
Analog: Operational

Miles of Plant: 349.0 (coaxial); 104.0 (fiber optic). Homes passed: 5,449.

President & Chief Executive Officer: Gregg Haskin. Technical Supervisor: Don Whittman. Customer Service Manager: Patricia Labnon.

Ownership: Waitsfield-Fayston Telephone Co.

WEST DOVER—Duncan Cable TV (formerly Area Telecable). Now served by WILMINGTON, VT [VT0017]. ICA: VT0016.

WHITINGHAM—Formerly served by Area Telecable. No longer in operation. ICA: VT0087.

WILLIAMSTOWN (portions)—Formerly served by North Valley Cable Systems Inc. No longer in operation. ICA: VT0084.

WILMINGTON—Duncan Cable TV Service, 48 Sunny Knoll Dr, PO Box 685, Wilmington, VT 05363-0685. Phone: 802-464-2233. Fax: 802-464-3232. E-mail: dctv8@sover.net. Web Site: http://www.duncancable.com. Also serves Wardsboro Twp. & West Dover. ICA: VT0017.

TV Market Ranking: Below 100 (Wardsboro Twp., West Dover, WILMINGTON). Franchise award date: N.A. Franchise expiration date: N.A. Began: January 1, 1966.

Channel capacity: N.A. Channels available but not in use: N.A.

Basic Service
Subscribers: N.A.

Programming (received off-air): WNNE (NBC) Hartford; WTEN (ABC) Albany; WVTA (PBS) Windsor; allband FM.

Programming (via microwave): WBZ-TV (CBS, Decades) Boston; WCVB-TV (ABC, MeTV) Boston; WFXT (FOX, Movies!) Boston; WGBH-TV (PBS) Boston; WHDH (NBC, This TV) Boston; WLVI (CW, The Country Network) Cambridge; WSBK-TV (MNT) Boston.

Programming (via satellite): A&E; AMC; CNBC; CNN; Discovery Channel; Disney Channel; ESPN; HGTV; Lifetime; Nickelodeon; QVC; Spike TV; Syfy; TBS; TLC; TNT; truTV; VH1.

Fee: $49.95 installation.

Pay Service 1
Pay Units: N.A.
Programming (via satellite): HBO.
Fee: $12.95 monthly.

Video-On-Demand: No

Internet Service
Operational: Yes, Dial-up. Began: April 1, 2002.
Broadband Service: Sovernet.
Fee: $39.95 monthly.

Telephone Service
None

Miles of Plant: 52.0 (coaxial); 12.0 (fiber optic).

General Manager: Clifford Duncan.
Ownership: Clifford Duncan.

VIRGINIA

Total Systems: . . . 44	Communities with Applications: . . . 0
Total Communities Served: . . . 454	Number of Basic Subscribers: . . . 980,497
Franchises Not Yet Operating: . . . 0	Number of Expanded Basic Subscribers: . . . 5,630
Applications Pending: . . . 0	Number of Pay Units: . . . 165

Top 100 Markets Represented: Norfolk-Newport News-Portsmouth-Hampton (44); Richmond-Petersburg (63); Roanoke-Lynchburg (70); Washington, DC (9).

For a list of cable communities in this section, see the Cable Community Index located in the back of Cable Volume 2.
For explanation of terms used in cable system listings, see p. D-11.

ALEXANDRIA—Comcast Cable. Now served by PRINCE WILLIAM COUNTY (portions), VA [VA0148]. ICA: VA0009.

ALTAVISTA—Formerly served by Adelphia Communications. Now served by Comcast Cable, DANVILLE, VA [VA0012]. ICA: VA0068.

AMELIA COUNTY (portions)—Comcast Cable. Now served by PETERSBURG, VA [VA0186]. ICA: VA0084.

AMHERST COUNTY (portions)—Comcast Cable. Now served by LYNCHBURG, VA [VA0013]. ICA: VA0039.

APPOMATTOX—Formerly served by Jet Broadband. Now served by Shentel, RUSTBURG, VA [VA0128]. ICA: VA0088.

ARLINGTON COUNTY (portions)—Comcast Cable. Now served by PRINCE WILLIAM COUNTY (portions), VA [VA0148]. ICA: VA0005.

AUSTINVILLE—Formerly served by Citizens Telephone Coop. No longer in operation. ICA: VA5301.

BARREN SPRINGS—Formerly served by Citizens Telephone Coop. No longer in operation. ICA: VA5302.

BASTIAN—Formerly served by Almega Cable. No longer in operation. ICA: VA0124.

BEDFORD—Formerly served by Charter Communications. Now served by Shentel, ROCKY MOUNT, VA [VA0196]. ICA: VA0048.

BELLE HAVEN—Charter Communications. Now served by ACCOMAC, VA [VA0158]. ICA: VA0046.

BEN HUR—Comcast Cable. Now served by KNOXVILLE, TN [TN0004]. ICA: VA0123.

BIRCHLEAF—Formerly served by R&S Communications LLC. No longer in operation. ICA: VA0184.

BISHOP—Formerly served by Bishop TV Club Inc. Now served by Time Warner Cable, RICHLANDS (town), VA [VA0041]. ICA: VA0118.

BLACKSBURG—Comcast Cable. Now served by SALEM, VA [VA0024]. ICA: VA0020.

BLACKSTONE—Formerly served by Nesbe Cable TV. Now served by Shentel, CREWE, VA [VA0099]. ICA: VA0081.

BOWLING GREEN—MetroCast. Now served by KING GEORGE, VA [VA0058]. ICA: VA0093.

BRISTOL—BVU OptiNet. Formerly [VA0190]. This cable system has converted to IPTV, 15022 Lee Hwy, Bristol, VA 24202. Phones: 276-821-6100; 866-835-1288. Fax: 276-821-6218. E-mail: help@bvu-optinet.com; info@bvu.net. Web Site: http://www.bvu-optinet.com. Also serves Abingdon (town), Hiltons & Washington County (unincorporated areas). ICA: VA5201.
TV Market Ranking: Below 100 (BRISTOL, Washington County (unincorporated areas)).
Channel capacity: N.A. Channels available but not in use: N.A.
Basic
Subscribers: 7,470.
Fee: $13.78 monthly. 28 channels - 20 in SD & 8 in HD.
Expanded
Subscribers: N.A.
Fee: $49.95 monthly 136 channels - 77 in SD & 59 in HD plus 46 music channels & one HD DVR.
Digital Essential
Subscribers: N.A.
Fee: $59.95 monthly. 136 channels - 77 in SD & 59 in HD plus 46 music channels & one HD DVR.
Family
Subscribers: N.A.
Fee: $74.95 monthly. 199 channels - 132 in SD & 74 in HD plus 46 music channels & one HD DVR.
Entertainment
Subscribers: N.A.
Fee: $89.95 monthly. 233 channels - 153 in SD & 74 in HD plus 46 music channels & one HD DVR.
Ultimate
Subscribers: N.A.
Fee: $119.95 monthly. 257 channels - 177 in SD & 80 in HD plus 46 music channels, one HD DVR, one whole home DVR & premium channels.
Internet Service
Operational: Yes.
Fee: $36.36-$259.95 monthly.
Telephone Service
Digital: Operational
Fee: $13.62-$14.64 monthly
Chief Operating Officer: Mike Bundy.
Ownership: BVU OptiNet.

BRISTOL—BVU OptiNet. This cable system has converted to IPTV. See BRISTOL, VA [VA5201]. ICA: VA0190.

BROOKNEAL—Comcast Cable. Now served by DANVILLE, VA [VA0012]. ICA: VA0125.

BROSVILLE—Chatmoss Cablevision, 12349 Martinsville Hwy, Danville, VA 24541-0855. Phone: 434-685-1521. Fax: 434-685-1803. E-mail: cs@chatmosscable.com. Web Site: http://chatmosscable.com. Also serves Axton, Bachelor's Hall, Cascade, Dry Fork, Tunstall (Pittsylvania County), Vandola & Whitmell. ICA: VA0075.
TV Market Ranking: Below 100 (Axton, Bachelor's Hall, BROSVILLE, Cascade, Dry Fork, Tunstall (Pittsylvania County), Vandola, Whitmell). Franchise award date: February 6, 1989. Franchise expiration date: N.A. Began: July 1, 1989.
Channel capacity: 22 (operating 2-way). Channels available but not in use: N.A.
Basic Service
Subscribers: 2,212.
Programming (received off-air): WBRA-TV (PBS) Roanoke; WDBJ (CBS, Decades, MNT) Roanoke; WFFP-TV (COZI TV, IND, Movies!) Danville; WFMY-TV (CBS) Greensboro; WFXR (CW, FOX) Roanoke; WGHP (Antenna TV, FOX) High Point; WGSR-LD (IND) Reidsville; WPXR-TV (ION) Roanoke; WSET-TV (ABC, Retro TV, WeatherNation) Lynchburg; WSLS-TV (MeTV, NBC) Roanoke; WUNL-TV (PBS) Winston-Salem; WXII-TV (MeTV, NBC) Winston-Salem; WXLV-TV (ABC, The Country Network) Winston-Salem; 24 FMs.
Programming (via satellite): A&E; AMC; BET; Cartoon Network; CMT; CNBC; CNN; Comcast SportsNet Mid-Atlantic; Comedy Central; C-SPAN; Discovery Channel; Disney Channel; ESPN; ESPN2; Freeform; HLN; Lifetime; MTV; Nickelodeon; QVC; Spike TV; Syfy; TBS; The Weather Channel; TLC; TNT; Trinity Broadcasting Network (TBN); USA Network; VH1; WGN America.
Fee: $35.00 installation; $16.00 monthly; $2.50 converter.
Pay Service 1
Pay Units: N.A.
Programming (via satellite): Cinemax; HBO; Showtime.
Fee: $8.95 monthly (Cinemax or Showtime), $9.95 monthly (HBO).
Video-On-Demand: No
Internet Service
Operational: Yes. Began: January 1, 2001.
Subscribers: 700.
Broadband Service: Fightstar.
Fee: $49.95 installation; $34.95 monthly; $10.00 modem lease; $250.00 modem purchase.
Telephone Service
None
Miles of Plant: 259.0 (coaxial); 48.0 (fiber optic). Homes passed: 3,200.
Secretary-Treasurer & General Manager: Charles F. Lewis. Customer Service Manager: Ida S. Lewis.
Ownership: John P. Shoemaker Jr.

BUCHANAN—Shentel, 500 Shentel Way, PO Box 459, Edinburg, VA 22824. Phones: 800-743-6835; 540-984-5224. Fax: 540-984-3438. E-mail: customer_service@shentel.net. Web Site: http://www.shentel.com. ICA: VA0126.
TV Market Ranking: 70 (BUCHANAN).
Channel capacity: 37 (not 2-way capable). Channels available but not in use: N.A.
Basic Service
Subscribers: 16.
Programming (received off-air): WBRA-TV (PBS) Roanoke; WDBJ (CBS, Decades, MNT) Roanoke; WFXR (CW, FOX) Roanoke; WPXR-TV (ION) Roanoke; WSET-TV (ABC, Retro TV, WeatherNation) Lynchburg; WSLS-TV (MeTV, NBC) Roanoke.
Programming (via satellite): A&E; AMC; CNN; Discovery Channel; Disney Channel; ESPN; ESPN2; Freeform; Great American Country; History; Lifetime; Nickelodeon; Spike TV; TBS; The Weather Channel; TLC; TNT; USA Network; WGN America.
Fee: $99.95 installation; $34.86 monthly.
Expanded Basic Service 1
Subscribers: 16.
Fee: $11.00 monthly.
Pay Service 1
Pay Units: N.A.
Programming (via satellite): HBO; Showtime; The Movie Channel.
Fee: $13.95 monthly (each).
Video-On-Demand: No
Internet Service
Operational: No.
Telephone Service
None
Miles of Plant: 39.0 (coaxial); None (fiber optic). Homes passed: 621.
Vice President, Industry Affairs & Regulatory: Chris Kyle. Assistant Secretary, Associate General Counsel: Ann Flowers.
Ownership: Shentel (MSO).

BUENA VISTA—Comcast Cable. Now served by CHARLOTTESVILLE, VA [VA0131]. ICA: VA0147.

BUENA VISTA—Formerly served by Adelphia Communications. Now served by Comcast Cable, BUENA VISTA, VA [VA0147]. ICA: VA0127.

CALLAGHAN—Formerly served by Clearview TV Cable. No longer in operation. ICA: VA0120.

CHARLES CITY COUNTY (portions)—Formerly served by Comcast Cable. No longer in operation. ICA: VA0078.

CHARLOTTESVILLE—Comcast Cable, 400 Westfield Rd, Charlottesville, VA 22901. Phones: 434-951-3800; 434-951-3700. Fax: 434-951-3705. Web Site: http://www.comcast.com. Also serves Caswell County (portions) & Yanceyville, NC; Altavista, Augusta County (portions), Barboursville, Bealeton, Bedford County (portions), Blacksburg, Blue Ridge, Botetourt

2017 Edition   D-801

Virginia—Cable Systems

County (portions), Boydton, Bridgewater, Bristow, Broadway, Brookneal, Buena Vista, Caroline County (portions), Catlett, Chase City, Chatham, Christiansburg, Cloverdale, Craigsville (town), Crimora, Crozet, Culpeper, Culpeper (town), Culpeper County (portions), Dale City, Daleville, Danville, Dayton, Dublin (town), Dumfries (town), Elkton, Fauquier County, Fincastle, Fishersville, Fluvanna County (portions), Fort Belvoir Army Base, Fort Myer Army Base, Fredericksburg, Gainesville, Garrisonville, Glasgow, Goodview, Gordonsville, Goshen, Greene County (portions), Gretna, Grottoes, Halifax, Halifax County (portions), Harrisonburg, Haymarket, Henry County (portions), Hot Springs, Huddleston, Hurt, King William (portions), La Crosse, Lacey Spring, Lake Monticello, Lake Ridge, Lexington, Locust Grove, Louisa, Louisa (town), Louisa County (portions), Luray, Madison, Madison County, Manassas, Manassas Park, Marine Corps Base Quantico, Martinsville, McGaheysville, Mecklenburg County, Mineral (town), Moneta, Montclair, Montgomery County (portions), Mount Clinton, Mount Crawford, Mount Sidney, Nokesville, Occoquan, Orange, Orange County (portions), Page County (portions), Palmyra, Patrick County (portions), Prince William County (portions), Pulaski, Pulaski County (portions), Quantico (town), Reston, Ridgeway, Roanoke County (portions), Rockbridge County (portions), Rockingham, Rockingham County (portions), Ruckersville, Ruther Glen, Salem, Shenandoah (town), Shenandoah County (portions), South Boston, South Hill, Spotsylvania County (portions), Stafford County (portions), Stanardsville, Stanley (town), Stanleytown, Staunton, Stuart, Stuarts Draft, Thaxton, The Plains, Timberville, Triangle, Troutville, Verona, Victoria, Warm Springs, Warrenton, Waynesboro, Weyers Cave, Woodbridge & Woodford, VA. ICA: VA0131.
TV Market Ranking: 47,73 (Caswell County (portions)); 63 (Caroline County (portions) (portions), Fluvanna County (portions) (portions), King William (portions), Locust Grove, Louisa County (portions) (portions), Ruther Glen); 70 (Altavista, Blacksburg, Blue Ridge, Brookneal, Buena Vista, Christiansburg, Cloverdale, Daleville, Fincastle, Glasgow, Goodview, Gretna, Halifax County (portions) (portions), Henry County (portions) (portions), Huddleston, Hurt, Lexington, Moneta, Montgomery County (portions), Patrick County (portions) (portions), Ridgeway, Roanoke County (portions), Rockbridge County (portions), Salem, Thaxton, Troutville); 9 (Bristow, Dale City, Dumfries (town), Fort Belvoir Army Base, Fort Myer Army Base, Gainesville, Haymarket, Lake Ridge, Manassas, Manassas Park, Marine Corps Base Quantico, Montclair, Nokesville, Occoquan, Prince William County (portions), Quantico (town), Reston, Stafford County (portions) (portions), Triangle, Woodbridge); Below 100 (Barboursville, Bealeton, Bedford County (portions), Botetourt County (portions), Bridgewater, Broadway, Catlett, CHARLOTTESVILLE, Chatham, Crimora, Crozet, Culpeper, Culpeper (town), Dayton, Dublin (town), Elkton, Fauquier County, Fishersville, Fredericksburg, Garrisonville, Greene County (portions), Grottoes, Halifax, Lacey Spring, Lake Monticello, Louisa, Louisa (town), Madison County, McGaheysville, Mineral (town), Mount Clinton, Mount Crawford, Mount Sidney, Orange, Orange County (portions), Page County (portions), Pulaski County (portions) (portions), Rockingham, Rockingham County (portions), Shenandoah (town), Shenandoah County (portions), Spotsylvania County (portions), Stanardsville, Stanley (town), Stanleytown, Stuarts Draft, The Plains, Timberville, Verona, Waynesboro, Weyers Cave, Woodford, Yanceyville, Culpeper County (portions), Danville, Gordonsville, Harrisonburg, Luray, Madison, Martinsville, Palmyra, Pulaski, Ruckersville, South Boston, Staunton, Warrenton, Caswell County (portions), Louisa County (portions) (portions), Halifax County (portions) (portions), Henry County (portions) (portions), Stafford County (portions) (portions)); Outside TV Markets (Boydton, Chase City, Craigsville (town), La Crosse, Mecklenburg County, Page County (portions), Pulaski County (portions) (portions), Shenandoah County (portions) (portions), Spotsylvania County (portions) (portions), Victoria, Warm Springs, Goshen, Hot Springs, South Hill, Stuart, Caroline County (portions) (portions), Fluvanna County (portions) (portions), Halifax County (portions) (portions), Patrick County (portions) (portions), Rockbridge County (portions) (portions)). Franchise award date: January 1, 1963. Franchise expiration date: N.A. Began: February 1, 1963.
Channel capacity: N.A. Channels available but not in use: N.A.

Basic Service
Subscribers: 258,229. Commercial subscribers: 2,649.
Programming (received off-air): WAHU-CD (FOX, This TV) Charlottesville; WCAV (CBS) Charlottesville; WHTJ (PBS) Charlottesville; WRIC-TV (ABC) Petersburg; WTTG (Buzzr, FOX) Washington; WVAW-LD (ABC) Charlottesville; WVIR-TV (CW, NBC, WeatherNation) Charlottesville; WVPT (PBS) Staunton; WWBT (Escape, MeTV, NBC) Richmond.
Programming (via satellite): C-SPAN; EVINE Live; QVC; Trinity Broadcasting Network (TBN).
Fee: $29.50-$46.00 installation; $50.00 monthly.

Expanded Basic Service 1
Subscribers: N.A.
Programming (via satellite): A&E; AMC; Animal Planet; BET; Bravo; Cartoon Network; CMT; CNBC; CNN; Comcast SportsNet Mid-Atlantic; Comedy Central; C-SPAN 2; Discovery Channel; Disney Channel; E! HD; ESPN; ESPN2; EWTN Global Catholic Network; Food Network; Fox News Channel; Freeform; FX; Golf Channel; Hallmark Channel; HGTV; History; HLN; Lifetime; MSNBC; MTV; Nickelodeon; Oxygen; Pop; Spike TV; Syfy; TBS; The Weather Channel; TLC; TNT; Travel Channel; truTV; Turner Classic Movies; TV Land; USA Network; VH1.
Fee: $15.00 installation; $6.50 monthly.

Digital Basic Service
Subscribers: N.A.
Programming (via satellite): BBC America; Bloomberg Television; CBS Sports Network; Discovery Digital Networks; Disney XD; DIY Network; ESPN Classic; ESPN HD; ESPN2 HD; ESPNews; Fox Sports 1; Fox Sports 2; Fuse; FXM; FYI; Great American Country; GSN; HD Theater; History International; HITS (Headend In The Sky); IFC; LMN; MC; NBCSN; NFL Network; Outdoor Channel; Sprout; Sundance TV; Tennis Channel; The Word Network; TNT HD; Trinity Broadcasting Network (TBN); WE tv.

Digital Pay Service 1
Pay Units: N.A.
Programming (via satellite): ART America; Cinemax (multiplexed); Flix; HBO (multiplexed); HBO HD; RTN; Showtime (multiplexed); Showtime HD; Starz (multiplexed); Starz Encore (multiplexed); The Filipino Channel; The Movie Channel (multiplexed); TV Asia; TV5, La Television International; Zee TV.
Video-On-Demand: No
Pay-Per-View
iN DEMAND (delivered digitally); Playboy TV (delivered digitally); Fresh (delivered digitally).
Internet Service
Operational: Yes.
Subscribers: 228,490.
Broadband Service: Comcast High Speed Internet.
Fee: $42.95 monthly.
Telephone Service
Digital: Operational
Subscribers: 148,572.
Miles of Plant: 19,286.0 (coaxial); 6,346.0 (fiber optic). Homes passed: 874,042.
Vice President & General Manager: Troy Fitzhugh. Technical Operations Director: Tom Jacobs. Marketing Director: Steve Miles. Marketing Coordinator: Cassie Cool.
Ownership: Comcast Cable Communications Inc. (MSO).

CHARLOTTESVILLE—Formerly served by NTELOS. No longer in operation. ICA: VA0163.

CHASE CITY—Formerly served by Adelphia Communications. Now served by Comcast Cable, SOUTH HILL, VA [VA0062]. ICA: VA0095.

CHESAPEAKE—Mediacom, 2854 Caratoke Hwy, Currituck, NC 27929. Phones: 845-695-2762; 800-239-8411. Web Site: http://www.mediacomcable.com. ICA: VA0183.
TV Market Ranking: 44 (CHESAPEAKE).
Channel capacity: N.A. Channels available but not in use: N.A.
Basic Service
Subscribers: 15.
Fee: $48.07 monthly.
Vice President, Financial Reporting: Kenneth J. Kohrs.
Ownership: Mediacom LLC (MSO).

CHESTERFIELD COUNTY—Formerly served by Comcast Cable. No longer in operation. ICA: VA0132.

CHINCOTEAGUE ISLAND—Charter Communications, 216 Moore Ave, PO Box 348, Suffolk, VA 23434. Phones: 314-543-2236; 636-207-5100 (Corporate office); 757-539-0713. Web Site: http://www.charter.com. ICA: VA0065.
TV Market Ranking: Below 100 (CHINCOTEAGUE ISLAND). Franchise award date: March 1, 1964. Franchise expiration date: N.A. Began: March 15, 1965.
Channel capacity: N.A. Channels available but not in use: N.A.
Digital Basic Service
Subscribers: 1,378.
Programming (via satellite): BBC America; Bloomberg Television; Discovery Life Channel; DIY Network; ESPN Classic; ESPNews; FOX College Sports Central; FOX College Sports Pacific; Fuse; FXM; FYI; GSN; History International; IFC; LMN; MC; Mid-Atlantic Sports Network (MASN); National Geographic Channel; Nick 2; Nick Jr.; Nicktoons; Sundance TV; TeenNick.
Fee: $49.99 installation; $26.99 monthly.
Digital Expanded Basic Service
Subscribers: N.A.
Programming (via satellite): A&E; AMC; Animal Planet; Cartoon Network; CMT; CNBC; CNN; Comcast SportsNet Mid-Atlantic; Comedy Central; Discovery Channel; Disney Channel; Disney XD; E! HD; ESPN; ESPN2; Fox News Channel; Fox Sports 1; Freeform; FX; HGTV; History; HLN; Lifetime; MSNBC; MTV; Nickelodeon; Spike TV; Syfy; TBS; The Weather Channel; TLC; TNT; Travel Channel; TV Land; USA Network; VH1.
Fee: $47.99 monthly.
Digital Pay Service 1
Pay Units: N.A.
Programming (via satellite): Cinemax (multiplexed); Flix; HBO (multiplexed); Showtime (multiplexed); Starz (multiplexed); Starz Encore; The Movie Channel (multiplexed).
Video-On-Demand: No
Pay-Per-View
iN DEMAND (delivered digitally); Playboy TV (delivered digitally); Fresh (delivered digitally); Shorteez (delivered digitally).
Internet Service
Operational: Yes.
Broadband Service: Charter Internet.
Fee: $19.99 monthly.
Telephone Service
None
Miles of Plant: 55.0 (coaxial); None (fiber optic). Homes passed: 3,860.
Vice President & General Manager: Anthony Pope. Operations Manager: Tom Ross. Marketing Director: Brooke Sinclair. Marketing Manager: LaRisa Scales. Accounting Director: David Sovanski.
Ownership: Charter Communications Inc. (MSO).

CLARAVILLE—Formerly served by Adelphia Communications. No longer in operation. ICA: VA0051.

CLARKSVILLE—Shentel, 500 Shentel Way, PO Box 459, Edinburg, VA 22824. Phones: 540-984-5224; 800-743-6835. Fax: 540-984-3438. E-mail: customer_service@shentel.net. Web Site: http://www.shentel.com. Also serves Mecklenburg County (portions). ICA: VA0101.
TV Market Ranking: Outside TV Markets (CLARKSVILLE, Mecklenburg County (portions)). Franchise award date: June 12, 1979. Franchise expiration date: N.A. Began: February 20, 1981.
Channel capacity: N.A. Channels available but not in use: N.A.
Basic Service
Subscribers: 49.
Programming (received off-air): WDBJ (CBS, Decades, MNT) Roanoke; WLFL (CW, The Country Network) Raleigh; WNCN (Antenna TV, CBS) Goldsboro; WRAL-TV (NBC, This TV) Raleigh; WRAY-TV (IND) Wilson; WRAZ (FOX, MeTV) Raleigh; WRDC (MNT) Durham; WRPX-TV (ION) Rocky Mount; WSET-TV (ABC, Retro TV, WeatherNation) Lynchburg; WSLS-TV (MeTV, NBC) Roanoke; WTVD (ABC, Live Well Network) Durham; WUNP-TV (PBS) Roanoke Rapids; 21 FMs.
Programming (via satellite): WGN America.
Fee: $99.95 installation; $33.98 monthly; $.75 converter.

Cable Systems—Virginia

Expanded Basic Service 1
Subscribers: N.A.
Programming (via satellite): A&E; AMC; Animal Planet; BET; Bravo; Cartoon Network; CMT; CNBC; CNN; Comedy Central; Discovery Channel; Disney Channel; E! HD; ESPN; ESPN2; Food Network; Fox News Channel; Fox Sports 1; Freeform; FX; Golf Channel; HGTV; History; HLN; INSP; Lifetime; MSNBC; MTV; Nickelodeon; Oxygen; QVC; Spike TV; Syfy; TBS; The Weather Channel; TLC; TNT; Travel Channel; truTV; Turner Classic Movies; TV Land; USA Network; VH1; WE tv.
Fee: $34.00 monthly.

Digital Basic Service
Subscribers: N.A.
Programming (via satellite): BBC America; Bloomberg Television; CMT; Discovery Kids Channel; Discovery Life Channel; Disney XD; DIY Network; DMX Music; ESPN Classic; ESPNews; FOX College Sports Central; FOX College Sports Pacific; Fuse; FXM; FYI; GSN; History International; IFC; Investigation Discovery; MTV Classic; MTV Hits; MTV Jams; MTV2; National Geographic Channel; Nick 2; Nick Jr.; Nicktoons; OWN; Oprah Winfrey Network; Science Channel; Sundance TV; TeenNick; Tr3s; TV Guide Interactive Inc.; VH1 Soul.
Fee: $13.00 monthly; $6.95 converter.

Digital Pay Service 1
Pay Units: N.A.
Programming (via satellite): Cinemax (multiplexed); Flix; HBO (multiplexed); Showtime (multiplexed); Starz (multiplexed); Starz Encore (multiplexed); The Movie Channel (multiplexed).
Fee: $20.00 installation; $13.00 monthly (Cinemax, HBO, Showtime/TMC/Flix or Starz/Encore).

Video-On-Demand: No

Pay-Per-View
iN DEMAND (delivered digitally); Playboy TV (delivered digitally); Fresh (delivered digitally); Shorteez (delivered digitally).

Internet Service
Operational: Yes.

Telephone Service
Digital: Operational
Miles of Plant: 30.0 (coaxial); None (fiber optic). Homes passed: 1,166.
Vice President, Industry Affairs & Regulatory: Chris Kyle. Assistant Secretary, Associate General Counsel: Ann Flowers.
Ownership: Shentel (MSO).

CLINTWOOD (town)—Formerly served by Adelphia Communications. Now served by Comcast Cable, KNOXVILLE, TN [TN0004]. ICA: VA0057.

COLONIAL BEACH—MetroCast. Now served by KING GEORGE, VA [VA0058]. ICA: VA0063.

COVINGTON—Shentel, 500 Shentel Way, PO Box 459, Edinburg, VA 22824. Phones: 800-743-6835; 540-984-5224. Fax: 540-984-3438. E-mail: customer_service@shentel.net. Web Site: http://www.shentel.com. Also serves Alleghany County, Clifton Forge & Iron Gate. ICA: VA0036.
TV Market Ranking: 70 (Alleghany County (portions), COVINGTON; Below 100 (Clifton Forge, Iron Gate); Outside TV Markets (Alleghany County (portions)). Franchise award date: July 10, 1962. Franchise expiration date: N.A. Began: December 19, 1963.
Channel capacity: N.A. Channels available but not in use: N.A.

Basic Service
Subscribers: 226.
Programming (received off-air): WBRA-TV (PBS) Roanoke; WDBJ (CBS, Decades, MNT) Roanoke; WFXR (CW, FOX) Roanoke; WPXR-TV (ION) Roanoke; WSET-TV (ABC, Retro TV, WeatherNation) Lynchburg; WSLS-TV (MeTV, NBC) Lynchburg; WWCW (CW, FOX) Lynchburg; 1 FM.
Programming (via satellite): A&E; AMC; Animal Planet; Cartoon Network; CMT; CNN; Comedy Central; Discovery Channel; ESPN; ESPN Classic; ESPN2; Food Network; Fox News Channel; FOX Sports Networks; Freeform; Hallmark Channel; HGTV; History; HLN; INSP; Lifetime; MSNBC; MTV; National Geographic Channel; Nickelodeon; QVC; Spike TV; Syfy; TBS; The Weather Channel; TLC; TNT; Travel Channel; TV Land; USA Network; VH1; WGN America.
Fee: $99.95 installation; $34.86 monthly; $2.16 converter.

Digital Basic Service
Subscribers: N.A.
Programming (via satellite): BBC America; Discovery Kids Channel; DMX Music; ESPNews; Fox Sports 1; FXM; FYI; Golf Channel; GSN; History International; LMN; Nick Jr.; Nicktoons; Outdoor Channel; Ovation; Starz Encore; Sundance TV; TeenNick; Turner Classic Movies.
Fee: $10.00 monthly.

Digital Pay Service 1
Pay Units: N.A.
Programming (via satellite): Cinemax (multiplexed); HBO (multiplexed); Showtime.

Video-On-Demand: No

Pay-Per-View
iN DEMAND; special events.

Internet Service
Operational: Yes.
Broadband Service: Rapid High Speed Internet.
Fee: $50.00 installation; $24.95 monthly.

Telephone Service
Digital: Operational
Miles of Plant: 160.0 (coaxial); 20.0 (fiber optic). Homes passed: 7,747.
Vice President, Industry Affairs & Regulatory: Chris Kyle. Assistant Secretary, Associate General Counsel: Ann Flowers.
Ownership: Shentel (MSO).

CRAIGSVILLE—Formerly served by Adelphia Communications. Now served by Comcast Cable, STAUNTON, VA [VA0026]. ICA: VA0133.

CRAWFORD MANOR—Crawford Manor Cable TV, 2806 NE Side Hwy, Elkton, VA 22827. Phone: 540-337-8450. ICA: VA0119.
TV Market Ranking: Below 100 (CRAWFORD MANOR). Franchise award date: N.A. Franchise expiration date: N.A. Began: August 1, 1982.
Channel capacity: N.A. Channels available but not in use: N.A.

Basic Service
Subscribers: N.A.
Programming (received off-air): WDCA (Heroes & Icons, MNT, Movies!, MundoMax) Washington; WHSV-TV (ABC, MeTV, MNT, This TV) Harrisonburg; WJLA-TV (ABC, MeTV, Retro TV) Washington; WTTG (Buzzr, FOX) Washington; WUSA (Bounce TV, CBS, WeatherNation) Washington; WVIR-TV (CW, NBC, WeatherNation) Charlottesville; WVPT (PBS) Staunton; WWBT (Escape, MeTV, NBC) Richmond.
Programming (via satellite): A&E; CNN; Disney Channel; ESPN; Freeform; TBS; TNT; USA Network.
Fee: $30.00 installation.

Pay Service 1
Pay Units: N.A.
Programming (via satellite): Showtime.
Fee: $9.00 monthly.

Video-On-Demand: No

Internet Service
Operational: No.

Telephone Service
None
Miles of Plant: 5.0 (coaxial); None (fiber optic). Homes passed: 250.
Vice President: Atville Lear.
Ownership: Crawford Manor Cable TV.

CREWE—Shentel, 500 Shentel Way, PO Box 459, Edinburg, VA 22824. Phones: 540-984-5224; 800-743-6835. Fax: 540-984-3438. E-mail: customer_service@shentel.net. Web Site: http://www.shentel.com. Also serves Blackstone, Burkeville, Kenbridge & Lunenburg County (portions). ICA: VA0099.
TV Market Ranking: 63 (Blackstone); Outside TV Markets (Burkeville, CREWE, Lunenburg County (portions), Kenbridge). Franchise award date: March 8, 1982. Franchise expiration date: N.A. Began: March 1, 1983.
Channel capacity: N.A. Channels available but not in use: N.A.

Basic Service
Subscribers: 55.
Programming (received off-air): WBRA-TV (PBS) Roanoke; WDBJ (CBS, Decades, MNT) Roanoke; WFFP-TV (COZI TV, IND, Movies!) Danville; WFXR (CW, FOX) Roanoke; WPXR-TV (ION) Roanoke; WSET-TV (ABC, Retro TV, WeatherNation) Lynchburg; WSLS-TV (MeTV, NBC) Roanoke; WWCW (CW, FOX) Lynchburg.
Programming (via satellite): WGN America.
Fee: $99.95 installation; $33.96 monthly.

Expanded Basic Service 1
Subscribers: N.A.
Programming (via satellite): A&E; AMC; Animal Planet; BET; Bravo; Cartoon Network; CMT; CNBC; CNN; Comcast SportsNet Mid-Atlantic; Comedy Central; C-SPAN; Discovery Channel; Disney Channel; Disney XD; E! HD; ESPN; ESPN2; Food Network; Fox News Channel; Fox Sports 1; Freeform; FX; FXM; Golf Channel; Great American Country; Hallmark Channel; HGTV; History; HLN; Lifetime; MSNBC; MTV; National Geographic Channel; Nickelodeon; Outdoor Channel; QVC; Spike TV; Syfy; TBS; The Weather Channel; TLC; TNT; Travel Channel; Trinity Broadcasting Network (TBN); truTV; Turner Classic Movies; TV Land; USA Network; VH1.
Fee: $34.00 monthly.

Digital Basic Service
Subscribers: N.A.
Programming (via satellite): BBC America; Cloo; CMT; Discovery Digital Networks; DIY Network; ESPN Classic; ESPN Deportes; ESPNews; ESPNU; Fuse; FYI; GSN; History International; IFC; LMN; MC; NBCSN; Nick Jr.; Nicktoons; Oxygen; TeenNick; Telemundo.
Fee: $13.00 monthly.

Digital Pay Service 1
Pay Units: N.A.
Programming (via satellite): Cinemax (multiplexed); Flix; HBO (multiplexed); Showtime (multiplexed); Starz (multiplexed); Starz Encore (multiplexed); The Movie Channel (multiplexed).
Fee: $11.95 monthly (Starz/Encore or Cinemax), $12.95 monthly (HBO or Showtime/TMC).

Video-On-Demand: No

Internet Service
Operational: Yes.
Broadband Service: JetBroadband.
Fee: $49.95 installation; $49.95 monthly; $5.00 modem lease.

Telephone Service
Digital: Operational
Miles of Plant: 22.0 (coaxial); None (fiber optic). Homes passed: 3,841.
Vice President, Industry Affairs & Regulatory: Chris Kyle. Assistant Secretary, Associate General Counsel: Ann Flowers.
Ownership: Shentel (MSO).

CROZET—Formerly served by Adelphia Communications. Now served by Comcast Cable, CHARLOTTESVILLE, VA [VA0131]. ICA: VA0097.

CULPEPER—Comcast Cable. Now served by CHARLOTTESVILLE, VA [VA0131]. ICA: VA0182.

CULPEPER (town)—Formerly served by Adelphia Communications. Now served by Comcast Cable, CULPEPPER, VA [VA0182]. ICA: VA0047.

DAMASCUS—Zito Media, 102 S Main St, PO Box 665, Coudersport, PA 16915. Phones: 814-260-9055; 800-365-6988. E-mail: info@zitomedia.com. Web Site: http://www.zitomedia.com. Also serves Washington County (portions). ICA: VA0134.
TV Market Ranking: Below 100 (DAMASCUS, Washington County (portions)).
Channel capacity: N.A. Channels available but not in use: N.A.

Basic Service
Subscribers: 120.
Programming (received off-air): WCYB-TV (CW, Decades, NBC) Bristol; WEMT (FOX, Movies!, This TV) Greeneville; WETP-TV (PBS) Sneedville; WJHL-TV (ABC, CBS, MeTV) Johnson City; WKPT-TV (COZI TV, Escape, MeTV, MNT) Kingsport; WSBN-TV (PBS) Norton.
Programming (via satellite): A&E; AMC; Animal Planet; Bravo; Cartoon Network; CMT; CNBC; CNN; Comedy Central; C-SPAN; C-SPAN 2; Discovery Channel; Disney Channel; E! HD; ESPN; ESPN2; Food Network; Fox News Channel; Fox Sports 1; Freeform; FX; Golf Channel; HGTV; History; HLN; INSP; Lifetime; MSNBC; MTV; Nickelodeon; Outdoor Channel; Oxygen; QVC; Spike TV; Syfy; TBS; The Weather Channel; TLC; TNT; Travel Channel; Trinity Broad-

2017 Edition

D-803

Virginia—Cable Systems

casting Network (TBN); truTV; Turner Classic Movies; TV Land; USA Network; VH1; WE tv.
Fee: $49.95 installation; $18.25 monthly.

Digital Basic Service
Subscribers: N.A.
Programming (via satellite): BBC America; Bloomberg Television; CMT; Discovery Digital Networks; DIY Network; FXM; FYI; GSN; History International; IFC; LMN; National Geographic Channel; Nick 2; Nick Jr.; Nicktoons; Sundance TV; TeenNick.

Digital Pay Service 1
Pay Units: N.A.
Programming (via satellite): Cinemax (multiplexed); Flix; HBO (multiplexed); LOGO; Showtime (multiplexed); Starz (multiplexed); Starz Encore; The Movie Channel (multiplexed).

Internet Service
Operational: Yes.
Subscribers: 34.

Telephone Service
Digital: Operational
Subscribers: 9.
Miles of Plant: 25.0 (coaxial); 5.0 (fiber optic). Homes passed: 350.
President: James Rigas.
Ownership: Zito Media (MSO).

DANVILLE—Comcast Cable. Now served by CHARLOTTESVILLE, VA [VA0131]. ICA: VA0012.

DELTAVILLE—MetroCast Communications, 70 East Lancaster Ave, Frazier, PA 19355. Phones: 800-952-1001; 804-758-3265; 804-758-5870; 804-435-2828. Web Site: http://www.metrocast.com. Also serves Irvington (town), Kilmarnock (town), Lancaster County, Middlesex County, Northumberland County (portions), Saluda, Urbanna & White Stone (town). ICA: VA0085.
TV Market Ranking: 44 (Middlesex County); Outside TV Markets (Irvington (town), Kilmarnock (town), Northumberland County (portions), Saluda, Urbanna, White Stone (town), Lancaster County). Franchise award date: March 1, 1983. Franchise expiration date: N.A. Began: April 2, 1984.
Channel capacity: N.A. Channels available but not in use: N.A.

Basic Service
Subscribers: 4,018.
Programming (received off-air): WAVY-TV (Bounce TV, NBC) Portsmouth; WCVE-TV (PBS) Richmond; WHRO-TV (PBS) Hampton-Norfolk; WRIC-TV (ABC) Petersburg; WRLH-TV (FOX, MNT, This TV) Richmond; WTKR (CBS) Norfolk; WTVR-TV (Antenna TV, CBS) Richmond; WUPV (Bounce TV, CW) Ashland; WVEC (ABC) Hampton; WWBT (Escape, MeTV, NBC) Richmond.
Programming (via satellite): A&E; AMC; Animal Planet; BET; Bravo; Cartoon Network; CNBC; CNN; Comcast SportsNet Mid-Atlantic; Comedy Central; C-SPAN; C-SPAN 2; Discovery Channel; Discovery Life Channel; Disney Channel; ESPN; ESPN Classic; ESPN2; Food Network; Fox News Channel; Fox Sports 1; Freeform; FX; Golf Channel; Hallmark Channel; HGTV; History; HLN; INSP; Lifetime; LMN; MSNBC; MTV; National Geographic Channel; Nickelodeon; Outdoor Channel; OWN: Oprah Winfrey Network; Oxygen; Pop; QVC; Spike TV; Syfy; TBS; The Weather Channel; TLC; TNT; Travel Channel; truTV; TV Land; USA Network; VH1; WGN America.
Fee: $49.95 installation; $33.95 monthly.

Digital Basic Service
Subscribers: N.A.
Programming (via satellite): AXS TV; BBC America; Bloomberg Television; CMT; Discovery Digital Networks; Disney XD; ESPN HD; ESPN2 HD; ESPNews; EVINE Live; FOX College Sports Central; FOX College Sports Pacific; Fuse; FXM; FYI; Great American Country; GSN; HD Theater; History International; IFC; NBCSN; Nick Jr.; Nicktoons; TeenNick; The Word Network; Trinity Broadcasting Network (TBN); WE tv.
Fee: $16.90 monthly.

Digital Pay Service 1
Pay Units: N.A.
Programming (via satellite): Cinemax (multiplexed); DMX Music; Flix; HBO (multiplexed); Showtime (multiplexed); Starz (multiplexed); Starz Encore (multiplexed); The Movie Channel (multiplexed).
Fee: $32.50 installation; $12.95 monthly (Cinemax), $16.50 monthly (Starz/Encore or Showtime/TMC), $19.00 monthly (HBO).

Video-On-Demand: No

Pay-Per-View
Hot Choice; iN DEMAND.

Internet Service
Operational: Yes.
Broadband Service: In-house.
Fee: $99.95 installation; $29.95 monthly; $2.00 modem lease; $99.00 modem purchase.

Telephone Service
Digital: Operational
Fee: $29.95 monthly
Miles of Plant: 224.0 (coaxial); 87.0 (fiber optic). Homes passed: 6,046.
Chief Financial Officer: Shawn P. Flannery. General Manager: Bill Newborg. Mid-Atlantic Regional Engineer: Jeff Shearer.
Ownership: Harron Communications LP (MSO).

DILLWYN—Comcast Cable. Now served by PETERSBURG, VA [VA0186]. ICA: VA0076.

DUFFIELD (town)—Formerly served by Adelphia Communications. Now served by Comcast Cable, KNOXVILLE, TN [TN0004]. ICA: VA0092.

EMPORIA—Comcast Cable. Now served by PETERSBURG, VA [VA0186]. ICA: VA0053.

EWING—Zito Media, 102 S Main St, PO Box 665, Coudersport, PA 16915. Phones: 814-260-9055; 800-365-6988. E-mail: info@zitomedia.com. Web Site: http://www.zitomedia.com. Also serves Lee County (portions) & Rose Hill. ICA: VA0137.
TV Market Ranking: Below 100 (EWING, Lee County (portions), Rose Hill). Franchise award date: May 6, 1976. Franchise expiration date: N.A. Began: March 1, 1976.
Channel capacity: N.A. Channels available but not in use: N.A.

Basic Service
Subscribers: 84.
Programming (received off-air): WBIR-TV (MeTV, NBC) Knoxville; WBXX-TV (CW, Escape) Crossville; WCYB-TV (CW, Decades, NBC) Bristol; WEMT (FOX, Movies!, This TV) Greeneville; WETP-TV (PBS) Sneedville; WJHL-TV (ABC, CBS, MeTV) Johnson City; WKPT-TV (COZI TV, Escape, MeTV, MNT) Kingsport; WLFG (IND, PBJ, Retro TV) Grundy; WSBN-TV (PBS) Norton; WVLT-TV (CBS, MNT) Knoxville.
Programming (via satellite): QVC; WGN America.
Fee: $49.95 installation; $21.95 monthly; $2.20 converter.

Expanded Basic Service 1
Subscribers: N.A.
Programming (via satellite): A&E; CMT; CNN; Discovery Channel; Disney Channel; ESPN; ESPN2; Freeform; Lifetime; Nickelodeon; Spike TV; TBS; TNT; Trinity Broadcasting Network (TBN); USA Network.
Fee: $19.95 monthly.

Digital Basic Service
Subscribers: N.A.
Programming (via satellite): BBC America; Cloo; Discovery Digital Networks; Disney XD; DMX Music; ESPN Classic; ESPNews; Fox Sports 1; Fuse; FYI; Golf Channel; GSN; History International; IFC; LMN; National Geographic Channel; NBCSN; Nick Jr.; Syfy; TeenNick; Turner Classic Movies; WE tv.

Digital Pay Service 1
Pay Units: N.A.
Programming (via satellite): Cinemax (multiplexed); Flix; HBO (multiplexed); Showtime (multiplexed); Starz (multiplexed); Starz Encore (multiplexed); The Movie Channel (multiplexed).

Video-On-Demand: No

Pay-Per-View
iN DEMAND (delivered digitally); Playboy TV (delivered digitally).

Internet Service
Operational: No.

Telephone Service
None
Miles of Plant: 47.0 (coaxial); None (fiber optic). Homes passed: 1,156.
President: James Rigas.
Ownership: Zito Media (MSO).

FAIRFAX COUNTY—Cox Communications, 6205 Peachtree Dunwoody Rd, 12th Floor, Atlanta, GA 30328. Phone: 404-269-6590. Web Site: http://www.cox.com. Also serves Alexandria (portions), Annandale, Burke, Centreville, Chantilly, Clifton, Fairfax, Fairfax Station, Falls Church, Great Falls, Herndon, Lorton, McLean, Oakton, Springfield & Vienna. ICA: VA0001.
TV Market Ranking: 9 (Alexandria (portions), Annandale, Burke, Centreville, Chantilly, Clifton, Fairfax, FAIRFAX COUNTY, Fairfax Station, Falls Church, Great Falls, Herndon, Lorton, McLean, Oakton, Springfield, Vienna). Franchise award date: September 1, 1983. Franchise expiration date: N.A. Began: August 1, 1983.
Channel capacity: N.A. Channels available but not in use: N.A.

Basic Service
Subscribers: 106,080. Commercial subscribers: 6,650.
Programming (received off-air): WDCA (Heroes & Icons, MNT, Movies!, Mundo-Max) Washington; WDCW (Antenna TV, CW, This TV) Washington; WETA-TV (PBS) Washington; WFDC-DT (getTV, UNV) Arlington; WHUT-TV (PBS) Washington; WJLA-TV (ABC, MeTV, Retro TV) Washington; WMPT (PBS) Annapolis; WNVC (ETV) Fairfax; WNVT (ETV) Goldvein; WPXW-TV (ION) Manassas; WRC-TV (COZI TV, NBC) Washington; WTTG (Buzzr, FOX) Washington; WUSA (Bounce TV, CBS, WeatherNation) Washington; 29 FMs.
Programming (via microwave): NewsChannel 8.
Programming (via satellite): C-SPAN; C-SPAN 2; EVINE Live; NASA TV; Pop; QVC; WGN America.
Fee: $29.99 installation; $21.99 monthly; $1.95 converter.

Expanded Basic Service 1
Subscribers: N.A.
Programming (via satellite): A&E; AMC; Animal Planet; BET; Bravo; Cartoon Network; CMT; CNBC; CNN; Comcast SportsNet Mid-Atlantic; Comedy Central; Discovery Channel; Disney Channel; E! HD; ESPN; ESPN2; EWTN Global Catholic Network; Food Network; Fox News Channel; Fox Sports 1; Freeform; FX; HGTV; History; HLN; Lifetime; Mid-Atlantic Sports Network (MASN); MSNBC; MTV; Nickelodeon; OWN: Oprah Winfrey Network; Oxygen; Spike TV; Syfy; TBS; Telemundo; The Weather Channel; TLC; TNT; Travel Channel; Trinity Broadcasting Network (TBN); truTV; Turner Classic Movies; TV Land; USA Network; VH1.
Fee: $27.70 monthly.

Digital Basic Service
Subscribers: N.A.
Programming (via satellite): BBC America; Bloomberg Television; Cooking Channel; Discovery Digital Networks; Disney XD; DIY Network; ESPN Classic; ESPNews; FYI; Golf Channel; GSN; Hallmark Channel; History International; HITS (Headend In The Sky); IFC; LMN; MC; NBCSN; Ovation; Sundance TV; WE tv.
Fee: $20.90 monthly.

Pay Service 1
Pay Units: N.A.
Programming (via satellite): Cinemax; HBO; Showtime; The Movie Channel.
Fee: $12.99 monthly (Cinemax), $13.99 monthly (HBO, Showtime or TMC).

Digital Pay Service 1
Pay Units: N.A.
Programming (via satellite): ART America; Cinemax (multiplexed); HBO (multiplexed); Korean Channel; Showtime (multiplexed); Starz (multiplexed); Starz Encore; The Filipino Channel; The Movie Channel (multiplexed); TV Asia.
Fee: $11.95 monthly (Filipino), $12.95 monthly (ART or Korean), $13.99 monthly (Cinemax, HBO, Showtime/TMC, or Starz/Encore), $14.95 monthly (TV Asia).

Video-On-Demand: Yes

Pay-Per-View
iN DEMAND; iN DEMAND (delivered digitally); NBA League Pass (delivered digitally); Playboy TV (delivered digitally); Fresh (delivered digitally); Shorteez (delivered digitally).

Internet Service
Operational: Yes.
Subscribers: 153,491.
Broadband Service: Cox High Speed Internet.
Fee: $99.95 installation; $44.95 monthly; $15.00 modem lease.

Telephone Service
Digital: Operational
Subscribers: 68,708.
Fee: $27.86 monthly
Miles of Plant: 7,101.0 (coaxial); 1,734.0 (fiber optic). Homes passed: 429,052.
Vice President & General Manager: Janet Branard. Vice President, Tax: Mary Vickers. Vice President, Network Development: Daryl Ladd. Marketing Manager: Byron Whitaker. Public Affairs Director: Alex Horwitz.
Ownership: Cox Communications Inc. (MSO).

Cable Systems—Virginia

FALLS CHURCH—RCN. This cable system has converted to IPTV. See WASHINGTON, DC (portions) [DC5001]. ICA: VA0194.

FARMVILLE—Shentel, 500 Shentel Way, PO Box 459, Edinburg, VA 22824. Phones: 540-984-5224; 800-743-6835. Fax: 540-984-3438. E-mail: info@shentel.net. Web Site: http://www.shentel.com. Also serves Charlotte County (eastern portion), Charlotte Court House, Cumberland County (southwestern portion), Drakes Branch, Hampden Sydney, Keysville, Phenix & Prince Edward County (northwestern portion). ICA: VA0050.
TV Market Ranking: 70 (Phenix); Outside TV Markets (Charlotte County (eastern portion), Charlotte Court House, Cumberland County (southwestern portion), Drakes Branch, FARMVILLE (portions), Hampden Sydney, KEYSVILLE, Prince Edward County (northwestern portion)). Franchise award date: January 10, 1991. Franchise expiration date: N.A. Began: November 11, 1979.
Channel capacity: N.A. Channels available but not in use: N.A.
Basic Service
Subscribers: 174.
Programming (received off-air): WCVE-TV (PBS) Richmond; WCVW (PBS) Richmond; WRIC-TV (ABC) Petersburg; WRLH-TV (FOX, MNT, This TV) Richmond; WSET-TV (ABC, Retro TV, WeatherNation) Lynchburg; WTVR-TV (Antenna TV, CBS) Richmond; WUPV (Bounce TV, CW) Ashland; WWBT (Escape, MeTV, NBC) Richmond; allband FM.
Programming (via satellite): C-SPAN; INSP; QVC; WGN America.
Fee: $99.95 installation; $33.96 monthly; $.75 converter.
Expanded Basic Service 1
Subscribers: N.A.
Programming (via satellite): A&E; AMC; Animal Planet; BET; Bravo; Cartoon Network; CMT; CNBC; CNN; Comcast SportsNet Mid-Atlantic; Comedy Central; Discovery Channel; Disney Channel; E! HD; ESPN; ESPN2; Food Network; Fox News Channel; Fox Sports 1; Freeform; FX; Golf Channel; HGTV; History; HLN; ION Television; Lifetime; MSNBC; MTV; Nickelodeon; Oxygen; Spike TV; Syfy; TBS; The Weather Channel; TLC; TNT; Travel Channel; truTV; Turner Classic Movies; TV Land; USA Network; VH1; WE tv.
Fee: $30.00 monthly.
Digital Basic Service
Subscribers: N.A.
Programming (via satellite): BBC America; Bloomberg Television; Discovery Life Channel; Disney XD; DIY Network; ESPN Classic; ESPNews; FOX College Sports Central; FOX College Sports Pacific; Fuse; FXM; FYI; GSN; History International; IFC; MC; National Geographic Channel; Nick 2; Nick Jr.; Nicktoons; Sundance TV; TeenNick; TV Guide Interactive Inc.
Fee: $13.00 monthly.
Digital Pay Service 1
Pay Units: N.A.
Programming (via satellite): Cinemax (multiplexed); Flix; HBO (multiplexed); Showtime (multiplexed); Starz (multiplexed); Starz Encore (multiplexed); The Movie Channel (multiplexed).
Fee: $14.95 installation; $11.50 monthly (HBO or Showtime).
Video-On-Demand: No

Pay-Per-View
iN DEMAND (delivered digitally); Playboy TV (delivered digitally); Fresh (delivered digitally); Shorteez (delivered digitally).
Internet Service
Operational: Yes.
Fee: $49.95 installation; $49.95 monthly.
Telephone Service
Digital: Operational
Miles of Plant: 73.0 (coaxial); None (fiber optic). Homes passed: 3,161.
President: Christopher French. Assistant Secretary, Associate General Counsel: Ann Flowers. Marketing Manager: Chris Ranson.
Ownership: Shentel (MSO).

FLOYD—Citizens Telephone Coop, 220 Webbs Mill Rd, PO Box 137, Floyd, VA 24091. Phones: 800-741-7525 (Technical Support); 540-745-2111; 800-941-0426. Fax: 540-745-3791. E-mail: gregsapp@citizens.coop. Web Site: http://citizens.coop. Also serves Floyd County (portions) & Fort Chiswell. ICA: VA0104.
TV Market Ranking: 70 (FLOYD, Floyd County (portions) (portions)); Below 100 (Fort Chiswell); Outside TV Markets (Floyd County (portions) (portions)). Franchise award date: August 13, 1983. Franchise expiration date: N.A. Began: December 1, 1986.
Channel capacity: N.A. Channels available but not in use: N.A.
Basic Service
Subscribers: 2,871.
Programming (received off-air): WBRA-TV (PBS) Roanoke; WDBJ (CBS, Decades, MNT) Roanoke; WFFP-TV (COZI TV, IND, Movies!) Danville; WFXR (CW, FOX) Roanoke; WPXR-TV (ION) Roanoke; WSET-TV (ABC, Retro TV, WeatherNation) Lynchburg; WSLS-TV (MeTV, NBC) Roanoke.
Programming (via satellite): C-SPAN; C-SPAN 2; EWTN Global Catholic Network; INSP; QVC; TBS; The Weather Channel; TLC; WGN America.
Fee: $99.00 installation; $15.95 monthly.
Expanded Basic Service 1
Subscribers: 2,713.
Programming (via satellite): A&E; Cartoon Network; CMT; CNBC; CNN; Comedy Central; Discovery Channel; Disney Channel; E! HD; ESPN; ESPN2; ESPNU; Food Network; Fox News Channel; Freeform; FX; Hallmark Channel; HGTV; History; HLN; Lifetime; MSNBC; MTV; Nickelodeon; RFD-TV; Spike TV; Syfy; TNT; truTV; Turner Classic Movies; TV Land; USA Network; VH1.
Fee: $24.00 monthly.
Digital Basic Service
Subscribers: 1,194.
Programming (via satellite): Animal Planet; BET; Bloomberg Television; CNN en Espanol; Comcast SportsNet Mid-Atlantic; Daystar TV Network; DMX Music; ESPN Classic; ESPNews; FamilyNet; LMN; Nick At Nite; Travel Channel; Trinity Broadcasting Network (TBN).
Fee: $25.00 monthly.
Digital Expanded Basic Service
Subscribers: 685.
Programming (via satellite): AMC; BBC America; Boomerang; Bravo; Church Channel; CNN International; Discovery Digital Networks; Disney XD; DIY Network; Family Friendly Entertainment; Flix; FOX College Sports Central; FOX College Sports Pacific; Fox Sports 1; Fox Sports 2; Fuse; FXM; FYI; Golf Channel; GolTV; Great American Country; GSN; History International;

IFC; National Geographic Channel; NBCSN; Nick 2; Nick Jr.; Nicktoons; Outdoor Channel; Oxygen; Starz Encore (multiplexed); Sundance TV; TeenNick; Univision Studios; WE tv.
Fee: $10.00 monthly.
Digital Pay Service 1
Pay Units: 16.
Programming (via satellite): Cinemax (multiplexed).
Fee: $12.95 monthly.
Digital Pay Service 2
Pay Units: 33.
Programming (via satellite): HBO (multiplexed).
Fee: $14.95 monthly.
Digital Pay Service 3
Pay Units: 10.
Programming (via satellite): Showtime (multiplexed).
Fee: $12.95 monthly.
Digital Pay Service 4
Pay Units: N.A.
Programming (via satellite): Starz (multiplexed); The Movie Channel (multiplexed).
Video-On-Demand: No
Internet Service
Operational: Yes, DSL & dial-up.
Telephone Service
Digital: Operational
Miles of Plant: 86.0 (coaxial); 70.0 (fiber optic). Homes passed: 6,000.
Chief Executive Officer & General Manager: J. Gregory Sapp. Assistant General Manager: Dennis Reece. Network Manager: Danny Vaughn. Marketing Director: Robert Weeks.
Ownership: Citizens Cablevision Inc. (VA) (MSO).

FORT A.P. HILL—Formerly served by MetroCast Communications. No longer in operation. ICA: VA0189.

FORT BELVOIR ARMY BASE—Comcast Cable. Now served by PRINCE WILLIAM COUNTY (portions), VA [VA0148]. ICA: VA0055.

FORT CHISWELL—Citizens Telephone Coop. Now served by FLOYD, VA [VA0104]. ICA: VA5303.

FORT CHISWELL—Citizens Telephone Coop. Now served by FLOYD, VA [VA0104]. ICA: VA0066.

FRANKLIN—Charter Communications. Now served by SUFFOLK, VA [VA0025]. ICA: VA0023.

FREDERICKSBURG—Cox Communications, 6205 Peachtree Dunwoody Rd, 12th Floor, Atlanta, GA 30328. Phone: 404-269-6590. Web Site: http://www.cox.com. Also serves Spotsylvania County & Stafford County (southern portion). ICA: VA0019.
Note: This system is an overbuild.
TV Market Ranking: Below 100 (FREDERICKSBURG, Spotsylvania County, Stafford County (southern portion)). Franchise award date: August 1, 1964. Franchise expiration date: N.A. Began: August 15, 1964.
Channel capacity: N.A. Channels available but not in use: N.A.
Basic Service
Subscribers: 10,797. Commercial subscribers: 596.
Programming (received off-air): WCVE-TV (PBS) Richmond; WDCA (Heroes & Icons, MNT, Movies!, MundoMax) Washington; WDCW (Antenna TV, CW, This TV) Washington; WETA-TV (PBS) Washington; WHUT-TV (PBS) Washington; WJLA-TV (ABC, MeTV, Retro TV) Washington; WNVC (ETV) Fairfax; WPXW-TV (ION) Manassas; WRC-TV (COZI TV, NBC) Washington; WRIC-TV (ABC) Petersburg; WTTG (Buzzr, FOX) Washington; WTVR-TV (Antenna TV, CBS) Richmond; WUSA (Bounce TV, CBS, WeatherNation) Washington; WWBT (Escape, MeTV, NBC) Richmond; 24 FMs.
Programming (via satellite): C-SPAN; C-SPAN 2; EVINE Live; EWTN Global Catholic Network; Pop; QVC; TBS.
Fee: $29.99 installation; $21.99 monthly; $2.00 converter.
Expanded Basic Service 1
Subscribers: N.A.
Programming (via satellite): A&E; AMC; Animal Planet; BET; Bravo; Cartoon Network; CMT; CNBC; CNN; Comcast SportsNet Mid-Atlantic; Comedy Central; Discovery Channel; Disney Channel; E! HD; ESPN; ESPN2; Food Network; Fox News Channel; Fox Sports 1; Freeform; FX; HGTV; History; HLN; Lifetime; MSNBC; MTV; Nickelodeon; OWN: Oprah Winfrey Network; Oxygen; Spike TV; Syfy; Telemundo; The Weather Channel; TLC; TNT; Travel Channel; Trinity Broadcasting Network (TBN); truTV; Turner Classic Movies; TV Land; USA Network; VH1.
Fee: $26.00 monthly.
Digital Basic Service
Subscribers: N.A.
Programming (via satellite): BBC America; Bloomberg Television; Cooking Channel; Discovery Digital Networks; Disney XD; DIY Network; ESPN Classic; ESPNews; Fuse; FXM; FYI; Golf Channel; GSN; Hallmark Channel; History International; IFC; LMN; Mid-Atlantic Sports Network (MASN); NBCSN; Sundance TV.
Fee: $14.95 monthly.
Pay Service 1
Pay Units: N.A.
Programming (via satellite): Cinemax; HBO; Showtime; The Movie Channel.
Fee: $3.50 installation; $10.45 monthly (each).
Digital Pay Service 1
Pay Units: N.A.
Programming (via satellite): Cinemax (multiplexed); DMX Music; HBO (multiplexed); HITS (Headend In The Sky); Showtime (multiplexed); Starz (multiplexed); Starz Encore (multiplexed); The Movie Channel (multiplexed).
Fee: $13.99 monthly (each).
Video-On-Demand: Yes

Virginia—Cable Systems

The industry bible...

Consumer Electronics Daily
Warren Communications News
Free 30-day trial—call 800-771-9202 or visit www.warren-news.com

Pay-Per-View
iN DEMAND; Shorteez (delivered digitally); iN DEMAND (delivered digitally); Hot Choice (delivered digitally); Playboy TV (delivered digitally); Fresh (delivered digitally).
Internet Service
Operational: Yes.
Subscribers: 11,311.
Broadband Service: Cox High Speed Internet.
Fee: $39.95 monthly.
Telephone Service
Digital: Operational
Subscribers: 6,127.
Miles of Plant: 765.0 (coaxial); 192.0 (fiber optic). Homes passed: 32,365.
Vice President & General Manager: Janet Branard. Vice President, Tax: Mary Vickers. Vice President, Network Development: Daryl Ladd. Marketing Coordinator: Stacy Thomas. Public Affairs Director: Alex Horwitz.
Ownership: Cox Communications Inc. (MSO).

FRONT ROYAL—Comcast Cable. Now served by FREDERICK COUNTY (portions), MD [MD0009]. ICA: VA0139.

GALAX—Comcast Cable. Now served by KNOXVILLE, TN [TN0004]. ICA: VA0140.

GATE CITY—Scott Telecom & Electronics, 149 Woodland St, PO Box 487, Gate City, VA 24251. Phones: 276-452-9119; 800-833-9823; 276-452-2201. E-mail: sctc@sctc.org. Web Site: http://www.sctc.org. Also serves Daniel Boone, Hiltons, Nickelsville, Weber City & Yuma. ICA: VA0054.
TV Market Ranking: Below 100 (Daniel Boone, GATE CITY, Hiltons, Nickelsville, Weber City, Yuma). Franchise award date: March 15, 1965. Franchise expiration date: N.A. Began: May 5, 1965.
Channel capacity: N.A. Channels available but not in use: N.A.
Basic Service
Subscribers: 3,200.
Programming (received off-air): WAPK-CD (Grit, Laff, MeTV) Kingsport; WCYB-TV (CW, Decades, NBC) Bristol; WEMT (FOX, Movies!, This TV) Greeneville; WETP-TV (PBS) Sneedville; WJHL-TV (ABC, CBS, MeTV) Johnson City; WKPT-TV (COZI TV, Escape, MeTV, MNT) Kingsport; WSBN-TV (PBS) Norton; allband FM.
Programming (via satellite): A&E; AMC; Animal Planet; BET; Cartoon Network; CMT; CNBC; CNN; Comcast SportsNet Mid-Atlantic; C-SPAN; C-SPAN 2; CW PLUS; Destination America; Discovery Channel; Discovery Life Channel; Disney Channel; Disney XD; DIY Network; E! HD; ESPN; ESPN Classic; ESPN2; Family Friendly Entertainment; Food Network; Fox News Channel; Fox Sports 1; Freeform; FX; FXM; Great American Country; GSN; Hallmark Channel; HGTV; History; HLN; INSP; ION Television; Lifetime; LMN; MoviePlex; MSNBC; MTV; National Geographic Channel; NBCSN; Nickelodeon; Outdoor Channel; OWN; Oprah Winfrey Network; QVC; RFD-TV; Science Channel; Spike TV; Syfy; TBS; The Weather Channel; TLC; TNT; Travel Channel; Trinity Broadcasting Network (TBN); truTV; TV Land; USA Network; VH1; WE tv; WGN America.
Fee: $45.50 installation; $28.00 monthly.
Digital Basic Service
Subscribers: N.A.
Programming (via satellite): BBC America; Bloomberg Television; Boomerang; CNN International; ESPNews; FamilyNet; FOX College Sports Central; FOX College Sports Pacific; Fuse; FYI; Golf Channel; History International; HRTV; Investigation Discovery; MC; Nick 2; Nick Jr.; Nicktoons; Oxygen; TeenNick; Tennis Channel; Turner Classic Movies.
Digital Pay Service 1
Pay Units: N.A.
Programming (via satellite): Cinemax (multiplexed); Flix; HBO (multiplexed); Showtime (multiplexed); Starz (multiplexed); Starz Encore (multiplexed); The Movie Channel (multiplexed).
Video-On-Demand: No
Internet Service
Operational: No, DSL.
Telephone Service
Analog: Operational
Miles of Plant: 130.0 (coaxial); None (fiber optic). Homes passed: 3,500.
General Manager: William J. Franklin. Marketing Director: Greg Hood. Chief Technician: Terry Holt.
Ownership: Scott County Telephone Cooperative.

GLADE SPRING—Comcast Cable. Now served by KNOXVILLE, TN [TN0004]. ICA: VA0032.

GLASGOW—Formerly served by Adelphia Communications. Now served by Comcast Cable, BUENA VISTA, VA [VA0147]. ICA: VA0103.

GLOUCESTER COUNTY—Cox Communications. Now served by HAMPTON ROADS (formerly Virginia Beach), VA [VA0002]. ICA: VA0031.

GORDONSVILLE—Comcast Cable. Now served by CULPEPER, VA [VA0182]. ICA: VA0102.

GOSHEN—Comcast Cable. Now served by BUENA VISTA, VA [VA0147]. ICA: VA0165.

GRUNDY (town)—Time Warner Cable. Now served by RICHLANDS (town), VA [VA0041]. ICA: VA0044.

HARRISONBURG—Comcast Cable. Now served by CHARLOTTESVILLE, VA [VA0131]. ICA: VA0016.

HARRISONBURG—Formerly served by NTELOS. No longer in operation. ICA: VA0179.

HAYSI—Formerly served by K & V Cable TV Co. No longer in operation. ICA: VA0116.

HENRICO COUNTY—Comcast Cable. Now served by PETERSBURG, VA [VA0186]. ICA: VA0003.

HOT SPRINGS—Comcast Cable. Now served by BUENA VISTA, VA [VA0147]. ICA: VA0096.

HURT—Formerly served by Adelphia Communications. Now served by Comcast Cable, DANVILLE, VA [VA0012]. ICA: VA0087.

INDEPENDENCE (town)—Formerly served by Adelphia Communications. Now served by Comcast Cable, KNOXVILLE, TN [TN0004]. ICA: VA0142.

IVANHOE—Citizens Telephone Coop. Now served by FORT CHISWELL, VA [VA0066]. ICA: VA5305.

JAMES CITY COUNTY—Cox Communications. Now served by HAMPTON ROADS (formerly Virginia Beach), VA [VA0002]. ICA: VA0027.

JARRATT—CWA Cable, 662 Blackridge Rd, La Crosse, VA 23950-2928. Phones: 800-448-0490; 434-636-6000. Fax: 434-636-2223. ICA: VA0114.
TV Market Ranking: 63 (JARRATT). Franchise award date: November 1, 1989. Franchise expiration date: N.A. Began: July 1, 1990.
Channel capacity: N.A. Channels available but not in use: N.A.
Basic Service
Subscribers: 30.
Programming (received off-air): WRAL-TV (NBC, This TV) Raleigh; WRIC-TV (ABC) Petersburg; WTVR-TV (Antenna TV, CBS) Richmond; WWBT (Escape, MeTV, NBC) Richmond.
Programming (via satellite): BET; CNN; C-SPAN; Discovery Channel; ESPN; Freeform; MTV; Nickelodeon; QVC; Spike TV; TBS; The Weather Channel; TNT; USA Network; WGN America.
Fee: $45.00 installation; $26.71 monthly.
Pay Service 1
Pay Units: 20.
Programming (via satellite): Cinemax.
Fee: $10.00 monthly.
Pay Service 2
Pay Units: 20.
Programming (via satellite): HBO.
Fee: $10.00 monthly.
Internet Service
Operational: No.
Telephone Service
None
Miles of Plant: 40.0 (coaxial); 24.0 (fiber optic). Homes passed: 400.
Ownership: Cathy Ashworth (MSO).

JONESVILLE (town)—Formerly served by CC & S Cable TV. Now served by Comcast Cable, KNOXVILLE, TN [TN0004]. ICA: VA0115.

KEEN MOUNTAIN—Time Warner Cable. Now served by RICHLANDS (town), VA [VA0041]. ICA: VA0083.

KENBRIDGE—Shentel. Now served by CREWE, VA [VA0099]. ICA: VA0110.

KEYSVILLE—Shentel. Now served by FARMVILLE, VA [VA0050]. ICA: VA0143.

KING GEORGE—MetroCast Communications, 70 East Lancaster Ave, Frazer, PA 19355. Phones: 800-952-1001; 540-775-0699; 804-758-5870. Web Site: http://www.metrocast.com. Also serves Essex County (portions), VT; Bowling Green, Caroline County, Caroline County (unincorporated areas), Colonial Beach, Dahlgren, Edgehill, Montross, Port Royal, Richmond County (portions), Sealston, Tappahannock, Warsaw, Westmoreland & Westmoreland County (unincorporated areas), VA. ICA: VA0058.
TV Market Ranking: 63 (Caroline County (portions), Caroline County (unincorporated areas) (portions)); Below 100 (Dahlgren, Port Royal, Bowling Green, Tappahannock, Caroline County (portions), Caroline County (unincorporated areas) (portions)); Outside TV Markets (Edgehill, KING GEORGE, Montross, Richmond County (portions), Sealston, Westmoreland, Westmoreland County (unincorporated areas), Colonial Beach, Warsaw, Caroline County (unincorporated areas) (portions)). Franchise award date: March 6, 1986. Franchise expiration date: N.A. Began: December 8, 1987.
Channel capacity: N.A. Channels available but not in use: N.A.

Basic Service
Subscribers: 6,289. Commercial subscribers: 351.
Programming (received off-air): WCVE-TV (PBS) Richmond; WDCA (Heroes & Icons, MNT, Movies!, MundoMax) Washington; WDCW (Antenna TV, CW, This TV) Washington; WETA-TV (PBS) Washington; WFDC-DT (getTV, UNV) Arlington; WJLA-TV (ABC, MeTV, Retro TV) Washington; WNVC (ETV) Fairfax; WNVT (ETV) Goldvein; WPXW-TV (ION) Manassas; WRC-TV (COZI TV, NBC) Washington; WTTG (Buzzr, FOX) Washington; WTVR-TV (Antenna TV, CBS) Richmond; WUSA (Bounce TV, CBS, WeatherNation) Washington; WWBT (Escape, MeTV, NBC) Richmond.
Programming (via satellite): C-SPAN; EWTN Global Catholic Network (multiplexed); QVC; TBS; Trinity Broadcasting Network (TBN).
Fee: $49.95 installation; $33.95 monthly.

Expanded Basic Service 1
Subscribers: 2,067.
Programming (via satellite): A&E; AMC; Animal Planet; BET; Bloomberg Television; Cartoon Network; CMT; CNBC; CNN; Comcast SportsNet Mid-Atlantic; Comedy Central; C-SPAN 2; Discovery Channel; Disney Channel; E! HD; ESPN; ESPN2; Food Network; Fox News Channel; Fox Sports 1; Freeform; FX; FXM; HGTV; History; HLN; Lifetime; MSNBC; MTV; NBCSN; Nickelodeon; Outdoor Channel; Spike TV; Syfy; The Weather Channel; TLC; TNT; Travel Channel; truTV; Turner Classic Movies; TV Land; USA Network; VH1; WE tv; WGN America.
Fee: $27.50 monthly.

Digital Basic Service
Subscribers: N.A.
Programming (via satellite): BBC America; Discovery Digital Networks; DMX Music; GSN; LMN; MTV Classic; National Geographic Channel; Nick Jr.; VH1 Country.
Fee: $8.95 monthly.

Digital Expanded Basic Service
Subscribers: N.A.
Programming (via satellite): Bravo; ESPN Classic; ESPNews; Golf Channel; IFC; Starz (multiplexed); Starz Encore (multiplexed); WE tv.
Fee: $8.95 monthly.

Cable Systems—Virginia

Digital Pay Service 1
Pay Units: N.A.
Programming (via satellite): Cinemax (multiplexed); HBO (multiplexed); Showtime (multiplexed).
Fee: $12.95 monthly (each).
Video-On-Demand: No
Pay-Per-View
iN DEMAND (delivered digitally).
Internet Service
Operational: Yes.
Fee: $29.95-$69.95 monthly.
Telephone Service
Digital: Operational
Fee: $44.95 monthly
Miles of Plant: 140.0 (coaxial); None (fiber optic).
Vice President, Programming & Marketing: Linda Stuchell-Leibert. Chief Financial Officer: Shawn P. Flannery. General Manager: Bill Newborg. Mid-Atlantic Regional Engineer: Jeff Shearer.
Ownership: Harron Communications LP (MSO).

KING WILLIAM (portions)—Comcast Cable. Now served by PRINCE WILLIAM COUNTY (portions), VA [VA0148]. ICA: VA0166.

LACEY SPRING—Formerly served by Adelphia Communications. Now served by Comcast Cable, HARRISONBURG, VA [VA0016]. ICA: VA0144.

LAKE GASTON—CWA Cable, 662 Blackridge Rd, La Crosse, VA 23950-2928. Phones: 800-448-0490; 434-636-6000. Fax: 434-636-2223. Also serves Bracey, Brunswick County (portions) & Mecklenburg County (portions). ICA: VA0170.
TV Market Ranking: Outside TV Markets (Bracey, Brunswick County (portions), LAKE GASTON, Mecklenburg County (portions)). Franchise award date: N.A. Franchise expiration date: N.A. Began: July 30, 1993.
Channel capacity: 60 (not 2-way capable). Channels available but not in use: N.A.
Basic Service
Subscribers: 800.
Programming (received off-air): WLFL (CW, The Country Network) Raleigh; WRAL-TV (NBC, This TV) Raleigh; WRDC (MNT) Durham; WRIC-TV (ABC) Petersburg; WTVD (ABC, Live Well Network) Durham; WUNP-TV (PBS) Roanoke Rapids.
Programming (via satellite): A&E; CNN; C-SPAN; C-SPAN 2; Discovery Channel; ESPN; Freeform; MTV; Nickelodeon; QVC; Spike TV; TBS; The Weather Channel; TNT; Travel Channel; USA Network; WGN America.
Fee: $45.00 installation; $32.95 monthly.
Pay Service 1
Pay Units: N.A.
Programming (via satellite): HBO.
Fee: $10.00 monthly.
Internet Service
Operational: No.
Telephone Service
None
Miles of Plant: 30.0 (coaxial); None (fiber optic).
Ownership: Cathy Ashworth (MSO).

LANCASTER COUNTY—MetroCast Communications. Now served by DELTAVILLE, VA [VA0085]. ICA: VA0146.

LANGLEY AFB—Cox Communications. Now served by HAMPTON ROADS (formerly Virginia Beach), VA [VA0002]. ICA: VA0008.

LAWRENCEVILLE—Shentel, 500 Shentel Way, PO Box 459, Edinburg, VA 22824. Phones: 540-984-5224; 800-743-6835. Fax: 540-984-3438. E-mail: info@shentel.net. Web Site: http://www.shentel.com. Also serves Alberta & Brunswick County. ICA: VA0089.
TV Market Ranking: 63 (Brunswick County (portions)); Outside TV Markets (Alberta, LAWRENCEVILLE, Brunswick County (portions)). Franchise award date: June 14, 1978. Franchise expiration date: N.A. Began: June 1, 1980.
Channel capacity: N.A. Channels available but not in use: N.A.
Basic Service
Subscribers: 45.
Programming (received off-air): WCVE-TV (PBS) Richmond; WCVW (PBS) Richmond; WRAL-TV (NBC, This TV) Raleigh; WRIC-TV (ABC) Petersburg; WRLH-TV (FOX, MNT, This TV) Richmond; WTVR-TV (Antenna TV, CBS) Richmond; WWBT (Escape, MeTV, NBC) Richmond; allband FM.
Programming (via satellite): C-SPAN; INSP; QVC.
Fee: $99.95 installation; $33.96 monthly; $.75 converter.
Expanded Basic Service 1
Subscribers: N.A.
Programming (via satellite): A&E; AMC; Animal Planet; BET; Bravo; Cartoon Network; CMT; CNBC; CNN; Comedy Central; Discovery Channel; Disney Channel; E! HD; ESPN; ESPN2; Food Network; Fox Sports 1; Freeform; FX; FXM; Golf Channel; HGTV; History; HLN; Lifetime; MSNBC; MTV; Nickelodeon; Oxygen; Spike TV; Syfy; TBS; The Weather Channel; TLC; TNT; Travel Channel; truTV; Turner Classic Movies; TV Land; USA Network; VH1; WE tv.
Fee: $55.95 monthly.
Digital Basic Service
Subscribers: N.A.
Programming (via satellite): BBC America; Bloomberg Television; Discovery Life Channel; Disney XD; DIY Network; ESPN Classic; ESPNews; FOX College Sports Central; FOX College Sports Pacific; Fuse; FXM; FYI; GSN; History International; IFC; MC; National Geographic Channel; Nick 2; Nick Jr.; Nicktoons; Sundance TV; TeenNick; TV Guide Interactive Inc.
Fee: $13.00 monthly.
Digital Pay Service 1
Pay Units: N.A.
Programming (via satellite): Cinemax (multiplexed); Flix; HBO (multiplexed); Showtime (multiplexed); Starz (multiplexed); Starz Encore (multiplexed); The Movie Channel (multiplexed).
Fee: $14.95 installation; $11.95 monthly (HBO).
Video-On-Demand: No
Pay-Per-View
iN DEMAND (delivered digitally); Playboy TV (delivered digitally); Fresh (delivered digitally); Shorteez (delivered digitally).
Internet Service
Operational: Yes.
Subscribers: 154.
Telephone Service
Digital: Operational
Subscribers: 94.
Miles of Plant: 61.0 (coaxial); 24.0 (fiber optic). Homes passed: 1,752.
President: Christopher French. Assistant Secretary, Associate General Counsel: Ann Flowers. Marketing Manager: Chris Ranson.
Ownership: Shentel (MSO).

LEBANON—Shentel, 500 Shentel Way, PO Box 459, Edinburg, VA 22824. Phones: 540-984-5224; 800-743-6835. Fax: 540-984-3438. E-mail: info@shentel.net. Web Site: http://www.shentel.com. Also serves Castlewood, Dante, Honaker, Russell County, St. Paul & Wise. ICA: VA0035.
TV Market Ranking: Below 100 (Castlewood, Dante, Honaker, LEBANON, Russell County, St. Paul, Wise). Franchise award date: N.A. Franchise expiration date: N.A. Began: October 1, 1964.
Channel capacity: N.A. Channels available but not in use: N.A.
Basic Service
Subscribers: 359.
Programming (received off-air): WAPK-CD (Grit, Laff, MeTV) Kingsport; WCYB-TV (CW, Decades, NBC) Bristol; WEMT (FOX, Movies!, This TV) Greeneville; WETP-TV (PBS) Sneedville; WJHL-TV (ABC, CBS, MeTV) Johnson City; WKPT-TV (COZI TV, Escape, MeTV, MNT) Kingsport; WLFG (IND, PBJ, Retro TV) Grundy; WSBN-TV (PBS) Norton; allband FM.
Programming (via satellite): C-SPAN; QVC; The Weather Channel; Trinity Broadcasting Network (TBN); WGN America.
Fee: $99.95 installation; $34.14 monthly.
Expanded Basic Service 1
Subscribers: N.A.
Programming (via satellite): A&E; Animal Planet; Cartoon Network; CMT; CNN; Comcast SportsNet Mid-Atlantic; Comedy Central; Discovery Channel; Disney Channel; E! HD; ESPN; ESPN2; Fox News Channel; Fox Sports 1; Freeform; FX; HGTV; History; HLN; Lifetime; MTV; Nickelodeon; Oxygen; Spike TV; Syfy; TBS; TLC; TNT; Travel Channel; Turner Classic Movies; TV Land; USA Network; VH1; WE tv.
Fee: $30.00 monthly.
Digital Basic Service
Subscribers: N.A.
Programming (via satellite): BBC America; Bloomberg Television; Discovery Digital Networks; Disney XD; DIY Network; FYI; GSN; History International; IFC; LMN; MC; Nick 2; Nick Jr.; Sundance TV; TeenNick; TV Guide Interactive Inc.
Fee: $11.00 monthly.
Digital Pay Service 1
Pay Units: N.A.
Programming (via satellite): Cinemax (multiplexed); Flix; HBO (multiplexed); Showtime (multiplexed); The Movie Channel (multiplexed).
Video-On-Demand: No
Pay-Per-View
Hot Choice (delivered digitally); iN DEMAND (delivered digitally).
Internet Service
Operational: Yes.
Broadband Service: JetBroadband.
Fee: $49.95 installation; $29.95 monthly.
Telephone Service
Digital: Operational
Miles of Plant: 175.0 (coaxial); None (fiber optic). Homes passed: 8,095.
President: Christopher French. Assistant Secretary, Associate General Counsel: Ann Flowers. Marketing Manager: Chris Ranson.
Ownership: Shentel (MSO).

LEBANON (portions)—Formerly served by Almega Cable. No longer in operation. ICA: VA0185.

LOUDOUN COUNTY (portions)—Comcast Cable. Now served by PRINCE WILLIAM COUNTY (portions), VA [VA0148]. ICA: VA0021.

LOUISA—Comcast Cable. Now served by CHARLOTTESVILLE, VA [VA0131]. ICA: VA0090.

LOVINGSTON/SHIPMAN—Nelson Cable, 380 Front St, Lovingston, VA 22949. Phone: 434-263-4805. Fax: 434-263-4821. E-mail: joeleemc@aol.com. Web Site: http://www.nelsoncable.com. Also serves Scottsville & Shipman. ICA: VA0192.
TV Market Ranking: 70 (SHIPMAN); Below 100 (Scottsville).
Channel capacity: N.A. Channels available but not in use: N.A.
Basic Service
Subscribers: 218.
Programming (received off-air): WCVE-TV (PBS) Richmond; WDBJ (CBS, Decades, MNT) Roanoke; WFFP-TV (COZI TV, IND, Movies!) Danville; WRIC-TV (ABC) Petersburg; WRLH-TV (FOX, MNT, This TV) Richmond; WSET-TV (ABC, Retro TV, WeatherNation) Lynchburg; WSLS-TV (MeTV, NBC) Roanoke; WTVR-TV (Antenna TV, CBS) Richmond; WVIR-TV (CW, NBC, WeatherNation) Charlottesville.
Programming (via satellite): A&E; AMC; BET; Cartoon Network; CMT; CNN; Discovery Channel; Disney Channel; ESPN; ESPN2; Freeform; Nickelodeon; Spike TV; TBS; The Weather Channel; TNT; Trinity Broadcasting Network (TBN).
Fee: $27.50 monthly.
Pay Service 1
Pay Units: N.A.
Programming (via satellite): Cinemax; HBO.
Fee: $7.00 monthly (Cinemax), $7.50 monthly (HBO).
Video-On-Demand: No
Internet Service
Operational: No.
Telephone Service
None
President: Joe Lee McClellan. Chief Technician: Terry Engelhardt.
Ownership: Nelson County Cablevision Corp. (MSO).

LURAY—Comcast Cable. Now served by HARRISONBURG, VA [VA0016]. ICA: VA0042.

LYNCHBURG—Comcast Cable, 400 Westfield Rd, Charlottesville, VA 22901. Phones: 434-951-3800; 434-951-3700. Fax: 434-951-3705. Web Site: http://www.comcast.com. Also serves Amherst, Amherst County (portions), Bedford County (portions) & Campbell County (portions). ICA: VA0013.
TV Market Ranking: 70 (Amherst, Amherst County (portions), Bedford County (portions), Campbell County (portions), LYNCHBURG). Franchise award date: January 1, 1972. Franchise expiration date: N.A. Began: June 1, 1977.
Channel capacity: N.A. Channels available but not in use: N.A.
Basic Service
Subscribers: 14,161. Commercial subscribers: 980.
Programming (received off-air): WBRA-TV (PBS) Roanoke; WDBJ (CBS, Decades, MNT) Roanoke; WFFP-TV (COZI TV, IND, Movies!) Danville; WFXR (CW, FOX) Roanoke; WPXR-TV (ION) Roanoke; WSET-TV (ABC, Retro TV, WeatherNation) Lynchburg; WSLS-TV (MeTV, NBC) Roanoke; WVPT (PBS) Staunton; WWCW (CW, FOX) Lynchburg.

2017 Edition   D-807

Virginia—Cable Systems

Programming (via satellite): C-SPAN 2; EVINE Live; Hallmark Channel; Pop; QVC; WGN America.
Fee: $29.50-$42.75 installation; $11.35 monthly.
Expanded Basic Service 1
Subscribers: N.A.
Programming (via satellite): A&E; AMC; Animal Planet; BET; Bravo; Cartoon Network; CMT; CNBC; CNN; Comcast SportsNet Mid-Atlantic; Comedy Central; C-SPAN; Discovery Channel; Disney Channel; E! HD; ESPN; ESPN2; Food Network; Fox News Channel; Freeform; FX; HGTV; History; HLN; INSP; Lifetime; MSNBC; MTV; Nickelodeon; Spike TV; Syfy; TBS; The Weather Channel; TLC; TNT; Travel Channel; truTV; Turner Classic Movies; TV Land; USA Network; VH1.
Digital Basic Service
Subscribers: N.A.
Programming (via satellite): BBC America; Bloomberg Television; CMT; Discovery Digital Networks; Disney XD; DIY Network; ESPN Classic; ESPNews; Flix; Fox Sports 1; Fuse; FXM; Great American Country; GSN; HITS (Headend In The Sky); LMN; LOGO; MC; National Geographic Channel; Nick 2; Nick Jr.; Nicktoons; TeenNick; The Word Network; Trinity Broadcasting Network (TBN); WE tv.
Digital Expanded Basic Service
Subscribers: N.A.
Programming (via satellite): CBS Sports Network; FOX College Sports Central; FOX College Sports Pacific; Fox Sports 2; FYI; Golf Channel; History International; IFC; NBCSN; NFL Network; Outdoor Channel; Sundance TV; Tennis Channel.
Digital Pay Service 1
Pay Units: N.A.
Programming (via satellite): ART America; Cinemax (multiplexed); Flix; HBO (multiplexed); RAI Italia; Showtime (multiplexed); Starz (multiplexed); Starz Encore (multiplexed); The Filipino Channel; The Movie Channel (multiplexed); TV Asia; TV5, La Television International.
Video-On-Demand: No
Pay-Per-View
Special events (delivered digitally); Playboy TV (delivered digitally); Fresh (delivered digitally); ESPN (delivered digitally); NHL Center Ice (delivered digitally); MLB Extra Innings (delivered digitally).
Internet Service
Operational: Yes.
Subscribers: 9,447.
Broadband Service: Comcast High Speed Internet.
Fee: $42.95 monthly; $7.00 modem lease.
Telephone Service
Digital: Operational
Subscribers: 6,524.
Miles of Plant: 994.0 (coaxial); 346.0 (fiber optic). Homes passed: 42,240.
Vice President & General Manager: Troy Fitzhugh. Technical Operations Director: Tom Jacobs. Technical Operations Manager: Mike Buckner. Marketing Director: Steve Miles.
Ownership: Comcast Cable Communications Inc. (MSO).

MADISON—Comcast Cable. Now served by CHARLOTTESVILLE, VA [VA0131]. ICA: VA0106.

MARION (town)—Comcast Cable. Now served by KNOXVILLE, TN [TN0004]. ICA: VA0149.

MARTINSVILLE—Comcast Cable. Now served by DANVILLE, VA [VA0012]. ICA: VA0150.

MATHEWS—MetroCast Communications, 10514 Buckley Hall Rd, Mathews, VA 23109. Phones: 877-959-4863; 800-952-1001; 804-529-6670; 804-435-2828; 804-758-5870. Fax: 804-725-1149. E-mail: administration@harron.com. Web Site: http://www.metrocast.com. Also serves Mathews County. ICA: VA0056.
TV Market Ranking: 44 (MATHEWS, Mathews County). Franchise award date: March 22, 1988. Franchise expiration date: N.A. Began: December 1, 1988.
Channel capacity: N.A. Channels available but not in use: N.A.
Basic Service
Subscribers: 981. Commercial subscribers: 15.
Programming (received off-air): WAVY-TV (Bounce TV, NBC) Portsmouth; WGNT (Antenna TV, CW) Portsmouth; WHRO-TV (PBS) Hampton-Norfolk; WTKR (CBS) Norfolk; WTVZ-TV (MNT, The Country Network) Norfolk; WVBT (FOX) Virginia Beach; WVEC (ABC) Hampton.
Programming (via satellite): C-SPAN; C-SPAN 2; INSP; LWS Local Weather Station; QVC; TBS.
Fee: $46.00 installation; $28.95 monthly.
Expanded Basic Service 1
Subscribers: N.A.
Programming (via satellite): A&E; BET; CMT; CNBC; CNN; Comcast SportsNet Mid-Atlantic; Discovery Channel; Disney Channel; ESPN; ESPN2; Fox News Channel; Freeform; History; HLN; Lifetime; MTV; Nickelodeon; Spike TV; Syfy; The Weather Channel; TNT; USA Network; VH1.
Fee: $17.00 monthly.
Digital Basic Service
Subscribers: N.A.
Programming (via satellite): BBC America; Bloomberg Television; Bravo; Discovery Life Channel; ESPN Classic; ESPNews; Fox Sports 1; FXM; Golf Channel; GSN; HGTV; MTV Classic; National Geographic Channel; NBCSN; Nick Jr.; Nicktoons; Outdoor Channel; Trinity Broadcasting Network (TBN); Turner Classic Movies; VH1 Country; WE tv.
Digital Pay Service 1
Pay Units: N.A.
Programming (via satellite): Cinemax (multiplexed); HBO (multiplexed); Showtime (multiplexed); Starz Encore; The Movie Channel (multiplexed).
Fee: $15.99 monthly (Starz, Cinemax, Showtime or TMC), $17.99 monthly (HBO).
Video-On-Demand: No

Pay-Per-View
Hits Movies & Events (delivered digitally); Fresh (delivered digitally); Playboy TV (delivered digitally).
Internet Service
Operational: No.
Telephone Service
None
Miles of Plant: 158.0 (coaxial); None (fiber optic).
Chief Financial Officer: Shawn P. Flannery. General Manager: Bill Newborg. Regional Engineer: Jeff Shearer.
Ownership: Harron Communications LP (MSO).

MAX MEADOWS—Citizens Telephone Coop. Now served by FORT CHISWELL, VA [VA0066]. ICA: VA5304.

MCKENNEY—Formerly served by Adelphia Communications. Now served by Comcast Cable, PETERSBURG, VA [VA0186]. ICA: VA0086.

MONTEREY—Formerly served by Highland Communications. No longer in operation. ICA: VA0113.

MOUNT CLINTON—Formerly served by Adelphia Communications. Now served by Comcast Cable, HARRISONBURG, VA [VA0016]. ICA: VA0153.

NEW CASTLE (town)—Citizens Telephone Coop, 220 Webbs Mill Rd, PO Box 137, Floyd, VA 24091. Phones: 800-741-7525 (Technical Support); 540-745-2111; 800-941-0426. Fax: 540-745-3791. Web Site: http://citizens.coop. Also serves Craig County (portions). ICA: VA0105.
TV Market Ranking: 70 (Craig County (portions), NEW CASTLE (TOWN)).
Channel capacity: N.A. Channels available but not in use: N.A.
Basic Service
Subscribers: 177.
Programming (received off-air): WBRA-TV (PBS) Roanoke; WDBJ (CBS, Decades, MNT) Roanoke; WFXR (CW, FOX) Roanoke; WPXR-TV (ION) Roanoke; WSET-TV (ABC, Retro TV, WeatherNation) Lynchburg; WSLS-TV (MeTV, NBC) Roanoke.
Programming (via satellite): C-SPAN; QVC; TBS; WGN America.
Fee: $99.00 installation; $15.95 monthly.
Expanded Basic Service 1
Subscribers: 149.
Programming (via satellite): CMT; CNN; Discovery Channel; Disney Channel; ESPN; ESPN2; Freeform; MSNBC; MTV; Nickelodeon; Spike TV; Syfy; The Weather Channel; TLC; TNT; Turner Classic Movies; USA Network.
Fee: $24.00 monthly.
Pay Service 1
Pay Units: 13.
Programming (via satellite): Cinemax.
Fee: $9.95 monthly.
Pay Service 2
Pay Units: 41.
Programming (via satellite): HBO.
Fee: $11.95 monthly.
Pay Service 3
Pay Units: 12.
Programming (via satellite): Showtime.
Fee: $9.95 monthly.
Video-On-Demand: No
Internet Service
Operational: Yes, DSL.

Telephone Service
None
Miles of Plant: 24.0 (coaxial); None (fiber optic). Homes passed: 746.
Chief Executive Officer & General Manager: J. Gregory Sapp. Network Manager: Danny Vaughn. Marketing Director: Robert Weeks. Executive Administrative Assistant: Amanda Souiers.
Ownership: Citizens Cablevision Inc. (VA) (MSO).

NEW KENT—Cox Communications. Now served by HAMPTON ROADS (formerly Virginia Beach), VA [VA0002]. ICA: VA0156.

NEWPORT—PemTel, 504 Snidow Street, PO Box 549, Pembroke, VA 24136. Phone: 540-626-7111. E-mail: pembroke@pemtel.net. Web Site: http://www.pemtel.com. Also serves Pembroke & Simmonsville. ICA: VA0197.
TV Market Ranking: 70 (NEWPORT, Pembroke, Simmonsville).
Channel capacity: N.A. Channels available but not in use: N.A.
Basic Service
Subscribers: 933.
Fee: $45.00 installation; $52.35 monthly.
General Manager: Lisa Epperley.
Ownership: Giles-Craig Communications Inc.

NICKELSVILLE—Formerly served by Scott Telecom & Electronics. No longer in operation. ICA: VA0187.

NORTHUMBERLAND COUNTY—MetroCast Communications, 129 Northumberland Highway, Callao, VA 22435. Phones: 800-952-1001; 804-758-3265; 804-435-2828; 804-758-5870. Web Site: http://www.metrocast.com. Also serves Burgess, Callao, Edwardsville, Heathsville, Lewisetta, Lottsburg, Ophelia, Reedville, Walmsley & Wicomico Church. ICA: VA0195.
TV Market Ranking: Outside TV Markets (Burgess, Callao, Edwardsville, Heathsville, Lewisetta, Lottsburg, NORTHUMBERLAND COUNTY, Ophelia, Reedville, Walmsley, Wicomico Church).
Channel capacity: N.A. Channels available but not in use: N.A.
Basic Service
Subscribers: 632.
Programming (received off-air): WAVY-TV (Bounce TV, NBC) Portsmouth; WCVE-TV (PBS) Richmond; WGNT (Antenna TV, CW) Portsmouth; WHRO-TV (PBS) Hampton-Norfolk; WRIC-TV (ABC) Petersburg; WRLH-TV (FOX, MNT, This TV) Richmond; WTVR-TV (Antenna TV, CBS) Richmond; WUPV (Bounce TV, CW) Ashland; WUSA (Bounce TV, CBS, WeatherNation) Washington; WWBT (Escape, MeTV, NBC) Richmond.
Programming (via satellite): BET; C-SPAN; C-SPAN 2; TBS; The Weather Channel.
Fee: $24.80 monthly.
Expanded Basic Service 1
Subscribers: N.A.
Programming (via satellite): A&E; CMT; CNBC; CNN; Comcast SportsNet Mid-Atlantic; Discovery Channel; Disney Channel; ESPN; ESPN2; Fox News Channel; Freeform; HGTV; HLN; Lifetime; MSNBC; MTV; Nickelodeon; QVC; Spike TV; TNT; TV Land; USA Network; VH1.
Digital Basic Service
Subscribers: N.A.
Programming (via satellite): BBC America; Bloomberg Television; Bravo; CMT; Discovery Digital Networks; DMX Music; ESPN

Cable Systems—Virginia

Classic; ESPNews; Fox Sports 1; FXM; Golf Channel; GSN; History; IFC; MTV Classic; National Geographic Channel; NBCSN; Nick Jr.; Nicktoons; Outdoor Channel; Trinity Broadcasting Network (TBN); Turner Classic Movies; WE tv.

Digital Pay Service 1
Pay Units: N.A.
Programming (via satellite): Cinemax (multiplexed); HBO (multiplexed); Showtime (multiplexed); Starz (multiplexed); Starz Encore (multiplexed); The Movie Channel (multiplexed).

Pay-Per-View
Special events (delivered digitally); Playboy TV (delivered digitally).

Internet Service
Operational: Yes.
Fee: $21.95-$58.95 monthly.

Telephone Service
Digital: Operational
Fee: $44.95 monthly
Miles of Plant: 220.0 (coaxial); None (fiber optic).
General Manager: Bill Newborg. Mid-Atlantic Regional Engineer: Jeff Shearer.
Ownership: Harron Communications LP (MSO).

NORTON—Comcast Cable. Now served by KNOXVILLE, TN [TN0004]. ICA: VA0157.

ONANCOCK—Charter Communications, 12405 Powerscourt Dr, St. Louis, MO 63131. Phones: 636-207-5100 (Corporate office); 757-539-0713. Fax: 757-539-1057. Web Site: http://www.charter.com. Also serves Accomac, Accomack County, Atlantic, Belle Haven, Bloxom, Cape Charles, Cheriton, Craddockville, Eastville, Exmore, Hallwood, Harborton, Keller, Mappsville, Melfa, Nassawadox, New Church, Northampton County, Oak Hall, Onley, Painter, Parksley, Pungoteague, Sanford, Saxis, Shadyside, Temperanceville, Wachapreague & Wattsville. ICA: VA0158.
TV Market Ranking: 44 (Cape Charles, Cheriton, Eastville, Northampton County (portions)); Below 100 (Accomack County (portions), Hallwood, Saxis, Northampton County (portions)); Outside TV Markets (Accomack County (portions), Atlantic, Belle Haven, Bloxom, Craddockville, Craddockville, Exmore, Keller, Mappsville, Melfa, Nassawadox, New Church, Oak Hall, ONANCOCK, Onley, Painter, Parksley, Pungoteague, Temperanceville, Wachapreague, Wattsville, Accomac, Northampton County (portions)). Franchise award date: N.A. Franchise expiration date: N.A. Began: June 5, 1970.
Channel capacity: 40 (not 2-way capable). Channels available but not in use: N.A.

Digital Basic Service
Subscribers: 2,015.
Programming (via satellite): BBC America; Bloomberg Television; Discovery Life Channel; Disney XD; DIY Network; ESPN Classic; ESPNews; FOX College Sports Central; FOX College Sports Pacific; Fuse; FXM; FYI; GSN; History International; IFC; LMN; MC; Mid-Atlantic Sports Network (MASN); National Geographic Channel; Nick 2; Nick Jr.; Sundance TV; TeenNick; TV Guide Interactive Inc.
Fee: $49.99 installation; $27.99 monthly.

Digital Expanded Basic Service
Subscribers: N.A.
Programming (via satellite): A&E; AMC; Cartoon Network; CMT; CNBC; CNN; Comedy Central; C-SPAN; Discovery Channel; Disney Channel; Fox News Channel; Freeform; FX; HGTV; History; HLN; MTV; Nickelodeon; Oxygen; Spike TV; Syfy; TBS; TLC; TNT; TV Land; USA Network; VH1; WE tv.
Fee: $47.99 monthly.

Digital Pay Service 1
Pay Units: N.A.
Programming (via satellite): Cinemax (multiplexed); Flix; HBO (multiplexed); Showtime (multiplexed); Starz (multiplexed); Starz Encore; The Movie Channel (multiplexed).

Video-On-Demand: No

Pay-Per-View
iN DEMAND (delivered digitally); Playboy TV (delivered digitally); Fresh (delivered digitally); Shorteez (delivered digitally).

Internet Service
Operational: No.

Telephone Service
None
Miles of Plant: 668.0 (coaxial); 121.0 (fiber optic). Homes passed: 13,451.
Vice President & General Manager: Anthony Pope. Operations Manager: Tom Ross. Marketing Director: Brooke Sinclair. Marketing Manager: LaRisa Scales. Accounting Director: David Sovanski.
Ownership: Charter Communications Inc. (MSO).

ORANGE—Comcast Cable. Now served by CULPEPER, VA [VA0182]. ICA: VA0073.

PALMYRA—Comcast Cable. Now served by CHARLOTTESVILLE, VA [VA0131]. ICA: VA0191.

PEARISBURG—Formerly served by Charter Communications. Now served by Suddenlink Communications, BECKLEY, WV [WV0005]. ICA: VA0043.

PENNINGTON GAP (town)—Formerly served by Adelphia Communications. Now served by Comcast Cable, KNOXVILLE, TN [TN0004]. ICA: VA0091.

PETERSBURG—Comcast Cable, 2033 East Whitehall Rd, Prince George, VA 23875-1249. Phones: 804-957-5739; 804-915-5400 (Richmond office). Fax: 804-957-5830. Web Site: http://www.comcast.com. Also serves Amelia County (portions), Ashland, Charles City County (portions), Chesterfield County (portions), Colonial Heights, Dillwyn, Dinwiddie, Emporia, Fort Lee, Goochland, Greensville County (portions), Hanover County (portions), Henrico County (portions), Hopewell, McKenney, Powhatan, Prince George & Richmond, VA; Bancroft (town), Barboursville, Buffalo (town), Cabell County (portions), Eleanor (town), Hometown, Huntington, Huntington (city), Kanawha County (portions), Lesage, Nitro (portions), Poca (town), Putnam County (portions), Red House, Scott Depot, St. Albans (portions), Wayne County (portions) & Winfield (town), WV. ICA: VA0186.
TV Market Ranking: 36 (Bancroft (town), Barboursville, Buffalo (town), Cabell County (portions), Eleanor (town), Hometown, Huntington, Huntington (city), Kanawha County (portions), Lesage, Nitro (portions), Poca (town), Putnam County (portions), Red House, Scott Depot, St. Albans (portions), Wayne County (portions), Winfield (town)); 63 (Amelia County (portions), Ashland, Chesterfield County (portions), Colonial Heights, Dinwiddie, Fort Lee, Goochland, Greensville County (portions) (portions), Hanover County (portions), Henrico County (portions), Hopewell, McKenney, PETERSBURG, Powhatan, Prince George, Richmond); Below 100 (Dillwyn, Wayne County (portions) (portions)); Outside TV Markets (Emporia, Amelia County (portions), Greensville County (portions) (portions)).
Channel capacity: N.A. Channels available but not in use: N.A.

Basic Service
Subscribers: 186,638. Commercial subscribers: 11,737.
Programming (received off-air): WCVE-TV (PBS) Richmond; WCVW (PBS) Richmond; WRIC-TV (ABC) Petersburg; WRLH-TV (FOX, MNT, This TV) Richmond; WTVR-TV (Antenna TV, CBS) Richmond; WUPV (Bounce TV, CW) Ashland; WWBT (Escape, MeTV, NBC) Richmond.
Programming (via satellite): E! HD; Freeform; INSP; Pop; QVC; WGN America.
Fee: $39.95-$49.95 installation; $28.20 monthly.

Expanded Basic Service 1
Subscribers: N.A.
Programming (via satellite): A&E; AMC; Animal Planet; BET; Bravo; Cartoon Network; CMT; CNBC; CNN; Comcast SportsNet Mid-Atlantic; Comedy Central; C-SPAN; C-SPAN 2; Discovery Channel; Disney Channel; ESPN; ESPN2; Food Network; Fox News Channel; FX; Great American Country; HGTV; History; HLN; ION Television; Lifetime; MSNBC; MTV; Nickelodeon; Spike TV; Syfy; TBS; The Weather Channel; TLC; TNT; Travel Channel; Trinity Broadcasting Network (TBN); truTV; Turner Classic Movies; TV Land; Univision Studios; USA Network; VH1.

Digital Basic Service
Subscribers: N.A.
Programming (via satellite): BBC America; Bloomberg Television; Discovery Life Channel; Disney XD; DIY Network; ESPN Classic; ESPNews; Fox Sports 1; Fuse; FYI; Golf Channel; GSN; History International; MC; Mid-Atlantic Sports Network (MASN); NBCSN; Outdoor Channel; Trinity Broadcasting Network (TBN); WE tv.

Digital Expanded Basic Service
Subscribers: N.A.
Programming (via satellite): National Geographic Channel; Nick Jr.

Pay Service 1
Pay Units: N.A.
Programming (via satellite): Cinemax; HBO.

Digital Pay Service 1
Pay Units: N.A.
Programming (via satellite): Cinemax (multiplexed); Flix; HBO (multiplexed); Showtime (multiplexed); Starz (multiplexed); Starz Encore (multiplexed); The Movie Channel (multiplexed).

Video-On-Demand: No

Pay-Per-View
Hot Choice (delivered digitally); Fresh (delivered digitally); HITS (delivered digitally); Playboy TV (delivered digitally).

Internet Service
Operational: Yes.
Subscribers: 83,435.
Broadband Service: Comcast High Speed Internet.
Fee: $42.95 monthly.

Telephone Service
Digital: Operational
Subscribers: 51,754.
Miles of Plant: 7,574.0 (coaxial); 2,376.0 (fiber optic). Homes passed: 365,268.
Technical Operations Director: Stephen Hill. Marketing Director: Erin Powell. Public Relations Director: Monica Smith-Callahan. Office Manager: Joyce Johnson.
Ownership: Comcast Cable Communications Inc. (MSO).

PETERSBURG—Comcast Cable. Now served by PETERSBURG, VA [VA0186]. ICA: VA0015.

POQUOSON—Cox Communications. Now served by HAMPTON ROADS (formerly Virginia Beach), VA [VA0002]. ICA: VA0180.

POWHATAN—Comcast Cable. Now served by PETERSBURG, VA [VA0186]. ICA: VA0100.

PRINCE GEORGE—Formerly served by Adelphia Communications. Now served by Comcast Cable, PETERSBURG, VA [VA0186]. ICA: VA0022.

PRINCE WILLIAM COUNTY (portions)—Comcast Cable. Now served by CHARLOTTESVILLE, VA [VA0131]. ICA: VA0148.

PULASKI—Comcast Cable. Now served by DANVILLE, VA [VA0012]. ICA: VA0159.

RADFORD—Shentel, 500 Shentel Way, PO Box 459, Edinburg, VA 22824. Phones: 540-984-5224; 800-743-6835. Fax: 540-984-3438. E-mail: info@shentel.net. Web Site: http://www.shentel.com. Also serves Christiansburg, Fairlawn, Montgomery County & Pulaski County (portions). ICA: VA0029.
TV Market Ranking: 70 (Christiansburg, Fairlawn, Montgomery County, Pulaski County (portions), RADFORD); Below 100 (Pulaski County (portions)); Outside TV Markets (Pulaski County (portions)). Franchise award date: N.A. Franchise expiration date: N.A. Began: January 1, 1970.
Channel capacity: N.A. Channels available but not in use: N.A.

Basic Service
Subscribers: 408.
Programming (received off-air): WBRA-TV (PBS) Roanoke; WDBJ (CBS, Decades, MNT) Roanoke; WFFP-TV (COZI TV, IND, Movies!) Danville; WFXR (CW, FOX) Roanoke; WPXR-TV (ION) Roanoke; WSET-TV (ABC, Retro TV, WeatherNation) Lynchburg; WSLS-TV (MeTV, NBC) Roanoke; allband FM.
Programming (via satellite): C-SPAN; INSP; Pop; QVC; TBS; Trinity Broadcasting Network (TBN); WGN America.
Fee: $99.95 installation; $34.86 monthly; $1.12 converter.

Expanded Basic Service 1
Subscribers: N.A.
Programming (via satellite): A&E; AMC; Animal Planet; BET; Bravo; Cartoon Network; CMT; CNBC; CNN; Comcast SportsNet Mid-Atlantic; Comedy Central; Discovery Channel; Disney Channel; ESPN; ESPN2; Fox News Channel; Fox Sports 1; Freeform; FX; HGTV; History; HLN; Lifetime; MSNBC; MTV; Nickelodeon; Spike TV; Syfy; The Weather Channel; TLC; TNT; Travel Channel; Turner Classic Movies; TV Land; USA Network; VH1.
Fee: $30.00 monthly.

Digital Basic Service
Subscribers: 1,354.
Programming (via satellite): BBC America; Discovery Digital Networks; DIY Network; FYI; History International; LMN; MC; Nick 2; Nick Jr.; Sundance TV; TeenNick.

2017 Edition

D-809

Virginia—Cable Systems

Digital Pay Service 1
Pay Units: N.A.
Programming (via satellite): Cinemax (multiplexed); Flix; HBO (multiplexed); Showtime (multiplexed); The Movie Channel (multiplexed).
Fee: $5.95 monthly (TMC), $7.00 monthly (Showtime & Flix), $10.00 monthly (HBO).
Video-On-Demand: No
Pay-Per-View
Hot Choice (delivered digitally); iN DEMAND (delivered digitally); Fresh (delivered digitally).
Internet Service
Operational: Yes.
Subscribers: 6,817.
Broadband Service: JetBroadband.
Fee: $49.95 installation; $29.95 monthly.
Telephone Service
Digital: Operational
Subscribers: 1,258.
Miles of Plant: 585.0 (coaxial); 135.0 (fiber optic). Homes passed: 21,314.
President: Christopher French. Assistant Secretary, Associate General Counsel: Ann Flowers. Marketing Manager: Chris Ranson.
Ownership: Shentel (MSO).

REDWOOD—Formerly served by Suddenlink Communications. No longer in operation. ICA: VA0033.

RESTON—Comcast Cable. Now served by PRINCE WILLIAM COUNTY (portions), VA [VA0148]. ICA: VA0017.

RICHLANDS (town)—Time Warner Cable, 1430 2nd St, Richlands, VA 24641-2455. Phone: 276-964-1150. Fax: 276-596-9046. Web Site: http://www.timewarnercable.com. Also serves Bandy, Big Rock, Bishop, Buchanan County (portions), Cedar Bluff (town), Doran, Gratton, Grundy (town), Harman, Hurley, Keen Mountain, Mavisdale, Maxie, North Tazewell, Oakwood, Paint Lick, Pilgrims Knob, Pounding Mill, Raven, Red Ash, Royal City, Russell County (portions), Stacy, Steelburg, Swords Creek, Tazewell (town), Tazewell County (portions), Tiptop, Vansant, Wardell, Whitewood & Wolford. ICA: VA0041.
TV Market Ranking: Below 100 (Bandy, Big Rock, Bishop, Buchanan County (portions) (portions), Cedar Bluff (town), Gratton, Harman, Hurley, Mavisdale, Maxie, North Tazewell, Oakwood, Paint Lick, Pilgrims Knob, Pounding Mill, Raven, Red Ash, RICHLANDS (TOWN), Royal City, Russell County (portions), Stacy, Tazewell (town), Tiptop, Vansant, Wardell, Whitewood, Wolford, Grundy (town), Keen Mountain); Outside TV Markets (Buchanan County (portions) (portions), Doran, Steelburg, Swords Creek). Franchise award date: N.A. Franchise expiration date: N.A. Began: January 1, 1952.
Channel capacity: N.A. Channels available but not in use: N.A.

Basic Service
Subscribers: 7,908.
Programming (received off-air): WCYB-TV (CW, Decades, NBC) Bristol; WDBJ (CBS, Decades, MNT) Roanoke; WKPT-TV (COZI TV, Escape, MeTV, MNT) Kingsport; WLFG (IND, PBJ, Retro TV) Grundy; WOAY-TV (ABC) Oak Hill; WSBN-TV (PBS) Norton; WVVA (CW, MeTV, NBC) Bluefield; allband FM.
Programming (via satellite): Concert TV; QVC.
Fee: $48.50 installation; $31.99 monthly; $3.25 converter.
Expanded Basic Service 1
Subscribers: N.A.
Programming (via satellite): A&E; AMC; Animal Planet; BET; Bravo; Cartoon Network; CMT; CNBC; CNN; Comcast SportsNet Mid-Atlantic; Comedy Central; C-SPAN; C-SPAN 2; Discovery Channel; Disney Channel; E! HD; ESPN; EVINE Live; Food Network; Freeform; FX; Hallmark Channel; HLN; Lifetime; MTV; Nickelodeon; Oxygen; Spike TV; TBS; The Weather Channel; TLC; TNT; Travel Channel; truTV; USA Network; VH1.
Fee: $27.25 monthly.
Digital Basic Service
Subscribers: N.A.
Programming (via satellite): BBC America; Bloomberg Television; Discovery Life Channel; Disney XD; ESPN Classic; ESPN2; ESPNews; Fox Sports 1; FXM; Golf Channel; GSN; HGTV; History; IFC; LMN; MC; MTV Classic; National Geographic Channel; NBCSN; Nick Jr.; Nicktoons; Outdoor Channel; Syfy; Trinity Broadcasting Network (TBN); Turner Classic Movies; TV Land; VH1 Country; WE tv.
Fee: $6.00 monthly (per tier).
Digital Pay Service 1
Pay Units: N.A.
Programming (via satellite): Cinemax (multiplexed); HBO (multiplexed); Showtime (multiplexed); Starz Encore; The Movie Channel (multiplexed).
Fee: $14.00 monthly (each).
Video-On-Demand: No
Pay-Per-View
Movies & Events (delivered digitally); Sports PPV (delivered digitally); Hot Choice (delivered digitally); Shorteez (delivered digitally); Fresh (delivered digitally); Playboy TV (delivered digitally).
Internet Service
Operational: Yes.
Subscribers: 8,407.
Broadband Service: Road Runner.
Fee: $44.95 monthly.
Telephone Service
Digital: Operational
Subscribers: 2,631.
Miles of Plant: 1,223.0 (coaxial); 67.0 (fiber optic). Homes passed: 22,056.
General Manager: C. K. Allen. Chief Technician: Danny Nelson. Marketing Manager: Mark Cole.
Ownership: Time Warner Cable (MSO).

RICHMOND—Comcast Cable. Now served by PETERSBURG, VA [VA0186]. ICA: VA0004.

RICHMOND—Formerly served by CavTel/Windstream. IPTV service no longer in operation. ICA: VA5000.

RICHMOND—Formerly served by NTELOS. No longer in operation. ICA: VA0181.

RIVER OAKS—Formerly served by Comcast Cable. No longer in operation. ICA: VA0178.

ROANOKE—Cox Communications, 6205 Peachtree Dunwoody Rd, 12th Floor, Atlanta, GA 30328. Phones: 404-269-6590; 540-776-3845. Web Site: http://www.cox.com. Also serves Roanoke County & Vinton. ICA: VA0007.
TV Market Ranking: 70 (ROANOKE, Roanoke County, Vinton). Franchise award date: January 20, 1975. Franchise expiration date: N.A. Began: November 18, 1976.
Channel capacity: N.A. Channels available but not in use: N.A.
Basic Service
Subscribers: 42,655. Commercial subscribers: 1,700.
Programming (received off-air): WBRA-TV (PBS) Roanoke; WDBJ (CBS, Decades, MNT) Roanoke; WFFP-TV (COZI TV, IND, Movies!) Danville; WFXR (CW, FOX) Roanoke; WPXR-TV (ION) Roanoke; WSET-TV (ABC, Retro TV, WeatherNation) Lynchburg; WSLS-TV (MeTV, NBC) Roanoke; 8 FMs.
Programming (via satellite): C-SPAN; C-SPAN 2; QVC; TBS; WGN America.
Fee: $38.95 installation; $21.99 monthly; $1.15 converter.
Expanded Basic Service 1
Subscribers: N.A.
Programming (via satellite): A&E; AMC; Animal Planet; BET; Bravo; Cartoon Network; CMT; CNBC; CNN; Comcast SportsNet Mid-Atlantic; Comedy Central; Discovery Channel; Disney Channel; E! HD; ESPN; ESPN2; EVINE Live; Food Network; Fox News Channel; Fox Sports 1; Freeform; FX; Hallmark Channel; HGTV; History; HLN; INSP; Lifetime; MSNBC; MTV; NBCSN; Nickelodeon; OWN: Oprah Winfrey Network; Oxygen; Pop; Spike TV; Syfy; The Weather Channel; TLC; TNT; Travel Channel; Trinity Broadcasting Network (TBN); truTV; TV Land; USA Network; VH1.
Fee: $18.99 installation; $32.04 monthly.
Digital Basic Service
Subscribers: N.A.
Programming (via satellite): BBC America; Bloomberg Television; Discovery Digital Networks; Disney XD; ESPN Classic; ESPNews; EWTN Global Catholic Network; FYI; Golf Channel; Great American Country; GSN; History International; IFC; LMN; MC; Mid-Atlantic Sports Network (MASN); Sundance TV; The Word Network; Turner Classic Movies; Univision Studios.
Fee: $7.95 monthly.
Pay Service 1
Pay Units: N.A.
Programming (via satellite): Cinemax (multiplexed); HBO (multiplexed); Showtime (multiplexed); Starz; Starz Encore; The Movie Channel.
Fee: $10.95 monthly (Cinemax, HBO, Showtime, Starz/Encore or TMC).
Digital Pay Service 1
Pay Units: N.A.
Programming (via satellite): Cinemax (multiplexed); Flix; HBO (multiplexed); Showtime (multiplexed); Starz (multiplexed); Starz Encore (multiplexed); Sundance TV; The Movie Channel (multiplexed).
Fee: $11.95 monthly (Cinemax, HBO, Flix/Showtime/Sundance/TMC, or Starz/Encore).
Video-On-Demand: Yes
Pay-Per-View
Vubiquity Inc.; ESPN Now (delivered digitally); iN DEMAND (delivered digitally); Playboy TV (delivered digitally); Fresh (delivered digitally).
Internet Service
Operational: Yes.
Subscribers: 41,514.
Broadband Service: Cox High Speed Internet.
Fee: $49.95 installation; $39.95 monthly; $10.00 modem lease; $39.95 modem purchase.
Telephone Service
Digital: Operational
Subscribers: 23,686.
Fee: $12.20 monthly
Miles of Plant: 1,965.0 (coaxial); 469.0 (fiber optic). Homes passed: 91,383.
Vice President, Tax: Mary Vickers. General Manager: Marilyn Burrows. Technical Operations Director: Rick Neilson. Marketing Director: Jodi Muller-Stotser. Public Relations Director: Mike Pedelty.
Ownership: Cox Communications Inc. (MSO).

ROANOKE—Formerly served by NTELOS. No longer in operation. ICA: VA0173.

ROCKINGHAM—Formerly served by Adelphia Communications. Now served by Comcast Cable, HARRISONBURG, VA [VA0016]. ICA: VA0151.

ROCKY MOUNT—Shentel, 500 Shentel Way, PO Box 459, Edinburg, VA 22824. Phones: 800-743-6835; 540-984-5224. Fax: 540-984-3438. E-mail: info@shentel.net. Web Site: http://www.shentel.com. Also serves Bedford, Bedford County (southwestern portion), Boones Mill & Franklin County. ICA: VA0196.
TV Market Ranking: 70 (Bedford, Boones Mill, Franklin County, ROCKY MOUNT).
Channel capacity: N.A. Channels available but not in use: N.A.
Basic Service
Subscribers: 505.
Fee: $99.95 installation; $34.86 monthly.
Digital Basic Service
Subscribers: 1,963.
Internet Service
Operational: Yes.
Subscribers: 6,864.
Telephone Service
Digital: Operational
Subscribers: 1,735.
Miles of Plant: 1,342.0 (coaxial); 393.0 (fiber optic). Homes passed: 23,688.
Assistant Secretary, Associate General Counsel: Ann Flowers.
Ownership: Shentel (MSO).

ROSEDALE—Cable Plus, 5162 Redbud Hwy, PO Box 1030, Honaker, VA 24260-1030. Phones: 866-670-4828; 276-873-4828. Fax: 276-873-4882. E-mail: officestaff@cableplus.tv. Also serves Belfast Mills & Russell County (portions). ICA: VA0161.
TV Market Ranking: Below 100 (Belfast Mills, ROSEDALE, Russell County (portions)). Franchise award date: N.A. Franchise expiration date: N.A. Began: June 1, 1977.
Channel capacity: 28 (not 2-way capable). Channels available but not in use: N.A.

Cable Systems—Virginia

Basic Service
Subscribers: N.A.
Programming (received off-air): WAPK-CD (Grit, Laff, MeTV) Kingsport; WCYB-TV (CW, Decades, NBC) Bristol; WEMT (FOX, Movies!, This TV) Greeneville; WJHL-TV (ABC, CBS, MeTV) Johnson City; WKPT-TV (COZI TV, Escape, MeTV, MNT) Kingsport; WSBN-TV (PBS) Norton; WVVA (CW, MeTV, NBC) Bluefield.
Programming (via satellite): A&E; Animal Planet; Bravo; Cartoon Network; CMT; CNBC; CNN; Comcast/Charter Sports Southeast (CSS); Comedy Central; C-SPAN; Discovery Channel; Disney Channel; Disney XD; E! HD; ESPN; ESPN Classic; ESPN2; Food Network; Fox News Channel; Fox Sports 1; Freeform; FX; Golf Channel; Hallmark Channel; HGTV; History; HLN; ION Television; Lifetime; MSNBC; MTV; National Geographic Channel; NFL Network; Nickelodeon; Outdoor Channel; Oxygen; QVC; RFD-TV; Spike TV; Syfy; TBS; The Weather Channel; TLC; TNT; Travel Channel; Trinity Broadcasting Network (TBN); Turner Classic Movies; TV Land; UP; USA Network; VH1; WE tv; WGN America.

Pay Service 1
Pay Units: N.A.
Programming (via satellite): Cinemax; HBO; Showtime; Starz Encore; The Movie Channel.
Video-On-Demand: No
Internet Service
Operational: Yes.
Fee: $29.95 monthly.
Telephone Service
None
Miles of Plant: 3.0 (coaxial); None (fiber optic).
General Manager: Jody Eaton.
Ownership: Cable Plus.

RUCKERSVILLE—Comcast Cable. Now served by CHARLOTTESVILLE, VA [VA0131]. ICA: VA0067.

RURAL RETREAT—Formerly served by Rural Retreat Cable TV Inc. No longer in operation. ICA: VA0109.

RUSTBURG—Shentel, 500 Shentel Way, PO Box 459, Edinburg, VA 22824. Phones: 540-984-5224; 800-743-6835. Fax: 540-984-3438. E-mail: info@shentel.net. Web Site: http://www.shentel.com. Also serves Alta Vista, Appomattox, Appomattox County (portions), Bedford County (northern portion), Campbell County (portions), Clarion, Concord, Evington, Forest, Goode, Pamplin & Timberlake. ICA: VA0128.
TV Market Ranking: 70 (Alta Vista, Appomattox, Appomattox County (portions), Bedford County (northern portion), Campbell County (portions), Clarion, Concord, Evington, Forest, Goode, Pamplin, RUSTBURG, Timberlake). Franchise award date: N.A. Franchise expiration date: N.A. Began: December 1, 1984.
Channel capacity: N.A. Channels available but not in use: N.A.

Basic Service
Subscribers: 489.
Programming (received off-air): WBRA-TV (PBS) Roanoke; WDBJ (CBS, Decades, MNT) Roanoke; WFFP-TV (COZI TV, IND, Movies!) Danville; WFXR (CW, FOX) Roanoke; WPXR-TV (ION) Roanoke; WSET-TV (ABC, Retro TV, WeatherNation) Lynchburg; WSLS-TV (MeTV, NBC) Roanoke; WWCW (CW, FOX) Lynchburg.

Programming (via satellite): WGN America.
Fee: $99.95 installation; $34.86 monthly.
Expanded Basic Service 1
Subscribers: N.A.
Programming (via satellite): A&E; AMC; Animal Planet; BET; Bravo; Cartoon Network; CMT; CNBC; CNN; Comcast SportsNet Mid-Atlantic; Comedy Central; C-SPAN; Discovery Channel; Disney Channel; Disney XD; E! HD; ESPN; ESPN2; Food Network; Fox News Channel; Fox Sports 1; Freeform; FX; FXM; Golf Channel; Great American Country; Hallmark Channel; HGTV; History; HLN; Lifetime; MSNBC; MTV; National Geographic Channel; Nickelodeon; Outdoor Channel; QVC; Spike TV; Syfy; TBS; The Weather Channel; TLC; TNT; Travel Channel; Trinity Broadcasting Network (TBN); truTV; Turner Classic Movies; TV Land; USA Network; VH1.
Fee: $30.00 monthly.
Digital Basic Service
Subscribers: 2,074.
Programming (via satellite): BBC America; Cloo; CMT; Discovery Digital Networks; DIY Network; DMX Music; ESPN Classic; ESPNews; ESPNU; Fuse; FYI; GSN; History International; IFC; LMN; NBCSN; Nick Jr.; Nicktoons; Oxygen; TeenNick.
Digital Pay Service 1
Pay Units: N.A.
Programming (via satellite): Cinemax (multiplexed); Flix; HBO (multiplexed); Showtime (multiplexed); Starz (multiplexed); Starz Encore (multiplexed); The Movie Channel (multiplexed).
Fee: $11.95 monthly (Cinemax or Starz/Encore), $12.95 monthly (HBO or Showtime/TMC).
Video-On-Demand: Planned
Pay-Per-View
iN DEMAND (delivered digitally); Hot Choice (delivered digitally); VaVoom (delivered digitally); Juicy (delivered digitally); SexSee (delivered digitally).
Internet Service
Operational: Yes.
Broadband Service: JetBroadband.
Fee: $49.95 installation; $29.95 monthly; $5.00 modem lease.
Telephone Service
Digital: Operational
Miles of Plant: 672.0 (coaxial); 60.0 (fiber optic). Homes passed: 24,213.
President: Christopher French. Assistant Secretary, Associate General Counsel: Ann Flowers. Marketing Manager: Chris Ranson.
Ownership: Shentel (MSO).

RUTHER GLEN—Comcast Cable. Now served by PRINCE WILLIAM COUNTY (portions), VA [VA0148]. ICA: VA0130.

SALEM—Comcast Cable. Now served by CHARLOTTESVILLE, VA [VA0131]. ICA: VA0024.

SANDY RIDGE—Scott Telecom & Electronics, 149 Woodland St, PO Box 487, Gate City, VA 24251. Phones: 800-833-9823; 276-452-9119. Fax: 276-452-2447. E-mail: sctc@sctc.org. Web Site: http://www.sctc.org. ICA: VA0188.
TV Market Ranking: Below 100 (SANDY RIDGE).
Channel capacity: N.A. Channels available but not in use: N.A.

Basic Service
Subscribers: N.A.
Programming (received off-air): WCYB-TV (CW, Decades, NBC) Bristol; WEMT (FOX, Movies!, This TV) Greeneville; WJHL-TV (ABC, CBS, MeTV) Johnson City; WLFG (IND, PBJ, Retro TV) Grundy; WSBN-TV (PBS) Norton.
Programming (via satellite): Animal Planet; CMT; CNN; Discovery Channel; Disney Channel; ESPN; Freeform; HLN; Spike TV; Syfy; TBS; TNT; Trinity Broadcasting Network (TBN); USA Network; WGN America.
Fee: $45.50 installation.

Pay Service 1
Pay Units: N.A.
Programming (via satellite): The Movie Channel.
Fee: $12.00 monthly.
Video-On-Demand: No
Internet Service
Operational: No, DSL.
Telephone Service
Analog: Operational
Miles of Plant: 18.0 (coaxial); None (fiber optic). Homes passed: 300.
General Manager: William J. Franklin. Chief Technician: Terry Holt. Marketing Director: Greg Hood.
Ownership: Scott County Telephone Cooperative (MSO).

SCOTTSVILLE—Nelson Cable. Now served by LOVINGSTON/SHIPMAN, VA [VA0192]. Also serves SCOTTSVILLE. ICA: VA0111.

SHENANDOAH—Formerly served by Adelphia Communications. Now served by Comcast Cable, HARRISONBURG, VA [VA0016]. ICA: VA0060.

SOUTH BOSTON—Comcast Cable. Now served by DANVILLE, VA [VA0012]. ICA: VA0040.

SOUTH HILL—Comcast Cable. Now served by CHARLOTTESVILLE, VA [VA0131]. ICA: VA0062.

SPEEDWELL—R&S Communications LLC, PO Box 261, Castlewood, VA 24224. Phone: 800-801-4078. Also serves Crockett & Rural Retreat (portions). ICA: VA0176. **Note:** This system is an overbuild.
TV Market Ranking: Below 100 (Crockett, Rural Retreat (portions), SPEEDWELL). Franchise award date: December 12, 1989. Franchise expiration date: N.A. Began: N.A.
Channel capacity: N.A. Channels available but not in use: N.A.

Basic Service
Subscribers: 11.
Programming (received off-air): WCYB-TV (CW, Decades, NBC) Bristol; WDBJ (CBS, Decades, MNT) Roanoke; WFXR (CW, FOX) Roanoke; WJHL-TV (ABC, CBS, MeTV) Johnson City; WKPT-TV (COZI TV, Escape, MeTV, MNT) Kingsport; WMSY-TV (PBS) Marion; WSLS-TV (MeTV, NBC) Roanoke; WVVA (CW, MeTV, NBC) Bluefield.
Programming (via satellite): CMT; CNN; C-SPAN; Discovery Channel; Disney Channel; E! HD; ESPN; ESPN2; Freeform; History; HLN; Nickelodeon; Outdoor Channel; QVC; Spike TV; TBS; The Weather Channel; TLC; TNT; Travel Channel; Trinity Broadcasting Network (TBN); Turner Classic Movies; USA Network; WGN America.
Fee: $40.00 installation; $31.95 monthly; $1.95 converter.

Pay Service 1
Pay Units: N.A.
Programming (via satellite): HBO; Showtime; The Movie Channel.

Fee: $12.95 monthly.
Video-On-Demand: No
Internet Service
Operational: Yes.
Fee: $29.95 monthly.
Telephone Service
None
Miles of Plant: 60.0 (coaxial); None (fiber optic). Homes passed: 527.
President & General Manager: Richard Beesmer. Vice President, Operations: James Bradley. Vice President, Sales: Mike DeRosa.

SPOTSYLVANIA—Formerly served by Comcast Cable. No longer in operation. ICA: VA0018.

STAUNTON—Comcast Cable. Now served by CHARLOTTESVILLE, VA [VA0131]. ICA: VA0026.

STUART—Comcast Cable. Now served by DANVILLE, VA [VA0012]. ICA: VA0069.

SUFFOLK—Charter Communications, 216 Moore Ave, PO Box 348, Suffolk, VA 23434. Phones: 314-543-2236; 636-207-5100 (Corporate office); 757-539-0713. Web Site: http://www.charter.com. Also serves Gates County (portions) & Gatesville, NC; Boykins, Branchville, Courtland, Franklin, Isle of Wight County, Ivor, Newsoms, Smithfield, Southampton County, Sussex County, Wakefield, Waverly & Windsor, VA. ICA: VA0025.
TV Market Ranking: 44 (Franklin, Gates County (portions) (portions), Isle of Wight County, Ivor, Smithfield, Southampton County (portions), SUFFOLK, Sussex County (portions), Wakefield, Waverly, Windsor); Outside TV Markets (Boykins, Branchville, Courtland, Gatesville, Newsoms, Gates County (portions) (portions), Southampton County (portions), Sussex County (portions)). Franchise award date: February 1, 1984. Franchise expiration date: N.A. Began: October 24, 1984.
Channel capacity: 75 (operating 2-way). Channels available but not in use: N.A.

Digital Basic Service
Subscribers: 22,114.
Programming (via satellite): AXS TV; BBC America; Bloomberg Television; Boomerang; CNN en Espanol; CNN International; Discovery Life Channel; DIY Network; ESPN; ESPN Classic; ESPNews; FOX College Sports Central; FOX College Sports Pacific; Fox Deportes; Fox Sports 2; FXM; FYI; Great American Country; History International; HITS (Headend In The Sky); IFC; LMN; MC; Mid-Atlantic Sports Network (MASN); NFL Network; Nick 2; Nick Jr.; Nicktoons; Outdoor Channel; Sundance TV; TeenNick; TV Guide Interactive Inc.
Fee: $49.99 installation; $26.99 monthly.

Digital Expanded Basic Service
Subscribers: N.A.
Programming (via satellite): A&E; AMC; Animal Planet; BET; Bravo; Cartoon Network; CMT; CNBC; CNN; Comcast SportsNet Mid-Atlantic; Comedy Central; Discovery Channel; Disney Channel; Disney XD; E! HD; ESPN; ESPN2; EVINE Live; Food Network; Fox News Channel; Fox Sports 1; Freeform; FX; Golf Channel; GSN; Hallmark Channel; HGTV; History; HLN; Lifetime; MSNBC; MTV; MTV2; National Geographic Channel; NBCSN; Nickelodeon; Oxygen; Pop; Spike TV; Syfy; TBS; The Weather Channel; TLC; TNT; Travel Channel; truTV; Turner Classic

2017 Edition

D-811

Virginia—Cable Systems

Movies; TV Land; USA Network; VH1; WE tv.
Fee: $47.99 monthly.
Digital Pay Service 1
Pay Units: N.A.
Programming (via satellite): Cinemax (multiplexed); Cinemax HD; HBO (multiplexed); HBO HD; Showtime (multiplexed); Showtime HD; Starz (multiplexed); Starz Encore (multiplexed); Starz HD; The Movie Channel (multiplexed).
Video-On-Demand: Yes
Pay-Per-View
iN DEMAND (delivered digitally); Playboy TV (delivered digitally); Fresh (delivered digitally); Shorteez (delivered digitally).
Internet Service
Operational: Yes. Began: September 1, 2001.
Subscribers: 22,941.
Broadband Service: Charter Internet.
Fee: $29.99 monthly.
Telephone Service
Digital: Operational
Subscribers: 13,063.
Miles of Plant: 2,878.0 (coaxial); 1,009.0 (fiber optic). Homes passed: 53,279.
Vice President & General Manager: Anthony Pope. Operations Manager: Tom Ross. Marketing Director: Brooke Sinclair. Sales & Marketing Manager: LaRisa Scales. Accounting Director: David Sovanski.
Ownership: Charter Communications Inc. (MSO).

TANGIER ISLAND—Formerly served by Charter Communications. No longer in operation. ICA: VA0117.

TAPPAHANNOCK—MetroCast Communications. Now served by KING GEORGE, VA [VA0058]. ICA: VA0080.

TAZEWELL (town)—Formerly served by Adelphia Communications. Now served by Time Warner Cable, RICHLANDS (town), VA [VA0041]. ICA: VA0045.

TROUTVILLE—Comcast Cable. Now served by SALEM, VA [VA0024]. ICA: VA0037.

VICTORIA—Formerly served by Adelphia Communications. Now served by Comcast Cable, SOUTH HILL, VA [VA0062]. ICA: VA0098.

VIRGINIA BEACH—Cox Communications, 6205 Peachtree Dunwoody Rd, 12th Floor, Atlanta, GA 30328. Phone: 404-269-6590. Web Site: http://www.cox.com. Also serves Chesapeake, Fort Eustis Army Base, Fort Monroe, Fort Story, Gloucester County, Grafton, Hampton, Hampton Roads, James City County, King & Queen County (portions), King William County (portions), Lanexa, Langley AFB, Mattaponi, New Kent, New Kent County (portions), Newport News, Norfolk, Norfolk Naval Base/Southside Hampton Roads, Poquoson, Portsmouth, Providence Forge, Quinton, Shacklefords, U.S. Coast Guard 5th District, U.S. Coast Guard Support Center, West Point, Williamsburg, York County, Yorktown & Yorktown Naval Weapons Station. ICA: VA0002.
TV Market Ranking: 44 (Chesapeake, Fort Eustis Army Base, Fort Monroe, Fort Story, Gloucester County (portions), Grafton, Hampton, Hampton Roads, James City County, Langley AFB, Newport News, Norfolk, Norfolk Naval Base/Southside Hampton Roads, Portsmouth, U.S. Coast Guard 5th District, U.S. Coast Guard Support Center, VIRGINIA BEACH, Williamsburg, York County, Yorktown, Yorktown Naval Weapons Station); 63 (King & Queen County (portions), King William County (portions) (portions), Lanexa, New Kent, New Kent County (portions), Providence Forge, Quinton, West Point (portions)); Below 100 (Poquoson); Outside TV Markets (Mattaponi, Shacklefords, Gloucester County (portions), King William County (portions) (portions), West Point (portions)). Franchise award date: N.A. Franchise expiration date: N.A. Began: January 16, 1978.
Channel capacity: 65 (operating 2-way). Channels available but not in use: N.A.
Basic Service
Subscribers: 283,166. Commercial subscribers: 11,817.
Programming (received off-air): WAVY-TV (Bounce TV, NBC) Portsmouth; WGNT (Antenna TV, CW) Portsmouth; WHRO-TV (PBS) Hampton-Norfolk; WPXV-TV (ION) Norfolk; WSKY-TV (Escape, IND, Laff) Manteo; WTKR (CBS) Norfolk; WTVZ-TV (MNT, The Country Network) Norfolk; WUNC-TV (PBS) Chapel Hill; WVBT (FOX) Virginia Beach; WVEC (ABC) Hampton.
Programming (via satellite): Animal Planet; C-SPAN; C-SPAN 2; Pop; QVC; TBS; Univision Studios; WGN America.
Fee: $40.00 installation; $21.99 monthly.
Expanded Basic Service 1
Subscribers: N.A.
Programming (via satellite): A&E; AMC; BET; Bravo; Cartoon Network; CMT; CNBC; CNN; Comcast SportsNet Mid-Atlantic; Comedy Central; Discovery Channel; Disney Channel; E! HD; ESPN; ESPN2; Food Network; Fox News Channel; Fox Sports 1; Freeform; FX; HGTV; History; HLN; International Television (ITV); Lifetime; MSNBC; MTV; NBCSN; Nickelodeon; OWN: Oprah Winfrey Network; Spike TV; Syfy; The Weather Channel; TLC; TNT; Travel Channel; truTV; TV Land; USA Network; VH1.
Fee: $41.99 monthly.
Digital Basic Service
Subscribers: N.A.
Programming (via satellite): BBC America; Bloomberg Television; Cooking Channel; Discovery Digital Networks; Disney XD; DIY Network; ESPN Classic; ESPNews; Flix; FYI; Golf Channel; GSN; Hallmark Channel; History International; IFC; LMN; LWS Local Weather Station; MC; Mid-Atlantic Sports Network (MASN); National Geographic Channel; NBA TV; Nick Jr.; Nicktoons; Oxygen; Starz Encore; Sundance TV; TeenNick; Turner Classic Movies.
Fee: $9.45 monthly.
Pay Service 1
Pay Units: N.A.
Programming (via satellite): Cinemax (multiplexed); HBO (multiplexed); Showtime; Starz; Starz Encore; The Movie Channel.
Fee: $15.00 installation; $12.00 monthly (each).
Digital Pay Service 1
Pay Units: N.A.
Programming (via satellite): Cinemax (multiplexed); HBO (multiplexed); Showtime (multiplexed); Starz (multiplexed); The Filipino Channel; The Movie Channel (multiplexed).
Video-On-Demand: Yes
Pay-Per-View
Hot Choice; iN DEMAND; special events; ESPN Now (delivered digitally); Adult PPV (delivered digitally); Sports PPV (delivered digitally).
Internet Service
Operational: Yes.
Subscribers: 306,346.
Broadband Service: Cox High Speed Internet.
Fee: $99.95 installation; $24.95 monthly; $15.00 modem lease; $299.00 modem purchase.
Telephone Service
Digital: Operational
Subscribers: 187,746.
Fee: $14.99 monthly.
Miles of Plant: 13,902.0 (coaxial); 2,866.0 (fiber optic). Homes passed: 727,708.
Vice President & Regional Manager: Gary McCollum. Vice President, Public & Government Affairs: Thom Prevette. Vice President, Tax: Mary Vickers. Public Affairs Manager: Pamela Marino.
Ownership: Cox Communications Inc. (MSO).

WARRENTON—Comcast Cable. Now served by PRINCE WILLIAM COUNTY (portions), VA [VA0148]. ICA: VA0034.

WARSAW—MetroCast Communications. Now served by KING GEORGE, VA [VA0058]. ICA: VA0094.

WESTMORELAND—MetroCast Communications. Now served by KING GEORGE, VA [VA0058]. ICA: VA0049.

WILLIAMSBURG—Cox Communications. Now served by HAMPTON ROADS (formerly Virginia Beach), VA [VA0002]. ICA: VA0177.

WINCHESTER—Comcast Cable. Now served by FREDERICK COUNTY (portions), MD [MD0009]. ICA: VA0014.

WINTERGREEN—Nelson Cable, 380 Front St, Lovingston, VA 22949. Phone: 434-263-4805. Fax: 434-263-4821. E-mail: joeleemc@aol.com. Web Site: http://www.nelsoncable.com. Also serves Augusta County (portions), Nelson County (portions) & Rockfish. ICA: VA0112.
TV Market Ranking: 70 (WINTERGREEN); Below 100 (Rockfish). Franchise award date: N.A. Franchise expiration date: N.A. Began: October 1, 1967.
Channel capacity: N.A. Channels available but not in use: N.A.
Basic Service
Subscribers: 756.
Programming (received off-air): WCVE-TV (PBS) Richmond; WDBJ (CBS, Decades, MNT) Roanoke; WRIC-TV (ABC) Petersburg; WSET-TV (ABC, Retro TV, WeatherNation) Lynchburg; WSLS-TV (MeTV, NBC) Roanoke; WTVR-TV (Antenna TV, CBS) Richmond; WWBT (Escape, MeTV, NBC) Richmond; WWCW (CW, FOX) Lynchburg; allband FM.
Programming (via satellite): CNN; Disney Channel; ESPN; Hallmark Channel; TBS.
Fee: $35.00 installation; $13.49 monthly.
Pay Service 1
Pay Units: N.A.
Programming (via satellite): Cinemax; HBO; Playboy TV; Showtime.
Fee: $10.00 monthly (each).
Video-On-Demand: No
Internet Service
Operational: Yes.
Fee: $44.00 monthly.
Telephone Service
None
Miles of Plant: 42.0 (coaxial); None (fiber optic). Homes passed: 1,000.
President: Joe Lee McClellan. Chief Technician: Terry Engelhardt.
Ownership: Nelson County Cablevision Corp. (MSO).

WOODSTOCK—Shentel, 500 Shentel Way, PO Box 459, Edinburg, VA 22824. Phones: 800-743-6835; 540-984-5224. Fax: 540-984-3438. Web Site: http://www.shentel.com. Also serves Basye, Edinburg, Maurertown, Mount Jackson, New Market, Shenandoah County, Strasburg & Toms Brook. ICA: VA0136.
TV Market Ranking: Below 100 (Mount Jackson, New Market, Shenandoah County (portions), Edinburg); Outside TV Markets (Basye, Maurertown, Shenandoah County (portions), Strasburg, Toms Brook, WOODSTOCK). Franchise award date: N.A. Franchise expiration date: N.A. Began: September 1, 1981.
Channel capacity: N.A. Channels available but not in use: N.A.
Basic Service
Subscribers: 463.
Programming (received off-air): WAZT-CD (IND) Woodstock; WDCA (Heroes & Icons, MNT, Movies!, MundoMax) Washington; WDCW (Antenna TV, CW, This TV) Washington; WHSV-TV (ABC, MeTV, MNT, This TV) Harrisonburg; WJLA-TV (ABC, MeTV, Retro TV) Washington; WRC-TV (COZI TV, NBC) Washington; WTTG (Buzzr, FOX) Washington; WUSA (Bounce TV, CBS, WeatherNation) Washington; WVPT (PBS) Staunton; WWPX-TV (ION) Martinsburg.
Programming (via satellite): Pop.
Fee: $99.95 installation; $32.81 monthly.
Expanded Basic Service 1
Subscribers: N.A.
Programming (via satellite): A&E; AMC; Animal Planet; BET; Bloomberg Television; Boomerang; Bravo; Cartoon Network; Chiller; CMT; CNBC; CNN; Comcast SportsNet Mid-Atlantic; Comedy Central; C-SPAN; C-SPAN 2; Discovery Channel; Disney Channel; E! HD; ESPN; ESPN Classic; ESPN2; EVINE Live; EWTN Global Catholic Network; FamilyNet; Food Network; Fox News Channel; Freeform; FX; Great American Country; Hallmark Channel; HGTV; History; HLN; Lifetime; MSNBC; MTV; National Geographic Channel; Nickelodeon; Outdoor Channel; OWN: Oprah Winfrey Network; Oxygen; QVC; RFD-TV; Spike TV; Syfy; TBS; The Weather Channel; TLC; TNT; Travel Channel; Trinity Broadcasting Network (TBN); truTV; Turner Classic Movies; TV Land; USA Network; VH1; WE tv; WGN America.
Fee: $26.00 monthly.
Digital Basic Service
Subscribers: 4,965.
Programming (via satellite): BBC America; Cloo; CMT; Cooking Channel; Destination America; Discovery Kids Channel; Discovery Life Channel; Disney XD; DIY Network; DMX Music; ESPNews; Fox Business Network; Fox Sports 2; FXM; FYI; GSN; History International; Investigation Discovery; MTV Classic; MTV Hits; MTV Jams; MTV2; Nat Geo WILD; NBCSN; Nick Jr.; Nicktoons; Science Channel; TeenNick; VH1 Soul.
Digital Expanded Basic Service
Subscribers: N.A.
Programming (via satellite): Cine Mexicano; CNN en Espanol; ESPN Deportes; FOX College Sports Central; FOX College Sports Pacific; Fox Deportes; Fox Sports 1; Golf Channel; History en Espanol; NBC Uni-

Cable Systems—Virginia

verso; Telemundo; Tennis Channel; Tr3s; ViendoMovies.
Fee: $4.95 monthly (sports package), $5.00 monthly (Spanish package).

Digital Expanded Basic Service 2
Subscribers: N.A.
Programming (via satellite): A&E HD; AXS TV; Bravo HD; CNBC HD+; Discovery Channel HD; ESPN HD; Food Network HD; FX HD; HGTV HD; History HD; National Geographic Channel HD; NFL Network HD; Syfy HD; TBS HD; TNT HD; Universal HD; USA Network HD.
Fee: $9.95 monthly.

Digital Pay Service 1
Pay Units: N.A.
Programming (via satellite): Cinemax (multiplexed); Cinemax HD; Flix; HBO (multiplexed); HBO HD; Showtime (multiplexed); Showtime HD; Starz (multiplexed); Starz Encore (multiplexed); Starz HD; The Movie Channel (multiplexed).
Fee: $6.95 monthly (Encore), $9.95 monthly (Cinemax or Showtime/TMC/Flix), $11.95 monthly (Starz/Encore), $12.95 monthly (HBO).

Video-On-Demand: No

Internet Service
Operational: Yes, DSL.

Telephone Service
Analog: Operational
Miles of Plant: 175.0 (coaxial); None (fiber optic).
Vice President, Customer Service: David Ferguson. Assistant Secretary, Associate General Counsel: Ann Flowers. Chief Technician: David Brock.
Ownership: Shentel.

WYTHE COUNTY—Citizens Telephone Coop. Now served by FORT CHISWELL, VA [VA0066]. ICA: VA5306.

WYTHEVILLE—Shentel, 500 Shentel Way, PO Box 459, Edinburg, VA 22824. Phones: 800-743-6835; 540-984-5224. Fax: 540-984-3438. E-mail: info@shentel.net. Web Site: http://www.shentel.com. Also serves Rural Retreat & Wythe County (portions). ICA: VA0061.
TV Market Ranking: Below 100 (Rural Retreat, Wythe County (portions), WYTHEVILLE). Franchise award date: N.A. Franchise expiration date: N.A. Began: December 1, 1969.
Channel capacity: N.A. Channels available but not in use: N.A.

Basic Service
Subscribers: 200.
Programming (received off-air): WBRA-TV (PBS) Roanoke; WDBJ (CBS, Decades, MNT) Roanoke; WKPT-TV (COZI TV, Escape, MeTV, MNT) Kingsport; WSET-TV (ABC, Retro TV, WeatherNation) Lynchburg; WSLS-TV (MeTV, NBC) Roanoke; WVVA (CW, MeTV, NBC) Bluefield; WWCW (CW, FOX) Lynchburg; allband FM.
Programming (via satellite): Cartoon Network; CMT; C-SPAN; C-SPAN 2; Discovery Channel; Freeform; INSP; MSNBC; QVC; TBS; The Weather Channel; Travel Channel; Trinity Broadcasting Network (TBN).
Fee: $99.95 installation; $34.96 monthly.

Expanded Basic Service 1
Subscribers: N.A.
Programming (via satellite): A&E; AMC; Animal Planet; CNN; Comedy Central; Disney Channel; E! HD; ESPN; ESPN2; Fox News Channel; FX; HGTV; HLN; Lifetime; MTV; Nickelodeon; Spike TV; Syfy; TLC; TNT; TV Land; USA Network.
Fee: $30.00 monthly.

Digital Basic Service
Subscribers: N.A.
Programming (via satellite): BBC America; Bravo; Discovery Digital Networks; DMX Music; GSN; History; IFC; MTV Classic; National Geographic Channel; Nick Jr.; Turner Classic Movies; VH1 Country; WE tv.
Fee: $13.00 monthly.

Digital Expanded Basic Service
Subscribers: N.A.
Programming (via satellite): ESPN Classic; ESPNews; Fox Sports 1; Golf Channel; NBCSN.
Fee: $4.00 monthly.

Digital Expanded Basic Service 2
Subscribers: N.A.
Programming (via satellite): Showtime (multiplexed); Starz Encore (multiplexed); The Movie Channel (multiplexed).
Fee: $9.00 monthly.

Digital Pay Service 1
Pay Units: N.A.
Programming (via satellite): Cinemax (multiplexed); HBO (multiplexed); Starz (multiplexed).
Fee: $12.95 installation; $13.00 monthly (each).

Video-On-Demand: No

Pay-Per-View
iN DEMAND (delivered digitally).

Internet Service
Operational: Yes.

Telephone Service
Digital: Operational
Miles of Plant: 125.0 (coaxial); None (fiber optic). Homes passed: 3,934.
President: Christopher French. Assistant Secretary, Associate General Counsel: Ann Flowers. Marketing Manager: Chris Ranson.
Ownership: Shentel (MSO).

YORKTOWN—Cox Communications. Now served by HAMPTON ROADS (formerly Virginia Beach), VA [VA0002]. ICA: VA0162.

FULLY SEARCHABLE • CONTINUOUSLY UPDATED • DISCOUNT RATES FOR PRINT PURCHASERS

For more information call **800-771-9202** or visit **www.warren-news.com**

WASHINGTON

Total Systems: 74	Communities with Applications: 0
Total Communities Served: 399	Number of Basic Subscribers: 1,259,394
Franchises Not Yet Operating: 0	Number of Expanded Basic Subscribers: 370
Applications Pending: 0	Number of Pay Units: 379

Top 100 Markets Represented: Seattle-Tacoma (20); Spokane (76).

For a list of cable communities in this section, see the Cable Community Index located in the back of Cable Volume 2.
For explanation of terms used in cable system listings, see p. D-11.

ABERDEEN TWP.—Comcast Cable, 410 Valley Ave NW, Ste 9, Puyallup, WA 98371. Phones: 253-864-4200; 425-398-6000 (Bothell office). Fax: 253-864-4352. Web Site: http://www.comcast.com. Also serves Cosmopolis, Elma, Grayland, Grays Harbor County (portions), Hoquaim, McCleary, Montesano, Pacific (Grays Harbor County), Tokeland, Tracyton, Westport & Wishkah. ICA: WA0003.

TV Market Ranking: 20 (Pacific (Grays Harbor County), Tracyton); Outside TV Markets (Cosmopolis, Elma, Grayland, Grays Harbor County (portions), Hoquaim, McCleary, Tokeland, Westport, Wishkah, ABERDEEN TWP, Montesano). Franchise award date: N.A. Franchise expiration date: N.A. Began: January 1, 1967.

Channel capacity: N.A. Channels available but not in use: N.A.

Basic Service
Subscribers: 12,325.
Programming (received off-air): KBTC-TV (PBS) Tacoma; KCPQ (Escape, FOX) Tacoma; KCTS-TV (PBS) Seattle; KFFV (Azteca America, COZI TV, MeTV) Seattle; KING-TV (NBC) Seattle; KIRO-TV (CBS, getTV, Retro TV) Seattle; KOMO-TV (ABC, This TV) Seattle; KONG (Mundo-Max) Everett; KSTW (CW, Decades) Tacoma; KTBW-TV (TBN) Tacoma; KUNS-TV (MundoMax, UNV) Bellevue; KWDK (Daystar TV, ETV) Tacoma; KWPX-TV (ION) Bellevue; KZJO (Antenna TV, MNT) Seattle; 24 FMs.
Programming (via satellite): C-SPAN; C-SPAN 2; Discovery Channel; Hallmark Channel; Jewelry Television; Northwest Cable News; Pop; QVC; The Weather Channel; TVW; Univision Studios.
Fee: $40.00 installation; $26.94 monthly.

Expanded Basic Service 1
Subscribers: N.A.
Programming (via satellite): A&E; AMC; Animal Planet; BET; Bravo; Cartoon Network; CMT; CNBC; CNN; Comedy Central; Disney Channel; E! HD; ESPN; ESPN2; Food Network; Fox News Channel; Fox Sports 1; Freeform; FX; History; HLN; Lifetime; MSNBC; MTV; MTV2; NBCSN; Nickelodeon; Oxygen; Spike TV; Syfy; TBS; TLC; TNT; Travel Channel; truTV; USA Network; VH1.
Fee: $27.74 monthly.

Digital Basic Service
Subscribers: N.A.
Programming (via satellite): ART America; BBC America; Bloomberg Television; Discovery Digital Networks; Disney XD; DMX Music; ESPN Classic; ESPNews; FSN Digital Atlantic; FSN Digital Central; FSN Digital Pacific; Fuse; FXM; FYI; Golf Channel; Great American Country; GSN; HGTV; History International; HITS (Headend In The Sky); IFC; Korean Channel; LMN; National Geographic Channel; Nick Jr.; Nicktoons; Outdoor Channel; Ovation; RAI Italia; RTN; Saigon Broadcasting Television Network (SBTN); Sundance TV; TeenNick; The Filipino Channel; The Word Network; Turner Classic Movies; TV Asia; TV Land; TV5MONDE USA; WE tv; Weatherscan; Zee TV.
Fee: $11.99 monthly.

Digital Pay Service 1
Pay Units: N.A.
Programming (via satellite): Cinemax (multiplexed); Flix; HBO (multiplexed); Showtime (multiplexed); Starz (multiplexed); Starz Encore (multiplexed); The Movie Channel (multiplexed).
Fee: $11.00 monthly (each).

Video-On-Demand: Yes

Pay-Per-View
Hot Choice (delivered digitally); Urban Xtra (delivered digitally); iN DEMAND (delivered digitally); Shorteez (delivered digitally); Playboy TV (delivered digitally); Fresh (delivered digitally); ESPN Now (delivered digitally); Sports PPV (delivered digitally).

Internet Service
Operational: Yes.
Subscribers: 12,446.
Broadband Service: Comcast High Speed Internet.
Fee: $42.95 monthly; $10.00 modem lease.

Telephone Service
Digital: Operational
Subscribers: 8,145.
Fee: $44.95 monthly.
Miles of Plant: 1,074.0 (coaxial); 200.0 (fiber optic). Homes passed: 33,919.
Area Vice President: Anne McMullen. Vice President, Engineering: Steve Taber. Vice President, Sales & Marketing: Tom Pierce. Marketing Manager: Jennifer Martinez. Public Relations Director: Steve Kipp.
Ownership: Comcast Cable Communications Inc. (MSO).

ABERDEEN TWP.—Comcast Cable. Now served by ABERDEEN, WA [WA0003]. ICA: WA0019.

ALMIRA—Formerly served by Almega Cable. No longer in operation. ICA: WA0143.

ANDERSON ISLAND—Wave Broadband. Now served by LAKE BAY, WA [WA0201]. ICA: WA0157.

ARLINGTON—Comcast Cable. Now served by SEATTLE, WA [WA0001]. ICA: WA0021.

AUBURN—Comcast Cable. Now served by SEATTLE, WA [WA0001]. ICA: WA0211.

BAINBRIDGE ISLAND—Comcast Cable. Now served by SEATTLE, WA [WA0001]. ICA: WA0024.

BAYVIEW—Wave Broadband. Now served by CAMANO ISLAND, WA [WA0046]. ICA: WA0149.

BELLEVUE—Comcast Cable. Now served by SEATTLE, WA [WA0001]. ICA: WA0212.

BELLINGHAM—Comcast Cable, 19909 120th Ave NE, Ste 200, Bothell, WA 98021. Phone: 425-398-6000. Fax: 425-398-6236. Web Site: http://www.comcast.com. Also serves Anacortes, Blaine, Burlington, Clinton, Coupeville, Deming, Everson, Ferndale, Freeland, Island County (portions), Kendall, Lake Samish, Langley, Lummi Indian Reservation, Lynden, Maple Falls, Mount Vernon, Nooksack, Oak Harbor, Sedro Woolley, Skagit, Skagit County (portions), Sudden Valley, Whatcom County (portions) & Whidbey Island Naval Air Station. ICA: WA0011.

TV Market Ranking: Below 100 (Anacortes, BELLINGHAM, Blaine, Clinton, Deming, Everson, Ferndale, Freeland, Island County (portions), Kendall, Lake Samish, Langley, Lummi Indian Reservation, Lynden, Maple Falls, Mount Vernon, Nooksack, Sedro Woolley, Skagit, Skagit County (portions), Whatcom County (portions), Whidbey Island Naval Air Station, Burlington, Coupeville, Oak Harbor; Outside TV Markets (Whatcom County (portions) (portions)). Franchise award date: N.A. Franchise expiration date: N.A. Began: February 1, 1949.

Channel capacity: N.A. Channels available but not in use: N.A.

Basic Service
Subscribers: 67,281.
Programming (received off-air): KBCB (Estrella TV) Bellingham; KCPQ (Escape, FOX) Tacoma; KCTS-TV (PBS) Seattle; KFFV (Azteca America, COZI TV, MeTV) Seattle; KING-TV (NBC) Seattle; KIRO-TV (CBS, getTV, Retro TV) Seattle; KOMO-TV (ABC, This TV) Seattle; KONG (MundoMax) Everett; KSTW (CW, Decades) Tacoma; KVOS-TV (MeTV, Movies!) Bellingham; KWDK (Daystar TV, ETV) Tacoma; KWPX-TV (ION) Bellevue; KZJO (Antenna TV, MNT) Seattle; 20 FMs.
Programming (via satellite): Comcast Network Philadelphia; C-SPAN; C-SPAN 2; Discovery Channel; Hallmark Channel; Northwest Cable News; QVC; Trinity Broadcasting Network (TBN); Univision Studios.
Fee: $40.00 installation; $29.16 monthly.

Expanded Basic Service 1
Subscribers: N.A.
Programming (via satellite): A&E; AMC; Animal Planet; BET; Bravo; Cartoon Network; CMT; CNBC; CNN; Comedy Central; Disney Channel; E! HD; ESPN; ESPN2; Food Network; Fox News Channel; Freeform; FX; History; HLN; Jewelry Television; Lifetime; MSNBC; MTV; MTV2; Nickelodeon; Oxygen; Pop; Spike TV; TBS; The Weather Channel; TLC; TNT; Travel Channel; truTV; USA Network; VH1.
Fee: $36.70 monthly.

Digital Basic Service
Subscribers: N.A.
Programming (via satellite): BBC America; Bloomberg Television; Discovery Digital Networks; Disney XD; DMX Music; ESPNews; Fox Sports 1; FSN Digital Atlantic; FSN Digital Central; FSN Digital Pacific; Fuse; FXM; FYI; Golf Channel; Great American Country; GSN; HGTV; History International; IFC; LMN; National Geographic Channel; NBCSN; Nick Jr.; Nicktoons; Outdoor Channel; Ovation; Sundance TV; Syfy; TeenNick; The Word Network; Turner Classic Movies; TV Land; WE tv; Weatherscan.
Fee: $11.99 monthly.

Digital Pay Service 1
Pay Units: N.A.
Programming (via satellite): ART America; Cinemax (multiplexed); Flix; HBO (multiplexed); HITS (Headend In The Sky); Korean Channel; RTN; Showtime (multiplexed); Starz (multiplexed); Starz Encore (multiplexed); The Filipino Channel; The Movie Channel (multiplexed); TV Asia; TV5MONDE USA.
Fee: $15.00 monthly (each).

Video-On-Demand: Yes

Pay-Per-View
ESPN Now (delivered digitally); Hot Choice (delivered digitally); iN DEMAND (delivered digitally); Playboy TV (delivered digitally); Fresh (delivered digitally); Shorteez (delivered digitally).

Internet Service
Operational: Yes.
Subscribers: 78,197.
Broadband Service: Comcast High Speed Internet.
Fee: $42.95 monthly.

Telephone Service
Digital: Operational
Subscribers: 43,486.
Fee: $44.95 monthly.
Miles of Plant: 3,505.0 (coaxial); 431.0 (fiber optic). Homes passed: 169,475.
Area Vice President: John Dietrich. Vice President, Engineering: Steve Taber. Vice President, Sales & Marketing: Tom Pierce. General Manager: Brett Fontes. Public Relations Director: Steve Kipp.
Ownership: Comcast Cable Communications Inc. (MSO).

BELLINGHAM—Wave Broadband, 401 Parkplace Center, Ste 500, Kirkland, WA 98033. Phones: 425-576-8200; 720-479-3558; 800-829-2225. Fax: 720-479-3585. E-mail: jpenney@wavebroadband.com. Web Site: http://www.wavebroadband.com. Also serves Whatcom County (portions). ICA: WA0080.

TV Market Ranking: Below 100 (BELLINGHAM, Whatcom County (portions)). Fran-

Cable Systems—Washington

chise award date: January 1, 1992. Franchise expiration date: N.A. Began: October 1, 1992.
Channel capacity: N.A. Channels available but not in use: N.A.

Basic Service
Subscribers: 515.
Programming (received off-air): KCPQ (Escape, FOX) Tacoma; KCTS-TV (PBS) Seattle; KING-TV (NBC) Seattle; KIRO-TV (CBS, getTV, Retro TV) Seattle; KOMO-TV (ABC, This TV) Seattle; KSTW (CW, Decades) Tacoma; KVOS-TV (MeTV, Movies!) Bellingham.
Programming (via satellite): A&E; AMC; CNN; C-SPAN; Discovery Channel; Disney Channel; ESPN; Freeform; History; HLN; Lifetime; MTV; Nickelodeon; Pop; QVC; Spike TV; Syfy; TBS; TLC; TNT; USA Network; VH1; WGN America.
Fee: $29.99 installation; $25.95 monthly; $3.00 converter.

Pay Service 1
Pay Units: N.A.
Programming (via satellite): HBO; Showtime.
Fee: $8.00 monthly (Showtime), $8.95 monthly (HBO).
Video-On-Demand: No

Internet Service
Operational: Yes.
Fee: $49.95 installation; $37.95 monthly.

Telephone Service
Digital: Operational
Fee: $39.99 monthly
Miles of Plant: 99.0 (coaxial); 10.0 (fiber optic). Homes passed: 1,500.
Chief Executive Officer: Steve Weed. Chief Financial Officer: Wayne Schattenkerk. President: Jim Penney. General Manager: Stephen J. George.
Ownership: WaveDivision Holdings LLC (MSO).

BIG LAKE—Wave Broadband. Now served by CAMANO ISLAND, WA [WA0046]. ICA: WA0085.

BREMERTON—Comcast Cable. Now served by SEATTLE, WA [WA0001]. ICA: WA0017.

BREWSTER—Formerly served by Wave Broadband. No longer in operation. ICA: WA0060.

BURIEN—Comcast Cable. Now served by SEATTLE, WA [WA0001]. ICA: WA0210.

BURLINGTON—Comcast Cable. Now served by BELLINGHAM, WA [WA0011]. ICA: WA0018.

CAMANO ISLAND—Wave Broadband, 401 Parkplace Center, Ste 500, Kirkland, WA 98033. Phones: 866-928-3123 (customer service); 804-648-5253; 360-399-1143; 800-442-8617. Web Site: http://www.wavebroadband.com. Also serves Bayview, Big Lake, Conway, La Conner, Lake McMurray, Seven Lakes, Shelter Bay, Skagit County (portions), Snohomish County (northwestern portion), Stanwood, Swinomish Indian Reservation, Utsalady & Whatcom County (southern portion). ICA: WA0046.
TV Market Ranking: 20 (CAMANO ISLAND (portions)); Below 100 (Bayview, Big Lake, Conway, La Conner, Lake McMurray, Seven Lakes, Shelter Bay, Skagit County (portions), Snohomish County (northwestern portion) (portions), Stanwood, Swinomish Indian Reservation, Utsalady, Whatcom County (southern portion), CA-MANO ISLAND (portions)); Outside TV Markets (Snohomish County (northwestern portion) (portions)). Franchise award date: January 1, 1968. Franchise expiration date: N.A. Began: June 1, 1980.
Channel capacity: 59 (not 2-way capable). Channels available but not in use: N.A.

Basic Service
Subscribers: 11,733.
Programming (received off-air): KCPQ (Escape, FOX) Tacoma; KCTS-TV (PBS) Seattle; KFFV (Azteca America, COZI TV, MeTV) Seattle; KING-TV (NBC) Seattle; KIRO-TV (CBS, getTV, Retro TV) Seattle; KOMO-TV (ABC, This TV) Seattle; KONG (MundoMax) Everett; KSTW (CW, Decades) Tacoma; KUNS-TV (MundoMax, UNV) Bellevue; KVOS-TV (MeTV, Movies!) Bellingham; KWPX-TV (ION) Bellevue; KZJO (Antenna TV, MNT) Seattle; allband FM.
Programming (via satellite): C-SPAN; EVINE Live; Jewelry Television; Pop; QVC; Trinity Broadcasting Network (TBN); TVW; various Canadian stations.
Fee: $29.99 installation; $25.95 monthly.

Expanded Basic Service 1
Subscribers: N.A.
Programming (via satellite): A&E; AMC; Animal Planet; BET; Bravo; Cartoon Network; CMT; CNBC; CNN; Comedy Central; Discovery Channel; Discovery Life Channel; Disney Channel; E! HD; ESPN; ESPN2; Food Network; Fox News Channel; FOX Sports Networks; Freeform; FX; FXM; Great American Country; Hallmark Channel; HGTV; History; HLN; INSP; Lifetime; MSNBC; MTV; National Geographic Channel; Nickelodeon; Northwest Cable News; Outdoor Channel; Oxygen; Spike TV; Syfy; TBS; The Weather Channel; TLC; TNT; Travel Channel; Turner Classic Movies; TV Land; USA Network; VH1.
Fee: $50.00 installation; $23.55 monthly.

Digital Basic Service
Subscribers: N.A.
Programming (via satellite): BBC America; BYUtv; Cloo; CMT; Destination America; Discovery Kids Channel; Disney XD; DMX Music; EWTN Global Catholic Network; Fox Business Network; FYI; History International; MTV Classic; MTV Hits; MTV Jams; MTV2; Nick Jr.; Nicktoons; OWN: Oprah Winfrey Network; Science Channel; Sprout; TeenNick; Tr3s; VH1 Soul.
Fee: $10.00 monthly.

Digital Expanded Basic Service
Subscribers: N.A.
Programming (via satellite): Bloomberg Television; Boomerang; Bravo; Cooking Channel; DIY Network; Fuse; GSN; Hallmark Movies & Mysteries; IFC; LMN; Ovation; truTV; WE tv.

Digital Expanded Basic Service 2
Subscribers: N.A.
Programming (via satellite): A&E HD; Animal Planet HD; AXS TV; Discovery Channel HD; Disney Channel HD; ESPN HD; ESPN2 HD; Food Network HD; FSN HD; HD Theater; HGTV HD; History HD; MGM HD; National Geographic Channel HD; NFL Network HD; Science HD; TBS HD; TLC HD; TNT HD; Travel Channel HD; Universal HD.

Digital Expanded Basic Service 3
Subscribers: N.A.
Programming (via satellite): CBS Sports Network; ESPN Classic; ESPNews; ESPNU; Fox Sports 1; FSN Digital Atlantic; FSN Digital Central; FSN Digital Pacific; Golf Channel; NBCSN; NFL Network; Tennis Channel.

Digital Pay Service 1
Pay Units: N.A.
Programming (via satellite): Cinemax (multiplexed); Cinemax HD; Flix; HBO (multiplexed); HBO HD; MoviePlex; Showtime (multiplexed); Showtime HD; Starz (multiplexed); Starz Encore (multiplexed); Starz HD; The Movie Channel (multiplexed); The Movie Channel HD.
Fee: $12.00 monthly (Showtime/TMC/Flix), $15.00 monthly (HBO, Cinemax or Starz/Encore).
Video-On-Demand: Yes

Pay-Per-View
Sports PPV (delivered digitally).

Internet Service
Operational: Yes.
Subscribers: 14,376.
Broadband Service: In-house.
Fee: $24.95-$74.95 monthly.

Telephone Service
Digital: Operational
Subscribers: 6,626.
Fee: $39.95 monthly
Miles of Plant: 1,216.0 (coaxial); 790.0 (fiber optic). Homes passed: 25,005.
Chief Financial Officer: Wayne Schattenkerk. General Manager: Jon Ulrich. Regional Office Manager: Bede Wells. Chief Technician: Ed Knipper. Marketing: Sue Campbell.
Ownership: WaveDivision Holdings LLC (MSO).

CARSON—Wave Broadband, 401 Parkplace Center, Ste 500, Kirkland, WA 98033. Phones: 425-576-8200; 720-479-3558; 800-829-2225. Fax: 720-479-3585. E-mail: jpenney@wavebroadband.com. Web Site: http://www.wavebroadband.com. Also serves Skamania County (portions) & Stevenson. ICA: WA0061.
TV Market Ranking: 29 (Skamania County (portions)); Outside TV Markets (CARSON, Stevenson). Franchise award date: N.A. Franchise expiration date: N.A. Began: January 1, 1953.
Channel capacity: N.A. Channels available but not in use: N.A.

Basic Service
Subscribers: 254.
Programming (received off-air): KATU (ABC, MeTV) Portland; KGW (Estrella TV, NBC) Portland; KOIN (CBS) Portland; KOPB-TV (PBS) Portland; KPDX (Escape, MNT) Vancouver; KPTV (COZI TV, FOX, Laff) Portland; allband FM.
Programming (via satellite): A&E; AMC; Animal Planet; CNN; C-SPAN; Discovery Channel; Disney Channel; ESPN; Fox News Channel; Freeform; HGTV; History; HLN; Lifetime; National Geographic Channel; Nickelodeon; Northwest Cable News; QVC; Spike TV; Syfy; TBS; The Weather Channel; TLC; TNT; Travel Channel; TV Land; USA Network; WGN America.
Fee: $29.95 installation; $25.95 monthly.

Digital Basic Service
Subscribers: N.A.
Programming (via satellite): A&E; BBC America; Bravo; Discovery Digital Networks; DMX Music; ESPN2; ESPNews; Fox Sports 1; Golf Channel; GSN; History International; IFC; LMN; NBCSN.
Fee: $18.35 monthly.

Digital Pay Service 1
Pay Units: N.A.
Programming (via satellite): Cinemax (multiplexed); HBO (multiplexed); Showtime (multiplexed); Starz (multiplexed); Starz Encore (multiplexed); The Movie Channel (multiplexed).
Fee: $6.00 monthly (each).
Video-On-Demand: No

Pay-Per-View
Playboy TV (delivered digitally); iN DEMAND (delivered digitally).

Internet Service
Operational: Yes.
Broadband Service: Millennium Cable-Speed.
Fee: $49.95 installation; $37.95 monthly.

Telephone Service
Digital: Operational
Fee: $39.99 monthly
Miles of Plant: 49.0 (coaxial); None (fiber optic). Homes passed: 1,520.
Chief Executive Officer: Steve Weed. Chief Financial Officer: Wayne Schattenkerk. President: Jim Penney. General Manager: Stephen J. George.
Ownership: WaveDivision Holdings LLC (MSO).

CENTRALIA-CHEHALIS—Comcast Cable. Now served by SEATTLE, WA [WA0001]. ICA: WA0022.

CHATTAROY—Formerly served by Almega Cable. No longer in operation. ICA: WA0181.

CHELAN—Wave Broadband, 401 Parkplace Center, Ste 500, Kirkland, WA 98033. Phones: 425-576-8200; 720-479-3558; 800-829-2225. Fax: 720-479-3585. E-mail: jpenney@wavebroadband.com. Web Site: http://www.wavebroadband.com. Also serves Chelan Falls, Entiat & Manson. ICA: WA0058.
TV Market Ranking: Outside TV Markets (CHELAN, Chelan Falls, Manson, Entiat). Franchise award date: N.A. Franchise expiration date: N.A. Began: May 1, 1954.
Channel capacity: 70 (operating 2-way). Channels available but not in use: N.A.

Basic Service
Subscribers: 881.
Programming (received off-air): KCPQ (Escape, FOX) Tacoma; KHQ-TV (NBC) Spokane; KING-TV (NBC) Seattle; KIRO-TV (CBS, getTV, Retro TV) Seattle; KOMO-TV (ABC, This TV) Seattle; KREM (CBS, TheCoolTV) Spokane; KSPS-TV (PBS) Spokane; KSTW (CW, Decades) Tacoma; KXLY-TV (ABC, MeTV) Spokane; KZJO (Antenna TV, MNT) Seattle; 8 FMs.
Programming (via satellite): A&E; AMC; CNBC; CNN; Comedy Central; C-SPAN; Discovery Channel; Disney Channel; ESPN; Fox News Channel; Freeform; History; HLN; Lifetime; National Geographic Channel; Nickelodeon; Northwest Cable News; QVC; Spike TV; TBS; TLC; TNT; Trinity Broadcasting Network (TBN); TVW; Univision Studios; USA Network.
Fee: $29.95 installation; $25.95 monthly.

Digital Basic Service
Subscribers: N.A.
Programming (via satellite): A&E; BBC America; Bravo; Discovery Digital Networks; DMX Music; ESPN2; ESPNews; Fox Sports 1; Golf Channel; GSN; HGTV; History International; HITS (Headend In The Sky); IFC; LMN; NBCSN; Starz Encore.
Fee: $13.40 monthly.

Digital Pay Service 1
Pay Units: N.A.
Programming (via satellite): Cinemax (multiplexed); HBO (multiplexed); Showtime (multiplexed).
Fee: $9.50 monthly (each).
Video-On-Demand: No

Pay-Per-View
iN DEMAND (delivered digitally); Playboy TV (delivered digitally).

Washington—Cable Systems

FULLY SEARCHABLE • CONTINUOUSLY UPDATED • DISCOUNT RATES FOR PRINT PURCHASERS

For more information call 800-771-9202 or visit www.warren-news.com

Internet Service
Operational: Yes.
Broadband Service: Millennium CableSpeed.
Fee: $49.95 installation; $24.95 monthly.
Telephone Service
Digital: Operational
Fee: $39.99 monthly
Miles of Plant: 1,691.0 (coaxial); 514.0 (fiber optic). Homes passed: 53,081.
Chief Executive Officer: Steve Weed. Chief Financial Officer: Wayne Schattenkerk. President: Jim Penney. General Manager: Stephen J. George.
Ownership: WaveDivision Holdings LLC (MSO).

CHENEY—Davis Communications, 1920 4th St., PO Box 117, Cheney, WA 99004. Phones: 509-235-5144; 509-624-7129. Fax: 509-235-5158. E-mail: questions@ daviscomm.net. Web Site: http://www. daviscomm.net. Also serves Four Lakes & Medical Lake. ICA: WA0217.
TV Market Ranking: 76 (CHENEY, Four Lakes, Medical Lake).
Channel capacity: 62 (not 2-way capable). Channels available but not in use: N.A.
Basic Service
Subscribers: 901.
Fee: $35.94 monthly.
Internet Service
Operational: Yes.
Subscribers: 1,136.
Telephone Service
Digital: Operational
Subscribers: 33.
Miles of Plant: 126.0 (coaxial); 47.0 (fiber optic). Homes passed: 7,000.
System Engineer: Tim Gainer. Project Manager: Robert Douthitt. Marketing Manager: Cheryl Reagan.
Ownership: Davis Communications Inc.

CHENEY—Formerly served by Wave Broadband. No longer in operation. ICA: WA0045.

CHINOOK—Chinook Progressive Club TV, PO Box 15, Chinook, WA 98614-0015. Phones: 360-777-8412; 360-244-5660. E-mail: chinooktv@yahoo.com. ICA: WA0146.
TV Market Ranking: Outside TV Markets (CHINOOK). Franchise award date: N.A. Franchise expiration date: N.A. Began: January 1, 1961.
Channel capacity: 12 (not 2-way capable). Channels available but not in use: N.A.
Basic Service
Subscribers: 194.
Programming (received off-air): KATU (ABC, MeTV) Portland; KGW (Estrella TV, NBC) Portland; KOIN (CBS) Portland; KOPB-TV (PBS) Portland; KPTV (COZI TV, FOX, Laff) Portland.
Programming (via satellite): A&E; CNN; C-SPAN; Discovery Channel; ESPN; Freeform; FX; QVC; Spike TV; TBS; The Weather Channel; TLC; TNT; Travel Channel; Trinity Broadcasting Network (TBN); USA Network.
Fee: $20.00 installation; $30.00 monthly.

Internet Service
Operational: No.
Telephone Service
None
Miles of Plant: 7.0 (coaxial); None (fiber optic). Homes passed: 300.
General Manager: Trophy W. Hughes. Chief Technician: Gary White. Bookkeeper: Luanne Anderson.
Ownership: Chinook Progressive Club TV Inc.

CHINOOK PASS—Formerly served by Almega Cable. No longer in operation. ICA: WA0109.

CLALLAM BAY—Formerly served by Wave Broadband. No longer in operation. ICA: WA0095.

CLE ELUM—R & R Cable, 103 South Second St, PO Box 610, Roslyn, WA 98941. Phones: 509-649-4638; 509-649-2211; 509-649-2212. E-mail: cable@inlandnet.com. Web Site: http://www.rrcable.com. Also serves Kittitas County (northern portion) & South Cle Elum. ICA: WA0068.
TV Market Ranking: Below 100 (Kittitas County (northern portion) (portions)); Outside TV Markets (CLE ELUM, Kittitas County (northern portion) (portions), South Cle Elum). Franchise award date: N.A. Franchise expiration date: N.A. Began: December 1, 1954.
Channel capacity: N.A. Channels available but not in use: N.A.
Basic Service
Subscribers: N.A.
Programming (received off-air): KAPP (ABC, MeTV, MNT) Yakima; KCYU-LD (FOX, This TV) Yakima; KIMA-TV (CBS, CW) Yakima; KNDO (NBC) Yakima; KYVE (PBS) Yakima; allband FM.
Programming (via microwave): KCPQ (Escape, FOX) Tacoma; KING-TV (NBC) Seattle; KIRO-TV (CBS, getTV, Retro TV) Seattle; KOMO-TV (ABC, This TV) Seattle.
Programming (via satellite): A&E; AMC; Animal Planet; Bravo; Cartoon Network; CMT; CNN; Comedy Central; C-SPAN; Discovery Channel; Discovery Life Channel; E! HD; ESPN; ESPN Classic; ESPN2; Food Network; Fox News Channel; Freeform; FX; Hallmark Channel; Lifetime; LMN; MSNBC; MTV; National Geographic Channel; Nickelodeon; Nicktoons; Northwest Cable News; Outdoor Channel; Pop; QVC; Spike TV; Syfy; TBS; The Weather Channel; TLC; TNT; Travel Channel; Trinity Broadcasting Network (TBN); truTV; TV Land; TVW; USA Network; VH1; WGN America; WSBK-TV (MNT) Boston.
Fee: $28.00 monthly.
Digital Basic Service
Subscribers: N.A.
Programming (via satellite): BBC America; Bloomberg Television; Cloo; Discovery Digital Networks; DMX Music; ESPNews; FOX College Sports Central; FOX College Sports Pacific; Fox Sports 1; Fuse; FXM; FYI; Golf Channel; Great American Country; GSN; HGTV; History; History International; IFC;

NBCSN; Nick Jr.; TeenNick; Turner Classic Movies; WE tv.
Fee: $7.00 monthly.
Digital Pay Service 1
Pay Units: N.A.
Programming (via satellite): Cinemax (multiplexed); HBO (multiplexed); Showtime (multiplexed); Starz (multiplexed); Starz Encore (multiplexed); The Movie Channel (multiplexed).
Fee: $7.00 monthly (Cinemax), $10.00 monthly (Starz & Encore), $12.00 monthly (Showtime & TMC), $13.00 monthly (HBO).
Video-On-Demand: No
Pay-Per-View
iN DEMAND (delivered digitally); Playboy TV (delivered digitally); Fresh (delivered digitally).
Internet Service
Operational: No, DSL.
Telephone Service
Analog: Operational
Miles of Plant: 23.0 (coaxial); None (fiber optic). Homes passed: 1,250.
General Manager: Doug Weiss. Chief Technician: Steven Vlahovich.
Ownership: Inland Telephone Co. (MSO).

COLFAX—Colfax Cable Co, PO Box 268, St. John, WA 99171. Phone: 509-648-3322. E-mail: service@stjohncable.com. Web Site: http://www.stjohncable.com. ICA: WA0075.
TV Market Ranking: Below 100 (COLFAX). Franchise award date: N.A. Franchise expiration date: N.A. Began: December 1, 1953.
Channel capacity: 42 (operating 2-way). Channels available but not in use: N.A.
Basic Service
Subscribers: 540.
Programming (received off-air): KAYU-TV (FOX, This TV) Spokane; KHQ-TV (NBC) Spokane; KLEW-TV (CBS) Lewiston; KREM (CBS, TheCoolTV) Spokane; KSKN (CW) Spokane; KSPS-TV (PBS) Spokane; KUID-TV (PBS) Moscow; KWSU-TV (PBS) Pullman; KXLY-TV (ABC, MeTV) Spokane; allband FM.
Programming (via satellite): A&E; AMC; CMT; CNBC; CNN; C-SPAN; C-SPAN 2; Discovery Channel; Disney Channel; Disney XD; E! HD; ESPN; ESPN Classic; ESPN2; EWTN Global Catholic Network; Food Network; Fox News Channel; Freeform; HGTV; History; HLN; ION Television; Lifetime; MTV; National Geographic Channel; Nickelodeon; Northwest Cable News; Outdoor Channel; Spike TV; Syfy; TBS; TLC; TNT; Travel Channel; Turner Classic Movies; USA Network; VH1; WGN America.
Fee: $52.00 monthly.
Digital Basic Service
Subscribers: N.A.
Programming (via satellite): BBC America; Bravo; Discovery Digital Networks; DMX Music; ESPN Classic; ESPN2; Fox Sports 1; Fuse; FYI; Golf Channel; GSN; History International; IFC; LMN; National Geographic Channel; NBCSN; WE tv.
Fee: $15.50 monthly.
Digital Pay Service 1
Pay Units: N.A.
Programming (via satellite): Cinemax (multiplexed); HBO (multiplexed); Showtime (multiplexed); Starz (multiplexed); Starz Encore (multiplexed); The Movie Channel (multiplexed).
Fee: $8.00 monthly (Cinemax), $9.50 monthly (Starz/Encore), $10 monthly (Showtime/TMC), $12.00 monthly (HBO).
Video-On-Demand: No

Pay-Per-View
iN DEMAND (delivered digitally); Playboy TV (delivered digitally).
Internet Service
Operational: Yes.
Broadband Service: St. John Cable.
Fee: $25.00 installation; $34.95-$45.00 monthly.
Telephone Service
Analog: Operational
Digital: Not Operational
Miles of Plant: 25.0 (coaxial); None (fiber optic).
General Manager: Gregory Morasch.
Ownership: Colfax Highline Cable Co.

COLVILLE—Charter Communications, 12405 Powerscourt Dr, St. Louis, MO 63131. Phones: 636-207-5100 (Corporate office); 360-828-6600; 360-828-6700. Fax: 360-828-6795. Web Site: http://www. charter.com. Also serves Arden & Kettle Falls. ICA: WA0038.
TV Market Ranking: Outside TV Markets (Arden, COLVILLE, Kettle Falls). Franchise award date: April 20, 1954. Franchise expiration date: N.A. Began: August 1, 1953.
Channel capacity: N.A. Channels available but not in use: N.A.
Digital Basic Service
Subscribers: 463.
Programming (via satellite): BBC America; Bloomberg Television; Bravo; Discovery Digital Networks; Disney XD; DMX Music; ESPN Classic; ESPNews; Fox Sports 1; Fuse; FXM; FYI; Golf Channel; GSN; History International; IFC; International Television (ITV); LMN; NBCSN; Nick Jr.; Outdoor Channel; Starz Encore (multiplexed); Sundance TV; TeenNick; Turner Classic Movies; TV Guide Interactive Inc.
Fee: $26.99 monthly.
Digital Expanded Basic Service
Subscribers: N.A.
Programming (via satellite): A&E; AMC; Animal Planet; Cartoon Network; CMT; CNBC; CNN; Comedy Central; Discovery Channel; Disney Channel; E! HD; ESPN; ESPN2; Food Network; Fox News Channel; Freeform; FX; Hallmark Channel; HGTV; History; HLN; Lifetime; MSNBC; MTV; National Geographic Channel; Nickelodeon; Northwest Cable News; Spike TV; Syfy; TLC; TNT; Travel Channel; TV Land; USA Network; VH1; WE tv.
Fee: $42.99 monthly.
Digital Pay Service 1
Pay Units: N.A.
Programming (via satellite): Cinemax (multiplexed); HBO (multiplexed); Showtime (multiplexed); Starz (multiplexed); The Movie Channel (multiplexed).
Fee: $25.95 installation; $10.95 monthly (Showtime or TMC), $11.95 monthly (HBO).
Video-On-Demand: No
Pay-Per-View
iN DEMAND (delivered digitally); Playboy TV (delivered digitally); Fresh (delivered digitally); Shorteez (delivered digitally).
Internet Service
Operational: No.
Telephone Service
None
Miles of Plant: 71.0 (coaxial); None (fiber optic). Homes passed: 3,070.
Vice President: Frank Antonovich. General Manager: Linda Kimberly. Technical Operations Director: Brian Lindholme. Marketing Director: Diane Long. Accounting Director: David Sovanski.
Ownership: Charter Communications Inc. (MSO).

D-816

TV & Cable Factbook No. 85

Cable Systems—Washington

CONCRETE—Wave Broadband, 401 Parkplace Center, Ste 500, Kirkland, WA 98033. Phones: 425-576-8200; 720-479-3558; 800-829-2225. Fax: 720-479-3585. E-mail: jpenney@wavebroadband.com. Web Site: http://www.wavebroadband.com. Also serves Hamilton, Lyman & Skagit County (portions). ICA: WA0069.

TV Market Ranking: Below 100 (Hamilton, Lyman, Skagit County (portions) (portions)); Outside TV Markets (CONCRETE, Skagit County (portions) (portions)). Franchise award date: N.A. Franchise expiration date: N.A. Began: January 1, 1966.

Channel capacity: N.A. Channels available but not in use: N.A.

Basic Service
Subscribers: 377.
Programming (received off-air): KCPQ (Escape, FOX) Tacoma; KCTS-TV (PBS) Seattle; KING-TV (NBC) Seattle; KIRO-TV (CBS, getTV, Retro TV) Seattle; KOMO-TV (ABC, This TV) Seattle; KVOS-TV (MeTV, Movies!) Bellingham; 1 FM.
Programming (via satellite): A&E; AMC; Bravo; Cartoon Network; CMT; CNN; C-SPAN; Discovery Channel; Disney Channel; E! HD; ESPN; Fox News Channel; Freeform; FX; History; HLN; Lifetime; National Geographic Channel; Northwest Cable News; QVC; Spike TV; Syfy; TBS; TLC; TNT; TV Land; USA Network; WGN America.
Fee: $29.95 installation; $25.95 monthly.

Digital Basic Service
Subscribers: N.A.
Programming (via satellite): A&E; BBC America; Discovery Digital Networks; DMX Music; ESPN2; ESPNews; Fox Sports 1; Golf Channel; GSN; HGTV; History International; IFC; LMN; NBCSN; Starz Encore.
Fee: $13.40 monthly.

Digital Pay Service 1
Pay Units: N.A.
Programming (via satellite): Cinemax (multiplexed); HBO (multiplexed); Showtime (multiplexed); The Movie Channel (multiplexed).
Fee: $10.00 monthly (each).

Video-On-Demand: No

Pay-Per-View
Playboy TV (delivered digitally); iN DEMAND (delivered digitally).

Internet Service
Operational: Yes.
Fee: $49.95 installation; $39.95 monthly.

Telephone Service
Digital: Operational
Fee: $39.99 monthly
Miles of Plant: 72.0 (coaxial); None (fiber optic).
Chief Executive Officer: Steve Weed. Chief Financial Officer: Wayne Schattenkerk. President: Jim Penney. General Manager: Stephen J. George.
Ownership: WaveDivision Holdings LLC (MSO).

CONNELL—Northstar Broadband, PO Box 2576, Post Falls, ID 83877. Phones: 208-262-9394; 800-572-0902. Fax: 208-262-9314. E-mail: j.webb@northstarbroadband.net. Web Site: http://www.northstarbroadband.net. ICA: WA0090.

TV Market Ranking: Below 100 (CONNELL). Franchise award date: September 13, 1988. Franchise expiration date: N.A. Began: December 23, 1955.

Channel capacity: 64 (2-way capable). Channels available but not in use: N.A.

Basic Service
Subscribers: 85.
Programming (received off-air): KEPR-TV (CBS, CW) Pasco; KHQ-TV (NBC) Spokane; KNDU (NBC) Richland; KSPS-TV (PBS) Spokane; KVEW (ABC, MeTV, MNT) Kennewick; 7 FMs.
Programming (via satellite): A&E; Animal Planet; Cartoon Network; CMT; Concert TV; C-SPAN; Discovery Channel; EVINE Live; EWTN Global Catholic Network; Food Network; Fox News Channel; Freeform; Hallmark Channel; History; HGTV; ION Television; MSNBC; NBCSN; Nickelodeon; OWN; Oprah Winfrey Network; Pop; QVC; TBS; TLC; Travel Channel; Trinity Broadcasting Network (TBN); TV Land; UniMas; WGN America.
Fee: $20.00 installation; $35.93 monthly.

Expanded Basic Service 1
Subscribers: N.A.
Programming (via satellite): AMC; Bravo; CNBC; CNN; Comedy Central; Disney Channel; Disney XD; E! HD; ESPN; ESPN Classic; ESPN2; Fox Sports 1; FX; HLN; Lifetime; MTV; National Geographic Channel; Northwest Cable News; Spike TV; Syfy; TNT; truTV; Turner Classic Movies; Univision; Univision Studios; USA Network; VH1.
Fee: $12.31 monthly.

Pay Service 1
Pay Units: N.A.
Programming (via satellite): Cinemax; HBO; Showtime.
Fee: $5.00 installation; $5.25 monthly (Cinemax), $8.65 monthly (Showtime), $9.60 monthly (HBO).

Video-On-Demand: No

Internet Service
Operational: Yes.

Telephone Service
None
Miles of Plant: 9.0 (coaxial); None (fiber optic). Homes passed: 902.
General Manager: Alisssa Freeman. Office Manager: Jennifer Webb. Operations Manager: Greg Lundwall.
Ownership: Northstar Broadband LLC (MSO).

COULEE CITY—Formerly served by Almega Cable. No longer in operation. ICA: WA0105.

COULEE DAM—Country Cable, 7520 North Washington St, Ste 14, Spokane, WA 99217. Phone: 509-633-2283. ICA: WA0092.

TV Market Ranking: Outside TV Markets (COULEE DAM). Franchise award date: September 1, 1954. Franchise expiration date: N.A. Began: September 1, 1954.

Channel capacity: N.A. Channels available but not in use: N.A.

Basic Service
Subscribers: 200.
Programming (received off-air): KAYU-TV (FOX, This TV) Spokane; KHQ-TV (NBC) Spokane; KREM (CBS, TheCoolTV) Spokane; KSPS-TV (PBS) Spokane; KXLY-TV (ABC, MeTV) Spokane; allband FM.
Programming (via satellite): CNN; Discovery Channel; ESPN; Spike TV; TBS; TNT.
Fee: $25.00 installation; $20.00 monthly.

Expanded Basic Service 1
Subscribers: 150.
Fee: $18.00 monthly.

Pay Service 1
Pay Units: 80.
Programming (via satellite): HBO.
Fee: $9.95 monthly.

Pay Service 2
Pay Units: 40.
Programming (via satellite): Starz.
Fee: $6.25 monthly.

Video-On-Demand: No

Internet Service
Operational: Yes.
Fee: $25.00 installation; $34.00 monthly.

Telephone Service
Digital: Operational
Miles of Plant: 8.0 (coaxial); None (fiber optic). Homes passed: 539.
Vice President: Carl Sherwood. General Manager & Chief Technician: Jon Cooke.
Ownership: Country Cable LLC (MSO).

COUPEVILLE—Comcast Cable. Now served by BELLINGHAM, WA [WA0011]. ICA: WA0071.

CRESTON—Formerly served by Wave Broadband. No longer in operation. ICA: WA0150.

DARRINGTON—Formerly served by Wave Broadband. No longer in operation. ICA: WA0078.

DAVENPORT—Northstar Broadband, PO Box 2576, Post Falls, ID 83877. Phones: 800-572-0902; 208-262-9394. Fax: 208-262-9314. E-mail: j.webb@northstarbroadband.net. Web Site: http://www.northstarbroadband.net. ICA: WA0089.

TV Market Ranking: Outside TV Markets (DAVENPORT).

Channel capacity: N.A. Channels available but not in use: N.A.

Basic Service
Subscribers: 66.
Programming (received off-air): KAYU-TV (FOX, This TV) Spokane; KGPX-TV (ION) Spokane; KHQ-TV (NBC) Spokane; KREM (CBS, TheCoolTV) Spokane; KSKN (CW) Spokane; KSPS-TV (PBS) Spokane; KXLY-TV (ABC, MeTV) Spokane.
Programming (via satellite): 3ABN; A&E; AMC; Animal Planet; Cartoon Network; CNBC; CNN; C-SPAN; C-SPAN 2; Discovery Channel; Disney Channel; E! HD; ESPN; ESPN2; Fox News Channel; FOX Sports West/Prime Ticket; Freeform; FX; Great American Country; HGTV; History; Lifetime; MTV; NBCSN; Nickelodeon; Northwest Cable News; OWN; Oprah Winfrey Network; QVC; Spike TV; Syfy; TBS; The Weather Channel; TLC; TNT; USA Network; VH1.
Fee: $60.00 installation; $56.95 monthly.

Pay Service 1
Pay Units: N.A.
Programming (via satellite): HBO.
Fee: $13.60 monthly.

Internet Service
Operational: Yes.

Telephone Service
None
Office Manager: Jennifer Webb. Operations Manager: Greg Lundwall.
Ownership: Northstar Broadband LLC (MSO).

DAYTON—Touchet Valley TV Inc, 107 South First St, PO Box 148, Dayton, WA 99328-0148. Phone: 509-382-2132. E-mail: tvcable@gmail.com. Web Site: http://www.touchetvalleytv.com. ICA: WA0070.

TV Market Ranking: Below 100 (DAYTON). Franchise award date: N.A. Franchise expiration date: N.A. Began: September 1, 1953.

Channel capacity: N.A. Channels available but not in use: N.A.

Basic Service
Subscribers: 285.
Programming (received off-air): KHQ-TV (NBC) Spokane; KREM (CBS, TheCoolTV) Spokane; KSKN (CW) Spokane; KSPS-TV (PBS) Spokane; KVEW (ABC, MeTV, MNT) Kennewick; allband FM.
Programming (via satellite): A&E; CMT; CNN; Discovery Channel; ESPN; Fox News Channel; Freeform; ION Television; Lifetime; Nickelodeon; Northwest Cable News; Outdoor Channel; QVC; Spike TV; Syfy; TBS; The Weather Channel; TNT; TV Land; Univision Studios; USA Network; VH1; WGN America.
Fee: $15.00 installation; $37.00 monthly.

Pay Service 1
Pay Units: N.A.
Programming (via satellite): HBO; Showtime.
Fee: $8.00 monthly (Showtime), $10.00 monthly (HBO).

Video-On-Demand: No

Internet Service
Operational: Yes.
Subscribers: 113.

Telephone Service
None
Miles of Plant: 24.0 (coaxial); None (fiber optic). Homes passed: 1,537.
General Manager: Ron Klingenstein. Chief Technician: Bob Truesdale.
Ownership: Ron Klingenstein.

DEER PARK—Northstar Broadband, PO Box 2576, Post Falls, ID 83877. Phones: 800-572-0902; 208-262-9394. Fax: 208-262-9314. E-mail: office@northstarbroadband.net. Web Site: http://www.northstarbroadband.net. ICA: WA0081.

TV Market Ranking: 76 (DEER PARK).

Channel capacity: N.A. Channels available but not in use: N.A.

Basic Service
Subscribers: 118.
Programming (received off-air): KAYU-TV (FOX, This TV) Spokane; KGPX-TV (ION) Spokane; KHQ-TV (NBC) Spokane; KQUP-LP Coeur d"Alene; KREM (CBS, TheCoolTV) Spokane; KSKN (CW) Spokane; KSPS-TV (PBS) Spokane; KXLY-TV (ABC, MeTV) Spokane.
Programming (via satellite): 3ABN; A&E; Animal Planet; Cartoon Network; C-SPAN; C-SPAN 2; Discovery Channel; Disney Channel; Disney XD; ESPN; ESPN Classic; ESPN2; EVINE Live; EWTN Global Catholic Network; Food Network; Fox News Channel; FOX Sports West/Prime Ticket; Freeform; Great American Country; Hallmark Channel; Hallmark Movies & Mysteries; HGTV; History; National Geographic Channel; Nickelodeon; QVC; TBS; The Weather Channel; TLC; Travel Channel; Trinity Broadcasting Network (TBN); TV Land; TVW; WGN America.
Fee: $60.00 installation; $35.93 monthly.

Expanded Basic Service 1
Subscribers: N.A.
Programming (via satellite): AMC; CNBC; CNN; Comedy Central; E! HD; Fox Sports 1; FX; FXM; Golf Channel; Lifetime; MTV; NBCSN; Northwest Cable News; Outdoor Channel; Spike TV; Syfy; TNT; Turner Classic Movies; USA Network; VH1.
Fee: $24.36 monthly.

Pay Service 1
Pay Units: N.A.
Programming (via satellite): Cinemax; HBO.
Fee: $12.15 monthly (Cinemax), $14.37 monthly (HBO).

Internet Service
Operational: Yes.

2017 Edition

Washington—Cable Systems

FULLY SEARCHABLE • CONTINUOUSLY UPDATED • DISCOUNT RATES FOR PRINT PURCHASERS
For more information call **800-771-9202** or visit **www.warren-news.com**

Telephone Service
None
General Manager: Alisssa Freeman. Office Manager: Jennifer Webb. Operations Manager: Greg Lundwall.
Ownership: Northstar Broadband LLC (MSO).

DIAMOND LAKE—Northstar Broadband, PO Box 2576, Post Falls, ID 83877. Phones: 800-572-0902; 208-262-9394. Fax: 208-262-9314. E-mail: j.webb@northstarbroadband.net. Web Site: http://www.northstarbroadband.net. ICA: WA0096.
TV Market Ranking: Outside TV Markets (DIAMOND LAKE).
Channel capacity: N.A. Channels available but not in use: N.A.

Basic Service
Subscribers: N.A.
Programming (received off-air): KAYU-TV (FOX, This TV) Spokane; KGPX-TV (ION) Spokane; KHQ-TV (NBC) Spokane; KREM (CBS, TheCoolTV) Spokane; KSKN (CW) Spokane; KSPS-TV (PBS) Spokane; KXLY-TV (ABC, MeTV) Spokane.
Programming (via satellite): 3ABN; A&E; CNN; C-SPAN; Discovery Channel; Disney Channel; ESPN; ESPN2; FOX Sports West/Prime Ticket; Freeform; Great American Country; HGTV; History; HLN; HSN; Lifetime; MTV; Nickelodeon; Northwest Cable News; Spike TV; Syfy; TBS; The Weather Channel; TLC; TNT; Turner Classic Movies; USA Network; VH1; WGN America.
Fee: $60.00 installation; $36.50 monthly.

Pay Service 1
Pay Units: N.A.
Programming (via satellite): HBO; Showtime; The Movie Channel.
Fee: $8.50 monthly (TMC), $11.50 monthly (Showtime), $12.95 monthly (HBO).

Internet Service
Operational: Yes.

Telephone Service
None
Office Manager: Jennifer Webb. Operations Manager: Greg Lundwall.
Ownership: Northstar Broadband LLC (MSO).

DUVALL—Wave Broadband, 401 Parkplace Center, Ste 500, Kirkland, WA 98033. Phones: 425-576-8200; 720-479-3558; 800-829-2225. Fax: 720-479-3585. E-mail: jpenney@wavebroadband.com. Web Site: http://www.wavebroadband.com. Also serves Carnation, Issaquah (southeastern portion), King County (portions), Redmond, Sahalee, Snoqualmie Valley & Woodinville. ICA: WA0043. **Note:** This system is an overbuild.
TV Market Ranking: 20 (Carnation, DUVALL, Issaquah (southeastern portion), King County (portions), Redmond, Sahalee, Snoqualmie Valley, Woodinville). Franchise award date: January 1, 1981. Franchise expiration date: N.A. Began: January 1, 1982.
Channel capacity: N.A. Channels available but not in use: N.A.

Basic Service
Subscribers: 2,541.
Programming (received off-air): KCPQ (Escape, FOX) Tacoma; KCTS-TV (PBS) Seattle; KFFV (Azteca America, COZI TV, MeTV) Seattle; KING-TV (NBC) Seattle; KIRO-TV (CBS, getTV, Retro TV) Seattle; KOMO-TV (ABC, This TV) Seattle; KONG (MundoMax) Everett; KSTW (CW, Decades) Tacoma; KTBW-TV (TBN) Tacoma; KUNS-TV (MundoMax, UNV) Bellevue; KWDK (Daystar TV, ETV) Tacoma; KWPX-TV (ION) Bellevue; KZJO (Antenna TV, MNT) Seattle.
Programming (via satellite): C-SPAN; EVINE Live; EWTN Global Catholic Network; Pop; QVC; TVW; various Canadian stations.
Fee: $29.95 installation; $25.95 monthly.

Expanded Basic Service 1
Subscribers: N.A.
Programming (via satellite): A&E; AMC; Animal Planet; BET; Bravo; Cartoon Network; Classic Arts Showcase; CMT; CNBC; CNN; Comedy Central; Cooking Channel; Discovery Channel; Disney Channel; E! HD; ESPN; ESPN Classic; ESPN2; Food Network; Fox News Channel; Freeform; FX; Golf Channel; GSN; HGTV; History; HLN; IFC; Lifetime; MSNBC; MTV; National Geographic Channel; Nickelodeon; Northwest Cable News; OWN; Oprah Winfrey Network; Spike TV; Syfy; TBS; Telemundo; The Weather Channel; TLC; TNT; Travel Channel; truTV; Turner Classic Movies; TV Land; USA Network; VH1; WE tv.
Fee: $30.00 monthly.

Digital Basic Service
Subscribers: N.A.
Programming (via satellite): AXS TV; BBC America; CMT; Destination America; Discovery Kids Channel; DIY Network; ESPN HD; Food Network HD; Hallmark Channel; HD Theater; HGTV HD; Investigation Discovery; MC; MTV Classic; MTV Hits; MTV Jams; MTV2; Nick 2; Nick Jr.; Nicktoons; Science Channel; Starz (multiplexed); Starz Encore (multiplexed); TeenNick; Tr3s; VH1 Soul.
Fee: $11.44 monthly.

Digital Expanded Basic Service
Subscribers: N.A.
Programming (via satellite): ESPNews; FOX College Sports Central; FOX College Sports Pacific; Fox Sports 1; NBCSN.
Fee: $5.99 monthly.

Digital Pay Service 1
Pay Units: N.A.
Programming (via satellite): Cinemax (multiplexed); Flix; HBO (multiplexed); Showtime (multiplexed); Sundance TV; The Movie Channel (multiplexed); Zee TV.
Fee: $5.50 monthly (HBO, Cinemax or Showtime/TMC), $14.95 monthly (Zee TV).

Video-On-Demand: No

Pay-Per-View
Special events (delivered digitally).

Internet Service
Operational: Yes.
Broadband Service: Millennium Cable-Speed.
Fee: $49.95 installation; $37.95 monthly.

Telephone Service
Digital: Operational
Fee: $39.99 monthly
Miles of Plant: 280.0 (coaxial); 113.0 (fiber optic). Homes passed: 5,000.
Chief Executive Officer: Steve Weed. Chief Financial Officer: Wayne Schattenkerk. President: Jim Penney. General Manager: Stephen J. George.
Ownership: WaveDivision Holdings LLC (MSO).

EASTON—Formerly served by Wave Broadband. No longer in operation. ICA: WA0203.

EATONVILLE—Rainier Cable, 104 Washington Ave N, PO Box 639, Eatonville, WA 98328-0639. Phones: 360-623-3278 (Customer service); 360-832-6161; 800-332-5725. Fax: 360-832-8817. E-mail: customerservice@rainierconnect.com. Web Site: http://www.rainierconnect.com. Also serves Graham, Pierce County (portions), Puyallup & University Place. ICA: WA0209. **Note:** This system is an overbuild.
TV Market Ranking: 20 (EATONVILLE, Graham, Pierce County (portions), Puyallup, University Place).
Channel capacity: 20 (operating 2-way). Channels available but not in use: N.A.

Basic Service
Subscribers: 964.
Programming (received off-air): KBTC-TV (PBS) Tacoma; KCPQ (Escape, FOX) Tacoma; KCTS-TV (PBS) Seattle; KING-TV (NBC) Seattle; KIRO-TV (CBS, getTV, Retro TV) Seattle; KOMO-TV (ABC, This TV) Seattle; KONG (MundoMax) Everett; KSTW (CW, Decades) Tacoma; KUNS-TV (MundoMax, UNV) Bellevue; KZJO (Antenna TV, MNT) Seattle.
Programming (via satellite): A&E; AMC; Animal Planet; AWE; BET; Boomerang; Bravo; BYUtv; Cartoon Network; CMT; CNBC; CNN; Comedy Central; C-SPAN; C-SPAN 2; Daystar TV Network; Discovery Channel; Disney Channel; DIY Network; E! HD; ESPN; ESPN Classic; ESPN2; Food Network; Fox News Channel; Fox Sports 1; Freeform; FX; Golf Channel; Hallmark Channel; HGTV; History; HLN; ION Television; Lifetime; MSNBC; MTV; National Geographic Channel; NBCSN; NFL Network; Nickelodeon; Northwest Cable News; Oxygen; Pop; QVC; Spike TV; Syfy; TBS; The Weather Channel; TLC; TNT; Travel Channel; Trinity Broadcasting Network (TBN); truTV; Turner Classic Movies; TV Land; TVW; USA Network; VH1; WE tv; WGN America.
Fee: $18.99 monthly.

Digital Basic Service
Subscribers: N.A.
Programming (via satellite): AXS TV; BBC America; Bloomberg Television; CBS Sports Network; Cinelatino; Cloo; CMT; CNN en Espanol; Destination America; Discovery Channel HD; Discovery Kids Channel; Disney XD; DMX Music; ESPN HD; ESPNews; Food Network HD; FOX College Sports Central; FOX College Sports Pacific; Fox Deportes; FXM; FYI; GSN; HGTV HD; History International; IFC; Investigation Discovery; MTV Classic; MTV Hits; MTV2; Nat Geo WILD; National Geographic Channel HD; Nick Jr.; Nicktoons; Outdoor Channel; Science Channel; Sprout; Starz Encore (multiplexed); Sundance TV; Teen-Nick; Toon Disney en Espanol; Tr3s; TVG Network; VH1 Soul; ViendoMovies.
Fee: $50.00 monthly.

Digital Pay Service 1
Pay Units: N.A.
Programming (via satellite): Cinemax (multiplexed); Cinemax HD; Flix; HBO (multiplexed); HBO en Espanol; HBO HD; Showtime (multiplexed); Showtime HD; Starz (multiplexed); Starz HD; The Filipino Channel; The Movie Channel (multiplexed).
Fee: $9.99 monthly (Starz), $10.99 monthly (Showtime, TMC & Flix), $11.99 monthly (Cinemax), $12.99 monthly (HBO).

Video-On-Demand: No

Pay-Per-View
iN DEMAND (delivered digitally).

Internet Service
Operational: Yes, DSL.
Broadband Service: Rainer Connect.
Fee: $99.95 installation; $29.95-$55.95 monthly; $10.00 modem lease.

Telephone Service
Digital: Operational
Fee: $19.99 monthly
Miles of Plant: 1,748.0 (coaxial); 595.0 (fiber optic). Homes passed: 110,330.
President & Chief Executive Officer: Brian Haynes. Vice President, Operations & Technology: Albert Weigand. Vice President, Sales & Marketing: Mike Villanueva. Marketing Manager: Debbie Reding.
Ownership: The Rainier Group (MSO).

ECHO LAKE/SNOHOMISH—Wave Broadband, 401 Parkplace Center, Ste 500, Kirkland, WA 98033. Phones: 425-576-8200; 720-479-3558; 800-829-2225. Fax: 720-479-3585. E-mail: jpenney@wavebroadband.com. Web Site: http://www.wavebroadband.com. Also serves Lake Roesiger & Snohomish County (southwestern portions). ICA: WA0205.
TV Market Ranking: 20 (ECHO LAKE/SNOHOMISH, Lake Roesiger, Snohomish County (southwestern portions)). Franchise award date: August 22, 1990. Franchise expiration date: N.A. Began: November 18, 1987.
Channel capacity: N.A. Channels available but not in use: N.A.

Basic Service
Subscribers: 1,440.
Programming (received off-air): KCPQ (Escape, FOX) Tacoma; KCTS-TV (PBS) Seattle; KING-TV (NBC) Seattle; KIRO-TV (CBS, getTV, Retro TV) Seattle; KOMO-TV (ABC, This TV) Seattle; KONG (MundoMax) Everett; KSTW (CW, Decades) Tacoma; KTBW-TV (TBN) Tacoma; KVOS-TV (MeTV, Movies!) Bellingham; KWPX-TV (ION) Bellevue; KZJO (Antenna TV, MNT) Seattle.
Programming (via satellite): A&E; AMC; Animal Planet; Cartoon Network; CMT; CNBC; CNN; Comedy Central; C-SPAN; Discovery Channel; Disney Channel; ESPN; ESPN2; Fox News Channel; Freeform; FX; FXM; HGTV; History; Lifetime; MTV; National Geographic Channel; Nickelodeon; Northwest Cable News; Outdoor Channel; QVC; Spike TV; Syfy; TBS; The Weather Channel; TLC; TNT; TV Land; USA Network; VH1.
Fee: $29.95 installation; $25.95 monthly.

Digital Basic Service
Subscribers: N.A.
Programming (via satellite): BBC America; Bravo; CMT; Destination America; Discovery Kids Channel; Disney XD; DMX Music; EVINE Live; FYI; Golf Channel; GSN; History International; IFC; Investigation Discovery; LMN; MTV Classic; MTV Hits; MTV2; Nick Jr.; Nicktoons; OWN; Oprah Winfrey Network; Science Channel; TeenNick; Turner Classic Movies; VH1 Soul; WE tv.

Cable Systems—Washington

Pay Service 1
Pay Units: N.A.
Programming (via satellite): Cinemax; HBO; Showtime; The Movie Channel.
Fee: $9.95 monthly (Showtime), $11.00 monthly (HBO or TMC), $11.95 monthly (Cinemax).
Digital Pay Service 1
Pay Units: N.A.
Programming (via satellite): Cinemax (multiplexed); Flix; HBO (multiplexed); Showtime (multiplexed); Starz (multiplexed); Starz Encore (multiplexed); The Movie Channel (multiplexed).
Video-On-Demand: No
Pay-Per-View
Special events (delivered digitally).
Internet Service
Operational: Yes.
Fee: $49.95 installation; $37.95 monthly.
Telephone Service
Digital: Operational
Fee: $39.99 monthly
Miles of Plant: 1,012.0 (coaxial); 15.0 (fiber optic). Homes passed: 2,880.
Chief Executive Officer: Steve Weed. Chief Financial Officer: Wayne Schattenkerk. President: Jim Penney. General Manager: Stephen J. George.
Ownership: WaveDivision Holdings LLC (MSO).

EDMONDS—Comcast Cable. Now served by SEATTLE, WA [WA0001]. ICA: WA0012.

ELLENSBURG—Charter Communications, 1105 East 10th Ave, Ellensburg, WA 98926. Phones: 636-207-5100 (Corporate office); 509-925-7469; 509-925-9210; 509-783-0132 (Kennewick office). Fax: 509-962-2034. Web Site: http://www.charter.com. Also serves Kittitas & Kittitas County (portions). ICA: WA0023.
TV Market Ranking: Below 100 (ELLENSBURG, Kittitas, Kittitas County (portions)). Franchise award date: N.A. Franchise expiration date: N.A. Began: August 1, 1954.
Channel capacity: N.A. Channels available but not in use: N.A.
Digital Basic Service
Subscribers: 3,443.
Programming (via satellite): BBC America; Bloomberg Television; Discovery Digital Networks; DIY Network; ESPN Classic; ESPNews; FOX College Sports Central; FOX College Sports Pacific; FOX Sports 2; Fuse; FXM; FYI; History International; IFC; International Television (ITV); LMN; MC; NFL Network; Nick 2; Nick Jr.; Nicktoons; Outdoor Channel; TeenNick; TV Guide Interactive Inc.
Fee: $49.99 installation; $26.99 monthly.
Digital Expanded Basic Service
Subscribers: N.A.
Programming (via satellite): A&E; AMC; Animal Planet; BET; Bravo; Cartoon Network; CMT; CNBC; CNN; Comedy Central; Discovery Channel; Discovery Life Channel; Disney Channel; Disney XD; E! HD; ESPN; ESPN2; Food Network; Fox News Channel; Fox Sports 1; Freeform; FX; Golf Channel; GSN; Hallmark Channel; HGTV; History; HLN; Lifetime; MSNBC; MTV; MTV2; National Geographic Channel; NBCSN; Nickelodeon; Northwest Cable News; Oxygen; Spike TV; Syfy; TBS; The Weather Channel; TLC; TNT; truTV; Turner Classic Movies; TV Land; Univision; USA Network; WE tv.
Fee: $50.99 monthly.
Digital Pay Service 1
Pay Units: N.A.
Programming (via satellite): Cinemax (multiplexed); Flix; HBO (multiplexed); Showtime (multiplexed); Starz (multiplexed); Starz Encore (multiplexed); The Movie Channel (multiplexed).
Video-On-Demand: No
Pay-Per-View
iN DEMAND (delivered digitally); en Espanol (delivered digitally); Playboy TV (delivered digitally); Fresh (delivered digitally); Shorteez (delivered digitally).
Internet Service
Operational: Yes. Began: June 1, 2002.
Subscribers: 4,471.
Broadband Service: Charter Internet.
Fee: $29.99 monthly.
Telephone Service
None
Miles of Plant: 252.0 (coaxial); 120.0 (fiber optic). Homes passed: 13,774. Miles of plant included in Kennewick
General Manager: Randy Lee. Technical Operations Manager: Jeff Hopkins. Chief Technician: Ron Graaff. Marketing Director: Diane Long. Program Director: Lloyd Swain. Accounting Director: Steve Lottmann.
Ownership: Charter Communications Inc. (MSO).

ENTIAT—Wave Broadband. Now served by CHELAN, WA [WA0058]. ICA: WA0116.

EPHRATA—Northland Cable Television, 254 North Fig St, PO Box T, Moses Lake, WA 98837. Phones: 888-667-8452; 509-765-6151. Fax: 509-765-5132. E-mail: moseslake@northlandcabletv.com. Web Site: http://www.yournorthland.com. Also serves Grant County (portions) & Soap Lake. ICA: WA0039.
TV Market Ranking: Below 100 (Grant County (portions) (portions)); Outside TV Markets (EPHRATA, Grant County (portions) (portions), Soap Lake). Franchise award date: N.A. Franchise expiration date: N.A. Began: January 1, 1953.
Channel capacity: N.A. Channels available but not in use: N.A.
Basic Service
Subscribers: 547.
Programming (received off-air): KAYU-TV (FOX, This TV) Spokane; KHQ-TV (NBC) Spokane; KREM (CBS, TheCoolTV) Spokane; KSKN (CW) Spokane; KSPS-TV (PBS) Spokane; KSTW (CW, Decades) Tacoma; KXLY-TV (ABC, MeTV) Spokane; 14 FMs.
Programming (via microwave): KING-TV (NBC) Seattle; KIRO-TV (CBS, getTV, Retro TV) Seattle; KOMO-TV (ABC, This TV) Seattle.
Programming (via satellite): A&E; Animal Planet; CNBC; CNN; C-SPAN; Discovery Channel; ESPN; ESPN2; Food Network; Fox News Channel; FX; Hallmark Channel; History; HLN; INSP; Lifetime; National Geographic Channel; Nickelodeon; Northwest Cable News; Pop; QVC; TBS; The Weather Channel; TLC; TNT; USA Network.
Fee: $75.00 installation; $47.64 monthly; $2.20 converter.
Expanded Basic Service 1
Subscribers: N.A.
Programming (via satellite): Cartoon Network; FXM; Great American Country; HGTV; Outdoor Channel; Spike TV; Syfy; Turner Classic Movies; VH1.
Fee: $5.00 monthly.
Digital Basic Service
Subscribers: N.A.
Programming (via satellite): BBC America; Bloomberg Television; Discovery Digital Networks; DMX Music; Fox Sports 1; GSN; NBCSN; Trinity Broadcasting Network (TBN); WE tv.
Fee: $14.50 monthly.
Pay Service 1
Pay Units: N.A.
Programming (via satellite): HBO; Showtime.
Fee: $9.25 monthly (Showtime), $12.30 monthly (HBO).
Digital Pay Service 1
Pay Units: N.A.
Programming (via satellite): Cinemax (multiplexed); Flix; HBO (multiplexed); Showtime (multiplexed); Starz (multiplexed); Starz Encore (multiplexed); The Movie Channel (multiplexed).
Fee: $14.75 monthly (HBO, Cinemax, Showtime/TMC/Flix or Starz/Encore).
Video-On-Demand: No
Pay-Per-View
Fresh (delivered digitally); Playboy TV (delivered digitally).
Internet Service
Operational: Yes. Began: December 1, 2002.
Broadband Service: Northland Express.
Fee: $42.95 monthly.
Telephone Service
Digital: Operational
Miles of Plant: 58.0 (coaxial); 1.0 (fiber optic). Homes passed: 5,184.
Executive Vice President: Richard I. Clark. General Manager: Jon Ulrich. Chief Technician: Kim Svetich.
Ownership: Northland Communications Corp. (MSO).

EVERETT—Comcast Cable. Now served by SEATTLE, WA [WA0001]. ICA: WA0213.

FAIRCHILD AFB—Formerly served by Cable Montana. Now served by Comcast Cable, SPOKANE, WA [WA0004]. ICA: WA0153.

FAIRFIELD—Formerly served by Elk River TV Cable Co. No longer in operation. ICA: WA0129.

FORKS—Formerly served by New Day Broadband. No longer in operation. ICA: WA0048.

FREELAND—Comcast Cable. Now served by SEATTLE, WA [WA0001]. ICA: WA0053.

FRIDAY HARBOR—Zito Media, 102 S Main St, PO Box 665, Coudersport, PA 16915. Phones: 814-260-9055; 800-365-6988. E-mail: info@zitomedia.com. Web Site: http://www.zitomedia.com. Also serves San Juan County (portions). ICA: WA0084.
TV Market Ranking: Below 100 (FRIDAY HARBOR, San Juan County (portions)). Franchise award date: N.A. Franchise expiration date: N.A. Began: December 15, 1974.
Channel capacity: N.A. Channels available but not in use: N.A.
Basic Service
Subscribers: 327.
Programming (received off-air): KCPQ (Escape, FOX) Tacoma; KCTS-TV (PBS) Seattle; KING-TV (NBC) Seattle; KIRO-TV (CBS, getTV, Retro TV) Seattle; KOMO-TV (ABC, This TV) Seattle; KSTW (CW, Decades) Tacoma; KVOS-TV (MeTV, Movies!) Bellingham; KWPX-TV (ION) Bellevue; KZJO (Antenna TV, MNT) Seattle; allband FM.
Programming (via satellite): C-SPAN; QVC; TBS; Trinity Broadcasting Network (TBN); various Canadian stations.
Fee: $49.95 installation; $18.02 monthly.
Expanded Basic Service 1
Subscribers: N.A.
Programming (via satellite): A&E; Cartoon Network; CMT; CNBC; CNN; Comedy Central; Discovery Channel; Disney Channel; E! HD; ESPN; ESPN2; Food Network; Fox News Channel; Freeform; FX; Hallmark Channel; HGTV; History; HLN; Lifetime; MTV; Nickelodeon; Northwest Cable News; Spike TV; Syfy; The Weather Channel; TLC; TNT; truTV; Turner Classic Movies; TV Land; USA Network; VH1.
Fee: $35.72 monthly.
Digital Basic Service
Subscribers: N.A.
Programming (via satellite): BBC America; Bloomberg Television; Bravo; CMT; Destination America; Discovery Kids Channel; ESPN Classic; ESPNews; Fuse; FYI; Golf Channel; GSN; History; History International; IFC; MC; MTV Classic; MTV Hits; MTV2; National Geographic Channel; NBCSN; Nick Jr.; Outdoor Channel; OWN; Oprah Winfrey Network; Science Channel; Sundance TV; TeenNick; WE tv.
Fee: $11.99 monthly.
Digital Pay Service 1
Pay Units: N.A.
Programming (via satellite): Cinemax (multiplexed); HBO (multiplexed); Showtime (multiplexed); Starz (multiplexed); Starz Encore (multiplexed); The Movie Channel (multiplexed).
Fee: $15.95 monthly (each).
Video-On-Demand: No
Pay-Per-View
iN DEMAND (delivered digitally).
Internet Service
Operational: Yes.
Subscribers: 238.
Fee: $24.95 installation; $19.95-$44.95 monthly.
Telephone Service
Digital: Operational
Subscribers: 63.
Miles of Plant: 47.0 (coaxial); 32.0 (fiber optic). Homes passed: 800.
President: James Rigas.
Ownership: Zito Media (MSO).

GARFIELD—Formerly served by Elk River TV Cable Co. No longer in operation. ICA: WA0117.

GOLDENDALE—J & N Cable, 614 South Columbus Ave, Goldendale, WA 98620-9006. Phones: 800-752-9809; 509-773-5359. Fax: 509-773-7900. E-mail: customersupport@jncable.net. Web Site: http://www.jncable.com. ICA: WA0063.
TV Market Ranking: Outside TV Markets (GOLDENDALE). Franchise award date:

Washington—Cable Systems

FULLY SEARCHABLE • CONTINUOUSLY UPDATED • DISCOUNT RATES FOR PRINT PURCHASERS

For more information call 800-771-9202 or visit www.warren-news.com

N.A. Franchise expiration date: N.A. Began: July 1, 1960.
Channel capacity: N.A. Channels available but not in use: N.A.

Basic Service
Subscribers: 200.
Programming (received off-air): KATU (ABC, MeTV) Portland; KGW (Estrella TV, NBC) Portland; KING-TV (NBC) Seattle; KOIN (CBS) Portland; KOMO-TV (ABC, This TV) Seattle; KOPB-TV (PBS) Portland; KPDX (Escape, MNT) Vancouver; KPTV (COZI TV, FOX, Laff) Portland; allband FM.
Programming (via satellite): A&E; Animal Planet; CNBC; CNN; Comedy Central; C-SPAN; Discovery Channel; Disney Channel; Disney XD; E! HD; ESPN; ESPN2; Fox News Channel; Freeform; FX; FXM; HGTV; History; HLN; Lifetime; MSNBC; MTV; Nickelodeon; Northwest Cable News; Pop; QVC; Spike TV; TBS; The Weather Channel; TLC; TNT; Trinity Broadcasting Network (TBN); Turner Classic Movies; TVW; USA Network; VH1; WGN America.
Fee: $35.00 installation; $17.95 monthly.

Digital Basic Service
Subscribers: N.A.
Programming (via satellite): American Heroes Channel; BBC America; Bravo; Cloo; Destination America; Discovery Family; ESPN Classic; ESPNews; FOX College Sports Central; FOX College Sports Pacific; Fox Sports 1; FYI; Golf Channel; GSN; History International; IFC; Investigation Discovery; LMN; National Geographic Channel; NBCSN; OWN: Oprah Winfrey Network; Science Channel; Starz Encore; The Word Network; WE tv.

Digital Pay Service 1
Pay Units: N.A.
Programming (via satellite): Cinemax (multiplexed); Flix; HBO (multiplexed); Showtime (multiplexed); Starz (multiplexed); The Movie Channel (multiplexed).

Video-On-Demand: No

Internet Service
Operational: No.

Telephone Service
None
Miles of Plant: 21.0 (coaxial); None (fiber optic). Homes passed: 1,400.
President & General Manager: John Kusky. Vice President & Marketing Manager: Nancy Kusky.
Ownership: J & N Cable Systems Inc. (MSO).

GRAND COULEE—Charter Communications, 12405 Powerscourt Dr, St. Louis, MO 63131. Phones: 636-207-5100 (Corporate office); 360-828-6700; 360-828-6600. Fax: 360-828-6795. Web Site: http://www.charter.com. Also serves Electric City, Elmer City & Grant County. ICA: WA0154.
TV Market Ranking: Outside TV Markets (Electric City, Elmer City, GRAND COULEE, Grant County). Franchise award date: N.A. Franchise expiration date: N.A. Began: August 1, 1980.
Channel capacity: N.A. Channels available but not in use: N.A.

Digital Basic Service
Subscribers: 126.
Programming (via satellite): BBC America; Bloomberg Television; Bravo; Discovery Life Channel; Disney XD; DMX Music; ESPN Classic; ESPNews; EVINE Live; Fox Sports 1; Fuse; FXM; FYI; Golf Channel; GSN; History; History International; IFC; LMN; NBCSN; Nick Jr.; Outdoor Channel; Syfy; TeenNick; Trinity Broadcasting Network (TBN); Turner Classic Movies; WE tv.
Fee: $26.99 monthly.

Digital Expanded Basic Service
Subscribers: N.A.
Programming (via satellite): A&E; AMC; Animal Planet; Cartoon Network; CNN; Disney Channel; E! HD; ESPN; ESPN2; Fox News Channel; Freeform; FX; HGTV; Lifetime; MSNBC; MTV; Nickelodeon; Spike TV; TLC; TNT; Travel Channel; USA Network.
Fee: $42.99 monthly.

Digital Pay Service 1
Pay Units: N.A.
Programming (via satellite): Cinemax (multiplexed); Flix; HBO (multiplexed); Showtime (multiplexed); Starz (multiplexed); Starz Encore (multiplexed); The Movie Channel (multiplexed).

Video-On-Demand: No

Pay-Per-View
iN DEMAND (delivered digitally); Hot Choice (delivered digitally); Playboy TV (delivered digitally); Fresh (delivered digitally); Shorteez (delivered digitally).

Internet Service
Operational: No.

Telephone Service
None
Miles of Plant: 39.0 (coaxial); 1.0 (fiber optic). Homes passed: 1,467.
Vice President: Frank Antonovich. General Manager: Linda Kimberly. Technical Operations Director: Brian Lindholme. Marketing Director: Diane Long. Accounting Director: David Sovanski.
Ownership: Charter Communications Inc. (MSO).

GRANDVIEW—Charter Communications. Now served by YAKIMA, WA [WA0009]. ICA: WA0047.

GREENBANK—Wave Broadband. Now served by WHIDBEY ISLAND, WA [WA0186]. ICA: WA0189.

GUEMES ISLAND—Formerly served by Index Cable TV Inc. No longer in operation. ICA: WA0207.

HARRINGTON—Formerly served by Elk River TV Cable Co. No longer in operation. ICA: WA0120.

HOOD CANAL—Wave Broadband. Now served by PORT ORCHARD, WA [WA0010]. ICA: WA0199.

INDEX—Formerly served by Iron Goat Networks LLC. No longer in operation. ICA: WA0193.

IONE—Northstar Broadband, PO Box 2576, Post Falls, ID 83877. Phones: 208-262-9394; 800-572-0902. Fax: 208-262-9314. E-mail: j.webb@northstarbroadband.net. Web Site: http://www.northstarbroadband.net. ICA: WA0155.
TV Market Ranking: Outside TV Markets (IONE). Franchise award date: September 13, 1988. Franchise expiration date: N.A. Began: December 1, 1978.
Channel capacity: 62 (2-way capable). Channels available but not in use: N.A.

Basic Service
Subscribers: 52.
Programming (received off-air): KAYU-TV (FOX, This TV) Spokane; KHQ-TV (NBC) Spokane; KREM (CBS, TheCoolTV) Spokane; KSPS-TV (PBS) Spokane; KXLY-TV (ABC, MeTV) Spokane.
Programming (via satellite): A&E; Animal Planet; Cartoon Network; CMT; C-SPAN; C-SPAN 2; Discovery Channel; EVINE Live; EWTN Global Catholic Network; Food Network; Fox News Channel; Freeform; Hallmark Channel; HGTV; History; ION Television; NBCSN; Nickelodeon; Ovation; OWN: Oprah Winfrey Network; Pop; QVC; TBS; TLC; Travel Channel; Trinity Broadcasting Network (TBN); truTV; TV Land; WGN America.
Fee: $20.00 installation; $32.97 monthly; $1.00 converter.

Expanded Basic Service 1
Subscribers: N.A.
Programming (via satellite): AMC; Bravo; CNBC; CNN; Comedy Central; Disney Channel; Disney XD; E! HD; ESPN; ESPN Classic; ESPN2; Fox Sports 1; FX; FXM; HLN; Lifetime; MoviePlex; MSNBC; MTV; Northwest Cable News; Outdoor Channel; Spike TV; Syfy; TNT; Turner Classic Movies; USA Network; VH1.
Fee: $16.02 monthly.

Pay Service 1
Pay Units: N.A.
Programming (via satellite): Cinemax; HBO; Showtime.
Fee: $5.00 installation; $5.25 monthly (Cinemax), $8.65 monthly (Showtime), $9.60 monthly (HBO).

Video-On-Demand: No

Internet Service
Operational: Yes.

Telephone Service
None
Miles of Plant: 49.0 (coaxial); None (fiber optic). Homes passed: 348.
Office Manager: Jennifer Webb. Operations Manager: Greg Lundwall.
Ownership: Northstar Broadband LLC (MSO).

KAHLOTUS—Formerly served by Community Cable Service. No longer in operation. ICA: WA0140.

KALA POINT—Wave Broadband. Now served by PORT TOWNSEND, WA [WA0027]. ICA: WA0156.

KENNEWICK—Charter Communications, 639 N Kellogg St, Kennewick, WA 99336. Phones: 636-207-5100 (Corporate office); 509-396-0613; 509-222-2500; 509-783-0132. Web Site: http://www.charter.com. Also serves Echo, Hermiston, Milton-Freewater, Pendleton, Stanfield & Umatilla County (portions), OR; Benton County, College Place, Dixie, Franklin County, Pasco, Richland, Waitsburg, Walla Walla, Walla Walla County, Walla Walla County (portions) & West Richland, WA. ICA: WA0008.
TV Market Ranking: Below 100 (Benton County, College Place, Echo, Franklin County (portions), Hermiston, KENNEWICK, Milton-Freewater, Pasco, Richland, Stanfield, Waitsburg, Walla Walla County, Pendleton, Walla Walla, West Richland); Outside TV Markets (Dixie, Franklin County (portions), Umatilla County (portions), Walla Walla County (portions)). Franchise award date: January 1, 1951. Franchise expiration date: N.A. Began: January 1, 1952.
Channel capacity: 82 (operating 2-way). Channels available but not in use: N.A.

Digital Basic Service
Subscribers: 40,498.
Programming (via satellite): 3ABN; AXS TV; BBC America; Bloomberg Television; Boomerang; BYUtv; CNN International; Discovery Life Channel; ESPN; ESPN Classic; ESPNews; FOX College Sports Central; FOX College Sports Pacific; Fox Sports 2; Fuse; FXM; FYI; Great American Country; HD Theater; History International; HITS (Headend In The Sky); IFC; INSP; International Television (ITV); LMN; MC; NFL Network; Nick 2; Nick Jr.; Nicktoons; Sundance TV; TeenNick.
Fee: $49.99 installation; $26.99 monthly.

Digital Expanded Basic Service
Subscribers: N.A.
Programming (via satellite): A&E; AMC; Animal Planet; BET; Bravo; Cartoon Network; CMT; CNBC; CNN; Comedy Central; Discovery Channel; Disney Channel; Disney XD; DIY Network; E! HD; ESPN; ESPN2; Food Network; Fox News Channel; Fox Sports 1; Freeform; FX; Golf Channel; GSN; Hallmark Channel; HGTV; History; HLN; Lifetime; MSNBC; MTV; MTV2; National Geographic Channel; NBCSN; Nickelodeon; Northwest Cable News; Outdoor Channel; Oxygen; Spike TV; Syfy; TBS; The Weather Channel; TLC; TNT; Travel Channel; truTV; Turner Classic Movies; TV Land; USA Network; VH1; WE tv.
Fee: $50.99 monthly.

Digital Pay Service 1
Pay Units: N.A.
Programming (via satellite): Cinemax (multiplexed); Cinemax HD; Flix; HBO (multiplexed); HBO HD; Showtime (multiplexed); Showtime HD; Starz (multiplexed); Starz Encore (multiplexed); Starz HD; The Movie Channel (multiplexed).

Video-On-Demand: Yes

Pay-Per-View
iN DEMAND (delivered digitally).

Internet Service
Operational: Yes. Began: December 1, 2002.
Subscribers: 54,055.
Broadband Service: Charter Internet.
Fee: $29.99 monthly.

Telephone Service
Digital: Operational
Subscribers: 14,940.
Miles of Plant: 2,961.0 (coaxial); 1,097.0 (fiber optic). Homes passed: 141,705. Miles of plant (fiber & coax combined) includes Ellensburg, Yakima, Burns OR, & La Grande OR
Vice President: Frank Antonovich. General Manager: Randy Lee. Technical Operations Manager: Jeff Hopkins. Marketing Director: Diane Long. Program Director: Lloyd Swain. Senior Accounting Director: Steve Lottmann.
Ownership: Charter Communications Inc. (MSO).

Cable Systems—Washington

LA CONNER—Wave Broadband. Now served by CAMANO ISLAND, WA [WA0046]. ICA: WA0158.

LAKE GOODWIN—Wave Broadband. Now served by CAMANO ISLAND, WA [WA0046]. ICA: WA0159.

LAKEBAY—Wave Broadband, 401 Parkplace Center, Ste 500, Kirkland, WA 98033. Phones: 425-576-8200; 720-479-3558; 800-829-2225. Fax: 720-479-3585. E-mail: jpenney@wavebroadband.com. Web Site: http://www.wavebroadband.com. Also serves Anderson Island, Herron Island & Key Peninsula. ICA: WA0201.
  TV Market Ranking: 12 (LAKEBAY); 20 (Anderson Island, Herron Island, Key Peninsula).
  Channel capacity: N.A. Channels available but not in use: N.A.
  Basic Service
    Subscribers: 353.
    Programming (received off-air): KBTC-TV (PBS) Tacoma; KCPQ (Escape, FOX) Tacoma; KCTS-TV (PBS) Seattle; KING-TV (NBC) Seattle; KIRO-TV (CBS, getTV, Retro TV) Seattle; KOMO-TV (ABC, This TV) Seattle; KONG (MundoMax) Everett; KSTW (CW, Decades) Tacoma; KTBW-TV (TBN) Tacoma; KZJO (Antenna TV, MNT) Seattle.
    Programming (via satellite): A&E; AMC; Animal Planet; Cartoon Network; CNBC; CNN; Comedy Central; C-SPAN; Discovery Channel; Disney Channel; ESPN; ESPN2; Food Network; Fox News Channel; FOX Sports North; Freeform; Hallmark Channel; HGTV; History; HLN; Lifetime; MTV; Nickelodeon; Northwest Cable News; QVC; Spike TV; Syfy; TBS; The Weather Channel; TLC; TNT; Travel Channel; USA Network; VH1.
    Fee: $29.95 installation; $25.95 monthly.
  Digital Basic Service
    Subscribers: N.A.
    Programming (via satellite): BBC America; Bloomberg Television; Bravo; CMT; Daystar TV Network; Destination America; Discovery Kids Channel; Discovery Life Channel; DMX Music; EVINE Live; FXM; FYI; Great American Country; GSN; History; History International; IFC; Investigation Discovery; LMN; MTV Classic; MTV Hits; MTV2; National Geographic Channel; Nick Jr.; Nicktoons; OWN: Oprah Winfrey Network; Science Channel; TeenNick; The Word Network; VH1 Soul.
    Fee: $13.40 monthly.
  Digital Expanded Basic Service
    Subscribers: N.A.
    Programming (via satellite): ESPNews; FOX College Sports Central; FOX College Sports Pacific; Fox Sports 1; Golf Channel; NBCSN; Outdoor Channel.
    Fee: $5.00 monthly.
  Pay Service 1
    Pay Units: N.A.
    Programming (via satellite): Cinemax; HBO; Showtime.
  Digital Pay Service 1
    Pay Units: N.A.
    Programming (via satellite): Cinemax (multiplexed); Flix; HBO (multiplexed); Showtime (multiplexed); Starz (multiplexed); Starz Encore (multiplexed); Sundance TV; The Movie Channel (multiplexed).
    Fee: $10.00 monthly (each).
  Video-On-Demand: No
  Pay-Per-View
    iN DEMAND (delivered digitally); Playboy TV (delivered digitally); Fresh (delivered digitally); Club Jenna (delivered digitally).

  Internet Service
    Operational: Yes.
    Broadband Service: Millennium Cable-Speed.
    Fee: $49.95 installation; $37.95 monthly.
  Telephone Service
    Digital: Operational
    Fee: $39.99 monthly
  Miles of Plant: 51.0 (coaxial); None (fiber optic).
  Chief Executive Officer: Steve Weed. Chief Financial Officer: Wayne Schattenkerk. President: Jim Penney. General Manager: Stephen J. George.
  Ownership: WaveDivision Holdings LLC (MSO).

LIBERTY LAKE—No longer in operation. ICA: WA0123.

LIND—Northstar Broadband, PO Box 2576, Post Falls, ID 83877. Phones: 208-262-9394; 800-572-0902. Fax: 208-262-9314. E-mail: j.webb@northstarbroadband.net. Web Site: http://www.northstarbroadband.net. ICA: WA0115.
  TV Market Ranking: Outside TV Markets (LIND). Franchise award date: N.A. Franchise expiration date: N.A. Began: December 1, 1953.
  Channel capacity: 62 (2-way capable). Channels available but not in use: N.A.
  Basic Service
    Subscribers: 4.
    Programming (received off-air): KAYU-TV (FOX, This TV) Spokane; KEPR-TV (CBS, CW) Pasco; KHQ-TV (NBC) Spokane; KREM (CBS, TheCoolTV) Spokane; KSKN (CW) Spokane; KSPS-TV (PBS) Spokane; KWSU-TV (PBS) Pullman; KXLY-TV (ABC, MeTV) Spokane; 8 FMs.
    Programming (via satellite): A&E; Animal Planet; Cartoon Network; CMT; C-SPAN; C-SPAN 2; Discovery Channel; EVINE Live; EWTN Global Catholic Network; Food Network; Fox News Channel; Freeform; Hallmark Channel; HGTV; History; ION Television; Nickelodeon; Ovation; OWN: Oprah Winfrey Network; QVC; TBS; TLC; Travel Channel; Trinity Broadcasting Network (TBN); truTV; TV Land; WGN America.
    Fee: $20.00 installation; $32.43 monthly; $35.00 converter.
  Expanded Basic Service 1
    Subscribers: N.A.
    Programming (via satellite): AMC; Bravo; CNBC; CNN; Comedy Central; Disney Channel; Disney XD; E! HD; ESPN; ESPN Classic; ESPN2; Fox Sports 1; FX; FXM; HLN; Lifetime; MoviePlex; MSNBC; MTV; Northwest Cable News; Outdoor Channel; Spike TV; Syfy; TNT; Turner Classic Movies; USA Network; VH1.
    Fee: $16.12 monthly.
  Pay Service 1
    Pay Units: N.A.
    Programming (via satellite): Cinemax; HBO; Showtime.
    Fee: $5.00 installation; $5.25 monthly (Cinemax), $8.65 monthly (Showtime), $9.60 monthly (HBO).
  Video-On-Demand: No
  Internet Service
    Operational: Yes.
  Telephone Service
    None
  Miles of Plant: 5.0 (coaxial); None (fiber optic). Homes passed: 230.
  Office Manager: Jennifer Webb. Operations Manager: Greg Lundwall.
  Ownership: Northstar Broadband LLC (MSO).

LONGVIEW—Comcast Cable. Now served by VANCOUVER, WA [WA0005]. ICA: WA0013.

LOOMIS—Formerly served by JKA Cable Systems. No longer in operation. ICA: WA0202.

LOON LAKE—Charter Communications. Now served by WENATCHEE, WA [WA0015]. ICA: WA0161.

LUMMI INDIAN RESERVATION—San Juan Cable & Construction, 2568 Mackenzie Rd, Bellingham, WA 98226-9204. Phone: 360-758-7879. ICA: WA0162.
  TV Market Ranking: Below 100 (LUMMI INDIAN RESERVATION).
  Channel capacity: 39 (not 2-way capable). Channels available but not in use: N.A.
  Basic Service
    Subscribers: N.A.
    Programming (received off-air): KCPQ (Escape, FOX) Tacoma; KCTS-TV (PBS) Seattle; KING-TV (NBC) Seattle; KIRO-TV (CBS, getTV, Retro TV) Seattle; KOMO-TV (ABC, This TV) Seattle; KSTW (CW, Decades) Tacoma; KVOS-TV (MeTV, Movies!) Bellingham.
    Fee: $24.95 monthly.
  Pay Service 1
    Pay Units: N.A.
    Programming (via satellite): HBO; Showtime.
    Fee: $7.00 monthly (each).
  Miles of Plant: 20.0 (coaxial); None (fiber optic). Homes passed: 850.
  General Manager: Roy Budde. Chief Technician: Ben Waldren. Marketing Director: Shaun Morgon. Program Director: Richard Warbus.
  Ownership: San Juan Cable & Construction.

LUMMI ISLAND—Lummi Island Cable, PO Box 29534, Bellingham, WA 98228. Phones: 877-396-3016; 360-966-7502. E-mail: info@mtbakercable.com. Web Site: http://www.mtbakercable.com. ICA: WA0216.
  TV Market Ranking: Below 100 (LUMMI ISLAND).
  Channel capacity: N.A. Channels available but not in use: N.A.
  Basic Service
    Subscribers: N.A.
    Programming (received off-air): KCPQ (Escape, FOX) Tacoma; KCTS-TV (PBS) Seattle; KING-TV (NBC) Seattle; KIRO-TV (CBS, getTV, Retro TV) Seattle; KOMO-TV (ABC, This TV) Seattle; KONG (MundoMax) Everett; KSTW (CW, Decades) Tacoma; KVOS-TV (MeTV, Movies!) Bellingham; various Canadian stations.
    Programming (via satellite): A&E; AMC; Animal Planet; Cartoon Network; Classic Arts Showcase; CMT; CNBC; CNN; Comedy Central; Cooking Channel; C-SPAN; Discovery Channel; Disney Channel; E! HD; ESPN; ESPN2; Food Network; Fox Business Network; Fox News Channel; Fox Sports 1; Freeform; FX; Hallmark Channel; HGTV; History; Lifetime; MSNBC; National Geographic Channel; Nickelodeon; Northwest Cable News; OWN: Oprah Winfrey Network; Pop; QVC; Root Sports Northwest; Spike TV; Syfy; TBS; The Weather Channel; TLC; TNT; Travel Channel; Trinity Broadcasting Network (TBN); TV Land; USA Network; VH1.
    Fee: $75.00 installation; $37.95 monthly; $3.00 converter.
  Pay Service 1
    Pay Units: N.A.
    Programming (via satellite): Cinemax; HBO; Showtime; Starz Encore.
    Fee: $5.00 monthly (Encore), $15.00 monthly (HBO, Cinemax or Showtime).
  Internet Service
    Operational: Yes.
  Telephone Service
    None
  General Manager: Dan Adams.
  Ownership: Mount Baker Cable (MSO).

LYLE—J & N Cable, 614 South Columbus Ave, Goldendale, WA 98620-9006. Phones: 800-752-9809; 509-773-5359. Fax: 509-773-7090. E-mail: customersupport@jncable.net. Web Site: http://www.jncable.com. ICA: WA0163.
  TV Market Ranking: Outside TV Markets (LYLE). Franchise award date: N.A. Franchise expiration date: N.A. Began: January 1, 1955.
  Channel capacity: N.A. Channels available but not in use: N.A.
  Basic Service
    Subscribers: N.A.
    Programming (received off-air): KATU (ABC, MeTV) Portland; KGW (Estrella TV, NBC) Portland; KOIN (CBS) Portland; KOPB-TV (PBS) Portland; KPDX (Escape, MNT) Vancouver; KPTV (COZI TV, FOX, Laff) Portland; allband FM.
    Programming (via satellite): AMC; CNN; Discovery Channel; Disney Channel; ESPN; ESPN2; Northwest Cable News; TBS.
    Fee: $25.00 installation.
  Video-On-Demand: No
  Internet Service
    Operational: No.
  Telephone Service
    None
  Miles of Plant: 5.0 (coaxial); None (fiber optic).
  President & General Manager: John Kusky. Vice President & Marketing Manager: Nancy Kusky.
  Ownership: J & N Cable Systems Inc. (MSO).

MALAGA—Formerly served by Almega Cable. No longer in operation. ICA: WA0164.

MANSFIELD—Formerly served by Wave Broadband. No longer in operation. ICA: WA0136.

MANSON—Formerly served by Millennium Digital Media. Now served by Wave Broadband, CHELAN, WA [WA0058]. ICA: WA0165.

MARBLEMOUNT—Formerly served by Wave Broadband. No longer in operation. ICA: WA0194.

2017 Edition

D-821

Washington—Cable Systems

FULLY SEARCHABLE • CONTINUOUSLY UPDATED • DISCOUNT RATES FOR PRINT PURCHASERS

For more information call 800-771-9202 or visit **www.warren-news.com**

MATTAWA—Formerly served by Almega Cable. No longer in operation. ICA: WA0098.

MAXWELTON—Formerly served by Comcast Cable. No longer in operation. ICA: WA0141.

McCHORD AIR FORCE BASE—Comcast Cable. Now served by SEATTLE, WA [WA0001]. ICA: WA0050.

MEDICAL LAKE—Formerly served by Wave Broadband. No longer in operation. ICA: WA0066.

METALINE FALLS—Northstar Broadband, PO Box 2576, Post Falls, ID 83877. Phones: 208-262-9394; 800-572-0902. Fax: 208-262-9314. E-mail: j.webb@northstarbroadband.net. Web Site: http://www.northstarbroadband.net. Also serves Metaline. ICA: WA0113.
TV Market Ranking: Outside TV Markets (Metaline, METALINE FALLS). Franchise award date: N.A. Franchise expiration date: N.A. Began: July 1, 1958.
Channel capacity: 35 (2-way capable). Channels available but not in use: N.A.
Basic Service
Subscribers: 17.
Programming (received off-air): KAYU-TV (FOX, This TV) Spokane; KHQ-TV (NBC) Spokane; KREM (CBS, TheCoolTV) Spokane; KSPS-TV (PBS) Spokane; KXLY-TV (ABC, MeTV) Spokane; allband FM.
Programming (via satellite): A&E; Animal Planet; Cartoon Network; CMT; C-SPAN; C-SPAN 2; Discovery Channel; EVINE Live; EWTN Global Catholic Network; Food Network; Fox News Channel; Freeform; Hallmark Channel; HGTV; History; ION Television; NBCSN; Nickelodeon; Ovation; OWN; Oprah Winfrey Network; QVC; Showtime; TBS; TLC; Travel Channel; Trinity Broadcasting Network (TBN); truTV; TV Land; WGN America.
Fee: $20.00 installation; $32.97 monthly; $1.00 converter.
Expanded Basic Service 1
Subscribers: N.A.
Programming (via satellite): AMC; Bravo; CNBC; CNN; Comedy Central; Disney Channel; Disney XD; E! HD; ESPN; ESPN Classic; ESPN2; Fox Sports 1; FOX Sports Networks; FX; FXM; HLN; Lifetime; MoviePlex; MSNBC; MTV; Northwest Cable News; Outdoor Channel; Spike TV; Syfy; TNT; Turner Classic Movies; USA Network; VH1.
Fee: $16.02 monthly.
Pay Service 1
Pay Units: N.A.
Programming (via satellite): Cinemax; HBO; Showtime.
Fee: $5.00 installation; $5.25 monthly (Cinemax), $8.65 monthly (Showtime), $9.60 monthly (HBO).
Video-On-Demand: No
Internet Service
Operational: Yes.
Telephone Service
None
Miles of Plant: 8.0 (coaxial); None (fiber optic). Homes passed: 348.
Office Manager: Jennifer Webb. Operations Manager: Greg Lundwall.
Ownership: Northstar Broadband LLC (MSO).

MINERAL—Comcast Cable, 410 Valley Ave NW, Ste 9, Puyallup, WA 98371. Phones: 253-864-4200; 425-398-6000 (Bothell office). Fax: 253-864-4352. Web Site: http://www.comcast.com. ICA: WA0132.
TV Market Ranking: Outside TV Markets (MINERAL). Franchise award date: N.A. Franchise expiration date: N.A. Began: June 1, 1984.
Channel capacity: N.A. Channels available but not in use: N.A.
Basic Service
Subscribers: 16.
Programming (received off-air): KCPQ (Escape, FOX) Tacoma; KCTS-TV (PBS) Seattle; KING-TV (NBC) Seattle; KIRO-TV (CBS, getTV, Retro TV) Seattle; KOMO-TV (ABC, This TV) Seattle; KSTW (CW, Decades) Tacoma; allband FM.
Programming (via satellite): AMC; Animal Planet; CNN; Discovery Channel; ESPN; Fox News Channel; Freeform; Spike TV; TNT; USA Network.
Fee: $40.00 installation; $25.99 monthly.
Pay Service 1
Pay Units: N.A.
Programming (via satellite): HBO; Showtime; Starz; Starz Encore.
Fee: $15.99 installation; $15.99 monthly (HBO, Showtime, or Starz/Encore).
Video-On-Demand: No
Internet Service
Operational: Yes.
Telephone Service
None
Miles of Plant: 9.0 (coaxial); None (fiber optic). Homes passed: 190.
Area Vice President: Anne McMullan. Vice President, Engineering: Steve Tabor. Public Relations Director: Steve Kipp. Vice President, Sales & Marketing: Tom Pierce.
Ownership: Comcast Cable Communications Inc. (MSO).

MONTESANO—Comcast Cable. Now served by ABERDEEN TWP., WA [WA0003]. ICA: WA0032.

MORTON—Wave Broadband, 401 Parkplace Center, Ste 500, Kirkland, WA 98033. Phones: 425-576-8200; 800-829-2225. Fax: 720-479-3585. E-mail: jpenney@wavebroadband.com. Web Site: http://www.wavebroadband.com. Also serves Lewis County. ICA: WA0082.
TV Market Ranking: Outside TV Markets (Lewis County, MORTON). Franchise award date: January 1, 1968. Franchise expiration date: N.A. Began: January 1, 1950.
Channel capacity: N.A. Channels available but not in use: N.A.
Basic Service
Subscribers: 174.
Programming (received off-air): KCPQ (Escape, FOX) Tacoma; KCTS-TV (PBS) Seattle; KING-TV (NBC) Seattle; KIRO-TV (CBS, getTV, Retro TV) Seattle; KOMO-TV (ABC, This TV) Seattle; KONG (MundoMax) Everett; KSTW (CW, Decades) Tacoma; allband FM.
Programming (via satellite): CMT; CNN; Discovery Channel; Freeform; HGTV; HLN; Nickelodeon; Northwest Cable News; Spike TV; TBS; WGN America.
Fee: $29.95 installation; $43.25 monthly.
Expanded Basic Service 1
Subscribers: N.A.
Programming (via satellite): A&E; Animal Planet; Comedy Central; Disney Channel; E! HD; ESPN; ESPN2; Fox News Channel; History; National Geographic Channel; Outdoor Channel; Syfy; TLC; TNT; Turner Classic Movies; USA Network.
Fee: $10.00 installation; $13.00 monthly.
Digital Basic Service
Subscribers: N.A.
Programming (via satellite): BBC America; Bloomberg Television; Cloo; Discovery Life Channel; Disney XD; DMX Music; ESPN Classic; ESPN2; ESPNews; EVINE Live; Fox Sports 1; FSN Digital Atlantic; FSN Digital Central; FSN Digital Pacific; Fuse; FXM; FYI; Golf Channel; Great American Country; GSN; HGTV; History; History International; IFC; National Geographic Channel; NBCSN; Outdoor Channel; Starz Encore (multiplexed); Syfy; Trinity Broadcasting Network (TBN); WE tv.
Pay Service 1
Pay Units: 81.
Programming (via satellite): HBO.
Fee: $20.00 installation; $10.95 monthly.
Digital Pay Service 1
Pay Units: N.A.
Programming (via satellite): Cinemax (multiplexed); HBO (multiplexed); Showtime (multiplexed); Starz (multiplexed); The Movie Channel (multiplexed).
Video-On-Demand: No
Pay-Per-View
iN DEMAND (delivered digitally); Playboy TV (delivered digitally); Fresh (delivered digitally).
Internet Service
Operational: No.
Telephone Service
None
Miles of Plant: 30.0 (coaxial); None (fiber optic). Homes passed: 780.
Chief Executive Officer: Steve Weed. Chief Financial Officer: Wayne Schattenkerk. President: Jim Penney. General Manager: Stephen J. George.
Ownership: WaveDivision Holdings LLC (MSO).

MOSES LAKE—Northland Cable Television, 254 North Fig St, PO Box T, Moses Lake, WA 98837. Phones: 888-667-8452; 509-765-6151. Fax: 509-765-5132. E-mail: moseslake@northlandcabletv.com. Web Site: http://www.yournorthland.com. Also serves Grant County (portions). ICA: WA0167.
TV Market Ranking: Below 100 (Grant County (portions) (portions)); Outside TV Markets (Grant County (portions) (portions), MOSES LAKE). Franchise award date: N.A. Franchise expiration date: N.A. Began: January 1, 1954.
Channel capacity: N.A. Channels available but not in use: N.A.
Basic Service
Subscribers: 2,390.
Programming (received off-air): KAYU-TV (FOX, This TV) Spokane; KHQ-TV (NBC) Spokane; KING-TV (NBC) Seattle; KIRO-TV (CBS, getTV, Retro TV) Seattle; KOMO-TV (ABC, This TV) Seattle; KREM (CBS, TheCoolTV) Spokane; KSKN (CW) Spokane; KSPS-TV (PBS) Spokane; KSTW (CW, Decades) Tacoma; KXLY-TV (ABC, MeTV) Spokane; 2 FMs.
Programming (via satellite): A&E; Animal Planet; Cartoon Network; CNBC; CNN; C-SPAN; Discovery Channel; ESPN; Food Network; Fox Deportes; Fox News Channel; Great American Country; Hallmark Channel; HGTV; HLN; INSP; Lifetime; National Geographic Channel; Northwest Cable News; Pop; QVC; TBS; Telemundo; The Weather Channel; TLC; TNT; Univision Studios; USA Network.
Fee: $75.00 installation; $47.64 monthly.
Expanded Basic Service 1
Subscribers: N.A.
Programming (via satellite): Comedy Central; ESPN2; FX; FXM; Golf Channel; History; MTV; Nickelodeon; Spike TV; Syfy; Turner Classic Movies.
Fee: $10.00 monthly.
Digital Basic Service
Subscribers: N.A.
Programming (via satellite): BBC America; Bloomberg Television; Bravo; Discovery Life Channel; DMX Music; Fox Sports 1; GSN; IFC; NBCSN; Outdoor Channel; Trinity Broadcasting Network (TBN); WE tv.
Fee: $10.50 monthly.
Pay Service 1
Pay Units: N.A.
Programming (via satellite): Cinemax; HBO.
Digital Pay Service 1
Pay Units: N.A.
Programming (via satellite): Cinemax (multiplexed); HBO (multiplexed); Showtime (multiplexed); Starz (multiplexed); Starz Encore (multiplexed); The Movie Channel (multiplexed).
Fee: $10.00 monthly (Cinemax, HBO or Showtime & TMC).
Video-On-Demand: No
Pay-Per-View
Fresh (delivered digitally); Playboy TV (delivered digitally).
Internet Service
Operational: Yes. Began: December 1, 2002.
Subscribers: 3,611.
Broadband Service: Northland Express.
Fee: $20.00 installation; $42.99 monthly.
Telephone Service
Analog: Not Operational
Digital: Operational
Subscribers: 917.
Fee: $29.99 monthly
Miles of Plant: 334.0 (coaxial); 39.0 (fiber optic). Homes passed: 14,022.
Executive Vice President: Richard I. Clark. General Manager: Jon Ulrich. Chief Technician: Kim Svetich.
Ownership: Northland Communications Corp. (MSO).

MOSSYROCK—Comcast Cable, 410 Valley Ave NW, Ste 9, Puyallup, WA 98371. Phones: 253-864-4200; 425-398-6000 (Bothell office). Fax: 253-864-4352. Web Site: http://www.comcast.com. Also serves Lewis County (portions). ICA: WA0091.
TV Market Ranking: Outside TV Markets (Lewis County (portions), MOSSYROCK). Franchise award date: N.A. Franchise ex-

Cable Systems—Washington

piration date: N.A. Began: January 1, 1981.
Channel capacity: N.A. Channels available but not in use: N.A.
Basic Service
Subscribers: 94.
Programming (received off-air): KCPQ (Escape, FOX) Tacoma; KCTS-TV (PBS) Seattle; KING-TV (NBC) Seattle; KIRO-TV (CBS, getTV, Retro TV) Seattle; KOMO-TV (ABC, This TV) Seattle; KSTW (CW, Decades) Tacoma; allband FM.
Programming (via satellite): A&E; AMC; Animal Planet; BET; Cartoon Network; CMT; CNBC; CNN; Comedy Central; Discovery Channel; Disney Channel; E! HD; ESPN; Food Network; Fox News Channel; Freeform; Hallmark Channel; HLN; Lifetime; MoviePlex; MSNBC; MTV; Nickelodeon; Northwest Cable News; QVC; Spike TV; TBS; TLC; TNT; Travel Channel; truTV; Univision Studios; USA Network; VH1.
Fee: $40.00 installation; $25.99 monthly.
Digital Basic Service
Subscribers: N.A.
Programming (via satellite): BBC America; Bravo; Discovery Kids Channel; DMX Music; ESPN Classic; ESPN2; ESPNews; Fuse; Golf Channel; Great American Country; GSN; HGTV; History; HITS (Headend In The Sky); IFC; National Geographic Channel; NBCSN; Nick Jr.; Nicktoons; OWN: Oprah Winfrey Network; Science Channel; Sprout; Syfy; TeenNick; The Word Network; Trinity Broadcasting Network (TBN); Turner Classic Movies; TV Land; WE tv.
Digital Expanded Basic Service
Subscribers: N.A.
Programming (via satellite): Urge; CMT; Destination America; Discovery Life Channel; Disney XD; FYI; History; History International; Investigation Discovery; LMN; MTV Hits; Starz Encore (multiplexed); Sundance TV.
Digital Pay Service 1
Pay Units: N.A.
Programming (via satellite): Cinemax (multiplexed); HBO (multiplexed); Showtime (multiplexed); Starz (multiplexed); The Movie Channel (multiplexed).
Video-On-Demand: No
Pay-Per-View
Special events (delivered digitally); Fresh (delivered digitally); Club Jenna (delivered digitally); Shorteez (delivered digitally); Playboy TV (delivered digitally); Hot Choice (delivered digitally).
Internet Service
Operational: Yes.
Telephone Service
None
Miles of Plant: 30.0 (coaxial); None (fiber optic). Homes passed: 629.
Area Vice President: Anne McMullen. Vice President, Sales & Marketing: Tom Pierce. Vice President, Engineering: Steve Tabor. Public Relations Director: Steve Kipp.
Ownership: Comcast Cable Communications Inc. (MSO).

NACHES—J & N Cable, 614 South Columbus Ave, Goldendale, WA 98620-9006. Phones: 800-752-9809; 509-773-5359. Fax: 509-773-7090. E-mail: customersupport@ jncable.net. Web Site: http://www.jncable. com. Also serves Cowiche, Gleed, Tieton & Yakima County (unincorporated areas). ICA: WA0059.
TV Market Ranking: Below 100 (Cowiche, Gleed, NACHES, Tieton, Yakima County (unincorporated areas)). Franchise award date: N.A. Franchise expiration date: N.A. Began: January 1, 1984.
Channel capacity: N.A. Channels available but not in use: N.A.
Basic Service
Subscribers: 100.
Programming (received off-air): KAPP (ABC, MeTV, MNT) Yakima; KCYU-LD (FOX, This TV) Yakima; KIMA-TV (CBS, CW) Yakima; KNDO (NBC) Yakima; KYVE (PBS) Yakima.
Programming (via satellite): A&E; Animal Planet; CNBC; CNN; C-SPAN; Discovery Channel; Disney Channel; Disney XD; E! HD; ESPN; Freeform; FX; FXM; History; HLN; Lifetime; MTV; Nickelodeon; QVC; Spike TV; TBS; TNT; Trinity Broadcasting Network (TBN); USA Network; VH1; WGN America.
Fee: $35.00 installation; $27.75 monthly.
Pay Service 1
Pay Units: N.A.
Programming (via satellite): HBO; Starz.
Video-On-Demand: No
Pay-Per-View
Pay-Per-View Channels (delivered digitally).
Internet Service
Operational: No.
Telephone Service
None
Miles of Plant: 72.0 (coaxial); None (fiber optic). Homes passed: 1,600.
President & General Manager: John Kusky. Vice President & Marketing Manager: Nancy Kusky.
Ownership: J & N Cable Systems Inc. (MSO).

NAPAVINE—Wave Broadband, 401 Parkplace Center, Ste 500, Kirkland, WA 98033. Phones: 425-576-8200; 720-479-3558; 800-829-2225. Fax: 720-479-3585. E-mail: jpenney@wavebroadband.com. Web Site: http://www.wavebroadband.com. ICA: WA0106.
TV Market Ranking: Outside TV Markets (NAPAVINE). Franchise award date: N.A. Franchise expiration date: N.A. Began: July 1, 1983.
Channel capacity: N.A. Channels available but not in use: N.A.
Basic Service
Subscribers: 72.
Programming (received off-air): KCKA (PBS) Centralia; KCPQ (Escape, FOX) Tacoma; KCTS-TV (PBS) Seattle; KING-TV (NBC) Seattle; KIRO-TV (CBS, getTV, Retro TV) Seattle; KOMO-TV (ABC, This TV) Seattle; KSTW (CW, Decades) Tacoma; KZJO (Antenna TV, MNT) Seattle.
Programming (via satellite): A&E; AMC; Animal Planet; Cartoon Network; CNN; Discovery Channel; Disney Channel; E! HD; ESPN; Fox News Channel; Freeform; FX; HGTV; History; HLN; Nickelodeon; Northwest Cable News; QVC; Spike TV; Syfy; TBS; The Weather Channel; TLC; TNT; TV Land; TVW; USA Network; WGN America.
Fee: $29.95 installation; $52.54 monthly.
Digital Basic Service
Subscribers: N.A.
Programming (via satellite): BBC America; Bravo; Discovery Digital Networks; DMX Music; FYI; GSN; History International; IFC; National Geographic Channel; Starz Encore (multiplexed); Turner Classic Movies.
Fee: $9.40 monthly.
Digital Expanded Basic Service
Subscribers: N.A.
Programming (via satellite): ESPN2; ESPNews; Fox Sports 1; Golf Channel; NBCSN.
Fee: $5.00 monthly.

FULLY SEARCHABLE • CONTINUOUSLY UPDATED • DISCOUNT RATES FOR PRINT PURCHASERS
For more information call 800-771-9202 or visit www.warren-news.com

Pay Service 1
Pay Units: N.A.
Programming (via satellite): HBO; Showtime.
Fee: $14.95 monthly (each).
Digital Pay Service 1
Pay Units: N.A.
Programming (via satellite): Cinemax (multiplexed); HBO (multiplexed); Showtime (multiplexed); The Movie Channel (multiplexed).
Fee: $10.00 monthly (each).
Video-On-Demand: No
Pay-Per-View
iN DEMAND (delivered digitally); Playboy TV (delivered digitally).
Internet Service
Operational: Yes.
Broadband Service: Millennium Cable-Speed.
Fee: $49.95 installation; $37.95 monthly.
Telephone Service
Digital: Operational
Fee: $39.99 monthly
Miles of Plant: 129.0 (coaxial); None (fiber optic).
Chief Executive Officer: Steve Weed. Chief Financial Officer: Wayne Schattenkerk. President: Jim Penney. General Manager: Stephen J. George.
Ownership: WaveDivision Holdings LLC (MSO).

NESPELEM—Formerly served by Country Cable. No longer in operation. ICA: WA0170.

NEWPORT—Concept Cable, 412 South Union Ave, PO Box 810, Newport, WA 99156-0810. Phone: 208-437-4544. Fax: 208-437-2740. E-mail: staff@conceptcable.com. Web Site: http://www.conceptcable.com. Also serves Bonner County (unincorporated areas), Clark Fork, Oldtown & Priest River, ID; Pend Oreille County, WA. ICA: WA0195.
TV Market Ranking: Outside TV Markets (Bonner County (unincorporated areas), Clark Fork, NEWPORT, Oldtown, Pend Oreille County, Priest River). Franchise award date: August 1, 1993. Franchise expiration date: N.A. Began: January 1, 1994.
Channel capacity: N.A. Channels available but not in use: N.A.
Basic Service
Subscribers: 1,206.
Programming (received off-air): KAYU-TV (FOX, This TV) Spokane; KCDT (PBS) Coeur d'Alene; KHQ-TV (NBC) Spokane; KQUP (IND) Pullman; KREM (CBS, The-CoolTV) Spokane; KSKN (CW) Spokane; KSPS-TV (PBS) Spokane; KXLY-TV (ABC, MeTV) Spokane.
Programming (via satellite): C-SPAN; Hallmark Channel; ION Television; Northwest Cable News; Pop; Trinity Broadcasting Network (TBN); Turner Classic Movies; WGN America.
Fee: $23.90 monthly; $.40 converter.
Expanded Basic Service 1
Subscribers: N.A.
Programming (via satellite): A&E; AMC; Animal Planet; Cartoon Network; CMT; CNBC; CNN; Comedy Central; Discovery Channel; Disney Channel; Disney XD; DIY Network; E! HD; ESPN; ESPN2; Food Network; Fox News Channel; Fox Sports 1; Freeform; FX; FXM; GSN; HGTV; History; HLN; Lifetime; MTV; National Geographic Channel; Nickelodeon; Outdoor Channel; OWN: Oprah Winfrey Network; Oxygen; Spike TV; Syfy; TBS; The Weather Channel; TLC; TNT; Travel Channel; truTV; TV Land; USA Network; VH1.
Fee: $40.95 monthly.
Digital Basic Service
Subscribers: N.A.
Programming (via satellite): Bloomberg Television; Bravo; CMT; Destination America; Discovery Kids Channel; ESPN Classic; ESPNews; Fuse; FYI; Golf Channel; History International; IFC; Investigation Discovery; LMN; MC; MTV Classic; MTV2; National Geographic Channel; NBCSN; Nick Jr.; Nicktoons; OWN: Oprah Winfrey Network; Science Channel; WE tv.
Digital Pay Service 1
Pay Units: N.A.
Programming (via satellite): Cinemax (multiplexed); Flix; HBO (multiplexed); Showtime (multiplexed); Starz (multiplexed); Starz Encore (multiplexed); The Movie Channel.
Fee: $9.95 monthly (Cinemax), $11.95 monthly (HBO, Starz/Encore or Showtime/TMC/Flix).
Video-On-Demand: No
Pay-Per-View
iN DEMAND (delivered digitally); Playboy TV (delivered digitally); Spice (delivered digitally).
Internet Service
Operational: Yes.
Fee: $19.95 installation; $24.95 monthly.
Telephone Service
None
Miles of Plant: 71.0 (coaxial); 10.0 (fiber optic). Homes passed: 1,800.
General Manager & Chief Technician: Keith Antcliff. Program & Marketing Director: Doris Dale.
Ownership: Keith Antcliff.

NORTH BONNEVILLE—Formerly served by North Bonneville Community Cable TV System. No longer in operation. ICA: WA0131.

NORTHPORT—Formerly served by Almega Cable. No longer in operation. ICA: WA0172.

OAK HARBOR—Comcast Cable. Now served by BELLINGHAM, WA [WA0011]. ICA: WA0218.

OAKESDALE—Formerly served by Elk River TV Cable Co. No longer in operation. ICA: WA0125.

OCEAN SHORES—Coast Communications Co. Inc, 349 Damon Rd NE, Ocean Shores, WA 98569-9226. Phones: 888-224-6502; 360-289-2252. Fax: 360-289-2750. E-mail: sales@coastaccess.com. Web Site: http://www.coastcommunications.com. Also serves Grays Harbor County & Pacific Beach. ICA: WA0042.

2017 Edition   D-823

Washington—Cable Systems

TV Market Ranking: Outside TV Markets (Grays Harbor County, OCEAN SHORES, Pacific Beach). Franchise award date: August 17, 1967. Franchise expiration date: N.A. Began: February 1, 1968.
Channel capacity: N.A. Channels available but not in use: N.A.

Basic Service
Subscribers: N.A.
Programming (via microwave): KCPQ (Escape, FOX) Tacoma; KCTS-TV (PBS) Seattle; KING-TV (NBC) Seattle; KIRO-TV (CBS, getTV, Retro TV) Seattle; KOMO-TV (ABC, This TV) Seattle; KONG (MundoMax) Everett; KSTW (CW, Decades) Tacoma; KZJO (Antenna TV, MNT) Seattle.
Programming (via satellite): C-SPAN; C-SPAN 2; Food Network; ION Television; Northwest Cable News; Ovation; QVC; TBS; Travel Channel; Trinity Broadcasting Network (TBN); TVW.
Fee: $45.00 installation; $2.95 converter.

Expanded Basic Service 1
Subscribers: N.A.
Programming (via satellite): A&E; Animal Planet; Bloomberg Television; Bravo; Cartoon Network; CNBC; CNN; Comedy Central; Discovery Channel; DIY Network; ESPN; ESPN Classic; ESPN2; Fox News Channel; FOX Sports Networks; Freeform; Great American Country; HGTV; History; HLN; Lifetime; National Geographic Channel; Pop; Syfy; The Weather Channel; TLC; TNT; truTV; Turner Classic Movies; TV Land; USA Network.
Fee: $22.00 monthly.

Digital Basic Service
Subscribers: N.A.
Programming (via satellite): BBC America; Discovery Digital Networks; ESPN; ESPN Classic; ESPN2; ESPNews; Fox Sports 1; FSN Digital Atlantic; FSN Digital Central; FYI; Golf Channel; HD Theater; History International; MTV; NBCSN; Nick 2; Nick Jr.; Nickelodeon; TeenNick.
Fee: $11.00 monthly.

Digital Pay Service 1
Pay Units: N.A.
Programming (via satellite): Cinemax (multiplexed); DMX Music; HBO; Showtime (multiplexed); Starz (multiplexed); Starz Encore (multiplexed); The Movie Channel (multiplexed).
Fee: $11.49 monthly (HBO, Cinemax/Starz, or Showtime/TMC).

Video-On-Demand: No

Pay-Per-View
iN DEMAND (delivered digitally).

Internet Service
Operational: Yes.
Broadband Service: Coast Access.
Fee: $42.95 monthly; $9.95 modem lease.

Telephone Service
Analog: Not Operational
Digital: Operational
Miles of Plant: 80.0 (coaxial); None (fiber optic). Homes passed: 3,500.
Vice President & General Manager: Ronald Thomasson.
Ownership: Edward Hewson (MSO).

ODESSA (town)—Northstar Broadband, PO Box 2576, Post Falls, ID 83877. Phones: 208-262-9394; 800-572-0902. Fax: 208-262-9314. E-mail: j.webb@northstarbroadband.net. Web Site: http://www.northstarbroadband.net. ICA: WA0173.
TV Market Ranking: Outside TV Markets (ODESSA (TOWN)).
Channel capacity: 62 (2-way capable). Channels available but not in use: N.A.

Basic Service
Subscribers: 90.
Programming (received off-air): KAYU-TV (FOX, This TV) Spokane; KHQ-TV (NBC) Spokane; KREM (CBS, TheCoolTV) Spokane; KSKN (CW) Spokane; KSPS-TV (PBS) Spokane; KXLY-TV (ABC, MeTV) Spokane.
Programming (via satellite): A&E; Animal Planet; Cartoon Network; CMT; C-SPAN; C-SPAN 2; Discovery Channel; EVINE Live; EWTN Global Catholic Network; Food Network; Fox News Channel; Freeform; Hallmark Channel; HGTV; History; ION Television; National Geographic Channel; Nickelodeon; Ovation; OWN: Oprah Winfrey Network; Pop; QVC; TBS; TLC; Travel Channel; Trinity Broadcasting Network (TBN); truTV; TV Land; WGN America.
Fee: $20.00 installation; $32.56 monthly; $1.00 converter.

Expanded Basic Service 1
Subscribers: N.A.
Programming (via satellite): AMC; Bravo; CNBC; CNN; Comedy Central; Disney Channel; Disney XD; E! HD; ESPN; ESPN Classic; ESPN2; Fox Sports 1; FX; FXM; Golf Channel; HLN; Lifetime; MoviePlex; MSNBC; MTV; NBCSN; Northwest Cable News; Spike TV; Syfy; TNT; Turner Classic Movies; USA Network; VH1.
Fee: $16.60 monthly.

Pay Service 1
Pay Units: N.A.
Programming (via satellite): Cinemax; HBO; Showtime.
Fee: $5.00 installation; $5.25 monthly (Cinemax), $8.65 monthly (Showtime), $9.60 monthly (HBO).

Video-On-Demand: No

Internet Service
Operational: Yes.

Telephone Service
None
Homes passed: 491.
Office Manager: Jennifer Webb. Operations Manager: Greg Lundwall.
Ownership: Northstar Broadband LLC (MSO).

OKANOGAN—Charter Communications. Now served by WENATCHEE, WA [WA0015]. ICA: WA0044.

OLYMPIA—Comcast Cable. Now served by SEATTLE, WA [WA0001]. ICA: WA0007.

ORCAS ISLAND—Formerly served by Almega Cable. No longer in operation. ICA: WA0083.

ORCAS ISLAND—Mt. Baker Cable, PO Box 29534, Bellingham, WA 98228. Phones: 877-396-3016; 360-966-7502. E-mail: info@mtbakercable.com. Web Site: http://www.mtbakercable.com. ICA: WA0215.
TV Market Ranking: Below 100 (ORCAS ISLAND). Franchise award date: N.A. Franchise expiration date: N.A. Began: August 15, 1989.
Channel capacity: N.A. Channels available but not in use: N.A.

Basic Service
Subscribers: N.A.
Programming (received off-air): KBCB (Estrella TV) Bellingham; KCPQ (Escape, FOX) Tacoma; KCTS-TV (PBS) Seattle; KING-TV (NBC) Seattle; KIRO-TV (CBS, getTV, Retro TV) Seattle; KOMO-TV (ABC, This TV) Seattle; KONG (MundoMax) Everett; KSTW (CW, Decades) Tacoma; KVOS-TV (MeTV, Movies!) Bellingham; KZJO (Antenna TV, MNT) Seattle.
Programming (via satellite): A&E; AMC; Animal Planet; CNBC; CNN; C-SPAN; Discovery Channel; Disney Channel; ESPN; ESPN2; Fox News Channel; FOX Sports Networks; Freeform; HGTV; History; MTV; NBCSN; Nickelodeon; Northwest Cable News; Spike TV; Syfy; TBS; The Weather Channel; TLC; TNT; USA Network; VH1.
Fee: $29.95 installation; $19.95 monthly.

Pay Service 1
Pay Units: N.A.
Programming (via satellite): Cinemax; HBO.

Video-On-Demand: No

Internet Service
Operational: Yes.

Telephone Service
None
General Manager: Dan Adams.
Ownership: Mount Baker Cable (MSO).

OROVILLE—Charter Communications. Now served by WENATCHEE, WA [WA0015]. ICA: WA0073.

OTHELLO—Northland Cable Television, 254 North Fig St, PO Box T, Moses Lake, WA 98837. Phones: 888-667-8452; 509-765-6151. Fax: 509-765-5132. E-mail: moseslake@northlandcabletv.com. Web Site: http://www.yournorthland.com. Also serves Adams County. ICA: WA0049.
TV Market Ranking: Outside TV Markets (Adams County, OTHELLO). Franchise award date: N.A. Franchise expiration date: N.A. Began: November 22, 1965.
Channel capacity: N.A. Channels available but not in use: N.A.

Basic Service
Subscribers: 315.
Programming (received off-air): KAYU-TV (FOX, This TV) Spokane; KEPR-TV (CBS, CW) Pasco; KHQ-TV (NBC) Spokane; KNDU (NBC) Richland; KREM (CBS, TheCoolTV) Spokane; KSKN (CW) Spokane; KSPS-TV (PBS) Spokane; KSTW (CW, Decades) Tacoma; KVEW (ABC, MeTV, MNT) Kennewick; KXLY-TV (ABC, MeTV) Spokane; 1 FM.
Programming (via microwave): KING-TV (NBC) Seattle; KIRO-TV (CBS, getTV, Retro TV) Seattle.
Programming (via satellite): A&E; Cartoon Network; CNN; Discovery Channel; ESPN; Fox Deportes; Fox News Channel; FX; Hallmark Channel; HGTV; HLN; INSP; Lifetime; National Geographic Channel; Northwest Cable News; Pop; QVC; TBS; Telemundo; The Weather Channel; TLC; TNT; Univision; Univision Studios; USA Network.
Fee: $75.00 installation; $47.64 monthly; $2.20 converter.

Expanded Basic Service 1
Subscribers: N.A.
Programming (via satellite): Animal Planet; Canal Sur; Cine Mexicano; Comedy Central; C-SPAN; ESPN2; Food Network; FXM; Golf Channel; History; MTV; Nickelodeon; Spike TV; Syfy; Turner Classic Movies.
Fee: $10.00 monthly.

Digital Basic Service
Subscribers: N.A.
Programming (via satellite): BBC America; Bloomberg Television; Destination America; Discovery Kids Channel; DMX Music; Fox Sports 1; GSN; LMN; NBCSN; Outdoor Channel; OWN: Oprah Winfrey Network; Science Channel; Trinity Broadcasting Network (TBN); WE tv.
Fee: $10.50 monthly.

Pay Service 1
Pay Units: N.A.
Programming (via satellite): HBO.

Digital Pay Service 1
Pay Units: N.A.
Programming (via satellite): Cinemax (multiplexed); Flix; HBO (multiplexed); Showtime (multiplexed); Starz (multiplexed); Starz Encore (multiplexed); The Movie Channel (multiplexed).
Fee: $14.75 monthly (HBO, Cinemax, Showtime/TMC/Flix, or Starz/Encore).

Video-On-Demand: No

Pay-Per-View
iN DEMAND (delivered digitally); Playboy TV (delivered digitally); Fresh (delivered digitally).

Internet Service
Operational: Yes. Began: December 1, 2002.
Subscribers: 445.
Broadband Service: Northland Express.
Fee: $42.99 monthly.

Telephone Service
Digital: Operational
Subscribers: 70.
Fee: $29.99 monthly
Miles of Plant: 63.0 (coaxial); 2.0 (fiber optic). Homes passed: 3,061.
General Manager: Jon Ulrich. Chief Technician: Kim Svetich.
Ownership: Northland Communications Corp. (MSO).

PACKWOOD—Wave Broadband, 401 Parkplace Center, Ste 500, Kirkland, WA 98033. Phones: 425-576-8200; 720-479-3558; 800-829-2225. Fax: 720-479-3585. E-mail: jpenney@wavebroadband.com. Web Site: http://www.wavebroadband.com. ICA: WA0074.
TV Market Ranking: Outside TV Markets (PACKWOOD). Franchise award date: N.A. Franchise expiration date: N.A. Began: December 1, 1983.
Channel capacity: N.A. Channels available but not in use: N.A.

Basic Service
Subscribers: 270.
Programming (received off-air): KCPQ (Escape, FOX) Tacoma; KCTS-TV (PBS) Seattle; KING-TV (NBC) Seattle; KIRO-TV (CBS, getTV, Retro TV) Seattle; KOMO-TV (ABC, This TV) Seattle.
Programming (via satellite): A&E; AMC; Animal Planet; CNN; Discovery Channel; Disney Channel; E! HD; ESPN; Fox News Channel; Freeform; Great American Country; HGTV; History; HLN; Lifetime; National Geographic Channel; Nickelodeon; Northwest Cable News; Pop; QVC; Spike TV; Syfy; TBS; TLC; TNT; USA Network; WGN America.
Fee: $29.95 installation; $22.08 monthly.

Digital Basic Service
Subscribers: N.A.
Programming (via satellite): BBC America; Bravo; Discovery Digital Networks; DMX Music; FYI; GSN; History International; IFC; LMN; Starz Encore (multiplexed).
Fee: $8.40 monthly.

Digital Expanded Basic Service
Subscribers: N.A.
Programming (via satellite): ESPN2; ESPNews; Fox Sports 1; Golf Channel; NBCSN.
Fee: $5.00 monthly.

Digital Pay Service 1
Pay Units: N.A.
Programming (via satellite): Cinemax (multiplexed); HBO (multiplexed); Showtime (multiplexed); The Movie Channel (multiplexed).

Cable Systems—Washington

Fee: $10.00 monthly (each).
Video-On-Demand: No
Pay-Per-View
iN DEMAND (delivered digitally); Playboy TV (delivered digitally).
Internet Service
Operational: Yes.
Fee: $49.95 installation; $39.95 monthly.
Telephone Service
None
Miles of Plant: 32.0 (coaxial); None (fiber optic). Homes passed: 1,030.
Chief Executive Officer: Steve Weed. Chief Financial Officer: Wayne Schattenkerk. President: Jim Penney. General Manager: Stephen J. George.
Ownership: WaveDivision Holdings LLC (MSO).

PE ELL—Formerly served by Wave Broadband. No longer in operation. ICA: WA0103.

POINT ROBERTS—Delta Cable, PO Box 869, Point Roberts, WA 98281-0869. Phones: 360-945-0456; 604-946-7676. Fax: 604-946-5627. E-mail: customerservice@deltacable.com. Web Site: http://www.deltacable.com. ICA: WA0076.
TV Market Ranking: Below 100 (POINT ROBERTS). Franchise award date: January 1, 1973. Franchise expiration date: N.A. Began: June 1, 1973.
Channel capacity: N.A. Channels available but not in use: N.A.
Basic Service
Subscribers: N.A.
Programming (received off-air): KBCB (Estrella TV) Bellingham; KCPQ (Escape, FOX) Tacoma; KCTS-TV (PBS) Seattle; KING-TV (NBC) Seattle; KIRO-TV (CBS, getTV, Retro TV) Seattle; KOMO-TV (ABC, This TV) Seattle; KSTW (CW, Decades) Tacoma; KVOS-TV (MeTV, Movies!) Bellingham; allband FM.
Programming (via satellite): A&E; CNN; C-SPAN; Discovery Channel; Disney Channel; E! HD; ESPN; ESPN Classic; Freeform; History; Northwest Cable News; Spike TV; TBS; TLC; TNT; Turner Classic Movies; USA Network; WGN America.
Fee: $18.00 installation; $5.00 converter.
Expanded Basic Service 1
Subscribers: N.A.
Programming (via satellite): Animal Planet; Bravo; Cartoon Network; Cooking Channel; DIY Network; Food Network; Fox Sports 1; Golf Channel; Hallmark Channel; HGTV; HLN; NBCSN; Syfy; truTV.
Fee: $10.00 monthly.
Pay Service 1
Pay Units: N.A.
Programming (via satellite): HBO.
Fee: $12.00 monthly.
Video-On-Demand: No
Internet Service
Operational: Yes.
Subscribers: 221.
Broadband Service: Delta Cable Communications.
Fee: $25.00 installation; $39.50 monthly.
Telephone Service
Digital: Operational
Miles of Plant: 30.0 (coaxial); 5.0 (fiber optic). Homes passed: 1,050.
President: John S. Thomas. General Manager: Larry Boule. Operations Manager: Craig Johnson. Regional Manager: Wayne Rothenberger. Engineering Manager: Gordie Duncan. Program Director: Adnan Hussain. Marketing Manager: Chris Rumbold. Customer Service Manager: Henri Wendel.
Ownership: Guiness Communications Inc.

POMEROY—Formerly served by Almega Cable. No longer in operation. ICA: WA0214.

PORT ANGELES—Wave Broadband, 401 Parkplace Center, Ste 500, Kirkland, WA 98033. Phones: 360-452-1278; 425-576-8200 (Administrative office); 866-928-3123 (Customer service); 360-452-8466; 800-244-7591. Web Site: http://www.wavebroadband.com. Also serves Clallam County (unincorporated areas) & Sequim. ICA: WA0020.
TV Market Ranking: Outside TV Markets (Clallam County (unincorporated areas), PORT ANGELES, Sequim). Franchise award date: May 1, 1960. Franchise expiration date: N.A. Began: May 1, 1960.
Channel capacity: N.A. Channels available but not in use: N.A.
Basic Service
Subscribers: 8,354.
Programming (received off-air): KBCB (Estrella TV) Bellingham; KCPQ (Escape, FOX) Tacoma; KCTS-TV (PBS) Seattle; KING-TV (NBC) Seattle; KIRO-TV (CBS, getTV, Retro TV) Seattle; KOMO-TV (ABC, This TV) Seattle; KONG (MundoMax) Everett; KSTW (CW, Decades) Tacoma; KVOS-TV (MeTV, Movies!) Bellingham; KWPX-TV (ION) Bellevue; KZJO (Antenna TV, MNT) Seattle; various Canadian stations.
Programming (via satellite): C-SPAN; Pop; QVC.
Fee: $29.95 installation; $25.95 monthly; $3.95 converter.
Expanded Basic Service 1
Subscribers: N.A.
Programming (via satellite): A&E; AMC; Animal Planet; Bravo; Cartoon Network; CMT; CNBC; CNN; Comedy Central; Discovery Channel; Disney Channel; E! HD; ESPN; ESPN2; Food Network; Fox News Channel; Freeform; FX; FXM; Golf Channel; Great American Country; Hallmark Channel; HGTV; History; HLN; Lifetime; MSNBC; MTV; National Geographic Channel; Nickelodeon; Northwest Cable News; Oxygen; Spike TV; Syfy; TBS; The Weather Channel; TLC; TNT; Travel Channel; truTV; Turner Classic Movies; TV Land; USA Network; VH1.
Fee: $50.00 installation; $23.55 monthly.
Digital Basic Service
Subscribers: N.A.
Programming (via satellite): BBC America; BYUtv; CMT; C-SPAN 2; Destination America; Discovery Kids Channel; Discovery Life Channel; Disney XD; EWTN Global Catholic Network; Fox Business Network; FYI; History International; Investigation Discovery; MC; MTV Classic; MTV Hits; MTV2; Nick Jr.; Nicktoons; OWN; Oprah Winfrey Network; Science Channel; Sprout; TeenNick; VH1 Soul.
Fee: $18.45 monthly.
Digital Expanded Basic Service
Subscribers: N.A.
Programming (via satellite): A&E HD; Animal Planet HD; AXS TV; Discovery Channel HD; Disney Channel HD; ESPN HD; ESPN2 HD; Food Network HD; FSN HD; HD Theater; HGTV HD; History HD; MGM HD; National Geographic Channel HD; NFL Network HD; Science HD; TBS HD; TLC HD; TNT HD; Travel Channel HD; Universal HD.
Digital Expanded Basic Service 2
Subscribers: N.A.
Programming (via satellite): Bloomberg Television; Boomerang; Bravo; Cooking Channel; DIY Network; Fuse; GSN; Hallmark Movies & Mysteries; IFC; LMN; Syfy; Trinity Broadcasting Network (TBN); WE tv.

Digital Expanded Basic Service 3
Subscribers: N.A.
Programming (via satellite): CBS Sports Network; ESPN Classic; ESPNews; ESPNU; Fox Sports 1; FSN Digital Atlantic; FSN Digital Central; FSN Digital Pacific; Golf Channel; NBCSN; NFL Network; Outdoor Channel; Tennis Channel.
Digital Pay Service 1
Pay Units: N.A.
Programming (via satellite): Cinemax (multiplexed); Cinemax HD; Flix; HBO (multiplexed); HBO HD; MoviePlex; Showtime (multiplexed); Showtime HD; Starz (multiplexed); Starz Encore (multiplexed); Starz HD; The Movie Channel (multiplexed); The Movie Channel HD.
Fee: $12.00 monthly (Showtime/TMC/Flix), $15.00 monthly (HBO, Cinemax or Starz/Encore).
Video-On-Demand: Yes
Pay-Per-View
Special events (delivered digitally); NBA League Pass; Sports PPV (delivered digitally).
Internet Service
Operational: Yes.
Subscribers: 12,093.
Broadband Service: Wave Broadband.
Fee: $24.95-$74.95 monthly.
Telephone Service
Digital: Operational
Subscribers: 4,578.
Fee: $29.95-$49.95 monthly
Miles of Plant: 828.0 (coaxial); 122.0 (fiber optic). Homes passed: 19,746.
Chief Financial Officer: Wayne Schattenkerk. General Manager: Jon Ulrich.
Ownership: WaveDivision Holdings LLC (MSO).

PORT ORCHARD—Wave Broadband, 401 Parkplace Center, Ste 500, Kirkland, WA 98033. Phones: 360-602-0183; 425-576-8200; 800-244-7591. Web Site: http://www.wavebroadband.com. Also serves Allyn (portions), Bangor Submarine Base, Belfair, Bremerton, Holly, Hood Canal, Jackson Park, Keyport, Keyport Naval Base, Kitsap Lake, Lake Symington, Manchester, Mason County, North Shore, Puget Sound Naval Shipyard, Seabeck, Silverdale, South Kitsap & Tahuya. ICA: WA0010.
TV Market Ranking: 20 (Allyn (portions), Bangor Submarine Base, Belfair, Bremerton, Holly, Hood Canal, Jackson Park, Keyport, Keyport Naval Base, Kitsap Lake, Lake Symington, Manchester, Mason County, North Shore, PORT ORCHARD, Puget Sound Naval Shipyard, Seabeck, Silverdale, South Kitsap, Tahuya). Franchise award date: N.A. Franchise expiration date: N.A. Began: January 1, 1971.
Channel capacity: 70 (operating 2-way). Channels available but not in use: N.A.
Basic Service
Subscribers: 23,019.
Programming (received off-air): KBTC-TV (PBS) Tacoma; KCPQ (Escape, FOX) Tacoma; KCTS-TV (PBS) Seattle; KING-TV (NBC) Seattle; KIRO-TV (CBS, getTV, Retro TV) Seattle; KOMO-TV (ABC, This TV) Seattle; KONG (MundoMax) Everett; KSTW (CW, Decades) Tacoma; KTBW-TV (TBN) Tacoma; KUNS-TV (MundoMax, UNV) Bellevue; KWDK (Daystar TV, ETV) Tacoma; KWPX-TV (ION) Bellevue; KZJO (Antenna TV, MNT) Seattle; allband FM.
Programming (via satellite): C-SPAN; INSP; Pop; QVC; WGN America.
Fee: $29.95 installation; $25.95 monthly; $2.50 converter.
Expanded Basic Service 1
Subscribers: N.A.
Programming (via satellite): A&E; AMC; Animal Planet; BET; Bravo; Cartoon Network; CMT; CNBC; CNN; Comedy Central; Discovery Channel; Discovery Life Channel; Disney Channel; Disney XD; E! HD; ESPN; ESPN2; Food Network; Fox News Channel; Fox Sports 1; Freeform; FX; Golf Channel; Great American Country; Hallmark Channel; HGTV; History; HLN; Lifetime; MSNBC; MTV; National Geographic Channel; Nickelodeon; Northwest Cable News; Outdoor Channel; Oxygen; Spike TV; Syfy; TBS; The Weather Channel; TLC; TNT; Travel Channel; Turner Classic Movies; TV Land; USA Network; VH1.
Fee: $28.00 monthly.
Digital Basic Service
Subscribers: N.A.
Programming (via satellite): BBC America; BYUtv; Cloo; CMT; Destination America; Discovery Kids Channel; EWTN Global Catholic Network; Fox Business Network; FYI; History International; Investigation Discovery; MC; MTV Classic; MTV Hits; MTV Jams; MTV2; Nick Jr.; Nicktoons; OWN; Oprah Winfrey Network; Science Channel; Sprout; TeenNick; Tr3s; VH1 Soul.
Fee: $10.00 monthly.
Digital Expanded Basic Service
Subscribers: N.A.
Programming (via satellite): Bloomberg Television; Boomerang; Cooking Channel; DIY Network; Fuse; FXM; GSN; Hallmark Movies & Mysteries; IFC; LMN; Ovation; truTV; WE tv.
Digital Expanded Basic Service 2
Subscribers: N.A.
Programming (via satellite): CBS Sports Network; ESPN Classic; ESPNews; ESPNU; FSN Digital Atlantic; FSN Digital Central; FSN Digital Pacific; NBCSN; NFL Network; Tennis Channel.
Digital Expanded Basic Service 3
Subscribers: N.A.
Programming (via satellite): A&E HD; AXS TV; Disney Channel HD; ESPN HD; ESPN2 HD; Food Network HD; FSN HD; HD Theater; HGTV HD; History HD; National Geographic Channel HD; NFL Network HD; Science HD; TBS HD; TNT HD; Travel Channel HD; Universal HD.
Digital Pay Service 1
Pay Units: N.A.
Programming (via satellite): Cinemax (multiplexed); Cinemax HD; Flix; HBO (multiplexed); HBO HD; here! TV; MoviePlex; Showtime (multiplexed); Showtime HD; Starz (multiplexed); Starz Encore (multiplexed); Starz HD; Sundance TV; The

2017 Edition   D-825

Washington—Cable Systems

Filipino Channel; The Movie Channel (multiplexed); The Movie Channel HD.
Fee: $20.00 installation; $10.95 monthly (Cinemax/Cinemax HD or Showtime/Showtime HD/Flix/Sundance/TMC/TMC HD), $11.95 monthly (HBO/HBO HD).

Video-On-Demand: Yes

Pay-Per-View
Hot Choice (delivered digitally); iN DEMAND (delivered digitally); Fresh (delivered digitally); Shorteez (delivered digitally); Sports PPV (delivered digitally).

Internet Service
Operational: Yes. Began: December 1, 2000.
Subscribers: 33,686.
Broadband Service: Wave Broadband.
Fee: $150.00 installation; $24.95-$74.95 monthly.

Telephone Service
Digital: Operational
Subscribers: 12,770.
Fee: $29.95-$49.95 monthly
Miles of Plant: 1,706.0 (coaxial); 519.0 (fiber optic). Homes passed: 68,459.
Chief Financial Officer: Wayne Schattenkerk. General Manager: Jerry Rotondo. Chief Technician: Richard Rumrill. Marketing Director: Keith Tyrrell.
Ownership: WaveDivision Holdings LLC (MSO).

PORT TOWNSEND—Wave Broadband, 401 Parkplace Center, Ste 500, Kirkland, WA 98033. Phones: 425-576-8200; 720-479-3558; 800-829-2225. Fax: 720-479-3585. E-mail: jpenney@wavebroadband.com. Web Site: http://www.wavebroadband.com. Also serves Kala Point, Port Hadlock, Port Ludlow & Quilcene. ICA: WA0027.
TV Market Ranking: 20 (Kala Point, Port Hadlock, Port Ludlow, Quilcene); Below 100 (PORT TOWNSEND). Franchise award date: January 1, 1977. Franchise expiration date: N.A. Began: December 28, 1977.
Channel capacity: N.A. Channels available but not in use: N.A.

Basic Service
Subscribers: 3,461.
Programming (received off-air): KCPQ (Escape, FOX) Tacoma; KCTS-TV (PBS) Seattle; KFFV (Azteca America, COZI TV, MeTV) Seattle; KING-TV (NBC) Seattle; KIRO-TV (CBS, getTV, Retro TV) Seattle; KOMO-TV (ABC, This TV) Seattle; KONG (MundoMax) Everett; KSTW (CW, Decades) Tacoma; KTBW-TV (TBN) Tacoma; KUNS-TV (MundoMax, UNV) Bellevue; KVOS-TV (MeTV, Movies!) Bellingham; KWDK (Daystar TV, ETV) Tacoma; KWPX-TV (ION) Bellevue; KZJO (Antenna TV, MNT) Seattle.
Programming (via satellite): EVINE Live; Pop; QVC; TVW; various Canadian stations.
Fee: $29.95 installation; $25.95 monthly.

Expanded Basic Service 1
Subscribers: N.A.
Programming (via satellite): A&E; AMC; Animal Planet; Cartoon Network; CMT; CNBC; CNN; Comedy Central; C-SPAN; Discovery Channel; Disney Channel; ESPN; ESPN Classic; ESPN2; Food Network; Fox News Channel; Freeform; FX; Hallmark Channel; HGTV; History; HLN; IFC; Lifetime; MTV; National Geographic Channel; Nickelodeon; Northwest Cable News; Spike TV; Syfy; TBS; TLC; TNT; Travel Channel; Turner Classic Movies; TV Land; USA Network.
Fee: $27.08 monthly.

Digital Basic Service
Subscribers: N.A.
Programming (via satellite): AXS TV; CMT; Discovery Digital Networks; DIY Network;

ESPN HD; Food Network HD; FOX College Sports Central; FOX College Sports Pacific; HD Theater; HGTV HD; MC; Nick Jr.; Nicktoons; Starz (multiplexed); Starz Encore (multiplexed); TeenNick; Turner Classic Movies.
Fee: $13.40 monthly.

Digital Expanded Basic Service
Subscribers: N.A.
Programming (via satellite): BBC America; ESPNews; Fox Sports 1; Golf Channel; NBCSN.
Fee: $5.00 monthly (Arts & Entertainment or Sports).

Digital Pay Service 1
Pay Units: N.A.
Programming (via satellite): Cinemax (multiplexed); Flix; HBO (multiplexed); Showtime (multiplexed); Sundance TV; The Movie Channel (multiplexed).
Fee: $5.50 monthly (each).

Video-On-Demand: No

Internet Service
Operational: Yes.
Broadband Service: Millennium CableSpeed.
Fee: $49.95 installation; $37.95 monthly.

Telephone Service
Digital: Operational
Fee: $39.99 monthly
Miles of Plant: 173.0 (coaxial); None (fiber optic). Homes passed: 6,100.
Chief Executive Officer: Steve Weed. Chief Financial Officer: Wayne Schattenkerk. President: Jim Penney. General Manager: Stephen J. George.
Ownership: WaveDivision Holdings LLC (MSO).

PRESCOTT—Formerly served by Charter Communications. No longer in operation. ICA: WA0133.

PULLMAN—Time Warner Cable, 828 West Pullman Rd, Moscow, ID 83843. Phones: 866-489-2669; 208-882-2832. Web Site: http://www.timewarnercable.com. Also serves Latah County (portions) & Moscow, ID; Albion & Whitman County (portions), WA. ICA: ID0081.
TV Market Ranking: Below 100 (Albion, Latah County (portions), Whitman County (portions), Moscow, PULLMAN). Franchise award date: N.A. Franchise expiration date: N.A. Began: May 1, 1953.
Channel capacity: 67 (operating 2-way). Channels available but not in use: N.A.

Basic Service
Subscribers: 6,078.
Programming (received off-air): KAYU-TV (FOX, This TV) Spokane; KHQ-TV (NBC) Spokane; KLEW-TV (CBS) Lewiston; KREM (CBS, TheCoolTV) Spokane; KSKN (CW) Spokane; KSPS-TV (PBS) Spokane; KUID-TV (PBS) Moscow; KWSU-TV (PBS) Pullman; KXLY-TV (ABC, MeTV) Spokane.
Programming (via satellite): C-SPAN; EWTN Global Catholic Network; INSP; International Television (ITV); ION Television; QVC.
Fee: $32.99 installation; $20.00 monthly.

Expanded Basic Service 1
Subscribers: N.A.
Programming (via satellite): A&E; AMC; Animal Planet; Bravo; Cartoon Network; CMT; CNBC; CNN; Comedy Central; Discovery Channel; Disney Channel; E! HD; ESPN; ESPN2; Fox News Channel; Freeform; FX; Hallmark Channel; HGTV; History; HLN; Lifetime; MTV; Nickelodeon; Northwest Cable News; Spike TV; Syfy; TBS; The Weather

Channel; TLC; TNT; Travel Channel; truTV; TV Land; USA Network; VH1.
Fee: $35.73 monthly.

Digital Basic Service
Subscribers: N.A.
Programming (via satellite): BBC America; Bloomberg Television; Discovery Life Channel; Disney XD; DIY Network; DMX Music; ESPN Classic; ESPNews; FOX College Sports Central; FOX College Sports Pacific; Fox Sports 1; FXM; FYI; Golf Channel; Great American Country; GSN; History International; IFC; National Geographic Channel; NBCSN; Nick Jr.; Outdoor Channel; Sundance TV; TeenNick; The Word Network; Trinity Broadcasting Network (TBN); Turner Classic Movies; WE tv.
Fee: $6.00 monthly (each tier).

Digital Pay Service 1
Pay Units: N.A.
Programming (via satellite): Cinemax (multiplexed); Flix; HBO (multiplexed); HITS (Headend In The Sky); RAI Italia; RTN; Showtime (multiplexed); Starz (multiplexed); Starz Encore (multiplexed); TAC TV; The Filipino Channel; The Movie Channel (multiplexed); TV Asia; TV5; La Television International; Zee TV.
Fee: $14.00 monthly (each).

Video-On-Demand: Planned

Pay-Per-View
Urban Extra (delivered digitally); Fresh (delivered digitally); Hot Choice (delivered digitally); Playboy TV (delivered digitally); HITS PPV 1-30 (delivered digitally).

Internet Service
Operational: Yes.
Subscribers: 11,139.
Broadband Service: RoadRunner.
Fee: $24.95 monthly.

Telephone Service
Digital: Operational
Subscribers: 1,738.
Fee: $24.95 monthly.
Miles of Plant: 346.0 (coaxial); 110.0 (fiber optic). Homes passed: 45,443.
Ownership: Time Warner Cable (MSO).

QUINCY—Formerly served by J & N Cable. No longer in operation. ICA: WA0057.

RANDLE—Wave Broadband, 401 Parkplace Center, Ste 500, Kirkland, WA 98033. Phones: 425-576-8200; 720-479-3558; 800-829-2225. Fax: 720-479-3585. E-mail: jpenney@wavebroadband.com. Web Site: http://www.wavebroadband.com. Also serves Glenoma. ICA: WA0208.
TV Market Ranking: Outside TV Markets (Glenoma, RANDLE).
Channel capacity: N.A. Channels available but not in use: N.A.

Basic Service
Subscribers: 64.
Programming (received off-air): KCTS-TV (PBS) Seattle; KING-TV (NBC) Seattle; KIRO-TV (CBS, getTV, Retro TV) Seattle; KOMO-TV (ABC, This TV) Seattle.
Programming (via satellite): A&E; AMC; CNN; Discovery Channel; Disney Channel; E! HD; ESPN; Fox News Channel; FOX Sports Networks; Freeform; Great American Country; HGTV; History; HLN; Lifetime; Nickelodeon; Northwest Cable News; Pop; QVC; Spike TV; Syfy; TBS; TLC; TNT; Trinity Broadcasting Network (TBN); Turner Classic Movies; USA Network; WGN America.
Fee: $29.95 installation; $22.08 monthly.

Digital Basic Service
Subscribers: N.A.
Programming (via satellite): BBC America; Bravo; Discovery Digital Networks; DMX

Music; FYI; GSN; History International; IFC; LMN; National Geographic Channel.
Fee: $13.40 monthly.

Digital Expanded Basic Service
Subscribers: N.A.
Programming (via satellite): ESPN2; ESPNews; Fox Sports 1; Golf Channel; NBCSN.
Fee: $5.00 monthly.

Digital Pay Service 1
Pay Units: N.A.
Programming (via satellite): Cinemax (multiplexed); HBO (multiplexed); Showtime (multiplexed); Starz (multiplexed); Starz Encore (multiplexed); The Movie Channel (multiplexed).
Fee: $10.00 monthly (each).

Video-On-Demand: No

Pay-Per-View
iN DEMAND (delivered digitally); Playboy TV (delivered digitally).

Internet Service
Operational: Yes.
Fee: $49.95 installation; $37.95 monthly.

Telephone Service
Digital: Operational
Fee: $39.99 monthly
Miles of Plant: 34.0 (coaxial); None (fiber optic).
Chief Executive Officer: Steve Weed. Chief Financial Officer: Wayne Schattenkerk. President: Jim Penney. General Manager: Stephen J. George.
Ownership: WaveDivision Holdings LLC (MSO).

RAYMOND—Comcast Cable, 600 West Wishkah St, Aberdeen, WA 98520. Phone: 877-824-2288. Web Site: http://www.comcast.com. Also serves Pacific County (portions) & South Bend. ICA: WA0040.
TV Market Ranking: Outside TV Markets (Pacific County (portions), South Bend, RAYMOND).
Channel capacity: N.A. Channels available but not in use: N.A.

Basic Service
Subscribers: 1,472.
Fee: $40.00 installation; $26.94 monthly.

Internet Service
Operational: Yes.

Telephone Service
Digital: Operational
Ownership: Comcast Cable Communications Inc.

REARDAN—Formerly served by Elk River Cable TV Co. No longer in operation. ICA: WA0121.

REDMOND—Comcast Cable. Now served by SEATTLE, WA [WA0001]. ICA: WA0034.

REPUBLIC—Television Assn. of Republic, 147-18 North Clark St, PO Box 555, Republic, WA 99166-0555. Phone: 509-775-3822. Fax: 509-775-3822. E-mail: billing@rcabletv.com. Web Site: http://www.rcabletv.com. ICA: WA0177.
TV Market Ranking: Outside TV Markets (REPUBLIC). Franchise award date: December 1, 1953. Franchise expiration date: N.A. Began: December 1, 1953.
Channel capacity: N.A. Channels available but not in use: N.A.

Basic Service
Subscribers: 276.
Programming (received off-air): KAYU-TV (FOX, This TV) Spokane; KHQ-TV (NBC) Spokane; KREM (CBS, TheCoolTV) Spokane; KSPS-TV (PBS) Spokane; KXLY-TV (ABC, MeTV) Spokane; various Canadian stations; allband FM.

Cable Systems—Washington

Programming (via satellite): A&E; AMC; Bravo; CNN; C-SPAN 2; Discovery Channel; Disney Channel; ESPN; ESPN2; Freeform; History; Lifetime; Nickelodeon; Northwest Cable News; Starz Encore; Syfy; TBS; TLC; TNT; Trinity Broadcasting Network (TBN); Turner Classic Movies; USA Network.
Fee: $40.00 installation; $39.00 monthly; $10.00 converter.

Expanded Basic Service 1
Subscribers: 220.
Programming (via satellite): Animal Planet; Cartoon Network; CMT; C-SPAN; Food Network; Fox News Channel; Fox Sports 1; Great American Country; HGTV; MTV; National Geographic Channel; NBCSN; Outdoor Channel; OWN: Oprah Winfrey Network; Spike TV; Travel Channel; TV Land; VH1; WGN America.
Fee: $6.50 monthly.

Pay Service 1
Pay Units: 79.
Programming (via satellite): HBO (multiplexed).
Fee: $10.50 monthly.

Internet Service
Operational: Yes. Began: October 1, 2000.
Broadband Service: In-house.
Fee: $60.00 installation; $30.50 monthly.

Telephone Service
None
Miles of Plant: 30.0 (coaxial); None (fiber optic).
General Manager: Jerry Larson. Secretary-Treasurer: Sheila Wellaert.
Ownership: Television Assn. of Republic.

RITZVILLE—Northstar Broadband, PO Box 2576, Post Falls, ID 83877. Phones: 208-262-9394; 800-572-0902. Fax: 208-262-9314. E-mail: j.webb@northstarbroadband.net. Web Site: http://www.northstarbroadband.net. ICA: WA0178.
TV Market Ranking: Outside TV Markets (RITZVILLE). Franchise award date: N.A. Franchise expiration date: N.A. Began: June 1, 1981.
Channel capacity: N.A. Channels available but not in use: N.A.

Basic Service
Subscribers: 120.
Programming (received off-air): KAYU-TV (FOX, This TV) Spokane; KHQ-TV (NBC) Spokane; KREM (CBS, TheCoolTV) Spokane; KSKN (CW) Spokane; KSPS-TV (PBS) Spokane; KWSU-TV (PBS) Pullman; KXLY-TV (ABC, MeTV) Spokane.
Programming (via satellite): A&E; Animal Planet; Cartoon Network; CMT; C-SPAN; C-SPAN 2; Discovery Channel; EVINE Live; EWTN Global Catholic Network; Food Network; Fox News Channel; Freeform; Hallmark Channel; HGTV; History; ION Television; MSNBC; National Geographic Channel; NBCSN; Nickelodeon; Ovation; OWN: Oprah Winfrey Network; Pop; QVC; TBS; TLC; Travel Channel; Trinity Broadcasting Network (TBN); truTV; TV Land; WGN America.
Fee: $20.00 installation; $56.95 monthly.

Expanded Basic Service 1
Subscribers: N.A.
Programming (via satellite): AMC; Bravo; CNBC; CNN; Comedy Central; Disney Channel; Disney XD; E! HD; ESPN; ESPN Classic; ESPN2; Fox Sports 1; FX; FXM; Golf Channel; HLN; Lifetime; MoviePlex; MTV; Northwest Cable News; Spike TV; Syfy; TNT; Turner Classic Movies; USA Network; VH1.
Fee: $16.41 monthly.

Pay Service 1
Pay Units: N.A.
Programming (via satellite): Cinemax (multiplexed); HBO (multiplexed); Showtime.
Fee: $5.00 installation; $5.25 monthly (Cinemax), $8.65 monthly (Showtime), $9.60 monthly (HBO).

Video-On-Demand: No

Internet Service
Operational: Yes, DSL.
Subscribers: 98.
Broadband Service: In-house.
Fee: $29.95 installation; $20.26 monthly.

Telephone Service
None
Miles of Plant: 50.0 (coaxial); None (fiber optic). Homes passed: 320.
Office Manager: Jennifer Webb. Operations Manager: Greg Lundwall.
Ownership: Northstar Broadband LLC (MSO).

ROCHESTER—Comcast Cable, 440 Yauger Way SW, Olympia, WA 98502. Phone: 877-824-2288. Web Site: http://www.comcast.com. Also serves Grays Harbor County (portions) & Oakville. ICA: WA0064.
TV Market Ranking: Outside TV Markets (Grays Harbor County (portions), Oakville, ROCHESTER).
Channel capacity: N.A. Channels available but not in use: N.A.

Basic Service
Subscribers: 286.
Fee: $40.00 installation; $28.22 monthly.

Internet Service
Operational: Yes.

Telephone Service
Digital: Operational
Ownership: Comcast Cable Communications Inc.

ROSALIA—Formerly served by Elk River TV Cable Co. No longer in operation. ICA: WA0122.

ROSLYN—R & R Cable, 103 South Second St, PO Box 610, Roslyn, WA 98941. Phones: 509-649-4638; 509-649-2211; 509-649-2212. Fax: 509-649-2555. E-mail: seth@inlandnet.com. Web Site: http://www.rrcable.com. Also serves KITTITAS COUNTY (portions), Lake Cle Elum & Ronald. ICA: WA0179.
TV Market Ranking: Below 100 (Lake Cle Elum); Outside TV Markets (Ronald, ROSLYN). Franchise award date: N.A. Franchise expiration date: N.A. Began: February 1, 1955.
Channel capacity: N.A. Channels available but not in use: N.A.

Basic Service
Subscribers: 1,180.
Programming (received off-air): KCPQ (Escape, FOX) Tacoma; KCYU-LD (FOX, This TV) Yakima; KING-TV (NBC) Seattle; KIRO-TV (CBS, getTV, Retro TV) Seattle; KOMO-TV (ABC, This TV) Seattle; allband FM.
Programming (via satellite): A&E; AMC; Animal Planet; Bravo; Cartoon Network; CMT; CNN; Comedy Central; C-SPAN; Discovery Channel; Discovery Life Channel; E! HD; ESPN; ESPN Classic; ESPN2; Food Network; Fox News Channel; Freeform; FX; Hallmark Channel; Lifetime; LMN; MSNBC; MTV; National Geographic Channel; Nickelodeon; Nicktoons; Northwest Cable News; Outdoor Channel; Pop; QVC; Spike TV; Syfy; TBS; The Weather Channel; TLC; TNT; Travel Channel; Trinity Broadcasting Network (TBN); truTV; TV Land; TVW; USA Network; VH1; WGN America; WSBK-TV (MNT) Boston.
Programming (via translator): KAPP (ABC, MeTV, MNT) Yakima; KIMA-TV (CBS, CW) Yakima; KNDO (NBC) Yakima; KYVE (PBS) Yakima.
Fee: $39.95 installation; $30.00 monthly.

Digital Basic Service
Subscribers: N.A.
Programming (via satellite): BBC America; Bloomberg Television; Cloo; Discovery Digital Networks; DMX Music; ESPNews; FOX College Sports Central; FOX College Sports Pacific; Fox Sports 1; Fuse; FXM; FYI; Golf Channel; Great American Country; GSN; HGTV; History; History International; IFC; NBCSN; Nick Jr.; TeenNick; Turner Classic Movies; WE tv.
Fee: $7.00 monthly.

Digital Pay Service 1
Pay Units: N.A.
Programming (via satellite): Cinemax (multiplexed); HBO (multiplexed); Showtime (multiplexed); Starz (multiplexed); Starz Encore (multiplexed); The Movie Channel (multiplexed).
Fee: $7.00 monthly (Cinemax), $10.00 monthly (Starz & Encore), $12.00 monthly (Showtime & TMC), $13.00 monthly (HBO).

Video-On-Demand: No

Pay-Per-View
iN DEMAND (delivered digitally); Playboy TV (delivered digitally); Fresh (delivered digitally).

Internet Service
Operational: No, DSL.

Telephone Service
Analog: Operational
Miles of Plant: 620.0 (coaxial); 88.0 (fiber optic). Homes passed: 2,830.
Secretary: Gregory A. Maras. General Manager: Doug Weiss. Technical Operations Manager: Seth M. Digby.
Ownership: Inland Telephone Co.

ROYAL CITY—Formerly served by Almega Cable. No longer in operation. ICA: WA0118.

RUSTON—Comcast Cable. Now served by SEATTLE, WA [WA0001]. ICA: WA0006.

RYDERWOOD—Comcast Cable, 410 Valley Ave NW, Ste 9, Puyallup, WA 98371. Phones: 253-864-4352; 425-398-6000 (Bothell office). Fax: 253-864-4352. Web Site: http://www.comcast.com. ICA: WA0127.
TV Market Ranking: Outside TV Markets (RYDERWOOD). Franchise award date: N.A. Franchise expiration date: N.A. Began: July 1, 1987.
Channel capacity: N.A. Channels available but not in use: N.A.

Basic Service
Subscribers: 68.
Programming (received off-air): KATU (ABC, MeTV) Portland; KCKA (PBS) Centralia; KCPQ (Escape, FOX) Tacoma; KGW (Estrella TV, NBC) Portland; KING-TV (NBC) Seattle; KIRO-TV (CBS, getTV, Retro TV) Seattle; KOIN (CBS) Portland; KOPB-TV (PBS) Portland; KPTV (COZI TV, FOX, Laff) Portland; allband FM.
Programming (via satellite): AMC; CNN; Discovery Channel; Disney Channel; E! HD; ESPN; Fox News Channel; FOX Sports Networks; Freeform; TBS; TNT; USA Network.
Fee: $40.00 installation; $25.99 monthly.

Pay Service 1
Pay Units: N.A.
Programming (via satellite): HBO; Starz; Starz Encore.

Video-On-Demand: No

Internet Service
Operational: Yes.

Telephone Service
None
Miles of Plant: 5.0 (coaxial); None (fiber optic).
Area Vice President: Anne McMullen. Vice President, Engineering: Steve Taber. Vice President, Sales & Marketing: Tom Pierce. Public Relations Director: Steve Kipp.
Ownership: Comcast Cable Communications Inc. (MSO).

SEATTLE—Comcast Cable, 19909 120th Ave NE, Ste 200, Bothell, WA 98021. Phone: 425-398-6000. Fax: 425-398-6236. E-mail: len_rozek@cable.comcast.com. Web Site: http://www.comcast.com. Also serves Algona, Arlington, Auburn, Bainbridge Island, Beaux Arts Village, Bellevue, Black Diamond, Bonney Lake, Bothell, Bremerton, Brier, Buckley, Burien, Carbonado, Carnation, Centralia, Chehalis, Clyde Hill, Covington, Des Moines, Du Pont, East Seattle, Eatonville, Edgewood, Edmonds, Enumclaw, Everett, Everett Naval Air Station, Fall City, Federal Way, Fife, Fircrest, Fort Lewis, Fox Island, Gig Harbor, Goldbar, Graham, Granite Falls, Hansville, Hunts Point, Indianola, Issaquah, Kenmore, Kent, King County (portions), Kingston, Kirkland, Kitsap County (portions), Lacey, Lake Forest Park, Lake Stevens, Lakebay, Lakewood, Lewis County (portions), Lynwood, Maple Valley, Marysville, Mason County (portions), McChord AFB, McKenna, Medina, Mercer Island, Mill Creek, Milton, Monroe, Mountlake Terrace, Mukiteo, Newcastle, Normandy Park, North Bend, Olympia, Orting, Pacific (King County), Pierce County (portions), Port Orchard, Poulsbo, Preston, Puget Sound (King County), Puget Sound (Kitsap County), Puyallup, Rainier, Redmond, Renton, Roy, Ruston, Sammamish, Seatac, Shelton, Shoreline, Silver Lake, Silverdale, Snohomish, Snohomish County (portions), Snoqualmie, South Prairie, South Tacoma, Startup, Steilacoom, Sultan, Sumner, Suquamish (unincorporated areas), Tacoma, Tenino, Thurston County (portions), Tukwila, Turnwater, University Place, Vashon Island, Wilkeson, Woodinville, Woods Creek, Woodway, Yarrow Point & Yelm. ICA: WA0001.
TV Market Ranking: 20 (Algona, Auburn, Bainbridge Island, Beaux Arts Village, Bellevue, Black Diamond, Bonney Lake, Bothell, Brier, Buckley, Burien, Carbonado, Carnation, Clyde Hill, Covington, Des Moines, Du Pont, East Seattle, Eatonville, Edgewood, Edmonds, Enumclaw, Everett, Everett Naval Air Station, Fall City, Federal Way, Fife, Fircrest, Fort Lewis,

2017 Edition   D-827

Washington—Cable Systems

Fox Island, Gig Harbor, Goldbar, Graham, Hansville, Hunts Point, Indianola, Issaquah, Kenmore, Kent, King County (portions) (portions), Kingston, Kirkland, Kitsap County (portions), Lacey, Lake Forest Park, Lake Stevens, Lakebay, Lakewood, Lewis County (portions) (portions), Lynwood, Maple Valley, Marysville, Mason County (portions) (portions), McChord AFB, McKenna, Medina, Mercer Island, Mill Creek, Milton, Monroe, Mountlake Terrace, Mukiteo, Newcastle, Normandy Park, North Bend, Olympia, Orting, Pacific (King County), Pierce County (portions) (portions), Port Orchard, Poulsbo, Preston, Puget Sound (King County), Puget Sound (Kitsap County), Puyallup, Rainier, Redmond, Renton, Roy, Ruston, Sammamish, Seatac, SEATTLE, Shelton, Shoreline, Silverdale, Snohomish, Snohomish County (portions) (portions), Snoqualmie, South Prairie, South Tacoma, Startup, Steilacoom, Sultan, Sumner, Suquamish (unincorporated areas), Tacoma, Tenino, Thurston County (portions) (portions), Tukwila, Tukwila, Turnwater, University Place, Vashon Island, Wilkeson, Woodinville, Woods Creek, Woodway, Yarrow Point, Yelm); Below 100 (Arlington, Granite Falls, King County (portions) (portions), Snohomish County (portions) (portions)); Outside TV Markets (Centralia, Chehalis, Silver Lake, King County (portions) (portions), Lewis County (portions) (portions), Mason County (portions) (portions), Pierce County (portions) (portions), Snohomish County (portions) (portions), Thurston County (portions) (portions)). Franchise award date: N.A. Franchise expiration date: N.A. Began: March 1, 1952.

Channel capacity: N.A. Channels available but not in use: N.A.

Basic Service
Subscribers: 836,009.
Programming (received off-air): KBCB (Estrella TV) Bellingham; KBTC-TV (PBS) Tacoma; KCPQ (Escape, FOX) Tacoma; KCTS-TV (PBS) Seattle; KFFV (Azteca America, COZI TV, MeTV) Seattle; KING-TV (NBC) Seattle; KIRO-TV (CBS, getTV, Retro TV) Seattle; KOMO-TV (ABC, This TV) Seattle; KONG (MundoMax) Everett; KSTW (CW, Decades) Tacoma; KTBW-TV (TBN) Tacoma; KUNS-TV (MundoMax, UNV) Bellevue; KWDK (Daystar TV, ETV) Tacoma; KWPX-TV (ION) Bellevue; KZJO (Antenna TV, MNT) Seattle; 28 FMs.
Programming (via satellite): C-SPAN; C-SPAN 2; Discovery Channel; Hallmark Channel; Jewelry Television; Northwest Cable News; Pop; The Weather Channel; Univision Studios.
Fee: $40.00 installation; $29.98 monthly; $1.00 converter.

Expanded Basic Service 1
Subscribers: N.A.
Programming (via satellite): A&E; AMC; Animal Planet; BET; Bravo; Cartoon Network; CMT; CNBC; CNN; Comedy Central; Disney Channel; E! HD; ESPN; ESPN2; Food Network; Fox News Channel; Fox Sports 1; Freeform; FX; Golf Channel; HGTV; History; HLN; International Television (ITV); Lifetime; MSNBC; MTV; MTV2; NBCSN; Nickelodeon; Oxygen; QVC; Spike TV; Syfy; TBS; TLC; TNT; Travel Channel; truTV; TVW; USA Network; VH1.
Fee: $36.70 monthly.

Digital Basic Service
Subscribers: N.A.
Programming (via satellite): BBC America; Bloomberg Television; BYUtv; Cooking Channel; Discovery Channel; Discovery Life Channel; Disney XD; DIY Network; DMX Music; ESPN; ESPN Classic; ESPNews; EWTN Global Catholic Network; FSN Digital Atlantic; FSN Digital Central; FSN Digital Pacific; Fuse; FXM; FYI; Great American Country; GSN; History International; IFC; iN DEMAND; LMN; MBC America; National Geographic Channel; NBA TV; NFL Network; Nick 2; Nick Jr.; Nicktoons; Outdoor Channel; Ovation; Sundance TV; TeenNick; The Word Network; Turner Classic Movies; TV Land; WE tv; Weatherscan.
Fee: $11.99 monthly.

Digital Pay Service 1
Pay Units: N.A.
Programming (via satellite): ART America; Cinemax; Flix; HBO; HITS (Headend In The Sky); Korean Channel; RTN; Saigon Broadcasting Television Network (SBTN); Showtime; Starz (multiplexed); Starz Encore (multiplexed); The Filipino Channel; The Movie Channel (multiplexed); TV Asia; TV5MONDE USA.
Fee: $39.95 installation; $15.00 monthly (each).

Video-On-Demand: Yes

Pay-Per-View
ESPN Now (delivered digitally); Hot Choice (delivered digitally); MLB Extra Innings (delivered digitally); iN DEMAND (delivered digitally); Playboy TV (delivered digitally); Fresh (delivered digitally); Shorteez (delivered digitally); Urban Xtra (delivered digitally); NBA League Pass (delivered digitally); NHL Center Ice (delivered digitally).

Internet Service
Operational: Yes.
Subscribers: 923,432.
Broadband Service: Comcast High Speed Internet.
Fee: $99.95 installation; $42.95 monthly.

Telephone Service
Digital: Operational
Subscribers: 459,945.
Fee: $44.95 monthly
Miles of Plant: 31,096.0 (coaxial); 3,704.0 (fiber optic). Homes passed: 1,863,091.
Area Senior Vice President: Len Rozek. Area Vice President: John Deitrech. Vice President, Engineering: Steve Tabor. Vice President, Marketing & Sales: Tom Pierce. Marketing Manager: Michelle Becker. Public Relations Director: Steve Kipp.
Ownership: Comcast Cable Communications Inc. (MSO).

SEATTLE—Formerly served by Sprint Corp. No longer in operation. ICA: WA0197.

SEATTLE (surrounding areas)—Wave Broadband, 401 Parkplace Center, Ste 500, Kirkland, WA 98033. Phones: 360-602-0183; 425-576-8200; 800-244-7591. Web Site: http://www.wavebroadband.com. Also serves Bellevue & Kenmore. ICA: WA0014.
Note: This system is an overbuild.
TV Market Ranking: 20 (Bellevue, Kenmore, SEATTLE (SURROUNDING AREAS)). Franchise award date: February 15, 1983. Franchise expiration date: N.A. Began: September 1, 1983.
Channel capacity: N.A. Channels available but not in use: N.A.

Basic Service
Subscribers: 7,651.
Programming (received off-air): KBTC-TV (PBS) Tacoma; KCPQ (Escape, FOX) Tacoma; KCTS-TV (PBS) Seattle; KFFV (Azteca America, COZI TV, MeTV) Seattle; KING-TV (NBC) Seattle; KIRO-TV (CBS, getTV, Retro TV) Seattle; KOMO-TV (ABC, This TV) Seattle; KONG (MundoMax) Everett; KSTW (CW, Decades) Tacoma; KTBW-TV (TBN) Tacoma; KUNS-TV (MundoMax, UNV) Bellevue; KWDK (Daystar TV, ETV) Tacoma; KWPX-TV (ION) Bellevue; KZJO (Antenna TV, MNT) Seattle; various Canadian stations.
Programming (via satellite): A&E; AMC; Animal Planet; BET; Bravo; Cartoon Network; CNBC; CNN; Comedy Central; Cooking Channel; C-SPAN; Discovery Channel; Disney Channel; E! HD; ESPN; ESPN2; EVINE Live; Food Network; Fox News Channel; Freeform; FX; HGTV; History; HLN; IFC; Lifetime; MSNBC; MTV; National Geographic Channel; Nickelodeon; Northwest Cable News; OWN: Oprah Winfrey Network; Pop; QVC; Spike TV; Syfy; TBS; Telemundo; The Weather Channel; TLC; TNT; Travel Channel; TVW; Univision Studios; USA Network; VH1; WE tv.
Fee: $29.95 installation; $25.95 monthly.

Digital Basic Service
Subscribers: N.A.
Programming (via satellite): BBC America; Discovery Digital Networks; DIY Network; DMX Music; ESPNews; Fox Sports 1; FSN Digital Atlantic; FSN Digital Central; FSN Digital Pacific; Golf Channel; NBCSN; Nick Jr.; Starz (multiplexed); Starz Encore (multiplexed); TeenNick; The Word Network.
Fee: $13.00 monthly.

Digital Pay Service 1
Pay Units: N.A.
Programming (via satellite): Cinemax (multiplexed); Flix; HBO (multiplexed); Showtime (multiplexed); Starz Encore (multiplexed); Sundance TV; The Movie Channel (multiplexed).
Fee: $5.50 monthly (each).

Video-On-Demand: Planned

Pay-Per-View
iN DEMAND; Fresh; special events.

Internet Service
Operational: Yes.
Subscribers: 8,746.
Broadband Service: Millennium Cable-Speed.
Fee: $19.95 installation; $29.95 monthly; $7.50 modem lease.

Telephone Service
Analog: Not Operational
Digital: Operational
Subscribers: 1,505.
Fee: $39.99 monthly
Miles of Plant: 243.0 (coaxial); 115.0 (fiber optic). Homes passed: 20,000.
Chief Financial Officer: Wayne Schattenkerk.
Ownership: WaveDivision Holdings LLC (MSO).

SEQUIM—Wave Broadband. Now served by PORT ANGELES, WA [WA0020]. ICA: WA0029.

SHELTON—Comcast Cable. Now served by SEATTLE, WA [WA0001]. ICA: WA0030.

SKAMOKAWA—Formerly served by Wright Cablevision. No longer in operation. ICA: WA0142.

SPANGLE—Formerly served by Elk River TV Cable Co. No longer in operation. ICA: WA0180.

SPOKANE—Comcast Cable, 19909 120th Ave NE, Ste 200, Bothell, WA 98021. Phone: 425-398-6000. Fax: 425-398-6236. Web Site: http://www.comcast.com. Also serves Airway Heights, Fairchild AFB, Liberty Lake, Millwood, Spokane County (portions) & Suncrest. ICA: WA0004.
TV Market Ranking: 76 (Airway Heights, Fairchild AFB, Liberty Lake, Millwood, SPOKANE, Spokane County (portions), Suncrest. Franchise award date: December 23, 1974. Franchise expiration date: N.A. Began: September 30, 1976.
Channel capacity: 72 (operating 2-way). Channels available but not in use: N.A.

Basic Service
Subscribers: 80,689.
Programming (received off-air): KAYU-TV (FOX, This TV) Spokane; KCDT (PBS) Coeur d'Alene; KHQ-TV (NBC) Spokane; KREM (CBS, TheCoolTV) Spokane; KSKN (CW) Spokane; KSPS-TV (PBS) Spokane; KXLY-TV (ABC, MeTV) Spokane.
Programming (via satellite): C-SPAN; C-SPAN 2; Hallmark Channel; Northwest Cable News; Pop; QVC; The Weather Channel; Trinity Broadcasting Network (TBN); TVW; WGN America.
Fee: $40.00 installation; $31.53 monthly.

Expanded Basic Service 1
Subscribers: N.A.
Programming (via satellite): A&E; AMC; Animal Planet; BET; Bravo; Cartoon Network; CMT; CNBC; CNN; Comedy Central; Discovery Channel; E! HD; ESPN; ESPN2; Food Network; Fox News Channel; Fox Sports 1; Freeform; FX; FXM; Golf Channel; HGTV; History; HLN; Jewelry Television; Lifetime; MSNBC; MTV; NBCSN; Nickelodeon; Spike TV; Syfy; TBS; TLC; TNT; Travel Channel; Turner Classic Movies; USA Network; VH1.
Fee: $30.50 monthly.

Digital Basic Service
Subscribers: N.A.
Programming (via satellite): BBC America; Discovery Digital Networks; Disney XD; DMX Music; ESPN Classic; ESPNews; Fuse; FYI; GSN; History International; HITS (Headend In The Sky); IFC; LMN; National Geographic Channel; Nick Jr.; Ovation; Starz Encore (multiplexed); Sundance TV; TeenNick; TV Land; WE tv.
Fee: $11.99 monthly.

Digital Pay Service 1
Pay Units: N.A.
Programming (via satellite): Cinemax (multiplexed); HBO (multiplexed); Showtime (multiplexed); Starz (multiplexed); The Movie Channel (multiplexed).
Fee: $3.00 installation; $15.00 monthly (each).

Video-On-Demand: Yes

Pay-Per-View
iN DEMAND (delivered digitally); Shorteez (delivered digitally); Playboy TV (delivered digitally).

Internet Service
Operational: Yes.
Subscribers: 91,525.
Broadband Service: Comcast High Speed Internet.
Fee: $42.95 monthly.

Telephone Service
Digital: Operational
Subscribers: 50,285.
Fee: $44.95 monthly
Miles of Plant: 3,425.0 (coaxial); 425.0 (fiber optic). Homes passed: 209,245.
Area Vice President: Ken Rhoades. Vice President, Engineering: Steve Tabor. Vice President, Sales & Marketing: Tom Pierce. General Manager: Kenneth Watts. Public Relations Director: Steve Kipp.
Ownership: Comcast Cable Communications Inc. (MSO).

Cable Systems—Washington

SPOKANE—Formerly served by Video Wave Television. No longer in operation. ICA: WA0190.

SPRAGUE—Formerly served by Elk River TV Cable Co. No longer in operation. ICA: WA0130.

SPRINGDALE—Formerly served by Elk River TV Cable Co. No longer in operation. ICA: WA0182.

ST. JOHN—St. John Cable Co. Inc, PO Box 268, St. John, WA 99171. Phone: 509-648-3322. Fax: 509-648-9900. E-mail: service@stjohncable.com. Web Site: http://www.stjohncable.com. Also serves Endicott & Lacrosse. ICA: WA0119.
TV Market Ranking: Below 100 (Endicott, Lacrosse, ST. JOHN). Franchise award date: N.A. Franchise expiration date: N.A. Began: January 1, 1983.
Channel capacity: 70 (operating 2-way). Channels available but not in use: N.A.
Basic Service
Subscribers: 283.
Programming (received off-air): KAYU-TV (FOX, This TV) Spokane; KGPX-TV (ION) Spokane; KHQ-TV (NBC) Spokane; KREM (CBS, TheCoolTV) Spokane; KSKN (CW) Spokane; KSPS-TV (PBS) Spokane; KUID-TV (PBS) Moscow; KWSU-TV (PBS) Pullman; KXLY-TV (ABC, MeTV) Spokane.
Programming (via satellite): A&E; AMC; Cartoon Network; CMT; CNBC; CNN; C-SPAN; C-SPAN 2; Discovery Channel; Disney Channel; E! HD; ESPN; ESPN Classic; ESPN2; Food Network; Fox News Channel; FOX Sports Networks; Freeform; HGTV; History; HLN; Lifetime; MTV; National Geographic Channel; Nickelodeon; Outdoor Channel; Spike TV; Syfy; TBS; TLC; TNT; Travel Channel; Turner Classic Movies; USA Network; VH1; WGN America.
Fee: $52.00 monthly.
Digital Basic Service
Subscribers: N.A.
Programming (via satellite): BBC America; Bravo; Discovery Digital Networks; DMX Music; ESPN Classic; ESPNews; Fox Sports 1; Fuse; FYI; Golf Channel; GSN; History International; IFC; LMN; National Geographic Channel; NBCSN; WE tv.
Fee: $15.00 monthly.
Pay Service 1
Pay Units: N.A.
Programming (via satellite): Cinemax; HBO.
Fee: $11.00 monthly.
Digital Pay Service 1
Pay Units: N.A.
Programming (via satellite): Cinemax (multiplexed); HBO (multiplexed); Showtime (multiplexed); Starz (multiplexed); Starz Encore (multiplexed); The Movie Channel (multiplexed).
Video-On-Demand: No
Pay-Per-View
iN DEMAND (delivered digitally); Playboy TV (delivered digitally).
Internet Service
Operational: Yes. Began: December 1, 2000.
Subscribers: 421.
Broadband Service: St. John Cable.
Fee: $30.00 monthly; $10.00 modem lease; $120.00 modem purchase.
Telephone Service
None
Miles of Plant: 53.0 (coaxial); 20.0 (fiber optic). Homes passed: 1,750.
General Manager: Greg Morasch. Chief Technician: Ole Olsen. Marketing Director: Donna Loomis.
Ownership: St. John Cable Co. Inc.

STARBUCK—Formerly served by Charter Communications. No longer in operation. ICA: WA0137.

SUDDEN VALLEY—Comcast Cable. Now served by BELLINGHAM, WA [WA0011]. ICA: WA0067.

SUMAS—City of Sumas TV Cable System, 433 Cherry St., PO Box 9, Sumas, WA 98295. Phone: 360-988-5711. Fax: 360-988-8855. Web Site: http://www.cityofsumas.com. ICA: WA0099.
TV Market Ranking: Below 100 (SUMAS). Franchise award date: N.A. Franchise expiration date: N.A. Began: March 1, 1953.
Channel capacity: N.A. Channels available but not in use: N.A.
Basic Service
Subscribers: 235.
Programming (received off-air): KCPQ (Escape, FOX) Tacoma; KCTS-TV (PBS) Seattle; KING-TV (NBC) Seattle; KIRO-TV (CBS, getTV, Retro TV) Seattle; KOMO-TV (ABC, This TV) Seattle; KONG (MundoMax) Everett; KVOS-TV (MeTV, Movies!) Bellingham; KZJO (Antenna TV, MNT) Seattle; 1 FM.
Programming (via satellite): A&E; CNN; C-SPAN; Discovery Channel; ESPN; FX; Hallmark Channel; HGTV; History; Nickelodeon; Northwest Cable News; Outdoor Channel; QVC; Spike TV; TBS; TLC; TNT; Trinity Broadcasting Network (TBN); Turner Classic Movies; TV Land.
Fee: $25.00 installation; $45.00 monthly.
Pay Service 1
Pay Units: 99.
Programming (via satellite): Showtime.
Fee: $15.00 installation; $8.00 monthly.
Video-On-Demand: No
Internet Service
Operational: No.
Telephone Service
None
Miles of Plant: 24.0 (coaxial); None (fiber optic). Homes passed: 500.
General Manager: Ruben Hernandez. Chief Technician: Brian Swanson. Deputy Clerk-Treasurer: Shelly Neitch.
Ownership: City of Sumas TV Cable System.

SUNCREST—Formerly served by TV Max. Now served by Comcast Cable, SPOKANE, WA [WA0004]. ICA: WA0086.

SUNNYSIDE—Charter Communications. Now served by YAKIMA, WA [WA0009]. ICA: WA0033.

TACOMA—Click! Network, 3628 South 35th St, Tacoma, WA 98409-3115. Phone: 253-502-8900. Fax: 253-502-8493. E-mail: customercare@click-network.com. Web Site: http://www.clickcabletv.com. Also serves Fife, Fircrest, Lakewood, Pierce County (portions) & University Place. ICA: WA0206. **Note:** This system is an overbuild.
TV Market Ranking: 20 (Fife, Fircrest, Lakewood, Pierce County (portions), TACOMA, University Place, University Place). Franchise award date: N.A. Franchise expiration date: N.A. Began: July 27, 1998.
Channel capacity: N.A. Channels available but not in use: N.A.

Basic Service
Subscribers: 18,276.
Programming (received off-air): KBTC-TV (PBS) Tacoma; KCPQ (Escape, FOX) Tacoma; KCTS-TV (PBS) Seattle; KFFV (Azteca America, COZI TV, MeTV) Seattle; KING-TV (NBC) Seattle; KIRO-TV (CBS, getTV, Retro TV) Seattle; KOMO-TV (ABC, This TV) Seattle; KONG (MundoMax) Everett; KSTW (CW, Decades) Tacoma; KTBW-TV (TBN) Tacoma; KUNS-TV (MundoMax, UNV) Bellevue; KWDK (Daystar TV, ETV) Tacoma; KWPX-TV (ION) Bellevue; KZJO (Antenna TV, MNT) Seattle.
Programming (via satellite): C-SPAN; Northwest Cable News; QVC; TVW.
Fee: $60.00 installation; $17.99 monthly.
Expanded Basic Service 1
Subscribers: N.A.
Programming (via satellite): A&E; AMC; Animal Planet; BBC America; BET; Bravo; Cartoon Network; CMT; CNBC; CNN; Comedy Central; C-SPAN 2; Discovery Channel; Disney Channel; Disney XD; E! HD; ESPN; ESPN2; Food Network; Fox News Channel; Fox Sports 1; Freeform; FX; FXM; Golf Channel; Hallmark Channel; HGTV; History; HLN; Lifetime; MSNBC; MTV; National Geographic Channel; NBCSN; Nickelodeon; Oxygen; Spike TV; Syfy; TBS; The Weather Channel; TLC; TNT; Travel Channel; truTV; Turner Classic Movies; TV Land; USA Network; various Canadian stations; VH1.
Fee: $37.50 monthly.
Digital Basic Service
Subscribers: N.A.
Programming (via satellite): Bloomberg Television; BYUtv; Cooking Channel; Discovery Digital Networks; DIY Network; ESPN Classic; ESPNews; EWTN Global Catholic Network; FOX College Sports Central; FOX College Sports Pacific; Fuse; FYI; Great American Country; GSN; History International; IFC; LMN; Nat Geo WILD; NFL Network; Nick Jr.; Nicktoons; Outdoor Channel; Starz Encore (multiplexed); TeenNick; The Word Network; WE tv.
Fee: $39.00 monthly.
Digital Expanded Basic Service
Subscribers: N.A.
Programming (via satellite): 3ABN; Boomerang; CBS Sports Network; C-SPAN 3; Fox Sports 2; Hallmark Channel; HRTV; Sprout; Tennis Channel; UP.
Fee: $5.99 monthly.
Digital Pay Service 1
Pay Units: N.A.
Programming (via satellite): Cinemax (multiplexed); Flix; HBO (multiplexed); Playboy TV; Showtime (multiplexed); Starz (multiplexed); Sundance TV; The Movie Channel (multiplexed).
Fee: $10.95 monthly (Cinemax), $11.25 monthly (Starz), $12.00 monthly (Playboy), $13.95 monthly (Flix, Showtime, Sundance, or TMC), $15.00 monthly (HBO).
Video-On-Demand: Yes
Pay-Per-View
Playboy TV; Fresh.

FULLY SEARCHABLE • CONTINUOUSLY UPDATED • DISCOUNT RATES FOR PRINT PURCHASERS
For more information call **800-771-9202** or visit **www.warren-news.com**

Internet Service
Operational: Yes. Began: December 1, 1999.
Subscribers: 18,627.
Broadband Service: Advanced Stream, HarborNet, Net-Venture.
Telephone Service
Digital: Operational
Subscribers: 626.
Miles of Plant: 1,454.0 (coaxial); 369.0 (fiber optic). Homes passed: 111,746.
General Manager: Tenzin Gyaltsen. Technical Operations Manager: Pat Bacon. Field Operations Manager: Rick Munson. Marketing Director: Diane Lachel. Network Services Manager: Terry Dillon. Ad Sales Manager: Carrie Harding.
Ownership: Tacoma Public Utilities.

TEKOA—Northstar Broadband, PO Box 2576, Post Falls, ID 83877. Phones: 208-262-9394; 800-572-0902. Fax: 208-262-9314. E-mail: j.webb@northstarbroadband.net. Web Site: http://www.northstarbroadband.net. ICA: WA0114.
TV Market Ranking: 76 (TEKOA). Franchise award date: N.A. Franchise expiration date: N.A. Began: February 1, 1975.
Channel capacity: 62 (2-way capable). Channels available but not in use: N.A.
Basic Service
Subscribers: 48.
Programming (received off-air): KAYU-TV (FOX, This TV) Spokane; KHQ-TV (NBC) Spokane; KREM (CBS, TheCoolTV) Spokane; KSKN (CW) Spokane; KSPS-TV (PBS) Spokane; KWSU-TV (PBS) Pullman; KXLY-TV (ABC, MeTV) Spokane; allband FM.
Programming (via satellite): A&E; Animal Planet; Cartoon Network; CMT; C-SPAN; C-SPAN 2; Discovery Channel; EVINE Live; EWTN Global Catholic Network; Food Network; Fox News Channel; Freeform; Hallmark Channel; HGTV; History; ION Television; Nickelodeon; Ovation; OWN; Oprah Winfrey Network; QVC; TBS; TLC; Travel Channel; Trinity Broadcasting Network (TBN); truTV; TV Land; TVW; WGN America.
Fee: $20.00 installation; $33.40 monthly.
Expanded Basic Service 1
Subscribers: N.A.
Programming (via satellite): AMC; Bravo; CNBC; CNN; Comedy Central; Disney Channel; Disney XD; E! HD; ESPN; ESPN Classic; ESPN2; Fox Sports 1; FX; FXM; HLN; Lifetime; MoviePlex; MSNBC; MTV; Northwest Cable News; Outdoor Channel; Spike TV; Syfy; TNT; Turner Classic Movies; USA Network; VH1.
Fee: $16.16 monthly.
Pay Service 1
Pay Units: N.A.
Programming (via satellite): Cinemax; HBO; Showtime.
Fee: $5.00 installation; $5.25 monthly (Cinemax), $8.65 monthly (Showtime), $9.60 monthly (HBO).
Video-On-Demand: No
Internet Service
Operational: Yes.

2017 Edition   **D-829**

Washington—Cable Systems

Telephone Service
None
Miles of Plant: 7.0 (coaxial); None (fiber optic). Homes passed: 441.
Office Manager: Jennifer Webb. Operations Manager: Greg Lundwall.
Ownership: Northstar Broadband LLC (MSO).

THORP—Formerly served by Wave Broadband. No longer in operation. ICA: WA0204.

TOLEDO—Formerly served by RGA Cable TV. No longer in operation. ICA: WA0107.

TULALIP INDIAN RESERVATION—
Tulalip Tribes Broadband, 8732 27th Ave Northeast, Tulalip, WA 98271. Phone: 360-716-3270. Fax: 360-716-3272. E-mail: cs@tulalipbroadband.net. Web Site: http://www.tulalipbroadband.com. ICA: WA0184.
TV Market Ranking: 20 (TULALIP INDIAN RESERVATION). Franchise award date: January 1, 1988. Franchise expiration date: N.A. Began: N.A.
Channel capacity: N.A. Channels available but not in use: N.A.
Basic Service
Subscribers: N.A.
Programming (received off-air): KCPQ (Escape, FOX) Tacoma; KCTS-TV (PBS) Seattle; KING-TV (NBC) Seattle; KIRO-TV (CBS, getTV, Retro TV) Seattle; KOMO-TV (ABC, This TV) Seattle; KONG (MundoMax) Everett; KSTW (CW, Decades) Tacoma; KTBW-TV (TBN) Tacoma; KVOS-TV (MeTV, Movies!) Bellingham; KZJO (Antenna TV, MNT) Seattle.
Programming (via satellite): A&E; AMC; Animal Planet; Bravo; Cartoon Network; CMT; CNN; Comedy Central; C-SPAN; C-SPAN 2; Discovery Channel; Disney Channel; ESPN; ESPN2; Food Network; Freeform; History; ION Television; Lifetime; MTV; National Geographic Channel; Nickelodeon; Northwest Cable News; Outdoor Channel; Pop; QVC; Spike TV; Syfy; TBS; TLC; TNT; Turner Classic Movies; TV Land; TVW; USA Network; VH1.
Fee: $78.00 installation; $2.00 converter.
Digital Basic Service
Subscribers: N.A.
Programming (via satellite): AZ TV; BBC America; Bloomberg Television; Cloo; CMT; Destination America; Discovery Kids Channel; Discovery Life Channel; Disney XD; DMX Music; ESPN Classic; ESPNews; Fox Sports 1; FXM; FYI; Golf Channel; GSN; HGTV; History International; IFC; Investigation Discovery; LMN; MTV Classic; MTV2; NBCSN; Nick Jr.; Ovation; OWN: Oprah Winfrey Network; Science Channel; TeenNick; VH1 Soul; WE tv.
Fee: $13.35 monthly.
Pay Service 1
Pay Units: N.A.
Programming (via satellite): HBO; Showtime.
Fee: $11.95 monthly (HBO), $10.95 monthly (Showtime).
Digital Pay Service 1
Pay Units: N.A.
Programming (via satellite): Cinemax (multiplexed); HBO (multiplexed); Showtime (multiplexed); Starz (multiplexed); Starz Encore (multiplexed); Sundance TV; The Movie Channel (multiplexed).
Video-On-Demand: No
Pay-Per-View
iN DEMAND (delivered digitally); Playboy TV (delivered digitally); Fresh (delivered digitally); Spice (delivered digitally); Spice 2 (delivered digitally).

Internet Service
Operational: Yes.
Fee: $40.95-$67.95 monthly.
Telephone Service
None
Miles of Plant: 100.0 (coaxial); None (fiber optic). Homes passed: 2,800.
Chief Engineer: Rick Dechenne. Office Supervisor: Angela M Miller. Director of Broadband Services: Richard A. Brown.
Ownership: The Tulalip Tribe Inc.

TWISP—Formerly served by Wave Broadband. No longer in operation. ICA: WA0101.

UNION—Hood Canal Communications, 300 East Dalby Rd, PO Box 249, Union, WA 98592. Phones: 800-356-9989; 360-898-2481. Fax: 360-898-2244. E-mail: info@hcc.net. Web Site: http://www.hcc.net. ICA: WA0052.
TV Market Ranking: 20 (UNION).
Channel capacity: N.A. Channels available but not in use: N.A.
Basic Service
Subscribers: 3,448.
Programming (received off-air): KTZZ; KBTC-TV (PBS) Tacoma; KCPQ (Escape, FOX) Tacoma; KCTS-TV (PBS) Seattle; KING-TV (NBC) Seattle; KIRO-TV (CBS, getTV, Retro TV) Seattle; KOMO-TV (ABC, This TV) Seattle; KONG (MundoMax) Everett; KSTW (CW, Decades) Tacoma.
Programming (via satellite): A&E; AMC; Cartoon Network; CNBC; CNN; Comedy Central; C-SPAN; Discovery Channel; E! HD; ESPN; Food Network; Fox News Channel; Freeform; History; HLN; ION Television; Lifetime; MTV; Nickelodeon; Northwest Cable News; Pop; QVC; Spike TV; Syfy; TBS; TLC; TNT; Trinity Broadcasting Network (TBN); TV Land; TVW; USA Network; VH1.
Fee: $35.00 installation; $56.95 monthly; $4.00 converter.
Digital Basic Service
Subscribers: N.A.
Programming (via satellite): BBC America; Bloomberg Television; Discovery Digital Networks; ESPN Classic; ESPN2; ESPNews; Fox Sports 1; FXM; FYI; Golf Channel; GSN; HGTV; History International; NBCSN; Nick Jr.; TeenNick; Turner Classic Movies; WE tv.
Fee: $10.00 monthly.
Digital Pay Service 1
Pay Units: N.A.
Programming (via satellite): Cinemax (multiplexed); HBO; Showtime (multiplexed); Starz (multiplexed); Starz Encore (multiplexed); The Movie Channel (multiplexed).
Fee: $7.00 monthly (Cinemax), $8.00 monthly (Showtime/TMC or Starz/Encore), $13.00 monthly (HBO).
Video-On-Demand: Yes
Pay-Per-View
Playboy TV (delivered digitally); Hot Network (delivered digitally); Spice (delivered digitally).
Internet Service
Operational: Yes. Began: March 1, 2001.
Broadband Service: In-house.
Fee: $26.95-$61.95 monthly.
Telephone Service
Digital: Operational
Fee: $22.00 monthly
Miles of Plant: 70.0 (coaxial); 100.0 (fiber optic).
President: Richard Buechel. Plant Supervisor: Mike Oblizalo. Marketing Director: Kellie Nielsen. Chief Technician: David Collins. Program Director: Kelle Oblizalo.
Ownership: Hood Canal Communications.

VADER—Formerly served by Millennium Digital Media. No longer in operation. ICA: WA0126.

VANCOUVER—Comcast Cable, 9605 Southwest Nimbus Ave, Beaverton, OR 97008-7198. Phone: 503-605-6000. Fax: 503-605-6226. Web Site: http://www.comcast.com. Also serves Battle Ground, Camas, Castle Rock, Clark County (portions), Cowlitz County (portions), Kalama, Kelso, La Center, Longview, Ridgefield, Toutle, Washougal & Woodland. ICA: WA0005.
TV Market Ranking: 29 (Battle Ground, Camas, Clark County (portions), Cowlitz County (portions) (portions), Kalama, La Center, Ridgefield, VANCOUVER, Washougal, Woodland); Below 100 (Cowlitz County (portions) (portions)); Outside TV Markets (Castle Rock, Kelso, Toutle, Longview, Cowlitz County (portions) (portions)). Franchise award date: November 26, 1981. Franchise expiration date: N.A. Began: October 1, 1982.
Channel capacity: N.A. Channels available but not in use: N.A.
Basic Service
Subscribers: 86,619.
Programming (received off-air): KATU (ABC, MeTV) Portland; KCTS-TV (PBS) Seattle; KGW (Estrella TV, NBC) Portland; KNMT (TBN) Portland; KOIN (CBS) Portland; KOPB-TV (PBS) Portland; KPDX (Escape, MNT) Vancouver; KPTV (COZI TV, FOX, Laff) Portland; KPXG-TV (ION) Salem; KRCW-TV (Antenna TV, CW, This TV) Salem.
Programming (via satellite): C-SPAN; C-SPAN 2; Discovery Channel; EVINE Live; Hallmark Channel; Pop; QVC; TVW; Univision Studios; WGN America.
Fee: $40.00 installation; $26.02 monthly; $1.60 converter.
Expanded Basic Service 1
Subscribers: N.A.
Programming (via satellite): A&E; AMC; Animal Planet; BET; Cartoon Network; CMT; CNBC; CNN; Comedy Central; Disney Channel; E! HD; ESPN; ESPN2; Food Network; Fox News Channel; Freeform; FX; Golf Channel; HGTV; History; HLN; International Television (ITV); Lifetime; MSNBC; MTV; Nickelodeon; Northwest Cable News; Oxygen; Spike TV; Syfy; TBS; The Weather Channel; TLC; TNT; Travel Channel; truTV; TV Land; USA Network; VH1.
Fee: $38.17 monthly.
Digital Basic Service
Subscribers: N.A.
Programming (via satellite): BBC America; Bloomberg Television; Bravo; Discovery Life Channel; Disney XD; DMX Music; ESPN Classic; ESPNews; EWTN Global Catholic Network; Fox Sports 1; FSN Digital Atlantic; FSN Digital Central; FSN Digital Pacific; Fuse; FXM; FYI; Great American Country; GSN; History International; HITS (Headend In The Sky); IFC; LMN; National Geographic Channel; NBCSN; Nick Jr.; Nicktoons; Outdoor Channel; Ovation; Sundance TV; TeenNick; The Word Network; Turner Classic Movies; WE tv; Weatherscan.
Fee: $10.95 monthly; $3.25 converter.
Digital Pay Service 1
Pay Units: N.A.
Programming (via satellite): Cinemax (multiplexed); Flix; HBO (multiplexed); RTN; Showtime (multiplexed); Starz (multiplexed); The Filipino Channel; The Movie Channel (multiplexed).
Fee: $18.05 monthly (each).
Video-On-Demand: Yes

Pay-Per-View
Fresh (delivered digitally); Sports PPV (delivered digitally); iN DEMAND (delivered digitally); Urban Xtra (delivered digitally); Shorteez (delivered digitally); Playboy TV (delivered digitally).
Internet Service
Operational: Yes.
Subscribers: 101,358.
Broadband Service: Comcast High Speed Internet.
Fee: $42.95 monthly; $3.00 modem lease.
Telephone Service
Digital: Operational
Subscribers: 54,010.
Fee: $44.95 monthly
Miles of Plant: 4,877.0 (coaxial); 627.0 (fiber optic). Homes passed: 215,272.
Vice President, Technical Operations: Mike Mason. Vice President, Marketing: Lars Lofas. General Manager: Hank Fore. Marketing Director: Brad Nosler. Public Relations Director: Theressa Davis. Ad Sales Manager: Tim Corken.
Ownership: Comcast Cable Communications Inc. (MSO).

WAITSBURG—Charter Communications. Now served by KENNEWICK, WA [WA0008]. ICA: WA0088.

WALLA WALLA—Charter Communications. Now served by KENNEWICK, WA [WA0008]. ICA: WA0016.

WARDEN—Northstar Broadband, PO Box 2576, Post Falls, ID 83877. Phones: 208-262-9394; 800-572-0902. Fax: 208-262-9314. E-mail: j.webb@northstarbroadband.net. Web Site: http://www.northstarbroadband.net. ICA: WA0185.
TV Market Ranking: Outside TV Markets (WARDEN).
Channel capacity: N.A. Channels available but not in use: N.A.
Basic Service
Subscribers: 91.
Programming (received off-air): KAYU-TV (FOX, This TV) Spokane; KEPR-TV (CBS, CW) Pasco; KHQ-TV (NBC) Spokane; KQUP (IND) Pullman; KREM (CBS, The CoolTV) Spokane; KSKN (CW) Spokane; KSPS-TV (PBS) Spokane; KXLY-TV (ABC, MeTV) Spokane.
Programming (via satellite): A&E; Animal Planet; Cartoon Network; CMT; C-SPAN; C-SPAN 2; Discovery Channel; EVINE Live; EWTN Global Catholic Network; Food Network; Fox News Channel; Freeform; Hallmark Channel; HGTV; History; ION Television; National Geographic Channel; Nickelodeon; OWN: Oprah Winfrey Network; Pop; QVC; TBS; TLC; Travel Channel; Trinity Broadcasting Network (TBN); truTV; TV Land; UniMas; Univision; Univision Studios; Vubiquity Inc.; WGN America.
Fee: $20.00 installation; $35.93 monthly; $1.00 converter.
Expanded Basic Service 1
Subscribers: N.A.
Programming (via satellite): AMC; Bravo; CNBC; CNN; Comedy Central; Disney Channel; Disney XD; E! HD; ESPN; ESPN2; Fox Sports 1; FX; FXM; HLN; Lifetime; MoviePlex; MSNBC; MTV; NBCSN; Northwest Cable News; Spike TV; Syfy; TNT; Turner Classic Movies; USA Network; VH1.
Fee: $5.00 installation; $15.15 monthly.
Pay Service 1
Pay Units: N.A.
Programming (via satellite): Cinemax; HBO; Showtime.

Fee: $5.00 installation; $5.25 monthly (Cinemax), $8.65 monthly (Showtime), $9.60 monthly (HBO).
Video-On-Demand: No
Internet Service
Operational: Yes, DSL.
Broadband Service: In-house.
Fee: $26.95 installation; $20.26 monthly; $2.00 modem lease; $25.00 modem purchase.
Telephone Service
None
Homes passed: 719.
Office Manager: Jennifer Webb. Operations Manager: Greg Lundwall.
Ownership: Northstar Broadband LLC (MSO).

WASHTUCNA—Formerly served by Charter Communications. No longer in operation. ICA: WA0134.

WATERVILLE—Formerly served by Wave Broadband. No longer in operation. ICA: WA0100.

WENATCHEE—Charter Communications, 12405 Powerscourt Dr, St. Louis, MO 63131. Phones: 636-207-5100 (Corporate office); 360-828-6700; 360-828-6600. Fax: 360-828-6795. Web Site: http://www.charter.com. Also serves Cashmere, Chelan County, Chewelah, Deer Lake, Douglas County, East Wenatchee, Leavenworth, Loon Lake, Okanogan, Okanogan County (unincorporated areas), Oroville & Rock Island. ICA: WA0015.
TV Market Ranking: 76 (Deer Lake, LOON LAKE); Below 100 (Chelan County (portions), Douglas County (portions)); Outside TV Markets (Cashmere, Chelan County (portions), Chewelah, Douglas County (portions), East Wenatchee, OKANOGAN, Okanogan County (unincorporated areas), OROVILLE, Rock Island, WENATCHEE). Franchise award date: January 1, 1953. Franchise expiration date: N.A. Began: August 1, 1953.
Channel capacity: N.A. Channels available but not in use: N.A.
Digital Basic Service
Subscribers: 9,024.
Programming (via satellite): 3ABN; A&E HD; AMC HD; Animal Planet HD; AXS TV; Bandamax; BBC America; Bloomberg Television; Boomerang; Bravo HD; BYUtv; Canal 22 Internacional; Cartoon Network HD; CBS Sports Network; Centric; Church Channel; Cine Mexicano; CMT; CNN en Espanol; CNN HD; CNN International; Comedy Central; Comedy Central HD; Cooking Channel; Daystar TV Network; De Pelicula; De Pelicula Clasico; Destination America; Discovery Channel HD; Discovery Family; Discovery Life Channel; Disney XD; Enlace USA; ESPN Clasico; ESPN Deportes; ESPN2 HD; ESPNews; ESPNU; FamilyNet; Food Network HD; Fox Business Network; FOX College Sports Central; FOX College Sports Pacific; Fox Life; Fox News HD; Fox Sports 2; Fuse; FX HD; FXM; FYI; Golf Channel HD; GolTV; Great American Country; Hallmark Movie Channel HD; HD Theater; HGTV HD; History en Espanol; History HD; History International; IFC; Infinito; INSP; Investigation Discovery; Jewelry Television; JUCE TV; Lifetime HD; LMN; LOGO; MavTV; MC; MLB Network HD; MTV Classic; MTV Hits; MTV Jams; MTV Live; mtvU; National Geographic Channel HD; NBC Universo; Nick Jr.; Nicktoons; Outdoor Channel; Outdoor Channel HD; OWN: Oprah Winfrey Network; Reelz; RFD-TV; Science Channel; Science HD; Smile of a Child TV; Smithsonian Channel HD; Sprout; Sundance TV; Syfy HD; TBS HD; TeenNick; Tennis Channel; The Sportsman Channel; The Weather Channel HD; TLC HD; TNT HD; Tr3s; Trinity Broadcasting Network (TBN); TVG Network; UniMas; Universal HD; Univision; UP; USA Network HD; Versus HD; VH1 Soul; VideoRola; WE tv; World Fishing Network.
Fee: $26.99 monthly.
Digital Expanded Basic Service
Subscribers: N.A.
Programming (via satellite): A&E; AMC; Animal Planet; BET; Bravo; Cartoon Network; CMT; CNBC; CNN; Comedy Central; Discovery Channel; Disney Channel; DIY Network; E! HD; ESPN; ESPN2; Flix; Food Network; Fox Deportes; Fox News Channel; Fox Sports 1; Freeform; FX; Golf Channel; GSN; Hallmark Channel; HGTV; History; HLN; Lifetime; MSNBC; MTV; MTV2; National Geographic Channel; NBCSN; Nickelodeon; Northwest Cable News; Oxygen; Root Sports Northwest; Spike TV; Syfy; TBS; Telemundo; TLC; TNT; Travel Channel; truTV; Turner Classic Movies; TV Land; TVW; USA Network; VH1.
Fee: $42.99 monthly.
Digital Pay Service 1
Pay Units: N.A.
Programming (via satellite): Cinemax (multiplexed); Cinemax HD; EPIX (multiplexed); HBO (multiplexed); HBO HD; Showtime (multiplexed); Showtime HD; Starz (multiplexed); Starz HD; The Movie Channel (multiplexed); The Movie Channel HD.
Fee: $13.15 monthly (Cinemax, HBO or Showtime).
Video-On-Demand: Yes
Pay-Per-View
iN DEMAND (delivered digitally); XTSY (delivered digitally); Playboy TV (delivered digitally); Fresh (delivered digitally); Spice: Xcess (delivered digitally).
Internet Service
Operational: Yes.
Broadband Service: Charter Internet.
Fee: $29.99 monthly.
Telephone Service
Digital: Operational
Fee: $29.99 monthly
Miles of Plant: 692.0 (coaxial); 142.0 (fiber optic). Homes passed: 38,219.
Vice President: Frank Antonovich. General Manager: Linda Kimberly. Technical Operations Director: Brian Lindholme. Marketing Director: Diane Long. Accounting Director: David Sovanski.
Ownership: Charter Communications Inc. (MSO).

WEST RICHLAND—Charter Communications. Now served by KENNEWICK, WA [WA0008]. ICA: WA0065.

WESTPORT—Comcast Cable. Now served by ABERDEEN, WA [WA0003]. ICA: WA0037.

WHIDBEY ISLAND—Wave Broadband, 401 Parkplace Center, Ste 500, Kirkland, WA 98033. Phones: 425-576-8200; 800-829-2225. Fax: 720-479-3585. E-mail: jpenney@wavebroadband.com. Web Site: http://www.wavebroadband.com. Also serves Greenbank. ICA: WA0186.
TV Market Ranking: 20 (Greenbank, WHIDBEY ISLAND). Franchise award date: January 1, 1990. Franchise expiration date: N.A. Began: February 1, 1991.
Channel capacity: N.A. Channels available but not in use: N.A.
Basic Service
Subscribers: 1,152.
Programming (received off-air): KCPQ (Escape, FOX) Tacoma; KCTS-TV (PBS) Seattle; KING-TV (NBC) Seattle; KIRO-TV (CBS, getTV, Retro TV) Seattle; KOMO-TV (ABC, This TV) Seattle; KONG (MundoMax) Everett; KSTW (CW, Decades) Tacoma; KTBW-TV (TBN) Tacoma; KVOS-TV (MeTV, Movies!) Bellingham; KWPX-TV (ION) Bellevue; KZJO (Antenna TV, MNT) Seattle.
Programming (via satellite): A&E; AMC; Cartoon Network; CNBC; CNN; Comedy Central; C-SPAN; Discovery Channel; Disney Channel; ESPN; ESPN2; Fox News Channel; Freeform; HGTV; HLN; Lifetime; Nickelodeon; QVC; Spike TV; Syfy; TLC; TNT; Trinity Broadcasting Network (TBN); Turner Classic Movies; USA Network.
Fee: $29.95 installation; $25.95 monthly.
Digital Basic Service
Subscribers: N.A.
Programming (via satellite): BBC America; Bloomberg Television; Bravo; Discovery Digital Networks; DMX Music; Fox Sports 1; Fuse; Golf Channel; GSN; History International; NBCSN; Outdoor Channel; Ovation; Trinity Broadcasting Network (TBN); WE tv.
Fee: $13.40 monthly.
Digital Pay Service 1
Pay Units: N.A.
Programming (via satellite): Cinemax (multiplexed); FXM; HBO (multiplexed); IFC; Showtime (multiplexed); Starz (multiplexed); Starz Encore (multiplexed); The Movie Channel (multiplexed).
Fee: $7.50 monthly (each).
Video-On-Demand: No
Pay-Per-View
ESPN Now; Hot Choice; iN DEMAND; Playboy TV; Fresh; Shorteez.
Internet Service
Operational: Yes.
Fee: $49.95 installation; $37.95 monthly.
Telephone Service
Digital: Operational
Fee: $49.99 monthly
Miles of Plant: 127.0 (coaxial); None (fiber optic). Homes passed: 1,600.
Chief Executive Officer: Steve Weed. Chief Financial Officer: Wayne Schattenkerk. President: Jim Penney. General Manager: Stephen J. George.
Ownership: WaveDivision Holdings LLC (MSO).

WILBUR—Formerly served by Northstar Broadband. No longer in operation. ICA: WA0102.

WILSON CREEK—Formerly served by Almega Cable. No longer in operation. ICA: WA0187.

WINLOCK—Comcast Cable, 410 Valley Ave NW, Ste 9, Puyallup, WA 98371. Phones: 253-864-4200; 425-398-6000 (Bothell office). Fax: 253-864-4352. Web Site: http://www.comcast.com. Also serves Lewis County (portions). ICA: WA0094.
TV Market Ranking: Outside TV Markets (WINLOCK). Franchise award date: N.A. Franchise expiration date: N.A. Began: December 1, 1971.
Channel capacity: N.A. Channels available but not in use: N.A.
Basic Service
Subscribers: 154.
Programming (received off-air): KCKA (PBS) Centralia; KCPQ (Escape, FOX) Tacoma; KCTS-TV (PBS) Seattle; KGW (Estrella TV, NBC) Portland; KING-TV (NBC) Seattle; KIRO-TV (CBS, getTV, Retro TV) Seattle; KOIN (CBS) Portland; KOMO-TV (ABC, This TV) Seattle; KPTV (COZI TV, FOX, Laff) Portland; KSTW (CW, Decades) Tacoma; allband FM.
Programming (via satellite): A&E; AMC; Animal Planet; BET; Cartoon Network; CMT; CNBC; CNN; Comedy Central; Discovery Channel; Disney Channel; E! HD; ESPN; Food Network; Fox News Channel; Freeform; Hallmark Channel; HLN; Lifetime; MSNBC; MTV; Nickelodeon; Northwest Cable News; QVC; Spike TV; TBS; TLC; TNT; Travel Channel; truTV; Univision Studios; USA Network; VH1.
Fee: $40.00 installation; $29.00 monthly.
Digital Basic Service
Subscribers: N.A.
Programming (via satellite): BBC America; Bravo; Discovery Life Channel; Disney XD; DMX Music; ESPN Classic; ESPN2; ESPNews; Fuse; FYI; Golf Channel; Great American Country; GSN; HGTV; History; History International; HITS (Headend In The Sky); IFC; LMN; MoviePlex; National Geographic Channel; NBCSN; Nick Jr.; Nicktoons; Sprout; Sundance TV; Syfy; TeenNick; The Word Network; Trinity Broadcasting Network (TBN); Turner Classic Movies; TV Land; WE tv.
Digital Pay Service 1
Pay Units: N.A.
Programming (via satellite): Cinemax (multiplexed); HBO (multiplexed); Showtime (multiplexed); Starz (multiplexed); Starz Encore (multiplexed); The Movie Channel (multiplexed).
Video-On-Demand: No
Pay-Per-View
Special events (delivered digitally); Fresh (delivered digitally); Shorteez (delivered digitally); Playboy TV (delivered digitally).
Internet Service
Operational: No.
Telephone Service
Digital: Operational
Miles of Plant: 14.0 (coaxial); None (fiber optic). Homes passed: 582.
Area Vice President: Anne McMullen. Vice President, Sales & Marketing: Tom Pierce. Vice President, Engineering: Steve Tabor. Public Relations Director: Steve Kipp.
Ownership: Comcast Cable Communications Inc. (MSO).

WISHRAM—Formerly served by J & N Cable. No longer in operation. ICA: WA0188.

Washington—Cable Systems

YACOLT—J & N Cable, 614 South Columbus Ave, Goldendale, WA 98620-9006. Phones: 800-752-9809; 509-773-5359. Fax: 509-773-7090. E-mail: customersupport@jncable.net. Web Site: http://www.jncable.com. ICA: WA0110.
TV Market Ranking: 29 (YACOLT). Franchise award date: November 1, 1988. Franchise expiration date: N.A. Began: July 1, 1989.
Channel capacity: N.A. Channels available but not in use: N.A.

Basic Service
Subscribers: N.A.
Programming (received off-air): KATU (ABC, MeTV) Portland; KGW (Estrella TV, NBC) Portland; KOIN (CBS) Portland; KOPB-TV (PBS) Portland; KPDX (Escape, MNT) Vancouver; KPTV (COZI TV, FOX, Laff) Portland; KRCW-TV (Antenna TV, CW, This TV) Salem.
Programming (via satellite): A&E; AMC; Animal Planet; Cartoon Network; CNBC; CNN; Comedy Central; C-SPAN; Discovery Channel; Disney Channel; DIY Network; ESPN; ESPN2; ESPNews; EVINE Live; EWTN Global Catholic Network; FamilyNet; Food Network; Fox News Channel; Fox Sports 1; FOX Sports Networks; Freeform; Great American Country; Hallmark Channel; HGTV; History; HLN; Lifetime; MSNBC; Northwest Cable News; Outdoor Channel; QVC; Syfy; TBS; The Weather Channel; TLC; TNT; Travel Channel; Trinity Broadcasting Network (TBN); truTV; Turner Classic Movies; USA Network.
Fee: $39.95 installation; $15.95 monthly.

Pay Service 1
Pay Units: N.A.
Programming (via satellite): HBO (multiplexed); Showtime (multiplexed); The Movie Channel.
Fee: $10.95 monthly (each).

Video-On-Demand: No

Internet Service
Operational: No.

Telephone Service
None

Miles of Plant: 4.0 (coaxial); None (fiber optic). Homes passed: 300.
President & General Manager: John Kusky. Vice President & Marketing Manager: Nancy Kusky.
Ownership: J & N Cable Systems Inc. (MSO).

YAKIMA—Charter Communications, 1005 N 16th St, Yakima, WA 98902. Phones: 636-207-5100 (Corporate office); 589-783-0132 (Kennewick office); 509-225-9645. Web Site: http://www.charter.com. Also serves Grandview, Granger, Mabton, Moxee City, Prosser, Selah, Sunnyside, Toppenish, Union Gap, Wapato, Yakima County (portions), Yakima Indian Reservation & Zillah. ICA: WA0009.
TV Market Ranking: Below 100 (Grandview, Granger, Mabton, Moxee City, Prosser, Selah, Sunnyside, Toppenish, Union Gap, Wapato, YAKIMA, Yakima County (portions), Yakima Indian Reservation, Zillah). Franchise award date: January 1, 1963. Franchise expiration date: N.A. Began: November 1, 1979.
Channel capacity: N.A. Channels available but not in use: N.A.

Digital Basic Service
Subscribers: 19,880.
Programming (via satellite): AXS TV; BBC America; Bloomberg Television; Boomerang; BYUtv; CNN en Espanol; CNN International; Discovery Life Channel; ESPN; ESPN Classic; ESPNews; FOX College Sports Central; FOX College Sports Pacific; Fox Deportes; Fox Sports 2; Fuse; FXM; FYI; Great American Country; GSN; History International; IFC; International Television (ITV); LMN; MC; NFL Network; Nick 2; Nick Jr.; Nicktoons; Sundance TV; TeenNick; Turner Classic Movies.
Fee: $49.99 installation; $26.99 monthly.

Digital Expanded Basic Service
Subscribers: N.A.
Programming (via satellite): A&E; AMC; Animal Planet; BET; Bravo; Cartoon Network; CMT; CNBC; CNN; Comedy Central; Discovery Channel; Disney Channel; Disney XD; DIY Network; E! HD; ESPN; ESPN2; Food Network; Fox News Channel; Fox Sports 1; Freeform; FX; Golf Channel; Hallmark Channel; HGTV; History; HLN; Lifetime; MSNBC; MTV; MTV2; National Geographic Channel; NBCSN; Nickelodeon; Northwest Cable News; Outdoor Channel; Oxygen; Spike TV; Syfy; TBS; The Weather Channel; TLC; TNT; Travel Channel; truTV; TV Land; Univision; USA Network; VH1; WE tv.
Fee: $50.99 monthly.

Digital Pay Service 1
Pay Units: N.A.
Programming (via satellite): Cinemax (multiplexed); HBO (multiplexed); Starz (multiplexed).

Video-On-Demand: Yes

Internet Service
Operational: Yes. Began: April 1, 2001.
Subscribers: 23,061.
Broadband Service: Charter Internet.
Fee: $29.99 monthly.

Telephone Service
Digital: Operational
Subscribers: 5,442.
Fee: $29.99 monthly

Miles of Plant: 1,522.0 (coaxial); 593.0 (fiber optic). Homes passed: 77,945. Miles of plant included in Kennewick
General Manager: Randy Lee. Technical Operations Manager: Jeff Hopkins. Marketing Director: Diane Long. Program Director: Lloyd Swain. Office Manager: Cathy Von Essen. Senior Accounting Director: Steve Lottmann.
Ownership: Charter Communications Inc. (MSO).

YAKIMA—Formerly served by Wireless Broadcasting Systems of Yakima Inc. No longer in operation. ICA: WA0191.

WEST VIRGINIA

Total Systems: 58	Communities with Applications: 0
Total Communities Served: 677	Number of Basic Subscribers: 318,914
Franchises Not Yet Operating: 0	Number of Expanded Basic Subscribers: 4,246
Applications Pending: 0	Number of Pay Units: 715

Top 100 Markets Represented: Charleston-Huntington (36); Wheeling, WV-Steubenville, OH (90).

For a list of cable communities in this section, see the Cable Community Index located in the back of Cable Volume 2.
For explanation of terms used in cable system listings, see p. D-11.

ALDERSON—Formerly served by Charter Communications. Now served by Suddenlink Communications, BECKLEY, WV [WV0005]. ICA: WV0091.

ALUM BRIDGE—Shentel. Now served by WESTON, WV [WV0034]. ICA: WV0119.

ANSTED—Shentel. Now served by SUMMERSVILLE, WV [WV0213]. ICA: WV0245.

ANTHONY CREEK—Crystal Broadband Networks, PO Box 180336, Chicago, IL 60618. Phones: 817-685-9588; 630-206-0447. E-mail: sales@crystalbn.com. Web Site: http://crystalbn.com. Also serves White Sulphur Springs. ICA: WV0254.
TV Market Ranking: Below 100 (ANTHONY CREEK, White Sulphur Springs).
Channel capacity: N.A. Channels available but not in use: N.A.
Basic Service
Subscribers: N.A.
Programming (received off-air): WFXR (CW, FOX) Roanoke; WOAY-TV (ABC) Oak Hill; WSWP-TV (PBS) Grandview; WVNS-TV (CBS, FOX) Lewisburg; WVVA (CW, MeTV, NBC) Bluefield.
Programming (via satellite): A&E; AMC; CMT; CNN; C-SPAN; Discovery Channel; Disney Channel; ESPN; ESPN2; Freeform; FX; Golf Channel; Lifetime; Nickelodeon; QVC; Spike TV; TBS; TLC; TNT; Trinity Broadcasting Network (TBN); USA Network; VH1; WGN America.
Fee: $39.95 installation; $55.34 monthly.
Digital Basic Service
Subscribers: N.A.
Programming (via satellite): BBC America; Bloomberg Television; Bravo; Discovery Digital Networks; ESPN Classic; ESPNews; Fox Sports 1; FXM; GSN; HGTV; History; IFC; MC; National Geographic Channel; NBCSN; Nick Jr.; Nicktoons; Outdoor Channel; Turner Classic Movies; WE tv.
Fee: $11.00 monthly.
Digital Pay Service 1
Pay Units: N.A.
Programming (via satellite): Cinemax (multiplexed); HBO (multiplexed); Showtime (multiplexed); Starz (multiplexed); Starz Encore (multiplexed); The Movie Channel (multiplexed).
Fee: $15.95 monthly (each).
Video-On-Demand: No
Pay-Per-View
Hits Movies & Events (delivered digitally); Fresh (delivered digitally).
Internet Service
Operational: No.
Telephone Service
None
General Manager: Ron Page. Program Manager: Shawn Smith.
Ownership: Crystal Broadband Networks (MSO).

APPLE GROVE—Formerly served by Vital Communications. No longer in operation. ICA: WV0186.

ARNETTSVILLE—Formerly served by Adelphia Communications. No longer in operation. ICA: WV0046.

ASBURY—Formerly served by Vital Communications. No longer in operation. ICA: WV0255.

AUBURN—Formerly served by Cebridge Connections. No longer in operation. ICA: WV0161.

AUGUSTA—Comcast Cable. Now served by KEYSER, WV [WV0020]. ICA: WV0117.

BALLARD—Formerly served by Vital Communications. No longer in operation. ICA: WV0113.

BECKLEY—Suddenlink Communications, 520 Maryville Centre Dr, Ste 300, St. Louis, MO 63141. Phones: 314-315-9400; 304-757-8001 (Scott Depot office). E-mail: Gene.Regan@suddenlink.com. Web Site: http://www.suddenlink.com. Also serves Giles County (portions), Glen Lyn, Narrows, Pearisburg, Pembroke & Rich Creek, VA; Alderson, Ameagle, Athens, Bradley, Colcord, Dorothy, Fayette County (portions), Fayetteville, Greenbrier County (portions), Hinton, Lansing, Lester, Lewisburg, Mabscott, Matoaka, Mercer County (portions), Monroe County, Mount Hope, Nimitz, Oak Hill, Pax, Peterstown, Pipestem, Princeton, Quinwood, Rainelle, Raleigh County (portions), Rhodell, Rupert, Sophia, Speedway, Stephenson, Summers County (unincorporated areas), White Sulphur Springs, Wyco & Wyoming County (portions), WV. ICA: WV0005.
TV Market Ranking: 36 (Fayette County (portions), Fayetteville); 70 (Giles County (portions)); Below 100 (Alderson, Ameagle, BECKLEY, Bradley, Colcord, Dorothy, Glen Lyn, Greenbrier County (portions), Hinton, Lansing, Lester, Lewisburg, Mabscott, Mercer County (portions), Monroe County, Mount Hope, Narrows, Nimitz, Oak Hill, Pax, Pearisburg, Pembroke, Peterstown, Pipestem, Quinwood, Rainelle, Rhodell, Rich Creek, Rupert, Sophia, Speedway, Stephenson, Summers County (unincorporated areas), White Sulphur Springs, Wyco). Franchise award date: N.A. Franchise expiration date: N.A. Began: October 1, 1964.
Channel capacity: 24 (operating 2-way). Channels available but not in use: N.A.
Basic Service
Subscribers: 40,364.
Programming (received off-air): WCHS-TV (ABC, Antenna TV) Charleston; WLFB (IND) Bluefield; WOAY-TV (ABC) Oak Hill; WSAZ-TV (MNT, NBC, This TV) Huntington; WSWP-TV (PBS) Grandview; WVAH-TV (FOX, The Country Network) Charleston; WVNS-TV (CBS, FOX) Lewisburg; WVVA (CW, MeTV, NBC) Bluefield; allband FM.
Programming (via satellite): C-SPAN; C-SPAN 2; EVINE Live; INSP; ION Television; Pop; QVC; Trinity Broadcasting Network (TBN).
Fee: $22.99 monthly.
Expanded Basic Service 1
Subscribers: N.A.
Programming (via satellite): A&E; AMC; Animal Planet; BET; Bravo; Cartoon Network; CMT; CNBC; CNN; Comedy Central; Discovery Channel; Disney Channel; Disney XD; E! HD; ESPN; ESPN2; Food Network; Fox News Channel; Fox Sports 1; Freeform; FX; Golf Channel; GSN; Hallmark Channel; HGTV; History; HLN; Lifetime; MSNBC; MTV; National Geographic Channel; NBCSN; Nickelodeon; Outdoor Channel; Oxygen; Root Sports Pittsburgh; Spike TV; Syfy; TBS; The Weather Channel; TLC; TNT; Travel Channel; truTV; Turner Classic Movies; TV Land; USA Network; VH1; WE tv.
Fee: $15.00 installation; $9.53 monthly.
Digital Basic Service
Subscribers: N.A.
Programming (via satellite): BBC America; Bloomberg Television; CBS Sports Network; Discovery Digital Networks; DIY Network; ESPN; ESPN Classic; ESPNews; FOX College Sports Central; FOX College Sports Pacific; Fox Deportes; Fox Sports 2; Fuse; FXM; FYI; Great American Country; HD Theater; History International; IFC; LMN; MC; NFL Network; Nick 2; Nick Jr.; Nicktoons; Sundance TV; TeenNick; TNT HD; TVG Network.
Digital Pay Service 1
Pay Units: N.A.
Programming (via satellite): Cinemax (multiplexed); Cinemax HD; Flix; HBO (multiplexed); HBO HD; LOGO; Showtime (multiplexed); Showtime HD; Starz (multiplexed); Starz Encore (multiplexed); Starz HD; The Movie Channel (multiplexed).
Video-On-Demand: Yes
Pay-Per-View
Playboy TV (delivered digitally); Fresh (delivered digitally); Shorteez (delivered digitally); iN DEMAND (delivered digitally); NHL Center Ice (delivered digitally); MLB Extra Innings (delivered digitally).
Internet Service
Operational: Yes.
Subscribers: 38,647.
Broadband Service: Suddenlink High Speed Internet.
Fee: $49.95 installation; $29.99 monthly.
Telephone Service
Digital: Operational
Subscribers: 26,992.
Miles of Plant: 1,856.0 (coaxial); 808.0 (fiber optic). Homes passed: 79,372.
Senior Vice President, Corporate Finance: Michael Pflantz. Vice President, Operations: David Bach. General Manager: Jack Ozminkowski. Marketing Director: Stan Howell. Technical Operations Director: Bob Legg. Technical Operations Manager: Ron Noor. Marketing Manager: Kenny Phillips. Office Manager: Susan Winston.
Ownership: Cequel Communications Holdings I LLC (MSO).

BEECH BOTTOM—Blue Devil Cable TV Inc, 116 South 4th St, Toronto, OH 43964-1368. Phones: 740-537-2030; 800-931-9392. Fax: 740-537-2802. Web Site: http://bluedevilcabletv.com. ICA: WV0114.
TV Market Ranking: 90 (BEECH BOTTOM). Franchise award date: N.A. Franchise expiration date: N.A. Began: January 1, 1952.
Channel capacity: 30 (not 2-way capable). Channels available but not in use: N.A.
Basic Service
Subscribers: 85.
Programming (received off-air): KDKA-TV (CBS, Decades) Pittsburgh; WNPB-TV (PBS) Morgantown; WPGH-TV (Antenna TV, FOX, The Country Network) Pittsburgh; WPXI (MeTV, NBC) Pittsburgh; WQED (PBS) Pittsburgh; WTAE-TV (ABC, This TV) Pittsburgh; WTOV-TV (MeTV, NBC) Steubenville; WTRF-TV (ABC, CBS, MNT) Wheeling; allband FM.
Programming (via satellite): CNN; ESPN; TBS; USA Network.
Fee: $25.00 installation; $8.00 monthly.
Pay Service 1
Pay Units: N.A.
Programming (via satellite): HBO.
Fee: $15.90 installation; $10.60 monthly.
Video-On-Demand: Planned
Internet Service
Operational: Yes.
Telephone Service
Digital: Operational
Miles of Plant: 10.0 (coaxial); None (fiber optic). Homes passed: 450.
Vice President: Joann Conner. General Manager: Bob Loveridge.
Ownership: Blue Devil Cable TV Inc. (MSO).

BEECH CREEK—Shentel, Shentel Center, 500 Shentel Way, Edinburg, VA 22824. Phones: 540-984-5224; 304-946-2871. Fax: 540-984-3438. E-mail: Angela.Washington@emp.shentel.com. Web Site: http://www.shentel.com. ICA: WV0272.
TV Market Ranking: Below 100 (BEECH CREEK).
Channel capacity: N.A. Channels available but not in use: N.A.
Basic Service
Subscribers: 111.
Programming (received off-air): WCHS-TV (ABC, Antenna TV) Charleston; WKPI-TV

2017 Edition   D-833

West Virginia—Cable Systems

(PBS) Pikeville; WOWK-TV (CBS) Huntington; WSAZ-TV (MNT, NBC, This TV) Huntington; WVPB-TV (PBS) Huntington; WVVA (CW, MeTV, NBC) Bluefield.
Programming (via satellite): QVC; TBS; Trinity Broadcasting Network (TBN); WGN America.
Fee: $40.00 installation; $26.57 monthly.

Expanded Basic Service 1
Subscribers: N.A.
Programming (via satellite): A&E; AMC; Animal Planet; Boomerang; Cartoon Network; CMT; CNN; Comedy Central; Discovery Channel; ESPN; ESPN2; Family Friendly Entertainment; FamilyNet; Fox Sports 1; Freeform; FX; Hallmark Channel; HGTV; History; HLN; Lifetime; Nickelodeon; Outdoor Channel; Spike TV; Syfy; The Weather Channel; TLC; TNT; TV Land; USA Network; VH1.
Fee: $27.45 monthly.

Pay Service 1
Pay Units: N.A. Included in Omar.
Programming (via satellite): HBO; Showtime; The Movie Channel.
Fee: $10.01 monthly (TMC), $10.54 monthly (Showtime) $12.66 monthly (HBO).

Internet Service
Operational: Yes.

Telephone Service
None
Homes passed & miles of plant included in Omar.
Operations Manager: Allen Siers. Vice President, Customer Service: Angela Washington.
Ownership: Colane Cable TV Inc. (MSO).

BELINGTON—Shentel, 500 Shentel Way, PO Box 459, Edinburg, VA 22824. Phones: 800-743-6835; 540-984-5224. Fax: 540-984-3438. E-mail: customer_service@shentel.net. Web Site: http://www.shentel.com. Also serves Barbour County & Junior. ICA: WV0077.
TV Market Ranking: Below 100 (Barbour County, BELINGTON, Junior). Franchise award date: N.A. Franchise expiration date: N.A. Began: June 1, 1956.
Channel capacity: N.A. Channels available but not in use: N.A.

Basic Service
Subscribers: 37.
Programming (received off-air): WBOY-TV (ABC, NBC) Clarksburg; WDTV (CBS) Weston; WNPB-TV (PBS) Morgantown; WTAE-TV (ABC, This TV) Pittsburgh; WVFX (CW, FOX) Clarksburg; allband FM.
Programming (via satellite): C-SPAN; C-SPAN 2; QVC; TV Guide Interactive Inc.
Fee: $49.95 installation; $31.27 monthly.

Expanded Basic Service 1
Subscribers: N.A.
Programming (via satellite): A&E; AMC; Animal Planet; Cartoon Network; CMT; CNBC; CNN; Comedy Central; Discovery Channel; Disney Channel; DMX Music; E! HD; ESPN; ESPN2; Fox News Channel; Fox Sports 1; Freeform; FX; HGTV; History; HLN; INSP; Lifetime; MTV; Nickelodeon; Oxygen; Root Sports Pittsburgh; Spike TV; TBS; The Weather Channel; TLC; TNT; Travel Channel; TV Land; USA Network; VH1.
Fee: $34.00 monthly.

Digital Basic Service
Subscribers: N.A.
Fee: $13.00 monthly.
Video-On-Demand: No

Pay-Per-View
Fresh (delivered digitally); Shorteez (delivered digitally); Playboy TV (delivered digitally); iN DEMAND (delivered digitally).

Internet Service
Operational: No.

Telephone Service
None
Miles of Plant: 25.0 (coaxial); None (fiber optic). Homes passed: 1,115.
Vice President, Industry Affairs & Regulations: Chris Kyle. Assistant Secretary, Associate General Counsel: Ann Flowers.
Ownership: Shentel (MSO).

BENS CREEK—Formerly served by Charter Communications. Now served by Colane Cable TV Inc., OMAR, WV [WV0191]. ICA: WV0135.

BERGOO—Formerly served by Charter Communications. Now served by Shentel, SUMMERSVILLE, WV [WV0213]. ICA: WV0163.

BETHANY—Comcast Cable. Now served by WHEELING, WV [WV0004]. ICA: WV0152.

BEVERLY—Suddenlink Communications, 520 Maryville Centre Dr, Ste 300, St. Louis, MO 63141. Phones: 304-636-2239; 314-315-9400. E-mail: Gene.Regan@suddenlink.com. Web Site: http://www.suddenlink.com. Also serves Dailey, East Dailey, Elkins, Hazelwood, Huttonsville, Mill Creek, Montrose, Randolph County (portions) & Valley Bend. ICA: WV0015.
TV Market Ranking: Below 100 (BEVERLY, Dailey, East Dailey, Elkins, Hazelwood, Huttonsville, Mill Creek, Randolph County (portions), Valley Bend); Outside TV Markets (Montrose). Franchise award date: December 14, 1979. Franchise expiration date: N.A. Began: December 1, 1979.
Channel capacity: 72 (operating 2-way). Channels available but not in use: N.A.

Basic Service
Subscribers: 4,546.
Programming (received off-air): KDKA-TV (CBS, Decades) Pittsburgh; WBOY-TV (ABC, NBC) Clarksburg; WCHS-TV (ABC, Antenna TV) Charleston; WDTV (CBS) Weston; WNPB-TV (PBS) Morgantown; WTAE-TV (ABC, This TV) Pittsburgh; WTRF-TV (ABC, CBS, MNT) Wheeling; WVFX (CW, FOX) Clarksburg.
Programming (via satellite): Classic Arts Showcase; C-SPAN; EWTN Global Catholic Network; Pop; QVC; The Weather Channel; Trinity Broadcasting Network (TBN); WGN America.
Fee: $22.99 monthly; $2.27 converter.

Expanded Basic Service 1
Subscribers: N.A.
Programming (via satellite): A&E; AMC; Animal Planet; BET; Cartoon Network; CNBC; CNN; Comedy Central; C-SPAN 2; Discovery Channel; Disney Channel; E! HD; ESPN; ESPN Classic; ESPN2; Food Network; Fox News Channel; Fox Sports 1; Freeform; FX; Great American Country; GSN; Hallmark Channel; HGTV; History; HLN; INSP; Lifetime; MSNBC; MTV; National Geographic Channel; Nickelodeon; Outdoor Channel; Root Sports Pittsburgh; Spike TV; Syfy; TBS; TLC; TNT; Travel Channel; TV Land; USA Network; VH1; WE tv.
Fee: $24.50 monthly.

Digital Basic Service
Subscribers: N.A.
Programming (via satellite): BBC America; Bloomberg Television; Discovery Digital Networks; Disney XD; DMX Music; ESPN News; EVINE Live; FOX College Sports Central; FOX College Sports Pacific; Fuse; FXM; FYI; Golf Channel; History International; IFC; LMN; NBCSN; Turner Classic Movies.
Fee: $13.95 monthly.

Pay Service 1
Pay Units: N.A.
Programming (via satellite): Cinemax; HBO; Showtime; The Movie Channel.
Fee: $17.50 installation; $7.95 monthly (Cinemax), $11.95 monthly (Showtime or HBO).

Digital Pay Service 1
Pay Units: N.A.
Programming (via satellite): Cinemax (multiplexed); HBO (multiplexed); Showtime (multiplexed); Starz (multiplexed); Starz Encore (multiplexed); The Movie Channel (multiplexed).
Video-On-Demand: No

Pay-Per-View
iN DEMAND (delivered digitally); Playboy TV (delivered digitally); Fresh (delivered digitally).

Internet Service
Operational: Yes. Began: April 26, 2004.
Subscribers: 4,620.
Broadband Service: Suddenlink High Speed Internet.
Fee: $49.95 installation; $29.99 monthly.

Telephone Service
Digital: Operational
Subscribers: 2,920.
Fee: $49.99 monthly
Miles of Plant: 221.0 (coaxial); 83.0 (fiber optic). Homes passed: 8,352.
Senior Vice President, Corporate Finance: Michael Pflantz. General Manager: Peter Brown.
Ownership: Cequel Communications Holdings I LLC (MSO).

BIRCH RIVER—Formerly served by Vital Communications. No longer in operation. ICA: WV0090.

BLUEFIELD—Comcast Cable, 1794 Old Gray Station Rd, Gray, TN 37615-3869. Phones: 423-282-1370; 866-922-0069; 866-774-3128. Fax: 423-283-4855. Web Site: http://www.comcast.com. Also serves Bland County (portions), Bluefield, Pocahontas, Rocky Gap & Tazewell County (portions), VA; Bluewell, Bramwell, Green Valley & Mercer County (portions), WV. ICA: WV0007.
TV Market Ranking: Below 100 (Bland County (portions), Bluefield, BLUEFIELD, Bluewell, Bramwell, Green Valley, Mercer County (portions), Pocahontas, Rocky Gap, Tazewell County (portions)). Franchise award date: February 26, 1954. Franchise expiration date: N.A. Began: January 1, 1956.
Channel capacity: N.A. Channels available but not in use: N.A.

Basic Service
Subscribers: 8,038. Commercial subscribers: 521.
Programming (received off-air): WBRA-TV (PBS) Roanoke; WDBJ (CBS, Decades, MNT) Roanoke; WLFB (IND) Bluefield; WOAY-TV (ABC) Oak Hill; WSWP-TV (PBS) Grandview; WVNS-TV (CBS, FOX) Lewisburg; WVVA (CW, MeTV, NBC) Bluefield.
Programming (via satellite): C-SPAN; ION Television; QVC; TBS.
Fee: $32.00-$49.95 installation; $24.20 monthly.

Expanded Basic Service 1
Subscribers: N.A.
Programming (via satellite): A&E; AMC; Animal Planet; BET; Cartoon Network; CMT; CNBC; CNN; Comcast/Charter Sports Southeast (CSS); Comedy Central; Discovery Channel; E! HD; ESPN; ESPN2; Food Network; Fox News Channel; Fox Sports 1; Freeform; FX; Golf Channel; Great American Country; GSN; Hallmark Channel; HGTV; History; HLN; Lifetime; MTV; NBCSN; Nickelodeon; OWN; Oprah Winfrey Network; Pop; Root Sports Pittsburgh; Spike TV; The Weather Channel; TLC; TNT; truTV; TV Land; USA Network; VH1.
Fee: $30.24 monthly.

Digital Basic Service
Subscribers: N.A.
Programming (via satellite): BBC America; Discovery Digital Networks; Disney Channel; Disney XD; ESPN HD; ESPNews; Flix; FYI; HD Theater; History International; MC; Nick 2; Nick Jr.; Nicktoons; Starz Encore (multiplexed); Sundance TV; TeenNick; TNT HD; WAM! America's Kidz Network; Weatherscan.

Digital Pay Service 1
Pay Units: N.A.
Programming (via satellite): Cinemax (multiplexed); Cinemax HD; HBO (multiplexed); HBO HD; Showtime (multiplexed); Showtime HD; Starz (multiplexed); Starz HD; The Movie Channel (multiplexed).
Fee: $13.95 monthly (each).
Video-On-Demand: No

Pay-Per-View
iN DEMAND (delivered digitally); Hot Choice (delivered digitally); Playboy TV (delivered digitally); Fresh (delivered digitally).

Internet Service
Operational: Yes.
Subscribers: 3,816.
Broadband Service: Comcast High Speed Internet.
Fee: $42.95 monthly.

Telephone Service
Digital: Operational
Subscribers: 2,636.
Miles of Plant: 770.0 (coaxial); 346.0 (fiber optic). Homes passed: 27,193.
Technical Operations Director: Tim Castor. Marketing Manager: Sandra Munsey.
Ownership: Comcast Cable Communications Inc. (MSO).

BOMONT—Formerly served by Vital Communications. No longer in operation. ICA: WV0265.

BOONE COUNTY (portions)—Armstrong Cable Services. Now served by ZELIENOPLE, PA [PA0053]. ICA: WV0274.

BRANDYWINE—Formerly served by Brandywine Cablevision. No longer in operation. ICA: WV0168.

BROAD RUN—Shentel. Now served by WESTON, WV [WV0034]. ICA: WV0155.

BROOKHAVEN—Formerly served by Adelphia Communications. No longer in operation. ICA: WV0170.

BRUNO—Shentel, Shentel Center, 500 Shentel Way, Edinburg, VA 22824. Phones: 540-984-5224; 304-946-2871. Fax: 540-984-3438. E-mail: Angela.Washington@emp.shentel.com. Web Site: http://www.shentel.com. ICA: WV0171.
TV Market Ranking: Below 100 (BRUNO). Franchise award date: October 1, 1991. Franchise expiration date: N.A. Began: N.A.
Channel capacity: N.A. Channels available but not in use: N.A.

Cable Systems—West Virginia

Basic Service
Subscribers: 155.
Programming (received off-air): WCHS-TV (ABC, Antenna TV) Charleston; WOWK-TV (CBS) Huntington; WSAZ-TV (MNT, NBC, This TV) Huntington; WSWP-TV (PBS) Grandview; WVAH-TV (FOX, The Country Network) Charleston; WVVA (CW, MeTV, NBC) Bluefield.
Programming (via satellite): CMT; CNN; ESPN; Freeform; MTV; Nickelodeon; Spike TV; TBS; TNT; USA Network; WGN America.
Fee: $40.00 installation; $26.57 monthly.

Pay Service 1
Pay Units: N.A. Included in Omar.
Programming (via satellite): HBO; Showtime; The Movie Channel.
Fee: $25.00 installation; $10.95 monthly (Showtime), $11.95 monthly (HBO).

Video-On-Demand: No

Internet Service
Operational: Yes.

Telephone Service
None
Homes passed & miles of plant included in Omar.
Operations Manager: Allen Siers. Vice President, Customer Service: Angela Washington.
Ownership: Colane Cable TV Inc. (MSO).

BUCKHANNON—Suddenlink Communications, 520 Maryville Centre Dr, Ste 300, St. Louis, MO 63141. Phones: 314-315-9400; 304-472-4193. Fax: 304-472-4193. E-mail: Gene.Regan@suddenlink.com. Web Site: http://www.suddenlink.com. Also serves Adrian, French Creek, Harrison County (portions), Hodgesville, Lewis County (northern portion), Lorentz, Lost Creek, McWhorter, Rock Cave, Upshur County & West Milford. ICA: WV0024.
TV Market Ranking: Below 100 (Adrian, BUCKHANNON, French Creek, Harrison County (portions), Hodgesville, Lewis County (northern portion), Lorentz, Lost Creek, McWhorter, Rock Cave, Upshur County, West Milford). Franchise award date: February 15, 1987. Franchise expiration date: N.A. Began: November 1, 1966.
Channel capacity: 50 (operating 2-way). Channels available but not in use: N.A.

Basic Service
Subscribers: 4,455. Commercial subscribers: 472.
Programming (received off-air): KDKA-TV (CBS, Decades) Pittsburgh; WBOY-TV (ABC, NBC) Clarksburg; WCHS-TV (ABC, Antenna TV) Charleston; WDTV (CBS) Weston; WNPB-TV (PBS) Morgantown; WTAE-TV (ABC, This TV) Pittsburgh; WTRF-TV (ABC, CBS, MNT) Wheeling; WVFX (CW, FOX) Clarksburg; allband FM.
Programming (via satellite): Classic Arts Showcase; C-SPAN; EWTN Global Catholic Network; Pop; QVC; The Weather Channel; Trinity Broadcasting Network (TBN); WGN America.
Fee: $22.99 monthly; $.65 converter.

Expanded Basic Service 1
Subscribers: N.A.
Programming (via satellite): A&E; AMC; Animal Planet; BET; Cartoon Network; Celebrity Shopping Network; CNBC; CNN; Comedy Central; C-SPAN 2; Discovery Channel; Disney Channel; E! HD; ESPN; ESPN Classic; ESPN2; Food Network; Fox News Channel; Fox Sports 1; Freeform; FX; Great American Country; GSN; Hallmark Channel; HGTV; History; HLN; INSP; Lifetime; MSNBC; MTV; National Geographic Channel; Nickelodeon; Outdoor Channel; Root Sports Pittsburgh; Spike TV; Syfy; TBS; TLC; TNT; Travel Channel; TV Land; USA Network; VH1; WE tv.
Fee: $23.00 monthly.

Digital Basic Service
Subscribers: N.A.
Programming (via satellite): BBC America; Bloomberg Television; CMT; Discovery Digital Networks; Disney XD; DMX Music; ESP-News; EVINE Live; FOX College Sports Central; FOX College Sports Pacific; Fuse; FXM; FYI; Golf Channel; History International; IFC; LMN; NBCSN; Nick Jr.; Nicktoons; Teen-Nick; Turner Classic Movies.
Fee: $13.95 monthly.

Pay Service 1
Pay Units: N.A.
Programming (via satellite): Cinemax; HBO; Showtime; The Movie Channel.
Fee: $10.00 installation.

Digital Pay Service 1
Pay Units: N.A.
Programming (via satellite): Cinemax (multiplexed); HBO (multiplexed); Showtime (multiplexed); Starz (multiplexed); Starz Encore (multiplexed); The Movie Channel (multiplexed).

Video-On-Demand: No

Pay-Per-View
iN DEMAND (delivered digitally); Playboy TV (delivered digitally); Fresh (delivered digitally).

Internet Service
Operational: Yes. Began: April 21, 2004.
Subscribers: 4,602.
Broadband Service: Suddenlink High Speed Internet.
Fee: $49.95 installation; $29.99 monthly.

Telephone Service
Digital: Operational
Subscribers: 2,932.
Fee: $49.99 monthly
Miles of Plant: 238.0 (coaxial); 77.0 (fiber optic). Homes passed: 10,222.
Senior Vice President, Corporate Finance: Michael Pflantz. Operations Director: Peter Brown.
Ownership: Cequel Communications Holdings I LLC (MSO).

BUD—Formerly served by Bud-Alpoca TV Cable Club Inc. No longer in operation. ICA: WV0138.

BURNSVILLE—Formerly served by Charter Communications. Now served by Shentel, WESTON, WV [WV0034]. ICA: WV0132.

CAIRO—Formerly served by Almega Cable. No longer in operation. ICA: WV0137.

CAMDEN ON GAULEY—Formerly served by Charter Communications. Now served by Shentel, SUMMERSVILLE, WV [WV0213]. ICA: WV0230.

CAMERON—Zito Media, 102 S Main St, PO Box 665, Coudersport, PA 16915. Phones: 814-260-9055; 800-365-6988. E-mail: info@zitomedia.com. Web Site: http://www.zitomedia.com. Also serves Marshall County (portions). ICA: WV0085.
TV Market Ranking: 90 (CAMERON, Marshall County (portions)). Franchise award date: N.A. Franchise expiration date: N.A. Began: January 1, 1950.
Channel capacity: 39 (not 2-way capable). Channels available but not in use: N.A.

Basic Service
Subscribers: 89.
Programming (received off-air): KDKA-TV (CBS, Decades) Pittsburgh; WOUC-TV (PBS) Cambridge; WPGH-TV (Antenna TV, FOX, The Country Network) Pittsburgh; WPXI (MeTV, NBC) Pittsburgh; WTAE-TV (ABC, This TV) Pittsburgh; WTOV-TV (MeTV, NBC) Steubenville; WTRF-TV (ABC, CBS, MNT) Wheeling; allband FM.
Programming (via satellite): C-SPAN; Trinity Broadcasting Network (TBN).
Fee: $49.95 installation; $24.49 monthly; $.73 converter.

Expanded Basic Service 1
Subscribers: N.A.
Programming (via satellite): A&E; AMC; CNN; Discovery Channel; Disney Channel; Disney XD; E! HD; ESPN; ESPN2; Fox News Channel; Freeform; Great American Country; HGTV; History; HLN; Lifetime; MSNBC; MTV; National Geographic Channel; Nickelodeon; Spike TV; Syfy; TBS; The Weather Channel; TNT; TV Land; USA Network; VH1.
Fee: $22.00 monthly.

Pay Service 1
Pay Units: N.A.
Programming (via satellite): Cinemax; HBO; Showtime; The Movie Channel.
Fee: $17.50 installation; $7.95 monthly (Cinemax), $11.95 monthly (Showtime or TMC), $11.99 monthly (HBO).

Video-On-Demand: No

Pay-Per-View
iN DEMAND (delivered digitally); Playboy TV (delivered digitally); Fresh (delivered digitally).

Internet Service
Operational: No.

Telephone Service
None
Miles of Plant: 24.0 (coaxial); None (fiber optic). Homes passed: 990.
President: James Rigas.
Ownership: Zito Media (MSO).

CANVAS—Formerly served by Econoco Inc. No longer in operation. ICA: WV0172.

CAPON BRIDGE—Formerly served by Valley Cable Systems. No longer in operation. ICA: WV0123.

CASS—Spruce Knob Seneca Rocks Telephone, 17009 Mountaineer Dr, PO Box 100, Riverton, WV 26814. Phones: 888-676-2121; 304-567-2121. E-mail: sksrt@spruceknob.net. Web Site: http://www.spruceknob.net. Also serves Durbin & Green Bank. ICA: WV0173.
TV Market Ranking: Outside TV Markets (CASS, Durbin). Franchise award date: N.A. Franchise expiration date: N.A. Began: N.A.
Channel capacity: N.A. Channels available but not in use: N.A.

Basic Service
Subscribers: 696.
Programming (received off-air): WDBJ (CBS, Decades, MNT) Roanoke; WDTV (CBS) Weston; WSLS-TV (MeTV, NBC) Roanoke.
Programming (via satellite): CNN; Disney Channel; ESPN; Freeform; HLN; TBS; TNT; Trinity Broadcasting Network (TBN); USA Network; WGN America.
Fee: $50.00 installation; $49.95 monthly.

Internet Service
Operational: No.

Telephone Service
None
General Manager: Vickie Colaw. Outside Plant Manager: Jason McAbee. Customer Care Coordinator: Janie Warner.
Ownership: Spruce Knob Seneca Rocks Telephone Inc. (MSO).

CHAPEL—Formerly served by Vital Communications. No longer in operation. ICA: WV0260.

CHARLESTON—Suddenlink Communications, 520 Maryville Centre Dr, Ste 300, St. Louis, MO 63141. Phones: 304-757-8001 (Scott Depot office); 314-315-9400. E-mail: Gene.Regan@suddenlink.com. Web Site: http://www.suddenlink.com. Also serves Alkol, Arnett, Barboursville, Belle, Bickmore, Boomer, Boone County (portions), Brownsville, Cabell County (portions), Campbells Creek, Cedar Grove, Chelyan, Chesapeake, Clay County (southern portion), Clendenin, Costa, Crabtree, Cross Lanes, Danville, Davis Creek, Dixie, Dunbar, East Bank, East Lynn, Echo, Fort Gay, Gauley Bridge, Glasgow, Handley, Hurricane, Indore, Institute, Jodie, Julian, Kanawha County, Lavalette, London, Loudendale, Madison, Marmet, Miami, Milton, Montgomery, Montgomery Heights, Morrisvale, Nicholas County (portions), Nitro, Paint Creek (portions), Poca, Pond Gap, Pratt, Prenter, Putnam County (portions), Racine, Rand, Ridgeview, Robson, Scott Depot, Seth, Smithers, South Charleston, St. Albans, Sylvester, Wayne & Whitesville. ICA: WV0006.
TV Market Ranking: 36 (Alkol, Barboursville, Belle, Bickmore, Boomer, Boone County (portions), Brownsville, Cabell County (portions), Campbells Creek, Cedar Grove, CHARLESTON, Chelyan, Chesapeake, Clay County (southern portion), Clendenin, Costa, Crabtree, Cross Lanes, Danville, Davis Creek, Dixie, Dunbar, East Bank, East Lynn, Echo, Fort Gay, Gauley Bridge, Glasgow, Handley, Holly, Hurricane, Indore, Institute, Jodie, Julian, Kanawha County, Lavalette, London, Loudendale, Madison, Marmet, Miami, Milton, Montgomery, Montgomery Heights, Morrisvale, Nitro, Paint Creek (portions), Poca, Pond Gap, Pratt, Prenter, Putnam County (portions), Racine, Rand, Ridgeview, Robson, Scott Depot, Seth, Smithers, South Charleston, St. Albans, Sylvester, Wayne, Whitesville); Below 100 (Arnett). Franchise award date: N.A. Franchise expiration date: N.A. Began: June 1, 1966.
Channel capacity: 24 (operating 2-way). Channels available but not in use: N.A.

Basic Service
Subscribers: 60,556.
Programming (received off-air): WCHS-TV (ABC, Antenna TV) Charleston; WLPX-TV (ION) Charleston; WOWK-TV (CBS) Huntington; WQCW (CW) Portsmouth; WSAZ-TV (MNT, NBC, This TV) Huntington; WTSF (Daystar TV) Ashland; WVAH-TV (FOX, The Country Network) Charleston; WVPB-TV (PBS) Huntington; WVPT (PBS) Staunton.
Programming (via satellite): C-SPAN; C-SPAN 2; EVINE Live; Pop; QVC; WGN America.
Fee: $35.50 installation; $22.99 monthly; $.93 converter.

Expanded Basic Service 1
Subscribers: N.A.
Programming (via satellite): A&E; AMC; Animal Planet; BET; Bravo; Cartoon Network; CMT; CNBC; CNN; Comedy Central; Discovery Channel; Disney Channel; Disney XD; E! HD; ESPN; ESPN Classic; ESPN2; Food Network; Fox News Channel; Fox Sports 1; Freeform; FX; Golf Channel; Hallmark Channel; HGTV; History; HLN; INSP; Lifetime; MSNBC; MTV; National Geographic Channel; NBCSN; Nickelodeon; Outdoor Channel; Oxygen; Root Sports

2017 Edition   D-835

West Virginia—Cable Systems

Pittsburgh; Spike TV; Syfy; TBS; The Weather Channel; TLC; TNT; Travel Channel; Trinity Broadcasting Network (TBN); truTV; Turner Classic Movies; TV Land; USA Network; VH1; WE tv.
Fee: $29.00 monthly.

Digital Basic Service
Subscribers: N.A.
Programming (via satellite): BBC America; Bloomberg Television; Discovery Digital Networks; DIY Network; Fox Deportes; FXM; FYI; Great American Country; History International; IFC; LMN; MC; Nick Jr.; Sundance TV; TeenNick.
Fee: $18.95 monthly.

Digital Pay Service 1
Pay Units: N.A.
Programming (via satellite): Cinemax (multiplexed); HBO (multiplexed); Showtime (multiplexed); Starz (multiplexed); Starz Encore (multiplexed); The Movie Channel (multiplexed).
Fee: $10.00 monthly (each).

Video-On-Demand: Yes

Pay-Per-View
iN DEMAND (delivered digitally); Playboy TV (delivered digitally); Fresh (delivered digitally); Shorteez (delivered digitally); Sports PPV (delivered digitally).

Internet Service
Operational: Yes.
Subscribers: 63,817.
Broadband Service: Suddenlink High Speed Internet.
Fee: $49.95 installation; $29.99 monthly.

Telephone Service
Digital: Operational
Subscribers: 38,140.
Fee: $49.99 monthly

Miles of Plant: 2,291.0 (coaxial); 891.0 (fiber optic). Homes passed: 134,880.
Senior Vice President, Corporate Finance: Michael Pflantz. Vice President, Operations: David Bach. General Manager: Patrick Barclay. Marketing Director: Stan Howell. Technical Operations Director: Bob Legg. Marketing Manager: Kenny Phillips.
Ownership: Cequel Communications Holdings I LLC (MSO).

CHATTAROY—Formerly served by Charter Communications. Now served by Suddenlink Communications, KERMIT, WV [WV0038]. ICA: WV0072.

CHESTER—Comcast Cable. Now served by WHEELING, WV [WV0004]. ICA: WV0032.

CLARKSBURG—Formerly served by Adelphia Communications. Now served by Comcast Cable, MORGANTOWN, WV [WV0198]. ICA: WV0174.

CLARKSBURG—Time Warner Cable, 507 Rosebud Plaza, Clarksburg, WV 26301-9380. Phones: 304-566-7586; 304-623-3933. Fax: 304-624-4805. Web Site: http://www.timewarnercable.com. Also serves Anmoore (town), Barrackville (town), Bridgeport, Fairmont, Harrison County (portions), Marion County (portions), Nutter Fort (town), Pleasant Valley, Stonewood & Taylor County (portions). ICA: WV0010.
TV Market Ranking: Below 100 (Anmoore (town), Barrackville (town), Bridgeport, CLARKSBURG, Fairmont, Harrison County (portions), Marion County (portions), Nutter Fort (town), Pleasant Valley, Stonewood, Taylor County (portions)). Franchise award date: N.A. Franchise expiration date: N.A. Began: July 1, 1953.
Channel capacity: N.A. Channels available but not in use: N.A.

Basic Service
Subscribers: 14,894.
Programming (received off-air): KDKA-TV (CBS, Decades) Pittsburgh; WBOY-TV (ABC, NBC) Clarksburg; WDTV (CBS) Weston; WNPB-TV (PBS) Morgantown; WTAE-TV (ABC, This TV) Pittsburgh; WVFX (CW, FOX) Clarksburg.
Programming (via satellite): ION Television; NASA TV; Pop; QVC.
Fee: $24.95-$61.55 installation; $24.50 monthly; $.57 converter.

Expanded Basic Service 1
Subscribers: N.A.
Programming (via satellite): A&E; AMC; Animal Planet; BET; Bravo; Cartoon Network; CMT; CNBC; CNN; Comedy Central; C-SPAN; C-SPAN 2; Discovery Channel; Discovery Life Channel; Disney Channel; E! HD; ESPN; ESPN Classic; ESPN2; EVINE Live; EWTN Global Catholic Network; Food Network; Fox News Channel; Freeform; FX; Great American Country; Hallmark Channel; HGTV; History; HLN; INSP; Lifetime; MSNBC; MTV; Nickelodeon; OWN: Oprah Winfrey Network; Oxygen; Root Sports Pittsburgh; Spike TV; TBS; The Weather Channel; TLC; TNT; Travel Channel; Trinity Broadcasting Network (TBN); truTV; TV Land; USA Network; VH1; WE tv.
Fee: $32.94 monthly.

Digital Basic Service
Subscribers: N.A.
Programming (via satellite): AXS TV; BBC America; Bloomberg Television; Cooking Channel; Discovery Channel; Disney XD; DIY Network; ESPN; ESPNews; Flix; Fox Sports 1; Fox Sports 2; FSN Digital Atlantic; FSN Digital Central; FSN Digital Pacific; Fuse; FYI; Golf Channel; GSN; History; IFC; iN DEMAND; LMN; MC; National Geographic Channel; NBA TV; NBCSN; Nick Jr.; Nicktoons; Outdoor Channel; Ovation; Syfy; TeenNick; Tennis Channel; TNT; Turner Classic Movies.
Fee: $6.00 monthly (each tier).

Digital Pay Service 1
Pay Units: N.A.
Programming (via satellite): Cinemax (multiplexed); HBO (multiplexed); HBO HD; Showtime (multiplexed); Showtime HD; Starz (multiplexed); The Movie Channel (multiplexed).
Fee: $14.00 monthly (each).

Video-On-Demand: Yes

Pay-Per-View
iN DEMAND (delivered digitally); Fresh (delivered digitally); Shorteez (delivered digitally); Playboy TV (delivered digitally); Hot Choice (delivered digitally).

Internet Service
Operational: Yes.
Subscribers: 15,459.
Broadband Service: Road Runner.
Fee: $99.95 installation; $44.95 monthly.

Telephone Service
Analog: Not Operational
Digital: Operational
Subscribers: 7,143.
Fee: $44.95 monthly

Miles of Plant: 894.0 (coaxial); 212.0 (fiber optic). Homes passed: 40,140. Miles of plant (coax) include miles of plant (fiber).
General Manager: Lenny Hannigan. Chief Technician: Brian Lewis. Marketing Manager: Mari Patterson. Advertising Sales Manager: Brenda Jasper.
Ownership: Time Warner Cable (MSO).

CLAY (town)—Formerly served by Vital Communications. No longer in operation. ICA: WV0063.

COALTON—Formerly served by Country Cable. No longer in operation. ICA: WV0176.

COLFAX—Formerly served by Comcast Cable. No longer in operation. ICA: WV0177.

COLLIERS—Formerly served by Blue Devil Cable TV Inc. No longer in operation. ICA: WV0146.

COTTAGEVILLE—Community Antenna Service, 1525 Dupont Rd, Parkersburg, WV 26101-9623. Phone: 304-420-2470. Fax: 304-420-2474. E-mail: info@cascable.com. Web Site: http://www.cascable.com. Also serves Jackson County (portions), Ravenswood & Ripley. ICA: WV0062.
TV Market Ranking: 36 (COTTAGEVILLE, Jackson County (portions), Ripley); Below 100 (Ravenswood). Franchise award date: N.A. Franchise expiration date: N.A. Began: November 1, 1981.
Channel capacity: N.A. Channels available but not in use: N.A.

Basic Service
Subscribers: 1,423.
Programming (received off-air): WCHS-TV (ABC, Antenna TV) Charleston; WOUB-TV (PBS) Athens; WOWK-TV (CBS) Huntington; WSAZ-TV (MNT, NBC, This TV) Huntington; WTAP-TV (FOX, MNT, NBC) Parkersburg; WVAH-TV (FOX, The Country Network) Charleston; WVPB-TV (PBS) Huntington.
Programming (via satellite): A&E; Animal Planet; Cartoon Network; CMT; CNBC; CNN; C-SPAN; C-SPAN 2; Discovery Channel; Disney Channel; ESPN; ESPN2; ESPNews; Fox News Channel; Fox Sports 1; Freeform; FX; Golf Channel; Great American Country; Hallmark Channel; HGTV; History; HLN; INSP; ION Television; Lifetime; MSNBC; National Geographic Channel; Nickelodeon; Outdoor Channel; OWN: Oprah Winfrey Network; Pop; QVC; Spike TV; Syfy; TBS; The Weather Channel; TLC; TNT; Travel Channel; Trinity Broadcasting Network (TBN); truTV; Turner Classic Movies; TV Land; USA Network; WGN America.
Fee: $45.00 installation; $61.00 monthly.

Pay Service 1
Pay Units: N.A.
Programming (via satellite): Cinemax; HBO; Starz; Starz Encore.
Fee: $10.90 monthly (Starz/Starz Encore), $10.95 monthly (Cinemax) & $13.95 monthly (HBO).

Video-On-Demand: No

Internet Service
Operational: Yes.
Broadband Service: In-house.
Fee: $19.95 monthly.

Telephone Service
Analog: Operational
Fee: $29.95-$39.95 monthly

Miles of Plant: 59.0 (coaxial); None (fiber optic). Homes passed: 1,685.
President & General Manager: Arthur R. Cooper. Chief Technician: Steve Defibaugh. Program & Marketing Director: Lisa Wilkinson.
Ownership: Arthur R. Cooper (MSO).

COWEN—Formerly served by Charter Communications. Now served by Shentel, SUMMERSVILLE, WV [WV0213]. ICA: WV0096.

CRAIGSVILLE—Shentel. Now served by SUMMERSVILLE, WV [WV0213]. ICA: WV0071.

CRAWLEY CREEK—Shentel, Shentel Center, 500 Shentel Way, Edinburg, VA 22824. Phones: 540-984-5224; 304-946-2871. Fax: 540-984-3438. E-mail: Angela.Washington@emp.shentel.com. Web Site: http://www.shentel.com. ICA: WV0236.
TV Market Ranking: Below 100 (CRAWLEY CREEK).
Channel capacity: N.A. Channels available but not in use: N.A.

Basic Service
Subscribers: 103.
Programming (received off-air): WCHS-TV (ABC, Antenna TV) Charleston; WOWK-TV (CBS) Huntington; WSAZ-TV (MNT, NBC, This TV) Huntington; WVAH-TV (FOX, The Country Network) Charleston; WVPB-TV (PBS) Huntington.
Programming (via satellite): A&E; Cartoon Network; CMT; CNN; Comedy Central; C-SPAN; Discovery Channel; ESPN; Freeform; HLN; Lifetime; MTV; Nickelodeon; QVC; Spike TV; Syfy; TBS; The Weather Channel; TNT; Trinity Broadcasting Network (TBN); USA Network; VH1; WGN America.
Fee: $40.00 installation; $34.90 monthly.

Pay Service 1
Pay Units: N.A.
Programming (via satellite): HBO.
Fee: $12.00 monthly.

Internet Service
Operational: No.

Telephone Service
None

Miles of Plant: 5.0 (coaxial); None (fiber optic). Homes passed: 400.
Operations Manager: Allen Siers. Vice President, Customer Service: Angela Washington.
Ownership: Colane Cable TV Inc. (MSO).

CROSSROADS—Formerly served by Crossroads TV Cable. No longer in operation. ICA: WV0235.

CURTIN—Formerly served by Charter Communications. Now served by Shentel, SUMMERSVILLE, WV [WV0213]. ICA: WV0164.

DAVIS—Atlantic Broadband, 201 South Mechanic St, Cumberland, MD 21502. Phone: 888-536-9600. Web Site: http://atlanticbb.com. Also serves Hambleton, Hendricks, Parsons, Thomas & Tucker County (portions). ICA: WV0282.
TV Market Ranking: Below 100 (Tucker County (portions)); Outside TV Markets (DAVIS, Hambleton, Hendricks, Parsons, Thomas, Tucker County (portions)).
Channel capacity: N.A. Channels available but not in use: N.A.

Basic Service
Subscribers: 466. Commercial subscribers: 28.
Fee: $40.00 installation; $33.23 monthly.
Miles of Plant: 112.0 (coaxial); 46.0 (fiber optic). Homes passed: 1,126.
Chief Financial Officer: Patrick Bratton. Senior Vice President & General Counsel: Leslie Brown.
Ownership: Atlantic Broadband (MSO).

DAWSON—Formerly served by Econoco Inc. No longer in operation. ICA: WV0271.

DELBARTON—Colane Cable TV Inc. Now served by OMAR, WV [WV0191]. ICA: WV0087.

DIANA—Formerly served by Country Cable. No longer in operation. ICA: WV0127.

Cable Systems—West Virginia

FULLY SEARCHABLE • CONTINUOUSLY UPDATED • DISCOUNT RATES FOR PRINT PURCHASERS

For more information call **800-771-9202** or visit **www.warren-news.com**

DINGESS—Armstrong Cable Services, 311 Main St, Hamlin, WV 25523. Phone: 540-984-5224. Web Site: http://armstrongonewire.com/television. Also serves Kiahsville, Logan County (portions), Midkiff, Mingo County (unincorporated areas) & Wayne County. ICA: WV0270.
  TV Market Ranking: 36 (Kiahsville, Logan County (portions), Midkiff, Wayne County); Outside TV Markets (Mingo County (unincorporated areas), DINGESS, Logan County (portions)).
  Channel capacity: N.A. Channels available but not in use: N.A.
  Basic Service
  Subscribers: 98.
  Programming (received off-air): WCHS-TV (ABC, Antenna TV) Charleston; WKPI-TV (PBS) Pikeville; WLPX-TV (ION) Charleston; WOWK-TV (CBS) Huntington; WQCW (CW) Portsmouth; WSAZ-TV (MNT, NBC, This TV) Huntington; WTSF (Daystar TV) Ashland; WVAH-TV (FOX, The Country Network) Charleston; WVPB-TV (PBS) Huntington.
  Programming (via satellite): C-SPAN; Pop; TBS; Trinity Broadcasting Network (TBN); WGN America.
  Fee: $35.00 installation; $17.75 monthly.
  Expanded Basic Service 1
  Subscribers: N.A.
  Programming (via satellite): A&E; AMC; Animal Planet; Cartoon Network; CMT; CNBC; CNN; Comedy Central; Discovery Channel; Disney Channel; E! HD; ESPN; ESPN2; Fox News Channel; Fox Sports 1; Freeform; FX; HGTV; History; HLN; Lifetime; MTV; Nickelodeon; Oxygen; Spike TV; Syfy; The Weather Channel; TLC; TNT; Turner Classic Movies; TV Land; USA Network; VH1.
  Fee: $15.86 monthly.
  Digital Basic Service
  Subscribers: N.A.
  Programming (via satellite): BBC America; Bloomberg Television; Discovery Digital Networks (multiplexed); Disney XD; DMX Music; ESPN Classic; ESPNews; Fuse; FXM; FYI; GSN; History International; IFC; LMN; Nick Jr.; Nicktoons; Sundance TV; TeenNick; WE tv.
  Digital Pay Service 1
  Pay Units: N.A.
  Programming (via satellite): Cinemax (multiplexed); Flix; HBO (multiplexed); Showtime (multiplexed); Starz (multiplexed); Starz Encore (multiplexed); The Movie Channel (multiplexed).
  Pay-Per-View
  iN DEMAND (delivered digitally); Fresh (delivered digitally); Shorteez (delivered digitally); Playboy TV (delivered digitally).
  Internet Service
  Operational: No.
  Telephone Service
  None
  Vice President, Financial Reporting: Mark Rankin.
  Ownership: Armstrong Group of Companies (MSO).

DINGESS—Armstrong Utilities Inc. Now served by DINGESS (formerly Harts), WV [WV0270]. ICA: WV0079.

DORCAS—C T & R Cable, 29 Water St, Petersburg, WV 26847-1544. Phone: 304-257-4891. Also serves Maysville. ICA: WV0224.
  TV Market Ranking: Outside TV Markets (DORCAS, Maysville). Franchise award date: N.A. Franchise expiration date: N.A. Began: May 15, 1991.
  Channel capacity: N.A. Channels available but not in use: N.A.
  Basic Service
  Subscribers: N.A.
  Programming (via satellite): Cartoon Network; Discovery Channel; ESPN; ESPN2; Fox News Channel; Freeform; Spike TV; TBS; TNT; USA Network; WGN America.
  Programming (via translator): WHSV-TV (ABC, MeTV, MNT, This TV) Harrisonburg; WJAC-TV (MeTV, NBC) Johnstown; WNPB-TV (PBS) Morgantown; WTTG (Buzzr, FOX) Washington; WUSA (Bounce TV, CBS, WeatherNation) Washington.
  Fee: $25.00 installation.
  Pay Service 1
  Pay Units: N.A.
  Programming (via satellite): Showtime.
  Fee: $9.00 monthly.
  Internet Service
  Operational: No.
  Telephone Service
  None
  Miles of Plant: 35.0 (coaxial); None (fiber optic).
  General Manager: Terry Hinkle. Chief Technician: Matt Alt.
  Ownership: C T & R Cable LLC (MSO).

DOROTHY—Formerly served by Charter Communications. Now served by Suddenlink Communications, BECKLEY, WV [WV0005]. ICA: WV0246.

DRENNEN—Shentel. Now served by SUMMERSVILLE, WV [WV0213]. ICA: WV0269.

DUNLOW—Formerly served by Almega Cable. No longer in operation. ICA: WV0179.

DURBIN—Spruce Knob Seneca Rocks Telephone. Now served by CASS, WV [WV0173]. ICA: WV0180.

EASTON—Formerly served by Adelphia Communications. No longer in operation. ICA: WV0181.

ELLAMORE—Formerly served by Vital Communications. No longer in operation. ICA: WV0125.

ELLENBORO—Formerly served by Charter Communications. Now served by Shentel, WESTON, WV [WV0034]. ICA: WV0247.

FAIRMONT—Time Warner Cable. Now served by CLARKSBURG, WV [WV0010]. ICA: WV0014.

FLAT ROCK—Formerly served by Windjammer Cable. No longer in operation. ICA: WV0108.

FLEMINGTON—Suddenlink Communications. Now served by SHINNSTON, WV [WV0029]. ICA: WV0074.

FOLSOM—Jones TV Cable & Satellite Systems Inc, RR 1 Box 8, Folsom, WV 26348-9725. Phone: 304-334-6504. Also serves Wallace. ICA: WV0141.
  TV Market Ranking: Below 100 (FOLSOM, Wallace). Franchise award date: N.A. Franchise expiration date: N.A. Began: April 1, 1985.
  Channel capacity: N.A. Channels available but not in use: N.A.
  Basic Service
  Subscribers: 200.
  Programming (received off-air): KDKA-TV (CBS, Decades) Pittsburgh; WBOY-TV (ABC, NBC) Clarksburg; WDTV (CBS) Weston; WNPB-TV (PBS) Morgantown; WTAE-TV (ABC, This TV) Pittsburgh; WTOV-TV (MeTV, NBC) Steubenville; WTRF-TV (ABC, CBS, MNT) Wheeling; WVFX (CW, FOX) Clarksburg.
  Programming (via satellite): A&E; CNN; Discovery Channel; Disney Channel; ESPN; ESPN2; Freeform; History; HLN; Spike TV; Syfy; TBS; TLC; Trinity Broadcasting Network (TBN); Turner Classic Movies; TV Land; USA Network; WGN America.
  Pay Service 1
  Pay Units: N.A.
  Programming (via satellite): HBO.
  Video-On-Demand: No
  Internet Service
  Operational: No.
  Telephone Service
  None
  Miles of Plant: 9.0 (coaxial); None (fiber optic). Homes passed: 215.
  General Manager & Chief Technician: Eugene Jones.
  Ownership: Eugene Jones.

FRAME—Formerly served by Vital Communications. No longer in operation. ICA: WV0276.

FRAMETOWN—Formerly served by Vital Communications. No longer in operation. ICA: WV0252.

FRANKFORD—Formerly served by Clearview TV Cable. No longer in operation. ICA: WV0098.

FRANKLIN—Shentel. Now served by PETERSBURG, WV [WV0064]. ICA: WV0095.

FRIENDLY—Formerly served by Vital Communications. No longer in operation. ICA: WV0133.

GANDEEVILLE—Formerly served by Econoco Inc. No longer in operation. ICA: WV0183.

GASSAWAY—Shentel. Now served by SUMMERSVILLE, WV [WV0213]. ICA: WV0061.

GENOA—Formerly served by Lycom Communications. No longer in operation. ICA: WV0214.

GILBERT—Shentel, 500 Shentel Way, PO Box 459, Edinburg, VA 22824. Phones: 540-984-5224; 800-743-6835; 304-946-2871. Fax: 540-984-3438. E-mail: Angela.Washington@emp.shentel.com. Web Site: http://www.shentel.com. Also serves Justice & Tamcliff. ICA: WV0075.
  TV Market Ranking: Below 100 (GILBERT, Justice, Tamcliff).
  Channel capacity: N.A. Channels available but not in use: N.A.
  Basic Service
  Subscribers: 323.
  Fee: $40.00 installation; $25.88 monthly.

Operations Manager: Allen Siers. Vice President, Customer Service: Angela Washington.
Ownership: Shentel (MSO).

GILBOA—Shentel. Now served by SUMMERSVILLE, WV [WV0213]. ICA: WV0268.

GLEN DALE—Comcast Cable. Now served by WHEELING, WV [WV0004]. ICA: WV0223.

GLENHAYES—Formerly served by Lycom Communications. No longer in operation. ICA: WV0139.

GLENVILLE—Shentel. Now served by WESTON, WV [WV0034]. ICA: WV0088.

GOLDTOWN—Formerly served by Econoco Inc. Now served by Suddenlink Communications, PARKERSBURG, WV [WV0003]. ICA: WV0184.

GRAFTON—Comcast Cable. Now served by TAYLOR COUNTY (portions), WV [WV0278]. ICA: WV0028.

GRANT TOWN—Atlantic Broadband, 320 Bailey Ave, Uniontown, PA 15401. Phones: 888-536-9600 (Customer service); 814-535-3506. Fax: 814-535-7749. E-mail: info@atlanticbb.com. Web Site: http://atlanticbb.com. Also serves Baxter, Fairview, Marion County (portions) & Monongalia County (portions). ICA: WV0083.
  TV Market Ranking: Below 100 (Baxter, Fairview, GRANT TOWN, Marion County (portions)). Franchise award date: N.A. Franchise expiration date: N.A. Began: January 1, 1968.
  Channel capacity: 21 (not 2-way capable). Channels available but not in use: N.A.
  Basic Service
  Subscribers: 207. Commercial subscribers: 3.
  Programming (received off-air): KDKA-TV (CBS, Decades) Pittsburgh; WBOY-TV (ABC, NBC) Clarksburg; WDTV (CBS) Weston; WNPB-TV (PBS) Morgantown; WPGH-TV (Antenna TV, FOX, The Country Network) Pittsburgh; WPXI (MeTV, NBC) Pittsburgh; WTAE-TV (ABC, This TV) Pittsburgh; WVFX (CW, FOX) Clarksburg; allband FM.
  Programming (via satellite): C-SPAN; QVC.
  Fee: $40.00 installation; $35.62 monthly.
  Expanded Basic Service 1
  Subscribers: N.A.
  Programming (via satellite): A&E; AMC; Animal Planet; Cartoon Network; CMT; CNBC; CNN; Comedy Central; Discovery Channel; Disney Channel; E! HD; ESPN; ESPN2; Food Network; Fox News Channel; Freeform; FX; GSN; Hallmark Channel; HGTV; History; HLN; Lifetime; MSNBC; MTV; National Geographic Channel; Nickelodeon; OWN: Oprah Winfrey Network; Oxygen; Root Sports Pittsburgh; Spike TV; Syfy; TBS; The Weather Channel; TLC; TNT; Trinity Broadcasting Network (TBN);

2017 Edition

D-837

West Virginia—Cable Systems

truTV; TV Guide; TV Land; USA Network; VH1.
Fee: $35.42 monthly.

Digital Basic Service
Subscribers: N.A.
Programming (via satellite): BBC America; Bloomberg Television; CMT; Cooking Channel; Destination America; Discovery Kids Channel; Discovery Life Channel; Disney XD; DMX Music; ESPN Classic; ESPNews; Fox Sports 1; Fuse; FYI; Golf Channel; History International; IFC; Investigation Discovery; LMN; MTV Classic; MTV2; Nick Jr.; Nicktoons; Outdoor Channel; Science Channel; Starz (multiplexed); Starz Encore (multiplexed); TeenNick; Trinity Broadcasting Network (TBN); Turner Classic Movies.
Fee: $21.90 monthly.

Digital Pay Service 1
Pay Units: N.A.
Programming (via satellite): Cinemax (multiplexed); HBO (multiplexed); Showtime (multiplexed); The Movie Channel (multiplexed).
Fee: $15.95 monthly (Cinemax, HBO or Showtime/TMC).

Video-On-Demand: No

Pay-Per-View
iN DEMAND (delivered digitally); Hot Choice (delivered digitally); Playboy TV (delivered digitally); Fresh (delivered digitally); Shorteez (delivered digitally).

Internet Service
Operational: Yes.

Telephone Service
None

Miles of Plant: 35.0 (coaxial); None (fiber optic). Homes passed: 1,479.
Senior Vice President & General Counsel: Leslie Brown. Vice President: David Dane. General Manager: Mike Papasergi. Technical Operations Director: Charles Sorchilla. Marketing & Customer Service Director: Dara Leslie. Marketing Manager: Natalie Kurchak.
Ownership: Atlantic Broadband (MSO).

GRANTSVILLE—Shentel, 500 Shentel Way, PO Box 459, Edinburg, VA 22824. Phones: 800-743-6835; 540-984-5224. Fax: 540-984-3438. E-mail: customer_service@shentel.net. Web Site: http://www.shentel.com. Also serves Calhoun County (portions) & Mount Zion. ICA: WV0099.
TV Market Ranking: Below 100 (GRANTSVILLE, Calhoun County (portions)); Outside TV Markets (Mount Zion, Calhoun County (portions)). Franchise award date: N.A. Franchise expiration date: N.A. Began: January 1, 1971.
Channel capacity: N.A. Channels available but not in use: N.A.

Basic Service
Subscribers: 22.
Programming (received off-air): WBOY-TV (ABC, NBC) Clarksburg; WCHS-TV (ABC, Antenna TV) Charleston; WDTV (CBS) Weston; WOWK-TV (CBS) Huntington; WSWP-TV (PBS) Grandview; WTAP-TV (FOX, MNT, NBC) Parkersburg; WVAH-TV (FOX, The Country Network) Charleston.
Programming (via satellite): Pop; QVC; Trinity Broadcasting Network (TBN); WGN America.
Fee: $99.95 installation; $35.14 monthly.

Expanded Basic Service 1
Subscribers: N.A.
Programming (via satellite): A&E; AMC; Animal Planet; Cartoon Network; CMT; CNBC; CNN; Comedy Central; C-SPAN; Discovery Channel; Disney Channel; E! HD; ESPN; ESPN2; Fox News Channel; Fox Sports 1;

Freeform; FX; Golf Channel; HGTV; History; HLN; Lifetime; MSNBC; MTV; Nickelodeon; Oxygen; Root Sports Pittsburgh; Spike TV; Syfy; TBS; The Weather Channel; TLC; TNT; Turner Classic Movies; TV Land; USA Network; VH1.
Fee: $34.00 monthly.

Digital Basic Service
Subscribers: N.A.
Programming (via satellite): BBC America; Bloomberg Television; Discovery Life Channel; Disney XD; DMX Music; ESPN Classic; ESPNews; FOX Sports Networks (multiplexed); Fuse; FXM; FYI; GSN; History International; IFC; LMN; Nick 2; Nick Jr.; Nicktoons; Sundance TV; TeenNick; WE tv.
Fee: $13.00 monthly.

Digital Pay Service 1
Pay Units: N.A.
Programming (via satellite): Cinemax (multiplexed); Flix; HBO; Showtime (multiplexed); Starz (multiplexed); Starz Encore; The Movie Channel.

Video-On-Demand: No

Pay-Per-View
iN DEMAND (delivered digitally); Pleasure (delivered digitally); Fresh (delivered digitally); Shorteez (delivered digitally); Playboy TV (delivered digitally).

Internet Service
Operational: No.

Telephone Service
None

Miles of Plant: 39.0 (coaxial); 18.0 (fiber optic). Homes passed: 980.
Vice President, Industry Affairs & Regulations: Chris Kyle.
Ownership: Shentel (MSO).

GRAYSVILLE—Formerly served by Vital Communications. No longer in operation. ICA: WV0185.

GREEN ACRES—Formerly served by Almega Cable. No longer in operation. ICA: WV0166.

HAMLIN—Armstrong Cable Services, 311 Main St, Hamlin, WV 25523. Phone: 304-824-5114. Fax: 304-824-7711. E-mail: info@zoominternet.net. Web Site: http://armstrongonewire.com/television. Also serves Big Creek, Boone County (portions), Branchland, Cabell County (unincorporated areas), Chapmanville, Cove Gap, Ferrellsburg, Harts, Lincoln County (portions), Ranger, Wayne & West Hamlin. ICA: WV0047.
TV Market Ranking: 36 (Big Creek, Boone County (portions), Branchland, Cabell County (unincorporated areas), Chapmanville, Cove Gap, Ferrellsburg, HAMLIN, Harts, Lincoln County (portions), Ranger, Wayne, West Hamlin). Franchise award date: December 2, 1968. Franchise expiration date: N.A. Began: January 1, 1971.
Channel capacity: N.A. Channels available but not in use: N.A.

Digital Basic Service
Subscribers: 3,575.
Programming (via satellite): A&E; AMC; Animal Planet; Bravo; Cartoon Network; CMT; CNBC; CNN; Comedy Central; C-SPAN; Discovery Channel; Disney Channel; E! HD; ESPN; ESPN Classic; ESPN2; EVINE Live; EWTN Global Catholic Network; Food Network; Fox News Channel; FOX Sports Ohio/Sports Time Ohio; Freeform; FX; HGTV; History; HLN; INSP; Lifetime; MC; MSNBC; MTV; Nickelodeon; Nicktoons; Pop; QVC; Root Sports Pittsburgh; Spike TV; Syfy; TBS; The Weather Channel; TLC;

TNT; Travel Channel; truTV; Turner Classic Movies; TV Land; USA Network; VH1.
Fee: $35.00 installation; $22.95 monthly.

Digital Expanded Basic Service
Subscribers: N.A.
Programming (via satellite): BBC America; Bloomberg Television; Boomerang; Chiller; Cloo; CMT; Cooking Channel; Destination America; Discovery Kids Channel; Discovery Life Channel; Disney XD; DIY Network; ESPN Classic; ESPNews; Fox Sports 1; FYI; Golf Channel; Great American Country; GSN; Hallmark Channel; Hallmark Movies & Mysteries; History International; HRTV; Investigation Discovery; Jewelry Television; LMN; MTV Classic; MTV Hits; MTV Jams; MTV2; National Geographic Channel; NBC Universo; NBCSN; NFL Network; NHL Network; Nick 2; Nick Jr.; Outdoor Channel; OWN: Oprah Winfrey Network; Oxygen; RFD-TV; Science Channel; Sprout; TeenNick; Tennis Channel; Tr3s; VH1 Soul; WE tv.
Fee: $12.00 monthly.

Digital Expanded Basic Service 2
Subscribers: N.A.
Programming (via satellite): A&E HD; Animal Planet HD; AXS TV; Bravo HD; CNN HD; Discovery Channel HD; Disney Channel HD; ESPN HD; ESPN2 HD; Food Network HD; Fox News HD; FX HD; Golf Channel HD; Hallmark Movie Channel HD; HD Theater; HGTV HD; History HD; MGM HD; MTV Live; National Geographic Channel HD; NFL Network HD; NHL Network HD; Outdoor Channel 2 HD; PBS HD; QVC HD; Science HD; Syfy HD; TBS HD; The Weather Channel HD; TLC HD; TNT HD; Universal HD; USA Network HD; Versus HD.
Fee: $9.00 monthly.

Digital Pay Service 1
Pay Units: N.A.
Programming (via satellite): Cinemax HD; Flix; HBO (multiplexed); HBO HD; Showtime (multiplexed); Showtime HD; Starz (multiplexed); Starz Encore (multiplexed); Starz HD; The Movie Channel (multiplexed); TV5MONDE USA.
Fee: $13.95 monthly (HBO, Cinemax, Showtime/TMC/Flix or Starz/Encore).

Video-On-Demand: Yes

Pay-Per-View
ESPN Now (delivered digitally); Hot Choice (delivered digitally); iN DEMAND (delivered digitally); ESPN Sports, NHL/MLB (delivered digitally).

Internet Service
Operational: Yes. Began: March 1, 2002.
Broadband Service: Armstrong Zoom.
Fee: $26.95-$39.95 monthly.

Telephone Service
Analog: Not Operational
Digital: Operational
Fee: $49.95 monthly
Miles of Plant: 70.0 (coaxial); None (fiber optic).
Vice President, Marketing: Jud D. Stewart. Vice President, Financial Reporting: Mark Rankin. General Manager: Todd L. Barrett. Chief Technician: Russ Mutter.
Ownership: Armstrong Group of Companies (MSO).

HAMPDEN—Colane Cable TV Inc. Now served by OMAR, WV [WV0191]. ICA: WV0232.

HANOVER—Shentel, 500 Shentel Way, PO Box 459, Edinburg, VA 22824. Phones: 540-984-5224; 800-743-6835; 304-946-2871. Fax: 540-984-3438. E-mail: Angela.Washington@emp.shentel.com. Web Site:

http://www.shentel.com. Also serves Wyoming County. ICA: WV0070.
TV Market Ranking: Below 100 (HANOVER, Wyoming County (portions)); Outside TV Markets (Wyoming County (portions)). Franchise award date: October 8, 1991. Franchise expiration date: N.A. Began: July 1, 1982.
Channel capacity: N.A. Channels available but not in use: N.A.

Basic Service
Subscribers: 431.
Programming (received off-air): WCHS-TV (ABC, Antenna TV) Charleston; WOAY-TV (ABC) Oak Hill; WOWK-TV (CBS) Huntington; WSAZ-TV (MNT, NBC, This TV) Huntington; WSWP-TV (PBS) Grandview; WVAH-TV (FOX, The Country Network) Charleston; WVPB-TV (PBS) Huntington; WVVA (CW, MeTV, NBC) Bluefield.
Programming (via satellite): CMT; CNN; Discovery Channel; Disney Channel; ESPN; Freeform; HLN; Lifetime; Nickelodeon; Spike TV; TBS; TNT; USA Network; WGN America.
Fee: $40.00 installation; $26.57 monthly.

Pay Service 1
Pay Units: N.A. Included in Omar.
Programming (via satellite): HBO; Showtime.
Fee: $25.00 installation; $10.95 monthly (Showtime), $11.95 monthly (HBO).

Internet Service
Operational: No.

Telephone Service
None

Homes passed & miles of plant included in Omar.
Operations Manager: Allen Siers. Vice President, Customer Service: Angela Washington.
Ownership: Shentel (MSO).

HARMAN—Formerly served by Harman Cable Corp. No longer in operation. ICA: WV0234.

HARRISVILLE—Formerly served by Rapid Cable. Now served by Shentel, WESTON, WV [WV0034]. ICA: WV0102.

HERNDON—Shentel. Now served by PINEVILLE, WV [WV0204]. ICA: WV0273.

HEWETT—Shentel, Shentel Center, 500 Shentel Way, Edinburg, VA 22824. Phones: 540-984-5224; 304-946-2871. Fax: 540-984-3438. E-mail: Angela.Washington@emp.shentel.com. Web Site: http://www.shentel.com. Also serves Jeffrey & Lake. ICA: WV0266.
TV Market Ranking: 36 (HEWETT, Jeffrey, Lake).
Channel capacity: N.A. Channels available but not in use: N.A.

Basic Service
Subscribers: 239.
Programming (received off-air): WCHS-TV (ABC, Antenna TV) Charleston; WLPX-TV (ION) Charleston; WOAY-TV (ABC) Oak Hill; WOWK-TV (CBS) Huntington; WSAZ-TV (MNT, NBC, This TV) Huntington; WSWP-TV (PBS) Grandview; WVAH-TV (FOX, The Country Network) Charleston; WVPB-TV (PBS) Huntington; WVVA (CW, MeTV, NBC) Bluefield.
Programming (via satellite): TBS; WGN America.
Fee: $40.00 installation; $24.18 monthly.

Expanded Basic Service 1
Subscribers: N.A.
Programming (via satellite): A&E; Cartoon Network; CMT; CNN; Comedy Central; C-

Cable Systems—West Virginia

SPAN; Discovery Channel; Disney Channel; ESPN; ESPN2; Freeform; FX; HLN; INSP; Lifetime; MTV; Nickelodeon; QVC; Spike TV; Syfy; The Weather Channel; TNT; Trinity Broadcasting Network (TBN); truTV; Turner Classic Movies; TV Land; USA Network; VH1.
Fee: $17.45 monthly.
Pay Service 1
Pay Units: 15.
Programming (via satellite): Cinemax.
Fee: $11.95 monthly.
Pay Service 2
Pay Units: 27.
Programming (via satellite): HBO.
Fee: $11.95 monthly.
Internet Service
Operational: Yes.
Telephone Service
None
Miles of Plant: 26.0 (coaxial); None (fiber optic). Homes passed: 918.
Operations Manager: Allen Siers. Vice President, Customer Service: Angela Washington.
Ownership: Colane Cable TV Inc. (MSO).

HINTON—Formerly served by Charter Communications. Now served by Suddenlink Communications, BECKLEY, WV [WV0005]. ICA: WV0059.

HUNTERSVILLE—Milestone Communications LP, 43 Herrn Lane, Castle Pines, CO 80108. Phone: 303-993-3557. Fax: 303-993-3559. Web Site: http://www.milestonecomminc.com. Also serves Minehaha Springs. ICA: WV0262.
TV Market Ranking: Below 100 (HUNTERSVILLE, Minehaha Springs). Franchise award date: N.A. Franchise expiration date: N.A. Began: N.A.
Channel capacity: N.A. Channels available but not in use: N.A.
Basic Service
Subscribers: 11.
Programming (received off-air): WDBJ (CBS, Decades, MNT) Roanoke; WSET-TV (ABC, Retro TV, WeatherNation) Lynchburg; WSLS-TV (MeTV, NBC) Roanoke; WVVA (CW, MeTV, NBC) Bluefield.
Programming (via satellite): CNN; ESPN; Freeform; Spike TV; TBS; TNT; Trinity Broadcasting Network (TBN); WGN America.
Fee: $50.00 installation; $24.95 monthly.
Internet Service
Operational: No.
Telephone Service
None
Miles of Plant: 6.0 (coaxial); None (fiber optic). Homes passed: 100.
Owner: Barbara Mock.
Ownership: Milestone Communications LP (MSO).

HUNTINGTON—Comcast Cable. Now served by PETERSBURG, VA [VA0186]. ICA: WV0002.

HUTCHINSON—Formerly served by Comcast Cable. No longer in operation. ICA: WV0094.

IAEGER—Shentel. Now served by PINEVILLE, WV [WV0204]. ICA: WV0039.

INWOOD—Formerly served by Adelphia Communications. Now served by Comcast Cable, JEFFERSON COUNTY (portions), WV [WV0016]. ICA: WV0021.

JEFFERSON COUNTY (portions)—Comcast Cable. Now served by FREDERICK COUNTY (portions), MD [MD0009]. ICA: WV0016.

JENKINJONES—Formerly served by Obey's TV Cable. No longer in operation. ICA: WV0226.

KERMIT—Suddenlink Communications, 520 Maryville Centre Dr, Ste 300, St. Louis, MO 63141. Phone: 314-315-9400. E-mail: Gene.Regan@suddenlink.com. Web Site: http://www.suddenlink.com. Also serves Aflex, Beauty, Burnwell, Davella, Debord, Elk Creek, Floyd County (portions), Forest Hills, Goody, Hardy, Hatfield, Hode, Huddy, Inez, Johnson County (portions), Lawrence County (portions), Lovely, Martin County (portions), Milo, Oppy, Paintsville, Pike County (unincorporated areas), Pilgrim, Pond Creek, Prestonsburg, Riverfront, Sharondale, South Williamson, Stone, Toler, Tomahawk, Turkey Creek, Warfield & Wolf Creek, KY; Belo, Bias, Blair, Boone County, Chapmanville, Chattaroy, Crum, East Kermit, East Lovely, Grey Eagle, Laurel Creek, Lenore, Logan, Logan County, Maher, Man, Merrimac, Mingo County (portions), Mitchell Heights, Mudfork, Myrtle, Naugatuck, Nolan, Ottawa, Rawl, Stonecoal, Tripp, West Logan, Williamson & Wyoming County (portions), WV. ICA: WV0038.
TV Market Ranking: 36 (Boone County (portions), Laurel Creek, Laurel Creek, Logan County (portions), Ottawa); Below 100 (Aflex, Burnwell, Floyd County (portions) (portions), Goody, Hardy, Huddy, Pike County (unincorporated areas), Pond Creek, Prestonsburg, Sharondale, South Williamson, Stone, Toler, Turkey Creek, Turkey Creek, Williamson, Boone County (portions), Logan County (portions)); Outside TV Markets (Beauty, Belo, Bias, Blair, Chapmanville, Crum, Davella, Debord, East Kermit, East Lovely, Elk Creek, Floyd County (portions) (portions), Grey Eagle, Hatfield, Hode, Inez, KERMIT, Lawrence County (portions), Lenore, Lovely, Maher, Man, Martin County (portions), Merrimac, Milo, Mingo County (portions), Mitchell Heights, Myrtle, Naugatuck, Nolan, Oppy, Paintsville, Pilgrim, Rawl, Riverfront, Tomahawk, Tripp, Warfield, West Logan, Wolf Creek, Stonecoal, Logan County (portions)). Franchise award date: November 1, 1985. Franchise expiration date: N.A. Began: N.A.
Channel capacity: 25 (operating 2-way). Channels available but not in use: N.A.
Basic Service
Subscribers: 18,865.
Programming (received off-air): WCHS-TV (ABC, Antenna TV) Charleston; WKPI-TV (PBS) Pikeville; WLPX-TV (ION) Charleston; WOWK-TV (CBS) Huntington; WQCW (CW) Portsmouth; WSAZ-TV (MNT, NBC, This TV) Huntington; WTSF (Daystar TV) Ashland; WVAH-TV (FOX, The Country Network) Charleston; WVPB-TV (PBS) Huntington; WYMT-TV (CBS, CW) Hazard.
Programming (via satellite): C-SPAN; C-SPAN 2; EVINE Live; QVC; WGN America.
Fee: $22.99 monthly; $1.24 converter.
Expanded Basic Service 1
Subscribers: N.A.
Programming (via satellite): A&E; AMC; Animal Planet; BET; Bravo; Cartoon Network; CMT; CNBC; CNN; Comedy Central; Discovery Channel; Disney Channel; Disney XD; E! HD; ESPN; ESPN Classic; ESPN2; Food Network; Fox News Channel; Fox Sports 1; Freeform; FX; Golf Channel; GSN; Hallmark Channel; HGTV; History; HLN; INSP; Lifetime; MSNBC; MTV; National Geographic Channel; NBCSN; Nickelodeon; Outdoor Channel; Oxygen; Root Sports Pittsburgh; Spike TV; Syfy; TBS; The Weather Channel; TLC; TNT; Travel Channel; truTV; Turner Classic Movies; TV Land; USA Network; VH1; WE tv.
Fee: $17.10 monthly.
Digital Basic Service
Subscribers: N.A.
Programming (via satellite): BBC America; Bloomberg Television; Discovery Digital Networks; DIY Network; ESPN; ESPNews; FOX College Sports Central; FOX College Sports Pacific; Fox Deportes; Fox Sports 2; Fuse; FXM; FYI; Great American Country; HD Theater; History International; IFC; LMN; MC; NFL Network; Nick 2; Nick Jr.; Nicktoons; Sundance TV; TeenNick; TVG Network.
Digital Pay Service 1
Pay Units: N.A.
Programming (via satellite): Cinemax (multiplexed); HBO (multiplexed); Showtime (multiplexed); Starz (multiplexed); Starz Encore (multiplexed); The Movie Channel (multiplexed).
Video-On-Demand: Yes
Pay-Per-View
Playboy TV (delivered digitally); Fresh (delivered digitally); Shorteez (delivered digitally); iN DEMAND (delivered digitally); NHL Center Ice (delivered digitally); MLB Extra Innings (delivered digitally).
Internet Service
Operational: Yes.
Subscribers: 17,542.
Broadband Service: Suddenlink High Speed Internet.
Fee: $49.95 installation; $29.99 monthly.
Telephone Service
Digital: Operational
Subscribers: 15,416.
Miles of Plant: 967.0 (coaxial); 577.0 (fiber optic). Homes passed: 38,557.
Vice President, Operations: David Bach. Vice President, Corporate Finance: Michael Pflantz. General Manager: Jack Ozminkowski. Chief Technician: Joe Davis. Marketing Director: Stan Howell. Office Supervisor: Donna Vance.
Ownership: Cequel Communications Holdings I LLC (MSO).

KEYSER—Comcast Cable, 15 Summit Park Dr, Pittsburgh, PA 15275. Phones: 412-747-6400; 304-788-2939 (Keyser office). Fax: 412-747-6401. Web Site: http://www.comcast.com. Also serves Allegany County (portions), Barton, Bloomington, Frostburg, Garrett County (portions), Lonaconing, Luke, McCoole, Midland, Midlothian & Westernport, MD; Augusta, Mineral County (portions), New Creek, Piedmont & Springfield, WV. ICA: WV0020.
TV Market Ranking: Below 100 (Augusta); Outside TV Markets (Allegany County (portions), Barton, Bloomington, Frostburg, Garrett County (portions), Garrett County (portions), KEYSER, Lonaconing, Luke, McCoole, Midland, Midlothian, Mineral County (portions), New Creek, Piedmont, Westernport, Springfield). Franchise award date: October 1, 1965. Franchise expiration date: N.A. Began: April 1, 1952. Channel capacity: N.A. Channels available but not in use: N.A.
Basic Service
Subscribers: 6,258. Commercial subscribers: 48.
Programming (received off-air): KDKA-TV (CBS, Decades) Pittsburgh; WJAC-TV (MeTV, NBC) Johnstown; allband FM.
Programming (via microwave): WDCA (Heroes & Icons, MNT, Movies!, Mundo-Max) Washington; WDCW (Antenna TV, CW, This TV) Washington; WHAG-TV (IND) Hagerstown; WJAL (IND) Hagerstown; WJLA-TV (ABC, MeTV, Retro TV) Washington; WJZ-TV (CBS, Decades) Baltimore; WTTG (Buzzr, FOX) Washington; WUSA (Bounce TV, CBS, WeatherNation) Washington; WWPB (PBS) Hagerstown.
Programming (via satellite): A&E; AMC; Animal Planet; BET; Cartoon Network; CMT; CNBC; CNN; Comcast SportsNet Mid-Atlantic; Comedy Central; C-SPAN; C-SPAN 2; Discovery Channel; Disney Channel; E! HD; ESPN; ESPN2; EWTN Global Catholic Network; Food Network; Fox News Channel; FOX Sports Networks; Freeform; FX; HGTV; History; HLN; ION Television; Lifetime; MSNBC; MTV; Nickelodeon; Outdoor Channel; QVC; Spike TV; TBS; The Weather Channel; TLC; TNT; Travel Channel; Trinity Broadcasting Network (TBN); truTV; TV Land; USA Network; VH1; WGN America.
Programming (via translator): WNPB-TV (PBS) Morgantown.
Fee: $29.50-$42.75 installation; $30.75 monthly.
Digital Basic Service
Subscribers: N.A.
Programming (via satellite): BBC America; Bloomberg Television; Bravo; CMT; Destination America; Discovery Kids Channel; Discovery Life Channel; Disney XD; ESPN Classic; ESPNews; FOX College Sports Central; FOX College Sports Pacific; Fox Sports 1; Fuse; FXM; FYI; Golf Channel; Great American Country; GSN; History; History International; IFC; Investigation Discovery; LMN; MTV Classic; MTV2; National Geographic Channel; Nick Jr.; Nicktoons; OWN: Oprah Winfrey Network; Science Channel; Syfy; TeenNick; The Word Network; Turner Classic Movies; UP; WE tv.
Fee: $10.95 monthly; $3.95 converter.
Digital Pay Service 1
Pay Units: N.A.
Programming (via satellite): Cinemax (multiplexed); HBO (multiplexed); Showtime (multiplexed); Starz (multiplexed); Starz Encore (multiplexed); The Movie Channel (multiplexed).
Fee: $15.95 monthly (each).
Video-On-Demand: No
Pay-Per-View
iN DEMAND (delivered digitally); Playboy TV (delivered digitally); Club Jenna (delivered digitally); Fresh (delivered digitally).
Internet Service
Operational: Yes.
Subscribers: 3,963.
Broadband Service: Comcast High Speed Internet.
Fee: $42.95 monthly.
Telephone Service
None
Miles of Plant: 460.0 (coaxial); 285.0 (fiber optic). Homes passed: 15,513.
Regional Vice President: Linda Hossinger. Vice President, Technical Operations: Randy Bender. Vice President, Marketing: Donna Corning. Vice President, Public Affairs: Jody Doherty. Chief Technician:

2017 Edition
D-839

West Virginia—Cable Systems

Roy Blanchard. Office Manager: Nancy Nesselrodt.
Ownership: Comcast Cable Communications Inc. (MSO).

KIMBALL—Formerly served by Comcast Cable. Now served by Shentel, PINEVILLE, WV [WV0204]. ICA: WV0121.

KINGWOOD—Atlantic Broadband, 107 1/2 B Pleasant Ave, Kingwood, WV 26537. Phones: 888-536-9600 (Customer service); 814-535-3506. Fax: 814-535-7749. E-mail: info@atlanticbb.com. Web Site: http://atlanticbb.com. Also serves Albright, Arthurdale, Bretz, Denver, Independence, Masontown, Newburg, Preston County (portions), Reedsville & Terra Alta. ICA: WV0189.
TV Market Ranking: Below 100 (Independence, Masontown, Newburg, Reedsville, Preston County (portions)); Outside TV Markets (Albright, Arthurdale, Bretz, KINGWOOD, Terra Alta, Preston County (portions)). Franchise award date: N.A. Franchise expiration date: N.A. Began: June 1, 1967.
Channel capacity: 66 (operating 2-way). Channels available but not in use: N.A.
Basic Service
Subscribers: 2,483. Commercial subscribers: 205.
Programming (received off-air): KDKA-TV (CBS, Decades) Pittsburgh; WBOY-TV (ABC, NBC) Clarksburg; WDTV (CBS) Weston; WNPB-TV (PBS) Morgantown; WPGH-TV (Antenna TV, FOX, The Country Network) Pittsburgh; WPNT (MNT) Pittsburgh; WPXI (MeTV, NBC) Pittsburgh; WTAE-TV (ABC, This TV) Pittsburgh; WVFX (CW, FOX) Clarksburg; WWCP-TV (FOX) Johnstown; allband FM.
Programming (via satellite): C-SPAN; C-SPAN 2; INSP; QVC; WGN America.
Fee: $40.00 installation; $34.36 monthly.
Expanded Basic Service 1
Subscribers: 2,283.
Programming (via satellite): A&E; AMC; Animal Planet; Bravo; Cartoon Network; CMT; CNBC; CNN; Comedy Central; Discovery Channel; Disney Channel; E! HD; ESPN; ESPN2; Food Network; Fox News Channel; Fox Sports 1; Freeform; FX; Golf Channel; Hallmark Channel; HGTV; History; HLN; Lifetime; MSNBC; MTV; National Geographic Channel; Nickelodeon; OWN: Oprah Winfrey Network; Oxygen; Root Sports Pittsburgh; Spike TV; Syfy; TBS; The Weather Channel; TLC; TNT; Travel Channel; truTV; TV Land; USA Network; VH1.
Fee: $43.18 monthly.
Digital Basic Service
Subscribers: N.A.
Programming (via satellite): A&E HD; BBC America; Bloomberg Television; Boomerang; CMT; Destination America; Discovery Kids Channel; Disney XD; DIY Network; ESPN Classic; ESPN HD; ESPNews; Fox Sports 2; FYI; Great American Country; HD Theater; History International; IFC; Investigation Discovery; LMN; MC; MTV Classic; MTV Hits; MTV Jams; MTV2; NFL Network; Nick 2; Nick Jr.; Nicktoons; Root Sports Pittsburgh; RTV; Science Channel; Starz (multiplexed); Starz Encore (multiplexed); Starz HD; TeenNick; TNT HD; Tr3s; VH1 Soul; WE tv; Weatherscan.
Fee: $18.95 monthly.
Digital Pay Service 1
Pay Units: N.A.
Programming (via satellite): Cinemax (multiplexed); Cinemax HD; Flix; HBO (multiplexed); HBO HD; Showtime (multiplexed); The Movie Channel (multiplexed).
Fee: $15.95 monthly (Cinemax, HBO or Showtime/Flix/TMC).
Video-On-Demand: No
Pay-Per-View
iN DEMAND (delivered digitally); Hot Choice (delivered digitally); Club Jenna (delivered digitally); Fresh (delivered digitally); Playboy TV (delivered digitally).
Internet Service
Operational: Yes.
Broadband Service: Atlantic Broadband High-Speed Internet.
Fee: $24.95-$57.95 monthly.
Telephone Service
Digital: Operational
Fee: $44.95 monthly
Homes passed: 7,008.
Chief Financial Officer: Patrick Bratton. Senior Vice President & General Counsel: Leslie Brown. Vice President: David Dane. General Manager: Mike Papasergi. Technical Operations Director: Charles Sorchilla. Marketing & Customer Service Director: Dara Leslie. Marketing Manager: Natalie Kurchak.
Ownership: Atlantic Broadband (MSO).

LEFT HAND—Formerly served by Econoco Inc. Now served by Suddenlink Communications, PARKERSBURG, WV [WV0003]. ICA: WV0190.

LENORE—Formerly served by Charter Communications. Now served by Suddenlink Communications, KERMIT, WV [WV0038]. ICA: WV0050.

LEON—Formerly served by Vital Communications. No longer in operation. ICA: WV0263.

LEWISBURG—Formerly served by Charter Communications. Now served by Suddenlink Communications, BECKLEY, WV [WV0005]. ICA: WV0033.

LITTLE OTTER—Shentel. Now served by SUMMERSVILLE, WV [WV0213]. ICA: WV0227.

LITTLETON—Zito Media, 102 S Main St, PO Box 665, Coudersport, PA 16915. Phones: 814-260-9055; 800-365-6988. E-mail: info@zitomedia.com. Web Site: http://www.zitomedia.com. Also serves Burton & Hundred. ICA: WV0106.
TV Market Ranking: 90 (Burton, Hundred, LITTLETON). Franchise award date: July 6, 1986. Franchise expiration date: N.A. Began: October 1, 1970.
Channel capacity: 35 (not 2-way capable). Channels available but not in use: N.A.
Basic Service
Subscribers: 99.
Programming (received off-air): KDKA-TV (CBS, Decades) Pittsburgh; WBOY-TV (ABC, NBC) Clarksburg; WDTV (CBS) Weston; WNPB-TV (PBS) Morgantown; WPGH-TV (Antenna TV, FOX, The Country Network) Pittsburgh; WPNT (MNT) Pittsburgh; WPXI (MeTV, NBC) Pittsburgh; WQED (PBS) Pittsburgh; WTAE-TV (ABC, This TV) Pittsburgh; WTOV-TV (MeTV, NBC) Steubenville; WTRF-TV (ABC, CBS, MNT) Wheeling; allband FM.
Fee: $49.95 installation; $22.95 monthly; $1.24 converter.
Expanded Basic Service 1
Subscribers: N.A.
Programming (via satellite): AMC; Animal Planet; CNN; Discovery Channel; Disney Channel; E! HD; ESPN; ESPN2; Freeform; Great American Country; Lifetime; Nickelodeon; Spike TV; Syfy; TBS; The Weather Channel; TNT; Trinity Broadcasting Network (TBN); USA Network; WGN America.
Fee: $23.00 monthly.
Pay Service 1
Pay Units: N.A.
Programming (via satellite): Cinemax; HBO; Showtime; The Movie Channel.
Fee: $10.00 installation; $7.95 monthly (Cinemax), $11.95 monthly (Showtime or TMC), $11.99 monthly (HBO).
Video-On-Demand: No
Internet Service
Operational: Yes.
Subscribers: 14.
Telephone Service
None
Miles of Plant: 34.0 (coaxial); 5.0 (fiber optic). Homes passed: 400.
President: James Rigas.
Ownership: Zito Media (MSO).

LOGAN—Formerly served by Charter Communications. Now served by Suddenlink Communications, KERMIT, WV [WV0038]. ICA: WV0017.

LOW GAP—Shentel, 500 Shentel Way, PO Box 459, Edinburg, VA 22824. Phones: 540-984-5224; 800-743-6835; 304-946-2871. Fax: 540-984-3438. E-mail: Angela.Washington@emp.shentel.com. Web Site: http://www.shentel.com. Also serves Haddleton. ICA: WV0280.
TV Market Ranking: 36 (Haddleton, LOW GAP).
Channel capacity: N.A. Channels available but not in use: N.A.
Basic Service
Subscribers: 85.
Fee: $40.00 installation; $24.18 monthly.
Operations Manager: Allen Siers. Vice President, Customer Service: Angela Washington.
Ownership: Shentel (MSO).

MADISON—Suddenlink Communications. Now served by CHARLESTON, WV [WV0006]. ICA: WV0192.

MANNINGTON—Formerly served by Mannington TV Inc. Now served by Comcast Cable, MORGANTOWN, WV [WV0198]. ICA: WV0067.

MARLINTON (town)—Shentel, 500 Shentel Way, PO Box 459, Edinburg, VA 22824. Phones: 800-743-6835; 540-984-5224. Fax: 540-984-3438. E-mail: customer_service@shentel.net. Web Site: http://www.shentel.com. Also serves Hillsboro & Pocahontas County (portions). ICA: WV0193.
TV Market Ranking: Below 100 (Hillsboro, MARLINTON (TOWN), Pocahontas County (portions)). Franchise award date: N.A. Franchise expiration date: N.A. Began: May 15, 1954.
Channel capacity: N.A. Channels available but not in use: N.A.
Basic Service
Subscribers: 30.
Programming (received off-air): WDBJ (CBS, Decades, MNT) Roanoke; WFFP-TV (COZI TV, IND, Movies!) Danville; WFXR (CW, FOX) Roanoke; WOAY-TV (ABC) Oak Hill; WSET-TV (ABC, Retro TV, WeatherNation) Lynchburg; WSLS-TV (MeTV, NBC) Roanoke; WSWP-TV (PBS) Grandview; WVNS-TV (CBS, FOX) Lewisburg; WVVA (CW, MeTV, NBC) Bluefield; allband FM.
Programming (via satellite): A&E; AMC; Animal Planet; Bravo; Cartoon Network; CMT; CNN; Comedy Central; C-SPAN; CW PLUS; Discovery Channel; Disney Channel; E! HD; ESPN; ESPN Classic; ESPN2; ESPNews; Fox News Channel; Fox Sports 1; Freeform; FX; Hallmark Channel; HGTV; History; HLN; Lifetime; MSNBC; MTV; Nickelodeon; Outdoor Channel; Pop; QVC; Root Sports Pittsburgh; Spike TV; Syfy; TBS; The Weather Channel; TLC; TNT; Travel Channel; Trinity Broadcasting Network (TBN); truTV; Turner Classic Movies; TV Land; USA Network; VH1; WE tv; WGN America.
Fee: $99.95 installation; $34.96 monthly; $30.00 converter.
Expanded Basic Service 1
Subscribers: N.A.
Fee: $34.00 monthly.
Digital Basic Service
Subscribers: N.A.
Programming (via satellite): BBC America; Bloomberg Television; CMT; Destination America; Discovery Life Channel; Discovery Kids Channel; Disney XD; FOX College Sports Central; FOX College Sports Pacific; Fuse; FXM; FYI; GSN; History International; IFC; Investigation Discovery; LMN; MTV Classic; MTV Hits; MTV Jams; MTV2; Nick 2; Nick Jr.; Nicktoons; OWN: Oprah Winfrey Network; Science Channel; Sundance TV; TeenNick; VH1 Soul; WE tv.
Fee: $13.00 monthly.
Digital Pay Service 1
Pay Units: N.A.
Programming (via satellite): Cinemax (multiplexed); Flix; HBO (multiplexed); Showtime (multiplexed); Starz (multiplexed); Starz Encore; The Movie Channel (multiplexed).
Video-On-Demand: No
Internet Service
Operational: No.
Telephone Service
None
Miles of Plant: 51.0 (coaxial); None (fiber optic). Homes passed: 1,225.
Vice President, Industry Affairs & Regulations: Chris Kyle. Assistant Secretary, Associate General Counsel: Ann Flowers.
Ownership: Shentel (MSO).

MARTINSBURG—Formerly served by Adelphia Communications. Now served by Comcast Cable, JEFFERSON COUNTY (portions), WV [WV0016]. ICA: WV0019.

MATEWAN—Formerly served by Charter Communications. No longer in operation. ICA: WV0073.

MAYSEL—Formerly served by Econoco Inc. No longer in operation. ICA: WV0195.

MEADOW BRIDGE—Formerly served by Vital Communications. No longer in operation. ICA: WV0089.

MEADOWDALE—Formerly served by Adelphia Communications. No longer in operation. ICA: WV0109.

MIDDLEBOURNE—Formerly served by Richards TV Cable. No longer in operation. ICA: WV0105.

MILTON—Suddenlink Communications. Now served by CHARLESTON, WV [WV0006]. ICA: WV0012.

Cable Systems—West Virginia

MONONGAH—Formerly served by Adelphia Communications. Now served by Comcast Cable, TAYLOR COUNTY (portions), WV [WV0278]. ICA: WV0055.

MOOREFIELD—Hardy Telecommunications, 2255 Kimseys Run Rd, Lost River, WV 26810. Phones: 800-838-2497; 304-897-9911 (Lost River office); 866-805-1827; 304-530-5000. Web Site: http://www.hardynet.net. Also serves Hardy County (portions) & Wardensville. ICA: WV0197.
TV Market Ranking: Below 100 (Hardy County (portions) (portions)); Outside TV Markets (Hardy County (portions) (portions), MOOREFIELD, Wardensville). Franchise award date: N.A. Franchise expiration date: N.A. Began: July 1, 1969.
Channel capacity: N.A. Channels available but not in use: N.A.
Basic Service
Subscribers: 121. Commercial subscribers: 22.
Programming (received off-air): WHAG-TV (IND) Hagerstown; WHSV-TV (ABC, MeTV, MNT, This TV) Harrisonburg; WJAC-TV (MeTV, NBC) Johnstown; WNPB-TV (PBS) Morgantown; WTTG (Buzzr, FOX) Washington; WUSA (Bounce TV, CBS, WeatherNation) Washington; WWCP-TV (FOX) Johnstown; WWPB (PBS) Hagerstown; WWPX-TV (ION) Martinsburg; allband FM.
Programming (via satellite): C-SPAN; QVC.
Fee: $40.00 installation; $29.05 monthly.
Expanded Basic Service 1
Subscribers: 111.
Programming (via satellite): A&E; AMC; CMT; CNN; Comedy Central; C-SPAN 2; Discovery Channel; Disney Channel; ESPN; ESPN2; Fox News Channel; Freeform; FX; HGTV; History; HLN; INSP; MTV; Nickelodeon; OWN: Oprah Winfrey Network; Spike TV; TBS; The Weather Channel; TNT; TV Land; USA Network; VH1.
Fee: $36.49 monthly.
Digital Basic Service
Subscribers: N.A.
Programming (via satellite): BBC America; Bloomberg Television; Cooking Channel; Discovery Kids Channel; Discovery Life Channel; Disney XD; DMX Music; ESPN Classic; ESPNews; Fuse; FYI; Golf Channel; GSN; History International; IFC; LMN; MTV2; Nick Jr.; Nicktoons; Outdoor Channel; Science Channel; Starz (multiplexed); Starz Encore (multiplexed); Trinity Broadcasting Network (TBN); Turner Classic Movies.
Fee: $21.90 monthly.
Digital Pay Service 1
Pay Units: N.A.
Programming (via satellite): Cinemax (multiplexed); HBO (multiplexed); Showtime (multiplexed).
Fee: $15.95 monthly (each).
Video-On-Demand: No
Pay-Per-View
iN DEMAND (delivered digitally); Hot Choice (delivered digitally); Playboy TV (delivered digitally); Fresh (delivered digitally); Shorteez (delivered digitally).
Internet Service
Operational: Yes.
Fee: $29.95-$89.95 monthly.
Telephone Service
Digital: Operational
Fee: $32.95 monthly
Miles of Plant: 51.0 (coaxial); None (fiber optic). Homes passed: 1,205.
President: Greg M. Zirk.
Ownership: Hardy Telecommunications Inc. (MSO).

MORGANTOWN—Comcast Cable, 15 Summit Park Dr, Pittsburgh, PA 15275. Phones: 412-747-6400; 304-292-6188 (Morgantown office). Fax: 412-747-6401. Web Site: http://www.comcast.com. Also serves Clarksburg, Core, Fairmont, Grafton, Granville, Maidsville, Mannington, Marion County (portions), Monongah, Monongalia County (portions), Osage, Pleasant Valley, Preston County (portions), Pursglove, Rachel, Rivesville, Rowlesburg, Star City, Taylor County (portions), Westover, Whitehall & Worthington. ICA: WV0198.
TV Market Ranking: Below 100 (Clarksburg, Core, Fairmont, Granville, Maidsville, Marion County (portions), Monongah, MORGANTOWN, Osage, Pleasant Valley, Pursglove, Rachel, Rivesville, Star City, Westover, Whitehall, Worthington, Taylor County (portions)); Outside TV Markets (Rowlesburg). Franchise award date: N.A. Franchise expiration date: N.A. Began: July 1, 1953.
Channel capacity: 116 (operating 2-way). Channels available but not in use: N.A.
Basic Service
Subscribers: 31,138. Commercial subscribers: 605.
Programming (received off-air): KDKA-TV (CBS, Decades) Pittsburgh; WBOY-TV (ABC, NBC) Clarksburg; WDTV (CBS) Weston; WNPB-TV (PBS) Morgantown; WPCB-TV (IND) Greensburg; WPGH-TV (Antenna TV, FOX, The Country Network) Pittsburgh; WPNT (MNT) Pittsburgh; WPXI (MeTV, NBC) Pittsburgh; WQED (PBS) Pittsburgh; WTAE-TV (ABC, This TV) Pittsburgh; WVFX (CW, FOX) Clarksburg; allband FM.
Programming (via satellite): A&E; C-SPAN; C-SPAN 2; EVINE Live; EWTN Global Catholic Network; Hallmark Network; HLN; Pop; QVC; Trinity Broadcasting Network (TBN); WGN America.
Fee: $29.50-$42.75 installation; $37.10 monthly.
Expanded Basic Service 1
Subscribers: N.A.
Programming (via satellite): AMC; Animal Planet; BET; Bravo; Cartoon Network; CMT; CNBC; CNN; Comedy Central; Discovery Channel; Disney Channel; E! HD; ESPN; ESPN2; Food Network; Fox News Channel; Fox Sports 1; Freeform; FX; HGTV; History; INSP; ION Television; Lifetime; MSNBC; MTV; MTV2; Nick Jr.; Nickelodeon; Oxygen; Root Sports Pittsburgh; Spike TV; Syfy; TBS; The Weather Channel; TLC; TNT; Travel Channel; truTV; TV Land; USA Network; VH1.
Fee: $28.00 monthly.
Digital Basic Service
Subscribers: N.A.
Programming (via satellite): BBC America; Bloomberg Television; Discovery Life Channel; Disney XD; DIY Network; ESPN Classic; ESPNews; Fuse; FXM; Golf Channel; Great American Country; GSN; History International; MC; NBCSN; Outdoor Channel; The Word Network; WE tv.
Fee: $10.95 monthly.
Digital Expanded Basic Service
Subscribers: N.A.
Programming (via satellite): FSN Digital Atlantic; FSN Digital Central; FSN Digital Pacific; FYI; IFC; National Geographic Channel; Nick 2; Nicktoons; TeenNick.
Fee: $6.95 monthly.
Digital Pay Service 1
Pay Units: N.A.
Programming (via satellite): ART America; Cinemax (multiplexed); Flix; HBO (multiplexed); HITS (Headend In The Sky); RAI Italia; RTN; Showtime (multiplexed); Starz (multiplexed); Starz Encore (multiplexed); The Filipino Channel; The Movie Channel (multiplexed); TV Asia; TV5MONDE USA; Zee TV.
Fee: $15.95 monthly (each).
Video-On-Demand: No
Pay-Per-View
Hot Choice (delivered digitally); Urban Xtra (delivered digitally); Playboy TV (delivered digitally); Fresh (delivered digitally); Shorteez (delivered digitally).
Internet Service
Operational: Yes.
Subscribers: 31,083.
Broadband Service: Comcast High Speed Internet.
Fee: $42.95 monthly.
Telephone Service
Digital: Operational
Subscribers: 14,709.
Miles of Plant: 1,600.0 (coaxial); 556.0 (fiber optic). Homes passed: 72,867.
Regional Vice President: Linda Hossinger. Vice President, Technical Operations: Randy Bender. Vice President, Marketing: Donna Corning. Vice President, Public Affairs: Jody Doherty. Chief Technician: Ed Hinkle. Customer Service Manager: Sheila Hall.
Ownership: Comcast Cable Communications Inc. (MSO).

MOUNDSVILLE—Comcast Cable. Now served by WHEELING, WV [WV0004]. ICA: WV0022.

MOUNT LOOKOUT—Formerly served by Econoco Inc. No longer in operation. ICA: WV0199.

MOUNT STORM—Formerly served by Almega Cable. No longer in operation. ICA: WV0257.

MUD RIVER—Shentel, Shentel Center, 500 Shentel Way, Edinburg, VA 22824. Phones: 540-984-5224; 304-946-2871. Fax: 540-984-3438. E-mail: Angela.Washington@emp.shentel.com. Web Site: http://www.shentel.com. ICA: WV0238.
TV Market Ranking: 36 (MUD RIVER).
Channel capacity: N.A. Channels available but not in use: N.A.
Basic Service
Subscribers: 39.
Programming (received off-air): WCHS-TV (ABC, Antenna TV) Charleston; WOWK-TV (CBS) Huntington; WSAZ-TV (MNT, NBC, This TV) Huntington; WVAH-TV (FOX, The Country Network) Charleston; WVPB-TV (PBS) Huntington.
Programming (via satellite): ESPN; Freeform; TNT; USA Network.
Fee: $40.00 installation; $24.18 monthly.
Pay Service 1
Pay Units: N.A.
Programming (via satellite): HBO.
Fee: $12.00 monthly.
Internet Service
Operational: No.
Telephone Service
None
Miles of Plant: 5.0 (coaxial); None (fiber optic). Homes passed: 150.
Operations Manager: Allen Siers. Vice President, Customer Service: Angela Washington.
Ownership: Colane Cable TV Inc. (MSO).

MULLENS—Formerly served by Jet Broadband. Now served by Shentel, PINEVILLE, WV [WV0204]. ICA: WV0086.

NEBO—Formerly served by Windjammer Cable. No longer in operation. ICA: WV0253.

NEIBERT—Shentel, Shentel Center, 500 Shentel Way, Edinburg, VA 22824. Phones: 540-984-5224; 304-946-2871. Fax: 540-984-3438. E-mail: Angela.Washington@emp.shentel.com. Web Site: http://www.shentel.com. Also serves Lyburn. ICA: WV0237.
TV Market Ranking: Below 100 (NEIBERT, Lyburn).
Channel capacity: N.A. Channels available but not in use: N.A.
Basic Service
Subscribers: 28.
Programming (received off-air): WCHS-TV (ABC, Antenna TV) Charleston; WOWK-TV (CBS) Huntington; WSAZ-TV (MNT, NBC, This TV) Huntington; WTSF (Daystar TV) Ashland; WVAH-TV (FOX, The Country Network) Charleston; WVPB-TV (PBS) Huntington.
Programming (via satellite): CMT; ESPN; Freeform; TBS; TNT; USA Network; WGN America.
Fee: $40.00 installation; $34.90 monthly.
Pay Service 1
Pay Units: N.A.
Programming (via satellite): HBO.
Fee: $12.00 monthly.
Internet Service
Operational: No.
Telephone Service
None
Miles of Plant: 5.0 (coaxial); None (fiber optic). Homes passed: 280.
Operations Manager: Allen Siers. Vice President, Customer Service: Angela Washington.
Ownership: Colane Cable TV Inc. (MSO).

NETTIE—Formerly served by Vital Communications. No longer in operation. ICA: WV0156.

NEW CUMBERLAND—Comcast Cable. Now served by STEUBENVILLE, OH [OH0048]. ICA: WV0069.

NEW MARTINSVILLE—Formerly served by Charter Communications. Now served by Suddenlink Communications, PARKERSBURG, WV [WV0003]. ICA: WV0025.

NITRO—Formerly served by Charter Communications. Now served by Suddenlink Communications, CHARLESTON, WV [WV0006]. ICA: WV0009.

NORTHFORK—Shentel. Now served by PINEVILLE, WV [WV0204]. ICA: WV0045.

NORTON—Formerly served by Vital Communications. No longer in operation. ICA: WV0256.

OAK HILL—Formerly served by Charter Communications. Now served by Suddenlink Communications, BECKLEY, WV [WV0005]. ICA: WV0023.

OAKVALE—Formerly served by Shentel. No longer in operation. ICA: WV0201.

OMAR—Shentel, Shentel Center, 500 Shentel Way, Edinburg, VA 22824. Phones: 540-984-5224; 304-946-2871. Fax: 540-984-3438.

West Virginia—Cable Systems

E-mail: Angela.Washington@emp.shentel.com. Web Site: http://www.shentel.com. Also serves Lawrence County (portions), Martin County (portions) & Pike County (portions), KY; Baisden, Barnabus, Bens Creek, Chauncey, Cow Creek, Delbarton, Gilbert Creek, Hampden, Hatfield, Micco, Mingo County (portions), Sarah Ann, Sharon Heights, Stirrat, Switzer, Varney & Wayne County (portions), WV. ICA: WV0191.

TV Market Ranking: Below 100 (Baisden, Barnabus, Chauncey, Cow Creek, Delbarton, Gilbert Creek, Hampden, Hatfield, Micco, OMAR, Sharon Heights, Stirrat, Switzer, Varney, Mingo County (portions), Sarah Ann); Outside TV Markets (Bens Creek, Lawrence County (portions), Martin County (portions), Pike County (portions), Wayne County (portions), Mingo County (portions)). Franchise award date: N.A. Franchise expiration date: N.A. Began: September 1, 1980.

Channel capacity: N.A. Channels available but not in use: N.A.

Basic Service
Subscribers: 1,032.
Programming (received off-air): WCHS-TV (ABC, Antenna TV) Charleston; WLPX-TV (ION) Charleston; WOWK-TV (CBS) Huntington; WQCW (CW) Portsmouth; WSAZ-TV (MNT, NBC, This TV) Huntington; WVAH-TV (FOX, The Country Network) Charleston; WVPB-TV (PBS) Huntington; WVVA (CW, MeTV, NBC) Bluefield.
Programming (via satellite): A&E; AMC; Boomerang; Cartoon Network; CMT; CNBC; CNN; C-SPAN; Discovery Channel; ESPN; ESPN2; ESPNews; Food Network; Fox News Channel; Fox Sports 1; FOX Sports Ohio/Sports Time Ohio; Freeform; FX; GSN; HGTV; History; HLN; Lifetime; MTV; Nickelodeon; Outdoor Channel; OWN: Oprah Winfrey Network; QVC; Spike TV; Syfy; TBS; The Weather Channel; TLC; TNT; Trinity Broadcasting Network (TBN); Turner Classic Movies; TV Land; USA Network; VH1; WE tv; WGN America.
Fee: $40.00 installation; $26.57 monthly.

Pay Service 1
Pay Units: 600 Includes Beech Creek, Bruno, & Hanover.
Programming (via satellite): HBO; Showtime; The Movie Channel.
Fee: $15.00 installation; $10.50 monthly (each).

Video-On-Demand: No
Internet Service
Operational: No.
Telephone Service
None
Miles of Plant: 102.0 (coaxial); None (fiber optic). Homes passed: 5,000. Homes passed and miles of plant includes Beech Creek, Bruno, & Hanover.
Operations Manager: Allen Siers. Vice President, Customer Service: Angela Washington.
Ownership: Colane Cable TV Inc. (MSO).

PAGE—Shentel. Now served by SUMMERSVILLE, WV [WV0213]. ICA: WV0248.

PANTHER—Formerly served by A & A Communications. No longer in operation. ICA: WV0101.

PARKERSBURG—Suddenlink Communications, 520 Maryville Centre Dr, Ste 300, St. Louis, MO 63141. Phones: 304-865-7225; 304-757-8001 (Scott Depot office); 314-315-9400; 800-972-5757 (Customer service). E-mail: Gene.Regan@suddenlink. com. Web Site: http://www.suddenlink.com. Also serves Addison Twp., Belpre, Cheshire, Cheshire Twp., Gallia County (portions), Gallipolis, Marietta, Meigs County (portions), Middleport, Minersville, Pomeroy, Racine, Reno, Rutland, Springfield Twp. & Syracuse, OH; Amma, Belmont, Boaz, Davisville, Elizabeth, Eureka, Gallipolis Ferry, Goldtown, Hartford, Henderson, Kenna, Left Hand, Mason, Mount Alto, New Haven, New Martinsville, Newton, North Hills, Paden City, Pleasants County, Point Pleasant, Ravenswood, Reno, Ripley, Sistersville, Spencer, St. Mary's, Tyler County (portions), Vienna, Waverly, Wetzel County (portions), Williamstown, Wirt County (portions) & Wood County, WV. ICA: WV0003.

TV Market Ranking: 36 (Amma, Gallia County (portions), Gallipolis, Gallipolis Ferry, Goldtown, Henderson, Kenna, Left Hand, Newton, Point Pleasant, Ripley, Spencer); 90 (New Martinsville, Paden City, Wetzel County (portions)); Below 100 (Belmont, Belpre, Boaz, Davisville, Elizabeth, Eureka, Hartford, Marietta, Mason, Meigs County (portions), Middleport, Minersville, Mount Alto, New Haven, North Hills, PARKERSBURG, Pomeroy, Racine, Ravenswood, Reno, Reno, Rutland, Sistersville, St. Mary's, Syracuse, Vienna, Waverly, Williamstown, Wirt County (portions), Wood County, Tyler County (portions)); Outside TV Markets (Addison Twp., Cheshire, Cheshire Twp., Springfield Twp., Tyler County (portions), Gallia County (portions)). Franchise award date: N.A. Franchise expiration date: N.A. Began: January 1, 1961.

Channel capacity: N.A. Channels available but not in use: N.A.

Basic Service
Subscribers: 44,150. Commercial subscribers: 2,364.
Programming (received off-air): WCHS-TV (ABC, Antenna TV) Charleston; WGN-TV (IND) Chicago; WOUB-TV (PBS) Athens; WOWK-TV (CBS) Huntington; WSAZ-TV (MNT, NBC, This TV) Huntington; WTAP-TV (FOX, MNT, NBC) Parkersburg; WVAH-TV (FOX, The Country Network) Charleston; WVPB-TV (PBS) Huntington; allband FM.
Programming (via microwave): WBNS-TV (Antenna TV, CBS, Decades) Columbus; WSYX (ABC, Antenna TV, MNT, This TV) Columbus.
Programming (via satellite): C-SPAN; C-SPAN 2; CW PLUS; EVINE Live; INSP; ION Television; QVC; Trinity Broadcasting Network (TBN).
Fee: $50.50 installation; $22.99 monthly; $2.00 converter.

Expanded Basic Service 1
Subscribers: N.A.
Programming (via satellite): A&E; AMC; Animal Planet; BET; Bravo; Cartoon Network; CMT; CNBC; CNN; Comedy Central; Discovery Channel; Disney Channel; Disney XD; E! HD; ESPN; ESPN2; Food Network; Fox News Channel; Fox Sports 1; Freeform; FX; Golf Channel; GSN; Hallmark Channel; HGTV; History; HLN; Lifetime; MSNBC; MTV; National Geographic Channel; NBCSN; Nickelodeon; Outdoor Channel; Oxygen; Pop; Root Sports Pittsburgh; Spike TV; Syfy; TBS; The Weather Channel; TLC; TNT; Travel Channel; truTV; Turner Classic Movies; TV Land; USA Network; VH1; WE tv.
Fee: $13.56 monthly.

Digital Basic Service
Subscribers: N.A.
Programming (via satellite): BBC America; Discovery Life Channel; DIY Network; DMX Music; ESPN; ESPN Classic; ESPNews; FOX College Sports Central; FOX College Sports Pacific; Fox Deportes; Fox Sports 2; Fuse; FXM; FYI; Great American Country; HD Theater; History International; IFC; LMN; MC; NFL Network; Nick 2; Nick Jr.; Nicktoons; Sundance TV; TeenNick; TVG Network.

Pay Service 1
Pay Units: N.A.
Programming (via satellite): Flix; Showtime (multiplexed); Starz Encore (multiplexed); The Movie Channel (multiplexed).

Digital Pay Service 1
Pay Units: N.A.
Programming (via satellite): Cinemax (multiplexed); HBO (multiplexed); HBO HD; Showtime; Starz (multiplexed).

Video-On-Demand: Yes
Pay-Per-View
Playboy TV (delivered digitally); Fresh (delivered digitally); Shorteez (delivered digitally).

Internet Service
Operational: Yes.
Subscribers: 42,872.
Broadband Service: Suddenlink High Speed Internet.
Fee: $49.95 installation; $29.99 monthly.

Telephone Service
Digital: Operational
Subscribers: 28,280.
Miles of Plant: 1,531.0 (coaxial); 496.0 (fiber optic). Homes passed: 89,254.
Senior Vice President, Corporate Finance: Michael Pflantz. Vice President, Operations: David Bach. General Manager: Patrick Barclay. Marketing Director: Stan Howell. Technical Operations Director: Bob Logg. Marketing Manager: Kenny Phillips.
Ownership: Cequel Communications Holdings I LLC (MSO).

PAW PAW—Atlantic Broadband, 201 South Mechanic St, Cumberland, MD 21502. Phones: 888-536-9600 (Customer service); 814-535-3506. Fax: 814-535-7749. E-mail: info@atlanticbb.com. Web Site: http://atlanticbb.com. ICA: WV0259.
TV Market Ranking: Outside TV Markets (PAW PAW).
Channel capacity: N.A. Channels available but not in use: N.A.

Basic Service
Subscribers: 47.
Programming (received off-air): WHAG-TV (IND) Hagerstown; WJLA-TV (ABC, MeTV, Retro TV) Washington; WNPB-TV (PBS) Morgantown; WTTG (Buzzr, FOX) Washington; WUSA (Bounce TV, CBS, WeatherNation) Washington.
Programming (via satellite): INSP; QVC.
Fee: $40.00 installation; $29.29 monthly.

Expanded Basic Service 1
Subscribers: 44.
Programming (via satellite): A&E; AMC; Animal Planet; Cartoon Network; CMT; CNN; Comedy Central; Discovery Channel; Disney Channel; E! HD; ESPN; Fox News Channel; FX; Hallmark Channel; History; Lifetime; MSNBC; Nickelodeon; OWN: Oprah Winfrey Network; Spike TV; Syfy; TBS; The Weather Channel; TLC; TNT; truTV; TV Land; USA Network; VH1.
Fee: $31.60 monthly.

Digital Basic Service
Subscribers: N.A.
Programming (via satellite): BBC America; Bloomberg Television; CMT; Cooking Channel; Destination America; Discovery Kids Channel; Discovery Life Channel; Disney XD; DMX Music; ESPN Classic; ESPN2; ESPNews; Fox Sports 1; Fuse; FYI; Golf Channel; GSN; History International; IFC; Investigation Discovery; LMN; MTV Classic; MTV2; National Geographic Channel; Nick Jr.; Nicktoons; Outdoor Channel; Science Channel; Starz (multiplexed); Starz Encore (multiplexed); Trinity Broadcasting Network (TBN); Turner Classic Movies.
Fee: $21.90 monthly.

Digital Pay Service 1
Pay Units: N.A.
Programming (via satellite): Cinemax (multiplexed); HBO (multiplexed); Showtime; The Movie Channel (multiplexed).
Fee: $15.95 monthly (Cinemax, HBO or Showtime/TMC).

Video-On-Demand: No
Pay-Per-View
iN DEMAND (delivered digitally).
Internet Service
Operational: Yes.
Telephone Service
None
Miles of Plant: 12.0 (coaxial); None (fiber optic). Homes passed: 223.
Chief Financial Officer: Patrick Bratton. Senior Vice President & General Counsel: Leslie Brown. Vice President: David Dane. General Manager: Mike Papasergi. Technical Operations Director: Charles Sorchilla. Marketing & Customer Service Director: Dara Leslie. Marketing Manager: Natalie Kurchak.
Ownership: Atlantic Broadband (MSO).

PAX—Formerly served by Charter Communications. Now served by Suddenlink Communications, BECKLEY, WV [WV0005]. ICA: WV0244.

PENNSBORO—Armstrong Cable Services. Now served by ZELIENOPLE, PA [PA0053]. ICA: WV0092.

PETERSBURG—Shentel, 500 Shentel Way, PO Box 459, Edinburg, VA 22824. Phones: 800-743-6835; 540-984-5224. Fax: 540-984-3438. E-mail: customer_service@shentel.net. Web Site: http://www.shentel.com. Also serves Franklin, Grant County (portions) & Pendleton County (portions). ICA: WV0064.

TV Market Ranking: Below 100 (Franklin, Pendleton County (portions)); Outside TV Markets (Grant County (portions), PETERSBURG, Pendleton County (portions)). Franchise award date: N.A. Franchise expiration date: N.A. Began: July 1, 1958.

Channel capacity: 38 (operating 2-way). Channels available but not in use: N.A.

Basic Service
Subscribers: 111.
Programming (received off-air): WHSV-TV (ABC, MeTV, MNT, This TV) Harrisonburg; WJAC-TV (MeTV, NBC) Johnstown; WNPB-TV (PBS) Morgantown; WTTG (Buzzr, FOX) Washington; WUSA (Bounce TV, CBS, WeatherNation) Washington; WWCP-TV (FOX) Johnstown; allband FM.
Programming (via satellite): C-SPAN; QVC; Trinity Broadcasting Network (TBN); WGN America.
Fee: $49.95 installation; $32.81 monthly; $1.24 converter.

Expanded Basic Service 1
Subscribers: N.A.
Programming (via satellite): A&E; AMC; CNN; Comedy Central; C-SPAN 2; Discovery Channel; Disney Channel; Disney XD; ESPN; ESPN Classic; ESPN2; Food Network; Fox News Channel; Fox Sports 1; Freeform; Great American Country; GSN; HLN; Lifetime; MSNBC; MTV; Nickelodeon;

Outdoor Channel; Root Sports Pittsburgh; Spike TV; Syfy; TBS; The Weather Channel; TLC; TNT; TV Land; USA Network; VH1; WE tv.
Fee: $32.00 monthly.

Digital Basic Service
Subscribers: N.A.
Programming (via satellite): BBC America; Bloomberg Television; Cloo; Discovery Digital Networks; ESPNews; EVINE Live; FOX College Sports Central; FOX College Sports Pacific; Fuse; FXM; FYI; Golf Channel; HGTV; History International; IFC; LMN; National Geographic Channel; NBCSN; Turner Classic Movies.
Fee: $12.00 monthly.

Pay Service 1
Pay Units: N.A.
Programming (via satellite): Cinemax; HBO; Showtime; Starz; Starz Encore; The Movie Channel.
Fee: $10.00 installation; $3.99 monthly (Encore), $7.95 monthly (Cinemax), $11.95 monthly (Showtime or TMC), $11.99 monthly (HBO).

Digital Pay Service 1
Pay Units: N.A.
Programming (via satellite): Cinemax (multiplexed); Flix; HBO (multiplexed); Showtime (multiplexed); Starz (multiplexed); Starz Encore (multiplexed); The Movie Channel (multiplexed).

Video-On-Demand: No

Pay-Per-View
iN DEMAND (delivered digitally); Playboy TV (delivered digitally); Fresh (delivered digitally).

Internet Service
Operational: Yes.

Telephone Service
Digital: Operational
Miles of Plant: 35.0 (coaxial); None (fiber optic). Homes passed: 1,797.
Vice President, Industry Affairs & Regulations: Chris Kyle.
Ownership: Shentel (MSO).

PETERSTOWN—Formerly served by Charter Communications. Now served by Suddenlink Communications, BECKLEY, WV [WV0005]. ICA: WV0251.

PHILIPPI—Philippi Communications System, 108 North Main St, PO Box 460, Philippi, WV 26416. Phone: 304-457-3700. Fax: 304-457-2703. Also serves Barbour County (portions). ICA: WV0054.
TV Market Ranking: Below 100 (Barbour County (portions), PHILIPPI). Franchise award date: March 1, 1985. Franchise expiration date: N.A. Began: March 1, 1986.
Channel capacity: N.A. Channels available but not in use: N.A.

Basic Service
Subscribers: 145.
Programming (received off-air): WBOY-TV (ABC, NBC) Clarksburg; WDTV (CBS) Weston; WNPB-TV (PBS) Morgantown; WTAE-TV (ABC, This TV) Pittsburgh; WVFX (CW, FOX) Clarksburg.
Programming (via satellite): C-SPAN; C-SPAN 2; HSN; QVC; The Weather Channel; Trinity Broadcasting Network (TBN); WGN America.
Fee: $50.00 installation; $16.84 monthly; $3.00 converter.

Expanded Basic Service 1
Subscribers: N.A.
Programming (via satellite): A&E; AMC; Animal Planet; Cartoon Network; CMT; CNBC; CNN; Comedy Central; C-SPAN 3; Discovery Channel; Disney Channel; ESPN; ESPN Classic; ESPN2; Food Network; Fox News Channel; Freeform; FX; Hallmark Channel; HGTV; History; HLN; Lifetime; LMN; MTV; National Geographic Channel; Nickelodeon; Outdoor Channel; Pop; Root Sports Pittsburgh; Spike TV; Syfy; TBS; TLC; TNT; Travel Channel; TV Land; USA Network; VH1.
Fee: $26.45 monthly.

Digital Basic Service
Subscribers: N.A.
Programming (via satellite): American Heroes Channel; BBC America; Chiller; Cloo; Destination America; Discovery Family; Discovery Life Channel; Disney XD; ESPNews; ESPNU; FYI; GSN; IFC; Investigation Discovery; MTV Classic; MTV Hits; MTV2; Nick Jr.; Nicktoons; OWN; Oprah Winfrey Network; Oxygen; Science Channel; Sprout; TeenNick; Turner Classic Movies; WE tv.
Fee: $9.00 monthly.

Digital Expanded Basic Service
Subscribers: N.A.
Programming (via satellite): Bloomberg Television; Boomerang; Cooking Channel; DIY Network; FamilyNet; FOX College Sports Central; FOX College Sports Pacific; Fox Sports 1; FXM; Golf Channel; Hallmark Movies & Mysteries; INSP; ION Television; MSNBC; NBCSN; RFD-TV; Tennis Channel; The Sportsman Channel; World Harvest Television.
Fee: $7.10 monthly.

Digital Expanded Basic Service 2
Subscribers: N.A.
Programming (via satellite): A&E HD; Animal Planet HD; AXS TV; Destination America HD; Discovery Channel HD; Disney Channel HD; ESPN HD; ESPN2 HD; Food Network HD; Fox News HD; Freeform HD; FX HD; HD Theater; HGTV HD; History HD; Lifetime HD; Lifetime Movie Network HD; National Geographic Channel HD; Outdoor Channel HD; Science HD; Syfy HD; TLC HD; TNT HD; Travel Channel HD; Universal HD; USA Network HD.
Fee: $7.95 monthly.

Digital Expanded Basic Service 3
Subscribers: N.A.
Programming (via satellite): Centric; CMT; DMX Music; Fuse; Great American Country; VH1 Soul.
Fee: $5.00 monthly.

Digital Pay Service 1
Pay Units: N.A.
Programming (via satellite): Cinemax (multiplexed); Flix; HBO (multiplexed); Showtime (multiplexed); Starz (multiplexed); Starz Encore (multiplexed); Sundance TV; The Movie Channel (multiplexed).
Fee: $14.75 monthly (Starz/Encore), $16.50 monthly (Showtime/TMC/Flix/Sundance), $19.50 monthly (HBO/Cinemax).

Video-On-Demand: No

Pay-Per-View
iN DEMAND (delivered digitally); XTSY (delivered digitally); Fresh (delivered digitally); Spice: Xcess (delivered digitally); Club Jenna (delivered digitally).

Internet Service
Operational: Yes.
Fee: $20.00-$60.00 monthly.

Telephone Service
None
Miles of Plant: 48.0 (coaxial); None (fiber optic). Homes passed: 2,000.
General Manager: Karen Weaver. Chief Technician: Carl Radcliff.
Ownership: City of Philippi.

PINE GROVE—Zito Media, 102 S Main St, PO Box 665, Coudersport, PA 16915. Phones: 814-260-9055; 800-365-6988. E-mail: info@zitomedia.com. Web Site: http://www.zitomedia.com. Also serves Hastings, Jacksonburg, Reader & Wetzel County. ICA: WV0081.
TV Market Ranking: 90 (Wetzel County (portions)); Below 100 (Hastings, Jacksonburg, PINE GROVE, Reader, Wetzel County (portions)). Franchise award date: N.A. Franchise expiration date: N.A. Began: January 1, 1954.
Channel capacity: 29 (not 2-way capable). Channels available but not in use: N.A.

Basic Service
Subscribers: 99.
Programming (received off-air): KDKA-TV (CBS, Decades) Pittsburgh; WBOY-TV (ABC, NBC) Clarksburg; WDTV (CBS) Weston; WNPB-TV (PBS) Morgantown; WTAE-TV (ABC, This TV) Pittsburgh; WTOV-TV (MeTV, NBC) Steubenville; WTRF-TV (ABC, CBS, MNT) Wheeling; WVFX (CW, FOX) Clarksburg; allband FM.
Programming (via satellite): The Weather Channel; WABC-TV (ABC, Live Well Network) New York; WGN America.
Fee: $49.95 installation; $22.95 monthly; $1.24 converter.

Expanded Basic Service 1
Subscribers: N.A.
Programming (via satellite): A&E; AMC; Animal Planet; Cartoon Network; CNN; C-SPAN; Discovery Channel; Disney Channel; E! HD; ESPN; ESPN2; Fox News Channel; Freeform; FX; Great American Country; Hallmark Channel; HGTV; History; Lifetime; Nickelodeon; Root Sports Pittsburgh; Spike TV; Syfy; TBS; TLC; TNT; TV Land; USA Network.
Fee: $22.00 monthly.

Digital Basic Service
Subscribers: N.A.
Programming (via satellite): BBC America; Bloomberg Television; Cloo; Discovery Digital Networks; Disney XD; DMX Music; ESPN Classic; ESPNews; EVINE Live; FOX College Sports Central; FOX College Sports Pacific; Fox Sports 1; Fuse; FXM; FYI; Golf Channel; GSN; History International; IFC; LMN; National Geographic Channel; NBCSN; Outdoor Channel; Trinity Broadcasting Network (TBN); Turner Classic Movies; WE tv.

Pay Service 1
Pay Units: N.A.
Programming (via satellite): HBO; Showtime.
Fee: $17.50 installation; $11.95 monthly (Showtime), $11.99 monthly (HBO).

Digital Pay Service 1
Pay Units: N.A.
Programming (via satellite): Cinemax (multiplexed); Flix; HBO (multiplexed); Showtime (multiplexed); Starz (multiplexed); Starz Encore (multiplexed); The Movie Channel (multiplexed).

Video-On-Demand: No

Pay-Per-View
iN DEMAND (delivered digitally); Playboy TV (delivered digitally); Fresh (delivered digitally).

Internet Service
Operational: No.

Telephone Service
None
Miles of Plant: 32.0 (coaxial); None (fiber optic). Homes passed: 1,059.
President: James Rigas.
Ownership: Zito Media (MSO).

PINEVILLE—Shentel, 500 Shentel Way, PO Box 459, Edinburg, VA 22824. Phones: 540-984-5224; 800-743-6835. Fax: 540-984-3438. E-mail: customer_service@shentel.net. Web Site: http://www.shentel.com. Also serves Amonate, VA; Alpoca (portions), Anawalt, Bradshaw, Brenton, Briar Creek, Bud (portions), Capels, Caretta, Clear Fork, Coalwood, Corinne, Covel, Cucumber, Cyclone, Davy, Fanrock, Garwood, Gary, Glen Fork, Glen Rogers, Havaco, Hemphill, Herndon, Hotchkiss, Iaeger, Itmann, Jesse, Keystone, Kimball, Kopperstown, Maben, Maitland-Superior, McDowell County (portions), McGraws, Mullens, New Richmond, North Welch, Northfork, Oceana, Pierpoint, Premier, Raleigh County (southwest portion), Ravencliff, Rock View, Sabine, Saulsville, Slab Fork, War, Welch & Wyoming County (portions), WV. ICA: WV0204.
TV Market Ranking: Below 100 (Alpoca (portions), Amonate, Anawalt, Bradshaw, Brenton, Briar Creek, Bud (portions), Capels, Caretta, Clear Fork, Coalwood, Corinne, Covel, Cucumber, Cyclone, Davy, Fanrock, Garwood, Gary, Glen Fork, Glen Rogers, Havaco, Hemphill, Hotchkiss, Itmann, Jesse, Keystone, Kimball, Kopperstown, Maben, Maitland-Superior, McDowell County (portions), McGraws, Mullens, New Richmond, North Welch, Oceana, Pierpoint, PINEVILLE, Premier, Raleigh County (southwest portion), Ravencliff, Rock View, Sabine, Saulsville, Slab Fork, Welch, Wyoming County (portions), Herndon, Iaeger, Northfork). Franchise award date: October 1, 1952. Franchise expiration date: N.A. Began: October 1, 1952.
Channel capacity: N.A. Channels available but not in use: N.A.

Basic Service
Subscribers: 513.
Programming (received off-air): WCHS-TV (ABC, Antenna TV) Charleston; WOAY-TV (ABC) Oak Hill; WSWP-TV (PBS) Grandview; WVNS-TV (CBS, FOX) Lewisburg; WVVA (CW, MeTV, NBC) Bluefield; 12 FMs.
Programming (via satellite): INSP; QVC; TBS; Trinity Broadcasting Network (TBN).
Fee: $99.95 installation; $32.49 monthly.

Expanded Basic Service 1
Subscribers: N.A.
Programming (via satellite): A&E; AMC; Animal Planet; Cartoon Network; CNBC; CNN; C-SPAN; Discovery Channel; Disney Channel; Disney XD; ESPN; ESPN2; Fox News Channel; Fox Sports 1; Freeform; FX; Golf Channel; Great American Country; HGTV;

West Virginia—Cable Systems

History; HLN; Lifetime; MSNBC; MTV; National Geographic Channel; Nickelodeon; Outdoor Channel; Root Sports Pittsburgh; Spike TV; Syfy; The Weather Channel; TLC; TNT; Travel Channel; Turner Classic Movies; TV Land; USA Network; VH1.
Fee: $32.00 monthly.

Digital Basic Service
Subscribers: 1,832.
Programming (via satellite): BBC America; Cloo; CMT; Destination America; Discovery Kids Channel; Discovery Life Channel; ESPN Classic; ESPNews; ESPNU; Fuse; FYI; GSN; History International; IFC; Investigation Discovery; LMN; MC; NBCSN; Nick Jr.; Nicktoons; OWN: Oprah Winfrey Network; Oxygen; Science Channel; TeenNick.

Pay Service 1
Pay Units: N.A.
Programming (via satellite): HBO; Showtime.
Fee: $10.90 monthly (Showtime), $11.95 monthly (HBO).

Digital Pay Service 1
Pay Units: N.A.
Programming (via satellite): Cinemax (multiplexed); Flix; HBO (multiplexed); Showtime (multiplexed); Starz (multiplexed); Starz Encore (multiplexed); The Movie Channel (multiplexed).
Fee: $11.95 monthly (Cinemax or Starz/Encore), $12.95 monthly (HBO or Showtime/TMC).

Video-On-Demand: No

Pay-Per-View
iN DEMAND (delivered digitally); Hot Choice (delivered digitally); VaVoom (delivered digitally); Juicy (delivered digitally); SexSee (delivered digitally).

Internet Service
Operational: Yes.

Telephone Service
Digital: Operational
Miles of Plant: 407.0 (coaxial); 167.0 (fiber optic). Homes passed: 9,486.
Vice President, Industry Affairs & Regulations: Chris Kyle. Assistant Secretary, Associate General Counsel: Ann Flowers.
Ownership: Shentel (MSO).

PIPESTEM—Suddenlink Communications. Now served by BECKLEY, WV [WV0005]. ICA: WV0118.

PLINY—Formerly served by Vital Communications. No longer in operation. ICA: WV0264.

POINT PLEASANT—Formerly served by Charter Communications. Now served by Suddenlink Communications, PARKERSBURG, WV [WV0003]. ICA: WV0008.

PRICETOWN—Formerly served by Cebridge Connections. No longer in operation. ICA: WV0205.

PRICHARD—Lycom Communications, 305 East Pike St, PO Box 1114, Louisa, KY 41230. Phones: 800-489-0640; 606-638-4278; 606-638-3600. Fax: 606-638-4278. E-mail: info@lycomonline.com. Web Site: http://lycomonline.com. Also serves Wayne County (unincorporated areas). ICA: KY0129.
TV Market Ranking: 36 (PRICHARD, Wayne County (unincorporated areas)). Franchise award date: N.A. Franchise expiration date: N.A. Began: January 1, 1983.
Channel capacity: N.A. Channels available but not in use: N.A.

Basic Service
Subscribers: 81.
Programming (received off-air): WCHS-TV (ABC, Antenna TV) Charleston; WKAS (PBS) Ashland; WOWK-TV (CBS) Huntington; WQCW (CW) Portsmouth; WSAZ-TV (MNT, NBC, This TV) Huntington; WTSF (Daystar TV) Ashland; WVAH-TV (FOX, The Country Network) Charleston; WVPB-TV (PBS) Huntington; WYMT-TV (CBS, CW) Hazard.
Programming (via satellite): QVC; WGN America.
Fee: $129.95 installation; $34.95 monthly.

Expanded Basic Service 1
Subscribers: 79.
Programming (via satellite): A&E; AMC; CMT; CNBC; CNN; Discovery Channel; Disney Channel; ESPN; ESPN2; Freeform; HLN; Lifetime; Nickelodeon; Spike TV; TBS; The Weather Channel; TLC; TNT; USA Network.
Fee: $20.00 monthly.

Digital Basic Service
Subscribers: 20.
Programming (via satellite): Bravo; ESPN Classic; HGTV; History; NBCSN; Syfy; WE tv.
Fee: $20.00 monthly.

Digital Pay Service 1
Pay Units: N.A.
Programming (via satellite): Cinemax (multiplexed); HBO (multiplexed); Showtime (multiplexed); Starz (multiplexed); Starz Encore (multiplexed); The Movie Channel (multiplexed).
Fee: $16.95 monthly (each).

Video-On-Demand: No

Pay-Per-View
iN DEMAND (delivered digitally); Club Jenna (delivered digitally).

Internet Service
Operational: No.

Telephone Service
Analog: Operational
Miles of Plant: 93.0 (coaxial); None (fiber optic). Homes passed: 2,122.
President: Steven J. Lycans. Chief Technician: Aaron Lycans.
Ownership: Lycom Communications Inc. (MSO).

PRINCETON—Formerly served by Charter Communications. Now served by Suddenlink Communications, BECKLEY, WV [WV0005]. ICA: WV0018.

PULLMAN—Formerly served by Cebridge Connections. No longer in operation. ICA: WV0159.

QUICK—Formerly served by Vital Communications. No longer in operation. ICA: WV0275.

RAVENCLIFF—Formerly served by Jet Broadband. Now served by Shentel, PINEVILLE, WV [WV0204]. ICA: WV0093.

RED HOUSE—Comcast Cable. Now served by HUNTINGTON, WV [WV0002]. ICA: WV0027.

RICHWOOD—Shentel. Now served by SUMMERSVILLE, WV [WV0213]. ICA: WV0058.

RIG—C T & R Cable, 29 Water St, Petersburg, WV 26847-1544. Phone: 304-257-4891. ICA: WV0225.
TV Market Ranking: Outside TV Markets (RIG). Franchise award date: N.A. Franchise expiration date: N.A. Began: May 15, 1988.
Channel capacity: N.A. Channels available but not in use: N.A.

Basic Service
Subscribers: N.A.
Programming (via satellite): Cartoon Network; Discovery Channel; ESPN; ESPN2; Fox News Channel; Freeform; Spike TV; TBS; TNT; USA Network; WGN America.
Programming (via translator): WHSV-TV (ABC, MeTV, MNT, This TV) Harrisonburg; WJAC-TV (MeTV, NBC) Johnstown; WNPB-TV (PBS) Morgantown; WTTG (Buzzr, FOX) Washington; WUSA (Bounce TV, CBS, WeatherNation) Washington.
Fee: $25.00 installation.

Pay Service 1
Pay Units: N.A.
Programming (via satellite): Showtime.
Fee: $9.00 monthly.

Internet Service
Operational: No.

Telephone Service
None
Miles of Plant: 8.0 (coaxial); None (fiber optic). Homes passed: 150.
General Manager: Terry Hinkle. Chief Technician: Matt Alt.
Ownership: C T & R Cable LLC (MSO).

ROBSON—Formerly served by Charter Communications. Now served by Suddenlink Communications, CHARLESTON, WV [WV0006]. ICA: WV0153.

RONCEVERTE—Shentel, 500 Shentel Way, PO Box 459, Edinburg, VA 22824. Phones: 800-743-6835; 252-943-3800. Fax: 540-984-3438. E-mail: customer_service@shentel.net. Web Site: http://www.shentel.com. Also serves Greenbrier County (portions). ICA: WV0208.
TV Market Ranking: Below 100 (Greenbrier County (portions), RONCEVERTE). Franchise award date: February 1, 1991. Franchise expiration date: N.A. Began: N.A.
Channel capacity: 36 (not 2-way capable). Channels available but not in use: N.A.

Basic Service
Subscribers: 26.
Programming (received off-air): WDBJ (CBS, Decades, MNT) Roanoke; WOAY-TV (ABC) Oak Hill; WSLS-TV (MeTV, NBC) Roanoke; WSWP-TV (PBS) Grandview; WVNS-TV (CBS, FOX) Lewisburg; WVVA (CW, MeTV, NBC) Bluefield; allband FM.
Programming (via satellite): A&E; CMT; CNN; Discovery Channel; ESPN; ESPN2; Freeform; Lifetime; Nickelodeon; Spike TV; Syfy; TBS; The Weather Channel; TLC; TNT; Trinity Broadcasting Network (TBN); Turner Classic Movies; USA Network; VH1; WGN America.
Fee: $99.95 installation; $32.49 monthly.

Pay Service 1
Pay Units: N.A.
Programming (via satellite): HBO.
Fee: $14.00 monthly.

Video-On-Demand: No

Internet Service
Operational: No.

Telephone Service
None
Miles of Plant: 36.0 (coaxial); None (fiber optic).
Vice President, Industry Affairs & Regulations: Chris Kyle. Assistant Secretary, Associate General Counsel: Ann Flowers.
Ownership: Shentel (MSO).

RUPERT—Formerly served by Charter Communications. Now served by Suddenlink Communications, BECKLEY, WV [WV0005]. ICA: WV0209.

SALEM—Shentel. Now served by WESTON, WV [WV0034]. ICA: WV0066.

SALEM COLLEGE—Formerly served by Basco Electronics Inc. No longer in operation. ICA: WV0110.

SALT ROCK—Formerly served by Armstrong Cable Services. No longer in operation. ICA: WV0084.

SAND FORK—Shentel. Now served by WESTON, WV [WV0034]. ICA: WV0147.

SANDYVILLE—Formerly served by Vital Communications. No longer in operation. ICA: WV0261.

SARAH ANN—Colane Cable TV Inc. Now served by OMAR, WV [WV0191]. ICA: WV0148.

SARDIS—Formerly served by Country Cable. No longer in operation. ICA: WV0175.

SCARBRO—Shentel. Now served by SUMMERSVILLE, WV [WV0213]. ICA: WV0031.

SHINNSTON—Suddenlink Communications, 520 Maryville Centre Dr, Ste 300, St. Louis, MO 63141. Phones: 314-315-9400; 304-472-4193. E-mail: gene.regan@suddenlink.com. Web Site: http://www.suddenlink.com. Also serves Adamsville, Barbour County (northeastern portion), Bethlehem, Boothsville, Brownton, Enterprise, Erie, Farmington, Flemington, Four States, Galloway, Gypsy, Harrison County (portions), Haywood, Hepzibah, Idamay, Lumberport, Marion County (portions), Meadowbrook, Rosemont, Simpson, Spelter & Taylor County (eastern portion). ICA: WV0029.
TV Market Ranking: Below 100 (Adamsville, Barbour County (northeastern portion), Bethlehem, Brownton, Enterprise, Erie, Farmington, Four States, Galloway, Gypsy, Harrison County (portions), Haywood, Hepzibah, Idamay, Lumberport, Marion County (portions), Meadowbrook, Rosemont, SHINNSTON, Simpson, Spelter, Taylor County (eastern portion), Flemington). Franchise award date: N.A. Franchise expiration date: N.A. Began: December 1, 1955.
Channel capacity: 36 (operating 2-way). Channels available but not in use: N.A.

Basic Service
Subscribers: 2,844. Commercial subscribers: 52.
Programming (received off-air): KDKA-TV (CBS, Decades) Pittsburgh; WBOY-TV (ABC, NBC) Clarksburg; WDTV (CBS) Weston; WNPB-TV (PBS) Morgantown; WTAE-TV (ABC, This TV) Pittsburgh; WTRF-TV (ABC, CBS, MNT) Wheeling; WVFX (CW, FOX) Clarksburg; allband FM.
Programming (via satellite): EWTN Global Catholic Network; QVC.
Fee: $22.99 monthly; $1.24 converter.

Expanded Basic Service 1
Subscribers: N.A.
Programming (via satellite): A&E; AMC; Animal Planet; Bravo; Cartoon Network; CNN; Comedy Central; C-SPAN; C-SPAN 2; Discovery Channel; Disney Channel; E! HD; ESPN; ESPN Classic; ESPN2; Food Network; Fox News Channel; Fox Sports 1; Freeform; FX; Great American Country; GSN; Hallmark Channel; HGTV; History; HLN; Lifetime; MSNBC; MTV; National Geographic Channel; Nickelodeon; Outdoor Channel; Pop; Root Sports Pittsburgh; Spike TV; Syfy; TBS; The Weather

Channel; TLC; TNT; Trinity Broadcasting Network (TBN); truTV; TV Land; USA Network; VH1; WE tv.
Fee: $26.00 monthly.
Digital Basic Service
Subscribers: N.A.
Programming (via satellite): BBC America; Bloomberg Television; Discovery Digital Networks; Disney XD; DMX Music; ESPNews; EVINE Live; FOX College Sports Central; FOX College Sports Pacific; Fuse; FXM; FYI; Golf Channel; History International; IFC; LMN; NBCSN; Turner Classic Movies.
Fee: $13.95 monthly.
Pay Service 1
Pay Units: N.A.
Programming (via satellite): Cinemax; HBO; Showtime; Starz Encore; The Movie Channel.
Fee: $17.50 installation; $3.99 monthly (Encore), $7.95 monthly (Cinemax), $11.95 monthly (Showtime & TMC), $11.99 monthly (HBO).
Digital Pay Service 1
Pay Units: N.A.
Programming (via satellite): Cinemax (multiplexed); HBO (multiplexed); Showtime (multiplexed); Starz (multiplexed); Starz Encore (multiplexed); The Movie Channel (multiplexed).
Video-On-Demand: No
Pay-Per-View
iN DEMAND (delivered digitally); Playboy TV (delivered digitally); Fresh (delivered digitally).
Internet Service
Operational: Yes. Began: May 27, 2004.
Broadband Service: Suddenlink High Speed Internet.
Fee: $49.95 installation; $29.99 monthly.
Telephone Service
Digital: Operational
Miles of Plant: 153.0 (coaxial); None (fiber optic). Homes passed: 6,429.
Senior Vice President, Corporate Finance: Michael Pflantz. Operations Director: Peter Brown.
Ownership: Cequel Communications Holdings I LLC (MSO).

SISSONVILLE—Suddenlink Communications, 520 Maryville Centre Dr, Ste 300, St. Louis, MO 63141. Phones: 304-472-8663; 314-315-9400; 304-472-4193. E-mail: Gene.Regan@suddenlink.com. Web Site: http://www.suddenlink.com. Also serves Alum Creek, Griffithsville, Guthrie, Jackson County (portions), Kanawha County (portions), Lincoln County (portions), Pocatalico, Sod, Sumerco, Tornado, Tyler Mountain & Yawkey. ICA: WV0036.
TV Market Ranking: 36 (Alum Creek, Alum Creek, Griffithsville, Griffithsville, Griffithsville, Guthrie, Kanawha County (portions), Lincoln County (portions), Pocatalico, SISSONVILLE, Sod, Sumerco, Tornado, Tyler Mountain, Yawkey). Franchise award date: N.A. Franchise expiration date: N.A. Began: January 1, 1982.
Channel capacity: N.A. Channels available but not in use: N.A.
Basic Service
Subscribers: 3,153. Commercial subscribers: 68.
Programming (received off-air): WCHS-TV (ABC, Antenna TV) Charleston; WLPX-TV (ION) Charleston; WOWK-TV (CBS) Huntington; WQCW (CW) Portsmouth; WSAZ-TV (MNT, NBC, This TV) Huntington; WVAH-TV (FOX, The Country Network) Charleston; WVPB-TV (PBS) Huntington.
Programming (via satellite): A&E; AMC; Animal Planet; Cartoon Network; Celebrity Shopping Network; CMT; CNN; C-SPAN; Discovery Channel; Disney Channel; E! HD; ESPN; ESPN2; Fox News Channel; Fox Sports 1; Freeform; FX; Hallmark Channel; HGTV; History; HLN; Lifetime; MTV; Nickelodeon; Outdoor Channel; QVC; Root Sports Pittsburgh; Spike TV; Syfy; TBS; The Weather Channel; TLC; TNT; Trinity Broadcasting Network (TBN); TV Land; USA Network; VH1; WGN America.
Fee: $67.81 monthly.
Digital Basic Service
Subscribers: N.A.
Programming (via satellite): BBC America; Bloomberg Television; C-SPAN 3; Discovery Digital Networks; Disney XD; DIY Network; ESPN Classic; ESPNews; FOX College Sports Central; FOX College Sports Pacific; Fuse; FXM; FYI; GSN; History International; IFC; LMN; MC; Sundance TV; WE tv.
Pay Service 1
Pay Units: N.A.
Programming (via satellite): Cinemax; HBO; Showtime.
Digital Pay Service 1
Pay Units: N.A.
Programming (via satellite): Cinemax (multiplexed); Flix; HBO (multiplexed); Showtime (multiplexed); Starz (multiplexed); Starz Encore; The Movie Channel (multiplexed).
Video-On-Demand: No
Pay-Per-View
iN DEMAND (delivered digitally); Playboy TV (delivered digitally).
Internet Service
Operational: Yes. Began: June 1, 2005.
Broadband Service: Suddenlink High Speed Internet.
Fee: $49.95 installation; $29.99 monthly.
Telephone Service
Digital: Operational
Fee: $49.99 monthly
Miles of Plant: 265.0 (coaxial); None (fiber optic). Homes passed: 5,547.
Senior Vice President, Corporate Finance: Michael Pflantz. General Manager: Peter Brown. Chief Technician: Steve Adkins.
Ownership: Cequel Communications Holdings I LLC (MSO).

SIX MILE ROAD—Shentel, Shentel Center, 500 Shentel Way, Edinburg, VA 22824. Phones: 540-984-5224; 304-946-2871. Fax: 540-984-3438. E-mail: Angela.Washington@emp.shentel.com. Web Site: http://www.shentel.com. ICA: WV0239.
TV Market Ranking: 36 (SIX MILE ROAD).
Channel capacity: N.A. Channels available but not in use: N.A.
Basic Service
Subscribers: 70.
Programming (received off-air): WCHS-TV (ABC, Antenna TV) Charleston; WOWK-TV (CBS) Huntington; WSAZ-TV (MNT, NBC, This TV) Huntington; WVAH-TV (FOX, The Country Network) Charleston; WVPB-TV (PBS) Huntington.
Programming (via satellite): A&E; Cartoon Network; CMT; CNN; Comedy Central; C-SPAN; Discovery Channel; ESPN; Freeform; HLN; Lifetime; MTV; Nickelodeon; QVC; Spike TV; Syfy; TBS; The Weather Channel; TNT; Trinity Broadcasting Network (TBN); USA Network; VH1; WGN America.
Fee: $40.00 installation; $24.22 monthly.
Pay Service 1
Pay Units: N.A.
Programming (via satellite): HBO.
Fee: $12.00 monthly.
Internet Service
Operational: No.

Communications Daily
Warren Communications News

Get the industry standard FREE —
For a no-obligation trial call 800-771-9202 or visit www.warren-news.com

Telephone Service
None
Miles of Plant: 5.0 (coaxial); None (fiber optic). Homes passed: 400.
Operations Manager: Allen Siers. Vice President, Customer Service: Angela Washington.
Ownership: Colane Cable TV Inc. (MSO).

SMITHFIELD—Formerly served by Almega Cable. No longer in operation. ICA: WV0157.

SNOWSHOE—Crystal Broadband Networks, PO Box 180336, Chicago, IL 60618. Phones: 817-685-9588; 630-206-0447. E-mail: sales@crystalbn.com. Web Site: http://crystalbn.com. ICA: WV0212.
TV Market Ranking: Outside TV Markets (SNOWSHOE). Franchise award date: N.A. Franchise expiration date: N.A. Began: December 1, 1982.
Channel capacity: N.A. Channels available but not in use: N.A.
Basic Service
Subscribers: 68.
Programming (received off-air): WCHS-TV (ABC, Antenna TV) Charleston; WDTV (CBS) Weston; WSLS-TV (MeTV, NBC) Roanoke; WVAH-TV (FOX, The Country Network) Charleston; WVPB-TV (PBS) Huntington.
Programming (via satellite): A&E; AMC; Animal Planet; Cartoon Network; CNBC; CNN; Comedy Central; Discovery Channel; ESPN; ESPN2; Fox News Channel; Freeform; FX; Golf Channel; HGTV; HLN; Lifetime; MTV; NBCSN; Nickelodeon; Pop; Spike TV; TBS; The Weather Channel; TNT; Travel Channel; USA Network; VH1; WGN America.
Fee: $29.95 installation; $37.05 monthly.
Digital Basic Service
Subscribers: N.A.
Programming (via satellite): BBC America; Bloomberg Television; Bravo; Discovery Kids Channel; ESPN Classic; ESPNews; FXM; GSN; History; IFC; MC; Nick Jr.; Nicktoons; Outdoor Channel; OWN; Oprah Winfrey Network; Science Channel; Syfy; Trinity Broadcasting Network (TBN); WE tv.
Fee: $12.00 monthly.
Pay Service 1
Pay Units: N.A.
Programming (via satellite): HBO.
Fee: $10.00 monthly.
Digital Pay Service 1
Pay Units: N.A.
Programming (via satellite): Cinemax (multiplexed); HBO (multiplexed); Showtime (multiplexed); Starz (multiplexed); Starz Encore (multiplexed); The Movie Channel (multiplexed).
Fee: $16.95 monthly (each).
Video-On-Demand: No
Pay-Per-View
iN DEMAND (delivered digitally); Club Jenna (delivered digitally); Fresh (delivered digitally).
Internet Service
Operational: No.

Telephone Service
None
Miles of Plant: 17.0 (coaxial); None (fiber optic). Homes passed: 1,506.
General Manager: Ron Page. Program Manager: Shawn Smith.
Ownership: Crystal Broadband Networks (MSO).

SPENCER—Formerly served by Charter Communications. Now served by Suddenlink Communications, PARKERSBURG, WV [WV0003]. ICA: WV0053.

SPRINGFIELD—Comcast Cable. Now served by KEYSER, WV [WV0020]. ICA: WV0258.

ST. MARY'S—Formerly served by Charter Communications. Now served by Suddenlink Communications, PARKERSBURG, WV [WV0003]. ICA: WV0057.

SUMMERSVILLE—Shentel, 500 Shentel Way, PO Box 459, Edinburg, VA 22824. Phones: 800-743-6835; 540-984-5224. Fax: 540-984-3438. E-mail: customer_service@shentel.net. Web Site: http://www.shentel.com. Also serves Ames Heights, Ansted, Bergoo, Braxton County, Camden (town), Camden on Gauley, Cottle, Cowen, Craigsville, Curtin, Dothan, Drennen, Enon, Fayette County (portions), Fenwick, Flatwoods, Gassaway, Gilboa, Glen Jean, Harvey, Hilltop, Holcomb, Ingram Branch, Johnson Branch, Kincaid, Kingston, Lansing, Little Otter, Lockwood, Mossy, New Hope, Nicholas County, North Page, Page, Parcoal, Poe, Redstar, Richwood, Scarbro, Sutton, Upperglade, Victor, Webster County (portions), Webster Springs, Wriston & Zela. ICA: WV0213.
TV Market Ranking: 36 (Ames Heights, Ansted, Dothan, Drennen, Enon, Fayette County (portions), Gilboa, Ingram Branch, Johnson Branch, Kincaid, Kingston, Lansing, Lockwood, Mossy, Nicholas County (portions), North Page, Page, Poe, Victor, Wriston); Below 100 (Braxton County (portions), Camden (town), Fenwick, Flatwoods, Glen Jean, Harvey, Hilltop, Holcomb, New Hope, Redstar, SUMMERSVILLE, Sutton, Zela, Gassaway, Little Otter, Richwood, Scarbro, Fayette County (portions), Nicholas County (portions)); Outside TV Markets (Bergoo, Braxton County (portions), Camden on Gauley, Cottle, Cowen, Curtin, Parcoal, Upperglade, Craigsville, Webster Springs, Nicholas County (portions)). Franchise award date: N.A. Franchise expiration date: N.A. Began: August 1, 1960.
Channel capacity: N.A. Channels available but not in use: N.A.
Digital Basic Service
Subscribers: 1,497.
Programming (received off-air): WCHS-TV (ABC, Antenna TV) Charleston; WDTV (CBS) Weston; WLPX-TV (ION) Charleston; WOAY-TV (ABC) Oak Hill; WOWK-TV (CBS) Huntington; WSAZ-TV (MNT, NBC, This TV) Huntington; WSWP-TV (PBS) Grandview;

2017 Edition

D-845

West Virginia—Cable Systems

WVAH-TV (FOX, The Country Network) Charleston; allband FM.
Programming (via satellite): C-SPAN; C-SPAN 2; Freeform; INSP; QVC; WGN America.
Fee: $99.95 installation; $35.34 monthly.
Digital Expanded Basic Service
Subscribers: 1,084.
Programming (via satellite): A&E; AMC; Animal Planet; Cartoon Network; CMT; CNBC; CNN; Comedy Central; Discovery Channel; Discovery Life Channel; Disney Channel; E! HD; ESPN; ESPN Classic; ESPN2; ESPNews; EWTN Global Catholic Network; Food Network; Fox News Channel; Fox Sports 1; FX; Hallmark Channel; HGTV; History; HLN; Lifetime; MSNBC; MTV; National Geographic Channel; Nickelodeon; Outdoor Channel; Oxygen; Root Sports Pittsburgh; Spike TV; Syfy; TBS; The Weather Channel; TLC; TNT; Travel Channel; truTV; TV Land; USA Network; VH1.
Fee: $38.00 monthly.
Digital Expanded Basic Service 2
Subscribers: 645.
Programming (via satellite): BBC America; Bloomberg Television; Bravo; CMT; Discovery Digital Networks; Disney XD; DMX Music; FOX College Sports Central; FOX College Sports Pacific; Fuse; FXM; FYI; Golf Channel; GSN; History International; IFC; LMN; NBCSN; Nick Jr.; Nicktoons; Sundance TV; TeenNick; Turner Classic Movies; WE tv.
Fee: $11.00 monthly.
Digital Pay Service 1
Pay Units: N.A.
Programming (via satellite): Cinemax (multiplexed); Flix; HBO (multiplexed); Showtime (multiplexed); Starz (multiplexed); Starz Encore (multiplexed); The Movie Channel (multiplexed).
Video-On-Demand: No
Internet Service
Operational: Yes.
Telephone Service
Digital: Operational
Miles of Plant: 32.0 (coaxial); None (fiber optic).
Vice President, Industry Affairs & Regulations: Chris Kyle. Assistant Secretary, Associate General Counsel: Ann Flowers.
Ownership: Shentel (MSO).

TALCOTT—Formerly served by Vital Communications. No longer in operation. ICA: WV0222.

TANNER—Formerly served by Vital Communications. No longer in operation. ICA: WV0149.

TAYLOR COUNTY (portions)—Comcast Cable. Now served by MORGANTOWN, WV [WV0198]. ICA: WV0278.

TUNNELTON—Formerly served by Community Antenna Service. No longer in operation. ICA: WV0112.

TURTLE CREEK—Colane Cable TV Inc. No longer in operation. ICA: WV0267.

UNION—Formerly served by Vital Communications. No longer in operation. ICA: WV0249.

UPPER TRACT—Formerly served by Cebridge Connections. No longer in operation. ICA: WV0136.

VAN—Shentel, 500 Shentel Way, PO Box 459, Edinburg, VA 22824. Phones: 540-984-5224; 800-743-6415; 304-946-2871. Fax: 540-984-3438. E-mail: Angela.Washington@emp.shentel.com. Web Site: http://www.shentel.com. Also serves Bald Knob, Barrett, Bim, Bob White, Boone County (portions), Gordon, Greenwood, Twilight, Wharton & Williams Mountain. ICA: WV0167.
TV Market Ranking: 36 (Bald Knob, Barrett, Bim, Bob White, Boone County (portions), Gordon, Greenwood, Twilight, VAN, Wharton, Williams Mountain). Franchise award date: N.A. Franchise expiration date: N.A. Began: January 1, 1979.
Channel capacity: N.A. Channels available but not in use: N.A.
Basic Service
Subscribers: 323.
Programming (received off-air): WCHS-TV (ABC, Antenna TV) Charleston; WLPX-TV (ION) Charleston; WOWK-TV (CBS) Huntington; WSAZ-TV (MNT, NBC, This TV) Huntington; WSWP-TV (PBS) Grandview; WVAH-TV (FOX, The Country Network) Charleston.
Programming (via satellite): C-SPAN; Disney Channel; Freeform; HLN; INSP; Lifetime; QVC; TBS; Trinity Broadcasting Network (TBN); truTV; USA Network; WGN America.
Fee: $40.00 installation; $24.18 monthly; $1.26 converter.
Expanded Basic Service 1
Subscribers: N.A.
Programming (via satellite): A&E; Cartoon Network; CMT; CNN; Comedy Central; Discovery Channel; ESPN; ESPN2; FX; History; MTV; Nickelodeon; Outdoor Channel; Root Sports Pittsburgh; Spike TV; Syfy; The Weather Channel; TNT; Turner Classic Movies; TV Land; VH1.
Fee: $29.95 monthly.
Pay Service 1
Pay Units: 56.
Programming (via satellite): HBO.
Fee: $11.95 monthly.
Pay Service 2
Pay Units: 17.
Programming (via satellite): Cinemax.
Fee: $11.95 monthly.
Internet Service
Operational: Yes.
Telephone Service
None
Miles of Plant: 54.0 (coaxial); None (fiber optic). Homes passed: 1,404.
Operations Manager: Allen Siers. Vice President, Customer Service: Angela Washington.
Ownership: Shentel.

VARNEY—Colane Cable TV Inc. Now served by OMAR, WV [WV0191]. ICA: WV0215.

WALKERSVILLE—Formerly served by Almega Cable. No longer in operation. ICA: WV0134.

WALTON—Formerly served by Windjammer Cable. No longer in operation. ICA: WV0277.

WAR—Formerly served by Suddenlink Communications. Now served by Shentel, NORTHFORK, WV [WV0045]. ICA: WV0048.

WARDENSVILLE—Formerly served by Valley Cable Systems. No longer in operation. ICA: WV0124.

WARWOOD—Centre TV Cable, 510 Warwood Ave, Wheeling, WV 26003-6842. Phone: 304-277-2811. Also serves Beech Bottom, RD No. 1 Trailer Courts, Short Creek & Windsor Heights. ICA: WV0043.
Note: This system is an overbuild.
TV Market Ranking: 10,90 (Beech Bottom, RD No. 1 Trailer Courts, Short Creek, WARWOOD, Windsor Heights). Franchise award date: N.A. Franchise expiration date: N.A. Began: January 1, 1950.
Channel capacity: 45 (not 2-way capable). Channels available but not in use: N.A.
Basic Service
Subscribers: 709.
Programming (received off-air): WFMJ-TV (CW, NBC) Youngstown; WKBN-TV (CBS) Youngstown; WNPB-TV (PBS) Morgantown; WPGH-TV (Antenna TV, FOX, The Country Network) Pittsburgh; WPNT (MNT) Pittsburgh; WQED (PBS) Pittsburgh; WTAE-TV (ABC, This TV) Pittsburgh; WTOV-TV (MeTV, NBC) Steubenville; WTRF-TV (ABC, CBS, MNT) Wheeling; WYTV (ABC, MNT) Youngstown; allband FM.
Programming (via satellite): A&E; Animal Planet; Cartoon Network; CMT; CNN; Comedy Central; CW PLUS; Discovery Channel; ESPN; ESPN2; EWTN Global Catholic Network; Food Network; Fox News Channel; Fox Sports 1; Freeform; FX; Great American Country; Hallmark Channel; HGTV; History; Lifetime; MTV; Nickelodeon; Outdoor Channel; Pop; QVC; Root Sports Pittsburgh; Spike TV; Syfy; TBS; The Weather Channel; TLC; TNT; Travel Channel; truTV; Turner Classic Movies; TV Land; USA Network; VH1; WGN America.
Fee: $50.67 monthly.
Pay Service 1
Pay Units: N.A.
Programming (via satellite): HBO (multiplexed); Starz Encore.
Fee: $25.00 installation; $7.75 monthly (Encore), $12.00 monthly (HBO).
Video-On-Demand: No
Internet Service
Operational: No.
Telephone Service
None
Miles of Plant: 15.0 (coaxial); None (fiber optic). Homes passed: 3,087.
President & General Manager: Kasmir Majewski.
Ownership: Centre TV Cable.

WASHINGTON—Community Antenna Service, 1525 Dupont Rd, Parkersburg, WV 26101-9623. Phone: 304-420-2470. Fax: 304-420-2474. E-mail: info@cascable.com. Web Site: http://www.cascable.com. Also serves Belleville, Dallison, Murphytown, Parkersburg (southern portion), Vienna, Walker & Williamstown. ICA: WV0200. **Note:** This system is an overbuild.
TV Market Ranking: Below 100 (Belleville, Dallison, Murphytown, Walker, WASHINGTON, Williamstown, Parkersburg (southern portion)). Franchise award date: N.A. Franchise expiration date: N.A. Began: June 1, 1981.
Channel capacity: 66 (not 2-way capable). Channels available but not in use: N.A.
Basic Service
Subscribers: 3,974.
Programming (received off-air): WCHS-TV (ABC, Antenna TV) Charleston; WOUB-TV (PBS) Athens; WOWK-TV (CBS) Huntington; WSAZ-TV (MNT, NBC, This TV) Huntington; WTAP-TV (FOX, MNT, NBC) Parkersburg; WVAH-TV (FOX, The Country Network) Charleston; WVPB-TV (PBS) Huntington.
Programming (via satellite): A&E; Animal Planet; Cartoon Network; CMT; CNBC; CNN; C-SPAN; C-SPAN 2; CW PLUS; Discovery Channel; Disney Channel; DIY Network; ESPN; ESPN2; ESPNews; Food Network; Fox News Channel; Fox Sports 1; FOX Sports Ohio/Sports Time Ohio; Freeform; FX; Golf Channel; Hallmark Channel; HGTV; History; HLN; INSP; ION Television; Lifetime; MSNBC; National Geographic Channel; Nickelodeon; Outdoor Channel; Ovation; OWN: Oprah Winfrey Network; Pop; Praise Television; QVC; Spike TV; Syfy; TBS; The Weather Channel; TLC; TNT; Travel Channel; Trinity Broadcasting Network (TBN); truTV; Turner Classic Movies; TV Land; USA Network; WGN America.
Fee: $45.00 installation; $61.00 monthly.
Digital Basic Service
Subscribers: N.A.
Programming (via satellite): MC; Starz Encore.
Fee: $15.80 monthly.
Pay Service 1
Pay Units: N.A.
Programming (via satellite): Cinemax; HBO; Showtime.
Fee: $10.95 monthly (Cinemax), $13.95 monthly (HBO or Showtime).
Digital Pay Service 1
Pay Units: N.A.
Programming (via satellite): Cinemax (multiplexed); Flix; HBO (multiplexed); Showtime (multiplexed); Sundance TV; The Movie Channel (multiplexed).
Fee: $10.95 monthly (Cinemax), $13.95 monthly (HBO or Flix/Showtime/Sundance/TMC).
Video-On-Demand: No
Internet Service
Operational: Yes.
Broadband Service: In-house.
Fee: $19.95 monthly.
Telephone Service
Digital: Operational
Fee: $29.95-$39.95 monthly
Miles of Plant: 113.0 (coaxial); None (fiber optic).
President & General Manager: Arthur R. Cooper. Program & Marketing Director: Lisa Wilkinson. Chief Technician: Steve Defibaugh.
Ownership: Arthur R. Cooper (MSO).

WAYNE—Suddenlink Communications. Now served by CHARLESTON, WV [WV0006]. ICA: WV0035.

WEBSTER SPRINGS—Shentel. Now served by SUMMERSVILLE, WV [WV0213]. ICA: WV0080.

WELCH—Shentel (formerly Jet Broadband). Now served by PINEVILLE, WV [WV0204]. ICA: WV0042.

WELLSBURG—Blue Devil Cable TV Inc, 116 South 4th St, Toronto, OH 43964-1368. Phone: 740-537-2214. Web Site: http://bluedevilcabletv.com. Also serves Colliers & Follansbee. ICA: WV0279.
TV Market Ranking: 10 (Colliers, Follansbee, WELLSBURG).
Channel capacity: N.A. Channels available but not in use: N.A.
Basic Service
Subscribers: 1,002.
Fee: $35.00 installation; $14.03 monthly.
Vice President: Joann Conner.
Ownership: Blue Devil Cable TV Inc. (MSO).

Cable Systems—West Virginia

WEST LIBERTY (town)—Comcast Cable. Now served by WHEELING, WV [WV0004]. ICA: WV0216.

WEST MILFORD—Formerly served by Cebridge Connections. Now served by Suddenlink Communications, BUCKHANNON, WV [WV0024]. ICA: WV0068.

WEST UNION—Armstrong Cable Services. Now served by ZELIENOPLE, PA [PA0053]. ICA: WV0104.

WESTON—Shentel, 500 Shentel Way, PO Box 459, Edinburg, VA 22824. Phones: 540-984-5224; 800-409-1203. Fax: 540-984-3438. E-mail: customer_service@shentel.net. Web Site: http://www.shentel.com. Also serves Alum Bridge, Braxton County (portions), Bristol, Broad Run, Burnsville, Camden, Doddridge County (northeast portion), Ellenboro, Gilmer County (portions), Glenville, Harrison County, Harrison County (portions), Harrisville, Industrial, Jane Lew, Lewis County (portions), Linn, Salem, Sand Fork & Troy. ICA: WV0034.

TV Market Ranking: Below 100 (Braxton County (portions), Bristol, Burnsville, Camden, Doddridge County (northeast portion), Ellenboro, Harrison County, Harrison County (portions), Harrisville, Industrial, Jane Lew, Lewis County (portions), Linn, Sand Fork, Troy, WESTON, Alum Bridge, Broad Run, Glenville, Salem). Franchise award date: N.A. Franchise expiration date: N.A. Began: January 1, 1954.

Channel capacity: N.A. Channels available but not in use: N.A.

Basic Service
Subscribers: 395.
Programming (received off-air): WBOY-TV (ABC, NBC) Clarksburg; WCHS-TV (ABC, Antenna TV) Charleston; WDTV (CBS) Weston; WNPB-TV (PBS) Morgantown; WTAE-TV (ABC, This TV) Pittsburgh; WVFX (CW, FOX) Clarksburg; 20 FMs.
Programming (via satellite): C-SPAN; C-SPAN 2; INSP; Pop; QVC; Trinity Broadcasting Network (TBN).
Fee: $99.95 installation; $31.27 monthly; $2.00 converter.

Expanded Basic Service 1
Subscribers: N.A.
Programming (via satellite): A&E; AMC; Animal Planet; Cartoon Network; CMT; CNBC; CNN; Comedy Central; Discovery Channel; Discovery Life Channel; Disney Channel; Disney XD; E! HD; ESPN; ESPN2; Food Network; Fox News Channel; Fox Sports 1; Freeform; FX; HGTV; History; HLN; Lifetime; MTV; National Geographic Channel; Nickelodeon; Outdoor Channel; Oxygen; Root Sports Pittsburgh; Spike TV; Syfy; TBS; The Weather Channel; TLC; TNT; Travel Channel; truTV; TV Land; USA Network.
Fee: $32.00 monthly.

Digital Basic Service
Subscribers: N.A.
Programming (via satellite): BBC America; Discovery Kids Channel; DMX Music; ESPN Classic; ESPNews; Golf Channel; GSN; IFC; NBCSN; OWN: Oprah Winfrey Network; Turner Classic Movies; TV Guide Interactive Inc.; WE tv.
Fee: $10.00 monthly.

Digital Pay Service 1
Pay Units: N.A.
Programming (via satellite): Cinemax (multiplexed); HBO (multiplexed); Showtime (multiplexed); Starz (multiplexed); Starz Encore (multiplexed); The Movie Channel (multiplexed).
Video-On-Demand: No
Pay-Per-View
iN DEMAND (delivered digitally); Playboy TV (delivered digitally).
Internet Service
Operational: Yes.
Fee: $50.00 installation; $39.95 monthly.
Telephone Service
Digital: Operational
Miles of Plant: 140.0 (coaxial); None (fiber optic).
Vice President, Industry Affairs & Regulations: Chris Kyle.
Ownership: Shentel (MSO).

WESTOVER—Formerly served by Adelphia Communications. Now served by Comcast Cable, MORGANTOWN, WV [WV0198]. ICA: WV0056.

WHARNCLIFFE—Shentel, 500 Shentel Way, PO Box 459, Edinburg, VA 22824. Phones: 540-984-5224; 800-743-6835; 304-946-2871. Fax: 540-984-3438. E-mail: Angela.Washington@emp.shentel.com. Web Site: http://www.shentel.com. ICA: WV0281.

TV Market Ranking: Outside TV Markets (WHARNCLIFFE).

Channel capacity: N.A. Channels available but not in use: N.A.

Basic Service
Subscribers: 66.
Fee: $40.00 installation; $25.88 monthly.
Operations Manager: Allen Siers. Vice President, Customer Service: Angela Washington.
Ownership: Shentel (MSO).

WHEELING—Comcast Cable, 15 Summit Park Dr, Pittsburgh, PA 15275. Phone: 412-747-6400. Fax: 412-747-6401. Web Site: http://www.comcast.com. Also serves Adena, Barnesville, Bellaire, Belmont County (portions), Bethesda, Blaine, Bridgeport, Brilliant, Brookside, Colerain Twp., Cross Creek Twp., Dillonvale, Fairpoint, Flushing, Glen Robbins, Goshen Twp. (Belmont County), Harrisville, Holloway, Island Creek Twp., Lafferty, Lansing, Martins Ferry, Mead Twp., Mingo Junction, Mount Pleasant, Mount Pleasant (village), Mount Pleasant Twp., Neffs, New Alexandria, Pease Twp. (Belmont County), Pultney, Pultney Twp., Rayland, Richland, Richland Twp., Richmond Twp., Salem Twp. (Jefferson County), Shadyside, Short Creek Twp., Smith Twp., Smithfield Twp. (Jefferson County), St. Clairsville, Steubenville, Steubenville Twp., Tiltonsville, Warren Twp. (Belmont County), Wheeling Twp., Wintersville & Yorkville, OH; Benwood, Bethany, Bethlehem, Brooke County (portions), Chester, Clearview, Follansbee, Glen Dale, Hancock County (portions), Lawrenceville, Marshall County (portions), McMechen, Moundsville, New Cumberland, New Manchester, Newell, Ohio County (portions), Triadelphia, Valley Grove, Warwood, Weirton, Wellsburg & West Liberty, WV. ICA: WV0004.

TV Market Ranking: 10 (Brilliant, Brooke County (portions), Follansbee, Mingo Junction, Mount Pleasant (village), Mount Pleasant Twp., New Alexandria, Steubenville, Steubenville Twp., Weirton, Wellsburg); 10,90 (Bethany, Chester, Hancock County (portions), Lawrenceville, New Cumberland, New Manchester, Newell); 90 (Adena, Barnesville, Bellaire, Belmont County (portions), Benwood, Bethesda, Bethlehem, Blaine, Bridgeport, Brookside, Clearview, Colerain Twp., Cross Creek Twp., Dillonvale, Fairpoint, Flushing, Glen Robbins, Goshen Twp. (Belmont County), Harrisville, Holloway, Island Creek Twp., Lafferty, Lansing, Marshall County (portions), Martins Ferry, McMechen, Mead Twp., Moundsville, Mount Pleasant, Neffs, Ohio County (portions), Pease Twp. (Belmont County), Pultney, Pultney Twp., Rayland, Richland, Richland Twp., Richmond Twp., Salem Twp. (Jefferson County), Shadyside, Short Creek Twp., Smith Twp., Smithfield Twp. (Jefferson County), St. Clairsville, Tiltonsville, Triadelphia, Valley Grove, Warren Twp. (Belmont County), Warwood, West Liberty, WHEELING, Wheeling Twp., Wintersville, Yorkville). Franchise award date: N.A. Franchise expiration date: N.A. Began: June 1, 1952.

Channel capacity: N.A. Channels available but not in use: N.A.

Basic Service
Subscribers: 56,487. Commercial subscribers: 480.
Programming (received off-air): WBWO (WBN) Wheeling; KDKA-TV (CBS, Decades) Pittsburgh; WNPB-TV (PBS) Morgantown; WPGH-TV (Antenna TV, FOX, The Country Network) Pittsburgh; WPXI (MeTV, NBC) Pittsburgh; WQED (PBS) Pittsburgh; WTAE-TV (ABC, This TV) Pittsburgh; WTOV-TV (MeTV, NBC) Steubenville; WTRF-TV (ABC, CBS, MNT) Wheeling; WYTV (ABC, MNT) Youngstown; 13 FMs.
Programming (via satellite): A&E; BET; Cartoon Network; CNBC; CNN; C-SPAN; Discovery Channel; Freeform; Hallmark Channel; HLN; Lifetime; MTV; Nickelodeon; QVC; TBS; The Weather Channel; TNT.
Fee: $29.95-$43.95 installation; $25.24 monthly; $4.00 converter.

Expanded Basic Service 1
Subscribers: N.A.
Programming (via satellite): AMC; Animal Planet; CMT; Comedy Central; C-SPAN 2; Disney Channel; E! HD; ESPN; ESPN2; EVINE Live; EWTN Global Catholic Network; Food Network; Fox News Channel; FX; HGTV; History; ION Television; MSNBC; Oxygen; Root Sports Pittsburgh; Spike TV; TLC; Travel Channel; truTV; TV Land; USA Network; VH1.
Fee: $37.99 monthly.

Digital Basic Service
Subscribers: N.A.
Programming (via satellite): BBC America; Bloomberg Television; Bravo; Discovery Digital Networks; Disney XD; DMX Music; ESPN Classic; ESPNews; EVINE Live; Fox Sports 1; FSN Digital Atlantic; FSN Digital Central; FSN Digital Pacific; Fuse; FXM; FYI; Golf Channel; Great American Country; GSN; History International; IFC; LMN; National Geographic Channel; NBCSN; Nick Jr.; Nicktoons; Outdoor Channel; Ovation; Sundance TV; Syfy; TeenNick; The Word Network; Trinity Broadcasting Network (TBN); Turner Classic Movies; WE tv; Weatherscan.
Fee: $10.95 monthly.

Digital Pay Service 1
Pay Units: N.A.
Programming (via satellite): Cinemax (multiplexed); Flix; HBO (multiplexed); Showtime (multiplexed); Starz (multiplexed); Starz Encore (multiplexed); The Movie Channel (multiplexed).
Video-On-Demand: Yes
Pay-Per-View
ESPN Now (delivered digitally); Sports PPV (delivered digitally); NBA TV (delivered digitally); iN DEMAND (delivered digitally); Urban Xtra (delivered digitally); Fresh (delivered digitally); Shorteez (delivered digitally); Playboy TV (delivered digitally); Hot Choice (delivered digitally).
Internet Service
Operational: Yes.
Subscribers: 48,299.
Broadband Service: Comcast High Speed Internet.
Fee: $42.95 monthly.
Telephone Service
Digital: Operational
Subscribers: 43,200.
Fee: $44.95 monthly
Miles of Plant: 2,439.0 (coaxial); 611.0 (fiber optic). Homes passed: 144,275.
Regional Vice President: Linda Hossinger. Vice President, Technical Operations: Randy Bender. Vice President, Marketing: Donna Corning. Vice President, Public Affairs: Jody Doherty.
Ownership: Comcast Cable Communications Inc. (MSO).

WHITE SULPHUR SPRINGS—Formerly served by Charter Communications. Now served by Suddenlink Communications, BECKLEY, WV [WV0005]. ICA: WV0217.

WHITEHALL—Formerly served by Adelphia Communications. Now served by Comcast Cable, MORGANTOWN, WV [WV0198]. ICA: WV0040.

WILEYVILLE—Formerly served by Almega Cable. No longer in operation. ICA: WV0165.

WILLIAMSON—Formerly served by Charter Communications. Now served by Suddenlink Communications, KERMIT, WV [WV0038]. ICA: WV0030.

WORTHINGTON—Formerly served by Adelphia Communications. Now served by Comcast Cable, MORGANTOWN, WV [WV0198]. ICA: WV0151.

WYATT—Formerly served by Country Cable. No longer in operation. ICA: WV0219.

WISCONSIN

Total Systems: 121	Communities with Applications: 0
Total Communities Served: 938	Number of Basic Subscribers: 807,757
Franchises Not Yet Operating: 0	Number of Expanded Basic Subscribers: 5,969
Applications Pending: 0	Number of Pay Units: 6,890

Top 100 Markets Represented: Minneapolis-St. Paul, MN (13); Milwaukee (23); Green Bay (62); Duluth, MN-Superior, WI (89); Madison (93); Rockford-Freeport, IL (97).

For a list of cable communities in this section, see the Cable Community Index located in the back of Cable Volume 2.
For explanation of terms used in cable system listings, see p. D-11.

ADAMS—Charter Communications, 165 Knights Way, Fond du Lac, WI 54935. Phones: 314-543-2236; 636-207-5100 (Corporate office); 920-907-7720. Web Site: http://www.charter.com. Also serves Adams (town), Friendship & Preston. ICA: WI0099.

TV Market Ranking: Outside TV Markets (ADAMS, Adams (town), Friendship, Preston). Franchise award date: N.A. Franchise expiration date: N.A. Began: July 31, 1981.

Channel capacity: 52 (not 2-way capable). Channels available but not in use: N.A.

Digital Basic Service
Subscribers: 384. Commercial subscribers: 9.
Programming (received off-air): WAOW (ABC, CW, This TV) Wausau; WEAU (NBC) Eau Claire; WHA-TV (PBS) Madison; WISC-TV (CBS, MNT) Madison; WKOW (ABC, MeTV, This TV) Madison; WMSN-TV (FOX, The Country Network) Madison; WMTV (CW, NBC) Madison; WSAW-TV (CBS, MNT) Wausau.
Programming (via satellite): C-SPAN; WGN America.
Fee: $49.99 installation; $21.99 monthly.

Digital Expanded Basic Service
Subscribers: N.A.
Programming (via satellite): A&E; AMC; Animal Planet; Bravo; CNN; C-SPAN 2; Discovery Channel; Disney Channel; ESPN; ESPN2; Freeform; HGTV; Lifetime; MSNBC; MTV; Nickelodeon; QVC; Spike TV; TBS; The Weather Channel; TLC; TNT; TV Land; USA Network.
Fee: $47.99 monthly.

Pay Service 1
Pay Units: N.A.
Programming (via satellite): Cinemax; HBO; Showtime.
Fee: $14.95 installation; $10.00 monthly (each).

Video-On-Demand: No

Internet Service
Operational: No.

Telephone Service
None

Miles of Plant: 610.0 (coaxial); 207.0 (fiber optic). Homes passed: 10,700.
Vice President & General Manager: Lisa Washa. Chief Technician: Jeff Gerner. Marketing Director: Traci Loonstra. Accounting Director: David Sovanski. Marketing Administrator: Rhonda Schelvan.
Ownership: Charter Communications Inc. (MSO).

ALBANY—Mediacom, 3033 Asbury Rd, Dubuque, IA 52001. Phones: 845-695-2762; 563-557-8025. Fax: 563-557-7413. Web Site: http://www.mediacomcable.com. Also serves Albany Twp. ICA: WI0152.

TV Market Ranking: 97 (ALBANY, Albany Twp.).
Channel capacity: N.A. Channels available but not in use: N.A.

Basic Service
Subscribers: 31.
Programming (received off-air): WHA-TV (PBS) Madison; WIFR (Antenna TV, CBS) Freeport; WISC-TV (CBS, MNT) Madison; WKOW (ABC, MeTV, This TV) Madison; WMSN-TV (FOX, The Country Network) Madison; WMTV (CW, NBC) Madison; WQRF-TV (Bounce TV, FOX) Rockford; WREX (CW, MeTV, NBC) Rockford; WTVO (ABC, MNT) Rockford.
Programming (via satellite): A&E; AMC; Animal Planet; Bravo; Cartoon Network; CMT; CNBC; CNN; Comedy Central; Discovery Channel; Discovery Life Channel; ESPN; ESPN2; Fox Sports 1; Freeform; HGTV; History; HLN; Lifetime; MTV; Nickelodeon; Oxygen; QVC; Spike TV; Syfy; TBS; The Weather Channel; TLC; TNT; Travel Channel; Trinity Broadcasting Network (TBN); truTV; TV Land; USA Network; VH1; WGN America.
Fee: $41.00 monthly.

Pay Service 1
Pay Units: N.A.
Programming (via satellite): HBO; Showtime.

Internet Service
Operational: No.

Telephone Service
None

Miles of plant included in Moline, IL.
Regional Vice President: Cari Fenzel. Vice President, Financial Reporting: Kenneth J. Kohrs. Area Manager: Kathleen McMullen. Engineering Director: Mitch Carlson. Marketing Director: Greg Evans. Technical Operations Manager: Darren Dean.
Ownership: Mediacom LLC (MSO).

ALMA—Midco, PO Box 5010, Sioux Falls, SD 57117. Phone: 800-888-1300. Web Site: http://www.midcocomm.com. Also serves Nelson & Pepin. ICA: WI0234.

TV Market Ranking: Below 100 (Pepin); Outside TV Markets (ALMA, Nelson). Franchise award date: N.A. Franchise expiration date: N.A. Began: January 1, 1960.
Channel capacity: N.A. Channels available but not in use: N.A.

Basic Service
Subscribers: N.A.
Programming (received off-air): KARE (NBC, WeatherNation) Minneapolis; KSTC-TV (Antenna TV, This TV) Minneapolis; KSTP-TV (ABC, MeTV) St. Paul; KTTC (CW, NBC) Rochester; WCCO-TV (CBS, Decades) Minneapolis; WEAU (NBC) Eau Claire; WFTC (MNT, Movies!) Minneapolis; WHLA-TV (PBS) La Crosse; WKBT-DT (CBS, MNT) La Crosse; WLAX (FOX, MeTV) La Crosse; WUCW (CW, The Country Network) Minneapolis; WXOW (ABC, CW, This TV) La Crosse.

Expanded Basic Service 1
Subscribers: N.A.
Programming (via satellite): A&E; Animal Planet; Bravo; Cartoon Network; CMT; CNBC; CNN; Comedy Central; C-SPAN; C-SPAN 2; Discovery Channel; E! HD; ESPN; ESPN2; EVINE Live; Food Network; Fox News Channel; Fox Sports 1; FOX Sports North; Freeform; FX; Great American Country; Hallmark Channel; History; HLN; Lifetime; MTV; National Geographic Channel; Nickelodeon; Spike TV; Syfy; TBS; TLC; TNT; Travel Channel; truTV; TV Land; USA Network; VH1.
Fee: $25.08 monthly.

Digital Basic Service
Subscribers: 208.
Programming (via satellite): BBC America; Bloomberg Television; Cloo; Discovery Digital Networks; Disney XD; DMX Music; ESPN Classic; ESPNews; EWTN Global Catholic Network; Fuse; Golf Channel; GSN; HGTV; IFC; LMN; MTV Classic; MTV2; NBCSN; Nick Jr.; QVC; TeenNick; The Weather Channel; Trinity Broadcasting Network (TBN); Turner Classic Movies; WE tv; WGN America.
Fee: $19.95 monthly.

Digital Expanded Basic Service
Subscribers: N.A.
Programming (via satellite): CMT; Discovery Life Channel; FXM; FYI; History; History International.
Fee: $2.95 monthly.

Digital Expanded Basic Service 2
Subscribers: N.A.
Programming (via satellite): NFL Network; Outdoor Channel.
Fee: $2.00 monthly.

Digital Pay Service 1
Pay Units: N.A.
Programming (via satellite): Cinemax (multiplexed); HBO (multiplexed); Showtime (multiplexed); Starz (multiplexed); The Movie Channel (multiplexed).
Fee: $6.95 monthly (Starz), $14.95 monthly (Cinemax, HBO, Showtime or TMC).

Video-On-Demand: No

Pay-Per-View
Fresh (delivered digitally) Playboy TV (delivered digitally); iN DEMAND (delivered digitally).

Internet Service
Operational: No.

Telephone Service
None

President & Chief Executive Officer: Pat McDaragh. Senior Vice President, Public Policy: Tom Simmons. Programming Director: Wynne Haakenstad.
Ownership: Midcontinent Communications (MSO).

ALMOND—Formerly served by New Century Communications. No longer in operation. ICA: WI0209.

AMBERG—Packerland Broadband, 105 Kent St., PO Box 885, Iron Mountain, MI 49801. Phone: 800-236-8434. Fax: 906-776-2811. E-mail: service@plbb.net; support@packerlandbroadband.com. Web Site: http://www.packerlandbroadband.com. ICA: WI0326.

Channel capacity: N.A. Channels available but not in use: N.A.

Basic Service
Subscribers: 16.
Fee: $24.95 monthly.
Ownership: Packerland Broadband.

AMERY—Northwest Community Communications, 116 Harriman Ave North, Amery, WI 54001. Phones: 715-268-6066; 715-268-7101. Fax: 715-268-9194. E-mail: info@nwcomm.net. Web Site: http://www.nwcomm.net. Also serves Clayton (Polk County), Deer Park, Polk County (portions) & Turtle Lake. ICA: WI0080.

TV Market Ranking: Outside TV Markets (AMERY, Clayton (Polk County), Deer Park, Turtle Lake). Franchise award date: N.A. Franchise expiration date: N.A. Began: September 1, 1984.

Channel capacity: N.A. Channels available but not in use: N.A.

Basic Service
Subscribers: 1,410.
Programming (received off-air): KARE (NBC, WeatherNation) Minneapolis; KMSP-TV (Bounce TV, Buzzr, FOX) Minneapolis; KPXM-TV (ION) St. Cloud; KSTC-TV (Antenna TV, This TV) Minneapolis; KSTP-TV (ABC, MeTV) St. Paul; KTCA-TV (PBS) St. Paul; KTCI-TV (PBS) St. Paul; WCCO-TV (CBS, Decades) Minneapolis; WEAU (NBC) Eau Claire; WEUX (FOX, MeTV) Chippewa Falls; WFTC (MNT, Movies!) Minneapolis; WHWC-TV (PBS) Menomonie; WQOW (ABC, CW, This TV) Eau Claire; WUCW (CW, The Country Network) Minneapolis.
Programming (via satellite): A&E; AMC; Animal Planet; BTN; CMT; CNBC; CNN; Comedy Central; C-SPAN; C-SPAN 2; Discovery Channel; Disney Channel; E! HD; ESPN; ESPN Classic; ESPN2; Food Network; Fox News Channel; Fox Sports 1; FOX Sports North; Freeform; FX; Golf Channel; Great American Country; Hallmark Channel; Hallmark Movies & Mysteries; HGTV; History; HLN; Lifetime; MTV; National Geographic Channel; Nickelodeon; Outdoor Channel; OWN: Oprah Winfrey Network; Pop; Spike

D-848   TV & Cable Factbook No. 85

Cable Systems—Wisconsin

TV; Syfy; TBS; The Weather Channel; TLC; TNT; Travel Channel; Turner Classic Movies; TV Land; USA Network; VH1; WGN America.

Fee: $50.00 installation; $28.74 monthly.

Digital Basic Service
Subscribers: N.A.
Programming (via satellite): BBC America; Bloomberg Television; Cloo; CMT; Destination America; Discovery Kids Channel; Discovery Life Channel; Disney XD; DMX Music; ESPN Classic; ESPNews; FSN Digital Atlantic; FSN Digital Central; FSN Digital Pacific; Fuse; FXM; FYI; Golf Channel; History International; IFC; Investigation Discovery; LMN; MTV Classic; MTV Hits; MTV2; NBCSN; Nick Jr.; Nicktoons; OWN: Oprah Winfrey Network; Science Channel; TeenNick; Trinity Broadcasting Network (TBN); UP; VH1 Soul; WE tv.
Fee: $17.95 monthly.

Digital Expanded Basic Service
Subscribers: N.A.
Programming (via satellite): A&E HD; AXS TV; BTN HD; Discovery Channel HD; ESPN HD; History HD; National Geographic Channel HD; Outdoor Channel 2 HD; PBS HD; Universal HD.
Fee: $13.95 monthly.

Pay Service 1
Pay Units: 54.
Programming (via satellite): Cinemax (multiplexed).
Fee: $10.95 monthly.

Pay Service 2
Pay Units: 224.
Programming (via satellite): HBO (multiplexed).
Fee: $12.95 monthly.

Pay Service 3
Pay Units: 121.
Programming (via satellite): Showtime (multiplexed); The Movie Channel.
Fee: $10.95 monthly.

Digital Pay Service 1
Pay Units: N.A.
Programming (via satellite): Cinemax (multiplexed); Flix; HBO (multiplexed); Showtime (multiplexed); Starz (multiplexed); Starz Encore (multiplexed); The Movie Channel.
Fee: $10.95 monthly (Cinemax, Showtime/TMC/Flix or Starz/Encore), $12.95 monthly (HBO).

Video-On-Demand: No

Internet Service
Operational: Yes.
Broadband Service: In-house.
Fee: $50.00 installation; $24.95-$49.95 monthly.

Telephone Service
Analog: Operational
Miles of Plant: 39.0 (coaxial); None (fiber optic).
Vice President: Scott Jensen. General Manager: Dwight Schmitt. Operations Manager: Myron Ranum.
Ownership: Northwest Community Communications (MSO).

AMHERST (village)—Amherst Telephone. This cable system has converted to IPTV. See AMHERST (village), WI [WI5372]. ICA: WI0144.

AMHERST (village)—Tomorrow Valley Video, 120 Mill St., PO Box 279, Amherst, WI 54406. Phone: 715-824-5529. Fax: 715-824-2050. Web Site: http://www.wi-net.com. Also serves Alban (town), Amherst (town), Amherst Junction (village), Buena Vista (town), Franzen (town), Harrison (town), Lanark (town), Nelsonville (village), New Hope (town), Rosholt (village), Sharon (town) & Stockton (town). ICA: WI5372.
Channel capacity: N.A. Channels available but not in use: N.A.

Basic
Subscribers: 1,707.
Fee: $240.00 installation; $48.98 monthly. Includes 60 channels plus music channels.

Expanded Basic
Subscribers: 1,573.
Fee: $61.43 monthly. Includes 110 channels plus music channels.

HD
Subscribers: N.A.
Fee: $7.95 monthly. Includes 61 channels.

Cinemax
Subscribers: N.A.
Fee: $11.95 monthly. Includes 3 channels.

HBO
Subscribers: N.A.
Fee: $15.95 monthly. Includes 4 channels.

Showtime/TMC/Flix
Subscribers: N.A.
Fee: $13.95 monthly. Includes 11 channels.

Starz/Encore
Subscribers: N.A.
Fee: $12.95 monthly. Includes 12 channels.

Internet Service
Operational: Yes.
Fee: $39.95-$79.95 monthly.

Telephone Service
Digital: Operational
Executive Vice President & General Manager: Richard Letto.
Ownership: Amherst Telephone Co.

ANGELICA—Formerly served by Packerland Broadband. No longer in operation. ICA: WI0330.

ANTIGO—Charter Communications. Now served by STEVENS POINT, WI [WI0019]. ICA: WI0052.

APPLETON—Time Warner Cable, 1001 West Kennedy Ave, PO Box 145, Kimberly, WI 54136-0145. Phones: 414-277-4032 (Milwaukee); 920-749-1400. Fax: 920-831-9372. Web Site: http://www.timewarnercable.com. Also serves Abrams (town), Algoma (town), Allouez, Ashwaubenon, Bellevue, Black Wolf (town), Brillion (town), Buchanan (town), Cato (town), Center, Chase, Clayton (Winnebago County), Combined Locks, Dale, De Pere, Ellington, Freedom, Grand Chute (town), Green Bay, Greenville (town), Harrison (town), Hilbert (village), Hobart, Holland (town), Howard (village), Kaukauna, Kaukauna (town), Kimberly, Lawrence (town), Ledgeview (town), Liberty (town), Little Chute, Little Suamico, Medina, Menasha (town), Neenah (town), Oconto County (portions), Oneida, Osborn, Oshkosh, Pittsfield, Reedsville, Rockland (town), Seymour, Sherwood (village), St. Nazianz, Stiles (town), Stockbridge (town), Stockbridge (village), Suamico, Valders, Vandenbroek, Vinland, Winchester (town), Woodville (town), Wrightstown (town) & Wrightstown (village). ICA: WI0006.
TV Market Ranking: 62 (Abrams (town), Algoma (town), Allouez, Ashwaubenon, Bellevue, Brillion (town), Buchanan (town), Cato (town), Center, Chase, Clayton (Winnebago County), Combined Locks, De Pere, Ellington, Freedom, Grand Chute (town), Green Bay, Greenville (town), Harrison (town), Hilbert (village), Hobart, Holland (town), Howard (village), Kaukauna, Kaukauna (town), Kimberly, Lawrence (town), Ledgeview (town), Little Chute, Little Suamico, Medina, Menasha (town), Neenah (town), Oconto County (portions), Oneida, Osborn, Pittsfield, Reedsville, Rockland (town), Seymour, Sherwood (village), St. Nazianz, Stiles (town), Stockbridge (town), Stockbridge (village), Suamico, Valders, Vandenbroek, Woodville (town), Wrightstown (town), Wrightstown (village)); Below 100 (Black Wolf (town), Dale, Liberty (town), Oshkosh, Vinland (town), Winchester (town)). Franchise award date: January 1, 1980. Franchise expiration date: N.A. Began: July 1, 1973.
Channel capacity: 65 (operating 2-way). Channels available but not in use: N.A.

Basic Service
Subscribers: 98,906.
Programming (received off-air): WACY-TV (Escape, Grit, Laff, MNT) Appleton; WBAY-TV (ABC) Green Bay; WCWF (CW) Suring; WFRV-TV (Bounce TV, CBS) Green Bay; WGBA-TV (MeTV, NBC) Green Bay; WLUK-TV (Antenna TV, FOX) Green Bay; WPNE-TV (PBS) Green Bay; WVTV (CW) Milwaukee.
Programming (via satellite): C-SPAN; EWTN Global Catholic Network; WGN America.
Fee: $99.95 installation; $27.21 monthly.

Expanded Basic Service 1
Subscribers: N.A.
Programming (via satellite): A&E; AMC; Animal Planet; Bravo; Cartoon Network; CMT; CNBC; CNN; Comedy Central; C-SPAN 2; Discovery Channel; Disney Channel; E! HD; ESPN; ESPN Classic; ESPN2; EVINE Live; Food Network; Fox News Channel; FOX Sports Networks; Freeform; FX; Golf Channel; Hallmark Channel; HGTV; History; HLN; Lifetime; LMN; MSNBC; MTV; National Geographic Channel; NBCSN; Nickelodeon; OWN: Oprah Winfrey Network; Oxygen; Pop; QVC; Spike TV; Syfy; TBS; The Weather Channel; TLC; TNT; Travel Channel; truTV; Turner Classic Movies; TV Land; Univision Studios; USA Network; VH1; WE tv.
Fee: $41.41 monthly.

Digital Basic Service
Subscribers: N.A.
Programming (via satellite): BBC America; Bloomberg Television; Cooking Channel; C-SPAN 3; Destination America; Discovery Kids Channel; Discovery Life Channel; Disney XD; DIY Network; ESPNews; Fox Sports 1; FSN Digital Atlantic; FSN Digital Central; FSN Digital Pacific; Fuse; FYI; Great American Country; GSN; History International; IFC; Investigation Discovery; MTV Classic; MTV2; NBA TV; Nick 2; Nick Jr.; Outdoor Channel; Ovation; Science Channel; TeenNick; Tennis Channel; Weatherscan.
Fee: $53.49 monthly.

Digital Pay Service 1
Pay Units: N.A.
Programming (via satellite): Cinemax (multiplexed); HBO (multiplexed); Showtime (multiplexed); Starz (multiplexed); Starz Encore (multiplexed); The Movie Channel (multiplexed).
Fee: $12.99 monthly (each).

Video-On-Demand: Yes

Pay-Per-View
iN DEMAND (delivered digitally); Playboy TV (delivered digitally); Club Jenna (delivered digitally); ESPN (delivered digitally).

Internet Service
Operational: Yes. Began: August 1, 2000.
Subscribers: 126,385.
Broadband Service: Road Runner.
Fee: $44.95 installation; $39.99 monthly; $7.00 modem lease.

Telephone Service
Digital: Operational
Subscribers: 61,052.
Miles of Plant: 5,977.0 (coaxial); 2,179.0 (fiber optic). Homes passed: 173,595. Homes passed & miles of plant (coax & fiber combined) include Marinette.
President: Jack Herbert. Vice President, Engineering: Randy Cicatello. Vice President, Marketing: Brenda Kinne. Vice President, Government & Public Affairs: Bev Greenburg. General Manager: Mike Fox. Public Affairs Manager: Bill Harken.
Ownership: Time Warner Cable (MSO).

ARGYLE—Mediacom, 3033 Asbury Rd, Dubuque, IA 52001. Phones: 845-695-2762; 309-797-2580 (Regional office); 563-557-8025. Fax: 563-557-7413. Web Site: http://www.mediacomcable.com. ICA: WI0175.
TV Market Ranking: 93 (ARGYLE).
Channel capacity: N.A. Channels available but not in use: N.A.

Basic Service
Subscribers: 24.
Fee: $70.95 monthly.

Internet Service
Operational: No.

Telephone Service
None
Miles of plant included in Moline, IL.
Regional Vice President: Cari Fenzel. Vice President, Financial Reporting: Kenneth J. Kohrs. Area Manager: Kathleen McMullen. Engineering Director: Mitch Carlson. Marketing Director: Greg Evans. Technical Operations Manager: Darren Dean.
Ownership: Mediacom LLC (MSO).

ARKANSAW—NTec (formerly Chippewa Valley Cable Co. Inc.), 318 Third Ave W, PO Box 228, Durand, WI 54736-0228. Phone: 715-672-4204. Fax: 715-672-4344. E-mail: admin@nelson-tel.net. Web Site: http://www.ntec.net. Also serves Durand, Mondovi & Plum City. ICA: WI0110.
TV Market Ranking: Below 100 (ARKANSAW, Durand, Mondovi); Outside TV Markets (Plum City). Franchise award date: January 1, 1968. Franchise expiration date: N.A. Began: September 1, 1968.
Channel capacity: N.A. Channels available but not in use: N.A.

Basic Service
Subscribers: 1,593.
Programming (received off-air): KARE (NBC, WeatherNation) Minneapolis; KSTC-TV (Antenna TV, This TV) Minneapolis; KSTP-TV (ABC, MeTV) St. Paul; KTCA-TV (PBS) St. Paul; WCCO-TV (CBS, Decades) Minneapolis; WEAU (NBC) Eau Claire; WEUX (FOX, MeTV) Chippewa Falls; WFTC (MNT, Movies!) Minneapolis; WKBT-DT (CBS, MNT) La Crosse; WQOW (ABC, CW, This TV) Eau Claire; WUCW (CW, The Country Network) Minneapolis; allband FM.
Programming (via satellite): A&E; AMC; Animal Planet; Cartoon Network; CMT; CNBC; CNN; Comedy Central; C-SPAN; Discovery Channel; DIY Network; ESPN; ESPN2; EWTN Global Catholic Network; Food Network; Fox News Channel; Fox Sports 1; FOX Sports North; Freeform; FX; Golf Channel; HGTV; History; HLN; Lifetime; LMN; MTV; National Geographic Channel; NFL Network; Nickelodeon; Outdoor Channel; Pop; QVC; Spike TV; Syfy;

2017 Edition D-849

Wisconsin—Cable Systems

TBS; The Weather Channel; TLC; TNT; TV Land; USA Network; VH1; WGN America.
Fee: $45.00 installation; $74.05 monthly.
Expanded Basic Service 1
Subscribers: N.A.
Fee: $4.95 monthly.
Digital Basic Service
Subscribers: N.A.
Programming (via satellite): Animal Planet HD; AXS TV; Bloomberg Television; Cloo; Discovery Channel HD; Discovery Kids Channel; DMX Music; ESPN HD; ESPNews; FSN HD; FYI; Golf Channel; GSN; Hallmark Channel; HD Theater; History International; Investigation Discovery; LMN; MTV Classic; MTV2; mtvU; NBCSN; Nick Jr.; Nicktoons; Outdoor Channel 2 HD; OWN; Oprah Winfrey Network; PBS HD; RFD-TV; Science Channel; TeenNick; TLC HD; Turner Classic Movies; WE tv.
Fee: $14.90 monthly.
Digital Pay Service 1
Pay Units: N.A.
Programming (via satellite): Cinemax (multiplexed); Cinemax HD; HBO (multiplexed); HBO HD; Showtime (multiplexed); Starz (multiplexed); Starz Encore (multiplexed); The Movie Channel (multiplexed).
Fee: $10.95 monthly (Cinemax), $12.95 monthly (Showtime or Starz/Starz Encore) or $18.95 monthly (HBO).
Video-On-Demand: No
Pay-Per-View
iN DEMAND (delivered digitally); Club Jenna (delivered digitally).
Internet Service
Operational: No, DSL & dial-up.
Telephone Service
Analog: Operational
Miles of Plant: 51.0 (coaxial); 4.0 (fiber optic). Homes passed: 2,313.
Executive Vice President & General Manager: Christy Berger. Chief Financial Officer: Laura Gullickson. Plant Manager: Dale Goss. Sales & Marketing: Larry Johnson.
Ownership: Nelson Telephone Cooperative.

ASHLAND—Charter Communications. Now served by EAU CLAIRE, WI [WI0011]. ICA: WI0047.

AUBURNDALE—Packerland Broadband, 105 Kent St., PO Box 885, Iron Mountain, MI 49801. Phones: 906-774-1291; 906-774-6621; 800-236-8434. Fax: 906-776-2811. E-mail: service@plbb.net; support@packerlandbroadband.com. Web Site: http://www.packerlandbroadband.com. Also serves Hewitt & Marshfield (portions). ICA: WI0166.
TV Market Ranking: Below 100 (AUBURNDALE, Hewitt, Marshfield (portions)).
Channel capacity: N.A. Channels available but not in use: N.A.
Basic Service
Subscribers: 50.
Programming (received off-air): WAOW (ABC, CW, This TV) Wausau; WEAU (NBC) Eau Claire; WFXS-DT Wittenberg; WHRM-TV (PBS) Wausau; WSAW-TV (CBS, MNT) Wausau.
Programming (via satellite): A&E; AMC; Animal Planet; CMT; CNBC; CNN; Discovery Channel; Disney Channel; ESPN; ESPN2; FOX Sports Networks; Freeform; History; Lifetime; MTV; Nickelodeon; Spike TV; Syfy; TBS; The Weather Channel; TLC; TNT; TV Land; USA Network; VH1; WGN America.
Fee: $45.00 installation; $25.95 monthly; $1.50 converter.
Pay Service 1
Pay Units: 35.
Programming (via satellite): HBO.
Fee: $14.95 installation; $10.95 monthly.
Video-On-Demand: No
Internet Service
Operational: Yes.
Fee: $26.95 monthly.
Telephone Service
None
Miles of Plant: 22.0 (coaxial); None (fiber optic). Homes passed: 639.
General Manager: Dan Plante. Technical Supervisor: Chad Kay.
Ownership: Packerland Broadband (MSO).

AUGUSTA—Packerland Broadband, 105 Kent St., PO Box 885, Iron Mountain, MI 49801. Phone: 800-236-8434. Fax: 906-776-2811. E-mail: service@plbb.net; support@packerlandbroadband.com. Web Site: http://www.packerlandbroadband.com. ICA: WI0141.
Channel capacity: N.A. Channels available but not in use: N.A.
Basic Service
Subscribers: 140.
Fee: $24.95 monthly.
Ownership: Packerland Broadband.

AVOCA—Packerland Broadband, 105 Kent St., PO Box 885, Iron Mountain, MI 49801. Phones: 906-774-1291; 800-236-8434; 906-774-6621. Fax: 906-776-2811. E-mail: service@plbb.net; support@packerlandbroadband.com. Web Site: http://www.packerlandbroadband.com. ICA: WI0237.
TV Market Ranking: Outside TV Markets (AVOCA).
Channel capacity: N.A. Channels available but not in use: N.A.
Basic Service
Subscribers: 19.
Programming (received off-air): WBUW (CW) Janesville; WHA-TV (PBS) Madison; WISC-TV (CBS, MNT) Madison; WKOW (ABC, MeTV, This TV) Madison; WMSN-TV (FOX, The Country Network) Madison; WMTV (CW, NBC) Madison.
Programming (via satellite): QVC; TBS; WGN America.
Fee: $75.00 installation; $55.95 monthly.
Expanded Basic Service 1
Subscribers: N.A.
Programming (via satellite): A&E; Animal Planet; CMT; CNN; Discovery Channel; Disney Channel; E! HD; ESPN; ESPN2; Freeform; History; HLN; Lifetime; Nickelodeon; Spike TV; The Weather Channel; TLC; TNT; Turner Classic Movies; USA Network.
Fee: $25.30 monthly.
Pay Service 1
Pay Units: N.A.
Programming (via satellite): HBO.
Fee: $14.95 monthly.
Video-On-Demand: No
Internet Service
Operational: No.
Telephone Service
None
Miles of Plant: 4.0 (coaxial); None (fiber optic). Homes passed: 293.
General Manager: Cory Heigl. Marketing Director: Andy Datta. Billing/Sales Manager: Jessica Kuhn. Finance: Catherine Faccin.
Ownership: Packerland Broadband (MSO).

BAGLEY (village)—Dairyland Cable Systems Inc, 2494 US Hwy 14 East, Richland Center, WI 53581-2983. Phones: 800-677-6383; 608-647-6383. Fax: 608-647-2093. ICA: WI0238.
TV Market Ranking: Below 100 (BAGLEY (VILLAGE)). Franchise award date: N.A. Franchise expiration date: N.A. Began: July 1, 1989.
Channel capacity: 13 (not 2-way capable). Channels available but not in use: N.A.
Basic Service
Subscribers: N.A.
Programming (received off-air): KCRG-TV (ABC, MNT) Cedar Rapids; KRIN (PBS) Waterloo; KWWL (CW, MeTV, NBC) Waterloo; WISC-TV (CBS, MNT) Madison; WKBT-DT (CBS, MNT) La Crosse.
Programming (via satellite): CNN; Discovery Channel; ESPN; TBS; TNT; USA Network; WGN America.
Fee: $25.00 installation.
Pay Service 1
Pay Units: N.A.
Programming (via satellite): The Movie Channel.
Fee: $10.50 monthly.
Video-On-Demand: No
Internet Service
Operational: No.
Telephone Service
None
General Manager: Jim Atkinson. Chief Technician: Rudy Marshall. Marketing Representative: Brian Sullivan.
Ownership: Dairyland Cable Systems Inc. (MSO).

BALDWIN TWP.—Baldwin Telecom Inc, 930 Maple St, PO Box 420, Baldwin, WI 54002. Phones: 877-684-3346; 715-684-3346. Fax: 715-684-4747. E-mail: info@baldwin-telecom.net; info@lswi.net. Web Site: http://www.baldwin-telecom.net. Also serves Baldwin (town), Baldwin (village), Eau Galle Twp., Emerald Twp., Erin Twp., Hammond (village), Hammond Twp., Hudson Twp., Knapp (village), Roberts (village), Troy Twp. & Woodville (village). ICA: WI0079.
Channel capacity: N.A. Channels available but not in use: N.A.
Basic Service
Subscribers: 4,677.
Fee: $79.95 installation; $24.95 monthly.
Pay Service 1
Pay Units: 1,045.
Programming (via satellite): HBO.
Fee: $8.95 monthly.
Internet Service
Operational: Yes.
Fee: $39.95-$49.90 monthly.
Telephone Service
Digital: Operational
General Manager: Matt Sparks. Cable TV Manager: Matt Knegendorf. Broadband Manager: Brad Mortel. Plant Manager: Duane Russett.
Ownership: Baldwin Telecom Inc.

BANCROFT—New Century Communications, 3588 Kennebec Dr, Eagan, MN 55122-1001. Phone: 651-688-2623. Fax: 651-688-2624. ICA: WI0215.
TV Market Ranking: Outside TV Markets (BANCROFT).
Channel capacity: N.A. Channels available but not in use: N.A.
Basic Service
Subscribers: N.A.
Programming (received off-air): WAOW (ABC, CW, This TV) Wausau; WEAU (NBC) Eau Claire; WFXS-DT Wittenberg; WHRM-TV (PBS) Wausau; WSAW-TV (CBS, MNT) Wausau.
Programming (via satellite): A&E; AMC; CNN; Discovery Channel; ESPN; Freeform; Lifetime; Nickelodeon; Showtime; Spike TV; TBS; TLC; TNT; Trinity Broadcasting Network (TBN); USA Network; WGN America.
Fee: $30.00 installation.
Video-On-Demand: No
Internet Service
Operational: No.
Telephone Service
None
Miles of Plant: 4.0 (coaxial); None (fiber optic). Homes passed: 163.
Executive Vice President: Marty Walch. General Manager & Chief Technician: Todd Anderson.
Ownership: New Century Communications (MSO).

BAY CITY—Midcontinent Communications. Now served by ELLSWORTH, WI [WI0248]. ICA: WI0239.

BEAR CREEK—Charter Communications. Now served by STEVENS POINT, WI [WI0019]. ICA: WI0240.

BELL CENTER—Formerly served by Richland-Grant Telephone Co-op. No longer in operation. ICA: WI0228.

BELL CENTER—Formerly served by Richland-Grant Telephone Co-op. No longer in operation. ICA: WI5364.

BELLEVILLE—Charter Communications. Now served by MADISON, WI [WI0002]. ICA: WI0138.

BLACK RIVER FALLS—Charter Communications. Now served by EAU CLAIRE, WI [WI0011]. ICA: WI0082.

BLANCHARDVILLE—Mediacom, 3033 Asbury Rd, Dubuque, IA 52001. Phones: 845-695-2762; 309-797-2580 (Regional office); 563-557-8025. Fax: 563-557-7413. Web Site: http://www.mediacomcable.com. ICA: WI0170.
TV Market Ranking: 93 (BLANCHARDVILLE).
Channel capacity: N.A. Channels available but not in use: N.A.
Basic Service
Subscribers: 9.
Programming (received off-air): WHA-TV (PBS) Madison; WISC-TV (CBS, MNT) Madison; WKOW (ABC, MeTV, This TV) Madison; WMSN-TV (FOX, The Country Network) Madison; WMTV (CW, NBC) Madison.
Programming (via satellite): A&E; AMC; Animal Planet; Bravo; Cartoon Network; CMT; CNBC; CNN; Comedy Central; C-SPAN; Discovery Channel; Discovery Life Channel; Disney Channel; ESPN; ESPN2; Food Network; Fox Sports 1; Freeform; Hallmark Channel; HGTV; History; HLN; INSP; Lifetime; MTV; Nickelodeon; Oxygen; QVC; Spike TV; Syfy; TBS; The Weather Channel; TLC; TNT; Travel Channel; Trinity Broadcasting Network (TBN); truTV; TV Land; USA Network; VH1; WGN America.
Fee: $69.95 monthly.
Pay Service 1
Pay Units: N.A.
Programming (via satellite): Cinemax; HBO; Showtime.
Internet Service
Operational: No.
Telephone Service
None
Miles of plant included in Moline, IL.
Regional Vice President: Cari Fenzel. Vice President, Financial Reporting: Kenneth J. Kohrs. Area Manager: Kathleen McMullen. Engineering Director: Mitch Carlson. Tech-

Cable Systems—Wisconsin

FULLY SEARCHABLE • CONTINUOUSLY UPDATED • DISCOUNT RATES FOR PRINT PURCHASERS

For more information call **800-771-9202** or visit **www.warren-news.com**

nical Operations Manager: Darren Dean. Marketing Director: Greg Evans.
Ownership: Mediacom LLC (MSO).

BLOOMINGDALE—Formerly served by Midwest Cable Inc. No longer in operation. ICA: WI0232.

BLUE RIVER (village)—Dairyland Cable Systems Inc, 2494 US Hwy 14 East, Richland Center, WI 53581-2983. Phone: 608-647-6383. Fax: 608-647-2093. ICA: WI0242.
TV Market Ranking: Outside TV Markets (BLUE RIVER (VILLAGE)). Franchise award date: N.A. Franchise expiration date: N.A. Began: November 1, 1989.
Channel capacity: 16 (not 2-way capable). Channels available but not in use: N.A.
Basic Service
Subscribers: N.A.
Programming (received off-air): WISC-TV (CBS, MNT) Madison; WKOW (ABC, MeTV, This TV) Madison; WMSN-TV (FOX, The Country Network) Madison; WMTV (CW, NBC) Madison; WMVS (PBS) Milwaukee.
Programming (via satellite): CNN; Discovery Channel; ESPN; Nickelodeon; TBS; TNT; USA Network; VH1; WGN America.
Fee: $25.00 installation.
Pay Service 1
Pay Units: N.A.
Programming (via satellite): The Movie Channel.
Fee: $10.50 monthly.
Video-On-Demand: No
Internet Service
Operational: No.
Telephone Service
None
General Manager: Jim Atkinson. Chief Technician: Randy Marshall. Marketing Representative: Brian Sullivan.
Ownership: Dairyland Cable Systems Inc. (MSO).

BLUFFVIEW MOBILE HOME PARK—Formerly served by HLM Cable Corp. Now served by Merrimac Cable, MERRIMAC, WI [WI0154]. ICA: WI0212.

BOAZ (village)—Village of Boaz, 25433 Jackson St, Muscoda, WI 53573. Phone: 608-536-3466. Fax: 608-536-3469. ICA: WI0229.
TV Market Ranking: Outside TV Markets (BOAZ (VILLAGE)).
Channel capacity: 20 (not 2-way capable). Channels available but not in use: N.A.
Basic Service
Subscribers: N.A.
Programming (received off-air): WHA-TV (PBS) Madison; WISC-TV (CBS, MNT) Madison; WKBT-DT (CBS, MNT) La Crosse; WKOW (ABC, MeTV, This TV) Madison; WMSN-TV (FOX, The Country Network) Madison; WMTV (CW, NBC) Madison.
Programming (via satellite): CW PLUS; Discovery Channel; ESPN; TBS; TNT; USA Network.
Internet Service
Operational: No.
Telephone Service
None
Miles of Plant: 3.0 (coaxial); None (fiber optic).
Chief Technician: Dan Schwarz. Village Clerk: Jean Welsh.
Ownership: Village of Boaz.

BONDUEL—Packerland Broadband, 105 Kent St., PO Box 885, Iron Mountain, MI 49801. Phone: 800-236-8434. Fax: 906-776-2811. E-mail: service@plbb.net; support@packerlandbroadband.com. Web Site: http://www.packerlandbroadband.com. ICA: WI0163.
Channel capacity: N.A. Channels available but not in use: N.A.
Ownership: Packerland Broadband.

BOSCOBEL—Mediacom, 4010 Alexandra Dr, Waterloo, IA 50702. Phones: 845-695-2762; 319-235-2197. Fax: 319-232-7841. Web Site: http://www.mediacomcable.com. Also serves Clayton, Elkader, Garnavillo, Guttenberg, Harpers Ferry, Lansing, Marquette, McGregor, Waukon & Waukon Junction, IA; Grant County (unincorporated areas), WI. ICA: WI0341.
TV Market Ranking: Below 100 (Grant County (unincorporated areas) (portions), Guttenberg, Lansing); Outside TV Markets (BOSCOBEL, Clayton, Elkader, Garnavillo, Grant County (unincorporated areas) (portions), Harpers Ferry, Marquette, McGregor, Waukon, Waukon Junction).
Channel capacity: N.A. Channels available but not in use: N.A.
Basic Service
Subscribers: 2,182.
Fee: $48.95 monthly.
Vice President, Financial Reporting: Kenneth J. Kohrs.
Ownership: Mediacom LLC (MSO).

BOULDER JUNCTION—Karban TV Systems Inc, 73A South Stevens St, Rhinelander, WI 54501. Phones: 715-550-7613; 800-236-0233. Fax: 715-277-2339. E-mail: sales@ktvs.net. Web Site: http://www.ktvs.net. ICA: WI0243.
TV Market Ranking: Below 100 (BOULDER JUNCTION). Franchise award date: N.A. Franchise expiration date: N.A. Began: August 1, 1990.
Channel capacity: 77 (2-way capable). Channels available but not in use: N.A.
Basic Service
Subscribers: N.A.
Programming (received off-air): WFXS-DT Wittenberg; WJFW-TV (Antenna TV, NBC) Rhinelander; WLEF-TV (PBS) Park Falls; WSAW-TV (CBS, MNT) Wausau; WYOW (ABC, CW, This TV) Eagle River.
Programming (via satellite): A&E; AMC; Animal Planet; CMT; CNBC; CNN; Comedy Central; C-SPAN; CW PLUS; Discovery Channel; Disney Channel; ESPN; ESPN2; EWTN Global Catholic Network; Food Network; Fox News Channel; Fox Sports 1; Freeform; FX; HGTV; History; HLN; Lifetime; MSNBC; NFL Network; Nickelodeon; Outdoor Channel; QVC; Spike TV; Syfy; TBS; The Weather Channel; TLC; TNT; Travel Channel; Trinity Broadcasting Network (TBN); Turner Classic Movies; TV Land; USA Network; VH1; WGN America.
Fee: $75.00 installation; $48.00 monthly.
Pay Service 1
Pay Units: N.A.
Programming (via satellite): Cinemax; HBO.
Fee: $10.00 monthly (each).
Video-On-Demand: No
Internet Service
Operational: Yes.
Telephone Service
None
Miles of Plant: 18.0 (coaxial); None (fiber optic). Homes passed: 200.
General Manager & Chief Technician: John Karban.
Ownership: Karban TV Systems Inc. (MSO).

BOYCEVILLE—Nextgen Communications, 234 East Oak St, PO Box 398, Glenwood City, WI 54013. Phones: 888-696-9146; 715-565-7742. Fax: 715-565-3001. E-mail: nextgen@nextgen-communications.net; nextgen@cltcomm.net. Web Site: http://www.nextgen-communications.net. Also serves Downing. ICA: WI0338.
TV Market Ranking: Below 100 (Downing, BOYCEVILLE).
Channel capacity: N.A. Channels available but not in use: N.A.
Basic Service
Subscribers: 4,654.
Programming (received off-air): KARE (NBC, WeatherNation) Minneapolis; KMSP-TV (Bounce TV, Buzzr, FOX) Minneapolis; KSTC-TV (Antenna TV, This TV) Minneapolis; KSTP-TV (ABC, MeTV) St. Paul; KTCA-TV (PBS) St. Paul; WCCO-TV (CBS, Decades) Minneapolis; WEAU (NBC) Eau Claire; WEUX (FOX, MeTV) Chippewa Falls; WFTC (MNT, Movies!) Minneapolis; WHWC-TV (PBS) Menomonie; WKBT-DT (CBS, MNT) La Crosse; WQOW (ABC, CW, This TV) Eau Claire; WUCW (CW, The Country Network) Minneapolis.
Programming (via satellite): C-SPAN; HSN; Pop; QVC; Trinity Broadcasting Network (TBN); WGN America.
Fee: $14.95 monthly.
Expanded Basic Service 1
Subscribers: N.A.
Programming (via satellite): A&E; AMC; Animal Planet; Bravo; BTN; Cartoon Network; CMT; CNBC; CNN; Comedy Central; Discovery Channel; Disney Channel; DIY Network; E! HD; ESPN; ESPN Classic; ESPN2; EWTN Global Catholic Network; Food Network; Fox News Channel; Fox Sports 1; FOX Sports North; Freeform; FX; Golf Channel; Great American Country; GSN; Hallmark Channel; HGTV; History; HLN; Lifetime; LMN; MLB Network; MSNBC; MTV; National Geographic Channel; NBCSN; NFL Network; Nickelodeon; Outdoor Channel; RFD-TV; Spike TV; Syfy; TBS; The Sportsman Channel; The Weather Channel; TLC; TNT; Travel Channel; truTV; Turner Classic Movies; TV Land; USA Network; VH1.
Fee: $35.00 monthly.
Digital Basic Service
Subscribers: N.A.
Programming (via satellite): American Heroes Channel; BBC America; Bloomberg Television; Centric; Church Channel; cloo; CMT; Cooking Channel; C-SPAN 2; Destination America; Discovery Kids Channel; Disney XD; DMX Music; EVINE Live; Fox Business Network; Fuse; FXM; FYI; Hallmark Movies & Mysteries; History International; IFC; INSP; Investigation Discovery; ION Television; Jewelry Television; JUCE TV; MTV Classic; MTV Hits; MTV Jams; MTV2; Nick Jr.; Nicktoons; OWN: Oprah Winfrey Network; Oxygen; Science Channel; Sprout; TeenNick; The Word Network; VH1 Soul; WE tv; Youtoo America.
Fee: $14.95 monthly.
Digital Expanded Basic Service
Subscribers: N.A.
Programming (received off-air): KARE (NBC, WeatherNation) Minneapolis; KMSP-TV (Bounce TV, Buzzr, FOX) Minneapolis; KSTP-TV (ABC, MeTV) St. Paul; WCCO-TV (CBS, Decades) Minneapolis; WEAU (NBC) Eau Claire; WHWC-TV (PBS) Menomonie; WQOW (ABC, CW, This TV) Eau Claire.
Programming (via satellite): A&E HD; Animal Planet HD; Discovery Channel HD; ESPN HD; ESPN2 HD; Food Network HD; HD Theater; HGTV HD; MLB Network HD; National Geographic Channel HD; Science HD; TLC HD; Universal HD.
Fee: $9.95 monthly.
Digital Expanded Basic Service 2
Subscribers: N.A.
Programming (via satellite): Discovery Life Channel; ESPNews; FOX College Sports Central; FOX College Sports Pacific; TVG Network.
Fee: $9.95 monthly.
Digital Pay Service 1
Pay Units: N.A.
Programming (via satellite): Cinemax (multiplexed); Flix; HBO (multiplexed); Showtime (multiplexed); Starz (multiplexed); Starz Encore (multiplexed); The Movie Channel (multiplexed).
Fee: $13.95 monthly (HBO, Cinemax, Starz/Encore or Showtime/TMC/Flix).
Pay-Per-View
iN DEMAND (delivered digitally).
Internet Service
Operational: Yes.
Fee: $19.95-$49.95 monthly.
Telephone Service
Analog: Operational
Miles of Plant: None (coaxial); 220.0 (fiber optic). Homes passed: 7,280. Homes passed, total homes in area & miles of plant included in Glenwood City.
President & General Manager: Mark Anderson. Technical Manager: Adrian Ocneanu. Product Management Director: Giovanni Mircea Barroso.
Ownership: Nextgen Communications (MSO).

BOYD/CADOTT—Charter Communications. Now served by EAU CLAIRE, WI [WI0011]. ICA: WI0131.

BRIGGSVILLE—New Century Communications, 3588 Kennebec Dr, Eagan, MN 55122-1001. Phone: 651-688-2623. Fax: 651-688-2624. ICA: WI0216.
TV Market Ranking: Outside TV Markets (BRIGGSVILLE).
Channel capacity: N.A. Channels available but not in use: N.A.
Basic Service
Subscribers: N.A.
Programming (received off-air): WHA-TV (PBS) Madison; WISC-TV (CBS, MNT) Madison; WKOW (ABC, MeTV, This TV) Madison; WMTV (CW, NBC) Madison.
Programming (via satellite): A&E; AMC; CNN; Discovery Channel; Disney Channel; ESPN; ESPN2; Freeform; History; QVC; Showtime (multiplexed); Spike TV; TBS;

2017 Edition

D-851

Wisconsin—Cable Systems

CABLE & TV STATION COVERAGE
Atlas 2017
The perfect companion to the Television & Cable Factbook
To order call 800-771-9202 or visit www.warren-news.com

TLC; TNT; Trinity Broadcasting Network (TBN); USA Network; WGN America.
Fee: $30.00 installation.
Video-On-Demand: No
Internet Service
Operational: No.
Telephone Service
None
Miles of Plant: 4.0 (coaxial); None (fiber optic). Homes passed: 152.
Executive Vice President: Marty Walch. General Manager & Chief Technician: Todd Anderson.
Ownership: New Century Communications (MSO).

BROOKFIELD—Time Warner Cable. Now served by MILWAUKEE, WI [WI0001]. ICA: WI0028.

BURLINGTON—Time Warner Cable. Now served by MILWAUKEE, WI [WI0001]. ICA: WI0023.

BUTTERNUT—Packerland Broadband, 105 Kent St., PO Box 885, Iron Mountain, MI 49801. Phone: 800-236-8434. Fax: 906-776-2811. E-mail: service@plbb.net; support@packerlandbroadband.com. Web Site: http://www.packerlandbroadband.com. ICA: WI0214.
Channel capacity: N.A. Channels available but not in use: N.A.
Basic Service
Subscribers: 97.
Fee: $58.95 monthly.
Ownership: Packerland Broadband.

CASCO—CenturyLink. Now served by NEW FRANKEN, WI [WI0269]. ICA: WI0115.

CAZENOVIA—Community Antenna System Inc, 1010 Lake St, Hillsboro, WI 54634-9019. Phone: 608-489-2321. Fax: 608-489-2321. E-mail: comant@comantenna.com. Web Site: http://comantenna.com. ICA: WI0222.
TV Market Ranking: Outside TV Markets (CAZENOVIA). Franchise award date: January 1, 1970. Franchise expiration date: N.A. Began: January 1, 1971.
Channel capacity: N.A. Channels available but not in use: N.A.
Basic Service
Subscribers: 17.
Programming (received off-air): WHA-TV (PBS) Madison; WISC-TV (CBS, MNT) Madison; WKBT-DT (CBS, MNT) La Crosse; WKOW (ABC, MeTV, This TV) Madison; WMSN-TV (FOX, The Country Network) Madison; WMTV (CW, NBC) Madison.
Programming (via satellite): ESPN; Freeform; Spike TV; TBS; TNT; WGN America.
Fee: $40.00 installation; $59.36 monthly.
Pay Service 1
Pay Units: N.A.
Programming (via satellite): Cinemax.
Fee: $6.95 monthly.
Internet Service
Operational: Yes.

Telephone Service
None
Miles of Plant: 2.0 (coaxial); None (fiber optic).
President & General Manager: Randall Kubarski. Chief Technician: Gregory Kubarski.
Ownership: Community Antenna System Inc. (MSO).

CECIL—Packerland Broadband, 105 Kent St., PO Box 885, Iron Mountain, MI 49801. Phone: 800-236-8434. Fax: 906-776-2811. E-mail: service@plbb.net; support@packerlandbroadband.com. Web Site: http://www.packerlandbroadband.com. ICA: WI0342.
Channel capacity: N.A. Channels available but not in use: N.A.
Basic Service
Subscribers: 174.
Fee: $24.95 monthly.
Ownership: Packerland Broadband.

CEDARBURG—Time Warner Cable. Now served by MILWAUKEE, WI [WI0001]. ICA: WI0031.

CHASEBURG—Mediacom. Now served by STODDARD, WI [WI0161]. ICA: WI0219.

CLEAR LAKE—CLT Communications, 316 3rd Ave, PO Box 47, Clear Lake, WI 54005. Phone: 715-263-2755. Fax: 715-263-2267. E-mail: info@cltcomm.net. Web Site: http://cltcomm.net. ICA: WI0340.
TV Market Ranking: Outside TV Markets (CLEAR LAKE).
Channel capacity: N.A. Channels available but not in use: N.A.
Basic Service
Subscribers: 173.
Fee: $73.32 monthly.
President: Matthew Anderson.
Ownership: CLT Communications LLC.

CLINTONVILLE—Charter Communications. Now served by STEVENS POINT, WI [WI0019]. ICA: WI0073.

COLEMAN—Packerland Broadband, 105 Kent St., PO Box 885, Iron Mountain, MI 49801. Phone: 800-236-8434. Fax: 906-776-2811. E-mail: service@plbb.net; support@packerlandbroadband.com. Web Site: http://www.packerlandbroadband.com. ICA: WI0173.
Channel capacity: N.A. Channels available but not in use: N.A.
Basic Service
Subscribers: 77.
Fee: $24.95 monthly.
Ownership: Packerland Broadband.

COON VALLEY—Mediacom. Now served by VIROQUA, WI [WI0068]. ICA: WI0171.

CRIVITZ—Howard Cable, 111 Pine St, PO Box 127, Peshtigo, WI 54157. Phones: 800-472-0576; 715-582-1141. Fax: 715-582-1142. E-mail: cableone@new.rr.com. ICA: WI0321.
TV Market Ranking: Below 100 (CRIVITZ). Franchise award date: January 1, 1986. Franchise expiration date: N.A. Began: January 1, 1985.
Channel capacity: N.A. Channels available but not in use: N.A.
Basic Service
Subscribers: 94.
Programming (received off-air): WACY-TV (Escape, Grit, Laff, MNT) Appleton; WBAY-TV (ABC) Green Bay; WCWF (CW) Suring; WFRV-TV (Bounce TV, CBS) Green Bay; WGBA-TV (MeTV, NBC) Green Bay; WLUK-TV (Antenna TV, FOX) Green Bay; WNMU (PBS) Marquette; WPNE-TV (PBS) Green Bay.
Programming (via satellite): EWTN Global Catholic Network; Freeform; HGTV; Lifetime; Nickelodeon; Spike TV; TNT; USA Network.
Fee: $24.95 monthly.
Expanded Basic Service 1
Subscribers: N.A.
Programming (via satellite): A&E; AMC; Animal Planet; Bloomberg Television; Bravo; Classic Arts Showcase; CMT; CNN; Comedy Central; Discovery Channel; Disney Channel; Disney XD; DIY Network; E! HD; ESPN; ESPN2; Food Network; Fox News Channel; FX; FXM; Great American Country; Hallmark Channel; History; HLN; MTV; National Geographic Channel; Outdoor Channel; QVC; Syfy; TBS; TLC; Travel Channel; Trinity Broadcasting Network (TBN); truTV; Turner Classic Movies; TV Land; VH1; WGN America.
Fee: $10.00 monthly.
Pay Service 1
Pay Units: N.A.
Programming (via satellite): HBO.
Fee: $10.95 monthly.
Video-On-Demand: No
Internet Service
Operational: No.
Telephone Service
None
Miles of Plant: 44.0 (coaxial); None (fiber optic). Homes passed: 994.
General Manager & Chief Technician: Howard C. Lock.
Ownership: Howard Lock (MSO).

CUBA CITY—Mediacom, 3900 26th Ave, Moline, IL 61265. Phones: 845-695-2762; 309-797-2580. Fax: 309-797-2414. Web Site: http://www.mediacomcable.com. Also serves Belmont, Benton, Darlington, Hazel Green, Potosi, Shullsburg & Tennyson. ICA: WI0334.
Channel capacity: N.A. Channels available but not in use: N.A.
Basic Service
Subscribers: 897.
Programming (received off-air): KFXA (FOX, The Country Network) Cedar Rapids; KWWL (CW, MeTV, NBC) Waterloo; WBUW (CW) Janesville; WHA-TV (PBS) Madison; WISC-TV (CBS, MNT) Madison; WKOW (ABC, MeTV, This TV) Madison; WMSN-TV (FOX, The Country Network) Madison; WMTV (CW, NBC) Madison.
Programming (via satellite): C-SPAN; C-SPAN 2; Discovery Channel; QVC; WGN America.
Fee: $45.00 monthly.
Expanded Basic Service 1
Subscribers: N.A.
Programming (via satellite): A&E; AMC; Bravo; BTN; Cartoon Network; CMT; CNBC; CNN; Comedy Central; Discovery Life Channel; Disney Channel; E! HD; ESPN; ESPN2; EWTN Global Catholic Network; Food Network; Fox News Channel; Fox Sports 1; FOX Sports Networks; Freeform; FX; Hallmark Channel; HGTV; History; HLN; INSP; Lifetime; MSNBC; MTV; NBCSN; Nickelodeon; Spike TV; Syfy; TBS; The Weather Channel; TLC; TNT; Travel Channel; Trinity Broadcasting Network (TBN); truTV; TV Land; USA Network; VH1; WE tv.
Fee: $34.00 monthly.
Digital Basic Service
Subscribers: N.A.
Programming (via satellite): BBC America; Bloomberg Television; Boomerang; CBS Sports Network; Chiller; Cloo; Destination America; Discovery Kids Channel; ESPNews; ESPNU; FOX College Sports Central; FOX College Sports Pacific; Fox Sports 2; Fuse; FXM; FYI; Golf Channel; GolTV; GSN; History International; IFC; Investigation Discovery; ION Television; LMN; MC; MTV Classic; MTV Hits; MTV2; Nat Geo WILD; National Geographic Channel; Nick Jr.; Nicktoons; Outdoor Channel; OWN: Oprah Winfrey Network; Qubo; Reelz; Science Channel; Sundance TV; TeenNick; Tennis Channel; TVG Network.
Fee: $22.95 monthly.
Digital Pay Service 1
Pay Units: N.A.
Programming (via satellite): Cinemax; Flix; HBO (multiplexed); HBO HD; Showtime (multiplexed); Showtime HD; Starz; Starz Encore (multiplexed); Starz HD; Sundance TV; The Movie Channel (multiplexed); The Movie Channel HD.
Fee: $9.00 monthly (Starz/Encore), $10.95 monthly (Cinemax or Showtime/TMC/Sundance/Flix), $14.95 monthly (HBO).
Video-On-Demand: No
Pay-Per-View
iN DEMAND (delivered digitally); Fresh (delivered digitally); Spice: Xcess (delivered digitally); Playboy TV (delivered digitally); SexSee (delivered digitally).
Internet Service
Operational: Yes.
Fee: $59.95 installation; $49.95 monthly.
Telephone Service
Digital: Operational
Miles of plant included in Moline, IL.
Regional Vice President: Cari Fenzel. Vice President, Financial Reporting: Kenneth J. Kohrs. Area Manager: Kathleen McMullen. Engineering Director: Mitch Carlson. Marketing Director: Greg Evans. Technical Operations Manager: Darren Dean.
Ownership: Mediacom LLC (MSO).

DALTON—Formerly served by New Century Communications. No longer in operation. ICA: WI0226.

DARIEN—Packerland Broadband, 105 Kent St., PO Box 885, Iron Mountain, MI 49801. Phones: 906-774-1291; 800-236-8434; 906-774-6621. Fax: 906-776-2811. E-mail: service@plbb.net; support@packerlandbroadband.com. Web Site: http://www.packerlandbroadband.com. ICA: WI0246.
TV Market Ranking: 97 (DARIEN). Franchise award date: N.A. Franchise expiration date: N.A. Began: December 1, 1988.
Channel capacity: N.A. Channels available but not in use: N.A.
Basic Service
Subscribers: 96.
Programming (received off-air): WBUW (CW) Janesville; WCGV-TV (MNT, The

D-852   TV & Cable Factbook No. 85

Cable Systems—Wisconsin

Country Network) Milwaukee; WDJT-TV (CBS, Decades) Milwaukee; WISC-TV (CBS, MNT) Madison; WISN-TV (ABC, Movies!) Milwaukee; WITI (Antenna TV, FOX) Milwaukee; WKOW (ABC, MeTV, This TV) Madison; WMTV (CW, NBC) Madison; WMVS (PBS) Milwaukee; WPXE-TV (ION) Kenosha; WTMJ-TV (COZI TV, Escape, Laff, NBC) Milwaukee; WVTV (CW) Milwaukee.
Programming (via satellite): A&E; AMC; CNN; Comedy Central; Discovery Channel; Disney Channel; ESPN; ESPN2; Freeform; History; Lifetime; MTV; Nickelodeon; Spike TV; Syfy; TBS; The Weather Channel; TLC; TNT; USA Network; VH1; WGN America.
Fee: $24.95 installation; $42.45 monthly; $1.50 converter.

Pay Service 1
Pay Units: 26.
Programming (via satellite): HBO.
Fee: $10.95 monthly.

Internet Service
Operational: Yes.
Fee: $34.95 monthly.

Telephone Service
Digital: Operational
Miles of Plant: 9.0 (coaxial); None (fiber optic). Homes passed: 463.
General Manager: Dan Plante. Technical Supervisor: Chad Kay.
Ownership: Packerland Broadband (MSO).

DELAVAN—Charter Communications. Now served by MADISON, WI [WI0002]. ICA: WI0329.

DODGE COUNTY (portions)—Packerland Broadband. Now served by LOMIRA, WI [WI0345]. ICA: WI0350.

DOYLESTOWN—Formerly served by New Century Communications. No longer in operation. ICA: WI0223.

DRESSER (village)—Charter Communications. Now served by EAU CLAIRE, WI [WI0011]. ICA: WI0087.

EAGLE RIVER—Charter Communications. Now served by STEVENS POINT, WI [WI0019]. ICA: WI0103.

EAU CLAIRE—Charter Communications, 12405 Powerscourt Dr, St. Louis, MO 63131. Phones: 636-207-5100 (Corporate office); 715-831-8930; 715-831-8940. Fax: 715-831-5862. Web Site: http://www.charter.com. Also serves Altura, Goodview, Hillsdale Twp., Homer, La Crescent, La Crescent (village), Lewiston, Minnesota City, Rollingstone, Stockton, Wilson & Winona, MN; Adams Twp., Altoona, Angelo, Anson Twp., Ashland, Bangor, Barksdale (town), Barre Twp., Barron, Barron (town), Barron Twp., Bass Lake Twp., Bayfield, Black River Falls, Bloomer, Boyd, Brockway Twp., Bruce (village), Brunswick Twp., Cadott (village), Cameron, Campbell Twp., Chetek, Chetek (town), Chetek Twp., Chippewa Falls, Colfax Twp., Cornell, Cumberland, Downsville, Dresser (village), Eagle Point, Eileen (town), Eisenstein (village), Elk Mound (village), Flambeau (town), Fountain City, Grant (Rusk County), Greenfield (town), Hallie, Hamilton Twp., Haugen, Hayward, Hayward Twp., Holland Twp., Holmen, La Crosse, La Grange Twp., Ladysmith, Lafayette, Lake Twp., Leon, Medary Twp., Melrose, Menomonie, Menomonie Twp., Mindoro (town), New Auburn, Oakdale, Onalaska, Osceola (town), Park Falls, Prairie Lake, Red Cedar Twp., Red Cliff Reservation, Rice Lake, Rockland, Sand Lake Twp., Shelby, Shell Lake, Sparta, Spooner, St. Croix Falls, Stanley, Stone Lake Twp., Tainter Twp., Tilden, Tomah, Tony (village), Union Twp. (Eau Claire County), Warrens, Washburn, West Salem, Wheaton Twp. & Wheeler (village), WI. ICA: WI0011.
TV Market Ranking: Below 100 (Adams Twp., Altoona, Angelo, Anson Twp., Bangor, Barre Twp., Bloomer, Boyd, Brunswick Twp., Cadott (village), Campbell Twp., Chetek, Chippewa Falls, Colfax Twp., Cornell, Downsville, Eagle Point, EAU CLAIRE, Elk Mound (village), Flambeau (town), Fountain City, Goodview, Greenfield (town), Hallie, Hamilton Twp., Hillsdale Twp., Holland Twp., Holmen, Homer, La Crosse, La Crosse, La Grange Twp., Lafayette, Leon, Lewiston, Medary Twp., Melrose, Menomonie, Menomonie Twp., Mindoro (town), Minnesota City, New Auburn, Onalaska, Red Cedar Twp., Rollingstone, Shelby, Sparta, Stanley, Tainter Twp., Tilden, Union Twp. (Eau Claire County), West Salem, Wheaton Twp., Wheeler (village), Wilson, Winona, Altura, Stockton); Outside TV Markets (Ashland, Barksdale (town), Barron, Barron (town), Barron Twp., Bass Lake Twp., Bayfield, Black River Falls, Brockway Twp., Bruce (village), Cameron, Cumberland, Dresser (village), EAU CLAIRE, Eileen (town), Eisenstein (village), Grant (Rusk County), Haugen, Hayward, Hayward Twp., Ladysmith, Lake Twp., Oakdale, Osceola (town), Park Falls, Prairie Lake, Red Cliff Reservation, Rice Lake, Sand Lake Twp., Shell Lake, Spooner, St. Croix Falls, Stone Lake Twp., Tomah, Tony (village), Warrens, Washburn). Franchise award date: N.A. Franchise expiration date: N.A. Began: January 1, 1961.
Channel capacity: 73 (operating 2-way). Channels available but not in use: N.A.

Digital Basic Service
Subscribers: 69,701.
Programming (via satellite): BBC America; Bravo; Discovery Digital Networks; DIY Network; Fuse; FYI; History International; LMN; MC; Nick 2; Nick Jr.; Sundance TV; TeenNick.
Fee: $14.99 monthly.

Digital Expanded Basic Service
Subscribers: N.A.
Programming (via satellite): A&E; AMC; Animal Planet; Cartoon Network; CMT; CNBC; CNN; Comedy Central; C-SPAN 2; Discovery Channel; Disney Channel; Disney XD; E! HD; ESPN; ESPN2; EWTN Global Catholic Network; Food Network; Fox News Channel; Fox Sports 1; FOX Sports North; Freeform; FX; Golf Channel; GSN; HGTV; History; HLN; Lifetime; MSNBC; MTV; National Geographic Channel; NBCSN; Nickelodeon; Outdoor Channel; Oxygen; QVC; Spike TV; Syfy; TBS; The Weather Channel; TLC; TNT; Travel Channel; Trinity Broadcasting Network (TBN); truTV; TV Land; USA Network; VH1.
Fee: $47.99 monthly.

Digital Pay Service 1
Pay Units: N.A.
Programming (via satellite): Cinemax (multiplexed); Flix; HBO (multiplexed); Showtime (multiplexed).
Fee: $15.00 installation; $10.00 monthly (Cinemax, HBO, Showtime, Flix/TMC or Starz/Encore).

Video-On-Demand: Yes

Pay-Per-View
iN DEMAND (delivered digitally); Playboy TV (delivered digitally); Fresh (delivered digitally); Shorteez (delivered digitally).

Communications Daily
Warren Communications News

Get the industry standard FREE —
For a no-obligation trial call 800-771-9202 or visit www.warren-news.com

Internet Service
Operational: Yes.
Subscribers: 74,123.
Broadband Service: Charter Internet.
Fee: $29.99 monthly; $4.95 modem lease.

Telephone Service
Digital: Operational
Subscribers: 38,048.
Fee: $29.99 monthly
Miles of Plant: 5,370.0 (coaxial); 2,556.0 (fiber optic). Homes passed: 198,478.
Vice President & General Manager: Lisa Washa. Marketing Director: Traci Loonstra. Engineering Director: Tim Normand. Accounting Director: David Sovanski. Construction Manager: Pat Anderson. Government Relations Manager: Mike Hill. Sales & Marketing Manager: Chris Putzkey. Operations Manager: Shirley Weibel.
Ownership: Charter Communications Inc. (MSO).

ELCHO (town)—Packerland Broadband, 105 Kent St., PO Box 885, Iron Mountain, MI 49801. Phones: 906-774-1291; 800-236-8434; 906-774-6621. Fax: 906-776-2811. E-mail: service@plbb.net; support@packerlandbroadband.com. Web Site: http://www.packerlandbroadband.com. Also serves Lake Lucerne & Oneida County (portions). ICA: WI0203.
TV Market Ranking: Below 100 (ELCHO (TOWN), Oneida County (portions)). Franchise award date: May 1, 1990. Franchise expiration date: N.A. Began: July 1, 1990.
Channel capacity: N.A. Channels available but not in use: N.A.

Basic Service
Subscribers: 204.
Programming (received off-air): WAOW (ABC, CW, This TV) Wausau; WFXS-DT Wittenberg; WHRM-TV (PBS) Wausau; WJFW-TV (Antenna TV, NBC) Rhinelander; WSAW-TV (CBS, MNT) Wausau.
Programming (via satellite): A&E; CMT; CNBC; CNN; C-SPAN; Discovery Channel; ESPN; ESPN2; EWTN Global Catholic Network; Food Network; Fox News Channel; Fox Sports 1; FOX Sports Networks; Freeform; FX; HGTV; History; HLN; Lifetime; MSNBC; MTV; Nickelodeon; QVC; Spike TV; TBS; The Weather Channel; TLC; TNT; Turner Classic Movies; TV Land; USA Network; VH1; WGN America.
Fee: $25.00 installation; $23.95 monthly.

Pay Service 1
Pay Units: N.A.
Programming (via satellite): Cinemax; HBO.
Fee: $11.55 monthly (each).

Video-On-Demand: No

Internet Service
Operational: Yes.
Fee: $26.95 monthly.

Telephone Service
None
Miles of Plant: 85.0 (coaxial); None (fiber optic). Homes passed: 1,500.
General Manager: Dan Plante. Technical Supervisor: Chad Kay.
Ownership: Packerland Broadband (MSO).

ELLSWORTH—Midco, PO Box 5010, Sioux Falls, SD 57117. Phone: 800-888-1300. Web Site: http://www.midcocomm.com. ICA: WI0248.
TV Market Ranking: 13 (ELLSWORTH). Franchise award date: N.A. Franchise expiration date: N.A. Began: February 1, 1986.
Channel capacity: N.A. Channels available but not in use: N.A.

Basic Service
Subscribers: N.A.
Programming (received off-air): KARE (NBC, WeatherNation) Minneapolis; KMSP-TV (Bounce TV, Buzzr, FOX) Minneapolis; KSTC-TV (Antenna TV, This TV) Minneapolis; KSTP-TV (ABC, MeTV) St. Paul; KTCA-TV (PBS) St. Paul; WCCO-TV (CBS, Decades) Minneapolis; WEAU (NBC) Eau Claire; WEUX (FOX, MeTV) Chippewa Falls; WHMC (PBS) Conway; WKBT-DT (CBS, MNT) La Crosse.
Programming (via satellite): A&E; Animal Planet; CMT; CNBC; CNN; Comedy Central; C-SPAN; Discovery Channel; Disney Channel; ESPN; ESPN2; Food Network; Fox News Channel; FOX Sports Networks; Freeform; History; HLN; Lifetime; MTV; Nickelodeon; QVC; Spike TV; TBS; The Weather Channel; TLC; TNT; Travel Channel; Turner Classic Movies; TV Land; USA Network; WGN America.

Digital Basic Service
Subscribers: 338.
Programming (via satellite): BBC America; Bloomberg Television; Bravo; Discovery Digital Networks; Disney XD; DMX Music; ESPN Classic; ESPNews; Fox Sports 1; Fuse; FXM; FYI; Golf Channel; GSN; HGTV; History International; IFC; LMN; NBCSN; Nick Jr.; Outdoor Channel; Starz Encore (multiplexed); Syfy; TeenNick; Trinity Broadcasting Network (TBN); WE tv.
Fee: $60.95 monthly.

Digital Pay Service 1
Pay Units: N.A. Included in Cambridge, MN.
Programming (via satellite): Cinemax (multiplexed); HBO (multiplexed); Showtime (multiplexed); Starz (multiplexed); The Movie Channel (multiplexed).
Fee: $6.95 monthly (Starz), $14.95 monthly (Cinemax, HBO, Showtime or TMC).

Video-On-Demand: No

Pay-Per-View
Fresh (delivered digitally); Playboy TV (delivered digitally); iN DEMAND (delivered digitally).

Internet Service
Operational: Yes.
Broadband Service: Warp Drive Online.
Fee: $42.95 monthly.

Telephone Service
None
Homes passed & miles of plant included in Cambridge, MN.
President & Chief Executive Officer: Pat McAdaragh. Senior Vice President, Public Policy: Tom Simmons. Programming Director: Wynne Haakenstad.
Ownership: Midcontinent Communications (MSO).

2017 Edition   **D-853**

Wisconsin—Cable Systems

ELMWOOD (village)—Video services provided by Celect Communications & available through Bloomer Tel, Bruce Tel, Celect Communications, NextGen & West WI Telcom. Formerly [WI0337]. This cable system has converted to IPTV, S131 McKay Ave, PO Box 189, Spring Valley, WI 54767-0189. Phones: 800-285-7993; 715-778-6121. Fax: 715-778-4798. E-mail: celecthelp@celectcom.net. Web Site: www.celectcom.net. Also serves Albany (town), Atlanta (town), Auburn (town), Big Bend (town), Birch Creek (town), Bloomer, Bloomer (town), Boyceville, Bruce (town), Burnzwick (town), Cady (town), Chetek (town), Cleveland (town), Colfax (town), Cooks Valley (town), Dovre (town), Downing, Doyle (town), Drammen, Dunn (town), Eau Claire, Eau Claire (town), El Paso (town), Elk Mound (town), Gilman (town), Grant (town), Hallie (town), Hallie (village), Hay River (town), Howard (town), Lucas (town), Martell (town), Menomonie, Menomonie (town), Murry (town), New Auburn (village), Otter Creek (town), Peru (town), Prairie Lake (town), Red Cedar (town), Rice Lake (town), Rock Creek (town), Rock Elm (town), Rusk (town), Sampson (town), Sherman (town), Sioux Creek (town), Spring Lake (town), Spring Valley (village), Springbrook (town), Springfield (town), Stanley (town), Stanton (town), Strickland (town), Stubbs (town), Sumner (town), Tainter (town), Thornapple (town), Tiffany (town), Tilden (town), Union (town), Washington (town), Waterville (town), Waubeek (town), Weston (town), Wheaton (town), Wilkinson (town), Wilson (town), Wilson (village) & Wood Mohr (town). ICA: WI5045.
TV Market Ranking: Below 100 (Bloomer (town), New Auburn (village), Prairie Lake (town)); Outside TV Markets (Bruce (town)).
Channel capacity: N.A. Channels available but not in use: N.A.
Digital Basic
Subscribers: 2,524.
Fee: $12.15 monthly.
Internet Service
Operational: Yes.
Telephone Service
None
General Manager: Mike Demarce.
Ownership: Celect Communications.

ELROY—Community Antenna System Inc, 1010 Lake St, Hillsboro, WI 54634-9019. Phone: 608-489-2321. Fax: 608-489-2321. E-mail: comant@comantenna.com. Web Site: http://comantenna.com. ICA: WI0132.
TV Market Ranking: Outside TV Markets (ELROY). Franchise award date: January 1, 1963. Franchise expiration date: N.A. Began: October 1, 1963.
Channel capacity: N.A. Channels available but not in use: N.A.
Basic Service
Subscribers: 194.
Programming (received off-air): WEAU (NBC) Eau Claire; WHA-TV (PBS) Madison; WISC-TV (CBS, MNT) Madison; WKBT-DT (CBS, MNT) La Crosse; WKOW (ABC, MeTV, This TV) Madison; WMSN-TV (FOX, The Country Network) Madison; WMTV (CW, NBC) Madison.
Programming (via satellite): ESPN; Freeform; Spike TV; TBS; TNT; WGN America.
Fee: $40.00 installation; $72.74 monthly.
Pay Service 1
Pay Units: 175.
Programming (via satellite): Cinemax.
Fee: $6.95 monthly.
Internet Service
Operational: Yes.
Broadband Service: In-house.
Fee: $27.99 monthly.
Telephone Service
None
Miles of Plant: 7.0 (coaxial); None (fiber optic). Homes passed: 656.
President & General Manager: Randall Kubarski. Chief Technician: Gregory Kubarski.
Ownership: Community Antenna System Inc. (MSO).

ENDEAVOR—Formerly served by New Century Communications. No longer in operation. ICA: WI0218.

ENTERPRISE—Packerland Broadband, 105 Kent St., PO Box 885, Iron Mountain, MI 49801. Phone: 800-236-8434. Fax: 906-776-2811. E-mail: service@plbb.net; support@packerlandbroadband.com. Web Site: http://www.packerlandbroadband.com. ICA: WI0343.
Channel capacity: N.A. Channels available but not in use: N.A.
Basic Service
Subscribers: 128.
Fee: $75.00 installation; $17.50 monthly.
Internet Service
Operational: Yes.
Fee: $40.95-$99.95 monthly.
Telephone Service
Digital: Operational
Fee: $24.95 monthly
Ownership: Packerland Broadband.

FAIRWATER—Formerly served by CenturyTel. No longer in operation. ICA: WI0220.

FALL CREEK—Packerland Broadband, 105 Kent St., PO Box 885, Iron Mountain, MI 49801. Phones: 906-774-1291; 800-236-8434; 906-774-6621. Fax: 906-776-2811. E-mail: service@plbb.net; support@packerlandbroadband.com. Web Site: http://www.packerlandbroadband.com. Also serves Augusta. ICA: WI0160.
TV Market Ranking: Below 100 (Augusta, FALL CREEK). Franchise award date: January 1, 1973. Franchise expiration date: N.A. Began: December 1, 1975.
Channel capacity: N.A. Channels available but not in use: N.A.
Basic Service
Subscribers: 151.
Programming (received off-air): WEAU (NBC) Eau Claire; WEUX (FOX, MeTV) Chippewa Falls; WHWC-TV (PBS) Menomonie; WKBT-DT (CBS, MNT) La Crosse; WQOW (ABC, CW, This TV) Eau Claire.
Programming (via satellite): A&E; Animal Planet; CMT; CNN; Comedy Central; Discovery Channel; ESPN; ESPN2; Fox News Channel; Fox Sports 1; FOX Sports Midwest; Freeform; Great American Country; Hallmark Channel; History; HLN; Lifetime; MTV; Nickelodeon; OWN: Oprah Winfrey Network; QVC; Spike TV; Syfy; TBS; The Weather Channel; TLC; TNT; Trinity Broadcasting Network (TBN); truTV; TV Land; USA Network; VH1; WGN America.
Fee: $15.00 installation; $24.95 monthly.
Pay Service 1
Pay Units: N.A.
Programming (via satellite): Flix; Showtime.
Fee: $9.95 monthly.
Video-On-Demand: No
Internet Service
Operational: Yes.
Fee: $26.95 monthly.
Telephone Service
None
Miles of Plant: 9.0 (coaxial); None (fiber optic). Homes passed: 450.
General Manager: Dan Plante. Technical Supervisor: Chad Kay.
Ownership: Packerland Broadband (MSO).

FENNIMORE—Mediacom. Now served by PRAIRIE DU CHIEN, WI [WI0066]. ICA: WI0335.

FIFIELD—Packerland Broadband, 105 Kent St., PO Box 885, Iron Mountain, MI 49801. Phones: 906-774-1291; 800-236-8434; 906-774-6621. Fax: 906-776-2811. E-mail: service@plbb.net; support@packerlandbroadband.com. Web Site: http://www.packerlandbroadband.com. Also serves Butternut. ICA: WI0250.
TV Market Ranking: Outside TV Markets (Butternut, FIFIELD). Franchise award date: January 1, 1991. Franchise expiration date: N.A. Began: N.A.
Channel capacity: N.A. Channels available but not in use: N.A.
Basic Service
Subscribers: 30.
Programming (received off-air): WAOW (ABC, CW, This TV) Wausau; WJFW-TV (Antenna TV, NBC) Rhinelander; WLEF-TV (PBS) Park Falls; WSAW-TV (CBS, MNT) Wausau.
Programming (via satellite): A&E; Animal Planet; CMT; CNN; Comedy Central; Discovery Channel; E! HD; ESPN; ESPN2; Fox Sports 1; Freeform; Hallmark Channel; History; HLN; MTV; Nickelodeon; QVC; Spike TV; Syfy; TBS; The Weather Channel; TLC; TNT; Trinity Broadcasting Network (TBN); TV Land; USA Network; VH1; WGN America.
Fee: $58.95 monthly.
Pay Service 1
Pay Units: N.A.
Programming (via satellite): Showtime.
Fee: $10.50 monthly.
Video-On-Demand: No
Internet Service
Operational: Yes.
Fee: $34.95 monthly.
Telephone Service
None
Miles of Plant: 4.0 (coaxial); None (fiber optic). Homes passed: 110.
General Manager: Dan Plante. Technical Supervisor: Chad Kay.
Ownership: Packerland Broadband (MSO).

FOND DU LAC—Charter Communications, 165 Knights Way, Fond du Lac, WI 54935. Phones: 636-207-5100 (Corporate office); 920-907-7720; 715-831-8940 (Altoona office). Web Site: http://www.charter.com. Also serves Algoma, Auburn, Aurora (town), Barton (town), Beaver Dam, Berlin, Black Wolf (town), Brandon, Brillion, Brooklyn (town), Brothertown, Burnett (town), Butte des Morts, Calamus, Calumet (town), Campbellsport, Carlton (town), Charlestown, Chester, Chilton, Clyman, Cooperstown (town), Denmark, Eden (village), Egg Harbor, Eldorado (town), Empire (town), Ephraim, Erin, Fish Creek, Fox Lake, Francis Creek, Friendship (town), Gibraltar (town), Gibson (town), Green Lake, Hartford, Horicon, Hubbard, Hubertus, Hustisford, Iron Ridge, Jackson, Jacksonport, Juneau, Kellnersville, Kewaskum, Kewaunee, Kiel, Kingston, Kohler, Kossuth (town), Lamartine, Liberty Grove (town), Lima (town), Lisbon (town), Lomira, Lowell, Manitowoc (town), Maribel, Markesan, Marquette, Mayville, Mishicot, Mount Calvary, Nasawapi, Nekimi (town), Neosho, New Holstein, North Fond du Lac, Oak Grove, Oakfield, Omro, Oshkosh, Pierce, Polk, Princeton, Randolph, Reeseville, Richfield, Ripon, Rosendale, Rubicon, Schleswig (town), Sevastapol, Sheboygan, Sheboygan Falls, Sister Bay, Slinger, St. Cloud, Sturgeon Bay, Taycheedah (town), Theresa, Trenton (town), Two Creeks, Utica (town), Van Dyne, Waupun, West Bend, Williamstown, Wilson & Winneconne (village). ICA: WI0018.
TV Market Ranking: 23 (Barton (town), Erin, Hartford, Hubertus, Jackson, Kewaskum, Lisbon (town), Polk, Richfield, Rubicon, Slinger, Trenton (town), West Bend); 62 (Algoma, Algoma, Brillion, Brothertown, Calumet (town), Carlton (town), Charlestown, Chilton, Cooperstown (town), Denmark, Francis Creek, Gibson (town), Kellnersville, Kewaunee, Kossuth (town), Manitowoc (town), Maribel, Mishicot, Oshkosh, Oshkosh, Pierce, Schleswig (town), Two Creeks, Utica (town)); 93 (Calamus, Lowell, Randolph, Reeseville); Below 100 (Auburn, Aurora (town), Beaver Dam, Berlin, Black Wolf (town), Brandon, Brooklyn (town), Burnett (town), Butte des Morts, Campbellsport, Chester, Clyman, Eden (village), Eldorado (town), Empire (town), FOND DU LAC, Fox Lake, Friendship (town), Gibraltar (town), Green Lake, Horicon, Hubbard, Iron Ridge, Juneau, Kiel, Kingston, Kohler, Lamartine, Liberty Grove (town), Lomira, Markesan, Mayville, Mount Calvary, Nekimi (town), Neosho, New Holstein, North Fond du Lac, Oak Grove, Oakfield, Omro, Princeton, Ripon, Rosendale, Sheboygan Falls, St. Cloud, Taycheedah (town), Theresa, Van Dyne, Waupun, Williamstown, Winneconne (village); Outside TV Markets (Egg Harbor, Ephraim, Fish Creek, Jacksonport, Lima (town), Nasawapi, Sevastapol, Hustisford, Sheboygan, Sister Bay, Sturgeon Bay). Franchise award date: N.A. Franchise expiration date: N.A. Began: November 1, 1979.
Channel capacity: 69 (operating 2-way). Channels available but not in use: N.A.

Digital Basic Service
Subscribers: 74,281.
Programming (via satellite): BBC America; Discovery Digital Networks; DIY Network; FYI; History International; MC; Nick 2; Nick Jr.; Nicktoons; Sundance TV; TeenNick; WE tv.
Fee: $49.99 installation; $26.99 monthly.

Cable Systems—Wisconsin

Digital Expanded Basic Service
Subscribers: N.A.
Programming (via satellite): A&E; AMC; Animal Planet; Bravo; Cartoon Network; CMT; CNBC; CNN; Comedy Central; Discovery Channel; Disney Channel; Disney XD; E! HD; ESPN; ESPN2; EWTN Global Catholic Network; Food Network; Fox News Channel; Fox Sports 1; FOX Sports North; Freeform; FX; Golf Channel; GSN; Hallmark Channel; HGTV; History; HLN; Lifetime; MSNBC; MTV; National Geographic Channel; NBCSN; Nickelodeon; Oxygen; Spike TV; Syfy; TBS; The Weather Channel; TLC; TNT; Travel Channel; truTV; Turner Classic Movies; TV Land; USA Network; VH1.
Fee: $47.99 monthly.

Digital Pay Service 1
Pay Units: N.A.
Programming (via satellite): Cinemax (multiplexed); Flix; HBO (multiplexed); Showtime (multiplexed); Starz; Starz Encore (multiplexed); The Movie Channel (multiplexed).
Fee: $10.00 monthly (Cinemax, HBO, Showtime, Flix/TMC or Starz/Encore).

Video-On-Demand: Yes

Pay-Per-View
Hot Choice (delivered digitally); Sports PPV (delivered digitally); Shorteez (delivered digitally); Fresh (delivered digitally); Playboy TV (delivered digitally); iN DEMAND (delivered digitally).

Internet Service
Operational: Yes.
Subscribers: 77,783.
Broadband Service: Charter Internet.
Fee: $29.99 monthly; $4.95 modem lease.

Telephone Service
Digital: Operational
Subscribers: 47,560.
Fee: $29.99 monthly
Miles of Plant: 6,124.0 (coaxial); 1,653.0 (fiber optic). Homes passed: 191,131.
Vice President: Lisa Washa. Accounting Director: David Sovanski. Chief Technician: Jeff Gerner. Marketing Administrator: Traci Loonstra.; Rhonda Schelvan.
Ownership: Charter Communications Inc. (MSO).

FORT McCOY—Mediacom, 4010 Alexandra Dr, Waterloo, IA 50702. Phones: 845-695-2762; 319-235-2197. Fax: 319-232-7841. Web Site: http://www.mediacomcable.com. ICA: WI0312.
TV Market Ranking: Below 100 (FORT McCOY). Franchise award date: March 24, 1995. Franchise expiration date: N.A. Began: February 1, 1996.
Channel capacity: N.A. Channels available but not in use: N.A.

Basic Service
Subscribers: 15.
Programming (received off-air): WEAU (NBC) Eau Claire; WHLA-TV (PBS) La Crosse; WKBT-DT (CBS, MNT) La Crosse; WLAX (FOX, MeTV) La Crosse; WXOW (ABC, CW, This TV) La Crosse.
Programming (via satellite): A&E; BET; CMT; CNN; Comedy Central; C-SPAN; C-SPAN 2; Discovery Channel; Disney Channel; E! HD; ESPN; ESPN2; Freeform; Hallmark Channel; History; HLN; MTV; NBCSN; Pop; RFD-TV; Spike TV; TBS; The Weather Channel; TLC; TNT; truTV; USA Network; VH1; WGN America.
Fee: $48.95 monthly.

Digital Basic Service
Subscribers: N.A.
Programming (via satellite): BBC America; Bloomberg Television; Cloo; Discovery Dig-

ital Networks; ESPNews; Fuse; FXM; FYI; Golf Channel; GSN; History International; IFC; LMN; MC; National Geographic Channel; Nick Jr.; Nicktoons; Outdoor Channel; TeenNick; Turner Classic Movies; TVG Network.

Digital Pay Service 1
Pay Units: N.A.
Programming (via satellite): Cinemax (multiplexed); Flix (multiplexed); HBO (multiplexed); Showtime (multiplexed); Starz (multiplexed); Starz Encore (multiplexed); Sundance TV (multiplexed); The Movie Channel (multiplexed).

Video-On-Demand: No

Pay-Per-View
ESPN (delivered digitally); Fresh (delivered digitally); Shorteez (delivered digitally); Playboy TV (delivered digitally); Pleasure (delivered digitally); SexSee (delivered digitally).

Internet Service
Operational: Yes.
Broadband Service: Mediacom High Speed Internet.

Telephone Service
None
Miles of Plant: 11.0 (coaxial); 12.0 (fiber optic). Homes passed: 1,475.
Regional Vice President: Doug Frank. Vice President, Financial Reporting: Kenneth J. Kohrs. General Manager: Doug Nix. Technical Operations Director: Greg Nank. Marketing Director: Steve Schuh. Marketing Coordinator: Joni Lindauer.
Ownership: Mediacom LLC (MSO).

FOUNTAIN CITY—Charter Communications. Now served by EAU CLAIRE, WI [WI0011]. ICA: WI0178.

FREMONT—Mediacom, 4010 Alexandra Dr, Waterloo, IA 50702. Phones: 845-695-2762; 319-235-2197. Fax: 319-232-7841. Web Site: http://www.mediacomcable.com. ICA: WI0172.
TV Market Ranking: Below 100 (FREMONT). Franchise award date: N.A. Franchise expiration date: N.A. Began: March 1, 1985.
Channel capacity: N.A. Channels available but not in use: N.A.

Basic Service
Subscribers: 11.
Programming (received off-air): WACY-TV (Escape, Grit, Laff, MNT) Appleton; WBAY-TV (ABC) Green Bay; WFRV-TV (Bounce TV, CBS) Green Bay; WGBA-TV (MeTV, NBC) Green Bay; WLUK-TV (Antenna TV, FOX) Green Bay; WPNE-TV (PBS) Green Bay; WSAW-TV (CBS, MNT) Wausau.
Programming (via satellite): A&E; Animal Planet; CMT; CNN; Comedy Central; Discovery Channel; ESPN; ESPN2; Freeform; FX; History; Lifetime; Nickelodeon; QVC; Spike TV; Syfy; TBS; The Weather Channel; TNT; USA Network; VH1; WGN America.
Fee: $45.00 installation; $40.00 monthly.

Pay Service 1
Pay Units: N.A.
Programming (via satellite): HBO; Showtime.
Fee: $11.99 monthly (each).

Video-On-Demand: No

Internet Service
Operational: No.

Telephone Service
None
Miles of Plant: 8.0 (coaxial); None (fiber optic). Homes passed: 394.
Regional Vice President: Doug Frank. Vice President, Financial Reporting: Kenneth J. Kohrs. General Manager: Doug Nix. Techni-

cal Operations Director: Greg Nank. Marketing Director: Steve Schuh. Marketing Coordinator: Joni Lindauer.
Ownership: Mediacom LLC (MSO).

GENOA CITY—Charter Communications. Now served by MADISON, WI [WI0002]. ICA: WI0039.

GILLETT—Packerland Broadband, 105 Kent St., PO Box 885, Iron Mountain, MI 49801. Phone: 800-236-8434. Fax: 906-776-2811. E-mail: service@plbb.net; support@packerlandbroadband.com. Web Site: http://www.packerlandbroadband.com. ICA: WI0181.
Channel capacity: N.A. Channels available but not in use: N.A.

Basic Service
Subscribers: 248.
Fee: $24.95 monthly.
Ownership: Packerland Broadband.

GILMAN—Formerly served by S & K TV Systems. No longer in operation. ICA: WI0333.

GLENWOOD CITY—Nextgen Communications, 234 East Oak St, PO Box 398, Glenwood City, WI 54013. Phones: 888-696-9146; 715-565-7742. Fax: 715-565-3001. E-mail: nextgen@nextgen-communications.net; nextgen@cltcomm.net. Web Site: http://www.nextgen-communications.net. ICA: WI0251.
TV Market Ranking: Outside TV Markets (GLENWOOD CITY). Franchise award date: January 1, 1968. Franchise expiration date: N.A. Began: January 1, 1968.
Channel capacity: N.A. Channels available but not in use: N.A.

Basic Service
Subscribers: 495.
Programming (received off-air): KARE (NBC, WeatherNation) Minneapolis; KMSP-TV (Bounce TV, Buzzr, FOX) Minneapolis; KSTC-TV (Antenna TV, This TV) Minneapolis; KSTP-TV (ABC, MeTV) St. Paul; KTCA-TV (PBS) St. Paul; KUCW (CW, Movies!, The Country Network) Ogden; WCCO-TV (CBS, Decades) Minneapolis; WEAU (NBC) Eau Claire; WEUX (FOX, MeTV) Chippewa Falls; WFTC (MNT, Movies!) Minneapolis; WHWC-TV (PBS) Menomonie; WKBT-DT (CBS, MNT) La Crosse; WQOW (ABC, CW, This TV) Eau Claire.
Programming (via satellite): A&E; AMC; Animal Planet; Bravo; Cartoon Network; CMT; CNN; Comedy Central; C-SPAN; C-SPAN 2; Discovery Channel; Disney Channel; E! HD; ESPN; ESPN Classic; ESPN2; Food Network; Fox News Channel; Fox Sports 1; FOX Sports Networks; Freeform; FX; Great American Country; GSN; Hallmark Channel; HGTV; History; HLN; ION Television; Lifetime; MSNBC; MTV; National Geographic Channel; Nickelodeon; Outdoor Channel; QVC; RFD-TV; Spike TV; Syfy; TBS; The Weather Channel; TLC; TNT; Travel Channel; Trinity Broadcasting Network (TBN);

truTV; TV Land; USA Network; VH1; WGN America.
Fee: $73.32 monthly; $1.50 converter.

Digital Basic Service
Subscribers: N.A.
Programming (via satellite): BBC America; Bloomberg Television; Bravo; Cloo; CMT; Discovery Digital Networks; DMX Music; ESPN Classic; ESPNews; Fox Sports 1; Fuse; FXM; FYI; Golf Channel; GSN; History International; IFC; LMN; National Geographic Channel; NBCSN; Nick Jr.; TeenNick; Trinity Broadcasting Network (TBN); Turner Classic Movies; WE tv.
Fee: $17.00 monthly.

Digital Pay Service 1
Pay Units: N.A.
Programming (via satellite): Cinemax (multiplexed); Flix (multiplexed); HBO (multiplexed); Showtime (multiplexed); Starz (multiplexed); Starz Encore (multiplexed); The Movie Channel.
Fee: $13.95 monthly (each).

Video-On-Demand: No

Pay-Per-View
iN DEMAND (delivered digitally).

Internet Service
Operational: Yes.
Subscribers: 206.
Fee: $29.95-$59.95 monthly.

Telephone Service
Analog: Operational
Fee: $25.45 monthly
Miles of Plant: 20.0 (coaxial); 2.0 (fiber optic). Homes passed: 536. Homes passed, total homes in area & miles of plant include Boyceville.
General Manager: Tim Kusilek. Product Management Director: Giovanni Mircea Barroso. Technical Manager: Adrian Ocneanu.
Ownership: Nextgen Communications (MSO).

GLIDDEN—Packerland Broadband, 105 Kent St., PO Box 885, Iron Mountain, MI 49801. Phones: 906-774-1291; 800-236-8434; 906-774-6621. Fax: 906-776-2811. E-mail: service@plbb.net; support@packerlandbroadband.com. Web Site: http://www.packerlandbroadband.com. ICA: WI0191.
TV Market Ranking: Outside TV Markets (GLIDDEN). Franchise award date: April 1, 1980. Franchise expiration date: N.A. Began: April 1, 1985.
Channel capacity: N.A. Channels available but not in use: N.A.

Basic Service
Subscribers: 69.
Programming (received off-air): KBJR-TV (CBS, MNT, NBC) Superior; KDLH (CBS, CW) Duluth; WDIO-DT (ABC, MeTV) Duluth; WJFW-TV (Antenna TV, NBC) Rhinelander; WLEF-TV (PBS) Park Falls; WSAW-TV (CBS, MNT) Wausau; WYOW (ABC, CW, This TV) Eagle River.
Programming (via satellite): A&E; Bloomberg Television; CNN; Discovery Channel; Disney Channel; ESPN; Freeform; History; MTV; Nickelodeon;

2017 Edition

D-855

Wisconsin—Cable Systems

Spike TV; Syfy; TBS; The Weather Channel; TNT; USA Network; VH1; WGN America.
Fee: $35.00 installation; $50.95 monthly.
Pay Service 1
Pay Units: N.A.
Programming (via satellite): The Movie Channel.
Fee: $10.00 installation; $12.00 monthly.
Video-On-Demand: No
Internet Service
Operational: No.
Telephone Service
None
Miles of Plant: 6.0 (coaxial); None (fiber optic). Homes passed: 300.
General Manager: Dan Plante. Technical Supervisor: Chad Kay.
Ownership: Packerland Broadband (MSO).

GOODMAN—Packerland Broadband, 105 Kent St., PO Box 885, Iron Mountain, MI 49801. Phone: 800-236-8434. Fax: 906-776-2811. E-mail: service@plbb.net; support@packerlandbroadband.com. Web Site: http://www.packerlandbroadband.com. ICA: WI0206.
Channel capacity: N.A. Channels available but not in use: N.A.
Basic Service
Subscribers: 46.
Fee: $24.95 monthly.
Ownership: Packerland Broadband.

GRANTON—New Century Communications, 3588 Kennebec Dr, Eagan, MN 55122-1001. Phone: 651-688-2623. Fax: 651-688-2624. ICA: WI0211.
TV Market Ranking: Outside TV Markets (GRANTON).
Channel capacity: N.A. Channels available but not in use: N.A.
Basic Service
Subscribers: N.A.
Programming (received off-air): WAOW (ABC, CW, This TV) Wausau; WEAU (NBC) Eau Claire; WHRM-TV (PBS) Wausau; WLAX (FOX, MeTV) La Crosse; WSAW-TV (CBS, MNT) Wausau.
Programming (via satellite): A&E; AMC; CNN; Discovery Channel; Disney Channel; ESPN; ESPN2; Freeform; History; Lifetime; Nickelodeon; Showtime; Spike TV; TBS; TLC; TNT; Trinity Broadcasting Network (TBN); USA Network; WGN America.
Fee: $30.00 installation.
Video-On-Demand: No
Internet Service
Operational: No.
Telephone Service
None
Miles of Plant: 4.0 (coaxial); None (fiber optic). Homes passed: 182.
Executive Vice President: Marty Walch. General Manager & Chief Technician: Todd Anderson.
Ownership: New Century Communications (MSO).

GRANTSBURG—Grantsburg Telcom, 139 West Madison Ave, PO Box 447, Grantsburg, WI 54840-0447. Phone: 715-463-5322. Fax: 715-463-5206. E-mail: office@grantsburgtelcom.com. Web Site: http://www.grantsburgtelcom.com. ICA: WI0252.
TV Market Ranking: Outside TV Markets (GRANTSBURG). Franchise award date: July 15, 1985. Franchise expiration date: N.A. Began: January 1, 1987.
Channel capacity: N.A. Channels available but not in use: N.A.
Basic Service
Subscribers: 293.
Programming (received off-air): KARE (NBC, WeatherNation) Minneapolis; KMSP-TV (Bounce TV, Buzzr, FOX) Minneapolis; KPXM-TV (ION) St. Cloud; KSTC-TV (Antenna TV, This TV) Minneapolis; KSTP-TV (ABC, MeTV) St. Paul; KTCA-TV (PBS) St. Paul; WCCO-TV (CBS, Decades) Minneapolis; WEAU (NBC) Eau Claire; WEUX (FOX, MeTV) Chippewa Falls; WFTC (MNT, Movies!) Minneapolis; WHWC-TV (PBS) Menomonie; WQOW (ABC, CW, This TV) Eau Claire; WUCW (CW, The Country Network) Minneapolis.
Programming (via satellite): A&E; AMC; Animal Planet; Cartoon Network; CMT; CNBC; CNN; Comedy Central; C-SPAN; C-SPAN 2; Discovery Channel; Disney Channel; DIY Network; E! HD; ESPN; ESPN Classic; ESPN2; EWTN Global Catholic Network; Food Network; Fox News Channel; Fox Sports 1; Freeform; FX; Golf Channel; Hallmark Channel; HGTV; History; HLN; Lifetime; LMN; Local Cable Weather; MTV; National Geographic Channel; NBCSN; Nickelodeon; Outdoor Channel; Oxygen; Pop; QVC; Spike TV; Syfy; TBS; The Weather Channel; TLC; TNT; Travel Channel; truTV; Turner Classic Movies; TV Land; USA Network; VH1; WGN America.
Fee: $24.95 installation; $74.95 monthly.
Digital Basic Service
Subscribers: N.A.
Programming (via satellite): AXS TV; BBC America; Cloo; CMT; Destination America; Discovery Kids Channel; Discovery Life Channel; Disney XD; DMX Music; ESPN HD; ESPNews; FXM; FYI; History International; Investigation Discovery; MTV Classic; MTV Hits; MTV2; Nick Jr.; Nicktoons; OWN; Oprah Winfrey Network; RFD-TV; Science Channel; TeenNick; Trinity Broadcasting Network (TBN); Universal HD; VH1 Soul; WE tv.
Fee: $49.95 installation; $21.00 monthly.
Pay Service 1
Pay Units: N.A.
Programming (via satellite): Cinemax; HBO; Showtime.
Fee: $9.00 monthly (each).
Digital Pay Service 1
Pay Units: N.A.
Programming (via satellite): Cinemax (multiplexed); Flix; HBO (multiplexed); Showtime (multiplexed); Starz (multiplexed); Starz Encore (multiplexed); The Movie Channel (multiplexed).
Fee: $11.95 monthly (each).
Video-On-Demand: No
Internet Service
Operational: Yes, DSL & dial-up.
Broadband Service: In-house.
Fee: $29.95 monthly.
Telephone Service
Digital: Operational
General Manager: Mark Anderson.
Ownership: Farmers Independent Telephone Co.

GREEN BAY—Formerly served by Sprint Corp. No longer in operation. ICA: WI0305.

GREENFIELD (Milwaukee County)—Time Warner Cable. Now served by MILWAUKEE, WI [WI0001]. ICA: WI0003.

GREENLEAF—Formerly served by CenturyTel. No longer in operation. ICA: WI0253.

GREENWOOD—Packerland Broadband, 105 Kent St., PO Box 885, Iron Mountain, MI 49801. Phones: 906-774-1291; 800-236-8434; 906-774-6621. Fax: 906-776-2811. E-mail: service@plbb.net; support@packerlandbroadband.com. Web Site: http://www.packerlandbroadband.com. ICA: WI0159.
TV Market Ranking: Outside TV Markets (GREENWOOD). Franchise award date: N.A. Franchise expiration date: N.A. Began: May 1, 1984.
Channel capacity: N.A. Channels available but not in use: N.A.
Basic Service
Subscribers: 80.
Programming (received off-air): WAOW (ABC, CW, This TV) Wausau; WEAU (NBC) Eau Claire; WEUX (FOX, MeTV) Chippewa Falls; WHRM-TV (PBS) Wausau; WKBT-DT (CBS, MNT) La Crosse; WSAW-TV (CBS, MNT) Wausau.
Programming (via satellite): A&E; Animal Planet; CMT; CNN; Comedy Central; Discovery Channel; ESPN; ESPN2; Fox News Channel; Fox Sports 1; Freeform; FX; Great American Country; Hallmark Channel; History; HLN; Lifetime; MTV; Nickelodeon; OWN: Oprah Winfrey Network; QVC; Spike TV; TBS; The Weather Channel; TLC; TNT; Travel Channel; Trinity Broadcasting Network (TBN); TV Land; USA Network; VH1; WGN America.
Fee: $25.00 installation; $25.95 monthly.
Pay Service 1
Pay Units: N.A.
Programming (via satellite): Flix; Showtime.
Fee: $9.95 monthly.
Video-On-Demand: No
Internet Service
Operational: No.
Telephone Service
None
Miles of Plant: 13.0 (coaxial); None (fiber optic). Homes passed: 450.
General Manager: Dan Plante. Technical Supervisor: Chad Kay.
Ownership: Packerland Broadband (MSO).

HAWKINS (village)—Packerland Broadband, 105 Kent St., PO Box 885, Iron Mountain, MI 49801. Phones: 906-774-1291; 800-236-8434; 906-774-6621. Fax: 906-776-2811. E-mail: service@plbb.net; support@packerlandbroadband.com. Web Site: http://www.packerlandbroadband.com. ICA: WI0254.
TV Market Ranking: Below 100 (HAWKINS (VILLAGE)).
Channel capacity: N.A. Channels available but not in use: N.A.
Basic Service
Subscribers: 33.
Programming (received off-air): WAOW (ABC, CW, This TV) Wausau; WEAU (NBC) Eau Claire; WEUX (FOX, MeTV) Chippewa Falls; WLEF-TV (PBS) Park Falls; WSAW-TV (CBS, MNT) Wausau.
Programming (via satellite): A&E; Bloomberg Television; CNN; Comedy Central; Discovery Channel; Disney Channel; ESPN; ESPN2; Freeform; History; MTV; Nickelodeon; Spike TV; Syfy; TBS; The Weather Channel; TNT; USA Network; VH1; WGN America.
Fee: $48.95 monthly.
Pay Service 1
Pay Units: N.A.
Programming (via satellite): Flix; Showtime.
Fee: $9.95 monthly.
Video-On-Demand: No
Internet Service
Operational: No.
Telephone Service
None
General Manager: Dan Plante. Technical Supervisor: Chad Kay.
Ownership: Packerland Broadband (MSO).

HAYWARD—Charter Communications. Now served by EAU CLAIRE, WI [WI0011]. ICA: WI0085.

HILLSBORO—Community Antenna System Inc, 1010 Lake St, Hillsboro, WI 54634-9019. Phone: 608-489-2321. E-mail: comant@comantenna.com. Web Site: http://comantenna.com. ICA: WI0135.
TV Market Ranking: Outside TV Markets (HILLSBORO). Franchise award date: N.A. Franchise expiration date: N.A. Began: January 1, 1959.
Channel capacity: N.A. Channels available but not in use: N.A.
Basic Service
Subscribers: 189.
Programming (received off-air): WEAU (NBC) Eau Claire; WHA-TV (PBS) Madison; WISC-TV (CBS, MNT) Madison; WKBT-DT (CBS, MNT) La Crosse; WKOW (ABC, MeTV, This TV) Madison; WMSN-TV (FOX, The Country Network) Madison; WMTV (CW, NBC) Madison.
Programming (via satellite): ESPN; Freeform; Spike TV; TBS; TNT; WGN America.
Fee: $40.00 installation; $72.74 monthly.
Pay Service 1
Pay Units: 98.
Programming (via satellite): Cinemax.
Fee: $6.95 monthly.
Internet Service
Operational: Yes.
Broadband Service: In-house.
Fee: $30.00 installation; $27.99 monthly.
Telephone Service
None
Miles of Plant: 5.0 (coaxial); None (fiber optic).
President & General Manager: Randall Kubarski. Chief Technician: Gregory Kubarski.
Ownership: Community Antenna System Inc. (MSO).

HOLCOMBE—S & K TV Systems, 508 Miner Ave West, Ladysmith, WI 54848. Phones: 715-532-7321; 800-924-7880. Fax: 715-532-7583. E-mail: dave@skcable.com. Web Site: http://www.skcable.com. ICA: WI0147.
TV Market Ranking: Outside TV Markets (HOLCOMBE). Franchise award date: January

Cable Systems—Wisconsin

1, 1989. Franchise expiration date: N.A. Began: March 1, 1990.
Channel capacity: N.A. Channels available but not in use: N.A.
Basic Service
Subscribers: N.A.
Programming (received off-air): WEAU (NBC) Eau Claire; WEUX (FOX, MeTV) Chippewa Falls; WHWC-TV (PBS) Menomonie; WKBT-DT (CBS, MNT) La Crosse; WQOW (ABC, CW, This TV) Eau Claire.
Programming (via satellite): A&E; AMC; Animal Planet; CMT; CNN; Discovery Channel; Disney Channel; ESPN; ESPN2; Freeform; Hallmark Channel; HGTV; History; HLN; Lifetime; MSNBC; Nickelodeon; Outdoor Channel; QVC; Spike TV; Syfy; TBS; The Weather Channel; TNT; Turner Classic Movies; TV Land; USA Network; WGN America.
Fee: $40.00 installation.
Digital Basic Service
Subscribers: N.A.
Programming (via satellite): Animal Planet; BBC America; Bloomberg Television; Cloo; Discovery Life Channel; DMX Music; ESPN Classic; ESPN2; ESPNews; Fox Sports 1; Fuse; FXM; FYI; Golf Channel; GSN; HGTV; History; History International; LMN; NBCSN; Nick Jr.; Nicktoons; Outdoor Channel; Syfy; TeenNick; TLC; Trinity Broadcasting Network (TBN); Turner Classic Movies; VH1.
Fee: $15.31 monthly.
Pay Service 1
Pay Units: N.A.
Programming (via satellite): Cinemax; HBO.
Fee: $10.00 installation; $7.95 monthly (Cinemax), $10.95 monthly (HBO).
Digital Pay Service 1
Pay Units: N.A.
Programming (via satellite): Cinemax (multiplexed); HBO (multiplexed); Showtime (multiplexed); Starz (multiplexed); Starz Encore (multiplexed); The Movie Channel (multiplexed).
Video-On-Demand: No
Internet Service
Operational: Yes.
Fee: $30.00 installation; $24.95-$39.95 monthly.
Telephone Service
None
Miles of Plant: 22.0 (coaxial); None (fiber optic). Homes passed: 500.
General Manager: Randy Scott. Office Manager: Dave Scott.
Ownership: S & K TV Systems Inc. (MSO).

HOLLANDALE—Packerland Broadband, 105 Kent St., PO Box 885, Iron Mountain, MI 49801. Phones: 906-774-1291; 800-236-8434; 906-774-6621. Fax: 906-776-2811. E-mail: service@plbb.net; support@packerlandbroadband.com. Web Site: http://www.packerlandbroadband.com. ICA: WI0278.
TV Market Ranking: 93 (HOLLANDALE). Franchise award date: N.A. Franchise expiration date: N.A. Began: June 1, 1989.
Channel capacity: N.A. Channels available but not in use: N.A.
Basic Service
Subscribers: 8.
Programming (received off-air): WBUW (CW) Janesville; WHA-TV (PBS) Madison; WISC-TV (CBS, MNT) Madison; WKOW (ABC, MeTV, This TV) Madison; WMSN-TV (FOX, The Country Network) Madison; WMTV (CW, NBC) Madison.

Programming (via satellite): A&E; QVC; TBS; WGN America.
Fee: $18.50 monthly.
Expanded Basic Service 1
Subscribers: N.A.
Programming (via satellite): CNN; Discovery Channel; Disney Channel; ESPN; ESPN2; FOX Sports North; Freeform; HLN; Nickelodeon; Spike TV; The Weather Channel; TLC; TNT; Turner Classic Movies; TV Land; USA Network.
Fee: $21.10 monthly.
Pay Service 1
Pay Units: N.A.
Programming (via satellite): HBO.
Fee: $13.95 monthly.
Video-On-Demand: No
Internet Service
Operational: No.
Telephone Service
None
Miles of Plant: 2.0 (coaxial); None (fiber optic). Homes passed: 115.
General Manager: Dan Plante. Technical Supervisor: Chad Kay.
Ownership: Packerland Broadband (MSO).

HOWARDS GROVE—Time Warner Cable. Now served by MILWAUKEE, WI [WI0001]. ICA: WI0097.

HUDSON (town)—Baldwin Telecom Inc. Now served by BALDWIN (town), WI [WI0079]. ICA: WI0126.

HUSTISFORD—Charter Communications. Now served by FOND DU LAC, WI [WI0018]. ICA: WI0005.

IOLA—Mediacom, 4010 Alexandra Dr, Waterloo, IA 50702. Phones: 845-695-2762; 319-235-2197. Fax: 319-232-7841. Web Site: http://www.mediacomcable.com. Also serves Scandinavia. ICA: WI0118.
TV Market Ranking: Outside TV Markets (IOLA, Scandinavia). Franchise award date: N.A. Franchise expiration date: N.A. Began: December 23, 1998.
Channel capacity: 42 (not 2-way capable). Channels available but not in use: N.A.
Basic Service
Subscribers: 37.
Programming (received off-air): WACY-TV (Escape, Grit, Laff, MNT) Appleton; WAOW (ABC, CW, This TV) Wausau; WBAY-TV (ABC) Green Bay; WFRV-TV (Bounce TV, CBS) Green Bay; WGBA-TV (MeTV, NBC) Green Bay; WLUK-TV (Antenna TV, FOX) Green Bay; WPNE-TV (PBS) Green Bay; WSAW-TV (CBS, MNT) Wausau.
Programming (via satellite): TBS; Trinity Broadcasting Network (TBN); WGN America.
Fee: $45.00 installation; $40.00 monthly.
Expanded Basic Service 1
Subscribers: N.A.
Programming (via satellite): A&E; AMC; Animal Planet; CMT; CNN; Discovery Channel; Disney Channel; ESPN; ESPN2; Freeform; HGTV; History; Lifetime; MTV; Nickelodeon; Spike TV; Syfy; The Weather Channel; TNT; Travel Channel; TV Land; USA Network.
Fee: $22.00 monthly.
Pay Service 1
Pay Units: N.A.
Programming (via satellite): Cinemax; HBO; Showtime.
Fee: $25.00 installation; $7.95 monthly (Cinemax), $11.99 monthly (HBO or Showtime).
Video-On-Demand: No

Internet Service
Operational: No.
Telephone Service
None
Miles of Plant: 18.0 (coaxial); None (fiber optic). Homes passed: 953.
Regional Vice President: Doug Frank. Vice President, Financial Reporting: Kenneth J. Kohrs. General Manager: Doug Nix. Technical Operations Director: Greg Nank. Marketing Director: Steve Schuh. Marketing Coordinator: Joni Lindauer.
Ownership: Mediacom LLC (MSO).

IRONTON—Formerly served by Dairyland Cable Systems Inc. No longer in operation. ICA: WI0256.

JANESVILLE—Charter Communications. Now served by MADISON, WI [WI0002]. ICA: WI0007.

JANESVILLE—Formerly served by Wireless Cable Systems Inc. No longer in operation. ICA: WI0307.

JUNCTION CITY—Packerland Broadband, 105 Kent St., PO Box 885, Iron Mountain, MI 49801. Phones: 906-774-1291; 906-774-6621; 800-236-8434. Fax: 906-776-2811. E-mail: service@plbb.net; support@packerlandbroadband.com. Web Site: http://www.packerlandbroadband.com. ICA: WI0257.
TV Market Ranking: Below 100 (JUNCTION CITY).
Channel capacity: N.A. Channels available but not in use: N.A.
Basic Service
Subscribers: 29.
Programming (received off-air): WAOW (ABC, CW, This TV) Wausau; WEAU (NBC) Eau Claire; WFXS-DT Wittenberg; WHRM-TV (PBS) Wausau; WJFW-TV (Antenna TV, NBC) Rhinelander; WSAW-TV (CBS, MNT) Wausau.
Programming (via satellite): A&E; AMC; Animal Planet; CMT; CNBC; CNN; Discovery Channel; Disney Channel; ESPN; ESPN2; FOX Sports Networks; Freeform; History; Lifetime; MTV; Nickelodeon; Spike TV; Syfy; TBS; The Weather Channel; TLC; TNT; TV Land; USA Network; VH1; WGN America.
Fee: $24.95 installation; $24.95 monthly; $1.50 converter.
Pay Service 1
Pay Units: 13.
Programming (via satellite): HBO.
Fee: $10.95 monthly.
Video-On-Demand: No
Internet Service
Operational: No.
Telephone Service
None
Miles of Plant: 5.0 (coaxial); None (fiber optic). Homes passed: 210.
General Manager: Dan Plante. Technical Supervisor: Chad Kay.
Ownership: Packerland Broadband (MSO).

KELLNERSVILLE—New Century Communications, 3588 Kennebec Dr, Eagan, MN 55122-1001. Phone: 651-688-2623. Fax: 651-688-2624. E-mail: i. ICA: WI0258.
TV Market Ranking: 62 (KELLNERSVILLE). Franchise award date: N.A. Franchise expiration date: N.A. Began: August 1, 1990.
Channel capacity: N.A. Channels available but not in use: N.A.
Basic Service
Subscribers: N.A.
Programming (received off-air): WACY-TV (Escape, Grit, Laff, MNT) Appleton; WBAY-TV (ABC) Green Bay; WEAU (NBC) Eau Claire; WFRV-TV (Bounce TV, CBS) Green Bay; WLUK-TV (Antenna TV, FOX) Green Bay; WPNE-TV (PBS) Green Bay.
Programming (via satellite): A&E; AMC; CNN; Discovery Channel; Disney Channel; ESPN; Freeform; Lifetime; Nickelodeon; Showtime; Spike TV; TBS; TLC; TNT; Trinity Broadcasting Network (TBN); USA Network; WGN America.
Fee: $30.00 installation.
Video-On-Demand: No
Internet Service
Operational: No.
Telephone Service
None
Miles of Plant: 2.0 (coaxial); None (fiber optic). Homes passed: 121.
Executive Vice President: Marty Walch. General Manager & Chief Technician: Todd Anderson.
Ownership: New Century Communications (MSO).

KENDALL—Community Antenna System Inc, 1010 Lake St, Hillsboro, WI 54634-9019. Phone: 608-489-2321. Fax: 608-489-2321. E-mail: comant@comantenna.com. Web Site: http://comantenna.com. ICA: WI0201.
TV Market Ranking: Outside TV Markets (KENDALL). Franchise award date: January 1, 1961. Franchise expiration date: N.A. Began: January 1, 1963.
Channel capacity: N.A. Channels available but not in use: N.A.
Basic Service
Subscribers: 49.
Programming (received off-air): WEAU (NBC) Eau Claire; WHA-TV (PBS) Madison; WISC-TV (CBS, MNT) Madison; WKBT-DT (CBS, MNT) La Crosse; WKOW (ABC, MeTV, This TV) Madison; WMSN-TV (FOX, The Country Network) Madison; WMTV (CW, NBC) Madison.
Programming (via satellite): ESPN; Freeform; Spike TV; TBS; TNT; WGN America.
Fee: $40.00 installation; $59.36 monthly.
Pay Service 1
Pay Units: 34.
Programming (via satellite): Cinemax.
Fee: $6.95 monthly.
Internet Service
Operational: Yes.
Telephone Service
None
Miles of Plant: 4.0 (coaxial); None (fiber optic). Homes passed: 225.

2017 Edition

D-857

Wisconsin—Cable Systems

President & General Manager: Randall Kubarski. Chief Technician: Gregory Kubarski.
Ownership: Community Antenna System Inc. (MSO).

KENOSHA—Time Warner Cable. Now served by MILWAUKEE, WI [WI0001]. ICA: WI0009.

KINGSTON—Formerly served by New Century Communications. No longer in operation. ICA: WI0213.

KNAPP (village)—Formerly served by Baldwin Telecom Inc. No longer in operation. ICA: WI0259.

KNOWLES—Packerland Broadband. Now served by LOMIRA, WI [WI0345]. ICA: WI0304.

KRAKOW—Packerland Broadband, 105 Kent St., PO Box 885, Iron Mountain, MI 49801. Phone: 800-236-8434. Fax: 906-776-2811. E-mail: service@plbb.net; support@packerlandbroadband.com. Web Site: http://www.packerlandbroadband.com. ICA: WI0327.
Channel capacity: N.A. Channels available but not in use: N.A.
Basic Service
Subscribers: 21.
Fee: $24.95 monthly.
Ownership: Packerland Broadband.

LA CROSSE—Charter Communications. Now served by EAU CLAIRE, WI [WI0011]. ICA: WI0017.

LA VALLE (village)—Packerland Broadband, 105 Kent St., PO Box 885, Iron Mountain, MI 49801. Phones: 906-774-1291; 800-236-8434; 906-774-6621. Fax: 906-776-2811. E-mail: service@plbb.net; support@packerlandbroadband.com. Web Site: http://www.packerlandbroadband.com. ICA: WI0260.
TV Market Ranking: Outside TV Markets (LA VALLE (VILLAGE)). Franchise award date: January 1, 1971. Franchise expiration date: N.A. Began: September 30, 1971.
Channel capacity: N.A. Channels available but not in use: N.A.
Basic Service
Subscribers: 34.
Programming (received off-air): WBUW (CW) Janesville; WHA-TV (PBS) Madison; WISC-TV (CBS, MNT) Madison; WKBT-DT (CBS, MNT) La Crosse; WKOW (ABC, MeTV, This TV) Madison; WMSN-TV (FOX, The Country Network) Madison; WMTV (CW, NBC) Madison.
Programming (via satellite): QVC; WGN America.
Fee: $49.95 installation; $27.95 monthly.
Expanded Basic Service 1
Subscribers: N.A.
Programming (received off-air): WBUW (CW) Janesville; WWRS-TV (TBN) Mayville.
Programming (via satellite): A&E; Animal Planet; CMT; CNN; Discovery Channel; Disney Channel; E! HD; ESPN; ESPN2; FOX Sports North; Freeform; History; HLN; MTV; Nickelodeon; Spike TV; TBS; The Weather Channel; TLC; TNT; Travel Channel; Turner Classic Movies; TV Land; USA Network.
Fee: $20.45 monthly.
Pay Service 1
Pay Units: N.A.
Programming (via satellite): HBO.
Fee: $13.95 monthly.
Video-On-Demand: No
Internet Service
Operational: No.
Telephone Service
None
Miles of Plant: 35.0 (coaxial); None (fiber optic). Homes passed: 633.
General Manager: Dan Plante. Technical Supervisor: Chad Kay.
Ownership: Packerland Broadband (MSO).

LAC DU FLAMBEAU—Formerly served by Gauthier Cablevision. No longer in operation. ICA: WI0182.

LADYSMITH—Charter Communications. Now served by EAU CLAIRE, WI [WI0011]. ICA: WI0081.

LAKE LUCERNE—Packerland Broadband, 105 Kent St., PO Box 885, Iron Mountain, MI 49801. Phone: 800-236-8434. Fax: 906-776-2811. E-mail: service@plbb.net; support@packerlandbroadband.com. Web Site: http://www.packerlandbroadband.com. ICA: WI0344.
Channel capacity: N.A. Channels available but not in use: N.A.
Basic Service
Subscribers: 28.
Fee: $23.95 monthly.
Ownership: Packerland Broadband.

LAKE NEBAGAMON—Charter Communications. Now served by DULUTH, MN [MN0006]. ICA: WI0133.

LANCASTER—Charter Communications, PO Box 124, Dodgeville, WI 53533. Phones: 314-543-2236; 636-207-5100 (Corporate office); 608-274-3822. Web Site: http://www.charter.com. Also serves Bloomington, Cassville, Dickeyville, Kieler & Patch Grove. ICA: WI0261.
TV Market Ranking: Below 100 (Bloomington, Cassville, Dickeyville, Kieler, LANCASTER, Patch Grove). Franchise award date: January 1, 1980. Franchise expiration date: N.A. Began: June 1, 1967.
Channel capacity: N.A. Channels available but not in use: N.A.
Digital Basic Service
Subscribers: 817.
Programming (received off-air): KCRG-TV (ABC, MNT) Cedar Rapids; KFXB-TV (Christian TV Network) Dubuque; KGAN (CBS) Cedar Rapids; KRIN (PBS) Waterloo; KWWL (CW, MeTV, NBC) Waterloo; WHA-TV (PBS) Madison; WISC-TV (CBS, MNT) Madison; WKOW (ABC, MeTV, This TV) Madison; WMSN-TV (FOX, The Country Network) Madison; WMTV (CW, NBC) Madison.
Programming (via satellite): A&E; WGN America.
Fee: $49.99 installation; $23.99 monthly.
Digital Expanded Basic Service
Subscribers: N.A.
Programming (via satellite): Animal Planet; Cartoon Network; CNN; C-SPAN; Discovery Channel; Disney Channel; ESPN; ESPN2; ESPNews; EWTN Global Catholic Network; FOX Sports North; Freeform; FX; Great American Country; HGTV; History; HLN; Lifetime; Nickelodeon; Spike TV; Syfy; TBS; The Weather Channel; TLC; TNT; Turner Classic Movies; TV Land; USA Network; VH1.
Fee: $19.99 monthly.
Pay Service 1
Pay Units: N.A.
Programming (via satellite): Cinemax; HBO.
Fee: $19.95 installation; $9.95 monthly (each).
Video-On-Demand: No
Pay-Per-View
Hot Network (delivered digitally); Hot Zone (delivered digitally); iN DEMAND (delivered digitally); Playboy TV (delivered digitally); Spice (delivered digitally); Spice2 (delivered digitally).
Internet Service
Operational: No.
Telephone Service
None
Miles of Plant: 56.0 (coaxial); None (fiber optic).
Vice President & General Manager: Lisa Washa. Technical Operations Director: Bruce Hummel. Marketing Director: Traci Loonstra. Engineering Director: Tim Sanderson. Accounting Director: David Sovanski. Government Relations Director: Tim Vowell.
Ownership: Charter Communications Inc. (MSO).

LAND O'LAKES—Karban TV Systems Inc, 73A South Stevens St, Rhinelander, WI 54501. Phones: 715-550-7613; 800-236-0233. Fax: 715-277-2339. E-mail: sales@ktvs.net. Web Site: http://www.ktvs.net. ICA: WI0262.
TV Market Ranking: Below 100 (LAND O'LAKES). Franchise award date: N.A. Franchise expiration date: N.A. Began: July 1, 1989.
Channel capacity: 77 (2-way capable). Channels available but not in use: N.A.
Basic Service
Subscribers: N.A.
Programming (received off-air): WFXS-DT Wittenberg; WJFW-TV (Antenna TV, NBC) Rhinelander; WLEF-TV (PBS) Park Falls; WSAW-TV (CBS, MNT) Wausau; WYOW (ABC, CW, This TV) Eagle River.
Programming (via satellite): A&E; AMC; Animal Planet; CMT; CNBC; CNN; Comedy Central; C-SPAN; CW PLUS; Discovery Channel; Disney Channel; ESPN; ESPN2; EWTN Global Catholic Network; Food Network; Fox News Channel; Fox Sports 1; Freeform; FX; HGTV; History; HLN; Lifetime; MSNBC; NFL Network; Nickelodeon; Outdoor Channel; QVC; Spike TV; Syfy; TBS; The Weather Channel; TLC; TNT; Travel Channel; Trinity Broadcasting Network (TBN); Turner Classic Movies; TV Land; USA Network; VH1; WGN America.
Fee: $75.00 installation; $48.00 monthly.
Pay Service 1
Pay Units: N.A.
Programming (via satellite): Cinemax; HBO.
Fee: $10.00 monthly (each).
Video-On-Demand: No
Internet Service
Operational: Yes.
Telephone Service
None
Miles of Plant: 8.0 (coaxial); None (fiber optic). Homes passed: 180.
General Manager & Chief Technician: John Karban.
Ownership: Karban TV Systems Inc. (MSO).

LAONA—Packerland Broadband, 105 Kent St., PO Box 885, Iron Mountain, MI 49801. Phone: 800-236-8434. Fax: 906-776-2811. E-mail: service@plbb.net; support@packerlandbroadband.com. Web Site: http://www.packerlandbroadband.com. ICA: WI0143.
Channel capacity: N.A. Channels available but not in use: N.A.
Basic Service
Subscribers: 197.
Fee: $23.95 monthly.
Miles of Plant: 37.0 (coaxial); 15.0 (fiber optic). Homes passed: 783.
Ownership: Packerland Broadband (MSO).

LENA—Packerland Broadband, 105 Kent St., PO Box 885, Iron Mountain, MI 49801. Phone: 800-236-8434. Fax: 906-776-2811. E-mail: service@plbb.net; support@packerlandbroadband.com. Web Site: http://www.packerlandbroadband.com. ICA: WI0204.
Channel capacity: N.A. Channels available but not in use: N.A.
Basic Service
Subscribers: 76.
Fee: $24.95 monthly.
Internet Service
Operational: Yes.
Subscribers: 34.
Telephone Service
Digital: Operational
Subscribers: 2.
Miles of Plant: 7.0 (coaxial); 16.0 (fiber optic). Homes passed: 323.
Ownership: Packerland Broadband.

LOGANVILLE (village)—Dairyland Cable Systems Inc, 2494 US Hwy 14 East, Richland Center, WI 53581-2983. Phone: 608-647-6383. Fax: 608-647-2093. ICA: WI0263.
TV Market Ranking: Outside TV Markets (LOGANVILLE (VILLAGE)). Franchise award date: N.A. Franchise expiration date: N.A. Began: September 1, 1989.
Channel capacity: 13 (not 2-way capable). Channels available but not in use: N.A.
Basic Service
Subscribers: N.A.
Programming (received off-air): WISC-TV (CBS, MNT) Madison; WKOW (ABC, MeTV, This TV) Madison; WMSN-TV (FOX, The Country Network) Madison; WMTV (CW, NBC) Madison; WMVS (PBS) Milwaukee.
Programming (via satellite): CNN; ESPN; Nickelodeon; Spike TV; TBS; TNT; USA Network; WGN America.
Fee: $25.00 installation.
Pay Service 1
Pay Units: N.A.
Programming (via satellite): HBO.
Fee: $10.50 monthly.
Video-On-Demand: No
Internet Service
Operational: No.
Telephone Service
None
General Manager: Jim Atkinson. Chief Technician: Randy Mardall. Marketing Representative: Brian Sullivan.
Ownership: Dairyland Cable Systems Inc. (MSO).

LOMIRA—Packerland Broadband, 105 Kent St., PO Box 885, Iron Mountain, MI 49801. Phone: 800-236-8434. Fax: 906-776-2811. E-mail: service@plbb.net; support@packerlandbroadband.com. Web Site: http://www.packerlandbroadband.com. Also serves Brownsville, Dodge County (portions), Farmersville, Kekoskee, Knowles, LeRoy & South Byron. ICA: WI0345.
TV Market Ranking: Below 100 (Brownsville, Farmersville, Kekoskee, LeRoy, South Byron).
Channel capacity: N.A. Channels available but not in use: N.A.

Cable Systems—Wisconsin

Basic Service
Subscribers: 150.
Fee: $27.95 monthly.
Ownership: Packerland Broadband.

LUCK (village)—Lakeland Communications, 825 Innovation Ave, PO Box 40, Milltown, WI 54858. Phones: 715-825-2171; 715-472-2101. Fax: 715-825-4299; 715-472-8880. E-mail: info@lakeland.ws. Web Site: http://www.lakeland.ws. Also serves Apple River (town), Balsam Lake (village), Balsam Lake Twp., Bone Lake (town), Centuria, Cushing, Eureka (town), Frederic, Georgetown (town), Laketown, Luck Twp., Milltown (village), Milltown Twp., St. Croix Falls (town), St. Croix Falls (village), Sterling (town), Trade Lake (town) & West Sweden (town). ICA: WI0104.
TV Market Ranking: Outside TV Markets (Balsam Lake Twp., Centuria, Frederic, LUCK (VILLAGE), Luck Twp.). Franchise award date: July 15, 1985. Franchise expiration date: N.A. Began: December 1, 1985.
Channel capacity: N.A. Channels available but not in use: N.A.

Digital Basic Service
Subscribers: 908.
Programming (received off-air): KARE (NBC, WeatherNation) Minneapolis; KMSP-TV (Bounce TV, Buzzr, FOX) Minneapolis; KPXM-TV (ION) St. Cloud; KSTC-TV (Antenna TV, This TV) Minneapolis; KSTP-TV (ABC, MeTV) St. Paul; KTCA-TV (PBS) St. Paul; WCCO-TV (CBS, Decades) Minneapolis; WEAU (NBC) Eau Claire; WEUX (FOX, MeTV) Chippewa Falls; WFTC (MNT, Movies!) Minneapolis; WHWC-TV (PBS) Menomonie; WQOW (ABC, CW, This TV) Eau Claire; WUCW (CW, The Country Network) Minneapolis.
Programming (via satellite): American Heroes Channel; BBC America; BTN; Cloo; CMT; Discovery Family; Disney XD; DMX Music; ESPNews; EWTN Global Catholic Network; FSN Digital Atlantic; FSN Digital Central; FSN Digital Pacific; FXM; FYI; History International; Investigation Discovery; MTV Classic; MTV Hits; MTV2; Nick Jr.; Nicktoons; OWN: Oprah Winfrey Network; QVC; Science Channel; TeenNick; The Weather Channel; Trinity Broadcasting Network (TBN); VH1 Soul; WE tv; WFTC (MNT, Movies!) Minneapolis; WGN America.
Fee: $42.49 monthly.

Digital Expanded Basic Service
Subscribers: N.A.
Programming (via satellite): A&E HD; AMC; Animal Planet HD; BTN; CMT; CNBC; CNN; Comedy Central; C-SPAN; C-SPAN 2; Discovery Channel HD; Disney Channel; DIY Network; E! HD; ESPN Classic; ESPN HD; ESPN2; FamilyNet; Food Network; Fox News Channel; Fox Sports 1; FOX Sports North; FSN HD; FX; Golf Channel HD; Hallmark Channel; HGTV; History HD; HLN; HSN; Lifetime; LMN; MTV; National Geographic Channel HD; NBCSN; Nickelodeon; Outdoor Channel HD; Oxygen; Pop; Spike TV; Syfy HD; TBS; The Weather Channel; TLC HD; TNT; Travel Channel; truTV; Turner Classic Movies; TV Land; USA Network; Velocity; VH1.
Fee: $46.25 monthly.

Digital Expanded Basic Service 2
Subscribers: N.A.
Planned programming (via satellite): AXS TV.
Programming (via satellite): Universal HD.
Fee: $10.00 monthly.

Digital Pay Service 1
Pay Units: N.A.
Programming (via satellite): Cinemax; Flix; HBO (multiplexed); Showtime (multiplexed); Starz (multiplexed); Starz Encore (multiplexed); The Movie Channel (multiplexed).
Fee: $11.99 monthly (Cinemax or Starz Encore), $14.99 monthly (Showtime/TMC/Flix), $20.99 monthly (HBO).

Video-On-Demand: No

Pay-Per-View
Club Jenna (delivered digitally); Fresh (delivered digitally).

Internet Service
Operational: Yes.
Fee: $59.99-$109.99 monthly.

Telephone Service
Digital: Operational
Miles of Plant: 57.0 (coaxial); 18.0 (fiber optic). Homes passed: 2,324.
President: John Klatt. System Manager: Shawn McGinnity. Plant Manager: Todd Roehm. Office Manager: Sheri Thorsbakken.
Ownership: Lakeland Communications.

MADISON—Charter Communications, 5618 Odana Rd, Ste 150, Madison, WI 53719. Phones: 314-543-2236; 636-207-5100 (Corporate office); 608-274-3822. Web Site: http://www.charter.com. Also serves Genoa, Harlem Twp., Harvard, Kingston, Manchester Twp., Marengo, Richmond (village), Riley, Rockton (village), Rockton Twp., Roscoe Twp., South Beloit & Union, IL; Afton, Albion, Arena (village), Arlington, Aztalan Twp., Baraboo, Baraboo (town), Barneveld, Belleville (village), Beloit, Black Earth, Blooming Grove, Blue Mounds, Bradford Twp., Bristol (town), Brodhead, Brooklyn (village), Buena Vista (town), Burke, Cambria, Cambridge, Center (town), Christiana, Clarno Twp., Clinton, Cobb, Columbus, Concord, Cottage Grove, Cross Plains (village), Dane (village), Darien, De Forest, Decatur Twp., Deerfield Twp., Dekorra (town), Delavan, Delton, Dodgeville, Dunkirk, Dunn, Edgerton, Elba (town), Elkhorn, Emmet, Evansville, Excelsior, Exeter (town), Fall River, Fitchburg, Fontana (village), Fort Atkinson, Fort Winnebago, Fulton Twp., Genoa City, Greenfield Twp., Harmony, Helenville, Highland, Indianford, Janesville, Jefferson, Johnson Creek, Koshkonong Twp., Lake Delton, Lake Mills, Lewiston, Linden, Linn Twp., Livingston, Lodi, Lone Rock, Lyndon Station, Machesney Park, Maple Bluff (village), Marshall, Mazomanie, McFarland (village), Medina, Middleton Twp., Milford Twp., Milton Twp., Mineral Point, Monona, Monroe, Montfort, Montrose, Mount Horeb, New Glarus, North Freedom, Oakland Twp., Oconomowoc, Oregon (village), Pacific, Palmyra, Pardeeville, Plain, Pleasant Springs Twp., Plymouth (town), Portage, Portland Twp., Poynette, Prairie du Sac (town), Reedsburg, Richland Center, Ridgeway, Rock, Rock Springs, Roxbury, Rutland, Sauk City, Sharon (village), Shorewood Hills (village), Spring Green, Springfield (town), Stoughton, Sullivan, Sumner Twp., Sun Prairie Twp., Turtle Twp., Twin Lakes (village), Union Twp. (Rock County), Verona (town), Vienna Twp., Walworth (village), Waterloo, Watertown, Watertown Twp., Waunakee, West Baraboo (village), West Point Twp., Westport Twp., Wheatland, Whitewater, Williams Bay, Windsor Twp., Wisconsin Dells & Wyocena, WI. ICA: WI0002.
TV Market Ranking: 23 (Johnson Creek, Oconomowoc, Palmyra, Portland Twp., Sullivan, Wheatland); 93 (Afton, Albion, Arena (village), Arlington, Aztalan Twp., Baraboo, Baraboo (town), Barneveld, Belleville (village), Black Earth, Blooming Grove, Blue Mounds, Bradford Twp., Bristol (town), Bristol (town), Brodhead, Brooklyn (village), Burke, Cambria, Cambridge, Center (town), Christiana, Clinton, Columbus, Concord, Cottage Grove, Cross Plains (village), Dane (village), De Forest, Decatur Twp., Deerfield Twp., Dekorra (town), Delton, Dunkirk, Dunn, Edgerton, Elba (town), Emmet, Evansville, Excelsior, Exeter (town), Fall River, Fitchburg, Fort Atkinson, Helenville, Indianford, Jefferson, Koshkonong Twp., Lake Mills, Lewiston, Lodi, MADISON, Maple Bluff (village), Marshall (viillage), Mazomanie, McFarland (village), Medina, Middleton Twp., Milford Twp., Milton Twp., Monona, Montrose, Mount Horeb, New Glarus, Oakland Twp., Oregon (village), Pacific, Pardeeville, Plain, Pleasant Springs Twp., Plymouth (town), Portage, Poynette, Prairie du Sac (town), Ridgeway, Roxbury, Rutland, Sauk City, Shorewood Hills (village), Spring Green, Springfield Twp., Stoughton, Sumner Twp., Sun Prairie Twp., Union Twp. (Rock County), Verona (town), Vienna Twp., Waterloo, Watertown Twp., Waunakee, West Baraboo (village), West Point Twp., Westport Twp., Windsor Twp., Wyocena); 93,97 (Harmony, Janesville, Monroe, Rock, Turtle Twp.); 97 (Beloit, Darien, Delavan, Elkhorn, Fontana (village), Fulton Twp., Genoa, Harlem Twp., Harvard, Kingston, Linn Twp., Machesney Park, Manchester Twp., Marengo, Rockton (village), Rockton Twp., Roscoe Twp., Sharon (village), South Beloit, Union, Walworth (village), Williams Bay); Below 100 (Genoa City, Livingston, Montfort, Richmond (village), Riley, Twin Lakes (village), Whitewater); Outside TV Markets (Buena Vista (town), Cobb, Dodgeville, Greenfield Twp., Highland, Lake Delton, Linden, Lone Rock, Mineral Point, North Freedom, Reedsburg, Richland Center, Rock Springs, Wisconsin Dells). Franchise award date: March 18, 1975. Franchise expiration date: N.A. Began: August 1, 1973.
Channel capacity: 69 (operating 2-way). Channels available but not in use: N.A.

Digital Basic Service
Subscribers: 162,967.
Programming (via satellite): BBC America; Discovery Digital Networks; DIY Network; ESPNews; EVINE Live; FOX Sports North; FYI; History International; HITS (Headend In The Sky); IFC; LMN; MC; Nick 2; Nick Jr.; Sundance TV; TeenNick.
Fee: $49.99 installation; $14.99 monthly.

Digital Expanded Basic Service
Subscribers: N.A.
Programming (via satellite): A&E; AMC; Animal Planet; BET; Bravo; Cartoon Network; CMT; CNBC; CNN; Comedy Central; Discovery Channel; Disney Channel; Disney XD; E! HD; ESPN; ESPN Classic; ESPN2; EWTN Global Catholic Network; Food Network; Fox News Channel; Fox Sports 1; Freeform; FX; Golf Channel; GSN; Hallmark Channel; HGTV; History; INSP; Lifetime; MSNBC; MTV; National Geographic Channel; NBCSN; Nickelodeon; Oxygen; Spike TV; Syfy; TBS; The Weather Channel; TLC; TNT; Travel Channel; truTV; Turner Classic Movies; TV Land; USA Network; VH1; WE tv.
Fee: $49.99 monthly.

Digital Pay Service 1
Pay Units: N.A.
Programming (via satellite): Cinemax (multiplexed); Flix; HBO (multiplexed); Showtime (multiplexed); Starz (multiplexed); Starz Encore (multiplexed); The Movie Channel (multiplexed).
Fee: $10.00 monthly (Cinemax, HBO, Showtime, Flix/TMC or Starz/Encore).

Video-On-Demand: Yes

Pay-Per-View
iN DEMAND (delivered digitally); Playboy TV (delivered digitally); Fresh (delivered digitally); Shorteez (delivered digitally).

Internet Service
Operational: Yes. Began: January 1, 2000.
Subscribers: 191,282.
Broadband Service: Charter Internet.
Fee: $49.95 installation; $39.99 monthly.

Telephone Service
Digital: Operational
Subscribers: 95,946.
Miles of Plant: 8,976.0 (coaxial); 2,624.0 (fiber optic). Homes passed: 475,498.
Vice President & General Manager: Lisa Washa. Technical Operations Director: Bruce Hummel. Marketing Director: Traci Loonstra. Accounting Director: David Sovanski. Government Relations Director: Tim Vowell.
Ownership: Charter Communications Inc. (MSO).

MANAWA—Manawa Telecom Video, 131 2nd St, PO Box 130, Manawa, WI 54949-0130. Phones: 800-872-5452; 920-596-2535. Fax: 920-596-3775. E-mail: manawa@wolfnet.net. Web Site: http://www.manawatelephone.com. Also serves Helvetia, Lebanon, Little Wolf, Ogdensburg, Royalton Twp., St. Lawrence & Union. ICA: WI0127.
TV Market Ranking: Below 100 (Helvetia, Lebanon, Little Wolf, MANAWA, Ogdensburg, Royalton Twp., St. Lawrence, Union). Franchise award date: December 6, 1982. Franchise expiration date: N.A. Began: November 1, 1984.
Channel capacity: N.A. Channels available but not in use: N.A.

Basic Service
Subscribers: 224.
Programming (received off-air): WACY-TV (Escape, Grit, Laff, MNT) Appleton; WAOW (ABC, CW, This TV) Wausau; WBAY-TV (ABC) Green Bay; WCWF (CW) Suring; WFRV-TV (Bounce TV, CBS) Green Bay; WGBA-TV (MeTV, NBC) Green Bay; WHRM-TV (PBS) Wausau; WLUK-TV (Antenna TV, FOX) Green Bay; WPNE-TV (PBS) Green Bay; WSAW-TV (CBS, MNT) Wausau; all-band FM.
Programming (via satellite): A&E; AMC; Animal Planet; Cartoon Network; CMT; CNBC; CNN; Comedy Central; C-SPAN; Discovery Channel; Disney Channel; E! HD; ESPN; ESPN Classic; ESPN2; Food Network; Fox News Channel; Fox Sports 1; FOX Sports North; Freeform; FX; GSN; Hallmark Channel; HGTV; History; HLN; Lifetime; MTV;

2017 Edition   D-859

Wisconsin—Cable Systems

National Geographic Channel; Nickelodeon; Outdoor Channel; Oxygen; QVC; Spike TV; Syfy; TBS; The Weather Channel; TLC; TNT; Travel Channel; Trinity Broadcasting Network (TBN); truTV; Turner Classic Movies; TV Land; USA Network; VH1; WGN America.
Fee: $75.00 installation; $61.45 monthly; $2.00 converter.

Digital Basic Service
Subscribers: N.A.
Programming (via satellite): A&E; AMC; Animal Planet; BTN; Cartoon Network; CMT; CNBC; CNN; Comedy Central; C-SPAN; CW PLUS; Discovery Channel; Discovery Kids Channel; Disney Channel; DMX Music; E! HD; ESPN; ESPN Classic; ESPN2; ESPNews; ESPNU; Food Network; Fox News Channel; Fox Sports 1; FOX Sports North; Freeform; FX; GSN; Hallmark Channel; HGTV; History; HLN; Lifetime; LMN; MTV; National Geographic Channel; NFL Network; Nickelodeon; Outdoor Channel; OWN; Oprah Winfrey Network; Oxygen; QVC; Science Channel; Spike TV; Syfy; TBS; The Weather Channel; TLC; TNT; Travel Channel; Trinity Broadcasting Network (TBN); truTV; Turner Classic Movies; TV Land; USA Network; VH1; WGN America.
Fee: $42.95 monthly.

Digital Expanded Basic Service
Subscribers: N.A.
Programming (via satellite): BBC America; Bloomberg Television; Boomerang; Bravo; CNN International; C-SPAN 2; Destination America; Discovery Life Channel; Disney XD; DIY Network; EWTN Global Catholic Network; FXM; FYI; Golf Channel; History International; Investigation Discovery; MSNBC; NBCSN; Ovation; RFD-TV; UP; WE tv.
Fee: $10.00 monthly.

Digital Expanded Basic Service 2
Subscribers: N.A.
Programming (via satellite): A&E HD; Discovery Channel HD; ESPN HD; ESPN2 HD; History HD; NFL Network HD; TNT HD.
Fee: $14.95 monthly.

Pay Service 1
Pay Units: 40.
Programming (via satellite): HBO.
Fee: $10.95 monthly.

Pay Service 2
Pay Units: 21.
Programming (via satellite): Showtime.
Fee: $10.95 monthly.

Digital Pay Service 1
Pay Units: N.A.
Programming (via satellite): Cinemax (multiplexed); Flix; HBO (multiplexed); Showtime (multiplexed); Starz (multiplexed); Starz Encore (multiplexed); Sundance TV; The Movie Channel (multiplexed).
Fee: $9.95 monthly (Cinemax), $11.95 monthly (HBO, Showtime/TMC/Sundance/Flix or Starz/Encore).

Video-On-Demand: No

Pay-Per-View
iN DEMAND (delivered digitally); Playboy TV (delivered digitally); Fresh (delivered digitally); Shorteez (delivered digitally).

Internet Service
Operational: No, DSL.

Telephone Service
Analog: Operational
Miles of Plant: 26.0 (coaxial); None (fiber optic). Homes passed: 775.
President: Tom Squires. Secretary-Treasurer: Brian J. Squires.
Ownership: Manawa Telecom Inc.

MANITOWOC—Comcast Cable. Now served by MINNEAPOLIS, MN [MN0001]. ICA: WI0021.

MARINETTE—Time Warner Cable, 1001 West Kennedy Ave, PO Box 145, Kimberly, WI 54136-0145. Phones: 920-749-1400; 414-277-4032 (Milwaukee). Fax: 920-831-9372. Web Site: http://www.timewarnercable.com. Also serves Ingallston Twp. & Menominee, MI; Menominee (town), Peshtigo (town) & Porterfield, WI. ICA: WI0025.
TV Market Ranking: Below 100 (Peshtigo (town), Porterfield); Outside TV Markets (Ingallston Twp., MARINETTE, Menominee, Menominee (town)). Franchise award date: August 9, 1966. Franchise expiration date: N.A. Began: March 1, 1970.
Channel capacity: N.A. Channels available but not in use: N.A.

Basic Service
Subscribers: 7,212.
Programming (received off-air): WACY-TV (Escape, Grit, Laff, MNT) Appleton; WBAY-TV (ABC) Green Bay; WCWF (CW) Suring; WFRV-TV (Bounce TV, CBS) Green Bay; WGBA-TV (MeTV, NBC) Green Bay; WGN-TV (IND) Chicago; WLUC-TV (FOX, NBC) Marquette; WLUK-TV (Antenna TV, FOX) Green Bay; WNMU (PBS) Marquette; WPNE-TV (PBS) Green Bay; allband FM.
Programming (via satellite): C-SPAN; TLC; WGN America.
Fee: $99.95 installation; $24.50 monthly.

Expanded Basic Service 1
Subscribers: N.A.
Programming (via satellite): A&E; AMC; Animal Planet; Bravo; Cartoon Network; CMT; CNBC; CNN; Comedy Central; C-SPAN 2; Discovery Channel; Disney Channel; E! HD; ESPN; ESPN Classic; ESPN2; EVINE Live; EWTN Global Catholic Network; Food Network; Fox News Channel; FOX Sports Networks; Freeform; FX; Golf Channel; Hallmark Channel; HGTV; History; HLN; Lifetime; LMN; MSNBC; MTV; National Geographic Channel; NBCSN; Nickelodeon; OWN; Oprah Winfrey Network; Oxygen; Pop; QVC; Spike TV; Syfy; TBS; TLC; TNT; Travel Channel; truTV; Turner Classic Movies; TV Land; Univision Studios; USA Network; VH1; WE tv.
Fee: $30.55 monthly.

Digital Basic Service
Subscribers: N.A.
Programming (via satellite): BBC America; Bloomberg Television; Cooking Channel; C-SPAN 3; Discovery Life Channel; Disney XD; DIY Network; ESPN Classic; ESPNews; Fox Sports 1; FSN Digital Atlantic; FSN Digital Central; FSN Digital Pacific; Fuse; FYI; Great American Country; GSN; History International; IFC; MTV Classic; MTV2; NBA TV; Nick 2; Nick Jr.; Outdoor Channel; Ovation; TeenNick; Tennis Channel; The Weather Channel; Weatherscan.
Fee: $8.00 ala carte.

Digital Pay Service 1
Pay Units: N.A.
Programming (via satellite): Cinemax (multiplexed); FXM; HBO (multiplexed); IFC; Showtime (multiplexed); Starz (multiplexed); Starz Encore (multiplexed); The Movie Channel (multiplexed).
Fee: $10.00 installation; $12.99 monthly (each).

Video-On-Demand: Yes

Pay-Per-View
iN DEMAND (delivered digitally); ESPN (delivered digitally); Playboy TV (delivered digitally); Club Jenna (delivered digitally); NBA League Pass (delivered digitally); NHL Center Ice (delivered digitally).

Internet Service
Operational: Yes, DSL.
Broadband Service: Road Runner, EarthLink, Internet.
Fee: $36.99 installation; $39.99 monthly.

Telephone Service
Digital: Operational
Fee: $39.95 monthly
Homes passed & miles of plant included in Appleton.
President: Jack Herbert. Vice President, Engineering: Randy Cicatello. Vice President, Government & Public Affairs: Bev Greenburg. Vice President, Marketing: Brenda Kinne. General Manager: Mike Fox. Public Affairs Manager: Bill Harke.
Ownership: Time Warner Cable (MSO).

MARQUETTE—New Century Communications, 3588 Kennebec Dr, Eagan, MN 55122-1001. Phone: 651-688-2623. Fax: 651-688-2624. ICA: WI0198.
TV Market Ranking: Below 100 (MARQUETTE).
Channel capacity: N.A. Channels available but not in use: N.A.

Basic Service
Subscribers: N.A.
Programming (received off-air): WHA-TV (PBS) Madison; WISC-TV (CBS, MNT) Madison; WKOW (ABC, MeTV, This TV) Madison; WMTV (CW, NBC) Madison.
Programming (via satellite): A&E; AMC; CMT; CNN; Discovery Channel; Disney Channel; ESPN; Freeform; Lifetime; Nickelodeon; Showtime; Spike TV; TBS; TLC; TNT; Trinity Broadcasting Network (TBN); TV Land; USA Network; WGN America.
Fee: $30.00 installation.

Video-On-Demand: No

Internet Service
Operational: No.

Telephone Service
None
Miles of Plant: 3.0 (coaxial); None (fiber optic). Homes passed: 232.
Executive Vice President: Marty Walch. General Manager & Chief Technician: Todd Anderson.
Ownership: New Century Communications (MSO).

MARSHFIELD—Charter Communications. Now served by STEVENS POINT, WI [WI0019]. ICA: WI0030.

MAUSTON—Mediacom, 4010 Alexandra Dr, Waterloo, IA 50702. Phones: 845-695-2762; 319-235-2197. Fax: 319-232-7841. Web Site: http://www.mediacomcable.com. Also serves Camp Douglas, Germantown, Hustler, Juneau County (unincorporated areas), Necedah, New Lisbon, Norwalk, Ontario & Wilton. ICA: WI0084.
TV Market Ranking: Below 100 (Norwalk, Ontario); Outside TV Markets (Camp Douglas, Germantown, Hustler, Juneau County (unincorporated areas), MAUSTON, Necedah, New Lisbon, Wilton). Franchise award date: N.A. Franchise expiration date: N.A. Began: April 1, 1977.
Channel capacity: N.A. Channels available but not in use: N.A.

Basic Service
Subscribers: 1,080.
Programming (received off-air): WEAU (NBC) Eau Claire; WHLA-TV (PBS) La Crosse; WISC-TV (CBS, MNT) Madison; WKBT-DT (CBS, MNT) La Crosse; WKOW (ABC, MeTV, This TV) Madison; WMSN-TV (FOX, The Country Network) Madison; WMTV (CW, NBC) Madison; allband FM.
Programming (via satellite): C-SPAN; C-SPAN 2; EWTN Global Catholic Network; Pop; QVC; Trinity Broadcasting Network (TBN); WGN America.
Fee: $35.16 installation; $43.00 monthly; $1.58 converter.

Expanded Basic Service 1
Subscribers: N.A.
Programming (via satellite): A&E; AMC; Animal Planet; Bravo; Cartoon Network; CMT; CNBC; CNN; Comedy Central; Discovery Channel; Disney Channel; E! HD; ESPN; ESPN2; Fox News Channel; Fox Sports 1; FOX Sports Networks; Freeform; FX; FXM; Hallmark Channel; HGTV; History; HLN; INSP; Lifetime; MSNBC; MTV; NBCSN; Nickelodeon; RFD-TV; Spike TV; Syfy; TBS; The Weather Channel; TLC; TNT; Travel Channel; truTV; TV Land; USA Network; VH1.
Fee: $14.91 monthly.

Digital Basic Service
Subscribers: N.A.
Programming (via satellite): AXS TV; BBC America; Bloomberg Television; Cloo; Discovery Digital Networks; ESPN; ESPN2; ESPNews; Fuse; FYI; Golf Channel; GSN; HD Theater; History International; IFC; LMN; MC; MTV; National Geographic Channel; Nick Jr.; Nicktoons; Outdoor Channel; TeenNick; Turner Classic Movies; TVG Network; Universal HD.

Digital Pay Service 1
Pay Units: N.A.
Programming (via satellite): Cinemax (multiplexed); Flix (multiplexed); HBO (multiplexed); HBO HD; Showtime (multiplexed); Showtime HD; Starz (multiplexed); Starz Encore (multiplexed); Starz HD; Sundance TV (multiplexed); The Movie Channel (multiplexed); The Movie Channel HD.

Video-On-Demand: No

Pay-Per-View
ESPN (delivered digitally); Fresh (delivered digitally); Shorteez (delivered digitally); Playboy TV (delivered digitally); Pleasure (delivered digitally); SexSee (delivered digitally).

Internet Service
Operational: Yes.
Broadband Service: Mediacom High Speed Internet.
Fee: $99.00 installation; $40.00 monthly.

Telephone Service
None
Miles of Plant: 55.0 (coaxial); None (fiber optic).
Regional Vice President: Doug Frank. Vice President, Financial Reporting: Kenneth J. Kohrs. General Manager: Doug Nix. Technical Operations Director: Greg Nank. Marketing Director: Steve Schuh. Marketing Coordinator: Joni Lindauer.
Ownership: Mediacom LLC (MSO).

MAZOMANIE—Charter Communications. Now served by MADISON, WI [WI0002]. ICA: WI0116.

MEDFORD—Charter Communications. Now served by STEVENS POINT, WI [WI0019]. ICA: WI0074.

MELLEN—Packerland Broadband, 105 Kent St., PO Box 885, Iron Mountain, MI 49801. Phones: 906-774-1291; 800-236-8434; 906-774-6621. Fax: 906-776-2811. E-mail: service@plbb.net; support@packerlandbroadband.com. Web Site: http://www.packerlandbroadband.com. ICA: WI0165.
TV Market Ranking: Outside TV Markets (MELLEN). Franchise award date: March

Cable Systems—Wisconsin

1, 1978. Franchise expiration date: N.A. Began: March 1, 1979.
Channel capacity: N.A. Channels available but not in use: N.A.
Basic Service
Subscribers: 136.
Programming (received off-air): KBJR-TV (CBS, MNT, NBC) Superior; KDLH (CBS, CW) Duluth; WDIO-DT (ABC, MeTV) Duluth; WJFW-TV (Antenna TV, NBC) Rhinelander; WLEF-TV (PBS) Park Falls.
Programming (via satellite): A&E; CNN; Comedy Central; Discovery Channel; ESPN; Freeform; History; Lifetime; MTV; Nickelodeon; Spike TV; Syfy; TBS; The Weather Channel; TLC; TNT; TV Land; USA Network; VH1; WGN America.
Fee: $56.95 monthly.
Pay Service 1
Pay Units: N.A.
Programming (via satellite): Flix; Showtime.
Fee: $9.95 monthly.
Video-On-Demand: No
Internet Service
Operational: No.
Telephone Service
None
Miles of Plant: 42.0 (coaxial); None (fiber optic). Homes passed: 400.
General Manager: Dan Plante. Technical Supervisor: Chad Kay.
Ownership: Packerland Broadband (MSO).

MELROSE—Charter Communications. Now served by EAU CLAIRE, WI [WI0011]. ICA: WI0202.

MELVINA—Formerly served by Midwest Cable Inc. No longer in operation. ICA: WI0231.

MENOMONEE FALLS—Time Warner Cable. Now served by MILWAUKEE, WI [WI0001]. ICA: WI0027.

MENOMONIE—Charter Communications. Now served by EAU CLAIRE, WI [WI0011]. ICA: WI0033.

MEQUON—Time Warner Cable. Now served by MILWAUKEE, WI [WI0001]. ICA: WI0041.

MERCER—Karban TV Systems Inc, 73A South Stevens St, Rhinelander, WI 54501. Phones: 715-550-7613; 800-236-0233. Fax: 715-277-2339. E-mail: sales@ktvs.net. Web Site: http://www.ktvs.net. ICA: WI0264.
TV Market Ranking: Outside TV Markets (MERCER). Franchise award date: N.A. Franchise expiration date: N.A. Began: March 1, 1988.
Channel capacity: 77 (not 2-way capable). Channels available but not in use: N.A.
Basic Service
Subscribers: N.A.
Programming (received off-air): WFXS-DT Wittenberg; WJFW-TV (Antenna TV, NBC) Rhinelander; WLEF-TV (PBS) Park Falls; WSAW-TV (CBS, MNT) Wausau; WYOW (ABC, CW, This TV) Eagle River.
Programming (via satellite): A&E; AMC; Animal Planet; CMT; CNBC; CNN; Comedy Central; C-SPAN; CW PLUS; Discovery Channel; Disney Channel; ESPN; ESPN2; EWTN Global Catholic Network; Food Network; Fox News Channel; Fox Sports 1; Freeform; FX; HGTV; History; HLN; Lifetime; MSNBC; NFL Network; Nickelodeon; Outdoor Channel; QVC; Spike TV; Syfy; TBS; The Weather Channel; TLC; TNT; Travel Channel; Trinity Broadcasting Net-

work (TBN); Turner Classic Movies; TV Land; USA Network; VH1; WGN America.
Fee: $75.00 installation; $48.00 monthly.
Pay Service 1
Pay Units: N.A.
Programming (via satellite): Cinemax; HBO.
Fee: $10.00 monthly (each).
Video-On-Demand: No
Internet Service
Operational: Yes.
Telephone Service
None
Miles of Plant: 16.0 (coaxial); None (fiber optic). Homes passed: 300.
General Manager & Chief Technician: John Karban.
Ownership: Karban TV Systems Inc. (MSO).

MERRILL—Charter Communications. Now served by STEVENS POINT, WI [WI0019]. ICA: WI0054.

MERRIMAC—Merrimac Cable, 327 Palisade St, PO Box 40, Merrimac, WI 53561. Phone: 608-493-9470. Fax: 608-493-9902. E-mail: office@merr.com; bart@merr.com. Web Site: http://www.merr.us. Also serves Caledonia (town), Mazomanie Twp., Merrimac (town), Prairie du Sac (village), Prairie du Sac Twp., Roxbury Twp., Sauk City, Sumpter (town) & West Point Twp. ICA: WI0154.
TV Market Ranking: 93 (Caledonia (town), Mazomanie Twp., MERRIMAC, Merrimac (town), Prairie du Sac (village), Prairie du Sac (village), Roxbury Twp., Sauk City, Sumpter (town), West Point Twp.). Franchise award date: March 1, 1984. Franchise expiration date: N.A. Began: October 1, 1984.
Channel capacity: 77 (operating 2-way). Channels available but not in use: N.A.
Basic Service
Subscribers: 1,201.
Programming (received off-air): WBUW (CW) Janesville; WCWF (CW) Suring; WHA-TV (PBS) Madison; WISC-TV (CBS, MNT) Madison; WKOW (ABC, MeTV, This TV) Madison; WMSN-TV (FOX, The Country Network) Madison; WMTV (CW, NBC) Madison; 5 FMs.
Programming (via satellite): C-SPAN; C-SPAN 2; Pop; QVC; WGN America.
Fee: $25.00 installation; $25.95 monthly.
Expanded Basic Service 1
Subscribers: 1,054.
Programming (via satellite): A&E; AMC; Animal Planet; AWE; Bravo; Cartoon Network; Classic Arts Showcase; CMT; CNBC; CNN; Comedy Central; Discovery Channel; Disney Channel; DIY Network; E! HD; ESPN; ESPN Classic; ESPN2; ESPNews; ESPNU; EVINE Live; EWTN Global Catholic Network; Food Network; Fox News Channel; Fox Sports 1; FOX Sports North; Freeform; FX; Hallmark Channel; HGTV; History; HLN; INSP; Jewelry Television; Lifetime; MSNBC; MTV; NASA TV; National Geographic Channel; NBCSN; Nickelodeon; Spike TV; Syfy; TBS; The Weather Channel; TLC; TNT; Travel Channel; Trinity Broadcasting Network (TBN); truTV; Turner Classic Movies; TV Land; USA Network; VH1; WE tv.
Digital Basic Service
Subscribers: N.A.
Programming (via satellite): A&E HD; AXS TV; BBC America; Bloomberg Television; Cloo; CMT; Cooking Channel; Destination America; Discovery Kids Channel; Discovery Life Channel; Disney XD; DMX Music; ESPN HD; ESPN2 HD; Food Network HD; Fox Business Network; Fuse; FXM; FYI;

Golf Channel; GSN; HD Theater; HGTV HD; History International; IFC; Investigation Discovery; MTV Classic; MTV Hits; MTV2; National Geographic Channel HD; Nick Jr.; Nicktoons; Outdoor Channel; OWN: Oprah Winfrey Network; RFD-TV; Science Channel; Sundance TV; TeenNick; Universal HD; VH1 Soul.
Fee: $11.95 monthly.
Digital Pay Service 1
Pay Units: N.A.
Programming (via satellite): Cinemax (multiplexed); Cinemax HD; Flix; HBO (multiplexed); HBO HD; Playboy TV; Showtime (multiplexed); Showtime HD; Starz (multiplexed); Starz Encore (multiplexed); Starz HD; The Movie Channel (multiplexed).
Fee: $9.95 monthly (Playboy or Cinemax), $13.95 monthly (Showtime/TMC/Flix or Starz/Encore), $14.95 monthly (HBO).
Video-On-Demand: No
Pay-Per-View
iN DEMAND (delivered digitally); Playboy TV (delivered digitally).
Internet Service
Operational: Yes, Dial-up.
Telephone Service
Analog: Not Operational
Digital: Operational
Fee: $14.99-$24.99 monthly
Miles of Plant: 51.0 (coaxial); 161.0 (fiber optic). Homes passed: 4,097.
President: Bartlett Olson. Chief Financial Officer: Jean Buelow. Office Manager: Michelle Hopp.
Ownership: Merrimac Communications Ltd.

MIKANA—S & K TV Systems, 508 Miner Ave West, Ladysmith, WI 54848. Phones: 715-532-7321; 800-924-7880. Fax: 715-532-7583. E-mail: techsupport@skcable.com. Web Site: http://www.skcable.com. Also serves Birchwood, Exeland, Radisson & Winter. ICA: WI0265.
TV Market Ranking: Outside TV Markets (Birchwood, Exeland, MIKANA, Winter, Radisson). Franchise award date: January 1, 1989. Franchise expiration date: N.A. Began: November 1, 1989.
Channel capacity: N.A. Channels available but not in use: N.A.
Basic Service
Subscribers: N.A.
Programming (received off-air): KQDS-TV (Antenna TV, FOX) Duluth; WCCO-TV (CBS, Decades) Minneapolis; WEAU (NBC) Eau Claire; WEUX (FOX, MeTV) Chippewa Falls; WHWC-TV (PBS) Menomonie; WQOW (ABC, CW, This TV) Eau Claire.
Programming (via satellite): A&E; AMC; Animal Planet; CMT; CNN; Discovery Channel; Disney Channel; ESPN; ESPN2; Freeform; Great American Country; Hallmark Channel; HGTV; History; HLN; Lifetime; MTV; Nickelodeon; Outdoor Channel; QVC; Spike TV; Syfy; TBS; The Weather Channel; TLC; TNT; Turner Classic Movies; TV Land; USA Network; VH1; WGN America.
Fee: $40.00 installation.

Digital Basic Service
Subscribers: N.A.
Programming (via satellite): BBC America; Bloomberg Television; CMT; Discovery Kids Channel; Discovery Life Channel; ESPN Classic; ESPN2; ESPNews; Fox Sports 1; Fuse; FXM; FYI; Golf Channel; GSN; HGTV; History; History International; Investigation Discovery; LMN; MTV Classic; MTV2; NBCSN; Nick Jr.; Nicktoons; Outdoor Channel; OWN: Oprah Winfrey Network; Science Channel; Syfy; TeenNick; Trinity Broadcasting Network (TBN); Turner Classic Movies.
Fee: $15.31 monthly.
Pay Service 1
Pay Units: N.A.
Programming (via satellite): Cinemax; HBO.
Fee: $7.95 monthly (Cinemax), $10.95 monthly (HBO).
Digital Pay Service 1
Pay Units: N.A.
Programming (via satellite): Cinemax (multiplexed); HBO (multiplexed); Showtime (multiplexed); Starz (multiplexed); Starz Encore (multiplexed); The Movie Channel (multiplexed).
Video-On-Demand: No
Internet Service
Operational: Yes.
Fee: $30.00 installation; $24.95-$39.95 monthly.
Telephone Service
None
Miles of Plant: 12.0 (coaxial); None (fiber optic).
General Manager: Randy Scott. Office Manager: Dave Scott.
Ownership: S & K TV Systems Inc. (MSO).

MILLADORE (town)—New Century Communications, 3588 Kennebec Dr, Eagan, MN 55122-1001. Phone: 651-688-2623. Fax: 651-688-2624. ICA: WI0221.
TV Market Ranking: Below 100 (MILLADORE (TOWN)).
Channel capacity: N.A. Channels available but not in use: N.A.
Basic Service
Subscribers: N.A.
Programming (received off-air): WAOW (ABC, CW, This TV) Wausau; WEAU (NBC) Eau Claire; WFXS-DT Wittenberg; WHRM-TV (PBS) Wausau; WSAW-TV (CBS, MNT) Wausau.
Programming (via satellite): A&E; AMC; CNN; Discovery Channel; ESPN; Freeform; Lifetime; Nickelodeon; Showtime; Spike TV; TBS; TLC; TNT; Trinity Broadcasting Network (TBN); TV Land; USA Network; WGN America.
Fee: $30.00 installation.
Video-On-Demand: No
Internet Service
Operational: No.
Telephone Service
None
Miles of Plant: 3.0 (coaxial); None (fiber optic). Homes passed: 113.

Wisconsin—Cable Systems

Executive Vice President: Marty Walch. General Manager & Chief Technician: Todd Anderson.
Ownership: New Century Communications (MSO).

MILWAUKEE—Time Warner Cable, 1320 North Dr Martin Luther King Dr, Milwaukee, WI 53212-4002. Phones: 414-908-4877; 414-277-4032; 414-277-4111. Fax: 414-277-8049. Web Site: http://www.timewarnercable.com. Also serves Adell (village), Ashippun (town), Bayside (village), Belgium (town), Big Bend (village), Bloomfield (town), Bristol (town), Brookfield, Brown Deer (village), Burlington, Butler (village), Caledonia (town), Cascade (village), Cedar Grove (village), Cedarburg, Cleveland (village), Cudahy, Delafield (town), Dousman (village), Dover (town), Eagle (town), East Troy (town), Elkhart Lake (village), Elm Grove (village), Elmwood Park (village), Fox Point (village), Franklin, Fredonia (town), Genesee (town), Geneva (town), Germantown, Glenbeulah (village), Glendale, Grafton (town), Greenbush (town), Greendale (village), Greenfield, Hales Corners (village), Hartland, Herman (town), Holland (town), Howards Grove (village), Ixonia (town), Kenosha, Lac La Belle, Lake Geneva, Lannon (village), Lima (town), Linn (town), Lisbon (town), Lyndon (town), Lyons (town), Menomonee Falls (village), Mequon, Merton (town), Mosel (town), Mount Pleasant (town), Mukwonago (village), Muskego, Nashota (village), New Berlin, Newburg (village), North Bay (village), North Prairie (village), Norway, Oak Creek, Oconomowoc (town), Oconomowoc Lake (village), Oostburg (village), Ottawa (town), Paddock Lake (village), Pewaukee (town), Pleasant Prairie (village), Plymouth, Port Washington, Racine, Randall (town), Random Lake (village), Raymond, Rhine (town), River Hills (village), Rochester (village), Salem (town), Saukville (village), Scott (town), Sherman (town), Shorewood (village), Silver Lake (village), Somers (town), South Milwaukee, Spring Prairie (town), St. Francis, Sturtevant (village), Sullivan (town), Summit (town), Sussex (village), Thiensville, Troy (town), Twin Lakes, Union Grove (village), Vernon (town), Waldo (village), Wales (town), Waterford (town), Waukesha, Wauwatosa, West Allis, West Milwaukee, Wheatland (town), Whitefish Bay (village), Wind Lake (town), Wind Point (village) & Yorkville (town). ICA: WI0001.
TV Market Ranking: 23 (Ashippun (town), Bayside (village), Belgium (town), Big Bend (village), Bristol (town), Brookfield, Brown Deer (village), Burlington, Butler (village), Caledonia (town), Cedarburg, Cudahy, Delafield (town), Dousman (village), Dover (town), Eagle (town), East Troy (town), Elm Grove (village), Elmwood Park (village), Fox Point (village), Franklin, Fredonia (town), Genesee (town), Germantown, Glendale, Grafton (town), Greendale (village), Greenfield, Hales Corners (village), Hartland, Holland (town), Ixonia (town), Kenosha, Lac La Belle, Lannon (village), Lisbon (town), Lyons (town), Menomonee Falls (village), Mequon, Merton (town), MILWAUKEE, Mount Pleasant (town), Mukwonago (village), Muskego, Nashota (village), New Berlin, Newburg (village), North Bay (village), North Prairie (village), Norway, Oak Creek, Oconomowoc (town), Oconomowoc Lake (village), Ottawa (town), Paddock Lake (village), Pewaukee (town), Port Washington, Racine, Random Lake (village), Raymond, River Hills (village), Rochester (village), Salem (town), Saukville (village), Shorewood (village), Somers (town), South Milwaukee, St. Francis, Sturtevant (village), Sullivan (town), Summit (town), Sussex (village), Thiensville, Troy (town), Union Grove (village), Vernon (town), Wales (village), Waterford (town), Waukesha, Wauwatosa, West Allis, West Milwaukee, Wheatland (town), Whitefish Bay (village), Wind Lake (town), Wind Point (village), Yorkville (town)); Below 100 (Adell (village), Bloomfield (town), Cascade (village), Cedar Grove (village), Elkhart Lake (village), Geneva (town), Glenbeulah (village), Greenbush (town), Howards Grove (village), Lake Geneva, Linn (town), Lyndon (town), Mosel (town), Oostburg (village), Plymouth, Rhine (town), Scott (town), Sherman (town), Silver Lake (village), Spring Prairie (town), Twin Lakes, Waldo (village)); Outside TV Markets (Cleveland (village), Herman (town), Lima (town), Randall (town)).
Franchise award date: June 1, 1983. Franchise expiration date: N.A. Began: December 11, 1984.
Channel capacity: 69 (operating 2-way). Channels available but not in use: N.A.

Basic Service
Subscribers: 275,895.
Programming (received off-air): WBME-CD (IND) Milwaukee; WCGV-TV (MNT, The Country Network) Milwaukee; WDJT-TV (CBS, Decades) Milwaukee; WISN-TV (ABC, Movies!) Milwaukee; WITI (Antenna TV, FOX) Milwaukee; WMLW-TV (Bounce TV, MeTV, TMO) Racine; WMVS (PBS) Milwaukee; WMVT (PBS) Milwaukee; WPXE-TV (ION) Kenosha; WTMJ-TV (COZI TV, Escape, Laff, NBC) Milwaukee; WVCY-TV (IND) Milwaukee; WVTV (CW) Milwaukee; WWRS-TV (TBN) Mayville; 5 FMs.
Programming (via satellite): BET; Cartoon Network; CNBC; C-SPAN 2; EVINE Live; HGTV; History; Jewelry Television; Lifetime; LMN; MoviePlex; MSNBC; MTV; National Geographic Channel; NBCSN; Nickelodeon; Oxygen; Pop; QVC; Spike TV; Syfy; TBS; Telemundo; The Weather Channel; TLC; VH1; WE tv; WGN America.
Fee: $99.95 installation; $27.21 monthly; $2.82 converter.

Expanded Basic Service 1
Subscribers: N.A.
Programming (via satellite): A&E; AMC; Animal Planet; Bravo; CNN; Comedy Central; Discovery Channel; Disney Channel; E! HD; ESPN; ESPN Classic; ESPN2; EWTN Global Catholic Network; Food Network; Fox News Channel; Freeform; FX; Golf Channel; Great American Country; Hallmark Channel; HLN; OWN: Oprah Winfrey Network; TNT; Travel Channel; truTV; Turner Classic Movies; TV Land; Univision Studios; USA Network.
Fee: $19.54 monthly.

Digital Basic Service
Subscribers: N.A.
Programming (via satellite): AXS TV; BBC America; Bloomberg Television; Boomerang; CBS Sports Network; Cloo; CMT; CNN International; Cooking Channel; C-SPAN 3; Discovery Life Channel; Disney Channel; Disney XD; DIY Network; ESPN; ESPNews; Fox Sports 1; Fox Sports 2; FOX Sports Networks; FSN Digital Atlantic; FSN Digital Central; FSN Digital Pacific; Fuse; FYI; GSN; HD Theater; History; HITS (Headend In The Sky); LWS Local Weather Station; MC; NBA TV; Nick Jr.; Nicktoons; Outdoor Channel; TeenNick; Tennis Channel; The Word Network; TNT HD; truTV.
Fee: $3.95 monthly.

Digital Pay Service 1
Pay Units: N.A.
Programming (via satellite): Cinemax; Flix (multiplexed); FXM; HBO; HBO HD (multiplexed); IFC; RAI Italia; Showtime; Showtime HD (multiplexed); Starz (multiplexed); Starz Encore (multiplexed); Sundance TV; The Movie Channel (multiplexed); TV Asia.
Fee: $12.99 monthly (each).

Video-On-Demand: Yes

Pay-Per-View
iN DEMAND (delivered digitally); Shorteez (delivered digitally); Sports PPV (delivered digitally); Playboy TV (delivered digitally); Juicy (delivered digitally); VaVoom (delivered digitally); NBA League Pass (delivered digitally); MLS Direct Kick (delivered digitally); NHL Center Ice (delivered digitally); MLB Extra Innings (delivered digitally).

Internet Service
Operational: Yes.
Subscribers: 358,385.
Broadband Service: Road Runner.
Fee: $79.95 installation; $44.95 monthly.

Telephone Service
Digital: Operational
Subscribers: 176,996.
Fee: $44.95 monthly
Miles of Plant: 17,370.0 (coaxial); 5,131.0 (fiber optic). Homes passed: 889,604.
President: Tom Adams. Vice President, Government Affairs: Celeste Flynn. Vice President, Operations: Mike Fox. Vice President, Technical Operations: Ralph Newcomb. Vice President, Sales & Marketing: Chuck Parshall. Vice President, Communications: Marci Pelzer.
Ownership: Time Warner Cable (MSO).

MINDORO—Charter Communications. Now served by EAU CLAIRE, WI [WI0011]. ICA: WI0310.

MINOCQUA—Charter Communications. Now served by STEVENS POINT, WI [WI0019]. ICA: WI0071.

MINONG—S & K TV Systems, 508 Miner Ave West, Ladysmith, WI 54848. Phones: 715-532-7321; 800-924-7880. Fax: 715-532-7583. E-mail: techsupport@skcable.com. Web Site: http://www.skcable.com. Also serves Trego. ICA: WI0317.
TV Market Ranking: Outside TV Markets (MINONG, Trego). Franchise award date: August 4, 1987. Franchise expiration date: N.A. Began: N.A.
Channel capacity: N.A. Channels available but not in use: N.A.

Basic Service
Subscribers: N.A.
Programming (received off-air): KBJR-TV (CBS, MNT, NBC) Superior; KDLH (CBS, CW) Duluth; KQDS-TV (Antenna TV, FOX) Duluth; KSTP-TV (ABC, MeTV) St. Paul; WDIO-DT (ABC, MeTV) Duluth; WDSE (PBS) Duluth.
Programming (via satellite): A&E; AMC; Animal Planet; CMT; CNN; Discovery Channel; Disney Channel; ESPN; ESPN2; Freeform; Hallmark Channel; HGTV; History; HLN; Lifetime; MTV; Nickelodeon; Outdoor Channel; Spike TV; Syfy; TBS; The Weather Channel; TLC; TNT; Turner Classic Movies; TV Land; USA Network; VH1; WGN America.
Fee: $40.00 installation.

Digital Basic Service
Subscribers: N.A.
Programming (via satellite): BBC America; Bloomberg Television; Discovery Life Channel; Disney XD; DMX Music; ESPN2; ESPNews; Fox Sports 1; Fuse; FXM; FYI; Golf Channel; GSN; HGTV; History; History International; LMN; NBCSN; Nick Jr.; Nicktoons; Outdoor Channel; Syfy; TeenNick; Trinity Broadcasting Network (TBN); Turner Classic Movies.
Fee: $15.31 monthly.

Pay Service 1
Pay Units: N.A.
Programming (via satellite): Cinemax; HBO.
Fee: $10.00 installation; $7.95 monthly (Cinemax), $10.95 monthly (HBO).

Digital Pay Service 1
Pay Units: N.A.
Programming (via satellite): Cinemax (multiplexed); HBO (multiplexed); Showtime (multiplexed); Starz (multiplexed); Starz Encore (multiplexed); The Movie Channel (multiplexed).

Video-On-Demand: No

Internet Service
Operational: No.

Telephone Service
None
Miles of Plant: 9.0 (coaxial); None (fiber optic).
General Manager: Randy Scott. Office Manager: Dave Scott.
Ownership: S & K TV Systems Inc. (MSO).

MONTELLO—Charter Communications, 165 Knights Way, Fond du Lac, WI 54935. Phones: 314-543-2236; 636-207-5100 (Corporate office); 920-907-7720. Web Site: http://www.charter.com. ICA: WI0122.
TV Market Ranking: Outside TV Markets (MONTELLO). Franchise award date: N.A. Franchise expiration date: N.A. Began: June 30, 1983.
Channel capacity: 40 (not 2-way capable). Channels available but not in use: N.A.

Digital Basic Service
Subscribers: 145.
Programming (received off-air): WFRV-TV (Bounce TV, CBS) Green Bay; WHA-TV (PBS) Madison; WISC-TV (CBS, MNT) Madison; WKOW (ABC, MeTV, This TV) Madison; WLUK-TV (Antenna TV, FOX) Green Bay; WMSN-TV (FOX, The Country Network) Madison; WMTV (CW, NBC) Madison; WVTV (CW) Milwaukee.
Programming (via satellite): QVC; WGN America.
Fee: $49.99 installation; $21.99 monthly.

Digital Expanded Basic Service
Subscribers: N.A.
Programming (via satellite): A&E; AMC; CNBC; CNN; Comedy Central; C-SPAN; Discovery Channel; Disney Channel; ESPN; ESPN2; EWTN Global Catholic Network; Freeform; HLN; Lifetime; MSNBC; MTV; Nickelodeon; Spike TV; TBS; The Weather Channel; TLC; TNT; USA Network; VH1.
Fee: $47.99 monthly.

Digital Pay Service 1
Pay Units: N.A.
Programming (via satellite): Cinemax; HBO; Showtime.

Video-On-Demand: No

Internet Service
Operational: No.

Telephone Service
None
Miles of Plant: 30.0 (coaxial); None (fiber optic). Homes passed: 986.
Vice President & General Manager: Lisa Washa. Accounting Director: David So-

Cable Systems—Wisconsin

vanski. Chief Technician: Jeff Gerner. Marketing Director: Traci Loonstra. Marketing Administrator: Rhonda Schelvan.
Ownership: Charter Communications Inc. (MSO).

MONTICELLO—Mediacom, 3900 26th Ave, Moline, IL 61265. Phones: 845-695-2762; 309-797-2580 (Moline regional office); 563-557-8025. Fax: 309-797-2414. Web Site: http://www.mediacomcable.com. ICA: WI0153.
TV Market Ranking: 97 (MONTICELLO). Franchise award date: N.A. Franchise expiration date: N.A. Began: June 18, 1984.
Channel capacity: N.A. Channels available but not in use: N.A.
Basic Service
  Subscribers: 16.
  Programming (received off-air): WHA-TV (PBS) Madison; WIFR (Antenna TV, CBS) Freeport; WISC-TV (CBS, MNT) Madison; WKOW (ABC, MeTV, This TV) Madison; WMSN-TV (FOX, The Country Network) Madison; WMTV (CW, NBC) Madison; WQRF-TV (Bounce TV, FOX) Rockford; WREX (CW, MeTV, NBC) Rockford; WTVO (ABC, MNT) Rockford.
  Programming (via satellite): A&E; AMC; Animal Planet; Cartoon Network; CMT; CNN; Discovery Channel; ESPN; ESPN2; Food Network; Freeform; HGTV; Lifetime; MTV; Nickelodeon; Spike TV; Syfy; TBS; TNT; Travel Channel; Trinity Broadcasting Network (TBN); USA Network; VH1; WGN America.
  Fee: $45.00 installation; $40.00 monthly.
Pay Service 1
  Pay Units: N.A.
  Programming (via satellite): Cinemax; HBO.
  Fee: $7.95 monthly (Cinemax), $11.99 monthly (HBO).
Video-On-Demand: No
Internet Service
  Operational: No.
Telephone Service
  None
Homes passed: 562. Miles of plant included in Moline, IL
Regional Vice President: Cari Fenzel. Vice President, Financial Reporting: Kenneth J. Kohrs. Area Manager: Kathleen McMullen. Engineering Director: Mitch Carlson. Marketing Director: Greg Evans. Technical Operations Manager: Darren Dean.
Ownership: Mediacom LLC (MSO).

MUSKEGO—Time Warner Cable. Now served by MILWAUKEE, WI [WI0001]. ICA: WI0051.

NEW BERLIN—Time Warner Cable. Now served by MILWAUKEE, WI [WI0001]. ICA: WI0026.

NEW FRANKEN—CenturyLink, PO Box 4065, Monroe, LA 71211. Phone: 920-837-7474. Web Site: http://www.centurylink.com. Also serves Casco (town), Casco (village), Forestville (village), Green Bay (town), Luxemburg (town), Luxemburg (village), Red River (town) & Scott (town). ICA: WI0269.
TV Market Ranking: 62 (Casco (town), Casco (village), Green Bay (town), Luxemburg (town), Luxemburg (village), NEW FRANKEN, Red River (town), Scott (town)). Franchise award date: February 1, 1983. Franchise expiration date: N.A. Began: February 1, 1983.
Channel capacity: N.A. Channels available but not in use: N.A.

Basic Service
  Subscribers: 1,100.
  Programming (received off-air): WACY-TV (Escape, Grit, Laff, MNT) Appleton; WBAY-TV (ABC) Green Bay; WCWF (CW) Suring; WFRV-TV (Bounce TV, CBS) Green Bay; WGBA-TV (MeTV, NBC) Green Bay; WLUK-TV (Antenna TV, FOX) Green Bay; WPNE-TV (PBS) Green Bay.
  Programming (via satellite): WGN America.
  Fee: $35.00 installation; $21.95 monthly.
Expanded Basic Service 1
  Subscribers: N.A.
  Programming (via satellite): A&E; AMC; Animal Planet; Cartoon Network; CMT; CNN; Comedy Central; Discovery Channel; Disney Channel; ESPN; ESPN2; EWTN Global Catholic Network; Food Network; Fox News Channel; FOX Sports North; Freeform; FX; Hallmark Channel; HGTV; History; Lifetime; MSNBC; MTV; Nickelodeon; QVC; Spike TV; Syfy; TBS; The Weather Channel; TLC; TNT; Travel Channel; Turner Classic Movies; TV Land; USA Network; VH1.
  Fee: $23.00 monthly.
Digital Basic Service
  Subscribers: N.A.
  Programming (via satellite): BBC America; Discovery Kids Channel; Discovery Life Channel; Disney XD; DMX Music; FYI; GSN; History International; International Television (ITV); MTV Classic; National Geographic Channel; Nick Jr.; Nicktoons; Ovation; TeenNick; Trinity Broadcasting Network (TBN); VH1 Country; WE tv.
  Fee: $5.00 monthly; $4.95 converter.
Digital Expanded Basic Service
  Subscribers: N.A.
  Programming (via satellite): ESPN Classic; ESPNews; Fox Sports 1; FXM; Golf Channel; IFC; LMN; NBCSN; Outdoor Channel.
  Fee: $3.00 monthly; $4.95 converter.
Digital Pay Service 1
  Pay Units: N.A.
  Programming (via satellite): Cinemax (multiplexed); HBO (multiplexed); Showtime (multiplexed); Starz (multiplexed); Starz Encore (multiplexed).
  Fee: $10.95 monthly (Cinemax), $11.95 monthly (Starz/Encore), $12.95 monthly (Showtime), $13.50 monthly (HBO), $20.95 monthly (Cinemax/HBO).
Pay-Per-View
  iN DEMAND (delivered digitally).
Internet Service
  Operational: Yes.
Telephone Service
  Digital: Operational
Miles of Plant: 68.0 (coaxial); 5.0 (fiber optic). Homes passed: 3,000.
Vice President, Operations: Robert Brown. Assistant Secretary: Joan Randazzo.
Ownership: CenturyLink (MSO).

NEW RICHMOND—Northwest Community Communications, 116 Harriman Ave North, Amery, WI 54001. Phones: 715-268-6066; 715-268-7101. Fax: 715-268-9194. E-mail: info@nwcomm.net. Web Site: http://www.nwcomm.net. Also serves Somerset (village), St. Joseph, Star Prairie (village) & Star Prairie (village). ICA: WI0077.
TV Market Ranking: 13 (NEW RICHMOND, Somerset (village), St. Joseph, Star Prairie (town), Star Prairie (village)). Franchise award date: March 1, 1983. Franchise expiration date: N.A. Began: February 1, 1984.
Channel capacity: N.A. Channels available but not in use: N.A.
Basic Service
  Subscribers: 1,445.
  Programming (received off-air): KARE (NBC, WeatherNation) Minneapolis; KMSP-TV (Bounce TV, Buzzr, FOX) Minneapolis; KSTP-TV (ABC, MeTV) St. Paul; KTCA-TV (PBS) St. Paul; WCCO-TV (CBS, Decades) Minneapolis; WEAU (NBC) Eau Claire; WFTC (MNT, Movies!) Minneapolis; WHWC-TV (PBS) Menomonie; WKBT-DT (CBS, MNT) La Crosse; WQOW (ABC, CW, This TV) Eau Claire; WUCW (CW, The Country Network) Minneapolis.
  Programming (via satellite): A&E; AMC; Animal Planet; Cartoon Network; CMT; CNN; Comedy Central; Discovery Channel; ESPN; ESPN Classic; ESPN2; Food Network; Fox News Channel; FOX Sports Networks; Freeform; Hallmark Channel; HGTV; History; HLN; INSP; Lifetime; MSNBC; MTV; National Geographic Channel; Nickelodeon; QVC; Spike TV; Syfy; TBS; The Weather Channel; TLC; TNT; Travel Channel; TV Land; USA Network; VH1; WGN America.
  Fee: $50.00 installation; $28.74 monthly.
Digital Basic Service
  Subscribers: N.A.
  Programming (via satellite): BBC America; Bloomberg Television; Discovery Kids Channel; DMX Music; ESPNews; Fox Sports 1; FXM; FYI; Golf Channel; GSN; History International; LMN; Nick Jr.; Nicktoons; Outdoor Channel; Ovation; Sundance TV; TeenNick; Turner Classic Movies.
  Fee: $12.95 monthly.
Pay Service 1
  Pay Units: N.A.
  Programming (via satellite): Cinemax; HBO; Showtime.
  Fee: $10.25 monthly (Cinemax), $10.75 monthly (HBO or Showtime).
Digital Pay Service 1
  Pay Units: N.A.
  Programming (via satellite): Cinemax (multiplexed); HBO (multiplexed); Showtime (multiplexed); Starz (multiplexed); Starz Encore (multiplexed); The Movie Channel (multiplexed).
  Fee: $12.50 monthly (HBO), $14.99 monthly (Showtime/TMC).
Video-On-Demand: No
Internet Service
  Operational: Yes.
  Fee: $29.95 installation; $39.95 monthly.
Telephone Service
  None
Miles of Plant: 15.0 (coaxial); None (fiber optic).
Vice President: Scott Jensen. General Manager: Dwight Schmitt. Operations Manager: Myron Ranum.
Ownership: Northwest Community Communications.

NEWBURG—Tiime Warner Cable. Now served by MILWAUKEE, WI [WI0001]. ICA: WI0270.

NIAGARA—Formerly served by Niagara Community TV Co-op. No longer in operation. ICA: WI0271.

NICHOLS—Packerland Broadband, 105 Kent St., PO Box 885, Iron Mountain, MI 49801. Phone: 800-236-8434. Fax: 906-776-2811. E-mail: service@plbb.net; support@packerlandbroadband.com. Web Site: http://www.packerlandbroadband.com. ICA: WI0328.
Channel capacity: N.A. Channels available but not in use: N.A.
Basic Service
  Subscribers: 18.
  Fee: $24.95 monthly.
Ownership: Packerland Broadband.

NORTH FREEDOM—Charter Communications. Now served by MADISON, WI [WI0002]. ICA: WI0325.

NORTH PRAIRIE—Time Warner Cable. Now served by MILWAUKEE, WI [WI0001]. ICA: WI0272.

NORWALK—Mediacom. Now served by MAUSTON, WI [WI0084]. ICA: WI0208.

OCONOMOWOC LAKE—Time Warner Cable. Now served by MILWAUKEE, WI [WI0001]. ICA: WI0273.

OCONTO—Formerly served by Charter Communications. No longer in operation. ICA: WI0075.

OCONTO FALLS—Formerly served by Oconto Falls Cable TV. Now served by Packerland Broadband, OCONTO FALLS, WI [WI0349]. ICA: WI0108.

OCONTO FALLS—Packerland Broadband, 105 Kent St., PO Box 885, Iron Mountain, MI 49801. Phone: 800-236-8434. Fax: 906-776-2811. E-mail: service@plbb.net; support@packerlandbroadband.com. Web Site: http://www.packerlandbroadband.com. ICA: WI0349.
Channel capacity: N.A. Channels available but not in use: N.A.
Miles of Plant: 26.0 (coaxial); None (fiber optic). Homes passed: 1,654.
Ownership: Packerland Broadband.

ONALASKA—Charter Communications. Now served by EAU CLAIRE, WI [WI0011]. ICA: WI0024.

ONTARIO—Mediacom. Now served by MAUSTON, WI [WI0084]. ICA: WI0303.

ORFORDVILLE—Mediacom, 3900 26th Ave, Moline, IL 61265. Phones: 845-695-2762; 309-797-2580 (Moline regional office); 563-557-8025 (Dubuque office). Fax: 309-797-2414. Web Site: http://www.mediacomcable.com. Also serves Footville. ICA: WI0130.
TV Market Ranking: 93,97 (Footville, ORFORDVILLE). Franchise award date: September 26, 1983. Franchise expiration date: N.A. Began: October 24, 1984.
Channel capacity: N.A. Channels available but not in use: N.A.

2017 Edition

D-863

Wisconsin—Cable Systems

Basic Service
Subscribers: 30.
Programming (received off-air): WHA-TV (PBS) Madison; WIFR (Antenna TV, CBS) Freeport; WISC-TV (CBS, MNT) Madison; WKOW (ABC, MeTV, This TV) Madison; WMSN-TV (FOX, The Country Network) Madison; WMTV (CW, NBC) Madison; WQRF-TV (Bounce TV, FOX) Rockford; WREX (CW, MeTV, NBC) Rockford; WTVO (ABC, MNT) Rockford.
Programming (via satellite): WGN America.
Fee: $45.00 installation; $40.00 monthly.

Expanded Basic Service 1
Subscribers: N.A.
Programming (via satellite): A&E; AMC; Animal Planet; Cartoon Network; CMT; CNN; Comedy Central; C-SPAN; Discovery Channel; Disney Channel; E! HD; ESPN; ESPN2; Freeform; FX; History; Lifetime; MTV; Nickelodeon; Spike TV; Syfy; TBS; The Weather Channel; TNT; Trinity Broadcasting Network (TBN); TV Land; USA Network.
Fee: $24.00 monthly.

Pay Service 1
Pay Units: N.A.
Programming (via satellite): Cinemax; HBO; Showtime; Starz; Starz Encore.
Fee: $5.99 monthly (Starz/Encore), $7.95 monthly (Cinemax), $11.99 monthly (HBO or Showtime).

Video-On-Demand: No

Internet Service
Operational: No.

Telephone Service
None
Homes passed: 890. Miles of plant included in Moline, IL.
Regional Vice President: Cari Fenzel. Vice President, Financial Reporting: Kenneth J. Kohrs. Area Manager: Kathleen McMullen. Engineering Director: Mitch Carlson. Marketing Director: Greg Evans. Technical Operations Manager: Darren Dean.
Ownership: Mediacom LLC (MSO).

OXFORD—New Century Communications, 3588 Kennebec Dr, Eagan, MN 55122-1001. Phone: 651-688-2623. Fax: 651-688-2624. ICA: WI0314.
TV Market Ranking: Outside TV Markets (OXFORD).
Channel capacity: N.A. Channels available but not in use: N.A.

Basic Service
Subscribers: N.A.
Programming (received off-air): WHA-TV (PBS) Madison; WISC-TV (CBS, MNT) Madison; WKOW (ABC, MeTV, This TV) Madison; WMTV (CW, NBC) Madison.
Programming (via satellite): A&E; AMC; Animal Planet; CMT; CNN; Comedy Central; Discovery Channel; Disney Channel; ESPN; ESPN2; FOX Sports Networks; Freeform; FX; History; Lifetime; Showtime (multiplexed); Spike TV; TBS; The Weather Channel; TLC; TNT; Trinity Broadcasting Network (TBN); TV Land; USA Network; WGN America.
Fee: $30.00 installation.

Pay Service 1
Pay Units: N.A.
Programming (via satellite): HBO.
Fee: $11.00 monthly.

Video-On-Demand: No

Internet Service
Operational: No.

Telephone Service
None
Executive Vice President: Marty Walch. General Manager & Chief Technician: Todd Anderson.
Ownership: New Century Communications (MSO).

PACKWAUKEE—New Century Communications, 3588 Kennebec Dr, Eagan, MN 55122-1001. Phone: 651-688-2623. Fax: 651-688-2624. ICA: WI0189.
TV Market Ranking: Outside TV Markets (PACKWAUKEE).
Channel capacity: N.A. Channels available but not in use: N.A.

Basic Service
Subscribers: N.A.
Programming (received off-air): WHA-TV (PBS) Madison; WISC-TV (CBS, MNT) Madison; WKOW (ABC, MeTV, This TV) Madison; WMTV (CW, NBC) Madison.
Programming (via satellite): A&E; AMC; CMT; CNN; Discovery Channel; Disney Channel; ESPN; ESPN2; FOX Sports Networks; Freeform; History; Lifetime; Showtime; Spike TV; TBS; TLC; TNT; Trinity Broadcasting Network (TBN); TV Land; USA Network; WGN America.
Fee: $30.00 installation.

Video-On-Demand: No

Internet Service
Operational: No.

Telephone Service
None
Miles of Plant: 10.0 (coaxial); None (fiber optic). Homes passed: 260.
Executive Vice President: Marty Walch. General Manager & Chief Technician: Todd Anderson.
Ownership: New Century Communications (MSO).

PARK FALLS—Charter Communications. Now served by EAU CLAIRE, WI [WI0011]. ICA: WI0086.

PEMBINE—Packerland Broadband, 105 Kent St., PO Box 885, Iron Mountain, MI 49801. Phone: 800-236-8434. Fax: 906-776-2811. E-mail: service@plbb.net; support@packerlandbroadband.com. Web Site: http://www.packerlandbroadband.com. ICA: WI0331.
Channel capacity: N.A. Channels available but not in use: N.A.

Basic Service
Subscribers: 82.
Fee: $24.95 monthly.
Ownership: Packerland Broadband.

PEPIN—Midcontinent Communications. Now served by ALMA, WI [WI0234]. ICA: WI0155.

PHELPS—Upper Peninsula Communications, 397 North US Hwy 41, Carney, MI 49812-9757. Phones: 906-639-2111; 906-639-2194. Fax: 906-639-9936. E-mail: louied@alphacomm.net. ICA: WI0176.
TV Market Ranking: Outside TV Markets (PHELPS).
Channel capacity: 40 (not 2-way capable). Channels available but not in use: N.A.

Basic Service
Subscribers: N.A.
Programming (received off-air): WAOW (ABC, CW, This TV) Wausau; WFXS-DT Wittenberg; WJFW-TV (Antenna TV, NBC) Rhinelander; WLEF-TV (PBS) Park Falls; WSAW-TV (CBS, MNT) Wausau; WYOW (ABC, CW, This TV) Eagle River.
Programming (via satellite): A&E; AMC; CMT; CNBC; CNN; C-SPAN; Discovery Channel; Disney Channel; ESPN; ESPN2; Freeform; HGTV; History; ION Television; Lifetime; Outdoor Channel; Spike TV; TBS; The Weather Channel; TLC; TNT; Trinity Broadcasting Network (TBN); TV Land; USA Network; WGN America.
Fee: $50.00 installation; $31.90 monthly.

Pay Service 1
Pay Units: N.A.
Programming (via satellite): Showtime.

Video-On-Demand: No

Internet Service
Operational: No.

Telephone Service
None
Miles of Plant: 16.0 (coaxial); None (fiber optic). Homes passed: 338.
General Manager & Chief Technician: Louis Dupont.
Ownership: Upper Peninsula Communications Inc. (MSO).

PHILLIPS—Price County Telephone Co. Formerly [WI0119]. This cable system has converted to IPTV, 105 N Avon Ave, PO Box 108, Phillips, WI 54555. Phone: 715-339-2151. Fax: 715-339-4512. Web Site: http://www.pctcnet.net. Also serves Eisenstein (town), Elk (town), Emery (town), Fifield (town), Flambeau (town), Hackett (town), Harmony (town), Lake (town), Park Falls, Prentice (town), Prentice (village), Winter (town) & Worcester (town). ICA: WI5049.
TV Market Ranking: Below 100 (Flambeau (town)); Outside TV Markets (Lake (town), Park Falls, PHILLIPS).
Channel capacity: N.A. Channels available but not in use: N.A.

Basic
Subscribers: 1,183.
Fee: $35.00 installation; $46.95 monthly. Includes 75+ channels plus 50 music channels & 1 STB.

Expanded
Subscribers: 1,041.
Fee: $53.95 monthly. Includes 100+ channels plus 50 music channels & 1 STB.

HD
Subscribers: N.A.
Fee: $9.95 monthly. Includes 30+ HD channels.

Cinemax
Subscribers: N.A.
Fee: $8.00 monthly. Includes 3 channels.

HBO
Subscribers: N.A.
Fee: $15.50 monthly. Includes 4 channels.

Showtime/TMC/Flix
Subscribers: N.A.
Fee: $13.50 monthly. Includes 8 channels.

Starz/Starz Encore
Subscribers: N.A.
Fee: $12.50 monthly. Includes 12 channels.

Video-On-Demand: No

Internet Service
Operational: Yes.
Fee: $39.95-$89.95 monthly.

Telephone Service
Digital: Operational
Fee: $10.50-$16.50 monthly
Ownership: Price County Telephone Co.

PHILLIPS—Price County Telephone Co. This cable system has converted to IPTV. See PHILLPS, WI [WI5049]. ICA: WI0119.

PITTSVILLE—Packerland Broadband, 105 Kent St., PO Box 885, Iron Mountain, MI 49801. Phones: 906-774-1291; 906-774-6621; 800-236-8434. Fax: 906-776-2811. E-mail: service@plbb.net; support@packerlandbroadband.com. Web Site: http://www.packerlandbroadband.com. ICA: WI0183.
TV Market Ranking: Outside TV Markets (PITTSVILLE). Franchise award date: January 1, 1987. Franchise expiration date: N.A. Began: January 1, 1988.
Channel capacity: N.A. Channels available but not in use: N.A.

Basic Service
Subscribers: 74.
Programming (received off-air): WAOW (ABC, CW, This TV) Wausau; WEAU (NBC) Eau Claire; WFXS-DT Wittenberg; WHRM-TV (PBS) Wausau; WSAW-TV (CBS, MNT) Wausau.
Programming (via satellite): A&E; Animal Planet; CMT; CNBC; CNN; Discovery Channel; Disney Channel; ESPN; ESPN2; FOX Sports Networks; Freeform; History; Lifetime; MTV; Nickelodeon; Spike TV; Syfy; TBS; The Weather Channel; TLC; TNT; TV Land; USA Network; VH1; WGN America.
Fee: $24.95 installation; $25.95 monthly.

Pay Service 1
Pay Units: 24.
Programming (via satellite): HBO.
Fee: $10.95 monthly (HBO).

Video-On-Demand: No

Internet Service
Operational: Yes.
Fee: $26.95 monthly.

Telephone Service
None
Miles of Plant: 11.0 (coaxial); None (fiber optic). Homes passed: 359.
General Manager: Dan Plante. Technical Supervisor: Chad Kay.
Ownership: Packerland Broadband (MSO).

PLATTEVILLE—CenturyLink Prism. This cable system has converted to IPTV, 135 North Bonson St, Platteville, WI 53818. Phones: 800-475-7526; 608-342-0123. Web Site: http://www.centurylink.com/prismtv. Also serves Belmont Twp., Evergreen Village Mobile Home Park & Platteville Twp. ICA: WI5387.
TV Market Ranking: Below 100 (Evergreen Village Mobile Home Park, PLATTEVILLE, Platteville Twp.). Franchise award date: August 1, 1965. Franchise expiration date: N.A. Began: January 1, 1966.
Channel capacity: N.A. Channels available but not in use: N.A.

Prism Essential
Subscribers: 1,572.
Programming (received off-air): KCRG-TV (ABC, MNT) Cedar Rapids; KFXB-TV (Christian TV Network) Dubuque; KGAN (CBS) Cedar Rapids; KWWL (CW, MeTV, NBC) Waterloo; WBUW (CW) Janesville; WHA-TV (PBS) Madison; WISC-TV (CBS, MNT) Madison; WKOW (ABC, MeTV, This TV) Madison; WMSN-TV (FOX, The Country Network) Madison; WMTV (CW, NBC) Madison.
Programming (via satellite): A&E; AMC; CMT; CNN; Comedy Central; Discovery Channel; Disney Channel; ESPN; ESPN2; Fox News Channel; FOX Sports North; Freeform; HGTV; History; Lifetime; MTV; Nickelodeon; QVC; Spike TV; TBS; The Weather Channel; TLC; TNT; Turner Classic Movies; TV Land; USA Network; VH1; WGN America.
Fee: $34.99 monthly. Includes 140+ channels including music channels.

Prism Complete
Subscribers: N.A.
Fee: $39.99 monthly. Includes 190+ channels including music channels.

Cable Systems—Wisconsin

Prism Preferred
Subscribers: N.A.
Fee: $49.99 monthly. Includes 290+ channels including Showtime/TMC & Starz/Encore.
Prism Premium
Subscribers: N.A.
Fee: $79.99 monthly. Includes 320+ channels including all premium movie channels.
Prism Paquette Latino
Subscribers: N.A.
Fee: $8.49 monthly.
Cinemax
Subscribers: N.A.
Fee: $12.99 monthly.
HBO
Subscribers: N.A.
Fee: $14.99 monthly.
Showtime/TMC
Subscribers: N.A.
Fee: $14.99 monthly.
Starz/Encore
Subscribers: N.A.
Fee: $12.99 monthly.
Internet Service
Operational: Yes.
Fee: $29.95 monthly.
Telephone Service
Digital: Operational
Vice President, Operations: Robert E. Brown.
Ownership: CenturyLink (MSO).

PLATTEVILLE—CenturyLink Prism. This cable system has converted to IPTV. See PLATTEVILLE, WI [WI5387]. ICA: WI0056.

PLATTEVILLE—Formerly served by Mediacom. No longer in operation. ICA: WI0320.

PLYMOUTH—Time Warner Cable. Now served by MILWAUKEE, WI [WI0001]. ICA: WI0064.

PRAIRIE DU CHIEN—Mediacom, 4010 Alexandra Dr, Waterloo, IA 50702. Phones: 845-695-2762; 319-235-2197. Fax: 319-232-7841. Web Site: http://www.mediacomcable.com. Also serves Clayton County, IA; Bridgeport (town), Fennimore, Muscoda & Muscoda Twp., WI. ICA: WI0066.
TV Market Ranking: Below 100 (Clayton County (portions), Crawford County (unincorporated areas) (portions), Fennimore); Outside TV Markets (Bridgeport (town), Clayton County (portions), Crawford County (unincorporated areas) (portions), PRAIRIE DU CHIEN). Franchise award date: N.A. Franchise expiration date: N.A. Began: February 1, 1968.
Channel capacity: N.A. Channels available but not in use: N.A.
Basic Service
Subscribers: 1,703.
Programming (received off-air): KCRG-TV (ABC, MNT) Cedar Rapids; KFXB-TV (Christian TV Network) Dubuque; KGAN (CBS) Cedar Rapids; KRIN (PBS) Waterloo; KWKB (The Works, This TV) Iowa City; KWWL (CW, MeTV, NBC) Waterloo; WHLA-TV (PBS) La Crosse; WKBT-DT (CBS, MNT) La Crosse; WLAX (FOX, MeTV) La Crosse; WMTV (CW, NBC) Madison; WXOW (ABC, CW, This TV) La Crosse; allband FM.
Fee: $43.00 monthly.
Expanded Basic Service 1
Subscribers: N.A.
Programming (via satellite): A&E; AMC; Animal Planet; Cartoon Network; CMT; CNBC; CNN; C-SPAN; Discovery Channel; Disney Channel; ESPN; ESPN2; EWTN Global Catholic Network; FOX Sports Midwest; Freeform; FXM; Hallmark Channel; HGTV; History; HLN; ION Television; Lifetime; MSNBC; Nickelodeon; Pop; Spike TV; Syfy; TBS; The Weather Channel; TLC; TNT; Travel Channel; Trinity Broadcasting Network (TBN); truTV; Turner Classic Movies; TV Land; USA Network; VH1; WGN America.
Digital Basic Service
Subscribers: N.A.
Programming (via satellite): BBC America; Bloomberg Television; Discovery Digital Networks; DMX Music; Fuse; FYI; Golf Channel; GSN; History International; IFC; LMN; Outdoor Channel.
Digital Pay Service 1
Pay Units: N.A.
Programming (via satellite): Cinemax (multiplexed); Flix; HBO (multiplexed); Showtime (multiplexed); Starz (multiplexed); Starz Encore (multiplexed); Sundance TV; The Movie Channel (multiplexed).
Fee: $20.00 installation; $10.00 monthly (Cinemax, HBO, Showtime, Flix, Sundance/TMC or Starz/Encore).
Video-On-Demand: No
Pay-Per-View
ESPN Now (delivered digitally); ETC (delivered digitally); Playboy TV (delivered digitally); Pleasure (delivered digitally); Fresh (delivered digitally); Shorteez (delivered digitally); Vubiquity Inc. (delivered digitally).
Internet Service
Operational: Yes.
Broadband Service: Mediacom High Speed Internet.
Telephone Service
None
Miles of Plant: 74.0 (coaxial); None (fiber optic).
Regional Vice President: Doug Frank. Vice President, Financial Reporting: Kenneth J. Kohrs. General Manager: Doug Nix. Technical Operations Director: Greg Nank. Marketing Director: Steve Schuh. Marketing Coordinator: Joni Lindauer.
Ownership: Mediacom LLC (MSO).

PRENTICE—Packerland Broadband, 105 Kent St., PO Box 885, Iron Mountain, MI 49801. Phones: 906-774-1291; 800-236-8434; 906-774-6621. Fax: 906-776-2811. E-mail: service@plbb.net; support@packerlandbroadband.com. Web Site: http://www.packerlandbroadband.com. ICA: WI0200.
TV Market Ranking: Outside TV Markets (PRENTICE). Franchise award date: January 1, 1985. Franchise expiration date: N.A. Began: May 1, 1986.
Channel capacity: N.A. Channels available but not in use: N.A.
Basic Service
Subscribers: 35.
Programming (received off-air): WAOW (ABC, CW, This TV) Wausau; WEAU (NBC) Eau Claire; WFXS-DT Wittenberg; WJFW-TV (Antenna TV, NBC) Rhinelander; WLEF-TV (PBS) Park Falls; WSAW-TV (CBS, MNT) Wausau.
Programming (via satellite): A&E; AMC; CNN; Comedy Central; Discovery Channel; ESPN; ESPN2; Freeform; History; MTV; Nickelodeon; OWN: Oprah Winfrey Network; Spike TV; Syfy; TBS; The Weather Channel; TLC; TNT; TV Land; USA Network; VH1; WGN America.
Fee: $35.00 installation; $48.95 monthly.

Pay Service 1
Pay Units: N.A.
Programming (via satellite): Flix; Showtime.
Fee: $9.95 monthly.
Video-On-Demand: No
Internet Service
Operational: No.
Telephone Service
None
Miles of Plant: 8.0 (coaxial); None (fiber optic). Homes passed: 250.
General Manager: Dan Plante. Technical Supervisor: Chad Kay.
Ownership: Packerland Broadband (MSO).

PULASKI—Nsight. Formerly [WI0114]. This cable system has converted to IPTV, 450 Security Blvd, Green Bay, WI 54313. Phones: 800-224-3308; 920-617-7000. Fax: 920-822-8665. E-mail: info@nsight.com. Web Site: http://www.nsight.com. ICA: WI5377.
Channel capacity: N.A. Channels available but not in use: N.A.
Tier 1
Subscribers: 1,359.
Fee: $61.90 monthly.
Tier 2
Subscribers: N.A.
Fee: $71.90 monthly.
Tier 3
Subscribers: N.A.
Fee: $79.90 monthly.
Cinemax
Subscribers: N.A.
Fee: $10.95 monthly. Includes 8 channels.
HBO
Subscribers: N.A.
Fee: $15.95 monthly. Includes 7 channels.
Showtime/TMC/Flix
Subscribers: N.A.
Fee: $13.95 monthly. Includes 11 channels.
Starz/Encore
Subscribers: N.A.
Fee: $13.95 monthly. Includes 16 channels.
Internet Service
Operational: Yes.
Fee: $31.00-$69.00 monthly.
Telephone Service
Digital: Operational
Fee: $24.95 monthly
President & Chief Executive Officer: Pat Riordan. Executive Vice President & Corporate Development Director: Rob Riordan. Vice President, Corporate Technical Services & Chief Technical Officer: Jim Lienau.
Ownership: Nsight Telservices.

PULASKI—Nsight. This cable system has converted to IPTV. See PULASKI, WI [WI5377]. ICA: WI0114.

RADISSON—S & K TV Systems. Now served by MIKANA, WI [WI0265]. ICA: WI0336.

RANDOLPH—CenturyLink, PO Box 4065, Monroe, LA 71211. Phone: 920-326-2226. Web Site: http://www.centurylink.com. Also serves Cambria (village), Courtland, Fall River (village), Fort Winnebago, Fountain Prairie, Fox Lake Twp., Friesland, Lowville, Marcellon, Otsego, Pacific, Pardeeville (village), Rio (village), Springvale, Westford & Wyocena. ICA: WI0048.
TV Market Ranking: 93 (Cambria (village), Fall River (village), Fort Winnebago, Fountain Prairie, Fox Lake Twp., Lowville, Marcellon, Otsego, Pacific, Pardeeville (village), Rio (village), Wyocena); Outside TV Markets (Courtland). Franchise award date: N.A. Franchise expiration date: N.A. Began: October 1, 1982.
Channel capacity: N.A. Channels available but not in use: N.A.
Basic Service
Subscribers: 656.
Programming (received off-air): WBUW (CW) Janesville; WHA-TV (PBS) Madison; WISC-TV (CBS, MNT) Madison; WKOW (ABC, MeTV, This TV) Madison; WMSN-TV (FOX, The Country Network) Madison; WMTV (CW, NBC) Madison; WMVS (PBS) Milwaukee.
Programming (via satellite): WGN America.
Fee: $35.00 installation; $21.95 monthly.
Expanded Basic Service 1
Subscribers: N.A.
Programming (via satellite): A&E; AMC; CMT; CNN; Comedy Central; C-SPAN; Discovery Channel; Disney Channel; ESPN; ESPN2; FOX Sports North; Freeform; Golf Channel; HGTV; History; Lifetime; Nickelodeon; Outdoor Channel; Spike TV; Syfy; TBS; The Weather Channel; TLC; TNT; TV Land; USA Network.
Fee: $23.00 monthly.
Pay Service 1
Pay Units: N.A.
Programming (via satellite): Cinemax; HBO; Showtime.
Fee: $10.95 monthly (Cinemax), $12.95 monthly (Showtime), $13.50 monthly (HBO).
Video-On-Demand: No
Internet Service
Operational: Yes.
Fee: $29.95 monthly.
Telephone Service
Digital: Operational
Miles of Plant: 104.0 (coaxial); 30.0 (fiber optic). Homes passed: 4,472.
Vice President, Operations: Robert E. Brown. Assistant Secretary: Joan Randazzo.
Ownership: CenturyLink (MSO).

RANDOM LAKE (village)—Time Warner Cable. Now served by MILWAUKEE, WI [WI0001]. ICA: WI0059.

RHINELANDER—Charter Communications. Now served by STEVENS POINT, WI [WI0019]. ICA: WI0037.

RIB LAKE—Formerly served by Citizens Communications. No longer in operation. ICA: WI0177.

RICE LAKE—Charter Communications. Now served by EAU CLAIRE, WI [WI0011]. ICA: WI0055.

2017 Edition

D-865

Wisconsin—Cable Systems

RICHLAND CENTER—Richland Center Cable TV, 2358 Gaetree Ln SE, Grand Rapids, MI 49546. E-mail: richlandcentercable@mail.com. ICA: WI0277.
TV Market Ranking: Franchise award date: N.A. Franchise expiration date: N.A. Began: August 1, 1954.
Channel capacity: N.A. Channels available but not in use: N.A.
Basic Service
Subscribers: 2,942.
Programming (received off-air): WHA-TV (PBS) Madison; WISC-TV (CBS, MNT) Madison; WKOW (ABC, MeTV, This TV) Madison; WMSN-TV (FOX, The Country Network) Madison; WMTV (CW, NBC) Madison.
Programming (via satellite): Bravo; C-SPAN; ION Television; Pop; QVC; Spike TV; TNT.
Fee: $42.95 installation; $13.95 monthly.
Expanded Basic Service 1
Subscribers: 2,055.
Programming (via satellite): A&E; AMC; BET; Bravo; Cartoon Network; CNBC; CNN; Comedy Central; Discovery Channel; Disney Channel; E! HD; ESPN; ESPN Classic; EWTN Global Catholic Network; Food Network; Fox News Channel; FOX Sports North; Freeform; FX; Golf Channel; GSN; History; HLN; INSP; Lifetime; MSNBC; National Geographic Channel; Nickelodeon; Oxygen; Syfy; TBS; The Weather Channel; TLC; Travel Channel; truTV; Turner Classic Movies; TV Land; Univision; USA Network; WE tv.
Fee: $29.95 monthly.
Digital Basic Service
Subscribers: 2,109.
Programming (via satellite): Animal Planet; BBC America; Destination America; Discovery Kids Channel; Disney XD; DIY Network; ESPN2; ESPNews; Fox Sports 1; FYI; HGTV; History International; IFC; Investigation Discovery; LMN; MC; MTV Hits; MTV Jams; Nick 2; Nick Jr.; Outdoor Channel; Science Channel; Sundance TV; TeenNick; Tr3s.
Digital Pay Service 1
Pay Units: 301.
Programming (via satellite): Cinemax (multiplexed).
Fee: $10.95 monthly.
Digital Pay Service 2
Pay Units: 242.
Programming (via satellite): HBO (multiplexed).
Fee: $10.95 monthly.
Digital Pay Service 3
Pay Units: 697.
Programming (via satellite): Starz (multiplexed); Starz Encore (multiplexed).
Fee: $11.95 monthly.
Digital Pay Service 4
Pay Units: 310.
Programming (via satellite): Flix; Showtime; The Movie Channel (multiplexed).
Fee: $9.95 monthly (Showtime or TMC/Flix).
Video-On-Demand: No
Pay-Per-View
iN DEMAND (delivered digitally); Shorteez (delivered digitally); Fresh (delivered digitally).
Internet Service
Operational: Yes.
Subscribers: 507.
Broadband Service: AOL for Broadband.
Fee: $49.95 installation.
Telephone Service
None
Miles of Plant: 49.0 (coaxial); None (fiber optic). Homes passed: 4,020.

General Manager: Josh Perkins. Marketing Director: Sylvia Morrison. Customer Service Manager: Chris McElroy.
Ownership: CYS Inc.

ROSHOLT—Formerly served by New Century Communications. No longer in operation. ICA: WI0280.

ROZELLVILLE—Formerly served by New Century Communications. No longer in operation. ICA: WI0281.

RUDOLPH—Charter Communications. Now served by STEVENS POINT, WI [WI0019]. ICA: WI0217.

SABIN—Formerly served by Richland-Grant Telephone Co-op. No longer in operation. ICA: WI5050.

SAND CREEK—Mosaic Telecom, 401 South First St, PO Box 664, Cameron, WI 54822. Phones: 800-924-3405; 715-458-5400. Fax: 715-458-2112. E-mail: chitel@mosaictelecom.net. Web Site: http://www.mosaictelecom.com. Also serves Almena, Cameron, Dallas, Prairie Farm & Ridgeland. ICA: WI0148. **Note:** This system is an overbuild.
TV Market Ranking: Below 100 (Ridgeland, SAND CREEK, Dallas); Outside TV Markets (Almena, Cameron, Prairie Farm). Franchise award date: N.A. Franchise expiration date: N.A. Began: March 1, 1980.
Channel capacity: 35 (not 2-way capable). Channels available but not in use: N.A.
Basic Service
Subscribers: 640.
Programming (received off-air): KARE (NBC, WeatherNation) Minneapolis; KMSP-TV (Bounce TV, Buzzr, FOX) Minneapolis; KSTP-TV (ABC, MeTV) St. Paul; KTCA-TV (PBS) St. Paul; WCCO-TV (CBS, Decades) Minneapolis; WEAU (NBC) Eau Claire; WEUX (FOX, MeTV) Chippewa Falls; WFTC (MNT, Movies!) Minneapolis; WHWC-TV (PBS) Menomonie; WKBT-DT (CBS, MNT) La Crosse; WQOW (ABC, CW, This TV) Eau Claire; WUCW (CW, The Country Network) Minneapolis.
Fee: $60.00 installation; $29.95 monthly.
Expanded Basic Service 1
Subscribers: N.A.
Programming (via satellite): A&E; AMC; Animal Planet; Bloomberg Television; CMT; CNBC; CNN; Comedy Central; C-SPAN; C-SPAN 2; Discovery Channel; Discovery Life Channel; Disney Channel; DIY Network; E! HD; ESPN; ESPN2; ESPNews; Flix; Fox News Channel; Freeform; FX; Golf Channel; HGTV; HLN; INSP; Lifetime; MTV; NBCSN; Nickelodeon; Outdoor Channel; QVC; Spike TV; Syfy; TBS; Telemundo; The Weather Channel; TLC; TNT; Trinity Broadcasting Network (TBN); truTV; TV Land; USA Network; VH1; WGN America.
Fee: $39.95 monthly.
Expanded Basic Service 2
Subscribers: N.A.
Programming (via satellite): Cartoon Network; Fox Sports 1; Great American Country; GSN; Hallmark Channel; History; Travel Channel; Turner Classic Movies; WE tv.
Fee: $5.95 monthly.
Pay Service 1
Pay Units: N.A.
Programming (via satellite): Cinemax (multiplexed); HBO (multiplexed) Showtime (multiplexed); The Movie Channel.

Fee: $11.95 monthly (Cinemax, Showtime or TMC), $9.00 monthly (HBO).
Video-On-Demand: Yes
Internet Service
Operational: Yes.
Telephone Service
Analog: Operational
Miles of Plant: 120.0 (coaxial); 50.0 (fiber optic).
Chief Executive Officer: N. Scott Behn; Rick Vergin. Technical Operations Officer: Scott Hickock.
Ownership: Chibardun Cable TV Corporation.

SAXEVILLE—New Century Communications, 3588 Kennebec Dr, Eagan, MN 55122-1001. Phone: 651-688-2623. Fax: 651-688-2624. ICA: WI0210.
TV Market Ranking: Below 100 (SAXEVILLE). Channel capacity: N.A. Channels available but not in use: N.A.
Basic Service
Subscribers: N.A.
Programming (received off-air): WACY-TV (Escape, Grit, Laff, MNT) Appleton; WBAY-TV (ABC) Green Bay; WFRV-TV (Bounce TV, CBS) Green Bay; WGBA-TV (MeTV, NBC) Green Bay; WLUK-TV (Antenna TV, FOX) Green Bay; WPNE-TV (PBS) Green Bay.
Programming (via satellite): A&E; AMC; Discovery Channel; Disney Channel; ESPN; Freeform; HLN; Lifetime; Nickelodeon; Showtime; Spike TV; TBS; TLC; TNT; Trinity Broadcasting Network (TBN); USA Network; WGN America.
Fee: $30.00 installation.
Video-On-Demand: No
Internet Service
Operational: No.
Telephone Service
None
Miles of Plant: 7.0 (coaxial); None (fiber optic). Homes passed: 183.
Executive Vice President: Marty Walch. General Manager & Chief Technician: Todd Anderson.
Ownership: New Century Communications (MSO).

SENECA (village)—Dairyland Cable Systems Inc, 2494 US Hwy 14 East, Richland Center, WI 53581-2983. Phone: 608-647-6383. Fax: 608-647-7394. Also serves Eastman (unincorporated areas), Lynxville (unincorporated areas) & Mount Sterling (unincorporated areas). ICA: WI0316.
TV Market Ranking: Outside TV Markets (Eastman (unincorporated areas), Lynxville (unincorporated areas), Mount Sterling (unincorporated areas), SENECA (VILLAGE)).
Channel capacity: 36 (not 2-way capable). Channels available but not in use: N.A.
Basic Service
Subscribers: N.A.
Programming (received off-air): KWWL (CW, MeTV, NBC) Waterloo; WHLA-TV (PBS) La Crosse; WKBT-DT (CBS, MNT) La Crosse; WLAX (FOX, MeTV) La Crosse; WMTV (CW, NBC) Madison; WQOW (ABC, CW, This TV) Eau Claire; WXOW (ABC, CW, This TV) La Crosse.
Programming (via satellite): A&E; AMC; Animal Planet; Bravo; CMT; CNN; Discovery Channel; Disney Channel; ESPN; ESPN2; Fox News Channel; Freeform; HGTV; History; Lifetime; Nickelodeon; Spike TV; TBS; TLC; TNT; Travel Channel; USA Network; WGN America.
Fee: $27.31 monthly.
Pay Service 1
Pay Units: N.A.
Programming (via satellite): HBO.

Fee: $10.50 monthly.
Video-On-Demand: No
Internet Service
Operational: No.
Telephone Service
None
Miles of Plant: 17.0 (coaxial); None (fiber optic). Homes passed: 425.
General Manager: Jim Atkinson. Chief Technician: Randy Marshall. Marketing Representative: Brian Sullivan.
Ownership: Dairyland Cable Systems Inc.

SHARON—Charter Communications. Now served by MADISON, WI [WI0002]. ICA: WI0140.

SHEBOYGAN—Charter Communications. Now served by FOND DU LAC, WI [WI0018]. ICA: WI0014.

SIREN—Siren Communications, 7723 Main St, PO Box 426, Siren, WI 54872. Phone: 715-349-2224. Fax: 715-349-2576. E-mail: sirentel@sirentel.net. Web Site: http://sirentel.com. ICA: WI0285.
TV Market Ranking: Outside TV Markets (SIREN). Franchise award date: July 1, 1986. Franchise expiration date: N.A. Began: June 1, 1987.
Channel capacity: N.A. Channels available but not in use: N.A.
Basic Service
Subscribers: 259.
Programming (received off-air): KARE (NBC, WeatherNation) Minneapolis; KMSP-TV (Bounce TV, Buzzr, FOX) Minneapolis; KPXM-TV (ION) St. Cloud; KSTP-TV (ABC, MeTV) St. Paul; KTCA-TV (PBS) St. Paul; WCCO-TV (CBS, Decades) Minneapolis; WEAU (NBC) Eau Claire; WEUX (FOX, MeTV) Chippewa Falls; WFTC (MNT, Movies!) Minneapolis; WHWC-TV (PBS) Menomonie; WQOW (ABC, CW, This TV) Eau Claire; WUCW (CW, The Country Network) Minneapolis.
Fee: $75.00 installation; $48.27 monthly.
Expanded Basic Service 1
Subscribers: 246.
Programming (via satellite): A&E; AMC; CNBC; CNN; C-SPAN; Discovery Channel; ESPN; ESPN2; FOX Sports Midwest; Freeform; HGTV; History; HLN; Lifetime; MTV; Nickelodeon; QVC; Spike TV; TBS; The Weather Channel; TLC; TNT; TV Land; USA Network; VH1; WGN America.
Fee: $76.25 monthly.
Video-On-Demand: No
Internet Service
Operational: Yes.
Broadband Service: In-house.
Fee: $99.00 installation; $43.75-$93.75 monthly.
Telephone Service
Digital: Operational
Fee: $32.00 monthly
Miles of Plant: 22.0 (coaxial); None (fiber optic). Homes passed: 547.
General Manager: Sid Sherstad. Treasurer: Karen Sherstad. Plant Manager: Kent Bassett.
Ownership: Siren Communications (MSO).

SISTER BAY—Charter Communications. Now served by FOND DU LAC, WI [WI0018]. ICA: WI0309.

SOLON SPRINGS—Northwest Community Communications, 116 Harriman Ave North, Amery, WI 54001. Phones: 715-268-6066; 715-268-7101. Fax: 715-268-9194. E-mail: info@nwcomm.net. Web Site: http://www.nwcomm.net. ICA: WI0286.

Cable Systems—Wisconsin

FULLY SEARCHABLE • CONTINUOUSLY UPDATED • DISCOUNT RATES FOR PRINT PURCHASERS

For more information call **800-771-9202** or visit **www.warren-news.com**

TV Market Ranking: 89 (SOLON SPRINGS). Franchise award date: N.A. Franchise expiration date: N.A. Began: January 1, 1989.
Channel capacity: 36 (not 2-way capable). Channels available but not in use: N.A.
Basic Service
Subscribers: 111.
Programming (received off-air): KARE (NBC, WeatherNation) Minneapolis; KMSP-TV (Bounce TV, Buzzr, FOX) Minneapolis; KPXM-TV (ION) St. Cloud; KSTP-TV (ABC, MeTV) St. Paul; KTCA-TV (PBS) St. Paul; WCCO-TV (CBS, Decades) Minneapolis; WEAU (NBC) Eau Claire; WEUX (FOX, MeTV) Chippewa Falls; WFTC (MNT, Movies!) Minneapolis; WHWC-TV (PBS) Menomonie; WQOW (ABC, CW, This TV) Eau Claire; WUCW (CW, The Country Network) Minneapolis.
Programming (via satellite): A&E; AMC; CNBC; CNN; C-SPAN; Discovery Channel; ESPN; ESPN2; FOX Sports Midwest; Freeform; HGTV; History; HLN; Lifetime; MTV; Nickelodeon; QVC; Spike TV; TBS; The Weather Channel; TLC; TNT; TV Land; USA Network; VH1; WGN America.
Fee: $39.50 installation; $47.99 monthly.
Pay Service 1
Pay Units: N.A.
Programming (via satellite): Cinemax; HBO; Showtime.
Fee: $9.00 monthly (each).
Internet Service
Operational: Yes.
Telephone Service
None
Miles of Plant: 22.0 (coaxial); None (fiber optic). Homes passed: 354.
General Manager: Dwight Schmitt. Operations Manager: Myron Ranum.
Ownership: Northwest Community Communications (MSO).

SOMERSET (village)—Northwest Community Communications. Now served by NEW RICHMOND, WI [WI0077]. ICA: WI0146.

SPARTA—Charter Communications. Now served by EAU CLAIRE, WI [WI0011]. ICA: WI0058.

SPENCER—Charter Communications. Now served by STEVENS POINT, WI [WI0019]. ICA: WI0034.

SPOONER—Charter Communications. Now served by EAU CLAIRE, WI [WI0011]. ICA: WI0096.

SPRING VALLEY—Celect Communications. This cable system has converted to IPTV. Now served by ELMWOOD (village), WI [WI5045]. ICA: WI0337.

ST. JOSEPH TWP.—Formerly served by Tele-Communications Cable Co. No longer in operation. ICA: WI0290.

STETSONVILLE—Charter Communications. Now served by STEVENS POINT, WI [WI0019]. ICA: WI0291.

STEUBEN—Formerly served by Steuben Community TV System. No longer in operation. ICA: WI0230.

STEVENS POINT—Charter Communications, 853 McIntosh St, Wausau, WI 54402. Phones: 636-207-5100 (Corporate office); 314-543-2236; 715-845-4223. Web Site: http://www.charter.com. Also serves Abbotsford, Aniwa (village), Antigo, Arbor Vitae, Argonne, Athens, Bear Creek, Belle Plaine, Bergen, Birnamwood, Biron, Black Creek, Bovina, Bowler (village), Bradley (town), Brokaw, Cameron (town), Carson, Cassian (town), Clintonville, Colby, Coloma, Crandon, Crescent, Dakota (town), Dale (town), Dayton (town), Dorchester, Eagle River, Edgar, Ellington, Embarrass, Farmington (town), Grand Rapids, Grant (Portage County), Granton, Gresham, Hancock, Hatley (village), Hazelhurst, Hortonia (town), Hortonville, Hull, Kronenwetter, Larrabee (town), Lebanon (town), Liberty (town), Lincoln, Lincoln (town), Lind (town), Linwood, Lohrville, Loyal, Maine, Maple Creek (town), Marathon City, Marion, Marion (town), Marshfield, Matteson (town), Mattoon (village), McMillan (town), Medford, Merrill, Milladore, Minocqua, Monico, Mosinee, Mukwa (town), Neillsville, Nekoosa, Neshkoro, New London, Newbold, Nokomis, Owen, Park Ridge (village), Pelican, Phelps, Pine Lake, Plainfield, Plover, Plover (village), Port Edwards, Port Edwards (village), Potter, Rantoul (town), Redgranite, Rhinelander, Rib Mountain, Richmond (town), Ringle (town), Rolling (town), Rothschild, Royalton (town), Rudolph, Rudolph (town), Saratoga, Schofield, Seneca, Shawano, Sherry, Shiocton, Spencer, Stella, Stetsonville, Stettin, Stockton (town), Stratford, Sugar Camp, Texas (town), Tomahawk, Two Rivers, Unity, Washington, Washington (town), Waukechon (town), Waupaca, Wausau, Wautoma, Wautoma (town), Wescott (town), Westfield, Weston, Weyauwega, Whiting (village), Wild Rose, Wisconsin Rapids, Withee, Woodboro (town) & Woodruff. ICA: WI0019.
TV Market Ranking: 23 (Farmington (town)); 62 (Belle Plaine, Black Creek, Bovina, Ellington, Embarrass, Maple Creek (town), Potter, Rantoul (town), Shawano, Shiocton, Two Rivers, Washington (town), Waukechon (town)); Below 100 (Abbotsford, Aniwa (village), Arbor Vitae, Argonne, Athens, Bergen, Birnamwood, Bowler (village), Bradley (town), Brokaw, Cameron (town), Carson, Cassian (town), Colby, Crandon, Crescent, Dale (town), Dorchester, Edgar, Granton, Gresham, Hatley (village), Hazelhurst, Hortonia (town), Hortonville, Hull, Kronenwetter, Larrabee (town), Lebanon (town), Liberty (town), Lincoln, Lincoln, Lind (town), Linwood, Maine, Marathon City, Marion, Marshfield, Matteson (town), Mattoon (village), McMillan (town), Milladore, Monico, Mosinee, Mukwa (town), Newbold, Nokomis, Park Ridge (village), Pelican, Pine Lake, Plover, Plover (village), Rib Mountain, Richmond (town), Ringle (town), Rolling (town), Rothschild, Royalton (town), Rudolph (town), Saratoga, Schofield, Sherry, Stella, Stettin, STEVENS POINT, Stockton (town), Stratford, Sugar Camp, Texas (town), Tomahawk, Unity, Washington, Waupaca, Wausau, Wescott (town), Weston, Weyauwega, Whiting (village), Wild Rose, Wisconsin Rapids, Withee, Medford, Spencer (portions), Woodruff, Antigo, Clintonville, Eagle River, Merrill, Minocqua, Rhinelander, Rudolph, Spencer (portions), Stetsonville); Outside TV Markets (Bear Creek, Biron, Coloma, Dakota (town), Dayton (town), Farmington (town), Grand Rapids, Grant (Portage County), Hancock, Lohrville, Loyal, Marion (town), Neillsville, Nekoosa, Neshkoro, Owen, Phelps, Phelps, Plainfield, Port Edwards, Port Edwards (village), Redgranite, Seneca, Wautoma (town), Westfield, Wild Rose, Wisconsin Rapids, Withee, Medford, Spencer (portions), Wautoma). Franchise award date: October 1, 1977. Franchise expiration date: N.A. Began: February 25, 1985.
Channel capacity: 69 (operating 2-way). Channels available but not in use: N.A.
Digital Basic Service
Subscribers: 69,342.
Programming (via satellite): AXS TV; BBC America; Discovery Digital Networks; DIY Network; ESPN; FOX College Sports Central; FOX College Sports Pacific; Fox Sports 2; Fuse; FYI; History International; LMN; MC; NFL Network; Nick 2; Nick Jr.; Nicktoons; Sundance TV; TeenNick; TV Guide Interactive Inc.
Fee: $49.99 installation; $26.99 monthly.
Digital Expanded Basic Service
Subscribers: N.A.
Programming (via satellite): A&E; AMC; Animal Planet; Bravo; Cartoon Network; CMT; CNBC; CNN; Comedy Central; Discovery Channel; Discovery Life Channel; Disney Channel; Disney XD; E! HD; ESPN; ESPN Classic; ESPN2; EVINE Live; EWTN Global Catholic Network; Food Network; Fox News Channel; Fox Sports 1; FOX Sports North; Freeform; FX; Golf Channel; Great American Country; GSN; Hallmark Channel; HGTV; History; HLN; INSP; ION Television; Lifetime; MSNBC; MTV; National Geographic Channel; NBCSN; Nickelodeon; Outdoor Channel; Oxygen; Pop; Spike TV; Syfy; TBS; The Weather Channel; TLC; TNT; Travel Channel; truTV; Turner Classic Movies; TV Land; USA Network; VH1; WE tv.
Fee: $33.84 monthly.
Digital Pay Service 1
Pay Units: N.A.
Programming (via satellite): Cinemax (multiplexed); Flix; HBO (multiplexed); HBO HD; Showtime (multiplexed); Showtime HD; Starz (multiplexed); Starz Encore (multiplexed); The Movie Channel (multiplexed).
Video-On-Demand: Yes
Pay-Per-View
iN DEMAND (delivered digitally); NHL Center Ice (delivered digitally); MLB Extra Innings (delivered digitally); Playboy TV (delivered digitally); Fresh (delivered digitally); Shorteez (delivered digitally).
Internet Service
Operational: Yes.
Subscribers: 68,492.
Broadband Service: Charter Internet.
Fee: $39.99 monthly; $3.95 modem lease.
Telephone Service
Digital: Operational
Subscribers: 41,037.
Fee: $29.99 monthly
Miles of Plant: 4,837.0 (coaxial); 2,035.0 (fiber optic). Homes passed: 188,323.
Vice President: Lisa Washa. Chief Technician: Bruce Wasleske. Marketing Director: Traci Loonstra. Accounting Director: David Sovanski.
Ownership: Charter Communications Inc. (MSO).

STODDARD—Mediacom, 4010 Alexandra Dr, Waterloo, IA 50702. Phones: 845-695-2762; 319-235-2197. Fax: 319-232-7841. Web Site: http://www.mediacomcable.com. Also serves Chaseburg, De Soto & Ferryville. ICA: WI0161.
TV Market Ranking: Below 100 (Chaseburg, De Soto, Ferryville, STODDARD).
Channel capacity: N.A. Channels available but not in use: N.A.
Basic Service
Subscribers: 104.
Fee: $43.00 monthly.
Vice President, Financial Reporting: Kenneth J. Kohrs.
Ownership: Mediacom LLC (MSO).

STURGEON BAY—Charter Communications. Now served by FOND DU LAC, WI [WI0018]. ICA: WI0043.

SUGAR CREEK (town)—Mediacom, 3900 26th Ave, Moline, IL 61265. Phones: 845-695-2762; 309-797-2580. Fax: 309-797-2414. Web Site: http://www.mediacomcable.com. Also serves Elkhorn, La Grange Twp. & Lafayette Twp. ICA: WI0292.
TV Market Ranking: 23 (SUGAR CREEK (TOWN)); Below 100 (Elkhorn, La Grange Twp., Lafayette Twp.).
Channel capacity: N.A. Channels available but not in use: N.A.
Basic Service
Subscribers: 30.
Programming (received off-air): WCGV-TV (MNT, The Country Network) Milwaukee; WDJT-TV (CBS, Decades) Milwaukee; WISN-TV (ABC, Movies!) Milwaukee; WITI (Antenna TV, FOX) Milwaukee; WMVS (PBS) Milwaukee; WTMJ-TV (COZI TV, Escape, Laff, NBC) Milwaukee; WVTV (CW) Milwaukee.
Programming (via satellite): A&E; AMC; CMT; CNBC; CNN; C-SPAN; Discovery Channel; Disney Channel; ESPN; ESPN2; Freeform; HLN; Lifetime; MTV; Nickelodeon; QVC; Spike TV; TBS; The Weather Channel; TLC; TNT; Trinity Broadcasting Network (TBN); USA Network; VH1; WGN America.
Fee: $45.00 installation; $69.95 monthly.
Pay Service 1
Pay Units: N.A.
Programming (via satellite): Showtime (multiplexed).
Fee: $9.95 monthly.
Video-On-Demand: No
Internet Service
Operational: No.
Telephone Service
None
Homes passed: 1,394. Miles of plant included in Moline, IL.
Regional Vice President: Cari Fenzel. Vice President, Financial Reporting: Kenneth J. Kohrs. Engineering Director: Mitch Carlson. Marketing Director: Greg Evans. Technical Operations Manager: Chris Toalson.
Ownership: Mediacom LLC (MSO).

SURING—Packerland Broadband, 105 Kent St, PO Box 885, Iron Mountain, MI 49801. Phone: 800-236-8434. Fax: 906-776-2811. E-mail: service@plbb.net;

Wisconsin—Cable Systems

support@packerlandbroadband.com. Web Site: http://www.packerlandbroadband.com. ICA: WI0346.
Channel capacity: N.A. Channels available but not in use: N.A.
Basic Service
  Subscribers: 68.
  Fee: $24.95 monthly.
  Ownership: Packerland Broadband.

THORP—CenturyLink, PO Box 4065, Monroe, LA 71211. Phones: 715-669-7108; 888-835-2485. Web Site: http://www.centurylink.com. ICA: WI0139.
  TV Market Ranking: Below 100 (THORP). Franchise award date: June 23, 1981. Franchise expiration date: N.A. Began: October 1, 1982.
  Channel capacity: N.A. Channels available but not in use: N.A.
Basic Service
  Subscribers: 216.
  Programming (received off-air): WAOW (ABC, CW, This TV) Wausau; WEAU (NBC) Eau Claire; WEUX (FOX, MeTV) Chippewa Falls; WHWC-TV (PBS) Menomonie; WKBT-DT (CBS, MNT) La Crosse; WQOW (ABC, CW, This TV) Eau Claire; WSAW-TV (CBS, MNT) Wausau.
  Programming (via satellite): WGN America.
  Fee: $20.95 monthly.
Expanded Basic Service 1
  Subscribers: N.A.
  Programming (via satellite): A&E; AMC; Animal Planet; Cartoon Network; CMT; CNN; Comedy Central; Discovery Channel; Disney Channel; ESPN; ESPN2; Food Network; Fox News Channel; Freeform; FX; Hallmark Channel; HGTV; History; Lifetime; MTV; Nickelodeon; QVC; Spike TV; Syfy; TBS; The Weather Channel; TLC; TNT; Travel Channel; Turner Classic Movies; TV Land; USA Network; VH1.
  Fee: $23.00 monthly.
Digital Basic Service
  Subscribers: N.A.
  Programming (via satellite): BBC America; Bloomberg Television; Bravo; Discovery Kids Channel; Discovery Life Channel; Disney XD; DMX Music; ESPN Classic; ESPNews; Fox Sports 1; FXM; FYI; Golf Channel; GSN; History International; IFC; International Television (ITV); LMN; National Geographic Channel; NBCSN; Nick Jr.; Nicktoons; Outdoor Channel; Ovation; TeenNick; Trinity Broadcasting Network (TBN); WE tv.
  Fee: $53.90 monthly.
Pay Service 1
  Pay Units: 68.
  Programming (via satellite): Cinemax; HBO.
  Fee: $15.95 monthly (each).
Pay Service 2
  Pay Units: 48.
  Programming (via satellite): Showtime; The Movie Channel.
  Fee: $11.95 monthly.
Pay Service 3
  Pay Units: N.A.
  Programming (via satellite): Starz; Starz Encore.
  Fee: $10.95 monthly.
Digital Pay Service 1
  Pay Units: N.A.
  Programming (via satellite): Cinemax (multiplexed); HBO (multiplexed); Showtime (multiplexed); Starz; Starz Encore; Sundance TV (multiplexed); The Movie Channel (multiplexed).
  Fee: $10.95 monthly (Cinemax), $11.95 monthly (Starz/Encore), $12.95 monthly (Showtime), $13.50 (HBO), $20.95 monthly (Cinemax/HBO).

Pay-Per-View
  iN DEMAND (delivered digitally).
Internet Service
  Operational: Yes.
Telephone Service
  Digital: Operational
  Miles of Plant: 14.0 (coaxial); None (fiber optic). Homes passed: 700.
  Vice President, Operations: Bob Brown. Assistant Secretary: Joan Randazzo.
  Ownership: CenturyLink (MSO).

THREE LAKES—Karban TV Systems Inc, 73A South Stevens St, Rhinelander, WI 54501. Phones: 715-493-7613; 800-200-0233. Fax: 715-277-2339. E-mail: sales@ktvs.net. Web Site: http://www.ktvs.net. ICA: WI0293.
  TV Market Ranking: Below 100 (THREE LAKES). Franchise award date: N.A. Franchise expiration date: N.A. Began: January 1, 1986.
  Channel capacity: 77 (2-way capable). Channels available but not in use: N.A.
Basic Service
  Subscribers: N.A.
  Programming (received off-air): WFXS-DT Wittenberg; WJFW-TV (Antenna TV, NBC) Rhinelander; WLEF-TV (PBS) Park Falls; WSAW-TV (CBS, MNT) Wausau; WYOW (ABC, CW, This TV) Eagle River.
  Programming (via satellite): A&E; AMC; Animal Planet; CMT; CNBC; CNN; Comedy Central; C-SPAN; CW PLUS; Discovery Channel; Disney Channel; ESPN; ESPN2; EWTN Global Catholic Network; Food Network; Fox News Channel; Fox Sports 1; Freeform; FX; HGTV; History; HLN; Lifetime; MSNBC; NFL Network; Nickelodeon; Outdoor Channel; QVC; Spike TV; Syfy; TBS; The Weather Channel; TLC; TNT; Travel Channel; Trinity Broadcasting Network (TBN); Turner Classic Movies; TV Land; USA Network; VH1; WGN America.
  Fee: $75.00 installation; $48.00 monthly.
Pay Service 1
  Pay Units: N.A.
  Programming (via satellite): Cinemax; HBO.
  Fee: $10.00 monthly (each).
Video-On-Demand: No
Internet Service
  Operational: Yes.
  Fee: $25.00-$65.00 monthly.
Telephone Service
  None
  Miles of Plant: 60.0 (coaxial); 15.0 (fiber optic). Homes passed: 1,200.
  General Manager & Chief Technician: John Karban.
  Ownership: Karban TV Systems Inc. (MSO).

TIGERTON—Wittenberg Cable TV. Now served by WITTENBERG, WI [WI0158]. ICA: WI0169.

TOMAH—Charter Communications. Now served by EAU CLAIRE, WI [WI0011]. ICA: WI0060.

TUSTIN—Formerly served by New Century Communications. No longer in operation. ICA: WI0225.

TWO RIVERS—Charter Communications. Now served by STEVENS POINT, WI [WI0019]. ICA: WI0035.

UPHAM—Packerland Broadband, 105 Kent St., PO Box 885, Iron Mountain, MI 49801. Phone: 800-236-8434. Fax: 906-776-2811. E-mail: service@plbb.net; support@packerlandbroadband.com. Web

Site: http://www.packerlandbroadband.com. ICA: WI0347.
Channel capacity: N.A. Channels available but not in use: N.A.
Basic Service
  Subscribers: 55.
  Fee: $23.95 monthly.
  Ownership: Packerland Broadband.

VESPER—Packerland Broadband, 105 Kent St., PO Box 885, Iron Mountain, MI 49801. Phones: 906-774-1291; 906-774-6621; 800-236-8434. Fax: 906-776-2811. E-mail: service@plbb.net; support@packerlandbroadband.com. Web Site: http://www.packerlandbroadband.com. Also serves Arpin (village). ICA: WI0295.
  TV Market Ranking: Below 100 (Arpin (village), VESPER).
  Channel capacity: N.A. Channels available but not in use: N.A.
Basic Service
  Subscribers: 46.
  Programming (received off-air): WAOW (ABC, CW, This TV) Wausau; WFXS-DT Wittenberg; WHRM-TV (PBS) Wausau; WSAW-TV (CBS, MNT) Wausau.
  Programming (via satellite): A&E; AMC; Animal Planet; CMT; CNBC; CNN; Discovery Channel; Disney Channel; ESPN; ESPN2; FOX Sports Networks; Freeform; History; Lifetime; MTV; Nickelodeon; Spike TV; Syfy; TBS; The Weather Channel; TLC; TNT; TV Land; USA Network; VH1; WGN America.
  Fee: $24.95 installation; $26.95 monthly; $1.50 converter.
Pay Service 1
  Pay Units: 24.
  Programming (via satellite): HBO.
  Fee: $14.95 installation; $10.95 monthly.
Video-On-Demand: No
Internet Service
  Operational: Yes.
  Fee: $26.95 monthly.
Telephone Service
  None
  Miles of Plant: 18.0 (coaxial); None (fiber optic). Homes passed: 474.
  General Manager: Dan Plante. Technical Supervisor: Chad Kay.
  Ownership: Packerland Broadband (MSO).

VIROQUA—Mediacom, 4010 Alexandra Dr, Waterloo, IA 50702. Phones: 845-695-2762; 319-235-2197. Fax: 319-232-7841. Web Site: http://www.mediacomcable.com. Also serves Brookview Trailer Court, Cashton, Coon Valley, Crawford County (portions), Gays Mills, Greenfield (La Crosse County), La Crosse, La Farge, Readstown, Shelby, Soldier's Grove, Vernon County (portions), Viola & Westby. ICA: WI0068.
  TV Market Ranking: Below 100 (Brookview Trailer Court, Greenfield (La Crosse County), La Crosse, La Farge, Shelby, Viola, VIROQUA, Westby, Cashton, Coon Valley, Vernon County (portions)); Outside TV Markets (Gays Mills, Readstown, Soldier's Grove, Vernon County (portions)). Franchise award date: N.A. Franchise expiration date: N.A. Began: January 1, 1968.
  Channel capacity: N.A. Channels available but not in use: N.A.
Basic Service
  Subscribers: 936.
  Programming (received off-air): WEAU (NBC) Eau Claire; WHLA-TV (PBS) La Crosse; WKBT-DT (CBS, MNT) La Crosse; WLAX (FOX, MeTV) La Crosse; WXOW (ABC, CW, This TV) La Crosse.

  Programming (via satellite): C-SPAN; C-SPAN 2; EWTN Global Catholic Network; Pop; QVC; Trinity Broadcasting Network (TBN); WGN America.
  Fee: $35.16 installation; $55.07 monthly; $1.58 converter.
Expanded Basic Service 1
  Subscribers: N.A.
  Programming (via satellite): A&E; AMC; Animal Planet; Bravo; Cartoon Network; CMT; CNBC; CNN; Comedy Central; Discovery Channel; Disney Channel; E! HD; ESPN; ESPN2; Food Network; Fox News Channel; Fox Sports 1; FOX Sports Networks; Freeform; FX; FXM; Hallmark Channel; HGTV; History; HLN; INSP; Lifetime; LMN; MSNBC; MTV; NBCSN; Nickelodeon; RFD-TV; Spike TV; Syfy; TBS; The Weather Channel; TLC; TNT; Travel Channel; truTV; Turner Classic Movies; TV Land; USA Network; VH1.
  Fee: $17.94 monthly.
Digital Basic Service
  Subscribers: N.A.
  Programming (via satellite): AXS TV; BBC America; Bloomberg Television; Cloo; Discovery Digital Networks; ESPN; ESPN2; ESPNews; Fuse; FYI; Golf Channel; GSN; HD Theater; History International; IFC; MC; National Geographic Channel; Nick Jr.; Nicktoons; Outdoor Channel; TeenNick; TVG Network; Universal HD.
Digital Pay Service 1
  Pay Units: N.A.
  Programming (via satellite): Cinemax (multiplexed); Flix (multiplexed); HBO (multiplexed); HBO HD; Showtime (multiplexed); Showtime HD; Starz (multiplexed); Starz Encore (multiplexed); Starz HD; Sundance TV (multiplexed); The Movie Channel (multiplexed); The Movie Channel HD.
Video-On-Demand: No
Pay-Per-View
  ESPN (delivered digitally); Fresh (delivered digitally); Shorteez (delivered digitally); Playboy TV (delivered digitally); Pleasure (delivered digitally); SexSee (delivered digitally).
Internet Service
  Operational: Yes.
  Broadband Service: Mediacom High Speed Internet.
Telephone Service
  None
  Miles of Plant: 108.0 (coaxial); None (fiber optic). Homes passed: 4,979.
  Regional Vice President: Doug Frank. Vice President, Financial Reporting: Kenneth J. Kohrs. General Manager: Doug Nix. Technical Operations Director: Greg Nank. Marketing Director: Steve Schuh. Marketing Coordinator: Joni Lindaur.
  Ownership: Mediacom LLC (MSO).

WABENO—Packerland Broadband, 105 Kent St., PO Box 885, Iron Mountain, MI 49801. Phone: 800-236-8434. Fax: 906-776-2811. E-mail: service@plbb.net; support@packerlandbroadband.com. Web Site: http://www.packerlandbroadband.com. ICA: WI0332.
  Channel capacity: N.A. Channels available but not in use: N.A.
Basic Service
  Subscribers: 92.
  Fee: $23.95 monthly.
  Ownership: Packerland Broadband.

WARRENS—Charter Communications. Now served by EAU CLAIRE, WI [WI0011]. ICA: WI0319.

Cable Systems—Wisconsin

WASHINGTON—Packerland Broadband, 105 Kent St., PO Box 885, Iron Mountain, MI 49801. Phone: 800-236-8434. Fax: 906-776-2811. E-mail: service@plbb.net; support@packerlandbroadband.com. Web Site: http://www.packerlandbroadband.com. ICA: WI0348.
Channel capacity: N.A. Channels available but not in use: N.A.
Basic Service
Subscribers: 135.
Fee: $24.95 monthly.
Ownership: Packerland Broadband.

WAUSAU—Charter Communications. Now served by STEVENS POINT, WI [WI0019]. ICA: WI0012.

WAUTOMA—Charter Communications. Now served by STEVENS POINT, WI [WI0019]. ICA: WI0057.

WAUWATOSA—Time Warner Cable. Now served by MILWAUKEE, WI [WI0001]. ICA: WI0004.

WAUZEKA—Packerland Broadband, 105 Kent St., PO Box 885, Iron Mountain, MI 49801. Phones: 906-774-1291; 800-236-8434; 906-774-6621. Fax: 906-776-2811. E-mail: service@plbb.net; support@packerlandbroadband.com. Web Site: http://www.packerlandbroadband.com. ICA: WI0324.
TV Market Ranking: Outside TV Markets (WAUZEKA).
Channel capacity: N.A. Channels available but not in use: N.A.
Basic Service
Subscribers: 37.
Programming (received off-air): KWWL (CW, MeTV, NBC) Waterloo; WHA-TV (PBS) Madison; WKBT-DT (CBS, MNT) La Crosse; WKOW (ABC, MeTV, This TV) Madison; WMSN-TV (FOX, The Country Network) Madison; WMTV (CW, NBC) Madison.
Programming (via satellite): CW PLUS; TBS; WGN America.
Fee: $27.95 monthly.
Expanded Basic Service 1
Subscribers: N.A.
Programming (via satellite): A&E; CMT; CNN; Discovery Channel; Disney Channel; E! HD; ESPN; ESPN2; FOX Sports North; Freeform; History; HLN; Nickelodeon; Spike TV; The Weather Channel; TLC; TNT; Turner Classic Movies; USA Network.
Fee: $20.45 monthly.
Pay Service 1
Pay Units: N.A.
Programming (via satellite): HBO.
Fee: $13.95 monthly.
Video-On-Demand: No
Internet Service
Operational: No.
Telephone Service
None
Miles of Plant: 5.0 (coaxial); None (fiber optic). Homes passed: 282.
General Manager: Dan Plante. Technical Supervisor: Chad Kay.
Ownership: Packerland Broadband (MSO).

WEST BEND—Charter Communications. Now served by FOND DU LAC, WI [WI0018]. ICA: WI0323.

WEYERHAEUSER—Formerly served by S & K TV Systems. No longer in operation. ICA: WI0297.

WHITE LAKE—Packerland Broadband, 105 Kent St., PO Box 885, Iron Mountain, MI 49801. Phones: 906-774-1291; 800-236-8434; 906-774-6621. Fax: 906-776-2811. E-mail: service@plbb.net; support@packerlandbroadband.com. Web Site: http://www.packerlandbroadband.com. ICA: WI0298.
TV Market Ranking: Below 100 (WHITE LAKE). Franchise award date: N.A. Franchise expiration date: N.A. Began: May 1, 1990.
Channel capacity: N.A. Channels available but not in use: N.A.
Basic Service
Subscribers: 23.
Programming (received off-air): WACY-TV (Escape, Grit, Laff, MNT) Appleton; WAOW (ABC, CW, This TV) Wausau; WBAY-TV (ABC) Green Bay; WFRV-TV (Bounce TV, CBS) Green Bay; WGBA-TV (MeTV, NBC) Green Bay; WJFW-TV (Antenna TV, NBC) Rhinelander; WLUK-TV (Antenna TV, FOX) Green Bay; WPNE-TV (PBS) Green Bay; WSAW-TV (CBS, MNT) Wausau.
Programming (via satellite): A&E; CNBC; CNN; C-SPAN; Discovery Channel; Disney Channel; ESPN; ESPN2; FOX Sports Networks; Freeform; History; MTV; Nickelodeon; QVC; Spike TV; TBS; The Weather Channel; TLC; TNT; Turner Classic Movies; USA Network; WGN America.
Fee: $25.00 installation; $53.95 monthly.
Pay Service 1
Pay Units: N.A.
Programming (via satellite): Cinemax; HBO.
Fee: $10.95 monthly (each) or $17.95 monthly (Cinemax/HBO).
Video-On-Demand: No
Internet Service
Operational: No.
Telephone Service
None
Miles of Plant: 7.0 (coaxial); None (fiber optic). Homes passed: 220.
General Manager: Dan Plante. Technical Supervisor: Chad Kay.
Ownership: Packerland Broadband (MSO).

WHITEHALL—Western Wisconsin Communications Cooperative, 417 5th Ave North, PO Box 578, Strum, WI 54770. Phones: 715-985-3101; 715-695-2691; 800-831-0610; 715-985-3101. Fax: 715-985-3261. E-mail: wwcc@triwest.net. Web Site: http://tccpro.net. Also serves Alma Center, Arcadia, Blair, Eleva, Ettrick, Fairchild, Galesville, Hixton, Humbird, Independence, Lincoln Twp., Merillan, Northfield, Osseo, Pigeon, Pigeon Falls, Strum, Taylor & Trempealeau County. ICA: WI0032.
TV Market Ranking: Below 100 (Arcadia, Blair, Eleva, Ettrick, Fairchild, Galesville, Independence, Lincoln Twp., Osseo, Pigeon, Pigeon Falls, Strum, Taylor, Trempealeau County (portions), WHITEHALL); Outside TV Markets (Alma Center, Hixton, Humbird, Merillan, Northfield, Trempealeau County (portions)). Franchise award date: January 1, 1977. Franchise expiration date: N.A. Began: January 1, 1980.
Channel capacity: 52 (operating 2-way). Channels available but not in use: N.A.
Basic Service
Subscribers: 4,799.
Programming (received off-air): WEAU (NBC) Eau Claire; WHLA-TV (PBS) La Crosse; WKBT-DT (CBS, MNT) La Crosse; WLAX (FOX, MeTV) La Crosse; WXOW (ABC, CW, This TV) La Crosse; allband FM.
Programming (via satellite): A&E; Animal Planet; BTN; Cartoon Network; CMT; CNN; Comedy Central; C-SPAN; CW PLUS; Discovery Channel; Disney Channel; ESPN; ESPN Classic; ESPN2; Food Network; Fox News Channel; FOX Sports North; Freeform; FX; Great American Country; HGTV; History; HLN; Lifetime; MSNBC; MTV; MyNetworkTV; NFL Network; Nickelodeon; Pop; Spike TV; Syfy; TBS; The Weather Channel; TLC; TNT; Travel Channel; Turner Classic Movies; TV Land; USA Network; VH1; Weatherscan; WGN America.
Fee: $25.00 installation; $56.14 monthly.
Digital Basic Service
Subscribers: N.A.
Programming (via satellite): BBC America; BBC World News; Bloomberg Television; Cloo; CMT; Destination America; Discovery Kids Channel; Discovery Life Channel; Disney XD; DIY Network; DMX Music; ESPNews; ESPNU; EWTN Global Catholic Network; Fox Sports 1; Fuse; FXM; FYI; Golf Channel; GSN; Hallmark Channel; History International; Investigation Discovery; LMN; MTV Classic; MTV2; National Geographic Channel; NBCSN; Nick Jr.; Nicktoons; Outdoor Channel; RFD-TV; Science Channel; TeenNick; Trinity Broadcasting Network (TBN); WE tv.
Fee: $25.00 installation; $16.00 monthly.
Digital Expanded Basic Service
Subscribers: N.A.
Programming (via satellite): A&E HD; Animal Planet HD; AXS TV; BTN HD; Discovery Channel HD; ESPN HD; ESPN2 HD; FSN HD; HD Theater; History HD; NFL Network HD; Outdoor Channel 2 HD; TBS HD; TNT HD.
Fee: $10.00 monthly.
Digital Expanded Basic Service 2
Subscribers: N.A.
Programming (via satellite): Cine Mexicano; Cinelatino; CNN en Espanol; ESPN Deportes; Fox Deportes; History en Espanol; NBC Universo; Tr3s; ViendoMovies.
Fee: $5.95 monthly.
Digital Pay Service 1
Pay Units: N.A.
Programming (via satellite): Cinemax (multiplexed); Cinemax HD; Flix; HBO (multiplexed); HBO HD; Showtime (multiplexed); Starz (multiplexed); Starz Encore (multiplexed); Sundance TV; The Movie Channel (multiplexed).
Fee: $16.99 monthly (Starz/Encore), $18.99 monthly (Showtime/TMC/Flix/Sundance), $19.99 monthly (Cinemax/Cinemax HD/HBO/HBO HD).
Video-On-Demand: No
Pay-Per-View
iN DEMAND (delivered digitally).
Internet Service
Operational: Yes.
Subscribers: 2,722.
Broadband Service: TriWest-Airstream.
Fee: $50.00 installation; $37.45-$53.45 monthly; $5.00 modem lease.
Telephone Service
Analog: Operational
Miles of Plant: 610.0 (coaxial); 213.0 (fiber optic). Homes passed: 10,700.
Chief Executive Officer: Fred Weier. Chief Operating Officer: Cheryl Rue. General Manager: Mark Schroeder. Chief Technician: Michael Flory.
Ownership: Tri-County Communications Cooperative Inc.

WHITEWATER—Charter Communications. Now served by MADISON, WI [WI0002]. ICA: WI0045.

WILTON—Mediacom. Now served by MAUSTON, WI [WI0084]. ICA: WI0302.

WISCONSIN RAPIDS—Charter Communications. Now served by STEVENS POINT, WI [WI0019]. ICA: WI0022.

WISCONSIN RAPIDS—Solarus, 440 East Grand Ave, PO Box 8045, Wisconsin Rapids, WI 54495. Phones: 800-421-9282; 715-421-8111. Fax: 715-421-6081. E-mail: support@solarus.net. Web Site: http://www.solarus.net. Also serves Armenia, Boron, Carson, Grand Rapids, Grant, Linwood, Nekoosa, Plover (town), Port Edwards, Rome Twp., Rudolph (town), Rudolph (village), Saratoga, Seneca, Sherry & Sigel. ICA: WI0279.
TV Market Ranking: Below 100 (Carson, Linwood, Plover (town), Rudolph (town), Rudolph (village), Saratoga, Sherry); Outside TV Markets (Armenia, Boron, Grand Rapids, Grant, Nekoosa, Port Edwards, Seneca, Sigel, Rome Twp., WISCONSIN RAPIDS). Franchise award date: N.A. Franchise expiration date: N.A. Began: January 1, 1984.
Channel capacity: N.A. Channels available but not in use: N.A.
Basic Service
Subscribers: 844.
Programming (received off-air): WAOW (ABC, CW, This TV) Wausau; WEAU (NBC) Eau Claire; WFXS-DT Wittenberg; WHRM-TV (PBS) Wausau; WSAW-TV (CBS, MNT) Wausau.
Programming (via satellite): Cartoon Network; CNN; Lifetime; Nickelodeon; TBS; Turner Classic Movies; USA Network; WGN America.
Fee: $25.00 installation; $23.99 monthly.
Pay Service 1
Pay Units: 80.
Programming (via satellite): Cinemax.
Fee: $8.00 monthly.
Pay Service 2
Pay Units: 127.
Programming (via satellite): HBO.
Fee: $10.00 monthly.
Video-On-Demand: No
Internet Service
Operational: Yes. Began: January 1, 2001.
Subscribers: 200.
Broadband Service: In-house.
Fee: $29.95 monthly; $6.95 modem lease.
Telephone Service
Analog: Operational
Miles of Plant: None (coaxial); 626.0 (fiber optic). Homes passed: 17,000.
Chief Executive Officer & General Manager: Douglas Wenzlaff. Operations Director:

Wisconsin—Cable Systems

Jamey Lysne. Sales & Marketing Director: Michael Meinel. Controller: Greg Krings. Ownership: Solarus.

WITTENBERG—Wittenberg Cable TV, 104 West Walker St, PO Box 160, Wittenberg, WI 54499-0160. Phones: 715-253-2111; 715-253-2828. Fax: 715-253-3497. E-mail: wittenbergtel@wittenbergnet.net. Web Site: http://www.wittenbergnet.net. Also serves Bevent, Eland, Elderdon, Galloway, Reid & Tigerton. ICA: WI0158.

TV Market Ranking: Below 100 (Bevent, Eland, ELDERDON, Galloway, Reid, WITTENBERG, Tigerton). Franchise award date: March 30, 1980. Franchise expiration date: N.A. Began: March 15, 1982.

Channel capacity: N.A. Channels available but not in use: N.A.

Basic Service
Subscribers: 671. Commercial subscribers: 88.
Programming (received off-air): WACY-TV (Escape, Grit, Laff, MNT) Appleton; WAOW (ABC, CW, This TV) Wausau; WBAY-TV (ABC) Green Bay; WFRV-TV (Bounce TV, CBS) Green Bay; WFXS-DT Wittenberg; WGBA-TV (MeTV, NBC) Green Bay; WHRM-TV (PBS) Wausau; WJFW-TV (Antenna TV, NBC) Rhinelander; WLUK-TV (Antenna TV, FOX) Green Bay; WSAW-TV (CBS, MNT) Wausau.
Programming (via satellite): A&E; AMC; Animal Planet; Bravo; CMT; CNN; Comedy Central; C-SPAN; Discovery Channel; Disney Channel; ESPN; ESPN Classic; ESPN2; Fox News Channel; Fox Sports 1; FOX Sports Networks; Freeform; FX; Hallmark Channel; HGTV; History; Lifetime; MTV; Nickelodeon; Outdoor Channel; RFD-TV; Spike TV; Syfy; TBS; The Weather Channel; TLC; TNT; Travel Channel; Turner Classic Movies; TV Land; USA Network; VH1; WGN America.
Fee: $50.00 installation; $62.90 monthly.

Pay Service 1
Pay Units: 116.
Programming (via satellite): HBO.
Fee: $7.50 installation; $12.75 monthly.

Pay Service 2
Pay Units: 36.
Programming (via satellite): Showtime.
Fee: $12.75 monthly.

Video-On-Demand: No

Internet Service
Operational: No, DSL.

Telephone Service
Analog: Operational
Miles of Plant: 67.0 (coaxial); 19.0 (fiber optic).
General Manager & Chief Technician: Allen Mahnke.
Ownership: Wittenberg Telephone Co. (MSO).

WOLF RIVER—New Century Communications, 3588 Kennebec Dr, Eagan, MN 55122-1001. Phone: 651-688-2623. Fax: 651-688-2624. ICA: WI0185.

TV Market Ranking: Below 100 (WOLF RIVER).
Channel capacity: N.A. Channels available but not in use: N.A.

Basic Service
Subscribers: N.A.
Programming (received off-air): WACY-TV (Escape, Grit, Laff, MNT) Appleton; WBAY-TV (ABC) Green Bay; WCWF (CW) Suring; WFRV-TV (Bounce TV, CBS) Green Bay; WGBA-TV (MeTV, NBC) Green Bay; WLUK-TV (Antenna TV, FOX) Green Bay; WPNE-TV (PBS) Green Bay.
Programming (via satellite): A&E; AMC; Animal Planet; CMT; CNN; Discovery Channel; Disney Channel; ESPN; ESPN2; Food Network; Fox Sports 1; FOX Sports North; Freeform; FX; Golf Channel; HGTV; History; Lifetime; MTV; Nickelodeon; Outdoor Channel; QVC; Spike TV; Syfy; TBS; The Weather Channel; TLC; TNT; TV Land; USA Network; VH1; WGN America.
Fee: $30.00 installation.

Digital Basic Service
Subscribers: N.A.
Programming (via satellite): BBC America; Bloomberg Television; Bravo; Cloo; CMT; Discovery Life Channel; Disney XD; DMX Music; ESPN Classic; ESPNews; Fuse; FXM; FYI; GSN; History; History International; IFC; LMN; MTV Classic; MTV2; NBCSN; Nick Jr.; Nicktoons; Science Channel; TeenNick; Trinity Broadcasting Network (TBN); Turner Classic Movies; UP; WE tv.
Fee: $11.00 monthly.

Digital Pay Service 1
Pay Units: N.A.
Programming (via satellite): Cinemax (multiplexed); HBO (multiplexed); Showtime (multiplexed); Starz (multiplexed); Starz Encore (multiplexed).
Fee: $9.95 monthly (Cinemax), $10.95 monthly (Starz/Encore), $12.95 monthly (Showtime), $13.95 monthly (HBO).

Video-On-Demand: No

Pay-Per-View
Playboy TV (delivered digitally); Spice (delivered digitally).

Internet Service
Operational: Yes.
Broadband Service: IBBS.
Fee: $49.95 installation; $34.95 monthly.

Telephone Service
None
Miles of Plant: 7.0 (coaxial); None (fiber optic). Homes passed: 298.
Executive Vice President: Marty Walch. General Manager & Chief Technician: Todd Anderson.
Ownership: New Century Communications (MSO).

WONEWOC—Packerland Broadband, 105 Kent St., PO Box 885, Iron Mountain, MI 49801. Phones: 906-774-1291; 800-236-8434; 906-774-6621. Fax: 906-776-2811. E-mail: service@plbb.net; support@packerlandbroadband.com. Web Site: http://www.packerlandbroadband.com. Also serves Union Center. ICA: WI0149.

TV Market Ranking: Outside TV Markets (Union Center, WONEWOC). Franchise award date: January 1, 1963. Franchise expiration date: N.A. Began: May 1, 1964.
Channel capacity: N.A. Channels available but not in use: N.A.

Basic Service
Subscribers: 77.
Programming (received off-air): WBUW (CW) Janesville; WEAU (NBC) Eau Claire; WHA-TV (PBS) Madison; WISC-TV (CBS, MNT) Madison; WKBT-DT (CBS, MNT) La Crosse; WKOW (ABC, MeTV, This TV) Madison; WMSN-TV (FOX, The Country Network) Madison; WMTV (CW, NBC) Madison.
Programming (via satellite): TBS; WGN America.
Fee: $28.95 monthly.

Expanded Basic Service 1
Subscribers: N.A.
Programming (via satellite): A&E; CMT; CNN; Discovery Channel; Disney Channel; E! HD; ESPN; ESPN2; FOX Sports North; Freeform; History; HLN; Nickelodeon; Spike TV; The Weather Channel; TLC; TNT; Turner Classic Movies; TV Land; USA Network.
Fee: $20.45 monthly.

Pay Service 1
Pay Units: N.A.
Programming (via satellite): HBO.
Fee: $13.95 monthly.

Video-On-Demand: No

Internet Service
Operational: No.

Telephone Service
None
Miles of Plant: 9.0 (coaxial); None (fiber optic). Homes passed: 646.
General Manager: Dan Plante. Technical Supervisor: Chad Kay.
Ownership: Packerland Broadband (MSO).

WOODMAN—Formerly served by Woodman TV Cable System. No longer in operation. ICA: WI0300.

WYOMING

Total Systems: 34	Communities with Applications: 0
Total Communities Served: 84	Number of Basic Subscribers: 86,237
Franchises Not Yet Operating: 0	Number of Expanded Basic Subscribers: 22,981
Applications Pending: 0	Number of Pay Units: 2,606

Top 100 Markets Represented: N.A.

For a list of cable communities in this section, see the Cable Community Index located in the back of Cable Volume 2.
For explanation of terms used in cable system listings, see p. D-11.

AFTON (town)—Formerly served by KLiP Interactive. No longer in operation. ICA: WY0030.

BASIN—TCT West Inc. This cable system has converted to IPTV, 1601 South Park Dr, Cody, WY 82414. Phones: 800-354-2911; 307-568-3800. Fax: 307-586-5450. E-mail: support@tctwest.net. Web Site: http://www.tctwest.net. Also serves Burlington, Byron, Cody, Cowley, Deaver, Emblem, Frannie, Greybull, Hyattville, Lovell, Manderson, Meeteese, Otto, Powell, Shell & Ten Sleep. ICA: WY5003.
 TV Market Ranking: Outside TV Markets (BASIN, Burlington, Byron, Cowley, Frannie, Greybull, Lovell, Manderson, Meeteese, Otto, Powell, Shell, Ten Sleep). Channel capacity: N.A. Channels available but not in use: N.A.
Basic
 Subscribers: 3,344.
 Fee: $47.99 monthly. Includes 80+ channels.
Value
 Subscribers: N.A.
 Fee: $75.99 monthly. Includes 125+ channels.
Expanded
 Subscribers: N.A.
 Fee: $83.99 monthly. Includes 160+ channels.
Cinemax
 Subscribers: N.A.
 Fee: $11.50 monthly. Includes 5 channels.
HBO
 Subscribers: N.A.
 Fee: $16.50 monthly. Includes 6 channels.
Showtime/TMC
 Subscribers: N.A.
 Fee: $11.50 monthly. Includes 8 channels.
Starz/Encore
 Subscribers: N.A.
 Fee: $11.50 monthly. Includes 9 channels.
Internet Service
 Operational: Yes.
 Fee: $35.50-$92.50 monthly.
Telephone Service
 Digital: Operational
 Fee: $31.42 monthly
 Miles of Plant: None (coaxial); 500.0 (fiber optic).
 Ownership: TCT West Inc.

BASIN—TCT West Inc. This cable system has converted to IPTV. See BASIN, WY [WY5003]. ICA: WY0072.

BUFFALO—Charter Communications, 12405 Powerscourt Dr, St. Louis, MO 63131. Phones: 636-207-5100 (Corporate office); 307-266-0034; 516-803-2300 (Corporate office); 866-213-6572; 877-273-7626. Web Site: http://www.charter.com. Also serves Johnson County (portions). ICA: WY0019.
 TV Market Ranking: Below 100 (BUFFALO, Johnson County (portions)); Outside TV Markets (Johnson County (portions)). Franchise award date: March 7, 1995. Franchise expiration date: N.A. Began: April 1, 1964.
 Channel capacity: N.A. Channels available but not in use: N.A.
Digital Basic Service
 Subscribers: 1,129.
 Programming (via satellite): A&E HD; AXS TV; BBC America; Bloomberg Television; Bravo; BYUtv; CBS Sports Network; CMT; Cooking Channel; Destination America; Discovery Kids Channel; Discovery Life Channel; Disney XD; DIY Network; DMX Music; ESPN Classic; ESPN HD; ESPN2 HD; ESPNews; FOX College Sports Central; FOX College Sports Pacific; Fox Sports 1; FSN HD; Fuse; FXM; FYI; Golf Channel; GSN; HD Theater; History International; HRTV; IFC; Investigation Discovery; ION Television; LMN; MTV Classic; MTV Hits; MTV Jams; MTV2; Nat Geo WILD; National Geographic Channel; National Geographic Channel HD; NBCSN; NFL Network; NFL Network HD; Nick 2; Nick Jr.; Nicktoons; Outdoor Channel; OWN: Oprah Winfrey Network; RFD-TV; Science Channel; Sprout; TeenNick; TNT HD; Tr3s; Trinity Broadcasting Network (TBN); Universal HD; UP; Versus HD; VH1 Soul.
 Fee: $26.99 monthly; $6.70 converter.
Digital Expanded Basic Service
 Subscribers: N.A.
 Programming (via satellite): A&E; Altitude Sports & Entertainment; AMC; Animal Planet; Cartoon Network; CMT; CNBC; CNN; Comedy Central; Discovery Channel; Disney Channel; E! HD; ESPN; ESPN2; Food Network; Fox News Channel; Freeform; FX; Great American Country; Hallmark Channel; HGTV; History; HLN; INSP; MSNBC; MTV; Nickelodeon; Oxygen; Root Sports Rocky Mountain; Spike TV; Syfy; The Weather Channel; TLC; TNT; Travel Channel; truTV; Turner Classic Movies; TV Land; USA Network; VH1.
 Fee: $36.40 monthly.
Digital Pay Service 1
 Pay Units: N.A.
 Programming (via satellite): Cinemax (multiplexed); HBO (multiplexed); HBO HD; Showtime (multiplexed); Showtime HD; Starz (multiplexed); Starz Encore (multiplexed); Starz HD; The Movie Channel (multiplexed).
 Fee: $49.99 installation; $12.00 monthly (Starz/Encore), $16.15 (Cinemax, HBO or Showtime/TMC).
Video-On-Demand: No
Pay-Per-View
 iN DEMAND (delivered digitally).
Internet Service
 Operational: Yes.
 Subscribers: 1,102.
 Broadband Service: Charter Internet.
 Fee: $29.95 monthly; $3.99 modem lease.
Telephone Service
 Digital: Operational
 Subscribers: 728.
 Fee: $46.99 monthly
 Miles of Plant: 69.0 (coaxial); 19.0 (fiber optic). Homes passed: 3,089.
 President & Chief Executive Officer: Tom Rutledge. General Manager: Clint Rodeman. Accounting Director: David Sovanski.
 Ownership: Charter Communications Inc. (MSO).

BURLINGTON—TCT West. This cable system has converted to IPTV. Now served by BASIN, WY [WY5033]. ICA: WY5004.

BURNS—Formerly served by B & C Cablevision Inc. No longer in operation. ICA: WY0070.

BYRON—Formerly served by Byron Cable TV. No longer in operation. ICA: WY0071.

BYRON—TCT West. This cable system has converted to IPTV. Now served by BASIN, WY [WY5033]. ICA: WY5019.

CASPER—Charter Communications, 12405 Powerscourt Dr, St. Louis, MO 63131. Phones: 636-207-5100 (Corporate office); 866-213-6572; 307-266-0034; 516-803-2300 (Corporate office); 877-273-7626. Web Site: http://www.charter.com. Also serves Bar Nunn, Evansville, Mills, Mountain View (Natrona County) & Natrona County. ICA: WY0001.
 TV Market Ranking: Below 100 (Bar Nunn, CASPER, Evansville, Mills, Natrona County (portions)); Outside TV Markets (Natrona County (portions)). Franchise award date: N.A. Franchise expiration date: N.A. Began: December 24, 1953.
 Channel capacity: N.A. Channels available but not in use: N.A.
Digital Basic Service
 Subscribers: 16,593.
 Programming (via satellite): A&E HD; Altitude Sports & Entertainment; Animal Planet HD; AXS TV; BBC America; Bloomberg Television; Bravo; CBS Sports Network; CMT; CNN HD; Cooking Channel; C-SPAN 3; Destination America; Discovery Channel HD; Discovery Kids Channel; Discovery Life Channel; Disney Channel HD; Disney XD; DIY Network; DMX Music; ESPN Classic; ESPN HD; ESPN2 HD; ESPNews; EVINE Live; Food Network HD; Fox Sports 1; Freeform HD; FSN HD; Fuse; FXM; FYI; Golf Channel; Great American Country; GSN; HD Theater; HGTV HD; History HD; History International; HRTV; IFC; Investigation Discovery; ION Television; Lifetime Movie Network HD; LMN; MTV Classic; MTV Hits; MTV2; Nat Geo WILD; National Geographic Channel; National Geographic Channel HD; NBC Universo; NBCSN; NFL Network HD; NHL Network; Nick Jr.; Nicktoons; Outdoor Channel; OWN: Oprah Winfrey Network; Qubo; RFD-TV; Science Channel; Science HD; Sprout; Syfy HD; TBS HD; TeenNick; The Weather Channel HD; TLC HD; TNT HD; Tr3s; Trinity Broadcasting Network (TBN); Universal HD; USA Network HD; Versus HD; VH1 Soul.
 Fee: $26.99 monthly; $6.70 converter.
Digital Expanded Basic Service
 Subscribers: 15,600.
 Programming (via satellite): A&E; Altitude Sports & Entertainment; AMC; Animal Planet; Cartoon Network; CMT; CNBC; CNN; Comedy Central; C-SPAN 2; Disney Channel; E! HD; ESPN; ESPN2; EWTN Global Catholic Network; Food Network; Fox News Channel; Freeform; FX; Hallmark Channel; HGTV; History; HLN; ION Television; Lifetime; MSNBC; MTV; Nickelodeon; Oxygen; Root Sports Rocky Mountain; Spike TV; Syfy; The Weather Channel; TLC; TNT; Travel Channel; truTV; Turner Classic Movies; TV Land; USA Network; VH1.
 Fee: $42.40 monthly.
Digital Pay Service 1
 Pay Units: N.A.
 Programming (via satellite): Cinemax (multiplexed); Cinemax HD; HBO (multiplexed); HBO HD; Showtime (multiplexed); Showtime HD; Starz (multiplexed); Starz Encore (multiplexed); Starz HD; The Movie Channel (multiplexed); The Movie Channel HD.
 Fee: $12.00 monthly (Starz/Encore), $16.15 (Cinemax, HBO or Showtime/TMC).
Video-On-Demand: Yes
Pay-Per-View
 iN DEMAND (delivered digitally); ESPN (delivered digitally); Fox Deportes (delivered digitally); NBC Universo (delivered digitally); Cinelatino (delivered digitally); History en Espanol (delivered digitally); Tr3s (delivered digitally); CNN en Espanol (delivered digitally); ESPN Deportes On Demand (delivered digitally); Cine Mexicano (delivered digitally); GolTV (delivered digitally); Bandamax (delivered digitally); De Pelicula (delivered digitally); De Pelicula Clasico (delivered digitally); Telehit (delivered digitally); Sports PPV (delivered digitally); MLS Direct Kick (delivered digitally); HBO on Demand (delivered digitally); Showtime on Demand (delivered digitally); Starz On Demand (delivered digitally); Free Speech TV on Demand (delivered digitally); The SPOT on Demand (delivered digitally); MLB Extra Innings (delivered digitally); NHL Center Ice (delivered digitally); FOX College Sports Central (delivered digitally); FOX College Sports Pacific (delivered digitally); ViendoMovies (delivered digitally).

2017 Edition D-871

Wyoming—Cable Systems

Internet Service
Operational: Yes.
Subscribers: 19,611.
Broadband Service: Charter Internet.
Fee: $49.99 installation; $29.95 monthly; $3.99 modem lease.

Telephone Service
Analog: Not Operational
Digital: Operational
Subscribers: 12,180.
Fee: $46.99 monthly
Miles of Plant: 675.0 (coaxial); 126.0 (fiber optic). Homes passed: 35,501.
President & Chief Executive Officer: Tom Rutledge. General Manager: Clint Rodeman. Accounting Director: David Sovanski.
Ownership: Charter Communications Inc. (MSO).

CHEYENNE—Charter Communications, 12405 Powerscourt Dr, St. Louis, MO 63131. Phones: 636-207-5100 (Corporate office); 866-213-6572; 516-803-2300 (Corporate office); 877-273-7626. Web Site: http://www.charter.com. Also serves Laramie County (portions) & Warren AFB. ICA: WY0002.
TV Market Ranking: Below 100 (CHEYENNE, Warren AFB, Laramie County (portions)); Outside TV Markets (Laramie County (portions)). Franchise award date: N.A. Franchise expiration date: N.A. Began: December 1, 1968.
Channel capacity: N.A. Channels available but not in use: N.A.

Digital Basic Service
Subscribers: 19,564.
Programming (received off-air): KLWY (FOX) Cheyenne.
Programming (via satellite): A&E HD; Altitude Sports & Entertainment; Animal Planet HD; AXS TV; BBC America; Bloomberg Television; BlueHighways TV; Bravo; BYUtv; CBS Sports Network; CMT; CNN HD; Cooking Channel; C-SPAN 3; Destination America; Discovery Channel HD; Discovery Kids Channel; Discovery Life Channel; Disney Channel HD; Disney XD; DIY Network; DMX Music; ESPN Classic; ESPN HD; ESPN2 HD; ESPNews; Food Network HD; Fox Sports 1; Freeform HD; FSN HD; Fuse; FXM; FYI; Golf Channel; GSN; HD Theater; HGTV HD; History; History HD; History International; HRTV; IFC; Investigation Discovery; ION Television; Lifetime Movie Network HD; LMN; MTV Classic; MTV Hits; MTV Jams; MTV2; Nat Geo WILD; National Geographic Channel; National Geographic Channel HD; NBC Universo; NBCSN; Nick 2; Nick Jr.; Nicktoons; Outdoor Channel; Outdoor Channel 2 HD; OWN: Oprah Winfrey Network; RFD-TV; Science Channel; Science HD; Sprout; Syfy HD; TBS HD; TeenNick; Tennis Channel; The Weather Channel HD; TLC HD; TNT HD; Tr3s; Trinity Broadcasting Network (TBN); UniMas; Universal HD; UP; USA Network HD; VH1 Soul.
Fee: $26.99 monthly; $6.70 converter.

Digital Expanded Basic Service
Subscribers: N.A.
Programming (via satellite): A&E; Altitude Sports & Entertainment; AMC; Animal Planet; BET; Cartoon Network; CMT; CNBC; CNN; Comedy Central; Discovery Channel; Disney Channel; E! HD; ESPN; ESPN2; Food Network; Fox News Channel; Freeform; FX; Great American Country; Hallmark Channel; HGTV; History; HLN; ION Television; MSNBC; MTV; Nickelodeon; Root Sports Rocky Mountain; Spike TV; Syfy; The Weather Channel; TLC; TNT; truTV; Turner Classic Movies; TV Land; USA Network; VH1.
Fee: $42.40 monthly.

Digital Pay Service 1
Pay Units: N.A.
Programming (via satellite): Cinemax (multiplexed); HBO (multiplexed); HBO HD; Showtime (multiplexed); Showtime HD; Starz (multiplexed); Starz Encore (multiplexed); Starz HD; The Movie Channel (multiplexed); The Movie Channel HD; Versus HD.
Fee: $12.00 monthly (Starz/Encore), $16.15 monthly (Cinemax, HBO or Showtime/TMC).

Video-On-Demand: Yes

Pay-Per-View
iN DEMAND (delivered digitally); ESPN (delivered digitally); NBC Universo (delivered digitally); Cinelatino (delivered digitally); History en Espanol (delivered digitally); Tr3s (delivered digitally); CNN en Espanol (delivered digitally); ESPN Deportes (delivered digitally); Cine Mexicano (delivered digitally); GolTV (delivered digitally); Bandamax (delivered digitally); De Pelicula (delivered digitally); De Pelicula Clasico (delivered digitally); Telehit (delivered digitally); Univision Studios (delivered digitally); NFL Network (delivered digitally); Cinemax On Demand (delivered digitally); HBO on Demand (delivered digitally); Showtime On Demand (delivered digitally); Starz On Demand (delivered digitally); Free Speech TV on Demand (delivered digitally); The SPOT On Demand (delivered digitally); careerSPOT On Demand (delivered digitally); homeSPOT On Demand (delivered digitally); NFL Network HD (delivered digitally); FOX College Sports Central (delivered digitally); FOX College Sports Pacific (delivered digitally); Viendo-Movies (delivered digitally); Fox Deportes (delivered digitally).

Internet Service
Operational: Yes.
Subscribers: 21,949.
Broadband Service: Charter Internet.
Fee: $49.99 installation; $29.95 monthly; $3.99 modem lease.

Telephone Service
Analog: Not Operational
Digital: Operational
Subscribers: 12,873.
Fee: $46.99 monthly
Miles of Plant: 935.0 (coaxial); 223.0 (fiber optic). Homes passed: 42,033.
President & Chief Executive Officer: Tom Rutledge. Regional Vice President: Clint Rodeman. General Manager: Wes Frost. Accounting Director: David Sovanski. Technical Operations Manager: Mitch Winter.
Ownership: Charter Communications Inc. (MSO).

CODY—Charter Communications, 12405 Powerscourt Dr, St. Louis, MO 63131. Phones: 636-207-5100 (Corporate office); 866-773-6303; 877-273-7626; 516-803-2300 (Corporate office). Web Site: http://www.charter.com. Also serves Park County (portions). ICA: WY0010.
TV Market Ranking: Outside TV Markets (CODY, Park County (portions)). Franchise award date: N.A. Franchise expiration date: N.A. Began: October 1, 1954.
Channel capacity: N.A. Channels available but not in use: N.A.

Digital Basic Service
Subscribers: 2,020.
Programming (via satellite): A&E HD; Altitude Sports & Entertainment; Animal Planet HD; AXS TV; BBC America; Bloomberg Television; CBS Sports Network; CMT; Cooking Channel; Destination America; Discovery Channel HD; Discovery Kids Channel; Discovery Life Channel; Disney XD; DIY Network; DMX Music; ESPN Classic; ESPN HD; ESPN2 HD; ESPNews; Fox Sports 1; FSN HD; Fuse; FXM; FYI; Golf Channel; GSN; HD Theater; History International; HRTV; IFC; Investigation Discovery; ION Television; LMN; MTV Classic; MTV Hits; MTV Jams; MTV2; Nat Geo WILD; National Geographic Channel; National Geographic Channel HD; NBCSN; Nick 2; Nick Jr.; Nicktoons; Outdoor Channel; OWN: Oprah Winfrey Network; RFD-TV; Science Channel; Science HD; Sprout; TeenNick; TLC HD; TNT HD; Tr3s; Trinity Broadcasting Network (TBN); Universal HD; UP; Versus HD; VH1 Soul.
Fee: $26.99 monthly; $6.70 converter.

Digital Expanded Basic Service
Subscribers: N.A.
Programming (via satellite): A&E; Altitude Sports & Entertainment; AMC; Animal Planet; Bravo; Cartoon Network; CMT; CNBC; CNN; Comedy Central; Discovery Channel; Disney Channel; E! HD; ESPN; ESPN2; EWTN Global Catholic Network; Food Network; Fox News Channel; Freeform; FX; Great American Country; Hallmark Channel; HGTV; History; HLN; INSP; MSNBC; MTV; Nickelodeon; Oxygen; Root Sports Rocky Mountain; Spike TV; Syfy; The Weather Channel; TLC; TNT; Travel Channel; truTV; Turner Classic Movies; TV Land; USA Network; VH1.
Fee: $42.34 monthly.

Digital Pay Service 1
Pay Units: N.A.
Programming (via satellite): Cinemax (multiplexed); HBO (multiplexed); HBO HD; Showtime (multiplexed); Showtime HD; Starz (multiplexed); Starz Encore (multiplexed); Starz HD; The Movie Channel (multiplexed).
Fee: $12.00 monthly (Starz/Encore), $16.15 monthly (Cinemax, HBO or Showtime/TMC).

Video-On-Demand: No

Pay-Per-View
ESPN (delivered digitally); iN DEMAND (delivered digitally).

Internet Service
Operational: Yes.
Broadband Service: Charter Internet.
Fee: $49.99 installation; $29.95 monthly; $3.99 modem lease.

Telephone Service
Analog: Not Operational
Digital: Operational
Fee: $46.99 monthly
Miles of Plant: 84.0 (coaxial); 15.0 (fiber optic). Homes passed: 4,800.
President & Chief Executive Officer: Tom Rutledge. Regional Vice President & General Manager: Clint Rodeman. Accounting Director: David Sovanski. Chief Technician: Dan Higgins.
Ownership: Charter Communications Inc. (MSO).

COKEVILLE—All West Communications. This cable system has converted to IPTV. See OAKLEY, UT [UT5034]. ICA: WY0054.

COWLEY—Formerly served by Cowley Telecable Inc. No longer in operation. ICA: WY0043.

COWLEY—TCT West. This cable system has converted to IPTV. Now served by BASIN, WY [WY5033]. ICA: WY5005.

DOUGLAS—Vyve Broadband, 234 North Windriver Dr, Douglas, WY 82633. Phones: 800-937-1397; 307-358-3833; 800-759-8448 (local access only); 307-358-3861. Web Site: http://vyvebroadband.com. Also serves Converse County (portions). ICA: WY0012.
TV Market Ranking: Outside TV Markets (Converse County (portions), DOUGLAS). Franchise award date: November 1, 1973. Franchise expiration date: N.A. Began: October 1, 1975.
Channel capacity: N.A. Channels available but not in use: N.A.

Basic Service
Subscribers: 966.
Programming (received off-air): KCWY-DT (CW, NBC) Casper; KFNB (FOX) Casper; KGWC-TV (CBS) Casper; KTWO-TV (ABC) Casper.
Programming (via microwave): KCNC-TV (CBS, Decades) Denver; KMGH-TV (ABC, Azteca America) Denver; KRMA-TV (PBS) Denver; KTVD (MeTV, MNT) Denver; KUSA (NBC, WeatherNation) Denver; KWGN-TV (CW, This TV) Denver.
Programming (via satellite): WGN America.
Fee: $59.95 installation; $25.00 monthly; $2.95 converter.

Expanded Basic Service 1
Subscribers: N.A.
Programming (via satellite): A&E; AMC; Animal Planet; Bravo; Cartoon Network; CMT; CNBC; CNN; Comedy Central; C-SPAN; C-SPAN 2; Discovery Channel; E! HD; ESPN; ESPN2; ESPNews; Food Network; Fox News Channel; Freeform; FX; Hallmark Channel; HGTV; History; HLN; Lifetime; MSNBC; MTV; Nick Jr.; Nickelodeon; Outdoor Channel; OWN: Oprah Winfrey Network; Pop; QVC; Root Sports Rocky Mountain; Spike TV; Syfy; TBS; The Weather Channel; TLC; TNT; Travel Channel; Trinity Broadcasting Network (TBN); truTV; TV Land; USA Network; VH1; WE tv.
Fee: $19.04 monthly.

Digital Basic Service
Subscribers: N.A.
Programming (via satellite): BBC America; Bloomberg Television; Bravo; Discovery Life Channel; DMX Music; ESPN Classic; ESPN2; ESPNews; EVINE Live; Fox Sports 1; FSN Digital Atlantic; FSN Digital Central; FSN Digital Pacific; Fuse; FXM; FYI; Golf Channel; Great American Country; GSN; HGTV; History; History International; IFC; International Television (ITV); LMN; MBC America; National Geographic Channel; NBCSN; Nick Jr.; Nicktoons; Outdoor Channel; Ovation; Sundance TV; Syfy; TeenNick; The Word Network; Trinity Broadcasting Network (TBN); Turner Classic Movies; TV Land; WE tv.
Fee: $11.95 monthly.

Digital Pay Service 1
Pay Units: N.A.
Programming (via satellite): Cinemax (multiplexed); Flix; HBO (multiplexed); Showtime (multiplexed); Starz (multiplexed); Starz Encore (multiplexed); The Movie Channel (multiplexed).
Fee: $11.95 monthly (Cinemax), $13.95 monthly (HBO, Starz/Encore, Showtime/Flix or TMC).

Video-On-Demand: No

Pay-Per-View
iN DEMAND (delivered digitally); Hot Choice (delivered digitally); Playboy TV (delivered digitally); Fresh (delivered digitally); Shorteez (delivered digitally).

Cable Systems—Wyoming

Internet Service
Operational: Yes. Began: August 1, 1998.
Broadband Service: Net Commander.
Fee: $39.95 installation; $51.95 monthly.
Telephone Service
Digital: Operational
Miles of Plant: 32.0 (coaxial); None (fiber optic). Homes passed: 2,800.
President & Chief Executive Officer: Jeffrey DeMond. Vice President, Residential Services: Vin Zachariah. Vice President, Marketing: Diane Quennoz. Senior Vice President, Financial Planning: Daniel White.
Ownership: Vyve Broadband LLC (MSO).

DUBOIS—Formerly served by KLiP Interactive. No longer in operation. ICA: WY0040.

EDGERTON—Formerly served by Tongue River Cable TV Inc. No longer in operation. ICA: WY0032.

EMBLEM—TCT West. This cable system has converted to IPTV. Now served by BASIN, WY [WY5033]. ICA: WY5006.

EVANSTON—All West Communications, 50 West 100 North, Kamas, UT 84036. Phones: 866-255-9378; 435-783-4361. Fax: 434-783-4928. E-mail: questions@allwest.net. Web Site: http://www.allwest.net. Also serves Uinta county (portions). ICA: WY0009.
TV Market Ranking: Outside TV Markets (Uinta County (portions), EVANSTON).
Channel capacity: N.A. Channels available but not in use: N.A.
Basic Service
Subscribers: 2,023.
Programming (received off-air): KBYU-TV (PBS) Provo; KCWC-DT (PBS) Lander; KJZZ-TV (IND) Salt Lake City; KSL-TV (NBC) Salt Lake City; KSTU (Antenna TV, FOX) Salt Lake City; KTVX (ABC, MeTV) Salt Lake City; KUCW (CW, Movies!, The Country Network) Ogden; KUED (PBS) Salt Lake City; KUEN (ETV) Ogden; KUTV (CBS, This TV) Salt Lake City.
Programming (via satellite): HSN; QVC; Telemundo; UniMas; Univision.
Fee: $32.35 monthly.
Expanded Basic Service 1
Subscribers: N.A.
Programming (via satellite): A&E; AMC; Animal Planet; Cartoon Network; CMT; CNBC; CNN; C-SPAN; Discovery Channel; Disney Channel; Disney XD; E! HD; ESPN; ESPN2; Food Network; Fox News Channel; Freeform; FX; Hallmark Channel; HGTV; History; Lifetime; MSNBC; MTV; National Geographic Channel; Nick At Nite; Nickelodeon; Root Sports Rocky Mountain; Spike TV; Syfy; TBS; The Weather Channel; TLC; TNT; truTV; TV Land; Univision; USA Network; VH1.
Internet Service
Operational: Yes.
Telephone Service
Digital: Operational
Fee: $18.95 monthly
President: Matthew Weller.
Ownership: All West Communications.

FRANNIE—TCT West. This cable system has converted to IPTV. Now served by BASIN, WY [WY5033]. ICA: WY5018.

GILLETTE—Charter Communications, 12405 Powerscourt Dr, St. Louis, MO 63131. Phones: 636-207-5100 (Corporate office); 307-257-2189; 307-265-3136; 800-788-9457. Fax: 307-266-6821. Web Site: http:// www.charter.com. Also serves Campbell County (portions). ICA: WY0005.
TV Market Ranking: Outside TV Markets (Campbell County (portions), GILLETTE). Franchise award date: August 1, 1992. Franchise expiration date: N.A. Began: April 1, 1964.
Channel capacity: N.A. Channels available but not in use: N.A.
Digital Basic Service
Subscribers: 7,744.
Programming (via satellite): A&E HD; Altitude Sports & Entertainment; AXS TV; BBC America; Bloomberg Television; Bravo; CBS Sports Network; CMT; Cooking Channel; Destination America; Discovery Kids Channel; Discovery Life Channel; Disney XD; DIY Network; DMX Music; ESPN Classic; ESPN HD; ESPN2 HD; ESPNews; EVINE Live; EWTN Global Catholic Network; Food Network HD; Fox Sports 1; FSN HD; Fuse; FXM; FYI; Golf Channel; Great American Country; GSN; HD Theater; HGTV HD; History HD; History International; HRTV; IFC; Investigation Discovery; ION Television; Lifetime Movie Network HD; LMN; MTV Classic; MTV Hits; MTV2; Nat Geo WILD; National Geographic Channel; National Geographic Channel HD; NBCSN; Nick Jr.; Nicktoons; Outdoor Channel; OWN: Oprah Winfrey Network; Qubo; RFD-TV; Science Channel; Sprout; Syfy HD; TBS HD; TeenNick; TNT HD; Trinity Broadcasting Network (TBN); Universal HD; UP; USA Network HD; Versus HD; VH1 Soul.
Fee: $26.99 monthly; $6.70 converter.
Digital Expanded Basic Service
Subscribers: 6,339.
Programming (via satellite): A&E; Altitude Sports & Entertainment; AMC; Animal Planet; Cartoon Network; CMT; CNBC; CNN; Comedy Central; Discovery Channel; Disney Channel; E! HD; ESPN; ESPN2; Food Network; Hallmark Channel; HGTV; History; HLN; MTV; Oxygen; Root Sports Rocky Mountain; Syfy; The Weather Channel; TNT; Travel Channel; truTV; Turner Classic Movies; TV Land; USA Network; VH1.
Fee: $41.25 monthly.
Digital Pay Service 1
Pay Units: N.A.
Programming (via satellite): Cinemax (multiplexed); HBO (multiplexed); HBO HD; Showtime (multiplexed); Showtime HD; Starz (multiplexed); Starz Encore (multiplexed); Starz HD (multiplexed); The Movie Channel (multiplexed); The Movie Channel HD.
Fee: $12.00 monthly (Starz/Encore), $16.15 monthly (Cinemax, HBO or Showtime/TMC).
Video-On-Demand: Yes
Pay-Per-View
iN DEMAND (delivered digitally); ESPN (delivered digitally); Cinemax On Demand (delivered digitally); HBO on Demand (delivered digitally); Showtime On Demand (delivered digitally); Starz On Demand (delivered digitally); Free Speech TV (delivered digitally); The SPOT On Demand (delivered digitally); careerOn Demand (delivered digitally); homeOn Demand (delivered digitally); NFL Network HD (delivered digitally).
Internet Service
Operational: Yes.
Subscribers: 8,894.
Broadband Service: Charter Internet.
Fee: $49.99 installation; $29.95 monthly; $3.99 modem lease.
Telephone Service
Digital: Operational
Subscribers: 4,919.
Fee: $46.99 monthly
Miles of Plant: 394.0 (coaxial); 83.0 (fiber optic). Homes passed: 16,481.
President & Chief Executive Officer: Tom Rutledge. General Manager: Clint Rodeman. Chief Technician: Dan Higgins. Accounting Director: David Sovanski.
Ownership: Charter Communications Inc. (MSO).

GLENDO—Formerly served by Communi-Comm Services. No longer in operation. ICA: WY0055.

GLENROCK—Vyve Broadband, 234 North Windriver Dr, Douglas, WY 82633. Phone: 855-367-8983. Web Site: http:// vyvebroadband.com. Also serves Rolling Hills. ICA: WY0018.
TV Market Ranking: Below 100 (GLENROCK, Rolling Hills). Franchise award date: June 1, 1972. Franchise expiration date: N.A. Began: February 3, 1974.
Channel capacity: N.A. Channels available but not in use: N.A.
Basic Service
Subscribers: 216.
Programming (received off-air): KCWC-DT (PBS) Lander; KFNB (FOX) Casper; KGWC-TV (CBS) Casper; KTWO-TV (ABC) Casper.
Programming (via microwave): KCWY-DT (CW, NBC) Casper.
Programming (via satellite): KUSA (NBC, WeatherNation) Denver; KWGN-TV (CW, This TV) Denver; QVC; WGN America.
Fee: $59.99 installation; $25.00 monthly.
Expanded Basic Service 1
Subscribers: N.A.
Programming (via satellite): A&E; AMC; Animal Planet; Bravo; Cartoon Network; CMT; CNBC; CNN; Comedy Central; C-SPAN; C-SPAN 2; Discovery Channel; E! HD; ESPN; ESPN Classic; ESPN2; ESPNews; Food Network; Fox News Channel; Freeform; FX; Great American Country; Hallmark Channel; HGTV; History; HLN; Lifetime; MSNBC; MTV; Nick Jr.; Nickelodeon; Outdoor Channel; OWN: Oprah Winfrey Network; Root Sports Rocky Mountain; Spike TV; Syfy; TBS; The Weather Channel; TLC; TNT; Travel Channel; Trinity Broadcasting Network (TBN); truTV; Turner Classic Movies; TV Land; USA Network; VH1; WE tv.
Fee: $19.04 monthly.
Digital Basic Service
Subscribers: N.A.
Programming (via satellite): BBC America; Bloomberg Television; Bravo; Discovery Life Channel; DMX Music; ESPN Classic; ESPN2; ESPNews; EVINE Live; Fox Sports 1; FSN Digital Atlantic; FSN Digital Central; FSN Digital Pacific; Fuse; FXM; FYI; Golf Channel; Great American Country; GSN; HGTV; History; History International; IFC; International Television (ITV); LMN; MBC America; National Geographic Channel; NBCSN; Nick Jr.; Nicktoons; Outdoor Channel; Ovation; Sundance TV; Syfy; TeenNick; The Word Network; Trinity Broadcasting Network (TBN); Turner Classic Movies; TV Land; WE tv.
Fee: $11.95 monthly.
Digital Pay Service 1
Pay Units: 117.
Programming (via satellite): Cinemax (multiplexed).
Fee: $11.95 monthly.
Digital Pay Service 2
Pay Units: 131.
Programming (via satellite): HBO (multiplexed).
Fee: $13.95 monthly.
Digital Pay Service 3
Pay Units: 135.
Programming (via satellite): Starz (multiplexed); Starz Encore (multiplexed).
Fee: $13.95 monthly.
Digital Pay Service 4
Pay Units: 44.
Programming (via satellite): Flix; Showtime (multiplexed); The Movie Channel (multiplexed).
Fee: $13.95 monthly (Showtime/Flix or TMC).
Video-On-Demand: No
Pay-Per-View
iN DEMAND (delivered digitally); Hot Choice (delivered digitally); Playboy TV (delivered digitally); Fresh (delivered digitally); Shorteez (delivered digitally).
Internet Service
Operational: Yes.
Broadband Service: Net Commander.
Fee: $39.95 installation; $51.95 monthly.
Telephone Service
None
Miles of Plant: 28.0 (coaxial); None (fiber optic). Homes passed: 1,352.
President & Chief Executive Officer: Jeffrey DeMond. Senior Vice President, Financial Planning: Daniel White. Vice President, Marketing: Diane Quennoz. Vice President, Residential Services: Vin Zachariah.
Ownership: Vyve Broadband LLC (MSO).

GREEN RIVER—Green River Cable TV. Now served by Sweetwater Cable TV, ROCK SPRINGS, WY [WY0004]. ICA: WY0008.

GREYBULL—Charter Communications, 12405 Powerscourt Dr, St. Louis, MO 63131. Phones: 636-207-5100 (Corporate office); 866-773-6303; 516-803-2300; 877-273-7626. Web Site: http://www.charter.com. Also serves Basin & Big Horn County. ICA: WY0022.
TV Market Ranking: Below 100 (Big Horn County (portions)); Outside TV Markets (Basin, Big Horn County (portions), GREYBULL). Franchise award date: N.A. Franchise expiration date: N.A. Began: March 1, 1956.
Channel capacity: N.A. Channels available but not in use: N.A.
Digital Basic Service
Subscribers: 296.
Programming (via satellite): A&E HD; Animal Planet HD; BBC America; Bloomberg Television; Bravo; CBS Sports Network; CMT; Destination America; Discovery Channel HD; Discovery Kids Channel; Discovery Life Channel; Disney Channel HD; Disney XD; DMX Music; ESPN Classic; ESPN HD; ESPNews; Food Network HD; Fox Sports 1; Freeform HD; Fuse; FXM; FYI; Golf Channel; GSN; HD Theater; HGTV HD; History HD; History International; HRTV; IFC; Investigation Discovery; ION Television; LMN; MTV Classic; MTV Hits; MTV2; Nat Geo WILD; National Geographic Channel; National Geographic Channel HD; NBCSN; Nick Jr.; Nicktoons; Outdoor Channel; OWN: Oprah Winfrey Network; RFD-TV; Science Channel; Science HD; Sprout; Syfy HD; TeenNick; Trinity Broadcasting Network (TBN); Universal HD; UP; USA Network HD; VH1 Soul.
Fee: $26.99 monthly; $6.70 converter.
Digital Expanded Basic Service
Subscribers: N.A.
Programming (via satellite): A&E; Altitude Sports & Entertainment; AMC; Animal Planet; BYUtv; Cartoon Network; CMT; CNBC; CNN; Comedy Central; Discovery Channel; Disney Channel; E! HD; ESPN;

2017 Edition
D-873

Wyoming—Cable Systems

FULLY SEARCHABLE • CONTINUOUSLY UPDATED • DISCOUNT RATES FOR PRINT PURCHASERS

For more information call 800-771-9202 or visit www.warren-news.com

ESPN2; Food Network; Fox News Channel; Freeform; FX; Great American Country; HGTV; History; HLN; INSP; ION Television; Lifetime; MSNBC; MTV; Nickelodeon; Oxygen; Root Sports Rocky Mountain; Spike TV; Syfy; The Weather Channel; TLC; TNT; Travel Channel; truTV; Turner Classic Movies; TV Land; USA Network; VH1.
Fee: $24.68 monthly.

Digital Pay Service 1
Pay Units: N.A.
Programming (via satellite): HBO (multiplexed); HBO HD; Showtime (multiplexed); Starz (multiplexed); Starz Encore (multiplexed); Starz HD; The Movie Channel (multiplexed).
Fee: $12.00 monthly (Encore or Starz/Starz HDTV), $16.15 monthly HBO/HBO HD or Showtime/TMC.

Video-On-Demand: No

Pay-Per-View
iN DEMAND (delivered digitally).

Internet Service
Operational: Yes.
Subscribers: 287.
Broadband Service: Charter Internet.
Fee: $49.99 installation; $29.95 monthly; $3.99 modem lease.

Telephone Service
Digital: Operational
Subscribers: 141.
Fee: $46.99 monthly
Miles of Plant: 40.0 (coaxial); 15.0 (fiber optic). Homes passed: 1,734.
President & Chief Executive Officer: Tom Rutledge. Regional Vice President & General Manager: Clint Rodeman. Chief Technician: Dan Higgins. Accounting Director: David Sovanski.
Ownership: Charter Communications Inc. (MSO).

GREYBULL—TCT West. This cable system has converted to IPTV. Now served by BASIN, WY [WY5033]. ICA: WY5007.

GUERNSEY—WinDBreak Cable, 1140 10th St, Gering, NE 69341-3239. Phones: 800-282-4650; 308-436-4650. Fax: 308-436-4779. E-mail: bill@intertech.net. Web Site: http://www.windbreak.com. Also serves Fort Laramie & Hartville. ICA: WY0026.
TV Market Ranking: Outside TV Markets (Fort Laramie, GUERNSEY, Hartville). Franchise award date: N.A. Franchise expiration date: N.A. Began: March 16, 1978.
Channel capacity: N.A. Channels available but not in use: N.A.

Basic Service
Subscribers: 153.
Programming (via microwave): KGWN-TV (CBS, CW) Cheyenne; KNEP (ABC) Scottsbluff; KSTF (CBS, CW) Scottsbluff; KTNE-TV (PBS) Alliance; KTWO-TV (ABC) Casper. Programming (via satellite): Cartoon Network; CNN; ESPN; Freeform; HLN; KCNC-TV (CBS, Decades) Denver; KMGH-TV (ABC, Azteca America) Denver; KRMA-TV (PBS) Denver; KUSA (NBC, WeatherNation) Denver; KWGN-TV (CW,

This TV) Denver; Spike TV; TBS; TNT; Turner Classic Movies; USA Network.
Fee: $34.95 installation; $39.00 monthly.

Pay Service 1
Pay Units: 33.
Programming (via satellite): HBO; Starz; Starz Encore.
Fee: $2.00 monthly (Encore), $11 monthly (Starz/Encore), $14 monthly (HBO).

Video-On-Demand: No

Internet Service
Operational: Yes.
Subscribers: 115.
Fee: $34.95 installation; $29.95 monthly.

Telephone Service
None
Miles of Plant: 16.0 (coaxial); None (fiber optic). Homes passed: 796.
General Manager & Chief Technician: Bill Bauer. Office Manager: Aubrey Luevano.
Ownership: WinDBreak Cable (MSO).

HULETT—Formerly served by Tongue River Communications. No longer in operation. ICA: WY0044.

HYATTVILLE—TCT West. This cable system has converted to IPTV. Now served by BASIN, WY [WY5033]. ICA: WY5008.

JACKSON (town)—Charter Communications, 12405 Powerscourt Dr, St. Louis, MO 63131. Phones: 636-207-5100 (Corporate office); 877-273-7626; 307-733-6030. Fax: 307-266-6821. Web Site: http://www.charter.com. Also serves Teton County (portions). ICA: WY0007.
TV Market Ranking: Below 100 (JACKSON (TOWN), Teton County (portions)). Franchise award date: N.A. Franchise expiration date: N.A. Began: December 1, 1954.
Channel capacity: N.A. Channels available but not in use: N.A.

Digital Basic Service
Subscribers: 5,038.
Programming (via satellite): A&E HD; Altitude Sports & Entertainment; AMC; Animal Planet HD; AXS TV; BBC America; Bloomberg Television; Bravo HD; CBS Sports Network; CMT; CNBC HD+; CNN HD; CNN International; Cooking Channel; C-SPAN 3; Destination America; Discovery Channel HD; Discovery Kids Channel; Discovery Life Channel; Disney Channel HD; Disney XD; DIY Network; DMX Music; ESPN Classic; ESPN HD; ESPN2 HD; ESPNews; Food Network HD; Fox Sports 1; Freeform HD; FSN HD; Fuse; FXM; FYI; Golf Channel; HD Theater; HGTV HD; History HD; History International; HRTV; IFC; Investigation Discovery; ION Television; Lifetime Movie Network HD; LMN; MTV Classic; MTV Hits; MTV Jams; MTV Live; MTV2; Nat Geo WILD; National Geographic Channel HD; NBC Universo; NBCSN; Nick 2; Nick Jr.; Nicktoons; Outdoor Channel; Outdoor Channel 2 HD; OWN: Oprah Winfrey Network; Qubo; RFD-TV; Science Channel; Science HD; Sprout; Syfy HD; TBS HD; TeenNick; The Weather Channel HD; TLC HD; TNT HD; Tr3s; Trinity Broadcasting

Network (TBN); Universal HD; UP; USA Network HD; Versus HD; VH1 Soul.
Fee: $26.99 monthly; $6.70 converter.

Digital Expanded Basic Service
Subscribers: N.A.
Programming (via satellite): A&E; Altitude Sports & Entertainment; AMC; Animal Planet; Bravo; Cartoon Network; CMT; CNBC; CNN; Comedy Central; Discovery Channel; Disney Channel; E! HD; ESPN; ESPN2; EWTN Global Catholic Network; Food Network; Fox News Channel; Freeform; FX; GSN; Hallmark Channel; HGTV; History; HLN; ION Television; MSNBC; MTV; Nickelodeon; Oxygen; Root Sports Rocky Mountain; Spike TV; Syfy; Tennis Channel; The Weather Channel; TLC; TNT; Travel Channel; truTV; Turner Classic Movies; TV Land; Univision Studios; USA Network; VH1.
Fee: $42.40 monthly.

Digital Pay Service 1
Pay Units: N.A.
Programming (via satellite): Cinemax (multiplexed); Cinemax HD; HBO (multiplexed); HBO HD; Showtime (multiplexed); Showtime HD; Starz (multiplexed); Starz Encore (multiplexed); Starz HD; The Movie Channel (multiplexed); The Movie Channel HD.
Fee: $12.00 monthly (Starz/Encore), $16.15 monthly (Cinemax, HBO or Showtime/TMC).

Video-On-Demand: No

Pay-Per-View
iN DEMAND (delivered digitally); ESPN (delivered digitally); Fox Deportes (delivered digitally); NBC Universo (delivered digitally); Cinelatino (delivered digitally); History en Espanol (delivered digitally); Tr3s (delivered digitally); CNN en Espanol (delivered digitally); ESPN Deportes (delivered digitally); Cine Mexicano (delivered digitally); MLB Extra Innings (delivered digitally); GolTV (delivered digitally); AYM Sports (delivered digitally); Bandamax (delivered digitally); De Pelicula (delivered digitally); De Pelicula Clasico (delivered digitally); Telehit (delivered digitally); NFL Network HD (delivered digitally); NHL Center Ice (delivered digitally); NFL Network (delivered digitally); FOX College Sports Central (delivered digitally); FOX College Sports Pacific (delivered digitally); NHL Network (delivered digitally); ViendoMovies (delivered digitally).

Internet Service
Operational: Yes. Began: July 1, 2003.
Broadband Service: Charter Internet.
Fee: $49.99 installation; $29.95 monthly; $3.99 modem lease.

Telephone Service
Digital: Operational
Fee: $46.99 monthly
Miles of Plant: 174.0 (coaxial); None (fiber optic). Homes passed: 10,000.
President & Chief Executive Officer: Tom Rutledge. General Manager: Clint Rodeman. Chief Technician: Dan Higgins. Accounting Director: David Sovanski.
Ownership: Charter Communications Inc. (MSO).

KEMMERER—Formerly served by KLiP Interactive. No longer in operation. ICA: WY0021.

LANDER—Formerly served by Bresnan Communications. Now served by Charter Communications, RIVERTON, WY [WY0059]. ICA: WY0056.

LARAMIE—Charter Communications, 12405 Powerscourt Dr, St. Louis, MO 63131. Phones: 636-207-5100 (Corporate office);

516-803-2300 (Corporate office); 877-273-7626. Web Site: http://www.charter.com. Also serves Albany County (portions). ICA: WY0003.
TV Market Ranking: Below 100 (LARAMIE, Albany County (portions)); Outside TV Markets (Albany County (portions)). Franchise award date: N.A. Franchise expiration date: N.A. Began: March 1, 1954.
Channel capacity: N.A. Channels available but not in use: N.A.

Digital Basic Service
Subscribers: 4,863.
Programming (via satellite): A&E HD; Altitude Sports & Entertainment; AMC; Animal Planet HD; AXS TV; BBC America; Bloomberg Television; BlueHighways TV; Bravo; Bravo HD; BYUtv; CMT; CNBC HD+; CNN HD; Cooking Channel; Destination America; Discovery Channel HD; Discovery Kids Channel; Discovery Life Channel; Disney Channel HD; Disney XD; DIY Network; DMX Music; ESPN Classic; ESPN HD; ESPN2 HD; ESPNews; Food Network HD; Fox Sports 1; Freeform HD; FSN HD; Fuse; FXM; FYI; Golf Channel; GSN; HD Theater; HGTV HD; History HD; History International; HRTV; IFC; Investigation Discovery; ION Television; Lifetime Movie Network HD; LMN; MTV Classic; MTV Hits; MTV Jams; MTV Live; MTV2; Nat Geo WILD; National Geographic Channel; National Geographic Channel HD; NBC Universo; NBCSN; Nick 2; Nick Jr.; Nicktoons; Outdoor Channel; Outdoor Channel 2 HD; OWN: Oprah Winfrey Network; Qubo; RFD-TV; Science Channel; Science HD; Sprout; Syfy HD; TBS HD; TeenNick; The Weather Channel HD; TLC HD; TNT HD; Tr3s; Trinity Broadcasting Network (TBN); Universal HD; UP; USA Network HD; Versus HD; VH1 Soul.
Fee: $26.99 monthly; $6.70 converter.

Digital Expanded Basic Service
Subscribers: N.A.
Programming (via satellite): A&E; Altitude Sports & Entertainment; AMC; Animal Planet; Cartoon Network; CBS Sports Network; CMT; CNBC; CNN; Comedy Central; Discovery Channel; Disney Channel; E! HD; ESPN; ESPN2; EWTN Global Catholic Network; Food Network; Fox News Channel; Freeform; FX; Hallmark Channel; HGTV; History; HLN; MSNBC; MTV; Nickelodeon; Oxygen; Root Sports Rocky Mountain; Spike TV; Syfy; The Weather Channel; TLC; TNT; Travel Channel; truTV; Turner Classic Movies; TV Land; Univision Studios; USA Network; VH1.
Fee: $42.40 monthly.

Digital Pay Service 1
Pay Units: N.A.
Programming (via satellite): Cinemax (multiplexed); Cinemax HD; HBO (multiplexed); HBO HD; Showtime (multiplexed); Showtime HD; Starz (multiplexed); Starz Encore (multiplexed); Starz HD; The Movie Channel (multiplexed); The Movie Channel HD.
Fee: $12.00 monthly (Starz/Encore), $16.15 monthly (Cinemax, HBO or Showtime/TMC).

Video-On-Demand: Yes

Pay-Per-View
iN DEMAND (delivered digitally); ESPN (delivered digitally); NHL Network (delivered digitally); ViendoMovies (delivered digitally); Fox Deportes (delivered digitally); NBC Universo (delivered digitally); Cinelatino (delivered digitally); History en Espanol (delivered digitally); Tr3s (delivered digitally); CNN en Espanol (delivered digitally); NBA League Pass (delivered digitally); ESPN Deportes (delivered digi-

Cable Systems—Wyoming

tally); Cine Mexicano (delivered digitally); GolTV (delivered digitally); Bandamax (delivered digitally); De Pelicula (delivered digitally); De Pelicula Clasico (delivered digitally); Telehit (delivered digitally); Univision Studios (delivered digitally); MLS Direct Kick (delivered digitally); Cinemax On Demand (delivered digitally); HBO on Demand (delivered digitally); Showtime On Demand (delivered digitally); Starz On Demand (delivered digitally); MLB Extra Innings (delivered digitally); Free Speech TV on Demand (delivered digitally); The SPOT On Demand (delivered digitally); careerSPOT On Demand (delivered digitally); homeSPOT On Demand (delivered digitally); NHL Center Ice (delivered digitally); NFL Network (delivered digitally); FOX College Sports Central (delivered digitally); FOX College Sports Pacific (delivered digitally).

Internet Service
Operational: Yes. Began: October 1, 2002.
Subscribers: 7,663.
Broadband Service: Charter Internet.
Fee: $49.99 installation; $29.95 monthly; $3.99 modem lease.

Telephone Service
Digital: Operational
Subscribers: 2,879.
Fee: $46.99 monthly
Miles of Plant: 219.0 (coaxial); 48.0 (fiber optic). Homes passed: 16,546.
President & Chief Executive Officer: Tom Rutledge. Regional Vice President & General Manager: Clint Rodeman. Technical Operations Manager: Mitch Winter. Accounting Director: David Sovanski.
Ownership: Charter Communications Inc. (MSO).

LOVELL—TCT West Inc. This cable system has converted to IPTV. Now served by BASIN, WY [WY5003]. ICA: WY0024.

LOVELL—TCT West. This cable system has converted to IPTV. Now served by BASIN, WY [WY5033]. ICA: WY5009.

LUSK—Vyve Broadband, 234 North Windriver Dr, Douglas, WY 82633. Phones: 800-937-1397; 307-358-3833; 800-759-8448; 307-358-3861. Web Site: http://vyvebroadband.com. ICA: WY0027.
TV Market Ranking: Outside TV Markets (LUSK). Franchise award date: November 1, 1978. Franchise expiration date: N.A. Began: May 1, 1980.
Channel capacity: N.A. Channels available but not in use: N.A.

Digital Basic Service
Subscribers: 150.
Programming (received off-air): KCWY-DT (CW, NBC) Casper; KNEP (ABC) Scottsbluff; KTWO-TV (ABC) Casper.
Programming (via microwave): KCNC-TV (CBS, Decades) Denver; KDVR (Antenna TV, FOX) Denver; KMGH-TV (ABC, Azteca America) Denver; KRMA-TV (PBS) Denver; KTVD (MeTV, MNT) Denver; KUSA (NBC, WeatherNation) Denver; KWGN-TV (CW, This TV) Denver.
Programming (via satellite): QVC; WGN America.
Fee: $59.99 installation; $25.00 monthly.

Digital Expanded Basic Service
Subscribers: 142.
Programming (via satellite): A&E; AMC; Animal Planet; Bravo; Cartoon Network; CMT; CNBC; CNN; Comedy Central; C-SPAN; C-SPAN 2; Discovery Channel; E! HD; ESPN; ESPN2; ESPNews; Food Net-

work; Fox News Channel; Freeform; FX; Hallmark Channel; HGTV; History; HLN; Lifetime; MSNBC; MTV; Nick Jr.; Nickelodeon; OWN: Oprah Winfrey Network; Root Sports Rocky Mountain; Spike TV; Syfy; TBS; The Weather Channel; TLC; TNT; Travel Channel; truTV; TV Land; USA Network; VH1; WE tv.
Fee: $22.99 monthly.

Digital Expanded Basic Service 2
Subscribers: N.A.
Programming (via satellite): BBC America; Bloomberg Television; Bravo; Discovery Life Channel; DMX Music; E! HD; ESPN Classic; ESPN2; ESPNews; EVINE Live; Fox Sports 1; FSN Digital Atlantic; FSN Digital Central; FSN Digital Pacific; Fuse; FXM; FYI; Golf Channel; Great American Country; GSN; HGTV; History; History International; IFC; International Television (ITV); LMN; MBC America; National Geographic Channel; NBCSN; Nick Jr.; Nicktoons; Outdoor Channel; Ovation; Sundance TV; Syfy; TeenNick; The Word Network; Trinity Broadcasting Network (TBN); Turner Classic Movies; TV Land; WE tv.
Fee: $11.95 monthly.

Digital Pay Service 1
Pay Units: 71.
Programming (via satellite): Cinemax (multiplexed).
Fee: $11.95 monthly.

Digital Pay Service 2
Pay Units: 81.
Programming (via satellite): HBO (multiplexed).
Fee: $13.95 monthly.

Digital Pay Service 3
Pay Units: 77.
Programming (via satellite): Starz (multiplexed); Starz Encore (multiplexed).
Fee: $10.95 monthly.

Digital Pay Service 4
Pay Units: 20.
Programming (via satellite): Flix; Showtime (multiplexed); The Movie Channel (multiplexed).
Fee: $13.95 monthly (Showtime/Flix or TMC).

Video-On-Demand: No

Pay-Per-View
iN DEMAND (delivered digitally); Hot Choice (delivered digitally); Playboy TV (delivered digitally); Fresh (delivered digitally); Shorteez (delivered digitally).

Internet Service
Operational: Yes.
Broadband Service: Net Commander.
Fee: $39.95 installation; $51.95 monthly.

Telephone Service
None
Miles of Plant: 17.0 (coaxial); None (fiber optic). Homes passed: 730.
President & Chief Executive Officer: Jeffrey DeMond. Senior Vice President, Financial Planning: Daniel White. Vice President, Marketing: Diane Quennoz. Vice President, Residential Services: Vin Zachariah.
Ownership: Vyve Broadband LLC (MSO).

MAMMOTH HOT SPRINGS—Formerly served by North Yellowstone Cable TV. No longer in operation. ICA: WY0048.

MANDERSON—TCT West. This cable system has converted to IPTV. Now served by BASIN, WY [WY5033]. ICA: WY5010.

MEDICINE BOW—Formerly served by Medicine Bow Cable. No longer in operation. ICA: WY0045.

MEETEETSE—Formerly served by KLiP Interactive. No longer in operation. ICA: WY0047.

MEETEETSE—TCT West. This cable system has converted to IPTV. Now served by BASIN, WY [WY5033]. ICA: WY5011.

MOORCROFT—Tongue River Communications, 620 Betty St, PO Box 759, Ranchester, WY 82839-0759. Phones: 800-953-9011; 307-665-9011. Fax: 307-655-9021. E-mail: trcatv@trcable.tv. Web Site: http://www.trcable.tv. ICA: WY0033.
TV Market Ranking: Outside TV Markets (MOORCROFT). Franchise award date: January 9, 1995. Franchise expiration date: N.A. Began: January 1, 1979.
Channel capacity: N.A. Channels available but not in use: N.A.

Basic Service
Subscribers: 68.
Programming (via satellite): A&E; Altitude Sports & Entertainment; AMC; Animal Planet; Cartoon Network; CNBC; CNN; C-SPAN; C-SPAN 2; Discovery Channel; Disney Channel; E! HD; ESPN; Freeform; HLN; KCNC-TV (CBS, Decades) Denver; KRMA-TV (PBS) Denver; KUSA (NBC, WeatherNation) Denver; Lifetime; MTV; Nickelodeon; QVC; Spike TV; TBS; The Weather Channel; TLC; TNT; Travel Channel; truTV; USA Network.
Programming (via translator): KGWC-TV (CBS) Casper; KHME (MeTV, This TV) Rapid City; KHSD-TV (ABC, FOX) Lead; KTWO-TV (ABC) Casper.
Fee: $40.95 installation; $44.99 monthly.

Pay Service 1
Pay Units: N.A.
Programming (via satellite): HBO; Starz Encore.
Fee: $14.95 installation; $1.75 monthly (Encore), $13.65 monthly (HBO).

Internet Service
Operational: No, DSL.

Telephone Service
None
Miles of Plant: 9.0 (coaxial); None (fiber optic). Homes passed: 466.
General Manager: Rob Hium.
Ownership: Lynda & Robert Jacobson (MSO).

MOUNTAIN VIEW (Uinta County)—Union Cable Co, 850 North Hwy 414, PO Box 160, Mountain View, WY 82939-0160. Phones: 888-926-2273; 307-782-6131. Fax: 307-787-7043. Web Site: http://uniontel.net. ICA: WY0023.
TV Market Ranking: Outside TV Markets (MOUNTAIN VIEW (UINTA COUNTY)). Franchise award date: N.A. Franchise expiration date: N.A. Began: December 1, 1962.
Channel capacity: N.A. Channels available but not in use: N.A.

Basic Service
Subscribers: 21.
Programming (via microwave): KJZZ-TV (IND) Salt Lake City; KSL-TV (NBC) Salt Lake City; KSTU (Antenna TV, FOX) Salt Lake City; KTVX (ABC, MeTV) Salt Lake

City; KTWO-TV (ABC) Casper; KUED (PBS) Salt Lake City; KUTV (CBS, This TV) Salt Lake City.
Programming (via satellite): CNN; Disney Channel; ESPN; Freeform; Spike TV; TBS; The Weather Channel; TNT; WGN America.
Fee: $35.00 installation; $18.00 monthly.

Expanded Basic Service 1
Subscribers: N.A.
Programming (via satellite): A&E; CMT; Discovery Channel; ESPN2; History; Nickelodeon; VH1.
Fee: $8.00 monthly.

Pay Service 1
Pay Units: N.A.
Programming (via satellite): FXM; HBO; Starz; Starz Encore.
Fee: $8.00 monthly.

Internet Service
Operational: Yes, DSL & dial-up.

Telephone Service
Analog: Operational
Miles of Plant: 15.0 (coaxial); None (fiber optic). Homes passed: 600.
General Manager & Chief Technician: Chuck Fagnant. Marketing Director: Rob Elwood.
Ownership: Union Telephone Co.-Mountain View, WY (MSO).

NEWCASTLE—Charter Communications, 12405 Powerscourt Dr, St. Louis, MO 63131. Phones: 636-207-5100 (Corporate office); 307-265-3136; 307-257-2189; 516-803-2300 (Corporate office); 877-273-7626. Web Site: http://www.charter.com. Also serves Weston County (portions). ICA: WY0020.
TV Market Ranking: Below 100 (Weston County (portions)); Outside TV Markets (NEWCASTLE, Weston County (portions)). Franchise award date: May 19, 1994. Franchise expiration date: N.A. Began: November 1, 1976.
Channel capacity: N.A. Channels available but not in use: N.A.

Digital Basic Service
Subscribers: 205.
Programming (via satellite): BBC America; Bloomberg Television; Bravo; CBS Sports Network; CMT; Destination America; Discovery Kids Channel; Discovery Life Channel; Disney XD; DMX Music; ESPN Classic; ESPNews; Fox Sports 1; Fuse; FXM; FYI; Golf Channel; GSN; History; History International; Investigation Discovery; LMN; MTV Classic; MTV2; National Geographic Channel; NBCSN; Nick Jr.; Nicktoons; Outdoor Channel; OWN: Oprah Winfrey Network; Science Channel; TeenNick; Trinity Broadcasting Network (TBN).
Fee: $26.99 monthly; $6.70 converter.

Digital Pay Service 1
Pay Units: N.A.
Programming (via satellite): Cinemax (multiplexed); HBO (multiplexed); Showtime; Starz (multiplexed); Starz Encore (multiplexed); The Movie Channel (multiplexed).
Fee: $12.00 monthly (Starz/Encore), $16.15 monthly (Cinemax, HBO or Showtime/TMC).

Video-On-Demand: No

Pay-Per-View
iN DEMAND.

ADVANCED TVFactbook
FULLY SEARCHABLE • CONTINUOUSLY UPDATED • DISCOUNT RATES FOR PRINT PURCHASERS
For more information call 800-771-9202 or visit www.warren-news.com

Wyoming—Cable Systems

Communications Daily
Warren Communications News

Get the industry standard FREE —
For a no-obligation trial call 800-771-9202 or visit www.warren-news.com

Internet Service
Operational: Yes.
Broadband Service: Charter Internet.
Fee: $39.95 monthly.
Telephone Service
Digital: Operational
Fee: $49.99 monthly
Miles of Plant: 38.0 (coaxial); None (fiber optic). Homes passed: 1,670.
President & Chief Executive Officer: Tom Rutledge. General Manager: Clint Rodeman. Chief Technician: Dan Higgins. Accounting Director: David Sovanski.
Ownership: Charter Communications Inc. (MSO).

OSAGE—Formerly served by Tongue River Cable TV Inc. No longer in operation. ICA: WY0049.

OTTO—TCT West. This cable system has converted to IPTV. Now served by BASIN, WY [WY5033]. ICA: WY5012.

PINE BLUFFS—WinDBreak Cable, 1140 10th St, Gering, NE 69341-3239. Phones: 800-282-4650; 308-436-4650. Fax: 308-436-4779. E-mail: bill@intertech.net. Web Site: http://www.windbreak.com. ICA: WY0031.
TV Market Ranking: Outside TV Markets (PINE BLUFFS). Franchise award date: November 7, 1962. Franchise expiration date: N.A. Began: July 1, 1957.
Channel capacity: N.A. Channels available but not in use: N.A.
Basic Service
Subscribers: 197.
Programming (via microwave): KCNC-TV (CBS, Decades) Denver; KGWN-TV (CBS, CW) Cheyenne; KMGH-TV (ABC, Azteca America) Denver; KNEP (ABC) Scottsbluff; KRMA-TV (PBS) Denver; KSTF (CBS, CW) Scottsbluff; KTNE-TV (PBS) Alliance; KTWO-TV (ABC) Casper; KUSA (NBC, WeatherNation) Denver; KWGN-TV (CW, This TV) Denver.
Programming (via satellite): CNN; ESPN; Freeform; TBS; TNT; USA Network.
Fee: $34.95 installation; $39.00 monthly.
Pay Service 1
Pay Units: 20.
Programming (via satellite): HBO; Starz; Starz Encore.
Fee: $2.00 monthly (Encore), $11.00 monthly (Starz/Encore), $14.00 monthly (HBO).
Video-On-Demand: No
Internet Service
Operational: Yes.
Subscribers: 130.
Fee: $34.95 installation; $29.95 monthly.
Telephone Service
None
Miles of Plant: 8.0 (coaxial); None (fiber optic). Homes passed: 950.
General Manager & Chief Technician: Bill Bauer. Office Manager: Sheryl McLean.
Ownership: WinDBreak Cable (MSO).

PINE HAVEN—Tongue River Communications, 620 Betty St, PO Box 759, Ranchester, WY 82839-0759. Phones: 800-953-9011; 307-655-9011. Fax: 307-655-9021. E-mail: trcatv@trcable.tv. Web Site: http://www.trcable.tv. ICA: WY0052.
TV Market Ranking: Outside TV Markets (PINE HAVEN). Franchise award date: September 1, 1987. Franchise expiration date: N.A. Began: October 1, 1987.
Channel capacity: N.A. Channels available but not in use: N.A.
Basic Service
Subscribers: N.A.
Programming (received off-air): KGWC-TV (CBS) Casper; KHME (MeTV, This TV) Rapid City; KOTA-TV (ABC, FOX) Rapid City; KPSD-TV (PBS) Eagle Butte.
Programming (via microwave): KCNC-TV (CBS, Decades) Denver; WWOR-TV (Bounce TV, Buzzr, Heroes & Icons, MNT) Secaucus.
Programming (via satellite): A&E; AMC; CMT; CNN; C-SPAN; Discovery Channel; Disney Channel; ESPN; Freeform; HLN; Lifetime; Nickelodeon; Spike TV; TBS; The Weather Channel; TNT; USA Network; WGN America.
Fee: $40.00 installation; $3.00 converter.
Pay Service 1
Pay Units: N.A.
Programming (via satellite): Cinemax; HBO; Starz Encore.
Fee: $10.00 installation; $3.00 monthly (Encore), $10.00 monthly (Cinemax), $12.00 monthly (HBO).
Internet Service
Operational: No.
Telephone Service
None
Miles of Plant: 6.0 (coaxial); None (fiber optic). Homes passed: 65.
General Manager: Rob Hium.
Ownership: Lynda & Robert Jacobson (MSO).

PINEDALE—Formerly served by KLiP Interactive. No longer in operation. ICA: WY0025.

POWELL—Charter Communications, 12405 Powerscourt Dr, St. Louis, MO 63131. Phones: 636-207-5100 (Corporate office); 866-773-6303; 516-803-2300 (Corporate office); 877-273-7626. Web Site: http://www.charter.com. Also serves Park County (portions). ICA: WY0015.
TV Market Ranking: Outside TV Markets (Park County (portions), POWELL). Franchise award date: N.A. Franchise expiration date: N.A. Began: December 1, 1965.
Channel capacity: N.A. Channels available but not in use: N.A.
Digital Basic Service
Subscribers: 1,000.
Programming (via satellite): A&E HD; Altitude Sports & Entertainment; Animal Planet HD; AXS TV; BBC America; Bloomberg Television; CBS Sports Network; CMT; Cooking Channel; Destination America; Discovery Channel HD; Discovery Life Channel; Disney XD; DIY Network; DMX Music; ESPN Classic; ESPN HD; ESPN2 HD; ESPNews; Fox Sports 1; FSN HD; Fuse; FXM; FYI; Golf Channel; GSN; HD Theater; History International; HRTV; IFC; Investigation Discovery; LMN; MTV Classic; MTV Hits; MTV Jams; MTV2; Nat Geo WILD; National Geographic Channel; National Geographic Channel HD; NBCSN; Nick 2; Nick Jr.; Nicktoons; Outdoor Channel; OWN: Oprah Winfrey Network; RFD-TV; Science Channel; Science HD; Sprout; TeenNick; TLC HD; TNT HD; Tr3s; Trinity Broadcasting Network (TBN); Universal HD; UP; Versus HD; VH1 Soul.
Fee: $26.99 monthly; $6.50 converter.
Digital Expanded Basic Service
Subscribers: N.A.
Programming (via satellite): A&E; Altitude Sports & Entertainment; AMC; Animal Planet; Bravo; Cartoon Network; Discovery Channel; Disney Channel; E! HD; ESPN; ESPN2; Food Network; Fox News Channel; FX; Great American Country; Hallmark Channel; HGTV; History; HLN; ION Television; Oxygen; Root Sports Rocky Mountain; Spike TV; Syfy; TLC; TNT; Travel Channel; truTV; Turner Classic Movies; TV Land; Univision Studios; USA Network.
Fee: $40.25 monthly.
Digital Pay Service 1
Pay Units: N.A.
Programming (via satellite): Cinemax (multiplexed); HBO (multiplexed); HBO HD (multiplexed); Showtime (multiplexed); Showtime HD; Starz (multiplexed); Starz Encore (multiplexed); Starz HD; The Movie Channel (multiplexed).
Fee: $12.00 monthly (Starz/Encore), $16.15 monthly (Cinemax, HBO or Showtime/TMC).
Video-On-Demand: No
Pay-Per-View
iN DEMAND (delivered digitally); NBA League Pass (delivered digitally); MLS Direct Kick (delivered digitally); NFL Network; NFL Network HD (delivered digitally); FOX College Sports Central (delivered digitally); FOX College Sports Pacific (delivered digitally).
Internet Service
Operational: Yes. Began: July 20, 2002.
Broadband Service: Charter Internet.
Fee: $49.99 installation; $29.95 monthly; $3.50 modem lease.
Telephone Service
Analog: Not Operational
Digital: Operational
Fee: $46.99 monthly
Miles of Plant: 40.0 (coaxial); 7.0 (fiber optic). Homes passed: 3,000.
President & Chief Executive Officer: Tom Rutledge. Regional Vice President & General Manager: Clint Rodeman. Chief Technician: Dan Higgins. Accounting Director: David Sovanski.
Ownership: Charter Communications Inc. (MSO).

POWELL—TCT West. This cable system has converted to IPTV. Now served by BASIN, WY [WY5033]. ICA: WY5015.

RANCHESTER—Tongue River Communications, 620 Betty St, PO Box 759, Ranchester, WY 82839-0759. Phones: 800-953-9011; 307-655-9011. Fax: 307-655-9021. E-mail: trcatv@trcable.tv. Web Site: http://www.trcable.tv. Also serves Dayton. ICA: WY0028.
TV Market Ranking: Below 100 (Dayton, RANCHESTER). Franchise award date: January 1, 1979. Franchise expiration date: N.A. Began: December 18, 1979.
Channel capacity: N.A. Channels available but not in use: N.A.
Basic Service
Subscribers: N.A.
Programming (received off-air): KCWC-DT (PBS) Lander; KGWC-TV (CBS) Casper; KHMT (FOX) Hardin; KSGW-TV (ABC, MeTV, This TV) Sheridan; KTVQ (CBS, CW, Grit) Billings; KTWO-TV (ABC) Casper.
Programming (via microwave): KCNC-TV (CBS, Decades) Denver; KRMA-TV (PBS) Denver; KTLA (Antenna TV, CW, This TV) Los Angeles; KUSA (NBC, WeatherNation) Denver; KWGN-TV (CW, This TV) Denver; WPIX (Antenna TV, CW, This TV) New York.
Programming (via satellite): A&E; AMC; Animal Planet; Cartoon Network; CMT; CNBC; CNN; C-SPAN; C-SPAN 2; Discovery Channel; Disney Channel; E! HD; ESPN; ESPN2; Freeform; HGTV; History; HLN; Lifetime; MSNBC; MTV; Nickelodeon; Outdoor Channel; Spike TV; Syfy; TBS; The Weather Channel; TLC; TNT; Travel Channel; Trinity Broadcasting Network (TBN); truTV; USA Network; VH1; WGN America.
Fee: $40.00 installation.
Pay Service 1
Pay Units: N.A.
Programming (via satellite): Cinemax; HBO; Starz Encore.
Fee: $10.00 installation; $12.00 monthly (HBO), $10.00 monthly (Cinemax), $3.00 monthly (Encore).
Video-On-Demand: No
Internet Service
Operational: Yes.
Broadband Service: In-house.
Fee: $45.00 monthly.
Telephone Service
Digital: Operational
Miles of Plant: 24.0 (coaxial); None (fiber optic). Homes passed: 710.
General Manager: Rob Hium.
Ownership: Lynda & Robert Jacobson (MSO).

RAWLINS—Charter Communications, 12405 Powerscourt Dr, St. Louis, MO 63131. Phones: 636-207-5100 (Corporate office); 866-213-6572; 307-266-0034; 516-803-2300 (Corporate office); 877-273-7626. Web Site: http://www.charter.com. Also serves Sinclair. ICA: WY0011.
TV Market Ranking: Below 100 (RAWLINS, Sinclair). Franchise award date: N.A. Franchise expiration date: N.A. Began: September 1, 1955.
Channel capacity: N.A. Channels available but not in use: N.A.
Digital Basic Service
Subscribers: 1,543.
Programming (via satellite): A&E HD; Altitude Sports & Entertainment; Animal Planet HD; AXS TV; BBC America; Bloomberg Television; Bravo; CBS Sports Network; CMT; CNN HD; Cooking Channel; Destination America; Discovery Channel HD; Discovery Kids Channel; Discovery Life Channel; Disney Channel HD; Disney XD; DIY Network; DMX Music; ESPN Classic; ESPN HD; ESPN2 HD; ESPNews; Food Network HD; Fox Sports 1; Freeform HD; FSN HD; Fuse; FXM; FYI; Golf Channel; GSN; HD Theater; HGTV HD; History HD; History International; HRTV; IFC; Investigation Discovery; Lifetime Movie Network HD; LMN; MTV Classic; MTV Hits; MTV Jams; MTV2; Nat Geo WILD; National Geographic Channel; National Geographic Channel HD; NBC Universo; NBCSN; Nick 2; Nick Jr.; Nicktoons; Outdoor Channel; OWN: Oprah Winfrey Network; RFD-TV; Science Channel; Science HD; Sprout; Syfy HD; TBS HD; TeenNick; The Weather Channel HD; TLC HD; TNT HD; Tr3s; Trinity Broadcasting Network (TBN);

D-876

TV & Cable Factbook No. 85

Cable Systems—Wyoming

FULLY SEARCHABLE • CONTINUOUSLY UPDATED • DISCOUNT RATES FOR PRINT PURCHASERS

For more information call **800-771-9202** or visit **www.warren-news.com**

Universal HD; UP; USA Network HD; Versus HD; VH1 Soul.
Fee: $26.99 monthly; $6.70 converter.
Digital Expanded Basic Service
Subscribers: N.A.
Programming (via satellite): A&E; Altitude Sports & Entertainment; AMC; Animal Planet; BYUtv; Cartoon Network; CMT; CNBC; CNN; Comedy Central; C-SPAN 2; Disney Channel; E! HD; ESPN; ESPN2; Food Network; Fox News Channel; Freeform; FX; Hallmark Channel; HGTV; History; HLN; INSP; Lifetime; MSNBC; MTV; Nickelodeon; Oxygen; Pop; QVC; Root Sports Rocky Mountain; Spike TV; Syfy; The Weather Channel; TLC; TNT; Travel Channel; truTV; Turner Classic Movies; TV Land; UniMas; Univision Studios; USA Network; VH1.
Fee: $42.00 monthly.
Digital Pay Service 1
Pay Units: N.A.
Programming (via satellite): Cinemax (multiplexed); Cinemax HD; HBO (multiplexed); HBO HD; Showtime (multiplexed); Showtime HD; Starz (multiplexed); Starz Encore (multiplexed); Starz HD; The Movie Channel (multiplexed); The Movie Channel HD.
Fee: $12.00 monthly (Starz/Encore), $16.15 monthly (Cinemax, HBO or Showtime/TMC).
Video-On-Demand: No
Pay-Per-View
iN DEMAND (delivered digitally); NFL Network (delivered digitally); History en Espanol (delivered digitally); Tr3s (delivered digitally); CNN en Espanol (delivered digitally); ESPN Deportes (delivered digitally); Cine Mexicano (delivered digitally); GolTV (delivered digitally); Bandamax (delivered digitally); De Pelicula (delivered digitally); De Pelicula Clasico (delivered digitally); Telehit (delivered digitally); Univision Studios (delivered digitally); UniMas (delivered digitally); NFL Network HD (delivered digitally); FOX College Sports Central (delivered digitally); FOX College Sports Pacific (delivered digitally); ViendoMovies (delivered digitally); Fox Deportes (delivered digitally); NBC Universo (delivered digitally); Cinelatino (delivered digitally).
Internet Service
Operational: Yes.
Broadband Service: Charter Internet.
Fee: $49.99 installation; $29.95 monthly; $3.99 modem lease.
Telephone Service
Digital: Operational
Fee: $46.99 monthly
Miles of Plant: 80.0 (coaxial); None (fiber optic). Homes passed: 4,800.
President & Chief Executive Officer: Tom Rutledge. General Manager: Clint Rodeman. Chief Technician: Mike Stypa. Accounting Director: David Sovanski.
Ownership: Charter Communications Inc. (MSO).

RIVERSIDE—Vyve Broadband, 234 North Windriver Dr, Douglas, WY 82633. Phones: 800-937-1397; 307-358-3833; 307-358-3861. Web Site: http://vyvebroadband.com. Also serves Encampment. ICA: WY0073.
TV Market Ranking: Outside TV Markets (RIVERSIDE, Encampment).
Channel capacity: N.A. Channels available but not in use: N.A.
Basic Service
Subscribers: 6.
Programming (via microwave): KCNC-TV (CBS, Decades) Denver; KDVR (Antenna TV, FOX) Denver; KMGH-TV (ABC, Azteca America) Denver; KTWO-TV (ABC) Casper; KUSA (NBC, WeatherNation) Denver; KWGN-TV (CW, This TV) Denver.
Programming (via satellite): Animal Planet; CMT; CNN; Discovery Channel; ESPN; Freeform; Nick Jr.; Nickelodeon; QVC; Spike TV; Syfy; TBS; TLC; TNT; Travel Channel; VH1; WGN America.
Fee: $64.95 installation; $44.99 monthly.
Pay Service 1
Pay Units: N.A.
Programming (via satellite): Cinemax; HBO.
Internet Service
Operational: No.
Telephone Service
None
President & Chief Executive Officer: Jeffrey DeMond. Senior Vice President, Financial Planning: Daniel White. Vice President, Marketing: Diane Quennoz. Vice President, Residential Services: Vin Zachariah.
Ownership: Vyve Broadband LLC (MSO).

RIVERTON—Charter Communications, 12405 Powerscourt Dr, St. Louis, MO 63131. Phones: 636-207-5100 (Corporate office); 866-213-6572; 307-266-0034; 877-273-7626; 516-803-2300 (Corporate office). Fax: 307-266-6821. Web Site: http://www.charter.com. Also serves Fremont County (portions) & Lander. ICA: WY0059.
TV Market Ranking: Below 100 (Fremont County (portions) (portions), Lander, RIVERTON); Outside TV Markets (Fremont County (portions) (portions)). Franchise award date: January 1, 1958. Franchise expiration date: N.A. Began: June 1, 1958.
Channel capacity: N.A. Channels available but not in use: N.A.
Digital Basic Service
Subscribers: 4,918.
Programming (via satellite): A&E HD; Altitude Sports & Entertainment; Animal Planet HD; AXS TV; BBC America; Bloomberg Television; CBS Sports Network; CMT; CNN HD; Cooking Channel; Destination America; Discovery Channel HD; Discovery Kids Channel; Discovery Life Channel; Disney Channel HD; Disney XD; DIY Network; DMX Music; ESPN Classic; ESPN HD; ESPN2 HD; ESPNews; Family Friendly Entertainment; Food Network HD; Fox Sports 1; Freeform HD; FSN HD; Fuse; FXM; FYI; Golf Channel; Great American Country; GSN; HD Theater; HGTV HD; History HD; History International; HRTV; IFC; Investigation Discovery; ION Television; Lifetime Movie Network HD; LMN; MTV Classic; MTV Hits; MTV Jams; MTV2; Nat Geo WILD; National Geographic Channel; National Geographic Channel HD; NBCSN; Nick 2; Nick Jr.; Nicktoons; OWN; Oprah Winfrey Network; Qubo; RFD-TV; Science Channel; Science HD; Sprout; Syfy HD; TBS HD; TeenNick; The Weather Channel HD; TLC HD; TNT HD; Tr3s; Trinity Broadcasting Network (TBN); Universal HD; USA Network HD; Versus HD; VH1 Soul.
Fee: $26.99 monthly; $6.70 converter.
Digital Pay Service 1
Pay Units: N.A.
Programming (via satellite): Cinemax (multiplexed); Cinemax HD; HBO (multiplexed); HBO HD; Showtime (multiplexed); Showtime HD; Starz (multiplexed); Starz Encore (multiplexed); Starz HD; The Movie Channel (multiplexed); The Movie Channel HD.
Fee: $12.00 monthly (Starz/Encore), $16.15 monthly (Cinemax, HBO or Showtime/TMC).
Video-On-Demand: No

Pay-Per-View
iN DEMAND (delivered digitally); ESPN (delivered digitally); NHL Network (delivered digitally); NFL Network HD (delivered digitally); NBA League Pass (delivered digitally); MLS Direct Kick (delivered digitally); MLB Extra Innings (delivered digitally); NHL Center Ice (delivered digitally); NFL Network (delivered digitally); FOX College Sports Central (delivered digitally); FOX College Sports Pacific (delivered digitally).
Internet Service
Operational: Yes.
Subscribers: 5,286.
Broadband Service: Charter Internet.
Fee: $49.99 installation; $29.95 monthly; $3.99 modem lease.
Telephone Service
Digital: Operational
Subscribers: 3,637.
Fee: $46.99 monthly
Miles of Plant: 227.0 (coaxial); 34.0 (fiber optic). Homes passed: 10,560.
President & Chief Executive Officer: Tom Rutledge. General Manager: Clint Rodeman. Chief Technician: Dan Higgins. Accounting Director: David Sovanski.
Ownership: Charter Communications Inc. (MSO).

ROCK SPRINGS—Sweetwater Cable TV Co. Inc, 602 Broadway St, Rock Springs, WY 82901-6348. Phone: 307-362-3773. Fax: 307-382-2781. E-mail: swtv@sweetwaterhsa.com. Web Site: http://www2.sweetwaterhsa.com. Also serves Green River, North Rock Springs, Reliance, Sweetwater County (portions) & Sweetwater County (unincorporated areas). ICA: WY0004.
TV Market Ranking: Below 100 (North Rock Springs, Reliance, ROCK SPRINGS, Sweetwater County (unincorporated areas) (portions), Green River, Sweetwater County (portions)); Outside TV Markets (Sweetwater County (unincorporated areas) (portions), Sweetwater County (portions)). Franchise award date: January 1, 1954. Franchise expiration date: N.A. Began: December 1, 1956.
Channel capacity: N.A. Channels available but not in use: N.A.
Digital Basic Service
Subscribers: 5,732.
Programming (received off-air): KGWR-TV (CBS) Rock Springs.
Programming (via microwave): KJZZ-TV (IND) Salt Lake City; KSL-TV (NBC) Salt Lake City; KSTV-LP (Azteca America) Sacramento; KTVX (ABC, MeTV) Salt Lake City; KTWO-TV (ABC) Casper; KUED (PBS) Salt Lake City; KUTV (CBS, This TV) Salt Lake City; KUWB-LD Bloomington.
Programming (via satellite): BYUtv; EWTN Global Catholic Network; INSP; Pop; QVC; TBS; The Weather Channel; Univision Studios.
Fee: $45.00 installation; $59.99 monthly; $25.00 converter.

Digital Expanded Basic Service
Subscribers: N.A.
Programming (via satellite): A&E; AMC; Animal Planet; Bravo; Cartoon Network; CBS Sports Network; CMT; CNBC; CNN; Comedy Central; C-SPAN; C-SPAN 2; Discovery Channel; Disney Channel; E! HD; ESPN; ESPN Classic; ESPN2; Food Network; Fox News Channel; Fox Sports 1; Freeform; FX; Hallmark Channel; HGTV; History; HLN; HSN; Investigation Discovery; Lifetime; MSNBC; MTV; National Geographic Channel; NFL Network; Nickelodeon; Outdoor Channel; Root Sports Rocky Mountain; Science Channel; Spike TV; Syfy; Telemundo; TLC; TNT; Travel Channel; truTV; TV Land; USA Network; VH1.
Fee: $27.95 monthly; $8.00 converter.
Digital Expanded Basic Service 2
Subscribers: N.A.
Programming (via satellite): 52MX; American Heroes Channel; BBC America; Bloomberg Television; Chiller; Cinelatino; Cloo; CMT; CNBC World; CNN en Espanol; Destination America; Discovery Family; Discovery Life Channel; Disney XD; DIY Network; DMX Music; ESPN Deportes; ESPNews; ESPNU; EVINE Live; Fox Business Network; Fox Deportes; FXM; FYI; Golf Channel; GSN; History en Espanol; History International; IFC; MTV Classic; MTV Hits; MTV2; NBCSN; Nick Jr.; Nicktoons; OWN; Oprah Winfrey Network; TeenNick; The Sportsman Channel; Trinity Broadcasting Network (TBN); Turner Classic Movies; VeneMovies; VH1 Soul.
Fee: $8.00 monthly.
Digital Expanded Basic Service 3
Subscribers: N.A.
Programming (via satellite): AXS TV; HD Theater; Universal HD.
Fee: $10.00 monthly.
Digital Pay Service 1
Pay Units: N.A.
Programming (via satellite): Cinemax (multiplexed); Flix; HBO (multiplexed); Showtime (multiplexed); Starz (multiplexed); Starz Encore (multiplexed); The Movie Channel (multiplexed).
Fee: $8.95 monthly (Cinemax), $10.95 monthly (Showtime/TMC or Starz/Encore), $13.95 monthly (HBO).
Video-On-Demand: No
Pay-Per-View
ESPN (delivered digitally); Spice: Xcess (delivered digitally); Hot Choice (delivered digitally); iN DEMAND (delivered digitally); Club Jenna (delivered digitally); Playboy TV (delivered digitally); Fresh (delivered digitally).
Internet Service
Operational: Yes. Began: March 4, 2001.
Subscribers: 4,148.
Broadband Service: ZCorum.
Fee: $49.00 installation; $29.95-$49.95 monthly; $64.95 modem purchase.
Telephone Service
Digital: Operational
Subscribers: 164.
Miles of Plant: 322.0 (coaxial); 95.0 (fiber optic). Homes passed: 14,000.

2017 Edition   D-877

Wyoming—Cable Systems

FULLY SEARCHABLE • CONTINUOUSLY UPDATED • DISCOUNT RATES FOR PRINT PURCHASERS

For more information call **800-771-9202** or visit **www.warren-news.com**

President & General Manager: Al Carollo Jr. Vice President & Marketing Manager: John Carollo. Chief Technician: Brian Jackson. Office Manager: Mandy Krueth. Ownership: Sweetwater Cable TV Co. Inc. (MSO).

SARATOGA—Vyve Broadband, 4 International Dr, Ste 330, Rye Brook, NY 10573. Phones: 800-937-1397; 307-358-3833; 800-759-8448 (Local access only); 307-358-3861. Web Site: http://vyvebroadband.com. Also serves Carbon County (portions) & Hanna. ICA: WY0016.
TV Market Ranking: Below 100 (Carbon County (portions), Hanna, SARATOGA); Outside TV Markets (Carbon County (portions)). Franchise award date: N.A. Franchise expiration date: N.A. Began: November 1, 1979.
Channel capacity: N.A. Channels available but not in use: N.A.

Basic Service
Subscribers: 98.
Programming (via microwave): KCNC-TV (CBS, Decades) Denver; KCWY-DT (CW, NBC) Casper; KDVR (Antenna TV, FOX) Denver; KMGH-TV (ABC, Azteca America) Denver; KRMA-TV (PBS) Denver; KTVD (MeTV, MNT) Denver; KTWO-TV (ABC) Casper; KUSA (NBC, WeatherNation) Denver; KWGN-TV (CW, This TV) Denver.
Programming (via satellite): A&E; AMC; Animal Planet; Bravo; Cartoon Network; CMT; CNBC; CNN; Comedy Central; C-SPAN; C-SPAN 2; Discovery Channel; Disney Channel; E! HD; ESPN; ESPN Classic; ESPN2; ESPNews; Food Network; Fox News Channel; FOX Sports Networks; Freeform; FX; Great American Country; Hallmark Channel; HGTV; History; HLN; Lifetime; MSNBC; MTV; Nick Jr.; Nickelodeon; Outdoor Channel; OWN: Oprah Winfrey Network; QVC; Spike TV; Syfy; TBS; The Weather Channel; TLC; TNT; Travel Channel; Trinity Broadcasting Network (TBN); truTV; Turner Classic Movies; TV Land; USA Network; VH1; WE tv; WGN America.
Fee: $59.99 installation; $25.00 monthly; $2.95 converter.

Digital Basic Service
Subscribers: N.A.
Programming (via satellite): BBC America; Bloomberg Television; Bravo; Discovery Life Channel; DMX Music; ESPN Classic; ESPN2; ESPNews; EVINE Live; Fox Sports 1; FSN Digital Atlantic; FSN Digital Central; FSN Digital Pacific; Fuse; FXM; FYI; Golf Channel; Great American Country; GSN; HGTV; History; History International; IFC; International Television (ITV); LMN; MBC America; National Geographic Channel; NBCSN; Nick Jr.; Nicktoons; Outdoor Channel; Ovation; Sundance TV; Syfy; TeenNick; The Word Network; Trinity Broadcasting Network (TBN); Turner Classic Movies; TV Land; WE tv.
Fee: $9.95 monthly.

Digital Pay Service 1
Pay Units: 6.
Programming (via satellite): Cinemax (multiplexed).
Fee: $13.95 monthly.
Digital Pay Service 2
Pay Units: 5.
Programming (via satellite): HBO (multiplexed).
Fee: $13.95 monthly.
Digital Pay Service 3
Pay Units: 1.
Programming (via satellite): Starz (multiplexed); Starz Encore (multiplexed).
Fee: $13.95 monthly.
Digital Pay Service 4
Pay Units: 24.
Programming (via satellite): Flix; Showtime (multiplexed); The Movie Channel (multiplexed).
Fee: $13.95 monthly (Showtime/Flix or TMC).
Video-On-Demand: No
Pay-Per-View
Hot Choice (delivered digitally); Playboy TV (delivered digitally); Fresh (delivered digitally); Shorteez (delivered digitally); iN DEMAND (delivered digitally).
Internet Service
Operational: Yes.
Broadband Service: Net Commander.
Fee: $39.95 installation; $51.95 monthly.
Telephone Service
None
Miles of Plant: 30.0 (coaxial); None (fiber optic). Homes passed: 1,001.
President & Chief Executive Officer: Jeffrey DeMond. Senior Vice President, Financial Planning: Daniel White. Vice President, Marketing: Diane Quennoz. Vice President, Residential Services: Vin Zachariah.
Ownership: Vyve Broadband LLC (MSO).

SHELL—TCT West. This cable system has converted to IPTV. Now served by BASIN, WY [WY5033]. ICA: WY5013.

SHERIDAN—Charter Communications, 12405 Powerscourt Dr, St. Louis, MO 63131. Phones: 636-207-5100 (Corporate office); 866-213-6572; 307-266-0034; 516-803-2300 (Corporate office); 877-273-7626. Fax: 307-266-6821. Web Site: http://www.charter.com. Also serves Sheridan County (portions). ICA: WY0006.
TV Market Ranking: Below 100 (SHERIDAN, Sheridan County (portions)); Outside TV Markets (Sheridan County (portions)). Franchise award date: N.A. Franchise expiration date: N.A. Began: September 1, 1955.
Channel capacity: N.A. Channels available but not in use: N.A.

Digital Basic Service
Subscribers: 4,972.
Programming (via satellite): A&E HD; AMC; Animal Planet HD; AXS TV; BBC America; Bloomberg Television; Bravo; Bravo HD; BYUtv; CBS Sports Network; CMT; CNBC HD+; CNN HD; Cooking Channel; Destination America; Discovery Channel HD; Discovery Kids Channel; Discovery Life Channel; Disney Channel HD; Disney XD; DIY Network; DMX Music; ESPN Classic; ESPN HD; ESPN2 HD; ESPNews; Fox Sports 1; Freeform HD; Fuse; FXM; FYI; Golf Channel; Great American Country; GSN; HD Theater; History HD; History International; HRTV; IFC; Investigation Discovery; ION Television; LMN; MTV Classic; MTV Hits; MTV Jams; MTV Live; MTV2; Nat Geo WILD; National Geographic Channel; National Geographic Channel HD; NBC Universo; Nick 2; Nick Jr.; Nicktoons; Outdoor Channel; Outdoor Channel 2 HD; OWN: Oprah Winfrey Network; Qubo; RFD-TV; Science Channel; Science HD; Sprout; TeenNick; The Weather Channel HD; TLC HD; TNT HD; Tr3s; Trinity Broadcasting Network (TBN); Universal HD; UP; Versus HD; VH1 Soul.
Fee: $12.99 monthly; $6.70 converter.

Digital Expanded Basic Service
Subscribers: N.A.
Programming (via satellite): A&E; AMC; Animal Planet; Cartoon Network; CMT; CNBC; CNN; Comedy Central; Discovery Channel; Disney Channel; E! HD; ESPN; ESPN2; EWTN Global Catholic Network; Food Network; Fox News Channel; Freeform; FX; Golf Channel; Hallmark Channel; HGTV; History; HLN; Lifetime; MSNBC; MTV; Nickelodeon; Pop; Root Sports Rocky Mountain; Spike TV; Syfy; TBS; The Weather Channel; TLC; TNT; Travel Channel; truTV; Turner Classic Movies; TV Land; USA Network; VH1.
Fee: $57.65 monthly.

Digital Pay Service 1
Pay Units: N.A.
Programming (via satellite): Cinemax (multiplexed); Cinemax HD; HBO (multiplexed); HBO HD; Showtime (multiplexed); Showtime HD; Starz (multiplexed); Starz Encore (multiplexed); Starz HD; The Movie Channel (multiplexed).
Fee: $12.00 monthly (Starz/Encore), $16.15 monthly (Cinemax, HBO or Showtime/TMC).
Video-On-Demand: No
Pay-Per-View
iN DEMAND (delivered digitally); NBA League Pass (delivered digitally); Viendo-Movies (delivered digitally); Fox Deportes (delivered digitally); NBC Universo (delivered digitally); Cinelatino (delivered digitally); History en Espanol (delivered digitally); Tr3s (delivered digitally); CNN en Espanol (delivered digitally); ESPN Deportes (delivered digitally); MLS Direct Kick (delivered digitally); Cine Mexicano (delivered digitally); NFL Network HD (delivered digitally); MLB Extra Innings (delivered digitally); NHL Center Ice (delivered digitally); NFL Network (delivered digitally); FOX College Sports Central (delivered digitally); FOX College Sports Pacific (delivered digitally); NHL Network (delivered digitally).

Internet Service
Operational: Yes.
Subscribers: 5,014.
Broadband Service: Charter Internet.
Fee: $49.99 installation; $29.95 monthly; $3.99 modem lease.
Telephone Service
Digital: Operational
Subscribers: 3,064.
Fee: $46.95 monthly
Miles of Plant: 238.0 (coaxial); 55.0 (fiber optic). Homes passed: 11,307.
President & Chief Executive Officer: Tom Rutledge. General Manager: Clint Rodeman.
Chief Technician: Shawn Jayne. Accounting Director: David Sovanski.
Ownership: Charter Communications Inc. (MSO).

SHERIDAN—Formerly served by Sprint Corp. No longer in operation. ICA: WY0068.

SHOSHONI—Formerly served by Winhill Corp. No longer in operation. ICA: WY0060.

STORY—Tongue River Communications, 620 Betty St, PO Box 759, Ranchester, WY 82839-0759. Phones: 800-953-9011; 307-655-9011. Fax: 307-655-9021. E-mail: trcatv@trcable.tv. Web Site: http://www.trcable.tv. ICA: WY0034.
TV Market Ranking: Below 100 (STORY). Franchise award date: N.A. Franchise expiration date: N.A. Began: July 1, 1980.
Channel capacity: N.A. Channels available but not in use: N.A.

Basic Service
Subscribers: N.A.
Programming (received off-air): KCWC-DT (PBS) Lander; KGWC-TV (CBS) Casper; KHMT (FOX) Hardin; KSGW-TV (ABC, MeTV, This TV) Sheridan; KTVQ (CBS, CW, Grit) Billings; KTWO-TV (ABC) Casper.
Programming (via microwave): KCNC-TV (CBS, Decades) Denver; KRMA-TV (PBS) Denver; KTLA (Antenna TV, CW, This TV) Los Angeles; KWGN-TV (CW, This TV) Denver; WPIX (Antenna TV, CW, This TV) New York.
Programming (via satellite): A&E; AMC; Animal Planet; Cartoon Network; CMT; CNBC; CNN; C-SPAN; C-SPAN 2; Discovery Channel; Disney Channel; E! HD; ESPN; ESPN2; Freeform; HGTV; History; HLN; KUSA (NBC, WeatherNation) Denver; Lifetime; MSNBC; MTV; Nickelodeon; Outdoor Channel; Spike TV; Syfy; TBS; The Weather Channel; TLC; TNT; Travel Channel; Trinity Broadcasting Network (TBN); truTV; USA Network; VH1; WGN America.
Fee: $40.00 installation.
Pay Service 1
Pay Units: N.A.
Programming (via satellite): Cinemax; HBO.
Fee: $10.00 installation; $10.00 monthly (Cinemax), $12.00 monthly (HBO).
Video-On-Demand: No
Internet Service
Operational: Yes.
Broadband Service: In-house.
Fee: $45.00 monthly.
Telephone Service
Digital: Operational
Miles of Plant: 13.0 (coaxial); None (fiber optic). Homes passed: 410.
General Manager: Rob Hium.
Ownership: Lynda & Robert Jacobson (MSO).

SUNDANCE—Tongue River Communications, 620 Betty St, PO Box 759, Ranchester, WY 82839-0759. Phones: 800-953-9011; 307-655-9011. Fax: 307-655-9021. E-mail: trcatv@trcable.tv. Web Site: http://www.trcable.tv. ICA: WY0061.
TV Market Ranking: Below 100 (SUNDANCE). Franchise award date: N.A. Franchise expiration date: N.A. Began: November 1, 1980.
Channel capacity: N.A. Channels available but not in use: N.A.

Basic Service
Subscribers: N.A.
Programming (received off-air): KCWC-DT (PBS) Lander; KGWC-TV (CBS) Casper; KHME (MeTV, This TV) Rapid City; KHSD-

D-878   TV & Cable Factbook No. 85

Cable Systems—Wyoming

TV (ABC, FOX) Lead; KPSD-TV (PBS) Eagle Butte; KTWO-TV (ABC) Casper.
Programming (via microwave): KCNC-TV (CBS, Decades) Denver; KTLA (Antenna TV, CW, This TV) Los Angeles; KUSA (NBC, WeatherNation) Denver; KWGN-TV (CW, This TV) Denver; WPIX (Antenna TV, CW, This TV) New York.
Programming (via satellite): A&E; AMC; Animal Planet; Cartoon Network; CMT; CNBC; CNN; C-SPAN; C-SPAN 2; Discovery Channel; Disney Channel; E! HD; ESPN; ESPN2; Freeform; HGTV; History; HLN; Lifetime; MSNBC; MTV; Nickelodeon; Outdoor Channel; Spike TV; Syfy; TBS; The Weather Channel; TLC; TNT; Travel Channel; Trinity Broadcasting Network (TBN); truTV; USA Network; VH1; WGN America.
Fee: $40.00 installation.
Pay Service 1
Pay Units: N.A.
Programming (via satellite): Cinemax; HBO; Starz Encore.
Fee: $10.00 installation; $3.00 monthly (Encore), $10.00 monthly (Cinemax), $12.00 monthly (HBO).
Video-On-Demand: No
Internet Service
Operational: Yes.
Broadband Service: In-house.
Fee: $45.00 monthly.
Telephone Service
Digital: Operational
Homes passed: 750.
General Manager: Rob Hium.
Ownership: Lynda & Robert Jacobson (MSO).

TEN SLEEP—TCT West. Now served by BASIN, WY [WY5003]. ICA: WY5017.

TEN SLEEP—TCT West. This cable system has converted to IPTV. Now served by BASIN, WY [WY5033]. ICA: WY0046.

THERMOPOLIS—Charter Communications, 12405 Powerscourt Dr, St. Louis, MO 63131. Phones: 636-207-5100 (Corporate office); 866-213-6572; 307-266-0034; 516-803-2300 (Corporate office); 307-856-3248 (Customer service). Web Site: http://www.charter.com. Also serves East Thermopolis & Hot Springs County (portions). ICA: WY0062.
TV Market Ranking: Below 100 (Hot Springs County (portions)); Outside TV Markets (East Thermopolis, THERMOPOLIS, Hot Springs County (portions)).
Channel capacity: N.A. Channels available but not in use: N.A.
Digital Basic Service
Subscribers: 767.
Programming (via satellite): A&E HD; Animal Planet HD; BBC America; Bloomberg Television; CBS Sports Network; CMT; Cooking Channel; Destination America; Discovery Channel HD; Discovery Kids Channel; Discovery Life Channel; DIY Network; DMX Music; ESPN Classic; ESPN HD; ESPNews; Food Network HD; Fox Sports 1; Fuse; FXM; FYI; Golf Channel; Great American Country; GSN; HD Theater; HGTV HD; History HD; History International; HRTV; IFC; Investigation Discovery; ION Television; LMN; MTV Classic; MTV Hits; MTV Jams; MTV2; Nat Geo WILD; National Geographic Channel; National Geographic Channel HD; NBCSN; Nick 2; Nick Jr.; Nicktoons; Outdoor Channel; OWN: Oprah Winfrey Network; RFD-TV; Science Channel; Science HD; Sprout; Syfy HD; TeenNick; Toon Disney; Tr3s; Trinity Broad-

casting Network (TBN); Universal HD; UP; USA Network HD; VH1 Soul.
Fee: $26.99 monthly; $6.70 converter.
Digital Expanded Basic Service
Subscribers: N.A.
Programming (via satellite): A&E; Altitude Sports & Entertainment; AMC; Animal Planet; Bravo; Cartoon Network; CMT; CNBC; Disney Channel; E! HD; ESPN; ESPN2; Food Network; Fox News Channel; FX; Hallmark Channel; HGTV; History; MSNBC; MTV; Oxygen; Pop; Root Sports Rocky Mountain; Spike TV; Syfy; The Weather Channel; TLC; TNT; Travel Channel; truTV; Turner Classic Movies; TV Land; USA Network; VH1.
Fee: $33.40 monthly.
Digital Pay Service 1
Pay Units: N.A.
Programming (via satellite): Cinemax (multiplexed); HBO (multiplexed); HBO HD; Showtime (multiplexed); Starz (multiplexed); Starz Encore (multiplexed); Starz HD; The Movie Channel (multiplexed).
Fee: $12.00 monthly (Starz/Encore), $16.15 monthly (Cinemax, HBO or Showtime/TMC).
Video-On-Demand: No
Pay-Per-View
iN DEMAND (delivered digitally); NFL Network (delivered digitally); FOX College Sports Central (delivered digitally); FOX College Sports Pacific (delivered digitally).
Internet Service
Operational: Yes.
Broadband Service: Charter Internet.
Fee: $49.99 installation; $29.95 monthly; $3.99 modem lease.
Telephone Service
Digital: Operational
Fee: $49.99 monthly
Miles of Plant: 19.0 (coaxial); 8.0 (fiber optic).
President & Chief Executive Officer: Tom Rutledge. General Manager: Clint Rodeman. Chief Technician: Dan Dorrell. Accounting Director: David Sovanski.
Ownership: Charter Communications Inc. (MSO).

TORRINGTON—Vyve Broadband, 234 North Windriver Dr, Douglas, WY 82633. Phone: 855-367-8983. Web Site: http://vyvebroadband.com. Also serves Goshen County (unincorporated areas) & Lingle. ICA: WY0014.
TV Market Ranking: Below 100 (Goshen County (unincorporated areas) (portions), TORRINGTON); Outside TV Markets (Goshen County (unincorporated areas) (portions), Lingle). Franchise award date: January 1, 1962. Franchise expiration date: N.A. Began: November 1, 1964.
Channel capacity: N.A. Channels available but not in use: N.A.
Basic Service
Subscribers: 984.
Programming (received off-air): KCWC-DT (PBS) Lander; KCWY-DT (CW, NBC) Casper; KGWN-TV (CBS, CW) Cheyenne; KLWY (FOX) Cheyenne; KNEP (ABC) Scottsbluff; KSTF (CBS, CW) Scottsbluff; KTNE-TV (PBS) Alliance.
Programming (via microwave): KCNC-TV (CBS, Decades) Denver; KMGH-TV (ABC, Azteca America) Denver; KTVD (MeTV, MNT) Denver; KUSA (NBC, WeatherNation) Denver; KWGN-TV (CW, This TV) Denver.
Programming (via satellite): QVC.
Fee: $59.99 installation; $25.00 monthly.

Expanded Basic Service 1
Subscribers: N.A.
Programming (via satellite): A&E; AMC; Animal Planet; Bravo; Cartoon Network; CMT; CNBC; CNN; Comedy Central; C-SPAN; C-SPAN 2; Discovery Channel; E! HD; ESPN; ESPN2; ESPNews; Food Network; Fox News Channel; Freeform; FX; Hallmark Channel; HGTV; History; HLN; Lifetime; MSNBC; MTV; Nick Jr.; Nickelodeon; Outdoor Channel; OWN: Oprah Winfrey Network; Pop; Root Sports Rocky Mountain; Spike TV; Syfy; TBS; The Weather Channel; TLC; TNT; Travel Channel; Trinity Broadcasting Network (TBN); truTV; TV Land; Univision Studios; USA Network; VH1; WE tv.
Fee: $19.04 monthly.
Digital Basic Service
Subscribers: N.A.
Programming (via satellite): BBC America; Bloomberg Television; Bravo; Discovery Life Channel; DMX Music; ESPN Classic; ESPN2; ESPNews; EVINE Live; Fox Sports 1; FSN Digital Atlantic; FSN Digital Central; FSN Digital Pacific; Fuse; FXM; FYI; Golf Channel; Great American Country; GSN; HGTV; History; History International; IFC; International Television (ITV); LMN; MBC America; National Geographic Channel; NBCSN; Nick Jr.; Nicktoons; Outdoor Channel; Ovation; Sundance TV; TeenNick; The Word Network; Turner Classic Movies; TV Land; WE tv.
Fee: $11.95 monthly.
Digital Pay Service 1
Pay Units: 384.
Programming (via satellite): Cinemax (multiplexed).
Fee: $11.95 monthly.
Digital Pay Service 2
Pay Units: 437.
Programming (via satellite): HBO (multiplexed).
Fee: $13.95 monthly.
Digital Pay Service 3
Pay Units: 417.
Programming (via satellite): Starz (multiplexed); Starz Encore (multiplexed).
Fee: $13.95 monthly.
Digital Pay Service 4
Pay Units: 74.
Programming (via satellite): Flix; Showtime (multiplexed); The Movie Channel (multiplexed).
Fee: $13.95 monthly (Showtime/Flix or TMC).
Video-On-Demand: No
Pay-Per-View
iN DEMAND (delivered digitally); Hot Choice (delivered digitally); Playboy TV (delivered digitally); Fresh (delivered digitally); Shorteez (delivered digitally).
Internet Service
Operational: Yes.
Subscribers: 1,225.
Broadband Service: Net Commander.
Fee: $39.95 installation; $51.95 monthly.
Telephone Service
None
Miles of Plant: 72.0 (coaxial); 12.0 (fiber optic). Homes passed: 4,298.

President & Chief Executive Officer: Jeffrey DeMond. Senior Vice President, Financial Planning: Daniel White. Vice President, Marketing: Diane Quennoz. Vice President, Residential Services: Vin Zachariah.
Ownership: Vyve Broadband LLC (MSO).

UPTON—Tongue River Communications, 620 Betty St, PO Box 759, Ranchester, WY 82839-0759. Phones: 800-953-9011; 307-665-9011. Fax: 307-655-9021. E-mail: trcatv@trcable.tv. Web Site: http://www.trcable.tv. ICA: WY0036.
TV Market Ranking: Outside TV Markets (UPTON). Franchise award date: June 7, 1990. Franchise expiration date: N.A. Began: November 1, 1978.
Channel capacity: N.A. Channels available but not in use: N.A.
Basic Service
Subscribers: 36.
Programming (received off-air): KHME (MeTV, This TV) Rapid City; KOTA-TV (ABC, FOX) Rapid City.
Programming (via microwave): KCNC-TV (CBS, Decades) Denver; KRMA-TV (PBS) Denver; KTWO-TV (ABC) Casper; KUSA (NBC, WeatherNation) Denver.
Programming (via satellite): A&E; Altitude Sports & Entertainment; AMC; Animal Planet; Cartoon Network; CNBC; CNN; C-SPAN; C-SPAN 2; CW PLUS; Discovery Channel; Disney Channel; E! HD; ESPN; Freeform; Hallmark Channel; HLN; ION Television; Lifetime; MSNBC; MTV; Nickelodeon; QVC; Spike TV; TBS; The Weather Channel; TLC; TNT; truTV; USA Network.
Fee: $40.95 installation; $1.65 converter.
Pay Service 1
Pay Units: N.A.
Programming (via satellite): HBO; Starz Encore.
Fee: $1.75 - $13.05 monthly (each).
Internet Service
Operational: No.
Telephone Service
None
Miles of Plant: 14.0 (coaxial); None (fiber optic). Homes passed: 343.
General Manager: Rob Hium.
Ownership: Lynda & Robert Jacobson (MSO).

WAMSUTTER—Formerly served by Sweetwater Cable TV Co. Inc. No longer in operation. ICA: WY0039.

WHEATLAND—Vyve Broadband, 234 North Windriver Dr, Douglas, WY 82633. Phones: 800-937-1397; 307-358-3833; 307-358-3861. Web Site: http://vyvebroadband.com. Also serves Platte County (unincorporated areas). ICA: WY0017.
TV Market Ranking: Outside TV Markets (Platte County (unincorporated areas), WHEATLAND). Franchise award date: January 1, 1962. Franchise expiration date: N.A. Began: September 1, 1963.
Channel capacity: N.A. Channels available but not in use: N.A.

Wyoming—Cable Systems

Get the industry standard FREE —
For a no-obligation trial call 800-771-9202 or visit www.warren-news.com

Communications Daily — Warren Communications News

Basic Service
Subscribers: 290.
Programming (via microwave): KCNC-TV (CBS, Decades) Denver; KCWC-DT (PBS) Lander; KCWY-DT (CW, NBC) Casper; KDVR (Antenna TV, FOX) Denver; KGWN-TV (CBS, CW) Cheyenne; KMGH-TV (ABC, Azteca America) Denver; KNEP (ABC) Scottsbluff; KSTF (CBS, CW) Scottsbluff; KTVD (MeTV, MNT) Denver; KUSA (NBC, WeatherNation) Denver; KWGN-TV (CW, This TV) Denver.
Fee: $59.99 installation; $25.00 monthly.

Expanded Basic Service 1
Subscribers: N.A.
Programming (via satellite): A&E; AMC; Animal Planet; Bravo; Cartoon Network; CMT; CNBC; CNN; C-SPAN; C-SPAN 2; Discovery Channel; E! HD; ESPN; ESPN2; ESPNews; Food Network; Fox News Channel; Freeform; FX; Hallmark Channel; HGTV; History; HLN; Lifetime; MSNBC; MTV; Nick Jr.; Nickelodeon; Outdoor Channel; OWN: Oprah Winfrey Network; Pop; QVC; Root Sports Rocky Mountain; Spike TV; Syfy; TBS; The Weather Channel; TLC; TNT; Travel Channel; Trinity Broadcasting Network (TBN); truTV; TV Land; Univision Studios; USA Network; VH1; WE tv; WGN America.
Fee: $36.54 monthly.

Digital Basic Service
Subscribers: N.A.
Programming (via satellite): BBC America; Bloomberg Television; Bravo; Discovery Life Channel; DMX Music; E! HD; ESPN Classic; ESPN2; ESPNews; EVINE Live; Fox Sports 1; FSN Digital Atlantic; FSN Digital Central; FSN Digital Pacific; Fuse; FXM; FYI; Golf Channel; Great American Country; GSN; HGTV; History; History International; IFC; International Television (ITV); LMN; MBC America; National Geographic Channel; NBCSN; Nick Jr.; Nicktoons; Outdoor Channel; Ovation; Sundance TV; Syfy; TeenNick; The Word Network; Trinity Broadcasting Network (TBN); Turner Classic Movies; TV Land; WE tv.
Fee: $11.95 monthly.

Digital Pay Service 1
Pay Units: 150.
Programming (via satellite): Cinemax (multiplexed).
Fee: $11.95 monthly.

Digital Pay Service 2
Pay Units: 174.
Programming (via satellite): HBO.
Fee: $13.95 monthly.

Digital Pay Service 3
Pay Units: 177.
Programming (via satellite): Starz (multiplexed); Starz Encore (multiplexed).
Fee: $13.95 monthly.

Digital Pay Service 4
Pay Units: 28.
Programming (via satellite): Flix; Showtime (multiplexed); The Movie Channel (multiplexed).
Fee: $13.95 monthly (Showtime/Flix or TMC).

Video-On-Demand: No

Internet Service
Operational: Yes. Began: August 1, 1998.
Broadband Service: Net Commander.
Fee: $39.95 installation; $51.95 monthly.

Telephone Service
None
Miles of Plant: 41.0 (coaxial); None (fiber optic). Homes passed: 1,956.
President & Chief Executive Officer: Jeffrey DeMond. Senior Vice President, Financial Planning: Daniel White. Vice President, Marketing: Diane Quennoz. Vice President, Residential Services: Vin Zachariah.
Ownership: Vyve Broadband LLC (MSO).

WORLAND—Charter Communications, 12405 Powerscourt Dr, St. Louis, MO 63131. Phones: 636-207-5100 (Corporate office); 307-347-3244; 877-273-7626; 516-803-2300 (Corporate office). Web Site: http://www.charter.com. Also serves Washakie County (portions). ICA: WY0013.
TV Market Ranking: Outside TV Markets (Washakie County (portions), WORLAND). Franchise award date: N.A. Franchise expiration date: N.A. Began: May 1, 1954.
Channel capacity: N.A. Channels available but not in use: N.A.

Digital Basic Service
Subscribers: 1,301.
Programming (via satellite): A&E HD; Animal Planet HD; BBC America; Bloomberg Television; CBS Sports Network; CMT; Cooking Channel; Destination America; Discovery Channel HD; Discovery Kids Channel; Discovery Life Channel; Disney Channel HD; Disney XD; DIY Network; DMX Music; ESPN Classic; ESPN HD; ESPNews; Food Network HD; Fox Sports 1; Freeform HD; Fuse; FXM; FYI; Golf Channel; GSN; HD Theater; HGTV HD; History HD; History International; HRTV; IFC; Investigation Discovery; LMN; MTV Classic; MTV Hits; MTV2; Nat Geo WILD; National Geographic Channel; National Geographic Channel HD; NBCSN; Nick Jr.; Nicktoons; Outdoor Channel; OWN: Oprah Winfrey Network; RFD-TV; Science Channel; Science HD; Sprout; Syfy HD; TeenNick; Tr3s; Trinity Broadcasting Network (TBN); Universal HD; UP; USA Network HD; VH1 Soul.
Fee: $26.99 monthly; $6.70 converter.

Digital Expanded Basic Service
Subscribers: 900.
Programming (via satellite): A&E; Altitude Sports & Entertainment; AMC; Animal Planet; Bravo; Cartoon Network; CMT; CNBC; CNN; Comedy Central; C-SPAN; Disney Channel; E! HD; ESPN; ESPN2; EWTN Global Catholic Network; Food Network; Fox News Channel; Freeform; FX; Hallmark Channel; HGTV; History; HLN; ION Television; Lifetime; MSNBC; MTV; Nickelodeon; Oxygen; Root Sports Rocky Mountain; Spike TV; Syfy; The Weather Channel; TLC; TNT; Travel Channel; truTV; Turner Classic Movies; TV Land; Univision Studios; USA Network; VH1.
Fee: $42.40 monthly.

Digital Pay Service 1
Pay Units: N.A.
Programming (via satellite): Cinemax (multiplexed); Flix; HBO (multiplexed); HBO HD; Showtime (multiplexed); Starz (multiplexed); Starz Encore (multiplexed); Starz HD; The Movie Channel (multiplexed).
Fee: $12.00 monthly (Starz/Encore), $16.15 monthly (Cinemax, HBO or Showtime/TMC).

Video-On-Demand: No

Pay-Per-View
iN DEMAND (delivered digitally); NFL Network (delivered digitally); History en Espanol (delivered digitally); Tr3s (delivered digitally); CNN en Espanol (delivered digitally); ESPN Deportes (delivered digitally); Cine Mexicano (delivered digitally); FOX College Sports Central (delivered digitally); FOX College Sports Pacific (delivered digitally); ViendoMovies (delivered digitally); Fox Deportes (delivered digitally); NBC Universo (delivered digitally); Cinelatino (delivered digitally).

Internet Service
Operational: Yes.
Broadband Service: Charter Internet.
Fee: $49.99 installation; $29.95 monthly; $3.99 modem lease.

Telephone Service
Digital: Operational
Fee: $46.99 monthly
Miles of Plant: 42.0 (coaxial); 6.0 (fiber optic). Homes passed: 2,967.
President & Chief Executive Officer: Tom Rutledge. Regional Vice President & General Manager: Clint Rodeman. Chief Technician: Dan Higgins. Accounting Director: David Sovanski.
Ownership: Charter Communications Inc. (MSO).

WRIGHT—Formerly served by Charter Communications. No longer in operation. ICA: WY0029.

WYODAK—Formerly served by Tongue River Cable TV Inc. No longer in operation. ICA: WY0035.

CUBA

Total Systems: 1	**Communities with Applications:** 0
Total Communities Served: 1	**Number of Basic Subscribers:** 0
Franchises Not Yet Operating: 0	**Number of Expanded Basic Subscribers:** 0
Applications Pending: 0	**Number of Pay Units:** 699

Top 100 Markets Represented: N.A.

For a list of cable communities in this section, see the Cable Community Index located in the back of Cable Volume 2.
For explanation of terms used in cable system listings, see p. D-11.

GUANTANAMO BAY—C H Comm LLC, 17 South Franklin Turnpike, Ramsey, NJ 07446. Phone: 201-825-9090. Fax: 201-825-8794. ICA: CU0001.
TV Market Ranking: Outside TV Markets (GUANTANAMO BAY). Franchise award date: December 5, 1986. Franchise expiration date: N.A. Began: March 1, 1987.
Channel capacity: N.A. Channels available but not in use: N.A.

Basic Service
Subscribers: N.A.
Programming (via satellite): A&E; BET; Cartoon Network; CMT; CNN; Comedy Central; C-SPAN; Discovery Channel; ESPN; ESPN2; Freeform; History; HLN; Lifetime; MTV; Nickelodeon; OpenTV; Pop; Spike TV; Syfy; TBS; Telemundo; TLC; TNT; Turner Classic Movies; TV Land; VH1; WGN America; WKRN-TV (ABC) Nashville; WNBC (COZI TV, NBC) New York; WPIX (Antenna TV, CW, This TV) New York; WSEE-TV (CBS, CW) Erie.
Fee: $10.00 installation; $1.68 converter.

Pay Service 1
Pay Units: 252.
Programming (via satellite): Cinemax.
Fee: $9.00 monthly.

Pay Service 2
Pay Units: 225.
Programming (via satellite): HBO.
Fee: $9.00 monthly.

Pay Service 3
Pay Units: 135.
Programming (via satellite): Showtime.
Fee: $9.00 monthly.

Pay Service 4
Pay Units: 87.
Programming (via satellite): The Movie Channel.
Fee: $9.00 monthly.
Video-On-Demand: No
Internet Service
Operational: Yes.
Telephone Service
None
Miles of Plant: 40.0 (coaxial); None (fiber optic). Homes passed: 3,000.
General Manager: Jim Feeney, Jr.
Ownership: C H Comm LLC (MSO).

GUAM

Total Systems: 1	Communities with Applications: 0
Total Communities Served: 20	Number of Basic Subscribers: 40,414
Franchises Not Yet Operating: 0	Number of Expanded Basic Subscribers: 0
Applications Pending: 0	Number of Pay Units: 0

Top 100 Markets Represented: N.A.

For a list of cable communities in this section, see the Cable Community Index located in the back of Cable Volume 2.
For explanation of terms used in cable system listings, see p. D-11.

AGANA—Docomo Pacific, 219 South Marine Corp Dr, Ste 206, Tamuning, GU 96913. Phones: 671-688-2273; 866-688-4826; 671-635-4628. Web Site: http://www.docomopacific.com. Also serves Agana Heights, Agat, Asan-Maina, Barrigada, Chalan Pago-Ordot, Dededo, Hagatna, Inarajan, Mangilao, Merizo, Mongmong-Toto-Maite, Piti, Santa Rita, Sinajana, Talofofo, Tamuning, Umatac, Yigo & Yona. ICA: GU0001.

TV Market Ranking: Below 100 (AGANA, Agana Heights, Agat, Asan-Maina, Barrigada, Chalan Pago-Ordot, Dededo, Hagatna, Inarajan, Mangilao, Merizo, Mongmong-Toto-Maite, Piti, Santa Rita, Sinajana, Talofofo, Tamuning, Umatac, Yigo, Yona). Franchise award date: N.A. Franchise expiration date: N.A. Began: October 1, 1970.

Channel capacity: N.A. Channels available but not in use: N.A.

Basic Service
Subscribers: 40,414.
Programming (received off-air): KGTF (PBS) Agana; KTGM (ABC) Tamuning; KUAM-TV (NBC) Hagatna; allband FM.
Programming (via satellite): A&E; AMC; Animal Planet; BET; Cartoon Network; CMT; CNBC World; CNN; CNN International; Comedy Central; Discovery Channel; Disney Channel; E! HD; ESPN; ESPN Classic; ESPN2; EWTN Global Catholic Network; Food Network; Fox News Channel; Freeform; FX; Golf Channel; HGTV; History; HLN; ION Television; Lifetime; MTV; Navy Office of Information (OI-03); Nickelodeon; Outdoor Channel; Pop; Spike TV; Syfy; The Weather Channel; TLC; TNT; Turner Classic Movies; TV Land; USA Network; VH1; WE tv.
Fee: $38.20 installation; $49.99 monthly; $4.95 converter.

Digital Basic Service
Subscribers: N.A.
Programming (via satellite): A&E HD; BBC America; BBC World News; Bravo; BYUtv; Destination America; Discovery Kids Channel; Disney XD; DIY Network; ESPN HD; ESPN2 HD; ESPNews; FOX College Sports Central; FOX College Sports Pacific; Fox Sports 1; FXM; FYI; Hallmark Channel; HD Theater; History International; Hope Channel; Investigation Discovery; JUCE TV; LMN; MC; MSNBC; MTV Classic; MTV Hits; MTV Jams; MTV2; NASA TV; National Geographic Channel; National Geographic Television; Nick Jr.; Nicktoons; OWN; Oprah Winfrey Network; Oxygen; Science Channel; TeenNick; Trinity Broadcasting Network (TBN); Universal HD.
Fee: $49.95 installation.

Pay Service 1
Pay Units: N.A.
Programming (via satellite): GMA Pinoy TV; Mix; The Filipino Channel.

Digital Pay Service 1
Pay Units: N.A.
Programming (via satellite): Cinemax; Flix; GMA Pinoy TV; HBO (multiplexed); MBC America; Mix; Showtime (multiplexed); Starz (multiplexed); Starz Encore (multiplexed); The Filipino Channel; The Movie Channel.

Video-On-Demand: Yes

Pay-Per-View
iN DEMAND (delivered digitally).

Internet Service
Operational: Yes.
Fee: $89.99 installation; $14.99-$79.99 monthly.

Telephone Service
Digital: Operational
Fee: $19.99 monthly

Miles of Plant: 709.0 (coaxial); 97.0 (fiber optic). Homes passed: 53,043.

President & Chief Executive Officer: Jonathan Kriegel. Chief Marketing Officer: Thomas Higa.

Ownership: Docomo Pacific (MSO).

MARIANA ISLANDS

Total Systems: 3	Communities with Applications: 0
Total Communities Served: 5	Number of Basic Subscribers: 4,766
Franchises Not Yet Operating: 0	Number of Expanded Basic Subscribers: 0
Applications Pending: 0	Number of Pay Units: 440

Top 100 Markets Represented: N.A.

For a list of cable communities in this section, see the Cable Community Index located in the back of Cable Volume 2.
For explanation of terms used in cable system listings, see p. D-11.

SAIPAN—CNMI Cablevision, PO Box 501298, Saipan, MP 96950. Phone: 670-235-4628. Fax: 670-235-0965. Web Site: http://www.docomopacific.com/cnmi. Also serves Rota & Tinian. ICA: MR0001.
TV Market Ranking: Below 100 (Rota, SAIPAN, Tinian). Franchise award date: N.A. Franchise expiration date: N.A. Began: June 1, 1976.
Channel capacity: N.A. Channels available but not in use: N.A.

Basic Service
Subscribers: N.A.
Programming (via microwave): KFVE (MNT) Honolulu; KGTF (PBS) Agana; KHNL (Antenna TV, NBC) Honolulu; KUAM-TV (NBC) Hagatna.
Programming (via satellite): CNBC World; CNN International; ESPN; Fox News Channel; Freeform; Korean Channel; Nickelodeon; The Weather Channel; USA Network.
Fee: $37.84 installation; $1.95 converter.

Expanded Basic Service 1
Subscribers: N.A.
Programming (via microwave): KHON-TV (CW, FOX) Honolulu.
Programming (via satellite): A&E; AMC; Animal Planet; Cartoon Network; Comedy Central; Discovery Channel; ESPN2; EWTN Global Catholic Network; Food Network; Golf Channel; HGTV; History; ION Television; Lifetime; MTV; Spike TV; Syfy; TLC; TNT; Turner Classic Movies; TV Land; VH1.
Fee: $13.55 monthly.

Pay Service 1
Pay Units: 440.
Programming (via satellite): Cinemax; HBO; Showtime; Starz; The Movie Channel.
Fee: $12.58 monthly (Cinemax, HBO or Starz), $15.74 monthly (Showtime/TMC/Sundance).

Pay Service 2
Pay Units: N.A.
Programming (via satellite): GMA Pinoy TV; The Filipino Channel.

Fee: $10.48 monthly (Japanese or Filipino channels), $22.10 monthly (Korean channel).
Video-On-Demand: No
Internet Service
Operational: Yes.
Broadband Service: In-house.
Fee: $62.95 monthly.
Telephone Service
None
Miles of Plant: 90.0 (coaxial); 20.0 (fiber optic). Homes passed: 10,000.
President & Chief Executive Officer: Jonathan Kriegel. Chief Marketing Officer: Thomas Higa.
Ownership: Docomo Pacific (MSO).

SINAPALO—CNMI Cablevision, PO Box 24728, Barrigada, GU 96921. Phone: 670-235-4628. Fax: 670-235-0965. E-mail: mcv.service@saipan.com. Web Site: http://www.docomopacific.com/cnmi. ICA: MR0003.
TV Market Ranking: Below 100 (SINAPALO).
Channel capacity: N.A. Channels available but not in use: N.A.

Basic Service
Subscribers: 126.
Fee: $30.00 monthly.
Chief Legal Officer: James W. Hofman, II. President & Chief Executive Officer: Jonathan Kriegel. Chief Marketing Officer: Thomas Higa.
Ownership: Docomo Pacific (MSO).

SUSUPE—CNMI Cablevision, PO Box 24728, Barrigada, GU 96921. Phone: 670-235-4628. Web Site: http://www.docomopacific.com/cnmi. ICA: MR0002.
TV Market Ranking: Below 100 (SUSUPE).
Channel capacity: N.A. Channels available but not in use: N.A.

Basic Service
Subscribers: 4,640.
Fee: $38.20 installation; $66.96 monthly.
President & Chief Executive Officer: Jonathan Kriegel. Chief Marketing Officer: Thomas Higa.
Ownership: Docomo Pacific (MSO).

PUERTO RICO

Total Systems: 6	Communities with Applications: 0
Total Communities Served: 87	Number of Basic Subscribers: 265,867
Franchises Not Yet Operating: 0	Number of Expanded Basic Subscribers: 0
Applications Pending: 0	Number of Pay Units: 0

Top 100 Markets Represented: N.A.

For a list of cable communities in this section, see the Cable Community Index located in the back of Cable Volume 2.
For explanation of terms used in cable system listings, see p. D-11.

BAYAMON—Liberty Cablevision, 1 Calle Manuel Camunas, PO Box 192296, San Juan, PR 00918. Phone: 787-355-3535. E-mail: info@libertypr.com. Web Site: http://www.libertypr.com. Also serves Carolina, Catano, Guaynabo, San Juan, Toa Alta, Toa Baja & Trujillo Alto. ICA: PR0002.
TV Market Ranking: Below 100 (Carolina, Catano, Guaynabo, Toa Alta, Toa Baja, Trujillo Alto, BAYAMON, San Juan).
Channel capacity: N.A. Channels available but not in use: N.A.
Basic Service
Subscribers: 126,981.
Fee: $34.00 installation; $15.00 monthly.
Internet Service
Operational: Yes.
Subscribers: 86,471.
Telephone Service
Digital: Operational
Subscribers: 36,737.
Miles of Plant: 2,950.0 (coaxial); 630.0 (fiber optic). Homes passed: 348,238.
Legal Representative: John F. Conrad.
Ownership: Liberty Cablevision of Puerto Rico LLC (MSO).

CAGUAS—Liberty Cablevision, 1 Calle Manuel Camunas, PO Box 192296, San Juan, PR 00919. Phone: 787-355-3535. E-mail: info@libertypr.com. Web Site: http://www.libertypr.com. Also serves Aguas Buenas, Aibonito, Barranquitas, Cayey, Cidra, Comerio, Gurabo, Humacao, Juncos, Las Piedras, Naranjito & Yabucoa. ICA: PR0004.
TV Market Ranking: Below 100 (Aguas Buenas, Aibonito, Barranquitas, CAGUAS, Cayey, Cidra, Comerio, Gurabo, Humacao, Juncos, Las Piedras, Naranjito, Yabucoa).
Channel capacity: N.A. Channels available but not in use: N.A.
Basic Service
Subscribers: 35,227.
Fee: $15.00 monthly.
Internet Service
Operational: Yes.
Subscribers: 8,599.
Telephone Service
Digital: Operational
Subscribers: 5,302.
Miles of Plant: 547.0 (coaxial); 284.0 (fiber optic). Homes passed: 40,622.
Legal Representative: John F. Conrad.
Ownership: Liberty Cablevision of Puerto Rico LLC.

CEIBA NAVAL BASE—Formerly served by Americable International. No longer in operation. ICA: PR0011.

CIALES—Liberty Cablevision, 1 Calle Manuel Camunas, PO Box 192296, San Juan, PR 00919. Phone: 787-355-3535. E-mail: info@libertypr.com. Web Site: http://www.libertypr.com. Also serves Arecibo, Corozal, Florida, Lares, Morovis, Orocovis, San Sebastion & Utuado. ICA: PR0012.
TV Market Ranking: Below 100 (Arecibo, CIALES, Corozal, Lares, Morovis, Orocovis, San Sebastion, Utuado).
Channel capacity: N.A. Channels available but not in use: N.A.
Basic Service
Subscribers: 34,300.
Fee: $15.00 monthly.
Legal Representative: John F. Conrad.
Ownership: Liberty Cablevision of Puerto Rico LLC (MSO).

LEVITTOWN—Liberty Cablevision. Now served by LUQUILLO, PR [PR0003]. ICA: PR0009.

LUQUILLO—Liberty Cablevision, 1 Calle Manuel Camunas, PO Box 192296, San Juan, PR 00919. Phones: 787-250-7780; 787-355-3535; 787-657-3050. E-mail: info@libertypr.com. Web Site: http://www.libertypr.com. Also serves Barceloneta, Caguas, Camuy, Canovanas, Ceiba, Dorado, Fajardo, Hatillo, Levittown, Loiza, Manati, Naguabo, Rio Grande, San Lorenzo, Vega Alta & Vega Baja. ICA: PR0003.
TV Market Ranking: Below 100 (Barceloneta, Caguas, Camuy, Canovanas, Ceiba, Dorado, Fajardo, Hatillo, Levittown, Loiza, LUQUILLO, Manati, Naguabo, Rio Grande, San Lorenzo, Vega Alta, Vega Baja). Franchise award date: N.A. Franchise expiration date: N.A. Began: December 1, 1985.
Channel capacity: N.A. Channels available but not in use: N.A.
Digital Basic Service
Subscribers: 23,175.
Programming (received off-air): WRFB (IND) Carolina; WSTE-DT (IND) Ponce.
Programming (via satellite): America CV Network LLC; GSN; QVC; Reelz; Telemundo Puerto Rico; Televisa; Univision Studios; WABC-TV (ABC, Live Well Network) New York; WCBS-TV (CBS, Decades) New York; WGN America; WNBC (COZI TV, NBC) New York; WPIX (Antenna TV, CW, This TV) New York.
Fee: $15.00 monthly.
Digital Expanded Basic Service
Subscribers: N.A.
Programming (via satellite): A&E; A&E HD; Animal Planet; Animal Planet HD; Antena 3 Internacional; Azteca; Bio HD; Bravo; Bravo HD; Caracol TV; Cartoon Network; CNBC; CNN; Comedy Central; Destination America HD; Discovery Channel; Discovery Channel HD; Disney Channel; Disney Channel HD; E! HD; ESPN; ESPN Deportes; ESPN HD; ESPN2; ESPN2 HD; ESPNU HD; Food Network; Freeform; FX; Golf Channel; GolTV; HD Theater; HGTV; History; History HD; HLN; Lifetime; MC; MSNBC; MTV; National Geographic Channel HD; NBC Universo; Nickelodeon; Science HD; Spike TV; Syfy; Syfy HD; TBS; The Weather Channel; TLC; TLC HD; TNT; Travel Channel; Travel Channel HD; truTV; TV Land; Universal HD; USA Network; USA Network HD; VH1; ViendoMovies; WGN America.
Fee: $42.99 monthly.
Digital Expanded Basic Service 2
Subscribers: N.A.
Programming (via satellite): BBC America; Bloomberg Television; Boomerang; Chiller; Cloo; CNN en Espanol; CNN International; Destination America; Discovery Kids Channel; Discovery Life Channel; Disney XD; DIY Network; ESPN Classic; ESPNews; ESPNU; EWTN Global Catholic Network; Fox Deportes; Fox Sports 1; Fuse; FYI; History International; IFC; Investigation Discovery; LMN; MTV Classic; MTV2; National Geographic Channel; NBCSN; Nick Jr.; Nicktoons; Outdoor Channel; OWN; Oprah Winfrey Network; Radar Channel; Science Channel; TeenNick; Tennis Channel; Tr3s; Turner Classic Movies; TVG Network; VH1 Country.
Fee: $14.99 monthly.
Digital Pay Service 1
Pay Units: N.A.
Programming (via satellite): Cinemax (multiplexed); Cinemax HD; HBO (multiplexed); HBO HD; Showtime (multiplexed); Showtime HD; Starz (multiplexed); Starz Encore (multiplexed); Starz HD; The Movie Channel (multiplexed); The Movie Channel HD.
Fee: $15.99 monthly (Cinemax, HBO, Showtime/TMC or Starz/Encore).
Video-On-Demand: Yes
Pay-Per-View
iN DEMAND (delivered digitally); Club Jenna (delivered digitally); Playboy TV (delivered digitally); Juicy (delivered digitally); Spice: Xcess (delivered digitally); MLB Extra Innings (delivered digitally).
Internet Service
Operational: Yes.
Subscribers: 8,599.
Broadband Service: In-house.
Telephone Service
Analog: Operational
Digital: Operational
Subscribers: 5,302.
Miles of Plant: 547.0 (coaxial); 284.0 (fiber optic). Homes passed: 40,622.
Executive Director: Naji Khoury. Vice President, Technical Operations: Ivan Rosa. Vice President, Sales & Marketing: Gabriel Palerm. Marketing Manager: Dalila Roldan. Legal Representative: John F. Conrad.
Ownership: Liberty Cablevision of Puerto Rico LLC.

MAYAGUEZ—Choice Cable, PO Box 204, Mercedita, PR 00715-0204. Phones: 787-355-3535; 877-717-0400. Fax: 787-651-9884. Web Site: http://www.choicecable.com. Also serves Aguada, Aguadilla, Anasco, Caba Rojo, Hormigueros, Isabela, Lajas, Las Marias, Moca, Quebradillas, Rincon & Sabanna Grande. ICA: PR0013.
TV Market Ranking: Below 100 (Aguada, Aguadilla, Anasco, Caba Rojo, Hormigueros, Isabela, Lajas, Las Marias, MAYAGUEZ, Moca, Quebradillas, Rincon, Sabanna Grande).
Channel capacity: 3 (not 2-way capable). Channels available but not in use: N.A.
Basic Service
Subscribers: 23,092.
Fee: $59.95 installation; $31.95 monthly.
Internet Service
Operational: Yes.
Subscribers: 19,379.
Telephone Service
Digital: Operational
Subscribers: 3,191.
Miles of Plant: 971.0 (coaxial); 172.0 (fiber optic). Homes passed: 82,033.
Vice President & Controller: John Rusak.
Ownership: Puerto Rico Cable Acquisition Co Inc (MSO).

MERCEDITA—Formerly served by Centennial de Puerto Rico. Now served by Choice Cable, PONCE, PR [PR0008]. ICA: PR0005.

PONCE—Choice Cable, PO Box 204, Mercedita, PR 00715-0204. Phones: 787-355-3535; 787-651-9867; 877-717-0400. Fax: 787-651-9884. Web Site: http://www.choicecable.com. Also serves Adjuntas, Arroyo, Coamo, Guanica, Guayama, Guayanilla, Jayuya, Juana Diaz, Maricao, Maunabo, Mercedita, Patillas, Penuelas, Playa de Ponce, Salinas, San German, Santa Isabel, Tallaboa, Villalba & Yauco. ICA: PR0008.
TV Market Ranking: Below 100 (Adjuntas, Adjuntas, Arroyo, Arroyo, Coamo, Coamo, Guanica, Guayama, Guayanilla, Jayuya, Jayuya, Juana Diaz, Juana Diaz, Maricao, Maunabo, Maunabo, Patillas, Penuelas, Playa de Ponce, PONCE, Salinas, San German, Santa Isabel, Tallaboa, Tallaboa, Villalba, Yauco). Franchise award date: June 1, 1984. Franchise expiration date: N.A. Began: June 16, 1986.
Channel capacity: 3 (operating 2-way). Channels available but not in use: N.A.
Digital Basic Service
Subscribers: 23,092.
Programming (received off-air): WAPA-TV (IND) San Juan; WCCV-TV (IND) Arecibo; WELU (ETV) Aguadilla; WIPM-TV (PBS) Mayaguez; WIRS (MundoMax) Yauco; WKAQ-TV (TMO) San Juan; WNJX-TV (IND) Mayaguez; WOLE-DT (IND, TMO) Aguadilla; WORA-TV (IND, UNV) Mayaguez; WPIX (Antenna TV, CW, This TV) New York; WQTO (PBS) Ponce; WSJU-TV (IND) San Juan; WSTE-DT (IND) Ponce; WSUR-DT (UNV) Ponce; WUJA (ETV)

Cable Systems—Puerto Rico

Caguas; WVEO (IND) Aguadilla; WVOZ-TV (IND) Ponce.

Programming (via satellite): A&E; AMC; Animal Planet; Bloomberg Television; Boomerang; Bravo; Cartoon Network; CNBC; CNN; CNN en Espanol; Comedy Central; C-SPAN; Discovery Channel; E! HD; ESPN; ESPN Classic; ESPN2; EWTN Global Catholic Network; Food Network; Fox Deportes; Fox News Channel; Freeform; Golf Channel; HGTV; History; HLN; HTV; Lifetime; LMN; MC; MSNBC; MTV; National Geographic Channel; Nickelodeon; Nicktoons; Outdoor Channel; OWN: Oprah Winfrey Network; QVC; Spike TV; Syfy; The Weather Channel; TLC; Travel Channel; Trinity Broadcasting Network (TBN); truTV; Turner Classic Movies; TV Land; USA Network; VH1; WE tv.

Fee: $31.95 monthly.

Digital Expanded Basic Service
Subscribers: N.A.
Programming (via satellite): BBC America; Destination America; Discovery Kids Channel; ESPN Deportes; ESPNews; Flix; FOX College Sports Central; FOX College Sports Pacific; FXM; FYI; History International; Investigation Discovery; MC; MoviePlex; MTV Classic; MTV Hits; MTV Jams; MTV2; NBCSN; Nick Jr.; Science Channel; TeenNick.

Digital Pay Service 1
Pay Units: N.A.
Programming (via satellite): Cinemax (multiplexed); HBO (multiplexed); Showtime (multiplexed); Starz (multiplexed); Starz Encore (multiplexed); The Movie Channel (multiplexed).

Video-On-Demand: Yes

Pay-Per-View
iN DEMAND (delivered digitally).

Internet Service
Operational: Yes.
Subscribers: 19,379.
Broadband Service: Choice OnLine.

Telephone Service
Digital: Operational
Subscribers: 3,191.
Miles of Plant: 971.0 (coaxial); 172.0 (fiber optic). Homes passed: 82,033.
President & General Manager: Michael Carrosquil. Vice President, Technical Operations & Chief of Operations: Jim Olanda. Vice President & Controller: John Rusak. Marketing Director: Tomas Montilla.
Ownership: Puerto Rico Cable Acquisition Co Inc (MSO).

SAN JUAN—Liberty Cablevision. Now served by BAYAMON, PR [PR0002]. ICA: PR0001.

VIRGIN ISLANDS

Total Systems: 2	Communities with Applications: 0
Total Communities Served: 3	Number of Basic Subscribers: 22,027
Franchises Not Yet Operating: 0	Number of Expanded Basic Subscribers: 8,650
Applications Pending: 0	Number of Pay Units: 16,845

Top 100 Markets Represented: N.A.

For a list of cable communities in this section, see the Cable Community Index located in the back of Cable Volume 2.
For explanation of terms used in cable system listings, see p. D-11.

ST. CROIX—St. Croix Cable TV, 4611 Tutu Park, Ste 200, St. Thomas, VI 00802. Phones: 340-779-9999; 866-240-2999; 340-712-5014. Fax: 340-778-3129. Web Site: http://www.innovativevi.net. ICA: VI0002.
TV Market Ranking: Below 100 (ST. CROIX). Franchise award date: January 1, 1981. Franchise expiration date: N.A. Began: April 1, 1981.
Channel capacity: N.A. Channels available but not in use: N.A.

Basic Service
Subscribers: 8,779.
Programming (received off-air): WCVI-TV (COZI TV, CW) Christiansted; WKAQ-TV (TMO) San Juan; WSVI (ABC) Christiansted; WTJX-TV (PBS) Charlotte Amalie; WVGN-LD (NBC) Charlotte Amalie; WVXF (This TV) Charlotte Amalie; 17 FMs.
Programming (via satellite): CNBC; Discovery Channel; EWTN Global Catholic Network; Freeform; Pop; QVC; TBS; The Weather Channel; TLC; Trinity Broadcasting Network (TBN); WGN America.
Fee: $34.71 installation; $11.53 monthly.

Expanded Basic Service 1
Subscribers: 8,650.
Programming (via satellite): A&E; Animal Planet; BET; Bravo; CNN; C-SPAN; C-SPAN 2; Disney Channel; E! HD; ESPN; ESPN2; History; HLN; Lifetime; MTV; Nickelodeon; Syfy; TBS; Tempo; TNT; Travel Channel; truTV; Turner Classic Movies; USA Network; VH1.
Fee: $43.25 monthly.

Digital Basic Service
Subscribers: N.A.
Programming (via satellite): 3ABN; BBC America; Boomerang; Cartoon Network; Cinelatino; CNN en Espanol; Comedy Central; Destination America; Discovery Kids Channel; DMX Music; ESPNews; Food Network; Fox Deportes; FOX Sports Networks; HGTV; History en Espanol; HRTV; Investigation Discovery; LMN; MTV Classic; MTV Hits; MTV2; NBA TV; NFL Network; Nick Jr.; Nicktoons; OWN: Oprah Winfrey Network; Science Channel; Spike TV; TeenNick; Tennis Channel; Toon Disney en Espanol; Tr3s; TV Land.

Digital Pay Service 1
Pay Units: 6,196.
Programming (via satellite): Cinemax (multiplexed); Flix; HBO (multiplexed); Showtime (multiplexed); The Movie Channel (multiplexed).
Fee: $40.00 installation.

Video-On-Demand: No

Pay-Per-View
Hot Network; iN DEMAND.

Internet Service
Operational: No, DSL & dial-up.

Telephone Service
Analog: Not Operational
Digital: Operational
Fee: $29.99 monthly
Miles of Plant: 480.0 (coaxial); None (fiber optic). Homes passed: 35,000.
Vice President, Public Relations: Jennifer Matarangas-King. Vice President, Cable TV Services: Graciela Rivera. Vice President, Cable Operations: Bernard Rey. Secretary-Treasurer: Mark Fortin.
Ownership: Innovative Communications Corp.

ST. THOMAS—Caribbean Communications Corp., 4611 Tutu Park, Ste 300, St. Thomas, VI 00802. Phones: 340-779-9999; 866-240-2999; 340-776-2150. Fax: 340-774-5029. Web Site: http://www.innovativevi.net. Also serves St. John. ICA: VI0001.
TV Market Ranking: Below 100 (St. John, ST. THOMAS). Franchise award date: October 21, 1985. Franchise expiration date: N.A. Began: January 1, 1966.
Channel capacity: N.A. Channels available but not in use: N.A.

Basic Service
Subscribers: 13,248.
Programming (received off-air): WCVI-TV (COZI TV, CW) Christiansted; WKAQ-TV (TMO) San Juan; WSVI (ABC) Christiansted; WTJX-TV (PBS) Charlotte Amalie; WVGN-LD (NBC) Charlotte Amalie; WVXF (This TV) Charlotte Amalie; 23 FMs.
Programming (via satellite): A&E; Bravo; CNBC; Comedy Central; C-SPAN; C-SPAN 2; Discovery Channel; EWTN Global Catholic Network; Freeform; Pop; QVC; The Weather Channel; TLC; Travel Channel; Trinity Broadcasting Network (TBN); TV2; WGN America.
Fee: $34.26 installation; $11.53 monthly; $3.05 converter.

Expanded Basic Service 1
Subscribers: N.A.
Programming (via satellite): AMC; Animal Planet; BET; Cartoon Network; CNN; Disney Channel; ESPN; ESPN Classic; ESPN2; Food Network; History; HLN; Lifetime; MTV; NFL Network; Nickelodeon; OWN: Oprah Winfrey Network; Spike TV; Syfy; TBS; Tempo; Tennis Channel; TNT; truTV; TV Land; USA Network; VH1; WE tv.
Fee: $2.00 installation; $43.25 monthly.

Digital Basic Service
Subscribers: N.A.
Programming (via satellite): 3ABN; BBC America; Discovery Digital Networks; Disney XD; E! HD; ESPN Deportes; ESPNews; HITS (Headend In The Sky); HRTV; INSP; LMN; NBA TV; Nick Jr.; Nicktoons; Oxygen; TeenNick.
Fee: $29.26 monthly.

Digital Pay Service 1
Pay Units: 10,649.
Programming (via satellite): Cinemax (multiplexed); Flix; HBO (multiplexed); Showtime (multiplexed); Starz (multiplexed); Starz Encore (multiplexed); Sundance TV; The Movie Channel (multiplexed).
Fee: $7.35 monthly (Cinemax), $9.45 monthly (Starz/Encore), $10.50 monthly (Showtime/TMC), $14.18 monthly (HBO).

Video-On-Demand: No

Pay-Per-View
iN DEMAND (delivered digitally); Playboy TV (delivered digitally); Fresh (delivered digitally); Shorteez (delivered digitally).

Internet Service
Operational: No.

Telephone Service
Digital: Operational
Miles of Plant: 386.0 (coaxial); 5.0 (fiber optic). Homes passed: 25,549.
Chief Executive Officer: Shawn O'Donnell. Vice President, Public Relations: Jennifer Matarangas-King. Vice President, Cable TV Services: Graciela Rivera. Vice President, Cable Operations: Bernard A. Rey. Secretary-Treasurer: Mark Fortin.
Ownership: Innovative Communications Corp. (MSO).

Ownership of Cable Systems in the United States

Comprises all persons or companies which have interest in cable systems or franchises. Ownership of all systems is assumed to be 100% unless otherwise noted.

3 RIVERS COMMUNICATIONS
PO Box 429
202 5th St. South
Fairfield, MT 59436
Phones: 406-467-2535; 800-796-4567
Fax: 406-467-3490
E-mail: 3rt@3rivers.net
Web site: http://www.3rivers.net
Officers:
David Gibson, General Manager
Bonnie Mayer, Human Resources Director
Sandi Oveson, Customer Operations Director
Brad Veis, Finance Director
Ron Warnick, Technical & Network Operations Director
Ownership: 3 Rivers Telephone Cooperative Inc..
Cable Systems (3):
Montana: CHOTEAU; CONRAD; SHELBY.

ACCESS CABLE TELEVISION INC.
302 Enterprise Dr.
Somerset, KY 42501
Phone: 606-677-2444
Fax: 606-677-2443
E-mail: roy@accesshsd.net
Web site: http://www.accesshsd.com
Officer:
Roy Baker, President
Cable Systems (6):
Kentucky: CUMBERLAND; GREENSBURG; HUSTONVILLE; McCREARY COUNTY (portions); WHITLEY COUNTY.
Tennessee: JELLICO.

ACENTEK
PO Box 360
207 East Cedar St.
Houston, MN 55943-0360
Phones: 507-896-3192; 888-404-4940
Fax: 507-896-2149
Web site: http://www.acentek.net/
Officers:
Todd Roesler, Chief Executive Officer
Jan Speer, Marketing Manager

Branch Offices:
Allendale
PO Box 509
6568 Lake Michigan Dr
Allendale, MI 49401
Phone: 616-895-9911
La Crescent
111 South Walnut St
La Crescent, MN 55947
Phone: 888-404-4940
Mesick
PO Box 69
5351 N M 37
Mesick, MI 49668
Phone: 800-361-8178
Traverse City
Old Mission - 14909 Peninsula Dr
Traverse City, MI 49686
Phone: 231-223-4211
Ownership: Ace Telephone Association.

Cable Systems (2):
Michigan: MESICK.
Minnesota: HOUSTON.

ADAMS CATV INC.
19 North Main St.
Carbondale, PA 18407-2303
Phones: 570-282-6121; 888-222-0077
Fax: 570-282-3787
E-mail: frontdesk@echoes.net
Web site: http://www.adamscable.com
Officers:
Dorotha T. Adams, President
Douglas V.R. Adams, Vice President
John Wallis, Engineering Director
Ownership: Dorotha T Adams.
Cable Systems (3):
New York: AFTON.
Pennsylvania: CARBONDALE TWP. (Lackawanna County); THOMPSON TWP..

ADAMS TELEPHONE CO-OPERATIVE
PO Box 248
405 Emminga Rd.
Golden, IL 62339
Phones: 217-696-4611; 877-696-4611
Fax: 217-696-4811
E-mail: sales@adams.net
Web site: http://www.adams.net
Officers:
Jim Broemmer, Chief Executive Officer
Walter Rowland, Chief Operating Officer
Dennis Cornwell, President
Vern Lubker, Vice President
Bill Scranton, Secretary-Treasurer
Cable Systems (2):
Illinois: BOWEN; CAMP POINT.
Other Holdings:
Cellular radio
Telephone

ADVANCE/NEWHOUSE PARTNERSHIP
5000 Campus Wood Dr.
East Syracuse, NY 13057-4250
Phone: 315-438-4100
Fax: 315-438-4643
E-mail: michael.mayer@mybrighthouse.com
Web site: http://www.timewarnercable.com/en/residential.html
Officers:
Steven A. Miron, President
Naomi M. Bergman, Executive Vice President, Strategy & Development
William A. Futera, Executive Vice President & Chief Financial Officer
Yixin J. Chen, Vice President, Advanced Technology
Kashif Haq, Vice President, Broadband Data Services
Mark A. Rinefierd, Vice President & Controller
Mark D. Wasserstrom, Vice President, Financial Planning
Ownership: Advance Publications, 61.24%; Newhouse Broadcasting Corp., 38.76%.
Represented (legal): Sabin, Bermant & Gould LLP.

Cable Systems (31):
California: BARSTOW.
Massachusetts: PITTSFIELD.
Nebraska: LINCOLN.
New York: ALBANY; DEWITT; JAMESTOWN.
North Carolina: CHARLOTTE; FARMVILLE; GREENSBORO; JACKSONVILLE; RALEIGH; WILMINGTON.
South Carolina: COLUMBIA; HILTON HEAD ISLAND.
Texas: AUSTIN; COLUMBUS; CORPUS CHRISTI; CRYSTAL CITY; DEL RIO; DILLEY; EAGLE PASS; EL PASO; GEORGE WEST; GONZALES; KERRVILLE; LAREDO; PHARR; PORT ARTHUR; SEADRIFT; UVALDE; WICHITA FALLS.
Cable Holdings:
Time Warner Entertainment Co. LP-Advance/Newhouse Partnership 33.3% interest; 26.3% of Bright House Networks LLC, see listing
Other Holdings:
Magazine: Golf Digest
Newspaper holdings

ADVOCATE COMMUNICATIONS INC.
12409 NW 35th St.
Coral Springs, FL 33065
Phone: 954-753-0100
Fax: 954-345-0783
Web site: http://www.advancedcable.net

Branch Office:
Weston Business Office
1274 Weston Rd
Weston, FL 33326
Cable Systems (2):
Florida: CORAL SPRINGS; WESTON.

ALGONA MUNICIPAL UTILITIES
PO Box 10
104 West Call St.
Algona, IA 50511
Phone: 515-295-3584
Fax: 515-295-3364
E-mail: info@netamu.com
Web site: http://www.netamu.com
Officer:
John Bilsten, General Manager
Cable Systems (1):
Iowa: ALGONA.

ALLEGHANY CABLEVISION INC.
Suite B
115 Atwood St.
Sparta, NC 28675
Phone: 336-657-0825
E-mail: alleghanycablevision@yahoo.com
Web site: http://www.alleghanycommunitytelevision.com
Officer:
George L. Sheets, President
Ownership: George L Sheets, President.
Cable Systems (1):
North Carolina: SPARTA.

ALLEN'S TV CABLE SERVICE INC.
PO Box 2643
800 Victor II Blvd.
Morgan City, LA 70380
Phone: 985-384-8335
Fax: 504-384-5243
E-mail: info@atvci.net
Web site: http://www.atvc.net
Officers:
Gregory A. Price, President
Chris Price, Vice President
Angela P. Governale, Secretary-Treasurer
Ownership: Elizabeth Price; Gregory A Price, jointly.
Represented (legal): Cole, Raywid & Braverman LLP.
Cable Systems (6):
Louisiana: ARNAUDVILLE; ASSUMPTION PARISH (portions); BAYOU L'OURSE; GRAND COTEAU; MORGAN CITY; PORT BARRE.

ALLIANCE COMMUNICATIONS
PO Box 349
612 3rd St.
Garretson, SD 57030
Phones: 605-594-3411; 605-772-644
Fax: 605-594-6776
E-mail: email@alliancecom.net
Web site: http://www.alliancecom.net
Officer:
Don Snyder, General Manager
Cable Systems (2):
South Dakota: GARRETSON; HOWARD.

ALL WEST COMMUNICATIONS
50 West 100 North
Kamas, UT 84036-9738
Phones: 435-783-4361; 866-255-9378
Fax: 435-783-4928
E-mail: questions@allwest.net; support@allwest.com
Web site: http://www.allwest.net
Officers:
Carl Clark, Chairman
Matthew Weller, President
Tony DiStefano, President, Operations
Lynne Pappas, President, Finance
Steve Taylor, Engineering Director
Ownership: Carl Clark, Principal.
Cable Systems (2):
Utah: OAKLEY.
Wyoming: EVANSTON.
Other Holdings:
Telephone

ALTA MUNICIPAL UTILITIES
223 Main St.
Alta, IA 51002
Phone: 712-200-1122
Fax: 712-200-9600
E-mail: altatec@alta-tec.net
Web site: http://www.alta-tec.net
Officers:
Kevin Walsh, Chairman, Board of Trustees
Randy Tilk, Utility Manager

Cable Owners

Cable Systems (1):
Iowa: ALTA.

ALTICE USA
1111 Stewart Ave.
Bethpage, NY 11714
Phone: 516-803-2300
Fax: 516-803-2368
Web site: http://alticeusa.com/
Officers:
Patrick Drahi, Founder
Dexter Goei, President, Altice NV & Chairman and Chief Executive Officer, Altice USA
Lisa Rosenblum, Vice Chairman
Hakim Boubazine, Co-President & Chief Operating Officer
Charles Stewart, Co-President & Chief Financial Officer
Terry Cordova, Chief Technology Officer
Paul Haddad, Global Chief Data Officer
Matthew Lake, Chief Marketing Officer
Victoria Mink, Chief Accounting Officer
Michael Schreiber, Chief Content Officer
Keith Sherwell, Chief Information Officer
Patrick Dolan, President, News 12 Networks
Ed Renicker, President, Media Sales
Kevin Stephens, President, Business Services
David Gilles, Head of Suddenlink Operations
Gregg Graff, Head of Residential Sales
Pragash Pillai, Head of Optimum Operations
Lee Schroeder, Head of Government Affairs
Colleen Schmidt, Head of Human Resources & Talent Development
David Connolly, Executive Vice President & General Counsel
Alan Dannenbaum, Senior Vice President, Programming
Ownership: Altice NV; BC Partners; Canadian Pension Plan Investment Board, jointly, 30%; ANV ownership; Patrick Drahi, 60.45%.
Cable Systems (31):
Connecticut: BRIDGEPORT; LITCHFIELD; NORWALK.
New Jersey: AVON-BY-THE-SEA; BAYONNE; BERGENFIELD; ELIZABETH; FREEHOLD; HAMILTON TWP. (Mercer County); HOBOKEN; MORRIS TWP.; NEWARK; OAKLAND; PATERSON; RARITAN; SEASIDE HEIGHTS.
New York: AMITYVILLE; BRONX; BROOKHAVEN; BROOKLYN; DOVER PLAINS; MAMARONECK; OSSINING; PORT CHESTER; RIVERHEAD; ROCKLAND; SUFFOLK COUNTY; WAPPINGERS FALLS; WARWICK; YONKERS; YORKTOWN.
Other Holdings:
Madison Square Garden, Radio City Music Hall
Cable advertising representative: Rainbow Advertising Sales Corp.
Common Carrier: Optimum Lightpath
Data service: IO: Interactive Optimum digital television, Optimum Online high-speed Internet, Optimum Voice digital voice-over-cable & Optimum Lightpath integrated business communications services
Newspaper holdings
Professional sports team: New York Knicks, Rangers and WNBA Liberty
Program source: News 12 Interactive; News 12 Hudson Valley; News 12 Brooklyn; News 12 Westchester; News 12 New Jersey; News 12 Long Island; News 12 Connecticut; News 12 Bronx
Telecommunications company: Lightpath CLEC

AMERICAN BROADBAND COMMUNICATIONS INC.
153 Dave Dugas Rd
Sulphur, LA 70665
Phone: 337-583-2111
Fax: 704-845-2299
E-mail: jduda@americanbb.com
Web site: http://www.americanbroadband.com
Officers:
Patrick L. Eudy, President & Chief Executive Officer
John P Duda, Executive Vice President & Chief Operating Officer
Cable Systems (8):
Louisiana: CARLYSS.
Missouri: MAITLAND; POMME DE TERRE; RICH HILL; SCHELL CITY.
Nebraska: BASSETT; BLAIR; WAYNE.

ANNE ARUNDEL BROADBAND LLC
Ste 201
406 Headquarters Dr.
Millersville, MD 21108
Phones: 866-950-2846; 410-987-9300
Fax: 410-987-4890
E-mail: customerserviceMD@broadstripe.com
Web site: http://www.broadstripe.com
Officer:
John Bjorn, Chief Executive Officer
Cable Systems (1):
Maryland: MILLERSVILLE.

KEITH ANTCLIFF
412 South Union Ave.
Newport, WA 99156
Phone: 208-437-4544
Fax: 208-437-2740
E-mail: staff@conceptcable.com
Web site: http://www.conceptcable.com
Cable Systems (1):
Washington: NEWPORT.

APPLIED COMMUNICATIONS TECHNOLOGY
PO Box 300
524 Nebraska Ave.
Arapahoe, NE 68922
Phones: 308-962-7298; 866-222-7873
Fax: 308-962-5373
E-mail: atccable@atcjet.net; support@atcjet.net
Web site: http://www.atcjet.net
Cable Systems (1):
Nebraska: ARAPAHOE.

ARGENT COMMUNICATIONS LLC
Ste 10, Box 235
10 Benning St.
West Lebanon, NH 03784
Phones: 603-922-7025; 877-295-1254
E-mail: service@argentcommunications.com
Web site: http://www.argentcommunications.com
Officer:
Andrew Bauer, Vice President, Business & Marketing
Cable Systems (5):
Maine: RANGELEY (town); TEMPLE (town).
New Hampshire: MILAN (town); SPOFFORD; TROY.

ARMSTRONG GROUP OF COMPANIES
One Armstrong Pl.
Butler, PA 16001
Phones: 724-283-0925; 877-277-5711
Fax: 724-283-9655
E-mail: info@zoominternet.net
Web site: http://armstrongonewire.com/television
Officers:
Jay L. Sedwick, Chairman
Kirby J. Campbell, Vice Chairman
Dru A. Sedwick, President & Chief Executive Officer
Jeffrey A. Ross, President, Armstrong Utilities Inc. (Broadband)
William C Stewart, Corporate Officer
Eric Aulbach, Chief Information Officer
Bryan Cipoletti, Chief Financial Officer
Christopher King, Executive Vice President, Financial & Accounting
David R Jamieson, General Counsel
Cable Systems (5):
Maryland: ABINGDON.
Ohio: VERNON TWP. (Trumbull County).
Pennsylvania: ZELIENOPLE.
West Virginia: DINGESS; HAMLIN.

ARTHUR MUTUAL TELEPHONE CO
21980 State Rte. 637
Defiance, OH 43512
Phone: 419-393-2233
Web site: http://www.artelco.net
Officers:
Eric Roughton, General Manager
Laureen Hill, Commercial Clerk
Cable Systems (1):
Ohio: DEFIANCE.

ASHLAND HOME NET
485 East Main St.
Ashland, OR 97520
Phone: 541-488-9207
E-mail: info@ashlandhome.net; customercare@ashlandhome.net
Web site: http://www.ashlandhome.net; http://www.ashlandtv.com
Officers:
Gary Nelson, President
Gary Knox, Operations Manager
Cable Systems (1):
Oregon: ASHLAND.

CATHY ASHWORTH
PO Box 1048
Littleton, NC 27850
Phone: 434-636-6000
Cable Systems (2):
Virginia: JARRATT; LAKE GASTON.
Other Holdings:
Cable construction: CWA Enterprises

ATC (ALMA, GA)
PO Box 2027
407 West 11th St.
Alma, GA 31510
Phones: 912-632-8603; 877-217-2842
Fax: 912-634-4519
E-mail: kbrooks@atc.cc; info@atcbroadband.com; sales@atcbroadband.com
Web site: http://www.atcbroadband.com
Officer:
Greg Davis, President

Branch Offices:
Baxley
371 W Parker St
Baxley, GA 31513
Phone: 912-705-5000
Blackshear
3349 Hwy. 84 W
Ste 104
Blackshear, GA 31516
Phone: 912-449-5443
Ownership: Alma Telephone Co..
Cable Systems (4):
Georgia: ALMA; BAXLEY; BLACKSHEAR; PATTERSON.

ATC COMMUNICATIONS
PO Box 98
225 West North St.
Albion, ID 83311
Phones: 208-673-5335; 208-673-1111
Web site: http://www.atcnet.net
Officers:
O'Deen Redman, President & Chief Executive Officer
Rich Redman, Vice President
Darla Redman, Executive Secretary
Barry Redman, Treasurer

Branch Offices:
Arco Office
205 Era Ave
Arco, ID 83213
Phone: 208-527-3249
Malad Office
89 N Main
Malad, ID 83252
Phone: 208-766-2882
Ownership: Albion Telephone Co..
Cable Systems (2):
Idaho: ARCO; MALAD CITY.

ATI NETWORKS INC.
PO Box 1558
344 South Cedar St.
Kalkaska, MI 49646
Phone: 231-518-0200
Fax: 231-518-0219
E-mail: info@atinetworks.net
Web site: http://atinetworks.net
Officers:
Gary John, President & Managing Partner
Shelly Narva, Office Manager
Cable Systems (1):
Michigan: BOARDMAN TWP. (southern portion).

ATKINS TELEPHONE CO.
PO Box 157
85 Main Ave.
Atkins, IA 52206
Phone: 319-446-7331
Fax: 319-446-9100
E-mail: jtraut@atkinstelephone.com
Web site: http://www.atkinstelephone.com
Officer:
Jody Traut, Manager
Cable Systems (1):
Iowa: ATKINS.

ATLANTIC BROADBAND
Ste 205
2 Batterymarch Park
Quincy, MA 02169
Phone: 617-786-8800
Fax: 617-786-8803
E-mail: info@atlanticbb.com
Web site: http://atlanticbb.com
Officers:
Louis Audet, President & Chief Executive Officer, Cogeco Cable
Richard Shea, President & Chief Executive Officer, US Operations
David Isenberg, President & Chief Revenue Officer
Christopher S. Daly, Chief Marketing Officer
Patrick Bratton, Senior Vice President & Chief Financial Officer
Leslie Brown, Senior Vice President & Legal Council
Joe Canavan, Senior Vice President, Business Services

Cable Owners

Donna Garofano, Senior Vice President, Government & Regulatory Affairs
David J Keefe, Senior Vice President & General Manager, Florida
Almis J Kuolas, Senior Vice President & Chief Technology Officer
Matthew M. Murphy, Senior Vice President, Corporate Development
Thomas F Roundtree, Senior Vice President, Human Resources
Jim Waldo, Senior Vice President & General Manager, Atlantic Broadband
Charles P Hanley, Vice President & General Manager, Connecticut
Curt Kosko, Vice President & General Manager, Pennsylvania
Courtney Long, Vice President, Customer Care
Heather McCallion, Vice President, Programming
Sam McGill, Vice President & General Manager, South Carolina and Maryland/Delaware
Ownership: Cogeco Cable Inc..
Cable Systems (26):
Connecticut: NEW LONDON.
Florida: MIAMI BEACH.
Maryland: CHESAPEAKE CITY; CUMBERLAND; PERRYVILLE; QUEENSTOWN.
New York: SALAMANCA.
Pennsylvania: ALTOONA; BRADFORD; CLEARFIELD; DERRY/DECATUR; JOHNSTOWN; McALEVYS FORT; MIFFLINBURG; NEW ENTERPRISE; SHIPPENVILLE; UNIONTOWN; WARREN.
South Carolina: AIKEN; ALLENDALE; BAMBERG; BARNWELL.
West Virginia: DAVIS; GRANT TOWN; KINGWOOD; PAW PAW.

ATLANTIC TELEPHONE MEMBERSHIP CORP.
PO Box 3198
640 Whiteville Rd. NW
Shallotte, NC 28459
Phones: 910-754-4311; 888-367-2862
Fax: 910-754-5499
E-mail: contact@atlantictelephone.org; contact@atmc.coop
Web site: http://www.atmc.net
Officers:
Lyle Ray King, President
Allen Russ, Chief Executive Officer & General Manager
Jackson Canady, Director, Engineering
Percy Woodard, Director, Marketing & Programming
Daphne Yarbrough-Jones, Public Relations Manager
Cable Systems (1):
North Carolina: SHALLOTTE.
Other Holdings:
Telephone holdings

ATWOOD CABLE SYSTEMS INC.
423 State St.
Atwood, KS 67730
Phone: 785-626-3261
Fax: 785-626-9005
E-mail: cableinfo@atwoodtv.net
Web site: http://www.atwoodcable.com
Officers:
Harold Dunker, President
Robert J. Dunker, Vice President
Kerry L. Dunker, Vice President, Operations
Ownership: Harold Dunker.
Cable Systems (1):
Kansas: ATWOOD.

AUBURN U.
300 Lem Morrison Dr.
OTI Dept
Auburn, AL 36849
Phone: 334-844-4000
Web site: http://www.auburn.edu
Cable Systems (1):
Alabama: AUBURN.

AUDREY HOMES LLC
PO Box 3015
Kalamazoo, MI 49003
Phone: 269-321-7912
Cable Systems (1):
Michigan: OSHTEMO.

AUGUSTA VIDEO INC.
115 East Capitol
Little Rock, AR 72201
Phone: 501-378-3400
Fax: 501-376-8594
Web site: http://wehco.com
Cable Systems (1):
Arkansas: AUGUSTA.

AYRSHIRE COMMUNICATIONS
PO Box 248
1405 Silver Lake Ave.
Ayrshire, IA 50515
Phone: 712-426-2800
Fax: 712-426-2008
Web site: http://www.ayrshireia.com
Officers:
John Higgins, President
William Myers, Vice President
Don Miller, General Manager
Eben Salton, Secretary
Ownership: Ayrshire Farmers Mutual Telephone Co.; AFMTC ownership; Northwest Communications Inc..
Cable Systems (1):
Iowa: GILLETT GROVE.

BAGLEY PUBLIC UTILITIES
PO Box M
18 Main Ave. South
Bagley, MN 56621-1012
Phone: 218-694-2300
Fax: 218-694-2865
E-mail: vfletcher@bagleymn.us; BagleyMinnesota@gmail.com
Web site: http://www.bagleymn.us
Officers:
Andrew Simons, Chairman
Dennis Merschmann, Secretary
Michael Jensen, General Manager
Ownership: Community owned--Bagley, MN.
Cable Systems (1):
Minnesota: BAGLEY.

BAILEY CABLE TV INC.
807 Church St.
Port Gibson, MS 39150
Phones: 601-437-8300; 601-892-5249
Fax: 601-437-6860
Web site: http://www.baileycable.net
Ownership: David A Bailey.
Cable Systems (15):
Louisiana: CLINTON; ETHEL; JACKSON; NORWOOD; ST. FRANCISVILLE.
Mississippi: CENTREVILLE; CRYSTAL SPRINGS; GLOSTER; HAZLEHURST; LIBERTY; MAGEE; MENDENHALL; PORT GIBSON; TERRY; WOODVILLE.

LEON M. BAILEY JR.
PO Box 368
115 North Main St.
Ripley, MS 38663
Phone: 662-837-4881
Fax: 662-837-9332
E-mail: leon@ripleycable.net
Web site: http://www.ripleycable.net
Cable Systems (1):
Mississippi: RIPLEY.

BALDWIN NASHVILLE TELEPHONE CO
PO Box 50
5075 Hwy. 64
Baldwin, IA 52207
Phone: 563-673-2001
Fax: 563-672-2241
Officer:
Larry Agnitch, President
Cable Systems (1):
Iowa: BALDWIN.

BALDWIN TELECOM INC.
PO Box 420
930 Maple St.
Baldwin, WI 54002
Phones: 715-684-3346; 877-684-3346
Fax: 715-684-4747
E-mail: info@baldwin-telecom.net; cabletv@baldwin-telecom.net
Web site: http://baldwinlightstream.com
Officers:
Matt Sparks, General Manager
Duane Russett, Plant Manager
Matt Knegendorf, CATV Manager
Ruthe Brenne, Office Manager
Brad Mortel, Broadband Manager
Ownership: Publicly held.
Cable Systems (1):
Wisconsin: BALDWIN TWP..
Other Holdings:
Cellular radio
Telephone

B & C CABLE
PO Box 548
Norwood, CO 81423
Phone: 970-327-4521
Fax: 970-327-4080
Officers:
Craig Greager, President, General Manager & Chief Technician
Mediatrica Greager, Vice President
Ownership: Craig Greager, 50%; Mediatrica Greager, 50%.
Cable Systems (1):
Colorado: NORWOOD.

BARBOURVILLE UTILITY COMMISSION
202 Daniel Boone Dr.
Barbourville, KY 40906
Phone: 606-546-3187
Fax: 606-546-4848
Web site: http://www.barbourville.com
Officers:
Randall Young, Superintendent
Wilhem Brewer, Assistant Superintendent
Josh Callihan, General Manager
Ownership: Community owned--Barbourville, KY.
Cable Systems (1):
Kentucky: BARBOURVILLE.

CITY OF BARDSTOWN
220 North 5th St.
Bardstown, KY 40004
Phone: 502-348-5947
Fax: 502-348-2433
E-mail: support@bardstowncable.net
Web site: http://www.bardstowncable.net
Officers:
Bill Sheckles, City Mayor
Mike Abell, Chief Financial Officer
Bobbie Blincoe, City Clerk
Lawrence Hamilton, Public Works & Engineering Director
Ownership: Community owned--Bardstown, KY.
Cable Systems (1):
Kentucky: BARDSTOWN.

CITY OF BARNESVILLE
PO Box 550
102 Front St. North
Barnesville, MN 56514
Phones: 218-354-2292; 800-354-2292
Fax: 218-354-2472
E-mail: klauer@bvillemn.net
Web site: http://www.barnesvillemn.com
Ownership: Community owned--Barnesville, MN.
Cable Systems (1):
Minnesota: BARNESVILLE.

BASCOM MUTUAL TELEPHONE CO.
PO Box 316
5990 West Tiffin St.
Bascom, OH 44809-0316
Phone: 419-937-2222
Fax: 419-937-2299
E-mail: contact@bascomtelephone.com
Web site: http://bascomtelephone.com
Officer:
Donna J. Siebenaller, Assistant Manager
Cable Systems (1):
Ohio: BASCOM.

CITY OF BAXTER SPRINGS
PO Box 577
1445 Military Ave.
Baxter Springs, KS 66713
Phone: 620-856-2114
Fax: 620-856-2460
Web site: http://www.lovesmalltownamerica.com/baxterspringsks.php
Ownership: Community owned--Baxter Springs, KS.
Cable Systems (1):
Kansas: BAXTER SPRINGS.

BAY COUNTRY COMMUNICATIONS
502 Maryland Ave.
Cambridge, MD 21613
Phone: 410-901-2224
Fax: 410-901-9116
E-mail: questions@bcctv.net
Web site: http://bcctv.com

Branch Office:
East New Market
47 Main St.
East New Market, MD 21631
Phone: 410-943-8311
Fax: 410-943-8430
Cable Systems (1):
Maryland: DORCHESTER COUNTY (portions).

BAYOU CABLE TV
378 Main St.
Marion, LA 71260
Phone: 318-292-4774
Fax: 318-292-4775
E-mail: admin@bayoucable.com
Web site: http://www2.bayoucable.com
Officers:
Allen Booker, President & Chief Executive Officer

2017 Edition   D-889

Cable Owners

Cathy Booker, Vice President & Secretary-Treasurer
Ownership: Allen Booker; Cathy Booker.
Cable Systems (5):
Arkansas: HUTTIG; STRONG.
Louisiana: MARION; ROCKY BRANCH; STERLINGTON.

BEAMSPEED LLC
2481 East Palo Verde St.
Yuma, AZ 85365
Phones: 928-343-0300; 928-317-6866
Fax: 928-726-8232
E-mail: support@beamspeed.net
Web site: http://www.beamspeed.com
Officers:
Harold Hendrick, General Manager
Hughie Williams, Chief Technician
Christi Weber, Marketing Director

Branch Office:
Calexico
640 S Imperial Ave
Suite 4
Calexico, CA 92231
Phone: 760-556-9000
Cable Systems (1):
Arizona: WELLTON.

BEAVER CREEK COOPERATIVE TELEPHONE CO.
15223 South Henrici Rd.
Oregon City, OR 97045
Phone: 503-632-3113
Fax: 503-632-4159
E-mail: support@bctonline.com
Web site: http://www.bctelco.com
Officers:
Paul Hauer, President
Mark Beaudry, Vice President, Operations
David Warner, Director, IT & Engineering
Tangee Summerhill-Bishop, Director, Marketing & Member Services
Cable Systems (1):
Oregon: BEAVERCREEK.

BEAVER VALLEY CABLE INC.
36150 Rte. 187
Rome, PA 18837
Phone: 570-247-2512
Fax: 570-247-2494
E-mail: bvc@cableracer.com
Web site: http://www.beavervalleycable.com
Officers:
Douglas Soden, Owner
Nancy Soden, Owner
Cable Systems (1):
Pennsylvania: ROME.

BEEHIVE BROADBAND LLC
2000 Sunset Rd.
Lake Point, UT 84074
Phones: 435-837-6000; 800-615-8021
Fax: 435-837-6109
E-mail: support@wirelessbeehive.com; support@beehive.net
Web site: http://beehive.net
Officer:
Wayne A. McCulley, Managing Member

Branch Offices:
1230 Aultman
Ely, NV 89301
Phone: 775-293-4040
Fax: 775-293-4036
Customer Service Centers
171 Silver St
Elko, NV 89801
Phone: 775-401-6650
Fax: 775-401-6653

Cable Systems (3):
Nevada: ELY; EUREKA; McGILL.

BEE LINE INC.
131 Lakewood Rd.
Madison, ME 04950
Phones: 207-474-2727; 800-439-4611
Fax: 207-474-0966
Web site: http://www.getbeeline.com
Officers:
Paul W. Hannigan, President
George C Allen, Vice President
Ownership: Paul W Hannigan, 5%.
Represented (legal): Garvey Schubert Barer.
Cable Systems (3):
Maine: FARMINGTON; MILLINOCKET; SKOWHEGAN.

BEK COMMUNICATIONS
PO Box 230
200 East Broadway
Steele, ND 58542
Phones: 701-475-2361; 888-475-2361
Fax: 701-475-2321
E-mail: bekcomm@bektel.com
Web site: http://www.bektel.com
Officers:
Brett Stroh, President
Tammy Birrenkott, Customer Service Manager
Cable Systems (1):
North Dakota: STEELE.

BELHAVEN CABLE TV INC.
PO Box 8
235 Pamlico St.
Belhaven, NC 27810-0008
Phone: 252-943-3736
Fax: 252-943-3738
Web site: http://www.belhavencabletv.com
Officers:
Guinn Leverett, Chairman & Chief Executive Officer
Ben Johnson, Chief Operating Officer
Corki Leverett, Secretary-Treasurer
Ownership: Corki Leverett.
Cable Systems (2):
North Carolina: BELHAVEN; OCRACOKE.

CITY OF BELLEVUE
106 North 3rd St.
Bellevue, IA 52031
Phone: 563-872-4456
Fax: 563-872-4094
E-mail: bellevue@ivuenet.com
Web site: http://www.bellevueia.gov
Ownership: Community owned--Bellevue, IA.
Cable Systems (1):
Iowa: BELLEVUE.

BENTON COOPERATIVE TELEPHONE CO.
2220 125th St. NW
Rice, MN 56367-9701
Phones: 320-393-2115; 800-683-0372
Fax: 320-393-2221
E-mail: bctc@bctelco.net
Web site: http://www.bctelco.net
Officers:
Dan Lieser, President
Ray Thompson, Vice President
Jim Young, Secretary-Treasurer
Cheryl Scapanski, General Manager
Duane Wentland, Operations Manager

Cable Systems (1):
Minnesota: RICE.

BENTON COUNTY CABLE
PO Box 430
Camden, TN 38320
Phones: 731-584-7100; 855-556-8423
Fax: 731-584-0913
E-mail: info@bentoncable.com
Web site: http://www.bentoncable.com
Cable Systems (1):
Tennessee: BENTON COUNTY (portions).

BENTON RIDGE TELEPHONE CO.
1805 North Dixie Hwy.
Lima, OH 45801-3255
Phone: 419-859-2144
Fax: 419-859-2150
E-mail: brtinfo@bright.net
Web site: http://www.brtelco.com
Officers:
Ken Williams, Chairman
Tom Knippen, Vice President & General Manager
Cable Systems (2):
Ohio: BENTON RIDGE; BROUGHTON.

BERESFORD CABLEVISION INC.
120 East Main St.
Beresford, SD 57004
Phones: 605-763-2500; 605-763-2008
Fax: 605-763-7112
E-mail: phone@bmtc.net
Web site: http://www.bmtc.net
Officers:
Todd Hanson, Manager
Dean Jacobson, Technician
Ownership: Community owned--Beresford, SD.
Cable Systems (1):
South Dakota: BERESFORD.

BEULAH LAND COMMUNICATIONS INC.
PO Box 188
8611 Central Ave.
Beulah, CO 81023-0188
Phone: 719-485-3400
Fax: 719-485-3500
E-mail: beulahland@socolo.net
Web site: http://www.pinedrivetel.com
Officer:
Richard J. Sellers, President
Ownership: Richard Sellers, Principal.
Cable Systems (1):
Colorado: BEULAH.

BEVCOMM
123 West 7th St.
Blue Earth, MN 56013
Phones: 507-526-2822; 800-473-1442
Fax: 507-553-6700
E-mail: info@bevcomm.net
Web site: http://www.bevcomm.net
Officer:
Bill Eckles, President & Chief Executive Officer

Branch Offices:
Minnesota Lake
208 Main St N
PO Box 188
Minnesota Lake, MN 56068
Phone: 888-846-8177
Morristown
100 2nd St SW
PO Box 86
Morristown, MN 55052
Phone: 800-390-6562

New Prague
115 Main St W
New Prague, MN 56071
Phone: 952-758-2501
Fax: 952-758-4343
Wells
191 2nd St SE
Wells, MN 56097
Phone: 507-553-3144
Winnebago
41 First Ave SE
PO Box 515
Winnebago, MN 56098
Phone: 507-893-3111
Cable Systems (4):
Minnesota: BLUE EARTH; MORRISTOWN; NEW PRAGUE; PINE ISLAND.

BIG SANDY BROADBAND
PO Box 586
510 Rte. 302 West
West Van Lear, KY 41268
Phones: 606-789-3455; 888-789-3455
E-mail: info@bigsandybb.com
Web site: http://www.bigsandybb.com
Officer:
Paul D. Butcher, Vice President
Cable Systems (1):
Kentucky: VAN LEAR.

BLAKELY CABLE TV INC.
65 Liberty St.
Blakely, GA 39823
Phone: 229-723-3555
Fax: 229-723-2000
Officer:
Charles Deloach Jr., President
Ownership: Charles Deloach Jr., 51%; Wayne R Foster, 49%.
Cable Systems (1):
Georgia: BLAKELY.

BLEDSOE TELEPHONE COOPERATIVE
PO Box 609
338 Cumberland Ave.
Pikeville, TN 37367
Phone: 423-447-2121
Fax: 423-447-2498
E-mail: bledsoe@bledsoe.net; customerservice@bledsoe.net
Web site: http://www.bledsoe.net
Officers:
John Lee Downey, President
Greg Anderson, General Manager
Nell Morgan, Secretary-Treasurer
Cable Systems (1):
Tennessee: PIKEVILLE.

BLOCK COMMUNICATIONS INC.
Ste 2100
405 Madison Ave.
Toledo, OH 43604
Phones: 419-724-6212; 419-724-6035
Fax: 419-724-6167
E-mail: askus@cablesystem.com
Web site: http://www.blockcommunications.com
Officers:
Allan J. Block, Chairman
John R. Block, Vice Chairman
Gary J. Blair, President
Joe Jensen, Executive Vice President, Cable & Telecommunications
David M. Beihoff, Vice President, Newspaper Operations

Cable Owners

Jodi L. Miehls, Assistant Secretary
Ownership: Allan J Block, 25%; John R Block, 25%; William Block Marital Trusts, Karen D Johnese, Trustee, 25%; Family Trust No. 2, William Block Jr, Chairperson of Trustees, 25%. votes.
Cable Systems (1):
Ohio: TOLEDO.
TV Stations:
Idaho: KTRV-TV Nampa.
Illinois: WAND Decatur.
Indiana: WMYO Salem.
Kentucky: WDRB Louisville.
Ohio: WLIO Lima.
LPTV Stations:
Illinois: W31BX-D Danville; W40CV-D Jacksonville.
Ohio: WFND-LD Findlay; WLMO-LP Lima; WLQP-LP Lima; WOHL-CD Lima.
Other Holdings:
Business Communications Provider: Line Systems Inc.
Construction: Metro Fiber & Cable Construction Co. (Toledo)
Newspaper holdings
Outdoor advertising: Community Communications Services, advertising distribution company
Telephone service: Buckeye Telesystem Inc. (Toledo)

BLOOMINGDALE COMMUNICATIONS
PO Box 187
101 West Kalamazoo St.
Bloomingdale, MI 49026
Phones: 269-521-7300; 800-377-3130
Fax: 269-521-7373
E-mail: staff@bloomingdalecom.net
Web site: http://www.bloomingdalecom.net
Officers:
Robert Remington, President
Mark Bahnson, General Manager
Dan Key, Facilities Manager

Branch Office:
Paw Paw
PO Box 205
114 S Kalamazoo St
Paw Paw, MI 49079
Phone: 269-415-0500
Ownership: William Godfrey, President.
Cable Systems (1):
Michigan: BLOOMINGDALE TWP. (Van Buren County).

BLUEBRIDGE MEDIA
231 South Cedar Ave
South Pittsburg, TN 37380
Phone: 423-837-2000
Web site: http://www.bluebridgemedia.com
Cable Systems (1):
Tennessee: ORME.

BLUE DEVIL CABLE TV INC.
116 South 4th St.
Toronto, OH 43964
Phones: 740-537-2030; 800-931-9392
Fax: 740-537-2802
E-mail: bdcable@brdband.com
Web site: http://bluedevilcabletv.com
Cable Systems (3):
Pennsylvania: BURGETTSTOWN.
West Virginia: BEECH BOTTOM; WELLSBURG.

BLUE MOUNTAIN TV CABLE CO.
PO Box 267
Mount Vernon, OR 97865
Phone: 541-932-4613
Fax: 541-932-4613
Web site: http://www.bmtvcable.com
Ownership: Jack McKenna.

Cable Systems (1):
Oregon: MOUNT VERNON.

BLUE VALLEY TELECOMMUNICATIONS
1559 Pony Express Hwy.
Home, KS 66438
Phones: 785-799-3311; 877-876-1228
E-mail: info@bluevalley.net
Web site: http://www.bluevalley.net
Officers:
Brian Thomason, General Manager & Chief Executive Officer
Candace Wright, Chief Financial Officer
Jada Ackerman, Public Relations & Community Development Director
Angie Armstrong, Marketing Supervisor
Kent Kucklelman, Network Operations Center Supervisor
Deb Runnebaum, Customer Service Supervisor
Cable Systems (1):
Kansas: AXTELL.

BOB & DIAN BOALDIN
610 S Cosmos
Elkhart, KS 67950
Phones: 620-697-2111; 800-544-4250
Web site: http://www.epictouch.com
Cable Systems (1):
Kansas: ELKHART.

VILLAGE OF BOAZ
Rte 1
Muscoda, WI 53573
Phone: 608-536-3493
E-mail: villofboaz@mwt.net
Ownership: Local investors.
Cable Systems (1):
Wisconsin: BOAZ (village).

DAN BOWLING
PO Box 522
652 Owls Nest Rd.
Hyden, KY 41749-0522
Phone: 606-672-3479
Cable Systems (1):
Kentucky: HYDEN.

BOYCOM CABLEVISION INC.
3467 Township Line Rd.
Poplar Bluff, MO 63901
Phones: 573-686-9101; 800-935-0255
Fax: 573-686-4722
E-mail: customer_service@boycomonline.com
Web site: http://www.boycom.com
Officers:
Steven D. Boyers, Chairman, President & Chief Executive & Operating Officer
Patricia Jo Boyers, Vice President, Secretary-Treasurer & Chief Financial Officer
Ownership: Steven D Boyers, 50%; Patricia Jo Boyers, 50%.
Cable Systems (7):
Missouri: DONIPHAN; FAIRDEALING; PIEDMONT; POPLAR BLUFF; PUXICO; VAN BUREN; WAPPAPELLO.

BRAINTREE ELECTRIC LIGHT DEPARTMENT
150 Potter Rd.
Braintree, MA 02184
Phone: 781-348-2353
Fax: 781-348-1002
E-mail: gm@beld.com
Web site: http://www.beld.com
Officers:

William G Bottiggi, General Manager
JoAnn Stak Bregnard, Marketing & Programming Director
Cable Systems (1):
Massachusetts: BRAINTREE.

BRIGHT HOUSE NETWORKS LLC
Ste 600
65 South Keller Rd.
Orlando, FL 32801
Phones: 407-291-2500; 855-222-0102
E-mail: stephen.colafrancesco@mybrighthouse.com
Web site: http://brighthouse.com
Officers:
Steven Miron, Chairman & Chief Executive Officer
Nomi Bergman, President
Kevin Hyman, Executive Vice President, Cable Operations
Leo Cloutier, Senior Vice President, Corporate Strategy & Business Development
Dick Amell, Corporate Vice President, Video Engineering & Operations
Pam Hagan, Corporate Vice President, Human Resources
Stephen Colafrancesco, Vice President, Marketing
Alan Mason, Vice President/General Manager, News & Local Programming
Jennifer Mooney, Vice President, Corporate Government & Public Affairs
Todd A Stewart, Vice President, Advertising Sales

Branch Office:
Central Florida
1670 E. Hwy. 50
Suite D
Clermont, FL 34711
Phone: 407-295-9119
Fax: 352-243-7592
Ownership: Charter Communications Inc., see listing, 73.7%; Advance/Newhouse Partnership, see listing, 26.3%. On May 26, 2015, Charter Communications Inc. announced it was merging with Time Warner Cable and acquiring Bright House Networks LLC (see listings for Charter and Time Warner Cable). FCC approved deals May 6, 2016. Deal closed May 18, 2016.
Cable Systems (19):
Alabama: BIRMINGHAM; CLIO; EUFAULA; GREENVILLE; WETUMPKA.
California: AVENAL; BAKERSFIELD.
Florida: BLOUNTSTOWN; BOWLING GREEN; CANTONMENT; CEDAR KEY; CHATTAHOOCHEE; CHIPLEY; DE FUNIAK SPRINGS; HILLSBOROUGH COUNTY (portions); ORLANDO.
Indiana: INDIANAPOLIS (portions); MARION.
Michigan: LIVONIA.

BRISTERS CABLE TV
107 Sleepy Oaks Rd.
Fort Walton Beach, FL 32548
Phone: 251-367-4243
Cable Systems (1):
Alabama: MOBILE.

BRISTOL BAY TELEPHONE COOPERATIVE INC.
PO Box 259
1 Main St.
King Salmon, AK 99613
Phones: 907-246-3403; 800-478-9100
Fax: 907-246-1115
E-mail: bbtcmanager@bristolbay.com; bbtccsr@bristolbay.com
Web site: http://www.bristolbay.com
Officer:

Todd Hoppe, General Manager
Ownership: Subscriber owned--Bristol Bay, AK.
Cable Systems (1):
Alaska: KING SALMON.

BRISTOL TENNESSEE ESSENTIAL SERVICES
2470 Volunteer Pkwy.
Bristol, TN 37620
Phone: 423-968-1526
Fax: 423-793-5520
E-mail: customerservice@btes.net
Web site: http://www.btes.net
Officers:
Dr. R Michael Browder, Chief Executive Officer
April L. Eads, Business Development Manager
Cable Systems (2):
Tennessee: BRISTOL; BRISTOL.

BROCKWAY TV INC.
501 Main St.
Brockway, PA 15824
Phone: 814-268-6565
Fax: 814-265-1300
E-mail: lwayne@brockwaytv.com
Web site: http://myaccount.brockwaytv.com
Officers:
Mike Arnold, Chairman
Tim Grieneisen, Vice Chairman
Laurie Wayne, Business Manager
Howard Olay, Head Technician
Ownership: Subscriber owned--Brockway, PA.
Represented (legal): Ferraro, Kruk & Ferraro LLP.
Cable Systems (1):
Pennsylvania: BROCKWAY.

BROKEN BOW TELEVISION CO.
210 North Park Dr.
Broken Bow, OK 74728
Phones: 580-584-3355; 580-584-5800
E-mail: info@pine-net.com; techsupport@pine-net.com
Web site: http://www.pine-net.com
Ownership: Jewel B Callaham Revocable Trust; Esta Callaham; John B Callaham; Angela G Wisenhunt, Trustees.
Cable Systems (1):
Oklahoma: BROKEN BOW.
LPTV Stations:
Oklahoma: K28DJ-D Broken Bow.
Other Holdings:
Telephone: Pine Telephone Co. Inc

BRYAN MUNICIPAL UTILITIES
841 East Edgerton St.
Bryan, OH 43506
Phones: 419-633-6100; 419-633-6130
Fax: 419-633-6105
E-mail: jferrell@cityofbryan.com
Web site: http://www.cityofbryan.net
Officer:
Lou Pendleton, Public Relations Director
Cable Systems (1):
Ohio: BRYAN.

BTC INC.
112 East Main St.
Breda, IA 51436
Phones: 712-673-2311; 888-508-2946
E-mail: customerservice@westianet.com
Web site: http://www.westianet.com
Ownership: Breda Telephone Corp.; BTC ownership:; Ott Boeckman, Principal.
Cable Systems (1):
Iowa: BREDA.
Other Holdings:
Telephone

2017 Edition

D-891

Cable Owners

BUFORD MEDIA GROUP LLC
6125 Paluxy Dr.
Tyler, TX 75703
Phone: 903-561-4411
Fax: 903-561-4031
E-mail: info@bufordmedia.com
Officers:
Ben W. Hooks Jr., Chief Executive Officer
Bennett Hooks III, President
Julie Newman, Vice President, Programming & Contract Compliance
Tony Swain, Engineering
Cable Systems (27):
Alabama: UNIONTOWN.
Arkansas: DES ARC; JUNCTION CITY; LAKE VIEW.
Louisiana: ARCADIA; BASILE; COLFAX; GIBSLAND; MERRYVILLE; MONTGOMERY; NATCHEZ; NEWELLTON; OLLA; WATERPROOF.
Mississippi: BASSFIELD; CROWDER; LEAKESVILLE; RICHTON; SHUBUTA.
Oklahoma: ANTLERS; WALTERS; WAURIKA.
Texas: COOPER; FREER; HEBBRONVILLE; JOURDANTON; LAKE CHEROKEE.
Other Holdings:
Manages Allegiance Communications, see listing

BULLDOG CABLE
455 Gees Mill Business Ct.
Conyers, GA 30013
Phone: 800-388-6577
Web site: http://www.bulldogcable.com
Officer:
Joe Sheehan, Chief Executive Officer
Cable Systems (15):
Georgia: ABBEVILLE; CHESTER; COLQUITT; DUDLEY; GORDON; NEWTON COUNTY; PUTNAM COUNTY; ROCHELLE; SPARTA; WRENS.
Montana: BIG SKY; PLENTYWOOD; POPLAR; SCOBEY; WEST YELLOWSTONE.

BULLOCH TELEPHONE COOPERATIVE
2903 Northside Dr. West
Statesboro, GA 30458
Phone: 912-865-1100
Fax: 912-865-2500
E-mail: bullnet@bulloch.net
Web site: http://www.bulloch.net
Officers:
W H Smith III, Chairman
William C Cromley III, Vice Chairman
Edwin Dale Smith, Secretary & Treasurer
Cable Systems (1):
Georgia: BROOKLET.

BUTLER-BREMER COMMUNICATIONS
PO Box 99
715 Main St.
Plainfield, IA 50666
Phones: 319-276-4458; 800-830-1146
Fax: 319-276-7530
E-mail: comments@butler-bremer.com
Web site: http://butler-bremer.com
Officers:
Gerome Bieneman, President
Richard Rettig, Secretary-Treasurer
Wayne R. Miller, General Manager
Cable Systems (1):
Iowa: TRIPOLI.

BVU OPTINET
c/o Bristol Virginia Utilities
15022 Lee Hwy.
Bristol, VA 24202
Phones: 276-821-6100; 866-835-1288
Fax: 276-821-6218
E-mail: help@bvu-optinet.com
Web site: http://www.bvu-optinet.com
Officers:
Wes Rosenbalm, President & Chief Executive Officer
Mike Bundy, Chief Operating Officer
Stacey Bright, Executive Vice President & Chief Financial Officer
Mark Lane, Chief Technical Officer
Brian Bolling, Vice President, Customer Service
David Copeland, Vice President, Field Operations
Kyle Hollifield, Vice President, Marketing & Business Development
Robert Snodgrass, Vice President, Operations
Cable Systems (1):
Virginia: BRISTOL.

BWTELCOM
607 Chief St.
Benkelman, NE 69021
Phone: 308-423-2000
Fax: 308-423-2399
E-mail: bwtelcom@bwtelcom.net
Web site: http://www.bwtelcom.net
Officer:
Randall J. Raille, Manager

Branch Office:
Wauneta
54 E Quachita St
Wauneta, NE 69045
Phone: 308-394-6000
Cable Systems (3):
Nebraska: BENKELMAN; HAIGLER; WAUNETA.

CABLEAMERICA CORP.
7822 East Gray Rd.
Mesa, AZ 85260
Phones: 480-315-1820; 480-558-7300
Fax: 480-315-1819
Web site: http://www.cableamerica.com
Officers:
Alan C. Jackson, Vice President
Eric W. Jackson, Vice President
William H. Lewis, Vice President
John A. Mori, Marketing Director

Branch Offices:
Houston/Licking and Surrounding Areas
115 E. Pine St.
Houston, MO 65483
Phone: 417-967-5571
Maryland Heights and Surrounding Areas
11422 Schenk Dr.
Maryland Heights, MO 63043
Phone: 314-995-4800
Mid-State Missouri
690 Missouri Ave
No 13
St. Robert, MO 65584
Phone: 573-336-5284
Republic, MO
655 Hillside Ave.
Republic, MO 65738
Phone: 417-732-7242
Ownership: William G Jackson, 90%; Gloria J Jackson, 10%.
Represented (legal): Cole, Raywid & Braverman LLP.
Cable Systems (11):
Arizona: GILA BEND.
Michigan: EAGLE HARBOR TWP.; GRAND MARAIS; REPUBLIC TWP.; SHINGLETON.
Missouri: LAKE SHERWOOD; LINN; MARYLAND HEIGHTS; PHELPS COUNTY (portions); REPUBLIC; ST. ROBERT.
Other Holdings:
SMATV

CABLE BAHAMAS LTD
PO Box CB 13050
Robinson & Old Trail Rd

Phones: 242-300-2200; 242-601-6780
Fax: 242-601-8900
E-mail: info@cablebahamas.com
Web site: http://www.cablebahamas.com
Officers:
Anthony Butler, President & Chief Executive Officer
Barry Williams, Senior Vice President, Finance
John Gomez, Vice President, Engineering
Blaine Schafer, Vice President, Information & Telecom Services
David Burrows, Director, Marketing
Ownership: Publicly held..
Cable Systems (1):
Florida: MARCO ISLAND.

CABLE COMMUNICATIONS OF WILLSBORO INC.
PO Box 625
3669 Essex Rd., Ste. 1
Willsboro, NY 12996
Phone: 518-963-4116
Fax: 518-963-7405
Officers:
Herb Longware, President
Shirley Longware, Chief Financial Officer
John Longware, General Manager & Marketing Director
Ownership: Herb Longware; Eileen Longware.
Cable Systems (1):
New York: WILLSBORO (town).

CABLE COOPERATIVE INC.
27 East College St.
Oberlin, OH 44074
Phone: 440-775-4001
Fax: 440-775-1635
E-mail: support@oberlin.net
Web site: http://www.oberlin.net
Officers:
Andrew Ruckman, Chairman
Ralph Potts, Chief Operating Officer
Dayton Livingston, Chief Financial Officer
Engle Smit, Engineering Director
Ownership: Subscriber-owned--Oberlin, OH.
Cable Systems (1):
Ohio: OBERLIN.

CABLE ONE INC.
210 East Earll Dr.
Phoenix, AZ 85012
Phones: 602-364-6000; 602-364-6372
Fax: 602-364-6011
E-mail: patricia.niemann@cableone.biz
Web site: http://www.cableone.net
Officers:
Thomas O. Might, Chief Executive Officer
Julia M. Laulis, President & Chief Operating Officer
Michael E. Bowker, Senior Vice President & Chief Sales and Marketing Officer
Kevin Coyle, Senior Vice President & Chief Financial Officer
Stephen A. Fox, Senior Vice President & Chief Network Officer
Lori Hall, Senior Vice President, Marketing
Charles McDonald, Senior Vice President, Operations
Alan H. Silverman, Senior Vice President, General Counsel & Secretary
T. Mitchell Bland, Vice President, Central Division
Michelle Cameron, Vice President, Customer Operations

Aldo Casartelli, Vice President, ISP
Patrick A. Dolohanty, Vice President & Treasurer
Joseph J Felbab, Vice President, Marketing
John D. Gosch, Vice President, West Division
Eric Lardy, Vice President, Finance & Strategy
Kishore Reddy, Vice President, Product Development & Support
Janiece St. Cyr, Vice President, Human Resources
Cary Westmark, Vice President, Information Technology
Ownership: Publicly held..
Cable Systems (48):
Alabama: ANNISTON.
Arizona: BISBEE; COTTONWOOD; GLOBE-MIAMI; PAGE; PRESCOTT; SAFFORD; SHOW LOW.
Idaho: BOISE; IDAHO FALLS; LEWISTON; POCATELLO; TWIN FALLS.
Iowa: SIOUX CITY.
Kansas: CHANUTE; EMPORIA; INDEPENDENCE; PARSONS.
Mississippi: BROOKHAVEN; CLARKSDALE; CLEVELAND; COLUMBUS; GRENADA; GULFPORT; NATCHEZ.
Missouri: JOPLIN; KIRKSVILLE.
Nebraska: NORFOLK.
New Mexico: RIO RANCHO; ROSWELL.
North Dakota: FARGO.
Oklahoma: ADA; ALTUS; ARDMORE; BARTLESVILLE; DUNCAN; ELK CITY; MIAMI; PONCA CITY; VINITA.
Tennessee: DYERSBURG; FRIENDSHIP.
Texas: ARANSAS PASS; BORGER; ODESSA; PORT LAVACA; SHERMAN; TEXARKANA.

CABLE PLUS
PO Box 1030
Honaker, VA 24260-1030
Phones: 276-873-4828; 866-670-4828
Fax: 276-873-4882
Cable Systems (1):
Virginia: ROSEDALE.

CABLE SERVICES INC.
PO Box 1995
Jamestown, ND 58402-1995
Phones: 701-252-5281; 701-252-2225
E-mail: info@csicable.com
Web site: http://csicable.com
Officer:
Roy A. Sheppard, Chief Executive & Operating Officer
Cable Systems (2):
North Dakota: JAMESTOWN; VALLEY CITY.

CABLESOUTH MEDIA3 LLC
PO Box 620
Milan, TN 38358
Phone: 866-257-2044
E-mail: customerservice@mymedia3.com
Web site: http://www.mymedia3.com
Cable Systems (26):
Arkansas: AUBREY; CLINTON; CROSSETT; FORDYCE; LEWISVILLE; LONOKE; MARSHALL; MAYFLOWER; PLUMERVILLE.
Louisiana: BERNICE; BOGALUSA; BUNKIE; FERRIDAY; JENA; JONESVILLE; KENTWOOD; MARKSVILLE; OAKDALE.
Mississippi: COAHOMA; COLLINS; COLUMBIA; LUMBERTON; MERIDIAN NAVAL AIR STATION; POPLARVILLE; SUMRALL; TYLERTOWN.

CABLESTAR INC.
PO Box 577
630 Main St.
Ragland, AL 35131-0577
Phone: 205-472-2141
Fax: 205-472-2145
E-mail: peggydickinson@ragland.net
Web site: http://www.ragland.net
Officer:

D-892   TV & Cable Factbook No. 85

Cable Owners

Peggy Dickinson, President
Ownership: Bob Dickinson; Peggy Dickinson, Principals.
Cable Systems (1):
Alabama: RAGLAND.
Other Holdings:
Telephone

CABLE TV OF STANTON
PO Box 716
1004 Ivy St.
Stanton, NE 68779
Phones: 800-411-2264; 402-439-2264
Fax: 402-439-7777
E-mail: info@stanton.net
Web site: http://www.stantontelecom.com
Officer:
Leona Paden, Secretary
Ownership: Leona Paden, 55%; John Paden, 15%; Richard A Paden, 15%; Robert J Paden, 15%.
Cable Systems (1):
Nebraska: STANTON.

CABLEVIEW COMMUNICATIONS
17214 Fremont St.
Esparto, CA 95627
Phones: 530-787-4656; 888-394-4772
E-mail: tech@cableview.tv; cs@cableview.tv
Web site: http://cableview.tv
Cable Systems (1):
California: ESPARTO.

CABLEVISION OF MARION COUNTY LLC
Ste 3
8296 SW 103rd St. Rd.
Ocala, FL 34481
Phone: 352-854-0408
Fax: 352-854-1829
E-mail: comc@lightningspeed.net
Web site: http://www.lightningspeed.net
Officers:
Jess R. King, President
Kerri L. King, Vice President, Customer Care
Richard Black, Vice President, Plant Services
Samson Massingill, Network Administrator
Louise Brush, Office Manager
Cable Systems (1):
Florida: MARION COUNTY (unincorporated areas).

CABLEVISION OF WALKER COUNTY
1304 10th St.
Huntsville, TX 77320
Phone: 936-291-2288
Fax: 936-291-0890
Cable Systems (2):
Texas: NEW WAVERLY; WATERWOOD.

CABLEVISION SERVICES INC.
1701 Cogswell Ave.
Pell City, AL 35125
Phones: 205-884-4545; 800-824-4773
Fax: 205-525-1585
Cable Systems (1):
Alabama: ODENVILLE.

CALIFORNIA-OREGON BROADCASTING INC.
PO Box 1489
125 South Fir St.
Medford, OR 97501
Phones: 541-779-5555; 1-800-821-8108
Fax: 541-779-1151
E-mail: comments@kobi5.com
Web site: http://www.kobi5.com

Officer:
Patricia C. Smullin, President & Owner
Ownership: Patricia C Smullin, President.
Represented (legal): Wiley Rein LLP.
Cable Systems (3):
Oregon: LA PINE; MADRAS; PRINEVILLE.
TV Stations:
Oregon: KLSR-TV Eugene; KOTI Klamath Falls; KOBI Medford; KPIC Roseburg.
LPTV Stations:
California: K34KJ-D Crescent City, etc.; K13HU Fort Jones, etc.; K05ET-D Likely; K47DV-D South Yreka; K04HE Yreka, etc..
Oregon: K07JT-D Brookings; K29KR-D Camas Valley; K43DI-D Canyonville; K07KT Canyonville, etc.; K07PZ-D Cave Junction; K06NS-D Chiloquin; K14MQ-D Coos Bay; K30BN-D Coos Bay; K36BX-D Coos Bay; K14GW-D Corvallis; KEVU-CD Eugene; K19GH-D Eugene, etc.; K26HO-D Glide; K25EN-D Gold Beach; K02FT Gold Hill; K50FW-D Grants Pass; K04EY Grants Pass, etc.; K07NR-D Lakeview, etc.; K32DY-D Medford; K36IB-D Midland, etc.; K49JE-D Murphy, etc.; K13HM-D Myrtle Creek; K08AK-D Port Orford, etc.; K38LQ-D Roseburg; K41JQ-D Roseburg; K11RM Silver Lake, etc.; K13MI-D Squaw Valley; K03EI Tolo, etc.; K11GH-D Tri-City, etc.; K07HS Williams; K32FI-D Yoncalla; K39CL-D Yoncalla.

CALNEVA BROADBAND LLC
PO Box 1470
322 Ash St.
Westwood, CA 96137
Phones: 530-256-2028; 866-330-2028
Fax: 530-256-3123
Web site: http://blog.calneva.org
Cable Systems (4):
California: FRAZIER PARK; LAKE ALMANOR; THE SEA RANCH.
Nevada: WINNEMUCCA.

C & W CABLE INC.
7920 Hwy. 30 West
Annville, KY 40402-9748
Phone: 606-364-5357
Officers:
Brett Williams, President & Chief Executive & Operating Officer
Viola Williams, Vice President, Secretary-Treasurer & Chief Financial Officer
Ownership: Don Williams; Judy C Williams.
Cable Systems (2):
Kentucky: BURNING SPRINGS; PEOPLES.

CARNEGIE CABLE
PO Box 96
25 South Colorado
Carnegie, OK 73015
Phone: 580-654-1002
Fax: 580-654-2699
E-mail: jpowers@carnegiecable.com
Web site: http://www.carnegietelco.com
Officers:
Lyn Johnson, President & Chief Executive Officer
Gary Woodruff, Vice President & Chief Operating Officer
Leslie Powers, Secretary & Treasurer
Darrin Cornelison, Central Officer Manager
James Powers, Operations Manager
Travis Ridgeway, Outside Plant Manager
Ownership: H. S Scott, 97%; Troy Scott, 1%; Wade Scott, 1%; Suzanne Scott, 1%.

Cable Systems (1):
Oklahoma: CARNEGIE.

CAROLINA MOUNTAIN CABLEVISION INC.
PO Box 298
4930 Jonathan Creek Rd.
Waynesville, NC 28785
Phones: 828-926-2288; 866-571-8671
Fax: 828-377-0006
Web site: http://www.cbvnol.com
Officers:
John Dixson, President
Terry Sersland, Chief Technology Officer
Ownership: Stewart Corbett; Gerald Aldridge; Ed Stark, Principals.
Cable Systems (4):
North Carolina: HAYWOOD COUNTY (portions).
Tennessee: DANDRIDGE; NEWPORT; TALBOTT.

CASCADE COMMUNICATIONS CO.
PO Box 250
106 Taylor St. SE
Cascade, IA 52033
Phone: 583-852-3710
Fax: 563-852-9935
E-mail: info@cascadecomm.com
Web site: http://www.cascadecomm.com
Officer:
David Gibson, Manager
Cable Systems (1):
Iowa: CASCADE.

CITY OF CASCADE LOCKS CABLE TV
PO Box 308
140 SW WaNaPa
Cascade Locks, OR 97014
Phone: 541-374-8484
Fax: 541-374-8752
E-mail: thupp@cascade-locks.or.us
Web site: http://www.clbb.net
Officers:
Robert Willoughby, General Manager
Ed Winnett, Chief Technology Officer
Ownership: Municipally owned--Cascade Locks, OR.
Cable Systems (1):
Oregon: CASCADE LOCKS.

CASEY MUTUAL TELEPHONE CO.
108 East Logan St.
Casey, IA 50048
Phone: 641-746-2222
Fax: 641-746-2221
E-mail: caseymutual@netins.net
Officer:
John Breining, Manager
Cable Systems (1):
Iowa: CASEY.

CASPIAN COMMUNITY TV CORP.
301 West Caspian Ave.
Caspian, MI 49915
Phone: 906-265-4747
Officers:
Vic Shepich, President
Chalmers McGreaham, Vice President
Robert Watts, Secretary-Treasurer
Albert Melchiori, Chief Technology Officer
Ownership: Subscriber owned--Caspian, MI.
Cable Systems (1):
Michigan: CASPIAN.

CASS CABLE TV INC.
PO Box 200
100 Redbud Rd.
Virginia, IL 62691

Phones: 217-452-7725; 800-252-1799
Fax: 217-452-7030
E-mail: solutions@casscomm.com
Web site: http://home.casscomm.com
Officers:
Gerald E. Gill, Chairman & President
Thomas D. Allen, Vice President & Chief Operating Officer
Gerald S. Gill, Vice President
Chad Winters, Cable TV Manager
Mike Reynolds, Internet & Phone Manager
Rick Koch, Head End Manager
Lance Allen, Chief Technical Officer
Casey French, Marketing & Public Relations Manager
John Plunkett, Production Manager
Laymon Carter, Advertising Director
Ownership: Gerald E. Gill. Gill owns Cass Telephone Co., Cass Long Distance, Cass Communications Management Inc. & has cellular telephone holdings.
Represented (legal): Cole, Raywid & Braverman LLP.
Cable Systems (2):
Illinois: BEARDSTOWN; PITTSFIELD.

CASTLE CABLE TV INC.
5 Avery Ave.
Alexandria Bay, NY 13607
Phones: 315-482-9975; 315-482-0691
Fax: 315-324-5917
E-mail: castlecable@cit-tele.com
Web site: http://www.castlecabletv.com
Officer:
Don Ceresoli Jr., President
Ownership: Citizens Telephone Co..
Cable Systems (1):
New York: ALEXANDRIA BAY.

CATALINA CABLE TV CO.
PO Box 2143
222 Metropole Ave.
Avalon, CA 90704
Phone: 310-510-0255
Web site: http://www.catalinaisp.com
Officer:
Ralph J. Morrow Jr., Chief Executive Officer
Ownership: Patricia L Morrow; Ralph J Morrow Jr..
Cable Systems (1):
California: AVALON/CATALINA ISLAND.

CATV SERVICE INC.
12099 NW 98th Ave.
Hialeah Gardens, FL 33018
Phone: 305-512-5601
Fax: 305-512-5606
E-mail: catvserv@ptd.net
Web site: http://www.catvservices.com
Officers:
Samuel Haulman, President & General Manager
Debra Bortel, Marketing Director
Beatrice DeSantis, Controller
William Hause, Chief Engineer
Dave Skelton, Sales Executive

Branch Offices:
Lewisburg
130 Buffalo Rd
Ste 209
Lewisburg, PA 17837
Phone: 570-523-3875
Fax: 570-523-9669
Milton/Watsontown
15 N Front St
Milton, PA 17847
Phone: 570-742-7421
Fax: 570-742-7568
Ownership: Margaret Walsonavich, Pres..

Cable Owners

Represented (legal): Womble Carlyle Sandridge & Rice LLP.
Cable Systems (1):
Pennsylvania: DANVILLE.

CEDAR FALLS MUNICIPAL COMMUNICATIONS UTILITY
PO Box 769
Cedar Falls, IA 50613
Phone: 319-266-1761
E-mail: cfu@cfunet.net
Web site: http://www.cfu.net
Officers:
Jim Krieg, General Manager
Ed Schultz, Operations Director
Betty Zeman, Marketing Manager
Steve Bernard, Director, Customer Services & Business Development
Ownership: Municipally owned--Cedar Falls, IA.
Cable Systems (1):
Iowa: CEDAR FALLS.

CELECT COMMUNICATIONS
PO Box 189
S131 McKay Ave.
Spring Valley, WI 54767
Phones: 715-778-6121; 800-285-7993
Fax: 715-778-5033
E-mail: celecthelp@celectcom.net
Web site: http://www.celectcom.net
Officers:
Randy Sailer, President
Max Downs, Vice President
Mike DeMarce, Chief Operating Officer
Jim Smart, Secretary
Dennis Bachman, Treasurer
Cable Systems (1):
Wisconsin: ELMWOOD (village).

CELINA CABLE COMMUNICATIONS
538 Cedar St.
McKenzie, TN 38201
Phone: 731-352-2980
Fax: 731-352-3533
Officer:
Gary Blount, Owner
Cable Systems (3):
Tennessee: BYRDSTOWN; CELINA; OVERTON COUNTY (portions).

CENTER CABLE TV
PO Box 117
Greeley, NE 68842
Phone: 308-428-2915
E-mail: greeleycitizen@centercable.tv
Officer:
Martin Callahan, Owner
Ownership: Martin Callahan, 50%; Thomas Callahan, 50%.
Cable Systems (1):
Nebraska: GREELEY.

CENTER JUNCTION TELEPHONE CO.
513 Main St.
Center Junction, IA 52212
Phone: 563-487-2631
Fax: 563-487-3701
Officers:
Dennis Orris, President
Judy Paulsen, Secretary-Treasurer
John Heiken, Manager

Cable Systems (1):
Iowa: CENTER JUNCTION.

CENTRAL SCOTT TELEPHONE
PO Box 260
125 North Second St.
Eldridge, IA 52748
Phone: 563-285-9611
Fax: 563-285-9648
Web site: http://centralscott.com
Officer:
Charles Rebman, President & Chief Operating Officer
Cable Systems (1):
Iowa: DIXON.

CENTRAL TELCOM SERVICES LLC
35 South State St.
Fairview, UT 84629
Phones: 435-427-3331; 800-427-8449
Fax: 435-427-3200
Web site: http://www.centracom.com
Officers:
Eddie Cox, General Manager
Kevin Arthur, Manager
Ownership: Lynch Interactive Corp..
Cable Systems (13):
Utah: CENTERFIELD; CENTRAL; DELTA; DUGWAY AFB; EPHRAIM; FILLMORE; MORONI; MOUNT PLEASANT; NEPHI; RICHFIELD; SALINA; SANTAQUIN; WENDOVER.

CENTRAL TEXAS COMMUNICATONS INC.
PO Box 627
1012 Reilley St.
Goldthwaite, TX 76844
Phones: 325-648-2237; 800-535-8904
Web site: http://www.centex.net
Cable Systems (1):
Texas: SAN SABA.

CENTRE TV CABLE
510 Warwood Ave.
Warwood, WV 26003-6893
Phone: 304-277-2811
Officers:
Kasmir Majewski, President
Edwaard Majewski, Vice President
Matthew Campbell, Treasurer
Cable Systems (1):
West Virginia: WARWOOD.

CENTURYLINK
100 CenturyLink Dr.
Monroe, LA 71203
Phones: 318-388-9000; 800-201-4099
Web site: http://www.centurylink.com
Officers:
Glen F. Post III, Chief Executive Officer & President
Karen A. Puckett, President, Global Markets
Girish K. Varma, President, Global IT Services & New Market Development
R. Stewart Ewing Jr, Executive Vice President, Chief Financial Officer & Assistant Secretary
Stacey W. Golf, Executive Vice President & General Counsel
Aamir Hussain, Executive Vice President & Chief Technology Officer
Maxine L. Moreau, Executive Vice President, Global Operations & Shared Services
Scott A. Trezise, Executive Vice President, Human Resources
William E. Bradley, Senior Vice President & Chief Information Officer
Ross Garrity, Senior Vice President, IT Solutions & Interim President, Global Markets

John Jones, Senior Vice President, Public Policy
Duane Ring, Senior Vice President, Global Field Operations
Ownership: Publicly held.
Cable Systems (9):
Arizona: SCOTTSDALE.
Colorado: EAGLE CITY.
Iowa: POSTVILLE.
Nebraska: OMAHA.
Utah: SOUTH JORDAN.
Wisconsin: NEW FRANKEN; PLATTEVILLE; RANDOLPH; THORP.

CEQUEL COMMUNICATIONS HOLDINGS I LLC
12444 Powerscourt Dr., Ste 450
dba Suddenlink Communications
St. Louis, MO 63131
Phones: 314-965-2020; 314-315-9400
Web site: http://www.suddenlink.com
Officers:
Dexter Goei, President, Altice NV & Chairman and Chief Executive Officer, Altice USA
Hakim Boubazine, Co-President & Chief Operating Officer, Altice USA
Charles F Stewart, Co-President & Chief Financial Officer, Altice USA
Kevin A. Stephens, President, Business Services, Altice USA
Dave Gilles, Head of Suddenlink Operations, Altice USA
Gregg Graff, Head of Residential Sales, Altice USA
Terry M Cordova, Senior Vice President & Chief Technology Officer
Peter M Abel, Senior Vice President, Corporate Communications
Justin Freesmeier, Senior Vice President, Sales & Fiscal Operations
John E Fuhler, Senior Vice President, Fiscal Operations
Gibbs Jones, Senior Vice President, Customer Experience
Ralph G Kelly, Senior Vice President, Treasurer
Tyler Nau, Senior Vice President, Commercial & Advertising Operations
Mike Pflantz, Senior Vice President, Corporate Finance & Accounting
Craig L Rosenthal, Senior Vice President, General Counsel
Douglas G Wiley, Senior Vice President, Human Resources
Phil Ahlschlager, Senior Vice President, Operations-North Carolina Region, Suddenlink
Dave Bach, Senior Vice President, Operations-Atlantic Region, Suddenlink
Todd Cruthird, Senior Vice President, Operations-Texoma Region, Suddenlink
Randy Goad, Senior Vice President, Operations-Mid South Region, Suddenlink
Pat O'Connor, Senior Vice President, Operations-Central Region, Suddenlink
Ownership: Altice NV, 70%; BC Partners, private equity firm, 15%. votes, 18.2% equity; CPP Investment Board, 15%. votes, 11.8% equity. On May 20, 2015, it was announced that Altice NV would acquire 70% interest in Suddenlink. Deal closed December 21, 2015.
Cable Systems (232):
Arizona: BULLHEAD CITY; FLAGSTAFF; KINGMAN; LAKE HAVASU CITY; PARKER; PAYSON (town); PINE; SEDONA.
Arkansas: ARKADELPHIA; ATKINS; BATESVILLE; BOONEVILLE; CABOT; CHARLESTON; CLARKSVILLE; DE WITT; DOVER; EL DORADO; GURDON; HAZEN; HEBER SPRINGS; HELENA; HOT SPRINGS VILLAGE; HOXIE; HUGHES; JONESBORO; LONDON; MAGNOLIA; MALVERN; MARVELL; MORRILTON; MOUNT IDA; MOUNTAIN HOME; NASHVILLE; NEWPORT; OZARK; PARIS; POCAHONTAS; RUSSELLVILLE; STUTTGART; WALDRON;

WHITEHALL.
California: BISHOP; BLYTHE; FORESTHILL; HUMBOLDT COUNTY (portions); LAKE OF THE PINES; MAMMOTH LAKES; MONTEREY; SHAVER LAKE; TRUCKEE.
Idaho: OROFINO; OSBURN; SPIRIT LAKE; ST. MARIES.
Kansas: ANTHONY; FORT SCOTT; PAOLA.
Kentucky: ADAIRVILLE; GRAYSON; PIKEVILLE; RUSSELLVILLE.
Louisiana: ALEXANDRIA; BASTROP; BOSSIER CITY; BOYCE; DE RIDDER; IBERIA PARISH (portions); IOWA; JONESBORO; LAKE CHARLES; LECOMPTE; LEESVILLE; MANY; MINDEN; MOREAUVILLE; NATCHITOCHES; RUSTON; SIBLEY; ST. JOSEPH; VILLE PLATTE; WINNFIELD.
Mississippi: GREENVILLE; GREENWOOD.
Missouri: BOONVILLE; BRANSON; BROOKFIELD; CARTHAGE; COLE COUNTY (portions); LAMAR; LEXINGTON; MARYVILLE; MONETT; NEOSHO; NIXA; ST. JOSEPH; TRENTON.
Nevada: LAUGHLIN; PAHRUMP.
New Mexico: CLOVIS.
North Carolina: GREENVILLE; KINSTON; MARTIN COUNTY (central portion); NEW BERN; ROCKY MOUNT; WASHINGTON (portions).
Ohio: BLOOMINGDALE; KNOX TWP. (Jefferson County); NELSON TWP.; SENECAVILLE.
Oklahoma: ALVA; ANADARKO; CHICKASHA; CUSHING; DRUMRIGHT; ENID; FAIRVIEW; FORT SILL; GROVE; HEALDTON; HEAVENER; HENRYETTA; HUGO; IDABEL; LINDSAY; MUSKOGEE; OKMULGEE; PAULS VALLEY; PERRY; POTEAU; PURCELL; SALLISAW; SEMINOLE; SPIRO; STILLWATER; WEATHERFORD; WEWOKA; WOODWARD.
Texas: ABILENE; ALBANY; AMARILLO; ANDREWS; ANSON; ATHENS; BIG LAKE; BIG SPRING; BRADY; BRECKENRIDGE; BRENHAM; BRYAN; BURKBURNETT; CALDWELL; CANADIAN; CENTER; CLARENDON; CLARKSVILLE; CONROE; CRANE; DAINGERFIELD; DIMMITT; EASTLAND; ELECTRA; GAINESVILLE; GATESVILLE; GEORGETOWN; GLADEWATER; GRAPELAND; HAMLIN; HAWKINS; HEARNE; HENDERSON; HENRIETTA; HUNTSVILLE; INGRAM; JACKSONVILLE; JARRELL; JUNCTION; KAUFMAN; KERMIT; KINGWOOD; KRUM; LAMPASAS; LEANDER; LOST PINES; LUBBOCK; LUFKIN; MIDLAND; MINEOLA; MINERAL WELLS; MONAHANS; MONT BELVIEU; MOUNT PLEASANT; MOUNT VERNON; NACOGDOCHES; NOCONA; OLNEY; ONALASKA; PADUCAH (town); PARIS; PECOS; PFLUGERVILLE; PILOT POINT; PITTSBURG; PLAINVIEW; PRAIRIE VIEW; QUANAH; ROCKDALE; ROTAN; RUSK; SAN ANGELO; SAN SABA; SEYMOUR; SHAMROCK; SNYDER; SONORA; SULPHUR SPRINGS; SWEETWATER; TERRELL; TYLER; VERNON; VICTORIA; WELLINGTON; WHITESBORO; WINNSBORO.
West Virginia: BECKLEY; BEVERLY; BUCKHANNON; CHARLESTON; KERMIT; PARKERSBURG; SHINNSTON; SISSONVILLE.

CHAMPAIGN TELEPHONE CO.
126 Scioto St.
Urbana, OH 43078
Phones: 937-653-4000; 937-653-2225
Fax: 937-652-1952
E-mail: customerservice@ctcommunications.com
Web site: http://www.ctcn.net
Officers:
Michael W. Conrad, President & General Manager
Tim Bolander, Vice President & Chief Technical Officer

Branch Office:
Store Address
731 Scioto St.
Urbana, OH 43078
Ownership: Consolidated Communications Inc., see listing.

Cable Owners

Cable Systems (1):
Ohio: URBANA.

CHAPARRAL CABLE CO.
320 McCombs Rd.
Chaparral, NM 88081
Phone: 575-824-4099
Fax: 575-824-1465
E-mail: chapcable2@chapcable.net
Web site: http://www.chaparralcable.com
Officers:
Ben Mossa, President
Gregory A. Groth, Vice President, Secretary & Treasurer
Adrian Valerio, Head Supervisor/Technician

Branch Offices:
Las Cruces Office
2000 West Hadley
Las Cruces, NM 88005
Phone: 575-636-2426
Fax: 575-636-2528
Santa Fe Office
5935 Agua Fria
Santa Fe, NM 87507
Phone: 505-473-9363
Fax: 505-473-1368
Ownership: Chaparral Holding Co. Inc..
Cable Systems (1):
New Mexico: CHAPARRAL.

CHARITON VALLEY TELECOM
PO Box 67
1213 East Briggs Dr.
Macon, MO 63552
Phones: 660-395-9000; 888-284-9830
Fax: 660-395-4403
E-mail: feedback@cvalley.net
Web site: http://www.cvalley.net
Officers:
James Simon, General Manager
Jesse Estevez, Network Operations Director
Ryan Johnson, Sales & Marketing Director
Tina Jordan, Finance Director
Ron Stone, Plant Operations Director
Jim Walker, Corporate Relations Director

Branch Office:
BUCKLIN
660 Oak St
Bucklin, MO 64631
Phone: 660-395-9000
Fax: 660-695-3606
Ownership: Chariton Valley Communications Corp.. Has telephone & cellular radio holdings.
Cable Systems (1):
Missouri: MACON.

CHARTER COMMUNICATIONS INC.
6th & 7th Fls.
400 Atlantic St.
Stamford, CT 06901
Phones: 203-316-9135; 203-905-7800
Web site: http://www.charter.com
Officers:
Tom Rutledge, Chairman & Chief Executive Officer
John Bickham, President & Chief Operating Officer
James M Heneghan, President, Charter Media
Philip Meeks, President, Business Enterprise Services
David G Ellen, Senior Executive Vice President
Tom Adams, Executive Vice President, Field Operations
Michael Bair, Executive Vice President, Spectrum Networks
Jim Blackley, Executive Vice President, Engineering & Information Technology
Catherine Bohigian, Executive Vice President, Government Affairs
Don Detampel, Executive Vice President, Technology & President, Commercial Services
Rich DiGeronimo, Executive Vice President, Product & Strategy
Richard Dykhouse, Executive Vice President, General Counsel & Corporate Secretary
Jonathan Hargis, Executive Vice President & Chief Marketing Officer
David Kline, Executive Vice President & President, Media Sales
Paul Marchand, Executive Vice President, Human Resources
Kathleen Mayo, Executive Vice President, Customer Operations
Tom Montemagno, Executive Vice President, Programming Acquisition
James Nuzzo, Executive Vice President, Business Planning
Scott Weber, Executive Vice President, Network Operations
Christopher Winfrey, Executive Vice President & Chief Financial Officer
Rhonda Crichlow, Chief Diversity Officer
Elizabeth Biley Andrion, Senior Vice President, Regulatory Affairs
Rocky Boler, Senior Vice President, Customer Care
Jay Carlson, Senior Vice President & Chief Information Officer, Information Technology
Craig Cowden, Senior Vice President, Wireless Technology
Alexander Dudley, Senior Vice President, Communications
Adam Falk, Senior Vice President, Government Affairs
Charlotte Field, Senior Vice President, Application Platform Operations
Charles Fisher, Senior Vice President, Corporate Finance
Clifford Harris, Senior Vice President, Law-Programming, Product & Regulatory
Alex Hoehn-Saric, Senior Vice President, Policy & External Affairs
Kevin D Howard, Senior Vice President, Controller & Chief Accounting Officer
Rob Klippel, Senior Vice President, Advanced Advertising Products & Strategy
Jim McGann, Senior Vice President, Charter Business
Jake Perlman, Seniior Vice President, Software Development
Abby Pfeiffer, Senior Vice President, Human Resources
Don Poulter, Senior Vice President, Commercial Operations
Jodi Robinson, Senior Vice President, User Experience Design & Development
Jay A Rolls, Senior Vice President & Chief Technology Officer, Advanced Engineering
Allan Sampson, Senior Vice President, Marketing
Gary Schanman, Senior Vice President, Video Products
Richard Schultz, Senior Vice President, Inbound Sales & Retention
Adam Weinstein, Senior Vice President, Programming Acquisitiion
Peter Brown, Vice President, User Experience Design
Paul Cancienne, Vice President, Legislative Affairs
Justin Colwell, Vice President, Wireless Products
Christianna Lewis Barnhart, Vice President, Regulatory Affairs
Tamara Lipper-Smith, Vice President, Government Affairs
Waldo McMillan, Vice President, Government Affairs
Marti Moore, Vice President, Technology Services
Justin Venech, Vice President, Communications
Jason Wyrick, Vice President, Application Development

Branch Offices:
Charter Alabama
2100 Columbiana Rd.
Vestavia Hills, AL 35216
Phone: 205-824-5400
Charter Central California
270 Bridge St.
San Luis Obispo, CA 93401
Phone: 805-544-1962
Charter Central States
941 Charter Commons Dr.
St. Louis, MO 63017
Phone: 636-207-7044
Charter East Michigan
7372 Davison Rd.
Davison, MI 48423
Phone: 810-652-1402
Charter Fort Worth
4800 Blue Mound Rd.
Forth Worth, TX 76106
Phone: 817-509-6272
Charter Georgia
1925 Breckinridge Plaza
Suite 100
Duluth, GA 30096
Phone: 770-806-7060
Charter Inland Empire
7337 Central Ave.
Riverside, CA 92504
Phone: 951-343-5100
Charter Los Angeles Metro
4781 Irwindale Ave.
Irwindale, CA 91706
Charter Louisiana
1304 Ridgefield Rd.
Thibodaux, LA 70301
Phone: 985-446-4941
Charter Minnesota & Nebraska
3380 Northern Valley Place NE
Rochester, MN 55906
Charter Nevada
9335 Prototype Way
Reno, NV 89521
Phone: 775-850-1200
Charter New England
95 Higgins St.
Worchester, MA 01606
Phone: 508-853-1515
Charter North Michigan
701 S. Airport Rd.
Traverse City, MI 49686
Phone: 231-947-5221
Charter North Wisconsin
165 Knights Way
Fon du Lac, WI 54935
Phone: 920-907-7751
Charter Northwest
521 NE 136th Ave.
Vancouver, WA 98684
Charter South Carolina
2 Digital Place
4th Floor
Simpsonville, SC 29681
Phone: 800-955-7766
Charter Southern Wisconsin
2701 Daniels St.
Madison, WI 53718
Phone: 608-274-3822
Charter Tennessee
1774 Henry G. Lane St.
Maryville, TN 37801
Phone: 865- 273-2701
Charter West Michigan
1433 Fulton St.
Grand Haven, MI 49417
Phone: 616-647-6201

Ownership: Liberty Broadband, 25%; Paul Allen, 2%. equity; 3% voting. On May 26, 2015, Charter announced it was merging with Time Warner Cable and acquiring Bright House Networks LLC (see listings for both). FCC approved deals May 6, 2016. Deals closed May 18, 2016.
Cable Systems (234):
Alabama: CULLMAN; CURRY; DADEVILLE; DECATUR; FAIRFIELD; FORT PAYNE; LAFAYETTE; LINEVILLE; MENTONE; MONTGOMERY; PELHAM; PHIL CAMPBELL; PIEDMONT; ROANOKE; SULLIGENT; TRINITY; WEDOWEE.
California: ALTURAS; CERRITOS; CRESCENT CITY; GILROY; GLENDALE; GREENFIELD; HESPERIA; KING CITY; LONG BEACH; LOS ANGELES COUNTY (portions); MALIBU; MOJAVE; MONTEREY COUNTY (portions); NORTH EDWARDS; PORTERVILLE; REDDING; RIVERSIDE; SAN LUIS OBISPO; SOLEDAD; THOUSAND OAKS; TURLOCK; VENTURA; WHITTIER; WRIGHTWOOD; YUCAIPA.
Colorado: ALAMOSA; BUENA VISTA; CANON CITY; CRAIG; DURANGO; DURANGO WEST; FORT MORGAN; GRAND JUNCTION; LA JUNTA; LEADVILLE; MEEKER; MONTROSE; PAONIA; RANGELY; SALIDA; STERLING; WALSENBURG.
Connecticut: ASHFORD; NEW MILFORD.
Georgia: ATHENS; CHATSWORTH; DALTON; DUBLIN; LAGRANGE; LAWRENCEVILLE; MILLEDGEVILLE; NEWNAN; RINGGOLD; SANDERSVILLE; STOCKBRIDGE; SUMMERVILLE; THOMASTON.
Louisiana: OPELOUSAS; SLIDELL; THIBODAUX.
Maryland: CRISFIELD.
Massachusetts: CHICOPEE; WESTPORT; WORCESTER.
Michigan: ALLENDALE TWP.; ALPENA; BILLINGS TWP.; BROOMFIELD TRAILER PARK; BUTMAN TWP.; CHESTER TWP. (Ottawa County); COLDWATER; COMSTOCK TWP.; CUSTER; FRENCHTOWN TWP.; GOODAR TWP.; GOODRICH; HALE; IRONWOOD; LAKEVIEW; MARQUETTE; MIDLAND; NEWBERRY; RICHFIELD TWP. (Roscommon County); SAGE TWP.; SAULT STE. MARIE; SEVILLE TWP.; SHERMAN TWP. (Isabella County); TRAVERSE CITY.
Minnesota: ALEXANDRIA; AUSTIN; BRAINERD; BUFFALO; DULUTH; FERGUS FALLS; MANKATO; OWATONNA; ROCHESTER; ROSEMOUNT; ST. CLOUD; WILLMAR.
Missouri: LOUISIANA; PERRYVILLE; ST. LOUIS.
Montana: ANACONDA; BIG TIMBER; BILLINGS; BOULDER; BOZEMAN; BUTTE; CASCADE; CHINOOK; CUT BANK; DEER LODGE; DILLON; FORT BENTON; GREAT FALLS; HAMILTON; HARLEM; HAVRE; HELENA; KALISPELL; LIVINGSTON (town); MALTA; MISSOULA; POLSON; RED LODGE; STEVENSVILLE; TOWNSEND.
Nebraska: BEATRICE; KEARNEY; KENESAW; NORTH PLATTE; SCOTTSBLUFF; SIDNEY (town); SPRINGFIELD.
Nevada: HAWTHORNE; RENO; YERINGTON.
New York: CHATHAM; PLATTSBURGH.
North Carolina: ANGIER; ASHEVILLE; BUXTON; HICKORY; KENLY; KILL DEVIL HILLS; ROANOKE RAPIDS; ROXBORO; TROY.
Oregon: ASTORIA; BURNS; COOS BAY; COTTAGE GROVE; DALLAS; FLORENCE; KLAMATH FALLS; LA GRANDE; LAKEVIEW; LINCOLN CITY; MEDFORD; ROSEBURG; THE DALLES.
South Carolina: SPARTANBURG.
Tennessee: ALCOA; CLARKSVILLE; CLEVELAND; COLUMBIA; COOKEVILLE; CROSSVILLE; JACKSON CITY; JASPER; KINGSPORT; LEBANON; MANCHESTER; MCEWEN; MORRISTOWN; TEN MILE.
Texas: CARROLLTON; DENTON; DUNCANVILLE; FORT WORTH (northern portions); MIDLOTHIAN; MONTGOMERY COUNTY (portions); ROCKWALL; UNIVERSITY PARK.
Vermont: ST. JOHNSBURY.

Cable Owners

Virginia: CHINCOTEAGUE ISLAND; ONANCOCK; SUFFOLK.
Washington: COLVILLE; ELLENSBURG; GRAND COULEE; KENNEWICK; WENATCHEE; YAKIMA.
Wisconsin: ADAMS; EAU CLAIRE; FOND DU LAC; LANCASTER; MADISON; MONTELLO; STEVENS POINT.
Wyoming: BUFFALO; CASPER; CHEYENNE; CODY; GILLETTE; GREYBULL; JACKSON (town); LARAMIE; NEWCASTLE; POWELL; RAWLINS; RIVERTON; SHERIDAN; THERMOPOLIS; WORLAND.
Cable Holdings:
Time Warner Cable, see listing.; 73.7% of Bright House Networks LLC, see listing.; 33% of GreatLand Connections Inc.
Other Holdings:
ActiveVideo: Has 35% interest.

C H COMM LLC
9507 Cherokee Trail
Crossville, TN 38572
Phone: 931-788-5261
Cable Systems (3):
Cuba: GUANTANAMO BAY.
New York: LONG LAKE; MINERVA (town).

CHEROKEE CABLEVISION INC.
PO Box 487
Cherokee, NC 28719
Phone: 828-497-4861
Fax: 828-497-4983
Ownership: Ken Blankenship, Pres..
Cable Systems (1):
North Carolina: CHEROKEE INDIAN RESERVATION.

CHEYENNE RIVER SIOUX TRIBE TELEPHONE AUTHORITY
PO Box 810
100 Main St.
Eagle Butte, SD 57625
Phones: 605-964-2600; 605-964-3307
Fax: 605-964-1000
E-mail: info@crstta.com
Web site: http://www.crstta.com
Officers:
J. D. Williams, General Manager
Mona Thompson, Assistant General Manager
Cable Systems (1):
South Dakota: EAGLE BUTTE.

CHIBARDUN CABLE TV CORPORATION
PO Box 664
401 South 1st St.
Cameron, WI 54822
Phones: 715-458-5400; 800-924-3405
Fax: 715-458-2112
E-mail: chitel@mosaictelecom.net
Web site: http://www.mosaictelecom.com
Officers:
Rick S. Vergin, Chief Executive Officer
Scott J. Hickok, Vice President, Programming & Chief Operating Officer

Branch Offices:
Amery
1074 Riverplace Mall
Amery, WI 54001
Phone: 715-268-5200
Barron
340 E. Division Street
Barron, WI 54812
Phone: 715-637-4282
Chetek
704 2nd St
Chetek, WI 54728
Phone: 715-924-2171

Dallas
110 N. 2nd Ave
Dallas, WI 54733
Phone: 715-837-1011
Ladysmith
200 W. 2nd St. N
Ladysmith, WI 54848
Phone: 715-532-8100
Rice Lake
2701 West Ave
Rice Lake, WI 54868
Phone: 715-434-4282
Cable Systems (1):
Wisconsin: SAND CREEK.

CHINOOK PROGRESSIVE CLUB TV INC.
PO Box 15
Chinook, WA 98614
Phone: 360-777-8412
Fax: 360-777-8255
Officers:
Terry Krager, President
Dale Hughes, Chief Executive Officer
Trophy W. Hughes, Chief Operating Officer
Rhoda Hughes, Secretary-Treasurer
Ownership: Subscriber owned--Chinook, WA.
Cable Systems (1):
Washington: CHINOOK.

CHRISTIAN ENTERPRISES
PO Box 300
Pioche, NV 89043
Phones: 775-962-5200; 775-962-5111
Officers:
John Christian, President
Paul Christian, Vice President
Cable Systems (2):
Nevada: ALAMO; PIOCHE.

CIM TEL CABLE INC.
PO Box 160
101 Cimarron St.
Mannford, OK 74044
Phones: 918-865-3311; 800-722-3979
Fax: 918-865-3187
E-mail: staff@cimtel.net
Web site: http://cimtel.net
Officers:
V. David Miller II, President
H. Gene Baldwin, Chief Executive Officer
Dan Overland, Chief Financial Officer
Ownership: Cimarron Telephone; CT ownership: MBO Corp.
Cable Systems (1):
Oklahoma: MANNFORD.

CINCINNATI BELL INC.
221 East Fourth St.
Cincinnati, OH 45202
Phones: 513-397-9900; 513-565-2210
Fax: 513-933-7208
Web site: http://www.cincinnatibell.com
Officers:
Theodore H Torbeck, President & Chief Executive Officer
Leigh Fox, Chief Financial Officer
David L Heimbach, Chief Operating Officer
Joshua T Duckworth, Vice President, Investor Relations & Controller
Christopher C Elma, Vice President, Treasury & Tax
Christopher J Wilson, Vice President & General Counsel

Cable Systems (1):
Ohio: LEBANON.

CIRCLE BAY YACHT CLUB CONDOMINIUM ASSOCIATION INC
1950 SW Palm City Rd.
Stuart, FL 34994
Phone: 772-287-0990
Fax: 772-205-3533
E-mail: office@circlebay.net
Web site: http://circlebay.net
Officers:
Grant Rawding, President
Frank Campbell, Vice President
Glenn Meyer, Secretary
Barry High, Treasurer
Ownership: Board of Directors.
Cable Systems (1):
Florida: STUART.

CITIZENS CABLE COMMUNICATIONS
PO Box 156
2748 State Rte. 982
Mammoth, PA 15664
Phone: 724-423-3000
Fax: 724-423-3003
E-mail: cable@wpa.net; telco@wpa.net
Web site: http://wpa.net
Cable Systems (1):
Pennsylvania: MAMMOTH.

CITIZENS CABLE TV
PO Box 465
134 North Bailey Ave.
Leslie, GA 31764
Phones: 229-853-1600; 229-268-2288
Fax: 229-877-2211
Web site: http://www.citizenscatv.com
Cable Systems (1):
Georgia: COBB.

CITIZENS CABLEVISION INC.
Box 217
26 South Main St.
Hammond, NY 13646
Phones: 315-324-5911; 315-324-6000
Fax: 315-324-5917
Web site: http://www.cit-tele.com
Officers:
Donald A Ceresoli Sr, Chairman
Donald A Ceresoli Jr, President
Mary Truskowski, Secretary-Treasurer
Ownership: Citizens Telephone Co..
Cable Systems (1):
New York: HAMMOND (town).

CITIZENS CABLEVISION INC. (VA)
PO Box 137
220 Webbs Mill Rd.
Floyd, VA 24091
Phones: 540-745-2111; 800-941-0426
Fax: 540-745-3791
Web site: http://citizens.coop
Officers:
Greg Sapp, Manager
Lori Worrell, Sales & Marketing Manager
Ownership: Citizens Telephone Cooperative Inc..
Cable Systems (2):
Virginia: FLOYD; NEW CASTLE (town).
Other Holdings:
Telephone.

CITIZENS MUTUAL TELEPHONE COOPERATIVE
114 West Jefferson St.
Bloomfield, IA 52537

Phones: 641-664-2074; 800-746-4268
E-mail: info@mycmtech.com
Web site: http://www.cmtel.com
Officers:
Joe Snyder, General Manager
Trent Gregory, Plant Manager
Cable Systems (1):
Iowa: BLOOMFIELD.

CITIZENS TELEPHONE CO. (MISSOURI)
PO Box 737
1905 Walnut St.
Higginsville, MO 64037
Phone: 800-321-4282
E-mail: customerservice@ctcis.net
Web site: http://www.ctcis.net
Officer:
Brian Cornelius, President
Ownership: Employee owned..
Cable Systems (1):
Missouri: HIGGINSVILLE.

CITIZENS TELEPHONE CORP.
PO Box 330
426 North Wayne St.
Warren, IN 46792
Phone: 260-375-2111
Fax: 260-375-2244
E-mail: info@citznet.com
Web site: http://www.citznet.com
Officers:
Gordon L. Laymon, President & Chief Executive Officer
Neil Laymon, Secretary-Treasurer
Ellen Laymon, Chief Financial Officer
Jack Roberts, Engineering Director
Cable Systems (1):
Indiana: WARREN.

CLARENCE TELEPHONE CO. INC.
608 Lombard St.
Clarence, IA 52216
Phone: 563-452-3852
Fax: 563-452-3883
E-mail: clarence@netins.net
Web site: http://www.clarencetelinc.com
Officers:
Curtis Eldrid, General Manager
Dan Sander, Technician
Chad Fall, Technician
Cable Systems (1):
Iowa: CLARENCE.

CLARENDON TV ASSOCIATION
PO Box 315
Clarendon, PA 16313
Phone: 814-726-3972
Officers:
Robert Jones, General Manager
Marlene Kay, Secretary-Treasurer
Ownership: Subscriber owned--Clarendon, PA.
Cable Systems (1):
Pennsylvania: CLARENDON.

CLARITY TELECOM
104 East Center St.
Sikeston, MO 63801-4108
Phones: 573-481-2264; 573-481-2770
E-mail: info@vastbroadband.com
Web site: http://www.claritycomm.net
Officers:
Jim Gleason, President & Chief Executive Officer
Larry Eby, Chief Operating Officer & Executive Vice President
Keith Davidson, Chief Financial Officer

Cable Owners

Kieran Donnelly, Business Development Manager
Rex Buettgenbach, General Manager, Vast Broadband
Ownership: Keith Davidson; Larry Eby; Jim Gleason; Pamlico Capital (Charlotte, NC).
Cable Systems (4):
Minnesota: ADRIAN; MARSHALL.
South Dakota: RAPID CITY; VIBORG.

CLEAR CREEK TELEPHONE & TELEVISION
18238 South Fischers Mill Rd.
Oregon City, OR 97045
Phone: 503-631-2101
Fax: 503-631-2098
E-mail: info@clearcreek.coop
Web site: http://www.ccmtc.com
Officer:
Mitchell Moore, President
Cable Systems (1):
Oregon: OREGON CITY (unincorporated areas).

CLEARVISION CABLE SYSTEMS INC.
1785 Rte. 40
Greenup, IL 62428
Phone: 217-923-5594
Fax: 217-923-5681
Cable Systems (18):
Illinois: ALLERTON (village); BEECHER CITY; BROCTON; COWDEN; DIETERICH; EDGEWOOD; GRANTFORK (village); HUME (village); JEWETT; KINMUNDY; MULBERRY GROVE; PATOKA; PIERRON; POCAHONTAS; SHUMWAY; SIDELL (village); ST. PETER; WATSON.

CLIMAX TELEPHONE CO.
13800 East Michigan Ave.
Galesburg, MI 49053
Phones: 269-746-4411; 800-627-5287
Fax: 269-746-9914
E-mail: info@ctstelecom.com
Web site: http://www.ctstelecom.com
Officers:
Jim Burnham, President & Chief Executive Officer
Bob Stewart, Vice President
Ginny Rutherford, Billing & Customer Services Supervisor
Ownership: CTS Communications Corp..
Cable Systems (1):
Michigan: CLIMAX TWP..

CLINTON CABLE INC.
PO Box 900
Clinton, AR 72031
Phone: 501-745-4040
Fax: 501-745-4663
E-mail: clintoncable@clintoncable.net
Web site: http://www.clintoncable.net
Officer:
John Hastings, Owner
Ownership: John Hastings.
Cable Systems (1):
Arkansas: CLINTON.

CLT COMMUNICATIONS LLC
PO Box 47
316 3rd Ave.
Clear Lake, WI 54005
Phone: 715-263-2755
Fax: 715-263-2267
E-mail: info@cltcomm.net; cltel@cltcomm.net
Web site: http://cltcomm.net

Cable Systems (1):
Wisconsin: CLEAR LAKE.

CND ACQUISITION CO. LLC
PO Box 880
Rossville, GA 30741
Phone: 706-866-0901
Fax: 706-866-0902
Web site: http://www.cabletvonline.net
Ownership: William J Cooke; David P Daniel, jointly.
Cable Systems (2):
North Carolina: ANDREWS; MURPHY.

COASTAL LINK COMMUNICATIONS LLC
314 West Texas St.
Brazoria, TX 77422
Phones: 979-798-2121; 979-798-5465
E-mail: customercare@btel.com
Web site: http://www.btel.com
Officer:
John H Greenberg, President
Ownership: Brazoria Telephone Co..
Cable Systems (1):
Texas: BRAZORIA.

COAXIAL CABLE TV CORP.
105 Walker Dr.
Edinboro, PA 16412
Phones: 814-734-1424; 800-684-1681
Fax: 814-734-8898
E-mail: info@coaxpa.com
Web site: http://www.coaxialcabletv.com
Officers:
Michael Mead, President
Edward M. Mead, Executive Vice President
Chris Lovell, General Manager
Ownership: Mead Newspapers. Mead Newspapers owns Erie (PA) News, Times & Times News; Warren (PA) Times-Observer.
Represented (legal): The McDonald Group LLP.
Cable Systems (1):
Pennsylvania: EDINBORO.

COAXIAL PROPERTIES INC.
Ste 805
4564 Telephone Rd.
Ventura, CA 93003
Phone: 805-658-1579
E-mail: commserv@cscable.net
Web site: http://cscable.net
Officer:
Phil Shockley, President
Cable Systems (1):
California: POINT MUGU NAVAL AIR STATION.

COLANE CABLE TV INC.
PO Box 610
Omar, WV 25638
Phone: 304-946-2871
Ownership: William Stark.
Cable Systems (8):
West Virginia: BEECH CREEK; BRUNO; CRAWLEY CREEK; HEWETT; MUD RIVER; NEIBERT; OMAR; SIX MILE ROAD.

COLDWATER BOARD OF PUBLIC UTILITIES
1 Grand St.
Coldwater, MI 49036
Phone: 517-279-9531
Fax: 517-279-0805
E-mail: jroyer@coldwater.org
Web site: http://www.coldwater.org/ProgramsAndServices/Cable_Internet_Phone_Menu.html

Officer:
David Sattler, Public Works
Cable Systems (1):
Michigan: COLDWATER.

COLFAX HIGHLINE CABLE CO.
North 301 Mill St.
Colfax, WA 99111
Phone: 509-397-2211
Fax: 509-397-2274
Ownership: St. John Cable Co. Inc., see listing, 50%; Ken Julian, 50%.
Cable Systems (1):
Washington: COLFAX.

COLO TELEPHONE CO.
PO Box 315
303 Main St.
Colo, IA 50056
Phone: 641-377-2202
Fax: 641-377-2209
E-mail: colo@netins.net
Web site: http://www.colotel.org
Officers:
Fred Cerka, President
Pete Heintz, Vice President
Edythe Lounsbury-Meller, Secretary
Larry Springer, Chief Executive Officer & General Manager
Cable Systems (1):
Iowa: COLO.

COLTONTEL
PO Box 68
20983 South Hwy. 211
Colton, OR 97017
Phone: 503-824-3211
Fax: 503-824-9944
Web site: http://www.coltontel.com
Officer:
Steve Krogue, General Manager
Cable Systems (1):
Oregon: COLTON.

COLUMBIA POWER & WATER SYSTEMS
201 Pickens Ln.
Columbia, TN 38401
Phone: 931-388-4833
Fax: 931-388-5287
E-mail: wes.kelley@cpws.com
Web site: http://www.cpws.com
Officers:
Wes Kelley, General Manager
Martha Mayberry, Office Manager
Cable Systems (1):
Tennessee: COLUMBIA.

COLUMBUS TELEPHONE CO.
224 South Kansas Ave.
Columbus, KS 66725
Phone: 620-429-3132
Fax: 620-429-1704
E-mail: coltelco@columbus-ks.com
Web site: http://columbus-telephone.com
Officers:
Ronald Boulware, President
Wes Houser, Vice President
Patricia Carroll, Secretary
Larry Prauser, Treasurer
Ownership: Community owned--Columbus, KS.
Cable Systems (1):
Kansas: COLUMBUS.

COMCAST CABLE COMMUNICATIONS INC.
1701 JFK Blvd.
Philadelphia, PA 19103

Phones: 215-286-1700; 215-981-7613
Fax: 215-286-7790
Web site: http://corporate.comcast.com
Officers:
Brian L. Roberts, Chairman & Chief Executive Officer, Comcast Corp.
Neil Smit, President & Chief Executive Officer
Tony G Werner, President, Technology & Product
Greg Butz, President, Comcast Mobile
Sree Kotay, Chief Technology Officer
D'Arcy F. Rudnay, Chief Communications Officer & Executive Vice President, Corporate Communications
David L Cohen, Senior Executive Vice President, Chief Diversity Officer
Catherine Avgiris, Executive Vice President & Chief Financial Officer
Robert Eatroff, Executive Vice President, Global Corporate Development & Strategy
Charlie Herrin, Executive Vice President, Customer Experience
Marcien Jenckes, Executive Vice President, Consumer Services
Peter Kiriacoulacos, Executive Vice President, Procurement
Chris Satchell, Executive Vice President & Chief Product Officer
John Schanz, Executive Vice President & Chief Network Officer
William Strahan, Executive Vice President, Human Resources
Matthew Strauss, Executive Vice President & General Manager, Video Services
Dave Watson, Executive Vice President & Chief Operating Officer
Susan Adams, Senior Vice President, Engineering & Operations
Rebecca Arbogast, Senior Vice President, Global Public Policy
Jason Armstrong, Senior Vice President, Investor Relations
C. Stephen Backstrom, Senior Vice President, Taxation
Michael Brady, Senior Vice President, State Regulatory Affairs
Ed Brassel, Senior Vice President, Business Intelligence
Francis Buono, Senior Vice President, Legal Regulatory Affairs & Senior Deputy General Counsel
Sherita T Ceasar, Senior Vice President, Engineering & Platform Services
Clem Chung, Senior Vice President, Human Resources, Sales & Marketing
Kristine Dankenbrink, Senior Vice President, Taxation
Noopur Davis, Senior Vice President, Product Security & Privacy, Technology & Product
Ruth Dawson, Senior Vice President, Comcast Innovation Labs & General Manager, Comcast Silicon Valley
Mike DeCandido, Senior Vice President, Call Center Operations
William E Dordelman, Senior Vice President & Treasurer
Karen Dougherty Buchholz, Senior Vice President, Administration
Kimberly Edmunds, Senior Vice President, Customer Care
Klayton Fennell, Senior Vice President, Government Affairs
Javier Garcia, Senior Vice President & General Manager, Multicultural Services
Todd Goodbinder, Senior Vice President, Comcast Business SMB Sales
Jan Hofmoeyr, Senior Vice President, X1 Platform
Rob Holmes, Senior Vice President, Advanced Advertising
Susan Jin Davis, Senior Vice President, Strategic Services, Communications & Data Services

2017 Edition
D-897

Cable Owners

Aljit Joy, Senior Vice President, Strategy & Communications Product Development
Jennifer Khoury, Senior Vice President, Corporate & Digital Communications
Grace Killelea, Senior Vice President, Talent
Bridget Kimball, Senior Vice President, Software Development & Engineering
Ken Klaer, Senior Vice President, Premises Technology
Kathryn Koles, Senior Vice President & Deputy General Counsel, Cable Legal Department
Shawn Leavitt, Senior Vice President, Global Benefits
Ebony Lee, Senior Vice President, Growth Development
Gerald Lewis, Senior Vice President, Chief Privacy Officer & Deputy General Counsel
Piers Lingle, Senior Vice President, Customer Experience
Tom Loretan, Senior Vice President & Executive Creative Director, User Experience & Product Design
David Marcus, Senior Vice President & Deputy General Counsel, Cable Legal Department
Melissa Maxfield, Senior Vice President, Congressional & Federal Government Affairs
Maggie McLean Suniewick, Senior Vice President, Strategic Integration
Elad Nafshi, Senior Vice President, Next Generation Access Networks
Michael Parker, Senior Vice President, Western New England
Melanie Penna, Senior Vice President, Human Resources Service Delivery
Ron Phillips, Senior Vice President, Employee Engagement
Tracy Pitcher, Senior Vice President, Small & Mid-Sized Business Operations, Comcast Business Services
Noam Raffaelli, Senior Vice President, IP & Communications Services
Luci Rainey, Senior Vice President, Consumer Marketing
Devesh Raj, Senior Vice President, Strategic & Financial Planning
Rick Rioboli, Senior Vice President, Metadata Productions & Search Services
Rebecca Scilingo, Senior Vice President, Enterprise Project Management Office
Inder Singh, Senior Vice President, Strategic Planning
Marc Sirota, Senior Vice President, Applied Analytics
Robert Slinkard, Senior Vice President, Product Management, Communications & Data Services
Rick Smotkin, Senior Vice President, Government Affairs
Sridhar Solur, Senior Vice President, Product Development, Xfinity Home & Internet of Things
Myrna Soto, Senior Vice President, Global Chief Information Security Officer
Amy Stipandic, Senior Vice President, Strategic Process, Design & Delivery
Fraser Stirling, Senior Vice President, Hardware Development
Tina Waters, Senior Vice President, Human Performance
Dalila Wilson-Scott, Senior Vice President, Community Investment & President, Comcast Foundation
Matt Zelesko, Senior Vice President, Software Development Engineering
Kathy Zachem, Senior Vice President, Regulatory & State Legislative Affairs
Beth Arnholt, Vice President, Integrated Talent Management
Daniel Carr, Vice President, Sales Operations, Comcast Business Services
Jennifer L Daley, Vice President & Assistant Treasurer
Julie Laine, Vice President, Chief Transaction Compliance Officer & Senior Deputy General Counsel
Dennis Mathew, Vice President, New Businesses, Communications & Data Services
James P McCue, Vice President & Assistant Treasurer
Daniel Murdock, Vice President-Corporate Controller
Sharmila Ravi, Vice President, Product Operations, Communications & Data Services
Thomas Wlodkowski, Vice President, Accessibility

Branch Offices:
CENTRAL DIVISION
600 Galleria Pkwy
Ste 1100
Atlanta, GA 30339
NORTHEAST DIVISION
676 Pond Island Rd
Manchester, NH 03109
WEST DIVISION
183 Inverness Dr W
Englewood, CO 80112
Ownership: Comcast Corp.; CC ownership:; BRCC Holdings LLC, 32%. votes; Remainder publicly held.; BRCCHLLC ownership:; Brian L Robert, Managing Member. votes, 28.8% assets; 1998 Grantor Retained Annuity Trust of Brian L. Roberts, 62.4%. assets; Irrevocable Deed of Trust of Brian L. Roberts for Children and Other Issue, 8.8%. assets; 1998GRAT & IDOT ownership:; Sheldon M Bonovitz, Sole Trustee. On February 13, 2014, Comcast announced it was acquiring Time Warner Cable for $45.2 billion, not including debt. Due to Department of Justice and Federal Communications Commission concerns, Comcast called off deal on April 24, 2015.
Represented (legal): LeBoeuf, Lamb, Greene & MacRae LLP.
Cable Systems (146):
Alabama: CLAYTON (town); MOBILE.
Arizona: TUCSON.
Arkansas: LITTLE ROCK.
California: COALINGA; FRESNO; HURON; LE GRAND; PATTERSON; PLANADA; SACRAMENTO; SAN FRANCISCO; WILLITS.
Colorado: CARBONDALE; COLORADO SPRINGS; DENVER; GLENWOOD SPRINGS; KREMMLING; LONGMONT; PARACHUTE; RIFLE; SILT; TRINIDAD.
Connecticut: NEW BRITAIN.
Florida: ARCHER; JACKSONVILLE; JASPER; MONTICELLO; SARASOTA; TALLAHASSEE; WAUCHULA; WEST PALM BEACH.
Georgia: ATLANTA; AUGUSTA; DARIEN; ELBERTON; GLENNVILLE; HOMERVILLE; MONTEZUMA; MOUNT VERNON; SAVANNAH; SOPERTON; WASHINGTON; WRIGHTSVILLE.
Illinois: CHAMPAIGN; CHICAGO; MONMOUTH; MOUNT PROSPECT; NEWMAN; PEORIA; PIPER CITY; SPRINGFIELD.
Indiana: HENDRICKS COUNTY (portions); TELL CITY.
Kentucky: ELIZABETHTOWN; GREENVILLE; HORSE CAVE.
Louisiana: SHREVEPORT.
Maryland: FREDERICK COUNTY (portions); TOWSON.
Massachusetts: BOSTON.
Michigan: DETROIT.
Minnesota: MINNEAPOLIS.
Mississippi: CORINTH; HATTIESBURG; JACKSON; TUPELO.
Missouri: INDEPENDENCE.
Montana: BROADUS.
New Jersey: AUDUBON; EATONTOWN BOROUGH; WEST ORANGE TWP..
New Mexico: ALBUQUERQUE; ANGEL FIRE (village); CIMARRON; DEMING; GALLUP; GRANTS; HATCH; LAS VEGAS; LOS ALAMOS; PECOS; PORTALES; QUESTA; RATON; RED RIVER; SPRINGER; TAOS; TUCUMCARI.
North Dakota: BEULAH; BISMARCK; BOWMAN; COOPERSTOWN (village); DEVILS LAKE; GRAND FORKS; LEEDS; MCCLUSKY; MINNEWAUKAN; MINOT; MOTT; SOUTH HEART; WAHPETON; WILLISTON.
Ohio: NEW MIDDLETOWN.
Oregon: PORTLAND.
Pennsylvania: BLAIRSVILLE; GREENSBURG; HARRISBURG; OIL CITY; PHILADELPHIA; PITTSBURGH; PUNXSUTAWNEY.
South Carolina: BEAUFORT USMC AIR STATION; LADY'S ISLAND; NEWBERRY; NORTH CHARLESTON.
South Dakota: ABERDEEN; FORT PIERRE; HURON; MITCHELL; SIOUX FALLS.
Tennessee: KNOXVILLE; LIVINGSTON; MEMPHIS; NASHVILLE.
Texas: HOUSTON.
Utah: SALT LAKE CITY.
Vermont: BURLINGTON.
Virginia: CHARLOTTESVILLE; LYNCHBURG; PETERSBURG.
Washington: ABERDEEN TWP.; BELLINGHAM; MINERAL; MOSSYROCK; RAYMOND; ROCHESTER; RYDERWOOD; SEATTLE; SPOKANE; VANCOUVER; WINLOCK.
West Virginia: BLUEFIELD; KEYSER; MORGANTOWN; WHEELING.
Other Holdings:
Equipment manufacturer: 5.1% of Arris.
Movie source: DreamWorks Animation SKG
Professional sports: Owns 66% of sports venture that includes Philadelphia Flyers (hockey team), Philadelphia 76ers (basketball team); CoreStates Center & CoreStates Spectrum (sports arenas); Phantoms of American Hockey League; Spectacor
Program source: 8.34% of MLB Network; 30% of Pittsburgh Cable News; 12.4% of Music Choice; 15.6% of NHL Network

COM-LINK INC.
1006 South Brundidge St.
Troy, AL 36081
Phones: 334-566-3310; 800-735-9546
Fax: 334-738-5555
E-mail: sales@comlinkinc.net
Web site: http://www.comlinkinc.net
Officer:
John Fischer, Chief Executive Officer
Ownership: Ropir Industries; Mrs. R. M. Pirnie, Principals. Pirnie has telephone holdings.
Cable Systems (2):
Alabama: LAKE MARTIN RESORT; UNION SPRINGS.

COMMUNICATIONS 1 NETWORK INC.
PO Box 20
105 South Main St.
Kanawha, IA 50447
Phones: 641-762-3772; 800-469-3772
Fax: 641-762-8201
E-mail: comm1net@comm1net.net
Web site: http://home.comm1net.net
Officer:
Randolph S. Yeakel, Chief Operating Officer & Director
Cable Systems (1):
Iowa: KANAWHA.
Other Holdings:
Cellular radio

COMMUNITY ANTENNA SYSTEM INC.
1010 Lake St.
Hillsboro, WI 54634
Phones: 608-489-2321; 888-394-4772
Fax: 608-489-2321
Web site: http://comantenna.com
Officers:
Bernice Kubarski, Chairman
Randall Kubarski, President
Gregory Kubarski, Vice President
Cable Systems (4):
Wisconsin: CAZENOVIA; ELROY; HILLSBORO; KENDALL.

COMMUNITY CABLE & BROADBAND INC.
PO Box 307
1550 West Rogers Blvd.
Skiatook, OK 74070-0307
Phone: 918-396-3019
Fax: 918-396-2081
E-mail: dennis.soule@ccbbi.com
Web site: http://www.communitycablebroadband.com
Officer:
Dennis Soule, President
Ownership: Ann E Hamilton; Georgie G Hamilton.
Cable Systems (8):
Oklahoma: AVANT; COPAN; HOMINY; OCHELATA; RAMONA; SKIATOOK; WYNONA; YALE.
Cable Holdings:
Community Cable & Broadband Inc.

COMMUNITY CABLE & BROADBAND LLC
PO Box 65
Meridian, MS 39302
Phones: 601-485-6980; 800-446-8698
Fax: 601-483-0103
E-mail: helpdesk@24hoursupport.com
Officer:
Granberry Holland Ward III, Manager
Ownership: Berry Ward. Formerly known as Sky Cablevision Ltd.
Cable Systems (7):
Alabama: BELLAMY; BOLIGEE; CENTREVILLE; EUTAW; FORKLAND; MARION; SWEET WATER.

COMMUNITY CABLE CORP. OF PENNSYLVANIA
4145 Rte. 549
Mansfield, PA 16933
Phones: 570-549-6737; 570-537-6737
Fax: 570-549-2500
E-mail: nptinfo@npacc.net
Web site: http://www.northpenntelephone.com
Officers:
Robert H. Wagner, President
Brian Wagner, Executive Vice President
Pete McClure, Vice President

Branch Office:
Prattsburgh
34 Main St
Prattsburgh, NY 14873
Phone: 800-338-3300
Ownership: North Penn Telephone Co..
Cable Systems (1):
Pennsylvania: EAST SMITHFIELD.
Other Holdings:
Telephone holdings

COMMUNITY CABLE TV CORP.
PO Box 489
102 South Eastern St.
Sanborn, IA 51248
Phone: 712-930-5593
Fax: 712-930-5595
E-mail: tca@tcaexpress.net
Web site: http://www.tcaexpress.com
Officer:
D. J. Weber, Manager
Ownership: Community owned--Sanborn, IA.

Cable Owners

Cable Systems (1):
Iowa: SANBORN.

COMMUNITY COMMUNICATIONS CO.
1920 Hwy. 425 North
Monticello, AR 71655
Phones: 870-367-7300; 800-272-2191
Fax: 870-367-9770
Web site: http://ccc-cable.com
Officer:
Paul Gardner, President
Ownership: Paul Gardner, Pres..
Cable Systems (7):
Arkansas: EUDORA; GOULD; MONTICELLO; RISON; TILLAR; WARREN.
Mississippi: ROSEDALE.

COMMUNITY NETWORK SERVICES
PO Box 1540
111 Victoria Pl.
Thomasville, GA 31799
Phone: 229-227-7001
Fax: 229-227-3366
E-mail: answers@cns-internet.com
Web site: http://www.cns-internet.com
Officers:
Mark Furhman, General Manager
Sherri Nix, Marketing Coordinator
Cable Systems (5):
Georgia: BACONTON; CAIRO; CAMILLA; MOULTRIE; THOMASVILLE.

COMMUNITY TELECOM SERVICES
PO Box 579
49 Hardwood Dr.
Monticello, KY 42633
Phone: 606-348-8416
Fax: 606-348-6397
E-mail: ads@ctsmediagroup.com
Web site: http://ctsmediagroup.com
Officer:
Jessie Fulton, General Manager
Cable Systems (1):
Kentucky: MONTICELLO.

COMMUNITY TV INC.
364 Riverview Dr.
Hazard, KY 41701
Phone: 606-436-4593
Officer:
Don Dresher, President
Ownership: Non-profit organization--Walkertown Station, KY.
Cable Systems (1):
Kentucky: WALKERTOWN.

COMMZOOM COMMUNICATIONS LLC
2438 Boardwalk
San Antonio, TX 78217-4429
Phone: 844-858-8500
Web site: http://www.commzoom.com
Cable Systems (9):
Texas: BANDERA; COMFORT; DEVINE; GOLIAD; HONDO; KENEDY; LA VERNIA; PLEASANTON; THREE RIVERS.

COMPORIUM COMMUNICATIONS
330 East Black St.
Rock Hill, SC 29730
Phones: 803-985-4040; 877-903-2200
Web site: http://www.comporium.com
Officer:
Dan Lehman, Vice President, Security, Monitoring & Automation
Ownership: Comporium Group.

Cable Systems (3):
North Carolina: BREVARD.
South Carolina: GILBERT; ROCK HILL.

COMSOUTH CORP.
PO Box 1298
99 Broad St.
Hawkinsville, GA 31036
Phone: 478-783-4001
Fax: 478-892-3055
E-mail: questions@comsouth.net
Web site: http://comsouth.net

Branch Offices:
Cochran
119 N Second Ave
Cochran, GA 31014
Phone: 478-783-4001
Fax: 478-278-4011
Fort Valley
128 E Main St
Fort Valley, GA 31030
Phone: 478-825-3626
Fax: 478-825-1639
Perry
1357-D Sam Nunn Blvd
Perry, GA 31069
Phone: 478-224-4001
Fax: 478-987-9932
Cable Systems (1):
Georgia: PERRY.

COMSTOCK COMMUNITY TV INC.
PO Box 9
Virginia City, NV 89440
Phone: 775-847-0572
Officers:
Marilou Walling, President
Gary Greenlund, Chief Technology Officer
Barbara Bowers, Secretary-Treasurer
Mark Blomstrom, Engineering Director
Ownership: Non-profit organization--Virginia City, NV.
Cable Systems (1):
Nevada: VIRGINIA CITY.

CONSOLIDATED TELCOM
PO Box 1408
507 South Main
Dickinson, ND 58601
Phones: 701-483-4000; 888-225-5282
Fax: 701-483-0001
Web site: http://www.ctctel.com
Officer:
Bryan Personne, Chief Operating Officer
Cable Systems (2):
North Dakota: DICKINSON; REGENT.

CONWAY CORP.
PO Box 99
1307 Prairie St.
Conway, AR 72034
Phone: 501-450-6000
Fax: 501-450-6099
E-mail: comments@conwaycorp.net
Web site: http://www.conwaycorp.net
Officers:
Barbara Money, Chairman
Richard Arnold, Chief Executive Officer
Tommy Shackelford, Chief Operating Officer
Bret Carroll, Chief Financial Officer
Earnest Hicks, Superintendent, Telecommunications
Ownership: Community owned--Conway, AR.

Cable Systems (1):
Arkansas: CONWAY.

COON CREEK TELEPHONE & CABLEVISION
PO Box 150
312 Locust St. NE
Blairstown, IA 52209-0150
Phones: 319-454-6234; 888-823-6234
Fax: 319-454-6480
E-mail: cooncrek@netins.net; csr@cooncreektelephone.com
Web site: http://www.cooncreektelephone.com
Cable Systems (1):
Iowa: BLAIRSTOWN.

COON RAPIDS MUNICIPAL CABLE SYSTEM
PO Box 207
123 3rd Ave. South
Coon Rapids, IA 50058
Phone: 712-999-2225
Fax: 712-999-5148
E-mail: info@crmu.net; crmuinfo@gmail.com
Web site: http://www.crmu.net/index-4.html
Officers:
Brad Honold, General Manager
Kevin Dorpinghaus, Technician
Ownership: Community owned--Coon Rapids, IA.
Cable Systems (1):
Iowa: COON RAPIDS.

COON VALLEY CABLEVISION
PO Box 108
516 Sherman St.
Menlo, IA 50164
Phone: 641-524-2111
Fax: 641-524-2112
Web site: http://www.coonvalleytelco.com
Officers:
Jim Nelson, General Manager
Michael Clarke, Technician
Cable Systems (1):
Iowa: MENLO.

ARTHUR R. COOPER
1525 Dupont Rd.
Parkersburg, WV 26101
Phones: 304-420-2470; 800-339-4002
Fax: 304-420-2474
E-mail: info@cascable.com
Web site: http://www.cascable.com
Cable Systems (2):
West Virginia: COTTAGEVILLE; WASHINGTON.

COPPER MOUNTAIN CONSOLIDATED METROPOLITAN DISTRICT
Box 3002
0800 Copper Rd.
Copper Mountain, CO 80443
Phone: 970-968-2537
Fax: 970-968-2932
E-mail: darnesen@cmcmdi.com
Web site: http://www.coppermtnmetro.org/cabletvinternet.html
Officers:
Thomas J. Malmgren, Chairman & Chief Executive Officer
Elizabeth Black, Chief Operating & Financial Officer
Dave Arnesen, Director, Cable Services
Ownership: Community owned--Copper Mountain, CO.

Cable Systems (1):
Colorado: COPPER MOUNTAIN.

CORN BELT TELEPHONE CO.
PO Box 445
108 Main St.
Wall Lake, IA 51466
Phone: 712-664-2221
Fax: 712-664-2083
E-mail: cornbeltpr@netins.net
Web site: http://www.cornbelttelephone.com
Cable Systems (1):
Iowa: WALL LAKE.

COUNCIL GROVE TELECOMMUNICATIONS
1410 Lilac Lake
Wamego, KS 66547
Phones: 785-456-2287; 620-767-5511
E-mail: tech@cablerocket.com
Web site: http://www.councilgrove.cablerocket.com
Cable Systems (1):
Kansas: COUNCIL GROVE.

COUNTRY CABLE LLC
Ste 14
7520 North Market St.
Spokane, WA 99217
Phones: 509-464-4906; 509-633-2283
Fax: 208-772-8576
E-mail: cs@couleedam.net
Web site: http://www.couleedam.net
Officer:
Carl Sherwood, Vice President
Ownership: Jon Cooke, 50%; Tim Devine, 50%.
Cable Systems (2):
Idaho: BONNERS FERRY.
Washington: COULEE DAM.

COUNTRY CABLE TV
196 South Main St.
Pleasant Gap, PA 16823
Phone: 814-359-3161
Fax: 814-359-2145
Ownership: Lee Dorman.
Cable Systems (1):
Pennsylvania: UNION TWP. (Centre County).

COX COMMUNICATIONS INC.
6205-B Peachtree Dunwoody Rd.
Atlanta, GA 30328
Phones: 404-843-5000; 866-961-0027
Fax: 404-843-5777
Web site: http://www.cox.com
Officers:
James C. Kennedy, Chairman, Cox Enterprises Inc.
Patrick J. Esser, President & Chief Executive Officer
Don Hallacy, Interim Chief Technology Officer
Leigh Woisard, Chief Communications Counsel
Len Barlik, Executive Vice President & Chief Human Resources Officer
Mark F. Bowser, Executive Vice President & Chief Financial Officer
Jill Campbell, Executive Vice President & Chief Operations Officer
Mark Greatrex, Executive Vice President & Chief Marketing and Sales Officer
Kevin Hart, Executive Vice President & Chief Technology Officer
Steve Necessary, Executive Vice President, Product Development & Management
Gregory S Rigdon, Executive Vice President, Corporate Development & Strategy
Asheesh Seksena, Executive Vice President & Chief Strategy Officer

Cable Owners

Rhonda Taylor, Executive Vice President & Chief People Officer
Andy Albert, Senior Vice President, Content Acquisition
Paul Cronin, Senior Vice President, Customer Service
Johannes Eckert, Senior Vice President, IT & Network
F. William Farina, Senior Vice President, Advertising Sales
Bill Fitzsimmons, Senior Vice President, Corporate Finance & Chief Accounting Officer
James A. Hatcher, Senior Vice President, Legal & Regulatory Affairs
Jennifer Hightower, Senior Vice President, Law & Policy
Claus F. Kroeger, Senior Vice President, Operations
Phil Meeks, Senior Vice President
Anthony Pope, Senior Vice President & Regional Manager, Louisiana
David Pugliese, Senior Vice President, Product Marketing
George Richter, Senior Vice President, Supply Chain Management
Janice Roberts, Senior Vice President, Field Services
Joseph J Rooney, Senior Vice President, Brand Marketing, Social Media & Advertising
Steve Rowley, Senior Vice President, Cox Business
Leigh Woisard, Senior Vice President, Corporate Communications & Public Affairs
John Wolfe, Senior Vice President & Regional Manager, Southwest
Keith Crandall, Vice President, Customer Care, Partner Performance
Kathryn Falk, Vice President, Market, Northern Virginia Operations
Kristine Faulkner, Vice President & General Manager, Home Security and Smart Home
Michael Grove, Vice President, Government Affairs
Carolyn Herbert, Vice President, Internal Communications, Public Affairs
Rose Kirkland, Vice President, Relationships, Requirements & Portfolio Management
Ken Kraft, Vice President, Cox Business Marketing
Mike Latino, Vice President, Service Infrastructure & Delivery
Tim McKinley, Vice President, Field Operations, East Region
Rob Smallwood, Vice President, Enterprise Development
Kelly Williams, Vice President, Wireless Product & Operations
Vince Groff, General Manager, Cox Home Security
Ownership: Cox Enterprises Inc.; CEI ownership;; Cox Family Voting Trust.
Cable Systems (38):
Arizona: PHOENIX; SIERRA VISTA; TUCSON.
Arkansas: BERRYVILLE; FORT SMITH; HARRISON; SPRINGDALE.
California: RANCHO PALOS VERDES; SAN DIEGO; SAN JUAN CAPISTRANO; SANTA BARBARA.
Connecticut: ENFIELD; MANCHESTER; MERIDEN.
Florida: GAINESVILLE; PENSACOLA.
Georgia: MACON.
Idaho: SUN VALLEY.
Kansas: DODGE CITY; GARDEN CITY; GREAT BEND; MANHATTAN; PITTSBURG; SALINA; TOPEKA; WICHITA.
Louisiana: BATON ROUGE; NEW ORLEANS.
Nebraska: OMAHA.
Nevada: LAS VEGAS.
Ohio: PARMA.
Oklahoma: OKLAHOMA CITY; TULSA.
Rhode Island: WEST WARWICK.

Virginia: FAIRFAX COUNTY; FREDERICKSBURG; ROANOKE; VIRGINIA BEACH.
Cable Holdings:
Australian cable interests
Other Holdings:
Cable advertising representative: Cablerep Advertising Inc.
Common Carrier: EasyTEL Communications--provides voice, data and video services.
Program source: QVC Network; 25% of Discovery Communications Inc.
Service company: K-Prime Partners/Prime Star satellite services

CRAIG CABLE TV INC.
PO Box 131
1301 Water Tower Rd.
Craig, AK 99921
Phone: 907-826-3470
Fax: 907-826-3469
E-mail: office@craigcabletv.com
Web site: http://www.craigcabletv.com
Officer:
Greg Ouelette, Manager
Cable Systems (1):
Alaska: CRAIG.

CRAWFORD MANOR CABLE TV
2806 NE Side Hwy.
Elkton, VA 22827
Phone: 540-337-8450
Cable Systems (1):
Virginia: CRAWFORD MANOR.

CRAW-KAN TELEPHONE COOPERATIVE
PO Box 100
200 North Ozark
Girard, KS 66743
Phones: 620-724-8235; 800-362-0316
Fax: 620-724-4099
Web site: http://web.ckt.net
Officer:
Craig Wilbert, General Manager
Ownership: Cooperative.
Cable Systems (3):
Kansas: EDNA; GIRARD; GIRARD.

CROSSLAKE COMMUNICATIONS
PO Box 70
35910 County Rd. 66
Crosslake, MN 56442
Phones: 218-692-2777; 800-992-8220
Fax: 218-692-2410
Web site: http://www.crosslake.net
Officer:
Paul Hoge, General Manager
Ownership: Community owned--Crosslake, MN.
Cable Systems (1):
Minnesota: CROSSLAKE.

CRYSTAL BROADBAND NETWORKS
5860 Main St.
Clay City, KY 40312
Phones: 630-206-0447; 877-319-0328
E-mail: sales@crystalbn.com; helpdesk@crystalbn.com
Web site: http://crystalbn.com
Cable Systems (23):
Arkansas: ASH FLAT; HORSESHOE BEND.
Indiana: PENN TWP.; PLYMOUTH.
Kentucky: BEATTYVILLE; HARDINSBURG; IRVINGTON; JACKSON; LESLIE COUNTY (northern portion); MOZELLE; STANTON.
North Carolina: HOLLISTER; MID LAKES TRAILER PARK; NASH COUNTY; OAK CITY; PINETOPS; WHITAKERS.
Ohio: AMSTERDAM; HANNIBAL; SALINEVILLE.

Oregon: ENTERPRISE.
West Virginia: ANTHONY CREEK; SNOWSHOE.

CITY OF CRYSTAL FALLS
401 Superior Ave.
Crystal Falls, MI 49920
Phone: 906-875-3212
Fax: 906-875-3767
E-mail: cfclerk@up.net; tpeltoma@crystalfalls.org
Web site: http://www.crystalfalls.org
Officers:
Dorothea Olson, City Manager
Dan Graff, CATV Technician
Ownership: Community owned--Crystal Falls, MI.
Cable Systems (1):
Michigan: CRYSTAL FALLS.

C T & R CABLE LLC
29 Water St.
Petersburg, WV 26847
Phone: 304-257-4891
Ownership: Matthew Alt, 50%; Terry Hinkle, 50%.
Cable Systems (2):
West Virginia: DORCAS; RIG.

CTC TELECOM
PO Box 88
130 North Superior St.
Cambridge, ID 83610
Phone: 208-253-3314
Fax: 208-257-3992
E-mail: support@ctcweb.net
Web site: http://ctcweb.net
Officers:
Richard Wiggins, General Manager
Jerry Piper, Marketing Director
Gordon Huff, Chief Technician
Cable Systems (2):
Idaho: CAMBRIDGE; COUNCIL.

CUNNINGHAM COMMUNICATIONS
220 West Main St.
Glen Elder, KS 67446
Phones: 785-545-3215; 800-287-8495
Fax: 785-527-3277
E-mail: brent@ctctelephony.tv
Web site: http://www.cunninghamtelephoneandcable.com
Officers:
John Cunningham, Owner & President
Terry Cunningham, Vice President & Outside Plant Supervisor

Branch Offices:
BELLEVILLE
1809 N St
Belleville, KS 66935
Phone: 785-527-2226
BELOIT
110 W Main St
Beloit, KS 67420
Phone: 785-534-1111
CONCORDIA
407 W 6th St
Concordia, KS 66901
Phone: 785-243-4068
Cable Systems (1):
Kansas: GLEN ELDER.

CUSTER TELEPHONE COOPERATIVE INC.
PO Box 324
1101 East Main Ave.
Challis, ID 83226
Phone: 208-879-2281
Web site: http://www.custertel.net

Cable Systems (2):
Idaho: CHALLIS; SALMON.

CYS INC.
2358 Gatetree Lane SE
Grand Rapids, MI 49546-7590
Officer:
Josh Perkins, Manager
Cable Systems (1):
Wisconsin: RICHLAND CENTER.
LPTV Stations:
Alabama: W08DC Birmingham.
California: K08LT Modesto.

DAIRYLAND CABLE SYSTEMS INC.
2494 Hwy. 14 East
Richland Center, WI 53581
Phone: 608-647-6383
Fax: 608-647-2093
Officer:
Frannie Hasburgh, Manager
Ownership: Lonnie Freeman, Principal.
Cable Systems (4):
Wisconsin: BAGLEY (village); BLUE RIVER (village); LOGANVILLE (village); SENECA (village).

DAKOTA CENTRAL TELECOMMUNICATIONS
PO Box 299
630 5th St. North
Carrington, ND 58421
Phones: 701-652-3184; 800-771-0974
Fax: 701-674-8121
E-mail: customerservice@daktel.com
Web site: http://www.daktel.com
Officers:
Keith A. Larson, General Manager & Chief Executive Officer
Paul Berg, Chief Plant Officer
Cindy Hewitt, Chief Financial Officer
Holly Utke, Chief Marketing Officer & Internal Operations Officer
Deedra Aasand, Customer Service Manager

Branch Office:
Jamestown
604 18th St SW
Jamestown, ND 58401
Phone: 701-952-1000
Fax: 701-952-1001
Ownership: Dakota Central Telecommunications Cooperative.
Represented (legal): Noack Law Office.
Cable Systems (2):
North Dakota: GLENFIELD; JAMESTOWN.

DALE-MEDIA INC.
1106-A Kingold Blvd.
Snow Hill, NC 28580
Phone: 252-747-5682
Fax: 252-747-3061
Cable Systems (1):
North Carolina: SNOW HILL.

DALTON TELEPHONE CO.
413 Elliot St.
Dalton, NE 69131
Phone: 866-542-6779
E-mail: dtc@daltontel.net; support@daltontel.net
Web site: http://www.daltontel.net
Officer:

Cable Owners

David Shipley, General Manager
Ownership: USConnect; USC ownership:; USConnect Holdings Inc.; USCHI ownership:; Brazoria Telephone Co., 17.357%; Dickey Rural Telephone Cooperative Inc. (see Dickey Rural Services Inc.), 17.357%; FTC Management Group, 17.357%; Golden West Telecommunications Cooperative (see Golden West Cablevision), 17.357%; Horry Telephone Cooperative Inc. (see listing), 17.357%; Leo Staurulakis, 3.33%; Manny Staurulakis, 3.33%; ML Star LLC, 3.24%; FTCMG ownership:; Farmers Telephone Cooperative Inc. (see listing); MLSLLC ownership:; Leo Staurulakis, 50%; Manny Staurulakis, 50%.
Cable Systems (1):
Nebraska: DALTON.

D & P COMMUNICATIONS INC.
PO Box 566
4200 Teal Rd.
Petersburg, MI 49270
Phones: 734-279-1339; 800-311-7340
Fax: 734-279-2640
E-mail: help@cass.net;
   servicedesk@d-pcomm.com
Web site: http://d-pcommunications.com

Branch Offices:
Adrian
100 E Church St
Adrian, MI 49221
Blissfield
137 S Lane St
Blissfield, MI 49228
Phone: 800-311-7340
Dundee
124 Tecumseh St
Dundee, MI 48131
Phone: 800-311-7340
Tecumseh
417 S Maumee St
Tecumseh, MI 49286
Cable Systems (1):
Michigan: PETERSBURG.

DARIEN COMMUNICATIONS
PO Box 575
1011 North Way
Darien, GA 31305
Phone: 912-437-4111
Fax: 912-437-7006
E-mail: dtcadmin@darientel.net
Web site: http://www.darientelephone.com
Officers:
Mary Lou Jackson Forsyth, President
Reginald V. Jackson, Vice President
Mary Alice Forsyth Thomas, Secretary-Treasurer
Cable Systems (1):
Georgia: DARIEN.

CHUCK DAVIS
Ste 106
501 Spur 316 Hwy.
Pottsboro, TX 75076
Phones: 903-786-7477; 888-815-0636
E-mail: tvcable@graysoncable.com
Web site: http://www.graysoncable.com
Cable Systems (4):
Texas: ECTOR; GORDONVILLE; GRAYSON COUNTY; POTTSBORO.

DAVIS COMMUNICATIONS INC.
PO Box 117
1920 4th. St
Cheney, WA 99004
Phones: 509-235-5144; 509-624-7129
Fax: 509-235-5158
E-mail: questions@daviscomm.net
Web site: http://www.daviscomm.net

Officers:
Thomas Davis, President
Cheryl Reagan, General Manager
Cable Systems (1):
Washington: CHENEY.

MICKEY DAVIS
PO Box 237
314 West Main St.
Mountain View, OK 73062
Phone: 800-980-7912
Fax: 580-347-2179
Cable Systems (2):
Oklahoma: FORT COBB; MOUNTAIN VIEW.

DONALD G. DEE
429 Court St.
Houlton, ME 04730-1958
Phones: 207-532-4451; 207-521-5666
Officer:
Donald G. Dee, Chairman & Chief Executive Officer
Cable Systems (1):
Maine: MATTAWAMKEAG (town).

DEMOPOLIS CATV CO.
PO Box 477
105 South Cedar St.
Demopolis, AL 36732
Phone: 334-289-0727
Fax: 334-289-2707
E-mail: lgoldman@demopoliscatv.com
Web site: http://www.demopoliscatv.com
Officers:
Lynn Goldman, President & Chief Executive Officer
Debbie Goldman, Vice President
Ownership: Lynn Goldman, 99.5%; Richard Manley, 0.5%.
Cable Systems (1):
Alabama: DEMOPOLIS.

DICKEY RURAL SERVICES INC.
PO Box 69
9628 Hwy. 281
Ellendale, ND 58436
Phones: 701-344-5000; 877-559-4692
Fax: 701-344-4300
E-mail: customerservice@drtel.com
Web site: http://www.drtel.com
Officers:
Ralph Neu, President
Robert K. Johnson, General Manager & Chief Executive Officer
Brunno Kinzler, Vice President
James Byerley, Engineering Manager
Janell Hauck, Marketing Manager
Kent Schimke, Plant Manager
Troy Schilling, Finance Manager
Duane Henrich, Secretary
Ownership: Dickey Rural Telephone Cooperative.
Cable Systems (1):
North Dakota: OAKES.
Other Holdings:
Telephone

DIODE CABLE CO. INC.
PO Box 236
300 Commercial St.
Diller, NE 68342
Phones: 402-793-5124; 877-668-9749
Fax: 402-793-5139
E-mail: customerservice@diodecom.net
Web site: http://diodecom.net
Ownership: Diller Telephone Co..
Cable Systems (2):
Nebraska: DILLER; HEBRON.
Other Holdings:
Telephone

DIRECT COMMUNICATIONS
PO Box 269
150 South Main St.
Rockland, ID 83271
Phones: 208-548-2345; 800-245-4329
Fax: 208-548-9911
E-mail: support@directcom.com;
   info@directcom.com
Web site: http://directcom.com
Officers:
Leonard May, President
Garrin Bott, General Manager
Jeremy Smith, General Manager, Starwest (Internet & Television)
Kip Wilson, General Manager, Direct Communications, Cedar Valley

Branch Offices:
Eagle Mountain (UT)
3726 E Campus Dr
Ste A
Eagle Mountain, UT 84005
Paris
648-1/2 N Main
Paris, ID 83261
Phone: 208-945-8035
Cable Systems (2):
Idaho: ABERDEEN TWP.; VICTOR.

DIVERSE COMMUNICATIONS INC.
246 North Division St.
Woodhull, IL 61490
Phone: 309-334-2150
Fax: 309-334-2989
E-mail: woodhulltel@yahoo.com
Web site: http://www.woodhulltel.com
Officers:
Jerry Krueger, President
Roscoe Lowrey, Executive Vice President
George Wirt, General Manager
Ownership: Woodhull Community Telephone Co..
Cable Systems (1):
Illinois: ALPHA.

DIXON TELEPHONE CO.
PO Box 10
608 Davenport St.
Dixon, IA 52745
Phone: 563-843-2901
Fax: 563-843-2481
E-mail: dixontel@netins.net
Officer:
Keith Steward, President
Cable Systems (1):
Iowa: DIXON.

DOCOMO PACIFIC
Ste 206
219 S Marine Corp. Dr.
Tamuning, MP 96913
Phones: 671-688-2273; 866-688-4826
Web site: http://www.docomopacific.com
Ownership: NTT Docomo.
Cable Systems (4):
Guam: AGANA.
Mariana Islands: SAIPAN; SINAPALO; SUSUPE.

CITY OF DOERUN
PO Box 37
223 West Broad Ave.
Doerun, GA 31744
Phone: 229-782-5444
Fax: 229-782-5224
Officer:

Herchel Finch, Manager & Chief Technician
Ownership: Community owned--Doerun, GA.
Cable Systems (1):
Georgia: DOERUN.

DOYLESTOWN COMMUNICATIONS INC.
81 North Portage St.
Doylestown, OH 44230
Phone: 330-658-2121
Fax: 330-658-2272
E-mail: info@doylestowntelephone.com
Web site: http://
   www.doylestowncommunications.com
Cable Systems (1):
Ohio: DOYLESTOWN.

DTC CABLE INC.
PO Box 271
107 Main St.
Delhi, NY 13753
Phones: 607-746-1500; 888-898-8006
Fax: 607-746-7991
E-mail: custserv@delhitel.com
Web site: http://www.delhitel.com
Officers:
Jason Miller, General Manager
Steve Oles, Business Office Manager
Cable Systems (4):
New York: BLOOMVILLE; BOVINA (town); DELHI (village); HAMDEN.

DUMONT TELEPHONE CO.
PO Box 349
506 Pine St.
Dumont, IA 50625
Phones: 641-857-3211; 319-267-2300
Fax: 641-857-3300
E-mail: dumontel@netins.net
Web site: http://www.dumonttelephone.com
Officers:
Roger Kregel, General Manager
Brooke Gulick, Office Manager
Terry Arenholz, Operations Manager
Stacy Miller, Technician
Ownership: Shareholder owned.
Cable Systems (1):
Iowa: DUMONT.

CLIFFORD DUNCAN
PO Box 685
Wilmington, VT 05363
Phone: 802-464-2233
Fax: 802-464-1289
E-mail: dctv8@sover.net
Web site: http://www.duncancable.com
Cable Systems (1):
Vermont: WILMINGTON.

DUNKERTON TELEPHONE COOPERATIVE
PO Box 188
701 South Canfield St.
Dunkerton, IA 50626
Phone: 319-822-4512
Fax: 319-822-2206
Web site: http://www.dunkerton.net
Officers:
Sue Bruns, General Manager
Brett Delagardelle, Plant Manager
Ownership: Ron Reil, Pres..

Cable Owners

Cable Systems (1):
Iowa: DUNKERTON (portions).

DUO COUNTY TELEPHONE COOPERATIVE
PO Box 80
2150 North Main St.
Jamestown, KY 42629
Phones: 270-343-3131; 270-378-4141
Fax: 270-343-3800
E-mail: duotel@duo-county.com
Web site: http://www.duo-county.com
Officers:
Tom Preston, Executive Vice President & Chief Executive Officer
Daryl Hammond, Vice President & Chief Financial Officer
Mark Henry, Vice President, Operations
Eric West, Marketing Director
Robert Lamb, Network Manager
Cable Systems (1):
Kentucky: RUSSELL SPRINGS.

RAY S. DYER JR.
PO Box 157
922 Main St.
Locke, NY 13092
Phone: 315-497-0444
Fax: 315-497-7653
E-mail: sbadman@sccinternet.com
Cable Systems (1):
New York: MORAVIA.

EAGLE CABLEVISION INC.
PO Box 39
205 1st Ave. NE
Remer, MN 56672
Phones: 218-566-2302; 800-903-1987
Officers:
Conrad Johnson, President
Ron Johnson, Vice President
Donna Gunderson, Secretary
Ownership: Conrad Johnson; Donna Johnson; Dwayne Johnson; Lowell Johnson; Ronald Johnson. Lowell & Ronald Johnson are executives with the Johnson Telephone Co., Remer, MN.
Cable Systems (1):
Minnesota: REMER.

EAGLE COMMUNICATIONS INC.
PO Box 817
2703 Hall St., Ste. 15
Hays, KS 67601
Phone: 785-625-4000
Fax: 785-625-3465
E-mail: support@eaglecom.net
Web site: http://www.eaglecom.net
Officers:
Robert E. Schmidt, Chairman
Gary Shorman, President & Chief Executive Officer
Ownership: Robert E Schmidt.
Represented (legal): Wiley Rein LLP.
Cable Systems (42):
Colorado: BURLINGTON; WRAY.
Kansas: ABILENE; ELLSWORTH; GOODLAND; HAYS; HOXIE; LINCOLN; MARION; McDONALD; MILFORD; MINNEAPOLIS; OBERLIN; RILEY; ST. FRANCIS.
Nebraska: ALBION (town); ALMA; BELLWOOD; BIG SPRINGS; BRULE; CEDAR RAPIDS; CENTRAL CITY; COLUMBUS; FRANKLIN; FULLERTON; GENOA; HUMPHREY; MONROE; NEWMAN GROVE; OSCEOLA; PALMER; PAXTON; PLATTE CENTER; POLK; RED CLOUD; RISING CITY; SCHUYLER; SHELBY; SILVER CREEK (village); SPALDING; ST. EDWARD; STROMSBURG.
Other Holdings:
Radio holdings

EAGLE VALLEY COMMUNICATIONS
PO Box 180
349 First St.
Richland, OR 97870
Phones: 541-893-6116; 800-366-0795
Fax: 541-893-6903
Web site: http://www.eagletelephone.com/services_eaglevalley.shtml
Ownership: Eagle Telephone System.
Cable Systems (1):
Oregon: RICHLAND.

EAST BUCHANAN TELEPHONE COOPERATIVE
PO Box 100
214 3rd St. North
Winthrop, IA 50682-0100
Phones: 319-935-3011; 866-327-2748
Fax: 319-935-3010
E-mail: ebtccw@netins.net; christy.wolfe@eastbuchanan.com
Web site: http://www.eastbuchanan.com
Officers:
Butch Rorabaugh, General Manager
Roger Olsen, Plant Manager
Christy Wolfe, Office Manager
Cable Systems (1):
Iowa: WINTHROP.

EAST CLEVELAND CABLE TV LLC
1395 Hayden Ave.
East Cleveland, OH 44112
Phone: 216-851-2215
Fax: 216-851-0231
E-mail: jimmy@ecctv.tv
Web site: http://www.ecctv.tv
Officer:
Pamela Bryson, Operations Manager
Ownership: Jerry Smart; Alan Thompson.
Cable Systems (1):
Ohio: EAST CLEVELAND.

EASTERN CABLE
PO Box 126
Corbin, KY 40702
Phone: 606-528-6400
Fax: 606-523-0427
E-mail: cablecsr@2geton.net
Web site: http://www.easterncable.net
Cable Systems (1):
Kentucky: GRAY.

EASTON UTILITIES COMMISSION
PO Box 1189
201 North Washington St.
Easton, MD 21601
Phone: 410-822-6110
Fax: 410-822-0743
E-mail: info@eastonutilities.com
Web site: http://www.eastonutilities.com
Officer:
Hugh E. Grunden, President & Chief Executive Officer
Cable Systems (1):
Maryland: EASTON.

E.COM TECHNOLOGIES LLC
PO Box 788
750 Liberty Dr.
Westfield, IN 46074
Phone: 317-569-2800
Officer:
Craig Kunkle, Vice President

Cable Systems (1):
Indiana: CARMEL.

ELGIN TV ASSN. INC.
PO Box 246
830 Adler
Elgin, OR 97827
Phone: 541-437-4575
Web site: http://elgin.elgintv.com
Officers:
Allen Williams, President
Harlan Scott, Vice President
Risa Hallgarth, Secretary-Treasurer
Mike Rutherford, Chief Technology Officer
Ownership: Subscriber owned--Elgin, OR.
Cable Systems (1):
Oregon: ELGIN.

ELLIJAY TELEPHONE CO.
224 Dalton St.
Ellijay, GA 30540
Phones: 706-276-2271; 800-660-6826
Fax: 706-276-9888
E-mail: info@ellijay.com
Web site: http://etcnow.com
Officers:
Albert E. Harrison, President
Marion Harrison, Secretary
Ownership: Albert E Harrison, 36.3%; Marion Harrison, 35.2%; John Harrison, 28.5%.
Cable Systems (1):
Georgia: ELLIJAY.

EMERY TELCOM
PO Box 629
445 East Hwy. 29
Orangeville, UT 84537
Phones: 435-748-2223; 888-749-1090
Web site: http://www.emerytelcom.com
Officer:
Brock Johansen, Chief Executive Officer & General Manager
Cable Systems (1):
Utah: EMERY.

EMILY COOPERATIVE TELEPHONE CO.
PO Box 100
40040 State Hwy. 6
Emily, MN 56447
Phones: 218-763-3000; 800-450-1036
Fax: 218-763-2042
E-mail: emilytel@emily.net
Web site: http://www.emily.net
Officers:
Bob Olson, General Manager
Charles Balk, Business Manager
Ownership: Subscriber owned--Emily, MN.
Represented (legal): Moss & Barnett.
Cable Systems (1):
Minnesota: EMILY.
Other Holdings:
Cellular radio

ENHANCED TELECOMMUNICATIONS CORP.
123 Nieman St.
Sunman, IN 47041
Phones: 812-623-2122; 866-382-4968
Fax: 812-622-4159
Web site: http://www.etczone.com
Officers:
Chad Miles, President & Chief Executive Officer
Mike Alig, Chief Financial Officer
Kevin McGuire, Chief Technical Officer
Mike Fledderman, Vice President, Operations
Matt Anderson, Network Operations Manager

Bruce Bauman, Outside Plant Manager, Sunman
Becky Brashear, Customer Service/Sales Manager
Lori Feldbauer, Business Development Manager
Anita Fledderman, Marketing Director
Ryan Ibold, Video Operations Manager
Dan Kirchgassner, Outside Plant Manager, Greensburg
Kevin Riehle, Outside Plant Manager, Batesville
Dave Smith, Facilities/Safety Manager

Branch Offices:
Batesville
244 SR 129 S
Batesville, IN 47006
Phone: 812-932-1000
Fax: 812-932-3299
Brookville
613 Main St
Brookville, IN 47012
Phone: 765-547-1000
Fax: 765-547-1429
Sunman
123 Nieman St
Sunman, IN 47041
Phone: 812-623-2122
Fax: 812-623-4159
Cable Systems (2):
Indiana: BROOKVILLE; SUNMAN.

EN-TOUCH SYSTEMS INC.
Ste 400
11011 Richmond
Houston, TX 77042
Phones: 281-225-1000; 888-765-6461
Fax: 281-225-0539
E-mail: marketing@entouch.net
Web site: http://www.entouch.net
Officer:
Matt Friesen, Manager
Cable Systems (1):
Texas: HOUSTON.

EPB
10 West M. L. King Blvd.
Chattanooga, TN 37402-1813
Phone: 423-648-1372
Web site: http://www.epb.net
Officers:
Harold DePriest, President & Chief Executive Officer
Dave Wade, Chief Operating Officer
Greg Eaves, Executive Vice President & Chief Financial Officer
Danna Bailey, Vice President, Corporate Communications
Diana Bullock, Vice President, Economic Development & Govt. Relations
Kathy Burns, Vice President, Customer Relations
Steve Clark, Vice President, Strategic Systems
Katie Espeth, Vice President, New Products
David Johnson, Vice President, IT
Ryan Keel, Vice President, Technical Operations
J. Ed Marston, Vice President, Marketing

Branch Offices:
Brainerd Location
830 Eastgate Loop
Chattanooga, TN 37421
Hixson Location
2124 Northpoint Blvd.
Chattanooga, TN 37343
Cable Systems (1):
Tennessee: CHATTANOOGA.

EVARTS TV INC.
PO Box 8
113 Yocum St.
Evarts, KY 40828
Phone: 606-837-2505
Fax: 606-837-3738

D-902   TV & Cable Factbook No. 85

Cable Owners

Cable Systems (1):
Kentucky: EVARTS.

EYECOM INC.
Ste 100
201 East 56th Ave.
Anchorage, AK 99518
Phone: 907-563-2003
Fax: 907-550-1675
E-mail: support@arctic.net
Web site: http://www.telalaska.com
Officers:
Brenda Shepard, Chief Executive Officer
David J. Goggins, Vice President, Operations

Branch Offices:
Nome
204 W First St
Nome, AK 99762

Seward
335 4th Ave
Seward, AK 99664
Phone: 907-224-5224

Unalaska
599 E Broadway
Unalaska, AK 99685
Phone: 907-581-1399
Ownership: TelAlaska Inc..
Represented (legal): Dorsey & Whitney LLP.
Cable Systems (2):
Alaska: GALENA; UNALASKA.

FAIRPOINT COMMUNICATIONS INC.
Ste 500
521 East Morehead St.
Charlotte, NC 28202
Phones: 704-344-8150; 866-984-2001
Fax: 704-344-8121
E-mail: information@fairpoint.com
Web site: http://www.fairpoint.com
Officers:
Paul H Sunu, Chief Executive Officer
John Lunny, Chief Technical Officer
Kenneth W Amburn, Executive Vice President, Operations & Engineering
Gregory Castle, Executive Vice President, Human Resources
Rose Hauer, Executive Vice President & Chief Information Officer
Shirley J Linn, Executive Vice President & General Counsel
Bruce Metge, Executive Vice President-Chief Legal Officer
Peter Nixon, Executive Vice President, External Affairs & Operational Support
Tony Tomae, Executive Vice President & Chief Revenue Officer
Karen D Turner, Executive Vice President & Chief Financial Officer
Edward D Horowitz, Chairman of the Board of Directors
Cable Systems (5):
New York: KINDERHOOK.
Ohio: COLUMBUS GROVE (village); LEIPSIC; ORWELL.
Pennsylvania: NORTH BETHLEHEM TWP..

FALCON BROADBAND
555 Hathaway Dr.
Colorado Springs, CO 80915
Phone: 719-573-5343
Fax: 719-886-7925
E-mail: info@falconbroadband.net; sales@falconbroadband.net
Web site: http://falconbroadband.net

Cable Systems (2):
Colorado: EL PASO COUNTY (eastern portions); PEYTON.

F & B COMMUNICATIONS
PO Box 309
103 Main St. North
Wheatland, IA 52777-0309
Phone: 563-374-1236
Fax: 563-374-1930
E-mail: info@fbc-tele.com
Web site: http://www.fbc-tele.com
Officers:
Ken Laursen, General Manager
Aaron Horman, Assistant General Manager
Brad Carpenter, Plant Manager
Julie Steines, Officer Manager
Cable Systems (1):
Iowa: WHEATLAND.

FARMERS & MERCHANTS MUTUAL TELEPHONE CO.
PO Box 247
210 West Main St.
Wayland, IA 52654
Phones: 319-256-2736; 800-822-2736
Fax: 319-256-7210
E-mail: manager@farmtel.com
Web site: http://www.farmtelcommunications.com
Cable Systems (2):
Iowa: OLDS; WAYLAND.

FARMERS COOPERATIVE TELEPHONE CO.
PO Box 280
322 Main St.
Dysart, IA 52224
Phone: 319-476-7800
Fax: 319-476-7911
E-mail: fctdysart@fctc.coop
Web site: http://www.fctc.coop
Officers:
Mark Harvey, General Manager
Don Callahan, Plant Manager
Glen Sailsbury, Technician
Cable Systems (1):
Iowa: CLUTIER.

FARMERS INDEPENDENT TELEPHONE CO.
PO Box 447
139 West Madison Ave.
Grantsburg, WI 54840
Phone: 715-463-5322
Fax: 715-463-5206
E-mail: dana@grantsburgtelcom.com; office@grantsburgtelcom.com
Web site: http://www.grantsburgtelcom.net
Officer:
Dana Olson, General Manager
Cable Systems (1):
Wisconsin: GRANTSBURG.

FARMERS MUTUAL COOPERATIVE TELEPHONE CO. (MOULTON, IA)
PO Box 38
101 N Main St.
Moulton, IA 52572
Phone: 641-642-3249
E-mail: fmtcmou@netins.net
Web site: http://www.farmersmutualcoop.com
Officer:
Tammy Wheeler, General Manager

Cable Systems (2):
Iowa: IRWIN; STANTON.

FARMERS MUTUAL TELEPHONE CO. (NORA SPRINGS)
608 East Congress
Nora Springs, IA 50458
Phones: 641-749-2531; 877-OmniTel
Fax: 641-749-9578
E-mail: question@omnitel.biz
Web site: http://www.omnitel.biz
Officer:
Ron Laudner, Chief Executive Officer
Cable Systems (2):
Iowa: RUDD; RUDD.

FARMERS TELEPHONE COOPERATIVE INC.
1101 East Main St.
Kingstree, SC 29556
Phones: 843-382-2333; 843-382-1387
E-mail: ftc_cs@ftc-i.net
Web site: http://www.ftc-i.net
Officers:
Newell Myers, Chairman
F Bradley Erwin, Chief Executive Officer
Jeffrey L Lawrimore, Chief Financial Officer
Roger L Flowers, Vice President
William E Brewer, Secretary

Branch Offices:
2389 Paxville Hwy
Manning, SC 29102-5076
235 N Ron McNair Blvd
Lake City, SC 29560-2437

104 E Church St
Bishopville, SC 29010-1726

255 W Wesmark Blvd.
Sumter, SC 29150-1989

1280 Peach Orchard Rd
Sumter, SC 29154-1365

631 N Pike W
Sumter, SC 29153-7920
Ownership: Farmers Telephone Cooperative Inc. has interests in Livingston Telephone Co. & Telcom Supply Inc., see listings.
Cable Systems (1):
South Carolina: TURBEVILLE.

FAYETTEVILLE PUBLIC UTILITIES
PO Box 120
408 West College St.
Fayetteville, TN 37334
Phones: 931-433-1522; 800-379-2534
Fax: 931-433-0646
E-mail: customerservice@fpu-tn.com
Web site: http://www.fpu-tn.com
Officers:
Britt Dye, Chief Executive Officer
Pete James, Telecommunications Director
Cable Systems (1):
Tennessee: FAYETTEVILLE.

FENTON COOPERATIVE TELEPHONE CO.
PO Box 77
300 2nd St.
Fenton, IA 50539
Phone: 515-889-2785
Fax: 515-889-2255
E-mail: fntn@netins.net
Officer:
Leroy E. Jacobsen, General Manager

Cable Systems (1):
Iowa: FENTON.

FIBERCAST CABLE
25 South Maple St.
Manchester, NH 03103
Phones: 603-689-0000; 603-689-0010
E-mail: support@fibercast.net; sales@fibercast.net
Web site: http://www.fibercastcable.com
Ownership: FiberCast Corp.; FCC ownership;: Gent Khav.
Cable Systems (3):
New Hampshire: NELSON (town); STODDARD; STRATFORD (town).

FIDELITY COMMUNICATIONS CO.
64 North Clark St.
Sullivan, MO 63080
Phones: 573-468-8081; 800-392-8070
Fax: 573-468-5440
E-mail: custserv@fidelitycommunications.com
Web site: http://www.fidelitycommunications.com
Cable Systems (16):
Arkansas: BEEBE; BENTON; HARDY; MAUMELLE; WEST PULASKI (portions).
Louisiana: NEW ROADS.
Missouri: EL DORADO SPRINGS; HARRISONVILLE; NEVADA; PHELPS COUNTY (portions); THAYER; WEST PLAINS.
Oklahoma: LAWTON (village).
Texas: ATLANTA; CARTHAGE; MARSHALL.

FLINT CABLE TELEVISION INC.
PO Box 669
Reynolds, GA 31076
Phone: 855-593-3278
Fax: 478-847-2010
E-mail: customerservice@flintcatv.com
Web site: http://www.flintrvr.com
Officers:
Donald E. Bond, President & General Manager
E. Kelly Bond, Vice President
Cable Systems (1):
Georgia: REYNOLDS.

FLORIDA FIBER NETWORKS
Ste 105
301 South Collins St
Plant City, FL 33563
Phones: 352-702-4990; 888-860-4088
E-mail: info@flfibernet.com; support@flfibernet.com
Web site: http://flfibernet.com

Branch Office:
Mailing Address
PO Box 498
Astor, FL 32102-2907
Ownership: David S Suarez, Chief Executive Officer & Managing Member; David R Orshan, Chief Marketing Officer & Managing Member.
Cable Systems (18):
Florida: ASTOR; BRONSON (town); CITRA; CLAY COUNTY (portions); FANNING SPRINGS; FLORAHOME; HAMPTON; HERNANDO COUNTY; LAWTEY; MARION COUNTY (southern portion); NORTH OLD TOWN; ORANGE SPRINGS; PAISLEY; PENNEY FARMS; PUTNAM COUNTY (eastern portion); PUTNAM COUNTY (western portion); SHARPES FERRY; ZELLWOOD.

FORSYTH CABLE
9 North Lee St.
Forsyth, GA 31029

2017 Edition
D-903

Cable Owners

Phones: 478-885-4111; 855-593-3278
Fax: 478-583-4999
E-mail: customerservice@forsythcable.com
Web site: http://www.forsythcable.com
Cable Systems (1):
Georgia: FORSYTH.

FORT JENNINGS TELEPHONE CO.
PO Box 146
65 West 3rd St.
Fort Jennings, OH 45844
Phone: 419-286-2181
Fax: 419-286-2193
E-mail: fjtc@bright.net
Web site: http://www.fjtelephone.com
Officer:
Mike Metzger, General Manager
Cable Systems (1):
Ohio: FORT JENNINGS.

FOSSIL COMMUNITY TV INC.
PO Box 209
401 Main St.
Fossil, OR 97830-0209
Phone: 541-763-2698
Officers:
Ron Deluca, Manager
Steve Conlee, Chief Technician
Cable Systems (1):
Oregon: FOSSIL.

CITY OF FOSSTON CABLE TV
PO Box 239
220 East First St.
Fosston, MN 56542
Phone: 218-435-1959
Fax: 218-435-1961
E-mail: chuck.lucken@fosston.com
Web site: http://www.fosston.com
Officer:
Russell W. Earls, Manager
Ownership: Community owned--Fosston, MN.
Cable Systems (1):
Minnesota: FOSSTON.

FRANKFORT PLANT BOARD
317 West 2nd St.
Frankfort, KY 40601
Phones: 502-352-4372; 888-312-4372
Fax: 502-223-4449
Web site: http://fpb.cc
Officers:
Joseph Smith, Chairman
Warner J. Caines, Chief Executive Officer
Adam Hellard, Chief Technology Officer
Ownership: Community owned--Frankfort, KY.
Cable Systems (1):
Kentucky: FRANKFORT.

FULL CHANNEL INC.
57 Everett St.
Warren, RI 02885
Phone: 401-247-1250
Web site: http://www.fullchannel.com
Officers:
Linda Jane Maaia, President & Chief Executive Officer
Levi C Maaia, Vice President
Mike Davis, General Manager
Brian Frazier, Engineering Director
Janna E. Meckowski, Programming Director
Matt Torrenti, Finance Director
Ownership: Hilda Donofrio Estate.
Represented (legal): William C. Maaia.
Cable Systems (1):
Rhode Island: WARREN.

GAINESBORO CATV INC.
PO Box 513
302 Minor St
Gainesboro, TN 38562-8502
Phone: 931-268-9612
Cable Systems (1):
Tennessee: GAINESBORO.

GALI ESTATE
PO Box 445
c/o Skyview TV Cable
Broadus, MT 59317
Phone: 406-436-2820
Cable Systems (1):
Montana: BROADUS.

GAP CABLE TV INC.
1 Washington Rd.
Annville, PA 17003
Phone: 717-865-0511
Officers:
Carolyn A. Bryce, President
George Bryce, Chief Operating Officer
Ray Funck, Vice President
Ruth Ann Funck, Secretary
Ownership: Carolyn A Bryce.
Cable Systems (1):
Pennsylvania: FORT INDIANTOWN GAP.

GARDEN VALLEY TELEPHONE CO.
PO Box 259
201 Ross Ave.
Erskine, MN 56535-0259
Phones: 218-687-5251; 800-448-8260
Fax: 218-687-2454
E-mail: gvtc@gvtel.com
Web site: http://www.gvtel.com
Officers:
George Fish, General Manager
Vernon Hamnes, President
Mark Klinkhammer, Finance Manager
Dave Hamre, Service & Operations Manager
Randy Versdahl, Facilities Manager & Safety Director
Julie Dahle, Marketing & PR Supervisor
Cable Systems (2):
Minnesota: McINTOSH; McINTOSH.

GCI CABLE INC.
Ste A3
701 West 36th Ave.
Anchorage, AK 99503
Phones: 907-265-5400; 800-800-4800
Fax: 907-265-5676
E-mail: support@gci.net; rcs@gci.com
Web site: http://www.gci.com
Officers:
Ronald A. Duncan, President & Chief Executive Officer
Wilson Hughes, President & Chief Executive Officer, The Alaska Wireless Network LLC
Gregory F. Chapados, Executive Vice President & Chief Operating Officer
William C. Behnke, Senior Vice President, Strategic Initiatives
Paul E Landes, Senior Vice President, Consumer Services
John M. Lowber, Senior Vice President & Chief Financial Officer
Tina Pidgeon, Senior Vice President, Governmental Affairs & General Counsel
Ownership: Publicly held. On June 5, 2012 Alaska Communications Systems & General Communication Inc. announced they would combine their wireless facilities under a new entity called The Alaska Wireless Network LLC. The transaction closed July 23, 2013.
Represented (legal): Hartig Rhodes LLC.
Cable Systems (21):
Alaska: ANCHORAGE; ANGOON; BARROW; BETHEL; CORDOVA; FAIRBANKS; FORT GREELY; GIRDWOOD; HOMER; JUNEAU; KENAI; KETCHIKAN; KODIAK; KOTZEBUE; NOME; PETERSBURG; SEWARD; SITKA; VALDEZ; WASILLA; WRANGELL.

GET REAL CABLE
412 West Blackwell Ave.
Blackwell, OK 74631-2859
Phone: 580-363-5580
Cable Systems (1):
Oklahoma: BLACKWELL.

GEUS
2810 Wesley St.
Greenville, TX 75401
Phone: 903-457-2800
Fax: 903-454-9249
E-mail: customerservices@geus.org
Web site: http://www.geus.org
Officers:
David McCalla, General Manager
Mark Stapp, Engineering & Operations Director
Alan Crane, Engineering Manager
Cable Systems (1):
Texas: GREENVILLE.

GIANT COMMUNICATIONS
Ste C
418 West 5th St.
Holton, KS 66436
Phones: 785-362-9331; 800-346-9084
Fax: 785-362-2144
E-mail: clientservices@giantcomm.net
Web site: http://www.giantcomm.net
Officer:
Gene Morris, General Manager

Branch Office:
Oskaloosa
324 Washington
Oskaloosa, KS
Ownership: Lict Corp..
Cable Systems (1):
Kansas: HOLTON.

GILES-CRAIG COMMUNICATIONS INC.
PO Box 549
504 Snidow St.
Pembroke, VA 24136
Phone: 540-626-7111
Fax: 540-626-3290
E-mail: pembroke@pemtel.net
Web site: http://www.pemtel.com
Officers:
Lisa W Epperley, General Manager
Jill S Williams, Office Manager
Cable Systems (1):
Virginia: NEWPORT.

GILMER CABLE
PO Box 1004
111 Marshall St.
Gilmer, TX 75644
Phone: 903-841-4955
Fax: 903-843-2045
E-mail: dpmooney@tatertv.com
Officers:
James T. Davis, Chief Financial Officer
Robbie C. Mooney, Marketing Director
Edwin LeFevere, Engineering Director
Ownership: David P. Mooney.
Represented (legal): Cole, Raywid & Braverman LLP.
Cable Systems (2):
Arkansas: HOPE; HOT SPRINGS.

GLASGOW ELECTRIC PLANT BOARD-CATV DIVISION
100 Mallory Dr.
Glasgow, KY 42141
Phone: 270-651-8341
Fax: 270-651-7572
Web site: http://www.glasgowepb.net/?page_id=9
Officers:
William J. Ray, President
Eddie Russell, Cable Operations Manager
Shelia Hogue, Marketing Director
Todd Barbour, Engineering Manager
Ownership: Community owned--Glasgow, KY.
Represented (legal): Herbert, Herbert & Pack.
Cable Systems (1):
Kentucky: GLASGOW.

GLENWOOD TELECOMMUNICATIONS
PO Box 97
510 West Gage St.
Blue Hill, NE 68930
Phones: 402-756-3131; 866-756-4746
Fax: 402-756-3134
E-mail: info@gtmc.net; info@shopglenwood.net
Web site: http://shopglenwood.net
Officers:
Phil Boyd, President
Ron Ostdiek, Secretary-Treasurer
Mark McFarland, System Engineer
Ownership: Glenwood Telephone Membership Corp..
Represented (legal): Dunmire, Fisher & Hastings.
Cable Systems (1):
Nebraska: BLUE HILL.
Other Holdings:
Telephone

GLW BROADBAND INC.
PO Box 67
993 Commerce Dr.
Grafton, OH 44044
Phone: 440-926-3230
Fax: 440-926-2889
E-mail: support@glwb.net
Web site: http://www.glwb.net

Branch Office:
Wellington
153 E. Herrick Ave
Wellington, OH 44090
Phone: 440-647-6445
Fax: 440-647-4183
Cable Systems (1):
Ohio: WELLINGTON.

GOLDEN BELT TELEPHONE ASSOCIATION INC.
PO Box 229
103 Lincoln
Rush Center, KS 67575
Phones: 785-372-4236; 800-432-7965
Fax: 785-372-4210
E-mail: custservice@gbta.net
Web site: http://www.gbta.net
Officers:
Beau Rebel, General Manager
Kirby Hagans, Plant Manager
Debra Tuzicka, Office Manager

Cable Owners

Branch Offices:
Ellis
101 W 9th
Ellis, KS 67637
Phone: 785-726-3200
Ness City
114 W Main
PO Box 264
Ness City, KS 67560
Phone: 785-798-3100
Ownership: Cooperative--Rush Center, KS.
Cable Systems (3):
Kansas: OFFERLE; RUSH CENTER; RUSH CENTER.

GOLDEN COMMUNICATIONS
PO Box 100
8800 Ferry St
Montague, MI 49437
Phone: 888-873-3353
Fax: 231-894-4960
Web site: http://goldcommcable.com
Cable Systems (1):
Michigan: MEARS.

GOLDEN RAIN FOUNDATION OF LAGUNA HILLS INC.
24351 El Torro Rd
Laguna Woods, CA 92637
Phones: 949-837-2670; 949-597-4200
Web site: http://www.lagunawoodsvillage.com/section.cfm?id=50
Ownership: Golden Rain Foundation, Non-Profit Corp..
Cable Systems (1):
California: LAGUNA WOODS.

GOLDEN VALLEY CABLE & COMMUNICATIONS INC.
4206 US Hwy. 68
Golden Valley, AZ 86413
Phone: 928-565-4190
E-mail: cs@goldenvalleycable.com
Web site: http://goldenvalleycable.com
Cable Systems (3):
Arizona: GOLDEN SHORES; GOLDEN VALLEY.
California: NEEDLES.

GOLDEN WEST CABLEVISION
PO Box 411
415 Crown St.
Wall, SD 57790-0411
Phones: 605-279-2727; 855-888-7777
Fax: 605-279-2727
E-mail: janschaefer@goldenwest.com
Web site: http://www.goldenwest.com
Officers:
Denny Law, Chief Executive Officer & General Manager
Jeff Nielsen, President
Gordon Kraut Jr., Chief Financial Officer
Duane Wood, Vice President
Kenneth Zickrick Jr., Secretary
Dale Guptill, Treasurer

Branch Offices:
Dell Rapids
525 East Fourth St
PO Box 98
Dell Rapids, SD 57022
Phone: 605-428-5421
Fax: 605-428-3132
Hartford
116 North Main Ave
PO Box 460
Hartford, SD 57033
Phone: 605-528-3211
Fax: 605-528-2266

Hot Springs
1510 National Ave
PO Box 571
Hot Springs, SD 57747
Phone: 605-745-3103
Fax: 605-745-5331
Ownership: Golden West Telecommunications. Golden West Telecommunications has interests in Livingston Communications & Telcom Supply Inc., see listings.
Represented (legal): Riter, Rogers, Wattier & Northrup LLP.
Cable Systems (6):
South Dakota: CUSTER; DELL RAPIDS; FREEMAN; PINE RIDGE; WALL; WINNER.
Other Holdings:
Cellular radio

GOLDFIELD COMMUNICATION SERVICES CORP.
PO Box 67
536 North Main
Goldfield, IA 50542
Phones: 515-825-3996; 800-825-9753
Fax: 515-825-3801
E-mail: gold@goldfieldaccess.net; gan1@goldfieldaccess.net
Web site: http://www.goldfieldaccess.net
Officers:
Kenneth Axon, President
Darrell L. Seaba, General Manager
Ownership: Goldfield Telephone Co..
Cable Systems (1):
Iowa: GOLDFIELD.
Other Holdings:
Cellular telephone

GORHAM TELEPHONE CO.
PO Box 235
100 Market St.
Gorham, KS 67640-0235
Phone: 785-637-5300
Fax: 785-637-5590
E-mail: gtc@gorhamtel.com
Web site: http://gorhamtel.com
Officers:
Michael Murphy, President
Tonya Murphy, Secretary-Treasurer
Ownership: Mike Murphy; Tonya Murphy.
Cable Systems (1):
Kansas: GORHAM.

GOVERNMENT CAMP CABLE
PO Box 10
Government Camp, OR 97028
Phone: 503-272-3333
Fax: 503-272-3800
Ownership: Charlie Sperr.
Cable Systems (1):
Oregon: GOVERNMENT CAMP.

GOWRIE CABLEVISION INC.
PO Box 145
1112 1/2 Beek St.
Gowrie, IA 50543
Phone: 515-352-5227
Ownership: Paul Johnson, Pres..
Cable Systems (1):
Iowa: GOWRIE.

GRANDE COMMUNICATIONS NETWORKS INC.
401 Carlson Cir.
San Marcos, TX 78666
Phones: 512-878-4000; 512-220-4600
Fax: 512-878-4010
E-mail: info@grandecom.com
Web site: http://mygrande.com
Officers:
Steve Simmons, Chairman
Jim Holanda, Chief Executive Officer
Matt Rohr, Vice President, Retail Operations & Interim Sr. Vice President, Operations/General Manager
Pete Drozdoff, Vice President, Marketing
Lamar Horton, Vice President, Network Operations & Engineering
Shane Schilling, Vice President, Technical Operations
Ownership: ABRY Partners, 75.3%. votes; Grande Holdings, 24.7%. votes. Sale to TPG Capital pends. Google Capital will hold minority interest. Deal is expected to close in first quarter of 2017. Jim Coulter is Co-Chief Executive Officer and founder of TPG Capital. Jim Holanda will continue as Chief Executive Officer.
Cable Systems (14):
Texas: AUSTIN; CORPUS CHRISTI; DALLAS (northwest suburbs); LITTLE RIVER-ACADEMY; MOODY; MORGAN'S POINT RESORT; ODESSA; ROGERS; SALADO; SAN ANTONIO; SAN MARCOS; TEMPLE; TROY; WACO.

GRAND MOUND COOPERATIVE TELEPHONE ASSN.
PO Box 316
705 Clinton St.
Grand Mound, IA 52751
Phone: 563-847-3000
Fax: 563-847-3001
E-mail: support@gmtel.net
Web site: http://www.gmtel.net
Officers:
Kurt Crosthwaite, President
Marcus Behnken, General Manager
Terri Bumann, Office Manager
Cable Systems (1):
Iowa: GRAND MOUND.

GREAT PLAINS COMMUNICATIONS INC.
PO Box 500
1635 Front St.
Blair, NE 68008
Phones: 855-853-1483; 888-343-8014
Fax: 402-456-6550
E-mail: billing@gpcom.com; localchannel@gpcom.com
Web site: http://www.gpcom.com
Cable Systems (13):
Nebraska: BANCROFT; BLOOMFIELD; BROKEN BOW; CHADRON; CHAPMAN; ELGIN; GRANT; McCOOK; NORTH BEND; PONCA; SUTHERLAND; TRENTON; WOLBACH.

GREENE COUNTY PARTNERS INC.
PO Box 200
100 Redbud Rd.
Virginia, IL 62691
Phones: 217-452-7725; 800-252-1799
Fax: 217-452-7030
E-mail: solutions@casscomm.com
Web site: http://www.casscomm.com
Officers:
Gerald E. Gill, Chairman & President
Gerald S. Gill, Vice President
Thomas D. Allen, Vice President & Chief Operating Officer
Lance Allen, Chief Technical Officer
Laymon Carter, Advertising Director
Cable Systems (1):
Illinois: WILLIAMSVILLE.

R. M. GREENE INC.
2400 Sportsman Dr.
dba Cable TV of East Alabama
Phenix City, AL 36867
Phone: 334-298-7000
Fax: 334-298-0833
E-mail: ofcmgr@ctvea.net
Web site: http://www.ctvea.net
Officers:
Roy M. Greene Sr., Chairman
Lynne G. Frakes, President
Cable Systems (1):
Alabama: PHENIX CITY.
LPTV Stations:
Alabama: W06BH Phenix City, etc..

GRIDLEY TELEPHONE
108 East 3rd St.
Gridley, IL 61744
Phones: 309-747-2221; 309-747-2324
E-mail: info@gridcom.net
Web site: http://www.gridtel.com
Officer:
Herb Fisher, General Manager
Ownership: Signal Telcom Partners.
Cable Systems (1):
Illinois: GRIDLEY.

GRISWOLD CO-OP TELEPHONE CO.
PO Box 640
607 Main St.
Griswold, IA 51535
Phone: 712-778-2121
E-mail: gctc@netins.net
Web site: http://www.griswoldtelco.com
Cable Systems (1):
Iowa: GRISWOLD.

GRUNDY CENTER MUNICIPAL LIGHT & POWER
PO Box 307
706 6th St.
Grundy Center, IA 50638
Phone: 319-825-5207
E-mail: gcmuni@gcmuni.net
Web site: http://www.gcmuni.net
Officers:
Jeff Carson, General Manager
Darrel Shuey, Cable TV
Cable Systems (1):
Iowa: GRUNDY CENTER.

GUINESS COMMUNICATIONS INC.
5381 48th Ave.
Delta, BC V4K 1W7
Phones: 604-946-1144; 604-946-7676
Fax: 604-946-5627
E-mail: customerservice@deltacable.com
Officers:
Larry Boule, General Manager
Monica Barrett, Finance Director
Cable Systems (1):
Washington: POINT ROBERTS.
Cable Holdings:
Canada: Delta, BC

GVTC COMMUNICATIONS
36101 FM 3159
New Braunfels, TX 78132-1604
Phones: 830-885-4411; 800-367-4882
Fax: 830-885-2100
E-mail: info@gvtc.com; webhelp@gvtc.com
Web site: http://www.gvtc.com
Officers:
Ritchie Sorrells, President & Chief Executive Officer
Robert Hunt, Vice President, Regulatory Affairs & Business Operations
Jeff Mnick, Vice President, Sales & Marketing
Mark Gitter, Chief Financial Officer

Cable Owners

Branch Office:
1221 S. Main St.
Boerne, TX 78006
Phone: 830-249-8181
Ownership: Community owned--Guadalupe Valley.
Cable Systems (1):
Texas: BOERNE.
Other Holdings:
Telephone holdings

HAEFELE TV INC.
PO Box 312
24 East Tioga St.
Spencer, NY 14883
Phones: 607-589-6235; 800-338-6330
E-mail: cs@htva.net
Web site: http://www.htva.net
Officer:
Denise Laue, Vice President
Ownership: Lee Haefele, Principal.
Cable Systems (5):
New York: BERKSHIRE; BURDETT; ENFIELD; SMITHVILLE; SPENCER.

HAINES & SKAGWAY CABLE TV
PO Box 1229
715 Main St.
Haines, AK 99827
Phone: 907-766-2337
Fax: 907-766-2345
Web site: http://hainescable.com
Ownership: Patty Campbell.
Cable Systems (2):
Alaska: HAINES; SKAGWAY.

HAMILTON COUNTY COMMUNICATIONS INC.
PO Box 40
Route 142 E
Dahlgren, IL 62828
Phones: 618-736-2211; 800-447-8725
Fax: 618-736-2616
Web site: http://www.hcc.coop
Officer:
Kevin Pyle, General Manager & Executive Vice President
Cable Systems (1):
Illinois: DAHLGREN.

HAMILTON COUNTY/GORE MOUNTAIN CABLE TV INC.
PO Box 275
1330 SR 30
Wells, NY 12190
Phones: 518-924-2013; 800-562-1560
Fax: 518-381-4833
Web site: http://www.hcctelevision.com
Officers:
Paul F. Schonewolf, President & Chief Operating Officer
George M. Williams, Chief Financial Officer
Brian Towers, Regional Manager
Ownership: Paul F Schonewolf, 80.1%; George M Williams, 19.9%.
Represented (legal): Koerner & Olender PC.
Cable Systems (3):
New York: INDIAN LAKE (town); JOHNSBURG (town); WELLS.

HANCEL INC.
PO Box 608
34 Read St.
Hancock, NY 13783-0608
Phones: 607-637-2568; 800-360-4664
Fax: 607-637-9999
E-mail: telco@hancock.net
Officers:
Robert C. Wrighter Sr., Chairman, President & Chief Operating Officer
Lewis Martin, Chief Financial Officer
Margaret Evanitsky, Customer Service
Ownership: Hancock Telephone Co..
Cable Systems (1):
New York: HANCOCK.

H & B CABLE SERVICE INC.
PO Box 108
108 North Main St.
Holyrood, KS 67450
Phones: 785-252-4000; 800-432-8296
Fax: 785-252-3229
E-mail: commentsquestions@hbcomm.net
Web site: http://www.hbcomm.net
Officers:
Robert Koch, President & General Manager
Don Nash, Vice President & Chief Financial Officer
Kathy Koch, Vice President
Del Jeane Nash, Secretary-Treasurer
Ownership: Betty Koch; Harold Koch.
Cable Systems (2):
Kansas: CHASE; HOLYROOD.

HANSON COMMUNICATIONS INC.
1700 Technology Dr. NE
Willmar, MN 56201
Phone: 320-235-2260
Fax: 320-847-7120
Web site: http://www.hcinet.net
Officer:
Bruce Hanson, President
Cable Systems (16):
Minnesota: BELVIEW; CLEMENTS; COMFREY; ECHO; HANLEY FALLS; LAKE LILLIAN; LAMBERTON; LUCAN; NICOLLET; RAYMOND; REVERE; WABASSO; WALNUT GROVE; WELCOME; WOOD LAKE.
South Dakota: TRIPP.

STEVEN HARAMOTO
500 West 10400 North
Elwood, UT 84337

Cable Systems (1):
Utah: HUNTSVILLE.

HARDY TELECOMMUNICATIONS INC.
2255 Kimseys Run Rd
Lost River, WV 26810
Phones: 304-897-9911; 800-838-2497
Web site: http://www.hardynet.net
Officers:
Greg M. Zirk, President
Loring E. Barry, Vice President
Victoria O. Dyer, Secretary
Harold K. Michael, Treasurer
Cable Systems (1):
West Virginia: MOOREFIELD.

HARGRAY COMMUNICATIONS GROUP INC.
PO Box 5986
856 William Hilton Pkwy.
Hilton Head Island, SC 29938
Phones: 843-842-4000; 843-341-1501
Fax: 843-341-1555
E-mail: info@hargray.com
Web site: http://www.hargray.com
Officers:
Michael Gottdenker, Chairman & Chief Executive Officer
Chris McCorkendale, Vice President, Operations, Engineering & Strategic Sales
Andrew J. Rein, Vice President, Sales & Marketing
Gwynne Lastinger, Director, Operations
Ownership: Quadrangle Group LLC. Formerly known as Hargray Telephone Co.
Cable Systems (3):
Georgia: GREENE COUNTY (unincorporated areas).
South Carolina: BLUFFTON (village); HILTON HEAD ISLAND.

HARLAN COMMUNITY TV INC.
PO Box 592
124 South 1st St.
Harlan, KY 40831
Phone: 606-573-2945
E-mail: hctv@harlanonline.net
Web site: http://www.harlantv.com
Officers:
Jack Hale, President & General Manager
Mark Lawrence, Vice President
Ownership: Subscriber owned--Harlan, KY.
Represented (legal): Greene & Forester.
Cable Systems (1):
Kentucky: HARLAN.

HARLAN MUNICIPAL UTILITIES
PO Box 71
2412 Southwest Ave.
Harlan, IA 51537
Phone: 712-755-5182
Fax: 712-755-2320
E-mail: hmu@harlannet.com
Web site: http://www.harlannet.com
Cable Systems (1):
Iowa: HARLAN.

HARMONY TELEPHONE CO
PO Box 308
35 First Ave. NE
Harmony, MN 55939
Phone: 507-886-2525
Fax: 507-886-2500
E-mail: info@harmonytel.com; custserv@harmonytel.net
Web site: http://www.harmonytel.com
Officers:
Lorren Tingesdal, Chief Executive Officer
Craig Otterness, Chief Financial Officer
Jill Fishbaugher, Marketing & Programming Director
Cable Systems (1):
Minnesota: HARMONY.

HARRON COMMUNICATIONS LP
70 East Lancaster Ave.
Frazer, PA 19355
Phones: 610-644-7500; 800-952-1001
Fax: 610-993-1100
E-mail: administration@harron.com
Web site: http://www.metrocast.com
Officers:
James J Bruder Jr., Chairman & Chief Executive Officer
Thomas M Marturano, President & Chief Operating Officer
Shawn P Flannery, Chief Financial Officer & Treasurer
Constance S Prince, Chief Administrative Officer
Ryan F Pearson, Executive Vice President & General Counsel
Steve A Murdough, Senior Vice President, Operations
Linda C Stuchell-Leibert, Senior Vice President, Programming
Joshua S Barstow, Vice President, Advanced Services
Brian Earnshaw, Vice President & Corporate Controller
Danny L Jobe, Vice President, System Operations
Emily R. Pollack, Vice President & Deputy General Counsel
Andrew J. Walton, Vice President, Marketing & Communications
Cable Systems (11):
Maine: SANFORD.
Maryland: LEONARDTOWN.
New Hampshire: BELMONT; ROCHESTER.
Pennsylvania: BERWICK; WEATHERLY.
South Carolina: BENNETTSVILLE.
Virginia: DELTAVILLE; KING GEORGE; MATHEWS; NORTHUMBERLAND COUNTY.

HART CABLE
PO Box 388
196 North Forest Ave.
Hartwell, GA 30643
Phones: 706-376-4701; 800-276-3925
Fax: 706-376-2009
Web site: http://www.htconline.net
Officer:
J. Lee Barton, President & Chief Executive Officer
Ownership: Lintel Inc..
Cable Systems (1):
Georgia: HART COUNTY.

HART ELECTRIC INC.
PO Box 282
102 South Main St.
Lostant, IL 61334
Phone: 815-368-3744
Fax: 815-368-3590
Web site: http://www.hihart.com
Cable Systems (2):
Illinois: LOSTANT; MALDEN.

HARTINGTON TELEPHONE CO.
PO Box 157
103 West Centre St.
Hartington, NE 68739
Phone: 402-254-3901
Fax: 402-254-2453
E-mail: htc@hartel.net
Web site: http://www.hartel.net
Cable Systems (1):
Nebraska: HARTINGTON.

JAMES DALE HASLETT
PO Box 386
Waldport, OR 97394
Phone: 541-563-4807
Fax: 541-563-7341
Cable Systems (1):
Oregon: WALDPORT.

HAVILAND TELEPHONE CO.
PO Box 308
104 North Main St.
Haviland, KS 67059
Phones: 620-862-5211; 800-339-8052
E-mail: custserv@havilandtelco.com
Web site: http://www.havilandtelco.com
Officers:
Mark Wade, General Manager & Vice President, Operations
Diane Thompson, Marketing Coordinator

Branch Office:
Conway Springs
211 W Spring
PO Box 277
Conway Springs, KS 67031
Phone: 620-456-2211

Cable Owners

Cable Systems (1):
Kansas: HAVILAND.

CITY OF HAWARDEN
1150 Central Ave.
Hawarden, IA 51023
Phone: 712-551-2565
Fax: 712-551-1117
E-mail: city@cityofhawarden.com
Web site: http://www.cityofhawarden.com
Officer:
Gary Tucker, City Administrator
Cable Systems (1):
Iowa: HAWARDEN.

JIM HAYS
PO Box 186
251 Broadway
Irvine, KY 40336
Phones: 606-723-4240; 606-723-3668
Fax: 606-723-4723
E-mail: irvtv@irvineonline.net
Web site: http://www.irvine-cable.net
Officers:
Jim Hays, Executive Vice President
Vicki Horn, Office Manager
Cable Systems (1):
Kentucky: IRVINE.

H C CABLE HOLDINGS LLC
2 A Jackson St.
Newnan, GA 30263
Phone: 770-683-6988
E-mail: info@nulinkdigital.com; customerservice@nulink.com
Web site: http://nulinkdigital.com
Officer:
John Brooks, Chairman & Chief Executive Officer
Ownership: Halyard Capital.
Cable Systems (1):
Georgia: NEWNAN.

HEARTLAND CABLE INC.
PO Box 7
156 West 5th
Minonk, IL 61760
Phones: 309-432-2075; 800-448-4320
Fax: 309-432-2500
Web site: http://www.hcable.net
Officers:
Steve Allen, Chief Executive & Operating Officer
Marshall Smith, Vice President
Jessica Meister, Secretary
Jaime Ruestman, Secretary
Ownership: Steve Allen; Ken Nevius; Marshall Smith, Principals.
Cable Systems (6):
Illinois: FLANAGAN; GRAND RIDGE; KENNEY; SIBLEY (village); SUBLETTE (village); TONICA.

HEART OF IOWA COMMUNICATIONS COOPERATIVE
PO Box 130
502 Main St.
Union, IA 50258-0130
Phones: 641-486-2211; 800-806-4482
Fax: 641-486-2205
E-mail: businessrelations@heartofiowa.coop
Web site: http://www.heartofiowa.coop
Officers:
Bryan Amundson, General Manager
Janell King-Squires, Marketing & Sales Director
Jay Duncan, Plant Manager
Heidi Mitchell, Customer Service Manager
Rich Trinkle, IT Manager

Branch Offices:
Conrad
123 Main St
Conrad, IA 50621
Phone: 641-922-7211
Fax: 641-939-7205
Eldora
1134 Edgington Ave
Eldora, IA 50627
Phone: 641-939-7211
Fax: 641-939-7205
Laurel
201 S Main St
Laurel, IA 50141
Phone: 641-476-3444
Fax: 641-476-3460
Cable Systems (1):
Iowa: UNION.
Other Holdings:
IPTV: IPTV owner

HERR CABLE CO.
RR 2
Paxinos, PA 17860
Phone: 570-435-2780
Ownership: Al Herr; Ralph Herr; Rita Herr; Barry Herr, jointly.
Cable Systems (1):
Pennsylvania: ELDRED TWP..

EDWARD HEWSON
349 Damon Rd. NE
Ocean Shores, WA 98569
Phones: 360-289-2252; 360-289-5760
E-mail: sales@coastaccess.com
Web site: http://www.coastcommunications.com
Cable Systems (1):
Washington: OCEAN SHORES.

HIAWATHA BROADBAND COMMUNICATIONS INC.
58 Johnson St.
Winona, MN 55987
Phones: 507-474-4000; 888-474-9995
Fax: 507-454-5878
E-mail: info@hbci.com
Web site: http://www.hbci.com

Branch Offices:
329 Hiawatha Dr. E
Suite One
Wabasha, MN 55981
Phone: 651-560-4000
1242 Whitewater Ave.
St. Charles, MN 55987
Phone: 507-932-8000
Cable Systems (1):
Minnesota: WINONA.

DEAN HILL CABLE
103 South Elm St.
Hamburg, AR 71661
Phone: 870-853-8387
Cable Systems (3):
Arkansas: MONTROSE; PORTLAND; WILMOT.

HINTON CATV CO.
126 West Main St.
Hinton, OK 73047
Phone: 405-542-3211
E-mail: hintoncatv@hintonet.net
Web site: http://www.hintontelephone.com
Officers:
Kenneth Doughty, President
Florene Doughty, Vice President
Kerry Allen, Secretary-Treasurer

Cable Systems (1):
Oklahoma: HINTON.

HOME TELECOM
PO Box 1194
579 Stoney Landing Rd.
Moncks Corner, SC 29461
Phones: 843-761-9101; 843-471-2200
Fax: 843-761-9120
Web site: http://www.homesc.com
Officers:
Robert L. Hemly Jr., Chief Executive Officer & Vice Chair
William S. Hemly Jr., President & Chief Operating Officer
H. Keith Oliver, Senior Vice President, Corporate Operations
Alan Smoak Jr., Controller
Robert P. Abbott Jr., Engineering Director
Judy S. Cronin, Sales & Business Development Director
Julie H. Forte, Customer Operations Director
Robert L. Hemly Jr., Support Operations Director
Caoimhe Higgins, Program Director
Eddie G. McGriff Jr., Plant Operations Director
Gina T. Shuler, Marketing Director
Denny Thompson, Administrative Services Director
Patrick Archibald, Information Services Manager
William Dangerfield, Switching & Networking Manager
Debra Ford, Regional Stores Manager
Thomas Higgins, Installation & Repair Manager
Luke Lapierre, Business Development Manager
Bernard Motte, Plant Support Manager
Victor Smith, Installation & Repair Manager
Ownership: Robert L. Helmly, President. Helmly is also President & General Manager of Home Telephone Co. Inc., Moncks Corner, SC.
Cable Systems (1):
South Carolina: DANIEL ISLAND.

HOMETEL ENTERTAINMENT INC.
Box 215
501 North Douglas
St Jacob, IL 62281
Phones: 618-644-2111; 618-644-2288
E-mail: admin@hometel.com
Web site: http://www.hometel.com
Ownership: Richard Schmidt.
Cable Systems (1):
Illinois: ST. JACOB.

HOOD CANAL COMMUNICATIONS
300 East Dalby Rd.
Union, WA 98592-0249
Phones: 360-898-2481; 800-356-9989
Fax: 360-898-2244
E-mail: rbuechel@hctc.com; info@hcc.net
Web site: http://www.hcc.net
Officers:
Brandi Edinger, Marketing Director
Rick Buechel, President

Branch Office:
Shelton
2218 Olympic Hwy. N
Shelton, WA 98584-2955
Phone: 360-462-4282
Fax: 360-898-2245
Cable Systems (1):
Washington: UNION.
Other Holdings:
Cellular radio

HORIZON CABLE TV INC.
PO Box 1240
520 Mesa Rd.
Point Reyes Station, CA 94956
Phones: 415-663-9610; 888-663-9610
Fax: 415-663-9608
Web site: http://www.horizoncable.com
Officer:
Kevin Daniel, President
Ownership: Ken Daniel, Principal.
Cable Systems (1):
California: POINT REYES STATION.

HORRY TELEPHONE COOPERATIVE INC.
PO Box 1820
3480 Hwy. 701 North
Conway, SC 29528
Phones: 843-365-2154; 800-824-6779
Fax: 843-365-0855
E-mail: customerservice@htcinc.net
Web site: http://www.htcinc.net
Officers:
Charles A. Whaley, President
Betty F. Jordam, Secretary
Cynthia J. Cannon, Treasurer
Sid Blackwelder, Information Operations
Lowell Carter, Plant Engineering
Brent D. Groome, Customer Operations
Carlton Lewis, Financial Operations
Glenda Page, Human Resources
Frank Sarvis, Network Engineering
Ownership: Subscriber owned--Homewood, SC.
Cable Systems (1):
South Carolina: HOMEWOOD.

HOT SPRINGS TELEPHONE CO.
PO Box 627
216 Main St.
Hot Springs, MT 59845
Phone: 406-741-2751
Web site: http://www.hotsprgs.net
Cable Systems (1):
Montana: HOT SPRINGS.

RUTH & RICK HOWARD
PO Box 229
Rte 40
Salyersville, KY 41465
Phone: 606-349-3317
Cable Systems (1):
Kentucky: SALYERSVILLE.

HTC CABLECOM
PO Box 142
107 2nd Ave. South
Hospers, IA 51238
Phones: 712-752-8100; 800-813-2023
E-mail: htc@hosperstel.com
Web site: http://www.hosperstel.com
Officers:
David Raak, General Manager
Gregg Andringa, Chief Technology Officer
Ownership: Hospers Telephone Exchange Inc..
Cable Systems (1):
Iowa: HOSPERS.

HUBBARD CO-OP CABLE
306 East Maple St.
Hubbard, IA 50122
Phone: 641-864-2216
Fax: 641-864-2666
E-mail: hubbard@netins.net

Cable Owners

Cable Systems (1):
Iowa: HUBBARD.

WALTER E. HUSSMAN JR.
2nd Fl.
115 East Capitol Ave.
Little Rock, AR 72201
Phone: 501-378-3400
Fax: 501-376-8594
E-mail: camdencabletvtech@cablelynx.com
Web site: http://www.wehco.com
Officers:
Walter E. Hussman Jr., President
Allen Berry, Chief Financial Officer
Cable Systems (1):
Arkansas: CAMDEN.
Cable Holdings:
WEHCO Video Inc., see listing

HUXLEY COMMUNICATIONS CORP.
102 North Main Ave.
Huxley, IA 50124
Phones: 515-597-2212; 515-597-2281
Fax: 515-597-2899
E-mail: huxtel@huxcomm.net
Web site: http://www.huxcomm.net
Officers:
Scott DeTar, President
Dave Halverson, Vice President
Steve Kovarik, Secretary-Treasurer
Gary Clark, General Manager
Terry Ferguson, Director, Operations
Ted Powell, Central Office/Network Administrator
Brant Strumpfer, Plant Manager
Mike Leeds, Sales & Marketing Specialist
Connie Patrick, Business Office Manager
Linda Grady, Customer Care Specialist
Ownership: Huxley Communications Cooperative.
Cable Systems (1):
Iowa: HUXLEY.

IDEATEK COMMUNICATIONS LLC
10400 East 69th St.
Buhler, KS 67522
Phone: 855-433-2835
E-mail: sales@idkcom.net
Web site: http://www.ideatek.com
Ownership: Daniel Friesen.
Cable Systems (1):
Kansas: BENTLEY.

IMON COMMUNICATIONS
Ste 100
625 First St. SE
Cedar Rapids, IA 52401
Phone: 319-298-6484
E-mail: support@ImOn.net
Web site: http://www.imon.net
Cable Systems (1):
Iowa: CEDAR RAPIDS.

INDCO CABLE TV
PO Box 3799
2700 North St. Louis
Batesville, AR 72503-3799
Phones: 870-793-4174; 800-364-0831
Fax: 870-793-7439
E-mail: indco@indco.net
Web site: http://www.indco.net
Officers:
J. D. Pierce, President
Boyce E. Barnett, Secretary-Treasurer
Ownership: J. D Pierce, 50%; Boyce E Barnett, 50%.
Cable Systems (13):
Arkansas: BLACK ROCK; BRADFORD; CALDWELL; CUSHMAN; EVENING SHADE; GUM SPRINGS; NEWARK; OIL TROUGH; PANGBURN; PFEIFFER; PLAINVIEW; PLEASANT PLAINS; TUMBLING SHOALS.

INDEPENDENCE LIGHT & POWER TELECOMMUNICATIONS
PO Box 754
700 7th Ave. NE
Independence, IA 50644
Phone: 319-332-0100
Fax: 319-332-0101
E-mail: rcurry@indytel.com
Web site: http://www.indytel.com
Officers:
Ron Curry, General Manager
Linda Kress, Office Manager
Cable Systems (1):
Iowa: INDEPENDENCE.

INFOSTRUCTURE INC.
314 North 22nd Ave.
Humboldt, TN 38343
Phone: 731-784-5000
Fax: 731-784-7474
E-mail: support@click1.net
Web site: http://www.clickone.net
Officers:
John Warmath, President
Mark Love, Engineering Director

Branch Office:
Medina
109 North Main St
Medina, TN 38355
Ownership: James C Warmath; John F Warmath. John F. Warmath also has microwave holdings.
Cable Systems (1):
Tennessee: HUMBOLDT.
Other Holdings:
Newspaper holdings
Radio holdings

INLAND TELEPHONE CO.
PO Box 171
103 South 2nd St.
Roslyn, WA 98941
Phones: 509-649-2211; 800-462-4578
Fax: 509-649-2555
E-mail: custserv@inlandnetworks.com
Web site: http://www.inlandnetworks.com
Officers:
Douglas W. Weis, President
Nathan R. Weis, Secretary-Treasurer

Branch Offices:
Cle Elum
218 East 1st St.
Cle Elum, WA 98922
Phone: 509-674-5940
Fax: 509-674-9606
Uniontown
211 Montgomery St.
PO Box 221
Uniontown, WA 99179
Phone: 509-229-2211
Fax: 509-229-3300
Ownership: Western Elite Inc. Services.
Cable Systems (2):
Washington: CLE ELUM; ROSLYN.

INNOVATIVE COMMUNICATIONS CORP.
PO Box 7450
4006 Estate Diamond
Christiansted, VI 00820
Phones: 340-779-9999; 866-240-3999
Fax: 340-778-6011
Web site: http://www.innovativevi.net
Cable Systems (2):
Virgin Islands: ST. CROIX; ST. THOMAS.

INSIDE CONNECT CABLE LLC
4890 Knob Creek Rd.
Brooks, KY 40109
Phone: 502-955-4882
Fax: 502-543-7553
E-mail: sales@insideconnect.net
Web site: http://iccable.com
Cable Systems (4):
Kentucky: BREMEN; BROOKS; HAWESVILLE; OWENTON.

INTEGRA TELECOM
4960 Colorado St. SE
Prior Lake, MN 55372
Phone: 952-226-7000
E-mail: prlcare@integratelecom.com; customerservice@integratelecom.com
Web site: http://www.integratelecom.com
Officers:
Marc Willency, Chief Executive Officer
Jim Huesgen, President
Jesse Selnick, Chief Financial Officer
Ken Smith, Executive Vice President, Sales
Karen Clauson, Senior Vice President & General Counsel
Joseph Harding, Senior Vice President, Marketing
Lisa Hillyer, Vice President, Human Resourcs
Martha Tate, Vice President, Wholesale Division
Cable Systems (1):
Minnesota: PRIOR LAKE.

INTERBEL TELEPHONE COOPERATIVE INC.
PO Box 648
300 Dewey Ave.
Eureka, MT 59917
Phone: 406-889-3311
Fax: 406-889-3787
E-mail: interbel@interbel.net
Web site: http://www.interbel.com
Cable Systems (1):
Montana: EUREKA.

INTER-COUNTY CABLE CO.
PO Box 578
127 Jackson St.
Brooklyn, IA 52211
Phone: 641-522-9211
Fax: 641-522-5001
Officer:
Tim Atkinson, General Manager
Ownership: Brooklyn Mutual Telephone Co..
Cable Systems (2):
Iowa: BROOKLYN; MALCOM.

INTER-MOUNTAIN CABLE INC.
PO Box 159
20 Laynesville Rd.
Harold, KY 41635
Phones: 606-478-9406; 800-635-7052
Fax: 606-478-1680
E-mail: hwiley@gearheart.com
Web site: http://www.imctv.com
Officers:
Paul R. Gearheart, President
Paul D. Gearheart, Vice President
Jefferson Thacker, Chief Engineer
Elaine Gearheart, Secretary-Treasurer
John . Schmold, Director, Operations
Lewis King, Chief Engineer
Roy Harlow, OSP Supervisor
Rebecca Walters, Customer Service & Billing Supervisor & Digital Coordinator
R. Heath Wiley, Director, Marketing
Ownership: Elaine Gearhart, 50%; Paul R Gearhart, 50%.
Cable Systems (2):
Kentucky: HAROLD; JENKINS.

INTERSTATE COMMUNICATIONS
404 Howland St.
Emerson, IA 51533
Phones: 712-824-7231; 800-765-3738
Fax: 641-765-4204
E-mail: customerservice@interstatecom.com
Web site: http://www.interstatecom.com

Branch Office:
Truro
105 N. West St.
Truro, IA 50257
Phone: 641-765-4201
Fax: 641-765-4204
Cable Systems (3):
Iowa: ANDREW; EMERSON; TRURO.
Other Holdings:
Telephone: Southwest Telephone Exchange Inc., Emerson, IA (affiliated with independent telephone cos.); Interstate '35' Telephone Co., Truro, IA;

INTERSTATE TELECOMMUNICATIONS COOPERATIVE INC.
PO Box 920
312 4th St. West
Clear Lake, SD 57226
Phones: 605-874-2181; 800-417-8667
Fax: 605-874-2014
E-mail: info@itctel.com
Web site: http://itc-web.com
Officer:
Jerry Heiberger, General Manager

Branch Offices:
Brookings
1022 South Main Ave
Brookings, SD 57006
Phone: 605-693-3211
Fax: 605-693-3
Webster
14 East Seventh Ave
Webster, SD 57274-1430
Phone: 605-345-4260
Fax: 605-345-3708
Cable Systems (1):
South Dakota: CLEAR LAKE.

IRON RIVER COOPERATIVE TV ANTENNA CORP.
316 North 2nd Ave.
Iron River, MI 49935
Phone: 906-265-3810
Fax: 906-265-3020
E-mail: ircable@ironriver.tv
Web site: http://www.ironriver.tv
Officers:
Pete Nocerini, President
Jerry Ward, Chief Technology Officer
Ownership: Subscriber owned--Iron River, MI.
Cable Systems (1):
Michigan: IRON RIVER.

JACKSON MUNICIPAL TV SYSTEM
80 West Ashley St.
Jackson, MN 56143
Phone: 507-847-3225
Fax: 507-847-5586
Officers:
Curt Egeland, General Manager
Steve Jenson, Chief Technology Officer
Ownership: Community owned--Jackson, MI.

Cable Owners

Cable Systems (1):
Minnesota: JACKSON.

LYNDA & ROBERT JACOBSON
PO Box 759
620 Betty St.
Ranchester, WY 82839
Phones: 307-655-9011; 800-953-9011
Fax: 307-655-9021
E-mail: trcatv@trcable.tv
Web site: http://www.trcable.tv
Officers:
Robert Jacobson, President
Lynda Lee Jacobson, Secretary-Treasurer
Cable Systems (6):
Wyoming: MOORCROFT; PINE HAVEN; RANCHESTER; STORY; SUNDANCE; UPTON.

JAGUAR COMMUNICATIONS
213 South Oak Ave.
Owatonna, MN 55060
Phones: 507-214-1000; 800-250-1517
E-mail: info@jagcom.net
Web site: http://www.jaguarcommunications.com
Officer:
E.T. Colson, Chief Executive Officer

Branch Offices:
Albert Lea Office
101 South Newton Ave
Albert Lea, MN 56007
Phone: 507-552-1000
Austin Office
507 1st St NW
Ste B
Austin, MN 55912
Phone: 507-355-1000
Northfield Office
205 Water St South
Ste 8
Northfield, MN 55057
Phone: 507-214-1000
Rochester Office
2109 S Broadway
Rochester, MN 55901
Phone: 507-361-1000
Cable Systems (2):
Minnesota: NEW MARKET; OWATONNA.

JAMES MOGG TV
PO Box 328
Cheyenne, OK 73628
Phone: 580-497-2182
Officers:
James M. Mogg, President
Lura Mae Mogg, Vice President
Ownership: James M Mogg, 50%; Lura Mae Mogg, 50%.
Cable Systems (1):
Oklahoma: CHEYENNE.

J & N CABLE SYSTEMS INC.
614 South Columbus Ave.
Goldendale, WA 98620-9006
Phones: 509-773-5359; 800-752-9809
Fax: 509-773-7090
E-mail: nancy@jncable.com
Officers:
John Kusky, President
Nancy Kusky, Vice President
Ownership: John Kusky; Nancy Kusky, 100% jointly.
Cable Systems (7):
Oregon: CONDON; MORO; RAINIER.

Washington: GOLDENDALE; LYLE; NACHES; YACOLT.

J. B. CABLE
PO Box 268
Minersville, PA 17954
Phone: 570-544-5582
Ownership: John Dunleavy, 50%; Thomas O'Brien, 50%.
Cable Systems (1):
Pennsylvania: CASS TWP. (Schuylkill County).

JEFFERSON COUNTY CABLE INC.
116 South 4th St.
Toronto, OH 43964
Phones: 740-537-2214; 800-931-9392
Fax: 740-537-2802
Web site: http://www.voiceflight.biz
Officer:
Bob Loveridge, General Manager
Ownership: Marvin L Bates Sr., Principal.
Cable Systems (3):
Ohio: EMPIRE; SMITHFIELD; TORONTO.

JEFFERSON TELEPHONE & CABLEVISION
105 West Harrison St.
Jefferson, IA 50129
Phone: 515-386-4141
Fax: 515-386-2600
E-mail: jtcobob@netins.net; info@jeffersontelecom.com
Web site: http://www.jeffersontelephone.com
Officer:
Jim Daubendiek, General Manager
Cable Systems (1):
Iowa: GRAND JUNCTION.

JESUP FARMER'S MUTUAL TELEPHONE CO.
PO Box 249
541 Young St.
Jesup, IA 50648-0249
Phone: 319-827-1151
Fax: 319-827-1110
E-mail: jesupfmt@jtt.net
Web site: http://www.jtt.net
Officers:
Robert Bloes, President
Tony Lang, Manager
Bob Venem, Engineering Director
Ownership: Cooperative.
Cable Systems (1):
Iowa: JESUP.

JOHNSONBURG COMMUNITY TV CO. INC.
PO Box 248
424 Center St.
Johnsonburg, PA 15845
Phone: 814-965-4888
Officers:
Archie Shuer, President
Harry Horne, Chief Operating Officer & Secretary
Sam Guaglianone, Chief Financial Officer
Ownership: Community owned--Johnsonburg, PA.
Cable Systems (1):
Pennsylvania: JOHNSONBURG.

EUGENE JONES
PO Box 8
Rte 1
Folsum, WV 26348
Phone: 304-334-6504
Fax: 304-334-6504

Cable Systems (1):
West Virginia: FOLSOM.

K2 COMMUNICATIONS
PO Box 232
339 Main St.
Mead, CO 80542
Phone: 970-535-6323
E-mail: info@k2cable.com
Web site: http://www.k2cable.com/cable-tv.html
Cable Systems (1):
Colorado: MEAD.

CITY OF KAHOKA
c/o Scott Groben
250 North Morgan
Kahoka, MO 63445-1433
Phone: 660-727-3711
Fax: 660-727-7891
E-mail: cityofkahoka@kahoka.com
Web site: http://www.kahokamo.com
Officers:
Jerry Webber, Mayor
Sandie Hopp, Cable Director
Scott Groben, Cable Manager
Ownership: Community owned--Kahoka, MO.
Cable Systems (1):
Missouri: KAHOKA.

KALIDA TELEPHONE CO.
PO Box 267
121 East Main St.
Kalida, OH 45853
Phone: 419-532-3218
Fax: 419-532-3300
E-mail: ktc@kalidatel.com
Web site: http://www.kalidatel.com
Officer:
Chris Phillips, Manager
Cable Systems (1):
Ohio: KALIDA.

KAPLAN TELEPHONE CO. INC.
220 North Cushing Ave.
Kaplan, LA 70548
Phones: 337-643-2255; 337-643-7171
Fax: 337-643-6000
Web site: http://ktcpace.com

Branch Office:
Abbeville
1730 Veterans Memorial Dr
Abbeville, LA 70510
Phone: 337-898-2255
Fax: 337-643-6000
Cable Systems (1):
Louisiana: KAPLAN.

KARBAN TV SYSTEMS INC.
73A South Stevens St.
Rhinelander, WI 54501
Phones: 715-493-7613; 800-236-0233
E-mail: sales@ktvs.net; jkarban@ktvs.net
Web site: http://www.ktvs.net
Officers:
John Karban
Jason Eichhorn
Jeff Brown
Ownership: John Karban.
Cable Systems (4):
Wisconsin: BOULDER JUNCTION; LAND O'LAKES; MERCER; THREE LAKES.

KENNEBEC TELEPHONE CO. INC.
PO Box 158
220 South Main St.
Kennebec, SD 57544-0158

Phones: 605-869-2220; 888-868-3390
Fax: 605-869-2221
E-mail: rodb@kennebectelephone.com
Web site: http://www.kennebectelephone.com
Officers:
Rod Bowar, President & Manager
Matt Collins, Plant Manager
Chris Zirpel, Office Manager
Jason Thiry, Marketing Manager
Ownership: Kennebec Telephone, Inc..
Cable Systems (1):
South Dakota: KENNEBEC.

KENTEC COMMUNICATIONS INC.
710 West Main St.
Sterling, CO 80751
Phone: 970-522-8107
Fax: 970-521-9457
E-mail: support@kci.net
Web site: http://www.kci.net
Cable Systems (1):
Colorado: MERINO.

KEYSTONE FARMERS COOPERATIVE TELEPHONE CO.
PO Box 277
86 Main St.
Keystone, IA 52249
Phones: 319-442-3241; 800-568-9584
E-mail: keystone@netins.net
Web site: http://www.keystonecommunications.com
Officers:
DuWayne Schirm, President
John C. Brady, General Manager
Cable Systems (1):
Iowa: KEYSTONE.
Other Holdings:
Cellular radio

KINGS BAY COMMUNICATIONS INC.
220 East King Ave.
Kingsland, GA 31548-6360
Phone: 912-729-3153
Cable Systems (1):
Georgia: KINGSLAND.

RON KLINGENSTEIN
PO Box 148
204 East Main St.
Dayton, WA 99328
Phone: 509-382-2132
E-mail: tvcable@gmail.com
Web site: http://www.touchetvalleytv.com
Cable Systems (1):
Washington: DAYTON.

KMHC INC.
PO Box 21
107 Jefferson
Kingston Mines, IL 61539
Phone: 309-389-5782
Ownership: Community owned--Kingston Mines, IL.
Cable Systems (1):
Illinois: KINGSTON MINES.

ARTHUR J. KRAUS
305 State St.
Manhattan, IL 60442
Phones: 815-478-4000; 800-442-2253
Web site: http://www.krausonline.com
Officer:
Arthur J. Kraus, President

2017 Edition
D-909

Cable Owners

Cable Systems (3):
Illinois: GARDNER; MANHATTAN; SENECA.

KUHN COMMUNICATIONS
PO Box 277
301 West Main St.
Walnut Bottom, PA 17266
Phones: 717-532-8857; 800-771-7072
E-mail: kuhncom1@kuhncom.net
Web site: http://www.kuhncom.net
Ownership: Earl Kuhn.
Cable Systems (5):
Pennsylvania: BLOSERVILLE; LANDISBURG; NEWBURG; ORRSTOWN; WALNUT BOTTOM.

BOROUGH OF KUTZTOWN
45 Railroad St.
Kutztown, PA 19530-1112
Phones: 610-683-5722; 610-683-5388
Fax: 610-683-6729
E-mail: telecom@kutztownboro.org
Web site: http://www.huhomenet.com
Officer:
Mark Arnold, Technical Director
Cable Systems (1):
Pennsylvania: KUTZTOWN.

LAKELAND CABLE TV INC.
PO Box 321
194 Telephone Rd.
Crowder, OK 74430
Phones: 918-334-3700; 888-527-3096
Fax: 918-334-3202
E-mail: cvstaff@cvok.net
Web site: http://cvok.net
Officers:
Charles O. Smith, Chairman
Janet Brooks, Secretary
Ownership: Charles Smith; Betty Smith; Orlean Smith, Principals. Charles Smith is Pres. & Gen. Mgr. and Betty Smith is exec. of the Canadian Valley Telephone Co., Crowder, OK.
Cable Systems (2):
Oklahoma: CANADIAN; CROWDER.

LAKELAND COMMUNICATIONS
PO Box 40
825 Innovation Ave.
Milltown, WI 54858
Phones: 715-825-2171; 715-472-2101
Fax: 715-825-4299; 715-472-8880
E-mail: info@lakeland.ws
Web site: http://www.lakeland.ws
Officer:
John K. Klatt, President & Chief Executive Officer
Cable Systems (1):
Wisconsin: LUCK (village).

LAMOTTE TELEPHONE CO. INC.
PO Box 8
400 Pine St.
LaMotte, IA 52054
Phones: 563-773-2213; 866-943-4375
Fax: 563-773-2345
E-mail: info@lamotte-telco.com
Web site: http://www.lamotte-telco.com
Officer:
JoAnne Gregorich, General Manager
Cable Systems (1):
Iowa: LAMOTTE.

LAUREL HIGHLAND TOTAL COMMUNICATIONS
PO Box 168
4157 Main St.
Stahlstown, PA 15687

Phones: 724-593-2411; 724-455-2411
Fax: 724-593-2423
Web site: http://www.lhtc.co
Officers:
James J Kail, President & Chief Executive Officer
Morgan F. Withrow, Vice President & Treasurer
Mary Lou Barnhart, Secretary

Branch Office:
868 Indian Creek Valley Rd
Indian Head, PA 15446
Phone: 724-455-2411
Ownership: J. Paul Kalp, 37%; M. Graham Hunter, 25%; Mary Lou Barnhart, 19%; Morgan F Withrow, 12%; William I Piper, 6%.
Cable Systems (1):
Pennsylvania: SALTLICK TWP..

LAURENS MUNICIPAL POWER & COMMUNICATIONS
272 North 3rd St.
Laurens, IA 50554
Phones: 712-841-4610; 712-841-4526
Fax: 712-841-4611
E-mail: lmpc@laurens-ia.com; bsmith@laurens-ia.com
Web site: http://www.laurens-ia.com
Officer:
Chad Cleveland, General Manager
Cable Systems (1):
Iowa: LAURENS.

DON T. LEAP
RR 96
Hyndman, PA 15545
Phone: 814-842-3370
Cable Systems (1):
Pennsylvania: LONDONDERRY TWP. (Bedford County).

LENOX MUNICIPAL CABLEVISION
205 South Main St.
Lenox, IA 50851
Phone: 641-333-2550
Fax: 641-333-2582
Web site: http://lenoxia.com/CityofLenox/Utility/LenoxMunicipalLight.htm
Cable Systems (1):
Iowa: LENOX.

LEWISTON COMMUNICATIONS
3250 South Van Wagoner Ave.
Fremont, MI 49412-8008
Phone: 989-607-9041
Fax: 231-924-4882
E-mail: help@lewistoncomm.com
Web site: http://portal.lewistoncomm.com
Cable Systems (1):
Michigan: LEWISTON.

LIBERTY CABLEVISION OF PUERTO RICO LLC
Road 992 KM. 0.2
Luquillo Industrial Park
Luquillo, PR 00773
Phones: 787-355-3535; 877-772-1518
Fax: 303-220-6601
Web site: http://www.libertypr.com
Officers:
Greg Maffei, Chief Executive Officer, Liberty Media
Mark Carleton, Chief Financial Officer, Liberty Media
Albert Rosenthaler, Chief Development Officer, Liberty Media

Christopher Shean, Senior Adviser, Liberty Media
Ownership: Liberty Global Inc., 60%; Searchlight Capital Partners LP, 40%; LGI ownership:; Liberty Media International; United Global Communications, jointly.
Cable Systems (4):
Puerto Rico: BAYAMON; CAGUAS; CIALES; LUQUILLO.

LIGHTHOUSE COMPUTERS INC.
Ste A
2972 West Eighth St.
Sault St. Marie, MI 49783
Phones: 906-632-1820; 888-883-3393
Web site: http://www.lighthouse.net/highspeed
Cable Systems (1):
Michigan: ENGADINE.

LINCOLN TELEPHONE CO.
111 Stemple Pass Rd.
Lincoln, MT 59639
Phone: 406-362-4216
Fax: 406-362-4606
E-mail: ltc@linctel.net
Web site: http://www.linctel.net
Ownership: Stockholder owned.
Cable Systems (1):
Montana: LINCOLN.

HOWARD LOCK
PO Box 127
111 Pine St.
Peshtigo, WI 54157
Phones: 715-582-1141; 800-472-0576
Fax: 715-582-1142
Represented (legal): Cinnamon Mueller.
Cable Systems (1):
Wisconsin: CRIVITZ.

LONE PINE TV INC.
223 Jackson St.
Lone Pine, CA 93545
Phone: 760-876-5461
Fax: 760-876-9101
E-mail: cs@lonepinetv.com
Web site: http://www.lonepinetv.com
Ownership: Bruce Branson, Chairman & President.
Cable Systems (1):
California: LONE PINE.

LONG LINES
PO Box 67
Sergeant Bluff, IA 51054
Phones: 712-271-4000; 866-901-5664
Fax: 712-271-2727
E-mail: info@longlines.biz
Web site: http://www.longlines.com
Officer:
Jon Winkel, Vice Chairman
Ownership: Publicly held..
Cable Systems (1):
Iowa: SALIX.
Other Holdings:
Mapleton Communications Inc., see listing

LOST NATION-ELWOOD TELEPHONE CO.
PO Box 97
304 Long Ave.
Lost Nation, IA 52254
Phone: 563-678-2470
Fax: 563-678-2300
E-mail: lnation@netins.net
Web site: http://www.lnetelco.com
Officers:

Glenn Short, General Manager
Crystal Burmeister, Bookkeeper
Gerald Wirth, President
Alvin Weirup, Vice President
Ownership: Lost Nation-Elwood Telephone.
Cable Systems (1):
Iowa: LOST NATION.
Other Holdings:
Telephone holdings

DEL LOTT
102 South Hayden St.
Belzoni, MS 39038
Phone: 662-247-1834
Fax: 662-247-3237
E-mail: office@belzonicable.com; stephen@belzonicable.com
Web site: http://www.belzonicable.com
Officers:
Del Lott, President
Genelle Lott, Secretary-Treasurer & Chief Financial Officer
Cable Systems (1):
Mississippi: BELZONI.

LOWELL COMMUNITY TV CORP.
PO Box 364
Water St.
Lowell, OH 45744
Phone: 740-896-2626
Officers:
Ron Bauerbach, President & Manager
Debbie Cline, Secretary-Treasurer
Ownership: Subscriber owned--Lowell, OH.
Cable Systems (1):
Ohio: LOWELL.

LYCOM COMMUNICATIONS INC.
PO Box 1114
305 East Pike St.
Louisa, KY 41230
Phone: 606-638-3600
Fax: 606-638-4278
E-mail: info@lycomonline.com
Web site: http://lycomonline.com
Ownership: Donna Lycans.
Cable Systems (4):
Kentucky: CHARLEY; LAWRENCE COUNTY (southern portion); LOUISA.
West Virginia: PRICHARD.

LYNNSTAR COMMUNICATIONS
3111 South Sheridan Rd.
Tulsa, OK 74145
Phones: 918-289-2155; 888-575-9230
Fax: 918-948-9910
Officers:
S. Gene Yarbrough, Chairman of the Board & Government Relations Director
Chris Romine, Chief Executive Officer, Executive Vice President & Co-Chairman of the Board
Steve Sizemore, Chief Operations Officer, Executive Vice President & Board Member
Gary Majors, Vice President & Business Development & Countertrade Director
Gus Salvino, Vice President & Programming & Vendor Relations Director
Daniel J. Sweeney, Vice President & Investor Relations Manager
Sheila Magness, Accounting Manager

Branch Office:
Fort Worth
4500 Mercantile Plz
Ste 300
Fort Worth, TX 76137
Phone: 682-730-0900
Fax: 682-730-6400
Cable Systems (12):
Texas: CLIFTON; COLEMAN; COMANCHE;

Cable Owners

EDEN; IRAAN; MART; MASON; MENARD; RANKIN; VALLEY MILLS; WEST; WHITNEY.

LYONS COMMUNICATIONS
PO Box 1403
Lyons, CO 80540
Phone: 303-823-5656
E-mail: lyonstv@gmail.com
Web site: http://www.lyonscomm.com
Officer:
Robert Jones, Owner
Ownership: Robert Jones.
Cable Systems (1):
Colorado: LYONS (town).

MADDOCK AREA DEVELOPMENT CORP.
306 Second St.
Maddock, ND 58348
Phone: 701-438-2541
Officers:
Beth Olson, Secretary
Rod Maddock, Treasurer
Cable Systems (1):
North Dakota: MADDOCK.

MADISON COMMUNICATIONS CO.
PO Box 29
Staunton, IL 62088
Phone: 800-422-4848
Fax: 618-635-7213
E-mail: infomtc@madisontelco.com
Web site: http://www.gomadison.com
Officers:
Robert W. Schwartz, Chairman
Len J. Schwartz, Chief Operating Officer
Mary J. Westernold, Chief Financial Officer
Cable Systems (1):
Illinois: STAUNTON.

MADISON COMMUNICATIONS INC.
216 South Marion St.
Athens, AL 35611-2504
Phone: 256-536-3724
Cable Systems (1):
Arkansas: HUNTSVILLE.

MAINSTAY COMMUNICATIONS
PO Box 487
1000 North Main St.
Henderson, NE 68371
Phones: 402-723-4848; 800-868-4848
Fax: 402-723-4451
E-mail: mainstay@mainstaycomm.net
Web site: http://www.mainstaycomm.net
Officer:
Matt Friesen, General Manager
Cable Systems (1):
Nebraska: HENDERSON.

MANAWA TELECOM INC.
PO Box 130
131 2nd St.
Manawa, WI 54949
Phones: 920-596-2535; 800-872-5452
Fax: 920-596-3775
E-mail: manawa@wolfnet.net
Web site: http://www.manawatelephone.com
Officers:
Thomas R. Squires, President
Robert E. Squires, Vice President
Brian J. Squires, Secretary-Treasurer
Ownership: Manawa Telecommunications Inc..
Cable Systems (1):
Wisconsin: MANAWA.
Other Holdings:
Telephone holdings

MANNING MUNICIPAL COMMUNICATION & TV SYSTEM UTILITY
PO Box 386
719 3rd St.
Manning, IA 51455
Phone: 712-655-2660
Fax: 712-655-3304
E-mail: info@mmctsu.com
Web site: http://www.mmctsu.com
Officer:
Kent Hilsabeck, Manager
Ownership: Community owned--Manning, IA.
Cable Systems (1):
Iowa: MANNING.

MARGARETVILLE TELEPHONE CO.
PO Box 260
50 Swart St.
Margaretville, NY 12455
Phones: 845-586-3311; 800-586-3387
Fax: 845-586-4050
E-mail: mtc@catskill.net
Web site: http://www.mtctelcom.com
Cable Systems (1):
New York: MARGARETVILLE.

MARNE & ELK HORN TELEPHONE CO.
PO Box 120
4242 Main St.
Elk Horn, IA 51531
Phones: 712-764-6161; 888-764-6141
Fax: 712-764-2773
E-mail: metc@metc.net
Web site: http://www.metc.net
Cable Systems (1):
Iowa: ELK HORN.

MARTELL CABLE SERVICE INC.
1597 Chowning Glen Dr.
Wixom, MI 48393
Phones: 248-755-1102; 248-960-5554
Ownership: Tony F Martell.
Cable Systems (1):
Michigan: NASHVILLE.

MARTELLE COOPERATIVE TELEPHONE ASSOCIATION
PO Box 128
204 South St.
Martelle, IA 52305
Phone: 319-482-2381
Fax: 319-482-3018
E-mail: martelle@netins.net
Web site: http://www.martellecom.com
Officers:
John O. Miller, President
Sandra Davis, System Manager
Richard Strother, Secretary-Treasurer
Ownership: Sandra Davis, Principal.
Cable Systems (1):
Iowa: MARTELLE.

MASTER VISION CABLE
PO Box 203
Cambridge Springs, PA 16403
Phones: 814-398-1946; 888-827-2259
E-mail: mastervision@mvbloomfield.net
Web site: http://www.canlakecable.net
Cable Systems (1):
Pennsylvania: CANADOHTA LAKE.

MAXXSOUTH BROADBAND
Ste 202-B
911 Hwy. 12 West
Starkville, MS 39759

Phone: 800-457-5351
Web site: http://www.maxxsouth.com
Officer:
Peter Kahelin, President & Chief Executive Officer
Cable Systems (6):
Mississippi: CARTHAGE; FOREST; KOSCIUSKO; PHILADELPHIA; PONTOTOC; RALEIGH.

MONTY MCCULLOUGH
PO Box 1115
Salem, AR 72576
Phone: 870-895-4993
Fax: 870-895-4905
Cable Systems (1):
Arkansas: SALEM.

MCNABB CABLE & SATELLITE INC.
PO Box 218
308 West Main St.
McNabb, IL 61335
Phone: 815-882-2201
Fax: 815-882-2141
E-mail: jsmith@nabbnet.com
Web site: http://www.nabbnet.com
Officer:
Jackie Smith, General Manager
Ownership: McNabb Telephone Co..
Cable Systems (1):
Illinois: MCNABB.

MCTV
PO Box 1000
Massillon, OH 44648-1000
Phones: 330-833-4134; 330-345-8114
Fax: 330-833-9775
Web site: http://www.mctvohio.com
Officers:
Richard W. Gessner, Chairman, Treasurer & Chief Financial Officer
Robert B. Gessner, President
David Hoffer, Chief Operating Officer
Susan R. Gessner, Secretary
Ownership: Richard W Gessner; Susan R Gessner, jointly, 54%; 100 stockholders, each with less than 5%.
Represented (legal): Womble Carlyle Sandridge & Rice LLP.
Cable Systems (2):
Ohio: MASSILLON; WOOSTER.

MECHANICSVILLE TELEPHONE CO.
PO Box 159
107 North John St.
Mechanicsville, IA 52306
Phone: 563-432-7221
Fax: 563-432-7721
E-mail: mtco@netins.net
Web site: http://www.mechanicsvilletel.net
Officers:
Norman Farrington, President
Robert G. Horner, Secretary-Treasurer
Hans Arwine, General Manager
Angie Entwisle, Office Coordinator
Cable Systems (1):
Iowa: MECHANICSVILLE.

MEDIACOM LLC
One Mediacom Way
Mediacom Park, NY 10918
Phones: 800-479-2082; 855-633-4226
Web site: http://www.mediacomcable.com
Officers:
Rocco B. Commisso, Chairman & Chief Executive Officer
Anush Prabhu, Managing Partner & Chief Strategy Partner

Italia Commisso Weinand, Executive Vice President, Programming & Human Resources
John G. Pascarelli, Executive Vice President, Operations
Mark E. Stephan, Executive Vice President & Chief Financial Officer
Charles J. Bartolotta, Senior Vice President, Customer Operations
Calvin Craib, Senior Vice President, Business Development
Tapan Dandnaik, Senior Vice President, Customer Service & Financial Operations
Thomas Larsen, Senior Vice President, Government & Public Relations
Peter Lyons, Senior Vice President, Information Technology
David M McNaughton, Senior Vice President, Marketing & Consumer Services
Edward S Pardini, Senior Vice President, Field Operations Group
Dan Templin, Senior Vice President, Mediacom Business
J R Walden, Senior Vice President, Technology
Brian M. Walsh, Senior Vice President & Corporate Controller
Joseph E. Young, Senior Vice President, General Counsel & Secretary
Joseph Commisso, Group Vice President, Corporate Finance
Joseph Selvage, Group Vice President, IP Networks
Suzanne Sosiewicz-Leggio, Vice President, Financial Services
Ownership: Rocco B Commisso.
Represented (legal): Dentons.
Cable Systems (239):
Alabama: ARDMORE; FAIRHOPE; GREENSBORO; MADISON COUNTY; MOBILE COUNTY; MONROEVILLE; ROBERTSDALE; THOMASVILLE; YORK.
Arizona: AJO; APACHE JUNCTION; NOGALES.
California: CLEARLAKE; KERN COUNTY (portions); RIDGECREST; SUN CITY; VALLEY CENTER.
Delaware: MILLSBORO.
Florida: EASTPOINT; GULF BREEZE; HAVANA (town); WALTON COUNTY (portions).
Georgia: ADEL; ALBANY; AMERICUS; BAINBRIDGE; COLUMBUS; CUTHBERT; EASTMAN; FITZGERALD; HAZLEHURST; THOMASVILLE; TIFTON; VALDOSTA.
Illinois: ALTAMONT; ARENZVILLE; ATLANTA; BELVIDERE TWP.; CARTHAGE; CHARLESTON; CHILLICOTHE; CLAY CITY; COFFEEN; CORTLAND (village); COULTERVILLE; DALLAS CITY; DELAVAN; EFFINGHAM; ELMWOOD; GENESEO; GERMAN VALLEY; GIBSON CITY; GOOD HOPE; GREENUP; HERRICK; INDUSTRY; IRVING; JACKSONVILLE; KINCAID; LE ROY; LOUISVILLE; MARTINSVILLE; MATTOON; MOLINE; MONTICELLO; MORRIS (town); MOUNT CARROLL; MURPHYSBORO; NEOGA; PONTIAC; RANTOUL; ROANOKE; ROBINSON; STREATOR; SUGAR GROVE; SULLIVAN; TAMPICO; TOWER HILL; TUSCOLA; VICTORIA; WASHINGTON PARK; WATSEKA; WYOMING; ZEIGLER.
Indiana: ANGOLA; AUBURN; DECATUR; KNOX; LAGRANGE; NEWTON COUNTY (portions); NORTH WEBSTER.
Iowa: ALBIA; AMANA; AMES; ANAMOSA; ATLANTIC; BELLE PLAINE; BURLINGTON; CALMAR; CARROLL; CEDAR RAPIDS; CHARITON; CHARLES CITY; CLINTON; DECORAH; DENISON; DES MOINES; DEXTER; DUBUQUE; EAGLE GROVE; ESTHERVILLE; FORT DODGE; FORT MADISON; GILMORE CITY; GLADBROOK; HAMILTON; HAMPTON; HUDSON; INDEPENDENCE; IOWA CITY; IOWA FALLS; KEOKUK; KEOTA; MAQUOKETA; MARSHALLTOWN; MASON CITY; NEW ALBIN; NEWTON; NORTH LIBERTY; NORWAY; OSAGE; OSKALOOSA; OTTUMWA; OXFORD JUNCTION; PRESTON; RED OAK; SPIRIT LAKE; STORM LAKE; SWEA CITY; VINTON; WASHINGTON; WATERLOO; WAVERLY;

Cable Owners

WILLIAMSBURG.
Kansas: ALTOONA; BURLINGTON; EUREKA; HAMILTON; MADISON; OSWEGO; THAYER; TORONTO.
Kentucky: BURKESVILLE; CADIZ; CANEYVILLE; HENDERSON COUNTY (portions); LINCOLN COUNTY (eastern portion); MARION; MARSHALL COUNTY; MORGANTOWN; NEBO; NORTONVILLE; PARK CITY; RUSSELL COUNTY (unincorporated areas); SUMMER SHADE; TRENTON; UPTON; WHITESVILLE.
Michigan: MARCELLUS; MATTAWAN; MENDON (village).
Minnesota: APPLETON; CALEDONIA; CALUMET; CANNON FALLS; CHATFIELD; CLOQUET; COOK; EVELETH; FRANKLIN; GRAND MARAIS; GRAND RAPIDS; HUTCHINSON; IVANHOE; LAKE CITY; MORRIS; MOUND; PAYNESVILLE; PRIOR LAKE; ST. PETER; WORTHINGTON.
Mississippi: BEAUMONT; LUCEDALE; ST. ANDREWS; WAVELAND.
Missouri: APPLETON CITY; ARCHIE; BRUNSWICK; BUTLER; CARL JUNCTION; CARROLLTON; CARUTHERSVILLE; CASSVILLE; COLUMBIA; DIAMOND; EVERTON; EXCELSIOR SPRINGS; HERMANN; JEFFERSON CITY; LIBERAL; LOWRY CITY; MARCELINE; OSCEOLA; SEYMOUR; SPRINGFIELD.
North Carolina: COLERAIN; CONWAY; CURRITUCK; EDENTON; PLYMOUTH (town).
Ohio: HICKSVILLE.
South Dakota: BROOKINGS.
Tennessee: HUNTLAND.
Virginia: CHESAPEAKE.
Wisconsin: ALBANY; ARGYLE; BLANCHARDVILLE; BOSCOBEL; CUBA CITY; FORT McCOY; FREMONT; IOLA; MAUSTON; MONTICELLO; ORFORDVILLE; PRAIRIE DU CHIEN; STODDARD; SUGAR CREEK (town); VIROQUA.

MEDIAPOLIS CABLEVISION CO.
652 Main St.
Mediapolis, IA 52637
Phones: 319-394-3456; 800-762-1527
Fax: 319-394-9155
E-mail: office@mepotelco.net
Web site: http://www.mtctech.net
Officers:
William R. Malcom, General Manager & Chief Executive Officer
Angie Rupe, Office Manager
Ownership: Mediapolis Telephone Co..
Cable Systems (1):
Iowa: MEDIAPOLIS.

SCOTT MERCER
PO Box 343
509 First St. East
Whitehall, MT 59759
Phone: 406-287-9326
Cable Systems (1):
Montana: WHITEHALL.

MERRIMAC COMMUNICATIONS LTD.
327 Palisade St.
Merrimac, WI 53561
Phone: 608-493-9470
Fax: 608-493-9902
E-mail: office@merr.com
Web site: http://www.merr.us
Officers:
Bartlett A. Olson, President & Chief Executive Officer
Jim Paul, Engineering Director
Charlotte A. Olson, Vice President & Secretary-Treasurer
Ownership: Bartlett Olson; Charlotte Olson, jointly.
Cable Systems (1):
Wisconsin: MERRIMAC.

MICOM
PO Box 100
Montague, MI 49437
Phone: 888-873-3353
Fax: 231-894-4960
Web site: http://www.micomcable.com
Ownership: Michigan Cable Partners Inc..
Cable Systems (7):
Michigan: BALDWIN (village); HIGHLAND PARK; MACKINAC ISLAND; MECOSTA; MIO; REMUS; RUTLAND TWP..

MI-CONNECTION
PO Box 90
435 South Broad St.
Mooresville, NC 28115
Phones: 704-660-3840; 704-662-3255
E-mail: manager@mi-connection.com
Web site: http://www.mi-connection.com
Officer:
Alan Hall, General Manager
Cable Systems (1):
North Carolina: MOORESVILLE.

MIDCONTINENT COMMUNICATIONS
PO Box 5010
Sioux Falls, SD 57117
Phone: 800-888-1300
E-mail: tom_simmons@mmi.net
Web site: http://www.midco.com
Officers:
Patrick McAdaragh, President & Chief Executive Officer
Steven E. Grosser, Chief Financial Officer
W. Tom Simmons, Senior Vice President, Public Policy
Scott Anderson, Vice President, Legal & General Counsel
Kent Johnson, Vice President, Finance
Trish McCann, Vice President, Marketing
Jon Pederson, Vice President, Technology
Mark Powell, Vice President, Business Solutions
Brad Schoenfelder, Vice President, Operations
Gary Shawd, Vice President, Information Services
Scott Smidt, Vice President, Business Engineering & Operations
Debbie Stang, Vice President, Human Resources
Ownership: Midcontinent Media, 50%; Comcast Corp., 50%; Midcontinent Media ownership:; Patrick McAdaragh, 33.33%; Steven Grosser, 33.33%; Richard Busch, 33.33%.
Represented (legal): Baker & Hostetler LLP.
Cable Systems (44):
Minnesota: BALATON; BEMIDJI; BREWSTER; CAMBRIDGE; CANBY; CANNON FALLS TWP.; CEYLON; DUNNELL; ELY; FAIRMONT; HERON LAKE; INTERNATIONAL FALLS; LITTLEFORK; NORTHROP; ROUND LAKE; STORDEN; WANAMINGO; WASECA COUNTY (portions); WOOD LAKE.
North Dakota: BEULAH; BISMARCK; BOWMAN; COOPERSTOWN (village); DEVILS LAKE; GRAND FORKS; LEEDS; McCLUSKY; MINNEWAUKAN; MINOT; MOTT; SOUTH HEART; WAHPETON; WEST FARGO; WILLISTON.
South Dakota: ABERDEEN; FORT PIERRE; HURON; MITCHELL; RAPID CITY; SIOUX FALLS; WATERTOWN; YANKTON.
Wisconsin: ALMA; ELLSWORTH.
Other Holdings:
Regional Cable Channel: Midco Sports Network.

MIDDLEBURGH TELEPHONE CO.
PO Box 191
103 Cliff St.
Middleburgh, NY 12122
Phones: 518-827-5211; 877-827-5211
Fax: 518-827-7600
E-mail: info@midtel.net
Web site: http://www.midtel.net
Officer:
Jason Becker, President
Cable Systems (1):
New York: BLENHEIM.

MIDDLE TENNESSEE BROADBAND
Box 99
College Grove, TN 37046
Phone: 877-368-2110
Web site: http://www.midtnbb.com
Cable Systems (1):
Tennessee: ROGERSVILLE.

MID-HUDSON CABLEVISION INC.
PO Box 399
200 Jefferson Heights
Catskill, NY 12414
Phones: 518-943-6600; 800-342-5400
Fax: 518-943-6603
E-mail: info@mhcable.com; cable@mid-hudson.com
Web site: http://www.mhcable.net
Officers:
James M. Reynolds, Chief Executive Officer
Jeff Rose, Chief Financial Officer
Stuart W. Smith, Operations Manager
Joanne Miller, Marketing & Programming Director
Edward D. Harter, Engineering Director
Cable Systems (2):
New York: CATSKILL; WINDHAM.

MID-KANSAS CABLE SERVICES INC.
805 North Main St.
McPherson, KS 67460-2839
Phones: 620-241-6955; 620-345-2831
Fax: 620-345-6106
Officers:
Carl Krehbiel, President
Kathryn Krehbiel, Secretary-Treasurer
Harry Weelborg, General Manager
Ownership: Carl C Krehbiel Trust, 50%; Kathryn Krehbiel Trust, 50%.
Cable Systems (1):
Kansas: MOUNDRIDGE.
Other Holdings:
Cellular radio
Telephone holdings

MID-RIVERS TELEPHONE COOPERATIVE INC.
PO Box 280
904 C Ave.
Circle, MT 59215
Phones: 406-485-3301; 800-452-2288
Fax: 406-485-2924
E-mail: customerservices@midrivers.com; tac@midrivers.coop
Web site: http://www.midrivers.com
Officers:
Bill Wade, General Manager
Aaron Arthur, Plant Manager
Ownership: Cooperative--Circle, MT.
Cable Systems (10):
Montana: BAKER; GLENDIVE; HARLOWTON; HYSHAM; JORDAN; LEWISTOWN; MILES CITY; ROUNDUP; SIDNEY (town); WIBAUX.
Other Holdings:
Cellular radio
Telephone holdings

MIDSTATE COMMUNICATIONS
PO Box 48
120 East 1st St.
Kimball, SD 57355
Phone: 605-778-6221
Fax: 605-778-8080
Web site: http://www.midstatesd.net
Branch Office:
Chamberlain
107 S. Main St
Chamberlain, SD 57325
Phone: 605-234-8000
Cable Systems (1):
South Dakota: WHITE LAKE.

MID-STATE COMMUNITY TV INC.
1001 12th St.
Aurora, NE 68818
Phones: 402-694-5101; 800-821-1831
Fax: 402-694-2848
E-mail: midstate@midstatetv.com
Web site: http://www.midstatetv.com
Officers:
Phillip C. Nelson, President
Betty Van Luchene, Secretary
Pat Phillips, Marketing Director
Tim Granfield, Engineering Director
Ownership: Phillip C Nelson. Nelson is Pres. of the Hamilton Telephone Co., Aurora, NE.
Cable Systems (6):
Nebraska: AURORA; DONIPHAN; GILTNER; HORDVILLE; MARQUETTE; TRUMBULL.

MIDSTATE TELEPHONE & COMMUNICATIONS
PO Box 400
215 Main St. South
Stanley, ND 58784
Phone: 701-628-2522
Fax: 701-628-3737
E-mail: drmm@midstatetel.com
Web site: http://www.midstatetel.com
Ownership: Wilhelmi Family..
Cable Systems (1):
North Dakota: STANLEY.

MIDVALE TELEPHONE EXCHANGE INC.
PO Box 7
2205 Keithly Creek Rd.
Midvale, ID 83645
Phones: 208-355-2211; 800-462-4523
Fax: 208-355-2222
E-mail: info@mtecom.net
Web site: http://www.mtecom.net
Officers:
Lane Williams, President & Chief Operating Officer
Mary Williams, Chief Financial Officer
John Stuart, Engineering Director
Cable Systems (1):
Idaho: MIDVALE.

MILAN INTERACTIVE COMMUNICATIONS
PO Box 240
312 South Main
Milan, MO 63556
Phone: 660-265-7174
Officers:
Rick Gardener, President & General Manager
Sara Gardener, Vice President
Cable Systems (3):
Missouri: CLARENCE; MILAN; RENICK.

MILESTONE COMMUNICATIONS LP
43 Herrn Ln.
Castle Rock, CO 80108
Phone: 303-993-3557
Fax: 303-993-3559
E-mail: mdrake@milestonecomminc.com

Cable Owners

Web site: http://www.milestonecomminc.com
Officer:
Michael Drake, President
Ownership: Michael W. Drake.
Represented (legal): Cinnamon Mueller.
Cable Systems (1):
West Virginia: HUNTERSVILLE.

MILFORD COMMUNICATIONS
906 Okoboji Ave.
Milford, IA 51351
Phone: 855-722-3450
E-mail: fbulk@milfordcomm.net;
 infoweb@milfordcomm.net
Web site: http://milfordcomm.net
Ownership: Frank Bulk.
Cable Systems (4):
Iowa: BLAIRSBURG; LIVERMORE; MILFORD; THOR.

MILLENNIUM TELCOM LLC
4700 Keller Hicks Rd.
Fort Worth, TX 76244
Phones: 817-745-2000; 877-210-3007
Fax: 817-745-2029
Officer:
Dorothy Young, Senior Manager, Business Compliance
Cable Systems (1):
Texas: KELLER.

RAY V. MILLER GROUP
9449 State Hwy. 197 S
Burnsville, NC 28714
Phones: 828-682-4074; 800-722-4074
Fax: 828-682-6895
Web site: http://ccvn.com
Officers:
Ray V. Miller, Chairman
Randall Miller, President
Bryan Hyder, Secretary-Treasurer
John Dickson, Chief Technology Officer
Represented (legal): Cole, Raywid & Braverman LLP.
Cable Systems (1):
North Carolina: BURNSVILLE.

V. DAVID & BILLIE LYNN MILLER
PO Box 509
Warner, OK 74469
Phone: 918-463-2921
Fax: 918-463-2551
Officers:
V. David Miller, President, Chief Executive & Operating Officer
Kim Collins, Chief Financial Officer
Billie L. Miller, Vice President & Secretary-Treasurer
V. David Miller II, Marketing Director
Edward Smith, Programming Director
Troy R. Duncan, Engineering Director
Represented (legal): Ronald Comingdeer.
Cable Systems (1):
Oklahoma: WARNER.

MILLHEIM TV TRANSMISSION CO.
PO Box 365
Millheim, PA 16854
Phone: 814-349-4837
Officers:
Earl Heckman, President
Harold Benfer, Secretary-Treasurer & Manager
Ownership: Subscriber owned--Millheim, PA.

Cable Systems (1):
Pennsylvania: MILLHEIM.

MINBURN CABLEVISION INC.
PO Box 206
416 Chestnut St.
Minburn, IA 50167-0206
Phones: 515-677-2264; 877-386-2933
Fax: 515-677-2007
E-mail: minburn@minburncomm.com
Web site: http://www.minburncomm.com
Officers:
Greg Burket, President
William Wright, Vice President
R. N. Flam, General Manager
Michele Blair, Secretary-Treasurer
David Book, Director
Greg Burket, Director

Branch Office:
Woodward
100 South Main St
PO Box 515
Woodward, IA 50276
Phone: 515-438-2200
Fax: 515-438-2933
Ownership: Minburn Telephone Co..
Cable Systems (1):
Iowa: MINBURN.

MINERVA VALLEY CABLEVISION INC.
PO Box 176
104 North Pine St.
Zearing, IA 50278
Phone: 641-487-7399
Fax: 641-487-7599
E-mail: minerva@netins.net
Web site: http://www.minervavalley.com
Cable Systems (1):
Iowa: ZEARING.

MITCHELL TELECOM
Ste 25
1801 North Main St.
Mitchell, SD 57301
Phone: 605-990-1000
Fax: 605-990-1010
E-mail: info@mitchelltelecom.com
Web site: http://www.mitchelltelecom.com
Officer:
Ryan Thompson, Chief Executive Officer & General Manager
Cable Systems (1):
South Dakota: MITCHELL.

MLGC
PO Box 66
301 Dewey St.
Enderlin, ND 58027
Phones: 701-437-3300; 877-893-6542
Fax: 701-437-3022
E-mail: mandl@mlgc.com
Web site: http://www.mlgc.com
Officer:
Tyler Kilder, Vice President

Branch Office:
Cooperstown
905 Lenham Ave SE
Cooperstown, ND 58425
Phone: 701-797-3300
Fax: 701-797-2541
Cable Systems (1):
North Dakota: ENDERLIN.

MM & G ENTERPRISES LLC
1910 Mockingbird Ln.
Paragould, AR 72450

Phone: 870-215-3456
Fax: 870-586-0675
E-mail: support@fusionmedia.tv
Web site: http://www.fusionmedia.tv
Cable Systems (1):
Arkansas: OAK GROVE HEIGHTS.

MOBIUS COMMUNICATIONS CO.
PO Box 246
523 Niobrara Ave.
Hemingford, NE 69348
Phones: 308-487-5500; 877-266-2487
E-mail: info@bbc.net
Web site: http://bbc.net
Ownership: Hemingford Cooperative Telephone Co..
Cable Systems (2):
Nebraska: CRAWFORD; HEMINGFORD.

CITY OF MONROE, WATER, LIGHT & GAS COMMISSION
PO Box 725
215 North Broad St.
Monroe, GA 30655
Phone: 770-267-3429
Fax: 770-267-3698
Web site: http://www.monroega.com/departments/utility-department
Officers:
Coleman P. Hood, Interim Superintendent
Bobby Morrow, Engineering & Operations Manager
Deborah M. Kirk, Administrative Assistant
Charlotte Hester, Clerk
Ownership: Community owned--Monroe, GA.
Represented (legal): Preston & Malcolm.
Cable Systems (1):
Georgia: MONROE.

MONTANASKY WEST LLC
PO Box 709
912 West 9th St.
Libby, MT 59923
Phone: 406-293-4335
E-mail: sales@montanasky.tv
Web site: http://www.montanasky.tv
Officer:
Frederick Weber, General Manager
Cable Systems (2):
Montana: LIBBY; TROY.

MONTEZUMA MUTUAL TELEPHONE CO.
PO Box 10
107 North 4th St.
Montezuma, IA 50171
Phone: 641-623-5654
Fax: 641-623-2199
E-mail: motel1@netins.net
Cable Systems (1):
Iowa: DEEP RIVER.

MOOSEHEAD ENTERPRISES INC.
3 Lakeview St.
Greenville, ME 04441
Phone: 207-695-3337
Fax: 207-695-3571
Officers:
Scott Richardson, Chairman & Chief Executive Officer
Earl Richardson Jr., President & Chief Operating & Financial Officer
Ownership: Earl Richardson.
Cable Systems (6):
Maine: BINGHAM; GREENVILLE; GUILFORD; JACKMAN; MONSON; ROCKWOOD.
Other Holdings:
SMATV

MOREHEAD STATE U.
Dept. of Telecommunications
110 Ginger Hall
Morehead, KY 40351
Phones: 606-783-9090; 800-585-6781
Web site: http://www.moreheadstate.edu
Cable Systems (1):
Kentucky: MOREHEAD STATE UNIVERSITY.

CITY OF MORGANTON
Ste A100
305 East Union St.
Morganton, NC 28655
Phone: 828-438-5353
Fax: 828-432-2532
E-mail: compasdept@ci.morganton.nc.us
Web site: http://compas.compascable.net
Officer:
Randy Loop, General Manager
Ownership: Community owned--Morganton, NC..
Cable Systems (1):
North Carolina: MORGANTON.

WAYNE E. MORGAN
85 Cordell Ln.
Coos Bay, OR 97420
Phone: 503-267-4788
Cable Systems (1):
Oregon: GREEN ACRES.

MORRIS COMMUNICATIONS CO LLC
725 Broad St.
Augusta, GA 30901
Phones: 800-622-6358; 706-724-0851
E-mail: morrisdigital@morris.com
Web site: http://www.morriscomm.com
Officers:
William S Morris III, Chairman & Chief Executive Officer
James C Currow, Executive Vice President, Newspapers
Craig S Mitchell, Senior Vice President, Finance & Secretary-Treasurer
Steve K Stone, Senior Vice President & Chief Financial Officer
Susan Morris Baker, Vice President
Terry K House Jr., Assistant Secretary & Tax Director
Ownership: Privately held..
Cable Systems (2):
North Carolina: HENDERSONVILLE; WEST JEFFERSON.
Other Holdings:
Juneau Empire, Peninsula Clarion (Kenai). Newspaper
Magazine: Publishes 21 periodicals through Morris Magazines plus 41 magazines and shoppers through Morris Publishing Group.
Outdoor advertising: Fairway Outdoor Advertising.
Publishing holdings: Globe Pequot Press
Radio holdings

MOULTRIE TELECOMMUNICATIONS INC.
PO Box 350
111 State & Broadway
Lovington, IL 61937
Phone: 217-873-5211
Fax: 217-873-4990
Web site: http://www.moultriemulticorp.com
Officers:
David A. Bowers, President & Chief Financial Officer
Jamie Frantz, Marketing Director
Represented (legal): John V. Freeman.

2017 Edition
D-913

Cable Owners

Cable Systems (1):
Illinois: LOVINGTON.

TOWN OF MOUNTAIN VILLAGE
Ste A
455 Mountain Village Blvd.
Mountain Village, CO 81435
Phone: 970-728-8000
E-mail: info@mvcable.net
Web site: http://townofmountainvillage.com/residents/utilities/cable/
Officers:
Kim Montgomery, Town Manager
Jackie Kennefick, Administartion Director/Town Clerk
Susan Johnston, Deputy Town Clerk
Steve Lehane, Broadband Services Director
Cable Systems (1):
Colorado: MOUNTAIN VILLAGE.

MOUNTAIN ZONE TV SYSTEMS
307 East Avenue E
Alpine, TX 79830
Phones: 432-837-2300; 432-837-5423
E-mail: mtnzone@sbcglobal.net
Web site: http://www.mountainzonetv.net
Officer:
Steve Neu, Manager
Represented (legal): Cinnamon Mueller.
Cable Systems (6):
Texas: BALMORHEA; FORT DAVIS; MARATHON; MARFA; PRESIDIO; SANDERSON.

MOUNT BAKER CABLE
PO Box 29534
Bellingham, WA 98228
Phones: 360-966-7502; 877-396-3016
E-mail: dan@mtbakercable.com
Web site: http://www.mtbakercable.com
Ownership: Dan Adams.
Cable Systems (2):
Washington: LUMMI ISLAND; ORCAS ISLAND.

MULLAN CABLE TV INC.
PO Box 615
202 North 2nd St.
Mullan, ID 83846
Phone: 208-744-1223
Fax: 208-556-5609
E-mail: cs@mctvusa.tv
Web site: http://www.mctvusa.tv
Officer:
James R. Dahl, Chairman & President
Ownership: James R. Dahl, Chmn. & Pres.
Cable Systems (1):
Idaho: MULLAN.

MURRAY ELECTRIC SYSTEM
PO Box 1095
401 Olive St.
Murray, KY 42071-1095
Phone: 270-753-5312
Fax: 270-753-6494
E-mail: murrayelectric@murray-ky.net
Web site: http://www2.murray-ky.net
Officers:
Tony Thompson, General Manager
David Richardson, Broadband Manager
Terry McCallon, Engineer
Brittney Houston, Sales & Marketing Coordinator
Cable Systems (1):
Kentucky: MURRAY.

MUSCATINE POWER & WATER
PO Box 899
3205 Cedar St.
Muscatine, IA 52761-0075

Phone: 563-263-2631
Fax: 563-262-3373
E-mail: onlinecs@mpw.org
Web site: http://www.mpw.org
Officer:
Salvatore L. LoBianco, General Manager
Cable Systems (1):
Iowa: MUSCATINE.

MUTUAL DATA SERVICES
319 North Clinton Ave.
St Johns, MI 48879
Phone: 989-224-6839
E-mail: mdssupport@mutualdata.com
Web site: http://www.mutualdata.com
Officer:
Barry C Buchholtz Jr, General Manager
Cable Systems (1):
Michigan: MAPLE RAPIDS.

MUTUAL TELEPHONE CO.
365 Main St.
Little River, KS 67457
Phones: 620-897-6200; 877-216-9951
Web site: http://mtc4me.com
Officers:
Jimmy Todd, General Manager
Heath Eberle, Operations Manager
Shayla Grasser, Marketing & Sales Manager
Cable Systems (1):
Kansas: MARQUETTE.

MWR CABLE
599 Tomales Rd.
Petaluma, CA 94952-5000
Phone: 707-765-7343
Fax: 707-765-7329
Officer:
Larry Streeter, Manager
Cable Systems (1):
California: PETALUMA COAST GUARD STATION.

NEBRASKA CENTRAL TELECOM INC.
PO Box 700
22 LaBarre St.
Gibbon, NE 68840
Phone: 888-873-6282
Fax: 308-468-9929
E-mail: customer-service@nctc.net
Web site: http://www.nctc.net
Cable Systems (1):
Nebraska: BURWELL.

CITY OF NEGAUNEE CABLE TV
225 North Pioneer Ave.
Negaunee, MI 49866
Phone: 906-464-6064
Fax: 906-475-9994
E-mail: utilitybilling@cityofnegaunee.com
Web site: http://www.negauneecable.com
Officers:
Tom Manninen, General Manager
Rick Kunath, Chief Technology Officer
Ownership: Community owned--Negaunee, MI.
Cable Systems (1):
Michigan: NEGAUNEE.

NELSON COUNTY CABLEVISION CORP.
PO Box 219
Nellysford, VA 22958
Phone: 434-263-4805
Fax: 434-263-4821
E-mail: info@cyberwind.net
Web site: http://www.nelsoncable.com
Officers:

Joe Lee McClellan, Chairman & President
W. Burkes Fortune, Vice President & Treasurer
Ownership: Joe Lee McClellan.
Cable Systems (2):
Virginia: LOVINGSTON/SHIPMAN; WINTERGREEN.

NELSON TELEPHONE COOPERATIVE
PO Box 228
318 3rd Ave. West
Durand, WI 54736
Phones: 715-672-4204; 855-672-6832
Fax: 715-672-4344
E-mail: admin@nelson-tel.net
Web site: http://www.ntec.net
Officers:
Christy Berger, Executive Vice President & General Manager
Laura Gullickson, Chief Financial Officer
Larry Johnson, Sales & Marketing
Cable Systems (1):
Wisconsin: ARKANSAW.

NELSONVILLE TV CABLE INC.
One West Columbus St.
Nelsonville, OH 45764
Phones: 740-753-2686; 740-767-2203
Fax: 740-753-3326
Web site: http://www.nelsonvilletv.com
Officers:
Eugene R. Edwards, President
Betty Edwards, Secretary-Treasurer
Ownership: Eugene R Edwards, 99.6%; Betty Edwards, 0.4%.
Cable Systems (1):
Ohio: NELSONVILLE.

NEMONT TELEPHONE COOP
PO Box 600
61 Hwy. 13 South
Scobey, MT 59263-0600
Phone: 800-636-6680
Fax: 406-783-5283
E-mail: nemont@nemont.coop
Web site: http://www.nemont.net
Officers:
Mike Kilgore, Chief Executive Officer
Remi Sun, Chief Financial Officer
Cable Systems (2):
Montana: GLASGOW; WOLF POINT.

NEW CENTURY COMMUNICATIONS
3588 Kennebec Dr.
Eagan, MN 55122
Phone: 651-688-2623
Fax: 651-688-2624
Officers:
Robert Smith, President
Richard Anderson, Vice President
Ownership: Cable Systems Services.
Cable Systems (14):
Iowa: DELHI (town); LUXEMBURG; WORTHINGTON.
Minnesota: ROUND LAKE TWP..
Wisconsin: BANCROFT; BRIGGSVILLE; GRANTON; KELLNERSVILLE; MARQUETTE; MILLADORE (town); OXFORD; PACKWAUKEE; SAXEVILLE; WOLF RIVER.

NEW HOPE TELEPHONE COOPERATIVE
PO Box 452
5415 Main Dr.
New Hope, AL 35760
Phones: 256-723-4211; 877-474-4211
Fax: 256-723-2800
E-mail: support@nehp.net; info@nehp.net
Web site: http://nhtc.coop

Officers:
Tom Wing, General Manager
Tammy Weeks, Office Manager
Steve Campbell, Central Office Manager
Cable Systems (1):
Alabama: NEW HOPE.

NEW KNOXVILLE TELEPHONE & CABLE CO.
PO Box 219
301 West South St.
New Knoxville, OH 45871
Phones: 419-753-5000; 419-629-1424
Fax: 419-753-2950
E-mail: info@nktelco.net
Web site: http://www.nktelco.net
Officers:
Preston Meyer, General Manager
Erin Brown, Sales & Marketing Director
Cable Systems (2):
Ohio: NEW KNOXVILLE; ST. HENRY.

TOM NEWMAN
PO Box 3
Waterfall, PA 16689
Phone: 814-685-3464
Cable Systems (1):
Pennsylvania: WATERFALL.

NEW PARIS TELEPHONE CO.
PO Box 47
19066 Market St.
New Paris, IN 46553
Phones: 574-831-2176; 574-831-2225
E-mail: qualcabl@bnin.net; info@nptel.com
Web site: http://www.nptel.com
Officers:
Mark Grady, Vice President
Myrna Rapp, Chief Financial Officer
Donald E. Johnson, Marketing Director
Dan Cox, Engineering Director
Cable Systems (1):
Indiana: NEW PARIS.

NEW RIVER CABLEVISION INC.
11401 SW State Rte. 231-235
Brooker, FL 32622
Phone: 352-485-1362
Fax: 352-485-1352
Officer:
Tom Hulett, President
Ownership: Cable Diversified Installations.
Cable Systems (1):
Florida: BROOKER.

NEW ULM TELECOM
PO Box 697
27 North Minnesota St.
New Ulm, MN 56073
Phones: 507-354-4111; 844-354-4111
Fax: 507-233-4242
E-mail: on-linecustservice@nu-telcom.net
Web site: http://www.nutelecom.net
Officers:
Bill Otis, President & Chief Executive Officer
Barbara Bornhoft, Chief Operating Officer & Vice President
Curtis Kawlweski, Chief Financial Officer & Treasurer
Branch Office:
Litchfield
421 S. CSAH 34
PO Box 678
Litchfield, MN 55355-0678
Phone: 320-593-2323
Ownership: New Ulm Telecom Inc..
Cable Systems (6):
Iowa: AURELIA.

D-914

TV & Cable Factbook No. 85

Cable Owners

Minnesota: COLOGNE; GLENCOE; JEFFERS; MAYER; NEW ULM.

NEWWAVE COMMUNICATIONS LLC
One Montgomery Plz., 4th Fl
Sikeston, MO 63801
Phones: 573-472-9500; 844-456-3278
Fax: 573-481-9809
E-mail: info@newwavecom.com
Web site: http://www.newwavecom.com
Officers:
Phil Spencer, President & Chief Executive Officer
Keith Davidson, Chief Financial Officer
Larry Eby, Senior Vice President, Operations
Cable Systems (62):
Arkansas: ASHDOWN.
Illinois: ANNA; ARGENTA; BENTON; CAIRO; EVANSVILLE; JERSEYVILLE; McLEANSBORO; MOWEAQUA; NEWTON; SPARTA; TAMMS; TAYLORVILLE; WESTVILLE.
Indiana: AVILLA; COVINGTON; ELBERFELD; FLORA; JASONVILLE; MONROEVILLE; MORGAN COUNTY (portions); MORGANTOWN; NEWPORT; SPENCER COUNTY (portions); VINCENNES.
Louisiana: BELLE CHASSE; BLANCHARD; CALHOUN; COLUMBIA; FARMERVILLE; HAYNESVILLE; LAKE PROVIDENCE; LOGANSPORT; MANSFIELD; MONROE; SPRINGHILL; WINNSBORO; WISNER.
Mississippi: ANGUILLA; ARCOLA; HOLLANDALE; LELAND; QUITMAN; WAYNESBORO.
Missouri: DEXTER; POPLAR BLUFF.
Texas: ANGLETON; BLACKWELL; CLEVELAND; GRAPE CREEK; HEMPSTEAD; JASPER; KINGSVILLE; LA GRANGE; MERKEL; ROBERT LEE; ROSCOE; SEALY; SOUR LAKE; TUSCOLA; WHARTON; WOODVILLE.

NEX-TECH
PO Box 158
145 North Main St.
Lenora, KS 67645-0158
Phones: 785-567-4281; 877-625-7872
Fax: 785-567-4401
E-mail: webmaster@nex-tech.com
Web site: http://www.nex-tech.com
Ownership: Rural Telephone Service Co., see listing.
Cable Systems (20):
Kansas: AGRA; ALMENA; BURR OAK; COURTLAND; EDMOND; GRAINFIELD; HILL CITY; KENSINGTON; KIRWIN; LEBANON; MUNJOR; NATOMA; NORCATUR; NORTON; PHILLIPSBURG; PLAINVILLE; SMITH CENTER; STOCKTON; VICTORIA; WOODSTON.

NEXTGEN COMMUNICATIONS
PO Box 398
234 East Oak St.
Glenwood City, WI 54013
Phones: 715-565-7742; 888-696-9146
Fax: 715-565-3001
E-mail: nextgen@nextgen-communications.net
Web site: http://nextgen-communications.net
Cable Systems (2):
Wisconsin: BOYCEVILLE; GLENWOOD CITY.

NITTANY MEDIA INC.
PO Box 111
18 Juniata St.
Lewistown, PA 17044-2048
Phones: 717-248-3733; 800-692-7401
Fax: 717-248-3732
E-mail: info@nittanymedia.com
Web site: http://www.nittanymedia.com
Ownership: Harry J Hain; Anna A Hain, Principals.

Cable Systems (2):
Pennsylvania: McCLURE; MIFFLINTOWN.

NORTEX COMMUNICATIONS
PO Box 587
205 North Walnut St.
Muenster, TX 76252
Phone: 940-759-2251
Fax: 940-759-5557
Web site: http://www.nortex.com
Officers:
Alvin M. Fuhrman, President
Joey Anderson, Vice President, Operations
Alan Rohmer, Vice President, Finance
Ownership: Alvin M Fuhrman, 50%; Ellen G Fuhrman, 50%. Fuhrmans are affiliated with the Nortex Communications Co., Muenster, TX.
Cable Systems (1):
Texas: VALLEY VIEW.

NORTH CENTRAL TELEPHONE COOPERATIVE
PO Box 70
872 Hwy. 52 Bypass East
Lafayette, TN 37083
Phones: 615-666-2151; 615-644-6282
Fax: 615-666-2182
E-mail: customersvc@nctc.com
Web site: http://www.nctc.com
Officers:
Nancy White, Chief Executive Officer
Johnny McClanahan, Vice President, Finance & Administrative Services
Cable Systems (1):
Kentucky: SCOTTSVILLE.

NORTHEAST IOWA TELEPHONE CO.
PO Box 835
800 South Main St.
Monona, IA 52159
Phones: 563-539-2122; 877-638-2122
Fax: 563-539-2003
E-mail: neitel@neitel.com; cabletv@neitel.com
Web site: http://neitel.com
Officers:
Keith Mohs, President
Arlyn Schroeder, Secretary-Treasurer
Cable Systems (1):
Iowa: MONONA.

NORTHEAST LOUISIANA TELEPHONE CO. INC.
PO Drawer 185
6402 Howell Ave.
Collinston, LA 71229
Phones: 318-874-7011; 888-318-1998
Fax: 318-874-2041
E-mail: info@ne-tel.com
Web site: http://www.northeasttel.net
Officers:
Rector L. Hopgood, President
William A. Norsworthy, Vice President
Dorothy Anne George, Secretary
Mike George, Treasurer
Ownership: Rector L Hopgood, 50%; William A Norsworthy, 50%.
Cable Systems (1):
Louisiana: COLLINSTON.

NORTHEAST NEBRASKA TELEPHONE CO.
PO Box 66
Jackson, NE 68743-0066
Phone: 888-397-4321
E-mail: egraffis@nntc.net

Web site: http://www.nntc.net
Officers:
Emory Graffis, General Manager
Pat McElroy, Assistant General Manager
Cable Systems (1):
Nebraska: CLARKS.

NORTHERN ARKANSAS TELEPHONE CO.
Box 209
301 East Main St.
Flippin, AR 72634
Phones: 870-453-8800; 800-775-6682
Fax: 870-453-7171
E-mail: steven@natconet.com
Web site: http://www.natconet.com
Officers:
Steve Smith, Business Manager
Travis Sullivan, Plant Manager
Meghan Ward, Marketing Coordinator
Cable Systems (1):
Arkansas: DIAMOND CITY.

NORTHLAND COMMUNICATIONS CORP.
Ste 700
101 Stewart St.
Seattle, WA 98101
Phone: 206-621-1351
Fax: 206-623-9015
Web site: http://www.yournorthland.com
Officers:
John S. Whetzell, Chairman & Chief Executive Officer
Gary S. Jones, President
Richard I. Clark, Executive Vice President
Richard J. Dyste, Senior Vice President & Technical Services
Rick J. McElwee, Vice President & Controller
H. Lee Johnson, Director & Vice President, Southeast Operations
Paul Milan, Vice President & Senior Counsel
John E. Iverson, Secretary
R. Gregory Ferrer, Treasurer

Branch Office:
32 E. Vine
Statesboro, GA 30458
Phone: 912-489-1065
Represented (legal): Cole, Raywid & Braverman LLP; Cairncross & Hempelman.
Cable Systems (31):
Alabama: ALICEVILLE.
California: COARSEGOLD; MARIPOSA; MOUNT SHASTA; OAKHURST; YREKA.
Georgia: STATESBORO; SWAINSBORO; VIDALIA.
Idaho: SANDPOINT.
North Carolina: FOREST CITY; HIGHLANDS.
South Carolina: EDGEFIELD; GREENWOOD; SALUDA; SENECA.
Texas: CORSICANA; CROCKETT; FAIRFIELD; HAMILTON; HILLSBORO; LAMESA; LLANO; MADISONVILLE; MARBLE FALLS; MARLIN; MEXIA; STEPHENVILLE.
Washington: EPHRATA; MOSES LAKE; OTHELLO.

NORTHSIDE TV CORP.
521 Vulcan St.
Iron Mountain, MI 49801-2333
Phone: 906-774-1351
E-mail: judyann@upnorthcable.com
Web site: http://www.upnorthcable.com
Ownership: Subscriber owned--Iron Mountain.
Cable Systems (1):
Michigan: IRON MOUNTAIN.

NORTHSTAR BROADBAND LLC
PO Box 2576
Post Falls, ID 83877

Phones: 208-262-9394; 800-572-0902
E-mail: j.webb@northstarbroadband.net
Web site: http://www.northstarbroadband.net
Officers:
Greg Lundwall, General Operations
Jennifer Webb, Office Manager
Cable Systems (11):
Washington: CONNELL; DAVENPORT; DEER PARK; DIAMOND LAKE; IONE; LIND; METALINE FALLS; ODESSA (town); RITZVILLE; TEKOA; WARDEN.

NORTHSTATE CABLEVISION CO.
PO Box 297
180 NE 2nd St.
Dufur, OR 97021
Phone: 541-467-2409
Officers:
J. W. Damon, President
Barbara Damon, Vice President
Helen Saunders, Secretary-Treasurer
Cable Systems (1):
Oregon: DUFUR.
Other Holdings:
Telephone holdings

NORTH TEXAS BROADBAND
PO Box 676
Aubery, TX 76227
Phones: 940-365-2030; 888-365-2930
E-mail: customerservice@northtxbroadband.com
Web site: http://northtxbroadband.com
Cable Systems (2):
Texas: CADDO PEAK; EGAN.

NORTHWEST COMMUNICATIONS COOPERATIVE
PO Box 38
111 Railroad Ave.
Ray, ND 58849
Phone: 800-245-5884
Fax: 701-568-7777
E-mail: ncc@nccray.com
Web site: http://www.nccray.com
Officer:
Dean Rustad, Operations Manager
Ownership: Estate of G. Russell Chambers, 33.3%; Francis E Martin, 33.3%; Thomas E Bird, 33.3%.
Cable Systems (1):
North Dakota: RAY.
Other Holdings:
Telephone

NORTHWEST COMMUNITY COMMUNICATIONS
116 Harriman Ave. North
Amery, WI 54001
Phone: 715-268-7101
Fax: 715-268-9194
E-mail: info@nwcomm.net
Web site: http://www.nwcomm.net
Ownership: Amery Telcom.
Cable Systems (3):
Wisconsin: AMERY; NEW RICHMOND; SOLON SPRINGS.
Other Holdings:
Telephone

NORTHWEST TELEPHONE COOPERATIVE ASSOCIATION
844 Wood St.
Havelock, IA 50546
Phones: 712-776-2222; 800-247-2776
Fax: 712-776-4444
E-mail: nis@ncn.net
Web site: http://northwest.coop
Officers:

2017 Edition

D-915

Cable Owners

Don Miller, Chief Executive Officer
Chase Cox, Chief Technical Officer
Sheila Akridge, Marketing/Customer Service Manager
Andy Wilta, Plant Manager
Cable Systems (1):
Iowa: HAVELOCK.
Cable Holdings:
Ayrshire Communications, see listing.

CITY OF NORWAY CATV
PO Box 99
1000 Saginaw St.
Norway, MI 49870
Phones: 906-563-9961; 906-563-9641
Fax: 906-563-7502
E-mail: catv@norwaymi.com
Web site: http://www.norwaymi.com/2173/Cable-Department
Officers:
Mark Isackson, Manager
James Bryner, Chief Technician
Ownership: Community owned--Norway, MI.
Cable Systems (1):
Michigan: NORWAY.

NORWOOD LIGHT BROADBAND
206 Central St.
Norwood, MA 02062
Phone: 781-948-1150
E-mail: business@norwoodlight.com
Web site: http://www.norwoodlight.com
Cable Systems (1):
Massachusetts: NORWOOD.

NOVA CABLEVISION INC.
PO Box 1412
677 West Main St.
Galesburg, IL 61402
Phones: 309-342-9681; 800-397-6682
Fax: 309-342-4408
E-mail: cableme@novalnet.com
Web site: http://www.novacablevision.com
Officers:
Robert G. Fischer Jr., Chief Executive, Operating & Financial Officer
Susan Ray, Marketing & Programming Director
Dave West, Engineering Director
Ownership: Robert G Fischer Jr., Chief Exec. & Operating Officer.
Cable Systems (12):
Illinois: CAMERON; GLADSTONE; IPAVA; KEITHSBURG; KIRKWOOD; LAKE BRACKEN; LITTLE YORK; NEW BOSTON; NORTH HENDERSON; TRIVOLI; VERMONT; WEE-MA-TUK HILLS.

RANDY NOVAKOVICH
215 North B St.
Bridger, MT 59014
Phone: 406-662-3516
E-mail: randy@brmt.net
Web site: http://www.brmt.net
Cable Systems (1):
Montana: BRIDGER.

RICHARD A NOWAK
PO Box 509
Bellaire, OH 43906
Phone: 740-676-6377
E-mail: cs@bellaire.tv
Web site: http://www.bellaire.tv
Cable Systems (1):
Ohio: WEST BELLAIRE.

STEPHEN NOWELL
PO Box 345
Hwy. 45
Trenton, TN 38382

Phone: 731-855-2808
Fax: 731-855-9512
Cable Systems (1):
Tennessee: TRENTON.

NSIGHT TELSERVICES
450 Security Blvd.
Green Bay, WI 54313
Phones: 920-617-7000; 800-826-5215
Fax: 920-826-5911
E-mail: tammy.vandenbusch@nsight.com
Web site: http://www.nsighttel.com
Officers:
Pat Riordan, President & Chief Executive Officer
Bob Riordan, Executive Vice President & Director of Corporate Development
Cable Systems (1):
Wisconsin: PULASKI.

NUSHAGAK COOPERATIVE INC.
PO Box 350
557 Kenny Wren Rd.
Dillingham, AK 99576
Phones: 907-842-5251; 800-478-5296
Fax: 907-842-2799
E-mail: nushtel@nushtel.com
Web site: http://www.nushtel.com
Officers:
Nick Wahl, President
Frank Corbin, Chief Executive Officer
Pete Andrew, Vice President
Rae Belle S. Whitcomb, Secretary
Mary Ford, Treasurer
Jana Lamb, Executive Secretary
Jim Timmerman, Board Member
Nancy Favors, Customer Service Manager
Mary Ford, Board Member
Matt Dinon, Board Member
Cable Systems (1):
Alaska: DILLINGHAM.

NU-TELECOM
PO Box 697
22 South Marshall
Springfield, MN 56087-0697
Phones: 507-723-4211; 888-873-6853
Fax: 507-723-4377
E-mail: on-linecustservice@nu-telcom.net
Web site: http://www.nutelecom.net
Officer:
Bill Otis, President & Chief Executive Officer

Branch Offices:
221 Main St
Aurelia, IA 51005
Phone: 712-434-5989
Fax: 712-434-5555
137 E 2nd St
Redwood Falls, MN 56283
Phone: 507-627-4111
Fax: 507-627-4110
22 S Marshall
Springfield, MN 56087
Phone: 507-723-4211
Fax: 507-723-4377
421 S CSAH 34
Litchfield, MN 55355-0678
Phone: 320-593-2323
Fax: 320-593-6211
235 Franklin St SW
PO Box 279
Hutchinson, MN 55350-0279
Phone: 320-587-2323
Fax: 320-587-6211

Cable Systems (2):
Minnesota: GOODHUE; SLEEPY EYE.

NWS COMMUNICATIONS
79 Mainline Dr.
Westfield, MA 01086-1416
Phone: 800-562-7081
Fax: 413-562-5415
E-mail: deleo@nwscorp.net; info@nwscorp.net
Web site: http://www.nwscorp.net
Officer:
Douglas J De Leo, Founder
Cable Systems (1):
California: SAN DIEGO NAVAL BASE.

OAK RUN ASSOCIATES LTD
10983 SW 89th Ave.
Ocala, FL 34481-9722
Phones: 352-854-3223; 866-917-4227
Web site: http://www.deccacable.net
Cable Systems (1):
Florida: OCALA/OAK RUN.

OGDEN TELEPHONE CO.
PO Box 457
202 West Walnut St.
Ogden, IA 50212
Phones: 515-275-2050; 877-818-2050
Fax: 515-275-2599
Web site: http://www.ogdentelephone.com
Officer:
Gerald R. Anderson, Manager
Cable Systems (1):
Iowa: OGDEN.

OKLAHOMA WESTERN TELEPHONE CO.
102 East Choctaw St.
Clayton, OK 74536
Phone: 918-569-4111
E-mail: ljones.owtc@yahoo.com
Web site: http://www.oklahomawesterntelephone.com
Officer:
Linda Jones, Marketing Director
Cable Systems (1):
Oklahoma: CLAYTON.

OLIN TELEPHONE & CABLEVISION CO.
318 Jackson St.
Olin, IA 52320
Phone: 319-484-2200
Fax: 319-484-2800
E-mail: olintel@netins.net
Web site: http://www.olintelephone.com
Officer:
Rodney Cozart, General Manager
Cable Systems (1):
Iowa: OLIN.

OMNI III CABLE TV INC.
PO Box 308
226 South 4th St.
Jay, OK 74346
Phone: 918-253-4545
Fax: 918-253-3400
E-mail: brixey@grand.net
Web site: http://www.grand.net
Officers:
Teresa A. Aubrey, President
Rex Ray Brixey, Executive Vice President & Treasurer
Tim Etris, Vice President, Operations & Assistant Manager

Norma R. Holt, Vice President, Industry Relations
Sherri Stephens, Secretary
Ownership: Teresa Aubrey, 51%; Norma Holt, 49%. Aubrey & Holt are execs. with the Grand Telephone Co., Jay, OK.
Cable Systems (1):
Oklahoma: DISNEY.
Other Holdings:
Cellular radio

ONEIDA CABLEVISION
PO Box 445
129 West Hwy. 34
Oneida, IL 61467
Phone: 309-483-3111
Fax: 309-483-7777
E-mail: info@oneidatel.net
Web site: http://oneidatel.com
Officers:
Gary Peterson, President
David Olson, General Manager
Cable Systems (1):
Illinois: ONEIDA.

ONSLOW COOPERATIVE TELEPHONE ASSOCIATION
PO Box 6
102 Anamosa Ave.
Onslow, IA 52321
Phone: 563-485-2833
Fax: 563-485-3891
Officer:
Ron Fagan, Chairman
Cable Systems (1):
Iowa: ONSLOW.

OPELIKA POWER SERVICES
600 Fox Run Pkwy.
Opelika, AL 36801
Phone: 334-705-5170
Web site: http://www.opelikapower.com
Cable Systems (1):
Alabama: OPELIKA.

OPP CABLEVISION
PO Box 34
Andalusia, AL 36420
Phone: 334-222-6464
Fax: 334-222-7226
E-mail: support@oppcatv.com
Web site: http://www.oppcatv.com
Ownership: Community owned--Opp, AL..
Cable Systems (1):
Alabama: OPP.

OSAGE MUNICIPAL UTILITIES
720 Chestnut St.
Osage, IA 50461
Phone: 641-832-3731
E-mail: support@osage.net
Web site: http://osage.net
Cable Systems (1):
Iowa: OSAGE.

OTEC COMMUNICATION CO.
PO Box 427
245 West 3rd St.
Ottoville, OH 45876-0427
Phone: 419-453-3324
Fax: 419-453-2468
E-mail: tomtc@bright.net
Web site: http://www.ottovillemutual.com
Officers:
Basil Alt, President
Ray Kaufman, Secretary-Treasurer
Bill Honigford, General Manager
Ownership: Non-profit organization--Ottoville, OH.

Cable Owners

Cable Systems (1):
Ohio: OTTOVILLE.

OTELCO
505 3rd Ave. East
Oneonta, AL 35121
Phones: 205-625-3591; 800-286-4600
Fax: 205-625-3523
E-mail: support@otelco.net
Web site: http://www.otelco.net
Officer:
Robert Souza, President

Branch Offices:
Arab
PO Box 130
113 S Main St
Arab, AL 35016
Phone: 256-586-2682
Fax: 256-586-2535
Blountsville
PO Box 1049
68959 Main St
Blountsville, AL 35031
Phone: 205-429-4141
Fax: 256-586-2535
Cable Systems (1):
Alabama: ONEONTA.

PACKERLAND BROADBAND
PO Box 885
105 Kent St.
Iron Mountain, MI 49801
Phones: 906-774-6621; 800-236-8434
Fax: 906-776-2811
E-mail: support@packerlandbroadband
Web site: http://
www.packerlandbroadband.com
Ownership: CCI Systems Inc..
Cable Systems (46):
Illinois: GEM SUBURBAN MOBILE HOME PARK; UNION.
Michigan: CARNEY/POWERS; DAGGETT; MELLEN TWP.; STEPHENSON.
Wisconsin: AMBERG; AUBURNDALE; AUGUSTA; AVOCA; BONDUEL; BUTTERNUT; CECIL; COLEMAN; DARIEN; ELCHO (town); ENTERPRISE; FALL CREEK; FIFIELD; GILLETT; GLIDDEN; GOODMAN; GREENWOOD; HAWKINS (village); HOLLANDALE; JUNCTION CITY; KRAKOW; LA VALLE (village); LAKE LUCERNE; LAONA; LENA; LOMIRA; MELLEN; NICHOLS; OCONTO FALLS; PEMBINE; PITTSVILLE; PRENTICE; SURING; UPHAM; VESPER; WABENO; WASHINGTON; WAUZEKA; WHITE LAKE; WONEWOC.

PALMER MUTUAL TELEPHONE CO.
PO Box 155
306 Main St.
Palmer, IA 50571
Phones: 712-359-2411; 800-685-7417
Fax: 712-359-2200
E-mail: palmerone@PalmerOne.com
Web site: http://www.palmerone.com
Officers:
Andy Lee Peterson, President
Steve Trimble, General Manager
Cable Systems (1):
Iowa: PALMER.

PALO COOPERATIVE TELEPHONE ASSN.
PO Box 169
807 2nd St.
Palo, IA 52324
Phone: 319-851-3431
Fax: 319-851-6970
E-mail: palocoop@netins.net
Web site: http://www.gopcta.com

Officers:
Danny Gardemann, President
Richard Minor, Vice President
Todd Christophersen, Manager
Carolyn Minor, Office Manager
Mike Kuba, Secretary
Doug Yates, Treasurer
Cable Systems (1):
Iowa: PALO.

P & W TV CABLE SYSTEMS INC.
109 Depot Rd.
Paintsville, KY 41240
Phone: 606-789-7603
Fax: 606-789-3391
Cable Systems (1):
Kentucky: TUTOR KEY.

PANHANDLE TELEPHONE COOPERATIVE INC.
2222 NW Hwy. 64
Guymon, OK 73942
Phones: 580-338-2556; 800-562-2556
Fax: 508-338-8260
E-mail: support@ptsi.net
Web site: http://www.ptsi.net
Officers:
Roger Edenborough, President
Hunter Novak, Vice President
Dennis Zimmerman, Secretary-Treasurer

Branch Offices:
115 W. Main St.
Boise City, OK 73933
2222 N.W. Hwy. 64
Guymon, OK 73942
7th & Oklahoma
Laverne, OK 73933
222 S. Amherst
Perryon, TX 79070
721 W. 7th
Spearman, TX 79081
115 Douglas St.
Beaver, OK 73932
Cable Systems (1):
Oklahoma: GUYMON.

PANORA COMMUNICATIONS COOPERATIVE
PO Box 189
114 East Main St.
Panora, IA 50216
Phone: 641-755-2424
Fax: 641-755-2425
E-mail: panora@netins.net
Web site: http://www.panoratelco.com
Officers:
Andrew M. Randol, General Manager
Bill Dorsett, Plant Manager
Cable Systems (1):
Iowa: PANORA.
Other Holdings:
Cellular radio
Telephone holdings

PARAGOULD LIGHT WATER & CABLE
PO Box 9
Paragould, AR 72451
Phone: 870-239-7700
Fax: 870-239-7727
E-mail: support@paragould.net
Web site: http://www.paragould.net

Cable Systems (1):
Arkansas: PARAGOULD.

PARISH COMMUNICATIONS
PO Box 10
Auburn, MI 48611
Phones: 989-662-6811; 800-466-6444
Web site: http://www.parishonline.net
Officer:
Floyd Grocholski, General Manager
Cable Systems (4):
Michigan: FRASER TWP.; HOPE; LEE TWP. (Midland County); SPRINGVALE TWP..

PARK TV & ELECTRONICS INC.
205 East Railroad Ave.
Cissna Park, IL 60924
Phones: 815-457-2659; 800-825-3882
Fax: 815-457-2735
Web site: http://parktvcable.com
Cable Systems (12):
Illinois: ARMSTRONG; BISMARCK; BUCKLEY (village); CISSNA PARK (village); POTOMAC (village); RANKIN (village); ROBERTS.
Indiana: BOSWELL; FOWLER; ROYAL CENTER; WALTON; WEST LEBANON.

PARTNER COMMUNICATIONS COOPERATIVE
PO Box 8
101 East Church St.
Gilman, IA 50106
Phones: 641-498-7701; 877-433-7701
Fax: 641-498-7308
E-mail: custsvc@partnercom.net; customercare@pcctel.net
Web site: http://www.pcctel.net
Officers:
J. Harry Scurr Jr., President
Bill Hotger, Vice President
Daniel Carnahan, Secretary

Branch Offices:
128 W Main St
State Center, IA 50247
Phone: 641-483-7701
PO Box 100
316 Railroad St
Kellogg, IA 50135
Phone: 641-526-8585
Cable Systems (1):
Iowa: GILMAN.

PATHWAY COMTEL
PO Box 1298
427 North Broadway
Joshua, TX 76058
Phone: 817-484-2222
Fax: 817-447-0169
Web site: http://www.usapathway.com
Officer:
Steve Allen, President
Cable Systems (1):
Texas: BURLESON.

PAUL BUNYAN COMMUNICATIONS
1831 Anne St. NW
Bemidji, MN 56601
Phones: 218-444-1234; 888-586-3100
Fax: 218-444-1121
E-mail: tv@paulbunyan.net; info@paulbunyan.net
Web site: http://www.paulbunyan.net
Officers:
Paul Freude, Chief Executive Officer
Gary Johnson, Chief Operating Officer & General Manager
Dave Schultz, Chief Financial Officer

Rob St. Clair, Plant Operations Manager
Bryan Marsh, Outside Plant Operations Manager

Branch Office:
Grand Rapids
1220 S Pokegama Ave
Central Square Mall
Grand Rapids, MN 55744
Phone: 218-999-1234
Ownership: Subscriber owned--Bemidji, MN.
Cable Systems (2):
Minnesota: MORSE TWP.; SOLWAY.

PC TELCORP
Ste 2
240 South Interocean Ave.
Holyoke, CO 80734
Phones: 970-854-2201; 866-854-2111
Fax: 970-854-2668
E-mail: customerservice@pctelcom.coop
Web site: http://www.pctelcom.coop
Officers:
Vincent Kropp, General Manager
Pete Markle, Director, Operations
Lonnie Krueger, Lead Network/Broadband Technician
Mark Smith, Marketing & Public Relations Manager
Cable Systems (1):
Colorado: HOLYOKE.

PENASCO VALLEY TELECOMMUNICATIONS
4011 West Main St.
Artesia, NM 88210
Phones: 575-748-1241; 800-505-4844
Fax: 575-746-4142
E-mail: pvtcsrs@pvt.com
Web site: http://www.pvt.com
Officers:
Glenn Lovelace, Chief Executive Officer
Terry Mullins, Vice President, Marketing & Sales
Sammy Reno, Vice President, Plant & Operations

Branch Offices:
1311 W. Main St.
Artersia, NM 88210
Phone: 575-746-9844
1101 W. Pierce
Calrsbad, NM 88220
Phone: 575-628-0604
2400 N. Grimes
Hobbs, NM 88240
Phone: 575-392-9958
4504 N Main St
Ste A
Roswell, NM 88201
Phone: 575-622-2006
Cable Systems (2):
New Mexico: ARTESIA; ELEPHANT BUTTE.

PENCOR SERVICES INC.
613 3rd St.
Palmerton, PA 18071
Phones: 610-826-9311; 610-826-2552
Fax: 610-826-7626
E-mail: custserv@corp.ptd.net
Web site: http://www.pencor.com
Officers:
Donald G. Reinhard, Chairman
Fred A. Reinhard, President
Richard Semmel, Vice President, Operations
Mark Masenheimer, Vice President & General Manager, Blue Ridge Communications
Jeff Gehman, Treasurer
Cable Systems (13):
Pennsylvania: BEACH LAKE; BENTLEY CREEK; EPHRATA; JACKSON TWP. (Tioga County);

Cable Owners

LEHIGHTON; MANSFIELD; MILFORD; MUNCY VALLEY; NEWBERRY TWP.; SOUTH CREEK TWP.; STROUDSBURG; TROY; TUNKHANNOCK.
Other Holdings:
Newspaper holdings
Telephone holdings: Palmerton Telephone Co.

PEOPLES RURAL TELEPHONE COOPERATIVE
1080 Main St. South
McKee, KY 40447
Phones: 606-287-7101; 606-593-5000
E-mail: prtccs@prtcnet.org
Web site: http://www.prtcnet.org
Officer:
Keith Gabbard, General Manager
Cable Systems (2):
Kentucky: BOONEVILLE; WANETA.

PEREGRINE COMMUNICATIONS
Ste 16A
14818 West 6th Ave.
Golden, CO 80401
Phones: 303-278-9660; 800-359-9660
Fax: 303-278-9685
E-mail: peregrine.info@perecom.com
Web site: http://www.perecom.com
Officers:
John Post, President & Chief Executive Officer
Marissa Schubert, Regional Sales Manager
Ownership: John Post, Pres. & Chief Exec. Officer.
Cable Systems (1):
Nebraska: STRATTON.

CITY OF PHILIPPI
PO Box 460
108 North Main St.
Philippi, WV 26416
Phone: 304-457-3700
Fax: 304-457-2703
Officer:
Carl Radcliff, Chief Engineer
Ownership: Community owned--Philippi, WV.
Cable Systems (1):
West Virginia: PHILIPPI.

PHONOSCOPE LTD.
6105 Westline Dr.
Houston, TX 77036
Phone: 713-272-4600
Fax: 713-271-4334
E-mail: trouble@phonoscope.com
Web site: http://www.phonoscopecable.com
Ownership: Partnership.
Cable Systems (1):
Texas: HOUSTON.
Other Holdings:
Data service: private data networks; Internet
Data Services: Private Fiber Networks; Digital Video Streaming; High Speed Internet; IP Telephony; Ethernet Circuits
Video production: Videoconferencing

PICKWICK CABLEVISION
PO Box 12
Pickwick Dam, TN 38365
Phone: 731-689-5722
Fax: 731-689-3632
Web site: http://www.pickwickcable.net
Ownership: Bob Campbell.
Cable Systems (1):
Tennessee: COUNCE.

PIEDMONT TELEPHONE MEMBERSHIP CORP.
191 Reeds Baptist Church Rd.
Lexington, NC 27295
Phone: 336-787-5433
Fax: 336-787-5246
E-mail: ptmc@ptmc.net
Web site: http://ptmc.net
Officers:
Gary L. Brown, President
Gilmer Jessup, Vice President
Ownership: Surry Telephone Membership Corp..
Represented (legal): Crisp, Page & Currin LLP.
Cable Systems (1):
North Carolina: CHURCHLAND.

PINE BELT TELEPHONE CO.
3984 County Road 32
Arlington, AL 36722
Phones: 334-385-2106; 888-810-4638
Fax: 334-385-2103
E-mail: contact@pinebelttalk.com
Web site: http://www.pinebelt.net; http://www.pinebelttalk.com
Officers:
John Nettles, President
Terry Smyly, Customer Service Manager, Landline
Brian Horton, Plant Operations Manager, Wireless
Randy Vick, Plant Operations Manager, Landline
Stephen Collins, Information Services Manager
Kevin Grass, Director, Sales & Marketing
Troy Harvill, Director, Finance & Accounting
Ownership: Nettles Family..
Cable Systems (2):
Alabama: BUTLER; GROVE HILL.

PINPOINT COMMUNICATIONS INC.
PO Box 490
611 Patterson
Cambridge, NE 69022
Phones: 308-697-7678; 800-793-2788
Fax: 308-697-3631
E-mail: info@pnpt.com
Web site: http://www.pnpt.com
Officer:
J. Richard Shoemaker, Chairman, PinPoint Holdings

Branch Office:
McCook
312 W. B St.
McCook, NE 69001
Phone: 308-345-3870
Ownership: PinPoint Holdings Inc..
Cable Systems (1):
Nebraska: CAMBRIDGE.

PIONEER BROADBAND
37 North St.
Houlton, ME 04730
Phone: 207-532-1254
Fax: 207-532-7195
E-mail: info@pioneerbroadband.net
Web site: http://www.pioneerbroadband.net
Cable Systems (1):
Maine: SHERMAN.

PIONEER COMMUNICATIONS
PO Box 707
120 West Kansas Ave.
Ulysses, KS 67880-2001
Phones: 620-356-3211; 800-308-7536
Fax: 620-356-3242
E-mail: marketing@pioncomm.net; info@pioncomm.net
Web site: http://www.pioncomm.net
Officers:
William Nicholas, President
Bill Boekhaus, Director
Catherine Moyer, General Manager
Lynda Caffey, Cable Television Programming

Branch Offices:
Hugoton
PO Box 460
114 E 6th
Hugoton, KS 67951
Phone: 620-544-4392
Johnson City
110 Chestnut
Johnson City, KS 67855
Phone: 620-492-6234
Lakin
PO Box 724
201 N Main
Lakin, KS 67860
Phone: 620-355-7355
Satanta
211 S Sequoyah
Satanta, KS 67870
Phone: 620-649-2225
Syracuse
PO Box 1445
210 N Main
Syracuse, KS 67878
Phone: 620-384-7721
Represented (legal): Lukas, Nace, Gutierrez & Sachs LLP.
Cable Systems (1):
Kansas: ULYSSES.

PIONEER TELEPHONE COOPERATIVE INC.
205 Harvey Ave.
Kingfisher, OK 73750
Phones: 405-375-0650; 405-375-4111
Web site: http://www.ptci.com
Officer:
Richard Ruhl, General Manager
Cable Systems (1):
Oklahoma: KINGFISHER.

PITCAIRN COMMUNITY ANTENNA SYSTEM
582 6th St.
Pitcairn, PA 15140
Phone: 412-372-6500
Fax: 412-349-0094
E-mail: pcc@pitcairnborough.us
Web site: http://www.pitcairnborough.us
Officers:
Orelio Vecchio, President
Gary Parks, Secretary-Treasurer
Philip Stevens
Ownership: Community owned--Pitcairn, PA.
Cable Systems (1):
Pennsylvania: PITCAIRN.

POLAR COMMUNICATIONS
PO Box 270
110 4th St. East
Park River, ND 58270
Phones: 701-284-7221; 800-284-7222
Fax: 701-284-7205
E-mail: info@polarcomm.com
Web site: http://www.polarcomm.com

Branch Office:
112 W Main St
Mayville, ND 58257
Phone: 701-788-7221
Fax: 701-284-9622
Ownership: David Drucker; Penny Drucker. Druckers also have interest in Cayo Hueso Networks LLC, Denver Digital Television LLC, Echonet Corp., GreenTV Corp. & Ketchikan TV LLC, see listings.
Cable Systems (1):
North Dakota: PARK RIVER.

PONDEROSA CABLEVISION
PO Box 21
O'Neals, CA 93645
Phones: 559-868-6000; 800-682-1878
E-mail: cherylf@ponderosatel.com; customercare@goponderosa.com
Web site: http://www.goponderosa.com

Branch Office:
Service & Engineering
47671 Rd 200
O'Neals, CA 93645
Phone: 559-868-6000
Cable Systems (1):
California: NORTH FORK.

POWHATAN POINT CABLE CO.
PO Box 67
140 1st St.
Powhatan, OH 43942
Phone: 614-795-5005
Ownership: Kasmir Majewski; Walter Matkovich.
Cable Systems (2):
Ohio: BARTON; POWHATAN POINT.

PRAIRIEBURG TELEPHONE CO INC
Ste 2
120 West Main St.
Prairieburg, IA 52219
Phone: 319-437-3611
Cable Systems (1):
Iowa: PRAIRIEBURG.

PREMIER COMMUNICATIONS INC.
339 1st Ave. NE
Sioux Center, IA 51250
Phones: 712-722-3451; 800-741-8351
Fax: 712-722-1113
E-mail: infoweb@mypremieronline.com
Web site: http://www.mypremieronline.com
Officer:
Ross K. Vernon, General Manager

Branch Office:
Le Mars
416 5th Ave SW
Le Mars, IA 51031
Phone: 712-546-7726
Fax: 712-722-4491
Cable Systems (3):
Iowa: LITTLE ROCK; MELVIN; SIOUX CENTER.
Other Holdings:
Telephone holdings

PROGRESSIVE RURAL TELEPHONE CO-OP INC.
PO Box 98
890 Simpson Ave.
Rentz, GA 31075-0098
Phones: 478-984-4201; 877-599-3939
Fax: 478-984-4205
E-mail: prtc@progressivetel.com
Web site: http://progressivetel.com
Officers:
Roger Lord, (At Large) President
Larry Sanders, Vice President
George Lindsey Sr., Treasurer
Kennon Smith, Secretary
Wayne Dixon, General Manager
Ron Chambers, Office Manager
Larry Stevenson, Central Office Supervisor
Nathaniel Nelson, Service Supervisor
Donnie Alligood, Outside Plant Supervisor
Russell Lane, Construction Supervisor

Cable Owners

Cable Systems (1):
Georgia: RENTZ.

CITY OF PROTIVIN
PO Box 53
117 North Main
Protivin, IA 52163
Phone: 563-569-8401
Ownership: Community owned--Protivin, IA..
Cable Systems (1):
Iowa: PROTIVIN.

PROVINCIAL CABLE & DATA
Ste A
123 West Main St.
Odessa, MO 64076
Phones: 816-633-1626; 866-284-3346
E-mail: mrunyan@provincial-cable.com
Web site: http://www.provincialcable.com
Cable Systems (5):
Missouri: ADRIAN; BUFFALO; COLE CAMP; SMITHTON; STURGEON.

PUERTO RICO CABLE ACQUISITION CO INC
Road 992 KM. 0.2
Luquillo Industrial Park
Luquillo, PR 00773
Phones: 787-355-3535; 877-772-1518
Fax: 303-220-6601
Web site: http://www.choicecable.com
Cable Systems (2):
Puerto Rico: MAYAGUEZ; PONCE.

PULASKI WHITE RURAL TELEPHONE COOPERATIVE
PO Box 408
306 South State Rd 39
Buffalo, IN 47925
Phones: 574-278-7121; 574-946-1377
Fax: 574-278-8448
E-mail: customerservice@pwrtc.net
Web site: http://www.lightstreamin.com
Officers:
Otto Leis, Chairman
Mike McCormick, Vice Chairman
Masrk A Dickerson, President & Chief Executive Officer
Laura Wheeler, Secretary
Wynemac Woodcock, Treasurer
Cable Systems (1):
Indiana: WINAMAC.

CITY OF QUITMAN
PO Box 208
100 West Screven St.
Quitman, GA 31643
Phone: 229-263-4166
E-mail: janice.jarvis@ymail.com
Web site: http://www.cityofquitmanga.com/CableTelevision.aspx
Officers:
J D Herring, City Manager
Janice Jarvis, City Clerk
Agnes Kimbrough, Administrative Assistant/Customer Service
Ownership: Community owned--Quitman, GA..
Cable Systems (1):
Georgia: QUITMAN.

RADCLIFFE CABLEVISION INC.
PO Box 140
202 Isabella St.
Radcliffe, IA 50230-7714
Phone: 515-899-2341
Fax: 515-899-2499
E-mail: info@radcliffetelephone.com
Web site: http://radcliffetelephone.com
Officer:
Ed Drake, General Manager
Cable Systems (1):
Iowa: RADCLIFFE.

RAINBOW COMMUNICATIONS
PO Box 147
608 Main St.
Everest, KS 66424
Phone: 800-892-0163
Fax: 785-548-7517
Web site: http://www.rainbowtel.net
Officers:
Vicky Ptomey, Customer Service Manager
Pat Streeter, Plant Manager

Branch Offices:
Hiawatha
628 Oregon St
Hiawatha, KS 66434
Phone: 785-548-7511
Fax: 785-742-2628
Horton
126 W 8th St
Horton, KS 66439
Phone: 785-548-7511
Fax: 785-486-3502
Seneca
513 Main St
Seneca, KS 66538
Phone: 785-548-7511
Fax: 785-334-7246
Ownership: Rainbow Telecommunications Association Inc..
Cable Systems (1):
Kansas: HIAWATHA.

THE RAINIER GROUP
PO Box 639
104 Washington Ave. North
Eatonville, WA 98328
Phones: 360-832-6161; 253-683-4100
Fax: 360-832-8817
Web site: http://www.rainierconnect.com
Ownership: Mashell Telecom.
Cable Systems (1):
Washington: EATONVILLE.

RANDOLPH TELEPHONE MEMBERSHIP CORP.
317 East Dixie Dr.
Asheboro, NC 27203
Phones: 336-879-5684; 336-622-7900
E-mail: csrep@rtmc.net
Web site: http://www.rtmc.net
Officer:
Frankie Cagle, General Manager & Chief Executive Officer

Branch Offices:
Liberty Office
211 West Swannanoa Ave
Liberty, NC 27298
Retail Office
177-H Specialty Shops - Hwy 42 N
Asheboro, NC 27203
Cable Systems (1):
North Carolina: LIBERTY.

RB3 LLC
PO Box 507
Arp, TX 75750
Phone: 800-687-1258
E-mail: support@reachbroadband.net
Web site: http://www.reachbroadband.net
Ownership: TS Communications Inc.; TSCI ownership:; Tom Semptimphelter.
Cable Systems (14):
New Mexico: SANTA ROSA.
Oklahoma: ERICK.
Texas: CROSBYTON; DE LEON; GORMAN; HART; LOCKNEY; MATADOR (town); McCAMEY; MEMPHIS; MULESHOE; RALLS; VAN HORN; WEST ODESSA.

RCN CORP.
650 College Road E
Princeton, NJ 08540
Phones: 609-681-2281; 609-452-8197
E-mail: cabletv@rcn.com
Web site: http://www.rcn.com
Officers:
Steve Simmons, Chairman
Jim Holanda, Chief Executive Officer
Chris Fenger, Chief Operating Officer
John Feehan, Chief Financial Officer
Felipe Alvarez, Senior Vice President & President, RCN Metro Optical Networks
Jackie Heitman, Senior Vice President, Marketing & Sales
Jeff Kramp, Senior Vice President, Secretary & General Counsel
Ownership: ABRY Partners LLC. Sale to TPG Capital pends. Google Capital will hold minority interest. Deal is expected to close in first quarter of 2017. Jim Coulter is Co-Chief Executive Officer and founder of TPG Capital. Jim Holanda will continue as Chief Executive Officer.
Cable Systems (6):
District of Columbia: WASHINGTON (portions).
Illinois: CHICAGO.
Massachusetts: BOSTON.
New York: NEW YORK CITY.
Pennsylvania: ALLENTOWN; RIDLEY PARK.

RC TECHNOLOGIES CORP.
205 Main St.
New Effington, SD 57255
Phones: 605-637-5211; 800-256-6854
Fax: 605-637-5302
E-mail: tnics@tnics.com
Web site: http://www.tnics.com
Officers:
Scott Bostrom, General Manager
Colin Bronson, Operations Manager
Rachel Bartnick, Marketing & Sales Manager
Paul Gravdahl, IT Manager
Ownership: Roberts County Telephone Cooperative Assn..
Cable Systems (2):
South Dakota: NEW EFFINGTON; SUMMIT.

REBELTEC COMMUNICATIONS LLC
PO Box 10
Kit Carson, CO 80825
Phones: 719-767-8902; 719-336-9066
Fax: 719-767-8906
E-mail: tech@rebeltec.net
Web site: http://www.rebeltec.net
Cable Systems (1):
Colorado: KIT CARSON.

RED RIVER CABLE TV
PO Box 674
Coushatta, LA 71019
Phone: 318-932-4991
Fax: 318-932-5123
Ownership: Jim Hardy, Principal.
Cable Systems (3):
Louisiana: CAMPTI; CLARENCE; COUSHATTA.

RED'S TV CABLE INC.
PO Box 202
601 West Horne Ave.
Farmville, NC 27828
Phone: 252-753-3074
E-mail: cable@redcable.com
Ownership: Frank Styers.
Cable Systems (1):
North Carolina: BATH (town).

RELIANCE CONNECTS
PO Box 357
301 South Broadway
Estacada, OR 97023
Phone: 503-630-4213
Fax: 503-630-4464
E-mail: info@rconnects.com; support@rconnects.com
Web site: http://relianceconnects.com
Officer:
Brenda Crosby, Manager
Ownership: Cascade Connects LLC.
Cable Systems (2):
Nevada: MESQUITE.
Oregon: ESTACADA.

RESERVATION TELEPHONE COOPERATIVE
PO Box 68
24 Main St. North
Parshall, ND 58770
Phones: 701-862-3115; 888-862-3115
Fax: 701-862-3008
E-mail: rtc@restel.com
Web site: http://rtc.coop
Officers:
Shane Hart, Chief Executive Officer & General Manager
David Aamot, Finance Manager
Chad Betz, Outside Plant Manager, East
Gretchen Edwards, Human Resources Manager
Brooks Goodall, Operations Manager
Kristin Jaeger, Marketing Manager
Tim Jarski, Construction Manager
Cory Johnson, Outside Plant Manager, West
Lisa Schenfisch, Customer Service Manager
Dan Schilla, Network Manager
Jeff Symens, Assistant Operations Manager
Cable Systems (1):
North Dakota: PARSHALL (portions).

RESERVE TELECOMMUNICATIONS
105 RTC Dr.
Reserve, LA 70084
Phones: 985-536-1111; 888-611-6111
E-mail: rtccustomercare@rtconline.com
Web site: http://www.rtconline.com
Officers:
William Ironside, President
Scott Small, Executive Vice President
Annette Faircloth, Vice President, Finance
Jeep Barrios, Customer Care Manager
Glenn Bourg, Facilities Manager
Darcey Delatte, Human Resources & Payroll Manager
Barry Farmin, Plant & Construction Manager
Luke Guillory, Network Operations Manager
Katie Klibert, Marketing Manager
Lisa Madere, Customer Care Manager
Chad Webb, Installation & Sales Manager
Ownership: The Reilly Family.
Cable Systems (2):
Louisiana: RESERVE; ST. JAMES PARISH (portions).

RESORTS CABLE TV
2190 South Hwy. 27
Somerset, KY 42501
Phone: 606-679-3427

Cable Owners

Cable Systems (1):
South Carolina: DAUFUSKIE ISLAND.

REVEILLE BROADBAND
PO Box 39
1008 Giddings St.
Lexington, TX 78947
Phones: 979-773-4700; 866-489-4739
Fax: 979-773-4733
E-mail: mariesullivan@reveillebroadband.com
Web site: http://www.reveillebroadband.com
Officers:
Marie Sullivan, Chairman & Chief Executive Officer
Jeff Sullivan, President
Cable Systems (5):
Texas: BARTLETT; BIRCH CREEK; LEXINGTON; LYONS; SMITHVILLE.

REYNOLDS CABLE TV INC.
PO Box 782
Swainsboro, GA 30401
Phone: 800-822-8650
E-mail: reynoldscable@reynoldscable.net
Web site: http://www.reynoldscable.net
Officers:
Terry Reynolds, Chairman, President & Chief Executive Officer
Randy Forehand, Marketing & Engineering Director
Ownership: Terry Reynolds, 51%; Randy Forehand, 44%; Bill McWhorter, 5%.
Represented (legal): Reddy, Begley & McCormick LLP.
Cable Systems (1):
Georgia: BOLINGBROKE.

RF CABLE LLC
19999 Hwy. 61
Rolling Fork, MS 39159
Phone: 662-873-6983
Fax: 662-873-6090
Officer:
Jerry Grant, Manager
Ownership: Mississippi Delta Wireless LLC; MDWLLC ownership:; George Martin; Johnny Sanders Sr..
Cable Systems (1):
Mississippi: ROLLING FORK.

RGW COMMUNICATIONS INC
1127 Leverett Rd.
Warner Robins, GA 31088
Phone: 478-922-9440
Web site: http://www.watsononline.net
Ownership: Watson Family.
Cable Systems (1):
Georgia: ROBINS AFB.

RIDGEWOOD CABLE
3700 South County Rd. 1316
Odessa, TX 79765
Phone: 432-563-4330
Fax: 432-563-0134
E-mail: support@ridgewoodcable.com; sales@ridgewoodcable.com
Web site: http://www.ridgewoodcable.com
Cable Systems (2):
Texas: ECTOR COUNTY (portions); GREENWOOD.

RINGSTED TELEPHONE CO.
PO Box 187
19 West Maple St.
Ringsted, IA 50578
Phone: 712-866-8000
Fax: 712-866-0002
E-mail: tjohnson@ringtelco.com
Web site: http://www.ringstedtelephone.com
Officers:
Dale Johansen, Chairman & Chief Executive Officer
Lavonne M. Tow, Office Manager
Represented (legal): Anderson, Pelzer & Hart.
Cable Systems (1):
Iowa: RINGSTED.
Other Holdings:
Cellular telephone
Telephone holdings

RITTER COMMUNICATIONS
2400 Ritter Dr.
Jonesboro, AR 72401
Phones: 870-336-3434; 888-336-4466
Web site: http://rittercommunications.com
Officers:
Paul Waits, President
John Strode, Vice President, External Affairs
Harold Kennel, Director, Cable Operations

Branch Offices:
Blytheville
646 East
Blytheville, AR 72315
Phone: 870-824-2249
Marked Tree
30 Elm St
Marked Tree, AR 72365
Phone: 870-358-4400
Millington
4880 Navy Rd
Millington, TN 38053
Phone: 901-872-7000
Munford
1464 Munford Ave
Munford, TN 38058
Cable Systems (3):
Arkansas: MARKED TREE; WESTERN GROVE.
Tennessee: MILLINGTON.

RIVER VALLEY TELECOMMUNICATIONS COOP
PO Box 250
106 E Robins Ave.
Graettinger, IA 51342
Phone: 712-859-3300
Fax: 712-859-3290
E-mail: questions@rvtc.net
Web site: http://www.rvtc.net
Officer:
Robert Louwagie, President
Cable Systems (1):
Iowa: GRAETTINGER.

RIVIERA UTILITIES CABLE TV
413 East Laurel Ave.
Foley, AL 36535
Phone: 251-943-5001
Fax: 251-943-5275
E-mail: mdugger@riviera-utilities.com
Web site: http://www.rivierautilities.com
Officers:
Michael M Dugger, Chief Executive Officer & General Manager
Thomas L. DeBell, Manager, Electric & CATV
Ownership: Community owned--Foley, AL.
Represented (legal): Bryan Cave LLP.
Cable Systems (1):
Alabama: FOLEY.

JIM ROBY
24285 State Hwy. 64 East
Canton, TX 75103
Phone: 903-567-2260
Fax: 903-567-4048
Web site: http://www.etcable.net

Cable Systems (2):
Texas: CANTON; SMITH COUNTY (portions).

ROCK PORT TELEPHONE CO.
PO Box 147
Rock Port, MO 64482
Phones: 660-744-5311; 877-202-1764
Fax: 660-744-2120
E-mail: rptel@rpt.coop
Web site: http://www.rptel.net
Officers:
Robert L. Stanton, President
Keith Ottmann, Vice President
Stanley Griffin, Secretary
Dan LaHue, Treasurer
Cable Systems (6):
Iowa: HAMBURG; MALVERN BOROUGH; SIDNEY (town); TABOR.
Missouri: MOUND CITY; ROCK PORT.

ROCKWELL COOPERATIVE TELEPHONE ASSOCIATION
PO Box 416
111 4th St. North
Rockwell, IA 50469-0416
Phone: 641-822-3211
Fax: 641-822-3550
E-mail: rockwell@netins.net
Web site: http://www.rockwellcoop.com/index.php
Officers:
Robert Amosson, President
Tom Worley, Vice President
Robert Corporon, Secretary
David Severin, General Manager
Ruth Reimers, Billing & Collection Manager
Cable Systems (2):
Iowa: MESERVEY; THORNTON.

ROYAL TELEPHONE CO.
PO Box 80
307 Main St.
Royal, IA 51357
Phone: 712-933-2615
Fax: 712-933-0015
E-mail: info@royaltelco.com
Web site: http://www.royaltelco.com
Cable Systems (1):
Iowa: ROYAL.

RTEC COMMUNICATIONS
PO Box 408
105 East Holland St.
Archbold, OH 43502
Phones: 419-267-8800; 800-362-2764
Fax: 419-267-8808
E-mail: info@rtecexpress.net; support@rtecexpress.net
Web site: http://www.rtecexpress.net
Officers:
David Gobrogge, General Manager
Ken Miller, Assistant General Manager
Brian Miller, Outside Plant Manager
Jayma Gobrogge, Marketing Manager & Business Account Coordinator
Ownership: Ridgeville Telephone Co..
Cable Systems (1):
Ohio: RIDGEVILLE CORNERS.

RUNESTONE TELECOM ASSOCIATION
PO Box 336
100 Runestone Dr.
Hoffman, MN 56339
Phone: 320-986-2013
Fax: 320-986-2050
E-mail: help@runestone.net
Web site: http://www.runestone.net
Officer:
Lee Maier, Manager
Cable Systems (1):
Minnesota: BARRETT.

RURAL ROUTE VIDEO
PO Box 640
360 Browning Ave.
Ignacio, CO 81137-0640
Phone: 970-563-9593
Fax: 970-563-9381
Officers:
Christopher L. May, President
Nancy Howley, Secretary
Cable Systems (1):
Colorado: SUNNYSIDE.

RURAL TELEPHONE CO.
892 West Madison Ave.
Glenns Ferry, ID 83623
Phones: 208-366-2614; 888-366-7821
Fax: 208-366-2615
E-mail: mark.martell@ruraltel.org
Web site: http://www.rtci.net
Ownership: James R Martell.
Cable Systems (1):
Idaho: GLENNS FERRY.

RURALWEST - WESTERN RURAL BROADBAND INC.
PO Box 52968
Bellevue, WA 98015-2968
Phone: 425-451-1470
Fax: 425-451-1471
E-mail: corporatestaff@ruralwest.com
Officer:
David Boland, Chief Operating Officer

Branch Offices:
Peterson Broadband
301 Mitchell St.
Colorado Springs, CO 80916
Phone: 719-597-0873
Fax: 719-597-0164
Vandenberg Broadband
PO Box 6009
Vandenberg AFB, CA 93437
Phone: 805-734-5578
Fax: 805-734-0158
Ownership: David Boland, 50%; Jim Hershey, 50%.
Cable Systems (2):
California: VANDENBERG AFB.
Colorado: PETERSON AFB.

RUSSELL MUNICIPAL CABLE TV
PO Box 408
Town Hall, 65 Main St.
Russell, MA 01071
Phone: 413-862-6204
Fax: 413-862-3103
E-mail: information@russellma.net
Web site: http://www.townofrussell.us
Officers:
Louis E. Garlo, Chief Executive Officer
Susan B. Maxwell, Chief Operating Officer
Richard Trusty, Chief Engineering Officer
Ownership: Community owned--Russell, MA.
Cable Systems (1):
Massachusetts: RUSSELL.

SAC COUNTY MUTUAL TELEPHONE CO.
PO Box 488
108 South Maple St.
Odebolt, IA 51458

Cable Owners

Phone: 712-668-2200
Fax: 712-668-2100
E-mail: odetelco@netins.net
Web site: http://www.scmtco.com
Officer:
Ronald Sorensen, Manager
Ownership: Publicly owned..
Cable Systems (3):
Iowa: ARTHUR; BATTLE CREEK; ODEBOLT.

ST. GEORGE CABLE INC.
PO Box 1090
St. George Island, FL 32328
Phone: 850-927-3200
Fax: 850-927-2060
E-mail: charles@stgeorgecable.com
Cable Systems (1):
Florida: ST. GEORGE ISLAND.

ST. JOHN CABLE CO. INC.
11 East Front St.
St. John, WA 99171
Phones: 509-648-3322; 800-875-0146
E-mail: service@stjohncable.com
Web site: http://www.stjohncable.com
Cable Systems (1):
Washington: ST. JOHN.
Other Holdings:
Cable: 50% interest in Colfax Highline Cable Co., see listing
Telephone holdings

SALTILLO TV CABLE CORP.
PO Box 89
Saltillo, PA 17253
Phone: 814-448-9182
Fax: 814-448-9182
Officers:
Rodney Thomas, President
Marsha M. Dell, Secretary-Treasurer
Cable Systems (1):
Pennsylvania: SALTILLO.

SAN BRUNO MUNICIPAL CABLE TV
398 El Camino Real
San Bruno, CA 94066
Phone: 650-616-3100
Fax: 650-871-5526
E-mail: info@sanbrunocable.com
Web site: http://www.sanbrunocable.com
Officers:
Al Johnson, System Engineer
Steve Firpo, Program & Technology Manager
Ownership: Municipally owned -- San Bruno, CA.
Cable Systems (1):
California: SAN BRUNO.

SAN CARLOS APACHE TELECOMMUNICATIONS UTILITY INC.
PO Box 1000
10 Telecom Ln.
Peridot, AZ 85542
Phone: 928-475-2433
Fax: 928-475-7047
Web site: http://www.scatui.net
Officer:
Richard Gomez, Chief Technology Officer
Ownership: Hal Williams, Court Trustee.
Cable Systems (1):
Arizona: SAN CARLOS.

S & K TV SYSTEMS INC.
508 Miner Ave. West
Ladysmith, WI 54848

Phones: 715-532-7321; 800-924-7880
Fax: 715-532-7583
Web site: http://www.skcable.com
Officer:
Randy Scott, Manager
Ownership: Randy Scott; Tom Krenz.
Cable Systems (3):
Wisconsin: HOLCOMBE; MIKANA; MINONG.

S & T COMMUNICATIONS INC.
PO Box 99
320 Kansas Ave.
Brewster, KS 67732
Phones: 785-694-2256; 800-432-8294
Web site: http://www.sttelcom.com
Officers:
Steve Richards, Chief Executive Officer
Fritz Doke, Outside Plant Manager
Clint Felzien, CATV Manager
Alicia Moore, Marketing Manager
Carolyn Somers, Chief Financial Officer
Cable Systems (2):
Kansas: BREWSTER; DIGHTON.

SAN JUAN CABLE & CONSTRUCTION
2568 MacKenzie Rd.
Bellingham, WA 98226-9204
Phone: 360-758-7879
Officers:
Fred J. Morgan, Chairman
Roy M. Budde, Chief Executive Officer
Edward Warner, Chief Operating Officer
Richard Warbus, Chief Financial Officer
Cable Systems (1):
Washington: LUMMI INDIAN RESERVATION.

SAN SIMEON COMMUNITY CABLE INC.
PO Box 544
Cambria, CA 93428
Phone: 805-927-5555
Web site: http://www.slocounty.ca.gov/PW/Franchise_Administration/SanSimeonCable.htm
Cable Systems (1):
California: SAN SIMEON ACRES.

SANTEL COMMUNICATIONS
PO Box 67
308 South Dumont Ave.
Woonsocket, SD 57385
Phones: 605-796-4411; 888-978-7777
Fax: 605-796-4419
E-mail: info@santel.net
Web site: http://www.santel.net
Officers:
Ryan Thompson, General Manager
Mark Wilson, Network Operations Manager
Cable Systems (1):
South Dakota: WOONSOCKET.

SATELLITE OPERATIONS INC.
PO Box 433
Dowagiac, MI 49047
Phone: 269-424-5737
E-mail: cs@sisterlakescable.com
Web site: http://www.sisterlakescable.com
Ownership: Tim Olmstead, 50%; Art Schmidt Jr., 50%.
Cable Systems (1):
Michigan: KEELER TWP..

SAT STAR COMMUNICATIONS LLC
11449 Challenger Ave.
Odessa, FL 33556

Phone: 800-445-1139
Fax: 813-249-2809
Web site: http://www.satstartech.com
Cable Systems (1):
Florida: RIVER RANCH.

SATVIEW BROADBAND LTD.
PO Box 18148
3550 Barron Way #13A
Reno, NV 89511-1852
Phones: 775-324-2198; 877-538-2662
Fax: 775-333-0255
E-mail: satviewreno@yahoo.com
Web site: http://www.satview.net
Officer:
Tariq Ahmad, President

Branch Office:
Elko
1250 Lamoille Hwy
Ste 1150
Elko, NV 89801
Phone: 775-738-2662
Ownership: WENR Corp.. See also Ngensolutions LLC.
Cable Systems (13):
Colorado: LAS ANIMAS; SPRINGFIELD.
Nevada: BATTLE MOUNTAIN; CARLIN; ELKO; JACKPOT; TOPAZ LAKE; WELLINGTON; WELLS.
New Mexico: CHAMA; DIXON; ESPANOLA; PENASCO.

SAVAGE COMMUNICATIONS INC.
PO Box 810
111 Tobies Mill Pl.
Hinckley, MN 55037-0810
Phones: 320-384-7442; 800-222-9809
Fax: 320-279-8085
E-mail: sales@scibroadband.com; support@scibroadband.com
Web site: http://www.scibroadband.com
Officers:
Ronald W. Savage, President
Mike Danielson, Vice President, Operations
Paula Savage, Secretary-Treasurer
Ownership: Ron Savage, Principal; Mike Danielson; Pat McCabe; Jerry Meier.
Cable Systems (12):
Minnesota: BARNUM; BOVEY; FLOODWOOD; GREENWAY TWP.; HILL CITY; ISLE; MC-GREGOR; PENGILLY; PILLAGER; SAGINAW; SANDSTONE; VERNDALE.

SBC-TELE
PO Box 226
Kinsman, OH 44428
Phones: 330-876-0294; 330-876-0500
Fax: 330-876-0294
Ownership: Scott Bryer.
Cable Systems (1):
Ohio: MOUNT ORAB.

SCHALLER TELEPHONE CO.
PO Box 9
111 West 2nd St.
Schaller, IA 51053
Phone: 712-275-4211
Fax: 712-275-4121
Web site: http://www.schallertel.net
Officers:
Missy Kestel, Manager
Robert Boeckman, Chief Financial Officer
Diana Myrtue, Programming Director
Ownership: Locally owned..

Cable Systems (1):
Iowa: SCHALLER.

SCHURZ COMMUNICATIONS INC.
1301 East Douglas Rd.
Mishawaka, IN 46545
Phone: 574-247-7237
Fax: 574-247-7238
E-mail: info@schurz.com
Web site: http://www.schurz.com
Officers:
Franklin D. Schurz Jr., Chairman
Scott C Schurz, Vice Chairman
Todd F Schurz, President & Chief Executive Officer
Marcia K. Burdick, Senior Vice President, Broadcasting
Gary N Hoipkemier, Senior Vice President, Chief Financial Officer, Secretary & Treasurer
Charles V Pittman, Senior Vice President, Publishing
David C Ray, Vice President
Martin D Switalski, Vice President, Human Resources & Administration
Judy A Felty, Assistant Secretary
Gesumino A Agostino, Assistant Treasurer
Ownership: Voting Trust Agreement dated July 22,2004, 75.2%. votes; David C Ray, 15.2%. votes, 9.5% assets; Robin S Bruni, 9.6%. votes, 10.3% assets; VTA ownership:; Franklin D. Schurz Jr.; Scott C. Schurz; Todd F. Schurz, Trustees.
Cable Systems (5):
Arizona: MARICOPA; ROBSON RANCH; SADDLEBROOKE; SUN LAKES.
Maryland: HAGERSTOWN.
TV Stations:
Missouri: KSPR Springfield.
Other Holdings:
Newspaper holdings

SCIO CABLEVISION INC.
PO Box 1100
38770 North Main St.
Scio, OR 97374
Phones: 503-394-3366; 503-394-2995
Fax: 503-394-3999
E-mail: scv@smt-net.com; smt@smt-net.com
Web site: http://www.smt-net.com
Officers:
Jim Nieuwstraten, Chairman
Dean Schrunk, Vice Chairman
Sandy Baggett, Secretary
Mark Wagner, Treasurer
Cable Systems (1):
Oregon: SCIO.
Other Holdings:
Telephone

SCOTT COUNTY TELEPHONE COOPERATIVE
PO Box 487
149 Woodland St.
Gate City, VA 24251
Phone: 276-452-9119
Fax: 276-452-4313
E-mail: sctc@sctc.org
Web site: http://www.sctc.org
Officers:
John Kilgore, President
William J. Franklin, Chief Executive Officer
Toby Hilton, Vice President
John Ferguson, Secretary
William Johnson, Treasurer
Cable Systems (2):
Virginia: GATE CITY; SANDY RIDGE.
Other Holdings:
Manufacturing

2017 Edition   D-921

Cable Owners

SCOTTSBORO ELECTRIC POWER BOARD
PO Box 550
404 East Willow St.
Scottsboro, AL 35768
Phones: 256-574-2680; 256-574-2682
Fax: 256-574-5085
E-mail: feedback@scottsboropower.com
Web site: http://www.scottsboropower.com
Cable Systems (1):
Alabama: SCOTTSBORO.

SCRANTON TELEPHONE CO.
PO Box 8
1200 Main St.
Scranton, IA 51462
Phone: 712-652-3355
Fax: 712-652-3777
E-mail: jingles@netins.net
Web site: http://www.scrantontelephone.com
Officer:
Sam Fengel, General Manager
Cable Systems (1):
Iowa: SCRANTON.

SEMO COMMUNICATIONS INC.
PO Box C
107 Semo Ln.
Sikeston, MO 63801
Phones: 573-471-6599; 800-635-8230
Fax: 573-471-6878
E-mail: semosupport@cablerocket.com
Web site: http://www.semocommunications.com
Officers:
Travis E. Garrett, Chairman
Tyrone Garrett, President
Shannon Garrett, Vice President & Secretary-Treasurer
Ownership: Tyrone Garrett, 50.1%; Shannon Garrett, 34.9%; Denise Antrobus, 15%.
Represented (legal): William Clayton Vandivort.
Cable Systems (1):
Missouri: ADVANCE.
Other Holdings:
Cable Consulting

SERVICE ELECTRIC CABLE TV INC.
PO Box 853
320 Sparta Ave.
Sparta, NJ 07871
Phone: 800-992-0132
Fax: 973-729-5635
E-mail: corporateoffice@secv.com
Web site: http://www.secable.com
Officers:
John M Walson, President
Mark Walter, Senior Vice President
Joe Macus, Vice President
Steve Salash, Marketing Director
Arlean Lilly, Regulatory Affairs Director
Ownership: Margaret Walson.
Represented (legal): Womble Carlyle Sandridge & Rice LLP.
Cable Systems (7):
New Jersey: HUNTERDON COUNTY; SPARTA.
Pennsylvania: ALLENTOWN; BIRDSBORO; HAZLETON; SUNBURY (village); WILKES-BARRE.
Other Holdings:
Common Carrier

SHADE GAP TV ASSN.
HC 83 Box 398
Shade Gap, PA 17255
Phone: 814-259-3673
Officers:
Richard Price, President
Mary McMullen, Secretary-Treasurer
Ownership: Community owned--Shade Gap.
Cable Systems (1):
Pennsylvania: SHADE GAP.

SHELLSBURG CABLEVISION INC.
PO Box 389
124 Main St.
Shellsburg, IA 52332
Phones: 319-436-2224; 800-248-8007
Fax: 319-436-2228
E-mail: webmaster@fmtcs.com
Web site: http://www.usacomm.coop
Officers:
Roy M. Fish, President
Rex Miller, Vice President
Robert H. Smith, Secretary
Warren Richart, Treasurer
Mark Harrison, General Manager
Ownership: Community owned--Shellsburg, IA.
Cable Systems (1):
Iowa: SHELLSBURG.
Other Holdings:
Telephone holdings

SHENTEL
PO Box 459
500 Shentel Way
Edinburg, VA 22824
Phones: 540-984-5224; 800-743-6835
Fax: 540-984-3438
Web site: http://www.shentel.com
Officers:
Christopher E French, President & Chief Executive Officer
Earle A MacKenzie, Chief Operating Officer & Executive Vice President
Adele M Skolits, Chief Financial Officer & Vice President, Finance
Edward McKay, Senior Vice President, Engineering & Network Planning
William L Pirtle, Senior Vice President, Marketing & Sales
Thomas Whitaker, Senior Vice President, Operations
Richard Baughman, Vice President, Information Technology
Kevin Folk, Vice President, Customer Services
Raymond Ostroski, Vice President, Legal & General Counsel
Cable Systems (26):
Maryland: OAKLAND.
Virginia: BUCHANAN; CLARKSVILLE; COVINGTON; CREWE; FARMVILLE; LAWRENCEVILLE; LEBANON; RADFORD; ROCKY MOUNT; RUSTBURG; WOODSTOCK; WYTHEVILLE.
West Virginia: BELINGTON; GILBERT; GRANTSVILLE; HANOVER; LOW GAP; MARLINTON (town); PETERSBURG; PINEVILLE; RONCEVERTE; SUMMERSVILLE; VAN; WESTON; WHARNCLIFFE.
Cable Holdings:
Shenandoah Cable Television LLC
Other Holdings:
Telephone holdings: Shenandoah Telephone Co.

JOHN P. SHOEMAKER JR.
PO Box 5064
Martinsville, VA 24115
Phone: 804-685-1521
Cable Systems (1):
Virginia: BROSVILLE.

SHREWSBURY'S COMMUNITY CABLEVISION
100 Maple Ave.
Shrewsbury, MA 01545
Phone: 508-841-8500
Fax: 508-842-9419
E-mail: customerservice@shrewsburyma.gov
Web site: http://www.selco.shrewsburyma.gov
Officers:
Jeff Black, Manager Digital Cable System
Joel Malaver, Cable Operations Manager
Jackie Pratt, Marketing Director
Ownership: Community owned--Shrewsbury, MA.
Cable Systems (1):
Massachusetts: SHREWSBURY.

SIERRA NEVADA COMMUNICATIONS
PO Box 281
Sonora, CA 95373
Phone: 209-588-9601
Fax: 209-532-6028
E-mail: cust@gosnc.com
Web site: http://gosnc.com
Cable Systems (3):
California: GROVELAND; LONG BARN; PINECREST.

SIGNAL INC.
PO Box 435
103 6th St. SE
West Bend, IA 50597
Phones: 515-887-4591; 515-302-3602
E-mail: msignal@ncn.net
Officers:
Michael Steil, President
David Carroll, Vice President
Cable Systems (1):
Iowa: LU VERNE.

SILVER STAR COMMUNICATIONS
PO Box 226
Freedom, WY 83120
Phones: 307-883-6684; 877-883-2411
E-mail: support@silverstar.com
Web site: http://www.silverstar.com
Cable Systems (2):
Idaho: SODA SPRINGS; VICTOR.

SIREN COMMUNICATIONS
PO Box 426
7723 Main St.
Siren, WI 54872
Phone: 715-349-2224
Fax: 715-349-2576
E-mail: sirentel@sirentel.net
Web site: http://sirentel.com
Officers:
Sid Sherstad, General Manager
Karen Sherstad, Treasurer
Kent Bassett, Plant Manager
Ownership: Siren Telephone Co..
Cable Systems (1):
Wisconsin: SIREN.

SITKA TV CABLE SYSTEM
964 Broadway Plaza
Paintsville, KY 41240
Phone: 606-789-3391
Cable Systems (1):
Kentucky: SITKA.

SIX MILE RUN TV ASSOCIATION
1171 Six Mile Run Rd.
Six Mile Run, PA 16679
Phone: 814-928-4897
Officers:
Richard W. White, President
Susan K. White, Secretary-Treasurer
Dale Roarbaugh, Manager
Harold Colbert, Chief Technology Officer
Ownership: Community owned--Six Mile Run, PA.
Cable Systems (1):
Pennsylvania: SIX MILE RUN.

SJOBERG'S CABLE TV INC.
315 Main Ave. North
Thief River Falls, MN 56701
Phones: 218-681-3044; 800-828-8808
E-mail: office1@mncable.net
Web site: http://trf.mncable.net
Officers:
Richard Sjoberg, President
Stan Sjoberg, Secretary-Treasurer
Ownership: Richard Sjoberg, 50%; Stan Sjoberg, 50%.
Represented (legal): Cole, Raywid & Braverman LLP.
Cable Systems (11):
Minnesota: BADGER; BAUDETTE; GREENBUSH; KARLSTAD; MIDDLE RIVER; NEWFOLDEN; RED LAKE FALLS; ROSEAU; THIEF RIVER FALLS; WARREN; WARROAD.

SLEDGE TELEPHONE CO.
124 Delta Ave.
Sunflower, MS 38778
Phones: 601-569-3311; 800-352-8156
E-mail: rsledge@deltaland.net
Web site: http://www.deltaland.net
Cable Systems (1):
Mississippi: SUNFLOWER.

SMR COMMUNICATIONS INC.
255B Bell Rd.
Niles, MI 49120
Phone: 269-591-8798
Fax: 269-683-7453
E-mail: info@michianasupernet
Web site: http://www.michianasupernet.com
Cable Systems (1):
Michigan: BAINBRIDGE TWP..

SOLARUS
PO Box 8045
440 East Grand Ave.
Wisconsin Rapids, WI 54495-8045
Phones: 715-421-8111; 800-421-9282
Fax: 715-421-6081
E-mail: support@solarus.net
Web site: http://www.solarus.net
Officers:
Douglas Wenzlaff, Chief Executive Officer & General Manager
Jamey Lysne, Director, Operations
Michael Meinel, Director, Sales & Marketing
Ownership: Cooperative.
Cable Systems (1):
Wisconsin: WISCONSIN RAPIDS.

SOMERFIELD CABLE TV CO.
6511 National Pike
Addison, PA 15411
Phone: 814-395-3084
E-mail: sc-tv@sc-tv.net
Web site: http://www.somerfield.biz
Officer:
Michael J. Diehl, Chairman, Chief Executive, Operating & Financial Officer
Ownership: Michael J Diehl, Chmn. & Chief Exec. Officer.

Cable Owners

Cable Systems (1):
Pennsylvania: ADDISON TWP. (southern portion).

SOUTH ARKANSAS TELEPHONE CO. INC.
PO Box 778
1st and Main St./Hwy 278
Hampton, AR 71744
Phone: 866-798-2201
Web site: http://www.sat-co.net
Cable Systems (1):
Arkansas: HAMPTON.

SOUTH CENTRAL COMMUNICATIONS
PO Box 555
45 North 100 West
Escalante, UT 84726
Phone: 888-826-4211
Fax: 435-826-4900
E-mail: customerservice@socen.com; support@scinternet.net
Web site: http://www.socen.com
Cable Systems (5):
Utah: ENOCH; ENTERPRISE; LYMAN; MILFORD; PANGUITCH.

SOUTHERN COASTAL CABLE
2101 South Frazer St.
Georgetown, SC 29440
Phone: 843-546-2200
E-mail: support@sccctv.net
Web site: http://www.southerncoastalcable.com
Cable Systems (1):
South Carolina: GEORGETOWN.

SOUTHERN KANSAS TELEPHONE CO.
PO Box 800
Clearwater, KS 67026-0800
Phones: 620-584-2255; 888-758-8976
Fax: 620-584-2260
E-mail: customerservice@sktc.net
Web site: http://www.sktmainstreet.com
Officers:
Kendall S. Mikesell, President
Gregory L. Mikesell, Controller

Branch Offices:
Belle Plaine
211 W 5th
Belle Plaine, KS 67013
Phone: 620-488-5999
Burden
408 W Fifth
Burden, KS 67019
Phone: 620-438-5999
Cable Systems (1):
Kansas: CLEARWATER.

SOUTHERN PLAINS CABLE
PO Box 165
Medicine Park, OK 73557
Phones: 580-529-5000; 800-218-1856
Fax: 580-529-5556
E-mail: office@spcisp.net
Web site: http://www.spcisp.net
Officers:
Douglas J. Hilliary, Chairman
Dustin J. Hilliary, President
Cable Systems (8):
Oklahoma: ALEX; APACHE; CEMENT; GRAND-FIELD; LAKE LAWTONKA; MEDICINE PARK; RUSH SPRINGS; STERLING.

SOUTHERN PLAINS TELEPHONE COOPERATIVE
PO Box 1379
Lubbock, TX 79408
Phone: 806-763-2301
E-mail: support@sptc.net
Web site: http://www.sptc.net
Officers:
Gary Harrell, President
Don Mimms, Vice President
Bill Sides, Secretary
Dan Houchin, Treasurer
Cable Systems (1):
Texas: WOODROW.

SOUTHERN VERMONT CABLE CO.
PO Box 166
Bondville, VT 05340-0166
Phone: 800-544-5931
Fax: 802-297-3714
E-mail: escialabba@svcable.net
Web site: http://www.svcable.net
Officers:
Herbert Scialabba, Chairman
Ernest Scialabba, President
Carol Scialabba, Secretary-Treasurer
Ownership: Ernest Scialabba; Herbert Scialabba.
Cable Systems (3):
Vermont: NEWFANE; PUTNEY; TOWNSHEND.

SOUTH HOLT CABLEVISION INC.
PO Box 227
Oregon, MO 64473
Phone: 816-446-3391
Officer:
Robert Williams, Chairman & Chief Executive Officer
Ownership: Robert Williams, Chmn. & Chief Exec. Officer.
Cable Systems (1):
Missouri: OREGON.

SOUTH SHORE CABLE TV INC.
6301 Broad Branch Rd.
Chevy Chase, MD 20815

Cable Systems (1):
Georgia: LUTHERSVILLE.

SOUTH SLOPE COOPERATIVE COMMUNICATIONS CO.
PO Box 19
980 North Front St.
North Liberty, IA 52317
Phones: 319-626-2211; 800-272-6449
Fax: 319-665-7000
E-mail: info@southslope.com
Web site: http://www.southslope.com
Officer:
Stephanie Rourke, Marketing Director
Ownership: South Slope Cooperative Telephone Co..
Cable Systems (1):
Iowa: ELY.

SPANISH FORK COMMUNITY NETWORK
65 South 630 W
Spanish Fork, UT 84660
Phones: 801-804-4500; 801-804-4503
E-mail: info@sfcn.org
Web site: http://www.sfcn.org
Officer:
John Bowcut, Manager
Ownership: City of Spanish Fork.
Cable Systems (1):
Utah: SPANISH FORK.

SPENCER MUNICIPAL UTILITIES
Ste 1
520 2nd Ave. East
Spencer, IA 51301
Phone: 712-580-5800
Fax: 712-580-5888
E-mail: jeffrey.rezabek@smunet.net
Web site: http://www.smunet.net
Officers:
Steve Pick, General Manager
Jeff Rezabek, Telecommunications Manager
Amanda Gloyd, Marketing & Community Relations Manager
Cable Systems (1):
Iowa: SPENCER.

SPILLWAY CABLEVISION INC.
10900 Highway 77
Maringouin, LA 70757
Phone: 225-625-2311
E-mail: cs@spillwaycable.com
Web site: http://www.spillwaycable.com
Officers:
Craig Greene, President
Mark Greene, Secretary-Treasurer
Ownership: Craig Greene; Mark Greene, Principals.
Cable Systems (4):
Louisiana: BUTTE LA ROSE; KROTZ SPRINGS; MARINGOUIN; MELVILLE.

SPIRIT BROADBAND
302 Woodlawn Rd.
Crossville, TN 38555
Phone: 877-368-2110
Fax: 615-368-2295
E-mail: info@spiritbb.com
Web site: http://www.spiritbb.com
Cable Systems (1):
Tennessee: CUMBERLAND COUNTY.

SPRING CITY CABLE TV INC.
PO Box 729
Spring City, TN 37381
Phone: 423-365-7288
Cable Systems (1):
Tennessee: SPRING CITY.

SPRING CREEK CABLE INC.
206 West Main St.
Montrose, CO 81401
Phone: 970-249-4506
Fax: 970-240-8122
E-mail: springcreek89@yahoo.com
Web site: http://www.springcreekcable.com
Cable Systems (2):
Colorado: MONTROSE; OLATHE.

SPRINGPORT TELEPHONE CO.
PO Box 208
400 East Main St.
Springport, MI 49284
Phones: 517-857-3100; 517-857-3500
Fax: 517-857-3329
E-mail: janet@springcom.com
Web site: http://www3.springcom.com
Cable Systems (1):
Michigan: SPRINGPORT TWP..

SPRINGVILLE COOPERATIVE TELEPHONE ASSN. INC.
PO Box 9
207 Broadway
Springville, IA 52336
Phones: 319-854-6107; 319-854-9960
Fax: 319-854-9010
E-mail: springvl@netins.net
Web site: http://www.springvilletelephone.com
Cable Systems (1):
Iowa: SPRINGVILLE.

SRT COMMUNICATIONS INC.
3615 North Broadway
Minot, ND 58703
Phones: 701-858-1200; 800-737-9130
Fax: 701-858-1428
E-mail: email@srt.com
Web site: http://www.srt.com
Officers:
Tom Wentz Jr., Board President
Steve Lysne, Chief Executive Officer & General Manager
John Reiser, Chief Operating Officer & Assistant General Manager
Cassidy Kersten, Corporate Communications Director
Ownership: Subscriber owned--Minot, ND..
Represented (legal): Pringle & Herigstad PC.
Cable Systems (1):
North Dakota: VELVA.
Other Holdings:
Telephone

STANDARD TOBACCO CO. INC.
PO Box 100
626 Forest Ave.
Maysville, KY 41056
Phones: 606-564-9220; 800-264-3572
Fax: 606-564-4291
E-mail: limestone@maysvilleky.net
Web site: http://www.limestonecable.com
Officers:
James A. Finch, Chairman, President & Chief Executive Officer
Ivan Cracraft, Chief Operating & Financial Officer
Ronald Buerkley, Vice President, Cable
Karen Campbell, Secretary
Jeffrey Cracraft, Marketing Director
Ownership: James A Finch Jr., 90%. Finch owns WFTM-AM-FM, Maysville, KY; Barbara Tucker, 10%.
Represented (legal): Royse, Zweigart, Kirk, Brammer & Caudill.
Cable Systems (2):
Kentucky: AUGUSTA; MAYSVILLE.
Other Holdings:
Radio holdings

STARVISION INC.
PO Box 348
3900 North US 421 Hwy.
Clinton, NC 28329
Phones: 910-564-4194; 800-706-6538
Fax: 910-564-5410
E-mail: adsales@stmc.net
Web site: http://www.starvision.tv
Officers:
Robert Hester, President
Randy Jacobs, General Manager
Lyman Horne, Chief Operating Officer
Robert Thornton, Secretary-Treasurer
Jeff Nethercutt, Chief Financial Officer

2017 Edition D-923

Cable Owners

Branch Office:
Elizabethtown
3112 Martin Luther King Dr.
Elizabethtown, NC 28337
Phone: 910-645-1111
Ownership: Star Telephone Membership Corp..
Represented (legal): Holland, Poole, Holland & Sanderson PA.
Cable Systems (1):
North Carolina: HALLS TWP..

STARWEST INC.
PO Box 98
Atkins, IA 52206
Phones: 319-293-6336; 800-568-4992
Fax: 319-446-7858
Ownership: John Stookesberry, Principal.
Cable Systems (6):
Iowa: BRIGHTON; FARMINGTON; FREMONT; HEDRICK; KEOSAUQUA; RICHLAND.

STOWE CABLEVISION INC.
PO Box 1522
Stowe, VT 05672
Phone: 802-253-9282
Fax: 802-253-7812
E-mail: stoweaccess@stoweaccess.com
Web site: http://www.stoweaccess.com
Ownership: Richard Landy.
Cable Systems (2):
Vermont: JEFFERSONVILLE; STOWE.

STRATA NETWORKS
211 East 200 North
Roosevelt, UT 84066
Phone: 435-622-5007
E-mail: company@stratanetworks.com; marketing@stratanetworks.com
Web site: http://www.stratanetworks.com
Officers:
Jeff Goodrich, Chief Operating Officer
Bruce Todd, Chief Executive Officer & General Manager
Tyler Rasmussen, Marketing Manager
Ownership: Formerly UBTA-UBET Communications.
Cable Systems (1):
Utah: DUCHESNE.

RICHARD STURTZ
PO Box 445
Broadus, MT 59317
Phone: 406-436-2820
Officers:
Richard Sturtz, President
Steve Kemmel, Vice President
Mary Sturtz, Secretary-Treasurer
Cable Systems (1):
Montana: BROADUS.

SUBURBAN CABLE LTD
4931 Mercer University Dr.
Macon, GA 31210
Phone: 478-477-6881
Cable Systems (1):
Georgia: BIBB COUNTY (portions).

CITY OF SUMAS TV CABLE SYSTEM
PO Box 9
433 Cherry St.
Sumas, WA 98295
Phone: 360-988-5711
Fax: 360-988-8855
Web site: http://cityofsumas.homestead.com
Officer:
Lawrence Silvis, Manager
Ownership: Community owned--Sumas, WA.

Cable Systems (1):
Washington: SUMAS.

SUMMIT DIGITAL
Box 465
107 West Bridge St.
Portland, MI 48875
Phone: 888-600-5040
Fax: 231-908-0039
E-mail: info@summitdigital.net
Web site: http://www.summitdigital.us
Officer:
Patty Coleman, General Manager
Ownership: Tom Nix.
Cable Systems (2):
Michigan: LE ROY; McBAIN.

SUMNER COMMUNICATIONS
117 West Harvey
Wellington, KS 67152
Phones: 620-326-8989; 877-773-8989
E-mail: sumnertv@sutv.com; support@sutv.com
Web site: http://sutv.com
Officer:
Philip Brown, Manager-Technician
Ownership: Jack Mitchell; Jeanne Mitchell.
Cable Systems (1):
Kansas: WELLINGTON.

SUNRISE COMMUNICATIONS LLC
PO Box 733
20938 Washington Ave.
Onaway, MI 49765
Phone: 989-733-8100
Fax: 989-733-8155
E-mail: info@src-mi.com
Web site: http://www.src-mi.com
Officer:
Angie Krajniak, Business Manager
Cable Systems (2):
Michigan: PICKFORD TWP.; POSEN.

SUPERVISION INC.
5450 A St.
Anchorage, AK 99518
Phones: 907-561-1674; 800-478-2020
Fax: 907-273-5322
E-mail: csr@yukontel.com
Web site: http://www.yukontel.com
Officer:
Don Eller, President & General Manager
Ownership: Clifton Eller.
Cable Systems (1):
Alaska: TANANA.

SWAYZEE COMMUNICATIONS CORP.
PO Box 97
214 South Washington St.
Swayzee, IN 46986
Phones: 765-922-7916; 800-435-8353
Fax: 765-922-7966
E-mail: swayzee@swayzee.com
Web site: http://swayzee.com
Officer:
S. M. Samuels, President
Cable Systems (8):
Indiana: FRANKTON; LA FONTAINE; LAPEL; MARKLE; SHERIDAN; SUMMITVILLE; SWAYZEE; VAN BUREN.
Other Holdings:
Telephone holdings

SWEETWATER CABLE TV CO. INC.
PO Box 8
602 Broadway
Rock Springs, WY 82901

Phone: 307-362-3773
E-mail: swtv@sweetwaterhsa.com
Web site: http://www2.sweetwaterhsa.com
Officers:
Albert M. Carollo Sr., Chairman
Albert M. Carollo Jr., President
John B. Carollo, Chief Operating Officer
James R. Carollo, Vice President
Leona Carollo, Secretary-Treasurer
Fred Pickett, Programming Director
Larry Gessner, Engineering Director
Ownership: Albert M Carollo Jr., 25%; James R Carollo, 25%; John B Carollo, 25%; Albert M Carollo Sr., 25%. Carollo family owns Pilot Butte Transmission Co. (Common Carrier) & TV Translator station in WY.
Represented (legal): Cole, Raywid & Braverman LLP.
Cable Systems (1):
Wyoming: ROCK SPRINGS.

TACOMA PUBLIC UTILITIES
PO Box 11007
3628 S 35th St.
Tacoma, WA 98409
Phones: 253-502-8000; 253-502-8900
Fax: 253-502-8493
E-mail: cservice@cityoftacoma.org
Web site: http://www.mytpu.org
Cable Systems (1):
Washington: TACOMA.

TALOGA CABLE TV
PO Box 218
Taloga, OK 73667
Phone: 405-328-5262
Ownership: Glenn Gore.
Cable Systems (1):
Oklahoma: TALOGA.

TCT WEST INC.
1601 South Park Dr.
Cody, WY 82414
Phones: 307-586-3800; 800-354-2911
Fax: 307-568-2506
E-mail: support@tctwest.net
Web site: http://www.tctwest.net
Officer:
Chris Davidson, CEO
Cable Systems (1):
Wyoming: BASIN.

TDS TELECOM
525 Junction Rd.
Madison, WI 53717
Phones: 608-664-4000; 866-571-6662
Fax: 608-830-5519
E-mail: comments@tdstelecom.com
Web site: http://www.tdstelecom.com
Officers:
Dave Wittwer, President & Chief Executive Officer
Mike Pandow, Senior Vice President, Human Resources & Administration
Mark Barder, Vice President, Cable Operations
DeAnne Boegli, National Public Relations Manager
Ownership: Telephone and Data Systems.
Cable Systems (22):
Colorado: CORTEZ; ESTES PARK; FORT CARSON; FORT COLLINS; TABLE MOUNTAIN; WOODLAND PARK.
Indiana: LINDEN.
New Hampshire: WARNER.
New Mexico: ALAMOGORDO; CARLSBAD; CARRIZOZO; JAL; LEA COUNTY (southern portion); LOVINGTON; RUIDOSO; SOCORRO; TRUTH OR CONSEQUENCES.

Texas: ALPINE; FORT STOCKTON; SEMINOLE.
Utah: CEDAR CITY; ST. GEORGE.

TEKSTAR COMMUNICATIONS INC.
Ste 100
150 2nd St. SW
Perham, MN 56573
Phones: 218-346-4227; 218-346-5500
Fax: 218-346-8829
E-mail: answers@arvig.com
Web site: http://www.arvig.com
Officers:
Allen Arvig, President
David Pratt, General Manager
Donna Ward, Vice President
Carmen Arvig, Secretary
Rick Vyskocil, Treasurer
Ownership: Arvig Enterprises Inc..
Cable Systems (7):
Minnesota: BIGFORK; GRAND MEADOW; MELROSE; PARKERS PRAIRIE; PELICAN RAPIDS; PERHAM; SAUK CENTRE.

TELAPEX INC.
Ste 700
1018 Highland Colony Pkwy.
Ridgeland, MS 39157
Phone: 601-355-1522
Fax: 601-353-0950
Web site: http://www.telapex.com
Officer:
L. Brooks Derryberry, Vice President
Ownership: Telapex Inc..
Cable Systems (3):
Mississippi: FLORA; MEADVILLE; WEIR.

TELECOM CABLE LLC
Ste 1020
1321 Louetta Rd.
Cypress, TX 77429
Phone: 888-240-4589
E-mail: information@telecomcable.net
Web site: http://www.telecomcable.net
Cable Systems (3):
Texas: CORRIGAN; OYSTER CREEK; WESTON LAKES.

TELE-MEDIA CORP.
PO Box 39
804 Jacksonville Rd.
Bellefonte, PA 16823
Phones: 814-353-2025; 800-704-4254
Fax: 814-359-5390
E-mail: techs@tele-media.com
Web site: http://www.tele-media.com
Officers:
Robert E. Tudek, Chairman & Chief Executive Officer
Tony S. Swain, President
Richard W. Shore, Senior Vice President, Corporate Development
Allen C. Jacobson, Senior Vice President, Legal Affairs & Secretary
Frank R. Vicente, Senior Vice President, Operations & Assistant Secretary
Robert D. Stemler, Senior Vice President, Finance & Treasurer
Russell G. Bamburger, Senior Vice President & President, Tele-Media Constructors Co.
Charles J. Hilderbrand, Vice President & Director, Purchasing
Randall S. Lewis, Vice President & General Sales Manager
Thomas T. Wolanski, Vice President, Tax Affairs
Steven E. Koval, Vice President, Information Technology
Jonathan P. Young, Vice President, Legal Affairs

Cable Owners

Dean Colbert III, Assistant Vice President & Assistant General Manager
Jean C. Brown, Administrative Vice President & Assistant Secretary
Elsie M. Tudek, Administrative Vice President & Assistant Secretary-Treasurer
Ownership: Robert E Tudek.
Cable Systems (3):
North Carolina: BALD HEAD ISLAND.
Pennsylvania: SNOW SHOE; ZION.

TELEPHONE AND DATA SYSTEMS
Ste 4000
30 North LaSalle St.
Chicago, IL 60602
Phone: 312-630-1900
Fax: 312-630-9299
E-mail: TDSinfo@tdsinc.com
Web site: http://www.teldta.com
Officers:
Walter C D Carlson, Chairman (non-executive)
LeRoy T Carlson Jr, President & Chief Executive Officer
Joseph R Hanley, Senior Vice President, Technology, Services & Strategy
Peter L Sereda, Senior Vice President, Finance & Treasurer
Douglas D Shuma, Senior Vice President & Controller
Kurt B Thaus, Senior Vice President & Chief Information Officer
Scott H Williamson, Senior Vice President, Acquisitions & Corporate Development
Ownership: The Voting Trust, 56.3%. votes. Comprised of 94.8% of TDS Series A Common Shares, 6% of outstanding TDS Common Shares.; TVT ownership:; LeRoy T Carlson Jr; Dr Letitia G C Carlson; Prudence E Carlson; Walter C D Carlson, Trustees.
Represented (legal): Holland & Knight LLP.
Cable Systems (2):
Oregon: BEND; SUNRIVER.
TV Stations:
Oregon: KOHD Bend.
LPTV Stations:
Oregon: KBNZ-LD Bend; K04BJ-D La Pine; K09YE-D La Pine; K34AI-D La Pine.
Cable Holdings:
TDS Baja Broadband LLC

TELEPHONE ELECTRONICS CORP. (TEC)
236 East Capitol St.
Jackson, MS 39201
Phone: 800-832-2515
Fax: 601-355-9746
E-mail: request@tec.com
Web site: http://www.tec.com
Officers:
Joseph D. Fail, Chairman & President
James H. Coakley Jr., Chief Operating Officer
Wayne Skelton, Secretary-Treasurer
Faye Lair, Marketing Director
Steve Hall, Programming & Engineering Director

Branch Offices:
Bay Springs
2988 Hwy 15
PO Box 409
Bay Springs, MS 39422
Phone: 601-764-2121
Fax: 601-764-2051
Bradford
224 E Main St
PO Box 10
Bradford, TN 38316
Phone: 731-742-2211
Fax: 731-742-2212

Cherokee
955 2nd St SW
PO Box 249
Cherokee, AL 35616
Phone: 256-359-4321
Fax: 256-359-6410
Friendship
563 Main St
PO Box 7
Friendship, TN 38034
Phone: 731-677-8181
Fax: 731-677-2161
Jackson
700 S West St
Jackson, MS 39201
Phone: 601-353-9118
Fax: 601-355-3746
Roanoke
950 Main St
Roanoke, AL 36274
Phone: 334-863-2111
Fax: 334-863-8624
Windermere
PO Box 556
Bay Springs, MS 39422
Phone: 601-375-2724
Cable Systems (2):
Mississippi: BAY SPRINGS.
Tennessee: ERIN.

TELEVISION ASSN. OF REPUBLIC
PO Box 555
147-10 North Clark
Republic, WA 99166
Phone: 509-775-3822
Web site: http://www.rcabletv.com
Officers:
Charles Sublett, Chairman & President
Sheila Welvaert, Secretary-Treasurer
Mahlon Gus Nickols III, Line Manager & Engineering Director
Ownership: Subscriber owned - Republic, WA.
Cable Systems (1):
Washington: REPUBLIC.

TEL-STAR CABLEVISION INC.
1295 Lourdes Rd.
Metamora, IL 61548-8416
Phone: 888-842-0258
Fax: 309-383-2657
Web site: http://www.telstar-online.net
Officers:
James Perley, Chairman & Chief Executive & Financial Officer
John Gregory, Engineering Director
Ownership: James L Perley, Chmn. & Chief Exec. Officer.
Cable Systems (2):
Illinois: METAMORA; WOODLAND HEIGHTS.

TEMPLETON TELEPHONE CO.
PO Box 77
115 North Main St.
Templeton, IA 51463
Phones: 712-669-3311; 888-669-3311
Fax: 712-669-3312
E-mail: citytemp@netins.net
Web site: http://www.templetoniowa.com
Officers:
Loretta Friedman, Chairman & President
Pat Snyder, General Manager
Cable Systems (2):
Iowa: DEDHAM; TEMPLETON.

THAMES VALLEY COMMUNICATIONS
295 Meridian St.
Groton, CT 06340
Phone: 860-446-4009
Fax: 860-446-4752

E-mail: info@tvcconnect.com
Web site: http://www.tvcconnect.com
Officer:
William H. Pearson, Chief Executive Officer
Cable Systems (1):
Connecticut: GROTON.

THREE RIVER DIGITAL CABLE LLC
PO Box 66
225 North 4th St.
Lynch, NE 68746
Phones: 402-569-2666; 866-569-2666
E-mail: info@threeriver.net
Web site: http://threeriver.net/newsite
Officers:
Neil K Classen, General Manager
Mike Gering, Marketing & Public Relations Director
Michael Swan, Outside Plant Supervisor/Springview
Ivan Keith Thompson, Outside Plant Supervisor/Lynch
Loree Boelter, Customer Service Representative Supervisor

Branch Offices:
Ainsworth
245 N Woodward
Ainsworth, NE 69210
Phone: 402-387-1353
Springview
PO Box 92
101 Main St
Springview, NE 68778
Phone: 402-497-4001
Cable Systems (1):
Nebraska: AINSWORTH.

TIME WARNER CABLE
17th Fl.
60 Columbus Cir.
New York, NY 10023
Phone: 212-364-8200
Fax: 203-328-0604
Web site: http://www.timewarnercable.com
Officers:
Marc Lawrence-Apfelbaum, Executive Vice President, General Counsel & Secretary
Gail G MacKinnon, Executive Vice President & Chief Government Relations Officer
William Osbourn, Co-Chief Financial Officer, Chief Accounting Officer & Senior Vice President, Controller
Matthew Siegel, Co-Chief Financial Officer & Senior Vice President-Treasurer
Christian Lee, Senior Vice President, Mergers & Acquisitions
--- Residential Services, ---
Jeff Hirsch, Executive Vice President & Chief Marketing & Sales Officer
Mark FitzPatrick, Senior Vice President & Chief Financial Officer, Residential Services
Deborah Picciolo, Senior Vice President, Technical Operations, Residential
--- Media Services, ---
--- Business Services, ---
Craig Collins, President
Gerry Campbell, Executive Vice President
Stephanie Anderson, Senior Vice President & Chief Marketing Officer
Brooks Borcherding, Senior Vice President, Enterprise & Carrier Sales
Craig Collins, Senior Vice President, Small & Medium Business Sales
Ken Fitzpatrick, Senior Vice President & Chief Operations and Transformation Officer
Henry Hryckiewicz, Senior Vice President, Field Network Operations
Greg King, Senior Vice President & Chief Product and Strategy Officer
Jeffrey Painting, Senior Vice President & Chief Sales Officer

---Technology & Network Operations, ---
Hamid Heidary, Executive Vice President & Chief Technology Officer
Jim Ludington, Executive Vice President, National Network Operations & Engineering
Frank Boncimino, Senior Vice President & Chief Information Officer
Dave Flessas, Senior Vice President, Network Operations Center & Operations Support
James Manchester, Senior Vice President, Applications Operations
Howard Pfeffer, Senior Vice President, Broadband Engineering & Technology
Matt Stanek, Senior Vice President, Core, Metro & Regional Network Operations
--- Finance, Communications & Human Resources, ---
Alan Lui, Senior Vice President, Human Resources
Chris Whitaker, Vice President, Learning Delivery, Human Resources

Branch Offices:
Advanced Technology Group
12101 Airport Way
Ste 100
Broomfield, CO 80021
Phone: 720-729-2810
Mid-Ohio Division
1266 Dublin Rd.
Columbus, OH 43215
Phone: 614-481-5000
Regional Office
13241 Woodland Park Rd
Herndon, VA 20171
Phone: 703-345-2400
Regional Office
7800 & 7910 Crescent Executive Dr
Charlotte, NC 28217
Phone: 704-731-3000
Ownership: Charter Communications Inc.. On May 26, 2015, Charter Communications Inc. announced it was merging with Time Warner Cable and acquiring Bright House Networks LLC (see listings for Charter and Bright House). FCC approved deals May 6, 2016. The deal closed May 18, 2016.
Represented (legal): Holland & Hart LLP.
Cable Systems (139):
Alabama: DALEVILLE; ENTERPRISE.
Arizona: YUMA (portions).
California: BANNING; BARSTOW; EL CENTRO; LOS ANGELES; LYTLE CREEK; PALM SPRINGS; SAN DIEGO.
Colorado: CRESTED BUTTE; TELLURIDE.
Hawaii: KAUAI ISLAND; KEALAKEKUA; MAUI ISLAND; OAHU ISLAND.
Idaho: COEUR D'ALENE.
Indiana: EVANSVILLE; MADISON; NEWBURGH; TERRE HAUTE.
Kentucky: ASHLAND; BOWLING GREEN; BULAN; CLAY (town); CORBIN; COVINGTON; DAWSON SPRINGS; LEBANON; LEXINGTON; LONDON; LOUISVILLE; MADISONVILLE; MAYFIELD; OWENSBORO; PROVIDENCE; RICHMOND; VANCEBURG.
Maine: DANFORTH; HOULTON; HOWLAND; ISLAND FALLS; MEDWAY; OAKFIELD; PORTLAND; PRESQUE ISLE.
Massachusetts: PITTSFIELD.
Missouri: KANSAS CITY.
Nebraska: LINCOLN.
New Hampshire: BERLIN; KEENE.
New Jersey: FORT LEE BOROUGH.
New York: ALBANY; BETHEL (town); BUFFALO; DEWITT; JAMESTOWN; MANHATTAN; MOUNT VERNON; STATEN ISLAND.
North Carolina: CHARLOTTE; ELIZABETH CITY; FARMVILLE; GREENSBORO; JACKSONVILLE; MURFREESBORO; RALEIGH; WILMINGTON.
Ohio: AMBERLEY (village); ASHLEY CORNER; ATHENS; BAINBRIDGE; BEVERLY; BOWERSTON; CADIZ; CALDWELL; CAMBRIDGE; CHILLICOTHE; CLEVELAND; COLUMBUS; COMMERCIAL POINT; COSHOCTON; DEFIANCE; DESHLER; HOPEDALE; JACKSON;

Cable Owners

JEWETT; LOGAN; MARION; MIDWAY; NEW HOLLAND; NEWARK; OAKLAND; PAULDING; PORT CLINTON; PORTSMOUTH; SCIO; SCIPIO TWP. (Meigs County); SUBURBANS MOTOR HOME PARK; TIFFIN; VAN WERT; VERSAILLES; WASHINGTON COURT HOUSE.
Oklahoma: ROGERS COUNTY (northern portion).
Pennsylvania: ERIE; FRANKLIN (Venango County).
South Carolina: COLUMBIA; HILTON HEAD ISLAND.
Tennessee: BOLIVAR (town); BROWNSVILLE.
Texas: AUSTIN; COLUMBUS; CORPUS CHRISTI; CRYSTAL CITY; DALLAS; DEL RIO; DILLEY; EAGLE PASS; EL PASO; GEORGE WEST; GONZALES; GREENVILLE; KERRVILLE; LAREDO; PHARR; PORT ARTHUR; ROCKPORT; SAN ANTONIO; SAN MARCOS; SEADRIFT; UVALDE; WICHITA FALLS; WINNIE.
Virginia: RICHLANDS (town).
Washington: PULLMAN.
West Virginia: CLARKSBURG.
Wisconsin: APPLETON; MARINETTE; MILWAUKEE.
Other Holdings:
Cable: 49.88% of Rhone Vision Cable S.A.S. (France); CiteReseau, S.A. (France)
Data service: 96.16% of Road Runner, Warner Brothers Online
Motion picture holdings: Warner Brothers International Theaters
Production: 50% of Bel-Air Entertainment, Looney Tunes, Telepictures Productions, Warner Bros. Television, Warner Bros. Television Animation, Warner Home Video, WarnerVision Entertainment, WB Television Network
Program source: NY1 News New York, NY; News 10 Now-Syracuse Syracuse, NY; Cinemax; Court TV; Home Box Office; 40% of HBO Asia; 23% of HBO Brasil; HBO Independent Productions; 33.46% of HBO Ole; HB TVKO Pay-Per-View; 50% of News 9 San Antonio San Antonio, TX; MetroSports; 33.3% of In Demand (held through TWE-A/N); Milwaukee News Channel Milwaukee, WI; Capital 9 News Albany, NY; R News Rochester, NY; News 14 Carolina-Raleigh Raleigh, NC; News 8 Austin Austin, TX; 50% of News 24 Houston Houston TX (held through TWE)
Publishing: 50% of DC Comics
Service Provider: DukeNet Communications
Telephone holdings

TITONKA TELEPHONE CO.
247 Main St. North
Titonka, IA 50480
Phones: 515-928-2110; 800-753-2016
Fax: 515-928-2897
E-mail: Titonka@TBCtel.com
Web site: http://www.tbctel.com
Officers:
Norman Cooper, President
Jim Mayland, General Manager
Vicky Nelson, Secretary-Treasurer
Cable Systems (1):
Iowa: TITONKA.
Other Holdings:
Telephone: The Burt Telephone Co.

TRANS-VIDEO INC.
56 Depot Sq.
Northfield, VT 05663
Phone: 802-485-3811
E-mail: info@trans-video.net
Web site: http://trans-video.net
Officers:
George L. Goodrich III, President
Jill Goodrich, Vice President
Ownership: George L Goodrich III, 51%; Jill Goodrich, 49%.

Cable Systems (1):
Vermont: NORTHFIELD (village).

TRI-COUNTY COMMUNICATIONS COOPERATIVE INC.
417 5th Ave. North
Strum, WI 54770
Phones: 715-695-2691; 715-985-3101
Fax: 715-695-3599
E-mail: info@tcc.coop
Web site: http://tccpro.net
Officers:
Fred Weier, Chief Executive Officer
Cheryl Rue, Chief Operating Officer
James Foss, President
Lynn Nelson, Secretary
Ownership:Company is the result of a merger of Western Wisconsin Communications Cooperative, Tri-County Telephone Cooperative and Tri-West Communications.
Cable Systems (1):
Wisconsin: WHITEHALL.

TRI-COUNTY COMMUNICATIONS INC.
PO Box 460
Belhaven, NC 27810
Phone: 252-964-2100
Fax: 252-964-2211
Officers:
Dennis M. Wallace Jr., Chief Executive Officer
Teresa M. Raupe, Subsidiary Products Manager
Jason Burleson, Video Systems Technician
Ownership: Tri-County Telephone Membership Corp..
Represented (legal): Harvey C. Raynor III.
Cable Systems (1):
North Carolina: BELHAVEN.

TRI-WAVE COMMUNICATIONS INC.
109 Depot Rd.
Paintsville, KY 41240
Phone: 606-789-7603
Fax: 606-789-3391
Officer:
Bart Ward, General Manager
Ownership: Bart Ward, General Manager & Owner.
Cable Systems (1):
Kentucky: LOWMANSVILLE.

TROY CABLEVISION
PO Box 1228
1006 South Brundidge St.
Troy, AL 36081
Phones: 334-566-3310; 800-735-9546
Fax: 334-566-3304
E-mail: support@troycable.net
Web site: http://www.troycable.net

Branch Offices:
Daleville
Daleville City Hall
Daleville, AL 36322
Phone: 334-598-1119
Elba
320 Simmons St
Elba, AL 36323
Phone: 334-853-3310
Enterprise
106 N Edwards St
Enterprise, AL 36330
Phone: 334-417-3310
Luverne
90 S Forest Ave
Luverne, AL 36049
Phone: 334-335-3435

Ozark
1298 Andrews Ave
Ozark, AL 36360
Phone: 334-443-3310
Ownership: Freeman Family.
Cable Systems (3):
Alabama: DALEVILLE; LUVERNE; TROY.

TRUVISTA COMMUNICATIONS
112 York St.
Chester, SC 29706
Phones: 803-385-2191; 800-768-1212
Fax: 803-581-2223
E-mail: ajohnson@truvista.biz
Web site: http://www.truvista.net
Officers:
Brian Singleton, President & Chief Executive Officer
David Brunt, Senior Vice President, Finance & Operations
Allison Jakubecy, Senior Vice President, Sales & Marketing
David Redys, Senior Vice President, Networks & Technology
Tom Harper, Vice President, Administration & Regulatory Affairs
Edward Hinson, Director, Business Operations
Tracy D Starnes, Senior Director, Field Operations
Patricia Joyner, Business Solutions Manager
Bob Wilkinson, Strategic Marketing Manager
Frank Young, Senior Director, Construction Services
Tony Helms, Manager, Switching & Video Services
Tony Miles, Manager, Purchasing & Property Services
Cheryl Wylie, Controller

Branch Offices:
Camden
1637 Springdale Dr
Camden, SC 29020
Phone: 803-432-3461
Great Falls
501 Dearborn St.
Great Falls, SC 29055
Phone: 803-482-2191
Ridgeway
295 S. Means St.
Ridgeway, SC 29180
Phone: 803-337-2291
Winnsboro
736 US Hwy. 321 Business S
Winnsboro, SC 29180
Phone: 803-635-6459
Cable Systems (7):
Georgia: CARNESVILLE; CLAYTON; FRANKLIN COUNTY; TOCCOA.
South Carolina: CAMDEN; CHESTER; WINNSBORO.

TSC COMMUNICATIONS INC.
PO Box 408
2 Willipie St.
Wapakoneta, OH 45895
Phones: 419-739-2200; 419-739-2300
Fax: 419-739-2299
E-mail: marketing@telserco.com
Web site: http://www.telserco.com

Branch Offices:
Middle Point Office
106 1/2 East Jackson St
Middle Point, OH 45863
Phone: 419-968-2000
Fax: 419-968-2701
St Marys Office
155 East High St
St Marys, OH 45885
Phone: 419-300-2300
Fax: 419-300-2499

Cable Systems (2):
Ohio: ST. MARYS TWP.; WAPAKONETA CITY.

THE TULALIP TRIBE INC.
2601 88th St. NE
Quil Ceda Village, WA 98271
Phone: 360-716-3270
Fax: 360-716-3272
Web site: http://www.tulalipbroadband.com
Officers:
Herman Williams, Jr., Chairman
Chris Henry, Chief Executive Officer
Richard Brown, Manager
Adrienne Calflooking, Bookkeeper
Sharon Contraro, Office Supervisor
Rick DeChenne, Head Technician
Merle Hayes, Technician
Cable Systems (1):
Washington: TULALIP INDIAN RESERVATION.

TV CABLE CO. OF ANDALUSIA INC.
PO Box 34
Andalusia, AL 36420
Phone: 334-222-6464
Fax: 334-222-7226
E-mail: jmike@andycable.com; support@andycable.com
Web site: http://www.andycable.com
Officers:
Ivan Bishop, President
J. Dige Bishop, Vice President
Ownership: Ivan Bishop, 23.35%; Linda Whitman, 18.82%; Julia H Bishop Trust, 16.09%; John Anderson, 9.86%; Jane Anthony, 7.42%; William H Albritton, 6.97%; Ophelia Albritton, 5.34%; Ann L Albritton, 4.25%; Harold & Virginia Broughton, 2.53%; Drew Cowen, 2.26%; Tyler Cowen, 2.26%; J. Dige Bishop Trust, 0.9%.
Cable Systems (5):
Alabama: ANDALUSIA; BEATRICE; CASTLEBERRY; HEATH; McKENZIE.

TV CABLE OF RENSSELAER INC.
PO Box 319
215 West Kellner Blvd., Ste. 19
Rensselaer, IN 47978-0319
Phones: 219-866-7101; 800-621-2344
E-mail: tvcable@rensselaer.tv
Web site: http://www.rensselaer.tv
Officers:
Eric Galbreath, Vice President & General Manager
Sue Shuey, Office Manager
Karen Maki, Marketing Director
Lisa Cawby, Customer Service Representative
Eric Sampson, Chief Technician
Cable Systems (2):
Indiana: MOROCCO; RENSSELAER (town).

TVC INC.
PO Box 329
3095 Sheridan Rd.
Lennon, MI 48449
Phones: 810-621-3363; 888-204-1077
Fax: 810-621-9600
E-mail: customerserv@lentel.com
Web site: http://www.lentel.com
Cable Systems (1):
Michigan: NEW LOTHROP.

TV SERVICE INC.
PO Box 1410
60 Communication Lane
Hindman, KY 41822
Phones: 606-785-9500; 800-624-2008
E-mail: tvs@tvscable.com; kenny@tvscable.com

Cable Owners

Web site: http://www.tvscable.com
Officers:
Robert C. Thacker, President, Chief Operating & Financial Officer
Archie W. Everage, Vice President, Operations
Junell Thacker, Secretary-Treasurer
Betty Thomas, Programming & Marketing Director
Ownership: Robert C Thacker. Thacker is part owner of Thacker-Grigsby Telephone Co., Hindman, KY.
Represented (legal): Slone & Bates.
Cable Systems (12):
Kentucky: BONNYMAN; BUSY; COWAN CREEK; HAYMOND; HINDMAN; JEREMIAH; LOTHAIR; MAYKING; MOUSIE; TOPMOST; VANCLEVE; VICCO.
Other Holdings:
Telephone holdings

TWIN VALLEY COMMUNICATIONS INC.
618 6th St.
Clay Center, KS 67432
Phones: 785-427-2288; 785-427-2211
Fax: 785-427-2216
E-mail: tvtinc@twinvalley.net
Web site: http://www.twinvalley.net
Officer:
Michael J. Foster, President

Branch Offices:
Clay Center
618 6th St
Clay Center, KS 67432
Miltonvale
22 West Spruce
Miltonvale, KS 67466
Ownership: John G. Foster, 11%; Joe Foster, 11%; Peggy S. Foster, 11%; Lulu R. Foster, 11%; Mildred H. Foster, 11%; Michael J. Foster, 11%; Jackie L. Foster, 11%; John F. Gisselbeck, 11%; Penny L. Gisselbeck, 11%. Michael J. Foster & John F. Gisselbeck are executives with the Twin Valley Telephone Co., Miltonvale, KS.
Cable Systems (1):
Kansas: MILTONVALE.

BILL TYLER
PO Box 110
Rte 2
Olney, TX 76374
Phones: 940-873-4563; 800-687-7311
Fax: 940-873-4563
E-mail: bill@tgncable.net
Officers:
Bill R. Tyler, Owner & Operator
Jan Tyler, Owner & Operator
Cable Systems (2):
Texas: LAKE GRAHAM; THROCKMORTON.
Cable Holdings:
TGN Cable Systems located in Throckmorton, Newcastle and Lake Graham, Texas.

TYLERSVILLE COMMUNITY TV ASSOCIATION INC.
1133 Summer Mountain Rd.
Loganton, PA 17747
Phone: 570-725-3865
Officer:
Jim Breon, President

Branch Office:
Loganton
3459 Narrows Rd
Loganton, PA 17747-9589
Ownership: Community owned--Tylersville, PA.

Cable Systems (1):
Pennsylvania: TYLERSVILLE.

UNEV COMMUNICATIONS INC.
760 8th St.
Lovelock, NV 89419
Phone: 702-273-2020
Ownership: Tom Mitchell.
Cable Systems (1):
Texas: OZONA.

UNION TELEPHONE CO.-MOUNTAIN VIEW, WY
PO Box 160
Mountain View, WY 82939
Phones: 888-926-2273; 307-782-7363
E-mail: webmaster@unionwireless.com
Web site: http://www.unionwireless.com
Cable Systems (1):
Wyoming: MOUNTAIN VIEW (Uinta County).

CITY OF UNIONVILLE CABLE TV
PO Box 255
1611 Grant St.
Unionville, MO 63565
Phone: 660-947-2437
Fax: 660-947-7756
Web site: http://www.unionvillemo.org
Officers:
Karl Klinginsmith, Mayor
Jerry Tilden, Chief Operating Officer
Cable Systems (1):
Missouri: UNIONVILLE.

UNITED COMMUNICATIONS ASSN. INC.
PO Box 117
1107 McArtor Rd.
Dodge City, KS 67801
Phones: 620-227-8641; 800-794-9999
Fax: 620-227-7032
E-mail: utasupport@unitedtelcom.net
Web site: http://www.unitedtelcom.net
Officers:
Laurence Vierthaler, President
Don Howell, Vice President
Craig Mock, General Manager
Sharon Batman, Secretary-Treasurer
Ownership: Subscriber owned--Dodge City, KS.
Cable Systems (1):
Kansas: CIMARRON.

UNITED TELEPHONE MUTUAL AID CORP.
PO Box 729
411 7th Ave.
Langdon, ND 58249
Phones: 701-256-5156; 800-844-9708
Fax: 701-256-5150
E-mail: info@utma.com
Web site: http://www.utma.com
Officers:
Thomas Eagan, President
Perry Oster, General Manager
Dennis Hansel, Assistant General Manager
Ross Feil, Facilities Manager
Kirsten Gendron, Customer Service Manager

Branch Offices:
Bottineau
538 11th St W
Ste 2
Bottineau, ND 58318
Phone: 701-228-1101

Rolla
617 Main Ave W
PO Box 238
Rolla, ND 58367
Phone: 701-477-1101
Ownership: Community cooperative--Munich, ND.
Represented (legal): Scott Stewart.
Cable Systems (3):
North Dakota: CAVALIER COUNTY (portions); MUNICH; TOWNER COUNTY (portions).

UPPER PENINSULA COMMUNICATIONS INC.
PO Box 66
Carney, MI 49812
Phone: 906-639-2194
Officers:
Louis DuPont, Acting President & Vice President, Operations
L. G. Matthews, Secretary-Treasurer
Ownership: Louis DuPont; L. G Matthews (Mrs.), Principals.
Cable Systems (5):
Michigan: ALPHA (village); AMASA; GARDEN TWP.; GERMFASK.
Wisconsin: PHELPS.

USA COMPANIES LP
Ste B
920 East 56th St.
Kearney, NE 68847
Phones: 308-236-1510; 877-234-0102
E-mail: support@usacommunications.tv; csr@usacommunications.tv
Web site: http://usacommunications.tv
Officers:
Chris Hilliard, Chief Executive Officer
Stuart Gilbertson, Corporate Engineer

Branch Office:
PO Box 1448
Kearney, NE 68848-1448
Ownership: Russell G. Hilliard.
Represented (legal): Cole, Raywid & Braverman LLP.
Cable Systems (24):
Alabama: LINCOLN; PELL CITY; TALLADEGA COUNTY (portions).
California: BOMBAY BEACH; BORREGO SPRINGS; CALIPATRIA; JULIAN; MECCA; NILAND; SALTON CITY; SALTON SEA BEACH.
Colorado: BAYFIELD; BLACK HAWK; CENTER; IGNACIO; LAKE CITY; NEDERLAND; PAGOSA SPRINGS; SAGUACHE; SOUTH FORK.
Montana: BILLINGS (western portion); COLSTRIP; FORSYTH; HARDIN.

UTE MOUNTAIN INDIAN TRIBE
PO Box 33
Towaoc, CO 81334
Phone: 303-565-9574
Cable Systems (1):
Colorado: TOWAOC.

VALLEY CABLE SYSTEMS
PO Box 78
Doylesburg, PA 17219
Phone: 717-349-7717
Officer:
Barry Kepner, Chairman
Ownership: Barry L Kepner, 50%; Sandy Kepner, 50%.
Cable Systems (2):
Pennsylvania: DOYLESBURG; METAL TWP..

VALLEY TV CO-OP INC.
PO Box 450
Parkdale, OR 97401

Phone: 503-352-6760
Cable Systems (2):
Oregon: ODELL; PARKDALE.

VALPARAISO COMMUNICATION SYSTEMS
PO Box 296
465 Valparaiso Pkwy.
Valparaiso, FL 32580
Phone: 850-729-5404
E-mail: support@valp.net
Web site: http://www.valp.net
Officers:
Burt B. Bennett, General Manager
Rick Howell, Chief Technology Officer
Helen J. Bourgeois, Chief Financial Officer & City Clerk
Ownership: Community owned--Valparaiso, FL.
Cable Systems (1):
Florida: VALPARAISO.

VAN HORNE TELEPHONE CO.
204 Main St.
Van Horne, IA 52346
Phone: 319-228-8791
Fax: 319-228-8784
E-mail: vanhorne@netins.net
Officers:
Ralph Petersen, President
Donald Whipple, Manager
Wayne Eichmeyer, Vice President
Patrice Smith, Secretary-Treasurer
Cable Systems (1):
Iowa: VAN HORNE.
Other Holdings:
Cellular radio: Navenroh Communications Inc.

VELOCITY TELEPHONE INC.
Ste 100
4050 Olson Memorial Hwy.
Golden Valley, MN 55422
Phone: 763-222-1000
Fax: 763-222-1001
E-mail: sales@velocitytelephone.com
Web site: http://www.velocitytelephone.com
Officers:
Jim Lundberg, Chief Executive Officer
Ron Cleven, Chief Technology Officer
Jim Hickle, President
Tom O'Brien, Director of Operations
Cable Systems (1):
California: WEAVERVILLE.

VENTURE COMMUNICATIONS COOPERATIVE
PO Box 157
218 Commercial Ave. SE
Highmore, SD 57345-0157
Phones: 605-852-2224; 800-824-7282
Fax: 605-852-2404
E-mail: venture@venturecomm.net
Web site: http://www.venturecomm.net
Officers:
Randy Houdek, Chief Executive Officer
Randy Olson, Assistant General Manager
Brad Ryan, Chief Technician
Represented (legal): Riter, Rogers, Wattier & Northrup LLP.
Cable Systems (9):
South Dakota: BRITTON; CRESBARD; FAULKTON; GETTYSBURG; HIGHMORE; ONIDA; ROSHOLT; SISSETON; WESSINGTON SPRINGS.
Other Holdings:
Cellular radio

Cable Owners

VERNONIA CATV INC.
536 South First Ave.
Vernonia, OR 97064
Phones: 503-427-8327; 503-429-5103
Officer:
Bud Foster, President
Ownership: Bud Foster, Pres..
Cable Systems (1):
Oregon: VERNONIA.

VIDEO SERVICES LTD.
PO Box 123
Bode, IA 50519
Phone: 515-379-1558
Ownership: Mark Steil, Principal.
Cable Systems (1):
Iowa: BODE.

VISION COMMUNICATIONS LLC (LOUISIANA)
115 West 10th Blvd.
Larose, LA 70373
Phone: 985-693-0123
Fax: 985-693-3049
E-mail: bchristian@wydctv.com
Web site: http://www.viscom.net/portal
Ownership: James Callahan.
Represented (legal): Arter & Hadden LLP.
Cable Systems (1):
Louisiana: GOLDEN MEADOW.

VI-TEL LLC
PO Box 789
223 Broadway
Davenport, OK 74026-0789
Phones: 918-377-2241; 800-252-8854
Fax: 918-377-2506
E-mail: info@cotc.net
Web site: http://www2.cotc.net
Officers:
Steven Guest, President
David Guest, Vice President
John Hart, Chief Financial Officer
Aaron Gardner, In-house Counsel
Ownership: Central Oklahoma Telephone Co..
Cable Systems (1):
Oklahoma: DAVENPORT.
Other Holdings:
Telephone holdings

VOGTMANN ENGINEERING INC.
6625 Maple Ridge Rd.
Alger, MI 48610
Phone: 989-836-8848
E-mail: moreinfo@algercable.com
Web site: http://www.veionline.com
Cable Systems (1):
Michigan: STERLING.

VOLCANO COMMUNICATIONS CO.
PO Box 1070
20000 Hwy. 88
Pine Grove, CA 95665
Phones: 209-296-7502; 888-865-2266
Fax: 209-296-4466
E-mail: info@volcanotel.com
Web site: http://www.volcanocommunications.com
Officers:
Sharon Lundgren, Chairman
Ray Crabtree, Manager
Ownership: Sharon Lundgren, Chmn. & Principal.
Represented (legal): Cooper, White & Cooper LLP.
Cable Systems (1):
California: IONE.
Other Holdings:
Cellular radio: Volcano Cellular Inc.
Telephone holdings

VYVE BROADBAND LLC
Ste 330
4 International Dr.
Rye Brook, NY 10573
Phone: 855-367-8983
E-mail: sbeqaj@bcimanagement.net
Web site: http://vyvebroadband.com
Officers:
Jeffrey S DeMond, President & Chief Executive Officer
Andrew Kober, Executive Vice President & Chief Financial Officer
Margot Bright, Senior Vice President & Treasurer
Marie Censoplano, Senior Vice President, General Counsel & Secretary
Angela Conklin, Senior Vice President, Human Resources
Dennis Davies, Senior Vice President, Engineering & Chief Technology Officer
John Gibbs, Senior Vice President, Business Services
Diane Quennoz, Senior Vice President, Marketing & Customer Experience
Daniel White, Senior Vice President, Financial Planning
Vin Zachariah, Senior Vice President, Residential Services
Shawn Beqaj, Vice President, Government & Regulatory Affairs
Jeffrey DeMedeiros, Vice President, Corporate Controller
Alex Harris, Vice President, Network Planning

Branch Offices:
Atchison
625 Commercial
Ste 1
Atchison, KS 66002
Dalhart
1619 Tennessee Blvd
Dalhart, TX 79022
Fort Riley
6422 Normandy Dr
Fort Riley, KS 66442
Guymon
215 NW 5th St
Guymon, OK 73942
McAlester
205 E Cherokee
McAlester, OK 74501
McGehee
501 E Ash St
McGehee, AR 71654
Medicine Lodge
108 N Main
Medicine Lodge, KS 67104
Mena
509 Mena St
Mena, AR 71953
New Boston
118 N West St
New Boston, TX 75570
Ottawa
118 W 15th St
Ottawa, KS 66067
Perryton
217 S Ash St
Perryton, TX 79070
Shawnee
1819 Airport Drive
Shawnee, OK 74804
Phone: 405-395-1104
Fax: 405-788-4314
Ownership: Jeffrey S DeMond; Andrew Kober; BBH Capital Partners, private equity fund sponsored by Brown Brothers Harriman & Co..
Cable Systems (92):
Arkansas: CORNING; DE QUEEN; FAIRFIELD BAY; McCRORY; McGEHEE; MENA; MURFREESBORO.
Colorado: OTIS (town).
Georgia: DOUGLAS; WAYCROSS.
Kansas: ATCHISON; ELLINWOOD; FORT RILEY; FREDONIA; GARNETT; HERINGTON; INMAN; MEADE; MEDICINE LODGE; OTTAWA; PEABODY; STAFFORD.
Louisiana: KINDER; LAKE ARTHUR; WESTLAKE.
Oklahoma: ACHILLE; ARPELAR; BRAGGS; BRISTOW; CHANDLER; COALGATE; CROMWELL; DEPEW; DURANT; EUFAULA; FORT GIBSON; GERONIMO; GOODWELL; GORE; GUYMON; HAILEYVILLE; HOLDENVILLE; HULBERT; KELLYVILLE; KEOTA; KETCHUM; KINGSTON; LANGSTON; McALESTER; MOUNDS; MOUNTAIN PARK; NEWKIRK; OKEMAH; PANAMA; PAWHUSKA; PECAN VALLEY; PORUM; PORUM LANDING; PRYOR; QUINTON; SALINA; SAVANNA; SHAWNEE; STIGLER; STILWELL; STRATFORD; STROUD; VIAN; WAGONER; WILBURTON.
Tennessee: NEW TAZEWELL.
Texas: BALLINGER; BOWIE; BRYSON; DALHART; DECATUR; GRAFORD; HUNTINGTON; JACKSBORO; NEW BOSTON; PERRYTON; POSSUM KINGDOM LAKE; PRESTON PENINSULA; SPRINGTOWN; WINTERS.
Wyoming: DOUGLAS; GLENROCK; LUSK; RIVERSIDE; SARATOGA; TORRINGTON; WHEATLAND.

WABASH INDEPENDENT NETWORKS
PO Box 719
113 Hagen Dr
Louisville, IL 62839
Phones: 618-665-3311; 618-662-3636
Fax: 618-665-4188
E-mail: winita@wabash.net
Web site: http://www.wabash.net
Officers:
David Grahn, President
Jeffrey Williams, Executive Vice President & General Manager
Tanya Wells, Controller
Cable Systems (1):
Illinois: FLORA.

WADSWORTH COMMUNICATIONS
120 Maple St.
Wadsworth, OH 44281
Phone: 330-335-2888
Fax: 330-335-2829
E-mail: support@wadsnet.com; support@wadsworthcitylink.com
Web site: http://www.wadsworthcitylink.com/city-link/citylink-cable-tv.html
Ownership: City of Wadsworth.
Cable Systems (1):
Ohio: WADSWORTH.

WAITSFIELD-FAYSTON TELEPHONE CO.
PO Box 9
Waitsfield, VT 05673
Phones: 802-496-3391; 800-496-3391
E-mail: ghaskin@wcvt.com
Web site: http://www.waitsfieldcable.com
Officers:
Dana Haskin, Chairman
Gregg Haskin, President & Chief Executive Officer
Roger Nishi, Vice President, Industry
Cable Systems (1):
Vermont: WAITSFIELD.

WALNUT COMMUNICATIONS
PO Box 346
510 Highland St.
Walnut, IA 51577-0346
Phones: 712-784-2211; 888-784-2211
Fax: 712-784-2010
E-mail: info@walnutel.net
Web site: http://www.walnutcommunications.com
Officer:
Bruce Heyne, General Manager

Branch Office:
Avoca
161 S Elm St.
Avoca, IA 51521-9000
Phone: 712-784-2211
Cable Systems (1):
Iowa: WALNUT.
Other Holdings:
Cellular radio

WAVEDIVISION HOLDINGS LLC
Ste 500
401 Kirkland Parkplace Ctr.
Kirkland, WA 98033
Phones: 425-576-8200; 866-928-3123
Fax: 425-576-8221
Web site: http://www.wavebroadband.com
Officers:
Steven Weed, Chief Executive Officer & Founder
Harold Zeitz, President & Chief Operating Officer
Colette Jelineo, Chief Marketing Officer
Steve Friedman, Executive Vice President of Fiber Design and Construction
Tim Klinefelter, Executive Vice President, Broadband Services
Patrick Knorr, Executive Vice President, IP & Business Services
Arah Peck, Executive Vice President, Strategic Development
Jim Penney, Executive Vice President, Business & legal Affairs
Ownership: Oak Hill Holdco; OHH ownership;; Oak Hill Capital Partners, majority interest; GI Partners; WaveDivision Capital LLC, Steven B Weed manager.
Cable Systems (27):
California: CONCORD; GARBERVILLE; PLACER COUNTY (southwestern portion); RIO VISTA; SAN FRANCISCO (southern portion); WEST SACRAMENTO.
Oregon: DEPOE BAY; SANDY; SILVERTON; TURNER.
Washington: BELLINGHAM; CAMANO ISLAND; CARSON; CHELAN; CONCRETE; DUVALL; ECHO LAKE/SNOHOMISH; LAKEBAY; MORTON; NAPAVINE; PACKWOOD; PORT ANGELES; PORT ORCHARD; PORT TOWNSEND; RANDLE; SEATTLE (surrounding areas); WHIDBEY ISLAND.

WAVE WIRELESS LLC
PO Box 921
2130 Corning Ave.
Parsons, KS 67357
Phone: 620-423-9283
E-mail: support@wavewls.com
Web site: http://www.wavewls.com
Cable Systems (1):
Kansas: ALTAMONT.

WEHCO VIDEO INC.
PO Box 2221
Little Rock, AR 72203
Phones: 501-378-3400; 800-903-0508
Fax: 501-376-8594
Web site: http://m.wehco.com
Officers:
Walter E. Hussman Jr., Chairman & Chief Executive Officer
J. P. Morbeck, Chief Operating Officer
Allen Berry, Chief Financial Officer
Jim Burk, Engineering Director

Cable Owners

Ownership: Walter E Hussman Jr., see listing, Principal; Camden News Publishing Company.
Represented (legal): Covington & Burling LLP.
Cable Systems (10):
Arkansas: BRINKLEY; CAMDEN; FORREST CITY; HOPE; HOT SPRINGS; PINE BLUFF; SEARCY.
Mississippi: VICKSBURG.
Oklahoma: TAHLEQUAH.
Texas: LONGVIEW.
Other Holdings:
Newspaper holdings

WEST ALABAMA TV CABLE CO. INC.
213 2nd Ave. NE
Fayette, AL 35555
Phone: 205-932-4700
E-mail: cable@watvc.com
Web site: http://www.watvc.com
Officer:
Stephen W. Vaughan, President
Ownership: Stephen W Vaughan, Pres..
Cable Systems (3):
Alabama: FAYETTE; HAMILTON; WINFIELD.

CITY OF WESTBROOK
PO Box 367
556 First Ave.
Westbrook, MN 56183
Phone: 507-274-6712
Fax: 507-274-5569
Officer:
Dennis Jutting, Superintendent
Cable Systems (1):
Minnesota: WESTBROOK.

WEST CENTRAL TELEPHONE ASSOCIATION
308 Frontage Rd.
Sebeka, MN 56477
Phones: 218-837-5151; 800-945-2163
Fax: 218-837-5001
E-mail: wcphone@wcta.net
Web site: http://www.wcta.net
Officers:
Anthony V. Mayer, Chief Executive Officer & Manager
Bruce Kinnunen, President
Dave Pulji, Vice President
Sheldon Sagedahl, Operations Director
Cable Systems (1):
Minnesota: MENAHGA.

WESTEL SYSTEMS
PO Box 330
012 East 3rd St.
Remsen, IA 51050
Phones: 712-786-1181; 800-352-0006
Fax: 712-786-2400
E-mail: support@westelsystems.com; acctinfo@westelsystems.com
Web site: http://www.westelsystems.com
Officer:
William H. Daubendiek II, Manager
Cable Systems (3):
Iowa: ANITA; MARCUS.
Nebraska: HOOPER.

WESTERN IOWA TELEPHONE
PO Box 38
202 Cedar St.
Lawton, IA 51030
Phones: 712-944-5711; 800-469-0811
Fax: 712-944-5722
E-mail: wiatel@wiatel.com
Web site: http://www.wiatel.com

Officers:
Phil Robinson, Operations Manager
Pam Clark, Marketing & Sales
Susan Kolker, Office Manager
Cable Systems (3):
Iowa: KINGSLEY; LAWTON (village); MOVILLE.

WESTERN MONTANA COMMUNITY TELEPHONE
312 Main St. SW
Ronan, MT 59864
Phone: 406-676-0798
Cable Systems (5):
Montana: PLAINS; SEELEY LAKE; ST. IGNATIUS; SUPERIOR; THOMPSON FALLS.

WESTFIELD COMMUNITY ANTENNA ASSN. INC.
121 Strang St.
Westfield, PA 16950
Phone: 814-367-5190
Fax: 814-367-5586
Officer:
Faun James, Office Manager
Ownership: Subscriber owned--Westfield, PA.
Cable Systems (1):
Pennsylvania: WESTFIELD.

WESTPA.NET INC.
PO Box 703
216 Pennsylvania Ave. W
Warren, PA 16365
Phone: 814-726-9462
Fax: 814-723-9585
E-mail: info@westpa.net
Web site: http://www.westpa.net
Cable Systems (1):
Pennsylvania: SHEFFIELD.

WEST RIVER COOPERATIVE TELEPHONE CO.
PO Box 39
801 Coleman Ave.
Bison, SD 57620
Phone: 605-244-5213
Fax: 605-244-7288
E-mail: westriver@sdplains.com
Web site: http://www.sdplains.com
Officers:
DeJon Bakken, President
Greg Fried, Vice President
Alice Holcomb, Secretary
Sandi Helms, Treasurer
Jerry Reisenauer, General Manager
Colgan Huber, Finance Director
Colle Nash, Operations Director
Cable Systems (2):
South Dakota: BISON; FAITH.

WEST TEXAS RURAL TELEPHONE COOPERATIVE
PO Box 1737
Hereford, TX 79045
Phone: 806-364-3331
Fax: 806-360-3790
Web site: http://www.wtrt.net
Officer:
Amy Linzey, Chief Executive Officer & General Manager
Cable Systems (1):
Texas: HEREFORD.

WETHERELL CABLE TV SYSTEM
407 West Grace St.
Cleghorn, IA 51014
Phone: 712-436-2266
Ownership: Ronald Wetherell; Todd Wetherell.

Cable Systems (1):
Iowa: CLEGHORN.

WHEAT STATE TELECABLE INC.
PO Box 320
106 West 1st St.
Udall, KS 67146
Phone: 800-442-6835
Fax: 620-782-3302
E-mail: support@wheatstate.com
Web site: http://www.wheatstate.com
Officers:
Greg Reed, Chairman, President & Chief Executive Officer
Arturo Macias, Chief Operating Officer & Secretary-Treasurer
Ownership: Golden Wheat Inc.. Also owns Wheat State Telephone Co.
Represented (legal): James M. Caplinger Chartered.
Cable Systems (1):
Kansas: UDALL.

TIMOTHY A. WHITNEY
PO Box 47
Keene Valley, NY 12943
Phone: 518-576-4510
Cable Systems (1):
New York: KEENE VALLEY.

WIDEOPENWEST LLC
Ste 1000
7887 East Belleview Ave.
Englewood, CO 80111
Phones: 720-479-3500; 720-479-3558
Fax: 720-479-3585
Web site: http://www.wowway.com
Officers:
Jeffrey Marcus, Chairman
Steven Cochran, President & Chief Executive Officer
Cash Hagen, Chief Operating Officer
Richard Fish, Chief Financial Officer
Scott Russell, Chief Marketing & Sales Officer
Cathy Kuo, Executive Vice President, Strategy & Engagement
Mark Dineen, Senior Vice President, Field Operations
Kelvin Fee, Senior Vice President, Midwest Region
Michael Furst, Senior Vice President, Customer Care
Mike Harry, Senior Vice President, Business Services
Scott Neesley, Senior Vice President, Central Region
Peter C Smith, Senior Vice President, Programming & Advertising Sales
Janice Turner, Senior Vice President, Human Resources
Craig Martin, General Counsel
Ownership: Avista Capital Partners, 65%. equity; Crestview Partners, 35%. equity.
Cable Systems (17):
Alabama: CHAMBERS COUNTY (portions); DOTHAN; HUNTSVILLE; MONTGOMERY.
Florida: PANAMA CITY BEACH; PINELLAS COUNTY (portions).
Georgia: AUGUSTA; COLUMBUS.
Illinois: NAPERVILLE.
Indiana: EVANSVILLE.
Kansas: LAWRENCE.
Michigan: DIMONDALE; PLYMOUTH.
Ohio: BEREA; COLUMBUS.
South Carolina: CHARLESTON.
Tennessee: KNOXVILLE.

WIKSTROM SYSTEMS LLC
PO Box 217
212 South Main St.
Karlstad, MN 56732-0217

Phones: 218-436-2121; 800-436-5222
Fax: 218-436-3100
E-mail: service@wiktel.com
Web site: http://www.wiktel.com
Officers:
Bryan Wixstrom, President & General Manager
Carrie Kern-Taggart, Controller
Cable Systems (7):
Minnesota: ALVARADO; ARGYLE; HALLOCK; KENNEDY; LAKE BRONSON; LANCASTER; STEPHEN.

WILCOP CABLE TV
PO Box 558
Brodhead, KY 40409
Phone: 606-758-8320
Ownership: Johnny Wilcop.
Cable Systems (1):
Kentucky: BRODHEAD.

TOM WILHELMI
PO Box 868
105 2nd St. NE
Beach, ND 58621
Phone: 701-629-1112
Cable Systems (1):
North Dakota: BEACH.

ANDY WILLIAMS
PO Box 2598
Starkville, MS 39759
Phone: 662-324-5121
Cable Systems (4):
Mississippi: EUPORA; MACON; OKTIBBEHA COUNTY; SCOOBA.

CITY OF WILLIAMSTOWN CABLE TV
PO Box 147
400 North Main St.
Williamstown, KY 41097
Phone: 859-824-3633
Fax: 859-824-6320
E-mail: jhartinger@wtownky.org
Web site: http://www.wtownky.org
Officers:
Chuck Hudson, Chairman, Chief Executive & Operating Officer
Michael E. Shoemaker, General Manager
Vivian Link, Chief Financial Officer
Tony Penick, Programming Director
Roy Osborne, Engineering Director
Ownership: Community owned--Williamstown, KY.
Cable Systems (1):
Kentucky: WILLIAMSTOWN.

WILSON COMMUNICATIONS
PO Box 190
2504 Ave. D
Wilson, KS 67490-0190
Phone: 800-432-7607
Fax: 785-658-3344
E-mail: customerservice@wilsoncom.us
Web site: http:// www.wilsoncommunications.us
Officers:
Brian Boisvert, General Manager
Scott Grauer, Vice President, Marketing
Gary Everett, Controller
Ownership: Bob Grauer; Eva Grauer; Scott Grauer.
Cable Systems (1):
Kansas: BROOKVILLE.

WINDBREAK CABLE
1140 10th St.
Gering, NE 69341

Cable Owners

Phone: 308-436-4650
Fax: 308-436-4779
E-mail: bill@intertech.net
Web site: http://www.windbreak.com
Officer:
William D. Bauer, President & Chief Executive Officer
Ownership: William D. Bauer, Pres. & Chief Exec. Officer.
Cable Systems (5):
Nebraska: HARRISON; LYMAN; OSHKOSH.
Wyoming: GUERNSEY; PINE BLUFFS.
Other Holdings:
Multimedia: InterTECH Corp.

WINDOM TELECOMMUNICATIONS
443 10th St.
Windom, MN 56101
Phone: 507-832-8000
Fax: 507-832-8010
E-mail: support@windomnet.com
Web site: http://www.windomnet.com
Officers:
Steven Nasby, City Administrator
Dennis Purrington, CATV Superintendent
Gene Sunstrom, Chief Technology Officer
Ownership: Community owned--Windom, MN.
Cable Systems (1):
Minnesota: WINDOM.

WINDSTREAM COMMUNICATIONS INC.
4001 Rodney Parham Rd.
Little Rock, AR 72212
Phones: 501-748-7000; 866-971-9463
Fax: 501-748-6392
E-mail: support@windstream.net
Web site: http://www.windstream.com
Officers:
Jeffrey Hinson, Chairman
Tony Thomas, President & Chief Executive Officer
Sarah Day, President, Consumer, Small & Medium Businesses
Mike Shippey, President, Carrier
David Works, President, Enterprise
Jarrod Berkshire, President, Operations, Georgia
Bob Gunderman, Chief Financial Officer
Ric Crane, Chief Marketing Officer & Executive Vice President
Lewis Langston, Chief Information Officer & Executive Vice President
Randy Nicklas, Chief Technical Officer & Executive Vice President, Engineering
Mark Faris, Executive Vice President, Operations
John Fletcher, Executive Vice President & Chief Counsel
Jeffrey Howe, Executive Vice President, Enterprise Sales
Susan Bradley, Senior Vice President, Human Resources
Rob Clancy, Senior Vice President & Treasurer
Matt Dement, Senior Vice President, Strategy, Corporate Development and Financial Planning & Analysis
Christie Grumbos, Senior Vice President & Treasurer
Kevin Halpin, Senior Vice President, Process Development & Improvement
Beth Lackey, Senior Vice President, Carrier Operations
Kristi Moody, Senior Vice President, Law & Corporate Secretary
Matt Preschern, Senior Vice President & Enterprise Chief Marketing Officer
Mike Rhoda, Senior Vice President, Governmental Affairs
Gregg Richey, Senior Vice President, Consumer Sales
Frank Schueneman, Senior Vice President, Network Services

Don Wilborne, Senior Vice President, Business Sales & Support
Ownership: Publicly held..
Cable Systems (6):
Georgia: DAHLONEGA; IRWINTON.
Missouri: BOLIVAR (town); STOCKTON.
North Carolina: LEXINGTON.
Pennsylvania: STATE COLLEGE.
Other Holdings:
Telephone holdings

WINDWAVE COMMUNICATIONS
PO Box 815
162 North Main St.
Heppner, OR 97836
Phone: 800-862-8508
Fax: 541-676-9655
E-mail: info@windwave.tc
Web site: http://www.windwave.org
Officers:
Nate Arbogast, President
Don Russel, Vice President
Gary Neal, Secretary-Treasurer
Randall Kowalke, Director
Cable Systems (1):
Oregon: HEPPNER.

SCOTT WINGER
210 North Main St.
Sweetser, IN 46987
Phone: 765-384-7873
E-mail: sweetser@comteck.com
Web site: http://www.comteck.com
Officer:
Scott Winger, President
Cable Systems (1):
Indiana: SWEETSER.

WINNEBAGO COOPERATIVE TELECOM ASSN.
704 East Main
Lake Mills, IA 50450
Phones: 641-592-6105; 800-592-6105
Fax: 641-592-6102
E-mail: wcta@wctatel.net
Web site: http://www.wctatel.net
Officers:
Mark Thoma, General Manager
Steve Savoy, Senior Network Administrator
Bob Klebsch, Plant Administrator
Ownership: Subscriber owned--Lake Mills, IA.
Cable Systems (1):
Iowa: LAKE MILLS.

WIRE TELE-VIEW CORP.
603 East Market St.
Pottsville, PA 17901
Phone: 570-622-4501
Fax: 570-622-8340
E-mail: customerserv@wtvaccess.com
Web site: http://www.wtvaccess.com
Officers:
Deborah A. Stabinsky, President
J. Richard Kirn, Secretary
Mary Louise Schoffstall, Treasurer
Ownership: Mary Louise Schoffstall, 30.4%; Deborah A Stabinsky, 12.2%; J. Richard Kirn, 9.6%; remainder undisclosed.
Cable Systems (2):
Pennsylvania: POTTSVILLE; TREMONT.

WITTENBERG TELEPHONE CO.
PO Box 160
104 West Walker St.
Wittenberg, WI 54499
Phone: 715-253-2111
Fax: 715-253-3497
E-mail: wittenbergtel@wittenbergnet.net

Web site: http://www.wittenbergnet.net
Officers:
Sydney R. Peterson, President
Allen Mahnke, Vice President
Lucy Lopez, Secretary
Larry Winter, Treasurer
Cable Systems (1):
Wisconsin: WITTENBERG.

CITY OF WOODSFIELD, OH
221 South Main St.
Woodsfield, OH 43793
Phone: 740-472-1865
Cable Systems (1):
Ohio: WOODSFIELD.

WOODSTOCK TELEPHONE CO.
PO Box C
337 Aetna St.
Ruthton, MN 56170
Phones: 507-658-3830; 800-752-9397
E-mail: wtcinfo@woodstocktel.net
Web site: http://www.woodstocktel.net
Officers:
Ken Knuth, Chief Executive & Financial Officer
Doug Folkerts, Chief Operating Officer
Ben Knuth, Marketing Director
Dave Berkowski, Engineering Director
Cable Systems (1):
Minnesota: RUTHTON.

WORTH CABLE SERVICES
PO Box 1733
Darien, GA 31305
Phone: 912-437-3422
Fax: 912-437-2065
Ownership: Dennis B Wortham.
Cable Systems (3):
Georgia: HOBOKEN; SURRENCY; UVALDA.

WTC COMMUNICATIONS INC.
1009 Lincoln St.
Wamego, KS 66547
Phones: 785-456-1000; 877-982-1912
Fax: 785-456-9903
E-mail: support@wamego.net; info@wtcks.com
Web site: http://www.wtcks.com
Officer:
Jeff Wick, General Manager
Cable Systems (2):
Kansas: WAMEGO; WAMEGO.

WYANDOTTE MUNICIPAL SERVICES
1st Fl.
3200 Biddle Ave.
Wyandotte, MI 48192
Phone: 734-324-7190
E-mail: stimcoe@wyan.org; talk2wms@wyan.org
Web site: http://www.wyan.org
Ownership: Community owned--Wyandotte, MI.
Cable Systems (1):
Michigan: WYANDOTTE.

XIT COMMUNICATIONS
PO Box 711
12324 US Hwy. 87
Dalhart, TX 79022
Phones: 806-384-3311; 800-232-3312
Fax: 806-384-3340
E-mail: xitcom@xit.net
Web site: http://www.xit.net
Officers:
J. W. McClellan Jr, President
Walter E. Lasley, Vice President
Gary Finch, Secretary-Treasurer

Darrell Dennis, General Manager
Kathy Duggan, Assistant Manager

Branch Offices:
1545 S Dumas Ave
Dumas, TX 79029
Phone: 806-935-8777
809 S 25 Mile Ave
Hereford, TX 79045
Phone: 806-364-1426

401 N 3rd
PO Box 1124
Stratford, TX 79084
Phone: 806-366-3355

1624 Tennessee Ave.
Dalhart, TX 79022
Phone: 806-244-3355
Cable Systems (2):
Texas: DALHART; VEGA.

YADKIN VALLEY TELEPHONE MEMBERSHIP CORP. INC.
PO Box 368
Yadkinville, NC 27055
Phone: 336-463-5022
E-mail: yadtel@yadtel.com; cstservice@yadtel.com
Web site: http://www.yadtel.com
Officer:
Mitzie Branon, Chief Executive Officer & General Manager
Cable Systems (1):
North Carolina: FARMINGTON.

YELCOT COMMUNICATIONS
225 North Mill St.
Yellville, AR 72687
Phones: 870-449-4211; 800-354-3360
Web site: http://www.yelcot.com
Cable Systems (6):
Arkansas: CALICO ROCK; GASSVILLE; MELBOURNE; MOUNT PLEASANT; MOUNTAIN VIEW; YELLVILLE.

YOUNGSVILLE TV CORP.
3 West Main St.
Youngsville, PA 16371
Phone: 814-563-3336
Fax: 814-563-7299
E-mail: ytv@eaglezip.net; info@youngsvilletv.com
Web site: http://youngsvilletv.com
Officers:
Richard Hutley, President
Samuel Walters, Vice President
Scott Barber Sr, General Manager
Ownership: Community owned--Youngsville, PA.
Cable Systems (1):
Pennsylvania: YOUNGSVILLE.

ZAMPELLI TV
PO Box 830
Lewistown, PA 17044
Phone: 717-248-1544
Fax: 717-248-4465
Ownership: Frank P Zampelli, Principal.
Cable Systems (4):
Pennsylvania: BELLEVILLE; LIVERPOOL; McVEYTOWN; MOUNT PLEASANT MILLS.

TOM ZELKA
PO Box 338
Hardin, MT 59034
Phone: 406-665-2103

Cable Owners

Cable Systems (1):
Montana: CROW AGENCY.

ZITO MEDIA
102 South Main St.
Coudersport, PA 16915
Phone: 800-365-6988
E-mail: info@zitomedia.net;
 support@zitomedia.net
Web site: http://www.zitomedia.com
Officer:
James Rigas, Manager
Ownership: The Rigas Family.

Cable Systems (95):
Alabama: BAILEYTON; CLANTON; COLUMBIANA; HALEYVILLE; HEFLIN; HENAGAR; LEIGHTON; RAINSVILLE; ROGERSVILLE; THORSBY.
California: BURNEY; SUSANVILLE.
Idaho: MOUNTAIN HOME.
Illinois: ALEXANDER COUNTY (portions); BUNCOMBE; CARRIER MILLS; FREEMAN SPUR; GOLCONDA; JACKSON COUNTY (portions); LAKE OF EGYPT; ROSICLARE; SALINE COUNTY (portions); WILLIAMSON COUNTY (portions).
Kansas: AMERICUS; BLUE RAPIDS; LIBERAL; ROSSVILLE; STRONG CITY.
Kentucky: BLACK MOUNTAIN; GRAVES COUNTY; HAZEL; HICKMAN; KUTTAWA; WALLINS CREEK; WHITLEY COUNTY (portions); WICKLIFFE.
Missouri: CHILLICOTHE; MARSHALL.
Nebraska: BRADSHAW; CERESCO; CHESTER; CLAY CENTER; DESHLER; GENEVA; GRAND ISLAND; GRETNA; MALCOLM; NELSON; PERU; SYRACUSE; VALPARAISO; WACO; WESTERN; WILBER.
North Carolina: BRYSON CITY; CRESTON (southern portion); ROBBINSVILLE.
Ohio: CORNING; DENMARK TWP.; GALLIPOLIS; ROCK CREEK; THOMPSON TWP. (Geauga County); WARNER.
Pennsylvania: BRAVE; CANTON; COGAN STATION; COUDERSPORT; HARRISON VALLEY; HAZEN; JOHNSONBURG; OSWAYO; RALSTON; SABULA; SPARTANSBURG; ST. MARY'S; TREASURE LAKE; WEEDVILLE; WILCOX.
Tennessee: CARTER COUNTY (portions); SNEEDVILLE.
Texas: BREMOND; CALVERT; CAMERON; CRAWFORD; FRANKLIN; GRAHAM; LOTT; NEWCASTLE; PALESTINE.
Virginia: DAMASCUS; EWING.
Washington: FRIDAY HARBOR.
West Virginia: CAMERON; LITTLETON; PINE GROVE.

ADVANCED TVFactbook
TELCO/IPTV • CABLE TV • TV STATIONS

Subscription pays for itself in just a few searches

Now you can access the entire contents of the Television & Cable Factbook instantly on your desktop or any Internet connection.

Your subscription to the *Advanced TV Factbook* online will provide you with access to over 1 million detailed records. Best of all, the database is continuously updated to ensure you always have the most current industry intelligence.

Save enormous amounts of time, effort & money

The user-friendly query interface allows you to perform fully customized data searches—so you can retrieve data in a number of ways, tailored to your precise needs. The search options are extensive and flexible, and will save you hours and hours of cumbersome research time.

You'll recover your subscription cost after just a few searches and continue to save enormous amounts of time, money and effort with every search.

See for yourself— take a risk free 7-day trial

Take a FREE 7-day trial —
See for yourself why the *Advanced TV Factbook* online is referred to as "an invaluable reference tool."

Sign up at **www.warren-news.com/factbookonline.htm**
You have **nothing to lose** and lots of time and money to save.

Continuously Updated • Easy Internet Access • Fully Searchable

Pay TV & Satellite Services

Total Subscribers are included only when they are provided by companies. Listings in *italics* are planned services.

PAY TV & SATELLITE SERVICES CROSS REFERENCE LISTS

AUDIO ONLY
DMX MUSIC
FMX CABLE FM SYSTEM
MC
MUSIC CHOICE
WALN CABLE RADIO
WKTV
YESTERDAY USA

CANADIAN
CBC/RADIO-CANADA
FIGHT NETWORK
FNTSY SPORTS NETWORK
PRIDEVISION TV
SLICE
TORSTAR MEDIA GROUP TELEVISION (TORONTO STAR TV)
TV5, LA TELEVISION INTERNATIONAL
WEATHER NETWORK
WILD TV

DIGITAL MULTICAST TELEVISION
24/7 NEWS CHANNEL
AAT TELEVISION
ALIENTO VISION
AVIVA TV
BLACK NETWORK TELEVISION
BOUNCE TV
BUENAVISION TV
COASTAL TELEVISION NETWORK
COZI TV
ENLACE USA
ESCAPE
ESPIRITU SANTO Y FUEGO NETWORK
FAMILIA TV
FIL AM TV
GCN
GEORGIA HIGHLANDS TELEVISION (GHTV)
GRIT
GUARDIAN TELEVISION NETWORK
HMONG TV NETWORK
HMONGUSA TV
IGLESIA JEMIR
INMIGRANTE TV
JANE.TV
KEMS
KENTUCKY EDUCATIONAL TELEVISION (KET)
KETKY
KET2
LAFF
LIVE WELL NETWORK
MANAVISION3
MC-TV
METV
MIAMI TEVE
MIRA TV
NACION TV
RED ADVENIR
REINO UNIDO TV
SNN: SUNCOAST NEWS NETWORK
SPANISH INDEPENDENT BROADCAST NETWORK
TANGO TRAFFIC
TELE VIDA ABUDANTE
TVC+ LATINO
TVHS
TVIDAVISION
VIDEO MIX TV
VIDEO ZONA TV
WOWT 6 NEWS

INTERACTIVE SERVICES
AMBERWATCH TV
BUZZTIME
MC PLAY
SWRV TV
TV GUIDE INTERACTIVE INC.

LOCAL NEWS SERVICES
5 NEWS
6 NEWS
10 NEWS 2
10 NEWS CHANNEL
ARIZONA NEWS CHANNEL
CAPITAL NEWS 9
CENTRAL FLORIDA NEWS 13
CLTV
NEW ENGLAND CABLE NEWS
NEWS 12 BRONX
NEWS 12 CONNECTICUT
NEWS 12 HUDSON VALLEY
NEWS 12 LONG ISLAND
NEWS 12 NEW JERSEY
NEWS 12 WESTCHESTER
NEWSCHANNEL 8
NEWSWATCH 15
NORTHWEST CABLE NEWS
NY1 RAIL & ROAD
PITTSBURGH CABLE NEWS CHANNEL
REGIONAL NEWS NETWORK
RHODE ISLAND NEWS CHANNEL
TIME WARNER CABLE NEWS (ANTELOPE VALLEY)
TIME WARNER CABLE NEWS (AUSTIN)
TIME WARNER CABLE NEWS (THE BRONX)
TIME WARNER CABLE NEWS (BROOKLYN)
TIME WARNER CABLE NEWS (BUFFALO)
TIME WARNER CABLE NEWS (CAPITAL REGION NY)
TIME WARNER CABLE NEWS (CENTRAL NY)
TIME WARNER CABLE NEWS (CENTRAL NC)
TIME WARNER CABLE NEWS (CHARLOTTE)
TIME WARNER CABLE NEWS (COASTAL NC)
TIME WARNER CABLE NEWS (HUDSON VALLEY)
TIME WARNER CABLE NEWS (JAMESTOWN)
TIME WARNER CABLE NEWS (MANHATTAN)
TIME WARNER CABLE NEWS (NORTHERN NY)
TIME WARNER CABLE NEWS NY1
TIME WARNER CABLE NEWS (QUEENS)
TIME WARNER CABLE NEWS (ROCHESTER)
TIME WARNER CABLE NEWS (SAN ANTONIO)
TIME WARNER CABLE NEWS (SOUTHERN TIER NY)
TIME WARNER CABLE NEWS (STATEN ISLAND)
TIME WARNER CABLE NEWS (TRIAD NC)

ONLINE SERVICES
ACC DIGITAL NETWORK
ASIA TRAVEL TV
ATV HOME CHANNEL (AMERICA)
BET PLAY
BTN2GO
CBS ALL ACCESS
CCTV-NEWS
CHINESE ENTERTAINMENT TELEVISION (CETV)
CMT LOADED
CNBC PRO
CNNGO
ENCORE PLAY
EPIX
ESPN360.COM
ESQUIRE TV NOW
FOX BUSINESS GO
FOX NEWS GO
FOX SOCCER 2GO
FOX SPORTS GO
FREE TO CHOOSE NETWORK
FXNOW
GUANGDONG SOUTHERN TELEVISION (TVS)
HBO GO
HBO NOW
HBO ON BROADBAND
HUNAN SATELLITE TV (HTV)
HWAZAN TV
IAVC
IDEA CHANNEL
INTERNATIONAL FAMILY TELEVISION
JIANGSU INTERNATIONAL CHANNEL
JIA YU CHANNEL
KUNLUN DRAMA
LEGISLATIVE COUNSEL BUREAU - BROADCAST AND PRODUCTION SERVICES
MACAU ASIA SATELLITE TV (MASTV)
MASSACHUSETTS SPANISH TV NETWORK (MASTV)
MAX GO
NTN BUZZTIME
PAC-12 NOW
PHOENIX NORTH AMERICA CHINESE CHANNEL
POKERTV NETWORK
SEC NETWORK+
SEESO
SHENZHEN SATELLITE TV
SKY LINK TV
SONY MOVIE CHANNEL EVERYWHERE
STARZ PLAY
SUDDENLINK2GO
TENNIS CHANNEL PLUS
TRAVEL CHANNEL BEYOND
UCTV
USA NOW
UVIDEOS
WATCH ABC FAMILY
WATCH DISNEY CHANNEL
WATCH DISNEY JUNIOR
WATCH DISNEY XD
WATCH ESPN
WATCH FOOD NETWORK
WATCH FREEFORM
WATCH TBS
WATCH TCM
WATCH TNT
WATCH TRUTV
WHEELSTV
XIAMEN TV
XTV
YANGTSE RIVER DRAMA
ZHEJIANG TV
Z LIVING GO

ONLINE VIDEO DISTRIBUTORS
3DGO!
BLOCKBUSTER ON DEMAND
CRACKLE
HULU
HULU LATINO
POPCORNFLIX.COM
URBAN MOVIE CHANNEL
VUDU

OTHER
CINEMOI NORTH AMERICA

PAY SERVICES
@MAX
5 STAR MAX
ART AMERICA
BAND INTERNACIONAL
BEIN SPORT
B4U MOVIES
BOLLYWOOD HITS ON DEMAND
CCTV-ENTERTAINMENT
CINE MEXICANO
CINEMAX
CINEMAX ON DEMAND
CNBC WORLD
COLORS KANNADA
CTC INTERNATIONAL
CYR TV (CHINESE YELLOW RIVER TV)
DIRECTV CINEMA
DOGTV
ENCORE LOVE
EPIX 2
EPIX 3
EPIX DRIVE-IN
EPIX HITS
EXXXOTICA
FITTV
FLIX
FOX MOVIE CHANNEL

2017 Edition   E-1

Pay TV & Satellite Services

FOX SOCCER PLUS
FUJIAN STRAITS TV
GAIAM TV FIT & YOGA
GRAN CINE
HBO 2
HBO
HBO COMEDY
HBO FAMILY
HBO LATINO
HBO SIGNATURE
HBO ZONE
HOME BOX OFFICE
HOME SHOPPING NETWORK
HOME SHOPPING NETWORK 2
IFC
I-LIFETV
INDIEPLEX
JADE CHANNEL
THE JEWISH CHANNEL
LONGHORN NETWORK
MAX LATINO
MEDIASET ITALIA
MORE MAX
THE MOVIE CHANNEL
THE MOVIE CHANNEL XTRA
MOVIE MAX
MOVIEPLEX
NESN NATIONAL
NESNPLUS
NEWS 10 NOW
NHK WORLD PREMIUM
NIPPON GOLDEN NETWORK
NOIRETV AFRICA
OUTER MAX
PENTHOUSE TV
PFC - O CANAL DO FUTEBOL
PHOENIX MOVIES CHANNEL
PIVOT
PLAYBOY EN ESPANOL
PLAYBOY TV
PLAYGIRL TV
PURSUIT CHANNEL
RAI ITALIA
RETROPLEX
RTP INTERNACIONAL
SHO2
SHOWTIME 2
SHO BEYOND
SHO EXTREME
SHO NEXT
SHORTSHD
SHO WOMEN
SHOWTIME
SHOWTIME FAMILYZONE
SHOWTIME SHOWCASE
SONY ENTERTAINMENT TELEVISION ASIA
STAR NEWS
STARZ
STARZ CINEMA
STARZ COMEDY
STARZ EDGE
STARZ ENCORE
STARZ ENCORE ACTION
STARZ ENCORE BLACK
STARZ ENCORE CLASSIC
STARZ ENCORE ESPANOL
STARZ ENCORE FAMILY
STARZ ENCORE SUSPENSE
STARZ IN BLACK
STARZ KIDS & FAMILY
THEBLAZE
THRILLER MAX
TV ASIA
TV GLOBO INTERNACIONAL
TV JAPAN
TV POLONIA
VIENDOMOVIES
VIVIDTV
WAPA AMERICA
WILLOW
XFINITY ON DEMAND
ZEE BUSINESS
ZEE KANNADA
ZEE MARATHI
ZEE PUNJABI
ZEE SMILE

PAY-PER-VIEW

BANG U
BRAZZERS TV
CLUB JENNA
FRESH
GAMEHD
HOT CHOICE
HUSTLER TV
IN DEMAND
IND PPV EN ESPANOL
JUICY
MLB EXTRA INNINGS
MLS DIRECT KICK
MOFOS
NBA LEAGUE PASS
NHL CENTER ICE
ONESPORTSPLUS
PLEASURE
REAL
REALITY KINGS TV (RKTV)
SEXSEE
SHORTEEZ
SPICE 2
SPICE
SPICE HOT
SPICE: XCESS
SPORTS PPV
STARZ ENCORE WESTERNS
TEAMHD
TEN
TIGERVISION
TRUE BLUE
VAVOOM
WORLD PICKS ON DEMAND (HINDI, LATINO, MANDARIN, RUSSIAN)
XTSY

PLANNED SERVICES

ACC NETWORK
ATLX (ATHLETICS TRAINING LIFESTYLE)
BLACK HERITAGE NETWORK
BLACK TELEVISION NEWS CHANNEL
BOXTV: THE BOXING CHANNEL
FSZ TV (FANTASY SPORTS ZONE TV)
HISPANIC PAY TV CHANNEL
ITALIANATION
LA1
LVES-TV
PBS KIDS
THE QUAD
THE SYZYGY NETWORK
UHD-1
U.S. MILITARY TV NETWORK
VRV

REGIONAL PROGRAMMING

ALTITUDE SPORTS & ENTERTAINMENT
ATLANTA INTERFAITH BROADCASTERS
BAY NEWS 9
BAY NEWS 9 EN ESPANOL
BEACHTV
BOSTON KIDS & FAMILY
BRIGHT HOUSE SPORTS NETWORK
BRIGHT HOUSE TRAVEL WEATHER NOW
CABLE TV NETWORK OF NEW JERSEY
CALIFORNIA CHANNEL
CAN TV
CATCH 47
CATHOLIC TELEVISION NETWORK
CET: COMCAST ENTERTAINMENT TELEVISION
CHANNEL 4 SAN DIEGO
CHICAGO ACCESS NETWORK TELEVISION
CN/2
CN8
CN100
COMCAST/CHARTER SPORTS SOUTHEAST (CSS)
COMCAST ENTERTAINMENT TELEVISION
COMCAST HOMETOWN NETWORK
COMCAST NETWORK PHILADELPHIA
COMCAST SPORTSNET BAY AREA
COMCAST SPORTSNET CALIFORNIA
COMCAST SPORTSNET CHICAGO
COMCAST SPORTSNET HOUSTON
COMCAST SPORTSNET MID-ATLANTIC
COMCAST SPORTSNET NEW ENGLAND
COMCAST SPORTSNET NORTHWEST
COMCAST SPORTSNET PHILADELPHIA
COMCAST SPORTSNET WASHINGTON
COMCAST SPORTSNET WEST
COMCAST SPORTS SOUTHWEST (CSS)
COMCAST TELEVISION (MICHIGAN)
COMCAST TELEVISION 2
COUNTY TELEVISION NETWORK SAN DIEGO
COX SPORTS TELEVISION
CREATV SAN JOSE
CT-N
CYCLONES.TV
DMTV7
DOLPHINS TELEVISION NETWORK
ECOLOGY CABLE SERVICE
ECUMENICAL TV CHANNEL
ENGLISH ON DEMAND
FIOS1 DALLAS
FIOS1 HIGH SCHOOL SPORTS WIDGET
FIOS1 LONG ISLAND
FIOS1 NEW JERSEY
FIOS1 POTOMAC
FLORIDA CHANNEL
FOX COLLEGE SPORTS ATLANTIC
FOX COLLEGE SPORTS CENTRAL
FOX COLLEGE SPORTS PACIFIC
FOX DEPORTES
FOX SPORTS ARIZONA
FOX SPORTS ARIZONA PLUS
FOX SPORTS DETROIT
FOX SPORTS FLORIDA/SUN SPORTS
FOX SPORTS HOUSTON
FOX SPORTS INDIANA
FOX SPORTS MIDWEST
FOX SPORTS NET NEW YORK
FOX SPORTS NET WEST 2
FOX SPORTS NETWORKS
FOX SPORTS NEW ORLEANS
FOX SPORTS NORTH
FOX SPORTS NORTH PLUS
FOX SPORTS OHIO/SPORTS TIME OHIO
FOX SPORTS OKLAHOMA
FOX SPORTS SAN DIEGO
FOX SPORTS SOUTH/SPORTSOUTH
FOX SPORTS SOUTHWEST
FOX SPORTS WEST/PRIME TICKET
FOX SPORTS WISCONSIN
GAVEL TO GAVEL ALASKA
GEORGIA PUBLIC BROADCASTING
GREEK CHANNEL
GTN
HAWKEYE NETWORK
HELENA CIVIC TELEVISION (HCT)
HOT TV (HISTORY OF TELEVISION)
HURRICANE VISION
ILLINOIS CHANNEL
INTERNATIONAL TELEVISION (ITV)
IOWA COMMUNICATIONS NETWORK
JTV
KANSAS NOW 22
KELSO LONGVIEW TELEVISION
KLRU CREATE
KLRU Q
KLTV
K-MTN TELEVISION
KOREA ONE: CHICAGOLAND KOREAN TV
LOCAL CABLE WEATHER
LOTTERY CHANNEL
LOUISIANA LEGISLATIVE NETWORK
LWS LOCAL WEATHER STATION
MAXXSOUTH SPORTS
METROCHANNELS
MID-ATLANTIC SPORTS NETWORK (MASN)
MIDCO SPORTS NETWORK
MIDWEST CHRISTIAN TELEVISION
MINNESOTA HOUSE & SENATE TELEVISION
MOVIES! CAROLINA
MSG 3D
MSG
MSG PLUS
NEW GREEK TV
NESN
NEW ENGLAND SPORTS NETWORK
NEW EVANGELIZATION TV
NEWS 8 AUSTIN
NEWS 12 BROOKLYN
NEWS 12 TRAFFIC & WEATHER
NEWS 14 CAROLINA
NEWS CHANNEL 3 ANYTIME
NEWS CHANNEL 5+
NEW YORK 1 NOTICIAS
NEW YORK NETWORK
NEW YORK RACING CHANNEL
NEW YORK STATE ASSEMBLY RADIO TELEVISION
NIPPON GOLDEN NETWORK 2
NIPPON GOLDEN NETWORK 3
NJTV
NORTHEAST OHIO NETWORK
NORTH SHORE-LIJ HEALTH TV
OC 16
OCEAN STATE NETWORKS
OC SPORTS
ODU-TV
OHIO CHANNEL
OKSTATE.TV
OLELO
OREGON PUBLIC AFFAIRS NETWORK
OUTV
PAC-12 ARIZONA
PAC-12 BAY AREA
PAC-12 LOS ANGELES
PAC-12 MOUNTAIN
PAC-12 NETWORKS
PAC-12 OREGON
PAC-12 WASHINGTON
PCTV
PENN NATIONAL RACING ALIVE
PENNSYLVANIA CABLE NETWORK
PIKES PEAK COMMUNITY COLLEGE
PORTUGUESE CHANNEL
POTTSTOWN COMMUNITY TV
PRIME TICKET
QUE HUONG
RCN TV
RHODE ISLAND STATEWIDE INTERCONNECT
ROOT SPORTS NORTHWEST
ROOT SPORTS PITTSBURGH
ROOT SPORTS ROCKY MOUNTAIN
ROOT SPORTS SOUTHWEST
ROOT SPORTS UTAH
SAINT CLOUD STATE UNIVERSITY CHANNEL
SAINT JOHNS COUNTY GOVERNMENT TELEVISION
SAN DIEGO NEWS CHANNEL 10
SINO TV
SNJ TODAY
SOONERVISION
THE SOUTH CAROLINA CHANNEL
SPORTSCHOICE
SPORTSNET NEW YORK
SPORTSOUTH
SPORTSTIME OHIO
SUN SPORTS
TELEMIAMI
TEMPO
TEXAS CHANNEL
TEXAS HOUSE OF REPRESENTATIVES VIDEO/AUDIO SERVICES
TIME WARNER CABLE COMMUNITY (SOCAL)
TIME WARNER CABLE SPORTSCHANNEL 2 (KANSAS CITY)

Pay TV & Satellite Services

TIME WARNER CABLE SPORTSCHANNEL (ALBANY)
TIME WARNER CABLE SPORTSCHANNEL (AUSTIN)
TIME WARNER CABLE SPORTSCHANNEL (BUFFALO)
TIME WARNER CABLE SPORTSCHANNEL (COLUMBIA)
TIME WARNER CABLE SPORTSCHANNEL (DALLAS)
TIME WARNER CABLE SPORTSCHANNEL (EASTERN NORTH CAROLINA)
TIME WARNER CABLE SPORTSCHANNEL (GREEN BAY)
TIME WARNER CABLE SPORTSCHANNEL (KANSAS CITY)
TIME WARNER CABLE SPORTSCHANNEL (LINCOLN)
TIME WARNER CABLE SPORTSCHANNEL (MID OHIO)
TIME WARNER CABLE SPORTSCHANNEL (MILWAUKEE)
TIME WARNER CABLE SPORTSCHANNEL (NORTHEAST OHIO)
TIME WARNER CABLE SPORTSCHANNEL (ROCHESTER)
TIME WARNER CABLE SPORTSCHANNEL (SOUTHWEST OHIO)
TIME WARNER CABLE SPORTSCHANNEL (SYRACUSE)
TIME WARNER CABLE SPORTSCHANNEL (WESTERN NORTH CAROLINA)
TIME WARNER CABLE SPORTSNET
TIME WARNER CABLE SPORTSNET LA
TKMI BROADCASTING
TOKYO TV
TRAVEL WEATHER NOW
TROJAN VISION
TV2
TVW
TW3
TWC TV NEW ENGLAND
VAN-TV
VIETNAMESE AMERICAN NETWORK TELEVISION
VSTV
WASHINGTON KOREAN TV
WCTY CHANNEL 16
WINK NEWS NOW 24/7
WISCONSINEYE
WKYT-TV
YANKEES ENTERTAINMENT & SPORTS
YUMA 77

RELIGIOUS PROGRAMMING

CORNERSTONE TELEVISION
GLC
GOD TV
SON BROADCASTING
TAIWAN MACROVIEW TV
TBN SALSA
TELECARE

SATELLITE PROGRAMMERS

3ABN
52MX
101 NETWORK
A&E
AAPKA COLORS
ABC FAMILY CHANNEL
ABP ANANDA
ABP NEWS
ACCUWEATHER NETWORK
ACTION MAX
ADULT SWIM
THE AFRICA CHANNEL
AFRICAN BOX OFFICE

AFRICAN TV NETWORK (ATVN)
AFRIQUE MUSIC TELEVISION
AFROTAINMENT MUSIC
AFROTAINMENT PLUS
AL KARMA TV
ALMAVISION
AMC
AMERICA TEVE
AMERICAN DESI
AMERICAN ED TV
AMERICAN HEROES CHANNEL
AMERICAN ICN TV NETWORK
AMERICANLIFE TV NETWORK
AMERICAN MOVIE CLASSICS
AMERICAN SPORTS NETWORK
AMERICA'S AUCTION NETWORK
AMGTV
AMRITA TV
ANGEL ONE
ANGEL TWO
ANHUI TV INTERNATIONAL
ANIMAL PLANET
ANIMAL PLANET HD
ANIME NETWORK
ANTENA 3 INTERNACIONAL
ANTENNA SATELLITE TV
ANTENNA TV
ARABIC CHANNEL
ARIANA AFGHANISTAN TV
ARIANA TV
ARIRANG DTV
ARMENIAN PUBLIC CHANNEL
ARMENIAN RUSSIAN TELEVISION NETWORK (ARTN)
ASC-TV
ASIANET
ASIANET MOVIES
ASIANET NEWS
ASIANET PLUS
ASPIRE
ASSYRIASAT
AUDIENCE NETWORK
THE AUTO CHANNEL
AUTOMOTIVE.TV
AWE
AXS TV
AYM SPORTS
AZ CLIC
AZTECA
AZ TV
BABYFIRST AMERICAS
BABYFIRSTTV
BABY TV
BBC AMERICA
BBC AMERICA ON DEMAND
BBC ARABIC
BBC WORLD NEWS
BEAUTY & FASHION CHANNEL
BEIJING TV
BET
BET GOSPEL
BET HIP HOP
BET J
BET SOUL
BIO
BIZ TV
BLOOMBERG TELEVISION
BLUEHIGHWAYS TV
BLUE OCEAN NETWORK
BOLIVIA TV
BONJOUR AMERICA TV
BOOK TV
BOOMERANG
BOSTEL
BOSTON CATHOLIC TELEVISION
BRAVO
BRIDGES TV
BTN
BUZZR TV
BYUTV
CANAL 44 (XHIJ-TV)
CANAL 22 INTERNACIONAL
CANAL 24 HORAS

CANAL SUR
CAPITAL OFF TRACK BETTING TELEVISION NETWORK
CARACOL TV
CAREER ENTERTAINMENT TELEVISION
CAROUSEL
CARS.TV
CARTOON NETWORK
CATHOLICTV
CB24
CBS SPORTS NETWORK
CCTV AMERICA
CCTV-DOCUMENTARY
CCTV-OPERA
CELEBRITY SHOPPING NETWORK
CENTRIC
CGNTV USA
CHANNEL ONE RUSSIA
CHILLER
CHINA MOVIE CHANNEL
CHRISTIAN TELEVISION NETWORK
CHURCH CHANNEL
CLASSIC ARTS SHOWCASE
CLOO
CMT
CMT PURE COUNTRY
CNBC
CNN
CNN EN ESPANOL
CNN INTERNATIONAL
COLLEGE SPORTS TELEVISION
COLORS MARATHI
COLOURS
COMEDY CENTRAL
COMEDY TIME
COMEDY.TV
COMET
CONCERT TV
COOKING CHANNEL
COUNTRY MUSIC TELEVISION
THE COUNTRY NETWORK
COURT TV
CREATE TV
CRIME & INVESTIGATION NETWORK
CRIME CHANNEL
CROSSINGS TV
CSN+
C-SPAN 2
C-SPAN 3
C-SPAN
C-SPAN EXTRA
CTI-ZHONG TIAN
CTNI
CUBANETWORK
CUBAPLAY TELEVISION
CW PLUS
DARE TO DREAM NETWORK
DAYSTAR TV NETWORK
DECADES
DELAHOYATV
DESTINATION AMERICA
DEUTSCHE WELLE TV
DISCOVERY CHANNEL
DISCOVERY FAMILIA
DISCOVERY FAMILY
DISCOVERY HEALTH CHANNEL
DISCOVERY HOME CHANNEL
DISCOVERY KIDS CHANNEL
DISCOVERY KIDS EN ESPANOL
DISCOVERY LIFE CHANNEL
DISCOVERY TIMES CHANNEL
DISCOVERY TRAVEL & LIVING (VIAJAR Y VIVIR)
DISNEY CHANNEL
DISNEY FAMILY MOVIES
DISNEY JUNIOR
DISNEY XD
DIYA TV
DIY NETWORK
DOCTOR TELEVISION CHANNEL (DRTV)
DOCUMENTARY CHANNEL
DOCU TVE
DODGERS ON DEMAND

DOM KINO
DOMINION SKY ANGEL
DRAGONTV
DRIVERTV
DUBAI TV
E!
EBRU TV
ECUAVISA INTERNACIONAL
E! ENTERTAINMENT TELEVISION
EL REY
EMIRATES DUBAI TELEVISION
EMPLOYMENT & CAREER CHANNEL
ENCORE MYSTERY
ENCORE WAM
ENGLISH CLUB
ENVISION TV
ESCAPES NETWORK
ESPN2
ESPN
ESPN BASES LOADED
ESPN BUZZER BEATER
ESPN CLASSIC
ESPN COLLEGE EXTRA
ESPNEWS
ESPN GOAL LINE
ESPN NOW
ESPNU
ESQUIRE NETWORK
ESTRELLA TV
ES.TV
ETERNAL WORD TV NETWORK
ET-GLOBAL
ET-NEWS
EUROCHANNEL
EUROCINEMA
EURONEWS
EVINE LIVE
EWTN GLOBAL CATHOLIC NETWORK
EXPO TV
FAITH TELEVISION NETWORK
THE FAMILY CHANNEL
FAMILY FRIENDLY ENTERTAINMENT
FAMILYNET
FASHION ONE 4K
FASHION ONE TELEVISION LTD.
FASHIONTV
FESTIVAL DIRECT
FIDOTV
FIGHT NOW TV
THE FILIPINO CHANNEL
FILM FESTIVAL CHANNEL
FIND IT ON DEMAND
FINE LIVING NETWORK
FIX & FOXI
FOOD NETWORK
FOX BUSINESS NETWORK
FOX LIFE
FOX NEWS CHANNEL
FOX REALITY CHANNEL
FOX SOCCER
FOX SPORTS 1
FOX SPORTS 2
FOX SPORTS CAROLINAS
FOX SPORTS KANSAS CITY
FOX SPORTS NET NORTHWEST
FOX SPORTS NET PITTSBURGH
FOX SPORTS NET ROCKY MOUNTAIN
FOX SPORTS NET UTAH
FOX SPORTS TENNESSEE
FOX SPORTS WORLD
FRANCE 24
FREEFORM
FREE SPEECH TV
FROST GREAT OUTDOORS
FUEL TV
FUNIMATION CHANNEL
FUSE
FUSION
FX
FXM
FXX
FYI
GALAVISION

2017 Edition E-3

Pay TV & Satellite Services

GAME SHOW NETWORK
GBTV
GEB AMERICA
GEM SHOPPING NETWORK
GEMSTV
GETTV
GLOBAL CHRISTIAN NETWORK
GMA LIFE TV
GMA PINOY TV
GMC
GMOVIES
GOLF CHANNEL
GOLTV
GOSCOUT HOMES
GOSPEL MUSIC CHANNEL
GREAT AMERICAN COUNTRY
GSN
H2
HALLMARK CHANNEL
HALLMARK MOVIES & MYSTERIES
HALOGEN TV
HAVOC TV
HAZARDOUS
HBO EN ESPANOL
HDNET
HDNET MOVIES
HD THEATER
HEADLINE NEWS
HEALTH & WELLNESS CHANNEL
HEALTHINATION
HEALTH ON DEMAND
HEARTLAND
HERE! TV
HEROES & ICONS
HGTV
HIGH 4K TV
HISTORY
HISTORY INTERNATIONAL
HITN
HITS (HEADEND IN THE SKY)
HLN
HOME & GARDEN TELEVISION
HOPE CHANNEL
HORSETV CHANNEL
HRTV
HSN2
HSN
HTV
HUB NETWORK
HUNT CHANNEL
IDRIVETV
I-HEALTH
IMETRO
IMPACT
THE IMPACT NETWORK
INDEPENDENT FILM CHANNEL
INDEPENDENT MUSIC NETWORK
INFINITO
INSP
INTELLICAST
INVESTIGATION DISCOVERY
ION LIFE
ION TELEVISION
I-PLAY
THE ISRAELI NETWORK
JCTV
JEWELRY TELEVISION
JEWISH BROADCASTING SERVICE
JEWISH LIFE TV
JTV DIRECT
JUCE TV
JUSTICE CENTRAL.TV
JUSTICE NETWORK
KABILLION
KABILLION GIRLS RULE
KARAOKE CHANNEL
KBS AMERICA
KOREAN EVERROCK MULTI-MEDIA SERVICE
KOREAN CHANNEL
KSTATEHD.TV
KTLA LOS ANGELES
KTV - KIDS & TEENS TELEVISION
LATV

LESEA BROADCASTING NETWORK
LIFE OK
LIFESTYLE FAMILY TELEVISION
LIFESTYLE NETWORK
LIFETIME
LIFETIME MOVIE NETWORK
LIFETIME REAL WOMEN
LINK TV
LIQUIDATION CHANNEL
LIVING FAITH TELEVISION
LMN
LOGO
LRW
LUXE.TV
MAC TV
MADISON SQUARE GARDEN NETWORK
MAG RACK
MARIAVISION
MASCHIC
MASMUSICA TEVE NETWORK
MAVTV
MBC ACTION
MBC AMERICA
MBCD
MBC DRAMA
MBC KIDS
MBC MASR
MBC TV
MDTV: MEDICAL NEWS NOW
MEADOWS RACING NETWORK
MEGA TV
MEXICANAL
MGM CHANNEL
MHZ NETWORKS
MHZ WORLDVIEW
MI MUSICA
MI CINE
MILITARY CHANNEL
MILITARY HISTORY
MISSION TV
MLB NETWORK
MLB NETWORK STRIKE ZONE
MNET
MOJO HD
MOMENTUM
MOTORS TV
MOVIES!
MSNBC
MTC PERSIAN TELEVISION
MTV2
MTV
MTV CLASSIC
MTV HITS
MTV JAMS
MTV LIVE
MTVU
MULTIMEDIOS TELEVISION
MUNDOMAX
MUN2
MUZIKA PERVOGO
MY COMBAT CHANNEL
MYDESTINATION.TV
MY FAMILY TV
MYNETWORKTV
MYX TV
NARRATIVE TELEVISION NETWORK
NASA TV
NASA TV UHD
NAT GEO WILD
NATIONAL GEOGRAPHIC CHANNEL
NATIONAL IRANIAN TELEVISION
NATIONAL JEWISH TV (NJT)
NATIONAL LAMPOON COLLEGE TELEVISION
NBA TV
NBC DEPORTES
NBCSN
NBC SPORTS NETWORK
NBC UNIVERSO
NEO CRICKET
THE NEW ENCORE
NEWS 12 INTERACTIVE
NEWSDAY TV
NEWSMAX TV

NEWSON
NEWSY
NEW TANG DYNASTY TV
NFL NETWORK
NFL REDZONE
NHK WORLD TV
NHL NETWORK
NICK 2
NICK AT NITE
NICKELODEON
NICK JR.
NICKMUSIC
NICKTOONS
NICKTOONS EN ESPANOL
NOGGIN
NONSTOP NETWORK
THE NOW NETWORK
NRB NETWORK
NTDTV
NTN24
NTV AMERICA
NUVOTV
OASIS TV
OLE TV
ONCE TV MEXICO
ONE AMERICA NEWS NETWORK
ONE CARIBBEAN TELEVISION
ONE WORLD SPORTS
ORBITA TV
OUI TV
OUTDOOR CHANNEL
OUTSIDE TELEVISION
OVATION
OWN: OPRAH WINFREY NETWORK
OXYGEN
PACVIA TV
PALLADIA
PARABLES TELEVISION NETWORK
PATRIOTS ON DEMAND
PBJ
PBS HD
PEACETV
PEGASUSTV
PETS.TV
PHOENIX INFONEWS
PIX11
PLANET GREEN
PLAYERS NETWORK (PNTV)
POKER CENTRAL
POP
PRAISE TELEVISION
PUBLIC INTEREST VIDEO NETWORK
PUNCH TV NETWORK
QUBO
QVC
QVC PLUS
RADAR CHANNEL
RANG-A-RANG TELEVISION
RCN NOVELAS
REACTV
REAL HIP-HOP NETWORK
REALTOR.COM CHANNEL
RECIPE.TV
REELZ
REV'N
REVOLT TV
RFD-TV
RIDE TV
RLTV
R NEWS
RSN RESORT TV
RT AMERICA
RTN
RTN+
RTR PLANETA
RTV
RTVI
RURAL TV
RUSSIAN KINO
RUSSIA TODAY
SAB TV
SAFE TV

SAIGON BROADCASTING TELEVISION NETWORK (SBTN)
SAIGON TV
SALAAM TV
SAUDITV
SBTN
SCIENCE CHANNEL
SCI-FI CHANNEL
SEC NETWORK
SETANTA SPORTS USA
SHALOM TV
SHARJAHTV
SHEPHERD'S CHAPEL NETWORK
SHOP AT HOME
SHOPHQ
SHOPNBC
SHOPTV
SI TV
SINOVISION
SIX NEWS NOW
THE SKI CHANNEL
SLEUTH
SMILE OF A CHILD TV
SMITHSONIAN CHANNEL
SNEAK PREVUE
SONLIFE BROADCASTING NETWORK
SONY MOVIE CHANNEL
SOUL OF THE SOUTH NETWORK
SOUNDTRACK CHANNEL
SOUTHEASTERN CHANNEL
SPEED
SPIKE TV
SPORTING CHANNEL
SPORTSKOOL
THE SPORTSMAN CHANNEL
SPORTS VIEW PLUS
SPROUT
STAR ONE
STAR CHINESE CHANNEL
STAR GOLD
STAR INDIA NEWS
STAR PLUS
STYLE NETWORK
SUN CHANNEL
SUNDANCE TV
SUPERENE
SUPERSTATION WGN
THE SURF CHANNEL
SYFY
TAC TV
TACH-TV
TALKLINE COMMUNICATIONS TV NETWORK
TAPESH TV
TAVSIR IRAN
TBS
TCT FAMILY
TCT
TEENNICK
TELECAFE
TELEFE INTERNACIONAL
TELEFORMULA
TELEFUTURA
TELEMUNDO
TELEMUNDO INTERNACIONAL
TELEMUNDO PUERTO RICO
TELENOSTALGIA
TELEVISION KOREA 24
TEN CRICKET
TENNIS CHANNEL
TFC
THECOOLTV
THE LEARNING CHANNEL
THE N
THIS TV
TIVI5MONDE
TLC
TOTAL LIVING NETWORK
TMC XTRA
TNN (THE NASHVILLE NETWORK)
TURNER NETWORK TELEVISION
TOO MUCH FOR TV ON DEMAND
TOON DISNEY
TOP CHANNEL TV

Pay TV & Satellite Services

TRACE SPORT STARS
TRAVEL CHANNEL
TRAVEL ON DEMAND
TR3S
TRINITY BROADCASTING NETWORK (TBN)
TRI-STATE CHRISTIAN TELEVISION
TRUTV
TUFF TV
TU INGLES TV
TURNER CLASSIC MOVIES
TNT
TURNER SOUTH
TV5MONDE USA
TV CHILE
TVGN
TVG NETWORK
TV GUIDE NETWORK
TVK (KOREAN)
TVK POP ON DEMAND
TVK2
TV LAND
TV MEX
TV ONE
TV 1000 RUSSIAN KINO
TV ORIENT
TVP INFO
TV RECORD
TV ROMANIA INTERNATIONAL
TV VENEZUELA
UBC-TV NETWORK
ULTRA FAMILIA
UNIMAS
UNIQUE BUSINESS NEWS
UNIQUE SATELLITE TV
UNIVERSAL HD
UNIVERSITY OF CALIFORNIA TV (UCTV)
UNIVISION
UNTAMED SPORTS TV
UP
UPLIFTV
USA NETWORK
UTILISIMA
VELOCITY
VENEMOVIES
VERIA LIVING
VERSUS
VH1
VH1 CLASSIC
VH1 COUNTRY
VH1 SOUL
VICELAND
VIDA VISION
VIDEO MUSIC CLUB
VIDEOROLA
VIVA TELEVISION NETWORK
VME KIDS
VREMYA
VU TELEVISION NETWORK
THEWALKTV
WAM! AMERICA'S KIDZ NETWORK
THE WEATHER CHANNEL
WEATHERNATION
WEATHERSCAN
WETA UK
WE TV
WGN
WGN AMERICA
WICKED ON DEMAND
WIZEBUYS TV
THE WORD NETWORK
THE WORKS
WORLD
WORLD FISHING NETWORK
WORLD HARVEST TELEVISION
WORSHIP NETWORK
WWE NETWORK
YES NETWORK
YNN ROCHESTER
YOUTOO AMERICA
ZEE CINEMA
ZEE TV
ZING NETWORKS LTD
Z LIVING

SPANISH LANGUAGE PROGRAMMING

3ABN LATINO
APLAUSO TV
ATRES SERIES
AZ CORAZON
BANDAMAX
BARCA TV
BEIN SPORT EN ESPANOL
C7 JALISCO
CABLE NOTICIAS
CANAL 10 DE CANCUN
CANAL 10 DE HONDURAS
CANAL 13 DE CHILE
CANAL ONCE
CARTOON NETWORK EN ESPANOL
CBEEBIES
CB TU TELEVISION MICHOACAN
CENTROAMERICA TV
CINE NOSTALGIA
CINE SONY TELEVISION
CINE CLASICO
CINE ESTELAR
CINELATINO
CLASICO TV
C13 DE CHILE
CUBAMAX TV
DAMAS TV
DE PELICULA
DE PELICULA CLASICO
DISCOVERY EN ESPANOL
DISNEY XD EN ESPANOL
DOMINICAN VIEW
ECTV
ECUADOR TV
EJTV
EL GARAGE TV USA
ELGOURMET
ENLACE JUVENIL
ESPN DEPORTES
ESPN DEPORTES+ POR ESPN3
ESTUDIO5
EWTN EN ESPANOL
FOROTV
HISTORY EN ESPANOL
HMX, EL CANAL DEL HOMBRE
HOLA! TV
INFOMAS
INTINETWORK
KLAVO
LA FAMILIA COSMOVISION
LATELE NOVELA NETWORK
LATIN AMERICAN SPORTS
LATINOAMERICA TELEVISION
LIFE DESIGN TV
LO MEJOR ON DEMAND
MEXICO TV
MILENIO TELEVISION
NAT GEO MUNDO
NEWS 12 THE BRONX EN ESPANOL
NEWS 12 NEW JERSEY EN ESPANOL
NICK EN ESPANOL
PASIONES
PERU MAGICO
PUERTO RICO NETWORK
PX TV
RCN NUESTRA TELE
REGIONAL MUSIC TELEVISION
RITMOSON
RUMBA TV
SEMILLITAS
SENAL DE VIDA
SHOWTIME EN ESPANOL
SORPRESA!
SUPER CANAL
SUR
SUR PERU
TBN ENLACE USA
TCT LA FUENTE
TELEAMAZONAS
TELECENTRO
TELE EL SALVADOR
TELEHIT
TELEKARIBE
TELEMICRO INTERNACIONAL
TELEMUNDO DEPORTES
TELE N
TELERITMO
TELE-ROMANTICA
TELEVEN AMERICA
TELEXITOS
TIME WARNER CABLE DEPORTES
TIME WARNER CABLE NEWS NY1 NOTICIAS
TV AGRO
TELEVISION DOMINICANA
TVE INTERNACIONAL
ULTRA CINE
ULTRA CLASICO
ULTRA DOCU
ULTRA FIESTA
ULTRA FILM
ULTRA HDPLEX
ULTRA KIDZ
ULTRA LUNA
ULTRA MACHO
ULTRA MEX
ULTRA TAINMENT
UNIVISION DEPORTES
UNIVISION DEPORTES DOS
UNIVISION TDN
UNIVISION TLNOVELAS
VASALLOVISION NETWORK
VMC
VME TV
XHIJ-TV

SUBSCRIPTION VIDEO ON DEMAND

NETFLIX

TEXT SERVICES

NEWS PLUS

PAY TV & SATELLITE SERVICES COMPANIES

@MAX — See Max Latino.

3ABN
PO Box 220
West Frankfort, IL 62896
Phone: 618-627-4651
Fax: 618-627-2726
E-mail: marketing@3abn.org
Web Site: http://www.3abn.org
Danny Shelton, President
Mollie Steenson, Vice President & General Manager
Moses Primo, Broadcasting Operations & Engineering Director
Type of service: Basic, streaming.
Operating hours/week: 168.
Operating areas: Available nationwide.
Programming: Focuses on recovery & rehabilitation, cooking & health, weight loss & smoking cessation, children & family issues, organic gardening, natural home remedies, gospel music & various Bible-themed programs.
Began: November 23, 1986.
Distribution method: Available to cable & satellite subscribers. Streaming available online.
Scrambled signal: Yes.
Ownership: Danny & Linda Shelton, Founders.

3ABN LATINO — See 3ABN.
Web Site: http://3abnlatino.org
John Dinzey, General Manager
Programming: Original 3ABN programming produced specifically for Spanish & Portuguese-speaking viewers.

3DGO!
1751 Richardson
Ste 4206
Montreal, QC H3K 1G6
Canada
Phone: 514-846-2022
E-mail: info@sensio.tv; support@3dgo.com
Web Site: http://sensio.tv; http://www.3dgo.com
Jacques Malo, Chairman
Nicholas Routhier, President & Chief Executive Officer
Richard LaBerge, Executive Vice President & Chief Marketing Officer
Eric Choquette, Chief Financial Officer
Jacques Patry, Vice President, Engineering
Marie-Claude Hamelin, Sales Director, Consumer Market
Chris Saito, General Manager

Branch Offices:
TOKYO: Roppongi KS Bldg. 6F, 3-16-12 Roppongi, Minato-Ku, Tokyo 106-0032, Japan. Phone: 81-3-3589-6221. Fax: 81-3-3589-6127.
Type of service: Video on demand.
Operating areas: Available nationwide.
Programming: Variety of 3D movies, including Hollywood studio titles.
Began: March 4, 2013.
Means of Support: Subscriber fees.
Distribution method: Available to all viewers with Vizio 3D sets.
Scrambled signal: Yes.
Ownership: SENSIO Technologies Inc.

4SD — See Channel 4 San Diego.

5 NEWS
318 N 13st St
Fort Smith, AR 72901
Phone: 479-783-3131
Fax: 479-783-3295
E-mail: van.comer@kfsm.com
Web Site: http://www.5newsonline.com
Van Comer, President & General Manager
Type of service: Basic.
Sales representative: Katz Continental Television.
Operating hours/week: 168.
Operating areas: Arkansas.
Programming: Local news channel.
Began: February 13, 1995.
Means of Support: Advertising.
Total subscribers: 46,000.
Distribution method: Available to cable & satellite subscribers.
Scrambled signal: Yes.
Ownership: Local TV Holdings LLC.

5 STAR MAX — See Cinemax.
c/o Home Box Office
1100 Avenue of the Americas
New York, NY 10036
Phone: 212-512-1000
Fax: 212-512-1166
Type of service: Pay, HD.
Operating hours/week: 168.
Operating areas: Available nationwide.
Programming: Modern classic movies.
Began: May 17, 2001.
Distribution method: Available to cable, IPTV & satellite subscribers.
Scrambled signal: Yes.
Ownership: Home Box Office Inc., a division of Time Warner.

Pay TV & Satellite Services

6 NEWS
644 New Hampshire
Lawrence, KS 66044
Phone: 785-832-6376
E-mail: news@6newslawrence.com
Web Site: http://www.6newslawrence.com
Ann Niccum, General Manager
Tabitha Mills, News Director
Barb Wells, Advertising Sales Manager
Type of service: Basic.
Distribution method: Available to cable subscribers.
Scrambled signal: Yes.
Ownership: WOW! Cable.

10 NEWS 2
WBIR TV-10
1513 Bill Williams Ave
Knoxville, TN 37917-3851
Phone: 865-637-1010
Fax: 865-637-6380
E-mail: manager@wbir.com
Web Site: http://www.wbir.com
Jeff Lee, General Manager
Beth Weissfeld, Sales Manager
Operating hours/week: 168.
Programming: 24-hour Knoxville news.
Total subscribers: 345,000.
Distribution method: Available to cable & satellite subscribers.
Scrambled signal: Yes.
Ownership: Gannett Company Inc.

10 NEWS CHANNEL
4600 Air Way
San Diego, CA 92102
Phone: 619-237-1010
Fax: 619-262-1302
E-mail: joel_davis@10news.com
Web Site: http://www.10news.com
Joel Davis, Station Manager
Tiffani Lupenski, News Director
Type of service: Digital.
Operating hours/week: 168.
Operating areas: Southern California.
Programming: Local news service.
Began: September 1, 1996, as News Channel 15; rebranded as 10 News Channel on January 25, 2006.
Means of Support: Advertising.
Total subscribers: 836,000.
Distribution method: Available to cable subscribers.
Scrambled signal: Yes.
Ownership: The E.W. Scripps Co.

24/7 NEWS CHANNEL
5407 West Fairview Ave
Boise, ID 83706
Phone: 208-375-7277
Fax: 208-375-7770
E-mail: ktvbnews@ktvb.com
Web Site: http://www.ktvb.com
Doug Armstrong, President & General Manager
Type of service: Basic, digital, over the air.
Operating hours/week: 168.
Programming: Local news.
Distribution method: Available over the air on digital sub-channels & to cable subscribers.
Scrambled signal: Yes.
Ownership: Belo Corp.

52MX
Blvd Puerto Aereo 486
Moctezuma the 2nd Sect
Mexico City 15530
Mexico
Phone: 52-55-5764-8100
Fax: 52-55-5764-83-53
E-mail: canal52@mvs.com
Web Site: http://52mx.tv; http://www.mvstelevision.com
Sandra Chavez, Sales Director, Latin America, MVS
Rafael Diaz Infantes C., Marketing Director, International, MVS
Type of service: Digital.
Programming: Spanish-language programming featuring original productions, sporting events, Mexican films & news.
Began: June 8, 2005.
Total subscribers: 5,000,000.
Distribution method: Available to satellite subscribers.
Scrambled signal: Yes.
Ownership: MVS Television. Distributed in the U.S. by Condista.

101 NETWORK — See Audience Network

A&E
235 E 45th St
New York, NY 10017
Phone: 212-210-1400
Fax: 212-692-9269
E-mail: aefeedback@aenetworks.com
Web Site: http://www.aetv.com
A+E NETWORKS:, -
Abbe Raven, Chairman Emeritus
Nancy Dubuc, President & Chief Executive Officer
Dan Suratt, President, Corporate Development, Strategy & Investments
David Zagin, President, Distribution
Mel Berning, Chief Revenue Officer
Amanda Hill, Chief Marketing Officer
Jim Hoffman, Executive Vice President, Program Partnerships & Strategic Initiatives
Peter Olsen, Executive Vice President, National Ad Sales
Lance Still, Senior Vice President, Branded Content
Michelle Strong, Senior Vice President, National Accounts
A& E:, -
Paul Buccieri, President, A&E & Lifetime
Rob Sharenow, Executive Vice President & General Manager, A&E & Lifetime
Elaine Frontain Bryant, Executive Vice President & Head of Programming
Mark Apter, Senior Vice President, Program Planning & Acquisition
Brian Joyce, Senior Vice President, Ad Sales, A&E, History & H2
Neil Klasky, Senior Vice President, West Coast Legal & Business Affairs
Gabriel Marano, Senior Vice President, Scripted Programming
Amy Savitsky, Senior Vice President, Development & Programming, Unscripted Series
Dan Silberman, Senior Vice President, Publicity, A&E & FYI
Drew Tappon, Senior Vice President, Development & Programming
Shelly Tatro, Senior Vice President, Development & Programming
Alexandra MacDowell, Vice President, Production Management
Dave Mace, Vice President, Non-Fiction & Alternative Programming
Fred Grinstein, Senior Director, Non-Fiction & Alternative Programming
Nicole Reed, Non-Fiction & Alternative Programming Director

Sales Offices:
CHICAGO: 111 E Wacker Dr, Ste 2208, Chicago, IL 60601. Phone: 312-819-0191.

DETROIT: 201 W Beaver Rd, Ste 1010, Troy, MI 48084. Phone: 248-740-1300. Fax: 248-740-2686.

LOS ANGELES: 2049 Century Park E, Los Angeles, CA 90067. Phone: 310-556-7500. Fax: 310-286-1240.
Type of service: Basic, HD, streaming, video on demand.
Satellites: Galaxy I, transponder 12.
Operating hours/week: 168.
Uplink: Stamford, CT.
Programming: Original series, biography, mysteries & special presentations.
Began: February 1, 1984, as Arts & Entertainment Network. Rebranded to A&E Network May 1995 & A&E in 1997. A&E HD began September 1, 2006.
Means of Support: Advertising, subscriber fees & program licensing fees.
Total subscribers: 10,000,000.
Distribution method: Available to cable, IPTV & satellite subscribers; online & mobile through website & app; video on demand (participating providers).
Scrambled signal: Yes.
Ownership: A+E Networks, a joint venture between Hearst Corp. (50%), The Walt Disney Co. (50%).

AAPKA COLORS
Viacom 18 Media Pvt. Ltd.
30-H, Simran Center, 3rd Fl, Parsi Panchay Rd
Andheri (E), Mumbai 400069
India
Phones: 91-022-42325300; 91-022-42325369
Fax: 91-022-67652663
Web Site: http://www.aapkacolors.com
Haresh Chawla, Group Chief Executive Officer, Viacom 18 & Network 18
Rajesh Kamat, Group Chief Operating Officer, Viacom 18 & Chief Executive Officer, Aapka Colors
Bhavneet Singh, Managing Director & Executive Vice President, Emerging Networks, MTV Networks International
Chris Kuelling, Vice President, International Programing, DISH Network
Sonia Huria, Senior Manager, Communications

Branch Offices:
DELHI: Viacom 18 Media Pvt. Ltd., Times Tower, 7th Fl, Sector- 28, Mg Rd, Opp. Gurgaon Central Mall, Gurgaon, Haryana 122002, India. Phone: 91-0124-4758800.
Programming: Scripted series, reality shows, game shows & blockbuster Bollywood films for the south Asian community.
Began: July 21, 2008, in India. January 27, 2010 in the U.S.
Total subscribers: 40,000,000 (worldwide).
Distribution method: Available to DISH Network subscribers.
Scrambled signal: Yes.
Ownership: Viacom 18 Media Pvt. Ltd., a joint venture between Viacom Inc. & Network 18.

AAT TELEVISION
3429 Fourth Ave S
Seattle, WA 98134
Phone: 206-447-2288
E-mail: info@aattv.com
Web Site: http://aattv.com
Steve Cho, Co-Founder
Jenny Kung, Co-Founder
David Cho, President
Type of service: Basic.
Operating hours/week: 168.
Operating areas: Washington.
Programming: Asian programming in Mandarin, Cantonese, Taiwanese and Vietnamese.
Began: March 27, 1995.
Means of Support: Advertising.
Total subscribers: 4,300,000.
Distribution method: Available over the air on digital sub-channels & to Comcast subscribers.
Scrambled signal: Yes.
Ownership: Steve Cho & Jenny Kung.

ABC FAMILY CHANNEL — See Freeform.

ABC NEWS/UNIVISION NETWORK — See Fusion.

ABP ANANDA — See ABP News.
Web Site: http://abpananda.abplive.in
Operating hours/week: 168.
Programming: Bengali language news.
Began: June 1, 2005, as STAR Ananda. Rebranded as ABP Ananda on June 1, 2012.
Distribution method: Available to DISH Network subscribers.
Scrambled signal: Yes.

ABP NEWS
301 Boston House, 3rd Fl
Suren Rd, Anheri-East
Mumbai 400093
India
Phone: 91-22-66160200
Fax: 91-22-66160243
E-mail: sales@abpnews.in
Web Site: http://www.abplive.in
Ashok Venkatramani, Chief Executive Officer, ABP News Network Pvt. Ltd.
Type of service: Expanded basic.
Operating hours/week: 168.
Operating areas: Available nationwide.
Programming: National Hindi news catering to North India.
Began: March 1, 2004, as STAR News. Rebranded ABP News on June 1, 2012.
Means of Support: Advertising and subscriber fees.
Total subscribers: 48,000,000 (worldwide.).
Distribution method: Available to Comcast, Time Warner & DirecTV subscribers.
Scrambled signal: Yes.
Ownership: ABP News Network Pvt. Ltd., an ABP Group company.

ACC DIGITAL NETWORK
4512 Weybridge Ln
Greensboro, NC 27407
Phone: 336-854-8787
Fax: 336-854-8797
Web Site: http://www.theacc.com
Jason Coyle, Chief Operating Officer, Silver Chalice Ventures
Ken Haines, President & Chief Executive Officer, Raycom Sports
John D. Swofford, ACC Commissioner
Michael Kelly, Associate Commissioner, Communications/Broadcasting & Football Operations
Amy Yakola, Associate Commissioner, Public Relations & Marketing
W Scott McBurney, Assistant Commissioner, Advanced Media
Lindsey Ross, Communications Director
Type of service: Streaming, video on demand.
Operating areas: Available nationwide.
Programming: ACC content through live television broadcasting, original programming, historical archives, mobile applications & social media.
Began: October 17, 2011.
Means of Support: Advertising.
Distribution method: Available online, mobile & on select video platforms.

Pay TV & Satellite Services

Scrambled signal: Yes.
Ownership: Raycom Sports & Silver Chalice Ventures.

ACC NETWORK
c/o ESPN, ESPN Plz
935 Middle St
Bristol, CT 06010
Phones: 860-766-2000; 888-549-3776
Fax: 860-766-2400
Web Site: http://www.espn.com
Programming: Plans live events, including regular season football games, menGÇÖs and womenGÇÖs basketball games, contests and tournaments from the ACC conferenceGÇÖs 27 sponsored sports plus news, information & original programming.
Scheduled to begin: Plans 2019.

ACCUWEATHER NETWORK
385 Science Park Rd
State College, PA 16803
Phones: 814-237-0309; 814-235-8650
Fax: 814-235-8609
E-mail: customerservice@accuweather.com
Web Site: http://www.accuweather.com
Dr. Joel Myers, Founder, Chairman & President
Barry Myers, Chief Executive Officer
Michael Smith, Chief Executive Officer, WeatherData Services Inc.
John Dokes, Chief Marketing Officer & General Manager
Jim Candor, Chief Strategy Officer
Steven Hickson, Chief Financial Officer
Steven Smith, Chief Digital Officer
Marie Svet, Chief Revenue Officer, Digital Media
Elliot Abrams, Senior Vice President & Chief Forecaster
Dr. Joe Sobel, Senior Vice President
Sarah Katt, Vice President, Product Development & Operations
Loren Tobia, Executive Director, Sales, Display Systems & Services Division
Justin Roberti, Campaign Director/PR Manager

Global Sales Office:
NEW YORK: 1270 Ave of the Americas, Ste 408, New York, NY 10020. Phone: 212-554-4750.
Type of service: Digital.
Operating hours/week: Plans 168.
Operating areas: Nationwide.
Programming: National, regional & local weather updates provided in context, reporting on top weather news and applying it to peoples' lives with topics such as family, safety, lifestyle, health, travel, business & more.
Began: March 17, 2015.
Means of Support: Advertising.
Distribution method: Available to Verizon FiOS subscribers.
Scrambled signal: Yes.
Ownership: AccuWeather Inc.

ACTION MAX — See Cinemax.
c/o Home Box Office
1100 Avenue of the Americas
New York, NY 10036
Phone: 212-512-1000
Fax: 212-512-1166
Type of service: Pay, HD.
Operating hours/week: 168.
Operating areas: Available nationwide.
Programming: Action movies, blockbusters, westerns, war movies & martial arts films.
Began: 1995 as Cinemax 3. Rebranded as Action Max in 1998.
Distribution method: Available to cable, IPTV & satellite subscribers.

Scrambled signal: Yes.
Ownership: Home Box Office Inc., a division of Time Warner.

ADULT SWIM
1050 Techwood Dr NW
Bldg 1000
Atlanta, GA 30318-5604
Phones: 404-827-1700; 404-885-2263
Fax: 404-885-4594
E-mail: advertisewithus@turner.com
Web Site: http://www.adultswim.com
Patty Gillette, Senior Vice President, Integrated Marketing, Turner Broadcasting Young Adults Group
Christina Miller, President & General Manager, Adult Swim, Cartoon Network & Boomerang
Michael Ouweleen, Chief Marketing Officer
Mike Lazzo, Executive Vice President & Creative Director
Keith Crofford, Vice President
Jason DeMarco, Vice President, On-Air & Creative Director
Type of service: Basic, streaming & video on demand.
Sales representative: Turner Network Sales.
Operating hours/week: 70, from 8 PM to 6 AM. Shares channel space with Cartoon Network.
Operating areas: Available nationwide.
Programming: Original and acquired animated and live-action series for young adults.
Began: September 1, 2001.
Total subscribers: 99,000,000 (Includes Cartoon Network subscribers.).
Distribution method: Available to most cable, IPTV & satellite providers; online & mobile through website or app; video on demand (participating providers).
Scrambled signal: Yes.
Ownership: Turner Broadcasting System Inc., a division of Time Warner.

ADVENTIST TELEVISION NETWORK — See Hope Channel.

THE AFRICA CHANNEL
5200 Lankershim Blvd
Ste 750
North Hollywood, CA 91601
Phone: 818-655-9977
Fax: 818-655-9944
E-mail: info@theafricachannel.com
Web Site: http://www.theafricachannel.com
Jacob Arback, Co-Founder
Richard E. Hammer, Co-Founder
James Makawa, Co-Founder
Elrick Williams, President & Chief Executive Officer
Genia Edelman, Executive Vice President, Sales & Marketing
Fred Paccone, Executive Vice President & Chief Financial Officer
Narenda Reddy, Senior Vice President, Programming & Production
Darrell Smith, Vice President, Community Development & Marketing
Lee Gaither, General Manager
Chelsea C. Hayes, Human Resources Director
Type of service: Expanded basic, HD.
Operating hours/week: 168.
Programming: Africa-centric news magazines, biographies, current business analysis, cultural & historical programming, travel & lifestyle series, talk shows, soap operas & feature films.
Began: September 1, 2005, The Africa Channel HD began August 2010.
Total subscribers: 10,000,000.

Distribution method: Available to Comcast, Cox & Time Warner cable subscribers in select markets.
Scrambled signal: Yes.

AFRICAN BOX OFFICE — See Afrotainment Plus.
Type of service: Pay.
Operating hours/week: 168.
Operating areas: Nationwide.
Programming: Top-rated English-language movies from Nollywood.
Distribution method: Available to DISH Network subscribers.

AFRICAN TV NETWORK (ATVN)
7376 Hickory Log Cir
Columbia, MD 21045
Phone: 443-498-8335
Web Site: http://www.africantvnetwork.com
Clement Afforo, Founder, President
Daniel Egbe, Chief Operating Officer
Bob Reid, Executive Vice President, Network General Manager
Cheryl Dorsey, Vice President Affiliate Sales, Western Division
Sherrice Smith, Vice President Affiliate Sales, Eastern Division
Stephanie King, Productions & Network Operations Director
Dagnet Worjloh, Affiliate Relations Director
Operating hours/week: 168.
Programming: Authentic African programs including news, sports & entertainment targeted to African & non-African audience.
Began: July 1, 2002.

AFRIQUE MUSIC TELEVISION
c/o Caspen Media
1629 K St NW, Ste 300
Washington, DC 20006
Phones: 202-559-8295; 202-378-0620
E-mail: partnerships@caspianmedia.com
Web Site: http://www.caspenmedia.com
Programming: Focuses on promoting African music content, playing music videos from African artists.
Distribution method: Available to cable subscribers.
Scrambled signal: Yes.
Ownership: Caspen Media.

AFROTAINMENT MUSIC — See Afrotainment Plus.
Type of service: Pay, streaming.
Operating areas: Cablevision service areas in Connecticut, New Jersey & New York. Nationwide for DISH.
Programming: Features music from the African continent. Programming includes music videos, live performances & entertainment programs.
Began: June 1, 2010.
Means of Support: Advertising & subscriber fees.
Distribution method: Available to Cablevision Systems & DISH Network subscribers. Streaming available online, on mobile & through app.
Scrambled signal: Yes.

AFROTAINMENT PLUS
36-01 37th Ave
Long Island City, NY 11101
Phone: 407-287-4127
E-mail: infos@afrotainment.us
Web Site: http://www.afrotainment.tv
Yves Bollanga, Creator & General Manager

Branch Offices:
OCOEE: 2910 Maguire Rd, Ocoee, FL 34761.
Type of service: Pay, streaming.

Operating areas: Cablevision service areas in Connecticut, New Jersey & New York. Nationwide for DISH.
Programming: The best of all Afrotainment programming, which includes African movies, series, reality shows, talk shows & African soccer.
Began: October 13, 2011.
Means of Support: Advertising and subscriber fees.
Distribution method: Available to Cablevision, DISH Network & Verizon FiOS subscribers. Streaming available through select providers.
Scrambled signal: Yes.
Ownership: Soundview Africa.

ALIENTO VISION
103-24 Roosevelt Ave, 3rd Fl
Ste 301
Corona, NY 11368
Phone: 718-205-1209
E-mail: marketing@alientovision.com
Web Site: http://www.alientovision.com
Type of service: Pay, over the air, streaming.
Operating hours/week: 168.
Programming: Spanish-language Christian programming.
Began: January 19, 2010.
Means of Support: Advertising, donations.
Distribution method: Available over the air on digital sub-channels. Streaming available through select providers.
Scrambled signal: Yes.

AL KARMA TV
PO Box 3610
Seal Beach, CA 90740
Phone: 714-709-4300
Fax: 925-226-4034
E-mail: info@alkarmatv.com
Web Site: http://www.alkarmatv.com
Type of service: Over the air, streaming.
Operating hours/week: 168.
Programming: Christian Arabic family programming.
Began: October 17, 2005.
Distribution method: Available over the air on select LPTV stations. Streaming available online.
Scrambled signal: Yes.

ALMAVISION
PO Box 26590
Santa Ana, CA 92799
Phones: 213-627-8711; 877-316-5159
Fax: 213-627-8712
E-mail: info@almavision.com
Web Site: http://www.almavision.com
Operating hours/week: 168.
Programming: Christian programming in Spanish.
Began: August 1, 2003.
Distribution method: Available to satellite subscribers.
Scrambled signal: Yes.

ALTITUDE SPORTS & ENTERTAINMENT
1000 Chopper Cir
Denver, CO 80204
Phones: 303-405-6100; 303-405-1100
Fax: 303-925-2994
E-mail: salesandmarketing@altitude.tv
Web Site: http://www.altitudesports.tv
Ben Boylan, President
Tom Philand, Executive Vice President & Chief Marketing Officer
Dave Fleck, Senior Vice President, Sales & Partnership Marketing
Phillip Mallios, Senior Vice President, Affiliate Sales & Marketing

2017 Edition

E-7

Pay TV & Satellite Services

CABLE & TV STATION COVERAGE
Atlas 2017
The perfect companion to the Television & Cable Factbook
To order call 800-771-9202 or visit www.warren-news.com

Dave Zur, Senior Vice President, Operations & Engineering
Billi Capra, Vice President, Broadcast Services
Michael Ceilley, Vice President, Strategic Partnerships
Type of service: Digital basic & video on demand.
Operating hours/week: 168.
Operating areas: Colorado, Idaho, Kansas, Montana, Nebraska, New Mexico, Nevada, South Dakota, Wyoming & Utah.
Programming: Regional high-school, college & professional sports, including basketball, soccer, hockey, baseball, lacrosse, boxing, cycling, outdoor & extreme sports. Official network of the Denver Nuggets, Colorado Avalanche, Colorado Mammoth & Colorado Rapids; broadcasting regular season & playoff games.
Began: September 4, 2004.
Total subscribers: 3,100,000.
Distribution method: Available to cable, DirecTV & DISH Network subscribers.
Scrambled signal: Yes.
Ownership: Stan Kroenke.

AMBERWATCH TV
3010 Old Ranch Pkwy
Ste 330
Seal Beach, CA 90740
Phone: 949-222-5880
Fax: 949-266-5604
E-mail: info@amberwatchfoundation.org
Web Site: http://www.amberwatchfoundation.org
Keith Jarrett, Chairman & Chief Executive Officer
Marc Penso, Secretary
Chip Damato, Treasurer
Type of service: Interactive on demand.
Operating hours/week: 168.
Operating areas: Connecticut, New Jersey & New York.
Programming: Offers entertainment & educational programming to keep kids safe & prevent abductions.
Began: November 15, 2011.
Distribution method: Available to Cablevision Systems Corp. subscribers.
Scrambled signal: No.
Ownership: AmberWatch Foundation.

AMC
11 Penn Plz
15th Fl
New York, NY 10001
Phones: 212-324-8500; 646-273-7105
E-mail: amccustomerservice@amctv.com
info-amc@amc.com
Web Site: http://www.amctv.com
Gregg Siebert, Vice Chairman, AMC Networks
Josh Sapan, President & Chief Executive Officer, AMC Networks
Ed Carroll, Chief Operating Officer, AMC Networks
Robert Broussard, President, AMC Networks Distribution
Rick Olshansky, Executive Vice President, Business Affairs, AMC Networks
Christian Wymbs, Executive Vice President & Chief Accounting Officer, AMC Networks
Valerie Cabrera, Senior Vice President, Distribution, AMC Networks
Melissa Landau, Senior Vice President, Business Affairs, AMC Networks
Bernadette Simpao, Vice President, Corporate Communications, AMC Networks
Charlie Collier, President & General Manager, AMC, Sundance TV & AMC Studios
Scott Collins, President, Advertising Sales
Joel Stillerman, President, Original Programming & Development, AMC & Sundance
Rick Olshansky, Co-Head, AMC Studios
Stefan Reinhardt, Co-Head, AMC Studios
Marnie Black, Executive Vice President, Public Relations
Susie Fitzgerald, Executive Vice President, Scripted Programming
Linda Schupack, Executive Vice President, Marketing
Drew Brown, Senior Vice President, Production
Michael Cagnazzi, Senior Vice President, Digital Product Development
Ben Davis, Senior Vice President, Scripted Programming
Eliot Goldberg, Senior Vice President, Unscripted Programming
Kristin Jones, Senior Vice President, International Programming, Development, Acquisitions & Co-Productions
Marc Krok, Senior Vice President, Advertising Sales
Scott Stein, Senior Vice President, Business Affairs
Melissa Wasserman, Senior Vice President, Client Solutions & Integrated Marketing
Bob Bel Bruno, Vice President, Advertising Sales
Joshua Berger, Vice President, Programming Operations, AMC & WEtv
Marco Bresaz, Vice President, Unscripted Programming
Kristi Felton, Vice President, Scripted Programming
Nancy Kane Leidersdorff, Vice President, Media Planning
Tracey Lentz, Vice President, Unscipted Programming
Gustavo Lopez, Vice President, Global Distribution & Business Development, Latin America, AMC & Sundance
Lisa Rogen, Vice President, Corporate Communications, AMC & IFC Films
Jaime Saberito, Vice President, Corporate Communications, AMC, WEtv & IFC
Type of service: Basic, HD, streaming & video on demand.
Satellites: Satcom C-4, transponder 1.
Sales representative: AMC Networks Advertising Sales.
Operating hours/week: 168.
Operating areas: Available nationwide.
Uplink: Floral Park, NY.
Programming: Features classic motion pictures, scripted & unscripted series & original specials.
Began: October 1, 1984, as American Movie Classics. Rebranded as AMC September 2002.
Means of Support: Subscriber fees.
Total subscribers: 96,600,000.
Distribution method: Available to cable, IPTV & satellite subscribers; online & mobile through the website or app (participating providers); video on demand (participating providers).
Scrambled signal: Yes. Equipment: VideoCipher II.
Ownership: AMC Networks Inc. Formerly Rainbow Media Holdings LLC owned by Cablevision Systems Corp., it became a publicly held company under the new name June 30, 2011.

AMERICA ONE TELEVISION — See Youtoo America.

AMERICA TEVE
13001 NW 107th Ave
Hialeah Gardens, FL 33018
Phones: 305-592-4141; 305-592-7141 x340
Fax: 305-592-3808
E-mail: info@americateve.com
Web Site: http://www.americateve.com
Omar Romey, President
Donny Hudson, Executive Vice President, Sales
Carlos Justo, Retail Sales & Paid Programming Director
Francisco Framil, National Sales Manager
Alba Eagan, Talent, Event & Media Relations
Gina Garcia, Sales Promotions
Type of service: Over the air, basic.
Operating hours/week: 168.
Operating areas: Florida, New York & Puerto Rico.
Programming: Spanish-language entertainment, sports, news, Caribbean cultural & lifestyle shows.
Began: August 13, 2012.
Means of Support: Advertising.
Distribution method: Available over the air on digital sub-channels & to cable, IPTV & satellite subscribers in Miami-Ft. Lauderdale, Puerto Rico & New York.
Scrambled signal: Yes.
Ownership: America CV Stations Group LLC.

AMERICAN DESI
120 Wood Ave S
Ste 300
Iselin, NJ 08830
Phone: 732-623-2220
Web Site: http://www.americandesi.tv
Vimal Verma, Chairman & Chief Executive Officer
Kenneth F. Gelb, Senior Vice President, Sales
Divya Ohri, Senior Vice President, Programming
Type of service: Basic.
Programming: 24-hour English-language television network for South Asians in America.
Began: January 1, 2005.

AMERICAN ED TV
3691 Gale Rd.
Granville, OH 43023
Phones: 740-587-4939; 877-966-3388
E-mail: mcacciato@americanedtv.com
Web Site: http://www.americanedtv.com
Matthew Cacciato, Co-Founder & President
Fred Cambria, Co-Founder
Jack Ford, Co-Founder
Patrick McDarrah, General Manager, Digital Media
Type of service: Video on demand.
Operating areas: Available nationwide.
Programming: The first network dedicated to the news, business and culture of American education.
Began: November 15, 2010.
Means of Support: Advertising.
Distribution method: Available to Verizon FiOS subscribers.
Scrambled signal: Yes.

AMERICAN HEROES CHANNEL — See Discovery Channel
c/o Discovery Communications
One Discovery Pl
Silver Spring, MD 20910-3354
Phone: 240-662-2000
Web Site: http://www.ahctv.com
Henry S. Schleiff, Group President, American Heroes Channels, Destination America & Investigation Discovery
Jane Latman, General Manager
Kevin Bennett, Executive Vice President, Programming
Sara Kozak, Senior Vice President, Production, American Heroes Channels, Destination America & Investigation Discovery
Doug Seybert, Senior Vice President, Marketing, American Heroes Channels, Destination America & Investigation Discovery
Sara Burns, Vice President, Programming, American Heroes & Investigation Discovery
Programming: Provides a rare glimpse into major events that shaped our world, visionary leaders and unexpected heroes who made a difference, and the great defenders of our freedom. Stories featured chronicle people & events that transcend time & place.
Began: September 13, 1999, as Discovery Wings Channel. Rebranded as Military Channel January 2005. Rebranded as American Heroes Channel March 2014.
Total subscribers: 62,000,000 (U.S. subscribers. 1,000,000 Canadian subscribers.).
Distribution method: Available to cable, IPTV & satellite subscribers.
Scrambled signal: Yes.
Ownership: Discovery Communications Inc.

AMERICAN ICN TV NETWORK
9550 Flair Dr
Ste 102
El Monte, CA 91731
Phone: 626-337-8889
Fax: 626-338-7666
Web Site: http://www.icntv.net

Branch Offices:

HOUSTON: 11122 Bellaire Blvd, Houston, TX 77072. Phone: 281-498-4310. Fax: 832-399-1355.

NEW YORK: 144 E 44th St, 7th Fl, New York, NY 10017. Phone: 212-818-9388. Fax: 212-818-9383.

SAN FRANCISCO: 8371 Central Ave, Newark, CA 94560. Phone: 510-573-1183. Fax: 510-573-1693.
Type of service: Basic, streaming.
Operating hours/week: 168.
Operating areas: California, New York, Texas & Washington.
Programming: Chinese-oriented television. Offers four channels in Chinese, one in English.
Distribution method: Available to Charter & Comcast cable system subscribers, satellite subscribers, over the air on digital sub-channels & online & mobile through website or app.
Scrambled signal: Yes.
Ownership: ICN.

AMERICANLIFE TV NETWORK — See Youtoo America.

Pay TV & Satellite Services

AMERICAN MOVIE CLASSICS — See AMC.

AMERICAN SPORTS NETWORK
1100 Fairfield Dr
West Palm Beach, FL 33401
Phone: 410-568-1500
Fax: 410-568-1533
E-mail: asnweb@sbgtv.com
Web Site: http://www.americansportsnet.com
Bill Lutzen, Vice President
Ibra Morales, Vice President, Operations
Todd Siegel, Vice President, Sales
Cliff Smith, Sales Director
Type of service: Over the air, basic, video on demand.
Operating areas: Nationwide.
Programming: Offers football, basketball & soccer plus additional sports from the Conference USA, the Colonial Athletic Association, Big South Conference, Southern Conference, Patriot League & Western Athletic Conference.
Began: August 30, 2014.
Means of Support: Advertising.
Total subscribers: 83,000,000 (for select games.).
Distribution method: Available on digital subchannels. Video on demand available online.
Scrambled signal: Yes.
Ownership: Sinclair Broadcast Group Inc.

AMERICA'S AUCTION NETWORK
289 34th St N
St. Petersburg, FL 33713
Phones: 727-231-5728; 800-269-9629
Web Site: http://www.aantv.com
Type of service: Basic, streaming.
Operating hours/week: 168.
Programming: Live TV auctions.
Distribution method: Available to BrightHouse, Time Warner, DISH Network & DirecTV subscribers. Streaming available online.
Scrambled signal: Yes.

AMGTV
202 Fifth Ave
Pittsburgh, PA 15222
Phone: 772-334-7252
Fax: 908-835-8139
E-mail: terry_elaqua@amgtv.tv
Web Site: http://www.amgtv.tv
Terry Elaqua, Chief Executive Officer & National Sales Manager
Michael Chandler, Programming Development Director
Shirley Bernard, Administrative Office Manager
Cristina Kalpa, Traffic Manager
Tammy Miller, Online Services
Type of service: Over the air, basic, streaming.
Satellites: Galaxy 19, transponder 7.
Operating hours/week: 168.
Operating areas: Available nationwide.
Programming: Family entertainment programming, including shows on home life, adventure, sports, drama, comedy, health, finance, instruction & travel plus children's programs.
Began: August 1, 2007.
Means of Support: Advertising.
Total subscribers: 40,000,000.
Distribution method: Available over the air & to cable subscribers. Streaming available through select providers.
Scrambled signal: Yes.
Ownership: Access Media Group.

AMRITA TV
Gandhi Nagar, Vazhuthacaud
Thiruvananthapuram-695014
India
Phones: 91-471-2321500; 91-471-2328901
Fax: 91-471-2328900
E-mail: info@amritatv.com
Web Site: http://www.amritatv.com
Sudhaka Jayaram, Director & Chief Executive Officer
Neelan, Chief Executive Officer
Shyamaprasad, President, Programs
Radhakrishnan, Senior Vice President, Sales
Anil Kumar, General Manager, Programs
Binoj, General Manager, Sales
Harikumar MG, General Manager, Human Resource & Administration
A. Sushil Kumar, Global Head, Marketing & Communications
G.P. Nair, Head of Engineering & IT

Branch Offices:
SAN RAMON: PO Box 68, San Ramon, CA 94583. Phone: 925-967-0221. Web site: http://http://www.amritatvusa.com.
Programming: Family entertainment, including dramas, musical performances, game shows, competitions & spiritual growth shows about the history of India.
Distribution method: Available to satellite subscribers.
Scrambled signal: Yes.

ANA TELEVISION NETWORK — No longer in operation. See MBC TV.

ANGEL ONE
1300 Goodlette Rd North
Naples, FL 34102
Phone: 800-759-2643
Web Site: http://www.angel1.tv
Programming: Christian programming.
Distribution method: Available to DISH subscribers.
Ownership: Sky Angel Networks LLC.

ANGEL TWO — See Angel One.
Web Site: http://www.angel2.tv
Programming: Christian programming.
Distribution method: Available to DISH subscribers.
Ownership: Sky Angel Network LLC.

ANHUI TV INTERNATIONAL
Anhui Maanshan
Rd. 38
Hefei 230009
China
Phones: 551-64678892; 551-64678847
Web Site: http://www.ahtv.cn
Type of service: Video on demand.
Operating areas: Available nationwide.
Programming: A variety channel offering overseas Chinese viewers programs in four categories: Anhui Today, Anhui Flavor, Entertaining and Home Theatre.
Means of Support: Advertising & subscriber fees.
Distribution method: Available to subscribers through KyLin's IPTV service.
Scrambled signal: Yes.

ANIMAL PLANET — See Discovery Channel.
c/o Discovery Communications
One Discovery Pl
Silver Spring, MD 20910-3354
Phone: 240-662-2000
Web Site: http://www.animalplanet.com
Rich Ross, President, Animal Planet, Discovery Channel & Science Channel
Rick Holzman, Executive Vice President & General Manager

FULLY SEARCHABLE • CONTINUOUSLY UPDATED • DISCOUNT RATES FOR PRINT PURCHASERS
For more information call **800-771-9202** or visit **www.warren-news.com**

Charlie Foley, Executive Vice President, Development
Victoria Lowell, Executive Vice President, Marketing & Operations, Animal Planet & TLC
Sharon O'Sullivan, Executive Vice President, National Ad Sales, Animal Planet, Discovery Fit & Health, Investigation Discover & TLC
Jason Carey, Senior Vice President, Production
Patricia Kollappalil, Senior Vice President, Communications & Talent Relations
Andy Weissberg, Senior Vice President, Programming
Andy Berg, Vice President, Development
Jamie Duger, Vice President, Creative
Michael Eisenbaum, Vice President, On-Air Creative & Branded Entertainment
Brian Eley, Vice President, Communications
Lauren Goodson, Vice President, Research
Kurt Tondorf, Vice President, Development
Erin Wanner, Vice President, Production
Tahli Kouperstein, Senior Director, Publicity
Keith Hoffman, Executive Producer
Lisa Lucas, Executive Producer
Melinda Toporoff, Executive Producer
Type of service: Basic, HD, video on demand.
Satellites: Satcom C-3., transponder 22.; West Coast Feed: AMC-10, transponder 14.
Operating hours/week: 168.
Operating areas: Available nationwide.
Programming: Offers animal lovers & pet owners access to a centralized online, television & mobile community for immersive, engaging, high-quality entertainment, information and enrichment. Programming highlights include Whale Wars, River Monsters, Fatal Attractions, Monsters Inside Me, Pit Bulls and Parolees and Dogs 101.
Began: June 1, 1996, Animal Planet HD began September 1, 2007.
Total subscribers: 96,000,000 (U.S. subscribers. 2,000,000 Canadian subscribers. 200,000,000 international subscribers.).
Distribution method: Available to cable, IPTV & satellite subscribers; online & mobile through the website; video on demand (participating providers).
Scrambled signal: Yes.
Ownership: Discovery Communications Inc.

ANIMAL PLANET HD — See Animal Planet.

ANIME NETWORK
10114 W Sam Houston Pkwy S
Houston, TX 77099
Phone: 713-341-7100
Fax: 713-587-0286
E-mail: info@theanimenetwork.com
Web Site: http://www.theanimenetwork.com
Mark Williams, General Manager & Chief Technology Officer
Kevin McFeeley, Vice President, Affiliate Sales & New Media
Stacey Dodson, Programming & Operations Director
Emily Olman, National Advertising Manager
Type of service: Digital basic, video on demand & mobile.
Operating hours/week: 168.

Programming: Animation from Japan. Also featuring J-pop & J-rock music videos & Asian movies.
Began: November 1, 2002.
Total subscribers: 31,500,000.
Scrambled signal: Yes.
Ownership: A.D. Vision Inc.

ANTENA 3 INTERNACIONAL
Avda. Isla Graciosa s/n
San Sebastian de los Reyes
E-28700 Madrid
Spain
Phone: 34-91-623-05-00
Fax: 34-91-654-8439
E-mail: sales@atresmedia.com
Web Site: http://www.antena3.com/internacional
Javier Badaji, General Manager, Atres Media
Type of service: Pay.
Operating areas: Nationwide.
Programming: Spanish-language series, miniseries & films.
Began: September 1, 1996, 2013 in the U.S.
Total subscribers: 1,500,000 (U.S. subscribers).
Distribution method: Available to DISH Network subscribers.
Scrambled signal: Yes.
Ownership: Atresmedia Television. Distributed in the U.S. by Condista.

ANTENNA SATELLITE TV
10-12 Kifisias Ave
Marousi, Athens 151 25
Greece
Phone: 30-210-6886490-2
Fax: 30-210-6893750
E-mail: satellite@antenna.gr
Web Site: http://www.antennasatellite.gr
Mike Kelly, Information Contact

Branch Offices:
NEW YORK: 645 Fifth Ave, Ste 406, New York, NY 10022. Phone: 212-688-5475. Fax: 212-688-8136. E-Mail: info@antennaus.com.
Type of service: Pay.
Satellites: Galaxy III, transponder 9.
Operating hours/week: 168.
Operating areas: Available nationwide.
Uplink: Orange, NJ.
Programming: Greek language programming.
Began: June 1, 1992.
Means of Support: Advertising & subscription fees.
Distribution method: Available to cable, IPTV & satellite subscribers.
Scrambled signal: Yes. Equipment: VideoCipher II Plus.

ANTENNA TV
2501 W Bradley Pl
Chicago, IL 60618-4718
Phone: 773-528-2311
E-mail: programming@antennatv.tv
Web Site: http://www.antennatv.tv
Dana Zimmer, President, Distribution, Tribune Broadcasting
Sean Compton, President, Strategic Programming & Acquisitions, Tribune Broadcasting & Antenna TV

Pay TV & Satellite Services

Type of service: Over the air, basic.
Operating areas: Nationwide.
Programming: Classic TV series & movies.
Began: January 1, 2011.
Total subscribers: 71,000,000.
Distribution method: Available over the air on digital sub-channels & to cable subscribers through local affiliate.
Scrambled signal: Yes.
Ownership: Tribune Broadcasting, a Tribune Media brand.

APLAUSO TV
c/o Olympusat Inc.
560 Village Blvd, Ste 250
West Palm Beach, FL 33409
Phone: 561-684-5657
Fax: 561-684-9690
E-mail: info@olympusat.com
Web Site: http://www.olympusat.com/networks/aplauso
Tom Mohler, Chief Executive Officer, Olympusat Holdings Inc.
Arturo Chavez, Senior Vice President, Hispanic Networks
Juan Bruno, New Programming Acquisitions & Contracts Director
John Baghdassarian, Head of Affiliate Sales, U.S.
Type of service: Pay.
Operating areas: Available in Mediacom's service area..
Programming: Spanish-language pop-culture entertainment.
Began: November 26, 2012.
Means of Support: Advertising.
Distribution method: Available to Mediacom subscribers.
Scrambled signal: Yes.
Ownership: Olympusat.

ARABIC CHANNEL — See TAC TV.

ARIANA AFGHANISTAN TV
18 Technology
Ste 132
Irvine, CA 92618
Phone: 949-825-7400
Fax: 949-825-7474
Web Site: http://www.arianaafgtv.com
Nabil G. Miskinyar, Founder, President & Executive Producer
Satellites: Telstar 5, transponder 8.
Operating hours/week: 168.
Programming: Cultural, religious, sporting, artistic & community-related shows.
Began: 2006 in U.S.
Distribution method: Available to satellite subscribers. Streaming available online.
Scrambled signal: Yes.

ARIANA TV
Darlaman St
Kabul
Afghanistan
Phone: 93-0-70-151515
E-mail: feedback@arianatelevision.com
Web Site: http://www.arianatelevision.com

Branch Offices:
FORT LEE: Parker Plz, 400 Kelby St, 16th Fl, Fort Lee, NJ 07024. Phone: 201-302-0400. Fax: 201-301-0406. E-Mail: ads@arianatelevision.com.
Type of service: Digital, streaming.
Operating hours/week: 168.
Programming: Afghani news & events in English, Pashto & Dari.
Distribution method: Available to satellite providers.
Scrambled signal: Yes.

ARIRANG DTV
3700 Wilshire Blvd
Ste 510
Los Angeles, CA 90010
Phone: 213-251-2000
E-mail: hannah@radiokorea.com
Web Site: http://www.arirang.co.kr
Sohn Jie-Ae, President & Chief Executive Officer
Hannah Kim, TV Programming & Production
Satellites: Intelsat 21.
Operating areas: California, Georgia, District of Columbia, Illinois & New York.
Programming: A public service agency that spreads the uniqueness of Korea to the world through cutting-edge broadcasting mediums.
Began: February 3, 1997, in Korea. June 1, 2009 in U.S.
Distribution method: Available over the air on digital sub-channels.
Scrambled signal: Yes.

ARIZONA NEWS CHANNEL
c/o KTVK
5555 N Seventh Ave
Phoenix, AZ 85010
Phones: 602-207-3333; 602-207-3304
Fax: 602-207-3477
E-mail: feedback@azfamily.com
Web Site: http://www.azfamily.com
Cameryn Beck, Executive News Director
Walcott Denison III, Technology Director
Blanca Esparza-Pap, Marketing Director
Traci Scott, Sales Director
Type of service: Digital, basic.
Operating hours/week: 168.
Operating areas: Arizona.
Programming: Simulcasts & rebroadcasts of KTVK local news; 24-hour news.
Began: November 4, 1996.
Means of Support: Advertising & subscriber fees.
Total subscribers: 630,000.
Distribution method: Available to Cox Digital subscribers in the Phoenix metropolitan area.
Scrambled signal: Yes.
Ownership: Joint venture of KTVK (owned by Meredith Corp.) & Cox Communications.

ARMENIAN PUBLIC CHANNEL
26 Gevorg Hovsepyan St
Yerevan, Nork
Armenia
Phones: 374-10-650015; 374-10-653751
E-mail: international@armtv.com
Web Site: http://www.armtv.com
Liana Haroyan, Deputy Executive Director & Head of Staff
Erik Antaranyan, Head of International Affairs
Operating hours/week: 168.
Operating areas: Los Angeles area & Verizon FiOS service areas.
Programming: Armenian language movies, game shows, soap operas, family & children's shows, cultural documentaries sporting events & news reports.
Distribution method: Available over the air on digital sub-channels in Los Angeles & to Verizon FiOS subscribers.
Scrambled signal: Yes.

ARMENIAN RUSSIAN TELEVISION NETWORK (ARTN)
4401 San Fernando Rd
Glendale, CA 91204
Phone: 818-553-3737
Fax: 818-552-3710
E-mail: info@artn.tv
Web Site: http://www.artn.tv
Robert Oglakhchyan, President & Chief Executive Officer

Type of service: Basic.
Operating hours/week: 168.
Programming: Armenian & Russian language shows including travel, food, children's & game shows, soap operas, cultural & entertainment shows featuring artists, politicians, lawyers & doctors.
Began: January 1, 1985.
Distribution method: Available to cable systems & satellite subscribers.
Scrambled signal: Yes.

ART AMERICA
(Arab Radio & Television)
PO Box 51668
Knoxville, TN 37950
Phone: 423-539-8260
Fax: 423-470-4320
E-mail: artamerica1@aol.com
Web Site: http://www.artonline.tv
Hani Gharbieh, General Manager
Fadi Gharbieh, Sales & Marketing
Salvatore Vecchuzzo, Public Relations & Marketing
Type of service: Pay.
Satellites: EchoStar I.
Operating hours/week: 48.
Programming: Arabic programming including news, movies, music videos, cultural documentaries, children's shows, sports & live events.
Began: March 3, 1996.
Means of Support: Subscription fees.
Distribution method: Available to satellite subscribers.
Scrambled signal: Yes.
Ownership: Arab Radio & Television.

ASC-TV
4332 Emerson St
Skokie, IL 60076
Phone: 847-679-2722
Web Site: http://www.asctvusa.com
Operating areas: Illinois.
Programming: South Asian programming.
Distribution method: Available to Comcast Cable subscribers in Illlinois.
Ownership: Asian Satellite Communications Inc.

ASIANET
TC 26/621, (1 to 13 No.s)
Puliyarakonam
Thiruvananthapuram, Kerala 695001
India
Phone: 91-0-471-3051305
Fax: 91-0-471-3051315
E-mail: contact@asianetworld.tv
Web Site: http://www.asianetglobal.com

Branch Offices:
COLLEGE PARK: 9920 Rhode Island Ave, College Park, MD 20740. Phone: 301-345-1139. Fax: 301-345-8160. E-Mail: info@asianetusa.tv.
Type of service: Expanded digital basic, streaming.
Operating areas: Available nationwide.
Programming: Malayalam-language movies, soaps, talk shows & music-based shows.
Distribution method: Available to DISH network subscribers. Streaming available online.
Scrambled signal: Yes.
Ownership: Asianet Communications Ltd., which is owned by STAR India, a 21st Century Fox subsidiary.

ASIANET MOVIES — See Asianet.
Type of service: Expanded digital basic, HD, streaming.
Operating hours/week: 168.

Programming: Malayalam-language movies.
Began: July 15, 2012.
Scrambled signal: Yes.

ASIANET NEWS — See Asianet.
Phones: 91-0-471-3092000; 91-0-471-3018666
Fax: 91-0-471-2338970
E-mail: webteam@asianetnews.in
Web Site: http://www.asianetnews.tv
Sathya Viswanath, President & Producer
Nandini Sikand, Assistant Producer
Type of service: Pay, streaming.
Satellites: SBS-6, transponder 13.
Operating hours/week: 168.
Programming: Malayalam-language news.
Began: September 1, 1993, relaunched in U.S. on May 1, 2003.
Means of Support: Advertising & subscription fees.
Total subscribers: 7,000.
Scrambled signal: Yes.

ASIANET PLUS — See Asianet.
Type of service: Expanded basic, streaming.
Operating hours/week: 168.
Programming: Malayalam-language movies, reality shows, music based programs, film based shows & movies targeted to family audiences.
Began: August 2005.
Scrambled signal: Yes.

ASIA TRAVEL TV
No 232, Dec 2
Bade Rd, 10th Fl
Taipei
Taiwan
Phone: 886-02-2772-8988
E-mail: service@asiadigital.com.tw
Web Site: http://www.asiadigital.com.tw
Type of service: Pay.
Programming: Travel shows.
Began: January 1, 2004.
Distribution method: Available to KyLin TV subscribers.
Scrambled signal: Yes.

ASPIRE
2077 Convention Center Concourse
Ste 300
Atlanta, GA 30337
Phones: 770-692-4559; 770-692-8890
Fax: 770-692-8895
Web Site: http://www.aspire.tv
Earvin 'Magic' Johnson Jr., Chairman & Chief Executive Officer
Ty Johnson, Vice President, Multicultural Sales

Advertising Sales:
NEW YORK: c/o UPtv, 1040 Ave of the Americas, New York, NY 10018. Phone: 212-613-4440. Fax: 212-564-1904. Matt Turner, Senior Vice President, Ad Sales, East Coast.
Type of service: Basic.
Operating hours/week: 168.
Operating areas: Available nationwide.
Programming: Offers enlightening, entertaining and positive programming to African-American families. Includes movies, documentaries, short films, music, comedy, visual and performing arts, and faith and inspirational programs.
Began: June 27, 2012.
Means of Support: Advertising.
Total subscribers: 21,000,000.
Distribution method: Available to Comcast & Time Warner cable and CenturyLink system subscribers.
Scrambled signal: Yes.
Ownership: Earvin 'Magic' Johnson Jr., majority owner.

Pay TV & Satellite Services

ASSYRIASAT
PO Box 4116
Modesto, CA 95352
Phone: 209-538-4130
Fax: 209-538-2795
E-mail: AssyriaSat@yahoo.com
Satellites: Galaxy 19, transponder 23.
Programming: Assyrian focused family programming, from news & general entertainment to cultural & educational shows.
Distribution method: Available to satellite subscribers.
Scrambled signal: Yes.
Ownership: Bet-Nahrain Inc.

ATLANTA INTERFAITH BROADCASTERS
1075 Spring St NW
Atlanta, GA 30309
Phone: 404-892-0454
Fax: 404-892-8687
E-mail: info@aibtv.com; aibsales@aibtv.com
Web Site: http://www.aibtv.com
Collie Burnett, Jr., President & Chief Executive Officer
Patsy E. Williams, Vice President, Operations
Dennis Mills, Information Director
Angela H. Rice, Senior Executive Producer
Type of service: Regional basic, streaming, video on demand.
Operating hours/week: 168.
Operating areas: Georgia.
Programming: Interfaith teaching, talk shows, worship & call-in shows.
Began: February 1, 1981.
Means of Support: Time sales, production fees & contributions.
Total subscribers: 850,000.
Distribution method: Available to Comcast & AT&T U-Verse subscribers in the Atlanta area. Streaming & video on demand available online.
Scrambled signal: Yes.
Ownership: Atlanta Interfaith Broadcasters Inc.

ATLX (ATHLETICS TRAINING LIFESTYLE)
5855-A Uplander Way
Culver City, CA 90230
E-mail: info@atlxtv.com
Web Site: http://www.atlxtv.com
Jacob Arback, Co-Founder, President & Chief Executive Officer
Mohamed Mohsen, Co-Founder
Bruce Luizzi, Executive Vice President, Corporate Development & Sales
John Moser, Executive Vice President, Programming & Production
Richard Wirthlin, Executive Vice President, Business Affairs
Sarah McWilliams, Digital Content Producer
Tony Cochi, Distribution Advisor
Nadim George, Production Advisor
Gary Grossman, Production Advisor
Scott Peyton, Financial Advisor
Denise Sanchez, Events & Network Promotions Advisor
Robb Weller, Programming & Production Advisor
Type of service: Plans basic.
Operating hours/week: Plans 168.
Operating areas: Plans nationwide.
Programming: Plans original entertainment & informational programming, including news, reality, biographies, documentaries, performance cooking, etc.
Scheduled to begin: Unannounced.
Means of Support: Plans to be advertiser supported.
Distribution method: Plans to be available to cable systems.
Scrambled signal: Yes.
Ownership: MUSL TV LLC, Nexos Capital Partners.

ATRES SERIES
Avda. Isla Graciosa 13
San Sebastian de los Reyes
E-28703 Madrid
Spain
Phone: 34-91-623-05-00
Fax: 34-91-654-8439
E-mail: sales@atresmedia.com
Web Site: http://www.antena3.com/series
Javier Bardaji, General Manager, Atresmedia Television
Operating hours/week: 168.
Programming: Spanish-language programming for the entire family.
Began: 2014 in the U.S.
Scrambled signal: Yes.
Ownership: Atresmedia Television. Distributed in the U.S. by Condista.

ATV HOME CHANNEL (AMERICA)
c/o EMO America
207 Canal St, 3rd Fl
New York, NY 10013
Phones: 212-844-9542; 646-652-1028
Web Site: http://www.hkatvusa.com
Operating hours/week: 168.
Programming: Cantonese channel providing a wide range of programming, including synchronization with the Hong Kong press reports and commentaries on current affairs as well as variety shows and classic series.
Distribution method: Available to satellite subscribers & to KyLin TV subscribers.
Scrambled signal: Yes.
Ownership: Asia Television Ltd.

AUDIENCE NETWORK
c/o DirecTV
2230 E Imperial Hwy
El Segundo, CA 90245
Phone: 310-535-5000
Fax: 310-535-5225
Web Site: http://www.directv.com
Daniel York, Chief Content Officer, ROOT Sports & Audience Network
Type of service: Basic, HD.
Operating hours/week: 168.
Operating areas: Available nationwide.
Programming: Original & acquired series, specials, movies & entertainment.
Began: November 25, 1999, as Freeview. Rebranded as The 101 Network on June 5, 2006 & Audience Network on June 1, 2011.
Total subscribers: 19,400,000.
Distribution method: Available to DirecTV subscribers.
Scrambled signal: Yes.
Ownership: DirecTV.

THE AUTO CHANNEL — See TACH-TV.

AUTOMOTIVE.TV
1925 Century Park E
Ste 1025
Los Angeles, CA 90067
Phone: 310-277-3500
Web Site: http://www.es.tv
Byron Allen, Founder, Chairman & Chief Executive Officer, Entertainment Studios
Type of service: Basic.
Operating hours/week: 168.
Operating areas: Nationwide.
Programming: Automotive programming.
Began: January 1, 2015.
Means of Support: Advertising.
Distribution method: Available over the air on digital sub-channels & cable subscribers.
Scrambled signal: Yes.
Ownership: Entertainment Studios.

AVIVA TV
13124 Ramona Blvd
Baldwin Park, CA 91706
Phone: 626-337-5700
E-mail: tvaviva3@gmail.com
Web Site: http://avivamedia.tv
Pastor Leonel Flores, Information Contact
Type of service: Basic.
Operating hours/week: 168.
Operating areas: California & Nevada.
Programming: Spanish language religious channel. Airs ministry programs, movies with religious themes as well as children's educational cartoons and music videos.
Distribution method: Available over the air on digital sub-channels.
Scrambled signal: Yes.
Ownership: Aviva Coorporativo.

AWE
c/o Herring Broadcasting Inc.
4757 Morena Blvd
San Diego, CA 92117
Phone: 858-270-6900
Fax: 858-270-6901
Web Site: http://www.awetv.com
Charles Herring, Sr., President & Chief Executive Officer
Eric Brown, Executive Vice President
Stephanie Gonzalez, Press Coordinator
Type of service: Basic digital, HD, 3D & video on demand.
Satellites: Galaxy 13.
Operating hours/week: 168.
Operating areas: Available nationwide.
Programming: Informative shows that provide insights on what every American dreams of, from travel secrets to fast cars, from better etiquette to better investing.
Began: June 1, 2004, as WealthTV. Wealth TV 3D began July 15, 2010. Rebranded as AWE & AWE 3D on October 1, 2013.
Means of Support: Advertising.
Total subscribers: 16,000,000.
Distribution method: Available to cable, IPTV & satellite subscribers.
Scrambled signal: Yes.
Ownership: Herring Broadcasting Inc.

AXS TV
320 S Walton St
Dallas, TX 75226
Phone: 214-698-3800
Fax: 214-571-9225
E-mail: viewer@axs.tv
Web Site: http://www.axs.tv
Mark Cuban, Chief Executive Officer & President
Philip Garvin, Chief Operating Officer & General Manager
Robert Thoele, Chief Financial Officer & General Counsel
Sue Hamilton, Executive Vice President, Distribution & Business Development
Fred Lutz, Executive Vice President, Operations & Administration
Michele M. Dix, Senior Vice President, Programming & Development
Tim Glomb, Vice President, Marketing & Social Media
Rachael Weaver, Vice President, Programming, Promotion, Scheduling & Traffic
Amy Pfister, Senior Director, Public Relations
Katie Gladstone, Programming & Scheduling Director
Carol McDaniel, Operations Director
Tiffany Comstock, Programming & Acquisitions Manager

Branch Offices:
DENVER: 8269 E 23rd Ave, Denver, CO 80238. Phone: 303-542-5600.
Operating areas: Available nationwide.
Programming: Provides viewers with exclusive behind-the-scenes access to live concerts and music festivals, red carpet premieres, award shows, parties, pop culture events, and in-depth interviews with people and artists from the entertainment industry.
Began: September 6, 2001, as HDNet. Rebranded to AXS TV July 2012.
Means of Support: Advertising.
Total subscribers: 40,000,000.
Distribution method: Available to AT&T U-verse, Charter, Comcast, DirecTV, DISH Network, Insight, Suddenlink & Verizon FiOS subscribers.
Scrambled signal: Yes.
Ownership: AEG, Creative Artists Agency, Mark Cuban Companies & Ryan Seacrest Media.

AYM SPORTS
c/o Alterna'TV
2020 Ponce de Leon Blvd, Ste 1107
Coral Gables, FL 33135
Phone: 786-609-9604
E-mail: management@alternatv.us
Web Site: http://www.aymsports.com.mx
Operating hours/week: 168.
Programming: Coverage of Mexican sports, including soccer, wrestling, boxing, college sports, rugby, etc.
Began: April 1, 2004, September 2006 in U.S.
Distribution method: Available on Charter, Grande Communications, San Bruno Municipal Cable, Time Warner Cable & Verzion FiOS systems.
Scrambled signal: Yes.
Ownership: AYM Sports SA de CV. Distributed in the U.S. by Alterna'tv.

AZ CLIC
Periferico Sur 4121
Col Fuentes del Pedregal CP 14141
Mexico
Phone: 55-5447-8844
E-mail: contacto@tvazteca.com
Web Site: http://www.aztvdepaga.com/azclic
Programming: Spanish-language music & entertainment programming geared towards younger adults.
Ownership: TV Azteca. Distributed in the U.S. by Condista.

AZ CORAZON
Periferico Sur 4121

Communications Daily — Warren Communications News
Get the industry standard FREE — For a no-obligation trial call 800-771-9202 or visit www.warren-news.com

2017 Edition E-11

Pay TV & Satellite Services

Col Fuentes del Pedregal CP 14141
Mexico
Phone: 55-5447-8844
E-mail: contacto@tvazteca.com
Web Site: http://www.aztvdepaga.com/azcorazon
Programming: Spanish-language telenovelas.
Ownership: TV Azteca. Distributed in the U.S. by Condista.

AZTECA
1139 Grand Central Ave
Glendale, CA 91201
Phone: 818-247-0400
Fax: 310-432-7907
Web Site: http://us.azteca.com
Benjamin Salinas, Chief Executive Officer
Martin K. Breidsprecher, Chief Operating Officer & Affiliate Relations Director
Ernesto Ortega, Chief Financial Officer
Craig Geller, Executive Vice President, Network Sales & Digital
Enrique Perez, Executive Vice President, Station Group
Court Stroud, Executive Vice President, Network Sales & Digital
Nicole Burri, Senior Vice President, National Sales
Greg Angel, Vice President, Sales
Margarita Black, Vice President, Programming
Horacio Medal, Vice President & Chief Legal Officer
Jose Luis Padilla, Vice President & General Manager, Los Angeles
Andrew Cain, Engineering & Operations Manager
Widad Leal, Marketing & Public Relations

Network & National Spot Sales:
NEW YORK: 1430 Broadway, 10th Fl, New York, NY 10018. Phone: 464-360-1788. Fax: 464-360-1785.
Type of service: Over the air, basic, HD.
Operating hours/week: 168.
Programming: Spanish language broadcast network for the U.S. Hispanic market, featuring news, sports & entertainment.
Began: January 1, 2001, as Azteca America in U.S. Rebranded Azteca May 13, 2014.
Total subscribers: 15,000,000.
Distribution method: Available over the air & to cable, IPTV & satellite subscribers.
Scrambled signal: Yes.
Ownership: Azteca International Corp.

AZ TV
AZ1011 M.Huseyn 1
Baku, Azerbaijan
Phone: 99-412-4923807
Fax: 99-412-4972020
E-mail: webmaster@aztv.az
Web Site: http://www.aztv.az
Arif Nizam Alishanov, Chairman
Faiq Nural son Husiyev, Deputy Chairman
Cavansir Muradkhan Cahangirov, Vice President
Ibrahim M. Mammadov, Vice President
Type of service: Basic.
Satellites: Galaxy 19.
Operating hours/week: 168.
Programming: News, serials, sports & musical events from Azerbaijan.
Distribution method: Available to satellite subscribers.
Scrambled signal: Yes.
Ownership: Azerbaijan Television & Radio Broadcasting Closed Joint-stock Co.

BABYFIRST AMERICAS
PO Box 25639
Los Angeles, CA 90024
Phone: 888-251-2229
Web Site: http://www.babyfirstamericas.com
Constantino Schwarz, Chairman & Chief Executive Officer
Guy Oranim, President & Founder
Mario Sollis-Marich, Vice President, Programming
Dr. Todd Eller, Chief Educational Advisor
Type of service: Basic.
Operating areas: Available nationwide.
Programming: Offers Latino parents the ability to help their children integrate into American society and provides an additional educational tool that meets families' needs whether they are currently bilingual or wanting to introduce their children to another language.
Began: April 1, 2012.
Total subscribers: 81,000,000 (Worldwide.).
Distribution method: Available to Comcast & Time Warner cable subscribers & DirecTV & DISH subscribers.
Scrambled signal: Yes.
Ownership: Guy Oranim, Founder.

BABYFIRSTTV
10390 Santa Monica Blvd
3rd Fl
Los Angeles, CA 90025
Phone: 888-251-2229
Web Site: http://www.babyfirsttv.com
Guy Oranim, Chief Executive Officer
Mary Jeanne Cavanagh, Executive Vice President, Advertising Sales
Sharon Rechter, Executive Vice President, Business Development & Marketing
Arik Kerman, Senior Vice President, Programming & Operations
Itamar Daube, Vice President, Creative
Arthur Pober, Chief Educational Advisor
Type of service: Basic & video on demand.
Satellites: Telstar, transponder 10.
Operating hours/week: 168.
Operating areas: Available nationwide.
Programming: Shows for babies & toddlers to age three.
Began: May 1, 2006.
Total subscribers: 50,000,000.
Distribution method: Available to BrightHouse, DirecTV, Dish Network, Comcast, Time Warner and AT&T U-verse customers.
Scrambled signal: Yes.
Ownership: Guy Oranim, Founder.

BABY TV
10 Hammersmith Grove
London W6 7AP
United Kingdom
Phone: 44-020-7751-7599
E-mail: info@babytvchannel.com
Web Site: http://www.babytv.com
Ron Isaak, Co-Founder & Creative Director
Maya Talit, Co-Founder & Global Marketing Director
Type of service: Expanded basic.
Operating hours/week: 168.
Operating areas: Available nationwide.
Programming: Short programs & music for children; programs are designed to promote learning, activity & interaction.
Began: December 4, 2003, in the U.K.; Began July 1, 2009 in the U.S.
Means of Support: Advertising.
Total subscribers: 30,000,000 (Viewers worldwide.).
Distribution method: Available to AT&T U-Verse, Cox & DISH subscribers.
Scrambled signal: Yes.
Ownership: Fox International Channels, a subsidiary of 21st Century Fox.

BANDAMAX — See Univision.
c/o Univision Communications Inc.

605 Third Ave, 12th Fl
New York, NY 10158
Phone: 212-455-5200
Web Site: http://www.televisanetworks.tv; http://corporate.univision.com
Beau Ferrari, Executive Vice President, Operations, Univision Networks
Satellites: AMC 10, transponder 4.
Operating areas: Available nationwide.
Programming: Features regional Mexican music videos as well as live original programming, the latest celebrity news and exclusive concerts.
Began: May 1, 2003.
Total subscribers: 2,000,000.
Distribution method: Available to cable, IPTV & satellite subscribers.
Scrambled signal: Yes.
Ownership: Televisa Networks. Univision Communications Inc. has an exclusive contract for this service.

BAND INTERNACIONAL
R. Radiantes 13
Morumbi
Sao Paulo 05699-900
Brazil
Phones: 55-11-3131-3903; 55-11-3131-7578
Fax: 55-11-3131-3905
Web Site: http://www.band.uol.com.br
Type of service: Pay.
Operating hours/week: 168.
Operating areas: Available nationwide.
Programming: Provides quality entertainment with news, sports, women's programs, talk shows, musicals and documentaries from three popular Brazilian channels.
Began: January 1, 2007.
Means of Support: Advertising and subscriber fees.
Distribution method: Available to Comcast cable subscribers.
Scrambled signal: Yes.
Ownership: Bandeirantes Communication Group.

BANG U
c/o Playboy Plus Entertainment
2300 W Empire Ave, 7th Fl
Burbank, CA 91504
Phone: 323-276-4000
Fax: 323-276-4500
E-mail: info.losangeles@mindgeek.com
Web Site: http://www.mindgeek.com
Type of service: Pay per view.
Programming: Adult entertainment.
Began: February 14, 1994, as Adam & Eve. Rebranded as Spice 2 on June 1, 1999, Shorteez & then Bang U.
Distribution method: Available to cable, IPTV & satellite subscribers.
Ownership: Playboy Plus Entertainment/Mindgeek.

BARCA TV
c/o FCB Barcelona
Aristides Maillol s/n
Barcelona 08028
Spain
Phone: 34-902-1899-00
Web Site: http://barcatv.fcbarcelona.com
Programming: FC Barcelona matches, news & information.
Began: July 27, 1999, as Canal Barca. Rebranded as Barca TV in 2004.
Scrambled signal: Yes.
Ownership: FC Barcelona. Distributed in the U.S. by Imagina U.S.

BAY NEWS 9
700 Carillon Pkwy
Ste 9

St. Petersburg, FL 33716
Phone: 727-329-2300
E-mail: comments@baynews9.com
Web Site: http://www.baynews9.com
Alan Mason, Vice President & General Manager, News & Local Programming
Sylvia Setheras, General Sales Manager
Mike Gautreau, Senior Director, News
Maggie Daniell, Business Affairs Director
Linda Granger, Marketing Director
Jason Bishop, Assistant News Director
Type of service: Basic, HD, streaming.
Operating hours/week: 168.
Operating areas: Tampa Bay region, Florida.
Programming: 24-hour news channel covering the Tampa Bay area. Spanish language available on Bay News 9 en Espanol.
Began: September 24, 1997.
Means of Support: Advertising.
Total subscribers: 1,000,000.
Distribution method: Available to Bright House subscribers in the Tampa Bay & Orlando area. Streaming available online or through app.
Scrambled signal: Yes.
Ownership: Bright House Networks.

BAY NEWS 9 EN ESPANOL — See Info-Mas.

BBC AMERICA
1120 Ave of the Americas
5th Fl
New York, NY 10036
Phone: 212-705-9300
Fax: 212-705-9420
Web Site: http://www.bbcamerica.com
Ann Sarnoff, President, BBC Worldwide North America
Sarah Barnett, President & General Manager
Sandy Ashendorf, Executive Vice President, Network Distribution, BBC Worldwide America, North America
Mark Gall, Executive Vice President, North American Ad Sales
Oswald Mendez, Executive Vice President, Marketing & Digital
Jo Petherbridge, Executive Vice President, Communications
Nena Rodrigue, Executive Vice President, Original Programming, Acquisitions & Production
Michael Ross, Executive Vice President, Business Affairs & Operations
Nick Ascheim, Senior Vice President, Consumer Digital
Valerie Bruce, Senior Vice President, Business Affairs
Richard De Croce, Senior Vice President, Programming
Mary Pratt-Henaghan, Senior Vice President, Operations & Administration
Matt Stein, Senior Vice President, Marketing, Promotion & Creative Services
Dawn Williamson, Senior Vice President, Advertising Sales, BBC Worldwide North America
Rachel Garcia, Vice President, Marketing & Social Media Strategy
Erin Jontow, Vice President, Scripted Programming
Ricky Kelehar, Vice President, Unscripted Programming
Courtney Thomasma, Vice President, Research
Tim Wastney, Vice President, Ad Sales, BBC Worldwide North America
Perry Simon, General Manager, Channels
Type of service: Basic, HD, streaming & video on demand.
Satellites: Satcom C-3, transponder 22.
Operating hours/week: 168.
Operating areas: Available nationwide.

Pay TV & Satellite Services

Programming: British entertainment, including news, comedy, drama, reality, movies, entertainment & science fiction.
Began: March 29, 1998.
Total subscribers: 81,000,000.
Distribution method: Available to cable, IPTV & satellite subscribers. Streaming available online & mobile through the website or app (participating providers); video on demand (participating providers).
Scrambled signal: Yes.
Ownership: British Broadcasting Corp., 50.1%; AMC Networks, 49.9%.

BBC AMERICA ON DEMAND — See BBC America.

BBC ARABIC — See BBC World News
Web Site: http://www.bbcarabic.com
Type of service: Basic, streaming.
Operating hours/week: 84.
Programming: News headlines & summaries.
Began: March 11, 2008.
Distribution method: Available to satellite subscribers; Streaming available online & mobile through the website or app (participating providers).
Scrambled signal: Yes.

BBC WORLD NEWS
BBC World Ltd.
Woodlands, 80 Wood Ln
London W12 0TT
United Kingdom
Phone: 44-0-20-8433-2000
Fax: 44-0-20-8749-0538
Web Site: http://www.bbc.com/news/world
Peter Horrocks, BBC World Service & Global News Director
Colin Lawrence, Commercial Director
Type of service: Digital.
Operating hours/week: 168.
Operating areas: Available nationwide.
Programming: Global news & events.
Began: March 11, 1991, in the U.K. April 30, 2006 in the U.S.
Total subscribers: 274,000,000 (Includes 2,300,000 U.S. subscribers).
Distribution method: Available to cable, IPTV & satellite subscribers.
Scrambled signal: Yes.

BEACHTV
1250 Bellflower Blvd
Long Beach, CA 90840
Phone: 562-985-4352
Web Site: http://cslbtv.amp.csulb.edu
Type of service: Basic.
Operating areas: California.
Programming: Campus, local, national & international news & entertainment.
Distribution method: Available to Charter, Time Warner & Verizon FiOS subscribers in the Long Beach area.
Scrambled signal: Yes.

BEAUTY & FASHION CHANNEL
4100 E Mississippi Ave
19th Fl
Glendale, CO 80246
Phone: 303-839-5303
Fax: 303-839-5335
Web Site: http://www.beautyfashiontv.com
Programming: Features news & trends in fashion & style.
Total subscribers: 32,000,000.
Distribution method: Available to cable & satellite subscribers.
Scrambled signal: Yes.
Ownership: Turner Media Group.

BEIJING TV
Jianguo Rd

Chaoyang District
Beijing, No. 98 100022
China
E-mail: btvsuggest@btv.com.cn
Web Site: http://www.btv.com.cn
Programming: Chinese language entertainment including culture, history, fashion, lifestyle, travel, sports & children.
Distribution method: Available to DISH Network subscribers.
Scrambled signal: Yes.
Ownership: Government owned.

BEIN SPORT
3 Columbus Cir
New York, NY 10019
Phone: 212-520-1945
E-mail: info@beinsport.tv
Web Site: http://www.beinsports.tv
Nasser Al Khelaifi, Chief Executive Officer
Antonio Briceno, Deputy Managing Director, North America
Roy Meyeringh, Vice President, Business Development & Affiliate Sales

Branch Offices:
MIAMI: 7291 NW 74th St, Miami, FL 33166.
Type of service: Premium, HD, streaming.
Operating hours/week: 168.
Operating areas: Available nationwide.
Programming: Soccer networks available in English and Spanish. Offers exclusive coverage of La Liga BBVA from Spain, as well as exclusive coverage of the Serie A from Italy and of Ligue 1 plus La Ligue UN (English-only) from France, Copa Italia, Super Copa Italia and the Capital One Cup as well as the Football League Championship. Coverage also includes Italian male volleyball, handball from Europe and rugby.
Began: August 15, 2012.
Means of Support: Advertising and subscriber fees.
Total subscribers: 80,000,000.
Distribution method: Available to cable, IPTV & satellite subscribers. Streaming available online & mobile through the website or app (participating providers).
Scrambled signal: Yes.
Ownership: Al Jazeera, which is owned by Qatar Media Corporation.

BEIN SPORT EN ESPANOL — See BeIN Sport.
Web Site: http://www.beinsports.com/us-es
Programming: Variety of sporting events including soccer, motorcross, cycling, rugby and boxing in Spanish.

BET
(Black Entertainment Television)
One BET Plz, 1235 W St NW
Washington, DC 20018
Phone: 202-608-2000
Fax: 202-608-2589
E-mail: adsales@bet.net
Web Site: http://www.bet.com
Debra L. Lee, Chairman & Chief Executive Officer
Louis Carr, President, Broadcast Media Sales
Stephen G. Hill, President, Programming
Michael Pickrum, Chief Financial Officer
Matthew Barnhill, Executive Vice President, Corporate Market Research
Peter Danielsen, Executive Vice President, Program Planning, Scheduling & Acquisitions
Kay Madati, Executive Vice President & Chief Digital Officer
Zola Mashariki, Executive Vice President & Head, Original Programming
Darrell E. Walker, Executive Vice President & General Counsel

Maureen Guthman, Senior Vice President, Programming & Acquisitions
Eddie Hill, Senior Vice President, Consumer Marketing & Brand Strategy
Jeanine Liburd, Senior Vice President, Corporate Communications & Corporate Social Responsibility
Reggie Williams, Senior Vice President, Programming, Music & Specials
Sean Gupta, Vice President, Program Strategy
Kevin Morrison, Senior Director, Development, Los Angeles
Shirley Salomon, Production for Development Director

Office Locations:
BET Productions: 2000 W Place NE, Washington, DC 20018. Phone: 202-608-2601.

Branch Offices:
ATLANTA: 3845 Pleasantdale Rd, Atlanta, GA 30340. Phone: 770-242-3899.

CENTURY CITY: 1840 Century Park E, Ste 600, Los Angeles, CA 90067. Phone: 310-552-8400. Fax: 310-552-8444.

CHICAGO: 180 N Stetson Ct, Ste 4350, Chicago, IL 60601. Phone: 312-819-8600. Fax: 312-819-8684.

NEW YORK: 380 Madison Ave, 20th Fl, New York, NY 10017. Phone: 212-697-5500. Fax: 212-697-2050.
Type of service: Basic, HD, streaming & video on demand.
Satellites: Galaxy V, transponder 20.
Operating hours/week: 168.
Operating areas: Available nationwide.
Programming: Entertainment, music, news and public affairs programming for the African-American audience.
Began: January 25, 1980, in U.S.; October 1, 1998 in Canada.
Means of Support: Advertising.
Total subscribers: 90,000,000 (in U.S.; 4,000,000 Canadian subscribers. 10,000,000 United Kingdom subscribers.).
Distribution method: Available to cable, IPTV & satellite subscribers; online & mobile through the website or app (participating providers); video on demand (participating providers).
Scrambled signal: Yes.
Ownership: Viacom Inc.

BET GOSPEL — See BET.
Programming: Gospel & inspirational programming.
Began: July 1, 2002.

BET HIP HOP — See BET.
Programming: Hip-rop & rap music videos & shows.
Began: July 1, 2002.

BET J — See Centric.

BET PLAY — See BET.
Type of service: Over the top, stand-alone streaming subscription service.
Operating areas: Nationwide.

Programming: BETGÇÖs signature award shows, current & classic TV series, documentaries, standup comedy, entertainment news and musical performances.
Began: 2016.
Distribution method: Available to subscribers through app.
Scrambled signal: Yes.

BET SOUL — See BET.
Programming: Music videos showcasing R&B, soul, hip hop, funk, jazz & Motown music from the 90s to today.
Began: 2000. Rebranded BET Soul December 28, 2015.

B4U MOVIES
c/o B4U US Inc.
39 W 32nd St, Ste 1401
New York, NY 10001
Phones: 917-414-1008; 315-510-6957
Fax: 212-564-3589
Web Site: http://www.b4utv.com
Type of service: Premium.
Operating areas: Available nationwide.
Programming: Bollywood network offering blockbuster, comedy, thriller & classic movies for every genre & the entire family; plus Bollywood gossip & star-studded interviews.
Began: January 1, 1999, in India. Began in the U.S. late 1999.
Means of Support: Subscriber fees.
Distribution method: Available to DISH subscribers.
Scrambled signal: Yes.
Ownership: B4U TV Ltd.

B4U MUSIC — See B4U Movies.
Web Site: http://b4umusic.us
Type of service: Premium digital.
Operating areas: Available nationwide.
Programming: Bollywood music videos, star interviews, artist profiles & concerts.
Distribution method: Available to DISH subscribers.
Scrambled signal: Yes.
Ownership: B4U TV Ltd.

BIG TEN NETWORK — See BTN.

BIO — See FYI.

BIZ TV
810 E Abram St
Arlington, TX 76010
Phone: 817-274-1609
Fax: 817-274-1609
E-mail: info@biztv.com
Web Site: http://www.biztv.com
Ed Frazier, President & Chief Executive Officer
Scott Miller, Executive Vice President
Mark MacGregor, Vice President, Affiliate Sales
Lisa McKibben, Marketing Director
Ryan Raines, Operations Director
Type of service: Over the air, basic, streaming.
Satellites: Galaxy 23, transponder 19.
Operating hours/week: 168.
Uplink: Media Gateway.

Pay TV & Satellite Services

CABLE & TV STATION COVERAGE
Atlas 2017
The perfect companion to the Television & Cable Factbook
To order call 800-771-9202 or visit www.warren-news.com

Programming: Offers shows appealing to entrepreneurs and small business owners.
Began: July 6, 2009.
Means of Support: Fees & advertising.
Distribution method: Available over the air on digital sub-channels & to cable & satellite subscribers. Streaming available online or app.
Scrambled signal: Yes.
Ownership: Centerpost Ltd.

BLACK HERITAGE NETWORK
2035 Federal St
Philadelphia, PA 19146
Phone: 215-385-3072
E-mail: info@bhn.tv
Web Site: http://www.bhn.tv
Richard Reingold, Co-Founder & Non-Executive Chairman
Hezekiah Lewis, President & Chief Executive Officer
Julianna T. Cole, Chief Digital & Operating Officer
Charles Grinker, Executive Vice President & Creative Director
Type of service: Plans digital basic.
Operating hours/week: Plans 168.
Operating areas: Nationwide.
Programming: True-to-life, non-fiction programming for African-Americans aged 25-54 & 50-plus.
Scheduled to begin: July 22, 2011, on YouTube. May 2013 on Roku. Plans to launch on cable & satellite.
Means of Support: Advertising.
Total subscribers: (Plans 7,000,000 subs at launch.).
Distribution method: Available on Roku & online. Plans to be available to cable & satellite subscribers.
Scrambled signal: Planned.
Ownership: Investors include Paul Besson, Tyrone Brown, Roger Ferguson, Steven Lerman & John Rogers.

BLACK NETWORK TELEVISION
1325 S Eugene St
Greensboro, NC 27406-1470
Phones: 336-235-0269; 336-908-2407
Fax: 336-272-8880
E-mail: sales@blacknetworktelevision.com
Web Site: http://blacknetworktelevision.com
Michael Woods, President & Chief Executive Officer
Ramona Woods, Chief Financial Officer
Kara Poole, Advertising
Lashawn Williamson, Advertising
Type of service: Basic.
Operating hours/week: 168.
Operating areas: North Carolina & Virginia.
Programming: Focuses on topics covering culture, entertainment and lifestyle from cultural destinations, to health and education, to popular trends.
Began: March 14, 2011.
Means of Support: Advertising.
Total subscribers: 4,200,000.
Distribution method: Available over the air on digital sub-channels.
Scrambled signal: Yes.
Ownership: Michael & Ramona Woods.

BLACK TELEVISION NEWS CHANNEL
1463 Market St
Tallahassee, FL 32312-1726
Phones: 850-906-9990; 877-469-2862
E-mail: fwatson@btnc.tv
Web Site: http://www.btnc.tv
J. C. Watts Jr, Chairman & Co-Manager
Robert Brillante, Co-Manager
Frank Watson, Vice President & General Manager
Steve Pruit, Vice President, Legislative & Regulatory Affairs
Type of service: Plans basic.
Operating hours/week: Plans 168.
Operating areas: Plans to launch in Atlanta, Baltimore, Chicago, Detroit, Miami, Philadelphia & Washington, DC.
Programming: Plans to launch as a public interest channel for first three years, then convert to a traditional for profit commercial channel, offering 12 hours of news, six hours of prime time programming and six hours of paid overnight gospel programming.
Scheduled to begin: Unannounced.
Total subscribers: 35,200,000 (Number based upon agreements).
Distribution method: Plans to be available to cable systems & satellite subscribers.
Scrambled signal: Yes.
Ownership: J.C. Watts Jr. & Robert Brilliante.

BLOCKBUSTER ON DEMAND
c/o DISH Digital LLC
9601 S Meridian Blvd
Englewood, CO 80112
Phone: 303-723-1000
E-mail: support@blockbusternow.com
Web Site: http://www.blockbusternow.com
Type of service: Video on demand.
Programming: Movie download service with content from film libraries spanning all genres: action, comedy, drama, family, foreign & classics.
Began: January 1, 2002, as Movielink. Acquired by Blockbuster & rebranded as Blockbuster on Demand in 2007.
Distribution method: Available through app.
Scrambled signal: Yes.
Ownership: DISH Digital LLC.

BLOOMBERG TELEVISION
731 Lexington Ave
New York, NY 10022
Phones: 212-617-2201; 212-318-2000
E-mail: inquiry1@bloomberg.net
Web Site: http://www.bloomberg.com/tv
Michael R. Bloomberg, Co-Founder, Chief Executive Officer & President, Bloomberg LP
Claudia Milne, Head of U.S. Live TV
Ted Fine, Head of Programming
Type of service: Basic, HD, mobile, streaming.
Satellites: HITS; Satcom C-3, transponder 8; G11.
Operating hours/week: 168.
Programming: Financial news from 126 news bureaus. Providing local, regional & international news that moves markets through live interviews & coverage of major events.
Began: February 1, 1994, as Bloomberg Information TV. Rebranded Bloomberg Television in 1998. Bloomberg Television HD began April 25, 2011.
Total subscribers: 48,000,000 (Includes full-time subscribers only; part-time subscribers comprise an additional 86,000,000).
Distribution method: Available to cable, IPTV & satellite subscribers. Streaming available online & through app.
Scrambled signal: Yes.
Ownership: Bloomberg L.P.

BLUEHIGHWAYS TV
1242 Old Hillsboro Rd
Franklin, TN 37069
Phone: 615-264-3292
E-mail: dhitchcock@bluehighwaystv.com
Web Site: http://www.bluehighwaystv.com
Stan Hitchcock, Founder & Chairman
Alan McLaughlin, Chief Operating Officer
Denise T. Hitchcock, Executive Vice President, Affiliate Relations & Marketing
Type of service: Basic digital, HD.
Satellites: AMC 10, transponder T-15.
Sales representative: Davida M. Shear.
Operating hours/week: 168.
Uplink: Atlanta, GA.
Programming: Americana programming featuring roots music, backroads travel, western & equestrian shows.
Began: July 1, 2004, on video on demand; linear channel launched March 11, 2007.
Total subscribers: 6,000,000 (reflects video on demand service).
Distribution method: Available to cable, IPTV & satellite subscribers.
Scrambled signal: No.
Ownership: Network Creative Group.

BLUE OCEAN NETWORK
The BON Bldg, CN16, Legend Town
No. 1 East Balizhuang
Chaoyang District, Beijing 10025
China
Phone: 86-10-5227-0888
Fax: 86-10-5227-0999
E-mail: bon@bon.tv
Web Site: http://www.bon.tv
Satellites: Galaxy 23 C-Band.
Operating hours/week: 168.
Operating areas: Available nationwide.
Programming: China-focused news & features, including business, technology, travel, art, creativity, health & living programming in English.
Began: 2010.
Distribution method: Available to DISH subscribers & through MHz Networks.

BOLIVIA TV
Av Camacho #1485 - Urban 6th Fl Bldg
Box 900
La Paz
Bolivia
Phone: 591-2-2203403
Fax: 591-2-2203973
Web Site: http://www.boliviatv.bo
Programming: Spanish-language general entertainment & news.
Scrambled signal: Yes.
Ownership: Empresa Nacional de Televisíon de Bolivia. Distributed in the U.S. by Condista.

BOLLYWOOD HITS ON DEMAND
c/o International Media Distribution
4100 E Dry Creek Rd
Centennial, CO 80122
Phones: 303-712-5400; 303-712-5401
Web Site: http://www.mybhod.com
Ken Naz, President, North America, Eros International PLC

Branch Offices:
LOS ANGELES: 5750 Wilshire Blvd, 3rd Fl, Los Angeles, CA 90036. Phone: 323-692-5348. Fax: 323-954-2991.

SEATTLE: 18 W Mercer, Ste 110, Seattle, WA 98119. Phone: 206-282-2762. Fax: 206-282-2763.
Type of service: Video on demand.
Programming: Bollywood movies & music videos.
Began: September 1, 2006.
Distribution method: Available to Bright House, Cablevision, Comcast, Cox, Time Warner, CenturyLink, RCN & Verizon FiOS subscribers.
Scrambled signal: Yes.
Ownership: Eros International PLC.

BONJOUR AMERICA TV
819 SW 10th Ave
Miami, FL 33130
Phone: 786-258-7848
E-mail: corporatepr@bonjouramericatv.com
Web Site: http://www.bonjouramericatv.com/
Victor Romero, President & Chief Executive Officer
Type of service: Basic.
Operating hours/week: 168.
Operating areas: Available nationwide.
Programming: Entertainment channel offering documentaries, concerts, drama, news, films & video clips broadcasting totally in French.
Began: September 11, 2016.
Means of Support: Advertising.
Total subscribers: 20,000,000 (Represents prospective audience.).
Scrambled signal: Yes.
Ownership: Bonjour America TV.

BOOK TV
400 N Capitol St NW
Ste 650
Washington, DC 20001
Phone: 202-737-3220
Fax: 202-737-0508
E-mail: booktv@c-span.org
Web Site: http://www.booktv.org
Robin Scullin, Media Relations Manager
Connie Doebele, Senior Executive Producer
Type of service: Basic.
Operating hours/week: 48. 8a.m. Sat.- 8a.m. Mon.
Uplink: Washington, D.C.
Programming: Featuring works of non-fiction authors and classics that have impacted public policy, history, or culture; historical fiction/non-fiction books for children and young adults; tours of unique bookstores & libraries; live call-in forums. Available on C-SPAN 2.
Began: December 9, 1998.
Total subscribers: 85,000,000.
Distribution method: Available to cable subscribers.
Scrambled signal: Yes.
Ownership: C-SPAN.

BOOMERANG
1050 Techwood Dr NW
Bldg 1000
Atlanta, GA 30318-5264
Phones: 404-827-1700; 404-885-2263
Fax: 404-885-4594
Web Site: http://www.boomeranggo.com
Christina Miller, President & General Manager, Adult Swim, Cartoon Network & Boomerang
Michael Ouweleen, Chief Marketing Officer
Vishnu Athreya, Vice President, Program Scheduling, Boomerang & Cartoon Network

E-14　　　　　　　　　　　　　　　　　　　　　　　　　　　　　　　　　　　TV & Cable Factbook No. 85

Pay TV & Satellite Services

Adina Pitt, Vice President, Content Acquisitions & Co-Productions, Boomerang & Cartoon Network
Type of service: Basic, video on demand.
Satellites: Galaxy I-R, transponder 15.
Operating hours/week: 168.
Operating areas: Available nationwide.
Programming: Classic cartoons. SAP where available.
Began: April 1, 2000, Boomerang on Demand began 2005.
Total subscribers: 18,000,000.
Distribution method: Available to cable, IPTV & satellite subscribers; video on demand (participating providers).
Scrambled signal: Yes.
Ownership: Turner Broadcasting System, division of Time Warner.

BOSTEL
Chicago, IL
Phone: 773-334-6200
E-mail: info@rtvbostel.com
Web Site: http://www.rtvbostel.com
ihad Mehanovic, Director
Operating hours/week: 168.
Programming: Traditional music, sports, business, art & technology focused shows for Bosnian community in U.S.
Began: January 1, 2001.

BOSTON CATHOLIC TELEVISION —
See CatholicTV.

BOSTON KIDS & FAMILY
One Guest St
Boston, MA 02135
Phone: 617-300-2000
Fax: 617-300-1026
Web Site: http://www.wgbh.org/kids/boston_kids_family
Type of service: Basic.
Operating areas: Boston, Massachusetts.
Programming: Educational programming for children during the day & history/cultural programming for adults in the evening.
Distribution method: Available to Comcast & RCN subscribers.
Scrambled signal: Yes.
Ownership: Collaboration between WCBH & the City of Boston.

BOUNCE TV
3500 Piedmont Rd
Ste 400
Atlanta, GA 30305
Phone: 770-672-6500
Fax: 404-577-1786
E-mail: jweiss@bouncetv.com
Web Site: http://www.bouncetv.com
Ryan Glover, President
Jonathan Katz, Chief Operating Officer
Maria Harvey, Chief Financial Officer
Jeffrey Wolf, Chief Distribution Officer
Elverage Allen, Executive Vice President, Advertising Sales
Cheryle Harrison, Senior Vice President, Sales Operations
Elizabeth Kealoha, Senior Vice President, Production & Programming Operations
Bryan Slonaker, Senior Vice President, Creative Services
Jim Weiss, Senior Vice President, Corporate Communications
Erick Asenjo, Vice President, Ad Sales
Celeste Castle, Vice President, Research
Ri-Karlo Handy, Vice President, Original Programming & Production
Calandria Meadows, Vice President, Social Media & Digital Content
Walter Naar, Vice President, Programming

Tracy Underwood, Vice President, Affiliate Relations
Mark Ward, Vice President, Operations
Sean Woodle, Vice President, West Coast Ad Sales
Gary Sarginario, Ad Sales Director
Type of service: Basic, over the air.
Operating areas: Available nationwide.
Programming: A mix of original & off-network series, theatrical motion pictures, documentaries, specials, live sports & more. Target audience is African Americans between the ages of 25-54.
Began: September 26, 2011.
Means of Support: Advertising.
Total subscribers: 65,000,000.
Distribution method: Over the air on digital sub-channels in all major markets.
Scrambled signal: No.

BOX — No longer in operation; see MTV2.

BOXTV: THE BOXING CHANNEL
1357 Broadway
Studio 211
New York, NY 10018-7107
Phone: 212-731-2151
Fax: 212-202-4265
E-mail: bricco@boxtv.org
Web Site: http://www.boxtv.org
Brian Ricco, President & Chief Executive Officer
Operating hours/week: Plans 168.
Operating areas: Plans to be available nationwide.
Scrambled signal: Yes.
Ownership: MultiVision Media Inc.

BRAVO
30 Rockefeller Plz
8th Fl E
New York, NY 10112
Phone: 212-664-4444
E-mail: bravofeedback@bravotv.com
Web Site: http://www.bravotv.com
NBCUNIVERSAL ENTERTAINMENT:, .
Bonnie Hammer, Chairman, NBCUniversal Cable Entertainment Group
Frances Berwick, President, Lifestyle Networks Group, NBCUniversal Cable Entertainment
David O'Connell, Executive Vice President, Production Management & Operations, Lifestyle Networks Group, NBCUniversal Cable Entertainment
BRAVO:, .
Holly Tang, Chief Financial Officer, Bravo & Oxygen Media
Lisa Hsia, Executive Vice President, Digital, Bravo & Oxygen Media
Jerry Leo, Executive Vice President, Program Strategy, Lifestyle Networks & Production, Bravo Media
Shari Levine, Executive Vice President, Current Production
Ellen Stone, Executive Vice President, Marketing, Bravo & Oxygen Media
Jamie Cutburth, Senior Vice President, Partnership Marketing, Bravo & Oxygen Media
Kathleen French, Senior Vice President, Production
Jennifer Geisser, Senior Vice President, Communications
Michael Haggerty, Senior Vice President, Research
Jonathan Hills, Senior Vice President, Bravo Digital Media
Maria Laino DeLuca, Senior Vice President, Trade & Consumer Marketing, Bravo Media
Jenn Levy, Senior Vice President, Production, Bravo Media
David O'Connell, Senior Vice President, Production Operations, Bravo & Oxygen Media

Ryan Pinette, Senior Vice President, Production & Operations, Bravo & Oxygen Media
Rachel Smith, Senior Vice President, Production
Lara Spotts, Senior Vice President, Development, Bravo Media
Amy Troiano, Senior Vice President, Creative & Brand Strategy, Bravo Media
Aimee Viles, Senior Vice President, Emerging Media, Bravo & Oxygen Media
David Brewer, Vice President, Program Strategy & Acquisitions, Bravo & Oxygen Media
Eric Cavanaugh, Vice President, Program Research, Bravo Media
Christy Dees, Vice President, Development, Bravo Media
Chloe Ellers, Vice President, Communications, Bravo & Oxygen Media
Ryan Flynn, Vice President, Current Production, Bravo Media
Nancy Jo, Vice President, Business Development & Digital Strategy, Bravo & Oxygen Media
Maria Jordan, Vice President, Financial Planning & Analysis
David Kaplan, Vice President, Ad Sales Research, Bravo Media
Rajal Lele, Vice President, Business Affairs, Bravo Media
Robert Mancini, Vice President, Content, Bravo Digital
Matt Reichman, Vice President, Current Production
Barry Rosenberg, Vice President, Communications, Bravo & Oxygen Media
Andrew Wang, Vice President, Scripted Development & Production, Bravo Media
Taryn Winkelman, Vice President, Consumer Marketing, Bravo Media
Suejin Yang, Vice President, Digital Media, Bravo Media
Emily Yeomans, Vice President, Communications, Bravo & Oxygen Media
Adam Zeller, Vice President, Social Media, Bravo & Oxygen Media

Regional Offices:
CHICAGO: NBC Tower, 454 N Columbus Dr, 3rd Fl, Chicago, IL 60611.

UNIVERSAL CITY: 200 Universal City Plz, Bldg 9128-3, Universal City, CA 91608.
Type of service: Basic, HD, streaming, video on demand.
Satellites: Satcom C4, transponder 7.
Operating hours/week: 168.
Operating areas: Available nationwide.
Programming: Drama & reality series, movies, comedy and music specials.
Began: December 1, 1980, Bravo HD began October 3, 2007.
Means of Support: Subscriber fees & advertising.
Total subscribers: 94,000,000.
Distribution method: Available to cable, IPTV & satellite subscribers; online & mobile through the website or app (participating providers); video on demand (participating providers).
Scrambled signal: Yes.
Ownership: NBCUniversal Cable Entertainment, a division of NBCUniversal LLC.

BRAZZERS TV
c/o MindGeek
7777 blvd Decarie, Ste 600
Montreal, PQ H4P 2H2
Canada
Phone: 514-359-3555
Fax: 514-359-3556
E-mail: info.montreal@mindgeek.com
Type of service: Pay per view.
Programming: Adult entertainment.
Began: May 1, 1989, as Spice. Rebranded to Fresh, then Brazzers TV.
Distribution method: Available to cable, IPTV & satellite subscribers.
Scrambled signal: Yes.
Ownership: Mindgeek.

BRIDGES TV
227 Thorn Ave
Studio V
Orchard Park, NY 14127
Phone: 716-662-3363
Fax: 716-961-3142
E-mail: info@bridgestv.com
Web Site: http://www.bridgestv.com
Muzzammil Hassan, President & Chief Executive Officer
Joan Lence, Program Director
Ambereen Shaikh, Advertising Sales
Samina Salahuddin, Media Relations
Type of service: Digital basic, streaming.
Programming: Programming for American Muslims focusing on entertainment, family, news, children's shows, sports & religion.
Began: December 14, 2004.
Means of Support: Subscribers, advertising.
Total subscribers: 1,000,000.
Distribution method: Available to cable & IPTV subscribers. Streaming available online.
Scrambled signal: Yes.

BRIGHT HOUSE SPORTS NETWORK
700 Carillon Pkwy
Ste 9
St. Petersburg, FL 33716
Phone: 727-497-2447
Fax: 727-329-2331
Web Site: http://www.bhsn.com
Chris Jadick, Director
Chris Elias, Sports Director
Lou Bruno, Engineering Manager
Glen Richard, Programming Manager
Mindy Smith, Accounting Manager
Mike Stanford, Marketing Manager

Branch Offices:
ORLANDO: 3767 All American Blvd, Orlando, FL 32810.
Type of service: Digital, video on demand.
Operating hours/week: 168.
Operating areas: Tampa & central Florida.
Programming: Regional sports network, including coverage of high school & college sports, fishing, auto racing, boxing, soccer & extreme sports.
Began: 2004 as Catch 47. Rebranded as Bright House Sports Network September 17, 2008.
Distribution method: Available to Bright House subscribers in Florida.
Scrambled signal: Yes.
Ownership: Bright House Networks.

Pay TV & Satellite Services

BRIGHT HOUSE TRAVEL WEATHER NOW — See Bay News 9.
700 Carillon Pkwy
Ste 9
St. Petersburg, FL 33716
Operating hours/week: 168.
Programming: 24-hour weather service.
Began: 1999 as Bay News 9 Weather Now. Rebranded Bay News 9 Travel Weather Now in 2004 & Bright House Travel Weather Now in 2009.
Distribution method: Available to Bright House Network subscribers.
Scrambled signal: Yes.
Ownership: Bright House Networks.

BTN
600 W Chicago
Ste 875
Chicago, IL 60654
Phone: 312-665-0700
Fax: 312-665-0740
E-mail: press@bigtennetwork.com
Web Site: http://btn.com
Mark Silverman, President
Mark Hulsey, Senior Vice President, Production & Executive Producer
Kim Beauvais, Vice President, Human Resources & Business Operations
Michael Calderon, Vice President, Programming & Digital Media
Elizabeth Conlisk, Vice President, Communications & University Relations
Erin Harvego, Vice President, Marketing
Jim Reeder, Vice President, Ad Sales
Type of service: Basic, HD, streaming & video on demand.
Operating hours/week: 168.
Operating areas: Available nationwide and across Canada.
Programming: Sports & other programming from 12-member Big Ten schools.
Began: August 30, 2007, as Big Ten Network. Big Ten Network HD began on the same day. Rebranded as BTN on May 31, 2011. BTN2Go began October 1, 2011.
Total subscribers: 90,000,000.
Distribution method: Available to cable, IPTV & satellite subscribers; online & mobile through the website or the BTN2go app (participating providers); video on demand (participating providers).
Scrambled signal: Yes.
Ownership: A joint venture between Fox Cable Networks (51%) & Big Ten Conference (49%).

BTN2GO — See BTN.
Programming: Live streaming of BTN telecasts.

BUENAVISION TV
904 23rd St
2nd Fl
Union City, NJ 07087
Phone: 646-558-6270
E-mail: contact@buenavisiontv.com
Web Site: http://buenavisiontv.com
Type of service: Pay, over the air.
Programming: Spanish-language programming from the Dominican Republic, Puerto Rico & Miami.
Scrambled signal: Yes.

BUZZR TV
c/o FremantleMedia North America
2900 W Alameda Ave, Ste 800
Burbank, CA 91505
Phone: 818-748-1100
E-mail: christine.shaw@fremantlemedia.com
Web Site: http://buzzrplay.com

Thom Beers, Chief Executive Officer, FremantleMedia North America
Ron Garfield, Executive Vice President & General Manager
Frank Cicha, Senior Vice President, Programming, Fox Television Stations
Christine Shaw, Senior Vice Preiddent, Communications & Marketing, FremantleMedia North America
Type of service: Basic, over the air.
Operating areas: Available nationwide.
Programming: Game show channel.
Began: June 1, 2015.
Means of Support: Advertising.
Total subscribers: 30,000,000.
Distribution method: Available over the air on digital sub-channels of Fox owned and operated stations.
Scrambled signal: Yes.
Ownership: Fox Television Stations Group.

BUZZTIME — See NTN Buzztime.

BYUTV
2000 Ironton Blvd
Provo, UT 84606
Phones: 866-662-9888; 801-422-8412
E-mail: byutv@byu.edu
Web Site: http://www.byutv.org
Derek Marquis, General Manager & Chief Executive Officer
Brandon Smith, Technical Operations Director
Type of service: Basic, streaming.
Operating hours/week: 168.
Operating areas: Arizona, California, Montana, Nevada, Utah, Washington & Wyoming.
Programming: Devotionals & forums, conference broadcasts, BYU sporting events, documentaries, musical performance. Aimed at alumni & friends of BYU & the LDS Church.
Began: January 1, 2000.
Means of Support: Viewer-supported.
Total subscribers: 53,000,000.
Distribution method: Available to cable & satellite subscribers. Streaming available online.
Scrambled signal: Yes.
Ownership: Brigham Young University & the Church of Jesus Christ of Latter-Day Saints.

C7 JALISCO
Francisco Rojas Gonzalez #155
Col. Ladron de Guervara
CP 44600 Guadalajara
Mexico
Phone: 52-33-30305300
Web Site: http://www.c7jalisco.com
Programming: Spanish-language news & general entertainment programming from Mexico.
Scrambled signal: Yes.
Ownership: Jalisco System Radio & Television. Distributed in the U.S. by Olympusat.

CABLE NOTICIAS
Ave Carrera 28
#36-41
Bogota
Columbia
Phone: 57-1-369-3700
E-mail: publicidad@cablenoticias.tv
Web Site: http://www.cablenoticias.tv
Type of service: Pay.
Operating hours/week: 168.
Programming: Spanish-language news, sports & entertainment.
Began: April 3, 2008.
Scrambled signal: Yes.
Ownership: Global Media Telecomunicaciones. Distributed in the U.S. by Olympusat.

CABLE TV NETWORK OF NEW JERSEY
124 W State S
Trenton, NJ 08608
Phone: 609-392-3223
Fax: 609-392-8682
James A. DeBold, Executive Director
Cliff Potent, Vice President, Engineering
Albert Stender, Vice President, Counsel
Mary Murphy, Sales Coordinator & Administrative Assistant
Type of service: Basic.
Operating hours/week: 168.
Operating areas: New Jersey.
Programming: Offers Gavel to Gavel, coverage of New Jersey State Senate & Assembly when in session, plus additional programming.
Began: January 17, 1983.
Means of Support: Advertising (program & spot).
Total subscribers: 1,800,000.
Distribution method: Available to cable subscribers.
Scrambled signal: Yes.

CALIFORNIA CHANNEL
1121 L St
Ste 110
Sacramento, CA 95814
Phone: 916-444-9792
Fax: 916-444-9812
E-mail: contact_us@calchannel.com
Web Site: http://www.calchannel.com
John Hancock, President
Jim Gualtieri, Broadcast Operations Director
Type of service: Basic.
Satellites: Satcom C-4, transponder 5.
Operating hours/week: 32.5.
Operating areas: California.
Programming: Statewide non-profit public affairs network providing gavel-to-gavel coverage of state government proceedings.
Began: February 1, 1991.
Total subscribers: 5,000,000.
Distribution method: Available to cable & satellite subscribers.
Scrambled signal: Yes.

CANAL 44 (XHIJ-TV)
Gomez Morin 8388, Bldg Canal44
Senecu Party
Juarez, Chihuahua 32540
Mexico
Phone: 52-656-648-3743
E-mail: noticieros@canal44.com
Web Site: http://www.canal44.com
Sergio Cabada Alvidrez, President & Chief Executive Officer
Alejandro Cabada Alvidrez, Production Director
Jesus Cabada Alvidrez, Administration Director
Armando Cabada Alvidrez, News Director
Edward Oates, Sales Director
Type of service: Pay.
Programming: Spanish news channel from Juarez, Mexico.
Began: October 16, 1980, Date of station launch. Service available in U.S. via Olympusat May 14, 2014.
Means of Support: Advertising.
Scrambled signal: Yes.
Ownership: Arnoldo Cabada de la O. Distributed in U.S by Olympusat.

CANAL 10 DE CANCUN
Av. Chichen Itza Sm. 38
Mza. 100 Lte. 3 Altos
Cancun Q. Roo C.P. 77507
Mexico
Phone: 52-99-88-43-65-00

E-mail: info@tucanal10.com
Web Site: http://canal10.tv

Branch Offices:
CHETUMAL: Av. San Salvador No. 471, Entre Privada San Salvador y Palermo, Chetumal Q. Roo. C.P. 77034, Mexico. Phone: 52-983-129-24-62.

COZUMEL: 50 Av. Norte x 1 Calle Sur, Col. Centro, Cozumel Q. Roo. C.P. 77600, Mexico. Phone: 52-987-872-67-18.

MERIDA: Prol. Paseo Montejo No.298, Frac. Campestre, Merida, Yucatan C.P. 97120, Mexico. Phone: 52-999-948-11-11.

PLAYA DEL CARMEN: Av. Norte No. 325, Frac. Xa Man Ha, Playa del carmen Q. Roo. C.P. 77710, Mexico. Phone: 52-984-803-20-53.
Type of service: Pay.
Programming: Spanish-language channel which covers the culture, life & people of the Yucatan Peninsula.
Began: January 1, 1980.
Means of Support: Advertising.
Scrambled signal: Yes.
Ownership: Promovision del Caribe SA de CV. Distributed in the U.S. by Olympusat.

CANAL 10 DE HONDURAS
Edificio Torrelibertad
Bulevar Suyapa
Tegucigalpa MDC
Honduras
Phone: 504-2239-7397
Fax: 504-2235-6615
E-mail: rwa@tencanal10.tv
Web Site: http://www.tencanal10.tv
Type of service: Pay.
Programming: Spanish-language educational programming from the Honduras.
Began: May 14, 2014, Date service available via Olympusat.
Scrambled signal: Yes.
Ownership: Distributed in U.S. by Olympusat.

CANAL 13 DE CHILE
InTs Matte Urrejola 0848
Santiago
Chile
Phone: 56-2-2251-4000
Web Site: http://www.13.cl
Cristian Bofill, Executive Director
Type of service: Pay, HD.
Programming: Spanish-language featuring original programming from Chile.
Began: August 21, 1959, in Chile.
Means of Support: Advertising.
Scrambled signal: Yes.
Ownership: A joint venture between the Luksic Group (67%) & the University of Chile (33%). Distributed in the U.S. by Olympusat.

CANAL 22 INTERNACIONAL
Atletas No. 2, Edificio Pedro Infante
Colonia Country Club
Delegacion Coyoacan CP 04220
Mexico
Phone: 52-21-22-96-80
Web Site: http://www.canal22.org.mx
Programming: Spanish-language documentaries, cultural newscasts & talk shows.
Began: 2004 in the U.S.
Distribution method: Available to cable, IPTV & satellite subscribers through Alterna'TV.
Scrambled signal: Yes.
Ownership: Canaculta. Distributed in the U.S. by Alterna'TV.

Pay TV & Satellite Services

CANAL 24 HORAS — See TVE International.

CANAL ONCE
National Polytechnic Institute
Col Carpio ext 475
Helmet Sto. Thomas CP 11340
Mexico
Phone: 55-5166-4000
E-mail: info@canalonce.ipn.mx
Web Site: http://oncetv-ipn.net
Rafael Lugo Sanchez, Chief Executive Officer
Clemente Cabello, General Manager, Alterna TV
Alejandro Penafiel, Programming Director, Alterna TV
Maricela Hernandez, Affiliate & Ad Sales Driector, Alterna TV
Raul Montalvo, Office Manager, Miami, Alterna TV
Operating areas: Available nationwide.
Programming: Family-friendly channel offering high quality and diverse Mexican programming that is suitable for all ages. Content is 100% Mexican.
Began: March 2, 1959, in Mexico. Began April 1, 2004 as Once TV Mexico, in the U.S. Rebranded as Canal Once in 2013.
Means of Support: Advertising & subscriber fees.
Distribution method: Available to cable, IPTV & satellite subscribers.
Scrambled signal: Yes.
Ownership: Instituto Politecnico Nacional. Distributed in the U.S. by Alterna'tv.

CANAL SUR — See Sur.
200 Crandon Blvd
Ste 316
Key Biscayne, FL 33149
Phone: 305-361-5271
Web Site: http://canalsur.tv
Programming: News, novelas, comedies, variety & reality programming.
Began: 1991 in U.S.
Scrambled signal: Yes.
Ownership: SUR LLC. Distributed in the U.S. by Condista.

CAN TV
(Chicago Access Network Television)
1309 S. Wood St
Chicago, IL 60608
Phone: 312-738-1400
Fax: 312-738-2519
E-mail: info@cantv.org
Web Site: http://www.cantv.org
Barbara Popovic, Executive Director
Mary M Stack, Associate Executive Director
Greg Boozell, Technology Director
Michael Jacobson, Marketing & Communications Director
Lesley Johnson, Program Director
Terrance N Morris, Operations Director
Type of service: Basic.
Operating areas: Chicago, IL area.
Programming: Offers five local, non-commercial channels. CAN TV19 offers local perspectives, arts, music & sports programming. CAN TV21 offers live, call-in programs as well as local politics & education programming. CAN TV27 offers community news & coverage of live events. CAN TV36 offers religious & inspirational programming. CAN TV42 offers on demand information on jobs, housing & health as well as audio from WDCB Jazz.
Began: January 1, 1983.
Means of Support: Grants, underwriting and funded partnerships plus support from Chicago area cable operators.
Total subscribers: 1,000,000.

Distribution method: Available to Comcast, WOW, AT&T U-Verse & RCN subscribers in Chicago.
Scrambled signal: Yes.
Ownership: Non-profit organization.

CAPITAL NEWS 9
104 Watervliet Ave Extension
Albany, NY 12206
Phone: 518-459-9999
Fax: 518-641-7025
E-mail: albanynews@ynn.com
Web Site: http://capitalregion.ynn.com
Al Marlin, General Manager
Chris Brunner, News Director
Cindy Griffo, Sales Manager, Capital Region
Derek Benedict, Sales Manager, Hudson Valley
Scott Christiansen, Marketing Manager
Type of service: Basic.
Sales representative: Advertising.
Operating hours/week: 168.
Programming: Local news channel.
Began: October 11, 2002.
Total subscribers: 320,000.
Scrambled signal: Yes.
Ownership: Time Warner Inc.

CAPITAL OFF TRACK BETTING TELEVISION NETWORK
510 Smith St
Schenectady, NY 12305
Phone: 518-344-5204
E-mail: marketingmail@capitalotb.com
Web Site: http://www.capitalotb.com
Programming: Live horse races & information on racing & betting for the Capital region of Upstate NY.
Began: July 1, 1974.

CARACOL TV
150 Alhambra Cir
Ste 1250
Coral Gables, FL 33134
Phone: 305-960-2018
Fax: 305-960-2017
E-mail: ventas@caracoltv.com.co
Web Site: http://www.caracolinternacional.com
Camilo Acuna, Vice President, Programming
Angelica Guerra, Vice President
Lisette Osorio, International Sales Director
Monica Ramon, Administrative & Marketing Coordinator
Roberto Corrente, Sales Executive, Eastern Europe & Asia
Berta Orozco, Sales Executive, Western Europe & Africa
Estefania Arteaga, Sales Assistant
Hector Ossa, Press Chief

Branch Offices:
COLOMBIA: Calle 103 No. 50-45, Bogota, Colombia. Phone: 57-1-6-430-430.
Satellites: PanamSat 9 6C.
Programming: Telenovelas, entertainment & series.
Began: September 1, 2003.
Total subscribers: 2,100,000.
Scrambled signal: Yes.
Ownership: Caracol Television Inc.

CAREER ENTERTAINMENT TELEVISION
10573 W Pico Blvd
Ste 168
Los Angeles, CA 90064-2348
Phone: 310-277-2388
Fax: 310-277-1037
E-mail: info@ce.tv
Web Site: http://www.ce.tv
Connie Johnson, Founder & President

Karen Barnes, Executive Vice President, Development & Programming
Samantha Brown, Senior Vice President, Affiliate Sales
Amy Cox, Senior Vice President, Marketing
Rick D'Andrea, Senior Vice President, Business Development
Jeffrey D. Torkelson, Senior Vice President, Communications
Darren E. Barker, Vice President, Finance
Hugh Cadden, Vice President, Programming & Development
Monica Deeter, Production Manager
Type of service: Digital basic & video on demand.
Programming: Entertainment & education-based programming devoted to work & the workplace.
Began: September 1, 2004.
Distribution method: Available to cable & satellite subscribers.
Scrambled signal: Yes.

CAROUSEL
19 Akademika Korolyova St
Moscow 127427
Russia
Phones: 7-495-617-55-80; 7-495-617-51-75
Fax: 7-495-617-51-14
E-mail: press@1tvrus.com
Web Site: http://www.karusel-tv.ru
Nikolay Dubovoy, Chief Executive Officer
Type of service: Premium.
Operating areas: Available in New Jersey & New York on cable & nationwide on DirecTV.
Programming: Russian language channel for children ages 3-14 and their parents.
Began: January 1, 2005.
Means of Support: Advertising & subscriber fees.
Total subscribers: 51,000,000 (Russian subscribers.).
Distribution method: Available to Time Warner & DirecTV subscribers.
Scrambled signal: Yes.
Ownership: Channel One. National Media Group, minority interest.

CARS.TV
1925 Century Park E
Ste 1025
Los Angeles, CA 90067
Phone: 310-277-3500
E-mail: eric@es.tv
Web Site: http://www.es.tv/networks/cars-tv
Byron Allen, Chairman & Chief Executive Officer
Darren Galatt, Vice President, Ad Sales
Type of service: Digital.
Operating hours/week: 168.
Operating areas: Available nationwide.
Programming: Features notable cars and the people who love them, showcasing the collectors, designers, innovators and the ultimate car enthusiasts.
Began: May 11, 2009.
Total subscribers: 1,900,000.
Distribution method: Available to cable & IPTV subscribers.
Scrambled signal: No.
Ownership: Entertainment Studios.

FULLY SEARCHABLE • CONTINUOUSLY UPDATED • DISCOUNT RATES FOR PRINT PURCHASERS
For more information call **800-771-9202** or visit **www.warren-news.com**

CARTOON NETWORK
1050 Techwood Dr NW
Bldg 1000
Atlanta, GA 30318-5264
Phones: 404-827-1717; 404-885-2263
Fax: 404-885-4594
E-mail: sgc2c@turner.com
Web Site: http://www.cartoonnetwork.com
TURNER BROADCASTING:, .
Stuart Snyder, President & Chief Operating Officer, Turner Broadcasting Animation, Young Adults & Kids Media Division
Josh Feldman, Senior Vice President & National Sales Manager, Turner Broadcasting, Young Adults Ad Sales
Patty Gillette, Senior Vice President, Integrated Marketing, Turner Broadcasting Young Adults Group
CARTOON NETWORK:, .
Christina Miller, President & General Manager, Adult Swim, Cartoon Network & Boomerang
Michael Ouweleen, Chief Marketing Officer
Robert Sorcher, Executive Vice President & Chief Content Officer
Brian Miller, Senior Vice President & General Manager, Cartoon Network Studios
Vishnu Athreya, Vice President, Program Scheduling, Boomerang & Cartoon Network
Molly Chase, Vice President & Executive Producer, New Media
Curtis Lelash, Vice President, Comedy Animation
Adina Pitt, Vice President, Content Acquisitions & Co-Productions, Boomerang & Cartoon Network
Deena Boykin, Senior Director, Retail Development & Brand Marketing
Type of service: Basic, HD, streaming & video on demand.
Satellites: Galaxy I/I-R, transponder 8.
Sales representative: Turner Network Sales.
Operating hours/week: 168.
Operating areas: Available nationwide.
Programming: Original, acquired and classic entertainment for kids and families. Cartoons from Hanna-Barbera, MGM, Warner Brothers & Paramount. Spanish-languarge available on Cartoon Network en Espanol.
Began: October 1, 1992, Cartoon Network HD began October 2007. Cartoon Network on Demand began in 2002.
Means of Support: Advertising.
Total subscribers: 99,000,000 (Includes Adult Swim subscribers.).
Distribution method: Available to most cable, IPTV & satellite subscribers; online & mobile through the website or app (participating providers); video on demand (participating providers).
Scrambled signal: Yes.
Ownership: Turner Broadcasting System, a division of Time Warner.

CARTOON NETWORK EN ESPANOL — See Cartoon Network.
Programming: Spanish-language programming from the Cartoon Network.

CASA CLUB TV — See MasChic.

2017 Edition

E-17

Pay TV & Satellite Services

CATCH 47 — See Bright House Sports Network.

CATHOLIC TELEVISION NETWORK
PO Box 301825
St. Thomas, VI 00803
Phone: 340-777-4828
Fax: 340-777-4828
Benny Gibbs, Director
Ronaldo A. Boschuite, Operations Director
Type of service: Basic.
Operating areas: U.S. Virgin Islands.
Programming: Mix of local religious programming with Trinity Broadcasting Network.
Distribution method: Available to cable subscribers.
Scrambled signal: Yes.

CATHOLICTV
PO Box 9196
34 Chestnut St
Watertown, MA 02471
Phone: 617-923-0220
Fax: 617-965-6587
E-mail: bctv@catholictv.org
Web Site: http://www.catholictv.com
Father Robert Reed, Interim President & Chief Executive Officer, iCatholic Media
Jay Fadden, General Manager
Helen C. Lee, VOD Content & Social Media Manager
Shannon Muldoon, Public Relations Manager
Bonnie Rodgers, Programming & Affiliate Relations
Kevin Nelson, Producer
Matthew Weber, Producer
Kate Andrews, Associate Producer
Andy Otto, Programming Associate
Type of service: Basic, digital.
Operating hours/week: 168.
Operating areas: Available nationwide.
Programming: Connecting people of faith through relevant, inspiring & prayerful programming; educating, teaching the Wisdom of God in the Catholic Tradition, endeavoring to move people of all ages, cultures & attitudes toward the Fullness of Life.
Began: January 1, 1983, 1957 over the air & 1983 on cable.
Means of Support: Sponsorship.
Distribution method: Available to over the air & to cable, IPTV & satellite in select areas. Streaming available online & on Roku.
Scrambled signal: Yes.
Ownership: iCatholic Media.

CB24
San Jose
Costa Rica
Phone: 506-4080-4646
E-mail: info@cb24tv
Web Site: http://cb24.tv
Carlos Alfred Garcia Ibanez, President
Programming: Spanish-language news from Central America.
Ownership: Central American Broadcasting, Carlos Alfredo Garcia Ibanez owner. Distributed in the U.S. by Condista.

CBC/RADIO-CANADA
PO Box 3220
Station C
Ottawa, ON K1Y 1E4
Canada
Phones: 613-288-6033; 866-220-6045
Fax: 613-288-6045
E-mail: liaison@radio-canada.ca
Web Site: http://www.cbc.radio-canada.ca
Timothy Casgrain, Chairman
Hubert T. Lacroix, President & Chief Executive Officer
Sylvain Lafrance, Executive Vice President, French Services
Richard Stursberg, Executive Vice President, English Services
Johanne Charbonneau, Vice President & Chief Financial Officer
Raymond Carnovale, Vice President & Chief Technology Officer
William B. Chambers, Vice President, Communications
Type of service: Over the air.
Operating areas: Canadian border states.
Ownership: Canadian Broadcasting Corp.

CBEEBIES
c/o BBC Worldwide Americas
135 San Lorenzo Ave, Ste 770
Coral Gables, FL 33146
Phone: 305-461-6999
Fax: 305-441-0035
Web Site: http://www.cbeebies.com/lat-am
William Graff, Vice President, Programming, BBC Worldwide Channels Latin America/US Hispanic
Nina Laricheva, Head of Channels Development, Global markets
Jessica Bishop, Affiliate Sales Manager

Branch Offices:
UNITED KINGDOM: c/o BBC Worldwide Ltd., Media Centre, 201 Wood Lane, London W12 7TQ, United Kingdom. Phone: 44-0-20-8433-2000.
Operating areas: Available nationwide.
Programming: Spanish language channel for pre-school children.
Began: February 11, 2002, in Europe. November 19, 2008 in the U.S.
Distribution method: Available to DISH Network subscribers.
Scrambled signal: Yes.
Ownership: BBC Worldwide.

CBS ALL ACCESS
235 Second St
San Francisco, CA 94105
Phone: 415-344-2000
Web Site: http://www.cbs.com/all-access
Marc DeBevoise, President & Chief Executive Officer, CBS Interactive
Julie McNamara, Executive Vice President, Original Content
Type of service: Streaming, video on demand.
Began: October 16, 2014.
Distribution method: Available online & through app or streaming devices (participating providers).
Ownership: CBS.

CBS SPORTS NETWORK
28 E 28th St
15th Fl
New York, NY 10016
Phone: 212-975-5100
Fax: 212-679-4657
Web Site: http://www.cbssportsnetwork.com
Sean McManus, Chairman, CBS Sports
David Berson, President, CBS Sports Network & President, CBS Sports
Ken Aagaard, Executive Vice President, Operations, Engineering & Production Services
Mike Aresco, Executive Vice President, Programming
Chris Bevilacqua, Executive Vice President
Patty Power, Executive Vice President, Operations & Engineering
Jeff Gerttula, Senior Vice President & General manager, CBS Sports Digital
Marty Kaye, Senior Vice President, Finance
Jennifer Sabatelle, Senior Vice President, Communications, CBS Sports
Dan Weinberg, Senior Vice President, Programming
Bess Barnes, Vice President, College Sports Programming
Ryan Briganti, Vice President, Ad Sales
Harold Bryant, Vice President, Production
Type of service: Basic, HD.
Programming: Live regular season & championship events across a broad spectrum of men's & women's sports including football, basketball, baseball, soccer, ice hockey & lacrosse.
Began: April 7, 2003, as College Sports Television. Rebranded as CBS College Sports on March 16, 2008. Rebranded as CBS Sports Network on February 15, 2011.
Total subscribers: 53,000,000.
Distribution method: Available to cable systems & satellite subscribers.
Scrambled signal: Yes.
Ownership: CBS Corp. CBS acquired network in January 2006 from founders Brian Bedol & Stephen D. Greenberg plus Chris Bevilacqua.

CB TU TELEVISION MICHOACAN
Av Lazaro Cardenas 1736
Col. Chapultepec Sur, Morelia
Michoacan CP 58260
Mexico
Phone: 52-443-314-3515
Fax: 52-443-315-6883
Web Site: http://www.cbtelevision.com.mx
Operating hours/week: 168.
Operating areas: Nationwide.
Programming: Locally focused shows covering economics, sports, tourism & news from the area of Michoacan, Mexico.
Began: September 1, 2004, in the U.S.
Means of Support: Advertising.
Distribution method: Available to Comcast, Grande Communications, San Bruno Cable & AT&T U-Verse subscribers.
Scrambled signal: Yes.
Ownership: Media Entertainment. Distributed in the U.S. by Alterna'tv.

CCTV-4 — See CCTV America.

CCTV-6 — See China Movie Channel.

CCTV-9 — See CCTV-Documentary.

CCTV-11 — See CCTV-Opera.

CCTV-13 — See CCTV-News.

CCTV AMERICA
1099 New York Ave NW
Ste 200
Washington, DC 20001
Phone: 202-639-4747
E-mail: digital.media@cctv-america.com
Web Site: http://www.cctv-america.com
Ma Jing, Director General
Bob Crawford, News Coverage Director
George Alexander, Senior Producer, General News
Barbara Dury, Senior Producer, Americas Now
Jim Laurie, Executive Consultant
Type of service: Basic, streaming.
Operating areas: Los Angeles, New York & Washington, DC on cable/IPTV. Nationwide on DISH Network.
Programming: English language all news channel.
Began: February 6, 2012, replacing CCTV-4 in the U.S.
Distribution method: Available to cable, IPTV & satellite subscribers. Streaming available online.
Scrambled signal: Yes.
Ownership: China Central Television.

CCTV-DOCUMENTARY
11B Fuxing Rd
Beijing 100038
China
Phone: 86-10-6-850-6517
E-mail: documentary@cctv.com; cctv-9@cctv.com
Web Site: http://cctv.cntv.cn/documentary
Satellites: Intelsat 21; Galaxy 3C.
Operating areas: Nationwide.
Programming: Chinese-language documentaries focusing on nature, history, the humanities & society.
Began: January 1, 2011, in China. February 15, 2011 in North America, Europe & Singapore.
Distribution method: Available to DirecTV, DISH, MHz Networks & KyLinTV subscribers.
Scrambled signal: No.
Ownership: China Central Television.

CCTV-ENTERTAINMENT — See CCTV-Documentary.
Web Site: http://cctv.cntv.cn
Satellites: Intelsat 21; Galaxy 3C; Echostar 7; Echostar 8; Echostar 9.
Programming: Mandarin Chinese-language variety & entertainment programming, including dramas, music, dance & arts.
Began: March 5, 2010, in China. October 1, 2007 in the U.S.
Distribution method: Available to DISH Network & KyLinTV subscribers.
Scrambled signal: Yes.

CCTV-NEWS — See CCTV-Documentary.
E-mail: cctvnews@cctv.com
Web Site: http://cctv.cntv.cn/cctvxinwen
Type of service: Pay.
Satellites: Intelsat 21; Galaxy 3C; Galaxy 17; Echostar 7, 8 & 9.
Operating hours/week: 168.
Programming: 24-hour Chinese news service.
Began: September 25, 2000.
Distribution method: Available to DirecTV, DISH, Verizon FiOS & KyLinTV subscribers. Streaming available online.
Scrambled signal: Yes.
Ownership: China Central Television.

CCTV-OPERA — See CCTV-Documentary.
Operating areas: Nationwide.
Programming: Mandarin Chinese-language local & global operas.
Began: July 9, 2001.
Distribution method: Available to DISH Network & KyLinTV subscribers.

CELEBRITY SHOPPING NETWORK
c/o Revenue Frontier LLC
3250 Ocean Park Blvd, Ste 200
Santa Monica, CA 90405
Phone: 310-584-9200
E-mail: info@revenuefrontier.tv
Type of service: Basic.
Programming: Beauty, fashion, health & style products from celebrity models & actors.
Distribution method: Satellite.

CENTRAL FLORIDA NEWS 13
20 N Orange Ave
Ste 13
Orlando, FL 32801
Phone: 407-513-1300
Fax: 407-513-1310
Web Site: http://www.cfnews13.com
Mike Gautreau, Senior Director, News
Rick Chattin, Finance Director
Stephen Chavarie, News Programming Director
Susan D'Astoli, News Director

Pay TV & Satellite Services

Deirdre Treacy, Marketing Director
Fletcher Christian, Operations Manager
Operating areas: Orlando-Daytona Beach-Melbourne, FL.
Programming: Regional 24-hour all local news channel.
Began: October 27, 1997.
Means of Support: Advertising & subscriber fees.
Total subscribers: 750,000.
Distribution method: Available to Bright House Networks subscribers.
Scrambled signal: No.
Ownership: Bright House Networks.

CENTRIC — See BET.
1 BET Plz
1235 W St NE
Washington, DC 20018
Phone: 202-608-2000
Fax: 202-269-9335
Web Site: http://www.centrictv.com
Paxton Baker, Executive Vice President & General Manager

Branch Offices:
NEW YORK: 1540 Broadway, 27th Fl, New York, NY 10037. Phone: 212-258-1000.
Type of service: Digital.
Satellites: Galaxy 11, transponder 3.
Operating hours/week: 168.
Operating areas: Available nationwide.
Programming: General interest entertainment network targeting African-Americans ages 25 to 54.
Began: January 15, 1996, as BET On Jazz. Re-launched as BET J on March 1, 2006. Re-launched as Centric September 28, 2009.
Means of Support: Advertising.
Total subscribers: 32,000,000.
Distribution method: Available to cable, IPTV & satellite subscribers.
Scrambled signal: Yes.
Ownership: BET Networks, a division of Viacom Inc.

CENTROAMERICA TV
c/o Hemisphere Media Group
2000 Ponce de Leon Blvd, Ste 500
Coral Gables, FL 33134
Phone: 305-421-6364
E-mail: info@centroamericatv.tv
Web Site: http://www.centroamericatv.tv
Alan J. Sokol, Chief Executive Officer, Hemisphere Media Group Inc.
Craig D. Fischer, Chief Financial Officer, Hemisphere Media Group Inc.
Antonio Briceno, General Manager
Operating areas: Available nationwide.
Programming: Spanish-language programming focusing on Central American communities.
Began: September 2004 in the U.S.
Total subscribers: 3,300,000.
Distribution method: Available to satellite subscribers.
Scrambled signal: Yes.
Ownership: Hemisphere Media Group.

CET: COMCAST ENTERTAINMENT TELEVISION
8000 E Iliff Ave
Denver, CO 80231
Phone: 303-603-2025
E-mail: denver_cet@cable.comcast.com
Web Site: http://www.comcastentertainmenttv.com
Cindy Parsons, Vice President, Public Relations
Brett Hatch, Content/TV Production Director
Type of service: Regional basic, video on demand.

Operating hours/week: 168.
Operating areas: Colorado.
Programming: Local high school, collegiate & regional sports, movies plus programs covering lifestyle & entertainment, documentaries & finance.
Began: September 1, 2004.
Means of Support: Advertising.
Total subscribers: 800,000.
Distribution method: Available to Comcast subscribers in Colorado.
Scrambled signal: Yes.
Ownership: Comcast Corp.

CGNTV USA
(Christian Global Network Television)
616 S Westmoreland Ave, Ste 408
Los Angeles, CA 90005
Phone: 323-932-1200
E-mail: cgntvusa@gmail.com
Web Site: http://us.cgntv.net
Yong-Jo Ha, Chief Director
Type of service: Basic.
Operating hours/week: 168.
Operating areas: Available nationwide.
Programming: A mission & education network for Korean missionaries abroad. The purpose was to supply Korean missionaries all over the world with spiritual training resources as well as help Korean Christian Diasporas maintain their spiritual walks with God.
Began: August 27, 2005.
Means of Support: Advertising.
Total subscribers: 19,000.
Distribution method: Available over the air digital sub-channels & to satellite subscribers.
Scrambled signal: Yes.

CHANNEL 4 SAN DIEGO
350 10th Ave
Ste 500
San Diego, CA 92101
Phone: 619-686-1900
Fax: 619-595-0168
Web Site: http://www.4sd.com
Tom Ceterski, Executive Producer & Director
Dan Novak, Vice President, Programming
Nick Davis, Senior Producer
Tom Morgigno, Station Manager
Type of service: Basic.
Operating areas: San Diego, CA region.
Programming: San Diego Padres major league baseball games, features and shows about baseball, the Padres ballclub, and the team's community activities, San Diego State U. football & basketball, local news magazine show & local biography shows.
Began: March 1, 1997.
Total subscribers: 500,000.
Distribution method: Available to Cox & Time Warner cable subscribers.
Scrambled signal: Yes.
Ownership: Cox Communications Inc.

CHANNEL ONE RUSSIA
19 Akademika Korolyova St
Moscow 127427
Russia
Phones: 7-495-617-55-88; 7-495-617-51-75
Fax: 7-495-617-51-14
E-mail: info@1tvrus.com
Web Site: http://eng.1tvrus.com
Nikolay Dubovoy, Director General
Type of service: Premium.
Operating areas: Nationwide.
Programming: Digital broadcasting in Russian, including news, entertainment (Russian & foreign), animated series (Russian & foreign) and soap operas.
Began: April 1, 1995, as Russian Public Television. Rebranded as Channel One Russia September 2, 2002.
Means of Support: Subscriber fees and advertising.
Total subscribers: 250,000,000 (subscribers worldwide.).
Distribution method: Available to cable & satellite subscribers.
Scrambled signal: Yes.
Ownership: National Media Group, minority interest.

CHICAGO ACCESS NETWORK TELEVISION — See CAN TV.

CHILLER
1221 Ave of the Americas
New York, NY 10019
Phone: 212-664-4444
E-mail: feedback@chillertv.com
Web Site: http://www.chillertv.com
Dave Howe, President, Strategy & Commercial Growth
Ted A'Zary, Senior Vice President, Research, Chiller & Syfy
Jeff Blackman, Senior Vice President, Creative, Syfy & Chiller
Katherine Nelson, Senior Vice President, Communications
Chris Regina, Senior Vice President, Program Strategy, Chiller & Syfy
Rob Spodek, Senior Vice President & Chief Financial Officer, Chiller & Syfy
Susan Lape, Vice President, Primary Research, Chiller & Syfy

Regional Offices:
CHICAGO: 454 N Columbus Dr, Chicago, IL 60611.

UNIVERSAL CITY: 100 Universal City Plz, Bldg 9128-3, Universal City, CA.
Type of service: Digital.
Satellites: AMC 11, transponder 24.
Programming: Classic drama and anthology series, documentaries and reality shows as well as films including feature-length premieres on the first Friday of each month.
Began: March 1, 2007.
Total subscribers: 41,000,000.
Distribution method: Available to cable & satellite subscribers.
Scrambled signal: Yes.
Ownership: NBCUniversal Cable Entertainment, a division of NBCUniversal LLC.

CHINA MOVIE CHANNEL — See CCTV-Documentary.
11B Fuxing Rd
Beijing 100038
China
Phone: 86-10-6-850-6517
Web Site: http://www.m1905.com
Programming: Chinese & foreign feature films, documentaries, science & educational films, cartoons, operas & TV plays as well as other relevant programs. (Also known as CCTV-6.).
Distribution method: Available to DISH Network & KyLinTV subscribers.
Scrambled signal: Yes.

Access the most current data instantly
FREE TRIAL @ ADVANCED TVFactbook
TELCO/IPTV • CABLE TV • TV STATIONS
www.warren-news.com/factbook.htm

CHINESE ENTERTAINMENT TELEVISION (CETV)
Block 8, Flat 5, Kingdee Software Park
2 Keji 12th Rd S, High-Tech Industrial Park
Nanshan District, Shenzhen 518057
China
Phone: 86-755-3332-0028
Fax: 86-775-3330-1928
E-mail: corp-comm@tomgroup.com
Web Site: http://www.cetv.com
Programming: 24-hour Putonghua general entertainment channel providing the latest and popular Asian and international entertainment programming.
Distribution method: Available to KyLinTV subscribers.
Scrambled signal: Yes.
Ownership: TOM Group & Turner Broadcasting System Asia Pacific Inc.

CHINESE TELEVISION NETWORK — See CTI-Zhong Tian.

CHRISTIAN TELEVISION NETWORK
6922 142nd Ave
Largo, FL 33771
Phone: 727-535-5622
Fax: 727-531-2497
E-mail: comments@ctnonline.com
Web Site: http://www.ctnonline.com
Bob D'Andrea, President & Founder
Paul Garber, Executive Director, CTNi

Branch Offices:
CTNi-Christian Television Network International: Carretera 861 Km. 4.4 Barrio Pina, Toa Alta, PR 00953. Phone: 787-200-1970. Web site: http://http://http://www.ctni.org.
Type of service: Basic.
Satellites: For CTNi–Intelsat IS-9.
Operating hours/week: 168.
Operating areas: Available nationwide.
Programming: Inspirational & Christian programming. CTNi offers similar programming in Spanish, Portuguese, French, and English.
Began: October 24, 1979, for CTN, 2004 for CTNi. September 7, 2013 CTNi broadcasts began from Puerto Rico.
Means of Support: Viewer supported.
Total subscribers: 15,000,000.
Distribution method: Available to cable & satellite subscribers.
Scrambled signal: Yes.

CHURCH CHANNEL
c/o TBN Networks
2442 Michelle Dr
Tustin, CA 92780
Phones: 714-665-2110; 714-832-2950
Fax: 714-832-0645
E-mail: jjones@tbn.org
Web Site: http://www.churchchannel.tv
Jan Crouch, President
Matthew Crouch, Vice President
Bob Fopma, Vice President, Production
Ben Miller, Vice President, Engineering
David Adcock, National Director, Cable & Satellite Relations
Jay Jones, Media Services
Colby May, Media Relations

2017 Edition E-19

Pay TV & Satellite Services

CABLE & TV STATION COVERAGE
Atlas 2017
The perfect companion to the Television & Cable Factbook
To order call 800-771-9202 or visit www.warren-news.com

Type of service: Over the air, digital basic, streaming.
Satellites: Galaxy 14, transponder 1; Galaxy 23, transponder 20 (Olympusat).
Operating hours/week: 168.
Operating areas: Available nationwide.
Programming: Features prominent & favorite church leaders from across the nation, traditional, contemporary & cutting edge programs.
Began: January 17, 2002.
Total subscribers: 15,776,000.
Distribution method: Available over the air on digital sub-channels and to cable, IPTV & satellite subscribers. Streaming available online.
Scrambled signal: Yes.
Ownership: TBN Networks, a non-profit corp.

CINE MEXICANO
c/o Olympusat Inc.
560 Village Blvd, Ste 250
West Palm Beach, FL 33409
Phone: 561-684-5657
Fax: 561-684-9690
Web Site: http://www.cinemexicano.tv
Tom Mohler, Chief Executive Officer, Olympusat Holdings Inc.
Chuck Mohler, Chief Operating Officer
Chris Williams, Chief Financial Officer
Colleen Glynn, Executive Vice President & General Counsel
Arturo Chavez, Senior Vice President, Hispanic Networks
Juan Bruno, New Programming Acquisitions & Contracts Director
John Baghdassarian, Head of Affiliate Sales, U.S.
Type of service: Pay.
Operating hours/week: 168.
Operating areas: Nationwide.
Programming: Spanish-language movie network featuring commercial free contemporary Mexican movies of various genres.
Began: November 1, 2004.
Means of Support: Subscriber fees.
Distribution method: Available to AT&T U-Verse, Buckeye, CableOne, Charter, Choice Cable, Comcast Xfinity, Consolidated Communications, Cox Communications, DirecTV, Frontier, Mediacom, Optimum, RCN, Suddenlink, Time Warner Cable & Verizon FiOS subscribers.
Scrambled signal: Yes.
Ownership: Olympusat.

CINE NOSTALGIA
2600 SW 3rd Ave
Miami, FL 33129
Phone: 305-856-7322
Web Site: http://www.cinenostalgia.tv
Carlos Vasallo, President & Chief Executive Officer
Operating hours/week: 168.
Operating areas: Available nationwide.
Programming: Offers black and white classic Mexican movies from the 20's to the 60's.
Began: September 9, 2008.
Distribution method: Available to DirecTV and Verizon FiOS subscribers.
Scrambled signal: Yes.
Ownership: Carlos Vasallo.

CINE SONY TELEVISION
c/o Sony Pictures Television
10202 W Washington Blvd
Culver City, CA 90232-3195
Phone: 310-244-4000
Fax: 310-244-1336
Web Site: http://www.cinesony.com
Superna Kalle, General Manager, Cine Sony Television & Senior Vice President, US Networks, Sony Pictures Television
Ron Garfield, Senior Vice President, Affiliate Sales, Cine Sony Television
Type of service: Pay.
Operating areas: Available nationwide.
Programming: Offers Hollywood films, music and TV series, presented uncensored and commercial free in Spanish.
Began: August 1, 2012.
Means of Support: Subscriber fees.
Distribution method: Available to Comcast Xfinity cable system subscribers.
Scrambled signal: Yes.
Ownership: Sony Pictures Television.

CINE CLASICO
c/o Olympusat Inc.
560 Village Blvd, Ste 250
West Palm Beach, FL 33409
Phone: 561-684-5657
Fax: 561-684-9690
E-mail: info@olympusat.com
Web Site: http://www.olympusat.com/networks/sorpresa
Tom Mohler, Chief Executive Officer, Olympusat Holdings Inc.
Arturo Chavez, Senior Vice President, Hispanic Networks
Juan Bruno, New Programming Acquisitions & Contracts Director
John Baghdassarian, Head of Affiliate Sales, U.S.
Type of service: Pay.
Operating areas: Available in the Mediacom service area.
Programming: Spanish-language classic movies from the golden age of Mexican & Spanish cinema.
Began: November 26, 2012.
Distribution method: Available to Mediacom subscribers.
Scrambled signal: Yes.
Ownership: Olympusat.

CINE ESTELAR
2600 SW 3rd Ave
Miami, FL 33129
Phone: 305-856-7322
Web Site: http://www.cinestelar.tv
Carlos Vasallo, President & Chief Executive Officer
Operating hours/week: 168.
Operating areas: Available nationwide.
Programming: Mexican movie channel showing films from the 60's, 70's, 80's & 90's.
Began: September 9, 2008.
Distribution method: Available to DirecTV and Verizon FiOS subscribers.
Scrambled signal: Yes.
Ownership: Carlos Vasallo.

CINELATINO
c/o MVS Multivision Digital
Blvd Puerto Aerei No 486
Montezuma 2a Secc, Distrito Fe 15530
Mexico
Phone: 52-55-5764-8100
Web Site: http://www.cinelatino.com/usa
James M. McNamara, Non-Executive Chairman
Sandra Austin, Chief Financial Officer
Carolina Bilbao, Creative Director
Katie Hamlin, Public Relations Director
Type of service: Premium.
Operating hours/week: 168.
Operating areas: Nationwide.
Programming: The latest movies and blockbusters from Mexico, Latin America and Spain.
Began: January 1, 1999.
Means of Support: Subscriber fees.
Total subscribers: 4,000,000.
Distribution method: Available to cable subscribers.
Scrambled signal: Yes.
Ownership: A joint venture between Hemisphere Media Group (50%) & MVS Television (50%).

CINEMAX
c/o Home Box Office
1100 Avenue of the Americas
New York, NY 10036
Phone: 212-512-1000
Fax: 212-512-1166
E-mail: contactmaxgo@hbo.com
Web Site: http://www.cinemax.com; http://www.maxgo.com
Kathy Antholis, President, Programming

Branch Offices
ATLANTA: 1000 Abernathy Rd, Ste 500, Atlanta, GA 30328. Phone: 404-239-6600. Fax: 404-261-4186.

CHICAGO: 6250 N River Rd, Ste 10-300, Rosemont, IL 60018. Phone: 847-318-5100. Fax: 847-825-1333.

DALLAS: 12750 Merit Dr, Ste 1105, Dallas, TX 75251. Phone: 972-450-1000. Fax: 972-387-5570.

DENVER: The Quadrant, 5445 DTC Pkwy, Ste 700, Englewood, CO 80111, 303-220-2900. Fax: 303-220-9668.

LOS ANGELES: 2049 Century Park E, Ste 4100, Los Angeles, CA 90067. Phone: 310-201-9200. Fax: 310-201-9310. Brad Saunders, Vice President, HBO Miniseries & Cinemax Programming.

PHILADELPHIA: 401 City Ave, Ste 620, Bala Cynwyd, PA 19004. Phone: 610-668-6500. Fax: 610-668-9318.

SAN FRANCISCO: 353 Sacramento St, 20th Floor, San Francisco, CA 94111. Phone: 415-785-7700. Fax: 415-788-0183.
Type of service: Pay, HD, streaming & video on demand.
Satellites: Galaxy 1-R, transponder 23 (Cinemax ETW); Galaxy 1-R, transponder 19 (Cinemax east); Galaxy V, transponder 16 (Cinemax west).
Operating hours/week: 168.
Operating areas: Available nationwide.
Uplink: Hauppauge, NY.
Programming: First-run films, movies & original programming.
Began: August 1, 1980, Cinemax HD began September 2008. Cinemax on Demand began 2002. Max GO began September 2010.
Means of Support: Subscriber fees.
Total subscribers: 43,000,000 (U.S. subscribers. 84,000,000 international subscribers. Subscriber counts includes HBO.).
Distribution method: Available to cable, IPTV & satellite subscribers; online & mobile through the Max GO website or app (participating providers); video on demand (participating providers).
Scrambled signal: Yes. Equipment: General Instrument.
Ownership: Time Warner.

CINEMAX ON DEMAND — See Cinemax.

CINEMOI NORTH AMERICA
1976 S La Cienega Blvd
Ste 248
Los Angeles, CA 90027
Phone: 310-271-7607
Web Site: http://www.cinemoius.com
Rod Sherwood, Chief Executive Officer
Daphna Edwards Ziman, President
Type of service: Pay.
Operating hours/week: 168.
Operating areas: Available nationwide.
Programming: Dedicated to curated films, high couture and stunning international lifestyle, primarily in English.
Began: September 17, 2012, on DirecTV; relaunched on Verizon FiOS January 29, 2014. Launched in Europe February 23, 2009.
Means of Support: Subscriber fees.
Total subscribers: 20,000,000.
Distribution method: Available to DirecTV & Verizon FiOS subscribers.
Scrambled signal: Yes.
Ownership: Oliver Bengough, Noreen Harrington, Rod Sherwood.

CLASICO TV
c/o Univision Communications Inc.
605 3rd Ave, 12th Fl
New York, NY 10158
Phone: 212-455-5200
E-mail: darodriguez@univision.net
Web Site: http://www.televisanetworks.tv
Monica Talan, Executive Vice President, Corporate Communications & Public Relations, Univision Communications
Satellites: AMC 1.
Operating areas: Nationwide.
Programming: Spanish language channel devoted to sitcoms from the 60s, 70s and 80s.
Began: May 1, 2007.
Distribution method: Available to cable & satellite subscribers.
Scrambled signal: Yes.
Ownership: Televisa Networks. Univision Communications Inc. has an exclusive contract for this service.

CLASSIC ARTS SHOWCASE
PO Box 828
Burbank, CA 91503
Phone: 323-878-0283
Fax: 323-878-0329
E-mail: casmail@sbcglobal.net
Web Site: http://www.classicartsshowcase.org
Jamie D. Rigler, President & Programming Director
Charlie Mount, General Manager
Peter Zeeman, Operations
Type of service: Basic.
Satellites: Galaxy 15, transponder 5.
Operating hours/week: 168.
Programming: All classic arts video featuring: animation, architectural art, ballet, chamber & choral music, dance, documentary, folk

Pay TV & Satellite Services

FULLY SEARCHABLE • CONTINUOUSLY UPDATED • DISCOUNT RATES FOR PRINT PURCHASERS

For more information call **800-771-9202** or visit **www.warren-news.com**

art, museum art, musical theatre, opera, orchestral, recital, solo instrumental & vocal & theatrical performance.
Began: May 3, 1994.
Means of Support: Underwritten by the Lloyd E. Rigler-Lawrence E. Deutsch Foundation.
Total subscribers: 48,000,000.
Distribution method: Available to cable & satellite subscribers.
Scrambled signal: Yes.
Ownership: Rigler-Deutsch Foundation, Lloyd E. Rigler & Lawrence Deutsch, founders.

CLOO
30 Rockefeller Plaza
21st Fl
New York, NY 10112
Phone: 212-664-4444
Web Site: http://www.cloo.com
Frank DeRose, Senior Vice President, Program Scheduling & Strategic Planning
Ryan Sharkey, Senior Vice President, Program Acquisitions & Administration
Type of service: Digital basic, video on demand.
Satellites: Galaxy 1R, transponder 24.
Operating hours/week: 168.
Operating areas: Hawaii, New York, North Carolina, Texas & Wisconsin.
Programming: Crime, mystery and suspense oriented series, movies & original programming.
Began: January 1, 2006, as Sleuth. Sleuth on demand began June 21, 2007. Rebranded cloo August 15, 2011.
Total subscribers: 38,000,000.
Distribution method: Available to cable & satellite subscribers.
Scrambled signal: Yes.
Ownership: NBCUniversal LLC.

CLTV
2501 W Bradley Pl
Chicago, IL 60618-4718
Phone: 773-528-2311
E-mail: programming@cltv.com
Web Site: http://www.cltv.com
Paul Rennie, President & General Manager
Ron Goldberg, Sales Director
Jennifer Lyons, News Director
Sandy Pudar, Assistant News Director
Type of service: Regional.
Operating hours/week: 168.
Operating areas: Chicago, IL area; Rockford, IL; and South Bend, IN.
Programming: Chicago area news & informational programming.
Began: January 1, 1993, as Chicagoland Television News. Rebranded as CLTV.
Means of Support: Advertising & subscriber fees.
Total subscribers: 1,500,000.
Distribution method: Available to Comcast, RCN & Medicacom subscribers in select Illinois & Indiana areas.
Scrambled signal: Yes.
Ownership: Tribune Media Co.

CLUB JENNA — See Reality Kings TV (RKTV).

CMT
330 Commerce St
Nashville, TN 37201
Phones: 615-457-8400; 615-457-8501
Fax: 615-457-8520
E-mail: cmtviewerservices@country.com
Web Site: http://www.cmt.com
VIACOM INC.:, .
Cyma Zarghami, President, Viacom Kids & Family Group
Richard Gay, Executive Vice President, Strategy & Business Operations, Viacom Music Group
David Giles, Executive Vice President, Strategic Insights & Research, Viacom Music Group
CMT:, .
Brian Philips, President
Jayson Dinsmore, Executive Vice President, Development & Programming
Neil Holt, Executive Vice President, Ad Sales
Anthony Barton, Senior Vice President, Consumer Marketing & Creative
Katie Buchanan, Senior Vice President, Programming, Strategy & Acquisitions
Leslie Fram, Senior Vice President, Music Strategy
Joe Livecchi, Senior Vice President, Program Development
Suzanne Norman, Senior Vice President, Strategy & Business Operations
Jennifer Ortega, Senior Vice President & Deputy General Counsel, Business & Legal Affairs
Lewis Bogach, Vice President, Development
Hector Campos, Vice President, Programming & Strategy
Cindy Finke, Vice President, Programm Publicity & Communications
Lucia Folk, Vice President, Public Affairs
Peter Mannes, Vice President, Creative Services
Morgan Selzer, Vice President, Development
Julia Silverton, Vice President, Development
Zena Van Ackeren, Vice President, Talent & Specialty Casting
Justin Wyatt, Vice President, Consumer Insights & Research
Quinn Brown, Executive Producer
Type of service: Basic, HD, video on demand.
Satellites: Satcom C-4, transponder 24.
Operating hours/week: 168.
Operating areas: Nationwide.
Programming: Country music videos, news, series, interviews & specials.
Began: March 6, 1983.
Means of Support: Advertising.
Total subscribers: 86,989,000.
Distribution method: Available to cable, IPTV & satellite subscribers; video on demand (participating providers).
Scrambled signal: Yes.
Ownership: Viacom Inc.

CMT LOADED — See CMT.
Type of service: Streaming.
Programming: Music, news, TV, movies & highlights from the CMT cable network.
Began: July 24, 2006.
Distribution method: Available online.
Scrambled signal: Yes.

CMT PURE COUNTRY — See CMT.
Programming: Country music videos from the 1980's to today.
Began: August 1, 1998, as VH1 Country. Rebranded CMT Pure Country May 26, 2006.
Total subscribers: 17,000,000.

CN/2
10170 Linn Station Rd
Ste 590
Louisville, KY 40223
Phone: 502-792-1100
Web Site: http://mycn2.com
Caroline Imler, Broadcast Operations Director
Type of service: Regional basic.
Operating areas: Indiana & Kentucky.
Programming: Offers 24-hour local news, weather and sports, plus political news and analysis.
Began: June 24, 2010.
Means of Support: Advertising.
Total subscribers: 600,000.
Distribution method: Available to Insight cable subscribers in the Louisville, KY region.
Scrambled signal: No.
Ownership: Insight Communications Co.

CN8 — See Comcast Network Philadelphia.

CN100
Comcast Greater Chicago Region
688 Industrial Dr
Elmhurst, IL 60126
Phone: 630-600-6117
Web Site: http://www.cn100.tv
Rebecca Cianci, Regional Programming Director
Type of service: Regional basic.
Operating areas: Illinois.
Programming: Local high school sports plus the Chicago Wolves of the American Hockey League. Also offers family entertainment, movies and shows covering local news and events.
Means of Support: Advertising.
Distribution method: Available to Comcast cable system subscribers.
Scrambled signal: Yes.
Ownership: Comcast Corp.

CNBC
900 Sylvan Ave
Englewood Cliffs, NJ 07632
Phone: 201-735-2622
Fax: 201-585-6244
Web Site: http://www.cnbc.com
Patricia Fill-Krushel, Chairman, NBCUniversal News Group
Mark Hoffman, Chief Executive Officer & President
Jodi Brenner, Chief Legal Officer & Senior Vice President, Legal & Business Affairs
K. C. Sullivan, President & Managing Director, CNBC International
Jim Ackerman, Senior Vice President, Primetime Alternative Programming
Scott Boyarsky, Senior Vice President, Technology
Thomas Clendenin, Senior Vice President, Marketing
Nikhil Deogun, Senior Vice President & Editor-in-Chief, Business News
Steven Fastook, Senior Vice President, Technical & Commercial Operations
Robert Foothorap, Senior Vice President, TV Network Advertising Sales
Brian W. Steel, Senior Vice President, Public Relations
Lou Tosto, Senior Vice President, Digital & Mobile Ad Sales
Tyler Benjamin, Vice President, Human Resources
Scott Drake, Vice President, Digital Technology & Products
Allen Wastler, Managing Editor, CNBC.com
Anna Gonzalez, Social Media Director
Marian Caracciolo, Sales Director, Direct Response
Jennifer Sobel, Finance Director

Branch Offices:
BURBANK: 3000 W Alameda Ave, Burbank, CA 91523-0002. Phone: 818-840-3214. Fax: 818-840-4181.

WASHINGTON, DC: 1025 Connecticut Ave NW, Washington, DC 20036. Phone: 202-467-5400. Fax: 202-467-6267.
Type of service: Basic, HD, streaming.
Satellites: Galaxy 5, transponder 13.
Operating hours/week: 168.
Programming: Provides financial news & information programming. On the weekends additional programming is offered.
Began: April 17, 1989, CNBC HD+ began October 1, 2007.
Means of Support: Advertising & license fees.
Total subscribers: 95,000,000.
Distribution method: Available to cable, IPTV & satellite subscribers; streaming available online & mobile through the website or app.
Scrambled signal: Yes. Equipment: VideoCipher.
Ownership: NBCUniversal News Group, a subsidiary of NBCUniversal LLC.

CNBC PRO — See CNBC.
Type of service: Streaming, video on demand.
Programming: Real-time financial data from over 100 stock exchanges, CNBC live streaming & video clips on demand.
Began: December 2010.
Means of Support: Subscription.
Distribution method: Available online or on mobile devices.
Scrambled signal: Yes.
Ownership: NBCUniversal LLC.

CNBC WORLD — See CNBC.
E-mail: cnbcworld@cnbc.com
K. C. Sullivan, President & Managing Director, CNBC International
Programming: Digital television network offering real-time coverage of global financial markets, live, worldwide. Combines the resources of CNBC Asia and CNBC Europe into a 24-hour a day, global business news network.
Began: July 1, 2001.
Total subscribers: 36,000,000.
Distribution method: Available to DirecTV, Google Fiber & Verizon FiOS subscribers.
Scrambled signal: Yes.

CNN
(Cable Network News)
One CNN Ctr
Atlanta, GA 30303
Phone: 404-827-1700
Web Site: http://www.cnn.com
CNN WORLDWIDE:, .
Jeff Zucker, President, CNN Worldwide
Katrina Cukaj, Executive Vice President, Ad Sales, CNN Worldwide
Rick Davis, Executive Vice President, News Standards & Practices, CNN Worldwide
Amy Entelis, Executive Vice President, Talent & Content Development, CNN Worldwide
Brad Ferrer, Executive Vice President, Finance & Administration, CNN Worldwide

2017 Edition

E-21

Pay TV & Satellite Services

Elizabeth Casanas, Senior Vice President, Human Resources, CNN Worldwide
Allison Gollust, Senior Vice President, Public Relations, CNN Worldwide
Parisa Khosravi, Senior Vice President, Global Relations, CNN Worldwide
Rick Lewchuk, Senior Vice President, Creative Marketing, CNN Worldwide
Leslie Picard, Senior Vice President, Sales & Branded Solutions, CNN Worldwide
Jack Womack, Senior Vice President, CNN Worldwide
Ramon Escobar, Vice President, Talent Recruitment & Development, CNN Worldwide
CNN:, .
Ken Jautz, Executive Vice President, CNN U.S.
Michael Bass, Senior Vice President, Programming
Jeff Collins, Senior Vice President, CNN Advertising Sales
Joseph Dugan, Senior Vice President, CNN Digital Advertising Sales
Sam Feist, Senior Vice President & Washington Bureau Chief
Robin Garfield, Senior Vice President, Research
Cynthia Hudson-Fernandez, Senior Vice President & General Manager, CNN en Espanol & Hispanic Strategy for CNN U.S.
Andrew Morse, Senior Vice President, CNN U.S. & General Manager, CNN Digital
E. Allen Wyke, Senior Vice President, Digital Technology & Product Development, CNN Digital
John Antonio, Vice President, Dayside Programming, CNN U.S.
Greg Asman, Vice President, Research & Analytics
Chris Berend, Vice President, Digital Video Development, CNN & CNN Digital
S Mitra Kalida, Vice President, Digital Programming
Lizzie Kerner, Vice President, Current Programming
Jim Murphy, Vice President, Daytime Programming
Stephen L. Pollack, Vice President & Sales Manager, Western Region
Eric Sherling, Vice President, Washington, DC Programming
Anne Woodward, Vice President, Technical Operations
CNN DIGITAL:, .
Karen DeGrammont, Vice President, Global Strategy & Business Intelligence, CNN Digital
Kitric Kerns, Vice President, Product Development & Operations, CNN Digital
Dewey Reid, Vice President & Executive Creative Director, CNN Digital
Mike Toppo, Vice President & Senior Editorial Director, CNN Digital
Alex Wellen, Chief Product Officer, CNN Digital
Meredith Artley, Editor in Chief, CNN Digital
Type of service: Basic, HD, video on demand.
Satellites: Galaxy I, transponder 7.
Sales representative: Turner Network Sales.
Operating hours/week: 168.
Operating areas: Nationwide.
Uplink: Atlanta, GA.
Programming: Coverage of major news stories & daily reports on business, finance, medicine, nutrition, sports, weather, fashion & entertainment. Spanish-language programming on CNN en Espanol.
Began: June 1, 1980, CNN HD began September 2007.
Means of Support: System pays 24-33 cents per subscriber; advertising.
Total subscribers: 98,000,000.
Distribution method: Available to cable, IPTV & satellite subscribers; video on demand (participating providers).

Scrambled signal: Yes. Equipment: VideoCipher II.
Ownership: Turner Broadcasting System, division of Time Warner.

CNN EN ESPANOL — See CNN.
Web Site: http://cnnespanol.cnn.com
Cynthia Hudson-Fernandez, Senior Vice President & General Manager, CNN en Espanol & Hispanic Strategy for CNN/US
Eduardo Suarez, Vice President, Programming & Production

Branch Offices:
MIAMI: Courvoisier Center II, 601 Brickell Jey Dr, Ste 403, Miami, FL 33131-4330. Phone: 305-603-2000. Fax: 305-603-2505.

ARGENTINA: Av. Eduardo Madero 1020, Piso 14, Buenos Aires C1106ACX, Argentina. Phone: 54-11-4312-9900. Fax: 54-11-4312-4581.

BRAZIL: Av. das Nacoes Unidas N, 12.901, 17 Andar CJ 1701 Chacara, Itaim, Sao Paulo 04578-000, Brazil. Phone: 55-11-5501-6700. Fax: 55-11-5507-7080.

MEXICO: Blvd. Manuel Avila Camacho No. 1, Piso 8, Despacho 805, Col. Chapultepec, Polanco DF 11009, Mexico. Phone: 52-55-5395-3066. Fax: 52-55-5395-3055.
Sales representative: Turner Network Sales.
Operating hours/week: 168.
Operating areas: Available nationwide.
Programming: Spanish language. Continuous news coverage of major world events, live breaking coverage supported by context and in-depth analysis, worldwide business and financial news, global weather updates, sports and feature programming on such topics as health, technology and entertainment.
Began: March 17, 1997.
Total subscribers: 7,000,000.
Distribution method: Available to most cable, IPTV & cable subscribers.
Scrambled signal: Yes.
Ownership: Turner Broadcasting System, division of Time Warner.

CNNGO — See CNN.
Type of service: Streaming.
Began: September 30, 2014.
Distribution method: Available online & mobile through participating providers & on Apple TV & Roku devices.

CNN INTERNATIONAL — See CNN.
Web Site: http://www.cnn.com/CNNI
Tony Maddox, Executive Vice President & Managing Director
Rani R. Raad, Executive Vice President & Chief Commercial Officer
Bill Galvin, Senior Vice President, Business Development & Sports Programming
Mike McCarthy, Senior Vice President, Programming
Peter Bale, Vice President & General Manager, CNN International Digital
Nick Wrenn, Vice President, Digital Services
Sales representative: Turner Network Sales.
Programming: News, business, sport and feature shows.
Began: September 1, 1985, in Europe. August 1989 in Asia-Pacific. 1991 in Latin America. July 2000 in South Asia. October 2000 in U.S.
Ownership: Turner Broadcasting Systems, a division of Time Warner.

COASTAL TELEVISION NETWORK
225 The Crossroads

Ste 183
Carmel, CA 93923
Phone: 831-899-2727
Fax: 831-899-2727
Web Site: http://www.coastaltvnetwork.com
Type of service: Regional.
Operating areas: Fresno, Monterey & Sacramento, CA.
Programming: Features programs about coastal California. Includes local history, sports and.
Means of Support: Advertising.
Distribution method: Available over the air on digital sub-channels.
Ownership: Monterey Bay LLC.

COLLEGE SPORTS TELEVISION — See CBS Sports Network.

COLORS KANNADA
c/o ETV Network
Ramoji Film City
Hyderabad 501 512
India
Phone: 91-08415-246555/111
E-mail: manohar.k@etv.co.in
Web Site: http://www.colorskannada.com
Type of service: Pay.
Operating areas: Nationwide.
Programming: Kannada-language Indian cultural, entertainment and informational programming.
Began: December 10, 2000, as ETV Kannada. Rebranded Colors Kannada April 26, 2015.
Distribution method: Available to DISH Network subscribers.
Scrambled signal: Yes.
Ownership: Eenadu Television Pvt. Ltd.

COLORS MARATHI — See Colors Kannada.
Programming: Marathi-language Indian cultural, entertainment & informational programming.
Began: As ETV Marathi. Rebranded Colors Marathi on April 26, 2015.

COLOURS
217 S Jackson St
Denver, CO 80209
Phone: 303-326-0088
Fax: 303-326-0087
E-mail: info@colourstv.org
Tracy Jenkins Winchester, President & Chief Executive Officer
Arthur O. Thomas, Executive Vice President
Programming: Multicultural & multi-ethnic programming offering movies, original series, short films, documentaries & sports.
Total subscribers: 14,000,000.
Ownership: Black Star Communications.

COMCAST/CHARTER SPORTS SOUTHEAST (CSS)
2925 Courtyards Dr
Norcross, GA 30071
Phone: 770-559-7800
E-mail: css@css-sports.com
Web Site: http://www.css-sports.com
Mark Fuhrman, Vice President & General Manager
Operating hours/week: 168.
Operating areas: AL, AR, FL, GA, KY, LA, MS, NC, SC, TN, TX, VA & WV.
Programming: Live sports, news & analysis geared toward the Southern sports fan.
Began: September 3, 1999.
Total subscribers: 6,000,000.
Scrambled signal: Yes.
Ownership: A joint venture between NBCUniversal Inc. (majority interest) & Charter Communications Inc.

COMCAST ENTERTAINMENT TELEVISION — See CET.

COMCAST HOMETOWN NETWORK
3055 Comcast Pl
Livermore, CA 94551
Phone: 415-252-6300
E-mail: Comcast_hometown@cable.comcast.com
Web Site: http://www.comcasthometown.com
Jeff Giles, Director
Bryan Byrd, Communications Director

Branch Offices:
HAYWARD: 23525 Clawiter Rd, Hayward, CA 94545. Phone: 510-266-3200.

SAN FRANCISCO: 2741 16th St, San Francisco, CA 94103. Phone: 415-863-8500.
Type of service: Digital basic, streaming, video on demand.
Operating hours/week: 168.
Operating areas: Northern & Central California.
Programming: Local & regional programming that showcases regional high school sports, Single A/Triple A baseball, Division I & II college sports, ECHL Hockey & regional community content in 6 DMAs throughout Northern California, from Fresno in the South Valley to Santa Maria on the Central Coast as well as the Bay Area & Central Valley.
Began: March 21, 2009.
Total subscribers: 2,000,000.
Distribution method: Available to Comcast cable system subscribers. Streaming available online.
Scrambled signal: Yes.
Ownership: Comcast Corp.

COMCAST NETWORK PHILADELPHIA
c/o Comcast SportsNet
3601 S Broad St
Philadelphia, PA 19148
Phone: 215-336-3500
E-mail: askcsn@comcastsportsnet.com
Web Site: http://csnphilly.com
Melissa Kennedy, Vice President, Marketing Communications

Studio Offices:
NEW CASTLE: 2215 N DuPont Hwy, New Castle, DE 19720. Phone: 302-661-4203. Fax: 302-661-4201.

PHILADELPHIA: 1351 S Columbus Blvd, Philadelphia, PA 19147. Phone: 215-468-2222. Fax: 215-463-5922.

TRENTON: 940 Prospect St, Trenton, NJ 08618. Phone: 609-394-3860. Fax: 609-394-6983.

UNION: 800 Rahway Ave, Union, NJ 07083. Phone: 732-602-7492. Fax: 908-851-8916.

Branch Offices:
MOORESTOWN: CN8 Creative, 650 Centerton Rd, Moorestown, NJ 08057. Phone: 856-638-4000. Fax: 856-206-0727.

OAKS: 200 Cresson Blvd, Oaks, PA 19456. Phone: 610-650-1000. Fax: 610-650-2909.
Type of service: Regional basic.
Operating hours/week: 168.
Operating areas: Delaware, New Jersey & Pennsylvania.
Programming: Mid-Atlantic regional programming featuring entertainment, sports, news

Pay TV & Satellite Services

and information & other locally produced programming.
Began: 1996 as CN8. Reorganized & rebranded as The Comcast Network January 2009.
Distribution method: Available to Comcast cable system subscribers.
Scrambled signal: Yes.
Ownership: NBCUniversal LLC.

COMCAST SPORTSNET BAY AREA
370 3rd St
Ste 200
San Francisco, CA 94107
Phone: 415-296-8900
Fax: 415-615-4793
E-mail: info@csnbayarea.com
Web Site: http://www.csnbayarea.com
Ted Griggs, Vice President & General Manager
John Feeley, Vice President, Sales & Syndication
Jen Franklin, Vice President, Digital Media
Tom Pellack, Vice President, Marketing
Peter Schofield, Vice President, Operations
Matt Butler, Senior Director, Traffic
Chris McDonald, Senior Director, Finance & Human Resources
David Koppett, Senior Executive Producer
Chris Olivere, News Director
Kyleen Bell, Programming Director
Jay Dela Cruz, Communications Director
Marisa Veroneau, Affiliate Marketing Manager
Type of service: Basic.
Satellites: GE-1, transponder 16.
Sales representative: Rasco.
Operating hours/week: 168.
Operating areas: Northern California & northern Nevada.
Programming: Regional sports service offering San Francisco Giants baseball, Golden State Warriors basketball, PAC 12 & Stanford U. sports, as well as original news sports programming – SportsNet Central and Chronicle Live. Formerly FSN Bay Area and SportChannel Pacific.
Began: April 4, 1990, as SportsChannel Bay Area. After July 1991 merger with Pacific Sports Network, rebranded SportsChannel Pacific. When company joined Fox Sports in January 1998, rebranded Fox Sports Bay Area. Once channel became part of Comcast SportsNet on March 31, 2009, rebranded Comcast SportsNet Bay Area.
Means of Support: Advertising & affiliate fees.
Total subscribers: 3,600,000.
Distribution method: Available to cable systems & satellite subscribers.
Scrambled signal: Yes.
Ownership: NBCUniversal LLC.

COMCAST SPORTSNET CALIFORNIA
4450 E Commerce Ave
2nd Fl
Sacramento, CA 95834
Phones: 415-296-8900; 415-296-8900
Fax: 915-515-2770
E-mail: info@csncalifornia.com
Web Site: http://www.csncalifornia.com
Larry Eldridge, Vice President & General Manager
John Feeley, Vice President, Sales & Syndication
Tom Pellack, Vice President, Marketing
Jen Franklin, Senior Director, Digital Media
Chris McDonald, Senior Director, Finance & Human Resources
Peter Schofield, Senior Director, Operations
Jay Dela Cruz, Communications Director
Richard Zinn, Executive Producer
Richard Leeson, Programming Director
Marisa Veroneau, Affiliate Marketing Manager

Type of service: Basic.
Operating areas: Northern California and portions of Nevada & Oregon.
Programming: Regional sports service offering Oakland Athletics baseball, Sacramento Kings basketball, San Jose Sharks hockey, San Jose Earthquakes soccer, and PAC 12 & U. of California Berkeley sports.
Began: November 2, 2004, as Comcast SportsNet West. Rebranded Comcast SportsNet California in 2008.
Total subscribers: 50,000,000 (Reflects combined total of Comcast SportsNet channels).
Distribution method: Available to Comcast and DISH Network subscribers.
Scrambled signal: Yes.

COMCAST SPORTSNET CHICAGO
350 N Orleans St
Ste S1-100
Chicago, IL 60654
Phone: 312-222-6000
Fax: 312-527-4028
E-mail: jnuich@comcastsportsnet.com
Web Site: http://www.csnchicago.com
Phil Bedella, General Manager & Vice President
Joyce Brewer, Senior Vice President, Finance
Greg Bowman, Vice President, Programming
Wesley Albury, Vice President, Engineering
Kevin Cross, Senior Director, News & Original Content
Jeff Nuich, Senior Director, Communications
Brian Sanderlin, Senior Director, Operations
Jim Corno Jr., Senior Executive Producer, Live Events
D. J. Maragos, Affiliate Marketing Director
Type of service: Basic, HD.
Operating hours/week: 168.
Programming: Regular, pre & post season games for the Blackhawks, Bulls, Cubs & White Sox; college sports events; sports-related news.
Began: October 1, 2004.
Total subscribers: 29,000,000 (Includes subscribers from all Comcast SportsNet channels.).
Distribution method: Available to cable, IPTV & satellite subscribers.
Scrambled signal: Yes.
Ownership: NBC Sports Group, a unit of NBCUniversal LLC; Bulls TV LLC; W Sports Media LLC; Sox TV LLC; Chicago Baseball Holdings LLC, 20% each.

COMCAST SPORTSNET HOUSTON —
See Root Sports Southwest.

COMCAST SPORTSNET MID-ATLANTIC
7700 Wisconsin Ave
Ste 200
Bethesda, MD 20814
Phone: 301-718-3200
Fax: 301-718-3300
E-mail: viewermail@csnwashington.com
Web Site: http://www.csnwashington.com;
http://www.csnbaltimore.com
Rebecca O'Sullivan-Schulte, President
Jeremy Howard, Vice President, Ad Sales
Mark Lapidus, Vice President, Digital Manager
George Psillos, Vice President, Finance & Business Administration
Mike Wargo, Digital Managing Editor
Cesar Aldama, Senior Director, News
Austin Krablin, Senior Director, Marketing & Creative Services
Brian H. Potter, Senior Director, Communications
Frank Crisafulli, News Director
Tom Pahnke, Operations Director

Lisa Pendleton, Programming Director
Glendalyn Junio, Marketing Coordinator
Lynne Cotton, Human Resources Specialist
Type of service: Regional basic.
Satellites: GE-3, transponder 6.
Operating hours/week: 168.
Operating areas: Delaware, District of Columbia, Maryland, North Carolina, Pennsylvania, Virginia & West Virginia.
Programming: The official sports network of the Washington Redskins, Baltimore Ravens, Washington Capitals, Washington Wizards, D.C. United, Atlantic Coast Conference and Colonial Athletic Association. Delivers more than 500 live sporting events per year, along with news, analysis and entertainment programming.
Began: April 4, 1984, as Home Team Sports. Rebranded as Comcast SportsNet Mid-Atlantic when acquired by Comcast April 4, 2001.
Means of Support: System fees & advertising.
Total subscribers: 4,700,000.
Distribution method: Available to Comcast, DirecTV & DISH Network subscribers.
Scrambled signal: Yes.
Ownership: NBCUniversal LLC.

COMCAST SPORTSNET NEW ENGLAND
42 Third Ave
Burlington, MA 01803
Phone: 781-270-7200
Fax: 781-221-7408
E-mail: fans@comcastportsnet.com
Web Site: http://www.csnne.com
Bill Bridgen, General Manager & Executive Vice President
Len Mead, Vice President, Production & Programming
Gregg Sanders, Vice President, Business Development & Marketing
Type of service: Basic.
Satellites: GE-1, transponder 14.
Sales representative: Rasco.
Operating areas: Connecticut, Maine, Massachusetts, New Hampshire, Rhode Island & Vermont.
Programming: Regional sports service offering Boston Celtics basketball, New England Revolution soccer, CT Suns women's basketball. PAC 10, Big 12 and CAA football and basketball. America East and A-10 basketball, plus nightly sports news, SportsNet Central.
Began: November 6, 1981, as PRISM New England. Rebranded as SportsChannel New England when acquired by Cablevision in 1983. Rebranded Fox Sports New England when service joined Fox Sports on January 28, 1998. Later named Fox Sports Net New England. Rebranded as Comcast SportsNet New England when Cablevision acquired Comcast on October 1, 2007.
Means of Support: Advertising & subscriber fees.
Total subscribers: 4,000,000.
Distribution method: Available to cable & satellite subscribers.
Scrambled signal: Yes.
Ownership: NBCUniversal LLC.

COMCAST SPORTSNET NORTHWEST
300 N Winning Way
Portland, OR 97227
Phone: 503-736-5140
Fax: 503-736-5135
Web Site: http://www.csnnw.com
Larry Eldridge, Vice President & General Manager
Casey Waage, Ad Sales Director
Ken Lotka, Programming Director
Satellites: Galaxy 14 (HD), transponder 4.
Operating areas: Alaska (portions), Idaho, Montana, Oregon & Washington.
Programming: Regional sports service providing NBA Portland Trail Blazers basketball and surrounding programming; NHL Vancouver Canucks hockey & other NHL; Emerald Downs horse racing; PAC-10 football & basketball; Big Sky football & basketball; Portland and Seattle sports radio; original outdoor programming: Outdoor GPS, Northwest Wild Country, WANTED, The Wild Life with Jeremy, Adrenaline Hunter and more.
Began: September 1, 1989.
Total subscribers: 2,400,000.
Distribution method: Available to cable & satellite subscribers.
Scrambled signal: Yes.
Ownership: NBCUniversal LLC.

COMCAST SPORTSNET PHILADELPHIA
3601 S Broad St
Wells Fargo Center
Philadelphia, PA 19148-5290
Phone: 215-336-3500
Fax: 215-952-5756
E-mail: askcsn@comcastsportsnet.com
Web Site: http://www.csnphilly.com
Joe Croce, Vice President, Advertising Sales
Cynthia Weiss, Vice President, Marketing
Todd Berman, Senior Director, Digital Media
Bo Koelle, Advertising Sales Director
Maureen Quilter, Communications Director
John Braun, National Sales Manager
Dan Rudley, Digital Sales Manager
Mike Garrity, Sponsorship Sales Manager
Type of service: Basic.
Operating hours/week: 168.
Operating areas: Philadelphia, southern New Jersey & Delaware.
Programming: Regional sports network. Provides local sports coverage, including more than 250 live game broadcasts of the NHL's Philadelphia Flyers, NBA's Philadelphia 76ers, MLB's Philadelphia Phillies, plus NCAA coverage, as well as sports news and analysis.
Began: January 1, 2009, as CN8. Reorganized in late 2008 & rebranded The Comcast Network in early 2009.
Total subscribers: 50,000,000 (Reflects combined total of Comcast SportsNet channels).
Distribution method: Available to cable & Verizon FiOS subscribers.
Scrambled signal: Yes.
Ownership: NBCUniversal LLC.

Pay TV & Satellite Services

COMCAST SPORTSNET WASHINGTON
7700 Wisconsin Ave
Ste 200
Bethesda, MD 20814
Phone: 240-223-6600
E-mail: csn@csnwashington.com
Web Site: http://www.csnwashington.com
Steve Lieberman, Advertising
Type of service: Regional basic.
Operating hours/week: 168.
Operating areas: District of Columbia, Maryland & Virginia.
Programming: Mid-Atlantic regional programming featuring entertainment, sports, news and information & other locally produced programming.
Began: January 1, 2009, as CN8. Reorganized in late 2008 and rebranded as The Comcast Network in early 2009.
Means of Support: Advertising.
Total subscribers: 4,500,000.
Distribution method: Available to Comcast cable system subscribers.
Scrambled signal: Yes.
Ownership: NBCUniversal LLC.

COMCAST SPORTSNET WEST — See Comcast SportsNet California

COMCAST SPORTS SOUTHWEST (CSS) — See Root Sports Southwest.

COMCAST TELEVISION (MICHIGAN)
27800 Franklin Rd
Southfield, MI 48034
Phones: 248-359-6516; 734-260-8188
E-mail: Rob_Ponto@cable.comcast.com
Brian Popa, Supervisor
Brett Hatch, Programming Manager
Rob Ponto, Public Relations Manager
Type of service: Regional basic.
Operating areas: Michigan.
Programming: Both channels offer public affairs, infomercials and local sports programming.
Began: March 1, 2008.
Means of Support: Advertising.
Distribution method: Available to Comcast cable system subscribers.
Scrambled signal: Yes.
Ownership: Comcast Corp.

COMCAST TELEVISION 2 — See Comcast Television (Michigan).
Began: August 15, 2008.

COMEDY CENTRAL
345 Hudson St
New York, NY 10014
Phone: 212-767-8600
Web Site: http://www.comedycentral.com
Doug Herzog, President, Viacom Music & Entertainment Group
Kent Alterman, President
Walter Levitt, Chief Marketing Officer
David Bernath, Executive Vice President, Program Strategy & Multi-platform Programming
John Cucci, Executive Vice President & Chief Operating Officer
Gary Gradinger, Executive Vice President & Deputy General Counsel, Business & Legal Affairs, Comedy Central & TV Land
Steve Albani, Senior Vice President, Communications
Sarah Babineau, Senior Vice President, Original Programming, East Coast
Melissa Bear, Senior Vice President, Business & Legal Affairs & General Counsel, Comedy Central & TV Land
Debbie Beiter, Senior Vice President, Production & Operations Brand Creative
Eric Blume, Senior Vice President, Movie Studio Production, Comedy Central & Spike
Lu Chekowsky, Senior Vice President, Brand Creative
Chanon Cook, Senior Vice President, Strategic Insights & Research
Steve Grimes, Senior Vice President, Multi-platform Programming & Strategy
Susie Kricena, Senior Vice President, Program Acquisitions
Jonas Larsen, Senior Vice President, Talent & Specials
Gary S. Mann, Senior Vice President, Original Programming & Development
Brooke Posch, Senior Vice President, Original Programming & Production, East Coast
Gerald Raines, Senior Vice President, Recreation Business Development
Steve Raizes, Senior Vice President, Enterprises
Megan Ring, Senior Vice President, Production
Bob Salazar, Senior Vice President & Executive Creator Director, Brand Creative
Jim Sharp, Executive Vice President, Original Programming & Development, West Coast
Don Steele, Senior Vice President, Fan Engagement/Mutli-platform Marketing
Sharon Alvardo, Vice President, Ad Sales Research, Comedy Central, Spike TV, MTV2
John Cassidy, Vice President & Creative Director, Brand Creative
Steve Dara, Vice President, Ad Sales, Comedy Central & Spike TV
Steve Elliott, Vice President, Branded Entertainment Development
JoAnn Grigioni, Vice President, Talent
Douglas P. Johnson, Vice President, Comedy Central Production, Short Form
Allison Kingsley, Vice President, Digital Development
Renata Luczak, Vice President, Communications
Christian McLaughlin, Vice President, Specials
Rob O'Neill, Vice President, Programming & Promotion Strategy
Jenni Runyan, Vice President, Communications
Chris Scarlata, Vice President, Design, Brand Creative
Jason Shafton, Vice President, Brand Marketing
Arian Sultan Rothman, Vice President, Business & Legal Affairs, East Coast
Beth Trentacost, Vice President, Movie Studio Production, Comedy Central & Spike TV
Ari Pearce, Original Programming & Development Director, East Coast

Branch Offices:
LOS ANGELES: 2600 Colorado Ave, Santa Monica, CA 90404. Phone: 310-752-8000.
Type of service: Basic, HD, streaming & video on demand.
Satellites: Galaxy I-R, transponder 1 (west coast); Satcom C-3, transponder 21 (east coast).
Operating hours/week: 168.
Programming: Original & syndicated comedy programming.
Began: April 1, 1991, as CTV: The Comedy Network. Channel merged with Viacom's Ha channel April 1, 1991. Rebranded Comedy Central June 1, 1991. Comedy Central HD began in 2009.
Means of Support: Advertising.
Total subscribers: 93,000,000.
Distribution method: Available to cable, IPTV & satellite subscribers; streaming available online & mobile through the website or app; video on demand (participating providers).
Scrambled signal: Yes.
Ownership: Viacom Inc.

COMEDY TIME
11812 San Vicente Blvd
4th Fl
Los Angeles, CA 90049
Phone: 310-841-2004
Fax: 310-287-2056
E-mail: info@comedy-time.com
Web Site: http://www.comedytime.tv
David Goldman, Chief Executive Officer
Michael Goldman, President
Type of service: Video on demand.
Operating areas: Available nationwide.
Programming: Short form comedy, including stand-up and sketch comedy. Also has special targeted segments including Chick Comedy (Women), Comedy Time Latino and Funny4Shizzle (Urban).
Began: July 1, 2004, on Sprint TV & Mobi TV; has since spread to traditional media.
Means of Support: Advertising.
Distribution method: Available to cable & satellite subscribers. Also available online & mobile.
Scrambled signal: Yes.
Ownership: Comedy Time Inc.

COMEDY.TV
1925 Century Park E
Ste 1025
Los Angeles, CA 90067
Phone: 310-277-3500
E-mail: eric@es.tv
Web Site: http://www.comedy.tv
Byron Allen, Chairman & Chief Executive Officer
Darren Galatt, Vice President, Ad Sales
Type of service: Digital broadband.
Operating hours/week: 168.
Operating areas: Available nationwide.
Programming: Offers comedians performing live and taped, as well as hosted talk and variety shows.
Began: May 11, 2009.
Total subscribers: 1,900,000.
Distribution method: Available to Verizon FiOS, Frontier Communications and Suddenlink cable system subscribers.
Scrambled signal: No.
Ownership: Entertainment Studios.

COMET
c/o Sinclair Broadcast Group Inc.
10706 Beaver Dam Rd
Cockeysville, MD 21030
Phone: 410-568-1500
E-mail: comments@sbgi.net
John Bryan, President, Domestic Television Distribution, MGM
Steve Pruett, Vice President & Co-Chief Operating Officer, Sinclair Television Group Inc.
Type of service: Basic.
Operating areas: Available nationwide.
Programming: Network features a mix of science fiction, fantasy and adventure programs from MGM plus movies.
Began: October 31, 2015.
Means of Support: Advertising.
Total subscribers: 65,000,000.
Distribution method: Available over the air on digital sub-channels on Sinclair, Titan and Tribune stations.
Scrambled signal: Yes.
Ownership: Sinclair Broadcast Group Inc. MGM handles programming aspects of service.

CONCERT TV
730 Wellington
Montreal, Quebec H3C 1T4
Canada
Phone: 514-664-1244
Fax: 514-664-1143
E-mail: info@concerttv.com
Web Site: http://www.concerttv.com
Brian Decker, Senior Vice President, Business Development
Programming: On demand music video service dedicated to delivering concerts featuring the well-known bands and artists. View free concert samples and order full length concerts from a vast selection of great music shows.
Began: 2003 in the U.S. Launched in Canada in 2011.
Total subscribers: 45,000,000.
Distribution method: Available to digital cable, IPTV & satellite subscribers.
Scrambled signal: Yes.
Ownership: Stingray Digital Group Inc.

CONNECTICUT NETWORK — See CTN.

COOKING CHANNEL
75 9th Ave
New York, NY 10011
Phone: 212-398-8836
Fax: 212-736-7716
Web Site: http://www.cookingchanneltv.com
Darren Campo, Senior Vice President, Program Strategy
Michael Smith, Senior Vice President & General Manager
Susie Fogelson, Senior Vice President, Marketing & Brand Strategy
Deirdre O'Hearn, Senior Vice President, Programming & Development
Bruce Seidel, Senior Vice President, Programming & Production
Jennifer Quainton, Vice President, Programming, Food Network & Cooking Channel
Type of service: Digital basic, video on demand.
Programming: Experts offer indepth and detailed information including unconventional how-tos, global cuisine, wines and spirits, international travel and classic favorites.
Began: March 1, 2002, as Fine Living Network. Rebranded as Cooking Channel May 31, 2010.
Total subscribers: 58,000,000.
Scrambled signal: Yes.
Ownership: Scripps Networks Interactive Inc.

CORNERSTONE TELEVISION
1 Signal Dr
Wall, PA 15148-1499
Phone: 412-824-3930
Fax: 412-824-5442
E-mail: info@ctvn.org
Web Site: http://www.ctvn.org
Jeffrey Kuster, President
Blake Richert, Vice President, Engineering
Tim Burgan, Vice President, Ministry
Satellites: AMC-4.
Operating hours/week: 168.
Programming: Offers multiple programs, including original in-house productions ministering salvation, encouragement & healing.
Began: April 15, 1979.
Total subscribers: 52,000,000.

COUNTRY MUSIC TELEVISION — See CMT.

THE COUNTRY NETWORK
6125 Airport Fwy
Haltom City, TX 76117
Phone: 817-834-6879
Web Site: http://tcncountry.net

Pay TV & Satellite Services

Steve Goldstein, Co-Founder & Chief Executive Officer
Chris Gannett, Chief Marketing Officer
Jamie Donnenfeld, Vice President, Ad Operations
Brooke Emerson, Vice President, New Business Development
Karma Gardner, Vice President, Strategic Sales

Branch Offices:
NASHVILLE: 209 Tenth Ave S, Ste 322, Nashville, TN 37203. Phone: 877-655-2351.
Type of service: Basic, over the air, streaming.
Operating hours/week: 168.
Operating areas: Available nationwide.
Programming: Country music videos.
Began: January 7, 2009, as the Artists & Fans Network. Rebranded the American Music Video Network August 2009 & then The Country Network June 15, 2010. Acquired by ZUUS Media Inc. early June 2013 and rebranded to ZUUS Country. Acquired by TCN Country LLC and rebranded as The Country Network May 2016.
Means of Support: Advertising.
Total subscribers: 33,000,000.
Distribution method: Available over the air on digital sub-channels & to cable, IPTV & satellite subscribers. Streaming available online.
Scrambled signal: Yes.
Ownership: TCN Country LLC.

COUNTY TELEVISION NETWORK SAN DIEGO
1600 Pacific Hwy
Rm 208
San Diego, CA 92101-2481
Phone: 619-595-4600
Fax: 619-557-4027
E-mail: michael.russo@sdcounty.ca.gov
Web Site: http://www.sandiegocounty.gov
Michael Workman, Director
Michael Russo, Program & Production Manager
Type of service: Basic.
Operating hours/week: 168.
Operating areas: San Diego, CA.
Programming: San Diego County government access programming.
Began: July 1, 1996.
Total subscribers: 725,000.
Scrambled signal: Yes.
Ownership: San Diego County.

COURT TV — See truTV.

COX SPORTS TELEVISION
2121 Airline Dr
Metairie, LA 70001
Phone: 504-304-2740
Fax: 504-304-2243
E-mail: coxsportstv@cox.com
Web Site: http://www.coxsportstv.com
Amaliya Lenz, Administrative Asst.
Satellites: Galaxy 23, transponder 1.
Operating areas: Texas, Arkansas, Louisiana, Florida, Georgia, Mississippi, Missouri, Oklahoma & Virginia.
Programming: A 24-hour local sports network that delivers exclusive programming, including both professional and collegiate sporting events. CST televises over 300 events per year. The exclusive regional sports network home of the New Orleans Saints and LSU Tigers.
Began: October 1, 2002.
Total subscribers: 2,000,000. Total systems served: 16.
Distribution method: Available to cable subscribers.

Scrambled signal: Yes.
Ownership: Cox Communications.

COZI TV
30 Rockefeller Plz
New York, NY 10112
Phone: 212-664-4444
Web Site: http://www.cozitv.com
Valari Staab, President, NBC Owned Television Stations
Meredith McGinn, Senior Vice President
John Durso Jr., Vice President, Community & Communications
Diane Petzke, Programming & Promotion Director

Branch Offices:
NBCUniversal Media Operations Center: 900 Sylvan Ave, Englewood Cliffs, NJ 07632-3312. Phone: 201-735-2700.
Type of service: Basic, over the air.
Operating hours/week: 168.
Operating areas: California, District of Columbia, Florida, Illinois, New York, Pennsylvania &Texas.
Programming: Classic TV series, hit movies plus original national and local programming.
Began: March 9, 2009, as Nonstop Network. Rebranded COZI TV December 20, 2012 on NBCs owned & operated stations. Launched nationwide January 1, 2013.
Means of Support: Advertising.
Total subscribers: 84,000,000.
Distribution method: Available over the air on digital sub-channels & to Verizon FiOS & cable subscribers.
Scrambled signal: Yes.
Ownership: NBCUniversal LLC.

CRACKLE
10202 W Washington Blvd
Culver City, CA 90232
Phone: 415-877-4800
Fax: 415-331-5501
Web Site: http://www.crackle.com
Eric Berger, Executive Vice President, Digital Media & General Manager
Type of service: Streaming, video on demand.
Programming: Original short form series & full-length traditional programming from Sony Pictures' vast library of television series & feature films. Genres include comedy, action, sci-fi, horror, music and reality.
Began: 2000s as Grouper. Rebranded as Crackle in 2007.
Distribution method: Available to Comcast subscribers, online & mobile.
Scrambled signal: Yes.
Ownership: Sony Pictures Entertainment Co.
Distributes TV, movies & original programming. Unit of Sony Pictures Television.

CREATE TV
c/o American Public Television
55 Summer St
Boston, MA 02110
Phone: 617-338-4455
Fax: 617-338-5369
Web Site: http://www.createtv.com
Cynthia A. Fenneman, President & Chief Executive Officer, APT
David Fournier, Vice President, Finance & Administration, APT
Chris Funkhouser, Vice President, Exchange Programming & Multicast Services, APT
Jamie Haines, Vice President, Communications, APT
Type of service: Digital, over the air.
Began: January 9, 2006, nationwide, initally launched in 2004 on WGBH-TV Boston and WLIW New York.

Means of Support: Donations to PBS.
Distribution method: Available over the air on digital sub-channels & to digital cable subscribers.
Ownership: American Public Television.

CREATV SAN JOSE
255 W Julian St
Ste 100
San Jose, CA 95110-2406
Phone: 408-295-8815
Fax: 408-295-8810
E-mail: suzanne@creatvsj.org
Web Site: http://www.creatvsj.org
Suzanne St John-Crane, Executive Director
Justin Cowgill, Chief Technology Officer
Luis Costa, Programming Director
Pam Kelly, Membership & Marketing Director
Alison Stewart, Operations Manager
Burton McKerchie, Engineer 1
Type of service: Regional basic.
Operating areas: California.
Programming: Inspires, educates and connects San Jose communities, using media to foster civic engagement.
Began: January 1, 2008.
Means of Support: Donations.
Distribution method: Available to Comcast Cable system subscribers.
Scrambled signal: Yes.
Ownership: Member-based, non-profit community media center that manages San Jose's public and education channels.

CRIME & INVESTIGATION NETWORK — See A&E.
235 E 45th St
New York, NY 10017
212-210-1400
Phone: 212-692-9269
Web Site: http://www.crimeandinvestigationnetwork.com
Type of service: Basic, HD.
Operating hours/week: 168.
Programming: Crime dramas & documentaries.
Began: 2005.
Distribution method: Available to cable, IPTV & satellite subscribers.
Scrambled signal: Yes.
Ownership: A+E Networks, a joint venture between Hearst Corp. (50%) & The Walt Disney Co. (50%).

CRIME CHANNEL
78206 Varner Rd
Ste D131
Palm Desert, CA 92211
Phone: 760-360-6151
Fax: 760-360-3258
E-mail: crimechannel@dc.rr.com
Web Site: http://www.thecrimechannel.com
Arnie Frank, President
Dan Blackburn, Senior Executive Vice President, Production
Wylie Drummond, Senior Executive Vice President, Sales & Marketing
Bill Immerman, Senior Executive Vice President, Legal & Business Affairs
Gary Miller, Senior Executive Vice President, Sales & Marketing
Type of service: Basic.

Satellites: Satcom C-1, transponder 11.
Operating hours/week: 2. Plans 168.
Uplink: Network I.
Programming: Crime-related programs.
Began: July 4, 1993.
Means of Support: Advertising.
Total subscribers: 16,000,000.
Distribution method: Available to cable & satellite subscribers.
Scrambled signal: Yes.
Ownership: Arnold Frank.

CROSSINGS TV
2030 W El Camino Blvd
Ste 263
Sacramento, CA 95833-1868
Phones: 916-226-1257; 888-901-5288
Fax: 888-878-8936
E-mail: info@crossingstv.com
Web Site: http://www.crossingstv.com
Daniel Sakaya, Marketing & Events
Paul Fisher, Sales & Advertising/Production
Lee Hudson, Programming & Master Control
Type of service: Basic, over the air.
Operating areas: Available in California, New Jersey, New York & Washington.
Programming: Provides multicultural programming for Chinese, Filipino, Hmong, Russian, South Asian & Vietnamese audiences.
Began: October 1, 2005.
Means of Support: Advertising.
Total subscribers: 2,250,000.
Distribution method: Available over the air on digital sub-channel of KBTV-CD in Sacramento, CA; on Comcast Cable serving Central Valley & San Francisco, CA; Chicago, IL & Seattle, WA and Time Warner Cable in New Jersey & York City, NY.
Scrambled signal: Yes.
Ownership: Crossings TV.

CSN+ — See regional Comcast SportsNet listings.

C-SPAN
400 N Capitol St NW
Ste 650
Washington, DC 20001
Phone: 202-737-3220
Fax: 202-737-3323
E-mail: pkiley@c-span.org
Web Site: http://www.c-span.org
Brian P. Lamb, Executive Chairman
Robert Kennedy, Co-Chief Executive Officer
Susan Swain, Co-Chief Executive Officer
Kathy Cahill, Vice President, Programming Operations
Bruce D. Collins, Vice President & General Counsel
Marty Dominguez, Vice President, Marketing
Roxane Kerr, Vice President, Corporate Engineering
Peter Kiley, Vice President, Affiliate Relations
Terry Murphy, Vice President, Programming
Richard Weinstein, Vice President, Digital Media
Type of service: Basic, HD, streaming.
Satellites: AMC 11, transponder 7.
Operating hours/week: 168.
Uplink: Fairfax County, VA.

Pay TV & Satellite Services

CABLE & TV STATION COVERAGE
Atlas 2017
The perfect companion to the Television & Cable Factbook
To order call 800-771-9202 or visit www.warren-news.com

Programming: Cable industry's cooperative for 24-hour public affairs programming including live coverage of U.S. House of Representatives, House & Senate hearings, press conferences, conventions and other public events from around the nation.
Began: March 19, 1979.
Means of Support: System fee per month. C-SPAN 2 & 3, free with C-SPAN.
Total subscribers: 100,000,000.
Distribution method: Available to cable, IPTV & satellite subscribers. Streaming available online through select providers.
Scrambled signal: Yes.
Ownership: Cable industry cooperative.

C-SPAN 2 — See C-SPAN.
Type of service: Basic, HD.
Operating hours/week: 168.
Began: June 2, 1986.
Scrambled signal: Yes.

C-SPAN 3 — See C-SPAN.
Type of service: Basic, HD.
Operating hours/week: 168.
Began: January 22, 2001, replacing C-SPAN Extra. C-SPAN 3 HD began June 28, 2010.
Scrambled signal: Yes.

C-SPAN EXTRA — See C-SPAN 3.

C13 DE CHILE — See Canal 13 de Chile.

CTC INTERNATIONAL
Monarch Business Center
31A Leningradsky Prospekt, Bld. 1
Moscow 125284
Russia
Phone: 7-495-797-4100
E-mail: info@ctcmedia.ru
Web Site: http://www.ctcmedia.ru
Anton Kudryashov, Chief Executive Officer
Viacheslav Murugov, Chief Content Officer & General Director
Boris Podolsky, Chief Financial Officer
Viacheslav Sinadski, Chief Strategy Officer
Maria Starovoyt, Head of PR & Press Secretary
Anna Zvereva, PR Manager
Type of service: Pay.
Operating hours/week: 168.
Operating areas: Available nationwide via satellite, New York City via cable.
Programming: Russian language family entertainment channel.
Began: December 21, 2009, in the U.S.
Means of Support: Advertising & subscriber fees.
Total subscribers: 175,000.
Distribution method: Available to DISH Network & Time Warner subscribers.
Scrambled signal: Yes.
Ownership: CTC Media Inc.

CTI-ZHONG TIAN
c/o International Media Distribution
4100 E Dry Creek Rd
Centennial, CO 80122
Phone: 303-712-5400
Fax: 303-712-5401
E-mail: service@ctitv.com.tw
Web Site: http://www.ctitv.com.tw
Type of service: Pay.
Operating hours/week: 168.
Programming: Mandarin Chinese-language news, variety, sports, dramas, entertainment & informational programming.
Began: August 1, 1999.
Distribution method: Available to cable & satellite subscribers.
Scrambled signal: Yes.
Ownership: CTI-ZTC.

CT-N
Capitol Place, 21 Oak St
Ste 605
Hartford, CT 06106
Phones: 860-246-1553; 860-240-8317
Fax: 860-246-1547
E-mail: paul.giguere@cga.ct.gov
Web Site: http://www.ct-n.com
Paul Giguere, Chief Executive Officer
William Bevacqua, Vice President, Administration & Communications
Dominique Avery, Programming Director
Thomas Paquette, Information Technology Director
Joseph Patriss, Engineering & Production Director
Paul Skaff, Education & Media Services Director
Mark Tyszka, Human Resources Director
Kirsten Faulkner, Office Manager
Type of service: Basic, digital & video on demand.
Operating hours/week: 168.
Programming: Gavel to gavel coverage of all three branches of Connecticut state government & other statewide public policy events.
Began: January 1, 1999.
Distribution method: Available to cable systems.

CTNI — See Christian Television Network.

CUBAMAX TV
1149 SW 27th Ave
#101
Miami, FL 33135
Phone: 305-575-1970
Amarilys Nunez, Director of Marketing
Type of service: Available to DISH Network & Sling Latino subscribers.
Operating hours/week: 168.
Operating areas: Nationwide.
Programming: General entertainment channel featuring shows, movies and cultural content from Cuba.
Began: June 15, 2016.
Means of Support: Advertising.
Distribution method: Available to DishLATINO and cable system subscribers.
Scrambled signal: Yes.
Ownership: Joint venture of Cuban Institute of Radio and Television, DISH Network & RTV Comercial.

CUBANETWORK
1040 N Las Palmas Ave
Bldg 25
Hollywood, CA 90038
Phone: 323-934-8283
E-mail: info@cubanetwork.com; contact@cubanetwork.com
Web Site: http://www.cubanetwork.com
Keith Bass, Founder & Chief Executive Officer
Liliana Samata, Chief Operating Officer
Marlene Braga, Head of Programming & Production
Starrett Berry, Senior Strategic Advisor
Type of service: Basic.
Operating areas: Available nationwide.
Programming: Delivers original Cuban programming in both English and Spanish.
Began: April 1, 2016.
Means of Support: Advertising.
Distribution method: Available over the air. Streaming available online & mobile.
Scrambled signal: Yes.
Ownership: Caribbean Broadcasting Network.

CUBAPLAY TELEVISION
c/o Olympusat Inc.
560 Village Blvd, Ste 250
West Palm Beach, FL 33409
Phone: 561-684-5657
Fax: 561-684-9690
E-mail: info@olympusat.com
Web Site: http://www.olympusat.com/networks/cubaplay
Tom Mohler, Chief Executive Officer, Olympusat Holdings Inc.
Arturo Chavez, Senior Vice President, Distribution
Juan Bruno, New Programming Acquisitions & Contracts Director
John Baghdassarian, Head of Affiliate Sales, U.S.
Type of service: Pay.
Programming: 100% original Cuban-produced television programming, never before seen in the U.S., including sports, movies, documentaries, children's programming, telenovelas & comedy.
Began: 2011.
Distribution method: Available to Choice Cable, Liberty Cable & Optimum subscribers.
Scrambled signal: Yes.
Ownership: Olympusat.

CW11 NEW YORK — See PIX11.

CW PLUS
411 N Hollywood Way
Bldg 2R
Burbank, CA 91505
Phone: 818-977-8480
Fax: 818-977-7949
Web Site: http://www.cwtv.com
Russell Myerson, Executive Vice President & General Manager
Steve Dornier, Senior Vice President, On-Air Promotion & Marketing
Merry Ewing, Senior Vice President, Affiliate Advertising Sales
Tad Vogels, Senior Vice President, Finance, Traffic & Administration
Type of service: Basic, over the air.
Operating hours/week: 168.
Programming: Shows from the CW network as well syndicated & brokered programs.
Began: September 20, 2006.
Distribution method: Available over the air on digital sub-channels & to cable & satellite subscribers.
Scrambled signal: Yes.
Ownership: A joint venture between CBS (50%) & Warner Brothers Entertainment (50%).

CYCLONES.TV
1800 S Fourth St
Jacobson Athletic Bldg
Ames, IA 50011-1140
Phones: 515-294-9240; 515-294-3662
E-mail: cytv@iastate.edu
Web Site: http://www.cyclones.com
Tom Kroeschell, Programming Director
Tyler Rutherford, Digital Media Director
John Walters, Broadcasting Director
Danielle Varley, Assistant Digital Media Director
Type of service: Expanded, HD, streaming.
Operating areas: Iowa.
Programming: Iowa State Cyclones women's basketball, volleyball, wrestling, soccer, gymnastics & softball, plus one football game & approximately 5-10 men's basketball games. In addition, carries various sports shows, live media conferences & archived classic replays.
Began: December 9, 2012.
Total subscribers: 500,000.
Distribution method: Available to Mediacom subscribers in Iowa. Streaming available online.
Scrambled signal: Yes.
Ownership: Iowa State University.

CYR TV (CHINESE YELLOW RIVER TV)
Shanxi Province
China
Programming: Offers programs in Mandarin Chinese which informs and teaches the viewer about Chinese culture.
Began: 1991 in China. June 1, 2004 in U.S.
Distribution method: Available to DISH & KyLinTV subscribers.
Scrambled signal: Yes.

DAMAS TV
c/o Olympusat Inc.
560 Village Blvd, Ste 250
West Palm Beach, FL 33409
Phone: 561-684-5657
Fax: 561-684-9690
E-mail: info@olympusat.com
Web Site: http://www.olympusat.com/networks/damas
Tom Mohler, Chief Executive Officer, Olympusat Holdings Inc.
Arturo Chavez, Senior Vice President, Hispanic Networks
Juan Bruno, New Programming Acquisitions & Contracts Director
John Baghdassarian, Head of Affiliate Sales, U.S.
Type of service: Pay.
Operating areas: Available in Mediacom's service area.
Programming: Spanish-language entertainment programming and telenovelas for the Latina audience.
Began: November 26, 2012.
Means of Support: Advertising.
Distribution method: Available to Mediacom subscribers.
Scrambled signal: Yes.
Ownership: Olympusat.

DARE TO DREAM NETWORK — See 3ABN.
PO Box 220
West Frankfort, IL
Phone: 618-627-4651
E-mail: mail@3abn.org
Web Site: http://d2dnetwork.tv
Yvonne Lewis, General Manager
Programming: Socially relevant programming to meet the needs of African Americans & other minorities who live in urban areas. Programming topics range from parenting to nutrition, health lifestyles to relationships, crime prevention to money management.

Pay TV & Satellite Services

Began: December 1, 2010, online. Began satellite broadcast January 1, 2012.
Scrambled signal: Yes.
Ownership: Three Angels Broadcasting Network Inc.

DAYSTAR TV NETWORK
PO Box 612066
Dallas, TX 75261-2066
Phone: 817-571-1229
Fax: 817-571-7458
E-mail: comments@daystar.com
Web Site: http://www.daystar.com
Marcus Lamb, Founder
Joni Lamb, Founder
Janice Smith, Vice President, Programming
Steve Wilhite, Regional Director, Affiliate Relations
Type of service: Basic, streaming, video on demand.
Operating hours/week: 168.
Programming: Contemporary, interdenominational, multi-cultural blend of Christian ministry & family-friendly programming including talk-shows, national ministries, children's programming & faith-based original series.
Began: December 31, 1997.
Total subscribers: 60,000,000.
Distribution method: Available to AT&T U-verse, Verizon FiOS, DISH Network, DirecTV, Glorystar & Sky Angel subscribers. Streaming & video on demand available online, on select streaming devices, mobile & through app.
Scrambled signal: Yes.

DECADES
c/o Weigel Broadcasting
26 N Halstead
Chicago, IL 60661
Phone: 312-705-2600
Web Site: http://www.decades.com
Peter Dunn, President, CBS Television Stations
Norman H. Shapiro, President, Weigle Broadcasting
Type of service: Basic, over the air.
Operating areas: Nationwide.
Programming: Iconic programming from the CBS library, including news and special events from the past.
Began: May 25, 2015, replacing CBSNY+.
Means of Support: Advertising.
Distribution method: Available over the air on digital sub-channels & to cable & IPTV subscribers.
Scrambled signal: Yes.
Ownership: A joint venture between CBS Television Station Group & Weigel Broadcasting.

DELAHOYATV
12605 Northwest 115th Ave
Ste 101
Medley, FL 33178
Web Site: http://www.delahoyatv.com
Jose Alberto Gomez, Executive Chairman
Oscar De La Hoya, Chairman
Victor Hugo Montero, Chief Executive Officer & General Manager
Operating areas: Nationwide.
Programming: Combat sports, news, analysis, special coverage and discussion of the major events in the world of boxing, MMA, wrestling, kickboxing, plus others.
Began: April 1, 2015.
Means of Support: Advertising.
Distribution method: Available to cable subscribers.
Scrambled signal: Yes.
Ownership: Oscar de la Hoya, Jose Alberto Gomez & Victor Hugo Montero.

DE PELICULA — See Univision.
c/o Univision Communications Inc.
605 Third Ave, 12th Fl
New York, NY 10158
Phone: 212-455-5200
Web Site: http://www.televisanetworks.tv; http://corporate.univision.com
Satellites: AMC 10, transponder 4.
Operating hours/week: 168.
Operating areas: Available nationwide.
Programming: Spanish-language movies including drama, comedy, westerns & musicals.
Began: May 1, 2003.
Total subscribers: 2,100,000.
Distribution method: Available to cable, IPTV & satellite subscribers.
Scrambled signal: Yes.
Ownership: Televisa Networks. Univision Communications Inc. has an exclusive contract for this service.

DE PELICULA CLASICO — See De Pelicula.
Satellites: AMC 10, transponder 4.
Operating hours/week: 168.
Operating areas: Available nationwide.
Programming: Spanish-language classic movies from the 40s & 50s.
Began: May 1, 2003.
Total subscribers: 2,000,000.
Distribution method: Available to cable, IPTV & satellite subscribers.
Scrambled signal: Yes.
Ownership: Televisa Networks. Univision Communications Inc. has an exclusive contract for this service.

DESTINATION AMERICA — See Discovery Channel.
c/o Discovery Communications
One Discovery Pl
Silver Spring, MD 20910-3354
Phone: 240-662-2000
Web Site: http://www.destinationamerica.com
Henry S. Schleiff, Group President, American Heroes Channels, Destination America & Investigation Discovery
Jane Latman, General Manager
Kevin Bennett, Executive Vice President, Programming
Sara Kozak, Senior Vice President, Production, American Heroes Channels, Destination America & Investigation Discovery
Doug Seybert, Senior Vice President, Marketing, American Heroes Channels, Destination America & Investigation Discovery
Sara Helman, Vice President, Development & Production
Caroline Perez, Vice President, Production & Development
Type of service: Digital, HD.
Programming: Features travel, food, adventure, home & natural history, with original content exploring the USA.
Began: 1998 as Discovery Home & Leisure. Rebranded as Discovery Home March 2004, Planet Green June 2008 & Destination America May 2012.
Total subscribers: 59,000,000.
Distribution method: Available to cable, IPTV & satellite subscribers.
Scrambled signal: Yes.
Ownership: Discovery Communications Inc.

DEUTSCHE WELLE TV
Washington Bureau
2000 M St, Ste 335
Washington, DC 20036
Phone: 202-785-5730
Fax: 202-785-5735
E-mail: news@dwelle-usa.com
Web Site: http://www.dw-world.de/english
Rudiger Lentz, Information Contact
Udo Bauer, Information Contact
Larz LaComa, Chief Engineer
Satellites: GE-1, transponder 22; Intelsat K, transponder 1; PAS-5 (digital), transponder 15 C.
Operating hours/week: 168.
Uplink: Berlin, Germany.
Programming: Current affairs television in English, German & Spanish.
Began: September 1, 1991.
Distribution method: Available to cable & satellite subscribers.
Scrambled signal: Yes.
Ownership: DW-TV.

DIRECTV CINEMA
2230 E Imperial Hwy
El Segundo, CA 90245
Phone: 310-964-5000
Web Site: http://www.directv.com/technology/directv_cinema
Dan York, Chief Content Officer
Paul Guyardo, Executive Vice President, Chief Revenue & Marketing Officer
Tony Goncalves, Senior Vice President, Digital Entertainment Products
Keith Kazerman, Senior Vice President, Ad Sales
Steven Roberts, Senior Vice President, New Media & Business Development
Robert Thun, Senior Vice President, Content & Programming
Type of service: Pay, streaming.
Operating areas: Nationwide.
Programming: Movies.
Began: July 1, 2010.
Means of Support: Subscriber fees.
Distribution method: Available to DirecTV subscribers. Streaming available online & mobile.
Scrambled signal: Yes.
Ownership: DIRECTV LLC, a subsidiary of AT&T.

DISCOVERY CHANNEL
One Discovery Pl
Silver Spring, MD 20910-3354
Phone: 240-662-2000
E-mail: viewer_relations@discovery.com
Web Site: http://dsc.discovery.com
DISCOVERY COMMUNICATIONS:, .
David Zaslav, President & Chief Executive Officer, Discovery Communications
Ben Price, President, Advertising Sales, Discovery Communications
Marc Graboff, President, Global Business & Legal Affairs, Production Management & Studios, Discovery Communications
Eric Phillips, President, Domestic Distribution, Discovery Communications
Adria Alpert-Romm, Chief Human Resources & Global Diversity Officer, Discovery Communications
Bruce Campbell, Chief Development, Distribution & Legal Officer, Discovery Communications
Paul Guyardo, Chief Commercial Officer, Discovery Communications
John Honeycutt, Chief Technology Officer, Discovery Communications
David Leavy, Chief Corporate Operations & Communications Officer, Discovery Communications
Simon Robinson, Chief Operating Officer, National Ad Sales, Discovery Communications
Doug Coblens, Executive Vice President, Business Strategy & New Media, Discovery Communications
Todd Davis, Executive Vice President, Tax & Treasury Worldwide, Discovery Communications
Charlie Foley, Executive Vice President, Original Content Group, Discovery Communications
Michael Lang, Executive Vice President, International Corporate Development & Digital
Karen Leever, Executive Vice President & General Manager, Digital Media, Discovery Communications
Glenn Oakley, Executive Vice President, Media Technology, Production & Operations, Discovery Communications
Gabe Vehovsky, Executive Vice President, Digital Strategy & Emerging Businesses, Discovery Communications
Jocelyn Egan, Senior Vice President, Discovery Solutions, Discovery Communications
Michelina Gauthier, Senior Vice President, Talent Business & Legal Affairs, Discovery Communications
Rebecca Glashow, Senior Vice President, Digital Distribution & Partnerships, Discovery Communications
Maria Kennedy, Senior Vice President, Advertising Sales, Direct Response, Discovery Communications
Jim McGrath, Senior Vice President, Global Media Engineering, Discovery Communications
Courtney Menzel, Senior Vice President, Domestic Distribution, Discovery Communications
Elizabeth Newell, Senior Vice President, Global Corporate Legal, Discovery Communications
Savalle Sims, Senior Vice President, Litigation & Intellectual Property, Discovery Communications
Robert Voltaggio, Senior Vice President, National Ad Sales & Planning, Discovery Communications
DISCOVERY CHANNEL:, .
Rich Ross, President, Animal Planet, Discovery Channel & Science Channel
Dolores Gavin, Executive Vice President, Development & Production, East, Discovery Channel
Laurie Goldberg, Executive Vice President, Discovery Channel, Science & Velocity
Paul Pastor, Executive Vice President, Network Strategy, Revenue & Operations
Marina Anglim, Senior Vice President, Marketing, Discovery & Science Channels
Camilla Carpenter, Senior Vice President, Strategy & Network Operations, Discovery & TLC Networks
Kelly Kane, Senior Vice President, Partner Marketing & National Accounts
Steve McGowan, Senior Vice President, Research, Discovery Channel

Pay TV & Satellite Services

Stephen Reverend, Senior Vice President, Development & Production for Specials & Events, Discovery Channel
Lara Richardson, Senior Vice President, Marketing-Creative, Discovery Channel
DISCOVERY INTERNATIONAL:, .
Doug Baker, Executive Vice President & Chief Financial Officer, Discovery Networks International
Elizabeth Hillman, Senior Vice President, International Communications, Discovery Networks International

Sales Offices:
ATLANTA: One Capital City Pl, 3350 Peachtree Rd NE, Ste 1630, Atlanta, GA 30326. Fred Norris, Vice President, Advertising Sales, Southeast Region, Discovery Communications.

CHARLOTTE: 4201 Congress St, Ste 425, Charlotte, NC 28209. Phone: 704-557-2400. Bill Goodwyn, President, Strategic Distribution, Discovery Communications & Chief Executive Officer, Discovery Education.

CHICAGO: 401 N Michigan Ave, Ste 3000, Chicago, IL 60611. Phone: 312-946-0909. Scott Kohn, Senior Vice President, Advertising Sales, Midwest Region, Discovery Communications.

LOS ANGELES: 10100 Santa Monica Blvd, Ste 1500, Los Angeles, CA 90067. Phone: 310-551-1611. Fax: 310-551-1684. Denise Contis, Executive Vice President, Production & Development, Discovery Channel; John Hoffman, Executive Vice President, Documentaries & Specials; Matthew Kelly, Vice President, Development & Production; Michael Sorensen, Vice President, Development & Production.

NEW YORK: 850 Third Ave, New York, NY 10022-7225. Phone: 212-548-5555. Scott Felenstein, Executive Vice President, Advertising Sales, American Heroes, Destination America, Discovery Channel, Science & Velocity; Evan Sternschein, Executive Vice President, Advertising Sales, Discovery Communications; Suzanne McDonnell, Senior Vice President, Sales Strategy & Client Solutions, Discovery Communications.

TROY: 101 W Big Beaver Rd, Ste 405, Troy, MI 48084-4169. Phone: 248-764-4400. Joe Paglino, Vice President, Advertising Sales, Midwest Region, Discovery Communications.

International Headquarters:
MIAMI: Latin America/U.S. Hispanic HQ, 6505 Blue Lagoon Dr, Ste 190, Miami, FL 33126. Phone: 786-273-4700. Enrique Martinez, President & Managing Director, Discovery Networks Latin America & U.S. Hispanic and Canada; Carolina Lightcap, Head of Content, Discovery Networks Latin America & U.S. Hispanic Group; Ivan Bargueiras, Executive Vice President, Advertising Sales, Discovery Networks Latin America/U.S. Hispanic; Allan Navarette, Executive Vice President, Discovery Networks Latin America & General Manager, Discovery en Espanol and Discovery Familia; Angela Recio Sondon, Vice President, Programming Strategy & Implementation, Discovery Networks Latin America & U.S. Hispanic.

POLAND: Central & Eastern Europe, Middle East & Africa HQ, 59 Zlota St, Zlota Tarasay, Lumen Bldg, Warsaw 00-120, Poland. Kasia Kieli, President & Managing Director, Discovery Networks CEEMEA.

SINGAPORE: Asia-Pacific HQ, 21 Media Cir, 08-01 138562, Singapore. Phone: 65-6510-7500. Web site: http://www.discoverychannelasia.com. Arjan Hoekstra, President & Managing Director, Discovery Networks Asia-Pacific.

UNITED KINGDOM: Western Europe HQ, Discovery House, Chiswick Park Bldg 2, 566 Chiswick High Rd, London W4 5YB, United Kingdom. Phone: 44-208-811-3000. J. B. Perrette, President, Discovery Networks International; Dee Forbes, President & Managing Director, Discovery Networks Western Europe; Marjorie Kaplan, President, Content, Discovery Networks International; Jean-Thierry Augustin, President, Sports Strategy & Development, Discovery Networks International.

Discovery Channel Canada:
TORONTO: c/o Bell Media, 50 Eglinton Ave E, Toronto, ON M4P 1A6, Canada. Phone: 416-924-6664. E-Mail: comments@discovery.ca. Web site: http://http://www.discovery.ca.
Type of service: Basic, HD.
Satellites: GE Satcom C-4, transponder 21 (east coast); Galaxy V, transponder 12 (west coast).
Operating hours/week: 168.
Operating areas: Nationwide.
Uplink: Stamford, CT.
Programming: Non-fiction entertainment covering nature, science & technology, history, adventure & world cultures.
Began: June 17, 1985, Discovery Channel HD began in 2005.
Means of Support: Advertising & subscriber fees.
Total subscribers: 98,000,000 (U.S. subscribers. 8,000,000 Canadian subscribers. 271,000,000 international subscribers.).
Distribution method: Available to cable, IPTV & satellite subscribers.
Scrambled signal: Yes. Equipment: VideoCipher II; VideoCipher II Plus.
Ownership: Discovery Communications Inc., owned by Liberty Media (66%), Advance/Newhouse (31%) & John Hendricks (1%).

DISCOVERY EN ESPANOL — See Discovery Channel.
Programming: Spanish-language non-fiction entertainment covering nature, science & technology, history, adventure & world cultures.
Began: February 1, 1994.
Total subscribers: 6,476,000.
Scrambled signal: Yes.

DISCOVERY FAMILIA — See Discovery Channel.
Web Site: http://tv.discoveryfamilia.com
Satellites: AMC 11, transponder 22.
Programming: Spanish language children's programming; lifestyle, food, travel, health & parenting shows.
Began: August 1, 2007, when Discovery Kids en Espanol & Discovery Travel & Living (Viajar Y Vivir) merged.
Total subscribers: 4,000,000.
Distribution method: Available to cable, IPTV & satellite subscribers.
Scrambled signal: Yes.
Ownership: Discovery Communications Inc.

DISCOVERY FAMILY
2950 N Hollywood Way
Ste 100
Burbank, CA 91505
Phone: 818-531-3600
Fax: 818-531-3601
Web Site: http://www.daytime.discoveryfamilychannel.com

Margaret Loesch, President & Chief Executive Officer
Tom Cosgrove, General Manager
Dena Kaplan, Chief Marketing Officer
Dan Pimentel, Chief Financial & Operations Officer
Joanna Dodd Massey, Senior Vice President, Corporate Communications & Publicity
Lou Fazio, Senior Vice President, Scheduling, Acquisitions & Planning
Brooke Goldstein, Senior Vice President, Ad Sales
Joshua Meyer, Senior Vice President, Business & Legal Affairs
Nikki Reed, Senior Vice President, Programming & Development
Jordan Beck, Vice President, Creative Services & On-Air Promotions
Ted Biaselli, Vice President, Programming
Sarah Davies, Vice President, Production & Development
Greg Heanue, Vice President, Marketing & Promotions
Alden Mitchell Budill, Vice President, Domestic Distribution & Strategy
Michael Grover, Executive Director, Consumer & Affiliate Marketing
Cindy Slocki, Executive Director, Integrated Marketing Solutions
J. J. Kawan, Operations Director
Stan Lim, Design Director
Type of service: Basic.
Operating hours/week: 168.
Operating areas: Nationwide.
Programming: Animated and live-action original and acquired series and specials programmed by Hasbro during the day. Adventure, history, nature and science from Discovery's video library in the evening.
Began: October 7, 1996, as Discovery Kids. Rebranded as The Hub on October 10, 2010. The Hub HD began October 10, 2010. Rebranded as Hub Network in 2013. Rebranded Discovery Family October 13, 2014.
Means of Support: Advertising.
Total subscribers: 72,000,000.
Distribution method: Available to cable, IPTV & satellite subscribers.
Scrambled signal: Yes.
Ownership: A joint venture between Discovery Communications (60%) & Hasbro Inc. (40%). Discovery acquired majority interest September 2014.

DISCOVERY FIT & HEALTH — See Discovery Life Channel.

DISCOVERY HEALTH CHANNEL — See OWN: Oprah Winfrey Network

DISCOVERY HOME CHANNEL — See Destination America.

DISCOVERY KIDS CHANNEL — See Discovery Family.

DISCOVERY KIDS EN ESPANOL — See Discovery Familia.

DISCOVERY LIFE CHANNEL — See Discovery Channel.
Web Site: http://www.discoverylife.com
Howard Lee, General Manager
Programming: Includes forensic mysteries, medical stories, emergency room dramas, baby and pregnancy programming, parenting challenges, and stories of extreme life conditions plus premiere series and specials.
Began: January 1, 2003, as FitTV. Rebranded as Discovery Fit & Health February 1, 2011. Rebranded as Discovery Life Channel January 15, 2015.
Total subscribers: 48,000,000.
Distribution method: Available to cable, IPTV & satellite subscribers.
Scrambled signal: Yes.
Ownership: Discovery Communications Inc.

DISCOVERY TIMES CHANNEL — See Investigation Discovery.

DISCOVERY TRAVEL & LIVING (VIAJAR Y VIVIR) — See Discovery Familia.

DISNEY CHANNEL
500 S Buena Vista St
Burbank, CA 91521
Phone: 818-569-7500
E-mail: dlr.media.relations@disney.com
Web Site: http://www.disneychannel.com
THE WALT DISNEY CO.:, .
Robert A. Iger, Chairman & Chief Executive Officer, The Walt Disney Co.
Andy Bird, Chairman, Walt Disney International, The Walt Disney Co.
Kevin Mayer, Senior Executive Vice President & Chief Strategy Officer
Christine McCarthy, Senior Executive Vice President & Chief Financial Officer
Zenia Mucha, Executive Vice President & Chief Communications Officer, The Walt Disney Co.
DISNEY/ABC TELEVISION GROUP:, .
Ben Sherwood, Co-Chair, Disney Media Networks & President, Disney|ABC Television Group
Channing Dungey, President, ABC Entertainment Group
Gary Marsh, President & Chief Creative Officer, Disney Channels Worldwide
Ben Pyne, President, Global Distribution, Disney Media Networks
Albert Cheng, Executive Vice President & Chief Product Officer, Disney|ABC Television Group
Sean Cocchia, Executive Vice President, Business Operations & General Manager, Disney Channels Worldwide
Rita Ferro, Executive Vice President, Disney Media Sales & Marketing
Susette Hsiung, Executive Vice President, Production, Disney|ABC Cable Networks Group
Vince Roberts, Executive Vice President, Global Operations & Chief Technology Officer, Disney|ABC Television Group
Peter Seymour, Executive Vice President & Chief Financial Officer, Disney|ABC Television Group
Renu Thomas, Executive Vice President, Media Operations, Engineering & IT, Disney|ABC Television Group
Chris Brush, Senior Vice President, Affiliate Sales & Marketing, Disney & ESPN Media Networks
Eric Coleman, Senior Vice President, Original Series, Disney Television Animation
Paul DeBenedittis, Senior Vice President, Program Strategy, Disney Channels Worldwide
Richard Loomis, Senior Vice President & Chief Marketing Officer, Disney Channels Worldwide
Karen Miller, Vice President, Acquisitions & Co-Productions & Worldwide Programming Strategy, Disney Channels Worldwide
James Rollins, Vice President, Digital Video Distribution, Disney & ESPN Media Networks
DISNEY CHANNEL:, .
Adam Bonnett, Executive Vice President, Original Programming, Disney Channel
Jonas Agin, Vice President, Original Series, Disney Channel & Disney XD

Pay TV & Satellite Services

Jennilee Cummings, Vice President, Original Series, Disney Channel & Disney XD
Dana Green, Vice President, Communications, Disney Channel
Lauren Kisilevsky, Vice President, Original Movies, Disney Channel
Katharine Linke, Vice President, Multi-Platform Programming, Disney Channel
Naketha Mattocks, Vice President, Original Movies, Disney Channel Worldwide
Jesus Rodriguez, Vice President, Marketing & Creative
DISNEY CHANNEL INTERACTIVE:, .
James Pitaro, President, Disney Interactive
Mark L. Walker, Senior Vice President & General Manager, Disney Interactive

Affiliate Sales Offices:
ATLANTA: 3343 Peachtree Rd NE, East Tower, Ste 600, Atlanta, GA 30326. Phone: 404-262-1227.

CHICAGO: 401 N Michigan Ave, Ste 2000, Chicago, IL 60611. Phone: 312-595-7600.

DALLAS: 5080 Spectrum Dr, Ste 1210 West Tower, Dallas, TX 75248. Phone: 972-851-6000.

NEW YORK: 500 Park Ave, 7th Fl, New York, NY 10022. Phone: 212-735-5380.
Type of service: Basic, pay, HD, streaming, video on demand.
Satellites: Galaxy I-R, transponder 7 (west coast); Galaxy V, transponder 1 (east coast).
Operating hours/week: 168.
Operating areas: Available nationwide.
Uplink: Burbank, CA.
Programming: Family-oriented programming, including original features, series & specials; acquisitions & Disney library classics.
Began: April 18, 1983, Disney Channel HD began March 19, 2008.
Means of Support: System fees and advertsing revenue.
Total subscribers: 99,000,000.
Distribution method: Available to cable, IPTV & satellite subscribers; streaming available online & mobile through the WATCH Disney website or app (participating providers); video on demand (participating providers).
Scrambled signal: Yes. Equipment: VideoCipher II.
Ownership: Disney Channels Worldwide.

DISNEY FAMILY MOVIES — See Disney Channel.
Web Site: http://disneyfamilymovies.dadt.com
Type of service: Video on demand.
Programming: Disney movies & short animated shows.
Began: December 10, 2008.
Distribution method: Available to cable & IPTV subscribers (through participating providers).
Scrambled signal: Yes.

DISNEY JUNIOR — See Disney Channel.
Web Site: http://disneyjunior.com
Nancy Kanter, Executive Vice President, Original Programming & General Manager
Joe D'Ambrosia, Senior Vice President, Original Programming
Emily Hart, Vice President, Original Programming
Type of service: Basic, HD, streaming, video on demand.
Operating hours/week: 168.
Operating areas: Available nationwide.
Programming: Offers programming for children ages 2 to 7.

Began: February 14, 2011, as a segment on the Disney Channel. Launched as a separate channel March 23, 2012.
Total subscribers: 63,000,000.
Distribution method: Available to cable, IPTV & satellite subscribers; streaming available online & mobile through the WATCH Disney Junior website or app (participating providers); video on demand (participating providers).
Scrambled signal: Yes.
Ownership: Disney Channels Worldwide.

DISNEY XD — See Disney XD.
Web Site: http://disneyxd.disney.com
Marc Buhaj, Senior Vice President, Programming & General Manager
Jennilee Cummings, Vice President, Disney Channel & Disney XD Original Series
Type of service: Basic, HD, streaming, video on demand.
Satellites: Galaxy VII, transponder 17.
Operating hours/week: 168.
Operating areas: Nationwide.
Uplink: Burbank, CA.
Programming: Animated kids shows plus some live action programs and movies. Spanish-language available on Disney XD en Espanol.
Began: April 18, 1998, as Toon Disney. Rebranded Disney XD February 13, 2009.
Means of Support: Subscriber fees.
Total subscribers: 82,000,000.
Distribution method: Available to cable, IPTV & satellite subscribers; online & mobile through the WATCH Disney XD website or app (participating providers); video on demand (participating providers).
Scrambled signal: Yes.
Ownership: Disney Channels Worldwide.

DISNEY XD EN ESPANOL — See Disney Channel.
Programming: Spanish-language programming from Disney XD.

DIYA TV
1640 Alum Rock Ave
San Jose, CA 95116-2429
Phone: 408-929-2800
E-mail: hello@diyatvinc.com
Web Site: http://www.diyatvusa
Ravi Kapur, Chief Executive Officer
Operating areas: Available in California, Illinois & Texas.
Programming: South Asian programming, rooted in news and investigative journalism, featuring programming in Hindi, Punjabi and English.
Began: January 1, 2009.
Means of Support: Advertising.
Total subscribers: 6,000,000.
Distribution method: Available over the air on digital sub-channels.

DIY NETWORK
9721 Sherrill Blvd
Knoxville, TN 37932
Phone: 865-694-2700
Fax: 865-985-7786
Web Site: http://www.diynetwork.com
Chad Youngblood, General Manager & Senior Vice President
John Feld, Senior Vice President, Programming & Production
Freddy James, Senior Vice President, Network Integrated Programming
Shannon Jamieson Driver, Senior Vice President, Network Marketing & Creative Services
Steven Lerner, Senior Vice President, Programming & Production

Cheryl Middleton Jones, Senior Vice President, International Human Resources
Julie Taylor, Senior Vice President, Program Planning
Alaka Williams, Senior Vice President, Network Human Resources
Cindy Brown, Vice President, Program Planning
Lynne A. Davis, Vice President, National Broadcast Media & Talent Relations
Gabriel Gordon, Vice President, Network Research
Heather Jagels, Vice President, Creative Services
Robert Liuag, Vice President, Research
Rob McCall, Vice President, Ad Sales, Midwest Region
Peter Moore, Vice President, Creative Services
Kendra Rudder, Vice President, Media Strategies
Julie Taylor, Vice President, Program Planning
Kent Takano, Executive Producer, Branded Entertainment
Christy Melton, Programming Director
Dean Melton, Programming Director
Dale Roy Robinson, Programming Director
Danny Tepper, Programming Director
Brandii Toby-Leon, Press & Public Relations Director

Branch Office:
NEW YORK: 1180 Avenue of the Americas, New York, NY 10036. Phone: 212-549-4488. Fax: 212-398-9319.
Type of service: Digital basic, HD, streaming, video on demand.
Satellites: Galaxy I-R, transponder 20.
Operating hours/week: 168.
Operating areas: Nationwide.
Uplink: Knoxville.
Programming: Programming covers a broad range of categories, including home improvement and landscaping.
Began: September 30, 1999, DIY Network HD began May 2010.
Means of Support: Advertising & subscriber fees.
Total subscribers: 56,000,000.
Distribution method: Available to cable, IPTV & satellite subscribers.
Scrambled signal: Yes.
Ownership: Scripps Networks Interactive.

DMTV7
400 Robert D Ray Dr
Des Moines, IA 50309
Phone: 515-283-4795
E-mail: pio@dmgov.org
Web Site: https://www.dmgov.org
Type of service: Basic, streaming.
Operating areas: Des Moines.
Programming: Programming for Des Moines run by the city's Public Information Office.
Total subscribers: 125,000.
Distribution method: Available to Mediacom subscribers. Streaming available online.
Scrambled signal: Yes.

DMX MUSIC
1703 W 5th St
Ste 600
Austin, TX 78701

FULLY SEARCHABLE • CONTINUOUSLY UPDATED • DISCOUNT RATES FOR PRINT PURCHASERS
For more information call **800-771-9202** or visit **www.warren-news.com**

Phone: 512-380-8500
Fax: 512-380-8501
E-mail: info@dmx.com
Web Site: http://www.dmx.com
R. Steven Hicks, Chairman
Paul D. Stone, President
John D. Cullen, Chief Executive Officer
Tim Seaton, Chief Operating Officer
Kimberly K. Shipman, Chief Financial Officer

Branch Offices:
ATLANTA: 3170 Reps Miller Rd, Ste 100, Norcross, GA 30071. Phone: 770-225-2500. Fax: 770-246-3941.

BOSTON: 77 Fourth Ave, 5th Fl, Waltham, MA 02451. Phone: 508-393-2591. Fax: 508-393-5137.

CHICAGO: 620 Enterprise Dr, Oak Brook, IL 60523. Phones: 847-930-3100; 800-640-2673. Fax: 847-930-3140.

LOS ANGELES: 11400 W Olympic Blvd, Ste 1100, Los Angeles, CA 90064-1507. Phones: 310-444-1744; 800-345-5000. Fax: 310-444-1717. E-Mail: musicideas@dmxmusic.com.

MIAMI: Latin American Offices, 1550 Biscayne Blvd, Miami, FL 33132. Phone: 305-894-2576. Fax: 305-894-4919. E-Mail: gustavo.tonelli@dmx.com.

SEATTLE: 411 First Ave S, Ste 501, Seattle, WA 98104. Phones: 206-329-1400; 800-345-5000. Fax: 206-329-9952.

BRAZIL: Rua Funchal 375, Ed. Sao Paulo Trade Bldg, 1 Andar, Vila Olimpica, Sao Paulo, Jardim Paulista 01424-001, Brazil. Phone: 55-11-3457-0654. Fax: 55-11-3457-0653. E-Mail: gustavo.tonelli@dmxmusic.com.

CANADA: 7260 12th St SE, Ste 120, Calgary, AB T2H 2S5, Canada. Phones: 403-640-8525; 800-350-0369. Fax: 888-823-0369. E-Mail: dmx.canada@dmx.com.

SOUTH AFRICA: Ground Floor Sandown Mews E, 88 Stella St., Sandown, Johannesburg, South Africa. Phone: 27-11-780-3000. Fax: 27-11-780-3001. E-Mail: info@dmx.co.za. Web site: http://www.dmx.co.za.

UNITED KINGDOM: Forest Lodge, Westerham Rd, Keston, Kent BR2 6HE, United Kingdom. Phone: 44-1689-882200. Fax: 44-1689-882288. E-Mail: marketing@dmxmusic.co.uk.
Type of service: Audio.
Satellites: Telstar 402-R; HITS; TVN; TDRSS; Galaxy 605.
Operating hours/week: 168.
Programming: Digital music service offering more than 100 channels of different music formats with on-screen song, artist & album information.
Total subscribers: 11,000,000.
Distribution method: Available to cable & satellite subscribers.
Scrambled signal: Yes. Equipment: Scientific-Atlanta; Comstream.
Ownership: Mood Media Corp.

Pay TV & Satellite Services

DOCTOR TELEVISION CHANNEL (DRTV)
2607 Success Dr
Ste C
Odessa, FL 33556
Phone: 727-375-2500
Fax: 727-375-5509
Web Site: http://drtvchannel.com
Jim West, President
Lee Miller, Communications Director
Type of service: Basic, over the air.
Operating hours/week: 168.
Operating areas: Nationwide.
Programming: Medical news, entertainment and medicine, plus stories on promoting healthy lifestyles, proper eating and living longer.
Began: January 6, 2014.
Means of Support: Advertising.
Total subscribers: 30,000,000 (Represents number of possible subscribers from current affiliation agreements.).
Distribution method: Available over the air on digital sub-channels & to cable subscribers.
Scrambled signal: Yes.

DOCUMENTARY CHANNEL — See Pivot.

DOCU TVE — See TVE Internacional.
Avda. Television Radio 4
Pozuelo de Alarco (Madrid) 28223
Spain
Phone: 34-91-581-70-00
E-mail: rtve.dircom@rtve.es
Web Site: http://www.rtve.es/television/tve-internacional
Programming: Documentaries, biographies & travel shows.
Began: January 1, 1999, in the U.S.
Total subscribers: 700,000 (U.S. subscribers).
Ownership: RTVE.

DODGERS ON DEMAND
c/o Time Warner Cable
4344 Eagle Rock Blvd
Los Angeles, CA 90041-3211
Phone: 323-258-3252
Fax: 323-255-1901
Type of service: Video on demand.
Operating areas: California.
Programming: Archived & new programming including game highlights, charity events & press conferences.
Began: August 9, 2006.
Total subscribers: 1,900,000.
Distribution method: Available to cable subscribers.
Scrambled signal: Yes.
Ownership: A joint venture between Time Warner & Los Angeles Dodgers.

DOGTV
955 Benecia Ave
Sunnyvale, CA 94085
Phone: 408-962-1582
E-mail: support@dogtv.com
Web Site: http://dogtv.com
Yossi Uzrad, Executive Chairman, President & Co-Founder
Ron Levi, Co-Founder & Chief Content Officer
Gilad Neumann, Chief Executive Officer
Aviv Messa, Chief Operating Officer
Zuri Guterman, Chief Marketing Officer
Beke Lubeach, Brand Partnerships & Alliances Director
Professor Nicholas Dodman, Chief Scientist
Type of service: Pay, streaming.
Operating hours/week: 168.
Operating areas: Nationwide.
Programming: Scientifically developed programming to provide the right company for dogs when left alone.
Began: February 13, 2012.
Means of Support: Subscriber fees.
Distribution method: Available to DirecTV subscribers. Streaming available online by subscription.
Scrambled signal: Yes.
Ownership: Jasmine TV, a subsidiary Jasmine International.

DOLPHINS TELEVISION NETWORK
347 Don Shula Dr
Miami Gardens, FL 33056
Phone: 305-943-8000
Web Site: http://www.miamidolphins.com/esp/news
Jim Rushton, Senior Vice President, Integrated Media & Corporate Partnerships
Bob Lynch, Vice President, Integrated Media Sales
Wayne Partello, Senior Director, Content & Creative
Type of service: Basic.
Operating areas: Southeast, southwest & central Florida.
Programming: Detailed and expanded coverage of Miami Dolphins football. Includes expanded preseason coverage plus pre- and post- game analysis.
Began: August 13, 2010.
Means of Support: Advertising.
Distribution method: Available to cable subscribers.
Scrambled signal: Yes.
Ownership: Miami Dolphins.

DOM KINO
19 Akademika Korolyova St
Moscow 127427
Russian Federation
Phones: 7-495-617-55-88; 7-495-617-51-75
Fax: 7-495-617-51-14
E-mail: info@1tvrus.com
Web Site: http://eng.1tvrus.com/domkino
Nikolay Dubovoy, Director General
Type of service: Premium.
Operating hours/week: 168.
Operating areas: Available in New Jersey & New York on cable & nationwide on DirecTV.
Programming: Russian movies.
Began: January 1, 2005.
Means of Support: Advertising & subscriber fees.
Total subscribers: 20,000,000 (subscribers worldwide.).
Distribution method: Available to DirecTV customers & Time Warner Cable system subscribers.
Scrambled signal: Yes.
Ownership: Channel One. National Media Group, minority interest.

DOMINICAN VIEW — See ULTRA HD-Plex.
Av Luperon 46
Distrito Nacional
Santo Domingo AP 3133
Dominican Republic
Phone: 809-531-3333
Fax: 809-473-6666
E-mail: inf@dominican-view.com
Web Site: http://www.dominican-view.com
Type of service: Pay, HD.
Operating areas: Available nationwide.
Programming: News, movies and shows from the Dominican Republic.
Means of Support: Subscriber fees.
Distribution method: Available to cable, IPTV & satellite subscribers.
Scrambled signal: Yes.
Ownership: Super Canal Group. Distributed in U.S. by Olympusat.

DOMINION SKY ANGEL — See Angel One.

DRAGONTV
c/o SMG
298 Weihai Rd
Shanghai 200041
China
Phone: 86-21-62565899
E-mail: support@dragontv.net
Web Site: http://www.dragontv.cn
Operating hours/week: 168.
Programming: News & entertainment.
Began: October 1998 as Shanghai Metropolitan TV. Rebranded October 29, 2003.
Distribution method: Available to satellite subscribers.
Scrambled signal: Yes.
Ownership: Shanghai Media Group.

DRIVERTV
435 Hudson St, 6th Fl
New York, NY 10014
Phone: 212-462-1630
E-mail: info@drivertv.com
Web Site: http://www.drivertv.com
Jan Renner, Founder & Chief Executive Officer
Adam Weiner, Chief Operating Officer
Type of service: Video on demand, broadband.
Programming: Research & comparison shopping for automobiles by brand, category or budget.
Began: November 1, 2005.
Total subscribers: 20,000,000.
Distribution method: Available to cable subscribers.
Scrambled signal: Yes.
Ownership: A joint venture between Radical Media & NBCUniversal LLC (minority interest, 6.5%).

DUBAI TV
PO Box 835
Dubai
United Arab Emirates
Phone: 971-4-336-9999
Fax: 971-4-336-0060
E-mail: info@dmi.ae
Web Site: http://www.dcn.ae/dubaitv
Programming: Arabic-language programming.
Began: June 1, 2004, replacing Emirates Dubai Television.
Distribution method: Available to satellite subscribers.
Scrambled signal: Yes.
Ownership: Dubai Media Inc.

E!
5750 Wilshire Blvd
Los Angeles, CA 90036-3709
Phone: 323-954-2400
Fax: 323-954-2660
Web Site: http://www.eonline.com
Frances Berwick, President, Lifestyle Network Group, NBCUniversal Cable Entertainment
Adam Stotsky, President
Donald C. Storm II, Chief Financial Officer, E! & Esquire Network
Cyndi McClellan, President, Network Strategy & E! News
Duccio Donati, Executive Vice President, E! & Esquire Network
Sheila Johnson, Executive Vice President, Business & Legal Affairs & General Counsel
John Najarian, Executive Vice President, News & Digital
David O'Connell, Executive Vice President, Production Management & Operations, Lifestyle Networks Group
Jeff Olde, Executive Vice President, Program Development
Gerald Abrahamian, Senior Vice President, Product, Technology & Operations, News & Digital
Blythe Asher, Senior Vice President, Talent Development & Casting
Damla Dogan, Senior Vice President, Programming & Development
Sarah Goldstein, Senior Vice President, Media Relations & Corporate Communications
Bryce Kristensen, Senior Vice President, Social & Interactive Experiences
Brent Mitchell, Senior Vice President, Consumer Marketing
Meeri Park Cunniff, Senior Vice President, Program Strategy & Acquisitions
Noah Pollack, Senior Vice President, Programming & Development
Romina Rosado, Senior Vice President, News & Digital Content
Edward Zarcoff, Senior Vice President, Digital Programming & Production
Leela Pon, Vice President, Programming & Development
Bryce Kristensen, Vice President, Social & Interactive Experiences

Ad Sales Office:
NEW YORK: 1221 Ave of the Americas, New York, NY 10020.

Branch Offices:
HARTFORD: 10 Columbus Blvd, 8th Floor, Hartford, CT 06106.
Type of service: Basic, HD, streaming, video on demand.
Satellites: AMC10, transponder C6; AMC11, transponder C8.
Operating hours/week: 168.
Operating areas: Nationwide.
Programming: Entertainment news, reality television & feature films.
Began: July 1987 as The Movietime Network. Rebranded to E! Entertainment Television June 1, 1990 following a management change. E! Entertainment HD began December 8, 2008. Rebranded as E! in July 2012.
Means of Support: Advertising, affiliate sales & international sales.
Total subscribers: 96,000,000.
Distribution method: Available to cable, IPTV & satellite subscribers. Streaming available through app. Video on demand available through participating providers.
Scrambled signal: Yes.
Ownership: NBCUniversal Cable Entertainment, a division of NBCUniversal LLC.

EBRU TV
300 Franklin Sq Dr
Somerset, NJ 08873
Phone: 732-560-0800
Fax: 732-560-0801
E-mail: jon@ebru.tv
Web Site: http://www.ebru.tv
Adem Kalac, President & Chief Executive Officer
Jon Omural, Vice President, Business Development & Human Resources
Type of service: Basic.
Satellites: Galaxy 25.
Operating hours/week: 168.
Operating areas: Nationwide.
Programming: Family oriented lifestyle and culture programming.
Began: November 1, 2006.
Distribution method: Available to cable subscribers.

Pay TV & Satellite Services

Scrambled signal: Yes.
Ownership: Samanyolu Broadcasting Co., majority interest.

ECOLOGY CABLE SERVICE
10763 Folkestone Way
Woodstock, MD 21163
Phone: 410-465-0480
Fax: 410-461-5840
E-mail: eric@ecology.com
Web Site: http://www.ecology.com
Eric McLamb, Founder & President
Shelley Duvall, Chairman & Chief Executive Officer
Ed Begley, Jr., Chairman, Environmental Advisory Board
John H. Hoagland Jr., Vice President & Secretary
Operating hours/week: 168.
Programming: Regional television service operating in affiliation with WETV-Canada. Environmental consumerism, lifestyles & news, home gardening & shopping, children's entertainment & environmental forums.
Began: May 1, 1997.
Scrambled signal: Yes.

ECTV
c/o Olympusat
560 Village Blvd, Ste 250
West Palm Beach, FL 33409
Phone: 561-684-5657
Fax: 561-684-9690
E-mail: info@olympusat.com
Tom Mohler, Chief Executive Officer, Olympusat Holdings Inc.
Kim Reed, Chief Operating Officer
Chris Williams, Chief Financial Officer
Colleen Glynn, Executive Vice President & General Counsel
Arturo Chavez, Senior Vice President, Hispanic Networks
Nick Fabrizio, Senior Vice President, Distribution

Ecuador TV Offices:
GUAYAQUIL: 9 de Octubre y Malecon, Edificio Previsora, Piso 27, Guayaquil, Ecuador. Phone: 593-042308241. Web site: http://www.ecuadortv.ec.

QUITO: San Salvador E6-49 y Eloy Alfaro, Edificio Medios Publicos, Quito, Ecuador. Phone: 593-023970800. Web site: http://www.ecuadortv.ec.
Operating areas: Nationwide.
Programming: News, sports, comedies, novelas, music and the Ecuadorian Soccer League.
Distribution method: Available to satellite subscribers.
Scrambled signal: Yes.
Ownership: Compania Television y Radio de Ecuador E.P. TRVECUADOR. Distributed in the U.S. by Olympusat Inc.

ECUADOR TV — See ECTV.

ECUAVISA INTERNACIONAL
Cerro del Carmen s/n
Guayquil
Ecuador
Phone: 593-4-2562-444
E-mail: ecuavisainternacional@ecuavisa.com
Web Site: http://www.ecuavisa.com
Vicente Maldonado, International Programming
Programming: News, telenovelas, comedy, travel, music, interviews, drama, lifestyle & general entertainment shows from Ecuador.

Scrambled signal: Yes.
Ownership: Corporacion Ecuatoriana de Television. Distributed in the U.S. by Alterna'TV.

ECUMENICAL TV CHANNEL
PO Box 430
Canfield, OH 44406-0430
Phone: 330-533-2243
E-mail: judyctny@aol.com
Web Site: http://www.doy.org
Bob Gavalier, General Manager
Judy Roberts, Operations Manager
Type of service: Regional.
Operating hours/week: 168.
Operating areas: Northeastern Ohio & western Pennsylvania.
Programming: Educational & family-oriented format representing 13 religious denominations.
Began: January 1, 1985.
Total subscribers: 502,100.
Distribution method: Available to cable subscribers.
Scrambled signal: Yes.
Ownership: Diocese of Youngstown.

E! ENTERTAINMENT TELEVISION — See E!

EJTV
2823 W Irving Blvd
Irving, TX 75061
Phone: 469-499-0820
Fax: 469-499-0836
E-mail: cesar@ejtv.tv; cespanol@enlace.org
Web Site: http://www.ejtv.tv
Rebecca Gonzalez, President
Cesar Espanol, National Director & Public Relations
David Adcock, Cable & Satellite Relations
Type of service: Basic, streaming.
Satellites: Intelsat 21, transponder DVB-S.
Operating hours/week: 168.
Operating areas: Nationwide.
Programming: Faith-based Hispanic music videos & entertaining programs produced by Hispanic youth from different nations, sharing their ideas for meeting today's challenges.
Began: Enlace Juvenil. Rebranded as EJTV in 2014.
Distribution method: Available to cable, IPTV & satellite subscribers. Streaming available online.
Scrambled signal: Yes.
Ownership: Enlace International & Enlace Christian Television, TBN Family of Networks.

EL GARAGE TV USA
c/o AMC Networks Intl. Latin America
800 Douglas Rd, North Tower, 10th Fl
Coral Gables, FL 33134
Phone: 305-445-4350
E-mail: contacto@elgarage.com
Web Site: http://www.elgarage.com
Eduardo Zulueta, Managing Director, AMC Networks Intl., Iberia & Latin America
Operating hours/week: 168.
Programming: Spanish-language automobile programming covering history, industry news, off-road & motorcycles.
Means of Support: Advertising.
Scrambled signal: Yes.
Ownership: AMC Networks International. Distributed in the U.S. by Olympusat.

ELGOURMET
c/o AMC Networks Intl. Latin America
800 Douglas Rd, North Tower, 10th Fl
Coral Gables, FL 33134

Access the most current data instantly
FREE TRIAL @ www.warren-news.com/factbook.htm

Phone: 305-445-4350
Web Site: http://elgourmet.com
Eduardo Zulueta, Managing Director, AMC Networks Intl., Iberia & Latin America
Programming: Spanish-language network dedicated to lovers of fine living.
Began: July 1, 2000, in Argentina.
Means of Support: Advertising.
Total subscribers: 12,800,000 (Worldwide).
Distribution method: Available to DirecTV subscribers.
Scrambled signal: Yes.
Ownership: AMC Networks International.

EL REY
c/o Tres Pistoleros Studios
4900 Old Manor Rd
Austin, TX 78723
Phone: 512-334-7777
E-mail: info@elreynetwork.com
Web Site: http://www.elreynetwork.com
Robert Rodriguez, Chairman & Co-Founder
John Fogelman, Co-Founder
Cristina Patwa, Co-Founder
Daniel Tibbets, President & General Manager
Chris Motsay, Chief Financial Officer
Chad Blankenship, Senior Vice President, Marketing & Communications
Skip Chaisson, Senior Vice President, Creative & On-Air Promotion
Michael Finn, Senior Vice President, Sales & Marketing
Jose Antonio Hernandez, Vice President, Marketing
Dawn Holliday-Mack, Vice President, Audience Strategy & Insights
Katie Lanegran, Vice President, Public Relations
Renee Mizrahi, Vice President, Integrated Marketing & Sales
Clarissa Colmenero, Executive Director, Public Relations & Communications
Chris Owen, Senior Account Executive
Melissa Viele Kearney, Account Executive

Branch Offices:
AUSTIN: Troublemaker Studios, 4900 Old Manor Rd, Austin, TX 78723. Phone: 512-334-7777.
Type of service: Basic.
Operating areas: Available nationwide.
Programming: English language service for Latino and general audiences that mixes reality, scripted and animated series, movies, documentaries, news, music, comedy and sports programming.
Began: December 15, 2013.
Means of Support: Advertising.
Total subscribers: 40,000,000.
Distribution method: Available to Comcast, Cox, Time Warner, DirecTV & Dish subscribers.
Scrambled signal: Yes.
Ownership: Robert Rodriguez & FactoryMade Ventures. Univision Communications Inc. has a 5% stake in venture to provide distribution and sales.

EMIRATES DUBAI TELEVISION — See Dubai TV.

EMPLOYMENT & CAREER CHANNEL
253 W 51st St
3rd Fl
New York, NY 10019
Phone: 212-445-0754
Fax: 212-445-0760
Web Site: http://www.employ.com
Broderick Byers, Chief Executive Officer
Eric D. Cunningham, Chief Financial Officer
Ernest Feiteira, Chief Operating Officer & General Manager
Jack Wagner, Vice President, Business Development
Type of service: Basic.
Programming: Creates & distributes employment & career development content in a digital video format for television & the Internet. Programming for all classes of workers, from first-time job seekers to high-income professionals & executives.
Means of Support: Advertising.
Scrambled signal: Yes.
Ownership: Private.

ENCORE — See Starz Encore.

ENCORE ACTION — See Starz Encore Action.

ENCORE BLACK — See Starz Encore Black.

ENCORE CLASSIC — See Starz Encore Classic.

ENCORE DRAMA — See Starz Encore Black.

ENCORE ESPANOL — See Starz Encore Espanol.

ENCORE FAMILY — See Starz Encore Family.

ENCORE LOVE — See Starz Encore Classic.

ENCORE MYSTERY — See Starz Encore Suspense.

ENCORE PLAY — See Starz Encore.
Type of service: Streaming.
Operating areas: Available nationwide.
Programming: Feature films & original programming from Starz Encore.
Distribution method: Available online & through app (participating providers).

ENCORE SUSPENSE — See Starz Encore Suspense.

ENCORE WAM — See Starz Encore Family.

ENCORE WESTERNS — See Starz Encore Westerns.

ENGLISH CLUB
6 St. David's Sq
Westferry Rd

Pay TV & Satellite Services

London E14 3WA
United Kingdom
Phone: 44-0-20-7515-6409
Fax: 44-0-20-7515-6490
E-mail: customer.support@english-club.tv
Web Site: http://www.english-club.tv
Type of service: HD, pay.
Programming: Educational programming allowing users to learn & practice English.
Scrambled signal: Yes.
Ownership: English Club TV Group. Distributed in the U.S. by Olympusat.

ENGLISH ON DEMAND
Comcast Corp
1500 Market St
Philadelphia, PA 19102
Phone: 215-665-1700
Type of service: Digital, video on demand.
Operating hours/week: 4.
Operating areas: Connecticut, Maine, Massachusetts, New Hampshire, Rhode Island, Vermont.
Programming: Basic English language skills. Also focuses on important areas of communication such as job & career advancement, managing family life, utilizing information & civic resources & emphasizes community participation.
Began: September 13, 2007.
Distribution method: Available to cable subscribers.
Scrambled signal: Yes.
Ownership: Comcast Corp.

ENLACE JUVENIL — See EJTV.

ENLACE USA
2823 W Irving Blvd
Irving, TX 75061
Phone: 469-499-0820
Fax: 469-499-0836
E-mail: cespanol@enlace.org
Web Site: http://www.enlace.org
Jonas Gonzalez, Chief Executive Officer
Cesar Espanol, National Director & Public Relations
David Adcock, National Director, Cable & Satellite Relations

Branch Offices:
Affiliate Relations & National Studios: TBN Networks Affiliate Relations, 2823 W Irving Blvd, Irving, TX 75061. Phone: 800-735-5542.

Media Services Agency: TBN Enlace USA, 14171 Chambers Rd, Tustin, CA 92780. Phone: 714-665-2110.

International Headquarters: PO Box 23-1200, San Jose, Costa Rica. Phone: 506-2220-3323. Fax: 506-2220-1597. Web site: http://www.enlace.org.
Type of service: Over the air, digital basic, streaming.
Satellites: Galaxy 14, transponder 1; Galaxy 23, transponder 6 (Olympusat).
Operating hours/week: 168.
Operating areas: Nationwide.

Programming: Spanish-language Christian programming, including church services, music videos, movies, children & family.
Began: May 1, 2002, in the U.S. as TBN Enlace USA. Rebranded Enlace USA in 2012.
Means of Support: Advertising.
Total subscribers: 30,000,000.
Distribution method: Available over the air on digital sub-channels and to cable, IPTV & satellite subscribers. Streaming available online.
Scrambled signal: Yes.
Ownership: Enlace International & Enlace Christian Television, TBN Family of Networks.

ENVISION TV
8560 West Sunset Blvd.
Ste 400
West Hollywood, CA 90069
Phone: 424-354-5015
E-mail: steve@fortuneroadmedia.com
Web Site: http://www.fortuneroadmedia.com
Sean O'Riordan, Company Partner, Fortune Road Media Inc.
Type of service: On demand.
Operating areas: Available nationwide.
Programming: Television network that brings together people from every discipline and culture who seek a deeper understanding of the world.
Began: March 2, 2016.
Means of Support: Advertising.
Total subscribers: 140,000,000 (Figure is total subscribers on all available platforms.).
Distribution method: Available to Comcast subscribers and Amazon Fire TV & online.
Scrambled signal: Yes.
Ownership: Fortune Road Media Inc.

EPIX
1545 Broadway
31st Floor
New York, NY 10036
Phone: 212-846-4004
Fax: 212-846-2194
E-mail: nryan@epixhd.com
Web Site: http://www.epixhd.com
Mark Greenberg, President & Chief Executive Officer
Rob Sussman, Executive Vice President, Business Operations & Strategy & General Manager
Jocelyn Diaz, Executive Vice President, Original Programming
Monty Sarhan, Executive Vice President, Programming, Acquisitions, Strategy & Enterprises
Jonathan Dakss, Chief Digital Officer
Kirk Iwanowski, Chief Marketing Officer
Ross Bernard, Senior Vice President, Live Events & Specials
Keary Hanan, Senior Vice President, Digital Programming & Production
Ian Puente, Senior Vice President, Business/Legal
Ben Tappan, Vice President, Scripted Programming
Type of service: Pay, HD, streaming, video on demand.
Operating areas: Nationwide.

Programming: New Hollywood titles plus classic feature films, original series, and music and comedy specials.
Began: May 2009 in Beta form. Officially launched October 30, 2009 along with EPIX HD & EPIX HD streaming.
Means of Support: Subscriber fees.
Total subscribers: 45,000,000.
Distribution method: Available to cable, IPTV & satellite subscribers. Streaming available online, mobile & through app (participating providers). Video on demand available through participating providers.
Scrambled signal: Yes.
Ownership: Studio 3 Partners, a joint venture between Viacom Inc. 42%; Lions Gate Entertainment Corp. 28.6%; Metro-Goldwyn-Mayer Inc. 28.6%.

EPIX 2 — See EPIX.
Type of service: Pay.
Operating areas: Available nationwide.
Programming: Movies, original series, comedies & concerts.
Began: May 12, 2010.
Distribution method: Available to cable, IPTV & satellite subscribers.
Scrambled signal: Yes.

EPIX 3 — See EPIX Hits.

EPIX DRIVE-IN — See EPIX.
Type of service: Pay.
Operating areas: Available nationwide.
Programming: Action, comedy, horror & science fiction movies.
Began: August 11, 2010, as The 3 from EPIX. Rebranded EPIX Drive-In December 2011.
Distribution method: Available to cable, IPTV & satellite subscribers.
Scrambled signal: Yes.

EPIX HITS — See EPIX.
Type of service: Pay.
Operating areas: Available nationwide.
Programming: Movies, first-run films & original series.
Began: January 1, 2012, as Epix 3. Rebranded EPIX Hits.
Distribution method: Available to cable, IPTV & satellite subscribers.
Scrambled signal: Yes.

THE EROTIC NETWORK — See TEN.

ESCAPE
c/o Katz Broadcasting LLC
3500 Piedmont Rd, Ste 400
Atlanta, GA 30305
Phones: 404-365-3075; 770-672-6500
Fax: 404-577-1786
E-mail: escape-info@katzbroadcasting.com
Web Site: http://www.escapetv.com
Jonathan Katz, President & Chief Executive Officer
Jeffrey Wolf, Chief Distribution Officer
Elverage Allen, Executive Vice President, Advertising Sales
Walter Naar, Vice President, Programming
Calandria Meadows, Vice President, Social Media & Digital Content
Operating areas: Available nationwide.
Programming: Targets women 25-54 with shows concentrating on crime and mystery stories.
Began: August 18, 2014.
Total subscribers: 77,000,000.
Distribution method: Available over the air on digital sub-channels of Univision stations in Chicago, Dallas, Houston, Los Angeles, Miami & New York.

Scrambled signal: Yes.
Ownership: Katz Broadcasting LLC.

ESCAPES NETWORK
25 S Monroe St
Ste 200
Monroe, MI 48161
Phone: 734-241-4410
Fax: 734-241-4416
Web Site: http://www.escapestv.com
Robert Oklejas, Chairman & President
Roy Radakovich, Chief Executive Officer
Jon Oswald, General Manager
Tim Larson, Vice President, Distribution
Alexander Zonjic, Artistic Director
Jennifer Bilski, Post-Production Manager
Mark Crittenden, Marketing & Strategic Planning Manager
Katherin Oklejas, Business Manager
Type of service: Basic.
Satellites: Galaxy 16, transponder 5.
Operating hours/week: 168.
Operating areas: Nationwide.
Programming: Fifteen-minute themed modules that include minimal edits, slow zooms, and pans of vistas ranging from lighthouses and cityscapes to ships at sea and tropical beaches, all scored with a soundtrack.
Began: March 17, 2011.
Distribution method: Available to cable, IPTV & satellite subscribers.
Scrambled signal: Yes.
Ownership: Robert Oklejas.

ESPIRITU SANTO Y FUEGO NETWORK
915 E Belmont Ave
Fresno, CA 93701
Phone: 559-981-5119
Jorge Gutierrez, Pastor & Founder
Type of service: Regional.
Operating areas: California.
Programming: Hispanic religious programming.
Means of Support: Donations.
Distribution method: Available over the air on digital sub-channels.
Scrambled signal: Yes.
Ownership: Iglesia Espiritu Santo y Fuego.

ESPN
ESPN Plz
935 Middle St
Bristol, CT 06010
Phones: 860-766-2000; 888-549-3776
Fax: 860-766-2400
Web Site: http://www.espn.com
John Skipper, Co-Chairman, Disney Media Networks & President, ESPN
Ed Erhardt, President, Global Sales & Marketing
Steve Anderson, Executive Vice President, Content Operations & Creative Services
Justin Connolly, Executive Vice President, Disney & ESPN Affiliate Sales & Marketing
Mary Donoghue, Executive Vice President, Global Strategy & Original Content
Christine Driessen, Executive Vice President & Chief Financial Officer
Edwin M. Durso, Executive Vice President, Administration
Eric Johnson, Executive Vice President, Global Multimedia Sales
John Kosner, Executive Vice President, ESPN Digital & Print Media
Aaron LaBerge, Executive Vice President & Chief Technology Officer
John Wildhack, Executive Vice President, Programming & Production
Norby Williamson, Executive Vice President, Production, Program Scheduling & Development

Pay TV & Satellite Services

FULLY SEARCHABLE • CONTINUOUSLY UPDATED • DISCOUNT RATES FOR PRINT PURCHASERS

For more information call **800-771-9202** or visit **www.warren-news.com**

Russell Wolff, Executive Vice President & Managing Director, ESPN International
Patricia Betron, Senior Vice President, Multimedia Sales
Christopher Brush, Senior Vice President, Affiliate Marketing
Brian Carr, Senior Vice President, Multimedia Sales
Oliver Dizon, Senior Vice President, Strategic Sales Planning & Revenue Enhancement
Vince Doria, Senior Vice President & News Director
Stephanie Druley, Senior Vice President, Production College Networks
Rosalyn Durant, Senior Vice President, College Networks
Bill Geist, Senior Vice President, Finance, Programming & Ad Sales
Matt Genore, Senior Vice President, Multimedia Sales
Laura Gentile, Senior Vice President, espnW & Women's Initiatives
Traug Keller, Senior Vice President, Production, Business Divisions - ESPN Audio, ESPN Local & ESPN Deportes
Chris LaPlace, Senior Vice President, Corporate Communications
Burke Magnus, Senior Vice President, Programming Acquisitions
Jodi Markley, Senior Vice President, Operations
Laurie Orlando, Senior Vice President, Talent Development & Planning
Wendell Scott, Senior Vice President, Multimedia Sales
Vikram Somaya, Senior Vice President & Chief Data Officer
Aaron Taylor, Senior Vice President, Marketing
Wanda Young, Senior Vice President, Marketing & Consumer Engagement
Freddy Rolon, Vice President & General Manager, ESPN Deportes
Robert Lipsyte, Ombudsman

Sales Offices:
ATLANTA: 5605 Glenridge Dr, Atlanta, GA 94111. Phone: 415-486-3053.

CHICAGO: 401 N Michigan Ave, Chicago, IL 60601. Phone: 312-245-4200.

DETROIT: 1000 Town Ctr, Southfield, MI 48075. Phone: 248-359-1030.

LOS ANGELES: 655 N Central Ave, Ste 1800, Glendale, CA 91203. Phone: 818-484-9884.

NEW YORK: 77 W 66th St, New York, NY 10023. Phone: 212-456-3654.

SAN FRANCISCO: 900 Front St, San Francisco, CA 94111, 415-486-3053.
Type of service: Basic, HD, streaming, video on demand.
Satellites: Galaxy V, transponder 9 (main feed); Galaxy I, transponder 14 (alternate feed).
Operating hours/week: 168.
Operating areas: Nationwide.
Uplink: Bristol, CT.
Programming: Sporting events including live & recorded telecasts, sports news & analysis as well as original programming.
Began: September 7, 1979, ESPN HD began March 2001.
Means of Support: Advertising & affiliate fees.
Total subscribers: 92,900,000.
Distribution method: Available to cable, IPTV & satellite subscribers; Streaming available online & mobile through the WATCH ESPN website or app (participating providers);
Video on demand available through participating providers.
Scrambled signal: Yes.
Ownership: A joint venture between The Walt Disney Co. (80%) & Hearst Corp. (20%).

ESPN2 — See ESPN.
Operating hours/week: 168.
Programming: Sports events, news & analysis.
Began: October 1, 1993.
Total subscribers: 99,000,000.
Scrambled signal: Yes.

ESPN3 — See WATCH ESPN.

ESPN360.COM — See ESPN3.

ESPN BASES LOADED — See ESPN.
Programming: Live cut-in & highlights of college baseball games as well as commentary & analysis. Only offered during the college baseball season.

ESPN BUZZER BEATER — See ESPN.
Programming: Live cut-in & highlights of various college basketball games as well as commentary & analysis. Only offered during college basketball season.
Began: September 4, 2010.
Scrambled signal: Yes.

ESPN CLASSIC — See ESPN.
Type of service: Basic, streaming, video on demand.
Operating hours/week: 168.
Programming: Reruns of classic sporting events, documentaries, series & movies.
Began: May 1995, as Classic Sports Network. Rebranded as ESPN Classic October 1997 after ESPN purchase.
Total subscribers: 31,000,000.
Scrambled signal: Yes.

ESPN COLLEGE EXTRA — See ESPN.
Programming: Over 600 live football, basketball & baseball events.
Began: August 28, 2015, announced. Began September 5, 2015, replacing ESPN Full Court & ESPN Game Plan.

ESPN DEPORTES — See ESPN.
Phone: 888-549-3776
Web Site: http://www.espndeportes.com
Traug Keller, Senior Vice President, Production, Business Divisions – EPSN Audio, ESPN Local & ESPN Deportes
Freddy Rolon, General Manager & Vice President, ESPN Deportes
Michelle Bella, Vice President, Sales & Consumer Marketing
John Fitzgerald, Vice President, Multimedia Sales, ESPN Deportes & ESPN Audio
Rodolfo Martinez, Vice President, Production, ESPN International & ESPN Deportes
Type of service: Basic, HD, video on demand.
Operating hours/week: 168.
Programming: Spanish-language sports events, news & analysis.
Began: January 2004. ESPN Deportes HD began April 2011.
Total subscribers: 5,900,000.
Distribution method: Available to cable, IPTV & satellite subscribers; online & mobile through the WATCH ESPN website or app (participating providers); video on demand (participating providers).
Scrambled signal: Yes.

ESPN DEPORTES+ POR ESPN3 —
See ESPN Deportes.
Type of service: Streaming.
Programming: Additional live Spanish-language sporting events.
Began: September 7, 2012.
Distribution method: Available on online and through ESPN3, WatchESPN & Xbox Live.
Scrambled signal: Yes.

ESPNEWS — See ESPN.
Programming: Sports news, information and highlights.
Began: November 1, 1996, ESPNews HD began March 30, 2008.
Total subscribers: 76,000,000.
Distribution method: Available to cable, IPTV & satellite subscribers; online & mobile through the WATCH ESPN website or app (participating providers).
Scrambled signal: Yes.

ESPN FULL COURT — See ESPN College Extra.

ESPN GAME PLAN — See ESPN College Extra.

ESPN GOAL LINE — See ESPN.
Programming: Live cut-in & highlights of various college football games as well as commentary & analysis. Only offered on Saturdays during the college football season.
Began: September 4, 2010.
Scrambled signal: Yes.

ESPN NOW — See WATCH ESPN.

ESPNU — See ESPN.
Rosalyn Durant, Vice President, College Sports Programming
Type of service: Basic, streaming.
Programming: College sports.
Began: March 2005.
Total subscribers: 76,000,000.
Distribution method: Available cable, IPTV & satellite subscribers. Streaming available online & mobile through the WATCH ESPN website or app.
Scrambled signal: Yes.

ESQUIRE NETWORK
5750 Wilshire Blvd
Los Angeles, CA 90036-3709
Phones: 323-954-2400; 323-954-6170
Fax: 323-954-2660
Web Site: http://tv.esquire.com
NBCUNIVERSAL CABLE ENTERTAINMENT GROUP:, .
Bonnie Hammer, Chairman
Frances Berwick, President, Lifestyle Networks Group
David O'Connell, Executive Vice President, Production Management & Operations, Lifestyle Networks Group
ESQUIRE NETWORK:, .
Adam Stotsky, President, E! & Esquire Network
Donald C. Storm II, Chief Financial Officer, E! & Esquire Network
Matt Hanna, Executive Vice President, Original Programming
Jen Neal, Executive Vice President, Marketing, E! & Esquire Network
Brent Mitchell, Senior Vice President, Consumer Marketing
Nidia Caceros Kilde, Vice President, Communications
Dave Serwatka, Vice President, Current Programming
Type of service: Basic, HD, streaming & video on demand.
Operating hours/week: 168.
Operating areas: Available nationwide.
Programming: A men's lifestyle and entertainment network featuring programming that speaks to classic and contemporary passions and interests, from fashion and style to food and drink, travel and women and relationships.
Began: September 23, 3013, replacing Style Network, which began October 1, 1998.
Means of Support: Advertising.
Total subscribers: 70,000,000.
Distribution method: Available to cable, IPTV & satellite subscribers. Streaming available through Esquire TV Now website or app.
Video on demand available through participating providers.
Scrambled signal: Yes.
Ownership: A joint venture between NBCUniversal Cable Entertainment (division of NBCUniversal LLC) & Hearst Magazines.

ESQUIRE TV NOW — See Esquire Network.
Web Site: http://tv.esquire.com/now
Type of service: Streaming.
Operating areas: Available nationwide.
Programming: Series from Esquire Network.
Began: May 30, 2014.
Distribution method: Available to online & through app (participating providers).

ESTRELLA TV
1845 Empire Ave
Burbank, CA 91504
Phone: 818-729-5300
E-mail: LBlinfo@lbimedia.com
Web Site: http://www.lbimedia.com
Jose Liberman, Co-Founder & Chairman
Lenard Liberman, Co-Founder & Executive Vice President, LBI Media
Winter Horton, Chief Operating Officer
Susan Malfi, Executive Vice President, National Advertising Sales & Marketing
Jim Baral, Senior Vice President, Integrated Sales, West Coast
Cathy Lewis Edgerton, Senior Vice President, Distribution & Affiliate Sales
Ibra Morales, Vice President, Network Operations
Type of service: Basic, over the air.
Satellites: AMC 3, transponder 23.
Sales representative: Spanish Media Rep Team.
Operating hours/week: 168.
Operating areas: Arizona, California, Florida, Nevada, New Mexico, New York, Oregon, Texas & Utah.
Uplink: Dallas, TX.
Programming: Spanish-language entertainment, including musical-variety, comedy, scripted drama, talk and game shows, and features top talent from the U.S., Mexico & Latin America.

Pay TV & Satellite Services

Began: September 14, 2009.
Means of Support: Advertising & subscriber fees.
Total subscribers: 17,000,000.
Distribution method: Available over the air on digital sub-channels & to satellite subscribers.
Scrambled signal: Yes. Equipment: Grass Valley, Thomson.
Ownership: Liberman Broadcasting Inc.

ESTUDIO5
c/o Condista, 200 Crandon Blvd
Ste 316
Key Biscayne, FL 33149
Phones: 786-331-9468; 305-510-6366
Web Site: http://www.estudio5.tv
Silvia Merino, Vice President, Programming
Nury Quevado, Marketing Director
Type of service: Premium.
Operating areas: Nationwide.
Programming: Offers series, movies and documentaries produced on five continents and spoken or subtitled in Spanish. Also offers live broadcasts of Mexican Ascenso League soccer matches.
Began: May 1, 2014.
Means of Support: Subscriber fees.
Distribution method: Available to DirecTV subscribers.
Scrambled signal: Yes.
Ownership: SUR LLC. Distributed in the U.S. by Condista.

ES.TV
1925 Century Park E
Ste 1025
Los Angeles, CA 90067
Phone: 310-277-3500
E-mail: eric@es.tv
Web Site: http://www.es.tv
Byron Allen, Chairman & Chief Executive Officer
Darren Galatt, Vice President, Ad Sales
Type of service: Digital.
Operating hours/week: 168.
Operating areas: Nationwide.
Programming: Features entertainment news, celebrity profiles and programming on entertainers, celebrities and others in the news.
Began: May 11, 2009.
Total subscribers: 1,900,000.
Distribution method: Available to Verizon FiOS and Frontier Communications cable system subscribers.
Scrambled signal: No.
Ownership: Entertainment Studios.

ETERNAL WORD TV NETWORK — See EWTN Global Catholic Network.

ET-GLOBAL
18430 E San Jose Ave
Ste A
City of Industry, CA 91748
Phones: 626-581-8899; 877-388-8787
Fax: 626-581-8877
E-mail: customer_service@ettvamerica.com
Web Site: http://www.ettvamerica.com
May Chiang, Executive Vice President, ETTV
Programming: Offers popular Taiwanese shows including traditional costume dramas, variety shows, continuing series, current affairs programs and local community news.
Means of Support: Subscriber fees.
Distribution method: Available to cable, IPTV & satellite subscribers.
Scrambled signal: No.
Ownership: ETTV America Corp.

ET-NEWS — See ET-GLOBAL.
Programming: Provides breaking international and domestic news for Taiwanese viewers.
Means of Support: Subscriber fees.
Distribution method: Available to cable, IPTV & satellite subscribers.
Scrambled signal: No.
Ownership: ETTV America Corp.

ETV KANNADA — See Colors Kannada.

ETV MARATHI — See Colors Marathi.

EUROCHANNEL
235 Lincoln Rd
Ste 201
Miami Beach, FL 33139
Phone: 305-531-1315
E-mail: joseph@eurochannel.com
Web Site: http://www.eurochannel.com
Gustavo Vainstein, Chairman & Chief Executive Officer
Alex Mihalev, Chief Technical Officer
Jesus Roldan, Chief Financial Officer
Joseph de Monvalier, Vice President, International Marketing & Sales
Christian Poccard, Vice President, Programming & Acquisitions
Sofia Martinez, International Marketing Manager
Type of service: Basic, video on demand.
Operating hours/week: 168.
Operating areas: Available nationwide.
Programming: A vast selection of modern entertainment from every corner of Europe. Eurochannel on Demand offers movies, documentaries & series on viewers own schedule.
Began: 1994 in Europe. April 30, 2008 in the U.S. Eurochannel on Demand began in the U.S. on November 20, 2012.
Means of Support: Advertising.
Total subscribers: 150,000.
Distribution method: Available to DISH Network subscribers. Video on demand available online.
Scrambled signal: Yes.
Ownership: Eurochannel Inc.

EUROCINEMA
1395 Brickell Ave
Ste 800
Miami, FL 33131
Phone: 305-529-6220
Fax: 305-529-6201
E-mail: contactus@eurocinema.com
Web Site: http://www.eurocinema.com
Sebastien Perioche, Chairman & Chief Executive Officer
Larry Namer, Senior Advisor & U.S. Operations Director
Steve Matela, Affiliate Sales & Marketing
Nicole Goesseringer, Media Relations

Branch Offices:
NEW YORK: 387 Park Ave S, 3rd Floor, New York, NY 10016. Phone: 212-763-5533.
Type of service: Basic, video on demand & pay-per-view.
Programming: Award-winning European & international films; documentaries, celebrity guests & coverage of major international film festivals.
Began: June 1, 2004.
Distribution method: Available to cable subscribers.
Scrambled signal: Yes.

EURONEWS
60 Chemin des Mouilles
BP 161-69131
Lyon Ecully Cedex
France
Phone: 33-4-72-18-80-00
Fax: 33-4-78-33-27-17
Web Site: http://www.euronews.net
Philippe Cayla, President
Michael Peters, Managing Director
Jill Grinda, Worldwide Distribution Director
Olivier de Montchenu, Sales & Marketing Director
Luis Rivas, News & Program Director
Type of service: Basic.
Satellites: Noorsat 2, transponder 120.
Operating hours/week: 168.
Programming: International all-news channel covering world events simultaneously in seven languages: English, French, German, Italian, Portuguese, Russian & Spanish.
Began: January 1, 1993.
Total subscribers: 1,605,000 (number includes U.S. subscribers only.).
Distribution method: Available to cable & satellite subscribers.
Scrambled signal: Yes.

EVINE LIVE
6740 Shady Oak Rd
Eden Prairie, MN 55344
Phone: 952-943-6000
Fax: 952-943-6011
Web Site: http://www.evine.com
John Buck, Chairman
Mark Bozek, Chief Executive Officer
Carol Steinberg, Chief Operating Officer
Russell Nuce, Chief Strategy Officer & Interim General Counsel
Tim Peterman, Chief Financial Officer & Executive Vice President
Mark Ahmann, Senior Vice President, Human Resources
Trish Mueller, Senior Vice President, Marketing
Robert Manning, Vice President, Affiliate Relations
Nathan Martin, Vice President, Fulfillment
Type of service: Basic.
Satellites: Galaxy G-1, transponder 12.
Operating hours/week: 168.
Operating areas: Nationwide.
Uplink: Minneapolis, MN.
Programming: Shop-at-home.
Began: October 15, 1991, as ValueVision. Rebranded as ShopNBC in 2011, ShopHQ in May 22, 2013 & EVINE Live in February 2015.
Means of Support: Product sales.
Total subscribers: 87,000,000.
Distribution method: Available to cable & satellite subscribers.
Scrambled signal: Yes.
Ownership: EVINE Live Inc.

EWTN EN ESPANOL — See EWTN Global Catholic Network.
Web Site: http://www.ewtn.com/espanol
Programming: Spanish-language programming from EWTN.

EWTN GLOBAL CATHOLIC NETWORK
5817 Old Leeds Rd
Irondale, AL 35210
Phones: 205-271-2900; 800-447-3986
Fax: 205-271-2925
E-mail: cwegemer@ewtn.com
Web Site: http://www.ewtn.com
Michael P. Warsaw, Chairman & Chief Executive Officer
Douglas Keck, President & Chief Operating Officer
Libby Isaack, Vice President & Chief Financial Officer
Terry Borders, Vice President, Engineering
Patti Connolly, Vice President, Human Resources
Enrique Duprat, Vice President, Spanish Language Production & Marketing
Peter Gagnon, Vice President, Programming & Production
Lisa Gould, Vice President, Viewer Services
John Manos, Vice President, Legal & Regulatory Activities & General Counsel
Len Marino, Vice President, Creative Services
Joseph O'Farrell, Vice President, Mission Advancement
Chris Wegemer, Vice President, Marketing
Michelle Johnson, Communications Director
Patrick Haygood, Human Resources Director
Fred Stok, Marketing Director, U.S.
Tom Wenzel, Marketing Director, North America
Walter Cordova, National Marketing Manager, Spanish Networks
Type of service: Basic, HD.
Satellites: Galaxy 15 (U.S.), transponder 5; IS 9 (Latin America), transponder 8-C; IS 10 (Africa, India), transponder 8-C; IS 8 (Pacific Rim), transponder 12-C; Hot Bird 4 (Europe), transponder III (Galaxy XI, Transponder 11-C (Channel 5-US English, Channel 4-Canada, Channel 3-US Spanish)).
Operating hours/week: 168.
Programming: Commercial-free family and religious programs from a Catholic perspective. Programs include live call-in talk shows, news programs, original series and documentaries, teaching series with noted theologians, children's shows, live coverage of the Pope and important Church events, a live daily Mass, devotions, concerts, music, and much more.
Began: August 15, 1981, EWTN HD began December 8, 2009.
Means of Support: Donations.
Total subscribers: 200,000,000 (Includes international subscribers).
Distribution method: Available to cable & DISH Network subscribers.
Scrambled signal: Yes.

EXPO TV
Expo Communications Inc.
15 W 18th St, 10th Fl
New York, NY 10011
Phone: 212-500-6600
Fax: 212-500-6601
E-mail: brian@expotv.com
Web Site: http://www.expotv.com
Daphne Kwon, Chief Executive Officer
Bill Hildebolt, President
David Rubenstein, Chief Revenue Officer
Thi Luu, Senior Vice President, Product & Technology
Jessica Thorpe, Vice President, Marketing
Type of service: Digital & video on demand.
Operating hours/week: 168.
Programming: Showcases a wide range of as seen on TV products ranging from fitness & entertainment to beauty & sports.
Began: March 1, 2005.
Means of Support: Advertising.
Total subscribers: 25,000,000.

EXXXOTICA
2319 E Valley Pkwy
Ste 127
Escondido, CA 92027
Phone: 800-557-5776
Fax: 619-749-8431
Dan Bender, President, Merlin-Sierra Inc.
Type of service: Pay & Pay-per-view.
Satellites: Telstar 405.
Operating hours/week: 168.
Programming: Adult movies.
Means of Support: Subscription fees.
Distribution method: Available to satellite subscribers.

Pay TV & Satellite Services

Scrambled signal: Yes.
Ownership: Merlin-Sierra Inc.

FAITH TELEVISION NETWORK — See The Family Channel.

FAMILIA TV
PO Box 102
9950 Westpark Dr, Ste 103
Houston, TX 77063
Phones: 713-469-5920; 713-589-9292
E-mail: familia_tv@yahoo.com
Web Site: http://www.ficmi.org
Jorge Gamboa, President & Chief Executive Officer
Jorge Aguilera, General Sales Manager
Type of service: Basic.
Operating areas: Texas.
Programming: Spanish-language network designed to meet the wide variety of cultural and denominational backgrounds within the Hispanic Community.
Began: April 8, 2010.
Means of Support: Advertising & donations.
Distribution method: Available over the air on digital sub-channels.
Scrambled signal: Yes.

THE FAMILY CHANNEL
225 East 8th St
Chattanooga, TN 37402
Phone: 423-468-5100
Web Site: http://www.famchannel.com
Timothy Harrington, Chief Executive Officer
Ken Gibson, Vice President, Affiliates
Chip Harwood, Vice President, Affiliate Sales & Marketing
Andrea Rhum, National & Direct Response Advertising Sales
Type of service: Basic.
Operating hours/week: 168.
Operating areas: Nationwide.
Programming: G-rated educational, entertaining & faith-based programming.
Began: August 2008 as Faith TV. Rebranded My Family TV December 15, 2008. Rebranded The Family Channel December 2013.
Means of Support: Advertising.
Total subscribers: 25,000,000.
Distribution method: Available on digital sub-channels.
Scrambled signal: Yes.
Ownership: Luken Communications LLC & ValCom Inc.

FAMILY FRIENDLY ENTERTAINMENT
PO Box 217
Gainesville, TX 76241
Phone: 800-665-2334
Web Site: http://www.familyfriendlye.com
Type of service: Basic.
Satellites: Telstar 7, transponder 20; Intelsat Americas 13, transponder 20.
Operating hours/week: 168.
Programming: Christian based family-centered television network with a focus on gospel music. Formerly Gospel Music TV.
Began: as Gospel Music TV. Rebranded Family Friendly Entertainment.
Means of Support: Advertising.
Scrambled signal: Yes.

FAMILYNET
49 Music Sq W
Nashville, TN 37203
Phone: 615-296-9282
Web Site: http://www.familynet.com
Patrick Gottsch, Founder & President
Dan Kripke, Senior Vice President & Sales Director, DRTV

Peter Clifford, Senior Vice President, Affiliate Sales
Type of service: Basic, HD.
Satellites: Intelsat 13, transponder 20.
Operating hours/week: 168.
Operating areas: Available nationwide.
Programming: Family entertainment, inspirational programs, sports & movies. Programming was combined with Rural TV on January 1, 2013.
Began: October 1, 1979, as the National Christian Network. Rebranded Liberty Broadcasting Network when acquired by Jerry Falwell in 1986. Rebranded FamilyNet April 4, 1988.
Means of Support: Advertising.
Total subscribers: 27,000,000.
Distribution method: Available over the air and to cable, IPTV & satellite subscribers.
Scrambled signal: Yes.
Ownership: Rural Media Group Inc.

FASHION ONE 4K
246 West Broadway
New York, NY 10013
Phone: 212-666-5000
Fax: 212-656-1828
E-mail: general@fashion4k.tv; press@fashion4k.tv
Web Site: http://www.fashion4k.tv
Gleb Livshits, Chief Operations Officer
Ferdinand Kayser, Chief Commercial Officer
Satellites: SES-3 (North America), transponder 22c; NSS-806 (Latin America), transponder 28/28; MEASAT-3a (Asia Pacific), transponder 11; ASTRA (Europe), transponder 1.043.
Operating hours/week: 168.
Operating areas: Nationwide.
Programming: 4k channel dedicated to fashion, entertainment and lifestyle.
Began: September 1, 2015.
Means of Support: Advertising.
Total subscribers: 253,000,000 (number of possible households worldwide via satellite).
Distribution method: Available to satellite subscribers.
Scrambled signal: Yes.
Ownership: Fashion One Television LLC.

FASHION ONE TELEVISION LTD.
207 Regent St.
3rd Floor
London W1B 3HH
United Kingdom
Phone: 44-20-3603-3270
E-mail: london@fashionone.com
Web Site: http://www.fashionone.com
Ashley Jordan, Chief Executive Officer, Bigfoot Entertainment
Andrew McMennamy, Head of Studios, Bigfoot Entertainment
Stephanie Manuel, Chief Human Resource Officer, Bigfoot Entertainment
Marivic Lu, Finance Manager, Bigfoot Entertainment
Carissa Marie Chiu, Marketing Supervisor, Bigfoot Entertainment
Sarah Walker, Studio & Location Director, Bigfoot Entertainment

Branch Offices:
HONG KONG: Asia Pacific HQ, 37 Hollywood Road, 13th Floor C. Wisdom Centre, Hong Kong, Hong Kong. Phone: 852-5808-3400.

UNITED ARAB EMIRATES: Middle East HQ, The Meydan, Glass Tower Offices, P.O. Box 333691, Dubai, United Arab Emirates. Phones: 971-4-81-3738; 971-50-1492200.
Satellites: Intelsat 805.
Operating hours/week: 168.

Operating areas: Available in Puerto Rico & the U.S. Virgin Islands.
Programming: Photography, street style and beauty tips, to designer retrospectives and the latest celebrity trends.
Began: April 8, 2010.
Means of Support: Advertising.
Total subscribers: 100,000,000 (viewers worldwide.).
Distribution method: Available to satellite subscribers.
Scrambled signal: Yes.
Ownership: Bigfoot Entertainment.

FASHIONTV
PO Box 3149
Road Town
Tortola
British Virgin Island
Phone: 43-1-5131267
Web Site: http://www.fashiontv.com
Programming: Fashion, beauty & lifestyle programming.
Distribution method: Available to satellite subscribers. Streaming available online.
Scrambled signal: Yes.
Ownership: FTV BVI Ltd.

FESTIVAL DIRECT — See Independent Film Channel.
200 Jericho Quadrangle
Jericho, NY 11753
Phone: 516-803-4500
Fax: 516-803-4506
E-mail: webmaster@ifctv.com
Web Site: http://www.ifc.com
Type of service: Viideo on demand.
Programming: Covers major film festivals in Cannes, Telluride, Toronto & Venice.
Began: February 29, 2008.
Distribution method: Available to cable subscribers.
Scrambled signal: Yes.
Ownership: AMC Networks.

FIDOTV
1110 Newport St
Denver, CO 80220
Phone: 720-648-2600
E-mail: info@fidotvchannel.com
Web Site: http://www.fidotvchannel.com
Tad Walden, Chief Executive Officer & Founder
Lauren Halpern, Chief Revenue Officer
Suzanne Doss, Senior Vice President, Distribution
Scott Hirsch, Senior Vice President, Programming/Production
Steve Walter, Senior Vice President, Distribution
Jonathan Sandak, Vice President, Advertising Sales
Type of service: Baasic.
Operating hours/week: 168.
Operating areas: Available nationwide.
Programming: TV entertainment and support services for dogs, including original & special live programming.
Began: October 14, 2015.
Means of Support: Advertising.
Total subscribers: 14,000,000.

Distribution method: Available to cable & DISH subscribers.
Scrambled signal: Yes.
Ownership: Tad Walden.

FIGHT NETWORK
2844 Dundas St W
2nd Fl
Toronto, ON M6P 1Y7
Canada
Phones: 416-987-7841; 888-726-0333
Fax: 647-343-4173
E-mail: anthony@fightnetwork.com
Web Site: http://www.fightnetwork.com
Leonard Asper, Chief Executive Officer
Anthony Cicione, General Manager
Chad Midgley, Vice President, Programming & Production
Mark Winokur, Vice President, Sales
Steve Duncan, Creative Director
Ariel Shnerer, Programming Manager
Rahonie Singh, Accounting
Type of service: Basic, pay-per-view & mobile.
Operating hours/week: 168.
Programming: News, movies, television series, documentaries & other entertainment related to boxing, wrestling, martial arts & other combatant styles.
Began: September 22, 2005.
Distribution method: Available to Cablevision Systems subscribers.
Scrambled signal: Yes.
Ownership: Anthem Media Group Inc.

FIGHT NOW TV
4055 W Sunset Rd
Las Vegas, NV 89118-3894
Phones: 702-616-0275; 702-616-1022
E-mail: info@fightnow.com
Web Site: http://www.fightnow.com
Mike Garrow, General Manager & Co-Founder
Cal Miller, Co-Founder
Romen Podzyhun, Co-Founder
Randy Couture, Spokesperson & Analyst
Type of service: Premium.
Operating hours/week: 168.
Operating areas: Connecticut, New Jersey and New York.
Programming: Combat sports.
Began: May 24, 2011.
Means of Support: Subscriber fees and advertising.
Total subscribers: 130,000 (Number of subscribers to Cablevision's iO Sports & Entertainment Pak).
Distribution method: Available to Cablevision Systems subscribers.
Scrambled signal: Yes.
Ownership: Channel Zero.

FIL AM TV
2014 Lincoln Ave
Pasadena, CA 91103-1323
Phone: 626-608-5007
Fax: 626-608-5005
E-mail: general@filamtv.com
Web Site: http://www.filamtv.com
Gilbert Dean Arcillas, Founder
Bill Ines, Chief Executive Officer
Nicole Parker, Office Manager
Type of service: Basic.

Pay TV & Satellite Services

Operating hours/week: 168.
Operating areas: California.
Programming: A celebration of the Filipino spirit, culture, values, arts and entertainment.
Began: January 1, 2011.
Total subscribers: 1,700,000.
Distribution method: Available over the air on digital sub-channels.
Scrambled signal: Yes.
Ownership: Filipino Media Group Inc.

THE FILIPINO CHANNEL
ABS-CBN International
150 Shoreline Dr
Redwood City, CA 94065-1400
Phones: 650-508-6000; 800-345-2465
Fax: 650-508-6001
E-mail: nclemente@abs-cbni.com
Web Site: http://www.abs-cbnglobal.com
Rafael Lopez, Managing Director & Chief Operating Officer
Zenon Carlos, Vice President, Operations
Menchi Orlina, Vice President & Chief Marketing Officer
Jun Del Rosario, North America Regional Marketing Head & Senior Director
Tom Consunji, Senior Director, Sales & Marketing
Marites Militar, Creative Broadcast Group Director
Type of service: Pay.
Satellites: Telstar 5.
Operating hours/week: 168.
Operating areas: California.
Programming: Showcases award-winning dramas, variety, comedy, news & public affairs programs from the dominant broadcasting company in the Philippines for the Filipino population.
Began: April 3, 1994.
Means of Support: Subscribers.
Total subscribers: 2,000,000 (Worldwide subscribers.).
Distribution method: Available to cable & IPTV subscribers (as The Filipino Channel) & to satellite subscribers (as TFC Direct).
Scrambled signal: Yes.
Ownership: ABS-CBN International.

FILM FESTIVAL CHANNEL
PO Box 39349
Los Angeles, CA 90039
Phones: 213-625-1242; 646-502-8625
E-mail: sundancechnladv@ifcsun.com
Lisa Henschel, President
Type of service: Basic & video on demand.
Programming: Focuses on film festivals; on-air competitions for new filmmakers.
Began: November 1, 2003, Video on demand began November 5, 2007.
Distribution method: Available to cable & IPTV subscribers.
Scrambled signal: Yes.

FIND IT ON DEMAND
c/o Time Warner Cable
60 Columbus Cir, 17th Fl
New York, NY 10023
Phone: 212-364-8200
E-mail: jeannette.castaneda@twcable.com
Joan Hogan Gillman, President, Time Warner Cable Media
Jeannette Castaneda, Public Relations Manager
Type of service: Video on demand.
Operating hours/week: 168.
Operating areas: Available nationwide.
Programming: Lookup service to Time Warner Cable's on demand channels.
Distribution method: Available to Time Warner Cable digital cable system subscribers.
Ownership: Time Warner Cable Inc.

FINE LIVING NETWORK — See Cooking Channel.

FIOS1 DALLAS
c/o Verizon Communications Inc.
701 Brazos St, Ste 600
Austin, TX 78701
Phone: 512-495-6713
Web Site: http://www.verizon.com/athomeblog
Shawne Angelle, President, Texas Operations
Harry J. Mitchell, Public Relations Director
Heather B. Wilner, Media Relations Manager
Type of service: Digital.
Operating areas: Texas.
Programming: Tape-delayed 'High School Football Game of the Week,' regular season football matches plus playoff games & boys' high school basketball games.
Began: November 7, 2011.
Distribution method: Available to Verizon FiOS subscribers.
Scrambled signal: Yes.
Ownership: Verizon Communications Inc.

FIOS1 HIGH SCHOOL SPORTS WIDGET
c/o Verizon Communications Inc.
701 Brazos St, Ste 600
Austin, TX 78701
Phone: 512-495-6713
Web Site: http://www.verizon.com/athomeblog
Shawne Angelle, President, Texas Operations
Rachel McGallian, Marketing Director, Texas
Deidre Mulcahy Hart, Media Relations Manager
Stefanie Scott, Contact Center Services Manager
Type of service: Digital.
Operating areas: Texas.
Programming: On-demand high school sports news, stats, photos and video highlights for area schools.
Began: September 2, 2011.
Total subscribers: 500,000.
Distribution method: Available to Verizon FiOS subscribers.
Scrambled signal: Yes.
Ownership: Verizon Communications Inc.

FIOS1 LONG ISLAND
c/o Verizon Communications Inc.
140 West St
New York, NY 10007
Phone: 888-553-1555
Web Site: http://fios1news.com/longisland
Marc Weiner, News Director
Michelle Webb, Programming Director
Type of service: Digital.
Operating areas: Long Island, NY.
Programming: Local news, sports, weather & community interest.
Began: June 22, 2009.
Distribution method: Available to Verizon FiOS subscribers.
Scrambled signal: Yes.
Ownership: Verizon Communications Inc.

FIOS1 NEW JERSEY — See FiOS Long Island.
Web Site: http://www.fios1news.com/NewJersey.php
Type of service: Digital.
Operating areas: Northern New Jersey.
Began: June 22, 2009.
Distribution method: Available to Verizon FiOS subscribers.
Scrambled signal: Yes.
Ownership: Verizon Communications Inc.

FIOS1 POTOMAC — See FiOS Long Island.
Web Site: http://www.fios1news.com/WashingtonDC.php
Type of service: Digital.
Operating areas: District of Columbia, Maryland & Virginia.
Programming: Local news, sports, weather & community interest.
Began: March 31, 2007.
Distribution method: Available to Verizon FiOS subscribers.
Scrambled signal: Yes.
Ownership: Verizon Communications Inc.

FITTV — See Discovery Life Channel.

FIX & FOXI
c/o Alterna'tv
2020 Ponce de Leon Blvd, Ste 1107
Coral Gables, FL 33134
Phone: 786-609 9604
Web Site: http://www.fixundfoxi.tv
Programming: Animated series.
Ownership: Your Family Entertainment. Distributed in the U.S. by Alterna'tv.

FLIX
Paramount Plaza Bldg
1633 Broadway
New York, NY 10019
Phone: 212-708-1600
Fax: 212-708-1212
E-mail: talk2@showtimeonline.com
Web Site: http:///www.sho.com
Matthew C. Blank, Chairman, Showtime Networks
David Nevins, Chief Executive Officer, Showtime Networks
Type of service: Pay, video on demand.
Satellites: AT&T Telstar 303, transponder 17.
Operating hours/week: 168.
Programming: Movie channel featuring films from the 60s, 70s, 80s & 90s, uncut & commercial-free.
Began: August 1, 1992.
Means of Support: Subscriber fees.
Scrambled signal: Yes. Equipment: VideoCipher II Plus.
Ownership: Showtime Networks.

FLORIDA CHANNEL
402 S Monroe St
Ste 901, The Capitol Bldg
Tallahassee, FL 32399-1300
Phone: 850-488-1281
Fax: 850-488-4876
E-mail: florida@wfsu.org
Web Site: http://thefloridachannel.org
Beth Switzer, Executive Director
Krysta Brown, News Director
Terry Longordo, Engineering Supervisor
Operating hours/week: 168.
Programming: A public service of the Florida Legislature, WFSU-TV and Florida State University that features programming covering all three branches of state government.
Scrambled signal: Yes.

FMX CABLE FM SYSTEM
c/o Channel & Communications
10715 Cherry Tree Ct
Adelphi, MD 20783
Phones: 301-595-3075; 301-595-5479
Fax: 301-577-4153
William L. Tucker, Jr., President & Chief Executive Officer
Brett-Lydle Martin, Vice President & Controller
Type of service: Pay, streaming.
Operating hours/week: 168.
Operating areas: Baltimore, MD & the District of Columbia.
Programming: Audio entertainment & information for cable subscribers & Internet users.
Began: January 1, 1995.
Means of Support: Subscriber fees & advertising.
Distribution method: Available to cable subscribers. Streaming available online.
Scrambled signal: Yes.

FNTSY SPORTS NETWORK
2844 Dundas St W
2nd Fl
Toronto, ON M6P 1Y7
Canada
Phones: 416-987-7841; 888-508-1143
Fax: 647-343-4173
Web Site: http://www.fantasysportsnetwork.com
Leonard Asper, Chief Executive Officer
Louis M. Maione, Executive Vice President
Chad Midgley, Vice President, Programming
Type of service: Basic.
Operating hours/week: 168.
Programming: The world's first 24-hour television and multi-platform channel dedicated to fantasy sports.
Began: March 4, 2014.
Means of Support: Advertising.
Total subscribers: 40,000,000 (Estimated size of potential audience).
Scrambled signal: Yes.
Ownership: Anthem Media Group Inc.

FOOD NETWORK
75 Ninth Ave
New York, NY 10011
Phone: 212-398-8836
Fax: 212-736-7716
Web Site: http://www.foodnetwork.com
Kenneth Lowe, Chairman & Chief Executive Officer
Ed Spray, President, Scripps Networks
Bob Tuschman, Senior Vice President & General Manager
Darren Campo, Senior Vice President, Program Strategy
Heidi Diamond, Senior Vice President, Marketing & Business Development
Susie Fogelson, Senior Vice President, Marketing & Brand Strategy
Karen Grinthal, Senior Vice President, Advertising Sales
Deirdre O'Hearn, Senior Vice President, Programming & Development
Eileen Opatut, Senior Vice President, Programming & Production
Bruce Seidel, Senior Vice President, Program Planning & Special Productions
Christine Barry, Vice President, Direct Response Ads
James Dowdle, Vice President, Midwestern Advertising Sales
Colleen Griffin, Vice President, Western Region, Advertising Sales
Bill Jarrett, Vice President, Engineering
Bill Kossman, Vice President, Program Planning
John Paruch, Vice President, Central Region, Advertising Sales
Jennifer Quainton, Vice President, Programming, Food Network & Cooking Channel
Carrie Welch, Vice President, Public Relations
Melissa Sheldon-Maurer, Ad Sales Research Director
Laura Health, Ad Sales Marketing Manager
Type of service: Basic, HD, streaming, video on demand.
Satellites: Galaxy I, transponder 4.
Operating hours/week: 168.

Pay TV & Satellite Services

Programming: All things food & related to food, such as nutrition, fitness & food-related features & films.
Began: August 30, 1993.
Means of Support: Advertising.
Total subscribers: 101,000,000.
Distribution method: Available to cable, IPTV & satellite subscribers. Streaming available online & through the WATCH Food Network app.
Scrambled signal: Yes.
Ownership: A joint venture between Scripps Networks Interactive (70%) & Tribune Media Co. (30%).

FOROTV — See Univision.
c/o Univision Communications Inc.
605 Third Ave, 12th Fl
New York, NY 10158
Phone: 212-455-5200
Web Site: http://www.televisanetworks.tv; http://corporate.univision.com
Beau Ferrari, Executive Vice President, Operations, Univision Networks
Type of service: Basic.
Satellites: AMC 10, transponder 4.
Operating hours/week: 168.
Operating areas: Available nationwide.
Programming: Spanish language news service customized for the U.S. offering viewers programming from a Latin perspective and a unique 'south of the border' point of view.
Began: May 3, 2012.
Means of Support: Advertising.
Distribution method: Available to satellite subscribers.
Scrambled signal: Yes.
Ownership: Televisa Networks. Univision Communications Inc. has an exclusive contract for this service.

FOX BUSINESS GO — See Fox Business Network.
Web Site: http://www.foxnewsgo.com
Type of service: Streaming.
Operating areas: Available nationwide.
Programming: Live programming & clips from Fox Business Network.
Distribution method: Available online & through app (participating providers.).

FOX BUSINESS NETWORK
1211 Ave of the Americas
12th Fl
New York, NY 10036
Phones: 212-607-7000; 888-369-4762
E-mail: john.mccann@foxnews.com
Web Site: http://www.foxbusiness.com
Rupert Murdoch, Chairman & Acting Chief Executive Officer
Dianne Brandi, Executive Vice President, Legal & Business Affairs
Irena Briganti, Executive Vice President, Corporate Communications, Fox News & Fox Business Network
Brian Jones, Executive Vice President, Operations
Neil Cavuto, Senior Vice President & Managing Editor, Fox News & Fox Business Network
Bruce Becker, Vice President, Business News, Washington, DC
Zach Friedman, Vice President, Digital Ad Sales, Fox News & Fox Business Network
Ray Lambiase, Vice President, Business Graphics
John McCann, Vice President, Ad Sales
Type of service: Basic, HD, streaming.
Satellites: Galaxy 17, transponder 8; Galaxy 17, transponder 2.
Operating hours/week: 168.
Operating areas: Available nationwide.
Programming: Business & financial market oriented news.
Began: October 15, 2007.
Total subscribers: 69,200,000.
Distribution method: Available to cable, IPTV & satellite subscribers. Streaming available online & through Fox Business app (participating providers).
Scrambled signal: Yes.
Ownership: 21st Century Fox.

FOX COLLEGE SPORTS ATLANTIC
c/o Fox Sports
10201 W Pico Blvd
Los Angeles, CA 90035
Phone: 310-369-1000
Web Site: http://www.foxsports.com/watch/fox-college-sports
Dan Bell, Vice President, Communications, FOX Sports
Ileana Pena, Communications Director, FOX Sports
Type of service: Basic, digital, streaming, video on demand.
Operating hours/week: 168.
Operating areas: Nationwide.
Programming: Features football, men's & women's basketball, baseball, softball, volleyball, lacrosse, ice hockey, wrestling & more from the Atlantic region.
Began: May 1, 2004.
Means of Support: Advertising.
Total subscribers: 65,000,000 (Includes subscribers for Atlantic, Central & Pacific Fox College Sports channels.).
Distribution method: Available to cable, IPTV & satellite subscribers. Streaming available online & through Fox Sports Go app (participating providers).
Scrambled signal: Yes.
Ownership: 21st Century Fox.

FOX COLLEGE SPORTS CENTRAL — See FOX College Sports Atlantic.
Programming: Features football, men's & women's basketball, baseball, softball, volleyball, lacrosse, ice hockey, wrestling & more from the Central region.

FOX COLLEGE SPORTS PACIFIC — See FOX College Sports Atlantic.
Programming: Features football, men's & women's basketball, baseball, softball, volleyball, lacrosse, ice hockey, wrestling & more from the Pacific region.

FOX DEPORTES
1211 Avenue of the Americas
31st Fl
New York, NY 10036
Phone: 212-822-9083
E-mail: support@foxhispanicmedia.com
Web Site: http://www.foxdeportes.com
FOX DEPORTES:, .
Carlos Sanchez, Executive Vice President & General Manager
Ruben Rocha, Operations Director
FOX HISPANIC MEDIA:, .
Tom Maney, Executive Vice President, Advertising Sales, Fox Hispanic Media
Juan Vallejo, Senior Vice President, Advertising Sales, Fox Hispanic Media
Type of service: Basic, digital, streaming, video on demand.
Satellites: Satcom C-1, transponder 16.
Operating hours/week: 168.
Operating areas: Nationwide.
Programming: National & international Spanish language sports network offering soccer, boxing, football, volleyball, surfing, tennis, auto & horse racing.
Began: March 1, 1995, as Fox Sports en Espanol. Rebranded as Fox Deports in October 2010.
Total subscribers: 21,000,000.
Distribution method: Available to cable, IPTV & satellite providers. Streaming available online & through Fox Sports Go app (participating providers).
Scrambled signal: Yes.
Ownership: 21st Century Fox.

FOX LIFE
1211 Avenue of the Americas
31st Fl
New York, NY 10036
Phone: 212-822-9083
E-mail: foxtv.info@fox.com
Web Site: http://www.foxlife.us/us; http://www.foxinternationalchannels.com/brands/utilisima
Carlos Martinez, President, Fox Networks Group, Latin America
Tom Maney, Executive Vice President, Advertising Sales, Fox Hispanic Media
Juan Vallejo, Senior Vice President, Advertising Sales, Fox Hispanic Media

Branch Offices:
ATLANTA: 3845 Pleasantdale Rd, Doraville, GA 30340-4205.

HOUSTON: 4000 Technology Forest Blvd, The Woodlands, TX 77381.

MIAMI: 2121 Ponce de Leon Blvd, Ste 1020, Coral Gables, FL 33134.

NEW YORK: 1211 Avenue of the Americas, New York, NY 10036.

WASHINGTON, DC: 1145 17th St NW, Washington, DC 20036.
Type of service: Basic, digital.
Operating areas: Nationwide.
Programming: Spanish language channel dedicated to food, health & family. Programming is heavily lifestyle-driven & showcases everything from cooking & personal style to decorating, do-it-yourself & home renovation.
Began: 1996 in Spain, as Utilisima. Began July 10, 2010 in the U.S. Rebranded Fox Life November, 4, 2013.
Total subscribers: 7,500,000.
Distribution method: Available to cable, IPTV & satellite subscribers.
Scrambled signal: Yes.
Ownership: Fox International Channels, a subsidiary of 21st Century Fox.

FOX MOVIE CHANNEL — See FXM.

FOX NEWS CHANNEL
1211 Ave of the Americas
2nd Fl
New York, NY 10036
Phones: 212-301-2000; 212-685-8400
Fax: 212-301-8274
Web Site: http://www.foxnews.com
Rupert Murdoch, Chairman
Jack Abernethy, Co-President
Bill Shine, Co-President
Dianne Brandi, Executive Vice President, Legal & Business Affairs
Irena Briganti, Executive Vice President, Corporate Communications, Fox News & Fox Business Report
Suzanne Scott, Executive Vice President, Programming & Development
Jay Wallace, Executive Vice President, News & Editorial
John Moody, Executive Vice President & Executive Editor
Paul Rittenburg, Executive Vice President, Advertising Sales
Sharri Berg, Senior Vice President, News Operations & Services
Neil Cavuto, Senior Vice President & Managing Editor, Fox News & Fox Business Network
Suzanne Scott, Senior Vice President, Programming & Development
Zach Friedman, Vice President, Digital Ad Sales, Fox News & Fox Business Network
Dom Rossi, Vice President, Eastern Sales
Frank Sorace, Vice President, Sales Planning & Commercial Operations
John Stack, Vice President, Newsgathering
Greg Ahlquist, Senior Director, Digital Media Productions
Richard O'Brien, Creative Director

Branch Offices:
LOS ANGELES: 2044 Armacost Ave, Los Angeles, CA 90025. Phone: 310-571-2000. Fax: 310-571-2009.

NEW YORK: 1211 Ave of the Americas, Concourse 1, New York, NY 10036. Phone: 212-301-3000. Fax: 212-301-4224.

WASHINGTON, DC: 400 N Capitol St NW, Ste 550, Washington, DC 20001. Phone: 202-824-6300. Fax: 202-824-6426.
Type of service: Basic, HD, streaming.
Satellites: Galaxy 17, transponder 6; Galaxy 15, transponder 2.
Operating hours/week: 168.
Operating areas: Available nationwide.
Programming: All news channel.
Began: October 7, 1996, Fox News HD launched May 1, 2008.
Means of Support: Advertising.
Total subscribers: 97,600,000.
Distribution method: Available to cable, IPTV & satellite providers. Streaming available online & through Fox News Go app (participating providers).
Scrambled signal: Yes.
Ownership: 21st Century Fox.

FOX NEWS GO — See Fox News Channel.
Web Site: http://www.foxnewsgo.com
Type of service: Streaming.
Operating areas: Available nationwide.
Programming: Live programming & clips from Fox News.
Distribution method: Available online & through app (participating providers).
Scrambled signal: Yes.

FOX REALITY CHANNEL — See Nat Geo WILD.

Pay TV & Satellite Services

FOX SOCCER — See Fox Soccer Plus.

FOX SOCCER PLUS
1440 S Sepulveda Blvd
Los Angeles, CA 90025
Phone: 310-444-8100
E-mail: comments@foxsoccer.com
Web Site: http://www.foxsoccerplus.com
David Nathanson, Executive Vice President & General Manager, FOX Sports 1 & FOX Sports 2
Jason Wormser, Vice President, Production
Type of service: Premium, HD, streaming, video on demand.
Operating areas: Nationwide.
Programming: Offers live, exclusive soccer matches from the best leagues in the world, including England's Barclays Premier League, the UEFA Champions League, England's FA Cup, Coca-Cola Championship, Carling Cup and England Men's National Team as well as Italy's Serie A.
Began: March 1, 2010, as a spin-off on the defunct Fox Soccer (formerly Fox Sport World).
Means of Support: Subscriber fees and advertising.
Distribution method: Available to cable, IPTV & satellite subscribers. Steaming & video on demand available online & through Fox Sports Soccer 2Go app.
Scrambled signal: Yes.
Ownership: 21st Century Fox.

FOX SOCCER 2GO — See Fox Soccer Plus.

FOX SPORTS 1
Fox Network Center
10201 W Pico Blvd, Bldg 101, 5th Fl
Los Angeles, CA 90064-2606
Phones: 310-369-9369; 310-369-9111
Web Site: http://www.foxsports.com/watch/foxsports1
FOX SPORTS:, .
Eric Shanks, President & Chief Operating Officer, FOX Sports
John Entz, President, Production, FOX Sports
Jamie Horowitz, President, FOX Sports National Networks
David Nathanson, Head of Business Operations, FOX Sports
Ed Delaney, Executive Vice President, Operations, FOX Sports
Barbara Blangiardi, Senior Vice President, Strategies & Creative Partnerships, FOX Sports
Mike Davies, Senior Vice President, Technical & Field Operations, FOX Sports
Sandy Gong, Senior Vice President, Production Management, FOX Sports
Aimee Leone, Senior Vice President, Talent, Fox Sports
Mark Pesavento, Senior Vice President, Content, FOX Sports Digital
Jack Simmons, Senior Vice President, Production, FOX Sports
Erik Arneson, Vice President, Media Relations, FOX Sports
Rod Conti, Vice President, Technical Operations & Production Management, FOX Sports
Gabe Goodein, Vice President, Cross-Platform Content
FOX SPORTS 1:, .
Charlie Dixon, Executive Vice President, Content, FOX Sports 1 & 2
Bill Battin, Senior Vice President, Marketing, FOX Sports 1
Whit Albohm, Vice President, Daily Studio Production
Type of service: Basic, HD, streaming, video on demand.
Satellites: Satcom C-4, transponder 11.
Operating hours/week: 168.
Operating areas: Available nationwide.
Programming: Offers college basketball & football, MLB, NASCAR, NFL (ancillary programs), soccer & UFC.
Began: February 23, 1996, as Speed Channel. Rebranded Fox Sports 1 August 17, 2013.
Means of Support: Advertising.
Total subscribers: 87,700,000.
Distribution method: Available to cable, IPTV & satellite subscribers. Streaming available online & through Fox Sports Go app (participating providers).
Scrambled signal: Yes.
Ownership: 21st Century Fox.

FOX SPORTS 2 — See FOX Sports 1.
Type of service: Basic, streaming, video on demand.
Operating hours/week: 168.
Operating areas: Available nationwide.
Programming: Adrenaline sports, entertainment & music.
Began: July 1, 2003, as Fuel TV. Rebranded as Fox Sports 2 August 17, 2013.
Total subscribers: 36,200,000.
Distribution method: Available to cable, IPTV & satellite subscribers. Streaming available online & through Fox Sports Go app (participating providers).
Scrambled signal: Yes.
Ownership: 21st Century Fox.

FOX SPORTS ARIZONA
One Renaissance Sq
2 N Central Ave, Ste 1700
Phoenix, AZ 85004
Phone: 602-257-9500
Fax: 602-257-0848
E-mail: fsnarizona@foxsports.com
Web Site: http://www.foxsports.com/arizona
Brian Hogan, Senior Vice President & General Manager
Brett Hansen, Communications & Marketing Director
Keith Warren, Local Sales Manager
Sarah Wells, Production Operations Manager
Type of service: Basic, HD, streaming, video on demand.
Operating areas: Arizona.
Programming: Regional coverage of the area's professional teams including Arizona Diamondbacks, Phoenix Suns, Arizona Cardinals & Phoenix Coyotes as well as coverage of ASU, U of A, NAU & New Mexico State sports.
Began: September 7, 1996, as Prime Sports Arizona. Rebranded Fox Sports Arizona November 1996.
Total subscribers: 2,800,000.
Distribution method: Available to cable & satellite subscribers. Steaming available online & through Fox Sports Go app (participating providers).
Scrambled signal: Yes.
Ownership: 21st Century Fox.

FOX SPORTS ARIZONA PLUS — See FOX Sports Arizona.
Programming: An alternate feed when events overlap; regional coverage of the area's professional & collegiate teams.

FOX SPORTS CAROLINAS
6000 Fairview Rd
Ste 1200
Charlotte, NC 28210
Phone: 704-552-3647
E-mail: fscarolinas@foxsports.net
Web Site: http://www.foxsports.com/carolinas
Jeff Genthner, Senior Vice President & General Manager, FOX Sports Carolinas, South & Tennessee
Type of service: Basic, HD, streaming, video on demand.
Operating areas: North & South Carolina.
Programming: Regional coverage of the area's professional teams including the Carolina Hurricanes, Carolina Panthers & Charlotte Hornets as well as ACC & SEC sports.
Began: October 27, 2008.
Means of Support: Advertising.
Total subscribers: 4,000,000.
Distribution method: Available to cable, IPTV & satellite subscribers. Streaming available online & through Fox Sports Go app (through participating providers).
Scrambled signal: Yes.
Ownership: 21st Century Fox.

FOX SPORTS DETROIT
26555 Evergreen
Ste 90
Southfield, MI 48076
Phone: 248-226-9700
Fax: 248-226-9740
E-mail: fsdetroit@foxsports.net
Web Site: http://www.foxsports.com/detroit
Greg Hammaren, Senior Vice President & General Manager
Marcia Turner, Vice President & General Sales Manager
Denise Bailet, Executive Director, Programming
John Gumina, Distribution Director
Karen Kanigowski, Finance Director
Lauren Pober, Marketing Director
Michael Happy, Digital Content Manager
Courtney Welch, Social Media Manager
John Tuohey, Executive Producer
Type of service: Basic, HD, streaming, video on demand.
Operating areas: Michigan, portions of northwestern Ohio & northern Indiana.
Programming: Regional coverage of the area's professional teams including Detroit Red Wings, Tigers, Pistons & the Lions football as well as Michigan Wolverines & Michigan State Spartans.
Began: September 17, 1997.
Total subscribers: 3,200,000.
Distribution method: Available to cable, IPTV & satellite subscribers. Streaming available online & through Fox Sports Go app (participating providers).
Scrambled signal: Yes.
Ownership: 21st Century Fox.

FOX SPORTS DETROIT PLUS — See FOX Sports Detroit.
Programming: An alternate feed when events overlap; regional coverage of the area's professional & collegiate teams.

FOX SPORTS FLORIDA/SUN SPORTS
500 E Broward Blvd
Ste 1300
Fort Lauderdale, FL 33394
Phone: 954-375-3634
Fax: 800-369-0073
E-mail: infofl@foxsports.net
Web Site: http://www.foxsports.com/florida
Steve Tello, Senior Vice President & General Manager
Marc LeSage, Vice President & General Sales Manager
Tim Ivy, Programming Director
Corenna Smith, Marketing & Communications Director
Brian De Los Santos, Digital Content Manager
Eric Esteban, Media Relations Manager
Marc Magnone, Local Sales Manager
A. J. Protash, National Sales Manager

Branch Offices:

ORLANDO: 1000 Legion Pl, Ste 1600, Orlando, FL 32801-1060. Phone: 407-648-1150. Fax: 407-245-2571.

TAMPA: 3001 N Rock Point Dr E, Ste 236, Tampa, FL 33607. Phone: 813-286-6185. Fax: 813-286-6185.
Type of service: Basic, HD, streaming, video on demand.
Satellites: GE-1, transponder 4.
Operating hours/week: 168.
Operating areas: Florida.
Programming: Regional coverage of the area's professional teams including Florida Panthers, Tampa Bay Lightening, Tampa Bay Buccaneers, Miami Dolphins, Jacksonville Jaguars, Tampa Bay Rays, Miami Marlins, Orlando Magic & Miami Heat as well as Florida Gators, Florida State Seminoles & Miami Hurricanes sports.
Began: January 1, 1997, as SportsChannel Florida. Rebranded as Fox Sports Florida on March 1, 2000.
Means of Support: Subscriber fees & advertising.
Total subscribers: 5,000,000.
Distribution method: Available to cable, IPTV & satellite subscribers. Streaming available online & through Fox Sports Go app (participating providers).
Scrambled signal: Yes. Equipment: DSR 4500X.
Ownership: 21st Century Fox.

FOX SPORTS FLORIDA PLUS — See FOX Sports Florida/Sun Sports.
Programming: An alternate feed when events overlap; regional coverage of the area's professional & collegiate teams.

FOX SPORTS GO — See Fox Sports Networks.
Web Site: http://www.foxsports.com/foxsportsgo
Brian Sullivan, President, Digital, Fox Networks Group
Type of service: Streaming.
Operating areas: Available nationwide.
Programming: Live & previously-aired programming from the Fox Sports Networks.
Distribution method: Available online & through app (participating providers).

FOX SPORTS HOUSTON — No longer in operation. See FOX Sports Southwest.

Pay TV & Satellite Services

FOX SPORTS INDIANA
135 N Pennsylvania St
Ste 720
Indianapolis, IN 46204
Phone: 317-684-5600
Web Site: http://www.foxsports.com/indiana
Jack Donovan, Senior Vice President & General Manager
Type of service: Basic, HD, streaming, video on demand.
Operating areas: Indiana.
Programming: Regional coverage of the area's profession teams including Indiana Pacers & Indiana Fever.
Began: November 1, 2006.
Means of Support: Advertising.
Total subscribers: 1,200,000.
Distribution method: Available to cable, IPTV & satellite subscribers. Streaming available online & through Fox Sports Go app (participating providers).
Scrambled signal: Yes.
Ownership: 21st Century Fox.

FOX SPORTS INDIANA PLUS — See FOX Sports Indiana.
Programming: An alternate feed when events overlap; regional coverage of the area's professional & collegiate teams.

FOX SPORTS KANSAS CITY — See FOX Sports Midwest.
E-mail: FSKansas.feedback@fox.com
Web Site: http://www.foxsports.com/kansas-city
Type of service: Basic, HD, streaming, video on demand.
Operating hours/week: 168.
Operating areas: Iowa, Kansas, Missouri & Nebraska.
Programming: Regional coverage of the area's professional teams including the Kansas City Royals & Kansas City Chiefs as well as K-State, KU & Mizzou basketball & football.
Began: April 1, 2008.
Means of Support: Advertising.
Total subscribers: 3,000,000.
Distribution method: Available to cable, IPTV & satellite subscribers. Streaming available online & though Fox Sports Go app (participating providers).
Scrambled signal: Yes.
Ownership: 21st Century Fox.

FOX SPORTS KANSAS CITY PLUS — See FOX Sports Kansas City.
Programming: An alternate feed when events overlap; regional coverage of the area's professional & collegiate teams.
Scrambled signal: Yes.

FOX SPORTS MIDWEST
333 S 18th St
Ste 300
St Louis, MO 63103-2256
Phone: 314-206-7000
Fax: 314-206-7070
E-mail: midwest@foxsports.net
Web Site: http://www.foxsports.com/midwest
Jack Donovan, Senior Vice President & General Manager
Robert Adelman, Vice President, Affiliate Sales & Marketing
Rick Powers, Programming Director
David Pokorny, Marketing Director
Robyn Althoff, Traffic Director
Matt Riordan, National Sales Manager
Ken Allgeyer, General Sales Manager
Geoff Goldman, Media Relations Manager
Larry Mago, Executive Producer
Gavin Bodell, Coordinating Producer
Max Leinwand, Coordinating Producer

Branch Offices:
INDIANAPOLIS: 135 N Pennsylvania St, First Indiana Plaza, Ste 720, Indianapolis, IN 46204. Phone: 317-684-5600. Fax: 317-684-5610.
Type of service: Basic, HD, video on demand.
Satellites: G7.
Operating hours/week: 168.
Operating areas: Illinois, Indiana, Iowa, Missouri, Nebraska & Kansas.
Programming: Local programming, including St. Louis Cardinals baseball, St. Louis Blues hockey, Kansas City Royals baseball, Indiana Pacers basketball, Indiana Fever basketball, Big 12 football, Big 12 women's basketball, Missouri Valley Conference athletics, U. of Missouri basketball & Kansas State U. sports.
Began: November 1, 1996.
Total subscribers: 6,000,000.
Distribution method: Available to cable, IPTV & satellite subscribers. Video on demand available through select providers.
Scrambled signal: Yes.
Ownership: Fox Entertainment Group.

FOX SPORTS MIDWEST PLUS — See FOX Sports Midwest.
Programming: An alternate feed when events overlap; regional coverage of the area's professional & collegiate teams.

FOX SPORTS NET NEW YORK — See MSG Plus.

FOX SPORTS NET NORTHWEST — See Root Sports Northwest.

FOX SPORTS NET PITTSBURGH — See Root Sports Pittsburgh.

FOX SPORTS NET ROCKY MOUNTAIN — See Root Sports Rocky Mountain.

FOX SPORTS NET UTAH — See Root Sports Rocky Mountain.

FOX SPORTS NET WEST 2 — See FOX Sports West/Prime Ticket.

FOX SPORTS NETWORKS — See regional FOX Sports Networks.
FOX SPORTS MEDIA GROUP:, .
Ed Goren, Vice Chairman, FOX Sports Media Group
Robert Gottlieb, Executive Vice President, Marketing, FOX Sports Media Group
Kai Dhaliwal, Senior Vice President, Business & Legal Affairs, FOX Sports Media Group
FOX SPORTS:, .
Eric Shanks, President, Chief Operating Officer & Executive Producer, FOX Sports
John Entz, President, Production, FOX Sports
Jamie Horowitz, President, FOX Sports National Networks, FOX Sports
Jeff Krolik, President, Fox Sports Regional Networks, FOX Sports
David Nathanson, Head of Business Operations, FOX Sports
Scott Ackerson, Executive Vice President, News, FOX Sports
Ed Delaney, Executive Vice President, Operations, FOX Sports
Robert Gottlieb, Executive Vice President, Marketing, FOX Sports
George Greenberg, Executive Vice President, Content Integration & Presentation, FOX Sports
Chris Hannan, Executive Vice President, Communications & Integration, FOX Sports
Gary Hartley, Executive Vice President, Graphics, FOX Sports
Larry Jones, Executive Vice President, Business, FOX Sports
Neil Mulcahy, Executive Vice President, Sports Sales, FOX Sports
Pete Vlastelica, Executive Vice President, Digital, FOX Sports
Bill Wanger, Executive Vice President, Programming, Research & Content Strategy, FOX Sports
Ben Gerst, Senior Vice President, Platform Development, FOX Sports
Clark Pierce, Senior Vice President, TV Everywhere, FOX Sports
Mike Davies, Senior Vice President, Technical & Field Operations, FOX Sports
Sandy Gong, Senior Vice President, Production Management, FOX Sports
Jack Simmons, Senior Vice President, Production, FOX Sports
Erik Arneson, Vice President, Media Relations, FOX Sports
Rod Conti, Vice President, Technical Operations & Production Management, FOX Sports
Began: November 1, 1996.
Total subscribers: 70,000,000 (Includes subscribers for 22 FSN regional networks.).

FOX SPORTS NEW ORLEANS — See FOX Sports Southwest.
Type of service: Basic, HD, streaming, video on demand.
Operating areas: Alabama, Florida, Louisiana, Mississippi & Texas.
Programming: Regional coverage of the area's professional teams including New Orleans Pelicans, Louisiana high school events, Texas Rangers baseball, Dallas Stars hockey, plus Big 12 Conference, Conference USA & PAC-12 Conference events.
Began: October 31, 2012.
Means of Support: Advertising.
Total subscribers: 1,600,000.
Distribution method: Available to cable, IPTV & satellite subscribers. Streaming available online & through Fox Sports Go app (participating providers).
Scrambled signal: Yes.
Ownership: 21st Century Fox.

FOX SPORTS NORTH
80 Lasalle Ave
Ste 200
Minneapolis, MN 55402
Phone: 612-332-2203
Fax: 612-486-9513
E-mail: fsnnorthinfo@foxsports.net
Web Site: http://www.foxsports.com/north
Mike Dimond, Senior Vice President & General Manager, FOX Sports North & FOX Sports Wisconsin
Type of service: Basic, HD, streaming, video on demand.
Operating hours/week: 168.
Operating areas: Iowa, Minnesota, North Dakota, South Dakota.
Programming: Regional coverage of the area's professional teams including Minnesota Vikings, Minnesota Timberwolves & Minnesota Twins as well as the Minnesota Wild, Minnesota Golden Gophers & Minnesota Lynx.
Began: January 1, 1989, as Midwest Sports Channel. Rebranded Fox Sports Net North in April 2001, then Fox Sports North in 2009.
Means of Support: Advertising.
Distribution method: Available to cable, IPTV & satellite subscribers. Streaming available online or through Fox Sports Go app (participating providers).
Scrambled signal: Yes.
Ownership: 21st Century Fox.

FOX SPORTS NORTH PLUS — See FOX Sports North.
Programming: An alternate feed when events overlap; regional coverage of the area's professional & collegiate teams.
Began: February 1, 2012.

FOX SPORTS OHIO/SPORTS TIME OHIO
9200 South Hills Blvd
Ste 200
Broadview Heights, OH 44147
Phone: 440-746-8000
Fax: 440-746-8700
E-mail: contactus-fso@foxsports.net
Web Site: http://www.foxsports.com/ohio
Francois McGillicuddy, Senior Vice President & General Manager
Tom Farmer, Vice President, Programming & Production
Charlie Knudson, Vice President & General Sales Manager
Alex Slemc, Marketing & Communications Director
Kate Zelasko, Public Relations Director
Type of service: Basic, HD, streaming, video on demand.
Satellites: GE-1, transponder 4.
Operating areas: Indiana, Kentucky, New York, Ohio, Pennsylvania & West Virginia.
Programming: Regional coverage of the area's professional teams including Cincinnati Reds, Cleveland Indians, Cleveland Cavaliers, Columbus Blue Jackets, Cleveland Browns & Cincinnati Bengals as well as Cincinnati Bearcats, Ohio State Buckeyes, U of Dayton & Xavier U sports.
Began: February 9, 1989, as Sports Channel Ohio. Rebranded FOX Sports Net in 2000, then FOX Sports Ohio in 2005. Sports Time Ohio began March 12, 2006.
Means of Support: Advertising.
Total subscribers: 5,000,000.
Distribution method: Available to cable, IPTV & satellite systems. Streaming available online & through the Fox Sports Go app (participating providers).
Scrambled signal: Yes.
Ownership: 21st Century Fox.

FOX SPORTS OHIO PLUS — See FOX Sports Ohio/Sports Time Ohio.
Programming: An alternate feed when events overlap; regional coverage of the area's professional & collegiate teams.

2017 Edition
E-39

Pay TV & Satellite Services

FOX SPORTS OKLAHOMA — See FOX Sports Southwest.
Type of service: Basic, HD, streaming, video on demand.
Operating areas: Oklahoma.
Programming: Regional coverage of the area's professional teams including Oklahoma City Thunder as well as U of Oklahoma & Oklahoma high school events, Texas Rangers baseball, Dallas Stars hockey, plus Big 12 Conference, Conference USA & Pac-12 Conference events.
Began: October 29, 2008.
Means of Support: Advertising.
Distribution method: Available to cable, IPTV & satellite subscribers. Streaming available online or through Fox Sports Go app (participating providers).
Scrambled signal: Yes.
Ownership: 21st Century Fox.

FOX SPORTS OKLAHOMA PLUS —
See FOX Sports Oklahoma.
Programming: An alternate feed when events overlap; regional coverage of the area's professional & collegiate teams.

FOX SPORTS SAN DIEGO
350 10th Ave
Ste 400
San Diego, CA 92101
Phone: 619-849-6324
E-mail: foxsportssandiego@foxsports.net
Web Site: http://www.foxsports.com/san-diego
Henry Ford, Senior President & General Manager
Wayne Guymon, Vice President & General Sales Manager
Kim Pletyak, Regional Operations Director
Trevor Arroyo, Programming Director
Megan Tolley, Marketing Director
Gema Tarango, Communications Manager
Jeff Byle, Executive Producer
Type of service: Basic, HD, streaming, video on demand.
Operating areas: Southern California, Arizona.
Programming: Regional coverage of the area's professional teams including the San Diego Padres, the San Diego Chargers, the Los Angeles Clippers & the Anaheim Ducks hockey as well as local college sports.
Began: March 17, 2012.
Means of Support: Subscriber fees and advertising.
Distribution method: Available to cable, IPTV & satellite subscribers. Streaming available online & through Fox Sports Go app (participating providers).
Scrambled signal: Yes.
Ownership: 21st Century Fox.

FOX SPORTS SOUTH/SPORTSOUTH
1175 Peachtree St NE
Bldg 100, Ste 200
Atlanta, GA 30361
Phone: 404-230-7300
Fax: 404-230-7199
E-mail: FSSouth@foxsports.net
Web Site: http://www.foxsports.com/south
Jeffrey Genthner, Vice President & General Manager
Brandon Howell, Vice President & General Sales Manager
Rolanda Gaines, Marketing & Communications Director
Type of service: Basic, HD, streaming & video on demand.
Satellites: Galaxy 11, transponder 4.
Operating hours/week: 168.
Operating areas: Alabama, Georgia, Kentucky & Mississippi.
Programming: Regional coverage of the area's professional teams including the Atlanta Hawks, the Atlanta Braves & the Atlanta Falcons as well as ACC & SEC events.
Began: August 29, 1990.
Means of Support: Advertising & subscriber fees.
Total subscribers: 7,000,000.
Distribution method: Available to cable, IPTV & satellite subscribers. Streaming available online or through Fox Sports Go app (participating providers).
Scrambled signal: Yes.
Ownership: 21st Century Fox.

FOX SPORTS SOUTH PLUS — See FOX Sports South/SportSouth.
Programming: An alternate feed when events overlap; regional coverage of the area's professional & collegiate teams.

FOX SPORTS SOUTHWEST
100 E Royal Ln
Ste 200
Irving, TX 75039
Phone: 972-868-1800
Fax: 972-868-1678
E-mail: ralvarez@foxsports.net
Web Site: http://www.foxsports.com/southwest
Jon Heidtke, Senior Vice President & General Manager
Mark Yates, Vice President & General Sales Manager
Ramon Alvarez, Public Relations Director
Brandon Davis, Affiliate Sales Director
Mary Hyink, Marketing Director
Tom Garnier, Programming Director
Kristi Roberts, Media Relations Manager
Type of service: Basic, HD, streaming, video on demand.
Operating hours/week: 168.
Operating areas: Arkansas, Louisiana, New Mexico, Oklahoma & Texas.
Programming: Regional coverage of the area's professional teams including Texas Rangers, Dallas Cowboys, Houston Texans, Dallas Stars, San Antonio Spurs, Dallas Mavericks, New Orleans Pelicans & Oklahoma City Thunder.
Began: January 4, 1983, as Home Sports Entertainment. Rebranded as Prime Sports Southwest in 1994, Fox Sports Southwest in 1996, Fox Sports Net Southwest in 2000, FSN Southwest in 2004 & Fox Sports Southwest in 2008.
Means of Support: Advertising.
Total subscribers: 7,600,000.
Distribution method: Available to cable, IPTV & satellite subscribers. Streaming available online & through Fox Sports Go app (participating providers).
Scrambled signal: Yes. Equipment: VideoCipher II.
Ownership: 21st Century Fox.

FOX SPORTS SOUTHWEST PLUS —
See FOX Sports Southwest.
Programming: An alternate feed when events overlap; regional coverage of the area's professional & collegiate teams.

FOX SPORTS TENNESSEE — See FOX Sports South/SportSouth.
E-mail: FSTennessee.feedback@fox.com
Web Site: http://www.foxsports.com/tennessee
Type of service: Basic, HD, streaming & video on demand.
Operating areas: Northern Alabama, eastern Arkansas, northeastern Mississippi, Tennessee.
Programming: Regional coverage of the area's professional teams including the Tennessee Titans, Memphis Grizzlies & Nashville Predators as well as the Tennessee Volunteers & SEC events.
Began: October 27, 2008.
Means of Support: Advertising.
Total subscribers: 1,800,000.
Distribution method: Available to cable, IPTV & satellite subscribers. Streaming available online & through FOX Sports Go app (participating providers).
Scrambled signal: Yes.
Ownership: 21st Century Fox.

FOX SPORTS WEST/PRIME TICKET
1100 S Flower St
Ste 2200
Los Angeles, CA 90015-2125
Phone: 213-743-7800
Fax: 310-286-6363
E-mail: communications@foxsports.net
Web Site: http://www.foxsports.com/west
Steve Simpson, Senior Vice President & General Manager
Melissa Dlin, Vice President & General Sales Manager
Whitney Burack, Communications Director
Debbie Chavez, Finance Director
Ian LaVallee, Marketing & OAP Director
Pete Stella, Digital Content Manager
Nick Davis, Executive Producer
Type of service: Basic, HD, streaming & video on demand.
Satellites: Satcom C-1, transponder 7 & 21.
Operating hours/week: 168.
Operating areas: California, Hawaii & Nevada.
Programming: Regional coverage of the area's professional teams including the Los Angeles Clippers, Los Angeles Kings, Los Angeles Angels as well as Big West, UCLA & USC events.
Began: October 19, 1985.
Means of Support: System fees & advertising.
Distribution method: Available to cable, IPTV & satellite subscribers. Streaming available online & through Fox Sports Go app (through participating providers).
Scrambled signal: Yes. Equipment: VideoCipher II.
Ownership: 21st Century Fox.

FOX SPORTS WEST PLUS — See FOX Sports West/Prime Ticket.
Programming: An alternate feed when events overlap; regional coverage of the area's professional & collegiate teams.

FOX SPORTS WISCONSIN — See FOX Sports North.
E-mail: fswisconsin.feedback@fox.com
Web Site: http://www.foxsports.com/wisconsin
Type of service: Basic, HD, streaming, video on demand.
Operating areas: Wisconsin.
Programming: Regional coverage of the area's professional teams including the Green Bay Packers, Milwaukee Brewers, the Milwaukee Bucks, as well as Wisconsin Badgers & Marquette Golden Eagle events.
Began: April 1, 2007.
Means of Support: Advertising.
Total subscribers: 1,500,000.
Distribution method: Available to cable, IPTV & satellite subscribers. Streaming available online or through Fox Sports Go app (through participating providers).
Scrambled signal: Yes.
Ownership: 21st Century Fox.

FOX SPORTS WISCONSIN PLUS —
See FOX Sports Wisconsin.
Programming: An alternate feed when events overlap; regional coverage of the area's professional & collegiate teams.

FOX SPORTS WORLD — See FOX Soccer PLUS.

FRANCE 24
5 rue des Nations Unies
Issy-les-Moulineaux 92130
France
Phone: 331-7301-2424
Fax: 331-7301-2456
E-mail: webdesk@france24.com
Web Site: http://www.france24.com
Alain de Pouzilhac, Chairman
Christine Ockrent, Chief Executive Officer
Patrice Begay, Chief Operating Officer, Advertising
Bruno Tezenas du Montcel, Chief Technology Officer
Philippe Rouxel, Vice President, Worldwide Distribution
Vincent Giret, General Manager
Albert Ripamonti, News Director
Anne Kacki, Legal Services Director
Nathalie Lenfant, Communications Director
Stanislas Leridon, Internet & New Media Director
Sophie Letierce, Human Resources Director
Cecile Maries, Administrative & Financial Director
Type of service: Basic, over the air.
Operating hours/week: 168.
Programming: International news channel covering world events from a French perspective and to convey French values throughout the world.
Began: December 6, 2006, in France. Began July 2009 in U.S.
Means of Support: Advertising.
Distribution method: Available over the air on digital sub-channels & to cable, IPTV & satellite subscribers.
Scrambled signal: Yes.
Ownership: Audiovisuel Exterieur de la France.

FREEFORM
500 S Buena Vista St
Burbank, CA 91521
Phone: 818-560-1000
E-mail: press@abcfamily.com
Web Site: http://abcfamily.go.com
Tom Ascheim, President
Laura Nathanson, President, Sales
Karey Burke, Executive Vice President, Programming & Development
Salaam Coleman Smith, Executive Vice President, Strategy & Programming
Eytan Keller, Executive Vice President, Alternative Programming
Nigel Cox-Hagen, Senior Vice President, Marketing, Creative & Branding
Laura Kuhn Nelson, Senior Vice President, Strategic Sales Insights
Kary McHoul, Senior Vice President, Programmimg & Development, Unscripted
Kenny Miller, Senior Vice President, Digital Programming & Product
Sabrina Padwa, Senior Vice President, Business Affairs
Mark Rejtig, Senior Vice President, National Sales
Simran Sethi, Senior Vice President, Original Programming & Development
Michelle Walenz, Senior Vice President, Marketing, Creative & Branding
Jori Arancio, Vice President, Media Relations
Elizabeth Boykewich, Vice President, Casting & Talent

Pay TV & Satellite Services

George Chen, Vice President, Strategy & Business Development
Jennifer Gersenblatt, Vice President, Current Programming
Kelly Goode, Vice President, Original Programming
Danielle Mullin, Vice President, Marketing
Jana Steele Helman, Vice President, Programming & Development
Type of service: Basic, digital, HD, steaming & video on demand.
Satellites: Galaxy V, transponder 11 (east coast); Satcom C-3, transponder 1 (west coast).
Operating hours/week: 168.
Programming: Family-oriented entertainment, including original series for kids.
Began: April 29, 1977, as CBN Satellite Service. Rebranded as CBN Cable Network in 1981, The CBN Family Channel in 1988 and The Family Channel in 1990. Rebranded as Fox Family Channel in 1998 after sale to News Corp. Rebranded as ABC Family on October 24, 2001 after sale to The Walt Disney Co. ABC Family HD began in 2008. Rebranded Freeform January 12, 2016.
Means of Support: Advertising & system fees.
Total subscribers: 94,400,000.
Distribution method: Available to cable, IPTV & satellite subscribers; online & mobile through the WATCH ABC Family website or app (participating providers); video on demand (participating providers).
Scrambled signal: Yes. Equipment: VideoCipher II.
Ownership: Disney-ABC Television Group.

FREE SPEECH TV
PO Box 44099
Denver, CO 80201
Phone: 303-442-8445
Fax: 303-442-6472
E-mail: jon@freespeech.org
Web Site: http://www.freespeech.org
Ron Williams, Executive Director
Jon Stout, General Manager
Yolanda Williams, Controller
Antoinette June, Online Director
Alexander Maness, Broadcast Media Director
Jason McKain, Development Director
Than Reeder, Operations Director
Type of service: Basic, streaming video on demand.
Satellites: Galaxy 18.
Operating hours/week: 168.
Programming: News & information programming that promotes under-represented voices & spotlights social, economic, environmental & racial justice issues. Programs include The Thom Hartmann Program, Democracy Now!, Al Jazeera English News, Gay USA & investigative documentaries.
Began: July 1, 1995.
Total subscribers: 22,000,000.
Distribution method: Available to cable, IPTV & satellite subscribers. Streaming available through select providers & online.
Scrambled signal: Yes.
Ownership: Public Communicators Inc.

FREE TO CHOOSE NETWORK
2002 Filmore Ave
Erie, PA 16506
Phones: 814-833-7107; 800-876-8930
Fax: 814-833-7415
E-mail: info@freetochoose.net
Web Site: http://www.freetochoose.net
Bob Chitester, President & Chief Executive Officer

Type of service: Basic.
Satellites: Galaxy III, transponder 23.
Operating hours/week: 1.
Programming: Uses accessible and entertaining media to build popular support for personal, economic and political freedom.
Began: October 1, 1992, as Idea Channel.
Means of Support: Advertising & investments.
Distribution method: Available to cable & satellite subscribers.
Scrambled signal: Yes.
Ownership: Bob Chitester.

FRESH — See Brazzers TV.

FROST GREAT OUTDOORS
PO Box 11409
Chattanooga, TN 37401
Phone: 423-468-5100
Fax: 423-468-5201
E-mail: info@luken.tv
Web Site: http://www.luken.tv
Henry Luken, Founder
Matt Winn, Vice President
Type of service: Basic.
Programming: Features hunting, camping, fishing and outdoor entertainment, plus home shopping through Frost Cutlery Co.
Began: August 1, 2011.
Means of Support: Advertising.
Distribution method: Available over-the-air on digital sub-channels.
Scrambled signal: Yes.
Ownership: A joint venture between Frost Cutlery Co. & Luken Communications LLC.

FSZ TV (FANTASY SPORTS ZONE TV)
6615 Boynton Beach Blvd
Ste 217
Boynton Beach, FL 33437
Phone: 800-851-8550
E-mail: paula@fsztv.com
Web Site: http://www.fsztv.com
Jeff Segansky, Co-Founder & Chairman
Steve Friedman, Co-Founder & President
Operating hours/week: Plans 168.
Operating areas: Plans nationwide.
Programming: Plans original programming devoted to professional and college fantasy sports, including baseball, basketball, NASCAR, hockey & golf.
Scheduled to begin: Unannounced.
Total subscribers: 35,000,000 (Size of target audience.).
Distribution method: Plans to be available to cable & satellite subscribers.
Scrambled signal: Yes.
Ownership: FSZ Media LLC.

FUEL TV — See Fox Sports 2.

FUJIAN STRAITS TV
c/o FMG
West Ring Rd
Fuzhou, Fujian 128 350004
China
Phones: 86-0-591-8331-0945; 86-0-591-335-3168
Web Site: http://www.fjtv.net
Programming: Provides a variety of Chinese programming in Fujianese dialect.
Began: October 1, 2005.
Distribution method: Available to KyLin TV & DISH Network subscribers.
Scrambled signal: Yes.
Ownership: Fujian Media Group.

FUNIMATION CHANNEL
560 Village Blvd
Ste 250
West Palm Beach, FL 33409
Phone: 561-684-5657

Fax: 561-684-9690
E-mail: kim@olympusat.com
Web Site: http://www.funimation.tv
Tom Mohler, Chief Executive Officer, Olympusat Holdings Inc.
Gen Fukunaga, Chief Executive Officer & President
Mauro Panzera, Chief Operating Officer, Olympusat Inc.
Bill Saltzgiver, Senior Vice President, Network Operations, Olympusat Inc.
Amanda Nanawa, Programming Director, FUNimation Channel, VOD Operations Director, Olympusat Inc.
Type of service: Digital, HD, streaming.
Satellites: Intelsat Galaxy 23.
Operating hours/week: 168.
Operating areas: Nationwide.
Programming: 24/7 anime.
Began: September 1, 2005.
Total subscribers: 40,000,000.
Distribution method: Available to cable & IPTV subscribers. Streaming available online.
Scrambled signal: Yes.
Ownership: A joint venture between Olympusat Inc. & FUNimation Entertainment.

FUSE
11 Penn Plz
17th Fl
New York, NY 10001
Phone: 212-465-6741
Fax: 212-324-3445
E-mail: fuseinfo@fuse.tv
Web Site: http://www.fuse.tv
Michael Schwimmer, Chief Executive Officer, Fuse Media
David Clark, Executive Vice President & General Manager
Matt Farber, Executive Vice President, Programming, Development & Digital
Brad Samuels, Executive Vice President, Content Distribution
Bob Dahill, Senior Vice President, Affiliate Sales & Marketing
Sharoan Harris, Senior Vice President, Pricing & Planning
Liana Huth Farnham, Senior Vice President, Partnerships & Events
Allan Infeld, Senior Vice President, Ad Sales
Marc Leonard, Senior Vice President, Content Strategy
Judi Lopez, Senior Vice President, Affiliate Distribution & Marketing
Jason Million, Senior Vice President, National Ad Sales
Amy Stevens, Senior Vice President, Strategic Alliances
Barry Watkins, Senior Vice President, Communications
Charlene Weisler, Senior Vice President, Research
Guy Cacciarelli, Vice President, Content Distribution, Western Region
Michael Goldstein, Vice President, Interactive Programming
Maggie Helm, Vice President, Ad Sales, West
Brian Hoffman, Vice President, Marketing Solutions
Marcelle Karp, Vice President, Creative Director Creative Services
Beth Lewand, Vice President, Digital Media

ADVANCED TVFactbook
FULLY SEARCHABLE • CONTINUOUSLY UPDATED • DISCOUNT RATES FOR PRINT PURCHASERS
For more information call **800-771-9202** or visit **www.warren-news.com**

Lauren Melone, Vice President, Public Relations
Bob Mitchell, Vice President, Consumer & Affiliate Marketing
Karen Ramspacher, Vice President, Research
Sue Rasmussen, Vice President, Direct-Response Advertising Sales
David Schafer, Vice President, Operations
Norm Schoenfeld, Vice President, Programming
Michelle Solomon, Vice President, Ad Sales Marketing
Peter Tulloch, Vice President, Content Distribution, Eastern Region
Carol Valentine, Vice President, Digital Media Sales
Kim Verkler, Vice President, Ad Sales, Midwest
Lori West, Vice President, Direct Response & Paid Programming
Donna Wolfe, Vice President, Production

Branch Offices:
LOS ANGELES: 700 N Central Ave, Ste 600, Glendale, CA 91203. Phone: 323-256-8900.
Type of service: Basic, digital, HD, streaming, video on demand.
Satellites: Loral Skynet Telstar 7, transponder 14.
Operating hours/week: 168.
Uplink: Belmont, NY.
Programming: Original programming that reflects a new attitude that is sexy, edgy, relevant and honest. Includes music videos, interviews & concerts.
Began: July 1, 1994, as MuchMusic USA. Rebranded as Fuse May 19, 2003. Fuse on Demand began June 1, 2003. NUVOtv was merged with Fuse September 30, 2015.
Means of Support: Advertising.
Total subscribers: 72,000,000 (18,000,000 on-demand subscribers.).
Distribution method: Available to cable, IPTV & satellite subscribers.
Scrambled signal: Yes. Equipment: VideoCipher II Plus.
Ownership: SiTV Media Inc.

FUSION
8551 NW 30th Ter
Doral, FL 33122
Phone: 305-714-7855
Web Site: http://www.fusion.net
Isaac Lee, Chief Executive Officer, Fusion and Chief News & Digital Officer, Univision Communications Inc.
Daniel Eilemberg, President & Chief Digital Officer
Wade Beckett, Chief Programming Officer
Boris Gartner, Senior Vice President & Chief Strategy Officer
John Hendler, Senior Vice President, Sales
George Lansbury, Senior Vice President, Production & Programming
Alexis Madrigal, Senior Vice President, Content & Editor-In-Chief
Keith Summa, Senior Vice President, Content & Programming
David Ford, Vice President, Corporate Communications & Public Relations
Eric Lieberman, Vice President & General Counsel

2017 Edition

E-41

Pay TV & Satellite Services

Mark Lima, Vice President, News
Arturo T. Luis, Vice President, Human Resources
Anhelo Reyes, Vice President, Marketing
Jorge Urrutia, Vice President, Digital Monetization
Hillary Frey, Global News Operations Director
Noreen Iqbal, Planning & Pricing Director
Margarita Noriega, Social Media Director
Kevin Roose, News Director
Laura Wides-Munoz, News Practices Director
Danilo Lauria, Social Video Manager
Maritza Puello, Managing Editor, Newscore
Alexis Madrigal, Editor-in-Chief
Jane Spencer, Editor in Chief, Digital Platforms
Dodai Stewart, Executive Editor
Joyce Tang, Managing Editor
Felix Samon, Senior Editor
Mariana Santos, Interactive Storytelling Editor
Type of service: Basic.
Operating hours/week: 168.
Operating areas: Available nationwide.
Programming: English language news channel for English-dominant and bilingual Hispanics. Offers information and lifestyle programming.
Began: October 28, 2013.
Means of Support: Advertising.
Total subscribers: 27,000,000 (Based on signed agreements.).
Distribution method: Available to AT&T U-verse, Cablevision, Charter, Cox, Dish and Google Fiber cable system subscribers.
Scrambled signal: Yes.
Ownership: Univision Communications Inc.

FX

10201 W Pico Blvd
Bldg 103
Los Angeles, CA 90064
Phone: 310-369-1000
E-mail: user@fxnetworks.com
Web Site: http://www.fxnetworks.com
FOX NETWORKS GROUP:, .
Peter Rice, Chairman & Chief Executive Officer, Fox Networks Group
Brian Sullivan, President, Digital, Fox Networks Group
Rita Tuzon, Executive Vice President & General Counsel, Fox Networks Group
FX NETWORKS:, .
John Landgraf, Chief Executive Officer, FX Networks & FX Productions
Chuck Saftler, President, Program Strategy & Chief Operating Officer, FX Networks
Nick Grad, President, Original Programming, FX Networks & FX Productions
Eric Schrier, President, Original Programming, FX Networks & FX Productions
Stephanie Gibbons, President, Marketing, Digital Media Marketing & On-Air Promotions, FX Networks
Gina Balian, Executive Vice President, Limited Series, FX Networks
Nicole Clemens, Executive Vice President, Series Development, FX Networks
Sally Daws, Executive Vice President, Marketing & Digital Media, FX Networks
Jonathan Frank, Executive Vice President, Current Programming, FX Networks
John Varvi, Executive Vice President, On-Air Promotions, FX Networks
Julie Piepenkotter, Executive Vice President, Research, FX Networks
Type of service: Basic, HD, streaming, video on demand.
Satellites: Galaxy VII, transponder 4 & 5.
Operating hours/week: 168.
Operating areas: Available nationwide.
Programming: Original entertainment programming, acquired series & movies.
Began: June 1, 1994.
Means of Support: Advertising & subscriber fees.
Total subscribers: 98,000,000.
Distribution method: Available to cable, IPTV & satellite subscribers. Streaming available online & mobile or through the FXNOW app (participating providers).
Scrambled signal: Yes.
Ownership: Fox Entertainment Group.

FXM — See FX.

Type of service: Pay, streaming, video on demand.
Operating areas: Available nationwide.
Programming: Films ranging from the great titles of the past to the blockbusters of today.
Began: October 31, 1994, as FXM Movies From FOX. Rebranded as Fox Movie Channel on March 1, 2000 & FXM on January 1, 2012.
Means of Support: Advertising & subscriber fees.
Total subscribers: 50,000,000.
Distribution method: Available to cable, IPTV & satellite subscribers. Streaming available online & mobile or through the FXNOW app (participating providers).
Scrambled signal: Yes.
Ownership: Fox Entertainment Group.

FXNOW — See FX.

Web Site: http://www.fxnetworks.com/fxnow
Type of service: Streaming.
Operating areas: Available nationwide.
Programming: Programming from FX, FXX & FXM.
Began: January 2014.
Distribution method: Available online & through app (participating providers).

FXX — See FX.

Type of service: Basic, HD, streaming, video on demand.
Sales representative: .
Operating hours/week: 168.
Operating areas: Available nationwide.
Programming: Original series, movies and acquired series appealing to adults 18 to 34.
Began: November 1997 as Fox Soccer. Rebranded as FXX September 2, 2013.
Means of Support: Advertising & subscriber fees.
Total subscribers: 72,000,000 (subscribers based on affiliate agreements.).
Distribution method: Available to cable, IPTV & satellite subscribers. Streaming available online & mobile or through the FXNOW app (participating providers).
Scrambled signal: Yes.
Ownership: Fox Entertainment Group.

FYI

235 E 45th St
New York, NY 10017
Phone: 212-210-1400
Fax: 212-692-9269
Web Site: http://www.fyi.tv
Paul Greenberg, Executive Vice President & General Manager
Amy Baker, Executive Vice President, FYI, Lifetime, LMN & LRW
Peter Tarshis, Executive Producer, Programming
Lisa Lucatuorto Mallen, Senior Vice President, National Ad Sales
Gena McCarthy, Senior Vice President, Programming
Thomas Moody, Senior Vice President, Programming Planning & Acquisitions
Dan Silberman, Senior Vice President, Publicity
James Bolosh, Vice President, Development & Programming
Liz Fine, Vice President, Development & Programming
Type of service: Digital & video on demand.
Satellites: Galaxy IX, transponder 23.
Programming: Reality series.
Began: December 1, 1998, as The Biography Channel. Rebranded as BIO July 16, 2007. Rebranded FYI July 8, 2014.
Total subscribers: 69,000,000.
Distribution method: Available to cable, IPTV & satellite subscribers. Video on demand available online & through app.
Scrambled signal: Yes.
Ownership: A joint venture between Hearst Corp. (50%) & The Walt Disney Co. (50%).

GAIAM TV FIT & YOGA

833 W South Boulder Rd
Louisville, CO 80027
Phones: 303-222-3600; 866-284-8058
Fax: 303-222-3700
E-mail: info@gaiamtv.com
Web Site: http://www.gaiamtv.com
Jirka Rysavy, Founder & Chairman
Lynn Powers, Chief Executive Officer
Bill Sondheim, President
Jaymi Bauer, Chief Marketing Officer
Steve Thomas, Chief Financial Officer

Branch Offices:
Distribution Center: 5455 West Chester Rd, West Chester, OH 45069.
Type of service: Video on demand.
Operating areas: Available nationwide.
Programming: Provides shows which empower yourself with knowledge, awareness and a choice in media. Content is designed to create an open-minded dialogue, and a welcoming space to explore your mind, body and soul.
Began: January 12, 2015.
Means of Support: Subscriber fees.
Distribution method: Available to Comcast & Verizon FiOS subscribers.
Scrambled signal: Yes.
Ownership: A joint venture between Comcast Corp. & Gaiam TV.

GALAVISION — See Univision.

9405 NW 41st St
Miami, FL 33178
Phone: 305-471-3900
Web Site: http://www.galavision.com; http://www.corporate.univision.com
Sebastian Trujillo, Senior Vice President, Operating Manager
Gerardo Lopez Gallo, Vice President, Programming & Production
Tim Spillane, Vice President, Affiliate Sales
Type of service: Basic, HD, video on demand.
Satellites: AMC 11, transponder 23.
Operating hours/week: 168.
Operating areas: Available nationwide.
Uplink: Miami, FL.
Programming: Spanish-language news, movies, novelas (soap operas), sports, comedy and variety.
Began: October 26, 1979, GalaVision HD began June 1, 2010.
Means of Support: Advertising.
Total subscribers: 68,100,000.
Distribution method: Available to cable, IPTV & satellite subscribers; video on demand (participating providers).
Scrambled signal: Yes.
Ownership: Univision Communications Inc.

GAMEHD — See iN DEMAND.

c/o iN DEMAND LLC
345 Hudson St, 17th Fl
New York, NY 10014
Phone: 646-638-8200
Fax: 646-486-0854
Web Site: http://www.indemand.com
Programming: On demand sports programming.

GAME SHOW NETWORK — See GSN.

GAS — See TeenNick.

GAVEL TO GAVEL ALASKA

360 Egan Dr
Juneau, AK 99801-1748
Phone: 907-586-1670
Web Site: http://gavelalaska.org
Bill Legere, General Manager
John Kelly, Control Room Director
David Waters, Control Room Director
Jeremy Hsieh, Producer
Type of service: Regional basic.
Operating areas: Alaska.
Programming: Provides unedited coverage of state government activities during the Legislative session.
Began: January 15, 1996, Had two week trial during First Session of Legislature in 1995.
Means of Support: Funded by the City and Borough of Juneau and private sector businesses and organizations.
Distribution method: Available to cable system subscribers.
Scrambled signal: Yes.
Ownership: 360 North/KTOO-TV, Juneau's public TV station.

GBTV — See TheBlaze.

GCN

4440 Tuck Rd
PO Box 3164
Loganville, GA 30052
Phones: 770-913-8035; 877-211-9331
E-mail: info@gcntv.org
Web Site: http://www.gcntv.us
Dr. Jaerock Lee, Chairman
Type of service: Basic.
Operating hours/week: 168.
Operating areas: Connecticut & New York.
Programming: Offers life-changing television with the message of Jesus Christ.
Distribution method: Available over the air on digital sub-channels.

GEB AMERICA

7777 S Lewis Ave
Tulsa, OK 74171
Phones: 918-495-7288; 800-255-4407
Fax: 918-495-7388
E-mail: golden-eagle@oru.edu
Web Site: http://www.gebamerica.com
Amy Calvert, Vice President, Marketing & Sales
Bill Lee, Engineering Director
Satellites: SES-1, transponder 1; DirecTV channel 363.
Operating hours/week: 168.
Programming: Focused on helping the 34 million baby boomers of faith to live well spirit, mind and body. Programming is well rounded, educational and culturally relevant showcasing the best inspirational voices in the world along with high value redemptive movies, series and entertainment.
Began: January 24, 1996, as Golden Eagle Broadcasting. Rebranded GEB America October 2012.
Means of Support: Non Commercial.
Distribution method: Available to cable & satellite subscribers.
Scrambled signal: Yes.

Pay TV & Satellite Services

GEM SHOPPING NETWORK
3414 Howell St
Duluth, GA 30096
Phone: 770-622-5505
Fax: 770-622-5503
E-mail: customerservice@gemshopping.com
Web Site: http://www.gemshopping.com
Operating hours/week: 168.
Programming: Television shopping channel offering fine gemstones & jewelry.
Began: May 10, 1997.
Total subscribers: 30,000,000.
Distribution method: Available to cable systems & satellite subscribers.
Scrambled signal: Yes.

GEMSTV
1190 Trademark Dr
Ste 107
Reno, NV 89521
Phone: 775-850-8080
Web Site: http://www.gemstv.com
Jason Wai, Chief Executive Officer
Wong Lai Kuen, Chief Financial Officer
Don Rene Kagen, President, Global Merchandising
Frankie Chow, Managing Director, Thailand
Kaori Miwa, Managing Director, GemsLondon
Diane Louie Schneiderjohn, Managing Director, GemsTV, USA
Karen Lesley Wenborn, Managing Director, GemsTV, UK
Type of service: Basic.
Operating hours/week: 168.
Programming: Jewelry & gemstone shopping channel.
Began: November 26, 2006, in U.S.
Total subscribers: 15,000,000 (U.S. subscribers.).
Distribution method: Available to cable & satellite subscribers.
Scrambled signal: Yes.

GEORGIA HIGHLANDS TELEVISION (GHTV)
Georgia Highlands College
Heritage Hall, 415 E Third Ave
Rome, GA 30161
Phones: 800-332-2406; 706-802-5301
E-mail: jbrown@highlands.edu
Web Site: http://www.highlands.edu
Jeff Brown, Channel Director
Type of service: Basic, over the air.
Operating areas: Georgia.
Programming: Educational.
Began: January 19, 1991.
Distribution method: Available over the air on digital sub-channels & to Comcast & AT&T U-verse subscribers.
Scrambled signal: Yes.
Ownership: Floyd County/City of Rome.

GEORGIA PUBLIC BROADCASTING
260 14th St NW
Atlanta, GA 30318
Phones: 404-685-2400; 800-222-6006
Fax: 404-685-2491
E-mail: ask@gpb.org
Web Site: http://www.gpb.org
Teya Ryan, President & Executive Director
Bonnie R. Bean, Chief Financial Officer
Mark Fehlig, Technical & Engineering Services Director
Melvin Jones, Human Resources Director
Michael E. Nixon, Education & Technology Services Director
Robert M. Olive, Assistant General Manager
Type of service: Satellite, streaming, open air.
Operating areas: Georgia.
Programming: Interactive distance learning for public schools, regional libraries & adult technical education centers.

Began: August 15, 1994.
Scrambled signal: Yes.
Ownership: Georgia Public Broadcasting.

GETTV
c/o Sony Pictures Television
10202 W Washington Blvd
Culver City, CA 90232
Phones: 310-244-4000; 310-244-7737 (press)
Fax: 310-244-2004
E-mail: contact@get.tv
Web Site: http://get.tv
Andy Kaplan, President, Worldwide Networks, Sony Pictures Television
Paula Askanas, Executive Vice President, Communications, Sony Pictures Television
Superna Kalle, General Manager, getTV & Senior Vice President, US Networks, Sony Pictures Television
Nathalie Lubensky, Senior Vice President, Marketing, Networks, Sony Pictures Television
Type of service: Basic.
Operating areas: Nationwide.
Programming: Classic Hollywood movies from Sony Pictures library.
Began: February 3, 2014.
Means of Support: Advertising.
Total subscribers: 50,000,000 (Number of households based on current affiliation agreements.).
Distribution method: Available over the air on digital sub-channels.
Scrambled signal: Yes.
Ownership: Sony Pictures Television Inc.

GLC
God's Learning Channel
12706 W Hwy 80 E
Odessa, TX 79765
Phones: 432-563-0420; 800-707-0420
Fax: 432-563-1736
E-mail: info@glc.us.com
Web Site: http://www.glc.us.com
Al Cooper, Founder
Tommie Cooper, Co-founder
Type of service: Basic, streaming.
Satellites: Galaxy 25; AMC-4.
Operating hours/week: 168.
Programming: Christian programming.

GLOBAL CHRISTIAN NETWORK — See GCN.

GMA LIFE TV — See GMA Pinoy TV.
Programming: Lifestyle programming from the Philippines.

GMA PINOY TV
GMA Network Center
EDSA Corner Timog Ave.
Diliman, Quezon City
Philippines
E-mail: gmapinoytv@gmanetwork.com
Web Site: http://www.gmapinoytv.com
Type of service: Digital.
Operating hours/week: 168.
Programming: News, entertainment & popular series from the Philippines.
Began: August 1, 2005, in U.S.

GMC — See UP.

GMOVIES
2077 Convention Center Concourse
Ste 300
Atlanta, GA 30337
Phone: 770-692-4559
Fax: 770-692-8895
Web Site: http://gmovies.com

Hal Rosenberg, Senior Vice President, Affiliate Sales
Type of service: Basic.
Operating areas: Nationwide.
Programming: More than 150 faith-friendly feature films of every genre, in addition to animated stories, television series and biblical documentaries.
Means of Support: Advertising.
Distribution method: Available to DISH Network subscribers.
Scrambled signal: Yes.
Ownership: InterMedia Partners majority interest, Magic Johnson.

GOD TV
Regional Office USA
PO Box 13206
Overland Park, KS 66282
Phone: 888-463-1365
Fax: 816-581-6001
E-mail: info.usa@god.tv
Web Site: http://www.god.tv

Branch Offices:
DENMARK: Box 12, DK 9800, Hjorring, Denmark. Phone: 45-98-90-91-50. Fax: 45-98-91-03-44.

GERMANY: Valentinskamp 24, 20354, Hamburg, Germany. Phone: 49-0-40-414-317-314. Fax: 49-0-40-3111-2616.

HONG KONG: Box 35216, King's Rd Post Office, Hong Kong. Phone: 852-3107-8877. Fax: 852-3107-8878.

INDIA: Box 3455, Anna Nagar, Chennai 600 040, India. Phone: 1600-44-2777. Fax: 91-44-5217-2928.

ISRAEL: Broadcast HQ, Box 7159, Jerusalem 91071, Israel.

SOUTH AFRICA: Box 79, Milnerton, Cape Town 7435, South Africa. Phone: 27-0-21-555-1206. Fax: 27-0-21-555-1207.

UNITED KINGDOM: Angel House, Borough Road, Sunderland SR1 1HW, United Kingdom. Phone: 44-0-870-60-70-446. Fax: 44-0-191-568-0879.
Type of service: Basic.
Operating areas: Nationwide.
Programming: International Christian programming, including conferences, in depth interviews, youth & music shows featuring prominent Christian leaders & artists from around the world.
Began: January 1, 1995.
Means of Support: Donations.
Total subscribers: 20,000,000.
Distribution method: Available to DirecTV subscribers.
Scrambled signal: Yes.
Ownership: Angel Christian Television Trust Inc., a non-profit Florida corporation.

GOLF CHANNEL
7580 Golf Channel Dr
Orlando, FL 32819
Phone: 407-355-4653

Fax: 407-363-7976
E-mail: customerservice@golfchannelsolutions.com
Web Site: http://www.golfchannel.com
Mike McCarley, President
Jay Madara, Chief Financial Officer
Jeff Foster, Senior Vice President, New Media Group
Tom Knapp, Senior Vice President, Programming
Will McIntosh, Senior Vice President, Business Development & Strategy
Christopher Murvin, Senior Vice President, Business Affairs & General Counsel
Geoff Russell, Senior Vice President & Executive Editor
Molly Solomon, Senior Vice President, Production & Operations and Executive Producer
Keith Allo, Vice President, Programming & Original Productions
Emily Ingram, Vice President, Human Resources
Regina O'Brien, Vice President, Marketing
David Schaefer, Vice President, Communications
Jeff Cravens, General Manager, Golf Channel Digital
Type of service: Basic, premium, digital, HD, streaming & video on demand.
Satellites: Galaxy 14; Galaxy 17.
Operating hours/week: 168.
Programming: Live golf tournaments, original programming, daily news shows, celebrity interviews, golf instruction, profiles and documentaries.
Began: January 17, 1995, Golf Channel HD began December 9, 2008.
Means of Support: National advertising & subscriber fees.
Total subscribers: 81,000,000.
Distribution method: Available to cable, IPTV & satellite subscribers. Streaming available online.
Scrambled signal: Yes.
Ownership: NBC Sports Group, a division of NBCUniversal LLC.

GOLTV
1666 JFK Cswy
Ste 402
North Bay Village, FL 33141
Phones: 305-864-9799; 866-644-6588
Fax: 305-864-7299
E-mail: info@goltv.tv
Web Site: http://www.goltv.tv
Francisco Casal, President
Enzo Francescoli, Chief Executive Officer
Rodrigo Lombello, Chief Operating Officer
Constantino Voulgaris, Executive Vice President, Programming
Ivan Perez, Vice President, Network Advertising Sales
Steve Soule, Vice President, Affiliate Sales
Jagdeep Wadhwani, Ad Sales Director
Type of service: Basic & video on demand.
Operating hours/week: 168.
Operating areas: Nationwide.
Programming: Soccer-exclusive bilingual network, offering over 800 live soccer matches & tournaments a year, plus soccer

Pay TV & Satellite Services

CABLE & TV STATION COVERAGE
Atlas 2017
The perfect companion to the Television & Cable Factbook
To order call 800-771-9202 or visit www.warren-news.com

newscasts & interviews. Available in both Spanish and English.
Began: February 1, 2003, in U.S. GolTV Movil began March 11, 2010, GolTV HD began August 1, 2010.
Total subscribers: 16,000,000 (includes 6500000 for english language feed).
Distribution method: Available to cable & satellite subscribers. Mobile available through GolTV Movile.
Scrambled signal: Yes.
Ownership: Gol TV Inc.

GOSCOUT HOMES
Cox Communications
1001 Summit Blvd, Ste 1200
Atlanta, GA 30319
Programming: Real estate listings available in select Cox Cable markets such as Omaha, NE & Phoenix, AZ.
Scrambled signal: Yes.
Ownership: Cox Media LLC.

GOSPEL MUSIC CHANNEL — See UP.

GOSPEL MUSIC TV — See Family Friendly Entertainment.

GRAN CINE
c/o Olympusat Inc.
560 Village Blvd, Ste 250
West Palm Beach, FL 33409
Phones: 561-684-5657; 866-940-2463
Fax: 561-684-9690
E-mail: info@olympusat.com
Web Site: http://www.olympusat.com/networks/gran-cine
Tom Mohler, Chief Executive Officer, Olympusat Holdings Inc.
Arturo Chavez, Senior Vice President, Hispanic Networks
Juan Bruno, New Programming Acquisitions & Contracts Director
John Baghdassarian, Head of Affiliate Sales, U.S.
Type of service: Pay.
Operating hours/week: 168.
Operating areas: Available nationwide.
Programming: Spanish-language movie network, including edgy, avant-garde & award-winning movies featuring top Latino talent from major telenovelas & feature films.
Began: April 18, 2012.
Means of Support: Subscriber fees.
Distribution method: Available to Choice Cable, Comcast, RCN & Verizon FiOS subscribers.
Scrambled signal: Yes.
Ownership: Ocean Holdings.

GREAT AMERICAN COUNTRY
9721 Sherrill Blvd
PO Box 51850
Knoxville, TN 37932
Phone: 865-694-2700
E-mail: mediarelations@scrippsnetworks.com
Web Site: http://www.gactv.com
John Feld, Senior Vice President, Programming & Production
Shannon Jamieson Driver, Senior Vice President, Network Marketing & Creative Services

Cheryl Middleton Jones, Senior Vice President, International Human Resources
Julie Taylor, Senior Vice President, Program Planning
Steven Lerner, Senior Vice President, Programming
Alaka Williams, Senior Vice President, Network Human Resources
Cindy Brown, Vice President, Program Planning
Bob Calandruccio, Vice President, Sales, Television Division
Gabriel Gordon, Vice President, Network Research
Type of service: Basic, digital, HD & video on demand.
Operating hours/week: 168.
Programming: Long-form programming concentrates on the family, home, food and travel; country music videos.
Began: December 31, 1995.
Means of Support: Advertising.
Total subscribers: 59,600,000.
Distribution method: Available to cable, IPTV & satellite subscribers.
Scrambled signal: Yes.
Ownership: Scripps Networks Interactive.

GREEK CHANNEL — See New Greek TV.

GRIT
c/o Katz Broadcasting LLC
3500 Piedmont Rd, Ste 400
Atlanta, GA 30305
Phones: 404-365-3075; 770-672-6500
Fax: 404-577-1786
E-mail: grit-info@katzbroadcasting.com
Web Site: http://www.grittv.com
Jonathan Katz, President & Chief Executive Officer
Jeffrey Wolf, Chief Distribution Officer
Elverage Allen, Executive Vice President, Advertising Sales
Bill Cox, Senior Vice President, Programming
Calandria Meadows, Vice President, Social Media & Digital Content
Operating hours/week: 168.
Operating areas: Available nationwide.
Programming: Reaches men 25-54 with concentration on western and war oriented action programming.
Began: August 18, 2014.
Total subscribers: 97,000,000.
Distribution method: Available on digital sub-channels of Sinclair and Univision stations.
Scrambled signal: Yes.
Ownership: Katz Broadcasting.

GSN
10202 W Washington Blvd
Culver City, CA 90232-3195
Phone: 310-244-2222
Fax: 310-244-2080
E-mail: programming@gsn.com
Web Site: http://www.gsn.com
David Goldhill, President & Chief Executive Officer
Chris Moseley, Executive Vice President & Chief Marketing Officer
Heidi Diamond, Executive Vice President

Amy Introcaso-Davis, Executive Vice President, Programming
Chad O'Hara, Executive Vice President, Business & Legal Affairs
Michael Kohn, Senior Vice President, Business & Legal Affairs
Jamie Roberts, Senior Vice President, Programming
John Zaccario, Senior Vice President, Advertising Sales
Marilyn Berryman, Vice President, National Accounts
Michael Bevan, Vice President, Original Programming
Dick Block, Vice President, Advertising Sales
Frank Cartwright, Vice President, Online Entertainment
Kim Cunningham, Vice President, Business Affairs
Anne Droste, Vice President, National Accounts
Linnea Hemenez, Vice President, Creative Services
Sandy McGill, Vice President, National Accounts
Sydney McQuoid, Vice President, Sales, Central Region
Marc Musicus, Vice President, Sales, Eastern Region
Russell H. Myerson, Vice President, Operations
Scott Perlmutter, Vice President, Affiliate Sales, Western Region
Ryan Tredennick, Vice President, Programming Services
Kenneth L. Warun, Vice President, On-Air Promotions
Jean Wiegman, Vice President, Production
Melissa Zimmerman, Vice President, Marketing Solutions
Adam S. Gaynor, Executive Director, Digital Media & Interactive Sales
Kim Caruso, Executive Director, Ad Sales Research
Joel McGee, Executive Director, Development
Leigh Primack, Executive Director, Distribution
Type of service: Basic.
Satellites: Galaxy VII; Galaxy XIII, transponder 13.
Operating hours/week: 168.
Programming: Contemporary & classic game shows, interactive during morning & prime-time hours.
Began: December 1, 1994, as Game Show Network. Rebranded as GSN March 2004. GSN HD began September 15, 2010.
Means of Support: Subscriber fees & advertising.
Total subscribers: 75,000,000.
Scrambled signal: Yes.
Ownership: A joint venture between Sony Pictures Entertainment & Liberty Media Corp.

GTN — See Guardian Television Network.

GUANGDONG SOUTHERN TELEVISION (TVS)
No. 331 Huan Shi Dong Road
Guangzhou 510066
China
Phone: 8620-6129-2727
Fax: 8620-8330-3629
Web Site: http://www.tvscn.com
Programming: Shows on Cantonese history, culture, social issues & Chinese news & entertainment.
Began: July 1, 2004.
Distribution method: Available to KyLin TV subscribers.
Scrambled signal: Yes.

GUARDIAN TELEVISION NETWORK
653 McCorkle Blvd
Ste P
Westerville, OH 43082
Phones: 614-416-6080; 800-517-5151
Fax: 614-416-6345
Web Site: http://gtn23.com
Richard Schilg, President
David C Wilson, Vice President, Programming & Operations
Type of service: Regional basic.
Operating hours/week: 168.
Operating areas: Ohio.
Programming: Offers classic programming and family movies.
Began: October 1, 2008.
Means of Support: Advertising.
Distribution method: Available over the air on digital sub-channels & to Insight and WideOpenWest cable subscribers.
Scrambled signal: Yes.
Ownership: Guardian Enterprise Group Inc.

H2 — See Viceland.

HALLMARK CHANNEL
12700 Ventura Blvd
Studio City, CA 91604
Phones: 818-755-2400; 800-522-5131
Fax: 818-755-2564
Web Site: http://www.hallmarkchannel.com
Bill Abbott, President & Chief Executive Officer
Edward Georger, President, Advertising Sales
Janice Arouh, Executive Vice President, Network Distribution & Services
Joan Gundlach, Executive Vice President, Distribution
Annie Howell, Executive Vice President, Corporate Communications & Media Relations
Laura Lee, Executive Vice President, Distribution
Laura Masse, Executive Vice President, Marketing
Susanne McAvoy, Executive Vice President, Marketing Creative & Communications
Kristen Roberts, Executive Vice President, Pricing Planning & Revenue Management
Charles Stanford, Executive Vice President & General Counsel
Brian Stewart, Executive Vice President & Chief Financial Officer
Michelle Vicary, Executive Vice President, Programming & Network Publicity
Harriet Beck, Senior Vice President, Legal Affairs
Chad Harris, Senior Vice President, Integrated Marketing & New Media
Mark J. Kern, Senior Vice President, Communications & Media Relations
Len Marino, Senior Vice President, Creative Services & On-Air Promotion
Susanne McAvoy, Senior Vice President, Network Operations
Todd McNulty, Senior Vice President, Creative Services
Darren Melameth, Senior Vice President, Program Plannings & Acquisitions
Randy Pope, Senior Vice President, Programming & Development
Laura Sillars, Senior Vice President, Lifestyle Programming
Pam Slay, Senior Vice President, Network Program Publicity
Amy Jo Wayne, Senior Vice President, National Advertising Sales, Crown Media Family Networks
Anthony White, Senior Vice President, Marketing
Jess Aguirre, Vice President, Research
Lisa Barroso, Vice President, Distribution
Donovan Batiste, Vice President, Research & Media Planning

Pay TV & Satellite Services

Bill Butte, Vice President, Direct Marketing
Roy Cowan, Vice President, Marketing
Shannon Dashiell-Rapp, Vice President, Design
Madeline Di Nonno, Vice President, Marketing Alliances
Cheryl Grimley, Vice President, Advertising Sales, Western Region
Shira Kalish, Vice President, Ad Sales & Alliance Marketing
Andy Karofsky, Vice President, Marketing
Sean Kelly, Vice President, Western Ad Sales
Holly Mauer, Vice President, Distribution
Erin McIlvain, Vice President, National Accounts
Randy Pope, Vice President, Programming
Hank Smith, Vice President, Human Resources
Ron Stark, Vice President, Affiliate Marketing
Tara Tzirlin, Vice President, Consumer Marketing
Claude Wells, Vice President, Network Distribution & Services
Bob Young, Vice President, Operations
Tara Donnelly, Senior Director, Consumer Marketing
Jaime Sabeirto, Senior Director, Corporate Communications
Shelly Bayne, Ad Sales Marketing Director
Allison Bennett, Corporate Communications & Media Relations Director
Melissa Davidson, Consumer Marketing Director
Laurie Ferneau, Programming Director, Scripted Series
Toni Lorusso, Ad Sales Marketing Director
Seema Patel, Pricing & Planning Director
Alexandra Smith, Programming Director
Type of service: Basic, HD.
Satellites: Satcom III-R, transponder 5.
Operating hours/week: 168.
Uplink: Denver, CO.
Programming: Family friendly programming.
Began: September 19, 1988, as Odyssey Network. Rebranded as Hallmark Channel on August 5, 2001. Hallmark HD began February 1, 2010.
Means of Support: Advertising & license fees.
Total subscribers: 87,500,000.
Distribution method: Available to cable, IPTV & satellite subscribers.
Scrambled signal: Yes.
Ownership: Hallmark Cards.

HALLMARK MOVIES & MYSTERIES — See Hallmark Channel.
Ayn Prince, Programming Director
Type of service: Digital, HD.
Programming: Suspense & mystery movies, original movies from the Hallmark Hall of Fame library, acquired series, new original movies & all-time classic holiday movies.
Began: 2008 as Hallmark Movie Channel. Hallmark Movie Channel HD began April 2008. Rebranded Hallmark Movies & Mysteries September 29, 2014.
Scrambled signal: Yes.

HALOGEN TV — See Pivot.

HAVOC TV
880 Apollo St
Ste 239
El Segundo, CA 90245
Phone: 310-524-9100
Fax: 310-524-1540
E-mail: support@havoctv.com
Web Site: http://havoc.tv
Bob Kresser, Chairman
Ryan Kresser, Chief Executive Officer & Founder
Dave deKadt, President & Founder

Mihai Crisan, Vice President, Marketing, Electronic Music
Jeff Cutler, Vice President, Action Sports
Jim Lindberg, Vice President, Marketing/Business Development, Indie Rock
Matt Muir, Vice President & Head of Programming
Clinton Cox, Original Programming/Production
Type of service: Video on demand.
Operating areas: Available nationwide.
Programming: New music videos, the latest action sports content & original content.
Began: January 1, 2002.
Means of Support: Advertising.
Total subscribers: 56,000,000.
Distribution method: Available to cable, IPTV & satellite subscribers; online & mobile through the website; video on demand (participating providers).
Scrambled signal: Yes.
Ownership: K2 Communications.

HAWKEYE NETWORK
105 Seashore Hall
The University of Iowa
Iowa City, IA 52242-1402
Phone: 319-335-2778
Fax: 319-335-2834
E-mail: scott-ketelsen@uiowa.edu
Scott Ketelsen, Director, Marketing & Media Production, UI Strategic Communications
Benjamin Hill, Creative Media Manager/Producer
Brian Gilbert, Creative Media Specialist
Type of service: Regional.
Operating areas: Iowa, portions of Nebraska & Wisconsin.
Programming: Offers University of Iowa sports plus academic and campus programming.
Began: February 1, 2013.
Means of Support: Advertising & donations.
Distribution method: Available to Mediacom cable system subscribers.
Scrambled signal: Yes.
Ownership: The University of Iowa.

HAZARDOUS — See NBCSN.

HBO
1100 Ave of the Americas
New York, NY 10036
Phone: 212-512-1000
Fax: 212-512-1166
E-mail: mr.admin@hbo.com
Web Site: http://www.homeboxoffice.com
Richard Plepler, Chairman & Chief Executive Officer
Len Amato, President, HBO Films
Kary Antholis, President, HBO Miniseries
Casey Bloys, President, HBO Programming
Bruce Grivetti, President, Film Programming & Executive Vice President, Business Affairs
Ken Hershman, President, HBO Sports
Sheila Nevins, President, HBO Documentaries & Family
Charles Schreger, President, Programming Sales
Simon Sutton, President, HBO International & Content Distribution
Tom Woodbury, President, Global Distribution
Shelley Wright Brindle, Executive Vice President, Domestic Network Distribution
Sofia Chang, Executive Vice President & General Manager, HBO Home Entertainment
Michael Ellenberg, Executive Vice President, HBO Programming
Susan Ennis, Executive Vice President, Program Planning & Strategy
Scott McElhone, Executive Vice President, Human Resources & Administration

Peter Nelson, Executive Vice President, HBO Sports
Robert Roth, Executive Vice President & Chief Financial Officer
Quentin Schaffer, Executive Vice President, Corporate Communications
David Levine, Senior Vice President, HBO Programming & Co-Head, Drama
Francesca Orsi, Senior Vice President, HBO Programming & Co-Head, Drama
Nora Skinner, Senior Vice President, Original Programming, Drama Series

Regional Offices:
ATLANTA: 1000 Abernathy Rd, Ste 500, Atlanta, GA 30328. Phone: 404-239-6600. Fax: 404-261-4185.

CHICAGO: 6250 N River Rd, Ste 10-300, Rosemont, IL 60018. Phone: 847-318-5100. Fax: 847-825-1333.

DALLAS: 12750 Merit Dr, Ste 1105, Dallas, TX 75251. Phone: 972-450-1000. Fax: 972-387-5670.

DENVER: The Quadrant, 5445 DTC Pkwy, Ste 700, Englewood, CO 80111. Phone: 303-220-2900. Fax: 303-220-9668.

LOS ANGELES: 2049 Century Park E, Ste 4100, Los Angeles, CA 90067. Phone: 310-201-9200. Fax: 310-201-9310.

PHILADELPHIA: 401 City Ave, Ste 620, Bala Cynwyd, PA 19004. Phone: 610-668-6500. Fax: 610-668-9318.

SAN FRANCISCO: 353 Sacramento St, 20th Floor, San Francisco, CA 94111. Phone: 415-765-7700. Fax: 415-788-0183.
Type of service: Pay, HD, streaming, video on demand.
Satellites: Galaxy V, transponder 8 (west coast); Galaxy 111-R, transponder 16 (east coast); Galaxy 111-R, transponder 20 (west coast); Galaxy 111-R, transponder 19 (east coast).
Operating hours/week: 168.
Operating areas: Nationwide.
Uplink: Smithtown, NY.
Programming: 24-hour variety programming including movies, entertainment specials, comedies, sports, special events, documentaries, children's programming & movies made for HBO. Spanish-language available on HBO Latino.
Began: November 8, 1972, HBO HD began March 1999. HBO on Demand began July 2001.
Means of Support: Subscriber fees.
Total subscribers: 43,000,000 (U.S. subscribers. 84,000,000 international subscribers. Subscriber counts include Cinemax.).
Distribution method: Available to cable, IPTV & satellite subscribers; online & mobile through the HBO Go or HBO Now website or app (participating providers); video on demand (participating providers).
Scrambled signal: Yes. Equipment: M/A-Com VideoCipher II.
Ownership: Time Warner.

FULLY SEARCHABLE • CONTINUOUSLY UPDATED • DISCOUNT RATES FOR PRINT PURCHASERS
For more information call **800-771-9202** or visit **www.warren-news.com**

HBO 2 — See HBO.
Type of service: Pay, HD.
Operating hours/week: 168.
Programming: Movies, original series, special events.
Began: 1991 as HBO2. Rebranded as HBO Plus October 1998 & HBO2 in 2002.
Scrambled signal: Yes.

HBO COMEDY — See HBO.
Type of service: Pay, HD.
Operating hours/week: 168.
Programming: Original comedy series, movies & stand-up specials.
Began: May 1, 1999.
Scrambled signal: Yes.

HBO EN ESPANOL — See HBO Latino.

HBO FAMILY — See HBO.
Delores Morris, Vice President, HBO Family & Documentary Programming
Type of service: Pay, HD.
Operating hours/week: 168.
Programming: Commercial-free, non-R/TVMA-rated programming geared to families & children of all ages.
Began: December 1996.

HBO GO — See HBO.
Web Site: http://play.hbogo.com
Type of service: Streaming.
Operating areas: Available nationwide.
Programming: Programming from HBO channels.
Began: February 2010.
Distribution method: Available online & through app (participating providers).

HBO LATINO — See HBO.
Type of service: Pay, HD.
Operating hours/week: 168.
Programming: Spanish-language films, documentaries, music videos, sports, original programming featuring entertainment & cultural issues & a mix of Hollywood movies.
Began: November 1, 2000, replacing HBO en Espanol, which began in 1989 as Selecciones en Espanol de HBO y Cinemax. Rebranded HBO en Espanol on September 27, 1993.
Scrambled signal: Yes.
Ownership: Time Warner.

HBO NOW — See HBO.
Web Site: https://order.hbonow.com
Type of service: Over the top, stand-alone streaming subscription service.
Operating areas: Nationwide.
Programming: HBO's original programming as well as the latest Hollywood hit movies, groundbreaking documentaries, sports, and exclusive comedy specials.
Began: April 7, 2015.
Total subscribers: 800,000.
Distribution method: Available to subscribers through participating providers.
Ownership: Time Warner.

HBO ON BROADBAND — No longer in operation. See HBO Go.

2017 Edition   E-45

Pay TV & Satellite Services

HBO SIGNATURE — See HBO.
Type of service: Pay, HD.
Operating hours/week: 168.
Programming: Documentaries, original series & movies targeted to women.
Began: 1995 as HBO 3. Rebranded as HBO Signature October 1998.
Scrambled signal: Yes.

HBO ZONE — See HBO.
Type of service: Pay, HD.
Operating hours/week: 168.
Programming: Mix of films, music videos & original HBO programming.
Began: May 1, 1999.
Scrambled signal: Yes.

HDNET — See AXS TV.

HDNET MOVIES — See AXS TV.

HD THEATER — See Velocity.

HEADLINE NEWS — See HLN.

HEALTH & WELLNESS CHANNEL
4000 NW 36th Ave
Miami, FL 33142-4210
Phone: 800-560-5148
E-mail: contact@hwchannel.com
Web Site: http://www.hwchannel.com
Drew Nederpelt, Founder
Jeff Dilley, Vice President, Finance
Randy Gruber, Vice President, Television Operations
Noley Keener, Vice President, Broadcast Technology
Mike Hickling, Production Coordinator
Type of service: Basic, streaming.
Programming: Aspirational and prescriptive broadcast network dedicated to all things life, love and longevity.
Began: September 17, 2015.
Means of Support: Advertising & retail sales.
Distribution method: Available to cable & satellite subscribers. Streaming available through participating providers.
Scrambled signal: Yes.

HEALTHINATION
50 W 17th St
17th Fl
New York, NY 10010
Phone: 212-633-0007
E-mail: diane@healthination.com
Web Site: http://www.healthination.com
Raj Amin, Chief Executive Officer & Co-Founder
Tony Estrella, Chief Operating Officer & Co-Founder
Holly Atkinson, MD, Chief Medical Officer
Brendan Anderer, Vice President, Programming
Stuart Rohrer, Vice President, Analytics & Technology
Scott Schappell, Vice President, Sales
Michael Stoeckel, Vice President, Client Services
Preeti Parikh, Medical Programming Director
Diane Hepps, Communications Director
Type of service: Basic, streaming, video on demand.
Operating areas: Available nationwide.
Programming: The channel that educates and inspires people to make healthier choices. The programs cover disease and condition education as well as lifestyle tips, diet and personal stories.
Began: January 30, 2007.
Means of Support: Advertising and subscriber fees.

Total subscribers: 32,000,000 (Also has over 40000000 unique users online.).
Distribution method: Available to cable systems and Verizon FiOS & AT&T U-verse subscribers.
Scrambled signal: Yes.
Ownership: Intel Capital & MK Capital.

HEALTH ON DEMAND
c/o Time Warner Cable
60 Columbus Cir, 17th Fl
New York, NY 10023
Phone: 212-364-8200
E-mail: jeannette.castaneda@twcable.com
Joan Hogan Gillman, President, Time Warner Cable Media
Patricia Karpas, Digital Strategy Officer
Jeannette Castaneda, Public Relations Manager
Scott Mowbry, Editor, Cooking Light
Type of service: Video on demand.
Operating hours/week: 168.
Operating areas: Nationwide.
Programming: 24 hour access to healthy lifestyle choices. Includes segments from Cooking Light and streaming video subscription service Gaiam TV.
Began: April 30, 2012.
Means of Support: Advertising.
Distribution method: Available to Time Warner Cable digital cable system subscribers.
Scrambled signal: Yes.
Ownership: Time Warner Cable Inc.

HEARTLAND
225 E Eighth St
Chattanooga, TN 37402
Phone: 423-468-5100
Web Site: http://www.watchheartlandtv.com
David Leach, President & Chief Executive Officer, Luken Communications
Doug Evans, Chief Operating Officer, Luken Communications
David Dornseif, Senior Vice President, Ad Sales, Luken Communications
Matt Wynn, Executive Vice President, Luken Communications
Dee Harlin, Vice President, Affiliate Sales
Tom Keegan, Vice President, Affiliate Sales
Tim Krass, Vice President, Affiliate Sales
Andrea Rhum, Senior Account Executive
Ben Kulikowski, National Account Executive

Mailing Address:
CHATTANOOGA: Box 11409, Chattanooga, TN 37401.
Type of service: Basic.
Operating hours/week: 168.
Operating areas: Nationwide.
Programming: A broad spectrum of true country music, including Bluegrass, Americana, Texas country and more.
Began: April 16, 2012, as a return of The Nashville Network, which aired from 1983 to 2000. Rebranded Heartland October 2013.
Means of Support: Advertising.
Distribution method: Available over the air on digital sub-channels & to cable & satellite subscribers.
Scrambled signal: Yes.
Ownership: Luken Communications LLC.

HELENA CIVIC TELEVISION (HCT)
1015 Poplar St
Helena, MT 59601
Phone: 406-447-1608
Fax: 406-447-1609
E-mail: hctv@bresnan.net
Web Site: http://www.helenacivictv.org
Kirsten Faubion, Executive Director
Jo McLean, Business Manager

Dave Clarke, Technical Operations
Operating hours/week: 168.
Programming: Unedited coverage of local & state government proceedings, public affairs & programs on culture, sports & religion.
Began: January 1, 2001.
Total subscribers: 14,000.

HERE! TV
10990 Wilshire Blvd
Penthouse
Los Angeles, CA 90024
Phone: 310-806-4298
Fax: 310-806-4268
E-mail: info@heretv.com
Web Site: http://www.heretv.com
Paul Colichman, Chief Executive Officer
Andrew Tow, Chief Operating Officer
Mark Reinhart, Executive Vice President, Distribution & Acquisition
Maria Dwyer, Senior Vice President, Distribution Sales & Marketing
Jeff Elgart, Senior Vice President, Corporate Ad Sales & Sponsorships
Stephen Macias, Senior Vice President, Corporate Communications, Public Relations & Consumer Marketing
John Mongiardo, Senior Vice President, Broadcast Operations
Josh Rosenzweig, Senior Vice President, Original Programming & Development
Meredith Kadlec, Vice President, Original Programming
Cory Sher, Distribution & Marketing Director
Billy Cogar, Development Director

Branch Offices:
NEW YORK: 245 W 17th St, 12th Floor, New York, NY 10011.
Type of service: Digital pay, video on demand.
Operating hours/week: 168.
Programming: Full-service network offering movies, original series & general entertainment programming targeted to broad-based gay & lesbian audience.
Began: August 29, 2003, here! On Demand began June 1, 2004.
Total subscribers: 40,000,000.
Scrambled signal: Yes.

HEROES & ICONS
c/o Weigel Broadcasting Co.
26 North Halsted
Chicago, IL 60661
Phone: 312-705-2600
Web Site: http://handitvnetwork.com
Neal Sabin, Vice Chairman, Weigel Broadcasting Co.
Type of service: Basic.
Operating areas: Nationwide.
Programming: Timeless classics to contemporary favorites, including action, westerns & police dramas.
Began: September 29, 2014.
Means of Support: Advertising.
Total subscribers: 29,000,000.
Distribution method: Available over the air on digital sub-channels and to cable subscribers.
Scrambled signal: Yes.
Ownership: Weigel Broadcasting Co.

HGTV
(Home & Garden Television)
9721 Sherrill Blvd
Knoxville, TN 37932
Phones: 865-694-2700; 865-694-7879
Fax: 865-531-8933
E-mail: online-ad@hgtv.com
Web Site: http://www.hgtv.com
Kenneth W. Lowe, President & Chief Executive Officer, E.W. Scripps

Richard A. Boehne, Chief Operating Officer, E.W. Scripps
Joseph G. NeCastro, Chief Finance & Administrative Officer, Scripps Networks Interactive
Susan Packard, President, New Ventures Group
Jim Samples, President, International
Bob Baskerville, Chief Operating Officer, International
Lori Asbury, Senior Vice President, Marketing & Creative Services
Mike Boyd, Senior Vice President, Consumer Marketing
Denise Conroy-Galley, Senior Vice President, Marketing & Creative Services
Sarah Cronan, Senior Vice President, Brand Management & Scheduling
A. B. Cruz, III, Senior Vice President & General Counsel
Michael Dingley, Senior Vice President, Programming, Content & Strategy
Lila Reinhard Everett, Senior Vice President, Marketing & Communications
John Feld, Senior Vice President, Programming & Production
Mark Hale, Senior Vice President, Technical Operations
Freddy P. James, Senior Vice President, Network Integrated Programming
Shannon Jamieson Driver, Senior Vice President, Network Marketing & Creative Services
Steven Lerner, Senior Vice President, Programming & Production
Jeff Meyer, Senior Vice President, Internet Sales
Cheryl Middleton Jones, Senior Vice President, International Human Resources
Donna Stephens, Senior Vice President, Ad Sales
Julie Taylor, Senior Vice President, Program Planning
Alaka Williams, Senior Vice President, Network Human Resources
Chad Youngblood, Senior Vice President, Home Category Initiatives
Audrey Adlam, Vice President, Communications
John E. Ajamie, Vice President, Network Operations & Duplication Services
Cindy Brown, Vice President, Program Planning
Annette Lindstrom Brun, Vice President, Consumer Marketing
Lynne A Davis, Vice President, National Broadcast Media & Talent Relations
Anna Gecan, Vice President, Programming
Gabriel Gordon, Vice President, Network Research
Paige Hardwick, Vice President, On-Air Strategy & Media Planning
Doug Hurst, Vice President, Affiliate Marketing
Heather Jagels, Vice President, Creatvie Services
Kristen Jordan, Vice President, International Development
Annette Lindstrom, Vice President, Marketing
Robert Liuag, Vice President, Research
Rob McCall, Vice President, Ad Sales, Midwest Region
Chris Moore, Vice President, Creative Director
Robin Pate, Vice President, Program Scheduling
Loren Ruch, Vice President, Programming Partnerships
Kendra Rudder, Vice President, Media Strategies
Dusty Schmidt, Vice President, Creative Services
Pamela Treacy, Vice President, New Business & Administration

Pay TV & Satellite Services

Karen Wishart, Vice President, Content Planning & Administration
Christy Melton, Programming Director
Dean Melton, Programming Director
Type of service: Basic, HD, video on demand.
Satellites: Galaxy I-R, transponder 20.
Operating hours/week: 168.
Programming: Features home repair & remodeling, home decorating, consumer audio, video, garden & lawn care.
Began: December 30, 1994.
Means of Support: Advertising & subscriber fees.
Total subscribers: 100,900,000.
Distribution method: Available to cable & satellite subscribers.
Scrambled signal: Yes.
Ownership: Scripps Networks Interactive.

HIGH 4K TV
The Seagram Bldg
375 Park Ave, Ste 2607
New York, NY 10152
Phone: 212-634-7482
Fax: 212-634-7474
E-mail: info@high4k.com
Web Site: http://www.high4k.com
Eric Klein, Chief Executive Officer

Branch Offices:
HONG KONG: Level 19 Two International Finance Center, 8 Finance Street Central, Hong Kong. Phone: 852-2251-1931.
Type of service: Basic.
Operating areas: Available nationwide.
Programming: Ultra high definition entertainment channel featuring a mix of travel, entertainment, lifestyle, sport & original content in 4K.
Began: June 1, 2014.
Means of Support: Advertising.
Distribution method: Available to cable & IPTV subscribers.
Scrambled signal: Yes.
Ownership: Footprint Media Holdings.

HISPANIC PAY TV CHANNEL
c/o Caracol Television
159 Alhambra Cir, Ste 1250
Coral Gables, FL 33134
305-960-2018
Fax: 305-960-2017
E-mail: losoriol@caracoltv.com.co
Web Site: http://www.caracolinternacional.com
Gonzalo Cordoba Mallarino, President, Caracol Television
Alberto Pecegueiro, General Director, Globosat
Type of service: Pay.
Operating areas: Plans nationwide.
Programming: Plans to offer content from both Caracol TV and Globosat, plus new Spanish-language productions.
Scheduled to begin: Plans 2015.
Means of Support: Plans subscriber fees.
Distribution method: Will be available to cable systems.
Scrambled signal: Yes.
Ownership: Caracol Television (Colombia) & Globosat (Brazil).

HISTORY
235 E 45th St
8th Fl
New York, NY 10017
Phone: 212-210-1400
Fax: 212-907-9481
E-mail: lynn.gardner@aetn.com
Web Site: http://www.history.com
Nancy Dubuc, President & Chief Executive Officer, A+E Networks
Jana Bennett, President & General Manager, History & H2
Paul Cabana, Executive Vice President & Head of Programming, History & H2
Marc Finnegan, Senior Vice President, Scheduling & Acquisitions
Peter Gaffney, Senior Vice President, Programming Strategy, Scheduling & Acquisitions
Lynn Gardner, Senior Vice President, Publicity
Matt Ginsberg, Vice President, Development & Programming
Julian Hobbs, Vice President, Development & Programming
Brian Joyce, Senior Vice President, Ad Sales, A&E, History & H2
Mike Stiller, Vice President, Development & Programming
Tim Healy, Vice President, Development & Programming
Russ McCarroll, Vice President, Development & Programming
Type of service: Basic cable, HD, streaming & video on demand.
Satellites: Satcom C-3, transponder 12 (analog east); Galaxy IX, transponder 23 (digital); Satcom C-4, transponder 6 (analog west).
Operating hours/week: 168.
Uplink: Stamford, CT.
Programming: Original non-fiction series, specials, event specials and mini-series.
Began: January 1, 1995, History HD began September 2007. Streaming began April 2014.
Means of Support: Advertiser & subscriber fees.
Total subscribers: 97,000,000.
Distribution method: Available to cable, IPTV & satellite subscribers. Streaming available online & through select providers. Video on demand available through select providers.
Scrambled signal: Yes.
Ownership: A+E Networks, a joint venture between Hearst Corp. (50%) & The Walt Disney Co. (50%).

HISTORY EN ESPANOL — See History.
Type of service: Basic & video on demand.
Operating hours/week: 168.
Programming: Spanish-language. Offers programs from History together with programs from the U.S. and Latin America spotlighting Latin roots and culture.
Began: June 1, 2004, in U.S.
Scrambled signal: Yes.

HISTORY INTERNATIONAL — See Viceland.

HITN
63 Flushing Ave, Bldg 292
Ste 211
Brooklyn, NY 11205
Phones: 212-966-5660; 877-391-4486
Fax: 212-966-5725; 718-797-2546
E-mail: programacion@hitn.org
Web Site: http://www.hitn.org
Jose Luis Rodriguez, President & Chief Executive Officer
Maryann Marrapodi, Chief Operating Officer
Eric Turpin, Vice President, Affiliate Sales & Distribution
Type of service: Basic & video on demand.
Operating hours/week: 168.
Operating areas: Nationwide.
Programming: Spanish-language, educational programming including documentaries, live interactive programs & original series.
Began: January 1, 1987.
Total subscribers: 38,000,000.
Distribution method: Available to DirecTV & DISH Network customers, AT&T U-verse, Charter, Comcast, Time Warner Cable & Verizon FiOS subscribers.
Scrambled signal: Yes.
Ownership: Privately held.

HITS (HEADEND IN THE SKY)
Comcast Wholesale
4100 E Dry Creek Rd
Centennial, CO 80122
Phone: 866-275-4487
E-mail: cmc_denver@cable.comcast.com
Web Site: http://www.HITS.com
Leslie E. Russell, Vice President & General Manager, HITS
Allison Olien, HITS Account Management Director
Programming: Provides digital programming packages to cable operators. Spanish-language available through HITS en Espanol service.
Scrambled signal: Yes.
Ownership: Comcast Wholesale, a division of Comcast Cable.

HLN
(Headline News)
One CNN Ctr
Atlanta, GA 30303
Phone: 404-827-1700
Web Site: http://www.hlntv.com
Keith Brown, Senior Vice President, Programming
Tim Mallon, Senior Vice President, Business Development & Operations
Kari Kim, Vice President, Program Development
Katie Caperton, Editor-in-Chief, HLNtv.com
Adrienne Lopez, Special Projects Director
Type of service: Basic, HD, streaming & video on demand.
Satellites: Galaxy I, transponder 8.
Sales representative: Turner Network Sales.
Operating hours/week: 168.
Operating areas: Nationwide.
Uplink: Atlanta, GA.
Programming: National, business, entertainment & weather news.
Began: December 31, 1981, as CNN2. Rebranded as CNN Headline News in 1983, HLN: Headline News in 1997 & HLN December 2008.
Total subscribers: 97,300,000.
Distribution method: Available to most cable, IPTV & satellite subscribers; streaming available online & mobile through the website or CNN app; video on demand through participating providers.
Scrambled signal: Yes. Equipment: VideoCipher.
Ownership: A CNN Worldwide Network, a division of Turner Broadcasting System (division of Time Warner).

HMONG TV NETWORK
1113 Daytona Ave
Ste 5
Clovis, CA 93612
Phones: 559-475-0045; 800-467-1258
Fax: 559-292-5824
E-mail: info@hmongtvnetwork.com
Web Site: http://hmongtvnetwork.com
Ying Fang, President
Type of service: Regional basic.
Operating hours/week: 168.
Operating areas: California.
Programming: Hmong news, entertainment and cultural programming.
Began: September 1, 2010, Launched online July 1, 2009.
Means of Support: Advertising & donations.
Total subscribers: 40,000.
Distribution method: Available over the air on digital sub-channels. Streaming available online.
Scrambled signal: Yes.
Ownership: Hmong TV Network Inc.

HMONGUSA TV
2515 E. Lamona Ave
Fresno, CA 93703
Phone: 559-292-4960
Fax: 559-292-4968
E-mail: info@hmongusatv.com
Web Site: http://hmongusatv.com
Yeu Cha, President & Chief Executive Officer
Thomas Herr, Vice President, Sales
Tong Xiong, Production Manager
Vue Xiong, IT, Web Developer
Type of service: Regional.
Operating hours/week: 100. 8 AM - Midnight M-F, 7 AM - Midnight Sat, 8 PM - 11 PM Sun.
Operating areas: California.
Programming: Offers news & entertainment for the Hmong community.
Means of Support: Advertising.
Distribution method: Available over the air on digital sub-channels as well as online and on Roku.
Scrambled signal: Yes.

HMX, EL CANAL DEL HOMBRE
Pedro Sainz de Baranda 139 COL. Avante
Delegate Coyoacan CP 0440
Mexico
Phones: 55-5550-1071; 55-8502-6969
E-mail: contact@hmx.tv; info@hmx.tv
Web Site: http://hmxtv.com
Tom Mohler, Chief Executive Officer, Olympusat
Operating areas: Nationwide.
Programming: Spanish-language men's channel featuring sports, game shows, and entertainment for adult males.
Began: May 14, 2014, Date service available via Olympusat.
Distribution method: Available to cable subscribers.
Scrambled signal: Yes.

HOLA! TV
c/o Imagina US
7291 NW 74th St
Miami, FL 33166
Phone: 305-777-1900
Fax: 305-820-9046
E-mail: comentarios@hola.tv
Web Site: http://hola.tv
Eduardo Sanchez Perez, Editor in Chief & General Manager, Hola! Magazine
Ignacio Sanz de Acedo, Chief Executive Officer & General Manager
Marcos Perez Salvador, Chief Financial Officer
Raul Garcia-Diez, Original Productions

Pay TV & Satellite Services

Patrick Ilabaca, Marketing, Communications & Creative Services
Maggie Salas-Amaro, Programming & Acquisitions
Type of service: Pay.
Operating hours/week: 168.
Operating areas: Available nationwide.
Programming: Programming about celebrities, royal families, lifestyle and fashion content in line with its printed publication Hola.
Began: September 2013 in Argentina, Chile, Colombia, Ecuador, Peru, Puerto Rico, Uruguay and Venezuela. Began May 1, 2014 in U.S.
Means of Support: Subscriber fees.
Total subscribers: 4,500,000 (Subscribers in the Caribbean and South America).
Distribution method: Available to DirecTV subscribers.
Scrambled signal: Yes.
Ownership: A joint venture between Atresmedia TV Group & Hola Magazine. Production based at Imagina Studios. Distributed in the U.S. by Condista.

HOME & GARDEN TELEVISION — See HGTV.

HOME BOX OFFICE — See HBO.

HOME SHOPPING NETWORK — See HSN.

HOME SHOPPING NETWORK 2 — See HSN2.

HOPE CHANNEL
12501 Old Columbia Pike
Silver Spring, MD 20904
Phones: 301-680-6689; 888-446-7388
Fax: 301-680-5147
E-mail: info@hopetv.org
Web Site: http://www.hopetv.org
Type of service: Basic.
Satellites: AMC-4.
Operating hours/week: 168.
Programming: Evangelical series, sermons & education, church news, meetings & sunday school study & programs on public health, family life & special events.
Distribution method: Available to cable systems & satellite subscribers.
Scrambled signal: Yes.
Ownership: Adventist Television Network.

HORSETV CHANNEL
4021 Anns Ln
Allen, TX 75002
Phone: 972-633-1133
Fax: 972-578-0675
Bernard Uechtritz, Executive Chairman
Type of service: Basic.
Operating hours/week: 168.
Programming: Equestrian documentaries, competitions & events; instructional programs; news.
Began: October 27, 2005, Service was shut down due to financial difficulties in December 2007. It was relaunched under new ownership in January 2009.
Distribution method: Available to cable systems & satellite subscribers.
Scrambled signal: Yes.
Ownership: Private Texas-based investment group.

HOT CHOICE
2029 Century Park E
Ste 2080
Los Angeles, CA 90067
Phone: 310-785-9194
Fax: 310-785-9769

E-mail: pressoffice@indemand.com
Web Site: http://www.indemand.com
Samuel L. Yates, Senior Vice President, Finance & Administration
Greg Rothberg, Vice President, Sales & Marketing
Sandra E. Landau, Vice President & General Counsel
Leigh Bolton, Vice President, Video Promotion
Terry Taylor, Vice President, Affiliate Relations
John Vartanian, Vice President, Technology & Operations
John Migliacci, Acquisitions Manager
Type of service: Pay-per-view.
Satellites: Satcom C-4, transponder 18.
Operating hours/week: 168.
Programming: Action-adventure and adult-appeal movies & special events.
Began: February 1, 1993.
Scrambled signal: Yes. Equipment: DigiCipher.
Ownership: A joint venture between Comcast, Cox Communications, AT&T Broadband & Internet Services/Liberty Media & Time Warner Cable.

HOT TV (HISTORY OF TELEVISION)
228 Kennedy Ct
Crowley, TX 76036
Phone: 817-986-9144
E-mail: bettertv@sbcglobal.net
Web Site: http://www.hottvchannel.com
Fred Hutton, Director
Type of service: Basic regional, over the air.
Operating hours/week: 168.
Operating areas: Texas.
Programming: Offers vintage wholesome programming for the whole family from the 50's and 60's.
Began: August 31, 2010.
Means of Support: Advertising.
Distribution method: Available over the air on digital sub-channels.
Scrambled signal: Yes.
Ownership: Fred Hutton.

HRTV
c/o Santa Anita Park
285 W Huntington Dr
Arcadia, CA 91007
Phones: 626-254-1300; 888-572-8883
E-mail: customerservice@hrtv.com
Web Site: http://www.hrtv.com
Scott Daruty, President & Chief Executive Officer
Amy Zimmerman, Executive Producer & Senior Vice President
Dennis Murphy, Senior Vice President, Advertising Sales
Christopher Swan, Senior Vice President, Distribution & Business Development
Phil Kubel, Vice President, Digital Media & Technology
Stephen Nagler, Vice President, Live Programming
Michael Canale, Senior Producer & Director, Remote Operations
Carolyn Conley, HRTV Director, Brand Management
Dotty Ewing, Marketing & Equestrian Programming
Type of service: Basic.
Operating hours/week: 168.
Programming: Thoroughbred and harness racing from top U.S. and international racetracks, as well as a wide range of world-class English and Western horse competitions.
Began: January 1, 2003.
Means of Support: Advertising.
Total subscribers: 19,000,000.
Scrambled signal: Yes.
Ownership: Betfair Group.

HSN
One HSN Dr.
St. Petersburg, FL 33729
Phone: 727-872-1000
Web Site: http://www.hsn.com
HSN INC:, .
Mindy Grossman, Chief Executive Officer & Director, HSN Inc.
Judy Schmeling, Chief Operating Officer, HSN Inc. & President, Cornerstone
Michael Attinella, Chief Financial Officer, HSN & Chief Accounting Officer, HSN Inc.
Bill Brand, President, HSN & Chief Marketing Officer, HSN Inc.
Karen Etzkorn, Chief Information Officer, HSN Inc.
Andy Sheldon, Chief Creative Officer, HSN Inc. & General Manager, HSN Productions
Greg Henchel, Chief Legal Officer & Secretary, HSN Inc.
Rob Solomon, Executive Vice President, Customer Care & Operations Administration, HSN Inc.
Bob Monti, Executive Vice President, Supply Chain & Logistics, HSN Inc.
HSN:, .
John Aylward, Executive Vice President & Chief Marketing Officer
Jennifer Cotter, Executive Vice President, Television & Content
Peter Ruben, Executive Vice President, Affiliate Relations
Type of service: Basic.
Satellites: Satcom C-4, transponder 10.
Operating hours/week: 168.
Programming: Live, discount shop-at-home service, featuring a range of products, from electronics & household items to beauty & fashion items.
Began: July 1, 1985, HSN HD began August 2009.
Means of Support: Commissions on merchandise sold.
Total subscribers: 96,000,000.
Distribution method: Available to cable, IPTV & satellite subscribers.
Scrambled signal: Yes.
Ownership: HSN Inc.

HSN2 — See HSN.
Type of service: Basic.
Operating hours/week: 168.
Operating areas: Available nationwide.
Programming: Shows mostly taped programs and products from HSN.
Began: August 1, 2010.
Total subscribers: 14,000,000.
Distribution method: Available to satellite subscribers.
Scrambled signal: Yes.

HTV
404 Washington Ave
Miami Beach, FL 33139
Phone: 305-887-8488
Fax: 305-887-0028
E-mail: contacto@htv.com
Web Site: http://www.htv.com
Daniel Sawicki, President & Chief Executive Officer
Jorge Escasena, Vice President, Affiliate Sales
Gustavo Tonelli, Marketing Director
Richard Taylor, Advertising Sales Director
Raquel Bretos Mendez, Programming Manager

Branch Offices:
ARGENTINA: Avenida Martin Garcia, Piso 7, Dto. A (1268), Buenos Aires, Argentina.
Phone: 54-1-307-2721.
Type of service: Basic.
Satellites: Intelsat 806, transponder 12A; GE-1, transponder 5; Hispasat, transponder 13.

Operating hours/week: 168.
Uplink: Miami, FL.
Programming: Spanish language music videos. Each hour of programming is divided into 4 blocks with different combinations of rhythms.
Began: August 25, 1995.
Means of Support: Advertising & subscriber fees.
Total subscribers: 8,100,000.
Distribution method: Available to cable systems.
Equipment: Scientific-Atlanta; VideoCipher II Plus.
Ownership: Daniel Sawicki & Robert Behar.

HUB NETWORK — See Discovery Family.

HULU
12312 W Olympic Blvd
Los Angeles, CA 90064
Phone: 310-571-4700
Fax: 310-571-4701
E-mail: media@hulu.com
Web Site: http://www.hulu.com
Mike Hopkins, Chief Executive Officer
Tian Lim, Chief Technical Officer
Julie DeTraglia, Head, Advertising Sales Research
Jean-Paul Colaco, Senior Vice President, Advertising
Craig Erwich, Senior Vice President, Content & Programming
John Foster, Senior Vice President, Talent & Organization
Chadwick Ho, Senior Vice President & General Counsel
Johannes Larcher, Senior Vice President, International
Peter Naylor, Senior Vice President, Sales
Elaine Paul, Senior Vice President & Chief Financial Officer
Ben Smith, Senior Vice President & Head of Experience
Jenny Wall, Senior Vice President & Head, Marketing
Eugene Wei, Senior Vice President, Audience
Reagan Feeney, Vice President, Network Partnerships
Richard Irving, Vice President, Product Management
Tim Connolly, Head of Distribution
Ben Smith, Head of Experience
Beatrice Springborn, Head of Originals
Type of service: Over the top, streaming subscription service.
Operating areas: Nationwide.
Programming: Full-length movies & TV series from Fox, NBC, Sony Pictures, MGM Studios & others. Spanish language available on Hulu Latino.
Began: October 29, 2007.
Means of Support: Advertising.
Total subscribers: 3,000,000 (Number represents paid subscribers.).
Distribution method: Available online & mobile.
Scrambled signal: Yes.
Ownership: A joint venture between NBCUniversal (30%), 21st Century Fox (30%), The Walt Disney Co. (30%) & Time Warner Inc. (10%).

HULU LATINO — See Hulu.
Began: December 12, 2011.

HUNAN SATELLITE TV (HTV)
Changsa, Hunan Golden Eagle
Hunan Intl Convention & Exhibition Ctr, 4th Fl
410003
China

Pay TV & Satellite Services

Phone: 86-0731-287-1680-8088
Fax: 86-0731-287-1686-8010
E-mail: media@hunantv.com
Web Site: http://news.hunantv.com/English
Programming: Offers Mandarin Chinese language news & entertainment programming.
Began: January 1, 1997, in China.
Distribution method: Available to KyLin TV subscribers.
Scrambled signal: Yes.

HUNT CHANNEL — See Angel Two.
1300 Goodlette Rd North
Naples, FL 34102
Phone: 800-759-2643
Web Site: http://huntchannel.tv
Merrill Sport, President
Stewart Thomas, Executive Vice President
Clint Norman, Vice President, Producer Services
Jimmy Sites, Vice President & Manager, Producer Relations
Tom Scott, Manager
Tiffany Bryan, Producer Services & Traffic Coordinator
Programming: Outdoor programming.
Distribution method: Available to DISH subscribers on Angel Two Channel.
Scrambled signal: Yes.
Ownership: Sky Angel Networks LLC.

HURRICANE VISION
The University of Tulsa
800 S Tucker Dr
Tulsa, OK 74104
Phone: 918-631-2381
Web Site: http://www.tulsahurricane.com/watch
Don Tomkalski, Senior Associate Athletic Director, Communications
Bruce Howard, Sports Broadcasting Director
Chris Becker, Video Services Director
Type of service: Video on demand.
Operating areas: Oklahoma.
Programming: Player profiles, interviews with players and coaches, game previews and coaches' shows.
Means of Support: Subscriber fees.
Distribution method: Available to Cox subscribers.
Scrambled signal: Yes.
Ownership: University of Tulsa.

HUSTLER TV
8484 Wilshire Blvd
Ste 900
Beverly Hills, CA 90211
Phone: 323-651-5400 x7130
Fax: 323-651-0651
E-mail: lmartin@lfp.com
Dave Josephson, Regional Vice President, Sales & Affiliate Marketing
James Donnellan, Regional Vice President, Sales & Affiliate Marketing
Patrick Harrell, Regional Vice President, Sales & Affiliate Marketing
Lillian Martin, Senior Vice President, Affiliate Sales & Marketing Director
Alexander Behrens, Vice President, Sales & Affiliate Marketing, Latin America
Daryl Boyd, Vice President, Programming
Marlon Gillett, Vice President, Operations
Amy Rowcliffe, Affiliate Sales & Marketing Director
Marilyn Taylor, New Media Services Director
Type of service: Video on demand & pay-per-view.
Satellites: Galaxy 15, transponder Transponder 10.
Programming: Adult entertainment.
Began: October 1, 2004.
Total subscribers: 55,000,000.

Distribution method: Available to cable & satellite subscribers.
Scrambled signal: Yes.
Ownership: LFP Broadcasting LLC.

HWAZAN TV
Taipei Nanjing East Rd 269
Lane 5, 6th Fl, B1
Taipei
Taiwan
Phone: 886-02-660-8968
Fax: 886-02-6600-9598
Web Site: http://www.hwazantv.com
Programming: Buddhist themed shows.
Distribution method: Available to KyLin TV subscribers.
Scrambled signal: Yes.

IAVC
9550 Flair Dr
Ste 102
El Monte, CA 91731
Phone: 626-337-8889
Web Site: http://www.iavcusa.com
Amanda Lee, Chief Executive Officer
Programming: Variety shows, entertainment & news from Taiwan.
Distribution method: Available through KyLin TV.
Scrambled signal: Yes.

ICTV — See ActiveVideo Networks in Management/Technical Services.

IDEA CHANNEL — See Free To Choose Network.

IDRIVETV
4100 E Mississippi Ave
Ste 1900
Glendale, CO 80246
Phone: 303-839-5303
Fax: 303-839-5335
E-mail: idrivetv@isafe.org
Programming: Interactive advertising channel focusing on cars, motor boats, motorbikes & airplanes.
Began: November 20, 2005.
Total subscribers: 15,000,000.
Distribution method: Available to DISH Network subscribers.
Scrambled signal: Yes.
Ownership: Networks Group.

IFC
11 Penn Plz
15th Fl
New York, NY 1001
Phone: 212-324-8500
E-mail: webmaster@ifc.com
Web Site: http://www.ifc.com
Ed Carroll, Chief Operating Officer, AMC Networks Inc.
Robert Broussard, President, AMC Networks Distribution
Jennifer Caserta, President & General Manager
Peter Aronson, Executive Vice President, Original Programming & Production
Blake Callaway, Executive Vice President, Marketing & Digital Media
Alan Klein, Executive Vice President, Partnerships & Operations
Vanessa Benfield, Senior Vice President, Sales
Allison Clarke, Senior Vice President, Advertising Sales, IFC & WE tv
Kim Granito, Senior Vice President, Digital Media & Integrated Marketing
Alan Klein, Senior Vice President, Partnerships & Licensing
Christine Lubrano, Senior Vice President, Original Programming

Sallie Schoneboom, Senior Vice President, Public Relations
Kevin Vitale, Senior Vice President, Brand Marketing
Lauren Burack, Vice President, Event Marketing & Promotions
Maura Madden, Vice President, Original Programming, New York City
Jeff Meyerson, Vice President, Original Programming, Los Angeles
Colin Moore, Vice President, Digital Media & Alternative Content
Andrew Siegal, Vice President, Production
Tony Song, Vice President, Sales & Partnerships
Sarah Takenaga, Vice President, Public Relations
Kim Volonakis Granito, Vice President, Integrated Marketing
Vincent Genovese, Editorial & Digital Production Manager

Branch Offices:
CENTRAL REGION: 205 N Michigan Ave, Ste 803, Chicago, IL 60601. Phone: 312-938-3134. Fax: 312-729-9370.

EASTERN REGION: 555 Fifth Ave, 3rd Floor, New York, NY 10017. Phone: 917-542-6300.

SOUTHERN/EASTERN REGION: 3 Village Cir, Ste 208, Westlake, TX 76262. Phone: 817-430-3589. Fax: 817-491-0435.

WESTERN REGION: 2425 W Olympic Blvd, Ste 5050 W, Santa Monica, CA 90404. Phone: 310-828-7005. Fax: 310-828-0375.
Type of service: Digital, HD, streaming & video on demand.
Satellites: Galaxy VII, transponder 14.
Sales representative: AMC Networks Advertising Sales.
Operating hours/week: 168.
Operating areas: Available nationwide.
Programming: Features domestic & international independent films to include documentaries, animation, comedies and other creative productions.
Began: September 1, 1994, as Independent Film Channel. Rebranded IFC January 9, 2014.
Total subscribers: 73,000,000.
Distribution method: Available to cable, IPTV & satellite subscribers; streaming available online & through the IFC app; video on demand through IFC Free (participating providers).
Scrambled signal: Yes.
Ownership: AMC Networks Inc. Formerly Rainbow Media Holdings LLC owned by Cablevision Systems Corp., it became a publicly held company under the new name June 30, 2011.

IGLESIA JEMIR
PO Box 223985
2929 S Westmoreland
Dallas, TX 75222
Phones: 214-330-8700; 866-481-8730
E-mail: info@jemir.org
Web Site: http://jemir.org

Pastor Roberto Gomez, President & Co-Founder
Elva Gomez, Co-Founder
Type of service: Basic.
Operating areas: Texas.
Programming: Spanish-language religious channel.
Began: February 9, 2006.
Means of Support: Donations & advertising.
Distribution method: Available over the air to digital sub-channels.
Scrambled signal: Yes.
Ownership: Iglesia Jesucristo Es Mi Refugio Inc.

I-HEALTH — See ION Life.

I-LIFETV — See Pivot.

ILLINOIS CHANNEL
PO Box 1856
Springfield, IL 62701
Phone: 217-741-9419
E-mail: illinoischannel@aol.com
Web Site: http://www.illinoischannel.org/index.htm
Terry Martin, Executive Director
Programming: Gavel to gavel coverage of the three branches of Illinois government.
Began: January 1, 2003.
Total subscribers: 860,000.

IMETRO — See ION Television.

IMPACT
c/o Comast Corp.
One Comcast Ctr
Philadelphia, PA 19103
Phone: 215-286-1700
Web Site: http://www.impactvod.com
Type of service: Video on demand.
Operating areas: Available nationwide.
Programming: Video on demand channel dedicated exclusively to action programming. Offers action movies & shows, including thrillers, spy, crime, westerns, war & martial arts films.
Began: August 1, 2008.
Distribution method: Available to cable subscribers.
Scrambled signal: Yes.
Ownership: A joint venture between Comcast Corp & Metro Goldwyn Mayer Studios.

THE IMPACT NETWORK
15738 Grand River Ave
Detroit, MI 48227
Phone: 313-243-1600
Fax: 866-455-4901
E-mail: info@watchimpact.com
Web Site: http://watchimpact.com
Dr. Beverly Y Jackson, Founder
Bishop Wayne T Jackson, Founder & President
Terry Arnold, Senior Vice President
Type of service: Premium.
Operating hours/week: 168.
Operating areas: Available nationwide.
Programming: Inspirational, informative & engaging family-oriented entertainment.
Began: January 15, 2011.

2017 Edition   E-49

Pay TV & Satellite Services

Means of Support: Subscriber fees and advertising.
Total subscribers: 30,000,000.
Distribution method: Available to Comcast & DISH subscribers.
Scrambled signal: Yes.
Ownership: The Impact Co. Bishop David Copeland, Bishop I. V. Hilliard, Bishop Wiley Jackson, Bishop Stanley Williams & the New Light Church.

IN DEMAND
345 Hudson St
17th Fl
New York, NY 10014
Phone: 646-638-8200
Fax: 646-486-0855
E-mail: business@indemand.com
Web Site: http://www.indemand.com
Robert G. Benya, President & Chief Executive Officer
Michael Berman, Executive Vice President, Programming & General Counsel
Stacie Gray, Executive Vice President & Chief Creative Director
Eric Petro, Executive Vice President, Business Development & Chief Financial Officer
Mark Boccardi, Senior Vice President, Programming & Business Development
Leigh Bolton, Senior Vice President, Video Promotion
Tony Dunaif, Senior Vice President, Digital Products
Claire Kostbar, Senior Vice President, Human Resources & Administration
Lauren LoFrisco, Senior Vice President, Affiliate Marketing
Emilio Nunez, Senior Vice President, Movies & Original Programming
John Vartanian, Senior Vice President & Chief Technology Officer
Ellen Cooper, Vice President, Corporate & Affiliate Communications
Michael Diana, Vice President, Affiliate Marketing
Craig Helmstetter, Vice President, Finance
David Ludder, Vice President, Technology
Maureen McBride, Vice Presdent, Human Resources
Sean Murray, Vice President, Audit
Doug Ohlandt, Vice President, Programming & Promotion
James Ra, Vice President, Software Coding & Management
Michael Raposa, Vice President, Infrastructure
John Schultz, Vice President, Broadcast Operations
Mark Troller, Vice President, Technology Solutions
Teresa Turano, Vice President, Transactional Database Management & Business Analysis
Bill Wolstromer, Vice President & Controller

Regional Offices:
ATLANTA: 5 Piedmont Ctr, Ste 402, Atlanta, GA 30305. Phone: 404-760-2843. Fax: 404-760-2841. Ray Monasterski, Information Contact.

LOS ANGELES: 2029 Century Park E, One Century Plaza, Ste 2080, Los Angeles, CA 90067. Phone: 310-785-9194. Fax: 310-785-9769.

Operations Center:
DENVER: 4100 E Dry Creek Rd, Centennial, CO 80120. Phone: 303-712-3360. Fax: 303-712-3360.
Type of service: Pay-per-view & video on demand.
Satellites: Satcom C-3; Loral T7, transponder 3; 2 (Chs. 1-22); Satcom C-4; Loral T7, transponder 18; 3 (Chs. 1-30); Telstar 7;
Loral T7, transponder 2,3,4; 4 (Chs. 1-34); GE-1, transponder 8,13,14.
Operating hours/week: 168.
Operating areas: Nationwide.
Uplink: Denver, CO.
Programming: Titles from all of the major Hollywood & independent studios, including sports & subscription sports packages & entertainment events. Also includes three digital barker channels.
Began: November 27, 1985, as Viewer's Choice. Rebranded as iN DEMAND January 1, 2000.
Means of Support: Pay-per-view & subscription fees.
Total subscribers: 29,000,000 (Figure represents addressable homes.).
Distribution method: Available to cable subscribers.
Scrambled signal: Yes. Equipment: VideoCipher II Plus; GI DigiCipher II.
Ownership: A joint venture between Bright House Networks; Comcast iN DEMAND Holdings Inc.; Cox Communications Holdings Inc. & Time Warner Cable Inc.

INDEPENDENT FILM CHANNEL — See IFC.

INDEPENDENT MUSIC NETWORK
8424 Santa Monica Blvd S
Ste 776
West Hollywood, CA 90069
Phone: 323-951-0674
Fax: 323-951-0674
E-mail: gary@independentmusicnetwork.com
Web Site: http://www.independentmusicnetwork.com
James Fallacaro, Chairman & President
Anthony L. Escamilla, Executive Vice President
Corinne Fallacaro, Secretary & Treasurer Director
Christopher Mauritz, Chief Technology Officer Director
Terry Shea, Public Relations & Marketing
Type of service: Basic.
Operating hours/week: 168.
Programming: Independent music video programming featuring amateur & professional musicians.
Began: June 1, 2000.
Distribution method: Available to cable & satellite subscribers.
Scrambled signal: Yes.

INDIEPLEX
8900 Liberty Cir
Englewood, CO 80112
Phone: 720-852-7700
Fax: 720-852-7710
E-mail: eric.becker@starz.com
Web Site: http://www.starz.com/channels/movieplex
Eric Becker, Vice President, Corporate Communications
Type of service: Pay, HD.
Operating areas: Nationwide.
Programming: Offers films on controversial topics and a creative point of view.
Began: April 4, 2006.
Means of Support: Subscriber fees.
Distribution method: Available to cable, IPTV & satellite subscribers.
Scrambled signal: Yes.
Ownership: Liberty Media Corp.

IND PPV EN ESPANOL — See iN DEMAND.
Type of service: Pay per View.
Operating areas: Available nationwide.
Programming: Spanish-language movies, music and comedy, documentaries, live and taped sports, reality & uncensored programming.
Began: December 1, 2012.

INFINITO
One CNN Center
Atlanta, GA 30303
Phone: 404-827-1700
E-mail: contacto@infinito.com
Web Site: http://www.infinito.com
Felipe De Stefani, Senior Vice President & General Manager
Celina Rossi, Media Channel Trends Manager, Turner Latin America
Operating hours/week: 168.
Operating areas: Nationwide.
Programming: New-age & spiritual lifestyle programming.
Began: March 1, 2003, in U.S.
Total subscribers: 15,800,000.
Distribution method: Available to cable & satellite subscribers.
Scrambled signal: Yes.
Ownership: Turner Broadcasting System Inc.

INFOMAS
700 Carillion Pkwy
Ste 9
St. Petersburg, FL 33716
Phone: 727-329-2300
Web Site: http://www.infomas.tv
Alan Mason, Vice President & General Manager, News & Local Programming
Type of service: Basic, HD.
Operating hours/week: 168.
Operating areas: Tampa & Orlando areas, Florida.
Programming: Regional Spanish-language news & information covering Tampa Bay & Central Florida.
Began: March 2002 as Bay News 9 en Espanol & December 2006 as Central Florida News en Espanol. Channels merged into InfoMas on July 12, 2011.
Means of Support: Advertising.
Distribution method: Available to Bright House cable subscribers.
Scrambled signal: Yes.
Ownership: Bright House Networks.

INMIGRANTE TV
6657 Navigation Blvd
Houston, TX 77011
Phones: 713-844-2700; 888-370-7022
Fax: 281-962-0233
Web Site: http://www.inmigrantetv.com
Type of service: Basic.
Operating areas: Arizona, California, Illinois & Texas.
Programming: Provides news, information and assistance for Hispanic immigrants.
Began: February 19, 2010.
Distribution method: Available over the air on digital sub-channels.
Ownership: Manuel Solis.

INSP
PO Box 7750
Charlotte, NC 28241
Phones: 803-578-1000; 800-725-4677
Fax: 803-578-1735
E-mail: info@insp.com
Web Site: http://www.insp.com
David Cerullo, Chairman & Chief Executive Officer
Dale Ardizzone, Chief Operating Officer
Robert I. Brace, Executive Vice President, Finance
Marc Favaro, Executive Vice President, Worldwide Sales
Doug Butts, Senior Vice President, Programming
Mark Kang, Senior Vice President, Worldwide Distribution
John Roos, Senior Vice President, Corporate Communications & Research
Samantha Adorno, Vice President, Digital Marketing
Tom Kingsley, Vice President, Broadcast Engineering & Information Technology
Craig Miller, Vice President, Original Programming
Shawn Nicholson, Vice President, Sales Operation
Christine Rodocker, Vice President, Affiliate Marketing
Gary Wheeler, Vice President, Original Movies
Type of service: Basic, digital, HD, video on demand.
Satellites: Galaxy 15, transponder 17; Galaxy I-R, transponder 17 (digital).
Operating hours/week: 168.
Uplink: Charlotte, NC.
Programming: Inspirational entertainment including children's programs, music videos, primetime specials, movies, concerts & selected ministry programs.
Began: September 1, 1990, as PTL - The Inspirational Network. Rebranded The Inspiration Network in 1990 & INSP in 2010.
Means of Support: Sale of airtime, advertising.
Total subscribers: 80,000,000 (6,000,000 on demand subscribers.).
Distribution method: Available to cable, IPTV & satellite subscribers.
Scrambled signal: Yes.
Ownership: The Inspiration Networks.

INTELLICAST — See The Weather Channel.

INTERNATIONAL FAMILY TELEVISION
PO Box 1568
Lomita, CA 90717
Phone: 310-719-9599
E-mail: info@iftv.tv
Web Site: http://www.iftv.tv
Programming: Dramas, music videos, cooking shows, cartoons, fitness & talk shows for adults & children available in English, Mandarin, Cantonese, Taiwanese, Japanese & Korean.
Distribution method: Available to KyLin TV subscribers.
Scrambled signal: Yes.

INTERNATIONAL TELEVISION (ITV)
PO Box 347
East Elmhurst, NY 11369
Phone: 718-784-8555
Fax: 718-784-8901
Web Site: http://www.itvgold.com
Sathya Viswanath, President & Producer
B. Viswanath, Vice President
Nandini Sikand, Co-Producer
Type of service: Basic, Digital.
Operating hours/week: 24.
Operating areas: New York.
Programming: Indian movies, news, serials, interviews & live shows.
Began: January 1, 1987.
Means of Support: Advertising.
Ownership: Deepak Viswanath, principal.

INTINETWORK
Av. Nahin Isaias y Miguel H Alcivar
Guayaquil
Ecuador

Pay TV & Satellite Services

Phones: 593-0-4-602-4840; 593-0-4-602-4825
Web Site: http://intinetwork.tv
Maria Kowalski-Alvarado, Content Director
Type of service: Pay.
Operating areas: Nationwide.
Programming: Offers a total experience, from the development of body, mind and spirit, social responsibility, fair trade, eco-tourism, culture and lifestyle of the connection with yourself and everything around us.
Began: July 1, 2013, in U.S.
Means of Support: Advertising and subscriber fees.
Distribution method: Available to satellite subscribers.
Scrambled signal: Yes.
Ownership: Ecuavisa. Distributed in the U.S. by Alterna'TV.

INVESTIGATION DISCOVERY — See Discovery Channel.
c/o Discovery Communications
One Discovery Pl
Silver Spring, MD 20910-3354
Phone: 240-662-2000
Web Site: http://www.investigationdiscovery.com
Henry S. Schleiff, Group President, American Heroes Channels, Destination America & Investigation Discovery
Kevin Bennett, General Manager & Executive Vice President, Programming
Sara Kozak, Senior Vice President, Production, American Heroes Channels, Destination America & Investigation Discovery
Jane Latman, Senior Vice President, Development
Doug Seybert, Senior Vice President, Marketing, American Heroes Channels, Destination America & Investigation Discovery
Sara Burn, Vice President, Programming, American Heroes & Investigation Discovery
Programming: A mystery & suspense network. Offers strong analytic, factual investigative & current affairs programming through original series like On the Case with Paula Zahn & Homicide Hunter: Lt. Joe Kenda and established investigative series, such as Dateline on ID & 48 Hours on ID.
Began: January 1, 1996, as Discovery Civilization Channel. Rebranded as Discovery Times Channel March 2003 & Investigation Discovery on January 27, 2008.
Total subscribers: 84,000,000 (U.S. subscribers. 1,000,000 Canadian subscribers. 74,000,000 international subscribers.).
Distribution method: Available to cable, IPTV & satellite subscribers.
Scrambled signal: Yes.
Ownership: Discovery Communications Inc.

ION LIFE — See ION Television.
Web Site: http://www.ionlife.tv
Programming: Healthy lifestyles & personal growth.
Began: February 19, 2007, Planned to launch as i-Health but changed to ION Life at launch.

ION TELEVISION
601 Clearwater Park Rd
West Palm Beach, FL 33401-6233
Phone: 561-659-4122
Fax: 561-659-4252
Web Site: http://www.ionline.tv
Brandon Burgess, Chairman & Chief Executive Officer
Steven P. Appel, President, Sales & Marketing
Jeff Quinn, Chief Financial Officer & Senior Vice President
Helen C. Karas, Senior Vice President, Network Sales
Adam K. Weinstein, Senior Vice President, Secretary & Chief Legal Officer
Curtis L. Brandon, Vice President, Controller
Emma Cordoba, Vice President & Human Resources Director
Henry J. Brandon, Director
Type of service: Basic, HD.
Satellites: GE-I, transponder 7.
Operating hours/week: 168.
Programming: Provides ION Television programming to cable systems unable to receive over-the-air signals from an ION Television affiliate.
Began: August 31, 1998, as PAX. Rebranded as i - Independent Television on September 25, 2005, then ION Television January 2007.
Means of Support: Advertising.
Total subscribers: 93,000,000.
Distribution method: Available to cable subscribers.
Scrambled signal: Yes.
Ownership: ION Media Networks.

IOWA COMMUNICATIONS NETWORK
400 E 14th St
Grimes State Office Bldg
Des Moines, IA 50319
Phones: 515-725-4692; 877-426-4692
Fax: 515-725-4727
Web Site: http://www.icn.state.ia.us
Bob Montgomery, General Advertising Sales Mgr.
Mike Woody, Local Advertising Sales Manager
Gail Ware, Local Program Manager
Type of service: Basic, microwave.
Operating hours/week: 168.
Operating areas: Iowa.
Programming: Special interest programming including public service shows, talk shows, area sporting events & coach commentary. Network alternately carries CNBC & CMT.
Began: January 1, 1980.
Total subscribers: 166,000.
Scrambled signal: Yes.
Ownership: Mediacom.

I-PLAY
100 Broadway
14th Fl
New York, NY 10005
Phone: 646-367-2020
Fax: 212-221-9240
Bob Hayes, President & Chief Operating Officer
Carl Hixon, Chief Technology Officer
Megan Barbour, Senior Vice President, Operations
Ginger Kraus, Senior Vice President, Global Partner Development & Revenue
Zach Koekemoer, Senior Vice President, Finance & Administration
Steve Hammer, Vice President, Marketing
Isaac Josephson, Vice President, Product Management & Merchandising

Branch Offices:
SEATTLE: 2101 4th Ave, Ste 1020, Seattle, WA 98121.
Type of service: Premium.
Operating hours/week: 168.
Operating areas: Available nationwide.
Programming: Interactive TV game service.
Began: February 3, 2010.
Means of Support: Subscriber fees.
Distribution method: Available to DISH Network subscribers.
Scrambled signal: Yes.
Ownership: Oberon Media, in license with The Tetris Company.

THE ISRAELI NETWORK
730 Columbus Ave
New York, NY 10025-6658
Phone: 646-438-9187
E-mail: shira@tin.tv
Web Site: http://tin.tv
Amit Ben Yehuda, Chief Executive Officer
Shira Vardi, Chief Operating Officer, U.S.
Niv Lior, Chief Financial Officer
Ofir Hagai, Head of Programming
Hagit Kaminetzky, Operations Manager & Assistant to Chief Executive Officer
Noa Miller, Interactive Manager, Subscribers, Marketing & Acquisition
Type of service: Pay.
Operating hours/week: 168.
Operating areas: Available nationwide.
Programming: Offers news and current affairs, Jewish culture, drama and entertainment, children's and sports programming.
Began: September 1, 2001.
Means of Support: Advertising & subscriber fees.
Distribution method: Available to DISH Network customers and Cablevision & Comcast cable system subscribers.
Scrambled signal: Yes.
Ownership: Kardan Communications of Kardan Group (Israel) & Monarchy Enterprises of Milchan Group (USA).

ITALIANATION
95 State Hwy 17
Paramus, NJ 07652
Phone: 201-712-5780
Fax: 201-712-5783
E-mail: tcgelio@italianation.com
Web Site: http://www.italianation.com
Tony Ceglio, Chief Executive Officer
Mark Kozaki, Chief Operating Officer & General Manager
Anthony Gianino, Chief Business Officer
Robert Russo, Chief Marketing Officer
Type of service: Digital.
Programming: Plans to feature shows about food, fashion, style, travel, music, contemporary issues and history as well as movies, sports, dramas, comedies, documentaries, biographies, reality programs, children's programs and adult education. Most programming will be in English, several in Italian with English subtitles as well as Italian language learning shows for preschoolers to adults.
Means of Support: Advertising.
Distribution method: Plans to be available to cable & satellite subscribers & online.
Scrambled signal: Yes.

JADE CHANNEL
c/o TVB (USA) Inc.
15411 Blackburn Ave
Norwalk, CA 90650
Phones: 562-802-0220; 877-893-8888
Fax: 562-802-5096
E-mail: jade@tvbusa.com
Philip Tam, Senior Vice President TVB-USA
Tracy Lee, Vice President, Advertising
Whayu Lin, Information Contact
Branch Office:
SAN FRANCISCO: 39 Dorman Ave, San Francisco, CA 94124. Phone: 415-282-8228. Fax: 415-282-8226. Karman Liu, Advertising.
Satellites: Galaxy IV.
Operating hours/week: 168.
Operating areas: Los Angeles, San Diego & San Francisco, CA.
Programming: Cantonese & Mandarin language programming.
Began: December 1, 1994.
Distribution method: Available to cable & satellite subscribers.
Scrambled signal: Yes.
Ownership: TVB (USA) Inc.

JANE.TV
5904 S Cooper
Ste 104 #128
Arlington, TX 76017
Phone: 817-323-7348
E-mail: admin@janemediagroup.com
Web Site: http://jane.tv
Jackie Dorman, Founder & President
Kimberly Heuser, Chief Executive Officer & Partner
Josh Heuser, Chief Operating Officer & Partner
Type of service: Regional basic.
Operating hours/week: 168.
Operating areas: Ohio.
Programming: Provides women with quality original programming that showcases the beauty of the female heart, the tenacity of the female will and the strength of the female spirit.
Began: November 18, 2011.
Means of Support: Advertising.
Distribution method: Available over the air on digital sub-channels.
Scrambled signal: Yes.
Ownership: Jackie Dorman, Josh Heuser & Kimberly Heuser.

JCTV — See JUCE TV.

JEWELRY TELEVISION
10001 Kingston Pike
Ste 57
Knoxville, TN 37922
Phones: 865-692-1368; 866-392-9524
Fax: 865-693-3688
E-mail: kelly.fletcher@jtv.com
Web Site: http://www.jtv.com
F. Robert Hall, Chairman & Chief Executive Officer, Multimedia Commerce Group Inc.
Charles A. Wagner, III, Vice Chairman
Tim Matthews, President & Chief Executive Officer
William C. Kouns, Chief Merchandising Officer
Crawford Wagner, Chief Financial Officer
Tim Engle, Senior Vice President, Strategic Initiatives
Andy Caldwell, Vice President, Affiliate Marketing
Stephen E. Roth, Vice President & General Counsel
Craig Shields, Vice President, E-Commerce
Type of service: Basic, over the air.
Satellites: Galaxy 11; Galaxy 23.
Operating hours/week: 168.
Operating areas: Available nationwide.

Pay TV & Satellite Services

Uplink: Knoxville, TN.
Programming: Home shopping network dedicated to jewelry & gemstones.
Began: October 15, 1993, as America's Collectibles Network. Rebranded Jewelry Television in 2004.
Means of Support: Shoppers.
Total subscribers: 65,000,000.
Distribution method: Available over the air on digital sub-channels & to cable subscribers. Available to satellite subscribers as JTV Direct.
Scrambled signal: No.
Ownership: Multimedia Commerce Group Inc.

JEWISH BROADCASTING SERVICE
PO Box 180
Riverdale Station
Bronx, NY 10471
Phone: 201-242-9460
Fax: 201-363-9241
E-mail: news@shalomtv.com
Web Site: http://www.shalomtv.com
Rabbi Mark Golub, President
Bradford N. Hammer, Chief Operating Officer
David Brugnone, Chief Marketing Officer
Dr. Evgueni Lvov, Vice President, Operations
Edith Samers, Vice President, Marketing
Alan E. Oirich, Production Director
Jan Weiss, Executive Assistant
Type of service: SD, HD, streaming, video on demand.
Satellites: Galaxy 16, transponder Transponder 5.
Operating hours/week: 168.
Operating areas: Nationwide.
Uplink: Fort Lee, NJ.
Programming: Daily news direct from Israel, live coverage of conferences & events, Live Shabbat & holiday services, children's programs & more.
Began: July 1, 2003, as Shalom TV. Rebranded Jewish Broadcasting Service September 24, 2014.
Means of Support: Viewer contributions, grants, private funding and sponsorships.
Total subscribers: 40,000,000.
Distribution method: Available to cable & IPTV subscribers. Streaming available online & through participating providers.
Scrambled signal: Yes.
Ownership: Shalom TV LLC.

THE JEWISH CHANNEL
151 W 30th St
7th Fl
New York, NY 10001
Phone: 212-643-9500
Web Site: http://tjctv.com
Elie Singer, Founder
Steven Weiss, Original Programming & New Media Director
Type of service: Pay.
Operating areas: New York.
Programming: Jewish news, documentaries, movies & entertainment.
Began: September 1, 2007.
Means of Support: Subscription fees.
Distribution method: Available to cable systems.

JEWISH LIFE TV
15060 Ventura Blvd
Ste 240
Sherman Oaks, CA 91403
Phone: 818-786-4000
Fax: 818-380-9232
E-mail: info@blazermediagroup.com; pblazer@jltv.tv
Web Site: http://www.jltv.tv
Phil Blazer, President & Chief Executive Officer
Allan Kass, Senior Vice President

Operating hours/week: 168.
Operating areas: Nationwide.
Programming: Jewish-themed news, sports, movies, music videos, documentaries & general entertainment.
Began: January 1, 2007.
Means of Support: Advertising.
Total subscribers: 40,000,000.
Distribution method: Available to Atlantic Broadband, Bright House Networks, Comcast, Time Warner & DirecTV subscribers.
Scrambled signal: Yes.

JIANGSU INTERNATIONAL CHANNEL
4 East Beijing Rd
Nanjing, Jiansu
China
Phones: 86-25-83188187; 86-25-8318815
Fax: 86-25-83188187
E-mail: info@jsbc.com
Web Site: http://www.jstv.com
Operating hours/week: 168.
Programming: Focuses on Wuyue culture.
Distribution method: Available to KyLin TV subscribers.
Scrambled signal: Yes.

JIA YU CHANNEL
No. 1-3,Jalan PJU 8/5H, Bandar Damansara Perd
47820 Petaling Jaya, Selangor Darul Ehsan
Malaysia
Phone: 60-3-7726-9593
Fax: 60-3-7710-9363
Web Site: http://www.jiayu.tv
Operating hours/week: 168.
Programming: Cantonese and Mandarin language channel from Malaysia offering general entertainment, news, animated & lifestyle programs.
Began: January 1, 2004.
Distribution method: Available through KyLin TV.
Scrambled signal: Yes.

JTV
Jackson Television
152 W Michigan Ave
Jackson, MI 49201
Phone: 517-787-8817
Fax: 517-783-5060
Web Site: http://www.jtv.tv
Bart Hawley, President
Kurt Baringer, General Manager
Andy Hawley, Sports Director
Type of service: Basic, HD.
Operating hours/week: 168.
Operating areas: Michigan.
Programming: Offers local daily talk show, cooking, home, design and health programs, plus extensive local high school sports coverage.
Began: July 1, 2000.
Means of Support: Advertising.
Distribution method: Available to cable subscribers.
Scrambled signal: Yes.

JTV DIRECT — See Jewelry Television.

JUCE TV
2442 Michelle Dr
Tustin, CA 92780
Phones: 714-832-2950 x2639; 714-665-3691
Fax: 714-832-0645
E-mail: jc-tv@jucetv.org
Web Site: http://www.jucetv.com
Jan Crouch, President
Matthew Crouch, Vice President
Bob Fopma, Vice President, Production
Bob Miller, Vice President, Engineering

David Adcock, National Director, Cable & Satellite Relations
Mark McCallie, Programming Director
Jay Jones, Media Services
Colby May, Media Relations
Type of service: Over the air, digital basic, streaming.
Satellites: Galaxy 14, transponder 1; Galaxy 23, transponder 20 (Olympusat).
Operating hours/week: 168.
Operating areas: Nationwide.
Programming: Music videos, concert specials, live events, comedy, movies, talk shows, sports, documentaries, faith-friendly for the 13-29 year-old age group.
Began: January 1, 2002, as JCTV. Rebranded as JUCE TV on January 1, 2014.
Distribution method: Available over the air on digital sub-channels. Available to cable, IPTV & satellite subscribers Streaming available online.
Scrambled signal: Yes.
Ownership: TBN Networks, a non-profit corp.

JUICY
c/o New Frontier Media
6000 Spine Rd, Ste 100
Boulder, CO 80301
Phones: 303-444-0900; 888-875-0632
Fax: 303-938-8388
Web Site: http://www.noof.com
Larry Flynt, Chief Executive Officer
Michael Klein, President
Chris Woodward, Chief Financial Officer
Type of service: Pay per view.
Operating areas: Available nationwide.
Programming: Adult programming.
Distribution method: Available to cable, IPTV & satellite subscribers.
Ownership: New Frontier Media.

JUSTICE CENTRAL.TV
1925 Century Park E
Ste 1025
Los Angeles, CA 90067
Phone: 310-277-3500
E-mail: eric@es.tv
Web Site: http://www.es.tv
Byron Allen, Chairman & Chief Executive Officer, Entertainment Studios
Eric Peterkofsky, Information Contact
Type of service: Digital.
Operating hours/week: 168.
Operating areas: Nationwide.
Programming: Legal and news network for court proceedings, talk and entertainment programming featuring the biggest names in law. Offers courtroom shows, legal news, and a broad range of law-oriented original programming.
Began: December 10, 2012.
Means of Support: Advertising.
Distribution method: Available to AT&T U-Verse customers.
Scrambled signal: Yes.
Ownership: Entertainment Studios.

JUSTICE NETWORK
c/o Steve Schiffman, CEO
150 Interstate North Pkwy SE
Atlanta, GA 30339
Phone: 770-955-1300
E-mail: info@justnettv.com
Web Site: http://www.justicenetworktv.com
Steve Schiffman, Chief Executive Officer
Wendy Brown, Chief Operating Officer
John Ford, Head of Programming
Barry Wallach, Head of Distribution
Brian Weiss, Distribution & Business Development Director
Type of service: Basic, over the air.
Operating areas: Nationwide.

Programming: Crime and mystery programs plus alerts on criminals and missing children.
Began: January 20, 2015.
Means of Support: Advertising.
Distribution method: Available over the air on digital sub-channels.
Scrambled signal: Yes.
Ownership: Justice Network LLC. Lonnie Cooper, majority stockholder; John Walsh.

KABILLION
c/o Splash Entertainment
21300 Oxnard St, Ste 100
Woodland Hills, CA 91367
Phone: 818-999-0062
Fax: 818-999-0172
E-mail: info@splashentertainment.com
Web Site: http://www.kabillion.com
David DiLorenzo, President
Steven Levy, Vice President, Productions & Global Operations
Type of service: Video on demand.
Operating areas: Nationwide.
Programming: High-quality animated & live-action series entertainment, games, music and chat.
Began: January 1, 2007.
Means of Support: Advertising.
Total subscribers: 50,000,000.
Distribution method: Available to Blue Ridge, Bresnan, Bright House Networks, Charter, Comcast, Time Warner & Verizon FiOS subscribers.
Scrambled signal: Yes.
Ownership: Splash Entertainment.

KABILLION GIRLS RULE — See Kabillion.
Programming: Animated entertainment geared towards girls.
Distribution method: Available to Blue Ridge, Bresnan, Bright House Networks, Charter, Comcast, Time Warner & Verizon FiOS subscribers.

KANSAS NOW 22
807 E Douglas
Wichita, KS 67202
Phone: 316-858-3300
Fax: 316-262-7484
Operating areas: Kansas, Missouri & Oklahoma.
Programming: Local news, national news, weather 24/7.
Total subscribers: 317,400.
Scrambled signal: Yes.
Ownership: Cox Communications Inc. & Gray Television Inc.

KARAOKE CHANNEL
6420-A1 Rea Rd
Ste 161
Charlotte, NC 28277
Phone: 704-817-1530
Fax: 866-932-9024
E-mail: support@thekaraokechannel.com
Web Site: http://www.thekaraokechannel.com
Brian Decker, Senior Vice President, Business Development

Branch Offices:
CANADA: Headquarters, 730 Wellington St, Montreal, PQ H3C 1T4, Canada.
Type of service: Basic & video on demand.
Operating areas: Nationwide.
Programming: Delivers more than 18,000 professional quality karaoke songs in English, French, Spanish, Dutch, German and Italian.
Began: November 4, 2008.
Total subscribers: 55,000,000.

Distribution method: Available to cable & satellite subscribers.
Scrambled signal: Yes.
Ownership: Stingray Digital Media.

KBS AMERICA
625 S Kingsley Dr
4th Fl
Los Angeles, CA 90005
Phone: 213-739-1111
Fax: 212-739-2729
E-mail: info@kbs-america.com
Web Site: http://www.kbs-america.com
Kyung Hee Kim, President & Chief Executive Officer
Richard Millet, Vice President
Sung Won Choi, Business Administration Director
Ki Gon Kim, Advertising Sales Director
Michael Kim, Content Business Director
Ken Lee, News, Programming & Production Director

Branch Offices:
JAPAN: Akasaka Jusan B/D 2F, 5-5-13 Akasaka, Minato-ku, Tokyo, Japaan. E-Mail: info@kbsjapan.co.jp. Web site: http://www.kbsworld.ne.jp.

SOUTH KOREA: Content Business Department, No. 18 Yeuido-dong Yeungdeungpo-gu, Seoul 150-790, South Korea.
Type of service: Basic.
Satellites: Intelsat 9.
Operating hours/week: 168.
Operating areas: Nationwide.
Programming: News, drama, entertainment and documentaries in Korean with English subtitles.
Began: July 16, 2004.
Means of Support: Advertising.
Distribution method: Available to Charter, Cox, Time Warner & DISH Network subscribers.
Scrambled signal: Yes.
Ownership: Korean Broadcasting System.

KELSO LONGVIEW TELEVISION
PO Box 702
1706 12th Ave
Longview, WA 98632
Phone: 360-636-3310
Fax: 360-636-1490
E-mail: kltv@kltv.org
Web Site: http://www.kltv.org
Barry Verrill, Executive Director
Gary Hill, Government Producer
Eric Anderson, Master Control Specialist
Brent Morvee, Information Technology Specialist
Corbin Riedel, Training Department Coordinator
Tory Fletcher, Mobile Production Technician
Mecheal Meskew, Membership Services
Operating areas: Cowlitz County, Washington.
Programming: Local channel offering entertaining, diverse, informative, challenging and interesting video that in the aggregate will appeal to a wide spectrum of the community.
Began: July 1, 1973.
Means of Support: Local sponsors.
Total subscribers: 40,000.
Distribution method: Available to cable subscribers.
Scrambled signal: Yes.
Ownership: Non-profit member owned.

KEMS
(Korean EverRock Multi-Media Service)
2102 Commerce Dr
San Jose, CA 95131
Phone: 408-433-0001
E-mail: info@kemstv.com
Web Site: http://www.kemstv.com
Taek Jong Ju, President
Type of service: Regional basic.
Operating hours/week: 168.
Operating areas: Available in Napa Valley, Oakland, San Francisco & San Jose, CA.
Programming: Airs locally produced news, and talk shows along with viewers favorite dramas, movies, sports and documentaries with English and select Chinese subtitles from major Korean television networks.
Began: January 1, 2007.
Total subscribers: 1,500,000.
Distribution method: Available over the air on digital sub-channels & to Comcast cable system subscribers.
Scrambled signal: Yes.
Ownership: Everrock Multimedia Inc.

KENTUCKY EDUCATIONAL TELEVISION (KET)
600 Cooper Dr
Lexington, KY 40502
Phones: 859-258-7000; 800-432-0951
Fax: 859-258-7399
E-mail: help@ket.org
Web Site: http://www.ket.org
Sahe Hopkins, Executive Director
Tim Biscoff, Senior Director, Marketing & Online Content
Mike Brower, Senior Director, Production Operations
Nancy Carpenter, Senior Director, Education
Craig Cornwell, Senior Director, Programming
Fred Engel, Senior Director, Technology
Linda Hume, Senior Director, Finance & Administration
Julie Schmidt, Senior Director, External Affairs
Type of service: Over the air, basic, digital basic, HD.
Programming: Locally produced Kentucky cultural & public information programs, primetime & kids series programming from PBS, how-to & adult education programs, GED programs & programs produced by independent Kentucky filmmakers.
Distribution method: Available over the air on digital sub-channels & to cable, IPTV & satellite subscribers.
Scrambled signal: Yes.
Ownership: Kentucky Authority for Educational Television.

KETKY — See Kentucky Educational Television (KET).
Type of service: Over the air, basic, digital basic.
Programming: Programs about Kentucky people, places, art & culture, history & issues.
Distribution method: Available over the air on digital sub-channels & to cable, IPTV & satellite subscribers.
Scrambled signal: Yes.

KET2 — See Kentucky Educational Television (KET).
Type of service: Over the air, basic, digital basic.
Programming: How-to programs, programs from PBS & PBS Kids & KET-produced programs about Kentucky.
Distribution method: Available over the air on digital sub-channels & to cable, IPTV & satellite subscribers.
Scrambled signal: Yes.

KLAVO
c/o Somos TV
2601 S Bayshore Dr, Ste 1250
Coconut Grove, FL 33133

FULLY SEARCHABLE • CONTINUOUSLY UPDATED • DISCOUNT RATES FOR PRINT PURCHASERS
For more information call **800-771-9202** or visit **www.warren-news.com**

Phone: 786-220-0280
Fax: 305-858-7188
E-mail: info@somostv.com
Web Site: http://www.somostv.com/es
Luis Villanueva, President & Chief Executive Officer, Somos TV
Operating areas: Nationwide.
Programming: Action-packed content, sports, thrilling and captivating series, movies plus adult after hour programming, all targeting Latino men.
Began: February 13, 2012.
Means of Support: Advertising.
Distribution method: Available to cable & satellite subscribers.
Scrambled signal: Yes.
Ownership: Somos TV.

KLRU CREATE — See KLRU-Q.
Programming: Do-it-yourself programming, including cooking, travel, arts & crafts, gardening, home improvement & other lifestyle interests.

KLRU Q
PO Box 7158
Austin, TX 78713
Phone: 512-471-4811
Fax: 512-475-9090
E-mail: info@klru.org
Web Site: http://www.klru.org
Bill Stotesbery, Chief Executive Officer & General Manager, KLRU
Type of service: Basic, over the air.
Operating areas: Texas.
Programming: Locally-programed channel featuring entertaining and inspiring shows about history, music, science, nature, food and more.
Began: July 1, 2009, replacing KLRU Too.
Distribution method: Available over the air on digital sub-channels & to cable subscribers.
Scrambled signal: Yes.
Ownership: Capital of Texas Public Telecommunications Council.

KLRU-TOO — See KLRU Q.

KLTV — See Kelso Longview Television.

K-MTN TELEVISION
2277 Lake Tahoe Blvd
South Lake Tahoe, CA 96150
Phone: 530-541-8686
Fax: 503-541-7469
Web Site: http://www.kmtn.com
Mike Conway, President
Renee Conway, Assistant
Type of service: Basic.
Operating hours/week: 168.
Operating areas: California & Nevada.
Programming: Focuses on entertainment, local events, family activities, ski reports & other seasonal recreation in the Lake Tahoe area.
Began: January 1, 1984.
Means of Support: Advertising.
Total subscribers: 2,665,000.
Distribution method: Available to cable & satellite subscribers.
Scrambled signal: Yes.
Ownership: Mike Conway.

KOREAN EVERROCK MULTI-MEDIA SERVICE — See KEMS.

KOREAN CHANNEL
18-38 131 St
College Point, NY 11356
Phone: 718-353-8970
Fax: 718-359-2067
E-mail: info@tkctv.com
Web Site: http://tkctv.com
Sang Ki Han, President
Jaehoo Han, Director
Sue Han, Information Contact
Type of service: Basic.
Operating hours/week: 168.
Programming: Korean entertainment, news, drama & movies.
Began: March 7, 1986.
Total subscribers: 1,000,000.

KOREA ONE: CHICAGOLAND KOREAN TV — See Washington Korean TV.

KSTATEHD.TV
c/o Kansas State Athletics
1800 College Ave, Bramlege Coliseum
Manhattan, KS 66502
Phones: 785-532-5180; 800-221-2287
Web Site: http://www.k-statehd.tv
John Currie, Athletic Director
Wyatt Thompson, Sportscasting & Public Relations Director
Brian Smoller, Sports Casting/Director, Powercat Vision
Robert Nelson, Chief Engineer
Type of service: Video on demand.
Operating areas: Nationwide.
Programming: Provides live athletics and academic events, classic games, press conferences, original programming, as well as on-campus performances and/or lectures.
Began: August 30, 2011.
Means of Support: Subscriber fees.
Distribution method: Available to cable subscribers.
Scrambled signal: Yes.
Ownership: Kansas State University.

KTLA LOS ANGELES
5800 Sunset Blvd
Los Angeles, CA 90028
Phone: 323-460-5500
Fax: 323-460-5994
E-mail: ktla-am-news@tribune.com
Web Site: http://www.ktla.com
Pete Boylan, President & Chief Operating Officer, TV Guide Inc.
Don Corsini, President & General Manager, KTLA
John Moczulski, Vice President, Programming Services
Type of service: Basic, over the air.
Satellites: GE 3, transponder 15.
Operating hours/week: 168.
Operating areas: Available over the air in the Los Angeles area. Cable & satellite are available nationwide.

Pay TV & Satellite Services

Programming: Antenna TV/CW/This TV affiliate in Los Angeles broadcasting movies, sports & syndicated programming.
Began: January 1, 1988.
Means of Support: System pays per subscriber.
Total subscribers: 10,300,000.
Distribution method: Available over the air on digital sub-channels & to cable, IPTV & satellite subscribers.
Scrambled signal: Yes. Equipment: VideoCipher II.
Ownership: Tribune Broadcasting.

KTV - KIDS & TEENS TELEVISION
1300 Goodlette Rd North
Naples, FL 34102
Phone: 800-759-2643
Web Site: http://www.ktvzone.com
Programming: Cartoons, animated shows, talk shows, Christian music videos, dramas & musicals as well as shows centered on creationism, social issues, history, as well as health and fitness geared towards kids & teens.
Distribution method: Available to DISH subscribers.
Ownership: Dominion Foundation Inc.

KUNLUN DRAMA
1600 Old Country Rd
Plainview, NY 11803
Phones: 888-591-2953; 516-622-8400
Web Site: http://www.kylintv.com/kylintv/us/eng/tv/kunlun-drama-hd
Programming: Offers male-oriented Chinese language programming.
Distribution method: Available to KyLin TV subscribers.
Scrambled signal: Yes.

LA FAMILIA COSMOVISION
6392 NW 84th Ave
Miami, FL 33166
Phones: 305-592-7077; 305-593-2727
Fax: 305-593-9608
E-mail: jorge@lfctelevision.com
Jorge Velasquez, Chief Executive Officer
Satellites: Olympusat I, transponder 6; Galaxy 13.
Programming: Hispanic family entertainment including live action & animated children's series, music, concerts, family novelas, news & sports.
Scrambled signal: Yes.
Ownership: The Inspiration Networks Inc.

LAFF
c/o Katz Media Group Inc.
125 W 55th St
New York, NY 10019
Phone: 212-424-6000
Web Site: http://www.laff.com
Jeffrey Wolf, Chief Distribution Officer, Katz Media Group Inc.
Calandria Meadows, Vice President, Social Media & Digital Content
Type of service: Over the air, basic.
Operating areas: Nationwide.
Programming: Features comedy programming.
Began: April 15, 2015.
Means of Support: Advertising.
Total subscribers: 72,400,000.
Distribution method: Available over the air on digital sub-channels.
Scrambled signal: Yes.
Ownership: Katz Broadcasting LLC.

LA1
9550 Firestone Blvd
Ste 105
Downey, CA 90241
Phone: 562-745-2300
Fax: 562-745-2341
Web Site: http://meruelogroup.com
Alex Meruelo, Chairman & Chief Executive Officer, Meruelo Group
Xavier A Gutierrez, Chief Investment Officer, Meruelo Group
Al Stoller, Chief Financial Officer, Meruelo Group
Mark Ernst, Corporate Vice President, Human Resources, Meruelo Group
Otto Padron, President, Meruelo Media Holdings
Rick Rodriguez, Chief Operating Officer, Meruelo Media Holdings
Type of service: Plans basic.
Operating areas: Plans superstation.
Programming: Plans to offer programming for the 18-49 demographic that will highlight Hollywood and the Los Angeles experience.
Scheduled to begin: Plans to launch in 2016.
Distribution method: Will be carried on digital sub-channel on KWHY-TV Los Angeles.
Ownership: Meruelo Media Holdings.

LATELE NOVELA NETWORK
c/o Dream House Entertainment
14750 NW 77 Ct, Ste 316
Miami Lakes, FL 33016
Web Site: http://www.dhetvmedia.com
Type of service: Pay.
Operating hours/week: 168.
Operating areas: Available nationwide.
Programming: Spanish-language network featuring great love stories & popular telenovelas produced from Latin America & Brazil.
Began: April 13, 2005.
Means of Support: Advertising.
Total subscribers: 750,000.
Distribution method: Available to AT&T U-verse subscribers.
Scrambled signal: Yes.
Ownership: Dream House Entertainment.

LATIN AMERICAN SPORTS
c/o AlternaTV
2020 Ponce de Leon Blvd, Ste 107
Coral Gables, FL 33134
Phone: 786-609-9604
E-mail: management@alternatv.us
Web Site: http://www.alternatv.us/index.php?art_id=211&categ=196
Alejandro Penafiel, Programming Director
Type of service: Pay.
Operating hours/week: 168.
Programming: Offers coverage of sports events and original productions from Puerto Rico, Cuba and Mexico. Includes baseball, soccer, basketball, volleyball, wrestling, boxing and Mexican rodeo.
Began: August 14, 2010, in U.S. September 21, 2010 in Puerto Rico.
Means of Support: Subscriber fees.
Distribution method: Available to cable, IPTV & satellite subscribers.
Scrambled signal: Yes.
Ownership: Distributed in the U.S. through AlternaTV.

LATINOAMERICA TELEVISION
2020 Ponce de Leon Blvd
Coral Gables, FL 33134
Phone: 786-609-9604
Web Site: http://www.alternatv.com.mx
Type of service: Pay.
Operating areas: Nationwide.
Programming: Regional news, soccer, entertainment, telenovelas, interviews, educational & kids' programming from Uruguay.
Began: January 1, 2006, in the U.S.
Distribution method: Available to satellite subscribers.
Scrambled signal: Yes.
Ownership: ACS Global TV.

LATV
2323 Corinth Ave
Los Angeles, CA 90064
Phone: 310-943-5288
Fax: 310-943-5299
E-mail: dcrowe@latv.com
Web Site: http://www.latv.com
Luca Bentivoglio, Chief Operating Officer & Head of Programming
David Morales, Vice President, Sales & Distribution
Natalia Barrios, Marketing & Affiliate Relations Manager

Branch Offices:
LOS ANGELES: 11835 W Olympic Blvd, Ste 450E, Los Angeles, CA 90064. Phone: 310-943-5303.
Operating hours/week: 168.
Operating areas: Nationwide.
Programming: Entertainment, lifestyle & information network targeting Latino youth aged 12-34.
Began: January 1, 2001, launched nationally April 23, 2007.
Total subscribers: 26,000,000.
Distribution method: Available over the air on digital sub-channels & to cable, IPTV & satellite subscribers.
Scrambled signal: Yes.
Ownership: LATV Networks LLC.

LEGISLATIVE COUNSEL BUREAU - BROADCAST AND PRODUCTION SERVICES
401 S Carson St
Carson City, NV 89701
Phone: 775-684-6990
Fax: 775-684-6988
E-mail: media@lcb.state.nv.us
Web Site: http://www.leg.state.nv.us
Programming: Coverage of Nevada state legislative session.
Scrambled signal: Yes.

LESEA BROADCASTING NETWORK —
See World Harvest Television.

LIFE DESIGN TV
CR 52
25-168 Ave Guayabal
Medellin
Colombia
Phone: 57-4-448-0506
E-mail: comunicaciones@lifedesigntv.com
Web Site: http://www.lifedesigntv.com

Branch Offices:
COLUMBIA: Carrera 52 #25-168, Avenida Guayabal, Medellin, Columbia. Phone: 47-4448 05 06.
Type of service: Basic.
Operating hours/week: 168.
Operating areas: Available nationwide.
Programming: Channel that teaches you how to live.
Scrambled signal: Yes.
Ownership: Life Design TV. Distributed by in the U.S. by Olympusat.

LIFE OK
c/o STAR India
Star House, Urmi Estate 95 Ganpat Rao, Kadam Marg Lower Parel
Mumbai 400013
India
Type of service: Premium, HD, streaming.
Operating areas: Available nationwide.
Programming: South Asian entertainment programs including lifestyle, dramas, comedies & games.
Began: December 18, 2011, Replacing Star One, which ceased operations on December 16, 2011.
Distribution method: Available to cable, IPTV & satellite subscribers. Streaming available online.
Scrambled signal: Yes.
Ownership: STAR India, a subsidiary of 21st Century Fox.

LIFESTYLE FAMILY TELEVISION
6922 142nd Ave
Largo, FL 33771
Phone: 727-535-5622
Fax: 727-531-2497
Web Site: http://www.ctnlifestyle.com
Robert D'Andrea, President
Type of service: Basic.
Operating areas: Available nationwide.
Programming: A safe television viewing experience with Christ-focused programming of all kinds. Shows that provide and create a Christian environment with no offensive promos or un-Biblical subject matter.
Means of Support: Donations.
Distribution method: Available over the air on digital sub-channels.
Ownership: Christian Television Network.

LIFESTYLE NETWORK
ABS-CBN International
150 Shoreline Dr
Redwood City, CA 94065-1400
Phones: 650-508-6000; 866-746-6988
Fax: 650-508-6001
E-mail: nclemente@abs-cbni.com
Web Site: http://www.lifestylenetwork.tv
Rafael Lopez, Managing Director & Chief Operating Officer
Zenon Carlos, Vice President, Operations
Menchi Orlina, Vice President & Chief Marketing Officer
Michael Scott, Vice President, Affiliate Sales & Marketing
Jun Del Rosario, North America Regional Marketing Head & Senior Director
Tom Consunji, Senior Director, Sales & Marketing
Marites Militar, Creative Broadcast Group Director
Type of service: Basic.
Operating areas: California & Hawaii.
Programming: Offers lifestyle and entertainment shows in English to Filipino Americans.
Began: January 11, 1999, in Philippines. Began April 29, 2013 in the U.S.
Means of Support: Advertising.
Total subscribers: 200,000.
Distribution method: Available to Bright House Networks & Time Warner Cable system subscribers plus DirecTV customers.
Scrambled signal: Yes.
Ownership: ABS-CBN International.

LIFETIME
235 45th St
New York, NY 10017
Phone: 212-424-7000
Fax: 212-957-4469
Web Site: http://www.mylifetime.com
Abbe Raven, Chairman Emeritus, A+E Networks
Nancy Dubuc, President & Chief Executive Officer, A+E Networks
Paul Buccieri, President, A&E & Lifetime
Rob Sharenow, Executive Vice President & General Manager
Amy Baker, Executive Vice President, FYI, Lifetime, LMN & LRW

Pay TV & Satellite Services

Liz Gateley, Executive Vice President, Programming
Mike Greco, Executive Vice President, Research
Rick Haskins, Executive Vice President, Marketing
Patricia Langer, Executive Vice President, Legal, Business Affairs & Human Resources
Kelly Abugov, Senior Vice President, Programming
Danielle Carrig, Senior Vice President, Publicity & Public Affairs
Mary Donahue, Senior Vice President, Non-Fiction Programming
Christian Drobnyk, Senior Vice President, Scheduling & Acquisition
Nina Lederman, Senior Vice President, Scripted Series
Tanya Lopez, Senior Vice President, Original Movies
Jessica Marshall, Senior Vice President & General Manager, Lifetime Online
Kimberly Chiseler Itskowitch, Vice President, Non-Fiction Programming
Mariana Flynn, Vice President, Non-fiction Programming
Paul Hardy, Vice President, Reality Programming
Teryl Brown, Vice President, National Ad Sales

Regional Offices:
CHICAGO: 444 N Michigan Ave, Ste 3270, Chicago, IL 60611. Phone: 312-464-1991.

LOS ANGELES: 2049 Century Park E, Ste 840, Los Angeles, CA 90067. Phone: 310-556-7500.
Type of service: Basic, HD, streaming, video on demand.
Satellites: AMC 11, transponder 4; Galaxy 14, transponder 21.
Operating hours/week: 168.
Operating areas: Available nationwide.
Uplink: Glenbrook, CT.
Programming: Scripted dramas, movies, reality, informational & entertainment programming targeted to women.
Began: February 1, 1984, by the merger of Daytime & Cable Health Network (CHN). Lifetime HD began April 17, 2008.
Means of Support: Advertising & affiliate fees.
Total subscribers: 100,000,000.
Distribution method: Available to cable, IPTV & satellite subscribers; streaming available online & mobile through the website or app (participating providers); video on demand (participating providers).
Scrambled signal: Yes. Equipment: VideoCipher II.
Ownership: A+E Television Networks, a joint venture of Hearst Corp. (50%) & Disney-ABC Television Group (50%).

LIFETIME MOVIE NETWORK — See LMN.

LIFETIME REAL WOMEN — See LRW.

LINK TV
PO Box 2008
San Francisco, CA 94126
Phone: 415-248-3950
Web Site: http://www.linktv.org
Paul S. Mason, President & Chief Executive Officer
Keith Chreston, Chief Financial Officer
Kim Spencer, Chief Content Officer
Hannah Eaves, Vice President, Digital & Engagement
Ben Fuller, Vice President, Business Development

Wendy Hanamura, Vice President, Strategy & General Manager
Lorraine Hess, Vice President, Programming
Janet Pailet, Vice President, Development
Type of service: Basic.
Operating hours/week: 168.
Operating areas: Nationwide.
Programming: Provides Americans with global perspectives on news, events and culture. with mix of uncompromising documentaries, international news analysis programs and diverse cultural programs.
Began: December 1, 1999.
Means of Support: Donations.
Total subscribers: 33,700,000.
Distribution method: Available to DirecTV and DISH Network subscribers.
Scrambled signal: Yes.
Ownership: Link Media Inc., a non-profit organization founded by Internews Network, the Independent Television Service (ITVS) and Internews Interactive (InterAct).

LIQUIDATION CHANNEL
100 Michael Angelo Way
Austin, TX 78728
Phone: 877-899-0078
E-mail: customerservice@liquidationchannel.com
Web Site: http://www.liquidationchannel.com
Programming: Home shopping network featuring jewelry and accessories. Operates in reverse auction format.
Began: December 1, 2008, replacing The Jewelry Channel, which launched April 2007.
Total subscribers: 60,000,000.
Scrambled signal: Yes.

LIVE WELL NETWORK
190 N State St
Chicago, IL 60601
Phone: 312-750-7777
Web Site: http://livewellnetwork.com
Rebecca Campbell, President, ABC Owned Television Stations Group
Type of service: Basic, over the air.
Operating areas: Fresno, Los Angeles & San Francisco, CA; Chicago, IL; New York, New York; Raleigh/Durham/Fayetteville, NC; Philadelphia, PA & Houston, TX.
Programming: Offers programming about the home, your health and a healthy lifestyle.
Began: April 27, 2009, Service ceased production of new programming mid-2015.
Distribution method: Available over the air on digital sub-channels of ABC owned and operated stations.
Scrambled signal: Yes.
Ownership: Disney Enterprises Inc.

LIVING FAITH TELEVISION
PO Box 1867
Abingdon, VA 24212
Phones: 276-676-3806; 888-275-9534
Fax: 276-676-3572
E-mail: info@livingfaithtv.com
Web Site: http://www.livingfaithtv.com
J R Linkous, Editor
Type of service: Basic.
Operating hours/week: 168.
Operating areas: Kentucky, North Carolina, Tennessee, Virginia & West Virginia.
Programming: Viewer supported Christian television.
Began: January 17, 1995.
Means of Support: Advertising & viewer supported.
Total subscribers: 1,600,000.
Distribution method: Available to cable & satellite subscribers.
Scrambled signal: Yes.
Ownership: Living Faith Broadcasting Inc.

LMN — See Lifetime.
Web Site: http://www.mylifetime.com/movies/lifetime-movie-network
Jana Bennett, President
Amy Baker, Executive Vice President, FYI, Lifetime, LMN & LRW
Patrick Guy, Senior Vice President, General & Legal Affairs
Thomas Moody, Senior Vice President, Programming, Planning & Acquisitions
Meredith Wanger, Senior Vice President, Public Affairs, Lifetime Entertainment Services
Richard Basso, Vice President, Pricing & Planning
Laura Fleury, Vice President, Programming & Development
Type of service: Expanded basic, HD, video on demand.
Satellites: Galaxy X, transponder 23.
Operating hours/week: 168.
Programming: Miniseries, made for TV movies & theatrical releases. SAP where available.
Began: June 29, 1998.
Means of Support: Advertising.
Total subscribers: 85,000,000.
Distribution method: Available to cable, IPTV & satellite subscribers; streaming available online & mobile through the website or app (participating providers); video on demand (participating providers) & on Lifetime Movie Club.
Scrambled signal: Yes.
Ownership: A+E Television Networks, a joint venture of Hearst Corp. (50%) & Disney-ABC Television Group (50%).

LOCAL CABLE WEATHER
385 Science Park Rd
State College, PA 16803
Phone: 814-235-8650
Fax: 814-235-8609
E-mail: info@accuwx.com
Web Site: http://www.accuweather.com
Joel N. Myers, President
Michael A. Steinberg, Senior Vice President
Joseph Montler, Television & Broadcasting Sales Director
Tom Burka, Cable Product Manager

Branch Office:
PHILADELPHIA: 2 Greenwood Sq, 331 Street Rd, Ste 440, Bensalem, PA 19020. Phone: 888-438-9847. Fax: 215-244-5329.
Type of service: Basic & digital.
Operating hours/week: 168.
Programming: Continuous local weather forecasts from AccuWeather.
Began: April 29, 1996.
Means of Support: Advertising.
Distribution method: Available to cable subscribers.
Scrambled signal: Yes.
Ownership: AccuWeather Inc.

LOGO
c/o MTV Networks
1775 Broadway, 11th Fl
New York, NY 10019
Phone: 212-846-7325
E-mail: jason.shumaker@logostaff.com
Web Site: http://www.logotv.com

Doug Herzog, President, Viacom Music & Entertainment Group
Chris McCarthy, President, VH1 & Logo
Amy Doyle, Executive Vice President, Live Programming & Events
Steve Agase, Senior Vice President, Music & Entertainment Ad Sales
Nancy Bennett, Senior Vice President, Creative & Content Development
Sarah Iooss, Senior Vice President, Digital Ad Sales, Music & Entertainment
Marc Leonard, Senior Vice President, Multi-platform Programming
Brent Zacky, Senior Vice President, Original Programming & Development
Michelle Auguste, Senior Director, Programming Research
Jason Shumaker, Communications & Public Affairs Director
Type of service: Basic & video on demand.
Programming: Entertainment programming for lesbians & gays. Original programming, movies, documentaries, news & specials. Also available in Mexico & Brazil in pay-per-view format.
Began: June 30, 2005.
Total subscribers: 50,000,000.
Distribution method: Available to cable & satellite subscribers.
Scrambled signal: Yes.
Ownership: Viacom Inc.

LO MEJOR ON DEMAND
c/o Time Warner Cable
290 Harbor Dr
Stamford, CT 06902
Phone: 203-328-0600
Monica Talan, Executive Vice President, Corporate Communications & Public Relations, Univision Communications
Type of service: Video on demand.
Operating hours/week: 168.
Operating areas: Available in California, New York & Texas.
Programming: The best in programming from Galavision, UniMas & Univision for Time Warner's digital cable customers.
Began: October 23, 2009.
Distribution method: Available to Time Warner Cable subscribers in Dallas, Los Angeles, New York, San Antonio & San Diego.
Scrambled signal: Yes.
Ownership: A joint venture between Time Warner Cable & Univision Communications Inc.

LONGHORN NETWORK
2312 San Gabriel St
Ste 200
Austin, TX 78705
Phones: 512-478-1833; 855-664-4676
Web Site: http://www.longhornnetwork.com
Michelle Druley, Senior Vice President, Production, College Networks
Dave Brown, Vice President, Programming & Acquisitions
Patricia Lorwy, Coordinating Producer II

Production Studio:
AUSTIN: 3300 N Interstate 35, Austin, TX 78705.
Type of service: Pay.

Pay TV & Satellite Services

Operating hours/week: 168.
Operating areas: Available nationwide.
Programming: Live athletic events, original series and studio shows, historical programming and academic and cultural happenings.
Began: August 26, 2011.
Means of Support: Advertising & subscriber fees.
Total subscribers: 3,900,000.
Distribution method: Available to cable, IPTV & satellite subscribers. Streaming available through WatchESPN.
Scrambled signal: Yes.
Ownership: A joint venture between ESPN, IMG College & U of Texas.

LOTTERY CHANNEL
425 Walnut St
Cincinnati, OH 45202
Phone: 513-381-0777
Fax: 513-721-6035
E-mail: info@lottery.com
Web Site: http://www.lottery.com
Roger Ach, Chairman & Chief Executive Officer
Carol Meinhardt, Executive Vice President
Jeffrey S. Perlee, Managing Director
Operating areas: Rhode Island.
Began: November 8, 1995.
Distribution method: Available to cable subscribers.
Scrambled signal: Yes.

LOUISIANA LEGISLATIVE NETWORK
900 N Third St
PO Box 94062
Baton Rouge, LA 70804
Phone: 225-342-0367
Fax: 225-342-3749
E-mail: pickensp@legis.state.la.us
Web Site: http://www.legis.state.la.us
Type of service: Basic, video on demand.
Operating hours/week: 28.
Operating areas: Louisiana.
Programming: Live & archived coverage of Louisiana legislature meetings & sessions year-round.
Distribution method: Available to cable subscribers. Video on demand available online.
Scrambled signal: Yes.

LRW — See Lifetime.
235 45th St
New York, NY 10017
Phone: 212-424-7000
Fax: 212-957-4469
Programming: Comedies, dramas, informative/instructional & reality programming.
Began: August 2001.
Total subscribers: 16,000,000.
Distribution method: Available to cable & IPTV subscribers.
Scrambled signal: Yes.

LUXE.TV
43 Zone op Zaemer
Bascharage (NidderkSerjeng) L-4959
Luxembourg
Phone: 352-26-50-48-1
Web Site: http://www.luxe.tv
Paul-Rene' Heinerscheid, Managing Director
Type of service: Pay.
Operating hours/week: 168.
Operating areas: Nationwide.
Programming: International TV channel dedicated to the world of luxury and lifestyle, broadcasting from Luxembourg in full HD.
Began: June 23, 2006, Began June 27, 2012 in the U.S.
Means of Support: Advertising, subscriber fees.

Total subscribers: 92,000,000 (Worldwide subscribers. Service is available in 107 countries.).
Distribution method: Available to DISH Network subscribers.
Scrambled signal: Yes.
Ownership: Opuntia S.A.

LVES-TV
PO Box 31571
Las Vegas, NV 89173
Phone: 702-765-5309
Web Site: http://www.lasvegasentsportstelevisioninc.com
Jon Astor-White, Founder, President & Chief Executive Officer
Type of service: Plans basic.
Operating areas: Plans nationwide.
Programming: Plans to feature original programming, weekly live musical concerts, weekly boxing/MMA competitions, entertainment and.
Distribution method: Plans to be available to cable subscribers.
Ownership: Jon Astor-White plus private investor capital.

LWS LOCAL WEATHER STATION
1950 N Meridian St
Indianapolis, IN 46202
Phone: 317-923-8888
Fax: 317-926-1144
E-mail: weather@wishtv.com
Web Site: http://www.wishtv.com
Lance Carwile, Program Director
Julie Zoumbaris, General Sales Manager
Carol Sergi, Market Development Director
Julie Gloyeske, Business Manager
Mike Lopez, Executive Producer
Type of service: Basic & expanded basic.
Operating hours/week: 168.
Operating areas: Illinois, Indiana, Michigan, Texas & Virginia.
Uplink: Local market.
Programming: Continuous local weather programming. Doppler Radar, weather forcasts, current conditions, travel updates & special coverage.
Began: January 1, 1994.
Means of Support: Advertising & subscriber fees.
Total subscribers: 1,423,982.
Distribution method: Available to cable subscribers in markets that have LIN stations.
Scrambled signal: Yes.
Ownership: LIN Television Corp.

MACAU ASIA SATELLITE TV (MASTV)
4,5 floor Macau Ave do Dr. Rodrigo Rodrigues
No 600E First Intl. Business Ctr
Andar
Macau
Phone: 853-28750080
Fax: 853-28750016
E-mail: administrator@mastv.cc
Web Site: http://www.imastv.com
Programming: News, global finance, world events, entertainment, cultural shows, sports from Macau. Also features Mandarin dramas & Korean variety shows.
Distribution method: Available to KyLin TV subscribers.
Scrambled signal: Yes.

MAC TV
No. 100, Lane 75
Kang-Ning Rd, Sec 3
Taipei 114
Taiwan, Republic of China
Phone: 8862-2630-1877

Fax: 8862-2630-1895
Satellites: JcSat-3A, transponder C3; AP-STAR IIR, transponder 7B-2; SuperBird-C, transponder 23D.
Operating hours/week: 168.
Programming: Diverse and refined programming to encourage mutual concern among overseas Chinese communities.
Began: March 1, 2000, in China.
Distribution method: Available to cable & satellite subscribers.
Scrambled signal: No.

MADISON SQUARE GARDEN NETWORK — See MSG.

MAG RACK
331 W 57th St
Ste 733
New York, NY 10019
Phone: 212-586-0860
E-mail: info@interactivation.com
Web Site: http://www.magrack.com
Joe Covey, Chief Executive Officer
Matthew Davidge, President
Type of service: Basic, video on demand.
Programming: Fitness, health & wellness, cooking, pet care, relationships and other topics.
Distribution method: Available to cable & satellite subscribers as a free service included with most basic cable packages.
Scrambled signal: Yes.
Ownership: Interactivation.

MANAVISION3
1340 Seventh St
Sanger, CA 93657
Phone: 559-240-5538
Web Site: http://www.manavision3.com
Ramon Pecina, President
Type of service: Regional.
Operating areas: California.
Programming: A family-oriented channel that carries a positive message to viewers.
Began: November 1, 2009.
Means of Support: Donations, advertising.
Distribution method: Available over the air on digital sub-channels.
Scrambled signal: Yes.
Ownership: Ramon Pecina.

MARIAVISION
Av Hildalgo No 110, Segiundo Piso
Centro, Zapopan
Jalisco CP 45100
Mexico
Phones: 52-01-900-849-3507; 52-33-3770-1800
E-mail: info@mariavision.com
Web Site: http://www.mariavision.com
Programming: Issues related to Catholicism.
Began: January 1, 2003, in U.S.
Ownership: Mariavision Partners.

MASCHIC
800 Douglas Rd
North Tower, 10th Fl
Coral Gables, FL 33134
Phone: 305-455-4350
Fax: 305-445-2058
Web Site: http://www.maschic.com
Programming: Fashion, beauty, home decor, cooking, lifestyle programming targeted to women.
Began: June 1, 2003, as Casa Club TV. Re-branded MasChic July 2015.
Scrambled signal: Yes.
Ownership: AMC Networks International.

MASMUSICA TEVE NETWORK
299 Alhambra Cir

Ste 510
Coral Gables, FL 33134
Phone: 305-648-0065
Fax: 305-648-0068
E-mail: rosamaria@caballero.com
Web Site: http://www.masmusica.tv

Branch Offices:
STUDIO: 3310 Keller Springs Rd, Ste 105, Carrollton, TX 75006. Phone: 972-503-6800. Fax: 972-503-6801.
Type of service: Basic.
Programming: 24-hour broadcast network featuring the latest youth-oriented Spanish-language music programming from a unique mix of the most popular Spanish music formats such as Regional Mexican, Latin Pop, Tropical and Rock en Espanol, including videos, concerts and interviews.
Means of Support: Advertising.
Scrambled signal: Yes.

MASSACHUSETTS SPANISH TV NETWORK (MASTV)
c/o El Plantea Media
311 Highland Ave
Somerville, MA 02144
Phone: 617-379-0216
Web Site: http://elplaneta.com
Operating areas: Massachusetts.
Programming: Spanish-language local news.
Distribution method: Available to Comcast subscribers in the Boston area.
Scrambled signal: Yes.
Ownership: MasTV/El Planeta Media Group.

MAVTV
302 N Sheridan St
Corona, CA 92880
Phone: 877-475-1711
E-mail: info@mavtv.net
Web Site: http://www.mavtv.com
Bob Patison, President
Mark Mitchell, Vice President, Sales Marketing & Business Development
Ed Niemi, Vice President, Distribution
Dan Teitscheid, Vice President, Content Distribution & Partner Marketing
Steve Grein, Executive Producer
Jason Patison, Programming Director
Rhonda Binckes, Billing

Branch Offices:
PLANO: Sales & Marketing, 5601 Democracy Dr, Ste 175, Plano, TX 75024. Phone: 972-403-3300.
Type of service: Premium, HD.
Satellites: Galaxy 11, transponder 21.
Operating hours/week: 168.
Operating areas: Available nationwide.
Uplink: Atlanta, GA—Encompass Digital Media.
Programming: High-action racings & motorsports along with automotive & motorcycle lifestyle.
Began: October 1, 2004.
Means of Support: Subscription, advertising, sponsorship.
Total subscribers: 42,000,000.
Distribution method: Available to cable, IPTV & DISH subscribers.
Scrambled signal: Yes.
Ownership: Lucas Oil Products Inc.

MAX GO — See Cinemax.
c/o Home Box Office
1100 Ave of the Americas
New York, NY 10036
Phone: 212-512-1000
Fax: 212-512-1166
Web Site: http://www.maxgo.com
Type of service: Streaming.
Operating areas: Nationwide.

Pay TV & Satellite Services

Programming: Programming from Cinemax channels.
Distribution method: Available online & through app (participating providers).

MAX LATINO — See Cinemax.
c/o Home Box Office
1100 Avenue of the Americas
New York, NY 10036
Phone: 212-512-1000
Fax: 212-512-1166
Type of service: Pay, HD.
Operating hours/week: 168.
Operating areas: Available nationwide.
Programming: Spanish-language simulcast of Cinemax.
Began: May 17, 2001, as @Max. Rebranded Max Latino June 2013.
Scrambled signal: Yes.
Ownership: Home Box Office Inc., a division of Time Warner.

MAXXSOUTH SPORTS
300 1/2 South Jackson St
Starkville, MS 39759
Phone: 800-457-5351
Web Site: http://www.maxxsouth.com
Peter Kahelin, President & Chief Executive Officer, MaxxSouth Broadband
Rick Ferrall, Regional General Manager, MaxxSouth Broadband
Type of service: Regional.
Operating areas: Mississippi.
Programming: High school and college sports from northern and central Mississippi.
Began: April 20, 2015.
Means of Support: Advertising.
Distribution method: Available to MaxxSouth subscribers.
Scrambled signal: Yes.
Ownership: MaxxSouth Broadband.

MBC ACTION — See MBC TV.
Programming: Action series, movies & reality shows as well as live football.
Scrambled signal: Yes.

MBC AMERICA
3400 W 6th St
4th Fl
Los Angeles, CA 90020
Phone: 213-487-2345
Fax: 213-736-1555
E-mail: contact@mbc24.com
Web Site: http://mbc-america.com
Bok Haeng Cho, President
Nam Jung Kim, General Director
Nahee Kim, Content Business & Planning Manager
Sung Ho Lee, Broadcast Engineering Manager
Yos Park, Production Manager
James Chong, Ad Manager
Type of service: Pay.
Operating hours/week: 168.
Programming: Popular South Korean soap operas, news broadcasts, dramas, current affairs, sports and cultural programs.
Began: September 1, 2002.
Distribution method: Available to cable & satellite subscribers.
Scrambled signal: Yes.
Ownership: Munwha Broadcasting Corp.

MBCD
3400 W. 6th St.
4th Floor
Los Angeles, CA 90020
Phone: 213-487-2345
Fax: 213-736-1555
Web Site: http://www.mbc-america.com/en
Operating hours/week: 168.
Operating areas: Atlanta, Chicago, Los Angeles, New York & San Francisco.
Programming: Korean-language dramas series, variety shows, documentaries, current issues & the local news.
Distribution method: Available over the air on digital sub-channels & to Time Warner subscribers in Los Angeles & New York.
Scrambled signal: Yes.

MBC DRAMA — See MBC America.
Type of service: Pay, HD, streaming.
Programming: Korean-language dramas as well as Korean box office hits, HD documentaries & K-pop music programs.
Distribution method: Available to Verizon FiOS & DirecTV subscribers. Streaming available online (participating providers).
Scrambled signal: Yes.

MBC DRAMA — See MBC TV.
Programming: Drama series from Egypt, Syria, Turkey, Mexico & India.
Began: November 27, 2010.

MBC KIDS — See MBC TV.
Programming: Pan-Arab children's education & entertainment programming.

MBC MASR — See MBC TV.
Programming: Arab & Egyptian dramas, series, movies & documentaries.
Began: November 9, 2012, in the Middle East.
Scrambled signal: Yes.

MBC TV
c/o Allied Media
5252 Cherokee Ave, Ste 200
Alexandria, VA 22312-2000
Phone: 703-333-2008
Fax: 703-997-7539
E-mail: mbc-tv@allied-media.com
Web Site: http://www.allied-media.com
M. Saout, Sales & Marketing Manager
Type of service: Pay.
Operating hours/week: 168.
Operating areas: Nationwide.
Programming: Pan-Arab news & entertainment.
Distribution method: Available to DISH Network subscribers.
Scrambled signal: Yes.
Ownership: Middle East Broadcasting Center.

MC
650 Dresher Rd
Horsham, PA 19044
Phone: 215-784-5840
Fax: 215-784-5869
E-mail: comments@musicchoice.com
Web Site: http://www.musicchoice.com
Dave Del Beccaro, President & Chief Executive Officer
Christina Tancredi, Chief Operating Officer
Rick Bergan, Senior Vice President, Distribution
Mark Melvin, Senior Vice President, National Ad Sales
Jeremy Rosenberg, Senior Vice President
Paula T. Calhoun, Vice President & General Counsel
Jim Coleson, Vice President, Commercial Dealer Operations
Tom Soper, Vice President, Distribution Sales
Anne Thiede, Vice President, Affiliate Sales & Operations
Damon Williams, Vice President, Programming & Production
Mike Corry, Senior Director, Ad Sales
Nolan Baynes, Marketing Director
Gerry Burke, Finance & Accounting Director

ADVANCED TVFactbook
FULLY SEARCHABLE • CONTINUOUSLY UPDATED • DISCOUNT RATES FOR PRINT PURCHASERS
For more information call 800-771-9202 or visit www.warren-news.com

Jason Guarracino, Web & Mobile Application Development Director
Mike Muccilo, Direct-Response Advertising Sales Director
Josefa Paganuzzi, Public Relations Director

Production Studio:
NEW YORK: 328 W 34th St, New York, NY 10001. Phone: 646-459-3300.
Type of service: Basic, video on demand & streaming.
Satellites: Satcom C-3, transponder 9; Satcom C-3, transponder 6; Galaxy 3-R (Latin America).
Operating hours/week: 168.
Programming: Commercial-free music & music oriented content.
Began: May 1, 1990, as Music Choice. Music Choice on Demand began November 1, 2004. Rebranded MC on February 1, 2012.
Total subscribers: 52,000,000 (51,000,000 on demand subscribers.).
Distribution method: Available to cable subscribers. Streaming available online & mobile.
Scrambled signal: Yes. Equipment: Jerrold.
Ownership: Joint venture between Comcast, Cox Communications, EMI Music, Microsoft, Motorola Mobility, Sony Corporation & Time Warner Cable.

MC-TV
(Midwest Christian Television)
262 E Golf Rd
Arlington Heights, IL 60005
Phone: 847-290-8282
Fax: 847-290-9992
E-mail: info@mc-tv.org
Web Site: http:///www.mc-tv.org
Kim Wang, Information Contact
Type of service: Regional basic.
Operating areas: Illinois.
Programming: Korean-language Christian programming.
Began: August 11, 2010.
Means of Support: Advertising.
Distribution method: Available on over the air digital sub-channels.
Scrambled signal: Yes.
Ownership: Kim Wang.

MC PLAY — See MC.
Web Site: http://www.swrv.tv
Type of service: Digital.
Operating hours/week: 168.
Operating areas: Nationwide.
Programming: Interactive music video network. Each show offers a unique way for viewers to impact what music videos will play next by voting, rating, or commenting via text message or online.
Began: February 10, 2010, as SWRV TV. Rebranded as MC Play October 15, 2013.
Total subscribers: 9,000,000.
Distribution method: Available to Cox, AT&T U-Verse, RCN & Verizon FiOS subscribers.
Scrambled signal: Yes.
Ownership: Joint venture between Comcast, Cox Communications, EMI Music, Microsoft, Motorola Mobility, Sony Corporation & Time Warner Cable.

MDTV: MEDICAL NEWS NOW
3 Mars Ct
Boonton Twp, NJ 07005
Phones: 973-334-6277; 800-985-6388
E-mail: pargen@mdtvnews.com
Web Site: http://mdtvnews.com
Paul G. Argen, Chief Executive Officer & Executive Producer
Maria Villalonga, RN, BSN, President
James Walsh, MS, Executive Director
Patrica Stark, Anchor
Type of service: Over the air, basic, streaming.
Programming: Presents technically advanced medical information in an easily understood format. Educates public on today's popular surgical procedures & highlights top surgeons.
Began: 1998.
Distribution method: Available over the air. Streaming available online & through participating providers.
Scrambled signal: Yes.
Ownership: MDTV Medical News Now, Inc., a non-profit company.

MEADOWS RACING NETWORK — See HRTV.

MEDIASET ITALIA
c/o International Media Distribution
4100 E Dry Creek Rd
Centennial, CO 80122
Phone: 303-712-5400
Fax: 303-712-5401
Web Site: http://www.imediadistribution.com
Scott Wheeler, Senior Vice President, Network Development
Mike Scott, Vice President, Affiliate Sales & Marketing
Shelly Kurtz, Executive Director, Affiliate Sales & Marketing
Kajsa Moe, Affiliate Sales & Marketing Director
Nicole Wang, Affiliate Sales & Marketing Manager
Type of service: Premium.
Operating hours/week: 168.
Operating areas: Nationwide.
Programming: Italian programming including drama series, comedies, news, and entertainment shows a few hours/days after airing on its mainstream local TV channels.
Began: June 8, 2011.
Means of Support: Subscriber fees.
Total subscribers: 3,000,000.
Distribution method: Available to cable subscribers.
Scrambled signal: Yes.
Ownership: Mediaset, owned by Silvio Berlusconi, former Prime Minister of Italy. Distributed in the U.S.by International Media Distribution.

MEGA TV
7007 NW 77th Ave
Miami, FL 33166
Phones: 305-441-6901; 305-644-4800
Fax: 786-470-1667
E-mail: info@mega.tv
Web Site: http://www.mega.tv

2017 Edition

E-57

Pay TV & Satellite Services

Raul Alarcon, Jr., Chairman, President & Chief Executive Officer
Pablo Raul Alarcon, Sr., Chairman Emeritus & Director
Joseph A. Garcia, Chief Financial Officer, Executive Vice President & Secretary
Marko Radlovic, Chief Operating Officer & Executive Vice President
Cynthia Hudson Fernandez, Chief Creative Officer & Executive Vice President, SBS; Managing Director, Mega TV
Berry Jasin, Senior Vice President, National Sales, Consolidated & Revenue Chief
Albert Rodriguez, General Manager
Rene Rodriguez, Sports Marketing Director
Camilo Bernal, Affiliate Relations Manager
Marilyn Navarro, Local Sales Manager
Operating hours/week: 168.
Operating areas: Nationwide.
Programming: Spanish-language programming, includes shows produced in Puerto Rico.
Began: March 1, 2006, Nationwide satellite launch date October 17, 2007.
Distribution method: Available over the air on digital sub-channels & to Bright House Network, Century Link, Comcast, Cox & satellite subscribers.
Scrambled signal: Yes.
Ownership: Spanish Broadcasting System Inc.

MELLI TV — See MTC Persian Television.

METROCHANNELS — See News 12 Interactive.

METRO SPORTS — See Time Warner Cable SportsChannel (Kansas City).

METRO SPORTS 2 — See Time Warner Cable SportsChannel 2 (Kansas City).

METV
26 North Halsted
Chicago, IL 60661
Phone: 512-804-2400
E-mail: info@metelevision.com
Web Site: http://www.metelevision.com
Neal Sabin, President, Content & Networks, Weigel Broadcasting Co.
Maura Cope, Vice President
Will Givens, Vice President, Network Marketing
Type of service: Basic, digital, over the air.
Operating hours/week: 168.
Operating areas: Nationwide.
Programming: Wide range of classic television programming from the libraries of CBS and 20th Century Fox as well as independent series.
Began: January 1, 2005, in the Chicago area. December 15, 2010, nationally.
Total subscribers: 98,000,000.
Distribution method: Available over the air on digital sub-channels & to cable & satellite subscribers.
Scrambled signal: Yes.
Ownership: Weigel Broadcasting Co. Distributed by Metro Goldwyn Mayer Studios Inc.

MEXICANAL
Av. Salvador Nava Martinez No. 2850
5to. Piso Fraccionamiento del Real
San Luis Potosi, SLP 78280
Mexico
Phones: 52-866-685-8007; 52-444-129-2929
Fax: 52-444-129-2930
E-mail: info@castaliacom.com
Web Site: http://www.mexicanal.com
Luis Torres-Bohl, President

Maruchi Urquiaga, Senior Vice President & General Manager
Chuck Wing, Senior Vice President, Syndication
Mark Henderson, Vice President, Affiliate Relations
Edwin Vidal, Operations Director
Israel Reyero, Assistant Director, Programming & Operations

Branch Offices:
CORPORATE OFFICE: Castalia Communications, 8097 Roswell Rd, Bldg. C, Ste 202, Atlanta, GA 30350. Phone: 770-396-7850. Fax: 770-396-3464.

DISTRIBUTION: Castalia Communications, 1532 Dunwoody Village Pkwy, Ste 203, Atlanta, GA 30338. Phone: 770-396-7850. Fax: 770-396-3464.
Programming: Regional news, sports news, baseball, interviews, debates, music, travel, kids' & women's shows.
Began: August 1, 2004.
Scrambled signal: Yes.
Ownership: Joint venture between Cablecom (Mexican cable operator) & Castalia Communications (Atlanta, GA distributor).

MEXICO TV
7311 NW 12th St
Ste 29
Miami, FL 33126-1924
Phones: 305-468-6602; 877-890-1787
Fax: 305-436-1953
Web Site: http://www.mexicotv.tv
Satellites: Galaxy 23, transponder 10C.
Operating areas: Available nationwide on satellite, California and Texas on cable.
Programming: Offering Mexicans living in the U.S. a full schedule of news, events, and entertainment programming.
Began: January 1, 1992.
Means of Support: Advertising and subscriber fees.
Total subscribers: 1,170,000.
Distribution method: Available to DirecTV & Time Warner Cable subscribers.
Scrambled signal: Yes.
Ownership: SUR LLC.

MGM CHANNEL
MGM Networks
10250 Constellation Blvd
Los Angeles, CA 90067
Phone: 310-449-3000
Web Site: http://www.mgmchannel.com
Gary Barber, Chairman & Chief Executive Officer
Roma Khanna, President, Television Group & Digital
Bruce Tuchman, Senior Vice President, MGM Channel Global
Steve Hendry, Senior Vice President, Television Operations, MGM
Courtney Williams, Vice President, Sales & Marketing
Steven Bernstein, Vice President, Business Development & Joint Ventures
Gracelyn Brown, Vice President, Programming
Doug Chalfant, Executive Creative Director
Mark Zelenz, Executive Director, Affiliate Sales
Elizabeth Squires, Programming & Marketing Director

Branch Offices:
NEW YORK: 655 Third Ave, New York, NY 10017. Phone: 212708-0300.
Operating hours/week: 168.
Programming: Popular movies from the MGM film library.
Began: 1999. MGM HD began October 10, 2007.

Distribution method: Available to cable, IPTV & satellite subscribers.
Scrambled signal: Yes.

MHZ NETWORKS
8101 A Lee Hwy
Falls Church, VA 22042
Phone: 703-770-7100
E-mail: fthomas@mhznetworks.org
Web Site: http://www.mhznetworks.org
Fred Thomas, General Manager
Stephanie Misar, Marketing Director
Type of service: Basic, over the air.
Operating hours/week: 168.
Programming: Independent, public television network focusing on international, educational & arts programming, including unedited international news broadcasts, documentaries, world sports & popular drama series.
Began: March 1, 1972.
Means of Support: Viewer supported.
Total subscribers: 4,900,000.
Distribution method: Available over the air on digital sub-channels & to cable, IPTV & satellite subscribers.
Scrambled signal: Yes.
Ownership: Commonwealth Public Broadcasting Corp.

MHZ WORLDVIEW — See MHz Networks.
Type of service: Basic, over the air.
Began: February 1, 2006.
Total subscribers: 42,000,000 (possible viewers.).
Distribution method: Available over the air on digital sub-channels & to cable, IPTV & satellite subscribers.
Scrambled signal: Yes.

MI MUSICA
c/o Latin Entertainment Group LLC
3300 NE 191st St, Park Central
Aventura, FL 33130
Phones: 786-863-8302; 202-465-4885
Web Site: http://www.canalmimusica.com/mimusica-television
Programming: Latin American music programming.
Scrambled signal: Yes.
Ownership: Latin Entertainment Group LLC. Distributed in the U.S. by Condista.

MIAMI TEVE
13001 NW 107th Ave
Hialeah Gardens, FL 33018
Phone: 305-592-4141
Fax: 305-592-3808
Web Site: http://www.miamitvchannel.com
Omar Romay, President & Chief Executive Officer, America CV Network
Andrea Gomez, Marketing Coordinator

Branch Offices:
PUERTO RICO: Calle Turquesa No. 2020, Urbanizacion Bucare, Guaynabo, PR 00969. Phone: 787-523-2406. Fax: 787-999-3201.
Type of service: Regional basic, over the air.
Operating areas: Southern Florida.
Programming: Hyper-local content celebrating the wide spectrum of colors and flavors of the Miami audience.
Began: January 28, 2013.
Means of Support: Advertising.
Distribution method: Available over the air to digital sub-channels and to Atlantic Broadband, AT&T U-verse & Comcast subscribers.
Scrambled signal: Yes.
Ownership: America CV Network.

MI CINE
c/o Alterna'TV
1500 San Ramos Ave, Ste 248
Coral Gables, FL 33146
Phone: 786-245-0484
Web Site: http://www.alternatv.us
Carlos Vasallo, Chief Executive Officer
Type of service: Pay.
Operating areas: Nationwide.
Programming: Mexican movies from the 1940s to today.
Began: June 1, 2007.
Means of Support: Advertising and subscriber fees.
Distribution method: Available to Comcast subscribers.
Scrambled signal: Yes.
Ownership: Mi Cine S.A. de C.V.

MID-ATLANTIC SPORTS NETWORK (MASN)
333 W Camden St
Baltimore, MD 21201-2435
Phone: 410-625-7100
E-mail: mhaley@masnsports.com
Web Site: http://www.masn.tv
Jim Cuddihy, Executive Vice President, Marketing, Programming & Affiliate Relations
Michael Hailey, Executive Vice President & Chief Financial Officer
John McGuinness, Senior Vice President & General Sales Manager
Chris Glass, Vice President, Executive Producer & Operations Director
Type of service: Basic.
Operating hours/week: 168.
Operating areas: Delaware, Maryland, North Carolina, Pennsylvania, Virginia, Washington, DC & West Virginia.
Programming: Regional sports coverage of major & NCAA league baseball, basketball & football games, shows & news. Coverage includes Washington Nationals, Baltimore Orioles, Baltimore Ravens & Georgetown University.
Began: July 31, 2006.
Total subscribers: 6,400,000.
Distribution method: Available to cable & satellite subscribers.
Scrambled signal: Yes.
Ownership: Washington Nationals & Baltimore Orioles.

MIDCO SPORTS NETWORK
3901 N Louise Ave
Sioux Falls, SD 57107
Phone: 605-274-7638
E-mail: laura_anderson@mmi.net
Web Site: http://www.midcosportsnet.com
Pat McAdaragh, President & Chief Executive Officer, Midcontinent Communications
Wynne Haakenstad, Programming Director
Tom Nieman, Programming Manager
Ron Peterson, Chief Broadcast Engineer
Type of service: Regional basic.
Operating areas: Available in Minnesota, North Dakota & South Dakota.
Programming: Regional sports broadcasts. Live high school, collegiate and professional sports coverage.
Began: August 18, 2010.
Total subscribers: 250,000.
Distribution method: Available to cable subscribers.
Scrambled signal: Yes.
Ownership: Midcontinent Communications.

MIDWEST CHRISTIAN TELEVISION — See MC-TV.

MILENIO TELEVISION
Paricutin y 5 de Febrero, No 312
Col. Roma

Pay TV & Satellite Services

Monterrey, Nuevo Leon 64700
Mexico
Phone: 52-81-8369-9919
Web Site: http://tv.milenio.com
Gustavo Mena, Cable & Satellite Distribution
Operating hours/week: 168.
Operating areas: Nationwide.
Programming: Mexican news channel.
Means of Support: Advertising.
Distribution method: Available to cable subscribers plus Verizon FiOS and AT&T U-verse subscribers.
Scrambled signal: Yes.
Ownership: Grupo Multimedios. Distributed in the U.S. by UNO Entertainment.

MILITARY CHANNEL — See American Heroes Channel.

MILITARY HISTORY — See History.
235 E 45th St
8th Fl
New York, NY 10017
Phone: 212-210-1400
Fax: 212-907-9481
Web Site: http://military.history.com
Programming: Documentaries & series pertaining to historical battles & wars and those who served as generals & soldiers.
Began: January 5, 2005, as Military History Channel. Rebranded Military History in March 2008.
Distribution method: Available to cable, IPTV & satellite subscribers.
Ownership: A+E Networks, a joint venture between Hearst Corp. (50%), The Walt Disney Co. (50%).

MINNESOTA HOUSE & SENATE TELEVISION
175 State Office Bldg
St. Paul, MN 55155-1298
Phones: 651-296-2146; 800-657-3550
Fax: 651-296-9029; 651-297-3800
Web Site: http://www.house.leg.state.mn.us
Barry LaGrave, House Television Director
Steve Senyk, Senate Media Services Director
Type of service: Basic.
Satellites: Telstar 5.
Operating hours/week: 45.
Operating areas: Minnesota.
Uplink: Group W Network Services.
Programming: Live and taped House & Senate committee & floor coverage.
Began: January 7, 1997.
Total subscribers: 200,000.
Distribution method: Available to cable subscribers.
Scrambled signal: Yes.
Ownership: Minnesota Legislature.

MIRA TV
2920 NW 7th St
Miami, FL 33125
Phone: 305-642-7777
E-mail: info@miratv.tv
Web Site: http://www.miratv.tv
Judith Prado, Vice President
Maria Jose Morla, Public Relations Specialist
Beatriz Moncayo, Assistant News Director
Type of service: Regional basic.
Operating hours/week: 168.
Operating areas: Florida.
Programming: Offers its viewers quality programming, focusing on shows that cover news, debate and entertainment.
Began: March 7, 2014.
Means of Support: Advertising.
Distribution method: Available over the air on digital sub-channels and to Bright House, Comcast, AT&T U-verse and Verizon FiOS subscribers.
Scrambled signal: Yes.

MISSION TV
PO Box 216
McDonald, TN 37353
Phone: 423-413-7321
E-mail: info@missiontv.com
Web Site: http://missiontv.com
David Gates, President, Gospel Ministries International
Operating hours/week: 168.
Programming: Channel devoted to the Great Commission of Matthew 28:17-20. Offers front line mission video adventures and interviews of missionaries who have been there.
Means of Support: Donations.
Scrambled signal: Yes.
Ownership: Gospel Ministries International & Jesus for Asia Inc.

MLB EXTRA INNINGS — See MLB Network.
Type of service: Pay per view.
Programming: Out-of-network MLB games.
Began: 2001.
Distribution method: Available to cable, IPTV & satellite subscribers.
Scrambled signal: Yes.

MLB NETWORK
One MLB Network Plz
Secaucus, NJ 07094
Phone: 201-520-6400
Web Site: http://mlb.mlb.com/network
Robert McGlarry, President
Bob Bowman, President, Business & Media, Major League Baseball
Mary Beck, Senior Vice President, Marketing & Promotion
Susan Stone, Senior Vice President, Operatins & Engineering
Brent Fisher, Vice President, Distribution, Affiliate Sales & Marketing
Type of service: Basic.
Operating hours/week: 168.
Operating areas: Nationwide.
Programming: Games & highlights, including out of market games.
Began: January 1, 2009.
Means of Support: Advertising.
Total subscribers: 71,000,000.
Distribution method: Available to cable & satellite subscribers.
Scrambled signal: Yes.
Ownership: A joint venture between Major League Baseball (7%), DirecTV LLC (16.67%), Comcast (5.44%), Cox (5.44%) & Time Warner Cable (5.44%).

MLB NETWORK STRIKE ZONE — See MLB Network.
Programming: Up-to-the-minute highlights & updates of live MLB games.
Began: April 10, 2012.

MLS DIRECT KICK
420 Fifth Ave
7th Fl
New York, NY 10018
Phone: 212-450-1200
Web Site: http://www.mlssoccer.com
Programming: Out-of-network MLS games & MLS Cup playoff matches.
Distribution method: Available to cable, IPTV & satellite subscribers.

MNET
3535 Hayden Ave
Ste 120
Culver City, CA 90232
Phone: 424-258-1900
Web Site: http://www.mnetamerica.com

Sang H. Cho, President & Chief Executive Officer
J. Edward Lee, Executive Vice President & Chief Operating Officer
Julie Choi, Senior Vice President, Programming & Development
David Chu, Senior Vice President, Programming & Production
Michael Huh, Vice President, Marketing & Strategic Development
Sung Lee, Vice President, Business Development
Thomas Pyun, Vice President, Ad Sales
Alexander Kim, General Counsel
Type of service: Basic, digital basic, streaming.
Operating areas: Nationwide.
Programming: Asian-American films, drama, series, sitcom, news, variety & game shows, children's programming, music videos, sports, documentaries.
Began: August 30, 2004, ImaginAsian TV. Rebranded as Mnet in 2011.
Means of Support: Advertising.
Total subscribers: 8,000,000.
Distribution method: Available to cable, IPTV & satellite subscribers. Streaming available online.
Scrambled signal: Yes.
Ownership: CJ Media.

MOFOS
c/o Playboy Plus Entertainment
2300 W Empire Ave, 7th Fl
Burbank, CA 91504
Phone: 323-276-4000
Fax: 323-276-4500
E-mail: info.losangeles@mindgeek.com
Type of service: Pay per view.
Programming: Adult entertainment.
Began as Hot Zone. Rebranded to Spice: Xcess, then MOFOS in 2012.
Distribution method: Available to cable, IPTV & satellite subscribers.
Ownership: Playboy Plus Entertainment/Mindgeek.

MOJO HD — See iN DEMAND.
Type of service: Video on demand.

MOMENTUM
Av. Bosques de la Reforma 495
Bosques de las Lomas
Delegacion Miguel Hidalgo DF 11700
Mexico
Phone: 52-55-5293-0550
Fax: 52-55-5589-7669
E-mail: mwnetworks@colorado.com.mx
Web Site: http://www.momentum.tv
Gilberto Leal, International Affiliate Sales
Julianna Garibay, U.S. Affiliate Sales-New York
Rozana Rotundo, U.S. Affiliate Sales-Miami
Satellites: SatMex 8.
Operating areas: Available nationwide.
Programming: Spanish-language documentaries, musicals, biographies, concerts, original shows & series.
Distribution method: Available to cable & satellite subscribers.
Scrambled signal: Yes.
Ownership: Colorado Inc.

MORE MAX — See Cinemax.
c/o Home Box Office
1100 Avenue of the Americas
New York, NY 10036
Phone: 212-512-1000
Fax: 212-512-1166
Type of service: Pay, HD.
Operating hours/week: 168.
Operating areas: Available nationwide.
Programming: Popular & rare films to complement Cinemax.
Began: 1991 as Cinemax 2. Rebranded as MoreMax in 1998.
Scrambled signal: Yes.
Ownership: Home Box Office Inc., a division of Time Warner.

MOTORS TV
4 John Prince's St
London W1G OJL
United Kingdom
Phone: 44-0-20-7612-1950
Web Site: https://northam.motorstv.com
Paul Bushell, Managing Director
Mike Gull, Sales Director
Programming: International motor sports.
Began: September 2000 in the U.K. Began in the U.S. in 2015.
Scrambled signal: Yes.
Ownership: Motors TV. Distributed in the U.S. by Alterna'TV.

THE MOVIE CHANNEL — See Showtime.
Paramount Plaza Bldg
1633 Broadway, 17th Fl
New York, NY 10019
212-708-1600
Phone: 212-708-1212
Web Site: http://www.sho.com
Type of service: Premium, HD, video on demand.
Began: April 1, 1973, as Star Channel. Rebranded The Movie Channel December 1979.
Distribution method: Available to cable, IPTV & satellite subscribers.
Ownership: CBS Corp.

THE MOVIE CHANNEL XTRA — See The Movie Channel.
Began: October 1997 as The Movie Channel 2. Rebranded as The Movie Channel Xtra in March 2001.

MOVIE MAX — See Cinemax.
c/o Home Box Office
1100 Avenue of the Americas
New York, NY 10036
Phone: 212-512-1000
Fax: 212-512-1166
Type of service: Pay, HD.
Operating hours/week: 168.
Operating areas: Available nationwide.
Programming: Family-oriented movies.
Began: May 17, 2001, as WMax. Rebranded as Movie Max on June 1, 2013.
Scrambled signal: Yes.
Ownership: Home Box Office Inc., a division of Time Warner.

Pay TV & Satellite Services

MOVIEPLEX
8900 Liberty Cir
Englewood, CO 80112
Phone: 720-852-7700
Fax: 720-852-7710
E-mail: eric.becker@starz.com
Web Site: http://www.starz.com/channels/movieplex
Eric Becker, Vice President, Corporate Communications
Type of service: Pay, HD, streaming, video on demand.
Satellites: Satcom C-4, transponder 5 (east/west/MTN).
Operating hours/week: 168.
Programming: Commercial free movies.
Began: October 1, 1994.
Means of Support: Subscriber fees.
Total subscribers: 5,600,000.
Distribution method: Available to cable, IPTV & satellite subscribers. Streaming available online & through app. Video on demand available through participating providers.
Scrambled signal: Yes. Equipment: Digital/DigiCipher II.
Ownership: Starz Inc.

MOVIES!
c/o Weigel Broadcasting Co.
26 North Halsted
Chicago, IL 60661
Phone: 312-705-2600
Web Site: http://moviestvnetwork.com
Neal Sabin, President, Content & Networks, Weigel Broadcasting Co.
Frank Cicha, Senior Vice President, Programming, Fox Television Stations
Will Givens, Vice President, Network Marketing
Type of service: Basic.
Operating hours/week: 168.
Operating areas: Nationwide.
Programming: Film-themed service that is 'fan-friendly'.
Began: May 27, 2013.
Means of Support: Advertising.
Total subscribers: 46,500,000 (Subscribers based on current affiliation agreements.).
Distribution method: Available over the air on digital sub-channels of Fox-owned stations and cable subscribers.
Scrambled signal: Yes.
Ownership: A joint venture between Fox Television Station Group & Weigel Broadcasting Co.

MOVIES! CAROLINA
Broadcast Pl
505 Rutherford St
Greenville, SC 29609
Phone: 864-242-4404
Fax: 864-240-5305
Web Site: http://www.wyff4.com
John R Soapes, President & General Manager, WYFF
Type of service: Regional basic.
Operating areas: South Carolina.
Programming: Has iconic films in prime time during the week and weekend movies feature different genres like Mystery Movies, Popcorn Movies or Saturday Night Love Movies.
Began: December 31, 2014.
Means of Support: Advertising.
Distribution method: Available over the air on digital subchannel and to cable system subscribers.
Scrambled signal: Yes.
Ownership: Hearst Television Inc.

MSG
2 Penn Plz
New York, NY 10121-0091
Phone: 212-465-6741
Fax: 212-465-6020
E-mail: mediainquiries@msg.com
Web Site: http://www.msg.com
MSG NETWORKS:, .
James Dolan, Executive Chairman, MSG Networks Inc.
Gregg Seibert, Vice Chairman, MSG Networks Inc.
Andrea Greenberg, President & Chief Executive Officer, MSG Networks Inc.
Bret Richter, Executive Vice President & Chief Financial Officer, MSG Networks Inc.
Lawrence Burian, Executive Vice President, General Counsel & Secretary, MSG Networks Inc.
Alison Hellman, Senior Vice President, Marketing & Promotion
MSG :, .
David Goodman, President, Productions & Live Entertainment
Ryan O'Hara, President, Content, Distribution & Sales
Melissa Ormond, President, MSG Entertainment
Hank Abate, Executive Vice President, Venue Management
Donna Coleman, Executive Vice President & Chief Financial Officer
Steve Collins, Executive Vice President, Facilities
Joel Fisher, Executive Vice President, Marquee Events & Operations
Scott Henry, Executive Vice President & Chief Technology Officer
Colin Ingram, Executive Vice President, MSG Productions
Andrew Lustgarten, Executive Vice President, Corporate Development & Strategy
Sharon Otterman, Executive Vice President & Chief Marketing Officer
Jordan Solomon, Executive Vice President, MSG Sports
Barry Watkins, Executive Vice President, Communications & Administration
Irene Baker, Senior Vice President, Government Affairs
Andrew Biggers, Senior Vice President, Content Distribution
Rich Claffey, Senior Vice President & General Manager, Madison Square Garden Arena
Kathryn Kerrigan, Senior Vice President, Planning & Analysis
Ocean MacAdams, Senior Vice President, Programming & Acquisitions
Jerry Passarro, Senior Vice President, Network Operations & Distribution
Donna Randazzo, Senior Vice President, Finance & Controller
Heather Pariseau, Vice President, Interactive Programming & Operations
Susan Schroeder, Vice President, Marketing Partnerships & Client Services
Peter Tulloch, Vice President, Advanced Services
Type of service: Regional, streaming & video on demand.
Satellites: GE-1, transponder 18.
Operating hours/week: 168.
Operating areas: Connecticut, New Jersey, New York & Pennsylvania (northeastern portion).
Programming: Sports & entertainment programming, including vintage & current concerts performed at Madison Square Garden.
Began: October 15, 1969.
Means of Support: Advertising & system fees.
Total subscribers: 11,200,000.
Distribution method: Available to cable, IPTV & satellite subscribers. Streaming available online. Video on demand through participating providers.
Scrambled signal: Yes.
Ownership: MSG Networks Inc. Publicly held.

MSG 3D — See MSG.
Began: March 24, 2010.
Distribution method: Available only to Cablevision Systems Inc. subscribers.

MSG PLUS
11 Penn Plz
New York, NY 10121
Phone: 212-465-6000
Fax: 212-465-6020
E-mail: msgnetpr@msg.com
Web Site: http://www.msg.com
Scott O'Neil, President, MSG Sports
Type of service: Regional.
Satellites: GE-1, transponder 18.
Operating hours/week: 168.
Operating areas: Connecticut (southern portion), New Jersey & New York.
Programming: Regional sports service offering New York Islanders hockey, New Jersey Devils hockey, plus college basketball & football, professional boxing, tennis, thoroughbred racing, motor racing & other sports programming.
Began: March 10, 2008, replacing Fox Sports Net New York.
Means of Support: System fees & advertising.
Total subscribers: 9,678,000.
Distribution method: Available to cable & satellite subscribers.
Scrambled signal: Yes.
Ownership: MSG Networks Inc. Publicly held.

MSNBC
30 Rockefeller Pl
New York, NY 10112
Phones: 212-664-4444; 212-664-6605
E-mail: mediainquiries@msnbc.com
Web Site: http://www.msnbc.com
Andy Lack, Chairman, MSNBC & NBC News
Phil Griffin, President
Errol Cockfield, Senior Vice President, MSNBC Communications
Deb Finan, Senior Vice President, Programming & Production
Yvette Miley, Senior Vice President, Talent
Sharon Otterman, Senior Vice President & Chief Marketing Officer
Barry Margolis, Vice President, NBC News Eastern Sales
Izzy Povich, Vice President, Talent & Development
Rachel Racusen, Vice President, Communications
Michael Rubin, Vice President, Long-Form Programming & Production
Lauren Skowronski, Vice President, Media Relations
Bill Wolff, Vice President, Primetime Programming
Marc Greenstein, Creative Director
Leslie Schwartz, Media Relations Director
Anne Keegan, Media Relations, MSNBC.com
John Reiss, Executive Producer, Political Programming

Branch Offices:
WASHINGTON, DC: 4001 Nebraska Ave NW, Washington, DC 20016.
Type of service: Basic, HD, streaming.
Satellites: 10.
Operating hours/week: 168.
Operating areas: Nationwide.
Programming: All news channel featuring packaged news reports, live remotes and analysis of breaking stories.
Began: July 15, 1996.
Means of Support: Advertising.
Total subscribers: 96,000,000.
Distribution method: Available to cable, IPTV & satellite subscribers. Streaming available online.
Scrambled signal: Yes. Equipment: Galaxy IR.
Ownership: NBCUniversal News Group, a subsidiary of NBCUniversal LLC.

MTC PERSIAN TELEVISION
21004 Nordhoff St
1st Fl, Ste A
Los Angeles, CA 91311
Phone: 818-703-8212
Fax: 818-887-6080
E-mail: info@mellitv.com
Web Site: http://www.mellitv.com
Operating hours/week: 168.
Programming: Persian variety, news, entertainment & cultural shows.
Distribution method: Available to cable & satellite subscribers.
Scrambled signal: Yes.

MTV
MTV Networks Inc.
1515 Broadway, 31st Fl
New York, NY 10036
Phone: 212-258-8000
Fax: 212-846-8759
Web Site: http://www.mtv.com
VIACOM MUSIC & ENTERTAINMENT GROUP:, .
Doug Herzog, President, Viacom Music & Entertainment Group
Kassie Canter, Executive Vice President, Communications, Viacom Music & Entertainment Group
John Cucci, Executive Vice President & Chief Operating Officer, Viacom Music & Entertainment Group
Tanya Giles, Executive Vice President, Strategic Insights & Research, Viacom Music & Entertainment Group
MTV:, .
Sean Atkins, Friedman, President
Robyn Demarco, Executive Vice President, Programming & Content Strategy
Lauren Dolgen, Executive Vice President, Series Development & Head, West Coast Reality Programming
Tina Exarhos, Executive Vice President, Marketing & Creative
Erik Flannigan, Executive Vice President, Music/Events Strategy & Development.
Kristin Frank, Executive Vice President, Strategy, Revenue & Operations
Michael Klein, Executive Vice President, Original Programming
Mina Lefevre, Executive Vice President & Head of Scripted Development
Eli Lerner, Executive Vice President, MTV2
Jacqueline Parkes, Executive Vice President, Marketing & Creative
Joanna Bomberg, Senior Vice President, Music & Talent Programming Strategy
Garrett English, Senior Vice President, MTV Programming, Events & Live Production
Jane Gould, Senior Vice President, Consumer Insights & Research
Colin Helms, Senior Vice President, Connected Content
Jeff Jacobs, Senior Vice President, Production Planning, Strategies & Operations
Mindy Stockfield, Senior Vice President, Marketing
Richard Turley, Senior Vice President, Visual Storytelling & Deputy Editorial Director, MTV
Laurel Weir, Senior Vice President, Strategic Insights & Research

Pay TV & Satellite Services

Type of service: Basic, streaming & video on demand.
Satellites: Galaxy III, transponder transponder 17.
Operating hours/week: 168.
Uplink: Network Operations Center, Smithtown, NY.
Programming: All-stereo video music channel including music news, specials, documentaries, original strip programming, promotions & interviews.
Began: August 1, 1981.
Means of Support: Advertising.
Total subscribers: 100,400,000.
Distribution method: Available to cable, IPTV & satellite subscribers. Streaming & video on demand through participating providers.
Scrambled signal: Yes. Equipment: VideoCipher II.
Ownership: Viacom Inc.

MTV2 — See MTV.
Paul Ricci, Senior Vice President & Head of Development, MTV2 & mtvU
Programming: Music, lifestyle & action sports programming.
Began: August 1, 1996.
Total subscribers: 71,000,000.
Scrambled signal: Yes.

MTV CLASSIC — See MTV.
Programming: Mainstream rock music videos & concert footage from the 1990s-2000s.
Scrambled signal: Yes.

MTV HITS — See NickMusic
Programming: Music videos.
Began: May 1, 2002.
Total subscribers: 28,000,000.

MTV JAMS — See MTV.
Programming: Hip hip & urban music videos.
Began: 1998, replacing MTVX.
Total subscribers: 29,000,000.
Scrambled signal: Yes.

MTV LIVE — See MTV.
Web Site: http://www.mtv.com/live
Type of service: Basic, HD.
Operating areas: Nationwide.
Programming: HD music channel focusing on concert programming.
Began: January 1, 2006, as MHD. Rebranded Palladia September 1, 2008 & rebranded MTV Live February 1, 2016.
Distribution method: Available to cable & satellite subscribers.
Scrambled signal: Yes.
Ownership: MTV Networks Inc.

MTVU — See MTV.
E-mail: feedback@mtvu.com
Web Site: http://www.mtvu.com
Paul Ricci, Senior Vice President & Head of Development, MTV2 & mtvU
Type of service: Basic.
Operating hours/week: 168.
Programming: Cable channel dedicated to every aspect of college life from music to news to campus life; broadcasts to over 720 colleges & universities.
Began: October 1, 2002, as College Television Network. Rebranded as mtvU January 20, 2004.
Total subscribers: 10,100,000 (7,500,000 on-campuses nationwide & 2,600,000 through cable & telco operators in college communities).
Scrambled signal: Yes.

MULTIMEDIOS TELEVISION
Paricutin y 5 de Febrero, No 312
Col. Roma
Monterrey, Nuevo Leon 64700
Mexico
Phone: 52-81-8369-9919
Web Site: http://www.multimedios.tv
Operating hours/week: 168.
Operating areas: Available nationwide.
Programming: Spanish-language news, sports, children's and entertainment programming. Local off-air affiliates also provide material as well.
Means of Support: Advertising and subscriber fees.
Distribution method: Available to over the air on digital sub-channels & to cable, IPTV & satellite subscribers.
Scrambled signal: Yes.
Ownership: Grupo Multimedios. Distributed in the U.S. by UNO Entertainment.

MUNDOFOX — See MundoMax.

MUNDOMAX
1440 S Sepulveda
Los Angeles, CA 90025
Phone: 310-444-8823
Web Site: http://www.mundomax.com
Jose I. Molina, Chief Financial Officer & Interim President
Nicolas J. Valls, Senior Vice President, Advertising Sales
Phillip R. Woodie, Senior Vice President, National Sales
Edward Jimenez, Vice President, National Sales
Javier Szerman, Vice President, Content Development
Type of service: Basic, over the air.
Operating areas: Nationwide.
Programming: Includes shows from RCN's Colombian TV network & outside suppliers of English- and Spanish-language programming, plus news.
Began: August 13, 2012, as MundoFOX. Relaunched MundoMax August 13, 2015.
Means of Support: Advertising.
Total subscribers: 26,000,000.
Distribution method: Available over the air on digital sub-channels & to cable, IPTV & satellite subscribers.
Scrambled signal: Yes.
Ownership: RCN Television Group Columbia.

MUN2 — See NBC Universo.

MUSIC CHOICE — See MC.

MUZIKA PERVOGO
19 Akademika Korolyova St
Moscow 127427
Russian Federation
Phones: 7-495-617-55-88; 7-495-617-51-75
Fax: 7-495-617-51-14
E-mail: info@1tvrus.com
Web Site: http://eng.1tvrus.com/muzika
Nikolay Dubovoy, Director General
Type of service: Premium.
Operating areas: Available in New Jersey & New York on cable & nationwide on DirecTV.
Programming: Russian music channel.
Began: January 1, 2005.
Means of Support: Advertising & subscriber fees.
Total subscribers: 20,000,000 (subscribers worldwide.).
Distribution method: Available to DirecTV & Time Warner Cable subscribers.
Scrambled signal: Yes.
Ownership: Channel One. National Media Group, minority interest.

MY COMBAT CHANNEL
301 N Canon Dr
Ste 208
Beverly Hills, CA 90210
Phones: 818-549-9988; 888-783-0014
E-mail: info@mycombatchannel.com
Leonard Asper, Chief Executive Officer
Type of service: Basic.
Operating hours/week: 168.
Operating areas: Nationwide.
Programming: 24/7 fight channel covering sports of combat including MMA, boxing, wrestling, and multiple martial arts disciplines such as Brazilian Jiu-Jitsu, Tae Kwon Do karate and amateur fights.
Began: January 1, 2011.
Means of Support: Advertising.
Distribution method: Available to cable subscribers.
Scrambled signal: Yes.
Ownership: Anthem Media Group Inc.

MYDESTINATION.TV
1925 Century Park E
Ste 1025
Los Angeles, CA 90067
Phone: 310-277-3500
E-mail: eric@es.tv
Web Site: http://www.mydestination.tv
Byron Allen, Chairman & Chief Executive Officer
Darren Galatt, Vice President, Ad Sales
Type of service: Digital, over the air.
Operating hours/week: 168.
Operating areas: Nationwide.
Programming: The best in luxury travel as well as fun, exciting, exotic destinations around the world.
Began: May 11, 2009.
Total subscribers: 1,900,000.
Distribution method: Available over the air on digital sub-channels & to cable subscribers.
Scrambled signal: No.
Ownership: Entertainment Studios.

MY FAMILY TV — See The Family Channel.

MYNETWORKTV
2121 Avenue of the Stars
Ste 2300
Los Angeles, CA 90013
Phone: 310-369-3293
Web Site: http://www.mynetworktv.com
Vinette Bond, Vice President, Business & Legal Affairs
Type of service: Basic, over the air.
Programming: Original, dramatic series & entertainment.
Began: September 4, 2006.
Distribution method: Available over the air through local affiliates.
Scrambled signal: Yes.
Ownership: 21st Century Fox.

MYX TV
150 Shoreline Dr
Redwood City, CA 94065
Phone: 650-508-6000
Web Site: http://myx.tv
Miguel Santos, Head of MYX TV
Joy Bovatsek, Head of Programming
Anthony Garcia, Head of Production
Ricky Resurreccion, Head of Ad Sales
Jun Del Rosario, Head of Distribution
Operating hours/week: 168.
Operating areas: Available in Boston, Chicago, Honolulu, Houston, Los Angeles, New York City, San Diego, San Francisco, Seattle, Washington, DC & Yuma, AZ.
Programming: Music entertainment and lifestyle channel dedicated to the Asian American community.
Began: July 22, 2007.
Means of Support: Advertising.
Total subscribers: 15,000,000.
Distribution method: Available to Time Warner & satellite subscribers.
Scrambled signal: Yes.
Ownership: ABS-CBN Corp.

NACION TV
10303 Northwest Fwy
Ste 435
Houston, TX 77092
Phone: 713-561-3746
E-mail: info@naciontv.org
Web Site: http://www.naciontv.org
Type of service: Basic.
Satellites: Galaxy 19, transponder 27.
Operating hours/week: 168.
Operating areas: Nationwide.
Programming: Programs for children, youths & adults that promote moral, social and cultural rights.
Distribution method: Available over the air on digital sub-channels & to satellite subscribers.
Scrambled signal: Yes.
Ownership: Nation TV.

NARRATIVE TELEVISION NETWORK
5840 S Memorial Dr
Ste 312
Tulsa, OK 74145-9082
Phones: 918-627-1000; 800-801-8184
Fax: 918-627-4101
E-mail: info@narrativetv.com
Web Site: http://www.narrativetv.com
Jim Stovall, President
Kathy Harper, Vice President
Kelly Morrison, Marketing Director
Clover Nuetzmann, Audience & Industry Relations Manager
Dorothy Thompson, Operations Manager
Type of service: Basic.
Satellites: Galaxy I, transponder 22.
Operating hours/week: 20.
Uplink: Alexandria, VA.
Programming: Programming accessible to blind & visually impaired viewers by adding the voice of a narrator to the existing programming sound track without interfering with any of the original audio and video.
Began: January 1, 1988.
Means of Support: Advertising.
Total subscribers: 35,000,000.
Distribution method: Available to cable & satellite subscribers.
Scrambled signal: Yes.

NASA TV
300 E St SW

Pay TV & Satellite Services

Code P
Washington, DC 20546
Phones: 202-358-1701; 202-358-0001
Fax: 202-358-4334; 202-358-4338
E-mail: public-inquiries@hq.nasa.gov
Web Site: http://www.nasa.gov/multimedia/nasatv/index.html
Joseph N. Benton, Executive Producer
Type of service: Digital, HD.
Satellites: AMC-6, transponder 17C; AMC-7, transponder 18C.
Operating hours/week: 168.
Programming: Digital coverage of NASA missions and events, as well as documentaries, archival and other special programming.
Began: July 1, 1990, NASA TV HD began February 17, 2012.
Distribution method: Available to cable & satellite subscribers.
Scrambled signal: Yes.
Ownership: National Aeronautics and Space Administration.

NASA TV UHD
300 E St SW
Ste 5R30
Washington, DC 20546
Phones: 202-358-0001; 202-358-1540
Fax: 202-358-4338
E-mail: karen.northon@nasa.gov
Web Site: http://www.nasa.gov
Charlie Bolden, Administrator
Dava Newman, Deputy Administrator
Robert M Lightfoot Jr, Associate Administrator
Lesa Roe, Deputy Associate Administrator
Karen Northon, Media Relations Officer
Type of service: Basic.
Satellites: SES AMC-18.
Operating areas: Available nationwide.
Programming: Showcases the breathtaking beauty and grandeur of space using high-resolution images and video generated on the International Space Station and other current NASA missions.
Began: November 1, 2015.
Distribution method: Available to cable & satellite subscribers.
Scrambled signal: Yes.
Ownership: National Aeronautics and Space Administration and Harmonic.

NAT GEO MUNDO
1211 Ave of the Americas
31st Fl
New York, NY 10036
Phone: 212-822-9083
E-mail: support@foxhispanicmedia.com
Web Site: http://www.natgeomundo.com; http://www.foxhispanicmedia.com
Declan Moore, Chief Executive Officer, National Geographic Partners
Ward Platt, Chief Operating Officer, National Geographic Partners
Courteney Monroe, Chief Executive Officer, National Geographic Global Networks
Tom Maney, Executive Vice President, Advertising Sales, Fox Hispanic Media
Jeffrey Schneider, Executive Vice President, Business & Legal Affairs, National Geographic Partners
Juan Vallejo, Senior Vice President, Advertising Sales, Fox Hispanic Media

Branch Offices:
CORAL GABLES: 2121 Ponce de Leon Blvd, Ste 1020, Coral Gables, FL 33134. Phone: 305-567-9788.
Type of service: Basic, digital.
Operating areas: Nationwide.
Programming: Non-fiction entertainment network for U.S. Hispanics that features high-quality original programming involving nature, science, culture & history.
Began: July 1, 2011.
Means of Support: Advertising.
Total subscribers: 4,000,000.
Distribution method: Available to cable, IPTV & satellite subscribers.
Scrambled signal: Yes.
Ownership: A joint venture between 21st Century Fox & National Geographic.

NAT GEO WILD
1145 17th St NW
Washington, DC 20036
Phones: 202-857-7027; 202-857-7700
E-mail: pressroom@ngs.com
Web Site: http://channel.nationalgeographic.com/wild
Declan Moore, Chief Executive Officer, National Geographic Partners
Ward Platt, Chief Operating Officer, National Geographic Partners
Courteney Monroe, Chief Executive Officer, National Geographic Global Networks
Jeffrey Schneider, Executive Vice President, Business & Legal Affairs, National Geographic Partners
Geoff Daniels, Executive Vice President & General Manager, Nat Geo Wild
Rich Goldfarb, Senior Vice President, Media Sales, National Geographic Channel & Nat Geo Wild
Hayes Tauber, Senior Vice President, Marketing, National Geographic Channel & Nat Geo Wild
Franklin Walker, Vice President, Business & Legal Affairs, National Geographic Channel & Nat Geo Wild
Dara Klatt, Senior Director, Corporate Communications, National Geographic Channel & Nat Geo Wild
Tyler Korba, Creative Director, National Geographic Channel & Nat Geo Wild
Type of service: Basic, HD, streaming, video on demand.
Operating hours/week: 168.
Operating areas: Available nationwide.
Programming: Natural history & animal-related programming.
Began: August 1, 2006, internationally. Began in U.S. on March 29, 2010, replacing Fox Reality Channel. Nat Geo Wild HD began on the same day.
Means of Support: Advertising.
Total subscribers: 58,000,000.
Distribution method: Available to cable, IPTV & satellite subscribers. Streaming available online & through app (participating providers).
Scrambled signal: Yes.
Ownership: National Geographic Partners, a joint venture between 21st Century Fox (73%) & National Geographic Society (27%).

NATIONAL GEOGRAPHIC CHANNEL
1145 17th St NW
Washington, DC 20036
Phones: 202-857-7000; 800-647-5463
Fax: 202-912-6602
E-mail: comments@natgeochannel.com
Web Site: http://channel.nationalgeographic.com
Declan Moore, Chief Executive Officer, National Geographic Partners
Ward Platt, Chief Operating Officer, National Geographic Partners
Claudia Malley, Chief Marketing & Brand Officer, National Geographic Partners
Jeffrey Schneider, Executive Vice President, Business & Legal Affairs, National Geographic Partners
Laura Nichols, Senior Vice President, Chief Communications Officer, National Geographic Partners
Courteney Monroe, Chief Executive Officer, National Geographic Global Networks
Tim Pastore, President, Original Programming & Production
Brooke Runnette, President, National Geographic Studios
Carolyn Bernstein, Executive Vice President & Head, Global Scripted Development & Production
Heather Moran, Executive Vice President, Programming & Strategy
Chris Albert, Senior Vice President, Communications & Talent Relations
John Campbell, Senior Vice President, Global Media
Brad Dancer, Senior Vice President, Programming Planning & Research
Alan Eyres, Senior Vice President, Programming Development, West Coast
Rich Goldfarb, Senior Vice President, Media Sales, National Geographic Channels & Nat Geo Wild
Dawn Rodney-Tranchitella, Senior Vice President, Marketing & Creative
Noel Siegel, Senior Vice President, Production & Development
Hayes Tauber, Senior Vice President, Marketing, National Geographic Channel & Nat Geo Wild
Paul Brake, Vice President, Finance
Allan Butler, Vice President, Development & Special Projects
Jennifer DeGuzman, Vice President, Communications & Talent Relations
John Fletcher, Vice President, Production Services & Network Operations
J. T. Ladt, Vice President, Programming & Development
Kevin Mohs, Vice President, Development & Production
Banafsheh Parsee, Vice President, Post Production & Broadcast Operations
Charlie Parsons, Vice President, Global Development
Joyce Romano, Vice President, Program Planning & Finance
Randy Rylander, Vice President, Programming
Lynn Sadofsky, Vice President, Production & Development, New York
Char Serwa, Vice President, Production
Franklin Walker, Vice President, Legal & Business Affairs, National Geographic Channel & Nat Geo Wild
David Friedlander, Executive Director, Research
Emily Cooper, Ad Sales, Marketing & Product Integration Director
Tyler Korba, Creative Director, National Geographic Channel & Nat Geo Wild
Dara Klatt, Senior Director, Corporate Communications, National Geographic Channel & Nat Geo Wild
Matthew Zymet, Digital Media Content Director
Brian Everett, Creative Director, Design
Kristin Montalbano, Digital Publicity & Media Relations Director
Type of service: Basic, HD, streaming, video on demand.
Operating hours/week: 168.
Operating areas: Available nationwide.
Programming: Non-fiction & documentaries about natural history, science, adventure, exploration & culture.
Began: January 1, 2001, National Geographic Channel HD began January 2006.
Total subscribers: 85,000,000.
Distribution method: Available to cable, IPTV & satellite subscribers. Streaming available online & through app (participating providers).
Scrambled signal: Yes.
Ownership: National Geographic Partners, a joint venture between 21st Century Fox (73%) & National Geographic Society (27%).

NEW GREEK TV
30-97 Steinway St
Astoria, NY 11103
Phone: 718-726-0900
Fax: 718-728-3328
E-mail: ngtv@ngtvonline.com
Web Site: http://www.ngtv.nyc
Demetris Kastanas, President
Norma Papamichael, Vice President
Type of service: Pay.
Operating hours/week: 168.
Programming: Greek & Greek-American language & culture programming including news, sports, talk shows, dramas, comedy series, movies & documentaries.
Began: September 1, 1975.
Distribution method: Available to cable subscribers.
Scrambled signal: Yes.

NATIONAL IRANIAN TELEVISION
6723 Variel Ave
Canoga Park, CA 91303
Phone: 818-835-9800
Fax: 818-835-9699
Web Site: http://www.nitv.tv
Zia Atabay, President & Chief Executive Officer
Noureddin Sabet Imani, Vice President & News Director
Type of service: Basic.
Programming: 24-hour Persian programming.
Began: March 1, 2000.

NATIONAL JEWISH TV (NJT)
PO Box 480
Wilton, CT 06897
Phone: 203-834-3799
Joel Levitch, President
Don Humphrey, Chief Executive Officer
Type of service: Basic.
Satellites: Satcom C-1, transponder 18.
Operating hours/week: 3. Sun., 1pm-4pm.
Programming: Cultural, religious & public affairs programming for the Jewish community.
Began: May 1, 1981.
Means of Support: Advertising.
Total subscribers: 10,000,000.

NATIONAL LAMPOON COLLEGE TELEVISION
254 W 54th St
Ste 800
New York, NY USA
Phone: 212-471-3532
E-mail: feedback@nationallampoon.com
Web Site: http://www.nationallampooncollege.com
Nick DeNinno, Vice President & General Manager
Type of service: Basic.
Operating hours/week: 12.
Programming: Programming aimed at college students (18-24) including comedy, sports, films & talk shows.
Began: January 17, 2003.
Total subscribers: 4,500,000.

NBA LEAGUE PASS — See NBA TV.
Type of service: Pay, streaming.
Programming: Out-of-market NBA games.
Scrambled signal: Yes.
Ownership: Available to cable, IPTV & satellite subscribers. Streaming available online & on mobile devices.

Pay TV & Satellite Services

NBA TV
Olympic Tower
645 Fifth Ave
New York, NY 10022
Phone: 212-407-8000
Fax: 212-223-5159
E-mail: nbatv@nba.com
Web Site: http://www.nba.com/nbatv
David Levy, President, Turner Sales, Distribution & Sports, Turner Broadcasting System Inc.
Mark Tatum, Deputy Commissioner & Chief Operating Officer, NBA
Bill Koenig, President, Global Media Distribution, NBA
Sal LaRocca, President, Global Operations & Merchandising, NBA
Danny Meiseles, President & Executive Producer, Content, NBA
Mike Bass, Executive Vice President, Communications, NBA
Thomas Carelli, Senior Vice President, Broadcasting, NBA
Tim Frank, Senior Vice President, Basketball Communications, NBA
Albert Vertino, Senior Vice President, Programming & General Manager, NBA Digital
Tatia Williams, Vice President, Business Affairs, NBA

Branch Offices:
PRODUCTION STUDIO: Turner Studios, 1050 Techwood Dr, Atlanta, GA 30318. Phone: 404-885-5331. Ken Brady, Vice President, Systems Technology & Digital Media, Turner Studios; Steve Mensch, Strategic Production Partnerships & Studio Operations, Turner Studios Director.

AFFILIATE CONTACT: Tatia Williams, Vice President, Business Affairs, E-mail: twilliams@nba.com. Phones: 212-407-8295; 202-669-9900 (cell). Fax: 646-264-4023.
Type of service: Digital, HD.
Operating hours/week: 168.
Programming: Everything NBA, including real time statistics, live look-ins of games in progress, vintage games, highlights, videos & specials.
Began: March 17, 1999, as NBA.com TV. Rebranded NBA TV on February 11, 2003.
Means of Support: Advertising.
Total subscribers: 45,000,000.
Distribution method: Available to cable, IPTV & satellite subscribers.
Scrambled signal: Yes.
Ownership: Service is jointly managed by the NBA & Turner Sports. Service is produced at Turner Studios.

NBC DEPORTES — See Telemundo Deportes

NBCSN
2 Stamford Plz, 9th Fl
281 Tresser Blvd
Stamford, CT 06901
Phone: 203-406-2500
Fax: 203-406-2530
Web Site: http://nbcsports.msnbc.com
NBC SPORTS GROUP:, .
Mark Lazarus, Chairman, NBC Sports Group
Jon Litner, President, NBC Sports Group
David Preschlack, President, NBC Sports Regional Networks & NBC Sports Group Platform & Content Strategy
Gary Zenkel, President, NBC Olympics & President, Operations & Strategies, NBC Sports Group
Jennifer Storms, Chief Marketing Officer, NBC Sports Group

Rick Cordella, Senior Vice President & General Manager, Digital Media, NBC Sports Group
Princell Hair, Senior Vice President, News & Talent, NBC Sports Group
Greg Hughes, Senior Vice President, Communications, NBC Sports Group
Tripp Dixon, Vice President, Creative Services, NBC Sports Group
NBCSN:, .
Jon Miller, President, Programming, NBC Sports & NBCSN
Sam Flood, Executive Producer, NBC Sports & NBCSN

Branch Offices:
CHICAGO: One IBM Plaza, 330 N Wabash Ave, Ste 2005, Chicago, IL 60611. Phone: 312-832-0808. Fax: 312-832-9485.

DETROIT: 401 S Woodward Ave, Ste 457, Birmingham, MI 48009. Phone: 248-594-0707. Fax: 248-594-1460.

HOUSTON: 133 N Friendswood Dr, Friendswood, TX 77548. Phone: 281-331-7787. Fax: 281-331-7262.

LOS ANGELES: 12100 W Olympic Blvd, Ste 200, Los Angeles, CA 90064. Phone: 310-979-2260. Fax: 310-979-2261.

NEW YORK: 1114 Avenue of the Americas, 20th Floor, New York, NY 10036. Phone: 914-931-1050. Fax: 212-687-1819.
Type of service: Expanded basic, streaming.
Satellites: Galaxy 11, transponder 21C.
Operating hours/week: 168.
Programming: Full-service sports network.
Began: July 1, 1995, as Outdoor Life Network. Rebranded as Versus on September 25, 2006. Versus HD launched January 2007. Rebranded as NBC Sports Network January 2, 2012. Rebranded as NBCSN Summer 2013.
Total subscribers: 86,000,000.
Distribution method: Available to cable, IPTV & satellite subscribers. Streaming available through the NCS Sports app.
Scrambled signal: Yes.
Ownership: NBCUniversal LLC.

NBC SPORTS NETWORK — See NBCSN.

NBC UNIVERSO
2290 W Eighth Ave
Hialeah, FL 33010
Phone: 305-884-8200
Web Site: http://www.nbcuniverso.com
Luis Silberwasser, President
Joe A Bernard, Senior Vice President, Advertising Sales
Chris Czarkowski, Senior Vice President, Hispanic Group Advertising Sales
Jeff Mayzurk, Senior Vice President, Operations & Technology
Alfredo Richard, Senior Vice President, Corporate Communications
Bilai Joa Silar, Senior Vice President, Programming & Production
Alex Alonso, Vice President, Marketing
Ricardo de Montreuil, Vice President & Creative Director
Peter Dobrow, Vice President, Communications
Fernando Gaston, Vice President, Production & Development
Jenny McNicholas, Vice President, Production & Operations
Margie Moreno, Vice President, Programming
Type of service: Basic.

Satellites: Spacenet 2, transponder 2; Galaxy 332-5, transponder 22; GE 1, transponder 5.
Operating hours/week: 112.
Programming: Bilingual general entertainment network for U.S. Hispanics aged 18-34, with original programming that reflects their lifestyles & relevant bilingual content.
Began: October 1, 2001, as mun2. Service rebranded as NBC Universo February 1, 2015.
Means of Support: Advertising & subscribers.
Total subscribers: 40,000,000.
Distribution method: Available to cable & satellite subscribers.
Scrambled signal: Yes. Equipment: DigiCipher.
Ownership: Telemundo Group, which is owned by NBCUniversal LLC.

NEO CRICKET
NIMBUS Centre
Oberoi Complex
Andheri West, Mumbai 400 053
India
Phones: 91-22-26352000 ext. 175; 9892438262
Fax: 91-22-26352123
E-mail: manishas@neosports.tv
Web Site: http://www.neosports.tv
Dr. Shan Chandrasekar, President & Chief Executive Officer
Vikram Das, Senior Vice President, International & Syndication
Manisha Sharma, Corporate Communications
Operating hours/week: 168.
Programming: Offers programming on and about cricket. Includes broadcasts of all cricket matches in India.
Began: April 2, 2008, in India. Began September 30, 2010 in the U.S.
Distribution method: Available to cable subscribers.
Ownership: NEO Sports Broadcast Pvt. Ltd.

NEON — See Time Warner Cable SportsChannel Ohio.

NESN — See New England Sports Network.

NESN NATIONAL — See New England Sports Network.
Type of service: Pay.
Programming: Similar programming to New England Sports Network although live broadcasts of Red Sox & Bruins games are not available due to league restrictions.
Began: September 30, 2010.

NESNPLUS — See New England Sports Network.
Type of service: Pay, HD.
Programming: Boston Red Sox or Boston Bruins game when both are on simultaneously or overlap time.
Scrambled signal: Yes.

NETFLIX
100 Winchester Cir
Los Gatos, CA 95032
Phones: 408-540-3700; 877-742-1480

E-mail: pr@netflix.com
Web Site: http://www.netflix.com
Reed Hastings, Co-Founder & Chief Executive Officer
Kelly Bennett, Chief Marketing Officer
Tawni Cranz, Chief Talent Officer
Jonathan Friedland, Chief Communications Officer
Neil Hunt, Chief Product Officer
Greg Peters, Chief Streaming & Partnerships Officer
Ted Sarandos, Chief Content Officer
David Wells, Chief Financial Officer
David Hyman, General Counsel
Cindy Holland, Vice President, Original Content
Anne Marie Squeo, Corporate Communications Director
Jane Wiseman, Senior Executive, Original Programming
Type of service: Pay, streaming.
Operating hours/week: 168.
Operating areas: Nationwide.
Programming: More than one billion hours of TV shows and movies, including original series.
Began: May 1, 2014, on TiVo boxes to MSO subscribers.
Means of Support: Subscriber fees.
Total subscribers: 46,970,000 (in US, 34,530,000 International.).
Distribution method: Available to cable & IPTV subscribers; online & mobile through the website or app.
Scrambled signal: Yes.
Ownership: Publicly held.

THE NEW ENCORE — See Starz Encore.

NEW ENGLAND CABLE NEWS
160 Wells Ave
Newton, MA 02459
Phone: 617-630-5000
Fax: 617-630-5055
E-mail: msegel@necn.com
Web Site: http://www.necn.com
Mike St. Peter, Senior Vice President & General Manager
Stacey Bronner, Vice President & Station Manager
Annie Peters, Vice President, Sales
Kenny Plotnik, Vice President, News
Type of service: Basic.
Operating hours/week: 168.
Operating areas: Connecticut, Maine, Massachusetts, New Hampshire, Rhode Island & Vermont.
Programming: National & local news, weather, sports, informational & talk programming.
Began: March 2, 1992.
Total subscribers: 3,700,000.
Distribution method: Available to cable subscribers.
Scrambled signal: Yes.
Ownership: NBCUniversal LLC.

NEW ENGLAND SPORTS NETWORK
480 Arsenal St
Bldg One
Watertown, MA 02472
Phone: 617-536-9233

2017 Edition

Pay TV & Satellite Services

Fax: 617-536-7814
E-mail: sports@nesn.com
Web Site: http://www.nesn.com
Sean McGrail, President & Chief Executive Officer
Raymond Guilbault, Chief Financial Officer
Susan McGrail, Vice President & General Manager
Joseph Maar, Vice President, Programming & Production and Executive Producer
Michael Hall, New Media Director
Jerry McAuliffe, Advertising Sales Director
Rick Booth, Creative Services Director
Peter Plaehn, Marketing Director
Donald J. Reilly, Business Affairs Director
John Slattery, Advertising & Promotion Director
Robert Whitelaw, Operations Director
Type of service: Pay, HD.
Satellites: AMC 11, transponder 14.
Sales representative: Group W Television Sales.
Operating hours/week: 168.
Operating areas: Connecticut (portions), Maine, Massachusetts, New Hampshire, Rhode Island & Vermont.
Uplink: Boston, MA.
Programming: Regional sports service offering Boston Bruins hockey, Boston Red Sox baseball, Hockey East college hockey, New England college football, basketball, soccer & lacrosse, Big Shot Candlepin Bowling, Beanpot Hockey Tournament, boxing, wrestling, outdoor specials, auto racing & sports specials.
Began: April 4, 1984.
Means of Support: Subscriber fees & advertising sales.
Total subscribers: 4,700,000.
Distribution method: Available to cable & satellite subscribers.
Scrambled signal: Yes. Equipment: VideoCipher II.
Ownership: Boston Red Sox; Boston Bruins.

NEW EVANGELIZATION TV
c/o Catholic Diocese of Brooklyn
1712 10th Ave
Brooklyn, NY 11215
Phones: 718-499-9705; 718-399-5900
Fax: 718-399-5957
Web Site: http://netny.net
M. J. Dempsey, Communications Director
Type of service: Regional.
Operating hours/week: 168.
Operating areas: Boroughs of Brooklyn & Queens, NY.
Programming: Daily mass & evening prayer, Christian music, Bible studies & shows on current events.
Began: March 15, 1988, as The Prayer Channel. Rebranded New Evangelization TV December 2008.
Total subscribers: 750,000.
Distribution method: Available to cable subscribers.
Scrambled signal: Yes.
Ownership: Office of Pastoral Communications, Catholic Diocese of Brooklyn.

NEWS 8 AUSTIN — See Time Warner Cable News (Austin).

NEWS 10 NOW — See Time Warner Cable News (Central NY).

NEWS 12 BRONX — See News 12 Interactive.
930 Soundview Ave
Bronx, NY 10473
Phone: 347-810-8013
E-mail: news12bx@news12.com
Web Site: http://bronx.news12.com
Type of service: Basic, HD.
Operating hours/week: 168.
Operating areas: New York.
Programming: Local news & information. Spanish-language on El Bronx en Espanol.
Began: June 1, 1998.
Means of Support: Advertising.
Total subscribers: 260,000.
Distribution method: Available to Optimum subscribers in the Bronx area.
Scrambled signal: Yes.
Ownership: Altice USA.

NEWS 12 THE BRONX EN ESPANOL — See News 12 Bronx
Operating areas: The Bronx, New York.
Programming: Spanish-language local news.
Began: 2011.
Distribution method: Available to Cablevision subscribers.

NEWS 12 BROOKLYN — See News 12 Interactive.
E 18th St & Ave Z
Brooklyn, NY 11235
Phones: 347-810-8013; 866-394-7236
E-mail: news12bkln@news12.com
Web Site: http://www.news12.com
Type of service: Basic, HD.
Operating hours/week: 168.
Operating areas: New York.
Programming: Local news & information.
Began: June 14, 2005.
Total subscribers: 400,000.
Distribution method: Available to Optimum & Time Warner subscribers in the Brooklyn area.
Scrambled signal: Yes.
Ownership: Altice USA.

NEWS 12 CONNECTICUT — See News 12 Interactive.
28 Cross St
Norwalk, CT 06851
Phone: 203-849-1321
Fax: 203-849-1327
E-mail: news12ct@news12.com
Web Site: http://www.news12.com
Type of service: Basic, HD.
Operating hours/week: 168.
Operating areas: Connecticut.
Programming: Local news & information.
Began: 1982 as a local origination channel. Became one of the News 12 channels on June 12, 1995.
Means of Support: Advertising.
Total subscribers: 200,000.
Distribution method: Available to Optimum subscribers in southwestern Connecticut.
Scrambled signal: Yes.
Ownership: Altice USA.

NEWS 12 HUDSON VALLEY — See News 12 Interactive.
235 W Nyack Rd
West Nyack, NY 10994
Phone: 842-624-8780
Fax: 845-735-1601
E-mail: news12hv@news12.com
Web Site: http://hudsonvalley.news12.com
Type of service: Basic, HD.
Operating hours/week: 168.
Operating areas: New York.
Programming: Local news & information.
Began: 2005.
Distribution method: Available to Optimum & Time Warner subscribers in Rockland & Orange Counties.
Scrambled signal: Yes.
Ownership: Altice USA.

NEWS 12 INTERACTIVE
One Media Crossways
Woodbury, NY 11797
Phone: 516-393-3638
Web Site: http://www.news12.com
Patrick Dolan, President, News 12 Networks
Steve Weinberg, Senior Vice President, Operations, News 12 Networks
Michael Felicetti, Vice President, Regional Sales, News 12 Networks
Deborah Koller-Feeny, Vice President, Marketing, News 12 Networks
David Kirschner, General Manager & News Director, News 12 Interactive
Type of service: Digital, streaming.
Operating areas: New Jersey, New York, Connecticut.
Programming: Interactive local news programming. Streaming available on mobile app.
Began: November 27, 2007.
Distribution method: Available to Optimum subscribers.
Scrambled signal: Yes.
Ownership: Altice USA.

NEWS 12 LONG ISLAND
One Media Crossways
Woodbury, NY 11797
Phone: 516-393-1200
Fax: 516-393-1456
E-mail: news12li@news12.com
Web Site: http://www.news12.com
Patrick Dolan, President, News 12 Networks & News Director, News 12 Long Island
Type of service: Basic.
Operating hours/week: 168.
Operating areas: New York.
Programming: Local news & information.
Began: December 15, 1986.
Means of Support: Advertising.
Total subscribers: 800,000.
Distribution method: Available to Optimum subscribers in Nassau & Suffolk Counties.
Scrambled signal: Yes.
Ownership: Altice USA.

NEWS 12 NEW JERSEY — See News 12 Interactive.
450 Raritan Center Pkwy
Edison, NJ 08837
Phone: 732-346-3200
Fax: 732-417-5155
E-mail: news12nj@news12.com
Web Site: http://www.newjersey.news12.com
Type of service: Basic.
Operating hours/week: 168.
Operating areas: New Jersey.
Programming: Local news & information. Spanish-language available on News 12 New Jersey en Espanol.
Began: March 25, 1996.
Means of Support: Advertising.
Total subscribers: 1,800,000.
Distribution method: Available to Comcast, Optimum, Time Warner & Service Electric subscribers in New Jersey.
Scrambled signal: Yes.
Ownership: Altice USA.

NEWS 12 NEW JERSEY EN ESPANOL — See News 12 New Jersey.
Operating areas: New Jersey.
Programming: Spanish-language local news.
Began: 2011.
Distribution method: Available to Cablevision subscribers.

NEWS 12 TRAFFIC & WEATHER —
See News 12 Interactive.
Type of service: Basic.
Operating hours/week: 168.
Operating areas: Connecticut, New Jersey & New York.
Programming: Local traffic, transit & weather.
Began: August 5, 1998, as News 12 Weather. Rebranded MSG MetroChannels in 198, then News 12 Traffic & Weather in 2005.
Means of Support: Advertising.
Total subscribers: 2,400,000.
Distribution method: Available to Cablevision subscribers.
Scrambled signal: Yes.
Ownership: Cablevision Systems Corp.

NEWS 12 WESTCHESTER — See News 12 Interactive.
6 Executive Plz
Yonkers, NY 10701
Phone: 914-378-8916
Fax: 914-378-8938
E-mail: news12wc@news12.com
Web Site: http://www.news12.com
Type of service: Basic, HD.
Operating hours/week: 168.
Operating areas: New York.
Programming: Local news & information.
Began: November 6, 1995.
Means of Support: Advertising.
Total subscribers: 240,000.
Distribution method: Available to Cablevision & Time Warner subscribers in Westchester County & Comcast subscribers in Putnam County.
Scrambled signal: Yes.
Ownership: Cablevision Systems Corp.

NEWS 14 CAROLINA
2505 Atlantic Ave
Ste 102
Raleigh, NC 27604-1411
Phones: 919-882-4040; 866-328-1414
Fax: 919-882-4045
E-mail: sales@news14.com
Web Site: http://news14.com
Rick Willis, News Director
Chuck Ward, Advertising Manager

Newsrooms:

CHARLOTTE: 316 E Morehead St, Ste 100, Charlotte, NC 28202. Phones: 704-973-5800; 866-249-6397. Fax: 704-731-2760.

GREENSBORO: 200 Centreport Dr, Ste 250, Greensboro, NC 27410. Phones: 336-856-9497; 866-907-9497. Fax: 336-662-0082.

NEWPORT: 500 Time Warner Dr, Newport, NC 28570. Phone: 866-963-9714. Fax: 252-223-6600.

WILMINGTON: 2321 Scientific Park Dr, Wilmington, NC 28405. Phone: 866-963-9714.
Type of service: Regional.
Operating areas: North Carolina.
Programming: 24-hour regional news in the Raleigh-Durham-Fayetteville / Charlotte / Greensboro-Winston-Salem-High Point markets.
Began: March 1, 2002.
Total subscribers: 485,000.
Distribution method: Available to Time Warner Cable subscribers.
Scrambled signal: Yes.
Ownership: Time Warner Cable.

NEWS CHANNEL 3 ANYTIME
c/o WREG
803 Channel 3 Dr
Memphis, TN 38103
Phone: 901-543-2333
Fax: 901-543-2198
Web Site: http://www.wreg.com
Ron Walter, General Manager

Pay TV & Satellite Services

FULLY SEARCHABLE • CONTINUOUSLY UPDATED • DISCOUNT RATES FOR PRINT PURCHASERS

For more information call **800-771-9202** or visit **www.warren-news.com**

Operating hours/week: 168.
Programming: Simulcasts & rebroadcasts of WREG's newscasts 24/7.
Began: January 1, 1992.
Scrambled signal: Yes.
Ownership: Partnership between WREG & Time Warner.

NEWS CHANNEL 5+
474 James Robertson Pkwy
Nashville, TN 37219
Phone: 615-248-5371
Fax: 615-248-5269
E-mail: plus@newschannel5.com
Web Site: http://www.newschannel5.com
Michelle Bonnett, Executive Director, News Channel 5+
Sandy Boonstra, News Director
Mark Binda, Programming Director
Natalie Ryman, Sales Manager
Programming: Local news, live call-in shows, weekly business show, public affairs; niche programs, outdoor show; consumer show.
Total subscribers: 500,000.
Ownership: Landmark Communications.

NEWSCHANNEL 8
1100 Wilson Blvd
6th Fl
Arlington, VA 22209
Phone: 703-236-9628
Fax: 703-236-2345
E-mail: mailus@news8.net
Web Site: http://www.news8.net
John D. Hillis, President
Wayne A. Lynch, Vice President, News & Programming
Dan Mellon, General Manager
Amy Wood, General Sales Manager
Jon DeFeo, News Director
Mitzi Freeberg, Human Resources Director
Eun-Hee Lee, Finance & Administration Director
Mark Olingy, Operations & Engineering Director
Robin Taylor, Marketing & Promotion Director
Type of service: Basic.
Operating hours/week: 168.
Operating areas: District of Columbia, Maryland & Virginia.
Programming: News coverage of the Washington, DC metropolitan area.
Began: October 7, 1991.
Means of Support: Advertising & subscriber fees.
Total subscribers: 2,000,000.
Distribution method: Available to cable subscribers.
Scrambled signal: Yes.
Ownership: Sinclair Broadcast Group Inc.

NEWSDAY TV
c/o Altice USA
1111 Stewart Ave
Bethpage, NY 11714
Phone: 866-575-8000
Web Site: http://www.cablevision.com
Operating hours/week: 168.
Programming: On-screen news subscription service and daily news shows.
Began: August 11, 2008.
Distribution method: Available to cable subscribers.
Scrambled signal: Yes.
Ownership: Altice USA.

NEWSMAX TV
PO Box 20989
West Palm Beach, FL 33416
Phones: 561-686-1165; 800-485-4350
Fax: 561-494-0922
Web Site: http://www.newsmaxtv.com
Christopher Ruddy, Chief Executive Officer, Newsmax Media

Branch Offices:
BOCA RATON: Newsmax Media Inc., 2200 NW Corporate Blvd, Boca Raton, FL 33431. Phone: 561-998-5336.
Type of service: Basic.
Operating hours/week: 168.
Operating areas: Available nationwide.
Programming: Independent news with a mainstream conservative tilt, while offering a balanced perspective and open to all points of view.
Began: June 16, 2014.
Means of Support: Advertising.
Total subscribers: 42,000,000.
Distribution method: Available to DirecTV, Dish & Verizon FiOS subscribers.
Scrambled signal: Yes.
Ownership: Newsmax Media Inc. NMI ownership: Christopher Ruddy 58%.

NEWSON
3390 Peachtree Rd
Ste 700
Atlanta, GA 30326
Phone: 800-385-6670
E-mail: info@newson.us
Web Site: http://newson.us/
Louis Gump, Chief Executive Officer
Craig Kirkland, Head of Product & Technology
Derek Van Nostran, Head of Marketing
Type of service: Basic.
Operating areas: Available nationwide.
Programming: Venture dedicated to distributing local news nationwide across multiple platforms.
Began: November 4, 2015.
Means of Support: Advertising.
Distribution method: Available on digital subchannels.
Ownership: The ABC Owned Television Station Group, Cox Media Group, Hearst Television, Hubbard Broadcasting, Media General & Raycom Media.

NEWS ON ONE - WOWT — See WOWT 6 News.

NEWS PLUS
The Free Range Group Inc.
628 Virginia Ave
Orlando, FL 32803
Phone: 407-896-7300
Fax: 407-896-7900
Timothy J. Brennan, President
Jeffrey B. Talbert, Vice President
Type of service: Text.
Satellites: Spacenet 3, transponder 4.
Operating hours/week: 168.
Programming: Full-color text and graphic news service, featuring world & national news, financial & business reports, sports scores & highlights; national & international weather conditions.
Began: January 1, 1985.
Means of Support: System pays according to number of subscribers.
Ownership: The Free Range Group Inc.

NEWSWATCH 15
1024 N Rampart St
New Orleans, LA 70116-2487
Phone: 504-529-4444
Fax: 504-529-6470
E-mail: tsmith@wwltv.com
Web Site: http://www.wwltv.com
Tod Smith, President & General Manager
Lourdes Keiffer, Sales Director
Type of service: Basic.
Sales representative: TeleRep Inc.
Operating hours/week: 168.
Operating areas: Louisiana.
Programming: Local news coverage every half hour.
Began: October 1, 1989.
Means of Support: Advertising.
Total subscribers: 289,530.
Distribution method: Available to cable subscribers.
Scrambled signal: Yes.
Ownership: A joint venture between WWL-TV & Cox Cable.

NEWSY
904 Elm St
Columbia, MO 65201
Phone: 513-977-3763
Web Site: http://www.newsy.com
Blake Sabatinelli, General Manager
Tony Brown, Vice President, Product
Christina Hartman, Vice President, News
Eric Svenson, Vice President, Marketing
Type of service: Basic.
Operating hours/week: 168.
Operating areas: Available in Ohio.
Programming: News network offering analysis and perspective on the dayÆs top stories, spanning world and national news, policy, culture, science and technology.
Began: Launched as OTT service in 2008, became available on cable September 2016.
Means of Support: Advertising.
Distribution method: Available to Cincinnati Bell Fioptics subscribers.
Ownership: The E. W. Scripps Co.

NEW TANG DYNASTY TV
229 W 28th St
Ste 700
New York, NY 10001
Phone: 212-736-8535
Fax: 212-736-8536
E-mail: feedback@ntdtv.com
Web Site: http://www.ntd.tv
Tang Zhong, President & Chief Executive Officer
Keran Feng, Senior Vice President, Marketing & Sales
Wanqing Huang, Senior Vice President, News
Samuel Zhou, Senior Vice President, External Affairs

Branch Offices:
CHICAGO: 234 W Cermak Rd, Ste 2F, Chicago, IL 60616. Phone: 312-791-9645. Fax: 312-791-9644.

LOS ANGELES: 9550 Flair Dr, Ste 112, El Monte, CA 91731. Phone: 626-443-2233. Fax: 626-443-2238.

SAN FRANCISCO: 1010 Corporation Way, Palo Alto, CA 94303. Phone: 408-656-6155. Fax: 408-904-5545.

WASHINGTON, DC: 8927 Shady Grove Ct, Gaithersburg, MD 20877. Phone: 202-449-9480. Fax: 202-449-8566.

CANADA: 420 Consumers Rd, Toronto M2J IP8, Canada. Phone: 416-787-1577. Fax: 416-787-6665.

TAIWAN: 6F-3 No. 9 Aiguo W Rd, Zhongzheng District, Taipei, Taiwan. Phone: 886-02-2268-3252. Fax: 886-02-2269-5556.
Type of service: Digital basic.
Satellites: Galaxy 19; EuroBird 9A; ST-2; KoreaSat 5; AMC10.
Operating hours/week: 168.
Operating areas: Nationwide.
Programming: Uncensored news, entertainment, health, travel, culture programming about China.
Began: February 15, 2002, in U.S.; July 2003 globally.
Total subscribers: 5,300,000.
Distribution method: Available to cable subscribers.
Scrambled signal: Yes.
Ownership: Not-for-profit 501 c (3).

NEW YORK 1 NOTICIAS — See Time Warner Cable News NY1.

NEW YORK NETWORK
Ste 146, S Concourse
Empire State Plz
Albany, NY 12223
Phone: 518-443-5333
Fax: 518-426-4198
E-mail: contact@nyn.suny.edu
Neil F. Satterly, Executive Director
Peg T. Palmiere, Finance Director
Steve Pingelski, Engineering Director
Dave Poplawski, Traffic Director
Type of service: Basic.
Programming: Provides live coverage of major events in Albany as well as instructional programming for educators, students & parents.
Scrambled signal: Yes.

NEW YORK RACING CHANNEL
PO Box 90
Jamaica, NY 11417
Phone: 718-641-4700
Fax: 516-488-6044
E-mail: nyra@nyrainc.com
Web Site: http://www.nyra.com
Rick Marks, Advertising
Bill Nader, Information Contact
Operating hours/week: 25.
Operating areas: Long Island & New York City.
Programming: Races, shows & payoffs.
Began: February 1, 1995.
Distribution method: Available to cable subscribers.
Scrambled signal: Yes.
Ownership: New York Racing Assn.

NEW YORK STATE ASSEMBLY RADIO TELEVISION
Room 102 LOB
Albany, NY 12248
Phone: 518-455-4557
Fax: 518-455-5136
E-mail: mergesm@assembly.state.ny.us
Web Site: http://www.assembly.state.ny.us
Type of service: Basic, streaming.
Operating hours/week: 168.

Pay TV & Satellite Services

Operating areas: New York.
Uplink: Fiber optic ring; internet connect.
Programming: Public affairs & gavel-to-gavel coverage of assembly sessions.
Began: January 1, 2002.
Distribution method: Available to Cablevision, Charter, Comcast, Mid-Hudson, MTC & Time Warner cable subscribers. Streaming available online.
Scrambled signal: Yes.
Ownership: New York State.

NFL NETWORK
280 Park Ave
New York, NY 10017
Phone: 212-450-2000
Fax: 212-681-7579
E-mail: jointheteam@nfl.com
Web Site: http://www.nfl.com/nflnetwork
Jordan Levin, Chief Content Officer, NFL
Brian Rolapp, Executive Vice President, Media, NFL
Ron Furman, Senior Vice President, Media Sales
Mark Quenzel, Senior Vice President, Programming & Production
Lorey Zlotnick, Senior Vice President, Marketing
Joel Chiodi, Vice President, Marketing & Promotions
Steven Graciano, Vice President, Marketing
Jennifer Love, Vice President, Coordinating Director
Dennis Johnson, Communications Director
Amanda Herald, Media Strategy & Business Development Director

Production Studio:
CULVER CITY: 10950 Washington Blvd, Ste 100, Culver City, CA 90232. Phone: 310-840-4635. Fax: 310-280-1132.
Type of service: Basic, HD.
Operating hours/week: 168.
Operating areas: Nationwide.
Programming: Dedicated solely to the NFL including original programming, NFL films & preseason games.
Began: November 4, 2003, NFL Network HD launched August 2004.
Total subscribers: 72,000,000.
Distribution method: Available to cable, IPTV & satellite subscribers.
Scrambled signal: Yes.
Ownership: National Football League.

NFL REDZONE — See NFL Network.
Web Site: http://www.nfl.com/redzonetv
Brian Rolapp, Executive Vice President
Type of service: Basic.
Operating areas: Nationwide.
Programming: Service that switches the viewer from game to game when a team is inside the 20-yard line, the 'Red Zone'.
Began: September 13, 2009.
Distribution method: Available to cable & satellite subscribers.
Scrambled signal: Yes.
Ownership: National Football League.

NHK WORLD PREMIUM — See NHK World TV.
Phone: 81-3-5458-6601
Fax: 81-3-5489-8401
Web Site: http://nhkworldpremium.com
Type of service: Pay.
Operating hours/week: 168.
Operating areas: Nationwide.
Programming: NHK news and information programs, dramas, children's, sports, entertainment, cultural and art programs.
Began: October 1, 1998.
Means of Support: Advertising and subscriber fees.

Distribution method: Available to cable & satellite subscribers.
Scrambled signal: Yes.

NHK WORLD TV
2-2-1 Jinnan
Shibuya-ku
Tokyo 150-8001
Japan
Fax: 81-3-5489-8401
E-mail: nhkworld@jibtv.com
Web Site: http://www3.nhk.or.jp/nhkworld/en/tv
Shigehiro Komaru, Chairman
Shigeo Fukuchi, President
Yoshinori Imai, Executive Vice President
Kenji Nagai, General Managing Director, Engineering
Shin Kanada, General Managing Director, Corporate Planning & Finance
Hyuge Hidemi, General Managing Director, Broadcasting
Type of service: Basic.
Satellites: Galaxy 13.
Operating hours/week: 168.
Operating areas: Nationwide.
Programming: English language news channel offering Japanese and Asian news and lifestyle programming.
Began: April 3, 1995, in Japan. Began August 5, 2013 in southern California.
Total subscribers: 260,000,000 (worldwide, 5600000 in southern California.).
Distribution method: Available over the air on digital sub-channels & to Time Warner & DISH Network subscribers.
Scrambled signal: Yes.
Ownership: Japan Broadcasting Corp. Japan International Broadcasting Inc. is distributor.

NHL CENTER ICE — See NHL Network.
Programming: Out-of-market NHL games.
Distribution method: Available to cable, IPTV & satellite subscribers.

NHL NETWORK
9 Channel Nine Ct
Scarborough, ON M1S 4B5
Canada
Phones: 416-384-5000; 800-559-2333
Fax: 416-384-4675
E-mail: info@nhlnetwork.ca
Web Site: http://www.nhlnetwork.com
Patti Fallick, Vice President, Media Operations & Planning
Jody Shapiro, Group Vice President, Television & Media Ventures

Branch Offices:
NEW YORK: NHL Network - USA, 1185 Avenue of the Americas, New York, NY 10020. Phone: 212-789-2000. Fax: 212-789-2020.
Type of service: Digital, HD, streaming, video on demand.
Satellites: Galaxy, transponder 15.
Operating hours/week: 168.
Programming: Offers viewers a 24-hour all-access pass to complete hockey coverage both on & off the ice, including live NHL games. The networks daily signature show - NHL On The Fly - offers fans exclusive live look-ins to NHL games, including goals, shootouts, features, interviews, pre- & post-game reports and expert analysis from a variety of hockey insiders & former players, plus special coverage from NHL events.
Began: 2001 in Canada. Began October 1, 2007 in U.S.
Total subscribers: 43,000,000.
Distribution method: Available to cable, IPTV & satellite subscribers. Streaming available

online. Video on demand available through participating providers.
Scrambled signal: Yes.
Ownership: A joint venture between National Hockey League (84.4%) & NBCUniversal (15.6%).

NICK 2 — See Nickelodeon.
Type of service: Digital.
Programming: Repackaged Eastern & Pacific time zone feeds. Also known as Nickelodeon/Nick@Nite (West).

NICK AT NITE — See Nickelodeon.
Programming: Popular sitcoms & original scripted series.
Began: July 1, 1985.
Total subscribers: 99,800,000.

NICKELODEON
c/o MTV Networks Inc.
1515 Broadway, 21st Fl
New York, NY 10036
Phone: 212-258-7500
Fax: 212-258-8329
Web Site: http://www.nick.com
Doug Cohn, Senior Vice President, Music Marketing & Talent, Nickelodeon, MTVN & Family Group
Kevin Ellman, Senior Vice President, Business & Legal Affairs, Nickelodeon, MTVN Kids & Family Group
Marianne Romano, Senior Vice President, Corporate Communications, Nickelodeon, MTVN & Family Group
VIACOM KIDS AND FAMILY GROUP:, .
Cyma Zarghami, President, Viacom Kids & Family Group
Sarah Kirshbaum Levy, Chief Operating Officer, Viacom Kids & Family Group
Lee Ann Chmielewski, Executive Vice President, Production, Viacom Kids & Family Group
Ron Geraci, Executive Vice President, Research & Planning, Viacom Kids & Family Group
Elizabeth Murray, Executive Vice President, Programming, Planning & Strategy, Viacom Kids & Family Group
Matthew Evans, Senior Vice President, Digital, Viacom Kids & Family Group
NICKELODEON GROUP:, .
Sharon Cohen, Executive Vice President, Partnership Marketing, Nickelodeon Group
Dan Martinsen, Executive Vice President, Corporate Communications, Nickelodeon Group
Anne Mullen, Executive Vice President, Creative Strategy, Nickelodeon Group
Andra Shapiro, Executive Vice President, Business Affairs & General Counsel, Nickelodeon Group
Dion Vlachos, Executive Vice President, Retail Sales, Marketing & Publishing, Nickelodeon Group
Andrea Fasulo, Executive Vice President, Retail & Movie Marketing, Nickelodeon Group
NICKELODEON :, .
Pam Kaufman, President & Chief Marketing Officer, Consumer Products, Nickelodeon
Keith Dawkins, Executive Vice President, Nicktoons & TeenNick
Marva Smalls, Executive Vice President, Public Affairs & Chief of Staff, Nickelodeon
Lauren Buerger, Senior Vice President, New Business Development, Nickelodeon
Damon Burrell, Senior Vice President, Consumer Marketing & Advertising, Nickelodeon
Jennifer Caveza, Senior Vice President, Toys & Business Development, Nickelodeon
Sergio Cuan, Senior Vice President, Creative Director, Nickelodeon

Jaime Dictenberg, Senior Vice President, Consumer Marketing, Nickelodeon
Jennifer Dodge, Senior Vice President, West Coast Development & Production, Nickelodeon Preschool
Jamie Drew, Senior Vice President, Strategy & Business Development, Nickelodeon
Karen Driscoll, Senior Vice President, Marketing & Strategic Planning, Nickelodeon
Matthew Duntemann, Senior Vice President, Creative Director & Brand Design, Nickelodeon
Lauren Elchoness, Senior Vice President, Integrated Marketing, Nickelodeon
Marc Epstein, Senior Vice President, Sports Recreation & New Business Integrated Marketing, Nickelodeon
Nancy Galeota, Senior Vice President, Preschool Current Series, Nickelodeon
John Paul Geurts, Senior Vice President, Experience Design, Nickelodeon
Jeffrey Imberman, Senior Vice President, Sales & Marketing, Nickelodeon
Tony Maxwell, Senior Vice President, Promotional Strategy & Creative, Nickelodeon
Sarah Noonan, Senior Vice President, Live Action Content & On-Air Promotions Creative Director, Nickelodeon
Bronwen O'Keefe, Senior Vice President, Content Strategy, Nickelodeon
Matthew Perreault, Senior Vice President, Nickelodeon Preschool Brand Creative
Antonious Porch, Senior Vice President & Deputy General Counsel, Digital Media, Nickelodeon
Jon Roman, Senior Vice President, Boys Toys & Business Development, Nickelodeon
Jason Root, Senior Vice President, Digital, Nick.com & Nickatnite.com
Jay Schmalholz, Senior Vice President, Live Event Television, Nickelodeon
Russ Spina, Senior Vice President, Character Art, Illustration & Media Product Design, Nickelodeon
Eric Squires, Senior Vice President, Creative Operations, Nickelodeon
Kristi Wasmer, Senior Vice President, Retail Sales, Nickelodeon Consumer Products
Megan Casey, Vice President, Current Series, Nickelodeon
Audrey Diehl, Vice President, Animation Development, Nickelodeon
Dave Perry, Vice President, Social Media
Claudia Spinelli, Vice President, Current Series, Nickelodeon

Branch Offices:
CENTRAL: 303 E Wacker Dr, Ste 428, Chicago, IL 60601. Phone: 312-565-2300.

EASTERN: 1775 Broadway, 4th Floor, New York, NY 10036. Phone: 212-713-6400. Amy Hyland, Executive Vice President, Ad Sales, New York, Nickelodeon Group; Jake Piasecki, Senior Vice President, Ad Sales, New York City.

SOUTHEASTERN: 3399 Peachtree Rd, Ste 990, Atlanta, GA 30326. Phone: 404-841-3090.

WESTERN: 10 Universal City Plz, 30th Fl, Universal City, CA 91608. Phone: 818-505-7800.
Type of service: Basic, HD, streaming & video on demand.
Satellites: Galaxy III, transponder 19 & 22.
Operating hours/week: 168.
Operating areas: Nationwide.
Uplink: Network Operations Center, Smithtown, NY.

Pay TV & Satellite Services

Programming: Age specific programming for pre-schoolers through teenagers. NickMusic offers music videos for kids.
Began: April 1, 1979, On September 9, 2016, MTV Hits became NickMusic.
Means of Support: Advertising.
Total subscribers: 101,400,000.
Distribution method: Available to cable, IPTV & satellite providers. Streaming available online & though app. Video on demand available through participating providers.
Scrambled signal: Yes. Equipment: VideoCipher II.
Ownership: Viacom Inc.

NICK EN ESPANOL — See Nickelodeon.
Began: 2005.

NICK JR. — See Nickelodeon.
Web Site: http://www.nickjr.com
Type of service: Basic, digital, HD, streaming.
Satellites: EchoStar.
Operating hours/week: 168.
Programming: Educational children's programming. Streaming available though Noggin app.
Began: February 2, 1999, as Noggin. Rebranded Nick Jr. on September 28, 2009. The Noggin app began March 5, 2015.
Means of Support: Merchandise sales.
Total subscribers: 72,700,000.
Distribution method: Available to cable, IPTV & satellite subscribers.
Scrambled signal: Yes.

NICKMUSIC — See Nickelodeon.
Operating hours/week: 168.
Programming: Top 40 hits for kids including artist-hosted programming blocks, concerts & series.
Began: May 1, 2002, as MTV Hits. Rebranded NickMusic September 9, 2016.
Total subscribers: 28,000,000.

NICKTOONS — See Nickelodeon.
Web Site: http://nicktoons.nick.com
Type of service: Digital.
Operating hours/week: 168.
Programming: Animated series. Spanish-language available on Nicktoons en Espanol.
Began: May 1, 2002, Nicktoons en Espanol began February 4, 2013.
Total subscribers: 57,600,000.
Distribution method: Available to cable, IPTV & satellite subscribers.
Scrambled signal: Yes.

NICKTOONS EN ESPANOL — See Nicktoons.

NIPPON GOLDEN NETWORK
2454 S Beretania St
Ste 301
Honolulu, HI 96826
Phone: 808-538-1966
Fax: 808-537-2024
Dr. Dennis M. Ogawa, President

Branch Office:
JAPAN: Higashi Ginza Bldg No. 9-18 Ginza, 3-Chome, Chuo-Ku, Tokyo, Japan.
Type of service: Digital.
Operating hours/week: 168.
Operating areas: Hawaii.
Programming: Japanese dramas, musical & variety shows, documentaries, educational programs & live sumo tournaments.
Began: January 1, 1982.
Means of Support: Subscriber fees & advertising.
Total subscribers: 16,762.

Distribution method: Available to Ocean Time Warner subscribers.
Scrambled signal: Yes.
Ownership: A joint venture between Nippon Hawaii Cablevision, The Seiyu Ltd., Dentsu Inc. & Television Tokyo Ltd.

NIPPON GOLDEN NETWORK 2 — See Nippon Golden Network.
Programming: Japanese programs from NHK via TV Japan.

NIPPON GOLDEN NETWORK 3 — See Nippon Golden Network.
Programming: Subtitled classic & modern Japanese movies.

NJTV
PO Box 5776
Englewood, NJ 07631
Phones: 609-777-0031; 800-882-6622
E-mail: answers@njtvonline.org
Web Site: http://www.njtvonline.org
Neal Shapiro, President & Chief Executive Officer, WNET
John Servidio, General Manager
Type of service: Basic.
Operating areas: New Jersey, New York & Pennsylvania.
Programming: Offers a lineup of local arts & culture and news & public affiars programming.
Began: 1971 NJN–New Jersey Network. Rebranded as NJTV on July 1, 2011.
Distribution method: Available to cable subscribers.
Scrambled signal: No.
Ownership: Thirteen/WNET, through the non-profit wholly-owned subsidiary Public Media NJ Inc.

NOGGIN — See Nick Jr.

NOIRETV AFRICA
3509 Connecticut Ave NW
Ste 1010
Washington, DC 20008
Phones: 202-559-8295; 202-681-4012
E-mail: partnerships@caspianmedia.com
Web Site: http://www.noiretv.com
Emeka Iwukemjika, Co-Founder
Dokun Adewole, Co-Founder
Type of service: Pay.
Operating hours/week: 168.
Operating areas: Connecticut, New Jersey & New York.
Programming: Provides viewers access to contemporary Nollywood film library, plus maintains a dedicated broadcast schedule of favorite African movies, series, reality shows, comedies, music videos and sports.
Began: October 10, 2011.
Means of Support: Advertising, subscriber fees.
Distribution method: Available to Cablevision Systems subscribers.
Ownership: Caspen Media.

NONSTOP NETWORK — See COZI TV.

NORTHEAST OHIO NETWORK — See Time Warner Cable SportsChannel (Northeast Ohio).

NORTH SHORE-LIJ HEALTH TV
125 Community Dr
Great Neck, NY 11021
Phones: 516-465-2600; 516-465-2640
E-mail: tlynam@nshs.edu
Web Site: https://www.northwell.edu/about/news/videos/focus-onhealth-tv

Michael Dowling, Chief Executive Officer
Terry Lynam, Vice President, Public Relations
Michelle Pinto, Media Relations Director
Type of service: Video on demand.
Operating areas: Long Island, the Bronx, Brooklyn, Westchester, Lower Hudson Valley, New Jersey and Connecticut.
Programming: Offers timely, vital health and wellness information from the North Shore-Long Island Jewish Health System.
Began: January 11, 2012.
Total subscribers: 3,000,000.
Distribution method: Available to Cablevision System subscribers.
Scrambled signal: No.
Ownership: North Shore-LIJ Health System.

NORTHWEST CABLE NEWS
333 Dexter Ave N
Seattle, WA 98109
Phone: 206-448-3600
Fax: 206-448-3797
E-mail: nwwebmaster@nwcn.com
Web Site: http://www.nwcn.com
Jim Rose, President & General Manager
Pam Guinn, General Sales Manager
Larry Blackstock, Operations Director
Kathryn Skinner, Marketing & Affiliate Relations Director
Guy Barbaro, Controller

Branch Offices:
BOISE: 5407 Fairview Ave, Boise, ID 83706. Phone: 208-321-5680.

PORTLAND: 1501 SW Jefferson St, Portland, OR 97201. Phone: 503-226-5615.

SPOKANE: 4103 S Regal St, Spokane, WA 99203. Phone: 509-838-7387.
Type of service: Basic.
Satellites: Satcom C-3.
Sales representative: National Cable Advertising Inc.
Operating areas: Alaska, California, Idaho, Montana, Oregon & Washington.
Programming: Regional all-news channel.
Began: December 18, 1995.
Total subscribers: 2,100,000.
Distribution method: Available to cable subscribers.
Scrambled signal: Yes.
Ownership: Belo Corp.

THE NOW NETWORK
133 Feritti Dr
Austin, TX 78734-5075
Phones: 864-498-6423; 800-409-5171
E-mail: programming@thenownetwork.org
Web Site: http://www.thenownetwork.org
Karen Simmons, Founder
Type of service: Basic, over the air, streaming.
Operating hours/week: 168.
Operating areas: Nationwide.
Programming: Religious programming.
Means of Support: Donations.
Distribution method: Available over the air on digital sub-channels. Streaming available online & mobile.
Scrambled signal: Yes.
Ownership: The NOW Network.

Access the most current data instantly
FREE TRIAL @
ADVANCED TVFactbook
TELCO/IPTV • CABLE TV • TV STATIONS
www.warren-news.com/factbook.htm

NRB NETWORK
404 BNA Dr
Bldg 200 Ste 400
Nashville, TN 37217
Phone: 615-866-2702
Fax: 615-348-1412
Web Site: http://www.nrbnetwork.tv
Troy A Miller, President & Chief Executive Officer
Allen Beckner, Channel Distribution Director
Tina Givens, Marketing Manager

Branch Offices:
WASHINGTON, DC: 9510 Technology Dr, Manassas, VA 20110. Phone: 703-330-7000. Fax: 703-330-7100.
Type of service: Basic.
Operating hours/week: 168.
Operating areas: Available nationwide.
Programming: Christian television that offers diverse lineup ranging from preaching and teaching programs on Sunday to shows about cooking, financial education, fitness, public policy, music, sports, travel, science & history the rest of the week.
Began: December 21, 2005.
Means of Support: Advertising & contributions.
Distribution method: Available to DirecTV subscribers.
Scrambled signal: Yes.
Ownership: National Religious Broadcasters Association.

NTDTV — See New Tang Dynasty TV.

NTN24
Canal Latino International Latino
Americas Av 65-82
Bogata, DC
Colombia
Phone: 571-426-9292
Fax: 571-426-9300
Web Site: http://www.ntn24.com
John de Armas, Vice President, World Direct, DirecTV
Operating hours/week: 168.
Operating areas: Nationwide.
Programming: 24-hour Spanish language international news channel.
Began: November 3, 2008, in Colombia. Began October 26, 2009, in the U.S.
Total subscribers: 8,500,000 (worldwide).
Distribution method: Available to DirecTV subscribers through their Mas service.
Scrambled signal: Yes.
Ownership: Radio Cadena Nacional. Majority stockholder Carlos Ardila Lulle. Distributed in the U.S. by Condista.

NTN BUZZTIME
2231 Rutherford Rd
Ste 200
Carlsbad, CA 92008
Phone: 760-438-7400
Fax: 760-438-3505
E-mail: kendra.berger@ntnbuzztime.com
Web Site: http://www.buzztime.com
Kendra Berger, Chief Financial Officer
Vladimir Edelman, Chief Content Officer
Christopher George, Chief Information Officer
Type of service: Pay.

2017 Edition E-67

Pay TV & Satellite Services

Programming: Interactive games & shows across many different platforms.
Began: January 1, 1985.
Total subscribers: 30,000 (Figure excludes satellite dish subscribers).
Distribution method: Available to cable & satellite subscribers.
Scrambled signal: Yes.

NTV AMERICA
One Marine Plz
Ste 305
North Bergen, NJ 07047
Phones: 201-556-8454; 201-965-9026
E-mail: info@ntvusa.net
Web Site: http://www.ntvamerica.ntv.ru
Programming: Russian-language news & entertainment.
Began: September 25, 2002.
Distribution method: Available to cable & satellite subscribers.
Scrambled signal: Yes.

NUVOTV — See Fuse.

NY1 — See Time Warner Cable News NY1.

NY1 NOTICIAS — See Time Warner Cable News NY1 Notices.

NY1 RAIL & ROAD
75 Ninth Ave
New York, NY 10011
Phone: 212-379-3311
Web Site: http://www.ny1.com/nyc/all-boroughs
Type of service: Regional basic, streaming.
Operating hours/week: 168.
Operating areas: New York.
Programming: Real-time traffic & commuter information for the metropolitan area.
Began: August 18, 2010.
Distribution method: Available to Time Warner cable subscribers. Streaming available online & through app.
Ownership: Time Warner Cable.

OASIS TV
2029 Century Park E
Ste 1400
Los Angeles, CA 90067
Phone: 310-553-4300
E-mail: info@watchotv.com
Web Site: http://www.otvlive.tv
Robert Schnitzer, President & Chief Executive Officer
Gerald Levin, Senior Advisor, Chairman-elect
Reinita Susman, Supervising Producer
Diannah Morgan, Webmaster/IT Director
Type of service: Basic, streaming, video on demand.
Operating areas: Nationwide.
Uplink: Avail-TVN.
Programming: Health & healing, metaphysics & spirituality, earth & environment, world peace & current affairs, visionary art & personal growth. Focuses on the following topics: personal growth, non-religious spirituality, alternative medicine, fitness, current affairs, green technology, love, sex and relationships.
Began: September 1, 1997.
Means of Support: Advertising sales & affiliate fees.
Total subscribers: 10,000,000.
Distribution method: Available to cable, IPTV & satellite subscribers. Streaming available online & mobile.
Scrambled signal: Yes.
Ownership: Elation Media.

OC 16
c/o Oceanic Time Warner Cable
200 Akamainui St
Mililani, HI 96789
Phone: 808-643-2100
Fax: 808-625-5888
Web Site: http://www.oc16.tv
Dave Vinton, Sports Director
Lianne Killion, Senior Programming Manager
Type of service: Regional.
Operating hours/week: 168.
Operating areas: Hawaii.
Programming: Offers a mix of locally produced shows that feature the unique people and places in Hawaii.
Began: January 1, 1989.
Distribution method: Available to Time Warner Cable subscribers.
Scrambled signal: Yes.
Ownership: Time Warner Cable.

OCEAN STATE NETWORKS
c/o WJAR
23 Kenney Dr
Cranston, RI 02920
Phone: 401-455-9100
E-mail: kreis@wjar.com
John Wolfe, Vice President, Government & Public Relations, Cox Communications
Eric Wagner, Public Relations Manager, Cox Communications
Kim Reis, Digital Media Marketing Director, WJAR

Branch Offices:
WEST WARWICK: Cox Communications Inc., 9 James P Murphy Hwy, West Warwick, RI 02893. Phone: 401-615-9100. Fax: 401-615-1581.
Type of service: Regional.
Operating areas: Rhode Island.
Programming: Offers sporting events from the Big East Conference, Providence College and the U of Rhode Island, Pawtucket Red Sox baseball plus coverage of Rhode Island Interscholastic League Championships and other local high school games.
Began: May 2, 2012.
Means of Support: Advertising.
Distribution method: Available to Cox Communications digital cable system subscribers.
Scrambled signal: No.
Ownership: A joint venture between Cox Communications Inc. & WJAR.

OC SPORTS
200 Akamainui St
Mililani, HI 96789-3999
Phone: 808-625-2100
Fax: 808-625-5888
Web Site: http://www.oceanic.com
Bob Barlow, President, Oceanic Time Warner Cable
Jim Donovan, Athletic Director, U of Hawaii
Type of service: Regional.
Operating areas: Hawaii.
Programming: Channel dedicated to U of Hawaii athletics.
Began: August 19, 2011.
Total subscribers: 400,000.
Distribution method: Available to Time Warner Cable subscribers.
Scrambled signal: Yes.
Ownership: Time Warner Cable.

ODU-TV
Intercollegiate Athletics
Jim Jarrett Athletic Administration Bldg
Norfolk, VA 23529-0201
Phone: 757-683-3373
E-mail: t2alexan@odu.edu
Debbie White, Senior Associate Athletic Director
Chuck Gray, General Manager, ODU Sports Properties
Ted Alexander, Broadcasting Director
Type of service: Video on demand.
Operating areas: Available in Hampton Roads, Northern Virginia and Roanoke.
Programming: Provides weekly highlight packages of all ODU sports action, replays and interviews with players and coaching staff.
Began: September 9, 2011.
Distribution method: Available to Cox Communications subscribers.
Scrambled signal: Yes.
Ownership: Old Dominion University.

OHIO CHANNEL
Ohio Government Telecommunications
Ohio Statehouse, Room 013
Columbus, OH 43215
Phones: 614-728-9814; 614-728-9791
E-mail: helpdesk@ohiochannel.org; dan@ohiochannel.org
Web Site: http://www.ohiochannel.org
Dan Shellenbarger, Executive Director
Type of service: Basic, streaming.
Operating hours/week: 42.
Programming: Public affairs, documentaries & gavel-to-gavel coverage of legislative session.
Began: January 1, 1996.
Total subscribers: 2,000,000.
Distribution method: Available to cable subscribers. Streaming available online.
Scrambled signal: Yes.

OKSTATE.TV
Athletics Center
Oklahoma State University
Stillwater, OK 74078
Phone: 405-744-7714
Fax: 405-744-7754
Web Site: http://www.okstate.com/sports/2015/8/6/live.aspx
Mike Holder, Athletics Director
Kevin Klintworth, Associate Athletic Director & Media Relations
Jeff Naple, Video Coordinator (Coaches)
C. J. Lickert, Media Requests
Type of service: Video on demand.
Operating areas: Oklahoma.
Programming: Game discussions with OSU football coach Bob Stoops, player interviews and profiles plus press conferences.
Began: September 16, 2011.
Means of Support: Subscriber fees.
Distribution method: Available to Cox Communications subscribers.
Scrambled signal: Yes.
Ownership: Oklahoma State University.

OLELO
1122 Mapunapuna St
Honolulu, HI 96819
Phone: 808-834-0007
Fax: 808-836-2546
E-mail: olelo@olelo.org
Web Site: http://www.olelo.org
Roy Amemiya Jr., President & Chief Executive Officer
Angela Angel, Communications & Media Services Director
Chris Lamb, Technology Services Director
Type of service: Basic.
Operating hours/week: 168.
Operating areas: Oahu, HI.
Programming: Public, educational & government access.
Began: January 1, 1991.
Means of Support: Cable franchise fees.
Total subscribers: 235,000.
Distribution method: Available to cable subscribers.
Scrambled signal: Yes.
Ownership: Non-profit organization.

OLE TV
PO Box 140567
Coral Gables, FL 33134
Phone: 305-570-9044
Fax: 305-856-3366
E-mail: info@oletv.tv
Web Site: http://www.oletv.tv
Jose Elejalde, President
Joseph Roses, Secretary
Gregory Pischner, Production
Amanda Guevara, Programming
Operating areas: South Florida.
Programming: 24/7 family-oriented, Hispanic arts, cultural and entertainment network.
Began: June 1, 1994.
Distribution method: Available to AT&T U-Verse & Charter subscribers.
Scrambled signal: Yes.

ONCE TV MEXICO — See Canal Once.

ONE AMERICA NEWS NETWORK
c/o Herring Broadcasting Inc.
4757 Morena Blvd
San Diego, CA 92117
Phone: 858-270-6900
Fax: 858-270-6901
Web Site: http://www.oneamericanews.com
Robert Herring Sr., Chief Executive Officer
Charles Herring, President
Sarah Nunez, Press Coordinator
Type of service: Basic.
Operating hours/week: 168.
Operating areas: Nationwide.
Programming: 24-hour news that appeals to viewers with self-described independent, conservative & libertarian values.
Began: July 4, 2013.
Means of Support: Advertising.
Total subscribers: 20,000,000.
Distribution method: Available to cable & IPTV subscribers.
Scrambled signal: Yes.
Ownership: Herring Broadcasting Inc.

ONE CARIBBEAN TELEVISION
3514 State St
Erie, PA 16508
Phone: 814-455-7575
E-mail: mwalton@onecaribbeantelevision.com
Web Site: http://www.onecaribbeantelevision.com
John Christianson, General Manager
Paula Randolph, Traffic Manager
Type of service: Premium.
Operating hours/week: 168.
Operating areas: Washington, DC; Chicago, IL; Boston, MA; New York, NY; Lehigh Valley & Philadelphia, PA.
Programming: Caribbean news, weather, sports, business, travel and entertainment.
Began: January 1, 2002, as Caribbean Weather Channel. Rebranded One Caribbean Television.
Means of Support: Advertising & subscriber fees.
Distribution method: Available to RCN subscribers.
Scrambled signal: Yes.
Ownership: Lilly Broadcasting LLC.

ONESPORTSPLUS
6125 Airport Fwy
Ste 202
Fort Worth, TX 76117-5396
Phone: 817-546-1400
Fax: 682-647-0756
E-mail: general@b-2networks.com

Preston Bornman, President, One Media Corp. Inc.
Bruce LeVine, Collegiate Programming Director, OneSportsPLUS.com
Type of service: Pay per view.
Operating areas: Nationwide.
Programming: More than 5,000 live and exclusive sporting events from over 100 U.S. colleges, 70 U.S. professional teams, and the top professional leagues in Europe and Asia.
Means of Support: Subscriber fees.
Distribution method: Available to cable subscribers.
Scrambled signal: Yes.
Ownership: One Media Corp. Inc.

ONE WORLD SPORTS
250 Harbor Dr
4th Fl
Stamford, CT 06902
Phone: 203-883-4493
E-mail: pr@oneworldsports.com
Web Site: http://www.oneworldsports.com
Alexander Brown, President & Chief Executive Officer
Ricardo Venegas, Chief Financial Officer
Randy Brown, Executive Vice President, Distribution
Joel Feld, Executive Vice President, Programming & Production
John Vilade, Executive Vice President, Ad Sales
Kristen McNeill, Senior Vice President, Western Division
Mark Romano, Senior Vice President, Eastern Division
Beth Sanford, Senior Vice President, Marketing
Todd Myers, Vice President, Programming, Acquisitions & Development
Rachel Gary, Media Strategy & Communications Director
Type of service: Digital basic, pay, HD.
Operating areas: Available nationwide.
Programming: Global sports.
Began: August 1, 2013, One World Sports HD began August 3, 2013.
Means of Support: Subscriber fees.
Total subscribers: 30,000,000 (worldwide).
Distribution method: Available to Charter Communications, Cablevision Optimum, DISH Network, Google Fiber, Mediacom Communications, NCTC (select systems), RCN & Verizon FiOS subscribers.
Scrambled signal: Yes.
Ownership: One Media Corp. Inc.

ORBITA TV
c/o Olympusat
560 Village Blvd, Ste 250
West Palm Beach, FL 33409
Phone: 561-684-5657
Fax: 561-684-9690
E-mail: info@olympusat.com
Web Site: http://www.orbitatv.com; http://www.olympusat.com
Programming: General entertainment geared towards Central American families in the U.S.
Scrambled signal: Yes.
Ownership: Distributed in the U.S. by Olympusat.

OREGON PUBLIC AFFAIRS NETWORK
PO Box 508
Salem, OR 97308
Phone: 541-737-2723
Fax: 541-737-3453
E-mail: operations@opan.org
Web Site: http://www.nwctv.com/OPAN/www.opan.org/index.html

Type of service: Basic, streaming.
Operating hours/week: 10.
Operating areas: Oregon.
Programming: Coverage of public affairs related programming, legislative committees, city clubs, university forums & debates.
Total subscribers: 4,000,000.
Distribution method: Available to cable subscribers. Streaming available to AT&T U-Verse & Comcast subscribers.
Scrambled signal: Yes.

OUI TV — See Afrotainment Plus.
36-01 37th Ave
Long Island, NY 11101
Phone: 407-287-4127
E-mail: infos@afrotainment.us
Web Site: http://www.afrotainment.tv
Type of service: Pay.
Operating areas: Nationwide.
Programming: French-language African sitcoms & drama series.
Distribution method: Available to DISH Network subscribers.
Ownership: Soundview Africa.

OUTDOOR CHANNEL
1000 Chopper Circle
Denver, CO 80204
Phones: 951-699-6991; 800-770-5750
Fax: 951-699-6313
E-mail: info@outdoorchannel.com
Web Site: http://www.outdoorchannel.com
Matt Hutchins, President & Chief Executive Officer, Kroenke Sports & Entertainment
Scott Long, President, Kroenke Sports & Entertainment Media Ventures
Jim Liberatore, President & Chief Executive Officer
Todd Merkow, President, Digital Media
Doug Langston, Chief Accounting Officer
Tom Allen, Executive Vice President & Chief Financial & Operating Officer
David Bolls, Executive Vice President, Business & Legal and Deputy General Counsel
Jason Brist, Executive Vice President, Advertising Sales
Greg Harrigan, Executive Vice President, Advertising Sales
Thomas H. Massie, Executive Vice President & Secretary
Steve Smith, Executive Vice President, Affiliate Sales & Marketing
Stephen Stieneker, Executive Vice President
Jeff Wayne, Executive Vice President, Programming
John Fabian, Senior Vice President, Advertising Sales, Eastern Region
Bill Osborne, Senior Vice President, Marketing
James Alexander, Vice President, Consumer Insights & Analytics
Chris Chaffin, Vice President, Public Relations & Conservation
Mark C. Corcoran, Vice President, Ad Sales
Michael Kim, Vice President, Affiliate Sales, Western Region
Scott Long, Vice President, Finance, Media
Scott Mann, Vice President, Outdoor Affinity Marketing
Paul Weaver, Vice President, Operations
Daniel Sloane, Regional Vice President, Central
Joe Stretesky, Regional Vice President, Western
Mike Kozdrey, Engineering Manager
Catherine Lee, General Counsel
Type of service: Basic, digital, HD, streaming video on demand.
Satellites: Galaxy 10-R, transponder 24.
Operating hours/week: 168.
Operating areas: Nationwide.

Programming: Focuses on fishing, hunting & all forms of outdoor activities & water sports.
Began: June 1, 1993, Outdoor Channel HD began June 28, 2010.
Means of Support: Advertising.
Total subscribers: 39,100,000 (8,150,000 Outdoor Channel HD subscribers.).
Distribution method: Available to cable, IPTV & satellite subscribers. Streaming available online.
Scrambled signal: Yes.
Ownership: Kroenke Sports & Entertainment.

OUTER MAX — See Cinemax.
c/o Home Box Office
1100 Avenue of the Americas
New York, NY 10036
Phone: 212-512-1000
Fax: 212-512-1166
Type of service: Pay, HD.
Operating hours/week: 168.
Operating areas: Available nationwide.
Programming: Sci-fi, horror & fantasy movies.
Began: May 1, 2001.
Scrambled signal: Yes.
Ownership: Home Box Office Inc., a division of Time Warner.

OUTSIDE TELEVISION
33 Riverside Ave
4th Fl
Westport, CT 06880
Phone: 203-221-9240
Fax: 203-221-9283
E-mail: info@outsidetv.com
Web Site: http://www.outsidetelevision.com
Mark Burchill, Chief Executive Officer
Jeff Dumais, Senior Vice President, Television Properties
Rob Faris, Senior Vice President, Programming & Production
Dennis Gillespie, Senior Vice President, Distribution
Carmine Parisi, Senior Vice President, Sales
Christopher Crowley, Executive Producer

Branch Offices:
NEW YORK: 420 Lexington Ave, Ste 440, New York, NY 10170. Phone: 212-922-2885. Fax: 212-922-1122.

PORTLAND: 7 Custom House St, Portland, ME 04101. Phone: 207-772-5000. Fax: 207-775-3658.
Type of service: Basic.
Operating areas: Available nationwide.
Programming: Active lifestyle entertainment for those passionate about the outdoors.
Began: January 1, 1985, as Resort Sports Network. Rebranded Outside Television in 1994. It became an independent service in 2011.
Means of Support: Advertising.
Total subscribers: 40,000,000.
Distribution method: Available to Comcast cable system subscribers.
Scrambled signal: Yes.

OUTV
Gaylord College of Journalism & Mass Communication

Pay TV & Satellite Services

FULLY SEARCHABLE • CONTINUOUSLY UPDATED • DISCOUNT RATES FOR PRINT PURCHASERS
For more information call **800-771-9202** or visit **www.warren-news.com**

395 W Lindsey
Norman, OK 73019
Phones: 405-325-0121; 405-325-2830
E-mail: tv@ou.edu
Web Site: http://www.ou.edu/tv
Lynn Franklin, Station Manager
Zach Sepanik, Assistant Station Manager
Malik Carter, Remote & Web Director
Hannah Jamil, Music Director
Mary Ann Maestre, Promotions Director
Elena Montes, Music Director
Doug Wilson, Operations Manager
Type of service: Video on demand.
Operating areas: Oklahoma.
Programming: Student run service offering music videos, sports and entertainment.
Began: September 16, 2011.
Total subscribers: 633,000.
Distribution method: Available to Cox Communications & AT&T U-verse subscribers.
Scrambled signal: Yes.
Ownership: Oklahoma University.

OVATION
2850 Ocean Park Blvd
#225
Santa Monica, CA 90405
Phone: 310-430-7575
E-mail: eforman@ovationtv.com
Web Site: http://www.ovationtv.com
Ken Solomon, Chairman
Charles Segars, Chief Executive Officer
Phil Gilligan, Chief Financial Officer
Rob Radner, General Counsel
Liz Janneman, Executive Vice President, Ad Sales
John Malkin, Executive Vice President, Content Distribution
Rob Canter, Senior Vice President, Production & Creative Services
Mike Kim, Senior Vice President, Content Distribution
Jodi Lipe, Senior Vice President, Marketing
David Wilderoe, Senior Vice President, Marketing & On-Air Promotions
Scott Woodward, Senior Vice President, Programming & Production
Jason Black, Vice President, Original Programming & Head of Digital Media
Lori Hall, Vice President, Program Scheduling
Ash Steffy, Vice President, Creative Services
Sonia Tower, Vice President, Community Relations
Ed Forman, Ad Sales Development & Planning Director
Type of service: Basic, digital, HD, video on demand & streaming.
Satellites: Galaxy VII, transponder 13.
Operating hours/week: 140.
Operating areas: Available nationwide.
Programming: Visual & performing arts.
Began: April 21, 1996, Re-launched June 20, 2007. Rebranded Ovation on March 1, 2010. Ovation HD began July 2010.
Means of Support: Advertising.
Total subscribers: 55,000,000.
Distribution method: Available to cable, IPTV & satellite subscribers.
Scrambled signal: Yes. Equipment: DigiCipher II.

Pay TV & Satellite Services

Ownership: A joint venture between Hubbard Media Group, Weinstein Co., Corporate Partners II, Perry Capital & Arcadia Investment Partners.

OWN: OPRAH WINFREY NETWORK
1041 North Formosa Ave
West Hollywood, CA 90046
Phone: 323-602-5500
Web Site: http://www.oprah.com/own
Oprah Winfrey, Chief Executive & Creative Officer
Erik Logan, President, OWN & Harpo Studios
Neal Kirsch, Chief Operating & Financial Officer
Harriet Seitler, Chief Marketing Officer & Executive Vice President
Kathleen Kayse, Executive Vice President, Ad Sales
Rita Mulllin, Executive Vice President, Programming & Development
Nicole Nichols, Executive Vice President, Communications & Strategy
Tina Perry, Executive Vice President, Business & Legal Affairs
Jill Dickerson, Senior Vice President, Programming & Development
Scott Garner, Senior Vice President, Scheduling & Acquisitions
Glenn Kaino, Senior Vice President, Digital
Meg Lowe, Senior Vice President, Distribution & Strategy
Mashawn Nix, Senior Vice President, Programming
Peggy Panosh, Senior Vice President, Consumer Marketing
Type of service: Basic.
Operating hours/week: 168.
Programming: A mix of original programs, specials, documentaries and acquired movies. Programming is focused on motivating people to lead healthy lives.
Began: January 1, 2011, replacing Discovery Health Channel. OWN HD began January 1, 2011.
Total subscribers: 83,000,000.
Distribution method: Available to cable & satellite subscribers.
Scrambled signal: Yes.
Ownership: A joint venture between Oprah Winfrey & Discovery Communications.

OXYGEN
30 Rockefeller Plz
New York, NY 10012
Phone: 212-651-2000
E-mail: o2_press@oxygen.com
Web Site: http://www.oxygen.com
Frances Berwick, President, Lifestyle Networks Group, NBCUniversal Cable Entertainment
Holly Tang, Chief Financial Officer
Rod Aissa, Executive Vice President, Original Programming & Development
Lisa Hsia, Executive Vice President, Digital, Bravo & Oxygen Media
Jerry Leo, Executive Vice President, Program Strategy & Acquisitions
David O'Connell, Executive Vice President, Production Management & Operations, Lifestyle Networks Group
Ellen Stone, Executive Vice President, Marketing, Bravo & Oxygen
Cori Abraham, Senior Vice President, Development & International
Jamie Cutburth, Senior Vice President, Partnership Marketing
Jennifer Geisser, Senior Vice President, Communications
Roger Guillen, Senior Vice President, Creative Director
Mike Haggerty, Senior Vice President, Research

Harleen Kahlon, Senior Vice President, Digital
Brian Katz, Senior Vice President, Oxygen Research
David O'Connell, Senior Vice President, Production Operations
Jane Olson, Senior Vice President, Marketing & Brand Strategy
Ryan Pinette, Senior Vice President, Production & Operations, Bravo & Oxygen Media
Sarah Tomassi Lindman, Senior Vice President, Program Strategy
David Brewer, Vice President, Program Strategy & Acquisitions
Brie Miranda Bryant, Vice President, Development & Production, Original Programming
Tony Carbone, Vice President, Digital
Sunil Chadda, Vice President & Chief Financial Officer
Chloe Ellers, Vice President, Communications
Trisha Espinoza, Vice President, Program Planning, Scheduling & Acquisitions
David Gross, Vice President, Development
Matthew Jarecki, Vice President, Advertising Sales
Teri Kennedy, Vice President, Current Programming
Jeff Nichols, Vice President, On-Air Promotions
Barry Rosenberg, Vice President, Communications
Joel K. Savitt, Vice President, Production & Operations
Jennifer Young, Vice President, Ad Sales Marketing
Adam Zeller, Vice President, Social Media
Type of service: Basic, HD & video on demand.
Satellites: Satcom C3, transponder 24.
Programming: A network targeted to women 18-34 with original series, specials & movies.
Began: February 2, 2000, Oxygen on Demand began August 1, 2003. Oxygen rebranded April 23, 2008 after sale to NBCUniversal. Oxygen HD launched March 2011.
Total subscribers: 76,000,000 (25,000,000 On Demand subscribers.).
Distribution method: Available to cable, IPTV & satellite subscribers; online & mobile through the website or app (participating providers); video on demand (participating providers).
Scrambled signal: Yes.
Ownership: NBCUniversal LLC.

PAC-12 ARIZONA — See PAC-12 Networks.
Programming: ASU & U of A sporting events; original programming.
Scrambled signal: Yes.

PAC-12 BAY AREA — See PAC-12 Networks.
Programming: California & Stanford sporting events; original programming.

PAC-12 LOS ANGELES — See PAC-12 Networks.
Programming: UCLA & USC sporting events; original programming.

PAC-12 MOUNTAIN — See PAC-12 Networks.
Programming: U of Colorado, Nevada & Utah sporting events; original programming.

PAC-12 NETWORKS
370 3rd St
3rd Fl
San Francisco, CA 94107
Phone: 415-580-4200
E-mail: pac-10@pac-10.org
Web Site: http://www.pac-12.com
Lydia Murphy-Stephans, President, Pac-12 Enterprises
Larry Scott, Commissioner
Kevin Weiberg, Deputy Commissioner & Chief Operating Officer
Bill Cella, Chief Revenue Officer
Danette Leighton, Chief Marketing Officer
Ron McQuate, Chief Financial Officer
Neil Davis, Executive Vice President, Sales
Jonathan Leess, Senior Vice President, Production Planning & Operations
Arturo Marquez, Senior Vice President, Affiliate Sales & Marketing
David Aufhauser, Vice President & General Manager, Digital Media
Woodie Dixon, Vice President, Business Affairs & General Counsel
Michael Harabin, Vice President, Engineering & Technology
Dave Hirsch, Vice President, Communications
Bob Keyser, Vice President, University Relations
Kirk Reynolds, Vice President, Public Relations
Scott Adametz, System Architecture & Technology Director
Kendall Ginsbach, Media Manager
Operating areas: Arizona, California, Colorado, Nevada, Oregon, Utah & Washington.
Programming: Covers men's & women's sporting events from the PAC-12 schools in their associated region.
Began: August 15, 2012.
Distribution method: Available to cable, IPTV & satellite subscribers. Streaming available online & through PAC-12 Now app.
Scrambled signal: Yes.
Ownership: Pacific-12 Media Enterprises, which is owned by the PAC-12 Conference.

PAC-12 NOW — See PAC-12 Networks.
Web Site: http://pac-12.com/content/pac-12-now-web-ios-android-apps
Type of service: Streaming.
Programming: Live games, shows, highlights, features & more from the PAC-12 Networks.
Distribution method: Available through app & participating providers.

PAC-12 OREGON — See PAC-12 Networks.
Programming: Oregon & Oregon State sporting events; original programming.

PAC-12 WASHINGTON — See PAC-12 Networks.
Programming: Washington & Washington State sporting events; original programming.

PACVIA TV
150 S Robles Ave
Ste 470
Pasadena, CA 91101
Phone: 626-304-2685
Web Site: http://www.pacviatv.com
Operating hours/week: 168.
Programming: Provides dramatic programming in Mandarin Chinese.

PALLADIA — See MTV Live.

PARABLES TELEVISION NETWORK
477 S Rosemary Ave
Ste 306
West Palm Beach, FL 33401
Phones: 561-684-5657; 888-724-2012
Fax: 561-684-9690
E-mail: info@parables.tv

Web Site: http://www.parables.tv
Mark Newmyer, President & Chief Executive Officer
Isaac Hernandez, Vice President, Programming & Syndication
Seta Goldstein, Manager, Syndication & Marketing
Type of service: Basic.
Operating hours/week: 168.
Operating areas: Available nationwide.
Programming: Faith-based network that features movies, documentaries & series.
Began: December 1, 2010.
Means of Support: Advertising.
Distribution method: Available to cable & satellite subscribers.
Scrambled signal: Yes.
Ownership: Parables HD LLC, a subsidiary of Olympusat Inc.

PASIONES
2000 Ponce de Leon Blvd
Ste 500
Coral Gables, FL 33134
Phone: 305-421-6364
Web Site: http://www.tvpasiones.com
Alan J. Sokol, Chief Executive Officer, Hemisphere Media Group Inc.
Craig D. Fischer, Chief Financial Officer, Hemisphere Media Group Inc.
Operating areas: Nationwide.
Programming: Spanish language soap operas.
Total subscribers: 11,000,000 (U.S. and Latin America).
Distribution method: Available to satellite subscribers.
Scrambled signal: Yes.
Ownership: Hemisphere Media Group Inc.

PATRIOTS ON DEMAND
c/o Comcast Corp.
1500 Market St
Philadelphia, PA 19102
Web Site: http://www.patriots.com
Type of service: Video on demand.
Programming: Daily team updates, news, analysis & game highlights of the New England Patriots.
Began: October 13, 2005.
Distribution method: Available to cable subscribers.
Scrambled signal: Yes.
Ownership: Comcast Corp.

PBJ
225 E 8th St
Ste 200
Chattanooga, TN 37402
Phones: 423-468-5100; 800-294-4800
E-mail: pbj@watchpbj.com
Web Site: http://watchpbj.com
David Leach, President & Chief Executive Officer, Luken Communications
Doug Evans, Chief Operating Officer, Luken Communications
David Dornseif, Senior Vice President, Ad Sales, Luken Communications
Type of service: Basic, over the air.
Operating hours/week: 168.
Operating areas: California, Colorado, Georgia, Kansas, Mississippi, Montana, Nevada, New Mexico, New York, N Carolina, Ohio, Pennsylvania, Tennessee & Utah.
Programming: Classic children & cartoon programming from the 1950's to the 1980's.
Began: September 3, 2011.
Means of Support: Advertising.
Distribution method: Available over-the-air on digital sub-channels.
Scrambled signal: No.
Ownership: Classic Media & Luken Communications LLC.

Pay TV & Satellite Services

PBS HD
2100 Crystal Dr
Arlington, VA 22202
Phone: 703-739-5000
Web Site: http://www.pbs.org
Paula Kerger, President & Chief Executive Officer
Jonathan Barzilay, Chief Operating Officer
Programming: A mix of new & archived HD & widescreen programs.
Began: March 1, 2004.

PBS KIDS
2100 Crystal Dr
Arlington, VA 22202
Phone: 703-739-5000
Web Site: http://pbskids.org
Type of service: Plans over the air, streaming.
Programming: Plans 24-hour children's programming.
Scheduled to begin: Plans to begin late 2016.
Distribution method: Plans over the air on digital sub-channels, streaming.
Scrambled signal: Yes.

PCTV
Warren & East Sts
Pottstown, PA 19464
Phone: 610-327-1866
Fax: 610-327-9681
E-mail: pctvpottstown@gmail.com
Web Site: http://www.thepctvnetwork.com
Type of service: Regional basic.
Operating hours/week: 168.
Operating areas: Pennsylvania (western Montgomery County, northern Chester County and eastern Berks County).
Programming: Offers local sports, business, and community affairs programs.
Began: January 1, 1983.
Means of Support: Advertising.
Total subscribers: 70,000.
Distribution method: Available to Comcast cable system subscribers.
Scrambled signal: Yes.
Ownership: Borough of Pottstown, PA. Operation is managed by TellisVisionLLC.

PEACETV
c/o Islamic Research Foundation
Quadrant Ct 48 Calthorpe Rd
Birmingham B15 1TH
United Kingdom
Phones: 44-0-2079-938470; 917-546-6836 in U.S.
Fax: 44-0-2033-726107
E-mail: admin@peacetv.tv
Web Site: http://www.peacetv.tv
Dr. Zakir Naik, Founder
Operating hours/week: 168.
Programming: Telecasting state-of-the-art TV programs in English, Urdu and Bangla promoting truth, justice, morality, harmony and wisdom for the whole of mankind.
Began: January 21, 2006.
Means of Support: Donations.
Total subscribers: 100,000,000 (viewers worldwide).
Distribution method: Available over the air on digital sub-channels and to satellite subscribers.
Scrambled signal: Yes.
Ownership: Dr. Zakir Naik.

PEGASUSTV
c/o Boot Media LLC
516 Villa Ave, Ste 2
Clovis, CA 93612
Phone: 805-630-2242
E-mail: info@pegasustv.com
Web Site: http://www.pegasustv.com
Sally Lasater, National Sales & Advertising
Lesley O'Connor, Texas Sales & Advertising
Charles Smallwood, California Sales & Advertising
Type of service: Over the air, streaming.
Operating hours/week: 168.
Programming: Deciated to equestrian pursuits and country lifestyles.
Began: April 15, 2011.
Means of Support: Advertising.
Total subscribers: 28,600,500.
Distribution method: Available to over the air. Streaming available online.
Scrambled signal: Yes.
Ownership: Boot Media LLC, majority equity holder and managing member.

PENN NATIONAL RACING ALIVE
(Telebet)
PO Box 32
Grantville, PA 17208
Phone: 717-469-2211
E-mail: fred.lipkin@pngaming.com
Web Site: http://www.bloodhorse.com/horseracing/racetracks/PEN/penn-national-race-course
Herb Grayek, President
P. T. O'Hara, Jr., Vice President, Operations
Type of service: Regional.
Satellites: Galaxy II (Four nights/week, Sunday afternoon.).
Operating areas: Pennsylvania.
Programming: Live thoroughbred racing with call-in betting.
Began: April 1, 1984.
Means of Support: Percentage of wagers; advertising.
Total subscribers: 400,000.
Equipment: Oak.

PENNSYLVANIA CABLE NETWORK
401 Fallowfield Rd
Camp Hill, PA 17011
Phone: 717-730-6000
Fax: 717-730-6009
Web Site: http://www.pcntv.com
Brian Lockman, President & Chief Executive Officer
Debra Kohr Sheppard, Senior Vice President & Chief Operating Officer
Joel Bechtel, Vice President, Marketing & Brand Development
Melissa Hiler, Vice President, Controller
Thierry Malley, Vice President, Strategic Partnerships
Corinna Vescey Wilson, Vice President, Programming
Satellites: GE-2, transponder 13C.
Operating hours/week: 168.
Operating areas: Pennsylvania.
Programming: State public affairs network, with live coverage of Pennsylvania House, Senate, and other governmental activities. Also features state events coverage, high school championship sports & educational programming.
Began: September 4, 1979.
Total subscribers: 3,300,000.

PENTHOUSE TV
c/o New Frontier Media
6000 Spine Rd, Ste 100
Boulder, CO 80301
Phones: 303-444-0900; 888-875-0632
Fax: 303-938-8388
Web Site: http://www.noof.com
Larry Flynt, Chief Executive Officer
Michael Klein, President
Chris Woodward, Chief Financial Officer
Type of service: Digital, pay per view, streaming, video on demand.
Satellites: Eutelsat Eurobird 9A.
Operating hours/week: 168.
Operating areas: Nationwide.
Programming: Adult programming.
Began: December 1, 2007.
Distribution method: Available to cable & satellite subscribers. Streaming available online & mobile.
Scrambled signal: Yes.
Ownership: New Frontier Media.

PERU MAGICO
Av. La Paz 1049
Piso 9 (Edificio Miracorp)
Miraflores, Lima
Peru
Phone: 511-207-4111
E-mail: perumagico@mnetworks.com.pe
Web Site: https://www.perumagico.pe; http://medianetworks.net
Fernando Espinoza, Commercial Ad Sales Director, Media Networks Sales
Type of service: Pay.
Operating areas: Nationwide.
Programming: Programs of and about Peru.
Means of Support: Advertising and subscriber fees.
Distribution method: Available to DirecTV subscribers.
Scrambled signal: Yes.
Ownership: Media Networks.

PETS.TV
1925 Century Park E
Ste 1025
Los Angeles, CA 90067
Phone: 310-277-3500
E-mail: eric@es.tv
Web Site: http://www.pets.tv
Byron Allen, Chairman & Chief Executive Officer
Lisa-Renee Ramirez, Executive Vice President & Director Producer
Darren Galatt, Vice President, Ad Sales
Type of service: Digital.
Operating hours/week: 168.
Operating areas: Nationwide.
Programming: Dedicated to pets and pet lovers, celebrating the best in show and the people who love them.
Began: May 11, 2009.
Total subscribers: 1,900,000.
Distribution method: Available to Verizon FiOS and Frontier Communications subscribers.
Scrambled signal: No.
Ownership: Entertainment Studios.

PFC - O CANAL DO FUTEBOL
Rua Itapiru 1209 - 4 andar
Rio Comprido
Rio de Janeiro RJ 20251-032
Brazil
Phone: 55-0-21-2563-0303
Fax: 55-0-21-2293-4311
Web Site: http://pfci.globo.com
Type of service: Pay.
Operating hours/week: 168.
Operating areas: Nationwide.
Programming: Portuguese language channel dedicated completely to Brazilian soccer.
Began: January 1, 2007, in Brazil.
Distribution method: Available to Bright House Networks, Comcast, RCN, Time Warner & DISH Network subscribers.
Scrambled signal: Yes.
Ownership: Globosat Programadora Ltd.

PHOENIX INFONEWS
c/o Phoenix Satellite TV (US) Inc.
3810 Durbin St
Irwindale, CA 91706
Phones: 626-388-1188; 866-287-2288
Fax: 626-388-1118
Web Site: http://ifengus.com
Type of service: HD.
Operating hours/week: 168.
Operating areas: Nationwide.
Programming: All news channel.
Began: January 1, 2001.
Distribution method: Available to cable, IPTV & satellite subscribers.
Scrambled signal: Yes.
Ownership: A joint venture between Today's Asia (37.5%), China Mobile (HK) Group. (19.9%), TPG China Media (12.15%), China Wise Intl. (8.3%) & others (22.15%).

PHOENIX MOVIES CHANNEL — See Phoenix Infonews.
Type of service: Premium.
Operating areas: Nationwide.
Programming: Non-stop family entertainment. 80% are Asian productions, the remainder from Hollywood and elsewhere.
Began: August 28, 1998.
Distribution method: Available to cable, IPTV & satellite subscribers.
Scrambled signal: Yes.

PHOENIX NORTH AMERICA CHINESE CHANNEL — See Phoenix Infonews.
Operating hours/week: 168.
Operating areas: Nationwide.
Programming: Provides news and entertainment shows from the Asian Pacific Region, including China, Hong Kong, Taiwan and others.
Began: January 1, 2000.
Distribution method: Available to cable & satellite subscribers.
Scrambled signal: Yes.

PIKES PEAK COMMUNITY COLLEGE
Distance Education
5675 S Academy Blvd, Campus Box 45
Colorado Springs, CO 80906
Phones: 719-540-7538; 800-456-6847
Fax: 719-540-7532
E-mail: lrc@ppcc.edu
Web Site: http://www.ppcc.edu
Julie Witherow, Distance Education Director
William Wright, Chief Engineer
Type of service: Basic.
Operating hours/week: 64.
Operating areas: Colorado.
Programming: Educational service carried on local cable systems.
Distribution method: Available to cable subscribers.
Scrambled signal: Yes.

PITTSBURGH CABLE NEWS CHANNEL
4145 Evergreen Rd
Pittsburgh, PA 15214-4145

Pay TV & Satellite Services

Phones: 412-237-1100; 800-237-9794
Fax: 412-237-1333
E-mail: mbarash@wpxi.com
Web Site: http://www.wpxi.com/s/pcnc
Ray Carter, Vice President & General Manager
Mark Barash, PCNC Station Manager
Mike Oliveira, News Director
Maureen O'Connor, Affiliate Relations Representative & Producer
Type of service: Basic & expanded basic.
Operating hours/week: 168.
Operating areas: Ohio, Pennsylvania, West Virginia.
Programming: Cable-exclusive 24-hour local news, talk & information.
Began: January 3, 1994.
Means of Support: Advertising & subscribers fees.
Total subscribers: 850,000. Total systems served: 3.
Distribution method: Available to cable & IPTV subscribers in select Ohio, Pennsylvania & West Virginia areas.
Scrambled signal: Yes.
Ownership: WPIX, part of the Cox Media Group.

PIVOT
331 Foothill Rd
Beverly Hills, CA 90210
Phone: 310-550-5100
Web Site: http://www.participantmedia.com
David Linde, Chief Executive Officer, Participant Media
Jeff Ivers, Chief Operating Officer
Kent Rees, General Manager
John Arianas, Executive Vice President, Advertising Sales & Partnerships
Belisa Balaban, Executive Vice President, Original Programming
Jerry Blake, Executive Vice President, Business & Legal Affairs
Kent Rees, Executive Vice President, Marketing, Scheduling & Operations
Stephanie Ruyle, Executive Vice President, Distribution
Holly Hines, Senior Vice President, Scripted Programming
Carla Lewis-Long, Senior Vice President, Distribution
Ben McLean, Senior Vice President, Legal Affairs & Business Development
Jennie Morris, Senior Vice President, Acquisitions & Operations
Craig Parks, Senior Vice President, Digital & Live Programming
Karen Ramspacher, Senior Vice President, Research & Insights
Type of service: Pay, streaming, video on demand.
Operating areas: Nationwide.
Programming: Original series, movies and documentaries.
Began: August 1, 2013, replacing the Documentary Channel & Halogen TV (which replaced i-Life TV).
Total subscribers: 50,000,000.
Distribution method: Available to cable, IPTV & satellite subscribers. Streaming available online. Video on demand available through participating providers.
Scrambled signal: Yes.
Ownership: Participant Media.

PIX11
220 E 42nd St
New York, NY 10017
Phone: 212-949-1100
Web Site: http://www.pix11.com
John Seminerio, Engineering Director
Debbie Presser, General Sales Manager
Type of service: Basic, over the air.
Satellites: Spacenet 3, transponder 5.
Operating hours/week: 168.
Programming: News, sports, local events & syndicated programming.
Began: May 1, 1984, as WPIX, a WB affiliate; re-launched on Sept. 20, 2006 as CW11. Rebranded PIX11 in 2008.
Means of Support: System pays per subscriber.
Total subscribers: 10,000,000 (Figure includes cable, Canadian, DTH & off-air).
Distribution method: Available over the air & to cable, IPTV & satellite subscribers.
Scrambled signal: Yes. Equipment: VideoCipher II.

PLANET GREEN — See Destination America.

PLAYBOY EN ESPANOL — See Playboy TV.
Began: January 1, 2000.

PLAYBOY TV
2300 W Empire Ave
7th Fl
Burbank, CA 91504-3350
Phone: 323-276-4000
Fax: 323-276-4050
E-mail: cable@playboy.com
Scott Flanders, Chief Operating Officer, Playboy Enterprises & President, Playboy Media
Hugh M Hefner, Chief Creative Officer & Editor-in-Chief, Playboy Enterprises
Matthew A. Nordby, President, Global Licensing & Chief Revenue Officer, Playboy Enterprises
Rachel Sagan, Executive Vice President, Business Affairs & General Counsel, Playboy Enterprises
Gary Rosenson, Senior Vice President & General Manager, Worldwide Television, Playboy Entertainment
Wendy Miller, Vice President, Development & Current Programming, Playboy TV
Darren Turbow, Vice President, Production & Post-Production, Playboy Entertainment

Branch Offices:
BEVERLY HILLS: 9242 Beverly Blvd, Beverly Hills, CA 90210.

LOS ANGELES: 2706 Media Center Dr, Los Angeles, CA 90065. Phone: 323-276-4000. Fax: 323-273-4500.

NEW YORK: 730 Fifth Ave, New York, NY 10019. Phone: 212-261-5000. Fax: 212-957-2900.

SANTA MONICA: 2112 Broadway, Santa Monica, CA 90404. Phone: 310-264-6600. Fax: 310-264-1994.
Type of service: Pay, video on demand.
Satellites: Galaxy V, transponder 2.
Operating hours/week: 168.
Uplink: Burbank, CA.
Programming: Features original programs & selected erotic films. Spanish-language available on Playboy en Espanol.
Began: November 1, 1982, Playboy TV on Demand began 2002.
Means of Support: Subscriber fees.
Total subscribers: 46,000,000.
Distribution method: Available to cable, IPTV & satellite subscribers.
Scrambled signal: Yes. Equipment: VideoCipher II Plus.
Ownership: Icon Acquisition Holdings L.P. Hugh M. Hefner & Scott Flanders are among the equity investors.

PLAYERS NETWORK (PNTV)
1771 E Flamingo Rd
Ste 201A
Las Vegas, NV 89119
Phone: 702-734-3457
Fax: 702-851-0746
E-mail: info@playersnetwork.com
Web Site: http://www.playersnetwork.com
Mark Bradley, Chief Executive Officer
Michael Berk, Chief Creative Officer
Leslie Thomas, Marketing & Operations Manager
Type of service: Basic, video on demand, pay-per-view.
Operating hours/week: 168.
Programming: Focuses on the gaming lifestyle.
Distribution method: Available to cable & satellite subscribers.
Scrambled signal: Yes.

PLAYGIRL TV
c/o Trans Digital Media LLC
801 2nd Ave
New York, NY 10017
Phone: 212-867-0234
Fax: 212-682-5278
Geoff Lurie, Chief Executive Officer
Type of service: Pay-per-view & video on demand.
Programming: Adult entertainment.
Began: January 1, 2004.
Total subscribers: 20,000,000.
Distribution method: Available to cable & satellite subscribers.
Scrambled signal: Yes.
Ownership: TransDigital Media.

PLEASURE
5435 Airport Blvd
Ste 100
Boulder, CO 80301
Phones: 303-786-8700; 888-728-9993
Fax: 303-938-8388
Mark Kreloff, President & Chief Executive Officer
Karyn Miller, Chief Financial & Operating Officer
Thomas Nyiri, Chief Technical Officer & Vice President, Broadband Communications
Michael Weiner, Executive Vice President, Business Affairs
Bill Mossa, Vice President, Affiliate Sales
John Chambliss, Programming Director
Mark Grant, Marketing Contact
Robin Rothman, Media Contact
Type of service: Pay-per-view.
Operating hours/week: 168.
Programming: Adult programming.
Began: June 1, 1999.
Means of Support: Pay-per-view; monthly subscription fee.
Distribution method: Available to cable & satellite subscribers.
Scrambled signal: Yes.
Ownership: New Frontier Media Inc.

POKER CENTRAL
3960 Howard Hughes Pkwy
Ste 500
Las Vegas, NV 89169
Phone: 702-858-9102
E-mail: syacura@pokercentral.com
Web Site: https://www.pokercentral.com
Daniel Stinchcomb, Chief Executive Officer
Sid Eshleman, Chief Distribution Officer
Dan Russell, Senior Vice President, Programming
John Matthews, Vice President, Distribution
Richard Blankenship, Advertising Sales
Sandra Yacura, Media Contact
Type of service: Video on demand.
Operating hours/week: 168.
Operating areas: Available nationwide.
Programming: An all-poker, all-the-time television network.
Began: October 1, 2015.
Means of Support: Advertising.
Total subscribers: 100,000,000 (Estimated).
Distribution method: Available to cable subscribers.
Scrambled signal: Yes.
Ownership: Daniel Negreanu.

POKERTV NETWORK
1555 Flamingo Rd
Ste 315
Las Vegas, NV 89119
Phone: 702-735-7588
Web Site: http://www.pokertvnetwork.com
Programming: News, information, travel, reality & talk shows related to the world of poker.
Began: December 1, 2005.

POP
5510 Lincoln Blvd
Ste 400
Playa Vista, CA 90094
Phone: 323-856-4035
E-mail: press@tvgn.tv
Web Site: http://www.tvgn.tv
Brad Schwartz, President
Dennis Miller, President, Operations
David Mandell, Chief Operating Officer & General Counsel
Debra Wichser, Chief Financial Officer
Michael Dupont, Executive Vice President, Advertising Sales
Justin Rosenblatt, Executive Vice President, Original Programming & Development
Nicole Sabatini, Executive Vice President, Marketing
Paul Adler, Senior Vice President, TV Development
Jack Carey, Senior Vice President, Operations
Leslie Furuta, Senior Vice President, Communications
Michael Kanner, Senior Vice President, Planning, Strategy & Operations
Michael Rissetto, Senior Vice President, Ad Sales Pricing & Planning
Lori West, Senior Vice President, Direct Response Ad Sales
Rich Browd, Vice President, Creative Director
Kristan Giordano, Vice President, Original Programming
Leslie Isaacs, Vice President, West Coast Sales
Takashi Nakano, Vice President, Content Distribution
Beecher Scarlett, Vice President, Ad Sales
Melissa Stone Mangham, Vice President, Marketing & Brand Strategy
Jessie Surovell, Vice President, Development

Branch Offices:
TULSA: 7140 S Lewis Ave, Tulsa, OK 74136.

NEW YORK: 11 W 42nd St, New York, NY 10036.
Type of service: Basic, HD, streaming, video on demand.
Satellites: Galaxy G-12, transponder 6.
Operating hours/week: 168.
Programming: Full-screen entertainment destination with programming that celebrates Hollywood, its stars and shows that fans love. Original series and specials.
Began: February 1, 1988, 1991 as Sneak Prevue. Rebranded Prevue Channel February 1, 1998, TV Guide Channel February 1, 1999, TV Guide Network June 4, 2007 & TVGN January 2013. Rebranded as Pop January 14, 2015.

Pay TV & Satellite Services

Means of Support: Subscriber fees & advertising.
Total subscribers: 88,000,000 (29,000,000 on demand subscribers.).
Distribution method: Available to cable systems & satellite subscribers.
Scrambled signal: Yes.
Ownership: A joint venture between Lionsgate Entertainment Corp. (50%) & CBS Corp. (50%).

POPCORNFLIX.COM
757 Third Ave
3rd Fl
New York, NY 10017
Phone: 212-308-1790
E-mail: info@popcornflix.com
Web Site: http://www.popcornflix.com
David Fannon, Executive Vice President, Screen Media Ventures
Donna Tracey, Vice President, Operations, Screen Media Ventures
Ben Saxton, Digital Distribution Manager
Type of service: Streaming.
Operating areas: Nationwide.
Programming: Movies & TV series.
Began: March 22, 2011.
Means of Support: Advertising and banner announcements.
Distribution method: Available online & through streaming devices, mobile & smart TVs.
Scrambled signal: Yes.
Ownership: Screen Media Ventures.

PORTUGUESE CHANNEL
1501 Achushnet Ave
New Bedford, MA 02746-0113
Phone: 508-997-3110
Fax: 508-990-1231
Eduardo Lima, General Manager
Cidolia Silva, Advertising Manager
Gary Emken, Accounting

Branch Offices:
STUDIO: 638 Mt. Pleasant St, New Bedford, MA 02745.
Type of service: Basic.
Operating hours/week: 105.
Operating areas: Massachusetts & Rhode Island.
Programming: Portuguese language programs from Brazil & Portugal.
Began: May 1, 1974.
Means of Support: Advertising.
Distribution method: Available to cable subscribers.
Scrambled signal: Yes.
Ownership: Eduardo Lima, Prinicpal.

POTTSTOWN COMMUNITY TV — See PCTV.

PPV EN ESPANOL — See iN DEMAND.

PRAISE TELEVISION
28059 US Hwy 19N
Ste 300
Clearwater, FL 33761
Phone: 727-536-0036
Fax: 727-530-0671
Web Site: http://www.praise-tv.com
Dustin Rubeck, President & Chief Executive Officer
Tim Brown, Vice President, News Media
Bob Shreffler, Vice President, Finance
Ken Gibson, Affiliates Director
Tim Rasmussen, Senior Producer
Satellites: GE-1, transponder 7.
Programming: Contemporary Christian music videos, music specials, movies & concerts.
Began: December 9, 1996.

Means of Support: Subscriber fees & advertising.
Distribution method: Available over the air & to cable & satellite subscribers.
Scrambled signal: Yes.
Ownership: Christian Network Inc.

PRIDEVISION TV — See OutTV.

PRIME TICKET — See FOX Sports West.
1100 S Flower St
Ste 2200
Los Angeles, CA 90015-2125
Phone: 213-743-7800
Fax: 310-286-6363
Web Site: http://www.foxsports.com/west
Began: October 1985 as Prime Ticket Network. Rebranded as Prime Sports West after sale to Liberty Media in 1994, then as Prime Ticket in 1996. On April 3, 2006, FSN West 2 was rebranded as FSN Prime Ticket, then Prime Ticket.
Means of Support: Advertising.

PUBLIC INTEREST VIDEO NETWORK
4704 Overbrook Rd
Bethesda, MD 20816
Phone: 301-656-7244
Arlen Slobodow, Director
Type of service: Basic.
Satellites: Westar IV; Satcom 3-R; Galaxy I, transponder varies.
Programming: Public affairs programming offered to public TV & cable systems on ad-hoc basis.
Began: January 1, 1979.

PUERTO RICO NETWORK
Avenida Hostos 570
Urb. Baldrich
Hato Rey, PR 00918
Phone: 787-766-0505
Pedro Rua, President
Type of service: Pay.
Operating hours/week: 168.
Operating areas: Connecticut, New Jersey & New York.
Programming: Offers special events and sports exclusives, as well as news, culture, variety, lifestyle, original documentaries and miniseries.
Means of Support: Advertising and subscriber fees.
Distribution method: Available to Cablevision Systems subscribers.
Ownership: Puerto Rico Corporation for Public Broadcasting.

PUNCH TV NETWORK
2698 Dawson Ave
Ste A
Signal Hill, CA 90755
Phone: 562-424-4597
E-mail: info@punchtvnetwork.com
Web Site: http://www.punchtvnetwork.com
Joseph Collins, Chief Executive Officer
Howard Messer, Chief Financial Officer
Mark C. Corcoran, Vice President, Distribution
Rachel Ramos, Vice President, Marketing
Type of service: Basic, over the air.
Satellites: Galaxy 3, transponder 18.
Operating hours/week: 168.
Operating areas: Nationwide.
Programming: 24-hour urban inspired family-friendly programming.
Began: October 19, 2011.
Means of Support: Advertising.
Total subscribers: 55,000,000.
Distribution method: Available over the air & to satellite subscribers.
Scrambled signal: Yes.

PURSUIT CHANNEL
122 S LeGrande Ave

Luverne, AL 36049
Phone: 334-335-6926
Fax: 334-335-3361
E-mail: rfaulk@pursuitchannel.com
Web Site: http://www.pursuitchannel.com
Rusty Faulk, Chief Executive Officer
Stewart Thomas, Operations Manager
Tiffany Bryan, Traffic Coordinator
Type of service: Basic.
Operating areas: Nationwide.
Programming: Hunting, shooting and fishing television network.
Began: April 23, 2008.
Means of Support: Advertising.
Total subscribers: 42,000,000.
Distribution method: Available over the air & to Shentel, DirecTV & DISH Network subscribers.
Scrambled signal: Yes.
Ownership: Anthem Media Group Inc. & Performance One Media, significant investors.

PX TV
Manuel M Ponce No 87
Col Guadalupe Inn Del Alvaro Obregon
Mexico City CP 01020
Mexico
Phone: 5563 8720 56
E-mail: info@pxtv.tv
Web Site: http://www.pxtv.tv
Dorig Bocquet, Content/Marketing Director
Programming: Sports including bicycle racing/BMX, motorcycle racing, skate boarding, surfing and others.
Began: May 26, 2012.
Means of Support: Advertising.
Distribution method: Available to cable subscribers.
Scrambled signal: Yes.
Ownership: Distributed in the U.S. by Alterna'TV.

THE QUAD
9123 W Sunset Blvd
West Hollywood, CA 90069
Phone: 310-499-2060
E-mail: info@thequadtv.com
Web Site: http://www.thequadtv.com
Garth Ancier, Chief Executive Officer
Michael Ross, Chief Operating & Financial Officer
Alan Goodman, Creative & Marketing
Diane Robina, Content Acquisition
Operating areas: Plans to be available nationwide.
Programming: Plans four separate channels, each carrying shows from a specific decade - the 60s, 70s, 80s & 90s.
Means of Support: Plans advertising.
Distribution method: Plans cable and satellite.
Scrambled signal: Yes.
Ownership: Zeus Media Partners.

QUBO
601 Clearwater Park Rd
West Palm Beach, FL 33401
Phones: 561-659-4252; 800-700-9789
Web Site: http://www.qubo.com
Brandon Burgess, Chief Executive Officer
Rick Rodriguez, President & General Manager
Stephen P. Appel, President, Sales & Marketing

Douglas C. Barker, President, Broadcast Distribution & Southern Region
Steven J. Friedman, President, Cable
Dean M. Goodman, President & Chief Executive Officer
Richard Garcia, Senior Vice President & Chief Financial Officer
Kerry J. Hughes, Senior Vice President, Advertising Sales & Sponsorships
Adam K. Weinstein, Senior Vice President, Secrtetary & Chief Legal Officer
Type of service: Digital & video on demand.
Operating hours/week: 168.
Programming: Children's oriented programming focusing on education, literacy & values.
Began: January 8, 2007, broadcast launch on Sept. 9, 2006.
Distribution method: Available to cable systems & satellite providers.
Scrambled signal: Yes.
Ownership: A joint venture between Ion Media Networks, Scholastic Corporation, Corus Entertainment Inc. (Nelvana Ltd.), Classic Media LLC & NBCUniversal Media LLC.

QUE HUONG
1630 Oakland Rd
Ste A109
San Jose, CA 95131
Phone: 408-645-5575
Fax: 408-645-5576
E-mail: qhradio@aol.com
Web Site: http://www.quehuongmedia.com
Khoi Nguyen, Information Contact
Type of service: Regional basic.
Operating areas: California.
Programming: Vietnamese programming.
Distribution method: Available over the air on digital sub-channels.
Ownership: Que Huong Media.

QVC
Studio Park
West Chester, PA 19380
Phones: 484-701-1000; 888-345-5788
Fax: 484-701-1350
E-mail: webmaster@qvc.com
Web Site: http://www.qvc.com
Michael George, President & Chief Executive Officer
Ted Jastrzebski, Chief Financial Officer
Tom Downs, Executive Vice President, Operations & Services
Beth Rubino, Executive Vice President, Human Resources & Workplace Services
Angie Simmons, Executive Vice President, Multichannel Platforms
John Sullivan, Executive Vice President & Chief Information Officer
Dave Apostolico, Senior Vice President, Affiliate Sales & Marketing
Robb Cardigan, Senior Vice President, Programming & Broadcasting
Jeff Charney, Senior Vice President, Marketing & Chief Marketing Officer
Francis Edwards, Senior Vice President, International
Rowland Gersen, Senior Vice President & Controller
Matthew Goldberg, Senior Vice President, Global Market Development

Pay TV & Satellite Services

Neal Grabell, Senior Vice President, General Counsel & Secretary
John Hunter, Senior Vice President, Customer Service
Ken O'Brien, Senior Vice President, Merchandising
Chuck Pulcini, Senior Vice President, Finance & Treasury
Dennis Reustle, Senior Vice President, Sales & Product Planning
Doug Rose, Senior Vice President, Multichannel Programming & Marketing
Beth Rubino, Senior Vice President, Human Resources
Glenn Thor, Senior Vice President, Finance & Treasury
Dave Caputo, Vice President, Content Production
Fausto Ceballos, Vice President, Creative Services
Andy Cellucci, Vice President, Affiliate Sales & Marketing
Tony Godonis, Vice President, Facilities & Planning
Cherie Grobbel, Vice President, International Finance
Doug Howe, Vice President, Merchandising, Fashion & Beauty
John Kelly, Vice President, Merchandising, Sales & Product Planning
Tim Megaw, Vice President, Broadcasting
Robert Palma, Vice President, Production
Ellen Robin, Vice President, Public Relations
Mark Stieber, Vice President, Corporate Marketing & Business Development
Type of service: Basic, HD.
Satellites: SatCom C4, transponder 9.
Operating hours/week: 168.
Operating areas: Nationwide.
Programming: Televised cable shopping, viewer games & sweepstakes.
Began: November 24, 1986.
Means of Support: Revenue from merchandise sold.
Total subscribers: 106,000,000 (U.S. subscribers; 250,000,000 subscribers worldwide.).
Distribution method: Available to cable, IPTV & satellite subscribers.
Scrambled signal: Yes.
Ownership: Liberty Interactive Corp.

QVC PLUS — See QVC.
Programming: Three hour delay rebroadcast of QVC plus additional special programming.
Began: August 22, 2013.
Distribution method: Available to Bright House Networks, Time Warner & DirecTV subscribers.
Scrambled signal: Yes.

RADAR CHANNEL
619 W College Ave
State College, PA 16801
Phone: 814-234-9601
Fax: 814-231-0453
E-mail: info@accuwx.com
Web Site: http://www.accuweather.com
Andy Hoover, Marketing Manager
Type of service: Basic.
Programming: Continuous weather radar.
Began: February 1, 1997.
Distribution method: Available to cable subscribers.
Scrambled signal: Yes.
Ownership: AccuWeather Inc.

RAI ITALIA
Viale Mazzini 14
Rome 00195
Italy
Phone: 39-06-87408197
E-mail: alessandra.sottile@rai.it
Web Site: http://www.rai.it
Anna Maria Tarantol, President
Luigi Gubitosi, Director General
Valerio Zingarelli, Chief Technology Officer
Type of service: Pay.
Satellites: Nimig 5; Anik F3.
Operating areas: Nationwide.
Programming: Italian programming, including soccer games, music, cultural events, movies & historical documentaries.
Began: January 1, 1992.
Means of Support: Subscription fees.
Distribution method: Available to cable & satellite subscribers.
Scrambled signal: Yes.
Ownership: RAI International. Distributed in the U.S. by Condista.

RANG-A-RANG TELEVISION
2221 Chain Bridge Rd
Vienna, VA 22182
Phone: 703-255-5500
Fax: 703-991-2184
Web Site: http://tv.rangarang.us
Davar Veiseh, Station Manager
Type of service: Basic.
Operating hours/week: 168.
Operating areas: Virginia, Maryland & District of Columbia.
Programming: Persian politics, history, culture, food & health shows.
Began: January 1, 1989.

RCN NOVELAS
Ave of the Americas #65-82
Bogata, DC
Colombia
Phone: 571-4-26-92-92
Web Site: http://www.canalrcn.com/telenovelas
Programming: Telenovelas.
Ownership: Radio Cadena Nacional. Majority stockholder Carlos Ardila Lulle. Distributed in the U.S. by Condista.

RCN NUESTRA TELE
Ave of the Americas 65-82
Bogata, DC
Colombia
Phone: 571-426-9393
Fax: 571-426-9300
E-mail: contacto@canalnuestratele.com
Web Site: http://www.canalnuestratele.com
Operating hours/week: 154. 22-hour broadcast day.
Operating areas: Nationwide.
Programming: News, sports, religious programming and telenovelas.
Began: July 10, 1998, as TV Colombia (as a privately owned broadcast service). Rebranded RCN Nuestra Tele.
Total subscribers: 9,000,000 (viewers worldwide in 28 countries).
Distribution method: Available to cable, IPTV & satellite subscribers.
Scrambled signal: Yes.
Ownership: Radio Cadena Nacional. Majority stockholder Carlos Ardila Lulle. Distributed in the U.S. by Condista.

RCN TV
7249 Airport Rd
Bath, PA 18014
Phones: 610-443-2909; 866-528-5793
Fax: 610-443-2774
E-mail: rcntv@rcn.net
Web Site: http://www.rcn.com/rcntv
Rick Geho, Studio Manager
Christopher Popik, Production Supervisor
Paul Lewis, Senior Editor
Glen Remaly, Chief Engineer
Walt Tindall, Master Control
Cathy Neelon, Advertising Associate
Kristin Vitovitch, Advertising Associate
Type of service: Regional.
Operating areas: Delaware Valley, Lehigh Valley, Washington, DC.
Programming: Offers coverage of local high-school sports, including football, basketball, soccer, tennis, baseball, softball and volleyball. Also carries Lafayette College Athletics, including football and basketball. Also community events, including parades, the Celtic Classic and the Great Allentown Fair.
Began: January 1, 1996.
Means of Support: Advertising.
Distribution method: Available to cable subscribers.
Scrambled signal: Yes.
Ownership: RCN Telecom Services LLC.

REACTV
c/o Maggio Media
10360 72nd St N, Ste 814
Largo, FL 33777
Phone: 727-800-3170
E-mail: info@reactv.com
Web Site: http://reactv.com
Frank Maggio, Founder & Chief Executive Officer
Type of service: Basic & broadband.
Operating hours/week: 168.
Programming: Specializes in creating entertaining reactive online and TV broadcast content that rewards an audience for verifying immersion in content and advertising.
Began: August 8, 2006.
Distribution method: Available to cable systems & online.
Scrambled signal: Yes.

REAL
c/o New Frontier Media
6000 Spine Rd, Ste 100
Boulder, CO 80301
Phones: 303-444-0900; 888-875-0632
Fax: 303-938-8388
Web Site: http://www.noof.com
Larry Flynt, Chief Executive Officer
Michael Klein, President
Chris Woodward, Chief Financial Officer
Type of service: Pay per view.
Operating areas: Available nationwide.
Programming: Adult programming.
Distribution method: Available to cable, IPTV & satellite subscribers.
Ownership: New Frontier Media.

REAL HIP-HOP NETWORK
1455 Pennsylvania Ave NW
Ste 400
Washington, DC 20004
Phones: 202-379-3115; 888-742-9993
Fax: 202-478-0832
E-mail: info@rhn.tv
Web Site: http://www.rhn.tv
Atonn Muhammad, Chief Executive Officer
Paul Waters, Chief Operating Officer
Jacqueline Lesane, Corporate Secretary
Kevin Brewer, Executive Vice President, Promotions & Marketing
Will Boisture, Executive Vice President, Creative Developing
Lucas Kuria, Executive Vice President, Programming & Development
Kendrick Lesane, Executive Vice President, Music & Talent
Jerome Leaks, Greater New York Regional Director
Type of service: Basic.
Operating hours/week: 168.
Uplink: TA Broadcasting.
Programming: Hip-Hop lifestyle.
Total subscribers: 21,000,000.
Distribution method: Available to cable & satellite subscribers.
Scrambled signal: Yes.

REALITY KINGS TV (RKTV)
c/o MindGeek
2300 W Empire Ave, 7th Fl
Burbank, CA 91504
Phone: 323-276-4000
Fax: 323-276-4500
E-mail: info.losangeles@mindgeek.com
Web Site: http://www.mindgeek.com
Type of service: Pay per view.
Programming: Adult entertainment.
Began: as Spice Hot. Rebranded to The Hot Network, then Club Jenna on November 1, 2006. Reality Kings replaced Club Jenna.
Distribution method: Available to cable, IPTV & satellite subscribers.
Ownership: MindGeek.

REALTOR.COM CHANNEL
c/o Move Inc.
910 E Hamilton Ave, 6th Fl
Campbell, CA 95008
Phones: 805-557-2300; 800-878-4166
Steve Berkowitz, Chief Executive Officer, Move Inc.
Steve Marques, Chief Executive Officer, RealBizMedia
Michele Conn, Vice President, Business Dvelopment, Move Inc.
Jennifer DuBois, Public Relations & Social Media Director, Move Inc.
Type of service: Basic.
Operating areas: Atlanta, GA & Las Vegas, NV. Plans nationwide.
Programming: Offers property listings that are displayed by price range and includes high quality photo-based videos and descriptions provided by agents.
Began: February 1, 2013, in Las Vegas, NV; April 26, 2013 in Atlanta, GA.
Means of Support: Advertising.
Distribution method: Available to Comcast cable system subscribers.
Scrambled signal: Yes.
Ownership: A joint venture between Move Inc. & RealBizMedia.

RECIPE.TV
1925 Century Park E
Ste 1025
Los Angeles, CA 90067
Phone: 310-277-3500
E-mail: eric@es.tv
Web Site: http://www.es.tv/networks/recipe-tv
Byron Allen, Chairman & Chief Executive Officer
Cat Santarosa, Executive Vice President & Director Producer
Darren Galatt, Vice President, Ad Sales
Type of service: Digital.
Operating hours/week: 168.
Operating areas: Nationwide.
Programming: Famous chefs, amazing recipes, food and cuisine from around the world.
Began: May 11, 2009.
Total subscribers: 1,900,000.
Distribution method: Available to Verizon FiOS and Frontier Communications subscribers.
Scrambled signal: No.
Ownership: Entertainment Studios.

RED ADVENIR
c/o Gospel Ministries International
PO Box 506
Collegedale, TN 37315

Pay TV & Satellite Services

Phone: 423-473-1841
Fax: 423-473-1846
E-mail: amigos@redadvenir.org
Web Site: http://www.gospelministry.org; http://redadvenir.org

Branch Offices:
HEADQUARTERS: Guatemala street number 232, Box 2400, Santa Cruz de la Sierra, Bolivia. Phone: 591-3-332-5000. Fax: 591-3-337-5050. Richard Carrera, Director.
Type of service: Basic.
Operating hours/week: 168.
Operating areas: Nationwide.
Programming: Christian television network dedicated to proclaiming the three angels message across the world.
Began: November 17, 2010.
Means of Support: Donations.
Distribution method: Available over the air to digital sub-channels & to satellite subscribers.
Scrambled signal: Yes.

REELZ
5650 University Blvd SE
Bldg D
Albuquerque, NM 87106
Phone: 505-212-8800
E-mail: info@reelz.com
Web Site: http://www.reelz.com
Roger Eman, Chief Operating Officer
Steve Cheskin, Senior Vice President, Programming
John deGarmo, Senior Vice President, Distribution
Lori Lung, Senior Vice President, Finance & Administration
Bill Rosolie, Senior Vice President, Advertising Sales
Artie Scheff, Senior Vice President, Marketing
Rob Swartz, Senior Vice President, Development & Current Programming
Christine Georgakakis, Vice President, Direct Response/Paid Programming Sales
Andrea Jomides, Vice President, Distribution
Andy Morris, Vice President, Research
Tim Shaw, Vice President, Ad Sales
Diane Villegas, Vice President, Affiliate Marketing
David Zaccaria, Vice President, Marketing & On-Air Promotion
Glenne Spell, Associate Director, Research
Jessica Trumble, Associate Director, Ad Sales & Marketing

Branch Office:
NEW YORK: 122 E 42nd St, Ste 1505, New York, NY 10168. Phone: 212-697-2024. Fax: 212-661-0096.
Type of service: Digital Basic, HD, video on demand.
Operating hours/week: 168.
Programming: Factual entertainment & reality programs, television events, mini-series, movies & series. Video on demand available through select providers.
Began: September 27, 2006, as ReelzChannel. ReelzChannel HD began August 1, 2010. Rebranded Reelz in 2012.
Means of Support: Ad supported.
Total subscribers: 70,000,000.
Distribution method: Available to cable, IPTV & satellite subscribers.
Scrambled signal: Yes.
Ownership: Hubbard Broadcasting Inc.

REGIONAL MUSIC TELEVISION
13345 S Saticoy St
North Hollywood, CA 91605
Phones: 818-555-1212; 561-684-5657
Fax: 561-684-9690
Type of service: Basic.

Operating hours/week: 84.
Operating areas: Nationwide.
Programming: Music video network that features the best in Mexican regional music.
Distribution method: Available to satellite subscribers.
Scrambled signal: Yes.

REGIONAL NEWS NETWORK
800 Westchester Ave
Ste S-640
Rye Brook, NY 10573
Phones: 914-417-2700; 914-417-2709 (Media)
Fax: 914-696-0276
E-mail: comments@rnntv.com
Web Site: http://www.rnntv.com
Richard French Jr., President & Chief Executive Officer
Richard French III, President, News & Programming
Christian French, Chief Operating Officer
Edward Van Sanders, Chief Financial Officer
Jeffrey L. Thompson, Senior Vice President, Business Development & General Manager, West Coast
Phil Corsentino, News Director

Branch Offices:
BEVERLY HILLS: 9465 Wilshire Blvd, Ste 300, Beverly Hills, CA 90210. Phone: 310-579-6650.
Operating hours/week: 168.
Operating areas: Connecticut, New Jersey & New York.
Programming: Regional news, information & children's educational programming.
Total subscribers: 5,000,000.
Ownership: RNNTV Limited Partnership.

REINO UNIDO TV
1215 Hartsdale Dr
Dallas, TX 75211
Phone: 214-850-2201
Web Site: http://www.ruweb.tv
Jose Rodolfo Villatoro, Information Contact
Type of service: Regional.
Operating areas: Texas.
Programming: Religious programming, including Sunday services.
Began: January 1, 1985, Reflects start of ministry.
Means of Support: Donations.
Distribution method: Available over the air on digital sub-channels.
Ownership: El Ministerio Internacional Lirios del Valle. Pastors Jose Rodolfo and Candida Villatroro, founders.

RETROPLEX
8900 Liberty Cir
Englewood, CO 80112
Phone: 720-852-7700
Fax: 720-852-7710
E-mail: eric.becker@starz.com
Eric Becker, Vice President, Corporate Communications
Type of service: Pay, HD.
Operating areas: Nationwide.
Programming: Classic movies.
Began: April 4, 2006, RetroPlex HD began February 10, 2010.
Distribution method: Available to cable, IPTV & satellite subscribers.
Scrambled signal: Yes.
Ownership: Liberty Media Corp.

RETRO TV NETWORK — See RTV.

REV'N
c/o Luken Communications
100 Martin Luther King Blvd., Ste 402
Chattanooga, TN 37402
Phone: 423-756-1200
Web Site: http://www.revntv.com
David Leach, President & Chief Executive Officer, Luken Communications
David Dornseif, Senior Vice President, Ad Sales, Luken Communications
Type of service: Basic, over the air.
Operating areas: Nationwide.
Programming: Automotive programming covering cars, trucks, motorcycles, boats, ATVs, snowmobiles, events & auctions.
Began: December 1, 2014.
Means of Support: Advertising.
Total subscribers: 55,000,000.
Distribution method: Available over the air on digital sub-channels & to cable subscribers.
Scrambled signal: Yes.
Ownership: Luken Communications.

REVOLT TV
1800 N Highland Ave
6th Fl
Los Angeles, CA 90028
Phone: 323-645-3000
E-mail: info@revolt.tv
Web Site: http://www.revolt.tv
Sean 'Diddy' Combs, Chairman
Keith Clinkscales, Chief Executive Officer
Key Kiarie, Chief Financial Officer
James Brown Jr, Executive Vice President, Content Distribution, Talent & Marketing
Michael Roche, Executive Vice President, Sales & Partnerships
Whitney-Gayle Benta, Senior Vice President, Music & Talent
Rahman Dukes, Senior Vice President, News Programming & Digital
Inga Dyer, Senior Vice President, Business & Legal Affairs
Bruce Perlmutter, Senior Vice President, Programming & Production
Angela Turner, Senior Vice President, Affiliate & Consumer Marketing
Dave Duff, Vice President, Content Distribution
Jake Katz, Vice President, Audience Insights & Strategy
Julie Pinkwater, Vice President, Client Development
Kai D. Wright, Vice President & Head of Communications & Public Relations
Operating areas: Nationwide.
Programming: Channel inspired by music and pop culture. Offers music videos, live performances, music news and interviews plus incorporate social media interaction for music, artists and fans.
Began: October 21, 2013.
Means of Support: Advertising.
Total subscribers: 50,000,000.
Distribution method: Available to Comcast, Time Warner & AT&T U-verse subscribers.
Scrambled signal: Yes.
Ownership: Combs Enterprises.

RFD-TV
921 Village Sq
Gretna, NE 68028
Phone: 402-289-2085
E-mail: info@rfdtv.com
Web Site: http://www.rfdtv.com

Patrick Gottsch, Founder & President, Rural Media Group
Ed Frazier, Chief Executive Officer, Rural Media Group
Brian Hughes, Chief Revenue & Strategy Officer and General Manager, Nashville Operations
Michael LaBroad, Chief Marketing Officer, Rural Media Group
Steve Campione, Chief Financial Officer
Gatsby Gottsch, Executive Vice President, Finance
Raquel Gottsch, Executive Vice President, Corporate Communications
Dave Randell, Senior Vice President, Advertising Sales
Terry Sekel, Senior Vice President, Advertising Sales
Andrew Eder, Vice President, Sales
Kelly Kantz, Vice President & General Manager
Sandy Lawson, Equine Sales Director
Heather Huston, PR
Type of service: Basic, HD.
Satellites: Galaxy 13, transponder 24.
Sales representative: Sony Picture Television Ad Sales.
Operating hours/week: 168.
Operating areas: US, Canada, & Brazil.
Uplink: G-13.
Programming: Services the needs & interests of rural America with programming focused on agriculture, equine & rural lifestyle, along with traditional country music & entertainment.
Began: December 1, 2000.
Means of Support: Carriage fee & advertising.
Total subscribers: 63,000,000.
Distribution method: Available to DISH Network and cable system subscribers.
Scrambled signal: Yes. Equipment: Scientific Atlanta.
Ownership: Rural Media Group Inc.

RHODE ISLAND NEWS CHANNEL
10 Orms St
Providence, RI 02904
Phone: 401-453-8000
Fax: 401-615-1559
E-mail: ctzianabos@abc6.com
Web Site: http://www.abc6.com
Chris Tzianabos, Vice President & General Manager, ABC 6
Nicole Moye, News Director
Michael Troiano, Sales Manager
Type of service: Basic.
Operating areas: Rhode Island.
Programming: Rhode Island 24-hour news channel.
Began: November 30, 1998.
Means of Support: Advertising.
Total subscribers: 290,000.
Distribution method: Available to cable subscribers.
Scrambled signal: Yes.
Ownership: Cox Communications Inc.

RHODE ISLAND STATEWIDE INTERCONNECT
c/o Rhode Island Public Utilities Commission
89 Jefferson Blvd
Warwick, RI 02888

2017 Edition E-75

Pay TV & Satellite Services

Phone: 401-941-4500
E-mail: kogut@dpuc.ri.gov
Web Site: http://www.ripuc.org
Thomas Ahern, Administrator
Type of service: Basic.
Operating hours/week: 133.
Operating areas: Rhode Island & seven Massachusetts communities.
Uplink: Johnston, RI.
Programming: State legislature, college credit courses, cultural, religious & public access of statewide interest.
Began: January 1, 1983.
Means of Support: Cable TV operators.
Total subscribers: 292,000.
Distribution method: Available to cable subscribers.
Scrambled signal: Yes.
Ownership: Rhode Island cable TV operators.

RIDE TV
1025 S Jennings Ave
Fort Worth, TX 76104
Phone: 817-984-3500
Fax: 817-369-5889
E-mail: info@ridetv.com
Web Site: http://www.ridetv.com
Michael Fletcher, Chief Executive Officer
Michael Trujillo, Vice President, Global Distribution
Operating hours/week: 168.
Operating areas: Ohio, Pennsylvania & West Virginia. Plans international distribution.
Programming: Network dedicated to the horse culture and lifestyle.
Began: October 13, 2014.
Distribution method: Available to Armstrong Utilities & Windstream subscribers. Streaming available online.
Scrambled signal: Yes.
Ownership: Michael Fletcher, co-founder, John Paul DeJoria, stockholder.

RITMOSON — See Univision.
c/o Univision Communications Inc.
605 Third Ave, 12th Fl
New York, NY 10158
Phone: 212-455-5200
Web Site: http://www2.esmas.com/ritmoson-latino/; http://www.corporate.univision.com
Beau Ferrari, Executive Vice President, Operations, Univision Networks
Satellites: AMC 10, transponder 4.
Operating hours/week: 168.
Operating areas: Available nationwide.
Uplink: Mexico City.
Programming: Spanish-language music and entertainment channel focusing on pop and alternative rhythms.
Began: May 1, 2003.
Means of Support: Advertising & subscriber fees.
Total subscribers: 400,000.
Distribution method: Available to cable, IPTV & satellite cable system subscribers.
Scrambled signal: Yes.
Ownership: Televisa Networks. Univision Communications Inc. has an exclusive contract for this service.

RLTV
(Retirement Living TV)
5525 Research Park Dr
Baltimore, MD 21228
Phones: 410-402-9601; 800-754-8464
Fax: 410-402-9691
E-mail: gbarton@rl.tv
Web Site: http://www.rl.tv
John Erickson, Founder & Chairman
Paul FitzPatrick, President & Chief Executive Officer

Elliot Jacobson, Chief Content Officer & Senior Vice President, Programming & Production
Patrick Baldwin, Senior Vice President, Affiliate Sales & Corporate Development
Hanna Grynwajg, Senior Vice President, Advertising Sales
Gig Barton, Vice President, Ad Sales
Roy Ennis, Vice President, Finance
Jonathan Lee, Vice President, Operations
Maria Mager, Integrated Network Manager
Sara Timmins, National Accounts Manager
Type of service: Basic & streaming.
Operating hours/week: 168.
Programming: Geared towards adults 50+; information and entertainment that inspires and enhances the perception of aging; health, finance, travel, reality, comedy and drama.
Began: September 5, 2006, RLTV HD began May 22, 2012.
Total subscribers: 29,000,000.
Distribution method: Available to cable & IPTV subscribers. Streaming available online.
Scrambled signal: Yes.
Ownership: A joint venture between John Erickson, Erickson Media & NBCUniversal LLC (20%).

R NEWS — See Time Warner Cable News (Rochester).

ROOT SPORTS NORTHWEST
3626 156th Ave SE
Bellevue, WA 98006
Phone: 425-748-3400
Web Site: http://northwest.rootsports.com
Patrick Crumb, President, DirecTV Sports Networks
Bob Aylward, Vice President, Business Operations, Seattle Mariners

Branch Offices:
Master Control: Managed by Encompass, 3845 Pleasantdale Rd, Atlanta, GA 30340.
Phone: 678-421-6600.
Operating areas: Alaska, Idaho, Montana, Oregon & Washington.
Programming: Home of the Seattle Mariners, Seattle Sounders FC, Portland Timbers and Gonzaga Bulldogs plus high school sports.
Began: 1987 as Northwest Cable Sports. Rebranded as Prime Sports Northwest in 1992, Fox Sports Northwest in 1996, FSN Northwest in 2004, Root Sports Northwest April 1, 2011.
Total subscribers: 3,200,000.
Scrambled signal: Yes.
Ownership: A joint venture between the Seattle Mariners baseball club (maj interest) & DirecTV Sports Networks (min interest). DirecTV provides day-to-day management.

ROOT SPORTS PITTSBURGH
323 N Shore Dr
Ste 200
Pittsburgh, PA 15212
Phone: 412-316-3800
Fax: 412-316-3892
E-mail: gesmith@directv.com
Web Site: http://pittsburgh.rootsports.com
Shawn McClintock, Senior Vice President & General Manager
Dale Albright, Affiliate Sales Director
Sharon Dowdell, Finance Director
Jim Huber, Programming Director
Kevin Gmiter, Senior Sales Manager
Jason Lewis, Sales Manager
Doug Johnson, Executive Producer

Branch Offices:
Master Control: Managed by Encompass, 3845 Pleasantdale Rd, Atlanta, GA 30340.
Phone: 678-421-6600.
Satellites: Primestar.
Operating hours/week: 168.
Operating areas: Pennsylvania, West Virginia, Ohio, New York & Maryland.
Programming: Regional sporting events including Pittsburgh Pirates, Pittsburgh Penguins, the WPIAL as well as select Big East Conference men's and women's basketball game telecasts.
Began: March 22, 1986, as KBL Entertainment Network. Rebranded Fox Sports Net Pittsburgh in 2006, then Root Sports Pittsburgh April 1, 2011.
Means of Support: Advertising & affiliate fees.
Total subscribers: 2,400,000.
Distribution method: Available to cable & satellite subscribers.
Scrambled signal: Yes. Equipment: Primestar IRD.
Ownership: DirecTV Sports Networks.

ROOT SPORTS ROCKY MOUNTAIN
44 Cook St
Ste 600
Denver, CO 80206
Phone: 303-267-7200
Fax: 303-267-7222
E-mail: twgriggs@directv.com
Web Site: http://rockymountain.rootsports.com
David Woodman, General Manager
Amy Turner, Public Relations Director
Dave Belmonte, General Sales Manager

Branch Offices:
Master Control: Managed by Encompass, 3845 Pleasantdale Rd, Atlanta, GA 30340.
Phone: 678-421-6600.
Operating areas: Colorado, Utah, Wyoming, Idaho, Kansas, Montana, Nebraska, Nevada, New Mexico & South Dakota.
Programming: Regional sports service providing Colorado Rockies, Utah Jazz, University of Colorado, University of Denver, as well as Big 12 football and women's basketball, Pac-10 football and basketball and ACC basketball.
Began: November 5, 1998, Prime Sports Rocky Mountain/Prime Sports Intermountain West. Rebranded as Fox Sports Rocky Mountain in 1996, then Roots Sports Rocky Mountain April 1, 2011.
Total subscribers: 2,600,000.
Distribution method: Available to cable subscribers.
Scrambled signal: Yes.
Ownership: DirecTV Sports Networks.

ROOT SPORTS SOUTHWEST
1201 San Jacinto St
Ste 200
Houston, TX 77002
Phones: 713-457-6700; 713-457-6304
Fax: 713-758-7315
Web Site: http://rssouthwest.itmwpb.com
Patrick Crumb, President, DirecTV Sports Networks
Bill Roberts, Vice President, Content, DirecTV Sports Networks
David Peart, General Manager
Operating areas: Arkansas, Louisiana, New Mexico (eastern portion), Oklahoma & Texas.
Programming: Offers Houston Astros baseball, Houston Rockets basketball & Houston Dynamo soccer plus Big Sky, Conference USA, Mountain West & Southern Confer-

ence college football games. Plans to offer Houston Dynamo professional soccer.
Began: September 1, 2009, as Comcast Sports Southwest. Replaced with Comcast SportsNet Houston on October 1, 2012. Per Chapter 11 bankruptcy reorganization, entity was purchased by AT&T/DirecTV & rebranded to Root Sports Southwest November 16, 2014.
Means of Support: Advertising & subscriber fees.
Total subscribers: 4,000,000.
Distribution method: Available to AT&T U-verse, Comcast & DirecTV subscribers.
Scrambled signal: Yes.
Ownership: DirecTV Sports Networks LLC.

ROOT SPORTS UTAH — See Root Sports Rocky Mountain.
Operating hours/week: 168.
Operating areas: Utah, Idaho, Wyoming & Montana.
Programming: Regional sports coverage.
Distribution method: Available to cable systems.

RSN RESORT TV — See Outside Television.

RT AMERICA
1325 G St NW
Washington, DC 20005
Phone: 202-681-7049
Fax: 202-942-7441
E-mail: rt-us@rttv.ru
Web Site: http://www.rt.com/usa
Satellites: Galaxy 19; Galaxy 23; Nimiq 5.
Operating areas: California, District of Columbia & suburbs, Illinois, Indiana, Maine, New Jersey, New York, North Carolina & South Carolina.
Programming: News reports, features and talk shows with an international/Russian perspective.
Began: January 1, 2010.
Means of Support: Advertising.
Total subscribers: 100,000.
Distribution method: Available to Buckeye, Comcast, Cox, Time Warner, RCN, Verizon FiOS & DISH Network subscribers.
Scrambled signal: Yes.
Ownership: ANO TV-Novosti.

RTN
Russian Media Group LLC
One Bridge Plaza North, Ste 145
Fort Lee, NJ 07024
Phones: 718-745-7000; 800-628-6634
E-mail: info@russianmediagroup.com
Web Site: http://www.russianmediagroup.com
Mark Golub, President & Chief Executive Officer
Evgueni Lvov, Vice President & Chief Operating Officer
Gary Flom, Vice President, Marketing
Vlada Khmelnitskaya, Programming Director & Manager, Production Department
Michael Paley, Information Technology Director
Serge Goldberg, Chief Engineer
Operating hours/week: 168.
Programming: Russian language newscasts plus concerts, sitcoms and entertainment programs.
Began: September 1, 1991.
Means of Support: Advertising.
Scrambled signal: Yes.
Ownership: Russian Media Group LLC.

RTN+ — See RTN.
Programming: Russian language movies.

Pay TV & Satellite Services

RTP INTERNACIONAL
Avenida Marechal Gomes da Costa, No. 37
Lisboa 1849 030
Portugal
Phone: 351-217-947-000
Fax: 351-217-947-570
Web Site: http://www.rtp.pt/rtpinternacional

Branch Offices:
WASHINGTON, DC: 2000 M St NW, Ste 372, Washington, DC 20036. Phone: 202-783-0095. Fax: 202-293-7204.
Type of service: Pay.
Operating hours/week: 168.
Operating areas: Nationwide.
Programming: Portuguese language channel offering news, drama, current affairs, talk shows, sports, Portuguese movies, Portuguese television series, educational and cultural programming.
Began: June 10, 1992, in Portugal.
Means of Support: Advertising and subscriber fees.
Distribution method: Available to Comcast & DISH Network subscribers.
Scrambled signal: Yes.
Ownership: Radio e Televisao de Portugal.

RTR PLANETA
5 Ul. Yamskogo Polya, 19/21
Moscow 125124
Russia
Phone: 7 495 250 05 11
Web Site: http://www.rtr-planeta.com
Dmitry Popov, Information Contact
Type of service: Premium.
Satellites: AsiaSat 5; Eutelsat Hot Bird 6.
Operating areas: New Jersey & New York on cable & nationwide on DirecTV.
Programming: Russian state television & broadcasting channel providing Russians abroad with Russian culture, history, art, theater, ballet & general entertainment.
Began: July 1, 2002.
Means of Support: Advertising & subscriber fees.
Distribution method: Available to Time Warner & DirecTV subscribers.
Scrambled signal: Yes.
Ownership: VGTRK. State-owned Russian enterprise.

RTV
225 E 8th St
Ste 500
Chattanooga, TN 37402
Phone: 423-468-5100
Fax: 423-468-5107
E-mail: rtn@myretrotv.com
Web Site: http://www.myretrotv.com
David Leach, President & Chief Executive Officer, Luken Communications
Doug Evans, Chief Operating Officer, Luken Communications
David Dornseif, Senior Vice President, Ad Sales, Luken Communications
Andrea Rhum, Senior Account Executive
Tom Faraday, Account Executive
Type of service: Basic digital.
Operating hours/week: 168.
Operating areas: Nationwide.
Programming: Classic television serials & shows.
Began: July 1, 2005, as RTN (Retro Television Network). Rebranded RTV in June 2009.
Total subscribers: 39,000,000.
Distribution method: Available over the air on digital sub-channels & to cable, IPTV & satellite subscribers.
Scrambled signal: Yes.
Ownership: Luken Communications LLC.

RTVI
304 Hudson St
New York, NY 10013
Phone: 646-292-0290
Web Site: http://www.rtvi.com
Nina Lepchenko, Chief Executive Officer
Katerina Kotrikadze, News Director
Aleksey Zyunkin, General Producer
Programming: Russian-language network providing six newscasts daily, latest TV-series, controversial talk-shows and movies.
Began: January 1, 1997.
Means of Support: Advertising.
Distribution method: Available to cable systems and DirecTV subscribers.

RUMBA TV
Carrera 73 #52-66
Barrio Los Colores
Medellin - Antioquia
Colombia
Phone: 57-4-448-2500
Fax: 57-4-266-7957
E-mail: rumbatv@globalmedia1.tv; info@olympusat.com
Web Site: http://www.canalrumbatv.com; http://www.olympusat.com
Yeison Grisales, Director
Type of service: Basic.
Operating areas: Nationwide.
Programming: Latin music videos; genres includes salsa, merengue, vallenato, reggaeton, pop, dance, clubbing & bachata.
Distribution method: Available to satellite subscribers.
Scrambled signal: Yes.
Ownership: Global Media Telecommunications SA. Distributed in the U.S. by Olympusat Inc.

RURAL TV
9500 W Dodge Rd
Ste 101
Omaha, NE 68114
Phone: 402-991-6290
Web Site: http://www.rfdtv.com
Patrick Gottsch, Founder & President, Rural Media Group
Ed Frazier, Chief Executive Officer, Rural Media Group
Michael LaBroad, Chief Marketing Officer, Rural Media Group
Dan Kripke, Senior Vice President, Sales Director, DRTV
Dave Randall, Senior Vice President, Advertising Sales
Tim Moan, Vice President, Midwest Sales
Laura Abel, Digital Media Strategy Director
Deb Hermann, Corporate Communciations Director
Type of service: Basic.
Sales representative: Sony Picture Television Ad Sales.
Operating hours/week: 168.
Operating areas: Available nationwide.
Programming: Features prime time news broadcasts focused on agribusiness and rural policy issues; world commodity markets; extensive event coverage; international farm and horse shows; expanded livestock auctions; plus independent productions.
Began: February 15, 2012.
Means of Support: Advertising.
Total subscribers: 63,000,000.
Distribution method: Available to DISH Network subscribers.
Ownership: Rural Media Group Inc.

RUSSIAN KINO — See TV 1000 Russian Kino.

RUSSIA TODAY — See RT.

ADVANCED TVFactbook
FULLY SEARCHABLE • CONTINUOUSLY UPDATED • DISCOUNT RATES FOR PRINT PURCHASERS
For more information call **800-771-9202** or visit **www.warren-news.com**

SAB TV
3rd Floor, Interface, Building No. 7
Off Malad Link Road, Malad (W)
Mumbai 400 064
India
Phone: 91-22-6708-1111
Fax: 91-22-6643-4748
E-mail: feedback.set@setindia.com
Web Site: http://www.sabtv.com
Anooj Kapoor, Executive Vice President & Business Head
Operating hours/week: 168.
Programming: India's only family comedy entertainment channel.
Began: April 23, 2000.
Means of Support: Advertising.
Scrambled signal: Yes.
Ownership: Multi Screen Media Pvt. Ltd.

SAFE TV
3556 Liberty Ave
Springdale, AR 72762
Phones: 479-361-2900; 888-777-9392
Fax: 479-361-2323
E-mail: feedback@safetv.org
Web Site: http://www.safetv.org
Carlos Pardeiro, President & Chief Executive Officer
Rudy Dolinsky, Chief Engineer
Dick Shadduck, Community Relations Director
Bonnie Dolinsky, Satellite Sales Coordinator
Darlene Doublehead, Administrative Secretary
Programming: Family & spiritual entertainment.
Distribution method: Available to cable & satellite subscribers.
Scrambled signal: Yes.

SAIGON BROADCASTING TELEVISION NETWORK (SBTN)
10517 Garden Grove Blvd
Garden Grove, CA 92843
Phones: 714-636-1121; 877-887-2612
Fax: 714-260-0236
E-mail: sbtn@sbtn.tv
Web Site: http://www.sbtn.tv
Truc Ho, Chief Executive Officer
Type of service: Pay.
Satellites: Galaxy 17, transponder 24.
Operating hours/week: 168.
Programming: Vietnamese news, talk shows, sports, children's programming, entertainment, variety, movies, culture & history.
Began: July 1, 2001.
Distribution method: Available to cable, IPTV & satellite subscribers.
Scrambled signal: Yes.
Ownership: A joint venture between Saigon Broadcasting (50%) & NBCUniversal LLC (50%).

SAIGON TV
14776 Moran St
Westminster, CA 92683-5553
Phone: 714-230-8476
Fax: 714-379-8083
E-mail: info@saigontivi.com
Web Site: http://www.saigontv.us; http://www.saigontivi.com
Type of service: Basic.
Satellites: Galaxy.
Operating areas: Nationwide.
Programming: News, special programs on community events plus new and creative shows such as: E-News, On the Beat, Cooking with the Pro, Travel Show, Film Review, What's Hot, A-Nation, Movies, Law, Financial & Community Events all in-language and bi-lingual.
Began: January 1, 2004.
Means of Support: Advertising.
Total subscribers: 5,800,000.
Distribution method: Available to Comcast & satellite subscribers.
Scrambled signal: Yes.
Ownership: Nam Nguyen, Diane Ai-Phuong Truong & Bao-Quoc Nguyen.

SAINT CLOUD STATE UNIVERSITY CHANNEL
Stewart Hall
720 Fourth Ave S, Ste 22
St. Cloud, MN 56301
Phone: 320-308-8887
Web Site: http://www.utvs.com
Joel Larsen, Interim Assistant Athletic Director, Marketing & Promotion
Chelsea Johnson, General Manager
Derrick Silvestri, Studio Manager
Matt Szymanski, Station Manager
Julia Allen, Marketing Director
Alec Ausmus, Sports Director
Justin Haugesag, Programming Director
Type of service: Basic.
Operating hours/week: 168.
Operating areas: Minnesota.
Programming: Offers expanded coverage of St. Cloud State's Division 1 hockey plus men's and women's basketball, football and other sports.
Began: October 4, 2013, Regular programming began October 21, 2013.
Means of Support: Membership fees paid by students to operate equipment.
Distribution method: Available to Charter cable system subscribers.
Ownership: St. Cloud State University.

SAINT JOHNS COUNTY GOVERNMENT TELEVISION
500 San Sebastian View
Saint Augustine, FL 32084
Phones: 904-209-0549; 877-475-2468
Fax: 904-209-0556
E-mail: mryan@sjcfl.us
Web Site: http://www.sjcfl.us/GTV
Michael Ryan, Communications Manager
Milton Soto, Communications Specialist
Type of service: Basic, streaming.
Operating areas: Florida.
Programming: Live and rebroadcasts of county commission meetings, planning and zoning meetings plus tourist development council meetings.
Distribution method: Available to AT&T U-Verse & Comcast Cable subscribers. Streaming available online.
Scrambled signal: Yes.
Ownership: Saint Johns County, FL.

SALAAM TV
PO Box 55066
Irvine, CA 92619
Phone: 949-297-8800

Pay TV & Satellite Services

Fax: 949-266-9006
E-mail: Salaam@Salaamtv.org
Web Site: http://www.salaamtv.com
Programming: Islamic programming.
Distribution method: Available to satellite subscribers.
Scrambled signal: Yes.

SAN DIEGO NEWS CHANNEL 10 — See 10 News Channel.

SAUDITV
PO Box 529
Riyadh 11421
Saudi Arabia
Phone: 966-1442-8400
Web Site: http://www.sauditv.sa
Programming: Arabic religion, culture, entertainment, music, drama, serials, news, current affairs & children's programming.
Distribution method: Available to satellite subscribers.
Scrambled signal: Yes.

SBTN — See Saigon Broadcasting Television Network.

SCIENCE CHANNEL
c/o Discovery Communications
One Discovery Pl
Silver Spring, MD 20910-3354
Phone: 240-662-2000
Web Site: http://www.sciencechannel.com
Rich Ross, President, Animal Planet, Discovery Channel & Science Channel
Marc Etkind, General Manager
Type of service: Pay, HD, video on demand.
Programming: Science-related series covering outer space, scientific exploration, new technology, earth science basics & more.
Began: October 1, 1996, as Discovery Science Network. Rebranded Science Channel in 2007. Science Channel HD began September 1, 2007. Rebranded Science June 8, 2011.
Total subscribers: 76,000,000 ((U.S. subscribers). 2,000,000 (Canadian subscribers). 82,000,000 (international subscribers)).
Distribution method: Available to cable, IPTV & satellite subscribers. Video on demand available through select providers.
Scrambled signal: Yes.
Ownership: Discovery Communications Inc.

SCI-FI CHANNEL — See Syfy.

SEC NETWORK
c/o ESPN Regional Television
11001 Rushmore Dr
Charlotte, NC 28277
Phone: 704-973-5000
Web Site: http://www.getsecnetwork.com
Stephanie Druley, Senior Vice President, Programming, College Networks
Dan Marguilis, Senior Director, College Sports Programming, ESPNU & SEC Network
Chris Turner, Senior Director, SEC Programming
John Stephens, Associate Director, Production Operations, SEC Network & ESPNU

Branch Offices:
BIRMINGHAM: 2210 Richard Arrington Blvd N, Birmingham, AL 35203. Phone: 205-458-3000. Fax: 205-458-3031.
Type of service: Basic.
Operating hours/week: 168.
Operating areas: Nationwide.
Programming: Offers sporting events from the Southeastern Conference.
Began: August 14, 2014.

Means of Support: Advertising.
Total subscribers: 91,000,000.
Distribution method: Available to cable, IPTV & satellite providers. Streaming available online & through WatchESPN app.
Scrambled signal: Yes.
Ownership: ESPN Inc.

SEC NETWORK+ — See SEC Network.
Type of service: Streaming.
Programming: Additional live SEC sporting events that aren't broadcast on TV.
Began: August 14, 2014.
Distribution method: Available online & through the WatchESPN app.
Scrambled signal: Yes.

SEESO
30 Rockefeller Plz
New York, NY 10112
Phones: 212-664-4444; 212-664-2432
E-mail: lauren.skowronski@nbcuni.com
Web Site: http://seeso.com
Evan Shapiro, Executive Vice President, NBCU Digital Enterprises
Patricia Parra Hadden, Head of Marketing, NBCU Digital Enterprises
Ben McLean, Head of Business Affairs, NBCU Digital Enterprises
Lauren Skowronski, NBCUniversal Corporate Communications
Type of service: Subscription video on demand.
Operating areas: Available nationwide.
Programming: Offers comedy entertainment, including comedy series, movies and stand-ups plus original productions.
Began: December 3, 2015, On Beta. Officially launched January 7, 2016.
Means of Support: Subscriber fees.
Distribution method: Available online & through participating providers.
Scrambled signal: Yes.
Ownership: NBCUniversal.

SEMILLITAS
2601 S Bayshore Dr
Ste 1250
Coconut Grove, FL 33133
Phone: 786-220-0280
Fax: 305-858-7188
E-mail: jespinal@somostv.net
Web Site: http://www.semillitas.tv
Luis Villanueva, President & Chief Executive Officer, SOMOS TV
Jose Antonio Espinal, Chief Operating Officer, SOMOS TV
Alejandro Parisca, General Manager, SOMOS TV
Type of service: Pay.
Operating hours/week: 168.
Operating areas: Nationwide.
Programming: 24-hour toddlers' and preschoolers' animation channel in Spanish.
Began: March 15, 2010.
Distribution method: Available to cable subscribers.
Scrambled signal: Yes.
Ownership: SOMOS TV.

SENAL DE VIDA — See ULTRA HDPlex.
Av Luperon 46
Distrito Nacional
Santo Domingo
Dominican Republic
Phone: 809-531-3333
Fax: 809-473-6666
Web Site: http://www.senaldevida.com
Type of service: Pay, HD.
Operating areas: Available nationwide.

Programming: Spanish-language Christian programming.
Distribution method: Available to cable, IPTV & satellite subscribers.
Scrambled signal: Yes.
Ownership: Super Canal Group. Distributed in the U.S. by Olympusat.

SETANTA SPORTS USA — No longer in operation as of February 2010. See FXX.

SEXSEE
c/o New Frontier Media
6000 Spine Rd, Ste 100
Boulder, CO 80301
Phones: 303-444-0900; 888-875-0632
Fax: 303-938-8388
Web Site: http://www.noof.com
Larry Flynt, Chief Executive Officer
Michael Klein, President
Chris Woodward, Chief Financial Officer
Type of service: Pay per view.
Operating areas: Available nationwide.
Programming: Adult programming.
Distribution method: Available to cable, IPTV & satellite subscribers.
Ownership: New Frontier Media.

SHALOM TV — See Jewish Broadcasting Service.

SHANGHAI DRAGON TV — See DragonTV.

SHARJAHTV
PO Box 111
Sharjah
United Arab Emirates
Phone: 971-0-6-566-1111
Web Site: http://www.sharjahtv.gov.ae
Programming: News, documentaries, movies & children's shows from the United Arab Emirates.
Distribution method: Available to satellite subscribers.
Scrambled signal: Yes.

SHENZHEN SATELLITE TV
Creative Park Creative Centre B201
Fuqiang Rd No 4001
Futitan District, Shenzhen 518000
China
Phone: 86-0755-22666000
Web Site: http://www.s1979.com
Operating hours/week: 168.
Programming: Offers programming that focuses on Hong Kong & Macao. Also provides news and entertainment shows plus some coverage of special events and sports.
Distribution method: Available to KyLin TV subscribers.
Scrambled signal: Yes.

SHEPHERD'S CHAPEL NETWORK
PO Box 416
Gravette, AR 72736
Phones: 479-787-6026; 479-787-6248
Web Site: http://www.shepherdschapel.com/index.cfm
Arnold Murray, President
Type of service: Basic.
Satellites: Galaxy IV, transponder 16.
Operating hours/week: 168.
Programming: All religious programming, featuring educational & call-in segments.
Began: April 1, 1987.
Means of Support: Donations.
Distribution method: Available to satellite subscribers.
Scrambled signal: Yes.
Ownership: Shepherd's Chapel.

SHO2 — See Showtime.
Type of service: Pay, HD.
Programming: Original series, movies & specials.
Began: October 1, 1991, as Showtime Too. Rebranded Showtime 2 & SHO2.
Scrambled signal: Yes.

SHOWTIME 2 — See SHO2.

SHO BEYOND — See Showtime.
Programming: Sci-fi, fantasy & horror.
Began: 1999 as Showtime Beyond. Rebranded SHO Beyond.

SHO EXTREME — See Showtime.
Type of service: Pay.
Programming: Action & martial arts films, gangster movies, thrillers, westerns, & boxing.
Began: March 1998 as Showtime Extreme. Rebranded SHO Extreme.
Scrambled signal: Yes.

SHO NEXT — See Showtime.
Type of service: Pay.
Programming: Movies, documentaries and specials aimed at the 18-34 year-old audience.
Began: March 2001 as Showtime Next. Rebranded SHO Next.

SHOP AT HOME — No longer in operation as of 2006. See Jewelry Television.

SHOPHQ — See EVINE Live.

SHOPNBC — See EVINE Live.

SHOPTV
601 Clearwater Park Rd
West Palm Beach, FL 33401-6223
Phone: 561-659-4122
Fax: 561-659-4252
E-mail: chrisaddeo@ionmedia.com
Web Site: http://www.shoptv.com
Brandon Burgess, Chairman & Chief Executive Officer
Chris Addeo, Vice President, Marketing
Type of service: Basic, over the air.
Operating hours/week: 168.
Operating areas: Nationwide.
Programming: Infomercials.
Began: April 1, 2012.
Means of Support: Advertising.
Total subscribers: 40,000,000.
Distribution method: Available over the air on digital sub channels.
Scrambled signal: Yes.
Ownership: ION Media Networks.

SHORTEEZ — See Bang U.

SHORTSHD
2716 Ocean Park Blvd
Ste 1091
Santa Monica, CA 90405
Phone: 310-452-1400
Fax: 310-288-6545
E-mail: marketing@shorts.tv; salesus@shorts.tv
Web Site: http://www.shorts.tv
Linda Olszewski, Acquisitions Consultant
Kalman Apple, Sales & Acquisitions Consultant
Type of service: Pay.
Programming: Short movies in a range of genres, including action, CGI, cartoon, comedy, drama and horror.
Began: July 20, 2009, in the U.S.
Means of Support: Subscriber fees.

Pay TV & Satellite Services

Distribution method: Available to DISH Network & U-verse subscribers.
Scrambled signal: Yes.

SHO WOMEN — See Showtime.
Type of service: Pay.
Programming: Feature films, original series and specials geared at a female audience.
Began: March 2001 as Showtime Women. Rebranded SHO Women.

SHOWTIME
Paramount Plaza Bldg
1633 Broadway, 17th Fl
New York, NY 10019
Phone: 212-708-1600
Fax: 212-708-1212
Web Site: http://www.sho.com
Matthew C. Blank, Chmn. & Chief Exec. Officer, Chairman, Showtime Networks
David Nevins, President & Chief Executive Officer, Showtime Networks
Tom Christie, Chief Operating Officer, Showtime Networks
Gary Levine, President, Programming, Showtime Networks
Donald Buckley, Executive Vice President, Program Marketing, Media, Promotions & Digital Services
Trisha Cardoso, Executive Vice President, Corporate Communications
Stephen Espinoza, Executive Vice President & General Manager, Showtime Sports & Event Programming
Gwen Marcus, Executive Vice President & General Counsel
Julia Veale, Executive Vice President, Business, Product Development & Management
Sharon Allen, Senior Vice President, Program Marketing & Advertising
Amy Britt, Senior Vice President, Talent & Casting
Chris DeBlasio, Senior Vice President, Sports Communications
Gary Garfinkel, Senior Vice President, Content Acquisitions
Robin Gurney, Senior Vice President, Original Programming
Amy Israel, Senior Vice President, Original Programming
Vinnie Malhotra, Senior Vice President, Documentaries, Unscripted & Sports Programming
Robin McMillan, Senior Vice President, Public Relations
Kent Sevener, Senior Vice President, Content Acquisitions and Business & Legal Affairs
Kjerstin Beatty, Vice President, Media
Susan Frank, Vice President, Program Marketing & Advertising
Johanna Fuentes, Vice President, Corporate Public Relations
Emily Gould, Vice President, Program Marketing & Advertising
Shari Kaufman, Vice President, Talent Relations & Special Events
Kate Meyer, Vice President, Awards & Film Festivals
Brian Swarth, Vice President & Group Director, Digital Services
Type of service: Pay, HD, video on demand.
Operating hours/week: 168.
Programming: Movies & original series.
Began: July 1, 1976.
Total subscribers: 21,300,000 (6,000,000 on demand subscribers, including TMC on Demand.).
Distribution method: Available to cable, IPTV & satellite subscribers; video on demand (participating providers). Spanish language available on Showtime en Espanol.
Scrambled signal: Yes.
Ownership: CBS Corp.

SHOWTIME BEYOND — See SHO Beyond

SHOWTIME EN ESPANOL — See Showtime.

SHOWTIME EXTREME — See SHO Extreme.

SHOWTIME FAMILYZONE — See Showtime.
Type of service: Pay.
Programming: Family-oriented programming, including movies and specials aimed at a younger audience.

SHOWTIME NEXT — See SHO Next

SHOWTIME SHOWCASE — See Showtime.
Type of service: Pay, HD.
Programming: Movies, first-run feature films and original made-for-cable films originally produced for Showtime.
Scrambled signal: Yes.

SHOWTIME WOMEN — See SHO Women.

SI TV — See Fuse.

SINO TV
Multicultural Radio Broadcasting Inc.
449 Broadway
New York, NY 10013
Phone: 212-966-1059
Fax: 212-966-9580
E-mail: tonyw@mrbi.net
Web Site: http://www.sinotv.us
Operating hours/week: 168.
Programming: Chinese-language news, sports & entertainment.
Distribution method: Available to cable subscribers.
Scrambled signal: Yes.

SINOVISION
15 E 40th St
New York, NY 10016
Phone: 212-213-6688
E-mail: info@sinovision.net
Web Site: http://www.sinovision.net
Janis Lam, Vice President
Yan Xia, Post Production
Type of service: Basic, over the air.
Operating hours/week: 168.
Operating areas: Connecticut, New Jersey, New York & Pennsylvania.
Programming: Chinese programming offering news and entertainment shows in Mandarin.
Began: January 1, 1990.
Means of Support: Advertising.
Distribution method: Available over the air & to cable system subscribers.
Scrambled signal: Yes.

SIX NEWS NOW — See SNN: Suncoast News Network.

THE SKI CHANNEL
881 Alma Real Dr
No T8
Pacific Palisades, CA 90272
Phone: 310-230-2050
E-mail: info@theskichannel.com
Web Site: http://www.theskichannel.com
Steve Bellamy, President & Chief Executive Officer
Type of service: Video on demand.
Operating areas: Nationwide.
Programming: Focused on year-round mountain sports including skiing, snowboarding, hiking, biking, climbing, caving, camping & kayaking.
Began: December 25, 2008.
Means of Support: Advertising.
Total subscribers: 45,000,000.
Distribution method: Available to cable & satellite subscribers.
Scrambled signal: Yes.
Ownership: Steve Bellamy.

SKY LINK TV
500 W Montebello Blvd
Rosemead, CA 91770
Phone: 323-888-0028
Fax: 323-888-0029
Web Site: http://www.skylinktv.us
Operating areas: Available in California over the air & cable. Available nationwide on satellite.
Programming: Mandarin language programming, including news, entertainment, music & documentaries.
Distribution method: Available over the air on digital sub-channels, cable & satellite subscribers & to KyLin TV subscribers.
Scrambled signal: Yes.

SLEUTH — See cloo.

SLICE
121 Bloor St E
Toronto, ON M4W 3M5
Canada
Phone: 416-967-1174
Fax: 416-960-0871
E-mail: corporate.inquiries@shawmedia.ca
Web Site: http://www.slice.ca
Paul Robertson, Group Vice President, Broadcasting
Dervin Kelly, Head of Corporate Communications & Network Publicity
Programming: Lifestyle and entertainment programming aimed at women in the form of reality television series, documentaries, talk shows and more.
Began: January 1, 1995, as Life Network; relaunched as Slice March 5, 2007.
Scrambled signal: Yes.
Ownership: Shaw Media.

SMILE OF A CHILD TV
c/o TBN Networks
2442 Michelle Dr
Tustin, CA 92780
Phone: 714-832-2950 x5518
Fax: 714-549-2990
E-mail: brossman@tbn.org
Web Site: http://www.smileofachildtv.org; http://www.tbnetworks.com
Jan Crouch, President
Matthew Crouch, Vice President
Bob Fopma, Vice President, Production
Ben Miller, Vice President, Engineering
David Adcock, National Director, Cable & Satellite Relations
Brenda Rossman, Programming Director, Smile of a Child
Jay Jones, Media Services
Colby May, Media Relations

Access the most current data instantly
FREE TRIAL @
ADVANCED TVFactbook
TELCO/IPTV • CABLE TV • TV STATIONS
www.warren-news.com/factbook.htm

Type of service: Over the air, digital basic, streaming.
Satellites: Galaxy 14, transponder 1; Galaxy 23, transponder 20 (Olympusat).
Operating hours/week: 168.
Operating areas: Available nationwide.
Programming: Commercial-free programming that emphasizes faith & values for kids from 2-12.
Began: December 24, 2005.
Total subscribers: 15,000,000.
Distribution method: Available over the air on digital sub-channels. Available to cable, IPTV & satellite subscribers. Streaming available online.
Scrambled signal: Yes.
Ownership: TBN Networks, a non-profit corp.

SMITHSONIAN CHANNEL
c/o Showtime Networks
1633 Broadway
New York, NY 10019
Phone: 212-708-1600
Fax: 212-708-1212
E-mail: contact@smithsoniannetworks.com
Web Site: http://www.smithsonianchannel.com
Tom Hayden, Executive Vice President & General Manager
David Royle, Executive Vice President, Programming & Production
Mary Ellen Bottone, Vice President, Ad Sales
Joanna Brahim, Vice President, Communications
Jeanny Kim, Vice President, Media Services, Smithsonian Business Ventures
Type of service: Basic, HD, video on demand.
Operating hours/week: 168.
Programming: Showcases the Smithsonian's archives & library of history, culture, Americana, music, art & aviation.
Began: September 26, 2007.
Total subscribers: 22,000,000.
Distribution method: Available to cable, IPTV & satellite subscribers; video on demand.
Scrambled signal: Yes.
Ownership: Showtime Networks & The Smithsonian Institution.

SNEAK PREVUE — See Pop.

SNJ TODAY
1101 Wheaton Ave
Millville, NJ 08332
Phone: 856-327-8800
Fax: 856-327-0408
Web Site: https://snjtoday.com
Ken Pustizzi, Owner
Frank DiMauro, Chief Financial & Operating Officer
Type of service: Basic.
Operating areas: Southern New Jersey.
Programming: Offers news, weather and sports for southern New Jersey.
Began: July 23, 2015.
Means of Support: Advrtising.
Distribution method: Available to Comcast subscribers and FiOS, DirecTV and Dish Network customers.
Ownership: Ken Pustizzi.

Pay TV & Satellite Services

SNN LOCAL NEWS — See SNN: Suncoast News Network.

SNN: SUNCOAST NEWS NETWORK
1741 Main St
Sarasota, FL 34236
Phones: 941-361-4600 (news); 941-361-4222 (sales)
Fax: 941-361-4699
E-mail: news@snn6.com
Web Site: http://www.snntv.com
Linda DesMarais, Executive Vice President & General Manager
Tom Conway, News Operations Manager
Valerie Rose-Schmidt, Business Manager
Dave Bunnell, Sales Manager
Type of service: Basic, over the air.
Operating hours/week: 168.
Operating areas: Florida.
Programming: Local news for the Sarasota area.
Began: July 17, 1995, as Six News Now. Rebranded SNN New 6 in 2002, SNN Local News 6 in 2009, SNN Local News in 2012 & SNN: Suncoast News Network March 2, 2014.
Means of Support: Advertising.
Total subscribers: 150,000.
Distribution method: Available over the air on digital sub-channels & to Comcast & Verizon FiOS subscribers.
Scrambled signal: Yes.
Ownership: Sarasota Herald Tribune.

SON BROADCASTING — See KCHF-TV in TV Stations.

SONLIFE BROADCASTING NETWORK
8919 World Ministries Ave
Baton Rouge, LA 70810
Phone: 225-768-8300
E-mail: info@jsm.com
Web Site: http://www.sonlifetv.com
Type of service: Basic.
Satellites: SBN Galaxy 19; Intelsat 21, transponder 7C.
Operating hours/week: 168.
Operating areas: Nationwide.
Programming: Christian network offering a variety of live & pre-recorded programs, specializing in music & teaching, that appeal to audiences of all generations & background.
Began: December 1, 2009.
Means of Support: Donations.
Total subscribers: 80,000,000.
Distribution method: Available over the air on digital sub-channels & to DISH Network & Verizon FiOS subscribers.
Scrambled signal: Yes.
Ownership: Jimmy Swaggart Ministries.

SONY ENTERTAINMENT TELEVISION ASIA
c/o MSM North America Inc
550 Madison Ave, 12th Fl, Rm 1259
New York, NY 10022
Phones: 212-833-7450; 212-833-7684
Fax: 212-833-7862
E-mail: viewer_infoUSA@spe.sony.com
Web Site: http://www.setasia.tv
Man Jit Singh, Chief Executive Officer, Sony Entertainment Network
Neeraj Arora, Executive Vice President & Head, International Business
Debarshi Pandit, Information Contact
Type of service: Digital.
Operating hours/week: 168.
Operating areas: California.
Programming: Focused on South Asian dramas, movies, reality-shows, comedies, soaps, talk & game shows.
Began: October 1995 in India. Began August 8, 2007 in the U.S.
Distribution method: Available to cable subscribers.
Scrambled signal: Yes.
Ownership: Sony Entertainment.

SONY MOVIE CHANNEL
c/o Sony Pictures Television
10202 W Washington Blvd
Culver City, CA 90232-3195
Phones: 310-244-4000; 310-244-5095
Fax: 310-244-2169
Web Site: http://www.sonymoviechannel.com
Andy Kaplan, President, Worldwide Networks, Sony Pictures Television
Paula Askanas, Executive Vice President, Communications, Sony Pictures Television
Superna Kalle, General Manager, Sony Movie Channel & Senior Vice President, Sony Pictures Television Networks
Ron Garfield, Senior Vice President, Affiliate Sales
Edward Zimmerman, Vice President, Media Production, Sony Pictures Television
Type of service: Basic, HD, video on demand.
Operating hours/week: 168.
Operating areas: Available nationwide.
Programming: Offers uncut and uninterrupted theatrical releases in high definition and 3D. Sony Movie Channel Everywhere allows Dish Network and DirecTV customers online access to over 3,500 Sony Pictures films.
Began: October 1, 2010, Sony Movie Channel Everywhere began October 4, 2011.
Distribution method: Available to cable, IPTV & satellite subscribers; video on demand through Sony Movie Channel Everywhere.
Scrambled signal: Yes.
Ownership: Sony Pictures Entertainment.

SONY MOVIE CHANNEL EVERYWHERE — See Sony Movie Channel.
Type of service: Streaming.
Operating areas: Nationwide.
Programming: Movies from Sony Movie Channel.
Distribution method: Available online to DirecTV & DISH Network subscribers.

SOONERVISION
c/o McClendon Center for Intercollegiate Athletics
180 W Brooks
Norman, OK 73019
Phone: 405-325-8200
E-mail: bmeier@ou.edu
Web Site: http://www.soonersports.com/school-bio/sooner-vision.html
Brandon Meier, Assistant Athletic Director, Broadcast Operations
Dan Cavanaugh, Broadcasting Director, Producer
Craig Moore, Engineering Director
Max Toperzer, Creative Director
Matt Jacques, Motion Graphic Designer
Type of service: Regional, streaming.
Operating areas: Oklahoma.
Programming: Provides broadcasts of basketball, wrestling, gymnastics, volleyball, softball and baseball plus press conferences, coaches' shows, practice videos, interviews, highlights and classic footage plus live streaming webcasts.
Began: January 1, 1997.
Means of Support: University funding.
Distribution method: Available to Cox subscribers. Streaming available online.
Scrambled signal: Yes.
Ownership: University of Oklahoma.

SORPRESA!
c/o Olympusat Inc.
560 Village Blvd, Ste 250
West Palm Beach, FL 33409
Phone: 561-684-5657
Fax: 561-684-9690
E-mail: info@olympusat.com
Web Site: http://www.sorpresatv.com
Tom Mohler, Chief Executive Officer, Olympusat Holdings Inc.
Chuck Mohler, Chief Operating Officer
Chris Williams, Chief Financial Officer
Colleen Glynn, Executive Vice President & General Counsel
Arturo Chavez, Senior Vice President, Hispanic Networks
Maria Luz Zuchella, Vice President, Programming & Acquisitions
John Baghdassarian, Head of Affiliate Sales, U.S.
Type of service: Basic.
Operating hours/week: 168.
Operating areas: Available nationwide.
Programming: Spanish-language children's network that offers programming from Latin America & around the world.
Began: December 1, 1999, as Hispanic Television Network. Began March 15, 2003 in the U.S.
Means of Support: Advertising.
Total subscribers: 1,600,000.
Distribution method: Available to Charter, Claro TV, Cox Communications, Frontier, Liberty Cable, Suddenlink & Time Warner Cable subscribers.
Scrambled signal: Yes.
Ownership: Ocean Holdings.

SOUL OF THE SOUTH NETWORK
One Shackleford Dr
Little Rock, AR 72211
Phone: 501-251-1800
Fax: 855-798-9897
E-mail: contact@ssn.tv
Web Site: http://www.ssn.tv
Richard Mays, Chairman
Doug McHenry, Chief Executive Officer
Larry Morton, Chief Strategic Officer
Christopher R. Clark, Executive Vice President, Business & Legal Affairs
Matthew Mixon, Vice President, Affiliate Relations
Type of service: Basic.
Operating hours/week: 168.
Operating areas: Nationwide.
Programming: Dedicated source for Black American news, information, entertainment and culture. Soul of the South features a unique mix of news, dramas, comedies, feature films, court shows, music, documentaries, and talk shows.
Began: May 27, 2013.
Means of Support: Advertising.
Total subscribers: 40,000,000.
Distribution method: Available over the air on digital sub channels and to Comcast, RCN & Time Warner subscribers.
Scrambled signal: Yes.
Ownership: SSN Media Group.

SOUNDTRACK CHANNEL
1335 4th St
Ste 400
Santa Monica, CA 90401
Phone: 310-899-1315
Fax: 310-587-3387
Web Site: https://soundtrackchannel.wordpress.com
William Lee, Chief Executive Officer & Co-Founder
Jeff Wishengrad, Co-Founder
Mike Miller, Co-Founder
Denis Leverson, Chief Operating Officer
Glenn Kopelson, Chief Financial Officer
Heather Hull, Affiliate Relations Director, STC U.S.
Type of service: Digital.
Operating hours/week: 168.
Programming: Music videos from movie soundtracks & entertainment-focused programming.
Began: March 1, 2002.
Total subscribers: 6,000,000.
Distribution method: Available to cable, IPTV & satellite subscribers.
Scrambled signal: Yes.

THE SOUTH CAROLINA CHANNEL
c/o South Carolina ETV & Radio
1041 George Rogers Blvd
Columbia, SC 29201
Phone: 803-737-3200
Web Site: http://scetv.org
Linda O'Bryon, President & Chief Executive Officer
Type of service: Regional basic.
Operating areas: South Carolina.
Programming: Features South Carolina-specific history, arts and nature programming, as well as the CreateTV block of crafts, cooking and home improvement programs.
Distribution method: Available to cable system subscribers.
Ownership: South Carolina ETV & Radio.

SOUTHEASTERN CHANNEL
c/o Southeastern Louisiana University
SLU Box 12872
Hammond, LA 70402
Phones: 985-549-2418; 800-222-SELU
E-mail: sechannel@selu.edu
Web Site: http://www2.selu.edu/thesoutheasternchannel
Rick Settoon, General Manager
Steve Zaffuto, Operations Manager
Type of service: Basic.
Operating hours/week: 168.
Operating areas: Louisiana.
Programming: Educational & community programming.
Began: July 9, 2002.
Distribution method: Available to cable subscribers.
Scrambled signal: Yes.

SPANISH INDEPENDENT BROADCAST NETWORK
5030 E Warner Rd
Ste 3
Phoenix, AZ 85044
Phone: 480-684-3802
Fax: 480-684-3804
E-mail: admin@38iztv.com
Web Site: http://www.38iztv.com
Adrian Quinones, Information Contact
Type of service: Basic.
Operating hours/week: 168.
Operating areas: Arizona.
Programming: Classic movies in Spanish, plus country music videos, extreme sports and music videos from the 60's, 70's, 80's & 90's.
Began: November 15, 1999.
Means of Support: Advertising.
Distribution method: Available over the air on digital sub-channels.
Scrambled signal: Yes.
Ownership: Adrian & Guadalupe Quinones.

SPEED — See Fox Sports 1.

SPICE — See Brazzers TV.

SPICE 2 — See Bang U.

Pay TV & Satellite Services

SPICE HOT — See Reality Kings TV (RKTV).

SPICE: XCESS — See MOFOS.

SPIKE TV
345 Hudson St
7th Fl
New York, NY 10024
Phone: 212-258-6000
Fax: 212-846-1923
Web Site: http://www.spike.com
Doug Herzog, President, Viacom Music & Entertainment Group
Kevin Kay, President, Spike TV
John Cucci, Executive Vice President & Chief Operating Officer
Kassie Canter, Executive Vice President, Communications
Sharon Levy, Executive Vice President, Original Series
Casey Patterson, Executive Vice President, Event Production, Talent & Studio Relations
Frank Tanki, Executive Vice President, Brand Marketing & Creative
Tom Zappala, Executive Vice President, Programming & Scheduling
Tim Duffy, Senior Vice President, Original Programming
Scott Fishman, Senior Vice President & Executive Producer
Cedric Foster, Senior Vice President, Brand Marketing, Digital & Fan Engagement Strategy
Ted Gold, Senior Vice President, Scripted Original Series
Terry Minogue, Senior Vice President, Brand Marketing & Creative
Ines Pluess, Senior Vice President, Brand Marketing & Creative
Chachi Senior, Senior Vice President, Original Series
Jon Slusser, Senior Vice President, Sports & Multi-Platform Events
Matt Califano, Vice President, Program Scheduling
Alex Eastburg, Vice President, Original Series
Cedric Foster, Vice President & General Manager, Digital Brand, Content & Programming Strategy
Justin Lacob, Vice President, Original Series
Debra Marseille, Vice President, Media Planning
Tori Socha, Vice President, Original Series
Jeff Saviano, Senior Director, Original Series

Sales, Mktg. & Affiliate Relations Office:
STAMFORD: Group W Satellite Communications, 250 Harbor Dr, Stamford, CT 06904. Phone: 203-965-6000. Fax: 203-965-6315.
Type of service: Basic, HD.
Satellites: Galaxy V, transponder 2.
Operating hours/week: 168.
Operating areas: Nationwide.
Programming: Acquired comedy & drama series, original series & movies geared towards males.
Began: March 7, 1983.
Means of Support: Advertising & subscriber fees.
Total subscribers: 98,700,000.
Distribution method: Available to cable, IPTV & satellite subscribers.
Scrambled signal: Yes.
Ownership: Viacom Inc.

SPORTING CHANNEL
7172 Hawthorn Ave
Ste 210
Los Angeles, CA 90046
Phone: 213-851-6375
Fax: 213-851-7134
Robert Crawford, Chief Executive Officer
Type of service: Basic & Pay-per-view.
Satellites: Columbia Communications/TDRSS G-7, transponder 10.
Operating hours/week: 4.
Uplink: Denver, CO.
Programming: International sports, including soccer, rugby, baseball, cricket & horse racing.
Began: October 22, 1994.
Means of Support: Advertising & subscribers.
Total subscribers: 6,000,000.
Distribution method: Available to cable & satellite subscribers.
Scrambled signal: Yes. Equipment: VideoCipher II Plus.

SPORTSCHOICE
c/o Oceanic Time Warner
PO Box 30050
Honolulu, HI 96820-0050
Phone: 808-625-2100
Fax: 808-625-5888
Web Site: http://www.oceanic.com
Type of service: Digital.
Operating areas: Hawaii.
Programming: Multiple streams of sports oriented video on a single, interactive tv screen.
Began: November 1, 2006.
Distribution method: Available to Oceanic Time Warner subscribers.
Scrambled signal: Yes.

SPORTSKOOL
100 Cathedral St
Ste 9
Annapolis, MD 21401
Phones: 410-280-8528; 888-490-6230
Fax: 888-446-5507
E-mail: andrew.walworth@gracecreek.com
Web Site: http://www.sportskool.com
Andrew Walworth, President
John Sorensen, Senior Producer
Type of service: Video on demand.
Programming: Network dedicated to delivering in-depth sports expert instruction and coaching for a wide range of sports and athletic activities.
Began: January 1, 2004.
Total subscribers: 25,000,000.
Distribution method: Available to cable subscribers.
Scrambled signal: Yes.
Ownership: Grace Creek Media.

THE SPORTSMAN CHANNEL
2855 S James Dr
Ste 101
New Berlin, WI 53151
Phones: 262-432-9100; 800-971-2330
Fax: 262-432-9101
E-mail: mscheuermann@thesportsmanchannel.com
Web Site: http://www.thesportsmanchannel.com
Jim Liberatore, President & Chief Executive Officer
Todd D. Hansen, Chief Operating Officer
Marc Fein, Executive Vice President, Programming & Production
Lisa Delligatti, Senior Vice President, Affiliate Sales
Michael Magnotta, Senior Vice President/Creative Director
Jeff Brown, Vice President, Affiliate Relations
Maura Fried, Vice President, Sales Operations
Graig Hale, Vice President, Business Development
Ben Lines, Vice President, Marketing
Jeff Nigl, Vice President, Finance
Mitch Petrie, Vice President, Programming
Sandi Castro, Affiliate Relations Director
Molly McFarland, Affiliate Sales Director
Michelle Scheuermann, Communications Director
Jim Seeley, Programming Director
Adam King, Affiliate Marketing Manager, Western Region
Alyse Ramer, Affiliate Relations Manager, Southeast Region
Lisa Swan, Affiliate Relations Manager, Eastern Region
Kimberly Hawkins, Senior Coordinator, Affiliate Relations
Type of service: Basic, HD, streaming, video on demand.
Operating hours/week: 168.
Uplink: Chandler, AZ.
Programming: Dedicated exclusively to hunting & fishing.
Began: April 7, 2003, The Sportsman Channel HD began February 10, 2010. The Sportsman Channel on Demand began August 17, 2011.
Total subscribers: 31,000,000.
Scrambled signal: Yes.
Ownership: Kroenke Sports & Entertainment.

SPORTSNET NEW YORK
75 Rockefeller Plz
29th Fl
New York, NY 10019
Phone: 212-485-4800
Fax: 212-485-4802
Web Site: http://www.sny.tv
Steve Raab, President
Curt Gowdy, Jr., Senior Vice President, Production & Executive Producer
Gary Morgenstern, Senior Vice President, Programming
Scott Weinfeld, Senior Vice President, Finance & Administration
Brad Como, Vice President, News Programming
Marie DeParis, Vice President, Marketing & Business Development
Andrew Fegyveresi, Vice President, Communications
Brian Erdlen, Chief Revenue Officer
Scott Wilpon, Senior Director, Business Development
Fred Harner, General Manager, Digital Media
Operating hours/week: 168.
Operating areas: New York, New Jersey, Connecticut & Pennsylvania.
Began: March 16, 2006.
Total subscribers: 12,000,000.
Distribution method: Available to cable, IPTV & satellite subscribers.
Scrambled signal: Yes.
Ownership: A joint venture between Sterling Entertainment Enterprises (65%), Time Warner Cable (27%), & Comcast (8%). Comcast operates & manages the service.

SPORTSOUTH — See FOX Sports South.
1175 Peachtree St NE
Bldg 100, Ste 200
Atlanta, GA 30361
Phone: 404-230-7300
Fax: 404-230-7339
E-mail: FSSouth@foxsports.net
Web Site: http://www.foxsports.com/south

FULLY SEARCHABLE • CONTINUOUSLY UPDATED • DISCOUNT RATES FOR PRINT PURCHASERS
For more information call 800-771-9202 or visit www.warren-news.com

Began: October 1, 1999, as Turner South; relaunched as SportSouth October 13, 2006.
Total subscribers: 8,900,000.

SPORTS PPV
4100 E Dry Creek Rd
Littleton, CO 80122
Phone: 303-486-3938
Fax: 303-486-3951
E-mail: rachel.ford@espn3.com
Web Site: http://www.hits.com
Jon Radloff, New Product Marketing Director
Type of service: Digital, pay-per-view.
Operating hours/week: 24.
Programming: Sports & sports barker channel. Part of headend HITS package.
Began: September 4, 1999.
Scrambled signal: Yes.
Ownership: ESPN Inc.

SPORTSTIME OHIO — See FOX Sports Ohio.

SPORTS VIEW PLUS
c/o Charter Communications
12405 Powerscourt Dr
St. Louis, MO 63131
Phone: 314-965-0555
Web Site: http://www.charter.com
Type of service: Digital.
Operating hours/week: 168.
Programming: Combines coverage of baseball, racing, hockey, football, basketball & other sports from cable channels and websites.
Began: March 2, 2009.
Distribution method: Available to Charter subscribers.
Scrambled signal: Yes.

SPROUT
PO Box 288
Fort Washington, PA 19034
Phone: 877-768-8411
E-mail: info@sproutonline.com
Web Site: http://www.sproutonline.com
Sandy Wax, President
Andrew Beecham, Senior Vice President, Programming
Amy Friedman, Senior Vice President, Programming & Development
Mark Sacher, Senior Vice President, Research
Jennifer Giddens, Vice President, Marketing
Jenni Glenn, Vice President, Communications & Marketing

Branch Office:
NEW YORK: 1790 Broadway, 16th Fl, New York, NY 10019. Phone: 212-708-3000.
Type of service: Digital, HD, video on demand.
Operating hours/week: 168.
Operating areas: Nationwide.
Programming: Popular preschooler series from PBS Kids, HIT Entertainment & Sesame Street.
Began: September 6, 1999, as PBS Kids. Service ceased operations October 1, 2005 and was replaced by PBS Kids Sprout. Sprout on Demand began April 1, 2005.
Total subscribers: 60,000,000 (Includes both basic & video on demand subscribers).

2017 Edition

E-81

Pay TV & Satellite Services

Distribution method: Available to cable & satellite subscribers.
Scrambled signal: Yes.
Ownership: NBCUniversal LLC. NBC bought out partners PBS and HIT Television Ventures (Apax Funds) November 2013.

STAR ONE — See Life OK.

STAR CHINESE CHANNEL
No 183, Sec 2, Tiding Bldg
Neihu District
Taipei City 114
Taiwan
Phone: 886-2-8752-8949
Programming: Provides a wide range of Mandarin-language general entertainment programs including talk shows, game shows, contemporary and costume dramas, lifestyle and variety shows.
Distribution method: Available to KyLin TV & satellite subscribers.
Scrambled signal: Yes.
Ownership: 21st Century Fox.

STAR GOLD — See STAR Plus.
Type of service: Expanded digital basic, HD.
Programming: Bollywood movies, including comedies, action, romance & family.
Began: 1991. STAR Gold HD began April 15, 2011.
Scrambled signal: Yes.

STAR INDIA NEWS — See ABP News.

STAR NEWS — See ABP News.

STAR PLUS
c/o STAR India
Star House, Urmi Estate 95 Ganpat Rao, Kadam Marg Lower Parel
Mumbai 400013
India
Web Site: http://www.startv.com
Type of service: Digital expanded basic, HD.
Operating areas: Available nationwide.
Programming: General entertainment including comedies, reality, family dramas & films.
Began: February 21, 1992, STAR India Plus HD began April 15, 2011.
Distribution method: Available to cable, IPTV & satellite subscribers. Streaming available online.
Scrambled signal: Yes.
Ownership: STAR India, a subsidiary of 21st Century Fox.

STARZ
8900 Liberty Cir
Englewood, CO 80112
Phone: 720-852-7700
Fax: 720-852-7710
E-mail: eric.becker@starz.com
Web Site: http://www.starz.com
Chris Albrecht, President & Chief Executive Officer
Jeffrey A Hirsch, Chief Operating Officer
Alison Hoffman, Chief Marketing Officer
Scott D Macdonald, Chief Financial Officer
John Penney, Chief Strategy Officer
David Weil, Chief Legal Officer
Glenn Curtis, President
Carmi Zlotnick, Managing Director, Original Programming
Kevin Kasha, Head of Acquisitions
Sheryl Anderson, Executive Vice President, Human Resources & Administration
Theano Apostolou, Executive Vice President, Corporate Communications
David Baldwin, Executive Vice President, Program Planning
Gene George, Executive Vice President, Worldwide Distribution
Joe Glennon, Executive Vice President, Affiliate Sales
Nancy McGee, Executive Vice President, Marketing
Ray Milius, Executive Vice President, Programming & IT Operations
Pamela Wolfe, Executive Vice President, Human Resources
Karen Bailey, Senior Vice President, Original Programming
Marc Barson, Senior Vice President, Business & Legal Affairs
Scott Barton, Senior Vice President, Branded Digital Content & Products
Eric Becker, Senior Vice President, Corporate Communications
Amy Bell, Senior Vice President, Brand Strategy & Marketing Communications
Bill Bergmann, Senior Vice President, Finance & Planning
Shannon Buck, Senior Vice President, Programming Publicity
Paul Campbell, Senior Vice President, Programming Publicity
Kevin Cross, Senior Vice President, Business & Legal Affairs
Colleen Curtis, Senior Vice President, Consumer & Digital Publicity
Janet Dickinson, Senior Vice President, Finance & Accounting and Controller
Carrie Dolce, Senior Vice President, Business & Legal Affairs
Debbie Egner, Senior Vice President, Affiliate Sales & Sales Operations
Marta Fernandez, Senior Vice President, Original Programming
Melissa Harper, Senior Vice President, Original Programming Production
Richter Hartig, Senior Vice President, Original Programming Production Finance
Todd Hoy, Senior Vice President, Business & Legal Affairs
Amy Kline, Senior Vice President, Programming Operations/Quality Control
Brad Martens, Senior Vice President, Broadcast Engineering
Randall McCurdy, Senior Vice President, Sales & Affiliate Marketing
Eric Neal, Senior Vice President, Program Planning
James Porter, Senior Vice President, Media Systems & IT Development
Russell Schwartz, Senior Vice President, Business & Legal Affairs
Ken Segna, Senior Vice President, Original Programming
Suzanne Sell, Senior Vice President, Research
Keno Thomas, Senior Vice President, Affiliate Sales
Michael Vamosy, Senior Vice President, Creative Services
Mara Winkour, Senior Vice President, Digital Media, Business Development & Strategy
Gavin Wise, Senior Vice President, Business & Legal Affairs
Jason Wyrick, Senior Vice President, Digital Platforms
Deanne Bloch, Vice President, Business & Legal Affairs
Brian Huggins, Vice President, Finance
John Martin, Vice President, Business & Legal Affairs, Production Labor Relations
Neal Massey, Vice President, Business & Consumer Insights, Research
Sue Provan, Vice President, Accounting
Lauren Reutz, Vice President, Media Strategy & Planning
Janine Scalise Boyd, Vice President, Business & Creative Affairs, Music
Joe Zamora, Vice President, Finance
John J. Sie, Founder
Type of service: Pay, HD, streaming, video on demand.
Satellites: Galaxy 13, transponder 15; Galaxy 13, transponder 9; Galaxy 14, transponder 12; Galaxy 15, transponder 13; Galaxy 15, transponder 3.
Operating hours/week: 168.
Programming: First run movies & original programming.
Began: February 1, 1994, Starz on Demand began September 2001. Starz HD began 2003. Starz stand-alone streaming service began April 2016.
Means of Support: Subscriber fees.
Total subscribers: 23,600,000 (Number includes all Starz channels. 3,700,000 on demand subscribers.).
Distribution method: Available to cable, IPTV & satellite subscribers; streaming available online & mobile through Starz Play (participating providers); video on demand available through participating providers.
Scrambled signal: Yes. Equipment: Digital/DigiCipher II.
Ownership: Starz LLC. On June 30, 2016 it was announced that Lionsgate would acquire Starz. Deal is expected to close by end of 2016.

STARZ CINEMA — See Starz.
Type of service: Pay, HD.
Programming: Independent & arthouse movies.
Began: May 1, 1999, Starz Cinema HD began June 23, 2010.
Scrambled signal: Yes.

STARZ COMEDY — See Starz.
Type of service: Pay, HD.
Programming: Comedy movies.
Began: May 1, 1999, Starz Comedy HD began in September 2007.
Scrambled signal: Yes.

STARZ EDGE — See Starz.
Type of service: Pay, HD.
Programming: Films & original programming geared towards 18-34 year-olds.
Began: March 15, 1996, as Starz 2. Rebranded Starz Edge in 2005. Starz Edge HD began in 2007.

STARZ ENCORE
8900 Liberty Cir
Englewood, CO 80112
Phones: 720-852-7700; 855-807-2989
Fax: 720-852-7710
Web Site: http://www.encoretv.com
Chris Albrecht, Chief Executive Officer, Starz LLC
Glenn Curtis, President, Starz LLC
Scott Macdonald, Chief Financial Officer, Starz LLC
John Penney, Chief Strategy Officer, Starz LLC
Carmi Zlotnik, Managing Director, Starz LLC
Sheryl Anderson, Executive Vice President, Human Resources & Administration, Starz LLC
Theano Apostolou, Executive Vice President, Communications, Starz LLC
David Baldwin, Executive Vice President, Program Planning, Starz LLC
Ray Milius, Executive Vice President, Programming & IT Operations, Starz LLC
David Weil, Executive Vice President & General Counsel, Starz LLC
Eric Becker, Senior Vice President, Corporate Communications, Starz LLC
Type of service: Pay, HD, streaming, video on demand.
Satellites: Galaxy 13, transponder 15; Galaxy 13, transponder 9; Galaxy 14, transponder 12; Galaxy 15, transponder 13; Galaxy 15, transponder 3.
Operating hours/week: 168.
Operating areas: Nationwide.
Programming: First-run & recent big hit movies, plus classic films, uncut & commercial free. The network focuses on high-quality movies that received box office success or critical acclaim & include notable stars and/or directors. Additionally, Encore features star interviews, movie trivia & original series.
Began: April 1, 1991, Encore HD began January 2003, then shut down in 2006. Relaunched in 2008. Encore on Demand began in 2000. Encore Play began October 8, 2012. Rebranded Starz Encore on April 5, 2016.
Means of Support: Subscriber fees.
Total subscribers: 32,200,000.
Distribution method: Available to cable, IPTV & satellite subscribers. Streaming available through Encore Play app. Video on demand available through participating providers.
Scrambled signal: Yes. Equipment: Digital/DigiCipher II.
Ownership: Starz LLC.

STARZ ENCORE ACTION — See Starz Encore.
Type of service: Pay, HD.
Operating areas: Nationwide.
Programming: Action movies.
Began: September 1, 1994, as Encore 5. Rebranded as Action & Encore Action in 2005. Encore Action HD began August 2011. Rebranded Starz Encore Action April 5, 2016.
Distribution method: Available to cable, IPTV & satellite subscribers.
Scrambled signal: Yes.

STARZ ENCORE BLACK — See Starz Encore.
Type of service: Pay, HD.
Operating areas: Available nationwide.
Programming: Movies, comedy & drama series.
Began: September 1, 1994, as Encore 6. Rebranded as True Stories & Drama & Encore Drama in March 2005. Encore Drama HD began August 2011. Rebranded Encore Black on December 2, 2013 & Starz Encore Black on April 5, 2016.
Distribution method: Available to cable, IPTV & satellite subscribers.
Scrambled signal: Yes.

STARZ ENCORE CLASSIC — See Starz Encore.
Type of service: Pay, HD.
Operating areas: Available nationwide.
Programming: Classic movies, comedy & drama series.
Began: April 1, 1991, as Encore 2. Rebranded as Love Stories, then Encore Love. Rebranded as Encore Classic on December 2, 2013. Encore Classic HD began December 2013. Rebranded Starz Encore Classic April 5, 2016.
Distribution method: Available to cable, IPTV & satellite subscribers.

STARZ ENCORE ESPANOL — See Starz Encore.
Type of service: Pay.
Operating areas: Available nationwide.
Programming: Imported & domestic Spanish-language films.
Began: August 1, 2011.
Distribution method: Available to cable, IPTV & satellite subscribers.

Pay TV & Satellite Services

STARZ ENCORE FAMILY — See Starz Encore.
Type of service: Pay.
Operating areas: Available nationwide.
Programming: Movies with no more than a PG-13 rating.
Began: September 1, 1994, as Encore 6, WAM! America's Youth Network, Encore Wam in 2005, Encore Family on August 1, 2011 & Starz Encore Family April 5, 2016.
Distribution method: Available to cable, IPTV & satellite subscribers.

STARZ ENCORE SUSPENSE — See Starz Encore.
Type of service: Pay, HD.
Operating areas: Available nationwide.
Programming: Mystery & suspense movies & series.
Began: 1994 as Mystery. Rebranded Encore Mystery in 2005 & Encore Suspense in 2011. Encore Suspense HD began December 2013. Rebranded Starz Encore Suspense April 5, 2016.
Distribution method: Available to cable, IPTV & satellite subscribers.

STARZ ENCORE WESTERNS — See Starz Encore.
Type of service: Pay.
Operating areas: Available nationwide.
Programming: Western movies & series.
Began: April 1, 1991, as Encore 3. Rebranded Westerns, Encore Westerns in 2005 & Starz Encore Westerns April 5, 2016.
Distribution method: Available to cable, IPTV & satellite subscribers.

STARZ IN BLACK — See Starz.
Type of service: Pay, HD.
Programming: Urban films & original programming.
Began: May 1, 1999, Starz In Black HD began on June 23, 2010.

STARZ KIDS & FAMILY — See Starz.
Type of service: Pay, HD.
Programming: Films & animated series geared towards families.
Began: May 1, 1999, Starz Kids & Family HD began September 1, 2007.

STARZ PLAY — See Starz.
Type of service: Streaming.
Operating areas: Nationwide.
Programming: Movies from Starz channels.
Distribution method: Available online & through app.

STREAMPIX
Comcast Ctr
1701 JFK Blvd
Philadelphia, PA 19103
Web Site: http://www.xfinity.com/streampix
Type of service: Streaming.
Distribution method: Available to Comcast Xfinity subscribers.
Scrambled signal: Yes.
Ownership: Comcast NBCUniversal.

STYLE NETWORK — See Esquire Network.

SUDDENLINK2GO
12444 Powerscourt Dr
St Louis, MO 63131
Phones: 314-965-2020; 314-315-9346
Web Site: http://www.suddenlink.com
Jerry Dow, Chief Marketing & Sales Officer
Type of service: Streaming.
Operating hours/week: 168.
Operating areas: Nationwide.
Programming: Features tens of thousands of full-length TV episodes and shorter video clips, plus more than 1,300 movies.
Began: June 8, 2011.
Distribution method: Available to Suddenlink subscribers.
Scrambled signal: Yes.
Ownership: Cequel Communications LLC.

SUN CHANNEL
c/o Olympusat Inc.
560 Village Blvd, Ste 250
West Palm Beach, FL 33409
Phone: 561-684-5657
Fax: 561-684-9690
E-mail: info@olympusat.com
Web Site: http://www.sunchanneltv.com; http://www.olympusat.com
Programming: Entertainment programming specializing in travel & tourism.
Scrambled signal: Yes.
Ownership: Sun Channel. Distributed in the U.S. by Olympsat.

SUNDANCE TV
11 Penn Plz
15th Fl
New York, NY 10001
Phone: 212-324-8500
E-mail: feedback@sundancechannel.com
Web Site: http://www.sundance.tv
Ed Carroll, Chief Operating Officer, AMC Networks Inc.
Robert Broussard, President, AMC Networks Distribution
Charlie Collier, President & General Manager, AMC & Sundance TV
Joel Stillerman, President, Original Programming & Development, AMC & Sundance
Susie Fitzgerald, Executive Vice President, Scripted Programming
Linda Schupack, Executive Vice President, Marketing
Vanessa Benfield, Senior Vice President, Partnership Sales & Integrated Solutions
Suzy Berkowitz Weksel, Senior Vice President, Public Relations
Monica Bloom, Senior Vice President, Marketing
Rob Friedman, Senior Vice President, Programming & Scheduling
Georgia Juvelis, Senior Vice President, Corporate Communications
Christian Vesper, Senior Vice President, International Programming, Development, Acquisitions & Co-Productions
Mark Williams, Senior Vice President, Brand Creative
Meg Bogdan, Vice President, Legal & Business Affairs
J. C. Cancedda, Vice President, Brand Strategy & Creative
Ilene Danuff, Vice President, Advertising Sales
Evan Fleischer, Vice President, Integrated Marketing & Branded Entertainment
Jessica Gleason, Vice President, On-Air Promotions & Branded Entertainment
Jordan Helman, Vice President, Development & Current Progamming
Gustavo Lopez, Vice President, Global Distribution & Business Development, Latin America
Drew Pisarra, Vice President, Digital Media & Marketing
Tony Song, Vice President, Sales & Partnerships
Denielle Webb, Vice President, Public Relations & Marketing
Lele Engler, Marketing & Media Director
Mark Zadroga, Digital Media Director
Type of service: Basic, HD, streaming & video on demand.
Satellites: Satcom C-3, transponder 24 (east); Galaxy 9, transponder 14 (west); HITS, transponder Pod 8.
Operating hours/week: 168.
Operating areas: Available nationwide.
Programming: Independent features, foreign films, documentaries, shorts, scripted & unscripted series, animation & experimental films without commercials.
Began: February 29, 1996, as Sundance Channel. Sundance TV HD began April 14, 2010. Rebranded Sundance TV February 3, 2014.
Means of Support: Advertising.
Total subscribers: 57,100,000.
Distribution method: Available to cable, IPTV & satellite subscribers. Streaming available online. Video on demand available through participating providers.
Scrambled signal: Yes.
Ownership: AMC Networks Inc. Formerly Rainbow Media Holdings LLC. It became a publicly held company under the new name June 30, 2011.

SUN SPORTS — See FOX Sports Florida/Sun Sports.

SUPER CANAL — See ULTRA HDPlex.
Av Luperon 46
Distrito Nacional
Santo Domingo AP 3133
Dominican Republic
Phone: 809-531-3333
Fax: 809-473-6666
E-mail: contact@supercanal.com
Web Site: http://www.supercanal.com
Frank Jorge Elias, President & Chief Executive Officer, Super Canal Group
Type of service: Pay, HD.
Satellites: AMC, transponder 3.
Operating hours/week: 168.
Operating areas: Available nationwide.
Programming: Spanish language general entertainment channel featuring news, music, sports, politics, and special events from the Dominican Republic.
Means of Support: Subscriber fees.
Distribution method: Available cable, IPTV & satellite subscribers.
Scrambled signal: Yes.
Ownership: Super Canal Group. Distributed in U.S. by Olympusat.

SUPERENE
c/o Condista, 409 N Pacific Coast Hwy
Ste 595
Redondo Beach, CA 90277
Phone: 323-554-6776
E-mail: info@condista.com
Web Site: http://www.superene.com
Programming: Spanish-language animated programming for children 4-12 years old.
Ownership: D'Ocon Films. Distributed in the U.S. by Condista.

SUPERSTATION WGN — See WGN America.

SUR
601 Brickell Key Dr
Ste 100
Miami, FL 33131
Phones: 305-530-3561; 786-236-2207
Fax: 305-373-7811
E-mail: jorge@condista.com
Web Site: http://www.canalsur.com
Arturo Delgado, Chief Executive Officer
Jose Garcia Conde, Chief Financial Officer
Rolando A. Figueroa, Vice President, Marketing
Rafael Manrique, Affiliate Relations

Branch Offices:
BOSTON: 911 Massachusetts Ave, Boston, MA 02118.

FALLS CHURCH: 150 S Washington St, Ste 401, Falls Church, VA 22046.

ST. PETERSBURG: 9455 Koger Blvd, Ste 113, St. Petersburg, FL 33702.
Type of service: Premium.
Satellites: Intelsat 705, transponder 5.
Operating hours/week: 168.
Operating areas: Nationwide.
Uplink: Lima, Peru.
Programming: Live newscasts, soccer games & family entertainment from Latin America.
Began: January 1, 1993, for Canal Sur.
Means of Support: Advertising.
Total subscribers: 1,500,000.
Distribution method: Available to Cablevision, Comcast, Time Warner, AT&T U-Verse, Verizon FiOS & DirecTV subscribers.
Scrambled signal: Yes.
Ownership: Sur Corp.

THE SURF CHANNEL
401 Wilshire Blvd
Ste 230
Santa Monica, CA 90401
Phone: 310-260-6434
E-mail: taylor@thesurfchannel.com
Web Site: http://www.thesurfchannel.com
Steve Bellamy, Founder
Shannon Marie Quirk, Editor-In-Chief, TheSurfChannel.com
Emily Bates, Athlete Coordinator
Type of service: Streaming, video on demand.
Operating areas: Available nationwide.
Programming: The first national television network dedicated to surfers, surfing & surf culture.
Began: August 16, 2012, online.
Means of Support: Advertising.
Total subscribers: 20,000,000 (Estimated number based on current carriage agreements.).
Distribution method: Available to Cablevision, Comcast, Cox Communications & DirecTV customers. Streaming available online.
Scrambled signal: Yes.
Ownership: Steve Bellamy.

SUR PERU — See Sur.
200 Crandon Blvd
Ste 316
Key Biscayne, FL 33149
Phone: 786-236-2207
Web Site: http://www.canalsur.com

Pay TV & Satellite Services

Programming: Spanish language news & entertainment from Peru.
Began: 2005.
Total subscribers: 1,600,000.
Scrambled signal: Yes.
Ownership: SUR LLC. Distributed in the U.S. by Condista.

SWRV TV — See MC.

SYFY
c/o USA Networks
1230 Avenue of the Americas
New York, NY 10020
Phone: 212-413-5236
Fax: 212-413-6515
Web Site: http://www.syfy.com
Dave Howe, President, Strategy & Commercial Growth
Bill McGoldrick, Executive Vice President, Scripted Content
Thomas P. Vitale, Executive Vice President, Programming & Original Movies, Syfy & Chiller
Ted A'Zary, Senior Vice President, Research, Syfy & Chiller
Jeff Blackman, Senior Vice President, Creative, Syfy & Chiller
Matthew Chiavelli, Senior Vice President, Digital
Sara Morgan Moscowitz, Senior Vice President, Strategic Marketing, Syfy
Katherine Nelson, Senior Vice President, Communications, Syfy & Chiller
Heather Olander, Senior Vice President, Alternative Series Development & Production, Syfy
Chris Regina, Senior Vice President, Program Strategy, Syfy & Chiller
Paul Shapiro, Senior Vice President, Original Content, Syfy
Rob Spodek, Senior Vice President & Chief Financial Officer, Syfy & Chiller
Andie Beckerman, Vice President, Alternative Development & Production, Syfy
Erika Kennair, Vice President, Original Programming & Development, Syfy
Dana Ortiz, Vice President, Brand Marketing, Syfy
Wayne Sampson, Vice President, Programming & Development, Syfy
Scott Vila, Vice President, Original Programming

Regional Offices:
CENTRAL: 401 N Michigan Ave, Ste 2550, Chicago, IL 60511. Phone: 312-644-5413.

WESTERN: 2049 Century Park E, Los Angeles, CA 90067. Phone: 310-201-2300.

AD SALES: 2000 Town Center, Ste 2460, Southfield, MI 40875. Phone: 313-353-1200.
Type of service: Basic, HD.
Satellites: Galaxy V, transponder 4.
Operating hours/week: 168.
Programming: Science-fiction/fact, horror & fantasy.
Began: September 24, 1992, as the Sci-Fi Channel. Sci-Fi Channel HD began October 3, 2007. Rebranded Syfy in 2009.
Total subscribers: 95,000,000.
Distribution method: Available to cable, IPTV & satellite subscribers.
Scrambled signal: Yes.
Ownership: NBCUniversal LLC.

THE SYZYGY NETWORK
593 Wrens Path
Akron, OH 44319
Phone: 330-472-0083
E-mail: info@syzygynetwork.com

Dave Andrews, Chief Executive Officer
Rob Weiss, President
Larry Nemecek, President, Publishing
Scott Brody, Vice President, Programming
Ron B. Moore, Visual Effects Director
David Reddick, Art Director
Type of service: Plans basic.
Operating areas: Plans nationwide.
Programming: Currently online only. Plans to offer a cable channel catering exclusively to the SciFi and Fantasy fan.
Scrambled signal: Yes.

TAC TV
c/o Allied Media Corp.
6723 Whittier Ave, Ste 204
McLean, VA 22101
Phone: 703-333-2008
Fax: 703-997-7539
E-mail: tac-tv@allied-media.com
Web Site: http://www.allied-media.com/ARABTV/the_arabic_channel_TACHist.html
Type of service: Basic, Pay, Digital.
Satellites: Telstar 5.
Sales representative: Allied Media Corp.
Operating hours/week: 168.
Operating areas: Greater New York City metropolitan area, including Jersey City & Bergen County, NJ & Mt. Vernon, NY.
Programming: Full-time family entertainment in the Arabic language (most programs subtitled in English).
Began: April 8, 1991.
Means of Support: Advertising & leased time programming.
Total subscribers: 1,250,000.
Distribution method: Available to cable, IPTV & satellite subscribers.
Scrambled signal: Yes.

TACH-TV
332 W Broadway
Ste 1604
Louisville, KY 40202
Phone: 502-992-0200
Fax: 502-992-0201
E-mail: bgordon@theautochannel.com
Web Site: http://www.theautochannel.com
Robert Jay Gordon, President
Marc J. Rauch, Executive Vice President
Mark E. Fulmer, Vice President & Editor in Chief
Carre Gordon, Affiliate Relations
Type of service: Basic, streaming.
Operating hours/week: 168.
Operating areas: Florida & Massachusetts. Expanding to Arizona, California & Pennsylvania.
Programming: TV & video programming produced over the years by The Auto Channel, along with select video content produced by independent producers and studios.
Began: January 1996 online. June 15, 2012 over the air.
Means of Support: Advertising.
Distribution method: Available over the air on digital sub channels. Streaming available online.
Scrambled signal: Yes.
Ownership: The Auto Channel LLC. Bob Gordon & Marc Rauch co-founders.

TAIWAN MACROVIEW TV — See MAC TV.

TALKLINE COMMUNICATIONS TV NETWORK
Park West Station
PO Box 20108
New York, NY 10025
Phones: 212-769-1925; 866-482-5554
Fax: 212-799-4195

E-mail: tcntalk@aol.com
Web Site: http://talklinecommunications.com
Zev Brenner, President
Type of service: Basic, over the air.
Satellites: Telstar 7.
Operating hours/week: 3.
Programming: Talk shows, news programs & music on & about Jewish life.
Began: August 1, 1981.
Means of Support: Advertising.
Distribution method: Available over the air on digital sub-channels & tp cable subscribers.
Scrambled signal: Yes.

TANGO TRAFFIC
147 Pennsylvania Ave
Malvern, PA 19355
Phones: 267-270-2470; 855-826-4655
E-mail: info@tangotraffic.com
Tim Chambers, Chief Executive Officer
John Acello, Vice President & General Manager
Suzanne Harris, Vice President, Marketing
Chris Cantz, Director
Type of service: Basic, over the air.
Operating hours/week: 168.
Operating areas: Pennsylvania.
Programming: Nation's first traffic network dedicated entirely to delivering 24/7 local on demand traffic information.
Began: January 1, 2011.
Distribution method: Available over the air on digital sub-channels and to Comcast & Verizon FiOS subscribers.
Scrambled signal: Yes.
Ownership: Tim Chambers, Vince Curran, Al McGowan & Kevin O'Kane.

TAPESH TV
26668 Agoura Rd
Calabasa, CA 91302
Phone: 818-610-0070
Fax: 818-593-4545
Web Site: http://www.tapesh.com
Programming: Persian news, movies, music, talk, children's & cooking shows.

TAVSIR IRAN
PO Box 1601
Simi Valley, CA 93062
Phone: 818-342-3399
E-mail: info@afnl.com
Web Site: http://www.afnl.com
Operating hours/week: 168.
Programming: Farsi-language news & entertainment for Iranian communities in the U.S.
Began: January 1, 1993.
Distribution method: Available to satellite subscribers.
Scrambled signal: Yes.

TBN ENLACE USA — See Enlace USA.

TBN SALSA
PO Box A
Santa Ana, CA 92711
Phone: 714-832-2950
Web Site: http://www.tbn-salsa.org
Type of service: Over the air, streaming.
Operating areas: Nationwide.
Programming: English-language contemporary worship & gospel music, church & ministry programming, talk shows highlighting issues and topics of interest to the Hispanic community, along with Latino-themed documentaries, sports shows, family-friendly movies and broadcast specials.
Began: June 1, 2015.
Distribution method: Available over the air on digital sub-channels. Streaming available online.

Scrambled signal: Yes.
Ownership: TBN Networks, a non-profit corp.

TBS
1050 Techwood Dr NW
Atlanta, GA 30318
Phone: 404-827-1717
Fax: 404-827-1947
E-mail: tbs.superstation@turner.com
Web Site: http://www.tbs.com
Kevin Reilly, President, TNT & TBS
Sandra Dewey, President, Productions & Business Affairs, TNT & TBS
Jeff Gregor, Chief Catalyst Officer, TNT & TBS
Michael Engleman, Executive Vice President, Entertainment Marketing & Brand Innovation, TNT & TBS
Patrick Kelly, Executive Vice President, Business Affairs, TNT & TBS
Brett Weitz, Executive Vice President, Original Programming, TBS
Dennis Adamovich, Senior Vice President, Digital, Affiliate, Lifestyle & Enterprise Commerce, TNT, TBS & TCM
David Eilenberg, Senior Vice President, Unscripted Development, TNT & TBS
Thom Hinkle, Senior Vice President, Original Programming
David Hudson, Senior Vice President, Late Night & Specials, TNT & TBS
Phil Oppenheim, Senior Vice President, Programming, TNT & TBS
Sandy Padula, Senior Vice President, Research, TNT & TBS
Mark Weissman, Senior Vice President, Production, TNT & TBS
Justin Williams, Senior Vice President, Digital Ventures, TNT & TBS
Rachel Brill, Vice President, Unscripted Programming, TNT & TBS
Jeff Carr, Vice President, Programming, TNT & TBS
Missy Chambless, Vice President, Unscripted Programming, TNT & TBS
Jimmy Jellinek, Vice President, Content Marketing & Digital Innovation, TNT & TBS
Lincoln Lopez, Vice President, Marketing, Digital & Social Media, TNT, TBS & TCM
Kristie Moomey, Vice President, Post Production, Unscripted Programming & Digital Extensions, TNT & TBS
Marie Moore, Vice President, Communications, TNT & TBS
Robin Pelleck, Vice President, Digital, TBS & TNT
Raghunadh Polavarapu, Vice President, Digital Operations, TNT, TBS & TCM
Nancy Rewis, Vice President, Commerce Enterprise, TNT, TBS & TCM
Type of service: Basic, HD, streaming & video on demand.
Satellites: Galaxy I, transponder 18.
Sales representative: Turner Network Sales.
Operating hours/week: 168.
Operating areas: Nationwide.
Uplink: Atlanta, GA.
Programming: Original scripted & acquired comedy series, late night talk, animation, movies, sports.
Began: December 17, 1976, TBS HD began September 2007.
Means of Support: System pays common carrier; advertising.
Total subscribers: 98,600,000.
Distribution method: Available to cable, IPTV & satellite subscribers. Streaming available online & mobile through website or the WATCH TBS app (participating providers). Video on demand available through participating providers.
Scrambled signal: Yes.
Ownership: Turner Broadcasting Systems, a division of Time Warner.

Pay TV & Satellite Services

TCT
PO Box 1010
11717 Rte 37 N
Marion, IL 62959
Phone: 618-997-4700
Fax: 618-993-9778
Web Site: http://www.tct.tv
Dr. Garth Coonce, President & Co-Founder
Tina Coonce, Co-Founder

Branch Offices:
CANADA: PO Box 1220, Fort Erie, ON L2A 5Y2, Canada.
Type of service: Basic, HD.
Satellites: SES-1.
Operating hours/week: 168.
Operating areas: Nationwide.
Programming: Commercial-free, inspirational programming designed to appeal to a wide variety of denominational and cultural backgrounds.
Began: May 20, 1977.
Means of Support: Donations.
Distribution method: Available over the air on digital sub-channels & to DirecTV subscribers.
Scrambled signal: Yes.
Ownership: Dr. Garth & Tina Coonce.

TCT FAMILY — See TCT.
Programming: Children's programming plus popular sitcoms from the past.
Began: March 30, 2009.

TCT LA FUENTE — See TCT.
Programming: Spanish-language inspirational programming from Colombia, Costa Rica, Peru, Venezuela & the U.S. for the Hispanic community.

TEAMHD — See iN DEMAND.
Programming: On demand sports programming.

TEENNICK
c/o MTV Networks
1515 Broadway, 21st Fl
New York, NY 10036
Phone: 212-258-8323
Fax: 212-258-8303
Web Site: http://www.teennick.com
Keith Dawkins, Executive Vice President
Type of service: Basic.
Operating hours/week: 168.
Programming: Original shows for pre-teen audience.
Began: April 1, 2002, as a programming block on The N. Launched as own channel December 2007, replacing GAS (Nickelodeon Game & Sports). Rebranded TeenNick September 28, 2009.
Total subscribers: 60,000,000.
Distribution method: Available to cable & satellite subscribers.
Scrambled signal: Yes.

TELE VIDA ABUDANTE
PO Box 6326
Santa Maria, CA 93456
Phones: 805-614-0730; 805-928-1030
Web Site: http://www.radiovidaabundante.com
Type of service: Basic, streaming.
Operating areas: Arizona, California, Colorado & Idaho.
Programming: Spanish language religious programming.
Began: January 1, 2004.
Distribution method: Available over the air on digital sub-channels. Streaming available online.
Scrambled signal: Yes.

TELEAMAZONAS
c/o Imagina US
7291 NW 74th St
Miami, FL 33166
Phone: 305-777-1900
Fax: 305-820-9046
Web Site: http://www.teleamazonas.com
Operating hours/week: 168.
Operating areas: Nationwide.
Programming: Spanish programming on and about Ecuador and neighboring regions. Also provides extensive soccer coverage.
Began: February 22, 1974.
Distribution method: Available to satellite subscribers.
Scrambled signal: Yes.

TELECAFE
19 Akademika Korolyova St
Moscow 127427
Russian Federation
Phones: 7-495-617-55-88; 7-495-617-51-75
Fax: 7-495-617-51-14
E-mail: info@1tvrus.com
Web Site: http://eng.1tvrus.com/telecafe
Nikolay Dubovoy, Director General
Type of service: Premium.
Operating areas: New Jersey & New York on cable; nationwide on DirecTV.
Programming: Russian food channel.
Began: January 1, 2005.
Means of Support: Advertising & subscriber fees.
Total subscribers: 20,000,000 (subscribers worldwide.).
Distribution method: Available to Time Warner & DirecTV subscribers.
Scrambled signal: Yes.
Ownership: Channel One. National Media Group, minority interest.

TELECARE
1200 Glenn Curtiss Blvd
Uniondale, NY 11553
Phone: 516-538-8700
Fax: 516-489-9701
E-mail: info@telecaretv.org
Web Site: http://www.telecaretv.org
James Vlaun, President & Chief Executive Officer
Joseph A. Perrone, General Manager
Type of service: Basic & Expanded basic.
Operating hours/week: 140.
Operating areas: New York.
Programming: Ecumenical, positive programming.
Began: January 1, 1976.
Distribution method: Available to cable subscribers.
Scrambled signal: Yes.
Ownership: Diocese of Rockville Centre.

TELECENTRO — See ULTRA HDPlex.
2600 SW Third Ave
Ste PH-B
Miami, FL 33129
Phones: 305-860-2036; 888-222-8025
Fax: 305-860-2102
E-mail: info@tvtelecentro.com
Web Site: http://www.tvtelecentro.com
Type of service: Pay, HD.
Operating hours/week: 168.
Operating areas: Available nationwide.
Programming: Offers news, sports & entertainment from Costa Rica, El Salvador, Guatemala, Honduras, Nicaragua & Panama.
Began: October 23, 2008.
Distribution method: Available to cable, IPTV & satellite subscribers.

Scrambled signal: Yes.
Ownership: Remigio Angel Gonzalez & Guillermo Canedo White. Distributed in the U.S. by Olympusat.

TELE EL SALVADOR — See ULTRA HDPlex.
Av Luperon 46
Distrito Nacional
Santo Domingo 3133
Dominican Republic
Phone: 809-531-3333
Fax: 809-473-6666
E-mail: contacto@teleelsalvador.com
Web Site: http://www.teleelsalvador.com
Marcos A. Jorge, Executive Vice President
Type of service: Pay, HD.
Operating hours/week: 168.
Operating areas: Available nationwide.
Programming: Spanish-language news & entertainment programming from El Salvador.
Means of Support: Subscriber fees.
Total subscribers: 2,500,000.
Distribution method: Available to cable, IPTV & satellite subscribers.
Scrambled signal: Yes.
Ownership: Super Canal Group. Distributed in the U.S. by Olympusat.

TELEFE INTERNACIONAL
Av Rivadavia 2358
5th Fl
Buenos Aires 1034
Argentina
Phone: 54-11-954-3670
Fax: 54-11-951-7992
E-mail: rcapone@telefe.com.ar
Web Site: http://www.telefeinternacional.com.ar
Roberto Capone, Administrative & Traffic Manager
Pablo Rabaiotti, Traffic Chief
Meca Salado Pizarro, Marketing Chief
Michelle Wasserman, International Business, Programming, Formats & Production Services Chief
Programming: Spanish-language entertainment from Argentina.
Began: January 1, 2001.
Scrambled signal: Yes.
Ownership: Telefonica. Distributed in the U.S. by Condista.

TELEFORMULA
c/o Condista, 200 Crandon Blvd
Ste 316
Key Biscayne, FL 33149
Phone: 305-361-5271
Web Site: http://www.teleformula.com.mx
Burke Berendes, West Coast Contact
Jorge Fiterre, East Coast Contact
Operating hours/week: 168.
Programming: Mexican service covering news, sports entertainment, women's issues, health plus financial and political issues.
Began: January 1, 2002.
Means of Support: Advertising.
Total subscribers: 1,800,000.
Distribution method: Available to satellite subscribers.

Scrambled signal: Yes.
Ownership: TeleFormula S.A. de C.V. Distributed in the U.S. by Condista.

TELEFUTURA — See UniMas.

TELEHIT — See Univision.
c/o Univision Communications Inc.
605 Third Ave, 12th Fl
New York, NY 10158
Phone: 212-455-5200
Web Site: http://www.telehit.com; http://corporate.univision.com
Beau Ferrari, Executive Vice President, Operations, Univision Networks
Satellites: AMC 10, transponder 4.
Operating areas: Available nationwide.
Programming: Spanish-language urban music & lifestyle shows for younger audiences.
Began: May 1, 2003.
Total subscribers: 1,900,000.
Distribution method: Available to cable, IPTV & satellite subscribers.
Scrambled signal: Yes.
Ownership: Televisa Networks. Univision Communications Inc. has an exclusive contract for this service.

TELEKARIBE
8 West Broad St
Hazleton, PA 18201
Phone: 570-299-0299
Web Site: http://telekaribehazleton.com
Max Garcia, Chief Executive Officer & Program Director
Operating hours/week: 168.
Operating areas: Available in New York, Pennsylvania and Puerto Rico.
Programming: Spanish-language, Dominican-oriented service offering comedy, general entertainment, movies, music, news, special programs, sports and weather.
Began: November 2, 2015.
Means of Support: Advertising.
Distribution method: Available to cable subscribers. Streaming available through participating providers.
Scrambled signal: Yes.

TELEMIAMI
2920 NW 7th St
Miami, FL 33121
Phone: 305-642-7777
Fax: 305-642-0077
E-mail: informacion@telemiami.com
Paul Stevens, President & Chief Executive Officer
Judith Prado, General Manager
Type of service: Basic.
Operating hours/week: 168.
Operating areas: Florida.
Programming: Entertainment, news, sports; 90% Spanish, 5% Italian, 5% Portuguese.
Began: January 1, 1984.
Means of Support: Advertising.
Total subscribers: 488,000.
Distribution method: Available to cable subscribers.
Scrambled signal: Yes.
Ownership: United Broadcasting Corp.

Pay TV & Satellite Services

TELEMICRO INTERNACIONAL
C/Mariano Cesteros esquina Enrique Henrfquez No. 1
Edificio Telemicro
Gazcue, Santo Domingo
Dominican Republic
Phone: 809-689-0555
Web Site: http://telemicro.com.do
Operating hours/week: 168.
Operating areas: Nationwide.
Programming: A 100% Dominican channel, with news, comedy, sports, and general entertainment.
Distribution method: Available to FiOS TV &cable system subscribers.
Scrambled signal: Yes.
Ownership: Groupo Telemicro. Distributed in the U.S. by Alterna'TV.

TELEMUNDO
2290 W Eighth Ave
Hialeah, FL 33010
Phone: 305-884-8200
E-mail: alfredo.richard@nbcuni.com
Web Site: http://www.telemundo.com
Jackie Hernandez, Chief Operating Officer, Telemundo Communications Group
Javier Maynulet, Chief Financial Officer
Luis Silberwasser, President, Telemundo
Manuel Martinez, President, Telemundo Stations Group
Patricio Wills, President, Producciones RTI Columbia
Peter Blacker, Executive Vice President, Digital Media & Emerging Businesses
Alina Falcon, Executive Vice President, News & Alternative Programming
Luis Fernandez, Executive Vice President, Network News
Stephen Levin, Executive Vice President, Sales
Mike Rosen, Executive Vice President, Ad Sales & Integrated Marketing
Susan Solano Villa, Executive Vice President, Marketing
Jesus Torres Viera, Executive Vice President, Entertainment
Aurelio Valcarcel, Executive Vice President, Telemundo Studios, Miami
Luis Carlos Velez, Executive Vice President, Network News
Mike Alvarez, Senior Vice President, Ad Sales
Aileen Angulo Merciel, Senior Vice President, Marketing & Creative
Mara Arakelian, Senior Vice President, Talent Management
Karen Barroeta, Senior Vice President, Interntional Cable Operations
Milagros Carrasquillo, Senior Vice President, Research
Anjelica Cohn, Senior Vice President, Business Affairs
Lee Flaster, Senior Vice President, Business Operations & Growth Strategy
Peach Gibson, Senior Vice President, Creative Services
Efrain Lopez, Senior Vice President, Strategy
Christine Maggiore-Escribano, Senior Vice President, Integrated Marketing Solutions
Rosy Marin, Senior Vice President, Regional Ad Sales
Patty Marrero, Senior Vice President, Client Partnership Development, Telemundo Media
Jeff Mayzurk, Senior Vice President, Operations & Technology
David McCormick, Senior Vice President, Standards, NBCUniversal News Group
Joe Navarro, Senior Vice President, Human Resources
Glenda Pacanins, Senior Vice President, Programming & Content
Borja Perez, Senior Vice President, Digital & Social Media
Mauricio Piccone, Senior Vice President, Reality Programming
Lynette Pinto, Senior Vice President, Marketing
Alfredo Richard, Senior Vice President, Communications & Talent Strategy
Mario Ruiz, Senior Vice President, Music & Entertainment Projects
Jose Sariego, Senior Vice President, Business & Legal Affairs
Lia Silkworth, Senior Vice President, Insights & Consumer Development
Lisette Simon, Senior Vice President, Human Resources
Leonor Sotillo, Senior Vice President, Programming Strategy
Eli Velazquez, Senior Vice President, Sports
Ken Wilkey, Senior Vice President, Broadcast Operations
Michelle Alban, Vice President, Corporate Communications & Public Affairs
Maureen Alliegro, Vice President, Network Sales
David Alvarado, Vice President, Entertainment Publicity
Andy Barnet, Vice President, National Sales
Hanna Bolte, Vice President, Media & Talent Relations, mun2/Telemundo
Yatisha Bothwell, Vice President, Insights & Strategy
Jack Brown, Vice President, Network Sales, Chicago
Carlos Collazo, Vice President, On Air Promotions
Daniel Cubillo, Vice President, Content Development
Angel Domenech, Vice President, Creative Strategy
Humberto Duran, Vice President, News Operations & Production Management
Maria Isabel Figueroa, Vice President, Marketing
Alonso Galvez, Vice President, Production
Ann Gaulke, Vice President, Affiliate Relations
Michael Guariglia, Vice President, Network Sales
Allan Infeld, Vice President, Client Development
Jose Nestor Marquez, Vice President, Digital Production & Development
Jose Morales, Vice President, Content
Joanna Popper, Vice President, Marketing
Christian Riehl, Vice President, Production
Latha Sarathy, Vice President, Digital Research
Roberto Stopello, Vice President, Novela Development
Eduardo Sunol, Vice President, Telemundo News Digital
Diego Tamayo, Vice President, On-Air Promotions
Ayan Valle, Vice President, Digital & Social Partnerships
Vincent L. Sandusky, Treasurer
Mirta Ojito, News Standards Director

Branch Offices:
EAST COAST: 1775 Broadway, Ste 300, New York, NY 10019. Phone: 212-492-5545.

WEST COAST: 6500 Wilshire Blvd, Ste 1200, Los Angeles, CA 90048. Phone: 323-852-5290.
Type of service: Basic.
Operating hours/week: 168.
Programming: Spanish language programming for the U.S. & international markets.
Began: January 1, 1987.
Means of Support: Advertising.
Total subscribers: 21,600,000.
Distribution method: Available to cable subscribers.
Scrambled signal: Yes.
Ownership: NBCUniversal LLC.

TELEMUNDO DEPORTES
2290 W Eighth Ave
Hialeah, FL 33010
Phone: 305-884-8200
Web Site: http://www.telemundodeportes.com
Ray Warren, President
Eli Velazquez, Executive Vice President, Sports, Hispanic Enterprises & Content
Operating areas: Available nationwide.
Programming: Spanish-language sports channel.
Began: 1987 as Deportes Telemundo. NBC Deportes replaced Deportes Telemundo in 2015. Service was rebranded back to Telemundo Deportes in 2016.
Means of Support: Advertising.
Distribution method: Available to cable system subscribers and satellite subscribers.
Scrambled signal: Yes.
Ownership: NBCUniversal.

TELEMUNDO INTERNACIONAL — See Telemundo.

TELEMUNDO PUERTO RICO — See Telemundo.
Type of service: Digital.
Programming: Live news broadcasts directly from Telemundo Puerto Rico (WKAQ-TV), popular Puerto Rican shows, series, sports, music videos, films & specials.
Began: February 1, 2005.
Total subscribers: 3,000,000.
Scrambled signal: Yes.

TELE N
c/o Olympusat Inc.
560 Village Blvd, Ste 250
West Palm Beach, FL 33409
Phone: 561-684-5657
Fax: 561-684-9690
E-mail: info@olympusat.com
Web Site: http://www.olympusat.com/node/1994
Tom Mohler, Chief Executive Officer, Olympusat Holdings Inc.
Arturo Chavez, Senior Vice President, Hispanic Networks
Juan Bruno, New Programming Acquisitions & Contracts Director
John Baghdassarian, Head of Affiliate Sales, U.S.
Type of service: Pay.
Operating areas: Available nationwide.
Programming: Spanish-language movie network featuring movies & major productions from the golden age of Mexican cinema & popular novels from Latin America & Brazil.
Distribution method: Available to cable & IPTV subscribers.
Scrambled signal: Yes.
Ownership: Olympusat.

TELENOSTALGIA
Carrera 73
52-66 Los Colores
Medellin
Colombia
Phone: 57-4-4482500
E-mail: telenostalgia@globalmedia1.tv
Web Site: http://www.canaltelenostalgia.com
Programming: Music videos & programs from 1960 to the present featuring the top Latin American stars of decades past.
Ownership: Global Media Telecommunications. Distributed in the U.S. by Olympusat.

TELERITMO
Paricutin y 5 de Febrero, No 312
Col. Roma
Monterrey, Nuevo Leon MX-64700
Mexico
Phone: 52-81-8369-9919
Web Site: http://www.multimedios.com/tv/envivo/teleritmo
Gustavo Mena, Cable & Satellite Distribution
Operating hours/week: 168.
Operating areas: Available nationwide.
Programming: Offers regional Mexican music direct from Monterrey.
Means of Support: Advertising.
Distribution method: Available to cable system subscribers plus Verizon FiOS and AT&T U-verse customers.
Scrambled signal: Yes.
Ownership: Grupo Multimedios. Distributed in the U.S. by UNO Entertainment.

TELE-ROMANTICA
c/o Condista, 200 Crandon Blvd
Ste 316
Key Biscayne, FL 33149
Phone: 305-361-5271
E-mail: info@dhetvmedia.com
Web Site: http://www.teleromantica.com
Mercedes Pedre-Fiore, President
Terry Planell, Vice President, Business Development & Marketing
Type of service: Basic.
Operating hours/week: 168.
Operating areas: Arizona, California, Florida, Illinois, Massachusetts, New York, Oklahoma, Puerto Rico, Tennessee, Texas & Washington.
Programming: Spanish-language telenovelas, films, series, documentaries & entertainment programs for women aged 18 to 35.
Began: May 2, 2012.
Means of Support: Advertising.
Distribution method: Available over the air on digital sub-channels.
Scrambled signal: Yes.
Ownership: DreamHouse Entertainment TV Media LLC. Distributed in the U.S. by Condista.

TELEVEN AMERICA
Avenida Romulo Gallegos con 4ta transversal de Horizonte
Edificio Televen
Caracas
Venezuela
Phones: 58-280-00-11; 58-280-00-12
Web Site: http://www.televen.com
Leonardo Bigott, Chief Executive Officer
Tom Mohler, President, Olympusat
Operating hours/week: 168.
Operating areas: Available nationwide.
Programming: Offers programming from Venezuela for an educated & affluent audience.
Began: July 3, 1988, in Venezuela. Began February 5, 2014 in the U.S.
Means of Support: Advertising.
Scrambled signal: Yes.
Ownership: Televen. Distributed in the U.S. by Olympusat.

TELEVISION KOREA 24
(tvK24)
3435 Wilshire Blvd, 19th Fl
Los Angeles, CA 90010
Phone: 213-382-9600
Fax: 213-382-9601
E-mail: info@tvk24.com
Web Site: http://www.tvk24.com
Eric Yoon, Founder & Chief Executive Officer
Heather Yoon, Executive Director
Taeo Cho, Broadcasting Operation Director
Taegsoo Cho, Broadcasting Supervisor

Pay TV & Satellite Services

Jenny Jang, Marketing Manager
Type of service: Digital basic & video on demand.
Operating hours/week: 168.
Programming: Korean language news, dramas, movies, sports, business, health, music, children's entertainment, educational programming & game shows.
Began: March 1, 2005.
Total subscribers: 500,000.
Distribution method: Available to cable systems & IPTV subscribers.
Scrambled signal: Yes.
Ownership: Eric Yoon, NBCUniversal LLC (minority interest).

TELEXITOS
7355 NW 41st St
Miami, FL 33166
Phone: 305-640-7600
E-mail: info@telemundostudios.com
Web Site: http://www.telexitos.com
Barbara Alfonso, Director
Type of service: Basic.
Operating hours/week: 168.
Operating areas: Available nationwide.
Programming: Spanish-language action and adventure series plus movies from the 1970s to 2000.
Began: January 2012 as Exitos. Rebranded Telexitos December 1, 2014.
Means of Support: Advertising.
Total subscribers: 20,000,000.
Distribution method: Available over the air on digital sub-channel.
Scrambled signal: Yes.
Ownership: Telemundo, a division of NBCUniversal.

TEMPO
Tempo Networks, LLC
58 Park Pl, Third Fl
Newark, NJ 07102
Phone: 973-508-1000
Web Site: http://www.gottempo.com
Frederick Morton, Senior Vice President & General Manager
Operating hours/week: 168.
Operating areas: Caribbean.
Programming: A mix of original & acquired Caribbean programming, including series, specials, movies, documentaries & sporting events.
Began: November 21, 2005.
Total subscribers: 1,600,000.
Ownership: Private investors.

TEN
c/o New Frontier Media
600 Spine Rd, Ste 100
Boulder, CO 80301
Phones: 303-444-0900; 888-875-0632
Fax: 303-938-8388
Web Site: http://www.noof.com
Larry Flynt, Chief Executive Officer
Michael Klein, President
Chris Woodward, Chief Financial Officer
Type of service: Pay per view.
Operating areas: Available nationwide.
Programming: Adult programming.
Distribution method: Available to cable, IPTV & satellite subscribers.
Ownership: New Frontier Media.

TEN CRICKET
Taj Television (India) Pvt. Ltd.
FC-9 Sector 16-A Film City
Noida UP 201 301
India
E-mail: prasenjit.basu@tensports.com
Web Site: http://www.tensports.com/tv-guide/cricket

Atul Pande, Chief Executive Officer
Sanjay Raina, Chief Operating Officer
Subhadip Bhattacharyya, Executive Vice President, Distribution
Operating hours/week: 168.
Operating areas: Available nationwide.
Programming: Channel dedicated to cricket.
Began: August 10, 2010, in India. Began August 2011 in the U.S.
Means of Support: Advertising.
Distribution method: Available to DISH Network subscribers.
Scrambled signal: Yes.
Ownership: Zee Entertainment Enterprises.

TENNIS CHANNEL
2850 Ocean Park Blvd
Ste 150
Santa Monica, CA 90405
Phone: 310-314-9400
Fax: 310-656-9433
E-mail: support@thetennischannel.com
Web Site: http://www.tennischannel.com
Ken Solomon, President
William Simon, Executive Vice President, Chief Operating & Financial Officer
Dean Hadaegh, Chief Technical Officer & Senior Vice President, Broadcast Operations
David Egdes, Senior Vice President, Tennis Industry Relations
Gary Herman, Senior Vice President, Ad Sales
Doug Martz, Senior Vice President, Ad Sales
Robyn Miller, Senior Vice President, Marketing
Peter Steckelman, Senior Vice President, Business & Legal Affairs
Adam Ware, Senior Vice President, Digital Media
Bob Whyley, Senior Vice President, Production & Executive Producer
Patrick Wilson, Senior Vice President, Distribution
Allison Bodenmann, Vice President, Advertising Sales
Laura Hockridge, Vice President, Original Programming
Jeremy Langer, Vice President, Programming
David Scott, Vice President, Programming

Branch Offices:
CULVER CITY: HD Technical Operations Center, 3555 Hayden Ave, Culver City, CA 90232.

NEW YORK: Ad Sales, 3 Park Ave, 25th Fl, New York, NY 10016. Phone: 212-808-0608.
Type of service: Basic, HD, streaming, video on demand.
Operating hours/week: 168.
Operating areas: Nationwide.
Programming: American & international tennis tournaments & matches, other original tennis-related programs.
Began: May 15, 2003, Tennis Channel HD began December 2007. Tennis Channel Plus began May 25, 2014.
Means of Support: Advertising.
Total subscribers: 47,000,000.
Distribution method: Available to cable & satellite subscribers. Streaming & video on demand available online, through app & through participating providers.
Scrambled signal: Yes.
Ownership: Sinclair Broadcast Group Inc.

TENNIS CHANNEL PLUS — See Tennis Channel.
Type of service: Subscription streaming.
Operating areas: Available nationwide.
Programming: Access to over 40 live tournaments a year plus access to classic matches and original programming from the Tennis Channel.
Began: May 25, 2014.
Means of Support: Subscriber fees.

Distribution method: Available online & through app (participating providers).
Scrambled signal: Yes.

TEXAS CHANNEL
c/o Time Warner Cable-Texas
1900 Blue Crest Dr
San Antonio, TX 78240
Phone: 210-710-0474
E-mail: melissa.sorola@twcable.com
Jon Gary Herrera, Vice President, Communications
Dick Kirby, Vice President, Programming, Time Warner Cable, Texas
Type of service: Regional.
Operating areas: Texas.
Programming: Offers a mix of syndicated and original local programming including high school and college athletics from Time Warner Cable Sports, the Big 12 Conference, and the Southland Conference, as well as special events and Texas-themed outdoor and lifestyle shows.
Means of Support: Advertising.
Total subscribers: 1,000,000.
Distribution method: Available to Time Warner Cable subscribers in Austin, Corpus Christi, Dallas, Laredo, Rio Grande Valley, San Antonio & Waco/Temple/Killeen.
Scrambled signal: Yes.
Ownership: Time Warner Cable.

TEXAS HOUSE OF REPRESENTATIVES VIDEO/AUDIO SERVICES
105 W 15th St
Austin, TX 78701
Phone: 512-463-0903
Fax: 512-463-5729
Web Site: http://www.house.state.tx.us
Type of service: Basic, streaming.
Programming: Coverage of House session and committee meetings.
Began: January 1, 1987.
Distribution method: Available to cable subscribers. Streaming available online.
Scrambled signal: Yes.

TFC — See The Filipino Channel.

THEBLAZE
1065 Ave of the Americas
12th Fl
New York, NY 10018
Phone: 212-730-8660
E-mail: contact@theblaze.com
Web Site: http://www.theblaze.com/tv
Chris Balfe, President & Chief Operating Officer, Mercury Radio Arts Inc.
Joel Cheatwood, President & Chief Content Officer
Eric Pearce, Senior Vice President, Television Operations
Scott Baker, Editor in Chief
Jonathon M Seidl, Assistant Editor
Meredith Jessup, Assistant Editor

Branch Offices:
IRVING:: Mercury Radio Arts - Dallas Studios, 6301 Riverside Dr, Irving, TX 75039-3531.
Type of service: Pay.
Operating hours/week: 168.
Operating areas: Nationwide.

Programming: Nightly panel discussions, reality programming and a children's show, plus The Glenn Beck Show.
Began: August 31, 2010, online. Began September 12, 2012 on DISH Network. GBTV merged into TheBlaze June 18, 2012.
Means of Support: Subscriber fees.
Total subscribers: 3,300,000.
Distribution method: Available to Cablevision Systems & DirecTV subscribers.
Scrambled signal: Yes.
Ownership: Mercury Radio Arts Inc.

THECOOLTV
PO Box 514
Lawrence, KS 66044
Phone: 888-342-8761
Fax: 773-439-8804
E-mail: info@thecooltv.com
Web Site: http://www.thecooltv.com
Joe Comparato, Chief Executive Officer
David Hampe, Chief Operating Officer
John (Digger) Pelaez, Senior Vice President & Co-Founder
Bobby Tarantino, Senior Vice President, Artist & Label Relations
Type of service: Basic, streaming.
Operating hours/week: 168.
Operating areas: Nationwide.
Programming: Music videos.
Began: March 2, 2009.
Means of Support: Advertising.
Total subscribers: 52,000,000.
Distribution method: Available over the air on digital sub-channels & to cable, IPTV & satellite subscribers. Streaming available online & mobile.
Scrambled signal: Yes.
Ownership: Cool Music Network LLC.

THE LEARNING CHANNEL — See TLC.

THE N — See TeenNick.

THIS TV
10250 Constellation Blvd
Los Angeles, CA 90067-6241
Phone: 310-499-3000
E-mail: comments@thistv.com
Web Site: http://www.thistv.com
Jim Packer, Co-President, MGM Worldwide TV
John Bryan, President, Domestic Television Distribution, MGM Television
Sean Compton, President, Programming, Tribune Broadcasting
Jim Marketti, Creative Director
Type of service: Digital.
Satellites: AMC-3.
Operating hours/week: 168.
Programming: Movies & TV shows from the MGM library & children's programming.
Began: November 1, 2008.
Means of Support: Advertising.
Total subscribers: 92,000,000.
Scrambled signal: Yes.
Ownership: A joint venture between Metro Goldwyn Mayer Studios Inc. (50%) & Tribune Media Co. (50%).

Pay TV & Satellite Services

THREE ANGELS BROADCASTING NETWORK — See 3ABN.

THRILLER MAX — See Cinemax.
c/o Home Box Office
1100 Avenue of the Americas
New York, NY 10036
Phone: 212-512-1000
Fax: 212-512-1166
Type of service: Pay, HD.
Operating hours/week: 168.
Operating areas: Available nationwide.
Programming: Mystery, suspense, horror & thriller movies, including recent box office hits & independent films.
Began: June 1, 1998.
Scrambled signal: Yes.
Ownership: Home Box Office Inc., a division of Time Warner.

TIGERVISION
c/o LSU Electronic Media
PO Box 25095
Baton Rouge, LA 70894-1797
Phone: 504-388-1797
Fax: 504-338-1861
E-mail: promotions@lsu.edu
Web Site: http://www.lsusports.net
Type of service: Pay-per-view.
Operating areas: Louisiana.
Programming: LSU football games.
Means of Support: Subscription fees.
Ownership: Louisiana State U.

TIME WARNER CABLE COMMUNITY (SOCAL)
(TWC Community)
3650 W Martin Luther King Blvd, Ste 521
Los Angeles, CA 90008
Phone: 888-892-2253
Web Site: http://www.twcsportschannel.com/ca/socal.html
Type of service: Regional.
Operating areas: Southern California.
Programming: Themed local channel that provides real-time traffic updates along with unique original local programming. The channel also offers information about Time Warner Cable services and local weather, news headlines and sports scores.
Began: as Time Warner Cable Socal 101. Rebranded TWC Community May 16, 2014.
Distribution method: Available to Time Warner Cable subscribers.
Scrambled signal: Yes.
Ownership: Time Warner Cable.

TIME WARNER CABLE DEPORTES
2345 Alaska Ave
El Segundo, CA 90245
Phones: 310-531-1400; 310-351-1550
E-mail: twcdeportes@twcable.com
Web Site: http://twcdeportes.com
Mark Shuken, Senior Vice President & General Manager, Time Warner Cable Sports Regional Networks
Deborah Picciolo, Regional Vice President, Operations, Time Warner Cable West Region
Pablo F. Urquiza, Vice President, Time Warner Cable Deportes
Type of service: Regional.
Operating areas: Southern California.
Programming: Carries in Spanish the Los Angeles Sparks of the WNBA, the LA Galaxy of the MLS and the Los Angeles Lakers of the NBA. Also has Mexican boxing and wrestling plus high school football teams in Hispanic communities.
Began: October 1, 2012.
Means of Support: Advertising and subscriber fees.

Distribution method: Available to Charter, Time Warner Cable, AT&T U-verse, Verizon FiOS & DirecTV subscribers.
Scrambled signal: Yes.
Ownership: Time Warner Cable.

TIME WARNER CABLE NEWS (ANTELOPE VALLEY)
41551 10th St NW
Palmdale, CA 93551
Phone: 661-272-0168
E-mail: twc.news@twcable.com
Web Site: http://www.ny1.com/ca/antelope-valley
Type of service: Regional basic.
Operating hours/week: 168.
Operating areas: California.
Programming: Local news, sports, traffic & politics from southern California.
Distribution method: Available to Time Warner cable subscribers.
Scrambled signal: Yes.
Ownership: Time Warner Cable.

TIME WARNER CABLE NEWS (AUSTIN)
1708 Colorado St
Austin, TX 78701-1209
Phone: 512-531-8800
Fax: 512-531-8008
E-mail: txnewsdesk@twcnews.com
Web Site: http://www.ny1.com/tx/austin
Michael Pearson, News Director
Type of service: Regional basic.
Operating hours/week: 168.
Operating areas: Texas.
Programming: Local news, sports, traffic & politics from the Austin area.
Began: September 13, 1999, as News 8 Austin. Rebranded YNN Austin January 2011 & Time Warner Cable News December 16, 2013.
Means of Support: Advertising.
Distribution method: Available to Time Warner cable subscribers.
Scrambled signal: Yes.
Ownership: Time Warner Cable.

TIME WARNER CABLE NEWS (THE BRONX) — See Time Warner Cable News NY1.
Web Site: http://www.ny1.com/nyc/bronx
Programming: Local news, sports, traffic & politics from the Bronx.

TIME WARNER CABLE NEWS (BROOKLYN) — See Time Warner Cable News NY1.
Web Site: http://www.ny1.com/nyc/brooklyn
Programming: Local news, sports, traffic & politics from Brooklyn.

TIME WARNER CABLE NEWS (BUFFALO)
355 Chicago St
Buffalo, NY 14204
Phone: 716-558-8999
Fax: 716-558-8501
E-mail: buffalo@twcnews.com
Web Site: http://www.twcnews.com/nys/buffalo
Ed Buttaccio, News Director
Type of service: Regional basic.
Operating hours/week: 168.
Operating areas: New York.
Programming: News, sports, traffic & politics from Western New York, including Buffalo-Niagara, the Genesee Valley & the Southern Tier.
Began: March 2009 YNN Buffalo. Rebranded Time Warner Cable News December 16, 2013.

Distribution method: Available to Time Warner cable subscribers.
Scrambled signal: Yes.
Ownership: Time Warner Cable.

TIME WARNER CABLE NEWS (CAPITAL REGION NY)
104 Watervliet Ave Ext
Albany, NY 12206
Phone: 518-459-9999
Fax: 518-641-7023
E-mail: albanynews@ynn.com
Web Site: http://www.ny1.com/nys/capital-region
Type of service: Regional basic.
Operating hours/week: 168.
Operating areas: Massachusetts & New York.
Programming: News, sports, traffic & politics from the Capital Region.
Began: October 11, 2002, as Capital 9 News. Rebranded YNN March 2010 & Time Warner Cable News December 16, 2013.
Distribution method: Available to Time Warner cable subscribers.
Scrambled signal: Yes.
Ownership: Time Warner Cable.

TIME WARNER CABLE NEWS (CENTRAL NY)
815 Erie Blvd E
Syracuse, NY 13210
Phone: 315-234-1000
Fax: 315-634-4270
E-mail: yournews@ynn.com
Web Site: http://www.ny1.com/nys/central-ny
Ron Lombard, News Director
Steve Osterhaus, Assistant News Director
Troy Shambaugh, Operations Manager
Type of service: Regional basic.
Operating hours/week: 168.
Operating areas: New York & Pennsylvania.
Programming: Local news, sports, traffic & politics from the metropolitan Syracuse area, Utica & the Mohawk Valley, the Adirondack Tri-Lakes area, Watertown & the St. Lawrence Seaway/Canadian border region.
Began: November 7, 2003, as News 10 Now. Rebranded YNN February 12, 2010. Rebranded Time Warner Cable News December 16, 2013.
Means of Support: Advertising.
Total subscribers: 600,000.
Distribution method: Available to Time Warner cable subscribers.
Scrambled signal: Yes.
Ownership: Time Warner Cable.

TIME WARNER CABLE NEWS (CENTRAL NC)
2505 Atlantic Ave
Ste 102
Raleigh, NC 27604-1411
Phone: 919-882-4000
Fax: 919-882-4045
E-mail: centralncnews@twcnews.com
Web Site: http://www.ny1.com/nc/triangle-sandhills
Type of service: Regional basic.
Operating hours/week: 168.
Operating areas: North Carolina.
Programming: Local news, sports, traffic & politics from the Raleigh area.
Began: March 22, 2002, as News 14 Carolina. Rebranded Time Warner Cable News December 16, 2013.
Distribution method: Available to Time Warner cable subscribers.
Scrambled signal: Yes.
Ownership: Time Warner Cable.

TIME WARNER CABLE NEWS (CHARLOTTE)
316 E Morehead St

Ste 100
Charlotte, NC 28202
Phone: 704-973-5800
Fax: 704-731-2760
E-mail: cltnews@twcnews.com
Web Site: http://www.ny1.com/nc/charlotte
Type of service: Regional basic.
Operating hours/week: 168.
Operating areas: North Carolina.
Programming: Local news, sports, traffic & politics from the Charlotte area, including Anson, Cabarrus, Cleveland, Gaston, Iredell, Richmond, Rowan, Stanly & Union counties.
Began: June 14, 2002, as News 14 Carolina. Rebranded Time Warner Cable News December 16, 2013.
Distribution method: Available to Time Warner cable subscribers.
Ownership: Time Warner Cable.

TIME WARNER CABLE NEWS (COASTAL NC)
2321 Scientific Park Dr
Wilmington, NC 28405
Phone: 866-963-9715
E-mail: coastalncnews@twcnews.com
Web Site: http://www.ny1.com/nc/coastal

Branch Offices:
NEWPORT:: 500 Time Warner Dr, Newport, NC 28570. Phone: 866-963-9714. Fax: 252-223-6600.
Type of service: Regional basic.
Operating hours/week: 168.
Operating areas: North Carolina.
Programming: Local news, sports, traffic & politics from the Coastal region.
Began: August 18, 2008, as News 14 Carolina. Rebranded Time Warner Cable News December 16, 2013.
Distribution method: Available to Time Warner cable subscribers.
Scrambled signal: Yes.
Ownership: Time Warner Cable.

TIME WARNER CABLE NEWS (HUDSON VALLEY) — See Time Warner Cable News (Capital Region NY).
E-mail: hvnews@twcnews.com
Web Site: http://www.ny1.com/nys/hudson-valley
Type of service: Regional basic.
Operating hours/week: 168.
Operating areas: New York.
Programming: News, sports, traffic & politics from the Hudson Valley & the Catskills.
Began: October 11, 2002, as Capital 9 News. Rebranded YNN March 2010 & Time Warner Cable News December 16, 2013.
Distribution method: Available to Time Warner cable subscribers.
Scrambled signal: Yes.
Ownership: Time Warner Cable.

TIME WARNER CABLE NEWS (JAMESTOWN)
355 Chicago St
Buffalo, NY 14204
Phone: 716-558-8999
Fax: 716-558-8501
E-mail: buffalo@twcnews.com
Web Site: http://www.ny1.com/nys/jamestown
Ed Buttaccio, News Director
Type of service: Regional basic.
Operating hours/week: 168.
Operating areas: New York.
Programming: Local news, sports, traffic & politics.
Began: March 25, 2009, as YNN. Rebranded Time Warner Cable News December 16, 2013.

Pay TV & Satellite Services

Distribution method: Available to Time Warner cable subscribers.
Ownership: Time Warner Cable.

TIME WARNER CABLE NEWS (MANHATTAN) — See Time Warner Cable News NY1.
Web Site: http://www.ny1.com/nyc/manhattan
Programming: Local news, sports, traffic & politics from Manhattan.

TIME WARNER CABLE NEWS (NORTHERN NY) — See Time Warner Cable News (Central NY).
Web Site: http://www.ny1.com/nys/watertown
Programming: Local news, sports, traffic & politics from the metropolitan Syracuse area, Utica & the Mohawk Valley, the Adirondack Tri-Lakes area, Watertown & the St. Lawrence Seaway/Canadian border region.
Began: November 7, 2003, as News 10 Now. Rebranded YNN North Country March 2010 & Time Warner Cable News December 16, 2003.

TIME WARNER CABLE NEWS NY1
75 Ninth Ave
6th Fl
New York, NY 10011
Phone: 212-379-3311
Fax: 212-379-3570
E-mail: ny1foryou@ny1.com
Web Site: http://www.ny1.com
Joe Truncale, Group Vice President, Operations, Time Warner Cable, Local News & Programming
Michael Chan, Vice President, Technical Operations
Dan Jacobson, News Director
Adam Rowe, Ad Sales Director
Nikia Redhead, Public Relations Manager
Type of service: Regional basic, HD, streaming.
Sales representative: National Cable Advertising Inc.
Operating hours/week: 168.
Operating areas: New Jersey, New York,.
Programming: Regional news service covering all five boroughs of New York City.
Began: September 8, 1992, As NY1. Rebranded Time Warner Cable News NY1 December 16, 2013.
Means of Support: Advertising.
Total subscribers: 2,100,000.
Distribution method: Available to Time Warner & Cablevision cable subscribers. Streaming available through app.
Scrambled signal: Yes.
Ownership: Time Warner Cable.

TIME WARNER CABLE NEWS NY1 NOTICIAS — Time Warner Cable News NY1.
Web Site: http://www.twcnews.com/nyc/twc-ny1-noticias.html
Programming: Spanish-language local news.
Began: June 30, 2003.

TIME WARNER CABLE NEWS (QUEENS) — See Time Warner Cable News NY1.
Web Site: http://www.ny1.com/nyc/queens
Programming: Local news, sports, traffic & politics from Queens.

TIME WARNER CABLE NEWS (ROCHESTER)
71 Mount Hope Ave
Rochester, NY 14620
Phones: 585-756-2424; 888-278-9889
Fax: 585-756-1673
E-mail: rochester@twcnews.com
Web Site: http://www.ny1.com/nys/rochester
Ed Buttaccio, News Director

Branch Offices:
BUFFALO: 355 Chicago St, Buffalo, NY 14204. Phones: 716-558-8999; 855-892-4966. Fax: 716-558-8501. E-Mail: news@buffalo.ynn.com. Web site: http://buffalo.ynn.com.
Type of service: Regional basic.
Operating hours/week: 168.
Operating areas: New York.
Programming: News, sports, traffic & politics from greater Rochester, the Finger Lakes & the Genesee Valley.
Began: January 1, 1990, as WGRC. Rebranded R News on July 4, 1995, YNN Rochester August 2009 & Time Warner Cable News December 16, 2013.
Distribution method: Available to Time Warner cable subscribers.
Scrambled signal: Yes.
Ownership: Time Warner Cable.

TIME WARNER CABLE NEWS (SAN ANTONIO)
403 Urban Loop
San Antonio, TX 78207
Phone: 210-582-9408
E-mail: txnewsdesk@twcnews.com
Web Site: http://www.ny1.com/tx/san-antonio
Michael Pearson, News Director
Type of service: Regional basic.
Operating hours/week: 168.
Operating areas: Texas.
Programming: Local news, sports, traffic & politics from San Antonio.
Began: June 2, 2014.
Means of Support: Advertising.
Total subscribers: 360,000.
Distribution method: Available to Time Warner cable subscribers.
Scrambled signal: Yes.
Ownership: Time Warner Cable.

TIME WARNER CABLE NEWS (SOUTHERN TIER NY) — See Time Warner Cable News (Central NY).
Web Site: http://www.ny1.com/nys/binghamton
Programming: News, sports, traffic & politics from the Southern Tier, including western Stueben County across the Elmira/Corning area, to Greater Binghamton, and along the Interstate-88 corridor through Oneonta, plus portions of the Northern Tier of Pennsylvania.
Began: November 7, 2003, as News 10 Now. Rebranded YNN Central New York March 2010 & Time Warner Cable News December 16, 2013.

TIME WARNER CABLE NEWS (STATEN ISLAND) — See Time Warner Cable News NY1.
Web Site: http://www.ny1.com/nyc/staten-island
Programming: Local news, sports, traffic & politics from Staten Island.

TIME WARNER CABLE NEWS (TRIAD NC)
200 Centreport Dr
Ste 250
Greensboro, NC 27410
Phones: 336-856-9497; 866-907-9497
Fax: 336-662-0082
E-mail: triadnews@twcnews.com
Web Site: http://www.ny1.com/nc/triad

Type of service: Regional basic.
Operating hours/week: 168.
Operating areas: North Carolina.
Programming: Local news, sports, traffic & politics from the Greensboro area.
Began: September 25, 2006, as News 14 Carolina. Rebranded Time Warner Cable News December 16, 2013.
Distribution method: Available to Time Warner cable subscribers.
Scrambled signal: Yes.
Ownership: Time Warner Cable.

TIME WARNER CABLE SPORTS 3 ALBANY — See Time Warner Cable SportsChannel (Albany).

TIME WARNER CABLE SPORTS CENTRAL NEW YORK — See Time Warner Cable SportsChannel (Syracuse).

TIME WARNER CABLE SPORTSCHANNEL 2 (KANSAS CITY)
Programming: Repeat viewings of sporting events & programs.
Began: March 1, 2010, as Metro Sports 2. Rebranded Time Warner Cable SportsChannel 2.

TIME WARNER CABLE SPORTSCHANNEL (ALBANY)
1021 High Bridge Rd
Schenectady, NY 12303
Phone: 866-321-2225
E-mail: sportschannelweb@twcable.com
Web Site: http://www.twcsportschannel.com/ny/albany
Steve Arvan, Senior Director, Local Sports Programming
Type of service: Regional basic, HD.
Operating areas: New York.
Programming: High school, college & professional sporting events, sports related news & entertainment.
Began: October 1, 2002.
Means of Support: Advertising.
Distribution method: Available to Time Warner cable subscribers.
Scrambled signal: Yes.
Ownership: Time Warner Cable.

TIME WARNER CABLE SPORTSCHANNEL (AUSTIN)
E-mail: sportschannelweb@twcable.com
Web Site: http://www.twcsportschannel.com/tx/austin
Type of service: Regional.
Operating areas: Texas.
Programming: High school sporting events including TAPPS games, soccer, college sporting evens & original programming.
Distribution method: Available to Time Warner cable subscribers.
Scrambled signal: Yes.
Ownership: Time Warner Cable.

TIME WARNER CABLE SPORTSCHANNEL (BUFFALO)
795 Indian Church Rd
West Seneca, NY 14224

FULLY SEARCHABLE • CONTINUOUSLY UPDATED • DISCOUNT RATES FOR PRINT PURCHASERS
For more information call **800-771-9202** or visit **www.warren-news.com**

Phone: 716-558-8881
E-mail: sportschannelweb@twcable.com
Web Site: http://www.twcsportschannel.com/ny/buffalo
Type of service: Regional basic, HD.
Operating areas: New York.
Programming: High school, college & professional sporting events, sports related news & entertainment.
Began: November 19, 2007.
Means of Support: Advertising.
Distribution method: Available to Time Warner cable subscribers.
Scrambled signal: Yes.
Ownership: Time Warner Cable.

TIME WARNER CABLE SPORTSCHANNEL (COLUMBIA) — See Time Warner Cable SportsChannel (Eastern North Carolina).
Web Site: http://www.twcsportschannel.com/sc/columbia

TIME WARNER CABLE SPORTSCHANNEL (DALLAS)
E-mail: sportschannelweb@twcable.com
Web Site: http://www.twcsportschannel.com/tx/dallas
Type of service: Regional basic, HD.
Operating hours/week: 168.
Operating areas: Texas.
Programming: High school sporting events including TAPPS games, soccer, college sporting evens & original programming.
Distribution method: Available to Time Warner cable subscribers.
Scrambled signal: Yes.
Ownership: Time Warner Cable.

TIME WARNER CABLE SPORTSCHANNEL (EASTERN NORTH CAROLINA)
2505 Atlantic Ave
Ste 102
Raleigh, NC
Phone: 919-882-4051
E-mail: sportschannelweb@twcable.com
Web Site: http://www.twcsportschannel.com/nc/easternnc
Type of service: Regional basic, HD.
Operating areas: North Carolina & South Carolina.
Programming: Sporting events including local high schools, Carolina Panthers & the Durham Bulls.
Distribution method: Available to Time Warner cable subscribers.
Scrambled signal: Yes.
Ownership: Time Warner Cable.

TIME WARNER CABLE SPORTSCHANNEL (GREEN BAY) — See Time Warner Cable SportsChannel (Milwaukee).
Web Site: http://www.twcsportschannel.com/wi/greenbay
Type of service: Regional basic, HD.
Operating areas: Wisconsin.
Programming: Live sporting events, tape-delayed games, other featured programming, high school, college, professional & amateur sports.

Pay TV & Satellite Services

Distribution method: Available to Time Warner cable subscribers.
Scrambled signal: Yes.
Ownership: Time Warner Cable.

TIME WARNER CABLE SPORTSCHANNEL (KANSAS CITY)
6550 Winchester Ave
Kansas City, MO 64133
Phones: 816-358-5360; 816-222-5500
Fax: 816-358-5479
E-mail: sportschannelweb@twcable.com
Web Site: http://www.twcsportschannel.com/mo/kansascity
Chris Huwe, General Manager
Type of service: Regional basic, HD.
Operating hours/week: 168.
Operating areas: Kansas City area & Nebraska.
Programming: Live & taped telecasts of high school & professional sporting events, studio shows, original documentary-style programs & other sports programming from the Kansas City area.
Began: December 12, 1996, as Metro Sports. Metro Sports HD began March 1, 2010. Rebranded Time Warner Cable SportsChannel.
Means of Support: Advertising.
Distribution method: Available to Comcast, WOW! & Time Warner Cable subscribers.
Scrambled signal: Yes.
Ownership: Time Warner Cable.

TIME WARNER CABLE SPORTSCHANNEL (LINCOLN)
5400 S 16th St
Lincoln, NE 68512
Phone: 402-421-0382
E-mail: sportschannelweb@twcable.com
Web Site: http://www.twcsportschannel.com/ne/lincoln
Type of service: Regional basic, HD.
Operating areas: Nebraska.
Programming: Sporting events & programming covering the Nebraska Huskers football and men's basketball teams, Eagle Raceway and local high school sports. Also covers some sports from the Kansas City metro area, including the Kansas Jayhawks and Kansas City Chiefs.
Distribution method: Available to Time Warner cable subscribers.
Scrambled signal: Yes.
Ownership: Time Warner Cable.

TIME WARNER CABLE SPORTSCHANNEL (MID OHIO) — See Time Warner Cable SportsChannel (Northeast Ohio).
Web Site: http://www.twcsportschannel.com/oh/midohio

TIME WARNER CABLE SPORTSCHANNEL (MILWAUKEE)
1320 N Dr Martin Luther King Dr
Milwaukee, WI 53212-3980
Phone: 414-908-4670
E-mail: TWCSportsWI@twcable.com
Web Site: http://www.twcsportschannel.com/wi/milwaukee
Tom Kurtz, Director & General Manager
Type of service: Regional basic, HD.
Operating areas: Wisconsin.
Programming: Live sporting events, tape-delayed games, other featured programming, high school, college, professional & amateur sports.
Began: February 1, 2007.
Means of Support: Advertising.

Distribution method: Available to Time Warner subscribers.
Scrambled signal: Yes.
Ownership: Time Warner Cable.

TIME WARNER CABLE SPORTSCHANNEL (NORTHEAST OHIO)
580 N Fourth St
Ste 350
Columbus, OH 43215
Phone: 614-384-2640
E-mail: sportschannelweb@twcable.com
Web Site: http://www.twcsportschannel.com/oh/northeastohio
Dave Stephany, Marketing Manager
Type of service: Regional basic, HD.
Operating hours/week: 168.
Operating areas: Ohio.
Programming: Statewide sports channel focusing on local high school and college athletics and other regional programming.
Began: August 1, 2012, replacing NEON.
Distribution method: Available to Time Warner Cable subscribers.
Scrambled signal: Yes.
Ownership: Time Warner Cable.

TIME WARNER CABLE SPORTSCHANNEL (ROCHESTER)
71 Mount Hope Ave
Rochester, NY 14620-1090
Phone: 585-756-5000
E-mail: sportschannelweb@twcable.com
Web Site: http://www.twcsportschannel.com/ny/rochester
Steve Arvan, Senior Director, Local Sports Programming
Type of service: Regional basic, HD.
Operating hours/week: 168.
Operating areas: Rochester, New York.
Programming: High school, college & professional sporting events, sports related news & entertainment.
Began: December 15, 2006.
Means of Support: Advertising.
Distribution method: Available to Time Warner Cable subscribers.
Scrambled signal: Yes.
Ownership: Time Warner Cable.

TIME WARNER CABLE SPORTSCHANNEL (SOUTHWEST OHIO) — See Time Warner Cable SportsChannel (Northeast Ohio).
Web Site: http://www.twcsportschannel.com/oh/southwestohio

TIME WARNER CABLE SPORTSCHANNEL (SYRACUSE)
6005 Fair Lakes Rd E
Syracuse, NY 13057
Phone: 315-634-6000
E-mail: sportschannelweb@twcable.com
Web Site: http://www.twcsportschannel.com/ny/syracuse
Steve Arvan, Senior Director, Local Sports Programming
Dave Perkins, Sales Manager
Type of service: Regional basic, HD.
Operating hours/week: 168.
Operating areas: New York.
Programming: High school, college & professional sporting events, sports related news & entertainment.
Distribution method: Available to Time Warner Cable subscribers.
Scrambled signal: Yes.
Ownership: Time Warner Cable.

TIME WARNER CABLE SPORTSCHANNEL (WESTERN NORTH CAROLINA) — See Time Warner Cable SportsChannel (Eastern North Carolina).
Fax: http://www.twcsportschannel.com/nc/westernnc

TIME WARNER CABLE SPORTSCHANNEL WISCONSIN — See Time Warner Cable SportsChannel (Milwaukee).

TIME WARNER CABLE SPORTSNET
2345 Alaska Ave
El Segundo, CA 90245
Phones: 310-531-1400; 310-351-1550
Web Site: http://twcsportsnet.com
Mark Shuken, Senior Vice President & General Manager, Time Warner Cable Sports Regional Networks
Deborah Picciolo, Regional Vice President, Operations, Time Warner Cable West Region
Larry Meyers, Vice President, Content & Executive Producer, Time Warner Cable Sports
Type of service: Regional pay.
Operating areas: Southern California.
Programming: Carries the Los Angeles Sparks of the WNBA, the LA Galaxy of the MLS and the Los Angeles Lakers of the NBA plus Mountain West Conference college football.
Began: October 1, 2012.
Means of Support: Advertising and subscriber fees.
Distribution method: Available to Charter, Time Warner, AT&T U-verse, Verizon FiOS & satellite subscribers.
Scrambled signal: Yes.
Ownership: Time Warner Cable.

TIME WARNER CABLE SPORTSNET BUFFALO — See Time Warner Cable SportsChannel (Buffalo).

TIME WARNER CABLE SPORTSNET LA
2345 Alaska Ave.
El Segundo, CA 90245
Phones: 310-531-1400; 310-531-1550
Web Site: http://www.sportsnetla.com
Mark R. Walter, Chief Executive Officer, Guggenheim Partners LLC & Chairman, Los Angeles Dodgers
Todd Boehly, President, Guggenheim Partners LLC
Mark Coleman, Vice President, Engineering & Operations, Time Warner Cable Sports
Larry Meyers, Vice President, Content & Executive Producer, Time Warner Cable Sports
Torie von Alt, Public Relations Director, Guggenheim Partners LLC
Type of service: Regional pay.
Operating hours/week: 168.
Operating areas: California.
Programming: Los Angeles Dodger baseball games.
Began: February 25, 2014.
Means of Support: Advertising, subscriber fees.
Total subscribers: 2,000,000 (Represents number of Time Warner subscribers in the Los Angeles area.).
Scrambled signal: Yes.
Ownership: A joint venture between American Media Productions & Time Warner Cable. TWC is charter distributor & provides non-game production/technical service.

TIME WARNER CABLE SPORTSNET ROCHESTER — See Time Warner Cable SportsChannel (Rochester)

TIVI5MONDE
8733 Sunset Blvd
Ste 202
West Hollywood, CA 90069
Phone: 800-737-0455
E-mail: toutsavoir@tv5monde.org
Web Site: http://www.tv5.org
Marie-Christine Saragosse, General Manager, TV5MONDE
Type of service: Pay.
Operating areas: Available nationwide.
Programming: French language channel devoted solely to children's programming. The channel is programmed to target children aged 4-14.
Began: January 26, 2012.
Means of Support: Subscriber fees.
Distribution method: Available to Dish Network subscribers.
Scrambled signal: Yes.

TKMI BROADCASTING
PO Box 46
101-115 Buffalo St
Mannington, WV 26582
Phones: 304-986-2896; 305-986-1595 (TV Dept.)
E-mail: tvtkmi@westco.net
Web Site: http://www.tkmi.org
Dr. Nicholas Lalli, Founder & President
Pamela Lalli, Vice President & Secretary
Lydia Shriver, Trustee
Kimberly Weir, Trustee
Type of service: Basic, streaming.
Operating hours/week: 168.
Operating areas: West Virginia.
Programming: Religious & inspirational; children & family; clean movies, sports & news.
Began: May 22, 2003.
Distribution method: Available over the air and to cable & IPTV subscribers. Mobile & streaming available online or through participating providers.
Scrambled signal: No.
Ownership: True Knowledge Ministries International.

TLC
c/o Discovery Communications
One Discovery Pl
Silver Spring, MD 20910
Phone: 240-662-0000
Web Site: http://www.tlc.com
Nancy Daniels, General Manager & Executive Vice President, TLC
Howard Lee, Executive Vice President, Development & Production
Victoria Lowell, Executive Vice President, Marketing, Animal Planet & TLC
Sharon O'Sullivan, Executive Vice President, National Ad Sales, Animal Planet, Discovery Fit & Health, Investigation Discover & TLC
Scott Lewers, Senior Vice President, Multi-Platform Strategy, TLC
Alon Ornstein, Senior Vice President, Production & Development, TLC, East Coast
Jennifer Sarlin, Senior Vice President, Marketing, TLC
Amy Savitsky, Senior Vice President, Program Development, TLC
Laura Staro, Senior Vice President, Research, TLC
Sandy Varo Jarrell, Senior Vice President, Production & Development, TLC, West Coast
Wendy Douglas, Vice President, Production, TLC, East Coast
Sara Helman, Vice President, Development & Production

Pay TV & Satellite Services

Marisa Levy, Vice President, Development, TLC, East Coast
Andrew Strauser, Vice President, Talent Development & Casting, TLC
Jack Tarantino, Vice President, Production, TLC, West Coast
Josh Trager, Vice President, National Sales, Ad Sales
Elvia Van Es Olivia, Vice President, Development, TLC, West Coast
Type of service: Basic, HD, streaming, video on demand.
Satellites: AMC 10, transponder 14.
Operating hours/week: 168.
Uplink: Stamford, CT.
Programming: Documentaries on history, human behavior & science; commercial-free/violence-free programs for preschoolers; how-to programming about cooking, fashion, gardening & home improvement.
Began: November 1, 1980, as The Learning Channel. Rebranded TLC in 1992. TLC HD began September 2007.
Means of Support: Subscribers & advertising.
Total subscribers: 95,000,000 (U.S. 907,000,000 international.).
Distribution method: Available to cable, IPTV & satellite subscribers. Streaming available online.
Scrambled signal: Yes.
Ownership: Discovery Communications Inc.

TOTAL LIVING NETWORK
25553 Wolf's Crossing
Ste A
Plainfield, IL 60585
Phone: 630-801-3838
Fax: 630-801-3839
E-mail: mail@tln.com
Web Site: http://www.tln.com
Jerry K. Rose, President
James R. Nichols, Vice President, Finance
Roy Pokorny, Vice President, Sales & Marketing
Dick Rolfe, Vice President, Strategic Initiatives
Peter Edgers, Network Operations Director
Bob Reed, Technical Operations Director
Type of service: Basic.
Satellites: Galaxy 1, transponder 5.
Operating hours/week: 168.
Operating areas: Available nationwide.
Programming: Christian television programming.
Began: August 31, 1998.
Means of Support: Advertising & donations.
Total subscribers: 8,000,000.
Distribution method: Available over the air on digital sub-channels, on Chicago area cable systems, on KTLN-TV Novato, CA & Sky Angel.
Scrambled signal: Yes.
Ownership: Christian Communications of Chicagoland Inc.

TMC — See The Movie Channel.

TMC XTRA — See The Movie Channel Xtra.

TNN (THE NASHVILLE NETWORK) — See Heartland.

TURNER NETWORK TELEVISION — See TNT.

TOKYO TV
1533 Bayshore Hwy
Burlingame, CA 94010
Phone: 650-552-9100
Fax: 650-552-9214
Web Site: http://www.ttvusa.com
Yoshimi Haruyama, President

Type of service: Basic.
Operating areas: California.
Programming: Broadcasts the latest Japanese programs, such as the daily morning news, documentaries, dramas and cooking shows.
Began: September 1, 1974.
Means of Support: Advertising.
Total subscribers: 7,200,000.
Distribution method: Broadcast on KCNS San Francisco, CA and available to area cable system subscribers.
Scrambled signal: Yes.
Ownership: Tokyo Television Broadcasting Corp.

TOO MUCH FOR TV ON DEMAND — See iN DEMAND.
Programming: On demand adult programming.

TOON DISNEY — See Disney XD.

TOP CHANNEL TV
International Cultural Center
Blv. Deshmoret e Kombit
Tirana
Albania
Phone: 355-4-2-253-177
Fax: 355-4-2-253-178
E-mail: info@top-channel.tv
Web Site: http://www.top-channel.tv
Programming: Albanian news, social & economic, films & sports.
Distribution method: Available to satellite subscribers.
Scrambled signal: Yes.

TORSTAR MEDIA GROUP TELEVISION (TORONTO STAR TV)
One Yonge St
9th Fl
Toronto, ON M5E 1E6
Canada
Phone: 416-869-4700
Fax: 416-869-4566
E-mail: production@tmgtv.ca
Mark Goodale, Vice President & General Manager
Heather Brunt, Operations Manager
Susan Gouvianakis, Traffic Manager
Deborah Kelly, Production Manager
Type of service: Basic.
Operating hours/week: 24.
Programming: Infomercial channel that airs short & long form infomercials for clients including The Toronto Star.
Began: October 17, 1997.
Means of Support: Advertising.
Total subscribers: 1,400,000.
Distribution method: Available to cable systems.
Ownership: Torstar Corporation.

TRACE SPORT STARS
73, rue Henri Barbusse
Clichy 92110
France
Phone: 33-0-1-77-68-05-20
Fax: 33-0-1-77-68-05-21
E-mail: info@trace.tv
Web Site: http://trace.tv
Programming: Entertainment channel dedicated to the lives of stars in the world of sports.
Ownership: Trace Partners. Distributed in the U.S. by Alterna'TV.

TRAVEL CHANNEL
9721 Sherrill Blvd
Knoxville, TN 37932
Phone: 865-694-2700

Web Site: http://www.travelchannel.com
Shannon O'Neill, President & Managing Director-Finance and Operations, US Networks
Andy Singer, General Manager
Patrick Lafferty, Chief Creative Officer
Ross Babbit, Senior Vice President, Programming & Development
Fred Graver, Senior Vice President, Programming
Eleo Hensleigh, Senior Vice President, Marketing & Communications
Marietta Hurwitz, Senior Vice President & General Manager, Digital
Robert Madden, Senior Vice President, Marketing, Creative, Communications & Brand Strategy
Brigitte McCray, Senior Vice President, Program Planning & Strategy
Lori McFarling, Senior Vice President, Distribution & Marketing
Greg Regis, Senior Vice President, Ad Sales
Patalia Tate, Senior Vice President, Marketing, Creative & Brand Strategy
Courtney White, Senior Vice President, Programming
Matthew Gould, Vice President, Development
Kerri Hannigan, Vice President, Marketing, Communications & Brand Strategy
Linette Hwu, Vice President, Legal Affairs
Brian Leonard, Vice President, Programming & Development
Mickey McKenzie, Vice President, Production
David W. Padrusch, Vice President, Production & Development
Rex Recka, Vice President, Business Affairs
Neil Regan, Vice President, Programming
Adam Sutherland, Vice President, Strategy & Business Development
Amelie Tseng, Vice President, Communications
Kay Robinson, Corporate Director, People Services
Doug Bailey, Production & Development Director
Rick Gomes, Communications Director
Bill Howard, Programming & Partnerships Director
Type of service: Basic, HD, streaming.
Satellites: Satcom F-1R, transponder 9; Satcom C-4, transponder 13; West Coast: AMC-10, transponder 14.
Operating hours/week: 126.
Programming: News & entertainment segments hosted by travel experts, authors, newsmakers & celebrities.
Began: February 1, 1987, Travel Channel HD launched January 14, 2008.
Means of Support: Advertising.
Total subscribers: 89,000,000.
Distribution method: Available to cable, IPTV & satellite subscribers. Streaming available online.
Scrambled signal: Yes. Equipment: VideoCipher II Plus.
Ownership: Scripps Networks Interactive Inc.

TRAVEL CHANNEL BEYOND — See Travel Channel.
Type of service: Broadband.

TRAVEL ON DEMAND
c/o Time Warner Cable
60 Columbus Cir, 17th Fl
New York, NY 10023
Phone: 212-364-8200
E-mail: jeannette.castaneda@twcable.com
Joan Hogan Gillman, President, Time Warner Cable Media
Jeannette Castaneda, Public Relations Manager
Type of service: Video on demand.
Operating hours/week: 168.
Operating areas: Available nationwide.
Programming: Offers programming on travel and related topics.
Distribution method: Available to Time Warner Cable digital cable system subscribers.
Ownership: Time Warner Cable Inc.

TRAVEL WEATHER NOW — See Bright House Travel Weather Now.

TR3S — See MTV.
MTV Networks
1515 Broadway
New York, NY 10036
Phones: 212-258-8000; 212-258-8760
E-mail: erica.saylor@vimn.com
Web Site: http://www.tr3s.com
Sofia Ioannu, Managing Director, Viacom International Media Networks, The Americas
Fernando Gaston, Senior Vice President, Content & Creative & Brand Manager
Charlie Singer, Senior Vice President, Content & Creative
Nancy Tellet, Senior Vice President, Research & Consumer Insights
Maria Badillo, Vice President, Programming & Production
Mario Cader-Frech, Vice President, Public Affairs & Corporate Responsibility
Luisa Fairborne, Vice President, Advertising Sales
Rene Rodriguez, Vice President, Digital Media
Sean Saylor, Vice President, Creative
Marc Zimet, Vice President, Music & Talent
Operating areas: Nationwide.
Programming: Lifestyle series, music videos, documentaries & other programming targeted toward bilingual Latinos & non-Latinos.
Began: September 25, 2006.
Means of Support: Advertising.
Total subscribers: 34,000,000.
Distribution method: Available to cable, IPTV & satellite subscribers.
Scrambled signal: Yes.
Ownership: Viacom International Media Networks.

TRINITY BROADCASTING NETWORK (TBN)
PO Box A
Santa Ana, CA 92711
Phones: 714-832-2950; 800-735-5542
E-mail: davidadcock@tbn.org
Web Site: http://www.tbn.org; http://www.tbnnetworks.com
Matthew Crouch, Chairman
Bob Fopma, Vice President, Production
Ben Miller, Vice President, Engineering

Pay TV & Satellite Services

David Adcock, National Director, Affiliate Sales & Relations
Jay Jones, Media Services; Media Relations
Type of service: Over the air, digital basic, HD, streaming.
Satellites: Galaxy 14, transponder 1; Galaxy 23, transponder 20 (Olympusat); AMC 18, transponder 21 (HITS).
Operating hours/week: 168.
Operating areas: Available nationwide.
Uplink: Tustin, CA.
Programming: Religious variety.
Began: May 28, 1973, via broadcast TV; May 1, 1978 via satellite. Trinity Broadcasting Network HD began December 15, 2009.
Means of Support: Donations.
Total subscribers: 64,718,049.
Distribution method: Available over the air through local affiliates. Available to cable, IPTV & satellite subscribers. Streaming available online.
Scrambled signal: Yes.
Ownership: TBN Networks, a non-profit corp.

TRI-STATE CHRISTIAN TELEVISION — See TCT.

TROJAN VISION
3131 S Figueroa St
Ste 110
Los Angeles, CA 90089-7756
Phone: 213-821-2176
Fax: 213-821-2149
E-mail: info@trojanvision.com
Web Site: http://www.trojanvision.com
Don Tillman, Executive Director
Nathaniel Schermerhorn, General Manager
Programming: Student-operated programming from USC.
Began: September 15, 1997.
Total subscribers: 1,800,000.

TRUE BLUE
5435 Airport Blvd
Ste 100
Boulder, CO 80301
Phone: 303-786-8700
Fax: 303-938-8388
Mark Kreloff, President & Chief Executive Officer
Karyn Miller, Chief Financial & Operating Officer
Michael Weiner, Executive Vice President, Business Affairs
Thomas Nyiri, Vice President, Broadband Communications & Chief Technical Offier
John Chambliss, Programming Director
Mark Grant, Marketing Contact
Robin Rothman, Media Contact
Type of service: Pay & Pay-per-view.
Satellites: Telstar 5, transponder 14.
Operating hours/week: 168.
Operating areas: Not available in Alabama, Mississippi, North Carolina, Oklahoma, Tennessee or Utah.
Uplink: Ottawa, ON.
Programming: Adult channel offering amateur films, talk shows & American classics.
Began: March 1, 1996.
Distribution method: Available to cable & satellite subscribers.
Scrambled signal: Yes. Equipment: Video Cipher II Plus.
Ownership: New Frontier Media Inc.

TRUTV
One Time Warner Center
New York, NY 10019-6038
Phone: 404-575-5577
Web Site: http://www.trutv.com
Chris Linn, President & Head of Programming

Marissa Ronca, Executive Vice President, Programming
Puja Vohra, Executive Vice President, Marketing & Digital
Michael Lanzillotta, Senior Vice President & General Manager
Mary Corigliano, Senior Vice President, Brand Strategy & Digital Content/Multi-Platform Development
Anthony Horn, Senior Vice President, Current Programming & Specials
Virginia Lazalde-McPherson, Senior Vice President, Business Affairs
Andrew Verderame, Senior Vice President, Creative Services
Angel Annussek, Vice President, Original Programming
Courtney Brown, Vice President, Integrated Brand Strategy
Raymond Doole, Vice President, Marketing
Mari Ghuneim, Vice President, Digital Strategy & Development
Lesley Goldman, Vice President, Development & Original Programming
Nancy McKenna, Vice President, Production Operations
Mark Powell, Vice President, Original Programming
Bryan Terry, Vice President, Development & Original Programming
Matt Stueland, Senior Director, Program Scheduling & Planning
Adam Dolgins, Executive Producer, Joker's Wild
Mitchell Rosenbaum, Executive Producer
Deb Savo, Executive Producer
Christine Walters, Executive Producer
Brian Silbert, Senior Producer

Western Regional Office:
BURBANK: 3000 W Alameda Ave, Ste C-185, Burbank, CA 91523. Phone: 818-840-3608.
Fax: 818-840-3112.
Type of service: Basic, HD, streaming & video on demand.
Satellites: Satcom C-3, transponder 6.
Sales representative: Turner Network Sales.
Operating hours/week: 168.
Operating areas: Nationwide.
Programming: Reality, comedy & entertainment.
Began: July 1, 1991, as Court TV; rebranded truTV on January 1, 2008.
Means of Support: Advertising.
Total subscribers: 90,800,000.
Distribution method: Available to most cable, IPTV & satellite subscribers. Streaming available online & mobile through the website or WATCH truTV app (participating providers). Video on demand through participating providers.
Scrambled signal: Yes.
Ownership: Turner Broadcasting System, a division of Time Warner.

TUFF TV
3340 Peachtree Rd, NE
Ste 1800
Atlanta, GA 30326
Phone: 404-230-9600
Fax: 404-230-5600
E-mail: seals@tufftv.com
Web Site: http://www.tufftv.com
David Leach, President & Chief Executive Officer, Luken Communications
Doug Evans, Chief Operating Officer, Luken Communications
Lou Seals, Founder, Chairman & Chief Executive Officer, TUFF TV Media Group LLC
John Bonner, Executive Vice President & Co-Founder
Chris Hannaford, Executive Vice President, Programming & Development

Chip Harwood, Vice President, Affiliate Sales & Marketing, TUFF TV Media Group LLC
Andrew Mearns, Programming Manager
Mike Snowden, Content Operations Manager
Cole Sweeton, Creative Services Manager
Andrea Rhum, Senior Account Manager, National Advertising Sales
Anthony Barrett, Account Executive, National Advertising Sales
Cathy Winters, Traffic Coordinator
Type of service: Basic, over the air.
Operating areas: Nationwide.
Uplink: Chattanooga, TN.
Programming: Programming targeted at men and the specific pursuits, interests, and hobbies, including sports, lifestyle, drama, reality, talk, specials, and movies.
Began: June 30, 2009.
Means of Support: Advertising.
Total subscribers: 38,000,000.
Distribution method: Available over the air on digital sub-channels.
Scrambled signal: Yes.
Ownership: TUFF TV Media Group LLC (Seals Entertainment Co.).

TU INGLES TV
c/o Olympusat Inc.
560 Village Blvd, Ste 250
West Palm Beach, FL 33409
Phone: 561-684-5657
Fax: 561-684-9690
E-mail: cursos@tuingles.tv
Web Site: http://www.tuingles.tv; http://www.olympusat.com
Programming: Offers courses at different levels of English in an entertaining, amusing and instructive environment.
Ownership: Distributed in the U.S. by Olympusat.

TURNER CLASSIC MOVIES
1050 Techwood Dr NW
Atlanta, GA 30318
Phone: 404-885-5535
Fax: 404-885-5536
Web Site: http://www.tcm.com
Jennifer Dorian, General Manager
Dennis Adamovich, Senior Vice President, Digital, Affiliate, Lifestyle & Enterprise Commerce, TNT, TBS & TCM
Charles Tabesh, Senior Vice President, Programming
Tom Brown, Vice President, Original Productions
Pola Changnon, Vice President & Creative Director
Darcy Hettrich, Vice President, Talent
Lincoln Lopez, Vice President, Marketing, Digital & Social Media, TNT, TBS & TCM
Genevieve McGillicuddy, Vice President, Brand Activation & Partnership
Raghunadh Polavarapu, Vice President, Digital Operations, TNT, TBS & TCM
Nancy Rewis, Vice President, Commerce Enterprise, TNT, TBS & TCM
Rachelle Savoia, Vice President, Communications
Type of service: Basic, HD, streaming & video on demand.
Sales representative: Turner Network Sales.
Operating areas: Nationwide.
Programming: Uncut films, commercial-free, from the largest film libraries; original documentaries and specials.
Began: April 14, 1994, Turner Classic Movies HD launched June 2009.
Total subscribers: 75,000,000.
Distribution method: Available to cable, IPTV & satellite subscribers. Streaming available online & mobile through the website or the WATCH TCM app (participating providers).

Video on demand available through participating providers.
Scrambled signal: Yes.
Ownership: Turner Broadcasting System, a division of Time Warner.

TNT
(Turner Network Television)
One CNN Center
Atlanta, GA 30348
Phones: 404-885-4570; 404-885-4647
Fax: 404-827-3368
Web Site: http://www.tntdrama.com
Kevin Reilly, President, TNT & TBS
Sandra Dewey, President, Productions & Business Affairs, TNT & TBS
Jeff Gregor, Chief Catalyst Officer, TNT & TBS
Sarah Aubrey, Executive Vice President, Original Programming, TNT
Michael Engleman, Executive Vice President, Entertainment Marketing & Brand Innovation, TNT & TBS
Patrick Kelly, Executive Vice President, Business Affairs, TNT & TBS
Dennis Adamovich, Senior Vice President, Digital, Affiliate, Lifestyle & Enterprise Commerce, TNT, TBS & TCM
Joey Chavez, Senior Vice President, Original Programming
David Eilenberg, Senior Vice President, Unscripted Development, TNT & TBS
David Hudson, Senior Vice President, Late Night & Specials, TNT & TBS
Sam Linsky, Senior Vice President, Original Programming, TNT
Lillah McCarthy, Senior Vice President, Original Programming, TNT
Phil Oppenheim, Senior Vice President, Programming, TNT & TBS
Sandy Padula, Senior Vice President, Research, TBS & TNT
Mark Weissman, Senior Vice President, Production, TNT & TBS
Justin Williams, Senior Vice President, Digital Ventures, TNT & TBS
Rachel Brill, Vice President, Unscripted Programming, TNT & TBS
Jeff Carr, Vice President, Programming, TNT & TBS
Missy Chambless, Vice President, Unscripted Series Marketing, TNT & TBS
Jimmy Jellinek, Vice President, Content Marketing & Digital Innovation, TNT & TBS
Lincoln Lopez, Vice President, Marketing, Digital & Social Media, TNT, TBS & TCM
Kristie Moomey, Vice President, Post Production, Unscripted Programming & Digital Extensions, TNT & TBS
Marie Moore, Vice President, Communications, TNT & TBS
Robin Pelleck, Vice President, Digital, TNT & TBS
Raghunadh Polavarapu, Vice President, Digital Operations, TNT, TBS & TCM
Nancy Rewis, Vice President, Commerce Enterprise, TNT, TBS & TCM
Meredith Zamsky, Vice President, Production

Branch Offices:
Chicago, IL; Dallas, TX; Detroit, MI; Los Angeles, CA; New York, NY.
Type of service: Basic, HD, streaming & video on demand.
Satellites: Satcom 3-R, transponder 18.
Sales representative: Turner Network Sales.
Operating hours/week: 168.
Operating areas: Available nationwide.
Programming: Offering original motion pictures, miniseries, original series, non-fiction specials & live events, contemporary films, NASCAR, NBA & NCAA & popular television series.
Began: October 3, 1988.

Pay TV & Satellite Services

Means of Support: Advertising.
Total subscribers: 97,500,000.
Distribution method: Available to cable, IPTV & satellite subscribers; online & mobile through the website or WATCH TNT app (participating providers); video on demand (participating providers).
Scrambled signal: Yes.
Ownership: Turner Broadcasting System, a division of Time Warner.

TURNER SOUTH — See SportSouth.

TV2
1045 Hamilton St
Allentown, PA 18101-1012
Phone: 610-434-7833
Fax: 610-432-6473
Web Site: http://www.tv2sports.com
Operating hours/week: 35.
Programming: Local sports coverage & sports oriented news & entertainment.
Began: January 1, 1969.
Ownership: Service Electric Cable.

TV5, LA TELEVISION INTERNATIONAL
TV5 Quebec Canada
1755 boul Rene-Levesque E, Bureau 101
Montreal, QC H2K 4P6
Canada
Phone: 514-522-5322
Fax: 514-522-6572
E-mail: info@tv5.ca
Web Site: http://www.tv5.ca
Suzanne Gouin, President & Chief Operating Officer
Ruby Dizeal, Chief of Operations
Nathalie D'Souza, Acquisitions & Coproductions Chief
Audrey Schelling, Communications Chief
Benoit Beaudoin, Vice President & General Manager
Denis Baby, Sales & Marketing Director
Regis Harrisson, Production & Technology Director
Pierre Gang, Program Director
Francine Grise, Finance & Administration Director
Christina Baldassare, Affiliate Relations Manager
Type of service: Basic.
Satellites: Anik E-2, transponder 10-A.
Operating hours/week: 168.
Uplink: Montreal, QC.
Programming: Rebroadcasts French language programs from Africa, Belgium, Canada, France & Switzerland.
Began: September 1, 1988, in Canada. June 1, 1998 in the U.S.
Means of Support: Subscriber fees, government support & advertising.
Total subscribers: 6,168,000.
Distribution method: Available to cable & satellite subscribers.
Scrambled signal: Yes.
Ownership: Consortium de Television Quebec Canada Inc.

TV5MONDE USA
8733 Sunset Blvd
Ste 202
West Hollywood, CA 90069
Phone: 800-737-0455
E-mail: toutsavoir@tv5monde.org
Web Site: http://www.tv5.org
Marie-Christine Saragosse, Director General
Jean Pierre Verines, Chief Technology Officer
Jamal Dajani, Vice President, Middle East & North Africa/Latin America & Caribbean
Frederic Groll-Bourel, Vice President Business Development & Marketing

Laura Strauss, Affiliate Sales & Marketing Director
Type of service: Pay.
Operating hours/week: 168.
Operating areas: Nationwide.
Programming: French-language news & entertainment.
Began: January 1, 1984, in Europe. 1998 in the U.S.
Means of Support: Advertising and subscriber fees.
Total subscribers: 350,000.
Distribution method: Available to cable & satellite subscribers.
Scrambled signal: Yes.

TV AGRO
Carrera 73 #52-66
Medellin - Antioquia
Colombia
Phone: 57-4-448-2500
Fax: 57-4-266-7957
E-mail: info@olympusat.com
Web Site: http://www.tvagro.tv
Type of service: Basic.
Operating areas: Nationwide.
Programming: Farming and agricultural programming.
Distribution method: Available to satellite subscribers.
Scrambled signal: Yes.
Ownership: Global Media Telecommunications SA. Distributed in the U.S. by Olympusat Inc.

TV ASIA
76 National Rd
Edison, NJ 08817
Phone: 732-650-1100
Fax: 732-650-1112
E-mail: info@tvasiausa.com
Web Site: http://www.tvasiausa.com
H.R. Shah, Founder
Lal Dadlaney, Senior Vice President, Business & Operations
Rohit Vyas, News Director
Type of service: Pay.
Satellites: Galaxy VI, transponder 12.
Operating hours/week: 168.
Operating areas: California & New Jersey.
Programming: Hindi, Urdu & English, with regional languages such as Punjabi, Gujurati, Bengali & Tamil.
Began: April 1, 1993.
Means of Support: Advertising & subscribers.
Total subscribers: 20,000.
Distribution method: Available to cable & satellite subscribers.
Scrambled signal: Yes.
Ownership: Asia Star Broadcasting Inc.

TVC+ LATINO
444 W Rialto Ave
Ste C
San Bernardino, CA 92401
Phone: 909-381-1877
E-mail: admin@tvclatino.net
Web Site: http://tvcmas.com
Karen Deaquino, Marketing Director
Samantha Folgar, Executive Assistant
Type of service: Over the air, basic, streaming.
Programming: Spanish & bilingual programming sports, movies, news and entertainment.
Began: December 1, 2011.
Means of Support: Advertising.
Distribution method: Available over the air to digital sub-channels and at AT&T U-verse, Mediacom & Verizon FiOS subscribers.
Scrambled signal: Yes.
Ownership: TVC Mas Latino Inc.

TV CHILE — See ULTRA HDPlex.
Bellevista 0990
Providencia, Santiago
Chile
Phones: 56-2-2707-7200; 56-2-2707-7240
Fax: 56-2-2707-7771
Web Site: http://www.tvchile.cl
Type of service: Pay, HD.
Operating areas: Available nationwide.
Programming: Spanish-language family entertainment, including sports, telenovelas, news & nature shows.
Began: January 1, 1999, in U.S.
Total subscribers: 2,400,000.
Distribution method: Available to cable, IPTV & satellite subscribers.
Scrambled signal: Yes.
Ownership: Television Nacional de Chile. Distributed in the U.S. by Olympusat.

TV COLOMBIA — See RCN Nuestra Tele.

TELEVISION DOMINICANA
2000 Ponce de Leon Blvd
Ste 500
Coral Gables, FL 33134
Phone: 305-421-6364
E-mail: info@televisiondominicana.tv
Web Site: http://www.televisiondominicana.tv
Alan J. Sokol, Chief Executive Officer, Hemisphere Media Group Inc.
Craig D. Fischer, Chief Financial Officer, Hemisphere Media Group Inc.
Operating areas: Nationwide.
Programming: Programs from the Dominican Republic.
Total subscribers: 2,200,000.
Distribution method: Available to satellite subscribers.
Scrambled signal: Yes.
Ownership: Hemisphere Media Group Inc.

TVE INTERNACIONAL
Avda Television Radio 4
Pozuelo de Alarco (Madrid) 28223
Spain
Phone: 34-91-581-70-00
E-mail: rtve.dircom@rtve.es
Web Site: http://www.rtve.es/television/tve-internacional
Leopoldo Gonzalez-Echenique, President, RTVE
Jose Ramon Diez, TVE Director
Type of service: Basic.
Satellites: AMC; Galaxy; Intelsat.
Operating hours/week: 168.
Programming: Spanish news, culture, education & entertainment.
Began: 1989.
Means of Support: State funding (Spain).
Distribution method: Available to satellite subscribers.
Scrambled signal: Yes.
Ownership: RTVE.

TV GLOBO INTERNACIONAL
Rua Evandro Carlos de Andrade, 160
Vila Cordeiro
Sao Paulo 04583-115
Brazil
Phones: 55-11-5112-4405; 55-115112-4018
Web Site: http://www.globotvinternational.com
Marcelo Spinola, Director
Bruno Assumpcao, Sales Executive
Carolina Krambeck, Sales Executive
Type of service: Pay.
Operating hours/week: 168.
Operating areas: Available nationwide.
Programming: Brazilian channel offering live news, live sport, telenovelas, miniseries, kids shows and variety shows.

Began: January 1, 1999, Began July 4, 2013 in the U.S.
Means of Support: Advertising and subscriber fees.
Total subscribers: 555,000 (worldwide subscribers.).
Distribution method: Available to Comcast and Verizon FiOS subscribers.
Scrambled signal: Yes.
Ownership: Organizacoes Globo.

TVGN — See Pop.

TVG NETWORK
19545 NW Von Neumann Dr
Ste 210
Beaverton, OR 97006
Phone: 888-752-9884
E-mail: comments@tvg.com; pr@tvg.com
Web Site: http://www.tvg.com
Kip Levin, Chief Executive Officer
John Hindman, Executive Vice President
Ben Evans, Senior Vice President, Programming & Marketing
Marci Miller, Vice President, Marketing
David Carrico, Vice President, Market Access
Kevin Plate, Vice President, Ad Sales
Rick Baedeker, Media Contact
Jason A. Bulger, Ad Sales Director
Type of service: Basic.
Satellites: GE-1, transponder 23.
Operating hours/week: 168.0.
Operating areas: Nationwide.
Programming: 24-hour sports entertainment network featuring five live horse races per hour on average, as well as sports news/commentary, behind-the-scenes footage, and programs with racing themes appealing to both the experienced and novice fan.
Began: July 14, 1999.
Total subscribers: 36,000,000.
Distribution method: Available to cable & satellite subscribers.
Scrambled signal: Yes.
Ownership: Betfair Group.

TV GUIDE INTERACTIVE INC.
7140 S Lewis Ave
Tulsa, OK 74136-5422
Phones: 918-488-4450; 800-447-7388
Fax: 918-499-6355
Web Site: http://www.tvguide.com
Jeff Shell, III, Chairman & Chief Executive Officer
Joachim Kiener, Vice Chairman
Charles Butler Ammann, Senior Vice President, Secretary & Gen. Counsel
Craig M. Waggy, Senior Vice President & Chief Financial Officer
Toby DeWeese, Vice President, Corporate Development
Gregory S. Taylor, Tax Officer
Marie-Claude Thomas, Assistant Secretary
Cindy Miles, Assistant Secretary
Satellites: Satcom IV-R, transponder 8.
Operating hours/week: 168.
Programming: Digital interactive program guide.
Began: June 1, 1997.
Means of Support: Subscription fees and ad revenue.
Total subscribers: 14,000,000.
Distribution method: Available to cable subscribers.
Scrambled signal: Yes.
Ownership: Rovi Corp.

TV GUIDE NETWORK — See Pop.

TVHS
829 Corporate Way
Fremont, CA 94539

Pay TV & Satellite Services

Phones: 510-353-1689; 510-585-8829
Andrew Kao, Information Contact
Type of service: Regional basic.
Operating hours/week: 168.
Operating areas: Northern California.
Programming: Taiwanese-language entertainment, news & educational programming.
Means of Support: Advertising.
Distribution method: Available over the air on digital sub-channels.
Scrambled signal: Yes.

TVIDAVISION
PO Box 1477
Porterville, CA 93257
Phone: 661-792-3232
E-mail: tvidavision@gmail.com
Rev. Zenaido G. Garza, President
Rev. Israel M. Reyna, Vice President
Jovita Castaneda, Secretary
Rev. Manolo Pineda, Treasurer

Branch Offices:
STUDIO: 1077 W Morton Ave, Ste 201, Porterville, CA 93257.
Type of service: Regional basic.
Operating hours/week: 168.
Operating areas: California (Central Valley area).
Programming: Alternative Spanish-language programming that promotes healthy family and spiritual values.
Began: January 1, 2005.
Means of Support: Advertising & donations.
Distribution method: Available over the air on digital sub-channels.
Scrambled signal: Yes.
Ownership: Rev. Jose Aparicio, Merced Ferrer, Rev. Elias Patino & Pastor Daniel Robles, founders.

TV JAPAN
100 Broadway
15th Floor
New York, NY 10005
Phone: 212-262-3377
Fax: 212-262-5577
E-mail: tvjapan@tvjapan.net
Web Site: http://www.tvjapan.net
Susumu Tanimura, Chief Executive Officer & President
Masao Watari, Executive Vice President, Programming
Yoshiaki Iida, Senior Vice President
Hiroyuki Yamamoto, Senior Vice President
Akio Yoshinaka, Senior Vice President, Treasurer & Secretary
Sonny Takahashi, Vice President, Sales & Marketing
Hacchi Morihata, Technical Operations Director
Helen Wood, Sales Coordinator

Branch Offices:
SANTA MONICA: 3130 Wilshire Blvd, Ste 360, Santa Monica, CA 90403. Phone: 310-829-5575. Fax: 310-829-5655.
Type of service: Premium.
Satellites: DISH Network.
Operating hours/week: 161.
Operating areas: Nationwide.
Programming: Japanese TV programming created by NHK, including news, sports, drama, education & children's programming.
Began: April 1, 1991.
Means of Support: Advertising & subscriber fees.
Total subscribers: 45,000.
Distribution method: Available to Charter, AT&T U-verse, DISH Network & Verizon FiOS customers subscribers.
Scrambled signal: Yes.

Ownership: Japan Network Group Inc., a joint venture of NHK Group & Itochu Group, in conjunction with 28 Japanese & American companies.

TVK (KOREAN)
3435 Wilshire Blvd
19th Fl
Los Angeles, CA 90010
Phone: 213-382-9600
Fax: 213-382-9601
E-mail: info@tvk24.com
Web Site: http://www.tvk24.com
Eric Yoon, Founder & Chief Executive Officer
Chris Park, Advertising Director
Type of service: Basic, video on demand.
Operating hours/week: 168.
Operating areas: Nationwide.
Programming: 24-hour Korean network serving first generation Korean-Americans.
Began: March 1, 2005.
Means of Support: Advertising.
Total subscribers: 26,000,000.
Distribution method: Available to cable & satellite subscribers.
Scrambled signal: Yes.
Ownership: Distributed in the U.S. by International Media Distribution.

TVK POP ON DEMAND — See TVK (Korean).
Programming: Korean music videos in a variety of genres including electropop, hip hop, pop, rock and R&B.
Began: 2012.

TVK2 — See TVK (Korean).
Programming: Korean network geared towards offering programming targeting the 1.5 and 2nd generation Koreans. News in English, plus movies, music videos & entertainment programming.
Began: November 11, 2009.
Scrambled signal: Yes.

TV LAND
1515 Broadway
48th Fl
New York, NY 10036
Phone: 212-258-8000
Fax: 212-258-1967
E-mail: postmaster@tvland.com
Web Site: http://www.tvland.com
Cyma Zarghami, President, Viacom Kids & Family Group
Keith Cox, President, Original Development & Production
John Cucci, Chief Operating Officer
Kassie Canter, Executive Vice President, Communications
Jaclyn Rann Cohen, Executive Vice President, Program Strategy & Acquisitions
Kim Rosenblum, Executive Vice President, Marketing & Creative
Steve Agase, Senior Vice President, Music & Entertainment Ad Sales
Ellen Dominus, Senior Vice President, Entertainment Sales, Music & Entertainment Ad Sales
Brad Gardner, Senior Vice President, Original Programming
Casey Patterson, Senior Vice President, Event Production & Talent Development
Rachel Sandler, Senior Vice President, Corporate Communications
Sharon Silverstein, Senior Vice President, Digital Ad Sales, Music & Entertainment
Caleb Weinstein, Senior Vice President, Strategy & Business Development, Entertainment Group
Maria Caulfield, Vice President, Affiliate Marketing

Rich Cornish, Vice President, Ad Sales Research
Kelleigh Dulany, Vice President, Public Responsibility
Scott Gregory, Vice President, Programming
Rose Catherine Pinkney, Vice President, Development & Original Programming
Dana Tuinier, Vice President, Development & Original Programming
Michael Waldron, Vice President, Creative Director, Design & Animation
Laurel Wichert, Vice President, Research
Rachel Lizerbram Sandler, Head of Communications

Branch Offices:
SANTA MONICA: 2600 Colorado Ave, 2nd Floor, Santa Monica, CA 90404. Fax: 310-752-8850.
Type of service: Expanded basic, HD.
Operating hours/week: 168.
Programming: Classic TV shows.
Began: April 29, 1996.
Means of Support: Advertising.
Total subscribers: 92,000,000.
Distribution method: Available to cable subscribers.
Scrambled signal: Yes.
Ownership: Viacom Inc.

TV MEX
468 N Camden Dr
Ste 250
Beverly Hills, CA 90210-4507
Phone: 310-598-5777
Fax: 310-860-5194
E-mail: mail@tv-mex.com
Web Site: http://www.tv-mex.com
Andrew Matviak, President
Jeremy Matviak, Vice President
Amy Hamilton, Manager
Gonzalo Gonzales, Information Contact
Pejman Partiyeli, Information Contact
Programming: The first 'ranchero' lifestyle network. The service combines all-original regional Mexican movies, shows, sports, events & music.
Began: As of July 2011 in Mexico.
Means of Support: Advertising.
Total subscribers: 2,000,000 (in Mexico.).
Scrambled signal: Yes.
Ownership: Plus Entertainment Inc.

TV ONE
1010 Wayne Ave
14th Fl
Silver Spring, MD 20910
Phone: 301-755-0400
Fax: 301-755-2883
Web Site: http://www.tvoneonline.com
Alfred Liggins, Chief Executive Officer
Brad Siegel, President
Keith Bowen, Chief Revenue Officer
Kenetta Bailey, Executive Vice President & Chief Marketing Officer
Susan Banks, Executive Vice President, Special Projects
Bob Buenting, Executive Vice President, Chief Financial Officer
Jody Drewer, Executive Vice President & Chief Financial Officer
Michelle Rice, Executive Vice President, Affiliate Sales & Marketing
Jay Schneider, Executive Vice President, Network Operations
Karen Wishart, Executive Vice President, Chief Legal Officer
Orlena Blanchard, Senior Vice President, Digital Marketing
Dexter Cole, Senior Vice President, Progeram Scheduling & Acquisitions
Linda Finney, Senior Vice President, Marketing
Lori Hall, Senior Vice President, Marketing

Kimberly Hulsey, Senior Vice President, Distribution & Strategy
Jeff Meier, Senior Vice President, Programming Strategy & Acquisitions
Scott Perkins, Senior Vice President, Creative Services
D'Angela Proctor, Senior Vice President, Programming & Production
Tosha Whitten-Griggs, Senior Vice President, Public Relations
Robyn Greene Arrington, Vice President, Original Programming & Production
Paul Duong, Vice President, Programming & Scheduling
Katrice Jones, Vice President, Digital Media
Toni Judkins, Vice President, Programming & Production
Tonia Lee, Vice President, Business Operations & Strategy
Laura Lipson, Vice President, Promotion & Marketing
Angelique Mais, Vice President, Creative Services
Jeff Meza, Vice President, Integrated Marketing
Kinyette Newman, Vice President, Production Management
Endi Piper, Vice President, Business & Legal Affairs
Seeta Zieger, Vice President, Advertising Sales, Western Region

Branch Offices:
CHICAGO: 180 N Stetson St, Ste 2850, Chicago, IL 60601. Phone: 312-861-4979.

LOS ANGELES: 5750 Wilshire Blvd, Los Angeles, CA 90036. Phone: 323-954-2822.

NEW YORK: 1114 Avenue of the Americas, 20th Floor, New York, NY 10036. Phone: 917-934-1023.
Type of service: Basic, HD.
Operating areas: Nationwide.
Programming: Targets African-American adults, offers entertainment & issue oriented original programs, classic series, movies, reality & game shows, entertainment news & music variety programs.
Began: January 19, 2004, TV One HD began December 17, 2008.
Total subscribers: 57,000,000 (14,000,000 (TV One HD)).
Distribution method: Available to cable, IPTV & satellite subscribers.
Scrambled signal: Yes.
Ownership: A joint venture between Radio One (51%) & NBCUniversal LLC (49%).

TV 1000 RUSSIAN KINO
Turgenev 15 of. 53
Kiev 01054
Ukraine
Phone: 380-044-498-5489
Web Site: http://viasat-channels.tv/channel/rufilms_tv1000
Type of service: Premium.
Operating areas: Available in southern California, New Jersey & New York on cable & nationwide on the DISH Network.
Programming: Provides viewers with original Russian movies, ranging from classic titles to more recent blockbusters.
Began: October 1, 2005, in the Baltic states, Russia, Moldova, Belarus, Ukraine, Georgia and Kazakhstan. Began November 2008 in the U.S.
Means of Support: Advertising & subscriber fees.
Distribution method: Available to to Time Warner & DISH Network subscribers.
Scrambled signal: Yes.
Ownership: Modern Times Group.

Pay TV & Satellite Services

TV ORIENT
25835 Southfield Rd
Southfield, MI 48075
Phone: 248-569-2020
E-mail: info@mbnamerica.net
Programming: Arabic-language entertainment, news, sports & cultural programs for viewers in the U.S.
Scrambled signal: Yes.

TVP INFO — See TV Polonia.
Programming: Polish news.

TV POLONIA
1350 Remington Rd
Schaumburg, IL 60173
Phone: 847-882-2000
Fax: 847-882-2002
E-mail: support@tvpolonia.com
Web Site: http://www.tvpolonia.com
Bob Spanski, President
Bob Pisarek, Vice President
Type of service: Pay.
Operating hours/week: 168.
Programming: Polish-language movies, sports, family entertainment, soap operas, documentaries, masterpiece theater, children's shows, educational programs & newscasts.
Scrambled signal: Yes.

TV RECORD
1221 Brickell Ave
Ste 900
Miami, FL 33131
Phone: 305-347-5131
Web Site: http://www.tvrecordusa.com
Alexandre Raposo, President
Operating areas: Nationwide.
Programming: Portuguese-language channel from Brazil with programming about culture and customs.
Began: September 27, 1953, in Brazil. Began Summer 2013 in the U.S.
Means of Support: Advertising.
Distribution method: Available to satellite subscribers.
Scrambled signal: Yes.
Ownership: Edir Macedo.

TV ROMANIA INTERNATIONAL
Dorobantilor Way 191
Sector 1
Bucharest 010 565
Romania
E-mail: tvr@tvr.ro
Web Site: http://www.tvr.ro
Programming: Public television; shows with Romanian point of view on cultural, social, economics & political events.

TV VENEZUELA
c/o Condista
200 Crandon Blvd, Ste 316
Key Biscayne, FL 33149
Phone: 305-361-5271
Web Site: http://canalsur.com/canales/sur-venezuela
Operating areas: Available nationwide on DirecTV & in AL, CA, CT, DC, FL, IL, MA, MD, MI, NY & RI on Comcast and Time Warner systems.
Programming: Offers shows from Venezuela.
Began: January 11, 2006.
Total subscribers: 1,700,000.
Distribution method: Available on Comcast, Time Warner & DirecTV subscribers.
Scrambled signal: Yes.
Ownership: SUR LLC. Distributed in the U.S. by Condista.

TVW
PO Box 25
Olympia, WA 98507-0025
Phone: 360-529-5310
Fax: 360-586-5678
E-mail: tvw@tvw.org
Web Site: http://www.tvw.org
Greg Lane, President & Chief Executive Officer
Mike Bay, Vice President, Programming
Marc Gerchak, Engineering Director
Carolyn Lindsey, Business Manager
Operating hours/week: 168.
Operating areas: Washington.
Programming: Unedited coverage of Washington State government deliberations, state Supreme Court, state agencies, boards, commissions & public policy events statewide.
Began: April 10, 1995.
Means of Support: Privately & publicly supported.
Total subscribers: 3,000,000.
Distribution method: Available to cable & satellite subscribers.
Scrambled signal: Yes.
Ownership: Non-profit organization.

TW3 — See Time Warner Cable Sports 3 Albany.

TWC TV NEW ENGLAND
83 Anthony Ave
Augusta, ME 04330
Phones: 207-253-2222; 800-833-2253
Fax: 207-253-2405
Web Site: http://www.twctv.net
Trudy DuBlois, Station Manager
Vinnie McGuire, Engineer
Type of service: Regional.
Operating areas: Maine & New Hampshire.
Programming: Covers local sports and offers programming on local events, issues and lifestyles.
Means of Support: Advertising.
Distribution method: Available to Time Warner Cable subscribers.
Ownership: Time Warner Cable.

TYC SPORTS
Avenida San Juan 1130
Buenos Aires 1147
Argentina
Phone: 54-11-4300-3800
Fax: 54-11-4300-3499
E-mail: contacto@tycsports.com.ar
Web Site: http://www.tycsports.com
Hernan Chiofalo, International Business Manager
Type of service: Premium & video on demand.
Satellites: Intelsat 11.
Operating hours/week: 168.
Operating areas: Florida.
Programming: Sports network from South America. Offers live coverage of the Argentine first-division league soccer league plus soccer from Chile & Paraguay plus boxing, Argentine basketball and auto racing.
Began: September 3, 1994.
Means of Support: Advertising & subscriber fees.
Total subscribers: 9,000,000 (worldwide).
Distribution method: Available to Comcast, Verizon FiOS and DirecTV subscribers.
Scrambled signal: Yes.
Ownership: Power Soccer. Distributed in the U.S. by Condista.

UBC-TV NETWORK
PO Box 1026
New York, NY 10027
Phone: 212-479-7837
E-mail: info@ubcnetwork.com
Web Site: http://www.ubctvnetwork.com
Peggy Dodson, President & Chief Executive Officer, Urban Broadcasting Co.
Type of service: Basic, streaming.
Operating areas: Nationwide.
Programming: Features cutting-edge, high quality, entertaining programming that celebrates the urban lifestyle, culture and experience.
Began: December 8, 2012.
Means of Support: Advertising & subscriber fees.
Total subscribers: 50,000,000 (Number based on carriage agreements.).
Distribution method: Available to cable & satellite subscribers. Streaming available online.
Scrambled signal: Yes.
Ownership: Urban Broadcasting Co.

UCTV
Phone: 886-07-2225612
Web Site: http://www.uctv.com.tw
Programming: Chinese-language Buddhist programming.
Distribution method: Available to KyLin TV subscribers.
Scrambled signal: Yes.

UHD-1
c/o Vivicast Media
1775 Moriah Woods Blvd, Ste 6
Memphis, TN 38117
Phone: 901-842-5340
E-mail: nfo@vivicast.com
Web Site: http://www.vivicast.com
Stuart Smitherman, President, Vivicast Media
Steve Corda, Vice President, North American Business Development
Marcus Payer, Corporate Communications
Type of service: Plans basic.
Satellites: SES-3.
Operating areas: Plans nationwide.
Programming: Plans to offer feature films, television series, exclusive concerts and documentaries for viewers in America and beyond.
Means of Support: Plans advertising.
Distribution method: Plans to be available to cable, IPTV & satellite subscribers.
Scrambled signal: Yes.
Ownership: Vivicast Media.

ULTRA CINE — See ULTRA HDPlex.
Programming: Spanish-language contemporary movies from Mexico, Spain & Latin America.
Distribution method: Available to Charter, Choice Cable, Claro TV & Verizon FiOS subscribers.
Scrambled signal: Yes.
Ownership: Olympusat.

ULTRA CLASICO — See ULTRA HDPlex.
Programming: Digitally-remastered classic Spanish-language movies in from the 1930s-1980s.
Distribution method: Available to Charter, Choice Cable, Liberty Cable & Verizon FiOS subscribers.
Scrambled signal: Yes.
Ownership: Olympusat.

ULTRA DOCU — See ULTRA HDPlex.
Programming: Spanish-language documentaries as well as lifestyle & human-interest programming.
Distribution method: Available to Charter, Choice Cable, Claro TV & Verizon FiOS subscribers.
Scrambled signal: Yes.
Ownership: Olympusat.

ULTRA FAMILIA — See ULTRA HDPlex.
Programming: Spanish-language family programming.
Distribution method: Available to Charter & Choice Cable subscribers.
Scrambled signal: Yes.
Ownership: Olympusat.

ULTRA FIESTA — See ULTRA HDPlex.
Programming: Latin music network featuring music videos, news, concerts, etc.
Distribution method: Available to Charter, Claro TV, Choice Cable & Verizon FiOS subscribers.
Scrambled signal: Yes.
Ownership: Olympusat.

ULTRA FILM — See ULTRA HDPlex.
Programming: Movie network featuring modern films from around the world, dubbed or originally produced in Spanish for the U.S. Latino audience.
Distribution method: Available to Choice Cable, Claro TV, Liberty Cable & Verizon FiOS subscribers.
Scrambled signal: Yes.
Ownership: Olympusat.

ULTRA HDPLEX
c/o Olympusat Inc
560 Village Blvd, Ste 250
West Palm Beach, FL 33409
Phone: 561-684-5657
Fax: 561-684-9690
E-mail: info@olympusat.com
Web Site: http://www.ultrahdplex.com
Tom Mohler, Chief Executive Officer, Olympusat Holdings Inc.
Chuck Mohler, Chief Operating Officer
Chris Williams, Chief Financial Officer
Colleen Glynn, Executive Vice President & General Counsel
Arturo Chavez, Senior Vice President, Hispanic Networks
Juan Bruno, New Programming Acquisitions & Contracts Director
John Baghdassarian, Head of Affiliate Sales, U.S.
Type of service: Pay, HD.
Operating hours/week: 168.
Operating areas: Available nationwide.
Programming: Package of HD Spanish-language channels distributed by Olympusat.
Began: April 30, 2012.
Means of Support: Subscriber fees.
Distribution method: Available to cable, IPTV & satellite subscribers.
Scrambled signal: Yes.

ULTRA KIDZ — See ULTRA HDPlex.
Programming: Spanish-language entertainment programming for pre-school, elementary & teenage children.
Distribution method: Available to Charter, Choice Cable, Claro TV, Liberty Cable & Verizon FiOS subscribers.
Scrambled signal: Yes.
Ownership: Olympusat.

ULTRA LUNA — See ULTRA HDPlex.
Programming: New & edgy telenovelas & series geared toward female audiences.
Distribution method: Available to Choice Cable & Verizon FiOS subscribers.
Scrambled signal: Yes.
Ownership: Olympusat.

2017 Edition   E-95

Pay TV & Satellite Services

ULTRA MACHO — See ULTRA HDPlex.
Programming: Spanish language sports programming, including Mexican wrestling, extreme sports & automobile sports.
Distribution method: Available to Charter, Choice Cable, Liberty Cable & Verizon FiOS subscribers.
Scrambled signal: Yes.
Ownership: Olympusat.

ULTRA MEX — See ULTRA HDPlex.
Programming: Spanish-language contemporary Mexican movies.
Distribution method: Available to Charter, Choice Cable & Verizon FiOS subscribers.
Scrambled signal: Yes.
Ownership: Olympusat.

ULTRA TAINMENT — See ULTRA HDPlex.
Programming: Spanish-language entertainment programming, including variety, talk, comedy, reality & sports.
Distribution method: Available to Choice Cable, Claro TV & Verizon FiOS subscribers.
Scrambled signal: Yes.
Ownership: Olympusat.

UNIMAS — See Univision.
c/o Univision Communications Inc.
9405 NW 41st St
Miami, FL 33178
Phone: 305-471-3900
Web Site: http://tv.univision.com/unimas; http://corporate.univision.com
Beau Ferrari, Executive Vice President, Operations, Univision Networks
Andres Mendoza, Vice President, Programming & Strategy
Type of service: Basic, HD.
Satellites: AMC 11, transponder 23.
Operating hours/week: 168.
Operating areas: Available nationwide.
Programming: Spanish-language general entertainment, drama series, movies and sports targeting a younger, more masculine audience.
Began: January 14, 2002, as TeleFutura. TeleFutura HD began April 28, 2010. Rebranded as UniMas January 7, 2012.
Means of Support: Advertising and fees from systems.
Total subscribers: 30,000,000.
Distribution method: Available to cable, IPTV & satellite subscribers.
Scrambled signal: Yes.
Ownership: Univision Communications Inc.

UNIQUE BUSINESS NEWS
No. 33-3, Lane 11
Guangfu N Rd
Taipei
Taiwan, Republic of China
Phone: 886-02-2766-2888
Fax: 886-02-2766-2910
Web Site: http://www.ustv.com.tw/UstvMedia
Programming: Business news from Republic of China.
Distribution method: Available to KyLin TV subscribers.
Scrambled signal: Yes.

UNIQUE SATELLITE TV
No. 33-3, Lane 11
Guangfu N Rd
Taipei
Taiwan
Phone: 886-02-2766-2888
Fax: 886-02-2766-2910
Web Site: http://www.ustv.com.tw/UstvMedia
Programming: Programming from Republic of China.

Distribution method: Available to KyLin TV subscribers.
Scrambled signal: No.

UNIVERSAL HD
900 Sylvan Ave
One CNBC Plz
Englewood Cliffs, NJ 07632
Web Site: http://www.universalhd.com
Frank DeRose, Senior Vice President, Program Scheduling & Strategic Planning
Ryan Sharkey, Senior Vice President, Program Acquisitions & Administration
Type of service: Digital.
Satellites: AMC 11, transponder 24.
Operating hours/week: 168.
Programming: Offers the best of NBC Universal in 100% 1080i HD, 24/7. Programming includes premiere sporting events, unedited and uninterrupted films and award winning series.
Began: December 1, 2004.
Total subscribers: 55,000,000.
Distribution method: Available to cable & satellite subscribers.
Scrambled signal: Yes.
Ownership: NBCUniversal LLC.

UNIVERSITY OF CALIFORNIA TV (UCTV)
9500 Gilman Dr
M/C 0176T
La Jolla, CA 92093-0176
Phone: 858-534-9412
E-mail: uctv@ucsd.edu
Web Site: http://www.uctv.tv
Lynn Burnstan, Managing Director
Steve Anderson, On-Air Operations
Melissa Weber, Web Developer
Type of service: Basic, streaming, video on demand.
Operating hours/week: 168.
Programming: Public affairs, science, health, humanities & arts programming drawn from 10 UC campuses & includes documentaries, faculty lectures, research symposiums & artistic performances.
Began: January 1, 2000.
Distribution method: Available to cable subscribers. Streaming & video on demand available through select providers, online & mobile app.
Scrambled signal: Yes.
Ownership: University of California.

UNIVISION
9405 NW 41st St
Miami, FL 33178
Phone: 305-471-3900
Fax: 305-471-4058
Web Site: http://corporate.univision.com
UNIVISION COMMUNICATIONS INC.:, .
Randy Falco, President & Chief Executive Officer
Isaac Lee, Chief News & Digital Officer
Francisco Lopez-Balboa, Chief Financial Officer
Daniel Coronell, President, News
Tonia O'Connor, President, Content Distribution & Chief Commercial Officer
Keith Turner, President, Advertising Sales & Marketing
Rick Alessandri, Executive Vice President
Carlos Deschapelles, Executive Vice President, Network & Digital Sales
John W. Eck, Executive Vice President, Technology, Operations & Engineering and Chief Local Media Officer
Beau Ferrari, Executive Vice President, Corporate Strategy & Development
Ruth Gaviria, Executive Vice President, Corporate Marketing
Roberto Llamas, Executive Vice President, Chief Human Resources & Empowerment Officer
Peter H. Lori, Executive Vice President, Finance & Chief Accounting and Interim Chief Financial Officer
Sarah Madigan, Executive Vice President, Content Distribution
Jed Meyer, Executive Vice President, Corporate Research
Jessica Rodriguez, Executive Vice President & Chief Marketing Office
Jonathan Schwartz, Executive Vice President, Government Relations & General Counsel
Jeff Browning, Senior Vice President, Network Sales
Carlos Deschappelles, Senior Vice President, Sports Sales
Glenn Dryfoos, Senior Vice President, Business Affairs
Sylvia Garcia, Senior Vice President, Media Planning & Multiplatform Strategy
Sara Hasson, Senior Vice President, Strategy & Insights - Automotive
Rosemary Mercedes, Senior Vice President, Corporate Communications
Ignacio Meyer, Senior Vice President, Enterprise Development
Mehul Nagrani, Senior Vice President & General Manager, Digital
Chris Pena, Senior Vice President, Local Media Television News
Jack Randall, Senior Vice President, Client Development Group
Peter J. Scanlon, Senior Vice President, Network Planning
Deborah Shinnick, Senior Vice President & Director, Network Sales & Strategy Research
Sandra Smester, Senior Vice President, Programming
Lourdes Torres, Senior Vice President, Political Coverage & Special Projects
Neil Brooks, Vice President, National Sales
Ana Ceppi, Vice President, Business Development - Healthcare & Financial
Ivelise Malave', Vice President, Consumer & Entertainment Public Relations
Jason Newman, Vice President, Sports Sales
UNIVISION NETWORK:, .
Patsy Loris, Executive Vice President, News & Executive News Director
Sandra Smester, Executive Vice President, Programming, Univision Network
Carlos Bardasano, Vice President, Original Content, Univision Networks

Branch Offices:
LOS ANGELES: 5999 Center Dr, Los Angeles, CA 90005. Phone: 310-348-3434. Greg Osborne, Vice President, Network Sales, Western Region, Univision Communications Inc.

MIAMI: 9405 NW 41st St, Miami, FL 33178. Phone: 305-471-3900.
Type of service: Basic, HD, streaming, video on demand.
Satellites: AMC 11, transponder 23.
Operating hours/week: 168.
Operating areas: Nationwide.
Uplink: Miami, FL.
Programming: Spanish language news, entertainment & information.
Began: September 1, 1961, as the Spanish International Network. Rebranded as Univision in 1986. Univision HD began January 1, 2010. UVideos (mobile & on-line service) began October 29, 2012 & will be discontinued in 2016.
Means of Support: Advertising.
Total subscribers: 13,000,000.
Distribution method: Available to cable, IPTV & satellite subscribers. Streaming available online & mobile through app. Video on demand through participating providers.
Scrambled signal: Yes.
Ownership: A joint venture between Univision Communications Inc. (95%) & Grupo Televisa (5%).

UNIVISION DEPORTES — See Univision.
9405 NW 41st St
Miami, FL 33178
Phone: 305-471-3900
Web Site: http://deportes.univision.com; http://corporate.univision.com
Juan Carlos Rodriguez, President
Eric Conrad, Senior Vice President, Programming & Acquisitions
Olek Loewenstein, Senior Vice President, Strategy & Operations
Marco Liceaga, Vice President, Marketing & Promotions
Type of service: Basic, HD, streaming.
Satellites: AMC 11, transponder 23.
Operating hours/week: 168.
Operating areas: Nationwide.
Programming: Spanish-language coverage of Mexico's national soccer team, the Mexican Soccer League, boxing, baseball, the NFL, NBA and UFC.
Began: April 7, 2014.
Means of Support: Advertising.
Total subscribers: 15,000,000 (DISH Network subscribers.).
Distribution method: Available to cable, IPTV & satellite subscribers. Streaming available online & mobile through the app (participating providers).
Scrambled signal: Yes.
Ownership: Univision Communications Inc.

UNIVISION DEPORTES DOS — See Univision Deportes.
Programming: Replays of sporting events on Univision Deportes.
Began: April 7, 2012.
Distribution method: Available to Dish subscribers only.

UNIVISION TDN — See Univision Deportes.

UNIVISION TLNOVELAS — See Univision.
9405 NW 41st St
Miami, FL 33178
Phone: 305-471-3900
Web Site: http://www.univisiontlnovelas.com; http://corporate.univision.com
Beau Ferrari, Executive Vice President, Operations, Univision Networks
Satellites: AMC 10, transponder 4.
Operating hours/week: 168.
Operating areas: Nationwide.
Uplink: Mexico City.
Programming: Handpicked selection of Televisa's all time, top-rated novelas.
Began: March 1, 2012.
Means of Support: Advertising & subscriber fees.
Distribution method: Available to cable & satellite subscribers.
Scrambled signal: No.
Ownership: Televisa Networks. Univision Communications Inc. has an exclusive contract for this service.

UNTAMED SPORTS TV
c/o Olympusat Inc
560 Village Blvd, Ste 250
West Palm Beach, FL 33409
Phone: 561-684-5657
Fax: 561-684-9690

Pay TV & Satellite Services

E-mail: feedback@untamedsportstv.com
Web Site: http://www.untamed.tv
Tom Mohler, Chief Executive Officer, Olympusat Holdings Inc.
Chuck Mohler, Chief Operating Officer
Chris Williams, Chief Financial Officer
Colleen Glynn, Executive Vice President & General Counsel
John Carter, Senior Vice President, Programming & Production
Mike Long, Senior Vice President, Sales & Marketing
John Baghdassarian, Head of Affiliate Sales, U.S.
Type of service: Digital basic, over the air.
Operating hours/week: 168.
Operating areas: Available nationwide.
Programming: Television gateway for the underserved adult demographic, which are devoted to, and aspire to participate in outdoor sports and activities.
Began: January 1, 2008.
Means of Support: Advertising.
Distribution method: Available over the air & to cable & IPTV subscribers.
Scrambled signal: Yes.
Ownership: Ocean Holdings.

UP
2077 Convention Ctr Concourse
Ste 300
Atlanta, GA 30337
Phone: 770-692-4559
Fax: 770-692-8895
E-mail: cburrows@uptv.com
Web Site: http://www.uptv.com
Charles Humbard, Founder, President & Chief Executive Officer
Leslie Glenn Chesloff, Executive Vice President, Programming
Amy Winter, Executive Vice President & General Manager
Paul Butler, Senior Vice President, General Counsel
Nancy Cohen, Senior Vice President, Ad Sales
Lisa Delligatti, Senior Vice President, Affiliate Sales
Genia Edelman, Senior Vice President, National Accounts
Barbara Fisher, Senior Vice President, Original Programming
Rex Humbard III, Senior Vice President, Production & Network Operations
Sophia Karteris Kelley, Senior Vice President, Programming
Richard Manwaring, Senior Vice President, Strategic Planning, Research & Technology
Wendy McCoy, Senior Vice President, Marketing
Reta J. Peery, Senior Vice President & General Counsel
Ron Plante, Senior Vice President, Research
Hal Rosenberg, Senior Vice President, Affiliate Sales
Richard Turner, Senior Vice President, Strategic Planning, Research & Technology
Kevin Wagner, Senior Vice President, Creative Services
Rick Bell, Vice President, Finance
Chelsye J. Burrows, Vice President, Public Relations
Angela Cannon, Vice President, Affiliate Marketing
Lisa Fischer, Vice President, Advertising Sales
Bill Keith, Vice President, Creative Services
Philip Manwaring, Vice President, Digital Media
Linda Ruffins, Vice President, Advertising Sales
Erin Sullivan, Vice President, West Coast Ad Sales
Matt Turner, Vice President, Eastern Region Ad Sales

Alvin Williams, Senior Director, Music, Talent & Acquisitions
Corey Prince, Human Resources Director
Michael Sinisi, Affiliate Marketing Director
Heather Symmes, Affiliate Marketing Director
Tiffany Thorpe, Production Operations Director
Tammi Weed, Music Industry Development & Program Acquisition Director
Ty Johnson, National Accounts Manager, Southeast
Tracey Tooks, Marketing Manager
Melissa Ingram, Counsel, Business Affairs

Branch Offices:
NEW YORK:: Advertising Sales, 29 W 35th St, 6th Fl, New York, NY 10001. Phone: 212-613-4440. Fax: 212-564-1904.
Type of service: Digital basic & video on demand.
Operating hours/week: 168.
Operating areas: Nationwide.
Programming: Uplifting music and entertainment network devoted to TV shows, movies, music videos, concert series & biographical documentaries.
Began: October 30, 2004, as Gospel Music Channel. Gospel Music Channel HD began November 27, 2009. Rebranded gmc on February 1, 2010, then UP on June 8, 2013.
Means of Support: Advertising.
Total subscribers: 67,000,000.
Distribution method: Available to cable, IPTV & satellite subscribers.
Scrambled signal: Yes.
Ownership: InterMedia Partners majority interest, Magic Johnson.

UPLIFTV
c/o Olympusat Inc.
560 Village Blvd, Ste 250
West Palm Beach, FL 33409
Phone: 561-684-5657
E-mail: info@upliftv.com
Web Site: http://www.upliftv.com
Tom Mohler, Chief Executive Officer, Olympusat Holdings
Chuck Mohler, Chief Operating Officer, Olympusat
Chris Williams, Chief Financial Officer
Colleen Glynn, Executive Vice President & General Counsel
Type of service: Basic.
Operating hours/week: 168.
Programming: Christian inspirational movies & documentaries with a variety of ministries and TV series for denominations of all ages.
Began: January 14, 2015.
Means of Support: Advertising.
Total subscribers: 15,500,000.
Distribution method: Available to cable & satellite subscribers.
Scrambled signal: Yes.
Ownership: Distributed by Olympusat Inc.

URBAN MOVIE CHANNEL
c/o RLJ Entertainment
The Trillium - East Tower, 6320 Canoga Ave, 8th Fl
Woodland Hills, CA 91367
Phones: 818-407-9100; 301-608-2115
Fax: 818-678-5025
E-mail: inquiries@rljentertainment.com
Web Site: https://urbanmoviechannel.com
Robert L. Johnson, Chairman, RLJ Entertainment
Miguel Penella, Chief Executive Officer, RLJ Entertainment
Mark Ward, Chief Acquisitions Officer, RLJ Entertainment

Traci Otey Blunt, Executive Vice President, Marketing & Corporate Affairs, RLJ Entertainment
Angela Northington, Senior Vice President, Content Acquisitions
Type of service: Streaming.
Operating areas: Nationwide.
Programming: Devoted to the development, production, and acquisition of feature films, comedy specials, stage plays, documentaries, music, and entertainment for the African American and urban audience.
Began: January 1, 2007, as One Village Entertainment. Rebranded Urban Movie Channel November 5, 2014.
Means of Support: Subscriber fees.
Distribution method: Available online.
Scrambled signal: Yes.
Ownership: RLJ Entertainment.

USA NETWORK
30 Rockefeller Plz
New York, NY 10112
Phone: 212-664-4444
Fax: 212-408-2711
Web Site: http://www.usanetwork.com
Bonnie Hammer, President, NBC Universal Entertainment & Cable Studio
Chris McCumber, President, Entertainment Networks
John Larrabee, Chief Information Officer
Mike Sileck, Chief Financial Officer
Dara Khosrowshahi, President, USAi
David Kissinger, President, Programming, Studios USA
Richard Sheingold, President, Sales
Jane Blaney, Executive Vice President, Programming, Acquisitions & Scheduling
Douglas Holloway, Executive Vice President, Network Distribution & Affiliate Relations
Rafael Pastor, Executive Vice President & Managing Director, USA Networks International
Alexandra Shapiro, Executive Vice President, Marketing & Digital
John Silvestri, Executive Vice President, Advertising Sales & General Sales Manager
Andrew Besch, Senior Vice President, Marketing
Stephen Brenner, Senior Vice President, USAi
Lonnie Burstein, Senior Vice President, First-Run Development
Frank DeRose, Senior Vice President, Program Scheduling & Strategic Planning
Ray Giacopelli, Senior Vice President, Research
Jeffrey Kaufman, Senior Vice President, Digital
Liz Korman, Senior Vice President, Advertising Sales
Heather Olander, Senior Vice President, Alternative Programming
Jesse Redniss, Senior Vice President, Digital
Dick Ross, Senior Vice President, Operations & Production
Donna Rothman, Senior Vice President, Emerging Networks
Peter Ruben, Senior Vice President, National Accounts & Western Division
Alex Sepiol, Senior Vice President, Original Scripted Series Programming
Adam Shapiro, Senior Vice President, Long-Form Programming
Ryan Sharkey, Senior Vice President, Program Acquisitions & Administration
Hilary Smith, Senior Vice President, Communications
Robert West, Senior Vice President, Programming & Scheduling
Scott Friedman, Vice President, Production, Alternative Programming
Jessica Sebastian, Vice President, Unscripted Series

Reena Singh, Vice President, Original Scripted Programming
Emily Spitale, Vice President, Communications
Tracy St. Pierre, Vice President, West Coast Communications

Regional Offices:
CHICAGO: 401 N Michigan Ave, Ste 3125, Chicago, IL 60611.

DETROIT: 2000 Town Center, Ste 2460, Southfield, MI 48075.

LOS ANGELES: 2049 Century Park E, Ste 2550, Los Angeles, CA 90067.
Type of service: Basic, HD.
Satellites: Galaxy 1R, transponder 24 (east coast); Galaxy 1R, transponder 24 (west coast).
Operating hours/week: 168.
Uplink: Smithtown, NY.
Programming: All entertainment, including original programs, game shows, sitcoms, movies & sports.
Began: April 1, 1977, as Madison Square Garden Network; renamed USA Network April 9, 1979.
Means of Support: System pays per subscriber; advertising.
Total subscribers: 101,200,000.
Distribution method: Available to cable, IPTV & satellite subscribers. Streaming available through USA Now app.
Scrambled signal: Yes.
Ownership: NBCUniversal LLC.

USA NOW — See USA Network.
Web Site: http://www.usanetwork.com/app
Type of service: Streaming.
Operating areas: Nationwide.
Programming: Programming from USA Network.
Distribution method: Available through app (participating providers).

U.S. MILITARY TV NETWORK
3650 Linda Vista Dr
Fallbrook, CA 92028
E-mail: lkelly@usmilitary.tv
Lauren Kelly, President & Chief Executive Officer

Branch Offices:
WASHINGTON, DC: Washington Sq, 1050 Connecticut Ave NW, Washington, DC 20036.
Operating hours/week: Plans 168.
Programming: Plans to focus on military personnel & their families through several programs including game shows, intramural sports, political commentary & live newscasts.
Scheduled to begin: Unannounced.
Distribution method: Plans to be available to cable & satellite providers.
Scrambled signal: Planned.

UTILISIMA — See Fox Life.

UVIDEOS — See Univision. Plans to be discontinued 2016.

VAN-TV
9798 Bellaire Blvd
Ste E
Houston, TX 77036
Phones: 281-840-8929; 800-729-5593
Fax: 713-995-6472
E-mail: vantvhouson@gmail.com
Ban Vu, Co-Founder
Bich Ngoc Nguyen, Co-Founder

2017 Edition
E-97

Pay TV & Satellite Services

Type of service: Regional basic.
Operating areas: Southeastern Texas.
Programming: Vietnamese language news, local talent shows & reality TV programs.
Began: May 1, 2009.
Means of Support: Advertising.
Distribution method: Available over the air on digital sub-channels.
Scrambled signal: Yes.
Ownership: Ban Vu & Bich Ngoc Nguyen.

VASALLOVISION NETWORK
2600 SW 3rd Ave
Miami, FL 33129
Phone: 305-856-7322
Web Site: http://www.vasallovision.tv
Operating areas: Colorado, Kentucky, Nevada and Texas.
Programming: The best shows from Mexico, including movies, telenovelas, talk shows, wrestling, biographies, plus programming about Mexican traditions, culture and music.
Began: October 22, 2009.
Means of Support: Advertising.
Scrambled signal: Yes.
Ownership: Carlos Vasallo.

VAVOOM
c/o New Frontier Media
6000 Spine Rd, Ste 100
Boulder, CO 80301
Phones: 303-444-0900; 888-875-0632
Fax: 303-938-8388
Web Site: http://www.noof.com
Larry Flynt, Chief Executive Officer
Michael Klein, President
Chris Woodward, Chief Financial Officer
Type of service: Pay per view.
Operating areas: Available nationwide.
Programming: Adult programming.
Distribution method: Available to cable, IPTV & satellite subscribers.
Ownership: New Frontier Media.

VELOCITY
c/o Discovery Communications
One Discovery Pl
Silver Spring, MD 20910-3354
Phone: 240-662-2000
Web Site: http://velocity.discovery.com
Marjorie Kaplan, Group President, Animal Planet, TLC & Velocity
Robert S. Scanlon, Executive Vice President & General Manager
Scott Felenstein, Executive Vice President, National Ad Sales
Laurie Goldberg, Executive Vice President, Discovery Channel, Science & Velocity
Roger Henry, Vice President, Programming
Operating hours/week: 168.
Operating areas: Nationwide.
Programming: Features more than 400 premiere hours of new and returning series and specials showcasing the best of the automotive, sports and leisure, adventure and travel genres.
Began: June 1, 2002, as HD Theater. Rebranded as Velocity on October 4, 2011.
Means of Support: Advertising.
Total subscribers: 56,000,000.
Distribution method: Available to cable, IPTV & satellite subscribers.
Scrambled signal: Yes.
Ownership: Discovery Communications Inc.

VENEMOVIES — See ViendoMovies.

VERIA LIVING — See Z Living.

VERSUS — See NBCSN.

VH1
MTV Networks Inc.
1515 Broadway, 22nd Fl
New York, NY 10036
Phone: 212-258-7800
E-mail: karen.keaney@mtvstaff.com
Web Site: http://www.vh1.com
Doug Herzog, President, Viacom Music & Entertainment Group
Chris McCarthy, President, VH1 & Logo
Nina Diaz, Executive Vice President & Head of Reality Programming and Development
Amy Doyle, Executive Vice President, Live Programming & Events
Carl D. Folta, Executive Vice President, Corporate Communications
Richard Gay, Executive Vice President, Strategy & Operations
Fred Graver, Executive Vice President, Programming
Rick Krim, Executive Vice President, Talent & Music Programming
Ben Zurier, Executive Vice President, Program Strategy
Robert Natter, Senior Counsel, Business & Legal Affairs
Steven Agase, Senior Vice President, Music & Entertainment Ad Sales
Stacy Alexander, Senior Vice President, Talent & Casting
Michael Benson, Senior Vice President, Promotion & Program Planning
Eddie Dalva, Senior Vice President, Programming, Co-Production & Creative Affairs
Reggie Fils-Aime, Senior Vice President, Marketing
Bill Flanagan, Senior Vice President, Editorial Director
David Giles, Senior Vice President, Research
Bruce Gillmer, Senior Vice President, Music & Talent Relations
Jason Hirschhorn, Senior Vice President & General Manager, VH1 Group
Tina Imm, Senior Vice President & General Manager, VH1 Digital
Sarah Iooss, Senior Vice President, Digital Ad Sales, Music & Entertainment
Susan Kantor, Senior Vice President, Creative Director
Joshua Katz, Senior Vice President, Marketing
John Kelley, Senior Vice President, Communications
George Moll, Senior Vice President, Production & Programming
Kiky Neumeyer, Senior Vice President, Development
Jill Newfield, Senior Vice President, Business Affairs & General Counsel
Paul Ricci, Senior Vice President, Head of Alternative Programming & Development
Caralene Robinson, Senior Vice President, Creative Group & Consumer Marketing
Trevor Rose, Senior Vice President, Talent & Series Development
Jeannie Scalzo, Senior Vice President, Music Sales, Music & Entertainment Ad Sales
Donald Silvey, Senior Vice President, Programming Enterprises & Business Development

Branch Offices:
Atlanta, GA; Dallas, TX; Detroit, MI; Los Angeles, CA; New York, NY.
Type of service: Basic, HD, streaming & video on demand.
Satellites: Galaxy III, transponder 15.
Operating hours/week: 168.
Uplink: Network Operations Center, Smithtown, NY.
Programming: Current & classic hit music videos for viewers 25-49.
Began: January 1, 1985.
Means of Support: Advertising.
Total subscribers: 98,000,000.
Distribution method: Available to cable, IPTV & satellite subscribers. Streaming available online. Video on demand through participating providers.
Scrambled signal: Yes. Equipment: M/A-Com; VideoCipher II.
Ownership: Viacom Inc.

VH1 CLASSIC — See MTV.

VH1 COUNTRY — See CMT Pure Country.

VH1 SOUL — See BET.

VICELAND
90 N 11th St
Brooklyn, NY 11211
Phone: 718-599-3101
E-mail: vice@vice.com
Web Site: https://www.viceland.com/en_us
Shane Smith, Chief Executive Officer
Spike Jonze, Co-President
Eddy Moretti, Co-President
Guy Slattery, General Manager
Type of service: Basic.
Operating areas: Nationwide.
Programming: Offers entertainment & lifestyle programming.
Began: 1996 as History International. Rebranded H2 in 2011. Replaced H2 February 29, 2016.
Total subscribers: 70,000,000.
Scrambled signal: Yes.
Ownership: Joint venture between Vice Media & A+E Networks. Disney has 10% interest in Vice Media, A+E Networks nearly 15%.

VIDA VISION
2264 NW 94th Ave
Miami, FL 33172
Phones: 305-513-4790; 786-426-9169
Fax: 786-331-8959
E-mail: info@nuestraraza.com
Ricardo Quintana, President
David R. Hurtado, Chief Operating Officer & Executive Vice President
Operating hours/week: 168.
Programming: Educational, informative & interactive Spanish-language programming for young Hispanic families.
Began: January 1, 2002.
Total subscribers: 100,000.
Distribution method: Available to cable & satellite subscribers.
Scrambled signal: Yes.

VIDEO MIX TV
18520 NW 67th Ave
Ste 288
Miami, FL 33015
Phone: 305-439-0477
Fax: 305-999-0949
E-mail: info@videomixtv.com
Web Site: http://www.videomixtv.com
Type of service: Basic.
Operating hours/week: 168.
Operating areas: Florida and Georgia.
Programming: Localized custom mix of music that plays in each market for 18 hours each day (10PM-4PM) along with a 6 hour (4PM-10PM) live broadcast that is simulcast to each market and online.
Began: January 1, 2000.
Means of Support: Advertising.
Total subscribers: 1,400,000.
Distribution method: Available over the air on digital sub-channels.
Scrambled signal: Yes.

VIDEO ZONA TV
1587 N Sanborn Rd
Ste 214
Salinas, CA 93905
Phone: 831-585-0875
E-mail: videozonatv@yahoo.com
Web Site: http://www.videozonatv.com
Marcial Estrada, President

Branch Offices:
PHOENIX: 2932 W Camelback Rd, Phoenix, AZ 85017-3339. Phone: 623-850-3365.
Type of service: Basic.
Operating hours/week: 168.
Operating areas: Arizona & California.
Programming: Offers regional Mexican videos.
Began: August 28, 2012.
Means of Support: Advertising.
Distribution method: Available over the air on digital sub-channels.
Ownership: Marcial Estrada.

VIDEO MUSIC CLUB — See VMC.

VIDEOROLA
Lazaro Cardenas 1710
Guadalajara, Jalisco 44900
Mexico
Phone: 52-333-750-0015
Fax: 52-333-750-0016
E-mail: atanaka@videorola.com
Web Site: http://www.videorola.com
Type of service: Basic.
Sales representative: US - Condista.
Programming: Regional Mexican music videos, interviews with top artists, live concerts, daily showbiz news, gossip programs & interactive call in-shows.
Began: April 1, 2001, in U.S.
Total subscribers: 1,850,000 (Mexico & U.S.).
Distribution method: Available to cable subscribers.
Scrambled signal: Yes.
Ownership: MegaCable. Distributed in the U.S. by Condista.

VIENDOMOVIES
2601 S Bayshore Dr
Ste 1250
Coconut Grove, FL 33133
Phone: 786-220-0280
Fax: 305-858-7188
E-mail: jespinal@somostv.net
Web Site: http://www.viendomovies.com
Luis Villanueva, President & Chief Executive Officer, SOMOS TV
Jose Antonio Espinal, Chief Operating Officer, SOMOS TV
Alejandro Parisca, General Manager, SOMOS TV
Type of service: Pay.
Operating hours/week: 168.
Operating areas: Nationwide.
Programming: 24-hour commercial free Spanish-language film channel.
Began: September 1, 2006, as VeneMovies. Rebranded ViendoMovies.
Means of Support: Subscriber fees.
Distribution method: Available to Bright House Networks & satellite subscribers.
Scrambled signal: Yes.
Ownership: SOMOS TV.

VIETNAMESE AMERICAN NETWORK TELEVISION — See VAN-TV.

VIVA TELEVISION NETWORK — See Vme TV.

VIVIDTV
3599 Cahuenga Blvd
4th Fl
Los Angeles, CA 90068-1397

Pay TV & Satellite Services

Phones: 323-845-4557; 800-423-4227
Bill Asher, Co-Chairman
Steven Hirsch, Co-Chairman
Michel Klein, President
Stephen E Walter, Senior Vice President, Business Development, Canada & Europe
Type of service: Pay and video on demand.
Operating areas: Nationwide.
Programming: Adult entertainment.
Began: August 24, 2012.
Means of Support: Advertising and subscriber fees.
Total subscribers: 20,000,000.
Distribution method: Available to cable & satellite subscribers.
Scrambled signal: Yes.
Ownership: Vivid Entertainment. Bill Asher, Steven Hirsch, David James owners.

VMC
c/o Olympusat Inc.
560 Village Blvd, Ste 250
West Palm Beach, FL 33409
Phone: 561-684-5657
Fax: 561-684-9690
E-mail: info@olympusat.com
Web Site: http://www.olympusat.com/networks/vmc
Tom Mohler, Chief Executive Officer, Olympusat Holdings Inc.
Arturo Chavez, Senior Vice President, Hispanic Networks
Juan Bruno, New Programming Acquisitions & Contracts Director
John Baghdassarian, Head of Affiliate Sales, U.S.
Type of service: Pay.
Operating areas: Available in Mediacom's service area.
Programming: Spanish-language music network featuring Latin American & Mexican music videos, concerts & interviews.
Began: November 26, 2012.
Distribution method: Available to Mediacom subscribers.
Scrambled signal: Yes.
Ownership: Olympusat.

VME KIDS
450 W 33rd St
New York, NY 10001
Phone: 212-560-1313
Web Site: http://www.vmetv.com/shows/vme-ninos
Eduardo Hauser, Chairman
Alvaro Garnica, General Manager
Andres Cardo, Chief Corporate Development Officer
Richard Taub, Vice President, Business Development
Type of service: Basic.
Operating hours/week: 168.
Operating areas: Nationwide.
Programming: Offers Spanish-language programming specifically for preschoolers.
Began: September 1, 2010.
Distribution method: Available to AT&T U-Verse customers.
Scrambled signal: No.
Ownership: V-me Media Inc. Eduardo Hauser, Juan Jose Rendon & Eligio Cedeno majority interest.

VME TV
450 W 33rd
11th Fl
New York, NY 10001
Phone: 212-273-4800
Fax: 212-273-6820
E-mail: info@vmetv.com
Web Site: http://www.vmetv.com
Alvaro Garnica, General Manager
Michael Bollo, Vice President, Sales & Sponsorship
Richard Taub, Vice President, Business Development
Ariel Martinez, Integrated Marketing & Digital Sales Director
Kim Fabian, Network Sales Manager
Mauricio Gallego, Post-Production Manager
Felix Martinez, IT & Operations Manager
Type of service: Basic, over the air.
Operating hours/week: 168.
Operating areas: Nationwide.
Programming: Spanish-language prime time drama, music, sports, current affairs & Latin cinema, along with world class kids, food, lifestyle & nature programs.
Began: March 5, 2007.
Total subscribers: 70,000,000.
Distribution method: Available over the air on digital sub-channels & to Comcast, DirecTV, DISH Network & AT&T U-verse subscribers.
Scrambled signal: Yes.
Ownership: V-me Media Inc. (Grupo Prisa, Syncom Funds, Baeza Group, WNET.org).

VREMYA
19 Akademika Korolyova St
Moscow 127427
Russian Federation
Phones: 7 495 617 55 88; 7 495 617 51 75
Fax: 7 495 617 51 14
E-mail: info@1tvrus.com
Web Site: http://eng.1tvrus.com/vremya
Nikolay Dubovoy, Director General
Type of service: Premium.
Operating areas: Available in New Jersey & New York on cable and nationwide on DirecTV.
Programming: Russian history and news channel.
Began: January 1, 2005.
Means of Support: Advertising & subscriber fees.
Total subscribers: 20,000,000 (subscribers worldwide.).
Distribution method: Available to DirecTV customers & Time Warner Cable system subscribers.
Ownership: Channel One. National Media Group, minority interest.

VRV
835 Market St
Ste 700
San Francisco, CA 94103
Phone: 415-796-3560
Web Site: http://www.ellation.com/
Tom Pickett, Chief Executive Officer, Ellation
Michael Aragon, General Manager
Type of service: Will offer both a premium SVOD service and an ad-supported VOD element.
Operating areas: Plans nationwide.
Programming: VRV will be a home where millennials can discover new channels to love, interact with fellow fans.
Scheduled to begin: Plans to launch in 2016.
Means of Support: Advertising.
Distribution method: Plans on being available on-line and cable systems.
Ownership: Ellation. Chernin Group and AT&T are investors.

VSTV
266 Meadow St
Rockport, ME 04856
Phone: 207-230-0354
E-mail: info@vstv.me
Web Site: http://www.vstv.me
Alan Hinsey, General Manager
Aaron Tibbetts, IT Manager
Steve Galvin, Chief Engineer
Type of service: Basic & video on demand.
Operating hours/week: 168.
Operating areas: Midcoast & Central Maine.
Programming: Offers local news, weather, and sports - plus politics, arts and culture, health and fitness, business and finance, local talk, food and entertainment, and more.
Began: February 1, 2015.
Means of Support: Advertising.
Total subscribers: 68,000.
Distribution method: Available over the air on digital subchannels & to Time Warner Cable subscribers.
Scrambled signal: Yes.
Ownership: Courier Publications LLC.

VUDU
600 W California Ave
Sunnyvale, CA 94086
Phone: 312-729-4068
E-mail: support@vudu.com
Web Site: http://www.vudu.com
Type of service: Video on demand.
Programming: Movies & TV series.
Scrambled signal: Yes.

VU TELEVISION NETWORK
c/o IC Punch Media Inc
1438 N Gower St
West Hollywood, CA 90028
Phone: 407-442-0309
E-mail: info@icplaces.com
Steve Samblis, Chairman & Chief Executive Officer, IC Punch Media Inc.
Gayle Dickie, President
James Allen Bradley, Executive Vice President, Production & Operations
Meredith Walters, Executive Vice President, Sales & Marketing Partnerships
Operating areas: Available nationwide.
Programming: Offers original programming plus local entertainment news and event offerings.
Began: September 23, 2013.
Scrambled signal: Yes.
Ownership: IC Punch Media Inc.

THEWALKTV
2607 Success Dr
Ste C
Odessa, FL 33556
Phone: 727-375-2500
Fax: 727-375-5509
E-mail: christi@thewalktv.com
Web Site: http://thewalktv.wordpress.com
Adam Armatas, Traffic, Program Specifications & Delivery
Christi Armatas, Advertising & Programming Sales
Jim West, Station Affiliation & Engineering Assistance
Mark Wilson, Engineering Assistance
Type of service: Basic, over the air.
Satellites: SBN Galaxy 19, transponder 7.
Operating hours/week: 168.
Operating areas: Nationwide.
Programming: Designed to educate viewers to better comprehend and appreciate their rich Judeo-Christian legacy and to apply such principles to their daily lives.
Began: January 11, 2010, as LegacyTV, renamed to TheWalktv November 1, 2012.
Means of Support: Advertising.
Total subscribers: 50,224,194.
Distribution method: Available over the air on digital sub-channels & to satellite subscribers.
Scrambled signal: Yes.

WALN CABLE RADIO
3028 S Pike Ave
Allentown, PA 18103
Phone: 610-791-1818
Fax: 610-791-9618
E-mail: info@walncableradio.com
Web Site: http://www.walncableradio.com
Type of service: Basic.
Operating hours/week: 168.
Operating areas: Eastern Pennsylvania & western New Jersey.
Programming: Blend of popular oldies & polka standards, love songs & ballads from the '40s through the '80s.
Means of Support: Advertising.

WAM! AMERICA'S KIDZ NETWORK — See Starz Encore Family.

WAPA AMERICA
2000 Ponce de Leon Blvd
6th Fl
Miami, FL 33134
Phone: 305-421-6375
E-mail: emily.love@wapa-tv.com
Web Site: http://www.wapa.tv
Alan Sokol, Chairman, WAPA-TV & Senior Partner, InterMedia Advisors
Rafael Perez-Subira, National Ad Sales Director

Branch Offices:
CHICOPEE:: Broadcast Headquarters, One Broadcast Ctr, Chicopee, MA 01013. Phones: 413-377-2054; 888-733-9272.
Type of service: Premium.
Operating areas: Nationwide.
Programming: Offers more than 40 hours a week of original, locally produced entertainment programs from Puerto Rico, plus news and sports events.
Began: August 23, 2004.
Total subscribers: 5,200,000.
Distribution method: Available to cable, IPTV & satellite subscribers.
Scrambled signal: Yes.
Ownership: Hemisphere Media Group, a joint venture between InterMedia Partners (73%) & Azteca Acquisition Corp. (27%).

WASHINGTON KOREAN TV
2931-G Eskridge Rd
Fairfax, VA 22031
Phone: 703-560-1590
E-mail: info@wktvusa.com
Web Site: http://www.wktvusa.com
Type of service: Digital.
Operating hours/week: 168.
Programming: Local news, dramas, sports & variety shows.
Began: January 1, 1985.
Distribution method: Available to cable subscribers.

WATCH ABC FAMILY — See WATCH Freeform.

WATCH DISNEY CHANNEL — See Disney Channel.
5000 S Buena Vista St
Burbank, CA 91521
Phone: 818-569-7500
Web Site: http://watchdisneychannel.go.com
Type of service: Streaming.
Operating areas: Available nationwide.
Programming: Live TV, full episodes, clips from Disney Channel.
Distribution method: Available online & through app (participating providers).
Scrambled signal: Yes.
Ownership: Disney Channels Worldwide.

WATCH DISNEY JUNIOR — See Disney Channel.
Web Site: http://watchdisneyjunior.go.com

Pay TV & Satellite Services

Type of service: Streaming.
Operating areas: Available nationwide.
Programming: Full episodes, clips & live TV.
Distribution method: Available online & through app (participating providers).
Scrambled signal: Yes.

WATCH DISNEY XD — See Disney Channel.
Web Site: http://watchdisneyxd.go.com
Type of service: Streaming.
Operating areas: Available nationwide.
Programming: Full episodes, clips & live TV.
Distribution method: Available online & through app (participating providers).
Scrambled signal: Yes.

WATCH ESPN — See ESPN.
ESPN Plz
935 Middle St
Bristol, CT 06010
Phones: 860-766-2000; 888-549-3776
Fax: 860-766-2400
Web Site: http://espn.go.com/watchespn
Type of service: Streaming.
Operating areas: Nationwide.
Programming: Living programming from ESPN networks.
Began: October 2010 & later rebranded WATCH ESPN. ESPN3, which began August 2005, was merged with WATCH ESPN August 2011.
Distribution method: Available online & through app (participating providers).
Scrambled signal: Yes.
Ownership: A joint venture between The Walt Disney Co. (80%) & Hearst Co. (20%).

WATCH FOOD NETWORK — See Food Network.
75 Ninth Ave
New York, NY 10011
Phone: 212-398-8836
Fax: 212-736-7716
Web Site: http://watch.foodnetwork.com/live
Type of service: Streaming.
Operating areas: Nationwide.
Programming: Programming from Food Network.
Distribution method: Available online & through app (participating providers).
Scrambled signal: Yes.
Ownership: A joint venture between Scripps Networks Interactive (70%) & Tribune Media Co. (30%).

WATCH FREEFORM — See Freeform.
500 S Buena Vista St
Burbank, CA 91521
Phone: 818-560-1000
Web Site: http://freeform.go.com/watch-live
Type of service: Streaming.
Operating areas: Nationwide.
Programming: Programming from Freeform.
Began: as WATCH ABC Family. Rebranded WATCH Freeform January 12, 2016.
Distribution method: Available online & through app (participating providers).
Ownership: Disney-ABC Television Group.

WATCH TBS — See TBS.
1050 Techwood Dr NW
Atlanta, GA 30318
Phone: 404-827-1717
Fax: 404-827-1947
E-mail: tbs.superstation@turner.com
Web Site: http://www.tbs.com/watchtbs
Type of service: Streaming.
Operating areas: Available nationwide.
Programming: Programming from TBS.
Distribution method: Available online & through app (participating providers).

Scrambled signal: Yes.
Ownership: Turner Broadcasting System, a division of Time Warner.

WATCH TCM — See Turner Classic Movies.
1050 Techwood Dr NW
Atlanta, GA 30318
Phone: 404-885-5535
Fax: 404-885-5536
Web Site: http://www.tcm.com/watchtcm
Type of service: Streaming.
Operating areas: Nationwide.
Programming: Programming from Turner Classic Movies.
Distribution method: Available online & through app (participating providers).
Ownership: Turner Broadcasting Network, a division of Time Warner.

WATCH TNT — See TNT.
One CNN Ctr
Atlanta, GA 30348
Phones: 404-885-4570; 404-885-4647
Fax: 404-827-3368
Web Site: http://www.tntdrama.com/watchtnt
Type of service: Streaming.
Operating areas: Nationwide.
Programming: Programming from TNT.
Distribution method: Available online & through app (participating providers).
Ownership: Turner Broadcasting System, a division of Time Warner.

WATCH TRUTV — See truTV.
One Time Warner Ctr
New York, NY
Phone: 404-575-5577
Web Site: http://www.trutv.com/live
Type of service: Streaming.
Operating areas: Nationwide.
Programming: Programming from TruTV.
Distribution method: Available online & through app (participating providers).
Ownership: Turner Broadcasting System, a division of Time Warner.

WCTY CHANNEL 16
200 E Washington St
Room G-22
Indianapolis, IN 46204
Phone: 317-327-2016
Fax: 317-327-2020
E-mail: kmontgom@indygov.org
Web Site: http://www.indygov.org/cable
Ken Montgomery, Station Manager
Angela Gilmer, Producer
Bradley K. Sims, Producer
Alan Dhayer, Systems Administrator
Nick Hess, Producer
Dave Lister, Programming & Promotions Coordinator
Operating hours/week: 168.
Programming: Live & archived coverage of local government meetings, deliberations & community affairs original programming.
Began: January 1, 1984.
Total subscribers: 250,000.

THE WEATHER CHANNEL
300 Interstate N Pkwy
Atlanta, GA 30339-2204
Phone: 770-226-0000
Fax: 770-226-2950
Web Site: http://www.weather.com
David Kenny, Chairman & Chief Executive Officer
Christopher Herbert, Chief Operating Officer, Product & Technology
Jennifer Dangar, Chief Strategy Officer & President, Distribution
David Jaye, Chief Marketing Officer

Bryson Koehler, Chief Information Officer
David Clark, President, TV Division
Cameron Clayton, President, Product & Technology
Mark Gildersleeve, President, Professional Division
Domenic Venuto, General Manager, AdFX
George Callard, Executive Vice President, General Counsel & Head of Government Affairs
Shirley Powell, Executive Vice President, Marketing & Communications
Barbara Bekkedahl, Senior Vice President, Ad Sales
D. J. Reali, Senior Vice President, National Ad Sales
David Shipps, Senior Vice President, Business & Alternative Revenue Development
Michael Finnerty, Senior Vice President & General Manager, Platform Products & Distribution
Megan Rock, Senior Vice President, Partnership Marketing
Michael Rubin, Senior Vice President, Original Programming
Brittany Smith, Senior Vice President, Distribution
Elliott Trice, Senior Vice President, Consumer Product
Indira Venkat, Senior Vice President, Research
Nora Zimmett, Senior Vice President, Live Programming
Sheri Bachstein, Vice President, Digital Operations
Rhonda Bitterman, Vice President, Agency Partnerships & Development
Lauren Frasca, Vice President, Original Programming
Jeremy Hlavacek, Vice President, Programmatic Sales
Mary Ellen Iwata, Vice President, Original Programming Development
Amol Jadhav, Vice President, Global Expansion
Neil Katz, Vice President & Editor in Chief, Digital
Sean Kearney, Vice President & Regional Manager, Multiplatform Sales
Chris Kuist, Vice President, Insights & Innovaton
Kristen Leone, Vice President, Sales Marketing
Sara Livingstone, Vice President, Enterprise Solutions & Measurement
Karen Marderosian, Vice President, Multiplatform Sales
Maureen Marshall, Vice President, Communications
Julie Michalowski, Vice President, Corporate Sales Partnerships & Development
Mark Mooney, Vice President, Multiplatform Sales
Alicia Muntzner, Vice President, Multiplatform Sales
Dan Owen, Vice President, Ad Sales, West Coast
Niki Santoro, Vice President, Product & Design
Randi Stipes, Vice President, Ad Sales Marketing & Solutions
Sandra Szahun, Vice President, Ad Sales Marketing
Piper Walker, Vice President, Digital Sales
Vikram Somaya, General Manager, AdFX & Analytics
Jeremy Steinberg, Head of Sales

Regional Offices:
CHICAGO: 180 N Stetson Ave, Ste 3030, Chicago, IL 60601. Phone: 312-946-0892.

DETROIT: 2690 Crooks Rd, Ste 217, Troy, MI 48084. Phone: 810-362-2290.

LOS ANGELES: 1875 Century Park E, Ste 900, Los Angeles, CA 90067. Phone: 310-785-0512.

MIAMI: 777 Brickell Ave, Ste 680, Miami, FL 33131. Phone: 305-375-6100. Fax: 305-375-6110.

NEW YORK: 845 3rd Ave, 11th Floor, New York, NY 10022. Phone: 212-893-2245.
Type of service: Basic, HD, video on demand.
Satellites: SES Americom AMC-10.
Sales representative: Patriot Media.
Operating hours/week: 168.
Operating areas: Nationwide.
Programming: Local, regional, national & international current & forecast weather information.
Began: May 2, 1982, The Weather Channel HD began October 1, 2007.
Means of Support: Subscriber fees & advertising.
Total subscribers: 101,700,000.
Distribution method: Available to cable, IPTV & satellite subscribers & select terrestrial LPTV stations. Video on demand available through select providers.
Scrambled signal: Yes.
Ownership: The Weather Company, a joint venture between NBCUniversal LLC, The Blackstone Group & Bain Capital.

WEATHERNATION
13276 E Fremont Pl
Centennial, CO 80112
Phone: 800-343-9516
Fax: 866-800-0351
E-mail: info@weathernationtv.com
Web Site: http://www.weathernationtv.com
Michael Norton, President
Tim Kelly, Senior Vice President, Digital
David Hampe, Vice President, Affiliate Relations
Harry Oates, Vice President, Production
Mike Witcher, Senior Meteorologist
Type of service: Basic, HD, over the air, streaming.
Operating hours/week: 168.
Operating areas: Available nationwide.
Programming: Continuous coverage of hyperlocal, local, regional & national weather events.
Began: June 11, 2011.
Distribution method: Available over the air on digital sub channels & to cable, IPTV & satellite subscribers. Streaming available online & through select providers.
Scrambled signal: Yes.
Ownership: WeatherNation TV Inc.

WEATHER NETWORK
2655 Bristol Cir
Oakville, ON L6H 7W1
Canada
Phone: 905-829-1156
Web Site: http://www.theweathernetwork.com
Kiko Grusecki, Broadcast Operations Director
Operating hours/week: 168.
Programming: Weather information & forecasting in both French & English broadcasts.
Distribution method: Available to cable & satellite providers.
Ownership: Pelmorex Communications Inc.

WEATHERSCAN
300 Interstate North Pkwy
Atlanta, GA 30339-2204
Phones: 770-226-0000; 770-226-2341
Fax: 770-226-2950
Web Site: http://www.weather.com
Felicia McDade, Business Development Director

Pay TV & Satellite Services

Branch Offices:
CHICAGO: 205 N Michigan Ave, Ste 1610, Chicago, IL 60601. Phone: 312-948-0892.

DETROIT: 2690 Crooks Rd, Ste 305, Troy, MI 48084. Phone: 810-362-2290.

LOS ANGELES: 1875 Century Park E, Ste 900, Los Angeles, CA 90067. Phone: 310-785-0512.

NEW YORK: 845 3rd Ave, 11th Floor, New York, NY 10022. Phone: 212-308-3055.
Satellites: Satcom C-3, transponder 13.
Operating hours/week: 168.
Programming: 24-hour, all-local weather available for digital carriage.
Began: July 1, 1998.
Total subscribers: 7,000,000.
Distribution method: Available to cable & satellite subscribers.
Scrambled signal: Yes.
Ownership: The Weather Company, a joint venture between NBCUniversal LLC, The Blackstone Group & Bain Capital.

WETA UK
3939 Campbell Ave
Arlington, VA 22206
Phone: 703-998-2600
Web Site: http://www.weta.org/tv/uk
Timothy C. Coughlin, Chairman
Ann Dibble Jordan, Vice Chairman & Secretary
Sharon Percy Rockefeller, President & Chief Executive Officer
Joseph B Bruns, Executive Vice President & Chief Operating Officer
Dalton Delan, Executive Vice President & Chief Programming Officer
Polly Povejsil Heath, Senior Vice President, Chief Financial Officer & Treasurer
Kevin Harris, Vice President & Station Manager, WETA-TV
Kari Waldack, Assistant Secretary
Type of service: Basic.
Operating hours/week: 168.
Operating areas: District of Columbia, Maryland & Virginia.
Programming: Features programming from British networks. The channel features classics, new favorites, and contemporary series currently airing in Britain.
Began: June 1, 2012, replacing WETA How-To (Create).
Distribution method: Available to Comcast, Cox & RCN cable system subscribers and on Verizon FiOS.
Scrambled signal: Yes.
Ownership: Greater Washington Educational Telecommunications Association Inc.

WE TV
11 Penn Plz
15th Fl
New York, NY 10001
Phone: 212-324-8500
E-mail: contactwe@rmhi.com
Web Site: http://www.we.tv
Ed Carroll, Chief Operating Officer, AMC Networks Inc.
Robert Broussard, President, AMC Networks Distribution
Marc Juris, President & General Manager
Lauren Gellert, Executive Vice President, Development & Original Programming
Dom Atteritano, Senior Vice President, Legal & Business Affairs
Cheryl Bloch, Senior Vice President, Scripted Programming
Allison Clarke, Senior Vice President, Advertising Sales, IFC & WE tv
Elizabeth Doree, Senior Vice President, Scheduling & Acquisitions
Mark Neschis, Senior Vice President, Public Relations
Theresa Patiri, Senior Vice President, Production & Business Affairs
Rosie Pisani, Senior Vice President, Marketing
Jennifer Robertson, Senior Vice President, Digital Media & Business Development
Joshua Berger, Vice President, Programming Operations, AMC & WE tv
CarolAnne Dolan, Vice President, Non-Fiction Development & Production
Suzanne Gladstone Murch, Vice President, Original Programming
Jennifer Kranz, Vice President, Marketing, Promotional Strategy & Planning
Andrea Bell Macey, Vice President, Digital Media & Business Development
Angela Malloy, Vice President, Development, Los Angeles
Tim Philbin, Vice President, Advertising Sales
Gary Pipa, Vice President, Program Planning & Scheduling
Sherry Pitkofsky, Vice President, Partnership Marketing, Promotions & Public Affairs
Jaime Saberito, Vice President, Corporate Communications, AMC, WE tv & IFC
Mary Scotti, Vice President, Business Affairs
Carole Smith, Vice President, Research
David Stefanou, Vice President, Development
Mike Walton, Vice President, Brand Creative
Stephanie Yates, Vice President, Research & Insights
Type of service: Basic, HD, streaming, video on demand.
Satellites: Satcom 3-R, transponder 14.
Sales representative: AMC Networks Advertising Sales.
Operating hours/week: 168.
Operating areas: Available nationwide.
Uplink: Belmont Racetrack, Long Island, NY.
Programming: Romantic movies, mini-series, celebrity interviews & lifestyle programs.
Began: January 1, 1997, as Romance Classics. Rebranded as WE: Women's Entertainment in 2001 & WE tv in 2006.
Means of Support: Subscriber fees.
Total subscribers: 86,000,000.
Distribution method: Available to cable, IPTV & satellite subscribers; online & mobile through the website; video on demand (participating providers).
Scrambled signal: Yes.
Ownership: AMC Networks Inc. Formerly Rainbow Media Holdings LLC owned by Cablevision Systems Corp. It became a publicly held company under the new name June 30, 2011.

WGN — See WGN America.

WGN AMERICA
2501 W Bradley Pl
Chicago, IL 60618-4718
Phone: 773-528-2311
Fax: 773-883-6299
E-mail: wgnamerica@tribune.com
Web Site: http://www.wgnamerica.com
Matt Cherniss, President & General Manager
David Rotem, Executive Vice President, Sales & Marketing
Jon Wax, Executive Vice President, Original Programming
Kevin Connor, Senior Vice President, Affiliate Sales & Marketing
Tom Huffman, Senior Vice President, Unscripted Programming
Brian Carr, Vice President, Strategic Sales & Planning
Marc Drazin, Engineering Director

Branch Offices:
HOLLYWOOD: 5800 Sunset Blvd, Bldg 21, Ste 12H, Hollywood, CA 90028. Phone: 323-460-3861. Fax: 323-460-5299.

NEW YORK: 220 E 42nd St, Ste 400, New York, NY 10017. Phone: 212-210-5900. Fax: 212-210-5905.
Type of service: Basic, HD.
Satellites: Galaxy 14, transponder 13C.
Operating hours/week: 168.
Operating areas: Nationwide.
Programming: Cable exclusives, first-run programs, blockbuster movies & live sports.
Began: November 8, 1978, as Superstation WGN. Rebranded as WGN America May 24, 2008. WGN America HD began July 19, 2008.
Means of Support: System pays per subscriber.
Total subscribers: 71,017,000 (Includes cable, satellite & Canadian viewers.).
Distribution method: Available to cable, IPTV & satellite subscribers.
Scrambled signal: Yes. Equipment: Scientific Atlanta Power Vue H.
Ownership: Tribune Media Co.

WHEELSTV
289 Great Rd
Ste 301
Acton, MA 01720
Phone: 978-264-4333
Fax: 978-264-9547
E-mail: contact@wheelstv.net
Web Site: http://wheelstvnetwork.com
Jim Barisano, Chairman & Founder

Branch Offices:
LOS ANGELES: 10642 Santa Monica Blvd, Ste 204, Los Angeles, CA 90025. Phone: 310-446-1960. Fax: 978-264-9547.
Type of service: Basic, broadband, IPTV, video on demand.
Operating hours/week: 168.
Programming: Automotive lifestyle entertainment, news & information. Original & acquired programming on cars, trucks & motorcycles; technology, history, international auto shows.
Began: January 1, 2004, reflects video on demand launch. IPTV service launched January 1, 2006.
Ownership: Automotive Networks LLC.

WICKED ON DEMAND
c/o Trans Digital Media LLC
801 2nd Ave
New York, NY 10017
Phone: 212-867-0234
Geoff Lurie, Chief Executive Officer
Type of service: Video on demand.
Programming: Adult entertainment.
Began: January 1, 2005.
Total subscribers: 17,500,000.
Distribution method: Available to cable subscribers.
Scrambled signal: Yes.
Ownership: A joint venture between TransDigital Media & Wicked Pictures.

WILD TV
11263 180th St
Edmonton, AB T5S 0B4
Canada
Phones: 780-444-1512; 877-294-5388
Fax: 780-443-4591
E-mail: info@wildtv.ca
Web Site: http://www.wildtv.ca
Operating hours/week: 168.
Programming: Hunting & fishing programs.

WILLOW
2225 E Bayshore Rd
Ste 200
Palo Alto, CA 94303-3220
E-mail: support@willow.tv
Web Site: http://www.willow.tv
Type of service: Pay.
Operating hours/week: 168.
Operating areas: Available nationwide.
Programming: Channel dedicated to the sport of cricket.
Began: January 1, 2010.
Means of Support: Subscriber fees.
Distribution method: Available to Bright House, Cablevision, Comcast, Cox and Time Warner cable subscribers plus DirecTV, DISH and Verizon FiOS customers.
Scrambled signal: Yes.
Ownership: Global Cricket Ventures Limited.

WINK NEWS NOW 24/7
2824 Palm Beach Blvd
Fort Myers, FL 33916-1590
Phone: 239-344-5000
E-mail: manager@winktv.com
Web Site: http://www.winknews.com
Wayne Simons, Vice President, General Manager & Sales Director
Russ Kilgore, News Director
Type of service: Basic.
Operating hours/week: 168.
Operating areas: Florida.
Programming: Offers local news plus updates, weather with graphics, and repeats of recent newscasts.
Began: February 20, 2012.
Means of Support: Advertising.
Distribution method: Available to Comcast cable system subscribers.
Ownership: Fort Myers Broadcasting Co.

WISCONSINEYE
122 W Washington Ave
Ste 200
Madison, WI 53703
Phones: 608-316-6850; 866-273-5755
Fax: 608-316-6868
E-mail: info@wiseye.org
Web Site: http://www.wiseye.org
Jon Henkes, President & Chief Executive Officer
Fred Woskoff, Operations Director
Claudia Looze, Program Manager
Type of service: Digital.
Operating areas: Wisconsin.
Programming: Statewide, private nonprofit public affairs network providing unbiased, unedited coverage of state government and public life on cable TV and the Internet.
Began: July 9, 2007.
Means of Support: Donations.
Distribution method: Available to cable systems and online.
Scrambled signal: Yes.
Ownership: Private, not for profit.

WIZEBUYS TV
1701 John F Kennedy Blvd
Ste 2510
Philadelphia, PA 19103
Phone: 215-405-2081
Fax: 610-696-8522
Web Site: http://www.wizebuys.tv
Ryan Mazur, Vice President, Network Sales & Operations
Jessica Braun, Operations Director
Type of service: Basic.
Operating hours/week: 168.
Programming: National infomercial network.
Began: October 1, 2002.
Total subscribers: 30,000,000.

Pay TV & Satellite Services

Distribution method: Available to satellite subscribers.
Scrambled signal: Yes.

WKTV
2931 Eskridge Rd
Ste G
Fairfax, VA 22031-2224
Phone: 703-560-1590
Fax: 703-560-1593
Web Site: http://wktvusa.com
Ron Chun, President & Chief Executive Officer
Type of service: Audio only.
Operating hours/week: 168.
Operating areas: Nationwide.
Programming: Delivers useful local information, high-quality programs, as well as news to Korean populations.
Began: January 1, 1986.
Means of Support: Advertising.
Total subscribers: 2,500,000.
Distribution method: Available to Comcast cable subscribers.
Scrambled signal: Yes.
Ownership: WKTV/KOREA ONE.

WKYT-TV
2851 Winchester Rd
Lexington, KY 40509
Phone: 859-299-0411
Fax: 859-2299-2494
E-mail: chris.mossman@wkyt.com
Web Site: http://www.wkyt.com
Chris Mossman, President & General Manager
Barbara Howard, Program Director
Type of service: Basic.
Programming: CBS & CW affiliate.
Began: May 1, 1995.
Means of Support: Advertising & subscriber fees.
Total subscribers: 445,000.
Scrambled signal: Yes.

THE WORD NETWORK
20733 W Ten Mile Rd
Southfield, MI 48075
Phones: 248-357-4566; 855-730-9673
Fax: 248-350-3422
E-mail: lewisg@thewordnetwork.org
Web Site: http://www.thewordnetwork.org
Kevin Adell, Chief Executive Officer
John Mattiello, Marketing Director
Paul Crouch Jr, Program Development Director
Thomas Ponsart, Engineering Director
Clara Childs, Affiliate Marketing Manager
Type of service: Basic.
Satellites: Galaxy 17, transponder 9C Horizontal.
Operating hours/week: 168.
Operating areas: Available nationwide.
Programming: Religious programming for the urban African-American community.
Began: February 1, 2000.
Means of Support: Non-profit organization.
Total subscribers: 85,000,000.
Distribution method: Available to home dish audiences and cable system subscribers.
Scrambled signal: Yes.
Ownership: Kevin Adell.

THE WORKS
245 North Beverly Ave
Beverly Hills, CA 90210
Phone: 310-449-3000
E-mail: relations@the-works.tv
Web Site: http://www.the-works.tv
John Bryant, President, MGM Domestic Television Distribution
Type of service: Digital basic, over the air.
Operating areas: Nationwide.
Programming: Programming from MGM library, news and shows from Huffington Post.
Began: April 1, 2014.
Means of Support: Advertising.
Distribution method: Available over the air on digital sub-channels.
Scrambled signal: Yes.
Ownership: A joint venture between Metro-Goldwyn-Mayer & Titan Broadcast Management.

WORLD
One Guest St
Boston, MA 02135
Phone: 617-300-5400
Fax: 617-300-1026
Web Site: http://worldcompass.org
Elizabeth Cheng, General Manager
Type of service: Basic & over the air.
Operating hours/week: 168.
Operating areas: Nationwide.
Programming: Non-fiction documentaries, science & news programming.
Began: January 1, 2004, was originally launched on Boston's WGBH & New York City's WNET as PBS World. Service became nationwide August 15, 2007.
Distribution method: Available over the air on digital sub-channels & to cable & IPTV subscribers.
Scrambled signal: Yes.
Ownership: Produced & distributed by WGBH, American Public Television & WNET in assoc. with Public Broadcasting Service & the National Educational Telecommunications Assn.

WORLD FISHING NETWORK
1000 Chopper Circle
Denver, CO 80204
Phone: 720-873-5020
E-mail: marketing@worldfishingnetwork.com
Web Site: http://www.worldfishingnetwork.com
Jim Liberatore, President & Chief Executive Officer
Sean Luxton, General Manager
Keri Mahe, Vice President, Sales & Sponsorship
Pam Stinson, Vice President, Marketing

Branch Offices:
TORONTO: 60 St Clair Ave E, Ste 400, Toronto, ON M4T 1N5, Canada. Phone: 416-593-0915.
Type of service: Basic.
Operating hours/week: 168.
Programming: Angling, saltwater & freshwater fishing, competitions & tournaments, advice & instructional shows & focus on travel destinations.
Began: December 1, 2005.
Means of Support: Advertising.
Total subscribers: 60,000,000.
Distribution method: Available to DISH Network customers AT&T U-verse, Comcast & Verizon FiOS cable system subscribers.
Scrambled signal: Yes.
Ownership: A joint venture between Kroenke Sports & Entertainment (Stan Kroenke) (50%) & Insight Sports Ltd. (50%).

WORLD HARVEST TELEVISION
61300 S Ironwood Rd
South Bend, IN 46614
Phone: 574-291-8200
Fax: 574-291-9043
E-mail: harvest@lesea.com
Web Site: http://www.lesea.com/wht
Peter Sumrall, President & General Manager
Steve Warnecke, General Manager, Affiliate Relations
David Hummel, Senior Program Executive
Type of service: Digital basic.
Satellites: Galaxy IV, transponder 15.
Sales representative: Landin Media Sales.
Operating hours/week: 168.
Programming: Family & religious.
Began: November 1, 2003.
Means of Support: Advertising.
Distribution method: Available to satellite subscribers.
Scrambled signal: Yes.
Ownership: LeSea Broadcasting.

WORLD PICKS ON DEMAND (HINDI, LATINO, MANDARIN, RUSSIAN)
c/o AMC Networks Inc.
11 Penn Plz
New York, NY 10001
Phone: 212-324-8500
Web Site: http://www.amcnetworks.com
Ellen Kroner, Executive Vice President, Communications & Marketing
Type of service: Pay per view.
Operating areas: Available in Connecticut, New Jersey & New York.
Programming: Offers 20 hours of Hindi, Latino, Mandarin and Russian-language subscription on demand programming every month.
Began: January 1, 2004.
Means of Support: Subscriber fees.
Distribution method: Available to Cablevision Systems subscribers.
Ownership: AMC Networks Inc.

WORSHIP NETWORK
PO Box 428
Safety Harbor, FL 34695
Phone: 800-728-8723
E-mail: info@worship.net
Web Site: http://www.worship.net
Bruce Koblish, President & Chief Executive Officer
Bob Shreffler, Vice President, Finance
Tim Brown, Vice President, News Media
Patricia Niedzielski, Vice President, Finance & Administration
Diana Nicholas, Producer
Type of service: Digital, over the air.
Satellites: GE-1, transponder 7.
Operating hours/week: 168.
Uplink: Clearwater, FL.
Programming: Worship & praise music set to scenic nature; music concert specials.
Began: September 28, 1992.
Means of Support: Viewers.
Total subscribers: 70,000,000.
Distribution method: Available over the air on digital sub-channels & to cable & satellite subscribers.
Scrambled signal: Yes.
Ownership: Christian Network Inc.

WOWT 6 NEWS
3501 Farnam St
Omaha, NE 68131-3301
Phone: 402-346-6666
Fax: 402-233-7880
E-mail: sixonline@wowt.com
Web Site: http://www.wowt.com
Vic Richards, Vice President & General Manager
Type of service: Basic, over the air.
Programming: Local news.
Began: 1995. Rebranded News 4 You in 2009, then WOWT 6 News October 2013.
Distribution method: Available over the air on digital sub-channels & to cable subscribers.
Ownership: Gray Television.

WWE NETWORK
1241 E Main St
Stamford, CT 06902
Phone: 203-352-8600
Web Site: http://corporate.wwe.com; http://wwe.com
Michael Luisi, President, WWE Studios
George Barrios, Chief Strategy & Financial Officer
Stephanie McMahon, Chief Brand Officer
Rajan Mehta, Chief Technology Officer
Michelle Wilson, Chief Revenue & Marketing Officer
John Brody, Executive Vice President, Global Sales & Partnerships
Casey Collins, Executive Vice President, Consumer Products
Kevin Dunn, Executive Vice President, Television Production
Gerrit Meier, Executive Vice President, International
Perkins Miller, Executive Vice President, Digital Media
Tandy O'Donoghue, Executive Vice President, Strategy & Analytics
Matthew Singerman, Executive Vice President, Programming
Barry McMullin, Senior Vice President, Sales & Partnership Marketing
Eric Pankowski, Senior Vice President, Creative & Development
Michael Pine, Senior Vice President, Global Sales & Partnership Marketing
Monty Sarhan, Senior Vice President & General Counsel
Patrick Tatty, Senior Vice President, Live Events
Tara Carraro, Vice President, Corporate Communications
Bill Hirsh, Vice President, Integrated Sales
Michele Martell, Vice President, Kids Entertainment
Ted Van Zelst, Vice President, Integrated Sales
Type of service: Basic and subscription streaming.
Programming: Offers wrestling plus original and animated programming.
Began: February 24, 2014, online; April 6, 2014 as a network.
Means of Support: Subscriber fees.
Distribution method: Available to cable & DISH Network subscribers. Streaming available online & app (participating providers).
Scrambled signal: Yes.
Ownership: World Wrestling Entertainment.

XFINITY ON DEMAND
One Comcast Center
Philadelphia, PA 19103
Phone: 215-286-1700
Web Site: http://tvgo.xfinity.com/ondemand
Programming: Comcast Interactive Media's collection of On Demand shows and movies available on TV and online. Programming is also available in Spanish through an internet portal.

XHIJ-TV — See Canal 44 (XHIJ-TV).

XIAMEN TV
c/o Xiamen Media Group
Radio & Television Bldg, 121 N Hubin Rd
Siming District, Xiamen City 36102
China
Phone: 86-592-5301301
Fax: 86-592-5301206
Web Site: http://www.xmg.com.cn/home
Operating hours/week: 168.
Programming: General entertainment channel broadcast in the Minnan dialect.
Distribution method: Available through KyLinTV.

Pay TV & Satellite Services

Scrambled signal: Yes.
Ownership: Xiamen Media Group.

XTSY
c/o New Frontier Media
6000 Spine Rd, Ste 100
Boulder, CO 80301
Phones: 303-444-0900; 888-875-0632
Fax: 303-938-8388
Web Site: http://www.noof.com
Larry Flynt, Chief Executive Officer
Michael Klein, President
Chris Woodward, Chief Financial Officer
Type of service: Pay per view.
Operating areas: Available nationwide.
Programming: Adult programming.
Distribution method: Available to cable, IPTV & satellite subscribers.
Ownership: New Frontier Media.

XTV
c/o Interactive TV Networks Inc.
23241 Ventura Blvd, Ste 217
Woodland Hills, CA 91364
Phone: 866-988-4988
Helen Wise, President
Carol Gorgichuk, Sales Representative
Type of service: Basic, pay-per-view, broadband & video on demand.
Programming: Adult programming including live TV, pay-per-view & interactive channels made available through IPTV technology.
Means of Support: Subscriber fees.
Distribution method: Available to cable & satellite providers.
Scrambled signal: Yes.

YANGTSE RIVER DRAMA
Programming: Offers female-oriented Chinese language programming. Available through KyLinTV.
Scrambled signal: Yes.

YANKEES ENTERTAINMENT & SPORTS — See YES Network.

YES NETWORK
805 Third Ave
30th Fl
New York, NY 10022
Phone: 646-487-3600
Fax: 646-487-3612
E-mail: info@yesnetwork.com
Web Site: http://web.yesnetwork.com
Jon Litner, President & Chief Executive Officer
John Filippelli, President, Production & Programming
Howard Levinson, Senior Vice President, Ad Sales
Woody Freiman, Vice President, Programming & Production
Eric Handler, Vice President, Communications
Michael Spirito, Vice President, Digital Media & Business Development
Mike Webb, Vice President, Broadcast Operations
Jamie Brokowsky, Controller
Daniel Guernsey, Senior Creative Director, On-Air Promotions
Rob Brinkmann, Studio & Production Planning Director
Joe Capobianco, National Sales Director
Type of service: Basic, HD, streaming, video on demand.
Operating hours/week: 168.
Operating areas: Available nationwide.
Programming: All New York Yankees baseball games, biography, interview & magazine programs covering the Yankees, as well as other professional & collegiate sports.
Began: March 19, 2002, A national feed of YES Network began April 1, 2009 to selected Bright House Networks systems in Orlando and Tampa, Florida. The service became available to California on March 1, 2012 and Birmingham, AL March 2, 2012.
Total subscribers: 24,000,000.
Distribution method: Available regionally to cable & IPTV subscribers as well as DirecTV. Streaming available online & through Fox Sports Go app (participating providers).
Scrambled signal: Yes.
Ownership: A joint venture between 21st Century Fox (80%) & Yankee Global Enterprises LLC (20%).

YESTERDAY USA
2001 Plymouth Rock
Richardson, TX 75081-3946
Phone: 972-889-9872
Fax: 972-889-2329
E-mail: bill46@yesterdayusa.com
Web Site: http://www.yesterdayusa.com
William J. Bragg, Founder
Satellites: Galaxy I, transponder 24; Galaxy V, transponder 7 (6.8 Wide Band Audio).
Operating hours/week: 168.
Programming: Commercial-free old-time radio shows & music.
Began: January 1, 1985.
Total subscribers: 3,800,000 (Figure includes satellite subscribers.).
Distribution method: Available to cable & satellite subscribers.
Scrambled signal: Yes.

YES2 — See YES Network.
Type of service: Basic, HD.
Programming: Alternate feed that broadcasts Nets games when the Nets & Yankee games overlap.
Scrambled signal: Yes.

YNN AUSTIN — See Time Warner Cable News (Austin).

YNN (CAPITAL REGION & HUDSON VALLEY, NY) — See Time Warner Cable News (Capital Region) & Time Warner Cable News (Hudson Valley).

YNN (CENTRAL, NORTHERN & SOUTHERN TIER, NY) — See Time Warner Cable News (Central NY), (Northern NY) & (Southern Tier NY).

YNN ROCHESTER — See Time Warner Cable News (Rochester).

YOUTOO AMERICA
808 E Abram St
Arlington, TX 76010
Phone: 817-274-1609
E-mail: info@youtoo.com
Web Site: http://www.youtoo.com
Edward Frazier, Chairman of the Board
Scott Miller, Executive Vice President
Tim Larson, Vice President, Distribution
Lisa McKibben, Marketing Director
Ryan Rains, Operations Director
Operating areas: Nationwide.
Programming: Social TV network. Allows users to be a part of the programming by submitting videos, texting to TV or voting in real time.
Began: February 1, 1985, as Nostalgia Television. Rebranded Goodlife TV then AmericanLife TV Network (ALN) on March 1, 2005. Rebranded Youtoo TV on September 27, 2011 then Youtoo America.
Means of Support: Fees to transfer links to friends & family members.
Total subscribers: 15,000,000.
Distribution method: Available to cable & satellite subscribers. Service is also accessible to those with smart phones, tablets or webcams.
Scrambled signal: Yes.
Ownership: CenterPost Networks LLC.

YUMA 77
198 S Main St
c/o Yuma County
Yuma, AZ 85364
Phone: 928-373-1010
Fax: 928-373-1120
Kevin Tunell, Communications Director
Bryan Longoria, Communications Specialist
Alberto Tansey, Cablecast Producer I
Type of service: Regional.
Operating hours/week: 168.
Operating areas: Arizona.
Programming: Provides county residents up-to-the-minute information on their county government and reports on community news.
Began: May 1, 2000.
Distribution method: Available to cable system subscribers.
Ownership: Yuma County.

ZEE BUSINESS — See Zee TV.
Web Site: http://zeenews.india.com/business/index.html
Type of service: Pay.
Operating areas: Available nationwide.
Programming: Business news, information and current affairs programs.
Began: November 1, 2004, in India. Began on August 30, 2011 in the U.S.
Means of Support: Advertising and subscriber fees.
Distribution method: Available to DISH Network customers.
Scrambled signal: Yes.
Ownership: Zee Entertainment Enterprises Ltd.

ZEE CINEMA — See Zee TV.
Programming: Bollywood films.

ZEE KANNADA
39 United Mansions
3rd Fl, M.G. Road
Bengalooru 560 001
India
Phones: 91-80-6610-9999; 646-745-9000
Fax: 91-80-2555-9432
E-mail: zeekannada@zeenetwork.com
Web Site: http://www.zeekannadatv.com
Siju Prabhakaran, Business Head
Raghavendra Hunsur, Programming Head
Prasad Alva, Distribution
Type of service: Pay.
Operating hours/week: 168.
Operating areas: Available nationwide.
Programming: Language specific service allowing Kannada-speaking populace to keep in touch with their culture.
Began: August 29, 2011.
Means of Support: Advertising and subscriber fees.
Distribution method: Available to DISH Network customers.
Scrambled signal: Yes.
Ownership: Zee Entertainment Enterprises Ltd.

ZEE MARATHI — See Zee TV.
E-mail: zeemarathi@zeenetwork.com
Web Site: http://www.zeemarathi.com
Type of service: Pay.
Operating hours/week: 168.
Operating areas: Available nationwide.
Programming: Language specific service allowing Marathi-speaking populace to keep in touch with their culture.
Began: August 29, 2011.
Means of Support: Advertising and subscriber fees.
Distribution method: Available to DISH Network customers.
Scrambled signal: Yes.
Ownership: Zee Entertainment Enterprises Ltd.

ZEE PUNJABI
Filmcity 19
Sector 16-A
Noida, Uttar Pradesh 201 301
India
Phone: 91-120-2511064
Fax: 91-120-2515240
E-mail: inews@zeemedia.esselgroup.com
Web Site: http://www.zeetv.co.uk/zeepunjabi
Sanjay Vohra, Editor & Business Head
Sanjeev Kumar, Vice President, Sales
Pramod Kaul, Assistant Vice President, Sales
Type of service: Pay.
Operating areas: Available nationwide.
Programming: Offers news, current affairs programs, music, devotional programs, interactive shows, magazine shows, Zee Punjabi Archives plus live events.
Began: August 30, 2011.
Means of Support: Advertising and subscriber fees.
Distribution method: Available to DISH Network customers.
Scrambled signal: Yes.
Ownership: Zee Entertainment Enterprises Ltd.

ZEE SMILE — See Zee TV.
Subhash Chandra, Non-Executive Chairman
Type of service: Pay.
Operating areas: Available nationwide.
Programming: Offers comedy entertainment.
Began: September 11, 2004, in India; Began August 30, 2011 in the U.S.
Means of Support: Advertising and subscriber fees.
Distribution method: Available to DISH Network customers.
Scrambled signal: Yes.
Ownership: Zee Entertainment Enterprises Ltd.

ZEE TV
Continental Bldg.
135 Dr Annie Besant Rd
Worli, Mumbai 400 018
India
Phone: 91-22-6697-1234
Fax: 91-22-2490-0302
E-mail: customerservice@zeetvusa.com
Web Site: http://www.zeetelevision.com
Punit Goenka, Chief Executive Officer & Managing Director
Ashish Sehgal, Chief Sales Officer
Mihir Modi, Chief Finance & Strategy Officer
Sharada Sunder, Executive Vice President, Regional Channels

Branch Offices:
NEW YORK: Zee TV USA, One Penn Plz, 250 W 34th St, Ste 3501, New York, NY 10119. Phone: 646-745-9000. Fax: 646-745-9090. E-Mail: customerservice@zeetvusa.com.
Type of service: Premium, HD.
Operating hours/week: 168.
Programming: Programming from India & Pakistan includes news, movies, dramas, children's programming, sports & talk shows aimed at serving the needs of South Asians living abroad.

Pay TV & Satellite Services

Began: January 1, 1999, October 1992 in Asia. Began July 18, 1998 in the U.S. Zee TV HD began September 2012.
Total subscribers: 500,000,000 (Worldwide).
Distribution method: Available to cable, IPTV & satellite subscribers.
Scrambled signal: Yes.
Ownership: Zee Entertainment Enterprises Ltd.

ZHEJIANG TV
No. 111 Moganshan Road
Hangzhou 310005
China
Web Site: http://www.zjstv.com
Operating hours/week: 168.
Programming: Mandarin-language children's programming, current affairs, education, entertainment and news.
Began: October 1, 1960.
Means of Support: Subscriber fees and advertising.
Scrambled signal: Yes.

ZHONG TIAN CHANNEL — See CTI-Zhong Tian.

ZING NETWORKS LTD
7B Shah Industrial Estate
Off. Veera Desai Road, Andheri West
Mumbai 400053
India
E-mail: zing@zeenetwork.com
Operating hours/week: 168.
Operating areas: Available nationwide.
Programming: Channel dedicated to South Asian music and entertainment.

Began: April 1, 2009, in India. Began on August 30, 2011 in the U.S.
Means of Support: Advertising.
Distribution method: Available to DISH Network customers.
Scrambled signal: Yes.
Ownership: Zee Entertainment Enterprises Ltd.

Z LIVING
One Penn Plz
250 W 34th St, Ste 3501
New York, NY 10119
Phones: 646-745-9090; 646-747-9101
Web Site: http://www.zliving.com
Eric Sherman, Chief Executive Officer
Rajeev Kheror, President, Strategy & Planning, International Business, Living Communications Inc.
David Cooper, Senior Vice President, Sales & Head of Advertising
Raymond Donahue, Senior Vice President, Head of Program Sales
Russell Maitland, Senior Vice President, Advertising Sales
Joseph Cho, Vice President, Digital
Andrew Struse, Vice President, Creative Services
Robert Washburn Jr., Vice President, Advertising Sales
Rafe Oller, General Manager
David Kutz, Executive in Charge, Production
Timothy Boell, Group Head, Distribution
Sandeep Krishnamurthy, Head of Over the Top Distribution
Gabriella Messina, Head of Programming
Colleen Cassel, Advertising Sales Director
Dennis Dunphy, Ad Sales Director, Central & Western Regions
Douglas Jost, Content Distribution & Marketing Director
Claire Verre, Direct Response Sales Representative
Jodi Chenoff Goldblatt, Senior Manager, Advertising Sales
Heidi Corn, Advertising Sales Manager
Barbara Ann Toffolo, Media

Branch Offices:
CHICAGO: 2010 N Halsted St, Chicago, IL 60014. Phone: 773-281-3467.

DALLAS: 4001 Highlander Blvd, Ste 149, Arlington, TX 76018. Phone: 817-557-1796.
Type of service: Basic.
Operating hours/week: 168.
Operating areas: Nationwide.
Programming: Media brand devoted to showcasing the best healthy lifestyle and wellness programming.
Began: October 1, 2007, as Veria TV, channel. Rebranded Veria Living September 26, 2011, Z Living October 2, 2014.
Total subscribers: 20,000,000.
Distribution method: Available to Cablevision Systems, DISH Network, Frontier Communications, RCN & Verizon FiOS subscribers.
Scrambled signal: Yes.
Ownership: Asia TV USA Ltd.

Z LIVING GO — See Z Living.
Web Site: http://go.zliving.com
Type of service: Subscription streaming.

Programming: Programming from Z Living.
Distribution method: Available online.

ZONETV
520 Broadway
Fl 3
Santa Monica, CA 90405
Phone: 855-966-3277
E-mail: support@zone.tv
Web Site: http://zone.tv
Doug Edwards, Executive Chairman
Jeff Weber, Chief Executive Officer
Mike Daymond, Chief Operating Officer
Stephen Massel, Chief Financial Officer
Bruce Rider, Media Consultant

Branch Offices:
Headquarters: 1795 Ironstone Manor, Ste 4, Pickering, Ontario L1W 3W9, Canada.

Office: 51 Wolseley St, Toronto, Ontario M5T 1A4, Canada.
Type of service: Pay.
Operating areas: Available nationwide.
Programming: Combines its advanced platform with the best digital first content and brands to deliver a mix of exciting and unique programming to millions of households through pay TV operators.
Began: September 1, 2013, Formerly known as ES3.
Means of Support: Subscriber fees.
Total subscribers: 8,500,000.
Scrambled signal: Yes.

ZUUS COUNTRY — See The Country Network.

Program Sources & Services

Offering live, film & tape recorders & commercials and production facilities to television stations and cable systems. These listings are based on data supplied by companies known to be serving TV & Cable systems.

@RADICAL MEDIA INC.
435 Hudson St
New York, NY 10014
Phone: 212-462-1500
Fax: 212-462-1600
Web Site: http://www.radicalmedia.com
Jon Karmen, Chairman & Chief Executive Officer
Michael Fiore, Chief Operating Officer & Chief Financial Officer
Evan Schnectman, Chief Technical Officer
India Hammer, Head of Operations & Human Resources

Branch Offices:
SANTA MONICA: 1630 12th St, Santa Monica, CA 90404. Phone: 310-664-4500. Fax: 310-664-4600. E-Mail: rubenstein@radicalmedia.com. Frank Scherma, President; Justin Wilkes, Vice President, Media & Entertainment; Liz Friesell-Mason, Managing Director, Post Production.

AUSTRALIA: 85 Commonwealth St, Surry Hills, NSW 2010, Australia. Phone: 61-0-2-9213-6300. Fax: 61-0-2-9213-6399. E-Mail: galluzzo@radicalmedia.com. Rob Galluzzo, Managing Director.

CHINA: 1508 Jiashan Lu, Highstreet Loft, Ste 2405, Shanghai 200031, China. Phone: 86-21-5466-5938. Fax: 86-21-5466-5939. E-Mail: spitzer@radicalmedia.com. Robb Spitzer, Managing Director.

GERMANY: Rueckerstr, Berlin D-10119, Germany. Phone: 49-0-30-233-229-0. Fax: 49-0-30-323-229-1. E-Mail: dressler@radicalmedia.com. Christine Dressler, Managing Director.

UNITED KINGDOM: Scriptor Ct, 155-157 Farringdon Rd, London WC1R 3AD, United Kingdom. Phone: 44-0-20-7462-4070. E-Mail: jodieb@radicalmedia.com. Jodie Brooks, Executive Producer, Sales.
Provides film production, new media, film development, TV programming & animation.

1-WORLD LLC
1605 S Jackson St
Seattle, WA 98144
Fax: 206-781-1401
E-mail: 1world@1worldfilms.com
Web Site: http://www.1worldfilms.com
Produces & distributes foreign motion pictures.

3 BALL ENTERTAINMENT
3650 Redondo Beach Ave
Redondo Beach, CA 90278
Phone: 424-236-7500
Fax: 424-236-7501
Web Site: http://3ballentertainment.com
Reinout Oerlemans, Chairman
J. D. Rothberg, Non-Executive Board Member & Co-Founder

Todd Nelson, Co-Chief Executive Officer & Co-Founder
Ross Weintraub, Co-Chief Executive Officer
Jeff Goldman, Chief Business Officer
Bryant Pinvidic, Chief Creative Officer
Produces reality & non-fiction programming for broadcast & cable.

62ND STREET PRODUCTIONS
2080 Peachtree Industrial Ct
Atlanta, GA 30341-2246
Phone: 770-455-3356
E-mail: steve@compro-atl.com
Kim A. Anderson, President
Nels A. Anderson, Director
Steve Brinson, Producer
Produces TV commercials; directors specialize in tabletop, fashion, cars, food, dialogue, humor, time lapse, kids, special effects & music videos.

89 EDIT
136 West 21st St
4th Fl
New York, NY 10011
Phone: 212-647-1300
Sharon Lew, Executive Producer
Juliet Conti, Producer
Janice Harryman, Mid-west Sales
Samantha Tuttlebee, Sales

AARP TV
601 E St NW
Washington, DC 20049
Phones: 202-434-3525; 888-687-2277
Web Site: http://www.aarp.org/tv
Jo Ann Jenkins, Chief Executive Officer
Scott Frisch, Chief Operating Officer
Martha M. Boudreau, Chief Communications & Marketing Officer
Produces programming geared towards viewers 50 years & older.

ABC NEWS
47 W 66th St
New York, NY 10023-6201
Phone: 212-456-7297
Web Site: http://www.abcnews.go.com
James Goldston, President
Tom Cibrowski, Senior Vice President, News Programs, News Gathering & Special Events
Subrata De, Vice President, Multi-Platform Newsgathering
Colby Smith, Vice President, ABC News Digital
Robin Sproul, Vice President, Public Affairs

ABC STUDIOS
500 S Buena Vista St
Burbank, CA 91521
Phone: 818-560-1000
Web Site: http://www.abc.com
Ayo Davis, Head, Talent & Casting, ABC Entertainment & ABC Studios
Patrick Moran, President, ABC Studios

Nne Ebong, Senior Vice President, Drama Development
Gary French, Senior Vice President, Production
Amy Hartwick, Senior Vice President, Creative Development
Stephanie Leifer, Senior Vice President, Current Programming
Dawn Soler, Senior Vice President, TV Music
Paula Warner, Senior Vice President, Post Production
Develops & produces TV programming.

ACCENTHEALTH
747 Third Ave
New York, NY 10017
Phone: 212-763-5102
Fax: 212-763-5200
E-mail: csr@accenthealth.com
Web Site: http://www.accenthealth.com
Daniel A. Stone, Chief Executive Officer

Branch Offices:
TAMPA: 5440 Beaumont Ctr Blvd, Ste 400, Tampa, FL 33634-5208. Phones: 813-349-7127; 800-235-4930. Fax: 813-349-7299.
Produces AccentHealth Waiting Room TV Network along with CNN. Programming features medical breakthroughs, condition-specific segments, parenting issues, nutrition, etc.

ACCENT MEDIA
1937 Reprise Ct
Vienna, VA 22182
Phone: 703-356-9427
E-mail: ceciliadomeyko@accentmediainc.com
Web Site: http://www.accentmediainc.com
Cecelia Domeyko, President & Writer/Director/Producer
Produces documentaries & training videos, public service announcements & information campaigns, video news releases, Spanish language productions, media training & museum videos.

ACCUWEATHER INC.
385 Science Park Rd
State College, PA 16803
Phones: 814-237-0809; 814-235-8650
Fax: 814-235-8609
E-mail: customerservice@accuweather.com
Web Site: http://www.accuweather.com
Dr. Joel N. Myers, Founder, Chairman & President
Barry Lee Myers, Chief Executive Officer
Michael R. Smith, Chief Executive Officer, WeatherData Services Inc.
Jim Candor, Chief Strategy Officer
John Dokes, Chief Marketing Officer
Steven Hickson, Chief Financial Officer
Steven Smith, Chief Digital Officer
Marie Svet, Chief Revenue Officer, Digital Media
Elliot Abrams, Senior Vice President & Chief Forecaster
Dr. Joe Sobel, Senior Vice President

Sarah Katt, Vice President, Product Development & Operations
Loren Tobia, Executive Director, Sales, Display Systems & Services Division

Branch Offices:
NEW YORK: Global Sales Office, 1270 Ave of the Americas, Ste 2330, New York, NY 10020. Phone: 212-554-4750.

WICHITA: WeatherData Services Inc., 100 N Broadway, Ste 750, Wichita, KS 67202. Phone: 316-266-8000.
Provides custom tailored weather forecasts, ready-for-air graphics, graphic access & display systems, real-time weather database & automated weather warning crawl generation system. Local Cable Weather & The Radar Channel give an automated turnkey local weather channel with live video capabilities.

AGENCY FOR INSTRUCTIONAL TECHNOLOGY
8111 Lee Paul Rd
Bloomington, IN 47404
Phones: 812-339-2203; 800-457-4509
Fax: 812-333-4218
E-mail: info@ait.net
Web Site: http://www.ait.net
Chuck Wilson, Executive Director
David Gudaitis, Production/Project Manager
Rolanda Kirkley, Warehouse & Facility Manager
Valerie French, Customer Service
Produces & distributes instructional materials including educational videos, computer programming, print materials (guides, workshop handbooks) & digital media; includes resources for Pre-K through adult learners & in all major curriculum areas.

AIRCRAFT MUSIC LIBRARY
162 Columbus Ave
Boston, MA 02116
Phones: 617-303-7600; 800-343-2514
Fax: 617-303-7666
E-mail: info@aircraftmusiclibrary.com
Web Site: http://www.aircraftmusiclibrary.com
Tim Reppert, Engineer, Composer & Producer
Distributes a comprehensive music package encompassing a wide variety of styles for the broadcast, non-broadcast, film & video industries.

ALDEN FILMS/FILMS OF THE NATIONS
PO Box 449
Clarksburg, NJ 08510
Phones: 732-462-3522; 800-832-0980
Fax: 732-294-0330
E-mail: info@aldenfilms.com

Program Sources & Services

Web Site: http://www.aldenfilms.com
Distributes Jewish, Scandinavian & children's film & video; produces art & flying saucer films & women's self-defense videos.

ALLEGRO PRODUCTIONS INC.
1000 Clint Moore Rd
Ste 108
Boca Raton, FL 33487
Phones: 561-994-9111; 800-232-2133
Fax: 561-241-0707
E-mail: scott@allegrovideo.com
Web Site: http://www.allegrovideo.com
Scott J. Forman, President
Glenn A. Forman, Vice President
Judith Sitkin, Business Manager
Provides film & video production, animation, CD-ROM/DVD authoring & duplication, high volume videotape duplication & fulfillment & custom music scoring.

ALLIANCE FOR CHRISTIAN MEDIA
644 W Peachtree St
Ste 300
Atlanta, GA 30308-1925
Phones: 404-815-0640; 800-229-3788
Fax: 404-815-0495
E-mail: contact@allianceforchristianmedia.org
Web Site: http://www.allianceforchristianmedia.org
Canon Louis C. Schueddig, President & Executive Director
Peter Wallace, Executive Producer & Day 1 Host
Tony Callaway, Development Director
Provides a wide selection of audio/visual resources for Christian education - audio books, videos, tapes & CDs.

ALLIED VAUGHN
7600 Parklawn Ave
Ste 300
Minneapolis, MN 55435
Phones: 952-832-3100; 800-323-0281
Fax: 952-832-3179
E-mail: avfsales@alliedvaughn.com
Web Site: http://www.alliedvaughn.com
Doug Olzenak, President
Richard Skillman, Vice President, Sales

Branch Offices:
ITASCA: 1310 W Thorndale, Itasca, IL 60143-1159. Phones: 630-919-2120; 800-759-4087. Fax: 847-595-8677.

LIVONIA: 11923 Brookfield, Livonia, MI 48150. Phones: 734-462-5543; 800-462-5543. Fax: 734-462-4004.

ORLANDO: 8812 Torrey Pines Terr, Orlando, FL 32819. Phones: 407-491-7737; 800-877-1778. Fax: 407-876-5388.
Provides video duplication, CD/DVD services, streaming services, Media On-Demand, MediaLinX Online Asset Management, MediaLinX Online Access Management, library management services, fulfillment & distribution services, audiotape duplication, broadcast equipment rental, post production & AVID suites.

ALL MOBILE VIDEO
221 W 26th St
New York, NY 10001
Phone: 212-727-1234
Fax: 212-255-6644
Web Site: http://www.allmobilevideo.com
Lenny Laxer, Vice President
Ken Smalley, Rentals, AMV Rentals
Eric Duke, Mobiles, AMV Mobile Division
Richard Duke, Post & Duplication, AMV Chelsea Post
Lenny Laxer, Transmission, AMV Transmission
Erik Thielking, Equipment Sales, AMV Broadcast Sales

Branch Offices:
CARTERET: AMV Gateway Teleport, 27 Randolph St, Carteret, NJ 07008. Phone: 732-969-3191. Fax: 732-541-2007.

LODI: AMV Field Operations, 272 State Rte 17 S, Lodi, NJ 07644. Phone: 201-488-4181. Fax: 201-488-3709.

NEW YORK: AMV Unitel, 515 W 57th St, New York, NY 10019. Phones: 212-265-3600; 212-586-8616.
Offers mobile production, post production & uplink solutions.

ALTERNA'TV
2020 Ponce de Leon Blvd
Ste 1107
Coral Gables, FL 33134
Phone: 786-609-9604
E-mail: aymeric.genty@alternatv.us
Web Site: http://www.alternatv.us
Aymeric Genty, Chief Executive Officer
Roberto Perez, Senior Director, Marketing & Distribution
Leonardo J Pinto, Senior Distribution Director, Latin America
Alejandro Penafiel Moreno, Content Director
Luis Jesus Zarate Gonzales, Marketing Supervisor
Delivers programming via its EUT113Wa satellite platform. Enables channel partners to reach a potential audience of more than 150 million pay-TV subscribers in more than 25 countries with a single video feed. Subsidiary of Eutelsat Americas.

AMAZON INC.
232 E Ohio St
3rd Fl
Chicago, IL 60611
Phone: 312-642-5400
Fax: 312-642-0142
E-mail: info@amazonedit.com
Web Site: http://www.amazonedit.com
Janice Rosenthal, President & AVID Editor
Steve Immer, AVID Editor
Provides offline editing services.

AMERICA CV NETWORK LLC
13001 NW 107th Ave
Hialeah Gardens, FL 33018
Phone: 305-592-4141
Fax: 305-592-3808
Web Site: http://www.americacv.com
Carlos Vasallo, President & Chief Executive
Herb Espino, Vice President, Sales
Gina Garcias, Sales Promotions & Events Director
Francisco Framil, National Sales Manager
Carlos Justo, Local Sales Manager
Produces 12 hours of Spanish language programming a day covering topics of local interest.

AMERICAN JEWISH COMMITTEE
PO Box 705
New York, NY 10150
Phone: 212-751-4000
Fax: 212-891-1450
E-Mail: sharbats@ajc.org
Web Site: http://www.ajc.org
E. Robert Goodkind, President
David A. Harris, Executive Director
Richard Foltin, National & Legislative Affairs Director
Produces original research, public opinion surveys & programming concerning the Jewish community.

AMERICAN PUBLIC TELEVISION (APTV)
55 Summer St
4th Fl
Boston, MA 02110
Phone: 617-338-4455
Fax: 617-338-5369
E-mail: info@aptonline.org
Web Site: http://www.aptonline.org
Cynthia Fenneman, President & Chief Executive Officer
Judy Barlow, Vice President, Business Development
David Fournier, Vice President, Finance & Administration
Chris Funkhouser, Vice President, Exchange Programming & Digital Services
Jamie Haines, Vice President, Communications
Eric Luskin, Vice President, Syndication & Premium Services
Terry Mena, Controller
Tom Davison, Business Development Director
Alan Gindelsky, PC/LAN Support Manager
Christi Collier, Program Development Executive, Premium Services
Syndicates & distributes programming for public TV stations in the U.S.

AMERICAN RELIGIOUS TOWN HALL MEETING INC.
PO Box 180118
Dallas, TX 75218
Phones: 214-328-9828; 800-783-9828
Fax: 214-328-3042
E-mail: tvtelecast@americanreligious.org
Web Site: http://www.americanreligious.org
Elizabeth Ann Leike, President & Chief Executive Officer
Jerry Lutz, Moderator
Produces & distributes interdenominational discussion programs for TV.

AMIT
817 Broadway
3rd Floor
New York, NY 10003
Phones: 212-477-4720; 800-989-2648
Fax: 212-353-2312
E-mail: info@amitchildren.org
Web Site: http://www.amitchildren.org
Francine S. Stein, President
Arnold Gerson, Executive Vice President

Branch Offices:
BALTIMORE: 2800 Stone Cliff Dr, Ste 112, Baltimore, MD 21202. Phone: 410-484-2223. E-Mail: robbiep@amitchildren.org.

HOLLYWOOD: 2700 N 29th Ave, Ste 203, Hollywood, FL 33020. Phone: 754-922-5100. E-Mail: amitfla@att.net.

LOS ANGELES: 1122 S Robertson Blvd, Ste 9, Los Angeles, CA 90035. Phone: 310-859-4885. Fax: 310-859-4875. E-Mail: jenniferl@amitchildren.org.

SKOKIE: 3856B W Oakton, Skokie, IL 60076. Phone: 847-677-3800. Fax: 847-982-0057. E-Mail: amitchicago@amitchildren.org.

WESTBOROUGH: Seven Brady Rd, Westborough, MA 01581. Phone: 508-870-1571. E-Mail: amitboston@charter.net.

ISRAEL: PO Box 71705, Jerusalem 93420, Israel. Phone: 972-02-673-8360. Fax: 972-02-673-8359. E-Mail: joffice@amit.org.il. Web site: http://www.amit.org.il.
Produces & distributes educational films & tape programs on Israel & AMIT facilities in Israel.

ANNENBERG CHANNEL
c/o Harvard-Smithsonian Center for Astrophysics
60 Garden St, MS 82
Cambridge, MA 02138
Phone: 800-228-8030
Fax: 617-496-7670
E-mail: channel@learner.org
Web Site: http://www.learner.org
Pete Neal, General Manager
Larisa M. Kirgan, Operations Officer
Michele McLeod, Senior Program Officer
Yolanda Odunsi, Interactive Services Manager
Kathryn Koczot, Administrative Assistant

Branch Office:
WASHINGTON: 401 9th St NW, Washington, DC 20004. Phone: 202-879-9654. Fax: 202-879-9696.
Adult educational programs & professional development series for K-12 educators.

ANOTHER COUNTRY
515 N State St
25th Fl
Chicago, IL 60654
Phone: 312-706-5800
Fax: 312-706-5801
E-mail: tim.konn@anothercountry.net
Web Site: http://www.anothercountry.net
Tim Konn, Producer
Sound design studio.

APA INTERNATIONAL FILM DISTRIBUTORS INC.
7400 SW 50th Terr
Ste 101
Miami, FL 33155
Phone: 305-667-4553
Fax: 305-234-7515
Rafael Fusaro, President
Maria Martinez, Senior Vice President
Beatriz Fusaro, Director
Distributes motion pictures, series & cartoons for all Spanish-speaking countries & other nations.

AP ENPS
1100 13th St
Ste 500
Washington, DC 20005
Phones: 202-641-9000; 800-821-4747
Fax: 202-370-2719
E-mail: info@enps.com
Web Site: http://www.enps.com
Provides a system that allows users to create content for broadcast or digital platforms. Users can send videos/photos, create & edit stories, access planning, rundowns, contacts, news wires & message coworkers from a tablet or smartphone.

AP RADIO NETWORK (APRN)
450 W 33rd St
New York, NY 10001
Phone: 212-621-1500
E-mail: info@ap.org
Web Site: http://www.ap.org
Provides audio news & information in a flexible, easy-to-use format that allows customization; delivers hundreds of audio cuts every day, covering the latest in news, sports, business & entertainment; offers

Program Sources & Services

three Special Events Channels for live, long-form coverage of press conferences, special events & major breaking news.

AP TELEVISION NEWS
The Interchange
Oval Rd
Camden Lock, London NW1 7DZ
United Kingdom
Phone: 44-0-20-7482-7400
Fax: 44-0-20-7413-8302
E-mail: aptninfo@ap.org
Web Site: http://www.aptn.com
Daisy Veerasingham, Vice President, EMEA Business Operations
Nigel Baker, Executive Director
Toby Hartwell, Marketing Director
Sandy MacIntyre, News Director

Branch Offices:
NEW YORK:. Phones: 212-621-7410; 212-621-7460. Fax: 212-621-7519. E-Mail: sgillesby@ap.org; rmerrill@ap.org. Sara Gillesby, New York Assignment Desk Manager; Robert Merrill, National Entertainment Video Manager.

WASHINGTON, DC:. Phones: 202-641-9700; 202-641-9720. E-Mail: dvance@ap.org. Denise Vance, Deputy Director, U.S. Broadcast.
Provides breaking global news, sports, entertainment, technology & human interest video content to broadcasters, online & mobile platforms; offices worldwide.

APTINET INC.
228 East 45th St
11th Floor
New York, NY 10017
Phone: 212-725-7255
Fax: 212-983-7591
E-mail: info@aptinet.com
Web Site: http://www.aptinet.com
Provides interactive & video services for ad agencies & businesses.

ARCHDIOCESE OF BALTIMORE
320 Cathedral St
Baltimore, MD 21201
Phones: 410-646-5102; 800-528-6822
Fax: 410-646-4806
E-mail: mediarch@archbalt.org
Web Site: http://www.archbalt.org
Julia Rogers, Media Director
Nancy Gordy, Media Assistant
Provides print & non-print resources, informational assistance, media consultation & technical assistance to parishes, schools, religious education programs & other organizations.

ARENAS
3375 Barham Blvd
Garden Level
Los Angeles, CA 90068
Phone: 323-785-5555
Fax: 323-785-5560
E-mail: general@arenasgroup.com
Web Site: http://www.arenasgroup.com
Santiago Pozo, Chief Executive Officer
Larry Gleason, President, Distribution
John Butkovich, Executive Vice President, Marketing
Dave Wong, Executive Vice President, Marketing
Isaac Cuevas, Vice President, Interactive Marketing
Leyla Fletcher, Vice President, Marketing Media

Branch Offices:
SPAIN: Estrella 15, 2 Izda, 28004 Madrid, Spain. Phone: 34-609-02-38-55.
Produces, acquires, markets & distributes films in all media including theatrical, video & TV.

ARCTEK SATELLITE PRODUCTIONS
PO Box 14976
Minneapolis, MN 55414
Phones: 612-623-1986; 866-623-1986
Fax: 612-331-2290
E-mail: bstanley@arcteksat.com
Web Site: http://www.arcteksat.com
Todd Hanks, Managing Partner
Brian Stanley, Sales/Operations
Provides video production & satellite transmission services - digital or analog.

ARMENIAN FILM FOUNDATION
2219 E Thousand Oaks Blvd
Ste 292
Thousand Oaks, CA 91362
Phone: 805-495-0717
Fax: 805-379-0667
E-mail: info@armenianfilm.org
Web Site: http://www.armenianfilm.org
J. Michael Hagopian, Chairman
Hratch Karakachian, Treasurer
Produces & distributes documentary & educational films on ethnic subjects concerning Middle Eastern & Armenian cultures.

ARMY & AIR FORCE HOMETOWN NEWS SERVICE — See Joint Hometown News Service

ARTBEATS SOFTWARE INC.
PO Box 709
1405 N Myrtle Rd
Myrtle Creek, OR 97457
Phones: 541-863-4429; 800-444-9392
Fax: 541-863-4547
E-mail: info@artbeats.com
Web Site: http://www.artbeats.com
Phil Bates, Founder & President
Provides royalty-free stock footage & still imagery for broadcast, film features, commercial, desktop video, game development & multimedia.

ASCENT MEDIA GROUP
520 Broadway
5th Fl
Santa Monica, CA 90401
Phone: 310-434-7000
E-mail: sales@ascentmedia.com
Web Site: http://www.ascentmedia.com
William Fitzgerald, Chief Executive Officer
Tom Kuehle, Executive Vice President, Strategic Solutions
William Niles, Executive Vice President, General Counsel & Secretary
Douglas Parish, Executive Vice President, Operations
George C. Platisa, Executive Vice President & Chief Financial Officer
David Pruitt, Senior Vice President, Business Development
Bill Romeo, Senior Vice President, Entertainment Television Sales, Creative Group
Provides solutions for the creation, management & distribution of content to major motion picture studios, independent producers, broadcast & programming networks & other companies; systems integration; consulting services; offices worldwide.

ASIA TV USA LTD.
One Penn Plz
Ste 3501
New York, NY 10119
Phone: 646-745-9000
Fax: 646-745-9090
Web Site: http://www.zeetvusa.com
Suresh Bala Iyer, Chief Executive Officer
Tom Marsillo, Senior Vice President, Advertising Sales
Distributes a wide variety of TV, entertainment & media content. Portfolio includes nine south Asian entertainment channels.

ASSOCIATED PRESS
450 W 33rd St
New York, NY 10001
Phones: 212-621-1500; 212-621-7103
E-mail: info@ap.org
Web Site: http://www.ap.org
Gary Pruitt, President & Chief Executive Officer
Jessica Bruce, Senior Vice President & Human Resources Director
Ken Dale, Senior Vice President & Chief Financial Officer
Dave Gwizdowski, Senior Vice President, Revenue - Americas
Ellen Hale, Senior Vice President & Corporate Communications Director
Karen Kaiser, Senior Vice President, General Counsel & Corporate Secretary
Jim Kennedy, Senior Vice President, Strategic Planning
Daisy Veerdsingham, Senior Vice President, Revenue - International
Mimi Polk Gitlin, Head, Media Development & Production
Global news network founded in 1846; delivers fast, unbiased news from every corner of the world to all media platforms & formats.

ASSOCIATED TELEVISION INTERNATIONAL
4401 Wilshire Blvd
Los Angeles, CA 90010
Phone: 323-556-5600
Fax: 323-556-5610
E-mail: sales@ati.la
Web Site: http://www.associatedtelevision.com
David McKenzie, President
Murray Drechsler, Chief Financial Officer
Richard Casares, Executive Vice President
Justin Pierce, Senior Vice President
David Stephan, Vice President, Aquisitions & Marketing
Ralitsa Trifonova, International Sales Director
Produces & distributes movies, TV, radio, interactive media, literature & music.

AWESOMENESS FILMS
11821 Mississippi Ave
Los Angeles, CA 90025
Phone: 310-601-1960
E-mail: media@awesomenesstv.com
Matt Kaplan, President
Produces & distributes feature-length films for young adults.

AWESOMENESSTV
11821 Mississippi Ave
Los Angeles, CA 90025
Phone: 310-601-1960
E-mail: media@awesomenesstv.com
Web Site: http://www.awesomenesstv.com
Brian Roberts, Chief Executive Officer
Samie Kim Falvey, Chief Content Officer, Programming Service
James Deutch, Creative Director, Branded Entertainment
Produces television series & theatrical films. DreamWorks Animation has 51% interest, Hearst Corp. & Verizon have 24.5% each.

BARBARY POST
435 Pacific Ave
Ste 300
San Francisco, CA 94133
Phone: 415-989-9123
Fax: 415-989-9124
E-mail: contact@barbarypost.com
Bob Spector, Director
Kristen Jenkins, Executive Producer
Nick Tomnay, Editor
Matt O'Donnell, Editor
Greg Gilmore, VFX Compositor
Kent Pritchett, Colorist
Provides post-production services; specializes in commercial editorial, visual effects & finishing for TV, web & theatrical.

BARON SERVICES INC.
4930 Research Dr
Huntsville, AL 35805
Phone: 256-881-8811
Fax: 256-881-8283
E-mail: sales@baronservices.com
Web Site: http://www.baronservices.com
Robert O. Baron, President & Chief Executive Officer
John W. Wessinger, Chief Operating Officer
Bob Baron, Jr., Chief Products Officer
Ardell Hill, President, Broadcast Operations
Tom Thompson, Executive Vice President, Software Development
Bob Dreiseverd, Vice President & Director, Forecast Services
Kim Grantham, Vice President, Marketing
Bill Walker, Vice President, Radar Division
Glen Denny, Director, Digital Sales
Provides weather sensing, weather display & meteorological analysis tools.

BATJAC PRODUCTIONS INC.
9595 Wilshire Blvd
Ste 610
Beverly Hills, CA 90212
Phone: 310-278-9870
Fax: 323-272-7381
Gretchen Wayne, President
Produces TV film & tape series & stock footage, mostly John Wayne films.

BBC WORLDWIDE LTD.
Media Ctr
201 Wood Ln
London W12 7TQ
United Kingdom
Phone: 44-0-20-8433-2000
Fax: 44-0-20-8749-0538
Web Site: http://www.bbcworldwide.com
Tony Hall, Chairman
Tim Davie, Chief Executive Officer & Global Director
Andrew Bott, Chief Financial Officer
Daniel Heaf, Chief Digital Officer
Helen Jackson, Chief Content Officer
Marcus Arthur, President, UK & ANZ
Paul Dempsey, President, Global Markets
Charlotte Elson, Communications Director

Branch Offices:
CORAL GABLES: 255 Alhambra Cir, 10th Fl, Coral Gables, FL 33134. Phone: 305-461-6999. Fax: 305-441-0035.

LOS ANGELES: 10351 Santa Monica Blvd, Ste 250, Los Angeles, CA 90025. Phone: 310-228-1001.

NEW YORK: 1120 Ave of the Americas, New York, NY 10036-6700. Phone: 212-705-9300. Fax: 212-888-0576. Ann Sarnoff, President, BBC Worldwide - North America.

BRAZIL: Ave das Nacoes Unidas 12551, 17 Andar Conjunto 1738, San Paulo 05428-002, Brazil. Phone: 55-11-3443-7482.

Program Sources & Services

CANADA: 409 King St W, 5th Fl, Toronto, ON M5V 1K1, Canada. Phone: 416-362-3223. Fax: 416-204-0500.

MEXICO: Paseoda la Reforma #115, Piso 9, Colonia Lomas de Chapultepe CP 11000, Mexico. Phone: 52-55-52-01-9807. Fax: 52-55-52-02-3243.
Distributes programming; offices worldwide

BEAMLY
350 Fifth Ave
Ste 1700
New York, NY 10018
E-mail: hello@beamly.com
Web Site: http://beamly.com
Elio Leoni-Sceti, Chairman
Ernesto Schmitt, Co-Founder & Chief Executive Officer
Anthony Rose, Co-Founder & Chief Technology Officer
Max Bleyleden, Chief Financial Officer & Head, Business Development
Alex Nunes, Engineering Director
Simon Miller, Chief, Product & Content Development
Jason Forbes, Executive Vice President, USA

Branch Offices:
NEW YORK: 84 Wooster St, Ste 703, New York, NY 10012.
Social TV platform that enables users to follow TV shows, celebrities & other users.

BEAST
18 E 16th St
6th Fl
New York, NY 10003
Phone: 212-206-0660
Fax: 212-206-0667
E-mail: ekrajewski@beast.tv
Web Site: http://www.beast.tv
Elizabeth Krajewski, Executive Producer

Branch Offices:
ATLANTA: 3399 Peachtree Rd NE, Ste 200, Atlanta, GA 30326. Phone: 404-237-9977. Fax: 404-237-3923. E-mail: molly.baroco@beast.tv. Molly Baroco, Executive Producer.

AUSTIN: 512 Rio Grande St, Austin, TX 78701. Phone: 512-583-4567. Fax: 512-610-4600. E-Mail: brent@beast.tv. Brent Holt, Executive Producer.

CHICAGO: 435 N Michigan, Ste 2200, Chicago, IL 60611. Phone: 312-573-2400. Fax: 312-573-2404. E-Mail: mthornley@beast.tv. Melissa Thornley, Executive Producer.

ROYAL OAK: 209 W Sixth St, Royal Oak, MI 48067. Phone: 248-837-2410. Fax: 248-837-2411. E-mail: laura.hochthanner@beast.tv. Laura Hochthanner, Executive Producer.

SANTA MONICA: 1222 Sixth St, Santa Monica, CA 90401. Phone: 310-576-6300. Fax: 310-576-6305. E-mail: jerry.sukys@beast.tv. Jerry Sukys, Executive Producer.

SAN FRANCISCO: 500 Sansome St, 7th Fl, San Francisco, CA 94111. Phone: 415-392-6300. Fax: 415-392-2600. E-mail: jettinger@beast.tv. Jon Ettinger, Executive Producer. Specializes in commercials, web virals & music videos.

DAVE BELL ASSOCIATES INC.
3211 Cahuenga Blvd W
Ste 200
Los Angeles, CA 90068-1372
Phone: 323-851-7801

Dave Bell, Producer
Produces motion picture features, TV movies & specials, documentaries, TV & cable series.

BELLUM ENTERTAINMENT
2901 W Alameda Ave
Ste 500
Burbank, CA 91505
Phone: 818-480-4600
E-mail: info@bellument.com
Web Site: http://www.bellument.com
Mary Carole McDonnell, Founder & President
Peter McDonnell, Vice President, Production
Rebecca Walker, Vice President, Sales
Mack Carroll, Digital Development Director
Produces & distributes TV projects for broadcast, cable, digital & ancillary markets.

BETTER LIFE MEDIA
5800 Democracy Dr
Plano, TX 75024
Phone: 877-929-0439
Fax: 817-442-1390
E-mail: customersupport@yoursuccessstore.com
Web Site: http://www.betterlifemedia.com
Michael Burgess, President
Tom Weise, Executive Vice President, Business Development
Linda Domholt, Vice President, Talent Relations

BIG SHOULDERS DIGITAL VIDEO PRODUCTIONS
875 N Michigan Ave
Ste 3750
Chicago, IL 60611
Phone: 312-540-5400
E-mail: info@bigshoulders.com
Web Site: http://www.bigshoulders.com
Frank Hanes, President
Dave Burkett, Vice President, Post Production
Brad Fox, Vice President
Angelo Bosco, Producer/Project Manager
Provides video production & post production services.

BIG SKY EDIT
10 E 40th St
Ste 1701
New York, NY 10016
Phone: 212-683-4004
Fax: 212-889-6220
E-mail: cheryl@bigskyedit.com
Web Site: http://www.bigskyedit.com
Cheryl Panek, Executive Producer
Provides film editing post production services with full 2D and 3D graphics, sound design and HD finishing.

BIKINI EDIT
64 Wooster St
6th Fl
New York, NY 10012
Phone: 212-925-4200
Fax: 212-925-6167
E-mail: g@bikinieditorial.com
Web Site: http://www.bikiniedit.com
Gina Pagano, Executive Producer
Provides offline editorial services.

BITESIZETV
6250 Hollywood Blvd
Ste 300
Los Angeles, CA 90028
Phone: 323-461-0822
Web Site: http://www.bitesizetv.com
Produces reality & unscripted entertainment programming ranging from live broadcast TV to short-form digital.

BLAST DIGITAL
575 Lexington Ave
22nd Fl
New York, NY 10022
Phone: 212-752-4143
Fax: 212-752-4152
Web Site: http://www.blastny.com
Carolyn Mandlavitz, Supervisor, Audio Post Production
Joe O'Connell, Mixer & Sound Designer
Mat Guido, Associate Mixer & Sound Designer
Gerard Collins, Associate Mixer & Sound Designer
Offers full-service audio post-production services, specializing in sound engineering, sound design & music production for national TV commercials.

BLUEROCK
575 Lexington Ave
26th Fl
New York, NY 10022
Phone: 212-752-3348
Fax: 212-752-0307
Web Site: http://www.bluerockny.com
Jennifer Lederman, Vice President & Managing Director
Kelly Salmon, Head of Sales
Provides creative editing services.

BONDED SERVICES
504 Jane St
Ft Lee, NJ 07024
Phone: 201-944-3700
Fax: 201-592-0727
Web Site: http://www.bonded.com

Branch Offices:
BURBANK: 3205 Burton Ave, Burbank, CA 91504. Phone: 818-848-9766. Fax: 818-848-9849.

INGLEWOOD: Freight Division, 441 N Oak St, Inglewood, CA 90302. Phone: 310-680-6830. Fax: 310-680-9099.

CANADA: 288 Judson St, Unit 10, Toronto, ON M8Z 5T6, Canada. Phone: 416-252-5081. Fax: 416-252-3955. E-Mail: darm@bondedservices.com.

FRANCE: 73 Rue du Volga, Paris 75020, France. Phone: 33-01-43-79-68-00.

HONG KONG: Tung Chun Industrial Bldg, 11-13 Tai Yuen St, Nos 7 & 8, 11th Fl, Block B, Kwai Chung, New Territories, Hong Kong. Phone: 852-2425-6036. Fax: 852-2480-5935. E-Mail: bsi@bonded.com.hk.

THE NETHERLANDS: Tokyostr 13-15, 1175 RB Lijnden, Amsterdam, The Netherlands. Phone: 31-20-6015-031. Fax: 31-20-6041-567. E-Mail: mark_grossouw@bonded.nl.

UNITED KINGDOM: Aerodrome Way, Carnford Lane, Hounslow, Middlesex TW5 9QB, United Kingdom. Phone: 44-0-20-8897-7973. Fax: 44-0-20-8897-5539. E-Mail: sales@ftsbonded.com.
Provides storage & distribution of motion picture features, industrial & educational films, picture shorts, foreign language films, TV film & tape series; exports films; film handlers; imports films & TV film series; film rejuvenation & tape evaluation and environmental storage of films & tapes.

BONNEVILLE INTERNATIONAL
55 North 300 West
Salt Lake City, UT 84101
Phone: 801-575-7500

Fax: 801-575-7541
Web Site: http://www.bonneville.com
Darrell K. Brown, President
Kent Nate, Vice President & Chief Financial Officer
Mike Dowdle, Vice President & General Counsel
Designs, produces & places advertising, public service spots & programs.

BOOSEY & HAWKES MUSIC PUBLISHERS LTD.
Aldwych House
71-91 Aldwych
London WC2B 4HN
United Kingdom
Phone: 44-0-20-7054-7200
E-mail: ukhire@boosey.com
Web Site: http://www.boosey.com
John Minch, President & Chief Executive Officer
Andre de Raaff, Director
Andrew Gummer, Business Affairs Director
Edward Knighton, Group Finance Director
Janis Susskino, Publishing Director
Denis Wigman, Director

Branch Offices:
NEW YORK: 35 E 21st St, New York, NY 10010-6212. Phone: 212-358-5300. Fax: 212-358-5305. E-Mail: info.ny@boosey.com. Marc Ostrow, General Manager.

GERMANY: Lutzowufer 26, Berlin 10787, Germany. Phone: 49-0-30-25001300. Fax: 49-0-30-25001399. E-Mail: musikverlag@boosey.com. Winfried Jacobs, Managing Director.
Provides complete music services for all media: from production music to public domain classical works to commercial catalogs & their recordings.

BOSCO PRODUCTIONS
160 E Grand Ave
Chicago, IL 60611
Phone: 312-644-8300
Fax: 312-644-1893
E-mail: angelo@boscoproductions.com
Web Site: http://www.boscoproductions.com
Angela Bosco, President & Chief Executive Officer
Iwona Awlasewicz, Video Production Manager
Betty Rake, Studio Manager
Digital audio production facility; provides casting, production, & trafficking services.

BREATHE EDITING INC.
PO Box 4957
New York, NY 10185
Phone: 212-947-1748
E-mail: kenny@thinkbreathelive.com
Web Site: http://www.thinkbreathelive.com
Kenny Pedini, Managing Director, Executive Producer
Michael Schwartz, Creative Director, Editor
Provides video content production and post production services.

BROADCAST MEDIA GROUP INC.
1012 N Jackson St
Starkville, MS 39759
Phones: 662-324-2489; 888-324-2489
Fax: 662-324-2486
E-mail: info@broadcastmediagroup.com
Web Site: http://www.broadcastmediagroup.com
Robbie C. Coblentz, President
Provides videography, editing, DVD creation & duplication services.

BROADCAST MUSIC INC. (BMI)
10 Music Square East

Program Sources & Services

Nashville, TN 37203
Phone: 615-401-2000
E-mail: nashville@bmi.com
Web Site: http://www.bmi.com
Paul Karpowicz, Chairman
Michael O'Neill, President & Chief Executive Officer
John E. Cody, Chief Operating Officer & Executive Vice President
Bruce A. Esworthy, Chief Financial Officer & Senior Vice President, Finance
Marvin L. Berenson, Senior Vice President & General Counsel
Fred Cannon, Senior Vice President, Government Relations
Ann Sweeney, Senior Vice President, Glocal Policy
Lauren Branson, Director, Public Relations

Branch Offices:
ATLANTA: 3340 Peachtree Rd NE, Ste 570, Atlanta, GA 30326. Phone: 404-261-5151.

MIAMI: 1691 Michigan Ave, Ste 350, Miami, FL 33139. Phone: 305-673-5148.

NASHVILLE: 10 Music Sq E, Nashville, TN 37203-4399. Phone: 615-401-2000.

SAN JUAN: 255 Ponce de Leon, MCS Plz, Ste 208, San Juan, PR 00917. Phone: 787-754-6490.

WEST HOLLYWOOD: 8730 Sunset Blvd, 3rd Fl W, West Hollywood, CA 90069-2211. Phone: 310-659-9109.

UNITED KINGDOM: 84 Harley House, Marylebone Rd, London NW1 5HN, United Kingdom. Phone: 44-207486-2036.
Provides music performing rights & copyright clearance services.

BROAD GREEN PICTURES
1040 N Las Palmas Ave
Bldg 1
Los Angeles, CA 90038
Phone: 323-688-1800
E-mail: info@broadgreen.com
Web Site: http://broadgreen.com
Gabriel Hammond, Chief Executive Officer
Daniel Hammond, Chief Creative Officer
Matt Alvarez, President, Production
Marc Danon, President, Acquisitions & Co-Productions
Victor Moyers, President, Physical Production
Finances, produces & distributes films.

BROADWAY TELEVISION NETWORK
690 Eighth Ave
6th Floor
New York, NY 10036
Phone: 212-471-6077
Fax: 212-471-6088
E-mail: bmb@broadwaytv.com
Web Site: http://www.broadwayonline.com
Kay Koplovitz, Chairman
Bruce Brandwen, Chief Executive Officer
Don Roy King, Creative Director
Jerry Zaks, Creative Director
Produces & distributes Direct From Broadway musicals.

BROADWAY VIDEO ENTERTAINMENT
1619 Broadway
New York, NY 10019-7412
Phone: 212-265-7600
Fax: 212-713-1535
Web Site: http://www.broadwayvideo.com
Lorne Michaels, Founder
Jack Sullivan, Chief Executive Officer
Joseph Brady, Chief Financial Officer

Britta von Schoeler, Senior Vice President & General Manager
Provides post-production services; produces TV & film.

BUG EDITORIAL INC.
PO Box 660
North Salem, NY 10560
Phone: 212-625-1313
Fax: 212-625-1414
E-mail: andreb@bugedit.com
Web Site: http://www.bugedit.com
Andre Betz, Owner & Editor
Jane Weintraub, Executive Producer, New York

Branch Offices:
SANTA MONICA: 225 Santa Monica Blvd, 9th Fl, Santa Monica, CA 90401-2209. Phone: 310-393-2300. Kim Nagel, Executive Producer, Los Angeles; Josh Towvim, Editor, Los Angeles.
Post-production editorial studios.

BUNIM-MURRAY PRODUCTIONS
6007 Sepulveda Blvd
Van Nuys, CA 91411
Phone: 818-756-5100
Fax: 818-756-5140
E-mail: contactus@bunim-murray.com
Web Site: http://www.bunim-murray.com
Gil Goldschein, Chairman & Chief Executive Officer
Scott Freeman, Executive Vice President, Current Programming & Development
Fabian Andre, Senior Vice President, Business Development
David Berson, Senior Vice President, Business & Legal Affairs
Jim Johnston, Vice President, Creative Affairs
Bart Peele, Vice President, Operations
Produces reality TV programming.

BURRUD PRODUCTIONS INC.
468 N Camden Dr
2nd Fl
Beverly Hills, CA 90210
Phone: 310-860-5158
Fax: 562-595-5986
E-mail: info@burrud.com
Web Site: http://www.burrud.com
John Burrud, President & Chief Executive Officer

Branch Offices:
LONG BEACH: 3620 Long Beach Blvd, Ste C1, Long Beach, CA 90807.
Produces film programs on order including documentaries, wildlife, adventure & children's programming; stock footage; multimedia.

BUZZCO ASSOCIATES INC.
33 Bleecker St
New York, NY 10012
Phone: 212-473-8800
Fax: 212-473-8891
E-mail: info@buzzzco.com
Web Site: http://www.buzzzco.com
Vincent Cafarelli, President & Creative Director
Marilyn Kraemer, Principal & General Manager
Candy Kugel, Principal & Producer
Produces film & tape spot commercials, film programs on order, industrial & educational films, open-end film commercials (made for TV), theatrical shorts & animation.

BUZZFEED MOTION PICTURES
200 5th Ave
8th Fl
New York, NY 10010
Phone: 212-431-7464

Fax: 212-431-7461
E-mail: pr@buzzfeed.com
Web Site: http://www.buzzfeed.com
Jonah Peretti, Founder & Chief Executive Officer
Produces & distributes original short & long-form series as well as feature-length films.

CAMPUS GROUP COMPANIES
415 Madison Ave
7th Fl
New York, NY 10017
Phones: 914-961-1900; 914-395-1010
Fax: 914-961-0882
E-mail: sales@campusgroup.com
Web Site: http://www.campusgroup.com
Steve Campus, President
Produces film & tape spot commercials, film programs on order, TV film & tape series, newsreels, slides, theatrical shorts & multimedia; produces & distributes industrial & educational films; news & teleconference producer/networker.

CAMRAC STUDIOS
1775 Kuenzli St
Reno, NV 89502-1117
Phone: 775-323-0965
Fax: 775-323-1099
E-mail: jim@camrac.com
Web Site: http://www.camrac.com
Jim Mitchell, President
Independent videotape & film production studio; produces & distributes home videos; production; editing; character generation; digital video effects; stereo audio & camera color artwork; duplication; graphics & other services.

CANDID CAMERA INC.
PO Box 827
Monterey, CA 93942
Phone: 831-324-4811
Fax: 831-324-0759
E-mail: comments@candidcamera.com
Web Site: http://www.candidcamera.com
Peter Funt, President & Host
Produces Candid Camera & hidden-camera programs & commercials for broadcast & cable outlets.

CANNELL STUDIOS
7083 Hollywood Blvd
Hollywood, CA 90028
Phone: 323-465-5800
Fax: 323-856-7390
E-mail: questions@cannell.com
Web Site: http://www.cannell.com
Stephen J. Cannell, Chief Executive Officer & Chairman
Syndicates & distributes TV programs.

CAPTION COLORADO
Plaza 25, 8300 East Maplewood Ave
Ste 300
Greenwood Village, CO 80111
Phones: 720-489-5662; 800-775-7838
Fax: 720-489-5664
Web Site: http://www.captioncolorado.com
R.T. Tad Polumbus, Chief Executive Officer
Troy Greenwood, Chief Operating Officer & Chief Technology Officer
Kurt Suppes, Chief Financial Officer
John Irwin, Senior Vice President, Sales & Marketing
Randy Holyfield, Vice President, Business Development
Mike Lyons, Vice President, Offline Division
Provides real-time closed captioning.

CAPTIONMAX
2438 27th Ave S

Minneapolis, MN 55406
Phone: 612-341-3566
Fax: 612-341-2345
E-mail: donna@captionmax.com
Web Site: http://www.captionmax.com
Gerald Freda, President & Chief Operating Officer
Max Duckler, Chief Executive Officer
Donna Horn, Executive Vice President, Business Development
Chris Leininger, Technology Director
Lindsay Beiriger, Business Development Manager
Emily Bell, Technical Sales & Services Manager
Maridelle B. Hannah, Business Development Manager
Nate Otterdahl, Real-time Services Manager

Branch Offices:
BURBANK: 441 N Varney, Burbank, CA 91502. Phone: 818-295-2500. Fax: 818-295-2509. Elizabeth Rojas, Project Manager.

NEW YORK: 159 W 25th St, Ste 1009, New York, NY 10001. Phone: 212-462-0060. Fax: 212-462-0061.

SOUTH RIDING: 26171 Glasgow Dr, South Riding, VA 20152. Phone: 703-327-7735. Fax: 703-327-7695.
Provides captioning, subtitling & audio description for all media; FTP services & in-house digital encoding.

CASTLE ROCK ENTERTAINMENT
335 N Maple Dr
Beverly Hills, CA 90210
Phone: 310-285-2300
Web Site: http://www.warnerbros.com
Martin Shafer, Chairman & Chief Executive Officer
Gregory M. Paul, President & Chief Operating Officer
Glenn Padnick, President, Castle Rock Television
Andrew Scheinman, Creative Director
Rob Reiner, Film Director
Produces feature films; a motion-picture production company. Division of Warner Bros. Pictures.

CATHOLIC COMMUNICATION CAMPAIGN
3211 Fourth St NE
Washington, DC 20017-1194
Phone: 202-541-3000
Fax: 202-541-3179
E-mail: ccc@usccb.org
Web Site: http://www.usccb.org/ccc
Thomas J. Costello, Chairman
Helen Osman, Communications Secretary
Funds & produces documentary & religious programs, public service messages & radio programs; programs available for sale & licensing.

CBC/RADIO-CANADA
PO Box 3220
Station C
Ottawa, ON K1Y 1E4
Canada
Phones: 613-288-6033; 866-220-6045
Fax: 613-288-6045
E-mail: liaison@radio-canada.ca
Web Site: http://www.cbc.radio-canada.ca
Timothy Casgrain, Chairman
Hubert T. Lacroix, President & Chief Executive Officer
Sylvain Lafrance, Executive Vice President, French Services
Richard Stursberg, Executive Vice President, English Services

2017 Edition   E-109

Program Sources & Services

Johanne Charbonneau, Vice President & Chief Financial Officer
Raymond Carnovale, Vice President & Chief Technology Officer
William B. Chambers, Vice President, Communications

C.B. DISTRIBUTION CO. — See listing for Jess S. Morgan & Co.

CBS NEWS INC.
555 W 57th St
New York, NY 10019
Phones: 212-975-3247; 800-777-8398
Fax: 212-975-1893
Web Site: http://www.cbsnews.com
David Rhodes, President
John Frazee, Senior Vice President, News Services
Sonya McNair, Senior Vice President, Communications
Ingrid Ciprian-Matthews, Vice President, News
Marsha Cooke, Vice President, News Services
Christopher Isham, Vice President & Bureau Chief, Washington DC
Chris Licht, Vice President, Programming & Executive Producer, CBS This Morning
Crystal Johns, Talent Development & Diversity Director

CBS TELEVISION DISTRIBUTION
2450 Colorado Ave
Ste 500E
Santa Monica, CA 90404
Phone: 310-264-3300
Web Site: http://www.cbstvd.com
Paul Franklin, President
Steven A. LoCascio, Chief Operating Officer
Stephen Hackett, President, Sales
Hillery Estey McLoughlin, President, Creative Affairs
Paul Montoya, President, Media Sales
Jonathan Bingaman, Executive Vice President, Domestic Cable Sales
Robert Schildhouse, Executive Vice President, Digital Licensing & Distribution

Branch Offices:
ATLANTA: 2002 Summit Blvd, Ste 875, Atlanta, GA 30319. Phone: 404-847-9989.

CHICAGO: 455 N Cityfront Plz Dr, Ste 2910, Chicago, IL 60611. Phone: 312-644-7500. Fax: 312-644-7506.

DALLAS: 12001 N Central Expwy, Ste 1300, Dallas, TX 75243. Phone: 972-701-8823.

LOS ANGELES: 2450 Colorado Ave, Ste 500E, Santa Monica, CA 90404. Phone: 310-264-3300.
Produces & distributes first-run series & offers worldwide television syndication. Unit of CBS Studios Inc.

CBS TELEVISION STUDIOS
5555 Melrose Ave
Los Angeles, CA 90038
Phone: 323-956-5000
Web Site: https://www.cbscorporation.com/portfolio/cbs-television-studios
Armando Nunez, President & Chief Executive Officer, CBS Studios International
Amy Powell, Jr., President, Paramount Television
Barry Chamberlain, President, Sales CBS Studios International
Glen Geller, Senior Vice President, Current Programming
Lauri Metrose, Senior Vice President, Communications

Bryan Seabury, Senior Vice President, Drama Development
The television production & distribution arm of CBS Corp.

CHANNEL Z EDIT
15 S Fifth St
Ste 616
Minneapolis, MN 55402
Phone: 612-370-0016
Fax: 612-370-0160
E-mail: ace@channelzedit.com
Web Site: http://www.channelzedit.com
Ace Allgood, Producer
Kelly Nelson, Producer
Provides creative, editorial & post-production services.

CHAPMAN/LEONARD STUDIO EQUIPMENT INC.
12950 Raymer St
Hollywood, CA 91605
Phones: 888-883-6559; 818-764-6726
Fax: 818-764-6730
E-mail: cristine@chapman-leonard.com
Web Site: http://www.chapman-leonard.com
Charles Huenergardt, Chief Operating Officer & Coordinator, Special Projects
Christine Chapman-Huenergardt, Vice President, Marketing Director & Sales Representative
Dana Kuprianczyk, Rental & Customer Service Manager
David Bullard, Equipment & Stage Rental Supervisor
Gilbert Alvarado, Shipping Coordinator
Annette Kiatpiriya, Leasing Coordinator

Branch Offices:
ALBUQUERQUE: 9201 Pan American Frwy NE, Albuquerque, NM 87118. Phone: 888-758-4826.

AUSTIN: 1901 E 51st St, Stage 3, Austin, TX 78723. Phones: 512-473-0084; 888-758-4826. Fax: 512-473-0042.

NEW ORLEANS: 660 Distributors Row, Elmwood Business Park, Sts C & D, New Orleans, LA 70123. Phones: 504-731-6050; 888-758-4826. Fax: 504-731-6051.

NORTH HOLLYWOOD: 12950 Raymer St, North Hollywood, CA 91605. Phones: 818-764-6726; 888-883-6559. Fax: 818-764-6728.

UNITED KINGDOM: Kingley Park, Station Road, Unit 5, Kings Langley WD4 8GW, United Kingdom. Phone: 44-0-1-92-326-5953. Fax: 44-0-1-92-326-8315. Michaela Barnes, Manager; Dennis Fraser, Managing Director.
Manufactures & rents camera support equipment for motion picture & TV use; also offers sound stage & production facility rentals.

CHERNIN ENTERTAINMENT
1733 Ocean Ave
Santa Monica, CA
Phone: 310-899-1205
Peter Chernin, Chairman
Dante Di Loreto, President, Television
Jenno Toppin, President, Film
Produces feature films & TV programs.

CHRISTIAN CHURCH (DISCIPLES OF CHRIST), COMMUNICATION MINISTRIES
PO Box 1986
Disciples Ctr
Indianapolis, IN 46206-1986

Phone: 317-635-3100
Fax: 317-713-2417
E-mail: chiggins@disciples.org
Web Site: http://www.disciples.org
Wanda Bryant-Wills, Executive Director
Christopher G. Higgins, Internet & New Media Manager

CHRISTIAN TELEVISION NETWORK
6922 142nd Ave
Largo, FL 33771
Phone: 727-535-5622
Fax: 727-531-2497
Web Site: http://www.ctnonline.com
Bob D'Andrea, President & Founder
Provides 24-hour Christian programming.

THE CHRISTOPHERS
5 Hanover Sq
11th Fl
New York, NY 10004
Phones: 212-759-4050; 888-298-4050
Fax: 212-838-5073
E-mail: mail@christophers.org
Web Site: http://www.christophers.org
Mary Ellen Robinson, Vice President
Produces & distributes syndicated half-hour radio series, one-minute radio spots & quarter-hour radio programs.

CHURCH FEDERATION OF GREATER INDIANAPOLIS INC.
1100 W 42nd St
Ste 345
Indianapolis, IN 46268
Phone: 317-926-5371
Fax: 317-926-5373
E-mail: churches@churchfederationindy.org
Web Site: http://www.churchfederationindy.org
Angelique Walker-Smith, Executive Director
Jim Miller, Associate Director, Programs & Community Ministries
Ray Marquette, Development & Membership
Produces religious TV programs.

THE CHURCH OF JESUS CHRIST OF LATTER-DAY SAINTS
50 E North Temple St
Salt Lake City, UT 84150
Phone: 801-240-1000
E-mail: 2010550-prs@ldschurch.org
Web Site: http://www.lds.org
Produces religious programming.

CHURCH WORLD SERVICE
PO Box 968
28606 Phillips St
Elkhart, IN 46515
Phones: 574-264-3102; 800-297-1516
Fax: 574-262-0966
E-mail: cwsinfo@cwsglobal.org
Web Site: http://www.cwsglobal.org
John L. McCullough, President & Chief Executive Officer
Joanne Rendall, Chief Financial Officer & Deputy Director, Operations
Maurice Bloem, Executive Vice President
William Wildey, Vice President, Development & Fundraising
Matthew Hackwork, Marketing & Communications Director
Ann Walle, Innovation & Strategic Affairs Director

Branch Offices:
NEW YORK: 475 Riverside Dr, Ste 700, New York, NY 10115. Phone: 212-870-2061. Fax: 212-870-3523. Lesley Crosson, Media Relations Officer.

WASHINGTON, DC: 110 Maryland Ave NE, Ste 401, Washington, DC 20002. Phone: 202-481-6937. Fax: 202-543-0653.
Produces film/tape spot commercials, development related films & slides.

CINECRAFT PRODUCTIONS INC.
2515 Franklin Blvd
Cleveland, OH 44113
Phone: 216-781-2300
Fax: 216-781-1067
E-mail: info@cinecraft.com
Web Site: http://www.cinecraft.com
Neil G. McCormick, Chairman
Maria E. Keckan, President
Daniel E. Keckan, Vice President, Sales & Marketing
Scott Minium, Executive Producer
Devon Collins, Producer & Editor
Kurt Albrecht, Senior Editor & Cameraman
Mark Conlon, Senior Programmer & IT Specialist
Provides video & film production, CD-ROM, DVD & web development.

CINEDIGM
1901 Ave of the Stars
12th Fl
Los Angeles, CA 90067
Phone: 424-281-5400
Web Site: http://www.cinedigm.com
Chris McGuirk, Chairman & Chief Executive Officer
Gary S. Loffredo, President, Digital Cinema Services, General Counsel & Secretary, Cinedigm
Adam Mizel, Chief Operating Officer
Jeffrey Edell, Chief Financial Officer
Susan Margolin, President, Docurama & Special Acquisitions
Bill Sondheim, President, Entertainment Group
Yolanda Macias, Executive Vice President, Acquisitions, Forecast, Planning & Digital Sales
Jill Newhouse, Executive Vice President, Marketing & Communications
Erick Opeka, Executive Vice President, Digital Networks
Norbert Hudak, Senior Vice President, Marketing & Brand Management
Bobbi Levinson, Senior Vice President, Production
Eric Trevore, Senior Vice President, Information Technology & Chief Information Officer

Branch Offices:
NEW YORK: 902 Broadway, 9th Fl, New York, NY 10010. Phones: 212-206-8600; 212-598-4898.
Distributes films & TV programming.

CINEGROUPE
3401 St-Antoine Ouest
Montreal, PQ H3Z 1X1
Canada
Phone: 514-524-7567
E-mail: distribution@cinegroupe.ca
Jacques Pettigrew, Founder, President & Chief Executive Officer
Creates, produces & distributes hit animation & CGI entertainment programming in all media for the worldwide marketplace.

CINELAN
407 Broome St
New York, NY 10013
Phone: 888-645-5551
E-mail: info@cinelan.com
Web Site: http://www.cinelan.com
Douglas Dicconson, Founder

Karol Martesko-Fenster, Founder
Produce & distribute short film programs.

CINEMA ARTS INC.
The Art Bldg
Huckleberry Hill
Angeles, PA 18460
Phone: 570-676-4152
Fax: 570-676-9194
John Allen, President
Beverly Allen, Vice President
Motion picture laboratory; produces optical transfers for 35mm, 16mm & super 16mm; enlargements & reductions including anamorphic & Vistavision formats; color & black & white; film-to-tape telecine transfer; specializes in shrunken & deteriorating film; stock footage 1895-1965.

CINE MAGNETICS DIGITAL & VIDEO LABORATORIES
100 Business Park Dr
Armonk, NY 10504
Phones: 914-273-7500; 800-431-1102
Fax: 914-273-7575
E-mail: sales@cinemagnetics.com
Web Site: http://www.cinemagnetics.com
Joseph J. Barber, Jr., President
Kenneth Wynne, Vice President & General Manager
Haitham Wahab, Chief Financial Officer

Branch Offices:
CHARLOTTE: 957 Whalley Rd, Charlotte, VT 05445. Phone: 800-431-1102. Fax: 914-273-7575.

OCEANSIDE: 5495 Parrolette Ct, Oceanside, CA 92057. Phone: 760-967-9523. Cindy Taylor, Sales/Client Services.

STUDIO CITY: 3765 Cahuenga Blvd W, Studio City, CA 91604-3504. Phone: 818-623-2560. Fax: 818-623-2565. Tim Willis, Technical Director.

Provides DVD authoring & compression, DVD & CD replication & duplication, video on demand, video streaming, digital asset management, video duplication, foreign language subtitling & language, replacement & custom design, printing & packaging services.

CISNEROS MEDIA DISTRIBUTION
121 Alhambra Plz
Ste 1400
Coral Gables, FL 33134
Phone: 305-442-3411
Fax: 305-446-4743
Web Site: http://www.cisnerosmediadist.com
Manuel Perez, Vice President & Chief Financial Officer
Cesar Diaz, Vice President, Sales
Rafael Garcia, Vice President, New Media Distribution
Jorge A. Pino, Vice President, Music
Hector Beltran, Sales Director, Central America
Todd Michael Jamison, Public Relations Director
Daniel Rodriguez, Sales Director, Latin America
Miguel Somoza, Regional Sales Director

Branch Offices:
SPAIN: c/o Juan Julio Baena, Maria Auxiliadora 26 Majadahonda, Madrid 28020, Spain. Phone: 34-91-639-3965. Fax: 34-91-399-1226.

VENEZUELA: Final Ave La Salle, Edf Antaraju, Stano Oficina #1, Colina de los Caobos, Caracas DF 1050, Venezuela. Phone: 58-212-708-9532. Fax: 58-212-782-3464. Jonathan Blum, Vice President & General Manager, Venevision; Fernando Aizaga, Vice President, Sales, Venevision; Soledad Leiva, International Acquisitions Manager, Venevision. Distributes TV programming to more than 100 countries & 20 languages; represents the products of Venevision Productions & Venevision, in addition to catalogues of third parties; distributes original Spanish-language films via Pay-Per-View, Video-On-Demand, DVD, cable, satellite and broadcast television in the U.S. & Caribbean. A Cisneros Company.

DICK CLARK PRODUCTIONS INC.
2900 Olympic Blvd
Santa Monica, CA 90404
Phone: 310-255-4600
Fax: 310-255-4601
Web Site: http://www.dickclark.com
Allen Shapiro, Chief Executive Officer
Michael Mahan, President
Amy Thurlow, Chief Operating Officer & Chief Financial Officer
Barry Adelman, Executive Vice President, Television
Michael Antinoro, Executive Vice President, Programming
Mark Bracco, Executive Vice President, Programming & Development
Tim Bock, Senior Vice President, Production
Produces TV, movies, radio programming & stage performances.

CNET NETWORKS INC.
235 Second St
San Francisco, CA 94105
Phone: 415-344-2000
Web Site: http://www.cnet.com
Scott Ard, Editor-in-Chief
Brian Cooley, Editor at Large, CNET TV

Branch Offices:
NEW YORK: 28 E 28th St, New York, NY 10016. Phone: 646-472-4000. Fax: 646-472-3912.

SOMERVILLE: 55 Davis Sq, Somerville, MA 02144. Phone: 617-284-8633. Fax: 617-284-8688.
Division of CBS Interactive Inc.

CNN NEWSOURCE SALES INC.
One CNN Center NW
Atlanta, GA 30303
Phones: 404-827-2085; 404-827-5032
Fax: 404-827-4959; 404-827-3640
Web Site: http://newsource.cnn.com
Provides sales & marketing of CNN Newsource & its services. Division of Turner Broadcasting System Inc.

COASTLINE COMMUNITY COLLEGE CENTER
11460 Warner Ave
Fountain Valley, CA 92708-2597
Phone: 714-546-7600
Web Site: http://www.coastline.edu
Ding-Jo Currie, President
Dan Jones, Instructional Systems Development Dean
Lynn Dahnke, Telecourse Marketing Director
Michelle Ma, Marketing & Public Relations Director
Laurie Melby, Telecourse Production & Telemedia Director
Produces & markets college courses by TV.

COLLEGE & SCHOOL NETWORK
c/o North American Catholic Educational Programming Foundation
2419 Hartford Ave
Johnston, RI 02919-1719
Phone: 401-934-1100
Fax: 401-934-2240
E-mail: tchodelka@nacepf.net
Web Site: http://www.csn-ed.net
John Primeau, Director
Offers distance learning, full semester educational courses to public, private & parochial schools & the general subscribing public.

COLLEGE BOWL CO.
5900 Canoga Ave
Ste 100
Woodland Hills, CA 91367-5009
Phones: 818-610-8225; 800-234-2695
Fax: 818-610-8230
E-mail: frank@collegebowl.com
Web Site: http://www.collegebowl.com
Richard Reid, President
Mary Oberembt, Vice President & General Manager
Franklin J. Gencur, Associate General Manager
Produces TV film & tape series.

COLUMBIA TRISTAR TELEVISION GROUP
— See listing for Sony Pictures Television.

COMPRO PRODUCTIONS INC.
2055 Boar Tusk Rd NE
Conyers, GA 30012-3801
Phone: 770-918-8163
E-mail: steve@compro-atl.com
Web Site: http://www.compro-atl.com
Nels A. Anderson, President & Director
Steve Brinson, Vice President & Producer
Kim Anderson, Chief Financial Officer & Executive Producer
Provides film & video production services; corporate & image films, documentaries, infomercials, episodic television; post production, DVD authoring, streaming video for web, extensive film & tape stock library - international & domestic scenics & culture; aerial & underwater production; outdoor & sports.

COMTEL VIDEO SERVICES INC.
PO Box 416
Ashland, OR 97520-0014
Phone: 541-708-5732
E-mail: bbeggs@comtelvideo.com
Web Site: http://www.comtelvideo.com
Robert C. Beggs, President
Provides video programming to TV stations & cable systems on Pacific islands.

CONCORDIA PUBLISHING HOUSE
3558 S Jefferson Ave
St Louis, MO 63118-3968
Phones: 314-268-1000; 800-325-3040
Fax: 800-490-9889
E-mail: order@cph.org
Web Site: http://www.cph.org
Bruce G. Kintz, President & Chief Executive Officer
Jonathan D. Schultz, Vice President & Corporate Counsel
Paul T. McCain, Publisher & Executive Director, Editorial
Peggy Anderson, Executive Director, Finance
Steve Harris, Executive Director, IT

FULLY SEARCHABLE • CONTINUOUSLY UPDATED • DISCOUNT RATES FOR PRINT PURCHASERS
For more information call **800-771-9202** or visit **www.warren-news.com**

Paul Brunette, Sales Director
Produces & distributes Christian films & videos.

CONDE NAST ENTERTAINMENT
One World Trade Ctr
New York, NY 10007
Phone: 212-286-2860
Web Site: http://www.condenast.com
Dawn Ostroff, President
Cameron Blanchard, Executive Vice President, Corporate Communications, Conde Nast
Sahar Elhabashi, Executive Vice President & Chief Operating Officer
Joe LaBracio, Executive Vice President, Alternative Programming
Jeremy Steckler, Executive Vice President, Motion Pictures
Lisa Valentino, Senior Vice President, Digital Sales, Conde Nast
Jonathan Koa, Vice President, Scripted Programming
Develops & distributes digital video, TV & film.

CONNECTICUT PUBLIC BROADCASTING INC.
1049 Asylum Ave
Hartford, CT 06105
Phones: 860-275-7550; 800-683-1899
E-mail: wherewelive@wnpr.org
Web Site: http://www.cpbn.org
Jerry Franklin, President & Chief Executive Officer
Nancy Bauer, Vice President, Sales & Corporate Sponsorship
Tanya Meck, Leadership Giving Director
Carol Sisco, Human Resources
Maria Zone, Media Relations

Branch Offices:
NEW HAVEN: 70 Audubon St, New Haven, CT 06510. Phone: 203-776-9677.
Produces public TV programming.

CONSULATE
536 Broadway
9th Fl
New York, NY 10012
Phone: 212-219-0020
Fax: 212-219-0590
E-mail: lisa@consulatefilm.com
Web Site: http://www.consulatefilm.com
Lisa Binassarie, Managing Director
Charlyn Derrick, Senior Producer
Provides film editing services.

CONTENT MEDIA CORP. LTD.
225 Arizona Ave
Ste 250
Santa Monica, CA 90401
Phone: 301-576-1059
Fax: 310-576-1859
E-mail: la@contentmediacorp.com
Web Site: http://www.contentmediacorp.com
Jamie Carmichael, President
Saralo MacGregor, Executive Vice President, Acquisitions, Development & Sales
Melissa Wohl, Senior Vice President, Worldwide Distribution
Harry White, Head of Sales
Owns & distributes film, TV & digital assets.

Program Sources & Services

CONTINENTAL FILM PRODUCTIONS CORP.
PO Box 5126
1466 Riverside Dr, Ste E
Chattanooga, TN 37406
Phone: 423-622-1193
Fax: 423-629-0853
E-mail: info@continentalfilm.com
Web Site: http://www.continentalfilm.com
Provides production services, including scripting & duplication.

CONTRADICTION FILMS
3103 Neilson Way
Ste C
Santa Monica, CA 90405
Phone: 310-396-8558
E-mail: jo@contradictionfilms.com
Web Site: http://www.contradictionfilms.com

Branch Offices:
AUSTIN: 100 Congress Ave, Austin, TX 78701. E-Mail: tomas@contradictionfilms.com. Tim Carter, Co-Owner, Writer & Producer.

CANADA: Quayside Tower One, 1033 Marinaside Crescent, Ste 3706, Vancouver, BC V6Z 3A3, Canada. Phone: 604-915-9646. E-Mail: tim@contradictionfilms.com. Tomas Harlan, Co-Owner.
Produces film, TV & new media programming.

COOKIE JAR ENTERTAINMENT INC.
266 King St W
2nd Fl
Toronto, ON M5V 1H8
Canada
Phone: 416-977-3238
E-mail: info@thecookiejarcompany.com
Web Site: http://www.cjar.com
Michael Hirsh, Chief Executive Officer
Toper Taylor, President & Chief Operating Officer
Aaron Ames, Chief Financial Officer
Jean-Michel Ciszewski, Senior Vice President, Sales & Distribution
Carrie Dumont, Senior Vice President, Business & Legal Affairs
Kenneth Locker, Senior Vice President, Digital Media
Tom Mazza, Worldwide TV Head

Branch Offices:
BURBANK: 4100 W Alameda Ave, Ste 201, Burbank, CA 91505. Phone: 818-955-5400.
Produces, distributes & markets quality children's & family programming; maintains dedicated operations involved in programs & product development/production, merchandising/licensing & marketing/distribution.

CORGAN MEDIA LAB
401 N Houston St
Dallas, TX 75202
Phone: 214-748-2000
Fax: 214-653-8281
E-mail: media.lab@corganmedialab.com
Web Site: http://www.corganmedialab.com
Fran Gaconnier, Executive Producer
Creates 3D elements & motion graphics for TV, broadcast & interactive experiences.

COSMO STREET
2036 Broadway
Santa Monica, CA 90404
Phone: 310-828-6666
Fax: 310-453-9699
E-mail: yvette@cosmostreet.com
Web Site: http://www.cosmostreet.com
Yvette Cobarrubias, Executive Producer

Branch Offices:
NEW YORK: 28 W 25th St, New York, NY 10010. Phone: 212-625-6800. Fax: 212-625-6888. Maura Woodward, Executive Producer.
Provides film & TV editing services

CRACKLE
10202 W Washington Blvd
Culver City, CA 90232
Phone: 415-877-4800
Fax: 415-331-5501
Web Site: http://www.crackle.com
Eric Berger, Executive Vice President, Digital Media & General Manager
Distributes TV, movies & original programming. Unit of Sony Pictures Television.

CRAVEN FILM
5 W 19th St
3rd Floor
New York, NY 10011
Phone: 212-463-7190
Fax: 212-627-4761
E-mail: info@cravenfilms.com
Web Site: http://www.cravenfilms.com
Full service audio-visual producer: industrial, training, educational, fund-raising, governmental, business & informational films & videos; commercials & public service announcements; motion picture shorts; foreign language productions.

CREW CUTS
28 W 44th St
22nd Fl
New York, NY 10036
Phone: 212-302-2828
Fax: 212-302-9846
E-mail: nancy@crewcuts.com
Web Site: http://www.crewcuts.com
Nancy Shames, Executive Producer
Dani Epstein, Sales Representative
Provides post-production editorial services.

CRITICAL CONTENT
1040 N Las Palmas Ave
Bldg 40
Los Angeles, CA 90038
Phone: 323-860-8600
Web Site: http://www.criticalcontent.com
Tom Forman, Chief Executive Officer
Andrew Marcus, President & Chief Operating Officer
Produced scripted & unscripted original programming for broadcast, cable & digital platforms.

CRN DIGITAL TALK RADIO
10487 Sunland Blvd
Sunland, CA 91040-1905
Phone: 818-352-7152
Fax: 818-352-3229
E-mail: info@crntalk.com
Web Site: http://www.crntalk.com
Michael Horn, President
Erin Farrell, Vice President, Affiliate Relations
Jennifer Horn, Vice President, Marketing & Sales
Paul Stern, Vice President, Operations
Erik Hines, Production Director
Provides talk radio programming for the telecommunications industry; develops new & unique talk talent & distributes it for use in cable audio packages & as VOD; provides cable systems with a personalized radio station designed to reach customers at the point of sale in a soothing & entertaining environment. Division of Cable Radio Networks.

CROSSPOINT
940 Wadsworth Blvd
2nd Fl
Lakewood, CO 80214
Phone: 303-233-2700
Fax: 303-232-6460
E-mail: info@crosspoint.com
Web Site: http://www.crosspoint.com
Kim Croy, General Manager
Jenn Bang, Client Services Manager
Corey Hayes, Business Development Manager
Shawn Roberts, Project Coordinator & Scheduler
Provides production & post-production services; HD production & editing facility; tape-to-tape color correction, non-linear off-line suites, digital image compositing, motion graphics & animation; audio suite for mix, edit, sweetening; local and remote VO record via ISDN, etc.; web site design, video to CD-ROM, CD-ROM duplication, interactive business cards, video for the web, DVD authoring.

CROSSROADS CHRISTIAN COMMUNICATIONS INC.
PO Box 5100
1295 N Service Rd
Burlington, ON L7R 4M2
Canada
Phone: 905-335-7100
Fax: 905-332-6655
E-mail: crossroads@crossroads.ca
Web Site: http://www.crossroads.ca
David Mainse, Founder
Norma-Jean Mainse, Co-founder

Branch Offices:
NEW YORK: PO Box 486, New York, NY 14302.
Provides Christian programming worldwide.

CROWN INTERNATIONAL PICTURES INC.
301 N Canon Dr
Ste 228
Beverly Hills, CA 90210
Phone: 310-657-6700
Fax: 310-657-4489
E-mail: crown@crownintlpictures.com
Web Site: http://www.crownintlpictures.com
Mark Tenser, President & Chief Executive Officer
Scott E. Schwimer, Senior Vice President
Lisa Agay, Publicity & Advertising Director
Produces & distributes theatrical feature films.

CRYSTAL CATHEDRAL MINISTRIES
13280 Chapman Ave
Garden Grove, CA 92840
Phone: 714-971-4000
E-mail: bonnie.balloch@hourofpower.org
Web Site: http://www.crystalcathedral.org
Robert H. Schuller, Founder
Michelle Cavinder, Learning Network & Women's Ministries Director
Sheila Coleman, Family Ministries Director
Jim Kok, Care Ministries Director
Maureen A. Winer, Congregational Life Ministry
Produces & distributes original Christian programming.

CRYSTAL PICTURES INC.
2000 Riverside Dr
Asheville, NC 28804
Phone: 828-285-9995
Fax: 828-285-9997
E-mail: cryspic@aol.com
Joshua Tager, President
Jane Ann Rolston, TV Sales Executive
Produces, distributes & syndicates features, documentaries & shorts.

CTV INC.
PO Box 9
Station O
Scarborough, ON M4A 2M9
Canada
Phones: 416-332-5000; 800-461-1542
Web Site: http://www.ctv.ca
Robert Hurst, President
Alexis Hood, Manager, Communications

Branch Offices:
CANADA: Nine Channel Nine Ct, Scarborough, ON M1S 4B5, Canada.
Produces newsreels; produces & distributes industrial & educational films & TV film/tape series; news; stock footage; imports TV film series.

CUT & RUN
Cinema House
93 Wardour St
London W1F 0UD
United Kingdom
Phone: 44-0-20-7432-9696
Fax: 44-0-20-7432-9697
Web Site: http://www.cutandrun.tv
James Tomkinson, Managing Director

Branch Offices:
NEW YORK: 599 Broadway, 12th Fl, New York, NY 10012. Phone: 212-260-8900. E-Mail: angie.aguilera@cutandrun.tv. Ran Martin, Executive Producer.

SANTA MONICA: 1635 12th St., Santa Monica, CA 90404. Phone: 310-450-1116. Fax: 310-450-1166. E-Mail: michelle@cutandrun.tv. Michelle Burke, Managing Director.

HONG KONG: 14/F One Hysan Ave, Causeway Bay, Hong Kong. Phone: 852-9184-4813. E-Mail: nick.diss@cutandrun.tv. Nick Diss, Contact.
Provides offline editing services.

CUTTERS
515 N State St
Ste 2500
Chicago, IL 60654
Phone: 312-644-2500
Fax: 312-644-2501
E-mail: craig@cutters.com
Web Site: http://www.cutters.com
Phil Barton, Chief Financial Officer
Chuck Silverman, Sales & Marketing Director
Cindy Duffy, Executive Producer
Nicole Visram, Executive Producer
Arnell Patscott, Chief Engineer

Branch Offices:
SANTA MONICA: 1657 Euclid St, Santa Monica, CA 90404. Phone: 310-309-3780. Fax: 310-309-3779. E-Mail: infola@cutters.com. Editorial boutique.

CWK NETWORK INC.
6849 Peachtree Dunwoody Rd
Building 4-150
Atlanta, GA 30328
Phones: 404-459-8081; 888-598-5437
E-mail: sales@cwknetwork.com
Web Site: http://connectwithkids.com
Stacey DeWitt, President, Chief Executive Officer & Director
Produces & syndicates programs focusing on the health, education & well-being of children.

DAPTV ASSOCIATES
820 Westbourne Dr
Ste 4
West Hollywood, CA 90069
Phone: 310-867-5881

Program Sources & Services

E-mail: dazars44@gmail.com
Web Site: http://www.daptv.com; http://www.ieditvideo.com
Don Azars, Writer, Director, Editor & Producer
Provides program & video development services & distributes film programs on order.

DAY 1
2715 Peachtree Rd NE
Atlanta, GA 30305
Phones: 888-411-DAY-1; 404-815-9110
Fax: 404-815-0495
E-mail: pwallace@day1.org
Web Site: http://day1.org
Thomas Keuneke, Chief Financial Officer
Peter M. Wallace, Executive Producer & Host
Donal A. Jones, Production Coordinator & Audio Engineer
C. Patricia Reagan, Philanthropy Director
Produces the religious radio program, Day 1 (formerly The Protestant Hour). Ministry of the Alliance for Christian Media Inc.

DAY OF DISCOVERY (RBC MINISTRIES)
3000 Kraft Ave SE
Grand Rapids, MI 49512
Phones: 616-974-2210; 800-653-8333
Fax: 616-957-5741
Web Site: http://www.rbc.org
Richard De Haan, President

Branch Offices:
CANADA: PO Box 1622, Windsor, ON N9A 6Z7, Canada. Phone: 519-979-1073. E-Mail: canada@rbc.org.
Produces & distributes religious programs; distributes TV film & tape series.

DEBMAR-MERCURY
225 Santa Monica Blvd
8th Fl
Santa Monica, CA 90401
Phone: 310-393-6000
Fax: 310-393-6110
Web Site: http://www.debmarmercury.com
Ira Bernstein, Co-President
Mort Marcus, Co-President
Lonnie Burstein, Executive Vice President, Programming & Production
Alexandra Jewett, Executive Vice President, Programming
Jim Kramer, Senior Vice President, Sales
Adam Lewis, Vice President, Marketing

Branch Offices:
NEW YORK: 75 Rockefeller Plz, 16th Fl, New York, NY 10010. Phone: 212-669-5025. Fax: 212-962-2872. Mike Chinery, Senior Vice President, Sales; Darren Doyle, Senior Vice President, Sales.
Provides production & distribution services; specializes in network, cable, syndication, VOD/pay-per-view & pay TV.

DEEP DISH TV
339 Lafayette St
New York, NY 10012
Phone: 212-473-8933
Fax: 212-420-8332
E-mail: deepdish@igc.org
Web Site: http://www.deepdishtv.org
Ron Davis, Chairman
Tom Poole, Vice President
Dee Dee Halleck, Development Coordinator
Distributes educational, social activist & arts programming linking independent producers, programmers & community-based activists.

DEFENSE MEDIA ACTIVITY
6700 Taylor Ave
Fort Meade, MD 20755
Phone: 301-222-6000
E-mail: dma.info@dma.mil
Web Site: http://www.dma.mil
Ray B. Shepherd, Director
Provides a broad range of multimedia products & services to inform, educate & entertain Department of Defense audiences around the world.

DELUXE ADVERTISING SERVICES
2130 North Hollywood Way
Burbank, CA 91505
Phone: 818-526-3700
Fax: 818-526-3701
E-mail: adservicesla@bydeluxe.com
Web Site: http://edelivery.bydeluxe.com/home
Steve McCoy, President

Branch Offices:
NEW YORK: 149 5th Ave, 6th Fl, New York, NY 10010. Phone: 212-459-0290. Fax: 212-459-0298. E-Mail: distributionny@bydeluxe.com.

SAN FRANCISCO: 500 Sansome St, 7th Fl, San Francisco, CA 94111. Phone: 415-394-2400. Fax: 415-397-8700. E-Mail: distributionsf@bydeluxe.com.
Formerly FilmCore. Provides video & non-linear editing, video duplication, trafficking & vault services.

DELUXE LABORATORIES INC.
2400 West Empire Ave
Burbank, CA 91504
Phone: 818-565-3600
Fax: 323-960-7016
E-mail: warren.stein@bydeluxe.com
Web Site: http://www.bydeluxe.com
Cyril Drabinsky, President & Chief Executive Officer, Deluxe Entertainment Services Group
Provides complete film laboratory, post production & digital lab facilities & services; offices worldwide.

DESTINATION EDUCATION
4910 S 75th St
Lincoln, NE 68516
Phone: 402-435-0110
Fax: 402-435-0110
E-mail: slenzen@shopdei.com
Web Site: http://www.shopdei.com
Steven Lenzen, Co-founder
Distributes & produces educational programming.

DEWOLFE MUSIC
37 West 17th St
7th floor, Ste E
New York, NY 10011
Phone: 212-259-0524
E-mail: info@dewolfemusicusa.com
Web Site: http://www.dewolfemusic.co.uk
Warren de Wolfe, Managing Director
Frank Barretta, Senior Sales Consultant
Steve Rosie, Senior Sales Consultant
John Connor, Sales, Licensing & Music

Branch Offices:
NEW YORK: 37 W 17th St, 7th Fl, Ste E, New York, NY 10011. Phone: 212-259-0524. E-Mail: info@dewolfemusicusa.com.
Music library & sound effects specialist for audio-visual & broadcast; classical music; voice recording & mix studio.

DIGIMATION INC.
1515 International Pkwy
Ste 2001
Lake Mary, FL 32746
Phone: 407-833-0600
E-mail: sales@digimation.com
Web Site: http://www.digimation.com
Provides 3D digital content, creative services & graphics software solutions.

DIGITAL FORCE
149 Madison Ave
12th Fl
New York, NY 10016
Phones: 212-252-9300; 877-347-2872
Fax: 212-252-7377
E-mail: frontdesk@digitalforce.com
Web Site: http://www.digitalforce.com
Jerome Bunke, President
Provides CD & DVD production services including CD & DVD duplication, replication & copying for audio CDs & data CDs.

DIGITAL JUICE INC.
600 Technology Park
Ste 104
Lake Mary, FL 32746
Phones: 407-531-5540; 800-525-2203
Fax: 407-358-5174
E-mail: info@digitaljuice.com
Web Site: http://www.digitaljuice.com
David Hebel, Chief Executive Officer
Viv Beason, President
Provides royalty-free professional animations, stock footage, music, layered graphics, clip art & templates.

DIGITAL POST SERVICES
712 Seward St
Hollywood, CA 90038
Phone: 310-312-9060
Fax: 310-479-5771
E-mail: sales@digitalpostservices.com
Web Site: http://www.digitalpostservices.com
Ryan Noto, Chief Executive Officer
International standards conversion & videotape duplication facility; provides film-to-tape transfers, post-production services & vault storage.

DILIGENT SYSTEMS INC.
726 Rte. 202 S
Ste 320
Bridgewater, NJ 08807
Phone: 800-978-7710 x101
E-mail: info@diligentsystems.com
Web Site: http://www.diligentsystems.com
Charles McMullin, Chief Executive Officer
Herbert Mischel, Chief Technology Officer
Peter Strub, Vice President, Business Development
Walt Laskowski, Sales Representative

Branch Offices:
LOS ANGELES: 1110 S Robertson Blvd, Los Angeles, CA 90035.
Digital matchback to repurpose TV content from SD to HD using OCN.

DISCOVERY DIGITAL NETWORKS
One Discovery Pl
Silver Spring, MD 20910-3354
Phone: 240-662-2000
Web Site: http://discoverydn.com
Karen Leever, Executive Vice President & General Manager, Digital Media
Suzanne Kolb, Executive Vice President & General Manager, Digital Networks
Nathan Brown, Senior Vice President, Development & Operations, Discovery Digital Networks
Produces & distributes digital programming.

DISCOVERY EDUCATION
One Discovery Pl
Silver Spring, MD 20910
Phone: 800-323-9084
Fax: 855-495-6542
Web Site: http://www.discoveryeducation.com
Bill Goodwyn, President, Global Distribution
Kelli Campbell, Senior Vice President, Product & Content Strategy
Mark Edwards, Senior Vice President, Digital Learning
Publishes & distributes high-quality digital educational resources.

DJM FILMS INC.
4 E 46th St
New York, NY 10017
Phone: 212-490-1113
Fax: 212-499-9081
Ed Friedman, Founder
Eileen Friedman, Senior Vice President & Operations Director
Danny Breen, Vice President, Operations
Wilson Converse, Editor & Smoke Artist
Joe Domilici, Editor
David Friedman, Editor
Charlie Weissman, Editor
Pete Serinita, Digital Audio Post
Provides editing & post-production services; audio recording & mixing; duplication & distribution.

DLT ENTERTAINMENT LTD.
124 E 55th St
New York, NY 10022
Phone: 212-245-4680
Fax: 212-315-1132
Web Site: http://www.dltentertainment.com
Don Taffner, President

Branch Offices:
UNITED KINGDOM: UK Headquarters, 10 Bedford Sq, London, England WC1B 3RA, United Kingdom. Phone: 44-0-20-7631-1184. Fax: 44-0-20-7636-4571.

UNITED KINGDOM: The Theatre of Comedy Co., Shaftesbury Theatre, 210 Shaftesbury Ave, London, England WC2H 8DP, United Kingdom. Phone: 44-0-20-7379-3345. Fax: 44-0-20-7836-8181.
Produces & distributes TV programs; first-run syndication; network development; co-production; international syndication sales.

DMX MUSIC
1703 W Fifth St
Ste 600
Austin, TX 78701
Phones: 512-380-8500; 800-345-5000
Fax: 512-380-8501
E-mail: info@dmx.com
Web Site: http://www.dmx.com
R. Steven Hicks, Chairman
Paul D. Stone, President
John D. Cullen, Chief Executive Officer
Tim Seaton, Chief Operating Officer
Kimberly K. Shipman, Chief Financial Officer

Branch Offices:
LOS ANGELES: 11150 W Olympic Blvd, Ste 770, Los Angeles, CA 90064. Phone: 310-575-3185.

MIAMI: Latin America Offices, 1550 Biscayne Blvd, Miami, FL 33132. Phone: 305-894-2576. Fax: 305-894-4919. E-Mail: gustavo.tonelli@dmx.com.

NORCROSS: 3170 Reps Miller Rd, Ste 100, Norcross, GA 30071. Phone: 770-225-2500. Fax: 770-246-3941.

Program Sources & Services

OAKBROOK: 620 Enterprise Dr, Oak Brook, IL 60523. Phones: 847-839-7890; 800-640-2673.

SEATTLE: 411 First Ave, Ste 501, Seattle, WA 94104. Phone: 800-345-5000.

WALTHAM: 77 Fourth Ave, 5th Fl, Waltham, MA 02451. Phone: 508-393-2591. Fax: 508-393-5137.

BRAZIL: Rua dos Bombeiros, 40, Ibirapuero, Sao Paulo 04001-100, Brazil. Phone: 55-11-3884-0150. E-Mail: atendimento@dmx.com. Web site: http://http://www.dmxmusic.com.br.

CANADA: 7260 12th St. SE, #120, Calgary, AB T2H 2S5, Canada. Phones: 403-640-8525; 800-350-0369. Fax: 888-823-0369. E-Mail: dmx.canada@dmx.com. Web site: http://www.dmx.ca.

SOUTH AFRICA: Ground Floor Sandown Mews E, 88 Stella St, Sandown, Johannesburg, South Africa. Phone: 27-11-780-3000. Fax: 27-11-780-3001. E-Mail: info@dmx.co.za. Web site: http://http://www.dmx.co.za. Provides sensory branding services including music design, new media, messaging & scent. Division of DMX Inc.

DOCURAMA FILMS
c/o Cinedigm
1901 Ave of the Stars, 12th Fl
Los Angeles, LA 90067
Phone: 424-281-5400
Web Site: http://www.docurama.com
Susan Margolin, President, Docurama & Special Acquisitions
Distributes documentaries covering an array of topics, including the performing and visual arts, history, politics, the environment and ethnic & gender interests.

DOVE BROADCASTING INC.
PO Box 1616
Greenville, SC 29602
Phone: 864-244-1616
Fax: 864-292-8481
E-mail: billyrainey16@gmail.com
Web Site: http://www.dovebroadcasting.com
Michele Loftis, Production Manager
Billy Rainey, Sales Manager
Produces Christian TV programming.

DOW JONES NEWSWIRES
1211 Ave of the Americas
7th Fl
New York, NY 10036
Phone: 800-223-2274
E-mail: service@dowjones.com
Web Site: http://www.dowjones.com
Neal Lipschutz, Senior Vice President & Managing Editor, Dow Jones Newswires
Provides real-time news services.

DREAMWORKS ANIMATION SKG
1000 Flower St
Glendale, CA 91201
Phone: 818-695-5000
Fax: 818-695-3510
Web Site: http://www.dreamworksanimation.com
Jeffrey Katzenburg, Chairman, DreamWorks New Media
Mark Zoradi, Chief Operating Officer
Michael R. Francis, Chief Global Brand Officer
Anne Globe, Chief Marketing Officer
Fazal Merchant, Chief Financial Officer
Heather O'Connor, Chief Accounting Officer
Andrew Chang, General Counsel & Corporate Secretary
Marjorie Cohn, Head of Television
Peter Gal, Head of TV Development
Dan Satterthwaite, Head of Human Resources
Mark Taylor, Head of TV Production

Branch Offices:
REDWOOD CITY: PDI/DreamWorks, 1800 Seaport Blvd, Redwood City, CA 94063. Produces & distributes computer-generated animation feature films. On April 28, 2016 Comcast announced it was acquiring DreamWorks Animation. Deal closed August 23, 2016.

DREAMWORKS STUDIOS SKG
100 Universal Plz
Universal City, CA 91608
Phone: 818-733-9600
E-mail: info@dreamworksstudios.com
Web Site: http://www.dreamworksstudios.com
Steven Spielberg, Principal Partner
Michael Wright, Chief Executive Officer
Holly Bario, Co-President, Production
Mark Sourian, Co-President, Production
Develops, produces & distributes films, video games & TV programming.

DREW ASSOCIATES INC.
5467 31st St Northwest
Washington, DC 20015
Phone: 202-525-8884
E-mail: jill@drewassociates.com
Web Site: http://www.drewassociates.net
Jill Drew, General Manager
Produces public affairs & entertainment documentaries, client films & corporate video newsletters.

DRIVER
115 W 27th St
12th Fl
New York, NY 10001
Phone: 212-675-2820
Fax: 212-675-2830
E-mail: jd@driver.tv
Web Site: http://www.driver.tv
Linda RaFoss, Partner & Managing Director
Scott Weitz, Executive Producer
J. D. Williams, Executive Producer

Branch Offices:
LOS ANGELES: 842 N Fairfax Ave, Los Angeles, CA 90046. Provides production services, including agency production, direct production services, in-house edit bays & graphic design; develops content for TV, film & new media.

DUART FILM & VIDEO
245 W 55th St
New York, NY 10019
Phones: 212-757-4580; 800-523-8278
Fax: 212-977-5609
E-mail: info@duart.com
Web Site: http://www.duart.com
Charles Darby, Chief Operating Officer
Steve Blakely, Vice President, Film Lab
Carmen Borgia, Vice President, Audio Production
Joe Monge, Vice President, Video Operations
Videotape post-production facility & film laboratory; provides video editing, tape duplication, film-to-tape & tape-to-film transfers, 16mm & 35mm processing & printing services.

EDITBAR
33 Union St
5th Floor
Boston, MA 02108
Phone: 617-572-3333
Fax: 617-572-3313
E-mail: info@editbar.com
Web Site: http://www.editbar.com
Provides editorial services & post-production management for advertising agencies, production companies & filmmakers.

RALPH EDWARDS PRODUCTIONS
6922 Hollywood Blvd
Ste 300
Hollywood, CA 90028
Phone: 323-462-2212
Fax: 323-461-1224
E-mail: info@ralphedwards.com
Web Site: http://www.ralphedwards.com
Barbara Dunn-Leonard, President
Produces & packages network & syndicated TV shows.

BERT ELLIOTT SOUND
1752 Harper St NW
Atlanta, GA 30318-3068
Phones: 404-626-9899; 404-351-9061
Fax: 404-351-6806
E-mail: bertesound@gmail.com
Web Site: http://www.bertelliottsound.com
Bert Elliott, President
Provides audio production; original music for film, video & multimedia productions; desktop audio & video production; 48-track facility.

ELLIS ENTERTAINMENT CORP.
7B Pleasant Blvd
Ste 960
Toronto, ON M4T 1K2
Canada
Phone: 416-444-7900
Fax: 416-444-2473
E-mail: info@ellisent.com
Web Site: http://www.ellisent.com
Stephen Ellis, President
Grace Lo, Manager, Client Service
Distributes non-fiction, wildlife & entertainment TV programming from Britain, Australia & the U.S.

ENCYCLOPAEDIA BRITANNICA INC.
331 N La Salle St
Chicago, IL 60654
Phones: 312-347-7159; 800-323-1229
Fax: 312-294-2104
Web Site: http://www.britannica.com
Michael Ross, Senior Vice President

Branch Offices:
AUSTRALIA: Encyclopaedia Britannica Australia Ltd., 9 Help St, Level 1, Chatswood, NSW 2067, Australia. Phone: 61-2-9915-8800. Fax: 61-2-9419-5247. E-Mail: sales@eb.com.au. Web site: http://www.britannica.com.au.

INDIA: Encyclopaedia Britannica India Pvt. Ltd., A-41, Mohan Cooperative Industrial Estate, Mathura Rd, New Delhi 110044, India. Phone: 91-11-4715-4100. Fax: 91-11-4715-4116. E-Mail: bcd@ebindia.com. Web site: http://www.britannicaindia.com.

ISRAEL: Britannica.com Israel Ltd., 16 Tozeret Ha'aretz St., Tel Aviv 67891, Israel. Phone: 972-3-607-0400. Fax: 972-3-607-0401. Web site: http://www.britannica.co.il.

JAPAN: Britannica Japan Co. Ltd., Da Vinci 2F, 8-3-16 Nishi-Gotanda, Shinagawa, Tokyo 141-0031, Japan. Phone: 81-3-5436-1388. Fax: 81-3-5436-1380. E-Mail: info@britannica.co.jp. Web site: http://www.britannica.co.jp.

SOUTH KOREA: Korea Britannica Corp., Youghan B/D 7F, 59-23 Chungmuro 3ga, Jung-gu, Seoul 100-013, South Korea. Phone: 82-1588-1768. Fax: 82-2-2278-9983. E-Mail: webmaster@britannica.co.kr.

TAIWAN: Sec 1, Chungching Rd South, Room 402, #10, Taipei City 100, Taiwan. Phone: 886-2-2311-2592. Fax: 886-2-2311-2595.

UNITED KINGDOM: Encyclopaedia Britannica (UK) Ltd., Mill St, Unity Wharf, 2nd Fl, London SE1 2BH, United Kingom. Phone: 44-20-7500-7800. Fax: 44-20-7500-7878. E-Mail: enquiries@britannica.co.uk. Web site: http://http://www.britannica.co.uk. Produces & distributes film & video materials for education, business & industry.

ENDEMOL SHINE NORTH AMERICA
9255 Sunset Blvd
Ste 1100
Los Angeles, CA 90069
Phone: 310-860-9914
Fax: 310-860-0073
Web Site: http://www.endemolusa.tv
Cris Abrego, Co-Chairman Endemol Shine Americas & Co-Chief Executive Officer, Endemol Shine North America
Charlie Corwin, Co-Chairman Endemol Shine Americas & Co-Chief Executive Officer, Endemol Shine North America
Ben Samek, Chief Operating Officer
Adrian Sexton, Chief Operating Officer, Endemol Beyond USA
Paul Jennings, Chief Financial Officer
Eden Gaha, President, Unscripted Television
Sharon Hall, President, Endemol Shine Studios
Bonnie Pan, President, Endemol Beyond USA
Vivi Zigler, President, Digital, Brand & Audience Development, Endemol Shine North America
John Farrell, General Counsel
Rob Day, Executive Vice President, Unscripted Production, Endemol Shine USA
Linda Giambrone, Executive Vice President, Head of Unscripted Production
Flavio Morales, Executive Vice President, US Initiatives, Endemol Shine Latino
Daniel Rodriguez, Co-Executive Vice President, Endemol Shine Latino
Rob Smith, Executive Vice President & Head of Unscripted Television
Michael Brooks, Senior Vice President, Programming, Endemol Shine USA
Jeff Browning, Senior Vice President, Sales, Endemol Beyond USA
Chris Culvenor, Senior Vice President, Unscripted Development, Endemol Shine USA
Rachel Dax, Senior Vice President, Unscripted Production, Endemol Shine USA
Robin Feinberg, Senior Vice President, Unscripted Programming, Endemol Shine USA
Michael Gifford, Senior Vice President, Business & Legal Affairs
Georgie Hurford-Jones, Senior Vice President, Unscripted Programming
Rico Martinez, Senior Vice President, Creative, Endemol Beyond USA
Tamaya Petteway, Senior Vice President, Brand & Licensing Partnership Division
Joe Schlosser, Senior Vice President, Communications
Michael Weinberg, Senior Vice President, Development
Laura Gibson, Vice President, Unscripted Development, Endemol Shine USA
Kelly C Hill, Vice President, Licensing Partnerships
Julie Holland, Vice President, Communications
Jenn Mancini, Vice President, East Coast Sales, Endemol Beyond USA

Program Sources & Services

Christopher Potts, Vice President, Unscripted Development, Endemol Shine USA
Ed Prince, Vice President, Business & Legal Affairs
Marjorie Williams, Vice President, Business & Legal Affairs
Produces TV & other audiovisual entertainment; scripted, non-scripted & digital media; offices worldwide. Division of Endemol Group.

ENOKI FILMS USA INC.
16430 Ventura Blvd
Ste 308
Encino, CA 91436
Phone: 818-907-6503
Fax: 818-907-6506
E-mail: yoshienokiusa@gmail.com
Web Site: http://www.enokifilmsusa.com
Zen Enoki, Chairman
Yoshi Enoki, President
Produces & distributes children's animated series & feature films.

ENVOY PRODUCTIONS
660 Mason Ridge Ctr Dr
St Louis, MO 63141
Phones: 314-317-4100; 888-229-7743
Fax: 314-317-4299
E-mail: contact@envoyproductions.com
Web Site: http://www.envoyproductions.com
Sandi Clement, Vice President, Sales & Programming
Kurt Sprenger, International Distributor, Life Media International
Produces, distributes & syndicates religious TV series & specials; produces & distributes foreign language TV series & specials; radio; radio syndicated talk show for women; Spanish & French programming.

ETC
1915 MacArthur Rd
Waukesha, WI 53188
Phones: 262-542-5600; 888-746-4382
Fax: 262-542-1524
E-mail: webmaster@etcia.com
Web Site: http://www.etcia.com
Dean W. Danner, President & Chief Executive Officer
Bonita M. Danner, Vice President, Engineering
Joseph A. Voight, Jr., Vice President, Sales & Marketing
Hazel Danner, Corporate Secretary & Human Resources Director
Supplies voice announcers & voice application platforms.

EUE/SCREEN GEMS STUDIOS
603 Greenwich St
New York, NY 10014
Phones: 212-450-1600; 212-450-7991
E-mail: nystudios@euescreengems.com
Web Site: http://www.screengemsstudios.com
Chris Cooney, President & Chief Operating Officer
Ed Branaccio, Chief Technical Officer
Merideth Shapiro, Senior Facility Manager
Paul Gilly, Studio Manager

Branch Offices:
WILMINGTON: 1223 23rd St N, Wilmington, NC 28405. Phone: 910-343-3500. E-Mail: info@screengemsstudios.com. Bill Vasser, Executive Vice President.
Provides video & film production; six sound stages in New York with lighting & grip equipment, two control rooms, prop room, camera room, casting stage, CMX edit room, 35mm & 16mm projection rooms & conference rooms.

FAITH FOR TODAY
PO Box 7729
Riverside, CA 92513
Phones: 805-955-7700; 888-940-0062
E-mail: info@faithfortoday.tv
Web Site: http://www.faithfortoday.tv
Michael Tucker, Executive Producer, Director & Co-Host
Produces Christian TV programming.

FAMILY THEATER PRODUCTIONS
7201 Sunset Blvd
Hollywood, CA 90046
Phones: 323-874-6633; 800-874-0999
Fax: 323-874-1168
E-mail: info@familytheater.org
Web Site: http://www.familytheater.org
Wilfred J. Raymond, National Director
Dan E. Pitre, Public Relations Director
Tony Sands, Administrator
David Guffey, Holy Cross Priest
Eleazar Bazini, Sound Engineer & Composer
Produces & distributes faith & values TV programming & films; produces public TV documentaries. Division of Holy Cross Family Ministries.

FARM JOURNAL MEDIA
1500 Market St
Ctr Sq W
Philadelphia, PA 19102
Phone: 215-557-8900
Fax: 215-568-4436
Web Site: http://www.farmjournalmedia.com
Jeff Pence, President
Andy Weber, Chief Executive Officer
Thomas C. Breslin, Chief Financial Officer & Executive Vice President
Steve Custer, Senior Vice President & Publisher
Produces, syndicates & distributes half-hour news, weather, markets & features programs focused on the agriculture industry; topics include production, pricing, food safety, new technologies & environmental matters.

FAST CUTS
1845 Woodall Rodgers Frwy
Ste 200
Dallas, TX 75201
Phone: 214-526-3278
Fax: 214-526-3290
Web Site: http://www.fastcuts.tv
Julie Koellner, Executive Producer
Mimi Hendrix, Senior Producer
Barbara Sanders, Senior Producer
P. K. Jones, Audio Producer
Provides post-production services.

THE FIELD
16 West 46th St
8th floor
New York, NY 10036
Phone: 212-253-2888
E-mail: michaelp@thefieldtv.com
Web Site: http://www.thefieldtv.com
Michael Porte, Founder
Barrett Heathcote, Editor
Fabrizio Rossetti, Editor
Mike Siedlecki, Editor
Provides editorial, production & design services for commercials, broadcast, broadband, cinema & emerging media.

FILMACK STUDIOS
3807 Kiess St
Glenview, IL 60026
Phones: 312-427-3395; 800-345-6225
Fax: 312-427-4866
E-mail: inquiries@filmack.com
Web Site: http://www.filmack.com
Robert Mack, President
Provides specialized 35mm film & video production & duplication services.

FILMCORE — See Deluxe Advertising Services.

FILMRISE
34 35th St
Brooklyn, NY 11232
Phone: 718-369-9090
E-mail: contact@filmrise.com
Web Site: http://www.filmrise.com
Alan Klingenstein, Chairman
Danny Fisher, Chief Executive Officer
Jack Fisher, President
Acquires & distributes films & TV programming.

FILMS AROUND THE WORLD INC.
Long Island City Art Ctr
44-02 23rd St-Studio 109 (Ground Floor)
Long Island City, NY 11101
Phone: 212-599-9500
Fax: 212-599-6040
E-mail: alexjr@pipeline.com
Web Site: http://www.filmsaroundtheworld.com
Alexander W. Kogan Jr., Personnel
Beverly Partridge, Personnel
Owns or co-owns with NBC 850 1950s/1960s long-format good copyright live kinescope-preserved programs. Related companies own/distribute more than 500 feature films & more than 2,500 hours of 1960s top-rated talk radio. These companies include Mr. Fat-W Video green & black or silver & blue, Mr. Fat-W Audio & Senor Fat-W Video.

FILMS OF INDIA — See listing for 1-World LLC.

FINAL CUT LTD.
118 West 22nd St
7th Floor
New York, NY 10011
Phone: 212-375-9800
E-mail: michelle_c@finalcut-uk.com
Web Site: http://www.finalcut-edit.com

Branch Offices:
NEW YORK: 118 W 22nd St, 7th Fl, New York, NY 10011. Phone: 212-375-9800. Fax: 212-375-0256. E-Mail: stephanie_a@finalcut-edit.com.

SANTA MONICA: 1634 Euclid St, Santa Monica, CA 90404-3724. Phone: 310-566-6600. Fax: 310-566-6601. E-Mail: saima_a@finalcut-edit.com.

FINE ART PRODUCTIONS, RICHIE SURACI PICTURES MULTIMEDIA, INTERACTIVE
67 Maple St
Newburgh, NY 12550-4034
Phones: 845-561-5866; 914-527-9740
Fax: 845-561-5866
Richie Suraci, Producer & Director
Produces & distributes film, video, DVD, CD & multimedia programs.

MICHAEL FIORE FILMS
12 W 31st St
Ground Fl
New York, NY 10001
Phone: 212-564-7163
E-mail: info@michaelfiorefilms.com
Web Site: http://www.michaelfiorefilms.com
Michael Fiore, President
Develops, finances & creates high-concept filmed content for the film, TV & ad world.

FIRESTONE COMMUNICATIONS INC.
6125 Airport Frwy
Ft Worth, TX 76117
Phone: 817-546-0670
Web Site: http://www.sorpresatv.com
Leonard L. Firestone, Chairman & Chief Executive Officer
Michael G. Fletcher, President
Christopher K. Firestone, Executive Vice President, Operations
J. Romer, Vice President
Francisco Cuevas, Creative Director
Operates SORPRESA, a U.S.-based 24-hr. network dedicated to America's Hispanic children; offers production & creative services.

FIREWORKS INTERNATIONAL
225 Arizona Ave
Ste 250
Santa Monica, CA 90401
Phone: 310-576-1059
Fax: 310-576-1859
E-mail: info@contentfilm.com
Web Site: http://www.contentfilm.com
Jonathan Ford, Executive Vice President, Digital Acquisitions & Distribution
Bob Kennedy, Executive Vice President, Non-Fiction Programming

Branch Offices:
SANTA MONICA: 225 Arizona Ave, Ste 250, Santa Monica, CA 90401. Phone: 310-576-1059. Fax: 310-576-1859. Saralo MacGregor, Executive Vice President, Worldwide Distribution; Melissa Wohl, Senior Vice President, Worldwide Distribution; Paul Lewis, Vice President, Development; Diana Zakis, Vice President, Sales, Latin America & Asia.

CANADA: 80 Richmond St W, Toronto, ON M5H 24A, Canada. Phone: 416-360-6103. Fax: 416-360-6065. Cameron Wallis, Director, Technical Operations.
International TV & distribution division of Content Film Co.

FIRST LIGHT VIDEO PUBLISHING
2321 Abbot Kinney Blvd
Ste 101
Venice, CA 90291
Phones: 310-577-8581; 800-262-8862
Fax: 310-574-0886
E-mail: sale@firstlightvideo.com
Web Site: http://www.firstlightvideo.com
Michael Bennett, President & Chief Executive Officer
Leslie Collins, Vice President, Sales & Marketing
Publishes & distributes instructional media arts programming developed specifically for the secondary & higher education markets; li-

---

Communications Daily
Warren Communications News

Get the industry standard FREE —
For a no-obligation trial call 800-771-9202 or visit www.warren-news.com

Program Sources & Services

brary contains over 400 craft-specific titles, including film & video production, radio & TV broadcasting, editing, media studies, writing, costuming, stagecraft for the theatre & many more topics for media arts courses.

FISCHER EDIT
219 North 2nd St
Ste 200
Minneapolis, MN 55401
Phone: 612-332-4914
Fax: 612-332-4910
E-mail: dorene@fischeredit.com
Web Site: http://www.fischeredit.com
Tony Fischer, President
Erica Leanna, Producer
Kathy Yerich, Producer
J. Matt Keil, Business Development
Charlotte Peterson, Business Development
Provides creative offline editing services; specializes in TV commercials.

FLATIRON FILM CO.
c/o Cinedigm
1901 Ave of the Stars, 12th Fl
Los Angeles, CA 90067
Phone: 424-281-5400
Distributes indie & foreign films.

FLUID
532 Broadway
5th Fl
New York, NY 10012
Phone: 212-431-4342
Fax: 212-431-6525
E-mail: katie@fluidny.com
Web Site: http://www.fluidny.com
Laura Relovsky, Executive Producer
Provides post-production services, including editorial, original music & sound design, visual effects and design & finishing for film, broadcast & web.

FOLLOW PRODUCTIONS
125 West End Ave
#7
New York, NY 10023
Phone: 212-691-1810
Fax: 212-691-1855
Web Site: http://www.followproductions.com
Gordon Elliott, Executive Producer
Mark Schneider, Managing Director
Produces TV series for the Food Network.

FOUNDATION
521 Live Oak Cir Dr
Calabasas, CA 91302
Phone: 424-238-0381
Web Site: http://www.foundationcontent.com
Samantha Hart, Executive Producer
Provides creative production services.

FOX STUDIOS AUSTRALIA — See listing for Granada Media.

FOX 21 TELEVISION STUDIOS
10351 Santa Monica Blvd
Beverly Hills, CA 90025
Phone: 310-295-3415
E-mail: leslie.oren@fox.com
Web Site: http://www.newscorp.com
Bert Salke, President
Leslie Oren, Senior Vice President, Corporate Communications
Andy Bourne, Vice President, Programming
Tara Flynn, Vice President, Creative Affairs
Produces TV programming for the U.S. & global markets. Division of 21st Century Fox. Company is a result of the merger of Fox 21 & Fox TV Studios.

SANDY FRANK ENTERTAINMENT INC.
910 Fifth Ave
New York, NY 10021
Phone: 212-772-1889
Fax: 212-772-2297
E-mail: filmsfe@aol.com
Web Site: http://www.sandyfrankentertainment.com
Sandy Frank, Chairman
Rosalie Perrone, Vice President, Business Affairs & Comptroller
Sandy Spidell, Vice President, Operations & Publicity
Nora Maria Diaz, Sales Director
Susan Piscitello, Creative Affairs Director
Steve Radosh, Creative Consulting Producer
Barbara Kalicinska, European Sales Representative
Independently produces & distributes syndicated series & format programming worldwide.

FREDERATOR STUDIOS
22 W 21st St
7th Fl
New York, NY 1010
Phone: 212-779-4133
E-mail: hey@frederator.com
Web Site: http://frederator.com
Fred Seibert, Founder & Chief Executive Officer
Matt Gielen, Vice President, Programming & Audience Development
Eric Homan, Vice President, Development
Jeremy Rosen, Vice President, Technology & Product
Produce cartoons for TV, movies & online.

FREMANTLE CORP.
23 Lesmill Rd
Ste 5
Toronto, ON M3B 2T3
Phone: 416-443-9204
Fax: 416-443-8685
Web Site: http://www.fremantlecorp.com
Randy Zalken, President
Diane Tripp, Managing Director, International Sales
Arlene Hay, Client Services & Contracts Manager
Karen Gregory, Accounting Manager

Branch Offices:
NEW YORK: 1501 Broadway, Ste 1902, New York, NY 10036. Phone: 212-840-6269. Fax: 212-398-9660.
Distributes TV movies, documentaries, tape series & international co-production. Division of Kaleidoscope Entertainment Inc.

FREMANTLEMEDIA LTD.
One Stephen St
London W1T 1AL
United Kingdom
Phone: 44-0-20-7691-6000
Fax: 44-0-20-7691-6100
E-mail: pressenquiries@fremantlemedia.com
Web Site: http://www.fremantlemedia.com
Cecile Frot-Coutaz, Chief Executive Officer
Sangeeta Desai, Chief Operating & Financial Officer
Craig Cegielski, Co-Chief Executive Officer, FremantleMedia North America
Jennifer Mullin, Co-Chief Executive Officer, FremantleMedia North America
Lee Rierson, Chief Operating Officer, FremantleMedia North America
Trish Kinane, President, Entertainment Programming
David Luner, President, Brand Partnerships & Franchise Management, FremantleMedia North America
Toby Gorman, Executive Vice President, Alternative Programming
Alex Demyanenko, Senior Vice President, Non-Fiction Development & Programming, FremantleMedia North America
Tony Opticon, Senior Vice President, Scripted Programming
Sean Hancock, Vice President, Reality, Game Show & Unscripted Development
Nicky Gray, Human Resources Director
Ian Ousey, Financial Director

Branch Offices:
BURBANK: FremantleMedia North America, 4000 W Alameda Ave, 3rd Fl, Burbank, CA 91505. Phone: 818-748-1100. Fax: 818-563-6410. Hayley Dickson, Vice President, Television Acquisitions & Development, Global Content; Holly Hines, Vice President, Scripted Development.

MIAMI: Fremantle Productions Latin America, Waterford Bldg, 5200 Blue Lagoon Dr, Ste 200, Miami, FL 33126. Phone: 305-267-0821.

NEW YORK: FremantleMedia North America, 1540 Broadway, 10th Fl, New York, NY 10036. Phone: 212-541-2800. Fax: 212-541-2810.

BRAZIL: FremantleMedia Brazil, Av Professor Manuel Jose Chavez 300, Alto Pinheiros, Sao Paulo 05463-070, Brazil. Phone: 55-11-3846-9100.

MEXICO: FremantleMedia Mexico, Camino al Ajusco #124, Three Col Jardines en la Montana, Tlapan CP 14210, Mexico. Phone: 52-5-55-631-2737.
Produces, licenses & distributes prime time, drama, serial drama & factual entertainment programming to broadcasters worldwide; also develops & produces media entertainment for mobile, broadband, game consoles & Internet protocol TV; company divisions include Fremantle International Distribution, FremantleMedia Interactive & FremantleMedia Licensing Group. Offices worldwide.

CHUCK FRIES PRODUCTIONS
10390 Santa Maria Blvd
Ste 360
Los Angeles, CA 90025
Phone: 310-203-9520
Fax: 310-203-9519
E-mail: friesfilms@aol.com; info@friesfilms.com
Charles W. Fries, Chairman & President
Produces & distributes theatrical, home video, TV & pay TV programming worldwide.

FUMC TELEVISION MINISTRIES
First United Methodist Church
500 Common St
Shreveport, LA 71101
Phone: 318-424-7771
Fax: 318-429-6888
E-mail: fumc@fumcshreveport.org
Web Site: http://www.fumcshreveport.org
Pat Day, Senior Pastor
Donna Bell, Finance Administrator
Jay Sawyer, Business Administrator
John Mark Wilcox, TV Coordinator
Produces the Sunday morning 11am Traditional Worship Service at FUMC, which airs live on KTBS Channel 3 and/or KTBS News Channel 3.3. Provides downloadable worship services as well as sermons on CD or DVD.

FUNNY OR DIE
167 Second Ave
San Mateo, CA 94401
Phone: 650-565-8566
Web Site: http://www.funnyordie.com
Produces film & TV programming.

FUTURE IS NOW (FIN)
32 W 10th St
4th Fl
New York, NY 10011
Phone: 917-293-0623
E-mail: gala@futurenyc.com
Web Site: http://www.futurenyc.com
Gala Verdugo, Founder
Provides professional AVID editing; specializes in commercials, promos, music videos, documentaries & short films.

GABBA MEDIA LLC
37 W37th St
12th Floor
New York, NY 10018
Phone: 212-741-9630
Fax: 212-741-9693
E-mail: info@gabbamedia.com
Web Site: http://www.gabbamedia.com
Gardiner Welch, Editor
Provides post-production services.

GARI MEDIA GROUP
1532 Falling Star Ave
Westlake Village, CA 91362
Phones: 818-707-4160; 888-424-0007
Fax: 818-707-4161
E-mail: antonio@garimediagroup.com
Web Site: http://www.garimediagroup.com
Frank Gari, President & Chief Executive Officer
Nick DiMinno, Vice President, GMG New York
Chris Gari, Vice President, Music & Creative Director
Kim Gari, Vice President, Licensing
Jon Herron, Vice President, New Media & Chief Technical Officer
Kyle King, Vice President, Sales
Larry McDaniel, Chief Marketing Officer
Antonio Corcella, Customer Relations Director

Branch Offices:
ATLANTA: 3575 Piedmont Rd, Atlanta, GA 30305. Phone: 404-924-4274. Fax: 404-467-1996.
Full-service creative agency; services includes production for sweep promotion, custom & syndicated music & graphic packages, media buying & strategic marketing.

GATEWAY FILMS/VISION VIDEO
PO Box 540
2030 Wentz Church Rd
Worcester, PA 19490
Phones: 610-584-3500; 800-523-0226
Fax: 610-584-4610
E-mail: info@visionvideo.com
Web Site: http://www.visionvideo.com
A. Kenneth Curtis, President
Produces & distributes Christian videos for family, church or school.

GERREN ENTERTAINMENT PRODUCTIONS
3640 W 63rd St
Ste 1A
Los Angeles, CA 90043
Phone: 323-292-1600
E-mail: latenitegano@gmail.com
Web Site: http://mindseedstudios.net
Produces & distributes films & cartoons to LPTV stations; rents audio & video equipment.

GLOBECAST AMERICA
10 E 40th St
11th Fl

Program Sources & Services

New York, NY 10016
Phone: 212-373-5140
Fax: 212-373-5454
Web Site: http://www.globecast.com
Philippe Bernard, Chairman & Chief Executive Officer, GlobeCast
Michele Gosetti, Interim Chief Executive Officer, GlobeCast Americas

Branch Offices:
CULVER CITY: GlobeCast America, 10525 W Washington Blvd, Culver City, CA 90232. Phone: 310-845-3900. Fax: 310-845-3904.

SUNRISE: 13801 NW 14th St, Sunrise, FL 33323. Phone: 954-514-5209. Fax: 954-514-5223.
Provides content management & worldwide transmission services for professional broadcast delivery; operates a secure global satellite & fiber network to manage and transport 10 million hours of video & other rich media each year, providing ingest, aggregation, transmission & re-purposing of content for delivery to direct-to-home satellite platforms; cable, IPTV, mobile & broadband headends. Offices worldwide. Subsidiary of France Telecom.

GLOBO INTERNATIONAL NY LTD.
157 Chambers St
15th Fl
New York, NY 10007
Phone: 917-551-3500
Amauri Soares, Chief Executive Officer
Produces & distributes series & specials.

GOOD LIFE BROADCASTING INC.
31 Skyline Dr
Lake Mary, FL 32746
Phone: 407-215-6745
Fax: 407-215-6789
E-mail: info@tv45.org
Web Site: http://www.tv45.org
Steve Stiger, President
Barbara Beck, Host
Doug Prusak, Production & Programming Manager
Provides religious, educational & family-oriented programming.

MARK GORDON CO
12200 W Olympic Blvd
Los Angeles, CA 90064
Phone: 310-943-6401
Produces film, network, cable & digital content.

GRACENOTE
40 Media Dr
Queensbury, NY 12804
Phones: 518-792-9914; 800-833-9581
E-mail: info@gracenote.com
Web Site: http://www.gracenote.com
Daniel Kazan, Chief Executive Officer
John B. Kelleher, President & Chief Operating Officer
Kathy Tolstrup, Senior Vice President, Sales

Branch Offices:
CHICAGO: 435 N Michigan, Ste 300, Chicago, IL 60611.

SAN FRANCISCO: 525 Brannan St, San Francisco, CA 94107-1650.

LOS ANGELES: Zap2it.com, Entertainment Bureau, 5800 Sunset Blvd, Los Angeles, CA 90028.

DEERFIELD BEACH: TMS International Entertainment Information, Data Operations, 333 SW 12th Ave, Deerfield Beach, FL 33442.

AMSTERDAM: TMS International Entertainment Information, Data Operations, Orlyplein 10, 25th FL, Amsterdam 1043 DP.
Creates, aggregates & distributes news, information & entertainment content that reaches users in print, online & on-screen. Subsidiary of The Tribune Co.

GRANADA MEDIA
US Office
Greenwich St, 9th Floor
New York, NY 10014
Phone: 212-905-1700
Web Site: http://www.granadamedia.com

Branch Offices:
LOS ANGELES: ITV Studios Inc., 15303 Ventura Blvd, Bldg C, Ste 800, Sherman Oaks, CA 91403. Phone: 818-455-4600. Web site: http://www.itv-america.com. Kevin Lygo, Managing Director, ITV Studios; Sam Zoda, Chief Operating Officer; Brent Montgomery, President, ITV Studios America; Philippe Maigret, President, Scripted Programming, ITV Studios America; Jenise Caiola, Executive Vice President, Human Resources, ITV Studios US Group; Bruce Robertson, Executive Vice President, Creative Strategy, ITV Studios America; Paul Reaney, Senior Vice President, Development, ITV Studios America; Brian Zagorski, Senior Vice President, Current & Programming, ITV Studios America; Colet Abedi, Vice President, Development.

NEW YORK: ITV Studios Inc., 609 Greenwich St, 9th Fl, New York, NY 10014. Phone: 212-905-1700. Web site: http://http://www.itv-america.com. Patrice Andrews, Chief Operating Officer, East Coast, ITV Studios America.

AUSTRALIA: Granada Australia, 38 Driver Ave, FSA #34, Level 1, Bldg 61, Moore Park, NSW 1363, Australia. Phone: 61-02-9383-4360. Web site: http://www.granadaproductions.com.au.

GERMANY: Granada Produktion fur Film & Fernsehen GmbH, Am Coloneum 6, Koln 50829, Germany. Phone: 49-0-221-492-048120. Web site: http://www.granadamedia.de.
Produces & distributes TV programming.

SHERRY GRANT ENTERPRISES INC.
18120 Sweet Elm Dr
Encino, CA 91316-4452
Phone: 818-705-2535
Sherry Grant, President
Produces & distributes short-form TV programs & other special entertainment projects.

GRB ENTERTAINMENT
13400 Riverside Dr
300
Sherman Oaks, CA 91423
Phone: 818-728-7600
Fax: 818-728-7601
E-mail: info@grbtv.com
Web Site: http://www.grbtv.com
Gary R. Benz, President & Chief Executive Officer
Michael Branton, Executive Vice President, Creative Affairs
James Cox, Senior Vice President, Development
Michael Lolato, Senior Vice President, International Distribution
Steven Montgomery, Senior Vice President & General Counsel
Karen M. Pinto, Senior Vice President, Production & Operations

Mitch Federer, Senior Counsel, Business & Legal Affairs
Produces unscripted alternative programming.

ROSS GREENBURG PRODUCTIONS
411 Theodore Fremd Ave
Ste 215
Rye, NY 10580
Phone: 914-967-0670
Web Site: http://www.rossgreenburgproductions.com
Ross Greenburg, Founder & President
Produces TV shows & films.

ALFRED HABER DISTRIBUTION INC.
111 Grand Ave
Ste 203
Palisades Park, NJ 07650
Phone: 201-224-8000
Fax: 201-947-4500
E-mail: info@haberinc.com
Web Site: http://www.alfredhaber.com
Alfred Haber, President
George Scanlon, Chief Financial Officer
Distributes network annual event programming & prime time series/specials, including unscripted reality, crime and investigation, clip shows, pop science, music events and films.

HARMONY GOLD USA INC.
7655 W. Sunset Blvd
Los Angeles, CA 90046-2700
Phones: 323-851-4900; 323-436-7204
Fax: 323-851-5599
E-mail: sales@harmonygold.com
Web Site: http://www.harmonygold.com
Kathryn Davolio, Reservations Coordinator
Produces & distributes animated programs, series, miniseries & documentaries, home video & merchandising; also provides screening room & theatre rentals.

HARPO PRODUCTIONS INC.
110 N Carpenter St
Chicago, IL 60607
Phone: 312-633-1000
Fax: 312-633-1979
Web Site: http://www.oprah.com
Sheri Salata, Co-President
Eric Logan, Co-President
Produces TV talk-shows and feature & made-for-TV films.

HARTLEY FILM FOUNDATION INC.
49 Richmondville Ave
Ste 204
Westport, CT 06880
Phones: 203-226-9500; 800-937-1819
Fax: 203-227-6938
E-mail: info@hartleyfoundation.org
Web Site: http://www.hartleyfoundation.org
Sarah Masters, Managing Director
Laura Healy, Office Manager
Non-profit organization; produces, cultivates, supports & distributes documentaries & audio mediations on world religions, spirituality, ethics & well-being.

HBO ENTERPRISES
1100 Ave of the Americas

FULLY SEARCHABLE • CONTINUOUSLY UPDATED • DISCOUNT RATES FOR PRINT PURCHASERS
For more information call **800-771-9202** or visit **www.warren-news.com**

New York, NY 10036
Phone: 212-512-1329
Web Site: http://www.homeboxoffice.com
Quentin Schaffer, Executive Vice President, Corporate Communications
Jeff Cusson, Senior Vice President, Corporate Affairs
Distributes entertainment TV programming worldwide.

HBO STUDIO PRODUCTIONS
120A E 23rd St
New York, NY 10010
Phone: 212-512-7800
Fax: 212-512-7788
Web Site: http://www.hbostudio.com
Provides video production & post-production services.

HEARST ENTERTAINMENT INC.
300 W 57th St
15th Fl
New York, NY 10019-5238
Phone: 212-969-7553
Fax: 646-280-1553
E-mail: svalenza@hearst.com
Web Site: http://hearstent.com
Neeraj Khemlani, Co-President
George Kliavkoff, Co-President
Stacey Valenza, Senior Vice President, Sales & Marketing
Produces & distributes made-for-TV movies, first-run entertainment, reality/documentary programming & animated series for the global marketplace.

HEARST TELEVISION INC. — See Hearst Entertainment Inc.

HENNINGER MEDIA SERVICES
320 N. Courthouse Rd
Ste 130
Arlington, VA 22201
Phones: 703-243-3444; 888-243-3444
Fax: 703-243-5697
E-mail: hmsinfo@henninger.com
Web Site: http://www.henninger.com
Robert L. Henninger, President & Chief Executive Officer
Eric Hansen, Executive Vice President & Chief Operating Officer
Sam Crawford, Engineering Director
Sue O'Hara, Production Manager
Full-service tele-production facility; provides creative design services; production & multimedia.

HIGH NOON ENTERTAINMENT
15303 Ventura Blvd
Ste C1100
Sherman Oaks, CA 91403
Phone: 818-646-2300
Web Site: http://www.highnoonentertainment.com
Jim Berger, Chief Executive Officer
Duke Hartman, Chief Operating Officer
Sonny Hutchinson, Chief Creative Officer
Pamela Healey, Senior Vice President, Development
Dana Eller Kopper, Vice President, Production

2017 Edition   E-117

Program Sources & Services

John Hardy, Vice President, Finance
Rachel Dax, Executive in Charge of Production

Branch Offices:
DENVER: 3035 S Parker Rd, Ste 500, Denver, CO 80014. Phone: 303-872-8700.

NEW YORK: 375 Greenwich St, 7th Fl, New York, NY 10013. Phone: 212-941-3878.
Independent production company; produces programming for VH1, TLC, Food Network, HGTV, DIY & History. An ITV Plc company.

THE HISTORYMAKERS
1900 S Michigan Ave
Ste 3
Chicago, IL 60616
Phone: 312-674-1900
Fax: 312-674-1915
E-mail: info@thehistorymakers.com
Web Site: http://www.thehistorymakers.com
Julieanna Richardson, Founder, Executive Director & Public Historian
Produces interviews detailing the untold personal stories of both well-known and unsung African Americans.

HOFFMAN COMMUNICATIONS INC.
2900 Washington Ave N
Minneapolis, MN 55411
Phone: 612-436-3600
Fax: 612-436-3619
Mark Hoffman, President
John Sands, Chief Financial Officer
Kathryn Johnson, Client Development Director
Larry King, Show Operations & Technical Director
Gary Oseid, IT Director
Karl Petersen, Production Director
Jeff Pauley, Business Development
Kelly Verner, Business Administrator
Production, creative & staging company; delivers communication solutions for events, training & multimedia production.

HOLLYWOOD VAULTS INC.
742 Seward St
Hollywood, CA 90038
Phones: 323-461-6464; 800-569-5336
Fax: 323-461-6479
E-mail: vault@hollywoodvaults.com
Web Site: http://www.hollywoodvaults.com
David Wexler, Owner & Founder
Julie Wexler, Vice President
Raymond Barber, Operations Manager
Provides preservation-quality storage of film, tape & digital media; temperature & humidity controlled, high-security, fire-proof storage with 24-hour access to private, individual vaults.

HOMESTEAD EDITORIAL INC.
56 West 22nd St
10th Floor
New York, NY 10010
Phone: 212-255-4440
Fax: 212-255-4494
E-mail: hello@lovehomestead.com
Web Site: http://www.homesteadedit.com
Lance Doty, Executive Producer
Provides post-production services.

HOMESTEAD FILMS
56 West 22nd St
10th Floor
New York, NY 10010
Phone: 212-255-4440
Fax: 212-255-4494
E-mail: michael@homesteadfilms.com
Web Site: http://www.homesteadfilms.com

Michael Garza, Executive Producer
Produces independent films.

HYENA EDITORIAL INC.
725 Arizona Ave
Ste 100
Santa Monica, CA 90401
Phone: 310-394-1048
Fax: 310-395-5868
E-mail: keith@hyenaedit.com
Web Site: http://www.hyenaedit.com
Keith Salmon, Founder & Editor
Kim Sprouse, Producer
Provides editorial & post-production services.

I-CUBED HYPERMEDIA
11 W Illinois
4th Fl
Chicago, IL 60654
Phone: 312-464-0911
Fax: 312-464-0511
E-mail: info@i3hypermedia.com
Web Site: http://www.i-cubedhypermedia.com
Provides production & post-production services.

IFC FILMS
11 Penn Plz
15th Fl
New York, NY 10001
Phone: 212-324-8500
E-mail: ifcfilmsinfo@ifcfilms.com
Web Site: http://www.ifcfilms.com
Jonathan Sehring, Co-President
Lisa Schwartz, Co-President

IMG WORLD
200 5th Ave
7th Floor
New York, NY 10010
Phone: 212-489-8300
Fax: 646-558-8399
Web Site: http://www.imgworld.com
Theodore J. Forstmann, Chairman & Chief Executive Officer
Ian Todd, President, IMG International

Branch Offices:
NEW YORK: 304 Park Ave S, New York, NY 10010. Phone: 212-489-8300. Fax: 212-246-1596.

SINGAPORE: One Scotts Rd #21-01/03, Shaw Ctr 228208, Singapore. Phone: 65-6505-9300. Fax: 65-6738-3617.

SPAIN: IMG (Overseas) Inc., Via Augusta 200, 4th Fl, Barcelona E-08021, Spain. Phone: 34-93-200-34-55. Fax: 34-93-200-59-24.

UNITED KINGDOM: McCormack House, Hogarth Business Park, Burlington Ln, Chiswick, London W4 2TH, United Kingdom. Phone: 44-208-233-5300. Fax: 44-208-233-5301.
Produces & distributes sports programming

IMPACT PRODUCTIONS
3939 S Harvard Ave
Ste 100
Tulsa, OK 74135
Phone: 918-877-2000
Fax: 918-877-0222
Web Site: http://www.impactprod.org
Tom Newman, Founder & President
Shane Harwell, Marketing Director
Evan Derrick, Chief Editor
Eric Newman, Lead Writer & Director
Cheryl Barnard, Business Development & Post-Production Producer

Jason Stafford, Line Producer & Assistant Director
Produces documentary dramas, TV programming, 3D animation & feature films.

INTERNATIONAL CONTACT INC.
351 15th St
Oakland, CA 94612
Phone: 510-836-1180
Fax: 510-835-1314
E-mail: info@intlcontact.com
Web Site: http://www.intlcontact.com
Carla Itzkowich, President
Provides translation, audio, web page localization, video & multimedia production, desktop publishing, research & consultation in all languages.

INTERNATIONAL MEDIA DISTRIBUTION (IMD)
4100 E Dry Creek Rd
Centennial, CO 80122
Phone: 303-712-5400
Fax: 303-712-5401
E-mail: info@imd.us.com
Web Site: http://www.imediadistribution.com
Scott Wheeler, Senior Vice President, Network Development
Mike Scott, Vice President, Affiliate Sales & Marketing
Kajsa Moe, Affiliate Sales & Marketing Director
Nicole Wang, Associate Director, Affiliate Sales & Marketing

Branch Offices:
LOS ANGELES: 5750 Wilshire Blvd, 3rd Fl, Los Angeles, CA 90036. Phone: 323-692-5348. Fax: 323-954-2991.

SEATTLE: 18 W Mercer, Ste 110, Seattle, WA 98119. Phone: 206-282-2762. Fax: 206-282-2763.
Provides in-language programming; represents over 30 TV channels including two SVOD services with content from a variety of international sources.

INTERNATIONAL PROGRAM CONSULTANTS INC.
52 E End Ave
Ste 24
New York, NY 10028
Phone: 212-734-9096
Russell Kagan, President
Produces & distributes TV programming.

INTERNATIONAL TELE-FILM
30 MacIntosh Blvd
Unit 7
Vaughan, ON L4K 4P1
Canada
Phones: 416-252-1173; 800-561-4300
Fax: 866-664-7545
Web Site: http://www.itf.ca
Teresa Machado, Account Manager
Susan Walklate, Business Manager
Represents training resource producers; resources are available on DVD & online; many programs are available in other languages.

IT IS WRITTEN INTERNATIONAL TELEVISION
PO Box 6
Chattanooga, TN 37401-0006
Phone: 844-974-8836
Fax: 877-507-3239
E-mail: iiw@iiw.org
Web Site: http://www.iiw.org
Shawn Boonstra, Director
Produces & distributes TV programs & video tapes.

IVANHOE BROADCAST NEWS INC.
2745 W Fairbanks Ave
Winter Park, FL 32789
Phone: 407-740-0789
Fax: 407-740-5320
E-mail: mthomas@ivanhoe.com
Web Site: http://www.ivanhoe.com
Marjorie Bekhaert Thomas, President & Publisher
John Cherry, President, Sales
Bette Bon Fleur, Chief Executive Officer Emeritus
Produces & syndicates programming on health, medicine & news for women ages 25-54.

JANUS FILMS CO.
215 Park Ave. S
5th Floor
New York, NY 10003
Phone: 212-756-8822
E-mail: booking@janusfilms.com
Web Site: http://www.janusfilms.com
Distributes motion picture features & shorts, foreign language films, TV film & tape series; stock footage; film buyer; imports films.

THE JIM HENSON COMPANY
1416 N LaBrea Ave
Hollywood, CA 90028
Phone: 323-802-1500
Fax: 323-802-1825
Web Site: http://www.henson.com
Brian Henson, Chairman
Lisa Henson, Chief Executive Officer
Peter Schube, President & Chief Operating Officer
Laurie Don, Executive Vice President, Operations & Finance
Dan Scharf, Executive Vice President, Business Affairs & General Counsel
Halle Stanford, Executive Vice President, Children Entertainment
Nicole Goldman, Vice President, Marketing & Public Relations

Branch Offices:
NEW YORK: 37-18 Northern Blvd, Ste 400, Long Island City, NY 11101. Phone: 212-794-2400. Fax: 212-439-7452.
Produces programming.

JOHNSON PUBLISHING CO. INC.
200 S Michigan Ave
#2000
Chicago, IL 60604
Phone: 312-322-9200
Web Site: http://www.johnsonpublishing.com
Linda Johnson Rice, Chairman & Chief Executive Officer
Anne Sempowskiward, President & Chief Operations Officer
Eunice W. Johnson, Secretary & Treasurer

Branch Offices:
NEW YORK: 1270 Ave of the Americas, Ste 1705, New York, NY 10020. Phone: 212-397-4500.

WASHINGTON, DC: 1750 Pennsylvania Ave NW, Ste 1201, Washington, DC 20006. Phone: 202-393-5860.
Produces TV programming.

JOINT HOMETOWN NEWS SERVICE
PO Box 3603
New Bern, NC 28564
Phones: 301-222-6287/6294; 301-222-6691
E-mail: admin@usafns.com
Web Site: http://jhns.dma.mil
Formerly known as Army & Air Force Hometown News Service. Produces & distributes

Program Sources & Services

free news & features about American men & women in uniform serving around the world; produces free annual holiday greetings; products distributed to TV stations in service members' hometown.

JUMP TV
463 King St W
3rd Fl
Toronto, ON M5V 1K4
Canada
Phone: 647-426-1310
E-mail: support@jumptv.com
Web Site: http://www.jumptv.com
Blair Baxter, Chief Financial Officer
Scott Paterson, Vice Chairman & President
Elmer Sotto, Vice President, Product & Business Operations
Jay Howard, Vice President & General Counsel

Branch Offices:
NEW YORK: 45 E 34th St, 5th Floor, New York, NY 10016.
Delivers content from several countries & channels through multiple Internet-enabled devices.

JUPITER ENTERTAINMENT
1250 Broadway
12th Fl
New York, NY 10001
Phone: 212-897-2185
E-mail: info@jupiterent.com
Web Site: http://www.jupiterent.com
Stephen Land, Chief Executive Officer & Executive Producer
Allison Wallach, President
Robert Twilley, Senior Vice President & General Manager
Deborah Allen, Vice President, Programming & Executive Producer
Todd Moss, Vice President, Programming & Executive Producer
Harris Land, Senior Director, Development
Julie Dean, Finance Director
John Kennedy, Operations Director
Steven McGovern, Production Director

Branch Offices:
KNOXVILLE: 8923 Linksvue Dr, Knoxville, TN 37922. Phone: 865-588-2626. Fax: 865-588-2202.
Produces unscripted, non-fiction programming, including docuseries, true crime thrillers, lifestyle formats & docu-soaps.

KABOOM! ENTERTAINMENT INC.
1867 Yonge St
Ste 650
Toronto, ON M4S 1Y5
Canada
Phones: 416-783-8383; 866-495-3650
Fax: 416-783-8384
E-mail: info@phase4films.com
Web Site: http://www.kaboom-ent.com
Berry Meyerowitz, President
David Richardson, Vice President, Sales
Lori Nytko, Operations Coordinator
Sells, markets, licenses & distributes DVDs, videos & ancillary merchandise. Nine offices in the U.S. & Canada.

KAMEN ENTERTAINMENT GROUP INC.
200 E 94th St
New York, NY 10128
Phone: 212-575-4660
Fax: 212-575-4799
E-mail: kamen@kamen.com
Web Site: http://www.kamen.com

Marina Kamen, Creative Director & Casting & Senior Music Producer
Roy Kamen, Senior Sound Designer, Radio Producer & Chief Mixer
Provides audio recording services; music library, original music, sound effects, voice-over casting, radio production & direction; 24-track recording studio; live shows.

KILLER TRACKS: NETWORK MUSIC
2110 Colorado Ave
Ste 110
Santa Monica, CA 90404
Phones: 310-865-4455; 800-454-5537
Fax: 310-865-4470
E-mail: sales@killertracks.com
Web Site: http://www.killertracks.com
Andy Donahue, Marketing Director
Produces & distributes music; sound effects libraries.

KINETIC CONTENT
11755 Wilshire Blvd
Ste 2000
Los Angeles, CA 90025
Phone: 310-883-7000
E-mail: psadighi@kineticcontent.com
Web Site: http://www.kineticcontent.com
Katie Griffin, Co-Head, Development & Programming
Produces TV series.

KING WORLD PRODUCTIONS INC. —
See listing for CBS Television Distribution

KLEIN &
8896 Carson St
Culver City, CA 90232
Phone: 310-317-9599
Fax: 310-456-7701
E-mail: bob@lafestival.org
Web Site: http://www.lafestival.org
Robert Klein, President
Markets & promotes electronic media, cable, TV; custom campaigns, including thematic concepts, music, animation & live action.

KULTUR INTERNATIONAL FILMS INC.
PO Box 755
Forked River, NJ 08731
Phone: 888-329-2580
E-mail: support@kultur.com
Web Site: http://www.kulturvideo.com
Dennis M. Hedlund, Chairman
Distributes performing arts home videos.

KUSA PRODUCTIONS
500 E. Speer Blvd
Denver, CO 80203
Phones: 303-871-9999; 303-871-1487
E-mail: kusa@9news.com
Web Site: http://www.9news.com
Mark Cornetta, President & General Manager
Provides film & video production & post-production; produces TV commercials, documentaries, industrials & programming.

KUSHNER LOCKE CO. INC.
280 S Beverly Dr
Ste 205
Beverly Hills, CA 90212
Phone: 310-275-7508
Fax: 310-275-7518
E-mail: info@kushnerlocke.com
Web Site: http://www.kushnerlocke.com
Donald Kushner, Co-Chairman, Co-Chief Executive Officer & Secretary
Peter Locke, Co-Chairman & Co-Chief Executive Officer
Bruce S. Lilliston, President & Chief Operations Officer

Brett Robinson, Chief Financial Officer & Senior Vice President
Distributes independent lower budget film & TV products; library includes 205 titles with over 1,000 hours of film & TV programming.

KYLINTV
1600 Old Country Rd
Plainview, NY 11803
Phones: 516-622-8454; 877-888-8598
Fax: 877-888-8597
E-mail: info@kylintv.com
Web Site: http://www.kylintv.com
Jianbing Duan, Chief Executive Officer
Richard N. Yelen, Vice President & Managing Director
Frieda Shieh, Marketing Director
Provides entertainment & news from China. Also offers SUN TV, a Japanese broadcasting service.

LATHAM FOUNDATION
1320 Harbor Bay Pkwy
Ste 200
Alameda, CA 94502
Phone: 510-521-0920
Fax: 510-521-9861
E-mail: info@latham.org
Web Site: http://www.latham.org
Produces & distributes educational programming, TV films & videos; humane & environmentally oriented; educational foundation; publishes a quarterly newsletter.

LEFTFIELD PICTURES
460 W 34th St
16th Fl
New York, NY 10001
Phone: 212-564-2607
Fax: 212-967-7573
Web Site: http://www.leftfieldpictures.com
Brent Montgomery, Owner & Executive Producer
Heath Banks, Chief Operating Officer
David George, President & Executive Producer
Adam Sher, Chief Creative Officer
Jerry DiMeglio, Chief Financial Officer
Chris Silvestri, General Counsel & Executive Vice President & Legal Affairs
Will Nothacker, Senior Vice President, Development
Ed Simpson, Senior Vice President, Business Development & International
Shawn Witt, Senior Vice President, Programming
Danielle Bibbo, Vice President, Production
Danielle DiStefano, Vice President, Post Production
Daniel Gingerich, Vice President, Finance
Simon Thomas, Vice President, Current Programming
Produces reality programming. A Leftfield Entertainment Co.

LEGENDARY ENTERTAINMENT
2900 W Alameda Ave
15th Fl
Burbank, CA 91505
Phone: 818-688-7003
E-mail: licensing@legendary.com; television@legendary.com
Web Site: http://www.legendary.com

Thomas Tull, Chairman & Chief Executive Officer
Owns, produces & distibutes film, TV & digital programming.

LESEA BROADCASTING NETWORK
61300 S Ironwood Rd
South Bend, IN 46614
Phone: 574-291-8200
Fax: 574-291-9043
Web Site: http://www.lesea.com
Peter Sumrall, President
Produces TV programs, infomercials, documentaries, commercials, corporate communications, live productions/programming & sporting events. Capabilities include video, audio, internet, satellite & multimedia.

LEAR LEVIN PRODUCTIONS INC.
16 W 88th St
New York, NY 10024
Phone: 212-595-5526
Lear Levin, President & Founder
Produces TV commercials.

LIFESTYLE MAGAZINE
PO Box 7729
Riverside, CA 92513
Phones: 805-955-7681; 888-940-0062
E-mail: info@lifestyle.org
Web Site: http://www.lifestyle.org
Michael L. Tucker, Executive Producer, Director & Co-Host
Gayle Tucker, Co-Host & Relationship Expert
Dr. Sharmini Long, Co-Host & Expert in Internal Medicine, Obesity Medicine and Endocrinology
Obi Obadike, Fitness & Nutrition Co-Host
Lynell LaMountain, Co-Host & Expert on Lifestyle Choices
Produces a half hour talk show that focuses on all aspects of whole life. Also produces The Evidence & McDougall MD.

LINCOLN SQUARE PRODUCTIONS
West End Ave
New York, NY 10023
Web Site: http://www.lincolnsquareproductions.com
Develops & produces non-fiction programming, including docuseries, topical specials, live events & scripted dramas.

LINSMAN FILM
5700 Wilshire Blvd
Ste 675
Los Angeles, CA 90036
Phone: 323-571-4535
Fax: 323-571-1378
E-mail: bill@linsman.com
Web Site: http://www.linsman.com
William D. Linsman, President & Director
Paula Panich, Vice President
Tim Goldberg, Representative
Produces TV commercials & programs. See also Ocean Park Pictures Inc.

LIONSGATE ENTERTAINMENT
2700 Colorado Ave
Santa Monica, CA 90404
Phone: 310-449-9200

Program Sources & Services

Fax: 310-255-3870
E-mail: general-inquiries@lionsgate.com
Web Site: http://www.lionsgate.com
Dr. Mark H. Rachesky, Chairman
Kevin Beggs, Chairman, Lionsgate Television Group
Michael Burns, Vice Chairman
Jon Feltheimer, Chief Executive Officer
Steve Beeks, Co-Chief Operating Officer & President, Motion Picture Group
Brian Goldsmith, Co-Chief Operating Officer
James W. Barge, Chief Financial Officer
Sean Kisker, Chief Strategy Officer & General Manager, Motion Picture Group
Wayne Levin, Chief Strategy Officer
Tim Palen, Chief Brand Officer
Peter Iacono, President, International Television & Digital Distribution
Peter Levin, President, Interactive Ventures & Games
Jim Packer, President, Worldwide Television & Digital Distribution
Ron Schwartz, President, Lionsgate Home Entertainment
Sandra Stern, President, Lionsgate Television Group
Thomas Hughes, Executive Vice President, Worldwide Digital Distribution
Agapy Kapouranis, Executive Vice President, Global SVOD
Jennifer O'Connell, Executive Vice President, Alternative Programming, Lionsgate Television Group
Ross Pollack, Executive Vice President & Chief Human Resources Officer
Lawrence Szabo, Executive Vice President, North American TV & SVOD Sales
James Marsh, Senior Vice President, Investor Relations

Branch Offices:
NEW YORK: 75 Rockefeller Plz, 16th Fl, New York, NY 10007. Phone: 212-577-2400.

CANADA: 2200-1055 W Hastings St., Vancouver, BC V6E 2E9, Canada. Phones: 604-983-5555; 877-848-3866. Fax: 604-983-5554.

AUSTRALIA: Lev 29, Chifley Tower, Two Chifley Sq, Sydney, NSW 2000, Australia.

UNITED KINGDOM: c/o Ariel House, 74A Charlotte St, London E1T 4QJ, United Kingdom. Phone: 44-0-20-7299-8800.
Produces & distributes motion pictures, TV programming, home entertainment, family entertainment & video-on-demand content.

LITTON ENTERTAINMENT
884 Allbritton Blvd
Ste 200
Mt Pleasant, SC 29464
Phone: 843-883-5060
Fax: 843-883-9957
E-mail: dwall@litton.tv
Web Site: http://www.litton.tv
Dave Morgan, Chief Executive Officer
Pete Sniderman, Chief Operating Officer
Tom Warner, Executive Vice President, Domestic Distribution
Kimi Serrano-Schenck, Senior Vice President, Syndication & New Media
Nancy Smeltzer, Vice President, Operations
Josh Levin, Program Development
Provides strip programming, weekly series, high impact TV specials, theatrical movies & news content; production studio; media sales.

LNS CAPTIONING
1123 SW Yamhill St
Portland, OR 97205
Phones: 503-299-6200; 800-366-6201
Fax: 503-299-6839
E-mail: cstudenmund@LNSCaptioning.com
Web Site: http://www.lnscaptioning.com
Carol Studenmund, President
Offers realtime & post-production closed captions for TV, video & webcasting, along with Internet realtime streaming & event captioning.

LOGIC GENERAL INC.
26200 SW 95th Ave
Ste 300
Wilsonville, OR 97070
Phone: 503-598-7747
Fax: 503-598-9375
Tara Hagman, Customer Service Manager

Branch Offices:
SEATTLE: 55 S Atlantic, Ste A-1, Seattle, WA 98134. Phone: 206-973-4200. Fax: 206-973-4201.

TEMPE: 1835 E Sixth St, Ste 1, Tempe, AZ 85281. Phone: 480-736-8959. Fax: 480-736-8961.
Manufactures CDs & DVDs; produces more than 90,000 units per day. Provides a combination of turnkey & media manufacturing resources.

LOOK & CO.
280 Park Ave S
New York, NY 10010
Phone: 212-629-7400
Fax: 212-629-3964
Produces original music & sound design for advertising, film & TV.

LOUD TV
460 W 34th St
5th Fl
New York, NY 10001
Phone: 646-459-8180
Fax: 212-967-7573
E-mail: info@loudtelevision.com
Web Site: http://www.loudtelevision.com
Nick Rigg, President
Jordana Hochman, Senior Vice President & Head of Programming
Produces a broad range of unscripted TV & digital content. A Leftfield Entertainment Co.

LX.TV
c/o NBC Local Media
30 Rockefeller Ctr
New York, NY 10112
Phone: 212-698-2000
E-mail: contact@lxtvn.com
Web Site: http://www.lxtv.com
Morgan Hertzan, Co-Founder
Joseph Varet, Co-Founder
Meredith McGinn, Senior Vice President
John Durso Jr., Vice President, Community & Communications

Branch Offices:
CHICAGO: 454 N Columbus Dr, 5th Fl, Chicago, IL 60611.

LOS ANGELES: 3000 W Alameda Ave, Bungalow 1585, Burbank, CA 91523.
Produces original lifestyle shows & specials.

LYNX IMAGES INC.
PO Box 2463
Station C
St John's, NL A1C 6E8
Canada
Phone: 709-576-3366
Fax: 709-576-3367
E-mail: website@lynximages.com
Web Site: http://www.lynximages.com
Russell Floren, President & Producer
Barbara Chisholm, Vice President, Production & Publishing
Andrea Gutsche, Vice President, Creative
Produces film, video & TV programming; documentaries include history, nature, travel video & books.

MAGINGLIA MEDIA
7925 Jones Branch Dr
Ste LL110
Tysons, VA 22102
Phones: 703-942-8011; 703-283-8532 (cell)
E-mail: frank@manigliamedia.com
Web Site: http://www.manigliamedia.com
Offers full service script & screen creative & branding; post-production services.

MAKER STUDIOS INC.
13428 Maxella Ave.
#525
Los Angeles, CA 90016
Phone: 310-606-2182
Web Site: http://www.makerstudios.com
Courtney Holt, Executive Vice President
Ryan Lissack, Chief Technology Officer
Chris M. Williams, Chief Audience Officer
Produces short-form video. Subsidiary of The Walt Disney Co.

MARYKNOLL WORLD PRODUCTIONS
PO Box 308
Walsh Bldg
Maryknoll, NY 10545
Phones: 914-941-7636 x2558; 800-258-5838
Fax: 914-945-0670
E-mail: syndication@maryknoll.org
Produces & distributes educational & religious films, documentary films/videos & TV tape series.

MAYSLES FILMS INC.
343 Lenox Ave
New York, NY 10027
Phone: 212-582-6050
Fax: 212-586-2057
E-mail: info@maysleșfilms.com
Web Site: http://www.maysleșfilms.com
Albert Maysles, Chief Executive Officer
K. A. Dilday, General Manager
Produces & distributes documentaries; produces commercials & corporate films.

MCGUANE STUDIO INC.
36 Horatio St
New York, NY 10014
Phone: 212-463-7259
Jim P. McGuane, President
Produces commercials, industrials, short features, documentaries & music videos.

MEADOWLANE ENTERPRISES INC.
15201 Burbank Blvd
Ste B
Van Nuys, CA 91411
Phone: 818-988-3830
Fax: 818-988-0276
E-mail: meadowlane@sbcglobal.net
Bill Allen, President
Licenses a library of classic TV series.

MEDIALINK WORLDWIDE INC.
The Video News Release Network
708 Third Ave
New York, NY 10017
Phones: 212-682-8300; 800-843-0677
Fax: 212-682-5260
E-mail: LearnMore@synapticdigital.com
Web Site: http://www.medialink.com
Michael Kassan, Chairman & Chief Executive Officer
Krish A. Menon, Chief Technology Officer
Lena Petersen, Chief Brand Officer
Dee Salomon, Chief Marketing Officer
Tom Morrissy, Executive Vice President, Sales
Daryl Evans, Senior Vice President, Mobile, Media & Advertising Strategy
Jennifer Kasper, Senior Vice President
Richard Kellner, Vice President, Finance
Andrew Lipson, Vice President, Operations
Matt Thomson, Managing Director, Europe

Branch Offices:
CHICAGO: 401 N Michigan Ave, Ste 2100, Chicago, IL 60611. Phone: 312-222-9850. Fax: 312-222-9810. E-Mail: zrobbins@medialink.com.

LOS ANGELES: 6404 Wilshire Blvd, Los Angeles, CA 90048. Phone: 323-653-8535. E-Mail: bmiddleton@medialink.com.

SAN FRANCISCO: 8 California St, Ste 500, San Francisco, CA 94111. Phone: 415-912-1650. E-Mail: sbratman@medialink.com.

WASHINGTON, DC: 529 14th St NW, Ste 450, Washington, DC 20045. Phone: 202-628-3800. Fax: 202-628-2377.

UNITED KINGDOM: 10-11 Percy St, London, England W1T1DN. Phone: 44-20-7580-8330.
Produces & distributes satellite video & audio news releases worldwide; satellite & radio media tours; corporate videos, Internet & newswire services.

MEDSTAR TELEVISION INC.
5920 Hamilton Blvd
Allentown, PA 18106
Phone: 610-395-1300
E-mail: Help@medstar.com
Web Site: http://www.medstar.com
Independently produces & syndicates medical news, health & wellness information programming.

LEE MENDELSON FILM PRODUCTIONS INC.
330 Primrose Rd
Ste 215
Burlingame, CA 94010-4028
Phone: 650-342-8284
Fax: 650-342-6170
E-mail: jason@mendelsonproductions.com
Web Site: http://www.mendelsonproductions.com
Produces industrial & educational films, open-end film commercials (made for TV), TV film & tape series & spot commercials, film programs on order & theatrical shorts.

MGM TELEVISION ENTERTAINMENT INC.
245 N Beverly Dr
Beverly Hills, CA 90210
Phone: 310-449-3000
E-mail: mgmonline@mgm.com
Web Site: http://www.mgm.com/tv
Gary Barber, Chairman & Chief Executive Officer, MGM
Kenneth Kay, Chief Financial Officer
Mark Burnett, President, MGM Television & Digital
John Bryan, President, Domestic Television Distribution
Kevin Conroy, President, Digital & New Platforms
Chris Ottinger, President, Worldwide Television Distribution & Acquisitions
Barry Poznick, President, Unscripted TV

E-120   TV & Cable Factbook No. 85

Steve Stark, President, Television Production & Development
LindsAy Sloane, Executive Vice President, Production & Development
Vicky Gregorian, Senior Vice President, Domestic Television Distribution
Susan Hummel, Senior Vice President, US Basic Cable & Canadian Television
Damien Marin, Senior Vice President, Pay Television & Digital Media
Vinicio Espinosa, Vice President, Latin American Television Distribution
Max Kisbye, Vice President, Television Production
Produces & distributes TV programming.

WARREN MILLER ENTERTAINMENT
5720 Flatiron Pkwy
Boulder, CO 80301
Phone: 303-253-6300
Fax: 303-253-6380
E-mail: wmfeedback@aimmedia.com
Web Site: http://www.skinet.com/warrenmiller
Jeffrey Moore, Senior Executive Producer
Ginger Sheehy, Development Manager
Josh Haskins, Producer
John Barcklay, Post Production Supervisor
Provides production & post-production services; fully capable in all media from digital video to full resolution HD; produces for both broadcast & broadband. Division of Bonnier Mountain Group.

MILNER-FENWICK INC.
119 Lakefront Dr
Hunt Valley, MD 21030-2216
Phones: 410-252-1700; 800-432-8433
Fax: 410-252-6316
E-mail: mail@milner-fenwick.com
Web Site: http://www.milner-fenwick.com
David Milner, President
Produces TV film & tape series and film programs on order; produces & distributes industrial & educational films; animation music library, recording facilities, studio facilities for rent & other services.

MIRAMAX
2450 Colorado Ave
Ste 100 East Tower
Santa Monica, CA 90404
Phone: 310-409-4321
E-mail: worldwidesales@miramax.com
Web Site: http://www.miramax.com
Steve Schoch, Chief Financial Officer & Interim Chief Executive Officer
Zanne Devine, Executive Vice President, Production & Development
Beth Minehart, Executive Vice President, Global Digital
Joe Patrick, Executive Vice President, Head of Worldwide Sales
Adrienne Gary, Senior Vice President, Organizational Strategy & Administration
Danny Goldman, Senior Vice President, Head of European Sales
Mitzi Reaugh, Senior Vice President, Strategy & Business Development
Daniel Pipski, Vice President, Television
Bob Cook, Strategic Adviser to Chief Executive Officer
Lindsay Gardner, Strategic Adviser to Chief Executive Officer
Produces & distributes motion picture films & television shows.

MODERN SOUND PICTURES INC.
1402 Howard St
Omaha, NE 68102
Phones: 402-341-8476; 800-228-9584
Fax: 402-341-8487
E-mail: info@modernsoundpictures.com
Web Site: http://www.modernsoundpictures.com
Sandra L. Smith, President
Distributes non-theatrical entertainment features & shorts; sells & rents audio/visual equipment.

MOFFITT-LEE PRODUCTIONS
1438 N Gower St
Ste 250
Los Angeles, CA 90028
Phone: 323-382-3469
John Moffitt, President
Produces TV film & tape series.

MONKEYLAND AUDIO INC.
1750 Flower St
Glendale, CA 91201
Phone: 818-553-0955
Fax: 818-553-1155
E-mail: info@monkeylandaudio.com
Web Site: http://www.monkeylandaudio.com
Trip Brock, Principal & Supervising Sound Editor
Rob Embrey, Scheduling & Operations Manager
Full-service, state-of-the-art digital audio post-production facility. Provides full post sound packages, including sound supervision, editorial, ADR, Foley & re-recording mixing services. Services the audio post-production needs of film studios, TV & cable networks.

JESS S. MORGAN & CO.
5900 Wilshire Blvd
Ste 2300
Los Angeles, CA 90036
Phone: 323-634-2400
Fax: 323-937-6532
E-mail: info@jsmco.com
Web Site: http://www.jsmco.com
Jess S. Morgan, Owner
Provides TV sales & syndication for Carol Burnett & Friends.

MOVIECRAFT INC.
PO Box 438
Orland Park, IL 60462-0438
Phone: 708-460-9082
E-mail: orders@moviecraft.com
Web Site: http://www.moviecraft.com
Larry Urbanski, President
Develops, produces & distributes programming for TV & home video; archival stock footage.

MULTICOM ENTERTAINMENT GROUP INC.
1575 Westwood Blvd
Ste 300
Los Angeles, CA 90024
Phone: 310-445-0700
Fax: 310-445-0703
E-mail: info@multicom.tv
Web Site: http://www.multicom.tv
Irv Holender, Chairman
Distributes content with a focus on the worldwide TV market, as well as digital media platforms including pay-per-view, Internet, mobile channels, co-productions, publishing, licensing & merchandising; co-produces original programming.

MUSCULAR DYSTROPHY ASSOCIATION
222 S. Riverside Plaza
Ste 1500
Chicago, IL 60606
Phone: 800-572-1717
E-mail: mda@mdausa.org
Web Site: http://www.mdausa.org
National voluntary health agency; produces the annual Jerry Lewis Labor Day Telethon.

MY DAMN CHANNEL
The Film Center
630 9th Ave, Ste 1012
New York, NY 10036
Phones: 212-582-2199; 310-734-6500
E-mail: info@mydamnchannel.com
Web Site: http://www.mydamnchannel.com
Rob Barnett, Co-Founder & Chief Executive Officer
Warren Chao, Co-Founder & Chief Operating Officer
Matt Kaplan, Chief Revenue Officer
Dork Alahydoian, Vice President, Business Development
Jesse Cowell, Content Director
Maria Alana Diokno, Social Media Director
Eric Mortensen, Programming & Acquisitions Director
Melissa Schneider, Production Director
Molly Templeton, Talent & Audience Development Director
Produces & distributes original series, including comedy, unscripted reality & live variety programming.

MYFOOTAGE.COM
244 Fifth Ave
Ste 2768
New York, NY 10001
Phone: 212-620-3955
Web Site: http://www.myfootage.com
Offers a stock footage library & stock photos.

NATIONAL CAPTIONING INSTITUTE
3725 Concorde Pkwy
Ste 100
Chantilly, VA 20151
Phone: 703-917-7600
Fax: 703-917-9853
E-mail: croney@ncicap.org
Web Site: http://www.ncicap.org
Gene Chao, Chairman, President & Chief Executive Officer
Drake Smith, Chief Technology Officer
Juan Mario Agudelo, Sales & Marketing Director
Beth Nubbe, Off-Line Captioning & Described Media Director
Marc Okrand, Administration & Live Captioning Director

Branch Offices:
BURBANK: 303 N Glenoaks Blvd, Ste 200, Burbank, CA 91502. Phone: 818-238-0068. Fax: 818-238-4266. E-Mail: esarna@ncicap.org. Elissa Sarna, West Coast Sales & Marketing Director.

DALLAS: 7610 N Stemmons Frwy, Ste 200, Dallas, TX 75247. Phone: 214-647-4360. Fax: 214-647-4386. E-Mail: croney@ncicap.org. Nonprofit firm that launched captioning in 1980; provides captioning & audio description services for broadcast, CATV, web streaming, DVD and government & corporate video programming. Provides subtitling & translation services in over 40 languages.

Program Sources & Services

Communications Daily
Warren Communications News

Get the industry standard FREE —
For a no-obligation trial call 800-771-9202 or visit www.warren-news.com

NATIONAL COUNCIL OF CHURCHES USA (NCC)
110 Maryland Ave NE
Ste 108
Washington, DC 20002-5603
Phone: 202-544-2350
Fax: 202-543-1297
E-mail: info@nationalcouncilofchurches.us
Web Site: http://www.nationalcouncilofchurches.us
Jim Winkler, General Secretary
Distributes religious films & TV film & tape series; produces network religious programs.

NATIONAL FILM BOARD OF CANADA
PO Box 6100
Station Centre-ville
Montreal, PQ H3C 3HS
Canada
Phones: 514-283-9000; 800-267-7710
Fax: 514-283-7564
Web Site: http://www.onf-nfb.gc.ca
Tom Perlmutter, Government Film Commissioner
Claude Joli-Coeur, Assistant Commissioner
Deborah Drisdell, Director General, Accessibility & Digital Enterprises
Luisa Frate, Director General, Finance, Operations & Technology
Monique Simard, Director General, French Program
Cindy Witten, Director General, English Program
Lily Robert, Communications Director
Distributes animation, motion picture shorts, foreign language films, theatrical shorts & individual program-documentaries for TV.

NATIONAL GEOGRAPHIC TELEVISION
PO Box 98199
Washington, DC 20090-8199
Phone: 800-647-5463
E-mail: pressroom@ngs.org
Web Site: http://www.nationalgeographic.com/tv
John Fahey, Chairman, Board of Trustees, National Geographic Society
Gary Knell, President & Chief Executive Officer, National Geographic Society
Brooke Runnette, President
Tim Pastore, Executive Vice President, Programming & Development
Produces nature, adventure & science films for commercial & non-commercial broadcast TV, CATV, home video & international TV/video.

NATIONAL TECHNICAL INFORMATION SERVICE
5301 Shawnee Rd
Alexandria, VA 22312
Phones: 703-605-6000; 800-553-6847
Fax: 703-605-6900
E-mail: info@ntis.gov
Web Site: http://www.ntis.gov
Bruce Borzino, Director
Distributes federally produced audiovisual programs including safety & health, medicine, history, social issues, dentistry & geography.

2017 Edition E-121

Program Sources & Services

NAVY OFFICE OF INFORMATION (OI-03)
1200 Navy Pentagon
Washington, DC 20350-1200
Phone: 703-697-5342
E-mail: chinfo.dutyoffic.fct@navy.mil
Web Site: http://www.navy.mil/local/chinfo
Terry Halverson, Chief Information Officer
Produces Dept. of Navy public affairs program.

NBC NEWS
30 Rockefeller Plz
New York, NY 10112
Phone: 212-664-4444
E-mail: nightly@nbc.com
Web Site: http://www.nbcnews.com
Andy Lack, Chairman, NBC News & MSNBC
Deborah Turness, President, NBC News
Mark Lukasiewicz, Senior Vice President, NBC News Specials
Produces global news & informational programming for the network's primetime, late-night & daytime schedules. Division of NBC Universal Inc.

NETFLIX
100 Winchester Cir
Los Gatos, CA 95032
Phones: 408-540-3700; 877-742-1480
E-mail: pr@netflix.com
Web Site: http://www.netflix.com
Reed Hastings, Co-Founder & Chief Executive Officer
Kelly Bennett, Chief Marketing Officer
Tawni Cranz, Chief Talent Officer
Jonathan Friedland, Chief Communications Officer
Neil Hunt, Chief Product Officer
Greg Peters, Chief Streaming & Partnerships Officer
Ted Sarandos, Chief Content Officer
David Wells, Chief Financial Officer
David Hyman, General Counsel
Cindy Holland, Vice President, Original Content
Anne Marie Squeo, Corporate Communications Director
Jane Wiseman, Senior Executive, Original Programming

NETHERLANDS CONSULATE GENERAL
Press & Cultural Section
One Rockefeller Pl, 11th Fl
New York, NY 10020-2094
Phone: 877-388-2443
Fax: 212-333-3603
E-mail: nyc-pcz@minbuza.nl
Web Site: http://www.cgny.org
Ferdinand Dorsman, General Director, Cultural Affairs
Robert Kloos, Visual Arts & Architecture Director
Arthur Kibbelaar, Press & Cultural Affairs Counsel

NEW FORM DIGITAL
2016 Broadway
Santa Monica, CA 90404
Phone: 310-586-0033
Web Site: http://newformdigital.com
Kathleen Grace, Chief Creative Officer
Melissa Schneider, Senior Vice President, Development & Production
J. C. Cangilla, Senior Vice President, Business Development
Produces original video content for digital platforms. Independent venture between Discovery Communications, Brian Grazer, Ron Howard, Craig Jacobson, Ed Wilson, Jim Wiatt, Michael Rosenberg & CAA.

NEWS BROADCAST NETWORK
451 Park Ave S
New York, NY 10016
Phones: 212-684-8910; 800-920-6397
Fax: 212-684-9650
E-mail: info@newsbroadcastnetwork.com
Web Site: http://www.newsbroadcastnetwork.com
Michael J. Hill, President
Tom Hill, Senior Vice President
Richard M. Neuman, Vice President, Broadcasting/Technology & Executive Producer, Live/Special Events
Steve Gold, NBN Healthcare Director
Laura Pair, Editorial Operations Director
Rick Vasta, Video Production Services Director
Bob Hill, Executive Producer
Produces & distributes video news releases, public service announcements, satellite media tours & marketing productions.

NEWTON MEDIA ASSOCIATES INC.
824 Greenbrier Pkwy
Ste 200
Chesapeake, VA 23320
Phone: 757-547-5400
Fax: 757-547-7383
E-mail: info@newtonmedia.com
Web Site: http://www.newtonmedia.com
Steven M. Newton, President & Chief Executive Officer
Janet Burke, Media Director
Aimee James, Media Buyer
Aubry Winfrey, Media Buyer
Steve Warnecke, New Business Development
Deborah Felmay, Account Executive
Specializes in creating & managing integrated TV, radio, print & interactive media campaigns for DRTV, corporate & charitable organizations.

NEW VISIONS SYNDICATION
44895 Hwy 82
Aspen, CO 81611
Phone: 970-366-2312
E-mail: kayla@newvisionssyndication.com
Web Site: http://www.newvisionssyndication.com
Rodney H. Jacobs, Chairman
Kayla B. Hoffman-Cook, Vice President, Syndication
Chris Laursen, Syndication Director
Produces & distributes entertainment, promotional & educational films; TV syndication, cable distribution, specials & series and stock footage.

NFL FILMS INC.
One Sabol Way
Mt Laurel, NJ 08054
Phone: 856-222-3500
Fax: 856-638-0754
E-mail: sales.facility@nfl.com
Web Site: http://www.nflfilms.com
Howard Katz, Chief Operating Officer
Produces educational films, motion picture shorts, TV film & tape series, film programs on order, stock footage & National Football League series, vignettes, footage, films & home video; provides laboratory facilities & services, music library, recording facilities & studio facilities for rent.

NORFLICKS PRODUCTIONS LTD.
124 Dupont St
Toronto, ON M5R 1V2
Canada
Phone: 416-351-7558
Fax: 416-351-8165
E-mail: mail@norflicks.com
Web Site: http://www.norflicks.com

Richard G. Nielsen, President
James Lau, Chief Financial Officer
Marc Ouellet, Manager, Corporate Affairs & Production
Patricia Joyes, Executive Assistant & Producer
Provides production consulting; produces TV series & feature films.

NORTHEAST VIDEO PRODUCTIONS
184 Birchcroft Rd
Leominster, MA 01453
Phone: 978-534-0882
E-mail: nevideo1@verizon.net
Web Site: http://www.nevideo.net
Henry Steiner, President
Provides full-service, script-to-screen video/film production.

NTV INTERNATIONAL CORP.
645 Fifth Ave
Ste 303
New York, NY 10022
Phone: 212-660-6900
Fax: 212-660-6998
E-mail: contact@ntvic.com
Web Site: http://www.ntvic.com
Jusaburo Hayashi, President & Chief Operating Officer
Tai Takeuchi, Chief Financial Officer & Human Resources
Leo Lahm, Technical Manager
News gathering bureau; provides production services & satellite transmission.

NW MEDIA
2117 Northeast Oregon St
#702
Portland, OR 97232
Phones: 503-223-5010; 800-547-2252
E-mail: contact@nwmedia.com
Web Site: http://www.nwmedia.com
Jeanne D. Alldredge, President
Stephen P. Wade, Sales Director
Mark Berry, Production Manager
Scott Thompson, Warehouse & Purchasing Manager
Provides complete solutions for CD/DVD manufacturing, digital printing, graphic design & multimedia.

OCEAN PARK PICTURES INC.
1223 Wilshire Blvd
#812
Santa Monica, CA 90402
Phone: 310-450-1220
Fax: 310-319-1342
E-mail: info@oceanparkpix.com
Web Site: http://www.oceanparkpix.com
Film production company; specializes in commercials.

THE OFFICE OF COMMUNICATION OF THE EPISCOPAL CHURCH
815 Second Ave
New York, NY 10017
Phones: 212-922-5385; 212-716-6000
E-mail: rudiganne75@gmail.com
Web Site: http://www.episcopalchurch.org
Anne Rudig, Director
Mary F. Brennan, Mission Communication Officer
Michael Collins, Multimedia Services Manager
Reverend Jake Dell, Digital Marketing & Advertising Sales Manager
Barry Merer, Web & Social Media Services Manager

OGLETREE PRODUCTIONS
24 Brentwood Cir
Lubbock, TX 79407
Phone: 806-791-2800

E-mail: oglepro@aol.com
Web Site: http://www.ogletreeproductions.com
Provides HD/SD videography & editing. Produces commercial & industrial videos and video crewing for national clients, broadcast, cable and corporate.

OGM PRODUCTION MUSIC
6464 Sunset Blvd
Ste 920
Hollywood, CA 90028
Phones: 323-461-2701; 323-868-2434
Fax: 323-461-1543
E-mail: ogmmusic@gmail.com
Web Site: http://www.ogmmusic.com
Ole Georg, President
Offers a library of music for every type of production, including film, TV, video, Internet, interactive & multimedia.

OLYMPUSAT INC.
560 Village Blvd
Ste 250
West Palm Beach, FL 33409
Phone: 561-684-5657
Fax: 561-684-9690
E-mail: seta@olympusat.com
Web Site: http://www.olympusat.com
Tom Mohler, Chief Executive Officer
Chuck Lavin, Chief Technology officer
Mauro Panzera, Chief Operating Officer
Kim Reed, Chief Business Development Officer
Chris Williams, Chief Financial Officer
Austin Powers, President, Olympusat Telecom
Colleen Glynn, Executive Vice President & General Counsel
Chuck Mohler, Executive Vice President
Arturo Chavez, Senior Vice President, Hispanic Networks
Nick Febrizio, Senior Vice President, Distribution
John Baghdassarian, Vice President, Distribution
Eric Bressler, Vice President, Technical Operations
Francisco Sibauste, Vice President, Sales & Business Development, US & International
Maria Luz Zucchella, Vice President, Programming & Acquisitions
Katie Beirne, Human Resources Director
Juan Bruno, New Programming Acquisitions & Contracts Director
Peter Savov, Information Technology Director
Shawn Copenhaver, Creative Services Director
Dean Broadhurst, General Manager, Network Operations
Fernando Vargas, General Manager, Mexico City
Luis Jairala, Network Manager, Music Networks
Laura Johnston, Controller
Distributes & provides independent programming networks to the cable, satellite & telco industry, in addition to multi-platforms (mobile, broadband, DVD); Spanish-language and Faith & Family offerings.

ON THE AIR STUDIOS
733 Third Ave
15th Fl
New York, NY 10017
Phone: 646-790-5792
E-mail: onair800@msn.com
Web Site: http://www.ontheairstudios.com
Richard Bianco, Owner & President
Provides demo tapes for voice-over radio, news, local commercials & radio commercials.

E-122

TV & Cable Factbook No. 85

Program Sources & Services

OPEN STUDENT TELEVISION NETWORK (OSTN)
1940 E 6th St
11th Fl
Cleveland, OH 44114
Phone: 216-586-9626
Fax: 217-586-9636
E-mail: info@ostn.tv
Web Site: http://www.ostn.tv
Arun Kumar, President & Chief Executive Officer
Rich Griffin, Executive Vice President & Director, Technology
Provides student & faculty produced original shows, projects & fine arts performances over over the Internet2 Network.

OPUS1 MUSIC LIBRARY
12711 Ventura Blvd
Ste 170
Studio City, CA 91604
Phones: 818-508-2040; 888-757-6787
Fax: 818-508-2044
E-mail: office@opus1musiclibrary.com
Web Site: http://www.opus1musiclibrary.com
Alan Ett, Chairman & Chief Executive Officer
Ryan Neill, Vice President, Production
Mitch Rabin, Vice President, Sales & Marketing
Marrsha Sill, Vice President, Film/TV Music
Levon Broussalian, Music Supervision Director
Production music library representing over 2,000 CDs; creates custom cues & scores.

ORION TELEVISION — See listing for MGM Television Entertainment Inc.

OUTPOST ENTERTAINMENT
11846 Ventura Blvd
Studio City, CA 91604
Phone: 818-583-2364
E-mail: info@outpostentertainment.com
Web Site: http://www.outpostentertainment.com
Jodi Flynn, President
Develops & produces unscripted TV programming. A Leftfield Entertainment Co.

EARL OWENSBY STUDIOS
One Motion Picture Blvd
Shelby, NC 28152
Phone: 704-487-0500
Fax: 704-487-4763
E-mail: earlowensby@bellsouth.net
Web Site: http://www.earlowensbystudios.com
Earl Owensby, President
Motion picture production facilities.

JIM OWENS ENTERTAINMENT INC.
1110 16th Ave S
Nashville, TN 37212
Phone: 615-256-7700
Fax: 615-256-7779
E-mail: jerryfox@aol.com
Web Site: http://www.crookandchase.com
Jim Owens, President
Jerry Fox, Sales Director
Produces & distributes music, entertainment & information programming for TV syndication & cable distribution.

PANTOMIME PICTURES INC.
12144 Riverside Dr
Valley Village, CA 91607-3829
Phone: 818-980-5555
Produces animation for commercial, educational & industrial use, specializes in animation design & conception.

PARAMOUNT LICENSING
5555 Melrose Ave
Hollywood, CA 90038
Phone: 323-956-2244
E-mail: licensing@paramount.com
Web Site: http://www.paramountlicensing.com
Michael Corcoan, President, Consumer Products & Recreation Group
Michael Bartok, Executive Vice President, Licensing
Charles Myers, Senior Vice President, Creative & Development
Lynda Cevallos, Vice President, Licensing
Ryan Gagerman, Vice President, International Licensing
Tom Renger, Vice President, Business Planning & Development
Darren Kyman, Executive Director, Marketing & Retail Development
Handles licensing rights worldwide for properties of Paramount Pictures, Paramount Vantage, Nickelodeon Movies & MTV Films. Division of Paramount Pictures Corp.

PARAMOUNT STUDIOS GROUP — See listing for The Studios at Paramount.

PARAMOUNT TELEVISION GROUP — See listing for CBS Television Studios.
5555 Melrose Ave
Hollywood, CA 90038
Phone: 323-956-5000
Web Site: http://www.paramount.com
Amy Powell, President
Jason Fisher, Head of Production
David Goldman, Head of Business Affairs
Jennifer Howell, Head of Comedy Development
Stephanie Love, Head of Finance
Annette Savitch, Head of Drama Development
Jessica Rovins, Executive Vice President, Communications
Produces TV series.

PATHE NEWS INC.
630 Ninth Ave
Ste 305
New York, NY 10036-4751
Phone: 212-489-8669
Fax: 212-489-1416
Provides TV production, stock footage & multimedia services.

PATTERSON STUDIOS INC.
600 Overlook Dr
Winter Haven, FL 33884
Phone: 863-324-3696
Fax: 863-324-0864
E-mail: admin@pattersonstudios.com
John D. Patterson, Founder, Director & Cameraman
Mike Palma, Post Production Supervisor
Kevin A. Tison, Marketing, Sales & Film Video Production
Produces TV dramas, industrial & documentary programming, commercials & theatrical films & video.

PAULIST PRODUCTIONS
6430 Sunset Blvd
Ste 1220
Los Angeles, CA 90028-7908
Phone: 310-454-0688
Fax: 310-459-6549
E-mail: paulistmail@paulistproductions.com
Web Site: http://www.paulistproductions.org
Chris Donahue, President
Joseph Kim, Vice President, Business Affairs
Marybeth Sprows, Vice President, Development & Production
Produces & distributes religious films.

Communications Daily
Warren Communications News
Get the industry standard FREE —
For a no-obligation trial call 800-771-9202 or visit www.warren-news.com

PBS INTERNATIONAL
10 Guest St
Boston, MA 02135
Phone: 617-208-0737
Fax: 617-779-7900
E-mail: bkleblanc@pbs.org
Web Site: http://pbsinternational.org
Tom Koch, Vice President, Distribution
Charles Schuerhoff, International Acquisitions Director
Betsy Leblanc, Senior Manager, International Sales
Nanci Barker, International Sales Manager
Andrew Campana, International Sales Manager
Jennifer Callahan, Project Manager, Program Development
Produces primetime programming for PBS in the U.S.

PEACOCK PRODUCTIONS
30 Rockefeller Plz
New York, NY 10012
Web Site: http://www.peacockproductions.tv
Benjamin Ringe, Executive Vice President & Executive Producer
Aretha Marshall, Senior Vice President, Casting & Talent Development & Executive Producer
Creates, develops & produces lifestyle & reality programs, documentaries & topical specials for broadcast, cable, syndication & emerging platforms.

PECKHAM PRODUCTIONS INC.
50 S Buckhout St
Irvington, NY 10533
Phone: 914-591-4140
Fax: 914-591-4149
E-mail: info@peckhampix.com
Web Site: http://www.peckhampix.com
Produces industrial, educational & documentary films, TV commercials, programs & promos.

PENNEBAKER ASSOCIATES INC.
262 W 91st St
New York, NY 10024
Phone: 212-496-8195
Fax: 212-496-8915
Web Site: http://phfilms.com
Fraze Pennebaker, Owner
Produces & distributes music, dance, theatrical drama & general performance films; theatre & TV features & shorts; stock footage.

PERENNIAL PICTURES FILM CORP.
2102 E 52nd St
Indianapolis, IN 46205
Phone: 317-253-1519
E-mail: mail@perennialpictures.com
Web Site: http://www.perennialpictures.com
G. Brian Reynolds, President
Russ Harris, Senior Vice President
Mike Ruggiero, Vice President
Produces animation for TV specials, series & features.

PHOENIX COMMUNICATIONS GROUP INC.
3 Empire Blvd
Ste 4
South Hackensack, NJ 07606
Phone: 201-807-0888
Produces Sports NewSatellite, a sports news & highlight feed; video news releases; satellite media tours for distribution.

PHOENIX ENTERTAINMENT GROUP
155 Pier Ave
Unit B
Hermosa Beach, CA 90254
Phone: 310-590-6406
E-mail: sean@phoenixentgroup.com
Tony Perez, Chief Executive Officer
Distributes specialty entertainment; produces, markets & distributes urban, Latino, horror & family/spiritual themed content.

PHOENIX FILMS & VIDEO
141 Millwell Dr
Ste A
St Louis, MO 63043
Phones: 314-569-0211 x104; 800-221-1274 x104
Fax: 314-569-2834
E-mail: info@phoenixlearninggroup.com
Web Site: http://www.phoenixlearninggroup.com
Distributes & produces educational programs. Film library for all ages from 2yrs old through adult. Library includes children's & entertainment programs, curriculum & educational films, documentaries, cultural & art films; programs available for digital streaming. Division of Phoenix Learning Group Inc.

PILOT PRODUCTIONS INC.
2123 McDaniel Ave
Evanston, IL 60201-2126
Phone: 847-328-3700
Fax: 847-328-3761
Produces video, multimedia & print for business.

PIXAR ANIMATION STUDIOS
1200 Park Ave
Emeryville, CA 94608
Phone: 510-922-3000
Fax: 510-922-3151
E-mail: rmancusp@pixar.com
Web Site: http://www.pixar.com
Dr. Ed Catmull, President
John A. Lasseter, Chief Creative Officer
Produces animated features. Subsidiary of Walt Disney Corp., Walt Disney Studios.

PLAYBOY ENTERTAINMENT GROUP INC.
2706 Media Center Dr
Los Angeles, CA 90065
Phone: 323-276-4000
Fax: 323-276-4500
Web Site: http://www.playboyenterprises.com
Hugh M. Hefner, Editor-in-Chief & Chief Creative Officer
Scott N. Flanders, Chief Executive Officer
David Israel, Chief Operating Officer & President, Playboy Media
Matthew Nordby, Executive Vice President & Chief Revenue Officer
Christopher Pachler, Executive Vice President & Chief Financial Officer

Program Sources & Services

Rachel Sagan, Executive Vice President, Business Affairs & General Counsel
Develops, produces, acquires & distributes a wide range of high-quality lifestyle & adult programming for domestic & international TV networks.

PLAY-IT PRODUCTIONS
735 Port Washington Blvd
Port Washington, NY 11050
Phones: 212-695-6530; 800-815-3444
Fax: 212-695-4304
E-mail: info@play-itproductions.net
Web Site: http://www.play-itproductions.net
Tony Tyler, President
Provides CD & DVD production services; CD-ROM production, authoring & consultation from I-200 CD-ROM or audio CD's overnight. Other services include mastering, replication, duplication, graphic design & printing.

PLAYON! SPORTS
2835 Brandywine Rd
McGill Bldg, Ste 102
Atlanta, GA 30341
Phone: 404-920-3190
Fax: 404-920-3199
E-mail: info@playonsports.com
Web Site: http://www.playonsports.com
David Rudolph, Chief Executive Officer
Robert Rothberg, President
Monisha Longacre, President, Subscription & Consumer Marketing
Mark Norman, Chief Operating Officer
Sandy Malcom, Chief Content Officer
Jay Sandhaus, Chief Technology Officer
Mike Carlton, Senior Vice President, Partner Development
Gary McCarthy, Senior Vice President, Finance & Strategy
Owen Shull, Senior Vice President & General Manager, PlayOn! Sports Properties
Mark Rothberg, Vice President, School Broadcast Program
Produces over 5,000 live sport events each year for TV & digital distribution. Also partners with high school associations to package media rights with marketing assets to create opportunities for local sponsors of high school sports.

POINT OF VIEW PRODUCTIONS
2477 Folsom St
San Francisco, CA 94110
Phone: 415-821-0435
Fax: 415-821-0434
E-mail: karil@karildaniels.com
Web Site: http://www.karildaniels.com
Karil Daniels, President
Provides cinematography, videography, photography, script supervision & other production services for corporate programs, commercials, TV shows & feature films.

PRESBYTERIAN CHURCH (U.S.A.)
100 Witherspoon St
Louisville, KY 40202-1396
Phones: 502-569-5000; 888-728-7228
Fax: 502-569-8005
E-mail: info@pcusa.org
Web Site: http://www.pcusa.org
Robert W. Maggs, Jr., President & Chief Executive Officer
Francis E. Maloney, Executive Vice President & Chief Operating Officer
Karen Babik, Public Relations & Marketing Communications

PRODUCTION STUDIO INC.
4930 Illinois Rd
Ste 1-F
Ft Wayne, IN 46804

Phone: 260-432-3601
Fax: 260-436-4800
E-mail: info@productionstudio.com
Web Site: http://www.productionstudio.com
Mark Douglas Fry, Financial Officer
Full service corporate communications company; provides video-film-multimedia beta-sp, 1 in., 0-2 formats, soft image non-linear editing, complete conference planning & design, remote taping, complete post production, graphics & animation.

PROMARK TELEVISION INC.
500 South Palm Canyon Dr
Ste 220
Palm Springs, CA 92264
Phones: 760-322-7776; 800-266-6662
Fax: 760-322-5149
E-mail: promarktv@promarktv.com
Web Site: http://www.promarktv.com
David Levine, Founder
TV syndication & national sales.

PSSI GLOBAL SERVICES/STRATEGIC TELEVISION
7030 Hayvenhurst Ave
Van Nuys, CA 91406
Phones: 310-575-4400; 800-728-5465
Fax: 310-575-4451
E-mail: operations@pssiglobal.com
Web Site: http://www.pssiglobal.com
Robert C Lamb, Chief Executive Officer, PSSI/Strategic Television
Matt Bridges, President, Strategic Television
Clint Bergeson, Project Manager

Branch Offices:
BIRMINGHAM: 6400 First Ave South, Birmingham, AL 35212. Phone: 818-933-7912. Matt Scalici, General Manager, PSSI.

SHREWSBURY: 786 Hartford Pike, Shrewsbury, MA 01545. Phone: 508-842-4328. Gavin Williams, Northeast Operations Manager.

LAS VEGAS: 4415 Wagon Tr Ave, Las Vegas, NV 89118. Phone: 702-798-0101. Fax: 702-895-7484. Brian Nelles, Senior Vice President, PSSI.
Provides global transmission & satellite services; has more than 40 Ku-Band, C-Band & C/Ku-Band Flyaway facilities based throughout the US, transportable HD fiber-encoding packages, hybrid full production-uplink trucks, multi-path transport, internet streaming, portable flyaway uplinks, downlinks, insert studios, teleport capabilities, distribution from Hawaii & Puerto Rico & communication systems over satellite.

PULSE FILMS
1645 Electric Ave
Los Angeles, CA 90291
Phone: 310-752-4350
E-mail: info@pulsefilms.com
Web Site: http://www.pulsefilms.com
Patrick Vien, President

Branch Offices:
BROOKLYN: 99 N 10th St, Brooklyn, NY 11249. Phone: 718-215-5790. E-Mail: info@pulsefilms.com.

LOS ANGELES: 1645 Electric Ave, Los Angeles, CA 90291. Phone: 310-752-4350. E-Mail: info@pulsefilms.com.
Provides production, distribution & talent management services. Produces fiction films, music & drama documentaries and scripted & unscripted television series.

PYRAMID MEDIA
3200 Airport Ave
Ste 19
Santa Monica, CA 90405
Phones: 310-398-6149; 800-421-2304
Fax: 310-398-7869
E-mail: info@pyramidmedia.com
Web Site: http://www.pyramidmedia.com
Distributes educational media, supplies stock footage & licenses programs to cable & pay TV.

QUARTET INTERNATIONAL INC.
20 Butternut Dr
Pearl River, NY 10965
Phone: 201-784-8488
Fax: 201-784-3993
E-mail: tvshowbizz@aol.com
Web Site: http://www.tvshowbiz.com
Harvey Chertok, President
Barbara A. Chertok, Vice President
Produces & distributes films, TV film & tape series; exports films, buys films & imports films & TV film series; TV rights.

RALEIGH STUDIOS
5300 Melrose Ave
Hollywood, CA 90038
Phones: 323-960-3456; 888-960-3456
E-mail: info@raleighstudios.com
Web Site: http://www.raleighstudios.com
Michael Moore, President
Karin Darrow, Executive Director, Leasing
Jim Fox, Facilities Director
Yolanda Montellano, Client Services Manager

Branch Offices:
BATON ROUGE: 10000 Mayfair Dr, Baton Rouge, LA 70809. Phone: 323-960-3456.

MANHATTAN BEACH: 1600 Rosencrans Ave, Manhattan Beach, CA 90266. Phones: 310-727-2700; 310-727-2710.

PLAYA VISTA: 5600 Campus Ctr Dr, Playa Vista, CA 90266. Phone: 323-960-3456. Willi Schmidt, Vice President, Studio Operations.
Leases film & TV facilities; provides grip & electrical services & post production facilities including screening rooms.

RAYCOM SPORTS INC.
1900 West Morehead St
Charlotte, NC 28208
Phone: 704-378-4400
Fax: 704-378-4465
E-mail: khaines@raycomsports.com
Web Site: http://www.raycomsports.com
Hunter Nickell, Chief Executive Officer
George Johnson, Senior Vice President
Wyatt Hicks, Vice President, Marketing & ACC Properties
Bill Lancaster, Vice President, Sales
Jimmy Rayborn, Vice President, Operations & Executive Producer
Peter Rolfe, Vice President, Production
Colin Smith, Vice President, Syndication & New Media
Syndicates, distributes & markets national & regional TV events with an emphasis on sporting events.

RCTV INTERNATIONAL
4380 NW 128th St
Miami, FL 33054
Phone: 305-688-7475
Fax: 305-685-5697
Web Site: http://www.rctvintl.com
Daniela Bergami, Chief Executive Officer
Guadalupe D'Agostino, Vice President & General Manager
Jorge Fernandez, Vice President, Finance & Administration

Haydee Pabon, International Sales Director
Marc Paneque, International Sales Director
Amina Galdo, Office Manager
Markets telenovelas, miniseries, movies, children's programming, series, documentaries & concerts to the international TV market.

RED RYDER ENTERPRISES INC.
5108 W Longfellow Ave
Tampa, FL 33629
Phone: 813-837-8773
Leases & licenses literary properties.

REEL MEDIA INTERNATIONAL
7000 Independence Pkwy
Ste 160-7
Plano, TX 75025
Phone: 214-521-3301
Fax: 214-522-3448
E-mail: reelmedia@aol.com
Web Site: http://www.reelmediainternational.com
Tom T. Moore, Chief Executive Officer
Dena Moore, Vice President
Distributes motion pictures, TV series & specials, including action & adventure films, science-fiction, animation, family, drama, horror & sports worldwide. Library of 2,000 classic movies and TV series with online database. (Reel Funds International Inc.).

REELTIME DISTRIBUTING CORP.
353 W 48th St
New York, NY 10036
Phone: 212-582-5380
Produces & distributes R-rated films for theater & video; sound recording.

RELATIVITY MEDIA
9242 Beverly Blvd
Ste 300
Beverly Hills, CA 90210
Phone: 310-724-7700
E-mail: pressrequests@relativitymedia.com
Web Site: http://www.relativitymedia.com
Ryan Kavanaugh, Chief Executive Officer
Carol Genis, Managing Director
Andy Levin, President, Legal & Human Resources

Branch Offices:
BEVERLY HILLS: 345 N Maple Dr, Ste 245, Beverly Hills, CA 90210.

HOLLYWOOD: 1040 N Las Palmas Ave, Bldg 40, Hollywood, CA 90038.

NEW YORK: 315 Park Ave S, 2nd FL, New York, NY 10010.

NORTHBROOK: 400 Skokie Blvd, Ste 280, Northbrook, IL 60062.

SAN FRANCISCO: 580 Pacific Ave, San Francisco, CA 94133.
Produces & distributes movies & TV programming.

REMBRANDT FILMS
34 Cross Pond Rd
Pound Ridge, NY 10576
Phones: 914-763-5817; 888-205-8778
E-mail: info@rembrandtfilms.com
Web Site: http://www.rembrandtfilms.com
Adam Snyder, Owner
Provides animation, video production, & business writing through Rembrandt Communications, Rembrandt Films Animation & Rembrandt Video Productions.

RENEGADE
10950 Gilroy Rd
Ste J

Program Sources & Services

FULLY SEARCHABLE • CONTINUOUSLY UPDATED • DISCOUNT RATES FOR PRINT PURCHASERS
For more information call **800-771-9202** or visit **www.warren-news.com**

Hunt Valley, MD 21031
Phone: 410-667-1400
Fax: 410-667-1482
E-mail: info@getrenegade.com
Web Site: http://www.getrenegade.com
Timothy J. Watkins, President & Chief Executive Officer
Jennifer Leo Stine, Executive Vice President & Chief Operating Officer
Chris Beutler, Vice President, Production & Executive Director, Creative
Robert Taylor, Chief Strategy Officer
Katrina Bartos, Account Services Director
Noah Thomason, Production Director
Terri Howard, Office Manager
Full-service advertising agency & production facility; supplies services to cable operators & programmers, including TV & radio spots, web and interactive campaigns, consumer direct mail & marketing, direct sales & customer service training videos and courses.

REVELATIONS ENTERTAINMENT
1221 Second St
#4
Santa Monica, CA 90401
Phone: 310-394-3131
Web Site: http://www.revelationsent.com
Morgan Freeman, Co-Founder & President
Lori McCreary, Co-Founder & Chief Executive Officer
James Younger, Executive Vice President, Factual Productions
Marcus Mucha, Vice President, Business Development
Tracy Mercer, Vice President, Development
Megan Parlen, Senior Director, Factual Productions
Produces film & TV programming.

REZN8
15452 Cabrito Rd
Studio 102
Van Nuys, CA 91406
Phone: 818-326-6018
E-mail: motion@rezn8.com
Web Site: http://www.rezn8.com
Jack Honour, Chairman
Herky Williams, President
Harvey Lowry, Chief Creative Officer
Paul Sidio, Special Projects Director
Provides design, motion graphics, animation & interface design services.

RINGSIDE CREATIVE
13320 Northend
Ste 3000
Oak Park, MI 48237
Phone: 248-548-2500
E-mail: info@ringsidecreative.com
Web Site: http://www.ringsidecreative.com
Steven Wild, President
Allan Rothfeder, Executive Vice President & Chief Financial Officer
Integrated media studio with expertise in creating visual, audio & interactive brand experiences.

RIOT CREATIVE
460 W 34th St
7th Fl
New York, NY 10001
Phone: 212-564-2607
Fax: 917-967-7573
E-mail: info@riotcreative.com
Web Site: http://riotcreative.com
Stephanie Angelides, President
Produces trendy, must-see programming for TV, OTT & digital. A Leftfield Entertainment Co.

RKO PICTURES
11301 West Olympic Blvd
Ste 510
Los Angeles, CA 90064
Phone: 310-277-0707
Fax: 310-566-8940
E-mail: info@rko.com
Web Site: http://www.rko.com
Ted Hartley, Chairman & Chief Executive Officer
Dina Merrill, Vice Chairman
Andrew Matthews, President
Vanessa Coifman, Executive Vice President, Production & Development
Kevin Cornish, Vice President, Development

Branch Offices:
NEW YORK: 750 Lexington Ave, Ste 2200, New York, NY 10022. Phone: 212-644-0600. Fax: 212-644-0384.
Provides multimedia programming, TV & motion picture production, operating entertainment centers & foreign rights sales/acquisitions.

PETER RODGERS ORGANIZATION
PO Box 2110
Hollywood, CA 90078
Phone: 323-962-1778
Fax: 323-962-7174
E-mail: info@profilms.com
Web Site: http://www.profilms.com
Stephen M. Rodgers, Chief Executive Officer
Ron Adler, Operations Director
Distributes TV films & programs worldwide; provides consulting services; representatives.

ROKU CHANNEL STORE
150 Winchester Circle
Los Gatos, CA 95032
Phone: 888-600-7658
Fax: 408-446-1734
E-mail: brian@roku.com
Web Site: http://www.roku.com
Anthony Wood, Founder & Chief Executive Officer
David Krall, President & Chief Operating Officer
Matthew Anderson, Chief Marketing Officer
Steve Louden, Chief Financial Officer
Mark Goodwin, Vice President, Engineering
Scott Rosenberg, Vice President, Business Development
Charles Seiber, Vice President, Marketing
James Wong, Vice President, Operations
Ann Hoover, Finance & Operations Director
Package of video services accessible through digital video player. Offers original programming, sports, video and photo sharing plus music.

ROLAND COMPANY INC.
1202 Bishopsgate Way
Reston, VA 20194
Phone: 703-450-6272
Fax: 703-444-3141
David Roland, President
Provides TV production & publishing services.

ROBERT ROSENHEIM ASSOCIATES
Five Gay St
Sharon, CT 06069
Phone: 860-364-0050
Fax: 860-364-5577
Web Site: http://www.rralc.com
Robert Rosenheim, President
Classic feature films & older TV series.

RTP-USA
283 E Kinney St
Newark, NJ 07105
Phone: 973-344-8888
Web Site: http://www.rtpusa.com

Anthony Seabra, President
Americo Seabra, Vice President
Adam Seabra, Manager

RUSSIAN MEDIA GROUP LLC
One Bridge Plz N
Ste 145
Fort Lee, NJ 07024
Phone: 800-222-2786
Web Site: http://www.russianmediagroup.com
Mark S. Golub, President & Chief Executifve Officer
Evguenei Lvov, Vice President & Chief Operating Officer
Serge Goldberg, Chief Engineer
Vlada Khmelnitskaya, Programming Director & Production Department Manager
Michael Paley, IT Department Director
Victoria Melnik, Marketing Manager
Provides Russian language TV services in the U.S.

RW PRODUCTIONS INC.
2630 Fountainview
Ste 218
Houston, TX 77057
Phones: 713-522-4701; 800-874-2745
Fax: 713-522-0426
E-mail: info@rwvideo.com
Web Site: http://www.rwvideo.com
Bob Willems, Owner
Produces film, video & TV programs; provides motion pictures DVD authoring & CD authoring.

SCENIC CABLE NETWORK & PRODUCTION
PO Box 5678
416 N Oates St
Dothan, AL 36303
Phone: 334-793-2722
Fax: 334-793-4171
Web Site: http://www.seniccable.com
Terry Duffie, President & General Manager
Mit Kirkland, Vice President, Operations
Angela Deloney, National Regional Sales Manager
Kim Gantt, General Sales Manager
Provides cable TV advertising & video production services.

SCREAM FACTORY
2015 S Westgate Ave
Los Angeles, CA 90025
Phone: 310-826-7126
Web Site: http://www.shoutfactory.com/tentpoles/scream-factory
Distributes horror & sci-fi films.

SEALS ENTERTAINMENT CO. INC.
3340 Peachtree Rd NE
Ste 1800
Atlanta, GA 30326
Phone: 404-222-6400
Fax: 404-230-5600
E-mail: info@sealsco.com
Web Site: http://www.sealsco.com
E. Lamar Seals, III, Chairman & Chief Executive Officer
John W. Bonner Jr., Executive Vice President & Chief Operating Officer

Produces programming; subjects include outdoors, motorsports, health & fitness, music, extreme & action sports, & a wide variety of youth, college & professional sporting events.

SEAR SOUND
353 W 48th St
Studio A/Studio C
New York, NY 10036
Phone: 212-582-5380
Fax: 212-581-2731
E-mail: waltersear@aol.com
Web Site: http://www.searsound.com
Roberta Findlay, Manager
Chris Allen, Chief Engineer
Ted Tuthill, Engineer
Grant Valentine, Assistant Engineer
Lim Wei, Assistant Engineer
Provides analog/digital sound recording & mixing services, recording for film/video & audio digital editing.

SENDTONEWS
535 Fifth Ave
#418
New York, NY 10017
Phones: 917-558-3108; 855-590-1991
E-mail: info@sendtonews.com
Web Site: http://www.sendtonews.com
Keith Wells, Founder & Vice President, Content Innovation
Matthew Watson, Executive Chairman
Arturo Aylesworth, Chairman
Sean Coutts, Chief Operating Officer
Philippe Guay, Executive Vice President, Sales & Strategic Partnerships
Mike John-Baptiste, Executive Vice President, Business Development
Peter Beblo, Vice President, Technology
David J. C. Davies, Vice President, Corporate Communications
Marc Hoelscher, Vice President, Marketing

Branch Offices:
SAN FRANCISCO: c/o RockerSpace Incubator, 181 Fremont St, San Francisco, CA 94105.
Distributes sports news video & highlights.

SEPTEMBER PRODUCTIONS
15 Madaket Rd
Nantucket, MA 02554
Phones: 508-228-8073; 508-332-3577
Fax: 508-228-3853
E-mail: info@september.com
Web Site: http://www.september.com
Sonta Giamber, Executive Producer
Jay Anderson, Midwest Contact
Michael Eha, East Coast Contact
Patricia O'Hara, West Coast Contact
Produces 35mm TV commercials.

SESAME WORKSHOP
One Lincoln Pl
New York, NY 10023
Phone: 212-595-3457
E-mail: dotorgmail@sesameworkshop.org
Web Site: http://www.sesameworkshop.org
H. Melvin Ming, President & Chief Executive Officer
Daryl Mintz, Chief Financial Officer

2017 Edition   E-125

Program Sources & Services

ADVANCED TVFactbook

FULLY SEARCHABLE • CONTINUOUSLY UPDATED • DISCOUNT RATES FOR PRINT PURCHASERS

For more information call **800-771-9202** or visit **www.warren-news.com**

Myung Kang-Huneke, Executive Vice President & General Counsel
Lewis Bernstein, Executive Vice President, Education & Research
Terry Fitzpatrick, Executive Vice President, Content Distribution
Sherri Rollins Westin, Executive Vice President & Chief Marketing Officer
Jeanette Betancourt, Senior Vice President, Outreach & Educational Practices
Charlotte Frances Cole, Senior Vice President, Global Education
Anita Stewart, Senior Vice President, Corporate Partnerships
Dr. Rosemarie Truglio, Senior Vice President, Education & Research
Jennifer Ahearn, Vice President, Licensing, Strategic Partner Relations
Erica Branch-Ridley, Vice President & Executive in Charge of Production, Sesame Learning
Lynn Chwatsky, Vice President, Outreach Initiatives & Partnerships
Jennifer Kotler Clarke, Vice President-Domestic Research
Juan Martinez, Vice President, Strategic Communications
Renee Mascara, Vice President, International Media Distribution
Produces & distributes entertaining & educational programming for children.

SEVENTH-DAY ADVENTIST CHURCH, COMMUNICATIONS DEPARTMENT
12501 Old Columbia Pike
Silver Spring, MD 20904-6600
Phone: 301-680-6300
Fax: 301-680-6312
Web Site: http://www.adventist.org/en
Andre Brink, Media Services Director
Garrett Caldwell, Public Relations Director
Ansel Oliver, Assistant Director, Adventist News Network
Andrew King, Assistant Director, Web Manager
Elizabeth Lechleitner, Editorial Coordinator
Provides media production services; coordinates activities on the Adventist News Network.

SFM ENTERTAINMENT
800 Westchester Ave
Ste N-345
New York, NY 10573
Phone: 212-398-4496
Fax: 212-398-5738
Web Site: http://www.sfment.com
Stanley Moger, President & Chief Executive Officer
Michael H. Maizes, Senior Vice President, In-House Counsel & Chief Financial Officer
Creates, sells & distributes programming for syndication.

SHOWCASE PRODUCTIONS INC. —
See Films Around the World Inc.

SHOWPLACE TELEVISION SYNDICATION
3023 N Clark St
Ste 890
Chicago, IL 60657-5261
Phone: 773-935-1572
Fax: 206-984-4179
E-mail: sales@showplaceonline.com
Web Site: http://www.showplaceonline.com
Hal Pontious, President
Daren Gaskill, Program Director
Domestic distributor & syndicator. Broadcasting division specializes in sales development, new media, program consulting, research, & database engineering for groups, networks and cable.

SIRENS MEDIA
8403 Colesville Rd
Ste 1600
Silver Spring, MD 20910
Phone: 310-920-9800
Web Site: http://www.sirensmedia.com
Rebecca Toth Diffenbach, Co-President & Executive Producer
Valerie Haselton, Co-President & Executive Producer
Stuart Zwagil, Chief Operating Officer
John Esteban, Executive Vice President, Finance
Lucilla D'Agostino, Senior Vice President, Content & Executive Producer
Jen Mayer Kulp, Senior Vice President, Talent & Development
Genevieve Croteau, Senior Director, Personnel
Nikki Rouiller, Senior Director, Production & Operations
Produces unscripted, reality & documentary programming. A Leftfield Entertainment Co.

SKOTLESKI PRODUCTIONS
1001 N Broad St
Ste A
Lansdale, PA 19446
Phones: 215-362-5880; 800-677-8433
Fax: 215-362-5881
E-mail: skotleski@skotleski.com
Web Site: http://www.skotleski.com
Ron Skotleski, President
Provides video production for international, regional & local broadcast & CATV advertising; provides creative strategy development & consulting services.

SKY ANGEL US LLC
3050 Horseshoe Drive N
Ste 290
Naples, FL 34104
Phone: 239-403-9130
Fax: 239-403-9105
E-mail: customerrelations@skyangel.com
Web Site: http://www.skyangel.com
Rob Johnson, Chief Executive Officer
Tom Scott, President & Chief Operating Officer
Brian Collins, Executive Vice President, Programming Acquisition & Sales

Branch Offices:
Network Operation Center: 4922 La Collina Way, Ooltewah, TN 37363. Phone: 423-396-8176. Fax: 423-396-8002. E-Mail: master.control@skyangel.com. Web site: http://www.skyangeltech.com.
Provides faith-based & family-friendly TV & radio programming

SMITH
439 Wellington St West
3rd Floor
Toronto, ON M5V 1E7
Canada
Phone: 416-593-1212
Web Site: http://callmesmith.com
John Stollar, Sales Director
Karen Huybers, Executive Producer
Provides post-production services for commercials, TV series & films. Formerly Axyz.

SOMAT PUBLISHING LTD.
250 W 57th
New York, NY 10107
Phone: 212-586-0660
Produces music.

SONY BMG MUSIC ENTERTAINMENT
550 Madison Ave
New York, NY 10022-3211
Phone: 212-833-8000
Fax: 212-833-4818
Web Site: http://www.sonymusic.com
Doug Morris, Chief Executive Officer
Kevin Kelleher, Executive Vice President & Chief Financial Officer
Music record label.

SONY PICTURES TELEVISION
10202 W Washington Blvd
Culver City, CA 90232
Phone: 310-244-4000
Fax: 310-244-2004
Web Site: http://www.sonypicturestelevision.com
Michael Lynton, Chief Executive Officer, Sony Entertainment
Jamie Erlicht, Co-President, Programming & Production
Zack Van Amburg, Co-President, U.S. Programming & Production
Amy Carney, President, Advertiser Sales & Research
Andy Kaplan, President, Worldwide Networks
Keith Le Goy, President, Distribution
John Weiser, President, U.S. Distribution
Andrea Wong, President, International Production
Glenn Adilman, Executive Vice President, U.S. Comedy Development
Paula Askanas, Executive Vice President, Communications
Thanda Belker, Executive Vice President, U.S. Pay Television
Eric Berger, Executive Vice President, Digital Networks, U.S. Distribution
Flory Bramnick, Executive Vice President, U.S. Cable Sales
Richard Burrus, Executive Vice President, Strategic Pricing & Analysis
George Chien, Executive Vice President, Networks, Asia-Pacific
Donna Cunningham, Executive Vice President, Operations & International Production
Christopher L. Elwell, Executive Vice President, U.S. Distribution
Jeff Frost, Executive Vice President, U.S. Business Affairs
Suzanne Patmore Gibbs, Executive Vice President, U.S. Drama Development
Holly Jacobs, Executive Vice President, US Reality & Syndicated Programming
Marie Jacobson, Executive Vice President, Programming & Production, International Networks
Sheraton Kalouria, Executive Vice President & Chief Marketing Officer
Ed Lammi, Executive Vice President, Production
Steve Maddox, Executive Vice President, Syndication Sales
Phillip Martzolf, Executive Vice President, U.S. Syndication Sales
T. C. Schultz, Executive Vice President, Networks, Latin America
Drew Shearer, Executive Vice President & Chief Financial Officer
Dawn Steinberg, Executive Vice President, U.S. Talent & Casting
Helen Verno, Executive Vice President, U.S. Movies & Miniseries
Mike Wald, Executive Vice President, International Distribution
Stuart Zimmerman, Executive Vice President, U.S. Advertiser Sales
Jordan Feiner, Senior Vice President, Scripted Programming
Lauren Moffat, Senior Vice President, Comedy Development
Produces & distributes TV film/tape series & film programs on order.

SPANISH BROADCASTING SYSTEM (SBS)
7007 NW 77th Ave
Miami, FL 33166
Phone: 305-441-6901
Fax: 305-883-3375
E-mail: sbscontact@sbscorporate.com
Web Site: http://www.spanishbroadcasting.com
Raul Alarcon, Chairman, President & Chief Executive Officer
Albert Rodriguez, Chief Operating Officer
Eric Garcia, Revenue Chief, Radio Division
Joe Mackay, Executive Vice President, National & Network Sales
Alex Aleman, Senior Vice President, Consolidated Operations
Donny Hudson, Vice President, Consolidated Sales, SBS
Berry Jasin, Vice President, National Sales, SBS Consolidated Operations
Richard Lom, Vice President, SBS Entertainment
Felix Lopez, Vice President, SBS Miami Radio/TV-Consolidated Sales
Jackie Nosti-Cambo, Vice President, Business Analytics
Eric Osuna, Vice President, Sales, SBS Los Angeles
Alfredo Schwarz, Vice President, Operations & Production, Mega TV
Bill Shadorf, Vice President, Corporate Sales & West Coast Market Manager
Euridice Ventura, Vice President, Affiliate Marketing, Consolidated Operations
Vladimir Gomez, Marketing & Communications Director
Produces programming for MEGA TV.

STEVENS DESIGN & ANIMATION LLC
PO Box 2893
Corrales, NM 87048
Phone: 505-200-2042
E-mail: tstevens@stevensanimation.com
Web Site: http://www.stevensanimation.com
Tim Stevens, Animator & Designer
Full-service animation & production house specializing in all things character.

MARTY STOUFFER PRODUCTIONS LTD.
15820 Euclid Ave
Chino, CA 91708
Phones: 970-925-5536; 888-925-5536
Fax: 970-920-3820
E-mail: customerservice@wildamerica.com
Web Site: http://www.wildamerica.com
Marty Stouffer, President
Produces film programs; wildlife & natural history subjects.

Program Sources & Services

THE STUDIOS AT PARAMOUNT
5555 Melrose Ave
Los Angeles, CA 90038
Phone: 323-956-5000
Web Site: http://www.paramountstudios.com
Randall Baumberger, President
TV & motion picture studio; provides art, production & post-production services. Division of Paramount Pictures Corp.

STX ENTERTAINMENT
3900 W Alameda Ave
32nd Fl
Burbank, CA 91505
Web Site: http://www.stxentertainment.com
Robert Simonds, Chairman & Chief Executive Officer
Thomas McGrath, Chief Operating Officer
Rich Sullivan, Chief Financial Officer
Adam Fogelson, Chairman, Motion Picture Group
Oren Aviv, President & Chief Content Officer
Kevin Grayson, President, Domestic Distribution
Kathy Savitt, President, Digital
Noah Fogelson, Executive Vice President & General Counsel
Produces, markets & distributes feature films & TV.

SUNDANCE SELECT
11 Penn Plz
15th Fl
New York, NY 10001
Phone: 212-324-8500
E-mail: ifcfilmsinfo@ifcfilms.com
Web Site: http://www.ifcfilms.com
Jonathan Sehring, Co-President
Lisa Schwartz, Co-President
Distributes American independent, documentaries and world cinema programming.

SUNRISE MEDIA LLC
200 Central Park South
12F
New York, NY 10019
Phone: 212-221-6310
Fax: 212-302-1854
E-mail: info@sunrisemedia.tv
Web Site: http://www.sunrisemedia.tv
Alvin H. Perlmutter, President
Joseph Schroeder, Production Coordinator
Lisa Zbar, Senior Producer & Healthcare Related Production
Morton Silverstein, Special Assignment Producer/Writer
Lorne Lieb, Producer/Administration
Elizabeth Benson, Business Administration
Produces programming for cable, commercial & public TV; home video production; corporate films & medical series. TV, film archives & production.

SWAIN FILM & VIDEO INC.
7214 N Leewynn Dr
Sarasota, FL 34240
Phone: 941-365-8433
Fax: 941-365-5359
E-mail: tony@swainmedia.com
Tony Swain, President
Mike Swain, Vice President
Richard Ramsdell, Creative Editor
Offers full service production & post-production facilities in digital video & BetaSP formats; non-linear post-production video for educational & industrial programming, documentaries & commercials; specializes in corporate image video productions; provides sales, marketing & training videos; end products include CD & DVD as well as video for websites.

2017 Edition

TECHNICOLOR INC./CFI
4050 Lankershim
North Hollywood, CA 91604
Phones: 818-754-5054; 818-505-2821
Fax: 818-761-4835
Web Site: http://www.technicolor.com
Luis Martinez Amago, President, Connected Home, North America
Provides lab services for filmmakers & commercial producers.

TELECOM PRODUCTIONS
2237 Creek Park Rd
Decatur, GA 30033-2715
Phones: 770-455-3569; 800-525-3051
Fax: 770-455-3938
Budd O. Libby, President
Sales promotion company; creator of Let's Go to the Races.

TELEFILM CANADA
360 Saint Jacques St
Ste 500
Montreal, PQ H2Y 1P5
Canada
Phones: 514-283-6363; 800-567-0890
Fax: 514-283-8212
E-mail: info@telefilm.gc.ca
Web Site: http://www.telefilm.gc.ca
Wayne Clarkson, Executive Director

Branch Offices:
BRITISH COLUMBIA: 609 Granville St, Ste 410, Vancouver, BC V7Y 1G5, Canada. Phones: 604-666-1566; 800-663-7771. Fax: 604-666-7754.

NOVA SCOTIA: 1717 Barrington St, 4th Fl, Halifax, NS B3J 2A4, Canada. Phones: 902-426-8425; 800-565-1773. Fax: 902-426-4445.

ONTARIO: 474 Bathurst St, Ste 100, Toronto, ON M5T 2S6, Canada. Phones: 416-973-4607; 800-463-4607. Fax: 416-973-8606.
Federal cultural agency dedicated to the development & promotion of the Canadian audiovisual industry. Provides financial support to the private sector to create Canadian productions that appeal to domestic & international audiences. The Corporation also administers the funding programs of the Canadian Television Fund.

TELEGENIC PROGRAMS INC.
161 Forest Hill Rd
Toronto, ON M5P 2N3
Canada
Phone: 416-484-8000
Fax: 416-484-8001
H. Lawrence Fein, President & Chief Executive Officer
TV program distribution company.

TELEMUNDO NETWORK GROUP
2290 West 8th Ave
Hialeah, FL 33010
Phone: 305-884-8200
Fax: 305-889-7950
Web Site: http://www.telemundo.com
Jackie Hernandez, Chief Operating Officer, Telemundo
Peter Blacker, Executive Vice President, Digital Media & Emerging Business
Jorge Hidalgo, Executive Vice President, Sports
Johanna Guerra, Senior Vice President, News
Eli Velazquez, Senior Vice President, Sports

Branch Offices:
CORAL GABLES: International Program Sales, 2745 de Leon Blvd, Coral Gables, FL 33134.

Phone: 305-774-0033. E-Mail: marcus.santana@nbcuni.com. Marcos Santana, President, Telemundo International.

NEW YORK: National Advertising Sales, 30 Rockefeller Plz, New York, NY 10112. Phone: 212-664-7417. E-Mail: michael.rodriguez@nbcuni.com.
Produces, distributes & imports Spanish-language programming worldwide.

TELEPICTURES PRODUCTIONS
4000 Warner Blvd
Burbank, CA 21522
Phone: 818-972-7073
Web Site: http://www.telepicturestv.com
David Decker, Executive Vice President, Business & legal Affairs
Stuart Krasnow, Executive Vice President, Creative Affairs
Donna Redier Linsk, Executive Vice President, Business Operations & Programming
Sheila Bouttier, Senior Vice President, Programming & Development
Jill Olsen, Senior Vice President, Finance & Administration
Tomii Crump, Development Director
Develops & produces reality & reality-based programming for the first-run syndication marketplace.

TELETECH COMMUNICATIONS
2358 Gatetree Ln SE
Grand Rapids, MI 49546
E-mail: teletechcomm@aol.com
John Jones, President
Alan Crispin, Vice President
Provides captioning services to the TV & film industries.

TELEVISA
Av. Vasco de Quiroga No. 2000
Edifico C, Piso 3
Col. Santa Fe, DF CP 01210
Mexico
Phone: 52-55-5261-2000
Fax: 52-55-5261-3213
E-mail: soportecnico@televisanetworks.tv
Web Site: http://www.televisanetworks.tv
Fernando Muniz, Director General
Paul Presburger, Managing Director, Televisa USA
Michael Garcia, Chief Creative Officer, Televisa USA
Ryan Likes, Chief of Operations & Business Affairs, Televisa USA
Chris Philip, Head, Production & Distribution Operations, Televisa USA
Bruce Boren, Vice President
Christian Cuadra, Administration & Finance Director
Santiago Kuribrena, Merchandising Director
Eduardo Jimenez Machorro, Technical Director
Ana Lydia Montoya, Programming Director
Produces Spanish language programming.

TELEVISION REPRESENTATIVES INC.
9720 Wilshire Blvd
Ste 202
Beverly Hills, CA 90212

Phone: 310-278-4050
TV syndication consultant; home video.

THE TELEVISION SYNDICATION CO. INC.
520 Sabal Lake Dr.
Ste 108
Longwood, FL 32779
Phone: 407-788-6407
Fax: 407-788-4397
E-mail: cassie@tvsco.com
Web Site: http://www.tvsco.com
Cassie M. Yde, President
Barbara DeMaio, Operations Manager
Mary E Joyce, International Sales Executive
Lisa Romine, Domestic Sales Executive
Brooke Smith, Administrative Assistant
Full-service syndication & distribution organization; provides new product from independent producers to broadcast television, digital platforms, in-flight entertainment, educational outlets worldwide; services include cash & barter market-by-market syndication in the U.S.; cash distribution abroad; acquisition of programs from domestic & international sources.

TERRITORY
22840 Woodward Ave
Ferndale, MI 48220
Phone: 248-548-1011
Fax: 248-548-1282
E-mail: jporter@territorypost.com
Web Site: http://www.territorypost.com
Joan Porter, Senior Producer
Formerly STS-Griot. Provides post-production services.

THIRTEEN/WNET
825 Eighth Ave
New York, NY 10019
Phones: 212-560-1313; 973-643-3315
Fax: 212-560-1314
E-mail: programming@thirteen.org
Web Site: http://www.thirteen.org
Neal Shapiro, President & Chief Executive Officer
Produces & broadcasts public TV.

THOMSON REUTERS CORP.
Three Times Sq
New York, NY 10036
Phone: 646-223-4000
E-mail: general.info@thomsonreuters.com
Web Site: http://thomsonreuters.com
David Thomson, Chairman
James C Smith, President & Chief Executive Officer
Andrew Rashbass, Chief Executive Officer, Reuters News Operation
Stephen J Adler, President & Editor In Chief, Reuters News Operation
Gustav Carlson, Executive Vice President & Chief Marketing Officer
Robert D Daleo, Executive Vice President & Chief Financial Officer
Stephen Dando, Executive Vice President & Chief Human Resources Officer
Deirdre Stanley, Executive Vice President & General Counsel
Formerly Reuters Group PLC. Provides intelligent information for businesses & profes-

Program Sources & Services

sionals in the media industry, as well as in financial, legal, tax & accounting, scientific & healthcare markets.

THREE THOUSAND EIGHT
3008 Ross Ave
Dallas, TX 75204
Phone: 214-922-9232
Fax: 214-922-8861
E-mail: ken@3008.com
Web Site: http://www.3008.com
Ken Skaggs, President & Partner
Brent Herrington, Partner & Editor
Anna Strock, Executive Producer
Provides post production services; specializes in high-end creative editorial.

TIMELESS MEDIA GROUP
2015 S Westgate Ave
Los Angeles, CA 90025
Phone: 310-826-7126
Web Site: http://www.shoutfactory.com/tent-poles/timeless-media-group
Distributes films, TV series & special interest programming. Subsidiary of Shout! Factory.

TM STUDIOS
2002 Academy Ln
Ste 110
Dallas, TX 75234-9220
Phone: 972-406-6800
Fax: 972-406-6890
E-mail: info@tmstudios.com
Web Site: http://www.tmstudios.com
Greg Clancy, General Manager & Vice President, Creative
John Kuykendall, Vice President, Facilities
Ricky Roo, Vice President & Creative Director
Provides custom & syndicated image packages & production libraries for TV. A Triton Co.

TODAY VIDEO
555 W 57th S
Ste 1420
New York, NY 10019
Phone: 212-307-0707
E-mail: todayvideo@aol.com
Web Site: http://www.todayvideo.com
David Seeger, Chief Executive Officer
Video & film boutique; provides creative solutions for all production & post-production needs, from concept to completion.

TOP KOPY
12 Skyline Dr
Hawthorne, NY 10532
Phone: 914-345-2650
Fax: 914-345-2617
E-mail: info@topkopy.com
Web Site: http://www.topkopy.com
Provides video duplication services for D2, D3, Digital Betacam, DV, one inch, Betacam (SP), MII, U-Matic (SP), VHS, S-VHS, HI-8, 8mm & Betamax formats.

TOUCHSTONE PICTURES/WALT DISNEY
500 S Buena Vista St
Burbank, CA 91521
Phone: 818-560-1000
Fax: 818-972-5402
Web Site: http://waltdisneystudios.com/corp/unit/264
Produces & distributes motion picture films.

TOUCHSTONE TELEVISION — See listing for ABC Studios.

TRANS WORLD INTERNATIONAL — See listing for IMG World.

TRAVELVIEW INTERNATIONAL
2000 Dairy Ashford
#480
Houston, TX 77077
Phones: 281-496-9799; 281-679-7619 ext. 204
Fax: 281-496-0760
Web Site: http://www.travelview.com
Darrell Turner, President & Editor-in-Chief
Jane Marie Turner, Editorial Director
Produces & distributes travel TV & video programs of destinations, hotels & attractions.

TRIANGLE INC.
420 Pearl St
Malden, MA 02148
Phone: 781-322-0400
Fax: 781-322-0410
E-mail: acarbone@triangle-inc.org
Web Site: http://www.triangle-inc.org
Michael A. Rodrigues, Chief Executive Officer
Thomas L. Marshall, Chief Operating Officer
Alisa Carbone, Media Producer
Produces Ablevision, a scripted, shot & hosted TV program created and produced entirely by people with disabilities.

TRIBECA FILM CENTER
375 Greenwich St
New York, NY 10013
Phone: 212-941-4000
Fax: 212-941-3997
E-mail: contactus@tribecafilm.com
Web Site: http://www.tribecafilm.com
Robert De Niro, Co-Founder
Jane Rosenthal, Co-Founder
Produces film & tape spot commercials; film handlers.

TRIBUNE MEDIA SERVICES INC. — See Gracenote.

TRIMARK TELEVISION — See listing for Lionsgate Entertainment.

TRISTAR TELEVISION — See listing for Sony Pictures Television.

TROMA ENTERTAINMENT INC.
36-40 11th St
Long Island City, NY 11106
Phone: 718-319-0110
Fax: 718-391-0255
E-mail: internationalsales@troma.com
Web Site: http://www.troma.com
Lloyd Kaufman, President
Independently produces, distributes & syndicates feature films to theatrical & ancillary markets worldwide.

TURNER BROADCASTING SYSTEM INC.
One CNN Ctr
Atlanta, GA 30303
Phone: 404-827-1700
Web Site: http://www.turner.com
Philip I. Kent, Chairman
John Martin, Chief Executive Officer
Kevin Reilly, President, Turner Broadcasting System & Chief Creative Officer, Turner Entertainment Networks
Lenny Daniels, President, Turner Sports
Sandra Dewey, President, Turner Broadcasting System Productions & Business Affairs
Ricky Ow, President, Turner Broadcasting System, Asia-Pacific
Donna Speciale, President, TV & Digital Sales
Gerhard Zeiler, President, Turner Broadcasting System International
Molly Battin, Chief Media & Business Insights Officer
Coleman Breland, Chief Operating Officer, Turner Network Sales
Jeremy Legg, Chief Technology Officer
Howard Shimmel, Chief Research Officer
Scott Teissler, Chief Technical Officer & Chief Digital Technical Strategist
Pascal Desroches, Executive Vice President & Chief Financial Officer
Jeff Gregor, Executive Vice President & Chief Marketing Officer
Matt Hong, Executive Vice President & General Manager, Turner Sports
Lauren Hurvitz, Executive Vice President & Chief Communications and Marketing Officer
Stephano Kim, Executive Vice President, Digital Strategy & Operations and Chief Data Strategist
Jennifer Mirgorod, Executive Vice President, Brand Distribution
Kelly Regal, Executive Vice President
Louise Sams, Executive Vice President & General Counsel
Angela Santone, Executive Vice President & Global Chief Human Resources Officer
Doug Shapiro, Executive Vice President & Chief Strategy Officer
Brett Weitz, Executive Vice President, Original Programming
Craig Barry, Senior Vice President, Production & Executive Creative Director, Turner Sports
Deborah K. Bradley, Senior Vice President, Program Acquisitions
Dennis Camlek, Senior Vice President, Turner Media Group
Amit Chaturvedi, Senior Vice President, Revenue Operations & Platforms
Andrea Ching, Senior Vice President, CNN & Turner Digital Ad Sales Marketing & Promotion
Loren Cooper, Senior Vice President, Finance & Accounting, Domestic Ad Sales, Domestic Distribution & Sports
David Eilenberg, Senior Vice President, Unscripted Development, TBS & TNT
Pete Galuskin, Senior Vice President & National Sales Manager, Young Adult Ad Sales
Shea Guinn, Senior Vice President, Turner Live Events, Ad Sales Division
John Harran, Senior Vice President, Business & Product Development, Turner Network Sales
Oliver Herrgesell, Senior Vice President, Communications, Turner Broadcasting System International
David Hudson, Senior Vice President, Late Night & Specials
Lisa Hyams, Senior Vice President, Nework Partnerships, US Network Operations
Shitiz Jain, Senior Vice President, Finance, Asia Pacific, Turner International Asia Pacific
Jill King, Senior Vice President, Sponsorship Group, Animation, Young Adults & Kids Media
Michael Luzzi, Senior Vice President, Technology & Operations, US Network Operations
Michael Marinello, Senior Vice President, Corporate Communications
Jeff Matteson, Senior Vice President, Communications
Christine Merrifield, Senior Vice President, Ad Sales Strategy & Monetization, Turner Ad Sales
Scott Miller, Senior Vice President, Associate General Counsel, Legal & Business Affairs, Turner Content Distribution
Sal Petruzzi, Senior Vice President, Domestic Communications Officer
Scott Porter, Senior Vice President, Human Resources, Corporate
Michael Quigley, Senior Vice President, Brand Distribution, Turner Network Sales
Veronica Sheehan, Senior Vice President, Global Network, Technology & Studio Operations
Michael Strober, Senior Vice President, Turner Entertainment Ad Sales
Frank Wall, Senior Vice President, National Sales Manager, Turner Sports Ad Sales
Laura Forti, Senior Vice President, Distribution, Turner Entertainment Networks
Natasha Hritzuk, Vice President, Client Insights & Content Partnerships Research
Mark Loughney, Vice President, Animation, Young Adults & Kids Media
Kristie Moomey, Vice President, Post Production, Unscripted Programming & Digital Extensions
Rachelle Savoia, Vice President, Communications
Dawn Simonton, Vice President, Network Partnerships
Creates & programs branded news, entertainment, animation & young adult media environments on TV & other platforms.

TURNER SPORTS
One CNN Center
Atlanta, GA 30303
Phone: 404-827-1700
Web Site: http://www.turner.com/locations
Lenny Daniels, President
Craig Barry, Executive Vice President, Production & Chief Content Officer
Louise Sams, Executive Vice President & General Counsel
Valerie Immele, Senior Vice President, Business
Tina Shah, Senior Vice President, Business Affairs & Associate General Counsel
Tara August, Vice President, Talent Relations
Hania Poole, Vice President, Business Operations, NCAA Digital
Produces televised & online sports programming. Television lineup includes the NBA, MLB, the NCAA Division I Men's Basketball Championship & professional golf. The digital portfolio includes Bleacher Report, NCAA.com and March Madness Live & PGA.com, as well as an accompanying collection of mobile websites & connected device apps. Turner Sports and the NBA also jointly manage NBA Digital.

TVO
PO Box 200
Station Q
Toronto, ON M4T 2T1
Canada
Phones: 416-484-2600; 800-613-0513
E-mail: asktvo@tvo.org
Web Site: http://www.tvo.org
Lisa de Wilde, Chief Executive Officer
Paul Dancy, Chief Financial Officer
Todd Slivinskas, Chief Technology Officer
Jiohn Ferri, Vice President, Current Affairs & Documentaries
Karen Grose, Vice President, Digital Education
Erika Kramer, Vice President, Distribution Services
Andrew Steele, Vice President, Strategy Marketing & Communications
Produces & distributes educational TV programming.

TWENTIETH CENTURY FOX FILM CORP.
PO Box 900
Beverly Hills, CA 90213
Phone: 310-277-2211
Fax: 310-203-1558
Web Site: http://www.foxmovies.com
Stacey Snider, Chairman & Chief Executive Officer, Twentieth Century Fox Film

Pamela Levine, President, Worldwide Theatrical Marketing
Chris Petri Kin, Senior Vice President, Corporate Communications
Finances, develops, produces, distributes & markets motion pictures, TV & home entertainment programming worldwide.

TWENTIETH CENTURY FOX HOME ENTERTAINMENT
PO Box 900
Beverly Hills, CA 90213-0900
Phone: 877-369-7867
Web Site: http://www.foxconnect.com
Markets, sells & distributes film & TV programming.

TWENTIETH CENTURY FOX TELEVISION
10201 W Pico Blvd
Bldg 103, Rm 5286
Los Angeles, CA 90064
Phone: 310-369-1000
Fax: 310-369-8726
Web Site: http://www.fox.com
Gary Newman, Co-Chairman & Co-Chief Executive Officer, Fox Television Group
Dana Walden, Co-Chairman & Co-Chief Executive Officer, Fox Television Group
Jonnie Davis, President, Creative Affairs
Howard Kurtzman, President, Business Operations
Angela Courtin, Chief Marketing Officer
Chris Alexander, Executive Vice President, Corporate Communications & Publicity
Bob Barron, Executive Vice President & Chief Finance Officer
Sharon Klein, Executive Vice President, Casting & Talent
Mark Pearson, Executive Vice President, Brand Management & Digital Media
Jim Sharp, Executive Vice President, Production
Michael Thorn, Executive Vice President, Development
Pam Baron, Senior Vice President, Business Affairs
Neal Baseman, Senior Vice President, Business Affairs
Geoff Bywater, Senior Vice President, TV Creative Music
Carolyn Cassidy, Senior Vice President, Current Programming
Nissa Diederich, Senior Vice President, Production
Gary Hall, Senior Vice President, Post Production
Jonathan Harris, Senior Vice President, Legal Affairs
Craig Hill, Senior Vice President, Production
Dana Honor, Senior Vice President, Comedy Development
Joel Hornstock, Senior Vice President, Production
Eileen Ige, Senior Vice President, Production Finance
Casey Kyber, Senior Vice President, Research
Bruce Margolis, Senior Vice President, Production
Steven Melnick, Senior Vice President, Marketing
Vibiana Molina, Senior Vice President, Business Affairs
Unju Paik, Senior Vice President, Legal Affairs
Marci Proietto, Senior Vice President, Animation
Steve Sicherman, Senior Vice President, Current Programming
Mike Walsh, Senior Vice President, Finance
Douglas Aaron, Vice President, Drama Production Accounting
Mark Ambrose, Vice President, Drama Development

Dan Brickman, Vice President, Production
Jennifer Carreras, Vice President, Comedy Development
Chloe Dan, Vice President, Drama Development
Carol Farhat, Vice President, Music Production & Administration
Michael Giordano, Vice President, Business Affairs
Grant Gish, Vice President, Animation
Ward Hake, Vice President, TV Creative Music
Stephanie Herman, Vice President, Casting
Beth Hoffman, Vice President, Business Affairs
Jan Kunesh, Vice President, Comedy Production Accounting
Sharon Merle-Lieberman, Vice President, Marketing & Promotions
Liz Paulson, Vice President, Casting
Sheri Rosenblum, Vice President, Media Relations
Dana Sharpless, Vice President, Current Programming
Mandy Summers, Vice President, Current Programming
Jen Weinberg, Vice President, Talent Relations & Special Events
Marc Wisot, Vice President, Legal Affairs
Supplies prime time network & cable series.

TWENTIETH TELEVISION
2121 Ave of the Stars
17th Fl
Los Angeles, CA 90067
Phone: 310-369-1000
Fax: 310-369-3899
Web Site: http://www.fox.com
Greg Meidel, President
Stephen Brown, Executive Vice President, Programming & Development
Joe Oulvey, Executive Vice President, Sales
Michael Teicher, Executive Vice President, Media Sales
Ken Lawson, Senior Vice President & General Sales Manager, Broadcast Syndication Sales
Les Eisner, Vice President, Media Relations
Rob Wussler, Vice President, Sales & Integrations
Produces & distributes a wide array of first-run & off-network programming, as well as feature film packages.

UNITED CHURCH OF CHRIST, OFFICE OF COMMUNICATIONS
700 Prospect Ave
Cleveland, OH 44115-1100
Phone: 216-736-2100
Fax: 216-736-2223
E-mail: guessb@ucc.org
Web Site: http://www.ucc.org
J. Bennett Guess, Executive Director
Cheryl Leanza, Policy Director
Barb Powell, Administration Director
Public relations, news, video, broadcast, radio & media advocacy.

UNITED FILM ENTERPRISES INC.
120 W Park Ave
Ste 309
Long Beach, NY 11561-3301
Phone: 516-431-2687
Fax: 516-431-2805
Nathan Podhorzer, President
Exports & imports films; film buyer; sales representative; producers' representative & purchasing agent for foreign distribution companies.

UNITED METHODIST COMMUNICATIONS
PO Box 320
Nashville, TN 37202-0320
Phone: 615-742-5400
Fax: 615-742-5423
E-mail: umcom@umcom.org
Web Site: http://www.umcom.org
Fran Coode, Strategic Project Coordinator, UMTV
Produces UMTV & a bi-monthly podcast as well as videos, audio & DVDs.

UNITED NATIONS — See listing for UN Multimedia.

UNITED PRESS INTERNATIONAL
1133 19th St NW
Washington, DC 20036
Phone: 202-898-8000
Fax: 202-898-8048
E-mail: ussales@upi.com
Web Site: http://www.upi.com
Chung Hwan Kwak, Chairman
Nicholas Chiaia, President
John Hendel, Executive Editor
Marc Oram, General Counsel
Ed Field, Licensing Director

Branch Offices:
CHILE: Nataniel Cox 47, Piso 9, Santiago, Chile. Phone: 56-2-6570874. Fax: 56-2-6986605. E-Mail: jmolina@upi.com. Juan Molina.

HONG KONG: Wui Tat Centre 18/F, 55 Connaught Rd W, Hong Kong. Phone: 852-2858-2774. Fax: 852-2858-2775.

JAPAN: AH 1 Bldg, 1-9-14 Azabudai, 8th Fl, Minato-ku, Tokyo 106-0041, Japan. Phone: 81-3-3586-2370. Fax: 81-3-3586-2373.

KOREA: 605 Yonhap News Agency Bldg, 85-1 Susong-dong, Chongro-gu, Seoul, Korea. Phone: 82-2-398-3654. Fax: 82-2-737-3654.

LEBANON: Gefinor Ctr, Bloc D, 3rd Fl, Ste 302, Clemenceau, Beirut, Lebanon. Phone: 961-1-745971. Fax: 961-1-745973. E-Mail: mideastsales@upi.com. Rabin Saade.
Provides critical information to media outlets, businesses, governments & researchers worldwide; licenses content directly to print outlets, online media & institutions of all types.

UNIVERSAL CABLE PRODUCTIONS
10 Universal City Pl
Universal City, CA 91608
Phone: 818-777-1000
Web Site: http://www.nbcuniversal.com
Bonnie Hammer, Chairman, NBCUniversal Cable Entertainment
Steve Dolcemaschio, Chief Operating Officer
Jeff Eachtel, Chief Content Officer, NBCUniversal Cable Entertainment & President, Universal Cable Productions
Mark Binke, Executive Vice President, Production
Dawn Olmstead, Executive Vice President, Development
Richard Rothstein, Executive Vice President, Current Programming

Nidia Caceros Kilde, Vice President, Communications
Produces original scripted & digital content for domestic & international distribution. Part of NBCUniversal Cable Entertainment, a division of NBC Universal.

UNIVERSAL MUSIC PUBLISHING GROUP (UMPG)
2100 Colorado Ave
Santa Monica, CA 90404
Phone: 310-235-4700
Fax: 310-235-4900
E-mail: umpg.newmedia@umusic.com
Web Site: http://www.umusicpub.com
Jody Gerson, Chairwoman & Chief Executive Officer
Marc Cimino, Chief Operating Officer
Evan Lamberg, President
Michael J. Sammis, Executive Vice President & Chief Financial Officer
Charity Roberts, Senior Vice President & Chief Technology Officer
Richard Conlon, Special Adviser, Performing Rights
Publishes music; offices worldwide.

UNIVERSAL TELEVISION
10 Universal City Plz
Universal City, CA 91608
Phone: 818-777-1000
Fax: 818-866-1430
Web Site: http://www.nbcuni.com/broadcast/universal-television
Pearlena Igbokwe, President
Mike Clement, Executive Vice President, Comedy Development
Jerry DiCanio, Executive Vice President, Production Operations
Jim Donnelly, Senior Vice President, Comedy Development
Curt King, Senior Vice President, Publicity
Beth Klein, Senior Vice President, Talent & Casting
Tracey Pakosta, Senior Vice President, Comedy
Russell Rothberg, Senior Vice President, Drama
Erin Underhill, Senior Vice President, Drama
Dan Shear, Vice President, Comedy Development
Stacey Silverman, Vice President, Drama Development
Andy Weil, Vice President, Comedy Development
Produces or co-produces series for broadcast networks & online outlets in a variety of dayparts & genres, including primetime, late-night, long form & reality programming. Subsidiary of NBCUniversal.

UNIVERSITY OF SOUTHERN CALIFORNIA: HUGH M. HEFNER MOVING IMAGE ARCHIVE
School of Cinematic Arts
University Park, NCT 100
Los Angeles, CA 90089-2211
Phone: 213-740-3182
Fax: 213-740-2920
E-mail: filmrequest@cinema.usc.edu
Web Site: http://cinema.usc.edu/about/movingimagearchive.cfm

Program Sources & Services

Dino Everett, Archivist
An archive for research & study by students & scholars; licenses of USC-produced materials.

UNIVISION STORY HOUSE
5999 Center Dr
Los Angeles, CA 90069
Phone: 310-216-3434
Camila Jimenez Villa, President & Chief Content Officer, Fusion Media Group
Christian Gabela, Vice President & General Manager
Silvanna Aguirre, Creative Director
Juan Rendon, Creative Director
Rosemary Mercedes, Information Contact
Produces original content for Univision Communication Inc's portfolio of owned networks as well as third party networks and platforms.

UNIVISION STUDIOS
5999 Center Dr
Los Angeles, CA 90045
Phone: 310-348-3434
Web Site: http://www.univision.net
German Perez Nahim, Vice President
Produces & co-produces reality shows, dramatic series & other programming formats for Univision Communications' platforms.

UN MULTIMEDIA
Rm S-805A
New York, NY 10017
Phones: 212-963-6953; 212-963-6939
Fax: 212-963-6869
Web Site: http://www.unmultimedia.org
Produces documentaries & TV series; provides live daily feeds.

UNUSUAL FILMS
c/o Bob Jones University
1700 Wade Hampton Blvd
Greenville, SC 29614
Phone: 864-241-1664
Fax: 864-242-5917
E-mail: films@bju.edu
Web Site: http://www.unusualfilms.com
Steve Ross, Manager
Produces & distributes motion picture features & shorts, promotional, educational, religious & foreign language films and animation.

UPA PRODUCTIONS OF AMERICA
8640 Wilshire Blvd
Beverly Hills, CA 90211
Phone: 310-659-6004
Fax: 310-659-4599
Produces & distributes TV programs, animated programs & feature films to cable, syndication, videocassette & foreign markets; produces industrial films & TV commercials; character licensing & merchandising.

U.S. DEPARTMENT OF AGRICULTURE, OFFICE OF COMMUNICATIONS
Broadcast Media & Technology Ctr
1400 Independence Ave SW, Room 1618-S
Washington, DC 20250-1300
Phone: 202-720-6072
Fax: 202-720-5773
E-mail: garth.clark@usda.gov
Web Site: http://www.usda.gov
Garth Clark, Center Director & Production Manager
Jordan Alexander, Resource Manager
Anthony Bouldin, Manager, Multimedia
Patrick O'Leary, Manager, TV Feature

Larry Holmes, Facility Engineer
Provides full-service digital production facilities to all agencies within the USDA & other federal agencies.

VENEVISION INTERNATIONAL INC. —
See Cisneros Media Distribution.

VENEVISION PRODUCTIONS
121 Alhambra Plz
Ste 1400
Coral Gables, FL 33134
Phone: 305-442-3411
Fax: 305-446-4743
Web Site: http://www.venevision.com
Juan Carlos Sosa, Executive Vice President, Operations
Produces Spanish-language programming in the U.S. A Cisneros Company.

VERITAS PRODUCTIONS INC.
269 Morehouse Hwy
Fairfield, CT 06825
Phone: 203-257-2667
Fax: 203-372-1141
E-mail: info@veritasproductions.com
Web Site: http://www.veritasproductions.com
Brian Thorne, Founder & Managing Member
Offers full studio production services.

VERTIGO PRODUCTIONS
1678 Lance Point Dr
Maumee, OH 43537
Phone: 416-891-2191
Fax: 416-891-2130
E-mail: contact@vertigocd.com
Provides replication services for CD-ROMS, audio CDs & DVDs.

VIACOM INC.
1515 Broadway
New York, NY 10036
Phone: 212-258-6000
Web Site: http://www.viacom.com
Bob Bakish, President & Chief Executive Officer, Viacom International Media Networks
Thomas Dooley, Chief Operating Officer
Wade Davis, Chief Financial Officer
Pierluigi Gazzolo, President, Americas Division, Viacom International Media Networks
Carl Folta, Executive Vice President, Corporate Communications
Michael D. Fricklas, Executive Vice President, General Counsel & Secretary
DeDe Lea, Executive Vice President, Government Affairs
Ross Martin, Executive Vice President, Marketing Strategy & Engagement, Viacom Media Networks
Scott Mills, Executive Vice President, Human Resources & Administration
Kern Schireson, Executive Vice President, Data Strategy & Consumer Intelligence
Develops, produces & distributes entertainment content.

VICE
90 N 11th St
Brooklyn, NY 11211
Phone: 718-599-3101
E-mail: vice@vice.com
Web Site: http://company.vice.com/en_us
Shane Smith, Founder & Chief Executive Officer
Suroosh Avi, Co-Founder
Andrew Creighton, President
Eddy Moretti, Chief Creative Officer
Tom Punch, Chief Commerical & Creative Officer
Ciel Hunter, Head of Content
Produces original series & films. Disney holds 10% interest in Vice Media.

VICTORY STUDIOS
2247 15th Ave W
Seattle, WA 98119
Phones: 206-282-1776; 888-282-1776
Fax: 206-282-3535
E-mail: info@victorystudios.com
Web Site: http://www.victorystudios.com
Conrad W. Denke, Chief Executive Officer & Owner
Laura Denke, Executive Vice President
Scott Thomas, Chief Engineer

Branch Offices:
NORTH HOLLYWOOD: 10911 Riverside Dr, Ste 100, North Hollywood, CA 91602. Phone: 818-769-1776. Fax: 818-760-1280. E-Mail: info@victorystudiosla.com.
Creative production & production services company; television program, Internet & remote productions from script to screen; production services include rental cameras and support gear, studios, editing, full audio services, graphics, color correction, DVD authoring & video transfers, compression and duplication.

VIDEO-CINEMA FILMS INC.
510 E 86th St
Apt 12C
New York, NY 10028
Phone: 212-734-1632
Distributes & licenses motion picture features for TV & video media.

VIDEO ENTERPRISES INC.
575 29th St
Manhattan Beach, CA 90266
Phone: 310-796-5555
Fax: 310-546-2921
E-mail: heidi@videoenterprisesinc.com
Web Site: http://www.videoenterprisesinc.com

Branch Offices:
NEW YORK:. Phone: 914-234-3725. Fax: 914-234-3725. E-mail: jody@videoenterprisesinc.com.
Provides promotional TV spots & prizes for game, talk, variety & sports shows.

VIDEO EXPRESS PRODUCTIONS
2B Normandy Sq Ct
Silver Spring, MD 20906
Phone: 301-598-6096
Fax: 301-598-6211
E-mail: info@videoexpresspro.com
Web Site: http://www.videoexpresspro.com
Julie Bargeski, President

Branch Offices:
ALEXANDRIA: 1044 N Royal, Alexandria, VA 22314. Phone: 703-836-7626.

MIDDLETOWN: Nine Groff Ct, Middletown, MD 21769. Phone: 301-371-9150.
Provides video production & produces programming.

VIDEO/FASHION NETWORK
611 Broadway
Ste 307
New York, NY 10012
Phone: 212-274-1600
Fax: 212-219-1969
E-mail: info@videofashion.com
Web Site: http://www.videofashion.com
Marlene Cardin, President & Chief Executive Officer
Produces & distributes fashion, beauty & lifestyle programming for all media markets.

VIP 2000
1200 Brickell Ave
Ste 1575
Miami, FL 33131
Phone: 305-373-2400
E-mail: vip2000@vip2000.tv
Web Site: http://vip2000.tv
Roxanna Rotundo, Chief Executive Officer
Rosaline Rotundo, Vice President, International
Adriana Delgado, Operations Director
Distributes film & TV programming.

VIRATECH.ORG
4719 Quail Lakes Dr
Ste G319
Stockton, CA 95207
Phone: 209-477-3030
E-mail: questions@viratech.org
Web Site: http://viratech.org
Formerly Imperia Entertainment Inc. Produces & distributes full-length feature films.

VISTA STREET ENTERTAINMENT
8700 Venice Blvd
Los Angeles, CA 90034
Phone: 310-280-1184
E-mail: vistastreet@sbcglobal.net
Web Site: http://www.vistastreet.com
Gerald Feifer, Information Contact
Produces cult, horror, witchcraft & action movies.

VITAC
101 Hillpointe Dr
Canonsburg, PA 15317-9503
Phones: 724-514-4000; 800-278-4822
Fax: 724-514-4111
E-mail: jim-b@vitac.com
Web Site: http://www.vitac.com
Patricia Prozzi, Chief Executive Officer & President
Dwight Wagner, Chief Systems & Technology Officer
Darryn Cleary, Vice President, Sales
Timothy Taylor, Vice President, Engineering & Facility Operations
Debbie Hammond, Client Services Manager

Branch Offices:
ARLINGTON: 1501 Wilson Blvd, Ste 1003, Arlington, VA 22209. Phone: 703-807-2766. Fax: 703-807-2761. E-Mail: heather-y@vitac.com. Bob Byer, General Manager; Heather York, Marketing Director.

NORTH HOLLYWOOD: 4605 Lankershim Blvd, Ste 250, North Hollywood, CA 91602. Phones: 818-755-0410; 888-528-4288. Fax: 818-755-0411. E-Mail: jim-b@vitac.com. Jim Ballard, Executive Vice President, Sales & Marketing; Maggie McDermott, West Coast Sales Director.
Provides captioning & subtitling services for all media formats, including broadcast, corporate & Internet video, subtitling & translation in over 45 languages, realtime English & Spanish captions, audio description, & Internet & streaming media captions.

VUBIQUITY INC.
3900 W Alameda Ave
Ste 1700
Burbank, CA 91505
Phone: 818-526-5000
Fax: 818-526-5001
Web Site: http://www.vubiquity.com
Darcy Antonellis, Chief Executive Officer
Doug Sylvester, President & Chief Operating Officer
William G. Arendt, Chief Financial Officer
Steve Holsten, Chief Legal Officer & General Counsel
Rob Jacobson, Chief Content Officer
James P. Riley, Chief Revenue Officer

Program Sources & Services

Branch Offices:
RESTON: 1881 Campus Commons Dr, Ste 101, Reston, VA 20191. Phone: 571-485-2760. Fax: 571-485-2690.

UNITED KINGDOM: 3 More London Riverside, London SE1 2AQ, United Kingdom. Phone: 44-0-20-2378-2500. Fax: 44-0-20-7378-2502.

Connects content owners & video providers to deliver entertainment to viewers on any screen; brings premium content to over 750 global video distributors.

WALLACH ENTERTAINMENT
1400 Braeridge Dr
Beverly Hills, CA 90210
Phone: 310-278-4574
George Wallach, President
Provides sports TV production & sports entertainment management.

WALT DISNEY ANIMATION STUDIOS
500 S Buena Vista St
Burbank, CA 91521
Phone: 818-560-1000
Fax: 818-560-1930
Web Site: http://www.disneyanimation.com
Ed Catmull, President
Formerly Walt Disney Feature Animation. Produces & distributes animated feature films.

WALT DISNEY PICTURES
500 S Buena Vista St
Burbank, CA 91521
Phone: 818-560-5151
Web Site: http://disney.go.com/disneypictures
Sean Bailey, President, Production, Walt Disney Studios Motion Picture Production
Alan Bergman, President, The Walt Disney Studios
Produces & distributes motion picture films.

WALT DISNEY STUDIOS
500 S Buena Vista St
Burbank, CA 91521
Phone: 818-560-5151
Web Site: http://waltdisneystudios.com
Alan Horn, Chairman
Sean Bailey, President, Walt Disney Studios Motion Picture Production
Alan Bergman, President, Walt Disney Studios
Dr Ed Catmull, President, Walt Disney & Pixar Animation Studios
Thomas Schumacher, President, Disney Theatrical Group
Ricky Strauss, President, Marketing, Walt Disney Studios
John Lasseter, Chief Creative Officer, Walt Disney & Pixar Animation Studios; Principal Creative Advisor, Walt Disney Imagineering
Ken Bunt, Executive Vice President, Disney Music Group
Christine Cadena, Senior Vice President, Multicultural Initiatives, Walt Disney Studios
Carolyn Wilson, Senior Vice President, Human Resources, The Walt Disney Studios
Paul Roeder, Vice President, Global Communications
Produces & acquires live-action, animated motion pictures, direct-to-DVD & Blu-ray programming, musical recording & live stage plays.

WARNER BROS. ANIMATION INC.
15301 Ventura Blvd
Ste 1200
Sherman Oaks, CA 91403
Phone: 818-977-8490
Web Site: http://www.warnerbros.com
Peter Roth, President, Warner Bros. Television Group President & Chief Content Officer
Sam Register, President, Warner Bros. Animation & Warner Digital Series
Ed Adams, Senior Vice President & General Manager
Jay Bastian, Senior Vice President, Series
Produces animation TV film/tape series, TV commercials & motion picture cartoon shorts.

WARNER BROS. DIGITAL NETWORKS
4000 Warner Blvd
Burbank, CA 91522-1703
Phone: 818-954-6000
Craig Hunegs, President
Produces digital programming.

WARNER BROS. DOMESTIC TELEVISION DISTRIBUTION
4000 Warner Blvd
Burbank, CA 91522-1184
Phone: 818-954-6000
Web Site: http://www.warnerbros
Ken Werner, President
David Decker, Executive Vice President, Cable & Subscription-Video-On-Demand Sales
Liz Huszarik, Executive Vice President, Media Research & Insights
Andy Lewis, Executive Vice President & General Manager
Gus Lucas, Executive Vice President, Strategic Sales & Planning
John O'Hara, Executive Vice President, Warner Brothers Brand Networks
Dan Menzel, Executive Vice President, Cable Sales
Distributes programming to the first-run & off-net syndication marketplaces.

WARNER BROS. INTERNATIONAL TELEVISION DISTRIBUTION
4000 Warner Blvd
Burbank, CA 91522
Phone: 818-954-6000
Fax: 212-954-7667
Web Site: http://www.wbitv.com
Jeffrey Schlesinger, President, Worldwide Television Distribution
Malcom Dudley-Smith, Executive Vice President, Sales & Business Development
Allen Etherton, Senior Vice President, Planning & Analysis, Worldwide Television Distribution
Andrew Shipps, Senior Vice President, Marketing
Licenses & distributes feature films, TV, programs & animation to the international TV marketplace.

WARNER BROS. PICTURES
4000 Warner Blvd
Burbank, CA 91522
Phone: 818-956-6000
Web Site: http://www.warnerbros.com/studio/divisions/warner-bros-pictures
Barry Meyer, Chairman
Kevin Tsujihara, Chief Executive Officer
Jeff Robinov, President, Warner Bros. Pictures Group & Office of the President
Lynne Frank, President, International Marketing & Worldwide Planning & Operations
Sue Kroll, President, Worldwide Marketing & International Distribution
Steve Papazian, President, Worldwide Physical Production
Blair Rich, President, Worldwide Marketing
Steven Spira, President, Worldwide Business Affairs
Thomas Gewecke, Chief Digital Officer, Warner Bros. Entertainment
Juli Goodwin, Executive Vice President, National Publicity
Dee Dee Myers, Executive Vice President, Worldwide Corporate Communications & Public Affairs
Loren Schwartz, Executive Vice President, Genre Marketing & Creative Advertising
Adam Keen, Senior Vice President, Publicity
Produces & distributes feature films.

WARNER BROS. PICTURES DOMESTIC DISTRIBUTION
4000 Warner Blvd
Burbank, CA 91522
Phone: 818-954-6000
Web Site: http://www.warnerbros.com/studio/divisions/television/warner-bros-domestic-television-distribution
Dan Fellman, President
Distributes theatrical first-run features, classic films, TV product & cartoons to non-theatrical markets; distributes classic films to the domestic theatrical market; sets the release schedule & all exhibition operations.

WARNER BROS. PICTURES INTERNATIONAL
4000 Warner Blvd
Burbank, CA 91522
Phone: 818-954-6222
Fax: 818-954-6488
Veronika Kwan-Rubinek, President, International Distribution
Sue Kroll, President, Worldwide Marketing
Angelina Speare, Executive Vice President, Operations & Finance
David Williamson, Senior Vice President, Finance
Distributes & markets feature films to the overseas marketplace.

WARNER BROS. TELEVISION GROUP
4000 Warner Blvd
Burbank, CA 91522-1703
Phone: 818-954-6000
Fax: 212-954-7667
Web Site: http://www.warnerbros.com/studio/divisions/television/television-group
Peter Roth, President & Chief Content Officer and President, Warner Bros. Television Studio
Mike Darnell, President, Unscripted & Alternative Programming
Craig Hunegs, President, Business & Strategy and President, Warner Bros. Digital Networks
Brett Paul, Co-President, Warner Horizon Scripted Television & Executive Vice President, Warner Brothers Television
Susan Rovner, Co-President, Warner Horizon Scripted Television & Executive Vice President, Development, Warner Brothers Television
Produces primetime series, tele-films & miniseries programming.

WARNER HOME VIDEO
4000 Warner Blvd
Burbank, CA 91522-0001
Phones: 818-954-6000; 866-373-4389
Fax: 818-954-6480
Web Site: http://www.warnerbros.com/studio/divisions/home-entertainment/warner-home-video
Ronald Sanders, President, Worldwide Home Entertainment Distribution
Mark Horak, President, North America Operations
Jeffrey Calman, Executive Vice President
David Hettler, Executive Vice President, Worldwide Finance & Infomation Technology
Jeff Baker, Senior Vice President, U.S. Sales
Rosemary Markson, Senior Vice President, TV & Special Interest Marketing
Releases & distributes current & library feature films; distributes TV series, direct-to-video hits & special interest lines.

WARNER INDEPENDENT PICTURES
4000 Warner Blvd
Burbank, CA 91522
Phone: 818-954-6000
Fax: 212-954-7667
Web Site: http://wip.warnerbros.com
Polly Cohen, President
Laura Kim, Executive Vice President, Marketing & Publicity
Produces & acquires smaller-budgeted films than those of its parent studio.

WEATHERNEWS INC.
Akabane Bridge Bldg
Tokyo Minato-ku 3-1-14
Tokyo 105-0014
Japan
Phone: 81-43-274-5550
E-mail: marketing@wni.com
Web Site: http://www.weathernews.com
Chihito Kusabiraki, President

Branch Offices:
NORMAN: Weathernews Americas Inc., 350 David L Boren Blvd, Ste 1000, Norman, OK 73072. Phone: 405-310-2800. Fax: 405-310-2804.

Provides weather forecasts, software & programming (including Internet service) to the broadcast industry, offices worldwide.

WEATHERVISION
1230 Raymond Rd
Box 800
Jackson, MS 39204
Phone: 601-665-7737
E-mail: edward@weathervision.com
Web Site: http://www.weathervision.com
Edward Saint Pe', President
Produces daily TV weathercasts for both large & small TV stations across the USA. The service provides TV stations that do not produce a local newscast a way to bring daily weather updates to their viewers.

EVAN WEINER PRODUCTIONS
370 Claremont Ave
Mount Vernon, NY 10552
Phones: 914-667-9070; 800-965-3347
Fax: 914-667-3043
E-mail: evan4256@aol.com
Evan Weiner, Executive Producer
Produces cable TV & TV station sports talk shows.

Communications Daily
Warren Communications News

Get the industry standard FREE —
For a no-obligation trial call 800-771-9202 or visit www.warren-news.com

Program Sources & Services

FULLY SEARCHABLE • CONTINUOUSLY UPDATED • DISCOUNT RATES FOR PRINT PURCHASERS
For more information call **800-771-9202** or visit **www.warren-news.com**

WESTCHESTER FILMS
245 W 55th St
Ste 1109
New York, NY 10019
Phone: 646-822-9229
E-mail: westchesttrfilms@gmail.com
Web Site: http://www.westchesterfilms.com
Restores classic motion pictures; distributes contemporary films for theatrical & non-theatrical releases.

WESTON WOODS STUDIOS INC.
143 Main St.
Norwalk, CT 06851-3709
Phones: 203-845-0197; 800-243-5020
Fax: 203-845-0498
Web Site: http://westonwoods.scholastic.com/products/westonwoods
Linda Lee, Vice President & General Manager
Paul Gagne, Production Director
Kim Hayes-Grimm, Associate Business Manager
Melanie Bishop, Operations Coordinator
Produces & distributes audio/visual materials based on children's books; distributes educational films & motion picture shorts; exports & imports children's films & video programs.

WORLD CLASS VIDEO
623 Wood Lot Tr
Annapolis, MD 21401
Phone: 410-224-0204
Fax: 410-224-0203
E-mail: bryan@worldclassvideo.com
Web Site: http://www.worldclassvideo.com
Bryan Mong, Founder, Director & Cameraman
TV production company; specializes in HD & in high-end film style video production of magazine features, documentaries & corporate communications; served news organizations, syndicated magazine shows, major broadcast & cable networks, corporations & agencies worldwide.

WORLD OF WONDER PRODUCTIONS
6650 Hollywood Blvd
Los Angeles, CA 90028
Phone: 323-603-6300
Web Site: http://worldofwonder.net
Produces film & TV programming.

WORLD PROPERTY CHANNEL
1221 Brickell Ave
Ste 900
Miami, FL 33131
Phone: 305-375-9292
E-mail: info@wpjnews.com
Web Site: http://www.worldpropertyjournal.com
Michael Gerrity, Founder & Chief Executive Officer
Publishes, distributes & syndicates on a daily basis residential, commercial and vacation real estate market news, investment trends, property cycles & listing information on a global scale; provides a real estate syndication service.

WORLDWIDE ENTERTAINMENT CORP.
135 S McCarty Dr
Ste 101
Beverly Hills, CA 90212
Phone: 310-858-1272
Fax: 310-858-3774
E-mail: jackhh@pacbell.net
Jack H. Harris, President & Owner
Judith Parker Harris, Vice President
Production, distribution, syndication, importation & exportation of theatrical feature films.

WORLD WRESTLING ENTERTAINMENT INC.
1241 E Main St
Stamford, CT 06902
Phone: 203-352-8600
Web Site: http://www.wwe.com
Vincent K. McMahon, Chairman & Chief Executive Officer
George Barrios, Chief Financial Officer
Michelle D. Wilson, Chief Marketing Officer
Kevin Dunn, Executive Vice President, TV Production
Brian Kalinowski, Executive Vice President, Digital Media
John Laurinaitis, Executive Vice President, Talent Relations
Michael Luisi, Executive Vice President, Business Development, General Counsel & Secretary
Stephanie McMahon, Executive Vice President, Creative Development & Operations
Mike Pavone, Executive Vice President, WWE Studios
Andrew Whitaker, Executive Vice President, International
Jim Connelly, Senior Vice President, Consumer Products

Branch Offices:
LOS ANGELES: Digital Sales, 12424 Wilshire Blvd, Ste 1400, Los Angeles, CA 90025. Phone: 310-481-9370.

NEW YORK: 780 Third Ave, Rm 1101, New York, NY 10017. Phone: 212-593-2228.

STAMFORD: TV Production Office, 120 Hamilton Ave, Stamford, CT 06902. Phone: 203-353-2900.

CANADA: Two Lansing Sq, Ste 1003, Willowdale, ON M2J 4PA, Canada. Phone: 418-497-8338.

CHINA: 18F Bund ctr, 22 Yarian Dong Rd, Shanghai 200002, China. Phone: 86-21-6132-3857.

JAPAN: Dongenzaka Imani Bldg 3F, 1-19-12 Gogenzaka, Shibya-ku, Tokyo 150-0043, Japan. Phone: 81-3-5456-6050.

SINGAPORE: Ubi Techpark, 10 Ubi Crescent #04-78 408564, Singapore. Phone: 65-6747-5651.

UNITED KINGDOM: Five Jubilee Pl, London 5W3 3TD, United Kingdom. Phone: 44-0-20-7349-1740.
Produces & distributes sports entertainment events & programs.

WPA FILM LIBRARY
16101 S 108th Ave
Orland Park, IL 60467
Phones: 708-873-3113; 800-323-0442
Fax: 708-460-0187
E-mail: sales@wpafilmlibrary.com
Web Site: http://www.wpafilmlibrary.com
Stock footage library, film archive.

WQED MULTIMEDIA
Content/Product Sales & Client Services
4802 Fifth Ave
Pittsburgh, PA 15213
Phone: 412-622-1300
Fax: 412-622-1488
E-mail: wqed@wqed.org
Web Site: http://www.wqed.org
Deborah L. Acklin, President & Chief Executive Officer
Provides motion picture & TV development services, including set construction, stock footage library, facility rental, studio & sound stage production facilities, post production & teleconference facilities.

WRS MOTION PICTURE & VIDEO LABORATORY
213 Tech Rd
Pittsburgh, PA 15205
Phone: 412-937-1200
Fax: 412-922-1200
E-mail: jackn@wrslabs.com
Web Site: http://www.wrslabs.com
Laboratory facilities & services, editing, processing & recording facilities, videotape-to-film & film-to-tape duplication and Macrovision anti-piracy process.

WTTW LOCAL PRODUCTIONS
5400 N St Louis Ave
Chicago, IL 60625
Phone: 773-583-5000
Web Site: http://www.wttw.com
Creates & distributes local programming. Division of Window to the World Communications Inc.

WTTW NATIONAL PRODUCTIONS
5400 N St Louis Ave
Chicago, IL 60625
Phone: 773-583-5000
Web Site: http://www.wttw.com
Parke Richeson, Senior Vice President & Executive in Charge
Produces original programming for public & commercial TV broadcasting. Division of Window to the World Inc.

YOUTUBE
901 Cherry Ave.
San Bruno, CA 94066
Phone: 650-253-0000
Fax: 650-253-0001
E-mail: press@youtube.com
Web Site: http://www.youtube.com
Susan Wojcick, Chief Executive Officer

ZEEBOX — See Beamly.

Brokerage & Financing

DAVID ABRAHAM & CO. LLC
265 Post Road West
Westport, CT 06880
Phone: 203-222-1919
E-mail: dabraham@daccapital.com
Web Site: http://www.daccapital.com
David Abraham, President
Provides private-market investment banking for media & communications; equity & debt private placements, merger & acquisition brokerage and financial advisory services.

ALTA COMMUNICATIONS
28 State St
Ste 1801
Boston, MA 02109
Phone: 617-262-7770
Fax: 617-262-9779
E-mail: jreed@altacomm.com
Web Site: http://www.altacomm.com
Timothy L. Dibble, Managing General Partner
Brian W. McNeill, Managing General Partner
Jessica Barry Reed, Vice President
Provides debt & equity financing to the media & telecommunications industries.

AUS CONSULTANTS
155 Gaither Dr
Ste A
Mt Laurel, NJ 08054
Phones: 856-234-9200; 800-925-4287
Fax: 856-234-8371
E-mail: aus@ausinc.com
Web Site: http://www.ausinc.com
John L. Ringwood, Chairman & Chief Executive Officer

Branch Offices:
CAMP HILL: 275 Grandview Ave, Ste 100, Camp Hill, PA 17011. Phone: 717-763-9890. Fax: 717-763-9931.

GREENFIELD: 8555 W Forest Home Ave, Ste 201, Greenfield, WI 53228. Phone: 414-529-5755. Fax: 414-529-5750.
Provides financial consulting services to the CATV industry; expert witness & testimony for presentations to regulatory agencies; valuation & survey research consulting.

AXA EQUITABLE
1290 Ave of the Americas
8th Fl
New York, NY 10104
Phones: 212-554-1234; 877-222-2144
Web Site: http://www.axa-equitable.com
Anthony Sages, Divisional President
Provides wealth protection, asset management & financial planning strategies to individuals & businesses.

BALBOA CAPITAL
2010 Main St
11th Fl
Irvine, CA 92614
Phones: 949-756-0800; 888-225-2621
Fax: 949-756-2565
E-mail: info@balboacapital.com
Web Site: http://www.balboacapital.com
Patrick Bryne, Chief Executive Officer
Phil Silva, President
Robert Rasmussen, Chief Operating Officer
David Chiurazzi, Chief Financial Officer
Susan Hooten, Regional Sales Manager

Branch Offices:
SAN FRANCISCO: 601 Montgomery St, Ste 1800, San Francisco, CA 94111. Phone: 800-950-7650.

SAN RAMON: 2410 Camino Ramon, Ste 175, San Ramon, CA 94583. Phone: 800-950-7650.

SCOTTSDALE: 14614 N Kierland Blvd, Ste N-200, Scottsdale, AZ 85254. Phone: 800-280-5624.
Provides equipment leasing & financing on audio/video, broadcast, computer & other capital equipment.

BANK OF AMERICA
333 S Hope St
13th Fl
Los Angeles, CA 90071
Phone: 213-621-7382
Fax: 213-621-3608
Web Site: http://www.bankofamerica.com
Provides commercial & investment banking services for entertainment & media industries.

BNY MELLON, MEDIA & TECHNOLOGY DIVISION
One Wall St
New York, NY 10286
Phone: 212-495-1784
Web Site: http://www.bnymellon.com
Robert P. Kelly, Chairman & Chief Executive Officer
Gerald L. Hassell, President

Branch Offices:
UNITED KINGDOM: One Canada Sq, London E14 5AL, United Kingdom. Phone: 44-20-7570-1784.
Provides financing for media companies.

BARCLAYS CAPITAL
Five The North Colonnade
Canary Wharf
London E14 4BB
United Kingdom
Phone: 44-0-20-7623-2323
E-mail: corporate.communications@barclayscapital.com
Web Site: http://www.barcap.com
Iain Abrahams, Managing Director, Risk, Liquidity & Private Equity
Gerald A. Donini, Managing Director & Head of Equities
Guglielmo Satori de Borgoricco, Managing Director & Head of Distribution

Branch Offices:
ATLANTA: 3344 Peachtree Rd, Ste 950, Atlanta, GA 30326. Phone: 404-262-4800.

BOSTON: 125 High St, Boston, MA 02110. Phone: 617-330-5800.

CHICAGO: 190 S LaSalle St, Chicago, IL 60603. Phone: 312-609-7200.

DALLAS: 200 Crescent Ct, Ste 400, Dallas, TX 75201. Phone: 214-720-9470.

HOUSTON: Fullbright Tower, 1301 McKinney St, Ste 400, Houston, TX 77010. Phone: 713-401-6800. Fax: 713-401-6752.

LOS ANGELES: 10250 Constellation Blvd, 24th Fl, Los Angeles, CA 90067. Phone: 310-481-2600.

MENLO PARK: 155 Linfield Dr, Menlo Park, CA 94025. Phone: 650-289-6000. Fax: 650-321-2207.

MIAMI: 1111 Brickell Ave, 12th Fl, Miami, FL 33131. Phone: 305-789-8700.

NEW YORK: 200 Park Ave, New York, NY 10166. Phone: 212-412-4000. Fax: 212-412-7300.

PORTLAND: 1001 SW Fifth Ave, Ste 1100, Portland, OR 97204. Phone: 503-535-8062. Fax: 503-535-0714.

SAN FRANCISCO: 555 California St, 30th Fl, San Francisco, CA 94104. Phone: 415-274-3300.

SANTA MONICA: Water Garden Bldg, 1620 26th St, Santa Monica, CA 90404. Phone: 310-907-0510.

SEATTLE: 701 Fifth Ave, Ste 7101, Seattle, WA 98104. Phone: 206-344-5870. Fax: 206-233-2817.

WASHINGTON, DC: 1501 K St NW, Ste 500, Washington, DC 20005. Phone: 202-452-4700.
Provides telecommunications & communications capital marketing & lending.

BARGER BROADCAST SERVICES INC.
8023 Vantage Dr
Ste 840
San Antonio, TX 78230
Phone: 210-340-7080
Fax: 210-341-1777
E-mail: jwbarger@sbcglobal.net
John Barger, President
Provides broadcast brokerage services, appraisals & management consulting.

BARKER CAPITAL LLC
10 Rockefeller Plz
Ste 910
New York, NY 10020
Phone: 212-332-4318
Fax: 212-332-4315
Web Site: http://www.barkercapital.com
Jacob J. Barker, Founding Partner
Robert B. Crossland III, Managing Director
Sara B. Gochberg, Managing Director
Dale E. Norton, Managing Director & Chief Financial Officer
Timothy P. Olson, Managing Director & General Counsel
Provides specialized investment banking services to underserved media companies with a focus on the broadcasting, publishing, & outdoor advertising sectors; manages an investment fund that provides senior capital to small- to medium-sized media companies & entrepreneurs.

BIA CAPITAL STRATEGIES LLC
14150 Parkeast Circle
Ste 110
Chantilly, VA 20151
Phone: 703-818-8115
Fax: 703-803-3299
E-mail: cwiebe@bia.com
Web Site: http://www.biacapital.com
Mike Andres, Managing Director
Thomas J. Buono, Managing Director
Gregg E. Johnson, Managing Director
Lloyd R. Sams, Managing Director
Charles A. Wiebe, Managing Director
Assists companies in the communications industry to establish strategic, financial & operating objectives and arrange equity, mezzanine & senior debt financing for acquisition & expansion opportunities. Provides clients financial advice, merger/acquisition consulting & access to capital.

BIA DIGITAL PARTNERSHIP LP
15120 Enterprise Ct
Ste 200
Chantilly, VA 20151
Phone: 703-227-9600
E-mail: contactdp@bia.com
Web Site: http://www.biadigitalpartners.com
Gregg E. Johnson, Managing Principal
Lloyd R. Sams, Managing Principal
Provides cost-effective junior capital to growing middle-market companies in the media, entertainment, telecommunications, information & business services sectors.

THE BIA KELSEY GROUP
14150 Parkeast Circle
Ste 110
Chantilly, VA 20151
Phones: 703-818-2425; 800-331-5086
Fax: 703-803-3299
E-mail: info@biakelsey.com
Web Site: http://www.bia.com
Tom J. Buono, Founder & Chief Executive Officerr
Mark A. Giannini, Chief Operating Officer & Senior Vice President

Brokerage & Financing

Rick Ducey, Chief Strategy Officer
Neal Polachek, President
Mark Fratrik, Vice President
Bobbi Loy-Luster, Vice President & Senior Analyst
Steve Passwaiter, Vice President, Business Development
Geoff Price, Vice President
Formerly BIA Financial Network LLC. Provides financial intelligence & investment resources to the media, telecommunications, technical & related industries; provides valuation & financial/strategic advisory services; publishes financial reports, yearbooks & pocket guides on the TV industry. Division of BIA Advisory Services.

BLACKBURN & CO. INC.
201 N Union St
Ste 340
Alexandria, VA 22314-2642
Phone: 703-519-3703
Fax: 703-519-9756
E-mail: jimblackburn@msn.com
James W. Blackburn, Jr., Chairman & Chief Executive Officer
Provides brokerage services to TV & radio station owners.

BMO CAPITAL MARKETS, MEDIA & COMMUNICATIONS GROUP
One First Canadian Pl
100 King St W
Toronto, ON M5X 1H3
Canada
Phones: 416-286-9992; 877-225-5266
Web Site: http://www.bmocm.com
Thomas V. Milroy, Chief Executive Officer
Eric C. Tripp, President
Robert S. Levine, Vice President
Darryl White, Executive Managing Director & Co-Head
Kevin J. Malone, Managing Director
Ashi Mathur, Co-Head

Branch Offices:
NEW YORK: Business Services & Media Group, Three Times Sq, New York, NY 10036. Sandra Andrews, Vice President; Susan Wolford, Managing Director & Group Head. Formerly BMO Financial Group. Offers comprehensive capital raising and M&A capabilities; provides investors with industry leading equity research, sales & trading for the media, communications & technology sectors.

BOND & PECARO INC.
1990 M St NW
Ste 400
Washington, DC 20036
Phone: 202-775-8870
Fax: 202-775-0175
E-mail: bp@bondpecaro.com
Web Site: http://www.bondpecaro.com
Timothy S. Pecaro, Principal
Jeffrey P. Anderson, Principal
Andrew R. Gefen, Principal
Matthew H. Lochte, Principal
John S. Sanders, Principal
Provides financial & management consulting services; specializes in asset appraisals, fair market valuations, expert testimony, impairment testing, feasibility studies, financial consulting, market research & related financial services for broadcasting, CATV, Internet, technology & other media; publishes The Television Industry: A Market-by-Market Review with the NAB.

BOWMAN VALUATION SERVICES LLC
706 Duke St
3rd Fl
Alexandria, VA 22314
Phone: 703-549-5681
Fax: 703-549-5682
Web Site: http://www.bowmanvaluation.com
Peter Bowman, Principal
Chip Snyder, Principal
Provides business valuation & appraisal services for the broadcasting & communications industry.

FRANK BOYLE & CO. LLC
2874 Main St.
#2
Stratford, CT 06614
Phone: 203-513-2402
Fax: 203-513-8189
E-mail: fboylebrkr@aol.com
Web Site: http://www.flboyle.com
Frank Boyle, President
Provides media brokerage & appraisals for the radio & TV industries.

BREAN MURRAY, CARRET & CO. LLC
1345 Avenue of the Americas
29th Floor
New York, NY 10105
Phone: 212-702-6500
Fax: 212-702-6649
Web Site: http://www.breanmurraycarret.com

Branch Offices:
CHICAGO: 225 W Washington St, 22nd Fl, #2210, Chicago, IL 60606. Phone: 312-924-2892.

SAN FRANCISCO: 580 California St, San Francisco, CA 94104. Phone: 415-283-3325.

CHINA: Capital Tower 3501, No 6 Jia Jianguomenwai Ave, Chaoyang District, Beijing, China. Phone: 86-5971-2880.
Full service, research-driven securities firm.

BULKLEY CAPITAL LP
5949 Sherry Ln
Ste 1616
Dallas, TX 75225
Phone: 214-692-5476
Fax: 214-692-9309
E-mail: info@bulkleycapital.com
Web Site: http://www.bulkleycapital.com
G. Bradford Bulkley, President & Founder
Lisa Bulkley, Vice President
Oliver Cone, Vice President
Gail Quick, Vice President
William Herdrich, Director
Richard W. Gilbert, Director & Advisory Board Member
John A. McKay, Director
William S. Skibitsky, Director
Nancy Wallin, General Manager
Craig R. Lentzsch, Advisory Board Member
William N. Case, Advisor

Branch Offices:
ATLANTA: 3500 Lenox Rd, Ste 1500, Atlanta, GA 30326. Phone: 404-843-2631. Fax: 404-843-2631.

COLUMBIA: 11276 Ridermark Rd, Columbia, MD 21044. Phone: 410-382-4622.
Provides mergers & acquisitions advisory services & private placement of senior & subordinated debt & equity for communications firms.

BV INVESTMENT PARTNERS LLC
125 High St
17th Fl
Boston, MA 02110-2003
Phone: 617-350-1500
Fax: 617-350-1509
E-mail: info@bvlp.com
Web Site: http://www.bvlp.com
Gerald S. Hobbs, Managing Director & Operating Partner
Louis V. Bertocci, Managing Director
Andrew C. Davis, Managing Director
Elizabeth Granville-Smith, Managing Director
Justin Harrison, Managing Director
Matthew J. Kinsey, Managing Director
Vikrant Raina, Managing Director
Provides equity & related capital for acquisitions, buyouts & expansions in TV, radio, cable, publishing, outdoor advertising, music and other communications & entertainment industries.

CHAISSON & CO. INC.
154 Indian Waters Dr
New Canaan, CT 06840
Phone: 203-966-6333
Fax: 203-966-1298
E-mail: rchaisco@aol.com
Robert A. Chaisson, President
Provides brokerage services to radio & TV sales, acquisitions & financing.

CHASE
270 Park Ave
New York, NY 10017-2070
Phone: 212-270-6000
Fax: 800-242-7324
Web Site: http://www.jpmorganchase.com
James Dimon, Chief Executive Officer

CITIBANK N.A.
399 Park Ave
New York, NY 10022
Phone: 800-627-3999
Fax: 212-559-7373
Web Site: http://www.online.citi.com
Provides radio, TV & cable financing.

CMS STATION BROKERAGE
1439 Denniston St
Pittsburgh, PA 15217
Phone: 412-421-2600
Fax: 412-421-6001
E-mail: roger@rafson.com
Web Site: http://www.cmsstationbrokerage.com
Roger Rafson, President
Provides station brokerage for small & medium-market broadcasters.

COBBCORP LLC
7400 Trail Blvd
Ste 102
Naples, FL 34108
Phones: 212-812-5020; 239-566-6051
Fax: 239-596-0660
E-mail: denisleclair@cobbcorp.com
Web Site: http://www.cobbcorp.com/team.htm
Brian E. Cobb, President
Denis LeClair, Vice President
Jeanette Kuszlyk, Controller
Provides brokerage, mergers & acquisition services, private equity, investment & merchant banking.

COMMUNICATIONS EQUITY ASSOCIATES
101 E Kennedy Blvd
Ste 3300
Tampa, FL 33602
Phone: 813-226-8844
Fax: 813-225-1513
E-mail: DMoyer@ceaworldwide.com
Web Site: http://www.ceaworldwide.com
J. Patrick Michaels, Jr., Chairman & Chief Executive Officer
Ming Jung, Senior Managing Director & Chief Financial Officer, CEA Cap Advisors
Ken Jones, Senior Vice President & General Counsel
Robert D. Berger, Managing Director
Raymond J Martin, Managing Director, Corporate Advisory Services & Investment Banking
Carsten Philipson, Managing Director
Donald Russell, Managing Director

Branch Offices:
CENTER VALLEY: Principal Advisors Group, 3477 Corporate Pkwy, Ste 100, Center Valley, PA 18034. Phone: 484-224-3429. Fax: 484-224-3501.

NEW YORK: 156 W 56th St, Ste 902, New York, NY 10019. Phone: 212-218-5085. Fax: 212-957-0620. Waldo Glasman, Managing Director; John Morrison, Managing Director; Alexander Rossi, Managing Director.

UNITED KINGDOM: Staple Ct, 11 Staple Inn Bldgs, London EC3A 7PT, WC1V 7Q4. Phone: 44-0-207-280-4899. Fax: 44-0-207-280-4899. Martin Farmer, Partner.
Provides investment banking & brokerage services to CATV, broadcasting, media & entertainment industries; acquisitions, divestitures, mergers & trades; financial placements for equity & debt; joint ventures; appraisals; consultation for tax & estate planning & shareholder negotiations.

CONLEY & ASSOCIATES LLC
1459 Interstate Loop
Bismarck, ND 58503-5560
Phone: 701-222-3902
Fax: 701-258-1937
E-mail: info@conleyassociates.net
Web Site: http://bis.midco.net/cbrg1/cbrg5/index.htm
Christopher J. Conley, Managing General Partner
Provides management & engineering consulting to the electronic media; specializes in appraisals & valuations; strategic planning & feasibility studies; financial planning & restructuring; contract management; operational evaluations & audits; engineering design & technical evaluations; marketing research & analysis; human resources development & training; franchising & refranchising; regulatory affairs & expert testimony.

COX & COX LLC
2454 Shiva Ct
St. Louis, MO 63011
Phones: 636-458-4780; 314-409-7180 (cell)
Fax: 636-458-6323
E-mail: bc@coxandcoxllc.com
Bob Cox, President
Linda Cox, Broker
Provides media brokerage services, specializing in media mergers & acquisitions.

CREDIT SUISSE
Paradeplatz 8
Zurich 8070
Switzerland
Phones: 41-44-212-16-16; 41-44-333-11-11
Fax: 41-44-333-25-87
Web Site: http://www.credit-suisse.com
Walter B. Kielholz, Chairman
Hans-Ulrich Doerig, Vice Chairman
Peter Brabeck-Letmathe, Vice Chairman

Branch Offices:
NEW YORK: 11 Madison Ave, New York, NY 10010-3629. Phone: 212-325-2000. Fax: 212-325-6665.

Brokerage & Financing

BRAZIL: Ave Brig Faria Lima, 3064 - 13 andar, Jardim Paulistano, San Paulo 01451-000, Brazil. Phone: 55-11-3841-6000. Fax: 55-11-3841-6900.

HONG KONG: Three Exchange Sq, Eight Connaught Pl Central, 22nd Fl, Hong Kong. Phone: 852-2101-6000. Fax: 852-2101-7990.

JAPAN: Izumi Garden Tower, 6-1 Roppongi 1-Chome, Minato-ku, Tokyo 106-6024, Japan. Phone: 81-3-4550-9000. Fax: 81-3-4550-9800.

SINGAPORE: One Raffles Link 05-02 039393, Singapore. Phone: 65-6212-6000. Fax: 65-6212-6200.

UNITED KINGDOM: One Cabot Sq, London E14 4QJ, United Kingdom. Phone: 44-20-7888-8888. Fax: 44-20-7888-1600. Provides investment & merchant bank services.

CVC CAPITAL CORP.
712 Fifth Ave
43rd Fl
New York, NY 10019
Phone: 212-265-6222
Fax: 212-265-6375
Web Site: http://www.cvc.com
Christopher Allen, Partner
Provides investment banking services.

DELOITTE & TOUCHE LLP
1633 Broadway
New York, NY 10019-6754
Phone: 212-489-1600
Fax: 212-489-1687
Web Site: http://www.deloitte.com
Sharon Allen, Chairman
Barry Salzberg, Chief Executive Officer
Provides assurance, advisory, tax & management consulting services; offices in more than 80 cities.

ENVEST MEDIA LLC
6802 Patterson Ave
Richmond, VA 23226
Phone: 804-282-5561
Fax: 804-282-5703
E-mail: mitt@envest.biz
Web Site: http://envest.biz
Mitt S. Younts, Managing Member

Branch Offices:
ATLANTA: One Glenlake Pkwy, 7th Fl, Ste 700, Alpharetta, GA 30328. Phones: 770-753-9650; 800-808-0130. Fax: 770-753-0089. Jesse Weatherby, Managing Director. Provides mergers, acquisitions, valuations, financing & strategic consulting services for the radio, TV, newspaper & media industries.

THE EXLINE CO.
17 Alipine Rd
Novato, CA 94945
Phone: 415-408-3324
E-mail: info@exlinecompany.com
Web Site: http://www.exlinecompany.com
Andrew McClure, President
Judi Lewis, Administrative Coordinator
Provides consulting services in operations, personnel & finance as well as brokerage & appraisals for radio & TV communications companies.

FBR CAPITAL MARKETS, TECHNOLOGY, MEDIA & TELECOMMUNICATIONS GROUP
1300 North 17th St.
Ste 1400
Arlington, VA 22209
Phones: 703-312-9500; 800-846-5050
Fax: 703-312-9501
E-mail: media@fbr.com
Web Site: http://www.fbr.com
David DeRuff, Senior Managing Director & Group Head
Provides creative capital raising, merger & acquisitions and corporate advisory services.

RICHARD A. FOREMAN ASSOCIATES INC.
330 Emery Dr E
Stamford, CT 06902
Phone: 203-327-2800
Fax: 203-967-9393
E-mail: raf@rafamedia.com
Web Site: http://www.rafamedia.com
Richard A. Foreman, President
Provides brokerage & consulting services to the radio, TV, digital & entertainment industries.

GAMMON MILLER LLC
1707 Thomas Cir
Suite B
Manhattan, KS 66502
Phone: 785-539-1700
Fax: 785-380-4628
E-mail: cmiller@gammonmiller.com
Web Site: http://www.gammonmiller.com
Christopher D. Miller, President & Chief Executive Officer
Douglas Padgett, Vice President
Formerly Gammon Media Brokers. Provides media investment banking. Experience in radio station, TV station & newspaper acquisitions or divestitures. Also offers relationship travel incentives for TV & radio stations as a form of new revenue generation.

CLIFTON GARDINER & CO. LLC
9541 E Jan Ave.
Mesa, AZ 85209
Phone: 623-336-7272
E-mail: cliff@cliftongardiner.com
Web Site: http://www.cliftongardiner.com
Clifton H. Gardiner, Managing Partner
Provides brokerage & investment banking services for media & communications companies.

GE CAPITAL SOLUTIONS
10 Riverview Dr.
Danbury, CT 06810
Phone: 203-749-6000
Web Site: http://www.ge.com/capitalsolutions
Provides equipment leasing & financial services for the entertainment industry.

W.B. GRIMES & CO.
24212 Muscari Ct
Gaithersburg, MD 20882
Phone: 301-253-5016
Fax: 240-358-0790
E-mail: lgrimes@mediamergers.com
Web Site: http://www.mediamergers.com
Larry Grimes, Owner & President

Branch Offices:
CAMDEN: 699 Channing Way, Camden, TN 38320. Phone: 731-694-2194. Fax: 731-584-4943. E-Mail: dennisr@usit.net. Dennis Richardson, Associate.

DES PLAINES: 765 Garland Pl, Des Plaines, IL 60016. Phone: 734-891-3008. E-Mail: peter.neill@comcast.net.

EAST GRAND FORKS: 1004 20th Ave SE, East Grand Forks, MN 56721. Phone: 218-230-8943. Fax: 218-335-7215. E-Mail: julie@wiktel.com. Julie Bergman, Senior Associate.

GOSHEN: 35 Ridge Rd, Goshen, NY 10924. Phone: 845-291-7367. E-Mail: jszefc@hvc.rr.com. Lewis Floyd, Senior Associate; John Szefc, Regional Manager.

GULF SHORES: 20050 Oak Rd E, Ste 1814, Gulf Shores, AL 36542. Phone: 850-290-5535. E-Mail: lfloydmedia@gmail.com. Peter Neill, Associate.

LOVELAND: 916 Scarsborough Dr, Loveland, CO 80538. Phone: 970-215-3060. E-Mail: ken.amundson@outlook.com. Ken Amundson, Regional Manager.

SPARTA: 59 Manor Sq, Sparta, NJ 07871. Phone: 973-729-7299. Fax: 973-729-0648. E-Mail: david8371@aol.com. David Slavin, Senior Associate.
Full service merger & acquisition firm.

HADDEN & ASSOCIATES
147 Eastpark Dr
Celebration, FL 34747
Phone: 321-939-3141
Fax: 321-939-3142
E-mail: hadden@haddenonline.com
Web Site: http://www.haddenonline.com
Doyle Hadden, President
Provides acquisition, divestiture, appraisal, consulting & financial assistance services.

HENSON MEDIA INC.
1930 Bishop Ln
Ste 1009
Louisville, KY 40218
Phone: 502-458-4222
Fax: 502-458-4999
E-mail: edhenson1@bellsouth.net
Web Site: http://www.hensonmedia.com
Ed Henson, President
Provides media brokerage services, assists clients in the buying & selling of radio stations & in doing valuations of broadcast facilities; specializes in the midwest & upper south.

R. MILLER HICKS & CO.
1011 W 11th St
Austin, TX 78703
Phone: 512-477-7000
Fax: 512-477-9697
R. Miller Hicks, President
Provides consultation services, appraisals, management & programming.

HOFFMAN-SCHUTZ MEDIA CAPITAL
1715 Soledad Way
San Diego, CA 92109
Phones: 908-291-9807; 619-291-7070
Web Site: http://www.hs-media.com
David E. Schutz, Founder & President
Provides broadcast station financing, appraisals, financial restructuring & litigation support.

HOLT MEDIA GROUP
PO Box 21985
Lehigh Valley, PA 18002-1985
Phone: 610-814-2821
Fax: 610-814-2826
E-mail: ArtHolt@holtmedia.com
Web Site: http://www.holtmedia.com
Arthur H. Holt, President & Chief Executive Officer
Christine Borger, Executive Vice President & Chief Financial Officer
Carl Strandell, Associate
Provides brokerage & acquisitions for internet, radio, TV & cable systems; fair market value, asset & liquidation appraisals; negotiation services & financial planning for sales & acquisitions; management & operations consulting; technical equipment sales & specifications; feasibility analysis & marketing planning for new ventures; expert witness & litigation consulting.

HPC PUCKETT & CO.
PO Box 9063
Rancho Santa Fe, CA 92067
Phone: 858-756-4915
Fax: 858-756-9779
Web Site: http://www.hpcpuckett.com
Thomas F. Puckett, Chairman
Hunter T. Puckett, Senior Vice President & General Counsel

Branch Offices:
TOPEKA: 5835 SW 29th St, Ste 203, Topeka, KS 66614. Phone: 785-273-0017. Fax: 785-273-5512. Jason A Meyer, Managing Director; Melissa L. Kramer, Vice President.
Provides brokerage services including acquisitions, divestiture, financing & investment banking; specializes in professional services with emphasis on legal procedures, financial analysis, closing procedures & community relations.

ING INVESTMENT MANAGEMENT
230 Park Ave
Ste 1800
New York, NY 10169
Phone: 212-338-4500
Web Site: https://www.nn-group.com
Robert G. Leary, Chairman & Chief Executive Officer
Jeffrey T. Becker, Vice Chairman, Chief Operating Officer & Chief Financial Officer
Frederic A. Nelson, Vice Chairman & Chief Investment Officer
Provides investment banking & corporate finance services.

JONES GROUP LTD.
9697 E Mineral Ave
Englewood, CO 80112-3408
Phones: 303-792-3111; 800-525-7002
Provides brokerage services to buyers & sellers in the communications industry.

JORGENSON BROADCAST BROKERAGE INC.
426 S River Rd
Tryon, NC 28782
Phone: 828-859-6982
Fax: 828-859-6831
E-mail: goradiotv@windstream.net
Web Site: http://www.goradiotv.com
Mark W. Jorgenson, Managing Partner

Brokerage & Financing

Branch Offices:
CUPERTINO: 19925 Stevens Creek Blvd, Cupertino, CA 95014-2358. Phone: 408-973-7292. Fax: 408-516-9526. E-Mail: pmieuli@att.net. Peter Mieuli, Partner.
Provides broadcast brokerage services nationwide.

KALIL & CO. INC.
2960 N Swan Rd
Ste 134
Tucson, AZ 85712
Phone: 520-795-1050
Fax: 520-322-0584
E-mail: kalil@kalilco.com
Web Site: http://www.kalilco.com
Frank Kalil, President
Steven R. Backerman, Chief Operations Officer
Provides media brokering services, trust & custodial services, appraisals & assistance with financing & consulting.

KANE REECE ASSOCIATES INC.
822 South Ave W
Westfield, NJ 07090-1460
Phones: 908-317-5757; 800-494-5263
Fax: 908-317-4434
Web Site: http://www.kanereece.com
John E. (Jack) Kane, Founder & Principal
Norval Reece, Co-Founder & Chairman Emeritus
Noah Gottdiener, Chief Executive Officer
Gerry Creagh, President
Dennis Elliott, Managing Director
Provides appraisals & valuations, business plans, engineering consulting, financial & technical due diligence, financing preparations, franchise renewals, litigation support, market/opinion research, management & management consulting, property tax compliance & control, solvency opinions, valuations for buy/sell agreements & workouts. Division of Duff & Phelps Corp.

KEPPER, TUPPER & CO.
2 Galleon
Ste 100
Hilton Head Island, SC 29928
Phone: 203-431-3366
E-mail: jtupper@kepper-tupper.com
Web Site: http://www.kepper-tupper.com
John B. Tupper, Chairman
James R. Kelly, President
Provides investment banking services including domestic & international brokerage of CATV systems & broadcast TV stations; appraisals of electronic media properties for tax & financial reporting; place financing; strategic planning & financial consulting.

KEYCORP.
127 Public Sq
Cleveland, OH 44114-1306
Phones: 216-689-6300; 800-539-2968
Fax: 216-689-0519
Web Site: http://www.key.com
Henry L. Meyer, III, Chairman, Chief Executive Officer & President
Thomas C. Stevens, Vice Chairman & Chief Administrative Officer

Beth Mooney, Vice Chairman, Key Community Banking
Charles S. Hyle, Chief Risk Officer
Provides specialized financing to meet the needs of the broad range of businesses, with specialized products & teams of experts dedicated to specific client segments.

KNOWLES MEDIA BROKERAGE SERVICES
PO Box 9698
Bakersfield, CA 93389
Phones: 661-833-3834; 661-333-9516 (cell phone)
Fax: 661-833-3845
E-mail: gregg.knowles@netzero.com
Web Site: http://www.media-broker.com
Gregg K. Knowles, Broker & Owner
Provides sales, consultation & appraisal services for print media owners nationwide.

KOZACKO MEDIA SERVICES
PO Box 90841
Raleigh, NC 27675
Phone: 607-733-7138
Fax: 607-733-1212
E-mail: dick@kozacko.com
Web Site: http://www.radio4sale.com
Richard L. Kozacko, President

Branch Offices:
TUCSON: PO Box 120-40, 6890 E Sunrise Dr, Tucson, AZ 85750. Phone: 520-299-4869. Fax: 520-844-8559. E-Mail: georgewkimble@aol.com. George W. Kimble, Associate; Pat Anderson, Associate.
Provides brokerage, appraisal & acquisition consulting services for TV & radio stations.

LAZARD
30 Rockefeller Pl
New York, NY 10112
Phone: 212-632-6000
Web Site: http://www.lazard.com
Bruce Wasserstein, Chairman & Chief Executive Officer
Steven J. Golub, Vice Chairman & Chairman, Financial Advisory Group
Charles G. Ward, III, President & Chairman, Asset Management Group
Michael J. Castellano, Chief Financial Officer
Scott D. Hoffman, General Counsel
Provides international financial advisory & asset management services.

MADISON DEARBORN PARTNERS LLC
70 W. Madison St.
Ste 4600
Chicago, IL 60602
Phone: 312-895-1000
Fax: 312-895-1001
E-mail: info@mdcp.com
Web Site: http://www.mdcp.com
John A. Canning, Jr., Chairman
Paul J. Finnegan, Co-Chief Executive Officer
Samuel M. Mencoff, Co-Chief Executive Officer
Provides venture capital for TV, radio, CATV, paging, cellular, PCS & SMR acquisitions.

THE MAHLMAN CO.
Four Midland Gardens
Ste 3F
Bronxville, NY 10708
Phone: 914-793-1577
Fax: 914-793-1587
E-mail: mahlmans@aol.com
Robert O. Mahlman, Founder
Nancy D. Mahlman, Founder
Bill Kehlbeck, Vice President
Specializes in radio station brokerage, appraisal & consulting.

MCG CAPITAL CORP.
1001 19th Street North
10th Floor
Arlington, VA 22209
Phone: 703-247-7500
Fax: 703-247-7505
Steven F. Tunney, President & Chief Executive Officer
Stephen J. Bacica, Executive Vice President & Chief Financial Officer
Samuel G. Rubenstein, Executive Vice President & General Counsel
B. Hagen Saville, Executive Vice President, Business Development
Derek Thomas, Executive Vice President, Risk Management & Underwriting
Tod K. Reichert, Senior Vice President, Chief Securities & Governance Counsel & Corporate Secretary
Provides capital to support the growth & value creation strategies of small- to mid-sized companies.

MCH ENTERPRISES INC.
8200 Stockdale Hwy
M-10, #164
Bakersfield, CA 93311
Phone: 805-769-8511
E-mail: mchenterprises@mchentinc.com
Web Site: http://www.mchentinc.com
Brett E. Miller, Founder
Rosario Miller, President
Sean Miller, Associate
Provides merger & acquisition support to buyers & sellers of broadcast & CATV properties; consulting services include station appraisals, financial planning, transactional management, project management, human resources consulting, website design & maintenance.

M/C VENTURE PARTNERS
75 State St
Ste 2500
Boston, MA 02109
Phone: 617-345-7200
Fax: 617-345-7201
E-mail: mcp@mcpartners.com
Web Site: http://www.mcpartners.com
David D. Croll, Managing General Partner
James F. Wade, Managing General Partner
John W. Watkins, Managing General Partner
John D. Patty, Vice President
Edward J. Keefe, Chief Financial Officer

Branch Offices:
SAN FRANCISCO: 235 Pine St, Ste 1675, San Francisco, CA 94104. Phone: 415-438-4875. Fax: 415-296-8901.

UNITED KINGDOM: Charles House, 18b Charles St, London W1J 5DU, United Kingdom. Phone: 44-0-20-7667-6838.
Provides equity financing & strategic guidance to entrepreneurial ventures in the media & telecommunications industries, including wireless telephony, CATV, broadcasting & publishing.

R.E. MEADOR & ASSOCIATES INC.
713 Bedfordshire Rd.
Louisville, KY 40222
Phone: 660-259-2544
Fax: 660-259-6424
Ralph E. Meador, President
Provides acquisitions & sales services; market studies & appraisals of broadcast properties.

MEDIA SERVICES GROUP INC.
149 S Roscoe Blvd
Ponte Vedra, FL 32082
Phone: 904-285-3239
Fax: 904-285-5618
E-mail: George@MediaServicesGroup.com
Web Site: http://www.mediaservicesgroup.com
George Reed, Managing Director

Branch Offices:
COLORADO SPRINGS: 2910 Electra Dr, Colorado Springs, CO 80906-1073. Phone: 719-630-3111. Fax: 719-630-1871. E-Mail: jbmccoy@mediaservicesgroup.com. Jody McCoy, Director.

HIGHLAND PARK: 147 Oak Knoll Ter, Highland Park, IL 60035. Phone: 847-266-9822. Fax: 847-266-9826. E-Mail: robertheymann@comcast.net. Robert L. Heymann, Jr., Director.

LOGAN: 1289 North 1500 East, Logan, UT 84341. Phone: 435-753-8090. E-Mail: merrill.greg@comcast.net. Greg Merrill, Director.

MORRILTON: 10 Wildewood Vista, Morrilton, AR 72110. Phone: 501-727-5100. Fax: 501-727-6475. Bill Cate, Director.

MORRISTOWN: 45 Park Pl S, Ste 146, Morristown, NJ 07960. Phone: 973-631-6612. Fax: 973-631-6633. E-Mail: rtmck2515@aol.com. Tom McKinley, Director.

PROVIDENCE: 170 Westminster St, Ste 701, Providence, RI 02903. Phone: 401-454-3130. Fax: 401-454-3131. E-Mail: rmaccini@cox.net. Bob Maccini, Director; Stephan Sloan, Director; Ted Clark, Analyst.

RICHARDSON: 1131 Rockingham Dr, Ste 209, Richardson, TX 75080. Phone: 972-231-4500. Fax: 972-231-4509. E-Mail: whitleytx@cs.com. Bill Whitley, Director.

ST. SIMONS ISLAND: 205 Marina Dr, St Simons Island, GA 31522. Phone: 912-634-6575. Fax: 912-634-5770. E-Mail: eddie@eddieesserman.com. Eddie Esserman, Director.
Provides brokerage services to media, entertainment & communications companies.

MEDIA VENTURE PARTNERS LLC
255 California St.
Ste 850
San Francisco, CA 94111
Phone: 415-391-4877
Fax: 415-549-0515
E-mail: pch@mediaventurepartners.com
Web Site: http://www.mediaventurepartners.com
Elliot Evers, Managing Director & Co-Founder
Greg Widroe, Managing Director & Founder, Telecom Group
Tim Beach, Vice President
Ari Citrin, Vice President
Renee Shaening, Vice President
Oliver Janssen, Managing Director
Kent Johnson, Associate
Ryan Carr, Analyst

Brokerage & Financing

Branch Offices:
BOULDER: 2033 11th St, Ste 6, Boulder, CO 80302. Phone: 303-284-3965. Fax: 415-549-0515. Brian Pryor, Managing Director; Paul Stapleton, Managing Director.

DEDHAM: 980-990 Washington St, Dedham, MA 02026. Phone: 617-345-7315. Fax: 617-549-0515. E-Mail: jhill@mediaventurepartners.com. Jason D. Hill, Managing Director & Co-Founder, Telecom Group; Bill Fanning, Managing Director.

KANSAS CITY: 435 Nichols Rd, Ste 200, Kansas City, MO 64112. Phone: 816-977-2822. Fax: 415-549-0515. E-Mail: cfunk@mediaventurepartners.com. Jason Nicolay, Vice President; R. Clayton Funk, Managing Director.

Provides strategic counsel & financial services, mergers/acquisitions, private equity/debt raises, financial, valuations & appraisals; focuses on clients in the media, telecom, technology & datacenter industries.

MILESTONE COMMUNICATIONS INC.
43 Herrn Ln
Castle Pines, CO 80108
Phones: 303-993-3557; 719-661-2478
Fax: 303-993-3559
E-mail: mdrake@milestonecomminc.com
Web Site: http://www.milestonecomminc.com
Michael W. Drake, President
Provides brokerage & consulting services, including acquisitions, divestitures & financing, to independent CATV operators.

MMTC MEDIA & TELECOM BROKERS
3636 16th St NW
Suite B-366
Washington, DC 20010
Phone: 202-332-0500
Fax: 202-332-0503
E-mail: info@mmtconline.org
Web Site: http://mmtconline.org/media-brokerage
David Honig, President
Provides media brokerage services; represents buyers & sellers of broadcast & telecom properties; NAMB member, minority-owned, non-profit.

MYMEDIABROKER.COM
407 Broadmoor
Portales, NM 88130
Phone: 505-356-2000
Fax: 505-356-2003
Web Site: http://www.mymediabroker.com
Sandi Bergman, Founder
Offers acquisition, appraisal & consulting services.

NATIONAL CITY CORP.
National City Ctr
1900 E Ninth St
Cleveland, OH 44114-3484
Phone: 216-222-2000
Web Site: http://www.nationalcity.com
David A. Daberko, Chairman & Chief Executive Officer
Jeffrey D. Kelly, Vice Chairman & Chief Financial Officer
William E. MacDonald, III, Vice Chairman
Peter E. Raskind, Vice Chairman, Consumer & Small Business Financial Services
Thomas A. Richlovsky, Senior Vice President & Treasurer
Provides commercial & retail banking, mortgage financing & servicing, consumer finance & asset management.

NEW COMMERCE COMMUNICATIONS (NCC)
259 Fields Terr
Port Charlotte, FL 33952
Phone: 239-282-5550
Fax: 414-755-1440
E-mail: tomm@com-broker.com; tom@millitzercapital.com
Web Site: http://www.com-broker.com
Tom Millitzer, President
Lisa Obrien, Vice President, Administration
Provides merger & acquisition services; focuses on telecom, hosting, cloud & data center industries.

NORMAN FISCHER & ASSOCIATES INC. (NFA INC.)
2520 Longview St
#313
Austin, TX 78705
Phone: 512-476-9457
Fax: 512-476-0540
E-mail: terrill@nfainc.com
Terrill Fischer, President
Provides management consulting, media brokerage & appraisals.

OPPENHEIMER & CO. INC.
85 Broad St.
New York, NY 10004
Phones: 212-668-8000; 800-221-5588
E-mail: info@opco.com
Web Site: http://www.opco.com
Albert Lowenthal, Chairman & Chief Executive Officer
Jeffrey J. Alfano, Executive Vice President & Chief Financial Officer
Provides financial services & advice to high net worth investors, individuals, businesses & institutions.

PATRICK COMMUNICATIONS LLC
6805 Douglas Legum Dr
Ste 100
Elkridge, MD 21075
Phone: 410-799-1740
Fax: 410-799-1705
E-mail: larry@patcomm.com
Web Site: http://www.patcomm.com
W. Lawrence Patrick, Managing Partner
Susan K. Patrick, Managing Partner
Gregory J. Guy, Managing Partner
Diana Wilkin, Partner
Jason James, Vice President
David Benton, Analysis Director
Provides station brokerage & investment banking services; fair market & asset appraisals; debt & equity placement; broadcast management & marketing consulting.

JOHN PIERCE & CO. LLC
PO Box 863
Florence, KY 41022
Phone: 859-647-0101
Fax: 859-647-2611
E-mail: info@johnpierceco.com
Web Site: http://www.johnpierceco.com
John Pierce, President
Tricia Burkhart, Vice President, Client Services
Kathryn Kegley, Associate Director
Provides brokerage, appraisal & consulting services to buyers & sellers of radio & TV properties.

PNC FINANCIAL SERVICES GROUP
Steel Plz Office
600 Grant St
Pittsburgh, PA 15219
Phones: 412-762-2000; 888-762-2265
Fax: 412-762-7568
Web Site: http://www.pnc.com

James E. Rohr, Chairman & Chief Executive Officer
Joseph C. Guyaux, President
Michael J. Hannon, Chief Credit Officer
Richard J. Johnson, Chief Financial Officer
Timothy G. Shack, Executive Vice President & Chief Information Officer
Thomas K. Whitford, Executive Vice President & Chief Administrative Officer
John J. Wixted, Jr., Senior Vice President & Chief Regulatory Officer
Provides financial services to communications companies nationwide.

PROVIDENCE EQUITY PARTNERS INC.
50 Kennedy Plz
18th Fl
Providence, RI 02903
Phone: 401-751-1700
Fax: 401-751-1790
Web Site: http://www.provequity.com
Jonathan M. Nelson, Chief Executive Officer
Gary S. Weinstein, Chief Operating Officer
Raymond M. Mathieu, Chief Financial Officer
Glenn M. Creamer, Senior Managing Director
Paul J. Salem, Senior Managing Director

Branch Offices:
LOS ANGELES: 1999 Avenue of the Stars, Ste 1250, Los Angeles, CA 90067. Phone: 310-228-5000. Fax: 310-228-5001.

NEW YORK: 9 W 57th St, 390 Park Ave, Ste 4799, New York, NY 10019. Phone: 212-588-5700. Fax: 212-588-6701.

HONG KONG: York House, 18th Fl, 15 Queens Rd, Central, Hong Kong, China. Phone: 852-3653-3800. Fax: 852-3653-3900.

INDIA: Birla Tower, 25 Barakhamba Rd, 6th Fl, New Delhi 110 001, India. Phone: 91-11-3041-9000. Fax: 91-11-3041-9090.

UNITED KINGDOM: 28 St George St, London W1S 2FA, United Kingdom. Phone: 44-0-20-7514-8800. Fax: 44-0-20-7629-2778. E-Mail: info@provequity.co.uk.
Private investment firm; specializes in equity investments in communications & media companies worldwide.

STAN RAYMOND & ASSOCIATES INC.
PO Box 8231
Longboat Key, FL 34228
Phone: 941-383-9404
Fax: 941-383-0132
E-mail: stnray@aol.com
Stan Raymond, President
Provides brokerage & consulting services for radio, TV & cable properties.

RBC DANIELS
3200 Cherry Creek S Dr
Ste 500
Denver, CO 80209
Phone: 303-778-5555
Fax: 303-778-5599
Web Site: http://www.danielsonline.com

Brian Deevy, Chairman & Chief Executive Officer
Brad Busse, President & Chief Operating Officer
Bill Fowler, Chief Financial Officer & Senior Managing Director
Bill Wedum, General Counsel
Greg Ainsworth, Senior Managing Director
Dave Rhodes, Senior Managing Director

Branch Offices:
LOS ANGELES: 11150 Santa Monica Blvd, Ste 1230, Los Angeles, CA 90025. Phone: 310-473-2300. Fax: 310-943-2052.

NEW YORK: 711 Fifth Ave, Ste 405, New York, NY 10022. Phone: 212-935-5900. Fax: 212-863-4859.
Provides mergers & acquisitions, corporate financing & financial advisory services to the cable telecommunications, media & technology industries; member NASD, SIPC.

ROBINSON/JEFFREY ASSOCIATES INC.
101 W Long Lake Rd
Bloomfield Hills, MI 48304
Phone: 248-644-0006
Fax: 248-647-2356
E-mail: robinsonjeffreyinc@msn.com
Peter Robinson, Principal
Michael Jeffrey, Principal
Provides investment banking & financial services for the broadband industry.

RUMBAUT & COMPANY
555 NE 34th St
Ste 2701
Miami, FL 33137-4060
Phone: 305-868-0000
Fax: 305-571-0433
E-mail: julio@rumbaut.com
Web Site: http://www.rumbaut.com
Julio Rumbaut, President
Provides media brokerage & consulting services.

SANDLER CAPITAL MANAGEMENT
711 Fifth Ave
15th Fl
New York, NY 10022
Phone: 212-754-8100
Fax: 212-826-0280; 212-826-0281
Web Site: http://www.sandlercap.com
Investment management firm; specializes in the communications industry, targeting public & private companies.

SATTERFIELD & PERRY INC.
7211 Fourth Ave S
St Petersburg, FL 33707
Phone: 727-439-4787
Fax: 727-345-3809
E-mail: eraust@prodigy.net
Web Site: http://www.satterfieldandperry.com
Robert Austin, President

Branch Offices:
AIKEN: 131 Inwood Dr, Aiken, SC 29803. Phone: 803-270-5613. Fax: 803-649-7786. John Willis, Secretary-Treasurer.

Brokerage & Financing

DENVER: 2020 S Monroe St, Ste 302, Denver, CO 80210. Phone: 303-758-1876. Fax: 303-756-1865. Joe Benkert, Vice President; Jim Birschbach, Vice President.

OVERLAND PARK: 4918 W 101st Ter, Overland Park, KS 66207. Phone: 913-649-5103. Doug Stephens, Vice President.

SALEM: 1159 Pawnee Circle SE, Salem, OR 97306. Phone: 503-990-7000. Dick McMahon, Vice President.

WETUMPKA: 169 Mountain Meadows Ln, Wetumpka, AL 36093. Phone: 334-514-2241. Fax: 334-514-2291. Ken Hawkins, Vice President.
Provides TV, cable & radio brokerage services; FDIC approved appraiser.

BURT SHERWOOD & ASSOCIATES INC.
6415 Midnight Pass Rd
Ste 206
Sarasota, FL 34242
Phone: 941-349-2165
Fax: 941-312-0974
Web Site: http://www.burtsherwood.com
Burt Sherwood, Owner, Chief Executive Officer & President
Jason W. Sherwood, Vice President
Provides media brokerage & appraisals for radio, TV & LPTV.

SNL FINANCIAL
One Lower Ragsdale Dr
Bldg 1, Ste 130
Monterey, CA 93940
Phone: 831-624-1536
Fax: 831-625-3225
E-mail: sales@snl.com
Web Site: http://www.snl.com
Derek Baine, Senior Vice President & Senior Analyst
Robin Flynn, Senior Vice President & Senior Analyst
Provides strategic financial planning, customized market & data analyses, regular fair market valuations of media properties.

SNOWDEN ASSOCIATES
PO Box 1966
Washington, NC 27889
Phone: 252-940-1680
Fax: 252-940-1682
Zoph Potts, President
Provides media brokerage services, valuations & consulting in Southeastern U.S.

STATE STREET CORP.
State Street Financial Ctr
One Lincoln St
Boston, MA 02111
Phone: 617-786-3000
E-mail: information@statestreet.com
Web Site: http://www.statestreet.com
Joseph L. Hooley, Chairman, President & Chief Executive Officer

Lends to cable, DBS, broadcasting, cellular & long distance resellers, publishing & other media & telecommunications industries; acquisition & expansion financing & refinancing; cash management, investment management, stock transfer, corporate trust & other financial services.

STONEGATE CAPITAL GROUP LLC
100 Pearl St.
12th Floor
Hartford, CT 06103
Phone: 860-493-2240
Web Site: http://www.stonegatecapitalgroup.com
Provides investment banking for the broadcast industry.

TD BANK
PO Box 9540
Two Portland Sq
Portland, ME 04112-9540
Phone: 800-462-3666
Web Site: http://www.tdbank.com
Bharat B. Masrani, President & Chief Executive Officer
Stephen J. Boyle, Executive Vice President, Finance & Chief Executive Officer
Walter J. Owens, Executive Vice President, Commercial Banking

Branch Offices:
CHERRY HILL: 1701 Rte 70 E, Cherry Hill, NJ 08034. Phone: 888-751-9000.
Provides commercial banking services.

TTV CAPITAL
1230 Peachtree St
Promenade II, Ste 1150
Atlanta, GA 30309
Phone: 404-347-8400
Fax: 404-347-8420
E-mail: info@ttvcapital.com
Web Site: http://www.ttvcapital.com
Gardiner W. Garrard III, Co-Founder & Managing Partner
W. Thomas Smith Jr., Co-Founder & Managing Partner
Mark A. Johnson, Partner
Sean M. Banks, Principal
Provides capital to early-to-late stage privately held companies.

UNUM PROVIDENT CORP.
One Fountain Sq
Chattanooga, TN 37402
Phones: 423-294-1011; 866-679-3054
Web Site: http://www.unumprovident.com
Thomas R. Watjen, President & Chief Executive Officer

Branch Offices:
COLUMBIA: 1200 Colonial Life Bldg, Columbia, SC 29230. Phone: 803-798-7000.

GLENDALE: 655 N Central Ave, Ste 900, Glendale, CA 91203. Phone: 800-424-2008.

PORTLAND: 2211 Congress St, Portland, ME 04122. Phone: 207-575-2211.

WORCESTER: 18 Chestnut St, Worcester, MA 01608. Phone: 774-437-4441.

UNITED KINGDOM: Milton Ct, Dorking, Surrey RH4 3LZ, United Kingdom. Phone: 44-1306-887766.
Provides group & individual disability income protection in the U.S. & the United Kingdom.

VALUATION RESEARCH CORP.
330 E Kilbourn Ave
Ste 1425
Milwaukee, WI 53202
Phone: 414-271-8662
Fax: 414-271-2294
Web Site: http://www.valuationresearch.com
Richard B. Nordberg, Senior Vice President, Business Development
Jeffrey N. Trader, Senior Vice President, Business Development

Branch Offices:
BOSTON: 101 Federal St, Ste 1900, Boston, MA 02110. Phone: 617-342-7366. Fax: 617-342-3606. Robert A. Schulte, Senior Vice President, Business Development; Glen J. Hartford, Senior Vice President.

CHICAGO: 200 W Madison St, Ste 2850, Chicago, IL 60606. Phone: 312-957-7500. Fax: 312-422-0035. William J. Hughes, Co-Chief Executive Officer, Managing Director & Senior Executive Vice President.

CINCINNATI: 105 E Fourth St, Ste 1005, Cincinnati, OH 45202. Phone: 513-579-9100. Fax: 513-579-9101. Lawrence E. Van Kirk, III, Senior Vice President; Thomas J. Courtright, Senior Vice President.

EWING: 200 Princeton S Corporate Ctr, Ste 200, Ewing, NJ 08628. Phone: 609-243-7000. Fax: 609-883-7651.

NEW YORK: 500 Fifth Ave, 39th Fl, New York, NY 10110. Phone: 212-983-3370. Fax: 212-278-0675.

SAN FRANCISCO: 50 California St, Ste 3050, San Francisco, CA 94111. Phone: 415-277-1800. Fax: 415-277-2948. Justin E. Johnson, Senior Vice President.

TAMPA: 777 S Harbour Island Blvd., Suite 980, Tampa, FL 33602. Phone: 813-463-8510. Fax: 813-273-6878. Steven Schuetz, Senior Vice President.
Provides fair market appraisals, fairness opinions, capital stock valuations, intangible-asset valuations, pre-acquisition feasibility studies & property tax appraisals.

VERONIS SUHLER STEVENSON
55 E 52nd St
33rd Fl

New York, NY 10055
Phone: 212-935-4990
Fax: 212-381-8168
E-mail: stevensonj@vss.com
Web Site: http://www.vss.com
John S. Suhler, Founding Partner & President
Jeffrey T. Stevenson, Managing Partner
John R. Sinatra, Chief Financial Officer & Managing Director
Marvin L. Shapiro, Managing Director

Branch Offices:
UNITED KINGDOM: Buchanan House, Three St James Sq, 8th Fl, London SW1Y 4JU, United Kingdom. Phone: 44-0-20-7484-1400. Fax: 44-0-20-7484-1401. E-mail: solim@vss.com.
Private equity & mezzanine capital fund management company dedicated to investing in the media, communications, information & education industries in the U.S. & Europe.

WACHOVIA CORP.
One Wachovia Ctr
301 S College St, Ste 4000
Charlotte, NC 28288-0013
Phones: 704-590-0000; 800-922-4684
Web Site: http://www.wachovia.com
Robert K. Steel, Chief Executive Officer
Thomas J. Wurtz, Chief Financial Officer
Provides financial services, including asset management, benefits & retirement, mergers & acquisition advisory, lending & financing, risk management, sales & trading; equity & debt offerings.

WALLER CAPITAL PARTNERS
One Rockefeller Plaza
23rd Floor
New York, NY 10020
Phone: 212-632-3600
Fax: 212-632-3607
E-mail: wallercapital@wallercc.com
Web Site: http://www.wallercc.com
John W. Waller, III, Chairman
Garrett M. Baker, President
William Bradley, Managing Director
Jeffrey A. Brandon, Managing Director
Matt Dahl, Managing Director
Michael McHugh, Managing Director
Steven R. Soraparu, Managing Director
Brian Stengel, Managing Director
Provides financing & investment services to the CATV industry; specializes in mergers & acquisitions, buy out financing, raising debt & equity and assisting in development & launching of new cable networks.

WELLS FARGO SECURITIES LLC
420 Montgomery St
San Francisco, CA 97104
Phone: 866-878-5865
Web Site: http://www.wellsfargo.com/securities
Provides equities & sales trading, investment banking & capital markets, fixed income sales sales & trading and integrated research & economics.

Management & Technical Services

ABI RESEARCH
249 South St
Oyster Bay, NY 11771
Phone: 516-624-2500
Fax: 516-624-2501
Web Site: http://www.abiresearch.com
Tim Archdeacon, President & Chief Executive Officer
Ed Rerisi, Chief Operating Officer
Stuart Carlaw, Chief Research Officer
Aaron Boyd, Chief Strategy Officer
Dominque Bonte, Vice President & Practice Director
Mitch Ferrer, Vice President, Business Development, North America
Marcia Lowenstein, Vice President
James Mielke, Vice President
Jake Saunder, Vice President & Practice Director

Branch Offices:
NEW YORK: 501 Seventh Ave, Ste 205A, New York, NY 10018. Phone: 646-383-8928.

SCOTTSDALE: Bay Colony E, 8777 E Via de Ventura, Ste 340, Scottsdale, AZ 85258. Phone: 480-346-1117.

SINGAPORE: 100 Beach Rd, No 16-04 Shaw Tower 189702, Singapore. Phone: 65-6592-0890. Fax: 65-6294-0991.

UNITED KINGDOM: 4-6 Staple In, 3rd Fl, Ste B, London WC1V 7QH, United Kingdom. Phone: 44-0-203-326-0140. Fax: 44-0-203-326-0141.
Assists wireless semiconductor component manufactures in understanding & entering new markets.

ACTIVEVIDEO
333 W San Carlos St
Ste 400
San Jose, CA 95110
Phones: 408-931-9200; 800-926-8398
Fax: 408-931-9100
E-mail: info@activevideo.com
Web Site: http://www.activevideo.com
Jeff Miller, President & Chief Executive Officer
Ronald Brockmann, Chief Technology Officer
Brian Sereda, Chief Financial Officer
Dave McElhatten, Senior Vice President, Studio & Services
Cliff Mercer, Senior Vice President, Engineering
Murali Nemani, Senior Vice President & Chief Marketing Officer
Michael Taylor, Senior Vice President, Business Development
Provides a cloud-based software platform enabling service providers, content aggregators, and consumer electronic (CE) manufacturers to rapidly deploy new services by virtualizing consumer premises equipment (CPE) functions in the cloud. Company is jointly owned by ARRIS Group Inc. and Charter Communications Inc.

THE AKER PARTNERS INC.
2801 M St NW
Washington, DC 20007
Phones: 202-719-8062; 202-223-4889
E-mail: aker@akerpartners.com
Web Site: http://www.akerpartners.com
Colburn Aker, Managing Partner
Carolyn Myles, Senior Partner
David Narsavage, Senior Partner
Sanda Pecina, Partner & Media Relations Director
Provides communications consulting, public relations & marketing services; specializes in marketing, media relations & public affairs.

ALLISON PAYMENT SYSTEMS LLC
2200 Production Dr
Indianapolis, IN 46241-4912
Phone: 800-755-2440
Fax: 317-808-2477
E-mail: sales@apsllc.com
Web Site: http://www.apsllc.com
Joseph H. Thomas, Chairman & Chief Executive Officer
Joseph P. Thomas, President & Chief Operating Officer
Dale J. Eland, Vice President, Manufacturing Services
Kevin W. Thomas, Vice President, Customer Relationship Management
Brad E. Turner, Vice President, Technical Services
Provides payment system products & services, including payment systems, print & mail statements & coupon books.

AMDOCS, BROADBAND CABLE & SATELLITE DIVISION
1390 Timberlake Manor Pkwy
Chesterfield, MO 63017
Phones: 314-212-7000; 877-878-2122
Fax: 314-212-7500
E-mail: info@amdocs.com
Web Site: http://www.amdocs.com
Brian Shephard, President, Broadband, Cable & Media
Provides customer management & billing services for video, broadband, telecommunications & utilities industries.

AMERICAN EUROPEAN CONSULTING CO. INC.
PO Box 19686
Houston, TX 77224
Phone: 713-464-8711
Fax: 713-464-8798
Web Site: http://www.aecchouston.com
Artur Krueger, Senior Consultant
Edward Kruger, Analyst
Provides management services, international market research & development.

ANCHOR PACIFIC CORP.
700 Laveca St
Ste 1400
Austin, TX 78701-3102
Phone: 512-334-6989
C. Ronald Dorchester, President & Chief Executive Officer
Provides management services for CATV, wireless video, etc.

ASCENT MEDIA GROUP
520 Broadway
5th Fl
Santa Monica, CA 90401
Phone: 310-434-7000
E-mail: sales@ascentmedia.com
Web Site: http://www.ascentmedia.com
William Fitzgerald, Chief Executive Officer
Tom Kuehle, Executive Vice President, Strategic Solutions
William Niles, Executive Vice President, General Counsel & Secretary
Douglas Parish, Executive Vice President, Operations
George C. Platisa, Executive Vice President & Chief Financial Officer
David Pruitt, Senior Vice President, Business Development
Bill Romeo, Senior Vice President, Entertainment Television Sales, Creative Group
Provides solutions for the creation, management & distribution of content to major motion picture studios, independent producers, broadcast & programming networks & other companies; systems integration; consulting services; offices worldwide.

ATV BROADCAST LLC
11650 Lantern Rd
Ste 104
Fishers, IN 46038
Phone: 317-566-1563
Fax: 317-843-2863
E-mail: DSmithCATV@aol.com
Web Site: http://www.atvbroadcast.tv
Michael N. Ruggiero, Chairman
Douglas A. Smith, Chief Executive Officer & President
Christopher A. Ruggiero, Vice President, Operations
Provides CATV relations for broadcasters; copyright reduction for cable; assists in solving effective competition; syndex & network non-duplication problems; FCC significant viewing filings; channel positioning & implementing Congressional cable bills; must-carry & retransmission consent solutions.

AUDIENCE RESEARCH & DEVELOPMENT LLC
2440 Lofton Terr
Fort Worth, TX 76109
Phone: 817-924-6922
Fax: 817-924-7539
E-mail: jgumbert@ar-d.com
Web Site: http://www.ar-d.com
Jerry Gumbert, President & Chief Executive Officer
Jim Willi, Principal & Senior Vice President, Multimedia Innovation
Earle Jones, Senior Vice President, Research
Terry Heaton, Senior Vice President, Media 2.0
Provides insight into the development of news, information & entertainment programs in regards to TV & Internet.

THE AUSTIN CO.
6095 Parkland Blvd
Cleveland, OH 44124
Phone: 440-544-2600
Fax: 440-544-2690
E-mail: austin@theaustin.com; ne@theaustin.com
Web Site: http://www.theaustin.com

Branch Offices:
ATLANTA: 300 Galleria Pkwy, Ste 1600, Atlanta, GA 30339. Phone: 404-564-3950. Fax: 404-564-3951. E-Mail: se@theaustin.com.

IRVINE: 6410 Oak Canyon, Ste 150, Irvine, CA 92618-5201. Phone: 949-451-9000. Fax: 949-451-9011. E-Mail: we@theaustin.com.

PORTAGE: 8135 Cox's Dr, Ste 213, Portage, MI 49002. Phone: 269-329-1170. Fax: 269-329-1417.

JAPAN: 5-11 Akasaka 6-Chome, Minato-ku, Tokyo 1078348, Japan. Phone: 81-090-1547-8903. Fax: 81-03-5544-1754. E-Mail: seiji.ishibashi@theaustin.com.
Consults, designs, engineers & constructs facilities for TV, radio, cable & motion pictures; specializes in broadcast/technical centers, network switching facilities, transmission facilities & executive/administrative facilities.

AZCAR USA INC.
121 Hillpointe Dr
Ste 700
Canonsburg, PA 15317
Phones: 724-873-0800; 888-873-0800
Fax: 724-873-4770
Stephen Pumple, Chairman & Chief Executive Officer
Gavin Schutz, President & Chief Operating Officer
William Frazier, Vice President, Business Development
Kenneth C. Fuller, Engineering Director
Provides broadcast & multimedia consulting & planning, project management, systems design & integration, equipment procurement & logistics, training and engineering & turnkey integration services; designs & constructs outside broadcast & satellite news gathering vehicles; resells digital audio-video products; offers financing solutions.

BACKCHANNELMEDIA INC.
105 South St
2nd Fl
Boston, MA 02111
Phones: 617-728-3626; 800-578-8283
Fax: 617-517-7777
E-mail: info@backchannelmedia.com

Management & Technical Services

Web Site: http://www.backchannelmedia.com
Daniel Hassan, Chairman & Co-Chief Executive Officer
Michael Kokernak, Co-Chief Executive Officer
Direct response media specialist agency; assists clients & media outlets to understand & capitalize on the changing TV advertising marketplace.

BAKER SCOTT & CO.
34 N Lenhome Dr
Ste 107
Cranford, NJ 07016
Phone: 973-263-3355
Fax: 973-263-9255
E-mail: exec.search@bakerscott.com
Web Site: http://www.bakerscott.com
Provides executive search & organization planning services.

THE BIA KELSEY GROUP
14150 Parkeast Circle
Ste 110
Chantilly, VA 20151
Phones: 703-818-2425; 800-331-5086
Fax: 703-803-3299
E-mail: info@biakelsey.com
Web Site: http://www.bia.com
Tom J. Buono, Founder & Chief Executive Officerr
Mark A. Giannini, Chief Operating Officer & Senior Vice President
Rick Ducey, Chief Strategy Officer
Neal Polachek, President
Mark Fratrik, Vice President
Bobbi Loy-Luster, Vice President & Senior Analyst
Steve Passwaiter, Vice President, Business Development
Geoff Price, Vice President
Formerly BIA Financial Network LLC. Provides financial intelligence & investment resources to the media, telecommunications, technical & related industries; provides valuation & financial/strategic advisory services; publishes financial reports, yearbooks & pocket guides on the TV industry. Division of BIA Advisory Services.

BITCENTRAL
4340 Von Karman Ave
Ste 400
Newport Beach, CA 92660
Phones: 949-253-9000; 800-214-2828
Fax: 949-253-9004
E-mail: info@bitcentral.com
Web Site: http://www.bitcentral.com
Fred Fourcher, President & Chief Executive Officer
Gary Coats, Chief Operating Officer
Cleve Cushing, Chief Financial Officer
Alex Keighley, Vice President, Sales
John King, Vice President, Professional Engineering Services
Lee Roquet, Vice President, Client Services
Ron Rosenthal, Vice President, Global Sales & Marketing
Rick Young, Vice President, Product Strategy
Consults, designs, procures & installs complete systems for the transmission & delivery of video, voice & data; provides video content management & distribution solutions.

BLACKMAGIC DESIGN USA
2875 Bayview Drive
Fremont, CA 94538
Phone: 408-954-0500
Fax: 408-954-0508
E-mail: info-usa@blackmagicdesign.com
Web Site: http://www.blackmagicdesign.com
Dan May, President, Video Production Sales

Branch Offices:
AUSTRALIA: 11 Gateway Ct, Port Melbourne, VIC 3207, Australia. Phone: 613-9682-4770. Fax: 613-9682-4790. E-Mail: info@blackmagic-design.com.

CHINA: Fortune Mansion, Room 906, No 18 Danling St, Haidian District, Beijing 100080, China. Phone: 86-10-5166-1116. Fax: 86-10-5166-1116, x108. E-Mail: leon_li@blackmagic-design.com. Leon Li, Video Product Sales.

JAPAN: 5F Sotokanda Bldg 4-13, Sotokanda 5-Chome, Chiyoda-ku, Tokyo 101-0021, Japan. Phone: 81-3-5846-6110. Fax: 81-3-5846-6120. E-Mail: info-jp@blackmagic-design.com. Ric Akashi, Video Product Sales.

SINGAPORE: 11 Stamford Rd, #03-05 Capitol Bldg 178884, Singapore. Phone: 65-6338-2696. Fax: 65-6338-2692. E-Mail: richardl@blackmagic-design.com. Richard Linn, Video Product Sales.

UNITED KINGDOM: Mere Hall Business Ctr, Unit 3, Bucklow Hill Ln, Mere, Knutsford, Cheshire WA16 6LE, United Kingdom. Phone: 44-0-1565-830049. Fax: 44-0-1565-830739. E-Mail: info-euro@blackmagic-design.com. Stuart Ashton, Video Product Sales, United Kingdom, Middle East & Africa.
Manufactures HD video editing technology; equipment includes video recorders, mini converters, broadcast videohubs, monitors & DeckLinks & multibridges.

BOERNER COMMUNICATIONS INC.
845 Third Ave, Ste 646
6th Fl
New York, NY 10022
Phone: 646-430-8280
E-mail: info@boernercommunications.com
Web Site: http://www.boernercommunications.com
Mary Ann Boerner, President & Chief Executive Officer
Louis Coppola, Vice President, Information Technology
Amy Gallagher, Vice President, Client Services
Hank Boerner, Senior Strategist & Advisor
Ken Cynar, Senior Strategist & Advisor
Provides executive management communications coaching & training; prepares spokespersons, provides seminars in TV news interviewing, government testimony; creative services for video tape presentations, sales & management communications, crisis management, video news releases & documentary production/distribution; Internet & web broadcasting platforms.

BOND & PECARO INC.
1990 M St NW
Ste 400
Washington, DC 20036
Phone: 202-775-8870
Fax: 202-775-0175
E-mail: bp@bondpecaro.com
Web Site: http://www.bondpecaro.com
Timothy S. Pecaro, Principal
Jeffrey P. Anderson, Principal
Andrew R. Gefen, Principal
Matthew H. Lochte, Principal
John S. Sanders, Principal
Provides financial & management consulting services; specializes in asset appraisals, fair market valuations, expert testimony, impairment testing, feasibility studies, financial consulting, market research & related financial services for broadcasting, CATV, Internet, technology & other media; publishes The Television Industry: A Market-by-Market Review with the NAB.

BOOZ, ALLEN & HAMILTON INC.
8283 Greensboro Dr
McLean, VA 22102
Phone: 703-902-5000
Fax: 703-902-3333
E-mail: communications@bah.com
Web Site: http://www.boozallen.com
Ralph W. Shrader, Chairman & Chief Executive Officer
Samuel R. Strickland, Executive Vice President & Chief Financial Officer
Provides consulting services to private & government sectors; specializes in strategic, organizational, technological, public management, productivity management & defense technology; offices worldwide.

BORTZ MEDIA & SPORTS GROUP
5105 DTC Pkwy
Ste 200
Greenwood Village, CO 80111
Phone: 303-893-9902
Fax: 303-893-9913
E-mail: info@bortz.com
Web Site: http://www.bortz.com
Arthur Steiker, Managing Director
James M. Trautman, Managing Director
Mark C. Wyche, Managing Director
Provides domestic & international consulting services for broadcast, cable, new media & professional sports industries; new business planning, fair market valuations of stations, cable systems & program networks; sports media rights analysis; market research & litigation support services.

BROADCAST SERVICES INC.
4801 Industrial Pkwy
Indianapolis, IN 46226
Phone: 317-895-9050
Fax: 317-895-2900
E-mail: dweaver@broadcastservicesinc.com
Web Site: http://www.broadcastservicesinc.com
Douglas S. Weaver, President & Chief Executive Officer
Peter Miller, Vice President & General Counsel
Clifford E. Thompson, Secretary-Treasurer
Provides broadcast & telecommunications antenna site design, development & management services.

BROADVIEW SOFTWARE INC.
110 Adelaide St E
3rd Floor
Toronto, ON M5C 1K9
Canada
Phone: 647-255-3500
Fax: 416-778-0648
E-mail: sales@broadviewsoftware.com
Web Site: http://www.broadviewsoftware.com
Arthur Drevnig, Sales & Marketing Director
Provides software that provides TV stations with an integrated solution for program acquisition, ad sales, program scheduling, traffic, master control automation interfacing & reporting.

STUART N. BROTMAN COMMUNICATIONS
47 Baskin Rd
Lexington, MA 02421-6928
Phone: 781-862-8257
Fax: 781-863-8260
E-mail: info@brotman.com
Web Site: http://brotman.com
Stuart N. Brotman, President

Provides senior management corporate strategy; financial, market, operations & regulatory planning in telecommunications, Internet, media, entertainment and sports.

CABLE AUDIT ASSOCIATES INC.
5340 S Quebec St
Greenwood Village, CO 80111-1910
Phone: 303-694-0444
Fax: 303-694-2559
E-mail: blazarus@mai-global.com
Web Site: http://www.mai-global.com
Bruce Lazarus, Chief Executive Officer
Raoul A. De Sota, Senior Vice President, Strategic Development
John MacDonald, Senior Vice President, Audit Operations
Mitchell Walker, Senior Vice President, Consulting & Technology Services
Greg Bryant, Vice President, Audit Operations & Staff Development
Dona Johnson, Vice President, Premium Services
Mary Miller, Vice President, Client Relations & Contract Compliance
Provides business to business auditing, assurance & revenue systems management services to companies in the media & entertainment industry.

CABLE SYSTEM SERVICES
3588 Kennebec Dr
Eagan, MN 55122
Phone: 651-688-2623
Fax: 651-688-2624
E-mail: gschmidt@cablesystemservices.com
Web Site: http://www.cablesystemservices.com
Provides broadband fiber design, installation & system management.

CAD DRAFTING SERVICES INC.
109 Bank St
Ashkum, IL 60911
Phone: 815-698-2564
Fax: 815-698-2263

CADENT NETWORK
1701 JFK Blvd
Ste 2510
Philadelphia, PA 19103
Phone: 215-568-7066
Fax: 215-564-5388
Web Site: http://cadentnetwork.tv
Lance Funston, Chairman Emeritus

Branch Offices:
CHICAGO: 410 N Michigan St, Ste N710, Chicago, IL 60611. Phone: 312-283-5045.

EL SEGUNDO: 2321 Rosecrans Ave, Ste 1290, El Segundo, CA 90245. Phone: 424-348-2000.

NEW YORK: 1450 Broadway, Ste 502, New York, NY 10018. Phone: 212-796-1960. Formerly Telamerica Media Inc. Operates a wireless cable network offering media buyers & advertisers an alternative to traditional national network cable buys.

CAPGEMINI, TELECOM, MEDIA & ENTERTAINMENT GROUP
623 Fifth Ave
33rd Fl
New York, NY 10022
Phone: 212-314-8000
Fax: 212-314-8001
Web Site: http://www.us.capgemini.com
Provides consulting, outsourcing & local professional services in more than 36 countries; publishes reports on the telecom, cable, media & entertainment industries.

Management & Technical Services

WILLIAM B. CARR & ASSOCIATES INC.
27 CR310
Dublin, TX 76446
Phone: 254-445-4200
Fax: 254-445-4201
William B. Carr, President
Offers consulting engineering services to the broadcasting & communication industries.

CB COMMUNICATIONS INC.
141 E 55th St
Ste 10-H
New York, NY 10022
Phone: 212-758-7880
Fax: 212-758-7881
Suzan Couch, President
Provides entertainment marketing, including strategic planning, advertising, promotion, traditional & online media and program packaging.

CCI SYSTEMS
PO Box 190
105 Kent St
Iron Mountain, MI 49801
Phones: 906-774-6621; 800-338-9299
Fax: 906-774-9120
Web Site: http://www.ccisystems.com
John P. Jamar, President & Chief Executive Officer
Jeff Culver, Vice President, Construction Operations
Rick J. Hurzeler, Vice President, Engineering Operations
Jeff Muraro, Vice President, Sales
Wayne M. Makela, Secretary-Treasurer
Bill Peters, Cable Sales Director
Provides mapping & design services, headend design & installation, IPTV, optical design & installation, SONET, Gig E, aerial, underground, coax & fiber optic construction; material supply & management; CMTS sales & installation, dispersion testing, coax & fusion splicing, activation, sweep & balance, ingress detection/repair & proof of performance testing. Complete turnkey project management.

CHADBOURN MARCATH INC.
3318 N Lakeshore Dr
Ste 100
Chicago, IL 60657-3959
Phones: 312-915-0300; 800-223-7828
Fax: 773-525-4898
E-mail: ccs@chadbourn.com
Web Site: http://www.chadbourn.com
James C. Weisberg, President & Chief Technology Officer
Elizabeth Eugenio, Vice President, Business Development
Shelia O'Shaughnessy, Vice President, Marketing
Todd Anderson, Customer Service Director
John Navarra, Systems & Programming Director
Provides telecommunications consulting services.

CHR SOLUTIONS INC.
9700 Bissonnet
Ste 2800
Houston, TX 77036-8014
Phone: 713-351-5111
Fax: 281-754-9170
E-mail: info@chrsolutions.com
Web Site: http://www.chrsolutions.com
Sean Fitzsimmons, Executive Vice President, Client Solutions
Gary Knee, Executive Vice President, Software Solutions
Fred Pratt, Executive Vice President, Client Services

Branch Offices:
AUSTIN: 5929 Balcones Dr, Ste 200, Austin, TX 78731-1639. Phone: 512-343-2544. Fax: 512-343-0119.

CAMDEN: 110 Harrison Ave SW, Camden, AR 71701. Phone: 870-836-9331. Fax: 870-836-2788.

DALLAS: 2711 LBJ Frwy, Ste 560, Dallas, TX 75234. Phone: 972-484-2323. Fax: 972-243-6139.

HOUSTON: Southwest Corporate Ctr, 9700 Bissonnet, Ste 2800, Houston, TX 77036.

LUBBOCK: 4747 S Loop 289, Lubbock, TX 79424. Phone: 806-722-7700. Fax: 806-722-7802.

MISSOULA: 3301 Great Northern Way, Ste 201, Missoula, MT 59808. Phone: 877-996-9646. Fax: 605-292-2250.

MITCHELL: 1515 N Sanborn Blvd, Mitchell, SD 57301-1021. Phones: 605-996-9646; 877-996-9646. Fax: 605-995-2577.

MOLALLA: 209 Marson Ct, PO Box 543, Molalla, OR 97038. Phones: 503-829-6660; 877-203-1442. Fax: 503-829-5648.

NASHVILLE: BNA Corp Ctr Bldg 100, 402 BNA Dr, Ste 409, Nashville, TN 37217-2542. Phone: 877-996-9646. Fax: 615-365-9052.

SIOUX FALLS: 110 N Minnesota, Ste 300, Sioux Falls, SD 57104-6460.
Provides business consulting, engineering services, software solutions & technology managed services to clients worldwide; helps clients grow revenues, reduce costs, improve operations, manage risk & align technology.

CNN NEWSOURCE SALES INC.
One CNN Center NW
Atlanta, GA 30303
Phones: 404-827-2085; 404-827-5032
Fax: 404-827-4959; 404-827-3640
Web Site: http://newsource.cnn.com
Provides sales & marketing of CNN Newsource & its services. Division of Turner Broadcasting System Inc.

COLUMBIA TELECOMMUNICATIONS CORP/CTC TECHNOLOGY & ENERGY
10613 Concord St
Kensington, MD 20895
Phone: 301-933-1488
Fax: 301-933-3340
E-mail: info@ctcnet.us
Web Site: http://www.ctcnet.us
Joanne S. Hovis, President
Andrew L. Afflerbach, PhD, Chief Executive Officer & Engineering Director
Provides communications engineering consulting services for public sector & non-profit clients nationwide.

COMMUNICATIONS ENGINEERING INC.
8500 Cinder Bed Rd
Ste 100
Newington, VA 22122
Phone: 703-550-5800
Fax: 703-550-5180
E-mail: sales@commeng.com
Web Site: http://www.commeng.com
Lawerence S. Brody, President & Chief Executive Officer
John Wesley Nash, Executive Vice President & Chief Operating Officer
Jim Conley, Senior Vice President, Engineering & Chief Technology Officer
David A. Giblin, Vice President & General Manager
Michael Jones, Vice President, Sales & Marketing
Designs & integrates broadcast & multimedia systems; provides expertise in SD & HD video, multi-format audio, high-speed data networking, asset-management, broadband video transmission, multimedia content, acoustics, space planning & mechanical (HVAC) systems.

COMMUNICATIONS EQUITY ASSOCIATES
101 E Kennedy Blvd
Ste 3300
Tampa, FL 33602
Phone: 813-226-8844
Fax: 813-225-1513
E-mail: DMoyer@ceaworldwide.com
Web Site: http://www.ceaworldwide.com
J. Patrick Michaels, Jr., Chairman & Chief Executive Officer
Ming Jung, Senior Managing Director & Chief Financial Officer, CEA Cap Advisors
Ken Jones, Senior Vice President & General Counsel
Robert D. Berger, Managing Director
Raymond J Martin, Managing Director, Corporate Advisory Services & Investment Banking
Carsten Philipson, Managing Director
Donald Russell, Managing Director

Branch Offices:
CENTER VALLEY: Principal Advisors Group, 3477 Corporate Pkwy, Ste 100, Center Valley, PA 18034. Phone: 484-224-3429. Fax: 484-224-3501.

NEW YORK: 156 W 56th St, Ste 902, New York, NY 10019. Phone: 212-218-5085. Fax: 212-957-0620. Waldo Glasman, Managing Director; John Morrison, Managing Director; Alexander Rossi, Managing Director.

UNITED KINGDOM: Staple Ct, 11 Staple Inn Bldgs, London EC3A 7PT, WC1V 7Q4. Phone: 44-0-207-280-4899. Fax: 44-0-207-280-4899. Martin Farmer, Partner.
Provides investment banking & brokerage services to CATV, broadcasting, media & entertainment industries; acquisitions, divestitures, mergers & trades; financial placements for equity & debt; joint ventures; appraisals; consultation for tax & estate planning & shareholder negotiations.

COMSEARCH
Janelia Technology Park
19700 Janelia Farm Blvd
Ashburn, VA 20147
Phones: 703-726-5500; 800-318-1234
Fax: 703-726-5600
E-mail: sales@comsearch.com
Web Site: http://www.comsearch.com
Douglass Hall, President
Chris Hardy, Vice President & General Manager
Tim Hardy, Vice President, Engineering Solutions
Mark Gibson, Senior Director, Business Development
Brian Downs, Government Solutions Director
Provides engineering services for mobile, PCS, microwave & satellite industries; includes engineering software, terrain digitizing, propagation analysis, interference analysis, network design, field studies, licensing assistance, demographic studies & market reports. Division of CommScope Inc.

COMSONICS INC.
PO Box 1106
1350 Port Republic Rd
Harrisonburg, VA 22801
Phones: 540-434-5965; 800-336-9681
Fax: 540-432-9794
E-mail: marketing@comsonics.com; info@comsonics.com
Web Site: http://www.comsonics.com
Jack A. Bryant III, Chief Executive Officer
Athena C. Hess, Chief Financial Officer
Bret V. Harrison, Marketing & Services Director
Manufactures cable test & measurement equipment; provides national repair services for distribution, headend, test, power supply & fiber optic equipment as well as onsite mobile calibration services throughout the contiguous U.S.

COMTEL VIDEO SERVICES INC.
PO Box 416
Ashland, OR 97520-0014
Phone: 541-708-5732
E-mail: bbeggs@comtelvideo.com
Web Site: http://www.comtelvideo.com
Robert C. Beggs, President
Provides video programming to TV stations & cable systems on Pacific islands.

CONLEY & ASSOCIATES LLC
1459 Interstate Loop
Bismarck, ND 58503-5560
Phone: 701-222-3902
Fax: 701-258-1937
E-mail: info@conleyassociates.net
Web Site: http://bis.midco.net/cbrg1/cbrg5/index.htm
Christopher J. Conley, Managing General Partner
Provides management & engineering consulting to the electronic media; specializes in appraisals & valuations; strategic planning & feasibility studies; financial planning & restructuring; contract management; operational evaluations & audits; engineering design & technical evaluations; marketing research & analysis; human resources development & training; franchising & refranchising; regulatory affairs & expert testimony.

CONTEC
1023 State St
Schenectady, NY 12307-1511
Phones: 518-382-8000; 800-382-2723
Fax: 518-382-7680
Web Site: http://www.gocontec.com

Branch Offices:
BROWNSVILLE: WorldWide Digital, 1900 Billy Mitchell Blvd, Brownsville, TX 78521. Phone: 956-541-0600. Fax: 956-831-8310.

SEATTLE: 1250 S 192nd St, Seattle, WA 98148. Phones: 206-244-0604; 888-266-8322. Fax: 206-244-4938.
Provides equipment repair to the broadband industry.

CORNWALL ASSOCIATES
234 N El Molino Ave
#100
Pasadena, CA 91101
Phone: 626-793-5782
Fax: 626-793-7956
E-mail: scornwall@sbcglobal.net
Kent Cornwall, President
J. Shirl Cornwall, Vice President
Provides architecture, interior & technical design & consulting services for production & broadcast facilities.

2017 Edition
E-141

Management & Technical Services

CREDIT PROTECTION ASSOCIATION INC.
13355 Noel Rd
Ste 2100
Dallas, TX 75240
Phones: 877-278-5106; 800-675-9579
E-mail: info@creditprotect.com
Web Site: http://www.creditprotect.com
Nate A. Levine, President & Chief Executive Officer
Ann E. Levine, Secretary
Douglas K. Bridges, Vice President & Chief Financial Officer
Full-service national collections company specializing in the CATV industry; offers complete automated submissions of write-off accounts through the major billing services, comprehensive client reports, on-line debtor status inquiry, pro-active.

CREWSTAR INC.
Southborough Ctr
One Boston Rd
Southborough, MA 01772
Phones: 508-481-2212; 888-746-6871
Fax: 508-481-7785
Lily Maiella, President
Joseph Maiella, Senior Vice President, Marketing & Sales
Provides clients with video & film crews around the world; provides personalized, accurate crew & talent payroll services for easy production payroll administration & to assure compliance with state & federal guidelines.

CRITICAL MENTION INC. (CLIP SYNDICATE)
1776 Broadway
24th Fl
New York, NY 10019
Phone: 212-400-8894
E-mail: ion@critical-media.com
Web Site: http://www.clipsyndicate.com
Sean Morgan, Founder & Chief Executive Officer
Michael Johnston, Vice President, Network Operations
Jim Pavoldi, Vice President, Business Development & Distribution
Donald Silvey, Vice President, Content Strategy
James Vaughn, Vice President, Software Engineering
Provides a web-based TV search & monitoring service.

CRYSTAL COMPUTER CORP.
4550 River Green Pkwy
Suite 220
Duluth, GA 30096
Phone: 770-932-0970
Fax: 775-719-3402
E-mail: sales@crystalcc.com
Web Site: http://www.crystalcc.com
Earl Franklin, Chairman
Roger Franklin, President & Chief Executive Officer
Rob Dowd, Senior Vice President, Sales & Marketing
Matthew Frei, Vice President

Tim Johnson, Sales Manager
Provides turnkey customer-tailored network management & control systems to the satellite & media transmission industries.

CSG SYSTEMS INC.
9555 Maroon Cir
Englewood, CO 80112
Phones: 303-200-2000; 800-366-2744
Fax: 303-200-3333
E-mail: sales@csgsystems.com
Web Site: http://www.csgsystems.com
Peter Kalan, President & Chief Executive Officer
Bret Griess, Executive Vice President & Chief Operating Officer
Joe Ruble, Executive Vice President, General Counsel & Chief Administration Officer
Brian Shepherd, Executive Vice President, CSG International & President, Global Broadband, Cable & Satellite
Randy Wiese, Executive Vice President & Chief Financial Officer

Branch Offices:
CHICAGO: 33 W Monroe St, Ste 900, Chicago, IL 60603. Phone: 312-660-5600.

OMAHA: North Park NP6, 2525 N 117th St, Omaha, NE 68164. Phone: 402-431-7000. Provides billing & customer management services for the converging communications industries.

DATAWORLD
14150 Parkeast Cir
Ste 110
Chantilly, VA 20151
Phones: 703-818-2425; 800-331-5086
Fax: 703-803-3299
E-mail: info@biakelsey.com
Web Site: http://www.bia.com/dataworld
Provides engineering & FCC business intelligence to communications industries via a range of data & information services, technical engineering studies & custom mapping. Division of BIA Kelsey Group.

DG FASTCHANNEL INC. — See Extreme Reach Inc.

DIVERSIFIED SYSTEMS INC.
363 Market St
Kenilworth, NJ 07033
Phone: 908-245-4833
Fax: 908-245-0011
E-mail: info@divsystems.com
Web Site: http://www.divsystems.com
Fred D'Alessandro, Founder, President & Chief Executive Officer
Kevin Collins, Executive Vice President & Chief Operating Officer
Mark M. S. Lee, Executive Vice President, International Growth Market
Duane Yoslov, Senior Vice President, Western Region

Branch Offices:
SANTA CLARA: 3275 Edward Ave, Santa Clara, CA 95054. Phone: 408-969-1972. Fax: 408-969-1985. E-Mail: d.yoslov@divsysinc.com. Duane Yoslov, Vice President, West Coast Operations.

SEATTLE: 4000 Aurora Ave N, Ste 225, Seattle, WA 98103. Phone: 206-547-0251. Fax: 206-547-0294. E-Mail: b.fisher@divsysinc.com.

WASHINGTON, DC: 23475 Rockhaven Way, Ste 140, Dulles, VA 20166. Phone: 703-661-8870. Fax: 703-661-1440. E-Mail: t.atkins@divsysinc.com.
Addresses the technical needs of the broadcast, presentation, cable & telecommunications industry. Provides system consultation, project budgeting, system design, architectural design, system documentation, equipment procurement, custom fabrication, system integration, project commissioning & system training.

EBS INTERNATIONAL (ENTERTAINMENT BUSINESS SERVICES)
1801 Century Park E
Ste 2400
Los Angeles, CA 90067
Phone: 310-284-8780
Fax: 310-284-3430
E-mail: info@ebsinternational.com
Michael R. Zerbib, Founder
Provides research & business services to foreign broadcasters, cable networks, TV & film producers, multimedia & online content developers. Services include film & TV programs acquisition, TV production development & broadband Internet content development.

EDX WIRELESS LLC
1400 Executive Pkwy
Ste 430
Eugene, OR 97401
Phone: 541-345-0019
Fax: 541-345-8145
E-mail: info@edx.com
Web Site: http://www.edx.com
Ted G. Hicks, Vice President, Product Management
Scott A. Blumberg, Executive Director, Software Development
Jennifer S. Duncan, Executive Director, Business Development & Strategy
Brian T. Cochran, Support Services Director
Provides cost effective & technologically advanced wireless network planning, design & management software tools for outdoor & indoor settings, across all frequency bands & in support of advanced air interface standards.

EFFROS COMMUNICATIONS
PO Box 8
Clifton, VA 20124
Phone: 703-631-2099
Fax: 703-631-6999
Web Site: http://www.effros.com
Stephen R. Effros, President
Provides legal consulting services, including strategic analysis & planning to cable & Internet companies.

EQUIDATA
PO Box 6610
724 Thimble Shoals Blvd
Newport News, VA 23606
Phones: 757-873-0519; 800-288-9809
Fax: 757-873-1224
E-mail: info@equidata.com
Web Site: http://www.equidata.com
Provides commercial collection services.

EXFO
400 Godin Ave
Quebec, QC G1M 2K2
Canada
Phones: 418-683-0211; 800-663-3936
Fax: 418-681-3986
E-mail: info@exfo.com
Web Site: http://www.exfo.com
Germain Lamonde, Chairman, President & Chief Executive Officer
Jon Bradley, Vice President, International Telecom Sales
Stephen Bull, Vice President, Research & Development
Etienne Gagnon, Vice President, Product Management & Marketing

Branch Offices:
RICHARDSON: 3400 Waterview Pkwy, Ste 100, Richardson, TX 75080. Phones: 972-761-9271; 800-663-3936. Fax: 972-761-9067.

SINGAPORE: Shaw Tower, 100, Beach Rd, No. 25-01/03 189702, Singapore. Phone: 65-6333-8241. Fax: 65-6333-8242.

UNITED KINGDOM: Omega Enterprise Park, Electron Way, Chandlers Ford, Eastleigh, Hampshire S053 4SE, United Kingdom. Phone: 44-2380-246-800. Fax: 44-2380-246-801.
Provides test & monitoring solutions for network service providers & equipment manufacturers in the global telecommunications industry.

THE EXLINE CO.
17 Alipine Rd
Novato, CA 94945
Phone: 415-408-3324
E-mail: info@exlinecompany.com
Web Site: http://www.exlinecompany.com
Andrew McClure, President
Judi Lewis, Administrative Coordinator
Provides consulting services in operations, personnel & finance as well as brokerage & appraisals for radio & TV communications companies.

EXTREME REACH INC.
75 Second Ave
Ste 720
Needham, MA 02494
Phones: 781-577-2016; 877-769-9382
E-mail: support@extremereach.com
Web Site: http://www.extremereach.com
John Roland, Co-Founder & Chief Executive Officer
Tim Conley, Co-Founder & Chief Operating Officer
Dan Brackett, Co-Founder & Chief Technology Officer
Avi Brown, Chief Digital Officer
Michael Greiner, Chief Financial Officer
Tim Hale, Chief Talent Officer
Patrick Hanavan, Chief Revenue Officer
Robert Haskitt, Chief Marketing Officer
Mark Burson, Channel Marketing Manager
Provides video advertising management & distribution solutions that span TV, digital & mobile. Activates, measures & optimizes video advertising campaigns across all screens & devices. Offices nationwide.

PAUL DEAN FORD
3775 W Dugger Ave
West Terre Haute, IN 47885
Phone: 812-535-1937
E-mail: wpfr@joink.com
Paul Dean Ford, PE
Provides broadcast engineering consulting services.

Management & Technical Services

FORRESTER RESEARCH INC.
60 Acorn Park Dr
Cambridge, MA 02140
Phone: 617-613-5730
Fax: 617-613-5200
Web Site: http://www.forrester.com
George F. Colony, Chairman & Chief Executive Officer
Charles Rutstein, Chief Operating Officer
Michael A. Doyle, Chief Financial Officer & Treasurer
Dwight Griesman, Chief Marketing Officer
Elizabeth A. Lemons, Chief People Officer
Gail S. Mann, Chief Legal Officer & Secretary
Greg Nelson, Chief Sales Officer
George M. Orlov, Chief Information & Chief Technology Officer
Mark R. Nemec, Managing Director, Technology Industry Client Group
Tom Pohlmann, Managing Director, Information Technology Client Group
Dennis van Lingen, Managing Director, Marketing & Strategy Client Group

Branch Offices:
DALLAS: 5001 Spring Valley Rd, Ste 200-E, Dallas, TX 75244. Phone: 469-221-5300.

NEW YORK: 160 5th Ave, New York, NY 10010. Phone: 212-857-0700.

SAN FRANCISCO: 150 Spear St, Ste 1100, San Francisco, CA 94105. Phone: 415-355-6000. Fax: 415-503-1936.

WASHINGTON, DC: 8180 Greensboro Dr, Ste 750, McLean, VA 22102. Phone: 703-584-2626.

FRANCE: Forrester Research SAS, 109-111 Rue Victor Hugo, Levallois Perret 92300, France. Phone: 33-01-4758-9300. Fax: 33-01-4758-9301.

GERMANY: Forrester Research GmbH & Co. KG, Eschersheimer Landstr 10, Frankfurt 60322, Germany. Phone: 49-69-9592980. Fax: 49-69-95929810.

THE NETHERLANDS: Forrester Research B.V., Rijnsburgstraat 9-11, Amsterdam 1059 AT, The Netherlands. Phone: 31-20-305-43-49. Fax: 31-20-305-43-333.

UNITED KINGDOM: 265 Strand, London WC2R 1BH, United Kingdom. Phone: 44-0-20-7631-0202. Fax: 44-0-20-7631-5252.
An independent technology & market research company; provides advice to global leaders in business & technology. Proprietary research, consulting, events & peer-to-peer executive programs.

FREEMAN CORP.
1600 Viceroy
Ste 100
Dallas, TX 75235
Phones: 214-445-1000; 888-508-5054
Fax: 214-445-0200
E-mail: pressroom@freemanco.com
Web Site: http://www.freemanco.com
Don Freeman, Chairman & Chief Executive Officer
Joe Popolo, Chief Executive Officer
Carrie Freeman Parsons, Vice Chair
John F. O'Connell Jr, President

Branch Offices:
ALEXANDRIA: 201 N Union St, Ste 210, Alexandria, VA 22314. Phone: 703-739-6620. Fax: 703-739-6627.

CHICAGO: 600 W Chicago Ave, Ste 125, Chicago, IL 60644. Phone: 312-654-8844. Fax: 312-654-8929.

GRAND PRAIRIE: 2940 114th St, Grand Prairie, TX 75050. Phone: 817-607-2600. Fax: 817-633-8392.

MOHAVE VALLEY: 9520 S Vanderslice Rd, Mohave Valley, AZ 86440. Phone: 928-788-4300. Fax: 928-768-6260.
Produces expositions, conventions, corporate events & exhibits

JIM FRENCH DESIGN SHOP
17 E Brady St
Tulsa, OK 74103
Phone: 918-583-2926
Fax: 918-583-5905
Jim French, President
Makes custom scenery, displays & props.

PETER FROEHLICH & CO.
111 Florine Ct
Weatherford, TX 76087
Phones: 817-594-9991; 800-742-4947
Fax: 817-594-1337
E-mail: pfsearch@flash.net
Peter Froehlich, Owner
Offers executive searches specializing in the communications industry; positions are filled at all levels & disciplines.

GELLER MEDIA INTERNATIONAL
666 W End Ave
Ste 11M
New York, NY 10025
Phone: 212-580-3385
Fax: 212-787-6279
E-mail: vgeller@aol.com
Web Site: http://www.gellermedia.com
Valerie Geller, President
Provides broadcasting consulting services; works with broadcasters throughout the world to create news/talk, information & personality radio.

GEOMART
139-B James Comeaux Rd
Ste 813
Lafayette, LA 70508
Phones: 970-416-8340; 800-248-6277
Fax: 970-416-8345; 800-321-6277
E-mail: sales@geomart.com
Web Site: http://www.geomart.com
Provides mapping services, including overnight delivery of any USGS topographic map; complete U.S. coverage of aerial photograph, custom mapping for line of site & cell tower placements, & custom aerial photography for flyovers.

GEORGIA U.S. DATA SERVICES INC.
5672 Peachtree Pkwy
Norcross, GA 30092
Phone: 770-734-0804
Offers subscriber billing services, including mail stream sort, zip + 4 barcode, post office certified reports, cable logo, scan line, sequence number, remarks insert key, insert printing, inserting & delivery to post office.

GORMAN & ASSOCIATES
1666 K St NW
Ste 500
Washington, DC 20006
Phone: 202-778-2108
Fax: 202-463-1927
E-mail: info@gormanandassociates.com
Web Site: http://www.gormanandassociates.com
Matthew A. Gorman, Founder & President

Patrick A. Gorman, Vice President
Provides consulting services; specializes in law & the legislative process, communications, government relations & operations.

GRAHAM BROCK INC.
5971 B New Jesup Hwy
Brunswick, GA 31523
Phones: 912-638-8028; 202-393-5133
Fax: 912-275-8869
E-mail: jeff@grahambrock.com; rsg@grahambrock.com
Web Site: http://www.grahambrock.com
R. Stuart Graham, President
Jefferson Brock, Vice President
Marilyn Matheny, Secretary-Treasurer
Provides technical broadcast consulting services for AM, FM & TV stations as well as auxiliary services (STL, RPU, LPTV, FM translators).

GREAT LAKES DATA SYSTEMS INC.
5954 Priestly Dr
Carlsbad, CA 92009
Phones: 800-882-7950; 760-602-1900
E-mail: sales@glds.com; support@glds.com
Web Site: http://www.glds.com
Laura Rosado, Chief Executive Officer
Garrick Russell, President & Chief Operating Officer
Kevin Kononchek, Business Development Manager

Branch Offices:
BEAVER DAM: 306 Seippel Blvd, Beaver Dam, WI 53916. Phones: 920-887-7651; 800-882-7950.
Provides billing, subscriber management & provisioning software.

F.P. HEALY & CO. INC.
307 E 44th St
Ste E
New York, NY 10017
Phone: 212-661-0366
Fax: 212-661-0383
E-mail: fphealy@aol.com
Web Site: http://www.fphealy.com
Frank P. Healy, President
Offers personalized executive & technical search services worldwide.

NORMAN HECHT RESEARCH INC.
20 Crossways Park Dr
Ste 400
Woodbury, NY 11797
Phone: 516-496-8866
Fax: 516-496-8165
E-mail: nhecht@normanhechtresearch.com
Web Site: http://www.normanhechtresearch.com
Norm Hecht, Chief Executive Officer
Laura Greenberg, Co-President & Chief Operating Officer
Dan Greenberg, Co-President
Dennis Regan, Senior Vice President, Research
Provides market & media research to the broadcast, cable, technology, commercial services & communications industries, including news programming & talent research.

FULLY SEARCHABLE • CONTINUOUSLY UPDATED • DISCOUNT RATES FOR PRINT PURCHASERS
For more information call **800-771-9202** or visit **www.warren-news.com**

HELLERSTEIN & ASSOCIATES
3001 Veazey Terr NW
Ste 1308
Washington, DC 20008
Phone: 202-362-5139
Fax: 646-365-5139
E-mail: judith@jhellerstein.com
Web Site: http://www.jhellerstein.com
Judith Hellerstein, Principal
Provides technology research services; helps companies & governments better understand their markets through ICT & E-Government strategies, market analysis, strategy consulting, next-generation technology strategies, technology assessments & regulatory impact analysis of ICT, telecom & technology issues.

R. MILLER HICKS & CO.
1011 W 11th St
Austin, TX 78703
Phone: 512-477-7000
Fax: 512-477-9697
R. Miller Hicks, President
Provides consultation services, appraisals, management & programming.

HLW INTERNATIONAL LLP
115 Fifth Ave
5th Fl
New York, NY 10003
Phone: 212-353-4600
Fax: 212-353-4666
E-mail: info.newyork@hlw.com
Web Site: http://www.hlw.com
John Gering, Managing Partner

Branch Offices:
LOS ANGELES: 1556 20th St, Ste B, Santa Monica, CA 90404. Phone: 310-453-2800.

CHINA: Jiushi Renaissance Mansion, 918 Huai Hai Rd, Section E, 14th Fl, Shanghai 200020, China. Phone: 86-21-6415-9437. Fax: 86-21-6415-9438.

UNITED KINGDOM: 29/31 Cowper St, London EC2A 4AT, United Kingdom. Phone: 44-207-566-6800. Fax: 44-207-253-4628.
Provides architectural & engineering planning, consulting & design services for the broadcast industry.

HORIZON MEDIA INC.
75 Varick St
New York, NY 10013
Phone: 212-220-5000
E-mail: shall@horizonmedia.com
Web Site: http://www.horizonmedia.com
Bill Koenigsberg, Founder, President & Chief Executive Officer
Rick Watrall, Chief Analytics Officer
Sarah Baehr, Executive Vice President, Digital Investment
Serena Duff, Executive Vice President & Managing Partner
Stan Fields, Executive Vice President & Managing Partner
Marianne Gambelli, Executive Vice President & Chief Investment Officer
Eva Kantrowitz, Executive Vice President & Managing Partner

2017 Edition

E-143

Management & Technical Services

Rich Simms, Executive Vice President & Managing Partner
Kimberly Aiello, Senior Vice President, Managing Director, Brand Strategy
Greg DePalma, Vice President, Advanced Video Analytics

Branch Offices:
LOS ANGELES: 1940 Century Park E, Los Angeles, CA 90067. Phone: 310-282-0909. Fax: 310-229-8104. Paul Santello, Executive Vice President & Managing Partner, Los Angeles.

ORLANDO: 1650 Sand Lake Rd, Ste 225, Orlando, FL 32809. Phone: 407-438-7945. Fax: 407-438-9989.

THE NETHERLANDS: Wilgenweg 28A, Amsterdam 1031 HV, The Netherlands. Phone: 31-20-344-66-33. Fax: 31-20-344-66-34. Provides brand management, channel planning, research, print negotiation, direct marketing, local market buying, national TV & radio buying.

J.C. HUMKE & ASSOCIATES INC.
5457 S Jericho Way
Centennial, CO 80015-3648
Phone: 303-489-1356
E-mail: joelhumke@comcast.net
Web Site: http://www.jchumke.com
Joel C. Humke, President
Provides design & installation services for radio communications users; services include detailed radio coverage & propagation studies from medium wave through microwave frequencies, antenna system design, interface resolution, antenna measurements, cellular telephone, expert witness testimony, TIS information stations, spectrum analysis, ANSI compliance measurements, facility planning, VHF-UHF-microwave & bid specification services.

IDC SERVICES INC.
Five Speen St
Framingham, MA 01701
Phone: 508-872-8200
E-mail: leads@idc.com
Web Site: http://www.idc.com
Kirk Campbell, President & Chief Executive Officer
Crawford Del Prete, Chief Research Officer & Executive Vice President, Worldwide Research Products
Mark Sullivan, Chief Financial Officer
Phillipe de Marcillac, Executive Vice President, International Business Units
John Gantz, Senior Vice President, Research
Frank Gens, Senior Vice President & Chief Analyst
Clare Gillan, Senior Vice President, Executive & Go-To-Market Programs
Vito Mabrucco, Senior Vice President, Worldwide Consulting & Managing Director, IDC Canada
Henry Morris, Senior Vice President, Integration, Development & Applications Strategies Solutions Research
Eric Prothero, Senior Vice President, Worldwide Tracker Research
Brad Thorpe, Senior Vice President, Worldwide Sales
Vernon Turner, Senior Vice President, Enterprise Computing Research
Meredith Whalen, Senior Vice President, U.S. Insights & Vertical Markets Research
Debra Bernardi, Vice President, Human Resources & Education
Ricardo Villate, Vice President, Latin American Operations

Branch Offices:
BOULDER: 1750 14th St, Ste 200, Boulder, CO 80302. Phone: 303-385-0327.

DENVER: 16 Market Square, 1400 16th St, Ste 400, Denver, CO 80202. Phone: 508-872-8200.

NEW YORK: 405 Lexington Ave, 25th Fl, New York, NY 10174. Phone: 212-907-6500.

RED BANK: 20 White St, Ste 2B, Red Bank, NJ 07701. Phone: 732-842-0791.

SAN MATEO: 155 Bovet Rd, Ste 800, San Mateo, CA 94402-3115. Phone: 650-653-7000.

WASHINGTON, DC: 211 N Union St, Ste 105, Alexandria, VA 22314. Phone: 571-296-8060.

CANADA: 33 Yonge St, Ste 420, Toronto, ON M5E 1G4, Canada. Phone: 416-369-0033. Fax: 416-369-0033.
Provides market intelligence, advisory services & events for the information, technology, telecommunications & consumer technology markets

INFONETICS RESEARCH
695 Campbell Technology Pkwy
Campbell, CA 95008
Phones: 408-583-0011; 800-447-2273
Fax: 408-583-0031
Web Site: http://www.infonetics.com
J'Amy Napolitan, Co-Founder & Chief Executive Officer
Michael Howard, Co-Founder & Principal Analyst, Carrier/Data Center Networks
Larry Howard, Vice President, Sales
Scott Coyne, Senior Account Director
George Stojsavljecic, Senior Account Director
Stephane Teral, Principal Analyst, Mobile & FMC Infrastructure
Jeff Wilson, Principal Analyst, Security

Branch Offices:
BOSTON: 91 Montvale Ave, Ste 102, Stoneham, MA 02180.

UNITED KINGDOM: Dorchester House, Station Rd, Ste 113, Letchworth Garden City SG6 3AW, United Kingdom. Phone: 44-1462-478900. Fax: 44-1462-482616.
Provides market research & consulting services; offers quarterly market share & forecasting, end-user survey research, service provider survey research & service provider capex analysis.

INFORMA TELECOMS & MEDIA
Mortimer House
37/41 Mortimer St
London W1T 3JH
United Kingdom
Phone: 44-20-7017-5537
Fax: 44-20-7017-4947
E-mail: telecoms.enquiries@informa.com
Web Site: http://www.informatm.com
Ian Hemming, Chief Executive Officer
Mark Bethell, Chief Financial Officer
Mark Newman, Chief Research Officer

Branch Offices:
WESTBOROUGH: One Research Dr, Westborough, MA 01581. Phone: 508-453-4894. E-Mail: charles.bowen@informa.com. Charles Bowen, Account Manager.

SINGAPORE: One Grange Rd, 08-02 Orchard Bldg, Singapore. Phone: 65-6835-5158. E-Mail: giovanni.cerrini@informa.com. Giovanni Cerrini, Director, Asia Pacific Business Development.
Provides strategic advice & forecasting on all aspects of converging mobile, fixed, entertainment & IT markets; publishes reports, magazine, books & directories covering global telecoms & media markets.

INFOSYS TECHNOLOGIES LTD.
Plot 44 & 97A
Hosur Rd
Electronics City, Bangalore 560 100
India
Phone: 91-80-28520261
Fax: 91-80-28520362
E-mail: askus@infosys.com
Web Site: http://www.infosys.com
K. Dinesh, Co-Founder & Board Member
N.R. Narayana Murthy, Chairman & Chief Mentor
S. Gopalakrishnan, Chief Executive Officer & Managing Director
S.D. Shibulal, Chief Operating Officer & Board Member

Branch Offices:
FREMONT: 6607 Kaiser Dr, Fremont, CA 94555. Phone: 510-724-3000. Fax: 510-742-3090.
Provides consulting & IT services

INITIATIVE MEDIA WORLDWIDE INC.
Manhattan Mall
100 West 33rd St
New York, NY 10001
Phone: 212-605-7000
Fax: 212-605-7200
E-mail: NewBusiness@initiative.com
Web Site: http://www.initiative.com
Richard Beaven, Chief Executive Officer
Mauricio Sabogal, President, World Markets
Eric Bader, President, G14 & Chief Strategy Officer, Worldwide
Provides media management & media planning/buying; offices worldwide.

INSIGHT RESEARCH CORP.
PO Box 2472
Durango, CO 81302
Phone: 973-541-9600
E-mail: info@insight-corp.com
Web Site: http://www.insight-corp.com
Provides market research & strategic analysis for the telecom industry; publishes market research reports, executive summaries & e-mail newsletters.

INTEGRATED ALLIANCE LP
5800 N Interstate 35
Ste 200B
Denton, TX 76207
Phone: 940-565-9415
Fax: 940-383-1876
E-mail: ryoung@integratedalliance.com
Web Site: http://www.integratedalliance.com
Randy Keylor, Chief Executive Officer
Russell Young, Vice President, Marketing
Liz Foster, Human Resources & Operations
Provides inbound & outbound call services for customer care, billing inquiries, technical support & sales/lead generation.

INTERNATIONAL CREATIVE MANAGEMENT INC.
10250 Constellation Blvd
Los Angeles, CA 90067
Phone: 310-550-4000
Fax: 310-555-4100
E-mail: webmaster@icmtalent.com
Web Site: http://www.icmtalent.com
Jeffrey Berg, Chairman & Chief Executive Officer
Richard B. Levy, Chief Operating Officer & General Counsel
Chris Silbermann, President
Esther Newberg, Senior Vice President

Branch Offices:
NEW YORK: 825 Eighth Ave, New York, NY 10019. Phone: 212-556-5600.

UNITED KINGDOM: 61 Frith St, London W1D 3JL, United Kingdom. Phone: 44-207-851-4853.
Represents creative & technical talent in the fields of motion pictures, TV, publishing, music, live performance, commercials & new media.

INTERNATIONAL TECHNOLOGY & TRADE ASSOCIATES INC.
1200 18th St NW
Ste 1002
Washington, DC 20036
Phone: 202-828-2614
Fax: 202-828-2617
Web Site: http://www.itta.com
Charles W. Dyke, Chairman & Chief Executive Officer
Eric D. Lundell, President & Chief Operating Officer
Constantine A. Pagedas, Executive Vice President
Provides international business consulting services; assists companies in developing & managing high-technology trades & investments; supports activities such as technology transfer, export promotion & foreign investment in industries including telecommunications, electronics & information technology.

ISUPPLI
1700 E Walnut Ave
Ste 600
El Segundo, CA 90245
Phone: 310-524-4000
Fax: 310-524-4050
E-mail: info@isuppli.com
Web Site: http://www.isuppli.com
Dale Ford, Senior Vice President, Market Intelligence
John Ward, Vice President, Marketing
Provides industry market intelligence & advice; offices worldwide.

JONES/NCTI — See NCTI.

KALBA INTERNATIONAL INC.
116 McKinley Ave
New Haven, CT 06515
Phone: 203-397-2199
Fax: 781-240-2657
E-mail: kas.kalba@kalbainternational.com
Web Site: http://www.kalbainternational.com
Kas Kalba, Co-founder
Dr. Yale Braunstein, Senior Advisor
Wes Vivian, Senior Technology Consultant
Provides a wide range of management consulting services covering broadband networks, mobile & internet access products & services, satellite communications & other telecom & multimedia businesses.

KANE REECE ASSOCIATES INC.
822 South Ave W
Westfield, NJ 07090-1460
Phones: 908-317-5757; 800-494-5263
Fax: 908-317-4434
Web Site: http://www.kanereece.com
John E. (Jack) Kane, Founder & Principal
Norval Reece, Co-Founder & Chairman Emeritus
Noah Gottdiener, Chief Executive Officer
Gerry Creagh, President

Dennis Elliott, Managing Director
Provides appraisals & valuations, business plans, engineering consulting, financial & technical due diligence, financing preparations, franchise renewals, litigation support, market/opinion research, management & management consulting, property tax compliance & control, solvency opinions, valuations for buy/sell agreements & workouts. Division of Duff & Phelps Corp.

LATIN WORLD ENTERTAINMENT
43470 NW 82nd Ave.
#670
Doral, FL 33122
Phone: 305-572-1515
Web Site: http://latinwe.com
Provides talent management & entertainment marketing services, including publicity, licensing, endorsements, brand integration, productions & content development.

LEHMANN STROBEL PC
3613 Anton Farms Rd
Baltimore, MD 21208
Phone: 443-352-8635
E-mail: info@lehmannstrobel.com
Web Site: http://www.lehmannstrobel.com
Walter G. Lehmann, Managing Partner
Sylvia L. Strobel, Senior Partner
Provides expert legal representation & business affairs services to film, TV, video, radio & multimedia professionals & companies.

ARTHUR D. LITTLE INC.
One Federal St.
Ste 2810
Boston, MA 02110
Phone: 617-532-9503
Fax: 617-261-6630
Web Site: http://www.adlittle-us.com
Michael Tram, Chief Executive Officer
Provides management, environmental, health & safety consulting services; technology & product development; offices worldwide.

FRANK N. MAGID ASSOCIATES INC.
One Research Ctr
Marion, IA 52302
Phone: 319-377-7345
Fax: 319-377-5861
E-mail: iowa@magid.com
Web Site: http://www.magid.com
Brent Magid, President & Chief Executive Officer
Steve Ridge, President, Media Strategies Group
Marv Danielski, Senior Vice President, Integrated Brand Development
Bill Hague, Senior Vice President
Jim Thomas, Vice President, Marketing

Branch Offices:
MINNEAPOLIS: 8500 Normandale Lake Blvd, Ste 630, Minneapolis, MN 55437. Phone: 952-835-4436. Fax: 952-835-3385. E-mail: mailmn@magid.com.

NEW YORK: 1775 Broadway, Ste 1401, New York, NY 10019. Phone: 212-515-4520. Fax: 212-515-4540. E-mail: mailny@magid.com.

SHERMAN OAKS: 15260 Ventura Blvd, Ste 1840, Sherman Oaks, CA 91403. Phone: 818-263-3300. Fax: 818-263-3311. E-mail: mailla@magid.com.
Provides custom attitudinal research & consultation services for all media; specializes in TV news & programming, audience surveys & complete implementation services including program evaluation, talent coaching & search; publishes daily newsletters & periodic syndicated research papers.

MAGNETIC IMAGE VIDEO
129 Jordan St
San Rafael, CA 94901-3919
Phone: 415-456-7900
Fax: 415-485-3874
E-mail: rentals@mivideo.com
Web Site: http://www.mivideo.com
Larry Kenworthy, President
Cael Hazard, Production Manager
Rents & repairs NTSC & PAL camera packages, monitors & projectors, equipment & lenses along with multicamera systems with or without crews.

M/A/R/C RESEARCH
7850 North Belt Line Rd.
Irving, TX 75063
Phone: 800-884-6272
Fax: 972-910-8904
E-mail: marketing@marcresearch.com
Web Site: http://www.marcresearch.com
Merrill Dubrow, President & Chief Executive Officer
Amy Barrentine, Executive Vice President & General Manager
Randall A. Wahl, Executive Vice President
Susan Hurry, Senior Vice President & General Manager
Betsy Sutherland, Senior Vice President & General Manager
Sherri Neuwirth, Senior Vice President

Branch Offices:
BRIDGETON: 3245 Smiley Rd, Bridgeton, MO 63044. Phone: 314-298-1516. Fax: 314-291-5586.

GREENSBORO: 202 CentrePoint Dr, Ste 300, Greensboro, NC 27409. Phone: 800-513-5700. Fax: 336-664-6705.
Provides brand development research & consulting services.

MARKET STRATEGIES
17430 College Pkwy
Livonia, MI 48152
Phone: 734-542-7600
Fax: 734-542-7620
Web Site: http://www.marketstrategies.com
Andrew James Morrison, Founder, Chairman & Chief Executive Officer
Reginald Baker, PhD, President & Chief Operating Officer
George Wilkerson, Executive Vice President, Communications & Energy Research Division
Leona Foster, Founder & Senior Vice President
Keri Christensen, Vice President, Communications Division
Paul Donagher, Vice President, Communications Division
Pamela S. McGill, Vice President, Communications Division

Branch Offices:
ATLANTA: 834 Inman Village Pkwy, Ste 200, Atlanta, GA 30307. Phone: 404-521-9955. Fax: 404-521-9263.

CLAREMONT: 250 W First St, Ste 304, Claremont, CA 91711. Phone: 909-626-2626. Fax: 909-626-1313.

LITTLE ROCK: 333 Executive Ct, Ste 100, Little Rock, AR 72205. Phone: 501-221-3303. Fax: 501-221-2554.

NEW PROVIDENCE: 571 Central Ave, Ste 115, New Providence, NJ 07974. Phone: 908-739-4500. Fax: 908-739-4519.

PORTLAND: 888 SW Fifth Ave, Ste 790, Portland, OR 97204. Phone: 503-225-0112. Fax: 503-225-8400.

UNITED KINGDOM: 15 Old Bailey, London EC4 M7EF, United Kingdom. Phone: 44-0-20-3178-3537. Fax: 44-0-20-3178-5179.
Provides custom & syndicated research & strategic consulting services.

MARSH & MCLENNAN COS. (MMC)
1166 Ave of the Americas
32nd Fl
New York, NY 10036
Phone: 212-345-5000
Fax: 212-345-8075
Web Site: http://www.mmc.com
Brian Duperreault, President & Chief Executive Officer
Matthew B. Bartley, Executive Vice President & Chief Financial Officer
Peter J. Beshar, Executive Vice President & General Counsel
Orlando D. Ashford, Senior Vice President, Human Resources
E. Scott Gilbert, Senior Vice President & Chief Compliance Officer
Provides management consulting & market research services; offices worldwide.

MAUCK & ASSOCIATES INC.
718 W Cactus Wren Dr
Phoenix, AZ 85021
Phone: 602-230-2537
Fax: 602-242-9449
Gary Mauck, President
Provides event management; specializes in trade shows, conferences & major promotional events.

B.K. MCINTYRE & ASSOCIATES
1250 24th St NW
Ste 350
Washington, DC 20037-1124
Phone: 202-785-5091
Fax: 202-785-5108
E-mail: bkm@bkmcintyre.com
Web Site: http://www.bkmcintyre.com
Bernice K. McIntyre, President
Meera Ahamed, Associate
Michael H. Pete, Associate
Provides management & regulatory consulting services & expertise to the communications & electric utilities industries.

MEDIASPAN ONLINE SERVICES
8687 Research Dr.
Ste 100
Irvine, CA 92618
Phones: 877-691-8888; 949-892-2929
Web Site: http://mediaspanonlineservices.com
F.R. Frank Campagnoni, President & Chief Executive Officer
William H. (Bud) Owen, Chief Financial Officer
Steven Barth, Executive Vice President & General Manager
Peter Cooper, Vice President, Marketing
Tobey Van Santvoord, Senior Manager

Management & Technical Services

Communications Daily
Warren Communications News
Get the industry standard FREE —
For a no-obligation trial call 800-771-9202 or visit www.warren-news.com

Branch Offices:
IRVINE: 8687 Research Dr, Ste 100, Irvine, CA 92618. Phone: 949-892-2929. Fax: 949-892-2930.

MELBOURNE: Media Software Ctr, 300 North Dr, Ste 100, Melbourne, FL 32934. Phone: 734-887-4400.

NEW YORK: Network Ctr, 41 E 11th St, 11th Fl, New York, NY 10003. Phone: 212-699-6472.
Provides online marketing solutions, including website management, streaming & podcasting tools that empower local media to grow audience & revenue.

MERIDIAN DESIGN ASSOCIATES ARCHITECTS
1140 Broadway
6th Fl
New York, NY 10001
Phone: 212-431-8643
Fax: 212-431-8775
E-mail: info@meridiandesign.com
Web Site: http://www.meridiandesign.com
Antonio Argibay, Lead AP Principal
Bice C. Wilson, Principal

Branch Offices:
MIAMI: 10630 NW 27th St, Miami, FL 33172. Phone: 305-362-7663. Fax: 305-362-7675.

BUENOS AIRES: Av Cordoba 1364, Piso 3D, Buenos Aires C1055AAQ, Argentina. Phone: 54-11-4-371-7130. Fax: 54-11-156-893-3722.

SWITZERLAND: 20, rue Boissonas, 1227 Acacias, Geneve, Switzerland. Phone: 41-22-560-88-88. Fax: 41-22-560-88-00. E-Mail: contact@meridiangroup8.com.
Designs media & communications workplaces.

MIDHUDSONMEDIA
315 S 3rd St
PO Box 515
Hudson, NY 12534
Phone: 518-828-2500
Fax: 518-828-0173
E-mail: adsales@midhudsonmedia.com
Web Site: http://midhudsonmedia.com
Provides marketing, media & Internet communications services, including video production, cable advertising sales, Internet broadcasting & integrated marketing.

MOBITV INC.
6425 Christie Ave
5th Fl
Emeryville, CA 94608
Phones: 510-438-6634; 510-450-5000
Fax: 510-450-5001
E-mail: press@mobitv.com
Web Site: http://www.mobitv.com
Charlie Nooney, Chairman & Chief Executive Officer
Paul Scanlan, President & Co-Founder
Bill Routt, Chief Operating Officer
Cedric Fernandes, Chief Technology Officer
Rick Herman, Chief Strategy Officer

2017 Edition   E-145

Management & Technical Services

Ellen McDonald, Chief Financial Officer & General Manager, Carrier Business
Delivers live & on-demand video to any screen with an end-to-end platform.

MULTICOMM SCIENCES INTERNATIONAL INC.
266 W Main St
Denville, NJ 07834
Phone: 973-627-7400
Fax: 973-215-2168
Web Site: http://www.multicommsciences.com
Offers wireless consulting engineering services from FCC frequency coordination, earth stations, path propagation, RF radiation level analysis & testing, design of microwave systems & mapping of fiber optic & microwave routes.

NATHAN ASSOCIATES INC.
1777 N. Kent St.
Ste 1400
Arlington, VA 22209
Phone: 703-516-7700
Fax: 703-351-6162
E-mail: jbeyer@nathaninc.com
Web Site: http://www.nathaninc.com
John C. Beyer, Chairman & Chief Executive Officer
Lakhbir Singh, President & Chief Operating Officer
Douglas Young, Principal Economist
Stephen Magiera, Principal Associate

Branch Offices:
IRVINE: 2010 Main St, Ste 700, Irvine, CA 92614. Phone: 949-955-9025. Fax: 949-474-4944. E-Mail: rmangum@nathaninc.com. Russell W. Mangum, III, Vice President & Director, South California Office.

MEMPHIS: 2151 Courtland Pl, Memphis, TN 38104. Phone: 901-725-6732. Fax: 901-725-6734. E-Mail: dsharp@nathaninc.com. David C. Sharp, Director, Memphis Office.

WARWICK: 39 Major Potter Rd, Warwick, RI 02886. Phone: 401-885-0648. Fax: 401-223-9771. E-Mail: sschneider@nathaninc.com. Stephen A. Schneider, Senior Vice President & Managing Director, South New England Office.

INDIA: 45 TTK Rd, George Pnnaiya Bldg, G-C, Ground Fl, Chennai 600 018, India. E-Mail: rtamara@nathaninc.com. Ram Tamara, Managing Director.

UNITED KINGDOM: 3 Millharbour, London E14 9XP, United Kingdom. Phone: 44-207-538-3111. E-Mail: ssinha@emergingmarkets.co.uk. Sunil Sinha, Managing Director.
Provides economic & management consultants services; demand & sales forecasting, market research, survey management, database design & implementation, financial analysis services & expert witness testimony to broadcasting, cable & telecommunications industries.

NATIONAL ECONOMIC RESEARCH ASSOCIATES INC. (NERA)
1166 Ave of the Americas
29th Fl
New York, NY 10036
Phone: 212-345-3000
Fax: 212-345-4650
Web Site: http://www.nera.com
Andrew Carron, President

Branch Offices:
AUSTIN: 1006 E 39th St, Austin, TX 78751. Phone: 512-371-8995. Fax: 512-371-9612.

BOSTON: 200 Clarendon St, 11th Fl, Boston, MA 02116. Phone: 617-927-4500. Fax: 617-927-4501. Dr. Augustin Ross, Vice President.

CHICAGO: 875 N Michigan Ave, Ste 3650, Chicago, IL 60611. Phone: 312-573-2800. Fax: 312-573-2810.

ITHACA: 308 N Cayuga St, Ithaca, NY 14850. Phone: 607-277-3007. Fax: 607-277-1581.

LOS ANGELES: 777 S Figueroa St, Ste 1950, Los Angeles, CA 90017. Phone: 213-346-3000. Fax: 213-346-3030.

PHILADELPHIA: Two Logan Sq, Ste 800, Philadelphia, PA 19103. Phone: 215-864-3880. Fax: 215-864-3840.

SAN FRANCISCO: One Front St, Ste 260, San Francisco, CA 94111. Phone: 415-291-1000. Fax: 415-291-1020. Dr. Alan Cox, Senior Vice President.

WASHINGTON, DC: 1255 23rd St NW, Ste 600, Washington, DC 20037. Phone: 202-466-3510. Fax: 202-466-3605. Dr. Chantale LaCasse, Senior Vice President; Dr. Richard Rozek, Senior Vice President.

WESTMINSTER: 10955 Westmoor Dr, Ste 400, Westminster, CO 80021. Phone: 303-465-6844. Fax: 303-465-6867.

WHITE PLAINS: 50 Main St, 14th Fl, White Plains, NY 10606. Phone: 914-448-4000. Fax: 914-448-4040.

CANADA: 161 Bay St, 16th Fl, PO Box 501, Toronto, ON M5J 2S5, Canada. Phone: 416-868-7310. Fax: 416-815-3332.
Provides economic research, analysis & consulting services for telephone, radio, TV, cable & common carriers; prepares analyses & expert testimony for judicial, legislative & regulatory proceedings; other services include antitrust, public utility & regulatory economics, public policy & managerial economics; offices worldwide.

NATIONAL TELECONSULTANTS INC.
550 N Brand Blvd
17th Fl
Glendale, CA 91203-1202
Phone: 818-265-4400
Fax: 818-265-4455
E-mail: information@ntc.com
Web Site: http://www.ntc.com
Eric Pohl, Chief Technology Officer
Chuck Phelan, Managing Partner

Branch Offices:
NEW YORK: 45 Rockefeller Plz, 20th Fl, New York, NY 10111-2000. Phone: 212-899-5454. Fax: 212-899-5455.
Provides strategic consulting & engineering design to the media industry.

NATIVE AMERICAN TELEVISION
PO Box 1754
Williamsburg, VA 23187
Phone: 703-554-2815
E-mail: rflood@natv.org
Web Site: http://www.natv.org
Provides education, training & professional certification to Native American students in Digital Studio/Field Production. Also offers educational courses in Journalism, Governmental Awareness and Environmental Studies.

NCTI
9697 E Mineral Ave
Centennial, CO 80112
Phones: 303-797-9393; 866-575-7206
Fax: 303-797-9394
E-mail: info@jonesncti.com
Web Site: http://www.jonesncti.com
Stacey Slaughter, Chief Executive & Financial Officer
Wayne Applehans, President & Chief Product Officer
Formerly Jones/NCTI. Provides workforce performance products, professional services & education to the cable & broadband industry. Products include performance tools & extensive training content in CD/DVD, instructor-led, paper-based & online delivery formats. Provides professional services such as custom curriculum development, e-learning development & conversion, product sales support & customer education & workforce assessments. Company was acquired by Stacey Slaughter in December 2015.

NORMAN FISCHER & ASSOCIATES INC. (NFA INC.)
2520 Longview St
#313
Austin, TX 78705
Phone: 512-476-9457
Fax: 512-476-0540
E-mail: terrill@nfainc.com
Terrill Fischer, President
Provides management consulting, media brokerage & appraisals.

NORTHSTAR TELESOLUTIONS
435 E Main St
Greenwood, IN 46143
Phones: 317-865-2400; 800-466-0900
Fax: 317-865-2411
E-mail: info@northstartele.com
Web Site: http://www.northstartele.com
Josh Thackery, President
Doug Clingman, Information Technology
Jenni Dick, Client Support
Denna Hughes, Business Development
Kelli Jones, Customer Service
Sherry Rose, Field Operations
Provides billing software & subscriber support services.

N.S. BIENSTOCK INC.
250 W 57th St
Ste 333
New York, NY 10107
Phone: 212-765-3040
Fax: 212-757-6411
E-mail: nsb@nsbtalent.com
Web Site: http://www.nsbtalent.com
Richard Leibner, President
Jonathan Leibner, General Counsel
Beverly Styles, Office Manager
Talent agency for reality TV & news.

ORC INTERNATIONAL
902 Carnegie Ctr
Ste 220
Princeton, NJ 08540
Phone: 800-444-4672
Web Site: http://www.orcinternational.com
Marc Litvinoff, President
Richard Cornelius, Managing Director, ORC International
Stacy S. Lee, Senior Vice President & Chief Financial Officer
David Magnani, Senior Vice President & General Manager
Jeffrey T. Resnick, Global Managing Director, Innovation & Partnerships
Greg Wayman, Regional Managing Director, Asia Pacific

Branch Offices:
BOSTON: 90 Canal St, Ste 600, Boston, MA 02114. Phone: 617-720-0174.

LOMBARD: 450 E 22nd St, Ste 155, Lombard, IL 60148. Phone: 630-424-6500.

MINNEAPOLIS: 2051 Killebrew Dr, Ste 210, Minneapolis, MN 55425. Phone: 800-367-8358.

WASHINGTON, DC: 900 17th St NW, Ste 850, Washington, DC 20006. Phone: 703-312-6004.
Formerly ORC Research Corp. Provides customized business research on client-specified aspects of TV & cable services industries, specializing in company, product, service or market studies. Confidential, narrow-focused or comprehensive research on merger & acquisition candidates, competitors, targeted markets, products & services, federal & state regulatory & policy activities.

OVATION DATA SERVICES INC.
14199 Westfair E Dr
Houston, TX 77041-1105
Phone: 713-464-1300
Fax: 713-464-1615
E-mail: info@ovationdata.com
Web Site: http://www.ovationdata.com

Branch Offices:
UNITED KINGDOM: UK Data Storage Group, 18 Soho Sq, London W1D 3QL, United Kingdom. Phone: 44-0-207-268-3826.

UNITED KINGDOM: Technology & Service Ctr, Crayfields Industrial Park, Main Rd, Unit 202, St. Paul's Cray, Kent BR5 3HP, United Kingdom. Phone: 44-0-1689-824-777.
Provides digital data management & preservation services; information technology systems.

PATRICK COMMUNICATIONS LLC
6805 Douglas Legum Dr
Ste 100
Elkridge, MD 21075
Phone: 410-799-1740
Fax: 410-799-1705
E-mail: larry@patcomm.com
Web Site: http://www.patcomm.com
W. Lawrence Patrick, Managing Partner
Susan K. Patrick, Managing Partner
Gregory J. Guy, Managing Partner
Diana Wilkin, Partner
Jason James, Vice President
David Benton, Analysis Director
Provides station brokerage & investment banking services; fair market & asset appraisals; debt & equity placement; broadcast management & marketing consulting.

PDI CONSTRUCTION
5001 W Watkins St
Phoenix, AZ 85043
Phones: 602-258-7544; 800-894-5601
Fax: 602-254-9309
E-mail: info@pdiconstruction.com
Web Site: http://www.pdiconstruction.com
Charles Campbell, III, President
Ed Campbell, Vice President
Troy Gronsky, Vice President
James Doughton, Technical Project Manager
Provides computer-aided system design, base & strand mapping & technical field support; sweep, proof-of-performance & CLI. Division of Paramount Designs Inc.

PEREGRINE COMMUNICATIONS
14818 W Sixth Ave
Ste 16A

Management & Technical Services

Golden, CO 80401
Phones: 303-278-9660; 800-359-9660
Fax: 303-278-9685
E-mail: peregrine.info@perecom.com
Web Site: http://www.perecom.com
John Post, President & Chief Executive Officer
Marissa Schubert, Manager, Regional Sales Systems Integrator.

PINNACLE MEDIA WORLDWIDE
931 S Mission Rd
#2
Fallbrook, CA 92028
Phone: 760-731-1141
Fax: 760-731-1187
E-mail: info@p-m-w.com
Mark Carlson, Vice President, Internet
Natalie Gonzalez, Business Manager
Provides strategic and tactical research & analysis services for media companies.

POHLY CO.
867 Boylston St
5th Floor
Boston, MA 02116
Phones: 617-451-1700; 800-383-0888
Fax: 617-338-7767
E-mail: info@pohlyco.com
Web Site: http://www.pohlyco.com
Diana Pohly, President & Chief Executive Officer
Paula Tennyson, Senior Director, Finance & Administration
Provides marketing & publishing services.

POINT OF VIEW PRODUCTIONS
2477 Folsom St
San Francisco, CA 94110
Phone: 415-821-0435
Fax: 415-821-0434
E-mail: karil@karildaniels.com
Web Site: http://www.karildaniels.com
Karil Daniels, President
Provides cinematography, videography, photography, script supervision & other production services for corporate programs, commercials, TV shows & feature films.

PRICEWATERHOUSECOOPERS (PWC)
300 Madison Ave
24th Fl
New York, NY 10017
Phone: 646-471-4000
Fax: 646-471-4444
Web Site: http://www.pwc.com
Samuel DiPiazza, Jr., Chief Executive Officer
Provides industry-focused services, including audit & insurance, crisis management, human resources, performance improvement, tax & transactions; offices nationwide.

QUALITY CABLE SERVICES INC.
9100 Jeffrey Dr
Cambridge, OH 43725
Phone: 800-804-4406
Fax: 740-439-1868
Web Site: http://qcsohio.com
Robert Van Fossen, Founder
Brian Van Fossen, President & General Manager
Josh Wagner, Sales Manager
Clayton Parks, Technical Supervisor
Repairs broadband cable TV & telephony equipment.

RCH CABLE
301 Commerce Dr
Moorestown, NJ 08057
Phone: 856-642-0008
Fax: 856-642-0781
E-mail: rch@rchcable.com

Robert Halgas, President & Chief Executive Officer
Peter Berkowitz, Chief Technical Officer
Paul Lutes, Chief Financial Officer
Steve Nolfi, Senior Vice President, Sales Operations
Erin Elmiger, Vice President, New Business Development
Provides custom support solutions, direct sales campaigns, field collections programs, audits of designated market areas or marketing research.

RCW ASSOCIATES
5667 San Pablo Dam Rd
El Sobrante, CA 94803-3414
Phone: 510-223-9700
Fax: 510-223-2390
Robert C. White, Owner & President
Provides collection services.

RFK ENGINEERING SOLUTIONS LLC
1229 19th St NW
Washington, DC 20036-2413
Phone: 202-463-1567
Fax: 202-463-0344
E-mail: info@rkf-eng.com
Web Site: http://rkf-eng.com
Philip A. Rubin, President
Ted Kaplan, Chief Operating Officer
Jeffrey Freedman, Chief Technical Officer
Alex Latker, Regulatory Affairs Director
Provides telecommunication consulting services addressing system engineering, technical analysis, supporting software development & ITU/FCC regulatory support.

RNL
1050 17th St
Ste A200
Denver, CO 80265
Phones: 303-295-1717; 800-826-7803
Fax: 303-292-0845
E-mail: denver@rnldesign.com
Web Site: http://www.rnldesign.com
John B. Rogers, Founder
H. Joshua Gould, Chief Executive Officer & Chairman
Richard L. von Luhrte, President
Michael Brendle, Design Director

Branch Offices:
LOS ANGELES: 800 Wilshire Blvd, Ste 400, Los Angeles, CA 90017. Phone: 213-955-9775. Fax: 213-955-9885. E-Mail: losangeles@rnldesign.com.

PHOENIX: 100 W Camelback Rd, Phoenix, AZ 85013. Phone: 602-212-1044. Fax: 602-212-0964. E-Mail: phoenix@rnldesign.com.
Offers architectural design & design/planning of TV & radio broadcasting facilities, including full-service feasibility & site studies, interior space planning, set design & systems integration.

SANTIAGO ROI
321 N. Pass Ave
Ste 168
Burbank, CA 91505
Phone: 818-509-5901
Web Site: http://www.santiagosolutionsgroup.com
Carlos Santiago, Founder, Chief Executive Officer, President & Chief Strategist
Steven Petroff, Strategic Planning Director
Dr. J. C. Alvarez, Retail Marketing & Community Relations Director
Formerly Santiago Solutions Group. Provides multi-cultural management consulting & business strategy development.

Access the most current data instantly
FREE TRIAL @ ADVANCED TVFactbook
TELCO/IPTV • CABLE TV • TV STATIONS
www.warren-news.com/factbook.htm

SIEMENS POWER TECHNOLOGIES INTL.
PO Box 1058
1482 Erie Blvd
Schenectady, NY 12301-1058
Phone: 518-395-5000
Fax: 518-346-2777
E-mail: pti-info.ptd@siemens.com
Web Site: http://www.pti-us.com
Dave Pacyna, President & Chief Executive Officer
Michael Edmonds, Vice President & General Manager

Branch Offices:
HOUSTON: 14521 Old Katy Rd, Ste 100, Houston, TX 77079. Phone: 281-497-2422. Fax: 281-497-0316.

LITTLETON: 7810 Shaffer Pkwy, Ste 100, Littleton, CO 80127. Phone: 303-568-7133. Fax: 303-568-7397.

MINNETONKA: 10900 Wayzata Blvd, Ste 400, Minnetonka, MN 55305. Phone: 952-607-2270. Fax: 952-607-2301.

MOUNTAIN VIEW: 1350 Shorebird Way, Mountain View, CA 94043-1338. Phone: 650-694-5096. Fax: 650-365-1356.

GERMANY: Freyeslebenstr 1, Erlangen 91058, Germany. Phone: 49-9131-734-444. Fax: 49-9131-734-445. E-Mail: power-technologies.ptd@siemens.com.

MALAYSIA: 13G Worldwide Business Centre, Block 1, Jalan Tinju 13/50, Shah Alam, Selangor 40675, Malaysia. Phone: 6-03-5511-4800. Fax: 6-03-5511-4801. E-Mail: pti-aps-support.ptd@siemens.com.

UNITED KINGDOM: Sir William Siemens House, Princess Rd, Manchester M20 2UR, United Kingdom. Phone: 44-0-161-446-5200. Fax: 44-0-161-446-6431. E-Mail: pti-service.ptd.uk@siemens.com.
Provides advanced technical consulting services, analytical software programs & professional education in power systems engineering.

SIGNASYS INC.
2158 Paragon Dr
San Jose, CA 95131-1305
Phone: 408-350-7200
Fax: 408-350-7299
Web Site: http://www.signasys.com
Roland Hoffman, President & Chief Executive Officer
Mark Brown, Executive Vice President & Chief Technical Officer
Roberta Friedman, Chief Financial Officer
Helps networks, broadcasters, producers & originators to advance their services/products, increase efficiencies, develop competitive advantages, comply with new legislation & train staff.

SMITH & FISHER
2237 Tacketts Mill Dr
Ste A

Lake Ridge, VA 22192
Phone: 703-494-2101
Fax: 703-494-2132
E-mail: kevin@smithandfisher.com
Web Site: http://www.smithandfisher.com
Neil M. Smith
Kevin T. Fisher
Jeanne F. Smith
Offers Longley-Rice studies, applications for new & changed FM, TV, DTV and LPTV facilities, mapping, expert-witness testimony, field measurement studies, FAA liaison & interference remedies.

SOFTWRIGHT LLC
PO Box 7205
Charlottesville, VA 22906
Phone: 800-728-4033
E-mail: sales@softwright.com
Web Site: http://www.softwright.com
Larry D. Ellis, PE, President
Kay Ward, Business Administrator
Curt Alway, Software Marketing & Sales
Michael Wiebe, Software Development
Develops software for evaluating transmitter site coverage; TV/FM, ITFS, PCS, microwave, cellular, paging, & two-way radio system design & site management.

SPANPRO INC.
5495 N Bend Rd
Ste 200
Burlington, KY 41005
Phones: 859-647-2736; 800-647-2790
Fax: 859-746-6245
Craig Wheeler, President
Dan Kerr, Vice President, Technology
Rick Weiss, Vice President, Operations
Dennis Hume, Business Development Director
Steve Sargent, Engineering Director
Provides telecommunications engineering construction, maintenance & related applications software development.

STERLING INSTITUTE INC.
11350 Random Hills Rd 6
Fairfax, VA 22030
Phones: 703-636-3232; 703-934-6089
Fax: 703-995-0862
E-mail: si@sterlinginstitute.com
Web Site: http://www.sterlinginstitute.com
Matt Livingston, President
Brandon Scott, Vice President, Learning Technologies
Danielle Lissak, Client Services Manager
Offers custom-designed executive, management & sales development programs for the broadcasting, cable & publishing industries.

STRATA MARKETING INC.
30 W Monroe St
Ste 1900
Chicago, IL 60603
Phone: 312-222-1555
Fax: 312-222-2510
E-mail: info@stratag.com
Web Site: http://www.stratag.com
John Shelton, President & Chief Executive Officer
Joy Baer, Executive Vice President
Michael Latulippe, Senior Vice President, Finance & Administration

Management & Technical Services

Michael Dehler, Vice President, Technical Infrastructure
David Drucker, Vice President & Agency Services Manager
Tom Gombas, Vice President, Cable Division
Paul Levy, Vice President, Custom Development
Mike McHugh, Vice President, Media Sales & Electronic Delivery
Peter Nason, Vice President, Contracts & Marketing
Francine Olson, Vice President, Major Accounts-Cable
David Prager, Vice President, e-Business Solutions & Program Management
Develops software for media buying departments, cable systems, TV & radio stations.

STRUCTURAL SYSTEMS TECHNOLOGY INC.
6867 Elm St
Ste 200
McLean, VA 22101-3870
Phones: 703-356-9765; 800-997-6555
Fax: 703-448-0979
Fred W. Purdy, PE, President
Kaveh Mehrnama, PE, Vice President, Engineering
Mary Acker, Executive Secretary & Office Manager
Greg Pleinka, National Sales Manager
Bryan Burton, Chief Designer & Draftsman

Branch Offices:
NEWPORT NEWS: 51 Lakeshore Dr, Newport News, VA 23608. Phones: 757-890-4505; 866-859-5505. Fax: 757-890-4506.
Designs, repairs, inspects & erects tall towers.

S2ONE INC.
9914 E Upriver Dr
Spokane, WA 99206-4415
Phones: 509-891-7362; 800-270-7050
Web Site: http://www.s2one.com
Mark Hills, President
Installs, maintains & repairs analog & digital transmission equipment throughout the U.S.

SYNTELLECT INC.
2095 W Pinnacle Peak Rd
Ste 110
Phoenix, AZ 85027
Phone: 602-789-2800
Fax: 602-789-2768
E-mail: info@syntellect.com
Web Site: http://www.syntellect.com
Steve Dodenhoff, President
Bruce Petillo, Marketing Manager

Branch Offices:
CHICAGO: 700 Commerce Dr, Oak Brook, IL 60523.

CANADA: 90 Nolan Ct, Ste 1A, Markham, ON L3R 4L9, Canada. Phone: 905-754-4100.

SINGAPORE: 371 Beach Rd #02-26, Keypoint 199597, Singapore. Phone: 65-6392-1833.

UNITED KINGDOM: Progression House, Turnhams Green Park, Pincents Lane, Fleet, Hamps, Berkshire RG31 4UH, United Kingdom. Phone: 44-0203-35-3000. Fax: 44-0110-972-8498.
Operates a transaction-based hosted services center.

SZABO ASSOCIATES INC.
3355 Lenox Rd NE
Ste 945
Atlanta, GA 30326
Phone: 404-266-2464
Fax: 404-266-2165
E-mail: info@szabo.com
Web Site: http://www.szabo.com
Robin Szabo, President
Nolan Childers, Division Manager, Television & Cable
Randy Neff, Division Manager, Radio
Sandi Garris, Legal Services Manager
Provides collection services exclusively for the media, advertising & entertainment industries; services include credit information system; A/R management; legal sources; corporate management reports; library resource center; bankruptcy assistance; EDI; international services.

TC SPECIALTIES
PO Box 192
17 S Main St
Coudersport, PA 16915
Phones: 814-274-8060; 800-458-6074
Fax: 814-274-0690
E-mail: sales@tcspecialties.com
Web Site: http://www.tcspecialties.com
Provides commercial printing services; coupon payment coupons; presort mail facility.

TELESTRATEGIES INC.
6845 Elm St
Ste 310
McLean, VA 22101
Phone: 703-734-7050
Fax: 703-893-3197
E-mail: info@telestrategies.com
Web Site: http://www.telestrategies.com
Offers telecommunication industry conferences, seminars, tutorials & trade shows.

TELETECH INC.
9197 S Peoria St
Englewood, CO 80112-5833
Phones: 303-397-8100; 800-835-3832
Fax: 303-397-8199
E-mail: media@teletech.com
Web Site: http://www.teletech.com
Kenneth Tuchman, Chairman & Chief Executive Officer
James Bartlett, Vice Chairman
Provides communications & media companies with solutions for integrated systems to grow revenue & increase customer retention.

TELVUE CORP.
16000 Horizon Way
Ste 500
Mount Laurel, NJ 08054
Phone: 800-885-8886
Fax: 856-866-7411
E-mail: sales@telvue.com
Web Site: http://www.telvue.com
Jesse Lerman, President & Chief Executive Officer
Paul Andrews, Vice President, Sales & Marketing
John Fell, Secretary & Treasurer
Helps hyperlocal TV channels achieve professional results at affordable prices. Provides products & solutions for: VOD, OTT, live streaming, linear broadcast & transcoding.

TIBA SOLUTIONS
201 Brookfield Pkwy
Ste 200
Greenville, SC 29607
Phone: 864-679-4800
Ken Brower, President & Chief Operating Officer
Kirk Gollwitzer, Executive Vice President
David Friedline, e-Government Solutions Director
Doris Rowland, Senior Account Executive
Provides in-house billing & subscriber management & total information systems, featuring order entry, dispatching, marketing support & analysis, sales analysis, outage analysis, addressability, pay-per-view control, receivables processing & inventory management.

TOWERS WATSON
335 Madison Ave
New York, NY 10017-4605
Phone: 212-309-3400
Fax: 212-309-0948
Web Site: http://www.towerswatson.com
Mark Mactas, Chairman & Chief Executive Officer
Bob Hogan, Chief Financial Officer
Kevin Young, Secretary & General Counsel
Jim Foreman, Managing Director, Human Capital Group
Tricia Guinn, Managing Director, Risk & Financial Services
Provides solutions to client issues in the areas of human resource strategy, design & management; actuarial & management consulting; reinsurance intermediary services; offices worldwide.

TRANSCOMM INC.
3601 Pickett Rd
No. 2845
Fairfax, VA 22031
Phone: 703-323-5150
Fax: 703-426-4527
E-mail: transcommusa1@gmail.com
Web Site: http://www.transcommusa.com
Norman C. Lerner, President
Provides consulting services; specializes in domestic & international financial solutions, economic & business development problems of high technology industries, with emphasis in telecommunications, energy & postal.

UNITED RECOVERY SYSTEMS
5800 N Course Dr
Houston, TX 77072
Phones: 713-977-1234; 800-568-0399
Fax: 713-977-0119
E-mail: sales@ursi.com
Web Site: http://www.unitedrecoverysystems.com
Jim Kelleher, President

Branch Offices:
BRYAN: 4001 E 29th St, Ste 130, Bryan, TX 77802.

TEMPE: 7340 S Kyrene, Tempe, AZ 85283.

TULSA: 6506 S Lewis Ave, Ste 260, Tulsa, OK 74136. Phones: 918-712-0077; 888-593-8401. Fax: 918-712-0606.
Provides adjustment & collection services, insurance services, business facilities oversight, business administration services & management support services.

USA 800 INC.
9808 E 66th Terr
Kansas City, MO 64133
Phones: 800-821-7539; 816-358-1303
Fax: 816-358-1303
E-mail: sales@usa-800.com
Web Site: http://www.usa-800.com
Tom Davis, President & Chief Executive Officer
Dan Quigley, Chief Operating & Financial Officer
Mike Douglas, Chief Information Officer
Corey Kramer, Vice President, Business Development
David Labatt, Vice President, Sales
Dan Lake, Vice President, Contact Centers
Mike Langel, Vice President, Technology
Michelle Melland, Vice President, Client Services
Jeanne Hicks, Operations Director

Branch Offices:
HALSTEAD: 327 Chestnut St, 2nd Fl, Halstead, KS 67056. Phone: 866-810-1499.

ST. JOSEPH: 5804 Corporate Dr, St. Joseph, MO 64507. Phones: 800-310-6762; 816-676-1020.
Provides customer care, sales & lead acquisition services.

U.S. DEPARTMENT OF COMMERCE
1401 Constitution Ave NW
Washington, DC 20230
Phones: 202-482-2000; 202-482-3548
Fax: 202-482-4128
E-mail: webmaster@doc.gov
Web Site: http://www.commerce.gov
Penny Pritzker, Commerce Secretary
Bruce H. Andrews, Deputy Commerce Secretary
Trade Development, International Trade Administration; government point of contact for the telecommunications, aerospace, aircraft & electronic components industries; measuring & controlling instruments, medical & dental; photographic, computer software & business equipment concerning market research, trade & business assistance.

VARVID INC.
1319 Commercial St
Ste 201
Bellingham, WA 98225
Phones: 360-738-7168; 855-827-8434
E-mail: info@varvid.com
Web Site: http://www.varvid.com
Aaron Booker, Chief Executive Officer
Mike Simmons, President
Provides video marketing services; helps clients leverage their existing online presence by way of video case studies, live event webcasting, social media integration & emerging online video portals.

T.J. VAUGHAN & ASSOCIATES
PO Box 440
Rye Beach, NH 03871
Phone: 603-964-6688
Fax: 603-964-5450
Thomas J. Vaughan, President
Provides HDTV feasibility studies, site selection, pattern & antenna analysis, antenna modification, pattern measurements & field tests; RFR measurements.

VIDCAD
2010 E Lohman Ave
Ste 2
Las Cruces, NM 88011
Phones: 575-522-0003; 800-843-2236
Fax: 575-635-4518
E-mail: sales@vidcad.com
Web Site: http://www.vidcad.com
Alex Sotelo, Vice President, Sales
Provides documentation automation software.

VISLINK SERVICES
101 Billerica Ave
Bldg 6
North Billerica, MA 01862
Phone: 800-490-5700
E-mail: info@vislink.com

Management & Technical Services

Web Site: http://www.vislink.com
Chris Gibbons, Vice President, Business Development
Mark Garcia, West Coast Operations Director
Specializes in wireless, video & IP technologies and their supporting management systems. Designs & manufactures radio, satellite transmission & wireless cameras.

VOZZCOM INC.
11768 W Sample Rd
Coral Springs, FL 33065
Phones: 954-753-8600; 866-254-8600
Fax: 954-753-5522
E-mail: sales@vozzcom.net
Web Site: http://www.vozzcom.net
Doreen Vozzola, President
David E. Vozzola, Chief Operating Officer
Mark Ecsedy, Vice President, Mid-Atlantic Region
Terry Board, Controller

Branch Offices:
CULVER CITY: 5601 W Slauson Ave, Ste 170, Culver City, CA 90230. Phone: 310-641-1500.
Provides support services to the broadband industry.

V-SOFT COMMUNICATIONS
401 Main St
Ste 213
Cedar Falls, IA 50613
Phones: 319-266-8402; 800-743-3684
Fax: 319-432-7275
E-mail: info@v-soft.com; consulting@v-soft.com
Web Site: http://www.v-soft.com
Doug Vernier, Chief Executive Officer & Owner
John Gray, Vice President, Owner & Research Director
Kate English, Broadcast Engineering Consultant
Gayle Vernier, Bookkeeper

Branch Offices:
KANSAS CITY:, 15233 W 153rd St, Olathe, KS 66062. Phone: 319-266-8402. Fax: 319-266-9212.

WEST PALM BEACH: 8893 Lakes Blvd, West Palm Beach, FL 33412. Phone: 319-266-8402. Fax: 319-266-9212.
Provides software & support for FCC AM, FM, TV/DTV & microwave allocations & propagation prediction software. Software to prepare custom FCC & Longley-Rice coverage & interference analysis maps, population & demographic studies & frequency searches; Software aids in the preparation of applications to the FCC for AM, FM, LPFM, TV, DTV, TV translators, microwave & other broadcast auxiliaries. Numerous census, terrain, land cover, world polygon mapping, market studies, microwave, AM, FM & TV databases.

WALTERS-STORYK DESIGN GROUP INC.
262 Martin Ave
Highland, NY 12528
Phone: 845-691-9300
Fax: 845-691-9361
E-mail: wsdginfo@wsdg.com
Web Site: http://www.wsdg.com
Beth Walters, Co-founder & Principal
John Storyk, Co-founder & Principal
Nancy Flannery, Chief Financial Officer
Romina Larregina, Senior Project Manager

Branch Offices:
NORTH MIAMI BEACH: 19585 NE 10th Ave, North Miami Beach, FL 33179. Phone: 305-479-2679.

SONOMA: 866 Virginia Ct, Sonoma, CA 95476. Phone: 415-407-6086.

ARGENTINA: Gascon 1364, Buenos Aires C1181 ACZ, Argentina. Phone: 54-11-4865-3111. E-Mail: sergio@wsdg.com. Sergio Molho, Director, International Relations & Partner.

BRAZIL: Rua Rio Grande de Norte 1560, Sala 1107, Savassi, Belo Horizonte MG CEP 30.130-131, Brazil. Phones: 55-31-3225-2766; 55-31-9195-9430. E-Mail: renato@wsdg.com. Renato C.R. Cipriano, Partner & General Manager.

HONG KONG: Ming Pao Industrial Ctr, 18 Ka Yip St, 1910-12, Block B, Chaiwan, Hong Kong. Phone: 852-2898-3133.

MEXICO CITY: Leibnitz 282, Col Nueva Anzures, Mexico City, DF 11590, Mexico. Phone: 52-55-5905-0500. Fax: 52-55-5905-0506.

SWITZERLAND: Dornacherstr 279, 4053 Basel, Switzerland. Phone: 41-61-903-13-40. Fax: 41-61-903-13-41. E-Mail: europe@wsdg.com. Dirk Noy, Partner & General Manager.
Full-service architectural & acoustic design firm; specializes in professional audio & video production facilities.

WARREN & MORRIS LTD.
48 Hua Nui Way
Lahaina, HI 96761
Phone: 619-520-9380
E-mail: cmorris@warrenmorrisltd.com
Web Site: http://www.warrenmorrisltd.com
Charles C. Morris, Senior Partner

Branch Offices:
EDEN: 3433 Big Piney Dr, Eden, UT 84301. Phone: 619-520-9380.
Provides executive search services to the digital media, broadband, cable & wireless industries.

WEBER SHANDWICK
919 3rd Ave
New York, NY 10022
Phone: 212-445-8000
E-mail: apolansky@webershandwick.com
Web Site: http://www.webershandwick.com
Jack Leslie, Chairman
Harris Diamond, Chief Executive Officer
Andy Polansky, President
Specializes in strategic marketing communications, media relations, public affairs, reputation & issues management & offers corporate communications counseling services; provides specialized integrated services including web relations, advocacy advertising, market research & visual communications; offices worldwide.

WIDEORBIT
1160 Battery St
Ste 300
San Francisco, CA 94111
Phone: 415-675-6700
Fax: 415-675-6755
E-mail: sales@wideorbit.com
Web Site: http://www.wideorbit.com
Eric Mathewson, Founder & Chief Executive Officer
Bruce Roberts, President
Nathan Gans, Chief Operations Officer
Margaret McCarthy, Chief Financial Officer
Eric Moe, Chief Technology Officer
Brian Burdick, Executive Vice President, Digital and Programmatic TV
William Offeman, Executive Vice President, Engineering
Mike Zinsmeister, Executive Vice President, Sales
Ian Ferreira, Senior Vice President, Programmatic TV

Branch Offices:
AGAWAM: 67 Hunt St, Ste 106, Agawam, ME 01001. Phone: 413-272-7220. Fax: 413-272-7222.

DALLAS: 601 Canyon Dr, Ste 101, Coppell, TX 75019. Phone: 214-451-4000.

DENVER: 700 17th St, Ste 1100, Denver, CO 80202. Phone: 720-224-9170. Fax: 720-224-9171.

LYNNWOOD: 3400 188th St SW, Ste 685, Lynnwood, WA 98037. Phone: 425-412-5300. Fax: 425-329-1119.

NEW YORK: 275 Seventh Ave, Ste 2301, New York, NY 10001. Phone: 415-675-6700.

CANADA: 13115 NE 4th St, Ste 140, Vancouver, WA 98684. Phone: 866-872-0781.

FRANCE: 23 Boulevard PoissonniFre, Paris 75002, France. Phone: 33-1-70-75-38-10.

SWEDEN: Lilla Bommen 3, 4th Floor, Goteborg 41104, Sweden. Phone: 46-31-23-34-50.

UNITED KINGDOM: 1 Northumberland Ave, Trafalgar Square, London WC2N 5BW, UK. Phone: 44-207-872-5746.
Provides business management software to media companies. Provides solutions for managing the business of broadcast & cable operations from proposal to order, scheduling to automation, billing & aging for linear, digital and programmatic advertising.

WILLIAM MORRIS ENDEAVOR ENTERTAINMENT
9601 Wilshire Blvd.
Beverly Hills, CA 90210
Phone: 310-285-9000
Fax: 310-285-9010
Web Site: http://www.wmeentertainment.com
Jim Wiatt, Chairman
Ariel Z. Emanuel, Chief Executive Officer
A talent & literary agency that represents clients in all segments of the entertainment industry.

WILLIAMS COMMUNICATIONS INC.
5524 Bee Cave Rd
Ste C-1
Austin, TX 78746
Phone: 512-328-2461
Fax: 512-328-3009
E-mail: info@catvdesign.com; info@wilcomm.com
Steve Williams, President
Provides engineering services worldwide, RF design, project management & drafting.

WSI CORP.
400 Minuteman Rd
Andover, MA 01810
Phone: 978-983-6300
Fax: 978-983-6400
E-mail: sales@wsi.com
Web Site: http://www.wsi.com
Mark Gildersleeve, President
Bill Dow, Vice President & General Manager, Media Division
John Caffery, Vice President, Human Resources
Linda Maynard, Vice President, Corporate Marketing
Jim Menard, Vice President, Digital Initiatives
Mark D. Miller, Vice President & General Manager, Decision Support
Dr. Peter P. Neilley, Vice President, Global Forecasting Services

Branch Offices:
UNITED KINGDOM: Edgbaston House, 3 Duchess Pl, Hagley Rd, 15th Fl, Birmingham B16 8HN, United Kingdom. Phone: 44-121-233-7600. Fax: 44-121-233-7666.
Provides worldwide weather & weather-related information, mission-critical systems, integration services & presentation services to customers in the media, aviation, industry, government & consumer markets.

JIM YOUNG & ASSOCIATES INC.
1424 Clear Lake Rd
Weatherford, TX 76086
Phone: 817-599-7623
Fax: 817-599-4483
Jim Young, President
Specializes in the placement of CATV, telecommunications, cellular telephone, RF engineering & satellite communications personnel.

Keep your key players on top of breaking telecom and media news.

Get them their own daily dose…

Take advantage of our **highly affordable multi-copy subscription** discounts and ensure all your key players are up to speed on business-critical regulatory activity, legislation, industry developments and competitive intelligence — **first thing, every business morning.**

No more waiting to receive a routed copy after the news cycle is over.

Now you can provide your team with breaking telecom news and analysis while the process can still be influenced.

Contact us today and eliminate the hassles of forwarding/routing while maintaining copyright compliance. Your account manager will help define a distribution package that **meets your intelligence needs and budget.**

Put your whole team in the know.

Communications Daily

Warren Communications News

Call **800-771-9202** today so we can help you find an affordable way to get Communications Daily on eveyone's desk tomorrow morning!

ESTIMATED GROWTH OF THE CABLE INDUSTRY

(as of January 1 of each year)

Year	Operating Systems	Total Basic Subscribers	Year	Operating Systems	Total Basic Subscribers*
1952	70	14,000	1987	7,900	41,000,000
1953	150	30,000	1988	8,500	44,000,000
1954	300	65,000	1989	9,050	47,500,000
1955	400	150,000	1990	9,575	50,000,000
1956	450	300,000	1991	10,704	51,000,000
1957	500	350,000	1992	11,035	53,000,000
1958	525	450,000	1993	11,108	54,200,000
1959	560	550,000	1994	11,214	55,300,000
1960	640	650,000	1995	11,218	56,500,000
1961	700	725,000	1996	11,119	60,280,000
1962	800	850,000	1997	10,050	64,050,000
1963	1,000	950,000	1998	10,845	64,170,000
1964	1,200	1,085,000	1999	10,700	65,500,000
1965	1,325	1,275,000	2000	10,400	66,500,000
1966	1,570	1,575,000	2001	10,300	67,200,000
1967	1,770	2,100,000	2002	9,900	64,500,000
1968	2,000	2,800,000	2003	9,400	64,800,000
1969	2,260	3,600,000	2004	8,875	65,250,000
1970	2,490	4,500,000	2005	8,400	65,300,000
1971	2,639	5,300,000	2006	8,000	64,900,000
1972	2,841	6,000,000	2007	7,100	66,000,000
1973	2,991	7,300,000	2008	6,585	65,190,000
1974	3,158	8,700,000	2009	6,050	65,500,000
1975	3,506	9,800,000	2010	6,150	65,800,000
1976	3,681	10,800,000	2011	6,016	77,750,000
1977	3,832	11,900,000	2012	5,575	77,655,000
1978	3,875	13,000,000	2013	5,202	67,350,197
1979	4,150	14,100,000	2014	4,800	55,377,499
1980	4,225	16,000,000	2015	4,155	58,716,159
1981	4,375	18,300,000	2016	3,699	55,743,965
1982	4,825	21,000,000	2017	3,325	49,075,500
1983	5,600	25,000,000			
1984	6,200	29,000,000			
1985	6,600	32,000,000			
1986	7,500	37,500,000			

Note: The change in the number of systems operating each year is determined by three factors: (1) New systems which began operation during the year; (2) older systems coming to the attention of Television & Cable Factbook for the first time and therefore included in the total for the first time; (3) the splitting, combining, or shutting down of systems by operators.

* Includes both analog and digital subscribers.

Cable Statistics

LARGEST U.S. CABLE SYSTEMS

(Those with 20,000 or more basic subscribers* as of October 2016)

System	Subscribers
BOSTON	1,541,850
SAN FRANCISCO	1,305,228
LOS ANGELES	1,206,754
DETROIT	997,611
HILLSBOROUGH COUNTY (portions)	897,463
SEATTLE	836,009
WEST PALM BEACH	813,001
MANHATTAN	751,966
ORLANDO	744,445
ATLANTA	741,462
CLEVELAND	650,104
AUDUBON	589,016
TOWSON	583,920
HARRISBURG	572,273
HOUSTON	568,447
PHOENIX	560,627
PEORIA	557,197
FREDERICK COUNTY (portions)	547,623
AMBERLEY (village)	511,686
PHILADELPHIA	505,915
MOUNT PROSPECT	504,711
MINNEAPOLIS	493,123
BUFFALO	489,148
DENVER	487,024
PORTLAND, OR (Comcast Cable)	441,379
DEWITT	438,766
NEW BRITAIN	433,700
EATONTOWN BOROUGH	418,966
HENDRICKS COUNTY (portions)	414,550
CHAMPAIGN	409,278
SACRAMENTO	408,548
RALEIGH	407,967
ST. LOUIS	407,772
AMITYVILLE	355,262
SAN DIEGO, CA (Cox Communications)	353,499
COLUMBUS, OH (Time Warner Cable)	346,044
PITTSBURGH	343,933
CHARLOTTE	339,334
LAS VEGAS	306,936
CHICAGO	305,109
DALLAS	304,828
SARASOTA	301,594
BROOKLYN	298,436
JACKSONVILLE, FL (Comcast Cable)	295,770
BRONX	289,019
VIRGINIA BEACH	283,166
ALBANY, NY (Time Warner Cable)	281,325
NASHVILLE	279,210
PORTLAND, ME (Time Warner Cable)	275,991
MILWAUKEE	275,895
GREENSBORO	271,244
AUSTIN	270,549
COLUMBIA, SC (Time Warner Cable)	270,436
BURLINGTON	267,429
KNOXVILLE	259,232
CHARLOTTESVILLE	258,229
SAN ANTONIO	238,706
WEST ORANGE TWP	234,790
SALT LAKE CITY	226,660
LOUISVILLE	222,024
OAHU ISLAND	205,932
WEST WARWICK	198,414
OKLAHOMA CITY	196,231
ZELIENOPLE	195,202
PETERSBURG	186,638
SAN JUAN CAPISTRANO	184,230
OAKLAND	177,037
KANSAS CITY	172,267
OMAHA	169,045
MADISON	162,967
FRESNO	161,999
MEMPHIS	160,090
NEW ORLEANS	155,526
SPARTANBURG	155,214
PLYMOUTH	150,949
SUFFOLK COUNTY	146,625
RARITAN	143,990
BATON ROUGE	142,513
ALBUQUERQUE	135,909
SAN DIEGO, CA (Time Warner Cable)	135,177
TULSA	131,062
BETHEL (town)	130,877
BAYAMON	126,981
CURRY	125,753
WORCESTER	124,930
WICHITA	123,955
TIFFIN	123,819
PELHAM	120,593
PENSACOLA	119,204
NORWALK	118,810
PHARR	113,851
COLORADO SPRINGS	113,704
LONGMONT	112,610
MIDLAND	109,746
TALLAHASSEE	108,700
FAIRFAX COUNTY	106,080
TUPELO	104,037
MORRIS TWP	102,310
APPLETON	98,906
TOLEDO	96,295
RENO	93,822
SAVANNAH	93,010
JACKSON	92,069
ALLENDALE TWP	92,058
HICKORY	91,183
COVINGTON	90,778
ARCHER	90,072
NORTH CHARLESTON	89,736
AVON-BY-THE-SEA	89,704
TUCSON, AZ (Cox Communications)	88,002
BRIDGEPORT	86,991
VANCOUVER	86,619
FORT WORTH (northern portions)	84,992
PALM SPRINGS	82,631
ALLENTOWN	81,438
SPOKANE	80,689
RIVERHEAD	77,841
WILMINGTON	77,688
FREEHOLD	77,523
BROOKHAVEN	76,779
BLAIRSVILLE	76,724
AUGUSTA	75,753
MAMARONECK	74,605
FOND DU LAC	74,281
GAINESVILLE	73,610
TRAVERSE CITY	71,951
LAWRENCEVILLE	71,914
EAU CLAIRE	69,701
STEVENS POINT	69,342
INDIANAPOLIS (portions)	68,772
LEXINGTON	68,618
BELLINGHAM	67,281
LINCOLN	66,788
BAKERSFIELD	65,691
LOS ANGELES COUNTY (portions)	65,672
WAPPINGERS FALLS	65,199
GOODRICH	64,849
COLUMBUS, OH (WOW! Internet, Cable & Phone)	64,306
SPRINGDALE	63,670
TUCSON, AZ (Comcast Cable)	63,519
EL PASO	62,820
SLIDELL	62,075
SPRINGFIELD, IL (Comcast Cable)	61,979
CHARLESTON	60,556
ASHEVILLE	60,329
INDEPENDENCE	59,999
JACKSONVILLE, NC (Time Warner Cable)	58,519
MOBILE	58,206

Cable Statistics

DES MOINES	58,194
MACON	58,065
PORT ARTHUR	56,894
NAPERVILLE	56,875
WHEELING	56,487
PHIL CAMPBELL	56,250
CHATTANOOGA	54,271
KINGSPORT	54,003
CORPUS CHRISTI	53,170
NEW MILFORD	52,414
LIVONIA	52,204
RIVERSIDE	51,961
ROCKLAND	50,519
ALCOA	50,502
OSSINING	49,819
MONTGOMERY, AL (Charter Communications)	49,448
DECATUR	49,055
LITTLE ROCK	48,722
GULFPORT	48,145
CHICOPEE	47,664
ANCHORAGE	47,574
RICHMOND	47,355
SANTA BARBARA	47,302
MANCHESTER	46,761
NEWARK, NJ (Cablevision)	46,403
BIRMINGHAM	46,298
ROCK HILL	45,981
HOMEWOOD	45,830
HATTIESBURG	45,741
GREENSBURG	45,259
EVANSVILLE, IN (Time Warner Cable)	45,161
YONKERS	44,997
HOBOKEN	44,527
STATEN ISLAND	44,427
PARKERSBURG	44,150
NEWNAN	44,119
ANGIER	43,996
PARMA	43,867
ROCHESTER, NH (MetroCast Communications)	43,420
JACKSON CITY	43,419
BERGENFIELD	43,065
STROUDSBURG	43,018
ROANOKE	42,655
HESPERIA	41,649
AMARILLO	41,619
KEALAKEKUA	40,813
MAUI ISLAND	40,683
KENNEWICK	40,498
AGANA	40,414
BECKLEY	40,364
BEREA	39,271
GLENDALE	39,205
SIOUX FALLS	38,158
SUNBURY (village)	38,056
SAN LUIS OBISPO	37,187
MOLINE	37,016
SHREVEPORT	35,591
BOISE	35,356
CAGUAS	35,227
MARQUETTE	34,952
LONG BEACH	34,808
CIALES	34,300
STOCKBRIDGE	34,190
CORBIN	34,110
MEDFORD	34,023
ELIZABETHTOWN	33,927
MIAMI BEACH	33,455
ROSEMOUNT	33,392
LAREDO	32,910
PITTSFIELD	32,884
COMSTOCK TWP.	32,087
BLUFFTON (village)	31,959
BEND	31,936
TOPEKA	31,660
YORKTOWN	31,269
MORGANTOWN	31,138
PORTSMOUTH	30,742
BISMARCK	30,526
LEHIGHTON	30,415
LUBBOCK	29,951
ROCHESTER, MN (Charter Communications)	29,657
HUNTSVILLE	29,569
OWENSBORO	29,394
ENFIELD	29,240
FORT SMITH	29,061
HAGERSTOWN	28,942
LAKE CHARLES	28,559
FORT LEE BOROUGH	28,405
SHALLOTTE	28,158
BILLINGS	28,141
MERIDEN	28,103
EPHRATA	27,702
BELMONT	27,119
ASHFORD	27,032
BIRDSBORO	27,017
TYLER	26,786
MILLSBORO	26,721
HAZLETON	26,321
KEARNEY	26,297
WARWICK	25,820
GRAND JUNCTION	25,658
CEDAR RAPIDS	25,214
ALTOONA	25,127
CLARKSVILLE	25,056
MASSILLON	25,038
ATHENS	24,461
LITCHFIELD	24,311
PATERSON	24,119
HAMILTON TWP. (Mercer County)	24,012
EVANSVILLE, IN (WOW! Internet, Cable & Phone)	23,995
BRYAN	23,864
MILFORD	23,785
BOWLING GREEN	23,763
SPARTA	23,692
KINGWOOD	23,631
GREENVILLE	23,543
ST. CLOUD	23,333
LUQUILLO	23,175
GRAND FORKS	23,112
MAYAGUEZ	23,092
PONCE	23,092
NEW LONDON	23,043
PORT ORCHARD	23,019
PONTOTOC	22,641
FARGO	22,449
COLUMBIA, TN (Charter Communications)	22,402
CAMBRIDGE	22,338
SUFFOLK	22,114
HUMBOLDT COUNTY (portions)	22,023
ALBANY, GA (Mediacom)	21,970
ELIZABETH	21,916
ALEXANDRIA	21,810
THIBODAUX	21,768
NEWARK, OH (Time Warner Cable)	21,451
SPRINGFIELD, MO (Mediacom)	21,234
ABINGDON	20,923
COLUMBUS, GA (WOW! Internet, Cable & Phone)	20,872
SAN ANGELO	20,656
MONTGOMERY, AL (WOW! Internet, Cable & Phone)	20,433
DIMONDALE	20,349

* Total analog and digital basic subscribers.

Nielsen Cable TV Household Estimates

Listed alphabetically by Nielsen Designated Market Area (DMA)

(Data as of October 2016)

DESIGNATED MARKET AREA	CABLE TV % RANK*	TV HSHLDS (Jan. 2017)	CABLE TV HSHLDS (Oct. 2016)	CABLE TV % of TV HSHLDS
Abilene-Sweetwater, TX	194	113,080	36,280	32
Albany, GA	171	142,800	52,450	37
Albany-Schenectady-Troy, NY	12	529,120	382,000	72
Albuquerque-Santa Fe, NM	205	677,590	166,930	25
Alexandria, LA	132	85,560	37,250	44
Alpena, MI	71	16,010	8,340	52
Amarillo, TX	166	190,240	72,290	38
Anchorage, AK	47	154,020	87,950	57
Atlanta, GA	53	2,412,730	1,354,100	56
Augusta, GA-Aiken, SC	104	260,840	125,550	48
Austin, TX	57	771,210	423,430	55
Bakersfield, CA	151	223,250	92,440	41
Baltimore, MD	9	1,119,480	830,490	74
Bangor, ME	166	133,310	50,800	38
Baton Rouge, LA	30	330,910	203,200	61
Beaumont-Port Arthur, TX	158	165,380	65,380	40
Bend, OR	104	67,430	32,410	48
Billings, MT	145	110,630	46,290	42
Biloxi-Gulfport, MS	139	130,030	56,420	43
Binghamton, NY	30	127,070	77,700	61
Birmingham (Anniston & Tuscaloosa), AL	123	696,380	320,780	46
Bluefield-Beckley-Oak Hill, WV	104	127,090	61,110	48
Boise, ID	210	270,200	34,750	13
Boston, MA (Manchester, NH)	1	2,424,240	2,066,190	85
Bowling Green, KY	30	80,230	48,560	61
Buffalo, NY	19	596,710	385,900	65
Burlington, VT-Plattsburgh, NY	86	307,470	153,930	50
Butte-Bozeman, MT	189	70,320	23,060	33
Casper-Riverton, WY	86	56,260	28,050	50
Cedar Rapids-Waterloo-Iowa City & Dubuque, IA	132	343,000	151,260	44
Champaign & Springfield-Decatur, IL	99	364,050	176,760	49
Charleston, SC	33	327,040	196,510	60
Charleston-Huntington, WV	123	431,150	200,220	46
Charlotte, NC	86	1,189,950	600,070	50
Charlottesville, VA	104	74,990	36,210	48
Chattanooga, TN	53	351,220	195,440	56
Cheyenne, WY-Scottsbluff, NE	60	56,120	30,200	54
Chicago, IL	44	3,463,060	2,008,050	58
Chico-Redding, CA	195	188,010	58,170	31
Cincinnati, OH	60	863,800	463,920	54
Clarksburg-Weston, WV	158	103,090	41,520	40
Cleveland-Akron (Canton), OH	33	1,498,960	897,530	60
Colorado Springs-Pueblo, CO	139	354,190	151,950	43
Columbia, SC	123	400,790	183,730	46
Columbia-Jefferson City, MO	195	171,330	52,360	31
Columbus, GA (Opelika, AL)	77	217,660	110,570	51
Columbus, OH	42	920,740	547,080	59
Columbus-Tupelo-West Point-Houston, MS	207	181,860	38,650	21
Corpus Christi, TX	115	209,760	97,780	47
Dallas-Fort Worth, TX	115	2,713,380	1,275,770	47
Davenport, IA-Rock Island-Moline, IL	145	294,680	123,330	42
Dayton, OH	77	466,040	237,620	51
Denver, CO	132	1,630,380	713,070	44
Des Moines-Ames, IA	189	433,950	143,150	33
Detroit, MI	17	1,853,030	1,214,410	66
Dothan, AL	145	97,960	40,960	42
Duluth, MN-Superior, WI	184	164,380	55,370	34
El Paso, TX (Las Cruces, NM)	171	333,270	122,950	37
Elmira (Corning), NY	53	90,550	50,270	56
Erie, PA	115	148,880	70,620	47
Eugene, OR	123	239,710	109,780	46
Eureka, CA	77	58,640	30,170	51
Evansville, IN	163	279,860	109,320	39
Fairbanks, AK	166	36,070	13,590	38
Fargo-Valley City, ND	86	249,010	125,200	50
Flint-Saginaw-Bay City, MI	57	423,010	234,580	55
Fort Myers-Naples, FL	28	518,730	319,880	62
Fort Smith-Fayetteville-Springdale-Rogers, AR	151	304,670	124,180	41
Fort Wayne, IN	177	262,990	94,150	36
Fresno-Visalia, CA	171	573,180	212,140	37
Gainesville, FL	132	126,400	56,060	44
Glendive, MT	60	4,370	2,350	54
Grand Junction-Montrose, CO	104	69,820	33,630	48
Grand Rapids-Kalamazoo-Battle Creek, MI	71	709,670	371,440	52
Great Falls, MT	189	63,720	21,080	33
Green Bay-Appleton, WI	132	438,070	194,080	44
Greensboro-High Point-Winston Salem, NC	99	690,050	340,160	49
Greenville-New Bern-Washington, NC	123	301,990	139,190	46
Greenville-Spartanburg-Anderson, SC-Asheville, NC	151	845,990	346,990	41
Greenwood-Greenville, MS	181	62,690	21,770	35
Harlingen-Weslaco-Brownsville-McAllen, TX	184	368,960	126,840	34
Harrisburg-Lancaster-Lebanon-York, PA	21	715,110	461,040	64
Harrisonburg, VA	69	89,730	47,780	53
Hartford & New Haven, CT	5	963,950	789,750	82
Hattiesburg-Laurel, MS	171	108,380	40,220	37
Helena, MT	139	28,110	12,200	43
Honolulu, HI	4	442,820	368,880	83
Houston, TX	104	2,450,800	1,182,370	48
Huntsville-Decatur (Florence), AL	99	385,470	189,180	49
Idaho Falls-Pocatello, ID (Jackson, WY)	209	123,170	24,740	20
Indianapolis, IN	60	1,086,310	589,360	54
Jackson, MS	166	321,830	123,210	38
Jackson, TN	99	89,970	43,720	49
Jacksonville, FL	47	688,500	392,170	57
Johnstown-Altoona-State College, PA	77	277,210	140,710	51
Jonesboro, AR	115	79,860	37,600	47
Joplin, MO-Pittsburg, KS	203	144,110	37,820	26
Juneau, AK	17	25,680	16,970	66
Kansas City, MO	86	919,020	458,940	50
Knoxville, TN	53	514,610	290,720	56
La Crosse-Eau Claire, WI	123	206,480	95,850	46
Lafayette, IN	33	69,180	41,270	60
Lafayette, LA	86	233,790	116,310	50
Lake Charles, LA	77	95,740	48,880	51
Lansing, MI	86	250,670	125,060	50
Laredo, TX	33	74,330	44,650	60
Las Vegas, NV	86	757,840	376,930	50
Lexington, KY	158	479,420	191,800	40
Lima, OH	33	66,570	40,100	60
Lincoln & Hastings-Kearney, NE	151	276,800	113,900	41
Little Rock-Pine Bluff, AR	177	547,950	195,130	36
Los Angeles, CA	77	5,476,830	2,772,670	51
Louisville, KY	60	662,170	355,110	54
Lubbock, TX	163	160,440	62,600	39
Macon, GA	171	232,910	86,080	37
Madison, WI	131	384,830	174,660	45
Mankato, MN	33	51,820	31,070	60
Marquette, MI	71	82,740	42,640	52
Medford-Klamath Falls, OR	181	168,710	58,430	35
Memphis, TN	145	633,930	264,870	42
Meridian, MS	195	65,300	20,540	31
Miami-Fort Lauderdale, FL	21	1,696,330	1,089,550	64
Milwaukee, WI	47	895,700	509,220	57
Minneapolis-St. Paul, MN	123	1,742,530	810,100	46
Minot-Bismarck-Dickinson (Williston), ND	60	167,010	90,060	54
Missoula, MT	199	115,020	34,080	30
Mobile, AL-Pensacola (Fort Walton Beach), FL	86	528,320	261,670	50
Monroe, LA-El Dorado, AR	189	170,890	56,060	33
Monterey-Salinas, CA	123	226,630	104,500	46
Montgomery-Selma, AL	71	230,420	120,470	52
Myrtle Beach-Florence, SC	44	291,680	168,780	58
Nashville, TN	71	1,011,570	522,450	52
New Orleans, LA	47	641,620	365,580	57
New York, NY	2	7,348,620	6,197,330	84
Norfolk-Portsmouth-Newport News, VA	25	717,170	451,660	63
North Platte, NE	115	14,370	6,690	47

Cable Statistics

DESIGNATED MARKET AREA	CABLE TV % RANK*	TV HSHLDS (Jan. 2017)	CABLE TV HSHLDS (Oct. 2016)	CABLE TV % of TV HSHLDS
Odessa-Midland, TX	104	163,450	78,280	48
Oklahoma City, OK	145	722,140	305,150	42
Omaha, NE	60	416,210	223,020	54
Orlando-Daytona Beach-Melbourne, FL	19	1,519,570	985,930	65
Ottumwa, IA-Kirksville, MO	158	44,690	17,670	40
Paducah, KY-Cape Girardeau, MO-Harrisburg, IL	177	369,390	132,510	36
Palm Springs, CA	25	158,010	100,280	63
Panama City, FL	104	141,740	68,510	48
Parkersburg, WV	28	60,620	37,520	62
Peoria-Bloomington, IL	104	235,690	112,270	48
Philadelphia, PA	6	2,942,800	2,369,790	81
Phoenix (Prescott), AZ	184	1,890,100	636,800	34
Pittsburgh, PA	13	1,160,220	818,980	71
Portland, OR	77	1,143,670	588,020	51
Portland-Auburn, ME	33	383,700	228,810	60
Presque Isle, ME	132	26,880	11,740	44
Providence, RI-New Bedford, MA	2	616,280	515,700	84
Quincy, IL-Hannibal, MO-Keokuk, IA	181	99,340	34,600	35
Raleigh-Durham (Fayetteville), NC	69	1,153,580	609,250	53
Rapid City, SD	115	99,170	47,080	47
Reno, NV	132	260,630	114,670	44
Richmond-Petersburg, VA	33	564,510	340,540	60
Roanoke-Lynchburg, VA	177	439,620	157,370	36
Rochester, MN-Mason City, IA-Austin, MN	115	141,920	67,340	47
Rochester, NY	33	404,170	243,540	60
Rockford, IL	71	170,480	88,810	52
Sacramento-Stockton-Modesto, CA	139	1,379,770	594,560	43
Salisbury, MD	21	162,050	103,360	64
Salt Lake City, UT	163	916,960	354,620	39
San Angelo, TX	77	56,680	28,790	51
San Antonio, TX	86	938,660	468,690	50
San Diego, CA	15	1,065,700	731,100	69
San Francisco-Oakland-San Jose, CA	25	2,488,090	1,561,850	63
Santa Barbara-Santa Maria-San Luis Obispo, CA	86	226,940	112,460	50
Savannah, GA	99	340,050	167,920	49
Seattle-Tacoma, WA	15	1,808,530	1,245,180	69
Sherman, TX-Ada, OK	207	126,050	25,930	21
Shreveport, LA	202	371,760	101,900	27
Sioux City, IA	139	150,790	64,170	43
Sioux Falls (Mitchell), SD	77	263,000	134,460	51
South Bend-Elkhart, IN	151	313,210	129,550	41
Spokane, WA	195	422,550	129,090	31
Springfield, MO	203	409,020	104,600	26
Springfield-Holyoke, MA	7	249,430	193,750	78
St. Joseph, MO	151	44,460	18,430	41
St. Louis, MO	86	1,215,570	604,610	50
Syracuse, NY	13	368,950	261,740	71
Tallahassee, FL-Thomasville, GA	104	268,390	127,730	48
Tampa-St. Petersburg (Sarasota), FL	8	1,908,590	1,459,670	76
Terre Haute, IN	184	133,780	45,270	34
Toledo, OH	60	400,170	216,580	54
Topeka, KS	104	172,470	82,590	48
Traverse City-Cadillac, MI	145	235,400	98,870	42
Tri-Cities, TN-VA	86	306,770	154,820	50
Tucson (Sierra Vista), AZ	151	425,860	174,420	41
Tulsa, OK	171	531,230	196,610	37
Twin Falls, ID	206	64,190	14,450	23
Tyler-Longview (Lufkin & Nacogdoches), TX	184	265,690	89,960	34
Utica, NY	21	99,190	63,900	64
Victoria, TX	139	32,930	14,010	43
Waco-Temple-Bryan, TX	158	357,720	144,720	40
Washington, DC (Hagerstown, MD)	9	2,476,680	1,823,310	74
Watertown, NY	42	88,070	51,640	59
Wausau-Rhinelander, WI	166	174,760	67,160	38
West Palm Beach-Fort Pierce, FL	9	824,920	609,180	74
Wheeling, WV-Steubenville, OH	60	128,720	69,060	54
Wichita Falls, TX & Lawton, OK	201	152,950	43,350	28
Wichita-Hutchinson, KS Plus	115	439,760	208,260	47
Wilkes Barre-Scranton-Hazleton, PA	57	554,660	305,320	55
Wilmington, NC	44	197,700	114,730	58
Yakima-Pasco-Richland-Kennewick, WA	200	230,950	66,310	29
Youngstown, OH	47	249,230	141,480	57
Yuma, AZ-El Centro, CA	189	109,930	36,090	33
Zanesville, OH	47	32,450	18,560	57

* Ranked by Cable TV Penetration, i.e Cable TV Households as % of TV Households.

Cable Statistics

A. C. Nielsen Co. Cable TV Household Estimates
Alphabetically by State

STATE	CABLE TV % RANK [1]	TV HOUSEHOLDS (Jan. 2017)	CABLE TV (Oct. 2016)	CABLE TV % OF TV HOUSEHOLDS
ALABAMA	38	1,794,810	829,710	46
ALASKA#	17	215,770	118,510	55
ARIZONA	47	2,390,460	831,840	35
ARKANSAS	45	1,097,040	404,290	37
CALIFORNIA	21	12,154,500	6,395,600	53
COLORADO	40	2,014,490	884,320	44
CONNECTICUT	3	1,288,430	1,075,900	84
DELAWARE	7	347,490	270,530	78
DIST. OF COLUMBIA	10	294,250	207,580	71
FLORIDA	12	7,771,940	5,194,620	67
GEORGIA	23	3,612,450	1,891,250	52
HAWAII	4	442,820	368,880	83
IDAHO	51	570,200	96,570	17
ILLINOIS	19	4,642,710	2,484,500	54
INDIANA	29	2,391,810	1,169,480	49
IOWA	43	1,180,130	466,300	40
KANSAS	27	1,057,190	536,940	51
KENTUCKY	32	1,644,710	790,370	48
LOUISIANA	23	1,694,640	880,500	52
MAINE	19	512,360	274,180	54
MARYLAND	8	2,172,650	1,618,980	75
MASSACHUSETTS	1	2,505,130	2,136,030	85
MICHIGAN	15	3,695,220	2,149,620	58
MINNESOTA	37	2,049,870	967,990	47
MISSISSIPPI	49	1,060,380	361,390	34
MISSOURI	42	2,269,920	952,280	42
MONTANA	47	397,340	137,180	35
NEBRASKA	29	707,170	343,510	49
NEVADA	32	1,014,000	484,610	48
NEW HAMPSHIRE	9	492,770	366,890	74
NEW JERSEY	5	3,087,810	2,537,320	82
NEW MEXICO	50	737,340	185,970	25
NEW YORK	6	6,959,020	5,488,380	79
NORTH CAROLINA	28	3,784,280	1,908,350	50
NORTH DAKOTA	17	301,980	165,280	55
OHIO	16	4,403,000	2,504,670	57
OKLAHOMA	45	1,460,340	546,440	37
OREGON	29	1,441,970	704,860	49
PENNSYLVANIA	11	4,793,660	3,321,600	69
RHODE ISLAND	1	404,620	344,120	85
SOUTH CAROLINA	32	1,821,570	879,200	48
SOUTH DAKOTA	23	321,860	166,820	52
TENNESSEE	21	2,416,400	1,273,770	53
TEXAS	38	9,480,830	4,350,970	46
UTAH	43	859,550	344,850	40
VERMONT	23	230,970	119,230	52
VIRGINIA	13	3,064,470	1,915,860	63
WASHINGTON	14	2,500,480	1,495,780	60
WEST VIRGINIA	32	710,600	337,770	48
WISCONSIN	32	2,213,920	1,064,720	48
WYOMING	41	217,810	92,920	43

[1] Ranked by cable TV penetration, i.e., cable TV households as % of TV households.
[2] Anchorage, Fairbanks and Juneau DMAs only.

U.S. CABLE PENETRATION STATE BY STATE

(As of October 2016)

Note: Figures reflect information supplied by system operators and do not include wireless cable systems.
* Basic subscribers, Expanded Basic subscribers, and Pay Unit totals include analog and digital subscribers. Some cable systems have converted to IPTV.

State	Systems	Communities Served	Basic Subscribers*	Expanded Basic Subscribers*	Pay Units*
Alabama	90	535	802,478	957	4,120
Alaska	30	55	88,922	6,780	35,487
Arizona	34	163	841,021	—	52,006
Arkansas	114	405	312,570	20,025	5,809
California	104	922	4,530,056	—	122,239
Colorado	67	268	793,044	3,991	5,621
Connecticut	11	210	876,515	—	—
Delaware	1	21	30,049	—	—
District of Columbia	1	24	33,231	—	—
Florida	56	673	3,626,593	34,945	4,035
Georgia	95	698	1,437,945	8,162	3,065
Hawaii	4	86	307,097	—	—
Idaho	26	156	99,741	1,327	374
Illinois	151	1,338	2,143,203	12,026	11,284
Indiana	53	557	641,319	324	1,492
Iowa	193	704	351,724	2,592	3,506
Kansas	110	373	332,549	13,849	22,080
Kentucky	110	908	751,675	14,671	2,658
Louisiana	89	404	575,842	9,485	347
Maine	23	367	304,400	—	1,812
Maryland	14	464	1,250,512	15,688	18,178
Massachusetts	10	368	1,817,403	—	—
Michigan	82	1,444	1,723,565	5,640	1,937
Minnesota	144	879	839,199	1,120	8,350
Mississippi	66	338	380,682	1,522	20
Missouri	86	704	798,681	5,242	130,517
Montana	63	128	124,500	45,221	1,200
Nebraska	99	337	318,883	1,747	54,465
Nevada	21	61	406,477	54,558	115
New Hampshire	11	89	102,428	—	360
New Jersey	19	701	2,124,455	10,232	194,734
New Mexico	37	122	182,958	107	3,564
New York	54	1,700	3,875,643	1,784	2,613
North Carolina	62	742	1,556,813	424	1,570
North Dakota	35	208	149,432	20,849	11,376
Ohio	91	2,102	2,178,861	4,646	9,310
Oklahoma	124	348	459,000	1,794	17,601
Oregon	47	261	601,063	176,250	197
Pennsylvania	107	2,593	2,364,881	85,716	42,583
Rhode Island	2	42	203,540	—	—
South Carolina	30	332	722,075	2,800	98,767
South Dakota	43	229	150,158	469	2,293
Tennessee	51	565	1,082,149	590	1,965
Texas	289	1,185	2,454,291	255,371	136,503
Utah	27	202	257,483	2,950	284
Vermont	10	271	283,972	826	—
Virginia	44	454	980,497	5,630	165
Washington	74	399	1,259,394	370	379
West Virginia	58	677	318,914	4,246	715
Wisconsin	121	938	807,757	5,969	6,890
Wyoming	34	84	86,237	22,981	2,606
Cuba	1	1	—	—	699
Guam	1	20	40,414	—	—
Marianas Islands	3	5	4,766	—	440
Puerto Rico	6	87	265,867	—	—
Virgin Islands	2	3	22,027	8,650	16,845
TOTAL	**3,330**	**27,950**	**49,074,951**	**872,526**	**1,043,176**

Commonly Used Initials and Abbreviations

AAAA—American Association of Advertising Agencies

A&E—Arts & Entertainment Network

AAF—American Advertising Federation

ABA—American Bar Association

ABC—American Broadcasting Co.

ABC—Australian Broadcasting Corp.

ABES—Association for Broadcast Engineering Standards

AC—alternating current

AC-3—Dolby Labs compression system for digital audio

ACA—American Cable Association

ACC—Association of Cable Communicators

ACLU—American Civil Liberties Union

ACRTF—Association Canadienne de la Radio et de la Television de Langue Francaise Inc.

ADI—Area of dominant influence

AFC—automatic frequency control

AFCCE—Association of Federal Communications Consulting Engineers

AFCEA—Armed Forces Communications & Electronics Association

AFL-CIO—American Federation of Labor & Congress of Industrial Organizations

AFM—American Federation of Musicians

AFRTS—American Forces Radio & Television Service

AFT—automatic fine tuning

AFTRA—American Federation of Television & Radio Artists

AFTS—American Forces Television Service

AGMA—American Guild of Musical Artists

AGVA—American Guild of Variety Artists

AIM—Accuracy in Media

AIT—Agency for Instructional Technology

ALS—Adult Learning Service (PBS) now

ALS—Advanced Launch System (Air Force)

AM—amplitude modulation

AMA—American Marketing Association

AMC—American Movie Classics

AMP—Association of Media Producers

AMPTP—Association of Motion Picture & Television Producers Inc.

ANA—Association of National Advertisers

ANG—American Newspaper Guild

ANPA—American Newspaper Publishers Association

AP—Associated Press

APA—Administrative Procedures Act

APBI—Associated Press Broadcasters Inc.

APRO—Association of Progressive Rental Organizations

APT—American Public Television

APTS—Association of Public TV Stations

ARF—Advertising Research Foundation

ARPA—Advanced Research Projects Agency

ARRL—American Radio Relay League

ASCAP—American Society of Composers, Authors & Publishers

ASIC—application-specific integrated circuit

ASNE—American Society of News Editors

ASTA—Advertiser Syndicated TV Association

ATAS—Academy of Television Arts & Sciences

ATIS—Automatic Transmitter Identification System (satellite)

ATSC—Advanced Television Systems Committee

ATV—Associated Television Ltd. (U.K.)

AV—audio-video, audio-visual

b&w—black & white

BAR—Broadcast Advertisers Reports

BBC—British Broadcasting Corporation

BBM—Bureau of Broadcast Measurement

BCFM—Broadcast Cable Financial Management Association

BEA—Broadcast Education Association

BEMA—Business Equipment Manufacturers Association

BET—Black Entertainment TV

BIAC—Broadcast Interassociation Council

BIB—Board for International Broadcasting

BICIAP—Broadcasting Industry Council to Improve American Productivity

BMI—Broadcast Music Inc.

BOC—Bell Operating Company

BPA—Broadcasters Promotion Association

BREMA—British Radio Equipment Manufacturers Association

BROADCAP—Broadcast Capital Fund Inc.

CAAA—Canadian Association of Advertising Agencies

CAB—Cabletelevision Advertising Bureau

CAB—Canadian Association of Broadcasters

CABLEPAC—Cable Industry Political Action Committee

CAMM—Catholic Apostolate of Mass Media

CARF—Canadian Advertising Research Foundation

CARS—Cable Television Relay Service

CARTA—Catholic Apostolate of Radio, Television & Advertising

CASA—Car Audio Specialists Association

CATV—community antenna TV, cable TV

CB—citizens band

CBA—Catholic Broadcasters Association

CBC—Canadian Broadcasting Corporation

CBO—Congressional Budget Office

CBS—formerly Columbia Broadcasting System

CC—closed captioned

CC—common carrier

CCBS—Clear Channel Broadcasting Service

CCC—Citizens Communications Center

CCD—charge-coupled device

CCIR—International Radio Consultative Committee

CCITT—International Telegraph & Telephone Consultative Committee

CCTA—Canadian Cable TV & Telecom Association

CCTV—closed-circuit television

CD—*Communications Daily*

CD—compact disc digital audio system

CD-E—erasable compact disc

CD+G—compact disc plus graphics

CD-I/CD-i—compact disc-interactive

CD-R—recordable compact disc

CD-ROM—compact disc read-only memory

CDMA—code division multiple access

CE—consumer electronics

CEA—Communications Equity Associates

CED—Committee for Economic Development

CED—*Consumer Electronics Daily*

CEDIA—Custom Electronic Design & Installation Association

CEA—Consumer Electronics Association (CEA)

CEN—Central Educational Network

CEO—chief executive officer

CEPT—Council of European Posts & Telegraph

CES—Consumer Electronics Show

CFA—Consumer Federation of America

CFO—chief financial officer

CHOB—Cannon House Office Building

CIRT—La Camera Nacional de la Industria de Radio y Televisión (Mexican Association of Broadcasters)

Abbreviations

CLeaR-TV—Christian Leaders for Responsible TV

cm—centimeter

CMA—Country Music Association

CMT—Country Music TV

CNN—Cable News Network

CNBC—Consumer News & Business Channel (NBCUniversal)

COLTAM—Committee On Local TV Audience Measurements

COMPO—Council of Motion Picture Organizations

CONTAM—Committee on Nationwide TV Audience Measurements

CONUS—contiguous U.S.

COO—chief operating officer

CP—construction permit

CPB—Corporation for Public Broadcasting

CPM—cost per thousand

CPSC—Consumer Product Safety Commission

CPU—central processing unit

CRP—circular polarization

CRT—cathode ray tube

CRTC—Canadian Radio-Television & Telecommunications Commission

CSG—Community Service Grant

C-SPAN—Cable-Satellite Public Affairs Network

CTAC—Cable Technical Advisory Committee

CTAM—Cable & Telecommunications Association for Marketing

CTIA—The Wireless Association

CTIC—Cable TV Information Center

CTPAA—Cable Television Public Affairs Association

CTV—Canadian TV Network

CTVHH—Cable TV Households

CTW—Children's Television Workshop

CU—Consumers Union

CWA—Communications Workers of America

D/A—digital-to-analog converter

DAB—digital audio broadcasting

DARS—digital audio radio service

dB—decibel

DBS—Direct Broadcast Satellite

DC—direct current

DCC—Digital Compact Cassette

DFS—Deutsches Fernsehen (Germany)

DGA—Directors Guild of America Inc.

DHS—Department of Homeland Security

DiMA—Digital Media Association

DJ—disc jockey

DMA—Designated Market Area

DMX—Digital Music Express

DoD—Department of Defense

DoJ—Department of Justice

DoT—Department of Transportation

DSA—Distinguished Service Award (NAB)

DSI—digital speech interpolation

DSOB—Dirksen Senate Office Building

DSP—digital signal processing

DSR—Statsradiofonien (Denmark)

DSRC—David Sarnoff Research Center

DSS—Digital Satellite System

DTH—direct to home (satellite transmission)

DTV—digital television

DVD—digital versatile disc

DVR—digital video recording, recorder

EBS—Educational Broadband Service

EBS—Emergency Broadcast System

EBS—Emergency Broadcasting Service

EBU—European Broadcasting Union

EEC—European Economic Community

EEN—Eastern Educational Network

EEO—Equal Employment Opportunity

EEOC—Equal Employment Opportunity Commission

EHF—extremely high frequency

EIA—Energy Information Administration

EIAJ—Electronic Industries Association of Japan

EIAK—Electronic Industries Association of Korea

EIRP—effective isotropically radiated power

EL—electro luminescence

EMRC—Electronic Media Rating Council

ENG—electronic news gathering

EP—extended play

EPA—Environmental Protection Agency

EPG—Electronic Program Guide

ERA—Electronics Representatives Association

ERP—effective radiated power

ESA—European Space Agency

ESPN—Entertainment & Sports Programming Network

ESRB—Entertainment Software Rating Board

ETNO—European Telecommunications Network Operators' Association

ETV—educational television

EUTELSAT—European Telecommunications Satellite Organization

EWTN—Eternal Word TV Network

FAA—Federal Aviation Administration

FAIR—Fairness & Accuracy in Reporting

FB—*Factbook*

FBA—Federal Bar Association

FBI—Federal Bureau of Investigation

FCBA—Federal Communications Bar Association

FCC—Federal Communications Commission

FDA—Food & Drug Administration

FEC—Federal Election Commission

FED—field emitter display

FET—field effect transistor

FM—frequency modulation

FOIA—Freedom of Information Act

FSI—free standing insert

FSS—fixed satellite service

FTC—Federal Trade Commission

FTTH—Fiber to the Home

GAO—Government Accountability Office

GATT—General Agreement on Tariffs & Trade

GDP—gross domestic product

GEC—General Electric Co. Ltd. (U.K.)

GEO—geostationary orbit

GHz—GigaHertz

GNP—gross national product

GPO—Government Printing Office

HBO—Home Box Office

HDTV—high definition television

HGTV—Home & Garden Television

HHS—Department of Health & Human Services

HITS—Headend in the Sky

HRRC—Home Recording Rights Coalition

HRTS—Hollywood Radio & TV Society

HSN—Home Shopping Network

HSOB—Hart Senate Office Building

HUD—Department of Housing & Urban Development

HUR—Households Using Radio

HUT—Households Using TV

Hz—Hertz (cycles per second)

IAAB—Inter-American Association of Broadcasters

IASU—International Association of Satellite Users

IATSE—International Alliance of Theatrical Stage Employees & Moving Picture Machine Operators

IBA—Independent Broadcasting Authority (U.K.)

IBEW—International Brotherhood of Electrical Workers

IBFM—Institute of Broadcasting Financial Management

IBM—International Business Machines

IC—integrated circuit

ICCE—International Conference on Consumer Electronics

ICT—Information & Communications Technology industry

IDSA—Interactive Digital Software Association

IEEE—Institute of Electrical & Electronic Engineers

IFA—Internationale Funkausstellung (Berlin consumer electronics show)

IFRB—International Frequency Registration Board

IIA—Information Industry Association

IMA—Interactive Multimedia Association

IMPPA—Independent Motion Picture Producers Association

Abbreviations

INMARSAT—International Maritime Satellite Organization

INTELSAT—International Telecommunication Satellite Organization

IPPV—Impulse Pay-Per-View

IPO—initial public offering

ips—inches per second

IPTV—Internet Protocol Television

IRAC—Interdepartment Radio Advisory Committee

IRD—integrated receiver/decoder for satellite reception

IRS—Internal Revenue Service

IRTS—International Radio & Television Society Inc.

ISA—Interactive Services Association

ISCET—International Society of Certified Electronics Technicians

ITA—International Trade Administration

ITC—Independent Television Corporation (U.K.)

ITC—International Trade Commission

ITFS—instructional television fixed service

ITN—Independent TV News Association (U.K.)

ITU—International Telecommunication Union

ITV—industrial TV, institutional TV, instructional TV, interactive TV

ITVA—Interactive TV Association

ITVA—International TV Association

IUE—International Union of Electrical Radio & Machine Workers

JCET—Joint Council on Educational Telecommunications

JEDEC—Joint Electron Device Engineering Council

JPEG—Joint Photographic Experts Group

JTAC—Joint Technical Advisory Council

JVC—Japan Victor Corporation

K—Kelvin (temperature)

kbps—kilobits per second

kHz—kilohertz

km—kilometer

kw—kilowatt

LAN—local area network

LCD—liquid crystal display

LEC—local exchange carrier

LED—light-emitting diode

LEO—low earth orbit

LF—low frequency

LG, LGE—formerly Lucky Goldstar & Goldstar Electronics

LHOB—Longworth House Office Building

LMAC—Land Mobile Advisory Committee

LMA—local marketing agreement

LMDS—Local Multipoint Distribution Service

LNA—low noise amplifier

LNB—low noise block (downconverter)

LPTV—low power TV

m—meter

MAC—multiplexed analog components

MAP—Media Access Project

MB—Media Bureau

Mbps—megabits per second

MCA—formerly Music Corporation of America

MDS—Multipoint Distribution Service

MDU—multiple dwelling unit

MECA—Matsushita Electric Corporation of America

MEI—Matsushita Electric Industries

MF—medium frequency

MFJ—Modified Final Judgment

MGM—Metro-Goldwyn-Mayer

MHz—megahertz

MITI—Ministry of International Trade & Industry (Japan)

mm—millimeter

MMCD—MultiMedia Compact Disc (Sony/Phillips DVD format)

MMDS—Multichannel Multipoint Distribution Service

MMTC—Minority Media & Telecommunications Council

MOS—metal oxide silicon

MPA—Motion Picture Association

MPAA—Motion Picture Association of America

MPC-1/MPC-2—Multimedia Personal Computer standard configurations

MPEG—Moving Picture Experts Group

MPR—Minnesota Public Radio

MPU—microprocessor unit

mR—milliroentgens

MSG—Madison Square Garden

MSO—multiple system operator (cable TV)

MSGN—Madison Square Garden Network

MTS—multichannel TV sound

MTV—Music Television

MUSE—Multiple Sub-Nyquist Encoding (Japanese high definition satellite transmission system)

NAACP—National Association for the Advancement of Colored People

NAB—National Association of Broadcasters

NABET—National Association of Broadcast Employees & Technicians

NABOB—National Association of Black-Owned Broadcasters

NABUG—National Association of Broadcast Unions & Guilds

NACo—National Association of Counties

NAD 27—North American Datum of 1927

NAFB—National Association of Farm Broadcasters

NAFTA—North American Free Trade Agreement

NAITPD—National Association of Independent Television Producers & Directors

NAM—National Association of Manufacturers

NAMM—National Association of Music Merchants

NAPAN—National Association of Public Affairs Networks

NARB—National Advertising Review Board

NARBA—North American Radio Broadcasting Agreement

NARDA—National Appliance & Radio-Electronic Dealers Association

NARDA—National Association of Retail Dealers of America

NARM—National Association of Recording Merchandisers

NARUC—National Association of Regulatory Utility Commissioners

NASA—National Aeronautics & Space Administration

NASB—National Association of Spanish Broadcasters

NASRC—National AM Stereo Radio Committee

NATAS—National Academy of Television Arts & Sciences

NATO—National Association of Theater Owners

NATOA—National Association of Telecommunications Officers & Advisers

NATPE—National Association of Television Program Executives

NATT—National Association of Towns & Townships

NAVA—National Audio-Visual Association Inc.

NAVD—National Association of Video Distributors

NBA—National Basketball Association

NBC—National Broadcasting Company

NBEA—National Broadcast Editorial Association

NBLC—National Black Lawyers Conference

NBMC—National Black Media Coalition

NBN—National Black Network

NCAA—National Collegiate Athletic Association

NCCB—National Citizens Committee for Broadcasting

NCCPTV—National Citizens Committee for Public TV

NCI—National Captioning Institute

NCPAC—National Conservative Political Action Committee

NCRP—National Council for Radiation Protection & Measurements

NCSL—National Conference of State Legislatures

NCTA—National Cable Telecommunications Association

NCTC—National Cable Television Cooperative

NEA—National Endowment for the Arts

NEC—Nippon Electric Corporation

NEDA—National Electrical Distributors Association

NEH—National Endowment for the Humanities

NEMA—National Electrical Manufacturers Association

NESDA—National Electronics Service Dealers Association

NESN—New England Sports Network

NET—National Educational Television

NETA—National Educational Telecommunications Association

Abbreviations

NEW—National Electronics Week (parts show)

NFA—National Federation of Advertising Agencies

NHK—Nippon Hoso Kyokai (Japan Broadcasting Corporation)

NIAC—National Industry Advisory Committee

NIH—National Institutes of Health

NIMLO—National Institute of Municipal Law Officers

NIST—National Institute for Science & Technology

NLC—National League of Cities

NLRB—National Labor Relations Board

NMPA—National Music Publishers' Association

NNA—National Newspaper Association

NoI—notice of inquiry

NORC—National Opinion & Research Center

NOW—National Organization of Women

NPC—National Press Club

NPR—National Public Radio

NPRM—notice of proposed rule making

NRB—National Religious Broadcasters

NRMA—National Retail Merchants Association

NRSC—National Radio Systems Committee

NRTC—National Rural Telecommunications Cooperative

NSI—Nielsen Station Index

NTA—National Translator Association

NTCA—National Telecommunications Cooperative Association

NTFC—National Television Film Council

NTI—Nielsen TV Index

NTIA—National Telecommunications & Information Administration (Department of Commerce)

NTIS—National Technical Information Service

NTSC—National Television System Committee

NUBA—National UHF Broadcasters Association

o-&-o—owned & operated stations (by network)

OEM—original equipment manufacturer

OEO—Office of Economic Opportunity

OET—Office of Engineering & Technology

OFS—Operational Fixed Service

OMB—Office of Management & Budget

OPP—Office of Strategic Planning & Policy Analysis

OSHA—Occupational Safety & Health Administration

OTA—Office of Technology Assessment

PA—public address (system)

PAL—phase alternation line (European color system)

PAX—PaxNet

PBR—Public Broadcasting Report

PBS—Public Broadcasting Service

PC—personal computer

PCS—personal communications system/service

PEG—public, educational, government cable access channels

PIB—Publishers Information Bureau

PIP—picture in picture

PMN—Pacific Mountain Network

POP—point-of-purchase

PPT—pay-per-transaction

PPV—pay-per-view

PR—public relations

PRI—Public Radio International

PSA—public service announcement

PSA—pre-sunrise authorization

PSHSB—Public Safety & Homeland Security Bureau of the FCC.

PSSC—Public Service Satellite Consortium

PTA—Parent Teachers Association

PTA—program test authorization

PTAR—prime time access rule

PTL—Public TV Library

PTV—projection TV

PTV—public TV

QVC—Quality, Value, Convenience Inc.

RAB—Radio Advertising Bureau

RADAR—Radio's All-Dimension Audience Research

RAI—Radiotelevisione Italiana

RAM—random access memory

R&D—research & development

RARC—Regional Administrative Radio Conference

RASO—Radio Allocations Study Organization

RF—radio frequency

RFA—Regulatory Flexibility Act

RFE—Radio Free Europe

RHC—regional holding company

RHOB—Rayburn House Office Building

RIAA—Recording Industry Association of America

RIO—Radio Information Office (NAB)

RISC—Reduced Instruction Set Computing

ROM—read-only memory

RSAC—Recreational Software Advisory Council

RSOB—Russell Senate Office Building

RTCA—Radio-Television Correspondents' Association

RTO—rent-to-own

RTDNA—Radio Television Digital News Association

SAG—Screen Actors Guild

SAP—Separate Audio Program (see MTS)

SBA—Small Business Administration

SBCA—Satellite Broadcasting & Communications Association

SBE—Society of Broadcast Engineers

SBRTC—Southern Baptist Radio-TV Commission

SCA—subsidiary communication authorization

SCTE—Society of Cable Telecommunications Engineers

SD—super density digital compact disk

SEC—Securities & Exchange Commission

SECA—Southern Educational Communications Association

SECAM—sequential couleur a memoire (French color TV system)

SESAC—music licensing society similar to ASCAP & BMI

SHF—super high frequency

SIA—Satellite Industry Association

SIMPP—Society of Independent Motion Picture Producers

SIP—Station Independence Program

SKU—stock-keeping unit

SMATV—Satellite Master Antenna Television

SMPTE—Society of Motion Picture & TV Engineers

SMR—specialized mobile radio

SMSA—Standard Metropolitan Statistical Area

SOB—Senate Office Building

SPA—Software Publishers Association

SPJ—Society of Professional Journalists

SRA—Station Representatives Association Inc.

SS—solid state

SSB—single side band

STA—special temporary authorization

STL—studio-to-transmitter link

S-VHS—Super VHS

SW—*Satellite Week* (See CD)

TARPAC—Television & Radio Political Action Committee

TARPEC—Television & Radio Political Education Committee

TASC—The Analytic Sciences Corp.

TASO—Television Allocations Study Organization

TBA—time brokerage agreement

TBC—time base corrector

TBN—Trinity Broadcasting Network

TBS—Turner Broadcasting System

3DO—a CD multimedia system and company

TI—Texas Instruments

TIA—Telecommunications Industry Association

TCM—Turner Classic Movies

TDMA—time division multiple access

TLC—The Learning Channel

TMC—The Movie Channel

TMO—Telemundo

TNE—The New Encore

TNT—Turner Network Television

TPG—Television Producers Guild

TPO—transmitter power output

TR—transponder

Abbreviations

TRAFCO—TV, Radio & Film Commission of Methodist Church

TV—television

TVB—Television Bureau of Advertising

TVHH—TV Households

TVI—TV interference

TVRO—TV receive-only earth station

TWC—The Weather Channel

TWTA—traveling wave tube amplifier

UE—United Electrical, Radio & Machine Workers of America

UHF—ultra high frequency

UHF-ICC—UHF Industry Coordinating Committee

UIT—See ITU

UK—United Kingdom

UL—Underwriters' Laboratories Inc.

UNESCO—United Nations Educational, Scientific and Cultural Organization

UNV—Univision

USIA—U.S. Information Agency

USTA—U.S. Telecommunications Association

USTR—United States Trade Representative

VBI—vertical blanking interval

VCPS—Video Copyright Protection Society

VCR—videocassette recorder

VDT—video display terminal

VH1—Video Hits One

VHF—very high frequency

VHS—Video Home System (a VCR format)

VHS-C—compact VHS

VLF—very low frequency

VOA—Voice of America

VOD—Video on-demand

VSB—vestigial sideband

VSDA—Video Software Dealers Association

VTR—videotape recording or video tape recorder

w—watt

"W"—widescreen picture when used in diagonal measurement

WARC—World Administrative Radio Conference

WCA—Wireless Communications Association

WE—Women's Entertainment

WESCON—Western Electronic Show & Convention

WGA—Writers Guild of America

WGAW—Writers Guild of America-West

WICT—Women in Cable Telecommunications

WID—*Washington Internet Daily*

W-VHS—Widescreen Video Home System (HDTV recording system)

WWE—World Wrestling Entertainment

XDS—extended data system

Glossary of Cable Television Terms

Derived in part from the glossaries of CableLabs and The National Cable & Telecommunications Association

Access Channels—Channels set aside by the cable operator for use by the public, educational institutions, municipal government or for lease on a non-discriminatory basis.

ACE—See CableACE.

Addressability—The capability of controlling the operation of individual cable subscriber terminals by sending commands from a central computer. See also Two-Way.

Aerial Plant—Cable that is suspended in the air generally on telephone or utility poles.

Affiliate—A TV station which carries, by contractual agreement, network programming. Also, the cable system to which a program service transmits its programming, usually by satellite.

Amplifier—A device that boosts the strength of an electronic signal. Amplifiers are spaced at regular intervals throughout a cable system to maintain the signal strength.

Analog—Transmission of audio and/or video signal by a continually variable waveform signal.

Bandwidth—The portion of the radio spectrum needed to transmit pictures, sound or both. Analog U.S. TV stations use a bandwidth of six million cycles per second (6 megahertz). 6 MHz is also used for digital TV channels since analog is much less prevelant.

Basic Cable—Usually the minimum amount of cable TV service available to a subscriber for a standard installation & monthly fee. It generally includes over-the-air broadcast signals & local originations.

Bi-directional—Two way cable communications.

Broadband—A transmission medium that allows transmission of voice, data & video simultaneously at rates of 1.544 Mbps or higher. Broadband transmission media generally can carry multiple channels—each at a different frequency or specific time slot.

C-band—Frequencies in the 4 & 6 GHz regions used in satellite earth station feeds in many television station configurations.

CableACE (Award for Cablecasting Excellence)—The cable TV industry's highest award for original, made-for-cable programming both locally & nationally.

CableCARD—A card that allows consumers to connect to cable TV without a set top box & can provide digital & high definition television service to HDTVs, PCs & DVRs.

Cablecasting—To originate programming over a cable system. Includes public access programming.

Cable Modem—A two-way device allowing the delivery & reception of broadband data to & from a subscriber's PC and other Internet protocol-connected devices via cable.

Cable Penetration—The percentage of TV homes subscribing to cable TV.

Cable System—Facility that provides cable service in a given geographic area, comprised of one or more headends.

Cable Television—A communications system that distributes broadcast TV signals plus satellite signals, original programming & other material by means of a coaxial and/or fiber optic cable.

Cable TV Households—An occupied dwelling unit with one or more television sets currently receiving cable television service.

CARS (Cable Television Relay Services)—A microwave system used to relay TV, FM radio, cablecasting & other signals to a terminal for distribution over cable.

Cash Flow—Cash flow is defined as operating income minus interest expense & it basically indicates the amount of cash available before taxes, capital expenditures & debt retirement.

CG (Character Generator)—A device which electronically displays letters & numbers on the TV screen.

Channel Capacity—The maximum number of channels that a system can carry simultaneously.

Churn—The percentage of cable TV subscribers that add or delete program services, or cable service entirely.

Class A Television Service—An FCC classification, created under a November 1999 Act of Congress, of certain qualifying low-power TV stations which have more interference protection from full service stations than most LPTV stations.

Coaxial Cable—An actual line of transmission for carrying TV signals. Its principal conductor is either a pure copper or copper-coated wire, surrounded by insulation & then encased in aluminum or copper.

Common Carrier—The generic name for any medium which carries messages prepared by others for a fee & is required by law to offer its services on a non-discriminatory basis. Common carriers are regulated by federal & state agencies and exercise no control over message content.

Compression—The act of reducing the amount of bandwidth needed to carry audio and/or video signals. Either analog or digital compression is technically possible.

Converter—A device that, associated with a TV set, can increase the channel capacity of the TV set or convert signals between analog & digital.

DBS (Direct Broadcast Satellite)—A system in which signals are transmitted directly from a satellite to a home receiving dish. DBS refers specifically to high-power transmissions in bands specified by the FCC.

Demographics—The breakdown by age, sex, income levels, education, race, etc. of TV viewers.

Descrambler—An electronic circuit that restores a scrambled video signal to its original form.

Digital—Binary number method for signal and/or data transmission.

Digital Service (contour)—See Noise Limited Contour.

Digital Transmission—A way of increasing channel capacity through digital compression rather than laying new cable. To receive the service, a subscriber needs a digital converter.

Dish—The installation, also called an earth station, for receiving and/or transmitting electronic signals between the earth & communications satellites.

Distant Signal—A TV channel from another market imported & carried by a cable TV system.

DMA (Designated Market Area)—The Nielsen definition of a viewing market for rating & sales purposes. A DMA market is composed of all counties in which commercial stations assigned to the market achieve the largest share of audience.

Downstream—The flow of signals from the cable system headend through the distribution network to the subscriber.

Drop Cable—The small-diameter cable feeding into the subscriber's home.

DVR (Digital Video Recorder)—An electronic device that records video in a digital format. Also referred to as a personal video recorder (PVR).

Earth Station—A structure, including satellite dishes, used for receiving and/or transmitting signals to or from a satellite.

Educational Broadband Service—Channels used to provide educational instruction and cultural & professional development in schools & other institutions, as well as other wireless services. The channels are often used for wireless communications.

Exclusivity—The contractual right to be the sole exhibitor of a program in a particular area during a particular time.

Expanded Basic—Additional cable service or services offered to the subscriber at a charge in addition to the basic cable service.

Fiber Optic Cable—Very thin & pliable cylinders of glass or plastic in a weather-resistant sheathing which carry data as light waves in wide bands of frequencies. Can be used to replace or supplement coaxial cable.

Franchise—The contractual agreement between a cable operator & a governmental body which defines the rights & responsibilities of each in the construction & operation of a cable TV system.

Franchising Authority—The governmental body (such as a local franchise authority) responsible for specifying the terms of a franchise, awarding it & regulating its operation. While the franchising authority is usually a local city or county body, some areas are regulated on the state level.

FTTx (Fiber to the X)—Generic term for a broadband telecommunications system based on fiber optic cables. Can be Fiber to the Node (FTTN), Fiber to the Curb (FTTC), Fiber to the Building (FTTB), Fiber to the Home (FTTH) or Fiber to the Premises (FTTP), which includes buildings & homes.

Governmental Cablecasting—An opportunity for federal, state & local officials to disseminate information to their constituents via cable TV.

Grandfathering—The situation that exists when a law is passed after a distribution system has begun operating, and the system may be exempt from that law.

Headend—The electronic control center of the cable system. This is the site of the receiving antenna & the signal processing equipment.

Homes Passed—The total number of homes passed by a cable system, thus having the potential of being served promptly.

Hubs—Local distribution centers where signals are taken from a master feed & transmitted over cable to subscribers.

Impulse Pay-Per-View—PPV programming which can be ordered instantly through a remote control or similar device.

Glossary of Terms

Independent—A cable TV system individually owned & operated, not affiliated with a multiple-system operator. Also, a TV station not affiliated with a major network.

Institutional Loop—The upstream transmission of signals from schools, libraries, etc., to the cable headend where the signals are added to the downstream distribution to subscribers. It also can be a separate, closed system interconnecting governmental agencies for sending & receiving voice and data.

Interactive—A sophisticated two-way system which has the capability of connecting more than two points.

Interconnect—The transmission of cable signals or advertising from one cable system to another so that programming & information may be shared.

IPTV (Internet Protocol Television)—Digital television service delivered via a broadband internet connection.

ITFS (Instructional Television Fixed Service)—See Educational Broadband Service.

Ku-band—Frequencies in the 12 GHz band used for business & video satellite services.

Leased access—Section 612 of the Communications Act of 1934, as amended, 47 U.S.C. § 532, and the Commission's leased access rules, 47 C.F.R. §§ 76.970 through 76.977 (October 2007 Edition), require a cable operator to set aside channel capacity for commercial use by unaffiliated video programmers. Commercial use means the provision of video programming, whether or not for profit.

Leased Channels—Any channel made available by the operator for a fee.

LMDS (Local Multipoint Distribution Service)—An MDS service which may be used to supplement capacity of wireless cable systems or for non-video data or other purposes.

Local Franchising Authority—Entity granted authority to regulate cable rates in a specified service area according to provisions in the FCC cable rules.

Local Origination Programming (LO)—Programming developed, leased or purchased by a cable TV system for the community it serves.

Local Signals—Over-the-air broadcast signals available within the community, usually carried on a cable system's minimum service level of programming.

Low-Power TV (LPTV)—A secondary broadcast television service licensed at a low power. Some LPTV stations provide original programming; some are affiliates of national or regional networks; others operate as translators for full-power TV stations. See also Class A Television Service.

LTE (Long-term Evolution)—Wireless broadband technology that will support speeds of over 300 Mbps downstream & 75 Mbps upstream.

MDS (Multipoint Distribution Service)—A private service utilizing a very high frequency to transmit one TV signal or other services. It is commonly used to broadcast pay TV or as part of a wireless phone system.

Microwave—A transmitting system that relays signals from one tower to another, linking cable systems or other services.

Miles of Plant—The total miles, to the nearest tenth, of coaxial and/or fiber optic cable in use to provide cable in each system's service area.

MMDS (Multichannel Multipoint Distribution Service)—An MDS service with the capability of transmitting more than one TV signal. Also known as wireless cable.

MSO (Multiple System Operator)—A company that owns & operates more than one cable system. Also called group operator.

Multiplexing—Practice of cable programmers, such as HBO & Showtime, of providing multiple channels of different programming simultaneously.

Must Carry—Provision in the Cable Act of 1992 by which a broadcast station is entitled to carriage of its signal by a cable system.

Narrowcasting—The delivery of specialized programming to a specific audience.

NCTA (National Cable & Telecommunications Association)—The major trade association for the cable TV industry. See index for complete listing.

Network—An entity that offers programming on a regular basis for 15 hours or more per week to either regional or national affiliates under contract. A network may be either broadcast or cable TV oriented; both are usually delivered via satellite.

Nielsen—A rating service which provides statistical information on viewing habits & demographics.

Non-duplication Rules—Restrictions placed on cable TV systems prohibiting them from importing distant programming which is simultaneously available from local TV stations.

Noise Limited Contour—The area where the predicted field strength of the station's signal exceeds the following levels (these are the levels at which reception of DTV service is limited by noise): Channels 2-6 28 dBu; Channels 7-13 36 dBu; Channels 14-69 41 dBu.

North American Datum of 1927 (NAD-27)—A system of latitude & longitude points established in 1927 which is the standard used by the FCC.

Off-air—Programming received at the cable system headend from over-the-air broadcast signals.

Open Cable—Interoperable digital set-top boxes which will provide greater access to interactive services.

Operating Income—Operating income is the difference between the revenues & direct operating expenses, before interest, depreciation & income taxes.

Ordinance—Enabling legislation passed by a local government to establish guidelines for the franchising process.

Overbuilder—A company that utilizes or builds on to existing infrastructure in areas where there is already cable service.

Pay-Per-View—Cable programming for which subscribers pay on a one-time basis for individual programs, such as prize fights, Broadway & movie premieres. See also Video On Demand.

Pay Programming—Movies, sports & other programs available to the cable subscriber for a charge in addition to the basic fee.

Pay Units—A total count of the number of individual pay subscriptions sold by a cable operator for one or more pay programming services.

Penetration—The ratio of the number of cable subscribers (or pay TV subscribers) to the total number of households passed by the system (or basic subscribers).

Pole Attachments—The multichannel video programming distributor hookups to telephone or utility poles.

Retransmission Consent—Negotiated agreement under terms specified in the Cable Act of 1992 by which a broadcast station may be entitled to some consideration in exchange for carriage of its signal by a multichannel video programming distributor.

RFP (Request for Proposals)—The document issued by the franchising authority for the applicant's use. It usually states proposed guidelines, outlines minimum requirements for each applicant & specifies application deadlines.

Satellite—A device in orbit that receives & transmits signals.

Security System—The capability of providing interactive services such as emergency rescue, burglar & fire alarm protection.

Shop-at-Home—Programs allowing subscribers to view products & order them by cable or telephone, including catalogs, shopping, shows, etc.

Significantly Viewed—Television stations achieving a 3% share of weekly viewing hours (2% for independent stations), and a net weekly circulation of 25% (5% for independent stations) in a given community.

Submarine Installation—The laying of cable underwater, as opposed to aerial suspension on poles.

Subscriber—A person who pays a multichannel video programming distributor for the reception of programs & other electronic services.

Syndicated Exclusivity (Syn Ex)—An FCC rule requiring cable systems to black out portions of distant signals in order to protect syndicated programming which local TV broadcasters have under an exclusive contract.

Television Households—An occupied dwelling unit with one or more television sets.

Tiered Programming—More than one cable service offered to the subscriber at a charge in addition to the basic cable service.

Total Households—All occupied dwelling units in a given area.

Translator—A small transmitter that picks up a distant TV signal, converts it to another channel to avoid interference & retransmits it into areas the original TV station could not reach.

Transponder—The part of the satellite that receives and re-transmits a signal.

TV Market Ranking—The 35-mile radius zone surrounding a community with an operating commercial station found in the markets listed in Sections 76.51 & 76.53 of the FCC cable rules.

Two-Way—A term used to describe a cable system that enables signals to pass in both directions between the headend and the subscriber.

Underground Installation—The burying of cable underground, as opposed to aerial suspension on poles.

Upstream—The flow of signals from the subscriber or remote origination point to the headend.

Video On-Demand (VOD)—Allows VCR-type control of video or movies offered on PPV basis.

Wide Area Network (WAN)—A computer network which usually spans larger geographic area, such as cities, counties, states & nations. WAN's usually employ telephone-type topologies, like T1, T2, T5, ATM, etc. The Internet is a WAN which is held together by Local Area Networks (LANs), which network computers.

Wideband—Typically, the term wideband represents a medium intermediate between narrowband & broadband. Wideband is capable of transmitting at more than 64 Kbps & less than 1.5 Mbps.

Wi-Fi (Wireless Fidelity)—A wireless technology brand owned by the Wi-Fi Alliance intended to improve the interoperability of wireless local area network products based on the IEEE 802.11 standards.

WiMAX (Worldwide Interoperability for Microwave Access)—Technology that uses fixed, local radio cells to provide high-speed Internet access via the air interface. A wireless broadband technology with a range of up to 80km and a bandwith of up to 75bps.

Cable Community Index

ALABAMA

ABBEVILLE—Comcast Cable. Now served by TALLAHASSEE, FL [FL0283]

ABERNANT—Formerly served by Comcast Cable. No longer in operation

ADAMSVILLE—See BIRMINGHAM, AL (AT&T U-verse. This is the regional video hub for the BIRMINGHAM area)

ADAMSVILLE—See PELHAM, AL (Charter Communications)

ADDISON—Charter Communications. Now served by PELHAM, AL [AL0192]

ADDISON—See BIRMINGHAM, AL (AT&T U-verse. This is the regional video hub for the BIRMINGHAM area)

ADDISON—See PELHAM, AL (Charter Communications)

AKRON (town)—Formerly served by CableSouth Inc. No longer in operation

ALABASTER—See BIRMINGHAM, AL (AT&T U-verse. This is the regional video hub for the BIRMINGHAM area)

ALABASTER—See PELHAM, AL (Charter Communications)

ALBERTVILLE—Charter Communications. Now served by DECATUR, AL [AL0184]

ALBERTVILLE—See BIRMINGHAM, AL (AT&T U-verse. This is the regional video hub for the BIRMINGHAM area)

ALBERTVILLE—See DECATUR, AL (Charter Communications)

ALEXANDER CITY—Charter Communications. Now served by PELHAM, AL [AL0192]

ALEXANDER CITY—See PELHAM, AL (Charter Communications)

ALEXANDRIA—See BIRMINGHAM, AL (AT&T U-verse. This is the regional video hub for the BIRMINGHAM area)

ALICEVILLE—Northland Cable Television

ALLGOOD—Formerly served by South-Tel Communications L.P. No longer in operation

ALLGOOD—See ONEONTA, AL (Otelco)

ALTOONA—Formerly served by Charter Communications. No longer in operation

ALTOONA—See ONEONTA, AL (Otelco)

ANDALUSIA—TV Cable Company of Andalusia

ANDERSON—See ROGERSVILLE, AL (Zito Media)

ANNISTON ARMY DEPOT—See ANNISTON, AL (Cable One)

ANNISTON—See BIRMINGHAM, AL (AT&T U-verse. This is the regional video hub for the BIRMINGHAM area)

ANNISTON—Cable One

ANTIOCH—See HEATH, AL (TV Cable Company of Andalusia)

APPLETON—Formerly served by Trust Cable. No longer in operation

ARAB—See DECATUR, AL (Charter Communications)

ARAB—See BAILEYTON, AL (Zito Media)

ARDMORE—Mediacom

ARDMORE—See ARDMORE, TN (Mediacom)

ARGO—See PELHAM, AL (Charter Communications)

ARITON—See CLIO, AL (Bright House Networks)

ARLEY—Formerly served by Zoom Media. No longer in operation

ARLEY—See BIRMINGHAM, AL (AT&T U-verse. This is the regional video hub for the BIRMINGHAM area)

ASHFORD—See DOTHAN, AL (WOW! Internet, Cable & Phone)

ASHLAND—See LINEVILLE, AL (Charter Communications)

ASHVILLE—Charter Communications. Now served by PELHAM, AL [AL0192]

ASHVILLE—See PELHAM, AL (Charter Communications)

ATHENS—Charter Communications. Now served by DECATUR, AL [AL0184]

ATHENS—Formerly served by Madison Communications. No longer in operation

ATHENS—Formerly served by WOW! Internet, Cable & Phone. No longer in operation

ATHENS—See BIRMINGHAM, AL (AT&T U-verse. This is the regional video hub for the BIRMINGHAM area)

ATHENS—See DECATUR, AL (Charter Communications)

ATHENS—See HUNTSVILLE, AL (WOW! Internet, Cable & Phone)

ATMORE—Mediacom. Now served by GULF BREEZE, FL [FL0070]

ATTALIA—See BIRMINGHAM, AL (AT&T U-verse. This is the regional video hub for the BIRMINGHAM area)

ATTALLA—Comcast Cable. Now served by TUPELO, MS [MS0009]

AUBURN—Charter Communications. Now served by PELHAM, AL [AL0192]

AUBURN—Auburn University Campus Cable System

AUBURN—See PELHAM, AL (Charter Communications)

AUTAUGA COUNTY (PORTIONS)—See MONTGOMERY, AL (WOW! Internet, Cable & Phone)

AUTAUGA COUNTY—See MONTGOMERY, AL (Charter Communications)

AUTAUGAVILLE—Formerly served by NewWave Communications. No longer in operation

AVON—See DOTHAN, AL (WOW! Internet, Cable & Phone)

AXIS—See MOBILE COUNTY, AL (Mediacom)

BABBIE—See HEATH, AL (TV Cable Company of Andalusia)

BAILEYTON—See BIRMINGHAM, AL (AT&T U-verse. This is the regional video hub for the BIRMINGHAM area)

BAILEYTON—Zito Media

BALDWIN COUNTY (northwestern portion)—Formerly served by Baldwin County Cable. No longer in operation

BALDWIN COUNTY (portions)—Mediacom. Now served by FAIRHOPE, AL [AL0124]

BALDWIN COUNTY (PORTIONS)—See FAIRHOPE, AL (Mediacom)

BALDWIN COUNTY (PORTIONS)—See ROBERTSDALE, AL (Mediacom)

BANKS—See TROY, AL (Troy Cablevision. Formerly [AL0032]. This cable system has converted to IPTV)

BARBOUR COUNTY (UNINCORPORATED AREAS)—See EUFAULA, AL (Bright House Networks)

BARNWELL—Mediacom. Now served by FAIRHOPE, AL [AL0124]

BARNWELL—See FAIRHOPE, AL (Mediacom)

BAY MINETTE—Mediacom. Now served by FAIRHOPE, AL [AL0124]

BAY MINETTE—See FAIRHOPE, AL (Mediacom)

BAYOU LA BATRE—See MOBILE COUNTY, AL (Mediacom)

BEAR CREEK—See HALEYVILLE, AL (Zito Media)

BEATRICE—TV Cable Company of Andalusia

BEAVERTON—See SULLIGENT, AL (Charter Communications)

BELK—See FAYETTE, AL (West Alabama TV Cable Co. Inc)

BELLAMY—Community Cable & Broadband LLC

BERRY—Formerly served by Almega Cable. No longer in operation

BESSEMER (PORTIONS)—See BIRMINGHAM, AL (Bright House Networks)

BESSEMER—See BIRMINGHAM, AL (AT&T U-verse. This is the regional video hub for the BIRMINGHAM area)

BESSEMER—See PELHAM, AL (Charter Communications)

BEULAH—Charter Communications. Now served by NEWNAN, GA [GA0042]

BIBB COUNTY (PORTIONS)—See CENTREVILLE, AL (Community Cable & Broadband LLC)

BIBB COUNTY (UNINCORPORATED AREAS)—See BIRMINGHAM, AL (AT&T U-verse. This is the regional video hub for the BIRMINGHAM area)

BIG COVE—Formerly served by Mediacom. No longer in operation

BIRMINGHAM (PORTIONS)—See PELHAM, AL (Charter Communications)

2017 Edition

Alabama—Cable Community Index

BIRMINGHAM—AT&T U-verse. This is the regional video hub for the BIRMINGHAM area

BIRMINGHAM—Bright House Networks

BLOUNT COUNTY (NORTHWESTERN PORTION)—See CULLMAN, AL (Charter Communications)

BLOUNT COUNTY (PORTIONS)—See ONEONTA, AL (Otelco)

BLOUNT COUNTY (UNINCORPORATED AREAS)—See BIRMINGHAM, AL (AT&T U-verse. This is the regional video hub for the BIRMINGHAM area)

BLOUNT COUNTY—Formerly served by Alabama Broadband LLC. Now served by Charter Communications, ASHVILLE, AL [AL0168]

BLOUNTSVILLE—Formerly served by Time Warner Cable. Now served by Charter Communications, CULLMAN, AL [AL0034]

BLOUNTSVILLE—See CULLMAN, AL (Charter Communications)

BLUFF PARK—See PELHAM, AL (Charter Communications)

BOAZ—See BIRMINGHAM, AL (AT&T U-verse. This is the regional video hub for the BIRMINGHAM area)

BOAZ—See DECATUR, AL (Charter Communications)

BOLIGEE—Sky Cablevision

BON AIR—See PELHAM, AL (Charter Communications)

BON SECOUR—See FOLEY, AL (Riviera Utilities Cable TV)

BOOTH—Formerly served by Zito Media. No longer in operation

BRACEVILLE (VILLAGE)—See ARDMORE, IL (Mediacom)

BRANCHVILLE—See ODENVILLE, AL (Cablevision Services Inc.)

BRANTLEY—See LUVERNE, AL (Crenshaw Cable)

BRENT—See CENTREVILLE, AL (Community Cable & Broadband LLC)

BREWTON—Mediacom. Now served by GULF BREEZE, FL [FL0070]

BRIDGEPORT—Charter Communications. Now served by JASPER, TN [TN0070]

BRIGHTON—See BIRMINGHAM, AL (AT&T U-verse. This is the regional video hub for the BIRMINGHAM area)

BRIGHTON—See BIRMINGHAM, AL (Bright House Networks)

BRILLIANT—See WINFIELD, AL (West Alabama TV Cable Co. Inc)

BROOKSIDE—See PELHAM, AL (Charter Communications)

BROOKWOOD—Charter Communications. Now served by PELHAM, AL [AL0192]

BROOKWOOD—See BIRMINGHAM, AL (AT&T U-verse. This is the regional video hub for the BIRMINGHAM area)

BROOKWOOD—See PELHAM, AL (Charter Communications)

BRUNDIDGE—See TROY, AL (Troy Cablevision. Formerly [AL0032]. This cable system has converted to IPTV)

BUHL—See PELHAM, AL (Charter Communications)

BUTLER COUNTY (PORTIONS)—See GREENVILLE, AL (Bright House Networks)

BUTLER—Pine Belt Broadband

CAHABA HEIGHTS—See PELHAM, AL (Charter Communications)

CALERA—See BIRMINGHAM, AL (AT&T U-verse. This is the regional video hub for the BIRMINGHAM area)

CALERA—See PELHAM, AL (Charter Communications)

CALHOUN COUNTY (UNINCORPORATED AREAS)—See BIRMINGHAM, AL (AT&T U-verse. This is the regional video hub for the BIRMINGHAM area)

CALHOUN COUNTY (UNINCORPORATED AREAS)—See ANNISTON, AL (Cable One)

CAMDEN—See MONROEVILLE, AL (Mediacom)

CAMP HILL—See PELHAM, AL (Charter Communications)

CAPSHAW—See MADISON COUNTY, AL (Mediacom)

CARBON HILL—See PELHAM, AL (Charter Communications)

CARDIFF—See PELHAM, AL (Charter Communications)

CARROLLTON—See BIRMINGHAM, AL (AT&T U-verse. This is the regional video hub for the BIRMINGHAM area)

CARROLLTON—See ALICEVILLE, AL (Northland Cable Television)

CASTLEBERRY—TV Cable Company of Andalusia

CEDAR BLUFF—Formerly served by Ridge Networks. No longer in operation

CENTER POINT—Charter Communications. Now served by PELHAM, AL [AL0192]

CENTER POINT—See BIRMINGHAM, AL (AT&T U-verse. This is the regional video hub for the BIRMINGHAM area)

CENTER POINT—See BIRMINGHAM, AL (Bright House Networks)

CENTER POINT—See PELHAM, AL (Charter Communications)

CENTER STAR—See ROGERSVILLE, AL (Zito Media)

CENTRE—Charter Communications. Now served by PIEDMONT, AL [AL0065]

CENTRE—See PIEDMONT, AL (Charter Communications)

CENTREVILLE—Community Cable & Broadband LLC

CHALKVILLE—See BIRMINGHAM, AL (AT&T U-verse. This is the regional video hub for the BIRMINGHAM area)

CHAMBERS COUNTY (PORTIONS)—See PELHAM, AL (Charter Communications)

CHAMBERS COUNTY (PORTIONS)—WOW! Internet, Cable & Phone

CHANCELLOR—Formerly served by TV Cable Company of Andalusia. No longer in operation

CHATOM—Formerly served by Community Cable & Broadband LLC. No longer in operation

CHELSEA—See BIRMINGHAM, AL (AT&T U-verse. This is the regional video hub for the BIRMINGHAM area)

CHELSEA—See PELHAM, AL (Charter Communications)

CHEROKEE COUNTY (PORTIONS)—See PIEDMONT, AL (Charter Communications)

CHEROKEE—Formerly served by Ramco Broadband Services. No longer in operation

CHICKASAW—See MOBILE, AL (Comcast Cable)

CHILDERSBURG—See PELHAM, AL (Charter Communications)

CHILTON COUNTY (PORTIONS)—See PELHAM, AL (Charter Communications)

CHILTON COUNTY (PORTIONS)—See CLANTON, AL (Zito Media)

CHILTON COUNTY (PORTIONS)—See THORSBY, AL (Zito Media)

CHILTON COUNTY (UNINCORPORATED AREAS)—See BIRMINGHAM, AL (AT&T U-verse. This is the regional video hub for the BIRMINGHAM area)

CHOCCOLOCCO—See BIRMINGHAM, AL (AT&T U-verse. This is the regional video hub for the BIRMINGHAM area)

CITRONELLE—See MOBILE COUNTY, AL (Mediacom)

CLANTON—See BIRMINGHAM, AL (AT&T U-verse. This is the regional video hub for the BIRMINGHAM area)

CLANTON—Zito Media

CLARKE COUNTY (PORTIONS)—See THOMASVILLE, AL (Mediacom)

CLARKE COUNTY (PORTIONS)—See GROVE HILL, AL (Pine Belt Broadband)

CLAY COUNTY (PORTIONS)—See PELHAM, AL (Charter Communications)

CLAY—See BIRMINGHAM, AL (AT&T U-verse. This is the regional video hub for the BIRMINGHAM area)

CLAYHATCHEE—See DALEVILLE, AL (Time Warner Cable)

CLAYHATCHEE—See TROY, AL (Troy Cablevision. Formerly [AL0032]. This cable system has converted to IPTV)

CLAYTON (TOWN)—Comcast Cable

CLEBURNE COUNTY (WESTERN PORTION)—See HEFLIN, AL (Zito Media)

CLERBURNE COUNTY (UNINCORPORATED AREAS)—See BIRMINGHAM, AL (AT&T U-verse. This is the regional video hub for the BIRMINGHAM area)

CLEVELAND—See ONEONTA, AL (Otelco)

CLIO—Bright House Networks

CLOVERDALE—Comcast Cable. Now served by TUPELO, MS [MS0009]

COALING—See BIRMINGHAM, AL (AT&T U-verse. This is the regional video hub for the BIRMINGHAM area)

COALING—See PELHAM, AL (Charter Communications)

CODEN—Formerly served by Mediacom. No longer in operation

COFFEE COUNTY (PORTIONS)—See ENTERPRISE, AL (Time Warner Cable)

COFFEEVILLE—Formerly served by Sky Cablevision. No longer in operation

COKER—See BIRMINGHAM, AL (AT&T U-verse. This is the regional video hub for the BIRMINGHAM area)

COKER—See PELHAM, AL (Charter Communications)

COLBERT COUNTY (PORTIONS)—See LEIGHTON, AL (Zito Media)

COLBERT COUNTY (UNINCORPORATED AREAS)—See BIRMINGHAM, AL (AT&T U-verse. This is the regional video hub for the BIRMINGHAM area)

COLBERT COUNTY—See DECATUR, AL (Charter Communications)

COLLINSVILLE—Formerly served by Collinsville TV Cable. No longer in operation

COLUMBIANA—See BIRMINGHAM, AL (AT&T U-verse. This is the regional video hub for the BIRMINGHAM area)

COLUMBIANA—Zito Media

CONCORD—See BIRMINGHAM, AL (AT&T U-verse. This is the regional video hub for the BIRMINGHAM area)

CONECUH COUNTY (PORTIONS)—See MONROEVILLE, AL (Mediacom)

COOSA COUNTY (PORTIONS)—See PELHAM, AL (Charter Communications)

COOSADA (TOWN)—See WETUMPKA, AL (Bright House Networks)

CORDOVA—See PELHAM, AL (Charter Communications)

Cable Community Index—Alabama

COTACO—See DECATUR, AL (Charter Communications)

COTTONDALE—See PELHAM, AL (Charter Communications)

COURTLAND—See LEIGHTON, AL (Zito Media)

COWARTS—See DOTHAN, AL (WOW! Internet, Cable & Phone)

CREOLA—See MOBILE COUNTY, AL (Mediacom)

CROSSVILLE—See DECATUR, AL (Charter Communications)

CUBA—Formerly served by Zoom Media. No longer in operation

CULLMAN COUNTY (PORTIONS)—See CULLMAN, AL (Charter Communications)

CULLMAN COUNTY (PORTIONS)—See BAILEYTON, AL (Zito Media)

CULLMAN COUNTY (UNINCORPORATED AREAS)—See BIRMINGHAM, AL (AT&T U-verse. This is the regional video hub for the BIRMINGHAM area)

CULLMAN—Formerly served by Alabama Broadband LLC. Now served by Charter Communications, CULLMAN, AL [AL0034]

CULLMAN—See BIRMINGHAM, AL (AT&T U-verse. This is the regional video hub for the BIRMINGHAM area)

CULLMAN—Charter Communications

CURRY—Charter Communications

DADEVILLE—Charter Communications

DALE COUNTY—See CLIO, AL (Bright House Networks)

DALE COUNTY—See ENTERPRISE, AL (Time Warner Cable)

DALEVILLE—Time Warner Cable

DALEVILLE—Troy Cable

DALEVILLE—See TROY, AL (Troy Cablevision. Formerly [AL0032]. This cable system has converted to IPTV)

DALLAS COUNTY—See MONTGOMERY, AL (Charter Communications)

DANVILLE—See DECATUR, AL (Charter Communications)

DAPHNE—Mediacom. Now served by FAIRHOPE, AL [AL0124]

DAPHNE—See FAIRHOPE, AL (Mediacom)

DAUPHIN ISLAND—Comcast Cable. Now served by MOBILE, AL [AL0002]

DAUPHIN ISLAND—See MOBILE, AL (Comcast Cable)

DEATSVILLE (TOWN)—See WETUMPKA, AL (Bright House Networks)

DECATUR—See BIRMINGHAM, AL (AT&T U-verse. This is the regional video hub for the BIRMINGHAM area)

DECATUR—Charter Communications

DEKALB COUNTY (PORTIONS)—See HENAGAR, AL (Zito Media)

DEKALB COUNTY (PORTIONS)—See RAINSVILLE, AL (Zito Media)

DEKALB COUNTY—See FORT PAYNE, AL (Charter Communications)

DEMOPOLIS—Demopolis CATV Co

DORA—See BIRMINGHAM, AL (AT&T U-verse. This is the regional video hub for the BIRMINGHAM area)

DORA—See PELHAM, AL (Charter Communications)

DOTHAN—Comcast Cable. Now served by TALLAHASSEE, FL [FL0283]

DOTHAN—See DALEVILLE, AL (Time Warner Cable)

DOTHAN—WOW! Internet, Cable & Phone

DOUBLE SPRINGS—Zito Media. Now served by HALEYVILLE, AL [AL0047]

DOUBLE SPRINGS—See HALEYVILLE, AL (Zito Media)

DOUGLAS—See BIRMINGHAM, AL (AT&T U-verse. This is the regional video hub for the BIRMINGHAM area)

DOUGLAS—See DECATUR, AL (Charter Communications)

DOZIER—See HEATH, AL (TV Cable Company of Andalusia)

DUNCANVILLE—See PELHAM, AL (Charter Communications)

DUTTON—See RAINSVILLE, AL (Zito Media)

EAST BROOKLYN (VILLAGE)—See ARDMORE, IL (Mediacom)

ECLECTIC (TOWN)—See WETUMPKA, AL (Bright House Networks)

EDGARD—See MOBILE, LA (Comcast Cable)

EDGEWATER—See BIRMINGHAM, AL (AT&T U-verse. This is the regional video hub for the BIRMINGHAM area)

EDWARDSVILLE—See HEFLIN, AL (Zito Media)

ELBA—Formerly served by Charter Communications. Now served by Troy Cablevision. This cable system has converted to IPTV. See TROY, AL [AL5091]

ELBA—See TROY, AL (Troy Cablevision. Formerly [AL0032]. This cable system has converted to IPTV)

ELBERTA—See FOLEY, AL (Riviera Utilities Cable TV)

ELDRIDGE—See PELHAM, AL (Charter Communications)

ELGIN—See ROGERSVILLE, AL (Zito Media)

ELKMONT—See BIRMINGHAM, AL (AT&T U-verse. This is the regional video hub for the BIRMINGHAM area)

ELKMONT—See DECATUR, AL (Charter Communications)

ELKTON—See ARDMORE, TN (Mediacom)

ELMORE (TOWN)—See WETUMPKA, AL (Bright House Networks)

ELMORE COUNTY (PORTIONS)—See WETUMPKA, AL (Bright House Networks)

ELMORE COUNTY—See MONTGOMERY, AL (Charter Communications)

ELROD—See PELHAM, AL (Charter Communications)

ENTERPRISE—Time Warner Cable

ENTERPRISE—See TROY, AL (Troy Cablevision. Formerly [AL0032]. This cable system has converted to IPTV)

ESSEX (VILLAGE)—See ARDMORE, IL (Mediacom)

ETOWAH COUNTY (PORTIONS)—See DECATUR, AL (Charter Communications)

ETOWAH COUNTY (PORTIONS)—See PIEDMONT, AL (Charter Communications)

ETOWAH COUNTY (UNINCORPORATED AREAS)—See BIRMINGHAM, AL (AT&T U-verse. This is the regional video hub for the BIRMINGHAM area)

ETOWAH—See PIEDMONT, AL (Charter Communications)

EUFAULA—Bright House Networks

EUTAW—Community Cable & Broadband LLC

EVA—See BIRMINGHAM, AL (AT&T U-verse. This is the regional video hub for the BIRMINGHAM area)

EVA—See BAILEYTON, AL (Zito Media)

EVERGREEN—See MONROEVILLE, AL (Mediacom)

EXCEL—See MONROEVILLE, AL (Mediacom)

FAIRFIELD (PORTIONS)—See BIRMINGHAM, AL (Bright House Networks)

FAIRFIELD—See BIRMINGHAM, AL (AT&T U-verse. This is the regional video hub for the BIRMINGHAM area)

FAIRFIELD—Charter Communications

FAIRHOPE—Mediacom

FAIRVIEW—See BIRMINGHAM, AL (AT&T U-verse. This is the regional video hub for the BIRMINGHAM area)

FAIRVIEW—See CULLMAN, AL (Charter Communications)

FALKVILLE—See BIRMINGHAM, AL (AT&T U-verse. This is the regional video hub for the BIRMINGHAM area)

FALKVILLE—See DECATUR, AL (Charter Communications)

FAYETTE—West Alabama TV Cable Co. Inc

FAYETTEVILLE—See BIRMINGHAM, TN (AT&T U-verse. This is the regional video hub for the BIRMINGHAM area)

FISH RIVER—See FAIRHOPE, AL (Mediacom)

FIVE POINTS—See DECATUR, AL (Charter Communications)

FLINT—See DECATUR, AL (Charter Communications)

FLORALA—Bright House Networks. Now served by DE FUNIAK SPRINGS, FL [FL0111]

FLORENCE—Comcast Cable. Now served by TUPELO, MS [MS0009]

FLORENCE—See BIRMINGHAM, AL (AT&T U-verse. This is the regional video hub for the BIRMINGHAM area)

FOLEY—See ROBERTSDALE, AL (Mediacom)

FOLEY—Riviera Utilities Cable TV

FORESTDALE—See BIRMINGHAM, AL (AT&T U-verse. This is the regional video hub for the BIRMINGHAM area)

FORESTDALE—See PELHAM, AL (Charter Communications)

FORKLAND—Sky Cablevision

FORT DEPOSIT—See GREENVILLE, AL (Bright House Networks)

FORT MITCHELL—See PHENIX CITY, AL (Phenix Cable TV)

FORT MORGAN—See ROBERTSDALE, AL (Mediacom)

FORT PAYNE—Charter Communications

FORT RUCKER—See DALEVILLE, AL (Time Warner Cable)

FRANKLIN COUNTY (PORTIONS)—See PHIL CAMPBELL, AL (Charter Communications)

FRANKLIN COUNTY—See DECATUR, AL (Charter Communications)

FREEMANVILLE—Formerly served by CableSouth Inc. No longer in operation

FRISCO CITY—See MONROEVILLE, AL (Mediacom)

FRUITHURST—See HEFLIN, AL (Zito Media)

FULTONDALE—See BIRMINGHAM, AL (AT&T U-verse. This is the regional video hub for the BIRMINGHAM area)

FULTONDALE—See PELHAM, AL (Charter Communications)

FYFFE—See RAINSVILLE, AL (Zito Media)

GADSDEN—Comcast Cable. Now served by TUPELO, MS [MS0009]

GADSDEN—See BIRMINGHAM, AL (AT&T U-verse. This is the regional video hub for the BIRMINGHAM area)

GANTT—See HEATH, AL (TV Cable Company of Andalusia)

GARDEN CITY—See CULLMAN, AL (Charter Communications)

GARDENDALE—See BIRMINGHAM, AL (AT&T U-verse. This is the regional video hub for the BIRMINGHAM area)

Alabama—Cable Community Index

GARDENDALE—See PELHAM, AL (Charter Communications)

GARYVILLE—See MOBILE, LA (Comcast Cable)

GENEVA COUNTY—See DALEVILLE, AL (Time Warner Cable)

GENEVA—Bright House Networks. Now served by CHIPLEY, FL [FL0126]

GEORGETOWN—See EUFAULA, GA (Bright House Networks)

GEORGIANA—See GREENVILLE, AL (Bright House Networks)

GERALDINE—See DECATUR, AL (Charter Communications)

GILES COUNTY—See ARDMORE, TN (Mediacom)

GLENCO—See BIRMINGHAM, AL (AT&T U-verse. This is the regional video hub for the BIRMINGHAM area)

GLENWOOD—See LUVERNE, AL (Crenshaw Cable)

GLENWOOD—See TROY, AL (Troy Cablevision. Formerly [AL0032]. This cable system has converted to IPTV)

GODLEY (VILLAGE)—See ARDMORE, IL (Mediacom)

GOOD HOPE—See BIRMINGHAM, AL (AT&T U-verse. This is the regional video hub for the BIRMINGHAM area)

GOODWATER—See PELHAM, AL (Charter Communications)

GORDO—See ALICEVILLE, AL (Northland Cable Television)

GORDON—Formerly served by Gordon Cable TV. No longer in operation

GOSHEN—See TROY, AL (Troy Cablevision. Formerly [AL0032]. This cable system has converted to IPTV)

GRAND BAY—See MOBILE COUNTY, AL (Mediacom)

GRANT—New Hope Telephone Cooperative. Now served by NEW HOPE, AL [AL0070]

GRANT—See NEW HOPE, AL (New Hope Telephone Cooperative)

GRAY—See MOBILE, LA (Comcast Cable)

GRAYSON VALLEY—See PELHAM, AL (Charter Communications)

GRAYSVILLE—See BIRMINGHAM, AL (AT&T U-verse. This is the regional video hub for the BIRMINGHAM area)

GRAYSVILLE—See PELHAM, AL (Charter Communications)

GREENE COUNTY (UNINCORPORATED AREAS)—See EUTAW, AL (Community Cable & Broadband LLC)

GREENSBORO—Mediacom

GREENVILLE—Bright House Networks

GRIMES—See DALEVILLE, AL (Time Warner Cable)

GROVE HILL—Pine Belt Broadband

GUIN—Charter Communications. Now served by SULLIGENT, AL [AL0084]

GUIN—See SULLIGENT, AL (Charter Communications)

GULF SHORES—Formerly served by Beyond Communications. No longer in operation

GULF SHORES—See ROBERTSDALE, AL (Mediacom)

GUNTERSVILLE—Charter Communications. Now served by DECATUR, AL [AL0184]

GUNTERSVILLE—See BIRMINGHAM, AL (AT&T U-verse. This is the regional video hub for the BIRMINGHAM area)

GUNTERSVILLE—See DECATUR, AL (Charter Communications)

GURLEY—Charter Communications. Now served by DECATUR, AL [AL0184]

GURLEY—See DECATUR, AL (Charter Communications)

HACKLEBURG—Formerly served by Mediastream. No longer in operation

HALE COUNTY (PORTIONS)—See GREENSBORO, AL (Mediacom)

HALEYVILLE—Zito Media

HAMILTON—West Alabama TV Cable Co. Inc

HAMMONDVILLE—See FORT PAYNE, AL (Charter Communications)

HANCEVILLE—See CULLMAN, AL (Charter Communications)

HARMONY—See HEATH, AL (TV Cable Company of Andalusia)

HARPERSVILLE—See BIRMINGHAM, AL (AT&T U-verse. This is the regional video hub for the BIRMINGHAM area)

HARPERSVILLE—See PELHAM, AL (Charter Communications)

HARTSELLE—Charter Communications. Now served by DECATUR, AL [AL0184]

HARTSELLE—See BIRMINGHAM, AL (AT&T U-verse. This is the regional video hub for the BIRMINGHAM area)

HARTSELLE—See DECATUR, AL (Charter Communications)

HARVEST—See BIRMINGHAM, AL (AT&T U-verse. This is the regional video hub for the BIRMINGHAM area)

HARVEST—See MADISON COUNTY, AL (Mediacom)

HATCHECHUBBEE—See PHENIX CITY, AL (Phenix Cable TV)

HAYDEN—See BIRMINGHAM, AL (AT&T U-verse. This is the regional video hub for the BIRMINGHAM area)

HAYNEVILLE—Formerly served by Alabama Broadband LLC. No longer in operation

HAZEL GREEN—See BIRMINGHAM, AL (AT&T U-verse. This is the regional video hub for the BIRMINGHAM area)

HEATH—TV Cable Company of Andalusia

HEFLIN—Zito Media

HELENA—See BIRMINGHAM, AL (AT&T U-verse. This is the regional video hub for the BIRMINGHAM area)

HELENA—See BIRMINGHAM, AL (Bright House Networks)

HELENA—See PELHAM, AL (Charter Communications)

HENAGAR—Zito Media

HENRY COUNTY (UNINCORPORATED AREAS)—See EUFAULA, AL (Bright House Networks)

HILLSBORO—Formerly served by Shoals Cable TV Inc. No longer in operation

HOBSON CITY—See ANNISTON, AL (Cable One)

HOG JAW—See BAILEYTON, AL (Zito Media)

HOKES BLUFF—See PIEDMONT, AL (Charter Communications)

HOLLIS CROSSROADS—Formerly served by Mediastream. No longer in operation

HOLLY POND—See BIRMINGHAM, AL (AT&T U-verse. This is the regional video hub for the BIRMINGHAM area)

HOLLY POND—See CULLMAN, AL (Charter Communications)

HOLLYWOOD—See DECATUR, AL (Charter Communications)

HOLT—See BIRMINGHAM, AL (AT&T U-verse. This is the regional video hub for the BIRMINGHAM area)

HOMEWOOD—See BIRMINGHAM, AL (AT&T U-verse. This is the regional video hub for the BIRMINGHAM area)

HOMEWOOD—See PELHAM, AL (Charter Communications)

HOOVER—Charter Communications. Now served by PELHAM, AL [AL0192]

HOOVER—See BIRMINGHAM, AL (AT&T U-verse. This is the regional video hub for the BIRMINGHAM area)

HOOVER—See BIRMINGHAM, AL (Bright House Networks)

HOOVER—See PELHAM, AL (Charter Communications)

HORN HILL—See OPP, AL (Opp Cablevision)

HORTON—See DECATUR, AL (Charter Communications)

HOUMA—See MOBILE, LA (Comcast Cable)

HOUSTON COUNTY—See DALEVILLE, AL (Time Warner Cable)

HUEYTOWN (PORTIONS)—See BIRMINGHAM, AL (Bright House Networks)

HUEYTOWN—See BIRMINGHAM, AL (AT&T U-verse. This is the regional video hub for the BIRMINGHAM area)

HUEYTOWN—See FAIRFIELD, AL (Charter Communications)

HULACO—See BAILEYTON, AL (Zito Media)

HUNTSVILLE—Comcast Cable. Now served by TUPELO, MS [MS0009]

HUNTSVILLE—See BIRMINGHAM, AL (AT&T U-verse. This is the regional video hub for the BIRMINGHAM area)

HUNTSVILLE—WOW! Internet, Cable & Phone

HURTSBORO—See PHENIX CITY, AL (Phenix Cable TV)

IDER—See HENAGAR, AL (Zito Media)

INDIAN SPRINGS VILLAGE—See PELHAM, AL (Charter Communications)

INDIAN SPRINGS—See BIRMINGHAM, AL (AT&T U-verse. This is the regional video hub for the BIRMINGHAM area)

IRONDALE—See BIRMINGHAM, AL (AT&T U-verse. This is the regional video hub for the BIRMINGHAM area)

IRONDALE—See BIRMINGHAM, AL (Bright House Networks)

IRONDALE—See PELHAM, AL (Charter Communications)

IRVINGTON—See MOBILE COUNTY, AL (Mediacom)

JACKSON COUNTY (PORTIONS)—See HENAGAR, AL (Zito Media)

JACKSON COUNTY—See DECATUR, AL (Charter Communications)

JACKSON—Mediacom. Now served by THOMASVILLE, AL [AL0080]

JACKSON—See THOMASVILLE, AL (Mediacom)

JACKSONS' GAP—See PELHAM, AL (Charter Communications)

JACKSONVILLE—See BIRMINGHAM, AL (AT&T U-verse. This is the regional video hub for the BIRMINGHAM area)

JACKSONVILLE—See ANNISTON, AL (Cable One)

JASPER—Charter Communications. Now served by PELHAM, AL [AL0192]

JASPER—Formerly served by Zoom Media. No longer in operation

JASPER—See BIRMINGHAM, AL (AT&T U-verse. This is the regional video hub for the BIRMINGHAM area)

JASPER—See PELHAM, AL (Charter Communications)

JEFFERSON COUNTY (PORTIONS)—See BIRMINGHAM, AL (Bright House Networks)

JEFFERSON COUNTY (PORTIONS)—See CULLMAN, AL (Charter Communications)

JEFFERSON COUNTY (PORTIONS)—See CENTREVILLE, AL (Community Cable & Broadband LLC)

JEFFERSON COUNTY (UNINCORPORATED AREAS)—See BIRMINGHAM, AL (AT&T U-verse. This is the regional video hub for the BIRMINGHAM area)

JEFFERSON COUNTY—See PELHAM, AL (Charter Communications)

JEMISON—See BIRMINGHAM, AL (AT&T U-verse. This is the regional video hub for the BIRMINGHAM area)

JEMISON—See THORSBY, AL (Zito Media)

JOPPA—See BAILEYTON, AL (Zito Media)

KANSAS—See PELHAM, AL (Charter Communications)

KELLYTON—See PELHAM, AL (Charter Communications)

KENNEDY—See ALICEVILLE, AL (Northland Cable Television)

KILLEN—See BIRMINGHAM, AL (AT&T U-verse. This is the regional video hub for the BIRMINGHAM area)

KILLEN—See ROGERSVILLE, AL (Zito Media)

KIMBERLY—See BIRMINGHAM, AL (AT&T U-verse. This is the regional video hub for the BIRMINGHAM area)

KIMBERLY—See CULLMAN, AL (Charter Communications)

KINSEY—See DOTHAN, AL (WOW! Internet, Cable & Phone)

KINSTON—See OPP, AL (Opp Cablevision)

LA PLACE—See MOBILE, LA (Comcast Cable)

LACEY'S SPRINGS—See ONEONTA, AL (Otelco)

LACEYS SPRING—See DECATUR, AL (Charter Communications)

LAFAYETTE—Charter Communications

LAFOURCHE PARISH (PORTIONS)—See MOBILE, LA (Comcast Cable)

LAKE MARTIN RESORT—Com-Link Inc

LAKE PURDY—See BIRMINGHAM, AL (AT&T U-verse. This is the regional video hub for the BIRMINGHAM area)

LAKEVIEW—See BIRMINGHAM, AL (AT&T U-verse. This is the regional video hub for the BIRMINGHAM area)

LAKEVIEW—See BIRMINGHAM, AL (Bright House Networks)

LAKEVIEW—See DECATUR, AL (Charter Communications)

LAMAR COUNTY (SOUTHERN PORTION)—See ALICEVILLE, AL (Northland Cable Television)

LANETT—See CHAMBERS COUNTY (portions), AL (WOW! Internet, Cable & Phone)

LAUDERDALE COUNTY (PORTIONS)—See ROGERSVILLE, AL (Zito Media)

LAUDERDALE COUNTY (UNINCORPORATED AREAS)—See BIRMINGHAM, AL (AT&T U-verse. This is the regional video hub for the BIRMINGHAM area)

LAWRENCE COUNTY (PORTIONS)—See DECATUR, AL (Charter Communications)

LAWRENCE COUNTY (PORTIONS)—See LEIGHTON, AL (Zito Media)

LAWRENCE COUNTY (UNINCORPORATED AREAS)—See BIRMINGHAM, AL (AT&T U-verse. This is the regional video hub for the BIRMINGHAM area)

LAY LAKE—Zito Media. Now served by COLUMBIANA, AL [AL0180]

LAY LAKE—See COLUMBIANA, AL (Zito Media)

LEE COUNTY (PORTIONS)—See PELHAM, AL (Charter Communications)

LEE COUNTY—See PHENIX CITY, AL (Phenix Cable TV)

LEEDS—See PELHAM, AL (Charter Communications)

LEESBURG—Formerly served by Ridge Networks. No longer in operation

LEIGHTON—Zito Media

LEVEL PLAINS—See DALEVILLE, AL (Time Warner Cable)

LEVEL PLAINS—See TROY, AL (Troy Cablevision. Formerly [AL0032]. This cable system has converted to IPTV)

LEXINGTON—See ROGERSVILLE, AL (Zito Media)

LILLIAN—See FAIRHOPE, AL (Mediacom)

LIMESTONE COUNTY (EASTERN PORTION)—See HUNTSVILLE, AL (WOW! Internet, Cable & Phone)

LIMESTONE COUNTY (portions)—Charter Communications. Now served by DECATUR, AL [AL0184]

LIMESTONE COUNTY (PORTIONS)—See DECATUR, AL (Charter Communications)

LIMESTONE COUNTY (UNINCORPORATED AREAS)—See BIRMINGHAM, AL (AT&T U-verse. This is the regional video hub for the BIRMINGHAM area)

LIMESTONE COUNTY—See ARDMORE, AL (Mediacom)

LINCOLN COUNTY (UNINCORPORATED AREAS)—See BIRMINGHAM, TN (AT&T U-verse. This is the regional video hub for the BIRMINGHAM area)

LINCOLN COUNTY—See ARDMORE, TN (Mediacom)

LINCOLN—USA Communications

LINDEN—Mediacom. Now served by GREENSBORO, AL [AL0110]

LINDEN—See GREENSBORO, AL (Mediacom)

LINEVILLE—Charter Communications

LIPSCOMB—See BIRMINGHAM, AL (AT&T U-verse. This is the regional video hub for the BIRMINGHAM area)

LIPSCOMB—See BIRMINGHAM, AL (Bright House Networks)

LISMAN—See BUTLER, AL (Pine Belt Broadband)

LITTLEVILLE—See DECATUR, AL (Charter Communications)

LIVINGSTON (TOWN)—See YORK, AL (Mediacom)

LOCUST FORK—Formerly served by Almega Cable. No longer in operation

LOCUST FORK—See BIRMINGHAM, AL (AT&T U-verse. This is the regional video hub for the BIRMINGHAM area)

LOUISVILLE—See CLIO, AL (Bright House Networks)

LOWNDES COUNTY—Formerly served by Alabama Broadband LLC. No longer in operation

LOXLEY—See ROBERTSDALE, AL (Mediacom)

LUVERNE—Crenshaw Cable

LUVERNE—See TROY, AL (Troy Cablevision. Formerly [AL0032]. This cable system has converted to IPTV)

MADISON COUNTY (PORTIONS)—See NEW HOPE, AL (New Hope Telephone Cooperative)

MADISON COUNTY (PORTIONS)—See HUNTSVILLE, AL (WOW! Internet, Cable & Phone)

MADISON COUNTY (UNINCORPORATED AREAS)—See BIRMINGHAM, AL (AT&T U-verse. This is the regional video hub for the BIRMINGHAM area)

MADISON COUNTY—See DECATUR, AL (Charter Communications)

MADISON COUNTY—Mediacom

MADISON—See BIRMINGHAM, AL (AT&T U-verse. This is the regional video hub for the BIRMINGHAM area)

MADISON—See HUNTSVILLE, AL (WOW! Internet, Cable & Phone)

MAGNOLIA SPRINGS—See FOLEY, AL (Riviera Utilities Cable TV)

MALVERN—See DALEVILLE, AL (Time Warner Cable)

MARGARET—Formerly served by Alabama Broadband LLC. Now served by Charter, ASHVILLE, AL [AL0168]

MARGARET—See PELHAM, AL (Charter Communications)

MARION COUNTY (PORTIONS)—See SULLIGENT, AL (Charter Communications)

MARION COUNTY (PORTIONS)—See HALEYVILLE, AL (Zito Media)

MARION—Community Cable & Broadband LLC

MARLOW—See FAIRHOPE, AL (Mediacom)

MARSHALL COUNTY (PORTIONS)—See NEW HOPE, AL (New Hope Telephone Cooperative)

MARSHALL COUNTY (PORTIONS)—See BAILEYTON, AL (Zito Media)

MARSHALL COUNTY—See DECATUR, AL (Charter Communications)

MAXWELL AFB—See MONTGOMERY, AL (WOW! Internet, Cable & Phone)

MAXWELL-GUNTER AFB—See WETUMPKA, AL (Bright House Networks)

MAYTOWN—See BIRMINGHAM, AL (AT&T U-verse. This is the regional video hub for the BIRMINGHAM area)

MAYTOWN—See PELHAM, AL (Charter Communications)

MCINTOSH—See MOBILE COUNTY, AL (Mediacom)

MCKENZIE—TV Cable Company of Andalusia

MEADOWBROOK—See BIRMINGHAM, AL (AT&T U-verse. This is the regional video hub for the BIRMINGHAM area)

MENTONE—Charter Communications

MERIDIANVILLE—See BIRMINGHAM, AL (AT&T U-verse. This is the regional video hub for the BIRMINGHAM area)

MEXIA—Formerly served by Galaxy Cablevision. No longer in operation

MIDFIELD—See BIRMINGHAM, AL (AT&T U-verse. This is the regional video hub for the BIRMINGHAM area)

MIDFIELD—See FAIRFIELD, AL (Charter Communications)

MIDLAND CITY—See DALEVILLE, AL (Time Warner Cable)

MIDLAND—See TROY, AL (Troy Cablevision. Formerly [AL0032]. This cable system has converted to IPTV)

MIDWAY—See UNION SPRINGS, AL (Union Springs Telephone Co)

MIFLIN—See FOLEY, AL (Riviera Utilities Cable TV)

MILLBROOK—See WETUMPKA, AL (Bright House Networks)

MILLPORT—Northland Cable Television. Now served by ALICEVILLE, AL [AL0055]

MILLPORT—See ALICEVILLE, AL (Northland Cable Television)

MILLRY—Formerly served by Sky Cablevision. No longer in operation

Alabama—Cable Community Index

MINOR—See BIRMINGHAM, AL (AT&T U-verse. This is the regional video hub for the BIRMINGHAM area)

MOBILE (PORTIONS)—See MOBILE COUNTY, AL (Mediacom)

MOBILE COUNTY (PORTIONS)—See MOBILE, AL (Comcast Cable)

MOBILE COUNTY—Formerly served by Charter Communications. No longer in operation

MOBILE COUNTY—Mediacom

MOBILE—Bristers Cable TV

MOBILE—Comcast Cable

MONROE COUNTY (PORTIONS)—See MONROEVILLE, AL (Mediacom)

MONROEVILLE—Mediacom. Now served by MONROEVILLE, AL [AL0112]

MONROEVILLE—Mediacom

MONTEVALLO—See BIRMINGHAM, AL (AT&T U-verse. This is the regional video hub for the BIRMINGHAM area)

MONTEVALLO—See PELHAM, AL (Charter Communications)

MONTGOMERY COUNTY—See WETUMPKA, AL (Bright House Networks)

MONTGOMERY COUNTY—See MONTGOMERY, AL (Charter Communications)

MONTGOMERY—Charter Communications

MONTGOMERY—WOW! Internet, Cable & Phone

MONTROSE—See FAIRHOPE, AL (Mediacom)

MOODY—See PELHAM, AL (Charter Communications)

MOORES MILL—See BIRMINGHAM, AL (AT&T U-verse. This is the regional video hub for the BIRMINGHAM area)

MORGAN CITY (portions)—Charter Communications. Now served by DECATUR, AL [AL0184]

MORGAN CITY (PORTIONS)—See DECATUR, AL (Charter Communications)

MORGAN CITY—See BAILEYTON, AL (Zito Media)

MORGAN COUNTY (PORTIONS)—See BAILEYTON, AL (Zito Media)

MORGAN COUNTY (UNINCORPORATED AREAS)—See BIRMINGHAM, AL (AT&T U-verse. This is the regional video hub for the BIRMINGHAM area)

MORGAN COUNTY—See DECATUR, AL (Charter Communications)

MORRIS—See BIRMINGHAM, AL (AT&T U-verse. This is the regional video hub for the BIRMINGHAM area)

MORRIS—See CULLMAN, AL (Charter Communications)

MOULTON—Charter Communications. Now served by DECATUR, AL [AL0184]

MOULTON—See BIRMINGHAM, AL (AT&T U-verse. This is the regional video hub for the BIRMINGHAM area)

MOULTON—See DECATUR, AL (Charter Communications)

MOUNDVILLE—See PELHAM, AL (Charter Communications)

MOUNT AIRY—See MOBILE, LA (Comcast Cable)

MOUNT OLIVE—See BIRMINGHAM, AL (AT&T U-verse. This is the regional video hub for the BIRMINGHAM area)

MOUNT OLIVE—See PELHAM, AL (Charter Communications)

MOUNT VERNON—See MOBILE COUNTY, AL (Mediacom)

MOUNTAIN BROOK—See BIRMINGHAM, AL (AT&T U-verse. This is the regional video hub for the BIRMINGHAM area)

MOUNTAIN BROOK—See PELHAM, AL (Charter Communications)

MOUNTAINBORO—See DECATUR, AL (Charter Communications)

MULGA—See PELHAM, AL (Charter Communications)

MUNFORD—See ANNISTON, AL (Cable One)

MUSCLE SHOALS—See BIRMINGHAM, AL (AT&T U-verse. This is the regional video hub for the BIRMINGHAM area)

NAPIER FIELD—See DALEVILLE, AL (Time Warner Cable)

NAPIER FIELD—See TROY, AL (Troy Cablevision. Formerly [AL0032]. This cable system has converted to IPTV)

NAUVOO—Formerly served by Zoom Media. No longer in operation

NECTAR—See ONEONTA, AL (Otelco)

NEW BROCKTON—See ENTERPRISE, AL (Time Warner Cable)

NEW BROCKTON—See TROY, AL (Troy Cablevision. Formerly [AL0032]. This cable system has converted to IPTV)

NEW HOPE—New Hope Telephone Cooperative

NEW MARKET—See BIRMINGHAM, AL (AT&T U-verse. This is the regional video hub for the BIRMINGHAM area)

NEW SITE—See PELHAM, AL (Charter Communications)

NEWTON—See DALEVILLE, AL (Time Warner Cable)

NEWTON—See TROY, AL (Troy Cablevision. Formerly [AL0032]. This cable system has converted to IPTV)

NORTH BREWTON—Formerly served by CableSouth Inc. No longer in operation

NORTH COURTLAND—See LEIGHTON, AL (Zito Media)

NORTH ROGERSVILLE—See ROGERSVILLE, AL (Zito Media)

NORTHPORT—See BIRMINGHAM, AL (AT&T U-verse. This is the regional video hub for the BIRMINGHAM area)

NORTHPORT—See PELHAM, AL (Charter Communications)

NOTASULGA—Formerly served by Com-Link Inc. No longer in operation

OAK GROVE—See PELHAM, AL (Charter Communications)

OAKMAN—Formerly served by Almega Cable. No longer in operation

OAKVILLE—See DECATUR, AL (Charter Communications)

ODENVILLE—Formerly served by Coosa Cable. No longer in operation

ODENVILLE—Cablevision Services Inc.

ODENVILLE—See PELHAM, AL (Charter Communications)

OHATCHEE—See ANNISTON, AL (Cable One)

OLEANDER—See DECATUR, AL (Charter Communications)

ONEONTA—Otelco

OPELIKA—See PELHAM, AL (Charter Communications)

OPELIKA—Opelika Power Services

OPP—Opp Cablevision

ORANGE BEACH—Formerly served by Beyond Communications. No longer in operation

ORANGE BEACH—See ROBERTSDALE, AL (Mediacom)

ORRVILLE—Formerly served by Zoom Media. No longer in operation

OWENS CROSS ROADS—New Hope Telephone Cooperative. Now served by NEW HOPE, AL [AL0070]

OWENS CROSS ROADS—See NEW HOPE, AL (New Hope Telephone Cooperative)

OXFORD—See BIRMINGHAM, AL (AT&T U-verse. This is the regional video hub for the BIRMINGHAM area)

OXFORD—See ANNISTON, AL (Cable One)

OZARK—Formerly served by Charter Communications. Now served by Troy Cablevision. This cable system has converted to IPTV. See TROY, AL [AL5091]

OZARK—See TROY, AL (Troy Cablevision. Formerly [AL0032]. This cable system has converted to IPTV)

PAINT ROCK—See DECATUR, AL (Charter Communications)

PARISH—See PELHAM, AL (Charter Communications)

PARRISH—See PELHAM, AL (Charter Communications)

PELHAM—See BIRMINGHAM, AL (AT&T U-verse. This is the regional video hub for the BIRMINGHAM area)

PELHAM—Charter Communications

PELL CITY—USA Communications

PENNINGTON—Formerly served by Zoom Media. No longer in operation

PERDIDO BEACH—Mediacom. Now served by ROBERTSDALE, AL [AL0019]

PERDIDO BEACH—See ROBERTSDALE, AL (Mediacom)

PERRY COUNTY (UNINCORPORATED AREAS)—See MARION, AL (Community Cable & Broadband LLC)

PERRY COUNTY—See UNIONTOWN, AL (Alliance Communications)

PETERSON—See PELHAM, AL (Charter Communications)

PETERSVILLE—See BIRMINGHAM, AL (AT&T U-verse. This is the regional video hub for the BIRMINGHAM area)

PETREY—See TROY, AL (Troy Cablevision. Formerly [AL0032]. This cable system has converted to IPTV)

PHENIX CITY—Phenix Cable TV

PHIL CAMPBELL—Charter Communications

PICKENS COUNTY (UNINCORPORATED AREAS)—See BIRMINGHAM, AL (AT&T U-verse. This is the regional video hub for the BIRMINGHAM area)

PICKENS COUNTY—See ALICEVILLE, AL (Northland Cable Television)

PICKENSVILLE—See BIRMINGHAM, AL (AT&T U-verse. This is the regional video hub for the BIRMINGHAM area)

PICKENSVILLE—See ALICEVILLE, AL (Northland Cable Television)

PIEDMONT—Charter Communications

PIKE ROAD—See MONTGOMERY, AL (Charter Communications)

PINCKARD—See DALEVILLE, AL (Time Warner Cable)

PINCKARD—See TROY, AL (Troy Cablevision. Formerly [AL0032]. This cable system has converted to IPTV)

PINE HILL—Formerly served by Zoom Media. No longer in operation

PINE RIDGE—See FORT PAYNE, AL (Charter Communications)

PINSON—See BIRMINGHAM, AL (AT&T U-verse. This is the regional video hub for the BIRMINGHAM area)

PINSON—See PELHAM, AL (Charter Communications)

PISGAH—See HENAGAR, AL (Zito Media)

PLEASANT GROVE—See BIRMINGHAM, AL (AT&T U-verse. This is the regional video hub for the BIRMINGHAM area)

Cable Community Index—Alabama

PLEASANT GROVE—See FAIRFIELD, AL (Charter Communications)

POINT CLEAR—See FAIRHOPE, AL (Mediacom)

POLLARD—Formerly served by CableSouth Inc. No longer in operation

PRATTVILLE—See WETUMPKA, AL (Bright House Networks)

PRATTVILLE—See MONTGOMERY, AL (Charter Communications)

PRATTVILLE—See MONTGOMERY, AL (WOW! Internet, Cable & Phone)

PRICEVILLE—See BIRMINGHAM, AL (AT&T U-verse. This is the regional video hub for the BIRMINGHAM area)

PRICEVILLE—See DECATUR, AL (Charter Communications)

PRICHARD—See MOBILE, AL (Comcast Cable)

PROSPECT—See ARDMORE, TN (Mediacom)

PROVIDENCE—Formerly served by Community Cable & Broadband LLC. No longer in operation

QUITMAN COUNTY—See EUFAULA, GA (Bright House Networks)

RAGLAND—Ragland Telephone Co

RAINBOW CITY—See BIRMINGHAM, AL (AT&T U-verse. This is the regional video hub for the BIRMINGHAM area)

RAINSVILLE—Zito Media

RANBURNE—Formerly served by Ranburne Cable. No longer in operation

RANDOLPH COUNTY—See ROANOKE, AL (Charter Communications)

RED BAY—MetroCast Communications. Now served by PONTOTOC, MS [MS0045]

RED LEVEL—See HEATH, AL (TV Cable Company of Andalusia)

REDSTONE ARSENAL—See HUNTSVILLE, AL (WOW! Internet, Cable & Phone)

REFORM—See ALICEVILLE, AL (Northland Cable Television)

REHOBETH—See DALEVILLE, AL (Time Warner Cable)

REPTON—See MONROEVILLE, AL (Mediacom)

RESERVE—See MOBILE, LA (Comcast Cable)

RIVER FALLS—See HEATH, AL (TV Cable Company of Andalusia)

RIVERCHASE—See PELHAM, AL (Charter Communications)

RIVERSIDE—See PELL CITY, AL (USA Communications)

ROANOKE—Charter Communications

ROBERTSDALE—Mediacom

ROCKFORD—See PELHAM, AL (Charter Communications)

ROGERSVILLE—Zito Media

ROOSEVELT CITY—See BIRMINGHAM, AL (Bright House Networks)

ROSA—See ONEONTA, AL (Otelco)

RUSSELL COUNTY—See PHENIX CITY, AL (Phenix Cable TV)

RUSSELLVILLE—Charter Communications. Now served by DECATUR, AL [AL0184]

RUSSELLVILLE—See DECATUR, AL (Charter Communications)

RUTH—See BAILEYTON, AL (Zito Media)

RUTLEDGE—See LUVERNE, AL (Crenshaw Cable)

RUTLEDGE—See TROY, AL (Troy Cablevision. Formerly [AL0032]. This cable system has converted to IPTV)

SALEM—See PHENIX CITY, AL (Phenix Cable TV)

SAMSON—Bright House Networks. Now served by CHIPLEY, FL [FL0126]

SANFORD—See HEATH, AL (TV Cable Company of Andalusia)

SARALAND (PORTIONS)—See MOBILE COUNTY, AL (Mediacom)

SARALAND—See MOBILE, AL (Comcast Cable)

SARDIS CITY—See DECATUR, AL (Charter Communications)

SATSUMA—See MOBILE COUNTY, AL (Mediacom)

SATSUMA—See MOBILE, AL (Comcast Cable)

SCHRIEVER—See MOBILE, LA (Comcast Cable)

SCOTTSBORO—Charter Communications. Now served by DECATUR, AL [AL0184]

SCOTTSBORO—See DECATUR, AL (Charter Communications)

SCOTTSBORO—Scottsboro Electric Power Board

SEALE—See PHENIX CITY, AL (Phenix Cable TV)

SECTION—See DECATUR, AL (Charter Communications)

SELBROOK—Formerly served by Alabama Broadband LLC. No longer in operation

SELMA—Charter Communications. Now served by MONTGOMERY, AL [AL0003]

SELMA—See MONTGOMERY, AL (Charter Communications)

SEMMES—See MOBILE COUNTY, AL (Mediacom)

SHEFFIELD—See BIRMINGHAM, AL (AT&T U-verse. This is the regional video hub for the BIRMINGHAM area)

SHELBY COUNTY (PORTIONS)—See PELHAM, AL (Charter Communications)

SHELBY COUNTY (PORTIONS)—See COLUMBIANA, AL (Zito Media)

SHELBY COUNTY (UNINCORPORATED AREAS)—See BIRMINGHAM, AL (AT&T U-verse. This is the regional video hub for the BIRMINGHAM area)

SHELBY LAKE—Zito Media. Now served by COLUMBIANA, AL [AL0180]

SHELBY LAKE—See COLUMBIANA, AL (Zito Media)

SHELBY—See BIRMINGHAM, AL (AT&T U-verse. This is the regional video hub for the BIRMINGHAM area)

SILVER HILL—See ROBERTSDALE, AL (Mediacom)

SIPSEY—See PELHAM, AL (Charter Communications)

SKYLINE—Formerly served by Almega Cable. No longer in operation

SMITHS—See PHENIX CITY, AL (Phenix Cable TV)

SMOKE RISE—See BIRMINGHAM, AL (AT&T U-verse. This is the regional video hub for the BIRMINGHAM area)

SNEAD—See ONEONTA, AL (Otelco)

SOMERVILLE—See DECATUR, AL (Charter Communications)

SOUTH VINEMONT—See BIRMINGHAM, AL (AT&T U-verse. This is the regional video hub for the BIRMINGHAM area)

SOUTHSIDE—Charter Communications. Now served by PIEDMONT, AL [AL0065]

SOUTHSIDE—See BIRMINGHAM, AL (AT&T U-verse. This is the regional video hub for the BIRMINGHAM area)

SOUTHSIDE—See PIEDMONT, AL (Charter Communications)

SPANISH COVE—Mediacom. Now served by FAIRHOPE, AL [AL0124]

SPANISH COVE—See FAIRHOPE, AL (Mediacom)

SPANISH FORT—See FAIRHOPE, AL (Mediacom)

SPRING VALLEY—See LEIGHTON, AL (Zito Media)

SPRINGVILLE—See PELHAM, AL (Charter Communications)

ST. CLAIR COUNTY (PORTIONS)—See ODENVILLE, AL (Cablevision Services Inc.)

ST. CLAIR COUNTY (PORTIONS)—See PELHAM, AL (Charter Communications)

ST. CLAIR COUNTY (PORTIONS)—See PELL CITY, AL (USA Communications)

ST. FLORIAN—See BIRMINGHAM, AL (AT&T U-verse. This is the regional video hub for the BIRMINGHAM area)

STAPLETON—Mediacom. Now served by FAIRHOPE, AL [AL0124]

STAPLETON—See FAIRHOPE, AL (Mediacom)

STEELE—See BIRMINGHAM, AL (AT&T U-verse. This is the regional video hub for the BIRMINGHAM area)

STRAUGHN—See HEATH, AL (TV Cable Company of Andalusia)

SULLIGENT—Charter Communications

SUMITON—See BIRMINGHAM, AL (AT&T U-verse. This is the regional video hub for the BIRMINGHAM area)

SUMITON—See PELHAM, AL (Charter Communications)

SUMMERDALE—See FOLEY, AL (Riviera Utilities Cable TV)

SUSAN MOORE—See ONEONTA, AL (Otelco)

SWEET WATER—Community Cable & Broadband LLC

SYCAMORE—See PELHAM, AL (Charter Communications)

SYLACAUGA—Charter Communications. Now served by PELHAM, AL [AL0192]

SYLACAUGA—See PELHAM, AL (Charter Communications)

SYLVAN SPRINGS—See BIRMINGHAM, AL (AT&T U-verse. This is the regional video hub for the BIRMINGHAM area)

SYLVAN SPRINGS—See PELHAM, AL (Charter Communications)

SYLVANIA—See HENAGAR, AL (Zito Media)

TALLADEGA COUNTY (PORTIONS)—See PELHAM, AL (Charter Communications)

TALLADEGA COUNTY (PORTIONS)—USA Communications

TALLADEGA COUNTY (UNINCORPORATED AREAS)—See BIRMINGHAM, AL (AT&T U-verse. This is the regional video hub for the BIRMINGHAM area)

TALLADEGA COUNTY (UNINCORPORATED AREAS)—See ANNISTON, AL (Cable One)

TALLADEGA—Charter Communications. Now served by PELHAM, AL [AL0192]

TALLADEGA—See PELHAM, AL (Charter Communications)

TALLAPOOSA COUNTY (PORTIONS)—See PELHAM, AL (Charter Communications)

TALLAPOOSA COUNTY (SOUTHERN PORTION)—See WETUMPKA, AL (Bright House Networks)

TALLASSEE—See WETUMPKA, AL (Bright House Networks)

TARRANT CITY—See PELHAM, AL (Charter Communications)

Alabama—Cable Community Index

TARRANT—See BIRMINGHAM, AL (AT&T U-verse. This is the regional video hub for the BIRMINGHAM area)

TAYLOR—See DALEVILLE, AL (Time Warner Cable)

TAYLORVILLE—See PELHAM, AL (Charter Communications)

THEODORE—See MOBILE COUNTY, AL (Mediacom)

THIBODAUX—See MOBILE, LA (Comcast Cable)

THOMASTON—Formerly served by Zoom Media. No longer in operation

THOMASVILLE—Mediacom

THORSBY—Zito Media

TILLMAN'S CORNER—See MOBILE COUNTY, AL (Mediacom)

TOWN CREEK—See LEIGHTON, AL (Zito Media)

TRAFFORD—Formerly served by Almega Cable. No longer in operation

TRIANA—See BIRMINGHAM, AL (AT&T U-verse. This is the regional video hub for the BIRMINGHAM area)

TRINITY—Formerly served by Coosa Cable. No longer in operation

TRINITY—See BIRMINGHAM, AL (AT&T U-verse. This is the regional video hub for the BIRMINGHAM area)

TRINITY—Charter Communications

TROY—Formerly served by Knology. Now served by Troy Cablevision. This cable system has converted to IPTV. See TROY, AL [AL5091]

TROY—Troy Cablevision. This cable system has converted to IPTV. See TROY, AL [AL5091]

TROY—Troy Cablevision. Formerly [AL0032]. This cable system has converted to IPTV

TRUSSVILLE—See BIRMINGHAM, AL (AT&T U-verse. This is the regional video hub for the BIRMINGHAM area)

TRUSSVILLE—See PELHAM, AL (Charter Communications)

TUSCALOOSA COUNTY (PORTIONS)—See PELHAM, AL (Charter Communications)

TUSCALOOSA COUNTY (PORTIONS)—See CENTREVILLE, AL (Community Cable & Broadband LLC)

TUSCALOOSA COUNTY (UNINCORPORATED AREAS)—See BIRMINGHAM, AL (AT&T U-verse. This is the regional video hub for the BIRMINGHAM area)

TUSCALOOSA COUNTY—Charter Communications. Now served by PELHAM, AL [AL0192]

TUSCALOOSA—Comcast Cable. Now served by TUPELO, MS [MS0009]

TUSCALOOSA—See BIRMINGHAM, AL (AT&T U-verse. This is the regional video hub for the BIRMINGHAM area)

TUSCALOOSA—See PELHAM, AL (Charter Communications)

TUSCUMBIA—See BIRMINGHAM, AL (AT&T U-verse. This is the regional video hub for the BIRMINGHAM area)

TUSKEGEE—Charter Communications. Now served by PELHAM, AL [AL0192]

TUSKEGEE—See PELHAM, AL (Charter Communications)

UNDERWOOD—See BIRMINGHAM, AL (AT&T U-verse. This is the regional video hub for the BIRMINGHAM area)

UNION GROVE—See DECATUR, AL (Charter Communications)

UNION GROVE—See ONEONTA, AL (Otelco)

UNION HILL—See DECATUR, AL (Charter Communications)

UNION SPRINGS—Union Springs Telephone Co

UNIONTOWN—Alliance Communications

VACHERIE—See MOBILE, LA (Comcast Cable)

VALHERMOSO SPRINGS—See DECATUR, AL (Charter Communications)

VALLEY GRANDE—See MONTGOMERY, AL (Charter Communications)

VALLEY HEAD—See FORT PAYNE, AL (Charter Communications)

VALLEY—See CHAMBERS COUNTY (portions), AL (WOW! Internet, Cable & Phone)

VANCE—See BIRMINGHAM, AL (AT&T U-verse. This is the regional video hub for the BIRMINGHAM area)

VANCE—See PELHAM, AL (Charter Communications)

VERNON—See SULLIGENT, AL (Charter Communications)

VESTAVIA HILLS—AT&T U-verse. This cable system has converted to IPTV. See BIRMINGHAM, AL [AL5004]

VESTAVIA HILLS—See BIRMINGHAM, AL (AT&T U-verse. This is the regional video hub for the BIRMINGHAM area)

VESTAVIA HILLS—See PELHAM, AL (Charter Communications)

VINCENT—See PELHAM, AL (Charter Communications)

VINEMONT—See CULLMAN, AL (Charter Communications)

WADLEY—Charter Communications. Now served by ROANOKE, AL [AL0023]

WADLEY—See ROANOKE, AL (Charter Communications)

WALKER COUNTY (PORTIONS)—See PELHAM, AL (Charter Communications)

WALKER COUNTY (UNINCORPORATED AREAS)—See BIRMINGHAM, AL (AT&T U-verse. This is the regional video hub for the BIRMINGHAM area)

WALLACE—See MOBILE, LA (Comcast Cable)

WALNUT GROVE—See ONEONTA, AL (Otelco)

WARRIOR—Formerly served by Time Warner Cable. Now served by Charter Communications, CULLMAN, AL [AL0034]

WARRIOR—See BIRMINGHAM, AL (AT&T U-verse. This is the regional video hub for the BIRMINGHAM area)

WARRIOR—See CULLMAN, AL (Charter Communications)

WASHINGTON COUNTY (UNINCORPORATED AREAS)—See MOBILE COUNTY, AL (Mediacom)

WATERLOO—Formerly served by North Crossroads Communications Inc. No longer in operation

WATERLOO—See BIRMINGHAM, AL (AT&T U-verse. This is the regional video hub for the BIRMINGHAM area)

WEAVER—See BIRMINGHAM, AL (AT&T U-verse. This is the regional video hub for the BIRMINGHAM area)

WEAVER—See ANNISTON, AL (Cable One)

WEBB—See DOTHAN, AL (WOW! Internet, Cable & Phone)

WEDOWEE—Charter Communications

WEST BLOCTON—Formerly served by Almega Cable. No longer in operation

WEST BLOCTON—See BIRMINGHAM, AL (AT&T U-verse. This is the regional video hub for the BIRMINGHAM area)

WEST BLOCTON—See CENTREVILLE, AL (Community Cable & Broadband LLC)

WEST END COBB—See BIRMINGHAM, AL (AT&T U-verse. This is the regional video hub for the BIRMINGHAM area)

WEST END—See PELHAM, AL (Charter Communications)

WEST JEFFERSON—See PELHAM, AL (Charter Communications)

WEST KILLEN—See ROGERSVILLE, AL (Zito Media)

WEST POINT—See BIRMINGHAM, AL (AT&T U-verse. This is the regional video hub for the BIRMINGHAM area)

WEST POINT—See CULLMAN, AL (Charter Communications)

WEST POINT—See CHAMBERS COUNTY (portions), GA (WOW! Internet, Cable & Phone)

WESTOVER—Charter Communications. Now served by PELHAM, AL [AL0192]

WESTOVER—See BIRMINGHAM, AL (AT&T U-verse. This is the regional video hub for the BIRMINGHAM area)

WESTOVER—See PELHAM, AL (Charter Communications)

WETUMPKA—Bright House Networks

WHATLEY—See GROVE HILL, AL (Pine Belt Broadband)

WHITES CHAPEL—See PELHAM, AL (Charter Communications)

WILCOX COUNTY (PORTIONS)—See MONROEVILLE, AL (Mediacom)

WILSONVILLE—See BIRMINGHAM, AL (AT&T U-verse. This is the regional video hub for the BIRMINGHAM area)

WILSONVILLE—See COLUMBIANA, AL (Zito Media)

WILTON—See BIRMINGHAM, AL (AT&T U-verse. This is the regional video hub for the BIRMINGHAM area)

WILTON—See PELHAM, AL (Charter Communications)

WINFIELD—West Alabama TV Cable Co. Inc

WINSTON COUNTY (PORTIONS)—See PELHAM, AL (Charter Communications)

WINSTON COUNTY (PORTIONS)—See HALEYVILLE, AL (Zito Media)

WINSTON COUNTY (UNINCORPORATED AREAS)—See BIRMINGHAM, AL (AT&T U-verse. This is the regional video hub for the BIRMINGHAM area)

WOODSTOCK—See BIRMINGHAM, AL (AT&T U-verse. This is the regional video hub for the BIRMINGHAM area)

WOODSTOCK—See CENTREVILLE, AL (Community Cable & Broadband LLC)

YORK—Mediacom

ALASKA

ADAK—Adak Cablevision. This cable system has converted to IPTV. See ADAK, AK [AK5003]

ADAK—Adak Cablevision. Formerly [AK0044]. This cable system has converted to IPTV

ANCHORAGE—Formerly served by ACS Television. No longer in operation

ANCHORAGE—Formerly served by Sprint Corp. No longer in operation

ANCHORAGE—GCI Cable Inc

ANGOON—GCI Cable Inc

AUKE BAY—See JUNEAU, AK (GCI Cable Inc)

BARROW—GCI Cable Inc

Cable Community Index—Arizona

BETHEL—GCI Cable Inc

CHUGIAK—See ANCHORAGE, AK (GCI Cable Inc)

CORDOVA—GCI Cable Inc

CRAIG—Craig Cable TV Inc

DILLINGHAM—Nushagak Cooperative Inc

DOUGLAS—See JUNEAU, AK (GCI Cable Inc)

EAGLE RIVER—See ANCHORAGE, AK (GCI Cable Inc)

ELELSON AFB—See FAIRBANKS, AK (GCI Cable Inc)

ELMENDORF AFB—See ANCHORAGE, AK (GCI Cable Inc)

FAIRBANKS COUNTY (UNINCORPORATED AREAS)—See FAIRBANKS, AK (GCI Cable Inc)

FAIRBANKS—GCI Cable Inc

FORT GREELY—GCI Cable Inc

FORT RICHARDSON—See ANCHORAGE, AK (GCI Cable Inc)

FORT WAINWRIGHT—See FAIRBANKS, AK (GCI Cable Inc)

GALENA—Eyecom Cable

GAMBELL—Formerly served by Frontier Cable Inc. No longer in operation

GIRDWOOD—GCI Cable Inc

HAINES—Haines Cable TV

HOMER—GCI Cable Inc

HOONAH—Formerly served by Hoonah Community TV. No longer in operation

HOOPER BAY—Formerly served by Frontier Cable Inc. No longer in operation

JUNEAU—GCI Cable Inc

KACHEMAK CITY—See HOMER, AK (GCI Cable Inc)

KENAI PENINSULA—See SEWARD, AK (GCI Cable Inc)

KENAI—GCI Cable Inc

KETCHIKAN GATEWAY BOROUGH—See KETCHIKAN, AK (GCI Cable Inc)

KETCHIKAN—GCI Cable Inc

KING COVE—Formerly served by Mount Dutton Cable Corp. No longer in operation

KING SALMON—Bay Cablevision

KIPNUK—Formerly served by Frontier Cable Inc. No longer in operation

KODIAK ISLAND BOROUGH—See KODIAK, AK (GCI Cable Inc)

KODIAK—GCI Cable Inc

KOTZEBUE—GCI Cable Inc

MATANUSKA VALLEY—See WASILLA, AK (GCI Cable Inc)

MOUNTAIN VILLAGE—Formerly served by Village Cable Co. No longer in operation

NAKNEK—See KING SALMON, AK (Bay Cablevision)

NOME—GCI Cable Inc

NORTH POLE—See FAIRBANKS, AK (GCI Cable Inc)

NORTH STAR BOROUGH—See FAIRBANKS, AK (GCI Cable Inc)

PALMER—See WASILLA, AK (GCI Cable Inc)

PETERS CREEK—See ANCHORAGE, AK (GCI Cable Inc)

PETERSBURG—GCI Cable Inc

PORT LIONS—Formerly served by Eyecom Cable. No longer in operation

QUINHAGAK—Formerly served by Frontier Cable Inc. No longer in operation

RIDGEWAY—See KENAI, AK (GCI Cable Inc)

SAVOONGA—Formerly served by Frontier Cable Inc. No longer in operation

SAXMAN—See KETCHIKAN, AK (GCI Cable Inc)

SEWARD—GCI Cable Inc

SITKA COUNTY—See SITKA, AK (GCI Cable Inc)

SITKA—GCI Cable Inc

SKAGWAY—Skagway Cable TV

SOLDOTNA—See KENAI, AK (GCI Cable Inc)

ST. MARY'S—Formerly served by Frontier Cable Inc. No longer in operation

TANANA—Supervision Inc

THORNE BAY—Formerly served by Thorne Bay Community TV Inc. No longer in operation

TOGIAK—Formerly served by Frontier Cable Inc. No longer in operation

TOKSOOK BAY—Formerly served by Frontier Cable Inc. No longer in operation

TUNUNAK—Formerly served by Frontier Cable Inc. No longer in operation

UNALAKLEET—Formerly served by Frontier Cable Inc. No longer in operation

UNALASKA—Eyecom Cable

VALDEZ—GCI Cable Inc

WARD COVE—See KETCHIKAN, AK (GCI Cable Inc)

WASILLA—GCI Cable Inc

WHITTIER—Supervision Inc. Now served by TANANA, AK [AK0031]

WHITTIER—See TANANA, AK (Supervision Inc)

WRANGELL—GCI Cable Inc

ARIZONA

AJO—Mediacom

ALPINE—Formerly served by Eagle West Communications Inc. No longer in operation

ANIMAS—See WILLCOX, NM (Valley Connections. Formerly [AZ0108]. This cable system has converted to IPTV.)

APACHE JUNCTION—See SCOTTSDALE, AZ (CenturyLink Prism)

APACHE JUNCTION—Mediacom

AVONDALE—Cox Communications. Now served by PHOENIX, AZ [AZ0001]

AVONDALE—See PHOENIX, AZ (Cox Communications)

BAGDAD—Formerly served by Eagle West Communications Inc. No longer in operation

BENSON—Cox Communications. Now served by TUCSON, AZ [AZ0002]

BENSON—See TUCSON, AZ (Cox Communications)

BISBEE—Cable One

BLACK CANYON CITY—Formerly served by RealStar Communications. No longer in operation

BONITA—See WILLCOX, AZ (Valley Connections. Formerly [AZ0108]. This cable system has converted to IPTV.)

BOWIE—See WILLCOX, AZ (Valley Connections. Formerly [AZ0108]. This cable system has converted to IPTV.)

BUCKEYE—See SCOTTSDALE, AZ (CenturyLink Prism)

BUCKEYE—See PHOENIX, AZ (Cox Communications)

BULLHEAD CITY—Suddenlink Communications

BUSHMAN ACRES—See SHOW LOW, AZ (Cable One)

BYLAS—San Carlos Apache Telecom. Now served by SAN CARLOS, AZ [AZ0046]

BYLAS—See SAN CARLOS, AZ (San Carlos Apache Telecom)

CAMP VERDE—See SEDONA, AZ (Suddenlink Communications)

CAREFREE—Cox Communications. Now served by PHOENIX, AZ [AZ0001]

CAREFREE—See PHOENIX, AZ (Cox Communications)

CASA GRANDE (northern portion)—Formerly served by RealStar Communications. No longer in operation

CASA GRANDE—Cox Communications. Now served by PHOENIX, AZ [AZ0001]

CASA GRANDE—See SCOTTSDALE, AZ (CenturyLink Prism)

CASA GRANDE—See PHOENIX, AZ (Cox Communications)

CASHION—See PHOENIX, AZ (Cox Communications)

CAVE CREEK—Formerly served by RealStar Communications. No longer in operation

CAVE CREEK—See PHOENIX, AZ (Cox Communications)

CHANDLER—See SCOTTSDALE, AZ (CenturyLink Prism)

CHANDLER—See PHOENIX, AZ (Cox Communications)

CHINLE—Formerly served by Frontier Communications. No longer in operation

CHINO VALLEY—See PRESCOTT, AZ (Cable One)

CLARKDALE—See COTTONWOOD, AZ (Cable One)

CLIFTON—Cable One. Now served by SAFFORD, AZ [AZ0021]

CLIFTON—See SAFFORD, AZ (Cable One)

CLIFTON—See WILLCOX, AZ (Valley Connections. Formerly [AZ0108]. This cable system has converted to IPTV.)

COCHISE COUNTY (PORTIONS)—See BISBEE, AZ (Cable One)

COCHISE COUNTY (PORTIONS)—See WILLCOX, AZ (Valley Connections. Formerly [AZ0108]. This cable system has converted to IPTV.)

COCONINO COUNTY—See PAGE, AZ (Cable One)

COCONINO COUNTY—See FLAGSTAFF, AZ (Suddenlink Communications)

COLORADO RIVER INDIAN RESERVATION—See PARKER, CA (Suddenlink Communications)

COLORADO RIVER INDIAN TRIBES—See PARKER, AZ (Suddenlink Communications)

COLUMBUS—See WILLCOX, NM (Valley Connections. Formerly [AZ0108]. This cable system has converted to IPTV.)

CONCHO VALLEY—Formerly served by Eagle West Communications Inc. No longer in operation

COOLIDGE—Formerly served by Cable America Corp. Now served by Cox Communications, PHOENIX, AZ [AZ0001]

COOLIDGE—See PHOENIX, AZ (Cox Communications)

CORDES LAKES—Formerly served by Cordes Lakes Cablevision. No longer in operation

CORNVILLE—See COTTONWOOD, AZ (Cable One)

COTTONWOOD (SOUTHEASTERN PORTIONS)—See SEDONA, AZ (Suddenlink Communications)

COTTONWOOD—Cable One

DAVIS-MONTHAN AFB—See TUCSON, AZ (Cox Communications)

DESERT HILLS—See LAKE HAVASU CITY, AZ (Suddenlink Communications)

DEWEY—See PRESCOTT, AZ (Cable One)

Arizona—Cable Community Index

DOUGLAS—Cox Communications. Now served by SIERRA VISTA, AZ [AZ0005]

DOUGLAS—See SIERRA VISTA, AZ (Cox Communications)

DUDLEYVILLE—Formerly served by RealStar Communications. No longer in operation

DUNCAN—See WILLCOX, AZ (Valley Connections. Formerly [AZ0108]. This cable system has converted to IPTV.)

EAGAR—Formerly served by RealStar Communications. No longer in operation

EAST MESA—Formerly served by Eagle West Communications Inc. No longer in operation

EL MIRAGE—See PHOENIX, AZ (Cox Communications)

ELFRIDA—See WILLCOX, AZ (Valley Connections. Formerly [AZ0108]. This cable system has converted to IPTV.)

ELOY—Formerly served by RealStar Communications. No longer in operation

FLAGSTAFF—Formerly served by Microwave Communication Services. No longer in operation

FLAGSTAFF—Suddenlink Communications

FLORENCE GARDEN MOBILE HOME PARK—Formerly served by Eagle West Communications Inc. No longer in operation

FLORENCE—See PHOENIX, AZ (Cox Communications)

FORT HUACHUCA—See SIERRA VISTA, AZ (Cox Communications)

FORT MOHAVE MESA—Formerly served by Americable International Arizona Inc. No longer in operation

FORT MOHAVE—See BULLHEAD CITY, AZ (Suddenlink Communications)

FOUNTAIN HILLS—See PHOENIX, AZ (Cox Communications)

FREDONIA—South Central Communications. Now served by PANGUITCH, UT [UT0043]

GILA BEND—CableAmerica (formerly Cox Communications). This cable system has converted to IPTV. See GILA BEND, AZ [AZ5021]

GILA BEND—CableAmerica (formerly Cox Communications). This cable system has converted to IPTV

GILA COUNTY (PORTIONS)—See SAN CARLOS, AZ (San Carlos Apache Telecom)

GILA COUNTY (PORTIONS)—See PAYSON (town), AZ (Suddenlink Communications)

GILA COUNTY (PORTIONS)—See PINE, AZ (Suddenlink Communications)

GILA COUNTY—San Carlos Apache Telecom. Now served by SAN CARLOS, AZ [AZ0046]

GILA COUNTY—See GLOBE-MIAMI, AZ (Cable One)

GILBERT—Cox Communications. Now served by PHOENIX, AZ [AZ0001]

GILBERT—See SCOTTSDALE, AZ (CenturyLink Prism)

GILBERT—See PHOENIX, AZ (Cox Communications)

GISELA—Formerly served by Indevideo Co. Inc. No longer in operation

GLENDALE (portions)—Formerly served by Qwest Choice TV. IPTV service has been discontinued

GLENDALE—See SCOTTSDALE, AZ (CenturyLink Prism)

GLENDALE—See PHOENIX, AZ (Cox Communications)

GLOBE-MIAMI—Cable One

GOLD CANYON—See APACHE JUNCTION, AZ (Mediacom)

GOLDEN SHORES—Golden Valley Cable

GOLDEN VALLEY—Golden Valley Cable & Communications

GOODYEAR—See SCOTTSDALE, AZ (CenturyLink Prism)

GOODYEAR—See PHOENIX, AZ (Cox Communications)

GRAHAM COUNTY (PORTIONS)—See WILLCOX, AZ (Valley Connections. Formerly [AZ0108]. This cable system has converted to IPTV.)

GRAHAM COUNTY—See SAFFORD, AZ (Cable One)

GRAND CANYON—Formerly served by Indevideo Co. Inc. No longer in operation

GRAND MISSOURI MOBILE HOME PARK—Formerly served by Sun Valley Cable Inc. No longer in operation

GREEN VALLEY—See TUCSON, AZ (Cox Communications)

GREENLEE COUNTY (PORTIONS)—See WILLCOX, AZ (Valley Connections. Formerly [AZ0108]. This cable system has converted to IPTV.)

GUADALUPE—See PHOENIX, AZ (Cox Communications)

HACHITA—See WILLCOX, NM (Valley Connections. Formerly [AZ0108]. This cable system has converted to IPTV.)

HEBER—Formerly served by RealStar Communications. No longer in operation

HOLBROOK—Cable One. Now served by SHOW LOW, AZ [AZ0014]

HOLBROOK—See SHOW LOW, AZ (Cable One)

HUACHUCA CITY—See SIERRA VISTA, AZ (Cox Communications)

HUMBOLDT—See PRESCOTT, AZ (Cable One)

JOSEPH CITY—See SHOW LOW, AZ (Cable One)

KAYENTA—Formerly served by Frontier Communications. No longer in operation

KEARNY—Formerly served by RealStar Communications. No longer in operation

KINGMAN—Suddenlink Communications

LA PAZ COUNTY (PORTIONS)—See PARKER, AZ (Suddenlink Communications)

LAKE HAVASU CITY—Suddenlink Communications

LAKE MONTEZUMA—See SEDONA, AZ (Suddenlink Communications)

LAKESIDE—See SHOW LOW, AZ (Cable One)

LEUPP—Formerly served by Indevideo Co. Inc. No longer in operation

LITCHFIELD PARK—See PHOENIX, AZ (Cox Communications)

LUKE AFB—Cox Communications. Now served by PHOENIX, AZ [AZ0001]

LUKE AFB—See PHOENIX, AZ (Cox Communications)

LUNA COUNTY (PORTIONS)—See WILLCOX, NM (Valley Connections. Formerly [AZ0108]. This cable system has converted to IPTV.)

MAMMOTH—Formerly served by RealStar Communications. No longer in operation

MARANA—See TUCSON, AZ (Comcast Cable)

MARICOPA CITY—See SCOTTSDALE, AZ (CenturyLink Prism)

MARICOPA COUNTY (PORTIONS)—See PHOENIX, AZ (Cox Communications)

MARICOPA COUNTY (UNINCORPORATED AREAS)—See SCOTTSDALE, AZ (CenturyLink Prism)

MARICOPA—Orbitel Communications

MARINE CORPS AIR STATION—See YUMA (portions), AZ (Time Warner Cable)

MAYER—See PRESCOTT, AZ (Cable One)

MCNEAL—See WILLCOX, AZ (Valley Connections. Formerly [AZ0108]. This cable system has converted to IPTV.)

MESA—Cox Communications. Now served by PHOENIX, AZ [AZ0001]

MESA—See SCOTTSDALE, AZ (CenturyLink Prism)

MESA—See PHOENIX, AZ (Cox Communications)

MILLER CANYON (UNINCORPORATED AREA)—See SIERRA VISTA, AZ (Cox Communications)

MOHAVE COUNTY (PORTIONS)—See BULLHEAD CITY, AZ (Suddenlink Communications)

MOHAVE COUNTY (PORTIONS)—See KINGMAN, AZ (Suddenlink Communications)

MOHAVE COUNTY (PORTIONS)—See LAKE HAVASU CITY, AZ (Suddenlink Communications)

MOHAVE VALLEY—See BULLHEAD CITY, AZ (Suddenlink Communications)

MORENCI—See SAFFORD, AZ (Cable One)

MORENCI—See WILLCOX, AZ (Valley Connections. Formerly [AZ0108]. This cable system has converted to IPTV.)

MUNDS PARK—Suddenlink Communications. Now served by SEDONA, AZ [AZ0025]

MUNDS PARK—See SEDONA, AZ (Suddenlink Communications)

NACO—See BISBEE, AZ (Cable One)

NAVAJO COUNTY (PORTIONS)—See SHOW LOW, AZ (Cable One)

NICKSVILLE—See SIERRA VISTA, AZ (Cox Communications)

NOGALES—Mediacom

OAK CREEK (VILLAGE)—See SEDONA, AZ (Suddenlink Communications)

ORACLE—Formerly served by RealStar Communications. No longer in operation

ORO VALLEY—See TUCSON, AZ (Comcast Cable)

PAGE SPRINGS—See COTTONWOOD, AZ (Cable One)

PAGE—Cable One

PARADISE VALLEY (portions)—Formerly served by Qwest Choice TV. IPTV service has been discontinued

PARADISE VALLEY—See SCOTTSDALE, AZ (CenturyLink Prism)

PARADISE VALLEY—See PHOENIX, AZ (Cox Communications)

PARKER—Suddenlink Communications

PATAGONIA—Cox Communications. Now served by SIERRA VISTA, AZ [AZ0005]

PATAGONIA—See SIERRA VISTA, AZ (Cox Communications)

PAULDEN—See PRESCOTT, AZ (Cable One)

PAYSON (TOWN)—Suddenlink Communications

PEACH SPRINGS—Formerly served by Eagle West Communications Inc. No longer in operation

PEARCE—See WILLCOX, AZ (Valley Connections. Formerly [AZ0108]. This cable system has converted to IPTV.)

PEORIA (portions)—Formerly served by Qwest Choice TV. Now served by CenturyLink Prism, SCOTTSDALE,

Cable Community Index—Arizona

AZ [AZ5019]. This cable system has converted to IPTV

PEORIA—See SCOTTSDALE, AZ (CenturyLink Prism)

PEORIA—See PHOENIX, AZ (Cox Communications)

PERIDOT—See SAN CARLOS, AZ (San Carlos Apache Telecom)

PERRYVILLE—Formerly served by Eagle West Communications Inc. No longer in operation

PHOENIX (portions)—CenturyLink (formerly Qwest). This cable system has converted to IPTV. See SCOTTSDALE, AZ [AZ5019]

PHOENIX—Formerly served by Sprint Corp. No longer in operation

PHOENIX—Formerly served by TV Max. No longer in operation

PHOENIX—See SCOTTSDALE, AZ (CenturyLink Prism)

PHOENIX—Cox Communications

PIMA COUNTY—See TUCSON, AZ (Comcast Cable)

PIMA COUNTY—See TUCSON, AZ (Cox Communications)

PIMA—See SAFFORD, AZ (Cable One)

PINAL COUNTY (PORTIONS)—See APACHE JUNCTION, AZ (Mediacom)

PINAL COUNTY (UNINCORPORATED AREAS)—See SCOTTSDALE, AZ (CenturyLink Prism)

PINAL COUNTY—See PHOENIX, AZ (Cox Communications)

PINE—Suddenlink Communications

PINETOP—See SHOW LOW, AZ (Cable One)

PINEVIEW—See SHOW LOW, AZ (Cable One)

PINEWOOD—See SEDONA, AZ (Suddenlink Communications)

PIRTLEVILLE—See SIERRA VISTA, AZ (Cox Communications)

PLAYAS—See WILLCOX, NM (Valley Connections. Formerly [AZ0108]. This cable system has converted to IPTV.)

POMERENE—Formerly served by Midvale Telephone Exchange Inc. No longer in operation

PORTAL—See WILLCOX, AZ (Valley Connections. Formerly [AZ0108]. This cable system has converted to IPTV.)

PRESCOTT VALLEY—See PRESCOTT, AZ (Cable One)

PRESCOTT—Cable One

QUARTZSITE—Formerly served by Americable International Arizona Inc. No longer in operation

QUEEN CREEK—See SCOTTSDALE, AZ (CenturyLink Prism)

QUEEN CREEK—See PHOENIX, AZ (Cox Communications)

QUEEN CREEK—See APACHE JUNCTION, AZ (Mediacom)

QUEEN VALLEY—See APACHE JUNCTION, AZ (Mediacom)

RAMSEY CANYON (UNINCORPORATED AREA)—See SIERRA VISTA, AZ (Cox Communications)

RIO RICO—See NOGALES, AZ (Mediacom)

RIO VERDE—Cox Communications. Now served by PHOENIX, AZ [AZ0001]

RIO VERDE—See PHOENIX, AZ (Cox Communications)

ROBSON RANCH—Orbitel Communications

ROCK SHADOWS—See APACHE JUNCTION, AZ (Mediacom)

RODEO—See WILLCOX, NM (Valley Connections. Formerly [AZ0108]. This cable system has converted to IPTV.)

ROOSEVELT TWP.—Formerly served by Salt River Cablevision. No longer in operation

SADDLE MOUNTAIN—Formerly served by Eagle West Communications Inc. No longer in operation

SADDLEBROOKE—Orbitel Communications

SAFFORD—Cable One

SAFFORD—See WILLCOX, AZ (Valley Connections. Formerly [AZ0108]. This cable system has converted to IPTV.)

SAHUARITA—See TUCSON, AZ (Cox Communications)

SALOME—Formerly served by San Carlos Cablevision. No longer in operation

SAN BERNARDINO COUNTY (PORTIONS)—See PARKER, CA (Suddenlink Communications)

SAN CARLOS—San Carlos Apache Telecom

SAN JUAN—Formerly served by RealStar Communications. No longer in operation

SAN LUIS—See YUMA (portions), AZ (Time Warner Cable)

SAN SIMEON—See WILLCOX, AZ (Valley Connections. Formerly [AZ0108]. This cable system has converted to IPTV.)

SANTA CRUZ COUNTY (PORTIONS)—See NOGALES, AZ (Mediacom)

SANTA RITA BEL AIRE—Cox Communications. Now served by TUCSON, AZ [AZ0002]

SANTA RITA BEL AIRE—See TUCSON, AZ (Cox Communications)

SCOTTSDALE—CenturyLink Prism

SCOTTSDALE—See PHOENIX, AZ (Cox Communications)

SEDONA—Suddenlink Communications

SELLS—Formerly served by Red Hawk Cable. No longer in operation

SHOW LOW—Cable One

SIERRA VISTA—Cox Communications

SNOWFLAKE—See SHOW LOW, AZ (Cable One)

SOLOMON—See SAFFORD, AZ (Cable One)

SOMERTON INDIAN RESERVATION—See YUMA (portions), AZ (Time Warner Cable)

SOMERTON—See YUMA (portions), AZ (Time Warner Cable)

SONOITA—See SIERRA VISTA, AZ (Cox Communications)

SOUTH TUCSON—See TUCSON, AZ (Cox Communications)

ST. DAVID—See SIERRA VISTA, AZ (Cox Communications)

ST. JOHNS—Formerly served by RealStar Communications. No longer in operation

STAR VALLEY—See PAYSON (town), AZ (Suddenlink Communications)

STRAWBERRY—See PINE, AZ (Suddenlink Communications)

STUMP CANYON (UNINCORPORATED AREA)—See SIERRA VISTA, AZ (Cox Communications)

SUN CITY WEST—See PHOENIX, AZ (Cox Communications)

SUN CITY—See PHOENIX, AZ (Cox Communications)

SUN LAKES—See PHOENIX, AZ (Cox Communications)

SUN LAKES—Orbitel Communications

SUNBIRD—See SUN LAKES, AZ (Orbitel Communications)

SUNIZONA—See WILLCOX, AZ (Valley Connections. Formerly [AZ0108]. This cable system has converted to IPTV.)

SUNSITES—See SIERRA VISTA, AZ (Cox Communications)

SUNSITES—See WILLCOX, AZ (Valley Connections. Formerly [AZ0108]. This cable system has converted to IPTV.)

SUPERIOR—Formerly served by RealStar Communications. No longer in operation

SURPRISE—See SCOTTSDALE, AZ (CenturyLink Prism)

SURPRISE—See PHOENIX, AZ (Cox Communications)

SWIFT TRAIL—See SAFFORD, AZ (Cable One)

TAYLOR—See SHOW LOW, AZ (Cable One)

TEMPE—See SCOTTSDALE, AZ (CenturyLink Prism)

TEMPE—See PHOENIX, AZ (Cox Communications)

THATCHER—See SAFFORD, AZ (Cable One)

THATCHER—See WILLCOX, AZ (Valley Connections. Formerly [AZ0108]. This cable system has converted to IPTV.)

TOLLESON—See PHOENIX, AZ (Cox Communications)

TOMBSTONE—See SIERRA VISTA, AZ (Cox Communications)

TOPOCK—See GOLDEN SHORES, AZ (Golden Valley Cable)

TORTOLITA—See TUCSON, AZ (Comcast Cable)

TSAILE—Formerly served by Frontier Communications. No longer in operation

TUBA CITY—Formerly served by Indevideo Co. Inc. No longer in operation

TUCSON ESTATES—Formerly served by Comcast Cable. No longer in operation

TUCSON—Formerly served by Sprint Corp. No longer in operation

TUCSON—Comcast Cable

TUCSON—Cox Communications

TUSAYAN—Formerly served by Indevideo Co. Inc. No longer in operation

VERDE VILLAGE—See SEDONA, AZ (Suddenlink Communications)

VIRDEN—See WILLCOX, NM (Valley Connections. Formerly [AZ0108]. This cable system has converted to IPTV.)

WELLTON—Beamspeed LLC

WHETSTONE—See SIERRA VISTA, AZ (Cox Communications)

WICKENBURG—Cox Communications. Now served by PHOENIX, AZ [AZ0001]

WICKENBURG—See PHOENIX, AZ (Cox Communications)

WILLCOX—Formerly served by Cox Communications. Now served by Valley Telecom Group. This cable system has converted to IPTV. See WILLCOX, AZ [AZ5009]

WILLCOX—Valley Connections. Formerly [AZ0108]. This cable system has converted to IPTV.

WILLIAMS—Formerly served by New Day Broadband. No longer in operation

WILLOW VALLEY—See BULLHEAD CITY, AZ (Suddenlink Communications)

WINSLOW—Cable One. Now served by SHOW LOW, AZ [AZ0014]

WINSLOW—See SHOW LOW, AZ (Cable One)

WINTERHAVEN—See YUMA (portions), CA (Time Warner Cable)

YARNELL—Formerly served by RealStar Communications. No longer in operation

Arizona—Cable Community Index

YAVAPAI COUNTY (NORTHEASTERN PORTION)—See COTTONWOOD, AZ (Cable One)

YAVAPAI COUNTY (PORTIONS)—See PRESCOTT, AZ (Cable One)

YAVAPAI-APACHE-CLARKSDALE RESERVATION—See COTTONWOOD, AZ (Cable One)

YORK VALLEY—See WILLCOX, AZ (Valley Connections. Formerly [AZ0108]. This cable system has converted to IPTV.)

YOUNGTOWN—See PHOENIX, AZ (Cox Communications)

YUMA (PORTIONS)—Time Warner Cable

YUMA COUNTY (PORTIONS)—See YUMA (portions), AZ (Time Warner Cable)

YUMA PROVING GROUND—See YUMA (portions), AZ (Time Warner Cable)

ARKANSAS

ALEXANDER—See LITTLE ROCK, AR (Comcast Cable)

ALEXANDER—See BENTON, AR (Fidelity Communications)

ALMA—See FORT SMITH, AR (Cox Communications)

ALMYRA—Formerly served by Cebridge Connections. No longer in operation

ALPENA—Ritter Communications. Now served by WESTERN GROVE, AR [AR0183]

ALPENA—See WESTERN GROVE, AR (Ritter Communications)

ALTHEIMER—Formerly served by Almega Cable. No longer in operation

ALTUS—See OZARK, AR (Suddenlink Communications)

AMITY—Formerly served by Cablevision of Amity. No longer in operation

ARBYRD—See MARKED TREE, MO (Ritter Communications)

ARKADELPHIA—Suddenlink Communications

ARKANSAS CITY—Formerly served by Cablevision of Arkansas City. No longer in operation

ARKOLA—See FORT SMITH, AR (Cox Communications)

ARKOMA—See FORT SMITH, OK (Cox Communications)

ASH FLAT—Crystal Broadband Networks

ASHDOWN—NewWave Communications

ASHLEY COUNTY (PORTIONS)—See CROSSETT, AR (Media3)

ATKINS—Suddenlink Communications

AUBREY—Media3

AUGUSTA—Augusta Video Inc

AUSTIN—See CABOT, AR (Suddenlink Communications)

AVOCA—See SPRINGDALE, AR (Cox Communications)

BALD KNOB—See SEARCY, AR (White County Cable TV)

BARLING—See FORT SMITH, AR (Cox Communications)

BASSETT—See MARKED TREE, AR (Ritter Communications)

BATESVILLE—Suddenlink Communications

BAUXITE—See BENTON, AR (Fidelity Communications)

BAXTER COUNTY (PORTIONS)—See MOUNTAIN HOME, AR (Suddenlink Communications)

BAXTER COUNTY (unincorporated areas)—Formerly served by Almega Cable. No longer in operation

BAY—See JONESBORO, AR (Suddenlink Communications)

BEARDEN—Formerly served by Zoom Media. No longer in operation

BEAVER LAKE—Cox Communications. Now served by SPRINGDALE, AR [AR0220]

BEAVER LAKE—See SPRINGDALE, AR (Cox Communications)

BEAVER SHORES—See SPRINGDALE, AR (Cox Communications)

BEAVER—See BERRYVILLE, AR (Cox Communications)

BEAVERAMA—See SPRINGDALE, AR (Cox Communications)

BEEBE—Fidelity Communications

BELLA VISTA—See SPRINGDALE, AR (Cox Communications)

BELLEFONTE—See HARRISON, AR (Cox Communications)

BENTON COUNTY—Cox Communications. Now served by SPRINGDALE, AR [AR0220]

BENTON COUNTY—See SPRINGDALE, AR (Cox Communications)

BENTON—Fidelity Communications

BENTONVILLE—See SPRINGDALE, AR (Cox Communications)

BERGMAN—See HARRISON, AR (Cox Communications)

BERRYVILLE—Cox Communications

BETHEL HEIGHTS TWP.—See SPRINGDALE, AR (Cox Communications)

BIGGERS—Formerly served by Boycom Cablevision Inc. No longer in operation

BISCOE—Formerly served by Cebridge Connections. No longer in operation

BISMARCK—Formerly served by Cablevision of Bismarck. No longer in operation

BLACK OAK—See MARKED TREE, AR (Ritter Communications)

BLACK ROCK—Indco Cable TV

BLYTHEVILLE—Ritter Communications. Now served by MARKED TREE, AR [AR0072]

BLYTHEVILLE—See MARKED TREE, AR (Ritter Communications)

BONANZA—See FORT SMITH, AR (Cox Communications)

BONO—Ritter Communications. Now served by MARKED TREE, AR [AR0072]

BONO—See OAK GROVE HEIGHTS, AR (Fusion Media)

BONO—See MARKED TREE, AR (Ritter Communications)

BOONE COUNTY—See HARRISON, AR (Cox Communications)

BOONEVILLE HUMAN DEVELOPMENT CENTER—Formerly served by Eagle Media. No longer in operation

BOONEVILLE—Suddenlink Communications

BRADFORD—Indco Cable TV

BRADLEY COUNTY—See WARREN, AR (Cablevision of Warren)

BRADLEY—Formerly served by Cebridge Connections. No longer in operation

BRIARCLIFF—Formerly served by Almega Cable. No longer in operation

BRINKLEY—East Arkansas Video Inc

BROOKLAND—See OAK GROVE HEIGHTS, AR (Fusion Media)

BROOKLAND—See MARKED TREE, AR (Ritter Communications)

BRYANT—See LITTLE ROCK, AR (Comcast Cable)

BRYANT—See BENTON, AR (Fidelity Communications)

BUCKNER—See LEWISVILLE, AR (Formerly served by Alliance Communications. Now served by Media3)

BULL SHOALS—See MOUNTAIN HOME, AR (Suddenlink Communications)

CABOT—Suddenlink Communications

CADDO VALLEY—See ARKADELPHIA, AR (Suddenlink Communications)

CALDWELL—Indco Cable TV

CALICO ROCK—Yelcot Communications

CAMDEN—Cam-Tel Co

CAMMACK VILLAGE—See LITTLE ROCK, AR (Comcast Cable)

CAMPBELL STATION—See NEWPORT, AR (Suddenlink Communications)

CARAWAY—See MARKED TREE, AR (Ritter Communications)

CARDWELL—See MARKED TREE, MO (Ritter Communications)

CARLISLE—See HAZEN, AR (Suddenlink Communications)

CARPENTER DAM—Formerly served by Cablevision of Carpenter Dam. No longer in operation

CARROLL COUNTY (PORTIONS)—See BERRYVILLE, AR (Cox Communications)

CARTHAGE—Formerly served by Almega Cable. No longer in operation

CARTHAGE—Formerly served by Almega Cable. No longer in operation

CASA—Formerly served by Eagle Media. No longer in operation

CASH—See MARKED TREE, AR (Ritter Communications)

CAVE CITY—See PFEIFFER, AR (Indco Cable TV)

CAVE SPRINGS—See SPRINGDALE, AR (Cox Communications)

CEDARVILLE—Cox Communications. Now served by FORT SMITH, AR [AR0003]

CEDARVILLE—See FORT SMITH, AR (Cox Communications)

CENTERTON—See SPRINGDALE, AR (Cox Communications)

CENTRAL CITY—See FORT SMITH, AR (Cox Communications)

CHARLESTON—Suddenlink Communications

CHEROKEE VILLAGE—See HARDY, AR (Fidelity Communications)

CHERRY VALLEY—See MARKED TREE, AR (Ritter Communications)

CHESTER—See FORT SMITH, AR (Cox Communications)

CHICOT COUNTY (PORTIONS)—See McGEHEE, AR (Vyve Broadband)

CHIDESTER—Formerly served by Almega Cable. No longer in operation

CLARENDON—Formerly served by Zoom Media. No longer in operation

CLARKSVILLE—Suddenlink Communications

CLAY COUNTY (PORTIONS)—See CORNING, AR (Vyve Broadband)

CLEBURNE COUNTY (PORTIONS)—See PANGBURN, AR (Indco Cable TV)

CLEBURNE COUNTY (PORTIONS)—See HEBER SPRINGS, AR (Suddenlink Communications)

CLEBURNE COUNTY (PORTIONS)—See FAIRFIELD BAY, AR (Vyve Broadband)

CLINTON—Clinton Cablevision Inc

CLINTON—Media3

COAL HILL—Formerly served by Suddenlink Communications. No longer in operation

COLLEGE CITY—See HOXIE, AR (Suddenlink Communications)

Cable Community Index—Arkansas

COLT—See CALDWELL, AR (Indco Cable TV)

COLUMBIA COUNTY—See MAGNOLIA, AR (Suddenlink Communications)

CONWAY COUNTY (PORTIONS)—See MORRILTON, AR (Suddenlink Communications)

CONWAY—Buford Media. Now served by GREENBRIER, AR [AR0077]

CONWAY—Formerly served by Alliance Communications. Now served by Media3, MAYFLOWER, AR [AR0049]

CONWAY—Conway Corp. C.T.S.

CONWAY—See MAYFLOWER, AR (Media3)

CORNING—Vyve Broadband

COTTER—See MOUNTAIN HOME, AR (Suddenlink Communications)

CRAIGHEAD COUNTY (NORTHWESTERN PORTION)—See MARKED TREE, AR (Ritter Communications)

CRAIGHEAD COUNTY (PORTIONS)—See OAK GROVE HEIGHTS, AR (Fusion Media)

CRAIGHEAD COUNTY (PORTIONS)—See JONESBORO, AR (Suddenlink Communications)

CRAWFORD COUNTY (UNINCORPORATED AREAS)—See SPRINGDALE, AR (Cox Communications)

CRAWFORD COUNTY—See FORT SMITH, AR (Cox Communications)

CRAWFORDSVILLE (portions)—Formerly served by Ritter Communications. No longer in operation

CRITTENDEN COUNTY (PORTIONS)—See HUGHES, AR (Suddenlink Communications)

CROSSETT—Media3

CRYSTAL HILL—See MAUMELLE, AR (Fidelity Communications)

CURTIS—Formerly served by Community Communications Co. No longer in operation

CUSHMAN—Indco Cable TV

DAMASCUS—See CLINTON, AR (Media3)

DANVILLE—Formerly served by Suddenlink Communications. No longer in operation

DARDANELLE—See RUSSELLVILLE, AR (Suddenlink Communications)

DE QUEEN—Vyve Broadband

DE VALLS BLUFF—See HAZEN, AR (Suddenlink Communications)

DE WITT—Suddenlink Communications

DECATUR—See SPRINGDALE, AR (Cox Communications)

DELIGHT—Formerly served by Almega Cable. No longer in operation

DELL—See MARKED TREE, AR (Ritter Communications)

DERMOTT—See McGEHEE, AR (Vyve Broadband)

DES ARC—Alliance Communications

DESHA COUNTY—See McGEHEE, AR (Vyve Broadband)

DESHA—See BATESVILLE, AR (Suddenlink Communications)

DIAMOND CITY—NATCO Communications Inc.

DIAZ—See NEWPORT, AR (Suddenlink Communications)

DIERKS—Formerly served by Allegiance Communications. No longer in operation

DOVER—Suddenlink Communications

DREW COUNTY—See MONTICELLO, AR (Cablevision of Monticello)

DUMAS—BCI Broadband. Now served by McGEHEE, AR [AR0262]

DUMAS—See McGEHEE, AR (Vyve Broadband)

DYER—See FORT SMITH, AR (Cox Communications)

DYESS—See MARKED TREE, AR (Ritter Communications)

EARLE—Comcast Cable. Now served by MEMPHIS, TN [TN0001]

EAST CAMDEN—Formerly served by Cablevision of East Camden. No longer in operation

EDEN ISLE—See HEBER SPRINGS, AR (Suddenlink Communications)

EL DORADO—Suddenlink Communications

ELAINE—See LAKE VIEW, AR (Alliance Communications)

ELKINS—See SPRINGDALE, AR (Cox Communications)

ELM SPRINGS—See SPRINGDALE, AR (Cox Communications)

EMERSON—Formerly served by Almega Cable. No longer in operation

EMMET—Formerly served by Almega Cable. No longer in operation

ENGLAND—Formerly served by Zoom Media. No longer in operation

EUDORA—Cablevision of Eudora

EUREKA SPRINGS—Cox Communications. Now served by BERRYVILLE, AR [AR0221]

EUREKA SPRINGS—See BERRYVILLE, AR (Cox Communications)

EVENING SHADE—Indco Cable TV

EVERTON—See WESTERN GROVE, AR (Ritter Communications)

EXCELSIOR—Cox Communications. Now served by FORT SMITH, AR [AR0003]

EXCELSIOR—See FORT SMITH, AR (Cox Communications)

FAIRFIELD BAY—Vyve Broadband

FARMINGTON—See SPRINGDALE, AR (Cox Communications)

FAULKNER COUNTY (PORTIONS)—See MAYFLOWER, AR (Media3)

FAULKNER COUNTY (PORTIONS)—See CABOT, AR (Suddenlink Communications)

FAYETTEVILLE—Cox Communications. Now served by SPRINGDALE, AR [AR0220]

FAYETTEVILLE—See SPRINGDALE, AR (Cox Communications)

FISHER—See MARKED TREE, AR (Ritter Communications)

FLIPPIN—See MOUNTAIN HOME, AR (Suddenlink Communications)

FORDYCE—Media3

FORREST CITY—East Arkansas Video Inc

FORT SMITH—Cox Communications

FOUKE—Cable One. Now served by TEXARKANA, TX [TX0031]

FOUNTAIN HILL—Formerly served by Almega Cable. No longer in operation

FRANKLIN COUNTY (WESTERN PORTION)—See FORT SMITH, AR (Cox Communications)

FRANKLIN—See HORSESHOE BEND, AR (Crystal Broadband Networks)

FRIENDSHIP—Formerly served by Community Communications Co. No longer in operation

FULTON—Formerly served by Allegiance Communications. No longer in operation

GARLAND CITY—Formerly served by Cebridge Connections. No longer in operation

GARLAND COUNTY (PORTIONS)—See HOT SPRINGS, AR (Resort TV Cable Co. Inc)

GARLAND COUNTY (PORTIONS)—See HOT SPRINGS VILLAGE, AR (Suddenlink Communications)

GASSVILLE—See MOUNTAIN HOME, AR (Suddenlink Communications)

GASSVILLE—Yelcot Communications

GENTRY—See SPRINGDALE, AR (Cox Communications)

GILLETT—Formerly served by Community Communications Co. No longer in operation

GILMORE—See MARKED TREE, AR (Ritter Communications)

GLENWOOD—Formerly served by Cablevision of Glenwood. No longer in operation

GOSHEN—See SPRINGDALE, AR (Cox Communications)

GOSNELL—Ritter Communications. Now served by MARKED TREE, AR [AR0072]

GOSNELL—See MARKED TREE, AR (Ritter Communications)

GOULD—Cablevision of Gould

GRADY—Formerly served by Cebridge Connections. No longer in operation

GRANT COUNTY (PORTIONS)—See WHITEHALL, AR (Suddenlink Communications)

GRAVETTE—See SPRINGDALE, AR (Cox Communications)

GREEN FOREST—See BERRYVILLE, AR (Cox Communications)

GREENBRIER—Formerly served by Alliance Communications. Now served by Media3, MAYFLOWER, AR [AR0049]

GREENBRIER—See MAYFLOWER, AR (Media3)

GREENE COUNTY (PORTIONS)—See OAK GROVE HEIGHTS, AR (Fusion Media)

GREENE COUNTY (unincorporated areas)—Formerly served by Indco Cable TV. No longer in operation

GREENLAND—See SPRINGDALE, AR (Cox Communications)

GREENWOOD—Formerly served by Eagle Media. No longer in operation

GREENWOOD—See FORT SMITH, AR (Cox Communications)

GREERS FERRY—Formerly served by Alliance Communications Network. No longer in operation

GRUBBS—See MARKED TREE, AR (Ritter Communications)

GUION—Formerly served by Indco Cable TV. No longer in operation

GUM SPRINGS—Indco Cable TV

GUM SPRINGS—See ARKADELPHIA, AR (Suddenlink Communications)

GURDON—Suddenlink Communications

GUY—See CLINTON, AR (Media3)

HACKETT—See FORT SMITH, AR (Cox Communications)

HAMBURG—Formerly served by Zoom Media. No longer in operation

HAMPTON—SATCO Cable TV

HARDIN—See WHITEHALL, AR (Suddenlink Communications)

HARDY—Fidelity Communications

HARMONY GROVE—Formerly served by Almega Cable. No longer in operation

HARRELL—Formerly served by Suddenlink Communications. No longer in operation

HARRELL—See HAMPTON, AR (SATCO Cable TV)

HARRISBURG—Ritter Communications. Now served by MARKED TREE, AR [AR0072]

HARRISBURG—See MARKED TREE, AR (Ritter Communications)

HARRISON—Cox Communications

2017 Edition

Cable Community Index-13

Arkansas—Cable Community Index

HARTFORD—See FORT SMITH, AR (Cox Communications)

HASKELL—See BENTON, AR (Fidelity Communications)

HATFIELD—Formerly served by Allegiance Communications. No longer in operation

HAYNES—See FORREST CITY, AR (East Arkansas Video Inc)

HAZEN—Suddenlink Communications

HEBER SPRINGS—Suddenlink Communications

HECTOR—Formerly served by Suddenlink Communications. No longer in operation

HELENA—Suddenlink Communications

HEMPSTEAD COUNTY (PORTIONS)—See NASHVILLE, AR (Suddenlink Communications)

HENSLEY—See BENTON, AR (Fidelity Communications)

HERMITAGE—Formerly served by Almega Cable. No longer in operation

HERMITAGE—See HAMPTON, AR (SATCO Cable TV)

HICKORY RIDGE—See MARKED TREE, AR (Ritter Communications)

HIGGINSON—White County Cable TV. Now served by SEARCY, AR [AR0017]

HIGGINSON—See SEARCY, AR (White County Cable TV)

HIGHLAND—See HARDY, AR (Fidelity Communications)

HOLIDAY ISLAND—See BERRYVILLE, AR (Cox Communications)

HOLLY GROVE—Formerly served by Cebridge Connections. No longer in operation

HOOKER/LADD—Formerly served by Community Communications Co. No longer in operation

HOPE—Hope Community TV

HORATIO—See DE QUEEN, AR (Vyve Broadband)

HORSESHOE BEND—Crystal Broadband Networks

HORSESHOE LAKE—See HUGHES, AR (Suddenlink Communications)

HOT SPRINGS VILLAGE—Suddenlink Communications

HOT SPRINGS—Resort TV Cable Co. Inc

HOXIE—Suddenlink Communications

HUGHES—Suddenlink Communications

HUMNOKE—Formerly served by Cebridge Connections. No longer in operation

HUMPHREY—Formerly served by Cebridge Connections. No longer in operation

HUNTINGTON—See FORT SMITH, AR (Cox Communications)

HUNTSVILLE—Madison County Cable

HUTTIG—Bayou Cable TV

IMBODEN—See BLACK ROCK, AR (Indco Cable TV)

INDEPENDENCE COUNTY (NORTHERN PORTION)—See PFEIFFER, AR (Indco Cable TV)

INDEPENDENCE COUNTY (PORTIONS)—See BATESVILLE, AR (Suddenlink Communications)

INDEPENDENCE COUNTY (UNINCORPORATED AREAS)—See PLEASANT PLAINS, AR (Indco Cable TV)

IZARD COUNTY—See HORSESHOE BEND, AR (Crystal Broadband Networks)

JACKSON COUNTY—See NEWPORT, AR (Suddenlink Communications)

JACKSONPORT—See NEWPORT, AR (Suddenlink Communications)

JACKSONVILLE—See LITTLE ROCK, AR (Comcast Cable)

JASPER—Ritter Communications. Now served by WESTERN GROVE, AR [AR0183]

JASPER—See WESTERN GROVE, AR (Ritter Communications)

JEFFERSON COUNTY (PORTIONS)—See PINE BLUFF, AR (Pine Bluff Cable TV Co. Inc)

JEFFERSON COUNTY (PORTIONS)—See WHITEHALL, AR (Suddenlink Communications)

JOHNSON—See SPRINGDALE, AR (Cox Communications)

JOINER—See MARKED TREE, AR (Ritter Communications)

JONES MILL—Formerly served by Cablevision of Jones Mill. No longer in operation

JONESBORO—See OAK GROVE HEIGHTS, AR (Fusion Media)

JONESBORO—See MARKED TREE, AR (Ritter Communications)

JONESBORO—Suddenlink Communications

JUDSONIA—See SEARCY, AR (White County Cable TV)

JUNCTION CITY—Alliance Communications

JUNCTION CITY—See JUNCTION CITY, LA (Alliance Communications)

KEISER—See MARKED TREE, AR (Ritter Communications)

KENSETT—See SEARCY, AR (White County Cable TV)

KIBLER—See FORT SMITH, AR (Cox Communications)

KNOBEL—Formerly served by Cebridge Connections. No longer in operation

KNOXVILLE—Formerly served by Quality Entertainment Corp. No longer in operation

LAFE—See OAK GROVE HEIGHTS, AR (Fusion Media)

LAGRANGE—See AUBREY, AR (Media3)

LAKE CITY—Ritter Communications. Now served by MARKED TREE, AR [AR0072]

LAKE CITY—See MARKED TREE, AR (Ritter Communications)

LAKE ERLING—Formerly served by Cebridge Connections. No longer in operation

LAKE VIEW—Alliance Communications

LAKE VILLAGE—BCI Broadband. Now served by McGEHEE, AR [AR0262]

LAKE VILLAGE—See McGEHEE, AR (Vyve Broadband)

LAKEVIEW—See MOUNTAIN HOME, AR (Suddenlink Communications)

LAMAR—See CLARKSVILLE, AR (Suddenlink Communications)

LANDMARK—See BENTON, AR (Fidelity Communications)

LAVACA—Cox Communications. Now served by FORT SMITH, AR [AR0003]

LAVACA—See FORT SMITH, AR (Cox Communications)

LAWRENCE COUNTY—See HOXIE, AR (Suddenlink Communications)

LE FLORE COUNTY (UNINCORPORATED AREAS)—See FORT SMITH, OK (Cox Communications)

LEACHVILLE—See MARKED TREE, AR (Ritter Communications)

LEAD HILL—See DIAMOND CITY, AR (NATCO Communications Inc.)

LEE COUNTY (PORTIONS)—See FORREST CITY, AR (East Arkansas Video Inc)

LEE COUNTY (SOUTHERN PORTION)—See AUBREY, AR (Media3)

LEOLA—Formerly served by Cebridge Connections. No longer in operation

LEPANTO—See MARKED TREE, AR (Ritter Communications)

LESLIE—Formerly served by Ritter Communications. No longer in operation

LETONA—See PANGBURN, AR (Indco Cable TV)

LEWISVILLE—Formerly served by Alliance Communications. Now served by Media3

LEXA—See HELENA, AR (Suddenlink Communications)

LINCOLN—See SPRINGDALE, AR (Cox Communications)

LITTLE FLOCK—See SPRINGDALE, AR (Cox Communications)

LITTLE RED RIVER—See HEBER SPRINGS, AR (Suddenlink Communications)

LITTLE RIVER COUNTY (PORTIONS)—See ASHDOWN, AR (NewWave Communications)

LITTLE ROCK AFB—See CABOT, AR (Suddenlink Communications)

LITTLE ROCK—Formerly served by Charter Communications. No longer in operation

LITTLE ROCK—Comcast Cable

LITTLE ROCK—See BENTON, AR (Fidelity Communications)

LOCKESBURG—Formerly served by Lockesburg Cablevision. No longer in operation

LOCUST BAYOU—Formerly served by Rapid Cable. No longer in operation

LONDON—Suddenlink Communications

LONOKE COUNTY (PORTIONS)—See CABOT, AR (Suddenlink Communications)

LONOKE—Media3

LOWELL—See SPRINGDALE, AR (Cox Communications)

LUXORA—See MARKED TREE, AR (Ritter Communications)

LYNN—Formerly served by Ritter Communications. No longer in operation

MABELVALE—See BENTON, AR (Fidelity Communications)

MACON—See CABOT, AR (Suddenlink Communications)

MADISON—See HUGHES, AR (Suddenlink Communications)

MAGAZINE—Formerly served by Almega Cable. No longer in operation

MAGIC SPRINGS—Formerly served by Cablevision of Magic Springs. No longer in operation

MAGNESS—See NEWARK, AR (Indco Cable TV)

MAGNOLIA—Suddenlink Communications

MALVERN—Suddenlink Communications

MANILA—Ritter Communications. Now served by MARKED TREE, AR [AR0072]

MANILA—See MARKED TREE, AR (Ritter Communications)

MANSFIELD—See FORT SMITH, AR (Cox Communications)

MARIANNA—See FORREST CITY, AR (East Arkansas Video Inc)

MARION COUNTY (PORTIONS)—See MOUNTAIN HOME, AR (Suddenlink Communications)

MARION COUNTY—See YELLVILLE, AR (Yelcot Communications)

MARKED TREE—Ritter Communications

MARMADUKE—See OAK GROVE HEIGHTS, AR (Fusion Media)

MARSHALL—Media3

Cable Community Index—Arkansas

MARVELL—Suddenlink Communications

MAUMELLE—Fidelity Communications

MAYFLOWER—Media3

McALMONT—Formerly served by Cobridge Communications. No longer in operation

McCASKILL—Formerly served by Allegiance Communications. No longer in operation

MCCRORY—Vyve Broadband

McDOUGAL—Formerly served by Almega Cable. No longer in operation

MCGEHEE—Vyve Broadband

MELBOURNE—Yelcot Communications

MENA—Vyve Broadband

MENIFEE—See PLUMERVILLE, AR (Media3)

MIDLAND—Cox Communications. Now served by FORT SMITH, AR [AR0003]

MIDLAND—See FORT SMITH, AR (Cox Communications)

MIDWAY—See MOUNTAIN HOME, AR (Suddenlink Communications)

MINERAL SPRINGS—Formerly served by Allegiance Communications. No longer in operation

MISSISSIPPI COUNTY (PORTIONS)—See MARKED TREE, AR (Ritter Communications)

MITCHELLVILLE—See McGEHEE, AR (Vyve Broadband)

MONETTE—See MARKED TREE, AR (Ritter Communications)

MONTGOMERY COUNTY (UNINCORPORATED AREAS)—See MOUNT IDA, AR (Suddenlink Communications)

MONTICELLO—Cablevision of Monticello

MONTROSE—Dean Hill Cable

MOOREFIELD—See BATESVILLE, AR (Suddenlink Communications)

MORO—Formerly served by Indco Cable TV. No longer in operation

MORRILTON—Suddenlink Communications

MOUNT IDA—Suddenlink Communications

MOUNT PLEASANT—Yelcot Communications

MOUNTAIN HARBOR RESORT—See MOUNT IDA, AR (Suddenlink Communications)

MOUNTAIN HOME—Suddenlink Communications

MOUNTAIN PINE—See HOT SPRINGS, AR (Resort TV Cable Co. Inc)

MOUNTAIN VIEW—Yelcot Communications

MOUNTAINBURG—See FORT SMITH, AR (Cox Communications)

MULBERRY—Cox Communications. Now served by FORT SMITH, AR [AR0003]

MULBERRY—See FORT SMITH, AR (Cox Communications)

MULDROW—See FORT SMITH, OK (Cox Communications)

MURFREESBORO—Vyve Broadband

NASHVILLE—Suddenlink Communications

NEWARK—Indco Cable TV

NEWPORT—Suddenlink Communications

NORMAN—Formerly served by Cablevision of Norman. No longer in operation

NORTH CROSSETT—See CROSSETT, AR (Media3)

NORTH LITTLE ROCK—See LITTLE ROCK, AR (Comcast Cable)

NORTH LITTLE ROCK—See MAUMELLE, AR (Fidelity Communications)

O'KEAN—Formerly served by Cebridge Connections. No longer in operation

OAK GROVE HEIGHTS—Fusion Media

OAK GROVE—See MAUMELLE, AR (Fidelity Communications)

OIL TROUGH—Indco Cable TV

OSCEOLA—Ritter Communications. Now served by MARKED TREE, AR [AR0072]

OSCEOLA—See MARKED TREE, AR (Ritter Communications)

OXFORD—Formerly served by Almega Cable. No longer in operation

OZARK ACRES—Formerly served by Cebridge Connections. No longer in operation

OZARK—Suddenlink Communications

PALESTINE—Formerly served by Almega Cable. No longer in operation

PANGBURN—Indco Cable TV

PARAGOULD—See OAK GROVE HEIGHTS, AR (Fusion Media)

PARAGOULD—Paragould City Light & Water Commission

PARIS—Suddenlink Communications

PARKDALE—See WILMOT, AR (Dean Hill Cable)

PATTERSON—See McCRORY, AR (Vyve Broadband)

PAYNEWAY—See MARKED TREE, AR (Ritter Communications)

PEA RIDGE—See SPRINGDALE, AR (Cox Communications)

PEARCY—Formerly served by Cablevision of Garland County. No longer in operation

PERLA—See MALVERN, AR (Suddenlink Communications)

PERRYVILLE—Formerly served by Alliance Communications Network. No longer in operation

PFEIFFER—Indco Cable TV

PHILLIPS COUNTY—See HELENA, AR (Suddenlink Communications)

PIKE COUNTY (portions)—Formerly served by Allegiance Communications. No longer in operation

PINE BLUFF (southern portion)—Formerly served by Almega Cable. No longer in operation

PINE BLUFF ARSENAL—See WHITEHALL, AR (Suddenlink Communications)

PINE BLUFF—Pine Bluff Cable TV Co. Inc

PINEBERGEN—Formerly served by Zoom Media. No longer in operation

PINEVILLE—See CALICO ROCK, AR (Yelcot Communications)

PLAINVIEW—Formerly served by Rapid Cable. No longer in operation

PLAINVIEW—Indco Cable TV

PLEASANT PLAINS—Indco Cable TV

PLUMERVILLE—Media3

POCAHONTAS—Suddenlink Communications

POCOLA—See FORT SMITH, OK (Cox Communications)

POINSETT COUNTY (PORTIONS)—See MARKED TREE, AR (Ritter Communications)

POLK COUNTY (PORTIONS)—See MENA, AR (Vyve Broadband)

POPE COUNTY (PORTIONS)—See ATKINS, AR (Suddenlink Communications)

POPE COUNTY (PORTIONS)—See LONDON, AR (Suddenlink Communications)

POPE COUNTY (PORTIONS)—See RUSSELLVILLE, AR (Suddenlink Communications)

POPE COUNTY (UNINCORPORATED AREAS)—See DOVER, AR (Suddenlink Communications)

POPLAR GROVE—See HELENA, AR (Suddenlink Communications)

PORTIA—See BLACK ROCK, AR (Indco Cable TV)

PORTLAND—Dean Hill Cable

POTTSVILLE—See RUSSELLVILLE, AR (Suddenlink Communications)

POWHATAN—See BLACK ROCK, AR (Indco Cable TV)

PRAIRIE COUNTY (PORTIONS)—See DES ARC, AR (Alliance Communications)

PRAIRIE COUNTY (UNINCORPORATED AREAS)—See HAZEN, AR (Suddenlink Communications)

PRAIRIE CREEK—See SPRINGDALE, AR (Cox Communications)

PRAIRIE GROVE—Cox Communications. Now served by SPRINGDALE, AR [AR0220]

PRAIRIE GROVE—See SPRINGDALE, AR (Cox Communications)

PRESCOTT—See HOPE, AR (Hope Community TV)

PULASKI COUNTY (PORTIONS)—See LITTLE ROCK, AR (Comcast Cable)

PULASKI COUNTY (PORTIONS)—See BENTON, AR (Fidelity Communications)

PULASKI COUNTY (PORTIONS)—See CABOT, AR (Suddenlink Communications)

QUITMAN—See CLINTON, AR (Media3)

RANDOLPH COUNTY (PORTIONS)—See POCAHONTAS, AR (Suddenlink Communications)

RATCLIFF—Formerly served by Eagle Media. No longer in operation

RAVENDEN SPRINGS—Formerly served by Cebridge Connections. No longer in operation

RAVENDEN—See BLACK ROCK, AR (Indco Cable TV)

RECTOR—NewWave Communications. Now served by DEXTER, MO [MO0039]

REDFIELD—See WHITEHALL, AR (Suddenlink Communications)

REED—See TILLAR, AR (Cablevision of Tillar Reed)

RISON—Cablevision of Rison

ROCKPORT—See MALVERN, AR (Suddenlink Communications)

ROGERS—Cox Communications. Now served by SPRINGDALE, AR [AR0220]

ROGERS—See SPRINGDALE, AR (Cox Communications)

ROLAND—See FORT SMITH, OK (Cox Communications)

RONDO—See AUBREY, AR (Media3)

ROYAL—Formerly served by Cablevision of Royal. No longer in operation

RUDY—Cox Communications. Now served by FORT SMITH, AR [AR0003]

RUDY—See FORT SMITH, AR (Cox Communications)

RUSSELL—Formerly served by Indco Cable TV. No longer in operation

RUSSELLVILLE—Suddenlink Communications

SALEM—Salem Cable Vision

SALINE COUNTY (PORTIONS)—See BENTON, AR (Fidelity Communications)

SALINE COUNTY (PORTIONS)—See HOT SPRINGS VILLAGE, AR (Suddenlink Communications)

Arkansas—Cable Community Index

SALINE COUNTY (unincorporated areas)—Formerly served by Community Cablevision. No longer in operation

SCRANTON—Formerly served by Eagle Media. No longer in operation

SEARCY—White County Cable TV

SEDGWICK—Formerly served by Cebridge Connections. No longer in operation

SEQUOYAH COUNTY (SOUTHERN PORTION)—See FORT SMITH, OK (Cox Communications)

SEVIER COUNTY—See DE QUEEN, AR (Vyve Broadband)

SHANNON HILLS—See BENTON, AR (Fidelity Communications)

SHERIDAN—Formerly served by Zoom Media. No longer in operation

SHERWOOD—See LITTLE ROCK, AR (Comcast Cable)

SHIRLEY—See FAIRFIELD BAY, AR (Vyve Broadband)

SIDNEY—Formerly served by Indco Cable TV. No longer in operation

SILOAM SPRINGS—Cox Communications. Now served by SPRINGDALE, AR [AR0220]

SILOAM SPRINGS—See SPRINGDALE, AR (Cox Communications)

SMACKOVER—Formerly served by Zoom Media. No longer in operation

SONORA—Cox Communications. Now served by SPRINGDALE, AR [AR0220]

SONORA—See SPRINGDALE, AR (Cox Communications)

SOUTH BEND—See CABOT, AR (Suddenlink Communications)

SOUTH SIDE—See BATESVILLE, AR (Suddenlink Communications)

SPRINGDALE—Cox Communications

ST. FRANCIS COUNTY—See CALDWELL, AR (Indco Cable TV)

STAMPS—See LEWISVILLE, AR (Formerly served by Alliance Communications. Now served by Media3)

STAR CITY—Formerly served by Cablevision of Star City. No longer in operation

STEPHENS—Formerly served by Zoom Media. No longer in operation

STRONG—Bayou Cable TV

STUTTGART—Suddenlink Communications

SUBIACO—Formerly served by Eagle Media. No longer in operation

SUGARLOAF LAKE—See FORT SMITH, AR (Cox Communications)

SULPHUR ROCK—See BATESVILLE, AR (Suddenlink Communications)

SUMMIT—See YELLVILLE, AR (Yelcot Communications)

SWIFTON—See MARKED TREE, AR (Ritter Communications)

TAYLOR—Formerly served by Cebridge Connections. No longer in operation

THORNTON—Formerly served by Almega Cable. No longer in operation

TILLAR—Cablevision of Tillar Reed

TONTITOWN—Cox Communications. Now served by SPRINGDALE, AR [AR0220]

TONTITOWN—See SPRINGDALE, AR (Cox Communications)

TRASKWOOD—Formerly served by Cebridge Connections. No longer in operation

TRUMANN—Ritter Communications. Now served by MARKED TREE, AR [AR0072]

TRUMANN—See MARKED TREE, AR (Ritter Communications)

TUCKERMAN—See NEWPORT, AR (Suddenlink Communications)

TULL—See BENTON, AR (Fidelity Communications)

TUMBLING SHOALS—Indco Cable TV

TUPELO—Formerly served by Indco Cable TV. No longer in operation

TURRELL—Ritter Communications. Now served by MARKED TREE, AR [AR0072]

TURRELL—See MARKED TREE, AR (Ritter Communications)

TYRONZA—See MARKED TREE, AR (Ritter Communications)

UNION COUNTY (PORTIONS)—See EL DORADO, AR (Suddenlink Communications)

VALLEY SPRINGS—See HARRISON, AR (Cox Communications)

VAN BUREN COUNTY (PORTIONS)—See CLINTON, AR (Clinton Cablevision Inc)

VAN BUREN COUNTY (PORTIONS)—See FAIRFIELD BAY, AR (Vyve Broadband)

VAN BUREN—Cox Communications. Now served by FORT SMITH, AR [AR0003]

VAN BUREN—See FORT SMITH, AR (Cox Communications)

VILONIA—Formerly served by Cobridge Communications. No longer in operation

VIOLA—Salem Cable Vision. Now served by SALEM, AR [AR0116]

VIOLA—See SALEM, AR (Salem Cable Vision)

WALCOTT—See OAK GROVE HEIGHTS, AR (Fusion Media)

WALDO—See MAGNOLIA, AR (Suddenlink Communications)

WALDRON—Suddenlink Communications

WALNUT RIDGE—See HOXIE, AR (Suddenlink Communications)

WARD—See CABOT, AR (Suddenlink Communications)

WARREN—Cablevision of Warren

WASHINGTON COUNTY—See SPRINGDALE, AR (Cox Communications)

WATSON—Formerly served by Cablevision of Watson. No longer in operation

WEINER—See MARKED TREE, AR (Ritter Communications)

WEST CROSSETT—See CROSSETT, AR (Media3)

WEST FORK—Cox Communications. Now served by SPRINGDALE, AR [AR0220]

WEST FORK—See SPRINGDALE, AR (Cox Communications)

WEST HELENA—See HELENA, AR (Suddenlink Communications)

WEST PULASKI (PORTIONS)—Fidelity Communications

WESTERN GROVE—Ritter Communications

WHEATLEY—Formerly served by Almega Cable. No longer in operation

WHITE COUNTY (PORTIONS)—See BEEBE, AR (Fidelity Communications)

WHITE COUNTY (PORTIONS)—See PLAINVIEW, AR (Indco Cable TV)

WHITEHALL—Suddenlink Communications

WIDENER—See HUGHES, AR (Suddenlink Communications)

WILMAR—Formerly served by Almega Cable. No longer in operation

WILMOT—Dean Hill Cable

WILSON—See MARKED TREE, AR (Ritter Communications)

WINSLOW—Cox Communications. Now served by SPRINGDALE, AR [AR0220]

WINSLOW—See SPRINGDALE, AR (Cox Communications)

WITCHERVILLE—Formerly served by Eagle Media. No longer in operation

WITCHERVILLE—See FORT SMITH, AR (Cox Communications)

WOOSTER—See MAYFLOWER, AR (Media3)

WRIGHTSVILLE—See BENTON, AR (Fidelity Communications)

WYNNE—See FORREST CITY, AR (East Arkansas Video Inc)

WYNNE—See MARKED TREE, AR (Ritter Communications)

YELLVILLE—Yelcot Communications

CALIFORNIA

ACAMPO—See SACRAMENTO, CA (Comcast Cable)

ACTON—See LOS ANGELES, CA (Time Warner Cable)

ADELANTO—See HESPERIA, CA (Charter Communications)

ADMIRAL HARTMAN NAVY HOUSING PROJECT—See SAN DIEGO, CA (Time Warner Cable)

ADOBE WELLS MOBILE HOME PARK—Formerly served by Comcast Cable. No longer in operation

AGOURA (PORTIONS)—See MALIBU, CA (Charter Communications)

AGOURA HILLS—Time Warner Cable. Now served by LOS ANGELES, CA [CA0009]

AGOURA HILLS—See MALIBU, CA (Charter Communications)

AGOURA HILLS—See LOS ANGELES, CA (Time Warner Cable)

AGOURA—See LOS ANGELES, CA (Time Warner Cable)

AHWAHNEE—See OAKHURST, CA (Northland Cable Television)

ALAMEDA NAVAL AIR STATION—See SAN FRANCISCO, CA (Comcast Cable)

ALAMEDA—Comcast Cable. Now served by SAN FRANCISCO, CA [CA0003]

ALAMEDA—Formerly served by Alameda Power & Telecom. Now served by Comcast Cable, SAN FRANCISCO, CA [CA0003]

ALAMEDA—See SAN FRANCISCO, CA (Comcast Cable)

ALBANY—See SAN FRANCISCO, CA (Comcast Cable)

ALHAMBRA—See LOS ANGELES COUNTY (portions), CA (Charter Communications)

ALISO VIEJO—See SAN JUAN CAPISTRANO, CA (Cox Communications)

ALTA SIERRA—See LAKE OF THE PINES, CA (Suddenlink Communications)

ALTADENA—See LOS ANGELES COUNTY (portions), CA (Charter Communications)

ALTURAS—Charter Communications

AMADOR COUNTY—See IONE, CA (Volcano Vision)

AMADOR—See SACRAMENTO, CA (Comcast Cable)

AMERICAN CANYON—See SAN FRANCISCO, CA (Comcast Cable)

ANAHEIM—Time Warner Cable. Now served by LOS ANGELES, CA [CA0009]

ANAHEIM—See LOS ANGELES, CA (Time Warner Cable)

Cable Community Index—California

ANDERSON—See REDDING, CA (Charter Communications)

ANGELS CAMP—See SACRAMENTO, CA (Comcast Cable)

ANGELUS OAKS—See HESPERIA, CA (Charter Communications)

ANTELOPE—See SACRAMENTO, CA (Consolidated Communications. Formerly [CA0459]. This cable system has converted to IPTV)

ANTIOCH—See SAN FRANCISCO, CA (Comcast Cable)

APPLE VALLEY—See HESPERIA, CA (Charter Communications)

ARBUCKLE—See SACRAMENTO, CA (Comcast Cable)

ARCADIA—See LOS ANGELES, CA (Time Warner Cable)

ARCATA—See HUMBOLDT COUNTY (portions), CA (Suddenlink Communications)

ARMONA—See FRESNO, CA (Comcast Cable)

ARROYO GRANDE—See SAN LUIS OBISPO, CA (Charter Communications)

ARTESIA—Formerly served by Comcast Cable. No longer in operation

ARTESIA—See LOS ANGELES, CA (Time Warner Cable)

ARVIN—See BAKERSFIELD, CA (Bright House Networks)

ATASCADERO—See SAN LUIS OBISPO, CA (Charter Communications)

ATHERTON—See SAN FRANCISCO, CA (Comcast Cable)

ATWATER—See FRESNO, CA (Comcast Cable)

AUBURN LAKE TRAILS—See SACRAMENTO, CA (Comcast Cable)

AUBURN—Wave Broadband. Now served by PLACER COUNTY (southwestern portion), CA [CA0131]

AUBURN—See LAKE OF THE PINES, CA (Suddenlink Communications)

AUBURN—See PLACER COUNTY (southwestern portion), CA (Wave Broadband)

AVALON/CATALINA ISLAND—Catalina Cable TV Co.

AVENAL—Bright House Networks

AVILA BEACH—See SAN LUIS OBISPO, CA (Charter Communications)

AZUSA—Charter Communications. Now served by LOS ANGELES COUNTY (portions), CA [CA0005]

AZUSA—See LOS ANGELES COUNTY (portions), CA (Charter Communications)

BAKERSFIELD—Bright House Networks. Now served by BAKERSFIELD, CA [CA0025]

BAKERSFIELD—Bright House Networks

BALDWIN PARK—See LOS ANGELES, CA (Time Warner Cable)

BALDY MESA—See WRIGHTWOOD, CA (Charter Communications)

BANNING—Time Warner Cable

BARSTOW—Time Warner Cable

BASS LAKE—See OAKHURST, CA (Northland Cable Television)

BAY POINT—See SAN FRANCISCO, CA (Comcast Cable)

BAYWOOD-LOS OSOS—See SAN LUIS OBISPO, CA (Charter Communications)

BEALE AFB—See SACRAMENTO, CA (Comcast Cable)

BEAR VALLEY—Formerly served by New Day Broadband. No longer in operation

BEAUMONT—See BANNING, CA (Time Warner Cable)

BELL CANYON—See LOS ANGELES, CA (Time Warner Cable)

BELL GARDENS—See LOS ANGELES, CA (Time Warner Cable)

BELL—Formerly served by Comcast Cable. No longer in operation

BELL—See LOS ANGELES, CA (Time Warner Cable)

BELLFLOWER—See LOS ANGELES, CA (Time Warner Cable)

BELMONT—See SAN FRANCISCO, CA (Comcast Cable)

BELVEDERE—See SAN FRANCISCO, CA (Comcast Cable)

BENBOW—See GARBERVILLE, CA (Wave Broadband)

BENICIA—Comcast Cable. Now served by SAN FRANCISCO, CA [CA0003]

BENICIA—See SAN FRANCISCO, CA (Comcast Cable)

BERKELEY—See SAN FRANCISCO, CA (Comcast Cable)

BEVERLY HILLS—See LOS ANGELES, CA (Time Warner Cable)

BIG BEAR CITY—See HESPERIA, CA (Charter Communications)

BIG BEAR LAKE—Charter Communications. Now served by HESPERIA, CA [CA0158]

BIG BEAR LAKE—See HESPERIA, CA (Charter Communications)

BIG BEAR—See HESPERIA, CA (Charter Communications)

BIG OAK FLAT—See GROVELAND, CA (SNC Cable)

BIG PINE—See BISHOP, CA (Suddenlink Communications)

BIGGS—See SACRAMENTO, CA (Comcast Cable)

BISHOP—Suddenlink Communications

BLOOMINGTON—See LOS ANGELES, CA (Time Warner Cable)

BLUE LAKE—See HUMBOLDT COUNTY (portions), CA (Suddenlink Communications)

BLYTHE—Suddenlink Communications

BODFISH—See KERN COUNTY (portions), CA (Mediacom)

BOMBAY BEACH—USA Communications

BONITA—See SAN DIEGO, CA (Cox Communications)

BONSALL—See SAN DIEGO, CA (Cox Communications)

BORON—Charter Communications. Now served by NORTH EDWARDS, CA [CA0404]

BORON—See NORTH EDWARDS, CA (Charter Communications)

BORREGO SPRINGS—USA Communications

BOX CANYON—Formerly served by Charter Communications. No longer in operation

BOYLE HEIGHTS—See LOS ANGELES, CA (Time Warner Cable)

BRADBURY—See LOS ANGELES, CA (Time Warner Cable)

BRAWLEY—See EL CENTRO, CA (Time Warner Cable)

BREA—Formerly served by Adelphia Communications. Now served by Time Warner Cable, LOS ANGELES, CA [CA0009]

BREA—See LOS ANGELES, CA (Time Warner Cable)

BRENTWOOD—Comcast Cable. Now served by SAN FRANCISCO, CA [CA0003]

BRENTWOOD—See SAN FRANCISCO, CA (Comcast Cable)

BRIDGEPORT—Formerly served by Satview Broadband. No longer in operation

BRISBANE—See SAN FRANCISCO, CA (Comcast Cable)

BROADMOOR—See SAN FRANCISCO, CA (Comcast Cable)

BROOKINGS—See CRESCENT CITY, OR (Charter Communications)

BUELLTON—See FRESNO, CA (Comcast Cable)

BUENA PARK—See LOS ANGELES, CA (Time Warner Cable)

BUENA VISTA—See IONE, CA (Volcano Vision)

BURBANK—See GLENDALE, CA (Charter Communications)

BURLINGAME—Comcast Cable. Now served by SAN FRANCISCO, CA [CA0003]

BURLINGAME—See SAN FRANCISCO, CA (Comcast Cable)

BURLINGAME—See SAN FRANCISCO (southern portion), CA (Wave Broadband)

BURNEY—Zito Media

BUTTE COUNTY (PORTIONS)—See SACRAMENTO, CA (Comcast Cable)

BUTTONWILLOW—See BAKERSFIELD, CA (Bright House Networks)

CABAZON—Formerly served by TV Max. No longer in operation

CALABASAS—Time Warner Cable. Now served by LOS ANGELES, CA [CA0009]

CALABASAS—See MALIBU, CA (Charter Communications)

CALABASAS—See LOS ANGELES, CA (Time Warner Cable)

CALAVERAS COUNTY (PORTIONS)—See SACRAMENTO, CA (Comcast Cable)

CALEXICO—See EL CENTRO, CA (Time Warner Cable)

CALIFORNIA CITY—Charter Communications. Now served by NORTH EDWARDS, CA [CA0404]

CALIFORNIA CITY—See NORTH EDWARDS, CA (Charter Communications)

CALIFORNIA HOT SPRINGS—Formerly served by Charter Communications. No longer in operation

CALIMESA—See LOS ANGELES, CA (Time Warner Cable)

CALIPATRIA—USA Communications

CALISTOGA—See SAN FRANCISCO, CA (Comcast Cable)

CAMARILLO—No longer in operation

CAMARILLO—Time Warner Cable. Now served by LOS ANGELES, CA [CA0009]

CAMARILLO—See LOS ANGELES, CA (Time Warner Cable)

CAMBRIA—See SAN LUIS OBISPO, CA (Charter Communications)

CAMP NELSON—See PORTERVILLE, CA (Charter Communications)

CAMP PENDLETON—See SAN DIEGO, CA (Cox Communications)

CAMPBELL—See SAN FRANCISCO, CA (Comcast Cable)

CANOGA PARK—See LOS ANGELES, CA (Time Warner Cable)

CANYON COUNTRY—Time Warner Cable. Now served by LOS ANGELES, CA [CA0009]

CANYON COUNTRY—See LOS ANGELES, CA (Time Warner Cable)

CANYON LAKE—See LOS ANGELES, CA (Time Warner Cable)

CAPE COD MOBILE HOME PARK—Formerly served by Comcast Cable. No longer in operation

CAPITOLA—See GILROY, CA (Charter Communications)

California—Cable Community Index

CARLSBAD—Time Warner Cable. Now served by SAN DIEGO, CA [CA0007]

CARLSBAD—See SAN DIEGO, CA (Time Warner Cable)

CARMEL HIGHLANDS—See MONTEREY COUNTY (portions), CA (Charter Communications)

CARMEL VALLEY (VILLAGE)—See SAN FRANCISCO, CA (Comcast Cable)

CARMEL-BY-THE-SEA—See SAN FRANCISCO, CA (Comcast Cable)

CARMICHAEL—See SACRAMENTO, CA (Consolidated Communications. Formerly [CA0459]. This cable system has converted to IPTV)

CARPINTERIA—See SANTA BARBARA, CA (Cox Communications)

CARSON—Formerly served by Wave Broadband. No longer in operation

CARSON—Time Warner Cable. Now served by LOS ANGELES, CA [CA0009]

CARSON—See LOS ANGELES, CA (Time Warner Cable)

CASA DE AMIGOS MOBILE HOME PARK—Formerly served by Comcast Cable. No longer in operation

CASTAIC—See LOS ANGELES, CA (Time Warner Cable)

CASTRO VALLEY—See SAN FRANCISCO, CA (Comcast Cable)

CASTROVILLE—See MONTEREY COUNTY (portions), CA (Charter Communications)

CATALINA ISLAND—See AVALON/CATALINA ISLAND, CA (Catalina Cable TV Co.)

CATHEDRAL CITY—See PALM SPRINGS, CA (Time Warner Cable)

CAYUCOS—See SAN LUIS OBISPO, CA (Charter Communications)

CBC NAVAL BASE—See LOS ANGELES, CA (Time Warner Cable)

CEDAR VALLEY—See OAKHURST, CA (Northland Cable Television)

CEDARVILLE—Formerly served by Almega Cable. No longer in operation

CENTRAL ORANGE COUNTY—Time Warner Cable. Now served by LOS ANGELES, CA [CA0009]

CENTRAL ORANGE COUNTY—See LOS ANGELES, CA (Time Warner Cable)

CERES—See TURLOCK, CA (Charter Communications)

CERRITOS—Charter Communications

CHALFANT VALLEY—Formerly served by Satview Broadband. No longer in operation

CHATSWORTH—Time Warner Cable. Now served by LOS ANGELES, CA [CA0009]

CHATSWORTH—See LOS ANGELES, CA (Time Warner Cable)

CHERRY VALLEY (PORTIONS)—See BANNING, CA (Time Warner Cable)

CHESTER—See LAKE ALMANOR, CA (CalNeva Broadband)

CHESTERTON NAVY HOUSING PROJECT—See SAN DIEGO, CA (Time Warner Cable)

CHICO—Comcast Cable. Now served by SACRAMENTO, CA [CA0002]

CHICO—See SACRAMENTO, CA (Comcast Cable)

CHINA LAKE NAVAL WEAPONS CENTER—See RIDGECREST, CA (Mediacom)

CHINO HILLS—See LOS ANGELES, CA (Time Warner Cable)

CHINO—Time Warner Cable. Now served by LOS ANGELES, CA [CA0009]

CHINO—See LOS ANGELES, CA (Time Warner Cable)

CHOWCHILLA—Comcast Cable. Now served by FRESNO, CA [CA0011]

CHOWCHILLA—See FRESNO, CA (Comcast Cable)

CHRISTIAN VALLEY—See LAKE OF THE PINES, CA (Suddenlink Communications)

CHULA VISTA—Formerly served by Access Cable. No longer in operation

CHULA VISTA—See SAN DIEGO, CA (Cox Communications)

CITRUS HEIGHTS—See SACRAMENTO, CA (Comcast Cable)

CITRUS HEIGHTS—See SACRAMENTO, CA (Consolidated Communications. Formerly [CA0459]. This cable system has converted to IPTV)

CLAREMONT—Time Warner Cable. Now served by LOS ANGELES, CA [CA0009]

CLAREMONT—See LOS ANGELES, CA (Time Warner Cable)

CLAYTON—See SAN FRANCISCO, CA (Comcast Cable)

CLEAR CREEK—See LAKE ALMANOR, CA (CalNeva Broadband)

CLEARLAKE OAKS—See CLEARLAKE, CA (Mediacom)

CLEARLAKE PARK—See CLEARLAKE, CA (Mediacom)

CLEARLAKE—Mediacom

CLOVERDALE—See SAN FRANCISCO, CA (Comcast Cable)

CLOVIS—See FRESNO, CA (Comcast Cable)

CLYDE—See SAN FRANCISCO, CA (Comcast Cable)

COACHELLA—See PALM SPRINGS, CA (Time Warner Cable)

COALINGA—Comcast Cable

COARSEGOLD—Northland Cable Television

COBB—See CLEARLAKE, CA (Mediacom)

COLD SPRINGS—See LONG BARN, CA (SNC Cable)

COLEVILLE—Formerly served by Satview Broadband. No longer in operation

COLFAX—See PLACER COUNTY (southwestern portion), CA (Wave Broadband)

COLMA—See SAN FRANCISCO, CA (Comcast Cable)

COLTON—Time Warner Cable. Now served by LOS ANGELES, CA [CA0009]

COLTON—See LOS ANGELES, CA (Time Warner Cable)

COLUSA COUNTY (PORTIONS)—See SACRAMENTO, CA (Comcast Cable)

COLUSA—See SACRAMENTO, CA (Comcast Cable)

COMMERCE—See LOS ANGELES COUNTY (portions), CA (Charter Communications)

COMPTON—Time Warner Cable. Now served by LOS ANGELES, CA [CA0009]

COMPTON—See LOS ANGELES, CA (Time Warner Cable)

CONCORD NAVAL WEAPONS STATION—See SAN FRANCISCO, CA (Comcast Cable)

CONCORD—Comcast Cable. Now served by SAN FRANCISCO, CA [CA0003]

CONCORD—Comcast Cable. Now served by SAN FRANCISCO, CA [CA0003]

CONCORD—See SAN FRANCISCO, CA (Comcast Cable)

CONCORD—Wave Broadband

CONTRA COSTA COUNTY (PORTIONS)—See SAN FRANCISCO, CA (Comcast Cable)

CONTRA COSTA COUNTY (UNINCORPORATED AREAS)—See CONCORD, CA (Wave Broadband)

COPPER COVE COPPEROPOLIS—Formerly served by Mountain View Cable. No longer in operation

CORCORAN—See FRESNO, CA (Comcast Cable)

CORNING—See SACRAMENTO, CA (Comcast Cable)

CORONA DEL MAR—See LOS ANGELES, CA (Time Warner Cable)

CORONA—Time Warner Cable. Now served by LOS ANGELES, CA [CA0009]

CORONA—See LOS ANGELES, CA (Time Warner Cable)

CORONADO—Time Warner Cable. Now served by SAN DIEGO, CA [CA0007]

CORONADO—See SAN DIEGO, CA (Time Warner Cable)

CORRALITOS—See GILROY, CA (Charter Communications)

CORTE MADERA—See SAN FRANCISCO, CA (Comcast Cable)

COSTA MESA—Time Warner Cable. Now served by LOS ANGELES, CA [CA0009]

COSTA MESA—See LOS ANGELES, CA (Time Warner Cable)

COTATI—See SAN FRANCISCO, CA (Comcast Cable)

COTO DE CAZA—See SAN JUAN CAPISTRANO, CA (Cox Communications)

COTTON CENTER—See PORTERVILLE, CA (Charter Communications)

COUNTRY CLUB ESTATES—See SAN LUIS OBISPO, CA (Charter Communications)

COVINA—Time Warner Cable. Now served by LOS ANGELES, CA [CA0009]

COVINA—See LOS ANGELES, CA (Time Warner Cable)

CRESCENT CITY—Charter Communications

CRESCENT MILLS—Formerly served by Wave Broadband. No longer in operation

CREST—See SAN DIEGO, CA (Cox Communications)

CROCKETT—See SAN FRANCISCO, CA (Comcast Cable)

CROW'S LANDING—See PATTERSON, CA (Comcast Cable)

CROWLEY LAKE—Formerly served by Satview Broadband. No longer in operation

CUDAHY—See LOS ANGELES, CA (Time Warner Cable)

CULVER CITY—See LOS ANGELES, CA (Time Warner Cable)

CUPERTINO—Comcast Cable. Now served by SAN FRANCISCO, CA [CA0003]

CUPERTINO—See SAN FRANCISCO, CA (Comcast Cable)

CURRY COUNTY (PORTIONS)—See CRESCENT CITY, OR (Charter Communications)

CYPRESS—Time Warner Cable. Now served by LOS ANGELES, CA [CA0009]

CYPRESS—See LOS ANGELES, CA (Time Warner Cable)

DALY CITY—See SAN FRANCISCO, CA (Comcast Cable)

DALY CITY—See SAN FRANCISCO (southern portion), CA (Wave Broadband)

Cable Community Index—California

DANA POINT—See SAN JUAN CAPISTRANO, CA (Cox Communications)

DANVILLE—See SAN FRANCISCO, CA (Comcast Cable)

DAVIS—Comcast Cable. Now served by SACRAMENTO, CA [CA0002]

DAVIS—See SACRAMENTO, CA (Comcast Cable)

DAY VALLEY—See GILROY, CA (Charter Communications)

DEL MAR—See SAN DIEGO, CA (Time Warner Cable)

DEL MONTE FOREST—See SAN FRANCISCO, CA (Comcast Cable)

DEL NORTE COUNTY—See CRESCENT CITY, CA (Charter Communications)

DEL REY OAKS—See SAN FRANCISCO, CA (Comcast Cable)

DEL REY OAKS—See MONTEREY, CA (Suddenlink Communications)

DELANO—See BAKERSFIELD, CA (Bright House Networks)

DESERT CENTER—Formerly served by American Pacific Co. No longer in operation

DESERT HOT SPRINGS—Time Warner Cable. Now served by PALM SPRINGS, CA [CA0036]

DESERT HOT SPRINGS—See PALM SPRINGS, CA (Time Warner Cable)

DIAMOND BAR—Time Warner Cable. Now served by LOS ANGELES, CA [CA0009]

DIAMOND BAR—See LOS ANGELES, CA (Time Warner Cable)

DILLON BEACH—See POINT REYES STATION, CA (Horizon Cable TV Inc)

DINUBA—See FRESNO, CA (Comcast Cable)

DIXON—See WEST SACRAMENTO, CA (Wave Broadband)

DONNER SUMMIT—See TRUCKEE, CA (Suddenlink Communications)

DORRIS—Formerly served by Almega Cable. No longer in operation

DOS PALOS—See FRESNO, CA (Comcast Cable)

DOWNEY—Formerly served by Comcast Cable. No longer in operation

DOWNEY—See LOS ANGELES, CA (Time Warner Cable)

DOWNIEVILLE—Formerly served by Downieville TV Corp. No longer in operation

DUARTE—See LOS ANGELES COUNTY (portions), CA (Charter Communications)

DUBLIN—See SAN FRANCISCO, CA (Comcast Cable)

DUNSMUIR—See MOUNT SHASTA, CA (Northland Cable Television)

DURHAM—See SACRAMENTO, CA (Comcast Cable)

EAGLE ROCK—Time Warner Cable. Now served by LOS ANGELES, CA [CA0009]

EAGLE ROCK—See LOS ANGELES, CA (Time Warner Cable)

EARLIMART—Charter Communications. Now served by PORTERVILLE, CA [CA0152]

EARLIMART—See PORTERVILLE, CA (Charter Communications)

EAST BLYTHE—See BLYTHE, CA (Suddenlink Communications)

EAST LOS ANGELES—Time Warner Cable. Now served by LOS ANGELES, CA [CA0009]

EAST LOS ANGELES—See LOS ANGELES, CA (Time Warner Cable)

EAST PALO ALTO—See SAN FRANCISCO, CA (Comcast Cable)

EAST SAN FERNANDO VALLEY—Time Warner Cable. Now served by LOS ANGELES, CA [CA0009]

EAST SAN FERNANDO VALLEY—See LOS ANGELES, CA (Time Warner Cable)

EASTVALE—See RIVERSIDE, CA (Charter Communications)

EASTVALE—See LOS ANGELES, CA (Time Warner Cable)

EDWARDS AFB—See LOS ANGELES, CA (Time Warner Cable)

EHRENBERG—See BLYTHE, AZ (Suddenlink Communications)

EL CAJON—See SAN DIEGO, CA (Cox Communications)

EL CENTRO NAF—See EL CENTRO, CA (Time Warner Cable)

EL CENTRO—Time Warner Cable

EL CERRITO—See SAN FRANCISCO, CA (Comcast Cable)

EL DORADO COUNTY (WESTERN PORTION)—See TRUCKEE, CA (Suddenlink Communications)

EL DORADO HILLS—See SACRAMENTO, CA (Comcast Cable)

EL DORADO—See SACRAMENTO, CA (Comcast Cable)

EL GRANADA—See SAN FRANCISCO, CA (Comcast Cable)

EL MONTE—Time Warner Cable. Now served by LOS ANGELES, CA [CA0009]

EL MONTE—See LOS ANGELES, CA (Time Warner Cable)

EL RIO—See LOS ANGELES, CA (Time Warner Cable)

EL SEGUNDO—See LOS ANGELES, CA (Time Warner Cable)

ELIZABETH LAKE—See LOS ANGELES, CA (Time Warner Cable)

ELK GROVE—See SACRAMENTO, CA (Comcast Cable)

ELK GROVE—See SACRAMENTO, CA (Consolidated Communications. Formerly [CA0459]. This cable system has converted to IPTV)

EMERYVILLE—See SAN FRANCISCO, CA (Comcast Cable)

ENCINITAS (PORTIONS)—See SAN DIEGO, CA (Time Warner Cable)

ENCINITAS—See SAN DIEGO, CA (Cox Communications)

ENCINO—See LOS ANGELES, CA (Time Warner Cable)

ESCALON—See TURLOCK, CA (Charter Communications)

ESCONDIDO—See SAN DIEGO, CA (Cox Communications)

ESPARTO—Cableview Communications

ETIWANDA—See LOS ANGELES, CA (Time Warner Cable)

ETNA—Formerly served by Siskiyou Cablevision Inc. No longer in operation

EUREKA—See HUMBOLDT COUNTY (portions), CA (Suddenlink Communications)

EXETER—See PORTERVILLE, CA (Charter Communications)

FAIRFAX—See SAN FRANCISCO, CA (Comcast Cable)

FAIRFIELD—Comcast Cable. Now served by SAN FRANCISCO, CA [CA0003]

FAIRFIELD—See SAN FRANCISCO, CA (Comcast Cable)

FALL RIVER MILLS—Formerly served by Almega Cable. No longer in operation

FARMERSVILLE—See PORTERVILLE, CA (Charter Communications)

FERNDALE—See HUMBOLDT COUNTY (portions), CA (Suddenlink Communications)

FILLMORE—See LOS ANGELES, CA (Time Warner Cable)

FIREBAUGH—See FRESNO, CA (Comcast Cable)

FISH CAMP—Formerly served by Northland Cable Television. No longer in operation

FOLSOM—See SACRAMENTO, CA (Comcast Cable)

FONTANA—See LOS ANGELES, CA (Time Warner Cable)

FOREST FALLS—See HESPERIA, CA (Charter Communications)

FOREST KNOLLS—See SAN FRANCISCO, CA (Comcast Cable)

FORESTHILL—Suddenlink Communications

FORT BRAGG—Comcast Cable. Now served by SAN FRANCISCO, CA [CA0003]

FORT BRAGG—See SAN FRANCISCO, CA (Comcast Cable)

FORT IRWIN—Formerly served by Total TV of Fort Irwin Inc. No longer in operation

FORTUNA—See HUMBOLDT COUNTY (portions), CA (Suddenlink Communications)

FOSTER CITY—Comcast Cable. Now served by SAN FRANCISCO, CA [CA0003]

FOSTER CITY—See SAN FRANCISCO, CA (Comcast Cable)

FOUNTAIN VALLEY—See LOS ANGELES, CA (Time Warner Cable)

FOWLER—See FRESNO, CA (Comcast Cable)

FRANCISCAN MOBILE HOME PARK—Formerly served by Comcast Cable. No longer in operation

FRAZIER PARK—CalNeva Broadband

FREEDOM—See GILROY, CA (Charter Communications)

FREMONT—Comcast Cable. Now served by SAN FRANCISCO, CA [CA0003]

FREMONT—See SAN FRANCISCO, CA (Comcast Cable)

FRESNO COUNTY (PORTIONS)—See FRESNO, CA (Comcast Cable)

FRESNO—Formerly served by Sprint Corp. No longer in operation

FRESNO—Comcast Cable

FULLERTON—See LOS ANGELES, CA (Time Warner Cable)

GALT—See SACRAMENTO, CA (Comcast Cable)

GARBERVILLE—Wave Broadband

GARDEN FARMS—See SAN LUIS OBISPO, CA (Charter Communications)

GARDEN GROVE—See LOS ANGELES, CA (Time Warner Cable)

GARDENA—See LOS ANGELES, CA (Time Warner Cable)

GASQUET—See CRESCENT CITY, CA (Charter Communications)

GEORGIAN MANOR MOBILE HOME PARK—Formerly served by Comcast Cable. No longer in operation

GILROY—Charter Communications

GLENDALE—Charter Communications

GLENDORA—Time Warner Cable. Now served by LOS ANGELES, CA [CA0009]

GLENDORA—See LOS ANGELES, CA (Time Warner Cable)

GLENHAVEN—See CLEARLAKE, CA (Mediacom)

GLENN COUNTY (PORTIONS)—See SACRAMENTO, CA (Comcast Cable)

GLENWOOD—Comcast Cable. Now served by SAN FRANCISCO, CA [CA0003]

California—Cable Community Index

GLENWOOD—See SAN FRANCISCO, CA (Comcast Cable)

GOLD BEACH—See CRESCENT CITY, OR (Charter Communications)

GOLETA—See SANTA BARBARA, CA (Cox Communications)

GONZALES—See SOLEDAD, CA (Charter Communications)

GRANADA HILLS—See LOS ANGELES, CA (Time Warner Cable)

GRAND TERRACE—See LOS ANGELES, CA (Time Warner Cable)

GRANITE BAY—See SACRAMENTO, CA (Consolidated Communications. Formerly [CA0459]. This cable system has converted to IPTV)

GRANITE BAY—See PLACER COUNTY (southwestern portion), CA (Wave Broadband)

GRASS VALLEY—Comcast Cable. Now served by SACRAMENTO, CA [CA0002]

GRASS VALLEY—See SACRAMENTO, CA (Comcast Cable)

GREEN VALLEY LAKE—See HESPERIA, CA (Charter Communications)

GREEN VALLEY—See LOS ANGELES, CA (Time Warner Cable)

GREENFIELD—Charter Communications

GRIDLEY—See SACRAMENTO, CA (Comcast Cable)

GROVELAND—SNC Cable

GROVER BEACH—See SAN LUIS OBISPO, CA (Charter Communications)

GUADALUPE—Charter Communications. Now served by SAN LUIS OBISPO, CA [CA0045]

GUADALUPE—See SAN LUIS OBISPO, CA (Charter Communications)

GUALALA—See THE SEA RANCH, CA (CalNeva Broadband)

GUSTINE—See PATTERSON, CA (Comcast Cable)

HACIENDA HEIGHTS—Time Warner Cable. Now served by LOS ANGELES, CA [CA0009]

HACIENDA HEIGHTS—Time Warner Cable. Now served by LOS ANGELES, CA [CA0009]

HACIENDA HEIGHTS—See LOS ANGELES, CA (Time Warner Cable)

HALF MOON BAY—Comcast Cable. Now served by SAN FRANCISCO, CA [CA0003]

HALF MOON BAY—See SAN FRANCISCO, CA (Comcast Cable)

HAMILTON BRANCH—See LAKE ALMANOR, CA (CalNeva Broadband)

HAMILTON CITY—See SACRAMENTO, CA (Comcast Cable)

HANFORD—See FRESNO, CA (Comcast Cable)

HAPPY CAMP—Formerly served by Almega Cable. No longer in operation

HARBOR CITY—See LOS ANGELES, CA (Time Warner Cable)

HAWAIIAN GARDENS—See LOS ANGELES, CA (Time Warner Cable)

HAWTHORNE—See LOS ANGELES, CA (Time Warner Cable)

HAYFORK—Formerly served by New Day Broadband. No longer in operation

HAYWARD—Comcast Cable. Now served by SAN FRANCISCO, CA [CA0003]

HAYWARD—See SAN FRANCISCO, CA (Comcast Cable)

HEALDSBURG—Comcast Cable. Now served by SAN FRANCISCO, CA [CA0003]

HEALDSBURG—See SAN FRANCISCO, CA (Comcast Cable)

HEMET—Time Warner Cable. Now served by LOS ANGELES, CA [CA0009]

HEMET—See LOS ANGELES, CA (Time Warner Cable)

HERCULES—See SAN FRANCISCO, CA (Comcast Cable)

HERITAGE RANCH—See SAN LUIS OBISPO, CA (Charter Communications)

HERLONG—Formerly served by Almega Cable. No longer in operation

HERMOSA BEACH—Time Warner Cable. Now served by LOS ANGELES, CA [CA0009]

HERMOSA BEACH—See LOS ANGELES, CA (Time Warner Cable)

HESPERIA—Charter Communications

HICKMAN—See TURLOCK, CA (Charter Communications)

HIDDEN HILLS—See MALIBU, CA (Charter Communications)

HIGHLAND—See LOS ANGELES, CA (Time Warner Cable)

HILLSBOROUGH—See SAN FRANCISCO, CA (Comcast Cable)

HIOUCHI—See CRESCENT CITY, CA (Charter Communications)

HOLLISTER—See GILROY, CA (Charter Communications)

HOLLYWOOD—See LOS ANGELES, CA (Time Warner Cable)

HOLTVILLE—See EL CENTRO, CA (Time Warner Cable)

HOMELAND—See LOS ANGELES, CA (Time Warner Cable)

HUGHSON—See TURLOCK, CA (Charter Communications)

HUMBOLDT COUNTY (PORTIONS)—Suddenlink Communications

HUNTINGTON BEACH—See LOS ANGELES, CA (Time Warner Cable)

HUNTINGTON PARK—See LOS ANGELES COUNTY (portions), CA (Charter Communications)

HURON—Comcast Cable

IDYLLWILD—See LOS ANGELES, CA (Time Warner Cable)

IMPERIAL BEACH—See SAN DIEGO, CA (Cox Communications)

IMPERIAL—See EL CENTRO, CA (Time Warner Cable)

INDEPENDENCE—See BISHOP, CA (Suddenlink Communications)

INDIAN WELLS—See PALM SPRINGS, CA (Time Warner Cable)

INDIO—See PALM SPRINGS, CA (Time Warner Cable)

INGLEWOOD—See LOS ANGELES, CA (Time Warner Cable)

INVERNESS—See POINT REYES STATION, CA (Horizon Cable TV Inc)

INYO COUNTY (PORTIONS)—See BISHOP, CA (Suddenlink Communications)

INYOKERN—See RIDGECREST, CA (Mediacom)

IONE—Volcano Vision

IRVINE—See SAN JUAN CAPISTRANO, CA (Cox Communications)

IRWINDALE—See LOS ANGELES COUNTY (portions), CA (Charter Communications)

ISLETON—Formerly served by Comcast Cable. No longer in operation

IVANHOE—See PORTERVILLE, CA (Charter Communications)

JACK RANCH/POSEY—Formerly served by Charter Communications. No longer in operation

JACKSON—See SACRAMENTO, CA (Comcast Cable)

JAMUL—See SAN DIEGO, CA (Cox Communications)

JANESVILLE—See SUSANVILLE, CA (Zito Media)

JOHNSON PARK—See BURNEY, CA (Zito Media)

JOSHUA TREE—See BANNING, CA (Time Warner Cable)

JULIAN—USA Communications

JUNE LAKE—Suddenlink Communications. Now served by MAMMOTH LAKES, CA [CA0358]

JUNE LAKE—See MAMMOTH LAKES, CA (Suddenlink Communications)

JURUPA VALLEY—See RIVERSIDE, CA (Charter Communications)

KAGEL CANYON—See LOS ANGELES, CA (Time Warner Cable)

KELSEYVILLE—See CLEARLAKE, CA (Mediacom)

KERMAN—See FRESNO, CA (Comcast Cable)

KERN COUNTY (PORTIONS)—Mediacom

KERN COUNTY (UNINCORPORATED AREAS)—See RIDGECREST, CA (Mediacom)

KERN COUNTY—See BAKERSFIELD, CA (Bright House Networks)

KERNVILLE—See KERN COUNTY (portions), CA (Mediacom)

KING CITY—Charter Communications

KINGS COUNTY (PORTIONS)—See FRESNO, CA (Comcast Cable)

KINGSBURG—See FRESNO, CA (Comcast Cable)

KIRKWOOD—See IONE, CA (Volcano Vision)

KLAMATH—Formerly served by Almega Cable. No longer in operation

KNIGHTSEN—Formerly served by Comcast Cable. No longer in operation

KYBURZ—Formerly served by Comcast Cable. No longer in operation

LA CANADA FLINTRIDGE—See LOS ANGELES COUNTY (portions), CA (Charter Communications)

LA CRESCENTA—See GLENDALE, CA (Charter Communications)

LA HABRA HEIGHTS—See LOS ANGELES, CA (Time Warner Cable)

LA HABRA—See LOS ANGELES, CA (Time Warner Cable)

LA HONDA—See SAN FRANCISCO, CA (Comcast Cable)

LA MESA—See SAN DIEGO, CA (Cox Communications)

LA MIRADA—See LOS ANGELES, CA (Time Warner Cable)

LA PALMA—See LOS ANGELES, CA (Time Warner Cable)

LA PAZ COUNTY (PORTIONS)—See BLYTHE, AZ (Suddenlink Communications)

LA PUENTE—See LOS ANGELES, CA (Time Warner Cable)

LA QUINTA—See PALM SPRINGS, CA (Time Warner Cable)

LA VERNE—See LOS ANGELES, CA (Time Warner Cable)

LAFAYETTE—See SAN FRANCISCO, CA (Comcast Cable)

LAGUNA BEACH—See SAN JUAN CAPISTRANO, CA (Cox Communications)

LAGUNA HILLS—See SAN JUAN CAPISTRANO, CA (Cox Communications)

LAGUNA NIGUEL—See SAN JUAN CAPISTRANO, CA (Cox Communications)

LAGUNA WOODS—See SAN JUAN CAPISTRANO, CA (Cox Communications)

Cable Community Index—California

LAGUNA WOODS—Golden Rain Foundation of Laguna Hills Inc.

LAKE ALMANOR—CalNeva Broadband

LAKE ARROWHEAD—Charter Communications. Now served by HESPERIA, CA [CA0158]

LAKE ARROWHEAD—See HESPERIA, CA (Charter Communications)

LAKE COUNTY—See CLEARLAKE, CA (Mediacom)

LAKE ELSINORE—Time Warner Cable. Now served by LOS ANGELES, CA [CA0009]

LAKE ELSINORE—See LOS ANGELES, CA (Time Warner Cable)

LAKE FOREST—See SAN JUAN CAPISTRANO, CA (Cox Communications)

LAKE HUGHES—Formerly served by Lake Hughes Cable TV Service. No longer in operation

LAKE ISABELLA—See KERN COUNTY (portions), CA (Mediacom)

LAKE LOS ANGELES—See LOS ANGELES, CA (Time Warner Cable)

LAKE OF THE PINES—Suddenlink Communications

LAKE WILDWOOD—Comcast Cable. Now served by SACRAMENTO, CA [CA0002]

LAKE WILDWOOD—See SACRAMENTO, CA (Comcast Cable)

LAKEPORT—See CLEARLAKE, CA (Mediacom)

LAKEWOOD—Formerly served by Time Warner Cable. No longer in operation

LAKEWOOD—See LOS ANGELES, CA (Time Warner Cable)

LAMONT—See BAKERSFIELD, CA (Bright House Networks)

LANCASTER—See LOS ANGELES, CA (Time Warner Cable)

LARKSPUR—See SAN FRANCISCO, CA (Comcast Cable)

LASSEN COUNTY—See SUSANVILLE, CA (Zito Media)

LATHROP—See SACRAMENTO, CA (Comcast Cable)

LATON—See FRESNO, CA (Comcast Cable)

LAWNDALE—See LOS ANGELES, CA (Time Warner Cable)

LE GRAND—Comcast Cable

LEE VINING—Formerly served by Satview Broadband. No longer in operation

LEMON COVE—See PORTERVILLE, CA (Charter Communications)

LEMON GROVE—See SAN DIEGO, CA (Cox Communications)

LEMOORE NAVAL AIR STATION—See FRESNO, CA (Comcast Cable)

LEMOORE—See FRESNO, CA (Comcast Cable)

LEONA VALLEY—See LOS ANGELES, CA (Time Warner Cable)

LEUCADIA—See SAN DIEGO, CA (Cox Communications)

LEWISTON—Formerly served by New Day Broadband. No longer in operation

LINCOLN—See SACRAMENTO, CA (Consolidated Communications. Formerly [CA0459]. This cable system has converted to IPTV)

LINCOLN—See PLACER COUNTY (southwestern portion), CA (Wave Broadband)

LINDA—See SACRAMENTO, CA (Comcast Cable)

LINDSAY—See PORTERVILLE, CA (Charter Communications)

LITTLEROCK—See LOS ANGELES, CA (Time Warner Cable)

LIVE OAK—See SACRAMENTO, CA (Comcast Cable)

LIVERMORE—See SAN FRANCISCO, CA (Comcast Cable)

LIVINGSTON—See TURLOCK, CA (Charter Communications)

LOCH LOMOND—See CLEARLAKE, CA (Mediacom)

LODI—Comcast Cable. Now served by SACRAMENTO, CA [CA0002]

LODI—See SACRAMENTO, CA (Comcast Cable)

LOMA LINDA—See LOS ANGELES, CA (Time Warner Cable)

LOMITA—See LOS ANGELES, CA (Time Warner Cable)

LOMPOC—Comcast Cable. Now served by FRESNO, CA [CA0011]

LOMPOC—See FRESNO, CA (Comcast Cable)

LONE PINE—Lone Pine TV Inc

LONG BARN—SNC Cable

LONG BEACH NAVAL BASE—Formerly served by Americable International. No longer in operation

LONG BEACH—Charter Communications

LOOMIS—See PLACER COUNTY (southwestern portion), CA (Wave Broadband)

LOS ALAMITOS—See LOS ANGELES, CA (Time Warner Cable)

LOS ALAMOS—Formerly served by Charter Communications. No longer in operation

LOS ALTOS HILLS—Comcast Cable. Now served by SAN FRANCISCO, CA [CA0003]

LOS ALTOS HILLS—See SAN FRANCISCO, CA (Comcast Cable)

LOS ALTOS—See SAN FRANCISCO, CA (Comcast Cable)

LOS ANGELES (south central portion)—Time Warner Cable. Now served by LOS ANGELES, CA [CA0009]

LOS ANGELES (UNINCORPORATED AREAS)—See MALIBU, CA (Charter Communications)

LOS ANGELES (western portion)—Time Warner Cable. Now served by LOS ANGELES, CA [CA0009]

LOS ANGELES COUNTY (PORTIONS)—Charter Communications

LOS ANGELES COUNTY (PORTIONS)—See LONG BEACH, CA (Charter Communications)

LOS ANGELES COUNTY (PORTIONS)—See MALIBU, CA (Charter Communications)

LOS ANGELES COUNTY (PORTIONS)—See RANCHO PALOS VERDES, CA (Cox Communications)

LOS ANGELES COUNTY (PORTIONS)—See LOS ANGELES, CA (Time Warner Cable)

LOS ANGELES—Time Warner Cable. Now served by LOS ANGELES, CA [CA0009]

LOS ANGELES—Time Warner Cable

LOS BANOS—Comcast Cable. Now served by FRESNO, CA [CA0011]

LOS BANOS—See FRESNO, CA (Comcast Cable)

LOS GATOS (unincorporated areas)—Comcast Cable. Now served by SAN FRANCISCO, CA [CA0003]

LOS GATOS—Comcast Cable. Now served by SAN FRANCISCO, CA [CA0003]

LOS GATOS—See SAN FRANCISCO, CA (Comcast Cable)

LOS OLIVOS—See FRESNO, CA (Comcast Cable)

LOS TRANCOS WOODS—Comcast Cable. Now served by SAN FRANCISCO, CA [CA0003]

LOS TRANCOS WOODS—See SAN FRANCISCO, CA (Comcast Cable)

LOWER LAKE—See CLEARLAKE, CA (Mediacom)

LOWER MOHAVE VALLEY—See NEEDLES, CA (Golden Valley Cable & Communications)

LUCERNE—See CLEARLAKE, CA (Mediacom)

LUSHMEADOWS—Formerly served by Northland Cable Television. No longer in operation

LYNWOOD—See LOS ANGELES, CA (Time Warner Cable)

LYTLE CREEK—Time Warner Cable

MADERA COUNTY (PORTIONS)—See FRESNO, CA (Comcast Cable)

MADERA—See FRESNO, CA (Comcast Cable)

MALIBU—Charter Communications

MAMMOTH LAKES—Suddenlink Communications

MANHATTAN BEACH—See LOS ANGELES, CA (Time Warner Cable)

MANTECA—Comcast Cable. Now served by SACRAMENTO, CA [CA0002]

MANTECA—See SACRAMENTO, CA (Comcast Cable)

MARCH AFB—See LOS ANGELES, CA (Time Warner Cable)

MARICOPA—See BAKERSFIELD, CA (Bright House Networks)

MARIN COUNTY (PORTIONS)—See SAN FRANCISCO, CA (Comcast Cable)

MARINA DEL RAY—See LOS ANGELES, CA (Time Warner Cable)

MARINA—See SAN FRANCISCO, CA (Comcast Cable)

MARINA—See MONTEREY, CA (Suddenlink Communications)

MARINE CORPS AIR STATION EL TORO—See SAN JUAN CAPISTRANO, CA (Cox Communications)

MARINE CORPS LOGISTICS BASE BARSTOW—See BARSTOW, CA (Time Warner Cable)

MARIPOSA—Northland Cable Television

MARSH CREEK MOTOR HOME PARK—Comcast Cable. Now served by SAN FRANCISCO, CA [CA0003]

MARSH CREEK MOTOR HOME PARK—See SAN FRANCISCO, CA (Comcast Cable)

MARTINEZ—See SAN FRANCISCO, CA (Comcast Cable)

MARYSVILLE—See SACRAMENTO, CA (Comcast Cable)

MAXWELL—See SACRAMENTO, CA (Comcast Cable)

MAYWOOD—See LOS ANGELES, CA (Time Warner Cable)

MCCLELLAN PARK—See SACRAMENTO, CA (Consolidated Communications. Formerly [CA0459]. This cable system has converted to IPTV)

MCCLOUD—See MOUNT SHASTA, CA (Northland Cable Television)

MCFARLAND—See BAKERSFIELD, CA (Bright House Networks)

MCKINLEYVILLE—See HUMBOLDT COUNTY (portions), CA (Suddenlink Communications)

MEADOW VISTA—Formerly served by Cebridge Connections. Now served by Suddenlink Communications, LAKE OF THE PINES, CA [CA0202]

MEADOW VISTA—See LAKE OF THE PINES, CA (Suddenlink Communications)

California—Cable Community Index

MECCA—USA Communications

MENDOCINO COUNTY (PORTIONS)—See SAN FRANCISCO, CA (Comcast Cable)

MENDOCINO COUNTY (PORTIONS)—See WILLITS, CA (Comcast Cable)

MENDOCINO—See SAN FRANCISCO, CA (Comcast Cable)

MENDOTA—See FRESNO, CA (Comcast Cable)

MENIFEE—See LOS ANGELES, CA (Time Warner Cable)

MENLO PARK—Comcast Cable. Now served by SAN FRANCISCO, CA [CA0003]

MENLO PARK—See SAN FRANCISCO, CA (Comcast Cable)

MENTONE—See LOS ANGELES, CA (Time Warner Cable)

MERCED COUNTY (PORTIONS)—See TURLOCK, CA (Charter Communications)

MERCED COUNTY (PORTIONS)—See FRESNO, CA (Comcast Cable)

MERCED—Comcast Cable. Now served by FRESNO, CA [CA0011]

MERCED—Formerly served by Sprint Corp. No longer in operation

MERCED—See FRESNO, CA (Comcast Cable)

MEYERS—Charter Communications. Now served by RENO, NV [NV0002]

MIDDLETOWN—See CLEARLAKE, CA (Mediacom)

MIDPINES—Formerly served by Timber TV. No longer in operation

MIDWAY CITY—See LOS ANGELES, CA (Time Warner Cable)

MILL VALLEY—See SAN FRANCISCO, CA (Comcast Cable)

MILLBRAE—See SAN FRANCISCO, CA (Comcast Cable)

MILPITAS—Comcast Cable. Now served by SAN FRANCISCO, CA [CA0003]

MILPITAS—See SAN FRANCISCO, CA (Comcast Cable)

MISSION BAY MOBILE HOME PARK—Formerly served by Comcast Cable. No longer in operation

MISSION HILLS (PORTIONS)—See LOS ANGELES, CA (Time Warner Cable)

MISSION HILLS—See FRESNO, CA (Comcast Cable)

MISSION HILLS—See LOS ANGELES, CA (Time Warner Cable)

MISSION VIEJO—See SAN JUAN CAPISTRANO, CA (Cox Communications)

MODESTO—Comcast Cable. Now served by SACRAMENTO, CA [CA0002]

MODESTO—See SACRAMENTO, CA (Comcast Cable)

MODJESKA CANYON—See SAN JUAN CAPISTRANO, CA (Cox Communications)

MODOC COUNTY (PORTIONS)—See ALTURAS, CA (Charter Communications)

MOFFETT FIELD NAVAL AIRSTATION—Formerly served by Americable International-Moffett Inc. No longer in operation

MOJAVE—Charter Communications

MOKELUMNE HILL—See SACRAMENTO, CA (Comcast Cable)

MONROVIA—See LOS ANGELES COUNTY (portions), CA (Charter Communications)

MONROVIA—See LOS ANGELES, CA (Time Warner Cable)

MONTAGUE—See YREKA, CA (Northland Cable Television)

MONTARA—See SAN FRANCISCO, CA (Comcast Cable)

MONTCLAIR—See LOS ANGELES, CA (Time Warner Cable)

MONTE SERENO—See SAN FRANCISCO, CA (Comcast Cable)

MONTEBELLO—See LOS ANGELES COUNTY (portions), CA (Charter Communications)

MONTEREY COUNTY (PORTIONS)—Charter Communications

MONTEREY COUNTY (PORTIONS)—See GREENFIELD, CA (Charter Communications)

MONTEREY COUNTY (PORTIONS)—See KING CITY, CA (Charter Communications)

MONTEREY COUNTY (PORTIONS)—See SOLEDAD, CA (Charter Communications)

MONTEREY PARK—See LOS ANGELES COUNTY (portions), CA (Charter Communications)

MONTEREY—Comcast Cable. Now served by SAN FRANCISCO, CA [CA0003]

MONTEREY—Formerly served by Sprint Corp. No longer in operation

MONTEREY—See SAN FRANCISCO, CA (Comcast Cable)

MONTEREY—Suddenlink Communications

MONTROSE—See GLENDALE, CA (Charter Communications)

MOORPARK—See LOS ANGELES, CA (Time Warner Cable)

MORAGA—See SAN FRANCISCO, CA (Comcast Cable)

MORENO VALLEY—See LOS ANGELES, CA (Time Warner Cable)

MORGAN HILL—Charter Communications. Now served by GILROY, CA [CA0425]

MORGAN HILL—See GILROY, CA (Charter Communications)

MORONGO VALLEY—See BANNING, CA (Time Warner Cable)

MORRO BAY—See SAN LUIS OBISPO, CA (Charter Communications)

MOSS BEACH—See SAN FRANCISCO, CA (Comcast Cable)

MOSS LANDING—See MONTEREY COUNTY (portions), CA (Charter Communications)

MOUNT SHASTA—Northland Cable Television

MOUNTAIN MEADOWS—Formerly served by Entertainment Express. No longer in operation

MOUNTAIN VIEW—Comcast Cable. Now served by SAN FRANCISCO, CA [CA0003]

MOUNTAIN VIEW—See SAN FRANCISCO, CA (Comcast Cable)

MURRIETA—See LOS ANGELES, CA (Time Warner Cable)

MUSCOY—See LOS ANGELES, CA (Time Warner Cable)

NAPA COUNTY (PORTIONS)—See SAN FRANCISCO, CA (Comcast Cable)

NAPA—Comcast Cable. Now served by SAN FRANCISCO, CA [CA0003]

NAPA—Comcast Cable. Now served by SAN FRANCISCO, CA [CA0003]

NAPA—See SAN FRANCISCO, CA (Comcast Cable)

NATIONAL CITY—See SAN DIEGO, CA (Cox Communications)

NATOMAS—See SACRAMENTO, CA (Consolidated Communications. Formerly [CA0459]. This cable system has converted to IPTV)

NEEDLES—Golden Valley Cable & Communications

NEVADA CITY—See SACRAMENTO, CA (Comcast Cable)

NEVADA COUNTY (PORTIONS)—See SACRAMENTO, CA (Comcast Cable)

NEW CUYAMA—Formerly served by Wave Broadband. No longer in operation

NEWARK—Comcast Cable. Now served by SAN FRANCISCO, CA [CA0003]

NEWARK—See SAN FRANCISCO, CA (Comcast Cable)

NEWBURY PARK—See LOS ANGELES, CA (Time Warner Cable)

NEWCASTLE—See PLACER COUNTY (southwestern portion), CA (Wave Broadband)

NEWHALL—See LOS ANGELES, CA (Time Warner Cable)

NEWMAN—See PATTERSON, CA (Comcast Cable)

NEWPORT BEACH—Formerly served by Adelphia Communications. Now served by Time Warner Cable, LOS ANGELES, CA [CA0009]

NEWPORT BEACH—See SAN JUAN CAPISTRANO, CA (Cox Communications)

NEWPORT BEACH—See LOS ANGELES, CA (Time Warner Cable)

NICE—See CLEARLAKE, CA (Mediacom)

NILAND—USA Communications

NIPOMO—See SAN LUIS OBISPO, CA (Charter Communications)

NORCO—See RIVERSIDE, CA (Charter Communications)

NORTH EDWARDS—Charter Communications

NORTH FORK—Ponderosa Cablevision

NORTH HILLS—See LOS ANGELES, CA (Time Warner Cable)

NORTH LAKEPORT—See CLEARLAKE, CA (Mediacom)

NORTH SMITH RIVER—See CRESCENT CITY, OR (Charter Communications)

NORTHRIDGE—See LOS ANGELES, CA (Time Warner Cable)

NORTHSTAR—Formerly served by Charter Communications. No longer in operation

NORWALK—See LOS ANGELES COUNTY (portions), CA (Charter Communications)

NOVATO—Comcast Cable. Now served by SAN FRANCISCO, CA [CA0003]

NOVATO—Formerly served by Horizon Cable TV Inc. No longer in operation

NOVATO—See SAN FRANCISCO, CA (Comcast Cable)

NUEVO—See LOS ANGELES, CA (Time Warner Cable)

OAK HILLS—See MONTEREY COUNTY (portions), CA (Charter Communications)

OAK PARK—See LOS ANGELES, CA (Time Warner Cable)

OAKDALE—See SACRAMENTO, CA (Comcast Cable)

OAKHURST—Northland Cable Television

OAKLAND—See SAN FRANCISCO, CA (Comcast Cable)

OAKLEY—See SAN FRANCISCO, CA (Comcast Cable)

OCEANO—See SAN LUIS OBISPO, CA (Charter Communications)

OCEANSIDE—See SAN DIEGO, CA (Cox Communications)

OCOTILLO—Formerly served by USA Communications. No longer in operation

OJAI—Time Warner Cable. Now served by LOS ANGELES, CA [CA0009]

Cable Community Index—California

OJAI—See LOS ANGELES, CA (Time Warner Cable)

OLEMA—See POINT REYES STATION, CA (Horizon Cable TV Inc)

OLINDA—Formerly served by Almega Cable. No longer in operation

OLIVEHURST—See SACRAMENTO, CA (Comcast Cable)

ONTARIO—Time Warner Cable. Now served by LOS ANGELES, CA [CA0009]

ONTARIO—See LOS ANGELES, CA (Time Warner Cable)

ONYX—See KERN COUNTY (portions), CA (Mediacom)

ORANGE CITY—See LOS ANGELES, CA (Time Warner Cable)

ORANGE COUNTY (UNINCORPORATED AREAS)—See LOS ANGELES, CA (Time Warner Cable)

ORANGE COUNTY (western portion)—Time Warner Cable. Now served by LOS ANGELES, CA [CA0009]

ORANGE COUNTY—See SAN JUAN CAPISTRANO, CA (Cox Communications)

ORANGE COVE—See PORTERVILLE, CA (Charter Communications)

ORANGEVALE—See SACRAMENTO, CA (Consolidated Communications. Formerly [CA0459]. This cable system has converted to IPTV)

ORCUTT—See FRESNO, CA (Comcast Cable)

ORICK—Formerly served by Almega Cable. No longer in operation

ORINDA—See SAN FRANCISCO, CA (Comcast Cable)

ORLAND—See SACRAMENTO, CA (Comcast Cable)

OROSI—See PORTERVILLE, CA (Charter Communications)

OROVILLE—Comcast Cable. Now served by SACRAMENTO, CA [CA0002]

OROVILLE—See SACRAMENTO, CA (Comcast Cable)

OXNARD—Time Warner Cable. Now served by LOS ANGELES, CA [CA0009]

OXNARD—See LOS ANGELES, CA (Time Warner Cable)

PACIFIC GROVE—See SAN FRANCISCO, CA (Comcast Cable)

PACIFIC PALISADES—See LOS ANGELES, CA (Time Warner Cable)

PACIFICA—Comcast Cable. Now served by SAN FRANCISCO, CA [CA0003]

PACIFICA—See SAN FRANCISCO, CA (Comcast Cable)

PACOIMA—See LOS ANGELES, CA (Time Warner Cable)

PAJARO DUNES—See GILROY, CA (Charter Communications)

PALM DESERT—See PALM SPRINGS, CA (Time Warner Cable)

PALM SPRINGS—Time Warner Cable

PALMDALE—Time Warner Cable. Now served by LOS ANGELES, CA [CA0009]

PALMDALE—See LOS ANGELES, CA (Time Warner Cable)

PALO ALTO—Comcast Cable. Now served by SAN FRANCISCO, CA [CA0003]

PALO ALTO—Comcast Cable. Now served by SAN FRANCISCO, CA [CA0003]

PALO ALTO—See SAN FRANCISCO, CA (Comcast Cable)

PALO CEDRO—Formerly served by New Day Broadband. No longer in operation

PALOS VERDES ESTATES—See RANCHO PALOS VERDES, CA (Cox Communications)

PALOS VERDES PENINSULA—Cox Communications. Now served by RANCHO PALOS VERDES, CA [CA0903]

PARADISE—See SACRAMENTO, CA (Comcast Cable)

PARAMOUNT—See LOS ANGELES, CA (Time Warner Cable)

PARLIER—See FRESNO, CA (Comcast Cable)

PASADENA—See LOS ANGELES COUNTY (portions), CA (Charter Communications)

PASO ROBLES—See SAN LUIS OBISPO, CA (Charter Communications)

PATTERSON—Comcast Cable

PAUMA VALLEY—See VALLEY CENTER, CA (Mediacom)

PEARBLOSSOM—See LOS ANGELES, CA (Time Warner Cable)

PENN VALLEY—See SACRAMENTO, CA (Comcast Cable)

PENRYN—See PLACER COUNTY (southwestern portion), CA (Wave Broadband)

PERRIS—Time Warner Cable. Now served by LOS ANGELES, CA [CA0009]

PERRIS—See LOS ANGELES, CA (Time Warner Cable)

PESCADERO—Comcast Cable. Now served by SAN FRANCISCO, CA [CA0003]

PESCADERO—See SAN FRANCISCO, CA (Comcast Cable)

PETALUMA COAST GUARD STATION—Compass Digital Media

PETALUMA—Comcast Cable. Now served by SAN FRANCISCO, CA [CA0003]

PETALUMA—See SAN FRANCISCO, CA (Comcast Cable)

PHELAN—See WRIGHTWOOD, CA (Charter Communications)

PICO RIVERA—See LOS ANGELES, CA (Time Warner Cable)

PIEDMONT—See SAN FRANCISCO, CA (Comcast Cable)

PINE GROVE—Volcano Vision. Now served by IONE, CA [CA0265]

PINE GROVE—See IONE, CA (Volcano Vision)

PINE VALLEY—See SAN DIEGO, CA (Cox Communications)

PINECREST—SNC Cable

PINOLE—Comcast Cable. Now served by SAN FRANCISCO, CA [CA0003]

PINOLE—Comcast Cable. Now served by SAN FRANCISCO, CA [CA0003]

PINOLE—See SAN FRANCISCO, CA (Comcast Cable)

PIONEER—See IONE, CA (Volcano Vision)

PIRU—See LOS ANGELES, CA (Time Warner Cable)

PISMO/SHELL BEACH—See SAN LUIS OBISPO, CA (Charter Communications)

PITTSBURG—Comcast Cable. Now served by SAN FRANCISCO, CA [CA0003]

PITTSBURG—See SAN FRANCISCO, CA (Comcast Cable)

PIXLEY—See PORTERVILLE, CA (Charter Communications)

PLACENTIA—See LOS ANGELES, CA (Time Warner Cable)

PLACER COUNTY (PORTIONS)—See SACRAMENTO, CA (Comcast Cable)

PLACER COUNTY (SOUTHWESTERN PORTION)—Wave Broadband

PLACER COUNTY (WESTERN PORTION)—See TRUCKEE, CA (Suddenlink Communications)

PLACER COUNTY (WESTERN PORTION)—See PLACER COUNTY (southwestern portion), CA (Wave Broadband)

PLACERVILLE—Comcast Cable. Now served by SACRAMENTO, CA [CA0002]

PLACERVILLE—See SACRAMENTO, CA (Comcast Cable)

PLAINVIEW—See PORTERVILLE, CA (Charter Communications)

PLANADA—Comcast Cable

PLANTATION-BY-THE-SEA—Formerly served by Cox Communications. No longer in operation

PLAYA DEL RAY—See LOS ANGELES, CA (Time Warner Cable)

PLAYA VISTA—See LOS ANGELES, CA (Time Warner Cable)

PLEASANT HILL—Comcast Cable. Now served by SAN FRANCISCO, CA [CA0003]

PLEASANT HILL—See SAN FRANCISCO, CA (Comcast Cable)

PLEASANT HILL—See CONCORD, CA (Wave Broadband)

PLEASANTON—Comcast Cable. Now served by SAN FRANCISCO, CA [CA0003]

PLEASANTON—See SAN FRANCISCO, CA (Comcast Cable)

PLYMOUTH—See SACRAMENTO, CA (Comcast Cable)

POINT MUGU NAVAL AIR STATION—Communication Services

POINT REYES STATION—Horizon Cable TV Inc

POMERADO TERRACE NAVY HOUSING—See SAN DIEGO, CA (Time Warner Cable)

POMONA—Time Warner Cable. Now served by LOS ANGELES, CA [CA0009]

POMONA—See LOS ANGELES, CA (Time Warner Cable)

POPLAR—See PORTERVILLE, CA (Charter Communications)

PORT COSTA—See SAN FRANCISCO, CA (Comcast Cable)

PORT HUENEME—See LOS ANGELES, CA (Time Warner Cable)

PORTERVILLE—Charter Communications

PORTOLA VALLEY—Comcast Cable. Now served by SAN FRANCISCO, CA [CA0003]

PORTOLA VALLEY—See SAN FRANCISCO, CA (Comcast Cable)

PORTOLA—Formerly served by New Day Broadband. No longer in operation

POWAY—See SAN DIEGO, CA (Cox Communications)

POWAY—See SAN DIEGO, CA (Time Warner Cable)

PRESIDIO OF MONTEREY—See MONTEREY, CA (Suddenlink Communications)

PRUNEDALE—See MONTEREY COUNTY (portions), CA (Charter Communications)

QUAIL VALLEY—See LOS ANGELES, CA (Time Warner Cable)

QUARTZ HILL—See LOS ANGELES, CA (Time Warner Cable)

QUINCY (portions)—Formerly served by New Day Broadband. No longer in operation

California—Cable Community Index

QUINCY—Formerly served by Quincy Community TV Assn. Inc. No longer in operation

RAINBOW—Formerly served by Venture Communications. No longer in operation

RAMONA—See SAN DIEGO, CA (Cox Communications)

RANCHO CORDOVA—Comcast Cable. Now served by SACRAMENTO, CA [CA0002]

RANCHO CORDOVA—See SACRAMENTO, CA (Comcast Cable)

RANCHO CORDOVA—See SACRAMENTO, CA (Consolidated Communications. Formerly [CA0459]. This cable system has converted to IPTV)

RANCHO CUCAMONGA—See RIVERSIDE, CA (Charter Communications)

RANCHO CUCAMONGA—See LOS ANGELES, CA (Time Warner Cable)

RANCHO MIRAGE—See PALM SPRINGS, CA (Time Warner Cable)

RANCHO PALOS VERDES—Cox Communications

RANCHO SAN DIEGO—See SAN DIEGO, CA (Cox Communications)

RANCHO SANTA FE—See SAN DIEGO, CA (Cox Communications)

RANCHO SANTA MARGARITA—See SAN JUAN CAPISTRANO, CA (Cox Communications)

RANCHO TIERRA GRANDE—See MONTEREY COUNTY (portions), CA (Charter Communications)

RANCHO YOLO MOBILE HOME PARK—Formerly served by Wave Broadband. No longer in operation

RASNOW—No longer in operation

RED BLUFF—Charter Communications. Now served by REDDING, CA [CA0058]

RED BLUFF—See REDDING, CA (Charter Communications)

REDDING—Formerly served by Sprint Corp. No longer in operation

REDDING—Charter Communications

REDLANDS—Time Warner Cable. Now served by LOS ANGELES, CA [CA0009]

REDLANDS—See LOS ANGELES, CA (Time Warner Cable)

REDONDO BEACH—Time Warner Cable. Now served by LOS ANGELES, CA [CA0009]

REDONDO BEACH—See LOS ANGELES, CA (Time Warner Cable)

REDWAY—See GARBERVILLE, CA (Wave Broadband)

REDWOOD CITY—See SAN FRANCISCO, CA (Comcast Cable)

REDWOOD CITY—See SAN FRANCISCO (southern portion), CA (Wave Broadband)

REEDLEY—See FRESNO, CA (Comcast Cable)

RESEDA—See LOS ANGELES, CA (Time Warner Cable)

RIALTO—See LOS ANGELES, CA (Time Warner Cable)

RICHMOND—See SAN FRANCISCO, CA (Comcast Cable)

RIDGECREST—Mediacom

RINCON—See VALLEY CENTER, CA (Mediacom)

RIO DELL—See HUMBOLDT COUNTY (portions), CA (Suddenlink Communications)

RIO VISTA—Comcast Cable. Now served by SAN FRANCISCO, CA [CA0003]

RIO VISTA—See SAN FRANCISCO, CA (Comcast Cable)

RIO VISTA—Wave Broadband

RIPON—See TURLOCK, CA (Charter Communications)

RIVERBANK—See TURLOCK, CA (Charter Communications)

RIVERDALE—Comcast Cable. Now served by FRESNO, CA [CA0011]

RIVERDALE—See FRESNO, CA (Comcast Cable)

RIVERSIDE COUNTY (EASTERN PORTION)—See BLYTHE, CA (Suddenlink Communications)

RIVERSIDE COUNTY (PORTIONS)—See RIVERSIDE, CA (Charter Communications)

RIVERSIDE COUNTY (PORTIONS)—See BANNING, CA (Time Warner Cable)

RIVERSIDE COUNTY (PORTIONS)—See LOS ANGELES, CA (Time Warner Cable)

RIVERSIDE COUNTY (PORTIONS)—See PALM SPRINGS, CA (Time Warner Cable)

RIVERSIDE COUNTY (WESTERN PORTION)—See SUN CITY, CA (Mediacom)

RIVERSIDE—Formerly served by Cross Country Wireless Cable. No longer in operation

RIVERSIDE—Charter Communications

ROCKLIN—See SACRAMENTO, CA (Consolidated Communications. Formerly [CA0459]. This cable system has converted to IPTV)

ROCKLIN—See PLACER COUNTY (southwestern portion), CA (Wave Broadband)

RODEO—See SAN FRANCISCO, CA (Comcast Cable)

ROHNERT PARK—Comcast Cable. Now served by SAN FRANCISCO, CA [CA0003]

ROHNERT PARK—See SAN FRANCISCO, CA (Comcast Cable)

ROLLING HILLS ESTATES—See RANCHO PALOS VERDES, CA (Cox Communications)

ROLLING HILLS—See RANCHO PALOS VERDES, CA (Cox Communications)

ROMOLAND—See LOS ANGELES, CA (Time Warner Cable)

ROSAMOND—See MOJAVE, CA (Charter Communications)

ROSEMEAD—See LOS ANGELES COUNTY (portions), CA (Charter Communications)

ROSEVILLE—Comcast Cable. Now served by SACRAMENTO, CA [CA0002]

ROSEVILLE—See SACRAMENTO, CA (Comcast Cable)

ROSEVILLE—See SACRAMENTO, CA (Consolidated Communications. Formerly [CA0459]. This cable system has converted to IPTV)

ROSS—See SAN FRANCISCO, CA (Comcast Cable)

ROSSMOOR—See LOS ANGELES, CA (Time Warner Cable)

ROUND VALLEY—See BISHOP, CA (Suddenlink Communications)

ROWLAND HEIGHTS—See LOS ANGELES, CA (Time Warner Cable)

SACRAMENTO COUNTY (PORTIONS)—See SACRAMENTO, CA (Comcast Cable)

SACRAMENTO—Formerly served by Wireless Broadcasting Services. No longer in operation

SACRAMENTO—SureWest Broadband. This cable system has converted to IPTV. See SACRAMENTO, CA [CA5597]

SACRAMENTO—Comcast Cable

SACRAMENTO—Consolidated Communications. Formerly [CA0459]. This cable system has converted to IPTV

SALINAS—See SAN FRANCISCO, CA (Comcast Cable)

SALTON CITY—USA Communications

SALTON SEA BEACH—USA Communications

SAN ANDREAS—Comcast Cable. Now served by SACRAMENTO, CA [CA0002]

SAN ANDREAS—See SACRAMENTO, CA (Comcast Cable)

SAN ANSELMO—See SAN FRANCISCO, CA (Comcast Cable)

SAN BENITO COUNTY (PORTIONS)—See GILROY, CA (Charter Communications)

SAN BERNARDINO COUNTY (PORTIONS)—See HESPERIA, CA (Charter Communications)

SAN BERNARDINO COUNTY (PORTIONS)—See RIVERSIDE, CA (Charter Communications)

SAN BERNARDINO COUNTY (PORTIONS)—See RIDGECREST, CA (Mediacom)

SAN BERNARDINO COUNTY (PORTIONS)—See BANNING, CA (Time Warner Cable)

SAN BERNARDINO COUNTY (PORTIONS)—See LOS ANGELES, CA (Time Warner Cable)

SAN BERNARDINO COUNTY—See BARSTOW, CA (Time Warner Cable)

SAN BERNARDINO—Charter Communications. Now served by RIVERSIDE, CA [CA0023]

SAN BERNARDINO—Time Warner Cable. Now served by LOS ANGELES, CA [CA0009]

SAN BERNARDINO—See RIVERSIDE, CA (Charter Communications)

SAN BERNARDINO—See LOS ANGELES, CA (Time Warner Cable)

SAN BRUNO—City of San Bruno Municipal Cable TV

SAN CARLOS—See SAN FRANCISCO, CA (Comcast Cable)

SAN CLEMENTE—See SAN JUAN CAPISTRANO, CA (Cox Communications)

SAN DIEGO (UNINCORPORATED AREAS)—See SAN DIEGO, CA (Cox Communications)

SAN DIEGO COUNTY—See SAN DIEGO, CA (Cox Communications)

SAN DIEGO COUNTY—See SAN DIEGO, CA (Time Warner Cable)

SAN DIEGO NAVAL BASE—NWS Communications

SAN DIEGO—Cox Communications

SAN DIEGO—Time Warner Cable

SAN DIMAS—See LOS ANGELES, CA (Time Warner Cable)

SAN FERNANDO—See LOS ANGELES, CA (Time Warner Cable)

SAN FRANCISCO (SOUTHERN PORTION)—Wave Broadband

SAN FRANCISCO—Formerly served by TV Max. No longer in operation

SAN FRANCISCO—Comcast Cable

SAN GABRIEL—See LOS ANGELES COUNTY (portions), CA (Charter Communications)

SAN JACINTO—See LOS ANGELES, CA (Time Warner Cable)

SAN JOAQUIN COUNTY (PORTIONS)—See TURLOCK, CA (Charter Communications)

SAN JOAQUIN COUNTY (PORTIONS)—See SACRAMENTO, CA (Comcast Cable)

SAN JOAQUIN—See FRESNO, CA (Comcast Cable)

Cable Community Index—California

SAN JOSE—Comcast Cable. Now served by SAN FRANCISCO, CA [CA0003]

SAN JOSE—Formerly served by Pacific Bell Video Services. No longer in operation

SAN JOSE—Formerly served by TV Max. No longer in operation

SAN JOSE—See SAN FRANCISCO, CA (Comcast Cable)

SAN JUAN BAUTISTA (PORTIONS)—See GILROY, CA (Charter Communications)

SAN JUAN CAPISTRANO—Cox Communications

SAN LEANDRO—See SAN FRANCISCO, CA (Comcast Cable)

SAN LORENZO—See SAN FRANCISCO, CA (Comcast Cable)

SAN LUIS OBISPO COUNTY (PORTIONS)—See SAN LUIS OBISPO, CA (Charter Communications)

SAN LUIS OBISPO—Formerly served by TVCN. No longer in operation

SAN LUIS OBISPO—Charter Communications

SAN MARCOS (PORTIONS)—See SAN DIEGO, CA (Time Warner Cable)

SAN MARCOS—See SAN DIEGO, CA (Cox Communications)

SAN MARINO—See LOS ANGELES, CA (Time Warner Cable)

SAN MATEO COUNTY (PORTIONS)—See SAN FRANCISCO, CA (Comcast Cable)

SAN MATEO—Comcast Cable. Now served by SAN FRANCISCO, CA [CA0003]

SAN MATEO—See SAN FRANCISCO, CA (Comcast Cable)

SAN MATEO—See SAN FRANCISCO (southern portion), CA (Wave Broadband)

SAN MIGUEL—See SAN LUIS OBISPO, CA (Charter Communications)

SAN PABLO—Comcast Cable. Now served by SAN FRANCISCO, CA [CA0003]

SAN PABLO—See SAN FRANCISCO, CA (Comcast Cable)

SAN PEDRO—See RANCHO PALOS VERDES, CA (Cox Communications)

SAN PEDRO—See LOS ANGELES, CA (Time Warner Cable)

SAN RAFAEL—Comcast Cable. Now served by SAN FRANCISCO, CA [CA0003]

SAN RAFAEL—See SAN FRANCISCO, CA (Comcast Cable)

SAN RAMON—See SAN FRANCISCO, CA (Comcast Cable)

SAN SIMEON ACRES—San Simeon Community Cable Inc

SAND CITY—See SAN FRANCISCO, CA (Comcast Cable)

SANGER—See FRESNO, CA (Comcast Cable)

SANTA ANA—Formerly served by Adelphia Communications. Now served by Time Warner Cable, LOS ANGELES, CA [CA0009]

SANTA ANA—See LOS ANGELES, CA (Time Warner Cable)

SANTA BARBARA COUNTY (PORTIONS)—See SANTA BARBARA, CA (Cox Communications)

SANTA BARBARA—Cox Communications

SANTA CLARA COUNTY (PORTIONS)—See GILROY, CA (Charter Communications)

SANTA CLARA COUNTY (PORTIONS)—See SAN FRANCISCO, CA (Comcast Cable)

SANTA CLARA—Comcast Cable. Now served by SAN FRANCISCO, CA [CA0003]

SANTA CLARA—See SAN FRANCISCO, CA (Comcast Cable)

SANTA CLARITA—Time Warner Cable. Now served by LOS ANGELES, CA [CA0009]

SANTA CLARITA—See LOS ANGELES, CA (Time Warner Cable)

SANTA CRUZ COUNTY (PORTIONS)—See GILROY, CA (Charter Communications)

SANTA CRUZ COUNTY (PORTIONS)—See SAN FRANCISCO, CA (Comcast Cable)

SANTA CRUZ—Comcast Cable. Now served by SAN FRANCISCO, CA [CA0003]

SANTA CRUZ—See SAN FRANCISCO, CA (Comcast Cable)

SANTA FE SPRINGS—See LOS ANGELES, CA (Time Warner Cable)

SANTA MARGARITA—See SAN LUIS OBISPO, CA (Charter Communications)

SANTA MARIA—Comcast Cable. Now served by FRESNO, CA [CA0011]

SANTA MARIA—See FRESNO, CA (Comcast Cable)

SANTA MONICA—Time Warner Cable. Now served by LOS ANGELES, CA [CA0009]

SANTA MONICA—See LOS ANGELES, CA (Time Warner Cable)

SANTA NELLA—See PATTERSON, CA (Comcast Cable)

SANTA PAULA—See LOS ANGELES, CA (Time Warner Cable)

SANTA ROSA—Comcast Cable. Now served by SAN FRANCISCO, CA [CA0003]

SANTA ROSA—See SAN FRANCISCO, CA (Comcast Cable)

SANTA YNEZ—See FRESNO, CA (Comcast Cable)

SANTEE—See SAN DIEGO, CA (Cox Communications)

SARATOGA—Comcast Cable. Now served by SAN FRANCISCO, CA [CA0003]

SARATOGA—See SAN FRANCISCO, CA (Comcast Cable)

SAUGUS—See LOS ANGELES, CA (Time Warner Cable)

SAUSALITO—See SAN FRANCISCO, CA (Comcast Cable)

SCOTTS VALLEY—See SAN FRANCISCO, CA (Comcast Cable)

SEAL BEACH NAVAL STATION—See LOS ANGELES, CA (Time Warner Cable)

SEAL BEACH—Formerly served by Adelphia Communications. Time Warner Cable. Now served by LOS ANGELES, CA [CA0009]

SEAL BEACH—See LOS ANGELES, CA (Time Warner Cable)

SEASIDE—See SAN FRANCISCO, CA (Comcast Cable)

SEASIDE—See MONTEREY, CA (Suddenlink Communications)

SEBASTOPOL—See SAN FRANCISCO, CA (Comcast Cable)

SEELEY—See EL CENTRO, CA (Time Warner Cable)

SELMA—See FRESNO, CA (Comcast Cable)

SHAFTER—See BAKERSFIELD, CA (Bright House Networks)

SHASTA COUNTY (PORTIONS)—See MOUNT SHASTA, CA (Northland Cable Television)

SHASTA COUNTY—See REDDING, CA (Charter Communications)

SHAVER LAKE—Suddenlink Communications

SHERMAN OAKS—Time Warner Cable. Now served by LOS ANGELES, CA [CA0009]

SHERMAN OAKS—See LOS ANGELES, CA (Time Warner Cable)

SIERRA DAWN ESTATES—Formerly served by Sierra Dawn Cablevision. No longer in operation

SIERRA MADRE—Time Warner Cable. Now served by LOS ANGELES, CA [CA0009]

SIERRA MADRE—See LOS ANGELES, CA (Time Warner Cable)

SIGNAL HILL—See LONG BEACH, CA (Charter Communications)

SILVER STRAND NAVY HOUSING—See SAN DIEGO, CA (Time Warner Cable)

SIMI VALLEY—Time Warner Cable. Now served by LOS ANGELES, CA [CA0009]

SIMI VALLEY—See LOS ANGELES, CA (Time Warner Cable)

SISKIYOU COUNTY (PORTIONS)—See MOUNT SHASTA, CA (Northland Cable Television)

SISKIYOU COUNTY (PORTIONS)—See YREKA, CA (Northland Cable Television)

SOLANA BEACH—See SAN DIEGO, CA (Cox Communications)

SOLANA BEACH—See SAN DIEGO, CA (Time Warner Cable)

SOLANO COUNTY (PORTIONS)—See SAN FRANCISCO, CA (Comcast Cable)

SOLANO COUNTY (WESTERN PORTIONS)—See SAN FRANCISCO, CA (Comcast Cable)

SOLANO—See SAN FRANCISCO, CA (Comcast Cable)

SOLEDAD—Charter Communications

SOLVANG—See FRESNO, CA (Comcast Cable)

SONOMA COUNTY (PORTIONS)—See SAN FRANCISCO, CA (Comcast Cable)

SONOMA—See SAN FRANCISCO, CA (Comcast Cable)

SONORA—Comcast Cable. Now served by SACRAMENTO, CA [CA0002]

SONORA—Comcast Cable. Now served by SACRAMENTO, CA [CA0002]

SONORA—See SACRAMENTO, CA (Comcast Cable)

SOUTH EL MONTE—See LOS ANGELES, CA (Time Warner Cable)

SOUTH GATE—Time Warner Cable. Now served by LOS ANGELES, CA [CA0009]

SOUTH GATE—See LOS ANGELES, CA (Time Warner Cable)

SOUTH LAKE TAHOE—Charter Communications. Now served by RENO, NV [NV0002]

SOUTH PASADENA—Time Warner Cable. Now served by LOS ANGELES, CA [CA0009]

SOUTH PASADENA—See LOS ANGELES, CA (Time Warner Cable)

SOUTH SAN FRANCISCO—Comcast Cable. Now served by SAN FRANCISCO, CA [CA0003]

SOUTH SAN FRANCISCO—See SAN FRANCISCO, CA (Comcast Cable)

SOUTH SAN FRANCISCO—See SAN FRANCISCO (southern portion), CA (Wave Broadband)

SOUTH SAN GABRIEL—See LOS ANGELES COUNTY (portions), CA (Charter Communications)

SOUTH WHITTIER—See LOS ANGELES, CA (Time Warner Cable)

California—Cable Community Index

SPANISH RANCH MOBILE HOME PARK—Formerly served by Comcast Cable. No longer in operation

SPRING VALLEY—See SAN DIEGO, CA (Cox Communications)

SPRINGVILLE—See PORTERVILLE, CA (Charter Communications)

ST. HELENA—See SAN FRANCISCO, CA (Comcast Cable)

STANFORD—See SAN FRANCISCO, CA (Comcast Cable)

STANISLAUS COUNTY (PORTIONS)—See TURLOCK, CA (Charter Communications)

STANISLAUS COUNTY (PORTIONS)—See PATTERSON, CA (Comcast Cable)

STANISLAUS COUNTY (PORTIONS)—See SACRAMENTO, CA (Comcast Cable)

STANTON—See LOS ANGELES, CA (Time Warner Cable)

STEVENSON RANCH—Time Warner Cable. Now served by LOS ANGELES, CA [CA0009]

STEVENSON RANCH—See LOS ANGELES, CA (Time Warner Cable)

STINSON BEACH—See POINT REYES STATION, CA (Horizon Cable TV Inc)

STOCKTON—Comcast Cable. Now served by SACRAMENTO, CA [CA0002]

STOCKTON—See SACRAMENTO, CA (Comcast Cable)

STRATHMORE—See PORTERVILLE, CA (Charter Communications)

STRAWBERRY—Formerly served by Comcast Cable. No longer in operation

STRAWBERRY—See PINECREST, CA (SNC Cable)

STUDIO CITY—Formerly served by Adelphia Communications. Now served by Time Warner Cable, LOS ANGELES, CA [CA0009]

STUDIO CITY—See LOS ANGELES, CA (Time Warner Cable)

SUISIN CITY—See SAN FRANCISCO, CA (Comcast Cable)

SUN CITY—Mediacom

SUN VALLEY—See LOS ANGELES, CA (Time Warner Cable)

SUNLAND—See LOS ANGELES, CA (Time Warner Cable)

SUNNYVALE—Comcast Cable. Now served by SAN FRANCISCO, CA [CA0003]

SUNNYVALE—See SAN FRANCISCO, CA (Comcast Cable)

SUNOL—See SAN FRANCISCO, CA (Comcast Cable)

SUNSET BEACH—See LOS ANGELES, CA (Time Warner Cable)

SUSANVILLE—Zito Media

SUTTER COUNTY (PORTIONS)—See SACRAMENTO, CA (Comcast Cable)

SUTTER CREEK—See SACRAMENTO, CA (Comcast Cable)

SYLMAR—See LOS ANGELES, CA (Time Warner Cable)

TAFT—See BAKERSFIELD, CA (Bright House Networks)

TAHOE CITY—See TRUCKEE, CA (Suddenlink Communications)

TARZANA—See LOS ANGELES, CA (Time Warner Cable)

TASSAJARA VALLEY—Formerly served by Comcast Cable. No longer in operation

TEHACHAPI—Bright House Networks. Now served by BAKERSFIELD, CA [CA0025]

TEHACHAPI—See BAKERSFIELD, CA (Bright House Networks)

TEHAMA COUNTY—See REDDING, CA (Charter Communications)

TEHAMA—Formerly served by New Day Broadband. No longer in operation

TEMECULA—See LOS ANGELES, CA (Time Warner Cable)

TEMPLE CITY—See LOS ANGELES COUNTY (portions), CA (Charter Communications)

TEMPLETON—See SAN LUIS OBISPO, CA (Charter Communications)

TERRA BELLA—See PORTERVILLE, CA (Charter Communications)

THE SEA RANCH—CalNeva Broadband

THERMAL—Formerly served by USA Communications. No longer in operation

THOUSAND OAKS—Time Warner Cable. Now served by LOS ANGELES, CA [CA0009]

THOUSAND OAKS—Charter Communications

THOUSAND OAKS—See LOS ANGELES, CA (Time Warner Cable)

THOUSAND PALMS—See PALM SPRINGS, CA (Time Warner Cable)

THREE RIVERS—See PORTERVILLE, CA (Charter Communications)

TIBURON—See SAN FRANCISCO, CA (Comcast Cable)

TIERRA BUENA—See SACRAMENTO, CA (Comcast Cable)

TIPTON—See PORTERVILLE, CA (Charter Communications)

TOPANGA—See MALIBU, CA (Charter Communications)

TORRANCE—Time Warner Cable. Now served by LOS ANGELES, CA [CA0009]

TORRANCE—See LOS ANGELES, CA (Time Warner Cable)

TOWER PARK—See SACRAMENTO, CA (Comcast Cable)

TRABUCO CANYON—See SAN JUAN CAPISTRANO, CA (Cox Communications)

TRACY—Comcast Cable. Now served by SACRAMENTO, CA [CA0002]

TRACY—See SACRAMENTO, CA (Comcast Cable)

TRAVIS AFB—Comcast Cable. Now served by SAN FRANCISCO, CA [CA0003]

TRAVIS AFB—See SAN FRANCISCO, CA (Comcast Cable)

TREASURE ISLAND NAVAL STATION—See SAN FRANCISCO, CA (Comcast Cable)

TRINIDAD—See HUMBOLDT COUNTY (portions), CA (Suddenlink Communications)

TRINITY CENTER—Formerly served by Almega Cable. No longer in operation

TRUCKEE—Suddenlink Communications

TUJUNGA—Time Warner Cable. Now served by LOS ANGELES, CA [CA0009]

TUJUNGA—See LOS ANGELES, CA (Time Warner Cable)

TULARE COUNTY (NORTHEASTERN PORTION)—See PORTERVILLE, CA (Charter Communications)

TULARE—See FRESNO, CA (Comcast Cable)

TULELAKE—Formerly served by Almega Cable. No longer in operation

TUOLUMNE COUNTY (PORTIONS)—See SACRAMENTO, CA (Comcast Cable)

TURLOCK—Charter Communications

TUSTIN—Time Warner Cable. Now served by LOS ANGELES, CA [CA0009]

TUSTIN—See SAN JUAN CAPISTRANO, CA (Cox Communications)

TUSTIN—See LOS ANGELES, CA (Time Warner Cable)

TWENTYNINE PALMS MARINE CORPS BASE—See BANNING, CA (Time Warner Cable)

TWENTYNINE PALMS—See BANNING, CA (Time Warner Cable)

UKIAH—Comcast Cable. Now served by SAN FRANCISCO, CA [CA0003]

UKIAH—See SAN FRANCISCO, CA (Comcast Cable)

UNION CITY—Comcast Cable. Now served by SAN FRANCISCO, CA [CA0003]

UNION CITY—See SAN FRANCISCO, CA (Comcast Cable)

UPLAND—See LOS ANGELES, CA (Time Warner Cable)

UPPER LAKE—See CLEARLAKE, CA (Mediacom)

VACAVILLE—Comcast Cable. Now served by SAN FRANCISCO, CA [CA0003]

VACAVILLE—See SAN FRANCISCO, CA (Comcast Cable)

VALENCIA—See LOS ANGELES, CA (Time Warner Cable)

VALLEJO—Comcast Cable. Now served by SAN FRANCISCO, CA [CA0003]

VALLEJO—See SAN FRANCISCO, CA (Comcast Cable)

VALLEY CENTER—Mediacom

VAN NUYS—Formerly served by Adelphia Communications. Now served by Time Warner, LOS ANGELES, CA [CA0009]

VAN NUYS—See LOS ANGELES, CA (Time Warner Cable)

VANDENBERG AFB—Vandenberg Broadband

VANDENBURG VILLAGE—See FRESNO, CA (Comcast Cable)

VENICE—See LOS ANGELES, CA (Time Warner Cable)

VENTURA COUNTY (PORTIONS)—See MALIBU, CA (Charter Communications)

VENTURA COUNTY (PORTIONS)—See LOS ANGELES, CA (Time Warner Cable)

VENTURA COUNTY (RINCON AREA)—See VENTURA, CA (Charter Communications)

VENTURA—Time Warner Cable. Now served by LOS ANGELES, CA [CA0009]

VENTURA—Charter Communications

VENTURA—See LOS ANGELES, CA (Time Warner Cable)

VICTORVILLE—Charter Communications. Now served by HESPERIA, CA [CA0158]

VICTORVILLE—See HESPERIA, CA (Charter Communications)

VILLA PARK—See LOS ANGELES, CA (Time Warner Cable)

VISALIA—Charter Communications. Now served by FRESNO, CA [CA0011]

VISALIA—Formerly served by Sprint Corp. No longer in operation

VISALIA—See FRESNO, CA (Comcast Cable)

VISTA—See SAN DIEGO, CA (Cox Communications)

VISTA—See SAN DIEGO, CA (Time Warner Cable)

WALNUT CREEK—Comcast Cable. Now served by SAN FRANCISCO, CA [CA0003]

WALNUT CREEK—See SAN FRANCISCO, CA (Comcast Cable)

Cable Community Index—Colorado

WALNUT CREEK—See CONCORD, CA (Wave Broadband)

WALNUT PARK—See LOS ANGELES, CA (Time Warner Cable)

WALNUT—See LOS ANGELES COUNTY (portions), CA (Charter Communications)

WASCO—See BAKERSFIELD, CA (Bright House Networks)

WATERFORD—See TURLOCK, CA (Charter Communications)

WATSONVILLE—Charter Communications. Now served by GILROY, CA [CA0425]

WATSONVILLE—See GILROY, CA (Charter Communications)

WEAVERVILLE—Velocity Telephone Inc

WEED—See MOUNT SHASTA, CA (Northland Cable Television)

WELDON—See KERN COUNTY (portions), CA (Mediacom)

WEST COVINA—See LOS ANGELES COUNTY (portions), CA (Charter Communications)

WEST HILLS—See LOS ANGELES, CA (Time Warner Cable)

WEST HOLLYWOOD—Time Warner Cable. Now served by LOS ANGELES, CA [CA0009]

WEST HOLLYWOOD—See LOS ANGELES, CA (Time Warner Cable)

WEST LOS ANGELES—Time Warner Cable. Now served by LOS ANGELES, CA [CA0009]

WEST LOS ANGELES—See LOS ANGELES, CA (Time Warner Cable)

WEST POINT—See IONE, CA (Volcano Vision)

WEST SACRAMENTO—Wave Broadband

WEST SAN FERNANDO VALLEY—See LOS ANGELES, CA (Time Warner Cable)

WESTLAKE VILLAGE—See LOS ANGELES, CA (Time Warner Cable)

WESTMINSTER—See LOS ANGELES, CA (Time Warner Cable)

WESTMORLAND—See EL CENTRO, CA (Time Warner Cable)

WESTWOOD—See LAKE ALMANOR, CA (CalNeva Broadband)

WHEATLAND—See SACRAMENTO, CA (Comcast Cable)

WHITTIER—Charter Communications

WILDOMAR—See LOS ANGELES, CA (Time Warner Cable)

WILLIAMS—Comcast Cable. Now served by SACRAMENTO, CA [CA0002]

WILLIAMS—See SACRAMENTO, CA (Comcast Cable)

WILLITS—Comcast Cable

WILLOW CREEK—Formerly served by Almega Cable. No longer in operation

WILLOW RANCH MOBILE HOME PARK—Formerly served by Comcast Cable. No longer in operation

WILLOWS—See SACRAMENTO, CA (Comcast Cable)

WILMINGTON—Time Warner Cable. Now served by LOS ANGELES, CA [CA0009]

WILMINGTON—See LOS ANGELES, CA (Time Warner Cable)

WINCHESTER—See LOS ANGELES, CA (Time Warner Cable)

WINDSOR—See SAN FRANCISCO, CA (Comcast Cable)

WINNETKA—See LOS ANGELES, CA (Time Warner Cable)

WINTERS—See WEST SACRAMENTO, CA (Wave Broadband)

WOFFORD HEIGHTS—See KERN COUNTY (portions), CA (Mediacom)

WOODLAKE—See PORTERVILLE, CA (Charter Communications)

WOODLAND HILLS—See LOS ANGELES, CA (Time Warner Cable)

WOODLAND—See WEST SACRAMENTO, CA (Wave Broadband)

WOODSIDE—See SAN FRANCISCO, CA (Comcast Cable)

WOODVILLE—See PORTERVILLE, CA (Charter Communications)

WRIGHTWOOD—Charter Communications

YORBA LINDA—Time Warner Cable. Now served by LOS ANGELES, CA [CA0009]

YORBA LINDA—See LOS ANGELES, CA (Time Warner Cable)

YOUNTVILLE—Comcast Cable. Now served by SAN FRANCISCO, CA [CA0003]

YOUNTVILLE—See SAN FRANCISCO, CA (Comcast Cable)

YREKA—Northland Cable Television

YUBA CITY—Comcast Cable. Now served by SACRAMENTO, CA [CA0002]

YUBA CITY—Formerly served by Sprint Corp. No longer in operation

YUBA CITY—See SACRAMENTO, CA (Comcast Cable)

YUCAIPA—Charter Communications

YUCAIPA—See LOS ANGELES, CA (Time Warner Cable)

YUCCA VALLEY—Time Warner Cable. Now served by BANNING, CA [CA0176]

YUCCA VALLEY—See BANNING, CA (Time Warner Cable)

COLORADO

ADAMS COUNTY (PORTIONS)—See DENVER, CO (Comcast Cable)

AKRON (town)—Mediastream. Now served by Vyve Broadband, OTIS (town), CO [CO0128]

AKRON—See OTIS (town), CO (Vyve Broadband)

ALAMOSA COUNTY—See ALAMOSA, CO (Charter Communications)

ALAMOSA EAST—See ALAMOSA, CO (Charter Communications)

ALAMOSA—Charter Communications

ANTONITO—Formerly served by Charter Communications. No longer in operation

APPLE TREE MOBILE HOME PARK—See SILT, CO (Comcast Cable)

ARAPAHOE COUNTY (PORTIONS)—See DENVER, CO (Comcast Cable)

ARCHULETA COUNTY—See PAGOSA SPRINGS, CO (USA Communications)

ARRIBA—Rebeltec Communications. Now served by KIT CARSON, CO [CO0152]

ARRIBA—See KIT CARSON, CO (Rebeltec Communications)

ARVADA—See TABLE MOUNTAIN, CO (Baja Broadband)

ARVADA—See DENVER, CO (Comcast Cable)

ASPEN—Comcast Cable. Now served by LONGMONT, CO [CO0011]

ASPEN—See LONGMONT, CO (Comcast Cable)

AULT—See FORT COLLINS, CO (Baja Broadband)

AURORA—See DENVER, CO (Comcast Cable)

AVON—Comcast Cable. Now served by LONGMONT, CO [CO0011]

AVON—See LONGMONT, CO (Comcast Cable)

BAILEY—Formerly served by US Cable of Coastal Texas LP. No longer in operation

BASALT—See LONGMONT, CO (Comcast Cable)

BATTLEMENT MESA—See PARACHUTE, CO (Comcast Cable)

BAYFIELD—USA Communications

BEAVER CREEK—See LONGMONT, CO (Comcast Cable)

BENNETT—Comcast Cable. Now served by DENVER, CO [CO0001]

BENNETT—See DENVER, CO (Comcast Cable)

BERTHOUD—See LONGMONT, CO (Comcast Cable)

BEULAH—Beulah Cable TV

BLACK FOREST—See COLORADO SPRINGS, CO (Comcast Cable)

BLACK HAWK—USA Communications

BLANCA—Formerly served by Jade Communications. No longer in operation

BLUE RIVER—See LONGMONT, CO (Comcast Cable)

BOULDER (portions)—Formerly served by Qwest Choice TV. No longer in operation

BOULDER COUNTY (PORTIONS)—See DENVER, CO (Comcast Cable)

BOULDER COUNTY (PORTIONS)—See LONGMONT, CO (Comcast Cable)

BOULDER—Comcast Cable. Now served by DENVER, CO [CO0001]

BOULDER—See DENVER, CO (Comcast Cable)

BOW MAR—See DENVER, CO (Comcast Cable)

BRECKENRIDGE—Comcast Cable. Now served by LONGMONT, CO [CO0011]

BRECKENRIDGE—See LONGMONT, CO (Comcast Cable)

BRIGHTON—Comcast Cable. Now served by DENVER, CO [CO0001]

BRIGHTON—See DENVER, CO (Comcast Cable)

BROOKSIDE—See CANON CITY, CO (Charter Communications)

BROOMFIELD—Comcast Cable. Now served by DENVER, CO [CO0001]

BROOMFIELD—See DENVER, CO (Comcast Cable)

BRUSH—See FORT MORGAN, CO (Charter Communications)

BUENA VISTA—Charter Communications

BURLINGTON—Eagle Communications

BYERS—See DENVER, CO (Comcast Cable)

CALHAN—Formerly served by FairPoint Communications. No longer in operation

CANON CITY—Charter Communications

CANTERBURY PARK—Formerly served by Island Cable. No longer in operation

CARBONDALE—Comcast Cable

CASCADE—See COLORADO SPRINGS, CO (Comcast Cable)

CASTLE PINES—See DENVER, CO (Comcast Cable)

CASTLE ROCK—Comcast Cable. Now served by DENVER, CO [CO0001]

CASTLE ROCK—See DENVER, CO (Comcast Cable)

CENTENNIAL—See DENVER, CO (Comcast Cable)

CENTER—Formerly served by Center Municipal Cable System. No longer in operation

Colorado—Cable Community Index

CENTER—USA Communications

CENTRAL CITY—USA Communications

CHAFFEE COUNTY (CENTRAL PORTION)—See BUENA VISTA, CO (Charter Communications)

CHAFFEE COUNTY (SOUTHEASTERN PORTION)—See SALIDA, CO (Charter Communications)

CHAPPELL—See HOLYOKE, NE (PC Telcom)

CHERRY HILLS VILLAGE—See DENVER, CO (Comcast Cable)

CHEYENNE WELLS—Formerly served by NexHorizon Communications. No longer in operation

CHIPITA PARK—See COLORADO SPRINGS, CO (Comcast Cable)

CLEAR CREEK COUNTY (PORTIONS)—See DENVER, CO (Comcast Cable)

CLOVERLEAF TRAILER PARK—See FORT COLLINS, CO (Baja Broadband)

COAL CREEK—See CANON CITY, CO (Charter Communications)

COLLBRAN (town)—Formerly served by KiRock Communications. No longer in operation

COLLINSAIRE TRAILER PARK—See FORT COLLINS, CO (Baja Broadband)

COLORADO CITY—Formerly served by Bresnan Communications. No longer in operation

COLORADO SPRINGS (PORTIONS)—See PEYTON, CO (Falcon Broadband)

COLORADO SPRINGS—Formerly served by Sprint Corp. No longer in operation

COLORADO SPRINGS—See FORT CARSON, CO (Baja Broadband)

COLORADO SPRINGS—Comcast Cable

COLUMBINE VALLEY—See DENVER, CO (Comcast Cable)

COMMERCE CITY—See DENVER, CO (Comcast Cable)

CONIFER—Formerly served by Baja Broadband. No longer in operation

COPPER MOUNTAIN—Copper Mountain Consolidated Metropolitan District

CORTEZ—Baja Broadband

CRAIG—Charter Communications

CREEDE—Formerly served by Cable USA. No longer in operation

CRESTED BUTTE—Time Warner Cable

CRIPPLE CREEK—Formerly served by Baja Broadband. No longer in operation

CUCHARA VALLEY—Formerly served by Westcom II LLC. No longer in operation

DACONO—See LONGMONT, CO (Comcast Cable)

DEER TRAIL—Formerly served by Champion Broadband. No longer in operation

DEL NORTE—Formerly served by Bresnan Communications. No longer in operation

DELTA COUNTY (EASTERN PORTION)—See PAONIA, CO (Charter Communications)

DELTA COUNTY (WESTERN PORTION)—See MONTROSE, CO (Charter Communications)

DELTA—Charter Communications. Now served by MONTROSE, CO [CO0028]

DELTA—See MONTROSE, CO (Charter Communications)

DENVER—Comcast Cable. Now served by DENVER, CO [CO0001]

DENVER—Formerly served by Sprint Corp. No longer in operation

DENVER—Comcast Cable

DILLON—Comcast Cable. Now served by LONGMONT, CO [CO0011]

DILLON—See LONGMONT, CO (Comcast Cable)

DOLORES—Charter Communications. Now served by DURANGO, CO [CO0023]

DOLORES—See DURANGO, CO (Charter Communications)

DOUGLAS COUNTY (PORTIONS)—See DENVER, CO (Comcast Cable)

DOVE CREEK—Formerly served by Bresnan Communications. No longer in operation

DUMONT—See DENVER, CO (Comcast Cable)

DURANGO WEST—Charter Communications

DURANGO—Charter Communications

EADS—Formerly served by NexHorizon Communications. No longer in operation

EAGLE CITY—CenturyLink Prism (formerly Qwest)

EAGLE COUNTY (PORTIONS)—See EAGLE CITY, CO (CenturyLink Prism (formerly Qwest))

EAGLE COUNTY (PORTIONS)—See LONGMONT, CO (Comcast Cable)

EAGLE—CenturyLink. This cable system has converted to IPTV. See EAGLE CITY, CO [CO5010]

EATON—Baja Broadband. Now served by FORT COLLINS, CO [CO0073]

EATON—See FORT COLLINS, CO (Baja Broadband)

EDGEWATER—See DENVER, CO (Comcast Cable)

EDWARDS—See EAGLE CITY, CO (CenturyLink Prism (formerly Qwest))

EDWARDS—See LONGMONT, CO (Comcast Cable)

EL PASO COUNTY (EASTERN PORTIONS)—See PEYTON, CO (Falcon Broadband)

EL PASO COUNTY (EASTERN PORTIONS)—Falcon PTC. Formerly Falcon, CO [CO0213]. This cable system has converted to IPTV

EL PASO COUNTY (PORTIONS)—See COLORADO SPRINGS, CO (Comcast Cable)

ELBERT COUNTY (PORTIONS)—See DENVER, CO (Comcast Cable)

ELIZABETH—See DENVER, CO (Comcast Cable)

EMPIRE—Comcast Cable. Now served by DENVER, CO [CO0001]

EMPIRE—See DENVER, CO (Comcast Cable)

ENGLEWOOD—See DENVER, CO (Comcast Cable)

ERIE—See LONGMONT, CO (Comcast Cable)

ESTES PARK—Baja Broadband

EVANS—See LONGMONT, CO (Comcast Cable)

EVANSTON—See LONGMONT, CO (Comcast Cable)

EVERGREEN—See DENVER, CO (Comcast Cable)

FAIRPLAY—Formerly served by Cebridge Connections. No longer in operation

FALCON—See COLORADO SPRINGS, CO (Comcast Cable)

FALCON—See PEYTON, CO (Falcon Broadband)

FEDERAL HEIGHTS—See DENVER, CO (Comcast Cable)

FIRESTONE—See LONGMONT, CO (Comcast Cable)

FLAGLER—Formerly served by NexHorizon Communications. No longer in operation

FLEMING—PC Telcom. Now served by HOLYOKE, CO [CO0165]

FLEMING—See HOLYOKE, CO (PC Telcom)

FLORENCE—See CANON CITY, CO (Charter Communications)

FORT CARSON—Baja Broadband

FORT COLLINS—Comcast Cable. Now served by LONGMONT, CO [CO0011]

FORT COLLINS—Formerly served by Sprint Corp. No longer in operation

FORT COLLINS—Baja Broadband

FORT COLLINS—See LONGMONT, CO (Comcast Cable)

FORT LUPTON—Comcast Cable. Now served by LONGMONT, CO [CO0011]

FORT LUPTON—See LONGMONT, CO (Comcast Cable)

FORT MORGAN—Charter Communications

FOUNTAIN—See COLORADO SPRINGS, CO (Comcast Cable)

FOWLER—Formerly served by Bresnan Communications. Now served by Charter Communications, LA JUNTA, CO [CO0040]

FOWLER—See LA JUNTA, CO (Charter Communications)

FOXFIELD—See DENVER, CO (Comcast Cable)

FRANKTOWN—See DENVER, CO (Comcast Cable)

FRASER—See LONGMONT, CO (Comcast Cable)

FREDERICK—Comcast Cable. Now served by LONGMONT, CO [CO0011]

FREDERICK—See LONGMONT, CO (Comcast Cable)

FREMONT COUNTY—See CANON CITY, CO (Charter Communications)

FRISCO—See LONGMONT, CO (Comcast Cable)

FRUITA—See GRAND JUNCTION, CO (Charter Communications)

GARDEN CITY—See LONGMONT, CO (Comcast Cable)

GARFIELD COUNTY (PORTIONS)—See CARBONDALE, CO (Comcast Cable)

GARFIELD COUNTY (PORTIONS)—See GLENWOOD SPRINGS, CO (Comcast Cable)

GARFIELD COUNTY (PORTIONS)—See LONGMONT, CO (Comcast Cable)

GARFIELD COUNTY (PORTIONS)—See RIFLE, CO (Comcast Cable)

GARFIELD COUNTY (PORTIONS)—See SILT, CO (Comcast Cable)

GENESEE—Comcast Cable. Now served by DENVER, CO [CO0001]

GENESEE—See DENVER, CO (Comcast Cable)

GEORGETOWN—See DENVER, CO (Comcast Cable)

GILCREST—Formerly served by Baja Broadband. No longer in operation

GILPIN COUNTY—Formerly served by CAMS Cable. No longer in operation

GLENDALE—See DENVER, CO (Comcast Cable)

GLENWOOD SPRINGS—Comcast Cable

GOLDEN—See DENVER, CO (Comcast Cable)

GRANADA—Formerly served by NexHorizon Communications. No longer in operation

GRANBY—Comcast Cable. Now served by LONGMONT, CO [CO0011]

GRANBY—See LONGMONT, CO (Comcast Cable)

GRAND COUNTY (PORTIONS)—See KREMMLING, CO (Comcast Cable)

GRAND COUNTY—See LONGMONT, CO (Comcast Cable)

28-Cable Community Index

TV & Cable Factbook No. 85

Cable Community Index—Colorado

GRAND JUNCTION—Charter Communications

GRAND LAKE—See LONGMONT, CO (Comcast Cable)

GREELEY—Comcast Cable. Now served by LONGMONT, CO [CO0011]

GREELEY—See LONGMONT, CO (Comcast Cable)

GREEN MOUNTAIN FALLS—See COLORADO SPRINGS, CO (Comcast Cable)

GREENWOOD VILLAGE—See DENVER, CO (Comcast Cable)

GUNNISON COUNTY—See CRESTED BUTTE, CO (Time Warner Cable)

GUNNISON—See CRESTED BUTTE, CO (Time Warner Cable)

GYPSUM—See EAGLE CITY, CO (CenturyLink Prism (formerly Qwest))

HAXTUN—See HOLYOKE, CO (PC Telcom)

HAYDEN—Formerly served by Bresnan Communications. Now served by Charter Communications, CRAIG, CO [CO0039]

HAYDEN—See CRAIG, CO (Charter Communications)

HERMOSA—Formerly served by Hermosa Cablevision Inc. Now served by Charter Communications, DURANGO, CO [CO0023]

HERMOSA—See DURANGO, CO (Charter Communications)

HIGHLANDS RANCH—Comcast Cable. Now served by DENVER, CO [CO0001]

HIGHLANDS RANCH—Formerly served by Qwest Choice TV. IPTV service has been discontinued

HIGHLANDS RANCH—Formerly served by Qwest Choice TV. IPTV service has been discontinued

HIGHLANDS RANCH—See DENVER, CO (Comcast Cable)

HOLIDAY VILLAGE—Formerly served by Island Cable. No longer in operation

HOLLY HILLS—See DENVER, CO (Comcast Cable)

HOLLY—Formerly served by NexHorizon Communications. No longer in operation

HOLYOKE—PC Telcom

HOT SULPHUR SPRINGS—See LONGMONT, CO (Comcast Cable)

HOTCHKISS—Formerly served by Rocky Mountain Cable. No longer in operation

HUDSON—Formerly served by US Cable of Coastal Texas LP. No longer in operation

HUERFANO COUNTY (PORTIONS)—See WALSENBURG, CO (Charter Communications)

HUGO—Formerly served by NexHorizon Communications. No longer in operation

IDAHO SPRINGS—Comcast Cable. Now served by DENVER, CO [CO0001]

IDAHO SPRINGS—See DENVER, CO (Comcast Cable)

IDLEDALE—See DENVER, CO (Comcast Cable)

IGNACIO—USA Communications

INDIAN HILLS—See DENVER, CO (Comcast Cable)

JEFFERSON COUNTY (PORTIONS)—See TABLE MOUNTAIN, CO (Baja Broadband)

JEFFERSON COUNTY (PORTIONS)—See DENVER, CO (Comcast Cable)

JOHNSTOWN—See FORT COLLINS, CO (Baja Broadband)

JULESBURG—PC Telcom. Now served by HOLYOKE, CO [CO0065]

JULESBURG—See HOLYOKE, CO (PC Telcom)

KERSEY—Formerly served by US Cable. No longer in operation

KEYSTONE—See LONGMONT, CO (Comcast Cable)

KIOWA—See DENVER, CO (Comcast Cable)

KIT CARSON—Rebeltec Communications

KITTREDGE—See DENVER, CO (Comcast Cable)

KREMMLING—Comcast Cable

LA JUNTA—Charter Communications

LA PLATA COUNTY—See DURANGO, CO (Charter Communications)

LA SALLE—See LONGMONT, CO (Comcast Cable)

LA VETA—Formerly served by Westcom II LLC. No longer in operation

LAFAYETTE—See LONGMONT, CO (Comcast Cable)

LAKE CITY—USA Communications

LAKE COUNTY—See LEADVILLE, CO (Charter Communications)

LAKEWOOD—Comcast Cable. Now served by DENVER, CO [CO0001]

LAKEWOOD—See DENVER, CO (Comcast Cable)

LAMAR—Charter Communications. Now served by LA JUNTA, CO [CO0040]

LAMAR—See LA JUNTA, CO (Charter Communications)

LAPORTE—Formerly served by Baja Broadband. No longer in operation

LARIMER COUNTY (PORTIONS)—See ESTES PARK, CO (Baja Broadband)

LARIMER COUNTY (PORTIONS)—See FORT COLLINS, CO (Baja Broadband)

LARIMER COUNTY (PORTIONS)—See LONGMONT, CO (Comcast Cable)

LARIMER COUNTY—Formerly served by NexHorizon Communications. No longer in operation

LARKSPUR—See DENVER, CO (Comcast Cable)

LAS ANIMAS COUNTY (PORTIONS)—See TRINIDAD, CO (Comcast Cable)

LAS ANIMAS—Satview Broadband

LEADVILLE NORTH—See LEADVILLE, CO (Charter Communications)

LEADVILLE—Charter Communications

LIMON—Formerly served by CAMS Cable. No longer in operation

LITTLETON—See DENVER, CO (Comcast Cable)

LOCHBUIE—See DENVER, CO (Comcast Cable)

LOG LANE VILLAGE—See FORT MORGAN, CO (Charter Communications)

LOGAN COUNTY—See STERLING, CO (Charter Communications)

LONE TREE—See DENVER, CO (Comcast Cable)

LONGMONT—Comcast Cable

LOUISVILLE—See LONGMONT, CO (Comcast Cable)

LOUVIERS—See DENVER, CO (Comcast Cable)

LOVELAND (Columbine Mobile Home Park)—Formerly served by US Cable of Coastal Texas LP. No longer in operation

LOVELAND—See LONGMONT, CO (Comcast Cable)

LYONS (TOWN)—Lyons Communications

MANASSA—Formerly served by Charter Communications. No longer in operation

MANCOS—Formerly served by Bresnan Communications. Now served by Charter Communications, DURANGO, CO [CO0023]

MANCOS—See DURANGO, CO (Charter Communications)

MANITOU SPRINGS—See COLORADO SPRINGS, CO (Comcast Cable)

MANZANOLA—Formerly served by Bresnan Communications. Now served by Charter Communications, LA JUNTA, CO [CO0040]

MANZANOLA—See LA JUNTA, CO (Charter Communications)

MEAD—K2 Communications

MEEKER—Charter Communications

MERINO—Kentec Communications

MESA COUNTY—See GRAND JUNCTION, CO (Charter Communications)

MILLIKEN—See FORT COLLINS, CO (Baja Broadband)

MINTURN—See LONGMONT, CO (Comcast Cable)

MOFFAT COUNTY—See CRAIG, CO (Charter Communications)

MONTE VISTA—Formerly served by Bresnan Communications. Now served by Charter Communications, ALAMOSA, CO [CO0035]

MONTE VISTA—See ALAMOSA, CO (Charter Communications)

MONTROSE COUNTY—See MONTROSE, CO (Charter Communications)

MONTROSE—Charter Communications

MONTROSE—Spring Creek Cable

MONUMENT—Formerly served by Adelphia Communications. Now served by Comcast Cable, COLORADO SPRINGS, CO [CO0003]

MONUMENT—See COLORADO SPRINGS, CO (Comcast Cable)

MORGAN COUNTY—See FORT MORGAN, CO (Charter Communications)

MORRISON—See DENVER, CO (Comcast Cable)

MOUNT CRESTED BUTTE—See CRESTED BUTTE, CO (Time Warner Cable)

MOUNTAIN VIEW—See DENVER, CO (Comcast Cable)

MOUNTAIN VILLAGE—Mountain Village Cable

MT. RANGE SHADOWS—See FORT COLLINS, CO (Baja Broadband)

NEDERLAND—USA Communications

NEW CASTLE (town)—Comcast Cable. Now served by SILT, CO [CO0108]

NEW CASTLE—See SILT, CO (Comcast Cable)

NORTHGLENN—See DENVER, CO (Comcast Cable)

NORWOOD—B & C Cablevision Inc

NUCLA—Formerly served by Charter Communications. No longer in operation

OAK CREEK—Formerly served by Westcom II LLC. No longer in operation

OLATHE—Formerly served by Cable USA. No longer in operation

OLATHE—Spring Creek Cable

OPHIR—See TELLURIDE, CO (Time Warner Cable)

ORDWAY—Formerly served by NexHorizon Communications. No longer in operation

OTERO COUNTY (UNINCORPORATED AREAS)—See LA JUNTA, CO (Charter Communications)

Colorado—Cable Community Index

OTIS (TOWN)—Vyve Broadband

OVID—See HOLYOKE, CO (PC Telcom)

PAGOSA SPRINGS—USA Communications

PALISADE—See GRAND JUNCTION, CO (Charter Communications)

PALMER LAKE—See COLORADO SPRINGS, CO (Comcast Cable)

PAONIA—Charter Communications

PARACHUTE—Comcast Cable

PARKER—See DENVER, CO (Comcast Cable)

PENROSE (unincorporated areas)—Formerly served by Bresnan Communications. Now served by Charter Communications, CANON CITY, CO [CO0016]

PENROSE—See CANON CITY, CO (Charter Communications)

PERRY PARK—See DENVER, CO (Comcast Cable)

PETERSON AFB—Peterson Broadband

PEYTON—Falcon Broadband

PIERCE—See FORT COLLINS, CO (Baja Broadband)

PITKIN COUNTY (PORTIONS)—See LONGMONT, CO (Comcast Cable)

PONCHA SPRINGS—See SALIDA, CO (Charter Communications)

POUDRE VALLEY—See FORT COLLINS, CO (Baja Broadband)

PROWERS COUNTY (UNINCORPORATED AREAS)—See LA JUNTA, CO (Charter Communications)

PTARMIGAN—See FORT COLLINS, CO (Baja Broadband)

PUEBLO COUNTY (PORTIONS)—See COLORADO SPRINGS, CO (Comcast Cable)

PUEBLO WEST—Comcast Cable. Now served by COLORADO SPRINGS, CO [CO0003]

PUEBLO WEST—See COLORADO SPRINGS, CO (Comcast Cable)

PUEBLO—Comcast Cable. Now served by COLORADO SPRINGS, CO [CO0003]

PUEBLO—See COLORADO SPRINGS, CO (Comcast Cable)

RANGELY—Charter Communications

RIFLE—Comcast Cable

RIO BLANCO COUNTY (EASTERN PORTION)—See MEEKER, CO (Charter Communications)

RIO BLANCO COUNTY (NORTHWESTERN PORTION)—See RANGELY, CO (Charter Communications)

RIO GRANDE COUNTY (PORTIONS)—See ALAMOSA, CO (Charter Communications)

ROCKVALE—See CANON CITY, CO (Charter Communications)

ROCKY FORD—Formerly served by Bresnan Communications. Now served by Charter Communications, LA JUNTA, CO [CO0040]

ROCKY FORD—See LA JUNTA, CO (Charter Communications)

ROUTT COUNTY (PORTIONS)—See LONGMONT, CO (Comcast Cable)

ROXBOROUGH PARK—See DENVER, CO (Comcast Cable)

ROXBOROUGH—See DENVER, CO (Comcast Cable)

SAGUACHE—USA Communications

SALIDA—Charter Communications

SAN LUIS—Formerly served by Charter Communications. No longer in operation

SAN MIGUEL COUNTY—See TELLURIDE, CO (Time Warner Cable)

SEDALIA—See DENVER, CO (Comcast Cable)

SEDGWICK—PC Telcom. Now served by HOLYOKE, CO [CO0065]

SEDGWICK—See HOLYOKE, CO (PC Telcom)

SEIBERT—Formerly served by B & C Cablevision Inc. No longer in operation

SEIBERT—See KIT CARSON, CO (Rebeltec Communications)

SEVERANCE—See FORT COLLINS, CO (Baja Broadband)

SHERIDAN—See DENVER, CO (Comcast Cable)

SILT—Comcast Cable

SILVER CREEK—See LONGMONT, CO (Comcast Cable)

SILVER PLUME—See DENVER, CO (Comcast Cable)

SILVERTHORNE—See LONGMONT, CO (Comcast Cable)

SILVERTON—Formerly served by Cable USA. No longer in operation

SIMLA—Formerly served by FairPoint Communications. No longer in operation

SNOWMASS VILLAGE—See LONGMONT, CO (Comcast Cable)

SOUTH FORK—USA Communications

SOUTHERN UTE INDIAN RESERVATION—See IGNACIO, CO (USA Communications)

SPRINGFIELD—Satview Broadband

STAGECOACH—Formerly served by Westcom II LLC. No longer in operation

STEAMBOAT SPRINGS—Comcast Cable. Now served by LONGMONT, CO [CO0011]

STEAMBOAT SPRINGS—See LONGMONT, CO (Comcast Cable)

STERLING—Charter Communications

STRASBURG—See DENVER, CO (Comcast Cable)

STRATTON—Formerly served by NexHorizon Communications. No longer in operation

SUGAR CITY—Formerly served by CableDirect. No longer in operation

SUMMIT COUNTY (PORTIONS)—See LONGMONT, CO (Comcast Cable)

SUNNYSIDE—Rural Route Video

SUNSET CREEK—Formerly served by Island Cable. No longer in operation

SUPERIOR—See LONGMONT, CO (Comcast Cable)

SWINK—See LA JUNTA, CO (Charter Communications)

TABLE MOUNTAIN—Baja Broadband

TELLER COUNTY (PORTIONS)—See WOODLAND PARK, CO (Baja Broadband)

TELLURIDE—Time Warner Cable

THE PINERY—See DENVER, CO (Comcast Cable)

THORNTON—See DENVER, CO (Comcast Cable)

TOWAOC—See CORTEZ, CO (Baja Broadband)

TOWAOC—Ute Mountain Cable TV

TRINIDAD—Comcast Cable

VAIL—See LONGMONT, CO (Comcast Cable)

VALDEZ—Formerly served by Wozniak TV. No longer in operation

VICTOR—Formerly served by Charter Communications. No longer in operation

WALDEN (village)—Formerly served by Charter Communications. No longer in operation

WALSENBURG—Charter Communications

WALSH—Formerly served by NexHorizon Communications. No longer in operation

WELD COUNTY (PORTIONS)—See FORT COLLINS, CO (Baja Broadband)

WELD COUNTY (PORTIONS)—See LONGMONT, CO (Comcast Cable)

WELD COUNTY—Formerly served by NexHorizon Communications. No longer in operation

WELLINGTON—See FORT COLLINS, CO (Baja Broadband)

WESTCLIFFE—Formerly served by NexHorizon Communications. No longer in operation

WESTMINSTER—See DENVER, CO (Comcast Cable)

WHEAT RIDGE—See DENVER, CO (Comcast Cable)

WIGGINS—Formerly served by Northern Colorado Communications Inc. No longer in operation

WILEY—Formerly served by NexHorizon Communications. No longer in operation

WILLIAMSBURG—See CANON CITY, CO (Charter Communications)

WINDSOR—See LONGMONT, CO (Comcast Cable)

WINTER PARK—Comcast Cable. Now served by LONGMONT, CO [CO0011]

WINTER PARK—See LONGMONT, CO (Comcast Cable)

WOODLAND PARK—Baja Broadband

WRAY—Eagle Communications

YUMA—Formerly served by Mediastream. Now served by Vyve Broadband, OTIS (town), CO [CO0128]

YUMA—See OTIS (town), CO (Vyve Broadband)

CONNECTICUT

ANDOVER—See NEW BRITAIN, CT (Comcast Cable)

ANSONIA—Comcast Cable. Now served by NEW BRITAIN, CT [CT0037]

ANSONIA—See NEW BRITAIN, CT (Comcast Cable)

ASHFORD—Charter Communications

AVON—See NEW BRITAIN, CT (Comcast Cable)

BARKHAMSTED—See NEW MILFORD, CT (Charter Communications)

BEACON FALLS—See NEW BRITAIN, CT (Comcast Cable)

BEEKMAN (TOWN)—See NEW BRITAIN, NY (Comcast Cable)

BERLIN—See NEW BRITAIN, CT (Comcast Cable)

BETHANY—See NEW BRITAIN, CT (Comcast Cable)

BETHEL—See NEW BRITAIN, CT (Comcast Cable)

BETHLEHEM—See NEW MILFORD, CT (Charter Communications)

BLOOMFIELD—See NEW BRITAIN, CT (Comcast Cable)

BOLTON—Comcast of Connecticut. Now served by NEW BRITAIN, CT [CT0037]

BOLTON—See NEW BRITAIN, CT (Comcast Cable)

BOZRAH—See NEW BRITAIN, CT (Comcast Cable)

BRANFORD—Comcast Cable. Now served by NEW BRITAIN, CT [CT0037]

BRANFORD—See NEW BRITAIN, CT (Comcast Cable)

BREWSTER (VILLAGE)—See NEW BRITAIN, NY (Comcast Cable)

BRIDGEPORT—Cablevision

Cable Community Index—Connecticut

BRIDGEWATER—See NEW MILFORD, CT (Charter Communications)

BRISTOL—See NEW BRITAIN, CT (Comcast Cable)

BROOKFIELD—See NEW MILFORD, CT (Charter Communications)

BROOKLYN—See ASHFORD, CT (Charter Communications)

BURLINGTON—See NEW BRITAIN, CT (Comcast Cable)

CANAAN—See NEW BRITAIN, CT (Comcast Cable)

CANTERBURY—See ASHFORD, CT (Charter Communications)

CANTON—See NEW BRITAIN, CT (Comcast Cable)

CARMEL—See NEW BRITAIN, NY (Comcast Cable)

CENTERBROOK—See NEW BRITAIN, CT (Comcast Cable)

CHAPLIN—See ASHFORD, CT (Charter Communications)

CHESHIRE—See MERIDEN, CT (Cox Communications)

CHESTER—See NEW BRITAIN, CT (Comcast Cable)

CLINTON—Comcast Cable. Now served by NEW BRITAIN, CT [CT0037]

CLINTON—See NEW BRITAIN, CT (Comcast Cable)

COLCHESTER—See NEW BRITAIN, CT (Comcast Cable)

COLEBROOK—See NEW MILFORD, CT (Charter Communications)

COLUMBIA—See ASHFORD, CT (Charter Communications)

CORNWALL—See LITCHFIELD, CT (Cablevision)

COVENTRY—See ASHFORD, CT (Charter Communications)

CROMWELL—See NEW BRITAIN, CT (Comcast Cable)

DANBURY—Comcast Cable. Now served by NEW BRITAIN, CT [CT0037]

DANBURY—See NEW BRITAIN, CT (Comcast Cable)

DANIELSON—See NEW LONDON, CT (Atlantic Broadband)

DARIEN—See NORWALK, CT (Cablevision)

DAYVILLE—See NEW LONDON, CT (Atlantic Broadband)

DEEP RIVER—See NEW BRITAIN, CT (Comcast Cable)

DERBY—See NEW BRITAIN, CT (Comcast Cable)

DURHAM—See NEW BRITAIN, CT (Comcast Cable)

EAST GLASTONBURY—See MANCHESTER, CT (Cox Communications)

EAST GRANBY—See ENFIELD, CT (Cox Communications)

EAST HADDAM—See NEW BRITAIN, CT (Comcast Cable)

EAST HAMPTON—See NEW BRITAIN, CT (Comcast Cable)

EAST HARTFORD—See NEW BRITAIN, CT (Comcast Cable)

EAST HAVEN—See NEW BRITAIN, CT (Comcast Cable)

EAST LYME—See NEW LONDON, CT (Atlantic Broadband)

EAST WINDSOR—See ENFIELD, CT (Cox Communications)

EASTFORD—See ASHFORD, CT (Charter Communications)

EASTON—See NORWALK, CT (Cablevision)

ELLINGTON—See NEW BRITAIN, CT (Comcast Cable)

ENFIELD—Cox Communications

ESSEX—See NEW BRITAIN, CT (Comcast Cable)

FAIRFIELD COUNTY—See BRIDGEPORT, CT (Cablevision)

FALLS VILLAGE—See NEW BRITAIN, CT (Comcast Cable)

FARMINGTON—See NEW BRITAIN, CT (Comcast Cable)

FRANKLIN—See NEW BRITAIN, CT (Comcast Cable)

GALES FERRY—See NEW BRITAIN, CT (Comcast Cable)

GLASTONBURY—See MANCHESTER, CT (Cox Communications)

GOSHEN—See LITCHFIELD, CT (Cablevision)

GRANBY—See ENFIELD, CT (Cox Communications)

GREENWICH—See NORWALK, CT (Cablevision)

GRISWOLD—See NEW LONDON, CT (Atlantic Broadband)

GROTON—Comcast Cable. Now served by NEW BRITAIN, CT [CT0037]

GROTON—See NEW BRITAIN, CT (Comcast Cable)

GROTON—Thames Valley Communications

GUILFORD—See NEW BRITAIN, CT (Comcast Cable)

HADDAM—See NEW BRITAIN, CT (Comcast Cable)

HAMDEN—See NEW BRITAIN, CT (Comcast Cable)

HAMPTON—See ASHFORD, CT (Charter Communications)

HARTFORD—Comcast Cable. Now served by NEW BRITAIN, CT [CT0037]

HARTFORD—See NEW BRITAIN, CT (Comcast Cable)

HARTLAND—See ENFIELD, CT (Cox Communications)

HARWINTON—See NEW MILFORD, CT (Charter Communications)

HEBRON—See NEW BRITAIN, CT (Comcast Cable)

HIGGANUM—See NEW BRITAIN, CT (Comcast Cable)

HOLLAND—See ENFIELD, MA (Cox Communications)

HUNTINGTON—See NEW BRITAIN, CT (Comcast Cable)

IVORYTON—See NEW BRITAIN, CT (Comcast Cable)

KENT (TOWN)—See NEW BRITAIN, NY (Comcast Cable)

KENT—See NEW MILFORD, CT (Charter Communications)

KILLINGLY—See NEW LONDON, CT (Atlantic Broadband)

KILLINGWORTH—See NEW BRITAIN, CT (Comcast Cable)

LAKEVILLE—Comcast Cable. Now served by NEW BRITAIN, CT [CT0037]

LAKEVILLE—See NEW BRITAIN, CT (Comcast Cable)

LEBANON—See ASHFORD, CT (Charter Communications)

LEDYARD—See NEW BRITAIN, CT (Comcast Cable)

LISBON—See NEW BRITAIN, CT (Comcast Cable)

LITCHFIELD—Cablevision

LYME—See NEW BRITAIN, CT (Comcast Cable)

MADISON—See NEW BRITAIN, CT (Comcast Cable)

MANCHESTER—Cox Communications

MANSFIELD—See ASHFORD, CT (Charter Communications)

MARLBOROUGH—See NEW BRITAIN, CT (Comcast Cable)

MERIDEN—Cox Communications

MIDDLEBURY—See NEW BRITAIN, CT (Comcast Cable)

MIDDLEFIELD—See NEW BRITAIN, CT (Comcast Cable)

MIDDLETOWN—Comcast Cable. Now served by NEW BRITAIN, CT [CT0037]

MIDDLETOWN—See NEW BRITAIN, CT (Comcast Cable)

MILFORD—See BRIDGEPORT, CT (Cablevision)

MONROE—See NEW MILFORD, CT (Charter Communications)

MONTVILLE—See NEW LONDON, CT (Atlantic Broadband)

MOOSUP—See NEW LONDON, CT (Atlantic Broadband)

MORRIS—See LITCHFIELD, CT (Cablevision)

MYSTIC—See NEW BRITAIN, CT (Comcast Cable)

NAUGATUCK—See NEW BRITAIN, CT (Comcast Cable)

NEW BRITAIN—Comcast Cable

NEW CANAAN—See NORWALK, CT (Cablevision)

NEW FAIRFIELD—See NEW MILFORD, CT (Charter Communications)

NEW HARTFORD—See NEW MILFORD, CT (Charter Communications)

NEW HAVEN—Comcast Cable. Now served by NEW BRITAIN, CT [CT0037]

NEW HAVEN—See NEW BRITAIN, CT (Comcast Cable)

NEW LONDON SUBMARINE BASE—See NEW BRITAIN, CT (Comcast Cable)

NEW LONDON—Atlantic Broadband

NEW MILFORD—Charter Communications

NEWINGTON—See MANCHESTER, CT (Cox Communications)

NEWTOWN (BOROUGH)—See NEW MILFORD, CT (Charter Communications)

NIANTIC—See NEW LONDON, CT (Atlantic Broadband)

NORFOLK—See NEW BRITAIN, CT (Comcast Cable)

NORTH BRANFORD—See NEW BRITAIN, CT (Comcast Cable)

NORTH CANAAN—See NEW BRITAIN, CT (Comcast Cable)

NORTH HAVEN—See NEW BRITAIN, CT (Comcast Cable)

NORTH STONINGTON—See NEW BRITAIN, CT (Comcast Cable)

NORWALK—Cablevision

NORWICH—Comcast Cable. Now served by NEW BRITAIN, CT [CT0037]

NORWICH—See NEW BRITAIN, CT (Comcast Cable)

OAKDALE—See NEW LONDON, CT (Atlantic Broadband)

OLD LYME—Comcast Cable. Now served by NEW BRITAIN, CT [CT0037]

OLD LYME—See NEW BRITAIN, CT (Comcast Cable)

OLD MYSTIC—See NEW BRITAIN, CT (Comcast Cable)

OLD SAYBROOK—See NEW BRITAIN, CT (Comcast Cable)

ONECO—See NEW LONDON, CT (Atlantic Broadband)

ORANGE—See BRIDGEPORT, CT (Cablevision)

OXFORD—See NEW BRITAIN, CT (Comcast Cable)

Connecticut—Cable Community Index

PATTERSON (TOWN)—See NEW BRITAIN, NY (Comcast Cable)

PAWCATUCK—See NEW BRITAIN, CT (Comcast Cable)

PAWLING (TOWN)—See NEW BRITAIN, NY (Comcast Cable)

PAWLING (VILLAGE)—See NEW BRITAIN, NY (Comcast Cable)

PEQUABUCK—See NEW BRITAIN, CT (Comcast Cable)

PLAINFIELD—Atlantic Broadband. Now served by NEW LONDON, CT [CT0008]

PLAINFIELD—See NEW LONDON, CT (Atlantic Broadband)

PLAINVILLE (TOWN)—See NEW BRITAIN, CT (Comcast Cable)

PLYMOUTH—See NEW BRITAIN, CT (Comcast Cable)

POMFRET—See ASHFORD, CT (Charter Communications)

PORTLAND—See NEW BRITAIN, CT (Comcast Cable)

PRESTON—See NEW BRITAIN, CT (Comcast Cable)

PROSPECT—See NEW BRITAIN, CT (Comcast Cable)

PUTNAM VALLEY (TOWN)—See NEW BRITAIN, NY (Comcast Cable)

PUTNAM—See NEW LONDON, CT (Atlantic Broadband)

QUAKER HILL—See NEW LONDON, CT (Atlantic Broadband)

REDDING—See NORWALK, CT (Cablevision)

RIDGEFIELD—See NEW BRITAIN, CT (Comcast Cable)

ROCKFALL—See NEW BRITAIN, CT (Comcast Cable)

ROCKY HILL—See MANCHESTER, CT (Cox Communications)

ROGERS—See NEW LONDON, CT (Atlantic Broadband)

ROXBURY—See NEW MILFORD, CT (Charter Communications)

SALEM—See NEW BRITAIN, CT (Comcast Cable)

SALISBURY—See NEW BRITAIN, CT (Comcast Cable)

SCOTLAND—See ASHFORD, CT (Charter Communications)

SEYMOUR—See NEW BRITAIN, CT (Comcast Cable)

SHARON—See NEW BRITAIN, CT (Comcast Cable)

SHELTON—See NEW BRITAIN, CT (Comcast Cable)

SHERMAN—See NEW MILFORD, CT (Charter Communications)

SIMSBURY—See NEW BRITAIN, CT (Comcast Cable)

SOMERS (TOWN)—See NEW BRITAIN, NY (Comcast Cable)

SOMERS—See ENFIELD, CT (Cox Communications)

SOUTH GLASTONBURY—See MANCHESTER, CT (Cox Communications)

SOUTH WINDSOR—See MANCHESTER, CT (Cox Communications)

SOUTHBURY—See NEW MILFORD, CT (Charter Communications)

SOUTHEAST (TOWN)—See NEW BRITAIN, NY (Comcast Cable)

SOUTHINGTON—See MERIDEN, CT (Cox Communications)

SPRAGUE—See NEW BRITAIN, CT (Comcast Cable)

STAFFORD—See ENFIELD, CT (Cox Communications)

STAMFORD—See NORWALK, CT (Cablevision)

STERLING—See NEW LONDON, CT (Atlantic Broadband)

STONINGTON—See NEW BRITAIN, CT (Comcast Cable)

STORRS (VILLAGE)—See ASHFORD, CT (Charter Communications)

STRATFORD—See BRIDGEPORT, CT (Cablevision)

SUFFIELD—See ENFIELD, CT (Cox Communications)

TERRYVILLE—See NEW BRITAIN, CT (Comcast Cable)

THOMASTON—See LITCHFIELD, CT (Cablevision)

THOMASTON—See NEW BRITAIN, CT (Comcast Cable)

THOMPSON—See ASHFORD, CT (Charter Communications)

TOLLAND—See NEW BRITAIN, CT (Comcast Cable)

TORRINGTON—See LITCHFIELD, CT (Cablevision)

TRUMBULL—See NEW MILFORD, CT (Charter Communications)

UNION—See ENFIELD, CT (Cox Communications)

VERNON—Comcast Cable. Now served by NEW BRITAIN, CT [CT0037]

VERNON—See NEW BRITAIN, CT (Comcast Cable)

VOLUNTOWN—See NEW BRITAIN, CT (Comcast Cable)

WALLINGFORD—See NEW BRITAIN, CT (Comcast Cable)

WARREN—See LITCHFIELD, CT (Cablevision)

WARREN—See NEW MILFORD, CT (Charter Communications)

WASHINGTON—See NEW MILFORD, CT (Charter Communications)

WATERBURY—Comcast Cable. Now served by NEW BRITAIN, CT [CT0037]

WATERBURY—See NEW BRITAIN, CT (Comcast Cable)

WATERFORD—See NEW LONDON, CT (Atlantic Broadband)

WATERTOWN—See LITCHFIELD, CT (Cablevision)

WAUREGAN—See NEW LONDON, CT (Atlantic Broadband)

WEST HARTFORD—See NEW BRITAIN, CT (Comcast Cable)

WEST HARTLAND—See NEW MILFORD, CT (Charter Communications)

WEST HAVEN—See NEW BRITAIN, CT (Comcast Cable)

WESTBROOK—See NEW BRITAIN, CT (Comcast Cable)

WESTON—See NORWALK, CT (Cablevision)

WESTPORT—See NORWALK, CT (Cablevision)

WETHERSFIELD—See MANCHESTER, CT (Cox Communications)

WILLIMANTIC—See ASHFORD, CT (Charter Communications)

WILLINGTON—See ASHFORD, CT (Charter Communications)

WILTON—See NORWALK, CT (Cablevision)

WINCHESTER—See NEW MILFORD, CT (Charter Communications)

WINDHAM—See ASHFORD, CT (Charter Communications)

WINDSOR LOCKS—See ENFIELD, CT (Cox Communications)

WINDSOR—See NEW BRITAIN, CT (Comcast Cable)

WINSTED—Charter Communications. Now served by NEW MILFORD, CT [CT0014]

WINSTED—See NEW MILFORD, CT (Charter Communications)

WOLCOTT—See NEW BRITAIN, CT (Comcast Cable)

WOODBRIDGE—See BRIDGEPORT, CT (Cablevision)

WOODBURY—See NEW MILFORD, CT (Charter Communications)

WOODSTOCK—See ASHFORD, CT (Charter Communications)

DELAWARE

BAYARD—See MILLSBORO, DE (Mediacom)

BETHANY BEACH—See MILLSBORO, DE (Mediacom)

BISHOPVILLE—See MILLSBORO, MD (Mediacom)

CLARKSVILLE—See MILLSBORO, DE (Mediacom)

DAGSBORO—See MILLSBORO, DE (Mediacom)

DOVER—Comcast Cable. Now served by TOWSON, MD [MD0003]

FRANKFORD—See MILLSBORO, DE (Mediacom)

LEWES—See MILLSBORO, DE (Mediacom)

MIDDLESEX BEACH—See MILLSBORO, DE (Mediacom)

MILFORD—Comcast Cable. Now served by TOWSON, MD [MD0003]

MILLSBORO—Mediacom

MILLVILLE—See MILLSBORO, DE (Mediacom)

OCEAN PINES—See MILLSBORO, MD (Mediacom)

OCEAN VIEW—See MILLSBORO, DE (Mediacom)

PITTSVILLE—See MILLSBORO, MD (Mediacom)

ROXANA—See MILLSBORO, DE (Mediacom)

SELBYVILLE—See MILLSBORO, DE (Mediacom)

SOUTH BETHANY—See MILLSBORO, DE (Mediacom)

SUSSEX COUNTY—See MILLSBORO, DE (Mediacom)

WHALEYSVILLE—See MILLSBORO, MD (Mediacom)

WICOMICO COUNTY (EASTERN PORTION)—See MILLSBORO, MD (Mediacom)

WILLARDS—See MILLSBORO, MD (Mediacom)

WILMINGTON—Comcast Cable. Now served by PHILADELPHIA, PA [PA0005]

WORCESTER COUNTY (PORTIONS)—See MILLSBORO, MD (Mediacom)

DISTRICT OF COLUMBIA

ADAMS MORGAN—See WASHINGTON (portions), DC (RCN. Formerly [DC0006]. This cable system has converted to IPTV)

AMERICAN UNIVERSITY PARK—See WASHINGTON (portions), DC (RCN. Formerly [DC0006]. This cable system has converted to IPTV)

ANACOSTIA—See WASHINGTON (portions), DC (RCN. Formerly [DC0006]. This cable system has converted to IPTV)

ARLINGTON—See WASHINGTON (portions), VA (RCN. Formerly [DC0006]. This cable system has converted to IPTV)

BENNING ROAD—See WASHINGTON (portions), DC (RCN. Formerly [DC0006]. This cable system has

Cable Community Index—District of Columbia

converted to IPTV)

BERKLEY—See WASHINGTON (portions), DC (RCN. Formerly [DC0006]. This cable system has converted to IPTV)

BETHESDA—See WASHINGTON (portions), MD (RCN. Formerly [DC0006]. This cable system has converted to IPTV)

BOLLING AFB—Comcast Cable. Now served by FREDERICK COUNTY (portions), MD [MD0009]

BOLLING AFB—Formerly served by Mid-Atlantic Communications. Now served by Comcast Cable, FREDERICK COUNTY, MD [MD0009]

BRIGHTWOOD—See WASHINGTON (portions), DC (RCN. Formerly [DC0006]. This cable system has converted to IPTV)

BROOKLAND—See WASHINGTON (portions), DC (RCN. Formerly [DC0006]. This cable system has converted to IPTV)

CAPITOL HILL—See WASHINGTON (portions), DC (RCN. Formerly [DC0006]. This cable system has converted to IPTV)

CHEVY CHASE—See WASHINGTON (portions), DC (RCN. Formerly [DC0006]. This cable system has converted to IPTV)

CHEVY CHASE—See WASHINGTON (portions), MD (RCN. Formerly [DC0006]. This cable system has converted to IPTV)

CHINATOWN—See WASHINGTON (portions), DC (RCN. Formerly [DC0006]. This cable system has converted to IPTV)

CLEVELAND PARK—See WASHINGTON (portions), DC (RCN. Formerly [DC0006]. This cable system has converted to IPTV)

COLLEGE PARK—See WASHINGTON (portions), MD (RCN. Formerly [DC0006]. This cable system has converted to IPTV)

COLONIAL VILLAGE—See WASHINGTON (portions), DC (RCN. Formerly [DC0006]. This cable system has converted to IPTV)

COLUMBIA HEIGHTS—See WASHINGTON (portions), DC (RCN. Formerly [DC0006]. This cable system has converted to IPTV)

CONGRESS HEIGHTS—See WASHINGTON (portions), DC (RCN. Formerly [DC0006]. This cable system has converted to IPTV)

DUPONT CIRCLE—See WASHINGTON (portions), DC (RCN. Formerly [DC0006]. This cable system has converted to IPTV)

EDGEWOOD—See WASHINGTON (portions), DC (RCN. Formerly [DC0006]. This cable system has converted to IPTV)

FALLS CHURCH—See WASHINGTON (portions), VA (RCN. Formerly [DC0006]. This cable system has converted to IPTV)

FOGGY BOTTOM—See WASHINGTON (portions), DC (RCN. Formerly [DC0006]. This cable system has converted to IPTV)

FORT DUPONT—See WASHINGTON (portions), DC (RCN. Formerly [DC0006]. This cable system has converted to IPTV)

FORT TOTTEN—See WASHINGTON (portions), DC (RCN. Formerly [DC0006]. This cable system has converted to IPTV)

FOXHALL—See WASHINGTON (portions), DC (RCN. Formerly [DC0006]. This cable system has converted to IPTV)

FRIENDSHIP HEIGHTS—See WASHINGTON (portions), DC (RCN. Formerly [DC0006]. This cable system has converted to IPTV)

GAITHERSBURG—See WASHINGTON (portions), MD (RCN. Formerly [DC0006]. This cable system has converted to IPTV)

GLOVER PARK—See WASHINGTON (portions), DC (RCN. Formerly [DC0006]. This cable system has converted to IPTV)

HILLCREST—See WASHINGTON (portions), DC (RCN. Formerly [DC0006]. This cable system has converted to IPTV)

IVY CITY—See WASHINGTON (portions), DC (RCN. Formerly [DC0006]. This cable system has converted to IPTV)

JUDICIARY SQUARE—See WASHINGTON (portions), DC (RCN. Formerly [DC0006]. This cable system has converted to IPTV)

KENILWORTH—See WASHINGTON (portions), DC (RCN. Formerly [DC0006]. This cable system has converted to IPTV)

KENT—See WASHINGTON (portions), DC (RCN. Formerly [DC0006]. This cable system has converted to IPTV)

LAMOND RIGGS—See WASHINGTON (portions), DC (RCN. Formerly [DC0006]. This cable system has converted to IPTV)

LANHAM—See WASHINGTON (portions), MD (RCN. Formerly [DC0006]. This cable system has converted to IPTV)

MANOR PARK—See WASHINGTON (portions), DC (RCN. Formerly [DC0006]. This cable system has converted to IPTV)

MCLEAN GARDENS—See WASHINGTON (portions), DC (RCN. Formerly [DC0006]. This cable system has converted to IPTV)

MICHIGAN PARK—See WASHINGTON (portions), DC (RCN. Formerly [DC0006]. This cable system has converted to IPTV)

MONTGOMERY COUNTY (PORTIONS)—See WASHINGTON (portions), MD (RCN. Formerly [DC0006]. This cable system has converted to IPTV)

MONTGOMERY VILLAGE—See WASHINGTON (portions), MD (RCN. Formerly [DC0006]. This cable system has converted to IPTV)

MOUNT PLEASANT—See WASHINGTON (portions), DC (RCN. Formerly [DC0006]. This cable system has converted to IPTV)

MOUNT VERNON SQUARE—See WASHINGTON (portions), DC (RCN. Formerly [DC0006]. This cable system has converted to IPTV)

PALISADES—See WASHINGTON (portions), DC (RCN. Formerly [DC0006]. This cable system has converted to IPTV)

PETWORTH—See WASHINGTON (portions), DC (RCN. Formerly [DC0006]. This cable system has converted to IPTV)

PLEASANT HILL—See WASHINGTON (portions), DC (RCN. Formerly [DC0006]. This cable system has converted to IPTV)

RIVER TERRACE—See WASHINGTON (portions), DC (RCN. Formerly [DC0006]. This cable system has converted to IPTV)

SHAW—See WASHINGTON (portions), DC (RCN. Formerly [DC0006]. This cable system has converted to IPTV)

SHEPHERD PARK—See WASHINGTON (portions), DC (RCN. Formerly [DC0006]. This cable system has converted to IPTV)

SILVER SPRING—See WASHINGTON (portions), MD (RCN. Formerly [DC0006]. This cable system has converted to IPTV)

SIXTEENTH STREET HEIGHTS—See WASHINGTON (portions), DC (RCN. Formerly [DC0006]. This cable system has converted to IPTV)

TAKOMA PARK—See WASHINGTON (portions), MD (RCN. Formerly [DC0006]. This cable system has converted to IPTV)

TENLEYTOWN—See WASHINGTON (portions), DC (RCN. Formerly [DC0006]. This cable system has converted to IPTV)

U.S. SOLDIERS' & AIRMEN'S HOME—Comcast Cable. Now served by FREDERICK COUNTY (portions), MD [MD0009]

U.S. SOLDIERS' & AIRMEN'S HOME—Formerly served by Chesapeake Cable Partners. Now served by Comcast Cable, FREDERICK COUNTY, MD [MD0009]

VAN NESS—See WASHINGTON (portions), DC (RCN. Formerly [DC0006]. This cable system has converted to IPTV)

WALTER REED ARMY MEDICAL CENTER—Comcast Cable. Now served by FREDERICK COUNTY (portions), MD [MD0009]

WASHINGTON (northwestern portion)—RCN. This cable system has converted to IPTV. See WASHINGTON, DC (portions) [DC5001]

WASHINGTON (portions)—Comcast Cable. Served by FREDERICK COUNTY (portions), MD [MD0009]

WASHINGTON (portions)—RCN. This cable system has converted to IPTV. See WASHINGTON, DC (portions) [DC5001]

WASHINGTON (PORTIONS)—RCN. Formerly [DC0006]. This cable system has converted to IPTV

WESLEY HEIGHTS—See WASHINGTON (portions), DC (RCN. Formerly [DC0006]. This cable system has

2017 Edition

District of Columbia—Cable Community Index

converted to IPTV)

WEST END—See WASHINGTON (portions), DC (RCN. Formerly [DC0006]. This cable system has converted to IPTV)

WOODLEY PARK—See WASHINGTON (portions), DC (RCN. Formerly [DC0006]. This cable system has converted to IPTV)

WOODRIDGE—See WASHINGTON (portions), DC (RCN. Formerly [DC0006]. This cable system has converted to IPTV)

FLORIDA

ABBEVILLE—See TALLAHASSEE, AL (Comcast Cable)

ADVENT CHRISTIAN VILLAGE—Formerly served by Advent Christian Village Cable TV. No longer in operation

ALACHUA COUNTY (PORTIONS)—See JACKSONVILLE, FL (Comcast Cable)

ALACHUA COUNTY (PORTIONS)—See GAINESVILLE, FL (Cox Communications)

ALACHUA—Formerly served by Altitude Communications. No longer in operation

ALACHUA—See GAINESVILLE, FL (Cox Communications)

ALFORD—See TALLAHASSEE, FL (Comcast Cable)

ALLAPATTAH—See MIAMI, FL (AT&T U-verse. This is the regional video hub for the MIAMI area)

ALLIGATOR POINT—Mediacom. Now served by EASTPOINT, FL [FL0180]

ALLIGATOR POINT—See EASTPOINT, FL (Mediacom)

ALTAMONTE SPRINGS—See ORLANDO, FL (Bright House Networks)

ALTOONA—See ASTOR, FL (Florida Fiber Networks)

ALVA—Comcast Cable. Now served by SARASOTA, FL [FL0017]

ALVA—See SARASOTA, FL (Comcast Cable)

ANNA MARIA—See HILLSBOROUGH COUNTY (portions), FL (Bright House Networks)

ANTHONY—See CITRA, FL (Florida Fiber Networks)

APALACHICOLA—Mediacom. Now served by EASTPOINT, FL [FL0180]

APALACHICOLA—See EASTPOINT, FL (Mediacom)

APOLLO BEACH—See HILLSBOROUGH COUNTY (portions), FL (Bright House Networks)

APOPKA—See ORLANDO, FL (Bright House Networks)

ARCADIA—Comcast Cable. Now served by SARASOTA, FL [FL0017]

ARCADIA—See SARASOTA, FL (Comcast Cable)

ARCH CREEK—See MIAMI, FL (AT&T U-verse. This is the regional video hub for the MIAMI area)

ARCHER—Comcast Cable

ARLINGTON—See JACKSONVILLE BEACH, FL (AT&T U-verse. Formerly [FL0358]. This cable system has converted to IPTV. This is the regional video hub for the JACKSONVILLE BEACH area)

ASHFORD—See TALLAHASSEE, AL (Comcast Cable)

ASTATULA—See ASTOR, FL (Florida Fiber Networks)

ASTOR—Florida Fiber Networks

ATLANTIC BEACH—See JACKSONVILLE BEACH, FL (AT&T U-verse. Formerly [FL0358]. This cable system has converted to IPTV. This is the regional video hub for the JACKSONVILLE BEACH area)

ATLANTIC BEACH—See JACKSONVILLE, FL (Comcast Cable)

ATLANTIS—See WEST PALM BEACH, FL (Comcast Cable)

ATMORE—See GULF BREEZE, AL (Mediacom)

AUBURNDALE—Bright House Networks. Now served by HILLSBOROUGH COUNTY (portions), FL [FL0003]

AUBURNDALE—See HILLSBOROUGH COUNTY (portions), FL (Bright House Networks)

AVENTURA—See MIAMI, FL (AT&T U-verse. This is the regional video hub for the MIAMI area)

AVENTURA—See MIAMI BEACH, FL (Atlantic Broadband)

AVENTURA—See WEST PALM BEACH, FL (Comcast Cable)

AVON PARK—See SARASOTA, FL (Comcast Cable)

AVON—See TALLAHASSEE, AL (Comcast Cable)

BAKER COUNTY (PORTIONS)—See JACKSONVILLE, FL (Comcast Cable)

BAKER—Mediacom. Now served by GULF BREEZE, FL [FL0070]

BAKER—See GULF BREEZE, FL (Mediacom)

BAL HARBOUR—See MIAMI, FL (AT&T U-verse. This is the regional video hub for the MIAMI area)

BAL HARBOUR—See MIAMI BEACH, FL (Atlantic Broadband)

BALDWIN COUNTY (PORTIONS)—See CANTONMENT, AL (Bright House Networks)

BALDWIN—See JACKSONVILLE BEACH, FL (AT&T U-verse. Formerly [FL0358]. This cable system has converted to IPTV. This is the regional video hub for the JACKSONVILLE BEACH area)

BALDWIN—See JACKSONVILLE, FL (Comcast Cable)

BAREFOOT BAY—See ORLANDO, FL (Bright House Networks)

BARTOW—Comcast Cable. Now served by SARASOTA, FL [FL0017]

BARTOW—See SARASOTA, FL (Comcast Cable)

BASCOM—See TALLAHASSEE, FL (Comcast Cable)

BAY COUNTY (PORTIONS)—See TALLAHASSEE, FL (Comcast Cable)

BAY COUNTY (PORTIONS)—See WALTON COUNTY (portions), FL (Mediacom)

BAY HARBOR ISLANDS—See MIAMI, FL (AT&T U-verse. This is the regional video hub for the MIAMI area)

BAY HARBOR ISLANDS—See MIAMI BEACH, FL (Atlantic Broadband)

BAY INDIES MOBILE HOME PARK—Formerly served by Mobile Home Properties Inc. No longer in operation

BAYONET—See HILLSBOROUGH COUNTY (portions), FL (Bright House Networks)

BELLE GLADE—Comcast Cable. Now served by WEST PALM BEACH, FL [FL0008]

BELLE GLADE—See WEST PALM BEACH, FL (Comcast Cable)

BELLE ISLE—See ORLANDO, FL (Bright House Networks)

BELLEAIR BEACH—See HILLSBOROUGH COUNTY (portions), FL (Bright House Networks)

BELLEAIR BLUFFS—See HILLSBOROUGH COUNTY (portions), FL (Bright House Networks)

BELLEAIR—See HILLSBOROUGH COUNTY (portions), FL (Bright House Networks)

BELLEVIEW—See ORLANDO, FL (Bright House Networks)

BEVERLY BEACH—Formerly served by TV Max. No longer in operation

BEVERLY BEACH—See ORLANDO, FL (Bright House Networks)

BEVERLY HILLS—See ARCHER, FL (Comcast Cable)

BIG COPPITT—See MIAMI, FL (AT&T U-verse. This is the regional video hub for the MIAMI area)

BIG CYPRESS SEMINOLE INDIAN RESERVATION—Formerly served by Comcast Cable. No longer in operation

BIG PINE KEY—See MIAMI, FL (AT&T U-verse. This is the regional video hub for the MIAMI area)

BISCAYNE PARK—See MIAMI, FL (AT&T U-verse. This is the regional video hub for the MIAMI area)

BISCAYNE PARK—See WEST PALM BEACH, FL (Comcast Cable)

BLACKSHEAR—See JACKSONVILLE BEACH, GA (AT&T U-verse. Formerly [FL0358]. This cable system has converted to IPTV. This is the regional video hub for the JACKSONVILLE BEACH area)

BLOUNTSTOWN—Bright House Networks

BOCA CHICA KEY—See MIAMI, FL (AT&T U-verse. This is the regional video hub for the MIAMI area)

BOCA GRANDE ISLAND—See SARASOTA, FL (Comcast Cable)

BOCA GRANDE—See SARASOTA, FL (Comcast Cable)

BOCA RATON—Comcast Cable. Now served by WEST PALM BEACH, FL [FL0008]

BOCA RATON—Comcast Cable. Now served by WEST PALM BEACH, FL [FL0008]

BOCA RATON—See WEST PALM BEACH, FL (Comcast Cable)

BONIFAY—Mediacom. Now served by WALTON COUNTY (portions), FL [FL0159]

BONIFAY—See WALTON COUNTY (portions), FL (Mediacom)

BONITA BEACH—See SARASOTA, FL (Comcast Cable)

BONITA SPRINGS—See SARASOTA, FL (Comcast Cable)

BOSTWICK—See PUTNAM COUNTY (eastern portion), FL (Florida Fiber Networks)

BOWLING GREEN—Bright House Networks

BOYNTON BEACH—See WEST PALM BEACH, FL (Comcast Cable)

BRADENTON (unincorporated areas)—Formerly served by Universal Cablevision Inc. No longer in operation

BRADENTON BEACH—See HILLSBOROUGH COUNTY (portions), FL (Bright House Networks)

BRADENTON—Bright House Networks. Now served by HILLSBOROUGH COUNTY (portions), FL [FL0003]

BRADENTON—Formerly served by Florida Cable. No longer in operation

BRADENTON—Formerly served by Sprint Corp. No longer in operation

BRADENTON—See HILLSBOROUGH COUNTY (portions), FL (Bright House Networks)

Cable Community Index—Florida

BRADFORD COUNTY (PORTIONS)—See JACKSONVILLE, FL (Comcast Cable)

BRADFORD COUNTY—See LAWTEY, FL (Florida Fiber Networks)

BRANDON—Comcast Cable. Now served by ARCHER, FL [FL0189]

BRANDON—See ARCHER, FL (Comcast Cable)

BRANFORD—Formerly served by Altitude Communications. No longer in operation

BRANTLEY COUNTY (UNINCORPORATED AREAS)—See JACKSONVILLE BEACH, GA (AT&T U-verse. Formerly [FL0358]. This cable system has converted to IPTV. This is the regional video hub for the JACKSONVILLE BEACH area)

BRATT—Formerly served by CableSouth Inc. No longer in operation

BREVARD COUNTY—See ORLANDO, FL (Bright House Networks)

BREWTON—See GULF BREEZE, AL (Mediacom)

BRIGHTON SEMINOLE RESERVE—Formerly served by Comcast Cable. No longer in operation

BRISTOL—See BLOUNTSTOWN, FL (Bright House Networks)

BROADVIEW PARK—See MIAMI, FL (AT&T U-verse. This is the regional video hub for the MIAMI area)

BRONSON (TOWN)—Florida Fiber Networks

BROOKER—New River Cablevision Inc

BROOKS COUNTY (PORTIONS)—See TALLAHASSEE, GA (Comcast Cable)

BROOKSVILLE (PORTIONS)—See HILLSBOROUGH COUNTY (portions), FL (Bright House Networks)

BROOKSVILLE—See HERNANDO COUNTY, FL (Florida Fiber Networks)

BROWARD COUNTY (portions)—Comcast Cable. Now served by WEST PALM BEACH, FL [FL0008]

BROWARD COUNTY (PORTIONS)—See CORAL SPRINGS, FL (Advanced Cable Communications)

BROWARD COUNTY (PORTIONS)—See WEST PALM BEACH, FL (Comcast Cable)

BROWARD COUNTY (UNINCORPORATED AREAS)—See MIAMI, FL (AT&T U-verse. This is the regional video hub for the MIAMI area)

BROWNSVILLE—See MIAMI, FL (AT&T U-verse. This is the regional video hub for the MIAMI area)

BRUNSWICK—See JACKSONVILLE BEACH, GA (AT&T U-verse. Formerly [FL0358]. This cable system has converted to IPTV. This is the regional video hub for the JACKSONVILLE BEACH area)

BRUNSWICK—See JACKSONVILLE, GA (Comcast Cable)

BUCKHEAD RIDGE—See WEST PALM BEACH, FL (Comcast Cable)

BUNNELL—See ORLANDO, FL (Bright House Networks)

BURNT STORE MARINA—See SARASOTA, FL (Comcast Cable)

BUSHNELL—See ORLANDO, FL (Bright House Networks)

CALHOUN COUNTY (PORTIONS)—See BLOUNTSTOWN, FL (Bright House Networks)

CALHOUN COUNTY (PORTIONS)—See TALLAHASSEE, FL (Comcast Cable)

CALLAHAN (town)—Comcast Cable. Now served by JACKSONVILLE, FL [FL0002]

CALLAHAN—See JACKSONVILLE BEACH, FL (AT&T U-verse. Formerly [FL0358]. This cable system has converted to IPTV. This is the regional video hub for the JACKSONVILLE BEACH area)

CALLAHAN—See JACKSONVILLE, FL (Comcast Cable)

CALLAWAY—See TALLAHASSEE, FL (Comcast Cable)

CALLAWAY—See PANAMA CITY BEACH, FL (WOW! Internet, Cable & Phone)

CAMDEN COUNTY (PORTIONS)—See JACKSONVILLE, GA (Comcast Cable)

CAMDEN COUNTY (UNINCORPORATED AREAS)—See JACKSONVILLE BEACH, GA (AT&T U-verse. Formerly [FL0358]. This cable system has converted to IPTV. This is the regional video hub for the JACKSONVILLE BEACH area)

CAMPBELLTON—Formerly served by Campbellton Cable. No longer in operation

CANTONMENT—Bright House Networks

CAPE CANAVERAL—See ORLANDO, FL (Bright House Networks)

CAPE CORAL—Comcast Cable. Now served by SARASOTA, FL [FL0017]

CAPE CORAL—See SARASOTA, FL (Comcast Cable)

CAPE HAZE—See SARASOTA, FL (Comcast Cable)

CAPE SAN BLAS—Mediacom. Now served by WALTON COUNTY (portions), FL [FL0159]

CAPE SAN BLAS—See WALTON COUNTY (portions), FL (Mediacom)

CAPTIVA ISLAND—See SARASOTA, FL (Comcast Cable)

CAROL CITY—See MIAMI, FL (AT&T U-verse. This is the regional video hub for the MIAMI area)

CARRABELLE—See EASTPOINT, FL (Mediacom)

CASSELBERRY—See ORLANDO, FL (Bright House Networks)

CEDAR GROVE—See TALLAHASSEE, FL (Comcast Cable)

CEDAR GROVE—See PANAMA CITY BEACH, FL (WOW! Internet, Cable & Phone)

CEDAR KEY—Bright House Networks

CELEBRATION—Comcast Cable. Now served by ARCHER, FL [FL0189]

CELEBRATION—See ARCHER, FL (Comcast Cable)

CENTER HILL—See ORLANDO, FL (Bright House Networks)

CENTURY—Bright House Networks. Now served by CANTONMENT [FL0090]

CENTURY—See CANTONMENT, FL (Bright House Networks)

CHARLOTTE COUNTY (PORTIONS)—See SARASOTA, FL (Comcast Cable)

CHARLOTTE HARBOR—See SARASOTA, FL (Comcast Cable)

CHARLTON COUNTY (PORTIONS)—See JACKSONVILLE, GA (Comcast Cable)

CHASEWOOD—Formerly served by Comcast Cable. No longer in operation

CHATTAHOOCHEE—Bright House Networks

CHIEFLAND—Formerly served by Altitude Communications. No longer in operation

CHIPLEY—Bright House Networks

CHRISTMAS—Formerly served by Florida Cable. No longer in operation

CINCO BAYOU—See PENSACOLA, FL (Cox Communications)

CITRA—Florida Fiber Networks

CITRUS COUNTY (NORTHERN PORTION)—See ARCHER, FL (Comcast Cable)

CITRUS COUNTY—See HILLSBOROUGH COUNTY (portions), FL (Bright House Networks)

CLAY COUNTY (PORTIONS)—See JACKSONVILLE, FL (Comcast Cable)

CLAY COUNTY (PORTIONS)—Florida Fiber Networks

CLAY COUNTY (UNINCORPORATED AREAS)—See JACKSONVILLE BEACH, FL (AT&T U-verse. Formerly [FL0358]. This cable system has converted to IPTV. This is the regional video hub for the JACKSONVILLE BEACH area)

CLAY COUNTY—See LAWTEY, FL (Florida Fiber Networks)

CLAY HILL—See CLAY COUNTY (portions), FL (Florida Fiber Networks)

CLEARWATER—See HILLSBOROUGH COUNTY (portions), FL (Bright House Networks)

CLEARWATER—See PINELLAS COUNTY (portions), FL (WOW! Internet, Cable & Phone)

CLERMONT—See ORLANDO, FL (Bright House Networks)

CLEVELAND—See SARASOTA, FL (Comcast Cable)

CLEWISTON—Comcast Cable. Now served by WEST PALM BEACH, FL [FL0008]

CLEWISTON—See WEST PALM BEACH, FL (Comcast Cable)

CLOUD LAKE—See WEST PALM BEACH, FL (Comcast Cable)

COCOA BEACH—See ORLANDO, FL (Bright House Networks)

COCOA—See ORLANDO, FL (Bright House Networks)

COCONUT CREEK—See MIAMI, FL (AT&T U-verse. This is the regional video hub for the MIAMI area)

COCONUT CREEK—See WEST PALM BEACH, FL (Comcast Cable)

COLEMAN—See ORLANDO, FL (Bright House Networks)

COLLIER COUNTY (PORTIONS)—See SARASOTA, FL (Comcast Cable)

COLUMBIA COUNTY (UNINCORPORATED AREAS)—See JACKSONVILLE BEACH, FL (AT&T U-verse. Formerly [FL0358]. This cable system has converted to IPTV. This is the regional video hub for the JACKSONVILLE BEACH area)

COLUMBIA—See JACKSONVILLE, FL (Comcast Cable)

COOPER CITY—See MIAMI, FL (AT&T U-verse. This is the regional video hub for the MIAMI area)

COOPER CITY—See WEST PALM BEACH, FL (Comcast Cable)

CORAL GABLES—See MIAMI, FL (AT&T U-verse. This is the regional video hub for the MIAMI area)

CORAL GABLES—See WEST PALM BEACH, FL (Comcast Cable)

CORAL SPRINGS—Advanced Cable Communications

CORAL SPRINGS—See MIAMI, FL (AT&T U-verse. This is the regional video hub for the MIAMI area)

COTTONDALE—See TALLAHASSEE, FL (Comcast Cable)

COTTONWOOD—See TALLAHASSEE, AL (Comcast Cable)

COWARTS—See TALLAHASSEE, AL (Comcast Cable)

CRAWFORDVILLE—Comcast Cable. Now served by TALLAHASSEE, FL [FL0283]

Florida—Cable Community Index

CRAWFORDVILLE—See TALLAHASSEE, FL (Comcast Cable)

CRESCENT BEACH—See JACKSONVILLE, FL (Comcast Cable)

CRESCENT CITY—Comcast Cable. Now served by JACKSONVILLE, FL [FL0002]

CRESCENT CITY—See JACKSONVILLE, FL (Comcast Cable)

CRESTVIEW—Cox Communications. Now served by PENSACOLA, FL [FL0018]

CRESTVIEW—See PENSACOLA, FL (Cox Communications)

CROSS CITY—Formerly served by Altitude Communications. No longer in operation

CRYSTAL RIVER—See HILLSBOROUGH COUNTY (portions), FL (Bright House Networks)

CUTLER BAY—See MIAMI, FL (AT&T U-verse. This is the regional video hub for the MIAMI area)

CUTLER BAY—See WEST PALM BEACH, FL (Comcast Cable)

DADE CITY—See HILLSBOROUGH COUNTY (portions), FL (Bright House Networks)

DADE COUNTY (PORTIONS)—See MIAMI BEACH, FL (Atlantic Broadband)

DADE COUNTY (PORTIONS)—See WEST PALM BEACH, FL (Comcast Cable)

DANIA BEACH—See MIAMI, FL (AT&T U-verse. This is the regional video hub for the MIAMI area)

DANIA—See WEST PALM BEACH, FL (Comcast Cable)

DAVENPORT—See HILLSBOROUGH COUNTY (portions), FL (Bright House Networks)

DAVIE—Comcast Cable. Now served by WEST PALM BEACH, FL [FL0008]

DAVIE—See MIAMI, FL (AT&T U-verse. This is the regional video hub for the MIAMI area)

DAVIE—See WEST PALM BEACH, FL (Comcast Cable)

DAYTONA BEACH SHORES—See ORLANDO, FL (Bright House Networks)

DAYTONA BEACH—See ORLANDO, FL (Bright House Networks)

DE BARY—See ORLANDO, FL (Bright House Networks)

DE FUNIAK SPRINGS—Bright House Networks

DE LAND—Formerly served by Bright House Networks. No longer in operation

DEBARY—Comcast Cable. Now served by ARCHER, FL [FL0189]

DEBARY—See ARCHER, FL (Comcast Cable)

DEENWOOD—See JACKSONVILLE BEACH, GA (AT&T U-verse. Formerly [FL0358]. This cable system has converted to IPTV. This is the regional video hub for the JACKSONVILLE BEACH area)

DEERFIELD BEACH—See MIAMI, FL (AT&T U-verse. This is the regional video hub for the MIAMI area)

DEERFIELD BEACH—See WEST PALM BEACH, FL (Comcast Cable)

DELAND—See ORLANDO, FL (Bright House Networks)

DELRAY BEACH—Comcast Cable. Now served by WEST PALM BEACH, FL [FL0008]

DELRAY BEACH—See WEST PALM BEACH, FL (Comcast Cable)

DELRAY SHORES—See WEST PALM BEACH, FL (Comcast Cable)

DELTONA—See ORLANDO, FL (Bright House Networks)

DESOTO COUNTY (PORTIONS)—See SARASOTA, FL (Comcast Cable)

DESTIN—See PENSACOLA, FL (Cox Communications)

DOCK JUNCTION—See JACKSONVILLE BEACH, GA (AT&T U-verse. Formerly [FL0358]. This cable system has converted to IPTV. This is the regional video hub for the JACKSONVILLE BEACH area)

DORAL—See MIAMI, FL (AT&T U-verse. This is the regional video hub for the MIAMI area)

DORAL—See WEST PALM BEACH, FL (Comcast Cable)

DOTHAN—See TALLAHASSEE, AL (Comcast Cable)

DOWLING PARK—Formerly served by KLiP Interactive. No longer in operation

DUCK KEY—See MIAMI, FL (AT&T U-verse. This is the regional video hub for the MIAMI area)

DUNDEE—See HILLSBOROUGH COUNTY (portions), FL (Bright House Networks)

DUNEDIN—See HILLSBOROUGH COUNTY (portions), FL (Bright House Networks)

DUNEDIN—See PINELLAS COUNTY (portions), FL (WOW! Internet, Cable & Phone)

DUNNELLON—Comcast Cable. Now served by ARCHER, FL [FL0189]

DUNNELLON—See ARCHER, FL (Comcast Cable)

DUVAL COUNTY (PORTIONS)—See JACKSONVILLE, FL (Comcast Cable)

DUVAL COUNTY (UNINCORPORATED AREAS)—See JACKSONVILLE BEACH, FL (AT&T U-verse. Formerly [FL0358]. This cable system has converted to IPTV. This is the regional video hub for the JACKSONVILLE BEACH area)

EAGLE LAKE—See HILLSBOROUGH COUNTY (portions), FL (Bright House Networks)

EAST BREWTON—See GULF BREEZE, AL (Mediacom)

EAST MILTON—Mediacom. Now served by GULF BREEZE, FL [FL0070]

EAST MILTON—See GULF BREEZE, FL (Mediacom)

EAST PALATKA—See JACKSONVILLE BEACH, FL (AT&T U-verse. Formerly [FL0358]. This cable system has converted to IPTV. This is the regional video hub for the JACKSONVILLE BEACH area)

EASTPOINT—Mediacom

EATONVILLE—See ORLANDO, FL (Bright House Networks)

EDGEWATER—See ORLANDO, FL (Bright House Networks)

EDGEWOOD—See ORLANDO, FL (Bright House Networks)

EGLIN AFB—See PENSACOLA, FL (Cox Communications)

EL JOBEAN—See SARASOTA, FL (Comcast Cable)

EL PORTAL—See MIAMI, FL (AT&T U-verse. This is the regional video hub for the MIAMI area)

EL PORTAL—See WEST PALM BEACH, FL (Comcast Cable)

ELFERS—See HILLSBOROUGH COUNTY (portions), FL (Bright House Networks)

ENGLEWOOD—Comcast Cable. Now served by SARASOTA, FL [FL0017]

ENGLEWOOD—See SARASOTA, FL (Comcast Cable)

ESCAMBIA COUNTY (PORTIONS)—See GULF BREEZE, FL (Mediacom)

ESCAMBIA COUNTY—See CANTONMENT, FL (Bright House Networks)

ESCAMBIA COUNTY—See PENSACOLA, FL (Cox Communications)

ESTERO—See SARASOTA, FL (Comcast Cable)

EUNOLA—See CHIPLEY, AL (Bright House Networks)

EUSTIS—See ARCHER, FL (Comcast Cable)

EUSTIS—See ASTOR, FL (Florida Fiber Networks)

EUSTIS—See MARION COUNTY (southern portion), FL (Florida Fiber Networks)

EVERGLADES CITY—Comcast Cable. Now served by SARASOTA, FL [FL0017]

EVERGLADES CITY—See SARASOTA, FL (Comcast Cable)

FAIRFIELD—See MARION COUNTY (unincorporated areas), FL (Cablevision of Marion County)

FANNING SPRINGS—Florida Fiber Networks

FELLSMERE—See WEST PALM BEACH, FL (Comcast Cable)

FERNANDINA BEACH—Comcast Cable. Now served by JACKSONVILLE, FL [FL0002]

FERNANDINA BEACH—See JACKSONVILLE BEACH, FL (AT&T U-verse. Formerly [FL0358]. This cable system has converted to IPTV. This is the regional video hub for the JACKSONVILLE BEACH area)

FERNANDINA BEACH—See JACKSONVILLE, FL (Comcast Cable)

FLAGLER BEACH—See ORLANDO, FL (Bright House Networks)

FLAGLER COUNTY—See ORLANDO, FL (Bright House Networks)

FLEMING ISLAND—See JACKSONVILLE BEACH, FL (AT&T U-verse. Formerly [FL0358]. This cable system has converted to IPTV. This is the regional video hub for the JACKSONVILLE BEACH area)

FLOMATON—See CANTONMENT, AL (Bright House Networks)

FLORAHOME—Florida Fiber Networks

FLORALA—See DE FUNIAK SPRINGS, AL (Bright House Networks)

FLORIDA CITY—See MIAMI, FL (AT&T U-verse. This is the regional video hub for the MIAMI area)

FLORIDA CITY—See WEST PALM BEACH, FL (Comcast Cable)

FLORIDA HIGHLANDS—Formerly served by KLiP Interactive. No longer in operation

FOLKSTON—See JACKSONVILLE, GA (Comcast Cable)

FOREST GLEN—Formerly served by Comcast Cable. No longer in operation

FORT GEORGE ISLAND—See JACKSONVILLE BEACH, FL (AT&T U-verse. Formerly [FL0358]. This cable system has converted to IPTV. This is the regional video hub for the JACKSONVILLE BEACH area)

FORT LAUDERDALE—Comcast Cable. Now served by WEST PALM BEACH, FL [FL0008]

FORT LAUDERDALE—See MIAMI, FL (AT&T U-verse. This is the regional video hub for the MIAMI area)

FORT LAUDERDALE—See WEST PALM BEACH, FL (Comcast Cable)

FORT MEADE—See SARASOTA, FL (Comcast Cable)

FORT MYERS BEACH—See SARASOTA, FL (Comcast Cable)

Cable Community Index—Florida

FORT MYERS—Comcast Cable. Now served by SARASOTA, FL [FL0017]

FORT MYERS—See SARASOTA, FL (Comcast Cable)

FORT OGDEN—See SARASOTA, FL (Comcast Cable)

FORT PIERCE—Comcast Cable. Now served by WEST PALM BEACH, FL [FL0008]

FORT PIERCE—Formerly served by Wireless Broadcasting of Fort Pierce. No longer in operation

FORT PIERCE—See WEST PALM BEACH, FL (Comcast Cable)

FORT WALTON BEACH—Cox Communications. Now served by PENSACOLA, FL [FL0018]

FORT WALTON BEACH—See PENSACOLA, FL (Cox Communications)

FRANKLIN COUNTY (PORTIONS)—See EASTPOINT, FL (Mediacom)

FREEPORT—Cox Communications. Now served by PENSACOLA, FL [FL0018]

FREEPORT—See PENSACOLA, FL (Cox Communications)

FROSTPROOF—See SARASOTA, FL (Comcast Cable)

FRUITLAND PARK—Comcast Cable. Now served by ARCHER, FL [FL0189]

FRUITLAND PARK—See ARCHER, FL (Comcast Cable)

FRUITLAND—See JACKSONVILLE, FL (Comcast Cable)

GADSDEN COUNTY (portions)—Mediacom. Now served by HAVANA (town), FL [FL0144]

GADSDEN COUNTY (PORTIONS)—See CHATTAHOOCHEE, FL (Bright House Networks)

GADSDEN COUNTY (PORTIONS)—See TALLAHASSEE, FL (Comcast Cable)

GADSDEN COUNTY (PORTIONS)—See HAVANA (town), FL (Mediacom)

GAINESVILLE—Formerly served by Brytlink. No longer in service

GAINESVILLE—Cox Communications

GENEVA COUNTY—See CHIPLEY, AL (Bright House Networks)

GENEVA—See CHIPLEY, AL (Bright House Networks)

GEORGETOWN—See JACKSONVILLE, FL (Comcast Cable)

GIBSONTON—See HILLSBOROUGH COUNTY (portions), FL (Bright House Networks)

GIFFORD—See WEST PALM BEACH, FL (Comcast Cable)

GILCHRIST COUNTY (PORTIONS)—See NORTH OLD TOWN, FL (Florida Fiber Networks)

GLADES COUNTY (PORTIONS)—See SARASOTA, FL (Comcast Cable)

GLEN RIDGE—See WEST PALM BEACH, FL (Comcast Cable)

GLEN ST. MARY—See JACKSONVILLE, FL (Comcast Cable)

GLYNN COUNTY (PORTIONS)—See JACKSONVILLE, GA (Comcast Cable)

GLYNN COUNTY (UNINCORPORATED AREAS)—See JACKSONVILLE BEACH, GA (AT&T U-verse. Formerly [FL0358]. This cable system has converted to IPTV. This is the regional video hub for the JACKSONVILLE BEACH area)

GOLDEN BEACH—See MIAMI, FL (AT&T U-verse. This is the regional video hub for the MIAMI area)

GOLDEN BEACH—See MIAMI BEACH, FL (Atlantic Broadband)

GOLDEN GATE—Comcast Cable. Now served by SARASOTA, FL [FL0017]

GOLDEN GATE—See SARASOTA, FL (Comcast Cable)

GOLDEN GLADES—See MIAMI, FL (AT&T U-verse. This is the regional video hub for the MIAMI area)

GOLF VILLAGE—Formerly served by Comcast Cable. No longer in operation

GOULDS—See MIAMI, FL (AT&T U-verse. This is the regional video hub for the MIAMI area)

GRACEVILLE—See CHIPLEY, FL (Bright House Networks)

GRAND ISLAND—See ORLANDO, FL (Bright House Networks)

GRAND RIDGE—See TALLAHASSEE, FL (Comcast Cable)

GRANDIN—See FLORAHOME, FL (Florida Fiber Networks)

GREEN COVE SPRINGS—See JACKSONVILLE BEACH, FL (AT&T U-verse. Formerly [FL0358]. This cable system has converted to IPTV. This is the regional video hub for the JACKSONVILLE BEACH area)

GREEN COVE SPRINGS—See JACKSONVILLE, FL (Comcast Cable)

GREENACRES CITY—Comcast Cable. Now served by WEST PALM BEACH, FL [FL0008]

GREENACRES—See WEST PALM BEACH, FL (Comcast Cable)

GREENSBORO—Mediacom. Now served by HAVANA (town), FL [FL0144]

GREENSBORO—See HAVANA (town), FL (Mediacom)

GREENVILLE—Formerly served by KLiP Interactive. No longer in operation

GREENWOOD—See TALLAHASSEE, FL (Comcast Cable)

GRETNA—Mediacom. Now served by HAVANA (town), FL [FL0144]

GRETNA—See HAVANA (town), FL (Mediacom)

GROVELAND—See ORLANDO, FL (Bright House Networks)

GULF BREEZE—Mediacom

GULF COUNTY (PORTIONS)—See WALTON COUNTY (portions), FL (Mediacom)

GULFPORT—See HILLSBOROUGH COUNTY (portions), FL (Bright House Networks)

HAINES CITY—See HILLSBOROUGH COUNTY (portions), FL (Bright House Networks)

HALLANDALE BEACH—See MIAMI, FL (AT&T U-verse. This is the regional video hub for the MIAMI area)

HALLANDALE—See WEST PALM BEACH, FL (Comcast Cable)

HAMILTON COUNTY (PORTIONS)—See JASPER, FL (Comcast Cable)

HAMPTON—Florida Fiber Networks

HARDEE COUNTY (PORTIONS)—See WAUCHULA, FL (Comcast Cable)

HARTFORD—See CHIPLEY, AL (Bright House Networks)

HASTINGS—Comcast Cable. Now served by JACKSONVILLE, FL [FL0002]

HASTINGS—See JACKSONVILLE, FL (Comcast Cable)

HAVANA (TOWN)—Mediacom

HAVERHILL—See WEST PALM BEACH, FL (Comcast Cable)

HAWTHORNE—Formerly served by Altitude Communications. No longer in operation

HAWTHORNE—See JACKSONVILLE BEACH, FL (AT&T U-verse. Formerly [FL0358]. This cable system has converted to IPTV. This is the regional video hub for the JACKSONVILLE BEACH area)

HAWTHORNE—See PUTNAM COUNTY (western portion), FL (Florida Fiber Networks)

HEADLAND—See TALLAHASSEE, AL (Comcast Cable)

HENDRY COUNTY (PORTIONS)—See SARASOTA, FL (Comcast Cable)

HENRY COUNTY (PORTIONS)—See TALLAHASSEE, AL (Comcast Cable)

HERNANDO COUNTY—Bright House Networks. Now served by HILLSBOROUGH COUNTY (portions), FL [FL0003]

HERNANDO COUNTY—See HILLSBOROUGH COUNTY (portions), FL (Bright House Networks)

HERNANDO COUNTY—Florida Fiber Networks

HIALEAH GARDENS—See MIAMI, FL (AT&T U-verse. This is the regional video hub for the MIAMI area)

HIALEAH GARDENS—See WEST PALM BEACH, FL (Comcast Cable)

HIALEAH—Comcast Cable. Now served by WEST PALM BEACH, FL [FL0008]

HIALEAH—See MIAMI, FL (AT&T U-verse. This is the regional video hub for the MIAMI area)

HIALEAH—See WEST PALM BEACH, FL (Comcast Cable)

HIDDEN ACRES—Formerly served by Comcast Cable. No longer in operation

HIDEAWAY MOBILE HOME PARK—See CITRA, FL (Florida Fiber Networks)

HIGH SPRINGS—Formerly served by Altitude Communications. No longer in operation

HIGHLAND BEACH—Comcast Cable. Now served by WEST PALM BEACH, FL [FL0008]

HIGHLAND BEACH—See WEST PALM BEACH, FL (Comcast Cable)

HIGHLANDS COUNTY (PORTIONS)—See SARASOTA, FL (Comcast Cable)

HILLCREST HEIGHTS—See SARASOTA, FL (Comcast Cable)

HILLCREST—See MIAMI, FL (AT&T U-verse. This is the regional video hub for the MIAMI area)

HILLIARD—Comcast Cable. Now served by JACKSONVILLE, FL [FL0002]

HILLIARD—See JACKSONVILLE, FL (Comcast Cable)

HILLSBORO BEACH—See MIAMI, FL (AT&T U-verse. This is the regional video hub for the MIAMI area)

HILLSBORO BEACH—See WEST PALM BEACH, FL (Comcast Cable)

HILLSBOROUGH COUNTY (PORTIONS)—Bright House Networks

HILLSBOROUGH COUNTY (PORTIONS)—See ARCHER, FL (Comcast Cable)

HOLIDAY—See HILLSBOROUGH COUNTY (portions), FL (Bright House Networks)

HOLLY HILL—See ORLANDO, FL (Bright House Networks)

HOLLYWOOD—Formerly served by Advanced Cable Communications. No longer in operation

HOLLYWOOD—See MIAMI, FL (AT&T U-verse. This is the regional video hub for the MIAMI area)

HOLLYWOOD—See WEST PALM BEACH, FL (Comcast Cable)

HOLMES BEACH—See HILLSBOROUGH COUNTY (portions), FL (Bright House Networks)

HOLMES COUNTY (PORTIONS)—See WALTON COUNTY (portions), FL (Mediacom)

Florida—Cable Community Index

HOLOPAW—Formerly served by Florida Cable. No longer in operation

HOLT—See GULF BREEZE, FL (Mediacom)

HOMELAND—See JACKSONVILLE, GA (Comcast Cable)

HOMESTEAD—See MIAMI, FL (AT&T U-verse. This is the regional video hub for the MIAMI area)

HOMESTEAD—See WEST PALM BEACH, FL (Comcast Cable)

HOMOSASSA—Formerly served by Bright House Networks. No longer in operation

HOSFORD—Formerly served by Southeast Cable TV Inc. No longer in operation

HOUSTON COUNTY (PORTIONS)—See TALLAHASSEE, AL (Comcast Cable)

HOWEY-IN-THE-HILLS—See ARCHER, FL (Comcast Cable)

HUDSON—See HILLSBOROUGH COUNTY (portions), FL (Bright House Networks)

HURLBURT FIELD—See PENSACOLA, FL (Cox Communications)

HYPOLUXO—See WEST PALM BEACH, FL (Comcast Cable)

IMMOKALEE SEMINOLE INDIAN RESERVATION—Formerly served by Comcast Cable. No longer in operation

IMMOKALEE—Comcast Cable. Now served by SARASOTA, FL [FL0017]

IMMOKALEE—See SARASOTA, FL (Comcast Cable)

INDIAN CREEK (VILLAGE)—See MIAMI, FL (AT&T U-verse. This is the regional video hub for the MIAMI area)

INDIAN HARBOUR BEACH—See ORLANDO, FL (Bright House Networks)

INDIAN RIVER COUNTY (PORTIONS)—See WEST PALM BEACH, FL (Comcast Cable)

INDIAN RIVER SHORES—See WEST PALM BEACH, FL (Comcast Cable)

INDIAN RIVER—See WEST PALM BEACH, FL (Comcast Cable)

INDIAN ROCKS BEACH—See HILLSBOROUGH COUNTY (portions), FL (Bright House Networks)

INDIAN SPRINGS—Formerly served by Formerly served by Comcast Cable. No longer in operation

INDIANTOWN—Comcast Cable. Now served by WEST PALM BEACH, FL [FL0008]

INDIANTOWN—See WEST PALM BEACH, FL (Comcast Cable)

INDIATLANTIC—See ORLANDO, FL (Bright House Networks)

INGLIS—See ARCHER, FL (Comcast Cable)

INTERLACHEN—See JACKSONVILLE, FL (Comcast Cable)

INVERNESS—Comcast Cable. Now served by ARCHER, FL [FL0189]

INVERNESS—See HILLSBOROUGH COUNTY (portions), FL (Bright House Networks)

INVERNESS—See ARCHER, FL (Comcast Cable)

ISLAMORADA (PORTIONS)—See WEST PALM BEACH, FL (Comcast Cable)

ISLAMORADA—See MIAMI, FL (AT&T U-verse. This is the regional video hub for the MIAMI area)

JACKSON COUNTY (PORTIONS)—See TALLAHASSEE, FL (Comcast Cable)

JACKSON COUNTY—See CHIPLEY, FL (Bright House Networks)

JACKSONVILLE BEACH—AT&T U-verse. Formerly [FL0358]. This cable system has converted to IPTV. This is the regional video hub for the JACKSONVILLE BEACH area

JACKSONVILLE BEACH—See JACKSONVILLE, FL (Comcast Cable)

JACKSONVILLE NAVAL AIR STATION—See JACKSONVILLE, FL (Comcast Cable)

JACKSONVILLE—AT&T U-verse. This cable system has converted to IPTV. See JACKSONVILLE BEACH, FL [FL5236]

JACKSONVILLE—Comcast Cable

JASPER—Comcast Cable

JAY—See CANTONMENT, FL (Bright House Networks)

JEFFERSON COUNTY (PORTIONS)—See MONTICELLO, FL (Comcast Cable)

JEKYLL ISLAND—See JACKSONVILLE BEACH, GA (AT&T U-verse. Formerly [FL0358]. This cable system has converted to IPTV. This is the regional video hub for the JACKSONVILLE BEACH area

JEKYLL ISLAND—See JACKSONVILLE, GA (Comcast Cable)

JENNINGS—Comcast Cable. Now served by JACKSONVILLE, FL [FL0002]

JENNINGS—See JACKSONVILLE, FL (Comcast Cable)

JENSEN BEACH—See WEST PALM BEACH, FL (Comcast Cable)

JOHNSON—See ORANGE SPRINGS, FL (Florida Fiber Networks)

JUNO BEACH—See WEST PALM BEACH, FL (Comcast Cable)

JUPITER INLET COLONY—See WEST PALM BEACH, FL (Comcast Cable)

JUPITER ISLAND—See WEST PALM BEACH, FL (Comcast Cable)

JUPITER—See WEST PALM BEACH, FL (Comcast Cable)

KEATON BEACH—Formerly served by Southeast Cable TV Inc. No longer in operation

KENANSVILLE—Formerly served by Florida Cable. No longer in operation

KENDALL—Comcast Cable. Now served by WEST PALM BEACH, FL [FL0008]

KENDALL—See MIAMI, FL (AT&T U-verse. This is the regional video hub for the MIAMI area)

KENDALL—See WEST PALM BEACH, FL (Comcast Cable)

KENNETH CITY—See HILLSBOROUGH COUNTY (portions), FL (Bright House Networks)

KEY BISCAYNE—See MIAMI, FL (AT&T U-verse. This is the regional video hub for the MIAMI area)

KEY BISCAYNE—See WEST PALM BEACH, FL (Comcast Cable)

KEY COLONY BEACH—Comcast Cable. Now served by WEST PALM BEACH, FL [FL0008]

KEY COLONY BEACH—See WEST PALM BEACH, FL (Comcast Cable)

KEY LARGO—Comcast Cable. Now served by WEST PALM BEACH, FL [FL0008]

KEY LARGO—See MIAMI, FL (AT&T U-verse. This is the regional video hub for the MIAMI area)

KEY LARGO—See WEST PALM BEACH, FL (Comcast Cable)

KEY WEST—Comcast Cable. Now served by WEST PALM BEACH, FL [FL0008]

KEY WEST—See MIAMI, FL (AT&T U-verse. This is the regional video hub for the MIAMI area)

KEY WEST—See WEST PALM BEACH, FL (Comcast Cable)

KEYSTONE HEIGHTS—See JACKSONVILLE BEACH, FL (AT&T U-verse. Formerly [FL0358]. This cable system has converted to IPTV. This is the regional video hub for the JACKSONVILLE BEACH area)

KEYSTONE HEIGHTS—See JACKSONVILLE, FL (Comcast Cable)

KEYSTONE HEIGHTS—See FLORAHOME, FL (Florida Fiber Networks)

KILLEARN LAKES—See TALLAHASSEE, FL (Comcast Cable)

KINGSLEY LAKE—See LAWTEY, FL (Florida Fiber Networks)

KINSEY—See TALLAHASSEE, AL (Comcast Cable)

KISSIMMEE—See ORLANDO, FL (Bright House Networks)

LA BELLE—Comcast Cable. Now served by SARASOTA, FL [FL0017]

LA BELLE—See SARASOTA, FL (Comcast Cable)

LADY LAKE—See ARCHER, FL (Comcast Cable)

LAKE ALFRED—See HILLSBOROUGH COUNTY (portions), FL (Bright House Networks)

LAKE BUTLER—Comcast Cable. Now served by JACKSONVILLE, FL [FL0002]

LAKE BUTLER—See JACKSONVILLE, FL (Comcast Cable)

LAKE CITY—Comcast Cable. Now served by JACKSONVILLE, FL [FL0002]

LAKE CITY—See JACKSONVILLE BEACH, FL (AT&T U-verse. Formerly [FL0358]. This cable system has converted to IPTV. This is the regional video hub for the JACKSONVILLE BEACH area)

LAKE CITY—See JACKSONVILLE, FL (Comcast Cable)

LAKE CLARKE SHORES—See WEST PALM BEACH, FL (Comcast Cable)

LAKE COUNTY (EASTERN PORTION)—See PAISLEY, FL (Florida Fiber Networks)

LAKE COUNTY (PORTIONS)—See ORLANDO, FL (Bright House Networks)

LAKE COUNTY (UNINCORPORATED AREAS)—See ARCHER, FL (Comcast Cable)

LAKE COUNTY (UNINCORPORATED AREAS)—See ASTOR, FL (Florida Fiber Networks)

LAKE FOREST—See MIAMI, FL (AT&T U-verse. This is the regional video hub for the MIAMI area)

LAKE HAMILTON—See HILLSBOROUGH COUNTY (portions), FL (Bright House Networks)

LAKE HELEN—See ORLANDO, FL (Bright House Networks)

LAKE MARY JANE—Formerly served by Florida Cable. No longer in operation

LAKE MARY—See ORLANDO, FL (Bright House Networks)

LAKE PARK—See WEST PALM BEACH, FL (Comcast Cable)

LAKE PLACID—Comcast Cablevision of West Florida Inc. Now served by SARASOTA, FL [FL0017]

LAKE PLACID—See SARASOTA, FL (Comcast Cable)

LAKE WALES—Comcast Cable. Now served by SARASOTA, FL [FL0017]

LAKE WALES—See HILLSBOROUGH COUNTY (portions), FL (Bright House Networks)

LAKE WALES—See SARASOTA, FL (Comcast Cable)

LAKE WORTH—See WEST PALM BEACH, FL (Comcast Cable)

Cable Community Index—Florida

LAKE YALE ESTATES—See MARION COUNTY (southern portion), FL (Florida Fiber Networks)

LAKELAND—See HILLSBOROUGH COUNTY (portions), FL (Bright House Networks)

LAKEPORT—See WEST PALM BEACH, FL (Comcast Cable)

LANARK VILLAGE—See EASTPOINT, FL (Mediacom)

LAND O' LAKES—See HILLSBOROUGH COUNTY (portions), FL (Bright House Networks)

LANTANA—See WEST PALM BEACH, FL (Comcast Cable)

LARGO—See HILLSBOROUGH COUNTY (portions), FL (Bright House Networks)

LARGO—See PINELLAS COUNTY (portions), FL (WOW! Internet, Cable & Phone)

LAUDERDALE LAKES—See MIAMI, FL (AT&T U-verse. This is the regional video hub for the MIAMI area)

LAUDERDALE LAKES—See WEST PALM BEACH, FL (Comcast Cable)

LAUDERDALE-BY-THE-SEA—See MIAMI, FL (AT&T U-verse. This is the regional video hub for the MIAMI area)

LAUDERDALE-BY-THE-SEA—See WEST PALM BEACH, FL (Comcast Cable)

LAUDERHILL—See MIAMI, FL (AT&T U-verse. This is the regional video hub for the MIAMI area)

LAUDERHILL—See WEST PALM BEACH, FL (Comcast Cable)

LAWTEY—Florida Fiber Networks

LAYTON—See WEST PALM BEACH, FL (Comcast Cable)

LAZY LAKE—See MIAMI, FL (AT&T U-verse. This is the regional video hub for the MIAMI area)

LAZY LAKE—See WEST PALM BEACH, FL (Comcast Cable)

LEE—Formerly served by KLiP Interactive. No longer in operation

LEESBURG (village)—Comcast Cable. Now served by ARCHER, FL [FL0189]

LEESBURG (VILLAGE)—See ARCHER, FL (Comcast Cable)

LEESBURG LAKESHORE MOBILE HOME PARK—Formerly served by Leesburg Lakeshore Mobile Home Park Inc. No longer in operation

LEHIGH ACRES—Comcast Cable. Now served by SARASOTA, FL [FL0017]

LEHIGH ACRES—See SARASOTA, FL (Comcast Cable)

LEISURE CITY—See MIAMI, FL (AT&T U-verse. This is the regional video hub for the MIAMI area)

LEON COUNTY (PORTIONS)—See TALLAHASSEE, FL (Comcast Cable)

LEVY COUNTY (PORTIONS)—See ARCHER, FL (Comcast Cable)

LEVY COUNTY—See BRONSON (town), FL (Florida Fiber Networks)

LIBERTY COUNTY—See BLOUNTSTOWN, FL (Bright House Networks)

LIGHTHOUSE POINT—See MIAMI, FL (AT&T U-verse. This is the regional video hub for the MIAMI area)

LIGHTHOUSE POINT—See WEST PALM BEACH, FL (Comcast Cable)

LITTLE TORCH KEY—Comcast Cable. Now served by WEST PALM BEACH, FL [FL0008]

LITTLE TORCH KEY—See WEST PALM BEACH, FL (Comcast Cable)

LIVE OAK—Comcast Cable. Now served by JACKSONVILLE, FL [FL0002]

LIVE OAK—Formerly served by Florida Cable. No longer in operation

LIVE OAK—Formerly served by KLiP Interactive. No longer in operation

LIVE OAK—See JACKSONVILLE, FL (Comcast Cable)

LOCKHART—See DE FUNIAK SPRINGS, AL (Bright House Networks)

LONGBOAT KEY—See SARASOTA, FL (Comcast Cable)

LONGWOOD—See ORLANDO, FL (Bright House Networks)

LYNN HAVEN—See TALLAHASSEE, FL (Comcast Cable)

LYNN HAVEN—See PANAMA CITY BEACH, FL (WOW! Internet, Cable & Phone)

MACCLENNY—Comcast Cable. Now served by JACKSONVILLE, FL [FL0002]

MACCLENNY—See JACKSONVILLE, FL (Comcast Cable)

MACDILL AFB—See HILLSBOROUGH COUNTY (portions), FL (Bright House Networks)

MADEIRA BEACH—See HILLSBOROUGH COUNTY (portions), FL (Bright House Networks)

MADISON COUNTY (PORTIONS)—See TALLAHASSEE, FL (Comcast Cable)

MADISON—Comcast Cable. Now served by TALLAHASSEE, FL [FL0283]

MADISON—See TALLAHASSEE, FL (Comcast Cable)

MADRID—See TALLAHASSEE, AL (Comcast Cable)

MAITLAND—See ORLANDO, FL (Bright House Networks)

MALABAR—See ORLANDO, FL (Bright House Networks)

MALONE—See TALLAHASSEE, FL (Comcast Cable)

MANALAPAN—See WEST PALM BEACH, FL (Comcast Cable)

MANATEE COUNTY (PORTIONS)—See SARASOTA, FL (Comcast Cable)

MANATEE COUNTY—See HILLSBOROUGH COUNTY (portions), FL (Bright House Networks)

MANGONIA PARK—See WEST PALM BEACH, FL (Comcast Cable)

MARATHON SHORES—See WEST PALM BEACH, FL (Comcast Cable)

MARATHON—See MIAMI, FL (AT&T U-verse. This is the regional video hub for the MIAMI area)

MARATHON—See WEST PALM BEACH, FL (Comcast Cable)

MARCO ISLAND—See SARASOTA, FL (Comcast Cable)

MARCO ISLAND—Marco Island Cable Inc

MARGATE—Comcast Cable. Now served by WEST PALM BEACH, FL [FL0008]

MARGATE—See MIAMI, FL (AT&T U-verse. This is the regional video hub for the MIAMI area)

MARGATE—See WEST PALM BEACH, FL (Comcast Cable)

MARIANNA—Comcast Cable. Now served by TALLAHASSEE, FL [FL0283]

MARIANNA—See TALLAHASSEE, FL (Comcast Cable)

MARION COUNTY (NORTHERN PORTION)—See CITRA, FL (Florida Fiber Networks)

MARION COUNTY (PORTIONS)—See ORLANDO, FL (Bright House Networks)

MARION COUNTY (PORTIONS)—See GAINESVILLE, FL (Cox Communications)

MARION COUNTY (PORTIONS)—See ORANGE SPRINGS, FL (Florida Fiber Networks)

MARION COUNTY (SOUTHERN PORTION)—Florida Fiber Networks

MARION COUNTY (SOUTHWESTERN PORTION)—See MARION COUNTY (unincorporated areas), FL (Cablevision of Marion County)

MARION COUNTY (SOUTHWESTERN PORTION)—See ARCHER, FL (Comcast Cable)

MARION COUNTY (UNINCORPORATED AREAS)—Cablevision of Marion County

MARION OAKS—See ORLANDO, FL (Bright House Networks)

MARTIN COUNTY (PORTIONS)—See WEST PALM BEACH, FL (Comcast Cable)

MARY ESTHER—See PENSACOLA, FL (Cox Communications)

MASCOTTE—See ORLANDO, FL (Bright House Networks)

MAXVILLE—See JACKSONVILLE BEACH, FL (AT&T U-verse. Formerly [FL0358]. This cable system has converted to IPTV. This is the regional video hub for the JACKSONVILLE BEACH area)

MAYO—Comcast Cable. Now served by JACKSONVILLE, FL [FL0002]

MAYO—See JACKSONVILLE, FL (Comcast Cable)

MAYPORT NAVAL AIR STATION—See JACKSONVILLE, FL (Comcast Cable)

MEDLEY—See MIAMI, FL (AT&T U-verse. This is the regional video hub for the MIAMI area)

MEDLEY—See WEST PALM BEACH, FL (Comcast Cable)

MELBOURNE BEACH—See ORLANDO, FL (Bright House Networks)

MELBOURNE VILLAGE—See ORLANDO, FL (Bright House Networks)

MELBOURNE—Bright House Networks. Now served by ORLANDO, FL [FL0001]

MELBOURNE—Formerly served by Wireless Broadcasting of Melbourne. No longer in operation

MELBOURNE—See ORLANDO, FL (Bright House Networks)

MEXICO BEACH—Mediacom. Now served by WALTON COUNTY (portions), FL [FL0159]

MEXICO BEACH—See WALTON COUNTY (portions), FL (Mediacom)

MIAMI (portions)—Formerly served by Bright House Networks. No longer in operation

MIAMI BEACH—See MIAMI, FL (AT&T U-verse. This is the regional video hub for the MIAMI area)

MIAMI BEACH—Atlantic Broadband

MIAMI GARDENS (BROWARD COUNTY)—See MIAMI, FL (AT&T U-verse. This is the regional video hub for the MIAMI area)

MIAMI GARDENS (MIAMI-DADE COUNTY)—See MIAMI, FL (AT&T U-verse. This is the regional video hub for the MIAMI area)

MIAMI LAKES—See MIAMI, FL (AT&T U-verse. This is the regional video hub for the MIAMI area)

MIAMI SHORES—See MIAMI, FL (AT&T U-verse. This is the regional video hub for the MIAMI area)

MIAMI SHORES—See WEST PALM BEACH, FL (Comcast Cable)

MIAMI SPRINGS—See MIAMI, FL (AT&T U-verse. This is the regional video hub for the MIAMI area)

Florida—Cable Community Index

MIAMI SPRINGS—See WEST PALM BEACH, FL (Comcast Cable)

MIAMI/DADE COUNTY—AT&T U-verse. This cable system has converted to IPTV. See MIAMI, FL [FL5430]

MIAMI-DADE COUNTY (UNINCORPORATED AREAS)—See MIAMI, FL (AT&T U-verse. This is the regional video hub for the MIAMI area)

MIAMI—Comcast Cable. Now served by WEST PALM BEACH, FL [FL0008]

MIAMI—Comcast Cable. Now served by WEST PALM BEACH, FL [FL0008]

MIAMI—AT&T U-verse. This is the regional video hub for the MIAMI area

MIAMI—See WEST PALM BEACH, FL (Comcast Cable)

MICANOPY (town)—Formerly served by CommuniComm Services. No longer in operation

MICCO—See WEST PALM BEACH, FL (Comcast Cable)

MIDDLEBURG—See JACKSONVILLE BEACH, FL (AT&T U-verse. Formerly [FL0358]. This cable system has converted to IPTV. This is the regional video hub for the JACKSONVILLE BEACH area)

MIDDLEBURG—See CLAY COUNTY (portions), FL (Florida Fiber Networks)

MIDWAY—Comcast Cablevision of Tallahassee Inc. Now served by TALLAHASSEE, FL [FL0283]

MIDWAY—See TALLAHASSEE, FL (Comcast Cable)

MILTON—Mediacom. Now served by GULF BREEZE, FL [FL0070]

MILTON—See GULF BREEZE, FL (Mediacom)

MIMS—Comcast Cable. Now served by WEST PALM BEACH, FL [FL0008]

MIMS—See WEST PALM BEACH, FL (Comcast Cable)

MINNEOLA—See ORLANDO, FL (Bright House Networks)

MIRAMAR—See MIAMI, FL (AT&T U-verse. This is the regional video hub for the MIAMI area)

MIRAMAR—See WEST PALM BEACH, FL (Comcast Cable)

MONROE COUNTY (UNINCORPORATED AREAS)—See MIAMI, FL (AT&T U-verse. This is the regional video hub for the MIAMI area)

MONT VERDE—See ARCHER, FL (Comcast Cable)

MONTICELLO—Comcast Cable

MOORE HAVEN—Comcast Cable. Now served by WEST PALM BEACH, FL [FL0008]

MOORE HAVEN—See WEST PALM BEACH, FL (Comcast Cable)

MOUNT DORA—See ORLANDO, FL (Bright House Networks)

MOUNT DORA—See ARCHER, FL (Comcast Cable)

MOUNT PLYMOUTH—See ARCHER, FL (Comcast Cable)

MULBERRY—See HILLSBOROUGH COUNTY (portions), FL (Bright House Networks)

MURDOCK—See SARASOTA, FL (Comcast Cable)

NAHUNTA—See JACKSONVILLE, GA (Comcast Cable)

NAPLES (town)—Comcast Cable. Now served by SARASOTA, FL [FL0017]

NAPLES (town)—Comcast Cable. Now served by SARASOTA, FL [FL0017]

NAPLES—See SARASOTA, FL (Comcast Cable)

NAPLES—See MARCO ISLAND, FL (Marco Island Cable Inc)

NARANJA—See MIAMI, FL (AT&T U-verse. This is the regional video hub for the MIAMI area)

NASSAU COUNTY (PORTIONS)—See JACKSONVILLE, FL (Comcast Cable)

NASSAU COUNTY (UNINCORPORATED AREAS)—See JACKSONVILLE BEACH, FL (AT&T U-verse. Formerly [FL0358]. This cable system has converted to IPTV. This is the regional video hub for the JACKSONVILLE BEACH area)

NAVARRE BEACH—See GULF BREEZE, FL (Mediacom)

NEPTUNE BEACH—See JACKSONVILLE BEACH, FL (AT&T U-verse. Formerly [FL0358]. This cable system has converted to IPTV. This is the regional video hub for the JACKSONVILLE BEACH area)

NEPTUNE BEACH—See JACKSONVILLE, FL (Comcast Cable)

NEW PORT RICHEY—See HILLSBOROUGH COUNTY (portions), FL (Bright House Networks)

NEW SMYRNA—See ORLANDO, FL (Bright House Networks)

NEWBERRY—Cox Communications. Now served by GAINESVILLE, FL [FL0027]

NEWBERRY—See GAINESVILLE, FL (Cox Communications)

NEWVILLE—See TALLAHASSEE, AL (Comcast Cable)

NICEVILLE—See PENSACOLA, FL (Cox Communications)

NOBLETON—See HERNANDO COUNTY, FL (Florida Fiber Networks)

NOMA—See TALLAHASSEE, FL (Comcast Cable)

NORLAND—See MIAMI, FL (AT&T U-verse. This is the regional video hub for the MIAMI area)

NORMANDY—See MIAMI, FL (AT&T U-verse. This is the regional video hub for the MIAMI area)

NORTH BAY VILLAGE—See MIAMI, FL (AT&T U-verse. This is the regional video hub for the MIAMI area)

NORTH BAY VILLAGE—See MIAMI BEACH, FL (Atlantic Broadband)

NORTH DADE COUNTY—Formerly served by Comcast Cable. No longer in operation

NORTH FORT MYERS—See SARASOTA, FL (Comcast Cable)

NORTH KEY LARGO—See MIAMI, FL (AT&T U-verse. This is the regional video hub for the MIAMI area)

NORTH LAUDERDALE—See MIAMI, FL (AT&T U-verse. This is the regional video hub for the MIAMI area)

NORTH LAUDERDALE—See WEST PALM BEACH, FL (Comcast Cable)

NORTH MIAMI BEACH—See MIAMI, FL (AT&T U-verse. This is the regional video hub for the MIAMI area)

NORTH MIAMI BEACH—See WEST PALM BEACH, FL (Comcast Cable)

NORTH MIAMI—See MIAMI, FL (AT&T U-verse. This is the regional video hub for the MIAMI area)

NORTH MIAMI—See WEST PALM BEACH, FL (Comcast Cable)

NORTH OLD TOWN—Florida Fiber Networks

NORTH PALM BEACH—See WEST PALM BEACH, FL (Comcast Cable)

NORTH PORT—See SARASOTA, FL (Comcast Cable)

NORTH REDINGTON BEACH—See HILLSBOROUGH COUNTY (portions), FL (Bright House Networks)

NORTHSIDE—See JACKSONVILLE BEACH, FL (AT&T U-verse. Formerly [FL0358]. This cable system has converted to IPTV. This is the regional video hub for the JACKSONVILLE BEACH area)

OAK HILL—See ORLANDO, FL (Bright House Networks)

OAKLAND PARK—See MIAMI, FL (AT&T U-verse. This is the regional video hub for the MIAMI area)

OAKLAND PARK—See WEST PALM BEACH, FL (Comcast Cable)

OAKLAND—See ORLANDO, FL (Bright House Networks)

OCALA/OAK RUN—Oak Run Associates LTD

OCALA—Cox Cable Greater Ocala. Now served by GAINESVILLE, FL [FL0027]

OCALA—See GAINESVILLE, FL (Cox Communications)

OCEAN BREEZE PARK—See WEST PALM BEACH, FL (Comcast Cable)

OCEAN REEF CLUB—See WEST PALM BEACH, FL (Comcast Cable)

OCEAN RIDGE—See WEST PALM BEACH, FL (Comcast Cable)

OCEANWAY—See JACKSONVILLE BEACH, FL (AT&T U-verse. Formerly [FL0358]. This cable system has converted to IPTV. This is the regional video hub for the JACKSONVILLE BEACH area)

OCOEE—See ORLANDO, FL (Bright House Networks)

OJUS—See MIAMI, FL (AT&T U-verse. This is the regional video hub for the MIAMI area)

OKALOOSA COUNTY (PORTIONS)—See PENSACOLA, FL (Cox Communications)

OKALOOSA ISLAND—See PENSACOLA, FL (Cox Communications)

OKEECHOBEE COUNTY (PORTIONS)—See WEST PALM BEACH, FL (Comcast Cable)

OKEECHOBEE—Comcast Cable. Now served by WEST PALM BEACH, FL [FL0008]

OKEECHOBEE—See WEST PALM BEACH, FL (Comcast Cable)

OLD TOWN—See FANNING SPRINGS, FL (Florida Fiber Networks)

OLDSMAR—See HILLSBOROUGH COUNTY (portions), FL (Bright House Networks)

OLDSMAR—See PINELLAS COUNTY (portions), FL (WOW! Internet, Cable & Phone)

OLYMPIA HEIGHTS—See MIAMI, FL (AT&T U-verse. This is the regional video hub for the MIAMI area)

OPA LOCKA—See MIAMI, FL (AT&T U-verse. This is the regional video hub for the MIAMI area)

OPA-LOCKA—See WEST PALM BEACH, FL (Comcast Cable)

ORANGE CITY—See ORLANDO, FL (Bright House Networks)

ORANGE COUNTY (unincorporated areas)—Comcast Cable. Now served by ARCHER, FL [FL0189]

ORANGE COUNTY (UNINCORPORATED AREAS)—See ARCHER, FL (Comcast Cable)

ORANGE COUNTY—See ORLANDO, FL (Bright House Networks)

ORANGE LAKE—Formerly served by Altitude Communications. No longer in operation

ORANGE PARK—Comcast Cable. Now served by JACKSONVILLE, FL [FL0002]

ORANGE PARK—See JACKSONVILLE BEACH, FL (AT&T U-verse. Formerly [FL0358]. This cable system has converted to IPTV. This is the regional video hub for the JACKSONVILLE

Cable Community Index—Florida

BEACH area)

ORANGE PARK—See JACKSONVILLE, FL (Comcast Cable)

ORANGE SPRINGS—Florida Fiber Networks

ORCHID—See WEST PALM BEACH, FL (Comcast Cable)

ORLANDO—Bright House Networks. Now served by ORLANDO, FL [FL0001]

ORLANDO—Bright House Networks

ORMOND BEACH—See ORLANDO, FL (Bright House Networks)

ORTONA—Formerly served by Comcast Cable. No longer in operation

OSCEOLA COUNTY (portions)—Comcast Cable. Now served by ARCHER, FL [FL0189]

OSCEOLA COUNTY (PORTIONS)—See ARCHER, FL (Comcast Cable)

OSCEOLA COUNTY (western portion)—Comcast Cable. Now served by ARCHER, FL [FL0189]

OSCEOLA COUNTY—See ORLANDO, FL (Bright House Networks)

OVIEDO—See ORLANDO, FL (Bright House Networks)

OZELLO—Formerly served by KLiP Interactive. No longer in operation

PACE—See GULF BREEZE, FL (Mediacom)

PAHOKEE—See WEST PALM BEACH, FL (Comcast Cable)

PAISLEY—Florida Fiber Networks

PALATKA—Comcast Cable. Now served by JACKSONVILLE, FL [FL0002]

PALATKA—See JACKSONVILLE BEACH, FL (AT&T U-verse. Formerly [FL0358]. This cable system has converted to IPTV. This is the regional video hub for the JACKSONVILLE BEACH area)

PALATKA—See JACKSONVILLE, FL (Comcast Cable)

PALATKA—See PUTNAM COUNTY (eastern portion), FL (Florida Fiber Networks)

PALM BAY—Comcast Cable. Now served by WEST PALM BEACH, FL [FL0008]

PALM BAY—See ORLANDO, FL (Bright House Networks)

PALM BAY—See WEST PALM BEACH, FL (Comcast Cable)

PALM BEACH (TOWN)—See WEST PALM BEACH, FL (Comcast Cable)

PALM BEACH CITY—See WEST PALM BEACH, FL (Comcast Cable)

PALM BEACH COUNTY (portions)—Comcast Cable. Now served by WEST PALM BEACH, FL [FL0008]

PALM BEACH COUNTY (PORTIONS)—See WEST PALM BEACH, FL (Comcast Cable)

PALM BEACH COUNTY (southeastern portion)—Comcast Cable. Now served by WEST PALM BEACH, FL [FL0008]

PALM BEACH GARDENS—Comcast Cable. Now served by WEST PALM BEACH, FL [FL0008]

PALM BEACH GARDENS—See WEST PALM BEACH, FL (Comcast Cable)

PALM BEACH SHORES—See WEST PALM BEACH, FL (Comcast Cable)

PALM CAY—Cablevision of Marion County. Now served by MARION COUNTY (unincorporated areas), FL [FL0368]

PALM CAY—See MARION COUNTY (unincorporated areas), FL (Cablevision of Marion County)

PALM CHASE—Formerly served by Comcast Cable. No longer in operation

PALM CITY—See WEST PALM BEACH, FL (Comcast Cable)

PALM COAST—Bright House Networks. Now served by ORLANDO, FL [FL0001]

PALM COAST—See ORLANDO, FL (Bright House Networks)

PALM SHORES MOBILE HOME PARK—See MARION COUNTY (southern portion), FL (Florida Fiber Networks)

PALM SHORES—See ORLANDO, FL (Bright House Networks)

PALM SPRINGS NORTH—See MIAMI, FL (AT&T U-verse. This is the regional video hub for the MIAMI area)

PALM SPRINGS—Comcast Cable. Now served by WEST PALM BEACH, FL [FL0008]

PALM SPRINGS—See WEST PALM BEACH, FL (Comcast Cable)

PALM VALLEY—See JACKSONVILLE BEACH, FL (AT&T U-verse. Formerly [FL0358]. This cable system has converted to IPTV. This is the regional video hub for the JACKSONVILLE BEACH area)

PALMETTO BAY—See MIAMI, FL (AT&T U-verse. This is the regional video hub for the MIAMI area)

PALMETTO BAY—See WEST PALM BEACH, FL (Comcast Cable)

PALMETTO—See HILLSBOROUGH COUNTY (portions), FL (Bright House Networks)

PANAMA CITY (PORTIONS)—See WALTON COUNTY (portions), FL (Mediacom)

PANAMA CITY BEACH—Comcast Cable. Now served by TALLAHASSEE, FL [FL0283]

PANAMA CITY BEACH—See TALLAHASSEE, FL (Comcast Cable)

PANAMA CITY BEACH—WOW! Internet, Cable & Phone

PANAMA CITY—Comcast Cable. Now served by TALLAHASSEE, FL [FL0283]

PANAMA CITY—See TALLAHASSEE, FL (Comcast Cable)

PANAMA CITY—See PANAMA CITY BEACH, FL (WOW! Internet, Cable & Phone)

PARKER—See TALLAHASSEE, FL (Comcast Cable)

PARKER—See PANAMA CITY BEACH, FL (WOW! Internet, Cable & Phone)

PARKLAND—See MIAMI, FL (AT&T U-verse. This is the regional video hub for the MIAMI area)

PARKLAND—See WEST PALM BEACH, FL (Comcast Cable)

PASCO COUNTY (central & eastern portions)—Bright House Networks. Now served by HILLSBOROUGH COUNTY (portions), FL [FL0003]

PASCO COUNTY (PORTIONS)—See HILLSBOROUGH COUNTY (portions), FL (Bright House Networks)

PASCO COUNTY (western portion)—Bright House Networks. Now served by HILLSBOROUGH COUNTY (portions), FL [FL0003]

PATRICK AFB—See ORLANDO, FL (Bright House Networks)

PAXTON—See DE FUNIAK SPRINGS, FL (Bright House Networks)

PEDRO—Cablevision of Marion County. Now served by MARION COUNTY (unincorporated areas), FL [FL0368]

PEDRO—See MARION COUNTY (unincorporated areas), FL (Cablevision of Marion County)

PEMBROKE PARK—See MIAMI, FL (AT&T U-verse. This is the regional video hub for the MIAMI area)

PEMBROKE PARK—See WEST PALM BEACH, FL (Comcast Cable)

PEMBROKE PINES—Comcast Cable. Now served by WEST PALM BEACH, FL [FL0008]

PEMBROKE PINES—See MIAMI, FL (AT&T U-verse. This is the regional video hub for the MIAMI area)

PEMBROKE PINES—See WEST PALM BEACH, FL (Comcast Cable)

PEMBROKE—See WEST PALM BEACH, FL (Comcast Cable)

PENNBROOKE—See ORLANDO, FL (Bright House Networks)

PENNEY FARMS—See JACKSONVILLE BEACH, FL (AT&T U-verse. Formerly [FL0358]. This cable system has converted to IPTV. This is the regional video hub for the JACKSONVILLE BEACH area)

PENNEY FARMS—Florida Fiber Networks

PENSACOLA BEACH—See GULF BREEZE, FL (Mediacom)

PENSACOLA—Cox Communications

PERRINE—See MIAMI, FL (AT&T U-verse. This is the regional video hub for the MIAMI area)

PERRY—Comcast Cable. Now served by TALLAHASSEE, FL [FL0283]

PERRY—See TALLAHASSEE, FL (Comcast Cable)

PIERSON—See ASTOR, FL (Florida Fiber Networks)

PINE ISLAND—See SARASOTA, FL (Comcast Cable)

PINE RUN—See OCALA/OAK RUN, FL (Oak Run Associates LTD)

PINECREST (MIAMI-DADE COUNTY)—See MIAMI, FL (AT&T U-verse. This is the regional video hub for the MIAMI area)

PINECREST (PORTIONS)—See MIAMI BEACH, FL (Atlantic Broadband)

PINECREST—See WEST PALM BEACH, FL (Comcast Cable)

PINELLAS COUNTY (portions)—Bright House Networks. Now served by HILLSBOROUGH COUNTY (portions), FL [FL0003]

PINELLAS COUNTY (PORTIONS)—See HILLSBOROUGH COUNTY (portions), FL (Bright House Networks)

PINELLAS COUNTY (PORTIONS)—WOW! Internet, Cable & Phone

PINELLAS PARK—See HILLSBOROUGH COUNTY (portions), FL (Bright House Networks)

PLANT CITY—See HILLSBOROUGH COUNTY (portions), FL (Bright House Networks)

PLANTATION (BROWARD COUNTY)—See WEST PALM BEACH, FL (Comcast Cable)

PLANTATION (SARASOTA COUNTY)—See SARASOTA, FL (Comcast Cable)

PLANTATION—See MIAMI, FL (AT&T U-verse. This is the regional video hub for the MIAMI area)

POINCIANA—See ORLANDO, FL (Bright House Networks)

POLK CITY—See HILLSBOROUGH COUNTY (portions), FL (Bright House Networks)

POLK COUNTY (portions)—Formerly served by People's Wireless Cable. No longer in operation

POLK COUNTY (PORTIONS)—See HILLSBOROUGH COUNTY (portions), FL (Bright House Networks)

POLK COUNTY (PORTIONS)—See ORLANDO, FL (Bright House Networks)

Florida—Cable Community Index

POLK COUNTY (PORTIONS)—See ARCHER, FL (Comcast Cable)

POMONA PARK—See JACKSONVILLE BEACH, FL (AT&T U-verse. Formerly [FL0358]. This cable system has converted to IPTV. This is the regional video hub for the JACKSONVILLE BEACH area)

POMONA PARK—See JACKSONVILLE, FL (Comcast Cable)

POMPANO BEACH—See MIAMI, FL (AT&T U-verse. This is the regional video hub for the MIAMI area)

POMPANO BEACH—See WEST PALM BEACH, FL (Comcast Cable)

PONCE INLET—See ORLANDO, FL (Bright House Networks)

PONTE VEDRA BEACH—See JACKSONVILLE BEACH, FL (AT&T U-verse. Formerly [FL0358]. This cable system has converted to IPTV. This is the regional video hub for the JACKSONVILLE BEACH area)

PORT CHARLOTTE—Comcast Cable. Now served by SARASOTA, FL [FL0017]

PORT CHARLOTTE—See SARASOTA, FL (Comcast Cable)

PORT ORANGE—See ORLANDO, FL (Bright House Networks)

PORT RICHEY—See HILLSBOROUGH COUNTY (portions), FL (Bright House Networks)

PORT ST. JOE—Mediacom. Now served by EASTPOINT, FL [FL0180]

PORT ST. JOE—See EASTPOINT, FL (Mediacom)

PORT ST. LUCIE—See WEST PALM BEACH, FL (Comcast Cable)

PRINCETON—See MIAMI, FL (AT&T U-verse. This is the regional video hub for the MIAMI area)

PUNTA GORDA—See SARASOTA, FL (Comcast Cable)

PUTNAM COUNTY (EASTERN PORTION)—Florida Fiber Networks

PUTNAM COUNTY (PORTIONS)—See JACKSONVILLE, FL (Comcast Cable)

PUTNAM COUNTY (UNINCORPORATED AREAS)—See JACKSONVILLE BEACH, FL (AT&T U-verse. Formerly [FL0358]. This cable system has converted to IPTV. This is the regional video hub for the JACKSONVILLE BEACH area)

PUTNAM COUNTY (WESTERN PORTION)—Florida Fiber Networks

PUTNAM COUNTY—Formerly served by Florida Cable. No longer in operation

QUINCY—Comcast Cable. Now served by TALLAHASSEE, FL [FL0283]

QUINCY—See TALLAHASSEE, FL (Comcast Cable)

QUITMAN—See TALLAHASSEE, GA (Comcast Cable)

RAIFORD—See LAWTEY, FL (Florida Fiber Networks)

REDINGTON SHORES—See HILLSBOROUGH COUNTY (portions), FL (Bright House Networks)

RICHMOND HEIGHTS—See MIAMI, FL (AT&T U-verse. This is the regional video hub for the MIAMI area)

RIVER RANCH—SAT STAR Communications

RIVERVIEW—See HILLSBOROUGH COUNTY (portions), FL (Bright House Networks)

RIVIERA BEACH—See WEST PALM BEACH, FL (Comcast Cable)

ROCKLEDGE—See ORLANDO, FL (Bright House Networks)

ROSELAND—See WEST PALM BEACH, FL (Comcast Cable)

ROYAL PALM BEACH—See WEST PALM BEACH, FL (Comcast Cable)

RUSKIN—See HILLSBOROUGH COUNTY (portions), FL (Bright House Networks)

SAFETY HARBOR—See HILLSBOROUGH COUNTY (portions), FL (Bright House Networks)

SAFETY HARBOR—See PINELLAS COUNTY (portions), FL (WOW! Internet, Cable & Phone)

SAMSON—See CHIPLEY, AL (Bright House Networks)

SAMSULA—Formerly served by Consolidated Cablevision. No longer in operation

SAN ANTONIO—See HILLSBOROUGH COUNTY (portions), FL (Bright House Networks)

SAN JOSE—See JACKSONVILLE BEACH, FL (AT&T U-verse. Formerly [FL0358]. This cable system has converted to IPTV. This is the regional video hub for the JACKSONVILLE BEACH area)

SAN MARCO—See JACKSONVILLE BEACH, FL (AT&T U-verse. Formerly [FL0358]. This cable system has converted to IPTV. This is the regional video hub for the JACKSONVILLE BEACH area)

SAN PABLO—See JACKSONVILLE BEACH, FL (AT&T U-verse. Formerly [FL0358]. This cable system has converted to IPTV. This is the regional video hub for the JACKSONVILLE BEACH area)

SAND-N-SEA—Formerly served by Formerly served by Comcast Cable. No longer in operation

SANDESTIN BEACH RESORT—Mediacom. Now served by WALTON COUNTY (portions), FL [FL0159]

SANDESTIN BEACH RESORT—See WALTON COUNTY (portions), FL (Mediacom)

SANDPIPER MOBILE HOME PARK—See MARION COUNTY (southern portion), FL (Florida Fiber Networks)

SANFORD—See ORLANDO, FL (Bright House Networks)

SANIBEL ISLAND—See SARASOTA, FL (Comcast Cable)

SANTA ROSA COUNTY (PORTIONS)—See GULF BREEZE, FL (Mediacom)

SANTA ROSA—See CANTONMENT, FL (Bright House Networks)

SARALAKE ESTATES MOBILE HOME PARK—Formerly served by Nalman Electronics. No longer in operation

SARASOTA COUNTY (PORTIONS)—See SARASOTA, FL (Comcast Cable)

SARASOTA—Comcast Cable

SATELLITE BEACH—See ORLANDO, FL (Bright House Networks)

SAWGRASS—See JACKSONVILLE BEACH, FL (AT&T U-verse. Formerly [FL0358]. This cable system has converted to IPTV. This is the regional video hub for the JACKSONVILLE BEACH area)

SEA RANCH LAKES—See MIAMI, FL (AT&T U-verse. This is the regional video hub for the MIAMI area)

SEA RANCH LAKES—See WEST PALM BEACH, FL (Comcast Cable)

SEBASTIAN—Comcast Cable. Now served by WEST PALM BEACH, FL [FL0008]

SEBASTIAN—See WEST PALM BEACH, FL (Comcast Cable)

SEBRING (village)—Comcast Cable. Now served by SARASOTA, FL [FL0017]

SEBRING (VILLAGE)—See SARASOTA, FL (Comcast Cable)

SEMINOLE COUNTY—See ORLANDO, FL (Bright House Networks)

SEMINOLE—See HILLSBOROUGH COUNTY (portions), FL (Bright House Networks)

SEMINOLE—See PINELLAS COUNTY (portions), FL (WOW! Internet, Cable & Phone)

SEWALL'S POINT—See WEST PALM BEACH, FL (Comcast Cable)

SHALIMAR—See PENSACOLA, FL (Cox Communications)

SHARPES FERRY—Florida Fiber Networks

SILVER SPRINGS SHORES—Formerly served by Comcast Cable. No longer in operation

SLOCOMB—See CHIPLEY, AL (Bright House Networks)

SMITH LAKE SHORES MOBILE HOME PARK—Formerly served by Florida Cable. No longer in operation

SNAPPER CREEK—See MIAMI, FL (AT&T U-verse. This is the regional video hub for the MIAMI area)

SNEADS—See TALLAHASSEE, FL (Comcast Cable)

SNUG HARBOR VILLAGE—See ORLANDO, FL (Bright House Networks)

SOPCHOPPY—See TALLAHASSEE, FL (Comcast Cable)

SORRENTO—See ARCHER, FL (Comcast Cable)

SORRENTO—See ASTOR, FL (Florida Fiber Networks)

SOUTH BAY—See WEST PALM BEACH, FL (Comcast Cable)

SOUTH BROWARD COUNTY—Formerly served by Comcast Cable. No longer in operation

SOUTH DAYTONA—See ORLANDO, FL (Bright House Networks)

SOUTH MIAMI HEIGHTS—See MIAMI, FL (AT&T U-verse. This is the regional video hub for the MIAMI area)

SOUTH MIAMI—See MIAMI, FL (AT&T U-verse. This is the regional video hub for the MIAMI area)

SOUTH MIAMI—See MIAMI BEACH, FL (Atlantic Broadband)

SOUTH PALM BEACH—See WEST PALM BEACH, FL (Comcast Cable)

SOUTH PASADENA—See HILLSBOROUGH COUNTY (portions), FL (Bright House Networks)

SOUTHGATE—See ORLANDO, FL (Bright House Networks)

SOUTHPORT—Mediacom. Now served by WALTON COUNTY (portions), FL [FL0159]

SOUTHPORT—See WALTON COUNTY (portions), FL (Mediacom)

SOUTHWEST RANCHES—See MIAMI, FL (AT&T U-verse. This is the regional video hub for the MIAMI area)

SOUTHWEST RANCHES—See WEST PALM BEACH, FL (Comcast Cable)

SPARR—See CITRA, FL (Florida Fiber Networks)

SPRING LAKE—Comcast Cable. Now served by WAUCHULA, FL [FL0288]

SPRING LAKE—See WAUCHULA, FL (Comcast Cable)

SPRINGFIELD—Formerly served by FiberCast Cable. No longer in operation

SPRINGFIELD—See TALLAHASSEE, FL (Comcast Cable)

SPRINGFIELD—See PANAMA CITY BEACH, FL (WOW! Internet, Cable & Phone)

SPRUCE CREEK NORTH—Formerly served by Galaxy Cablevision. No longer in operation

Cable Community Index—Florida

SPRUCE CREEK—See MARION COUNTY (unincorporated areas), FL (Cablevision of Marion County)

ST. AUGUSTINE BEACH—See JACKSONVILLE BEACH, FL (AT&T U-verse. Formerly [FL0358]. This cable system has converted to IPTV. This is the regional video hub for the JACKSONVILLE BEACH area)

ST. AUGUSTINE BEACH—See JACKSONVILLE, FL (Comcast Cable)

ST. AUGUSTINE—Comcast Cable. Now served by JACKSONVILLE, FL [FL0002]

ST. AUGUSTINE—See JACKSONVILLE BEACH, FL (AT&T U-verse. Formerly [FL0358]. This cable system has converted to IPTV. This is the regional video hub for the JACKSONVILLE BEACH area)

ST. AUGUSTINE—See JACKSONVILLE, FL (Comcast Cable)

ST. CLOUD—See ORLANDO, FL (Bright House Networks)

ST. GEORGE ISLAND—See EASTPOINT, FL (Mediacom)

ST. GEORGE ISLAND—St. George Cable Inc

ST. JOHNS COUNTY (PORTIONS)—See JACKSONVILLE, FL (Comcast Cable)

ST. JOHNS COUNTY (UNINCORPORATED AREAS)—See JACKSONVILLE BEACH, FL (AT&T U-verse. Formerly [FL0358]. This cable system has converted to IPTV. This is the regional video hub for the JACKSONVILLE BEACH area)

ST. LEO—See HILLSBOROUGH COUNTY (portions), FL (Bright House Networks)

ST. LUCIE COUNTY (PORTIONS)—See WEST PALM BEACH, FL (Comcast Cable)

ST. LUCIE VILLAGE—See WEST PALM BEACH, FL (Comcast Cable)

ST. LUCIE WEST—See WEST PALM BEACH, FL (Comcast Cable)

ST. MARK'S—See TALLAHASSEE, FL (Comcast Cable)

ST. MARY'S—See JACKSONVILLE, GA (Comcast Cable)

ST. PETERSBURG BEACH—See HILLSBOROUGH COUNTY (portions), FL (Bright House Networks)

ST. PETERSBURG—See HILLSBOROUGH COUNTY (portions), FL (Bright House Networks)

ST. PETERSBURG—See PINELLAS COUNTY (portions), FL (WOW! Internet, Cable & Phone)

ST. SIMONS ISLAND—See JACKSONVILLE BEACH, GA (AT&T U-verse. Formerly [FL0358]. This cable system has converted to IPTV. This is the regional video hub for the JACKSONVILLE BEACH area)

STARKE—See JACKSONVILLE, FL (Comcast Cable)

STARKE—See HAMPTON, FL (Florida Fiber Networks)

STEINHATCHEE—Formerly served by Altitude Communications. No longer in operation

STOCK ISLAND—See MIAMI, FL (AT&T U-verse. This is the regional video hub for the MIAMI area)

STUART—Comcast Cable. Now served by WEST PALM BEACH, FL [FL0008]

STUART—Circle Bay Yacht Club Condo Assoc Inc

STUART—See WEST PALM BEACH, FL (Comcast Cable)

SUGARLOAF KEY—See MIAMI, FL (AT&T U-verse. This is the regional video hub for the MIAMI area)

SUMMERFIELD—See MARION COUNTY (unincorporated areas), FL (Cablevision of Marion County)

SUMMERLAND KEY—See WEST PALM BEACH, FL (Comcast Cable)

SUMTER COUNTY (PORTIONS)—See ORLANDO, FL (Bright House Networks)

SUMTER COUNTY (UNINCORPORATED AREAS)—See ARCHER, FL (Comcast Cable)

SUMTER COUNTY—Formerly served by Florida Cable. Now served by Florida Fiber Networks, HERNANDO COUNTY, FL [FL0148]

SUMTER COUNTY—See HERNANDO COUNTY, FL (Florida Fiber Networks)

SUN CITY CENTER—See HILLSBOROUGH COUNTY (portions), FL (Bright House Networks)

SUNNY HILLS—Formerly served by Community Cable. No longer in operation

SUNNY ISLES BEACH—See MIAMI, FL (AT&T U-verse. This is the regional video hub for the MIAMI area)

SUNNY ISLES—See MIAMI BEACH, FL (Atlantic Broadband)

SUNRISE—See MIAMI, FL (AT&T U-verse. This is the regional video hub for the MIAMI area)

SUNRISE—See WEST PALM BEACH, FL (Comcast Cable)

SURFSIDE—See MIAMI, FL (AT&T U-verse. This is the regional video hub for the MIAMI area)

SURFSIDE—See MIAMI BEACH, FL (Atlantic Broadband)

SUWANNEE CAMPGROUND—Formerly served by KLiP Interactive. No longer in operation

SUWANNEE COUNTY (PORTIONS)—See JACKSONVILLE, FL (Comcast Cable)

SWEETWATER GOLF & TENNIS CLUB EAST—Formerly served by Sweetwater Golf & Tennis Club East Inc. No longer in operation

SWEETWATER OAKS—Formerly served by Galaxy Cablevision. No longer in operation

SWEETWATER—See MIAMI, FL (AT&T U-verse. This is the regional video hub for the MIAMI area)

SWEETWATER—See WEST PALM BEACH, FL (Comcast Cable)

TALLAHASSEE—Comcast Cable

TAMARAC—See MIAMI, FL (AT&T U-verse. This is the regional video hub for the MIAMI area)

TAMARAC—See WEST PALM BEACH, FL (Comcast Cable)

TAMPA (PORTIONS)—See ARCHER, FL (Comcast Cable)

TAMPA—Formerly served by V TV Video Television. No longer in operation

TAMPA—See HILLSBOROUGH COUNTY (portions), FL (Bright House Networks)

TARPON SPRINGS—See HILLSBOROUGH COUNTY (portions), FL (Bright House Networks)

TARPON SPRINGS—See PINELLAS COUNTY (portions), FL (WOW! Internet, Cable & Phone)

TAVARES—See ARCHER, FL (Comcast Cable)

TAVERNIER—See MIAMI, FL (AT&T U-verse. This is the regional video hub for the MIAMI area)

TAYLOR COUNTY (PORTIONS)—See TALLAHASSEE, FL (Comcast Cable)

TEMPLE TERRACE—See HILLSBOROUGH COUNTY (portions), FL (Bright House Networks)

TEQUESTA—Comcast Cable. Now served by WEST PALM BEACH, FL [FL0008]

TEQUESTA—See WEST PALM BEACH, FL (Comcast Cable)

THE VILLAGES—See ARCHER, FL (Comcast Cable)

TITUSVILLE—See ORLANDO, FL (Bright House Networks)

TREASURE ISLAND—See HILLSBOROUGH COUNTY (portions), FL (Bright House Networks)

TRENTON—Comcast Cable. Now served by ARCHER, FL [FL0189]

TRENTON—See ARCHER, FL (Comcast Cable)

TYNDALL AFB—Mediacom. Now served by WALTON COUNTY (portions), FL [FL0159]

TYNDALL AFB—See WALTON COUNTY (portions), FL (Mediacom)

UMATILLA—See ARCHER, FL (Comcast Cable)

UMATILLA—See MARION COUNTY (southern portion), FL (Florida Fiber Networks)

UNION COUNTY (PORTIONS)—See JACKSONVILLE, FL (Comcast Cable)

UNION COUNTY—See LAWTEY, FL (Florida Fiber Networks)

UNIVERSITY OF WEST FLORIDA—See PENSACOLA, FL (Cox Communications)

VACA KEY—See MIAMI, FL (AT&T U-verse. This is the regional video hub for the MIAMI area)

VALPARAISO—Valparaiso Communications System

VENICE—Comcast Cable. Now served by SARASOTA, FL [FL0017]

VENICE—See SARASOTA, FL (Comcast Cable)

VERNON—See WALTON COUNTY (portions), FL (Mediacom)

VERO BEACH—Comcast Cable. Now served by WEST PALM BEACH, FL [FL0008]

VERO BEACH—See WEST PALM BEACH, FL (Comcast Cable)

VIRGINIA GARDENS—See WEST PALM BEACH, FL (Comcast Cable)

VOLUSIA COUNTY (UNINCORPORATED AREAS)—See ARCHER, FL (Comcast Cable)

VOLUSIA COUNTY (UNINCORPORATED AREAS)—See ASTOR, FL (Florida Fiber Networks)

VOLUSIA COUNTY—See ORLANDO, FL (Bright House Networks)

VOLUSIA—See ASTOR, FL (Florida Fiber Networks)

WAKULLA—See TALLAHASSEE, FL (Comcast Cable)

WALDO—Comcast Cable. Now served by JACKSONVILLE, FL [FL0002]

WALDO—See JACKSONVILLE, FL (Comcast Cable)

WALTON COUNTY (PORTIONS)—See DE FUNIAK SPRINGS, FL (Bright House Networks)

WALTON COUNTY (PORTIONS)—See PENSACOLA, FL (Cox Communications)

WALTON COUNTY (PORTIONS)—Mediacom

WARE COUNTY (UNINCORPORATED AREAS)—See JACKSONVILLE BEACH, GA (AT&T U-verse. Formerly [FL0358]. This cable system has converted to IPTV. This is the regional video hub for the JACKSONVILLE BEACH area)

WASHINGTON COUNTY—See CHIPLEY, FL (Bright House Networks)

Florida—Cable Community Index

WATERFORD—See SARASOTA, FL (Comcast Cable)

WATERTOWN—See JACKSONVILLE BEACH, FL (AT&T U-verse. Formerly [FL0358]. This cable system has converted to IPTV. This is the regional video hub for the JACKSONVILLE BEACH area)

WAUCHULA—Comcast Cable

WAYCROSS—See JACKSONVILLE BEACH, GA (AT&T U-verse. Formerly [FL0358]. This cable system has converted to IPTV. This is the regional video hub for the JACKSONVILLE BEACH area)

WAYNESVILLE—See JACKSONVILLE, GA (Comcast Cable)

WEBSTER—See ORLANDO, FL (Bright House Networks)

WEBSTER—See HERNANDO COUNTY, FL (Florida Fiber Networks)

WELAKA (town)—Comcast Cable. Now served by JACKSONVILLE, FL [FL0002]

WELAKA (TOWN)—See JACKSONVILLE, FL (Comcast Cable)

WELAKA—See JACKSONVILLE BEACH, FL (AT&T U-verse. Formerly [FL0358]. This cable system has converted to IPTV. This is the regional video hub for the JACKSONVILLE BEACH area)

WELLINGTON—Formerly served by Bright House Networks. No longer in operation

WELLINGTON—See WEST PALM BEACH, FL (Comcast Cable)

WESCONNETT—See JACKSONVILLE BEACH, FL (AT&T U-verse. Formerly [FL0358]. This cable system has converted to IPTV. This is the regional video hub for the JACKSONVILLE BEACH area)

WESLEY CHAPEL—See HILLSBOROUGH COUNTY (portions), FL (Bright House Networks)

WEST ARCADIA—See SARASOTA, FL (Comcast Cable)

WEST HOLLYWOOD—See MIAMI, FL (AT&T U-verse. This is the regional video hub for the MIAMI area)

WEST MELBOURNE—See ORLANDO, FL (Bright House Networks)

WEST MIAMI—See MIAMI, FL (AT&T U-verse. This is the regional video hub for the MIAMI area)

WEST MIAMI—See WEST PALM BEACH, FL (Comcast Cable)

WEST PALM BEACH—Comcast Cable

WEST PARK—See MIAMI, FL (AT&T U-verse. This is the regional video hub for the MIAMI area)

WESTON—Advocate Communications

WESTON—See MIAMI, FL (AT&T U-verse. This is the regional video hub for the MIAMI area)

WESTON—See WEST PALM BEACH, FL (Comcast Cable)

WESTVILLE—Formerly served by Community Cable. No longer in operation

WESTWOOD LAKES—See MIAMI, FL (AT&T U-verse. This is the regional video hub for the MIAMI area)

WEWAHITCHKA—See WALTON COUNTY (portions), FL (Mediacom)

WHITE SPRINGS—Formerly served by Southeast Cable TV Inc. No longer in operation

WHITING FIELD NAVAL AIR STATION—See GULF BREEZE, FL (Mediacom)

WILDWOOD—Bright House Networks. Now served by ORLANDO, FL [FL0001]

WILDWOOD—See ORLANDO, FL (Bright House Networks)

WILLISTON—Comcast Cable. Now served by ARCHER, FL [FL0189]

WILLISTON—See ARCHER, FL (Comcast Cable)

WILTON MANORS—See MIAMI, FL (AT&T U-verse. This is the regional video hub for the MIAMI area)

WILTON MANORS—See WEST PALM BEACH, FL (Comcast Cable)

WIMAUMA—See HILLSBOROUGH COUNTY (portions), FL (Bright House Networks)

WINDERMERE—See ORLANDO, FL (Bright House Networks)

WINTER GARDEN—See ORLANDO, FL (Bright House Networks)

WINTER HAVEN—See HILLSBOROUGH COUNTY (portions), FL (Bright House Networks)

WINTER PARK—See ORLANDO, FL (Bright House Networks)

WINTER SPRINGS—See ORLANDO, FL (Bright House Networks)

WOODBINE—See JACKSONVILLE, GA (Comcast Cable)

WOODFIELD—Formerly served by Formerly served by Comcast Cable. No longer in operation

WORTHINGTON SPRINGS—See BROOKER, FL (New River Cablevision Inc)

WYNMOOR VILLAGE—Comcast Cable. Now served by WEST PALM BEACH, FL [FL0008]

WYNMOOR VILLAGE—See WEST PALM BEACH, FL (Comcast Cable)

YANKEETOWN—Comcast Cable. Now served by ARCHER, FL [FL0189]

YANKEETOWN—See ARCHER, FL (Comcast Cable)

YULEE—Comcast Cable. Now served by JACKSONVILLE, FL [FL0002]

YULEE—See JACKSONVILLE BEACH, FL (AT&T U-verse. Formerly [FL0358]. This cable system has converted to IPTV. This is the regional video hub for the JACKSONVILLE BEACH area)

YULEE—See JACKSONVILLE, FL (Comcast Cable)

ZELLWOOD—Florida Fiber Networks

ZEPHYRHILLS—See HILLSBOROUGH COUNTY (portions), FL (Bright House Networks)

ZOLFO SPRINGS—See WAUCHULA, FL (Comcast Cable)

GEORGIA

ABBEVILLE COUNTY (PORTIONS)—See ELBERTON, SC (Comcast Cable)

ABBEVILLE—Bulldog Cable

ACWORTH—Formerly served by KLiP Interactive. No longer in operation

ACWORTH—See ATLANTA, GA (Comcast Cable)

ADAIRSVILLE—See ATLANTA, GA (Comcast Cable)

ADEL—Mediacom

ADRIAN—Comcast Cable. Now served by SAVANNAH, GA [GA0005]

ADRIAN—See SAVANNAH, GA (Comcast Cable)

ADRIAN—See METTER, GA (Pineland Telephone Coop. This cable system has converted to IPTV)

AIKEN COUNTY (PORTIONS)—See AUGUSTA, SC (Comcast Cable)

AILEY—See MOUNT VERNON, GA (Comcast Cable)

ALAMO—See MOUNT VERNON, GA (Comcast Cable)

ALAPAHA—See ADEL, GA (Mediacom)

ALBANY—Mediacom

ALDORA—See STOCKBRIDGE, GA (Charter Communications)

ALLENHURST—See SAVANNAH, GA (Comcast Cable)

ALLENTOWN—Formerly served by KLiP Interactive. No longer in operation

ALMA—Dixie Cable TV

ALPHARETTA—See ATLANTA, GA (Comcast Cable)

ALTO—See DAHLONEGA, GA (Windstream Teleview)

AMBROSE—See DOUGLAS, GA (Vyve Broadband)

AMERICUS—Mediacom

ANDERSONVILLE—Formerly served by Andersonville Cable. No longer in operation

APPLING COUNTY (UNINCORPORATED AREAS)—See SURRENCY, GA (Worth Cable)

ARABI—Formerly served by Citizens Cable TV. No longer in operation

ARAGON—See NEWNAN, GA (Charter Communications)

ARCADE—See ATLANTA, GA (Comcast Cable)

ARCADE—See DAHLONEGA, GA (Windstream Teleview)

ARGYLE—See HOMERVILLE, GA (Comcast Cable)

ARLINGTON—See CUTHBERT, GA (Mediacom)

ARNOLDSVILLE—Formerly served by Allegiance Communications. No longer in operation

ARNOLDSVILLE—See ATHENS, GA (Charter Communications)

ASHBURN—See TIFTON, GA (Mediacom)

ATHENS—Charter Communications

ATLANTA (metro area 2)—Formerly served by BellSouth Entertainment. No longer in operation

ATLANTA (metro area)—Comcast Cable. Now served by ATLANTA, GA [GA0017]

ATLANTA (northern portion)—Comcast Cable. Now served by ATLANTA, GA [GA0017]

ATLANTA (perimeter north)—Comcast Cable. Now served by ATLANTA, GA [GA0017]

ATLANTA—Comcast Cable

ATTAPULGUS—Formerly served by KLiP Interactive. No longer in operation

AUBURN—See ATLANTA, GA (Comcast Cable)

AUBURN—See COLUMBUS, AL (WOW! Internet, Cable & Phone)

AUGUSTA—Comcast Cable

AUGUSTA—WOW! Internet, Cable & Phone

AUSTELL—See ATLANTA, GA (Comcast Cable)

AVALON—Formerly served by Galaxy Cablevision. Now served by Hart Communications, HART COUNTY, GA [GA0293]

AVALON—See HART COUNTY, GA (Hart Communications)

AVERA—Formerly served by National Cable Inc. No longer in operation

AVONDALE ESTATES—See ATLANTA, GA (Comcast Cable)

BACONTON—CNS

BAINBRIDGE—Mediacom

BALDWIN COUNTY (eastern portion)—Formerly served by KLiP Interactive. No longer in operation

BALDWIN COUNTY (NORTHERN PORTION)—See PUTNAM COUNTY, GA (Bulldog Cable)

Cable Community Index—Georgia

BALDWIN COUNTY—See MILLEDGEVILLE, GA (Charter Communications)

BALDWIN—See DAHLONEGA, GA (Windstream Teleview)

BALL GROUND—See ELLIJAY, GA (Community Cable Television Co)

BANKS COUNTY (PORTIONS)—See ATLANTA, GA (Comcast Cable)

BANKS COUNTY (PORTIONS)—See DAHLONEGA, GA (Windstream Teleview)

BARNESVILLE—See STOCKBRIDGE, GA (Charter Communications)

BARROW COUNTY (PORTIONS)—See ATLANTA, GA (Comcast Cable)

BARTOW COUNTY (PORTIONS)—See ATLANTA, GA (Comcast Cable)

BARTOW—See AUGUSTA, GA (Comcast Cable)

BARTOW—See METTER, GA (Pineland Telephone Coop. This cable system has converted to IPTV)

BAXLEY—ATC Broadband

BEECH ISLAND—See AUGUSTA, SC (Comcast Cable)

BELLVILLE—See SAVANNAH, GA (Comcast Cable)

BEN HILL COUNTY (PORTIONS)—See FITZGERALD, GA (Mediacom)

BENT TREE—Ellijay Telephone Cooperative. Now served by ELLIJAY, GA [GA0044]

BENT TREE—See ELLIJAY, GA (Community Cable Television Co)

BERKELEY LAKE—See ATLANTA, GA (Comcast Cable)

BERLIN—Formerly served by Mega Cable LLC. No longer in operation

BERRIEN COUNTY (PORTIONS)—See ADEL, GA (Mediacom)

BETHLEHEM—See ATLANTA, GA (Comcast Cable)

BETWEEN—See ATLANTA, GA (Comcast Cable)

BETWEEN—See MONROE, GA (Monroe Utilities Network)

BEULAH—See NEWNAN, AL (Charter Communications)

BIBB CITY—See NEWNAN, GA (Charter Communications)

BIBB COUNTY (PORTIONS)—Suburban Cable

BIBB COUNTY—See MACON, GA (Cox Communications)

BIG CANOE—Teleview. Now served by DAHLONEGA, GA [GA0099]

BIG CANOE—See DAHLONEGA, GA (Windstream Teleview)

BISHOP—Formerly served by KLiP Interactive. No longer in operation

BLACKSHEAR—ATC Broadband

BLAIRSVILLE—Teleview. Now served by DAHLONEGA, GA [GA0099]

BLAIRSVILLE—See DAHLONEGA, GA (Windstream Teleview)

BLAKELY—Blakely Cable TV Inc

BLECKLEY COUNTY (PORTIONS)—See PERRY, GA (ComSouth Telesys Inc)

BLITCHTON COUNTY (PORTIONS)—See SAVANNAH, GA (Comcast Cable)

BLOOMINGDALE—See SAVANNAH, GA (Comcast Cable)

BLUE RIDGE—Community Cable Television Co. Now served by ELLIJAY, GA [GA0044]

BLUE RIDGE—See ELLIJAY, GA (Community Cable Television Co)

BLYTHE—See AUGUSTA, GA (Comcast Cable)

BOGART—See ATHENS, GA (Charter Communications)

BOLINGBROKE—Reynolds Cable TV Inc

BONAIRE—See PERRY, GA (ComSouth Telesys Inc)

BOSTON—Formerly served by Southeast Cable TV Inc. No longer in operation

BOSTWICK—See MONROE, GA (Monroe Utilities Network)

BOWDON—See NEWNAN, GA (Charter Communications)

BOWERSVILLE—See FRANKLIN COUNTY, GA (TruVista Communications)

BOWMAN—Comcast Cablevision of the South. Now served by ELBERTON, GA [GA0192]

BOWMAN—See ELBERTON, GA (Comcast Cable)

BOX SPRINGS—See REYNOLDS, GA (Flint Cable TV)

BRANTLEY COUNTY (UNINCORPORATED AREAS)—See HOBOKEN, GA (Worth Cable)

BRASELTON—See ATLANTA, GA (Comcast Cable)

BRASWELL—See ATLANTA, GA (Comcast Cable)

BREMEN—See NEWNAN, GA (Charter Communications)

BREMEN—See ATLANTA, GA (Comcast Cable)

BRONWOOD—Formerly served by Citizens Cable TV. No longer in operation

BROOKLET—Bulloch Telephone

BROOKLET—See STATESBORO, GA (Northland Cable Television)

BROOKS COUNTY (EASTERN PORTION)—See VALDOSTA, GA (Mediacom)

BROOKS—See ATLANTA, GA (Comcast Cable)

BROWNS CROSSING—Formerly served by National Cable Inc. No longer in operation

BROXTON—See DOUGLAS, GA (Vyve Broadband)

BRUNSWICK—Comcast Cable. Now served by JACKSONVILLE, FL [FL0002]

BRYAN COUNTY (PORTIONS)—See SAVANNAH, GA (Comcast Cable)

BUCHANAN—See NEWNAN, GA (Charter Communications)

BUENA VISTA—Flint Cable TV. Now served by REYNOLDS, GA [GA0236]

BUENA VISTA—See REYNOLDS, GA (Flint Cable TV)

BUFORD—See LAWRENCEVILLE, GA (Charter Communications)

BULLOCH COUNTY (PORTIONS)—See STATESBORO, GA (Northland Cable Television)

BURKE COUNTY (PORTIONS)—See AUGUSTA, GA (Comcast Cable)

BURNETTOWN—See AUGUSTA, SC (Comcast Cable)

BUTLER—Flint Cable TV. Now served by REYNOLDS, GA [GA0236]

BUTLER—See REYNOLDS, GA (Flint Cable TV)

BUTTS COUNTY (PORTIONS)—See STOCKBRIDGE, GA (Charter Communications)

BUTTS COUNTY—See NEWTON COUNTY, GA (Bulldog Cable)

BYRON—See MACON, GA (Cox Communications)

CADWELL—See RENTZ, GA (Progressive Rural Telephone. This cable system has converted to IPTV.)

CAIRO—CNS

CAIRO—See THOMASVILLE, GA (Mediacom)

CALHOUN FALLS—See ELBERTON, SC (Comcast Cable)

CALHOUN—See ATLANTA, GA (Comcast Cable)

CAMAK—See AUGUSTA, GA (Comcast Cable)

CAMDEN COUNTY (PORTIONS)—See KINGSLAND, GA (Kings Bay Communications Inc)

CAMILLA—Mediacom. Now served by ALBANY, GA [GA0011]

CAMILLA—CNS

CAMILLA—See ALBANY, GA (Mediacom)

CANDLER COUNTY (PORTIONS)—See SAVANNAH, GA (Comcast Cable)

CANON—See FRANKLIN COUNTY, GA (TruVista Communications)

CANTON—See ATLANTA, GA (Comcast Cable)

CARL (TOWN)—See ATLANTA, GA (Comcast Cable)

CARNESVILLE—TruVista Communications

CARROLL COUNTY (PORTIONS)—See ATLANTA, GA (Comcast Cable)

CARROLL COUNTY—See NEWNAN, GA (Charter Communications)

CARROLLTON—Charter Communications. Now served by NEWNAN, GA [GA0042]

CARROLLTON—See NEWNAN, GA (Charter Communications)

CARROLLTON—See ATLANTA, GA (Comcast Cable)

CARTERSVILLE—Comcast Cable. Now served by ATLANTA, GA [GA0017]

CARTERSVILLE—See ATLANTA, GA (Comcast Cable)

CATAULA—See COLUMBUS, GA (Mediacom)

CATOOSA COUNTY—See RINGGOLD, GA (Charter Communications)

CAVE SPRING—See NEWNAN, GA (Charter Communications)

CECIL—See VALDOSTA, GA (Mediacom)

CEDARTOWN—Charter Communications. Now served by NEWNAN, GA [GA0042]

CEDARTOWN—See NEWNAN, GA (Charter Communications)

CENTERVILLE—See MACON, GA (Cox Communications)

CENTRALHATCHEE—See LAGRANGE, GA (Charter Communications)

CHALYBEATE SPRINGS—See LAGRANGE, GA (Charter Communications)

CHAMBERS COUNTY (PORTIONS)—See NEWNAN, AL (Charter Communications)

CHAMBLEE—See ATLANTA, GA (Comcast Cable)

CHATHAM COUNTY (PORTIONS)—See SAVANNAH, GA (Comcast Cable)

CHATSWORTH—Charter Communications

CHATTAHOOCHEE HILLS—See ATLANTA, GA (Comcast Cable)

CHATTOOGA COUNTY—See SUMMERVILLE, GA (Charter Communications)

CHAUNCEY—Formerly served by KLiP Interactive. No longer in operation

CHEROKEE COUNTY (PORTIONS)—See ATLANTA, GA (Comcast Cable)

CHEROKEE COUNTY (PORTIONS)—See ELLIJAY, GA (Community Cable Television Co)

CHESTER—Bulldog Cable

CHESTER—See RENTZ, GA (Progressive Rural Telephone. This cable system has converted to IPTV.)

CLARKE COUNTY (PORTIONS)—See ATHENS, GA (Charter Communications)

Georgia—Cable Community Index

CLARKE COUNTY (PORTIONS)—See ATLANTA, GA (Comcast Cable)

CLARKESVILLE—See DAHLONEGA, GA (Windstream Teleview)

CLARKSTON—See ATLANTA, GA (Comcast Cable)

CLAXTON—Comcast Cable. Now served by SAVANNAH, GA [GA0005]

CLAXTON—See SAVANNAH, GA (Comcast Cable)

CLAY COUNTY (WESTERN PORTIONS)—See DAHLONEGA, NC (Windstream Teleview)

CLAYTON COUNTY (PORTIONS)—See STOCKBRIDGE, GA (Charter Communications)

CLAYTON—See ATLANTA, GA (Comcast Cable)

CLAYTON—TruVista Communications

CLERMONT—Comcast Cable. Now served by ATLANTA, GA [GA0017]

CLERMONT—See ATLANTA, GA (Comcast Cable)

CLEVELAND—Teleview. Now served by DAHLONEGA, GA [GA0099]

CLEVELAND—See DAHLONEGA, GA (Windstream Teleview)

CLIMAX—Formerly served by KLiP Interactive. No longer in operation

CLINCH COUNTY (PORTIONS)—See HOMERVILLE, GA (Comcast Cable)

COBB COUNTY (PORTIONS)—See ATLANTA, GA (Comcast Cable)

COBB COUNTY—See LAWRENCEVILLE, GA (Charter Communications)

COBB—Citizens Cable TV

COBBTOWN—See METTER, GA (Pineland Telephone Coop. This cable system has converted to IPTV)

COCHRAN—See PERRY, GA (ComSouth Telesys Inc)

COFFEE COUNTY (UNINCORPORATED AREAS)—See DOUGLAS, GA (Vyve Broadband)

COHUTTA—See DALTON, GA (Charter Communications)

COLBERT—See ATHENS, GA (Charter Communications)

COLLEGE PARK—See ATLANTA, GA (Comcast Cable)

COLLINS—Formerly served by Worth Cable. No longer in operation

COLONELS ISLAND—Comcast Cable. Now served by SAVANNAH, GA [GA0005]

COLONELS ISLAND—See SAVANNAH, GA (Comcast Cable)

COLQUITT COUNTY (PORTIONS)—See TIFTON, GA (Mediacom)

COLQUITT—Bulldog Cable

COLUMBIA COUNTY (PORTIONS)—See AUGUSTA, GA (Comcast Cable)

COLUMBIA COUNTY (PORTIONS)—See AUGUSTA, GA (WOW! Internet, Cable & Phone)

COLUMBIA—See BLAKELY, AL (Blakely Cable TV Inc)

COLUMBUS—Charter Communications. Now served by NEWNAN, GA [GA0042]

COLUMBUS—See NEWNAN, GA (Charter Communications)

COLUMBUS—Mediacom

COLUMBUS—WOW! Internet, Cable & Phone

COMER—Charter Communications. Now served by ATHENS, GA [GA0014]

COMER—See ATHENS, GA (Charter Communications)

COMMERCE—See DAHLONEGA, GA (Windstream Teleview)

CONCORD—Formerly served by Georgia Broadband. No longer in operation

CONLEY—See ATLANTA, GA (Comcast Cable)

CONYERS—See ATLANTA, GA (Comcast Cable)

COOK COUNTY (PORTIONS)—See ADEL, GA (Mediacom)

COOLIDGE—Formerly served by Southeast Cable TV Inc. No longer in operation

COPPERHILL—See ELLIJAY, TN (Community Cable Television Co)

CORDELE—Mediacom. Now served by FITZGERALD, GA [GA0052]

CORDELE—See FITZGERALD, GA (Mediacom)

CORINTH—See LAGRANGE, GA (Charter Communications)

CORNELIA—Windstream Teleview. Now served by DAHLONEGA, GA [GA0099]

CORNELIA—See DAHLONEGA, GA (Windstream Teleview)

COVINGTON—Charter Communications. Now served by STOCKBRIDGE, GA [GA0083]

COVINGTON—See STOCKBRIDGE, GA (Charter Communications)

COWETA COUNTY (PORTIONS)—See ATLANTA, GA (Comcast Cable)

COWETA COUNTY (PORTIONS)—See NEWNAN, GA (NuLink Digital)

COWETA COUNTY—See NEWNAN, GA (Charter Communications)

CRAWFORD COUNTY (Eastern portion)—Formerly served by Piedmont Cable Corp. No longer in operation

CRAWFORD COUNTY (PORTIONS)—See REYNOLDS, GA (Flint Cable TV)

CRAWFORD—Formerly served by Allegiance Communications. No longer in operation

CRAWFORDVILLE—Formerly served by CommuniComm Services. No longer in operation

CRESCENT—See DARIEN, GA (Comcast Cable)

CRISP COUNTY (PORTIONS)—See FITZGERALD, GA (Mediacom)

CRISP COUNTY (SOUTHERN PORTION)—See COBB, GA (Citizens Cable TV)

CULLODEN—See REYNOLDS, GA (Flint Cable TV)

CUMMING—Comcast Cable. Now served by ATLANTA, GA [GA0017]

CUMMING—See ATLANTA, GA (Comcast Cable)

CUSSETA—Formerly served by Almega Cable. No longer in operation

CUTHBERT—Mediacom

DACULA—See LAWRENCEVILLE, GA (Charter Communications)

DAHLONEGA—Windstream Teleview. Now served by DAHLONEGA, GA [GA0099]

DAHLONEGA—Windstream Teleview

DAISY—See SAVANNAH, GA (Comcast Cable)

DALLAS—See ATLANTA, GA (Comcast Cable)

DALTON—Charter Communications

DANIELSVILLE—See ATHENS, GA (Charter Communications)

DARIEN—Comcast Cable

DARIEN—Darien Communications

DAVISBORO—Formerly served by Walker Cablevision. No longer in operation

DAVISBORO—See METTER, GA (Pineland Telephone Coop. This cable system has converted to IPTV)

DAWSON COUNTY (PORTIONS)—See DAHLONEGA, GA (Windstream Teleview)

DAWSON—See ALBANY, GA (Mediacom)

DAWSONVILLE—Windstream Teleview. Now served by DAHLONEGA, GA [GA0099]

DAWSONVILLE—See DAHLONEGA, GA (Windstream Teleview)

DE SOTO—See COBB, GA (Citizens Cable TV)

DEARING—See AUGUSTA, GA (Comcast Cable)

DECATUR COUNTY (PORTIONS)—See BAINBRIDGE, GA (Mediacom)

DECATUR—See ATLANTA, GA (Comcast Cable)

DEKALB COUNTY (PORTIONS)—See ATLANTA, GA (Comcast Cable)

DEMOREST—See DAHLONEGA, GA (Windstream Teleview)

DEXTER—See CHESTER, GA (Bulldog Cable)

DEXTER—See RENTZ, GA (Progressive Rural Telephone. This cable system has converted to IPTV.)

DILLARD—See CLAYTON, GA (TruVista Communications)

DOBBINS AIR FORCE BASE—See ATLANTA, GA (Comcast Cable)

DODGE COUNTY (PORTIONS)—See EASTMAN, GA (Mediacom)

DOERUN—Doerun Cable TV

DONALSONVILLE—Mediacom. Now served by BAINBRIDGE, GA [GA0060]

DONALSONVILLE—See BAINBRIDGE, GA (Mediacom)

DOOLY COUNTY (PORTIONS)—See COBB, GA (Citizens Cable TV)

DOOLY COUNTY (PORTIONS)—See PERRY, GA (ComSouth Telesys Inc)

DOOLY COUNTY (PORTIONS)—See FITZGERALD, GA (Mediacom)

DORAVILLE—See ATLANTA, GA (Comcast Cable)

DOUGHERTY COUNTY (PORTIONS)—See ALBANY, GA (Mediacom)

DOUGLAS COUNTY (PORTIONS)—See ATLANTA, GA (Comcast Cable)

DOUGLAS—Vyve Broadband

DOUGLASVILLE—See ATLANTA, GA (Comcast Cable)

DRAYTON—See COBB, GA (Citizens Cable TV)

DRY BRANCH—Formerly served by KLiP Interactive. No longer in operation

DUBLIN—Charter Communications

DUCKTOWN—See ELLIJAY, TN (Community Cable Television Co)

DUDLEY—Bulldog Cable

DUDLEY—See RENTZ, GA (Progressive Rural Telephone. This cable system has converted to IPTV.)

DULUTH—See LAWRENCEVILLE, GA (Charter Communications)

DULUTH—See ATLANTA, GA (Comcast Cable)

DUNWOODY—See ATLANTA, GA (Comcast Cable)

DUTCH ISLAND—See SAVANNAH, GA (Comcast Cable)

EAST DUBLIN—Charter Communications. Now served by DUBLIN, GA [GA0043]

EAST DUBLIN—Formerly served by Bulldog Cable. No longer in operation

EAST DUBLIN—See DUBLIN, GA (Charter Communications)

EAST ELLIJAY—See ELLIJAY, GA (Community Cable Television Co)

EAST POINT—See ATLANTA, GA (Comcast Cable)

Cable Community Index—Georgia

EASTMAN—Mediacom

EATONTON—Charter Communications. Now served by MILLEDGEVILLE, GA [GA0046]

EATONTON—See MILLEDGEVILLE, GA (Charter Communications)

EDGEFIELD—See AUGUSTA, SC (Comcast Cable)

EDISON—See CUTHBERT, GA (Mediacom)

EFFINGHAM COUNTY (PORTIONS)—See SAVANNAH, GA (Comcast Cable)

ELBERT COUNTY (PORTIONS)—See ELBERTON, GA (Comcast Cable)

ELBERTON—ElbertonNET. This cable system has converted to IPTV. See ELBERTON, GA [GA5280]

ELBERTON—Comcast Cable

ELBERTON—ElbertonNET. Formerly [GA0304]. This cable system has converted to IPTV

ELLABELLE—See SAVANNAH, GA (Comcast Cable)

ELLAVILLE—See AMERICUS, GA (Mediacom)

ELLENWOOD—See ATLANTA, GA (Comcast Cable)

ELLERSLIE—See COLUMBUS, GA (Mediacom)

ELLIJAY—Community Cable Television Co

EMANUEL COUNTY (PORTIONS)—See SAVANNAH, GA (Comcast Cable)

EMANUEL COUNTY (PORTIONS)—See SWAINSBORO, GA (Northland Cable Television)

EMERSON—See ATLANTA, GA (Comcast Cable)

ENIGMA—Mediacom. Now served by ADEL, GA [GA0063]

ENIGMA—See ADEL, GA (Mediacom)

ETON—See CHATSWORTH, GA (Charter Communications)

EUHARLEE—See ATLANTA, GA (Comcast Cable)

EULONIA—Comcast Cable. Now served by DARIEN, GA [GA0117]

EULONIA—See DARIEN, GA (Comcast Cable)

EVANS COUNTY (PORTIONS)—See SAVANNAH, GA (Comcast Cable)

EVANS—See SAVANNAH, GA (Comcast Cable)

FAIRBURN—Comcast Cable. Now served by ATLANTA, GA [GA0017]

FAIRBURN—See ATLANTA, GA (Comcast Cable)

FAIRFAX—See NEWNAN, AL (Charter Communications)

FAIRMOUNT—See ATLANTA, GA (Comcast Cable)

FANNIN COUNTY (PORTIONS)—See ELLIJAY, GA (Community Cable Television Co)

FAYETTE COUNTY (PORTIONS)—See ATLANTA, GA (Comcast Cable)

FAYETTEVILLE—See ATLANTA, GA (Comcast Cable)

FITZGERALD—Mediacom

FLEMING—See SAVANNAH, GA (Comcast Cable)

FLEMINGTON—See SAVANNAH, GA (Comcast Cable)

FLINT RIVER—Formerly served by KLiP Interactive. No longer in operation

FLOVILLA—See STOCKBRIDGE, GA (Charter Communications)

FLOWERY BRANCH—See LAWRENCEVILLE, GA (Charter Communications)

FLOYD COUNTY (PORTIONS)—See ATLANTA, GA (Comcast Cable)

FLOYD COUNTY—See NEWNAN, GA (Charter Communications)

FOLKSTON—Comcast Cable. Now served by JACKSONVILLE, FL [FL0002]

FOREST PARK—See ATLANTA, GA (Comcast Cable)

FORSYTH COUNTY (PORTIONS)—See ATLANTA, GA (Comcast Cable)

FORSYTH—Forsyth CableNet

FORT BENNING—Charter Communications. Now served by NEWNAN, GA [GA0042]

FORT BENNING—See NEWNAN, GA (Charter Communications)

FORT GAINES—See CUTHBERT, GA (Mediacom)

FORT GILLEM—See ATLANTA, GA (Comcast Cable)

FORT GORDON—WOW! Internet, Cable & Phone. Now served by AUGUSTA, GA [GA0288]

FORT GORDON—See AUGUSTA, GA (WOW! Internet, Cable & Phone)

FORT MCPHERSON—See ATLANTA, GA (Comcast Cable)

FORT STEWART—See SAVANNAH, GA (Comcast Cable)

FORT VALLEY—ComSouth. Now served by PERRY, GA [GA0229]

FORT VALLEY—Flint Cable TV. Now served by REYNOLDS, GA [GA0236]

FORT VALLEY—See PERRY, GA (ComSouth Telesys Inc)

FORT VALLEY—See REYNOLDS, GA (Flint Cable TV)

FRANKLIN COUNTY (NORTHERN PORTION)—See HART COUNTY, GA (Hart Communications)

FRANKLIN COUNTY (PORTIONS)—See CARNESVILLE, GA (TruVista Communications)

FRANKLIN COUNTY—TruVista Communications

FRANKLIN SPRINGS—See FRANKLIN COUNTY, GA (TruVista Communications)

FRANKLIN—See LAGRANGE, GA (Charter Communications)

FULTON COUNTY (PORTIONS)—See ATLANTA, GA (Comcast Cable)

FUNSTON—Formerly served by Wainwright Cable Inc. No longer in operation

GAINESVILLE—Charter Communications. Now served by LAWRENCEVILLE, GA [GA0009]

GAINESVILLE—See LAWRENCEVILLE, GA (Charter Communications)

GARDEN CITY—See SAVANNAH, GA (Comcast Cable)

GARFIELD—See METTER, GA (Pineland Telephone Coop. This cable system has converted to IPTV)

GIBSON—Formerly served by KLiP Interactive. No longer in operation

GILLSVILLE—See ATLANTA, GA (Comcast Cable)

GILMER COUNTY—See ELLIJAY, GA (Community Cable Television Co)

GLENNVILLE—Comcast Cable

GLENWOOD—See MOUNT VERNON, GA (Comcast Cable)

GOOD HOPE—See MONROE, GA (Monroe Utilities Network)

GORDON COUNTY (PORTIONS)—See ATLANTA, GA (Comcast Cable)

GORDON—Bulldog Cable

GORDON—See IRWINTON, GA (Windstream Teleview)

GRADY COUNTY—See THOMASVILLE, GA (Mediacom)

GRANTVILLE—See ATLANTA, GA (Comcast Cable)

GRAY—Formerly served by Allegiance Communications. No longer in operation

GRAY—See MILLEDGEVILLE, GA (Charter Communications)

GRAYSON—See ATLANTA, GA (Comcast Cable)

GREENE COUNTY (PORTIONS)—See MILLEDGEVILLE, GA (Charter Communications)

GREENE COUNTY (UNINCORPORATED AREAS)—Plantation Cablevision Inc

GREENSBORO—Formerly served by Allegiance Communications. Now served by Charter Communications, MILLEDGEVILLE, GA [GA0046]

GREENSBORO—See MILLEDGEVILLE, GA (Charter Communications)

GREENVILLE—Formerly served by Almega Cable. No longer in operation

GREENVILLE—Formerly served by Charter Communications. No longer in operation

GREENVILLE—Formerly served by Georgia Broadband. No longer in operation

GRIFFIN—Comcast Cable. Now served by ATLANTA, GA [GA0017]

GRIFFIN—See ATLANTA, GA (Comcast Cable)

GROVETOWN—See AUGUSTA, GA (WOW! Internet, Cable & Phone)

GUMBRANCH—See SAVANNAH, GA (Comcast Cable)

GUYTON—Comcast Cable. Now served by SAVANNAH, GA [GA0005]

GUYTON—See SAVANNAH, GA (Comcast Cable)

GWINNETT COUNTY (PORTIONS)—See LAWRENCEVILLE, GA (Charter Communications)

GWINNETT COUNTY (PORTIONS)—See ATLANTA, GA (Comcast Cable)

GWINNETT COUNTY—See LAWRENCEVILLE, GA (Charter Communications)

HABERSHAM COUNTY (PORTIONS)—See DAHLONEGA, GA (Windstream Teleview)

HADDOCK—Formerly served by KLiP Interactive. No longer in operation

HAGAN—See SAVANNAH, GA (Comcast Cable)

HAHIRA—See VALDOSTA, GA (Mediacom)

HALL COUNTY (PORTIONS)—See ATLANTA, GA (Comcast Cable)

HALL COUNTY—See LAWRENCEVILLE, GA (Charter Communications)

HAMILTON—See NEWNAN, GA (Charter Communications)

HAMPTON—See STOCKBRIDGE, GA (Charter Communications)

HANCOCK COUNTY—See SPARTA, GA (Bulldog Cable)

HAPEVILLE—See ATLANTA, GA (Comcast Cable)

HARALSON COUNTY (PORTIONS)—See ATLANTA, GA (Comcast Cable)

HARALSON COUNTY—See NEWNAN, GA (Charter Communications)

HARLEM—See AUGUSTA, GA (WOW! Internet, Cable & Phone)

HARRIS COUNTY (PORTIONS)—See LAGRANGE, GA (Charter Communications)

HARRIS COUNTY (PORTIONS)—See NEWNAN, GA (Charter Communications)

HARRIS COUNTY (PORTIONS)—See COLUMBUS, GA (WOW! Internet, Cable & Phone)

HARRIS COUNTY (SOUTHERN PORTION)—See COLUMBUS, GA (Mediacom)

2017 Edition

Cable Community Index-47

Georgia—Cable Community Index

HARRISON—Formerly served by Walker Cablevision. No longer in operation

HART COUNTY (PORTIONS)—See ELBERTON, GA (Comcast Cable)

HART COUNTY (PORTIONS)—See FRANKLIN COUNTY, GA (TruVista Communications)

HART COUNTY—Hart Communications

HARTWELL—Comcast Cablevision of the South. Now served by ELBERTON, GA [GA0192]

HARTWELL—See ELBERTON, GA (Comcast Cable)

HARTWELL—See HART COUNTY, GA (Hart Communications)

HAWKINSVILLE—ComSouth Telesys Inc. Now served by PERRY, GA [GA0229]

HAWKINSVILLE—See PERRY, GA (ComSouth Telesys Inc)

HAYESVILLE—See DAHLONEGA, NC (Windstream Teleview)

HAYNEVILLE—ComSouth Telesys Inc. Now served by PERRY, GA [GA0229]

HAYNEVILLE—See PERRY, GA (ComSouth Telesys Inc)

HAZLEHURST—Mediacom

HEARD COUNTY (PORTIONS)—See LAGRANGE, GA (Charter Communications)

HEARD COUNTY (PORTIONS)—See NEWNAN, GA (Charter Communications)

HELEN—Teleview. Now served by DAHLONEGA, GA [GA0099]

HELEN—See DAHLONEGA, GA (Windstream Teleview)

HELENA—See EASTMAN, GA (Mediacom)

HENRY COUNTY (PORTIONS)—See ATLANTA, GA (Comcast Cable)

HENRY COUNTY—See STOCKBRIDGE, GA (Charter Communications)

HEPHZIBAH—See AUGUSTA, GA (Comcast Cable)

HIAWASSEE—Windstream Teleview. Now served by DAHLONEGA, GA [GA0099]

HIAWASSEE—See DAHLONEGA, GA (Windstream Teleview)

HIGGSTON—See VIDALIA, GA (Northland Cable Television)

HIGHLAND WOODS MOTOR HOME PARK—See SAVANNAH, GA (Comcast Cable)

HILTONIA—See AUGUSTA, GA (Comcast Cable)

HINESVILLE—Comcast Cable. Now served by SAVANNAH, GA [GA0005]

HINESVILLE—See SAVANNAH, GA (Comcast Cable)

HIRAM—See ATLANTA, GA (Comcast Cable)

HOBOKEN—Worth Cable

HOGANSVILLE—See ATLANTA, GA (Comcast Cable)

HOLLY SPRINGS—See ATLANTA, GA (Comcast Cable)

HOMER—See DAHLONEGA, GA (Windstream Teleview)

HOMERVILLE—Comcast Cable

HOSCHTON—See ATLANTA, GA (Comcast Cable)

HOUSTON COUNTY (PORTIONS)—See PERRY, GA (ComSouth Telesys Inc)

HOUSTON COUNTY—See MACON, GA (Cox Communications)

HUGULEY—See NEWNAN, AL (Charter Communications)

HULL—See ATHENS, GA (Charter Communications)

HUNTER ARMY AIRFIELD—See SAVANNAH, GA (Comcast Cable)

IRON CITY—Formerly served by KLiP Interactive. No longer in operation

IRWIN COUNTY (PORTIONS)—See FITZGERALD, GA (Mediacom)

IRWINTON—Windstream Teleview

IVEY—See IRWINTON, GA (Windstream Teleview)

JACKSON COUNTY (portions)—Comcast Cable. Now served by ATLANTA, GA [GA0017]

JACKSON COUNTY (PORTIONS)—See ATLANTA, GA (Comcast Cable)

JACKSON COUNTY (PORTIONS)—See DAHLONEGA, GA (Windstream Teleview)

JACKSON—See STOCKBRIDGE, GA (Charter Communications)

JASPER COUNTY—See NEWTON COUNTY, GA (Bulldog Cable)

JASPER—See ELLIJAY, GA (Community Cable Television Co)

JEFF DAVIS COUNTY (PORTIONS)—See HAZLEHURST, GA (Mediacom)

JEFFERSON COUNTY (PORTIONS)—See AUGUSTA, GA (Comcast Cable)

JEFFERSON—Windstream Teleview. Now served by DAHLONEGA, GA [GA0099]

JEFFERSON—See DAHLONEGA, GA (Windstream Teleview)

JEFFERSONVILLE—Formerly served by Windstream Teleview. No longer in operation

JEKYLL ISLAND—Comcast Cable. Now served by JACKSONVILLE, FL [FL0002]

JENKINS COUNTY (PORTIONS)—See AUGUSTA, GA (Comcast Cable)

JENKINSBURG—See STOCKBRIDGE, GA (Charter Communications)

JERSEY—See ATLANTA, GA (Comcast Cable)

JESUP—Comcast Cable. Now served by AUGUSTA, GA [GA0004]

JESUP—See SAVANNAH, GA (Comcast Cable)

JOHNS CREEK—See LAWRENCEVILLE, GA (Charter Communications)

JOHNSON COUNTY (PORTIONS)—See WRIGHTSVILLE, GA (Comcast Cable)

JONES COUNTY (PORTIONS)—See MILLEDGEVILLE, GA (Charter Communications)

JONES COUNTY (PORTIONS)—See MACON, GA (Cox Communications)

JONESBORO—See ATLANTA, GA (Comcast Cable)

KATHLEEN—See PERRY, GA (ComSouth Telesys Inc)

KENNESAW—See ATLANTA, GA (Comcast Cable)

KINGSLAND—Kings Bay Communications Inc

KINGSTON—See ATLANTA, GA (Comcast Cable)

KITE—Formerly served by Walker Cablevision. No longer in operation

KITE—See METTER, GA (Pineland Telephone Coop. This cable system has converted to IPTV)

LAFAYETTE—Comcast Cable. Now served by KNOXVILLE, TN [TN0004]

LAFAYETTE—See NEWNAN, AL (Charter Communications)

LAGRANGE—Charter Communications

LAKE CITY—See ATLANTA, GA (Comcast Cable)

LAKE GEORGE—See SAVANNAH, GA (Comcast Cable)

LAKE OCONEE—See GREENE COUNTY (unincorporated areas), GA (Plantation Cablevision Inc)

LAKE PARK—Formerly served by Altitude Communications. No longer in operation

LAKE RABUN—See CLAYTON, GA (TruVista Communications)

LAKELAND—Mediacom. Now served by ADEL, GA [GA0063]

LAKELAND—See ADEL, GA (Mediacom)

LAMAR COUNTY—See STOCKBRIDGE, GA (Charter Communications)

LANETT—See NEWNAN, AL (Charter Communications)

LAURENS COUNTY (PORTIONS)—See DUDLEY, GA (Bulldog Cable)

LAURENS COUNTY (PORTIONS)—See RENTZ, GA (Progressive Rural Telephone. This cable system has converted to IPTV.)

LAURENS COUNTY—See DUBLIN, GA (Charter Communications)

LAVONIA—See CARNESVILLE, GA (TruVista Communications)

LAWRENCEVILLE—Charter Communications

LAWRENCEVILLE—See ATLANTA, GA (Comcast Cable)

LEARY—Formerly served by Blakely Cable TV Inc. No longer in operation

LEE COUNTY (PORTIONS)—See ALBANY, GA (Mediacom)

LEESBURG—See ALBANY, GA (Mediacom)

LENOX—See ADEL, GA (Mediacom)

LESLIE—Citizens Cable TV. Now served by COBB, GA [GA0150]

LESLIE—See COBB, GA (Citizens Cable TV)

LEXINGTON—See ATHENS, GA (Charter Communications)

LEXSY—See METTER, GA (Pineland Telephone Coop. This cable system has converted to IPTV)

LIBERTY COUNTY (PORTIONS)—See SAVANNAH, GA (Comcast Cable)

LILBURN—See ATLANTA, GA (Comcast Cable)

LILLY—See COBB, GA (Citizens Cable TV)

LINCOLN COUNTY (PORTIONS)—See WASHINGTON, GA (Comcast Cable)

LINCOLNTON—Comcast Cable. Now served by WASHINGTON, GA [GA0260]

LINCOLNTON—Formerly served by KLiP Interactive. No longer in operation

LINCOLNTON—See WASHINGTON, GA (Comcast Cable)

LITHONIA—See ATLANTA, GA (Comcast Cable)

LIZELLA—Flint Cable TV. Now served by REYNOLDS, GA [GA0236]

LIZELLA—See REYNOLDS, GA (Flint Cable TV)

LOCUST GROVE—See STOCKBRIDGE, GA (Charter Communications)

LOGANVILLE—See ATLANTA, GA (Comcast Cable)

LONE OAK—See NEWNAN, GA (Charter Communications)

LONG COUNTY (PORTIONS)—See SAVANNAH, GA (Comcast Cable)

LOUISVILLE—Comcast Cable. Now served by AUGUSTA, GA [GA0004]

LOUISVILLE—See AUGUSTA, GA (Comcast Cable)

LOVEJOY—See ATLANTA, GA (Comcast Cable)

LOWNDES COUNTY—See VALDOSTA, GA (Mediacom)

LUDOWICI—See SAVANNAH, GA (Comcast Cable)

LULA—Comcast Cable. Now served by ATLANTA, GA [GA0017]

Cable Community Index—Georgia

LULA—See ATLANTA, GA (Comcast Cable)

LUMBER CITY—See HAZLEHURST, GA (Mediacom)

LUMPKIN COUNTY (PORTIONS)—See DAHLONEGA, GA (Windstream Teleview)

LUMPKIN—See CUTHBERT, GA (Mediacom)

LUTHERSVILLE—See NEWNAN, GA (Charter Communications)

LUTHERSVILLE—Luthersville Cablevision

LYERLY—See SUMMERVILLE, GA (Charter Communications)

LYONS—See VIDALIA, GA (Northland Cable Television)

MACON COUNTY (PORTIONS)—See MONTEZUMA, GA (Comcast Cable)

MACON—Cox Communications

MADISON COUNTY—See ATHENS, GA (Charter Communications)

MADISON—See MILLEDGEVILLE, GA (Charter Communications)

MANCHESTER—Charter Communications. Now served by LaGRANGE, GA [GA0208]

MANCHESTER—See LAGRANGE, GA (Charter Communications)

MANSFIELD—See ATLANTA, GA (Comcast Cable)

MARIETTA—See ATLANTA, GA (Comcast Cable)

MARSHALLVILLE—See PERRY, GA (ComSouth Telesys Inc)

MARTIN—See HART COUNTY, GA (Hart Communications)

MARTIN—See CARNESVILLE, GA (TruVista Communications)

MAUK—See REYNOLDS, GA (Flint Cable TV)

MAYSVILLE—See ATLANTA, GA (Comcast Cable)

MCCAYSVILLE—See ELLIJAY, GA (Community Cable Television Co)

MCDONOUGH—See STOCKBRIDGE, GA (Charter Communications)

MCDUFFIE COUNTY (PORTIONS)—See AUGUSTA, GA (Comcast Cable)

MCINTOSH COUNTY (PORTIONS)—See DARIEN, GA (Comcast Cable)

MCINTOSH COUNTY—See DARIEN, GA (Darien Communications)

MCINTYRE—See IRWINTON, GA (Windstream Teleview)

McRAE—Mediacom. Now served by EASTMAN, GA [GA0076]

MCRAE—See EASTMAN, GA (Mediacom)

MEIGS—See ALBANY, GA (Mediacom)

MENLO—See SUMMERVILLE, GA (Charter Communications)

MERIWETHER COUNTY (PORTIONS)—See LAGRANGE, GA (Charter Communications)

MERIWETHER COUNTY (PORTIONS)—See NEWNAN, GA (Charter Communications)

MERIWETHER COUNTY—See LUTHERSVILLE, GA (Luthersville Cablevision)

METTER—Comcast Cable. Now served by SAVANNAH, GA [GA0005]

METTER—Pineland Telephone Coop. Inc. This cable system has converted to IPTV. Now served by METTER, GA [GA5005]

METTER—See SAVANNAH, GA (Comcast Cable)

METTER—Pineland Telephone Coop. This cable system has converted to IPTV

MIDVILLE—Pineland Telephone Coop. Inc. This cable system has converted to IPTV. Now served by METTER, GA [GA5005]

MIDVILLE—See METTER, GA (Pineland Telephone Coop. This cable system has converted to IPTV)

MIDWAY—See SAVANNAH, GA (Comcast Cable)

MILAN—Formerly served by Bulldog Cable. No longer in operation

MILLEDGEVILLE—Charter Communications

MILLEN—Comcast Cable. Now served by AUGUSTA, GA [GA0004]

MILLEN—See AUGUSTA, GA (Comcast Cable)

MILLER COUNTY (PORTIONS)—See COLQUITT, GA (Bulldog Cable)

MILNER—See STOCKBRIDGE, GA (Charter Communications)

MINERAL BLUFF—See ELLIJAY, GA (Community Cable Television Co)

MITCHELL COUNTY (PORTIONS)—See ALBANY, GA (Mediacom)

MONROE COUNTY (PORTIONS)—See MACON, GA (Cox Communications)

MONROE COUNTY (PORTIONS)—See REYNOLDS, GA (Flint Cable TV)

MONROE COUNTY (PORTIONS)—See FORSYTH, GA (Forsyth CableNet)

MONROE—Monroe Utilities Network

MONTEZUMA—Comcast Cable

MONTGOMERY COUNTY (PORTIONS)—See MOUNT VERNON, GA (Comcast Cable)

MONTGOMERY COUNTY (PORTIONS)—See VIDALIA, GA (Northland Cable Television)

MONTGOMERY COUNTY (PORTIONS)—See UVALDA, GA (Worth Cable)

MONTICELLO—See ATLANTA, GA (Comcast Cable)

MORELAND—See NEWNAN, GA (Charter Communications)

MORGAN COUNTY (PORTIONS)—See MILLEDGEVILLE, GA (Charter Communications)

MORGAN—Formerly served by Blakely Cable TV Inc. No longer in operation

MORGANTON—See ELLIJAY, GA (Community Cable Television Co)

MORROW—See ATLANTA, GA (Comcast Cable)

MOULTRIE—Mediacom. Now served by TIFTON, GA [GA0032]

MOULTRIE—CNS

MOULTRIE—See TIFTON, GA (Mediacom)

MOUNT AIRY—See DAHLONEGA, GA (Windstream Teleview)

MOUNT VERNON—Comcast Cable

MOUNT ZION—See ATLANTA, GA (Comcast Cable)

MOUNTAIN CITY—See CLAYTON, GA (TruVista Communications)

MOUNTAIN PARK—See LAWRENCEVILLE, GA (Charter Communications)

MURRAY COUNTY (CENTRAL PORTION)—See CHATSWORTH, GA (Charter Communications)

NAHUNTA—Comcast Cable. Now served by JACKSONVILLE, FL [FL0002]

NASHVILLE—See ADEL, GA (Mediacom)

NELSON—See ELLIJAY, GA (Community Cable Television Co)

NEWBORN—See ATLANTA, GA (Comcast Cable)

NEWINGTON—Formerly served by Planters Telephone Cooperative. No longer in operation

NEWNAN—Charter Communications

NEWNAN—NuLink Digital

NEWTON COUNTY (PORTIONS)—See ATLANTA, GA (Comcast Cable)

NEWTON COUNTY (southern portion)—Formerly served by KLiP Interactive. No longer in operation

NEWTON COUNTY—Bulldog Cable

NEWTON COUNTY—See STOCKBRIDGE, GA (Charter Communications)

NEWTON—Formerly served by Blakely Cable TV Inc. No longer in operation

NICHOLLS—See DOUGLAS, GA (Vyve Broadband)

NICHOLSON—See DAHLONEGA, GA (Windstream Teleview)

NORCROSS—See ATLANTA, GA (Comcast Cable)

NORMAN PARK—Formerly served by Wainwright Cable Inc. No longer in operation

NORTH AUGUSTA—See AUGUSTA, SC (Comcast Cable)

NUNEZ—See METTER, GA (Pineland Telephone Coop. This cable system has converted to IPTV)

OAK PARK—Pineland Telephone Coop. Inc. This cable system has converted to IPTV. Now served by METTER, GA [GA5005]

OAK PARK—See METTER, GA (Pineland Telephone Coop. This cable system has converted to IPTV)

OAKWOOD—See LAWRENCEVILLE, GA (Charter Communications)

OCHLOCKNEE—Formerly served by Southeast Cable TV Inc. No longer in operation

OCILLA—See FITZGERALD, GA (Mediacom)

OCONEE COUNTY—See ATHENS, GA (Charter Communications)

OCONEE COUNTY—See ATLANTA, GA (Comcast Cable)

OCONEE—Formerly served by National Cable Inc. No longer in operation

ODUM—See SAVANNAH, GA (Comcast Cable)

OFFERMAN—See PATTERSON, GA (ATC Broadband)

OGLETHORPE COUNTY (PORTIONS)—See ATHENS, GA (Charter Communications)

OGLETHORPE—See MONTEZUMA, GA (Comcast Cable)

OMEGA—Formerly served by Plant Telenet. No longer in operation.

OMEGA—See TIFTON, GA (Mediacom)

ORCHARD HILL—See ATLANTA, GA (Comcast Cable)

OXFORD—See STOCKBRIDGE, GA (Charter Communications)

PALMETTO—See ATLANTA, GA (Comcast Cable)

PALMETTO—See NEWNAN, GA (NuLink Digital)

PATTERSON—ATC Broadband

PAULDING COUNTY (PORTIONS)—See ATLANTA, GA (Comcast Cable)

PAVO—Formerly served by Southeast Cable TV Inc. No longer in operation

PAYNE CITY—See MACON, GA (Cox Communications)

PEACH COUNTY (PORTIONS)—See MACON, GA (Cox Communications)

PEACH COUNTY—See PERRY, GA (ComSouth Telesys Inc)

PEACHTREE CITY—See ATLANTA, GA (Comcast Cable)

PEACHTREE CITY—See NEWNAN, GA (NuLink Digital)

Georgia—Cable Community Index

PEARSON—See ADEL, GA (Mediacom)

PELHAM—See ALBANY, GA (Mediacom)

PEMBROKE—Comcast Cable. Now served by SAVANNAH, GA [GA0005]

PEMBROKE—See SAVANNAH, GA (Comcast Cable)

PENDERGRASS—See ATLANTA, GA (Comcast Cable)

PERRY—ComSouth Telesys Inc

PERRY—See MACON, GA (Cox Communications)

PICKENS COUNTY (PORTIONS)—See ELLIJAY, GA (Community Cable Television Co)

PINE GLEN—See ALBANY, GA (Mediacom)

PINE LAKE—See ATLANTA, GA (Comcast Cable)

PINE MOUNTAIN VALLEY—See NEWNAN, GA (Charter Communications)

PINE MOUNTAIN—Charter Communications. Now served by NEWNAN, GA [GA0042]

PINE MOUNTAIN—See NEWNAN, GA (Charter Communications)

PINEHURST—ComSouth Telesys Inc. Now served by PERRY, GA [GA0229]

PINEHURST—See PERRY, GA (ComSouth Telesys Inc)

PINEVIEW—Formerly served by KLiP Interactive. No longer in operation

PITTS—Formerly served by KLiP Interactive. No longer in operation

PLAINS—Citizens Cable TV. Now served by COBB, GA [GA0150]

PLAINS—See COBB, GA (Citizens Cable TV)

PLAINVILLE—See ATLANTA, GA (Comcast Cable)

POLK COUNTY (PORTIONS)—See ATLANTA, GA (Comcast Cable)

POLK COUNTY—See NEWNAN, GA (Charter Communications)

POOLER—Hargray. Now served by BLUFFTON (village), SC [SC0020]

POOLER—See SAVANNAH, GA (Comcast Cable)

PORT WENTWORTH (portions)—Comcast Cable. Now served by SAVANNAH, GA [GA0005]

PORT WENTWORTH—See SAVANNAH, GA (Comcast Cable)

PORTAL—Formerly served by KLiP Interactive. No longer in operation

PORTAL—See BROOKLET, GA (Bulloch Telephone)

PORTERDALE—See STOCKBRIDGE, GA (Charter Communications)

POULAN—See ALBANY, GA (Mediacom)

POWDER SPRINGS—See ATLANTA, GA (Comcast Cable)

PRESTON—Formerly served by Citizens Cable TV. No longer in operation

PULASKI COUNTY (PORTIONS)—See PERRY, GA (ComSouth Telesys Inc)

PULASKI—See METTER, GA (Pineland Telephone Coop. This cable system has converted to IPTV)

PUTNAM COUNTY (PORTIONS)—See MILLEDGEVILLE, GA (Charter Communications)

PUTNAM COUNTY (UNINCORPORATED AREAS)—See GREENE COUNTY (unincorporated areas), GA (Plantation Cablevision Inc)

PUTNAM COUNTY—Bulldog Cable

PUTNEY—See ALBANY, GA (Mediacom)

QUITMAN—Comcast Cable. Now served by TALLAHASSEE, FL [FL0283]

QUITMAN—Camellia City Cable

RABUN COUNTY (PORTIONS)—See CLAYTON, GA (TruVista Communications)

RANDOLPH COUNTY (PORTIONS)—See CUTHBERT, GA (Mediacom)

RANGER—Formerly served by 3D Cable Inc. No longer in operation

RAY CITY—See ADEL, GA (Mediacom)

RAYLE—Formerly served by KLiP Interactive. No longer in operation

RAYSVILLE—Formerly served by KLiP Interactive. No longer in operation

REBECCA—Formerly served by KLiP Interactive. No longer in operation

RECOVERY—Formerly served by KLiP Interactive. No longer in operation

REGENCY MOTOR HOME PARK—See SAVANNAH, GA (Comcast Cable)

REIDSVILLE—Hargray. Now served by BLUFFTON (village), SC [SC0020]

REMERTON—See VALDOSTA, GA (Mediacom)

RENTZ—Progressive Rural Telephone. This cable system has converted to IPTV. See RENTZ, GA [GA5268]

RENTZ—Progressive Rural Telephone. This cable system has converted to IPTV.

RESACA—See ATLANTA, GA (Comcast Cable)

REST HAVEN—See LAWRENCEVILLE, GA (Charter Communications)

REYNOLDS—Flint Cable TV

RHINE—Formerly served by KLiP Interactive. No longer in operation

RICEBORO—See SAVANNAH, GA (Comcast Cable)

RICHLAND—See CUTHBERT, GA (Mediacom)

RICHMOND COUNTY (PORTIONS)—See AUGUSTA, GA (WOW! Internet, Cable & Phone)

RICHMOND HILL—See SAVANNAH, GA (Comcast Cable)

RINCON—See SAVANNAH, GA (Comcast Cable)

RINGGOLD—Formerly served by Ringgold Telephone. No longer in operation

RINGGOLD—Charter Communications

RIVERDALE—See ATLANTA, GA (Comcast Cable)

ROBERTA—Flint Cable TV. Now served by REYNOLDS, GA [GA0236]

ROBERTA—See REYNOLDS, GA (Flint Cable TV)

ROBINS AFB—See MACON, GA (Cox Communications)

ROBINS AFB—Watson Cable

ROCHELLE—Bulldog Cable

ROCKDALE COUNTY (PORTIONS)—See ATLANTA, GA (Comcast Cable)

ROCKDALE COUNTY (UNINCORPORATED AREAS)—See STOCKBRIDGE, GA (Charter Communications)

ROCKMART—Charter Communications. Now served by NEWNAN, GA [GA0042]

ROCKMART—See NEWNAN, GA (Charter Communications)

ROME—See ATLANTA, GA (Comcast Cable)

ROSSVILLE—Comcast Cable. Now served by KNOXVILLE, TN [TN0004]

ROSWELL—Charter Communications. Now served by LAWRENCEVILLE, GA [GA0009]

ROSWELL—See LAWRENCEVILLE, GA (Charter Communications)

ROSWELL—See ATLANTA, GA (Comcast Cable)

ROYSTON—See TOCCOA, GA (TruVista Communications)

RUTLEDGE—See MILLEDGEVILLE, GA (Charter Communications)

SANDERSVILLE—Charter Communications

SANFORD—Formerly served by KLiP Interactive. No longer in operation

SANTA CLAUS—See VIDALIA, GA (Northland Cable Television)

SARDIS—Formerly served by KLiP Interactive. No longer in operation

SASSER—Formerly served by Citizens Cable TV. No longer in operation

SAVANNAH—Comcast Cable

SCHLEY COUNTY (PORTIONS)—See AMERICUS, GA (Mediacom)

SCOTLAND—See EASTMAN, GA (Mediacom)

SCREVEN COUNTY (PORTIONS)—See AUGUSTA, GA (Comcast Cable)

SCREVEN—See SAVANNAH, GA (Comcast Cable)

SEMINOLE COUNTY (PORTIONS)—See BAINBRIDGE, GA (Mediacom)

SEMINOLE COUNTY—Formerly served by Bulldog Cable. No longer in operation

SENOIA—See ATLANTA, GA (Comcast Cable)

SHARPSBURG—See NEWNAN, GA (Charter Communications)

SHARPSBURG—See NEWNAN, GA (NuLink Digital)

SHELLMAN BLUFF—See DARIEN, GA (Comcast Cable)

SHELLMAN—See CUTHBERT, GA (Mediacom)

SHILOH—See LAGRANGE, GA (Charter Communications)

SILVERWOOD PLANTATION—See SAVANNAH, GA (Comcast Cable)

SKIDAWAY ISLAND—Formerly served by US Cable of Coastal Texas LP. Now served by Comcast Cable, SAVANNAH, GA [GA0005]

SKIDAWAY ISLAND—See SAVANNAH, GA (Comcast Cable)

SMITHVILLE—Citizens Cable TV. Now served by COBB, GA [GA0150]

SMITHVILLE—See COBB, GA (Citizens Cable TV)

SMYRNA—Charter Communications. Now served by LAWRENCEVILLE, GA [GA0009]

SMYRNA—See LAWRENCEVILLE, GA (Charter Communications)

SMYRNA—See ATLANTA, GA (Comcast Cable)

SNELLVILLE—See ATLANTA, GA (Comcast Cable)

SOCIAL CIRCLE—See ATLANTA, GA (Comcast Cable)

SOCIAL CIRCLE—See MONROE, GA (Monroe Utilities Network)

SOPERTON—Comcast Cable

SOUTHBRIDGE—Formerly served by Comcast Cable. No longer in operation

SPALDING COUNTY (PORTIONS)—See ATLANTA, GA (Comcast Cable)

SPARKS—See ADEL, GA (Mediacom)

SPARTA—Bulldog Cable

SPRINGFIELD—See SAVANNAH, GA (Comcast Cable)

ST. MARY'S—Comcast Cable. Now served by JACKSONVILLE, FL [FL0002]

STAPLETON—Formerly served by KLiP Interactive. No longer in operation

STATESBORO—Northland Cable Television

Cable Community Index—Georgia

STATHAM—Comcast Cable. Now served by ATLANTA, GA [GA0017]

STATHAM—See ATLANTA, GA (Comcast Cable)

STEPHENS COUNTY—See TOCCOA, GA (TruVista Communications)

STILLMORE—Pineland Telephone Coop. Inc. This cable system has converted to IPTV. Now served by METTER, GA [GA5005]

STILLMORE—See METTER, GA (Pineland Telephone Coop. This cable system has converted to IPTV)

STOCKBRIDGE—Charter Communications

STOCKBRIDGE—See ATLANTA, GA (Comcast Cable)

STONE MOUNTAIN—See ATLANTA, GA (Comcast Cable)

SUGAR HILL—See LAWRENCEVILLE, GA (Charter Communications)

SUMMERVILLE—Charter Communications

SUMTER COUNTY (PORTIONS)—See COBB, GA (Citizens Cable TV)

SUMTER COUNTY (PORTIONS)—See AMERICUS, GA (Mediacom)

SUNNY SIDE—See ATLANTA, GA (Comcast Cable)

SURRENCY—Worth Cable

SUWANEE—See LAWRENCEVILLE, GA (Charter Communications)

SWAINSBORO—Northland Cable Television

SWAINSBORO—See METTER, GA (Pineland Telephone Coop. This cable system has converted to IPTV)

SYCAMORE—See TIFTON, GA (Mediacom)

SYLVANIA—Comcast Cable. Now served by AUGUSTA, GA [GA0004]

SYLVANIA—See AUGUSTA, GA (Comcast Cable)

SYLVESTER—See ALBANY, GA (Mediacom)

TALBOT COUNTY—See LAGRANGE, GA (Charter Communications)

TALBOTTON—See LAGRANGE, GA (Charter Communications)

TALKING ROCK—See ELLIJAY, GA (Community Cable Television Co)

TALLAPOOSA—Comcast Cable. Now served by ATLANTA, GA [GA0017]

TALLAPOOSA—See ATLANTA, GA (Comcast Cable)

TALMO—See ATLANTA, GA (Comcast Cable)

TATE—See ELLIJAY, GA (Community Cable Television Co)

TATTNALL COUNTY (PORTIONS)—See GLENNVILLE, GA (Comcast Cable)

TAYLORSVILLE—See ATLANTA, GA (Comcast Cable)

TELFAIR COUNTY (PORTIONS)—See EASTMAN, GA (Mediacom)

TEMPLE—See NEWNAN, GA (Charter Communications)

TENNILLE—See SANDERSVILLE, GA (Charter Communications)

TERRELL COUNTY (SOUTHERN PORTION)—See ALBANY, GA (Mediacom)

THOMAS COUNTY (PORTIONS)—See ALBANY, GA (Mediacom)

THOMAS COUNTY—See THOMASVILLE, GA (Mediacom)

THOMASTON—Charter Communications

THOMASVILLE—CNS

THOMASVILLE—Mediacom

THOMSON—See AUGUSTA, GA (Comcast Cable)

THUNDERBOLT—See SAVANNAH, GA (Comcast Cable)

TIFT COUNTY (PORTIONS)—See ADEL, GA (Mediacom)

TIFTON—Mediacom

TIGER—See CLAYTON, GA (TruVista Communications)

TIGNALL—Formerly served by Almega Cable. No longer in operation

TOCCOA FALLS—See TOCCOA, GA (TruVista Communications)

TOCCOA—TruVista Communications

TOOMBS COUNTY (PORTIONS)—See VIDALIA, GA (Northland Cable Television)

TOOMBS COUNTY (PORTIONS)—See UVALDA, GA (Worth Cable)

TOOMSBORO—Formerly served by KLiP Interactive. Now served by Windstream Teleview, IRWINTON, GA [GA0300]

TOOMSBORO—See IRWINTON, GA (Windstream Teleview)

TOWNS COUNTY (PORTIONS)—See DAHLONEGA, GA (Windstream Teleview)

TOWNSEND—See DARIEN, GA (Comcast Cable)

TOWNSEND—See DARIEN, GA (Darien Communications)

TRENTON—Charter Communications. Now served by JASPER, TN [TN0070]

TRENTON—See AUGUSTA, SC (Comcast Cable)

TREUTLEN COUNTY (PORTIONS)—See SOPERTON, GA (Comcast Cable)

TRION—See SUMMERVILLE, GA (Charter Communications)

TROUP COUNTY (PORTIONS)—See LAGRANGE, GA (Charter Communications)

TROUP COUNTY (PORTIONS)—See NEWNAN, GA (Charter Communications)

TROUP COUNTY (PORTIONS)—See ATLANTA, GA (Comcast Cable)

TUNNEL HILL—See DALTON, GA (Charter Communications)

TURIN—See NEWNAN, GA (Charter Communications)

TURNER COUNTY (SOUTHERN PORTION)—See TIFTON, GA (Mediacom)

TWIN CITY—Comcast Cable. Now served by SAVANNAH, GA [GA0005]

TWIN CITY—See SAVANNAH, GA (Comcast Cable)

TWIN CITY—See METTER, GA (Pineland Telephone Coop. This cable system has converted to IPTV)

TY TY—See TIFTON, GA (Mediacom)

TYBEE ISLAND—Comcast Cable. Now served by SAVANNAH, GA [GA0005]

TYBEE ISLAND—See SAVANNAH, GA (Comcast Cable)

TYRONE—See ATLANTA, GA (Comcast Cable)

TYRONE—See NEWNAN, GA (NuLink Digital)

U.S. MARINE LOGISTICS BASE (GOVERNMENT RESERVE)—See ALBANY, GA (Mediacom)

UNADILLA—Formerly served by CommuniComm Services. Now served by ComSouth Telesys Inc., PERRY, GA [GA0229]

UNADILLA—See PERRY, GA (ComSouth Telesys Inc)

UNION CITY—See ATLANTA, GA (Comcast Cable)

UNION COUNTY (PORTIONS)—See DAHLONEGA, GA (Windstream Teleview)

UNION POINT—See MILLEDGEVILLE, GA (Charter Communications)

UPSON COUNTY (PORTIONS)—See REYNOLDS, GA (Flint Cable TV)

UPSON COUNTY (UNINCORPORATED AREAS)—See THOMASTON, GA (Charter Communications)

UVALDA—Worth Cable

VALDOSTA—Mediacom

VALLEY—See NEWNAN, AL (Charter Communications)

VARNELL—See DALTON, GA (Charter Communications)

VERNONBURG—See SAVANNAH, GA (Comcast Cable)

VIDALIA—Northland Cable Television

VIENNA—See COBB, GA (Citizens Cable TV)

VIENNA—See FITZGERALD, GA (Mediacom)

VILLA RICA—Charter Communications. Now served by NEWNAN, GA [GA0042]

VILLA RICA—See NEWNAN, GA (Charter Communications)

VILLA RICA—See ATLANTA, GA (Comcast Cable)

WACO—See ATLANTA, GA (Comcast Cable)

WADLEY—See AUGUSTA, GA (Comcast Cable)

WALESKA—See ATLANTA, GA (Comcast Cable)

WALNUT GROVE—See ATLANTA, GA (Comcast Cable)

WALTHOURVILLE—See SAVANNAH, GA (Comcast Cable)

WALTON COUNTY (PORTIONS)—See ATLANTA, GA (Comcast Cable)

WARE COUNTY (EASTERN PORTION)—See WAYCROSS, GA (Vyve Broadband)

WARM SPRINGS—See LAGRANGE, GA (Charter Communications)

WARNER ROBINS—See PERRY, GA (ComSouth Telesys Inc)

WARNER ROBINS—See MACON, GA (Cox Communications)

WARREN COUNTY (PORTIONS)—See AUGUSTA, GA (Comcast Cable)

WARRENTON—Comcast Cable. Now served by AUGUSTA, GA [GA0004]

WARRENTON—See AUGUSTA, GA (Comcast Cable)

WARWICK—Citizens Cable TV. Now served by COBB, GA [GA0150]

WARWICK—See COBB, GA (Citizens Cable TV)

WASHINGTON COUNTY (PORTIONS)—See SANDERSVILLE, GA (Charter Communications)

WASHINGTON—Comcast Cable

WATKINSVILLE—See ATHENS, GA (Charter Communications)

WAVERLY HALL—Charter Communications. Now served by NEWNAN, GA [GA0042]

WAVERLY HALL—See NEWNAN, GA (Charter Communications)

WAYCROSS—Vyve Broadband

WAYNE COUNTY (PORTIONS)—See SAVANNAH, GA (Comcast Cable)

WAYNESBORO—Comcast Cablevision of the South. Now served by AUGUSTA, GA [GA0004]

WAYNESBORO—See AUGUSTA, GA (Comcast Cable)

WAYNESVILLE—Comcast Cable. Now served by JACKSONVILLE, FL [FL0002]

Georgia—Cable Community Index

WEST POINT—Charter Communications. Now served by NEWNAN, GA [GA0042]

WEST POINT—See NEWNAN, GA (Charter Communications)

WHEELER COUNTY (PORTIONS)—See MOUNT VERNON, GA (Comcast Cable)

WHIGHAM—Formerly served by KLiP Interactive. No longer in operation

WHITE COUNTY (PORTIONS)—See DAHLONEGA, GA (Windstream Teleview)

WHITE—See ATLANTA, GA (Comcast Cable)

WHITESBURG—See ATLANTA, GA (Comcast Cable)

WHITFIELD COUNTY—See DALTON, GA (Charter Communications)

WILEY ACRES—Citizens Cable TV. Now served by COBB, GA [GA0150]

WILEY ACRES—See COBB, GA (Citizens Cable TV)

WILKES COUNTY (PORTIONS)—See WASHINGTON, GA (Comcast Cable)

WILKINSON COUNTY (portions)—Windstream Teleview. Now served by IRWINTON, GA [GA0300]

WILKINSON COUNTY (PORTIONS)—See IRWINTON, GA (Windstream Teleview)

WILLACOOCHEE—See ADEL, GA (Mediacom)

WILLIAMSON—Formerly served by Georgia Broadband. No longer in operation

WINDER—Comcast Cable. Now served by ATLANTA, GA [GA0017]

WINDER—See ATLANTA, GA (Comcast Cable)

WINTERVILLE—See ATHENS, GA (Charter Communications)

WOODBINE—Comcast Cable. Now served by JACKSONVILLE, FL [FL0002]

WOODBURY—Formerly served by Almega Cable. No longer in operation

WOODBURY—Formerly served by Georgia Broadband. No longer in operation

WOODLAND LAKES RESORT—See SAVANNAH, GA (Comcast Cable)

WOODLAND—See LAGRANGE, GA (Charter Communications)

WOODSTOCK—See ATLANTA, GA (Comcast Cable)

WOODVILLE—See MILLEDGEVILLE, GA (Charter Communications)

WOOLSEY—See ATLANTA, GA (Comcast Cable)

WORTH COUNTY (EASTERN PORTION)—See ALBANY, GA (Mediacom)

WORTH COUNTY (PORTIONS)—See COBB, GA (Citizens Cable TV)

WRENS—Bulldog Cable

WRIGHTSVILLE—Comcast Cable

YATESVILLE—Flint Cable TV. Now served by REYNOLDS, GA [GA0236]

YATESVILLE—See REYNOLDS, GA (Flint Cable TV)

YOUNG HARRIS—See DAHLONEGA, GA (Windstream Teleview)

ZEBULON—Formerly served by Georgia Broadband. No longer in operation

HAWAII

AHUIMANU—See OAHU ISLAND, HI (Oceanic Time Warner Cable)

ALIAMANU GOVERNMENT RESERVE—See OAHU ISLAND, HI (Oceanic Time Warner Cable)

BARKING SANDS NAVAL BASE—See KAUAI ISLAND, HI (Oceanic Time Warner Cable)

BELLOWS AFB—Oceanic Time Warner Cable. Now served by OAHU ISLAND, HI [HI0001]

BELLOWS AFB—See OAHU ISLAND, HI (Oceanic Time Warner Cable)

CAPTAIN COOK—See KEALAKEKUA, HI (Oceanic Time Warner Cable)

EAST HONOLULU—See OAHU ISLAND, HI (Oceanic Time Warner Cable)

ENCHANTED HILLS—See OAHU ISLAND, HI (Oceanic Time Warner Cable)

EWA BEACH—See OAHU ISLAND, HI (Oceanic Time Warner Cable)

EWA—See OAHU ISLAND, HI (Oceanic Time Warner Cable)

HALEIWA—See OAHU ISLAND, HI (Oceanic Time Warner Cable)

HANA—See MAUI ISLAND, HI (Oceanic Time Warner Cable)

HAU—See KEALAKEKUA, HI (Oceanic Time Warner Cable)

HAUULA—See OAHU ISLAND, HI (Oceanic Time Warner Cable)

HAWAII KAI—Oceanic Time Warner Cable. Now served by OAHU ISLAND, HI [HI0001]

HAWAII KAI—See OAHU ISLAND, HI (Oceanic Time Warner Cable)

HAWAII—See KEALAKEKUA, HI (Oceanic Time Warner Cable)

HAWI—Oceanic Time Warner Cable. Now served by KEALAKEKUA (formerly KONA), HI [HI0011]

HAWI—See KEALAKEKUA, HI (Oceanic Time Warner Cable)

HICKAM AFB—Formerly served by Cable TV Services. No longer in operation

HICKAM AFB—See OAHU ISLAND, HI (Oceanic Time Warner Cable)

HILO—Oceanic Time Warner Cable. Now served by KEALAKEKUA (formerly KONA), HI [HI0011]

HILO—See KEALAKEKUA, HI (Oceanic Time Warner Cable)

HOLUALOA—See KEALAKEKUA, HI (Oceanic Time Warner Cable)

HONAUNAU—See KEALAKEKUA, HI (Oceanic Time Warner Cable)

HONOKAA—See KEALAKEKUA, HI (Oceanic Time Warner Cable)

HONOLULU—Formerly served by Craig Wireless Honolulu Inc. No longer in operation

HONOLULU—See OAHU ISLAND, HI (Oceanic Time Warner Cable)

HONOMU—See KEALAKEKUA, HI (Oceanic Time Warner Cable)

IWELEI—See OAHU ISLAND, HI (Oceanic Time Warner Cable)

KAAAWA—See OAHU ISLAND, HI (Oceanic Time Warner Cable)

KAHALUU—See OAHU ISLAND, HI (Oceanic Time Warner Cable)

KAHULUI—See MAUI ISLAND, HI (Oceanic Time Warner Cable)

KAILUA (PORTIONS)—See KEALAKEKUA, HI (Oceanic Time Warner Cable)

KAILUA (PORTIONS)—See OAHU ISLAND, HI (Oceanic Time Warner Cable)

KAIMUKI—See OAHU ISLAND, HI (Oceanic Time Warner Cable)

KALAOA—See KEALAKEKUA, HI (Oceanic Time Warner Cable)

KALAUPAPA—See MAUI ISLAND, HI (Oceanic Time Warner Cable)

KALIHI—See OAHU ISLAND, HI (Oceanic Time Warner Cable)

KAMUELA—See KEALAKEKUA, HI (Oceanic Time Warner Cable)

KANEOHE BAY MARINE CORPS BASE—See OAHU ISLAND, HI (Oceanic Time Warner Cable)

KANEOHE—See OAHU ISLAND, HI (Oceanic Time Warner Cable)

KAPAHULU—See OAHU ISLAND, HI (Oceanic Time Warner Cable)

KAU—See KEALAKEKUA, HI (Oceanic Time Warner Cable)

KAUAI ISLAND—Oceanic Time Warner Cable

KAUNAKAKAI—See MAUI ISLAND, HI (Oceanic Time Warner Cable)

KAWAIABE—See KEALAKEKUA, HI (Oceanic Time Warner Cable)

KAWAIHAE—See KEALAKEKUA, HI (Oceanic Time Warner Cable)

KEALAKEKUA—Oceanic Time Warner Cable

KEAUHOU—See KEALAKEKUA, HI (Oceanic Time Warner Cable)

KEEAU—See KEALAKEKUA, HI (Oceanic Time Warner Cable)

KIHEI—See MAUI ISLAND, HI (Oceanic Time Warner Cable)

KONA—See KEALAKEKUA, HI (Oceanic Time Warner Cable)

KULA—See MAUI ISLAND, HI (Oceanic Time Warner Cable)

KURTISTOWN—See KEALAKEKUA, HI (Oceanic Time Warner Cable)

LAHAINA—See MAUI ISLAND, HI (Oceanic Time Warner Cable)

LAIE—See OAHU ISLAND, HI (Oceanic Time Warner Cable)

LANAI CITY—See MAUI ISLAND, HI (Oceanic Time Warner Cable)

LAUPAHOEHOE—See KEALAKEKUA, HI (Oceanic Time Warner Cable)

MAALAEA—See MAUI ISLAND, HI (Oceanic Time Warner Cable)

MAKAHA—See OAHU ISLAND, HI (Oceanic Time Warner Cable)

MAKAWAO—See MAUI ISLAND, HI (Oceanic Time Warner Cable)

MAUI ISLAND—Oceanic Time Warner Cable

MAUI—Formerly served by Hawaiian Cablevision. Now served by Oceanic Time Warner Cable, MAUI ISLAND, HI [HI0013]

MAUI—Formerly served by Maui Cablevision Corp. No longer in operation

MAUNA KEA—See KEALAKEKUA, HI (Oceanic Time Warner Cable)

MAUNA LANI—See KEALAKEKUA, HI (Oceanic Time Warner Cable)

MAUNAWILI—See OAHU ISLAND, HI (Oceanic Time Warner Cable)

MILIANI—See OAHU ISLAND, HI (Oceanic Time Warner Cable)

MOANALUA—See OAHU ISLAND, HI (Oceanic Time Warner Cable)

MOUNTAIN VIEW—See KEALAKEKUA, HI (Oceanic Time Warner Cable)

NORTH KOHALA DISTRICT—See KEALAKEKUA, HI (Oceanic Time Warner Cable)

NORTH SHORE—See OAHU ISLAND, HI (Oceanic Time Warner Cable)

OAHU ISLAND—Oceanic Time Warner Cable

PAAUILO—See KEALAKEKUA, HI (Oceanic Time Warner Cable)

PAHALA—Formerly served by Time Warner Cable. No longer in operation

PAHOA—See KEALAKEKUA, HI (Oceanic Time Warner Cable)

PAIA—See MAUI ISLAND, HI (Oceanic Time Warner Cable)

PALOLO—See OAHU ISLAND, HI (Oceanic Time Warner Cable)

Cable Community Index—Idaho

PAPAALOA—See KEALAKEKUA, HI (Oceanic Time Warner Cable)

PAPAIKOU—See KEALAKEKUA, HI (Oceanic Time Warner Cable)

PEARL HARBOR GOVERNMENT RESERVE—See OAHU ISLAND, HI (Oceanic Time Warner Cable)

PEPEEKEO—See KEALAKEKUA, HI (Oceanic Time Warner Cable)

PUAKO—See KEALAKEKUA, HI (Oceanic Time Warner Cable)

PUKALANI—See MAUI ISLAND, HI (Oceanic Time Warner Cable)

PUNA—See KEALAKEKUA, HI (Oceanic Time Warner Cable)

SALT LAKE—See OAHU ISLAND, HI (Oceanic Time Warner Cable)

VOLCANO VILLAGE—See KEALAKEKUA, HI (Oceanic Time Warner Cable)

WAHIAWA—See OAHU ISLAND, HI (Oceanic Time Warner Cable)

WAIALUA—See OAHU ISLAND, HI (Oceanic Time Warner Cable)

WAIANAE—See OAHU ISLAND, HI (Oceanic Time Warner Cable)

WAIKOLOA RESORT—See KEALAKEKUA, HI (Oceanic Time Warner Cable)

WAIKOLOA VILLAGE—See KEALAKEKUA, HI (Oceanic Time Warner Cable)

WAILEA—See MAUI ISLAND, HI (Oceanic Time Warner Cable)

WAILUKU—See MAUI ISLAND, HI (Oceanic Time Warner Cable)

WAIMANALO—See OAHU ISLAND, HI (Oceanic Time Warner Cable)

WAIPIO—See OAHU ISLAND, HI (Oceanic Time Warner Cable)

IDAHO

ABERDEEN TWP.—Direct Communications

ADA COUNTY (PORTIONS)—See BOISE, ID (Cable One)

ADA COUNTY (unincorporated areas)—Formerly served by Ada Cable Vision Inc. No longer in operation

ALBION (town)—Formerly served by Telsat Systems Inc. No longer in operation

AMERICAN FALLS—Cable One. Now served by POCATELLO, ID [ID0004]

AMERICAN FALLS—See POCATELLO, ID (Cable One)

AMMON—See IDAHO FALLS, ID (Cable One)

ARCO—ATC Communications

ASHTON—Formerly served by Silver Star Broadband. No longer in operation

ASOTIN COUNTY—See LEWISTON, WA (Cable One)

ASOTIN—See LEWISTON, WA (Cable One)

ATHOL—See COEUR D'ALENE, ID (Time Warner Cable)

AVERY—Formerly served by Rapid Cable. No longer in operation

BANCROFT—See SODA SPRINGS, ID (Silver Star Communications)

BANNOCK COUNTY—See POCATELLO, ID (Cable One)

BASALT—See IDAHO FALLS, ID (Cable One)

BAYVIEW—See COEUR D'ALENE, ID (Time Warner Cable)

BELLEVUE—See SUN VALLEY, ID (Cox Communications)

BINGHAM COUNTY—See IDAHO FALLS, ID (Cable One)

BLACKFOOT—See IDAHO FALLS, ID (Cable One)

BLAINE COUNTY—See SUN VALLEY, ID (Cox Communications)

BOISE—Formerly served by Wireless Broadcasting Systems. No longer in operation

BOISE—Cable One

BONNER COUNTY (PORTIONS)—See SANDPOINT, ID (Northland Cable Television)

BONNERS FERRY—Country Cable

BONNEVILLE COUNTY—See IDAHO FALLS, ID (Cable One)

BOUNDARY COUNTY—See BONNERS FERRY, ID (Country Cable)

BOVILL—Formerly served by Adelphia Communications. No longer in operation

BOVILL—Formerly served by Elk River TV Cable Co. No longer in operation

BUHL—Formerly served by Millennium Digital Media. Now served by Cable One, TWIN FALLS, ID [ID0088]

BUHL—See TWIN FALLS, ID (Cable One)

BURLEY—See TWIN FALLS, ID (Cable One)

CALDWELL—Cable One. Now served by BOISE, ID [ID0001]

CALDWELL—See BOISE, ID (Cable One)

CAMBRIDGE—Cambridge Cable TV

CANYON COUNTY (PORTIONS)—See BOISE, ID (Cable One)

CASCADE—Cable One. Now served by BOISE, ID [ID0001]

CASCADE—See BOISE, ID (Cable One)

CASSIA COUNTY (NORTHERN PORTION)—See TWIN FALLS, ID (Cable One)

CASTLEFORD—Formerly served by WDB Communications. No longer in operation

CATALDO—Suddenlink Communications. Now served by OSBURN, ID [ID0015]

CATALDO—See OSBURN, ID (Suddenlink Communications)

CHALLIS—Custer Telephone Broadband Services

CHUBBOCK—See POCATELLO, ID (Cable One)

CLARKSTON—See LEWISTON, WA (Cable One)

COEUR D'ALENE—Time Warner Cable

COTTONWOOD—See OROFINO, ID (Suddenlink Communications)

COUNCIL—Cambridge Cable TV

COUNCIL—See CAMBRIDGE, ID (Cambridge Cable TV)

CULDESAC—Formerly served by Rapid Cable. No longer in operation

DALTON GARDENS—See COEUR D'ALENE, ID (Time Warner Cable)

DEARY—Formerly served by Elk River TV Cable Co. No longer in operation

DONNELLY—Cable One. Now served by BOISE, ID [ID0001]

DONNELLY—See BOISE, ID (Cable One)

DOVER—See SANDPOINT, ID (Northland Cable Television)

DOWNEY—Formerly served by Independent Cable. Now served by Silver Star Communications, SODA SPRINGS, ID [ID0022]

DOWNEY—See SODA SPRINGS, ID (Silver Star Communications)

DRIGGS—Formerly served by Independent Cable. Now served by Silver Star Broadband, VICTOR, ID [ID0062]

DRIGGS—See VICTOR, ID (Silver Star Broadband)

EAGLE—See BOISE, ID (Cable One)

ELIZABETH PARK—See OSBURN, ID (Suddenlink Communications)

ELK RIVER—Formerly served by Elk River TV Cable Co. No longer in operation

ELMORE COUNTY—See MOUNTAIN HOME, ID (Zito Media)

EMMETT—Cable One. Now served by BOISE, ID [ID0001]

EMMETT—See BOISE, ID (Cable One)

ENAVILLE—See OSBURN, ID (Suddenlink Communications)

FERNAN LAKE—See COEUR D'ALENE, ID (Time Warner Cable)

FILER—Formerly served by Filer Mutual Telephone. No longer in operation

FILER—See TWIN FALLS, ID (Cable One)

FIRTH—See IDAHO FALLS, ID (Cable One)

FISH HAVEN—Formerly served by Independent Cable. Now served by Silver Star Communications, SODA SPRINGS, ID [ID0022]

FISH HAVEN—See SODA SPRINGS, ID (Silver Star Communications)

FREMONT COUNTY (SOUTHERN PORTION)—See IDAHO FALLS, ID (Cable One)

FRUITLAND—See BOISE, ID (Cable One)

GARDEN CITY—See BOISE, ID (Cable One)

GARDEN CITY—See SODA SPRINGS, UT (Silver Star Communications)

GEM COUNTY (PORTIONS)—See BOISE, ID (Cable One)

GEORGETOWN—See SODA SPRINGS, ID (Silver Star Communications)

GLENNS FERRY—RTI-Rural Telecom

GOODING COUNTY (PORTIONS)—See TWIN FALLS, ID (Cable One)

GOODING—See TWIN FALLS, ID (Cable One)

GRACE—See SODA SPRINGS, ID (Silver Star Communications)

GRANGEVILLE—See OROFINO, ID (Suddenlink Communications)

GREENLEAF—See BOISE, ID (Cable One)

HAGERMAN—See TWIN FALLS, ID (Cable One)

HAILEY—See SUN VALLEY, ID (Cox Communications)

HANSEN—See TWIN FALLS, ID (Cable One)

HARRISON—Formerly served by Rapid Cable. No longer in operation

HAUSER LAKE—See COEUR D'ALENE, ID (Time Warner Cable)

HAYDEN LAKE—See COEUR D'ALENE, ID (Time Warner Cable)

HAYDEN—See COEUR D'ALENE, ID (Time Warner Cable)

HAZELTON—Formerly served by WDB Communications. No longer in operation

HEYBURN—See TWIN FALLS, ID (Cable One)

HOMEDALE—See BOISE, ID (Cable One)

HORSESHOE BEND—See BOISE, ID (Cable One)

HUETTER—See COEUR D'ALENE, ID (Time Warner Cable)

IDAHO CITY—Formerly served by Idaho City Cable TV. No longer in operation

IDAHO FALLS—Cable One

INKOM—See POCATELLO, ID (Cable One)

Idaho—Cable Community Index

IONA—See IDAHO FALLS, ID (Cable One)

JEFFERSON COUNTY—See IDAHO FALLS, ID (Cable One)

JEROME—See TWIN FALLS, ID (Cable One)

KAMIAH—See OROFINO, ID (Suddenlink Communications)

KELLOGG—See OSBURN, ID (Suddenlink Communications)

KETCHUM—See SUN VALLEY, ID (Cox Communications)

KIMBERLY—See TWIN FALLS, ID (Cable One)

KINGSTON—See OSBURN, ID (Suddenlink Communications)

KOOSKIA—Formerly served by Rapid Cable. No longer in operation

KOOTENAI COUNTY (portions)—Formerly served by Rapid Cable. No longer in operation

KOOTENAI COUNTY (PORTIONS)—See COEUR D'ALENE, ID (Time Warner Cable)

KOOTENAI—See SANDPOINT, ID (Northland Cable Television)

KUNA—See BOISE, ID (Cable One)

LAVA HOT SPRINGS—Formerly served by Independent Cable. Now served by Silver Star Communications, SODA SPRINGS, ID [ID0022]

LAVA HOT SPRINGS—See SODA SPRINGS, ID (Silver Star Communications)

LEWISTON—Cable One

MACKAY—Formerly served by Independent Cable. Now served by ATC Communications, ARCO, ID [ID0030]

MACKAY—See ARCO, ID (ATC Communications)

MADISON COUNTY (NORTHERN PORTION)—See IDAHO FALLS, ID (Cable One)

MALAD CITY—ATC Communications

MALHEUR COUNTY (PORTIONS)—See BOISE, OR (Cable One)

MARSING—See BOISE, ID (Cable One)

McCALL—Cable One. Now served by BOISE, ID [ID0001]

MCCALL—See BOISE, ID (Cable One)

McCAMMON—Formerly served by Independent Cable. Now served by Silver Star Communications, SODA SPRINGS, ID [ID0022]

MCCAMMON—See SODA SPRINGS, ID (Silver Star Communications)

MERIDIAN—See BOISE, ID (Cable One)

MIDDLETON—See BOISE, ID (Cable One)

MIDVALE—Midvale Telephone Exchange Inc.

MINIDOKA COUNTY (SOUTHERN PORTION)—See TWIN FALLS, ID (Cable One)

MONTPELIER—See SODA SPRINGS, ID (Silver Star Communications)

MOUNTAIN HOME AFB—See MOUNTAIN HOME, ID (Zito Media)

MOUNTAIN HOME—Zito Media

MULLAN—Mullan Cable TV Inc

MURRAY—Formerly served by Rapid Cable. No longer in operation

NAMPA—See BOISE, ID (Cable One)

NEW MEADOWS—Cable One. Now served by BOISE, ID [ID0001]

NEW MEADOWS—See BOISE, ID (Cable One)

NEW PLYMOUTH—See BOISE, ID (Cable One)

NEZ PERCE COUNTY (PORTIONS)—See LEWISTON, ID (Cable One)

NOTUS—See BOISE, ID (Cable One)

NYSSA—See BOISE, OR (Cable One)

ONTARIO—See BOISE, OR (Cable One)

OROFINO—Suddenlink Communications

OSBURN—Suddenlink Communications

OWYHEE COUNTY (NORTHWESTERN PORTION)—See BOISE, ID (Cable One)

PARIS—See SODA SPRINGS, ID (Silver Star Communications)

PARMA—See BOISE, ID (Cable One)

PAUL—See TWIN FALLS, ID (Cable One)

PAYETTE—See BOISE, ID (Cable One)

PINEHURST—See OSBURN, ID (Suddenlink Communications)

POCATELLO—Cable One

PONDERAY—See SANDPOINT, ID (Northland Cable Television)

POST FALLS—See COEUR D'ALENE, ID (Time Warner Cable)

PRESTON—Formerly served by Direct Communications. Now served by Silver Star Communications, SODA SPRINGS, ID [ID0022]

PRESTON—See SODA SPRINGS, ID (Silver Star Communications)

PRICHARD—Formerly served by Rapid Cable. No longer in operation

PURPLE SAGE—See BOISE, ID (Cable One)

RATHDRUM—See COEUR D'ALENE, ID (Time Warner Cable)

REXBURG—See IDAHO FALLS, ID (Cable One)

RICHFIELD—Formerly served by WDB Communications. No longer in operation

RIGBY—See IDAHO FALLS, ID (Cable One)

RIGGINS—Formerly served by Elk River TV Cable Co. No longer in operation

RIRIE—See IDAHO FALLS, ID (Cable One)

ROCKFORD—See IDAHO FALLS, ID (Cable One)

RUPERT—See TWIN FALLS, ID (Cable One)

SALMON—Custer Telephone Broadband Services

SANDPOINT (UNINCORPORATED AREAS)—See SANDPOINT, ID (Northland Cable Television)

SANDPOINT—Northland Cable Television

SHELLEY—See IDAHO FALLS, ID (Cable One)

SHOSHONE—Formerly served by Millennium Digital Media. Now served by Cable One, TWIN FALLS, ID [ID0088]

SHOSHONE—See TWIN FALLS, ID (Cable One)

SILVERTON—See OSBURN, ID (Suddenlink Communications)

SMELTERVILLE—See OSBURN, ID (Suddenlink Communications)

SODA SPRINGS—Silver Star Communications

SPIRIT LAKE—Formerly served by Cebridge Connections. Now served by Suddenlink Communications, SPIRIT LAKE, ID [ID0092]

SPIRIT LAKE—Suddenlink Communications

ST. ANTHONY—See IDAHO FALLS, ID (Cable One)

ST. CHARLES—See SODA SPRINGS, ID (Silver Star Communications)

ST. MARIES—Suddenlink Communications

STAR—See BOISE, ID (Cable One)

SUGAR CITY—See IDAHO FALLS, ID (Cable One)

SUN VALLEY—Cox Communications

TETON—See IDAHO FALLS, ID (Cable One)

TROY—Formerly served by Elk River TV Cable Co. No longer in operation

TWIN FALLS COUNTY (PORTIONS)—See TWIN FALLS, ID (Cable One)

TWIN FALLS—Cable One

TWIN LAKES—See SPIRIT LAKE, ID (Suddenlink Communications)

UCON—See IDAHO FALLS, ID (Cable One)

VALE—See BOISE, OR (Cable One)

VICTOR—Silver Star Broadband

WALLACE—See OSBURN, ID (Suddenlink Communications)

WARDNER—See OSBURN, ID (Suddenlink Communications)

WEISER—Cable One. Now served by BOISE, ID [ID0001]

WEISER—See BOISE, ID (Cable One)

WENDELL—See TWIN FALLS, ID (Cable One)

WILDER—See BOISE, ID (Cable One)

WORLEY—Formerly served by Elk River TV Cable Co. No longer in operation

ILLINOIS

ABINGDON—Mediacom. Now served by ELMWOOD, IL [IL0205]

ABINGDON—See ELMWOOD, IL (Mediacom)

ADAIR (unincorporated areas)—Formerly served by CableDirect. No longer in operation

ADAMS COUNTY (PORTIONS)—See PEORIA, IL (Comcast Cable)

ADDIEVILLE—Charter Communications. Now served by ST. LOUIS, MO [MO0009]

ADDISON—See PEORIA, IL (Comcast Cable)

AKRON—See CHAMPAIGN, IN (Comcast Cable)

ALBANY TWP.—See MOUNT CARROLL, WI (Mediacom)

ALBANY—See MOUNT CARROLL, WI (Mediacom)

ALBION (TOWN)—See McLEANSBORO, IL (NewWave Communications)

ALBION—NewWave Communications. Now served by McLEANSBORO, IL [IL0177]

ALDO (UNINCORPORATED AREAS)—See ONEIDA, IL (Oneida Cablevision Inc. Formerly [IL0361]. This cable system has converted to IPTV)

ALEDO—See GENESEO, IL (Mediacom)

ALEXANDER COUNTY (PORTIONS)—Zito Media

ALEXIS—Mediacom. Now served by GENESEO, IL [IL0170]

ALEXIS—See GENESEO, IL (Mediacom)

ALGONQUIN—See MOUNT PROSPECT, IL (Comcast Cable)

ALHAMBRA—Madison Communications. Now served by STAUNTON, IL [IL0171]

ALHAMBRA—See STAUNTON, IL (Madison Communications)

ALLERTON (VILLAGE)—Clearvision Cable Systems Inc

ALMA—See KINMUNDY, IL (Clearvision Cable Systems Inc)

ALPHA—Diverse Communications Inc.

ALPHA—See ONEIDA, IL (Oneida Cablevision Inc. Formerly [IL0361]. This cable system has converted to IPTV)

Cable Community Index—Illinois

ALSEY TWP.—Formerly served by Longview Communications. No longer in operation

ALSIP—See CHAMPAIGN, IL (Comcast Cable)

ALTAMONT—Mediacom

ALTO PASS—See ZEIGLER, IL (Mediacom)

ALTONA (village)—Mediacom. Now served by GENESEO, IL [IL0170]

ALTONA—See GENESEO, IL (Mediacom)

ALTONA—See ELLISVILLE, IL (Mid Century Communications)

ALTONA—See ONEIDA, IL (Oneida Cablevision Inc. Formerly [IL0361]. This cable system has converted to IPTV)

AMBOY—Comcast Cable. Now served by MOUNT PROSPECT, IL [IL0036]

AMBOY—See MOUNT PROSPECT, IL (Comcast Cable)

ANDALUSIA TWP.—See MOLINE, IL (Mediacom)

ANDALUSIA—See MOLINE, IL (Mediacom)

ANDERSONVILLE—See CHICAGO, IL (RCN Corp. Formerly [IL0661]. This cable system has converted to IPTV)

ANDOVER—See GENESEO, IL (Mediacom)

ANNA—NewWave Communications

ANNAWAN—See GENESEO, IL (Mediacom)

ANTIOCH—See MOUNT PROSPECT, IL (Comcast Cable)

APOLLO ACRES—Mediacom. Now served by ROANOKE, IL [IL0068]

APOLLO ACRES—See ROANOKE, IL (Mediacom)

APPLE RIVER—See MOUNT CARROLL, IL (Mediacom)

ARCOLA—See TUSCOLA, IL (Mediacom)

ARENZVILLE—Mediacom

ARGENTA—NewWave Communications

ARGYLE—See BELVIDERE TWP., IL (Mediacom)

ARGYLE—See MOUNT CARROLL, WI (Mediacom)

ARLINGTON HEIGHTS—See MOUNT PROSPECT, IL (Comcast Cable)

ARLINGTON HEIGHTS—See NAPERVILLE, IL (WOW! Internet, Cable & Phone)

ARMINGTON—Formerly served by Heartland Cable Inc. No longer in operation

ARMSTRONG—Park TV & Electronics Inc

AROMA PARK—See CHAMPAIGN, IL (Comcast Cable)

AROMA—See CHAMPAIGN, IL (Comcast Cable)

ARTHUR—See TUSCOLA, IL (Mediacom)

ASHKUM—See CHAMPAIGN, IL (Comcast Cable)

ASHLAND—See BEARDSTOWN, IL (Cass Cable TV Inc)

ASHMORE—See CHARLESTON, IL (Mediacom)

ASHTON—See MOUNT PROSPECT, IL (Comcast Cable)

ASSUMPTION—See MOWEAQUA, IL (NewWave Communications)

ASTORIA—Formerly served by Mediacom. Now served by Nova Cablevision, IPAVA, IL [IL0357]

ASTORIA—See IPAVA, IL (Nova1Net)

ATHENS—See WILLIAMSVILLE, IL (Greene County Partners Inc)

ATKINSON—See GENESEO, IL (Mediacom)

ATLANTA—Mediacom

ATWOOD—See TUSCOLA, IL (Mediacom)

AUBURN—See TAYLORVILLE, IL (NewWave Communications)

AUGUSTA—Adams Telcom. Now served by BOWDEN, IL [IL0702]

AUGUSTA—See BOWEN, IL (Adams Telcom)

AURORA—Comcast Cable. Now served by PEORIA, IL [IL0012]

AURORA—See PEORIA, IL (Comcast Cable)

AVA—Formerly served by Longview Communications. No longer in operation

AVON—Mediacom. Now served by ELMWOOD, IL [IL0205]

AVON—See ELMWOOD, IL (Mediacom)

AVONDALE—See CHICAGO, IL (RCN Corp. Formerly [IL0661]. This cable system has converted to IPTV)

BAINBRIDGE TWP.—See CHAMPAIGN, MI (Comcast Cable)

BALL TWP.—See SPRINGFIELD, IL (Comcast Cable)

BANNOCKBURN—See MOUNT PROSPECT, IL (Comcast Cable)

BARDOLPH—Formerly served by CableDirect. No longer in operation

BARODA (VILLAGE)—See CHAMPAIGN, MI (Comcast Cable)

BARODA TWP.—See CHAMPAIGN, MI (Comcast Cable)

BARRINGTON HILLS—Comcast Cable. Now served by MOUNT PROSPECT, IL [IL0036]

BARRINGTON HILLS—See MOUNT PROSPECT, IL (Comcast Cable)

BARRINGTON—See MOUNT PROSPECT, IL (Comcast Cable)

BARRY—Formerly served by Crystal Broadband Networks. No longer in operation

BARSTOW—See MOLINE, IL (Mediacom)

BARTELSO—Formerly served by CableDirect. No longer in operation

BARTLETT—See MOUNT PROSPECT, IL (Comcast Cable)

BARTONVILLE—See PEORIA, IL (Comcast Cable)

BATAVIA—Comcast Cable. Now served by PEORIA, IL [IL0012]

BATAVIA—See PEORIA, IL (Comcast Cable)

BATH—See BEARDSTOWN, IL (Cass Cable TV Inc)

BAYLES LAKE—See RANTOUL, IL (Mediacom)

BAYLIS (village)—Formerly served by Cass Cable TV Inc. No longer in operation

BAYVIEW GARDENS—See ROANOKE, IL (Mediacom)

BEACH PARK—See MOUNT PROSPECT, IL (Comcast Cable)

BEARDSTOWN—Cass Cable TV Inc

BEAVERVILLE TWP.—Formerly served by CableDirect. No longer in operation

BEDFORD PARK—See PEORIA, IL (Comcast Cable)

BEECHER CITY—Clearvision Cable Systems Inc

BEECHER—See CHAMPAIGN, IL (Comcast Cable)

BELGIUM—See WESTVILLE, IL (NewWave Communications)

BELLE RIVE—Formerly served by Longview Communications. No longer in operation

BELLE RIVE—See DAHLGREN, IL (Hamilton County Communications. Formerly [IL0381]. This cable system has converted to IPTV)

BELLEVILLE—Charter Communications. Now served by ST. LOUIS, MO [MO0009]

BELLEVUE—See PEORIA, IL (Comcast Cable)

BELLFLOWER—See LE ROY, IL (Mediacom)

BELLMONT—Formerly served by CableDirect. No longer in operation

BELLWOOD—See PEORIA, IL (Comcast Cable)

BELMONT HARBOR—See CHICAGO, IL (RCN Corp. Formerly [IL0661]. This cable system has converted to IPTV)

BELVIDERE TWP.—Mediacom. Now served by BELVIDERE TWP. (formerly POPLAR GROVE), IL [IL0282]

BELVIDERE TWP.—Mediacom

BELVIDERE—Formerly served by Insight Communications. Now served by Comcast Cable, MOUNT PROSPECT, IL [IL0036]

BELVIDERE—See MOUNT PROSPECT, IL (Comcast Cable)

BEMENT—See MONTICELLO, IL (Mediacom)

BENLD—See STAUNTON, IL (Madison Communications)

BENSENVILLE—See PEORIA, IL (Comcast Cable)

BENSON—See ROANOKE, IL (Mediacom)

BENTON HARBOR—See CHAMPAIGN, MI (Comcast Cable)

BENTON TWP. (BERRIEN COUNTY)—See CHAMPAIGN, MI (Comcast Cable)

BENTON—NewWave Communications

BERKELEY—See PEORIA, IL (Comcast Cable)

BERRIEN SPRINGS (VILLAGE)—See CHAMPAIGN, MI (Comcast Cable)

BERRIEN TWP.—See CHAMPAIGN, MI (Comcast Cable)

BERTRAND TWP.—See CHAMPAIGN, MI (Comcast Cable)

BERWYN—See PEORIA, IL (Comcast Cable)

BETHANY—Formerly served by Suddenlink Communications. Now served by NewWave Communications, MOWEAQUA, IL [IL0185]

BETHANY—See MOWEAQUA, IL (NewWave Communications)

BETTENDORF—See MOLINE, IA (Mediacom)

BEVERLY SHORES—See CHAMPAIGN, IN (Comcast Cable)

BIBLE GROVE—See FLORA, IL (Wabash Independent Networks)

BIG ROCK—See SUGAR GROVE, IL (Mediacom)

BIGGSVILLE—Formerly served by CableDirect. No longer in operation

BIRDS—Formerly served by Park TV & Electronics Inc. No longer in operation

BISHOP HILL—See ELLISVILLE, IL (Mid Century Communications)

BISHOP HILL—See ONEIDA, IL (Oneida Cablevision Inc. Formerly [IL0361]. This cable system has converted to IPTV)

BISMARCK—Park TV & Electronics Inc

BISSEL—See SPRINGFIELD, IL (Comcast Cable)

BLAIRSVILLE—See ZEIGLER, IL (Mediacom)

Illinois—Cable Community Index

BLANCHARDVILLE—See MOUNT CARROLL, WI (Mediacom)

BLANDINSVILLE (VILLAGE)—See PEORIA, IL (Comcast Cable)

BLOOMINGDALE—See PEORIA, IL (Comcast Cable)

BLOOMINGTON—Comcast Cable. Now served by PEORIA, IL [IL0012]

BLOOMINGTON—See PEORIA, IL (Comcast Cable)

BLUE GRASS—See MOLINE, IA (Mediacom)

BLUE ISLAND—See CHAMPAIGN, IL (Comcast Cable)

BLUE MOUND—Formerly served by Suddenlink Communications. Now served by NewWave Communications, MOWEAQUA, IL [IL0185]

BLUE MOUND—See MOWEAQUA, IL (NewWave Communications)

BLUFF CITY—See TAYLORVILLE, IL (NewWave Communications)

BLUFF SPRINGS—See BEARDSTOWN, IL (Cass Cable TV Inc)

BLUFFS—Formerly served by Crystal Broadband Networks. No longer in operation

BLUFORD—Formerly served by Longview Communications. No longer in operation

BODEN—See GENESEO, IL (Mediacom)

BOLINGBROOK—See PEORIA, IL (Comcast Cable)

BOND COUNTY (PORTIONS)—See TAYLORVILLE, IL (NewWave Communications)

BONDVILLE—See CHAMPAIGN, IL (Comcast Cable)

BONE GAP—Formerly served by CableDirect. No longer in operation

BONE GAP—See FLORA, IL (Wabash Independent Networks)

BONFIELD (village)—Formerly served by CableDirect. No longer in operation

BONNIE—Formerly served by Longview Communications. No longer in operation

BOODY—Formerly served by CableDirect. No longer in operation

BOONE COUNTY (PORTIONS)—See MOUNT PROSPECT, IL (Comcast Cable)

BOULDER HILL—See PEORIA, IL (Comcast Cable)

BOURBONAIS—See CHAMPAIGN, IL (Comcast Cable)

BOWEN—Adams Telcom

BRADFORD—Mediacom. Now served by WYOMING, IL [IL0196]

BRADFORD—See WYOMING, IL (Mediacom)

BRADLEY—See CHAMPAIGN, IL (Comcast Cable)

BRAIDWOOD—See PEORIA, IL (Comcast Cable)

BREESE—Charter Communications. Now served by ST. LOUIS, MO [MO0009]

BRIDGEPORT—See CHICAGO, IL (RCN Corp. Formerly [IL0661]. This cable system has converted to IPTV

BRIDGEVIEW—See PEORIA, IL (Comcast Cable)

BRIDGMAN—See CHAMPAIGN, MI (Comcast Cable)

BRIGHTON—Formerly served by Greene County Partners. Now served by NewWave Communications, JERSEYVILLE, IL [IL0130]

BRIGHTON—See JERSEYVILLE, IL (NewWave Communications)

BRIMFIELD—Mediacom. Now served by CHILLICOTHE, IL [IL0118]

BRIMFIELD—Mediacom. Now served by CHILLICOTHE, IL [IL0118]

BRIMFIELD—See CHILLICOTHE, IL (Mediacom)

BRIMFIELD—See METAMORA, IL (TelStar Cablevision Inc)

BRISTOL—See PEORIA, IL (Comcast Cable)

BRISTOL—See CHAMPAIGN, IN (Comcast Cable)

BROADLANDS—See NEWMAN, IL (Comcast Cable)

BROADVIEW—See PEORIA, IL (Comcast Cable)

BROCTON—Clearvision Cable Systems Inc

BRONZEVILLE—See CHICAGO, IL (RCN Corp. Formerly [IL0661]. This cable system has converted to IPTV

BROOK—See WATSEKA, IN (Mediacom)

BROOKFIELD—See PEORIA, IL (Comcast Cable)

BROUGHTON—See DAHLGREN, IL (Hamilton County Communications. Formerly [IL0381]. This cable system has converted to IPTV)

BROWNS—See FLORA, IL (Wabash Independent Networks)

BROWNSTOWN—See TAYLORVILLE, IL (NewWave Communications)

BROWNTOWN—See MOUNT CARROLL, WI (Mediacom)

BRUCE TWP.—See STREATOR, IL (Mediacom)

BRYANT (village)—Formerly served by CableDirect. No longer in operation

BUCHANAN TWP.—See CHAMPAIGN, MI (Comcast Cable)

BUCHANAN—See CHAMPAIGN, MI (Comcast Cable)

BUCKLEY (VILLAGE)—Park TV & Electronics Inc

BUCKNER—See BENTON, IL (NewWave Communications)

BUDA—See GENESEO, IL (Mediacom)

BUENA PARK—See CHICAGO, IL (RCN Corp. Formerly [IL0661]. This cable system has converted to IPTV

BUFFALO GROVE—See MOUNT PROSPECT, IL (Comcast Cable)

BUFFALO—Mediacom. Now served by KINCAID, IL [IL0176]

BUFFALO—See MOLINE, IA (Mediacom)

BUFFALO—See KINCAID, IL (Mediacom)

BULPITT—See KINCAID, IL (Mediacom)

BUNCOMBE—Zito Media

BUNKER HILL—See STAUNTON, IL (Madison Communications)

BURBANK—See PEORIA, IL (Comcast Cable)

BUREAU COUNTY (PORTIONS)—See MOUNT PROSPECT, IL (Comcast Cable)

BUREAU—Mediacom. Now served by MOUNT PROSPECT, IL [IL0036]

BUREAU—See CHILLICOTHE, IL (Mediacom)

BURKET—See CHAMPAIGN, IN (Comcast Cable)

BURLINGTON (village)—Formerly served by Mediacom. No longer in operation

BURNHAM—See CHAMPAIGN, IL (Comcast Cable)

BURNS HARBOR—See CHAMPAIGN, IN (Comcast Cable)

BURR RIDGE—See PEORIA, IL (Comcast Cable)

BUSH—See ZEIGLER, IL (Mediacom)

BUSHNELL—Formerly served by Insight Communications. Now served by Comcast Cable, PEORIA, IL [IL0012]

BUSHNELL—See PEORIA, IL (Comcast Cable)

BUZZVILLE—See BEARDSTOWN, IL (Cass Cable TV Inc)

BYRON—See MOUNT PROSPECT, IL (Comcast Cable)

CAHOKIA—Charter Communications. Now served by ST. LOUIS, MO [MO0009]

CAIRO—NewWave Communications

CALEDONIA—Mediacom. Now served by BELVIDERE TWP., IL [IL0282]

CALEDONIA—See BELVIDERE TWP., IL (Mediacom)

CALHOUN COUNTY (portions)—Formerly served by CableDirect. No longer in operation

CALUMET CITY—See CHAMPAIGN, IL (Comcast Cable)

CALUMET CITY—See NAPERVILLE, IL (WOW! Internet, Cable & Phone)

CALUMET PARK—See CHAMPAIGN, IL (Comcast Cable)

CALVIN TWP.—See CHAMPAIGN, MI (Comcast Cable)

CAMARGO—See TUSCOLA, IL (Mediacom)

CAMBRIA—See ZEIGLER, IL (Mediacom)

CAMBRIDGE—See GENESEO, IL (Mediacom)

CAMERON—Nova1Net

CAMERON—See ONEIDA, IL (Oneida Cablevision Inc. Formerly [IL0361]. This cable system has converted to IPTV)

CAMP POINT—Adams Telephone. This cable system has converted to IPTV. See CAMP POINT, IL [IL5313]

CAMP POINT—Adams Telcom. Formerly [IL0206]. This cable system has converted to IPTV

CAMPBELLS ISLAND—See MOLINE, IL (Mediacom)

CAMPTON HILLS—See PEORIA, IL (Comcast Cable)

CAMPTON TWP.—Formerly served by Comcast Cable. No longer in operation

CANDLEWICK LAKE—See BELVIDERE TWP., IL (Mediacom)

CANTON—Comcast Cable. Now served by PEORIA, IL [IL0012]

CANTON—See PEORIA, IL (Comcast Cable)

CANTON—See ONEIDA, IL (Oneida Cablevision Inc. Formerly [IL0361]. This cable system has converted to IPTV)

CANTRALL—Mediacom. Now served by DELEVAN, IL [IL0172]

CANTRALL—See DELAVAN, IL (Mediacom)

CAPRON—See BELVIDERE TWP., IL (Mediacom)

CARBON CLIFF—See MOLINE, IL (Mediacom)

CARBON HILL—See PEORIA, IL (Comcast Cable)

CARBONDALE TWP.—See MURPHYSBORO, IL (Mediacom)

CARBONDALE—See MURPHYSBORO, IL (Mediacom)

CARLINVILLE—NewWave Communications. Now served by TAYLORVILLE, IL [IL0098]

CARLINVILLE—See TAYLORVILLE, IL (NewWave Communications)

CARLOCK—Formerly served by CableDirect. No longer in operation

Cable Community Index—Illinois

CARLYLE—Charter Communications. Now served by ST. LOUIS, MO [MO0009]

CARMI—Formerly served by Charter Communications. No longer in operation

CARMI—See McLEANSBORO, IL (NewWave Communications)

CAROL STREAM—See PEORIA, IL (Comcast Cable)

CARPENTERSVILLE—Comcast Cable. Now served by MOUNT PROSPECT, IL [IL0036]

CARPENTERSVILLE—See MOUNT PROSPECT, IL (Comcast Cable)

CARRIER MILLS—Zito Media

CARROLL COUNTY (WESTERN PORTION)—See MOUNT CARROLL, IL (Mediacom)

CARROLLTON—NewWave Communications. Now served by JERSEYVILLE, IL [IL0130]

CARROLLTON—See JERSEYVILLE, IL (NewWave Communications)

CARTERVILLE—See MURPHYSBORO, IL (Mediacom)

CARTHAGE—Mediacom

CARY—See MOUNT PROSPECT, IL (Comcast Cable)

CASEY—Mediacom. Now served by MARTINSVILLE, IL [IL0217]

CASEY—See MARTINSVILLE, IL (Mediacom)

CASSOPOLIS—See CHAMPAIGN, MI (Comcast Cable)

CATLIN—See WESTVILLE, IL (NewWave Communications)

CAVE-IN-ROCK—Formerly served by Vital Communications. No longer in operation

CAYUGA—See CHAMPAIGN, IN (Comcast Cable)

CEDAR GROVE—See FREEMAN SPUR, IL (Zito Media)

CEDAR LAKE—See CHAMPAIGN, IN (Comcast Cable)

CEDAR POINT—Formerly served by McNabb Cable & Satellite Inc. No longer in operation

CEDARVILLE—See MOUNT PROSPECT, IL (Comcast Cable)

CERRO GORDO—Mediacom. Now served by SULLIVAN, IL [IL0154]

CERRO GORDO—See SULLIVAN, IL (Mediacom)

CHADWICK—See MOUNT CARROLL, IL (Mediacom)

CHAMPAIGN COUNTY (PORTIONS)—See CHAMPAIGN, IL (Comcast Cable)

CHAMPAIGN COUNTY (PORTIONS)—See RANTOUL, IL (Mediacom)

CHAMPAIGN—Comcast Cable

CHANDLERVILLE—See BEARDSTOWN, IL (Cass Cable TV Inc)

CHANNAHON—Comcast Cable. Now served by PEORIA, IL [IL0012]

CHANNAHON—See PEORIA, IL (Comcast Cable)

CHAPIN—Mediacom. Now served by JACKSONVILLE, IL [IL0065]

CHAPIN—See JACKSONVILLE, IL (Mediacom)

CHARLESTON—Mediacom

CHATHAM—Formerly served by Insight Communications. Now served by Comcast Cable, SPRINGFIELD, IL [IL0016]

CHATHAM—See SPRINGFIELD, IL (Comcast Cable)

CHATSWORTH—See ROANOKE, IL (Mediacom)

CHEBANSE—See CHAMPAIGN, IL (Comcast Cable)

CHEMUNG—Mediacom. Now served by BELVIDERE TWP., IL [IL0282]

CHEMUNG—See BELVIDERE TWP., IL (Mediacom)

CHENOA—See ROANOKE, IL (Mediacom)

CHERRY VALLEY—See MOUNT PROSPECT, IL (Comcast Cable)

CHERRY—See MOUNT PROSPECT, IL (Comcast Cable)

CHESTER—Formerly served by Charter Communications. Now served by NewWave Communications, SPARTA, IL [IL0147]

CHESTER—See SPARTA, IL (NewWave Communications)

CHESTERFIELD (village)—Formerly served by CableDirect. No longer in operation

CHESTERTON—See CHAMPAIGN, IN (Comcast Cable)

CHICAGO (Area 4)—Comcast Cable. Now served by CHICAGO, IL [IL0001]

CHICAGO (Area 5)—Comcast Cable. Now served by CHICAGO, IL [IL0001]

CHICAGO (Areas 1, 4 & 5)—Comcast Cable. Now served by CHICAGO, IL [IL0001]

CHICAGO (portions)—RCN Corp. This cable system has converted to IPTV. See CHICAGO, IL [IL5236]

CHICAGO (southern portion)—WOW! Internet, Cable & Phone. Now served by NAPERVILLE, IL [IL0655]

CHICAGO (SOUTHERN PORTION)—See NAPERVILLE, IL (WOW! Internet, Cable & Phone)

CHICAGO HEIGHTS—See CHAMPAIGN, IL (Comcast Cable)

CHICAGO HEIGHTS—See NAPERVILLE, IL (WOW! Internet, Cable & Phone)

CHICAGO RIDGE—See CHAMPAIGN, IL (Comcast Cable)

CHICAGO—Formerly served by Preferred Entertainment of Chicago. No longer in operation

CHICAGO—Comcast Cable

CHICAGO—RCN Corp. Formerly [IL0661]. This cable system has converted to IPTV

CHIKAMING TWP.—See CHAMPAIGN, MI (Comcast Cable)

CHILLICOTHE—Mediacom

CHRISMAN—See CHAMPAIGN, IL (Comcast Cable)

CHRISTIAN COUNTY (PORTIONS)—See TAYLORVILLE, IL (NewWave Communications)

CHRISTOPHER—See BENTON, IL (NewWave Communications)

CICERO—See PEORIA, IL (Comcast Cable)

CISCO (village)—Formerly served by Longview Communications. No longer in operation

CISNE—Wabash Independent Networks. Now served by FLORA, IL [IL0140]

CISNE—See FLORA, IL (Wabash Independent Networks)

CISSNA PARK (VILLAGE)—Park TV & Electronics Inc

CLAREMONT—Formerly served by CableDirect. No longer in operation

CLARENDON HILLS—See PEORIA, IL (Comcast Cable)

CLARK COUNTY—See MARTINSVILLE, IL (Mediacom)

CLAY CITY—Mediacom

CLAY COUNTY (PORTIONS)—See FLORA, IL (Wabash Independent Networks)

CLAYTON—See CAMP POINT, IL (Adams Telcom. Formerly [IL0206]. This cable system has converted to IPTV)

CLEAR LAKE (VILLAGE)—See KINCAID, IL (Mediacom)

CLEAR LAKE—See ELMWOOD, IN (Mediacom)

CLEVELAND—See MOLINE, IL (Mediacom)

CLIFTON—See CHAMPAIGN, IL (Comcast Cable)

CLINTON—Mediacom. Now served by RANTOUL, IL [IL0089]

CLINTON—See RANTOUL, IL (Mediacom)

CLYBOURN CORRIDOR—See CHICAGO, IL (RCN Corp. Formerly [IL0661]. This cable system has converted to IPTV)

COAL CITY—See PEORIA, IL (Comcast Cable)

COAL VALLEY—See MOLINE, IL (Mediacom)

COALTON—See TAYLORVILLE, IL (NewWave Communications)

COATSBURG—See BOWEN, IL (Adams Telcom)

COBDEN—Mediacom. Now served by ZEIGLER, IL [IL0123]

COBDEN—See ZEIGLER, IL (Mediacom)

COFFEEN—Mediacom

COLCHESTER—See PEORIA, IL (Comcast Cable)

COLES COUNTY—See MATTOON, IL (Mediacom)

COLFAX—Mediacom. Now served by LE ROY, IL [IL0539]

COLFAX—See LE ROY, IL (Mediacom)

COLOMA TWP.—See MOUNT PROSPECT, IL (Comcast Cable)

COLOMA TWP.—See CHAMPAIGN, MI (Comcast Cable)

COLOMA—See CHAMPAIGN, MI (Comcast Cable)

COLONA—See MOLINE, IL (Mediacom)

COLP (VILLAGE)—See MURPHYSBORO, IL (Mediacom)

COMPTON—Formerly served by Compton Cable TV Co. No longer in operation

COMPTON—Formerly served by Heartland Cable Broadband. No longer in operation

CONGERVILLE—Tel-Star Cablevision Inc. Now served by METAMORA, IL [IL0326]

CONGERVILLE—See METAMORA, IL (Tel-Star Cablevision Inc)

COOK COUNTY (PORTIONS)—See CHAMPAIGN, IL (Comcast Cable)

COOK COUNTY (PORTIONS)—See MOUNT PROSPECT, IL (Comcast Cable)

COOK COUNTY (PORTIONS)—See PEORIA, IL (Comcast Cable)

CORDOVA—See GENESEO, IL (Mediacom)

CORNELL—Mediacom. Now served by PONTIAC, IL [IL0109]

CORNELL—See PONTIAC, IL (Mediacom)

CORTLAND (VILLAGE)—Mediacom

COULTERVILLE—Mediacom. Now served by COULTERVILLE (formerly RED BUD), IL [IL0152]

COULTERVILLE—Mediacom

COUNTRY CLUB HILLS—See CHAMPAIGN, IL (Comcast Cable)

COUNTRYSIDE—See PEORIA, IL (Comcast Cable)

COWDEN—Clearvision Cable Systems Inc

Illinois—Cable Community Index

CRAINVILLE—See MURPHYSBORO, IL (Mediacom)

CRAWFORD COUNTY—See ROBINSON, IL (Mediacom)

CREAL SPRINGS—See LAKE OF EGYPT, IL (Zito Media)

CRESCENT CITY—See WATSEKA, IL (Mediacom)

CREST HILL—See PEORIA, IL (Comcast Cable)

CRESTON—See MOUNT PROSPECT, IL (Comcast Cable)

CRESTWOOD—See CHAMPAIGN, IL (Comcast Cable)

CRESTWOOD—See NAPERVILLE, IL (WOW! Internet, Cable & Phone)

CRETE—See CHAMPAIGN, IL (Comcast Cable)

CREVE COEUR—See PEORIA, IL (Comcast Cable)

CROSSVILLE—See McLEANSBORO, IL (NewWave Communications)

CROWN POINT—See CHAMPAIGN, IN (Comcast Cable)

CRYSTAL LAKE—See MOUNT PROSPECT, IL (Comcast Cable)

CUBA—See PEORIA, IL (Comcast Cable)

CUBA—See ONEIDA, IL (Oneida Cablevision Inc. Formerly [IL0361]. This cable system has converted to IPTV)

CULLOM—Mediacom. Now served by PONTIAC, IL [IL0109]

CULLOM—See PONTIAC, IL (Mediacom)

CURRAN—See SPRINGFIELD, IL (Comcast Cable)

CUSTER PARK—Comcast Cable. Now served by PEORIA, IL [IL0012]

CUSTER PARK—See PEORIA, IL (Comcast Cable)

DAHLGREN—Hamilton County Communications. This cable system has converted to IPTV. See DAHLGREN, IL [IL5024]

DAHLGREN—Hamilton County Communications. Formerly [IL0381]. This cable system has converted to IPTV

DAKOTA—See MOUNT CARROLL, IL (Mediacom)

DALLAS CITY—Mediacom. Now served by DALLAS CITY (formerly Roseville), IL [IL0274]

DALLAS CITY—Mediacom

DALTON CITY—See MOWEAQUA, IL (NewWave Communications)

DALZELL—See MOUNT PROSPECT, IL (Comcast Cable)

DANFORTH—See SPRINGFIELD, IL (Comcast Cable)

DANVERS—Mediacom. Now served by ROANOKE, IL [IL0068]

DANVERS—See ROANOKE, IL (Mediacom)

DANVILLE—Formerly served by Insight Communications. Now served by Comcast Cable, CHAMPAIGN, IL [IL0019]

DANVILLE—See CHAMPAIGN, IL (Comcast Cable)

DANVILLE—See WESTVILLE, IL (NewWave Communications)

DARIEN—See PEORIA, IL (Comcast Cable)

DAVENPORT—See MOLINE, IA (Mediacom)

DAVIESS COUNTY (PORTIONS)—See NEWTON, IN (NewWave Communications)

DAVIS JUNCTION—See CORTLAND (village), IL (Mediacom)

DAVIS—See MOUNT CARROLL, IL (Mediacom)

DAWSON—See KINCAID, IL (Mediacom)

DAYTON TWP.—See STREATOR, IL (Mediacom)

DE LAND—See RANTOUL, IL (Mediacom)

DE SOTO—See MURPHYSBORO, IL (Mediacom)

DECATUR—Formerly served by Insight Communications. Now served by Comcast Cable, SPRINGFIELD, IL [IL0016]

DECATUR—See SPRINGFIELD, IL (Comcast Cable)

DEER CREEK—Mediacom. Now served by ROANOKE, IL [IL0068]

DEER CREEK—See ROANOKE, IL (Mediacom)

DEER PARK—See MOUNT PROSPECT, IL (Comcast Cable)

DEERFIELD—See MOUNT PROSPECT, IL (Comcast Cable)

DEKALB COUNTY (PORTIONS)—See CORTLAND (village), IL (Mediacom)

DEKALB COUNTY (PORTIONS)—See SUGAR GROVE, IL (Mediacom)

DEKALB—Comcast Cable. Now served by MOUNT PROSPECT, IL [IL0036]

DEKALB—See MOUNT PROSPECT, IL (Comcast Cable)

DEL MAR WOODS—See MOUNT PROSPECT, IL (Comcast Cable)

DELAVAN—Mediacom

DEMOTTE—See CHAMPAIGN, IN (Comcast Cable)

DEPUE—See MOUNT PROSPECT, IL (Comcast Cable)

DES PLAINES—See MOUNT PROSPECT, IL (Comcast Cable)

DES PLAINES—See NAPERVILLE, IL (WOW! Internet, Cable & Phone)

DIAMOND—See PEORIA, IL (Comcast Cable)

DIETERICH—Clearvision Cable Systems Inc

DIVERNON—See SPRINGFIELD, IL (Comcast Cable)

DIX—Formerly served by Beck's Cable Systems. No longer in operation

DIXMOOR—See CHAMPAIGN, IL (Comcast Cable)

DIXON—Comcast Cable. Now served by MOUNT PROSPECT, IL [IL0036]

DIXON—See MOUNT PROSPECT, IL (Comcast Cable)

DOLTON—Comcast Cable. Now served by CHAMPAIGN, IL [IL0019]

DOLTON—See CHAMPAIGN, IL (Comcast Cable)

DONGOLA—Formerly served by Longview Communications. No longer in operation

DONOVAN TWP.—Formerly served by CableDirect. No longer in operation

DOUGLAS COUNTY (PORTIONS)—See NEWMAN, IL (Comcast Cable)

DOUGLAS COUNTY (PORTIONS)—See TUSCOLA, IL (Mediacom)

DOWAGIAC—See CHAMPAIGN, MI (Comcast Cable)

DOWELL—See ZEIGLER, IL (Mediacom)

DOWNERS GROVE—See PEORIA, IL (Comcast Cable)

DOWNS—See LE ROY, IL (Mediacom)

DU PAGE COUNTY (UNINCORPORATED AREAS)—See PEORIA, IL (Comcast Cable)

DU QUOIN—See BENTON, IL (NewWave Communications)

DUNE ACRES—See CHAMPAIGN, IN (Comcast Cable)

DUNELAND BEACH—See CHAMPAIGN, IN (Comcast Cable)

DUNFERMLINE—See ELMWOOD, IL (Mediacom)

DUNLAP—Mediacom. Now served by CHILLICOTHE, IL [IL0118]

DUNLAP—See CHILLICOTHE, IL (Mediacom)

DUPAGE COUNTY (portions)—Comcast Cable. Now served by PEORIA, IL [IL0012]

DUPAGE COUNTY (PORTIONS)—See MOUNT PROSPECT, IL (Comcast Cable)

DUPAGE COUNTY (PORTIONS)—See PEORIA, IL (Comcast Cable)

DUPAGE COUNTY (PORTIONS)—See NAPERVILLE, IL (WOW! Internet, Cable & Phone)

DUPAGE COUNTY (SOUTHWESTERN PORTION)—See PEORIA, IL (Comcast Cable)

DURAND (village)—Mediacom. Now served by LENA, IL [IL0223]

DURAND—See MOUNT CARROLL, IL (Mediacom)

DURANT—See MOLINE, IA (Mediacom)

DWIGHT—Mediacom. Now served by PONTIAC, IL [IL0109]

DWIGHT—See PONTIAC, IL (Mediacom)

DYER—See CHAMPAIGN, IN (Comcast Cable)

EAGLE TWP.—See STREATOR, IL (Mediacom)

EARLVILLE—See SUGAR GROVE, IL (Mediacom)

EAST CAPE GIRARDEAU—See ALEXANDER COUNTY (portions), IL (Zito Media)

EAST CHICAGO—See CHAMPAIGN, IN (Comcast Cable)

EAST DUBUQUE—Mediacom. Now served by DUBUQUE, IA [IA0007]

EAST DUNDEE—See MOUNT PROSPECT, IL (Comcast Cable)

EAST GALESBURG—See PEORIA, IL (Comcast Cable)

EAST GILLESPIE—See TAYLORVILLE, IL (NewWave Communications)

EAST HAZEL CREST—See CHAMPAIGN, IL (Comcast Cable)

EAST MOLINE—See MOLINE, IL (Mediacom)

EAST PEORIA—See PEORIA, IL (Comcast Cable)

EAST ST. LOUIS—Charter Communications. Now served by ST. LOUIS, MO [MO0009]

EASTON—See BEARDSTOWN, IL (Cass Cable TV Inc)

EDGAR COUNTY (PORTIONS)—See WESTVILLE, IL (NewWave Communications)

EDGEWATER—See CHICAGO, IL (RCN Corp. Formerly [IL0661]. This cable system has converted to IPTV)

EDGEWOOD—Clearvision Cable Systems Inc

EDINBURG—See KINCAID, IL (Mediacom)

EDWARDS—See METAMORA, IL (TelStar Cablevision Inc)

EDWARDSBURG—See CHAMPAIGN, MI (Comcast Cable)

EFFINGHAM COUNTY (PORTIONS)—See ALTAMONT, IL (Mediacom)

EFFINGHAM COUNTY (UNINCORPORATED AREAS)—See EFFINGHAM, IL (Mediacom)

EFFINGHAM COUNTY—See WATSON, IL (Clearvision Cable Systems Inc)

EFFINGHAM—Mediacom

Cable Community Index—Illinois

EL PASO—See ROANOKE, IL (Mediacom)

ELBURN—See SUGAR GROVE, IL (Mediacom)

ELDORADO—See MURPHYSBORO, IL (Mediacom)

ELDRED—Formerly served by Longview Communications. No longer in operation

ELDRIDGE—See MOLINE, IA (Mediacom)

ELGIN TWP.—See PEORIA, IL (Comcast Cable)

ELGIN—Comcast Cable. Now served by PEORIA, IL [IL0012]

ELGIN—See PEORIA, IL (Comcast Cable)

ELGIN—See NAPERVILLE, IL (WOW! Internet, Cable & Phone)

ELIZABETH—Mediacom. Now served by LENA, IL [IL0223]

ELIZABETH—See MOUNT CARROLL, IL (Mediacom)

ELIZABETHTOWN—See ROSICLARE, IL (Zito Media)

ELK GROVE—See MOUNT PROSPECT, IL (Comcast Cable)

ELKHART COUNTY (PORTIONS)—See CHAMPAIGN, IN (Comcast Cable)

ELKHART TWP.—Formerly served by Mediacom. No longer in operation

ELKHART—See CHAMPAIGN, IN (Comcast Cable)

ELKHART—See DELAVAN, IL (Mediacom)

ELKVILLE—See ZEIGLER, IL (Mediacom)

ELLIOTT—See SIBLEY (village), IL (Heartland Cable Inc)

ELLISVILLE—Mid Century Communications

ELLISVILLE—See ONEIDA, IL (Oneida Cablevision Inc. Formerly [IL0361]. This cable system has converted to IPTV)

ELLSWORTH—See SIBLEY (village), IL (Heartland Cable Inc)

ELMHURST—Comcast Cable. Now served by PEORIA, IL [IL0012]

ELMHURST—See PEORIA, IL (Comcast Cable)

ELMWOOD PARK—See PEORIA, IL (Comcast Cable)

ELMWOOD—Mediacom

ELNORA—See NEWTON, IN (NewWave Communications)

ELWOOD—See MANHATTAN, IL (Kraus Electronics Systems Inc)

EMDEN—See DELAVAN, IL (Mediacom)

ENERGY—See MURPHYSBORO, IL (Mediacom)

ENFIELD—NewWave Communications. Now served by McLEANSBORO, IL [IL0177]

ENFIELD—See McLEANSBORO, IL (NewWave Communications)

ETNA GREEN—See CHAMPAIGN, IN (Comcast Cable)

EUGENE—See CHAMPAIGN, IL (Comcast Cable)

EUREKA—See ROANOKE, IL (Mediacom)

EUREKA—See METAMORA, IL (Tel-Star Cablevision Inc)

EVANSTON—See MOUNT PROSPECT, IL (Comcast Cable)

EVANSTON—See CHICAGO, IL (RCN Corp. Formerly [IL0661]. This cable system has converted to IPTV)

EVANSVILLE—NewWave Communications

EVERGREEN PARK—See CHAMPAIGN, IL (Comcast Cable)

EWING—See DAHLGREN, IL (Hamilton County Communications. Formerly [IL0381]. This cable system has converted to IPTV)

EWING—See BENTON, IL (NewWave Communications)

FAIRBURY—Mediacom. Now served by ROANOKE, IL [IL0068]

FAIRBURY—Mediacom. Now served by ROANOKE, IL [IL0068]

FAIRBURY—See ROANOKE, IL (Mediacom)

FAIRFIELD—NewWave Communications. Now served by McLEANSBORO, IL [IL0177]

FAIRFIELD—See McLEANSBORO, IL (NewWave Communications)

FAIRMONT CITY—See WASHINGTON PARK, IL (Mediacom)

FAIRMOUNT—See CHAMPAIGN, IL (Comcast Cable)

FAIRVIEW—Mediacom. Now served by ELMWOOD, IL [IL0205]

FAIRVIEW—See ELMWOOD, IL (Mediacom)

FAIRVIEW—See ELLISVILLE, IL (Mid Century Communications)

FAIRVIEW—See ONEIDA, IL (Oneida Cablevision Inc. Formerly [IL0361]. This cable system has converted to IPTV)

FAR HILLS—See ROANOKE, IL (Mediacom)

FARINA—See LOUISVILLE, IL (Mediacom)

FARMER CITY—Mediacom. Now served by RANTOUL, IL [IL0089]

FARMER CITY—See RANTOUL, IL (Mediacom)

FARMERSVILLE—NewWave Communications. Now served by TAYLORVILLE, IL [IL0098]

FARMERSVILLE—See TAYLORVILLE, IL (NewWave Communications)

FARMINGTON—See ELMWOOD, IL (Mediacom)

FAYETTE COUNTY (PORTIONS)—See ALTAMONT, IL (Mediacom)

FAYETTEVILLE—Formerly served by CableDirect. No longer in operation

FIATT—See WEE-MA-TUK HILLS, IL (Nova1Net)

FIATT—See ONEIDA, IL (Oneida Cablevision Inc. Formerly [IL0361]. This cable system has converted to IPTV)

FIELDON—Formerly served by CableDirect. No longer in operation

FILLMORE—Formerly served by CableDirect. No longer in operation

FINDLAY—Formerly served by Almega Cable. No longer in operation

FISHER—See RANTOUL, IL (Mediacom)

FITHIAN—See CHAMPAIGN, IL (Comcast Cable)

FLANAGAN—Heartland Cable Inc

FLORA—Wabash Independent Networks

FLOSSMOOR—See CHAMPAIGN, IL (Comcast Cable)

FORD HEIGHTS—See CHAMPAIGN, IL (Comcast Cable)

FOREST CITY—See BEARDSTOWN, IL (Cass Cable TV Inc)

FOREST PARK—See PEORIA, IL (Comcast Cable)

FOREST VIEW—See PEORIA, IL (Comcast Cable)

FORREST—See ROANOKE, IL (Mediacom)

FORRESTON—See MOUNT PROSPECT, IL (Comcast Cable)

FORSYTH (VILLAGE)—See SPRINGFIELD, IL (Comcast Cable)

FORT SHERIDAN—See MOUNT PROSPECT, IL (Comcast Cable)

FOWLER—See BOWEN, IL (Adams Telcom)

FOX CREEK—See METAMORA, IL (Tel-Star Cablevision Inc)

FOX LAKE—See MOUNT PROSPECT, IL (Comcast Cable)

FOX RIVER GROVE—See MOUNT PROSPECT, IL (Comcast Cable)

FRANKFORT (VILLAGE)—See PEORIA, IL (Comcast Cable)

FRANKFORT TWP.—See PEORIA, IL (Comcast Cable)

FRANKLIN COUNTY (PORTIONS)—See BENTON, IL (NewWave Communications)

FRANKLIN COUNTY—See ZEIGLER, IL (Mediacom)

FRANKLIN COUNTY—See FREEMAN SPUR, IL (Zito Media)

FRANKLIN GROVE—Comcast Cable. Now served by MOUNT PROSPECT, IL [IL0036]

FRANKLIN GROVE—See MOUNT PROSPECT, IL (Comcast Cable)

FRANKLIN PARK—See PEORIA, IL (Comcast Cable)

FREEMAN SPUR—Zito Media

FREEPORT—Comcast Cable. Now served by MOUNT PROSPECT, IL [IL0036]

FREEPORT—See MOUNT PROSPECT, IL (Comcast Cable)

FRYE LAKE—See GENESEO, IL (Mediacom)

FULTON COUNTY (PORTIONS)—See PEORIA, IL (Comcast Cable)

FULTON COUNTY (PORTIONS)—See CHAMPAIGN, IN (Comcast Cable)

FULTON COUNTY (UNINCORPORATED AREAS)—See ELLISVILLE, IL (Mid Century Communications)

GALATIA—See DAHLGREN, IL (Hamilton County Communications. Formerly [IL0381]. This cable system has converted to IPTV)

GALATIA—See SALINE COUNTY (portions), IL (Zito Media)

GALENA—Mediacom. Now served by DUBUQUE, IA [IA0007]

GALESBURG—Comcast Cable. Now served by PEORIA, IL [IL0012]

GALESBURG—See PEORIA, IL (Comcast Cable)

GALVA—See GENESEO, IL (Mediacom)

GARDEN PRAIRIE—Mediacom. Now served by BELVIDERE TWP., IL [IL0282]

GARDEN PRAIRIE—See BELVIDERE TWP., IL (Mediacom)

GARDNER TWP.—See SPRINGFIELD, IL (Comcast Cable)

GARDNER—Gardner Cable TV Co.

GARRETT—See TUSCOLA, IL (Mediacom)

GARY—See CHAMPAIGN, IN (Comcast Cable)

GAYS (village)—Formerly served by CableDirect. No longer in operation

GEFF—Wabash Independent Networks. Now served by FLORA, IL [IL0140]

GEFF—See FLORA, IL (Wabash Independent Networks)

GEM SUBURBAN MOBILE HOME PARK—Packerland Broadband

GENESEO—Mediacom

GENEVA—See PEORIA, IL (Comcast Cable)

GENOA—Charter Communications. Now served by MADISON, WI [WI0002]

Illinois—Cable Community Index

GEORGETOWN—See WESTVILLE, IL (NewWave Communications)

GERMAN VALLEY—Mediacom

GERMANTOWN HILLS—See ROANOKE, IL (Mediacom)

GIBSON CITY—Mediacom

GIFFORD (VILLAGE)—See RANTOUL, IL (Mediacom)

GILBERTS—Mediacom. Now served by CORTLAND (village), IL [IL0485]

GILBERTS—See CORTLAND (village), IL (Mediacom)

GILLESPIE—NewWave Communications. Now served by TAYLORVILLE, IL [IL0098]

GILLESPIE—See TAYLORVILLE, IL (NewWave Communications)

GILMAN—See SPRINGFIELD, IL (Comcast Cable)

GILSON—See ELLISVILLE, IL (Mid Century Communications)

GILSON—See ONEIDA, IL (Oneida Cablevision Inc. Formerly [IL0361]. This cable system has converted to IPTV)

GINGER RIDGE—Formerly served by Universal Cable Inc. No longer in operation

GIRARD—See TAYLORVILLE, IL (NewWave Communications)

GLADSTONE—Nova1Net

GLADSTONE—See ONEIDA, IL (Oneida Cablevision Inc. Formerly [IL0361]. This cable system has converted to IPTV)

GLASFORD—Mediacom. Now served by ELMWOOD, IL [IL0205]

GLASFORD—See ELMWOOD, IL (Mediacom)

GLASFORD—See METAMORA, IL (Tel-Star Cablevision Inc)

GLEN ELLYN—See PEORIA, IL (Comcast Cable)

GLEN ELLYN—See NAPERVILLE, IL (WOW! Internet, Cable & Phone)

GLENARM—See SPRINGFIELD, IL (Comcast Cable)

GLENCOE—See MOUNT PROSPECT, IL (Comcast Cable)

GLENDALE HEIGHTS—Comcast Cable. Now served by PEORIA, IL [IL0012]

GLENDALE HEIGHTS—See PEORIA, IL (Comcast Cable)

GLENDALE HEIGHTS—See NAPERVILLE, IL (WOW! Internet, Cable & Phone)

GLENVIEW NAVAL AIR STATION—See MOUNT PROSPECT, IL (Comcast Cable)

GLENVIEW—Comcast Cable. Now served by MOUNT PROSPECT, IL [IL0036]

GLENVIEW—See MOUNT PROSPECT, IL (Comcast Cable)

GLENVIEW—See NAPERVILLE, IL (WOW! Internet, Cable & Phone)

GLENWOOD—See CHAMPAIGN, IL (Comcast Cable)

GOLCONDA—Zito Media

GOLD COAST—See CHICAGO, IL (RCN Corp. Formerly [IL0661]. This cable system has converted to IPTV)

GOLDEN—Adams Telcom. Now served by BOWDEN, IL [IL0702]

GOLDEN—See BOWEN, IL (Adams Telcom)

GOLF—See MOUNT PROSPECT, IL (Comcast Cable)

GOOD HOPE—Mediacom

GOODFIELD—See ROANOKE, IL (Mediacom)

GOODFIELD—See METAMORA, IL (Tel-Star Cablevision Inc)

GOODLAND—See WATSEKA, IN (Mediacom)

GOOFY RIDGE—See BEARDSTOWN, IL (Cass Cable TV Inc)

GOOSE LAKE—See PEORIA, IL (Comcast Cable)

GOREVILLE—See LAKE OF EGYPT, IL (Zito Media)

GORHAM TWP.—Formerly served by CableDirect. No longer in operation

GOSHEN—See CHAMPAIGN, IN (Comcast Cable)

GRAFTON—Formerly served by Almega Cable. No longer in operation

GRAND BEACH—See CHAMPAIGN, MI (Comcast Cable)

GRAND RIDGE—Heartland Cable Inc

GRAND TOWER (village)—Formerly served by CableDirect. No longer in operation

GRANDVIEW—See SPRINGFIELD, IL (Comcast Cable)

GRANT PARK (village)—Mediacom. Now served by NEWTON COUNTY (portions), IN [IN0316]

GRANTFORK (VILLAGE)—Clearvision Cable Systems Inc

GRANVILLE—See CHILLICOTHE, IL (Mediacom)

GRAYSLAKE—See MOUNT PROSPECT, IL (Comcast Cable)

GRAYVILLE—NewWave Communications. Now served by McLEANSBORO, IL [IL0177]

GRAYVILLE—See McLEANSBORO, IL (NewWave Communications)

GREAT LAKES NAVAL TRAINING CENTER—Comcast Cable. Now served by MOUNT PROSPECT, IL [IL0036]

GREAT LAKES NAVAL TRAINING CENTER—See MOUNT PROSPECT, IL (Comcast Cable)

GREEN OAKS—See MOUNT PROSPECT, IL (Comcast Cable)

GREEN ROCK—See MOLINE, IL (Mediacom)

GREEN VALLEY—See DELAVAN, IL (Mediacom)

GREENFIELD—Formerly served by BrightGreen Cable. No longer in operation

GREENUP—Mediacom

GREENVIEW—Mediacom. Now served by DELAVAN, IL [IL0172]

GREENVIEW—See DELAVAN, IL (Mediacom)

GREENVILLE—NewWave Communications. Now served by TAYLORVILLE, IL [IL0098]

GREENVILLE—See TAYLORVILLE, IL (NewWave Communications)

GRIDLEY—Gridley Cable

GRIFFITH—See CHAMPAIGN, IN (Comcast Cable)

GRIGGSVILLE—Cass Cable TV Inc. Now served by PITTSFIELD, IL [IL0158]

GRIGGSVILLE—See PITTSFIELD, IL (Cass Cable TV Inc)

GROVELAND—See PEORIA, IL (Comcast Cable)

GRUNDY COUNTY (PORTIONS)—See PEORIA, IL (Comcast Cable)

GURNEE—See MOUNT PROSPECT, IL (Comcast Cable)

HAGAR TWP.—See CHAMPAIGN, MI (Comcast Cable)

HAINESVILLE—See MOUNT PROSPECT, IL (Comcast Cable)

HAMEL—Madison Communications. Now served by STAUNTON, IL [IL0171]

HAMEL—See STAUNTON, IL (Madison Communications)

HAMMOND—See CHAMPAIGN, IN (Comcast Cable)

HAMMOND—See TUSCOLA, IL (Mediacom)

HAMMOND—See NAPERVILLE, IN (WOW! Internet, Cable & Phone)

HAMPSHIRE—Mediacom. Now served by CORTLAND (village), IL [IL0485]

HAMPSHIRE—See CORTLAND (village), IL (Mediacom)

HAMPTON—See MOLINE, IL (Mediacom)

HANNA CITY—See ELMWOOD, IL (Mediacom)

HANOVER PARK—See MOUNT PROSPECT, IL (Comcast Cable)

HANOVER—Mediacom. Now served by LENA, IL [IL0223]

HANOVER—See MOUNT CARROLL, IL (Mediacom)

HARDIN COUNTY—See ROSICLARE, IL (Zito Media)

HARDIN—Formerly served by Bright-Green Cable. No longer in operation

HARRISBURG—Mediacom. Now served by MARION, IL [IL0083]

HARRISBURG—See MURPHYSBORO, IL (Mediacom)

HARRISTOWN (VILLAGE)—See SPRINGFIELD, IL (Comcast Cable)

HARTFORD TWP.—See CHAMPAIGN, MI (Comcast Cable)

HARTSBURG—Mediacom. Now served by DELAVAN, IL [IL0172]

HARTSBURG—See DELAVAN, IL (Mediacom)

HARVARD—Charter Communications. Now served by MADISON, WI [WI0002]

HARVEL—Mediacom. Now served by KINCAID, IL [IL0176]

HARVEL—See KINCAID, IL (Mediacom)

HARVEY—Comcast Cable. Now served by CHAMPAIGN, IL [IL0019]

HARVEY—See CHAMPAIGN, IL (Comcast Cable)

HARWOOD HEIGHTS—See PEORIA, IL (Comcast Cable)

HAVANA—See BEARDSTOWN, IL (Cass Cable TV Inc)

HAWTHORNE WOODS—See MOUNT PROSPECT, IL (Comcast Cable)

HAZEL CREST—See CHAMPAIGN, IL (Comcast Cable)

HEARTVILLE—See WATSON, IL (Clearvision Cable Systems Inc)

HEBRON (village)—Mediacom. Now served by BELVIDERE TWP., IL [IL0282]

HEBRON (VILLAGE)—See BELVIDERE TWP., IL (Mediacom)

HEBRON—See CHAMPAIGN, IN (Comcast Cable)

HECKER—See COULTERVILLE, IL (Mediacom)

HEGELER—See WESTVILLE, IL (NewWave Communications)

HENDERSON—See GENESEO, IL (Mediacom)

HENNEPIN—See CHILLICOTHE, IL (Mediacom)

HENNING—Formerly served by CableDirect. No longer in operation

HENRY COUNTY (NORTHWESTERN PORTION)—See MOLINE, IL (Mediacom)

HENRY COUNTY (PORTIONS)—See MOUNT PROSPECT, IL (Comcast Cable)

Cable Community Index—Illinois

HENRY COUNTY (UNINCORPORATED AREAS)—See GENESEO, IL (Mediacom)

HENRY COUNTY (UNINCORPORATED AREAS)—See ELLISVILLE, IL (Mid Century Communications)

HENRY—See CHILLICOTHE, IL (Mediacom)

HERITAGE LAKE—Tel-Star Cablevision Inc. Now served by METAMORA, IL [IL0326]

HERITAGE LAKE—See METAMORA, IL (Tel-Star Cablevision Inc)

HERRICK—Mediacom

HERRIN—Mediacom. Now served by MARION, IL [IL0083]

HERRIN—See MURPHYSBORO, IL (Mediacom)

HERSCHER—Comcast Cable. Now served by CHAMPAIGN, IL [IL0019]

HERSCHER—See CHAMPAIGN, IL (Comcast Cable)

HETTICK (village)—Formerly served by CableDirect. No longer in operation

HEWITTVILLE—See TAYLORVILLE, IL (NewWave Communications)

HEYWORTH—Mediacom. Now served by ATLANTA, IL [IL0197]

HEYWORTH—See ATLANTA, IL (Mediacom)

HICKORY HILLS—Comcast Cable. Now served by CHAMPAIGN, IL [IL0019]

HICKORY HILLS—See CHAMPAIGN, IL (Comcast Cable)

HIGHLAND PARK—Comcast Cable. Now served by MOUNT PROSPECT, IL [IL0036]

HIGHLAND PARK—See MOUNT PROSPECT, IL (Comcast Cable)

HIGHLAND—See CHAMPAIGN, IN (Comcast Cable)

HIGHWOOD—See MOUNT PROSPECT, IL (Comcast Cable)

HILLCREST—See MOUNT PROSPECT, IL (Comcast Cable)

HILLSBORO—NewWave Communications. Now served by TAYLORVILLE, IL [IL0098]

HILLSBORO—See TAYLORVILLE, IL (NewWave Communications)

HILLSDALE—See GENESEO, IL (Mediacom)

HILLSIDE—See PEORIA, IL (Comcast Cable)

HINCKLEY—See SUGAR GROVE, IL (Mediacom)

HINDSBORO—See TUSCOLA, IL (Mediacom)

HINSDALE—See PEORIA, IL (Comcast Cable)

HOBART—See CHAMPAIGN, IN (Comcast Cable)

HODGKINS—See PEORIA, IL (Comcast Cable)

HOFFMAN ESTATES—See MOUNT PROSPECT, IL (Comcast Cable)

HOFFMAN—Formerly served by CableDirect. No longer in operation

HOLIDAY HILLS—See MOUNT PROSPECT, IL (Comcast Cable)

HOLIDAY SHORES—See STAUNTON, IL (Madison Communications)

HOLLYWOOD PARK—See CHICAGO, IL (RCN Corp. Formerly [IL0661]. This cable system has converted to IPTV)

HOMER TWP.—See PEORIA, IL (Comcast Cable)

HOMER—See CHAMPAIGN, IL (Comcast Cable)

HOMETOWN—See CHAMPAIGN, IL (Comcast Cable)

HOMEWOOD—Comcast Cable. Now served by CHAMPAIGN, IL [IL0019]

HOMEWOOD—See CHAMPAIGN, IL (Comcast Cable)

HOOPESTON—Formerly served by Avenue Broadband Communications. Now served by NewWave Communications, WESTVILLE, IL [IL0079]

HOOPESTON—See WESTVILLE, IL (NewWave Communications)

HOOPPOLE—Formerly served by CableDirect. No longer in operation

HOPEDALE—See ROANOKE, IL (Mediacom)

HOPEWELL—See CHILLICOTHE, IL (Mediacom)

HOPKINS TWP.—See MOUNT PROSPECT, IL (Comcast Cable)

HOWARD TWP.—See CHAMPAIGN, MI (Comcast Cable)

HOYLETON—Formerly served by CableDirect. No longer in operation

HUDSON—Mediacom. Now served by ROANOKE, IL [IL0068]

HUDSON—See ROANOKE, IL (Mediacom)

HUMBOLDT—See TUSCOLA, IL (Mediacom)

HUME (VILLAGE)—Clearvision Cable Systems Inc

HUNTLEY—See MOUNT PROSPECT, IL (Comcast Cable)

HURST—See ZEIGLER, IL (Mediacom)

HUTSONVILLE—See ROBINSON, IL (Mediacom)

HYDE PARK—See CHICAGO, IL (RCN Corp. Formerly [IL0661]. This cable system has converted to IPTV)

ILLIOPOLIS (VILLAGE)—See SPRINGFIELD, IL (Comcast Cable)

INA—Formerly served by Longview Communications. No longer in operation

INDIAN CREEK—See MOUNT PROSPECT, IL (Comcast Cable)

INDIAN HEAD PARK—See PEORIA, IL (Comcast Cable)

INDIANOLA—See CHAMPAIGN, IL (Comcast Cable)

INDUSTRY—Mediacom

INVERNESS—See MOUNT PROSPECT, IL (Comcast Cable)

IPAVA—Nova1Net

IROQUOIS (village)—Formerly served by CableDirect. No longer in operation

IROQUOIS COUNTY (PORTIONS)—See CHAMPAIGN, IL (Comcast Cable)

IROQUOIS COUNTY (PORTIONS)—See WATSEKA, IL (Mediacom)

IRVING PARK—See CHICAGO, IL (RCN Corp. Formerly [IL0661]. This cable system has converted to IPTV)

IRVING—Mediacom. Now served by IRVING, IL [IL0687]

IRVING—Mediacom

ISLAND LAKE—See MOUNT PROSPECT, IL (Comcast Cable)

ITASCA—See PEORIA, IL (Comcast Cable)

IUKA—Formerly served by Advanced Technologies & Technical Resources Inc. No longer in operation

IVESDALE—See TUSCOLA, IL (Mediacom)

JACKSON COUNTY (PORTIONS)—See MURPHYSBORO, IL (Mediacom)

JACKSON COUNTY (PORTIONS)—See ZEIGLER, IL (Mediacom)

JACKSON COUNTY (PORTIONS)—Zito Media

JACKSONVILLE—Mediacom

JASPER COUNTY (PORTIONS)—See CHAMPAIGN, IN (Comcast Cable)

JASPER COUNTY (SOUTHERN PORTION)—See NEWTON, IL (NewWave Communications)

JEFFERSON TWP. (CASS COUNTY)—See CHAMPAIGN, MI (Comcast Cable)

JEFFERSON TWP.—See CHAMPAIGN, IN (Comcast Cable)

JEISYVILLE—See KINCAID, IL (Mediacom)

JEROME—See SPRINGFIELD, IL (Comcast Cable)

JERSEY COUNTY (PORTIONS)—See JERSEYVILLE, IL (NewWave Communications)

JERSEYVILLE—NewWave Communications

JEWETT—Clearvision Cable Systems Inc

JOHNSBURG—See MOUNT PROSPECT, IL (Comcast Cable)

JOHNSON COUNTY (NORTHERN PORTION)—See LAKE OF EGYPT, IL (Zito Media)

JOHNSON COUNTY (PORTIONS)—See BUNCOMBE, IL (Zito Media)

JOHNSTON CITY—See MURPHYSBORO, IL (Mediacom)

JOLIET—See PEORIA, IL (Comcast Cable)

JONESBORO—See ANNA, IL (NewWave Communications)

JOY—See ONEIDA, IL (Oneida Cablevision Inc. Formerly [IL0361]. This cable system has converted to IPTV)

JUSTICE—See PEORIA, IL (Comcast Cable)

KAMPSVILLE (village)—Formerly served by Cass Cable TV Inc. No longer in operation

KANE COUNTY (PORTIONS)—See MOUNT PROSPECT, IL (Comcast Cable)

KANE COUNTY (PORTIONS)—See PEORIA, IL (Comcast Cable)

KANE COUNTY—See SUGAR GROVE, IL (Mediacom)

KANEVILLE—See SUGAR GROVE, IL (Mediacom)

KANGLEY—See STREATOR, IL (Mediacom)

KANKAKEE—Comcast Cable. Now served by CHAMPAIGN, IL [IL0019]

KANKAKEE—See CHAMPAIGN, IL (Comcast Cable)

KANSAS—See CHARLESTON, IL (Mediacom)

KARNAK—Formerly served by Longview Communications. No longer in operation

KEITHSBURG—Nova1Net

KEITHSBURG—See ONEIDA, IL (Oneida Cablevision Inc. Formerly [IL0361]. This cable system has converted to IPTV)

KENDALL COUNTY (PORTIONS)—See PEORIA, IL (Comcast Cable)

KENILWORTH—See MOUNT PROSPECT, IL (Comcast Cable)

KENNEY—Heartland Cable Inc

KENTLAND—See WATSEKA, IN (Mediacom)

KEWANEE TWP.—See MOUNT PROSPECT, IL (Comcast Cable)

KEWANEE—Comcast Cable. Now served by MOUNT PROSPECT, IL [IL0036]

KEWANEE—See MOUNT PROSPECT, IL (Comcast Cable)

KEYESPORT—Formerly served by CableDirect. No longer in operation

KICKAPOO—See METAMORA, IL (Tel-Star Cablevision Inc)

Illinois—Cable Community Index

KILBOURNE—See BEARDSTOWN, IL (Cass Cable TV Inc)

KILDEER—See MOUNT PROSPECT, IL (Comcast Cable)

KINCAID—Mediacom

KINDERHOOK—Formerly served by Almega Cable. No longer in operation

KINGSBURY—See CHAMPAIGN, IN (Comcast Cable)

KINGSFORD HEIGHTS—See CHAMPAIGN, IN (Comcast Cable)

KINGSTON MINES—KMHC Inc

KINGSTON—Formerly served by Kingston Cable TV Co. No longer in operation

KINMUNDY—Clearvision Cable Systems Inc

KIRKLAND—Mediacom. Now served by CORTLAND (village), IL [IL0485]

KIRKLAND—See CORTLAND (village), IL (Mediacom)

KIRKWOOD—Nova1Net

KIRKWOOD—See ONEIDA, IL (Oneida Cablevision Inc. Formerly [IL0361]. This cable system has converted to IPTV)

KNOX COUNTY (PORTIONS)—See NEWTON, IN (NewWave Communications)

KNOX COUNTY (UNINCORPORATED AREAS)—See ELLISVILLE, IL (Mid Century Communications)

KNOXVILLE—See PEORIA, IL (Comcast Cable)

KOSCIUSKO COUNTY (PORTIONS)—See CHAMPAIGN, IN (Comcast Cable)

LA GRANGE PARK—See PEORIA, IL (Comcast Cable)

LA GRANGE—Comcast Cable. Now served by PEORIA, IL [IL0012]

LA GRANGE—See PEORIA, IL (Comcast Cable)

LA HARPE—Formerly served by Insight Communications. Now served by Comcast Cable, PEORIA, IL [IL0012]

LA HARPE—See PEORIA, IL (Comcast Cable)

LA MOILLE (village)—Formerly served by CableDirect. No longer in operation

LA PLACE—Formerly served by Longview Communications. No longer in operation

LA PORTE COUNTY (PORTIONS)—See CHAMPAIGN, IN (Comcast Cable)

LA PORTE—See CHAMPAIGN, IN (Comcast Cable)

LA ROSE—Formerly served by Tel-Star Cablevision Inc. No longer in operation

LA SALLE TWP.—See STREATOR, IL (Mediacom)

LA SALLE—See MOUNT PROSPECT, IL (Comcast Cable)

LACON—Mediacom. Now served by ROANOKE, IL [IL0068]

LACON—Mediacom. Now served by ROANOKE, IL [IL0068]

LACON—See ROANOKE, IL (Mediacom)

LADD—Comcast Cable. Now served by MOUNT PROSPECT, IL [IL0036]

LADD—See MOUNT PROSPECT, IL (Comcast Cable)

LAFAYETTE—See ELLISVILLE, IL (Mid Century Communications)

LAFAYETTE—See ONEIDA, IL (Oneida Cablevision Inc. Formerly [IL0361]. This cable system has converted to IPTV)

LAGRANGE TWP.—See CHAMPAIGN, MI (Comcast Cable)

LAKE BARRINGTON—See MOUNT PROSPECT, IL (Comcast Cable)

LAKE BLUFF—See MOUNT PROSPECT, IL (Comcast Cable)

LAKE BRACKEN—Nova1Net

LAKE BRACKEN—See ONEIDA, IL (Oneida Cablevision Inc. Formerly [IL0361]. This cable system has converted to IPTV)

LAKE CAMELOT—Tel-Star Cablevision Inc. Now served by METAMORA, IL [IL0326]

LAKE CAMELOT—See METAMORA, IL (Tel-Star Cablevision Inc)

LAKE COUNTY (PORTIONS)—See MOUNT PROSPECT, IL (Comcast Cable)

LAKE COUNTY (PORTIONS)—See CHAMPAIGN, IN (Comcast Cable)

LAKE FOREST—See MOUNT PROSPECT, IL (Comcast Cable)

LAKE HOLIDAY—Comcast Cable. Now served by PEORIA, IL [IL0012]

LAKE HOLIDAY—See PEORIA, IL (Comcast Cable)

LAKE IN THE HILLS—See MOUNT PROSPECT, IL (Comcast Cable)

LAKE OF EGYPT—Zito Media

LAKE OF THE WOODS—See RANTOUL, IL (Mediacom)

LAKE SARA—See EFFINGHAM, IL (Mediacom)

LAKE STATION—See CHAMPAIGN, IN (Comcast Cable)

LAKE SUMMERSET—See MOUNT CARROLL, IL (Mediacom)

LAKE TWP.—See CHAMPAIGN, MI (Comcast Cable)

LAKE VILLA—See MOUNT PROSPECT, IL (Comcast Cable)

LAKE WARREN—See ONEIDA, IL (Oneida Cablevision Inc. Formerly [IL0361]. This cable system has converted to IPTV)

LAKE WINDERMERE—See METAMORA, IL (Tel-Star Cablevision Inc)

LAKE ZURICH—Comcast Cable. Now served by MOUNT PROSPECT, IL [IL0036]

LAKE ZURICH—See MOUNT PROSPECT, IL (Comcast Cable)

LAKEMOOR—See MOUNT PROSPECT, IL (Comcast Cable)

LAKES OF THE FOUR SEASONS—See CHAMPAIGN, IN (Comcast Cable)

LAKEVIEW—See CHICAGO, IL (RCN Corp. Formerly [IL0661]. This cable system has converted to IPTV)

LAKEWOOD—See MOUNT PROSPECT, IL (Comcast Cable)

LAMPLIGHTER—See ROANOKE, IL (Mediacom)

LANARK—See MOUNT CARROLL, IL (Mediacom)

LANSING—Comcast Cable. Now served by CHAMPAIGN, IL [IL0019]

LANSING—See CHAMPAIGN, IL (Comcast Cable)

LAWRENCEVILLE—NewWave Communications. Now served by VINCENNES, IN [IN0035]

LE CLAIRE—See MOLINE, IA (Mediacom)

LE ROY—Mediacom

LEAF RIVER—Formerly served by Grand River Cablevision. No longer in operation

LELAND GROVE—See SPRINGFIELD, IL (Comcast Cable)

LELAND—See SUGAR GROVE, IL (Mediacom)

LEMONT—See PEORIA, IL (Comcast Cable)

LENA—See MOUNT CARROLL, IL (Mediacom)

LENZBURG—See SPARTA, IL (NewWave Communications)

LEONORE—Formerly served by HI Cablevision. No longer in operation

LERNA—Formerly served by CableDirect. No longer in operation

LEWISTOWN—Formerly served by Insight Communications. Now served by Comcast Cable, PEORIA, IL [IL0012]

LEWISTOWN—See PEORIA, IL (Comcast Cable)

LEXINGTON—Mediacom. Now served by ROANOKE, IL [IL0068]

LEXINGTON—See ROANOKE, IL (Mediacom)

LIBERTY—Adams Telcom. Now served by BOWDEN, IL [IL0702]

LIBERTYVILLE—Comcast Cable. Now served by MOUNT PROSPECT, IL [IL0036]

LIBERTYVILLE—See MOUNT PROSPECT, IL (Comcast Cable)

LILY LAKE (VILLAGE)—See PEORIA, IL (Comcast Cable)

LIMA—See BOWEN, IL (Adams Telcom)

LIMESTONE—See CHAMPAIGN, IL (Comcast Cable)

LINCOLN PARK—See CHICAGO, IL (RCN Corp. Formerly [IL0661]. This cable system has converted to IPTV)

LINCOLN TWP. (BERRIEN COUNTY)—See CHAMPAIGN, MI (Comcast Cable)

LINCOLN—Formerly served by Insight Communications. Now served by Comcast Cable, SPRINGFIELD, IL [IL0016]

LINCOLN—See SPRINGFIELD, IL (Comcast Cable)

LINCOLNSHIRE—See MOUNT PROSPECT, IL (Comcast Cable)

LINDENHURST—See MOUNT PROSPECT, IL (Comcast Cable)

LISLE—Comcast Cable. Now served by PEORIA, IL [IL0012]

LISLE—See PEORIA, IL (Comcast Cable)

LITCHFIELD—NewWave Communications. Now served by TAYLORVILLE, IL [IL0098]

LITCHFIELD—See TAYLORVILLE, IL (NewWave Communications)

LITTLE YORK—Nova1Net

LITTLE YORK—See ONEIDA, IL (Oneida Cablevision Inc. Formerly [IL0361]. This cable system has converted to IPTV)

LIVINGSTON COUNTY (PORTIONS)—See PONTIAC, IL (Mediacom)

LIVINGSTON—See STAUNTON, IL (Madison Communications)

LOAMI—Mediacom. Now served by KINCAID, IL [IL0176]

LOAMI—See KINCAID, IL (Mediacom)

LOCKPORT TWP.—See PEORIA, IL (Comcast Cable)

LOCKPORT—See PEORIA, IL (Comcast Cable)

LODA—See RANTOUL, IL (Mediacom)

LODI—See CHAMPAIGN, IN (Comcast Cable)

LOGAN COUNTY (PORTIONS)—See SPRINGFIELD, IL (Comcast Cable)

LOMAX—See DALLAS CITY, IL (Mediacom)

LOMBARD—See PEORIA, IL (Comcast Cable)

Cable Community Index—Illinois

LONDON MILLS—Mediacom. Now served by ELMWOOD, IL [IL0205]

LONDON MILLS—See ELMWOOD, IL (Mediacom)

LONG BEACH—See CHAMPAIGN, IN (Comcast Cable)

LONG CREEK (VILLAGE)—See SPRINGFIELD, IL (Comcast Cable)

LONG GROVE—See MOUNT PROSPECT, IL (Comcast Cable)

LONG GROVE—See MOLINE, IA (Mediacom)

LONG POINT (village)—Formerly served by Longview Communications. No longer in operation

LORAINE—See BOWEN, IL (Adams Telcom)

LOSTANT—HI Cablevision

LOUISVILLE—Wabash Independent Networks. Now served by FLORA, IL [IL0140]

LOUISVILLE—Mediacom

LOUISVILLE—See FLORA, IL (Wabash Independent Networks)

LOVES PARK—See MOUNT PROSPECT, IL (Comcast Cable)

LOVINGTON—Moultrie Telecommunications

LOWELL—See CHAMPAIGN, IN (Comcast Cable)

LOWPOINT—Formerly served by Tel-Star Cablevision Inc. No longer in operation

LUDLOW (VILLAGE)—See RANTOUL, IL (Mediacom)

LYNWOOD—See CHAMPAIGN, IL (Comcast Cable)

LYONS—See PEORIA, IL (Comcast Cable)

MACEDONIA—See DAHLGREN, IL (Hamilton County Communications. Formerly [IL0381]. This cable system has converted to IPTV)

MACHESNEY PARK—See MOUNT PROSPECT, IL (Comcast Cable)

MACKINAW TRAILER PARK—See ROANOKE, IL (Mediacom)

MACKINAW—See ROANOKE, IL (Mediacom)

MACKINAW—See METAMORA, IL (Tel-Star Cablevision Inc)

MACOMB—Comcast Cable. Now served by PEORIA, IL [IL0012]

MACOMB—See PEORIA, IL (Comcast Cable)

MACON COUNTY (PORTIONS)—See SPRINGFIELD, IL (Comcast Cable)

MACON COUNTY (PORTIONS)—See ARGENTA, IL (NewWave Communications)

MACON—See MOWEAQUA, IL (NewWave Communications)

MACOUPIN COUNTY (PORTIONS)—See TAYLORVILLE, IL (NewWave Communications)

MADISON COUNTY—See WASHINGTON PARK, IL (Mediacom)

MAHOMET—Mediacom. Now served by RANTOUL, IL [IL0089]

MAHOMET—See RANTOUL, IL (Mediacom)

MAINE TWP.—See MOUNT PROSPECT, IL (Comcast Cable)

MALDEN—HI Cablevision

MALTA—Mediacom. Now served by KIRKLAND, IL [IL0277]

MALTA—See CORTLAND (village), IL (Mediacom)

MANCHESTER (village)—Formerly served by Longview Communications. No longer in operation

MANCHESTER—See JERSEYVILLE, IL (NewWave Communications)

MANHATTAN—Kraus Electronics Systems Inc

MANITO—Cass Cable TV Inc. Now served by BEARDSTOWN, IL [IL0598]

MANITO—See BEARDSTOWN, IL (Cass Cable TV Inc)

MANLIUS (village)—Mediacom. Now served by GENESEO, IL [IL0170]

MANLIUS (VILLAGE)—See GENESEO, IL (Mediacom)

MANSFIELD—Mediacom. Now served by RANTOUL, IL [IL0089]

MANSFIELD—See RANTOUL, IL (Mediacom)

MANTENO—See CHAMPAIGN, IL (Comcast Cable)

MAPLE PARK (VILLAGE)—See CORTLAND (village), IL (Mediacom)

MAPLETON—See METAMORA, IL (Tel-Star Cablevision Inc)

MAQUON—Mediacom. Now served by ELMWOOD, IL [IL0205]

MAQUON—See ELMWOOD, IL (Mediacom)

MAQUON—See ELLISVILLE, IL (Mid Century Communications)

MAQUON—See ONEIDA, IL (Oneida Cablevision Inc. Formerly [IL0361]. This cable system has converted to IPTV)

MARCELLINE—See BOWEN, IL (Adams Telcom)

MARIETTA—See ELLISVILLE, IL (Mid Century Communications)

MARIETTA—See ONEIDA, IL (Oneida Cablevision Inc. Formerly [IL0361]. This cable system has converted to IPTV)

MARION—Mediacom. Now served by MURPHYSBORO, IL [IL0059]

MARION—See MURPHYSBORO, IL (Mediacom)

MARISSA—See SPARTA, IL (NewWave Communications)

MARK—See CHILLICOTHE, IL (Mediacom)

MARKHAM—See CHAMPAIGN, IL (Comcast Cable)

MAROA—Formerly served by Crystal Broadband Networks. No longer in operation

MARQUETTE HEIGHTS—See PEORIA, IL (Comcast Cable)

MARSEILLES—See STREATOR, IL (Mediacom)

MARSHALL COUNTY (PORTIONS)—See CHAMPAIGN, IN (Comcast Cable)

MARSHALL—See MARTINSVILLE, IL (Mediacom)

MARTINSVILLE—Mediacom

MARTINTON (village)—Formerly served by CableDirect. No longer in operation

MARTINTOWN—See MOUNT CARROLL, WI (Mediacom)

MARYVILLE—Charter Communications. Now served by ST. LOUIS, MO [MO0009]

MASON CITY—Formerly served by Greene County Cable. Now served by Cass Cable TV Inc., BEARDSTOWN, IL [IL0598]

MASON CITY—See BEARDSTOWN, IL (Cass Cable TV Inc)

MASON TWP. (CASS COUNTY)—See CHAMPAIGN, MI (Comcast Cable)

MASON TWP.—See CHAMPAIGN, MI (Comcast Cable)

MASON—See EDGEWOOD, IL (Clearvision Cable Systems Inc)

MATHERVILLE—See GENESEO, IL (Mediacom)

MATTESON—Comcast Cable. Now served by CHAMPAIGN, IL [IL0019]

MATTESON—See CHAMPAIGN, IL (Comcast Cable)

MATTOON—Mediacom

MAYWOOD—Comcast Cable. Now served by PEORIA, IL [IL0012]

MAYWOOD—See PEORIA, IL (Comcast Cable)

MAZON (village)—Formerly served by CableDirect. No longer in operation

MAZON (VILLAGE)—See PEORIA, IL (Comcast Cable)

MCCLURE—See ALEXANDER COUNTY (portions), IL (Zito Media)

MCCOLLUM LAKE—See MOUNT PROSPECT, IL (Comcast Cable)

MCCONNELL—See MOUNT CARROLL, IL (Mediacom)

MCCOOK—See PEORIA, IL (Comcast Cable)

MCDONOUGH COUNTY (PORTIONS)—See PEORIA, IL (Comcast Cable)

MCDONOUGH COUNTY (UNINCORPORATED AREAS)—See ELLISVILLE, IL (Mid Century Communications)

MCHENRY COUNTY (PORTIONS)—See MOUNT PROSPECT, IL (Comcast Cable)

MCHENRY COUNTY (PORTIONS)—See BELVIDERE TWP., IL (Mediacom)

MCHENRY—Comcast Cable. Now served by MOUNT PROSPECT, IL [IL0036]

MCHENRY—See MOUNT PROSPECT, IL (Comcast Cable)

MCLEAN COUNTY (PORTIONS)—See PEORIA, IL (Comcast Cable)

MCLEAN COUNTY (PORTIONS)—See LE ROY, IL (Mediacom)

MCLEAN—See ATLANTA, IL (Mediacom)

MCLEANSBORO—See DAHLGREN, IL (Hamilton County Communications. Formerly [IL0381]. This cable system has converted to IPTV)

MCLEANSBORO—NewWave Communications

MCNABB—McNabb TV Cable

MECHANICSBURG—See KINCAID, IL (Mediacom)

MEDORA—Formerly served by CableDirect. No longer in operation

MELROSE PARK—See PEORIA, IL (Comcast Cable)

MELVIN—Mediacom. Now served by RANTOUL, IL [IL0089]

MELVIN—See RANTOUL, IL (Mediacom)

MENARD COUNTY (PORTIONS)—See WILLIAMSVILLE, IL (Greene County Partners Inc)

MENDON—See BOWEN, IL (Adams Telcom)

MENDOTA—Comcast Cable. Now served by MOUNT PROSPECT, IL [IL0036]

MENDOTA—See MOUNT PROSPECT, IL (Comcast Cable)

MENTONE—See CHAMPAIGN, IN (Comcast Cable)

MERRILLVILLE—See CHAMPAIGN, IN (Comcast Cable)

MERRIONETTE PARK—See CHAMPAIGN, IL (Comcast Cable)

METAMORA—See ROANOKE, IL (Mediacom)

METAMORA—Tel-Star Cablevision Inc

METCALF (VILLAGE)—See HUME (village), IL (Clearvision Cable Systems Inc)

METTAWA—See MOUNT PROSPECT, IL (Comcast Cable)

Illinois—Cable Community Index

MICHIANA SHORES—See CHAMPAIGN, IN (Comcast Cable)

MICHIANA—See CHAMPAIGN, MI (Comcast Cable)

MICHIGAN CITY—See CHAMPAIGN, IN (Comcast Cable)

MIDDLEBURY—See CHAMPAIGN, IN (Comcast Cable)

MIDDLETOWN—Mediacom. Now served by DELAVAN, IL [IL0172]

MIDDLETOWN—See DELAVAN, IL (Mediacom)

MIDLOTHIAN—See CHAMPAIGN, IL (Comcast Cable)

MILAN (UNINCORPORATED AREAS)—See ONEIDA, IL (Oneida Cablevision Inc. Formerly [IL0361]. This cable system has converted to IPTV)

MILAN—See MOLINE, IL (Mediacom)

MILFORD—See WESTVILLE, IL (NewWave Communications)

MILL SHOALS—Formerly served by CableDirect. No longer in operation

MILLEDGEVILLE—See MOUNT CARROLL, IL (Mediacom)

MILLINGTON—Comcast Cable. Now served by PEORIA, IL [IL0012]

MILLINGTON—See PEORIA, IL (Comcast Cable)

MILTON TWP. (CASS COUNTY)—See CHAMPAIGN, MI (Comcast Cable)

MILTON—Formerly served by Cass Cable TV Inc. No longer in operation

MINERAL—See GENESEO, IL (Mediacom)

MINIER—Mediacom. Now served by ROANOKE, IL [IL0068]

MINIER—See ROANOKE, IL (Mediacom)

MINONK—See ROANOKE, IL (Mediacom)

MINOOKA—Comcast Cable. Now served by PEORIA, IL [IL0012]

MINOOKA—See PEORIA, IL (Comcast Cable)

MINOOKA—See MORRIS (town), IL (Mediacom)

MISHAWAKA—See CHAMPAIGN, IN (Comcast Cable)

MOBET—See GENESEO, IL (Mediacom)

MOKENA—See PEORIA, IL (Comcast Cable)

MOLINE—Mediacom

MOMENCE—Mediacom. Now served by NEWTON COUNTY (portions), IN [IN0316]

MONEE—See CHAMPAIGN, IL (Comcast Cable)

MONMOUTH—Comcast Cable

MONROE CENTER—Mediacom. Now served by KIRKLAND, IL [IL0277]

MONROE CENTER—See CORTLAND (village), IL (Mediacom)

MONROE COUNTY (PORTIONS)—See COULTERVILLE, IL (Mediacom)

MONTGOMERY COUNTY (PORTIONS)—See TAYLORVILLE, IL (NewWave Communications)

MONTGOMERY—See PEORIA, IL (Comcast Cable)

MONTICELLO—Mediacom

MONTMORENCY TWP.—See MOUNT PROSPECT, IL (Comcast Cable)

MONTROSE—See DIETERICH, IL (Clearvision Cable Systems Inc)

MORGAN COUNTY (PORTIONS)—See JACKSONVILLE, IL (Mediacom)

MORRIS (town)—Comcast Cable. Now served by PEORIA, IL [IL0012]

MORRIS (TOWN)—Mediacom

MORRIS—See PEORIA, IL (Comcast Cable)

MORRISONVILLE—Mediacom. Now served by KINCAID, IL [IL0176]

MORRISONVILLE—See KINCAID, IL (Mediacom)

MORTON GROVE—Comcast Cable. Now served by MOUNT PROSPECT, IL [IL0036]

MORTON GROVE—See MOUNT PROSPECT, IL (Comcast Cable)

MORTON GROVE—See CHICAGO, IL (RCN Corp. Formerly [IL0661]. This cable system has converted to IPTV)

MORTON—See PEORIA, IL (Comcast Cable)

MORTON—See METAMORA, IL (TelStar Cablevision Inc)

MOUND CITY—See ZEIGLER, IL (Mediacom)

MOUNDS—Mediacom. Now served by ZEIGLER, IL [IL0123]

MOUNDS—See ZEIGLER, IL (Mediacom)

MOUNT AUBURN—Mediacom. Now served by KINCAID, IL [IL0176]

MOUNT AUBURN—See KINCAID, IL (Mediacom)

MOUNT CARMEL—NewWave Communications. Now served by McLEANSBORO, IL [IL0177]

MOUNT CARMEL—See McLEANSBORO, IL (NewWave Communications)

MOUNT CARROLL—Mediacom. Now served by LENA, IL [IL0223]

MOUNT CARROLL—Mediacom

MOUNT CLARE—See STAUNTON, IL (Madison Communications)

MOUNT JOY—See MOLINE, IA (Mediacom)

MOUNT MORRIS—See MOUNT PROSPECT, IL (Comcast Cable)

MOUNT OLIVE—See STAUNTON, IL (Madison Communications)

MOUNT PROSPECT—Comcast Cable

MOUNT PROSPECT—See NAPERVILLE, IL (WOW! Internet, Cable & Phone)

MOUNT PULASKI—Formerly served by Insight Communications. Now served by Comcast Cable, SPRINGFIELD, IL [IL0016]

MOUNT PULASKI—See SPRINGFIELD, IL (Comcast Cable)

MOUNT STERLING—Cass Cable TV Inc. Now served by BEARDSTOWN, IL [IL0598]

MOUNT STERLING—See BEARDSTOWN, IL (Cass Cable TV Inc)

MOUNT ZION (VILLAGE)—See SPRINGFIELD, IL (Comcast Cable)

MOWEAQUA—NewWave Communications

MULBERRY GROVE—Clearvision Cable Systems Inc

MULKEYTOWN—See BENTON, IL (NewWave Communications)

MUNCIE—See CHAMPAIGN, IL (Comcast Cable)

MUNDELEIN—See MOUNT PROSPECT, IL (Comcast Cable)

MUNSTER—See CHAMPAIGN, IN (Comcast Cable)

MURPHYSBORO—Mediacom

MURRAYVILLE—Formerly served by Almega Cable. No longer in operation

NAPERVILLE—Comcast Cable. Now served by PEORIA, IL [IL0012]

NAPERVILLE—See PEORIA, IL (Comcast Cable)

NAPERVILLE—WOW! Internet, Cable & Phone

NAPLATE—See STREATOR, IL (Mediacom)

NAUVOO—Medicom. Now served by DALLAS CITY, IL [IL0274]

NAUVOO—See DALLAS CITY, IL (Mediacom)

NEOGA—Mediacom

NEPONSET—See GENESEO, IL (Mediacom)

NEW ATHENS—See SPARTA, IL (NewWave Communications)

NEW BERLIN—Mediacom. Now served by KINCAID, IL [IL0176]

NEW BERLIN—See KINCAID, IL (Mediacom)

NEW BOSTON—Nova1Net

NEW BOSTON—See ONEIDA, IL (Oneida Cablevision Inc. Formerly [IL0361]. This cable system has converted to IPTV)

NEW BUFFALO TWP.—See CHAMPAIGN, MI (Comcast Cable)

NEW BUFFALO—See CHAMPAIGN, MI (Comcast Cable)

NEW CARLISLE (TOWN)—See CHAMPAIGN, IN (Comcast Cable)

NEW CHICAGO—See CHAMPAIGN, IN (Comcast Cable)

NEW DOUGLAS—Madison Communications. Now served by STAUNTON, IL [IL0171]

NEW DOUGLAS—Madison Communications. Now served by STAUNTON, IL [IL0171]

NEW DOUGLAS—See STAUNTON, IL (Madison Communications)

NEW HARMONY—See McLEANSBORO, IN (NewWave Communications)

NEW HAVEN (village)—Formerly served by CableDirect. No longer in operation

NEW HOLLAND—Mediacom. Now served by DELAVAN, IL [IL0172]

NEW HOLLAND—See DELAVAN, IL (Mediacom)

NEW LENOX TWP.—See PEORIA, IL (Comcast Cable)

NEW LENOX—See PEORIA, IL (Comcast Cable)

NEW MILFORD—See MOUNT PROSPECT, IL (Comcast Cable)

NEW TRIER TWP.—See MOUNT PROSPECT, IL (Comcast Cable)

NEW WINDSOR—See ONEIDA, IL (Oneida Cablevision Inc. Formerly [IL0361]. This cable system has converted to IPTV)

NEWARK—See PEORIA, IL (Comcast Cable)

NEWBERRY—See NEWTON, IN (NewWave Communications)

NEWMAN—Comcast Cable

NEWTON—NewWave Communications

NIANTIC (VILLAGE)—See SPRINGFIELD, IL (Comcast Cable)

NILES TWP.—See CHAMPAIGN, MI (Comcast Cable)

NILES—See MOUNT PROSPECT, IL (Comcast Cable)

NILES—See CHAMPAIGN, MI (Comcast Cable)

NILWOOD—See TAYLORVILLE, IL (NewWave Communications)

NOBLE—Wabash Independent Networks. Now served by FLORA, IL [IL0140]

NOBLE—See FLORA, IL (Wabash Independent Networks)

NOKOMIS—NewWave Communications. Now served by TAYLORVILLE, IL [IL0098]

NOKOMIS—See TAYLORVILLE, IL (NewWave Communications)

Cable Community Index—Illinois

NORMAL—See PEORIA, IL (Comcast Cable)

NORRIDGE—See PEORIA, IL (Comcast Cable)

NORRIS CITY—NewWave Communications. Now served by McLEANSBORO, IL [IL0177]

NORRIS CITY—See McLEANSBORO, IL (NewWave Communications)

NORRIS—Formerly served by Insight Communications. Now served by Comcast Cable, PEORIA, IL [IL0012]

NORRIS—See PEORIA, IL (Comcast Cable)

NORTH AURORA—See PEORIA, IL (Comcast Cable)

NORTH BARRINGTON (VILLAGE)—See MOUNT PROSPECT, IL (Comcast Cable)

NORTH CHICAGO—See MOUNT PROSPECT, IL (Comcast Cable)

NORTH CITY—See BENTON, IL (NewWave Communications)

NORTH HENDERSON—Nova1Net

NORTH HENDERSON—See ONEIDA, IL (Oneida Cablevision Inc. Formerly [IL0361]. This cable system has converted to IPTV)

NORTH PEKIN—See PEORIA, IL (Comcast Cable)

NORTH RIVERSIDE—See PEORIA, IL (Comcast Cable)

NORTH UTICA—See MOUNT PROSPECT, IL (Comcast Cable)

NORTHBROOK—See MOUNT PROSPECT, IL (Comcast Cable)

NORTHFIELD—See MOUNT PROSPECT, IL (Comcast Cable)

NORTHLAKE—See PEORIA, IL (Comcast Cable)

NORWOOD—See PEORIA, IL (Comcast Cable)

NOTRE DAME—See CHAMPAIGN, IN (Comcast Cable)

OAK BROOK—See PEORIA, IL (Comcast Cable)

OAK FOREST—Comcast Cable. Now served by CHAMPAIGN, IL [IL0019]

OAK FOREST—See CHAMPAIGN, IL (Comcast Cable)

OAK FOREST—See NAPERVILLE, IL (WOW! Internet, Cable & Phone)

OAK GROVE—See MOLINE, IL (Mediacom)

OAK LAWN—Comcast Cable. Now served by CHAMPAIGN, IL [IL0019]

OAK LAWN—See CHAMPAIGN, IL (Comcast Cable)

OAK PARK ESTATES—See CHILLICOTHE, IL (Mediacom)

OAK PARK—See PEORIA, IL (Comcast Cable)

OAKBROOK TERRACE—See PEORIA, IL (Comcast Cable)

OAKFORD (VILLAGE)—See BEARDSTOWN, IL (Cass Cable TV Inc)

OAKLAND—See TUSCOLA, IL (Mediacom)

OAKWOOD HILLS—See MOUNT PROSPECT, IL (Comcast Cable)

OAKWOOD—See CHAMPAIGN, IL (Comcast Cable)

OBLONG—See ROBINSON, IL (Mediacom)

OCONEE—Formerly served by Mediacom. No longer in operation

ODELL—Mediacom. Now served by PONTIAC, IL [IL0109]

ODELL—See PONTIAC, IL (Mediacom)

ODON—See NEWTON, IN (NewWave Communications)

OGDEN DUNES—See CHAMPAIGN, IN (Comcast Cable)

OGDEN—See CHAMPAIGN, IL (Comcast Cable)

OGLE COUNTY (PORTIONS)—See MOUNT PROSPECT, IL (Comcast Cable)

OGLESBY—See MOUNT PROSPECT, IL (Comcast Cable)

OKAWVILLE—Charter Communications. Now served by ST. LOUIS, MO [MO0009]

OLD TOWN—See CHICAGO, IL (RCN Corp. Formerly [IL0661]. This cable system has converted to IPTV)

OLIVET—See CHAMPAIGN, IL (Comcast Cable)

OLNEY—NewWave Communications. Now served by NEWTON, IL [IL0559]

OLNEY—See NEWTON, IL (NewWave Communications)

OLYMPIA FIELDS—See CHAMPAIGN, IL (Comcast Cable)

OMAHA—Formerly served by CableDirect. No longer in operation

ONARGA—Comcast Cable. Now served by SPRINGFIELD, IL [IL0016]

ONARGA—See SPRINGFIELD, IL (Comcast Cable)

ONEIDA—Oneida Cablevision Inc. This cable system has converted to IPTV. See ONEIDA, IL [IL5332]

ONEIDA—Oneida Cablevision Inc. Formerly [IL0361]. This cable system has converted to IPTV

ONTWA TWP.—See CHAMPAIGN, MI (Comcast Cable)

OPDYKE—See DAHLGREN, IL (Hamilton County Communications. Formerly [IL0381]. This cable system has converted to IPTV)

OPHIEM—See ALPHA, IL (Diverse Communications Inc.)

OQUAWKA—Mediacom. Now served by DALLAS CITY, IL [IL0274]

OQUAWKA—See DALLAS CITY, IL (Mediacom)

ORANGEVILLE—See MOUNT CARROLL, IL (Mediacom)

OREANA—See ARGENTA, IL (NewWave Communications)

OREGON—Formerly served by Insight Communications. No longer in operation

OREGON—See MOUNT PROSPECT, IL (Comcast Cable)

ORIENT—See FREEMAN SPUR, IL (Zito Media)

ORION—See MOLINE, IL (Mediacom)

ORLAND HILLS—See CHAMPAIGN, IL (Comcast Cable)

ORLAND PARK—Comcast Cable. Now served by CHAMPAIGN, IL [IL0019]

ORLAND PARK—Comcast Cable. Now served by CHAMPAIGN, IL [IL0019]

ORLAND PARK—See CHAMPAIGN, IL (Comcast Cable)

ORONOKO TWP.—See CHAMPAIGN, MI (Comcast Cable)

OSCEOLA—See CHAMPAIGN, IN (Comcast Cable)

OSCO TWP.—See GENESEO, IL (Mediacom)

OSWEGO—Comcast Cable. Now served by PEORIA, IL [IL0012]

OSWEGO—See PEORIA, IL (Comcast Cable)

OTTAWA—Mediacom. Now served by STREATOR, IL [IL0069]

OTTAWA—See STREATOR, IL (Mediacom)

OTTER CREEK TWP.—See STREATOR, IL (Mediacom)

OTTO—See CHAMPAIGN, IL (Comcast Cable)

OWANECO—See TAYLORVILLE, IL (NewWave Communications)

PALATINE—See MOUNT PROSPECT, IL (Comcast Cable)

PALESTINE—See ROBINSON, IL (Mediacom)

PALMER—Mediacom. Now served by KINCAID, IL [IL0176]

PALMER—See KINCAID, IL (Mediacom)

PALMYRA—Formerly served by Almega Cable. No longer in operation

PALOMA—See BOWEN, IL (Adams Telcom)

PALOS HEIGHTS—See CHAMPAIGN, IL (Comcast Cable)

PALOS HILLS—See CHAMPAIGN, IL (Comcast Cable)

PALOS PARK—Formerly served by TV Max. No longer in operation

PALOS PARK—See CHAMPAIGN, IL (Comcast Cable)

PALOS PARK—See NAPERVILLE, IL (WOW! Internet, Cable & Phone)

PANA—NewWave Communications. Now served by TAYLORVILLE, IL [IL0098]

PANA—See TAYLORVILLE, IL (NewWave Communications)

PANAMA—Formerly served by Beck's Cable Systems. No longer in operation

PANORAMA PARK—See MOLINE, IA (Mediacom)

PARIS—Formerly served by Avenue Broadband Communications. Now served by NewWave Communications, WESTVILLE, IL [IL0079]

PARIS—See WESTVILLE, IL (NewWave Communications)

PARK CITY—See MOUNT PROSPECT, IL (Comcast Cable)

PARK FOREST (COOK COUNTY)—See CHAMPAIGN, IL (Comcast Cable)

PARK FOREST (WILL COUNTY)—See CHAMPAIGN, IL (Comcast Cable)

PARK FOREST—Comcast Cable. Now served by CHAMPAIGN, IL [IL0019]

PARK RIDGE—See MOUNT PROSPECT, IL (Comcast Cable)

PARK TWP.—See CHAMPAIGN, MI (Comcast Cable)

PARK VIEW—See MOLINE, IA (Mediacom)

PARKERSBURG—Formerly served by CableDirect. No longer in operation

PATOKA—Clearvision Cable Systems Inc

PAWNEE—See SPRINGFIELD, IL (Comcast Cable)

PAXTON—See RANTOUL, IL (Mediacom)

PAYSON—Formerly served by Adams Telcom. No longer in operation

PEARL CITY (village)—Mediacom. Now served by LENA, IL [IL0223]

PEARL CITY (VILLAGE)—See MOUNT CARROLL, IL (Mediacom)

PECATONICA—Mediacom. Now served by LENA, IL [IL0223]

PECATONICA—See MOUNT CARROLL, IL (Mediacom)

PEKIN—Comcast Cable. Now served by PEORIA, IL [IL0012]

PEKIN—See PEORIA, IL (Comcast Cable)

PENFIELD—Formerly served by CableDirect. No longer in operation

PENN TWP. (PORTIONS)—See CHAMPAIGN, MI (Comcast Cable)

PEORIA COUNTY (PORTIONS)—See PEORIA, IL (Comcast Cable)

Illinois—Cable Community Index

PEORIA COUNTY (PORTIONS)—See METAMORA, IL (Tel-Star Cablevision Inc)

PEORIA COUNTY (UNINCORPORATED AREAS)—See ELLISVILLE, IL (Mid Century Communications)

PEORIA COUNTY—See CHILLICOTHE, IL (Mediacom)

PEORIA HEIGHTS—See PEORIA, IL (Comcast Cable)

PEORIA—Comcast Cable

PEOTONE—Comcast Cable. Now served by CHAMPAIGN, IL [IL0019]

PEOTONE—See CHAMPAIGN, IL (Comcast Cable)

PERCY—See SPARTA, IL (NewWave Communications)

PERRY COUNTY (PORTIONS)—See BENTON, IL (NewWave Communications)

PERRY COUNTY—See ZEIGLER, IL (Mediacom)

PERU—See MOUNT PROSPECT, IL (Comcast Cable)

PESOTUM—See MONTICELLO, IL (Mediacom)

PETERSBURG—See WILLIAMSVILLE, IL (Greene County Partners Inc)

PHILO—See CHAMPAIGN, IL (Comcast Cable)

PHOENIX—See CHAMPAIGN, IL (Comcast Cable)

PIERRON—Clearvision Cable Systems Inc

PIERSON—See TUSCOLA, IL (Mediacom)

PINCKNEYVILLE—See BENTON, IL (NewWave Communications)

PINES TWP.—See CHAMPAIGN, IN (Comcast Cable)

PINGREE GROVE—See MOUNT PROSPECT, IL (Comcast Cable)

PIPER CITY—Comcast Cable

PIPESTONE TWP.—See CHAMPAIGN, MI (Comcast Cable)

PITTSBURG—See WILLIAMSON COUNTY (portions), IL (Zito Media)

PITTSFIELD—Cass Cable TV Inc

PLAINFIELD TWP.—See PEORIA, IL (Comcast Cable)

PLAINFIELD—Comcast Cable. Now served by PEORIA, IL [IL0012]

PLAINFIELD—See PEORIA, IL (Comcast Cable)

PLAINVILLE—See NEWTON, IN (NewWave Communications)

PLANO—Comcast Cable. Now served by PEORIA, IL [IL0012]

PLANO—See PEORIA, IL (Comcast Cable)

PLEASANT HILL—Formerly served by Crystal Broadband Networks. No longer in operation

PLEASANT PLAINS—See BEARDSTOWN, IL (Cass Cable TV Inc)

PLEASANT VALLEY—See MOLINE, IA (Mediacom)

PLYMOUTH—See BOWEN, IL (Adams Telcom)

PLYMOUTH—See CHAMPAIGN, IN (Comcast Cable)

POCAHONTAS—Clearvision Cable Systems Inc

POKAGON TWP.—See CHAMPAIGN, MI (Comcast Cable)

POLO—See MOUNT PROSPECT, IL (Comcast Cable)

PONTIAC—Mediacom

PONTOOSUC—See DALLAS CITY, IL (Mediacom)

POPLAR GROVE—See MOUNT PROSPECT, IL (Comcast Cable)

POPLAR GROVE—See BELVIDERE TWP., IL (Mediacom)

PORT BARRINGTON—See MOUNT PROSPECT, IL (Comcast Cable)

PORT BRYON—See GENESEO, IL (Mediacom)

PORTAGE—See CHAMPAIGN, IN (Comcast Cable)

PORTER COUNTY (PORTIONS)—See CHAMPAIGN, IN (Comcast Cable)

PORTER TWP.—See CHAMPAIGN, MI (Comcast Cable)

PORTER—See CHAMPAIGN, IN (Comcast Cable)

POSEN—See CHAMPAIGN, IL (Comcast Cable)

POSEN—See NAPERVILLE, IL (WOW! Internet, Cable & Phone)

POSEY COUNTY (PORTIONS)—See McLEANSBORO, IN (NewWave Communications)

POTOMAC (VILLAGE)—Park TV & Electronics Inc

POTTAWATTOMIE PARK—See CHAMPAIGN, IN (Comcast Cable)

PRAIRIE CITY—Formerly served by CableDirect. No longer in operation

PRAIRIE CITY—See GOOD HOPE, IL (Mediacom)

PRAIRIE DU ROCHER—See EVANSVILLE, IL (NewWave Communications)

PRAIRIE GROVE—See MOUNT PROSPECT, IL (Comcast Cable)

PREEMPTION—See GENESEO, IL (Mediacom)

PRINCETON—Comcast Cable. Now served by MOUNT PROSPECT, IL [IL0036]

PRINCETON—See MOUNT PROSPECT, IL (Comcast Cable)

PRINCETON—See MOLINE, IA (Mediacom)

PRINCEVILLE—Mediacom. Now served by CHILLICOTHE, IL [IL0118]

PRINCEVILLE—See CHILLICOTHE, IL (Mediacom)

PROSPECT HEIGHTS—See MOUNT PROSPECT, IL (Comcast Cable)

PROSPECT HEIGHTS—See NAPERVILLE, IL (WOW! Internet, Cable & Phone)

PROVISO TWP.—See PEORIA, IL (Comcast Cable)

PULASKI COUNTY (PORTIONS)—See ZEIGLER, IL (Mediacom)

PULASKI COUNTY—See ALEXANDER COUNTY (portions), IL (Zito Media)

PULASKI—See ALEXANDER COUNTY (portions), IL (Zito Media)

PUTNAM COUNTY (NORTHEASTERN PORTION)—See CHILLICOTHE, IL (Mediacom)

QUINCY—Comcast Cable. Now served by PEORIA, IL [IL0012]

QUINCY—See BOWEN, IL (Adams Telcom)

QUINCY—See PEORIA, IL (Comcast Cable)

QUIVER TWP.—See BEARDSTOWN, IL (Cass Cable TV Inc)

RALEIGH—See SALINE COUNTY (portions), IL (Zito Media)

RAMSEY—NewWave Communications. Now served by TAYLORVILLE, IL [IL0098]

RAMSEY—See TAYLORVILLE, IL (NewWave Communications)

RANDOLPH COUNTY (PORTIONS)—See SPARTA, IL (NewWave Communications)

RANKIN (VILLAGE)—Park TV & Electronics Inc

RANSOM—See GRAND RIDGE, IL (Heartland Cable Inc)

RANTOUL—Mediacom

RAPIDS CITY—See GENESEO, IL (Mediacom)

RAVENSWOOD—See CHICAGO, IL (RCN Corp. Formerly [IL0661]. This cable system has converted to IPTV)

RAYMOND—NewWave Communications. Now served by TAYLORVILLE, IL [IL0098]

RAYMOND—See TAYLORVILLE, IL (NewWave Communications)

READING TWP.—See STREATOR, IL (Mediacom)

RED BUD—See COULTERVILLE, IL (Mediacom)

REDMON—Formerly served by CableDirect. No longer in operation

REYNOLDS—See GENESEO, IL (Mediacom)

REYNOLDS—See ONEIDA, IL (Oneida Cablevision Inc. Formerly [IL0361]. This cable system has converted to IPTV)

RICHLAND COUNTY (PORTIONS)—See NEWTON, IL (NewWave Communications)

RICHMOND—See BELVIDERE TWP., IL (Mediacom)

RICHTON PARK—See CHAMPAIGN, IL (Comcast Cable)

RICHVIEW—Formerly served by CableDirect. No longer in operation

RIDGE FARM—Formerly served by Insight Communications. Now served by Comcast Cable, CHAMPAIGN, IL [IL0019]

RIDGE FARM—See CHAMPAIGN, IL (Comcast Cable)

RIDOTT TWP.—See GERMAN VALLEY, IL (Mediacom)

RINGWOOD—See BELVIDERE TWP., IL (Mediacom)

RIO—Formerly served by Nova Cablevision Inc. No longer in operation

RIO—See ONEIDA, IL (Oneida Cablevision Inc. Formerly [IL0361]. This cable system has converted to IPTV)

RIVER FOREST—See PEORIA, IL (Comcast Cable)

RIVER GROVE—See PEORIA, IL (Comcast Cable)

RIVER NORTH—See CHICAGO, IL (RCN Corp. Formerly [IL0661]. This cable system has converted to IPTV)

RIVER OAKS (village)—Mediacom. Now served by KINCAID, IL [IL0176]

RIVER OAKS (VILLAGE)—See KINCAID, IL (Mediacom)

RIVERDALE—See CHAMPAIGN, IL (Comcast Cable)

RIVERDALE—See MOLINE, IA (Mediacom)

RIVERSIDE—See PEORIA, IL (Comcast Cable)

RIVERTON—See WILLIAMSVILLE, IL (Greene County Partners Inc)

RIVERWOODS—See MOUNT PROSPECT, IL (Comcast Cable)

ROANOKE—Mediacom

ROBBINS (VILLAGE)—See CHAMPAIGN, IL (Comcast Cable)

ROBBINS—Comcast Cable. Now served by CHAMPAIGN, IL [IL0019]

ROBBINS—See NAPERVILLE, IL (WOW! Internet, Cable & Phone)

ROBERTS—Park TV & Electronics Inc

ROBINSON—Mediacom

ROCHELLE—See MOUNT PROSPECT, IL (Comcast Cable)

ROCHESTER TWP.—See SPRINGFIELD, IL (Comcast Cable)

Cable Community Index—Illinois

ROCHESTER—See SPRINGFIELD, IL (Comcast Cable)

ROCHESTER—See CHAMPAIGN, IN (Comcast Cable)

ROCK CITY—See MOUNT CARROLL, IL (Mediacom)

ROCK FALLS—See MOUNT PROSPECT, IL (Comcast Cable)

ROCK ISLAND ARSENAL—See MOLINE, IL (Mediacom)

ROCK ISLAND COUNTY—See MOLINE, IL (Mediacom)

ROCK ISLAND—Mediacom. Now served by MOLINE, IL [IL0011]

ROCK ISLAND—See MOLINE, IL (Mediacom)

ROCKDALE—See PEORIA, IL (Comcast Cable)

ROCKFORD (UNINCORPORATED AREAS)—See BELVIDERE TWP., IL (Mediacom)

ROCKFORD—Comcast Cable. Now served by MOUNT PROSPECT, IL [IL0036]

ROCKFORD—Formerly served by Wireless Cable Systems Inc. No longer in operation

ROCKFORD—See MOUNT PROSPECT, IL (Comcast Cable)

ROGERS PARK (PORTIONS)—See CHICAGO, IL (RCN Corp. Formerly [IL0661]. This cable system has converted to IPTV)

ROLLING MEADOWS MOBILE HOME PARK—See CORTLAND (village), IL (Mediacom)

ROLLING MEADOWS—Comcast Cable. Now served by MOUNT PROSPECT, IL [IL0036]

ROLLING MEADOWS—See MOUNT PROSPECT, IL (Comcast Cable)

ROME—See CHILLICOTHE, IL (Mediacom)

ROMEOVILLE—Comcast Cable. Now served by PEORIA, IL [IL0012]

ROMEOVILLE—See PEORIA, IL (Comcast Cable)

ROODHOUSE—See JERSEYVILLE, IL (NewWave Communications)

ROSAMOND—Formerly served by Beck's Cable Systems. No longer in operation

ROSCOE VILLAGE—See CHICAGO, IL (RCN Corp. Formerly [IL0661]. This cable system has converted to IPTV)

ROSELAND—See CHAMPAIGN, IN (Comcast Cable)

ROSELLE—See PEORIA, IL (Comcast Cable)

ROSEMONT—See PEORIA, IL (Comcast Cable)

ROSEVILLE—See DALLAS CITY, IL (Mediacom)

ROSICLARE—Zito Media

ROSSVILLE—See WESTVILLE, IL (NewWave Communications)

ROUND LAKE BEACH—See MOUNT PROSPECT, IL (Comcast Cable)

ROUND LAKE HEIGHTS—See MOUNT PROSPECT, IL (Comcast Cable)

ROUND LAKE PARK—See MOUNT PROSPECT, IL (Comcast Cable)

ROUND LAKE—See MOUNT PROSPECT, IL (Comcast Cable)

ROXANA—Charter Communications. Now served by ST. LOUIS, MO [MO0009]

ROYAL—Formerly served by CableDirect. No longer in operation

ROYALTON TWP.—See CHAMPAIGN, MI (Comcast Cable)

ROYALTON—See ZEIGLER, IL (Mediacom)

RUMA—See EVANSVILLE, IL (NewWave Communications)

RUSHVILLE—Cass Cable TV Inc. Now served by BEARDSTOWN, IL [IL0598]

RUSHVILLE—See BEARDSTOWN, IL (Cass Cable TV Inc)

RUTLAND—See FLANAGAN, IL (Heartland Cable Inc)

SADORUS—Formerly served by Longview Communications. No longer in operation

SALEM—Charter Communications. Now served by ST. LOUIS, MO [MO0009]

SALINE COUNTY (PORTIONS)—Zito Media

SALINE COUNTY (PORTIONS)—See CARRIER MILLS, IL (Zito Media)

SAN JOSE—See DELAVAN, IL (Mediacom)

SANDBORN—See NEWTON, IN (NewWave Communications)

SANDWICH—See PEORIA, IL (Comcast Cable)

SANGAMON COUNTY (PORTIONS)—See SPRINGFIELD, IL (Comcast Cable)

SANGAMON COUNTY (PORTIONS)—See DELAVAN, IL (Mediacom)

SAUK VILLAGE—See CHAMPAIGN, IL (Comcast Cable)

SAUNEMIN—See PONTIAC, IL (Mediacom)

SAVOY—See CHAMPAIGN, IL (Comcast Cable)

SAWYERVILLE—See STAUNTON, IL (Madison Communications)

SAYBROOK—Mediacom. Now served by LE ROY, IL [IL0539]

SAYBROOK—See LE ROY, IL (Mediacom)

SCALES MOUND—Mediacom. Now served by MOUNT CARROLL, IL [IL0223]

SCALES MOUND—See MOUNT CARROLL, IL (Mediacom)

SCHAUMBURG—See MOUNT PROSPECT, IL (Comcast Cable)

SCHAUMBURG—See NAPERVILLE, IL (WOW! Internet, Cable & Phone)

SCHERERVILLE—See CHAMPAIGN, IN (Comcast Cable)

SCHILLER PARK—See PEORIA, IL (Comcast Cable)

SCHRAM CITY—See TAYLORVILLE, IL (NewWave Communications)

SCOTT AFB—Charter Communications. Now served by ST. LOUIS, MO [MO0009]

SCOTT COUNTY (PORTIONS)—See MOLINE, IA (Mediacom)

SEATONVILLE (village)—Formerly served by CableDirect. No longer in operation

SECOR—See ROANOKE, IL (Mediacom)

SENECA—Kraus Electronics Systems Inc

SESSER—NewWave Communications. Now served by McLEANSBORO, IL [IL0177]

SESSER—See McLEANSBORO, IL (NewWave Communications)

SHABBONA—See SUGAR GROVE, IL (Mediacom)

SHADY OAKS TRAILER PARK—See MORRIS (town), IL (Mediacom)

SHANNON—See MOUNT CARROLL, IL (Mediacom)

SHAWNEETOWN—Time Warner Cable. Now served by OWENSBORO, KY [KY0004]

SHEFFIELD—See GENESEO, IL (Mediacom)

SHELBY COUNTY (PORTIONS)—See TAYLORVILLE, IL (NewWave Communications)

SHELBYVILLE—NewWave Communications. Now served by TAYLORVILLE, IL [IL0098]

SHELBYVILLE—See TAYLORVILLE, IL (NewWave Communications)

SHELDON—See WATSEKA, IL (Mediacom)

SHERIDAN (village)—Mediacom. Now served by STREATOR, IL [IL0069]

SHERIDAN—See STREATOR, IL (Mediacom)

SHERMAN—See WILLIAMSVILLE, IL (Greene County Partners Inc)

SHERRARD—See GENESEO, IL (Mediacom)

SHIPMAN—Formerly served by Mediacom. Now served by Madison Communications, STAUNTON, IL [IL0171]

SHIPMAN—See STAUNTON, IL (Madison Communications)

SHOREHAM (VILLAGE)—See CHAMPAIGN, MI (Comcast Cable)

SHOREWOOD—See PEORIA, IL (Comcast Cable)

SHUMWAY—Clearvision Cable Systems Inc

SIBLEY (VILLAGE)—Heartland Cable Inc

SIDELL (VILLAGE)—Clearvision Cable Systems Inc

SIDNEY—See CHAMPAIGN, IL (Comcast Cable)

SIGEL—See EFFINGHAM, IL (Mediacom)

SILVER CREEK TWP.—See CHAMPAIGN, MI (Comcast Cable)

SILVER LAKE—See CHAMPAIGN, IN (Comcast Cable)

SILVERWOOD—See CHAMPAIGN, IN (Comcast Cable)

SILVIS—See MOLINE, IL (Mediacom)

SIMS—Formerly served by CableDirect. No longer in operation

SKOKIE—Comcast Cable. Now served by MOUNT PROSPECT, IL [IL0036]

SKOKIE—Formerly served by RCN Corp. No longer in operation

SKOKIE—See MOUNT PROSPECT, IL (Comcast Cable)

SKOKIE—See CHICAGO, IL (RCN Corp. Formerly [IL0661]. This cable system has converted to IPTV)

SLEEPY HOLLOW—See MOUNT PROSPECT, IL (Comcast Cable)

SMITHFIELD—Formerly served by CableDirect. No longer in operation

SMITHFIELD—See ELLISVILLE, IL (Mid Century Communications)

SMITHFIELD—See ONEIDA, IL (Oneida Cablevision Inc. Formerly [IL0361]. This cable system has converted to IPTV)

SMITHTON—See COULTERVILLE, IL (Mediacom)

SMITHVILLE—See ELMWOOD, IL (Mediacom)

SODUS TWP.—See CHAMPAIGN, MI (Comcast Cable)

SOMONAUK—See SUGAR GROVE, IL (Mediacom)

SOUTH BARRINGTON—See MOUNT PROSPECT, IL (Comcast Cable)

SOUTH BEND—See CHAMPAIGN, IN (Comcast Cable)

SOUTH CHICAGO HEIGHTS—See CHAMPAIGN, IL (Comcast Cable)

SOUTH ELGIN—See PEORIA, IL (Comcast Cable)

SOUTH HOLLAND—Comcast Cable. Now served by CHAMPAIGN, IL [IL0019]

Illinois—Cable Community Index

SOUTH HOLLAND—See CHAMPAIGN, IL (Comcast Cable)

SOUTH HOLLAND—See NAPERVILLE, IL (WOW! Internet, Cable & Phone)

SOUTH JACKSONVILLE—See JACKSONVILLE, IL (Mediacom)

SOUTH OTTAWA TWP.—See STREATOR, IL (Mediacom)

SOUTH PEKIN—See PEORIA, IL (Comcast Cable)

SOUTH WAYNE—See MOUNT CARROLL, WI (Mediacom)

SOUTH WILMINGTON (village)—Mediacom. Now served by PONTIAC, IL [IL0109]

SOUTH WILMINGTON (VILLAGE)—See PONTIAC, IL (Mediacom)

SOUTHERN VIEW—See SPRINGFIELD, IL (Comcast Cable)

SOUTHPORT CORRIDOR—See CHICAGO, IL (RCN Corp. Formerly [IL0661]. This cable system has converted to IPTV)

SPARLAND—See CHILLICOTHE, IL (Mediacom)

SPARTA—NewWave Communications

SPAULDING—See SPRINGFIELD, IL (Comcast Cable)

SPRING BAY—See ROANOKE, IL (Mediacom)

SPRING GROVE (village)—Mediacom. Now served by BELVIDERE TWP., IL [IL0282]

SPRING GROVE (VILLAGE)—See BELVIDERE TWP., IL (Mediacom)

SPRING VALLEY—See MOUNT PROSPECT, IL (Comcast Cable)

SPRINGERTON—See DAHLGREN, IL (Hamilton County Communications. Formerly [IL0381]. This cable system has converted to IPTV)

SPRINGFIELD TWP.—See SPRINGFIELD, IL (Comcast Cable)

SPRINGFIELD—Comcast Cable

ST. ANNE—See CHAMPAIGN, IL (Comcast Cable)

ST. AUGUSTINE—See ELMWOOD, IL (Mediacom)

ST. CHARLES—See PEORIA, IL (Comcast Cable)

ST. CLAIR COUNTY (PORTIONS)—See SPARTA, IL (NewWave Communications)

ST. CLAIR COUNTY (UNINCORPORATED PORTIONS)—See WASHINGTON PARK, IL (Mediacom)

ST. CLAIR TWP.—See WASHINGTON PARK, IL (Mediacom)

ST. DAVID—Mediacom. Now served by ELMWOOD, IL [IL0205]

ST. DAVID—See ELMWOOD, IL (Mediacom)

ST. ELMO—See ALTAMONT, IL (Mediacom)

ST. FRANCISVILLE—NewWave Communications. Now served by VINCENNES, IN [IN0035]

ST. JACOB—HomeTel Cable TV

ST. JOHN—See CHAMPAIGN, IN (Comcast Cable)

ST. JOHNS (VILLAGE)—See BENTON, IL (NewWave Communications)

ST. JOSEPH COUNTY (PORTIONS)—See CHAMPAIGN, IN (Comcast Cable)

ST. JOSEPH COUNTY (UNINCORPORATED AREAS)—See CHAMPAIGN, IN (Comcast Cable)

ST. JOSEPH TWP.—See CHAMPAIGN, MI (Comcast Cable)

ST. JOSEPH—See CHAMPAIGN, IL (Comcast Cable)

ST. JOSEPH—See CHAMPAIGN, MI (Comcast Cable)

ST. LIBORY—Formerly served by CableDirect. No longer in operation

ST. PETER—Clearvision Cable Systems Inc

STANDARD—See CHILLICOTHE, IL (Mediacom)

STANFORD—See ROANOKE, IL (Mediacom)

STARK COUNTY (UNINCORPORATED AREAS)—See ELLISVILLE, IL (Mid Century Communications)

STAUNTON—Madison Communications

STE. MARIE TWP.—Formerly served by Advanced Technologies & Technical Resources Inc. No longer in operation

STEELEVILLE—See SPARTA, IL (NewWave Communications)

STEGER—See CHAMPAIGN, IL (Comcast Cable)

STEPHENSON COUNTY—See MOUNT PROSPECT, IL (Comcast Cable)

STEPHENSON COUNTY—See MOUNT CARROLL, IL (Mediacom)

STERLING TWP.—See MOUNT PROSPECT, IL (Comcast Cable)

STERLING—Comcast Cable. Now served by MOUNT PROSPECT, IL [IL0036]

STERLING—See MOUNT PROSPECT, IL (Comcast Cable)

STEVENSVILLE (VILLAGE)—See CHAMPAIGN, MI (Comcast Cable)

STEWARDSON—See NEOGA, IL (Mediacom)

STICKNEY—See PEORIA, IL (Comcast Cable)

STILLMAN VALLEY—See MOUNT PROSPECT, IL (Comcast Cable)

STOCKTON—Mediacom. Now served by LENA, IL [IL0223]

STOCKTON—See MOUNT CARROLL, IL (Mediacom)

STONE PARK—See PEORIA, IL (Comcast Cable)

STONINGTON—See MOWEAQUA, IL (NewWave Communications)

STRASBURG—Mediacom. Now served by NEOGA, IL [IL0249]

STRASBURG—See NEOGA, IL (Mediacom)

STREAMWOOD—Comcast Cable. Now served by MOUNT PROSPECT, IL [IL0036]

STREAMWOOD—See MOUNT PROSPECT, IL (Comcast Cable)

STREAMWOOD—See NAPERVILLE, IL (WOW! Internet, Cable & Phone)

STREATOR—Mediacom

STREETERVILLE—See CHICAGO, IL (RCN Corp. Formerly [IL0661]. This cable system has converted to IPTV)

STRONGHURST—Mediacom. Now served by DALLAS CITY, IL [IL0274]

STRONGHURST—See DALLAS CITY, IL (Mediacom)

SUBLETTE (VILLAGE)—Heartland Cable Broadband

SUGAR GROVE—Mediacom

SULLIVAN—Mediacom

SUMMIT—See PEORIA, IL (Comcast Cable)

SUMMUM—See ELLISVILLE, IL (Mid Century Communications)

SUMMUM—See ONEIDA, IL (Oneida Cablevision Inc. Formerly [IL0361]. This cable system has converted to IPTV)

SUMNER—NewWave Communications. Now served by VINCENNES, IN [IN0035]

SUN RIVER TERRACE—See CHAMPAIGN, IL (Comcast Cable)

SUNSET LAKE—See TAYLORVILLE, IL (NewWave Communications)

SYCAMORE—See MOUNT PROSPECT, IL (Comcast Cable)

TABLE GROVE—Mid Century Telephone Cooperative. Formerly [IL0587]. This cable system has converted to IPTV. Now served by ELLISVILLE, IL [IL5238]

TABLE GROVE—Mid Century Telephone Cooperative. This cable system has converted to IPTV. Now served by ELLISVILLE, IL [IL5238]

TABLE GROVE—See ELLISVILLE, IL (Mid Century Communications)

TABLE GROVE—See ONEIDA, IL (Oneida Cablevision Inc. Formerly [IL0361]. This cable system has converted to IPTV)

TALBOTT—See BEARDSTOWN, IL (Cass Cable TV Inc)

TALLULA—See BEARDSTOWN, IL (Cass Cable TV Inc)

TAMAROA—See BENTON, IL (NewWave Communications)

TAMMS—NewWave Communications

TAMPICO—Mediacom

TAYLOR RIDGE (UNINCORPORATED AREAS)—See ONEIDA, IL (Oneida Cablevision Inc. Formerly [IL0361]. This cable system has converted to IPTV)

TAYLOR RIDGE—See MOLINE, IL (Mediacom)

TAYLOR SPRINGS—See TAYLORVILLE, IL (NewWave Communications)

TAYLORVILLE—NewWave Communications

TAZEWELL COUNTY (PORTIONS)—See PEORIA, IL (Comcast Cable)

TEUTOPOLIS—See EFFINGHAM, IL (Mediacom)

THAWVILLE—Formerly served by CableDirect. No longer in operation

THAYER—See TAYLORVILLE, IL (NewWave Communications)

THE LOOP—See CHICAGO, IL (RCN Corp. Formerly [IL0661]. This cable system has converted to IPTV)

THEBES—See ALEXANDER COUNTY (portions), IL (Zito Media)

THIRD LAKE—See MOUNT PROSPECT, IL (Comcast Cable)

THOMASBORO—See RANTOUL, IL (Mediacom)

THOMPSONVILLE—See DAHLGREN, IL (Hamilton County Communications. Formerly [IL0381]. This cable system has converted to IPTV)

THORNTON TWP.—See CHAMPAIGN, IL (Comcast Cable)

THORNTON—See CHAMPAIGN, IL (Comcast Cable)

THREE OAKS TWP.—See CHAMPAIGN, MI (Comcast Cable)

THREE OAKS—See CHAMPAIGN, MI (Comcast Cable)

TILDEN—See COULTERVILLE, IL (Mediacom)

TILTON—See WESTVILLE, IL (NewWave Communications)

TIMBER RIDGE—See ROANOKE, IL (Mediacom)

TINLEY PARK—See CHAMPAIGN, IL (Comcast Cable)

TISKILWA—See MOUNT PROSPECT, IL (Comcast Cable)

TOLEDO—See GREENUP, IL (Mediacom)

TOLONO—Mediacom. Now served by TUSCOLA, IL [IL0135]

Cable Community Index—Illinois

TOLONO—See MONTICELLO, IL (Mediacom)

TOLUCA—See ROANOKE, IL (Mediacom)

TONICA—Heartland Cable Inc

TOULON—See WYOMING, IL (Mediacom)

TOVEY—See KINCAID, IL (Mediacom)

TOWANDA—See ROANOKE, IL (Mediacom)

TOWER HILL—Mediacom

TOWER LAKES—See MOUNT PROSPECT, IL (Comcast Cable)

TRAIL CREEK—See CHAMPAIGN, IN (Comcast Cable)

TREMONT—See PEORIA, IL (Comcast Cable)

TREMONT—See METAMORA, IL (Tel-Star Cablevision Inc)

TRIANGLE MOBILE HOME PARK—See RANTOUL, IL (Mediacom)

TRIVOLI—Nova1Net

TROY GROVE (village)—Formerly served by CableDirect. No longer in operation

TROY TWP.—See PEORIA, IL (Comcast Cable)

TUSCOLA—Mediacom

ULLIN—See ALEXANDER COUNTY (portions), IL (Zito Media)

UNION COUNTY (PORTIONS)—See ZEIGLER, IL (Mediacom)

UNION COUNTY (PORTIONS)—See ANNA, IL (NewWave Communications)

UNION—Packerland Broadband

UNIVERSITY PARK—See CHAMPAIGN, IL (Comcast Cable)

UPTOWN—See CHICAGO, IL (RCN Corp. Formerly [IL0661]. This cable system has converted to IPTV)

URBANA—See CHAMPAIGN, IL (Comcast Cable)

URSA—See BOWEN, IL (Adams Telcom)

VALIER—See McLEANSBORO, IL (NewWave Communications)

VALPARAISO—See CHAMPAIGN, IN (Comcast Cable)

VANDALIA—NewWave Communications. Now served by TAYLORVILLE, IL [IL0098]

VANDALIA—See TAYLORVILLE, IL (NewWave Communications)

VANDERBURGH COUNTY (WESTERN PORTION)—See McLEANSBORO, IN (NewWave Communications)

VARNA—See ROANOKE, IL (Mediacom)

VERA—See TAYLORVILLE, IL (NewWave Communications)

VERGENNES—Formerly served by CableDirect. No longer in operation

VERMILION COUNTY (PORTIONS)—See CHAMPAIGN, IL (Comcast Cable)

VERMILION COUNTY (PORTIONS)—See WESTVILLE, IL (NewWave Communications)

VERMILLION (village)—Formerly served by CableDirect. No longer in operation

VERMONT—Nova1Net

VERNON HILLS—See MOUNT PROSPECT, IL (Comcast Cable)

VERNON—See PATOKA, IL (Clearvision Cable Systems Inc)

VERSAILLES—Cass Cable TV Inc. Now served by BEARDSTOWN, IL [IL0598]

VERSAILLES—See BEARDSTOWN, IL (Cass Cable TV Inc)

VICTORIA—Mediacom

VICTORIA—See ELLISVILLE, IL (Mid Century Communications)

VICTORIA—See ONEIDA, IL (Oneida Cablevision Inc. Formerly [IL0361]. This cable system has converted to IPTV)

VIENNA—See BUNCOMBE, IL (Zito Media)

VILLA GROVE—See TUSCOLA, IL (Mediacom)

VILLA PARK—Comcast Cable. Now served by PEORIA, IL [IL0012]

VILLA PARK—See PEORIA, IL (Comcast Cable)

VIOLA—See GENESEO, IL (Mediacom)

VIOLA—See ONEIDA, IL (Oneida Cablevision Inc. Formerly [IL0361]. This cable system has converted to IPTV)

VIRDEN—NewWave Communications. Now served by TAYLORVILLE, IL [IL0098]

VIRDEN—See TAYLORVILLE, IL (NewWave Communications)

VIRGINIA—See BEARDSTOWN, IL (Cass Cable TV Inc)

VOLO—See MOUNT PROSPECT, IL (Comcast Cable)

WABASH COUNTY (PORTIONS)—See McLEANSBORO, IL (NewWave Communications)

WADSWORTH—See MOUNT PROSPECT, IL (Comcast Cable)

WAKARUSA—See CHAMPAIGN, IN (Comcast Cable)

WALCOTT—See MOLINE, IA (Mediacom)

WALNUT—Mediacom. Now served by GENESEO, IL [IL0170]

WALNUT—See GENESEO, IL (Mediacom)

WALTONVILLE—Formerly served by Longview Communications. No longer in operation

WAPELLA—See ATLANTA, IL (Mediacom)

WARREN COUNTY (PORTIONS)—See MONMOUTH, IL (Comcast Cable)

WARREN—Mediacom. Now served by LENA, IL [IL0223]

WARREN—See MOUNT CARROLL, IL (Mediacom)

WARRENSBURG—Formerly served by Crystal Broadband Networks. No longer in operation

WARRENVILLE—See PEORIA, IL (Comcast Cable)

WARSAW—See CHAMPAIGN, IN (Comcast Cable)

WASHBURN—See ROANOKE, IL (Mediacom)

WASHINGTON PARK—Mediacom

WASHINGTON TWP. (MACOMB COUNTY)—See CHAMPAIGN, MI (Comcast Cable)

WASHINGTON TWP.—See CHAMPAIGN, MI (Comcast Cable)

WASHINGTON—See PEORIA, IL (Comcast Cable)

WASHINGTON—See METAMORA, IL (Tel-Star Cablevision Inc)

WATAGA—Mediacom. Now served by GENESEO, IL [IL0170]

WATAGA—See GENESEO, IL (Mediacom)

WATERLOO—Charter Communications. Now served by ST. LOUIS, MO [MO0009]

WATERMAN—See SUGAR GROVE, IL (Mediacom)

WATERVLIET TWP.—See CHAMPAIGN, MI (Comcast Cable)

WATERVLIET—See CHAMPAIGN, MI (Comcast Cable)

WATSEKA—Mediacom

WATSON—Clearvision Cable Systems Inc

WAUCONDA—See MOUNT PROSPECT, IL (Comcast Cable)

WAUKEGAN—Comcast Cable. Now served by MOUNT PROSPECT, IL [IL0036]

WAUKEGAN—See MOUNT PROSPECT, IL (Comcast Cable)

WAYNE CITY—NewWave Communications. Now served by McLEANSBORO, IL [IL0177]

WAYNE CITY—See DAHLGREN, IL (Hamilton County Communications. Formerly [IL0381]. This cable system has converted to IPTV)

WAYNE CITY—See McLEANSBORO, IL (NewWave Communications)

WAYNE COUNTY (PORTIONS)—See McLEANSBORO, IL (NewWave Communications)

WAYNE TWP.—See CHAMPAIGN, MI (Comcast Cable)

WAYNESVILLE—See ATLANTA, IL (Mediacom)

WEE-MA-TUK HILLS—Nova1Net

WEESAW—See CHAMPAIGN, MI (Comcast Cable)

WELDON—Mediacom. Now served by RANTOUL, IL [IL0089]

WELDON—See RANTOUL, IL (Mediacom)

WELLINGTON—See WESTVILLE, IL (NewWave Communications)

WENONA—See ROANOKE, IL (Mediacom)

WEST CHICAGO—Comcast Cable. Now served by PEORIA, IL [IL0012]

WEST CHICAGO—See PEORIA, IL (Comcast Cable)

WEST CITY (VILLAGE)—See BENTON, IL (NewWave Communications)

WEST DUNDEE—See MOUNT PROSPECT, IL (Comcast Cable)

WEST FRANKFORT—See MURPHYSBORO, IL (Mediacom)

WEST PEORIA—See PEORIA, IL (Comcast Cable)

WEST SALEM—Formerly served by Park TV & Electronics Inc. No longer in operation

WEST UNION—Formerly served by Longview Communications. No longer in operation

WESTCHESTER—See PEORIA, IL (Comcast Cable)

WESTERN SPRINGS—Comcast Cable. Now served by PEORIA, IL [IL0012]

WESTERN SPRINGS—See PEORIA, IL (Comcast Cable)

WESTFIELD—See CHARLESTON, IL (Mediacom)

WESTMONT—See PEORIA, IL (Comcast Cable)

WESTVILLE—NewWave Communications

WHEATON—See PEORIA, IL (Comcast Cable)

WHEELING—See MOUNT PROSPECT, IL (Comcast Cable)

WHITE COUNTY—See McLEANSBORO, IL (NewWave Communications)

WHITE HALL—See JERSEYVILLE, IL (NewWave Communications)

WHITE HEATH—Formerly served by Park TV & Electronics Inc. No longer in operation

WHITEASH—See MURPHYSBORO, IL (Mediacom)

WHITING—See CHAMPAIGN, IN (Comcast Cable)

WILL COUNTY (NORTHWESTERN PORTION)—See CHAMPAIGN, IL (Comcast Cable)

Illinois—Cable Community Index

WILL COUNTY (PORTIONS)—See CHAMPAIGN, IL (Comcast Cable)

WILL COUNTY (PORTIONS)—See PEORIA, IL (Comcast Cable)

WILL—See CHAMPAIGN, IL (Comcast Cable)

WILLIAMSFIELD—Mediacom. Now served by WYOMING, IL [IL0196]

WILLIAMSFIELD—See WYOMING, IL (Mediacom)

WILLIAMSFIELD—See ELLISVILLE, IL (Mid Century Communications)

WILLIAMSFIELD—See ONEIDA, IL (Oneida Cablevision Inc. Formerly [IL0361]. This cable system has converted to IPTV)

WILLIAMSON COUNTY (PORTIONS)—See MURPHYSBORO, IL (Mediacom)

WILLIAMSON COUNTY (PORTIONS)—See ZEIGLER, IL (Mediacom)

WILLIAMSON COUNTY (PORTIONS)—Zito Media

WILLIAMSON COUNTY (SOUTHERN PORTION)—See LAKE OF EGYPT, IL (Zito Media)

WILLIAMSON—See STAUNTON, IL (Madison Communications)

WILLIAMSVILLE—Greene County Partners Inc

WILLOW HILL TWP.—Formerly served by Advanced Technologies & Technical Resources Inc. No longer in operation

WILLOW SPRINGS—See PEORIA, IL (Comcast Cable)

WILLOWBROOK—See PEORIA, IL (Comcast Cable)

WILMETTE—See MOUNT PROSPECT, IL (Comcast Cable)

WILMINGTON—Comcast Cable. Now served by PEORIA, IL [IL0012]

WILMINGTON—See PEORIA, IL (Comcast Cable)

WILSONVILLE—Formerly served by Mediacom. Now served by Madison Communications, STAUNTON, IL [IL0171]

WILSONVILLE—See STAUNTON, IL (Madison Communications)

WILTON—See MOLINE, IA (Mediacom)

WINCHESTER—Formerly served by Crystal Broadband Networks. No longer in operation

WINDSOR—Mediacom. Now served by NEOGA, IL [IL0249]

WINDSOR—See NEOGA, IL (Mediacom)

WINFIELD—See PEORIA, IL (Comcast Cable)

WINFIELD—See CHAMPAIGN, IN (Comcast Cable)

WINNEBAGO COUNTY (PORTIONS)—See MOUNT PROSPECT, IL (Comcast Cable)

WINNEBAGO COUNTY (PORTIONS)—See MOUNT CARROLL, IL (Mediacom)

WINNETKA—See MOUNT PROSPECT, IL (Comcast Cable)

WINONA LAKE—See CHAMPAIGN, IN (Comcast Cable)

WINSLOW—Mediacom. Now served by LENA, IL [IL0223]

WINSLOW—See MOUNT CARROLL, IL (Mediacom)

WINTHROP HARBOR—See MOUNT PROSPECT, IL (Comcast Cable)

WITT—See TAYLORVILLE, IL (NewWave Communications)

WOLF LAKE—Formerly served by CableDirect. No longer in operation

WONDER LAKE—See MOUNT PROSPECT, IL (Comcast Cable)

WOOD DALE—See PEORIA, IL (Comcast Cable)

WOODFORD COUNTY—See ROANOKE, IL (Mediacom)

WOODHULL—See ALPHA, IL (Diverse Communications Inc.)

WOODHULL—See ONEIDA, IL (Oneida Cablevision Inc. Formerly [IL0361]. This cable system has converted to IPTV)

WOODLAND (VILLAGE)—See WATSEKA, IL (Mediacom)

WOODLAND HEIGHTS—Tel-Star Cablevision Inc

WOODLAWN—Charter Communications. Now served by ST. LOUIS, MO [MO0009]

WOODLAWN—Charter Communications. Now served by ST. LOUIS, MO [MO0009]

WOODRIDGE—See PEORIA, IL (Comcast Cable)

WOODSIDE TWP.—See SPRINGFIELD, IL (Comcast Cable)

WOODSTOCK—Comcast Cable. Now served by MOUNT PROSPECT, IL [IL0036]

WOODSTOCK—See MOUNT PROSPECT, IL (Comcast Cable)

WORDEN—Madison Communications. Now served by STAUNTON, IL [IL0171]

WORDEN—See STAUNTON, IL (Madison Communications)

WORTH—See CHAMPAIGN, IL (Comcast Cable)

WRIGLEYVILLE—See CHICAGO, IL (RCN Corp. Formerly [IL0661]. This cable system has converted to IPTV)

WYANET—See MOUNT PROSPECT, IL (Comcast Cable)

WYOMING—Mediacom

XENIA—Wabash Independent Networks. Now served by FLORA, IL [IL0140]

XENIA—See FLORA, IL (Wabash Independent Networks)

YATES CITY—See ELMWOOD, IL (Mediacom)

YATES CITY—See ELLISVILLE, IL (Mid Century Communications)

YATES CITY—See ONEIDA, IL (Oneida Cablevision Inc. Formerly [IL0361]. This cable system has converted to IPTV)

YORKVILLE—See PEORIA, IL (Comcast Cable)

ZEIGLER—Mediacom

ZION—See MOUNT PROSPECT, IL (Comcast Cable)

INDIANA

ADAMS LAKE—See AUBURN, IN (Mediacom)

AKRON (town)—Comcast Cable. Now served by CHAMPAIGN, IL [IL0019]

ALBANY—See HENDRICKS COUNTY (portions), IN (Comcast Cable)

ALBION—See AUBURN, IN (Mediacom)

ALEXANDRIA—See HENDRICKS COUNTY (portions), IN (Comcast Cable)

ALLEN COUNTY (PORTIONS)—See HENDRICKS COUNTY (portions), IN (Comcast Cable)

ALLEN COUNTY—Mediacom. Now served by AUBURN, IN [IN0066]

ALLEN COUNTY—See AUBURN, IN (Mediacom)

AMBOY—Formerly served by CableDirect. No longer in operation

AMO—See VINCENNES, IN (NewWave Communications)

ANDERSON—Comcast Cable. Now served by HENDRICKS COUNTY (portions), IN [IN0001]

ANDERSON—Formerly served by Broadcast Cable Inc. No longer in operation

ANDERSON—See HENDRICKS COUNTY (portions), IN (Comcast Cable)

ANDREWS—Formerly served by Longview Communications. No longer in operation

ANDREWS—See HENDRICKS COUNTY (portions), IN (Comcast Cable)

ANGOLA—Mediacom

ARCADIA—See HENDRICKS COUNTY (portions), IN (Comcast Cable)

ARGOS—Mediacom. Now served by NORTH WEBSTER, IN [IN0038]

ARGOS—See NORTH WEBSTER, IN (Mediacom)

ASHLEY—Formerly served by Longview Communications. No longer in operation

ATLANTA—See HENDRICKS COUNTY (portions), IN (Comcast Cable)

ATTICA (VILLAGE)—See HENDRICKS COUNTY (portions), IN (Comcast Cable)

AUBURN—Mediacom

AURORA—See HENDRICKS COUNTY (portions), IN (Comcast Cable)

AVILLA—NewWave Communications

BAINBRIDGE—Formerly served by Global Com Inc. No longer in operation

BARGERSVILLE—See HENDRICKS COUNTY (portions), IN (Comcast Cable)

BARTHOLOMEW COUNTY (PORTIONS)—See HENDRICKS COUNTY (portions), IN (Comcast Cable)

BARTHOLOMEW COUNTY (PORTIONS)—See VINCENNES, IN (NewWave Communications)

BATESVILLE—Formerly served by Comcast Cable. Now served by Enhanced Telecommunications Corp., BROOKVILLE, IN [IN0108]

BATESVILLE—See BROOKVILLE, IN (Enhanced Telecommunications Corp)

BATTLE GROUND—See HENDRICKS COUNTY (portions), IN (Comcast Cable)

BEDFORD—Comcast Cable. Now served by HENDRICKS COUNTY (portions), IN [IN0001]

BEDFORD—See HENDRICKS COUNTY (portions), IN (Comcast Cable)

BEDFORD—See VINCENNES, IN (NewWave Communications)

BEECH GROVE—See HENDRICKS COUNTY (portions), IN (Comcast Cable)

BENTON COUNTY (PORTIONS)—See HENDRICKS COUNTY (portions), IN (Comcast Cable)

BENTON TWP.—See NEW PARIS, IN (Quality Cablevision)

BERNE—See HENDRICKS COUNTY (portions), IN (Comcast Cable)

BICKNELL—Formerly served by Charter Communications. Now served by NewWave Communications, VINCENNES, IN [IN0035]

BICKNELL—See VINCENNES, IN (NewWave Communications)

BIRDSEYE—Formerly served by CableDirect. No longer in operation

BLACKFORD COUNTY (PORTIONS)—See HENDRICKS COUNTY (portions), IN (Comcast Cable)

Cable Community Index—Indiana

BLOOMFIELD—Formerly served by Insight Communications. Now served by Comcast Cable, HENDRICKS COUNTY (portions), IN [IN0001]

BLOOMFIELD—See HENDRICKS COUNTY (portions), IN (Comcast Cable)

BLOOMINGDALE—See JASONVILLE, IN (NewWave Communications)

BLOOMINGTON—Comcast Cable. Now served by HENDRICKS COUNTY (portions), IN [IN0001]

BLOOMINGTON—See HENDRICKS COUNTY (portions), IN (Comcast Cable)

BLOUNTSVILLE—See HENDRICKS COUNTY (portions), IN (Comcast Cable)

BLUFFTON (VILLAGE)—See DECATUR, IN (Mediacom)

BOONE COUNTY (PORTIONS)—See HENDRICKS COUNTY (portions), IN (Comcast Cable)

BOONE COUNTY—See INDIANAPOLIS (portions), IN (Bright House Networks)

BOONVILLE—Time Warner Cable. Now served by EVANSVILLE, IN [IN0006]

BOONVILLE—See EVANSVILLE, IN (Time Warner Cable)

BOONVILLE—See EVANSVILLE, IN (WOW! Internet, Cable & Phone)

BOSWELL—Benton County Cable Co

BOURBON—Mediacom. Now served by NORTH WEBSTER, IN [IN0038]

BOURBON—See NORTH WEBSTER, IN (Mediacom)

BRAZIL—NewWave Communications. Now served by VINCENNES, IN [IN0035]

BRAZIL—See VINCENNES, IN (NewWave Communications)

BREMEN—Mediacom. Now served by NORTH WEBSTER, IN [IN0038]

BREMEN—See NORTH WEBSTER, IN (Mediacom)

BRIDGEPORT—See VINCENNES, IL (NewWave Communications)

BRINGHURST—See FLORA, IN (NewWave Communications)

BRISTOL—Comcast Cable. Now served by CHAMPAIGN, IL [IL0019]

BROOKLYN—Formerly served by CableDirect. No longer in operation

BROOKSTON—See HENDRICKS COUNTY (portions), IN (Comcast Cable)

BROOKVILLE—Enhanced Telecommunications Corp

BROWN COUNTY (NORTHWEST PORTION)—See HENDRICKS COUNTY (portions), IN (Comcast Cable)

BROWN COUNTY—See VINCENNES, IN (NewWave Communications)

BROWNSBURG—See HENDRICKS COUNTY (portions), IN (Comcast Cable)

BROWNSTOWN—Comcast Cable. Now served by HENDRICKS COUNTY (portions), IN [IN0001]

BROWNSTOWN—See HENDRICKS COUNTY (portions), IN (Comcast Cable)

BRUCE LAKE—See WINAMAC, IN (LightStream)

BRUCEVILLE—See VINCENNES, IN (NewWave Communications)

BRYANT—See HENDRICKS COUNTY (portions), IN (Comcast Cable)

BUFFALO—See HENDRICKS COUNTY (portions), IN (Comcast Cable)

BUNKER HILL—See HENDRICKS COUNTY (portions), IN (Comcast Cable)

BURLINGTON—See FLORA, IN (NewWave Communications)

BURNETTSVILLE—See HENDRICKS COUNTY (portions), IN (Comcast Cable)

BUTLER—Mediacom. Now served by ANGOLA, IN [IN0034]

BUTLER—See ANGOLA, IN (Mediacom)

CADIZ—See HENDRICKS COUNTY (portions), IN (Comcast Cable)

CAMBRIDGE CITY—See HENDRICKS COUNTY (portions), IN (Comcast Cable)

CAMBY—See MORGAN COUNTY (portions), IN (NewWave Communications)

CAMDEN—See FLORA, IN (NewWave Communications)

CAMPBELLSBURG—Formerly served by Insight Communications. Now served by Time Warner Cable, LOUISVILLE, KY [KY0001]

CANNELTON—See TELL CITY, IN (Comcast Cable)

CARBON—NewWave Communications. Now served by VINCENNES, IN [IN0035]

CARBON—See VINCENNES, IN (NewWave Communications)

CARLISLE—Formerly served by Almega Cable. No longer in operation

CARMEL—See INDIANAPOLIS (portions), IN (Bright House Networks)

CARMEL—FirstMile Technologies

CARROLL COUNTY (PORTIONS)—See HENDRICKS COUNTY (portions), IN (Comcast Cable)

CARROLL COUNTY (PORTIONS)—See FLORA, IN (NewWave Communications)

CARTHAGE—See HENDRICKS COUNTY (portions), IN (Comcast Cable)

CASS COUNTY (PORTIONS)—See HENDRICKS COUNTY (portions), IN (Comcast Cable)

CATARACT LAKE—Formerly served by Longview Communications. No longer in operation

CEDARVILLE—See AUBURN, IN (Mediacom)

CENTER POINT—Formerly served by CableDirect. No longer in operation

CENTERTON—NewWave Communications. Now served by MORGAN COUNTY (portions), IN [IN0098]

CENTERTON—See MORGAN COUNTY (portions), IN (NewWave Communications)

CENTERVILLE—See HENDRICKS COUNTY (portions), IN (Comcast Cable)

CHALMERS—See HENDRICKS COUNTY (portions), IN (Comcast Cable)

CHANDLER—See EVANSVILLE, IN (WOW! Internet, Cable & Phone)

CHARLOTTESVILLE—See HENDRICKS COUNTY (portions), IN (Comcast Cable)

CHESTERFIELD—See HENDRICKS COUNTY (portions), IN (Comcast Cable)

CHRISNEY—Formerly served by CableDirect. No longer in operation

CHURUBUSCO—See AUBURN, IN (Mediacom)

CICERO—See HENDRICKS COUNTY (portions), IN (Comcast Cable)

CLARKS HILL—See HENDRICKS COUNTY (portions), IN (Comcast Cable)

CLAY CITY—Formerly served by Global Com Inc. No longer in operation

CLAY COUNTY (NORTH CENTRAL PORTION)—See VINCENNES, IN (NewWave Communications)

CLAYTON—See VINCENNES, IN (NewWave Communications)

CLEAR LAKE—Mediacom. Now served by ELMWOOD, IL [IL0205]

CLERMONT—See HENDRICKS COUNTY (portions), IN (Comcast Cable)

CLIFFORD—See HENDRICKS COUNTY (portions), IN (Comcast Cable)

CLINTON COUNTY (PORTIONS)—See HENDRICKS COUNTY (portions), IN (Comcast Cable)

CLINTON—NewWave Communications. Now served by VINCENNES, IN [IN0035]

CLINTON—See VINCENNES, IN (NewWave Communications)

CLOVERDALE—Formerly served by Indiana Communications. No longer in operation

COAL CITY—Formerly served by CableDirect. No longer in operation

COALMONT—See JASONVILLE, IN (NewWave Communications)

COATESVILLE—NewWave Communications. Now served by VINCENNES, IN [IN0035]

COATESVILLE—See VINCENNES, IN (NewWave Communications)

COLFAX—See LINDEN, IN (Tri-County Communications)

COLUMBIA CITY—See AUBURN, IN (Mediacom)

COLUMBUS—Comcast Cable. Now served by HENDRICKS COUNTY (portions), IN [IN0001]

COLUMBUS—See HENDRICKS COUNTY (portions), IN (Comcast Cable)

CONNERSVILLE—Comcast Cable. Now served by HENDRICKS COUNTY (portions), IN [IN0001]

CONNERSVILLE—See HENDRICKS COUNTY (portions), IN (Comcast Cable)

CONVERSE—See SWEETSER, IN (Oak Hill Cablevision Inc)

CONVOY—See MONROEVILLE, OH (NewWave Communications)

CORDRY LAKE—See VINCENNES, IN (NewWave Communications)

CORUNNA—Formerly served by CableDirect. No longer in operation

COVINGTON—NewWave Communications

COWAN—See HENDRICKS COUNTY (portions), IN (Comcast Cable)

CRAIGVILLE—See DECATUR, IN (Mediacom)

CRAWFORD COUNTY (portions)—Formerly served by NewWave Communications. No longer in operation

CRAWFORDSVILLE—Comcast Cable. Now served by HENDRICKS COUNTY (portions), IN [IN0001]

CRAWFORDSVILLE—Formerly served by Accelplus. Now served by Metronet, GREENCASTLE, IN [IN5142]

CRAWFORDSVILLE—See HENDRICKS COUNTY (portions), IN (Comcast Cable)

CROMWELL—See AUBURN, IN (Mediacom)

CULVER—See KNOX, IN (Mediacom)

CUMBERLAND (TOWN)—See HENDRICKS COUNTY (portions), IN (Comcast Cable)

CYNTHIANA—Time Warner Cable. Now served by EVANSVILLE, IN [IN0006]

CYNTHIANA—See EVANSVILLE, IN (Time Warner Cable)

DALE—See SPENCER COUNTY (portions), IN (NewWave Communications)

DALEVILLE—See HENDRICKS COUNTY (portions), IN (Comcast Cable)

Indiana—Cable Community Index

DANVILLE—See HENDRICKS COUNTY (portions), IN (Comcast Cable)

DARLINGTON—Formerly served by Indiana Communications. No longer in operation

DARMSTADT—See EVANSVILLE, IN (Time Warner Cable)

DAVIESS COUNTY—See VINCENNES, IN (NewWave Communications)

DAYTON—See HENDRICKS COUNTY (portions), IN (Comcast Cable)

DEARBORN COUNTY (PORTIONS)—See HENDRICKS COUNTY (portions), IN (Comcast Cable)

DECATUR COUNTY (PORTIONS)—See HENDRICKS COUNTY (portions), IN (Comcast Cable)

DECATUR—Mediacom

DECKER—Formerly served by CableDirect. No longer in operation

DEKALB COUNTY—See AUBURN, IN (Mediacom)

DELAWARE COUNTY (PORTIONS)—See HENDRICKS COUNTY (portions), IN (Comcast Cable)

DELPHI—See FLORA, IN (NewWave Communications)

DENVER—See HENDRICKS COUNTY (portions), IN (Comcast Cable)

DESOTO—Comcast Cable. Now served by HENDRICKS COUNTY (portions), IN [IN0001]

DESOTO—See HENDRICKS COUNTY (portions), IN (Comcast Cable)

DILLSBORO—See HENDRICKS COUNTY (portions), IN (Comcast Cable)

DISTRICT OF SWEETWATER—Formerly served by NewWave Communications. No longer in operation

DUBLIN—See HENDRICKS COUNTY (portions), IN (Comcast Cable)

DUBOIS COUNTY (PORTIONS)—See EVANSVILLE, IN (Time Warner Cable)

DUBOIS COUNTY—Formerly served by CableDirect. No longer in operation

DUGGER—See JASONVILLE, IN (NewWave Communications)

DUNKIRK—See HENDRICKS COUNTY (portions), IN (Comcast Cable)

DUNREITH—See HENDRICKS COUNTY (portions), IN (Comcast Cable)

DUPONT—Formerly served by CableDirect. No longer in operation

EATON—See HENDRICKS COUNTY (portions), IN (Comcast Cable)

ECONOMY—Formerly served by CableDirect. No longer in operation

EDGEWOOD—See HENDRICKS COUNTY (portions), IN (Comcast Cable)

EDINBURGH—Formerly served by Avenue Broadband Communications. Now served by NewWave Communications, VINCENNES, IN [IN0035]

EDINBURGH—See VINCENNES, IN (NewWave Communications)

EDWARDSPORT—See VINCENNES, IN (NewWave Communications)

ELBERFELD—NewWave Communications

ELIZABETH (town)—Formerly served by Windjammer Cable. No longer in operation

ELIZABETHTOWN—See HENDRICKS COUNTY (portions), IN (Comcast Cable)

ELKHART COUNTY (PORTIONS)—See NORTH WEBSTER, IN (Mediacom)

ELKHART—Comcast Cable. Now served by CHAMPAIGN, IL [IL0019]

ELLETTSVILLE—See HENDRICKS COUNTY (portions), IN (Comcast Cable)

ELWOOD—See HENDRICKS COUNTY (portions), IN (Comcast Cable)

ENGLISH—Formerly served by NewWave Communications. No longer in operation

EVANSVILLE—Time Warner Cable

EVANSVILLE—WOW! Internet, Cable & Phone

FAIRMOUNT—See HENDRICKS COUNTY (portions), IN (Comcast Cable)

FAIRVIEW PARK—See VINCENNES, IN (NewWave Communications)

FARMERSBURG—See JASONVILLE, IN (NewWave Communications)

FARMLAND—See HENDRICKS COUNTY (portions), IN (Comcast Cable)

FAYETTE COUNTY (PORTIONS)—See HENDRICKS COUNTY (portions), IN (Comcast Cable)

FERDINAND—NewWave Communications. Now served by SPENCER COUNTY (portions), IN [IN0089]

FERDINAND—See SPENCER COUNTY (portions), IN (NewWave Communications)

FILLMORE—Formerly served by Global Com Inc. No longer in operation

FISH LAKE—Formerly served by CableDirect. No longer in operation

FISHERS—See INDIANAPOLIS (portions), IN (Bright House Networks)

FISHERS—See HENDRICKS COUNTY (portions), IN (Comcast Cable)

FISHERS—See CARMEL, IN (FirstMile Technologies)

FLAT ROCK—Formerly served by Comcast Cable. No longer in operation

FLAT ROCK—See BROOKVILLE, IN (Enhanced Telecommunications Corp)

FLORA—NewWave Communications

FORT BRANCH—Time Warner Cable. Now served by EVANSVILLE, IN [IN0006]

FORT BRANCH—See EVANSVILLE, IN (Time Warner Cable)

FORT RECOVERY—See HENDRICKS COUNTY (portions), OH (Comcast Cable)

FORT WAYNE—Comcast Cable. Now served by HENDRICKS COUNTY (portions), IN [IN0001]

FORT WAYNE—See HENDRICKS COUNTY (portions), IN (Comcast Cable)

FORTVILLE—See INDIANAPOLIS (portions), IN (Bright House Networks)

FOUNTAIN CITY—See HENDRICKS COUNTY (portions), IN (Comcast Cable)

FOUNTAIN COUNTY (PORTIONS)—See HENDRICKS COUNTY (portions), IN (Comcast Cable)

FOUNTAIN COUNTY (PORTIONS)—See COVINGTON, IN (NewWave Communications)

FOWLER—Benton County Cable Inc.

FOWLERTON—See HENDRICKS COUNTY (portions), IN (Comcast Cable)

FRANCESVILLE—Mediacom. Now served by KNOX, IN [IN0060]

FRANCESVILLE—See KNOX, IN (Mediacom)

FRANCISCO—Formerly served by Almega Cable. No longer in operation

FRANKFORT—Comcast Cable. Now served by HENDRICKS COUNTY (portions), IN [IN0001]

FRANKFORT—See HENDRICKS COUNTY (portions), IN (Comcast Cable)

FRANKLIN—Formerly served by Insight Communications. Now served by Comcast Cable, HENDRICKS COUNTY (portions), IN [IN0001]

FRANKLIN—See HENDRICKS COUNTY (portions), IN (Comcast Cable)

FRANKTON—Swayzee Communications

FREELANDVILLE—See VINCENNES, IN (NewWave Communications)

FREETOWN—Formerly served by CableDirect. No longer in operation

FREMONT—See ANGOLA, IN (Mediacom)

FRENCH LICK—Formerly served by Avenue Broadband Communications. Now served by NewWave Communications, VINCENNES, IN [IN0035]

FRENCH LICK—See VINCENNES, IN (NewWave Communications)

FULTON COUNTY (WESTERN PORTION)—See WINAMAC, IN (LightStream)

GALVESTON—See HENDRICKS COUNTY (portions), IN (Comcast Cable)

GARRETT—See AUBURN, IN (Mediacom)

GARY—Comcast Cable. Now served by CHAMPAIGN, IL [IL0019]

GAS CITY—See MARION, IN (Bright House Networks)

GASTON—Formerly served by Longview Communications. No longer in operation

GENEVA—See HENDRICKS COUNTY (portions), IN (Comcast Cable)

GIBSON COUNTY (PORTIONS)—See VINCENNES, IN (NewWave Communications)

GIBSON COUNTY (PORTIONS)—See EVANSVILLE, IN (Time Warner Cable)

GLENWOOD—Formerly served by CableDirect. No longer in operation

GOLDEN LAKE—Formerly served by CableDirect. No longer in operation

GOSHEN—See NEW PARIS, IN (Quality Cablevision)

GOSPORT—Formerly served by Insight Communications. Now served by Comcast Cable, HENDRICKS COUNTY (portions), IN [IN0001]

GOSPORT—See HENDRICKS COUNTY (portions), IN (Comcast Cable)

GRABILL—See AUBURN, IN (Mediacom)

GRANT COUNTY (PORTIONS)—See HENDRICKS COUNTY (portions), IN (Comcast Cable)

GRANT COUNTY—See MARION, IN (Bright House Networks)

GRANT PARK (VILLAGE)—See NEWTON COUNTY (portions), IL (Mediacom)

GREENCASTLE—Comcast Cable. Now served by HENDRICKS COUNTY (portions), IN [IN0001]

GREENCASTLE—See HENDRICKS COUNTY (portions), IN (Comcast Cable)

GREENDALE—See HENDRICKS COUNTY (portions), IN (Comcast Cable)

GREENE COUNTY (PORTIONS)—See HENDRICKS COUNTY (portions), IN (Comcast Cable)

GREENE COUNTY (WESTERN PORTION)—See JASONVILLE, IN (NewWave Communications)

GREENE TWP.—See PENN TWP., IN (Crystal Broadband Networks)

GREENFIELD—See HENDRICKS COUNTY (portions), IN (Comcast Cable)

GREENS FORK—Formerly served by CableDirect. No longer in operation

Cable Community Index—Indiana

GREENSBORO—See HENDRICKS COUNTY (portions), IN (Comcast Cable)

GREENSBURG—Comcast Cable. Now served by HENDRICKS COUNTY (portions), IN [IN0001]

GREENSBURG—See HENDRICKS COUNTY (portions), IN (Comcast Cable)

GREENTOWN—See HENDRICKS COUNTY (portions), IN (Comcast Cable)

GREENWOOD—Comcast Cable. Now served by HENDRICKS COUNTY (portions), IN [IN0001]

GREENWOOD—See HENDRICKS COUNTY (portions), IN (Comcast Cable)

GRIFFIN (town)—Formerly served by CableDirect. No longer in operation

GRISSOM AFB—See HENDRICKS COUNTY (portions), IN (Comcast Cable)

GROVERTOWN—See KNOX, IN (Mediacom)

GUILFORD—See HENDRICKS COUNTY (portions), IN (Comcast Cable)

HAGERSTOWN—See HENDRICKS COUNTY (portions), IN (Comcast Cable)

HAMILTON COUNTY (PORTIONS)—See INDIANAPOLIS (portions), IN (Bright House Networks)

HAMILTON COUNTY (PORTIONS)—See HENDRICKS COUNTY (portions), IN (Comcast Cable)

HAMILTON—See ANGOLA, IN (Mediacom)

HAMLET—Formerly served by CableDirect. No longer in operation

HAMMOND—Comcast Cable. Now served by CHAMPAIGN, IL [IL0019]

HAMMOND—WOW! Internet, Cable & Phone. Now served by NAPERVILLE, IL [IL0655]

HANCOCK COUNTY (PORTIONS)—See INDIANAPOLIS (portions), IN (Bright House Networks)

HANCOCK COUNTY (PORTIONS)—See HENDRICKS COUNTY (portions), IN (Comcast Cable)

HANOVER (TOWN)—See MADISON, IN (Time Warner Cable)

HARDINSBURG—Formerly served by CableDirect. No longer in operation

HARLAN—See AUBURN, IN (Mediacom)

HARMONY—NewWave Communications. Now served by VINCENNES, IN [IN0035]

HARMONY—See VINCENNES, IN (NewWave Communications)

HARTFORD CITY—Comcast Cable. Now served by HENDRICKS COUNTY (portions), IN [IN0001]

HARTFORD CITY—See HENDRICKS COUNTY (portions), IN (Comcast Cable)

HARTSVILLE—See HENDRICKS COUNTY (portions), IN (Comcast Cable)

HATFIELD—Time Warner Cable. Now served by OWENSBORO, KY [KY0004]

HAUBSTADT—See EVANSVILLE, IN (Time Warner Cable)

HAYDEN—Formerly served by CableDirect. No longer in operation

HEBRON—Comcast Cable. Now served by CHAMPAIGN, IL [IL0019]

HENDERSON COUNTY (PORTIONS)—See EVANSVILLE, KY (Time Warner Cable)

HENDERSON—See EVANSVILLE, KY (Time Warner Cable)

HENDRICKS COUNTY (PORTIONS)—See INDIANAPOLIS (portions), IN (Bright House Networks)

HENDRICKS COUNTY (PORTIONS)—Comcast Cable

HENDRICKS COUNTY (PORTIONS)—See MORGAN COUNTY (portions), IN (NewWave Communications)

HENDRICKS COUNTY (SOUTHERN PORTION)—See VINCENNES, IN (NewWave Communications)

HENRY COUNTY (PORTIONS)—See HENDRICKS COUNTY (portions), IN (Comcast Cable)

HERITAGE LAKE—Formerly served by Global Com Inc. No longer in operation

HIDDEN VALLEY LAKE—See HENDRICKS COUNTY (portions), IN (Comcast Cable)

HILLSBORO—Formerly served by Longview Communications. No longer in operation

HILLSDALE TWP.—Formerly served by CableDirect. No longer in operation

HOAGLAND—Formerly served by CableDirect. No longer in operation

HOLLAND—Formerly served by CableDirect. No longer in operation

HOLTON—Formerly served by CableDirect. No longer in operation

HOMECROFT—See HENDRICKS COUNTY (portions), IN (Comcast Cable)

HOPE—See HENDRICKS COUNTY (portions), IN (Comcast Cable)

HOWARD COUNTY (PORTIONS)—See HENDRICKS COUNTY (portions), IN (Comcast Cable)

HOWE—See LAGRANGE, IN (Mediacom)

HUNTERTOWN—See HENDRICKS COUNTY (portions), IN (Comcast Cable)

HUNTINGBURG—See EVANSVILLE, IN (Time Warner Cable)

HUNTINGTON COUNTY (PORTIONS)—See HENDRICKS COUNTY (portions), IN (Comcast Cable)

HUNTINGTON—Comcast Cable. Now served by HENDRICKS COUNTY (portions), IN [IN0001]

HUNTINGTON—See HENDRICKS COUNTY (portions), IN (Comcast Cable)

HUNTINGTON—See WARREN, IN (Warren Cable)

HYMERA—See JASONVILLE, IN (NewWave Communications)

IDAVILLE—See HENDRICKS COUNTY (portions), IN (Comcast Cable)

INDIANAPOLIS (PORTIONS)—Bright House Networks

INDIANAPOLIS—Formerly served by Sprint Corp. No longer in operation

INDIANAPOLIS—See HENDRICKS COUNTY (portions), IN (Comcast Cable)

INGALLS—See INDIANAPOLIS (portions), IN (Bright House Networks)

JACKSON COUNTY (PORTIONS)—See HENDRICKS COUNTY (portions), IN (Comcast Cable)

JALAPA—See SWEETSER, IN (Oak Hill Cablevision Inc)

JAMESTOWN—Formerly served by Indiana Communications. No longer in operation

JASONVILLE—NewWave Communications

JASPER COUNTY (PORTIONS)—See RENSSELAER (town), IN (TV Cable of Rensselaer Inc)

JASPER COUNTY (WESTERN PORTION)—See NEWTON COUNTY (portions), IN (Mediacom)

JASPER—Formerly served by NewWave Communications. No longer in operation

JASPER—Time Warner Cable. Now served by EVANSVILLE, IN [IN0006]

JASPER—See EVANSVILLE, IN (Time Warner Cable)

JAY COUNTY (PORTIONS)—See HENDRICKS COUNTY (portions), IN (Comcast Cable)

JEFFERSON TWP.—Comcast Cable. Now served by CHAMPAIGN, IL [IL0019]

JEFFERSON TWP.—See MADISON, IN (Time Warner Cable)

JEFFERSONVILLE—Time Warner Cable. Now served by LOUISVILLE, KY [KY0001]

JENNINGS COUNTY (PORTIONS)—See HENDRICKS COUNTY (portions), IN (Comcast Cable)

JOHNSON COUNTY (PORTIONS)—See HENDRICKS COUNTY (portions), IN (Comcast Cable)

JONESBORO—See MARION, IN (Bright House Networks)

JONESVILLE—See HENDRICKS COUNTY (portions), IN (Comcast Cable)

KANKAKEE COUNTY—See NEWTON COUNTY (portions), IL (Mediacom)

KEMPTON—Formerly served by Country Cablevision Ltd. No longer in operation

KENDALLVILLE—See AUBURN, IN (Mediacom)

KENNARD—See HENDRICKS COUNTY (portions), IN (Comcast Cable)

KENTLAND—Mediacom. Now served by WATSEKA, IL [IL0092]

KEWANNA—Formerly served by CableDirect. No longer in operation

KIMMEL—Formerly served by CableDirect. No longer in operation

KINGMAN—Formerly served by CableDirect. No longer in operation

KINGSLAND—See DECATUR, IN (Mediacom)

KNIGHTSTOWN—Formerly served by Insight Communications. Now served by Comcast Cable, HENDRICKS COUNTY (portions), IN [IN0001]

KNIGHTSTOWN—See HENDRICKS COUNTY (portions), IN (Comcast Cable)

KNIGHTSVILLE—NewWave Communications. Now served by VINCENNES, IN [IN0035]

KNIGHTSVILLE—See VINCENNES, IN (NewWave Communications)

KNOX COUNTY—See VINCENNES, IN (NewWave Communications)

KNOX—Mediacom

KOKOMO—Comcast Cable. Now served by HENDRICKS COUNTY (portions), IN [IN0001]

KOKOMO—See HENDRICKS COUNTY (portions), IN (Comcast Cable)

KOONTZ LAKE—See KNOX, IN (Mediacom)

KOSCIUSKO COUNTY—See NORTH WEBSTER, IN (Mediacom)

KOUTS—Mediacom. Now served by NEWTON COUNTY (portions), IN [IN0316]

KOUTS—See NEWTON COUNTY (portions), IN (Mediacom)

LA CROSSE—See NEWTON COUNTY (portions), IN (Mediacom)

LA FONTAINE—Swayzee Communications

LA PAZ—See KNOX, IN (Mediacom)

LA PORTE MOBILE HOME PARK—Formerly served by North American Cablevision. Now served by Comcast Cable, CHAMPAIGN, IL [IL0019]

Indiana—Cable Community Index

LA PORTE—Comcast Cable. Now served by CHAMPAIGN, IL [IL0019]

LAFAYETTE—Comcast Cable. Now served by HENDRICKS COUNTY (portions), IN [IN0001]

LAFAYETTE—See HENDRICKS COUNTY (portions), IN (Comcast Cable)

LAGRANGE COUNTY (PORTIONS)—See LAGRANGE, IN (Mediacom)

LAGRANGE—Mediacom

LAGRO—Formerly served by CableDirect. No longer in operation

LAKE CICOTT—Formerly served by Insight Communications. Now served by Comcast Cable, HENDRICKS COUNTY (portions), IN [IN0001]

LAKE CICOTT—See HENDRICKS COUNTY (portions), IN (Comcast Cable)

LAKE COUNTY (SOUTHERN PORTION)—See NEWTON COUNTY (portions), IN (Mediacom)

LAKE SANTEE—Formerly served by CableDirect. No longer in operation

LAKE VILLAGE—See NEWTON COUNTY (portions), IN (Mediacom)

LAKES OF THE FOUR SEASONS—Comcast Cable. Now served by CHAMPAIGN, IL [IL0019]

LAKETON—See AUBURN, IN (Mediacom)

LAKEVILLE—Mediacom. Now served by KNOX, IN [IN0060]

LAKEVILLE—See KNOX, IN (Mediacom)

LAOTTO—See AUBURN, IN (Mediacom)

LAPEL—Swayzee Communications

LAPORTE COUNTY (PORTIONS)—See KNOX, IN (Mediacom)

LARWILL—Formerly served by CableDirect. No longer in operation

LAUREL TWP.—Formerly served by CableDirect. No longer in operation

LAWRENCE COUNTY (PORTIONS)—See HENDRICKS COUNTY (portions), IN (Comcast Cable)

LAWRENCE COUNTY (PORTIONS)—See VINCENNES, IL (NewWave Communications)

LAWRENCE COUNTY (UNINCORPORATED AREAS)—See VINCENNES, IN (NewWave Communications)

LAWRENCE—See HENDRICKS COUNTY (portions), IN (Comcast Cable)

LAWRENCEBURG—Comcast Cable. Now served by HENDRICKS COUNTY (portions), IN [IN0001]

LAWRENCEBURG—See HENDRICKS COUNTY (portions), IN (Comcast Cable)

LAWRENCEVILLE—See VINCENNES, IL (NewWave Communications)

LEAVENWORTH—Formerly served by CableDirect. No longer in operation

LEBANON—Comcast Cable. Now served by HENDRICKS COUNTY (portions), IN [IN0001]

LEBANON—See HENDRICKS COUNTY (portions), IN (Comcast Cable)

LEESBURG—See NORTH WEBSTER, IN (Mediacom)

LEITERS FORD—Formerly served by CableDirect. No longer in operation

LEO—See AUBURN, IN (Mediacom)

LEWISVILLE—See HENDRICKS COUNTY (portions), IN (Comcast Cable)

LIBERTY CENTER—See DECATUR, IN (Mediacom)

LIBERTY MILLS—Formerly served by CableDirect. No longer in operation

LIBERTY—Formerly served by Comcast Cable. Now served by Enhanced Telecommunications Corp., BROOKVILLE, IN [IN0108]

LIBERTY—See BROOKVILLE, IN (Enhanced Telecommunications Corp)

LIGONIER—LigTel Communications. This cable system has converted to IPTV. See LIGONIER, IN [IN5133]

LIGONIER—Mediacom. Now served by AUBURN, IN [IN0066]

LIGONIER—LigTel Communications. This cable system has converted to IPTV

LIGONIER—See AUBURN, IN (Mediacom)

LINDEN—Tri-County Communications

LINTON—Comcast Cable. Now served by BLOOMINGTON, IN [IN0016]

LINTON—See HENDRICKS COUNTY (portions), IN (Comcast Cable)

LIZTON—See INDIANAPOLIS (portions), IN (Bright House Networks)

LOGANSPORT—Comcast Cable. Now served by HENDRICKS COUNTY (portions), IN [IN0001]

LOGANSPORT—See HENDRICKS COUNTY (portions), IN (Comcast Cable)

LOOGOOTEE—Formerly served by Avenue Broadband Communications. Now served by NewWave Communications, VINCENNES, IN [IN0035]

LOOGOOTEE—See VINCENNES, IN (NewWave Communications)

LOON LAKE—Formerly served by CableDirect. No longer in operation

LOSANTVILLE—See HENDRICKS COUNTY (portions), IN (Comcast Cable)

LYNN—See HENDRICKS COUNTY (portions), IN (Comcast Cable)

LYNNVILLE—Formerly served by Avenue Broadband Communications. No longer in operation

LYONS—Formerly served by Insight Communications. Now served by Comcast Cable, HENDRICKS COUNTY (portions), IN [IN0001]

LYONS—See HENDRICKS COUNTY (portions), IN (Comcast Cable)

MACY—Formerly served by Longview Communications. No longer in operation

MADISON COUNTY (PORTIONS)—See INDIANAPOLIS (portions), IN (Bright House Networks)

MADISON COUNTY (PORTIONS)—See HENDRICKS COUNTY (portions), IN (Comcast Cable)

MADISON—Time Warner Cable

MAGLEY—See DECATUR, IN (Mediacom)

MALDEN—See NEWTON COUNTY (portions), IN (Mediacom)

MANILLA—Formerly served by CableDirect. No longer in operation

MARENGO—Formerly served by NewWave Communications. No longer in operation

MARIAH HILL—See SPENCER COUNTY (portions), IN (NewWave Communications)

MARION—Bright House Networks

MARKLE—Swayzee Communications

MARKLEVILLE—See HENDRICKS COUNTY (portions), IN (Comcast Cable)

MARSHALL COUNTY (PORTIONS)—See PLYMOUTH, IN (Crystal Broadband Network)

MARSHALL COUNTY—Formerly served by Windjammer Cable. No longer in operation

MARSHALL COUNTY—See KNOX, IN (Mediacom)

MARSHALL—See JASONVILLE, IN (NewWave Communications)

MARTIN COUNTY (PORTIONS)—See VINCENNES, IN (NewWave Communications)

MARTINSVILLE—Comcast Cable. Now served by HENDRICKS COUNTY (portions), IN [IN0001]

MARTINSVILLE—See HENDRICKS COUNTY (portions), IN (Comcast Cable)

MCCORDSVILLE—See INDIANAPOLIS (portions), IN (Bright House Networks)

MCCORDSVILLE—See HENDRICKS COUNTY (portions), IN (Comcast Cable)

MECCA—See JASONVILLE, IN (NewWave Communications)

MEDARYVILLE—See KNOX, IN (Mediacom)

MEDORA—Formerly served by Insight Communications. Now served by Comcast Cable, HENDRICKS COUNTY (portions), IN [IN0001]

MEDORA—See HENDRICKS COUNTY (portions), IN (Comcast Cable)

MENTONE—Formerly served by Longview Communications. No longer in operation

MERIDIAN HILLS—See HENDRICKS COUNTY (portions), IN (Comcast Cable)

MEROM—Formerly served by CableDirect. No longer in operation

MERRILLVILLE—Comcast Cable. Now served by CHAMPAIGN, IL [IL0019]

METAMORA—Formerly served by CableDirect. No longer in operation

MEXICO—See HENDRICKS COUNTY (portions), IN (Comcast Cable)

MIAMI COUNTY (PORTIONS)—See HENDRICKS COUNTY (portions), IN (Comcast Cable)

MIAMI—Formerly served by CableDirect. No longer in operation

MICHIANA—Formerly served by Sprint Corp. No longer in operation

MICHIGAN CITY—Comcast Cable. Now served by CHAMPAIGN, IL [IL0019]

MICHIGANTOWN—Formerly served by Country Cablevision Ltd. No longer in operation

MIDDLEBURY—Comcast Cable. Now served by CHAMPAIGN, IL [IL0019]

MIDDLETOWN (town)—Formerly served by Insight Communications. Now served by Comcast Cable, HENDRICKS COUNTY (portions), IN [IN0001]

MIDDLETOWN—See HENDRICKS COUNTY (portions), IN (Comcast Cable)

MIDLAND—See JASONVILLE, IN (NewWave Communications)

MILAN—See HENDRICKS COUNTY (portions), IN (Comcast Cable)

MILFORD—See NORTH WEBSTER, IN (Mediacom)

MILLERSBURG—See NEW PARIS, IN (Quality Cablevision)

MILROY—Formerly served by CableDirect. No longer in operation

MILTON—See HENDRICKS COUNTY (portions), IN (Comcast Cable)

MITCHELL—NewWave Communications. Now served by VINCENNES, IN [IN0035]

MITCHELL—See VINCENNES, IN (NewWave Communications)

MODOC—See HENDRICKS COUNTY (portions), IN (Comcast Cable)

MOMENCE—See NEWTON COUNTY (portions), IL (Mediacom)

Cable Community Index—Indiana

MONMOUTH—See DECATUR, IN (Mediacom)

MONON—See HENDRICKS COUNTY (portions), IN (Comcast Cable)

MONROE CITY—Formerly served by Cebridge Connections. Now served by NewWave Communications, VINCENNES, IN [IN0035]

MONROE CITY—See VINCENNES, IN (NewWave Communications)

MONROE COUNTY (PORTIONS)—See HENDRICKS COUNTY (portions), IN (Comcast Cable)

MONROE—See DECATUR, IN (Mediacom)

MONROEVILLE—NewWave Communications

MONROVIA—See MORGAN COUNTY (portions), IN (NewWave Communications)

MONTEREY—Formerly served by CableDirect. No longer in operation

MONTEZUMA—Formerly served by Indiana Communications. Now served by JASONVILLE, IN [IN0106]

MONTEZUMA—See JASONVILLE, IN (NewWave Communications)

MONTGOMERY COUNTY (PORTIONS)—See HENDRICKS COUNTY (portions), IN (Comcast Cable)

MONTGOMERY TWP. (Indiana County)—Formerly served by CableDirect. No longer in operation

MONTICELLO—Comcast Cable. Now served by HENDRICKS COUNTY (portions), IN [IN0001]

MONTICELLO—See HENDRICKS COUNTY (portions), IN (Comcast Cable)

MONTPELIER—Formerly served by Comcast Cable. No longer in operation

MOORELAND—See HENDRICKS COUNTY (portions), IN (Comcast Cable)

MOORES HILL—See HENDRICKS COUNTY (portions), IN (Comcast Cable)

MOORESVILLE—See HENDRICKS COUNTY (portions), IN (Comcast Cable)

MOORESVILLE—See MORGAN COUNTY (portions), IN (NewWave Communications)

MORGAN COUNTY (PORTIONS)—See HENDRICKS COUNTY (portions), IN (Comcast Cable)

MORGAN COUNTY (PORTIONS)—NewWave Communications

MORGANTOWN—NewWave Communications

MOROCCO—TV Cable of Rensselaer Inc

MORRISTOWN—Formerly served by Longview Communications. No longer in operation

MOUNT AUBURN—See HENDRICKS COUNTY (portions), IN (Comcast Cable)

MOUNT SUMMIT—Comcast Cable. Now served by HENDRICKS COUNTY (portions), IN [IN0001]

MOUNT SUMMIT—See HENDRICKS COUNTY (portions), IN (Comcast Cable)

MOUNT VERNON—Time Warner Cable. Now served by EVANSVILLE, IN [IN0006]

MOUNT VERNON—See EVANSVILLE, IN (Time Warner Cable)

MOUNT VERNON—See EVANSVILLE, IN (WOW! Internet, Cable & Phone)

MULBERRY—See HENDRICKS COUNTY (portions), IN (Comcast Cable)

MUNCIE—Comcast Cable. Now served by HENDRICKS COUNTY (portions), IN [IN0001]

MUNCIE—See HENDRICKS COUNTY (portions), IN (Comcast Cable)

MURRAY—See DECATUR, IN (Mediacom)

NAPOLEON—See SUNMAN, IN (Enhanced Telecommunications Corp)

NAPPANEE—See NORTH WEBSTER, IN (Mediacom)

NASHVILLE—NewWave Communications. Now served by VINCENNES, IN [IN0035]

NASHVILLE—See VINCENNES, IN (NewWave Communications)

NEW ALBANY—Formerly served by Insight Communications. Now served by Time Warner Cable, LOUISVILLE, KY [KY0001]

NEW CASTLE—Formerly served by Insight Communications. Now served by Comcast Cable, HENDRICKS COUNTY (portions), IN [IN0001]

NEW CASTLE—See HENDRICKS COUNTY (portions), IN (Comcast Cable)

NEW DURHAM TWP.—See NEWTON COUNTY (portions), IN (Mediacom)

NEW HAVEN—See HENDRICKS COUNTY (portions), IN (Comcast Cable)

NEW MARKET—Formerly served by Indiana Communications. No longer in operation

NEW PALESTINE—See HENDRICKS COUNTY (portions), IN (Comcast Cable)

NEW PARIS—Quality Cablevision

NEW RICHMOND—See LINDEN, IN (Tri-County Communications)

NEW WAVERLY—See HENDRICKS COUNTY (portions), IN (Comcast Cable)

NEW WHITELAND—See HENDRICKS COUNTY (portions), IN (Comcast Cable)

NEWBURGH—Time Warner Cable

NEWBURGH—See EVANSVILLE, IN (WOW! Internet, Cable & Phone)

NEWPORT—NewWave Communications

NEWTON COUNTY (PORTIONS)—Mediacom

NINEVEH—See VINCENNES, IN (NewWave Communications)

NOBLE COUNTY (PORTIONS)—See AUBURN, IN (Mediacom)

NOBLE COUNTY (PORTIONS)—See AVILLA, IN (NewWave Communications)

NOBLESVILLE—Comcast Cable. Now served by HENDRICKS COUNTY (portions), IN [IN0001]

NOBLESVILLE—See HENDRICKS COUNTY (portions), IN (Comcast Cable)

NORTH JUDSON—See KNOX, IN (Mediacom)

NORTH LIBERTY—See KNOX, IN (Mediacom)

NORTH MANCHESTER—Mediacom. Now served by AUBURN, IN [IN0066]

NORTH MANCHESTER—See AUBURN, IN (Mediacom)

NORTH VERNON—Comcast Cable. Now served by HENDRICKS COUNTY (portions), IN [IN0001]

NORTH VERNON—See HENDRICKS COUNTY (portions), IN (Comcast Cable)

NORTH WEBSTER—Mediacom

OAKLAND CITY—Formerly served by Charter Communications. Now served by NewWave Communications, VINCENNES, IN [IN0035]

OAKLAND CITY—See VINCENNES, IN (NewWave Communications)

OAKTOWN—Formerly served by Almega Cable. No longer in operation

OAKVILLE—See HENDRICKS COUNTY (portions), IN (Comcast Cable)

ODON—Formerly served by Suddenlink Communications. Now served by NewWave Communications, NEWTON, IL [IL0559]

OHIO COUNTY (PORTIONS)—See HENDRICKS COUNTY (portions), IN (Comcast Cable)

OHIO TWP. (EASTERN PORTION)—See NEWBURGH, IN (Time Warner Cable)

OLIVER LAKE—Formerly served by CableDirect. No longer in operation

OOLITIC—See HENDRICKS COUNTY (portions), IN (Comcast Cable)

ORANGE COUNTY (UNINCORPORATED AREAS)—See VINCENNES, IN (NewWave Communications)

ORESTES—See HENDRICKS COUNTY (portions), IN (Comcast Cable)

ORLEANS—See VINCENNES, IN (NewWave Communications)

OSGOOD—See HENDRICKS COUNTY (portions), IN (Comcast Cable)

OSSIAN—See HENDRICKS COUNTY (portions), IN (Comcast Cable)

OTTER LAKE—Formerly served by CableDirect. No longer in operation

OTTERBEIN—See HENDRICKS COUNTY (portions), IN (Comcast Cable)

OTWELL—Formerly served by CableDirect. No longer in operation

OWEN COUNTY (PORTIONS)—See HENDRICKS COUNTY (portions), IN (Comcast Cable)

OWENSBURG—Formerly served by CableDirect. No longer in operation

OWENSVILLE (village)—Formerly served by Sigecom. Now served by Time Warner Cable, EVANSVILLE, IN [IN0006]

OWENSVILLE—See EVANSVILLE, IN (Time Warner Cable)

OXFORD—Formerly served by Indiana Communications. No longer in operation

PAINT MILL LAKE—Formerly served by CableDirect. No longer in operation

PAOLI—See VINCENNES, IN (NewWave Communications)

PARAGON—See MORGAN COUNTY (portions), IN (NewWave Communications)

PARKE COUNTY (PORTIONS)—See VINCENNES, IN (NewWave Communications)

PARKE COUNTY—See JASONVILLE, IN (NewWave Communications)

PARKER CITY—See HENDRICKS COUNTY (portions), IN (Comcast Cable)

PATOKA—Formerly served by Almega Cable. No longer in operation

PATOKA—See EVANSVILLE, IN (Time Warner Cable)

PATRICKSBURG—Formerly served by CableDirect. No longer in operation

PAYNE—See MONROEVILLE, OH (NewWave Communications)

PEKIN—Time Warner Cable. Now served by LOUISVILLE, KY [KY0001]

PENDLETON—See HENDRICKS COUNTY (portions), IN (Comcast Cable)

PENN TWP.—Crystal Broadband Networks

PENNVILLE—See HENDRICKS COUNTY (portions), IN (Comcast Cable)

Indiana—Cable Community Index

PERRY COUNTY (PORTIONS)—See TELL CITY, IN (Comcast Cable)

PERRYSVILLE—Formerly served by Indiana Communications. Now served by NewWave Communications, NEWPORT, IN [IN0304]

PERRYSVILLE—See NEWPORT, IN (NewWave Communications)

PERSHING—See HENDRICKS COUNTY (portions), IN (Comcast Cable)

PERU—See HENDRICKS COUNTY (portions), IN (Comcast Cable)

PETERSBURG—See VINCENNES, IN (NewWave Communications)

PIERCETON—See NORTH WEBSTER, IN (Mediacom)

PIKE COUNTY (PORTIONS)—See VINCENNES, IN (NewWave Communications)

PINE VILLAGE—Formerly served by CableDirect. No longer in operation

PITTSBORO—See INDIANAPOLIS (portions), IN (Bright House Networks)

PITTSBURG—See FLORA, IN (NewWave Communications)

PLAINFIELD—See INDIANAPOLIS (portions), IN (Bright House Networks)

PLAINFIELD—See HENDRICKS COUNTY (portions), IN (Comcast Cable)

PLEASANT MILLS—See DECATUR, IN (Mediacom)

PLYMOUTH—Crystal Broadband Network

PONETO—See DECATUR, IN (Mediacom)

PORTAGE—Comcast Cable. Now served by CHAMPAIGN, IL [IL0019]

PORTLAND—Comcast Cable. Now served by HENDRICKS COUNTY (portions), IN [IN0001]

PORTLAND—See HENDRICKS COUNTY (portions), IN (Comcast Cable)

POSEY COUNTY (PORTIONS)—See EVANSVILLE, IN (Time Warner Cable)

POSEYVILLE—Time Warner Cable. Now served by EVANSVILLE, IN [IN0006]

POSEYVILLE—See EVANSVILLE, IN (Time Warner Cable)

PREBLE—See DECATUR, IN (Mediacom)

PRETTY LAKE—Formerly served by Longview Communications. No longer in operation

PRINCES LAKES—Formerly served by Avenue Broadband Communications. Now served by NewWave Communications, VINCENNES, IN [IN0035]

PRINCES LAKES—See VINCENNES, IN (NewWave Communications)

PRINCETON—Time Warner Cable. Now served by EVANSVILLE, IN [IN0006]

PRINCETON—See EVANSVILLE, IN (Time Warner Cable)

PULASKI COUNTY (SOUTHERN PORTION)—See WINAMAC, IN (LightStream)

PUTNAM COUNTY (PORTIONS)—See HENDRICKS COUNTY (portions), IN (Comcast Cable)

RANDOLPH COUNTY (PORTIONS)—See HENDRICKS COUNTY (portions), IN (Comcast Cable)

REDKEY—See HENDRICKS COUNTY (portions), IN (Comcast Cable)

REMINGTON—See HENDRICKS COUNTY (portions), IN (Comcast Cable)

RENSSELAER (TOWN)—TV Cable of Rensselaer Inc

REYNOLDS—See HENDRICKS COUNTY (portions), IN (Comcast Cable)

RICHLAND—Formerly served by Time Warner Cable. No longer in operation

RICHMOND—Comcast Cable. Now served by HENDRICKS COUNTY (portions), IN [IN0001]

RICHMOND—See HENDRICKS COUNTY (portions), IN (Comcast Cable)

RIDGEVILLE—See HENDRICKS COUNTY (portions), IN (Comcast Cable)

RILEY—See TERRE HAUTE, IN (Time Warner Cable)

RIPLEY COUNTY (PORTIONS)—See HENDRICKS COUNTY (portions), IN (Comcast Cable)

RISING SUN—See HENDRICKS COUNTY (portions), IN (Comcast Cable)

ROACHDALE—Formerly served by Indiana Communications. No longer in operation

ROANN—Formerly served by CableDirect. No longer in operation

ROANOKE—See HENDRICKS COUNTY (portions), IN (Comcast Cable)

ROCKFIELD—See FLORA, IN (NewWave Communications)

ROCKPORT—Time Warner Cable. Now served by OWENSBORO, KY [KY0004]

ROCKVILLE—Formerly served by Cequel Communications. Now served by JASONVILLE, IN [IN0106]

ROCKVILLE—See JASONVILLE, IN (NewWave Communications)

ROME CITY—Mediacom. Now served by AUBURN, IN [IN0066]

ROME CITY—See AUBURN, IN (Mediacom)

ROMNEY—See LINDEN, IN (Tri-County Communications)

ROSEDALE—Formerly served by Rapid Cable. Now served by NewWave Communications, VINCENNES, IN [IN0035]

ROSEDALE—See VINCENNES, IN (NewWave Communications)

ROSELAWN—See NEWTON COUNTY (portions), IN (Mediacom)

ROSEWOOD MANOR—See NEWTON COUNTY (portions), IN (Mediacom)

ROYAL CENTER—Park TV & Electronics Inc

RUSH COUNTY (PORTIONS)—See HENDRICKS COUNTY (portions), IN (Comcast Cable)

RUSHVILLE—Comcast Cable. Now served by HENDRICKS COUNTY (portions), IN [IN0001]

RUSHVILLE—See HENDRICKS COUNTY (portions), IN (Comcast Cable)

RUSSELLVILLE—Formerly served by CableDirect. No longer in operation

RUSSIAVILLE—See HENDRICKS COUNTY (portions), IN (Comcast Cable)

SALEM—Formerly served by Insight Communications. No longer in operation

SAN PIERRE—Mediacom. Now served by KNOX, IN [IN0060]

SAN PIERRE—See KNOX, IN (Mediacom)

SANTA CLAUS—See SPENCER COUNTY (portions), IN (NewWave Communications)

SARATOGA—See HENDRICKS COUNTY (portions), IN (Comcast Cable)

SCHNEIDER—See NEWTON COUNTY (portions), IN (Mediacom)

SCOTTSBURG—Formerly served by Insight Communications. Now served by Time Warner Cable, LOUISVILLE, KY [KY0001]

SEELYVILLE—See VINCENNES, IN (NewWave Communications)

SELMA—See HENDRICKS COUNTY (portions), IN (Comcast Cable)

SEYMOUR—Comcast Cable. Now served by HENDRICKS COUNTY (portions), IN [IN0001]

SEYMOUR—See HENDRICKS COUNTY (portions), IN (Comcast Cable)

SHADELAND—See HENDRICKS COUNTY (portions), IN (Comcast Cable)

SHAMROCK—See HENDRICKS COUNTY (portions), IN (Comcast Cable)

SHARPSVILLE—See HENDRICKS COUNTY (portions), IN (Comcast Cable)

SHELBURN—See JASONVILLE, IN (NewWave Communications)

SHELBY COUNTY (PORTIONS)—See HENDRICKS COUNTY (portions), IN (Comcast Cable)

SHELBYVILLE—Comcast Cable. Now served by HENDRICKS COUNTY (portions), IN [IN0001]

SHELBYVILLE—See HENDRICKS COUNTY (portions), IN (Comcast Cable)

SHERIDAN—Swayzee Communications

SHIPSHEWANA—Formerly served by Longview Communications. No longer in operation

SHIRLEY—See HENDRICKS COUNTY (portions), IN (Comcast Cable)

SHOALS—Formerly served by Almega Cable. No longer in operation

SHOALS—See VINCENNES, IN (NewWave Communications)

SILVER LAKE—Comcast Cable. Now served by CHAMPAIGN, IL [IL0019]

SKINNER LAKE—See AUBURN, IN (Mediacom)

SOMERSET (village)—Formerly served by CableDirect. No longer in operation

SOUTH BEND—Comcast Cable. Now served by CHAMPAIGN, IL [IL0019]

SOUTH BEND—Formerly served by Sprint Corp. No longer in operation

SOUTH WHITLEY—Mediacom. Now served by AUBURN, IN [IN0066]

SOUTH WHITLEY—See AUBURN, IN (Mediacom)

SOUTHPORT—See HENDRICKS COUNTY (portions), IN (Comcast Cable)

SPEEDWAY—See HENDRICKS COUNTY (portions), IN (Comcast Cable)

SPENCER COUNTY (PORTIONS)—NewWave Communications

SPENCER—Formerly served by Insight Communications. Now served by Comcast Cable, HENDRICKS COUNTY (portions), IN [IN0001]

SPENCER—See HENDRICKS COUNTY (portions), IN (Comcast Cable)

SPENCERVILLE—See AUBURN, IN (Mediacom)

SPICELAND—See HENDRICKS COUNTY (portions), IN (Comcast Cable)

SPRING GROVE—See HENDRICKS COUNTY (portions), IN (Comcast Cable)

SPRING LAKE—See HENDRICKS COUNTY (portions), IN (Comcast Cable)

SPRINGPORT—See HENDRICKS COUNTY (portions), IN (Comcast Cable)

SPURGEON—Formerly served by CableDirect. No longer in operation

ST. FRANCISVILLE—See VINCENNES, IL (NewWave Communications)

ST. JOE—See AUBURN, IN (Mediacom)

Cable Community Index—Indiana

ST. JOSEPH COUNTY (PORTIONS)—See PENN TWP., IN (Crystal Broadband Networks)

ST. JOSEPH COUNTY—See KNOX, IN (Mediacom)

ST. LEON—See SUNMAN, IN (Enhanced Telecommunications Corp)

ST. PAUL—Formerly served by Longview Communications. No longer in operation

STAR CITY—See WINAMAC, IN (LightStream)

STARKE COUNTY—See KNOX, IN (Mediacom)

STAUNTON—See VINCENNES, IN (NewWave Communications)

STEUBEN COUNTY (PORTIONS)—See ANGOLA, IN (Mediacom)

STILESVILLE—See VINCENNES, IN (NewWave Communications)

STINESVILLE—See HENDRICKS COUNTY (portions), IN (Comcast Cable)

STRAUGHN—See HENDRICKS COUNTY (portions), IN (Comcast Cable)

SULLIVAN COUNTY (PORTIONS)—See HENDRICKS COUNTY (portions), IN (Comcast Cable)

SULLIVAN—Formerly served by Insight Communications. Now served by Comcast Cable, HENDRICKS COUNTY (portions), IN [IN0001]

SULLIVAN—See HENDRICKS COUNTY (portions), IN (Comcast Cable)

SULPHUR SPRINGS—See HENDRICKS COUNTY (portions), IN (Comcast Cable)

SUMAVA RESORTS—See NEWTON COUNTY (portions), IN (Mediacom)

SUMMITVILLE—Swayzee Communications

SUMNER—See VINCENNES, IL (NewWave Communications)

SUNMAN—Enhanced Telecommunications Corp

SWAYZEE—The Swayzee Telephone Co

SWEETSER—Oak Hill Cablevision Inc

SWITZERLAND COUNTY (PORTIONS)—See HENDRICKS COUNTY (portions), IN (Comcast Cable)

SYRACUSE—Mediacom. Now served by NORTH WEBSTER, IN [IN0038]

SYRACUSE—See NORTH WEBSTER, IN (Mediacom)

TALMA—Formerly served by CableDirect. No longer in operation

TELL CITY—Comcast Cable

TERRE HAUTE CITY—See VINCENNES, IN (NewWave Communications)

TERRE HAUTE—Time Warner Cable

THAYER—See NEWTON COUNTY (portions), IN (Mediacom)

THORNTOWN—Comcast Cable. Now served by HENDRICKS COUNTY (portions), IN [IN0001]

THORNTOWN—See HENDRICKS COUNTY (portions), IN (Comcast Cable)

TIPPECANOE COUNTY (PORTIONS)—See HENDRICKS COUNTY (portions), IN (Comcast Cable)

TIPPECANOE COUNTY (PORTIONS)—See FLORA, IN (NewWave Communications)

TIPPECANOE COUNTY (SOUTHERN PORTION)—See LINDEN, IN (Tri-County Communications)

TIPPECANOE—See NORTH WEBSTER, IN (Mediacom)

TIPTON (portions)—Formerly served by Country Cablevision Ltd. No longer in operation

TIPTON COUNTY (PORTIONS)—See HENDRICKS COUNTY (portions), IN (Comcast Cable)

TIPTON—See HENDRICKS COUNTY (portions), IN (Comcast Cable)

TOCSIN—See DECATUR, IN (Mediacom)

TOPEKA—Formerly served by Lig TV. No longer in operation

TRAFALGAR—Formerly served by CableDirect. No longer in operation

TRI-LAKES—See AUBURN, IN (Mediacom)

TROY—Formerly served by Avenue Broadband Communications. No longer in operation

TWELVE MILE—Formerly served by CableDirect. No longer in operation

TWIN LAKES—Formerly served by CableDirect. No longer in operation

ULEN—See HENDRICKS COUNTY (portions), IN (Comcast Cable)

UNION CITY—Time Warner Cable. Now served by AMBERLEY (village), OH [OH0001]

UNIONDALE—See DECATUR, IN (Mediacom)

UNIVERSAL—See VINCENNES, IN (NewWave Communications)

UPLAND—See HENDRICKS COUNTY (portions), IN (Comcast Cable)

URBANA—Formerly served by CableDirect. No longer in operation

VAN BUREN—Swayzee Communications

VANDERBURGH COUNTY (PORTIONS)—See EVANSVILLE, IN (Time Warner Cable)

VANDERBURGH COUNTY (PORTIONS)—See EVANSVILLE, IN (WOW! Internet, Cable & Phone)

VEEDERSBURG—NewWave Communications. Now served by COVINGTON, IN [IN0124]

VEEDERSBURG—See COVINGTON, IN (NewWave Communications)

VERA CRUZ—See DECATUR, IN (Mediacom)

VERMILLION COUNTY (PORTIONS)—See VINCENNES, IN (NewWave Communications)

VERNON—See HENDRICKS COUNTY (portions), IN (Comcast Cable)

VERSAILLES—See HENDRICKS COUNTY (portions), IN (Comcast Cable)

VEVAY (TOWN)—See MADISON, IN (Time Warner Cable)

VEVAY—Formerly served by Adelphia Communications. Now served by Time Warner Cable, MADISON, IN [IN0046]

VIGO COUNTY (PORTIONS)—See VINCENNES, IN (NewWave Communications)

VIGO COUNTY (PORTIONS)—See TERRE HAUTE, IN (Time Warner Cable)

VIGO—See JASONVILLE, IN (NewWave Communications)

VINCENNES—NewWave Communications

WABASH COUNTY (PORTIONS)—See HENDRICKS COUNTY (portions), IN (Comcast Cable)

WABASH—Comcast Cable. Now served by HENDRICKS COUNTY (portions), IN [IN0001]

WABASH—See HENDRICKS COUNTY (portions), IN (Comcast Cable)

WABASH—See AUBURN, IN (Mediacom)

WADESVILLE—Formerly served by NewWave Communications. No longer in operation

WAKARUSA—Comcast Cable. Now served by CHAMPAIGN, IL [IL0019]

WALKERTON—Mediacom. Now served by KNOX, IN [IN0060]

WALKERTON—See KNOX, IN (Mediacom)

WALTON—Park TV & Electronics Inc

WANATAH—Mediacom. Now served by NEWTON COUNTY (portions), IN [IN0316]

WANATAH—See NEWTON COUNTY (portions), IN (Mediacom)

WARREN COUNTY (PORTIONS)—See HENDRICKS COUNTY (portions), IN (Comcast Cable)

WARREN PARK—See HENDRICKS COUNTY (portions), IN (Comcast Cable)

WARREN—Warren Cable

WARRICK COUNTY (PORTIONS)—See ELBERFELD, IN (NewWave Communications)

WARRICK COUNTY (PORTIONS)—See EVANSVILLE, IN (Time Warner Cable)

WARRICK COUNTY (PORTIONS)—See EVANSVILLE, IN (WOW! Internet, Cable & Phone)

WARRICK COUNTY—See NEWBURGH, IN (Time Warner Cable)

WARSAW—Comcast Cable. Now served by CHAMPAIGN, IL [IL0019]

WASHINGTON—Formerly served by Charter Communications. Now served by NewWave Communications, VINCENNES, IN [IN0035]

WASHINGTON—See VINCENNES, IN (NewWave Communications)

WATERLOO—See AUBURN, IN (Mediacom)

WAVELAND—Formerly served by CableDirect. No longer in operation

WAYNE COUNTY (PORTIONS)—See HENDRICKS COUNTY (portions), IN (Comcast Cable)

WAYNETOWN—Formerly served by Indiana Communications. No longer in operation

WELLS COUNTY (PORTIONS)—See HENDRICKS COUNTY (portions), IN (Comcast Cable)

WELLS COUNTY—See DECATUR, IN (Mediacom)

WEST BADEN SPRINGS—See VINCENNES, IN (NewWave Communications)

WEST LAFAYETTE—See HENDRICKS COUNTY (portions), IN (Comcast Cable)

WEST LEBANON—Park TV & Electronics Inc

WEST TERRE HAUTE—See TERRE HAUTE, IN (Time Warner Cable)

WESTFIELD—See HENDRICKS COUNTY (portions), IN (Comcast Cable)

WESTFIELD—See CARMEL, IN (First-Mile Technologies)

WESTPORT—Comcast Cable. Now served by HENDRICKS COUNTY (portions), IN [IN0001]

WESTPORT—See HENDRICKS COUNTY (portions), IN (Comcast Cable)

WESTVILLE—See NEWTON COUNTY (portions), IN (Mediacom)

WHEATFIELD—Mediacom. Now served by NEWTON COUNTY (portions), IN [IN0316]

WHEATFIELD—See NEWTON COUNTY (portions), IN (Mediacom)

WHEATLAND—See VINCENNES, IN (NewWave Communications)

WHITE COUNTY (PORTIONS)—See HENDRICKS COUNTY (portions), IN (Comcast Cable)

Indiana—Cable Community Index

WHITELAND—See HENDRICKS COUNTY (portions), IN (Comcast Cable)

WHITESTOWN—Formerly served by Longview Communications. No longer in operation

WHITESTOWN—See INDIANAPOLIS (portions), IN (Bright House Networks)

WHITLEY COUNTY (PORTIONS)—See HENDRICKS COUNTY (portions), IN (Comcast Cable)

WILFRED—See JASONVILLE, IN (NewWave Communications)

WILKINSON—Formerly served by Insight Communications. Now served by Comcast Cable, HENDRICKS COUNTY (portions), IN [IN0001]

WILKINSON—See HENDRICKS COUNTY (portions), IN (Comcast Cable)

WILLIAMS CREEK—See HENDRICKS COUNTY (portions), IN (Comcast Cable)

WILLIAMSBURG—Formerly served by CableDirect. No longer in operation

WILLIAMSBURG—Formerly served by Vital Communications. No longer in operation

WILLIAMSPORT—See HENDRICKS COUNTY (portions), IN (Comcast Cable)

WINAMAC—LightStream

WINCHESTER—Comcast Cable. Now served by HENDRICKS COUNTY (portions), IN [IN0001]

WINCHESTER—See HENDRICKS COUNTY (portions), IN (Comcast Cable)

WINDFALL—See HENDRICKS COUNTY (portions), IN (Comcast Cable)

WINGATE—See LINDEN, IN (Tri-County Communications)

WINSLOW—NewWave Communications. Now served by VINCENNES, IN [IN0035]

WINSLOW—See VINCENNES, IN (NewWave Communications)

WOLCOTT—See HENDRICKS COUNTY (portions), IN (Comcast Cable)

WOLCOTTVILLE—See AUBURN, IN (Mediacom)

WOODBURN—See HENDRICKS COUNTY (portions), IN (Comcast Cable)

WORTHINGTON—Formerly served by Indiana Communications. Now served by JASONVILLE, IN [IN0106]

WORTHINGTON—See JASONVILLE, IN (NewWave Communications)

WYNNEDALE—See HENDRICKS COUNTY (portions), IN (Comcast Cable)

YANKEETOWN—Formerly served by Time Warner Cable. No longer in operation

YORKTOWN—See HENDRICKS COUNTY (portions), IN (Comcast Cable)

YOUNG AMERICA—Formerly served by CableDirect. No longer in operation

ZANESVILLE—Formerly served by CableDirect. No longer in operation

ZIONSVILLE—See INDIANAPOLIS (portions), IN (Bright House Networks)

ZIONSVILLE—See CARMEL, IN (FirstMile Technologies)

IOWA

ACKLEY—See IOWA FALLS, IA (Mediacom)

ADAIR—Formerly served by B & L Technologies LLC. No longer in operation

ADEL—Mediacom. Now served by DEXTER, IA [IA0015]

ADEL—See DEXTER, IA (Mediacom)

AFTON—Formerly served by B & L Technologies LLC. No longer in operation

AGENCY—See OTTUMWA, IA (Mediacom)

AINSWORTH—Formerly served by Starwest Inc. No longer in operation

AKRON—Premier Communications. Now served by SIOUX CENTER, IA [IA0076]

AKRON—See SIOUX CENTER, IA (Premier Communications)

ALBANY—See CLINTON, IL (Mediacom)

ALBIA—Mediacom

ALBION—Heart of Iowa Telecommunications. This cable system has converted to IPTV. See UNION, IA [IA5001]

ALBION—See UNION, IA (Heart of Iowa Communications. Formerly [IA0521]. This cable system has converted to IPTV.)

ALBURNETT—See SHELLSBURG, IA (USA Communications)

ALDEN—Formerly served by Latimer/Coulter Cablevision. No longer in operation

ALEXANDER—Formerly served by CableDirect. No longer in operation

ALGONA—Mediacom. Now served by FORT DODGE, IA [IA0011]

ALGONA—Algona Municipal Utilities

ALGONA—See FORT DODGE, IA (Mediacom)

ALLAMAKEE COUNTY (PORTIONS)—See POSTVILLE, IA (CenturyLink)

ALLEMAN—Formerly served by Huxley Communications Corp. No longer in operation

ALLERTON—Formerly served by Longview Communications. No longer in operation

ALLERTON—See MURRAY, IA (GRM Networks)

ALLISON—See DUMONT, IA (Dumont Cablevision)

ALTA VISTA (town)—Formerly served by Alta Vista Municipal Cable. No longer in operation

ALTA—ALTA-TEC

ALTA—See STORM LAKE, IA (Mediacom)

ALTON—See MARCUS, IA (WesTel Systems)

ALTOONA—See DES MOINES, IA (Mediacom)

AMANA—Mediacom

AMANA—See ELY, IA (South Slope Coop. Communications Co. Formerly served by NORTH LIBERTY, IA [IA0432]. This cable system has converted to IPTV)

AMES—Mediacom

ANAMOSA—Mediacom

ANDREW—Andrew Telephone Co. Inc

ANITA—WesTel Systems

ANKENY—See DES MOINES, IA (Mediacom)

ANTHON—Long Lines. Now served by SALIX, IA [IA0510]

ANTHON—See SALIX, IA (Long Lines)

APLINGTON—See WAVERLY, IA (Mediacom)

APPANOOSE COUNTY—See ALBIA, IA (Mediacom)

ARCADIA—See BREDA, IA (Western Iowa Networks)

ARLINGTON—Formerly served by Alpine Communications LC. No longer in operation

ARNOLDS PARK—See SPIRIT LAKE, IA (Mediacom)

ARTHUR—Sac County Mutual Telco

ASBURY—See DUBUQUE, IA (Mediacom)

ASHTON—Formerly served by Premier Communications. Now served by HTC Communications, HOSPERS, IA [IA0060]

ASHTON—See HOSPERS, IA (HTC Communications)

ATALISSA—See NORTH LIBERTY, IA (Mediacom)

ATKINS—Atkins Telephone

ATLANTIC—Mediacom

AUBURN—See BREDA, IA (Western Iowa Networks)

AUDUBON—See CARROLL, IA (Mediacom)

AURELIA—NU-Telecom. This cable system has converted to IPTV. See AURELIA, IA [IA5021]

AURELIA—NU-Telecom. Formerly [IA0212]. This cable system has converted to IPTV

AURORA—Formerly served by Alpine Communications LC. No longer in operation

AVOCA—See DENISON, IA (Mediacom)

AVOCA—See WALNUT, IA (Walnut Communications)

AYRSHIRE—ATC Cablevision. Now served by GILLETT GROVE, IA [IA0386]

AYRSHIRE—See GILLETT GROVE, IA (ATC Cablevision)

BADGER—Formerly served by Goldfield Communication Services Corp. No longer in operation

BAGLEY—Panora Communications Cooperative. Now served by PANORA, IA [IA0108]

BAGLEY—See PANORA, IA (Panora Communications Cooperative)

BALDWIN—Baldwin Nashville Telephone Co

BANCROFT—See SWEA CITY, IA (Mediacom)

BARNES CITY—See DEEP RIVER, IA (Montezuma Mutual Telephone & Cable Co.)

BARNUM—See FORT DODGE, IA (Mediacom)

BATAVIA—Formerly served by Westcom. No longer in operation

BATTLE CREEK—Sac County Mutual Telco

BAXTER—See GILMAN, IA (Partner Communications)

BAYARD—Formerly served by Tele-Services Ltd. No longer in operation

BEACON—See OSKALOOSA, IA (Mediacom)

BEAMAN—See UNION, IA (Heart of Iowa Communications. Formerly [IA0521]. This cable system has converted to IPTV.)

BEAMAN—See GLADBROOK, IA (Mediacom)

BEDFORD—See RED OAK, IA (Mediacom)

BELLE PLAINE—See BLAIRSTOWN, IA (Coon Creek Telephone & Cablevision)

BELLE PLAINE—Mediacom

BELLEVUE (VILLAGE)—See LAMOTTE, IA (LaMotte Telephone Co)

BELLEVUE—IVUE Network. This cable system has converted to IPTV. See BELLEVUE, IA [IA5033]

Cable Community Index—Iowa

BELLEVUE—IVUE Network. Formerly [IA0553]. This cable system has converted to IPTV

BELMOND—See FORT DODGE, IA (Mediacom)

BENNETT—F&B Communications. This cable system has converted to IPTV. Now served by WHEATLAND, IA [IA5105]

BENNETT—See WHEATLAND, IA (F&B Communications. Formerly [IA0529]. This cable system has converted to IPTV.)

BERTRAM—See CEDAR RAPIDS, IA (Mediacom)

BETHANY—See MURRAY, MO (GRM Networks)

BIRMINGHAM—Starwest Inc. Now served by KEOSAUQUA, IA [IA0186]

BIRMINGHAM—See KEOSAUQUA, IA (Starwest Inc)

BLACK HAWK COUNTY (PORTIONS)—See WATERLOO, IA (Mediacom)

BLAIRSBURG—Milford Cable TV

BLAIRSTOWN—Coon Creek Telephone & Cablevision

BLAKESBURG—Formerly served by Telnet South LC. No longer in operation

BLENCOE—Formerly served by Sky Scan Cable Co. No longer in operation

BLENCOE—Long Lines. Now served by SALIX, IA [IA0510]

BLENCOE—See SALIX, IA (Long Lines)

BLOCKTON—Formerly served by B & L Technologies LLC. No longer in operation

BLOOMFIELD—Citizens Mutual Telephone

BLOOMFIELD—See ALBIA, IA (Mediacom)

BLUE GRASS—Mediacom. Now served by MOLINE, IL [IL0011]

BODE—Video Services Ltd

BONAPARTE—Formerly served by Mediacom. Now served by Starwest Inc., KEOSAUQUA, IA [IA0186]

BONAPARTE—See KEOSAUQUA, IA (Starwest Inc)

BONDURANT—See DES MOINES, IA (Mediacom)

BOONE COUNTY (EASTERN PORTION)—See AMES, IA (Mediacom)

BOONE COUNTY (SOUTHERN PORTION)—See AMES, IA (Mediacom)

BOONE—See AMES, IA (Mediacom)

BOONEVILLE—See DEXTER, IA (Mediacom)

BOYDEN—Premier Communications. Now served by SIOUX CENTER, IA [IA0076]

BOYDEN—See SIOUX CENTER, IA (Premier Communications)

BRADDYVILLE—Formerly served by CableDirect. No longer in operation

BRANDON—Formerly served by New Path Communications LC. No longer in operation

BRAYTON—See ELK HORN, IA (Marne & Elk Horn Telephone Co)

BREDA—Western Iowa Networks

BRIGHTON—Starwest Inc

BRISTOW—Formerly served by Dumont Cablevision. No longer in operation

BRITT—See MASON CITY, IA (Mediacom)

BRONSON—Formerly served by TelePartners. Now served by Wiatel, LAWTON (village), IA [IA0330]

BRONSON—See LAWTON (village), IA (Wiatel)

BROOKLYN—Inter-County Cable Co

BUENA VISTA COUNTY—See STORM LAKE, IA (Mediacom)

BUFFALO CENTER—Mediacom. Now served by SWEA CITY, IA [IA0226]

BUFFALO CENTER—Winnebago Cooperative Telephone Assn. Now served by LAKE MILLS, IA [IA0590]

BUFFALO CENTER—See SWEA CITY, IA (Mediacom)

BUFFALO CENTER—See LAKE MILLS, IA (Winnebago Cooperative Telecom Assn)

BURLINGTON—Mediacom

BURT—See SWEA CITY, IA (Mediacom)

BUSSEY—See HAMILTON, IA (Mediacom)

CALAMUS—F&B Communications. This cable system has converted to IPTV. Now served by WHEATLAND, IA [IA5105]

CALAMUS—See DIXON, IA (Dixon Telephone Co)

CALAMUS—See WHEATLAND, IA (F&B Communications. Formerly [IA0529]. This cable system has converted to IPTV.)

CALHOUN COUNTY (portions)—Formerly served by Gowrie Cablevision. No longer in operation

CALHOUN COUNTY (PORTIONS)—See FORT DODGE, IA (Mediacom)

CALLENDER—See LEHIGH, IA (Lehigh Valley Cooperative Telephone Assn. Formerly LEHIGH, IA [IA0464]. This cable system has converted to IPTV)

CALMAR—Mediacom

CALUMET—See MARCUS, IA (WesTel Systems)

CAMANCHE—See CLINTON, IA (Mediacom)

CAMBRIDGE—Huxley Communications Corp. Now served by HUXLEY, IA [IA0595]

CAMBRIDGE—See HUXLEY, IA (Huxley Communications Corp)

CANTRIL—See KEOSAUQUA, IA (Starwest Inc)

CARLISLE—See DES MOINES, IA (Mediacom)

CARROLL COUNTY (PORTIONS)—See CLINTON, IL (Mediacom)

CARROLL—Western Iowa Networks. Now served by BREDA, IA [IA0318]

CARROLL—Mediacom

CARROLL—See BREDA, IA (Western Iowa Networks)

CARSON—Formerly served by Interstate Communications. No longer in operation

CASCADE—Cascade Communications

CASEY—Casey Cable Co

CEDAR FALLS—Cedar Falls Municipal Communications Utility

CEDAR FALLS—See WATERLOO, IA (Mediacom)

CEDAR RAPIDS (PORTIONS)—See ELY, IA (South Slope Coop. Communications Co. Formerly served by NORTH LIBERTY, IA [IA0432]. This cable system has converted to IPTV

CEDAR RAPIDS—ImOn Communications

CEDAR RAPIDS—Mediacom

CENTER JUNCTION—Center Junction Telephone Co

CENTER POINT—See SHELLSBURG, IA (USA Communications)

CENTERVILLE—See ALBIA, IA (Mediacom)

CENTRAL CITY—USA Communications. Now served by SHELLSBURG, IA [IA0255]

CENTRAL CITY—See SHELLSBURG, IA (USA Communications)

CERRO GORDO—See MASON CITY, IA (Mediacom)

CHARITON—Mediacom

CHARLES CITY—Mediacom

CHARLOTTE—See PRESTON, IA (Mediacom)

CHARTER OAK—Formerly served by Tip Top Communication. No longer in operation

CHEROKEE—See STORM LAKE, IA (Mediacom)

CHESTER—Formerly served by CableDirect. No longer in operation

CHURDAN—Formerly served by Western Iowa Networks. No longer in operation

CINCINNATI—Formerly served by B & L Technologies LLC. No longer in operation

CLARE—See FORT DODGE, IA (Mediacom)

CLARENCE—Clarence Cablevision

CLARINDA—See RED OAK, IA (Mediacom)

CLARION—See GOLDFIELD, IA (Goldfield Communication Services Corp)

CLARION—See FORT DODGE, IA (Mediacom)

CLARKSVILLE—See TRIPOLI, IA (Butler-Bremer Communications)

CLAYTON COUNTY (PORTIONS)—See POSTVILLE, IA (CenturyLink)

CLEAR LAKE—See MASON CITY, IA (Mediacom)

CLEARFIELD—Formerly served by B & L Technologies LLC. No longer in operation

CLEGHORN—Wetherell Cable TV System

CLEMONS—See ZEARING, IA (Minerva Valley Cablevision)

CLERMONT—Formerly served by Alpine Communications LC. No longer in operation

CLINTON COUNTY—See CLINTON, IA (Mediacom)

CLINTON—Mediacom

CLIVE—See CHARITON, IA (Mediacom)

CLUTIER—FCTC. This cable system has converted to IPTV. See CLUTIER, IA [IA5077]

CLUTIER—FCTC. Formerly [IA0413]. This cable system has converted to IPTV

COALVILLE—See FORT DODGE, IA (Mediacom)

COGGON—USA Communications. Now served by SHELLSBURG, IA [IA0255]

COGGON—See SHELLSBURG, IA (USA Communications)

COLESBURG—Formerly served by Alpine Communications LC. No longer in operation

COLFAX—See NEWTON, IA (Mediacom)

COLLINS—Formerly served by Huxley Communications Corp. No longer in operation

COLO—Colo Telephone Co. This cable system has converted to IPTV. See COLO, IA [IA5003]

COLO—Colo Telephone Co. Formerly [IA0416]. This cable system has converted to IPTV

COLUMBUS CITY—See BURLINGTON, IA (Mediacom)

COLUMBUS JUNCTION—Mediacom. Now served by BURLINGTON, IA [IA0405]

Iowa—Cable Community Index

COLUMBUS JUNCTION—See BURLINGTON, IA (Mediacom)

CONRAD—See UNION, IA (Heart of Iowa Communications. Formerly [IA0521]. This cable system has converted to IPTV.)

CONRAD—See GLADBROOK, IA (Mediacom)

COON RAPIDS—Coon Rapids Municipal Cable System

CORALVILLE (PORTIONS)—See ELY, IA (South Slope Coop. Communications Co. Formerly served by NORTH LIBERTY, IA [IA0432]. This cable system has converted to IPTV)

CORALVILLE—See IOWA CITY, IA (Mediacom)

CORLEY—See IRWIN, IA (Mutual Communications Services)

CORNELIA—See FORT DODGE, IA (Mediacom)

CORNING—See RED OAK, IA (Mediacom)

CORRECTIONVILLE—See SALIX, IA (Long Lines)

CORWITH—Comm1. Now served by KANAWHA, IA [IA5095]

CORWITH—See KANAWHA, IA (Comm1. Formerly [IA0229]. This cable system has converted to IPTV)

CORYDON—See CHARITON, IA (Mediacom)

COULTER—Formerly served by Latimer/Coulter Cablevision. No longer in operation

CRAWFORD COUNTY (SOUTHERN PORTION)—See DENISON, IA (Mediacom)

CRESCO—Mediacom. Now served by OSAGE, IA [IA0085]

CRESCO—See OSAGE, IA (Mediacom)

CRESTON—Mediacom. Now served by CHARITON, IA [IA0017]

CRESTON—See CHARITON, IA (Mediacom)

CUSHING—See SCHALLER, IA (Comserv Ltd)

CYLINDER—Formerly served by ATC Cablevision. No longer in operation

DAKOTA CITY—See SIOUX CITY, NE (Cable One)

DAKOTA CITY—See FORT DODGE, IA (Mediacom)

DAKOTA COUNTY (PORTIONS)—See SIOUX CITY, NE (Cable One)

DAKOTA DUNES—See SIOUX CITY, SD (Cable One)

DAKOTA DUNES—See SALIX, SD (Long Lines)

DALLAS CENTER—See DEXTER, IA (Mediacom)

DALLAS COUNTY—See DEXTER, IA (Mediacom)

DALLAS—See DES MOINES, IA (Mediacom)

DANBURY—Long Lines. Now served by SALIX, IA [IA0510]

DANBURY—See SALIX, IA (Long Lines)

DANVILLE—See BURLINGTON, IA (Mediacom)

DAVIS CITY—Formerly served by Telnet South LC. No longer in operation

DAYTON—Lehigh Services Inc. Now served by LEHIGH, IA [IA5319]

DAYTON—See LEHIGH, IA (Lehigh Valley Cooperative Telephone Assn. Formerly LEHIGH, IA [IA0464]. This cable system has converted to IPTV)

DE WITT—See GRAND MOUND, IA (Grand Mound Communications Corp.)

DECATUR—Formerly served by Telnet South LC. Now served by Mediacom, CHARITON, IA [IA0017]

DECATUR—See CHARITON, IA (Mediacom)

DECORAH—Mediacom

DEDHAM—Templeton Telephone Co.

DEEP RIVER—Montezuma Mutual Telephone & Cable Co.

DEFIANCE—Formerly served by Farmers Mutual Telephone Co. Now served by Mutual Communications Services, IRWIN, IA [IA0302]

DEFIANCE—See IRWIN, IA (Mutual Communications Services)

DELAWARE COUNTY (PORTIONS)—See WAVERLY, IA (Mediacom)

DELHI (TOWN)—New Century Communications

DELMAR—F&B Communications. This cable system has converted to IPTV. Now served by WHEATLAND, IA [IA5105]

DELMAR—See WHEATLAND, IA (F&B Communications. Formerly [IA0529]. This cable system has converted to IPTV.)

DELOIT—Formerly served by Tip Top Communications. No longer in operation

DELTA—Formerly served by Longview Communications. No longer in operation

DENISON—Mediacom

DENMARK—Formerly served by Longview Communications. No longer in operation

DENVER—See WAVERLY, IA (Mediacom)

DES MOINES COUNTY (PORTIONS)—See BURLINGTON, IA (Mediacom)

DES MOINES—Mediacom

DESOTO—See DEXTER, IA (Mediacom)

DEWAR—See WATERLOO, IA (Mediacom)

DEWITT—See CLINTON, IA (Mediacom)

DEXTER—Mediacom

DIAGONAL—Formerly served by B & L Technologies LLC. No longer in operation

DICKENS—Premier Communications. Now served by SIOUX CENTER, IA [IA0076]

DICKENS—See SIOUX CENTER, IA (Premier Communications)

DICKINSON COUNTY (PORTIONS)—See SPIRIT LAKE, IA (Mediacom)

DIKE—See WAVERLY, IA (Mediacom)

DIXON—Central Scott Telephone

DIXON—Dixon Telephone Co

DONAHUE—Dixon Telephone Co. Now served by DIXON, IA [IA0358]

DONAHUE—See DIXON, IA (Central Scott Telephone)

DONAHUE—See DIXON, IA (Dixon Telephone Co)

DONNELLSON—Formerly served by Longview Communications. No longer in operation

DOON—See SIOUX CENTER, IA (Premier Communications)

DOW CITY—Formerly served by Tip Top Communications. No longer in operation

DOWS—Formerly served by Dows Cablevision. No longer in operation

DRAKESVILLE—See BLOOMFIELD, IA (Citizens Mutual Telephone)

DUBUQUE COUNTY—See DUBUQUE, IA (Mediacom)

DUBUQUE—Mediacom

DUMONT—Dumont Cablevision

DUNCAN—See MASON CITY, IA (Mediacom)

DUNKERTON (PORTIONS)—Dunkerton Telephone Coop

DUNLAP—Formerly served by Tip Top Communications. No longer in operation

DYERSVILLE—See DUBUQUE, IA (Mediacom)

DYSART—See CLUTIER, IA (FCTC. Formerly [IA0413]. This cable system has converted to IPTV)

DYSART—See AMES, IA (Mediacom)

EAGLE GROVE—Mediacom

EARLHAM—See DEXTER, IA (Mediacom)

EARLING—See IRWIN, IA (Mutual Communications Services)

EARLVILLE—Formerly served by Alpine Communications LC. No longer in operation

EARLY—See CLEGHORN, IA (Wetherell Cable TV System)

EAST DUBUQUE—See DUBUQUE, IL (Mediacom)

EDDYVILLE—Mediacom. Now served by ALBIA, IA [IA0039]

EDDYVILLE—See ALBIA, IA (Mediacom)

EDGEWOOD—See WAVERLY, IA (Mediacom)

ELDON—Mediacom. Now served by ALBIA, IA [IA0039]

ELDON—See ALBIA, IA (Mediacom)

ELDORA—See UNION, IA (Heart of Iowa Communications. Formerly [IA0521]. This cable system has converted to IPTV.)

ELDORA—See GLADBROOK, IA (Mediacom)

ELGIN—See CALMAR, IA (Mediacom)

ELK HORN—Marne & Elk Horn Telephone Co

ELK RUN HEIGHTS—See WATERLOO, IA (Mediacom)

ELKHART—Huxley Communications Corp. Now served by HUXLEY, IA [IA0595]

ELKHART—See HUXLEY, IA (Huxley Communications Corp)

ELLIOT—See GRISWOLD, IA (Griswold Cable TV)

ELMA—See OSAGE, IA (Mediacom)

ELMA—See RUDD, IA (Omnitel Communications. This system has converted to IPTV)

ELWOOD—See LOST NATION, IA (LN Satellite. Formerly [IA0279]. This cable system has converted to IPTV)

ELY—South Slope Coop. Communications Co. Formerly served by NORTH LIBERTY, IA [IA0432]. This cable system has converted to IPTV

EMERSON—Interstate Communications

EMMET COUNTY (PORTIONS)—See ESTHERVILLE, IA (Mediacom)

EMMETSBURG—See ESTHERVILLE, IA (Mediacom)

EPWORTH—See DUBUQUE, IA (Mediacom)

ERIE—See CLINTON, IL (Mediacom)

ESSEX—See RED OAK, IA (Mediacom)

ESTHERVILLE—Mediacom

EVANSDALE—See WATERLOO, IA (Mediacom)

EXIRA—Marne & Elk Horn Telephone Co. Now served by ELK HORN, IA [IA0123]

EXIRA—See ELK HORN, IA (Marne & Elk Horn Telephone Co)

Cable Community Index—Iowa

FAIRBANK—Mediacom. Now served by WAVERLY, IA [IA0021]

FAIRBANK—See WAVERLY, IA (Mediacom)

FAIRFAX—Formerly served by Starwest Inc. No longer in operation

FAIRFAX—See CEDAR RAPIDS, IA (Mediacom)

FAIRFAX—See ELY, IA (South Slope Coop. Communications Co. Formerly served by NORTH LIBERTY, IA [IA0432]. This cable system has converted to IPTV)

FAIRFIELD—See OTTUMWA, IA (Mediacom)

FAIRVIEW—See MARTELLE, IA (Martelle Communications Co-op)

FARLEY—See DUBUQUE, IA (Mediacom)

FARMERSBURG—See MONONA, IA (Northeast Iowa Telephone Co)

FARMINGTON—Starwest Inc

FARRAGUT—Formerly served by Western Iowa Networks. No longer in operation

FAYETTE COUNTY (PORTIONS)—See WAVERLY, IA (Mediacom)

FAYETTE—See CALMAR, IA (Mediacom)

FENTON—Fenton Cablevision

FERGUSON—See UNION, IA (Heart of Iowa Communications. Formerly [IA0521]. This cable system has converted to IPTV.)

FERTILE—Formerly served by Westcom. No longer in operation

FLORIS—See BLOOMFIELD, IA (Citizens Mutual Telephone)

FLOYD COUNTY (PORTIONS)—See CHARLES CITY, IA (Mediacom)

FLOYD—See RUDD, IA (Omnitel Communications. This system has converted to IPTV)

FLOYD—See RUDD, IA (Omnitel Communications)

FONDA—Formerly served by TelePartners. No longer in operation

FONTANELLE—Formerly served by B & L Technologies LLC. No longer in operation

FOREST CITY—Winnebago Cooperative Telephone Assn. Now served by LAKE MILLS, IA [IA0590]

FOREST CITY—See MASON CITY, IA (Mediacom)

FOREST CITY—See LAKE MILLS, IA (Winnebago Cooperative Telecom Assn)

FORT ATKINSON—See CALMAR, IA (Mediacom)

FORT DODGE—Mediacom

FORT MADISON—Mediacom

FOSTORIA—See MILFORD, IA (Milford Cable TV)

FOSTORIA—See SPENCER, IA (SMU Cable TV)

FREDERICKSBURG—See CALMAR, IA (Mediacom)

FREDERIKA—See TRIPOLI, IA (Butler-Bremer Communications)

FREDONIA—See BURLINGTON, IA (Mediacom)

FREMONT—Starwest Inc

FRUITLAND—See MUSCATINE, IA (MPW Cable)

FULTON—See CLINTON, IL (Mediacom)

GALENA—See DUBUQUE, IL (Mediacom)

GALVA—See SCHALLER, IA (Comserv Ltd)

GALVA—See CLEGHORN, IA (Wetherell Cable TV System)

GARBER—Formerly served by Alpine Communications LC. No longer in operation

GARNAVILLO—Mediacom. Now served by BOSCOBEL, WI [WI0341]

GARNER—See MASON CITY, IA (Mediacom)

GARWIN—See UNION, IA (Heart of Iowa Communications. Formerly [IA0521]. This cable system has converted to IPTV.)

GARWIN—See GLADBROOK, IA (Mediacom)

GENEVA—Formerly served by Dumont Cablevision. No longer in operation

GEORGE—Formerly served by Siebring Cable TV. Now served by Premier Communications, SIOUX CENTER, IA [IA0076]

GEORGE—See SIOUX CENTER, IA (Premier Communications)

GILBERT—See STRATFORD, IA (Stratford Mutual Telephone)

GILBERTVILLE—See WATERLOO, IA (Mediacom)

GILLETT GROVE—ATC Cablevision

GILMAN—Partner Communications

GILMORE CITY—Mediacom

GLADBROOK—Mediacom

GLENWOOD—See RED OAK, IA (Mediacom)

GLIDDEN—See CARROLL, IA (Mediacom)

GOLDFIELD—Goldfield Communication Services Corp

GOODELL (village)—Formerly served by New Path Communications LC. No longer in operation

GOOSE LAKE—See PRESTON, IA (Mediacom)

GOWRIE—Gowrie Cablevision

GRAETTINGER—See ESTHERVILLE, IA (Mediacom)

GRAETTINGER—River Valley Telecommunications Coop

GRAFTON—Formerly served by Westcom. No longer in operation

GRAND JUNCTION—Jefferson Telecom

GRAND MOUND—Grand Mound Communications Corp.

GRAND RIVER—Formerly served by B & L Technologies LLC. No longer in operation

GRAND RIVER—See MURRAY, IA (GRM Networks)

GRANGER—See DEXTER, IA (Mediacom)

GRANT—See GRISWOLD, IA (Griswold Cable TV)

GRANVILLE—Premier Communications. Now served by SIOUX CENTER, IA [IA0076]

GRANVILLE—See SIOUX CENTER, IA (Premier Communications)

GRAVITY—Formerly served by CableDirect. No longer in operation

GREELEY—Formerly served by Alpine Communications LC. No longer in operation

GREEN MOUNTAIN—See MARSHALLTOWN, IA (Mediacom)

GREENE (town)—Formerly served by Mediacom. No longer in operation

GREENE COUNTY—See AMES, IA (Mediacom)

GREENE—See RUDD, IA (Omnitel Communications)

GREENFIELD—See CHARITON, IA (Mediacom)

GRIMES—See DES MOINES, IA (Mediacom)

GRINNELL—See NEWTON, IA (Mediacom)

GRISWOLD—Griswold Cable TV

GRUNDY CENTER—Grundy Center Municipal Utilities

GRUNDY CENTER—See GLADBROOK, IA (Mediacom)

GRUNDY COUNTY (UNINCORPORATED AREAS)—See UNION, IA (Heart of Iowa Communications. Formerly [IA0521]. This cable system has converted to IPTV.)

GUTHRIE CENTER—See PANORA, IA (Panora Communications Cooperative)

HAMBURG—Rock Port Cablevision

HAMILTON COUNTY (PORTIONS)—See KEOKUK, IA (Mediacom)

HAMILTON COUNTY—See FORT DODGE, IA (Mediacom)

HAMILTON—Mediacom

HAMILTON—See KEOKUK, IL (Mediacom)

HAMPTON—Mediacom

HANCOCK COUNTY (PORTIONS)—See KEOKUK, IL (Mediacom)

HANCOCK—See IRWIN, IA (Mutual Communications Services)

HARCOURT—See LEHIGH, IA (Lehigh Valley Cooperative Telephone Assn. Formerly LEHIGH, IA [IA0464]. This cable system has converted to IPTV)

HARDIN COUNTY (UNINCORPORATED AREAS)—See UNION, IA (Heart of Iowa Communications. Formerly [IA0521]. This cable system has converted to IPTV.)

HARDIN COUNTY—See GLADBROOK, IA (Mediacom)

HARLAN—Harlan Municipal Utilities

HARLAN—See DENISON, IA (Mediacom)

HARRIS—See SPIRIT LAKE, IA (Mediacom)

HARTFORD—Formerly served by Telnet South LC. Now served by Mediacom, DES MOINES, IA [IA0001]

HARTFORD—See DES MOINES, IA (Mediacom)

HARTLEY—See SANBORN, IA (Community Cable TV Agency of O'Brien County)

HARVESTER COMMUNITY—See GILMAN, IA (Partner Communications)

HAVELOCK—Northwest Telephone Cooperative Association

HAVERHILL—See UNION, IA (Heart of Iowa Communications. Formerly [IA0521]. This cable system has converted to IPTV.)

HAWARDEN—Formerly served by Premier Communications. No longer in operation

HAWARDEN—HiTec Cable

HAWKEYE—Hawkeye Telephone Co. This cable system has converted to IPTV. See HAWKEYE, IA [IA5322]

HAWKEYE—Hawkeye Telephone Co. This cable system has converted to IPTV

HAZLETON—See WAVERLY, IA (Mediacom)

HEDRICK—Starwest Inc

HENRY COUNTY—See FORT MADISON, IA (Mediacom)

HIAWATHA—See CEDAR RAPIDS, IA (ImOn Communications)

HIAWATHA—See CEDAR RAPIDS, IA (Mediacom)

HILLS—See IOWA CITY, IA (Mediacom)

Iowa—Cable Community Index

HINTON—Premier Communications. Now served by SIOUX CENTER, IA [IA0076]

HINTON—See SIOUX CENTER, IA (Premier Communications)

HOLLAND—Formerly served by CableDirect. No longer in operation

HOLSTEIN—See SALIX, IA (Long Lines)

HOLY CROSS—See LUXEMBURG, IA (New Century Communications)

HOPKINTON—Formerly served by New Century Communications. No longer in operation

HORNICK—Formerly served by Telepartners. Now served by Wiatel, LAWTON (village), IA [IA0330]

HORNICK—See LAWTON (village), IA (Wiatel)

HOSPERS—HTC Communications. Now served by HOSPERS, IA [IA0060]

HOSPERS—HTC Communications

HUBBARD—Hubbard Co-op Cable

HUDSON—Mediacom

HULL—See SIOUX CENTER, IA (Premier Communications)

HUMBOLDT—See GOLDFIELD, IA (Goldfield Communication Services Corp)

HUMBOLDT—See FORT DODGE, IA (Mediacom)

HUMESTON—Formerly served by B & L Technologies LLC. No longer in operation

HUXLEY—Huxley Communications Corp

HUXLEY—See AMES, IA (Mediacom)

IDA GROVE—See SALIX, IA (Long Lines)

INDEPENDENCE—Independence Light & Power Telecommunications

INDEPENDENCE—Mediacom

INDIANOLA—See DES MOINES, IA (Mediacom)

INWOOD—Alliance Communications. Now served by GARRETSON, SD [SD0016]

IONIA—Formerly served by Mid-American Cable Systems. No longer in operation

IOWA ARMY MUNITIONS PLANT—See BURLINGTON, IA (Mediacom)

IOWA CITY—Mediacom

IOWA FALLS—Mediacom

IRETON—Premier Communications. Now served by SIOUX CENTER, IA [IA0076]

IRETON—See SIOUX CENTER, IA (Premier Communications)

IRWIN—Mutual Communications Services

JACKSON COUNTY—See PRESTON, IA (Mediacom)

JACKSONVILLE—See IRWIN, IA (Mutual Communications Services)

JAMAICA—Panora Cooperative Cablevision Assn. Inc. Now served by PANORA, IA [IA0108]

JAMAICA—See PANORA, IA (Panora Communications Cooperative)

JANESVILLE—See WAVERLY, IA (Mediacom)

JASPER COUNTY (CENTRAL PORTION)—See NEWTON, IA (Mediacom)

JEFFERSON COUNTY—See OTTUMWA, IA (Mediacom)

JEFFERSON—Mediacom. Now served by AMES, IA [IA0008]

JEFFERSON—See SALIX, SD (Long Lines)

JEFFERSON—See AMES, IA (Mediacom)

JESUP—Jesup Cablevision

JEWELL—See STRATFORD, IA (Stratford Mutual Telephone)

JO DAVIESS COUNTY—See DUBUQUE, IL (Mediacom)

JOHNSON COUNTY (PORTIONS)—See NORTH LIBERTY, IA (Mediacom)

JOHNSTON—See DES MOINES, IA (Mediacom)

JOICE (village)—Formerly served by Westcom. No longer in operation

JONES COUNTY (PORTIONS)—See ANAMOSA, IA (Mediacom)

KALONA—See WASHINGTON, IA (Mediacom)

KANAWHA—Comm1. This cable system has converted to IPTV. See KANAWHA, IA [IA5095]

KANAWHA—Comm1. Formerly [IA0229]. This cable system has converted to IPTV

KELLERTON—Formerly served by Telnet South LC. Now served by Mediacom, CHARITON, IA [IA0017]

KELLERTON—See CHARITON, IA (Mediacom)

KELLEY—Huxley Communications Corp. Now served by HUXLEY, IA [IA0595]

KELLEY—See HUXLEY, IA (Huxley Communications Corp)

KELLOGG—See GILMAN, IA (Partner Communications)

KENSETT—See MASON CITY, IA (Mediacom)

KEOKUK—Mediacom

KEOSAUQUA—Starwest Inc

KEOTA—Mediacom

KESWICK—Formerly served by Longview Communications. No longer in operation

KEYSTONE—Keystone Communications

KIMBALLTON—See ELK HORN, IA (Marne & Elk Horn Telephone Co)

KINGSLEY—Wiatel

KIRKMAN—See IRWIN, IA (Mutual Communications Services)

KIRON—See SCHALLER, IA (Comserv Ltd)

KLEMME—Comm1. Now served by KANAWHA, IA [IA5095]

KLEMME—See KANAWHA, IA (Comm1. Formerly [IA0229]. This cable system has converted to IPTV)

KNOXVILLE (unincorporated areas)—Formerly served by Telnet South LC. Now served by Mediacom, HAMILTON, IA [IA0018]

KNOXVILLE—Mediacom. Now served by HAMILTON, IA [IA0018]

KNOXVILLE—See HAMILTON, IA (Mediacom)

LA PORTE—See WAVERLY, IA (Mediacom)

LACONA—Formerly served by Telnet South LC. No longer in operation

LAKE CITY—See FORT DODGE, IA (Mediacom)

LAKE MILLS—Winnebago Cooperative Telecom Assn

LAKE PANORAMA—See PANORA, IA (Panora Communications Cooperative)

LAKE PARK—Mediacom. Now served by SPIRIT LAKE, IA [IA0036]

LAKE PARK—See SPIRIT LAKE, IA (Mediacom)

LAKE VIEW—Corn Belt Telephone Co. Now served by WALL LAKE, IA [IA0256]

LAKE VIEW—See WALL LAKE, IA (Corn Belt Telephone Co)

LAKESIDE—See STORM LAKE, IA (Mediacom)

LAKOTA—Formerly served by Heck's TV & Cable. No longer in operation

LAKOTA—See FORT DODGE, IA (Mediacom)

LAMBS GROVE—See NEWTON, IA (Mediacom)

LAMONI—Formerly served by Telnet South LC. Now served by Mediacom, CHARITON, IA [IA0017]

LAMONI—See CHARITON, IA (Mediacom)

LAMONT—Formerly served by Alpine Communications LC. No longer in operation

LAMOTTE—LaMotte Telephone Co

LANSING—Mediacom. Now served by BOSCOBEL, WI [WI0341]

LARCHWOOD—Alliance Communications. Now served by GARRETSON, SD [SD0016]

LATIMER—Formerly served by Latimer/Coulter Cablevision. No longer in operation

LAUREL—See UNION, IA (Heart of Iowa Communications. Formerly [IA0521]. This cable system has converted to IPTV.)

LAUREL—See GILMAN, IA (Partner Communications)

LAURENS—Laurens Municipal Power & Communications

LAURENS—See FORT DODGE, IA (Mediacom)

LAWLER—Formerly served by Alpine Communications LC. No longer in operation

LAWTON (VILLAGE)—Wiatel

LE GRAND—See MARSHALLTOWN, IA (Mediacom)

LE MARS—Premier Communications. Now served by SIOUX CENTER, IA [IA0076]

LE MARS—See SIOUX CENTER, IA (Premier Communications)

LEDYARD (village)—Formerly served by New Path Communications LC. No longer in operation

LEE COUNTY (PORTIONS)—See FORT MADISON, IA (Mediacom)

LEE COUNTY (PORTIONS)—See KEOKUK, IA (Mediacom)

LEHIGH—Lehigh Valley Cooperative Telephone Assn. This cable system has converted to IPTV. See LEHIGH, IA [IA5318]

LEHIGH—Lehigh Valley Cooperative Telephone Assn. Formerly LEHIGH, IA [IA0464]. This cable system has converted to IPTV

LELAND—See MASON CITY, IA (Mediacom)

LENOX—Lenox Municipal Cablevision

LEON—See MURRAY, IA (GRM Networks)

LEON—See CHARITON, IA (Mediacom)

LEWIS—See GRISWOLD, IA (Griswold Cable TV)

LIBERTYVILLE—Formerly served by Westcom. No longer in operation

LIDDERDALE—See BREDA, IA (Western Iowa Networks)

LIME SPRINGS—See OSAGE, IA (Mediacom)

LIME SPRINGS—See RUDD, IA (Omnitel Communications. This system has converted to IPTV)

LIME SPRINGS—See RUDD, IA (Omnitel Communications)

LINDEN—See PANORA, IA (Panora Communications Cooperative)

LINEVILLE—See MURRAY, IA (GRM Networks)

Cable Community Index—Iowa

LINN COUNTY (PORTIONS)—See CEDAR RAPIDS, IA (ImOn Communications)

LINN COUNTY (UNINCORPORATED AREAS)—See CEDAR RAPIDS, IA (Mediacom)

LISBON—See NORTH LIBERTY, IA (Mediacom)

LISCOMB—Formerly served by New Path Communications LC. No longer in operation

LISCOMB—See UNION, IA (Heart of Iowa Communications. Formerly [IA0521]. This cable system has converted to IPTV.)

LITTLE CEDAR—See RUDD, IA (Omnitel Communications. This system has converted to IPTV)

LITTLE ROCK—Premier Communications

LITTLE SIOUX—Formerly served by TelePartners. No longer in operation

LITTLETON—Formerly served by Farmers Mutual Cooperative Telephone Co. Now served by Jesup Cablevision, JESUP, IA [IA0116]

LITTLETON—See JESUP, IA (Jesup Cablevision)

LIVERMORE—Livermore Cable

LOCKRIDGE—Formerly served by Westcom. No longer in operation

LOGAN—Long Lines. Now served by SALIX, IA [IA0510]

LOGAN—See SALIX, IA (Long Lines)

LOHRVILLE—Formerly served by Tele-Services Ltd. No longer in operation

LONE TREE—See WASHINGTON, IA (Mediacom)

LORIMOR—See MURRAY, IA (GRM Networks)

LOST NATION—Lost Nation-Elwood Telephone Co. This cable system has converted to IPTV. See LOST NATION, IA [IA5107]

LOST NATION—LN Satellite. Formerly [IA0279]. This cable system has converted to IPTV

LOUISA COUNTY—See BURLINGTON, IA (Mediacom)

LOUISA COUNTY—See MUSCATINE, IA (MPW Cable)

LOVILIA—See HAMILTON, IA (Mediacom)

LOW MOOR—See CLINTON, IA (Mediacom)

LOWDEN—See WHEATLAND, IA (F&B Communications. Formerly [IA0529]. This cable system has converted to IPTV.)

LU VERNE—Signal Inc

LUANA—See MONONA, IA (Northeast Iowa Telephone Co)

LUCAS—Formerly served by Telnet South LC. Now served by Mediacom, CHARITON, IA [IA0017]

LUCAS—See CHARITON, IA (Mediacom)

LUXEMBURG—New Century Communications

LYMAN—See GRISWOLD, IA (Griswold Cable TV)

LYNDON—See CLINTON, IL (Mediacom)

LYNNVILLE—See NEWTON, IA (Mediacom)

LYTTON—Formerly served by TelePartners. No longer in operation

MADRID—See AMES, IA (Mediacom)

MAGNOLIA—See SALIX, IA (Long Lines)

MALCOM—Inter-County Cable Co

MALLARD—See HAVELOCK, IA (Northwest Telephone Cooperative Association)

MALVERN BOROUGH—Rock Port Cablevision

MANCHESTER—See WAVERLY, IA (Mediacom)

MANILLA—Formerly served by Manilla Municipal Cable. Now served by Mutual Communications Services, IRWIN, IA [IA0302]

MANILLA—See IRWIN, IA (Mutual Communications Services)

MANLY—See MASON CITY, IA (Mediacom)

MANNING—Manning Municipal Cable TV

MANSON—See FORT DODGE, IA (Mediacom)

MAPLETON—Long Lines. Now served by SALIX, IA [IA0510]

MAPLETON—See SALIX, IA (Long Lines)

MAQUOKETA—Mediacom

MARATHON—See CLEGHORN, IA (Wetherell Cable TV System)

MARBLE ROCK—Omnitel Communications. Now served by RUDD, IA [IA0503]

MARBLE ROCK—See RUDD, IA (Omnitel Communications. This system has converted to IPTV)

MARBLE ROCK—See RUDD, IA (Omnitel Communications)

MARCUS—WesTel Systems

MARENGO—See BLAIRSTOWN, IA (Coon Creek Telephone & Cablevision)

MARENGO—See BELLE PLAINE, IA (Mediacom)

MARION COUNTY—See HAMILTON, IA (Mediacom)

MARION—See CEDAR RAPIDS, IA (ImOn Communications)

MARION—See CEDAR RAPIDS, IA (Mediacom)

MARNE—See ELK HORN, IA (Marne & Elk Horn Telephone Co)

MARSHALL COUNTY (UNINCORPORATED AREAS)—See UNION, IA (Heart of Iowa Communications. Formerly [IA0521]. This cable system has converted to IPTV.)

MARSHALL COUNTY—See MARSHALLTOWN, IA (Mediacom)

MARSHALLTOWN—See UNION, IA (Heart of Iowa Communications. Formerly [IA0521]. This cable system has converted to IPTV.)

MARSHALLTOWN—Mediacom

MARTELLE—Martelle Communications Co-op

MARTENSDALE—Interstate Communications. Now served by TRURO, IA [IA0344]

MARTENSDALE—See TRURO, IA (Interstate Communications)

MASON CITY—Mediacom

MASSENA—Formerly served by B & L Technologies LLC. No longer in operation

MAURICE—Premier Communications. Now served by SIOUX CENTER, IA [IA0076]

MAURICE—See SIOUX CENTER, IA (Premier Communications)

MAXWELL—Formerly served by Huxley Communications Corp. No longer in operation

MAYNARD—Mediacom. Now served by WAVERLY, IA [IA0021]

MAYNARD—See WAVERLY, IA (Mediacom)

MAYSVILLE—Dixon Telephone Co. Now served by DIXON, IA [IA0358]

MAYSVILLE—See DIXON, IA (Central Scott Telephone)

MAYSVILLE—See DIXON, IA (Dixon Telephone Co)

MCCALLSBURG—See ZEARING, IA (Minerva Valley Cablevision)

MCCAUSLAND—See CLINTON, IA (Mediacom)

MCCLELLAND—See WALNUT, IA (Walnut Communications)

MCINTIRE—See RUDD, IA (Omnitel Communications. This system has converted to IPTV)

MECHANICSVILLE—Mechanicsville Telephone

MEDIAPOLIS—See MUSCATINE, IA (MPW Cable)

MEDIAPOLIS—MTC Technologies

MELBOURNE—See GILMAN, IA (Partner Communications)

MELCHER—See HAMILTON, IA (Mediacom)

MELVIN—Premier Communications

MENLO—Coon Valley Cooperative Telephone

MERIDEN—See CLEGHORN, IA (Wetherell Cable TV System)

MERRILL—Premier Communications. Now served by SIOUX CENTER, IA [IA0076]

MERRILL—See SIOUX CENTER, IA (Premier Communications)

MESERVEY—Rockwell Communications Systems Inc

MIDDLETOWN—See BURLINGTON, IA (Mediacom)

MILES—See PRESTON, IA (Mediacom)

MILFORD—Milford Cable TV

MILLERTON—See MURRAY, IA (GRM Networks)

MILLS COUNTY (EASTERN PORTION)—See RED OAK, IA (Mediacom)

MILO—Formerly served by Telnet South LC. No longer in operation

MILTON—Starwest Inc. Now served by KEOSAUQUA, IA [IA0186]

MILTON—See KEOSAUQUA, IA (Starwest Inc)

MINBURN—Minburn Cablevision Inc.

MINDEN—Walnut Communications. Now served by WALNUT, IA [IA0241]

MINDEN—See WALNUT, IA (Walnut Communications)

MINGO—Formerly served by Huxley Communications Corp. No longer in operation

MISSOURI VALLEY—Long Lines. Now served by SALIX, IA [IA0510]

MISSOURI VALLEY—See SALIX, IA (Long Lines)

MITCHELLVILLE—See NEWTON, IA (Mediacom)

MODALE—Formerly served by TelePartners. No longer in operation

MONDAMIN—Formerly served by TelePartners. No longer in operation

MONMOUTH—See BALDWIN, IA (Baldwin Nashville Telephone Co)

MONONA—Northeast Iowa Telephone Co

MONROE COUNTY (PORTIONS)—See ALBIA, IA (Mediacom)

MONROE—Formerly served by Telnet South LC. Now served by Mediacom, NEWTON, IA [IA0016]

MONROE—See NEWTON, IA (Mediacom)

Iowa—Cable Community Index

MONTEZUMA—See DEEP RIVER, IA (Montezuma Mutual Telephone & Cable Co.)

MONTICELLO—See CEDAR RAPIDS, IA (Mediacom)

MONTOUR—See GILMAN, IA (Partner Communications)

MONTROSE—Mediacom. Now served by KEOKUK, IA [IA0612]

MONTROSE—See KEOKUK, IA (Mediacom)

MOORHEAD—Formerly served by Soldier Valley Telephone. Now served by Long Lines, SALIX, IA [IA0510]

MOORHEAD—Long Lines. Now served by SALIX, IA [IA0510]

MOORHEAD—See SALIX, IA (Long Lines)

MOORLAND—See FORT DODGE, IA (Mediacom)

MORAVIA—Formerly served by B & L Communications LLC. No longer in operation

MORLEY—See MARTELLE, IA (Martelle Communications Co-op)

MORNING SUN—See BURLINGTON, IA (Mediacom)

MORRISON—See CLINTON, IL (Mediacom)

MOULTON—Formerly served by B & L Technologies LLC. No longer in operation

MOUNT AYR—See CHARITON, IA (Mediacom)

MOUNT PLEASANT—See FORT MADISON, IA (Mediacom)

MOUNT VERNON—See NORTH LIBERTY, IA (Mediacom)

MOVILLE—Wiatel

MOVILLE—See LAWTON (village), IA (Wiatel)

MURRAY—Formerly served by Interstate Communications. This cable system has converted to IPTV. Now served by GRM Networks, MURRAY, IA [IA5135]

MURRAY—GRM Networks

MUSCATINE COUNTY—See MUSCATINE, IA (MPW Cable)

MUSCATINE—MPW Cable. Now served by MUSCATINE, IA [IA0587]

MUSCATINE—MPW Cable

MYSTIC—Formerly served by B & L Technologies LLC. No longer in operation

NASHUA—See TRIPOLI, IA (Butler-Bremer Communications)

NEOLA—Walnut Communications. Now served by WALNUT, IA [IA0241]

NEOLA—See WALNUT, IA (Walnut Communications)

NEVADA—See AMES, IA (Mediacom)

NEW ALBIN—Mediacom

NEW HAMPTON—See MURRAY, MO (GRM Networks)

NEW HAMPTON—See CALMAR, IA (Mediacom)

NEW HARTFORD—See WAVERLY, IA (Mediacom)

NEW HAVEN—See RUDD, IA (Omnitel Communications. This system has converted to IPTV)

NEW LIBERTY—Dixon Telephone Co. Now served by DIXON, IA [IA0358]

NEW LIBERTY—See DIXON, IA (Central Scott Telephone)

NEW LIBERTY—See DIXON, IA (Dixon Telephone Co)

NEW LONDON—See FORT MADISON, IA (Mediacom)

NEW MARKET—Farmers Mutual Telephone Co. Now served by STANTON, IA [IA0264]

NEW MARKET—See STANTON, IA (Farmers Mutual Telephone Co)

NEW PROVIDENCE—See UNION, IA (Heart of Iowa Communications. Formerly [IA0521]. This cable system has converted to IPTV.)

NEW SHARON—See OSKALOOSA, IA (Mediacom)

NEW VIENNA—See LUXEMBURG, IA (New Century Communications)

NEW VIRGINIA—Interstate Communications. Now served by TRURO, IA [IA0344]

NEW VIRGINIA—See TRURO, IA (Interstate Communications)

NEWELL—Formerly served by TelePartners. No longer in operation

NEWHALL—See VINTON, IA (Mediacom)

NEWHALL—See ELY, IA (South Slope Coop. Communications Co. Formerly served by NORTH LIBERTY, IA [IA0432]. This cable system has converted to IPTV)

NEWTON—Mediacom

NICHOLS—Formerly served by PEC Cablevision. No longer in operation

NORA SPRINGS—See RUDD, IA (Omnitel Communications. This system has converted to IPTV)

NORA SPRINGS—See RUDD, IA (Omnitel Communications)

NORTH ENGLISH—See WILLIAMSBURG, IA (Mediacom)

NORTH LIBERTY—South Slope Communications Co. This cable system has converted to IPTV. Now served by ELY, IA [IA5004]

NORTH LIBERTY—Mediacom

NORTH LIBERTY—See ELY, IA (South Slope Coop. Communications Co. Formerly served by NORTH LIBERTY, IA [IA0432]. This cable system has converted to IPTV)

NORTH SIOUX CITY—See SIOUX CITY, SD (Cable One)

NORTHWOOD—Mediacom. Now served by MASON CITY, IA [IA0010]

NORTHWOOD—See MASON CITY, IA (Mediacom)

NORWALK—See DES MOINES, IA (Mediacom)

NORWAY—Mediacom

NORWAY—See ELY, IA (South Slope Coop. Communications Co. Formerly served by NORTH LIBERTY, IA [IA0432]. This cable system has converted to IPTV)

OAKLAND ACRES—See GILMAN, IA (Partner Communications)

OAKLAND—Formerly served by Our Cable. No longer in operation

OAKVILLE—Formerly served by Longview Communications. No longer in operation

OCHEYEDAN—HTC Communications. Now served by HOSPERS, IA [IA0060]

OCHEYEDAN—See HOSPERS, IA (HTC Communications)

ODEBOLT—Sac County Mutual Telco

OELWEIN—Mediacom. Now served by WAVERLY, IA [IA0021]

OELWEIN—See WAVERLY, IA (Mediacom)

OGDEN—Ogden Telephone Co. Cablevision

OKOBOJI—See SPIRIT LAKE, IA (Mediacom)

OLDS—Farmers & Merchants Mutual Telephone. Formerly served by Wayland, IA [IA0525]. This cable system has converted to IPTV

OLIN—Olin Telephone & Cablevision Co

ONAWA—Long Lines. Now served by SALIX, IA [IA0510]

ONAWA—See SALIX, IA (Long Lines)

ONSLOW—Onslow Cooperative Telephone Assn

ORANGE CITY—Formerly served by Orange City Communications. Now served by Long Lines, SALIX, IA [IA0510]

ORANGE CITY—Premier Communications. Now served by SIOUX CENTER, IA [IA0076]

ORANGE CITY—See SALIX, IA (Long Lines)

ORANGE CITY—See SIOUX CENTER, IA (Premier Communications)

ORLEANS—See SPIRIT LAKE, IA (Mediacom)

OSAGE—Mediacom

OSAGE—See RUDD, IA (Omnitel Communications)

OSAGE—Osage Municipal Utilities

OSCEOLA—See CHARITON, IA (Mediacom)

OSKALOOSA—Mediacom

OSSIAN—See CALMAR, IA (Mediacom)

OTHO—See LEHIGH, IA (Lehigh Valley Cooperative Telephone Assn. Formerly LEHIGH, IA [IA0464]. This cable system has converted to IPTV)

OTO—See LAWTON (village), IA (Wiatel)

OTTUMWA—Mediacom

OXFORD JUNCTION—See LOST NATION, IA (LN Satellite. Formerly [IA0279]. This cable system has converted to IPTV)

OXFORD JUNCTION—Mediacom

OXFORD—See NORTH LIBERTY, IA (Mediacom)

OXFORD—See ELY, IA (South Slope Coop. Communications Co. Formerly served by NORTH LIBERTY, IA [IA0432]. This cable system has converted to IPTV)

OYENS—See MARCUS, IA (WesTel Systems)

PALMER—Palmer Mutual Telephone Co

PALO—Palo Cooperative Telephone Association

PANAMA—See IRWIN, IA (Mutual Communications Services)

PANORA—Panora Communications Cooperative

PARALTA—See SPRINGVILLE, IA (Springville Cooperative Telephone Assn Inc)

PARKERSBURG—See WAVERLY, IA (Mediacom)

PATON—Gowrie Cablevision. Now served by GOWRIE, IA [IA0439]

PATON—See GOWRIE, IA (Gowrie Cablevision)

PAULINA—Formerly served by WesTel Systems. Now served by Community Cable TV Agency of O'Brien County, SANBORN, IA [IA0104]

PAULINA—See SANBORN, IA (Community Cable TV Agency of O'Brien County)

PELLA—See NEWTON, IA (Mediacom)

PEOSTA—See DUBUQUE, IA (Mediacom)

PERRY—See DEXTER, IA (Mediacom)

PERRY—See MINBURN, IA (Minburn Cablevision Inc.)

Cable Community Index—Iowa

PERSIA—Formerly served by TelePartners. Now served by Walnut Communications, WALNUT, IA [IA0241]

PERSIA—See WALNUT, IA (Walnut Communications)

PETERSON—WesTel Systems. Now served by MARCUS, IA [IA0171]

PETERSON—See MARCUS, IA (WesTel Systems)

PIERSON—See CLEGHORN, IA (Wetherell Cable TV System)

PISGAH—Formerly served by TelePartners. No longer in operation

PLAINFIELD—See TRIPOLI, IA (Butler-Bremer Communications)

PLEASANT HILL—See DES MOINES, IA (Mediacom)

PLEASANTVILLE—See HAMILTON, IA (Mediacom)

PLOVER—See HAVELOCK, IA (Northwest Telephone Cooperative Association)

PLYMOUTH COUNTY—See SIOUX CENTER, IA (Premier Communications)

PLYMOUTH—OmniTel Communications. This system has converted to IPTV. See PLYMOUTH, IA [IA5127]

PLYMOUTH—See RUDD, IA (Omnitel Communications. This system has converted to IPTV)

POCAHONTAS—See FORT DODGE, IA (Mediacom)

POLK CITY—See AMES, IA (Mediacom)

POLK COUNTY (NORTHWESTERN PORTION)—See AMES, IA (Mediacom)

POLK—See DES MOINES, IA (Mediacom)

POMEROY—Formerly served by TelePartners. No longer in operation

POSTVILLE—CenturyLink

POWERSVILLE (VILLAGE)—See MURRAY, MO (GRM Networks)

POWESHIEK COUNTY (PORTIONS)—See NEWTON, IA (Mediacom)

PRAIRIE CITY—See NEWTON, IA (Mediacom)

PRAIRIEBURG—Prairieburg Telephone Co

PRESTON—Mediacom

PRIMGHAR—See SANBORN, IA (Community Cable TV Agency of O'Brien County)

PRINCETON—See MURRAY, IA (GRM Networks)

PROPHETSTOWN—See CLINTON, IL (Mediacom)

PROTIVIN—Protivin Cablevision

PULASKI—See BLOOMFIELD, IA (Citizens Mutual Telephone)

QUASQUETON—See WINTHROP, IA (East Buchanan Telephone Cooperative)

QUIMBY—See MARCUS, IA (WesTel Systems)

RADCLIFFE—Radcliffe Cablevision. This cable system has converted to IPTV. See RADCLIFFE, IA [IA5020]

RADCLIFFE—Radcliffe Cablevision. Formerly [IA0265]. This cable system has converted to IPTV

RANDALL—See AMES, IA (Mediacom)

RANDOLPH—Formerly served by Westcom. No longer in operation

RAYMOND—See WATERLOO, IA (Mediacom)

READLYN—RTC Communications (formerly Readlyn Telephone Co.) This cable system has converted to IPTV. See READLYN, IA [IA5325]

READLYN—RTC Communications. This cable system has converted to IPTV

RED OAK—Mediacom

REDFIELD—See DEXTER, IA (Mediacom)

REINBECK—See WAVERLY, IA (Mediacom)

REMBRANDT—See CLEGHORN, IA (Wetherell Cable TV System)

REMSEN—See MARCUS, IA (WesTel Systems)

RENWICK—Formerly served by Heck's TV & Cable. Now served by Goldfield Communication Services, GOLDFIELD, IA [IA0252]

RENWICK—See GOLDFIELD, IA (Goldfield Communication Services Corp)

RHODES—See GILMAN, IA (Partner Communications)

RICEVILLE—See RUDD, IA (Omnitel Communications. This system has converted to IPTV)

RICHLAND—Starwest Inc

RINGSTED—Ringsted Cablevision

RIVERSIDE—See WASHINGTON, IA (Mediacom)

ROBINS—See SHELLSBURG, IA (USA Communications)

ROCK CREEK LAKE—See GILMAN, IA (Partner Communications)

ROCK FALLS—See RUDD, IA (Omnitel Communications. This system has converted to IPTV)

ROCK RAPIDS—Premier Communications. Now served by SIOUX CENTER, IA [IA0076]

ROCK RAPIDS—See SIOUX CENTER, IA (Premier Communications)

ROCK VALLEY—See SIOUX CENTER, IA (Premier Communications)

ROCKFORD—See RUDD, IA (Omnitel Communications)

ROCKWELL CITY—See FORT DODGE, IA (Mediacom)

ROCKWELL—See HAMPTON, IA (Mediacom)

RODNEY—See LAWTON (village), IA (Wiatel)

ROLAND—See STRATFORD, IA (Stratford Mutual Telephone)

ROLFE—See HAVELOCK, IA (Northwest Telephone Cooperative Association)

ROWLEY (village)—Formerly served by New Path Communications LC. No longer in operation

ROYAL—Royal Telephone Co

RUDD—Omnitel Communications. This system has converted to IPTV

RUDD—Omnitel Communications

RUNNELLS—Formerly served by Telnet South LC. No longer in operation

RUSSELL—Formerly served by Longview Communications. No longer in operation

RUTHVEN—Formerly served by Terril Cable Systems. No longer in operation

RYAN—USA Communications. Now served by SHELLSBURG, IA [IA0255]

RYAN—See SHELLSBURG, IA (USA Communications)

SABULA—See CLINTON, IA (Mediacom)

SAC CITY—See FORT DODGE, IA (Mediacom)

SAGEVILLE—See DUBUQUE, IA (Mediacom)

SALEM—Formerly served by Longview Communications. No longer in operation

SALIX—Long Lines

SANBORN—Community Cable TV Agency of O'Brien County

SANBORN—See SIOUX CENTER, IA (Premier Communications)

SAVANNA—See CLINTON, IL (Mediacom)

SCHALLER—Comserv Ltd

SCHLESWIG—Formerly served by Tip Top Communications. No longer in operation

SCRANTON—Scranton Community Antenna Television

SERGEANT BLUFF—See SIOUX CITY, IA (Cable One)

SERGEANT BLUFF—See SALIX, IA (Long Lines)

SEYMOUR—Formerly served by Longview Communications. No longer in operation

SHEFFIELD—See HAMPTON, IA (Mediacom)

SHELBY—Walnut Communications. Now served by WALNUT, IA [IA0241]

SHELBY—See WALNUT, IA (Walnut Communications)

SHELDAHL—See AMES, IA (Mediacom)

SHELDON—See HOSPERS, IA (HTC Communications)

SHELL ROCK—See WAVERLY, IA (Mediacom)

SHELLSBURG—USA Communications

SHENANDOAH—See RED OAK, IA (Mediacom)

SHERRILL—Formerly served by Alpine Communications LC. No longer in operation

SHUEYVILLE—See NORTH LIBERTY, IA (Mediacom)

SHUEYVILLE—See ELY, IA (South Slope Coop. Communications Co. Formerly served by NORTH LIBERTY, IA [IA0432]. This cable system has converted to IPTV)

SIBLEY—HTC Communications. Now served by HOSPERS, IA [IA0060]

SIBLEY—See HOSPERS, IA (HTC Communications)

SIDNEY (TOWN)—Rock Port Cablevision

SIGOURNEY—Mediacom. Now served by KEOTA, IA [IA0632]

SIGOURNEY—See KEOTA, IA (Mediacom)

SILVER CITY—Formerly served by Interstate Communications. No longer in operation

SIOUX CENTER—Premier Communications

SIOUX CITY—Cable One

SIOUX RAPIDS—WesTel Systems. Now served by MARCUS, IA [IA0171]

SIOUX RAPIDS—See MARCUS, IA (WesTel Systems)

SLATER—See AMES, IA (Mediacom)

SLOAN—See SALIX, IA (Long Lines)

SMITHLAND—Formerly served by TelePartners. Now served by Wiatel, LAWTON (village), IA [IA0330]

SMITHLAND—See LAWTON (village), IA (Wiatel)

SOLDIER—Formerly served by Soldier Valley Telephone. Now served by Long Lines, SALIX, IA [IA0510]

SOLDIER—Long Lines. Now served by SALIX, IA [IA0510]

SOLDIER—See SALIX, IA (Long Lines)

SOLON MILLS—See NORTH LIBERTY, IL (Mediacom)

SOLON—See ELY, IA (South Slope Coop. Communications Co. Formerly served by NORTH LIBERTY, IA [IA0432]. This cable system has converted to IPTV)

SOUTH SIOUX CITY—See SIOUX CITY, NE (Cable One)

Iowa—Cable Community Index

SOUTH SIOUX CITY—See SALIX, NE (Long Lines)

SPENCER—See ESTHERVILLE, IA (Mediacom)

SPENCER—SMU Cable TV

SPILLVILLE—See CALMAR, IA (Mediacom)

SPIRIT LAKE—Mediacom

SPRINGVILLE—Springville Cooperative Telephone Assn Inc

ST. ANSGAR—See RUDD, IA (Omnitel Communications. This system has converted to IPTV)

ST. ANTHONY—See ZEARING, IA (Minerva Valley Cablevision)

ST. CHARLES—Interstate Communications. Now served by TRURO, IA [IA0344]

ST. CHARLES—See TRURO, IA (Interstate Communications)

ST. DONATUS—See LAMOTTE, IA (LaMotte Telephone Co)

ST. LUCAS—Formerly served by Alpine Communications LC. No longer in operation

ST. MARYS—See TRURO, IA (Interstate Communications)

ST. OLAF—See MONONA, IA (Northeast Iowa Telephone Co)

STACEYVILLE—See RUDD, IA (Omnitel Communications)

STACYVILLE—See RUDD, IA (Omnitel Communications. This system has converted to IPTV)

STANTON—Farmers Mutual Telephone Co

STANWOOD—Clarence Cablevision. Now served by CLARENCE, IA [IA0213]

STANWOOD—See CLARENCE, IA (Clarence Cablevision)

STATE CENTER—Partner Communications. Now served by GILMAN, IA [IA0128]

STATE CENTER—See GILMAN, IA (Partner Communications)

STEAMBOAT ROCK—Formerly served by Steamboat Rock Cablevision. No longer in operation

STEAMBOAT ROCK—See UNION, IA (Heart of Iowa Communications. Formerly [IA0521]. This cable system has converted to IPTV.)

STOCKPORT—See KEOSAUQUA, IA (Starwest Inc)

STONE CITY—See MARTELLE, IA (Martelle Communications Co-op)

STORM LAKE—Clarity Telecom. Now served by VIBORG, SD [SD0071]

STORM LAKE—Mediacom

STORY CITY—See AMES, IA (Mediacom)

STORY COUNTY—See AMES, IA (Mediacom)

STRATFORD—Stratford Mutual Telephone. This cable system has converted to IPTV. See STRATFORD, IA [IA5024]

STRATFORD—Stratford Mutual Telephone

STRAWBERRY POINT—Mediacom. Now served by WAVERLY, IA [IA0021]

STRAWBERRY POINT—See WAVERLY, IA (Mediacom)

STUART—See DEXTER, IA (Mediacom)

SULLY—See NEWTON, IA (Mediacom)

SUMNER—See CALMAR, IA (Mediacom)

SUN VALLEY LAKE—Formerly served by Interstate Communications. This cable system has converted to IPTV. Now served by GRM Networks, MURRAY, IA [IA5135]

SUN VALLEY LAKE—See MURRAY, IA (GRM Networks)

SUTHERLAND—WesTel Systems. Now served by MARCUS, IA [IA0171]

SUTHERLAND—See MARCUS, IA (WesTel Systems)

SWALEDALE (village)—Formerly served by New Path Communications LC. No longer in operation

SWEA CITY—Mediacom

SWISHER—See NORTH LIBERTY, IA (Mediacom)

SWISHER—See ELY, IA (South Slope Coop. Communications Co. Formerly served by NORTH LIBERTY, IA [IA0432]. This cable system has converted to IPTV)

TABOR—Rock Port Cablevision

TAMA COUNTY (PORTIONS)—See GLADBROOK, IA (Mediacom)

TAMA—See GLADBROOK, IA (Mediacom)

TEMPLETON—Templeton Telephone Co

TENNANT—See IRWIN, IA (Mutual Communications Services)

TERRIL—Terril Telephone Cooperative. This cable system has converted to IPTV. See TERRIL, IA [IA5327]

TERRIL—Terril Telephone Cooperative

THOMPSON—Winnebago Cooperative Telecom Assn. Now served by LAKE MILLS, IA [IA0590]

THOMPSON—See LAKE MILLS, IA (Winnebago Cooperative Telecom Assn)

THOMSON—See CLINTON, IL (Mediacom)

THOR—Milford Cable TV

THORNTON—Rockwell Communications Systems Inc

THURMAN—Formerly served by Tele-Services Ltd. No longer in operation

TIFFIN—See NORTH LIBERTY, IA (Mediacom)

TIFFIN—See ELY, IA (South Slope Coop. Communications Co. Formerly served by NORTH LIBERTY, IA [IA0432]. This cable system has converted to IPTV)

TIPTON—See OXFORD JUNCTION, IA (Mediacom)

TITONKA—Titonka-Burt Communications

TOLEDO—Mediacom. Now served by AMES, IA [IA0008]

TOLEDO—See AMES, IA (Mediacom)

TORONTO—Formerly served by F&B Communications. No longer in operation

TRAER—Mediacom. Now served by AMES, IA [IA0008]

TRAER—See AMES, IA (Mediacom)

TREYNOR—Formerly served by Our Cable. No longer in operation

TRIPOLI—Butler-Bremer Communications

TRURO—Interstate Communications

UNDERWOOD—Formerly served by TelePartners. Now served by Walnut Communications, WALNUT, IA [IA0241]

UNDERWOOD—See WALNUT, IA (Walnut Communications)

UNION COUNTY (PORTIONS)—See SIOUX CITY, SD (Cable One)

UNION GROVE VILLAGE—Heart of Iowa Telecommunications. This cable system has converted to IPTV. See UNION, IA [IA5001]

UNION—Heart of Iowa Communications. Formerly [IA0521]. This cable system has converted to IPTV.

UNIVERSITY HEIGHTS—See IOWA CITY, IA (Mediacom)

UNIVERSITY PARK—See OSKALOOSA, IA (Mediacom)

URBANA—See SHELLSBURG, IA (USA Communications)

URBANDALE—See DES MOINES, IA (Mediacom)

UTE—Long Lines. Now served by SALIX, IA [IA0510]

UTE—See SALIX, IA (Long Lines)

VAIL—Formerly served by Tip Top Communications. No longer in operation

VAN HORNE—Van Horne Telephone Co

VAN METER—See DEXTER, IA (Mediacom)

VAN WERT—Formerly served by B & L Technologies LLC. No longer in operation

VENTURA—See MASON CITY, IA (Mediacom)

VILLISCA—See RED OAK, IA (Mediacom)

VINCENT—See THOR, IA (Milford Cable TV)

VINTON—Mediacom

VIOLA—See SPRINGVILLE, IA (Springville Cooperative Telephone Assn Inc)

VOLGA—Formerly served by Alpine Communications LC. No longer in operation

WADENA (village)—Formerly served by Alpine Communications LC. No longer in operation

WAHPETON—See SPIRIT LAKE, IA (Mediacom)

WALFORD—See ELY, IA (South Slope Coop. Communications Co. Formerly served by NORTH LIBERTY, IA [IA0432]. This cable system has converted to IPTV)

WALKER—Formerly served by Mid American Cable Systems. No longer in operation

WALL LAKE—Corn Belt Telephone Co

WALLINGFORD—See ESTHERVILLE, IA (Mediacom)

WALLINGFORD—See GRAETTINGER, IA (River Valley Telecommunications Coop)

WALNUT—Walnut Communications

WAPELLO COUNTY—See OTTUMWA, IA (Mediacom)

WAPPELLO—See BURLINGTON, IA (Mediacom)

WARREN COUNTY (PORTIONS)—See DES MOINES, IA (Mediacom)

WARSAW—See KEOKUK, IL (Mediacom)

WASHBURN—See WATERLOO, IA (Mediacom)

WASHINGTON—Mediacom

WASHTA—See CLEGHORN, IA (Wetherell Cable TV System)

WATERLOO—Formerly served by Wireless Cable TV of Waterloo. No longer in operation

WATERLOO—Mediacom

WATKINS—See ELY, IA (South Slope Coop. Communications Co. Formerly served by NORTH LIBERTY, IA [IA0432]. This cable system has converted to IPTV)

WAUKEE—See DES MOINES, IA (Mediacom)

WAVERLY—Mediacom

WAYLAND—Farmers & Merchants Mutual Telephone. This cable system has converted to IPTV. See WAYLAND, IA [IA5076]

WAYLAND—Farmers & Merchants Mutual Telephone. Formerly served by Wayland, IA [IA0525]. This cable system has converted to IPTV

WAYNE COUNTY (PORTIONS)—See CHARITON, IA (Mediacom)

WEBB—See SIOUX CENTER, IA (Premier Communications)

WEBSTER CITY—See FORT DODGE, IA (Mediacom)

WEBSTER COUNTY—See FORT DODGE, IA (Mediacom)

WELLMAN—See WASHINGTON, IA (Mediacom)

WELLSBURG—Formerly served by Union Cablevision. No longer in operation

WESLEY—Formerly served by Comm1. No longer in operation

WESLEY—Formerly served by Comm1. No longer in operation

WEST BEND—See HAVELOCK, IA (Northwest Telephone Cooperative Association)

WEST BRANCH—See NORTH LIBERTY, IA (Mediacom)

WEST BURLINGTON—See BURLINGTON, IA (Mediacom)

WEST DES MOINES—See DES MOINES, IA (Mediacom)

WEST LIBERTY—See NORTH LIBERTY, IA (Mediacom)

WEST OKOBOJI—See SPIRIT LAKE, IA (Mediacom)

WEST POINT—See FORT MADISON, IA (Mediacom)

WEST UNION—See CALMAR, IA (Mediacom)

WESTGATE (village)—Formerly served by Alpine Communications LC. No longer in operation

WESTPHALIA—See IRWIN, IA (Mutual Communications Services)

WESTSIDE—Western Iowa Networks. Now served by BREDA, IA [IA0318]

WESTSIDE—See BREDA, IA (Western Iowa Networks)

WESTWOOD—See FORT MADISON, IA (Mediacom)

WHAT CHEER—See KEOTA, IA (Mediacom)

WHEATLAND—F&B Communications. This cable system has converted to IPTV. Now served by WHEATLAND, IA [IA5105]

WHEATLAND—F&B Communications. Formerly [IA0529]. This cable system has converted to IPTV.

WHITESIDE COUNTY (PORTIONS)—See CLINTON, IL (Mediacom)

WHITING—Long Lines. Now served by SALIX, IA [IA0510]

WHITING—See SALIX, IA (Long Lines)

WHITTEMORE—ATC Cablevision. Now served by GILLETT GROVE, IA [IA0386]

WHITTEMORE—See GILLETT GROVE, IA (ATC Cablevision)

WHITTEN—See UNION, IA (Heart of Iowa Communications. Formerly [IA0521]. This cable system has converted to IPTV.)

WHITTIER—See SPRINGVILLE, IA (Springville Cooperative Telephone Assn Inc)

WILLIAMS—Formerly served by Williams Cablevision. No longer in operation

WILLIAMSBURG—Mediacom

WILTON—See MUSCATINE, IA (MPW Cable)

WINDSOR HEIGHTS—See DES MOINES, IA (Mediacom)

WINFIELD—Formerly served by Longview Communications. No longer in operation

WINTERSET—See CHARITON, IA (Mediacom)

WINTHROP—East Buchanan Telephone Cooperative

WODEN—Formerly served by Heck's TV & Cable. No longer in operation

WOODBINE—See SALIX, IA (Long Lines)

WOODBURN—Formerly served by Telnet South LC. Now served by Mediacom, CHARITON, IA [IA0017]

WOODBURN—See CHARITON, IA (Mediacom)

WOODBURY COUNTY—See SIOUX CITY, IA (Cable One)

WOODWARD—See AMES, IA (Mediacom)

WOODWARD—See MINBURN, IA (Minburn Cablevision Inc.)

WOOLSTOCK—Goldfield Communication Services Corp. Now served by GOLDFIELD, IA [IA0252]

WOOLSTOCK—See GOLDFIELD, IA (Goldfield Communication Services Corp)

WORTHINGTON—New Century Communications. Now served by WORTHINGTON, IA [IA0613]

WORTHINGTON—New Century Communications

WRIGHT COUNTY (CENTRAL PORTION)—See FORT DODGE, IA (Mediacom)

WYOMING—See OXFORD JUNCTION, IA (Mediacom)

YALE—See PANORA, IA (Panora Communications Cooperative)

ZEARING—Minerva Valley Cablevision

ZWINGLE—See LAMOTTE, IA (LaMotte Telephone Co)

KANSAS

ABBYVILLE—Formerly served by Cox Communications. No longer in operation

ABILENE—Eagle Communications

AGRA—Nex-Tech. Formerly served by LENORA, KS [KS0450]. This cable system has converted to IPTV

ALBERT (RURAL PORTIONS)—See RUSH CENTER, KS (GBT Communications Inc)

ALBERT—See RUSH CENTER, KS (GBT Communications Inc)

ALEXANDER (RURAL PORTIONS)—See RUSH CENTER, KS (GBT Communications Inc)

ALEXANDER—See RUSH CENTER, KS (GBT Communications Inc)

ALLEN COUNTY (PORTIONS)—See PITTSBURG, KS (Cox Communications)

ALMA—Formerly served by Zito Media. No longer in operation

ALMENA—Nex-Tech. This cable system has converted to IPTV. See ALMENA, KS [KS5146]

ALMENA—Nex-Tech. Formerly [KS0360]. This cable system has converted to IPTV

ALTA VISTA—Formerly served by Galaxy Cablevision. No longer in operation

ALTAMONT—Wave Wireless

ALTON—See WOODSTON, KS (Nex-Tech. Formerly [KS0306]. This cable system has converted to IPTV)

ALTOONA—Mediacom

AMERICUS—Zito Media

AMORET—See GIRARD, MO (Craw-Kan)

AMSTERDAM—See GIRARD, MO (Craw-Kan)

ANDALE—Formerly served by Almega Cable. No longer in operation

ANDOVER—See WICHITA, KS (Cox Communications)

ANTHONY—Suddenlink Communications

ARCADIA—Formerly served by National Cable Inc. No longer in operation

ARCADIA—See GIRARD, KS (Craw-Kan)

ARGONIA—Formerly served by Almega Cable. No longer in operation

ARKANSAS CITY—See WICHITA, KS (Cox Communications)

ARLINGTON—Formerly served by Almega Cable. No longer in operation

ARMA—See PITTSBURG, KS (Cox Communications)

ARMA—See GIRARD, KS (Craw-Kan)

ASBURY—See GIRARD, MO (Craw-Kan)

ASHLAND—Formerly served by Cebridge Connections. Now served by United Communications Assn. Inc., CIMARRON, KS [KS0126]

ASHLAND—See CIMARRON, KS (United Communications Assn. Inc)

ASSARIA—Home Communications Inc. Formerly [KS0363]. This cable system has converted to IPTV. Now served by GALVA, KS [KS5068]

ASSARIA—Home Communications Inc. This cable system has converted to IPTV. Now served by GALVA, KS [KS5068]

ASSARIA—See GALVA, KS (Home Communications Inc)

ATCHISON COUNTY (PORTIONS)—See ATCHISON, KS (Vyve Broadband)

ATCHISON—Vyve Broadband

ATLANTA—See CLEARWATER, KS (SKT Entertainment)

ATTICA (village)—Formerly served by Almega Cable. No longer in operation

ATWOOD—Atwood Cable Systems Inc

AUBURN—See TOPEKA, KS (Cox Communications)

AUGUSTA—See WICHITA, KS (Cox Communications)

AURORA—See MILTONVALE, KS (Twin Valley Communications. Formerly served by BENNINGTON, KS [KS0214]. This cable system has converted to IPTV)

AXTELL—Blue Valley Tele-Communications. Now served by AXTELL (formerly Frankfort & Home), KS [KS0424]

AXTELL—Blue Valley Tele-Communications

BAILEYVILLE—Formerly served by Rainbow Communications. No longer in operation

BALDWIN CITY—Mediacom. Now served by BURLINGTON, KS [KS0064]

BALDWIN CITY—See BURLINGTON, KS (Mediacom)

BARBER COUNTY (PORTIONS)—See MEDICINE LODGE, KS (Vyve Broadband)

BARNARD—See MILTONVALE, KS (Twin Valley Communications. Formerly served by BENNINGTON, KS [KS0214]. This cable system has

Kansas—Cable Community Index

converted to IPTV)

BARNES—Formerly served by Eagle Communications. No longer in operation

BARTLETT—See GIRARD, KS (Craw-Kan)

BARTON COUNTY—See GREAT BEND, KS (Cox Communications)

BASEHOR—Formerly served by Knology (formerly Sunflower Broadband). Now served by WOW! Internet, Cable & Phone, LAWRENCE, KS [KS0004]

BASEHOR—See LAWRENCE, KS (WOW! Internet, Cable & Phone)

BAXTER SPRINGS—City of Baxter Springs

BAZINE (RURAL PORTIONS)—See RUSH CENTER, KS (GBT Communications Inc)

BAZINE—Formerly served by Cebridge Connections. Now served by GBT Communications Inc., RUSH CENTER, KS [KS5143]

BAZINE—See RUSH CENTER, KS (GBT Communications Inc)

BEATTIE—Formerly served by Allegiance Communications. No longer in operation

BEELER (RURAL PORTIONS)—See RUSH CENTER, KS (GBT Communications Inc)

BEELER—See RUSH CENTER, KS (GBT Communications Inc)

BEL AIRE—See WICHITA, KS (Cox Communications)

BELLE PLAINE—SKT Entertainment. Now served by CLEARWATER, KS [KS0136]

BELLE PLAINE—See CLEARWATER, KS (SKT Entertainment)

BELLEVILLE—Cunningham Cable TV. Now served by GLEN ELDER, KS [KS0228]

BELLEVILLE—See GLEN ELDER, KS (Cunningham Cable)

BELOIT—Cunningham Cable TV. Now served by GLEN ELDER, KS [KS0228]

BELOIT—See GLEN ELDER, KS (Cunningham Cable)

BELVUE—Formerly served by Giant Communications. No longer in operation

BELVUE—See WAMEGO, KS (WTC Communications)

BELVUE—See WAMEGO, KS (WTC Communications)

BENNINGTON—Twin Valley Communications. This system has converted to IPTV. Now served by MILTONVALE, KS [KS5032]

BENNINGTON—See MINNEAPOLIS, KS (Eagle Communications)

BENNINGTON—See MILTONVALE, KS (Twin Valley Communications. Formerly served by BENNINGTON, KS [KS0214]. This cable system has converted to IPTV)

BENTLEY—IdeaTek Communications LLC

BERN—Formerly served by Rainbow Communications. No longer in operation

BERRYTON—See TOPEKA, KS (Cox Communications)

BEVERLY—See MILTONVALE, KS (Twin Valley Communications. Formerly served by BENNINGTON, KS [KS0214]. This cable system has converted to IPTV)

BIG BOW—See ULYSSES, KS (Pioneer Communications)

BIRD CITY—See McDONALD, KS (Eagle Communications)

BISON (RURAL PORTIONS)—See RUSH CENTER, KS (GBT Communications Inc)

BISON—See RUSH CENTER, KS (GBT Communications Inc)

BLUE MOUND—Formerly served by National Cable Inc. No longer in operation

BLUE RAPIDS—Zito Media

BOURBON COUNTY (UNINCORPORATED AREAS)—See FORT SCOTT, KS (Suddenlink Communications)

BRAZILTON—See GIRARD, KS (Craw-Kan)

BREWSTER—S&T Cable

BRIDGEPORT—See GALVA, KS (Home Communications Inc)

BRONSON—See GIRARD, KS (Craw-Kan)

BROOKVILLE—Wilson Communications. Now served by BROOKVILLE, KS [KS0162]

BROOKVILLE—Wilson Communications

BROWNELL (RURAL PORTIONS)—See RUSH CENTER, KS (GBT Communications Inc)

BROWNELL—See RUSH CENTER, KS (GBT Communications Inc)

BUCHANAN COUNTY—See ATCHISON, MO (Vyve Broadband)

BUCKLIN—United Communications Assn. Inc. Now served by CIMARRON, KS [KS0126]

BUCKLIN—See CIMARRON, KS (United Communications Assn. Inc)

BUFFALO—Formerly served by National Cable Inc. No longer in operation

BUHLER—Formerly served by Vyve Broadband. No longer in operation

BURDEN—SKT Entertainment. Now served by CLEARWATER, KS [KS0136]

BURDEN—See CLEARWATER, KS (SKT Entertainment)

BURDETT (RURAL PORTIONS)—See RUSH CENTER, KS (GBT Communications Inc)

BURDETT—See RUSH CENTER, KS (GBT Communications Inc)

BURLINGAME—See BURLINGTON, KS (Mediacom)

BURLINGTON—Mediacom

BURNS—Formerly served by Blue Sky Cable LLC. No longer in operation

BURR OAK—Nex-Tech. This cable system has converted to IPTV. See BURR OAK, KS [KS5042]

BURR OAK—Nex-Tech. Formerly [KS0265]. This cable system has converted to IPTV

BURRTON—Formerly served by Cebridge Connections. No longer in operation

BURRTON—Formerly served by Cebridge Connections. No longer in operation

BURRTON—See WICHITA, KS (Cox Communications)

BUSHTON (RURAL)—See HOLYROOD, KS (H&B Communications. This system has converted to IPTV)

BUSHTON—See HOLYROOD, KS (H&B Communications. This system has converted to IPTV)

BUTLER COUNTY (PORTIONS)—See WICHITA, KS (Cox Communications)

BUTLER COUNTY (PORTIONS)—See UDALL, KS (Wheat State Telecable Inc.)

CALDWELL—Formerly served by Almega Cable. No longer in operation

CANEY—See PITTSBURG, KS (Cox Communications)

CANTON—Formerly served by Cox Communications. No longer in operation

CANTON—Formerly served by Home Communications Inc. No longer in operation

CANTON—See GALVA, KS (Home Communications Inc)

CARBONDALE—See BURLINGTON, KS (Mediacom)

CASSODAY—See UDALL, KS (Wheat State Telecable Inc.)

CAWKER CITY—Formerly served by City of Cawker City. Now served by Blue Valley Tele-Communications, GLEN ELDER, KS [KS0228]

CAWKER CITY—See GLEN ELDER, KS (Cunningham Cable)

CEDAR VALE—See CLEARWATER, KS (SKT Entertainment)

CENTRALIA—Blue Valley Tele-Communications. Now served by AXTELL (formerly Frankfort & Home), KS [KS0424]

CENTRALIA—See AXTELL, KS (Blue Valley Tele-Communications)

CHANUTE—Cable One

CHAPMAN—Eagle Communications. Now served by ABILENE, KS [KS0034]

CHAPMAN—See ABILENE, KS (Eagle Communications)

CHASE COUNTY (PORTIONS)—See UDALL, KS (Wheat State Telecable Inc.)

CHASE—H&B Communications

CHENEY—See WICHITA, KS (Cox Communications)

CHEROKEE COUNTY (NORTHERN PORTION)—See PITTSBURG, KS (Cox Communications)

CHEROKEE—See GIRARD, KS (Craw-Kan)

CHERRYVALE—See PITTSBURG, KS (Cox Communications)

CHETOPA—Formerly served by Allegiance Communications. No longer in operation

CHICOPEE—See PITTSBURG, KS (Cox Communications)

CIMARRON—United Communications Assn. Inc

CIRCLEVILLE—See HOLTON, KS (Giant Communications)

CLAFLIN—See HOLYROOD, KS (H&B Communications. This system has converted to IPTV)

CLAY CENTER—Eagle Communications. Now served by ABILENE, KS [KS0034]

CLAY CENTER—See ABILENE, KS (Eagle Communications)

CLAY CENTER—See MILTONVALE, KS (Twin Valley Communications. Formerly served by BENNINGTON, KS [KS0214]. This cable system has converted to IPTV)

CLAY COUNTY (PORTIONS)—See ABILENE, KS (Eagle Communications)

CLEARWATER—SKT Entertainment

CLIFTON—Formerly served by Zito Media. No longer in operation

CLIFTON—See MILTONVALE, KS (Twin Valley Communications. Formerly served by BENNINGTON, KS [KS0214]. This cable system has converted to IPTV)

CLYDE—See MILTONVALE, KS (Twin Valley Communications. Formerly served by BENNINGTON, KS [KS0214]. This cable system has converted to IPTV)

COFFEYVILLE—Cox Communications. Now served by PITTSBURG, KS [KS0011]

Cable Community Index—Kansas

COFFEYVILLE—See PITTSBURG, KS (Cox Communications)

COLBY—S&T Cable. Now served by BREWSTER, KS [KS0315]

COLBY—See BREWSTER, KS (S&T Cable)

COLDWATER—United Communications Assn. Inc. Now served by CIMARRON, KS [KS0126]

COLDWATER—See CIMARRON, KS (United Communications Assn. Inc)

COLLYER—See GRAINFIELD, KS (Nex-Tech. Formerly [KS0381]. This cable system has converted to IPTV)

COLUMBUS—Columbus Telephone Co. This cable system has converted to IPTV. See COLUMBUS, KS [KS5041]

COLUMBUS—Columbus Telephone Co. Formerly [KS0056]. This cable system has converted to IPTV

COLUMBUS—See GIRARD, KS (Craw-Kan)

COLWICH—Formerly served by Almega Cable. No longer in operation

CONCORDIA—Cunningham Cable TV. Now served by GLEN ELDER, KS [KS0228]

CONCORDIA—See GLEN ELDER, KS (Cunningham Cable)

CONWAY SPRINGS—Formerly served by Allegiance Communications. No longer in operation

COOLIDGE—See ULYSSES, KS (Pioneer Communications)

COPELAND—United Communications Assn. Inc. Now served by CIMARRON, KS [KS0126]

COPELAND—See CIMARRON, KS (United Communications Assn. Inc)

COTTONWOOD FALLS—See STRONG CITY, KS (Zito Media)

COUNCIL GROVE—Tri-County Telecom (TCT). This cable system has converted to IPTV. See COUNCIL GROVE, KS [KS5218]

COUNCIL GROVE—TCT. This cable system has converted to IPTV

COURTLAND—Nex-Tech. This cable system has converted to IPTV. See COURTLAND, KS [KS5043]

COURTLAND—Nex-Tech. Formerly [KS0271]. This cable system has converted to IPTV

CRAWFORD COUNTY (EASTERN PORTION)—See PITTSBURG, KS (Cox Communications)

CUBA—Formerly served by Eagle Communications. No longer in operation

CUNNINGHAM—Cox Communications. Now served by WICHITA, KS [KS0001]

CUNNINGHAM—See WICHITA, KS (Cox Communications)

DEARING—Formerly served by SKT Entertainment. Now served by Cox Communications, PITTSBURG, KS [KS0011]

DEARING—See PITTSBURG, KS (Cox Communications)

DEERFIELD—See ULYSSES, KS (Pioneer Communications)

DELPHOS—Formerly served by Cunningham Cable TV. No longer in operation

DELPHOS—See MILTONVALE, KS (Twin Valley Communications. Formerly served by BENNINGTON, KS [KS0214]. This cable system has converted to IPTV)

DENISON—Formerly served by Rainbow Communications. No longer in operation

DENSMORE—See EDMOND, KS (Nex-Tech. Formerly served by LENORA, KS [KS0450]. This cable system has converted to IPTV)

DERBY—See WICHITA, KS (Cox Communications)

DEXTER—See CLEARWATER, KS (SKT Entertainment)

DICKINSON COUNTY (PORTIONS)—See HERINGTON, KS (Vyve Broadband)

DICKINSON COUNTY—See ABILENE, KS (Eagle Communications)

DIGHTON—S&T Cable

DODGE CITY—Cox Communications

DORRANCE (RURAL)—See HOLYROOD, KS (H&B Communications. This system has converted to IPTV)

DORRANCE—See CHASE, KS (H&B Communications)

DOUGLAS COUNTY (UNINCORPORATED AREAS)—See LAWRENCE, KS (WOW! Internet, Cable & Phone)

DOUGLASS—Formerly served by Allegiance Communications. No longer in operation

DOWNS—Cunningham Cable TV. Now served by GLEN ELDER, KS [KS0228]

DOWNS—Formerly served by Cebridge Connections. No longer in operation

DOWNS—See GLEN ELDER, KS (Cunningham Cable)

DUBUQUE—See HOLYROOD, KS (H&B Communications. This system has converted to IPTV)

DURHAM—Formerly served by Eagle Communications. No longer in operation

DWIGHT—Formerly served by Eagle Communications. No longer in operation

EASTBOROUGH—See WICHITA, KS (Cox Communications)

EASTON—Formerly served by Giant Communications. No longer in operation

EDGERTON—See BURLINGTON, KS (Mediacom)

EDMOND—Nex-Tech. Formerly served by LENORA, KS [KS0450]. This cable system has converted to IPTV

EDNA—Craw-Kan. Now served by GIRARD, KS [KS0446]

EDNA—See GIRARD, KS (Craw-Kan)

EDNA—Formerly served by GIRARD, KS [KS0446]. Craw-Kan Telephone Co-op. This cable system has converted to IPTV

EFFINGHAM—Rainbow Communications. No longer in operation

EL DORADO—See WICHITA, KS (Cox Communications)

ELK CITY—Formerly served by SKT Entertainment. No longer in operation

ELK COUNTY—See CLEARWATER, KS (SKT Entertainment)

ELKHART—Epic Touch Co

ELLINWOOD—See HOLYROOD, KS (H&B Communications. This system has converted to IPTV)

ELLINWOOD—Vyve Broadband

ELLIS (RURAL PORTIONS)—See RUSH CENTER, KS (GBT Communications Inc)

ELLIS—See HAYS, KS (Eagle Communications)

ELLIS—See RUSH CENTER, KS (GBT Communications Inc)

ELLSWORTH—Eagle Communications

ELWOOD—See HIAWATHA, KS (Rainbow Communications)

EMMETT—Formerly served by Rainbow Communications. No longer in operation

EMPORIA—Cable One

ENSIGN—United Communications Assn. Inc. Now served by CIMARRON, KS [KS0126]

ENSIGN—See CIMARRON, KS (United Communications Assn. Inc)

ENTERPRISE—See ABILENE, KS (Eagle Communications)

ERIE—See PITTSBURG, KS (Cox Communications)

ESBON—See LEBANON, KS (Nex-Tech. Formerly [KS0397]. This cable system has converted to IPTV)

ESKRIDGE—Formerly served by Zito Media. No longer in operation

EUDORA—See LAWRENCE, KS (WOW! Internet, Cable & Phone)

EUREKA—Mediacom

EVEREST—See HIAWATHA, KS (Rainbow Communications)

FAIRVIEW—Formerly served by Carson Communications. Now served by Rainbow Communications, HIAWATHA, KS [KS0059]

FAIRVIEW—See HIAWATHA, KS (Rainbow Communications)

FAIRWAY—See LENEXA, KS (SureWest Communications. Formerly [KS0462]. This cable system has converted to IPTV)

FALUN—See GALVA, KS (Home Communications Inc)

FARLINGTON—See GIRARD, KS (Craw-Kan)

FINNEY COUNTY (PORTIONS)—See GARDEN CITY, KS (Cox Communications)

FLORENCE—See MARION, KS (Eagle Communications)

FORD COUNTY—See DODGE CITY, KS (Cox Communications)

FORD—United Communications Assn. Inc. Now served by CIMARRON, KS [KS0126]

FORD—See CIMARRON, KS (United Communications Assn. Inc)

FORMOSO—Cunningham Cable TV. Now served by GLEN ELDER, KS [KS0228]

FORMOSO—See GLEN ELDER, KS (Cunningham Cable)

FORT RILEY—Vyve Broadband

FORT SCOTT—Suddenlink Communications

FOWLER—See MEADE, KS (Vyve Broadband)

FRANKFORT—Blue Valley Tele-Communications. Now served by AXTELL, KS [KS0424]

FRANKFORT—See AXTELL, KS (Blue Valley Tele-Communications)

FRANKLIN—See PITTSBURG, KS (Cox Communications)

FREDONIA—Vyve Broadband

FRONTENAC—Formerly served by Almega Cable. No longer in operation

FRONTENAC—See PITTSBURG, KS (Cox Communications)

GALENA—Mediacom. Now served by CARL JUNCTION, MO [MO0094]

GALESBURG—See GIRARD, KS (Craw-Kan)

GALVA—Formerly served by Home Communications Inc. No longer in operation

GALVA—Home Communications Inc

GARDEN CITY—Cox Communications

GARDEN PLAIN (PORTIONS)—See WICHITA, KS (Cox Communications)

GARDEN PLAIN—Formerly served by Cebridge Connections. No longer in operation

Kansas—Cable Community Index

GARFIELD (RURAL PORTIONS)—See RUSH CENTER, KS (GBT Communications Inc)

GARFIELD—See RUSH CENTER, KS (GBT Communications Inc)

GARNETT—Vyve Broadband

GAS—See PITTSBURG, KS (Cox Communications)

GAYLORD—See WOODSTON, KS (Nex-Tech. Formerly [KS0306]. This cable system has converted to IPTV)

GENESEO—Formerly served by Eagle Communications. No longer in operation

GENESEO—See GALVA, KS (Home Communications Inc)

GIRARD—Formerly served by Craw-Kan Telephone Co-op. No longer in operation

GIRARD—Craw-Kan

GIRARD—Craw-Kan

GLASCO—Formerly served by Cunningham Cable TV. No longer in operation

GLASCO—See MILTONVALE, KS (Twin Valley Communications. Formerly served by BENNINGTON, KS [KS0214]. This cable system has converted to IPTV)

GLEN ELDER—Cunningham Cable

GODDARD—See WICHITA, KS (Cox Communications)

GOESSEL—Mid-Kansas Cable Services Inc. Now served by MOUNDRIDGE, KS [KS0133]

GOESSEL—See MOUNDRIDGE, KS (Mid-Kansas Cable Services Inc.)

GOFF—Formerly served by Rainbow Communications. No longer in operation

GOODLAND—S&T Cable. Now served by BREWSTER, KS [KS0315]

GOODLAND—Eagle Communications

GOODLAND—See BREWSTER, KS (S&T Cable)

GORHAM—Gorham Tele-Com (formerly Nex-Tech). This cable system has converted to IPTV. See GORHAM, KS [KS5164]

GORHAM—Gorham Tele-Com. Formerly [KS0380]. This cable system has converted to IPTV

GOVE—See GRAINFIELD, KS (Nex-Tech. Formerly [KS0381]. This cable system has converted to IPTV)

GRAINFIELD—Nex-Tech. This cable system has converted to IPTV. See GRAINFIELD, KS [KS5071]

GRAINFIELD—Nex-Tech. Formerly [KS0381]. This cable system has converted to IPTV

GRANDVIEW PLAZA—See MANHATTAN, KS (Cox Communications)

GRANTVILLE—Formerly served by Cox Communications. No longer in operation

GREAT BEND—Cox Communications

GREELEY COUNTY (PORTIONS)—See ULYSSES, KS (Pioneer Communications)

GREEN—Formerly served by Eagle Communications. No longer in operation

GREEN—See MILTONVALE, KS (Twin Valley Communications. Formerly served by BENNINGTON, KS [KS0214]. This cable system has converted to IPTV)

GREENLEAF—Formerly served by Allegiance Communications. No longer in operation

GREENLEAF—See MILTONVALE, KS (Twin Valley Communications. Formerly served by BENNINGTON, KS [KS0214]. This cable system has converted to IPTV)

GREENSBURG—Formerly served by Allegiance Communications. No longer in operation

GREENWOOD COUNTY (PORTIONS)—See UDALL, KS (Wheat State Telecable Inc.)

GRENOLA—See CLEARWATER, KS (SKT Entertainment)

GRIDLEY—See BURLINGTON, KS (Mediacom)

GRINNELL—See BREWSTER, KS (S&T Cable)

GYPSUM—Home Communications Inc. This cable system has converted to IPTV. Now served by GALVA, KS [KS5068]

GYPSUM—See GALVA, KS (Home Communications Inc)

HADDAM—Formerly served by Westcom. No longer in operation

HALSTEAD—See WICHITA, KS (Cox Communications)

HAMILTON—Mediacom

HANOVER—Blue Valley Tele-Communications. Now served by AXTELL (formerly Frankfort & Home), KS [KS0424]

HANOVER—See AXTELL, KS (Blue Valley Tele-Communications)

HANSTON—United Communications Assn. Inc. Now served by CIMARRON, KS [KS0126]

HANSTON—See CIMARRON, KS (United Communications Assn. Inc)

HARPER—Formerly served by Allegiance Communications. No longer in operation

HARTFORD—Formerly served by Zito Media. No longer in operation

HARVEY COUNTY (UNINCORPORATED AREAS)—See WICHITA, KS (Cox Communications)

HARVEYVILLE—Formerly served by Galaxy Cablevision. No longer in operation

HAVEN—Formerly served by Allegiance Communications. No longer in operation

HAVENSVILLE—Formerly served by Blue Valley Tele-Communications. No longer in operation

HAVENSVILLE—Formerly served by Rainbow Communications. No longer in operation

HAVILAND—Haviland Cable-Vision

HAYS—Eagle Communications

HAYSVILLE—See WICHITA, KS (Cox Communications)

HEALY—S&T Cable. Now served by DIGHTON, KS [KS0144]

HEALY—See DIGHTON, KS (S&T Cable)

HEPLER—See GIRARD, KS (Craw-Kan)

HERINGTON—Vyve Broadband

HERNDON—Formerly served by Pinpoint Cable TV. No longer in operation

HESSTON—See WICHITA, KS (Cox Communications)

HIATTVILLE—See GIRARD, KS (Craw-Kan)

HIAWATHA—Rainbow Communications

HICKOK—See ULYSSES, KS (Pioneer Communications)

HIGHLAND—See HIAWATHA, KS (Rainbow Communications)

HILL CITY—Nex-Tech

HILLSBORO—See MARION, KS (Eagle Communications)

HITSCHMAN—See HOLYROOD, KS (H&B Communications. This system has converted to IPTV)

HOISINGTON—See GREAT BEND, KS (Cox Communications)

HOLCOMB—See ULYSSES, KS (Pioneer Communications)

HOLTON—Giant Communications

HOLYROOD—H&B Communications. This cable system has converted to IPTV. See HOLYROOD, KS [KS5105]

HOLYROOD—H&B Communications. This system has converted to IPTV

HOPE—Formerly served by Eagle Communications. No longer in operation

HORACE—See ULYSSES, KS (Pioneer Communications)

HORTON—See HIAWATHA, KS (Rainbow Communications)

HOWARD—See CLEARWATER, KS (SKT Entertainment)

HOXIE—Eagle Communications

HOYT—Giant Communications. Now served by HOLTON, KS [KS0066]

HOYT—See HOLTON, KS (Giant Communications)

HUGOTON—See ULYSSES, KS (Pioneer Communications)

HUMBOLDT—See PITTSBURG, KS (Cox Communications)

HUME—See GIRARD, MO (Craw-Kan)

HUTCHINSON—Cox Communications. Now served by WICHITA, KS [KS0001]

HUTCHINSON—See WICHITA, KS (Cox Communications)

INDEPENDENCE—Cable One

INGALLS—United Communications Assn. Inc. Now served by CIMARRON, KS [KS0126]

INGALLS—See CIMARRON, KS (United Communications Assn. Inc)

INMAN—Vyve Broadband

IOLA—Cox Communications. Now served by PITTSBURG, KS [KS0011]

IOLA—See PITTSBURG, KS (Cox Communications)

IUKA—Formerly served by Cox Communications. No longer in operation

JAMESTOWN—Cunningham Cable TV. Now served by GLEN ELDER, KS [KS0228]

JAMESTOWN—See GLEN ELDER, KS (Cunningham Cable)

JEFFERSON COUNTY (PORTIONS)—See TOPEKA, KS (Cox Communications)

JENNINGS—See EDMOND, KS (Nex-Tech. Formerly served by LENORA, KS [KS0450]. This cable system has converted to IPTV)

JETMORE—United Communications Assn. Inc. Now served by CIMARRON, KS [KS0126]

JETMORE—See CIMARRON, KS (United Communications Assn. Inc)

JEWELL—Cunningham Cable TV. Now served by GLEN ELDER, KS [KS0228]

JEWELL—See GLEN ELDER, KS (Cunningham Cable)

JOHNSON CITY—See ULYSSES, KS (Pioneer Communications)

JOHNSON COUNTY (portions)—Comcast Cable. Now served by INDEPENDENCE, MO [MO0004]

JOHNSON COUNTY (SOUTHERN PORTION)—See PAOLA, KS (Suddenlink Communications)

JUNCTION CITY—See MANHATTAN, KS (Cox Communications)

KANOPOLIS—See ELLSWORTH, KS (Eagle Communications)

KANORADO—See BREWSTER, KS (S&T Cable)

KANSAS CITY (unincorporated areas)—Formerly served by Char-

Cable Community Index—Kansas

ter Communications. Now served by WOW! Internet, Cable & Phone, LAWRENCE, KS [KS0004]

KANSAS CITY (UNINCORPORATED AREAS)—See LAWRENCE, KS (WOW! Internet, Cable & Phone)

KANSAS CITY—See LENEXA, KS (SureWest Communications. Formerly [KS0462]. This cable system has converted to IPTV)

KANSAS CITY—See LENEXA, MO (SureWest Communications. Formerly [KS0462]. This cable system has converted to IPTV)

KANSAS STATE UNIVERSITY—See MANHATTAN, KS (Cox Communications)

KECHI—See WICHITA, KS (Cox Communications)

KENDALL—See ULYSSES, KS (Pioneer Communications)

KENSINGTON—Formerly served by Cunningham Cable TV. No longer in operation

KENSINGTON—Nex-Tech. Formerly served by LENORA, KS [KS0450]. This cable system has converted to IPTV

KEYES—See ELKHART, OK (Epic Touch Co)

KINGMAN COUNTY—See WICHITA, KS (Cox Communications)

KINGMAN—See WICHITA, KS (Cox Communications)

KINSLEY—Cox Communications. Now served by DODGE CITY, KS [KS0015]

KINSLEY—See DODGE CITY, KS (Cox Communications)

KIOWA—Formerly served by Almega Cable. No longer in operation

KIRWIN—Nex-Tech

KISMET—See MEADE, KS (Vyve Broadband)

LA CROSSE—Formerly served by Cox Communications. Now served by GBT Communications Inc., RUSH CENTER, KS [KS0418]

LA CROSSE—See RUSH CENTER, KS (GBT Communications Inc)

LA CYGNE—Formerly served by Almega Cable. No longer in operation

LA HARPE—Formerly served by CableDirect. No longer in operation

LAKE DABINAWA—Formerly served by Rainbow Communications. No longer in operation

LAKE OF THE FOREST—Time Warner Cable. Now served by KANSAS CITY, MO [MO0001]

LAKE WABAUNSEE—Formerly served by Galaxy Cablevision. No longer in operation

LAKIN—See ULYSSES, KS (Pioneer Communications)

LANCASTER—See ATCHISON, KS (Vyve Broadband)

LANE—Formerly served by National Cable Inc. No longer in operation

LANSING—See LAWRENCE, KS (WOW! Internet, Cable & Phone)

LARNED—See GREAT BEND, KS (Cox Communications)

LAWRENCE—WOW! Internet, Cable & Phone

LEAVENWORTH COUNTY (UNINCORPORATED AREAS)—See LAWRENCE, KS (WOW! Internet, Cable & Phone)

LEBANON—Nex-Tech. This cable system has converted to IPTV. See LEBANON, KS [KS5049]

LEBANON—Nex-Tech. Formerly [KS0397]. This cable system has converted to IPTV

LEBO—See BURLINGTON, KS (Mediacom)

LECOMPTON—See TOPEKA, KS (Cox Communications)

LEHIGH—Formerly served by Eagle Communications. No longer in operation

LENEXA—SureWest Broadband. This cable system has converted to IPTV. See LENEXA, KS [KS5122]

LENEXA—SureWest Communications. Formerly [KS0462]. This cable system has converted to IPTV

LENORA—Nex-Tech. This cable system has converted to IPTV. Now served by EDMOND, KS [KS5045]

LENORA—See EDMOND, KS (Nex-Tech. Formerly served by LENORA, KS [KS0450]. This cable system has converted to IPTV)

LEON—See CLEARWATER, KS (SKT Entertainment)

LEONARDVILLE—Formerly served by Giant Communications. No longer in operation

LEONARDVILLE—See MILTONVALE, KS (Twin Valley Communications. Formerly served by BENNINGTON, KS [KS0214]. This cable system has converted to IPTV)

LEOTI—Formerly served by Cebridge Connections. Now served by Pioneer Communications, ULYSSES, KS [KS0044]

LEOTI—See ULYSSES, KS (Pioneer Communications)

LEROY—See BURLINGTON, KS (Mediacom)

LEWIS & CLARK VILLAGE—See ATCHISON, MO (Vyve Broadband)

LEWIS (RURAL PORTIONS)—See RUSH CENTER, KS (GBT Communications Inc)

LEWIS—See RUSH CENTER, KS (GBT Communications Inc)

LIBERAL—Zito Media

LIEBENTHAL—See RUSH CENTER, KS (GBT Communications Inc)

LINCOLN—Eagle Communications

LINCOLNVILLE—See MARION, KS (Eagle Communications)

LINN—Formerly served by Allegiance Communications. No longer in operation

LINSBORG—Cox Communications. Now served by WICHITA, KS [KS0001]

LINSBORG—See WICHITA, KS (Cox Communications)

LINWOOD—See LAWRENCE, KS (WOW! Internet, Cable & Phone)

LOGAN—See EDMOND, KS (Nex-Tech. Formerly served by LENORA, KS [KS0450]. This cable system has converted to IPTV)

LONGFORD—See MILTONVALE, KS (Twin Valley Communications. Formerly served by BENNINGTON, KS [KS0214]. This cable system has converted to IPTV)

LONGTON—See CLEARWATER, KS (SKT Entertainment)

LORRAINE—See CHASE, KS (H&B Communications)

LOUISBURG—Formerly served by Almega Cable. No longer in operation

LOUISVILLE—WTC Communications. Now served by WAMEGO, KS [KS5017]

LOUISVILLE—See WAMEGO, KS (WTC Communications)

LOUISVILLE—See WAMEGO, KS (WTC Communications)

LOWELL—Formerly served by Riverton-Lowell Cablevision. No longer in operation

LUCAS—Wilson Communications. Now served by BROOKVILLE, KS [KS0162]

LUCAS—See BROOKVILLE, KS (Wilson Communications)

LURAY—Gorham Tele-Com (formerly Nex-Tech). This cable system has converted to IPTV. See GORHAM, KS [KS5164]

LURAY—See GORHAM, KS (Gorham Tele-Com. Formerly [KS0380]. This cable system has converted to IPTV)

LYNDON—See BURLINGTON, KS (Mediacom)

LYON COUNTY (PORTIONS)—See UDALL, KS (Wheat State Telecable Inc.)

LYON COUNTY—Formerly served by Galaxy Cablevision. No longer in operation

LYON COUNTY—See EMPORIA, KS (Cable One)

LYONS—Cox Communications. Now served by GREAT BEND, KS [KS0012]

LYONS—See GREAT BEND, KS (Cox Communications)

MACKSVILLE—Formerly served by Almega Cable. No longer in operation

MACKSVILLE—See RUSH CENTER, KS (GBT Communications Inc)

MADISON—Mediacom

MAHASKA—Formerly served by Westcom. No longer in operation

MAIZE—See WICHITA, KS (Cox Communications)

MANHATTAN—Cox Communications

MANKATO—Cunningham Cable TV. Now served by GLEN ELDER, KS [KS0228]

MANKATO—See GLEN ELDER, KS (Cunningham Cable)

MANTER—See ULYSSES, KS (Pioneer Communications)

MAPLE HILL—Formerly served by Zito Media. No longer in operation

MARIENTHAL—See ULYSSES, KS (Pioneer Communications)

MARION COUNTY (PORTIONS)—See MARION, KS (Eagle Communications)

MARION COUNTY (SOUTHERN PORTION)—See WICHITA, KS (Cox Communications)

MARION—Eagle Communications

MARQUETTE—MTC

MARYSVILLE—Blue Valley Tele-Communications. Now served by AXTELL (formerly Frankfort & Home), KS [KS0424]

MARYSVILLE—See AXTELL, KS (Blue Valley Tele-Communications)

MATFIELD GREEN—See UDALL, KS (Wheat State Telecable Inc.)

MAYETTA—Giant Communications. Now served by HOLTON, KS [KS0066]

MAYETTA—See HOLTON, KS (Giant Communications)

MCCONNELL AFB—See WICHITA, KS (Cox Communications)

MCCRACKEN (RURAL PORTIONS)—See RUSH CENTER, KS (GBT Communications Inc)

MCCRACKEN—See RUSH CENTER, KS (GBT Communications Inc)

McCUNE—Formerly served by Craw-Kan Telephone Co-op. No longer in operation

2017 Edition

Kansas—Cable Community Index

MCCUNE—See GIRARD, KS (Craw-Kan)

MCDONALD—Eagle Communications

McFARLAND—Formerly served by Galaxy Cablevision. No longer in operation

McLOUTH—Giant Communications. Now served by HOLTON, KS [KS0066]

MCLOUTH—See HOLTON, KS (Giant Communications)

MCPHERSON COUNTY (PORTIONS)—See WICHITA, KS (Cox Communications)

McPHERSON—Cox Communications. Now served by WICHITA, KS [KS0001]

MCPHERSON—See WICHITA, KS (Cox Communications)

MEADE—Vyve Broadband

MEDICINE LODGE—Vyve Broadband

MELVERN—Formerly served by Zito Media. No longer in operation

MENTOR—See GALVA, KS (Home Communications Inc)

MERIDEN—Formerly served by SCI Cable. Now served by Cox Communications, TOPEKA, KS [KS0002]

MERIDEN—See TOPEKA, KS (Cox Communications)

MERRIAM—See LENEXA, KS (SureWest Communications. Formerly [KS0462]. This cable system has converted to IPTV)

MIAMI COUNTY (UNINCORPORATED AREAS)—See PAOLA, KS (Suddenlink Communications)

MILFORD (PORTIONS)—See MANHATTAN, KS (Cox Communications)

MILFORD—Eagle Communications

MILFORD—See MILTONVALE, KS (Twin Valley Communications. Formerly served by BENNINGTON, KS [KS0214]. This cable system has converted to IPTV)

MILTONVALE—Twin Valley Communications. Formerly served by BENNINGTON, KS [KS0214]. This cable system has converted to IPTV

MINNEAPOLIS—Eagle Communications

MINNEOLA—See MEADE, KS (Vyve Broadband)

MISSION WOODS—See LENEXA, KS (SureWest Communications. Formerly [KS0462]. This cable system has converted to IPTV)

MISSION—See LENEXA, KS (SureWest Communications. Formerly [KS0462]. This cable system has converted to IPTV)

MITCHELL COUNTY (PORTIONS)—See GLEN ELDER, KS (Cunningham Cable)

MOLINE—See CLEARWATER, KS (SKT Entertainment)

MONTEZUMA—United Communications Assn. Inc. Now served by CIMARRON, KS [KS0126]

MONTEZUMA—See CIMARRON, KS (United Communications Assn. Inc)

MONTGOMERY COUNTY (PORTIONS)—See INDEPENDENCE, KS (Cable One)

MONTGOMERY COUNTY (PORTIONS)—See PITTSBURG, KS (Cox Communications)

MORGANVILLE—Formerly served by Eagle Communications. No longer in operation

MORGANVILLE—See MILTONVALE, KS (Twin Valley Communications. Formerly served by BENNINGTON, KS [KS0214]. This cable system has converted to IPTV)

MORRILL—Formerly served by Rainbow Communications. No longer in operation

MORRIS COUNTY (PORTIONS)—See COUNCIL GROVE, KS (TCT. This cable system has converted to IPTV)

MORROWVILLE—Formerly served by Diode Cable Co. No longer in operation

MOSCOW—See ULYSSES, KS (Pioneer Communications)

MOUND VALLEY—Formerly served by National Cable Inc. No longer in operation

MOUNDRIDGE—Mid-Kansas Cable Services Inc.

MOUNT HOPE—Formerly served by Almega Cable. No longer in operation

MULBERRY—See GIRARD, KS (Craw-Kan)

MULLINVILLE—Formerly served by Mullinville Cable TV. No longer in operation

MULVANE (unincorporated areas)—Formerly served by CableDirect. No longer in operation

MULVANE—Cox Communications. Now served by WICHITA, KS [KS0001]

MULVANE—See WICHITA, KS (Cox Communications)

MUNDEN—Formerly served by Westcom. No longer in operation

MUNJOR—Nex-Tech. This cable system has converted to IPTV. See MUNJOR, KS [KS5193]

MUNJOR—See HAYS, KS (Eagle Communications)

MUNJOR—Nex-Tech. Formerly [KS0473]. This cable system has converted to IPTV

MUSCOTAH—Rainbow Communications. This cable system has converted to IPTV. Now served by WILLIS, SD [KS5177]

NARKA—Formerly served by Westcom. No longer in operation

NATOMA—Formerly served by Eagle Communications. No longer in operation

NATOMA—Nex-Tech. Formerly served by LENORA, KS [KS0450]. This cable system has converted to IPTV

NEODESHA—Cable One. Now served by INDEPENDENCE, KS [KS0022]

NEODESHA—See INDEPENDENCE, KS (Cable One)

NEOSHO COUNTY (PORTIONS)—See CHANUTE, KS (Cable One)

NEOSHO COUNTY (PORTIONS)—See PITTSBURG, KS (Cox Communications)

NEOSHO RAPIDS—Formerly served by Zito Media. No longer in operation

NESS CITY (RURAL PORTIONS)—See RUSH CENTER, KS (GBT Communications Inc)

NESS CITY—Formerly served by Cebridge Connections. Now served by GBT Communications Inc., RUSH CENTER, KS [KS0418]

NESS CITY—See RUSH CENTER, KS (GBT Communications Inc)

NETAWAKA—See HOLTON, KS (Giant Communications)

NEW STRAWN—See BURLINGTON, KS (Mediacom)

NEWTON—Cox Communications. Now served by WICHITA, KS [KS0001]

NEWTON—See WICHITA, KS (Cox Communications)

NICKERSON—See WICHITA, KS (Cox Communications)

NORCATUR—Nex-Tech (formerly Pinpoint Cable TV) This cable system has converted to IPTV

NORCATUR—Nex-Tech. Formerly [KS0314]. This cable system has converted to IPTV

NORTH NEWTON—See WICHITA, KS (Cox Communications)

NORTON—See ALMENA, KS (Nex-Tech. Formerly [KS0360]. This cable system has converted to IPTV)

NORTON—Nex-Tech

NORTONVILLE—Giant Communications. Now served by HOLTON, KS [KS0066]

NORTONVILLE—See HOLTON, KS (Giant Communications)

NORWICH—Formerly served by Almega Cable. No longer in operation

OAKLEY—S&T Cable. Now served by BREWSTER, KS [KS0315]

OAKLEY—See BREWSTER, KS (S&T Cable)

OBERLIN—Eagle Communications

ODIN—See HOLYROOD, KS (H&B Communications. This system has converted to IPTV)

OFFERLE—GBT Communications Inc

OGDEN—See MANHATTAN, KS (Cox Communications)

OLATHE—See LENEXA, KS (SureWest Communications. Formerly [KS0462]. This cable system has converted to IPTV)

OLPE—Formerly served by Zito Media. No longer in operation

OLPE—See UDALL, KS (Wheat State Telecable Inc.)

OLSBURG—Formerly served by Giant Communications. No longer in operation

OLSBURG—See MILTONVALE, KS (Twin Valley Communications. Formerly served by BENNINGTON, KS [KS0214]. This cable system has converted to IPTV)

ONAGA—Blue Valley Tele-Communications. Now served by AXTELL (formerly Frankfort & Home), KS [KS0424]

ONAGA—See AXTELL, KS (Blue Valley Tele-Communications)

OSAGE CITY—Mediacom. Now served by BURLINGTON, KS [KS0064]

OSAGE CITY—See BURLINGTON, KS (Mediacom)

OSAGE COUNTY—Formerly served by Galaxy Cablevision. No longer in operation

OSAWATOMIE—See PAOLA, KS (Suddenlink Communications)

OSBORNE—See WOODSTON, KS (Nex-Tech. Formerly [KS0306]. This cable system has converted to IPTV)

OSKALOOSA—Giant Communications. Now served by HOLTON, KS [KS0066]

OSKALOOSA—See HOLTON, KS (Giant Communications)

OSWEGO—Mediacom

OTIS (RURAL PORTIONS)—See RUSH CENTER, KS (GBT Communications Inc)

OTTAWA—Vyve Broadband

OVERBROOK—Formerly served by Zito Media. No longer in operation

OVERLAND PARK—Formerly served by Time Warner Cable of Johnson County. No longer in operation

OVERLAND PARK—See LENEXA, KS (SureWest Communications. Formerly [KS0462]. This cable system has converted to IPTV)

Cable Community Index—Kansas

OXFORD—Formerly served by Allegiance Communications. No longer in operation

OZAWKIE—Giant Communications. Now served by HOLTON, KS [KS0066]

OZAWKIE—See HOLTON, KS (Giant Communications)

PALMER—Formerly served by Eagle Communications. No longer in operation

PAOLA—Suddenlink Communications

PARADISE—See GORHAM, KS (Gorham Tele-Com. Formerly [KS0380]. This cable system has converted to IPTV)

PARK CITY—See WICHITA, KS (Cox Communications)

PARK—See GRAINFIELD, KS (Nex-Tech. Formerly [KS0381]. This cable system has converted to IPTV)

PARKER—Formerly served by National Cable Inc. No longer in operation

PARSONS—Cable One

PARTRIDGE—Formerly served by CableDirect. No longer in operation

PAULINE—See TOPEKA, KS (Cox Communications)

PAWNEE ROCK—GBT Communications Inc. Now served by RUSH CENTER, KS [KS0418]

PAWNEE ROCK—See RUSH CENTER, KS (GBT Communications Inc)

PAXICO—Formerly served by Zito Media. No longer in operation

PAXICO—See WAMEGO, KS (WTC Communications)

PAXICO—See WAMEGO, KS (WTC Communications)

PEABODY—Vyve Broadband

PERRY—Cox Communications. Now served by TOPEKA, KS [KS0002]

PERRY—See TOPEKA, KS (Cox Communications)

PHILLIPSBURG—Nex-Tech. This cable system has converted to IPTV. See PHLLIPSBURG, KA [KS5201]

PHILLIPSBURG—Nex-Tech. Formerly [KS0060]. This cable system has converted to IPTV

PITTSBURG—Cox Communications

PLAINS—See MEADE, KS (Vyve Broadband)

PLAINVILLE—Nex-Tech. This cable system has converted to IPTV. See PLAINVILLE, KS [KS5202]

PLAINVILLE—Nex-Tech. Formerly [KS0445]. This cable system has converted to IPTV

PLATTE COUNTY (WESTERN PORTION)—See ATCHISON, MO (Vyve Broadband)

PLEASANTON—Formerly served by Almega Cable. No longer in operation

PLEASANTON—See GIRARD, KS (Craw-Kan)

POMONA—Formerly served by Zito Media. No longer in operation

POTTAWATOMIE COUNTY (portions)—WTC Communications. Now served by WAMEGO, KS [KS5017]

POTTAWATOMIE COUNTY (SOUTHEASTERN PORTION)—See MANHATTAN, KS (Cox Communications)

POTTAWATOMIE COUNTY (UNINCORPORATED AREAS)—See WAMEGO, KS (WTC Communications)

POTTAWATOMIE COUNTY (UNINCORPORATED AREAS)—See WAMEGO, KS (WTC Communications)

POTWIN—See UDALL, KS (Wheat State Telecable Inc.)

PRAIRIE VILLAGE—See LENEXA, KS (SureWest Communications. Formerly [KS0462]. This cable system has converted to IPTV)

PRATT COUNTY—See WICHITA, KS (Cox Communications)

PRATT—Cox Communications. Now served by WICHITA, KS [KS0001]

PRATT—See WICHITA, KS (Cox Communications)

PRESCOTT—Craw-Kan Telephone Co-op. This cable system has converted to IPTV. Now served by GIRARD, KS [KS5099]

PRESCOTT—See GIRARD, KS (Craw-Kan)

PRETTY PRAIRIE—Formerly served by Almega Cable. No longer in operation

PRINCETON—Formerly served by CableDirect. No longer in operation

PROTECTION—United Communications Assn. Inc. Now served by CIMARRON, KS [KS0126]

PROTECTION—See CIMARRON, KS (United Communications Assn. Inc)

PURCELL—See GIRARD, MO (Craw-Kan)

QUENEMO—Formerly served by Galaxy Cablevision. No longer in operation

QUINTER—Formerly served by Quinter Cable Co. No longer in operation

QUINTER—See GRAINFIELD, KS (Nex-Tech. Formerly [KS0381]. This cable system has converted to IPTV)

RANDALL—Cunningham Cable TV. Now served by GLEN ELDER, KS [KS0228]

RANDALL—See GLEN ELDER, KS (Cunningham Cable)

RANDOLPH—Formerly served by Rainbow Communications. No longer in operation

RANSOM (RURAL PORTIONS)—See RUSH CENTER, KS (GBT Communications Inc)

RANSOM—See RUSH CENTER, KS (GBT Communications Inc)

READING—Formerly served by Galaxy Cablevision. No longer in operation

RENO COUNTY (PORTIONS)—See WICHITA, KS (Cox Communications)

REPUBLIC—Formerly served by Diode Cable Co. No longer in operation

RESERVE TWP.—Formerly served by Rainbow Communications. No longer in operation

REXFORD—See EDMOND, KS (Nex-Tech. Formerly served by LENORA, KS [KS0450]. This cable system has converted to IPTV)

RICE COUNTY—See GREAT BEND, KS (Cox Communications)

RICHFIELD—See ULYSSES, KS (Pioneer Communications)

RICHMOND—Formerly served by Zito Media. No longer in operation

RILEY COUNTY (SOUTHERN PORTION)—See MANHATTAN, KS (Cox Communications)

RILEY—Eagle Communications

RILEY—See MILTONVALE, KS (Twin Valley Communications. Formerly served by BENNINGTON, KS [KS0214]. This cable system has converted to IPTV)

ROBINSON—See HIAWATHA, KS (Rainbow Communications)

ROELAND PARK—See LENEXA, KS (SureWest Communications. Formerly [KS0462]. This cable system has converted to IPTV)

ROLLA—See ULYSSES, KS (Pioneer Communications)

ROSALIA—Formerly served by CableDirect. No longer in operation

ROSE HILL—See WICHITA, KS (Cox Communications)

ROSSVILLE—Zito Media

ROZEL (RURAL PORTIONS)—See RUSH CENTER, KS (GBT Communications Inc)

ROZEL—See RUSH CENTER, KS (GBT Communications Inc)

RUSH CENTER—GBT Communications Inc

RUSH CENTER—GBT Communications Inc

RUSHVILLE—See ATCHISON, MO (Vyve Broadband)

RUSSELL—Eagle Communications. Now served by HAYS, KS [KS0384]

RUSSELL—See HAYS, KS (Eagle Communications)

SABETHA—See HIAWATHA, KS (Rainbow Communications)

SALEMSBORG—See GALVA, KS (Home Communications Inc)

SALINA (SOUTHWEST RURAL PORTIONS)—See GALVA, KS (Home Communications Inc)

SALINA—Formerly served by TVCN. No longer in operation

SALINA—Cox Communications

SALINE COUNTY (PORTIONS)—See SALINA, KS (Cox Communications)

SATANTA—See ULYSSES, KS (Pioneer Communications)

SAVONBURG—See GIRARD, KS (Craw-Kan)

SCANDIA—Cunningham Cable TV. Now served by GLEN ELDER, KS [KS0228]

SCANDIA—See GLEN ELDER, KS (Cunningham Cable)

SCHOENCHEN—See RUSH CENTER, KS (GBT Communications Inc)

SCOTT CITY—Pioneer Communications. Now served by ULYSSES, KS [KS0044]

SCOTT CITY—See ULYSSES, KS (Pioneer Communications)

SCRANTON—See BURLINGTON, KS (Mediacom)

SEDAN—Formerly served by Allegiance Communications. No longer in operation

SEDGWICK COUNTY (portions)—Formerly served by Westcom. No longer in operation

SEDGWICK COUNTY (PORTIONS)—See WICHITA, KS (Cox Communications)

SEDGWICK COUNTY (PORTIONS)—See CLEARWATER, KS (SKT Entertainment)

SEDGWICK—See WICHITA, KS (Cox Communications)

SELDEN—See EDMOND, KS (Nex-Tech. Formerly served by LENORA, KS [KS0450]. This cable system has converted to IPTV)

SENECA—Formerly served by Carson Communications. Now served by Rainbow Communications, HIAWATHA, KS [KS0059]

SENECA—See HIAWATHA, KS (Rainbow Communications)

SEVERY—See CLEARWATER, KS (SKT Entertainment)

SEWARD COUNTY (PORTIONS)—See MEADE, KS (Vyve Broadband)

SHARON SPRINGS—Formerly served by Cebridge Connections. Now served by Pioneer Communications, ULYSSES, KS [KS0044]

SHARON SPRINGS—See ULYSSES, KS (Pioneer Communications)

Kansas—Cable Community Index

SHARON—Formerly served by Allegiance Communications. No longer in operation

SHAWNEE COUNTY—See TOPEKA, KS (Cox Communications)

SHAWNEE—See LENEXA, KS (SureWest Communications. Formerly [KS0462]. This cable system has converted to IPTV)

SILVER LAKE—See TOPEKA, KS (Cox Communications)

SILVER LAKE—See ROSSVILLE, KS (Zito Media)

SMITH CENTER—Nex-Tech. This cable system has converted to IPTV. See SMITH CENTER, KS [KS5204]

SMITH CENTER—Nex-Tech. Formerly [KS0102]. This cable system has converted to IPTV

SMOLAN—Formerly served by Home Communications Inc. No longer in operation

SMOLAN—See GALVA, KS (Home Communications Inc)

SOLOMON—Eagle Communications. Now served by ABILENE, KS [KS0034]

SOLOMON—See ABILENE, KS (Eagle Communications)

SOUTH COFFEYVILLE—See PITTSBURG, OK (Cox Communications)

SOUTH HAVEN—Formerly served by Almega Cable. No longer in operation

SOUTH HUTCHINSON—See WICHITA, KS (Cox Communications)

SPEARVILLE—United Communications Assn. Inc. Now served by CIMARRON, KS [KS0126]

SPEARVILLE—See CIMARRON, KS (United Communications Assn. Inc)

SPRING HILL—Formerly served by Cebridge Connections. Now served by Suddenlink Communications, PAOLA, KS [KS0029]

SPRING HILL—See PAOLA, KS (Suddenlink Communications)

ST. FRANCIS—Eagle Communications

ST. GEORGE—Formerly served by Kansas Cable. Now served by Cox Communications, MANHATTAN, KS [KS0006]

ST. GEORGE—See MANHATTAN, KS (Cox Communications)

ST. GEORGE—See WAMEGO, KS (WTC Communications)

ST. GEORGE—See WAMEGO, KS (WTC Communications)

ST. JOHN—See RUSH CENTER, KS (GBT Communications Inc)

ST. MARY'S—WTC Communications. Now served by WAMEGO, KS [KS5017]

ST. MARY'S—See WAMEGO, KS (WTC Communications)

ST. MARYS—See WAMEGO, KS (WTC Communications)

ST. PAUL—Formerly served by Cable TV of St. Paul. No longer in operation

STAFFORD—Vyve Broadband

STERLING—Formerly served by Eagle Communications. Now served by Cox Communications, GREAT BEND, KS [KS0012]

STERLING—See GREAT BEND, KS (Cox Communications)

STOCKTON—Nex-Tech. This cable system has converted to IPTV. See STOCKTON, KS [KS5055]

STOCKTON—Nex-Tech. Formerly [KS0051]. This cable system has converted to IPTV

STRONG CITY—Zito Media

SUBLETTE—See ULYSSES, KS (Pioneer Communications)

SUMMERFIELD—Blue Valley Tele-Communications. Now served by AXTELL (formerly Frankfort & Home), KS [KS0424]

SUMNER COUNTY (PORTIONS)—See CLEARWATER, KS (SKT Entertainment)

SYLVAN GROVE—Wilson Communications. Now served by BROOKVILLE, KS [KS0162]

SYLVAN GROVE—See BROOKVILLE, KS (Wilson Communications)

SYLVIA—Formerly served by Cox Communications. No longer in operation

SYRACUSE—See ULYSSES, KS (Pioneer Communications)

TAMPA—Formerly served by Eagle Communications. No longer in operation

TESCOTT—See MILTONVALE, KS (Twin Valley Communications. Formerly served by BENNINGTON, KS [KS0214]. This cable system has converted to IPTV)

THAYER—Mediacom

TIMKEN (RURAL PORTIONS)—See RUSH CENTER, KS (GBT Communications Inc)

TIMKEN—See RUSH CENTER, KS (GBT Communications Inc)

TIPTON—Wilson Communications. Now served by BROOKVILLE, KS [KS0162]

TIPTON—See BROOKVILLE, KS (Wilson Communications)

TONGANOXIE—See LAWRENCE, KS (WOW! Internet, Cable & Phone)

TOPEKA—Cox Communications

TORONTO—Mediacom

TOWANDA—See WICHITA, KS (Cox Communications)

TRIBUNE—Formerly served by Cebridge Connections. Now served by Pioneer Communications, ULYSSES, KS [KS0044]

TRIBUNE—See ULYSSES, KS (Pioneer Communications)

TROY—See HIAWATHA, KS (Rainbow Communications)

TURON—Formerly served by Cox Communications. No longer in operation

TYRO—See PITTSBURG, KS (Cox Communications)

UDALL—Wheat State Telecable Inc.

ULYSSES—Pioneer Communications

UNIONTOWN—Craw-Kan Telephone Co-op. This cable system has converted to IPTV. Now served by GIRARD, KS [KS5099]

UNIONTOWN—See GIRARD, KS (Craw-Kan)

UTICA—See RUSH CENTER, KS (GBT Communications Inc)

VALLEY CENTER—See WICHITA, KS (Cox Communications)

VALLEY FALLS—Giant Communications. Now served by HOLTON, KS [KS0066]

VALLEY FALLS—See HOLTON, KS (Giant Communications)

VERMILLION—Blue Valley Tele-Communications. Now served by AXTELL (formerly Frankfort & Home), KS [KS0424]

VICTORIA—See HAYS, KS (Eagle Communications)

VICTORIA—Nex-Tech

VIOLA—See CLEARWATER, KS (SKT Entertainment)

WABAUNSEE COUNTY (UNINCORPORATED AREAS)—See WAMEGO, KS (WTC Communications)

WABAUNSEE COUNTY (UNINCORPORATED AREAS)—See WAMEGO, KS (WTC Communications)

WAKEENEY—Eagle Communications. Now served by HAYS, KS [KS0384]

WAKEENEY—See HAYS, KS (Eagle Communications)

WAKEFIELD—Eagle Communications. Now served by ABILENE, KS [KS0034]

WAKEFIELD—See ABILENE, KS (Eagle Communications)

WAKEFIELD—See MILTONVALE, KS (Twin Valley Communications. Formerly served by BENNINGTON, KS [KS0214]. This cable system has converted to IPTV)

WALDO—See GORHAM, KS (Gorham Tele-Com. Formerly [KS0380]. This cable system has converted to IPTV)

WALNUT—Craw-Kan Telephone Co-op. This cable system has converted to IPTV. Now served by GIRARD, KS [KS5099]

WALNUT—See GIRARD, KS (Craw-Kan)

WALTON—Formerly served by Galaxy Cablevision. No longer in operation

WAMEGO—WTC Communications

WAMEGO—WTC Communications

WASHINGTON—Formerly served by Cunningham Cable TV. Now served by Blue Valley Tele-Communications, AXTELL, KS [KS0424]

WASHINGTON—See AXTELL, KS (Blue Valley Tele-Communications)

WATERVILLE—Blue Valley Tele-Communications. Now served by AXTELL (formerly Frankfort & Home), KS [KS0424]

WATERVILLE—See AXTELL, KS (Blue Valley Tele-Communications)

WATHENA—See HIAWATHA, KS (Rainbow Communications)

WAVERLY—Formerly served by Zito Media. No longer in operation

WEIR—Formerly served by WSC Cablevision. No longer in operation

WEIR—See GIRARD, KS (Craw-Kan)

WELLINGTON—Sumner Cable TV Inc.

WELLSVILLE—See BURLINGTON, KS (Mediacom)

WEST MINERAL—See GIRARD, KS (Craw-Kan)

WESTMORELAND—Formerly served by Giant Communications. No longer in operation

WESTMORELAND—See AXTELL, KS (Blue Valley Tele-Communications)

WESTWOOD HILLS—See LENEXA, KS (SureWest Communications. Formerly [KS0462]. This cable system has converted to IPTV)

WESTWOOD—See LENEXA, KS (SureWest Communications. Formerly [KS0462]. This cable system has converted to IPTV)

WETMORE—Rainbow Communications. No longer in operation

WETMORE—See HOLTON, KS (Giant Communications)

WHEATON—See AXTELL, KS (Blue Valley Tele-Communications)

WHITE CITY—Formerly served by Eagle Communications. No longer in operation

WHITE CLOUD—Formerly served by Rainbow Communications. No longer in operation

Cable Community Index—Kentucky

WHITING—Formerly served by Rainbow Communications. No longer in operation

WICHITA—Formerly served by Sprint Corp. No longer in operation

WICHITA—Cox Communications

WILLIAMSBURG—Formerly served by Zito Media. No longer in operation

WILLOWBROOK—See WICHITA, KS (Cox Communications)

WILSEY—Formerly served by CableDirect. No longer in operation

WILSON COUNTY—See FREDONIA, KS (Vyve Broadband)

WILSON—See BROOKVILLE, KS (Wilson Communications)

WINCHESTER—Giant Communications. Now served by HOLTON, KS [KS0066]

WINCHESTER—See HOLTON, KS (Giant Communications)

WINFIELD—See WICHITA, KS (Cox Communications)

WINONA—See BREWSTER, KS (S&T Cable)

WOODBINE—Formerly served by Eagle Communications. No longer in operation

WOODSTON—Nex-Tech. This cable system has converted to IPTV. See WOODSTON, KS [KS5088]

WOODSTON—Nex-Tech. Formerly [KS0306]. This cable system has converted to IPTV

WYANDOTTE COUNTY (PORTIONS)—See LAWRENCE, KS (WOW! Internet, Cable & Phone)

YATES CENTER—See PITTSBURG, KS (Cox Communications)

KENTUCKY

ADAIR COUNTY (PORTIONS)—See RUSSELL SPRINGS, KY (Duo County Telecom)

ADAIRVILLE—Suddenlink Communications

ALBANY—Mediacom. Now served by SUMMER SHADE, KY [KY0092]

ALBANY—See SUMMER SHADE, KY (Mediacom)

ALEXANDRIA—See COVINGTON, KY (Time Warner Cable)

ALLEN COUNTY (UNINCORPORATED AREAS)—See SCOTTSVILLE, KY (NCTC. Formerly [KY0073]. This cable system has converted to IPTV)

ALLEN—See HAROLD, KY (Inter Mountain Cable Inc)

ALLOCK—See VICCO, KY (TVS Cable)

ALTRO—Formerly served by Altro TV Inc. No longer in operation

ANCHORAGE—See LOUISVILLE, KY (Time Warner Cable)

ANDERSON COUNTY (EASTERN PORTION)—See RICHMOND, KY (Time Warner Cable)

ANNVILLE—See PEOPLES, KY (C & W Cable)

ARGO—See HAROLD, KY (Inter Mountain Cable Inc)

ARJAY—See CORBIN, KY (Time Warner Cable)

ARLINGTON—See WICKLIFFE, KY (Zito Media)

ARTEMUS—See BARBOURVILLE, KY (Barbourville Utility Commission)

ASHLAND—Formerly served by Adelphia Communications. No longer in operation

ASHLAND—Time Warner Cable

AUBURN—Suddenlink Communications. Now served by RUSSELLVILLE, KY [KY0032]

AUBURN—See RUSSELLVILLE, KY (Suddenlink Communications)

AUDUBON PARK—See LOUISVILLE, KY (Time Warner Cable)

AUGUSTA—Formerly served by Bracken County Cablevision Inc. Now served by Limestone Bracken Cablevision, AUGUSTA, KY [KY0316]

AUGUSTA—Limestone Bracken Cablevision

AUSTIN—See LOUISVILLE, IN (Time Warner Cable)

AUXIER—See VAN LEAR, KY (Big Sandy Broadband)

BALLARD COUNTY (PORTIONS)—See GRAVES COUNTY, KY (Zito Media)

BANCROFT—See LOUISVILLE, KY (Time Warner Cable)

BANNER—See HAROLD, KY (Inter Mountain Cable Inc)

BARBOURMEADE—See LOUISVILLE, KY (Time Warner Cable)

BARBOURVILLE—Barbourville Utility Commission

BARBOURVILLE—See GRAY, KY (Eastern Cable Corp)

BARDSTOWN—Bardstown Cable TV

BARDWELL—See WICKLIFFE, KY (Zito Media)

BARLOW—See WICKLIFFE, KY (Zito Media)

BARREN COUNTY (PORTIONS)—See SUMMER SHADE, KY (Mediacom)

BASKETT—See OWENSBORO, KY (Time Warner Cable)

BATH COUNTY (PORTIONS)—See RICHMOND, KY (Time Warner Cable)

BAUGHMAN—See CORBIN, KY (Time Warner Cable)

BAXTER—See HARLAN, KY (Harlan Community TV Inc)

BAXTER—See BLACK MOUNTAIN, KY (Zito Media)

BEATTYVILLE—Crystal Broadband Networks

BEAVER DAM—Time Warner Cable. Now served by MADISONVILLE, KY [KY0013]

BEAVER DAM—See MADISONVILLE, KY (Time Warner Cable)

BEDFORD—See LOUISVILLE, KY (Time Warner Cable)

BEECHWOOD VILLAGE—See LOUISVILLE, KY (Time Warner Cable)

BELFRY—See HAROLD, KY (Inter Mountain Cable Inc)

BELL COUNTY (PORTIONS)—See CORBIN, KY (Time Warner Cable)

BELLEFONTE—See ASHLAND, KY (Time Warner Cable)

BELLEMEADE—See LOUISVILLE, KY (Time Warner Cable)

BELLEVUE—See COVINGTON, KY (Time Warner Cable)

BELLEWOOD—See LOUISVILLE, KY (Time Warner Cable)

BENHAM—Access Cable Television Inc. Now served by CUMBERLAND, KY [KY0075]

BENHAM—See CUMBERLAND, KY (Access Cable Television Inc)

BENTON—Formerly served by Charter Communications. Now served by Time Warner Cable, MAYFIELD, KY [KY0037]

BENTON—See MAYFIELD, KY (Time Warner Cable)

BEREA—See RICHMOND, KY (Time Warner Cable)

BETSY LAYNE—See HAROLD, KY (Inter Mountain Cable Inc)

BEVINSVILLE—See HAROLD, KY (Inter Mountain Cable Inc)

BIG CLIFTY—Mediacom. Now served by CANEYVILLE, KY [KY0291]

BIG CLIFTY—See CANEYVILLE, KY (Mediacom)

BIG CREEK—See CORBIN, KY (Time Warner Cable)

BIMBLE—See CORBIN, KY (Time Warner Cable)

BLACK MOUNTAIN—Zito Media

BLACKBERRY CITY—See HAROLD, WV (Inter Mountain Cable Inc)

BLACKBERRY CREEK—See HAROLD, KY (Inter Mountain Cable Inc)

BLACKEY—See JEREMIAH, KY (TVS Cable)

BLAINE—Formerly served by Lycom Communications. No longer in operation

BLAIR TOWN—See HAROLD, KY (Inter Mountain Cable Inc)

BLAIR—See CUMBERLAND, KY (Access Cable Television Inc)

BLEDSOE—See MOZELLE, KY (Crystal Broadband Networks)

BLOOMFIELD—Formerly served by Insight Communications. No longer in operation

BLUE BANK—See RICHMOND, KY (Time Warner Cable)

BLUE RIDGE MANOR—See LOUISVILLE, KY (Time Warner Cable)

BLUE RIVER—See HAROLD, KY (Inter Mountain Cable Inc)

BOLDMAN—See HAROLD, KY (Inter Mountain Cable Inc)

BOND—See PEOPLES, KY (C & W Cable)

BONNIEVILLE—See UPTON, KY (Mediacom)

BONNYMAN—TVS Cable

BOONE COUNTY (PORTIONS)—See COVINGTON, KY (Time Warner Cable)

BOONEVILLE—See BEATTYVILLE, KY (Crystal Broadband Networks)

BOONEVILLE—Peoples Telecom

BOONS CAMP—See VAN LEAR, KY (Big Sandy Broadband)

BORDEN—See LOUISVILLE, IN (Time Warner Cable)

BOTTOM—See JENKINS, KY (Inter Mountain Cable Inc)

BOURBON COUNTY (PORTIONS)—See RICHMOND, KY (Time Warner Cable)

BOWLING GREEN—Time Warner Cable

BOYD COUNTY (PORTIONS)—See GRAYSON, KY (Suddenlink Communications)

BOYD COUNTY (PORTIONS)—See ASHLAND, KY (Time Warner Cable)

BOYLE COUNTY (PORTIONS)—See RICHMOND, KY (Time Warner Cable)

BRACKEN COUNTY (PORTIONS)—See AUGUSTA, KY (Limestone Bracken Cablevision)

BRADFORD—See MAYFIELD, TN (Time Warner Cable)

BRADFORDSVILLE—Formerly served by Charter Communications. No longer in operation

BRANDENBURG—See LOUISVILLE, KY (Time Warner Cable)

BREATHITT COUNTY (PORTIONS)—See BULAN, KY (Time Warner Cable)

BRECKINRIDGE COUNTY (PORTIONS)—See CANEYVILLE, KY (Mediacom)

BRECKINRIDGE COUNTY—See HARDINSBURG, KY (Crystal Broadband Networks)

BREMEN—Inside Connect Cable

Kentucky—Cable Community Index

BRIARWOOD—See LOUISVILLE, KY (Time Warner Cable)

BRINKLEY—See HINDMAN, KY (TVS Cable)

BROAD BOTTOM—See HAROLD, KY (Inter Mountain Cable Inc)

BROAD FIELDS—See LOUISVILLE, KY (Time Warner Cable)

BRODHEAD—See LINCOLN COUNTY (eastern portion), KY (Mediacom)

BRODHEAD—Wilcop Cable TV

BROECK POINTE—See LOUISVILLE, KY (Time Warner Cable)

BROMLEY—See COVINGTON, KY (Time Warner Cable)

BRONSTON—See CORBIN, KY (Time Warner Cable)

BROOKPORT—See ELIZABETHTOWN, IL (Comcast Cable)

BROOKS—Inside Connect Cable

BROOKSIDE—See BLACK MOUNTAIN, KY (Zito Media)

BROOKSVILLE—Formerly served by Bracken County Cablevision Inc. Now served by Limestone Bracken Cablevision, AUGUSTA, KY [KY0316]

BROOKSVILLE—See AUGUSTA, KY (Limestone Bracken Cablevision)

BROWNS FORK—See BONNYMAN, KY (TVS Cable)

BROWNSBORO FARM—See LOUISVILLE, KY (Time Warner Cable)

BROWNSBORO VILLAGE—See LOUISVILLE, KY (Time Warner Cable)

BROWNSVILLE—Mediacom. Now served by MORGANTOWN, KY [KY0096]

BROWNSVILLE—See MORGANTOWN, KY (Mediacom)

BRYANTSVILLE—Formerly served by Charter Communications. No longer in operation

BUCHANAN COUNTY—See HAROLD, VA (Inter Mountain Cable Inc)

BUCKNER—See LOUISVILLE, KY (Time Warner Cable)

BULAN—Time Warner Cable

BULLITT COUNTY (PORTIONS)—See LOUISVILLE, KY (Time Warner Cable)

BULLSKIN CREEK—Formerly served by Bullskin Cable TV. No longer in operation

BURDINE—See JENKINS, KY (Inter Mountain Cable Inc)

BURGIN—See RICHMOND, KY (Time Warner Cable)

BURKESVILLE—Mediacom

BURNING SPRINGS—C & W Cable

BURNSIDE—Formerly served by Charter Communications. Now served by Time Warner Cable, CORBIN, KY [KY0030]

BURNSIDE—See CORBIN, KY (Time Warner Cable)

BURTONVILLE—See RICHMOND, KY (Time Warner Cable)

BUSY—TVS Cable

BUTLER COUNTY (PORTIONS)—See MORGANTOWN, KY (Mediacom)

BUTLER—See COVINGTON, KY (Time Warner Cable)

BUTTERFLY—See BUSY, KY (TVS Cable)

CADIZ—Mediacom

CALDWELL COUNTY (PORTIONS)—See DAWSON SPRINGS, KY (Time Warner Cable)

CALDWELL COUNTY—See MARION, KY (Mediacom)

CALHOUN—See OWENSBORO, KY (Time Warner Cable)

CALIFORNIA—See COVINGTON, KY (Time Warner Cable)

CALLOWAY COUNTY (PORTIONS)—See MARSHALL COUNTY, KY (Mediacom)

CALLOWAY COUNTY—Mediacom. Now served by MARSHALL COUNTY, KY [KY0035]

CALLOWAY COUNTY—See MAYFIELD, KY (Time Warner Cable)

CALVERT CITY—Formerly served by Charter Communications. Now served by Time Warner Cable, MAYFIELD, KY [KY0037]

CALVERT CITY—See MAYFIELD, KY (Time Warner Cable)

CALVIN—See CORBIN, KY (Time Warner Cable)

CAMARGO—See RICHMOND, KY (Time Warner Cable)

CAMBRIDGE—See LOUISVILLE, KY (Time Warner Cable)

CAMPBELL COUNTY (PORTIONS)—See COVINGTON, KY (Time Warner Cable)

CAMPBELLSBURG—See LOUISVILLE, IN (Time Warner Cable)

CAMPBELLSBURG—See LOUISVILLE, KY (Time Warner Cable)

CAMPBELLSVILLE—Comcast Cablevision of the South. Now served by ELIZABETHTOWN, KY [KY0012]

CAMPBELLSVILLE—See ELIZABETHTOWN, KY (Comcast Cable)

CAMPTON—MTTV. This cable system has converted to IPTV. Now served by WEST LIBERTY, KY [KY5013]

CAMPTON—See WEST LIBERTY, KY (MTTV. Formerly [KY0090]. This cable system has converted to IPTV.)

CANADA—See HAROLD, KY (Inter Mountain Cable Inc)

CANEYVILLE—Mediacom

CANNEL CITY—See WEST LIBERTY, KY (MTTV. Formerly [KY0090]. This cable system has converted to IPTV.)

CANNON—See GRAY, KY (Eastern Cable Corp)

CARCASSONNE—See JEREMIAH, KY (TVS Cable)

CARLISLE COUNTY (PORTIONS)—See GRAVES COUNTY, KY (Zito Media)

CARLISLE COUNTY—See WICKLIFFE, KY (Zito Media)

CARLISLE—Time Warner Cable. Now served by RICHMOND, KY [KY0008]

CARLISLE—See RICHMOND, KY (Time Warner Cable)

CARRIE—See HINDMAN, KY (TVS Cable)

CARROLL COUNTY (PORTIONS)—See LOUISVILLE, KY (Time Warner Cable)

CARROLLTON—See LOUISVILLE, KY (Time Warner Cable)

CARTER COUNTY (PORTIONS)—See GRAYSON, KY (Suddenlink Communications)

CARTER COUNTY (SOUTHWESTERN PORTION)—See RICHMOND, KY (Time Warner Cable)

CASEY COUNTY (portions)—Mediacom. Now served by RUSSELL COUNTY, KY [KY0114]

CASEY COUNTY (PORTIONS)—See CORBIN, KY (Time Warner Cable)

CASEY COUNTY (SOUTHERN PORTION)—See RUSSELL COUNTY (unincorporated areas), KY (Mediacom)

CAVE CITY—See HORSE CAVE, KY (Comcast Cable)

CAWOOD—See BLACK MOUNTAIN, KY (Zito Media)

CENTERTOWN—See MADISONVILLE, KY (Time Warner Cable)

CENTRAL CITY—See GREENVILLE, KY (Comcast Cable)

CENTRAL CITY—See BREMEN, KY (Inside Connect Cable)

CHARLESTOWN—See LOUISVILLE, IN (Time Warner Cable)

CHARLEY—Lycom Communications

CHAVIES—See BONNYMAN, KY (TVS Cable)

CHERRYWOOD VILLAGE—See LOUISVILLE, KY (Time Warner Cable)

CHEVROLET—See BLACK MOUNTAIN, KY (Zito Media)

CHRISTIAN COUNTY (PORTIONS)—See MADISONVILLE, KY (Time Warner Cable)

CHRISTIAN COUNTY—See NORTONVILLE, KY (Mediacom)

CHRISTIAN COUNTY—See TRENTON, KY (Mediacom)

CHRISTOPHER—See LOTHAIR, KY (TVS Cable)

CLAIBORNE COUNTY (PORTIONS)—See CORBIN, TN (Time Warner Cable)

CLARK COUNTY (PORTIONS)—See LOUISVILLE, IN (Time Warner Cable)

CLARK COUNTY (PORTIONS)—See RICHMOND, KY (Time Warner Cable)

CLARKSON—See ELIZABETHTOWN, KY (Comcast Cable)

CLARKSVILLE—See LOUISVILLE, IN (Time Warner Cable)

CLAY (town)—Time Warner Cable. Now served by CLAY (town) (formerly Dixon), KY [KY0218]

CLAY (TOWN)—Time Warner Cable

CLAY CITY—See STANTON, KY (Crystal Broadband Networks)

CLEAR CREEK—See CORBIN, KY (Time Warner Cable)

CLINTON COUNTY (PORTIONS)—See SUMMER SHADE, KY (Mediacom)

CLINTON COUNTY—Mediacom. Now served by SUMMER SHADE, KY [KY0092]

CLINTON—See WICKLIFFE, KY (Zito Media)

CLOVER BOTTOM—Formerly served by McKee TV Enterprises Inc. No longer in operation

CLOVERPORT—Formerly served by Inside Connect Cable (formerly Crystal Broadband). No longer in operation

COAL GROVE (VILLAGE)—See ASHLAND, OH (Time Warner Cable)

COAL RUN—See HAROLD, KY (Inter Mountain Cable Inc)

COALGOOD—See BLACK MOUNTAIN, KY (Zito Media)

COLD SPRING—See COVINGTON, KY (Time Warner Cable)

COLDIRON—See HARLAN, KY (Harlan Community TV Inc)

COLDIRON—See WALLINS CREEK, KY (Zito Media)

COLDSTREAM—See LOUISVILLE, KY (Time Warner Cable)

COLLIER CREEK—See JENKINS, KY (Inter Mountain Cable Inc)

COLONY—See LONDON, KY (Time Warner Cable)

COLSON—See JEREMIAH, KY (TVS Cable)

COLUMBIA (PORTIONS)—See RUSSELL SPRINGS, KY (Duo County Telecom)

COLUMBIA—Duo County Telephone. Now served by RUSSELL SPRINGS, KY [KY0243]

CONWAY—See CORBIN, KY (Time Warner Cable)

CORBIN—Time Warner Cable

Cable Community Index—Kentucky

CORINTH—Formerly served by City of Williamstown. No longer in operation

CORYDON—Time Warner Cable. Now served by OWENSBORO, KY [KY0004]

CORYDON—See LOUISVILLE, IN (Time Warner Cable)

CORYDON—See OWENSBORO, KY (Time Warner Cable)

COVINGTON—Time Warner Cable

COWAN CREEK—TVS Cable

CRAB ORCHARD—Wilcop Cable TV. Now served by BRODHEAD, KY [KY0173]

CRAB ORCHARD—See BRODHEAD, KY (Wilcop Cable TV)

CRANKS—See BLACK MOUNTAIN, KY (Zito Media)

CREEKSIDE—See LOUISVILLE, KY (Time Warner Cable)

CRESCENT PARK—See COVINGTON, KY (Time Warner Cable)

CRESCENT SPRINGS—See COVINGTON, KY (Time Warner Cable)

CRESTVIEW HILLS—See COVINGTON, KY (Time Warner Cable)

CRESTVIEW—See COVINGTON, KY (Time Warner Cable)

CRESTWOOD—See LOUISVILLE, KY (Time Warner Cable)

CRITTENDEN COUNTY—See MARION, KY (Mediacom)

CRITTENDEN—Formerly served by Insight Communications. Now served by Time Warner Cable, COVINGTON, KY [KY0002]

CRITTENDEN—See COVINGTON, KY (Time Warner Cable)

CROFTON—See NORTONVILLE, KY (Mediacom)

CROMONA—See HAYMOND, KY (TVS Cable)

CROMWELL—Formerly served by Vital Communications. No longer in operation

CROSSGATE—See LOUISVILLE, KY (Time Warner Cable)

CROTHERSVILLE—See LOUISVILLE, IN (Time Warner Cable)

CRUMMIES—See BLACK MOUNTAIN, KY (Zito Media)

CUBAGE—See CORBIN, KY (Time Warner Cable)

CUMBERLAND COUNTY (PORTIONS)—See RUSSELL SPRINGS, KY (Duo County Telecom)

CUMBERLAND COUNTY (PORTIONS)—See BURKESVILLE, KY (Mediacom)

CUMBERLAND—Access Cable Television Inc

CUNNINGHAM—See GRAVES COUNTY, KY (Zito Media)

CUTSHIN—Formerly served by Craft Cable Service. Now served by TVS Cable, VICCO, KY [KY0339]

CUTSHIN—See VICCO, KY (TVS Cable)

CYNTHIANA—Time Warner Cable. Now served by RICHMOND, KY [KY0008]

CYNTHIANA—See RICHMOND, KY (Time Warner Cable)

DANVILLE—Time Warner Cable. Now served by RICHMOND, KY [KY0008]

DANVILLE—See RICHMOND, KY (Time Warner Cable)

DARFORK—See BULAN, KY (Time Warner Cable)

DAVID—See HAROLD, KY (Inter Mountain Cable Inc)

DAVIESS COUNTY (PORTIONS)—See WHITESVILLE, KY (Mediacom)

DAVIESS COUNTY (PORTIONS)—See OWENSBORO, KY (Time Warner Cable)

DAWSON SPRINGS—Time Warner Cable

DAYHOIT—See HARLAN, KY (Harlan Community TV Inc)

DAYHOIT—See WALLINS CREEK, KY (Zito Media)

DAYTON—See COVINGTON, KY (Time Warner Cable)

DEANE—See JENKINS, KY (Inter Mountain Cable Inc)

DEFEATED—See SCOTTSVILLE, TN (NCTC. Formerly [KY0073]. This cable system has converted to IPTV)

DEMA—See TOPMOST, KY (TVS Cable)

DENVER—See VAN LEAR, KY (Big Sandy Broadband)

DEWITT—See CORBIN, KY (Time Warner Cable)

DEXTER—See MARSHALL COUNTY, KY (Mediacom)

DIXON—See CLAY (town), KY (Time Warner Cable)

DIZNEY—See BLACK MOUNTAIN, KY (Zito Media)

DOE VALLEY—See LOUISVILLE, KY (Time Warner Cable)

DORTON—See HAROLD, KY (Inter Mountain Cable Inc)

DOUGLASS HILLS—See LOUISVILLE, KY (Time Warner Cable)

DOVER—See TRENTON, TN (Mediacom)

DRAKESBORO—See GREENVILLE, KY (Comcast Cable)

DRUID HILLS—See LOUISVILLE, KY (Time Warner Cable)

DRY RIDGE—See COVINGTON, KY (Time Warner Cable)

DUNMOR—Formerly served by Windjammer Cable. No longer in operation

DWALE—See HAROLD, KY (Inter Mountain Cable Inc)

DYER—See MAYFIELD, TN (Time Warner Cable)

EARLINGTON—See MADISONVILLE, KY (Time Warner Cable)

EAST BERNSTADT—See LONDON, KY (Time Warner Cable)

EAST PINEVILLE—See CORBIN, KY (Time Warner Cable)

EAST POINT—See VAN LEAR, KY (Big Sandy Broadband)

EASTERN—See HAROLD, KY (Inter Mountain Cable Inc)

EDDYVILLE—See KUTTAWA, KY (Zito Media)

EDGEWOOD—See COVINGTON, KY (Time Warner Cable)

EDMONSON COUNTY—See MORGANTOWN, KY (Mediacom)

EDMONTON—See SUMMER SHADE, KY (Mediacom)

EIGHTY EIGHT—See SUMMER SHADE, KY (Mediacom)

ELIZABETHTOWN—Comcast Cable

ELIZAVILLE—See RICHMOND, KY (Time Warner Cable)

ELKHORN CITY—Formerly served by Cebridge Connections. Now served by Suddenlink Communications, PIKEVILLE, KY [KY0045]

ELKHORN CITY—See PIKEVILLE, KY (Suddenlink Communications)

ELKTON—Mediacom. Now served by TRENTON, KY [KY0101]

ELKTON—See TRENTON, KY (Mediacom)

ELLIOTT COUNTY (UNINCORPORATED AREAS)—See WEST LIBERTY, KY (MTTV. Formerly [KY0090]. This cable system has converted to IPTV.)

ELSMERE—See COVINGTON, KY (Time Warner Cable)

EMINENCE—See LOUISVILLE, KY (Time Warner Cable)

EMMA—See HAROLD, KY (Inter Mountain Cable Inc)

ENTERPRISE—See RICHMOND, KY (Time Warner Cable)

EOLIA—Formerly served by Charter Communications. Now served by Inter Mountain Cable Inc., JENKINS, KY [KY0041]

EOLIA—See JENKINS, KY (Inter Mountain Cable Inc)

EPWORTH—See RICHMOND, KY (Time Warner Cable)

EQUALITY (VILLAGE)—See OWENSBORO, IL (Time Warner Cable)

ERLANGER—See COVINGTON, KY (Time Warner Cable)

ERMINE—See MAYKING, KY (TVS Cable)

ESTILL COUNTY (PORTIONS)—See HINDMAN, KY (TVS Cable)

ESTILL COUNTY—See IRVINE, KY (Irvine Community TV Inc)

EUBANK—See CORBIN, KY (Time Warner Cable)

EVARTS—Evarts TV Inc

EVERSOLE—See JENKINS, KY (Inter Mountain Cable Inc)

EWING—See RICHMOND, KY (Time Warner Cable)

EZEL—See WEST LIBERTY, KY (MTTV. Formerly [KY0090]. This cable system has converted to IPTV.)

FABER—See CORBIN, KY (Time Warner Cable)

FAIRMEADE—See LOUISVILLE, KY (Time Warner Cable)

FAIRVIEW—See COVINGTON, KY (Time Warner Cable)

FALCON—See SALYERSVILLE, KY (Howard's TV Cable)

FALLSBURG—Formerly served by Lycom Communications. No longer in operation

FALMOUTH—Formerly served by Insight Communications. Now served by Time Warner Cable, COVINGTON, KY [KY0002]

FALMOUTH—See COVINGTON, KY (Time Warner Cable)

FANCY FARM—See GRAVES COUNTY, KY (Zito Media)

FAYETTE COUNTY (PORTIONS)—See LEXINGTON, KY (Time Warner Cable)

FAYETTE TWP.—See ASHLAND, OH (Time Warner Cable)

FEDSCREEK—Formerly served by Fuller's TV. Now served by Inter Mountain Cable Inc., HAROLD, KY [KY0006]

FEDSCREEK—See HAROLD, KY (Inter Mountain Cable Inc)

FERGUSON—See CORBIN, KY (Time Warner Cable)

FINCASTLE—See LOUISVILLE, KY (Time Warner Cable)

FISTY—See BULAN, KY (Time Warner Cable)

FITCH—See RICHMOND, KY (Time Warner Cable)

FIVE STAR—Formerly served by Insight Communications. No longer in operation

FLAT LICK—Time Warner Cable. Now served by CORBIN, KY [KY0030]

FLAT LICK—See CORBIN, KY (Time Warner Cable)

FLATWOODS—See ASHLAND, KY (Time Warner Cable)

Kentucky—Cable Community Index

FLEMING COUNTY (PORTIONS)—See RICHMOND, KY (Time Warner Cable)

FLEMING—See JENKINS, KY (Inter Mountain Cable Inc)

FLEMINGSBURG—Formerly served by Adelphia Communications. Now served by Time Warner Cable, RICHMOND, KY [KY0008]

FLEMINGSBURG—See RICHMOND, KY (Time Warner Cable)

FLORENCE—See COVINGTON, KY (Time Warner Cable)

FLOYD COUNTY (PORTIONS)—See LOUISVILLE, IN (Time Warner Cable)

FLOYD COUNTY—See HAROLD, KY (Inter Mountain Cable Inc)

FLOYDS KNOBS—See LOUISVILLE, IN (Time Warner Cable)

FOGERTOWN—See CORBIN, KY (Time Warner Cable)

FORDSVILLE—See WHITESVILLE, KY (Mediacom)

FOREST HILLS—See LOUISVILLE, KY (Time Warner Cable)

FORT CAMPBELL—Comcast Cable. Now served by NASHVILLE, TN [TN0002]

FORT KNOX—See LOUISVILLE, KY (Time Warner Cable)

FORT MITCHELL—See COVINGTON, KY (Time Warner Cable)

FORT THOMAS—See COVINGTON, KY (Time Warner Cable)

FORT WRIGHT—See COVINGTON, KY (Time Warner Cable)

FOURMILE—See CORBIN, KY (Time Warner Cable)

FOXPORT—See RICHMOND, KY (Time Warner Cable)

FRAKES—Formerly served by Suddenlink Communications. No longer in operation

FRANKFORT/STONEWALL—Formerly served by Vital Communications. No longer in operation

FRANKFORT—Frankfort Plant Board Cable Service

FRANKLIN COUNTY (SOUTHERN PORTION)—See RICHMOND, KY (Time Warner Cable)

FRANKLIN FURNACE—See ASHLAND, OH (Time Warner Cable)

FRANKLIN—Comcast Cable. Now served by NASHVILLE, TN [TN0002]

FREDERICKTOWN—See BARDSTOWN, KY (Bardstown Cable TV)

FREDONIA—See MARION, KY (Mediacom)

FREEBURN—See HAROLD, KY (Inter Mountain Cable Inc)

FRENCHBURG—MTTV. This cable system has converted to IPTV.

Now served by WEST LIBERTY, KY [KY5013]

FRENCHBURG—See WEST LIBERTY, KY (MTTV. Formerly [KY0090]. This cable system has converted to IPTV.)

FULTON—Time Warner Cable. Now served by MAYFIELD, KY [KY0037]

FULTON—See MAYFIELD, KY (Time Warner Cable)

GALLATIN COUNTY (PORTIONS)—See COVINGTON, KY (Time Warner Cable)

GALLATIN COUNTY (PORTIONS)—See OWENSBORO, KY (Time Warner Cable)

GALVESTON—See HAROLD, KY (Inter Mountain Cable Inc)

GAMALIEL—See SUMMER SHADE, KY (Mediacom)

GARRARD COUNTY (PORTIONS)—See RICHMOND, KY (Time Warner Cable)

GARRARD—Time Warner Cable. Now served by CORBIN, KY [KY0030]

GARRARD—See CORBIN, KY (Time Warner Cable)

GARRETT—See HAROLD, KY (Inter Mountain Cable Inc)

GARRISON—Formerly served by Adelphia Communications. Now served by Time Warner Cable, VANCEBURG, KY [KY0286]

GARRISON—See VANCEBURG, KY (Time Warner Cable)

GEORGETOWN—Time Warner Cable. Now served by RICHMOND, KY [KY0008]

GEORGETOWN—See LOUISVILLE, IN (Time Warner Cable)

GEORGETOWN—See RICHMOND, KY (Time Warner Cable)

GERMANTOWN—See AUGUSTA, KY (Limestone Bracken Cablevision)

GHENT—See LOUISVILLE, KY (Time Warner Cable)

GIBBO—See JENKINS, KY (Inter Mountain Cable Inc)

GIBSON COUNTY—See MAYFIELD, TN (Time Warner Cable)

GIRDLER—See GRAY, KY (Eastern Cable Corp)

GIRDLER—See CORBIN, KY (Time Warner Cable)

GLASGOW—Glasgow Electric Power Board-CATV Division. This cable system has converted to IPTV. See GLASGOW, KY [KY5022]

GLASGOW—Glasgow EPB. Formerly [KY0038]. This cable system has converted to IPTV

GLENVIEW HILLS—See LOUISVILLE, KY (Time Warner Cable)

GLENVIEW MANOR—See LOUISVILLE, KY (Time Warner Cable)

GLENVIEW—See LOUISVILLE, KY (Time Warner Cable)

GLOBE—See RICHMOND, KY (Time Warner Cable)

GOOSE CREEK—See LOUISVILLE, KY (Time Warner Cable)

GOOSE ROCK—See CORBIN, KY (Time Warner Cable)

GORDON—See COWAN CREEK, KY (TVS Cable)

GRAND RIVERS—See KUTTAWA, KY (Zito Media)

GRANT COUNTY (PORTIONS)—See COVINGTON, KY (Time Warner Cable)

GRAPEVINE—See BONNYMAN, KY (TVS Cable)

GRAVES COUNTY (PORTIONS)—See MAYFIELD, KY (Time Warner Cable)

GRAVES COUNTY—Zito Media

GRAY HAWK—See WANETA, KY (Peoples Telecom)

GRAY—Eastern Cable Corp

GRAYMOOR-DEVONDALE—See LOUISVILLE, KY (Time Warner Cable)

GRAYS KNOB—See HARLAN, KY (Harlan Community TV Inc)

GRAYSON COUNTY (PORTIONS)—See ELIZABETHTOWN, KY (Comcast Cable)

GRAYSON COUNTY (PORTIONS)—See CANEYVILLE, KY (Mediacom)

GRAYSON—Suddenlink Communications

GREASY CREEK—Formerly served by Suddenlink Communications. No longer in operation

GREASY CREEK—See LESLIE COUNTY (northern portion), KY (Crystal Broadband Networks)

GREEN COUNTY (PORTIONS)—See GREENSBURG, KY (Access Cable Television Inc)

GREEN SPRING—See LOUISVILLE, KY (Time Warner Cable)

GREEN TWP. (SCIOTO COUNTY)—See ASHLAND, OH (Time Warner Cable)

GREENMOUNT—See PEOPLES, KY (C & W Cable)

GREENSBURG—Access Cable Television Inc

GREENUP COUNTY (PORTIONS)—See ASHLAND, KY (Time Warner Cable)

GREENUP—Formerly served by Charter Communications. Now served by Armstrong Cable Services, ZELIENOPLE, PA [PA0053]

GREENVILLE—Comcast Cable

GREENVILLE—See LOUISVILLE, IN (Time Warner Cable)

GRETHEL—See HAROLD, KY (Inter Mountain Cable Inc)

GUTHRIE—See TRENTON, KY (Mediacom)

HAGERHILL—See VAN LEAR, KY (Big Sandy Broadband)

HALDEMAN—See RICHMOND, KY (Time Warner Cable)

HAMILTON TWP. (LAWRENCE COUNTY)—See ASHLAND, OH (Time Warner Cable)

HANCOCK COUNTY (PORTIONS)—See HAWESVILLE, KY (Inside Connect Cable)

HANGING ROCK (VILLAGE)—See ASHLAND, OH (Time Warner Cable)

HANGING ROCK—See ASHLAND, OH (Time Warner Cable)

HANSON—See MADISONVILLE, KY (Time Warner Cable)

HARDBURLY—See BULAN, KY (Time Warner Cable)

HARDIN COUNTY (PORTIONS)—See ELIZABETHTOWN, KY (Comcast Cable)

HARDIN COUNTY (PORTIONS)—See LOUISVILLE, KY (Time Warner Cable)

HARDIN COUNTY (SOUTHEASTERN PORTION)—See UPTON, KY (Mediacom)

HARDIN—See MARSHALL COUNTY, KY (Mediacom)

HARDINSBURG—Crystal Broadband Networks

HARDSHELL—See BULAN, KY (Time Warner Cable)

HARDY—See HAROLD, KY (Inter Mountain Cable Inc)

HARLAN COUNTY (PORTIONS)—See CUMBERLAND, KY (Access Cable Television Inc)

HARLAN COUNTY (UNINCORPORATED AREAS)—See EVARTS, KY (Evarts TV Inc)

HARLAN COUNTY—See HARLAN, KY (Harlan Community TV Inc)

HARLAN—Harlan Community TV Inc

HARLAN—See CORBIN, KY (Time Warner Cable)

HAROLD—Inter Mountain Cable Inc

HARRISON COUNTY (PORTIONS)—See LOUISVILLE, IN (Time Warner Cable)

HARRISON COUNTY (PORTIONS)—See RICHMOND, KY (Time Warner Cable)

HARRODSBURG—Time Warner Cable. Now served by RICHMOND, KY [KY0008]

HARRODSBURG—See RICHMOND, KY (Time Warner Cable)

HART COUNTY—See UPTON, KY (Mediacom)

HARTFORD—See MADISONVILLE, KY (Time Warner Cable)

HATFIELD BOTTOM—See HAROLD, WV (Inter Mountain Cable Inc)

Cable Community Index—Kentucky

HATFIELD—See OWENSBORO, IN (Time Warner Cable)

HAWESVILLE—Inside Connect Cable

HAYMOND—TVS Cable

HAZARD—Formerly served by Hazard TV Cable Co. Inc. No longer in operation

HAZEL GREEN—See WEST LIBERTY, KY (MTTV. Formerly [KY0090]. This cable system has converted to IPTV.)

HAZEL—Zito Media

HEIDRICK—See BARBOURVILLE, KY (Barbourville Utility Commission)

HELTON—See MOZELLE, KY (Crystal Broadband Networks)

HENDERSON (portions)—Time Warner Cable. Now served by EVANSVILLE, IN [IN0006]

HENDERSON (town)—Time Warner Cable. Now served by OWENSBORO, KY [KY0004]

HENDERSON (TOWN)—See OWENSBORO, KY (Time Warner Cable)

HENDERSON COUNTY (PORTIONS)—Mediacom

HENDERSON COUNTY (PORTIONS)—See OWENSBORO, KY (Time Warner Cable)

HENDERSON—See HENDERSON COUNTY (portions), KY (Mediacom)

HENRY COUNTY (PORTIONS)—See LOUISVILLE, KY (Time Warner Cable)

HENRYVILLE—See LOUISVILLE, KY (Time Warner Cable)

HERITAGE CREEK—See LOUISVILLE, KY (Time Warner Cable)

HI HAT—See HAROLD, KY (Inter Mountain Cable Inc)

HICKMAN—Zito Media

HICKORY HILL—See LOUISVILLE, KY (Time Warner Cable)

HICKORY—See GRAVES COUNTY, KY (Zito Media)

HIGHLAND HEIGHTS—See COVINGTON, KY (Time Warner Cable)

HILLS AND DALES—See LOUISVILLE, KY (Time Warner Cable)

HILLSBORO—See RICHMOND, KY (Time Warner Cable)

HILLVIEW—See LOUISVILLE, KY (Time Warner Cable)

HIMA—See CORBIN, KY (Time Warner Cable)

HINDMAN—TVS Cable

HINKLE—See CORBIN, KY (Time Warner Cable)

HIPPO—See HAROLD, KY (Inter Mountain Cable Inc)

HIRAM—See CUMBERLAND, KY (Access Cable Television Inc)

HISEVILLE—See HORSE CAVE, KY (Comcast Cable)

HITE—See HAROLD, KY (Inter Mountain Cable Inc)

HODGENVILLE—Comcast Cablevision of the South. Now served by ELIZABETHTOWN, KY [KY0012]

HODGENVILLE—See ELIZABETHTOWN, KY (Comcast Cable)

HOLLOW CREEK—See LOUISVILLE, KY (Time Warner Cable)

HOLLYVILLA—See LOUISVILLE, KY (Time Warner Cable)

HOLMES MILL—See BLACK MOUNTAIN, KY (Zito Media)

HOPKINS COUNTY (PORTIONS)—See NORTONVILLE, KY (Mediacom)

HOPKINS COUNTY (PORTIONS)—See DAWSON SPRINGS, KY (Time Warner Cable)

HOPKINS COUNTY (UNINCORPORATED AREAS)—See MADISONVILLE, KY (Time Warner Cable)

HOPKINS COUNTY—See NEBO, KY (Mediacom)

HOPKINSVILLE—Time Warner Cable. Now served by MADISONVILLE, KY [KY0013]

HOPKINSVILLE—See TRENTON, KY (Mediacom)

HOPKINSVILLE—See MADISONVILLE, KY (Time Warner Cable)

HORNBEAK—See MAYFIELD, TN (Time Warner Cable)

HORSE CAVE—Comcast Cable

HOUSTON ACRES—See LOUISVILLE, KY (Time Warner Cable)

HUEYSVILLE—See HAROLD, KY (Inter Mountain Cable Inc)

HUNTER—See HAROLD, KY (Inter Mountain Cable Inc)

HUNTERS HOLLOW—See LOUISVILLE, KY (Time Warner Cable)

HURLEY—See HAROLD, VA (Inter Mountain Cable Inc)

HURSTBOURNE ACRES—See LOUISVILLE, KY (Time Warner Cable)

HURSTBOURNE—See LOUISVILLE, KY (Time Warner Cable)

HUSTONVILLE—Access Cable Television Inc

HYDEN—Bowling Cable TV

INDEPENDENCE—See COVINGTON, KY (Time Warner Cable)

INDEX—See WEST LIBERTY, KY (MTTV. Formerly [KY0090]. This cable system has converted to IPTV.)

INDIAN HILLS-CHEROKEE—See LOUISVILLE, KY (Time Warner Cable)

INDIAN HILLS—See LOUISVILLE, KY (Time Warner Cable)

INEZ—Formerly served by Charter Communications. Now served by Suddenlink Communications, KERMIT, WV [WV0038]

IRONTON—See ASHLAND, OH (Time Warner Cable)

IRVINE—Irvine Community TV Inc

IRVINGTON (VILLAGE)—See IRVINGTON, KY (Crystal Broadband Networks)

IRVINGTON—Crystal Broadband Networks

ISLAND CITY—Formerly served by City TV Cable. No longer in operation

ISLAND CREEK—See HAROLD, KY (Inter Mountain Cable Inc)

ISLAND—Formerly served by Crystal Broadband Networks. No longer in operation

ISOM—See JEREMIAH, KY (TVS Cable)

IVEL—See HAROLD, KY (Inter Mountain Cable Inc)

IVYTON—See SALYERSVILLE, KY (Howard's TV Cable)

JACKHORN—See JENKINS, KY (Inter Mountain Cable Inc)

JACKSON COUNTY (PORTIONS)—See PEOPLES, KY (C & W Cable)

JACKSON COUNTY (PORTIONS)—See LOUISVILLE, IN (Time Warner Cable)

JACKSON COUNTY—See WANETA, KY (Peoples Telecom)

JACKSON—Crystal Broadband Networks

JAMESTOWN (PORTIONS)—See RUSSELL SPRINGS, KY (Duo County Telecom)

JEFF—See LOTHAIR, KY (TVS Cable)

JEFFERSON COUNTY (PORTIONS)—See LOUISVILLE, KY (Time Warner Cable)

JEFFERSONTOWN—See LOUISVILLE, KY (Time Warner Cable)

JEFFERSONVILLE (PORTIONS)—See LOUISVILLE, KY (Time Warner Cable)

JEFFERSONVILLE (PORTIONS)—See RICHMOND, KY (Time Warner Cable)

JEFFERSONVILLE—See LOUISVILLE, IN (Time Warner Cable)

JENKINS—Inter Mountain Cable Inc

JEREMIAH—TVS Cable

JESSAMINE COUNTY (NORTHERN PORTION)—See LEXINGTON, KY (Time Warner Cable)

JESSAMINE COUNTY (PORTIONS)—See RICHMOND, KY (Time Warner Cable)

JOHNNY YOUNG BRANCH—See HAROLD, KY (Inter Mountain Cable Inc)

JOHNSON COUNTY—See HAROLD, KY (Inter Mountain Cable Inc)

JUNCTION (VILLAGE)—See OWENSBORO, IL (Time Warner Cable)

JUNCTION CITY (BOYLE COUNTY)—See RICHMOND, KY (Time Warner Cable)

JUNCTION CITY (LINCOLN COUNTY)—See RICHMOND, KY (Time Warner Cable)

KEAVY—See LONDON, KY (Time Warner Cable)

KEENELAND—See LOUISVILLE, KY (Time Warner Cable)

KEITH—See WALLINS CREEK, KY (Zito Media)

KENTON COUNTY (PORTIONS)—See COVINGTON, KY (Time Warner Cable)

KENTON VALE—See COVINGTON, KY (Time Warner Cable)

KENTON—See MAYFIELD, TN (Time Warner Cable)

KETTLE ISLAND—See CORBIN, KY (Time Warner Cable)

KEVIL—See ELIZABETHTOWN, KY (Comcast Cable)

KIMPER—See HAROLD, KY (Inter Mountain Cable Inc)

KINGSLEY—See LOUISVILLE, KY (Time Warner Cable)

KINGSTON—See RICHMOND, KY (Time Warner Cable)

KIRKSVILLE—See RICHMOND, KY (Time Warner Cable)

KITE—See TOPMOST, KY (TVS Cable)

KNOTT COUNTY (PORTIONS)—See HAROLD, KY (Inter Mountain Cable Inc)

KNOTT COUNTY (PORTIONS)—See BULAN, KY (Time Warner Cable)

KNOTT COUNTY—See HINDMAN, KY (TVS Cable)

KNOX COUNTY (PORTIONS)—See CORBIN, KY (Time Warner Cable)

KNOX COUNTY (PORTIONS)—See WHITLEY COUNTY (portions), KY (Zito Media)

KNOX COUNTY—See BARBOURVILLE, KY (Barbourville Utility Commission)

KRYPTON—See BUSY, KY (TVS Cable)

KUTTAWA—Zito Media

LA CENTER—See WICKLIFFE, KY (Zito Media)

LA GRANGE—See LOUISVILLE, KY (Time Warner Cable)

LAFAYETTE—Formerly served by Adelphia Communications. No longer in operation

LAFAYETTE—See SCOTTSVILLE, TN (NCTC. Formerly [KY0073]. This cable system has converted to IPTV)

LAKE COUNTY (PORTIONS)—See MAYFIELD, TN (Time Warner Cable)

LAKESIDE PARK—See COVINGTON, KY (Time Warner Cable)

LAKEVIEW HEIGHTS—See RICHMOND, KY (Time Warner Cable)

Kentucky—Cable Community Index

LANCASTER—See RICHMOND, KY (Time Warner Cable)

LANDSAW—See WEST LIBERTY, KY (MTTV. Formerly [KY0090]. This cable system has converted to IPTV.)

LANESVILLE—See LOUISVILLE, IN (Time Warner Cable)

LANGDON PLACE—See LOUISVILLE, KY (Time Warner Cable)

LARUE COUNTY (PORTIONS)—See ELIZABETHTOWN, KY (Comcast Cable)

LARUE COUNTY (PORTIONS)—See RICHMOND, KY (Time Warner Cable)

LARUE COUNTY (WESTERN PORTION)—See UPTON, KY (Mediacom)

LATONIA LAKES—See COVINGTON, KY (Time Warner Cable)

LAUREL COUNTY (PORTIONS)—See PEOPLES, KY (C & W Cable)

LAUREL COUNTY (PORTIONS)—See CORBIN, KY (Time Warner Cable)

LAUREL COUNTY (WESTERN PORTION)—See LONDON, KY (Time Warner Cable)

LAWRENCE COUNTY (SOUTHERN PORTION)—Lycom Communications

LAWRENCE TWP.—See ASHLAND, OH (Time Warner Cable)

LAWRENCEBURG—Time Warner Cable. Now served by RICHMOND, KY [KY0008]

LAWRENCEBURG—See RICHMOND, KY (Time Warner Cable)

LAWTON—See RICHMOND, KY (Time Warner Cable)

LEATHERWOOD—See LOTHAIR, KY (TVS Cable)

LEBANON JUNCTION—See LOUISVILLE, KY (Time Warner Cable)

LEBANON—Time Warner Cable

LEBURN—See HINDMAN, KY (TVS Cable)

LEDBETTER—See ELIZABETHTOWN, KY (Comcast Cable)

LEE CITY—See VANCLEVE, KY (TVS Cable)

LEITCHFIELD—Comcast Cable. Now served by ELIZABETHTOWN, KY [KY0012]

LEITCHFIELD—See ELIZABETHTOWN, KY (Comcast Cable)

LEJUNIOR—See BLACK MOUNTAIN, KY (Zito Media)

LEROSE—Formerly served by Phil's Cablevision. No longer in operation

LESLIE COUNTY (NORTHERN PORTION)—Crystal Broadband Networks

LESLIE COUNTY (PORTIONS)—See HYDEN, KY (Bowling Cable TV)

LESLIE COUNTY (PORTIONS)—See CORBIN, KY (Time Warner Cable)

LETCHER COUNTY (PORTIONS)—See JEREMIAH, KY (TVS Cable)

LEWIS COUNTY (WESTERN PORTION)—See RICHMOND, KY (Time Warner Cable)

LEWIS CREEK—See JENKINS, KY (Inter Mountain Cable Inc)

LEWISBURG—See RUSSELLVILLE, KY (Suddenlink Communications)

LEWISPORT—Formerly served by Crystal Broadband Networks. Now served by Inside Connect Cable, HAWESVILLE, KY [KY0232]

LEWISPORT—See HAWESVILLE, KY (Inside Connect Cable)

LEXINGTON—Formerly served by Wireless Associates L.P. No longer in operation

LEXINGTON—See LOUISVILLE, IN (Time Warner Cable)

LEXINGTON—Time Warner Cable

LIBERTY—Time Warner Cable. Now served by CORBIN, KY [KY0030]

LIBERTY—See CORBIN, KY (Time Warner Cable)

LICKBURG—See SALYERSVILLE, KY (Howard's TV Cable)

LILY—See CORBIN, KY (Time Warner Cable)

LIMESTONE—See RICHMOND, KY (Time Warner Cable)

LINCOLN COUNTY (EASTERN PORTION)—Mediacom

LINCOLN COUNTY (NORTHERN PORTION)—See RICHMOND, KY (Time Warner Cable)

LINCOLN COUNTY (PORTIONS)—See HUSTONVILLE, KY (Access Cable Television Inc)

LINCOLNSHIRE—See LOUISVILLE, KY (Time Warner Cable)

LINEFORK—See COWAN CREEK, KY (TVS Cable)

LITTCARR—See HINDMAN, KY (TVS Cable)

LITTLE MUD CREEK—See HAROLD, KY (Inter Mountain Cable Inc)

LITTLE ROBINSON—See HAROLD, KY (Inter Mountain Cable Inc)

LIVERMORE—Time Warner Cable. Now served by OWENSBORO, KY [KY0004]

LIVERMORE—See OWENSBORO, KY (Time Warner Cable)

LIVINGSTON COUNTY (PORTIONS)—See KUTTAWA, KY (Zito Media)

LOG MOUNTAIN—See CORBIN, KY (Time Warner Cable)

LOGAN COUNTY (PORTIONS)—See RUSSELLVILLE, KY (Suddenlink Communications)

LONDON—Time Warner Cable

LONE OAK (GRAYSON COUNTY)—See ELIZABETHTOWN, KY (Comcast Cable)

LORETTO—See LEBANON, KY (Time Warner Cable)

LOTHAIR—TVS Cable

LOUELLEN—See BLACK MOUNTAIN, KY (Zito Media)

LOUISA—Lycom Communications

LOUISVILLE—No longer in operation

LOUISVILLE—Time Warner Cable

LOVELACEVILLE—See GRAVES COUNTY, KY (Zito Media)

LOWMANSVILLE—Tri-Wave Communications Inc

LOYALL—See HARLAN, KY (Harlan Community TV Inc)

LUDLOW—See COVINGTON, KY (Time Warner Cable)

LYNCH—Formerly served by Tri-Star Communications. No longer in operation

LYNCH—See CUMBERLAND, KY (Access Cable Television Inc)

LYNDON—See LOUISVILLE, KY (Time Warner Cable)

LYNN—See HAROLD, WV (Inter Mountain Cable Inc)

LYNNVIEW—See LOUISVILLE, KY (Time Warner Cable)

LYON COUNTY—See KUTTAWA, KY (Zito Media)

MADISON COUNTY (PORTIONS)—See RICHMOND, KY (Time Warner Cable)

MADISONVILLE—Time Warner Cable

MAGOFFIN COUNTY—See SALYERSVILLE, KY (Howard's TV Cable)

MAGOFFIN—See HAROLD, KY (Inter Mountain Cable Inc)

MAJESTIC—See HAROLD, KY (Inter Mountain Cable Inc)

MALLIE—See HINDMAN, KY (TVS Cable)

MALONE—See WEST LIBERTY, KY (MTTV. Formerly [KY0090]. This cable system has converted to IPTV.)

MALONETON—Time Warner Cable. Now served by VANCEBURG, KY [KY0286]

MALONETON—See VANCEBURG, KY (Time Warner Cable)

MANCHESTER—Formerly served by C & W Cable. No longer in operation

MANOR CREEK—See LOUISVILLE, KY (Time Warner Cable)

MANTON—See HAROLD, KY (Inter Mountain Cable Inc)

MARION COUNTY (PORTIONS)—See LEBANON, KY (Time Warner Cable)

MARION—Mediacom

MARROWBONE—See BURKESVILLE, KY (Mediacom)

MARSHALL COUNTY—Mediacom

MARTIN—See HAROLD, KY (Inter Mountain Cable Inc)

MARTINS FORK—Formerly served by Tri-State Cable TV. No longer in operation

MARY ALICE—See HARLAN, KY (Harlan Community TV Inc)

MARYHILL ESTATES—See LOUISVILLE, KY (Time Warner Cable)

MASON COUNTY—See MAYSVILLE, KY (Limestone Bracken Cablevision)

MASSAC COUNTY (PORTIONS)—See ELIZABETHTOWN, IL (Comcast Cable)

MATEWAN—See HAROLD, WV (Inter Mountain Cable Inc)

MAYFIELD—Time Warner Cable

MAYFIELD—See GRAVES COUNTY, KY (Zito Media)

MAYKING—TVS Cable

MAYSVILLE—Limestone Bracken Cablevision

MAYTOWN—See HAROLD, KY (Inter Mountain Cable Inc)

MCCARR—See HAROLD, KY (Inter Mountain Cable Inc)

MCCRACKEN COUNTY (PORTIONS)—See ELIZABETHTOWN, KY (Comcast Cable)

MCCREARY COUNTY (PORTIONS)—Access Cable Television Inc

MCHENRY—See MADISONVILLE, KY (Time Warner Cable)

MCKEE—See WANETA, KY (Peoples Telecom)

MCKINNEY—Time Warner Cable. Now served by CORBIN, KY [KY0030]

MCKINNEY—See CORBIN, KY (Time Warner Cable)

MCLEAN COUNTY (PORTIONS)—See OWENSBORO, KY (Time Warner Cable)

MCROBERTS—See JENKINS, KY (Inter Mountain Cable Inc)

MCVEIGH—See HAROLD, KY (Inter Mountain Cable Inc)

MEADE COUNTY (PORTIONS)—See LOUISVILLE, KY (Time Warner Cable)

MEADOW VALE—See LOUISVILLE, KY (Time Warner Cable)

MEADOWBROOK FARM—See LOUISVILLE, KY (Time Warner Cable)

MEADOWVIEW ESTATES—See LOUISVILLE, KY (Time Warner Cable)

MEALLY—See VAN LEAR, KY (Big Sandy Broadband)

MEANS—See WEST LIBERTY, KY (MTTV. Formerly [KY0090]. This cable system has converted to IPTV.)

Cable Community Index—Kentucky

MELBOURNE—See COVINGTON, KY (Time Warner Cable)

MELVIN—See HAROLD, KY (Inter Mountain Cable Inc)

MENIFEE COUNTY (UNINCORPORATED AREAS)—See WEST LIBERTY, KY (MTTV. Formerly [KY0090]. This cable system has converted to IPTV.)

MENTOR—See COVINGTON, KY (Time Warner Cable)

MERCER COUNTY (PORTIONS)—See RICHMOND, KY (Time Warner Cable)

META—See HAROLD, KY (Inter Mountain Cable Inc)

METROPOLIS—See ELIZABETHTOWN, IL (Comcast Cable)

MIDDLEBURG—See CORBIN, KY (Time Warner Cable)

MIDDLESBORO—Time Warner Cable. Now served by CORBIN, KY [KY0030]

MIDDLESBORO—See CORBIN, KY (Time Warner Cable)

MIDDLETOWN—See LOUISVILLE, KY (Time Warner Cable)

MIDWAY—Time Warner Cable. Now served by RICHMOND, KY [KY0008]

MIDWAY—See RICHMOND, KY (Time Warner Cable)

MILLERSBURG—See RICHMOND, KY (Time Warner Cable)

MILLSTONE—See HAYMOND, KY (TVS Cable)

MILLVILLE—Formerly served by Chumley's Antenna Systems Inc. No longer in operation

MILLWOOD—See CANEYVILLE, KY (Mediacom)

MILTON—See LOUISVILLE, KY (Time Warner Cable)

MINGO COUNTY—See HAROLD, WV (Inter Mountain Cable Inc)

MINOR LANE HEIGHTS—See LOUISVILLE, KY (Time Warner Cable)

MIRACLE—See CORBIN, KY (Time Warner Cable)

MIZE—See WEST LIBERTY, KY (MTTV. Formerly [KY0090]. This cable system has converted to IPTV.)

MOCKINGBIRD VALLEY—See LOUISVILLE, KY (Time Warner Cable)

MONROE COUNTY (PORTIONS)—See SUMMER SHADE, KY (Mediacom)

MONROE—See LOUISVILLE, KY (Time Warner Cable)

MONTGOMERY COUNTY (PORTIONS)—See RICHMOND, KY (Time Warner Cable)

MONTICELLO—Community Telecom Services

MOORLAND—See LOUISVILLE, KY (Time Warner Cable)

MOREHEAD STATE UNIVERSITY—Morehead State University

MOREHEAD—Time Warner Cable. Now served by RICHMOND, KY [KY0008]

MOREHEAD—See RICHMOND, KY (Time Warner Cable)

MORELAND—See HUSTONVILLE, KY (Access Cable Television Inc)

MORGAN COUNTY (UNINCORPORATED AREAS)—See WEST LIBERTY, KY (MTTV. Formerly [KY0090]. This cable system has converted to IPTV.)

MORGANFIELD—See OWENSBORO, KY (Time Warner Cable)

MORGANTOWN—Mediacom

MORNING VIEW—See COVINGTON, KY (Time Warner Cable)

MORTONS GAP—See MADISONVILLE, KY (Time Warner Cable)

MOUNT CARMEL—See RICHMOND, KY (Time Warner Cable)

MOUNT OLIVET—See AUGUSTA, KY (Limestone Bracken Cablevision)

MOUNT STERLING—Time Warner Cable. Now served by RICHMOND, KY [KY0008]

MOUNT STERLING—See RICHMOND, KY (Time Warner Cable)

MOUNT VERNON—Formerly served by Charter Communications. Now served by Time Warner Cable, CORBIN, KY [KY0030]

MOUNT VERNON—See CORBIN, KY (Time Warner Cable)

MOUNT WASHINGTON—See LOUISVILLE, KY (Time Warner Cable)

MOUSIE—TVS Cable

MOZELLE—Crystal Broadband Networks

MUHLENBERG COUNTY—See GREENVILLE, KY (Comcast Cable)

MULDRAUGH—See LOUISVILLE, KY (Time Warner Cable)

MUNFORDVILLE—See UPTON, KY (Mediacom)

MURRAY HILL—See LOUISVILLE, KY (Time Warner Cable)

MURRAY—Time Warner Cable. Now served by MAYFIELD, KY [KY0037]

MURRAY—Murray Electric System

MURRAY—See MAYFIELD, KY (Time Warner Cable)

MYRA—See HAROLD, KY (Inter Mountain Cable Inc)

NANCY—See CORBIN, KY (Time Warner Cable)

NAVAL ORDNANCE STATION LOUISVILLE—See LOUISVILLE, KY (Time Warner Cable)

NEBO—Mediacom

NELSON COUNTY (PORTIONS)—See BARDSTOWN, KY (Bardstown Cable TV)

NELSON COUNTY (PORTIONS)—See LEBANON, KY (Time Warner Cable)

NELSON—Formerly served by Time Warner Cable. No longer in operation

NEON—See JENKINS, KY (Inter Mountain Cable Inc)

NEPTON—See RICHMOND, KY (Time Warner Cable)

NEW ALBANY—See LOUISVILLE, IN (Time Warner Cable)

NEW CASTLE—See LOUISVILLE, KY (Time Warner Cable)

NEW HAVEN—Formerly served by Adelphia Communications. Now served by Time Warner Cable, LEBANON, KY [KY0049]

NEW HAVEN—See LEBANON, KY (Time Warner Cable)

NEW PEKIN—See LOUISVILLE, IN (Time Warner Cable)

NEW WASHINGTON—See LOUISVILLE, KY (Time Warner Cable)

NEWPORT—Formerly served by Insight Communications. Now served by Time Warner Cable, COVINGTON, KY [KY0002]

NEWPORT—See COVINGTON, KY (Time Warner Cable)

NEWTOWN—See HAROLD, WV (Inter Mountain Cable Inc)

NICHOLAS COUNTY (PORTIONS)—See RICHMOND, KY (Time Warner Cable)

NICHOLASVILLE—Time Warner Cable. Now served by RICHMOND, KY [KY0008]

NICHOLASVILLE—See RICHMOND, KY (Time Warner Cable)

NORBOURNE ESTATES—See LOUISVILLE, KY (Time Warner Cable)

NORTH MATEWAN—See HAROLD, WV (Inter Mountain Cable Inc)

NORTH MIDDLETOWN—Time Warner Cable. Now served by RICHMOND, KY [KY0008]

NORTH MIDDLETOWN—See RICHMOND, KY (Time Warner Cable)

NORTHFIELD—See LOUISVILLE, KY (Time Warner Cable)

NORTONVILLE—Mediacom

NORWOOD—See LOUISVILLE, KY (Time Warner Cable)

OAK GROVE—Mediacom. Now served by TRENTON, KY [KY0101]

OAK GROVE—See TRENTON, KY (Mediacom)

OAKLAND—See BOWLING GREEN, KY (Time Warner Cable)

OBION COUNTY (PORTIONS)—See MAYFIELD, TN (Time Warner Cable)

OHIO COUNTY (PORTIONS)—See WHITESVILLE, KY (Mediacom)

OHIO COUNTY (PORTIONS)—See MADISONVILLE, KY (Time Warner Cable)

OLD BROWNSBORO PLACE—See LOUISVILLE, KY (Time Warner Cable)

OLD SHAWNEETOWN (VILLAGE)—See OWENSBORO, IL (Time Warner Cable)

OLDHAM COUNTY (PORTIONS)—See LOUISVILLE, KY (Time Warner Cable)

OLIVE HILL—Time Warner Cable. Now served by RICHMOND, KY [KY0008]

OLIVE HILL—See RICHMOND, KY (Time Warner Cable)

ONEIDA—See CORBIN, KY (Time Warner Cable)

ORCHARD GRASS HILLS—See LOUISVILLE, KY (Time Warner Cable)

OVEN FORK—See JENKINS, KY (Inter Mountain Cable Inc)

OWEN COUNTY (PORTIONS)—See OWENTON, KY (Inside Connect Cable (formerly Kentucky Ridge Country Communications))

OWENSBORO—Time Warner Cable

OWENTON—Inside Connect Cable (formerly Kentucky Ridge Country Communications)

OWINGSVILLE—Time Warner Cable. Now served by RICHMOND, KY [KY0008]

OWINGSVILLE—See RICHMOND, KY (Time Warner Cable)

OWSLEY COUNTY (NORTHERN PORTION)—See BEATTYVILLE, KY (Crystal Broadband Networks)

OWSLEY COUNTY (PORTIONS)—See BOONEVILLE, KY (Peoples Telecom)

PADUCAH (town)—Comcast Cable. Now served by ELIZABETHTOWN, KY [KY0012]

PADUCAH (town)—Formerly served by NDW II Inc. No longer in operation

PADUCAH—See ELIZABETHTOWN, KY (Comcast Cable)

PAINTSVILLE—Formerly served by Charter Communications. Now served by Suddenlink Communications, KERMIT, WV [WV0038]

PALMYRA—See LOUISVILLE, IN (Time Warner Cable)

PARIS—Time Warner Cable. Now served by RICHMOND, KY [KY0008]

PARIS—See RICHMOND, KY (Time Warner Cable)

PARK CITY—Mediacom

PARK HILLS—See COVINGTON, KY (Time Warner Cable)

PARKSVILLE—Formerly served by Charter Communications. No longer in operation

Kentucky—Cable Community Index

PARKWAY VILLAGE—See LOUISVILLE, KY (Time Warner Cable)

PARTRIDGE—See JENKINS, KY (Inter Mountain Cable Inc)

PATHFORK—Formerly served by Suddenlink Communications. No longer in operation

PAYNE GAP—See JENKINS, KY (Inter Mountain Cable Inc)

PEKIN—See LOUISVILLE, IN (Time Warner Cable)

PEMBROKE—See TRENTON, KY (Mediacom)

PENDLETON COUNTY (PORTIONS)—See COVINGTON, KY (Time Warner Cable)

PEOPLES—C & W Cable

PERRY COUNTY (PORTIONS)—See LESLIE COUNTY (northern portion), KY (Crystal Broadband Networks)

PERRY COUNTY (PORTIONS)—See BULAN, KY (Time Warner Cable)

PERRY COUNTY (PORTIONS)—See HINDMAN, KY (TVS Cable)

PERRY TWP. (LAWRENCE COUNTY)—See ASHLAND, OH (Time Warner Cable)

PERRYVILLE—Time Warner Cable. Now served by RICHMOND, KY [KY0008]

PERRYVILLE—See RICHMOND, KY (Time Warner Cable)

PETER FORK—See HAROLD, KY (Inter Mountain Cable Inc)

PEWEE VALLEY—See LOUISVILLE, KY (Time Warner Cable)

PHELPS—See HAROLD, KY (Inter Mountain Cable Inc)

PHYLLIS—See HAROLD, KY (Inter Mountain Cable Inc)

PICKETT COUNTY (PORTIONS)—See SUMMER SHADE, TN (Mediacom)

PIKE COUNTY (PORTIONS)—See PIKEVILLE, KY (Suddenlink Communications)

PIKE COUNTY—See HAROLD, KY (Inter Mountain Cable Inc)

PIKEVILLE—See HAROLD, KY (Inter Mountain Cable Inc)

PIKEVILLE—Suddenlink Communications

PINE HILL—Time Warner Cable. Now served by RICHMOND, KY [KY0008]

PINE HILL—See RICHMOND, KY (Time Warner Cable)

PINE TOP—See HINDMAN, KY (TVS Cable)

PINEVILLE—Formerly served by NewWave Communications. Now served by Time Warner Cable, CORBIN, KY [KY0030]

PINEVILLE—Time Warner Cable. Now served by CORBIN, KY [KY0030]

PINEVILLE—See CORBIN, KY (Time Warner Cable)

PINSONFORK—See HAROLD, KY (Inter Mountain Cable Inc)

PIONEER VILLAGE—See LOUISVILLE, KY (Time Warner Cable)

PIPPA PASSES—See HINDMAN, KY (TVS Cable)

PLANTATION—See LOUISVILLE, KY (Time Warner Cable)

PLEASANT HILL—See SALYERSVILLE, KY (Howard's TV Cable)

PLEASANT RIDGE—Formerly served by Vital Communications. No longer in operation

PLEASUREVILLE—See LOUISVILLE, KY (Time Warner Cable)

PLUM SPRINGS—See BOWLING GREEN, KY (Time Warner Cable)

PLYMOUTH VILLAGE—See LOUISVILLE, KY (Time Warner Cable)

POUND—See JENKINS, VA (Inter Mountain Cable Inc)

POWDERLY—See GREENVILLE, KY (Comcast Cable)

POWELL COUNTY (UNINCORPORATED AREAS)—See STANTON, KY (Crystal Broadband Networks)

PRATER CREEK—See HAROLD, KY (Inter Mountain Cable Inc)

PRATER FORK—See HAROLD, KY (Inter Mountain Cable Inc)

PREMIUM—See JEREMIAH, KY (TVS Cable)

PRESTONSBURG—Suddenlink Communications. Now served by KERMIT, WV [WV0038]

PRESTONSBURG—See HAROLD, KY (Inter Mountain Cable Inc)

PRESTONVILLE—See LOUISVILLE, KY (Time Warner Cable)

PRINCETON—Mediacom. Now served by MARION, KY [KY0071]

PRINCETON—See MARION, KY (Mediacom)

PRINTER—See HAROLD, KY (Inter Mountain Cable Inc)

PROSPECT—See LOUISVILLE, KY (Time Warner Cable)

PROVIDENCE—Time Warner Cable

PRYORSBURG—See GRAVES COUNTY, KY (Zito Media)

PULASKI COUNTY (PORTIONS)—See CORBIN, KY (Time Warner Cable)

PURYEAR—See HAZEL, TN (Zito Media)

PUTNEY—See BLACK MOUNTAIN, KY (Zito Media)

PYRAMID—See HAROLD, KY (Inter Mountain Cable Inc)

RACELAND—See ASHLAND, KY (Time Warner Cable)

RADCLIFF—See ELIZABETHTOWN, KY (Comcast Cable)

RADCLIFF—See LOUISVILLE, KY (Time Warner Cable)

RADO HOLLOW—See JENKINS, KY (Inter Mountain Cable Inc)

RANSOM—See HAROLD, KY (Inter Mountain Cable Inc)

RAVEN—See TOPMOST, KY (TVS Cable)

RAVENNA—See IRVINE, KY (Irvine Community TV Inc)

RED BOILING SPRINGS—See SCOTTSVILLE, TN (NCTC. Formerly [KY0073]. This cable system has converted to IPTV)

RED JACKET—See HAROLD, WV (Inter Mountain Cable Inc)

REDFOX—See JEREMIAH, KY (TVS Cable)

RENFRO VALLEY—See CORBIN, KY (Time Warner Cable)

RIBOLT—See RICHMOND, KY (Time Warner Cable)

RICHLAWN—See LOUISVILLE, KY (Time Warner Cable)

RICHMOND—Time Warner Cable

RIDGELY—See MAYFIELD, TN (Time Warner Cable)

RIDGWAY (VILLAGE)—See OWENSBORO, IL (Time Warner Cable)

RINGOS MILLS—See RICHMOND, KY (Time Warner Cable)

RISNER—See HAROLD, KY (Inter Mountain Cable Inc)

RIVER BLUFF—See LOUISVILLE, KY (Time Warner Cable)

RIVERWOOD—See LOUISVILLE, KY (Time Warner Cable)

ROBARDS—See OWENSBORO, KY (Time Warner Cable)

ROBERTS BRANCH—See JENKINS, KY (Inter Mountain Cable Inc)

ROBINETTE KNOB—See HAROLD, KY (Inter Mountain Cable Inc)

ROBINSON CREEK—See HAROLD, KY (Inter Mountain Cable Inc)

ROBINSWOOD—See LOUISVILLE, KY (Time Warner Cable)

ROCHESTER—Formerly served by Vital Communications. No longer in operation

ROCKCASTLE COUNTY (PORTIONS)—See CORBIN, KY (Time Warner Cable)

ROCKCASTLE COUNTY (WESTERN PORTION)—See LINCOLN COUNTY (eastern portion), KY (Mediacom)

ROCKHOLDS—See CORBIN, KY (Time Warner Cable)

ROCKHOUSE—See HAROLD, KY (Inter Mountain Cable Inc)

ROCKPORT—See OWENSBORO, IN (Time Warner Cable)

ROCKPORT—See MADISONVILLE, KY (Time Warner Cable)

ROLLING FIELDS—See LOUISVILLE, KY (Time Warner Cable)

ROLLING HILLS—See LOUISVILLE, KY (Time Warner Cable)

ROSSPOINT—See BLACK MOUNTAIN, KY (Zito Media)

ROUGH RIVER DAM—Formerly served by Mediacom. No longer in operation

ROWAN COUNTY (PORTIONS)—See RICHMOND, KY (Time Warner Cable)

ROWDY—See BULAN, KY (Time Warner Cable)

RUSSELL COUNTY (PORTIONS)—See RUSSELL SPRINGS, KY (Duo County Telecom)

RUSSELL COUNTY (UNINCORPORATED AREAS)—Mediacom

RUSSELL SPRINGS—Duo County Telecom

RUSSELL—See ASHLAND, KY (Time Warner Cable)

RUSSELLVILLE—Suddenlink Communications

RUTHERFORD—See MAYFIELD, TN (Time Warner Cable)

RYLAND HEIGHTS—See COVINGTON, KY (Time Warner Cable)

SACRAMENTO—See BREMEN, KY (Inside Connect Cable)

SALEM—See MARION, KY (Mediacom)

SALEM—See LOUISVILLE, IN (Time Warner Cable)

SALT GUM—See CORBIN, KY (Time Warner Cable)

SALT LICK—See RICHMOND, KY (Time Warner Cable)

SALTILLO—See LOUISVILLE, IN (Time Warner Cable)

SALYERSVILLE—Howard's TV Cable

SAMBURG—See MAYFIELD, TN (Time Warner Cable)

SANDY HOOK—Formerly served by Windjammer Cable. No longer in operation

SANDY HOOK—See WEST LIBERTY, KY (MTTV. Formerly [KY0090]. This cable system has converted to IPTV.)

SASSAFRAS—See VICCO, KY (TVS Cable)

SCALF—See CORBIN, KY (Time Warner Cable)

SCIENCE HILL—See CORBIN, KY (Time Warner Cable)

SCOTT COUNTY (PORTIONS)—See LOUISVILLE, IN (Time Warner Cable)

SCOTT COUNTY (PORTIONS)—See RICHMOND, KY (Time Warner Cable)

SCOTTSBURG—See LOUISVILLE, IN (Time Warner Cable)

Cable Community Index—Kentucky

SCOTTSVILLE—NCTC. This cable system has converted to IPTV. See SCOTTSVILLE, KY [KY5016]

SCOTTSVILLE—NCTC. Formerly [KY0073]. This cable system has converted to IPTV

SEBREE—Time Warner Cable. Now served by MADISONVILLE, KY [KY0013]

SEBREE—See MADISONVILLE, KY (Time Warner Cable)

SECO—See HAYMOND, KY (TVS Cable)

SEDALIA—See GRAVES COUNTY, KY (Zito Media)

SELLERSBURG—See LOUISVILLE, IN (Time Warner Cable)

SENECA GARDENS—See LOUISVILLE, KY (Time Warner Cable)

SHARKEY—See RICHMOND, KY (Time Warner Cable)

SHARPSBURG—Formerly served by Adelphia Communications. Now served by Time Warner Cable, RICHMOND, KY [KY0008]

SHARPSBURG—See RICHMOND, KY (Time Warner Cable)

SHAWNEETOWN—See OWENSBORO, IL (Time Warner Cable)

SHELBY COUNTY (PORTIONS)—See LOUISVILLE, KY (Time Warner Cable)

SHELBY GAP—See HAROLD, KY (Inter Mountain Cable Inc)

SHELBYVILLE—Formerly served by Insight Communications. Now served by Time Warner Cable, LOUISVILLE, KY [KY0001]

SHELBYVILLE—See LOUISVILLE, KY (Time Warner Cable)

SHEPHERDSVILLE—Inside Connect Cable. Now served by BROOKS, KY [KY0199]

SHEPHERDSVILLE—See BROOKS, KY (Inside Connect Cable)

SHEPHERDSVILLE—See LOUISVILLE, KY (Time Warner Cable)

SHIVELY—See LOUISVILLE, KY (Time Warner Cable)

SIBERT—See CORBIN, KY (Time Warner Cable)

SILOAM—See SCOTTSVILLE, TN (NCTC. Formerly [KY0073]. This cable system has converted to IPTV)

SILVER GROVE—See COVINGTON, KY (Time Warner Cable)

SIMPSONVILLE—See LOUISVILLE, KY (Time Warner Cable)

SITKA—Sitka TV Cable

SLAUGHTERS—Formerly served by Vital Communications. No longer in operation

SLOANS VALLEY—See CORBIN, KY (Time Warner Cable)

SMITHFIELD—See LOUISVILLE, KY (Time Warner Cable)

SMITHLAND—See KUTTAWA, KY (Zito Media)

SMITHS GROVE—See BOWLING GREEN, KY (Time Warner Cable)

SOLDIER—Time Warner Cable. Now served by RICHMOND, KY [KY0008]

SOLDIER—See RICHMOND, KY (Time Warner Cable)

SOMERSET (village)—Time Warner Cable. Now served by CORBIN, KY [KY0030]

SOMERSET—See CORBIN, KY (Time Warner Cable)

SONORA—See UPTON, KY (Mediacom)

SOUTH CARROLLTON—See GREENVILLE, KY (Comcast Cable)

SOUTH FULTON—See MAYFIELD, TN (Time Warner Cable)

SOUTH PARK VIEW—See LOUISVILLE, KY (Time Warner Cable)

SOUTH PIKEVILLE—See PIKEVILLE, KY (Suddenlink Communications)

SOUTHGATE—See COVINGTON, KY (Time Warner Cable)

SPENCER COUNTY (PORTIONS)—See OWENSBORO, IN (Time Warner Cable)

SPENCER COUNTY (PORTIONS)—See LOUISVILLE, KY (Time Warner Cable)

SPRING VALLEY—See LOUISVILLE, KY (Time Warner Cable)

SPRINGFIELD—See LEBANON, KY (Time Warner Cable)

SPRINGLEE—See LOUISVILLE, KY (Time Warner Cable)

ST. CHARLES—See DAWSON SPRINGS, KY (Time Warner Cable)

ST. MATTHEWS—See LOUISVILLE, KY (Time Warner Cable)

ST. PAUL—See CANEYVILLE, KY (Mediacom)

ST. REGIS PARK—See LOUISVILLE, KY (Time Warner Cable)

STAMPING GROUND—See RICHMOND, KY (Time Warner Cable)

STANFORD—Time Warner Cable. Now served by RICHMOND, KY [KY0008]

STANFORD—See RICHMOND, KY (Time Warner Cable)

STANTON—Crystal Broadband Networks

STANVILLE—See HAROLD, KY (Inter Mountain Cable Inc)

STEWART COUNTY—See TRENTON, TN (Mediacom)

STINNETT—See LESLIE COUNTY (northern portion), KY (Crystal Broadband Networks)

STONE COAL—See HAROLD, KY (Inter Mountain Cable Inc)

STONEY FORK—See CORBIN, KY (Time Warner Cable)

STOPOVER—See HAROLD, KY (Inter Mountain Cable Inc)

STRAIGHT CREEK—See CORBIN, KY (Time Warner Cable)

STRATHMOOR GARDENS—See LOUISVILLE, KY (Time Warner Cable)

STRATHMOOR MANOR—See LOUISVILLE, KY (Time Warner Cable)

STRATHMOOR VILLAGE—See LOUISVILLE, KY (Time Warner Cable)

STURGIS—Time Warner Cable. Now served by OWENSBORO, KY [KY0004]

STURGIS—See OWENSBORO, KY (Time Warner Cable)

SUMMER SHADE—Mediacom. Now served by SUMMER SHADE, KY [KY0092]

SUMMER SHADE—Mediacom

SUMMERSVILLE—Formerly served by NewWave Communications. No longer in operation

SUMMERSVILLE—See GREENSBURG, KY (Access Cable Television Inc)

SYCAMORE CREEK—Formerly served by Inter Mountain Cable Inc. No longer in operation

SYCAMORE—See LOUISVILLE, KY (Time Warner Cable)

SYMSONIA—See GRAVES COUNTY, KY (Zito Media)

TATEVILLE—See CORBIN, KY (Time Warner Cable)

TAYLOR COUNTY (PORTIONS)—See ELIZABETHTOWN, KY (Comcast Cable)

TAYLOR MILL—See COVINGTON, KY (Time Warner Cable)

TAYLORSVILLE—Formerly served by Insight Communications. Now served by Time Warner Cable, LOUISVILLE, KY [KY0001]

TAYLORSVILLE—See LOUISVILLE, KY (Time Warner Cable)

TEABERRY—See HAROLD, KY (Inter Mountain Cable Inc)

TEN BROECK—See LOUISVILLE, KY (Time Warner Cable)

THACKER—See HAROLD, WV (Inter Mountain Cable Inc)

THORNHILL—See LOUISVILLE, KY (Time Warner Cable)

THORNTON—See MAYKING, KY (TVS Cable)

TIPTONVILLE—See MAYFIELD, TN (Time Warner Cable)

TODD COUNTY—See TRENTON, KY (Mediacom)

TOLER CREEK—See HAROLD, KY (Inter Mountain Cable Inc)

TOLLESBORO—Formerly served by Adelphia Communications. Now served by Time Warner Cable, RICHMOND, KY [KY0008]

TOLLESBORO—See RICHMOND, KY (Time Warner Cable)

TOMPKINSVILLE—See SUMMER SHADE, KY (Mediacom)

TOPMOST—TVS Cable

TOTZ—See BLACK MOUNTAIN, KY (Zito Media)

TRAM—See HAROLD, KY (Inter Mountain Cable Inc)

TRENTON—Mediacom

TRIBBEY—See BULAN, KY (Time Warner Cable)

TRIGG COUNTY—See CADIZ, KY (Mediacom)

TRIMBLE COUNTY (PORTIONS)—See LOUISVILLE, KY (Time Warner Cable)

TUTOR KEY—P & W TV Cable

TYNER—See PEOPLES, KY (C & W Cable)

TYPO—See BONNYMAN, KY (TVS Cable)

UNION COUNTY (PORTIONS)—See OWENSBORO, KY (Time Warner Cable)

UNION TWP. (LAWRENCE COUNTY)—See ASHLAND, OH (Time Warner Cable)

UNION—See COVINGTON, KY (Time Warner Cable)

UNIONTOWN—See OWENSBORO, KY (Time Warner Cable)

UPPER JOHNS CREEK—See HAROLD, KY (Inter Mountain Cable Inc)

UPPER TWP.—See ASHLAND, OH (Time Warner Cable)

UPPER TYGART—See RICHMOND, KY (Time Warner Cable)

UPTON/SONORA—Mediacom. Now served by UPTON (formerly Munfordville), KY [KY0086]

UPTON—Mediacom

UTICA—See LOUISVILLE, IN (Time Warner Cable)

VAN LEAR—Big Sandy Broadband

VANCEBURG—Time Warner Cable

VANCLEVE—TVS Cable

VARNEY—Inter Mountain Cable Inc. Now served by HAROLD, KY [KY0006]

VARNEY—See HAROLD, KY (Inter Mountain Cable Inc)

VERSAILLES—Time Warner Cable. Now served by RICHMOND, KY [KY0008]

VERSAILLES—See RICHMOND, KY (Time Warner Cable)

VEST—See HINDMAN, KY (TVS Cable)

Kentucky—Cable Community Index

VICCO—TVS Cable

VIENNA—See LOUISVILLE, IN (Time Warner Cable)

VILLA HILLS—See COVINGTON, KY (Time Warner Cable)

VINE GROVE—See ELIZABETHTOWN, KY (Comcast Cable)

VIPER—See LOTHAIR, KY (TVS Cable)

WACO—See RICHMOND, KY (Time Warner Cable)

WALKER—See CORBIN, KY (Time Warner Cable)

WALKERTOWN—Walkertown Cable

WALLINGFORD—See RICHMOND, KY (Time Warner Cable)

WALLINS CREEK—Zito Media

WALLINS—See HARLAN, KY (Harlan Community TV Inc)

WALLINS—See WALLINS CREEK, KY (Zito Media)

WALTON—See COVINGTON, KY (Time Warner Cable)

WANETA—Peoples Telecom

WARREN COUNTY (PORTIONS)—See BOWLING GREEN, KY (Time Warner Cable)

WARSAW—Time Warner Cable. Now served by COVINGTON, KY [KY0002]

WARSAW—See COVINGTON, KY (Time Warner Cable)

WASHINGTON COUNTY (PORTIONS)—See LOUISVILLE, IN (Time Warner Cable)

WASHINGTON COUNTY (PORTIONS)—See RICHMOND, KY (Time Warner Cable)

WATERGAP—See HAROLD, KY (Inter Mountain Cable Inc)

WATTERSON PARK—See LOUISVILLE, KY (Time Warner Cable)

WAVERLY—See OWENSBORO, KY (Time Warner Cable)

WAYLAND—See TOPMOST, KY (TVS Cable)

WAYNE COUNTY—See MONTICELLO, KY (Community Telecom Services)

WAYNESBURG—See CORBIN, KY (Time Warner Cable)

WEBSTER COUNTY (PORTIONS)—See CLAY (town), KY (Time Warner Cable)

WEBSTER COUNTY (PORTIONS)—See OWENSBORO, KY (Time Warner Cable)

WEBSTER COUNTY (PORTIONS)—See PROVIDENCE, KY (Time Warner Cable)

WEEKSBURY—See HAROLD, KY (Inter Mountain Cable Inc)

WELCHS CREEK—Formerly served by Vital Communications. No longer in operation

WELLINGTON—See LOUISVILLE, KY (Time Warner Cable)

WELLS ADDITION—See HAROLD, KY (Inter Mountain Cable Inc)

WEST BUECHEL—See LOUISVILLE, KY (Time Warner Cable)

WEST LIBERTY—MTTV. This cable system has converted to IPTV. Now served by WEST LIBERTY, KY [KY5013]

WEST LIBERTY—MTTV. Formerly [KY0090]. This cable system has converted to IPTV.

WEST POINT—See BROOKS, KY (Inside Connect Cable)

WEST POINT—See LOUISVILLE, KY (Time Warner Cable)

WEST PRESTONSBURG—See HAROLD, KY (Inter Mountain Cable Inc)

WEST VAN LEAR—See VAN LEAR, KY (Big Sandy Broadband)

WESTMORELAND—See SCOTTSVILLE, TN (NCTC. Formerly [KY0073]. This cable system has converted to IPTV)

WESTWOOD—See ASHLAND, KY (Time Warner Cable)

WHEATCROFT—See CLAY (town), KY (Time Warner Cable)

WHEELWRIGHT—See HAROLD, KY (Inter Mountain Cable Inc)

WHIPPS MILLGATE—See LOUISVILLE, KY (Time Warner Cable)

WHITCO—See COWAN CREEK, KY (TVS Cable)

WHITE HALL—See RICHMOND, KY (Time Warner Cable)

WHITE PLAINS—See MADISONVILLE, KY (Time Warner Cable)

WHITESBURG—Formerly served by Comcast Cable. No longer in operation

WHITESBURG—See HAYMOND, KY (TVS Cable)

WHITESVILLE—Mediacom

WHITLEY CITY—Access Cable Television Inc. Now served by McCREARY COUNTY, KY [KY0331]

WHITLEY COUNTY (PORTIONS)—See CORBIN, KY (Time Warner Cable)

WHITLEY COUNTY (PORTIONS)—Zito Media

WHITLEY COUNTY—Access Cable Television Inc

WICKLIFFE—Zito Media

WILDER—See COVINGTON, KY (Time Warner Cable)

WILDWOOD—See LOUISVILLE, KY (Time Warner Cable)

WILLIAMSBURG—Time Warner Cable. Now served by CORBIN, KY [KY0030]

WILLIAMSBURG—See WHITLEY COUNTY, KY (Access Cable Television Inc)

WILLIAMSBURG—See CORBIN, KY (Time Warner Cable)

WILLIAMSPORT—See VAN LEAR, KY (Big Sandy Broadband)

WILLIAMSTOWN—Williamstown Cable

WILLISBURG—Formerly served by Windjammer Cable. No longer in operation

WILMORE—See RICHMOND, KY (Time Warner Cable)

WINCHESTER—Time Warner Cable. Now served by RICHMOND, KY [KY0008]

WINCHESTER—See RICHMOND, KY (Time Warner Cable)

WINDING FALLS—See LOUISVILLE, KY (Time Warner Cable)

WINDSOR—See RUSSELL COUNTY (unincorporated areas), KY (Mediacom)

WINDY HILLS—See LOUISVILLE, KY (Time Warner Cable)

WINGO—See GRAVES COUNTY, KY (Zito Media)

WISE COUNTY (NORTHERN PORTION)—See JENKINS, VA (Inter Mountain Cable Inc)

WOLFE COUNTY (UNINCORPORATED AREAS)—See WEST LIBERTY, KY (MTTV. Formerly [KY0090]. This cable system has converted to IPTV.)

WOODBINE—See CORBIN, KY (Time Warner Cable)

WOODBURN—See BOWLING GREEN, KY (Time Warner Cable)

WOODFORD COUNTY (EASTERN PORTION)—See RICHMOND, KY (Time Warner Cable)

WOODLAND HILLS—See LOUISVILLE, KY (Time Warner Cable)

WOODLAWN PARK—See LOUISVILLE, KY (Time Warner Cable)

WOODLAWN—See COVINGTON, KY (Time Warner Cable)

WOOTON—See LESLIE COUNTY (northern portion), KY (Crystal Broadband Networks)

WORTHINGTON HILLS—See LOUISVILLE, KY (Time Warner Cable)

WORTHINGTON—See ASHLAND, KY (Time Warner Cable)

WORTHVILLE—See LOUISVILLE, KY (Time Warner Cable)

WYNNBURG—See MAYFIELD, TN (Time Warner Cable)

YERKES—See BUSY, KY (TVS Cable)

YOSEMITE—See CORBIN, KY (Time Warner Cable)

ZEBULON—See HAROLD, KY (Inter Mountain Cable Inc)

LOUISIANA

ABBEVILLE—Cox Communications. Now served by BATON ROUGE, LA [LA0003]

ABBEVILLE—See BATON ROUGE, LA (Cox Communications)

ABITA SPRINGS—See SLIDELL, LA (Charter Communications)

ACADIA PARISH (portions)—Formerly served by Almega Cable. No longer in operation

ACADIA PARISH (PORTIONS)—See OPELOUSAS, LA (Charter Communications)

ADDIS—See BATON ROUGE, LA (Cox Communications)

ALBANY—See SLIDELL, LA (Charter Communications)

ALEXANDRIA—Suddenlink Communications

ALLEN PARISH (PORTIONS)—See KINDER, LA (Vyve Broadband)

ALLEN PARISH—See OAKDALE, LA (Media3)

AMA—See NEW ORLEANS, LA (Cox Communications)

AMELIA—See THIBODAUX, LA (Charter Communications)

AMITE CITY—See SLIDELL, LA (Charter Communications)

ANACOCO—See LEESVILLE, LA (Suddenlink Communications)

ANGOLA—Formerly served by Bailey Cable TV Inc. No longer in operation

ARABI—See NEW ORLEANS, LA (Cox Communications)

ARCADIA—Alliance Communications

ARNAUDVILLE—Allen's TV Cable Service Inc

ASCENSION PARISH—See BATON ROUGE, LA (Cox Communications)

ASSUMPTION PARISH (PORTIONS)—Allen's TV Cable Service Inc

ASSUMPTION PARISH (PORTIONS)—See BAYOU L'OURSE, LA (Allen's TV Cable Service Inc)

ASSUMPTION PARISH (SOUTHERN PORTION)—See THIBODAUX, LA (Charter Communications)

AVONDALE—See NEW ORLEANS, LA (Cox Communications)

AVOYELLES PARISH (PORTIONS)—See MARKSVILLE, LA (Media3)

AVOYELLES PARISH—See MOREAUVILLE, LA (Suddenlink Communications)

BAKER—See BATON ROUGE, LA (Cox Communications)

BALDWIN—See BATON ROUGE, LA (Cox Communications)

BALL—See ALEXANDRIA, LA (Suddenlink Communications)

BANKS SPRINGS—See COLUMBIA, LA (NewWave Communications)

Cable Community Index—Louisiana

BARATARIA—See NEW ORLEANS, LA (Cox Communications)

BARKSDALE AFB—See BOSSIER CITY, LA (Suddenlink Communications)

BASILE—Alliance Communications

BASTROP—Suddenlink Communications

BATON ROUGE—Cox Communications

BAYOU L'OURSE—Allen's TV Cable Service Inc

BAYOU PIGEON—See BATON ROUGE, LA (Cox Communications)

BAYOU SORREL—See BATON ROUGE, LA (Cox Communications)

BAYOU VISTA—See BATON ROUGE, LA (Cox Communications)

BEAUREGARD PARISH (PORTIONS)—See DE RIDDER, LA (Suddenlink Communications)

BELCHER—See SHREVEPORT, LA (Comcast Cable)

BELLE CHASSE—See NEW ORLEANS, LA (Cox Communications)

BELLE CHASSE—NewWave Communications

BELLE RIVER—See ASSUMPTION PARISH (portions), LA (Allen's TV Cable Service Inc)

BENTON—Formerly served by Zoom Media. No longer in operation

BERNICE—Media3

BERWICK—See MORGAN CITY, LA (Allen's TV Cable Service Inc)

BIENVILLE PARISH (PORTIONS)—See ARCADIA, LA (Alliance Communications)

BLANCHARD—NewWave Communications

BOGALUSA—Media3

BONITA—See COLLINSTON, LA (Northeast Tel)

BORDELONVILLE—See MOREAUVILLE, LA (Suddenlink Communications)

BOSSIER CITY—Suddenlink Communications

BOSSIER PARISH—See BOSSIER CITY, LA (Suddenlink Communications)

BOURG—Charter Communications. Now served by THIBODAUX, LA [LA0011]

BOURG—See THIBODAUX, LA (Charter Communications)

BOUTTE—See NEW ORLEANS, LA (Cox Communications)

BOYCE—Suddenlink Communications

BRAITHWAITE—Formerly served by CMA Cablevision. No longer in operation

BRAITHWAITE—See NEW ORLEANS, LA (Cox Communications)

BREAUX BRIDGE—See BATON ROUGE, LA (Cox Communications)

BRIDGE CITY—See NEW ORLEANS, LA (Cox Communications)

BROUILLETTE—Formerly served by Almega Cable. No longer in operation

BROUSSARD—See BATON ROUGE, LA (Cox Communications)

BRUSLY—See BATON ROUGE, LA (Cox Communications)

BUNKIE—Media3

BUTTE LA ROSE—Spillway Cablevision Inc

CADDO PARISH (PORTIONS)—See SHREVEPORT, LA (Comcast Cable)

CADDO PARISH—See BLANCHARD, LA (NewWave Communications)

CALCASIEU PARISH (PORTIONS)—See IOWA, LA (Suddenlink Communications)

CALCASIEU PARISH (PORTIONS)—See WESTLAKE, LA (Vyve Broadband)

CALCASIEU PARISH—See LAKE CHARLES, LA (Suddenlink Communications)

CALHOUN—NewWave Communications

CALVIN—Formerly served by Cebridge Connections. No longer in operation

CAMERON—Formerly served by Charter Communications. No longer in operation

CAMERON—See CARLYSS, LA (Cameron Communications. Formerly [LA0063]. This cable system has converted to IPTV.)

CAMPTI—Red River Cable TV

CARENCRO—See BATON ROUGE, LA (Cox Communications)

CARLYSS—Cameron Communications. This cable system has converted to IPTV. See CARLYSS, LA [LA5000]

CARLYSS—Cameron Communications. Formerly [LA0063]. This cable system has converted to IPTV.

CARRIERRE—See SLIDELL, MS (Charter Communications)

CARVILLE—See BATON ROUGE, LA (Cox Communications)

CATAHOULA PARISH (PORTIONS)—See JONESVILLE, LA (Media3)

CECELIA—See BATON ROUGE, LA (Cox Communications)

CECILIA (northern portion)—Formerly served by Trust Cable. No longer in operation

CENTERVILLE—See BATON ROUGE, LA (Cox Communications)

CENTRAL—See BATON ROUGE, LA (Cox Communications)

CHALMETTE—See NEW ORLEANS, LA (Cox Communications)

CHARENTON—See BATON ROUGE, LA (Cox Communications)

CHATAIGNIER—See OPELOUSAS, LA (Charter Communications)

CHATHAM—Formerly served by Chatham CATV. No longer in operation

CHAUVIN—See THIBODAUX, LA (Charter Communications)

CHENEYVILLE—See LECOMPTE, LA (Suddenlink Communications)

CHOUDRANT—Formerly served by Almega Cable. No longer in operation

CHURCH POINT—See OPELOUSAS, LA (Charter Communications)

CLARENCE—Red River Cable TV

CLARKS—See COLUMBIA, LA (NewWave Communications)

CLAYTON (town)—Formerly served by Zoom Media. No longer in operation

CLINTON—Bailey Cable TV Inc

CLOUTIERVILLE—Formerly served by Almega Cable. No longer in operation

COLFAX—Alliance Communications

COLLINSTON—Northeast Tel

COLLINSTON—See BASTROP, LA (Suddenlink Communications)

COLUMBIA HEIGHTS—See COLUMBIA, LA (NewWave Communications)

COLUMBIA—NewWave Communications

CONCORDIA PARISH—See FERRIDAY, LA (Media3)

CONVENT—See ST. JAMES PARISH (portions), LA (Reserve Telecommunications)

COTEAU HOLMES—Formerly served by Trust Cable. No longer in operation

COTTON VALLEY—Formerly served by Zoom Media. No longer in operation

COTTONPORT—See MOREAUVILLE, LA (Suddenlink Communications)

COUSHATTA—Red River Cable TV

COVINGTON—See SLIDELL, LA (Charter Communications)

CREOLA—See ALEXANDRIA, LA (Suddenlink Communications)

CREOLE—See CARLYSS, LA (Cameron Communications. Formerly [LA0063]. This cable system has converted to IPTV.)

CROWLEY—Cox Communications. Now served by BATON ROUGE, LA [LA0003]

CROWLEY—See BATON ROUGE, LA (Cox Communications)

CROWN POINT—See NEW ORLEANS, LA (Cox Communications)

CULLEN—See SPRINGHILL, LA (NewWave Communications)

CUT OFF—See GOLDEN MEADOW, LA (Vision Communications)

DE QUINCY—Formerly served by Mediastream. No longer in operation

DE QUINCY—See WESTLAKE, LA (Vyve Broadband)

DE RIDDER—Suddenlink Communications

DE SOTO PARISH (PORTIONS)—See SHREVEPORT, LA (Comcast Cable)

DELCAMBRE—See BATON ROUGE, LA (Cox Communications)

DELHI (town)—NewWave Communications. Now served by MONROE, LA [LA0049]

DELHI (TOWN)—See MONROE, LA (NewWave Communications)

DENHAM SPRINGS—See BATON ROUGE, LA (Cox Communications)

DES ALLEMANDS—See NEW ORLEANS, LA (Cox Communications)

DESTREHAN—See NEW ORLEANS, LA (Cox Communications)

DIXIE INN—Formerly served by PC One Cable. No longer in operation

DODSON—Formerly served by Cebridge Connections. No longer in operation

DONALDSONVILLE—See BATON ROUGE, LA (Cox Communications)

DONNER—See THIBODAUX, LA (Charter Communications)

DOYLINE—See SIBLEY, LA (Suddenlink Communications)

DRY PRONG—Formerly served by Zoom Media. No longer in operation

DUBACH—See BERNICE, LA (Media3)

DUBBERLY—See SIBLEY, LA (Suddenlink Communications)

DUPLESSIS—See BATON ROUGE, LA (Cox Communications)

DUSON—See BATON ROUGE, LA (Cox Communications)

EAST BATON ROUGE PARISH—See BATON ROUGE, LA (Cox Communications)

EAST HODGE—See JONESBORO, LA (Suddenlink Communications)

ECHO—See MOREAUVILLE, LA (Suddenlink Communications)

EFFIE—Formerly served by Zoom Media. No longer in operation

EGAN—Formerly served by Trust Cable. No longer in operation

ELIZABETH—See CARLYSS, LA (Cameron Communications. Formerly [LA0063]. This cable system has converted to IPTV.)

ELIZABETH—See OAKDALE, LA (Media3)

ELTON—See KINDER, LA (Vyve Broadband)

ERATH—See BATON ROUGE, LA (Cox Communications)

ERWINVILLE—See BATON ROUGE, LA (Cox Communications)

Louisiana—Cable Community Index

ESTHERWOOD—Formerly served by Alliance Communications Network. No longer in operation

ETHEL—Bailey Cable TV Inc

EUNICE—See OPELOUSAS, LA (Charter Communications)

EVANGELINE PARISH (PORTIONS)—See OPELOUSAS, LA (Charter Communications)

EVANGELINE PARISH—See VILLE PLATTE, LA (Suddenlink Communications)

EVERGREEN—See BUNKIE, LA (Media3)

FARMERVILLE—NewWave Communications

FERRIDAY—Media3

FILLMORE—See BOSSIER CITY, LA (Suddenlink Communications)

FISHER—See LEESVILLE, LA (Suddenlink Communications)

FLORIEN—See LEESVILLE, LA (Suddenlink Communications)

FOLSOM—Charter Communications. Now served by SLIDELL, LA [LA0182]

FOLSOM—See SLIDELL, LA (Charter Communications)

FORDOCHE—See MARINGOUIN, LA (Spillway Cablevision Inc)

FOREST HILL—See LECOMPTE, LA (Suddenlink Communications)

FORKED ISLAND—Formerly served by Kaplan Telephone Co., KAPLAN, LA [LA0162]. No longer in operation

FORT POLK—Suddenlink Communications. Now served by LEESVILLE, LA [LA0035]

FORT POLK—See LEESVILLE, LA (Suddenlink Communications)

FOUR CORNERS—Formerly served by CableSouth Inc. No longer in operation

FOURCHON—See GOLDEN MEADOW, LA (Vision Communications)

FRANKLIN—Cox Communications. Now served by BATON ROUGE, LA [LA0003]

FRANKLIN—See BATON ROUGE, LA (Cox Communications)

FRANKLINTON—See BOGALUSA, LA (Media3)

FRENCH SETTLEMENT—See SLIDELL, LA (Charter Communications)

GALLIANO—See GOLDEN MEADOW, LA (Vision Communications)

GARDEN CITY—See BATON ROUGE, LA (Cox Communications)

GEORGETOWN—Formerly served by Almega Cable. No longer in operation

GHEENS—See GOLDEN MEADOW, LA (Vision Communications)

GIBSLAND—Alliance Communications

GIBSON—See THIBODAUX, LA (Charter Communications)

GILBERT—See WISNER, LA (NewWave Communications)

GILCHRIST—See CARLYSS, TX (Cameron Communications. Formerly [LA0063]. This cable system has converted to IPTV.)

GILLIAM—See SHREVEPORT, LA (Comcast Cable)

GLENMORA—See LECOMPTE, LA (Suddenlink Communications)

GOLDEN MEADOW—Vision Communications

GONZALES—See BATON ROUGE, LA (Cox Communications)

GOOD PINE—See JENA, LA (Media3)

GRAMBLING—See RUSTON, LA (Suddenlink Communications)

GRAMERCY—Cox Communications. Now served by BATON ROUGE, LA [LA0003]

GRAMERCY—See BATON ROUGE, LA (Cox Communications)

GRAND CHENIER—Formerly served by CableSouth Inc. Now served by Cameron Communications, CARLYSS, LA [LA5000]. This cable system has converted to IPTV

GRAND CHENIER—See CARLYSS, LA (Cameron Communications. Formerly [LA0063]. This cable system has converted to IPTV.)

GRAND COTEAU—Allen's TV Cable Service Inc

GRAND ISLE—See GOLDEN MEADOW, LA (Vision Communications)

GRAND LAKE—Formerly served by CableSouth Inc. Now served by Cameron Communications, CARLYSS, LA [LA5000]. This cable system has converted to IPTV

GRAND LAKE—See CARLYSS, LA (Cameron Communications. Formerly [LA0063]. This cable system has converted to IPTV.)

GRANT PARISH (PORTIONS)—See ALEXANDRIA, LA (Suddenlink Communications)

GRAYSON—See COLUMBIA, LA (NewWave Communications)

GREENSBURG—Formerly served by Almega Cable. No longer in operation

GREENWOOD—See SHREVEPORT, LA (Comcast Cable)

GRETNA—See NEW ORLEANS, LA (Cox Communications)

GROSSE TETE—See BATON ROUGE, LA (Cox Communications)

GUEYDAN—See LAKE ARTHUR, LA (Vyve Broadband)

HACKBERRY—Formerly served by Charter Communications. No longer in operation

HACKBERRY—See CARLYSS, LA (Cameron Communications. Formerly [LA0063]. This cable system has converted to IPTV.)

HAHNVILLE—See NEW ORLEANS, LA (Cox Communications)

HALL SUMMIT—Formerly served by Red River Cable TV. No longer in operation

HAMMOND—Charter Communications. Now served by SLIDELL, LA [LA0182]

HAMMOND—See SLIDELL, LA (Charter Communications)

HARAHAN—See NEW ORLEANS, LA (Cox Communications)

HARRISON COUNTY (PORTIONS)—See SHREVEPORT, TX (Comcast Cable)

HARVEY—See NEW ORLEANS, LA (Cox Communications)

HAUGHTON—Formerly served by Cebridge Connections. No longer in operation

HAUGHTON—See BOSSIER CITY, LA (Suddenlink Communications)

HAYNESVILLE—NewWave Communications

HEFLIN—See SIBLEY, LA (Suddenlink Communications)

HEMPHILL—See MANY, LA (Suddenlink Communications)

HENDERSON—See BATON ROUGE, LA (Cox Communications)

HENRY—Formerly served by CableSouth Inc. No longer in operation

HESSMER—See MARKSVILLE, LA (Media3)

HESTER—See ST. JAMES PARISH (portions), LA (Reserve Telecommunications)

HIGH ISLAND—See CARLYSS, TX (Cameron Communications. Formerly [LA0063]. This cable system has converted to IPTV.)

HILLY—See RUSTON, LA (Suddenlink Communications)

HODGE—See JONESBORO, LA (Suddenlink Communications)

HOMER—NewWave Communications. Now served by HAYNESVILLE, LA [LA0076]

HOMER—See HAYNESVILLE, LA (NewWave Communications)

HORNBECK—See LEESVILLE, LA (Suddenlink Communications)

HOSSTON—Comcast Cable. Now served by SHREVEPORT, LA [LA0004]

HOSSTON—See SHREVEPORT, LA (Comcast Cable)

HOTWELLS—See BOYCE, LA (Suddenlink Communications)

HOUMA—Comcast Cable. Now served by MOBILE, AL [AL0002]

IBERIA PARISH (PORTIONS)—Suddenlink Communications

IBERIA PARISH—See BATON ROUGE, LA (Cox Communications)

IBERVILLE PARISH (PORTIONS)—See MARINGOUIN, LA (Spillway Cablevision Inc)

IBERVILLE PARISH—See BATON ROUGE, LA (Cox Communications)

IBERVILLE—See BATON ROUGE, LA (Cox Communications)

INDEPENDENCE—See SLIDELL, LA (Charter Communications)

INNIS—Formerly served by Spillway Communications Inc. No longer in operation

IOTA—Charter Communications. Now served by OPELOUSAS, LA [LA0022]

IOTA—See OPELOUSAS, LA (Charter Communications)

IOWA—Suddenlink Communications

JACKSON PARISH (PORTIONS)—See JONESBORO, LA (Suddenlink Communications)

JACKSON—Bailey Cable TV Inc

JEAN LAFITTE—See NEW ORLEANS, LA (Cox Communications)

JEANERETTE—See BATON ROUGE, LA (Cox Communications)

JEFFERSON DAVIS PARISH (PORTIONS)—See OPELOUSAS, LA (Charter Communications)

JEFFERSON DAVIS PARISH (PORTIONS)—See IOWA, LA (Suddenlink Communications)

JEFFERSON DAVIS PARISH (PORTIONS)—See LAKE ARTHUR, LA (Vyve Broadband)

JEFFERSON PARISH (PORTIONS)—See NEW ORLEANS, LA (Cox Communications)

JENA—Media3

JENNINGS—See OPELOUSAS, LA (Charter Communications)

JOHNSON BAYOU—See CARLYSS, LA (Cameron Communications. Formerly [LA0063]. This cable system has converted to IPTV.)

JONESBORO—Suddenlink Communications

JONESVILLE—Media3

JOYCE—See WINNFIELD, LA (Suddenlink Communications)

KAPLAN—Kaplan Telephone Co. This cable system has converted to IPTV. See KAPLAN, LA [LA5021]

Cable Community Index—Louisiana

KAPLAN—See BATON ROUGE, LA (Cox Communications)

KAPLAN—KTC Pace. Formerly [LA0162]. This cable system has converted to IPTV

KENNER—See NEW ORLEANS, LA (Cox Communications)

KENTWOOD—Media3

KILBOURNE—Formerly served by Community Communications Co. No longer in operation

KILLIAN—See SLIDELL, LA (Charter Communications)

KINDER—Vyve Broadband

KOLIN—See LECOMPTE, LA (Suddenlink Communications)

KROTZ SPRINGS—Spillway Cablevision Inc

LA PLACE—Comcast Cable. Now served by MOBILE, AL [AL0002]

LA SALLE PARISH (PORTIONS)—See OLLA, LA (Alliance Communications)

LA SALLE PARISH—See JENA, LA (Media3)

LACOMBE—See SLIDELL, LA (Charter Communications)

LAFAYETTE PARISH—See BATON ROUGE, LA (Cox Communications)

LAFAYETTE—Cox Communications. Now served by BATON ROUGE, LA [LA0003]

LAFAYETTE—See BATON ROUGE, LA (Cox Communications)

LAFOURCHE PARISH (WESTERN PORTION)—See THIBODAUX, LA (Charter Communications)

LAFOURCHE PARISH—See GOLDEN MEADOW, LA (Vision Communications)

LAKE ARTHUR—Vyve Broadband

LAKE BISTINEAU—See SIBLEY, LA (Suddenlink Communications)

LAKE BRUIN—See ST. JOSEPH, LA (Suddenlink Communications)

LAKE CHARLES—Suddenlink Communications

LAKE CLAIBORNE—Formerly served by Almega Cable. No longer in operation

LAKE PROVIDENCE—NewWave Communications

LAKE ST. JOHN—Formerly served by Almega Cable. No longer in operation

LAROSE—See GOLDEN MEADOW, LA (Vision Communications)

LECOMPTE—Suddenlink Communications

LEESVILLE—Suddenlink Communications

LEEVILLE—See GOLDEN MEADOW, LA (Vision Communications)

LEONVILLE—See OPELOUSAS, LA (Charter Communications)

LINCOLN PARISH (PORTIONS)—See BERNICE, LA (Media3)

LINCOLN PARISH—See RUSTON, LA (Suddenlink Communications)

LIVINGSTON PARISH (PORTIONS)—See SLIDELL, LA (Charter Communications)

LIVINGSTON—See SLIDELL, LA (Charter Communications)

LIVONIA—See MARINGOUIN, LA (Spillway Cablevision Inc)

LOCKPORT—See GOLDEN MEADOW, LA (Vision Communications)

LOGANSPORT—NewWave Communications

LOREAUVILLE—See BATON ROUGE, LA (Cox Communications)

LULING—See NEW ORLEANS, LA (Cox Communications)

LUTCHER—See BATON ROUGE, LA (Cox Communications)

MADISON PARISH (PORTIONS)—See MONROE, LA (NewWave Communications)

MADISONVILLE—See SLIDELL, LA (Charter Communications)

MAMOU—See VILLE PLATTE, LA (Suddenlink Communications)

MANDEVILLE—See SLIDELL, LA (Charter Communications)

MANGHAM—Formerly served by Almega Cable. No longer in operation

MANSFIELD—NewWave Communications

MANSURA—See MARKSVILLE, LA (Media3)

MANY—Suddenlink Communications

MARINGOUIN—Spillway Cablevision Inc

MARION—Bayou Cable TV

MARKSVILLE—Formerly served by Zoom Media. No longer in operation

MARKSVILLE—Media3

MARRERO—See NEW ORLEANS, LA (Cox Communications)

MATHEWS—See GOLDEN MEADOW, LA (Vision Communications)

MAURICE—See BATON ROUGE, LA (Cox Communications)

MCINTYRE—Formerly served by Almega Cable. No longer in operation

MCNARY—See LECOMPTE, LA (Suddenlink Communications)

MCNEILL—See SLIDELL, MS (Charter Communications)

MELVILLE—Spillway Cablevision Inc

MER ROUGE—See BASTROP, LA (Suddenlink Communications)

MERAUX—See NEW ORLEANS, LA (Cox Communications)

MERRYVILLE—Alliance Communications

METAIRIE—See NEW ORLEANS, LA (Cox Communications)

MIDWAY—See JENA, LA (Media3)

MILTON—See BATON ROUGE, LA (Cox Communications)

MINDEN—Suddenlink Communications

MIRE—Formerly served by Trust Cable. No longer in operation

MONROE—NewWave Communications

MONTEREY—Formerly served by Almega Cable. No longer in operation

MONTGOMERY—Alliance Communications

MOORINGSPORT—See BLANCHARD, LA (NewWave Communications)

MOREAUVILLE—Suddenlink Communications

MOREHOUSE PARISH (PORTIONS)—See BASTROP, LA (Suddenlink Communications)

MORGAN CITY—Allen's TV Cable Service Inc

MORGANZA (VILLAGE)—See NEW ROADS, LA (Fidelity Communications)

MOSS BLUFF—See CARLYSS, LA (Cameron Communications. Formerly [LA0063]. This cable system has converted to IPTV.)

MOSS BLUFF—See WESTLAKE, LA (Vyve Broadband)

NAPOLEONVILLE—See THIBODAUX, LA (Charter Communications)

NATCHEZ—Alliance Communications

NATCHITOCHES (portions)—Formerly served by Rapid Cable. Now served by Suddenlink Communications, NATCHITOCHES, LA [LA0029]

NATCHITOCHES PARISH—See NATCHITOCHES, LA (Suddenlink Communications)

NATCHITOCHES—Suddenlink Communications

NAVAL AIR STATION JOINT RESERVE BASE—See BELLE CHASSE, LA (NewWave Communications)

NEGREET—See MANY, LA (Suddenlink Communications)

NEW IBERIA—Cox Communications. Now served by BATON ROUGE, LA [LA0003]

NEW IBERIA—See BATON ROUGE, LA (Cox Communications)

NEW IBERIA—See IBERIA PARISH (portions), LA (Suddenlink Communications)

NEW LLANO—See LEESVILLE, LA (Suddenlink Communications)

NEW ORLEANS—Cox Communications

NEW ROADS—Fidelity Communications

NEWELLTON—Alliance Communications

NOME—See CARLYSS, TX (Cameron Communications. Formerly [LA0063]. This cable system has converted to IPTV.)

NORTH HODGE—See JONESBORO, LA (Suddenlink Communications)

NORWOOD—Bailey Cable TV Inc

OAK GROVE—NewWave Communications. Now served by LAKE PROVIDENCE, LA [LA0053]

OAK GROVE—See LAKE PROVIDENCE, LA (NewWave Communications)

OAK RIDGE—Formerly served by Charter Communications. No longer in operation

OAKDALE—Media3

OBERLIN—See KINDER, LA (Vyve Broadband)

OIL CITY—See BLANCHARD, LA (NewWave Communications)

OLLA—Alliance Communications

OPELOUSAS—Charter Communications

ORLEANS PARISH—See NEW ORLEANS, LA (Cox Communications)

OUACHITA PARISH (PORTIONS)—See MONROE, LA (NewWave Communications)

PALMETTO—Formerly served by Village Cable Co. No longer in operation

PANOLA COUNTY (PORTIONS)—See SHREVEPORT, TX (Comcast Cable)

PARKS—See BATON ROUGE, LA (Cox Communications)

PATTERSON—See BATON ROUGE, LA (Cox Communications)

PAULINA—See ST. JAMES PARISH (portions), LA (Reserve Telecommunications)

PEARL RIVER COUNTY—See SLIDELL, MS (Charter Communications)

PEARL RIVER—See SLIDELL, LA (Charter Communications)

PECANIERE—Formerly served by CableSouth Inc. No longer in operation

PICAYUNE—See SLIDELL, MS (Charter Communications)

PIERRE PART—Allen's TV Cable Service Inc. Now served by ASSUMPTION PARISH (portions), LA [LA0240]

PIERRE PART—See ASSUMPTION PARISH (portions), LA (Allen's TV Cable Service Inc)

PINE PRAIRIE—Formerly served by Charter Communications. Now served by Media3, OAKDALE, LA [LA0241]

PINE PRAIRIE—See OAKDALE, LA (Media3)

PINEVILLE—See ALEXANDRIA, LA (Suddenlink Communications)

PITKIN—See CARLYSS, LA (Cameron Communications. Formerly [LA0063].

2017 Edition

Cable Community Index-107

Louisiana—Cable Community Index

This cable system has converted to IPTV.)

PLAIN DEALING—Formerly served by Alliance Communications Network. No longer in operation

PLAQUEMINE—See BATON ROUGE, LA (Cox Communications)

PLAQUEMINES PARISH (PORTIONS)—See NEW ORLEANS, LA (Cox Communications)

PLAUCHEVILLE—See MOREAUVILLE, LA (Suddenlink Communications)

POINT PLACE—See NATCHEZ, LA (Alliance Communications)

POINTE A LA HACHE—Formerly served by CMA Cablevision. No longer in operation

POINTE COUPEE PARISH—See NEW ROADS, LA (Fidelity Communications)

POINTE COUPEE PARISH—See MARINGOUIN, LA (Spillway Cablevision Inc)

POLLOCK—See ALEXANDRIA, LA (Suddenlink Communications)

PONCHATOULA—See SLIDELL, LA (Charter Communications)

PORT ALLEN—See BATON ROUGE, LA (Cox Communications)

PORT BARRE—Allen's TV Cable Service Inc

PORT SULPHUR—See BELLE CHASSE, LA (NewWave Communications)

PORT VINCENT—See SLIDELL, LA (Charter Communications)

PORTERVILLE—See SPRINGHILL, LA (NewWave Communications)

POYDRAS—See NEW ORLEANS, LA (Cox Communications)

PRINCETON—See BOSSIER CITY, LA (Suddenlink Communications)

QUITMAN—See JONESBORO, LA (Suddenlink Communications)

RAPIDES PARISH (PORTIONS)—See LECOMPTE, LA (Suddenlink Communications)

RAPIDES PARISH (PORTIONS)—See MOREAUVILLE, LA (Suddenlink Communications)

RAPIDES PARISH—See ALEXANDRIA, LA (Suddenlink Communications)

RAYNE—See BATON ROUGE, LA (Cox Communications)

RAYVILLE—Formerly served by Cotton Country Cable. No longer in operation

RAYVILLE—See MONROE, LA (NewWave Communications)

RESERVE—Reserve Telecommunications

RIDGECREST—See FERRIDAY, LA (Media3)

RINGGOLD—See SIBLEY, LA (Suddenlink Communications)

RIVER RIDGE—See NEW ORLEANS, LA (Cox Communications)

ROANOKE—See LAKE ARTHUR, LA (Vyve Broadband)

ROBELINE—Formerly served by MAR-BAC Communications. No longer in operation

ROCKY BRANCH—Bayou Cable TV

RODESSA—Formerly served by Almega Cable. No longer in operation

ROSEDALE—See BATON ROUGE, LA (Cox Communications)

ROSELAND—See SLIDELL, LA (Charter Communications)

ROSEPINE—See DE RIDDER, LA (Suddenlink Communications)

RUSTON—Suddenlink Communications

SABINE PARISH (PORTIONS)—See LEESVILLE, LA (Suddenlink Communications)

SABINE PARISH (PORTIONS)—See MANY, LA (Suddenlink Communications)

SCOTT—See BATON ROUGE, LA (Cox Communications)

SHREVEPORT—Comcast Cable

SIBLEY—Suddenlink Communications

SICILY ISLAND—Formerly served by Almega Cable. No longer in operation

SIMMESPORT—See MOREAUVILLE, LA (Suddenlink Communications)

SIMPSON—Formerly served by Zoom Media. No longer in operation

SIMSBORO—See RUSTON, LA (Suddenlink Communications)

SLAUGHTER—See BATON ROUGE, LA (Cox Communications)

SLIDELL—Charter Communications

SORRENTO—See BATON ROUGE, LA (Cox Communications)

SPRINGFIELD—See SLIDELL, LA (Charter Communications)

SPRINGHILL—NewWave Communications

ST. BERNARD PARISH—Cox Communications. Now served by NEW ORLEANS, LA [LA0001]

ST. BERNARD PARISH—See NEW ORLEANS, LA (Cox Communications)

ST. CHARLES PARISH (PORTIONS)—See NEW ORLEANS, LA (Cox Communications)

ST. FRANCISVILLE—Bailey Cable TV Inc

ST. GABRIEL—See BATON ROUGE, LA (Cox Communications)

ST. JAMES PARISH (PORTIONS)—Reserve Telecommunications

ST. JAMES PARISH—See BATON ROUGE, LA (Cox Communications)

ST. JOSEPH—Suddenlink Communications

ST. LANDRY PARISH (PORTIONS)—See ARNAUDVILLE, LA (Allen's TV Cable Service Inc)

ST. LANDRY PARISH (PORTIONS)—See GRAND COTEAU, LA (Allen's TV Cable Service Inc)

ST. LANDRY PARISH (PORTIONS)—See PORT BARRE, LA (Allen's TV Cable Service Inc)

ST. LANDRY PARISH (PORTIONS)—See OPELOUSAS, LA (Charter Communications)

ST. LANDRY PARISH (PORTIONS)—See KROTZ SPRINGS, LA (Spillway Cablevision Inc)

ST. MARTIN PARISH (PORTIONS)—See ARNAUDVILLE, LA (Allen's TV Cable Service Inc)

ST. MARTIN PARISH (PORTIONS)—See IBERIA PARISH (portions), LA (Suddenlink Communications)

ST. MARTIN PARISH (SOUTHERN PORTION)—See MORGAN CITY, LA (Allen's TV Cable Service Inc)

ST. MARTIN PARISH—See BATON ROUGE, LA (Cox Communications)

ST. MARTINVILLE—Cox Communications. Now served by BATON ROUGE, LA [LA0003]

ST. MARTINVILLE—See BATON ROUGE, LA (Cox Communications)

ST. MARY PARISH (PORTIONS)—See MORGAN CITY, LA (Allen's TV Cable Service Inc)

ST. MARY PARISH—See THIBODAUX, LA (Charter Communications)

ST. MARY PARISH—See BATON ROUGE, LA (Cox Communications)

ST. ROSE—See NEW ORLEANS, LA (Cox Communications)

ST. TAMMANY PARISH (UNINCORPORATED AREAS)—See SLIDELL, LA (Charter Communications)

START—Formerly served by Almega Cable. No longer in operation

STEPHENSVILLE—See MORGAN CITY, LA (Allen's TV Cable Service Inc)

STERLINGTON—Bayou Cable TV

STONEWALL—See SHREVEPORT, LA (Comcast Cable)

SUGARTOWN—See CARLYSS, LA (Cameron Communications. Formerly [LA0063]. This cable system has converted to IPTV.)

SULPHUR—Suddenlink Communications. Now served by LAKE CHARLES, LA [LA0007]

SULPHUR—See LAKE CHARLES, LA (Suddenlink Communications)

SUNSET—See GRAND COTEAU, LA (Allen's TV Cable Service Inc)

SUNSHINE—See BATON ROUGE, LA (Cox Communications)

SWEETWATER—Formerly served by Charter Communications. No longer in operation

TALLULAH—NewWave Communications. Now served by MONROE, LA [LA0049]

TALLULAH—See MONROE, LA (NewWave Communications)

TANGIPAHOA PARISH—See SLIDELL, LA (Charter Communications)

TANGIPAHOA—Formerly served by Almega Cable. No longer in operation

TENSAS PARISH (PORTIONS)—See ST. JOSEPH, LA (Suddenlink Communications)

TERREBONNE PARISH (PORTIONS)—See THIBODAUX, LA (Charter Communications)

TERRYTOWN—See NEW ORLEANS, LA (Cox Communications)

THIBODAUX—Charter Communications

TICKFAW—See SLIDELL, LA (Charter Communications)

TULLOS—See OLLA, LA (Alliance Communications)

TURKEY CREEK—Formerly served by Alliance Communications Network. No longer in operation

UNION PARISH (PORTIONS)—See BERNICE, LA (Media3)

URANIA—See OLLA, LA (Alliance Communications)

VACHERIE—See THIBODAUX, LA (Charter Communications)

VACHERIE—See ST. JAMES PARISH (portions), LA (Reserve Telecommunications)

VARNADO—Formerly served by Charter Communications. No longer in operation

VERDUNVILLE—See BATON ROUGE, LA (Cox Communications)

VERMILION PARISH (PORTIONS)—See IBERIA PARISH (portions), LA (Suddenlink Communications)

VERMILION PARISH (RURAL AREAS)—See KAPLAN, LA (KTC Pace. Formerly [LA0162]. This cable system has converted to IPTV.)

VERMILION PARISH—See BATON ROUGE, LA (Cox Communications)

VERNON PARISH (PORTIONS)—See DE RIDDER, LA (Suddenlink Communications)

VERNON PARISH (PORTIONS)—See LEESVILLE, LA (Suddenlink Communications)

VERNON PARISH (PORTIONS)—See MANY, LA (Suddenlink Communications)

VIENNA—See RUSTON, LA (Suddenlink Communications)

VILLE PLATTE—Suddenlink Communications

Cable Community Index—Maine

VINTON—Formerly served by Allegiance Communications. Now served by Vyve Broadband, WESTLAKE, LA [LA0025]

VINTON—See WESTLAKE, LA (Vyve Broadband)

VIOLET—See NEW ORLEANS, LA (Cox Communications)

VIVIAN—See BLANCHARD, LA (NewWave Communications)

WALKER (PORTIONS)—See BATON ROUGE, LA (Cox Communications)

WALLACE RIDGE—Formerly served by Zoom Media. No longer in operation

WASHINGTON PARISH—See BOGALUSA, LA (Media3)

WASHINGTON—See OPELOUSAS, LA (Charter Communications)

WASKOM—See SHREVEPORT, TX (Comcast Cable)

WATERPROOF—Alliance Communications

WATSON—See BATON ROUGE, LA (Cox Communications)

WEBSTER PARISH (SOUTHERN PORTION)—See SIBLEY, LA (Suddenlink Communications)

WEBSTER PARISH—See MINDEN, LA (Suddenlink Communications)

WELSH—Formerly served by CommuniComm Services. Now served by Vyve Broadband, LAKE ARTHUR, LA [LA0078]

WELSH—See LAKE ARTHUR, LA (Vyve Broadband)

WEST BATON ROUGE PARISH—See BATON ROUGE, LA (Cox Communications)

WEST FELICIANA PARISH (PORTIONS)—See ST. FRANCISVILLE, LA (Bailey Cable TV Inc)

WEST MONROE—Comcast Cable. Now served by JACKSON, MS [MS0001]

WESTLAKE—Vyve Broadband

WESTWEGO—See NEW ORLEANS, LA (Cox Communications)

WHITE CASTLE—See BATON ROUGE, LA (Cox Communications)

WILSON—Formerly served by Trust Cable. No longer in operation

WINN PARISH—See WINNFIELD, LA (Suddenlink Communications)

WINNFIELD—Suddenlink Communications

WINNSBORO TWP.—See WINNSBORO, LA (NewWave Communications)

WINNSBORO—NewWave Communications

WISNER—NewWave Communications

WOODWORTH—See LECOMPTE, LA (Suddenlink Communications)

YOUNGSVILLE—See BATON ROUGE, LA (Cox Communications)

ZACHARY—See BATON ROUGE, LA (Cox Communications)

ZWOLLE—See MANY, LA (Suddenlink Communications)

MAINE

ACTON (TOWN)—See PORTLAND, ME (Time Warner Cable)

ACTON—See SANFORD, ME (MetroCast Cablevision)

ADDISON (town)—Time Warner Cable. Now served by PORTLAND, ME [ME0001]

ADDISON (TOWN)—See PORTLAND, ME (Time Warner Cable)

ALBANY—See PORTLAND, NH (Time Warner Cable)

ALBION—See PORTLAND, ME (Time Warner Cable)

ALFRED—See PORTLAND, ME (Time Warner Cable)

ALLAGASH (TOWN)—See PRESQUE ISLE, ME (Time Warner Cable)

ALLAGASH—See PRESQUE ISLE, ME (Time Warner Cable)

ALNA—See LINCOLNVILLE, ME (Lincolnville Communications. Formerly [ME0094]. This cable system has converted to IPTV)

ALNA—See PORTLAND, ME (Time Warner Cable)

ANDOVER—See PORTLAND, ME (Time Warner Cable)

ANSON—See SKOWHEGAN, ME (Bee Line Cable TV)

APPLETON—See LINCOLNVILLE, ME (Lincolnville Communications. Formerly [ME0094]. This cable system has converted to IPTV)

AROOSTOOK COUNTY (PORTIONS)—See HOULTON, ME (Time Warner Cable)

AROOSTOOK COUNTY—See PRESQUE ISLE, ME (Time Warner Cable)

ARUNDEL—See PORTLAND, ME (Time Warner Cable)

ASHLAND—Time Warner Cable. Now served by PRESQUE ISLE, ME [ME0008]

ASHLAND—See PRESQUE ISLE, ME (Time Warner Cable)

AUBURN—Formerly served by Oxford Networks. No longer in operation

AUBURN—See PORTLAND, ME (Time Warner Cable)

AUGUSTA—Time Warner Cable. Now served by PORTLAND, ME [ME0001]

AUGUSTA—See PORTLAND, ME (Time Warner Cable)

AVON—Time Warner Cable. Now served by PORTLAND, ME [ME0001]

AVON—See PORTLAND, ME (Time Warner Cable)

BAILEYVILLE—See PORTLAND, ME (Time Warner Cable)

BALDWIN—See PORTLAND, ME (Time Warner Cable)

BANGOR—Time Warner Cable. Now served by PORTLAND, ME [ME0001]

BANGOR—See PORTLAND, ME (Time Warner Cable)

BAR HARBOR—See PORTLAND, ME (Time Warner Cable)

BAR MILLS—See PORTLAND, ME (Time Warner Cable)

BARING—See PORTLAND, ME (Time Warner Cable)

BARTLETT—See PORTLAND, NH (Time Warner Cable)

BASS HARBOR—See PORTLAND, ME (Time Warner Cable)

BEALS ISLAND—See PORTLAND, ME (Time Warner Cable)

BELFAST—See PORTLAND, ME (Time Warner Cable)

BELGRADE (TOWN)—See PORTLAND, ME (Time Warner Cable)

BELGRADE LAKES—See PORTLAND, ME (Time Warner Cable)

BELGRADE—Time Warner Cable. Now served by PORTLAND, ME [ME0001]

BELMONT (TOWN)—See PORTLAND, ME (Time Warner Cable)

BENTON—See PORTLAND, ME (Time Warner Cable)

BERNARD—See PORTLAND, ME (Time Warner Cable)

BETHEL—Formerly served by Adelphia Communications. Now served by Time Warner Cable, PORTLAND, ME [ME0001]

BETHEL—See PORTLAND, ME (Time Warner Cable)

BIDDEFORD—See PORTLAND, ME (Time Warner Cable)

BINGHAM—Moosehead Enterprises

BLAINE—See PRESQUE ISLE, ME (Time Warner Cable)

BLUE HILL (town)—Formerly served by Adelphia Communications. Now served by Time Warner Cable, PORTLAND, ME [ME0001]

BLUE HILL (TOWN)—See PORTLAND, ME (Time Warner Cable)

BOOTHBAY HARBOR—See LINCOLNVILLE, ME (Lincolnville Communications. Formerly [ME0094]. This cable system has converted to IPTV)

BOOTHBAY HARBOR—See PORTLAND, ME (Time Warner Cable)

BOOTHBAY—Formerly served by Adelphia Communications. Now served by Time Warner Cable, PORTLAND, ME [ME0001]

BOOTHBAY—See PORTLAND, ME (Time Warner Cable)

BRADLEY—See PORTLAND, ME (Time Warner Cable)

BREWER—See PORTLAND, ME (Time Warner Cable)

BRIDGEWATER (TOWN)—See HOULTON, ME (Time Warner Cable)

BRIDGTON—Time Warner Cable. Now served by PORTLAND, ME [ME0001]

BRIDGTON—See PORTLAND, ME (Time Warner Cable)

BRISTOL (TOWN)—See PORTLAND, ME (Time Warner Cable)

BRISTOL—Time Warner Cable. Now served by PORTLAND, ME [ME0001]

BROOKFIELD (TOWN)—See PORTLAND, NH (Time Warner Cable)

BROWNVILLE—See PORTLAND, ME (Time Warner Cable)

BRUNSWICK (town)—Comcast Cable. Now served by BOSTON, MA [MA0001]

BRYANT POND—See PORTLAND, ME (Time Warner Cable)

BUCKFIELD (TOWN)—See PORTLAND, ME (Time Warner Cable)

BUCKFIELD—Time Warner Cable. Now served by PORTLAND, ME [ME0001]

BUCKSPORT—See PORTLAND, ME (Time Warner Cable)

BURNHAM—See PORTLAND, ME (Time Warner Cable)

BUXTON—Time Warner Cable. Now served by PORTLAND, ME [ME0001]

BUXTON—See PORTLAND, ME (Time Warner Cable)

CALAIS—Time Warner Cable. Now served by PORTLAND, ME [ME0001]

CALAIS—See PORTLAND, ME (Time Warner Cable)

CAMDEN—See PORTLAND, ME (Time Warner Cable)

CANAAN—See PORTLAND, ME (Time Warner Cable)

CANTON (town)—Time Warner Cable. Now served by PORTLAND, ME [ME0001]

CANTON (TOWN)—See PORTLAND, ME (Time Warner Cable)

CAPE ELIZABETH—See PORTLAND, ME (Time Warner Cable)

CAPE PORPOISE—See PORTLAND, ME (Time Warner Cable)

CARIBOU—See PRESQUE ISLE, ME (Time Warner Cable)

Maine—Cable Community Index

CARMEL—See PORTLAND, ME (Time Warner Cable)

CARRABASSETT VALLEY—Time Warner Cable. Now served by PORTLAND, ME [ME0001]

CARRABASSETT VALLEY—See PORTLAND, ME (Time Warner Cable)

CASCO—See PORTLAND, ME (Time Warner Cable)

CASTINE—Formerly served by Adelphia Communications. Now served by Time Warner Cable, PORTLAND, ME [ME0001]

CASTINE—See PORTLAND, ME (Time Warner Cable)

CASTLE HILL—Time Warner Cable. Now served by PRESQUE ISLE, ME [ME0008]

CASTLE HILL—See PRESQUE ISLE, ME (Time Warner Cable)

CASWELL (TOWN)—See PRESQUE ISLE, ME (Time Warner Cable)

CENTER OSSIPEE—See PORTLAND, NH (Time Warner Cable)

CHELSEA—See PORTLAND, ME (Time Warner Cable)

CHERRYFIELD—Time Warner Cable. Now served by PORTLAND, ME [ME0001]

CHERRYFIELD—See PORTLAND, ME (Time Warner Cable)

CHINA—See PORTLAND, ME (Time Warner Cable)

CLINTON—See PORTLAND, ME (Time Warner Cable)

COLUMBIA FALLS—See PORTLAND, ME (Time Warner Cable)

CONNOR (PORTIONS)—See PRESQUE ISLE, ME (Time Warner Cable)

CONWAY—See PORTLAND, NH (Time Warner Cable)

COPLIN—See PORTLAND, ME (Time Warner Cable)

CORINNA—See PORTLAND, ME (Time Warner Cable)

CORINTH (TOWN)—See PORTLAND, ME (Time Warner Cable)

CORNISH (town)—Time Warner Cable. Now served by PORTLAND, ME [ME0001]

CORNISH (TOWN)—See PORTLAND, ME (Time Warner Cable)

CUMBERLAND—See PORTLAND, ME (Time Warner Cable)

CUSHING (TOWN)—See PORTLAND, ME (Time Warner Cable)

CUTLER—See PORTLAND, ME (Time Warner Cable)

DAMARISCOTTA—See LINCOLNVILLE, ME (Lincolnville Communications. Formerly [ME0094]. This cable system has converted to IPTV)

DAMARISCOTTA—See PORTLAND, ME (Time Warner Cable)

DANFORTH—Time Warner Cable

DAYTON—See PORTLAND, ME (Time Warner Cable)

DEDHAM (TOWN)—See PORTLAND, ME (Time Warner Cable)

DEER ISLE (TOWN)—See PORTLAND, ME (Time Warner Cable)

DENMARK (TOWN)—See PORTLAND, ME (Time Warner Cable)

DENMARK—Time Warner Cable. Now served by PORTLAND, ME [ME0001]

DENNYSVILLE—See PORTLAND, ME (Time Warner Cable)

DETROIT (TOWN)—See PORTLAND, ME (Time Warner Cable)

DEXTER—See PORTLAND, ME (Time Warner Cable)

DIXFIELD—See PORTLAND, ME (Time Warner Cable)

DOVER-FOXCROFT—See PORTLAND, ME (Time Warner Cable)

DRESDEN—See PORTLAND, ME (Time Warner Cable)

DYER BROOK—See OAKFIELD, ME (Time Warner Cable)

EAGLE LAKE—Formerly served by Adelphia Communications. Now served by Time Warner Cable, PRESQUE ISLE, ME [ME0008]

EAGLE LAKE—See PRESQUE ISLE, ME (Time Warner Cable)

EAST BALDWIN—See PORTLAND, ME (Time Warner Cable)

EAST BOOTHBAY—See PORTLAND, ME (Time Warner Cable)

EAST DIXFIELD—See PORTLAND, ME (Time Warner Cable)

EAST LEBANON—See SANFORD, ME (MetroCast Cablevision)

EAST MACHIAS—Formerly served by Pine Tree Cablevision. No longer in operation

EAST MACHIAS—See PORTLAND, ME (Time Warner Cable)

EAST MILLINOCKET—See MILLINOCKET, ME (Bee Line Cable TV)

EASTON—Time Warner Cable. Now served by PRESQUE ISLE, ME [ME0008]

EASTON—See PRESQUE ISLE, ME (Time Warner Cable)

EASTPORT—See PORTLAND, ME (Time Warner Cable)

EATON (TOWN)—See PORTLAND, NH (Time Warner Cable)

EDDINGTON—See PORTLAND, ME (Time Warner Cable)

EDGECOMB—See LINCOLNVILLE, ME (Lincolnville Communications. Formerly [ME0094]. This cable system has converted to IPTV)

EDGECOMB—See PORTLAND, ME (Time Warner Cable)

EDMUNDS TWP.—See PORTLAND, ME (Time Warner Cable)

EFFINGHAM—See PORTLAND, NH (Time Warner Cable)

ELLSWORTH—See PORTLAND, ME (Time Warner Cable)

EMBDEN—See PORTLAND, ME (Time Warner Cable)

ENFIELD—See HOWLAND, ME (Time Warner Cable)

EUSTIS—See PORTLAND, ME (Time Warner Cable)

FAIRFIELD—See PORTLAND, ME (Time Warner Cable)

FALMOUTH—See PORTLAND, ME (Time Warner Cable)

FARMINGDALE—See PORTLAND, ME (Time Warner Cable)

FARMINGTON—Bee Line Cable TV

FAYETTE—See PORTLAND, ME (Time Warner Cable)

FORT FAIRFIELD—See PRESQUE ISLE, ME (Time Warner Cable)

FORT KENT—Formerly served by Adelphia Communications. Now served by Time Warner Cable, PRESQUE ISLE, ME [ME0008]

FORT KENT—See PRESQUE ISLE, ME (Time Warner Cable)

FRANKLIN (town)—Time Warner Cable. Now served by, PORTLAND, ME [ME0001]

FRANKLIN (TOWN)—See PORTLAND, ME (Time Warner Cable)

FRANKLIN—See PORTLAND, ME (Time Warner Cable)

FREEDOM (TOWN)—See PORTLAND, NH (Time Warner Cable)

FRENCHVILLE—See PRESQUE ISLE, ME (Time Warner Cable)

FRIENDSHIP (town)—Time Warner Cable. Now served by PORTLAND, ME [ME0001]

FRIENDSHIP (TOWN)—See PORTLAND, ME (Time Warner Cable)

FRYEBURG—See PORTLAND, ME (Time Warner Cable)

GARDINER—See PORTLAND, ME (Time Warner Cable)

GLEN—See PORTLAND, NH (Time Warner Cable)

GLENBURN—Time Warner Cable. Now served by PORTLAND, ME [ME0001]

GLENBURN—See PORTLAND, ME (Time Warner Cable)

GORHAM—See PORTLAND, ME (Time Warner Cable)

GOULDSBORO—See PORTLAND, ME (Time Warner Cable)

GRAND ISLE—See PRESQUE ISLE, ME (Time Warner Cable)

GRAY (TOWN)—See PORTLAND, ME (Time Warner Cable)

GREENBUSH (town)—Formerly served by Argent Communications. No longer in operation

GREENE (town)—Time Warner Cable. Now served by PORTLAND, ME [ME0001]

GREENE (TOWN)—See PORTLAND, ME (Time Warner Cable)

GREENVILLE—Moosehead Enterprises

GREENWOOD—See PORTLAND, ME (Time Warner Cable)

GUILFORD—Moosehead Enterprises

HALLOWELL—See PORTLAND, ME (Time Warner Cable)

HAMLIN (TOWN)—See PRESQUE ISLE, ME (Time Warner Cable)

HAMPDEN—See PORTLAND, ME (Time Warner Cable)

HANCOCK—Time Warner Cable. Now served by PORTLAND, ME [ME0001]

HANCOCK—See PORTLAND, ME (Time Warner Cable)

HANOVER (TOWN)—See PORTLAND, ME (Time Warner Cable)

HARRINGTON—See PORTLAND, ME (Time Warner Cable)

HARRISON—See PORTLAND, ME (Time Warner Cable)

HARTLAND—See PORTLAND, ME (Time Warner Cable)

HERMON—Time Warner Cable. Now served by PORTLAND, ME [ME0001]

HERMON—See PORTLAND, ME (Time Warner Cable)

HINKLEY—See PORTLAND, ME (Time Warner Cable)

HIRAM—See PORTLAND, ME (Time Warner Cable)

HODGDON—See HOULTON, ME (Time Warner Cable)

HOLDEN—See PORTLAND, ME (Time Warner Cable)

HOLLIS—See PORTLAND, ME (Time Warner Cable)

HOPE—See LINCOLNVILLE, ME (Lincolnville Communications. Formerly [ME0094]. This cable system has converted to IPTV)

HOULTON—Time Warner Cable

HOWLAND—Time Warner Cable

INDUSTRY—See FARMINGTON, ME (Bee Line Cable TV)

ISLAND FALLS—Time Warner Cable

JACKMAN—Moosehead Enterprises

Cable Community Index—Maine

JACKSON—See PORTLAND, NH (Time Warner Cable)

JAY—Time Warner Cable. Now served by PORTLAND, ME [ME0001]

JAY—See PORTLAND, ME (Time Warner Cable)

JEFFERSON (TOWN)—See PORTLAND, ME (Time Warner Cable)

JEFFERSON—See LINCOLNVILLE, ME (Lincolnville Communications. Formerly [ME0094]. This cable system has converted to IPTV)

JEFFERSON—See PORTLAND, NH (Time Warner Cable)

JONESPORT—Time Warner Cable. Now served by PORTLAND, ME [ME0001]

JONESPORT—See PORTLAND, ME (Time Warner Cable)

KEARSARGE—See PORTLAND, NH (Time Warner Cable)

KENDUSKEAG—Time Warner Cable. Now served by PORTLAND, ME [ME0001]

KENDUSKEAG—See PORTLAND, ME (Time Warner Cable)

KENNEBUNK—Time Warner Cable. Now served by PORTLAND, ME [ME0001]

KENNEBUNK—See PORTLAND, ME (Time Warner Cable)

KENNEBUNKPORT—See PORTLAND, ME (Time Warner Cable)

KEZAR FALLS—See PORTLAND, ME (Time Warner Cable)

KINGFIELD—See PORTLAND, ME (Time Warner Cable)

LAMOINE—See PORTLAND, ME (Time Warner Cable)

LEEDS—See PORTLAND, ME (Time Warner Cable)

LEVANT—See PORTLAND, ME (Time Warner Cable)

LEWISTON—Time Warner Cable. Now served by PORTLAND, ME [ME0001]

LEWISTON—See PORTLAND, ME (Time Warner Cable)

LIMERICK—See PORTLAND, ME (Time Warner Cable)

LIMESTONE—See PRESQUE ISLE, ME (Time Warner Cable)

LIMINGTON—See PORTLAND, ME (Time Warner Cable)

LINCOLN—Time Warner Cable. Now served by PORTLAND, ME [ME0001]

LINCOLN—See PORTLAND, ME (Time Warner Cable)

LINCOLNVILLE—Lincolnville Communications. This cable system has converted to IPTV. See LINCOLNVILLE, ME [ME5003]

LINCOLNVILLE—Lincolnville Communications. Formerly [ME0094]. This cable system has converted to IPTV

LISBON FALLS—See PORTLAND, ME (Time Warner Cable)

LISBON—See PORTLAND, ME (Time Warner Cable)

LITCHFIELD—See PORTLAND, ME (Time Warner Cable)

LITTLETON (TOWN)—See HOULTON, ME (Time Warner Cable)

LIVERMORE FALLS—See PORTLAND, ME (Time Warner Cable)

LIVERMORE—See PORTLAND, ME (Time Warner Cable)

LOCKE MILLS—See PORTLAND, ME (Time Warner Cable)

LOVELL (town)—Time Warner Cable. Now served by PORTLAND, ME [ME0001]

LOVELL (TOWN)—See PORTLAND, ME (Time Warner Cable)

LUBEC—Formerly served by Pine Tree Cablevision. No longer in operation

LUBEC—See PORTLAND, ME (Time Warner Cable)

LYMAN—See PORTLAND, ME (Time Warner Cable)

MACHIAS—Formerly served by Pine Tree Cablevision. No longer in operation

MACHIAS—See PORTLAND, ME (Time Warner Cable)

MACHIASPORT—See PORTLAND, ME (Time Warner Cable)

MADAWASKA—Time Warner Cable. Now served by PRESQUE ISLE, ME [ME0008]

MADAWASKA—See PRESQUE ISLE, ME (Time Warner Cable)

MADISON (TOWN)—See PORTLAND, NH (Time Warner Cable)

MADISON—See SKOWHEGAN, ME (Bee Line Cable TV)

MANCHESTER—See PORTLAND, ME (Time Warner Cable)

MANSET—See PORTLAND, ME (Time Warner Cable)

MAPLETON—See PRESQUE ISLE, ME (Time Warner Cable)

MARS HILL—Time Warner Cable. Now served by PRESQUE ISLE, ME [ME0008]

MARS HILL—See PRESQUE ISLE, ME (Time Warner Cable)

MARSHFIELD—See PORTLAND, ME (Time Warner Cable)

MATTAWAMKEAG (TOWN)—Mattawamkeag Cablevision

MATTAWAMKEAG—See MATTAWAMKEAG (town), ME (Mattawamkeag Cablevision)

MECHANIC FALLS—See PORTLAND, ME (Time Warner Cable)

MEDWAY—Time Warner Cable

MERRILL—See OAKFIELD, ME (Time Warner Cable)

MEXICO—See PORTLAND, ME (Time Warner Cable)

MIDDLETON (TOWN)—See PORTLAND, NH (Time Warner Cable)

MILBRIDGE—See PORTLAND, ME (Time Warner Cable)

MILFORD—See PORTLAND, ME (Time Warner Cable)

MILLINOCKET—Bee Line Cable TV

MILO—Time Warner Cable. Now served by PORTLAND, ME [ME0001]

MILO—See PORTLAND, ME (Time Warner Cable)

MINOT—See PORTLAND, ME (Time Warner Cable)

MONMOUTH—See PORTLAND, ME (Time Warner Cable)

MONSON—Moosehead Enterprises

MONTICELLO (town)—Formerly served by Polaris Cable Services. Now served by Time Warner Cable, HOULTON, ME [ME0025]

MONTICELLO (TOWN)—See HOULTON, ME (Time Warner Cable)

MONTICELLO—See HOULTON, ME (Time Warner Cable)

MOODY—See PORTLAND, ME (Time Warner Cable)

MOULTONBOROUGH (TOWN)—See PORTLAND, NH (Time Warner Cable)

MOUNT DESERT (town)—Time Warner Cable. Now served by PORTLAND, ME [ME0001]

MOUNT DESERT (TOWN)—See PORTLAND, ME (Time Warner Cable)

MOUNT VERNON (TOWN)—See PORTLAND, ME (Time Warner Cable)

NAPLES—See PORTLAND, ME (Time Warner Cable)

NEW GLOUCESTER (TOWN)—See PORTLAND, ME (Time Warner Cable)

NEW HARBOR—See PORTLAND, ME (Time Warner Cable)

NEW PORTLAND—See PORTLAND, ME (Time Warner Cable)

NEW SHARON (town)—Formerly served by Argent Communications. No longer in operation

NEW SWEDEN (PORTIONS)—See PRESQUE ISLE, ME (Time Warner Cable)

NEW VINEYARD—See PORTLAND, ME (Time Warner Cable)

NEWCASTLE—Time Warner Cable. Now served by PORTLAND, ME [ME0001]

NEWCASTLE—See LINCOLNVILLE, ME (Lincolnville Communications. Formerly [ME0094]. This cable system has converted to IPTV)

NEWCASTLE—See PORTLAND, ME (Time Warner Cable)

NEWFIELD—See SANFORD, ME (MetroCast Cablevision)

NEWPORT—See PORTLAND, ME (Time Warner Cable)

NEWRY—See PORTLAND, ME (Time Warner Cable)

NOBLEBORO—See LINCOLNVILLE, ME (Lincolnville Communications. Formerly [ME0094]. This cable system has converted to IPTV)

NOBLEBORO—See PORTLAND, ME (Time Warner Cable)

NORRIDGEWOCK—See PORTLAND, ME (Time Warner Cable)

NORTH ANSON—Time Warner Cable. Now served by PORTLAND, ME [ME0001]

NORTH ANSON—See PORTLAND, ME (Time Warner Cable)

NORTH BERWICK—See PORTLAND, ME (Time Warner Cable)

NORTH CONWAY—See PORTLAND, NH (Time Warner Cable)

NORTH HAVEN—See PORTLAND, ME (Time Warner Cable)

NORTH MONMOUTH—See PORTLAND, ME (Time Warner Cable)

NORTH NEW PORTLAND—See PORTLAND, ME (Time Warner Cable)

NORTH VASSALBORO—See PORTLAND, ME (Time Warner Cable)

NORTH YARMOUTH—See PORTLAND, ME (Time Warner Cable)

NORWAY—Time Warner Cable. Now served by PORTLAND, ME [ME0001]

NORWAY—See PORTLAND, ME (Time Warner Cable)

OAKFIELD—Time Warner Cable

OAKLAND—See PORTLAND, ME (Time Warner Cable)

OGUNQUIT—See PORTLAND, ME (Time Warner Cable)

OLD ORCHARD BEACH—See PORTLAND, ME (Time Warner Cable)

OLD TOWN—See PORTLAND, ME (Time Warner Cable)

ORLAND—See PORTLAND, ME (Time Warner Cable)

ORONO—See PORTLAND, ME (Time Warner Cable)

ORRINGTON—See PORTLAND, ME (Time Warner Cable)

OSSIPEE (TOWN)—See PORTLAND, NH (Time Warner Cable)

OWLS HEAD—See PORTLAND, ME (Time Warner Cable)

OXFORD—See PORTLAND, ME (Time Warner Cable)

2017 Edition

Cable Community Index-111

Maine—Cable Community Index

PALERMO—See PORTLAND, ME (Time Warner Cable)

PALMYRA—See PORTLAND, ME (Time Warner Cable)

PARIS—See PORTLAND, ME (Time Warner Cable)

PARSONFIELD—See PORTLAND, ME (Time Warner Cable)

PASSADUMKEAG—See HOWLAND, ME (Time Warner Cable)

PATTEN—Formerly served by Polaris Cable Services. Now served by Time Warner Cable, ISLAND FALLS, ME [ME0108]

PATTEN—See ISLAND FALLS, ME (Time Warner Cable)

PEAKS ISLAND—See PORTLAND, ME (Time Warner Cable)

PEMAQUID—See PORTLAND, ME (Time Warner Cable)

PEMBROKE—Formerly served by Pine Tree Cablevision. No longer in operation

PEMBROKE—See PORTLAND, ME (Time Warner Cable)

PENOBSCOT INDIAN ISLAND RESERVATION—See PORTLAND, ME (Time Warner Cable)

PERRY—See PORTLAND, ME (Time Warner Cable)

PERU—See PORTLAND, ME (Time Warner Cable)

PHILLIPS—See PORTLAND, ME (Time Warner Cable)

PITTSFIELD—Time Warner Cable. Now served by PORTLAND, ME [ME0001]

PITTSFIELD—See PORTLAND, ME (Time Warner Cable)

PITTSTON—See PORTLAND, ME (Time Warner Cable)

PLANTATION ST. JOHN—See PRESQUE ISLE, ME (Time Warner Cable)

PLEASANT RIDGE PLANTATION—Formerly served by Pleasant Ridge Cablevision Inc. No longer in operation

POLAND—Formerly served by Adelphia Communications. No longer in operation

POLAND—See PORTLAND, ME (Time Warner Cable)

PORT CLYDGE—See PORTLAND, ME (Time Warner Cable)

PORTAGE LAKE—See PRESQUE ISLE, ME (Time Warner Cable)

PORTAGE—Time Warner Cable. Now served by PRESQUE ISLE, ME [ME0008]

PORTAGE—See PRESQUE ISLE, ME (Time Warner Cable)

PORTER—See PORTLAND, ME (Time Warner Cable)

PORTLAND—Time Warner Cable

POWNAL—See PORTLAND, ME (Time Warner Cable)

PRESQUE ISLE—Time Warner Cable

PRINCETON—See PORTLAND, ME (Time Warner Cable)

RANDOLPH—See PORTLAND, ME (Time Warner Cable)

RANGELEY (TOWN)—Argent Communications

RAYMOND—See PORTLAND, ME (Time Warner Cable)

READFIELD (TOWN)—See PORTLAND, ME (Time Warner Cable)

RICHMOND—See PORTLAND, ME (Time Warner Cable)

ROCKLAND—Time Warner Cable. Now served by PORTLAND, ME [ME0001]

ROCKLAND—See PORTLAND, ME (Time Warner Cable)

ROCKPORT (TOWN)—See PORTLAND, ME (Time Warner Cable)

ROCKWOOD—Moosehead Enterprises

ROME (TOWN)—See PORTLAND, ME (Time Warner Cable)

ROQUE BLUFFS—See PORTLAND, ME (Time Warner Cable)

ROUND POND—See PORTLAND, ME (Time Warner Cable)

ROXBURY (TOWN)—See PORTLAND, ME (Time Warner Cable)

RUMFORD—Formerly served by Adelphia Communications. Now served by Time Warner Cable, PORTLAND, ME [ME0001]

RUMFORD—See PORTLAND, ME (Time Warner Cable)

SABATTUS—See PORTLAND, ME (Time Warner Cable)

SACO—See PORTLAND, ME (Time Warner Cable)

SANBORNVILLE—See PORTLAND, NH (Time Warner Cable)

SANFORD—MetroCast Cablevision

SCARBOROUGH—See PORTLAND, ME (Time Warner Cable)

SEARSMONT—Formerly served by Argent Communications. No longer in operation

SEARSMONT—See LINCOLNVILLE, ME (Lincolnville Communications. Formerly [ME0094]. This cable system has converted to IPTV)

SEARSPORT—See PORTLAND, ME (Time Warner Cable)

SEBAGO (town)—Time Warner Cable. Now served by PORTLAND, ME [ME0001]

SEBAGO (TOWN)—See PORTLAND, ME (Time Warner Cable)

SHAPLEIGH—See SANFORD, ME (MetroCast Cablevision)

SHAWMUT—See PORTLAND, ME (Time Warner Cable)

SHELBURNE—See PORTLAND, NH (Time Warner Cable)

SHERMAN MILLS—See SHERMAN, ME (Pioneer Broadband)

SHERMAN—Pioneer Broadband

SIDNEY (town)—Time Warner Cable. Now served by PORTLAND, ME [ME0001]

SIDNEY (TOWN)—See PORTLAND, ME (Time Warner Cable)

SINCLAIR—See PRESQUE ISLE, ME (Time Warner Cable)

SKOWHEGAN—Bee Line Cable TV

SMITHFIELD (town)—Time Warner Cable. Now served by PORTLAND, ME [ME0001]

SMITHFIELD (TOWN)—See PORTLAND, ME (Time Warner Cable)

SMYRNA—See OAKFIELD, ME (Time Warner Cable)

SOLON—See PORTLAND, ME (Time Warner Cable)

SORRENTO—Time Warner Cable. Now served by PORTLAND, ME [ME0001]

SORRENTO—See PORTLAND, ME (Time Warner Cable)

SOUTH BERWICK—See PORTLAND, ME (Time Warner Cable)

SOUTH BRISTOL (TOWN)—See PORTLAND, ME (Time Warner Cable)

SOUTH BRISTOL—See LINCOLNVILLE, ME (Lincolnville Communications. Formerly [ME0094]. This cable system has converted to IPTV)

SOUTH PARIS—See PORTLAND, ME (Time Warner Cable)

SOUTH PORTLAND—See PORTLAND, ME (Time Warner Cable)

SOUTH THOMASTON (TOWN)—See PORTLAND, ME (Time Warner Cable)

SOUTHPORT (TOWN)—See PORTLAND, ME (Time Warner Cable)

SOUTHWEST HARBOR—See PORTLAND, ME (Time Warner Cable)

SPRINGVALE—See SANFORD, ME (MetroCast Cablevision)

SPRUCE HEAD—See PORTLAND, ME (Time Warner Cable)

ST. AGATHA—See PRESQUE ISLE, ME (Time Warner Cable)

ST. ALBANS—See PORTLAND, ME (Time Warner Cable)

ST. FRANCIS TWP.—See PRESQUE ISLE, ME (Time Warner Cable)

ST. FRANCIS—Formerly served by Adelphia Communications. Now served by Time Warner Cable, PRESQUE ISLE, ME [ME0008]

ST. FRANCIS—See PRESQUE ISLE, ME (Time Warner Cable)

ST. GEORGE (TOWN)—See PORTLAND, ME (Time Warner Cable)

ST. JOHN—See PRESQUE ISLE, ME (Time Warner Cable)

STACYVILLE—See SHERMAN, ME (Pioneer Broadband)

STANDISH—See PORTLAND, ME (Time Warner Cable)

STEEP FALLS—See PORTLAND, ME (Time Warner Cable)

STOCKHOLM (town)—Formerly served by Argent Communications. No longer in operations

STOCKTON SPRINGS—Time Warner Cable. Now served by PORTLAND, ME [ME0001]

STOCKTON SPRINGS—See PORTLAND, ME (Time Warner Cable)

STONINGTON—Formerly served by Adelphia Communications. Now served by Time Warner Cable, PORTLAND, ME [ME0001]

STONINGTON—See PORTLAND, ME (Time Warner Cable)

STRATTON—See PORTLAND, ME (Time Warner Cable)

STRONG—See PORTLAND, ME (Time Warner Cable)

SULLIVAN—See PORTLAND, ME (Time Warner Cable)

SURRY—See PORTLAND, ME (Time Warner Cable)

TAMWORTH (TOWN)—See PORTLAND, NH (Time Warner Cable)

TEMPLE (TOWN)—Argent Communications

TENANTS HARBOR—See PORTLAND, ME (Time Warner Cable)

THOMASTON—See PORTLAND, ME (Time Warner Cable)

THORNDIKE—See PORTLAND, ME (Time Warner Cable)

TREMONT—See PORTLAND, ME (Time Warner Cable)

TRENTON—Time Warner Cable. Now served by PORTLAND, ME [ME0001]

TRENTON—See PORTLAND, ME (Time Warner Cable)

TREVETT—See PORTLAND, ME (Time Warner Cable)

TUFTONBORO (TOWN)—See PORTLAND, NH (Time Warner Cable)

TURNER—See PORTLAND, ME (Time Warner Cable)

UNION (town)—Time Warner Cable. Now served by PORTLAND, ME [ME0001]

UNION (TOWN)—See PORTLAND, ME (Time Warner Cable)

UNITY—Formerly served by FrontierVision. No longer in operation

Cable Community Index—Maryland

UNITY—See PORTLAND, ME (Time Warner Cable)

VAN BUREN—Time Warner Cable. Now served by PRESQUE ISLE, ME [ME0008]

VAN BUREN—See PRESQUE ISLE, ME (Time Warner Cable)

VASSALBORO—See PORTLAND, ME (Time Warner Cable)

VEAZIE—See PORTLAND, ME (Time Warner Cable)

VERONA—See PORTLAND, ME (Time Warner Cable)

VINALHAVEN—Time Warner Cable. Now served by PORTLAND, ME [ME0001]

VINALHAVEN—See PORTLAND, ME (Time Warner Cable)

WAKEFIELD (TOWN)—See PORTLAND, NH (Time Warner Cable)

WALDOBORO—See PORTLAND, ME (Time Warner Cable)

WALES—See PORTLAND, ME (Time Warner Cable)

WALLAGRASS—See PRESQUE ISLE, ME (Time Warner Cable)

WARREN (town)—Time Warner Cable. Now served by PORTLAND, ME [ME0001]

WARREN (TOWN)—See PORTLAND, ME (Time Warner Cable)

WASHBURN—Time Warner Cable. Now served by PRESQUE ISLE, ME [ME0008]

WASHBURN—See PRESQUE ISLE, ME (Time Warner Cable)

WATERBORO—See PORTLAND, ME (Time Warner Cable)

WATERFORD (TOWN)—See PORTLAND, ME (Time Warner Cable)

WATERVILLE VALLEY—See PORTLAND, NH (Time Warner Cable)

WATERVILLE—Time Warner Cable. Now served by PORTLAND, ME [ME0001]

WATERVILLE—See PORTLAND, ME (Time Warner Cable)

WAYNE—See PORTLAND, ME (Time Warner Cable)

WELD—Formerly served by Argent Communications. No longer in operation

WELLS—See PORTLAND, ME (Time Warner Cable)

WEST BALDWIN—See PORTLAND, ME (Time Warner Cable)

WEST ENFIELD—See HOWLAND, ME (Time Warner Cable)

WEST GARDINER—See PORTLAND, ME (Time Warner Cable)

WEST PARIS—See PORTLAND, ME (Time Warner Cable)

WEST SOUTHPORT—See PORTLAND, ME (Time Warner Cable)

WESTBROOK—See PORTLAND, ME (Time Warner Cable)

WESTFIELD—See PRESQUE ISLE, ME (Time Warner Cable)

WESTON—See DANFORTH, ME (Time Warner Cable)

WESTPORT—See PORTLAND, ME (Time Warner Cable)

WHITEFIELD (TOWN)—See PORTLAND, ME (Time Warner Cable)

WHITING—See PORTLAND, ME (Time Warner Cable)

WHITNEYVILLE—See PORTLAND, ME (Time Warner Cable)

WILTON—See FARMINGTON, ME (Bee Line Cable TV)

WINDHAM—Time Warner Cable. Now served by PORTLAND, ME [ME0001]

WINDHAM—See PORTLAND, ME (Time Warner Cable)

WINDSOR (TOWN)—See PORTLAND, ME (Time Warner Cable)

WINN—See MATTAWAMKEAG (town), ME (Mattawamkeag Cablevision)

WINSLOW—See PORTLAND, ME (Time Warner Cable)

WINTER HARBOR—Formerly served by Pine Tree Cablevision. Now served by Time Warner Cable, PORTLAND, ME [ME0001]

WINTER HARBOR—See PORTLAND, ME (Time Warner Cable)

WINTERPORT—See PORTLAND, ME (Time Warner Cable)

WINTHROP—See PORTLAND, ME (Time Warner Cable)

WISCASSET—See PORTLAND, ME (Time Warner Cable)

WOODLAND—See PRESQUE ISLE, ME (Time Warner Cable)

WOODSTOCK—See PORTLAND, ME (Time Warner Cable)

WYMAN—See PORTLAND, ME (Time Warner Cable)

YARMOUTH—See PORTLAND, ME (Time Warner Cable)

YORK—Time Warner Cable. Now served by PORTLAND, ME [ME0001]

YORK—See PORTLAND, ME (Time Warner Cable)

MARYLAND

ABELL—See LEONARDTOWN, MD (MetroCast Communications)

ABERDEEN/EDGEWOOD PROVING GROUND—See TOWSON, MD (Comcast Cable)

ABERDEEN—See TOWSON, MD (Comcast Cable)

ABINGDON—Armstrong Cable Services

ABINGDON—See TOWSON, MD (Comcast Cable)

ADAMSTOWN—See FREDERICK COUNTY (portions), MD (Comcast Cable)

ALEXANDRIA—See FREDERICK COUNTY (portions), VA (Comcast Cable)

ALLEGANY COUNTY—See CUMBERLAND, MD (Atlantic Broadband)

ANDREWS AFB—See FREDERICK COUNTY (portions), MD (Comcast Cable)

ANNAPOLIS JUNCTION—See MILLERSVILLE, MD (Broadstripe)

ANNAPOLIS—Comcast Cable. Now served by TOWSON, MD [MD0003]

ANNAPOLIS—See TOWSON, MD (Comcast Cable)

ANNE ARUNDEL COUNTY (NORTHERN PORTION)—See MILLERSVILLE, MD (Broadstripe)

ANNE ARUNDEL COUNTY (PORTIONS)—See TOWSON, MD (Comcast Cable)

ARBUTUS—See TOWSON, MD (Comcast Cable)

ARLINGTON COUNTY (PORTIONS)—See FREDERICK COUNTY (portions), VA (Comcast Cable)

ARNOLD—See MILLERSVILLE, MD (Broadstripe)

ARNOLD—See TOWSON, MD (Comcast Cable)

ASHBURN—See FREDERICK COUNTY (portions), VA (Comcast Cable)

AVENUE—See LEONARDTOWN, MD (MetroCast Communications)

BALDWIN—See TOWSON, MD (Comcast Cable)

BALTIMORE (Inner Harbor)—Formerly served by Flight Systems Cablevision. No longer in operation

BALTIMORE COUNTY (UNINCORPORATED AREAS)—See TOWSON, MD (Comcast Cable)

BALTIMORE—Comcast Cable. Now served by TOWSON, MD [MD0003]

BALTIMORE—Formerly served by Sprint Corp. No longer in operation

BALTIMORE—See TOWSON, MD (Comcast Cable)

BARCLAY—See QUEENSTOWN, MD (Atlantic Broadband)

BARNESVILLE—See FREDERICK COUNTY (portions), MD (Comcast Cable)

BATH (TOWN)—See FREDERICK COUNTY (portions), WV (Comcast Cable)

BAYARD—See OAKLAND, WV (Shentel)

BEL AIR—See ABINGDON, MD (Armstrong Cable Services)

BEL AIR—See TOWSON, MD (Comcast Cable)

BELCAMP—See TOWSON, MD (Comcast Cable)

BENEDICT—See TOWSON, MD (Comcast Cable)

BERKELEY COUNTY (PORTIONS)—See FREDERICK COUNTY (portions), WV (Comcast Cable)

BERKELEY SPRINGS—See FREDERICK COUNTY (portions), WV (Comcast Cable)

BERLIN—See TOWSON, MD (Comcast Cable)

BERRYVILLE (TOWN)—See FREDERICK COUNTY (portions), VA (Comcast Cable)

BERWYN HEIGHTS—See FREDERICK COUNTY (portions), MD (Comcast Cable)

BETHEL—See TOWSON, DE (Comcast Cable)

BETHESDA—See FREDERICK COUNTY (portions), MD (Comcast Cable)

BETHLEHEM—See TOWSON, MD (Comcast Cable)

BETTERTON—See QUEENSTOWN, MD (Atlantic Broadband)

BIVALVE—See TOWSON, MD (Comcast Cable)

BLADENSBURG—See FREDERICK COUNTY (portions), MD (Comcast Cable)

BLADES—See TOWSON, DE (Comcast Cable)

BLAINE—See OAKLAND, WV (Shentel)

BOLIVAR—See HAGERSTOWN, MD (Antietam Cable Television Inc)

BOLIVAR—See FREDERICK COUNTY (portions), WV (Comcast Cable)

BOLLING AFB—See FREDERICK COUNTY (portions), DC (Comcast Cable)

BOONSBORO—See HAGERSTOWN, MD (Antietam Cable Television Inc)

BOWERS BEACH—See TOWSON, DE (Comcast Cable)

BOWIE—See FREDERICK COUNTY (portions), MD (Comcast Cable)

BOYCE—See FREDERICK COUNTY (portions), VA (Comcast Cable)

BOYDS—See FREDERICK COUNTY (portions), MD (Comcast Cable)

BRENTWOOD—See FREDERICK COUNTY (portions), MD (Comcast Cable)

BRIDGEVILLE—See TOWSON, DE (Comcast Cable)

BROADKILL BEACH—See TOWSON, DE (Comcast Cable)

BROOKEVILLE—See FREDERICK COUNTY (portions), MD (Comcast Cable)

BROOKVIEW—See TOWSON, MD (Comcast Cable)

Maryland—Cable Community Index

BRUNSWICK—See FREDERICK COUNTY (portions), MD (Comcast Cable)

BURKITTSVILLE—See FREDERICK COUNTY (portions), MD (Comcast Cable)

BURTONSVILLE—See FREDERICK COUNTY (portions), MD (Comcast Cable)

BUSHWOOD—See LEONARDTOWN, MD (MetroCast Communications)

CABIN JOHN—See FREDERICK COUNTY (portions), MD (Comcast Cable)

CALIFORNIA—See LEONARDTOWN, MD (MetroCast Communications)

CALLAWAY—See LEONARDTOWN, MD (MetroCast Communications)

CALVERT BEACH—See TOWSON, MD (Comcast Cable)

CAMBRIDGE—Comcast Cable. Now served by TOWSON, MD [MD0003]

CAMBRIDGE—See DORCHESTER COUNTY (portions), MD (Bay Country Communications)

CAMBRIDGE—See TOWSON, MD (Comcast Cable)

CAMDEN—See TOWSON, DE (Comcast Cable)

CAPE ST. CLAIRE—See TOWSON, MD (Comcast Cable)

CAPITOL HEIGHTS—See FREDERICK COUNTY (portions), MD (Comcast Cable)

CARDIFF—See ABINGDON, MD (Armstrong Cable Services)

CAROLINE COUNTY (PORTIONS)—See QUEENSTOWN, MD (Atlantic Broadband)

CAROLINE COUNTY (PORTIONS)—See TOWSON, MD (Comcast Cable)

CARPENDALE—See CUMBERLAND, WV (Atlantic Broadband)

CARROLL COUNTY (PORTIONS)—See TOWSON, MD (Comcast Cable)

CASTLETON—See ABINGDON, MD (Armstrong Cable Services)

CATONSVILLE—See TOWSON, MD (Comcast Cable)

CECIL COUNTY (PORTIONS)—See ABINGDON, MD (Armstrong Cable Services)

CECIL COUNTY (PORTIONS)—See CHESAPEAKE CITY, MD (Atlantic Broadband)

CECIL COUNTY (PORTIONS)—See PERRYVILLE, MD (Atlantic Broadband)

CECIL COUNTY (PORTIONS)—See TOWSON, MD (Comcast Cable)

CECILTON—Comcast Cable. Now served by TOWSON, MD [MD0003]

CECILTON—See TOWSON, MD (Comcast Cable)

CENTREVILLE—See QUEENSTOWN, MD (Atlantic Broadband)

CHAPTICO—See LEONARDTOWN, MD (MetroCast Communications)

CHARLES COUNTY (portions)—Comcast Cable. Now served by TOWSON, MD [MD0003]

CHARLES COUNTY (PORTIONS)—See TOWSON, MD (Comcast Cable)

CHARLES TOWN—See FREDERICK COUNTY (portions), WV (Comcast Cable)

CHARLESTOWN—See TOWSON, MD (Comcast Cable)

CHARLOTTE HALL—See TOWSON, MD (Comcast Cable)

CHESAPEAKE BEACH—Comcast Cable. Now served by TOWSON, MD [MD0003]

CHESAPEAKE BEACH—See TOWSON, MD (Comcast Cable)

CHESAPEAKE CITY—Atlantic Broadband

CHESAPEAKE CITY—See TOWSON, MD (Comcast Cable)

CHESTERTOWN—See QUEENSTOWN, MD (Atlantic Broadband)

CHESWOLD—See TOWSON, DE (Comcast Cable)

CHEVERLY—See FREDERICK COUNTY (portions), MD (Comcast Cable)

CHEVY CHASE—See FREDERICK COUNTY (portions), MD (Comcast Cable)

CHURCH CREEK—See TOWSON, MD (Comcast Cable)

CHURCH HILL—See QUEENSTOWN, MD (Atlantic Broadband)

CHURCHVILLE—See TOWSON, MD (Comcast Cable)

CLARKE COUNTY (PORTIONS)—See FREDERICK COUNTY (portions), VA (Comcast Cable)

CLARKSVILLE—See TOWSON, MD (Comcast Cable)

CLAYTON—See TOWSON, DE (Comcast Cable)

CLEAR SPRING—See HAGERSTOWN, MD (Antietam Cable Television Inc)

CLEMENTS—See LEONARDTOWN, MD (MetroCast Communications)

COBB ISLAND—See TOWSON, MD (Comcast Cable)

COCKEYSVILLE—See TOWSON, MD (Comcast Cable)

COLD SPRING—See TOWSON, MD (Comcast Cable)

COLLEGE PARK—See FREDERICK COUNTY (portions), MD (Comcast Cable)

COLMAR MANOR—See FREDERICK COUNTY (portions), MD (Comcast Cable)

COLTONS POINT—See LEONARDTOWN, MD (MetroCast Communications)

COLUMBIA—See TOWSON, MD (Comcast Cable)

COMPTON—See LEONARDTOWN, MD (MetroCast Communications)

COOKSVILLE—See TOWSON, MD (Comcast Cable)

COTTAGE CITY—See FREDERICK COUNTY (portions), MD (Comcast Cable)

CRISFIELD—Charter Communications

CROFTON—See TOWSON, MD (Comcast Cable)

CROWNSVILLE—See TOWSON, MD (Comcast Cable)

CRUMPTON—See QUEENSTOWN, MD (Atlantic Broadband)

CUMBERLAND VALLEY TWP.—See CUMBERLAND, PA (Atlantic Broadband)

CUMBERLAND—Atlantic Broadband

CURTIS BAY—See TOWSON, MD (Comcast Cable)

DAMASCUS—See FREDERICK COUNTY (portions), MD (Comcast Cable)

DAMERON—See LEONARDTOWN, MD (MetroCast Communications)

DARLINGTON—See ABINGDON, MD (Armstrong Cable Services)

DAVIDSONVILLE—See TOWSON, MD (Comcast Cable)

DAYTON—See TOWSON, MD (Comcast Cable)

DEAL ISLAND—See TOWSON, MD (Comcast Cable)

DEALE—See TOWSON, MD (Comcast Cable)

DEEP CREEK LAKE—Formerly served by Comcast Cable. No longer in operation

DEEP CREEK—See OAKLAND, MD (Shentel)

DEER PARK—See OAKLAND, MD (Shentel)

DELAWARE CITY—See CHESAPEAKE CITY, DE (Atlantic Broadband)

DELMAR—See TOWSON, DE (Comcast Cable)

DELMAR—See TOWSON, MD (Comcast Cable)

DENTON—See TOWSON, MD (Comcast Cable)

DERWOOD—See FREDERICK COUNTY (portions), MD (Comcast Cable)

DEWEY BEACH—See TOWSON, DE (Comcast Cable)

DISTRICT HEIGHTS—See FREDERICK COUNTY (portions), MD (Comcast Cable)

DORCHESTER COUNTY (PORTIONS)—Bay Country Communications

DORCHESTER COUNTY (WESTERN PORTION)—See TOWSON, MD (Comcast Cable)

DOVER AFB—See TOWSON, DE (Comcast Cable)

DOVER—See TOWSON, DE (Comcast Cable)

DRYDEN—See LEONARDTOWN, MD (MetroCast Communications)

DUBLIN—See ABINGDON, MD (Armstrong Cable Services)

DUNDALK—See TOWSON, MD (Comcast Cable)

DUNKIRK—See TOWSON, MD (Comcast Cable)

EARLEVILLE—See TOWSON, MD (Comcast Cable)

EAST NEW MARKET—See TOWSON, MD (Comcast Cable)

EAST NOTTINGHAM TWP.—See ABINGDON, PA (Armstrong Cable Services)

EASTON—Easton Cable

EDGEMERE—See TOWSON, MD (Comcast Cable)

EDGEWOOD ARSENAL—See TOWSON, MD (Comcast Cable)

EDMONDSTON—See FREDERICK COUNTY (portions), MD (Comcast Cable)

ELK GARDEN—See OAKLAND, WV (Shentel)

ELK TWP. (CHESTER COUNTY)—See ABINGDON, PA (Armstrong Cable Services)

ELKRIDGE—See TOWSON, MD (Comcast Cable)

ELKTON—Comcast Cable. Now served by TOWSON, MD [MD0003]

ELKTON—See TOWSON, MD (Comcast Cable)

ELLENDALE—See TOWSON, DE (Comcast Cable)

ELLICOTT CITY—See TOWSON, MD (Comcast Cable)

EMMITSBURG—See FREDERICK COUNTY (portions), MD (Comcast Cable)

ESSEX—See TOWSON, MD (Comcast Cable)

FAIRFAX COUNTY (PORTIONS)—See FREDERICK COUNTY (portions), VA (Comcast Cable)

FAIRLEE—See QUEENSTOWN, MD (Atlantic Broadband)

FAIRMOUNT HEIGHTS—See FREDERICK COUNTY (portions), MD (Comcast Cable)

FALLSTON—See TOWSON, MD (Comcast Cable)

FARMINGTON—See TOWSON, DE (Comcast Cable)

FEDERALSBURG—See TOWSON, MD (Comcast Cable)

Cable Community Index—Maryland

FELTON—See TOWSON, DE (Comcast Cable)

FENWICK ISLAND—See TOWSON, DE (Comcast Cable)

FOREST HEIGHTS—See FREDERICK COUNTY (portions), MD (Comcast Cable)

FOREST HILL—See ABINGDON, MD (Armstrong Cable Services)

FOREST HILL—See TOWSON, MD (Comcast Cable)

FORT DETRICK—See FREDERICK COUNTY (portions), MD (Comcast Cable)

FORT MEADE—See TOWSON, MD (Comcast Cable)

FOXVILLE—See HAGERSTOWN, MD (Antietam Cable Television Inc)

FREDERICA—See TOWSON, DE (Comcast Cable)

FREDERICK COUNTY (PORTIONS)—Comcast Cable

FREDERICK COUNTY (PORTIONS)—See FREDERICK COUNTY (portions), VA (Comcast Cable)

FREDERICK—See FREDERICK COUNTY (portions), MD (Comcast Cable)

FRONT ROYAL—See FREDERICK COUNTY (portions), VA (Comcast Cable)

FRUITLAND—See TOWSON, MD (Comcast Cable)

FULTON COUNTY (PORTIONS)—See FREDERICK COUNTY (portions), PA (Comcast Cable)

FULTON—See TOWSON, MD (Comcast Cable)

FUNKSTOWN—See HAGERSTOWN, MD (Antietam Cable Television Inc)

GAITHERSBURG—See FREDERICK COUNTY (portions), MD (Comcast Cable)

GALENA—See TOWSON, MD (Comcast Cable)

GALESTOWN—See TOWSON, MD (Comcast Cable)

GALESVILLE—See TOWSON, MD (Comcast Cable)

GAMBRILLS—See MILLERSVILLE, MD (Broadstripe)

GAMBRILLS—See TOWSON, MD (Comcast Cable)

GARRETT COUNTY (PORTIONS)—See OAKLAND, MD (Shentel)

GARRETT PARK—See FREDERICK COUNTY (portions), MD (Comcast Cable)

GEORGETOWN—See TOWSON, DE (Comcast Cable)

GERMANTOWN—See FREDERICK COUNTY (portions), MD (Comcast Cable)

GLEN BURNIE—See MILLERSVILLE, MD (Broadstripe)

GLEN BURNIE—See TOWSON, MD (Comcast Cable)

GLEN ECHO—See FREDERICK COUNTY (portions), MD (Comcast Cable)

GLENARDEN—See FREDERICK COUNTY (portions), MD (Comcast Cable)

GLENELG—See TOWSON, MD (Comcast Cable)

GLENWOOD—See TOWSON, MD (Comcast Cable)

GOLDSBORO—See TOWSON, MD (Comcast Cable)

GORMAN—See OAKLAND, MD (Shentel)

GORMANIA—See OAKLAND, WV (Shentel)

GRANT COUNTY (PORTIONS)—See OAKLAND, WV (Shentel)

GRANTSVILLE—Comcast Cable. Now served by BLAIRSVILLE, PA [PA0320]

GRASONVILLE—See QUEENSTOWN, MD (Atlantic Broadband)

GREAT CACAPON—See FREDERICK COUNTY (portions), WV (Comcast Cable)

GREAT MILLS—See LEONARDTOWN, MD (MetroCast Communications)

GREENBELT—See FREDERICK COUNTY (portions), MD (Comcast Cable)

GREENHILLS—See TOWSON, MD (Comcast Cable)

GREENSBORO—See TOWSON, MD (Comcast Cable)

GREENWOOD—See TOWSON, DE (Comcast Cable)

HAGERSTOWN—Antietam Cable Television Inc

HAMILTON—See FREDERICK COUNTY (portions), VA (Comcast Cable)

HAMPSHIRE COUNTY—See CUMBERLAND, WV (Atlantic Broadband)

HAMPSTEAD—See TOWSON, MD (Comcast Cable)

HANCOCK—Comcast Cable. Now served by FREDERICK COUNTY (portions), MD [MD0009]

HANCOCK—See FREDERICK COUNTY (portions), MD (Comcast Cable)

HANOVER—See MILLERSVILLE, MD (Broadstripe)

HANOVER—See TOWSON, MD (Comcast Cable)

HARFORD COUNTY (portions)—Comcast Cable. Now served by TOWSON, MD [MD0003]

HARFORD COUNTY (PORTIONS)—See ABINGDON, MD (Armstrong Cable Services)

HARFORD COUNTY (PORTIONS)—See TOWSON, MD (Comcast Cable)

HARMANS—See MILLERSVILLE, MD (Broadstripe)

HARMANS—See TOWSON, MD (Comcast Cable)

HARMONY—See TOWSON, MD (Comcast Cable)

HARPERS FERRY—See FREDERICK COUNTY (portions), WV (Comcast Cable)

HARRINGTON—See TOWSON, DE (Comcast Cable)

HARTLY—See TOWSON, DE (Comcast Cable)

HAVRE DE GRACE—See TOWSON, MD (Comcast Cable)

HEBRON—See TOWSON, MD (Comcast Cable)

HEDGESVILLE—See FREDERICK COUNTY (portions), WV (Comcast Cable)

HELEN—See LEONARDTOWN, MD (MetroCast Communications)

HENDERSON—See TOWSON, MD (Comcast Cable)

HENLOPEN ACRES—See TOWSON, DE (Comcast Cable)

HIGHLAND TWP. (CHESTER COUNTY)—See ABINGDON, PA (Armstrong Cable Services)

HIGHLAND—See TOWSON, MD (Comcast Cable)

HILLSBORO—See TOWSON, MD (Comcast Cable)

HOLLYWOOD—See LEONARDTOWN, MD (MetroCast Communications)

HOUSTON—See TOWSON, DE (Comcast Cable)

HOWARD COUNTY (portions)—Formerly served by Mid-Atlantic Communications. Now served by Comcast Cable, TOWSON, MD [MD0003]

HOWARD COUNTY (PORTIONS)—See TOWSON, MD (Comcast Cable)

HUGHESVILLE—See TOWSON, MD (Comcast Cable)

HURLOCK—See TOWSON, MD (Comcast Cable)

HYATTSVILLE—See FREDERICK COUNTY (portions), MD (Comcast Cable)

INDIAN HEAD—See TOWSON, MD (Comcast Cable)

JARRETTSVILLE—See ABINGDON, MD (Armstrong Cable Services)

JEFFERSON COUNTY (PORTIONS)—See FREDERICK COUNTY (portions), WV (Comcast Cable)

JEFFERSON—See FREDERICK COUNTY (portions), MD (Comcast Cable)

JESSUP—See MILLERSVILLE, MD (Broadstripe)

JESSUP—See TOWSON, MD (Comcast Cable)

JOPPA—See TOWSON, MD (Comcast Cable)

KEEDYSVILLE—See FREDERICK COUNTY (portions), MD (Comcast Cable)

KENNEDYVILLE—See QUEENSTOWN, MD (Atlantic Broadband)

KENSINGTON—See FREDERICK COUNTY (portions), MD (Comcast Cable)

KENT COUNTY (PORTIONS)—See CHESAPEAKE CITY, MD (Atlantic Broadband)

KENT COUNTY (PORTIONS)—See QUEENSTOWN, MD (Atlantic Broadband)

KENT COUNTY (PORTIONS)—See TOWSON, DE (Comcast Cable)

KENT COUNTY (PORTIONS)—See TOWSON, MD (Comcast Cable)

KENT ISLAND—See QUEENSTOWN, MD (Atlantic Broadband)

KINGSVILLE—See TOWSON, MD (Comcast Cable)

KITZMILLER—See OAKLAND, MD (Shentel)

LA PLATA—See TOWSON, MD (Comcast Cable)

LANDOVER HILLS—See FREDERICK COUNTY (portions), MD (Comcast Cable)

LANSDOWNE—See TOWSON, MD (Comcast Cable)

LARGO—See FREDERICK COUNTY (portions), MD (Comcast Cable)

LAUREL (PORTIONS)—See FREDERICK COUNTY (portions), MD (Comcast Cable)

LAUREL (PORTIONS)—See TOWSON, MD (Comcast Cable)

LAUREL—See MILLERSVILLE, MD (Broadstripe)

LAUREL—See TOWSON, DE (Comcast Cable)

LAYTONSVILLE—See FREDERICK COUNTY (portions), MD (Comcast Cable)

LEESBURG—See FREDERICK COUNTY (portions), VA (Comcast Cable)

LEIPSIC—See TOWSON, DE (Comcast Cable)

LEONARDTOWN—MetroCast Communications

LEWES—See TOWSON, DE (Comcast Cable)

LEXINGTON PARK—Formerly served by GMP Cable TV. Now served by MetroCast Communications, LEONARDTOWN, MD [MD0024]

LEXINGTON PARK—See LEONARDTOWN, MD (MetroCast Communications)

2017 Edition

Cable Community Index-115

Maryland—Cable Community Index

LIBERTYTOWN—See FREDERICK COUNTY (portions), MD (Comcast Cable)

LINCOLN—See TOWSON, DE (Comcast Cable)

LINTHICUM—See MILLERSVILLE, MD (Broadstripe)

LINTHICUM—See TOWSON, MD (Comcast Cable)

LISBON—See TOWSON, MD (Comcast Cable)

LITTLE CREEK—See TOWSON, DE (Comcast Cable)

LOCH LYNN HEIGHTS—See OAKLAND, MD (Shentel)

LONDONDERRY TWP. (BEDFORD COUNTY)—See CUMBERLAND, PA (Atlantic Broadband)

LONDONDERRY TWP. (CHESTER COUNTY)—See ABINGDON, PA (Armstrong Cable Services)

LOTHIAN—Comcast Cable. Now served by TOWSON, MD [MD0003]

LOTHIAN—See TOWSON, MD (Comcast Cable)

LOUDOUN COUNTY (PORTIONS)—See FREDERICK COUNTY (portions), VA (Comcast Cable)

LOVETTSVILLE—See FREDERICK COUNTY (portions), VA (Comcast Cable)

LOVEVILLE—See LEONARDTOWN, MD (MetroCast Communications)

LOWER OXFORD TWP.—See ABINGDON, PA (Armstrong Cable Services)

LYNCH—See QUEENSTOWN, MD (Atlantic Broadband)

MAGNOLIA—See TOWSON, DE (Comcast Cable)

MANCHESTER (TOWN)—See TOWSON, MD (Comcast Cable)

MARDELA SPRINGS—See TOWSON, MD (Comcast Cable)

MARRIOTTSVILLE—See TOWSON, MD (Comcast Cable)

MARTINSBURG—See FREDERICK COUNTY (portions), WV (Comcast Cable)

MARYDEL—See TOWSON, MD (Comcast Cable)

MARYLAND CITY—See TOWSON, MD (Comcast Cable)

MECHANICSVILLE—See TOWSON, MD (Comcast Cable)

MECHANICSVILLE—See LEONARDTOWN, MD (MetroCast Communications)

MIDDLE RIVER—See TOWSON, MD (Comcast Cable)

MIDDLEBURG—See FREDERICK COUNTY (portions), VA (Comcast Cable)

MIDDLETON (TOWN)—See FREDERICK COUNTY (portions), VA (Comcast Cable)

MIDDLETOWN (TOWN)—See CHESAPEAKE CITY, DE (Atlantic Broadband)

MIDDLETOWN—See FREDERICK COUNTY (portions), MD (Comcast Cable)

MILFORD—See TOWSON, DE (Comcast Cable)

MILLERSVILLE—Broadstripe

MILLERSVILLE—See TOWSON, MD (Comcast Cable)

MILLINGTON—See QUEENSTOWN, MD (Atlantic Broadband)

MILTON—See TOWSON, DE (Comcast Cable)

MINERAL COUNTY (PORTIONS)—See OAKLAND, WV (Shentel)

MINERAL COUNTY—See CUMBERLAND, WV (Atlantic Broadband)

MONTGOMERY COUNTY (portions)—Comcast Cable. Now served by FREDERICK COUNTY (portions), MD [MD0009]

MONTGOMERY COUNTY (portions)—RCN. This cable system has converted to IPTV. See WASHINGTON, DC (portions) [DC5001]

MONTGOMERY COUNTY (PORTIONS)—See FREDERICK COUNTY (portions), MD (Comcast Cable)

MORGAN COUNTY (PORTIONS)—See FREDERICK COUNTY (portions), WV (Comcast Cable)

MORGANZA—See LEONARDTOWN, MD (MetroCast Communications)

MORNINGSIDE—See FREDERICK COUNTY (portions), MD (Comcast Cable)

MOUNT AIRY (CARROLL COUNTY)—See TOWSON, MD (Comcast Cable)

MOUNT AIRY (FREDERICK COUNTY)—See FREDERICK COUNTY (portions), MD (Comcast Cable)

MOUNT JOY—See TOWSON, PA (Comcast Cable)

MOUNT RAINIER—See FREDERICK COUNTY (portions), MD (Comcast Cable)

MOUNTAIN LAKE PARK—See OAKLAND, MD (Shentel)

MYERSVILLE—See FREDERICK COUNTY (portions), MD (Comcast Cable)

NANTICOKE—See TOWSON, MD (Comcast Cable)

NAVAL AIR STATION PATUXENT RIVER—See LEONARDTOWN, MD (MetroCast Communications)

NEW CARROLLTON—See FREDERICK COUNTY (portions), MD (Comcast Cable)

NEW CASTLE COUNTY (PORTIONS)—See CHESAPEAKE CITY, DE (Atlantic Broadband)

NEW CASTLE COUNTY (PORTIONS)—See TOWSON, DE (Comcast Cable)

NEW MARKET—See FREDERICK COUNTY (portions), MD (Comcast Cable)

NEW WINDSOR—See TOWSON, MD (Comcast Cable)

NEWBURG—See TOWSON, MD (Comcast Cable)

NORRISVILLE—See ABINGDON, MD (Armstrong Cable Services)

NORTH BEACH—See TOWSON, MD (Comcast Cable)

NORTH BRENTWOOD—See FREDERICK COUNTY (portions), MD (Comcast Cable)

NORTH EAST—See TOWSON, MD (Comcast Cable)

OAKLAND—Shentel

OCEAN CITY—Comcast Cable. Now served by TOWSON, MD [MD0003]

OCEAN CITY—See TOWSON, MD (Comcast Cable)

ODENTON—See MILLERSVILLE, MD (Broadstripe)

ODENTON—See TOWSON, MD (Comcast Cable)

ODESSA—See CHESAPEAKE CITY, DE (Atlantic Broadband)

OLDTOWN—Formerly served by Oldtown Community Systems Inc. No longer in operation

OLNEY—See FREDERICK COUNTY (portions), MD (Comcast Cable)

OVERLEA—See TOWSON, MD (Comcast Cable)

OWINGS MILLS—See TOWSON, MD (Comcast Cable)

OXFORD (TOWN)—See ABINGDON, PA (Armstrong Cable Services)

OXFORD—See QUEENSTOWN, MD (Atlantic Broadband)

OXON HILL—See FREDERICK COUNTY (portions), MD (Comcast Cable)

PAEONIEN SPRINGS—See FREDERICK COUNTY (portions), VA (Comcast Cable)

PARK HALL—See LEONARDTOWN, MD (MetroCast Communications)

PARKVILLE—See TOWSON, MD (Comcast Cable)

PASADENA—See MILLERSVILLE, MD (Broadstripe)

PASADENA—See TOWSON, MD (Comcast Cable)

PATUXENT HEIGHTS—See LEONARDTOWN, MD (MetroCast Communications)

PATUXENT RIVER—See LEONARDTOWN, MD (MetroCast Communications)

PERRY HALL—See TOWSON, MD (Comcast Cable)

PERRY POINT—See CHESAPEAKE CITY, MD (Atlantic Broadband)

PERRYMAN—See TOWSON, MD (Comcast Cable)

PERRYVILLE—Atlantic Broadband

PIKESVILLE—See TOWSON, MD (Comcast Cable)

PINEY POINT—See LEONARDTOWN, MD (MetroCast Communications)

POCOMOKE—Comcast Cable. Now served by TOWSON, MD [MD0003]

POCOMOKE—See TOWSON, MD (Comcast Cable)

POINT OF ROCKS—See FREDERICK COUNTY (portions), MD (Comcast Cable)

POMFRET—See TOWSON, MD (Comcast Cable)

POOLESVILLE—See FREDERICK COUNTY (portions), MD (Comcast Cable)

PORT DEPOSIT—See PERRYVILLE, MD (Atlantic Broadband)

POTOMAC—See FREDERICK COUNTY (portions), MD (Comcast Cable)

PRESTON—See TOWSON, MD (Comcast Cable)

PRINCE FREDERICK—Comcast Cable. Now served by TOWSON, MD [MD0003]

PRINCE FREDERICK—See TOWSON, MD (Comcast Cable)

PRINCE GEORGE'S COUNTY (northern portion)—Comcast Cable. Now served by FREDERICK COUNTY (portions), MD [MD0009]

PRINCE GEORGE'S COUNTY (portions)—Comcast Cable. Now served by FREDERICK COUNTY (portions), MD [MD0009]

PRINCE GEORGE'S COUNTY (PORTIONS)—See FREDERICK COUNTY (portions), MD (Comcast Cable)

PRINCESS ANNE—See TOWSON, MD (Comcast Cable)

PURCELLVILLE—See FREDERICK COUNTY (portions), VA (Comcast Cable)

PYLESVILLE—See ABINGDON, MD (Armstrong Cable Services)

QUEEN ANNE'S COUNTY (PORTIONS)—See QUEENSTOWN, MD (Atlantic Broadband)

QUEEN ANNE—See TOWSON, MD (Comcast Cable)

QUEENSTOWN—Atlantic Broadband

Cable Community Index—Maryland

RANDALLSTOWN—See TOWSON, MD (Comcast Cable)

RANSON—See FREDERICK COUNTY (portions), WV (Comcast Cable)

RAPPAHANNOCK COUNTY (PORTIONS)—See FREDERICK COUNTY (portions), VA (Comcast Cable)

REHOBOTH BEACH—See TOWSON, DE (Comcast Cable)

REIDS GROVE—See TOWSON, MD (Comcast Cable)

REISTERSTOWN—See TOWSON, MD (Comcast Cable)

REMINGTON—See FREDERICK COUNTY (portions), VA (Comcast Cable)

RIDGE—See LEONARDTOWN, MD (MetroCast Communications)

RIDGELEY—See CUMBERLAND, WV (Atlantic Broadband)

RIDGELY—See TOWSON, MD (Comcast Cable)

RIO VISTA—See QUEENSTOWN, MD (Atlantic Broadband)

RISING SUN—Armstrong Cable Services. Now served by ABINGDON, MD [MD0019]

RISING SUN—See ABINGDON, MD (Armstrong Cable Services)

RIVERDALE—See FREDERICK COUNTY (portions), MD (Comcast Cable)

ROCK HALL—See QUEENSTOWN, MD (Atlantic Broadband)

ROCKVILLE—See FREDERICK COUNTY (portions), MD (Comcast Cable)

ROMNEY—See CUMBERLAND, WV (Atlantic Broadband)

ROSEDALE—See TOWSON, MD (Comcast Cable)

ROSEMONT (VILLAGE)—See FREDERICK COUNTY (portions), MD (Comcast Cable)

ROUND HILL—See FREDERICK COUNTY (portions), VA (Comcast Cable)

SALISBURY—Comcast Cable. Now served by TOWSON, MD [MD0003]

SALISBURY—See TOWSON, MD (Comcast Cable)

SAVAGE—See TOWSON, MD (Comcast Cable)

SEAFORD—See TOWSON, DE (Comcast Cable)

SEAT PLEASANT—See FREDERICK COUNTY (portions), MD (Comcast Cable)

SECRETARY—See TOWSON, MD (Comcast Cable)

SEVERN—See MILLERSVILLE, MD (Broadstripe)

SEVERN—See TOWSON, MD (Comcast Cable)

SEVERNA PARK—See MILLERSVILLE, MD (Broadstripe)

SEVERNA PARK—See TOWSON, MD (Comcast Cable)

SHARPSBURG—See FREDERICK COUNTY (portions), MD (Comcast Cable)

SHARPTOWN—See TOWSON, MD (Comcast Cable)

SHEPERDSTOWN—See FREDERICK COUNTY (portions), WV (Comcast Cable)

SHERWOOD FOREST—See TOWSON, MD (Comcast Cable)

SILVER SPRING—See FREDERICK COUNTY (portions), MD (Comcast Cable)

SIMPSONVILLE—See TOWSON, MD (Comcast Cable)

SLAUGHTER BEACH—See TOWSON, DE (Comcast Cable)

SMITHSBURG—See HAGERSTOWN, MD (Antietam Cable Television Inc)

SMYRNA—See TOWSON, DE (Comcast Cable)

SNOW HILL—See TOWSON, MD (Comcast Cable)

SOMERSET COUNTY (PORTIONS)—See CRISFIELD, MD (Charter Communications)

SOMERSET COUNTY (PORTIONS)—See TOWSON, MD (Comcast Cable)

SOMERSET—See FREDERICK COUNTY (portions), MD (Comcast Cable)

SOUTH RIDING—See FREDERICK COUNTY (portions), VA (Comcast Cable)

SOUTHAMPTON TWP. (BEDFORD COUNTY)—See CUMBERLAND, PA (Atlantic Broadband)

ST. GEORGES—See CHESAPEAKE CITY, DE (Atlantic Broadband)

ST. INIGOES—See LEONARDTOWN, MD (MetroCast Communications)

ST. MARY'S CITY—See TOWSON, MD (Comcast Cable)

ST. MARY'S COUNTY—See LEONARDTOWN, MD (MetroCast Communications)

ST. MICHAELS—See QUEENSTOWN, MD (Atlantic Broadband)

STEPHENS CITY—See FREDERICK COUNTY (portions), VA (Comcast Cable)

STEPHENSON—See FREDERICK COUNTY (portions), VA (Comcast Cable)

STERLING—See FREDERICK COUNTY (portions), VA (Comcast Cable)

STEVENSVILLE—See QUEENSTOWN, MD (Atlantic Broadband)

STILL POND—See QUEENSTOWN, MD (Atlantic Broadband)

STREET—See ABINGDON, MD (Armstrong Cable Services)

SUDLERSVILLE—See QUEENSTOWN, MD (Atlantic Broadband)

SUSSEX COUNTY (PORTIONS)—See TOWSON, DE (Comcast Cable)

SYKESVILLE—See TOWSON, MD (Comcast Cable)

TAKOMA PARK—See FREDERICK COUNTY (portions), MD (Comcast Cable)

TALBOT COUNTY (PORTIONS)—See QUEENSTOWN, MD (Atlantic Broadband)

TALL TIMBERS—See LEONARDTOWN, MD (MetroCast Communications)

TANEYTOWN—See TOWSON, MD (Comcast Cable)

TANYARD—See TOWSON, MD (Comcast Cable)

TEMPLEVILLE—See QUEENSTOWN, MD (Atlantic Broadband)

THURMONT—See FREDERICK COUNTY (portions), MD (Comcast Cable)

TIMONIUM-LUTHERVILLE—See TOWSON, MD (Comcast Cable)

TOWNSEND—See CHESAPEAKE CITY, DE (Atlantic Broadband)

TOWSON—Comcast Cable

TRAPPE—See QUEENSTOWN, MD (Atlantic Broadband)

U.S. SOLDIERS' & AIRMEN'S HOME—See FREDERICK COUNTY (portions), DC (Comcast Cable)

UNION BRIDGE—See TOWSON, MD (Comcast Cable)

UNIVERSITY PARK—See FREDERICK COUNTY (portions), MD (Comcast Cable)

UPPER MARLBORO—See FREDERICK COUNTY (portions), MD (Comcast Cable)

UPPER OXFORD TWP.—See ABINGDON, PA (Armstrong Cable Services)

VALLEY LEE—See LEONARDTOWN, MD (MetroCast Communications)

VIENNA—See TOWSON, MD (Comcast Cable)

VIOLA—See TOWSON, DE (Comcast Cable)

WALDORF—See TOWSON, MD (Comcast Cable)

WALKERSVILLE—See FREDERICK COUNTY (portions), MD (Comcast Cable)

WALTER REED ARMY MEDICAL CENTER—See FREDERICK COUNTY (portions), DC (Comcast Cable)

WARREN COUNTY (PORTIONS)—See FREDERICK COUNTY (portions), VA (Comcast Cable)

WARTON—See QUEENSTOWN, MD (Atlantic Broadband)

WARWICK—Formerly served by Mid-Atlantic Communications. Now served by Comcast Cable, TOWSON, MD [MD0003]

WARWICK—See TOWSON, MD (Comcast Cable)

WASHINGTON (PORTIONS)—See FREDERICK COUNTY (portions), DC (Comcast Cable)

WASHINGTON COUNTY (PORTIONS)—See FREDERICK COUNTY (portions), MD (Comcast Cable)

WASHINGTON COUNTY—See HAGERSTOWN, MD (Antietam Cable Television Inc)

WASHINGTON GROVE—See FREDERICK COUNTY (portions), MD (Comcast Cable)

WASHINGTON—See FREDERICK COUNTY (portions), VA (Comcast Cable)

WEST BETHESDA—See FREDERICK COUNTY (portions), MD (Comcast Cable)

WEST FALLOWFIELD TWP.—See ABINGDON, PA (Armstrong Cable Services)

WEST FRIENDSHIP—See TOWSON, MD (Comcast Cable)

WEST NOTTINGHAM TWP.—See ABINGDON, PA (Armstrong Cable Services)

WESTMINSTER—Comcast Cable. Now served by TOWSON, MD [MD0003]

WESTMINSTER—See TOWSON, MD (Comcast Cable)

WHEATON—See FREDERICK COUNTY (portions), MD (Comcast Cable)

WHITEFORD—See ABINGDON, MD (Armstrong Cable Services)

WICOMICO COUNTY (PORTIONS)—See TOWSON, MD (Comcast Cable)

WICOMICO COUNTY (SOUTHWESTERN PORTION)—See TOWSON, MD (Comcast Cable)

WILLIAMSPORT—See HAGERSTOWN, MD (Antietam Cable Television Inc)

WINCHESTER—See FREDERICK COUNTY (portions), VA (Comcast Cable)

WOODBINE—See TOWSON, MD (Comcast Cable)

WOODLAWN—See TOWSON, MD (Comcast Cable)

WOODSBORO—See FREDERICK COUNTY (portions), MD (Comcast Cable)

WOODSIDE—See TOWSON, DE (Comcast Cable)

WOODSTOCK—See TOWSON, MD (Comcast Cable)

WORCESTER COUNTY (PORTIONS)—See TOWSON, MD (Comcast Cable)

WYOMING—See TOWSON, DE (Comcast Cable)

Massachusetts—Cable Community Index

MASSACHUSETTS

ABINGTON—See BOSTON, MA (Comcast Cable)

ACTON—See BOSTON, MA (Comcast Cable)

ACUSHNET—See BOSTON, MA (Comcast Cable)

ADAMS—See PITTSFIELD, MA (Time Warner Cable)

ALLENSTOWN—See BOSTON, NH (Comcast Cable)

ALLSTON—See BOSTON, MA (Comcast Cable)

ALLSTON—See BOSTON, MA (RCN Corp. Formerly [MA0105]. This cable system has converted to IPTV)

AMESBURY—Comcast Cable. Now served by BOSTON, MA [MA0001]

AMESBURY—See BOSTON, MA (Comcast Cable)

AMHERST—Comcast Cable. Now served by BURLINGTON, VT [VT0001]

AMHERST—See BOSTON, NH (Comcast Cable)

ANDOVER—Comcast Cable. Now served by BOSTON, MA [MA0001]

ANDOVER—See BOSTON, MA (Comcast Cable)

ANTRIM—See BOSTON, NH (Comcast Cable)

AQUINNAH—See BOSTON, MA (Comcast Cable)

ARLINGTON—Comcast Cable. Now served by BOSTON, MA [MA0001]

ARLINGTON—See BOSTON, MA (Comcast Cable)

ARLINGTON—See BOSTON, MA (RCN Corp. Formerly [MA0105]. This cable system has converted to IPTV)

ASHBURNHAM—See BOSTON, MA (Comcast Cable)

ASHBY (TOWN)—See BOSTON, MA (Comcast Cable)

ASHLAND—See BOSTON, MA (Comcast Cable)

ATHOL—Time Warner Cable. Now served by KEENE, NH [NH0009]

ATKINSON—See BOSTON, NH (Comcast Cable)

ATTLEBORO—See BOSTON, MA (Comcast Cable)

AUBURN—See WORCESTER, MA (Charter Communications)

AUBURN—See BOSTON, NH (Comcast Cable)

AUBURNDALE—See BOSTON, MA (RCN Corp. Formerly [MA0105]. This cable system has converted to IPTV)

AVON—See BOSTON, MA (Comcast Cable)

AYER—See BOSTON, MA (Comcast Cable)

BACK BAY—See BOSTON, MA (RCN Corp. Formerly [MA0105]. This cable system has converted to IPTV)

BARNSTABLE—See BOSTON, MA (Comcast Cable)

BARRE (TOWN)—See WORCESTER, MA (Charter Communications)

BATH—See BOSTON, ME (Comcast Cable)

BAY VILLAGE—See BOSTON, MA (RCN Corp. Formerly [MA0105]. This cable system has converted to IPTV)

BEACON HILL—See BOSTON, MA (RCN Corp. Formerly [MA0105]. This cable system has converted to IPTV)

BEDFORD—See BOSTON, MA (Comcast Cable)

BEDFORD—See BOSTON, NH (Comcast Cable)

BELCHERTOWN—Charter Communications. Now served by CHICOPEE, MA [MA0082]

BELCHERTOWN—See CHICOPEE, MA (Charter Communications)

BELLINGHAM—See BOSTON, MA (Comcast Cable)

BELMONT—See BOSTON, MA (Comcast Cable)

BENNINGTON—See BOSTON, NH (Comcast Cable)

BERKLEY—See BOSTON, MA (Comcast Cable)

BERLIN—See WORCESTER, MA (Charter Communications)

BERNARDSTON—Comcast Cable. Now served by BURLINGTON, VT [VT0001]

BERWICK—See BOSTON, ME (Comcast Cable)

BEVERLY—Comcast Cable. Now served by BOSTON, MA [MA0001]

BEVERLY—See BOSTON, MA (Comcast Cable)

BILLERICA—See BOSTON, MA (Comcast Cable)

BLACKSTONE—See BOSTON, MA (Comcast Cable)

BOLTON—See BOSTON, MA (Comcast Cable)

BOSCAWEN—See BOSTON, NH (Comcast Cable)

BOSTON—RCN Corp. This cable system has converted to IPTV. See BOSTON, MA [MA5096]

BOSTON—Comcast Cable

BOSTON—RCN Corp. Formerly [MA0105]. This cable system has converted to IPTV

BOURNE—See BOSTON, MA (Comcast Cable)

BOW—See BOSTON, NH (Comcast Cable)

BOWDOIN (TOWN)—See BOSTON, ME (Comcast Cable)

BOWDOINHAM (TOWN)—See BOSTON, ME (Comcast Cable)

BOXBOROUGH—See BOSTON, MA (Comcast Cable)

BOXFORD—See BOSTON, MA (Comcast Cable)

BOYLSTON—See WORCESTER, MA (Charter Communications)

BRAINTREE—Comcast Cable. Now served by BOSTON, MA [MA0001]

BRAINTREE—BELD Broadband

BRAINTREE—See BOSTON, MA (Comcast Cable)

BRENTWOOD—See BOSTON, NH (Comcast Cable)

BREWSTER—See BOSTON, MA (Comcast Cable)

BRIDGEWATER—See BOSTON, MA (Comcast Cable)

BRIGHTON—See BOSTON, MA (Comcast Cable)

BRIGHTON—See BOSTON, MA (RCN Corp. Formerly [MA0105]. This cable system has converted to IPTV)

BRIMFIELD—See CHICOPEE, MA (Charter Communications)

BROCKTON—Comcast Cable. Now served by BOSTON, MA [MA0001]

BROCKTON—See BOSTON, MA (Comcast Cable)

BROOKFIELD—See WORCESTER, MA (Charter Communications)

BROOKLINE—See WORCESTER, NH (Charter Communications)

BROOKLINE—See BOSTON, MA (Comcast Cable)

BROOKLINE—See BOSTON, MA (RCN Corp. Formerly [MA0105]. This cable system has converted to IPTV)

BRUNSWICK (TOWN)—See BOSTON, ME (Comcast Cable)

BURLINGTON—See BOSTON, MA (Comcast Cable)

BURLINGTON—See BOSTON, MA (RCN Corp. Formerly [MA0105]. This cable system has converted to IPTV)

CAMBRIDGE—See BOSTON, MA (Comcast Cable)

CAMBRIDGE—See BOSTON, MA (RCN Corp. Formerly [MA0105]. This cable system has converted to IPTV)

CANDIA—See BOSTON, NH (Comcast Cable)

CANTERBURY—See BOSTON, NH (Comcast Cable)

CANTON—See BOSTON, MA (Comcast Cable)

CARLISLE (TOWN)—See BOSTON, MA (Comcast Cable)

CARVER—See BOSTON, MA (Comcast Cable)

CHARLESTOWN—See BOSTON, MA (Comcast Cable)

CHARLESTOWN—See BOSTON, MA (RCN Corp. Formerly [MA0105]. This cable system has converted to IPTV)

CHARLTON—Charter Communications. Now served by WORCESTER, MA [MA0002]

CHARLTON—See WORCESTER, MA (Charter Communications)

CHATHAM—See BOSTON, MA (Comcast Cable)

CHELMSFORD—See BOSTON, MA (Comcast Cable)

CHELSEA—See BOSTON, MA (Comcast Cable)

CHESHIRE—See PITTSFIELD, MA (Time Warner Cable)

CHESTER—Comcast Cable. Now served by BURLINGTON, VT [VT0001]

CHESTER—See BOSTON, NH (Comcast Cable)

CHESTNUT HILL—See BOSTON, MA (RCN Corp. Formerly [MA0105]. This cable system has converted to IPTV)

CHICHESTER—See BOSTON, NH (Comcast Cable)

CHICOPEE—Charter Communications

CHILMARK—See BOSTON, MA (Comcast Cable)

CLARKSBURG—See PITTSFIELD, MA (Time Warner Cable)

CLINTON—See BOSTON, MA (Comcast Cable)

COHASSET—See BOSTON, MA (Comcast Cable)

CONCORD—See BOSTON, MA (Comcast Cable)

CONCORD—See BOSTON, NH (Comcast Cable)

CONWAY—Comcast Cable. Now served by BURLINGTON, VT [VT0001]

DALTON—See PITTSFIELD, MA (Time Warner Cable)

DANVERS—Comcast Cable. Now served by BOSTON, MA [MA0001]

DANVERS—See BOSTON, MA (Comcast Cable)

DANVILLE—See BOSTON, NH (Comcast Cable)

DARTMOUTH—See BOSTON, MA (Comcast Cable)

DEDHAM—Comcast Cable. Now served by BOSTON, MA [MA0001]

DEDHAM—See BOSTON, MA (Comcast Cable)

DEDHAM—See BOSTON, MA (RCN Corp. Formerly [MA0105]. This cable system has converted to IPTV)

DEERING—See BOSTON, NH (Comcast Cable)

DENNIS—See BOSTON, MA (Comcast Cable)

Cable Community Index—Massachusetts

DERRY—See BOSTON, NH (Comcast Cable)

DIGHTON—See BOSTON, MA (Comcast Cable)

DORCHESTER—See BOSTON, MA (Comcast Cable)

DOUGLAS (TOWN)—See WORCESTER, MA (Charter Communications)

DOVER—See BOSTON, MA (Comcast Cable)

DOVER—See BOSTON, NH (Comcast Cable)

DRACUT—See BOSTON, MA (Comcast Cable)

DUDLEY—See WORCESTER, MA (Charter Communications)

DUNSTABLE—See WORCESTER, MA (Charter Communications)

DURHAM (TOWN)—See BOSTON, ME (Comcast Cable)

DURHAM—See BOSTON, NH (Comcast Cable)

DUXBURY—See BOSTON, MA (Comcast Cable)

EAST BOSTON—See BOSTON, MA (Comcast Cable)

EAST BRIDGEWATER—See BOSTON, MA (Comcast Cable)

EAST BROOKFIELD (TOWN)—See WORCESTER, MA (Charter Communications)

EAST BROOKFIELD—See WORCESTER, MA (Charter Communications)

EAST FALMOUTH—See BOSTON, MA (Comcast Cable)

EAST KINGSTON—See BOSTON, NH (Comcast Cable)

EAST LONGMEADOW—See CHICOPEE, MA (Charter Communications)

EASTHAM—See BOSTON, MA (Comcast Cable)

EASTHAMPTON—See CHICOPEE, MA (Charter Communications)

EASTON—See BOSTON, MA (Comcast Cable)

EDGARTOWN—See BOSTON, MA (Comcast Cable)

ELIOT—See BOSTON, ME (Comcast Cable)

EPPING—See BOSTON, NH (Comcast Cable)

ESSEX—See BOSTON, MA (Comcast Cable)

EVERETT—See BOSTON, MA (Comcast Cable)

EXETER—See BOSTON, NH (Comcast Cable)

FAIRHAVEN—Comcast Cable. Now served by NEW BOSTON, MA [MA0001]

FAIRHAVEN—See BOSTON, MA (Comcast Cable)

FALL RIVER—See BOSTON, MA (Comcast Cable)

FALMOUTH—See BOSTON, MA (Comcast Cable)

FENWAY-KENMORE—See BOSTON, MA (RCN Corp. Formerly [MA0105]. This cable system has converted to IPTV)

FITCHBURG—See BOSTON, MA (Comcast Cable)

FORT DEVONS—Formerly served by Americable International. No longer in operation

FOXBOROUGH—Comcast Cable. Now served by BOSTON, MA [MA0001]

FOXBOROUGH—See BOSTON, MA (Comcast Cable)

FRAMINGHAM—Comcast Cable. Now served by BOSTON, MA [MA0001]

FRAMINGHAM—See BOSTON, MA (Comcast Cable)

FRAMINGHAM—See BOSTON, MA (RCN Corp. Formerly [MA0105]. This cable system has converted to IPTV)

FRANCESTOWN—See BOSTON, NH (Comcast Cable)

FRANKLIN—See BOSTON, MA (Comcast Cable)

FREEPORT (TOWN)—See BOSTON, ME (Comcast Cable)

FREETOWN—See BOSTON, MA (Comcast Cable)

FREMONT—See BOSTON, NH (Comcast Cable)

GARDNER—See BOSTON, MA (Comcast Cable)

GEORGETOWN—See BOSTON, MA (Comcast Cable)

GLOUCESTER—Comcast Cable. Now served by BOSTON, MA [MA0001]

GLOUCESTER—See BOSTON, MA (Comcast Cable)

GOFFSTOWN—See BOSTON, NH (Comcast Cable)

GRAFTON—See WORCESTER, MA (Charter Communications)

GREAT BARRINGTON—See PITTSFIELD, MA (Time Warner Cable)

GREENLAND—See BOSTON, NH (Comcast Cable)

GREENVILLE—See BOSTON, NH (Comcast Cable)

GROTON—See WORCESTER, MA (Charter Communications)

GROVELAND—See BOSTON, MA (Comcast Cable)

HADLEY—See CHICOPEE, MA (Charter Communications)

HALIFAX—See BOSTON, MA (Comcast Cable)

HAMILTON—See BOSTON, MA (Comcast Cable)

HAMPDEN—See CHICOPEE, MA (Charter Communications)

HAMPSTEAD—See BOSTON, NH (Comcast Cable)

HAMPTON FALLS—See BOSTON, NH (Comcast Cable)

HAMPTON—See BOSTON, NH (Comcast Cable)

HANCOCK—See BOSTON, NH (Comcast Cable)

HANOVER—See BOSTON, MA (Comcast Cable)

HANSCOM AFB—See BOSTON, MA (Comcast Cable)

HANSON—See BOSTON, MA (Comcast Cable)

HARPSWELL—See BOSTON, ME (Comcast Cable)

HARVARD—See WORCESTER, MA (Charter Communications)

HARWICH—See BOSTON, MA (Comcast Cable)

HAVERHILL—Comcast Cable. Now served by BOSTON, MA [MA0001]

HAVERHILL—See BOSTON, MA (Comcast Cable)

HENNIKER—See BOSTON, NH (Comcast Cable)

HILLSBOROUGH—See BOSTON, NH (Comcast Cable)

HINGHAM—See BOSTON, MA (Comcast Cable)

HINSDALE—Charter Communications. Now served by CHATHAM, NY [NY0088]

HOLBROOK—See BOSTON, MA (Comcast Cable)

HOLDEN—See WORCESTER, MA (Charter Communications)

HOLLAND—Cox Communications. Now served by ENFIELD, CT [CT0011]

HOLLIS—See WORCESTER, NH (Charter Communications)

HOLLISTON—See BOSTON, MA (Comcast Cable)

HOOKSETT—See BOSTON, NH (Comcast Cable)

HOPEDALE—See BOSTON, MA (Comcast Cable)

HOPKINTON—Comcast Cable. Now served by BOSTON, MA [MA0001]

HOPKINTON—See BOSTON, MA (Comcast Cable)

HOPKINTON—See BOSTON, NH (Comcast Cable)

HOUSATONIC—See PITTSFIELD, MA (Time Warner Cable)

HUBBARDSTON—See WORCESTER, MA (Charter Communications)

HUDSON—See BOSTON, MA (Comcast Cable)

HUDSON—See BOSTON, NH (Comcast Cable)

HULL—See BOSTON, MA (Comcast Cable)

HYDE PARK—See BOSTON, MA (Comcast Cable)

HYDE PARK—See BOSTON, MA (RCN Corp. Formerly [MA0105]. This cable system has converted to IPTV)

IPSWICH—See BOSTON, MA (Comcast Cable)

JAFFREY—See BOSTON, NH (Comcast Cable)

JAMAICA PLAIN—See BOSTON, MA (Comcast Cable)

JAMAICA PLAIN—See BOSTON, MA (RCN Corp. Formerly [MA0105]. This cable system has converted to IPTV)

KENSINGTON—See BOSTON, NH (Comcast Cable)

KINGSTON—See BOSTON, MA (Comcast Cable)

KINGSTON—See BOSTON, NH (Comcast Cable)

KITTERY—See BOSTON, ME (Comcast Cable)

LAKEVILLE—See BOSTON, MA (Comcast Cable)

LANCASTER—See BOSTON, MA (Comcast Cable)

LANESBORO—Formerly served by Charter Communications. No longer in operation

LAWRENCE—Comcast Cable. Now served by BOSTON, MA [MA0001]

LAWRENCE—See BOSTON, MA (Comcast Cable)

LEE—Time Warner Cable. Now served by PITTSFIELD, MA [MA0090]

LEE—See BOSTON, NH (Comcast Cable)

LEE—See PITTSFIELD, MA (Time Warner Cable)

LEICESTER—See WORCESTER, MA (Charter Communications)

LENOX—See PITTSFIELD, MA (Time Warner Cable)

LEOMINSTER—Comcast Cable. Now served by BOSTON, MA [MA0001]

LEOMINSTER—See BOSTON, MA (Comcast Cable)

LEXINGTON—Comcast Cable. Now served by BOSTON, MA [MA0001]

LEXINGTON—See BOSTON, MA (Comcast Cable)

LEXINGTON—See BOSTON, MA (RCN Corp. Formerly [MA0105]. This cable system has converted to IPTV)

LINCOLN (TOWN)—See BOSTON, MA (Comcast Cable)

LITCHFIELD—See BOSTON, NH (Comcast Cable)

LITTLETON (TOWN)—See BOSTON, MA (Comcast Cable)

Massachusetts—Cable Community Index

LONDONDERRY—See BOSTON, NH (Comcast Cable)

LONGMEADOW—Comcast Cable. Now served by BURLINGTON, VT [VT0001]

LOUDON—See BOSTON, NH (Comcast Cable)

LOWELL—Comcast Cable. Now served by BOSTON, MA [MA0001]

LOWELL—See BOSTON, MA (Comcast Cable)

LUDLOW—See CHICOPEE, MA (Charter Communications)

LUNENBURG—See BOSTON, MA (Comcast Cable)

LYNN—See BOSTON, MA (Comcast Cable)

LYNNFIELD—See BOSTON, MA (Comcast Cable)

MADBURY—See BOSTON, NH (Comcast Cable)

MALDEN—Comcast Cable. Now served by BOSTON, MA [MA0001]

MALDEN—See BOSTON, MA (Comcast Cable)

MANCHESTER-BY-THE-SEA (TOWN)—See BOSTON, MA (Comcast Cable)

MANCHESTER—See BOSTON, NH (Comcast Cable)

MANSFIELD—See BOSTON, MA (Comcast Cable)

MARBLEHEAD—See BOSTON, MA (Comcast Cable)

MARION—Comcast Cable. Now served by BOSTON, MA [MA0001]

MARION—See BOSTON, MA (Comcast Cable)

MARLBOROUGH—Comcast Cable. Now served by BOSTON, MA [MA0001]

MARLBOROUGH—See BOSTON, MA (Comcast Cable)

MARSHFIELD—Comcast Cable. Now served by BOSTON, MA [MA0001]

MARSHFIELD—See BOSTON, MA (Comcast Cable)

MARTHA'S VINEYARD—Formerly served by Comcast Cable. No longer in operation

MASHPEE—Comcast Cable. Now served by BOSTON, MA [MA0001]

MASHPEE—See BOSTON, MA (Comcast Cable)

MATTAPAN—See BOSTON, MA (Comcast Cable)

MATTAPAN—See BOSTON, MA (RCN Corp. Formerly [MA0105]. This cable system has converted to IPTV)

MATTAPOISETT—See BOSTON, MA (Comcast Cable)

MAYNARD—Comcast Cable. Now served by BOSTON, MA [MA0001]

MAYNARD—See BOSTON, MA (Comcast Cable)

MEDFIELD—See BOSTON, MA (Comcast Cable)

MEDFORD—See BOSTON, MA (Comcast Cable)

MEDFORD—See BOSTON, MA (RCN Corp. Formerly [MA0105]. This cable system has converted to IPTV)

MEDWAY—See BOSTON, MA (Comcast Cable)

MELROSE—See BOSTON, MA (Comcast Cable)

MENDON—See BOSTON, MA (Comcast Cable)

MERRIMAC—See BOSTON, MA (Comcast Cable)

MERRIMACK—See BOSTON, NH (Comcast Cable)

METHUEN—See BOSTON, MA (Comcast Cable)

MIDDLEBOROUGH—Comcast Cable. Now served by BOSTON, MA [MA0001]

MIDDLEBOROUGH—See BOSTON, MA (Comcast Cable)

MIDDLETON—See BOSTON, MA (Comcast Cable)

MILFORD—Comcast Cable. Now served by BOSTON, MA [MA0001]

MILFORD—See BOSTON, MA (Comcast Cable)

MILFORD—See BOSTON, NH (Comcast Cable)

MILLBURY—See WORCESTER, MA (Charter Communications)

MILLIS—See BOSTON, MA (Comcast Cable)

MILLVILLE—See WORCESTER, MA (Charter Communications)

MILTON—See BOSTON, MA (Comcast Cable)

MILTON—See BOSTON, MA (RCN Corp. Formerly [MA0105]. This cable system has converted to IPTV)

MISSION HILL—See BOSTON, MA (RCN Corp. Formerly [MA0105]. This cable system has converted to IPTV)

MOUNT VERNON—See BOSTON, NH (Comcast Cable)

NAHANT—See BOSTON, MA (Comcast Cable)

NANTUCKET—Comcast Cable. Now served by BOSTON, MA [MA0001]

NANTUCKET—See BOSTON, MA (Comcast Cable)

NASHUA—See BOSTON, NH (Comcast Cable)

NATICK—Comcast Cable. Now served by BOSTON, MA [MA0001]

NATICK—See BOSTON, MA (Comcast Cable)

NATICK—See BOSTON, MA (RCN Corp. Formerly [MA0105]. This cable system has converted to IPTV)

NEEDHAM HEIGHTS—See BOSTON, MA (RCN Corp. Formerly [MA0105]. This cable system has converted to IPTV)

NEEDHAM—Comcast Cable. Now served by BOSTON, MA [MA0001]

NEEDHAM—See BOSTON, MA (Comcast Cable)

NEEDHAM—See BOSTON, MA (RCN Corp. Formerly [MA0105]. This cable system has converted to IPTV)

NEW BEDFORD—Comcast Cable. Now served by BOSTON, MA [MA0001]

NEW BEDFORD—See BOSTON, MA (Comcast Cable)

NEW BOSTON—See BOSTON, NH (Comcast Cable)

NEW CASTLE—See BOSTON, NH (Comcast Cable)

NEW IPSWICH—See BOSTON, NH (Comcast Cable)

NEWBURY—See BOSTON, MA (Comcast Cable)

NEWBURYPORT—Comcast Cable. Now served by BOSTON, MA [MA0001]

NEWBURYPORT—See BOSTON, MA (Comcast Cable)

NEWFIELDS—See BOSTON, NH (Comcast Cable)

NEWINGTON—See BOSTON, NH (Comcast Cable)

NEWMARKET—See BOSTON, NH (Comcast Cable)

NEWTON CENTER—See BOSTON, MA (RCN Corp. Formerly [MA0105]. This cable system has converted to IPTV)

NEWTON HIGHLANDS—See BOSTON, MA (RCN Corp. Formerly [MA0105]. This cable system has converted to IPTV)

NEWTON LOWER FALLS—See BOSTON, MA (RCN Corp. Formerly [MA0105]. This cable system has converted to IPTV)

NEWTON UPPER FALLS—See BOSTON, MA (RCN Corp. Formerly [MA0105]. This cable system has converted to IPTV)

NEWTON—See BOSTON, MA (Comcast Cable)

NEWTON—See BOSTON, NH (Comcast Cable)

NEWTON—See BOSTON, MA (RCN Corp. Formerly [MA0105]. This cable system has converted to IPTV)

NEWTONVILLE—See BOSTON, MA (RCN Corp. Formerly [MA0105]. This cable system has converted to IPTV)

NORFOLK—See BOSTON, MA (Comcast Cable)

NORTH ADAMS—Time Warner Cable. Now served by PITTSFIELD, MA [MA0090]

NORTH ADAMS—See PITTSFIELD, MA (Time Warner Cable)

NORTH ANDOVER—Comcast Cable. Now served by BOSTON, MA [MA0001]

NORTH ANDOVER—See BOSTON, MA (Comcast Cable)

NORTH ATTLEBORO—See BOSTON, MA (Comcast Cable)

NORTH BROOKFIELD (TOWN)—See WORCESTER, MA (Charter Communications)

NORTH BROOKFIELD—See WORCESTER, MA (Charter Communications)

NORTH END—See BOSTON, MA (RCN Corp. Formerly [MA0105]. This cable system has converted to IPTV)

NORTH HAMPTON—See BOSTON, NH (Comcast Cable)

NORTH READING—See BOSTON, MA (Comcast Cable)

NORTHAMPTON—Comcast Communications. Now served by BURLINGTON, VT [VT0001]

NORTHBOROUGH—See WORCESTER, MA (Charter Communications)

NORTHBRIDGE—See WORCESTER, MA (Charter Communications)

NORTON—See BOSTON, MA (Comcast Cable)

NORWELL—See BOSTON, MA (Comcast Cable)

NORWOOD—Comcast Cable. Now served by BOSTON, MA [MA0001]

NORWOOD—See BOSTON, MA (Comcast Cable)

NORWOOD—Norwood Light Broadband

NOTTINGHAM—See BOSTON, NH (Comcast Cable)

OAK BLUFFS—See BOSTON, MA (Comcast Cable)

OAKHAM—See WORCESTER, MA (Charter Communications)

ORLEANS—Comcast Cable. Now served by BOSTON, MA [MA0001]

ORLEANS—See BOSTON, MA (Comcast Cable)

OTIS AIR NATIONAL GUARD—See BOSTON, MA (Comcast Cable)

OXFORD—See WORCESTER, MA (Charter Communications)

PAXTON—See WORCESTER, MA (Charter Communications)

PEABODY—Comcast Cable. Now served by BOSTON, MA [MA0001]

PEABODY—See BOSTON, MA (Comcast Cable)

PELHAM—See BOSTON, NH (Comcast Cable)

PEMBROKE—Comcast Cable. Now served by BOSTON, MA [MA0001]

Cable Community Index—Massachusetts

PEMBROKE—See BOSTON, MA (Comcast Cable)

PEMBROKE—See BOSTON, NH (Comcast Cable)

PEPPERELL—Charter Communications. Now served by WORCESTER, MA [MA0002]

PEPPERELL—See WORCESTER, MA (Charter Communications)

PETERBOROUGH—See BOSTON, NH (Comcast Cable)

PHILLIPSTON—Comcast Cable. Now served by BOSTON, MA [MA0001]

PHILLIPSTON—See BOSTON, MA (Comcast Cable)

PHIPPSBURG (TOWN)—See BOSTON, ME (Comcast Cable)

PITTSFIELD—Time Warner Cable

PLAINVILLE—See BOSTON, MA (Comcast Cable)

PLAISTOW—See BOSTON, NH (Comcast Cable)

PLYMOUTH—Comcast Cable. Now served by BOSTON, MA [MA0001]

PLYMOUTH—See BOSTON, MA (Comcast Cable)

PLYMPTON—See BOSTON, MA (Comcast Cable)

PORTSMOUTH—See BOSTON, NH (Comcast Cable)

PROVINCETOWN—See BOSTON, MA (Comcast Cable)

QUINCY—Comcast Cable. Now served by BOSTON, MA [MA0001]

QUINCY—See BOSTON, MA (Comcast Cable)

QUINCY—See BOSTON, MA (RCN Corp. Formerly [MA0105]. This cable system has converted to IPTV)

RANDOLPH—See BOSTON, MA (Comcast Cable)

RAYMOND—See BOSTON, NH (Comcast Cable)

RAYNHAM—See BOSTON, MA (Comcast Cable)

READING—See BOSTON, MA (Comcast Cable)

REHOBOTH—Comcast Cable. Now served by BOSTON, MA [MA0001]

REHOBOTH—See BOSTON, MA (Comcast Cable)

REVERE—See BOSTON, MA (Comcast Cable)

RICHMOND—See PITTSFIELD, MA (Time Warner Cable)

ROCHESTER—See BOSTON, MA (Comcast Cable)

ROCKLAND—See BOSTON, MA (Comcast Cable)

ROCKPORT—See BOSTON, MA (Comcast Cable)

ROLLINSFORD—See BOSTON, NH (Comcast Cable)

ROSLINDALE—See BOSTON, MA (Comcast Cable)

ROSLINDALE—See BOSTON, MA (RCN Corp. Formerly [MA0105]. This cable system has converted to IPTV)

ROWLEY—See BOSTON, MA (Comcast Cable)

ROXBURY—See BOSTON, MA (Comcast Cable)

ROXBURY—See BOSTON, MA (RCN Corp. Formerly [MA0105]. This cable system has converted to IPTV)

RUSSELL—Russell Municipal Cable TV

RUTLAND (town)—Charter Communications. Now served by WORCESTER, MA [MA0002]

RUTLAND (TOWN)—See WORCESTER, MA (Charter Communications)

RYE—See BOSTON, NH (Comcast Cable)

SALEM (TOWN)—See BOSTON, NH (Comcast Cable)

SALEM—See BOSTON, MA (Comcast Cable)

SALISBURY—See BOSTON, MA (Comcast Cable)

SANDOWN—See BOSTON, NH (Comcast Cable)

SANDWICH—See BOSTON, MA (Comcast Cable)

SAUGUS—Comcast Cable. Now served by BOSTON, MA [MA0001]

SAUGUS—See BOSTON, MA (Comcast Cable)

SCITUATE—Comcast Cable. Now served by BOSTON, MA [MA0001]

SCITUATE—See BOSTON, MA (Comcast Cable)

SEABROOK—See BOSTON, NH (Comcast Cable)

SEEKONK—See BOSTON, MA (Comcast Cable)

SHARON—See BOSTON, MA (Comcast Cable)

SHEFFIELD (TOWN)—See PITTSFIELD, MA (Time Warner Cable)

SHERBORN—See BOSTON, MA (Comcast Cable)

SHIRLEY (TOWN)—See BOSTON, MA (Comcast Cable)

SHREWSBURY—Shrewsbury's Community Cablevision

SOMERSET—See BOSTON, MA (Comcast Cable)

SOMERSWORTH—See BOSTON, NH (Comcast Cable)

SOMERVILLE—See BOSTON, MA (Comcast Cable)

SOMERVILLE—See BOSTON, MA (RCN Corp. Formerly [MA0105]. This cable system has converted to IPTV)

SOUTH BERWICK—See BOSTON, ME (Comcast Cable)

SOUTH BOSTON—See BOSTON, MA (Comcast Cable)

SOUTH BOSTON—See BOSTON, MA (RCN Corp. Formerly [MA0105]. This cable system has converted to IPTV)

SOUTH HAMPTON—See BOSTON, NH (Comcast Cable)

SOUTH YARMOUTH—Comcast Cable. Now served by BOSTON, MA [MA0001]

SOUTH YARMOUTH—See BOSTON, MA (Comcast Cable)

SOUTHAMPTON—See CHICOPEE, MA (Charter Communications)

SOUTHBOROUGH—See WORCESTER, MA (Charter Communications)

SOUTHBRIDGE—See WORCESTER, MA (Charter Communications)

SPENCER—See WORCESTER, MA (Charter Communications)

SPRINGFIELD—Comcast Cable. Now served by BURLINGTON, VT [VT0001]

STERLING—Comcast Cable. Now served by BOSTON, MA [MA0001]

STERLING—See BOSTON, MA (Comcast Cable)

STOCKBRIDGE—See PITTSFIELD, MA (Time Warner Cable)

STONEHAM—See BOSTON, MA (Comcast Cable)

STONEHAM—See BOSTON, MA (RCN Corp. Formerly [MA0105]. This cable system has converted to IPTV)

STOUGHTON—Comcast Cable. Now served by BOSTON, MA [MA0001]

STOUGHTON—See BOSTON, MA (Comcast Cable)

STOW—See BOSTON, MA (Comcast Cable)

STRATHAM—See BOSTON, NH (Comcast Cable)

STURBRIDGE—See WORCESTER, MA (Charter Communications)

SUDBURY—See BOSTON, MA (Comcast Cable)

SUTTON—See WORCESTER, MA (Charter Communications)

SWAMPSCOTT—See BOSTON, MA (Comcast Cable)

SWANSEA—See BOSTON, MA (Comcast Cable)

TAUNTON—Comcast Cable. Now served by BOSTON, MA [MA0001]

TAUNTON—See BOSTON, MA (Comcast Cable)

TEMPLE—See BOSTON, NH (Comcast Cable)

TEMPLETON—See BOSTON, MA (Comcast Cable)

TEWKSBURY—See BOSTON, MA (Comcast Cable)

TISBURY—Comcast Cable. Now served by BOSTON, MA [MA0001]

TISBURY—See BOSTON, MA (Comcast Cable)

TOPSFIELD—See BOSTON, MA (Comcast Cable)

TOPSHAM—See BOSTON, ME (Comcast Cable)

TOWNSEND (TOWN)—See BOSTON, MA (Comcast Cable)

TRURO—See BOSTON, MA (Comcast Cable)

TYNGSBOROUGH—See BOSTON, MA (Comcast Cable)

UPTON—See WORCESTER, MA (Charter Communications)

UPTON—See BOSTON, MA (Comcast Cable)

UXBRIDGE—Charter Communications. Now served by WORCESTER, MA [MA0002]

UXBRIDGE—See WORCESTER, MA (Charter Communications)

VINEYARD HAVEN—See BOSTON, MA (Comcast Cable)

WABAN—See BOSTON, MA (RCN Corp. Formerly [MA0105]. This cable system has converted to IPTV)

WAKEFIELD—See BOSTON, MA (Comcast Cable)

WAKEFIELD—See BOSTON, MA (RCN Corp. Formerly [MA0105]. This cable system has converted to IPTV)

WALES—Charter Communications. Now served by CHICOPEE, MA [MA0082]

WALES—See CHICOPEE, MA (Charter Communications)

WALPOLE—See BOSTON, MA (Comcast Cable)

WALTHAM—Comcast Cable. Now served by BOSTON, MA [MA0001]

WALTHAM—See BOSTON, MA (Comcast Cable)

WALTHAM—See BOSTON, MA (RCN Corp. Formerly [MA0105]. This cable system has converted to IPTV)

WAREHAM—See BOSTON, MA (Comcast Cable)

WATERTOWN—Comcast Cable. Now served by BOSTON, MA [MA0001]

WATERTOWN—See BOSTON, MA (Comcast Cable)

WATERTOWN—See BOSTON, MA (RCN Corp. Formerly [MA0105]. This cable system has converted to IPTV)

WAYLAND—See BOSTON, MA (Comcast Cable)

WEARE—See BOSTON, NH (Comcast Cable)

WEBSTER—See WORCESTER, MA (Charter Communications)

Massachusetts—Cable Community Index

WELLESLEY—See BOSTON, MA (Comcast Cable)

WELLFLEET—See BOSTON, MA (Comcast Cable)

WENHAM—See BOSTON, MA (Comcast Cable)

WEST BATH—See BOSTON, ME (Comcast Cable)

WEST BOYLSTON—See WORCESTER, MA (Charter Communications)

WEST BRIDGEWATER—See BOSTON, MA (Comcast Cable)

WEST BROOKFIELD—See WORCESTER, MA (Charter Communications)

WEST NEWBURY—See BOSTON, MA (Comcast Cable)

WEST NEWTON—See BOSTON, MA (RCN Corp. Formerly [MA0105]. This cable system has converted to IPTV)

WEST ROXBURY—See BOSTON, MA (Comcast Cable)

WEST ROXBURY—See BOSTON, MA (RCN Corp. Formerly [MA0105]. This cable system has converted to IPTV)

WEST STOCKBRIDGE—Charter Communications. Now served by CHATHAM, NY [NY0088]

WEST TISBURY—See BOSTON, MA (Comcast Cable)

WESTBOROUGH—See WORCESTER, MA (Charter Communications)

WESTFIELD—Comcast Cable. Now served by BURLINGTON, VT [VT0001]

WESTFORD—Comcast Cable. Now served by BOSTON, MA [MA0001]

WESTFORD—See BOSTON, MA (Comcast Cable)

WESTMINSTER—See BOSTON, MA (Comcast Cable)

WESTON—See BOSTON, MA (Comcast Cable)

WESTPORT—Charter Communications

WESTWOOD—See BOSTON, MA (Comcast Cable)

WESTWOOD—See BOSTON, MA (RCN Corp. Formerly [MA0105]. This cable system has converted to IPTV)

WEYMOUTH—Comcast Cable. Now served by BOSTON, MA [MA0001]

WEYMOUTH—See BOSTON, MA (Comcast Cable)

WHITMAN—See BOSTON, MA (Comcast Cable)

WILBRAHAM—See CHICOPEE, MA (Charter Communications)

WILLIAMSTOWN—See PITTSFIELD, MA (Time Warner Cable)

WILMINGTON—See BOSTON, MA (Comcast Cable)

WILTON—See BOSTON, NH (Comcast Cable)

WINCHENDON—Comcast Cable. Now served by BOSTON, MA [MA0001]

WINCHENDON—See BOSTON, MA (Comcast Cable)

WINCHESTER—See BOSTON, MA (Comcast Cable)

WINDHAM—See BOSTON, NH (Comcast Cable)

WINTHROP—See BOSTON, MA (Comcast Cable)

WOBURN—Comcast Cable. Now served by BOSTON, MA [MA0001]

WOBURN—See BOSTON, MA (Comcast Cable)

WOBURN—See BOSTON, MA (RCN Corp. Formerly [MA0105]. This cable system has converted to IPTV)

WOOLWICH—See BOSTON, ME (Comcast Cable)

WORCESTER—Charter Communications

WRENTHAM—See BOSTON, MA (Comcast Cable)

YARMOUTH (TOWN)—See BOSTON, MA (Comcast Cable)

YARMOUTH—See BOSTON, MA (Comcast Cable)

MICHIGAN

ACADIA TWP.—See TRAVERSE CITY, MI (Charter Communications)

ACME (VILLAGE)—See TRAVERSE CITY, MI (Charter Communications)

ACME TWP.—See TRAVERSE CITY, MI (Charter Communications)

ADA TWP.—See DETROIT, MI (Comcast Cable)

ADAMS TWP. (HILLSDALE COUNTY)—See DETROIT, MI (Comcast Cable)

ADAMS TWP. (HOUGHTON COUNTY)—See MARQUETTE, MI (Charter Communications)

ADDISON (village)—Comcast Cable. Now served by DETROIT, MI [MI0001]

ADDISON (VILLAGE)—See DETROIT, MI (Comcast Cable)

ADDISON TWP.—See GOODRICH, MI (Charter Communications)

ADRIAN—Comcast Cable. Now served by DETROIT, MI [MI0001]

ADRIAN—See DETROIT, MI (Comcast Cable)

ADRIAN—See PETERSBURG, MI (D & P Cable)

AETNA TWP. (MECOSTA COUNTY)—See ALLENDALE TWP., MI (Charter Communications)

AGATE HARBOR—See EAGLE HARBOR TWP., MI (Cable America Corp)

AHMEEK—See MARQUETTE, MI (Charter Communications)

AKRON/FAIRGROVE—Formerly served by Pine River Cable. No longer in operation

ALABASTER TWP.—See MIDLAND, MI (Charter Communications)

ALAIEDON TWP.—See DETROIT, MI (Comcast Cable)

ALAIEDON TWP.—See DIMONDALE, MI (WOW! Internet, Cable & Phone)

ALAMO TWP.—See ALLENDALE TWP., MI (Charter Communications)

ALAMO TWP.—See COMSTOCK TWP., MI (Charter Communications)

ALANSON TWP.—See TRAVERSE CITY, MI (Charter Communications)

ALBA—Charter Communications. Now served by TRAVERSE CITY, MI [MI0026]

ALBA—See TRAVERSE CITY, MI (Charter Communications)

ALBEE TWP.—See MIDLAND, MI (Charter Communications)

ALBERT TWP.—See LEWISTON, MI (Lewiston Communications)

ALBION TWP.—See DIMONDALE, MI (WOW! Internet, Cable & Phone)

ALBION—See DIMONDALE, MI (WOW! Internet, Cable & Phone)

ALCONA TWP.—See ALPENA, MI (Charter Communications)

ALCONA TWP.—See MIDLAND, MI (Charter Communications)

ALGANSEE TWP.—See COLDWATER, MI (Charter Communications)

ALGOMA TWP.—See ALLENDALE TWP., MI (Charter Communications)

ALGONAC—See DETROIT, MI (Comcast Cable)

ALLEGAN COUNTY (PORTIONS)—See ALLENDALE TWP., MI (Charter Communications)

ALLEGAN TWP.—See ALLENDALE TWP., MI (Charter Communications)

ALLEGAN—Charter Communications. Now served by ALLENDALE TWP., MI [MI0094]

ALLEGAN—See ALLENDALE TWP., MI (Charter Communications)

ALLEN (village)—Formerly served by CableDirect. No longer in operation

ALLEN PARK—Comcast Cable. Now served by DETROIT, MI [MI0001]

ALLEN PARK—See DETROIT, MI (Comcast Cable)

ALLEN PARK—See PLYMOUTH, MI (WOW! Internet, Cable & Phone)

ALLEN TWP.—See COLDWATER, MI (Charter Communications)

ALLEN TWP.—See DETROIT, MI (Comcast Cable)

ALLENDALE TWP.—Charter Communications

ALLENDALE—AcenTek (formerly Allendale Communications). Now served by AcenTek, MESICK, MI [MI5074]

ALLENDALE—See MESICK, MI (AcenTek (formerly Ace Communications). This system has converted to IPTV)

ALLOUEZ TWP.—See MARQUETTE, MI (Charter Communications)

ALMA—Charter Communications. Now served by MIDLAND, MI [MI0030]

ALMA—See MIDLAND, MI (Charter Communications)

ALMENA TWP.—See DETROIT, MI (Comcast Cable)

ALMENA TWP.—See MATTAWAN, MI (Mediacom)

ALMER TWP.—See GOODRICH, MI (Charter Communications)

ALMIRA TWP.—See TRAVERSE CITY, MI (Charter Communications)

ALMONT TWP.—See GOODRICH, MI (Charter Communications)

ALMONT—Charter Communications. Now served by GOODRICH, MI [MI0290]

ALMONT—See GOODRICH, MI (Charter Communications)

ALOHA TWP.—See TRAVERSE CITY, MI (Charter Communications)

ALPENA TWP.—See ALPENA, MI (Charter Communications)

ALPENA—Charter Communications

ALPHA (VILLAGE)—Upper Peninsula Communications

ALPINE TWP.—See ALLENDALE TWP., MI (Charter Communications)

ALPINE TWP.—See DETROIT, MI (Comcast Cable)

AMASA—Upper Peninsula Communications

AMBER TWP.—See ALLENDALE TWP., MI (Charter Communications)

AMBOY TWP.—Formerly served by CableDirect. No longer in operation

ANN ARBOR TWP.—See DETROIT, MI (Comcast Cable)

ANN ARBOR—Comcast Cable. Now served by DETROIT, MI [MI0001]

ANN ARBOR—See DETROIT, MI (Comcast Cable)

ANTIOCH TWP.—See MESICK, MI (AcenTek (formerly Ace Communications). This system has converted to IPTV)

ANTWERP TWP.—See DETROIT, MI (Comcast Cable)

ANTWERP TWP.—See MATTAWAN, MI (Mediacom)

APPLEGATE—Formerly served by Cablevision Systems Corp. No longer in operation

ARBELA TWP.—See GOODRICH, MI (Charter Communications)

ARCADA TWP.—See MIDLAND, MI (Charter Communications)

Cable Community Index—Michigan

ARCADIA TWP. (LAPEER COUNTY)—See GOODRICH, MI (Charter Communications)

ARENAC TWP.—See MIDLAND, MI (Charter Communications)

ARGENTINE TWP.—See GOODRICH, MI (Charter Communications)

ARLINGTON TWP.—See BLOOMINGDALE TWP. (Van Buren County), MI (Bloomingdale Communications)

ARLINGTON TWP.—See DETROIT, MI (Comcast Cable)

ARMADA (VILLAGE)—See DETROIT, MI (Comcast Cable)

ARMADA TWP.—See DETROIT, MI (Comcast Cable)

ARNOLD LAKE—Formerly served by Charter Communications. No longer in operation

ASH TWP.—See FRENCHTOWN TWP., MI (Charter Communications)

ASHLAND TWP.—See ALLENDALE TWP., MI (Charter Communications)

ASHLEY—Formerly served by Pine River Cable. No longer in operation

ASHTON—See LE ROY, MI (Summit Digital)

ATHENS TWP.—See DIMONDALE, MI (WOW! Internet, Cable & Phone)

ATHENS—See DIMONDALE, MI (WOW! Internet, Cable & Phone)

ATLANTA—Formerly served by Northwoods Cable Inc. No longer in operation

ATLAS TWP.—See GOODRICH, MI (Charter Communications)

ATTICA TWP.—Charter Communications. Now served by GOODRICH, MI [MI0290]

ATTICA TWP.—See GOODRICH, MI (Charter Communications)

AU GRES—Charter Communications. Now served by MIDLAND, MI [MI0030]

AU GRES—See MIDLAND, MI (Charter Communications)

AU SABLE TWP. (IOSCO COUNTY)—See MIDLAND, MI (Charter Communications)

AU TRAIN TWP.—See MARQUETTE, MI (Charter Communications)

AUBURN HILLS—Comcast Cable. Now served by DETROIT, MI [MI0001]

AUBURN HILLS—See DETROIT, MI (Comcast Cable)

AUBURN—See MIDLAND, MI (Charter Communications)

AUGUSTA (VILLAGE)—See DETROIT, MI (Comcast Cable)

AUGUSTA TWP.—See DETROIT, MI (Comcast Cable)

AUGUSTA—See DETROIT, MI (Comcast Cable)

AURELIUS TWP.—See DIMONDALE, MI (WOW! Internet, Cable & Phone)

AURORA—See MARQUETTE, WI (Charter Communications)

AUSTIN TWP. (MECOSTA COUNTY)—See ALLENDALE TWP., MI (Charter Communications)

AUSTIN TWP. (MECOSTA COUNTY)—See IRON MOUNTAIN, MI (Northside T.V. Corp)

BACKUS TWP.—See RICHFIELD TWP. (Roscommon County), MI (Charter Communications)

BAD AXE—Comcast Cable. Now served by DETROIT, MI [MI0001]

BAD AXE—See DETROIT, MI (Comcast Cable)

BAGLEY TWP.—See TRAVERSE CITY, MI (Charter Communications)

BAINBRIDGE TWP.—Michiana Supernet

BALDWIN (VILLAGE)—MIcom

BALDWIN TWP. (IOSCO COUNTY)—See MIDLAND, MI (Charter Communications)

BANCROFT—See GOODRICH, MI (Charter Communications)

BANGOR TWP. (BAY COUNTY)—See MIDLAND, MI (Charter Communications)

BANGOR—See DETROIT, MI (Comcast Cable)

BANKS TWP.—See TRAVERSE CITY, MI (Charter Communications)

BARAGA—See MARQUETTE, MI (Charter Communications)

BARK RIVER TWP.—See MARQUETTE, MI (Charter Communications)

BARRY TWP.—See DETROIT, MI (Comcast Cable)

BARRYTON—Formerly served by Pine River Cable. No longer in operation

BARTON CITY—Formerly served by Pine River Cable. No longer in operation

BARTON HILLS (VILLAGE)—See DETROIT, MI (Comcast Cable)

BATAVIA TWP.—See COLDWATER, MI (Charter Communications)

BATES TWP.—See IRON RIVER, MI (Iron River Cable)

BATH TWP.—See DIMONDALE, MI (WOW! Internet, Cable & Phone)

BATTLE CREEK—Comcast Cable. Now served by DETROIT, MI [MI0001]

BATTLE CREEK—See DETROIT, MI (Comcast Cable)

BAY CITY—Charter Communications. Now served by MIDLAND, MI [MI0030]

BAY CITY—See MIDLAND, MI (Charter Communications)

BAY MILLS TWP.—See SAULT STE. MARIE, MI (Charter Communications)

BAY PORT VILLAGE—See DETROIT, MI (Comcast Cable)

BAY SHORE—See TRAVERSE CITY, MI (Charter Communications)

BAY TWP.—See TRAVERSE CITY, MI (Charter Communications)

BAY VIEW—See TRAVERSE CITY, MI (Charter Communications)

BEAR CREEK TWP.—See TRAVERSE CITY, MI (Charter Communications)

BEAR LAKE (VILLAGE)—See TRAVERSE CITY, MI (Charter Communications)

BEAR LAKE TWP.—See TRAVERSE CITY, MI (Charter Communications)

BEAR LAKE—Charter Communications. Now served by TRAVERSE CITY, MI [MI0026]

BEAR LAKE—See TRAVERSE CITY, MI (Charter Communications)

BEAUGRAND (VILLAGE)—See TRAVERSE CITY, MI (Charter Communications)

BEAVER CREEK TWP.—See RICHFIELD TWP. (Roscommon County), MI (Charter Communications)

BEAVER ISLAND—Formerly served by Pine River Cable. No longer in operation

BEAVER TWP. (Bay County)—Charter Communications. Now served by MIDLAND, MI [MI0030]

BEAVER TWP. (BAY COUNTY)—See MIDLAND, MI (Charter Communications)

BEAVERTON—See RICHFIELD TWP. (Roscommon County), MI (Charter Communications)

BEDFORD TWP. (CALHOUN COUNTY)—See DETROIT, MI (Comcast Cable)

BEDFORD TWP. (MONROE COUNTY)—See FRENCHTOWN TWP., MI (Charter Communications)

BELDING—See ALLENDALE TWP., MI (Charter Communications)

BELLAIRE (VILLAGE)—See TRAVERSE CITY, MI (Charter Communications)

BELLEVILLE—See DETROIT, MI (Comcast Cable)

BELLEVUE—See DIMONDALE, MI (WOW! Internet, Cable & Phone)

BELVIDERE TWP.—See LAKEVIEW, MI (Charter Communications)

BENNINGTON TWP.—See MIDLAND, MI (Charter Communications)

BENTON TWP. (CHEBOYGAN COUNTY)—See TRAVERSE CITY, MI (Charter Communications)

BENTON TWP. (EATON COUNTY)—See DIMONDALE, MI (WOW! Internet, Cable & Phone)

BENZIE COUNTY (PORTIONS)—See TRAVERSE CITY, MI (Charter Communications)

BENZONIA (VILLAGE)—See TRAVERSE CITY, MI (Charter Communications)

BENZONIA TWP.—See TRAVERSE CITY, MI (Charter Communications)

BERGLAND TWP.—See IRONWOOD, MI (Charter Communications)

BERGLAND—Charter Communications. Now served by IRONWOOD, MI [MI0064]

BERGLAND—See IRONWOOD, MI (Charter Communications)

BERKLEY—See DETROIT, MI (Comcast Cable)

BERKLEY—See PLYMOUTH, MI (WOW! Internet, Cable & Phone)

BERLIN TWP. (IONIA COUNTY)—See ALLENDALE TWP., MI (Charter Communications)

BERLIN TWP. (IONIA COUNTY)—See DIMONDALE, MI (WOW! Internet, Cable & Phone)

BERLIN TWP. (MONROE COUNTY)—See FRENCHTOWN TWP., MI (Charter Communications)

BERLIN TWP. (MONROE COUNTY)—See DETROIT, MI (Comcast Cable)

BERLIN TWP. (St. Clair County)—Formerly served by Charter Communications. No longer in operation

BESSEMER—See IRONWOOD, MI (Charter Communications)

BETHANY TWP.—See MIDLAND, MI (Charter Communications)

BETHEL TWP.—See COLDWATER, MI (Charter Communications)

BEULAH—See TRAVERSE CITY, MI (Charter Communications)

BEVERLY HILLS (VILLAGE)—See DETROIT, MI (Comcast Cable)

BEVERLY HILLS—See PLYMOUTH, MI (WOW! Internet, Cable & Phone)

BIG CREEK TWP.—See MIO, MI (MIcom)

BIG PRAIRIE TWP.—MIcom. Now served by BALDWIN (village), MI [MI0214]

BIG PRAIRIE TWP.—See BALDWIN (village), MI (MIcom)

BIG RAPIDS—Charter Communications. Now served by ALLENDALE TWP., MI [MI0094]

BIG RAPIDS—See ALLENDALE TWP., MI (Charter Communications)

BIG STAR LAKE—Formerly served by MIcom. No longer in operation

BILLINGS TWP.—Charter Communications

BINGHAM FARMS (VILLAGE)—See DETROIT, MI (Comcast Cable)

BINGHAM TWP. (LEELANAU COUNTY)—See TRAVERSE CITY, MI (Charter Communications)

BINGHAM TWP.—See MIDLAND, MI (Charter Communications)

Michigan—Cable Community Index

BIRCH RUN—See MIDLAND, MI (Charter Communications)

BIRMINGHAM—Comcast Cable. Now served by DETROIT, MI [MI0001]

BIRMINGHAM—See DETROIT, MI (Comcast Cable)

BIRMINGHAM—See PLYMOUTH, MI (WOW! Internet, Cable & Phone)

BLACKMAN TWP.—See DETROIT, MI (Comcast Cable)

BLAIR TWP.—See TRAVERSE CITY, MI (Charter Communications)

BLENDON TWP.—See ALLENDALE TWP., MI (Charter Communications)

BLISSFIELD—See PETERSBURG, MI (D & P Cable)

BLOOMFIELD HILLS—See DETROIT, MI (Comcast Cable)

BLOOMFIELD TWP. (OAKLAND COUNTY)—See DETROIT, MI (Comcast Cable)

BLOOMINGDALE (VILLAGE)—See BLOOMINGDALE TWP. (Van Buren County), MI (Bloomingdale Communications)

BLOOMINGDALE TWP. (VAN BUREN COUNTY)—Bloomingdale Communications

BLUE LAKE TWP. (MUSKEGON COUNTY)—See ALLENDALE TWP., MI (Charter Communications)

BLUE LAKE TWP.—See TRAVERSE CITY, MI (Charter Communications)

BLUMFIELD TWP.—See MIDLAND, MI (Charter Communications)

BOARDMAN TWP. (SOUTHERN PORTION)—ATI Networks Inc.

BOARDMAN TWP.—See MESICK, MI (AcenTek (formerly Ace Communications). This system has converted to IPTV)

BOSTON TWP.—See DIMONDALE, MI (WOW! Internet, Cable & Phone)

BOURRET TWP.—See BUTMAN TWP., MI (Charter Communications)

BOWNE TWP.—See ALLENDALE TWP., MI (Charter Communications)

BOYNE CITY—See TRAVERSE CITY, MI (Charter Communications)

BOYNE FALLS (VILLAGE)—See TRAVERSE CITY, MI (Charter Communications)

BOYNE VALLEY TWP.—See TRAVERSE CITY, MI (Charter Communications)

BRADY TWP. (KALAMAZOO COUNTY)—See DETROIT, MI (Comcast Cable)

BRADY TWP. (SAGINAW COUNTY)—See MIDLAND, MI (Charter Communications)

BRAMPTON TWP.—See MARQUETTE, MI (Charter Communications)

BRANCH TWP. (MASON COUNTY)—See CUSTER, MI (Charter Communications)

BRANDON TWP.—See GOODRICH, MI (Charter Communications)

BRECKENRIDGE—See MIDLAND, MI (Charter Communications)

BREITUNG TWP.—See MARQUETTE, MI (Charter Communications)

BRETHREN—Formerly served by Pine River Cable. No longer in operation

BRIDGEHAMPTON TWP.—See DETROIT, MI (Comcast Cable)

BRIDGEPORT (PORTIONS)—See MIDLAND, MI (Charter Communications)

BRIDGEPORT TWP.—Charter Communications. Now served by MIDLAND, MI [MI0030]

BRIDGEPORT TWP.—See MIDLAND, MI (Charter Communications)

BRIGHTON TWP.—See DETROIT, MI (Comcast Cable)

BRIGHTON—Comcast Cable. Now served by DETROIT, MI [MI0001]

BRIGHTON—See DETROIT, MI (Comcast Cable)

BRIMLEY—See SAULT STE. MARIE, MI (Charter Communications)

BRITTON (VILLAGE)—See DETROIT, MI (Comcast Cable)

BRITTON—See PETERSBURG, MI (D & P Cable)

BROCKWAY TWP.—See DETROIT, MI (Comcast Cable)

BRONSON TWP. (portions)—Formerly served by CableDirect. No longer in operation

BRONSON—See COLDWATER, MI (Charter Communications)

BROOKFIELD TWP. (EATON COUNTY)—See SPRINGPORT TWP., MI (Springport Telephone Co)

BROOKFIELD TWP.—See DETROIT, MI (Comcast Cable)

BROOKLYN (IRISH HILLS)—Comcast Cable. Now served by SUMMIT TWP. (Jackson County), MI [MI0039]

BROOKLYN (IRISH HILLS)—See DETROIT, MI (Comcast Cable)

BROOKS TWP. (PORTIONS)—See ALLENDALE TWP., MI (Charter Communications)

BROOKS TWP.—See DETROIT, MI (Comcast Cable)

BROOMFIELD TRAILER PARK—Charter Communications

BROOMFIELD TWP.—See SHERMAN TWP. (Isabella County), MI (Charter Communications)

BROWN CITY—Comcast Cable. Now served by DETROIT, MI [MI0001]

BROWN CITY—See DETROIT, MI (Comcast Cable)

BROWNSTOWN TWP.—See DETROIT, MI (Comcast Cable)

BRUCE TWP. (MACOMB COUNTY)—See DETROIT, MI (Comcast Cable)

BRUTUS—Formerly served by CenturyLink. No longer in service

BUCKEYE TWP.—See RICHFIELD TWP. (Roscommon County), MI (Charter Communications)

BUCKLEY (VILLAGE)—See TRAVERSE CITY, MI (Charter Communications)

BUCKLEY—See MESICK, MI (AcenTek (formerly Ace Communications). This system has converted to IPTV)

BUEL TWP.—See DETROIT, MI (Comcast Cable)

BUENA VISTA TWP.—See MIDLAND, MI (Charter Communications)

BUNKER HILL TWP.—See DIMONDALE, MI (WOW! Internet, Cable & Phone)

BURLEIGH TWP.—See MIDLAND, MI (Charter Communications)

BURLINGTON (VILLAGE)—See COLDWATER, MI (Charter Communications)

BURLINGTON TWP.—See DIMONDALE, MI (WOW! Internet, Cable & Phone)

BURNS TWP.—See GOODRICH, MI (Charter Communications)

BURR OAK—See COLDWATER, MI (Charter Communications)

BURT TWP.—See TRAVERSE CITY, MI (Charter Communications)

BURT—Charter Communications. Now served by TRAVERSE CITY, MI [MI0026]

BURTCHVILLE TWP.—See DETROIT, MI (Comcast Cable)

BURTON—Comcast Cable. Now served by DETROIT, MI [MI0001]

BURTON—See DETROIT, MI (Comcast Cable)

BUTMAN TWP.—Charter Communications

BYRON TWP.—See DETROIT, MI (Comcast Cable)

BYRON—See GOODRICH, MI (Charter Communications)

CADILLAC—Charter Communications. Now served by TRAVERSE CITY, MI [MI0026]

CADILLAC—See TRAVERSE CITY, MI (Charter Communications)

CALDWELL TWP.—See TRAVERSE CITY, MI (Charter Communications)

CALEDONIA TWP. (ALCONA COUNTY)—See ALPENA, MI (Charter Communications)

CALEDONIA TWP. (KENT COUNTY)—See ALLENDALE TWP., MI (Charter Communications)

CALEDONIA TWP. (SHIAWASSEE COUNTY)—See MIDLAND, MI (Charter Communications)

CALEDONIA—See ALLENDALE TWP., MI (Charter Communications)

CALEDONIA—See DETROIT, MI (Comcast Cable)

CALUMET—See MARQUETTE, MI (Charter Communications)

CALVIN TWP.—See DETROIT, MI (Comcast Cable)

CAMBRIA TWP.—Formerly served by CableDirect. No longer in operation

CAMBRIA—See DETROIT, MI (Comcast Cable)

CAMBRIDGE TWP.—See DETROIT, MI (Comcast Cable)

CAMPBELL TWP.—See DIMONDALE, MI (WOW! Internet, Cable & Phone)

CANADIAN LAKES—Formerly served by Charter Communications. No longer in operation

CANNON TWP.—See DETROIT, MI (Comcast Cable)

CANNON—See ALLENDALE TWP., MI (Charter Communications)

CANTON TWP.—See DETROIT, MI (Comcast Cable)

CANTON TWP.—See PLYMOUTH, MI (WOW! Internet, Cable & Phone)

CARLETON (VILLAGE)—See FRENCHTOWN TWP., MI (Charter Communications)

CARLTON TWP.—See DIMONDALE, MI (WOW! Internet, Cable & Phone)

CARMEL TWP.—See DIMONDALE, MI (WOW! Internet, Cable & Phone)

CARNEY/POWERS—Packerland Broadband

CARO—Charter Communications. Now served by GOODRICH, MI [MI0290]

CARO—See GOODRICH, MI (Charter Communications)

CARP LAKE TWP.—See TRAVERSE CITY, MI (Charter Communications)

CARP LAKE—See IRONWOOD, MI (Charter Communications)

CARPAC—Comcast Cable. Now served by DETROIT, MI [MI0001]

CARPAC—See DETROIT, MI (Comcast Cable)

CARROLLTON—See MIDLAND, MI (Charter Communications)

CARSON CITY—Formerly served by Pine River Cable. No longer in operation

CARSONVILLE—See DETROIT, MI (Comcast Cable)

CASCADE TWP.—See ALLENDALE TWP., MI (Charter Communications)

CASCADE TWP.—See DETROIT, MI (Comcast Cable)

CASCO TWP. (ALLEGAN COUNTY)—See DETROIT, MI (Comcast Cable)

CASCO TWP. (ST. CLAIR COUNTY)—See DETROIT, MI (Comcast Cable)

Cable Community Index—Michigan

CASEVILLE—Comcast Cable. Now served by DETROIT, MI [MI0001]

CASEVILLE—See DETROIT, MI (Comcast Cable)

CASNOVIA (VILLAGE)—See ALLENDALE TWP., MI (Charter Communications)

CASPIAN—Caspian Community TV Corp

CASS CITY—Charter Communications. Now served by GOODRICH, MI [MI0290]

CASS CITY—See GOODRICH, MI (Charter Communications)

CASSOPOLIS—Comcast Cable. Now served by CHAMPAIGN, IL [IL0019]

CATO TWP.—See LAKEVIEW, MI (Charter Communications)

CEDAR CREEK TWP. (MUSKEGON COUNTY)—See DETROIT, MI (Comcast Cable)

CEDAR CREEK TWP.—See TRAVERSE CITY, MI (Charter Communications)

CEDAR SPRINGS—See ALLENDALE TWP., MI (Charter Communications)

CEDAR—See TRAVERSE CITY, MI (Charter Communications)

CEMENT CITY—See DETROIT, MI (Comcast Cable)

CENTER LINE—See DETROIT, MI (Comcast Cable)

CENTER LINE—See PLYMOUTH, MI (WOW! Internet, Cable & Phone)

CENTERVILLE TWP.—See TRAVERSE CITY, MI (Charter Communications)

CENTRAL LAKE (VILLAGE)—See TRAVERSE CITY, MI (Charter Communications)

CENTRAL LAKE TWP.—See TRAVERSE CITY, MI (Charter Communications)

CENTREVILLE—See DETROIT, MI (Comcast Cable)

CHAMPION TWP.—Formerly served by Upper Peninsula Communications. Now served by Cable America Corp., REPUBLIC, MI [MI0216].

CHAMPION TWP.—See REPUBLIC TWP., MI (Cable America Corp)

CHARLESTON TWP. (PORTIONS)—See CLIMAX TWP., MI (Climax Telephone Co)

CHARLESTON TWP. (PORTIONS)—See DETROIT, MI (Comcast Cable)

CHARLEVOIX TWP.—See TRAVERSE CITY, MI (Charter Communications)

CHARLEVOIX—Charter Communications. Now served by TRAVERSE CITY, MI [MI0026]

CHARLEVOIX—See TRAVERSE CITY, MI (Charter Communications)

CHARLOTTE—See DIMONDALE, MI (WOW! Internet, Cable & Phone)

CHASSELL TWP.—See MARQUETTE, MI (Charter Communications)

CHATHAM—See MARQUETTE, MI (Charter Communications)

CHEBOYGAN—Charter Communications. Now served by TRAVERSE CITY, MI [MI0026]

CHEBOYGAN—See TRAVERSE CITY, MI (Charter Communications)

CHELSEA—See DETROIT, MI (Comcast Cable)

CHERRY GROVE TWP.—See TRAVERSE CITY, MI (Charter Communications)

CHESANING—Charter Communications. Now served by MIDLAND, MI [MI0030]

CHESANING—See MIDLAND, MI (Charter Communications)

CHESHIRE TWP.—See BLOOMINGDALE TWP. (Van Buren County), MI (Bloomingdale Communications)

CHESTER TWP. (OTTAWA COUNTY)—Charter Communications

CHESTER TWP.—See TRAVERSE CITY, MI (Charter Communications)

CHESTERFIELD TWP.—Comcast Cable. Now served by DETROIT, MI [MI0001]

CHESTERFIELD TWP.—See DETROIT, MI (Comcast Cable)

CHESTONIA TWP.—See TRAVERSE CITY, MI (Charter Communications)

CHINA TWP.—See DETROIT, MI (Comcast Cable)

CHIPPEWA TWP. (Isabella County)—Charter Communications. Now served by MIDLAND, MI [MI0030]

CHIPPEWA TWP. (ISABELLA COUNTY)—See MIDLAND, MI (Charter Communications)

CHIPPEWA TWP. (MECOSTA COUNTY)—See IRON MOUNTAIN, MI (Northside T.V. Corp)

CHOCOLAY TWP.—See MARQUETTE, MI (Charter Communications)

CHRISTMAS—See MARQUETTE, MI (Charter Communications)

CHURCHILL TWP.—See RICHFIELD TWP. (Roscommon County), MI (Charter Communications)

CLAM LAKE TWP.—See TRAVERSE CITY, MI (Charter Communications)

CLARE—Charter Communications. Now served by MIDLAND, MI [MI0030]

CLARE—See MIDLAND, MI (Charter Communications)

CLARENCE TWP.—See SPRINGPORT TWP., MI (Springport Telephone Co)

CLARK TWP.—Formerly served by Northwoods Cable Inc. No longer in operation

CLARKSTON—Comcast Cable. Now served by DETROIT, MI [MI0001]

CLARKSTON—See DETROIT, MI (Comcast Cable)

CLARKSVILLE—See DIMONDALE, MI (WOW! Internet, Cable & Phone)

CLAWSON—See DETROIT, MI (Comcast Cable)

CLAWSON—See PLYMOUTH, MI (WOW! Internet, Cable & Phone)

CLAY TWP.—See DETROIT, MI (Comcast Cable)

CLAYTON TWP. (GENESEE COUNTY)—See GOODRICH, MI (Charter Communications)

CLAYTON TWP. (GENESEE COUNTY)—See NEW LOTHROP, MI (TVC Cable)

CLAYTON—See STERLING, MI (Vogtmann Engineering Inc)

CLEARWATER TWP.—See TRAVERSE CITY, MI (Charter Communications)

CLEMENT TWP.—See BUTMAN TWP., MI (Charter Communications)

CLEON TWP.—Ace Communications. Formerly served by THOMPSONVILLE, MI [MI0230]. This cable system has converted to IPTV. Now served by MESICK, MI [MI5074]

CLEON TWP.—See MESICK, MI (AcenTek (formerly Ace Communications). This system has converted to IPTV)

CLEVELAND TWP.—See TRAVERSE CITY, MI (Charter Communications)

CLIFFORD—See GOODRICH, MI (Charter Communications)

CLIMAX TWP.—Climax Telephone Co

CLINTON TWP.—See DETROIT, MI (Comcast Cable)

CLINTON—See DETROIT, MI (Comcast Cable)

CLINTON—See PLYMOUTH, MI (WOW! Internet, Cable & Phone)

CLIO—See DETROIT, MI (Comcast Cable)

CLYDE TWP. (ALLEGAN COUNTY)—See DETROIT, MI (Comcast Cable)

CLYDE TWP. (ST. CLAIR COUNTY)—See DETROIT, MI (Comcast Cable)

COE TWP.—See MIDLAND, MI (Charter Communications)

COLD SPRINGS TWP.—See TRAVERSE CITY, MI (Charter Communications)

COLDWATER—Charter Communications

COLDWATER—Coldwater Board of Public Utilities

COLEMAN—Charter Communications. Now served by MIDLAND, MI [MI0030]

COLEMAN—See MIDLAND, MI (Charter Communications)

COLFAX TWP.—See MESICK, MI (AcenTek (formerly Ace Communications). This system has converted to IPTV)

COLFAX TWP.—See DETROIT, MI (Comcast Cable)

COLON—See COLDWATER, MI (Charter Communications)

COLUMBIA TWP.—See DETROIT, MI (Comcast Cable)

COLUMBIAVILLE—See GOODRICH, MI (Charter Communications)

COLUMBUS TWP. (ST. CLAIR COUNTY)—See DETROIT, MI (Comcast Cable)

COMINS TWP.—See MIO, MI (MIcom)

COMMERCE TWP.—Comcast Cable. Now served by DETROIT, MI [MI0001]

COMMERCE TWP.—See DETROIT, MI (Comcast Cable)

COMMONWEALTH—See MARQUETTE, WI (Charter Communications)

COMSTOCK TWP. (PORTIONS)—See CLIMAX TWP., MI (Climax Telephone Co)

COMSTOCK TWP.—Charter Communications

COMSTOCK TWP.—See DETROIT, MI (Comcast Cable)

CONCORD TWP.—See DIMONDALE, MI (WOW! Internet, Cable & Phone)

CONCORD—See DIMONDALE, MI (WOW! Internet, Cable & Phone)

CONSTANTINE—See DETROIT, MI (Comcast Cable)

CONVIS TWP.—See DIMONDALE, MI (WOW! Internet, Cable & Phone)

CONWAY—See TRAVERSE CITY, MI (Charter Communications)

COOPER TWP.—See COMSTOCK TWP., MI (Charter Communications)

COOPERSVILLE—See MESICK, MI (AcenTek (formerly Ace Communications). This system has converted to IPTV)

COOPERSVILLE—See ALLENDALE TWP., MI (Charter Communications)

COPEMISH—Ace Communications. Formerly served by THOMPSONVILLE, MI [MI0230]. This cable system has converted to IPTV. Now served by MESICK, MI [MI5074]

COPEMISH—See MESICK, MI (AcenTek (formerly Ace Communications). This system has converted to IPTV)

COPPER CITY—See MARQUETTE, MI (Charter Communications)

CORUNNA—See MIDLAND, MI (Charter Communications)

CORWITH TWP.—See TRAVERSE CITY, MI (Charter Communications)

COTTRELLVILLE TWP.—See DETROIT, MI (Comcast Cable)

COUNTRY ACRES MOBILE HOME PARK—See ALLENDALE TWP., MI (Charter Communications)

Michigan—Cable Community Index

COUNTRY ACRES—Charter Communications. Now served by ALLENDALE TWP., MI [MI0094]

COURTLAND TWP.—See ALLENDALE TWP., MI (Charter Communications)

COVERT TWP.—See DETROIT, MI (Comcast Cable)

CROCKERY TWP.—See ALLENDALE TWP., MI (Charter Communications)

CROSWELL—See DETROIT, MI (Comcast Cable)

CROTON TWP.—MIcom. Now served by BALDWIN (village), MI [MI0214]

CROTON TWP.—See BALDWIN (village), MI (MIcom)

CRYSTAL FALLS—City of Crystal Falls

CRYSTAL LAKE—See TRAVERSE CITY, MI (Charter Communications)

CRYSTAL TWP.—Formerly served by Great Lakes Communication. No longer in operation

CUMMING TWP.—See GOODAR TWP., MI (Charter Communications)

CUSTER—Charter Communications

DAFTER TWP.—See SAULT STE. MARIE, MI (Charter Communications)

DAGGETT—Packerland Broadband

DALTON TWP. (PORTIONS)—See ALLENDALE TWP., MI (Charter Communications)

DALTON TWP.—See DETROIT, MI (Comcast Cable)

DANBY TWP.—See DIMONDALE, MI (WOW! Internet, Cable & Phone)

DANSVILLE (VILLAGE)—See DIMONDALE, MI (WOW! Internet, Cable & Phone)

DAVISON—See GOODRICH, MI (Charter Communications)

DAY TWP.—See ALLENDALE TWP., MI (Charter Communications)

DAYTON TWP. (NEWAYGO COUNTY)—See DETROIT, MI (Comcast Cable)

DAYTON TWP. (TUSCOLA COUNTY)—See GOODRICH, MI (Charter Communications)

DE TOUR (village)—Formerly served by Upper Peninsula Communications. No longer in operation

DE WITT TWP.—See DETROIT, MI (Comcast Cable)

DE WITT—See DETROIT, MI (Comcast Cable)

DEARBORN HEIGHTS—Comcast Cable. Now served by DETROIT, MI [MI0001]

DEARBORN HEIGHTS—See DETROIT, MI (Comcast Cable)

DEARBORN HEIGHTS—See PLYMOUTH, MI (WOW! Internet, Cable & Phone)

DEARBORN—Comcast Cable. Now served by DETROIT, MI [MI0001]

DEARBORN—See DETROIT, MI (Comcast Cable)

DEARBORN—See PLYMOUTH, MI (WOW! Internet, Cable & Phone)

DECATUR (VILLAGE)—See DETROIT, MI (Comcast Cable)

DECKERVILLE—Comcast Cable. Now served by DETROIT, MI [MI0001]

DECKERVILLE—See DETROIT, MI (Comcast Cable)

DEEP RIVER TWP.—See MIDLAND, MI (Charter Communications)

DEEP RIVER—See STERLING, MI (Vogtmann Engineering Inc)

DEERFIELD TWP. (ISABELLA COUNTY)—See SHERMAN TWP. (Isabella County), MI (Charter Communications)

DEERFIELD TWP. (LAPEER COUNTY)—See GOODRICH, MI (Charter Communications)

DEERFIELD TWP. (MECOSTA COUNTY)—See ALLENDALE TWP., MI (Charter Communications)

DEERFIELD—See GOODRICH, MI (Charter Communications)

DEERFIELD—See PETERSBURG, MI (D & P Cable)

DELHI TWP.—See DIMONDALE, MI (WOW! Internet, Cable & Phone)

DELTA TWP.—See DETROIT, MI (Comcast Cable)

DELTON—Formerly served by MIcom. No longer in operation

DENMARK TWP.—See MIDLAND, MI (Charter Communications)

DENTON TWP.—See RICHFIELD TWP. (Roscommon County), MI (Charter Communications)

DENVER TWP. (ISABELLA COUNTY)—See MIDLAND, MI (Charter Communications)

DENVER TWP.—See BALDWIN (village), MI (MIcom)

DETROIT—Formerly served by Sprint Corp. No longer in operation

DETROIT—Comcast Cable

DEXTER TWP.—See GOODRICH, MI (Charter Communications)

DEXTER—See DETROIT, MI (Comcast Cable)

DIMONDALE—WOW! Internet, Cable & Phone

DOLLAR BAY—See MARQUETTE, MI (Charter Communications)

DORR TWP. (PORTIONS)—See ALLENDALE TWP., MI (Charter Communications)

DORR TWP.—See DETROIT, MI (Comcast Cable)

DOUGLAS (VILLAGE)—See DETROIT, MI (Comcast Cable)

DOUGLASS TWP.—See ALLENDALE TWP., MI (Charter Communications)

DOVER TWP. (OTSEGO COUNTY)—See TRAVERSE CITY, MI (Charter Communications)

DOVER TWP.—See DETROIT, MI (Comcast Cable)

DOWAGIAC—Comcast Cable. Now served by CHAMPAIGN, IL [IL0019]

DRUMMOND ISLAND—Formerly served by Northwoods Cable Inc. No longer in operation

DRYDEN TWP.—See GOODRICH, MI (Charter Communications)

DRYDEN—See GOODRICH, MI (Charter Communications)

DUNDEE TWP.—See FRENCHTOWN TWP., MI (Charter Communications)

DUNDEE—See DETROIT, MI (Comcast Cable)

DUNDEE—See PETERSBURG, MI (D & P Cable)

DURAND—Charter Communications. Now served by GOODRICH, MI [MI0290]

DURAND—See GOODRICH, MI (Charter Communications)

DURAND—See NEW LOTHROP, MI (TVC Cable)

DWIGHT TWP.—See DETROIT, MI (Comcast Cable)

EAGLE (VILLAGE)—See DIMONDALE, MI (WOW! Internet, Cable & Phone)

EAGLE HARBOR TWP.—Cable America Corp

EAGLE TWP.—See DIMONDALE, MI (WOW! Internet, Cable & Phone)

EAST BAY TWP.—See TRAVERSE CITY, MI (Charter Communications)

EAST CHINA TWP.—See DETROIT, MI (Comcast Cable)

EAST GRAND RAPIDS—See DETROIT, MI (Comcast Cable)

EAST JORDAN—Charter Communications. Now served by TRAVERSE CITY, MI [MI0026]

EAST JORDAN—See TRAVERSE CITY, MI (Charter Communications)

EAST LAKE—See TRAVERSE CITY, MI (Charter Communications)

EAST LANSING—Comcast Cable. Now served by DETROIT, MI [MI0001]

EAST LANSING—See DETROIT, MI (Comcast Cable)

EAST TAWAS—See MIDLAND, MI (Charter Communications)

EASTON TWP.—See ALLENDALE TWP., MI (Charter Communications)

EASTPOINTE—See DETROIT, MI (Comcast Cable)

EASTPOINTE—See PLYMOUTH, MI (WOW! Internet, Cable & Phone)

EATON RAPIDS TWP.—See DIMONDALE, MI (WOW! Internet, Cable & Phone)

EATON RAPIDS—Comcast Cable. Now served by DETROIT, MI [MI0001]

EATON RAPIDS—See DETROIT, MI (Comcast Cable)

EATON TWP.—See DIMONDALE, MI (WOW! Internet, Cable & Phone)

EBEN JUNCTION—See MARQUETTE, MI (Charter Communications)

ECKFORD TWP.—See DIMONDALE, MI (WOW! Internet, Cable & Phone)

ECORSE—See DETROIT, MI (Comcast Cable)

EDENVILLE TWP.—See MIDLAND, MI (Charter Communications)

EDMORE—See ALLENDALE TWP., MI (Charter Communications)

EDWARDSBURG—Comcast Cable. Now served by CHAMPAIGN, IL [IL0019]

EGELSTON TWP.—See DETROIT, MI (Comcast Cable)

ELBA TWP. (LAPEER COUNTY)—See GOODRICH, MI (Charter Communications)

ELBERTA—See TRAVERSE CITY, MI (Charter Communications)

ELK RAPIDS (VILLAGE)—See TRAVERSE CITY, MI (Charter Communications)

ELK RAPIDS TWP.—See TRAVERSE CITY, MI (Charter Communications)

ELK TWP.—See DETROIT, MI (Comcast Cable)

ELKHART COUNTY (PORTIONS)—See DETROIT, IN (Comcast Cable)

ELKLAND TWP.—See GOODRICH, MI (Charter Communications)

ELKTON—See DETROIT, MI (Comcast Cable)

ELLINGTON TWP.—See GOODRICH, MI (Charter Communications)

ELLSWORTH—See TRAVERSE CITY, MI (Charter Communications)

ELMER TWP.—See MIO, MI (MIcom)

ELMIRA TWP.—See TRAVERSE CITY, MI (Charter Communications)

ELMWOOD TWP. (LEELANAU COUNTY)—See TRAVERSE CITY, MI (Charter Communications)

ELMWOOD TWP.—See DETROIT, MI (Comcast Cable)

ELSIE—Charter Communications. Now served by MIDLAND, MI [MI0030]

ELSIE—See MIDLAND, MI (Charter Communications)

ELY TWP.—See MARQUETTE, MI (Charter Communications)

EMERSON TWP.—See MIDLAND, MI (Charter Communications)

EMMETT TWP.—See DETROIT, MI (Comcast Cable)

Cable Community Index—Michigan

EMPIRE (VILLAGE)—See TRAVERSE CITY, MI (Charter Communications)

EMPIRE TWP.—See TRAVERSE CITY, MI (Charter Communications)

ENGADINE—Lighthouse Computers Inc.

ENSLEY TWP.—See ALLENDALE TWP., MI (Charter Communications)

ERIE TWP.—See FRENCHTOWN TWP., MI (Charter Communications)

ERWIN TWP.—See IRONWOOD, MI (Charter Communications)

ESCANABA—Charter Communications. Now served by MARQUETTE, MI [MI0033]

ESCANABA—See MARQUETTE, MI (Charter Communications)

ESSEXVILLE—See MIDLAND, MI (Charter Communications)

ESTRAL BEACH—See FRENCHTOWN TWP., MI (Charter Communications)

EUREKA TWP.—See ALLENDALE TWP., MI (Charter Communications)

EVANGELINE TWP.—See TRAVERSE CITY, MI (Charter Communications)

EVART—Charter Communications. Now served by ALLENDALE TWP., MI [MI0094]

EVART—See ALLENDALE TWP., MI (Charter Communications)

EVELINE TWP.—See TRAVERSE CITY, MI (Charter Communications)

EVERETT TWP.—See ALLENDALE TWP., MI (Charter Communications)

EVERETT TWP.—See BALDWIN (village), MI (MIcom)

EVERGREEN TWP.—See ALLENDALE TWP., MI (Charter Communications)

EWEN—Charter Communications. Now served by IRONWOOD, MI [MI0064]

EWEN—See IRONWOOD, MI (Charter Communications)

EXCELSIOR TWP.—See TRAVERSE CITY, MI (Charter Communications)

EXETER TWP.—See FRENCHTOWN TWP., MI (Charter Communications)

EXETER TWP.—See DETROIT, MI (Comcast Cable)

FABIUS—See DETROIT, MI (Comcast Cable)

FAIRFIELD TWP.—See DETROIT, MI (Comcast Cable)

FAIRHAVEN TWP.—See DETROIT, MI (Comcast Cable)

FAIRVIEW—See MIO, MI (MIcom)

FALMOUTH—Formerly served by Pine River Cable. No longer in operation

FARMINGTON HILLS—See LIVONIA, MI (Bright House Networks)

FARMINGTON—Bright House Networks. Now served by LIVONIA, MI [MI0019]

FARMINGTON—See LIVONIA, MI (Bright House Networks)

FARWELL—See MIDLAND, MI (Charter Communications)

FAWN RIVER TWP.—See COLDWATER, MI (Charter Communications)

FAYETTE TWP.—See DETROIT, MI (Comcast Cable)

FENNVILLE—See DETROIT, MI (Comcast Cable)

FENTON TWP.—See GOODRICH, MI (Charter Communications)

FENTON—Charter Communications. Now served by GOODRICH, MI [MI0290]

FENTON—See GOODRICH, MI (Charter Communications)

FERNDALE—See DETROIT, MI (Comcast Cable)

FERNDALE—See PLYMOUTH, MI (WOW! Internet, Cable & Phone)

FERRYSBURG—See DETROIT, MI (Comcast Cable)

FIFE LAKE (VILLAGE)—See TRAVERSE CITY, MI (Charter Communications)

FIFE LAKE TWP.—See TRAVERSE CITY, MI (Charter Communications)

FIFE LAKE—Charter Communications. Now served by TRAVERSE CITY, MI [MI0026]

FILER CITY TWP.—See TRAVERSE CITY, MI (Charter Communications)

FILLMORE TWP. (NORTHWEST PORTION)—See ALLENDALE TWP., MI (Charter Communications)

FINE LAKE—Formerly served by Pine River Cable. No longer in operation

FLAT ROCK—See DETROIT, MI (Comcast Cable)

FLINT TWP.—See DETROIT, MI (Comcast Cable)

FLINT—See DETROIT, MI (Comcast Cable)

FLORENCE—See MARQUETTE, WI (Charter Communications)

FLOWERFIELD—See DETROIT, MI (Comcast Cable)

FLUSHING TWP.—See DETROIT, MI (Comcast Cable)

FLUSHING—See DETROIT, MI (Comcast Cable)

FORD RIVER TWP.—See MARQUETTE, MI (Charter Communications)

FOREST HOME TWP.—See TRAVERSE CITY, MI (Charter Communications)

FOREST TWP. (GENESEE COUNTY)—See GOODRICH, MI (Charter Communications)

FOREST TWP.—See TRAVERSE CITY, MI (Charter Communications)

FORESTER TWP.—Formerly served by Cablevision Systems Corp. No longer in operation

FORESTVILLE—Formerly served by Cablevision Systems Corp. No longer in operation

FORSYTH TWP.—See MARQUETTE, MI (Charter Communications)

FORT GRATIOT TWP.—See DETROIT, MI (Comcast Cable)

FOUNTAIN—See CUSTER, MI (Charter Communications)

FOWLER—Charter Communications. Now served by MIDLAND, MI [MI0030]

FOWLER—See MIDLAND, MI (Charter Communications)

FOWLERVILLE—See DIMONDALE, MI (WOW! Internet, Cable & Phone)

FRANKENLUST TWP.—See MIDLAND, MI (Charter Communications)

FRANKENMUTH—See MIDLAND, MI (Charter Communications)

FRANKFORT—See TRAVERSE CITY, MI (Charter Communications)

FRANKLIN (VILLAGE)—See DETROIT, MI (Comcast Cable)

FRANKLIN TWP.—See DETROIT, MI (Comcast Cable)

FRASER TWP.—Formerly served by MIcom. No longer in operation

FRASER TWP.—Parish Communications

FRASER—See DETROIT, MI (Comcast Cable)

FRASER—See PLYMOUTH, MI (WOW! Internet, Cable & Phone)

FREDERIC TWP.—Formerly served by Charter Communications. No longer in operation

FREDERICK—See TRAVERSE CITY, MI (Charter Communications)

FREDONIA TWP.—See COLDWATER, MI (Charter Communications)

FREDONIA TWP.—See DIMONDALE, MI (WOW! Internet, Cable & Phone)

FREE SOIL—Formerly served by Charter Communications. No longer in operation

FREELAND—See MIDLAND, MI (Charter Communications)

FREEMAN TWP.—See ALLENDALE TWP., MI (Charter Communications)

FREEMONT TWP.—See GOODRICH, MI (Charter Communications)

FREEPORT—Formerly served by Lewiston Communications. No longer in operation

FREEPORT—See DIMONDALE, MI (WOW! Internet, Cable & Phone)

FREMONT—See DETROIT, MI (Comcast Cable)

FRENCHTOWN TWP.—Charter Communications

FRENCHTOWN TWP.—See DETROIT, MI (Comcast Cable)

FRIENDSHIP TWP.—See TRAVERSE CITY, MI (Charter Communications)

FROST TWP.—Charter Communications. Now served by MIDLAND, MI [MI0030]

FROST TWP.—See MIDLAND, MI (Charter Communications)

FRUITLAND TWP.—See DETROIT, MI (Comcast Cable)

FRUITLAND—See ALLENDALE TWP., MI (Charter Communications)

FRUITPORT CHARTER TWP. (PORTIONS)—See ALLENDALE TWP., MI (Charter Communications)

FRUITPORT CHARTER TWP.—See DETROIT, MI (Comcast Cable)

FRUITPORT VILLAGE—See ALLENDALE TWP., MI (Charter Communications)

GAASTRA—See CASPIAN, MI (Caspian Community TV Corp)

GAGETOWN—Comcast Cable. Now served by DETROIT, MI [MI0001]

GAGETOWN—See DETROIT, MI (Comcast Cable)

GAINES TWP. (GENESEE COUNTY)—See GOODRICH, MI (Charter Communications)

GAINES TWP. (GENESEE COUNTY)—See DETROIT, MI (Comcast Cable)

GAINES TWP. (GENESEE COUNTY)—See NEW LOTHROP, MI (TVC Cable)

GAINES TWP. (KENT COUNTY)—See ALLENDALE TWP., MI (Charter Communications)

GAINES TWP. (KENT COUNTY)—See DETROIT, MI (Comcast Cable)

GAINES—See GOODRICH, MI (Charter Communications)

GALESBURG—See DETROIT, MI (Comcast Cable)

GANGES TWP.—See DETROIT, MI (Comcast Cable)

GARDEN CITY—See DETROIT, MI (Comcast Cable)

GARDEN CITY—See PLYMOUTH, MI (WOW! Internet, Cable & Phone)

GARDEN TWP.—Upper Peninsula Communications

GARFIELD TWP. (Clare County)—Charter Communications. Now served by MIDLAND, MI [MI0030]

GARFIELD TWP. (CLARE COUNTY)—See MIDLAND, MI (Charter Communications)

GARFIELD TWP. (GRAND TRAVERSE COUNTY)—See TRAVERSE CITY, MI (Charter Communications)

GARFIELD TWP. (NEWAYGO COUNTY)—See ALLENDALE TWP., MI (Charter Communications)

GARFIELD TWP. (NEWAYGO COUNTY)—See DETROIT, MI (Comcast Cable)

GARFIELD TWP.—See MIDLAND, MI (Charter Communications)

Michigan—Cable Community Index

GARFIELD—See MESICK, MI (AcenTek (formerly Ace Communications). This system has converted to IPTV)

GAYLORD—Charter Communications. Now served by TRAVERSE CITY, MI [MI0026]

GAYLORD—See TRAVERSE CITY, MI (Charter Communications)

GENESEE COUNTY (PORTIONS)—See GOODRICH, MI (Charter Communications)

GENESEE TWP.—See DETROIT, MI (Comcast Cable)

GENEVA TWP. (MIDLAND COUNTY)—See MIDLAND, MI (Charter Communications)

GENEVA TWP. (VAN BUREN COUNTY)—See DETROIT, MI (Comcast Cable)

GENOA TWP.—See DETROIT, MI (Comcast Cable)

GEORGETOWN TWP.—See DETROIT, MI (Comcast Cable)

GEORGETOWN—See MESICK, MI (AcenTek (formerly Ace Communications). This system has converted to IPTV)

GERMFASK—Upper Peninsula Communications

GERRISH TWP. (PORTIONS)—See RICHFIELD TWP. (Roscommon County), MI (Charter Communications)

GERRISH TWP.—See RICHFIELD TWP. (Roscommon County), MI (Charter Communications)

GIBRALTAR—See DETROIT, MI (Comcast Cable)

GILEAD—Formerly served by CableDirect. No longer in operation

GILMORE TWP. (BENZIE COUNTY)—See TRAVERSE CITY, MI (Charter Communications)

GILMORE TWP. (Isabella County)—Charter Communications. Now served by MIDLAND, MI [MI0030]

GILMORE TWP. (ISABELLA COUNTY)—See MIDLAND, MI (Charter Communications)

GIRARD TWP.—See COLDWATER, MI (Charter Communications)

GLADSTONE—See MARQUETTE, MI (Charter Communications)

GLADWIN—See RICHFIELD TWP. (Roscommon County), MI (Charter Communications)

GLEN ARBOR TWP.—See TRAVERSE CITY, MI (Charter Communications)

GLENN—See DETROIT, MI (Comcast Cable)

GLENNIE (village)—Formerly served by CenturyLink. No longer in operation

GOBLES CITY—See ALLENDALE TWP., MI (Charter Communications)

GOLDEN TWP.—See MEARS, MI (Golden Communications)

GOODAR TWP.—Charter Communications

GOODELLS—Formerly served by Cablevision Systems Corp. No longer in operation

GOODRICH—Charter Communications

GORE TWP.—See DETROIT, MI (Comcast Cable)

GRAND BLANC TWP.—See DETROIT, MI (Comcast Cable)

GRAND BLANC—See DETROIT, MI (Comcast Cable)

GRAND HAVEN—See ALLENDALE TWP., MI (Charter Communications)

GRAND ISLAND TWP.—See MARQUETTE, MI (Charter Communications)

GRAND LAKE—Formerly served by Charter Communications. No longer in operation

GRAND LEDGE—See DETROIT, MI (Comcast Cable)

GRAND MARAIS—Cable America Corp

GRAND RAPIDS TWP.—See DETROIT, MI (Comcast Cable)

GRAND RAPIDS—Comcast Cable. Now served by DETROIT, MI [MI0001]

GRAND RAPIDS—See DETROIT, MI (Comcast Cable)

GRANDVILLE—See DETROIT, MI (Comcast Cable)

GRANT TWP. (GRAND TRAVERSE COUNTY)—See TRAVERSE CITY, MI (Charter Communications)

GRANT TWP. (IOSCO COUNTY)—See MIDLAND, MI (Charter Communications)

GRANT TWP. (NEWAYGO COUNTY)—See ALLENDALE TWP., MI (Charter Communications)

GRANT TWP. (OCEANA COUNTY)—See ALLENDALE TWP., MI (Charter Communications)

GRANT TWP. (PORTIONS)—See MIDLAND, MI (Charter Communications)

GRANT TWP.—See MESICK, MI (AcenTek (formerly Ace Communications). This system has converted to IPTV)

GRANT—Charter Communications. Now served by ALLENDALE TWP., MI [MI0094]

GRANT—See ALLENDALE TWP., MI (Charter Communications)

GRASS LAKE TWP.—See DIMONDALE, MI (WOW! Internet, Cable & Phone)

GRASS LAKE—Formerly served by Millennium Digital Media. Now served by WOW! Internet Cable & Phone, DIMONDALE, MI [MI0136]

GRASS LAKE—See DIMONDALE, MI (WOW! Internet, Cable & Phone)

GRATTAN TWP.—See DETROIT, MI (Comcast Cable)

GRAYLING—Charter Communications. Now served by RICHFIELD TWP. (Roscommon County), MI [MI0116]

GRAYLING—See RICHFIELD TWP. (Roscommon County), MI (Charter Communications)

GREEN LAKE TWP.—See TRAVERSE CITY, MI (Charter Communications)

GREEN OAK TWP.—See GOODRICH, MI (Charter Communications)

GREEN OAK TWP.—See DETROIT, MI (Comcast Cable)

GREEN OAK TWP.—See DIMONDALE, MI (WOW! Internet, Cable & Phone)

GREEN TWP. (ALPENA COUNTY)—See ALPENA, MI (Charter Communications)

GREEN TWP. (MECOSTA COUNTY)—See ALLENDALE TWP., MI (Charter Communications)

GREENBUSH TWP. (ALCONA COUNTY)—See MIDLAND, MI (Charter Communications)

GREENDALE TWP.—See MIDLAND, MI (Charter Communications)

GREENLAND TWP.—See IRONWOOD, MI (Charter Communications)

GREENVILLE—Charter Communications. Now served by ALLENDALE TWP., MI [MI0094]

GREENVILLE—See ALLENDALE TWP., MI (Charter Communications)

GREENWOOD TWP. (OSCODA COUNTY)—See LEWISTON, MI (Lewiston Communications)

GROSSE ILE—See DETROIT, MI (Comcast Cable)

GROSSE ILE—See PLYMOUTH, MI (WOW! Internet, Cable & Phone)

GROSSE POINTE FARMS—See DETROIT, MI (Comcast Cable)

GROSSE POINTE PARK—See DETROIT, MI (Comcast Cable)

GROSSE POINTE SHORES—See DETROIT, MI (Comcast Cable)

GROSSE POINTE WOODS—See DETROIT, MI (Comcast Cable)

GROSSE POINTE—See DETROIT, MI (Comcast Cable)

GROUT TWP.—See SAGE TWP., MI (Charter Communications)

GROVELAND TWP.—See DETROIT, MI (Comcast Cable)

GUNPLAIN TWP.—See ALLENDALE TWP., MI (Charter Communications)

GWINN—See MARQUETTE, MI (Charter Communications)

HADLEY TWP.—See GOODRICH, MI (Charter Communications)

HALE—Charter Communications

HAMBURG TWP.—See GOODRICH, MI (Charter Communications)

HAMILTON TWP. (CLARE COUNTY)—See SAGE TWP., MI (Charter Communications)

HAMILTON TWP. (VAN BUREN COUNTY)—See DETROIT, MI (Comcast Cable)

HAMLIN TWP. (EATON COUNTY)—See SPRINGPORT TWP., MI (Springport Telephone Co)

HAMLIN TWP. (Mason County)—Charter Communications. Now served by ALLENDALE TWP., MI [MI0094]

HAMLIN TWP. (MASON COUNTY)—See ALLENDALE TWP., MI (Charter Communications)

HAMLIN TWP.—See DETROIT, MI (Comcast Cable)

HAMPTON TWP.—See MIDLAND, MI (Charter Communications)

HAMTRAMCK—See DETROIT, MI (Comcast Cable)

HANCOCK—See MARQUETTE, MI (Charter Communications)

HANDY TWP.—See DIMONDALE, MI (WOW! Internet, Cable & Phone)

HANOVER TWP.—See MESICK, MI (AcenTek (formerly Ace Communications). This system has converted to IPTV)

HANOVER TWP.—See TRAVERSE CITY, MI (Charter Communications)

HANOVER TWP.—See DIMONDALE, MI (WOW! Internet, Cable & Phone)

HANOVER—See DIMONDALE, MI (WOW! Internet, Cable & Phone)

HARBOR BEACH—Comcast Cable. Now served by DETROIT, MI [MI0001]

HARBOR BEACH—See DETROIT, MI (Comcast Cable)

HARBOR SPRINGS—See TRAVERSE CITY, MI (Charter Communications)

HARING TWP.—See TRAVERSE CITY, MI (Charter Communications)

HARPER WOODS—See DETROIT, MI (Comcast Cable)

HARPER WOODS—See PLYMOUTH, MI (WOW! Internet, Cable & Phone)

HARRIS TWP.—See MARQUETTE, MI (Charter Communications)

HARRISON TWP.—See DETROIT, MI (Comcast Cable)

HARRISON TWP.—See PLYMOUTH, MI (WOW! Internet, Cable & Phone)

HARRISON—See MIDLAND, MI (Charter Communications)

HARRISVILLE—See MIDLAND, MI (Charter Communications)

HART TWP.—See ALLENDALE TWP., MI (Charter Communications)

Cable Community Index—Michigan

HART—Charter Communications. Now served by ALLENDALE TWP., MI [MI0094]

HART—See ALLENDALE TWP., MI (Charter Communications)

HARTFORD—See DETROIT, MI (Comcast Cable)

HARTLAND TWP.—Comcast Cable. Now served by DETROIT, MI [MI0001]

HARTLAND TWP.—See DETROIT, MI (Comcast Cable)

HARVEY—See MARQUETTE, MI (Charter Communications)

HASTINGS TWP.—See DIMONDALE, MI (WOW! Internet, Cable & Phone)

HASTINGS—See DIMONDALE, MI (WOW! Internet, Cable & Phone)

HATTON TWP.—See MIDLAND, MI (Charter Communications)

HAWES TWP. (PORTIONS)—See ALPENA, MI (Charter Communications)

HAWES TWP. (PORTIONS)—See MIDLAND, MI (Charter Communications)

HAY TWP.—See BILLINGS TWP., MI (Charter Communications)

HAYES TWP. (CLARE COUNTY)—See MIDLAND, MI (Charter Communications)

HAYES TWP.—See TRAVERSE CITY, MI (Charter Communications)

HAZEL PARK—Comcast Cable. Now served by DETROIT, MI [MI0001]

HAZEL PARK—See DETROIT, MI (Comcast Cable)

HAZEL PARK—See PLYMOUTH, MI (WOW! Internet, Cable & Phone)

HAZELTON TWP.—See NEW LOTHROP, MI (TVC Cable)

HEATH TWP.—See ALLENDALE TWP., MI (Charter Communications)

HELENA TWP.—See TRAVERSE CITY, MI (Charter Communications)

HENRIETTA TWP.—See DIMONDALE, MI (WOW! Internet, Cable & Phone)

HERMANSVILLE—See MARQUETTE, MI (Charter Communications)

HERSEY—See ALLENDALE TWP., MI (Charter Communications)

HESPERIA—MIcom. Now served by BALDWIN (village), MI [MI0214]

HESPERIA—See BALDWIN (village), MI (MIcom)

HIAWATHA TWP.—See MARQUETTE, MI (Charter Communications)

HIGGINS TWP.—Charter Communications. Now served by RICHFIELD TWP. (Roscommon County), MI [MI0116]

HIGGINS TWP.—See RICHFIELD TWP. (Roscommon County), MI (Charter Communications)

HIGHLAND PARK—MIcom

HIGHLAND TWP. (OAKLAND COUNTY)—See DETROIT, MI (Comcast Cable)

HILL TWP.—See GOODAR TWP., MI (Charter Communications)

HILLMAN TWP.—Formerly served by Northwoods Cable Inc. No longer in operation

HILLSDALE—Comcast Cable. Now served by DETROIT, MI [MI0001]

HILLSDALE—See DETROIT, MI (Comcast Cable)

HOLLAND CHARTER TWP.—See MESICK, MI (AcenTek (formerly Ace Communications). This system has converted to IPTV)

HOLLAND TWP.—See ALLENDALE TWP., MI (Charter Communications)

HOLLAND—Comcast Cable. Now served by DETROIT, MI [MI0001]

HOLLAND—See DETROIT, MI (Comcast Cable)

HOLLY TWP.—See DETROIT, MI (Comcast Cable)

HOLLY VILLAGE—See DETROIT, MI (Comcast Cable)

HOLTON TWP.—See DETROIT, MI (Comcast Cable)

HOME TWP.—See ALLENDALE TWP., MI (Charter Communications)

HOMER—See DIMONDALE, MI (WOW! Internet, Cable & Phone)

HOMESTEAD TWP.—See TRAVERSE CITY, MI (Charter Communications)

HONOR (VILLAGE)—See TRAVERSE CITY, MI (Charter Communications)

HOPE TWP. (Midland County)—Formerly served by MIcom. No longer in operation

HOPE—Parish Communications

HOPKINS—See ALLENDALE TWP., MI (Charter Communications)

HORTON—See DIMONDALE, MI (WOW! Internet, Cable & Phone)

HOUGHTON LAKE—Formerly served by Charter Communications. No longer in operation

HOUGHTON—Charter Communications. Now served by MARQUETTE, MI [MI0033]

HOUGHTON—See MARQUETTE, MI (Charter Communications)

HOWARD CITY—Charter Communications. Now served by ALLENDALE TWP., MI [MI0094]

HOWARD CITY—See ALLENDALE TWP., MI (Charter Communications)

HOWELL—See GOODRICH, MI (Charter Communications)

HOWELL—See DETROIT, MI (Comcast Cable)

HOXEYVILLE—See MESICK, MI (AcenTek (formerly Ace Communications). This system has converted to IPTV)

HUBBARDSTON—See DIMONDALE, MI (WOW! Internet, Cable & Phone)

HUDSON TWP.—See DETROIT, MI (Comcast Cable)

HUDSON—Comcast Cable. Now served by DETROIT, MI [MI0001]

HUDSON—See PETERSBURG, MI (D & P Cable)

HUDSONVILLE—See ALLENDALE TWP., MI (Charter Communications)

HUMBOLDT TWP.—See REPUBLIC TWP., MI (Cable America Corp)

HUME TWP.—See DETROIT, MI (Comcast Cable)

HUNTINGTON WOODS—See DETROIT, MI (Comcast Cable)

HUNTINGTON WOODS—See PLYMOUTH, MI (WOW! Internet, Cable & Phone)

HURLEY—See IRONWOOD, WI (Charter Communications)

HURON TWP. (WAYNE COUNTY)—See FRENCHTOWN TWP., MI (Charter Communications)

HURON TWP.—See DETROIT, MI (Comcast Cable)

IDA TWP.—See FRENCHTOWN TWP., MI (Charter Communications)

IDA TWP.—See PETERSBURG, MI (D & P Cable)

IMLAY CITY—Charter Communications. Now served by GOODRICH, MI [MI0290]

IMLAY CITY—See GOODRICH, MI (Charter Communications)

IMLAY TWP.—See GOODRICH, MI (Charter Communications)

INDEPENDENCE TWP.—See DETROIT, MI (Comcast Cable)

INDIAN RIVER—Charter Communications. Now served by TRAVERSE CITY, MI [MI0026]

INDIAN RIVER—See TRAVERSE CITY, MI (Charter Communications)

INDIANFIELDS TWP.—See GOODRICH, MI (Charter Communications)

INGERSOLL TWP.—See MIDLAND, MI (Charter Communications)

INGHAM TWP.—See DIMONDALE, MI (WOW! Internet, Cable & Phone)

INKSTER—See DETROIT, MI (Comcast Cable)

INLAND TWP.—See TRAVERSE CITY, MI (Charter Communications)

INVERNESS TWP.—See TRAVERSE CITY, MI (Charter Communications)

IONIA TWP.—See ALLENDALE TWP., MI (Charter Communications)

IONIA—Charter Communications. Now served by ALLENDALE TWP., MI [MI0094]

IONIA—See ALLENDALE TWP., MI (Charter Communications)

IRA TWP.—See DETROIT, MI (Comcast Cable)

IRON MOUNTAIN—Charter Communications. Now served by MARQUETTE, MI [MI0033]

IRON MOUNTAIN—See MARQUETTE, MI (Charter Communications)

IRON MOUNTAIN—Northside T.V. Corp

IRON RIVER TWP.—See IRON RIVER, MI (Iron River Cable)

IRON RIVER—Iron River Cable

IRONWOOD—Charter Communications

ISABELLA TWP.—See MIDLAND, MI (Charter Communications)

ISHPEMING—See MARQUETTE, MI (Charter Communications)

ITHACA—See MIDLAND, MI (Charter Communications)

JACKSON—Comcast Cable. Now served by DETROIT, MI [MI0001]

JACKSON—Formerly served by Wireless Cable Systems Inc. No longer in operation

JACKSON—See DETROIT, MI (Comcast Cable)

JAMES TWP.—See MIDLAND, MI (Charter Communications)

JAMESTOWN TWP. (PORTIONS)—See ALLENDALE TWP., MI (Charter Communications)

JAMESTOWN TWP.—Charter Communications. Now served by ALLENDALE TWP., MI [MI0094]

JAMESTOWN TWP.—See DETROIT, MI (Comcast Cable)

JEFFERSON TWP. (HILLSDALE COUNTY)—See DETROIT, MI (Comcast Cable)

JEFFERSON—See DETROIT, MI (Comcast Cable)

JONES—Comcast Cable. Now served by DETROIT, MI [MI0001]

JONES—See DETROIT, MI (Comcast Cable)

JONESFIELD TWP.—See MIDLAND, MI (Charter Communications)

JONESVILLE—See DETROIT, MI (Comcast Cable)

JOYFIELD TWP.—See TRAVERSE CITY, MI (Charter Communications)

KALAMAZOO TWP. (WESTERN PORTION)—See COMSTOCK TWP., MI (Charter Communications)

KALAMAZOO—See COMSTOCK TWP., MI (Charter Communications)

KALEVA (village)—Formerly served by Pine River Cable. No longer in operation

KALKASKA (VILLAGE)—See TRAVERSE CITY, MI (Charter Communications)

Michigan—Cable Community Index

KALKASKA COUNTY (PORTIONS)—See BOARDMAN TWP. (southern portion), MI (ATI Networks Inc.)

KALKASKA TWP.—See TRAVERSE CITY, MI (Charter Communications)

KASSON TWP.—See TRAVERSE CITY, MI (Charter Communications)

KAWKAWLIN TWP. (SOUTHERN PORTION)—See MIDLAND, MI (Charter Communications)

KEARNEY TWP.—See TRAVERSE CITY, MI (Charter Communications)

KEEGO HARBOR—See DETROIT, MI (Comcast Cable)

KEELER TWP.—Sister Lakes Cable TV

KENT CITY—See ALLENDALE TWP., MI (Charter Communications)

KENTWOOD—See DETROIT, MI (Comcast Cable)

KEWEENAW COUNTY (PORTIONS)—See EAGLE HARBOR TWP., MI (Cable America Corp)

KIMBALL TWP.—See DETROIT, MI (Comcast Cable)

KINCHELOE—Formerly served by Charter Communications. No longer in operation

KINDE—See DETROIT, MI (Comcast Cable)

KINDERHOOK TWP.—Formerly served by CableDirect. No longer in operation

KINDERHOOK TWP.—See COLDWATER, MI (Charter Communications)

KINGSFORD—See MARQUETTE, MI (Charter Communications)

KINGSLEY (VILLAGE)—See TRAVERSE CITY, MI (Charter Communications)

KINGSTON (VILLAGE)—See GOODRICH, MI (Charter Communications)

KINGSTON TWP.—Charter Communications. Now served by GOODRICH, MI [MI0290]

KINGSTON TWP.—See GOODRICH, MI (Charter Communications)

KINROSS—See SAULT STE. MARIE, MI (Charter Communications)

KNIGHT (TOWN)—See IRONWOOD, WI

KOCHVILLE TWP. (PORTIONS)—See MIDLAND, MI (Charter Communications)

KOYLTON TWP.—See GOODRICH, MI (Charter Communications)

KRAKOW TWP.—See ALPENA, MI (Charter Communications)

L'ANSE—See MARQUETTE, MI (Charter Communications)

LA SALLE TWP.—See FRENCHTOWN TWP., MI (Charter Communications)

LAGRANGE COUNTY—See DETROIT, IN (Comcast Cable)

LAINGSBURG—See DIMONDALE, MI (WOW! Internet, Cable & Phone)

LAKE ANGELUS—See DETROIT, MI (Comcast Cable)

LAKE ANN (VILLAGE)—See TRAVERSE CITY, MI (Charter Communications)

LAKE CITY—See TRAVERSE CITY, MI (Charter Communications)

LAKE GEORGE—Formerly served by Charter Communications. No longer in operation

LAKE LINDEN—See MARQUETTE, MI (Charter Communications)

LAKE ODESSA—See DIMONDALE, MI (WOW! Internet, Cable & Phone)

LAKE ORION (VILLAGE)—See DETROIT, MI (Comcast Cable)

LAKE TWP. (ROSCOMMON COUNTY)—See RICHFIELD TWP. (Roscommon County), MI (Charter Communications)

LAKE TWP.—See TRAVERSE CITY, MI (Charter Communications)

LAKETON TWP.—See DETROIT, MI (Comcast Cable)

LAKETOWN TWP.—See ALLENDALE TWP., MI (Charter Communications)

LAKEVIEW—Charter Communications

LAKEWOOD (VILLAGE)—See ALLENDALE TWP., MI (Charter Communications)

LANSING TWP.—See DETROIT, MI (Comcast Cable)

LANSING—Comcast Cable. Now served by DETROIT, MI [MI0001]

LANSING—Formerly served by Sprint Corp. No longer in operation

LANSING—See DETROIT, MI (Comcast Cable)

LAPEER TWP.—See GOODRICH, MI (Charter Communications)

LAPEER—Charter Communications. Now served by GOODRICH, MI [MI0290]

LAPEER—See GOODRICH, MI (Charter Communications)

LARKIN TWP.—See MIDLAND, MI (Charter Communications)

LATHRUP VILLAGE—See DETROIT, MI (Comcast Cable)

LATHRUP VILLAGE—See PLYMOUTH, MI (WOW! Internet, Cable & Phone)

LAURIUM—See MARQUETTE, MI (Charter Communications)

LAWRENCE TWP.—See DETROIT, MI (Comcast Cable)

LAWRENCE—See DETROIT, MI (Comcast Cable)

LAWTON (village)—Comcast Cable. Now served by DETROIT, MI [MI0001]

LAWTON (VILLAGE)—See DETROIT, MI (Comcast Cable)

LAWTON—See DETROIT, MI (Comcast Cable)

LE ROY—Summit Digital

LEBANON TWP.—See DIMONDALE, MI (WOW! Internet, Cable & Phone)

LEE TWP. (ALLEGAN COUNTY)—See BLOOMINGDALE TWP. (Van Buren County), MI (Bloomingdale Communications)

LEE TWP. (MIDLAND COUNTY)—Parish Communications

LEE TWP.—See MIDLAND, MI (Charter Communications)

LEELANAU TWP.—See TRAVERSE CITY, MI (Charter Communications)

LEIGHTON TWP.—See ALLENDALE TWP., MI (Charter Communications)

LELAND TWP.—See TRAVERSE CITY, MI (Charter Communications)

LENNON—See GOODRICH, MI (Charter Communications)

LENNON—See NEW LOTHROP, MI (TVC Cable)

LENOX TWP.—See DETROIT, MI (Comcast Cable)

LEONARD—See GOODRICH, MI (Charter Communications)

LEONI TWP.—See DETROIT, MI (Comcast Cable)

LEROY TWP.—See DETROIT, MI (Comcast Cable)

LEROY TWP.—See DIMONDALE, MI (WOW! Internet, Cable & Phone)

LESLIE TWP.—See DIMONDALE, MI (WOW! Internet, Cable & Phone)

LESLIE—See DIMONDALE, MI (WOW! Internet, Cable & Phone)

LEVERING—Charter Communications. Now served by TRAVERSE CITY, MI [MI0026]

LEVERING—See TRAVERSE CITY, MI (Charter Communications)

LEWISTON—Lewiston Communications

LEXINGTON (village)—Comcast Cable. Now served by DETROIT, MI [MI0001]

LEXINGTON (VILLAGE)—See DETROIT, MI (Comcast Cable)

LEXINGTON TWP.—See DETROIT, MI (Comcast Cable)

LIBERTY TWP. (JACKSON COUNTY)—See DETROIT, MI (Comcast Cable)

LIBERTY TWP.—See TRAVERSE CITY, MI (Charter Communications)

LIBERTY TWP.—See DIMONDALE, MI (WOW! Internet, Cable & Phone)

LILLEY TWP.—Formerly served by Charter Communications. No longer in operation

LILLEY TWP.—See BALDWIN (village), MI (MIcom)

LIMA TWP.—See DETROIT, MI (Comcast Cable)

LINCOLN PARK—See DETROIT, MI (Comcast Cable)

LINCOLN PARK—See PLYMOUTH, MI (WOW! Internet, Cable & Phone)

LINCOLN TWP.—See MIDLAND, MI (Charter Communications)

LINCOLN—See MIDLAND, MI (Charter Communications)

LINDEN—See GOODRICH, MI (Charter Communications)

LITCHFIELD—See COLDWATER, MI (Charter Communications)

LITTLE LAKE—See MARQUETTE, MI (Charter Communications)

LITTLE TRAVERSE TWP.—See TRAVERSE CITY, MI (Charter Communications)

LITTLEFIELD TWP.—See TRAVERSE CITY, MI (Charter Communications)

LIVINGSTON COUNTY (portions)—Charter Communications. Now served by GOODRICH, MI [MI0290]

LIVINGSTON COUNTY (PORTIONS)—See GOODRICH, MI (Charter Communications)

LIVINGSTON TWP.—See TRAVERSE CITY, MI (Charter Communications)

LIVONIA—Bright House Networks

LOCKPORT—See DETROIT, MI (Comcast Cable)

LODI TWP.—See DETROIT, MI (Comcast Cable)

LOGAN TWP.—See RICHFIELD TWP. (Roscommon County), MI (Charter Communications)

LONDON TWP.—See FRENCHTOWN TWP., MI (Charter Communications)

LONDON TWP.—See DETROIT, MI (Comcast Cable)

LONG LAKE TWP.—See TRAVERSE CITY, MI (Charter Communications)

LONG RAPIDS TWP.—See ALPENA, MI (Charter Communications)

LOWELL TWP.—See DETROIT, MI (Comcast Cable)

LOWELL—Comcast Cable. Now served by DETROIT, MI [MI0001]

LOWELL—See DETROIT, MI (Comcast Cable)

LUDINGTON—Charter Communications. Now served by ALLENDALE TWP., MI [MI0094]

LUDINGTON—See ALLENDALE TWP., MI (Charter Communications)

LUNA PIER—See FRENCHTOWN TWP., MI (Charter Communications)

LUTHER—See LE ROY, MI (Summit Digital)

LUZERNE—Formerly served by Pine River Cable. No longer in operation

LYON TWP. (OAKLAND COUNTY)—See DETROIT, MI (Comcast Cable)

Cable Community Index—Michigan

LYON TWP. (ROSCOMMON COUNTY)—See RICHFIELD TWP. (Roscommon County), MI (Charter Communications)

LYONS TWP.—See ALLENDALE TWP., MI (Charter Communications)

LYONS TWP.—See DIMONDALE, MI (WOW! Internet, Cable & Phone)

LYONS VILLAGE—See ALLENDALE TWP., MI (Charter Communications)

MACKINAC ISLAND—MIcom

MACKINAW CITY—Charter Communications. Now served by TRAVERSE CITY, MI [MI0026]

MACKINAW CITY—See TRAVERSE CITY, MI (Charter Communications)

MACKINAW TWP.—See TRAVERSE CITY, MI (Charter Communications)

MACOMB TWP.—See DETROIT, MI (Comcast Cable)

MADISON HEIGHTS—Comcast Cable. Now served by DETROIT, MI [MI0001]

MADISON HEIGHTS—See DETROIT, MI (Comcast Cable)

MADISON HEIGHTS—See PLYMOUTH, MI (WOW! Internet, Cable & Phone)

MADISON TWP.—See DETROIT, MI (Comcast Cable)

MANCELONA TWP.—See TRAVERSE CITY, MI (Charter Communications)

MANCELONA—Charter Communications. Now served by TRAVERSE CITY, MI [MI0026]

MANCELONA—See TRAVERSE CITY, MI (Charter Communications)

MANCHESTER—See DETROIT, MI (Comcast Cable)

MANISTEE TWP.—See TRAVERSE CITY, MI (Charter Communications)

MANISTEE—Charter Communications. Now served by TRAVERSE CITY, MI [MI0026]

MANISTEE—See TRAVERSE CITY, MI (Charter Communications)

MANISTIQUE—See MARQUETTE, MI (Charter Communications)

MANLIUS TWP.—See ALLENDALE TWP., MI (Charter Communications)

MANLIUS TWP.—See DETROIT, MI (Comcast Cable)

MANTON—Charter Communications. Now served by TRAVERSE CITY, MI [MI0026]

MANTON—See TRAVERSE CITY, MI (Charter Communications)

MAPLE CITY—See TRAVERSE CITY, MI (Charter Communications)

MAPLE GROVE TWP.—See MIDLAND, MI (Charter Communications)

MAPLE RAPIDS—Mutual Data Services

MAPLE RIDGE TWP. (ALPENA COUNTY)—See ALPENA, MI (Charter Communications)

MAPLE VALLEY TWP. (MONTCALM COUNTY)—See ALLENDALE TWP., MI (Charter Communications)

MARATHON TWP.—See GOODRICH, MI (Charter Communications)

MARATHON—See GOODRICH, MI (Charter Communications)

MARCELLUS TWP.—See DETROIT, MI (Comcast Cable)

MARCELLUS TWP.—See MARCELLUS, MI (Mediacom)

MARCELLUS—Mediacom

MARENGO TWP.—See DIMONDALE, MI (WOW! Internet, Cable & Phone)

MARENISCO TWP.—Formerly served by Upper Peninsula Communications. No longer in operation

MARILLA—See MESICK, MI (AcenTek (formerly Ace Communications). This system has converted to IPTV)

MARINE CITY—See DETROIT, MI (Comcast Cable)

MARION TWP. (LIVINGSTON COUNTY)—See GOODRICH, MI (Charter Communications)

MARION TWP. (SANILAC COUNTY)—See DETROIT, MI (Comcast Cable)

MARION TWP.—See TRAVERSE CITY, MI (Charter Communications)

MARION—Formerly served by Pine River Cable. No longer in operation

MARKEY TWP.—See RICHFIELD TWP. (Roscommon County), MI (Charter Communications)

MARLETTE (VILLAGE)—See DETROIT, MI (Comcast Cable)

MARQUETTE—Charter Communications

MARSHALL TWP.—See DIMONDALE, MI (WOW! Internet, Cable & Phone)

MARSHALL—See DETROIT, MI (Comcast Cable)

MARSHALL—See DIMONDALE, MI (WOW! Internet, Cable & Phone)

MARTIN (VILLAGE)—See ALLENDALE TWP., MI (Charter Communications)

MARTIN TWP.—See ALLENDALE TWP., MI (Charter Communications)

MARTINY TWP. (SOUTHERN PORTION)—See IRON MOUNTAIN, MI (Northside T.V. Corp)

MARTINY TWP.—See MECOSTA, MI (MIcom)

MARYSVILLE—See DETROIT, MI (Comcast Cable)

MASON TWP. (ARENAC COUNTY)—See MIDLAND, MI (Charter Communications)

MASON—See DIMONDALE, MI (WOW! Internet, Cable & Phone)

MASONVILLE TWP. (SOUTHERN PORTION)—See MARQUETTE, MI (Charter Communications)

MASS CITY—Formerly served by Charter Communications. No longer in operation

MATHERTON—See DIMONDALE, MI (WOW! Internet, Cable & Phone)

MATTAWAN—Mediacom

MAYBEE—See FRENCHTOWN TWP., MI (Charter Communications)

MAYFIELD TWP. (GRAND TRAVERSE COUNTY)—See TRAVERSE CITY, MI (Charter Communications)

MAYFIELD TWP. (LAPEER COUNTY)—See GOODRICH, MI (Charter Communications)

MAYFIELD—See MESICK, MI (AcenTek (formerly Ace Communications). This system has converted to IPTV)

MAYFIELD—See TRAVERSE CITY, MI (Charter Communications)

MAYVILLE—Charter Communications. Now served by GOODRICH, MI [MI0290]

MAYVILLE—See GOODRICH, MI (Charter Communications)

MCBAIN—Summit Digital

MCBRIDES VILLAGE—See ALLENDALE TWP., MI (Charter Communications)

MCKINLEY TWP.—See TRAVERSE CITY, MI (Charter Communications)

MCKINLEY TWP.—See DETROIT, MI (Comcast Cable)

MCMILLAN TWP. (LUCE COUNTY)—See NEWBERRY, MI (Charter Communications)

MEADE—See DETROIT, MI (Comcast Cable)

MEARS—Golden Communications

MECOSTA—MIcom

MELLEN TWP.—Packerland Broadband

MELROSE TWP.—See TRAVERSE CITY, MI (Charter Communications)

MELVINDALE—See DETROIT, MI (Comcast Cable)

MELVINDALE—See PLYMOUTH, MI (WOW! Internet, Cable & Phone)

MEMPHIS—See DETROIT, MI (Comcast Cable)

MENDON (VILLAGE)—Mediacom

MENDON TWP.—See MENDON (village), MI (Mediacom)

MENDON—See DETROIT, MI (Comcast Cable)

MENTOR TWP.—See MIO, MI (MIcom)

MERIDIAN TWP.—See DETROIT, MI (Comcast Cable)

MERRILL—See MIDLAND, MI (Charter Communications)

MERRITT TWP.—Formerly served by Cablevision Systems Corp. No longer in operation

MESICK—Formerly served by Pine River Cable. No longer in operation

MESICK—AcenTek (formerly Ace Communications). This system has converted to IPTV

METAMORA TWP.—See GOODRICH, MI (Charter Communications)

METAMORA—See GOODRICH, MI (Charter Communications)

MEYER TWP.—See MARQUETTE, MI (Charter Communications)

MICHIGAMME—Formerly served by Upper Peninsula Communications. No longer in operation

MICHIGAMME—See REPUBLIC TWP., MI (Cable America Corp)

MIDDLEBURY TWP.—See MIDLAND, MI (Charter Communications)

MIDDLEVILLE/CALEDONIA—Charter Communications. Now served by ALLENDALE TWP., MI [MI0094]

MIDDLEVILLE—See ALLENDALE TWP., MI (Charter Communications)

MIDLAND TWP.—See MIDLAND, MI (Charter Communications)

MIDLAND—Charter Communications

MIKADO TWP.—Formerly served by Pine River Cable. No longer in operation

MILFORD (VILLAGE)—See DETROIT, MI (Comcast Cable)

MILFORD TWP.—See DETROIT, MI (Comcast Cable)

MILLINGTON TWP.—See GOODRICH, MI (Charter Communications)

MILLINGTON—See GOODRICH, MI (Charter Communications)

MILLS TWP. (OGEMAW COUNTY)—See RICHFIELD TWP. (Roscommon County), MI (Charter Communications)

MILTON TWP. (ANTRIM COUNTY)—See TRAVERSE CITY, MI (Charter Communications)

MINDEN CITY—Formerly served by Cablevision Systems Corp. No longer in operation

MIO—MIcom

MISSAUKEE COUNTY (PORTIONS)—See TRAVERSE CITY, MI (Charter Communications)

MISSAUKEE COUNTY (unincorporated areas)—Formerly served by Pine River Cable. No longer in operation

MOFFATT—See STERLING, MI (Vogtmann Engineering Inc)

MOLTKE TWP.—See ALPENA, MI (Charter Communications)

MONITOR TWP.—See MIDLAND, MI (Charter Communications)

MONROE TWP. (MONROE COUNTY)—See FRENCHTOWN TWP., MI (Charter Communications)

Michigan—Cable Community Index

MONROE TWP.—See DETROIT, MI (Comcast Cable)

MONROE—Comcast Cable. Now served by DETROIT, MI [MI0001]

MONROE—See FRENCHTOWN TWP., MI (Charter Communications)

MONROE—See DETROIT, MI (Comcast Cable)

MONTAGUE—See ALLENDALE TWP., MI (Charter Communications)

MONTCALM TWP. (NORTHERN PORTION)—See ALLENDALE TWP., MI (Charter Communications)

MONTCALM TWP.—See ALLENDALE TWP., MI (Charter Communications)

MONTMORENCY COUNTY—See LEWISTON, MI (Lewiston Communications)

MONTREAL—See IRONWOOD, WI (Charter Communications)

MONTROSE TWP.—See MIDLAND, MI (Charter Communications)

MONTROSE—Charter Communications. Now served by MIDLAND, MI [MI0030]

MONTROSE—See MIDLAND, MI (Charter Communications)

MORAN—See SAULT STE. MARIE, MI (Charter Communications)

MORENCI—See PETERSBURG, MI (D & P Cable)

MORLEY—See ALLENDALE TWP., MI (Charter Communications)

MORRICE—See DIMONDALE, MI (WOW! Internet, Cable & Phone)

MORTON TWP.—See IRON MOUNTAIN, MI (Northside T.V. Corp)

MOTTVILLE—See DETROIT, MI (Comcast Cable)

MOUNT CLEMENS—See DETROIT, MI (Comcast Cable)

MOUNT CLEMENS—See PLYMOUTH, MI (WOW! Internet, Cable & Phone)

MOUNT HALEY TWP.—See MIDLAND, MI (Charter Communications)

MOUNT MORRIS TWP.—See DETROIT, MI (Comcast Cable)

MOUNT MORRIS—See DETROIT, MI (Comcast Cable)

MOUNT PLEASANT—Charter Communications. Now served by MIDLAND, MI [MI0030]

MOUNT PLEASANT—See MIDLAND, MI (Charter Communications)

MUIR—See ALLENDALE TWP., MI (Charter Communications)

MULLET LAKE TWP.—See TRAVERSE CITY, MI (Charter Communications)

MULLETT TWP.—Formerly served by Northwoods Cable Inc. No longer in operation

MULLIKEN—See DIMONDALE, MI (WOW! Internet, Cable & Phone)

MUNDY TWP.—See DETROIT, MI (Comcast Cable)

MUNISING—See MARQUETTE, MI (Charter Communications)

MUNITH—See DIMONDALE, MI (WOW! Internet, Cable & Phone)

MUSKEGON HEIGHTS—See DETROIT, MI (Comcast Cable)

MUSKEGON—Comcast Cable. Now served by DETROIT, MI [MI0001]

MUSKEGON—See DETROIT, MI (Comcast Cable)

NADEAU—See CARNEY/POWERS, MI (Packerland Broadband)

NAPOLEON TWP.—See DETROIT, MI (Comcast Cable)

NASHVILLE—Martell Cable

NAUBINWAY—See ENGADINE, MI (Lighthouse Computers Inc.)

NEGAUNEE—See MARQUETTE, MI (Charter Communications)

NEGAUNEE—City of Negaunee Cable TV

NELSON TWP. (PORTIONS)—See ALLENDALE TWP., MI (Charter Communications)

NEW BALTIMORE—See DETROIT, MI (Comcast Cable)

NEW ERA (VILLAGE)—See ALLENDALE TWP., MI (Charter Communications)

NEW HAVEN—See DETROIT, MI (Comcast Cable)

NEW LOTHROP—TVC Cable

NEWARK TWP.—See MIDLAND, MI (Charter Communications)

NEWAYGO—See ALLENDALE TWP., MI (Charter Communications)

NEWBERG TWP.—See DETROIT, MI (Comcast Cable)

NEWBERRY—Charter Communications

NEWFIELD TWP.—See BALDWIN (village), MI (MIcom)

NEWTON TWP.—See DETROIT, MI (Comcast Cable)

NILES—Comcast Cable. Now served by CHAMPAIGN, IL [IL0019]

NORTH ADAMS—See DETROIT, MI (Comcast Cable)

NORTH BRANCH (VILLAGE)—See GOODRICH, MI (Charter Communications)

NORTH BRANCH TWP.—Charter Communications. Now served by GOODRICH, MI [MI0290]

NORTH BRANCH TWP.—See GOODRICH, MI (Charter Communications)

NORTH MUSKEGON—See DETROIT, MI (Comcast Cable)

NORTH PLAINS TWP.—See DIMONDALE, MI (WOW! Internet, Cable & Phone)

NORTHFIELD TWP.—See GOODRICH, MI (Charter Communications)

NORTHPORT (VILLAGE)—See TRAVERSE CITY, MI (Charter Communications)

NORTHVILLE TWP.—See DETROIT, MI (Comcast Cable)

NORTHVILLE TWP.—See PLYMOUTH, MI (WOW! Internet, Cable & Phone)

NORTHVILLE—See DETROIT, MI (Comcast Cable)

NORTHVILLE—See PLYMOUTH, MI (WOW! Internet, Cable & Phone)

NORTON SHORES—See DETROIT, MI (Comcast Cable)

NORVELL TWP.—See DETROIT, MI (Comcast Cable)

NORWAY TWP.—See NORWAY, MI (City of Norway CATV)

NORWAY—City of Norway CATV

NORWOOD TWP.—See TRAVERSE CITY, MI (Charter Communications)

NOTTAWA TWP. (ISABELLA COUNTY)—See SHERMAN TWP. (Isabella County), MI (Charter Communications)

NOTTAWA—See DETROIT, MI (Comcast Cable)

NOVESTA TWP.—See GOODRICH, MI (Charter Communications)

NOVI TWP.—See LIVONIA, MI (Bright House Networks)

NOVI—See LIVONIA, MI (Bright House Networks)

NOVI—See DETROIT, MI (Comcast Cable)

NUNDA TWP.—See TRAVERSE CITY, MI (Charter Communications)

OAK PARK—See DETROIT, MI (Comcast Cable)

OAKLAND TWP.—See DETROIT, MI (Comcast Cable)

OAKLEY (VILLAGE)—See MIDLAND, MI (Charter Communications)

OCEOLA TWP.—See DETROIT, MI (Comcast Cable)

ODEN—See TRAVERSE CITY, MI (Charter Communications)

ODESSA TWP.—See DIMONDALE, MI (WOW! Internet, Cable & Phone)

OLIVE TWP. (Ottawa County)—Charter Communications. Now served by ALLENDALE TWP., MI [MI0094]

OLIVE TWP. (OTTAWA COUNTY)—See ALLENDALE TWP., MI (Charter Communications)

OLIVE—See MESICK, MI (AcenTek (formerly Ace Communications). This system has converted to IPTV)

OLIVER TWP.—See DETROIT, MI (Comcast Cable)

OLIVET—See DIMONDALE, MI (WOW! Internet, Cable & Phone)

OMER—Charter Communications. Now served by MIDLAND, MI [MI0030]

OMER—See MIDLAND, MI (Charter Communications)

ONAWAY—Formerly served by Northwoods Cable Inc. No longer in operation

ONEIDA CHARTER TWP.—See DIMONDALE, MI (WOW! Internet, Cable & Phone)

ONEIDA TWP.—See DETROIT, MI (Comcast Cable)

ONEKAMA (VILLAGE)—See TRAVERSE CITY, MI (Charter Communications)

ONEKAMA TWP.—See TRAVERSE CITY, MI (Charter Communications)

ONONDAGA TWP.—See DIMONDALE, MI (WOW! Internet, Cable & Phone)

ONSTED—See DETROIT, MI (Comcast Cable)

ONTONAGON—Charter Communications. Now served by IRONWOOD, MI [MI0064]

ONTONAGON—See IRONWOOD, MI (Charter Communications)

ORANGE TWP. (KALKASKA COUNTY)—See BOARDMAN TWP. (southern portion), MI (ATI Networks Inc.)

ORANGE TWP.—See MESICK, MI (AcenTek (formerly Ace Communications). This system has converted to IPTV)

ORANGEVILLE TWP.—See ALLENDALE TWP., MI (Charter Communications)

ORCHARD LAKE—See DETROIT, MI (Comcast Cable)

OREGON TWP.—See GOODRICH, MI (Charter Communications)

ORION TWP.—See DETROIT, MI (Comcast Cable)

ORLEANS TWP. (PORTIONS)—See ALLENDALE TWP., MI (Charter Communications)

ORTONVILLE—See GOODRICH, MI (Charter Communications)

OSCEOLA TWP. (HOUGHTON COUNTY)—See MARQUETTE, MI (Charter Communications)

OSCEOLA TWP. (OSCEOLA COUNTY)—See ALLENDALE TWP., MI (Charter Communications)

OSCODA TWP.—See MIDLAND, MI (Charter Communications)

OSCODA—Charter Communications. Now served by MIDLAND, MI [MI0030]

OSCODA—See MIDLAND, MI (Charter Communications)

OSHTEMO TWP.—Comcast Cable. Now served by DETROIT, MI [MI0001]

OSHTEMO TWP.—See COMSTOCK TWP., MI (Charter Communications)

Cable Community Index—Michigan

OSHTEMO TWP.—See DETROIT, MI (Comcast Cable)

OSHTEMO TWP.—See MATTAWAN, MI (Mediacom)

OSHTEMO—Audrey Homes LLC

OSSINEKE TWP.—See ALPENA, MI (Charter Communications)

OTISCO TWP.—See ALLENDALE TWP., MI (Charter Communications)

OTISVILLE—See GOODRICH, MI (Charter Communications)

OTSEGO CITY—See ALLENDALE TWP., MI (Charter Communications)

OTTER LAKE—See GOODRICH, MI (Charter Communications)

OVERISEL TWP.—See ALLENDALE TWP., MI (Charter Communications)

OVERISEL—See MESICK, MI (AcenTek (formerly Ace Communications). This system has converted to IPTV)

OVID TWP.—See COLDWATER, MI (Charter Communications)

OVID VILLAGE—See MIDLAND, MI (Charter Communications)

OWENDALE—See DETROIT, MI (Comcast Cable)

OWOSSO TWP.—See MIDLAND, MI (Charter Communications)

OWOSSO—Charter Communications. Now served by MIDLAND, MI [MI0030]

OWOSSO—See MIDLAND, MI (Charter Communications)

OXFORD (VILLAGE)—See GOODRICH, MI (Charter Communications)

OXFORD TWP.—See GOODRICH, MI (Charter Communications)

OXFORD—Charter Communications. Now served by GOODRICH, MI [MI0290]

OXFORD—See GOODRICH, MI (Charter Communications)

PALMER—See MARQUETTE, MI (Charter Communications)

PALMYRA TWP.—See DETROIT, MI (Comcast Cable)

PALMYRA TWP.—See PETERSBURG, MI (D & P Cable)

PARADISE TWP.—See TRAVERSE CITY, MI (Charter Communications)

PARCHMENT—See COMSTOCK TWP., MI (Charter Communications)

PARK TWP. (OTTAWA COUNTY)—See ALLENDALE TWP., MI (Charter Communications)

PARK—See MESICK, MI (AcenTek (formerly Ace Communications). This system has converted to IPTV)

PARMA TWP.—See SPRINGPORT TWP., MI (Springport Telephone Co)

PARMA TWP.—See DIMONDALE, MI (WOW! Internet, Cable & Phone)

PARMA—See DIMONDALE, MI (WOW! Internet, Cable & Phone)

PAVILION TWP. (PORTIONS)—See CLIMAX TWP., MI (Climax Telephone Co)

PAVILION TWP.—See COMSTOCK TWP., MI (Charter Communications)

PAVILION—See DETROIT, MI (Comcast Cable)

PAW PAW (VILLAGE)—See DETROIT, MI (Comcast Cable)

PAW PAW TWP.—See DETROIT, MI (Comcast Cable)

PECK—See DETROIT, MI (Comcast Cable)

PELLSTON—Charter Communications. Now served by TRAVERSE CITY, MI [MI0026]

PELLSTON—See TRAVERSE CITY, MI (Charter Communications)

PENCE—See IRONWOOD, WI (Charter Communications)

PENINSULA TWP.—See TRAVERSE CITY, MI (Charter Communications)

PENN TWP. (PORTIONS)—See DETROIT, MI (Comcast Cable)

PENNFIELD TWP.—See DETROIT, MI (Comcast Cable)

PENTLAND TWP.—See NEWBERRY, MI (Charter Communications)

PENTWATER—Charter Communications. Now served by ALLENDALE TWP., MI [MI0094]

PENTWATER—See ALLENDALE TWP., MI (Charter Communications)

PERE MARQUETTE TWP.—See ALLENDALE TWP., MI (Charter Communications)

PERRINTON—Formerly served by Pine River Cable. No longer in operation

PERRY TWP.—See DIMONDALE, MI (WOW! Internet, Cable & Phone)

PERRY—See DIMONDALE, MI (WOW! Internet, Cable & Phone)

PETERSBURG—D & P Cable

PETOSKEY—Charter Communications. Now served by TRAVERSE CITY, MI [MI0026]

PETOSKEY—See TRAVERSE CITY, MI (Charter Communications)

PEWAMO—See DIMONDALE, MI (WOW! Internet, Cable & Phone)

PICKFORD TWP.—Sunrise Communications LLC

PIERSON (VILLAGE)—See ALLENDALE TWP., MI (Charter Communications)

PIGEON—Comcast Cable. Now served by DETROIT, MI [MI0001]

PIGEON—See DETROIT, MI (Comcast Cable)

PINCKNEY—See GOODRICH, MI (Charter Communications)

PINCONNING TWP.—See MIDLAND, MI (Charter Communications)

PINCONNING—See MIDLAND, MI (Charter Communications)

PINE GROVE TWP.—See ALLENDALE TWP., MI (Charter Communications)

PINE RIVER TWP.—See MIDLAND, MI (Charter Communications)

PINE TWP.—See ALLENDALE TWP., MI (Charter Communications)

PIPESTONE TWP.—See BAINBRIDGE TWP., MI (Michiana Supernet)

PITTSFIELD TWP.—See DETROIT, MI (Comcast Cable)

PITTSFORD TWP.—See DETROIT, MI (Comcast Cable)

PLAINFIELD TWP. (IOSCO COUNTY)—See GOODAR TWP., MI (Charter Communications)

PLAINFIELD TWP. (KENT COUNTY)—See ALLENDALE TWP., MI (Charter Communications)

PLAINFIELD TWP. (KENT COUNTY)—See DETROIT, MI (Comcast Cable)

PLAINWELL CITY—See ALLENDALE TWP., MI (Charter Communications)

PLEASANT LAKE—See DIMONDALE, MI (WOW! Internet, Cable & Phone)

PLEASANT RIDGE—See DETROIT, MI (Comcast Cable)

PLEASANT RIDGE—See PLYMOUTH, MI (WOW! Internet, Cable & Phone)

PLEASANTON TWP.—See TRAVERSE CITY, MI (Charter Communications)

PLEASANTVIEW TWP.—See TRAVERSE CITY, MI (Charter Communications)

PLYMOUTH TWP.—See DETROIT, MI (Comcast Cable)

PLYMOUTH TWP.—See PLYMOUTH, MI (WOW! Internet, Cable & Phone)

PLYMOUTH—See DETROIT, MI (Comcast Cable)

PLYMOUTH—WOW! Internet, Cable & Phone

POLKTON TWP.—See ALLENDALE TWP., MI (Charter Communications)

POLKTON—See MESICK, MI (AcenTek (formerly Ace Communications). This system has converted to IPTV)

PONTIAC—Comcast Cable. Now served by DETROIT, MI [MI0001]

PONTIAC—See DETROIT, MI (Comcast Cable)

PORT AUSTIN—Comcast Cable. Now served by DETROIT, MI [MI0001]

PORT AUSTIN—See DETROIT, MI (Comcast Cable)

PORT HOPE—Comcast Cable. Now served by DETROIT, MI [MI0001]

PORT HOPE—See DETROIT, MI (Comcast Cable)

PORT HURON TWP.—See DETROIT, MI (Comcast Cable)

PORT HURON—See DETROIT, MI (Comcast Cable)

PORT SANILAC—See DETROIT, MI (Comcast Cable)

PORT SHELDON TWP.—See ALLENDALE TWP., MI (Charter Communications)

PORTAGE (NORTHEASTERN PORTION)—See COMSTOCK TWP., MI (Charter Communications)

PORTAGE TWP. (Mackinac County)—Formerly served by Upper Peninsula Communications. Now served by Lighthouse Computers Inc., ENGADINE, MI [MI0297]

PORTAGE TWP. (MACKINAC COUNTY)—See ENGADINE, MI (Lighthouse Computers Inc.)

PORTAGE—See DETROIT, MI (Comcast Cable)

PORTER TWP. (CASS COUNTY)—See DETROIT, MI (Comcast Cable)

PORTER TWP. (VAN BUREN COUNTY)—See DETROIT, MI (Comcast Cable)

PORTLAND TWP.—See DIMONDALE, MI (WOW! Internet, Cable & Phone)

PORTLAND—See DIMONDALE, MI (WOW! Internet, Cable & Phone)

PORTSMOUTH TWP.—See MIDLAND, MI (Charter Communications)

POSEN—Sunrise Communications LLC

POTTERVILLE—See DIMONDALE, MI (WOW! Internet, Cable & Phone)

PRAIRIE RONDE—See DETROIT, MI (Comcast Cable)

PRAIRIEVILLE—See DETROIT, MI (Comcast Cable)

PRESCOTT (village)—Formerly served by Charter Communications. No longer in operation

PRINCETON—See MARQUETTE, MI (Charter Communications)

PULASKI TWP.—See POSEN, MI (Sunrise Communications LLC)

PULASKI TWP.—See DIMONDALE, MI (WOW! Internet, Cable & Phone)

PUTNAM TWP.—See GOODRICH, MI (Charter Communications)

QUINCY—See COLDWATER, MI (Charter Communications)

RAISIN TWP.—See DETROIT, MI (Comcast Cable)

RAISINVILLE TWP.—See FRENCHTOWN TWP., MI (Charter Communications)

RAISINVILLE TWP.—See DETROIT, MI (Comcast Cable)

RAPID RIVER TWP.—See TRAVERSE CITY, MI (Charter Communications)

RAPID RIVER—See TRAVERSE CITY, MI (Charter Communications)

RAVENNA TWP.—See CHESTER TWP. (Ottawa County), MI (Charter Communications)

Michigan—Cable Community Index

RAVENNA—See CHESTER TWP. (Ottawa County), MI (Charter Communications)

RAY TWP.—See DETROIT, MI (Comcast Cable)

READING—See COLDWATER, MI (Charter Communications)

REDFORD TWP.—See PLYMOUTH, MI (WOW! Internet, Cable & Phone)

REDFORD—Bright House Networks. Now served by LIVONIA, MI [MI0019]

REDFORD—See LIVONIA, MI (Bright House Networks)

REED CITY—Charter Communications. Now served by ALLENDALE TWP., MI [MI0094]

REED CITY—See ALLENDALE TWP., MI (Charter Communications)

REEDER TWP.—See TRAVERSE CITY, MI (Charter Communications)

REESE—Charter Communications. Now served by MIDLAND, MI [MI0030]

REESE—See MIDLAND, MI (Charter Communications)

REMUS—MIcom

REPUBLIC TWP.—Cable America Corp

RESORT TWP.—See TRAVERSE CITY, MI (Charter Communications)

REYNOLDS TWP.—See ALLENDALE TWP., MI (Charter Communications)

RICHFIELD TWP. (GENESEE COUNTY)—See GOODRICH, MI (Charter Communications)

RICHFIELD TWP. (GENESEE COUNTY)—See DETROIT, MI (Comcast Cable)

RICHFIELD TWP. (ROSCOMMON COUNTY)—Charter Communications

RICHLAND (VILLAGE)—See DETROIT, MI (Comcast Cable)

RICHLAND TWP. (MISSAUKEE COUNTY)—See TRAVERSE CITY, MI (Charter Communications)

RICHLAND TWP. (MONTCALM COUNTY)—See SEVILLE TWP., MI (Charter Communications)

RICHLAND TWP. (SAGINAW COUNTY)—See MIDLAND, MI (Charter Communications)

RICHLAND TWP.—Comcast Cable. Now served by DETROIT, MI [MI0001]

RICHLAND TWP.—See DETROIT, MI (Comcast Cable)

RICHLAND TWP.—See STERLING, MI (Vogtmann Engineering Inc)

RICHLAND—Comcast Cable. Now served by DETROIT, MI [MI0001]

RICHMOND TWP. (MACOMB COUNTY)—See DETROIT, MI (Comcast Cable)

RICHMOND TWP. (OSCEOLA COUNTY)—See ALLENDALE TWP., MI (Charter Communications)

RICHMOND—See DETROIT, MI (Comcast Cable)

RIDGEWAY TWP.—See DETROIT, MI (Comcast Cable)

RIDGEWAY TWP.—See PETERSBURG, MI (D & P Cable)

RIGA TWP.—See PETERSBURG, MI (D & P Cable)

RIVER ROUGE—See DETROIT, MI (Comcast Cable)

RIVERDALE—See SEVILLE TWP., MI (Charter Communications)

RIVERSIDE TWP.—See McBAIN, MI (Summit Digital)

RIVERVIEW—See DETROIT, MI (Comcast Cable)

RIVERVIEW—See PLYMOUTH, MI (WOW! Internet, Cable & Phone)

RIVES JUNCTION—Formerly served by Cablevision Systems Corp. No longer in operation

RIVES JUNCTION—See DETROIT, MI (Comcast Cable)

ROBINSON TWP.—See ALLENDALE TWP., MI (Charter Communications)

ROBINSON—See MESICK, MI (AcenTek (formerly Ace Communications). This system has converted to IPTV)

ROCHESTER HILLS—See DETROIT, MI (Comcast Cable)

ROCHESTER HILLS—See PLYMOUTH, MI (WOW! Internet, Cable & Phone)

ROCHESTER—See DETROIT, MI (Comcast Cable)

ROCHESTER—See PLYMOUTH, MI (WOW! Internet, Cable & Phone)

ROCK RIVER TWP.—See MARQUETTE, MI (Charter Communications)

ROCKFORD—Charter Communications. Now served by ALLENDALE TWP., MI [MI0094]

ROCKFORD—See ALLENDALE TWP., MI (Charter Communications)

ROCKLAND TWP.—See IRONWOOD, MI (Charter Communications)

ROCKWOOD—See DETROIT, MI (Comcast Cable)

ROGERS CITY—Charter Communications. Now served by ALPENA, MI [MI0061]

ROGERS CITY—See ALPENA, MI (Charter Communications)

ROGERS TWP.—See ALPENA, MI (Charter Communications)

ROLLAND TWP.—Formerly served by Blanchard Cable Inc. No longer in operation

ROLLIN—See DETROIT, MI (Comcast Cable)

ROMEO—See DETROIT, MI (Comcast Cable)

ROMULUS—Comcast Cable. Now served by DETROIT, MI [MI0001]

ROMULUS—See DETROIT, MI (Comcast Cable)

RONALD TWP.—See ALLENDALE TWP., MI (Charter Communications)

ROOSEVELT PARK—See DETROIT, MI (Comcast Cable)

ROSCOMMON (VILLAGE)—See RICHFIELD TWP. (Roscommon County), MI (Charter Communications)

ROSCOMMON—Charter Communications. Now served by RICHFIELD TWP. (Roscommon County), MI [MI0116]

ROSCOMMON—See RICHFIELD TWP. (Roscommon County), MI (Charter Communications)

ROSE CITY—See GOODAR TWP., MI (Charter Communications)

ROSE TWP. (OAKLAND COUNTY)—See DETROIT, MI (Comcast Cable)

ROSE TWP. (OGEMAW COUNTY)—See GOODAR TWP., MI (Charter Communications)

ROSEBUSH—Charter Communications. Now served by MIDLAND, MI [MI0030]

ROSEBUSH—See MIDLAND, MI (Charter Communications)

ROSEVILLE—Comcast Cable. Now served by DETROIT, MI [MI0001]

ROSEVILLE—See DETROIT, MI (Comcast Cable)

ROSEVILLE—See PLYMOUTH, MI (WOW! Internet, Cable & Phone)

ROSS TWP.—See DETROIT, MI (Comcast Cable)

ROTHBURY—See ALLENDALE TWP., MI (Charter Communications)

ROXANNE TWP.—See DIMONDALE, MI (WOW! Internet, Cable & Phone)

ROYAL OAK TWP.—See DETROIT, MI (Comcast Cable)

ROYAL OAK—See DETROIT, MI (Comcast Cable)

ROYAL OAK—See PLYMOUTH, MI (WOW! Internet, Cable & Phone)

RUBICON TWP.—See DETROIT, MI (Comcast Cable)

RUDYARD TWP.—See SAULT STE. MARIE, MI (Charter Communications)

RUSH TWP.—See MIDLAND, MI (Charter Communications)

RUTLAND TWP.—MIcom

SAGE TWP.—Charter Communications

SAGINAW TWP.—See MIDLAND, MI (Charter Communications)

SAGINAW—Charter Communications. Now served by MIDLAND, MI [MI0030]

SAGINAW—See MIDLAND, MI (Charter Communications)

SAGOLA TWP.—See MARQUETTE, MI (Charter Communications)

SALEM TWP. (WASHTENAW COUNTY)—See GOODRICH, MI (Charter Communications)

SALEM—See MESICK, MI (AcenTek (formerly Ace Communications). This system has converted to IPTV)

SALINE TWP.—See DETROIT, MI (Comcast Cable)

SALINE—Comcast Cable. Now served by DETROIT, MI [MI0001]

SALINE—See DETROIT, MI (Comcast Cable)

SANBORN TWP.—See ALPENA, MI (Charter Communications)

SAND BEACH TWP.—See DETROIT, MI (Comcast Cable)

SAND LAKE—See ALLENDALE TWP., MI (Charter Communications)

SANDS TWP.—See MARQUETTE, MI (Charter Communications)

SANDSTONE TWP.—See DETROIT, MI (Comcast Cable)

SANDUSKY—Comcast Cable. Now served by DETROIT, MI [MI0001]

SANDUSKY—See DETROIT, MI (Comcast Cable)

SANFORD—Formerly served by Charter Communications. No longer in operation

SANILAC TWP.—See DETROIT, MI (Comcast Cable)

SARANAC—See DIMONDALE, MI (WOW! Internet, Cable & Phone)

SAUGATUCK TWP.—See DETROIT, MI (Comcast Cable)

SAUGATUCK—Comcast Cable. Now served by DETROIT, MI [MI0001]

SAULT STE. MARIE—Charter Communications

SCHOOLCRAFT TWP.—See DETROIT, MI (Comcast Cable)

SCHOOLCRAFT—See DETROIT, MI (Comcast Cable)

SCIO TWP.—See DETROIT, MI (Comcast Cable)

SCIOTA TWP.—See DIMONDALE, MI (WOW! Internet, Cable & Phone)

SCIPIO TWP.—See DETROIT, MI (Comcast Cable)

SCOTTS—See CLIMAX TWP., MI (Climax Telephone Co)

SCOTTVILLE—See ALLENDALE TWP., MI (Charter Communications)

SEBEWAING—Comcast Cable. Now served by DETROIT, MI [MI0001]

SEBEWAING—See DETROIT, MI (Comcast Cable)

SECORD TWP.—See BUTMAN TWP., MI (Charter Communications)

SELFRIDGE AFB—See DETROIT, MI (Comcast Cable)

Cable Community Index—Michigan

SELMA TWP.—See TRAVERSE CITY, MI (Charter Communications)

SENECA TWP.—See PETERSBURG, MI (D & P Cable)

SENEY—Formerly served by Cable America Corp. No longer in operation

SEVILLE TWP.—Charter Communications

SHAFTSBURG—See DIMONDALE, MI (WOW! Internet, Cable & Phone)

SHELBY (UNINCORPORATED AREAS)—See ALLENDALE TWP., MI (Charter Communications)

SHELBY TWP.—See DETROIT, MI (Comcast Cable)

SHELBY TWP.—See PLYMOUTH, MI (WOW! Internet, Cable & Phone)

SHEPHERD—See MIDLAND, MI (Charter Communications)

SHERIDAN TWP. (CALHOUN COUNTY)—See SPRINGPORT TWP., MI (Springport Telephone Co)

SHERIDAN TWP. (NEWAYGO COUNTY)—See DETROIT, MI (Comcast Cable)

SHERIDAN TWP.—See DIMONDALE, MI (WOW! Internet, Cable & Phone)

SHERIDAN—See ALLENDALE TWP., MI (Charter Communications)

SHERMAN TWP. (ISABELLA COUNTY)—Charter Communications

SHERMAN TWP. (MASON COUNTY)—See CUSTER, MI (Charter Communications)

SHERMAN TWP. (NEWAYGO COUNTY)—See DETROIT, MI (Comcast Cable)

SHERMAN TWP. (ST. JOSEPH COUNTY)—See COLDWATER, MI (Charter Communications)

SHERMAN TWP. (ST. JOSEPH COUNTY)—See DETROIT, MI (Comcast Cable)

SHERMAN TWP.—See BALDWIN (village), MI (MIcom)

SHERWOOD TWP.—Formerly served by CableDirect. No longer in operation

SHERWOOD—See DIMONDALE, MI (WOW! Internet, Cable & Phone)

SHIAWASSEE TWP.—See GOODRICH, MI (Charter Communications)

SHINGLETON—Cable America Corp

SIDNEY TWP.—See ALLENDALE TWP., MI (Charter Communications)

SILVER CREEK TWP.—See KEELER TWP., MI (Sister Lakes Cable TV)

SIMS TWP.—See MIDLAND, MI (Charter Communications)

SISTER LAKES—See KEELER TWP., MI (Sister Lakes Cable TV)

SKANDIA TWP.—See MARQUETTE, MI (Charter Communications)

SKIDWAY LAKE—Formerly served by Charter Communications. No longer in operation

SLAGLE TWP.—See MESICK, MI (AcenTek (formerly Ace Communications). This system has converted to IPTV)

SOLON TWP. (KENT COUNTY)—See ALLENDALE TWP., MI (Charter Communications)

SOLON TWP. (LEELANAU COUNTY)—See TRAVERSE CITY, MI (Charter Communications)

SOMERSET TWP.—See DETROIT, MI (Comcast Cable)

SOO TWP.—See SAULT STE. MARIE, MI (Charter Communications)

SOUTH ARM TWP.—See TRAVERSE CITY, MI (Charter Communications)

SOUTH BOARDMAN—See MESICK, MI (AcenTek (formerly Ace Communications). This system has converted to IPTV)

SOUTH BRANCH TWP.—See MESICK, MI (AcenTek (formerly Ace Communications). This system has converted to IPTV)

SOUTH BRANCH TWP.—See RICHFIELD TWP. (Roscommon County), MI (Charter Communications)

SOUTH HAVEN TWP.—See DETROIT, MI (Comcast Cable)

SOUTH HAVEN—Comcast Cable. Now served by DETROIT, MI [MI0001]

SOUTH HAVEN—See DETROIT, MI (Comcast Cable)

SOUTH LYON—See DIMONDALE, MI (WOW! Internet, Cable & Phone)

SOUTH RANGE—See MARQUETTE, MI (Charter Communications)

SOUTH ROCKWOOD—See DETROIT, MI (Comcast Cable)

SOUTHFIELD—Comcast Cable. Now served by DETROIT, MI [MI0001]

SOUTHFIELD—See DETROIT, MI (Comcast Cable)

SOUTHGATE—See DETROIT, MI (Comcast Cable)

SOUTHGATE—See PLYMOUTH, MI (WOW! Internet, Cable & Phone)

SPARTA TWP.—See ALLENDALE TWP., MI (Charter Communications)

SPARTA TWP.—See DETROIT, MI (Comcast Cable)

SPARTA—See ALLENDALE TWP., MI (Charter Communications)

SPAULDING TWP.—See MIDLAND, MI (Charter Communications)

SPEAKER TWP.—See DETROIT, MI (Comcast Cable)

SPENCER TWP.—See ALLENDALE TWP., MI (Charter Communications)

SPREAD EAGLE—See MARQUETTE, WI (Charter Communications)

SPRING ARBOR TWP.—See DETROIT, MI (Comcast Cable)

SPRING ARBOR TWP.—See DIMONDALE, MI (WOW! Internet, Cable & Phone)

SPRING LAKE TWP.—See DETROIT, MI (Comcast Cable)

SPRING LAKE—See ALLENDALE TWP., MI (Charter Communications)

SPRINGDALE TWP.—Ace Communications. Formerly served by THOMPSONVILLE, MI [MI0230]. This cable system has converted to IPTV. Now served by MESICK, MI [MI5074]

SPRINGDALE TWP.—See MESICK, MI (AcenTek (formerly Ace Communications). This system has converted to IPTV)

SPRINGFIELD TWP. (Oakland County)—Comcast Cable. Now served by DETROIT, MI [MI0001]

SPRINGFIELD TWP.—See MESICK, MI (AcenTek (formerly Ace Communications). This system has converted to IPTV)

SPRINGFIELD TWP.—See TRAVERSE CITY, MI (Charter Communications)

SPRINGFIELD TWP.—See DETROIT, MI (Comcast Cable)

SPRINGFIELD—See DETROIT, MI (Comcast Cable)

SPRINGPORT (VILLAGE)—See SPRINGPORT TWP., MI (Springport Telephone Co)

SPRINGPORT TWP.—Springport Telephone Co

SPRINGVALE TWP.—See TRAVERSE CITY, MI (Charter Communications)

SPRINGVALE TWP.—Parish Communications

ST. CHARLES (VILLAGE)—See MIDLAND, MI (Charter Communications)

ST. CHARLES TWP.—See MIDLAND, MI (Charter Communications)

ST. CLAIR SHORES—See DETROIT, MI (Comcast Cable)

ST. CLAIR SHORES—See PLYMOUTH, MI (WOW! Internet, Cable & Phone)

ST. CLAIR TWP.—See DETROIT, MI (Comcast Cable)

ST. CLAIR—See DETROIT, MI (Comcast Cable)

ST. IGNACE TWP.—See SAULT STE. MARIE, MI (Charter Communications)

ST. IGNACE—Charter Communications. Now served by SAULT STE. MARIE, MI [MI0090]

ST. IGNACE—See SAULT STE. MARIE, MI (Charter Communications)

ST. JOHNS—Charter Communications. Now served by MIDLAND, MI [MI0030]

ST. JOHNS—See MIDLAND, MI (Charter Communications)

ST. JOSEPH—Comcast Cable. Now served by CHAMPAIGN, IL [IL0019]

ST. LOUIS—See MIDLAND, MI (Charter Communications)

STAMBAUGH—See CASPIAN, MI (Caspian Community TV Corp)

STANDISH TWP.—See MIDLAND, MI (Charter Communications)

STANDISH—Charter Communications. Now served by MIDLAND, MI [MI0030]

STANDISH—See MIDLAND, MI (Charter Communications)

STANNARD TWP.—See IRONWOOD, MI (Charter Communications)

STANTON—Charter Communications. Now served by ALLENDALE TWP., MI [MI0094]

STANTON—See ALLENDALE TWP., MI (Charter Communications)

STANWOOD—See ALLENDALE TWP., MI (Charter Communications)

STAR TWP.—See TRAVERSE CITY, MI (Charter Communications)

STEPHENSON—Packerland Broadband

STERLING HEIGHTS—Comcast Cable. Now served by DETROIT, MI [MI0001]

STERLING HEIGHTS—See DETROIT, MI (Comcast Cable)

STERLING HEIGHTS—See PLYMOUTH, MI (WOW! Internet, Cable & Phone)

STERLING VILLAGE—See STERLING, MI (Vogtmann Engineering Inc)

STERLING—Vogtmann Engineering Inc

STOCKBRIDGE TWP.—See DIMONDALE, MI (WOW! Internet, Cable & Phone)

STOCKBRIDGE—See DIMONDALE, MI (WOW! Internet, Cable & Phone)

STRONACH TWP.—See TRAVERSE CITY, MI (Charter Communications)

STURGIS—See COLDWATER, MI (Charter Communications)

SULLIVAN TWP.—See DETROIT, MI (Comcast Cable)

SUMMERFIELD TWP. (MONROE COUNTY)—See FRENCHTOWN TWP., MI (Charter Communications)

SUMMERFIELD TWP.—See PETERSBURG, MI (D & P Cable)

SUMMIT TWP. (Jackson County)—Comcast Cable. Now served by DETROIT, MI [MI0001]

SUMMIT TWP. (JACKSON COUNTY)—See DETROIT, MI (Comcast Cable)

SUMMIT TWP. (MASON CO.)—See ALLENDALE TWP., MI (Charter Communications)

Michigan—Cable Community Index

SUMMIT-LEONI—See DETROIT, MI (Comcast Cable)

SUMNER TWP. (PORTIONS)—See MIDLAND, MI (Charter Communications)

SUMNER TWP. (PORTIONS)—See SEVILLE TWP., MI (Charter Communications)

SUMPTER TWP.—See DETROIT, MI (Comcast Cable)

SUNFIELD TWP.—See DIMONDALE, MI (WOW! Internet, Cable & Phone)

SUNFIELD—See DIMONDALE, MI (WOW! Internet, Cable & Phone)

SUPERIOR TWP. (WASHTENAW COUNTY)—See DETROIT, MI (Comcast Cable)

SURREY TWP.—See MIDLAND, MI (Charter Communications)

SUTTONS BAY TWP.—See TRAVERSE CITY, MI (Charter Communications)

SUTTONS BAY—See TRAVERSE CITY, MI (Charter Communications)

SWAN CREEK TWP.—See MIDLAND, MI (Charter Communications)

SWARTZ CREEK—See DETROIT, MI (Comcast Cable)

SWEETWATER TWP. (LAKE COUNTY)—See CUSTER, MI (Charter Communications)

SYLVAN LAKE—See DETROIT, MI (Comcast Cable)

SYLVAN TWP.—See DETROIT, MI (Comcast Cable)

TALLMADGE TWP.—See ALLENDALE TWP., MI (Charter Communications)

TALLMADGE TWP.—See DETROIT, MI (Comcast Cable)

TAWAS CITY—See MIDLAND, MI (Charter Communications)

TAWAS TWP.—See MIDLAND, MI (Charter Communications)

TAYLOR—See DETROIT, MI (Comcast Cable)

TAYLOR—See PLYMOUTH, MI (WOW! Internet, Cable & Phone)

TAYMOUTH TWP.—See MIDLAND, MI (Charter Communications)

TECUMSEH—See DETROIT, MI (Comcast Cable)

TECUMSEH—See PETERSBURG, MI (D & P Cable)

TEKONSHA—See COLDWATER, MI (Charter Communications)

TEXAS TWP.—See DETROIT, MI (Comcast Cable)

THE HOMESTEAD—See TRAVERSE CITY, MI (Charter Communications)

THETFORD TWP.—Charter Communications. Now served by GOODRICH, MI [MI0290]

THETFORD TWP.—See GOODRICH, MI (Charter Communications)

THOMAS TWP.—Charter Communications. Now served by MIDLAND, MI [MI0030]

THOMAS TWP.—See MIDLAND, MI (Charter Communications)

THOMPSON TWP.—See MARQUETTE, MI (Charter Communications)

THOMPSONVILLE—Ace Communications. This cable system has converted to IPTV. Now served by MESICK, MI [MI5074]

THOMPSONVILLE—See MESICK, MI (AcenTek (formerly Ace Communications). This system has converted to IPTV)

THORNAPPLE TWP.—See ALLENDALE TWP., MI (Charter Communications)

THREE OAKS—Comcast Cable. Now served by CHAMPAIGN, IL [IL0019]

THREE OAKS—Comcast Cable. Now served by CHAMPAIGN, IL [IL0019]

THREE RIVERS—Comcast Cable. Now served by DETROIT, MI [MI0001]

THREE RIVERS—See DETROIT, MI (Comcast Cable)

TILDEN TWP.—See MARQUETTE, MI (Charter Communications)

TITTABAWASSEE TWP.—See MIDLAND, MI (Charter Communications)

TOBACCO TWP.—See BILLINGS TWP., MI (Charter Communications)

TORCH LAKE TWP. (ANTRIM COUNTY)—See TRAVERSE CITY, MI (Charter Communications)

TORCH LAKE TWP. (HOUGHTON COUNTY)—See MARQUETTE, MI (Charter Communications)

TRAVERSE CITY—Charter Communications

TRENTON—See DETROIT, MI (Comcast Cable)

TRENTON—See PLYMOUTH, MI (WOW! Internet, Cable & Phone)

TROWBRIDGE TWP.—See ALLENDALE TWP., MI (Charter Communications)

TROY—See DETROIT, MI (Comcast Cable)

TROY—See PLYMOUTH, MI (WOW! Internet, Cable & Phone)

TURNER TWP.—See MIDLAND, MI (Charter Communications)

TURNER VILLAGE—See MIDLAND, MI (Charter Communications)

TUSCARORA TWP.—See TRAVERSE CITY, MI (Charter Communications)

TUSCOLA TWP.—See GOODRICH, MI (Charter Communications)

TUSTIN—See LE ROY, MI (Summit Digital)

TWINING—See MIDLAND, MI (Charter Communications)

TYRONE TWP. (KENT COUNTY)—See ALLENDALE TWP., MI (Charter Communications)

TYRONE TWP. (LIVINGSTON COUNTY)—See GOODRICH, MI (Charter Communications)

UBLY—Comcast Cable. Now served by DETROIT, MI [MI0001]

UBLY—See DETROIT, MI (Comcast Cable)

UNADILLA TWP.—See GOODRICH, MI (Charter Communications)

UNION CITY—WOW! Internet, Cable & Phone. Now served by DIMONDALE, MI [MI0136]

UNION CITY—See DIMONDALE, MI (WOW! Internet, Cable & Phone)

UNION TWP. (ISABELLA COUNTY)—See MIDLAND, MI (Charter Communications)

UNIONVILLE—Formerly served by Pine River Cable. No longer in operation

UTICA—See DETROIT, MI (Comcast Cable)

UTICA—See PLYMOUTH, MI (WOW! Internet, Cable & Phone)

VALLEY TWP.—See ALLENDALE TWP., MI (Charter Communications)

VAN BUREN COUNTY (PORTIONS)—See BLOOMINGDALE TWP. (Van Buren County), MI (Bloomingdale Communications)

VAN BUREN—See DETROIT, MI (Comcast Cable)

VANDALIA—See DETROIT, MI (Comcast Cable)

VANDERBILT—See TRAVERSE CITY, MI (Charter Communications)

VASSAR TWP.—See GOODRICH, MI (Charter Communications)

VASSAR—Charter Communications. Now served by GOODRICH, MI [MI0290]

VASSAR—See GOODRICH, MI (Charter Communications)

VENICE TWP.—See GOODRICH, MI (Charter Communications)

VENICE TWP.—See NEW LOTHROP, MI (TVC Cable)

VERGENNES TWP.—See DETROIT, MI (Comcast Cable)

VERMONTVILLE—Formerly served by WOW! Internet, Cable & Phone. No longer in operation

VERMONTVILLE—See NASHVILLE, MI (Martell Cable)

VERNON (VILLAGE)—See GOODRICH, MI (Charter Communications)

VERNON TWP. (SHIAWASSEE COUNTY)—See GOODRICH, MI (Charter Communications)

VERNON TWP.—See MIDLAND, MI (Charter Communications)

VERNON TWP.—See NEW LOTHROP, MI (TVC Cable)

VERONA TWP.—See DETROIT, MI (Comcast Cable)

VEVAY TWP.—See DIMONDALE, MI (WOW! Internet, Cable & Phone)

VICKSBURG—See DETROIT, MI (Comcast Cable)

VICTOR TWP.—See DIMONDALE, MI (WOW! Internet, Cable & Phone)

VIENNA TWP. (GENESEE COUNTY)—See DETROIT, MI (Comcast Cable)

VOLINIA TWP.—See DETROIT, MI (Comcast Cable)

WAKEFIELD—See IRONWOOD, MI (Charter Communications)

WALDRON—Comcast Cable. Now served by DETROIT, MI [MI0001]

WALDRON—See DETROIT, MI (Comcast Cable)

WALKER—See DETROIT, MI (Comcast Cable)

WALLACE—See STEPHENSON, MI (Packerland Broadband)

WALLED LAKE—See DETROIT, MI (Comcast Cable)

WALTON TWP.—See DIMONDALE, MI (WOW! Internet, Cable & Phone)

WARREN TWP.—See MIDLAND, MI (Charter Communications)

WARREN—See DETROIT, MI (Comcast Cable)

WARREN—See PLYMOUTH, MI (WOW! Internet, Cable & Phone)

WASHINGTON TWP. (MACOMB COUNTY)—See DETROIT, MI (Comcast Cable)

WATERFORD TWP.—See DETROIT, MI (Comcast Cable)

WATERLOO TWP.—See DIMONDALE, MI (WOW! Internet, Cable & Phone)

WATERSMEET—Charter Communications. Now served by IRONWOOD, MI [MI0064]

WATERSMEET—See IRONWOOD, MI (Charter Communications)

WATERTOWN TWP. (CLINTON COUNTY)—See DETROIT, MI (Comcast Cable)

WATERTOWN TWP. (CLINTON COUNTY)—See DIMONDALE, MI (WOW! Internet, Cable & Phone)

WATERTOWN TWP. (SANILAC COUNTY)—See DETROIT, MI (Comcast Cable)

WATERTOWN TWP. (TUSCOLA COUNTY)—See GOODRICH, MI (Charter Communications)

WATERVLIET—Comcast Cable. Now served by CHAMPAIGN, IL [IL0019]

WATSON TWP.—See ALLENDALE TWP., MI (Charter Communications)

WAUCEDAH TWP.—See MARQUETTE, MI (Charter Communications)

Cable Community Index—Minnesota

WAVERLY TWP. (VAN BUREN COUNTY)—See BLOOMINGDALE TWP. (Van Buren County), MI (Bloomingdale Communications)

WAVERLY TWP. (VAN BUREN COUNTY)—See DETROIT, MI (Comcast Cable)

WAWATAM TWP.—See TRAVERSE CITY, MI (Charter Communications)

WAYLAND—See ALLENDALE TWP., MI (Charter Communications)

WAYNE—Comcast Cable. Now served by CHAMPAIGN, IL [IL0019]

WAYNE—See DETROIT, MI (Comcast Cable)

WAYNE—See PLYMOUTH, MI (WOW! Internet, Cable & Phone)

WEARE TWP.—See ALLENDALE TWP., MI (Charter Communications)

WEBBERVILLE—See DIMONDALE, MI (WOW! Internet, Cable & Phone)

WEBSTER TWP.—See GOODRICH, MI (Charter Communications)

WELDON—See MESICK, MI (AcenTek (formerly Ace Communications). This system has converted to IPTV)

WELLS TWP.—See MARQUETTE, MI (Charter Communications)

WELLSTON—Formerly served by Pine River Cable. No longer in operation

WEST BLOOMFIELD TWP.—Comcast Cable. Now served by DETROIT, MI [MI0001]

WEST BLOOMFIELD TWP.—See DETROIT, MI (Comcast Cable)

WEST BRANCH—Charter Communications. Now served by RICHFIELD TWP. (Roscommon County), MI [MI0116]

WEST BRANCH—See RICHFIELD TWP. (Roscommon County), MI (Charter Communications)

WEST TRAVERSE TWP.—See TRAVERSE CITY, MI (Charter Communications)

WESTLAND—Comcast Cable. Now served by DETROIT, MI [MI0001]

WESTLAND—See DETROIT, MI (Comcast Cable)

WESTLAND—See PLYMOUTH, MI (WOW! Internet, Cable & Phone)

WESTPHALIA—See DIMONDALE, MI (WOW! Internet, Cable & Phone)

WETMORE—See MARQUETTE, MI (Charter Communications)

WEXFORD TWP.—See MESICK, MI (AcenTek (formerly Ace Communications). This system has converted to IPTV)

WHEATFIELD TWP.—See DIMONDALE, MI (WOW! Internet, Cable & Phone)

WHEATFIELD—See DETROIT, MI (Comcast Cable)

WHEATLAND TWP. (MECOSTA COUNTY)—See REMUS, MI (MIcom)

WHEELER TWP.—See MIDLAND, MI (Charter Communications)

WHITE CLOUD—MIcom. Now served by BALDWIN (village), MI [MI0214]

WHITE CLOUD—See BALDWIN (village), MI (MIcom)

WHITE LAKE TWP.—See DETROIT, MI (Comcast Cable)

WHITE PIGEON (VILLAGE)—See DETROIT, MI (Comcast Cable)

WHITE PIGEON TWP. (EASTERN PORTION)—See COLDWATER, MI (Charter Communications)

WHITE PIGEON—See DETROIT, MI (Comcast Cable)

WHITE RIVER TWP.—See ALLENDALE TWP., MI (Charter Communications)

WHITEHALL—Charter Communications. Now served by ALLENDALE TWP., MI [MI0094]

WHITEHALL—See ALLENDALE TWP., MI (Charter Communications)

WHITEWATER TWP.—See TRAVERSE CITY, MI (Charter Communications)

WHITNEY TWP.—See MIDLAND, MI (Charter Communications)

WHITTEMORE—Charter Communications. Now served by MIDLAND, MI [MI0030]

WHITTEMORE—See MIDLAND, MI (Charter Communications)

WILBER TWP.—See MIDLAND, MI (Charter Communications)

WILCOX TWP.—See BALDWIN (village), MI (MIcom)

WILDWOOD—See DETROIT, MI (Comcast Cable)

WILLIAMS TWP. (EASTERN PORTION)—See MIDLAND, MI (Charter Communications)

WILLIAMS TWP. (WESTERN PORTION)—See MIDLAND, MI (Charter Communications)

WILLIAMSTON—See DIMONDALE, MI (WOW! Internet, Cable & Phone)

WILLIAMSTOWN TWP.—See DIMONDALE, MI (WOW! Internet, Cable & Phone)

WILSON TWP. (ALPENA COUNTY)—See ALPENA, MI (Charter Communications)

WILSON TWP. (CHARLEVOIX COUNTY)—See TRAVERSE CITY, MI (Charter Communications)

WINDSOR CHARTER TWP.—See DETROIT, MI (Comcast Cable)

WINDSOR TWP.—See DIMONDALE, MI (WOW! Internet, Cable & Phone)

WINFIELD TWP.—See ALLENDALE TWP., MI (Charter Communications)

WINSOR TWP.—See DETROIT, MI (Comcast Cable)

WISE TWP.—See MIDLAND, MI (Charter Communications)

WISNER (village)—Formerly served by Northwoods Cable Inc. No longer in operation

WIXOM—See DETROIT, MI (Comcast Cable)

WOLF LAKE—Summit Digital. Now served by LE ROY, MI [MI0198]

WOLF LAKE—See LE ROY, MI (Summit Digital)

WOLVERINE (village)—Formerly served by Upper Peninsula Communications. No longer in operation

WOLVERINE LAKE (VILLAGE)—See DETROIT, MI (Comcast Cable)

WOODHAVEN—Comcast Cable. Now served by DETROIT, MI [MI0001]

WOODHAVEN—See DETROIT, MI (Comcast Cable)

WOODHAVEN—See PLYMOUTH, MI (WOW! Internet, Cable & Phone)

WOODHULL TWP.—See DIMONDALE, MI (WOW! Internet, Cable & Phone)

WOODLAND (village)—Formerly served by Pine River Cable. No longer in operation

WOODLAND TWP.—See DIMONDALE, MI (WOW! Internet, Cable & Phone)

WOODSTOCK TWP.—See DETROIT, MI (Comcast Cable)

WORTH TWP.—See DETROIT, MI (Comcast Cable)

WRIGHT TWP. (HILLSDALE COUNTY)—See DETROIT, MI (Comcast Cable)

WRIGHT TWP. (OTTAWA COUNTY)—See DETROIT, MI (Comcast Cable)

WRIGHT TWP. (PORTIONS)—See ALLENDALE TWP., MI (Charter Communications)

WYANDOTTE—Wyandotte Municipal Services

WYOMING—See DETROIT, MI (Comcast Cable)

YALE—Comcast Cable. Now served by DETROIT, MI [MI0001]

YALE—See DETROIT, MI (Comcast Cable)

YANKEE SPRINGS TWP.—See ALLENDALE TWP., MI (Charter Communications)

YORK TWP.—Comcast Cable. Now served by DETROIT, MI [MI0001]

YORK TWP.—See DETROIT, MI (Comcast Cable)

YPSILANTI TWP.—See DETROIT, MI (Comcast Cable)

YPSILANTI—See DETROIT, MI (Comcast Cable)

ZEELAND CHARTER TWP.—See MESICK, MI (AcenTek (formerly Ace Communications). This system has converted to IPTV)

ZEELAND TWP.—See ALLENDALE TWP., MI (Charter Communications)

ZILWAUKEE—See MIDLAND, MI (Charter Communications)

MINNESOTA

ADA—See PELICAN RAPIDS, MN (Arvig)

ADAMS—Mediacom. Now served by CHATFIELD, MN [MN0111]

ADAMS—See CHATFIELD, MN (Mediacom)

ADRIAN—Clarity Telcom

AFTON—See MINNEAPOLIS, MN (Comcast Cable)

AITKIN—Charter Communications. Now served by BRAINERD, MN [MN0022]

AITKIN—See BRAINERD, MN (Charter Communications)

AKELEY TWP.—See PERHAM, MN (Arvig)

AKELEY—See PERHAM, MN (Arvig)

ALASKA TWP.—See SOLWAY, MN (Paul Bunyan Communications)

ALBANY—Charter Communications. Now served by ST. CLOUD, MN [MN0011]

ALBANY—See ST. CLOUD, MN (Charter Communications)

ALBERT LEA—Charter Communications. Now served by AUSTIN, MN [MN0019]

ALBERT LEA—See AUSTIN, MN (Charter Communications)

ALBERT LEA—See OWATONNA, MN (Jaguar Communications)

ALBERTVILLE—See BUFFALO, MN (Charter Communications)

ALDEN—See WASECA COUNTY (portions), MN (Midco)

ALEXANDRIA TWP.—See ALEXANDRIA, MN (Charter Communications)

ALEXANDRIA—Formerly served by Viking Vision. No longer in operation

ALEXANDRIA—Charter Communications

ALTURA—Formerly served by Midcontinent Communications. Now served by Charter Communications, EAU CLAIRE, WI [WI0011]

ALVARADO—Wikstrom Cable LLC

ALVWOOD TWP.—See MORSE TWP., MN (Paul Bunyan Communications)

AMOR TWP.—See PERHAM, MN (Arvig)

ANDOVER—See MINNEAPOLIS, MN (Comcast Cable)

Minnesota—Cable Community Index

ANNANDALE—Formerly served by Heart of the Lakes Cable System Inc. No longer in operation

ANOKA—See MINNEAPOLIS, MN (Comcast Cable)

APPLE VALLEY—See ROSEMOUNT, MN (Charter Communications)

APPLETON—Mediacom

ARBO TWP.—See MORSE TWP., MN (Paul Bunyan Communications)

ARDEN HILLS—See MINNEAPOLIS, MN (Comcast Cable)

ARDENHURST TWP.—See MORSE TWP., MN (Paul Bunyan Communications)

ARGYLE—Wikstrom Cable LLC

ARLINGTON—See FRANKLIN, MN (Mediacom)

ASHBY—See DALTON, MN (Otter Tail Telcom)

ASKOV—See SANDSTONE, MN (SCI Broadband)

ATLANTA TWP.—See PERHAM, MN (Arvig)

ATWATER—See PAYNESVILLE, MN (Mediacom)

AUDUBON TWP.—See PERHAM, MN (Arvig)

AUDUBON—See PERHAM, MN (Arvig)

AURDAL TWP.—See FERGUS FALLS, MN (Charter Communications)

AURDAL TWP.—See DALTON, MN (Otter Tail Telcom)

AURORA—See EVELETH, MN (Mediacom)

AUSTIN—Charter Communications

AUSTIN—See OWATONNA, MN (Jaguar Communications)

AVON TWP.—See CAMBRIDGE, MN (Midco)

AVON—Formerly served by US Cable of Coastal Texas LP. Now served by Midco, CAMBRIDGE, MN [MN0016]

AVON—See CAMBRIDGE, MN (Midco)

BABBITT—Midcontinent Communications. Now served by ELY, MN [MN0060]

BABBITT—See ELY, MN (Midco)

BACKUS—See BRAINERD, MN (Charter Communications)

BADGER TWP. (PORTIONS)—See McINTOSH, MN (Garden Valley Telephone Co)

BADGER TWP. (PORTIONS)—See McINTOSH, MN (Garden Valley Telephone Co)

BADGER—Sjoberg's Cable TV Inc

BADOURA TWP.—See PERHAM, MN (Arvig)

BAGLEY—Bagley Public Utilities

BAGLEY—See McINTOSH, MN (Garden Valley Telephone Co)

BALATON—Midco

BALDWIN TWP.—See CAMBRIDGE, MN (Midco)

BALL CLUB—See MORSE TWP., MN (Paul Bunyan Communications)

BARCLAY TWP.—See BRAINERD, MN (Charter Communications)

BARNESVILLE—Formerly served by Sprint Corp. No longer in operation

BARNESVILLE—Barnesville Cable TV

BARNUM—SCI Broadband

BARRETT—Runestone Cable TV

BASS BROOK TWP.—See GRAND RAPIDS, MN (Mediacom)

BATTLE LAKE—See PERHAM, MN (Arvig)

BATTLE TWP.—See SOLWAY, MN (Paul Bunyan Communications)

BAUDETTE—Sjoberg's Cable TV Inc

BAXTER—See BRAINERD, MN (Charter Communications)

BAXTER—See RANDALL, MN (Consolidated Telecommunications Co. Formerly [MN0202]. This cable system has converted to IPTV)

BAY CITY—See PINE ISLAND, WI (BEVCOMM. Formerly [MN0089]. This cable system has converted to IPTV)

BAY LAKE—See BRAINERD, MN (Charter Communications)

BAYPORT—See MINNEAPOLIS, MN (Comcast Cable)

BAYTOWN TWP.—See MINNEAPOLIS, MN (Comcast Cable)

BEAR CREEK—See McINTOSH, MN (Garden Valley Telephone Co)

BEAR PARK TWP.—See McINTOSH, MN (Garden Valley Telephone Co)

BEAVER BAY—See CLOQUET, MN (Mediacom)

BECIDA—See SOLWAY, MN (Paul Bunyan Communications)

BECKER—See CAMBRIDGE, MN (Midco)

BEJOU TWP.—See McINTOSH, MN (Garden Valley Telephone Co)

BELGRADE TWP.—See MANKATO, MN (Charter Communications)

BELGRADE—Mediacom. Now served by MORRIS, MN [MN0210]

BELGRADE—See MORRIS, MN (Mediacom)

BELLE PLAINE—Mediacom. Now served by ST. PETER (formerly Waseca), MN [MN0043]

BELLE PLAINE—See ST. PETER, MN (Mediacom)

BELLE PRAIRIE TWP.—See ST. CLOUD, MN (Charter Communications)

BELLECHESTER—See GOODHUE, MN (NU-Telecom. Formerly [MN0208]. This cable system has converted to IPTV)

BELTRAMI COUNTY (PORTIONS)—See BEMIDJI, MN (Midco)

BELTRAMI—See McINTOSH, MN (Garden Valley Telephone Co)

BELVIEW—Clara City Telephone Co

BEMIDJI TWP.—See SOLWAY, MN (Paul Bunyan Communications)

BEMIDJI—Midco

BEMIDJI—See SOLWAY, MN (Paul Bunyan Communications)

BENSON—Charter Communications. Now served by WILLMAR, MN [MN0018]

BENSON—See WILLMAR, MN (Charter Communications)

BENVILLE TWP.—See McINTOSH, MN (Garden Valley Telephone Co)

BERTHA TWP.—See PERHAM, MN (Arvig)

BETHEL—See CAMBRIDGE, MN (Midco)

BEULAH TWP.—See EMILY, MN (Emily Cooperative Telephone. Formerly [MS0081]. This cable system has converted to IPTV)

BIG FALLS—Formerly served by Arvig. No longer in operation

BIG LAKE—See BUFFALO, MN (Charter Communications)

BIGELOW—Formerly served by American Telecasting of America Inc. No longer in operation

BIGFORK—Arvig

BIRCH TWP.—See SOLWAY, MN (Paul Bunyan Communications)

BIRCHDALE TWP.—See MELROSE, MN (Arvig)

BIRCHWOOD VILLAGE—See MINNEAPOLIS, MN (Comcast Cable)

BIRD ISLAND—See FRANKLIN, MN (Mediacom)

BIWABIK—See EVELETH, MN (Mediacom)

BLACK RIVER TWP.—See McINTOSH, MN (Garden Valley Telephone Co)

BLACKDUCK—Paul Bunyan Communications. This cable system has converted to IPTV. Now served by SOLWAY, MN [MN5083]

BLACKDUCK—See SOLWAY, MN (Paul Bunyan Communications)

BLAINE—See MINNEAPOLIS, MN (Comcast Cable)

BLOOMFIELD TWP.—See CALEDONIA, MN (Mediacom)

BLOOMING PRAIRIE—Mediacom. Now served by CANNON FALLS, MN [MN0076]

BLOOMING PRAIRIE—See OWATONNA, MN (Jaguar Communications)

BLOOMING PRAIRIE—See CANNON FALLS, MN (Mediacom)

BLOOMINGTON—Formerly served by Time Warner Cable. Now served by Comcast Cable, MINNEAPOLIS, MN [MN0001]

BLOOMINGTON—See MINNEAPOLIS, MN (Comcast Cable)

BLUE EARTH—BEVCOMM

BLUE HILL TWP.—See CAMBRIDGE, MN (Midco)

BLUEBERRY TWP.—See MENAHGA, MN (West Central Telephone Assn. This cable system has converted to IPTV)

BLUFFTON TWP.—See PERHAM, MN (Arvig)

BLUFFTON—See PERHAM, MN (Arvig)

BORUP—See PELICAN RAPIDS, MN (Arvig)

BOVEY—SCI Broadband

BOY LAKE TWP.—See PERHAM, MN (Arvig)

BOYD—FMTC/Acira

BRADFORD TWP.—See CAMBRIDGE, MN (Midco)

BRAHAM—See CAMBRIDGE, MN (Midco)

BRAINERD—Charter Communications

BRAINERD—See RANDALL, MN (Consolidated Telecommunications Co. Formerly [MN0202]. This cable system has converted to IPTV)

BRANDSVOLD TWP.—See McINTOSH, MN (Garden Valley Telephone Co)

BRANSVOLD TWP. (PORTIONS)—See McINTOSH, MN (Garden Valley Telephone Co)

BRAY TWP.—See McINTOSH, MN (Garden Valley Telephone Co)

BREEZY POINT—See BRAINERD, MN (Charter Communications)

BREITUNG TWP.—See ELY, MN (Midco)

BREWSTER—Midco

BRICELYN—See NEW PRAGUE, MN (BEVCOMM. Formerly [MN0337]. This cable system has converted to IPTV)

BRISTOL TWP.—See HOUSTON, MN (AcenTek)

BROOKLYN CENTER—Comcast Cable. Now served by MINNEAPOLIS, MI [MN0001]

BROOKLYN CENTER—See MINNEAPOLIS, MN (Comcast Cable)

BROOKLYN PARK—Comcast Cable. Now served by MINNEAPOLIS, MN [MN0001]

Cable Community Index—Minnesota

BROOKLYN PARK—See MINNEAPOLIS, MN (Comcast Cable)

BROOKS—See McINTOSH, MN (Garden Valley Telephone Co)

BROOTEN—Mediacom. Now served by MORRIS, MN [MN0210]

BROOTEN—See MORRIS, MN (Mediacom)

BROWERVILLE—Charter Communications. Now served by BRAINERD, MN [MN0022]

BROWERVILLE—See BRAINERD, MN (Charter Communications)

BROWNS CREEK TWP.—See McINTOSH, MN (Garden Valley Telephone Co)

BROWNS VALLEY—Formerly served by Midcontinent Communications. No longer in operation

BROWNSDALE—See CANNON FALLS, MN (Mediacom)

BROWNSVILLE—Mediacom. Now served by CALEDONIA, MN [MN0086]

BROWNSVILLE—See HOUSTON, MN (AcenTek)

BROWNSVILLE—See CALEDONIA, MN (Mediacom)

BROWNTON—See HUTCHINSON, MN (Mediacom)

BUFFALO CITY—See WINONA, WI (Hiawatha Broadband. Formerly Winona, MN [MN0398]. This cable system has converted to IPTV)

BUFFALO LAKE—See HUTCHINSON, MN (Mediacom)

BUFFALO—Charter Communications

BUHL—See EVELETH, MN (Mediacom)

BURLINGTON TWP.—See PERHAM, MN (Arvig)

BURNHAMVILLE TWP.—See MELROSE, MN (Arvig)

BURNSVILLE—See MINNEAPOLIS, MN (Comcast Cable)

BURTRUM—See MELROSE, MN (Arvig)

BUSE TWP.—See FERGUS FALLS, MN (Charter Communications)

BUTLER TWP.—See PERHAM, MN (Arvig)

BUTTERFIELD—See ST. PETER, MN (Mediacom)

BUZZLE TWP.—See McINTOSH, MN (Garden Valley Telephone Co)

BUZZLE TWP.—See SOLWAY, MN (Paul Bunyan Communications)

BYRON—See ROCHESTER, MN (Charter Communications)

CALEDONIA—See HOUSTON, MN (AcenTek)

CALEDONIA—Mediacom

CALLAWAY—See PERHAM, MN (Arvig)

CALUMET—Mediacom

CAMBRIDGE TWP.—See CAMBRIDGE, MN (Midco)

CAMBRIDGE—Midco

CANBY—Midco

CANDOR TWP.—See PERHAM, MN (Arvig)

CANNON FALLS TWP.—Midco

CANNON FALLS—Mediacom

CANTERBURY ESTATES—See PRIOR LAKE, MN (Mediacom)

CANTON—Mediacom. Now served by CALEDONIA, MN [MN0086]

CANTON—See HOUSTON, MN (AcenTek)

CANTON—See CALEDONIA, MN (Mediacom)

CARLOS—Arvig. Now served by PARKERS PRAIRIE, MN [MN0346]

CARLOS—See PARKERS PRAIRIE, MN (Arvig)

CARLOS—See ALEXANDRIA, MN (Charter Communications)

CARLTON—See CLOQUET, MN (Mediacom)

CARVER—See MINNEAPOLIS, MN (Comcast Cable)

CASCADE TWP.—See ROCHESTER, MN (Charter Communications)

CASS LAKE—See BEMIDJI, MN (Midco)

CASS LAKE—See SOLWAY, MN (Paul Bunyan Communications)

CASTALIA—See HOUSTON, IA (AcenTek)

CATO—See MINNEAPOLIS, WI (Comcast Cable)

CEDAR LAKE TWP.—See PRIOR LAKE, MN (Integra Telecom)

CENTER CITY—See CAMBRIDGE, MN (Midco)

CENTER TWP.—See BRAINERD, MN (Charter Communications)

CENTERVILLE—See MINNEAPOLIS, MN (Comcast Cable)

CEYLON—Midco

CHAMPLIN—See MINNEAPOLIS, MN (Comcast Cable)

CHANHASSEN—See MOUND, MN (Mediacom)

CHASKA—Formerly served by Time Warner Cable. Now served by Comcast Cable, MINNEAPOLIS, MN [MN0001]

CHASKA—See MINNEAPOLIS, MN (Comcast Cable)

CHATFIELD—Mediacom

CHATHAM TWP.—See BUFFALO, MN (Charter Communications)

CHESTER TWP.—See McINTOSH, MN (Garden Valley Telephone Co)

CHISAGO CITY—Midcontinent Communications. Now served by CAMBRIDGE, MN [MN0016]

CHISAGO CITY—See CAMBRIDGE, MN (Midco)

CHISHOLM—See EVELETH, MN (Mediacom)

CHOKIO—See MORRIS, MN (Mediacom)

CIRCLE PINES—See MINNEAPOLIS, MN (Comcast Cable)

CLARA CITY—See PAYNESVILLE, MN (Mediacom)

CLAREMONT—See OWATONNA, MN (Jaguar Communications)

CLAREMONT—See WASECA COUNTY (portions), MN (Midco)

CLARISSA—See BRAINERD, MN (Charter Communications)

CLARKFIELD—See WOOD LAKE, MN (Midco)

CLARKS GROVE—See OWATONNA, MN (Jaguar Communications)

CLARKS GROVE—See WASECA COUNTY (portions), MN (Midco)

CLAY TWP.—See PERHAM, MN (Arvig)

CLEAR LAKE TWP.—See CAMBRIDGE, MN (Midco)

CLEAR LAKE—See CAMBRIDGE, MN (Midco)

CLEARBROOK—Garden Valley Telephone Co. Now served by McINTOSH, MN [MN0105]

CLEARBROOK—See McINTOSH, MN (Garden Valley Telephone Co)

CLEARBROOK—See McINTOSH, MN (Garden Valley Telephone Co)

CLEARWATER—See CAMBRIDGE, MN (Midco)

CLEMENTS—Clara City Telephone Co

CLERMONT—See HOUSTON, IA (AcenTek)

CLEVELAND—See ST. PETER, MN (Mediacom)

CLINTON—Mediacom. Now served by APPLETON, MN [MN0106]

CLINTON—See APPLETON, MN (Mediacom)

CLITHERALL TWP.—See PERHAM, MN (Arvig)

CLITHERALL—See PERHAM, MN (Arvig)

CLOQUET—Mediacom

CLOVER TWP.—See McINTOSH, MN (Garden Valley Telephone Co)

CLOVERLEAF TWP.—See McINTOSH, MN (Garden Valley Telephone Co)

COATES—See CANNON FALLS TWP., MN (Midco)

COCHRANE—See WINONA, WI (Hiawatha Broadband. Formerly Winona, MN [MN0398]. This cable system has converted to IPTV)

COHASSET—See MORSE TWP., MN (Paul Bunyan Communications)

COKATO—See BUFFALO, MN (Charter Communications)

COLD SPRING—See CAMBRIDGE, MN (Midco)

COLERAINE—Formerly served by North American Communications Corp. Now served by SCI Broadband, BOVEY, MN [MN0112]

COLERAINE—See BOVEY, MN (SCI Broadband)

COLLINWOOD TWP.—See HUTCHINSON, MN (Mediacom)

COLOGNE—NU-Telecom

COLUMBIA HEIGHTS—See MINNEAPOLIS, MN (Comcast Cable)

COLUMBIA TWP.—See McINTOSH, MN (Garden Valley Telephone Co)

COLUMBUS TWP.—See CAMBRIDGE, MN (Midco)

COMFREY—Clara City Telephone Co

CONCORD—Formerly served by Mediacom. No longer in operation

COOK—Mediacom

COON RAPIDS—See MINNEAPOLIS, MN (Comcast Cable)

COPLEY TWP.—See McINTOSH, MN (Garden Valley Telephone Co)

CORCORAN—See MINNEAPOLIS, MN (Comcast Cable)

CORLISS TWP.—See PERHAM, MN (Arvig)

CORMANT TWP.—See SOLWAY, MN (Paul Bunyan Communications)

CORMORANT TWP.—See PELICAN RAPIDS, MN (Arvig)

COSMOS—Mediacom. Now served by PAYNESVILLE, MN [MN0125]

COSMOS—See PAYNESVILLE, MN (Mediacom)

COTTAGE GROVE—See MINNEAPOLIS, MN (Comcast Cable)

COTTONWOOD—Charter Communications. Now served by WILLMAR, MN [MN0018]

COTTONWOOD—See WILLMAR, MN (Charter Communications)

COURTLAND—See NEW ULM, MN (NU-Telecom. Formerly [MN0285]. This cable system has converted to IPTV)

CREDIT RIVER TWP.—See PRIOR LAKE, MN (Mediacom)

CREDIT RIVER—See PRIOR LAKE, MN (Integra Telecom)

CROOKED LAKE TWP.—See EMILY, MN (Emily Cooperative Telephone. For-

Minnesota—Cable Community Index

merly [MS0081]. This cable system has converted to IPTV)

CROOKSTON—Midco. Now served by GRAND FORKS, ND [ND0003]

CROSBY—See BRAINERD, MN (Charter Communications)

CROSBY—See RANDALL, MN (Consolidated Telecommunications Co. Formerly [MN0202]. This cable system has converted to IPTV)

CROSSLAKE—Crosslake Communications

CROW WING COUNTY (NORTHERN PORTION)—See BRAINERD, MN (Charter Communications)

CROW WING COUNTY (UNINCORPORATED AREAS)—See BRAINERD, MN (Charter Communications)

CRYSTAL—See MINNEAPOLIS, MN (Comcast Cable)

CURRIE—See MARSHALL, MN (Clarity Telcom)

CUYUNA—See BRAINERD, MN (Charter Communications)

CYRUS—See BARRETT, MN (Runestone Cable TV)

DAKOTA—Mediacom. Now served by CALEDONIA, MN [MN0086]

DAKOTA—See HOUSTON, MN (AcenTek)

DAKOTA—See CALEDONIA, MN (Mediacom)

DALTON—Otter Tail Telcom

DANE PRAIRIE TWP.—See FERGUS FALLS, MN (Charter Communications)

DANUBE—See FRANKLIN, MN (Mediacom)

DARWIN—See HUTCHINSON, MN (Mediacom)

DASSEL TWP.—See HUTCHINSON, MN (Mediacom)

DASSEL—See BUFFALO, MN (Charter Communications)

DAWSON—Mediacom. Now served by APPLETON, MN [MN0106]

DAWSON—See APPLETON, MN (Mediacom)

DAYTON—See BUFFALO, MN (Charter Communications)

DEAD LAKE TWP.—See PERHAM, MN (Arvig)

DECORIA TWP.—See MANKATO, MN (Charter Communications)

DEEPHAVEN—See MOUND, MN (Mediacom)

DEER CREEK—See PERHAM, MN (Arvig)

DEER PARK TWP.—See McINTOSH, MN (Garden Valley Telephone Co)

DEER RIVER TWP.—See MORSE TWP., MN (Paul Bunyan Communications)

DEER RIVER—Paul Bunyan Communications. This cable system has converted to IPTV. Now served by MORSE TWP., MN [MN5068]

DEER RIVER—See MORSE TWP., MN (Paul Bunyan Communications)

DEERWOOD TWP.—See KARLSTAD, MN (Sjoberg's Cable TV Inc)

DEERWOOD—See BRAINERD, MN (Charter Communications)

DELANO—See BUFFALO, MN (Charter Communications)

DELAVAN—BEVCOMM. This cable system has converted to IPTV. Now served by NEW PRAGUE, MN [MN5366]

DELAVAN—See NEW PRAGUE, MN (BEVCOMM. Formerly [MN0337]. This cable system has converted to IPTV)

DELLWOOD—See MINNEAPOLIS, MN (Comcast Cable)

DENMARK TWP.—See MINNEAPOLIS, MN (Comcast Cable)

DENT—See PERHAM, MN (Arvig)

DETROIT LAKES—See PERHAM, MN (Arvig)

DETROIT TWP.—See PERHAM, MN (Arvig)

DEXTER—Formerly served by North American Communications Corp. This cable system has converted to IPTV. Now served by Jaguar Communications, OWATONNA, MN [MN5121]

DEXTER—See OWATONNA, MN (Jaguar Communications)

DILWORTH—Formerly served by Loretel Cablevision. Now served by Cable One, FARGO, ND [ND0001]

DODGE CENTER—Mediacom. Now served by CANNON FALLS, MN [MN0076]

DODGE CENTER—See CANNON FALLS, MN (Mediacom)

DONNELLY—See BARRETT, MN (Runestone Cable TV)

DORA TWP.—See PERHAM, MN (Arvig)

DORCHESTER—See HOUSTON, IA (AcenTek)

DOVER TWP.—See CHATFIELD, MN (Mediacom)

DOVER—See WINONA, MN (Hiawatha Broadband. Formerly Winona, MN [MN0398]. This cable system has converted to IPTV)

DOVER—See CHATFIELD, MN (Mediacom)

DRESBACH—See CALEDONIA, MN (Mediacom)

DUDLEY TWP.—See McINTOSH, MN (Garden Valley Telephone Co)

DULUTH (UNINCORPORATED AREAS)—See SAGINAW, MN (SCI Broadband)

DULUTH—Charter Communications

DUNDAS—See ROSEMOUNT, MN (Charter Communications)

DUNDAS—See NEW MARKET, MN (Jaguar Communications)

DUNDEE (village)—Formerly served by American Telecasting of America Inc. No longer in operation

DUNN TWP.—See PELICAN RAPIDS, MN (Arvig)

DUNNELL—Midco

DURAND TWP.—See SOLWAY, MN (Paul Bunyan Communications)

EAGAN—Comcast Cable. Now served by MINNEAPOLIS, MN [MN0001]

EAGAN—See MINNEAPOLIS, MN (Comcast Cable)

EAGLE LAKE—See MANKATO, MN (Charter Communications)

EAST BETHEL—See CAMBRIDGE, MN (Midco)

EAST GULL LAKE—SCI Broadband. Now served by PILLAGER, MN [MN0230]

EAST GULL LAKE—See PILLAGER, MN (SCI Broadband)

EAST SIDE TWP.—See ISLE, MN (SCI Broadband)

EASTON—BEVCOMM. This cable system has converted to IPTV. Now served by NEW PRAGUE, MN [MN5366]

EASTON—See NEW PRAGUE, MN (BEVCOMM. Formerly [MN0337]. This cable system has converted to IPTV)

ECHO—Clara City Telephone Co

ECKLES TWP.—See SOLWAY, MN (Paul Bunyan Communications)

ECKLES—See BEMIDJI, MN (Midco)

ECKVOLD TWP.—See McINTOSH, MN (Garden Valley Telephone Co)

EDDY TWP.—See McINTOSH, MN (Garden Valley Telephone Co)

EDEN LAKE TWP.—See MELROSE, MN (Arvig)

EDEN PRAIRIE—See MINNEAPOLIS, MN (Comcast Cable)

EDEN TWP.—See McINTOSH, MN (Garden Valley Telephone Co)

EDEN VALLEY—See MELROSE, MN (Arvig)

EDGERTON—See ADRIAN, MN (Clarity Telcom)

EDINA—See MINNEAPOLIS, MN (Comcast Cable)

EDNA TWP.—See PERHAM, MN (Arvig)

EITZEN—Ace Communications. Formerly [MN0294]. This cable system has converted to IPTV. Now served by HOUSTON, MN [MN5105]

EITZEN—Ace Communications. Formerly [MN0294]. This cable system has converted to IPTV. Now served by HOUSTON, MN [MN5105]

EITZEN—See HOUSTON, MN (AcenTek)

ELBOW LAKE—Runestone Cable TV. Now served by BARRETT, MN [MN0233]

ELBOW LAKE—See BARRETT, MN (Runestone Cable TV)

ELGIN TWP.—See CAMBRIDGE, MN (Midco)

ELGIN—See WINONA, MN (Hiawatha Broadband. Formerly Winona, MN [MN0398]. This cable system has converted to IPTV)

ELGIN—See CAMBRIDGE, MN (Midco)

ELIZABETH TWP.—See DALTON, MN (Otter Tail Telcom)

ELK RIVER—See BUFFALO, MN (Charter Communications)

ELKO NEW MARKET—See PRIOR LAKE, MN (Integra Telecom)

ELKO—Mediacom. Now served by PRIOR LAKE, MN [MN0039]

ELKO—See PRIOR LAKE, MN (Mediacom)

ELLENDALE—See OWATONNA, MN (Jaguar Communications)

ELLENDALE—See WASECA COUNTY (portions), MN (Midco)

ELLSWORTH TWP.—See HUTCHINSON, MN (Mediacom)

ELLSWORTH—Clarity Telcom. Now served by ADRIAN, MN [MN0158]

ELLSWORTH—See ADRIAN, MN (Clarity Telcom)

ELMORE—See BLUE EARTH, MN (BEVCOMM)

ELY—Midco

ELYSIAN—See WASECA COUNTY (portions), MN (Midco)

EMARDVILLE TWP.—See McINTOSH, MN (Garden Valley Telephone Co)

EMILY—Emily Cooperative Telephone. This cable system has converted to IPTV. See EMILY, MN [MN5256]

EMILY—Emily Cooperative Telephone. Formerly [MS0081]. This cable system has converted to IPTV

EMMONS—Formerly served by Heck's TV & Cable. No longer in operation

EMPIRE TWP.—See ROSEMOUNT, MN (Charter Communications)

ENSTROM TWP.—See WARROAD, MN (Sjoberg's Cable TV Inc)

EQUALITY TWP.—See McINTOSH, MN (Garden Valley Telephone Co)

ERDAHL—See BARRETT, MN (Runestone Cable TV)

Cable Community Index—Minnesota

ERHARD—See DALTON, MN (Otter Tail Telcom)

ERIE TWP.—See PERHAM, MN (Arvig)

ERSKINE (VILLAGE)—See McINTOSH, MN (Garden Valley Telephone Co)

ERSKINE (VILLAGE)—See McINTOSH, MN (Garden Valley Telephone Co)

ERSKINE—See McINTOSH, MN (Garden Valley Telephone Co)

ERSKINE—See McINTOSH, MN (Garden Valley Telephone Co)

ESKO—See CLOQUET, MN (Mediacom)

ESPELIE TWP.—See McINTOSH, MN (Garden Valley Telephone Co)

ESSIG—See NEW ULM, MN (NU-Telecom. Formerly [MN0285]. This cable system has converted to IPTV)

EVELETH—Mediacom

EVERTS TWP.—See PERHAM, MN (Arvig)

EXCELSIOR—See MOUND, MN (Mediacom)

EYOTA—See ROCHESTER, MN (Charter Communications)

EYOTA—See WINONA, MN (Hiawatha Broadband. Formerly Winona, MN [MN0398]. This cable system has converted to IPTV)

FAIRFAX—See FRANKLIN, MN (Mediacom)

FAIRFIELD TWP.—See EMILY, MN (Emily Cooperative Telephone. Formerly [MS0081]. This cable system has converted to IPTV)

FAIRHAVEN TWP.—See MELROSE, MN (Arvig)

FAIRMONT—Midco

FALCON HEIGHTS—See MINNEAPOLIS, MN (Comcast Cable)

FALK TWP.—See McINTOSH, MN (Garden Valley Telephone Co)

FARDEN TWP.—See PERHAM, MN (Arvig)

FARDEN TWP.—See SOLWAY, MN (Paul Bunyan Communications)

FARIBAULT—Charter Communications. Now served by OWATONNA, MN [MN0023]

FARIBAULT—See OWATONNA, MN (Charter Communications)

FARIBAULT—See NEW MARKET, MN (Jaguar Communications)

FARMING TWP.—See MELROSE, MN (Arvig)

FARMINGTON—See ROSEMOUNT, MN (Charter Communications)

FAYAL TWP.—See EVELETH, MN (Mediacom)

FERGUS FALLS TWP.—See FERGUS FALLS, MN (Charter Communications)

FERGUS FALLS—Charter Communications

FERGUS FALLS—See DALTON, MN (Otter Tail Telcom)

FERN TWP.—See SOLWAY, MN (Paul Bunyan Communications)

FERTILE—Garden Valley Telephone Co. Now served by McINTOSH, MN [MN0105]

FERTILE—See McINTOSH, MN (Garden Valley Telephone Co)

FERTILE—See McINTOSH, MN (Garden Valley Telephone Co)

FIFTY LAKES—See CROSSLAKE, MN (Crosslake Communications)

FIFTY LAKES—See EMILY, MN (Emily Cooperative Telephone. Formerly [MS0081]. This cable system has converted to IPTV)

FINLAND—Formerly served by New Century Communications. No longer in operation

FINLAYSON—See SANDSTONE, MN (SCI Broadband)

FLOODWOOD—SCI Broadband

FLORENCE TWP.—See LAKE CITY, MN (Mediacom)

FOLEY—See CAMBRIDGE, MN (Midco)

FOREST LAKE—See CAMBRIDGE, MN (Midco)

FOREST PRAIRIE TWP.—See MELROSE, MN (Arvig)

FORESTON—See CAMBRIDGE, MN (Midco)

FORT ATKINSON—See HOUSTON, IA (AcenTek)

FOSSTON—City of Fosston Cable TV

FOSSTON—See McINTOSH, MN (Garden Valley Telephone Co)

FOUNTAIN—Formerly served by Arvig. No longer in operation

FRANKLIN TWP.—See BUFFALO, MN (Charter Communications)

FRANKLIN—Mediacom

FRAZEE—See PERHAM, MN (Arvig)

FREEBORN—See NEW PRAGUE, MN (BEVCOMM. Formerly [MN0337]. This cable system has converted to IPTV)

FREEBORN—See WASECA COUNTY (portions), MN (Midco)

FREEDHEM—See RANDALL, MN (Consolidated Telecommunications Co. Formerly [MN0202]. This cable system has converted to IPTV)

FRENCH RIVER TWP.—Formerly served by New Century Communications. No longer in operation

FRIDLEY—Formerly served by Time Warner Cable. Now served by Comcast Cable, MINNEAPOLIS, MN [MN0001]

FRIDLEY—See MINNEAPOLIS, MN (Comcast Cable)

FROHN TWP.—See BEMIDJI, MN (Midco)

FROHN TWP.—See SOLWAY, MN (Paul Bunyan Communications)

FRONTENAC—See LAKE CITY, MN (Mediacom)

FROST—See NEW PRAGUE, MN (BEVCOMM. Formerly [MN0337]. This cable system has converted to IPTV)

FULDA—Mediacom. Now served by IVANHOE, MN [MN0189]

FULDA—See IVANHOE, MN (Mediacom)

GARDEN CITY—Formerly served by North American Communications Corp. This cable system has converted to IPTV. Now served by Jaguar Communications, OWATONNA, MN [MN5121]

GARDEN CITY—See OWATONNA, MN (Jaguar Communications)

GARDEN TWP.—See McINTOSH, MN (Garden Valley Telephone Co)

GARFIELD TWP.—See McINTOSH, MN (Garden Valley Telephone Co)

GARNES TWP.—See McINTOSH, MN (Garden Valley Telephone Co)

GARY—Formerly served by Loretel Cablevision. Now served by Arvig, PERHAM, MN [MN0050]

GARY—See PERHAM, MN (Arvig)

GATZKE—See McINTOSH, MN (Garden Valley Telephone Co)

GAYLORD—Mediacom. Now served by FRANKLIN, MN [MN0057]

GAYLORD—See FRANKLIN, MN (Mediacom)

GEM LAKE—See MINNEAPOLIS, MN (Comcast Cable)

GENEVA—See WASECA COUNTY (portions), MN (Midco)

GENTILLY TWP.—See McINTOSH, MN (Garden Valley Telephone Co)

GERVAIS TWP.—See McINTOSH, MN (Garden Valley Telephone Co)

GETTY TWP.—See MELROSE, MN (Arvig)

GHENT—See WOOD LAKE, MN (Midco)

GIBBON—See FRANKLIN, MN (Mediacom)

GILBERT—See EVELETH, MN (Mediacom)

GIRARD TWP.—See PERHAM, MN (Arvig)

GLENCOE TWP.—See GLENCOE, MN (NU-Telecom)

GLENCOE—NU-Telecom

GLENVILLE—Midco. Now served by WASECA COUNTY (portions), MN [MN0266]

GLENVILLE—See WASECA COUNTY (portions), MN (Midco)

GLENWOOD—Charter Communications. Now served by ALEXANDRIA, MN [MN0031]

GLENWOOD—See ALEXANDRIA, MN (Charter Communications)

GLYNDON TWP.—See PELICAN RAPIDS, MN (Arvig)

GLYNDON—See PELICAN RAPIDS, MN (Arvig)

GODFREY TWP. (PORTIONS)—See McINTOSH, MN (Garden Valley Telephone Co)

GODFREY TWP.—See McINTOSH, MN (Garden Valley Telephone Co)

GOLDEN VALLEY—See MINNEAPOLIS, MN (Comcast Cable)

GONVICK—See McINTOSH, MN (Garden Valley Telephone Co)

GONVICK—See McINTOSH, MN (Garden Valley Telephone Co)

GOOD HOPE TWP.—See MORSE TWP., MN (Paul Bunyan Communications)

GOOD THUNDER—Formerly served by Woodstock LLC. No longer in operation

GOODHUE—Nu-Telecom (formerly Sleepy Eye Telephone). This cable system has converted to IPTV. See GOODHUE, MN [MN5120]

GOODHUE—NU-Telecom. Formerly [MN0208]. This cable system has converted to IPTV

GOODRIDGE TWP.—See McINTOSH, MN (Garden Valley Telephone Co)

GOODRIDGE—See McINTOSH, MN (Garden Valley Telephone Co)

GOODVIEW—Hiawatha Broadband. This cable system has converted to IPTV. Now served by WINONA, MN [MN5161]

GOODVIEW—See WINONA, MN (Hiawatha Broadband. Formerly Winona, MN [MN0398]. This cable system has converted to IPTV)

GOOSE PRAIRIE TWP.—See PERHAM, MN (Arvig)

GORMAN TWP.—See PERHAM, MN (Arvig)

GRACEVILLE—Mediacom. Now served by APPLETON, MN [MN0106]

GRACEVILLE—See APPLETON, MN (Mediacom)

GRANADA—Formerly served by Midcontinent Communications. Now served by BEVCOMM. This cable system has converted to IPTV. See NEW PRAGUE, MN [MN5366]

GRANADA—See NEW PRAGUE, MN (BEVCOMM. Formerly [MN0337]. This cable system has converted to IPTV)

Minnesota—Cable Community Index

GRAND MARAIS—Mediacom

GRAND MEADOW—Arvig

GRAND PLAIN TWP.—See McINTOSH, MN (Garden Valley Telephone Co)

GRAND PRAIRIE—See GRAND RAPIDS, MN (Mediacom)

GRAND RAPIDS TWP.—See GRAND RAPIDS, MN (Mediacom)

GRAND RAPIDS TWP.—See MORSE TWP., MN (Paul Bunyan Communications)

GRAND RAPIDS—Mediacom

GRAND RAPIDS—See MORSE TWP., MN (Paul Bunyan Communications)

GRANITE FALLS—Mediacom. Now served by PAYNESVILLE, MN [MN0125]

GRANITE FALLS—See PAYNESVILLE, MN (Mediacom)

GRANT TWP.—See MINNEAPOLIS, MN (Comcast Cable)

GRANT VALLEY TWP.—See BEMIDJI, MN (Midco)

GRANT VALLEY TWP.—See SOLWAY, MN (Paul Bunyan Communications)

GRATTAN TWP.—See MORSE TWP., MN (Paul Bunyan Communications)

GREEN ISLE—Formerly served by North American Communications Corp. This cable system has converted to IPTV. Now served by Jaguar Communications, NEW MARKET, MN [MN5374]

GREEN ISLE—See NEW MARKET, MN (Jaguar Communications)

GREEN LAKE TWP.—See WILLMAR, MN (Charter Communications)

GREEN PRAIRIE TWP.—See ST. CLOUD, MN (Charter Communications)

GREENBUSH—Sjoberg's Cable TV Inc

GREENFIELD TWP.—See CAMBRIDGE, MN (Midco)

GREENWALD—See MELROSE, MN (Arvig)

GREENWAY TWP.—SCI Broadband

GREENWOOD TWP.—See McINTOSH, MN (Garden Valley Telephone Co)

GREENWOOD—See MOUND, MN (Mediacom)

GREGORY TWP.—See McINTOSH, MN (Garden Valley Telephone Co)

GREY CLOUD ISLAND TWP.—See MINNEAPOLIS, MN (Comcast Cable)

GREY EAGLE—Arvig (formerly diversiCOM). This cable system has converted to IPTV. See MELROSE, MN [MN5017]

GREY EAGLE—See MELROSE, MN (Arvig)

GROVE CITY—Mediacom. Now served by PAYNESVILLE, MN [MN0125]

GROVE CITY—See PAYNESVILLE, MN (Mediacom)

GROVE PARK TWP. (PORTIONS)—See McINTOSH, MN (Garden Valley Telephone Co)

GROVE PARK TWP.—See McINTOSH, MN (Garden Valley Telephone Co)

GROVE TWP.—See MELROSE, MN (Arvig)

GRYGLA—Garden Valley Telephone Co. Now served by McINTOSH, MN [MN0105]

GRYGLA—See McINTOSH, MN (Garden Valley Telephone Co)

GRYGLA—See McINTOSH, MN (Garden Valley Telephone Co)

GULLY TWP.—See McINTOSH, MN (Garden Valley Telephone Co)

GULLY—See McINTOSH, MN (Garden Valley Telephone Co)

GUTHRIE TWP.—See SOLWAY, MN (Paul Bunyan Communications)

HACKENSACK—See BRAINERD, MN (Charter Communications)

HADLEY—See IVANHOE, MN (Mediacom)

HAGALI TWP.—See SOLWAY, MN (Paul Bunyan Communications)

HAGER CITY—Scc PINE ISLAND, WI (BEVCOMM. Formerly [MN0089]. This cable system has converted to IPTV)

HALLOCK—Wikstrom Cable LLC

HAM LAKE—See MINNEAPOLIS, MN (Comcast Cable)

HAMBURG—See MOUND, MN (Mediacom)

HAMMOND—See McINTOSH, MN (Garden Valley Telephone Co)

HAMPTON TWP.—See CANNON FALLS TWP., MN (Midco)

HAMPTON—Formerly served by Cannon Valley Cablevision. Now served by Midcontinent Communications, CANNON FALLS TWP., MN [MN0391]

HAMPTON—See CANNON FALLS TWP., MN (Midco)

HAMRE TWP.—See McINTOSH, MN (Garden Valley Telephone Co)

HANCOCK—Mediacom. Now served by MORRIS, MN [MN0210]

HANCOCK—See MORRIS, MN (Mediacom)

HANGAARD TWP.—See McINTOSH, MN (Garden Valley Telephone Co)

HANLEY FALLS—Clara City Telephone Co

HANOVER—See MINNEAPOLIS, MN (Comcast Cable)

HANSKA—Formerly served by Clara City Telephone Co. No longer in operation

HARMONY—Harmony Telephone Co

HARRIS TWP.—See GRAND RAPIDS, MN (Mediacom)

HARRIS—See CAMBRIDGE, MN (Midco)

HARRISON TWP.—See WILLMAR, MN (Charter Communications)

HART LAKE TWP.—See SOLWAY, MN (Paul Bunyan Communications)

HARTLAND—See WASECA COUNTY (portions), MN (Midco)

HASSAN TWP.—See BUFFALO, MN (Charter Communications)

HASSEN VALLEY TWP.—See HUTCHINSON, MN (Mediacom)

HASTINGS—See MINNEAPOLIS, MN (Comcast Cable)

HAUGEN TWP.—See ROUND LAKE TWP., MN (New Century Communications)

HAVEN TWP.—See ST. CLOUD, MN (Charter Communications)

HAVEN TWP.—See CAMBRIDGE, MN (Midco)

HAVERHILL TWP.—See ROCHESTER, MN (Charter Communications)

HAWLEY—Formerly served by Loretel Cablevision. Now served by Arvig, PERHAM, MN [MN0050]

HAWLEY—See PERHAM, MN (Arvig)

HAY CREEK TWP.—See ROSEMOUNT, MN (Charter Communications)

HAYFIELD—Mediacom. Now served by CANNON FALLS, MN [MN0076]

HAYFIELD—See OWATONNA, MN (Jaguar Communications)

HAYFIELD—See CANNON FALLS, MN (Mediacom)

HAYWARD—Formerly served by North American Communications Corp. This cable system has converted to IPTV. Now served by Jaguar Communications, OWATONNA, MN [MN5121]

HAYWARD—See OWATONNA, MN (Jaguar Communications)

HECTOR—Mediacom. Now served by HUTCHINSON, MN [MN0145]

HECTOR—See HUTCHINSON, MN (Mediacom)

HEIER TWP.—See McINTOSH, MN (Garden Valley Telephone Co)

HELENA TWP.—See MINNEAPOLIS, MN (Comcast Cable)

HELGA TWP.—See SOLWAY, MN (Paul Bunyan Communications)

HENDERSON—See ST. PETER, MN (Mediacom)

HENDRICKS—Formerly served by US Cable of Coastal Texas LP. No longer in operation

HENDRICKSON TWP.—See SOLWAY, MN (Paul Bunyan Communications)

HENNING TWP.—See PERHAM, MN (Arvig)

HENNING—See PERHAM, MN (Arvig)

HENRIETTA TWP.—See PERHAM, MN (Arvig)

HEREIM TWP.—See GREENBUSH, MN (Sjoberg's Cable TV Inc)

HERMAN—See BARRETT, MN (Runestone Cable TV)

HERMANTOWN—See CLOQUET, MN (Mediacom)

HERON LAKE—Midco

HEWITT—See PERHAM, MN (Arvig)

HIBBING—See CALUMET, MN (Mediacom)

HICKORY TWP.—See McINTOSH, MN (Garden Valley Telephone Co)

HIGH LANDING TWP.—See McINTOSH, MN (Garden Valley Telephone Co)

HILL CITY—SCI Broadband

HILL RIVER TWP. (PORTIONS)—See McINTOSH, MN (Garden Valley Telephone Co)

HILL RIVER TWP.—See McINTOSH, MN (Garden Valley Telephone Co)

HILLS—Alliance Communications. Now served by GARRETSON, SD [SD0016]

HILLSDALE—See WINONA, MN (Hiawatha Broadband. Formerly Winona, MN [MN0398]. This cable system has converted to IPTV)

HILLTOP—See MINNEAPOLIS, MN (Comcast Cable)

HINCKLEY—See SANDSTONE, MN (SCI Broadband)

HINES TWP.—See SOLWAY, MN (Paul Bunyan Communications)

HIRAM TWP.—See PERHAM, MN (Arvig)

HIRAM TWP.—See BRAINERD, MN (Charter Communications)

HOBART TWP.—See PERHAM, MN (Arvig)

HOFFMAN—See BARRETT, MN (Runestone Cable TV)

HOKAH—Mediacom. Now served by CALEDONIA, MN [MN0086]

HOKAH—See HOUSTON, MN (AcenTek)

HOKAH—See CALEDONIA, MN (Mediacom)

HOLDINGFORD—See CAMBRIDGE, MN (Midco)

HOLLAND—See RUTHTON, MN (Woodstock Communications)

HOLLANDALE—See WASECA COUNTY (portions), MN (Midco)

HOLMESVILLE TWP.—See PERHAM, MN (Arvig)

HOLST TWP.—See McINTOSH, MN (Garden Valley Telephone Co)

Cable Community Index—Minnesota

HOLT—See THIEF RIVER FALLS, MN (Sjoberg's Cable TV Inc)

HOMER—Hiawatha Broadband. This cable system has converted to IPTV. Now served by WINONA, MN [MN5161]

HOMER—See WINONA, MN (Hiawatha Broadband. Formerly Winona, MN [MN0398]. This cable system has converted to IPTV)

HOMESTEAD TWP.—See PERHAM, MN (Arvig)

HOPE TWP.—See IVANHOE, MN (Mediacom)

HOPKINS—See MINNEAPOLIS, MN (Comcast Cable)

HORNET TWP.—See SOLWAY, MN (Paul Bunyan Communications)

HOUSTON—Mediacom. Now served by CALEDONIA, MN [MN0086]

HOUSTON—AcenTek

HOUSTON—See CALEDONIA, MN (Mediacom)

HOWARD LAKE—Mediacom. Now served by HUTCHINSON, MN [MN0145]

HOWARD LAKE—See HUTCHINSON, MN (Mediacom)

HOYT LAKES—See EVELETH, MN (Mediacom)

HUDSON—See MINNEAPOLIS, WI (Comcast Cable)

HUGO—See MINNEAPOLIS, MN (Comcast Cable)

HUNTLEY—See NEW PRAGUE, MN (BEVCOMM. Formerly [MN0337]. This cable system has converted to IPTV)

HUTCHINSON—Mediacom. Now served by HUTCHINSON, MN [MN0145]

HUTCHINSON—Mediacom

IDEAL TWP.—See BRAINERD, MN (Charter Communications)

INDEPENDENCE—See MOUND, MN (Mediacom)

INGER—See MORSE TWP., MN (Paul Bunyan Communications)

INGUADONA—See PERHAM, MN (Arvig)

INTERNATIONAL FALLS—Midco

INVER GROVE HEIGHTS—See MINNEAPOLIS, MN (Comcast Cable)

IONA—Formerly served by American Telecasting of America Inc. No longer in operation

IRONDALE—See BRAINERD, MN (Charter Communications)

IRONTON—See BRAINERD, MN (Charter Communications)

IRONTON—See RANDALL, MN (Consolidated Telecommunications Co. Formerly [MN0202]. This cable system has converted to IPTV)

IRVING TWP.—See WILLMAR, MN (Charter Communications)

ISANTI TWP.—See CAMBRIDGE, MN (Midco)

ISANTI—See CAMBRIDGE, MN (Midco)

ISLAND LAKE TWP.—See McINTOSH, MN (Garden Valley Telephone Co)

ISLE HARBOR—See ISLE, MN (SCI Broadband)

ISLE—SCI Broadband

ITASCA COUNTY (UNORGANIZED TOWNSHIPS)—See MORSE TWP., MN (Paul Bunyan Communications)

ITASCA TWP.—See McINTOSH, MN (Garden Valley Telephone Co)

ITASCA TWP.—See SOLWAY, MN (Paul Bunyan Communications)

IVANHOE—Mediacom

JACKSON TWP.—See MINNEAPOLIS, MN (Comcast Cable)

JACKSON—Jackson Municipal TV System

JADIS TWP.—See ROSEAU, MN (Sjoberg's Cable TV Inc)

JANESVILLE—Mediacom. Now served by ST. PETER (formerly Waseca), MN [MN0043]

JANESVILLE—See ST. PETER, MN (Mediacom)

JASPER—Clarity Telcom. Now served by ADRIAN, MN [MN0158]

JASPER—See JASPER, MN (Clarity Telcom. Now served by ADRIAN, MN [MN0158])

JASPER—See ADRIAN, MN (Clarity Telcom)

JEFFERS—NU-Telecom

JENKINS—See BRAINERD, MN (Charter Communications)

JOHNSON TWP.—See McINTOSH, MN (Garden Valley Telephone Co)

JONES TWP.—See McINTOSH, MN (Garden Valley Telephone Co)

JONES TWP.—See SOLWAY, MN (Paul Bunyan Communications)

JORDAN—Formerly served by Time Warner Cable. Now served by Comcast Cable, MINNEAPOLIS, MN [MN0001]

JORDAN—See MINNEAPOLIS, MN (Comcast Cable)

KANDIYOHI—See WILLMAR, MN (Charter Communications)

KANDOTA TWP.—See SAUK CENTRE, MN (Arvig)

KARLSTAD—Sjoberg's Cable TV Inc

KASOTA—See OWATONNA, MN (Jaguar Communications)

KASOTA—See ST. PETER, MN (Mediacom)

KASSON—See ROCHESTER, MN (Charter Communications)

KATHIO TWP.—See ISLE, MN (SCI Broadband)

KEEWATIN—Mediacom. Now served by GRAND RAPIDS, MN [MN0038]

KEEWATIN—See GRAND RAPIDS, MN (Mediacom)

KEGO TWP.—See PERHAM, MN (Arvig)

KELLIHER TWP.—See SOLWAY, MN (Paul Bunyan Communications)

KELLIHER—Formerly served by North American Communications Corp. No longer in operation

KELLIHER—See SOLWAY, MN (Paul Bunyan Communications)

KELLOGG—See CAMBRIDGE, MN (Midco)

KENNEDY—Wikstrom Cable LLC

KENSINGTON—See BARRETT, MN (Runestone Cable TV)

KENYON—Mediacom. Now served by CANNON FALLS, MN [MN0076]

KENYON—See CANNON FALLS, MN (Mediacom)

KERKHOVEN—Charter Communications. Now served by WILLMAR, MN [MN0018]

KERKHOVEN—See WILLMAR, MN (Charter Communications)

KIESTER—See BLUE EARTH, MN (BEVCOMM)

KIMBALL—See MELROSE, MN (Arvig)

KING TWP. (PORTIONS)—See McINTOSH, MN (Garden Valley Telephone Co)

KING TWP.—See McINTOSH, MN (Garden Valley Telephone Co)

KINGHURST TWP.—See MORSE TWP., MN (Paul Bunyan Communications)

KINGSTON—See MELROSE, MN (Arvig)

KINGSTON TWP.—See MELROSE, MN (Arvig)

KINNEY—See EVELETH, MN (Mediacom)

KLOSSNER—See NEW ULM, MN (NU-Telecom. Formerly [MN0285]. This cable system has converted to IPTV)

KNIFE LAKE TWP.—Formerly served by New Century Communications. No longer in operation

KNIFE RIVER—Formerly served by Mediacom. No longer in operation

KNUTE TWP.—See McINTOSH, MN (Garden Valley Telephone Co)

KNUTE TWP.—See McINTOSH, MN (Garden Valley Telephone Co)

KOOCHICHING COUNTY (PORTIONS)—See INTERNATIONAL FALLS, MN (Midco)

KOOCHICHING COUNTY (UNORGANIZED TOWNSHIPS)—See MORSE TWP., MN (Paul Bunyan Communications)

KRATKA TWP.—See McINTOSH, MN (Garden Valley Telephone Co)

LA CRESCENT—See HOUSTON, MN (AcenTek)

LA GARDE TWP.—See PERHAM, MN (Arvig)

LA GRAND TWP.—See ALEXANDRIA, MN (Charter Communications)

LA PRAIRIE TWP.—See McINTOSH, MN (Garden Valley Telephone Co)

LA PRAIRIE TWP.—See GRAND RAPIDS, MN (Mediacom)

LA PRAIRIE—See MORSE TWP., MN (Paul Bunyan Communications)

LAFAYETTE—Mediacom. Now served by ST. PETER (formerly Waseca), MN [MN0043]

LAFAYETTE—See ST. PETER, MN (Mediacom)

LAKE ALICE TWP.—See SOLWAY, MN (Paul Bunyan Communications)

LAKE BENTON—See IVANHOE, MN (Mediacom)

LAKE BRONSON—Wikstrom Cable LLC

LAKE CITY—See WINONA, MN (Hiawatha Broadband. Formerly Winona, MN [MN0398]. This cable system has converted to IPTV)

LAKE CITY—Mediacom

LAKE COUNTY (WESTERN PORTION)—See EVELETH, MN (Mediacom)

LAKE COUNTY—See CLOQUET, MN (Mediacom)

LAKE CRYSTAL—Mediacom. Now served by ST. PETER (formerly Waseca), MN [MN0043]

LAKE CRYSTAL—See ST. PETER, MN (Mediacom)

LAKE ELMO—See MINNEAPOLIS, MN (Comcast Cable)

LAKE EUNICE TWP.—See PERHAM, MN (Arvig)

LAKE GEORGE TWP.—See SOLWAY, MN (Paul Bunyan Communications)

LAKE GROVE TWP.—See PERHAM, MN (Arvig)

LAKE HATTIE TWP.—See SOLWAY, MN (Paul Bunyan Communications)

LAKE LILLIAN—Clara City Telephone Co

LAKE NEBAGAMON—See DULUTH, WI (Charter Communications)

LAKE PARK TWP.—See PERHAM, MN (Arvig)

LAKE PARK—See PERHAM, MN (Arvig)

LAKE PLEASANT TWP.—See McINTOSH, MN (Garden Valley Telephone Co)

Minnesota—Cable Community Index

LAKE SHORE—See BRAINERD, MN (Charter Communications)

LAKE ST. CROIX BEACH—See MINNEAPOLIS, MN (Comcast Cable)

LAKE TWP.—See LAKE CITY, MN (Mediacom)

LAKE TWP.—See WARROAD, MN (Sjoberg's Cable TV Inc)

LAKE VALLEY—See APPLETON, MN (Mediacom)

LAKE WILSON—See ADRIAN, MN (Clarity Telcom)

LAKEFIELD—Formerly served by Lakefield Public TV. No longer in operation

LAKELAND SHORES—See MINNEAPOLIS, MN (Comcast Cable)

LAKELAND—See MINNEAPOLIS, MN (Comcast Cable)

LAKEPORT TWP.—See SOLWAY, MN (Paul Bunyan Communications)

LAKESIDE TWP.—See ISLE, MN (SCI Broadband)

LAKEVIEW TWP.—See PERHAM, MN (Arvig)

LAKEVILLE—See ROSEMOUNT, MN (Charter Communications)

LAMBERT TWP.—See McINTOSH, MN (Garden Valley Telephone Co)

LAMBERTON—Clara City Telephone Co

LAMMERS TWP.—See McINTOSH, MN (Garden Valley Telephone Co)

LAMMERS TWP.—See SOLWAY, MN (Paul Bunyan Communications)

LANCASTER—Wikstrom Cable LLC

LANDFALL—See MINNEAPOLIS, MN (Comcast Cable)

LANESBORO—Mediacom. Now served by CHATFIELD, MN [MN0111]

LANESBORO—See HOUSTON, MN (AcenTek)

LANESBORO—See CHATFIELD, MN (Mediacom)

LANESBURGH TWP.—See MINNEAPOLIS, MN (Comcast Cable)

LANGOR TWP.—See SOLWAY, MN (Paul Bunyan Communications)

LANSING—See OWATONNA, MN (Jaguar Communications)

LAPORTE—See SOLWAY, MN (Paul Bunyan Communications)

LAUDERDALE—See MINNEAPOLIS, MN (Comcast Cable)

LE CENTER—See WASECA COUNTY (portions), MN (Midco)

LE ROY—Mediacom. Now served by CHATFIELD, MN [MN0111]

LE ROY—See CHATFIELD, MN (Mediacom)

LE SAUK TWP.—See ST. CLOUD, MN (Charter Communications)

LE SUEUR—Mediacom. Now served by ST. PETER (formerly Waseca), MN [MN0043]

LE SUEUR—See ST. PETER, MN (Mediacom)

LEAF LAKE TWP.—See PERHAM, MN (Arvig)

LEE TWP.—See McINTOSH, MN (Garden Valley Telephone Co)

LEECH LAKE TWP.—See PERHAM, MN (Arvig)

LENGBY—See McINTOSH, MN (Garden Valley Telephone Co)

LENT TWP.—See CAMBRIDGE, MN (Midco)

LEON TWP. (PORTIONS)—See McINTOSH, MN (Garden Valley Telephone Co)

LEON TWP.—See McINTOSH, MN (Garden Valley Telephone Co)

LEONARD—See McINTOSH, MN (Garden Valley Telephone Co)

LEONIDAS—See EVELETH, MN (Mediacom)

LEOTA—Formerly served by American Telecasting of America Inc. No longer in operation

LESSOR TWP. (PORTIONS)—See McINTOSH, MN (Garden Valley Telephone Co)

LESSOR TWP.—See McINTOSH, MN (Garden Valley Telephone Co)

LESTER PRAIRIE—Mediacom. Now served by HUTCHINSON, MN [MN0145]

LESTER PRAIRIE—See HUTCHINSON, MN (Mediacom)

LEWISTON—Hiawatha Broadband. This cable system has converted to IPTV. Now served by WINONA, MN [MN5161]

LEWISTON—See WINONA, MN (Hiawatha Broadband. Formerly Winona, MN [MN0398]. This cable system has converted to IPTV)

LEWISVILLE—Formerly served by North American Communications Corp. No longer in operation

LEXINGTON—See MINNEAPOLIS, MN (Comcast Cable)

LIBERTY TWP.—See McINTOSH, MN (Garden Valley Telephone Co)

LIBERTY TWP.—See SOLWAY, MN (Paul Bunyan Communications)

LIDA TWP.—See PERHAM, MN (Arvig)

LILYDALE—See MINNEAPOLIS, MN (Comcast Cable)

LIME TWP.—See MANKATO, MN (Charter Communications)

LINCOLN—See RANDALL, MN (Consolidated Telecommunications Co. Formerly [MN0202]. This cable system has converted to IPTV)

LINDSTROM—See CAMBRIDGE, MN (Midco)

LINO LAKES—See MINNEAPOLIS, MN (Comcast Cable)

LINWOOD TWP.—See CAMBRIDGE, MN (Midco)

LINWOOD—See CAMBRIDGE, MN (Midco)

LISMORE—Formerly served by K-Communications Inc. No longer in operation

LITCHFIELD TWP.—See HUTCHINSON, MN (Mediacom)

LITCHFIELD—Mediacom. Now served by HUTCHINSON, MN [MN0145]

LITCHFIELD—See HUTCHINSON, MN (Mediacom)

LITTLE CANADA—See MINNEAPOLIS, MN (Comcast Cable)

LITTLE ELBOW TWP.—See PERHAM, MN (Arvig)

LITTLE FALLS TWP.—See ST. CLOUD, MN (Charter Communications)

LITTLE FALLS—Charter Communications. Now served by ST. CLOUD, MN [MN0011]

LITTLE FALLS—See ST. CLOUD, MN (Charter Communications)

LITTLE PINE TWP.—See EMILY, MN (Emily Cooperative Telephone. Formerly [MS0081]. This cable system has converted to IPTV)

LITTLEFORK—Midco

LIVONIA TWP.—See CAMBRIDGE, MN (Midco)

LOCKHART TWP.—See McINTOSH, MN (Garden Valley Telephone Co)

LONE PINE TWP.—See GREENWAY TWP., MN (SCI Broadband)

LONG BEACH—See ALEXANDRIA, MN (Charter Communications)

LONG LAKE—Formerly served by New Century Communications. Now served by Mediacom, MOUND, MN [MN0010]

LONG LAKE—See MOUND, MN (Mediacom)

LONG PRAIRIE—Charter Communications. Now served by BRAINERD, MN [MN0022]

LONG PRAIRIE—See BRAINERD, MN (Charter Communications)

LONGVILLE—See PERHAM, MN (Arvig)

LONSDALE—See ST. PETER, MN (Mediacom)

LORETTO—See MOUND, MN (Mediacom)

LOUISVILLE TWP. (SCOTT COUNTY)—See MINNEAPOLIS, MN (Comcast Cable)

LOUISVILLE TWP.—See McINTOSH, MN (Garden Valley Telephone Co)

LOWER SIOUX—See FRANKLIN, MN (Mediacom)

LOWRY—Formerly served by Lowry Telephone Co. Now served by Runestone Cable TV, BARRETT, MN [MN0233]

LOWRY—See BARRETT, MN (Runestone Cable TV)

LUCAN—Clara City Telephone Co

LUVERNE—Mediacom. Now served by WORTHINGTON, MN [MN0041]

LUVERNE—See ADRIAN, MN (Clarity Telcom)

LUVERNE—See WORTHINGTON, MN (Mediacom)

LUXEMBURG TWP.—See MELROSE, MN (Arvig)

LYLE—No longer in operation

LYLE—See CHATFIELD, MN (Mediacom)

LYND—See WOOD LAKE, MN (Midco)

MABEL—Mediacom. Now served by CALEDONIA, MN [MN0086]

MABEL—See CALEDONIA, MN (Mediacom)

MADELIA—Formerly served by Time Warner Cable. Now served by Comcast Cable, MINNEAPOLIS, MN [MN0001]

MADELIA—See MINNEAPOLIS, MN (Comcast Cable)

MADISON LAKE—Formerly served by North American Communications Corp. This cable system has converted to IPTV. Now served by Jaguar Communications, OWATONNA, MN [MN5121]

MADISON LAKE—See OWATONNA, MN (Jaguar Communications)

MADISON—Mediacom. Now served by APPLETON, MN [MN0106]

MADISON—See APPLETON, MN (Mediacom)

MAGNOLIA—Formerly served by American Telecasting of America Inc. No longer in operation

MAHNOMEN—Formerly served by Loretel Cablevision. Now served by Arvig, PERHAM, MN [MN0050]

MAHNOMEN—See PERHAM, MN (Arvig)

MAHTOMEDI—See MINNEAPOLIS, MN (Comcast Cable)

MAINE PRAIRIE TWP.—See MELROSE, MN (Arvig)

MAINE TWP.—See PERHAM, MN (Arvig)

MAINE TWP.—See DALTON, MN (Otter Tail Telcom)

MANANNAH TWP.—See MELROSE, MN (Arvig)

Cable Community Index—Minnesota

MANHATTAN BEACH—See CROSSLAKE, MN (Crosslake Communications)

MANITOWOC (TOWN)—See MINNEAPOLIS, WI (Comcast Cable)

MANITOWOC RAPIDS—See MINNEAPOLIS, WI (Comcast Cable)

MANITOWOC—See MINNEAPOLIS, WI (Comcast Cable)

MANKATO TWP.—See MANKATO, MN (Charter Communications)

MANKATO—Charter Communications

MANTORVILLE—See CANNON FALLS, MN (Mediacom)

MANTRAP TWP.—See PERHAM, MN (Arvig)

MAPLE GROVE—See MINNEAPOLIS, MN (Comcast Cable)

MAPLE LAKE—See BUFFALO, MN (Charter Communications)

MAPLE PLAIN—See MOUND, MN (Mediacom)

MAPLE RIDGE TWP.—See SOLWAY, MN (Paul Bunyan Communications)

MAPLETON—See WASECA COUNTY (portions), MN (Midco)

MAPLEVIEW—Formerly served by North American Communications Corp. This cable system has converted to IPTV. Now served by Jaguar Communications, OWATONNA, MN [MN5121]

MAPLEVIEW—See OWATONNA, MN (Jaguar Communications)

MAPLEWOOD—See MINNEAPOLIS, MN (Comcast Cable)

MARBLE—Formerly served by Marble Cable TV Systems. Now served by Mediacom, CALUMET, MN [MN0027]

MARBLE—See CALUMET, MN (Mediacom)

MARINE ON THE ST. CROIX—See CAMBRIDGE, MN (Midco)

MARION TWP.—See ROCHESTER, MN (Charter Communications)

MARSHALL—Charter Communications. Now served by WILLMAR, MN [MN0018]

MARSHALL—See WILLMAR, MN (Charter Communications)

MARSHALL—Clarity Telcom

MARSHAN TWP.—See CANNON FALLS TWP., MN (Midco)

MAX TWP.—See MORSE TWP., MN (Paul Bunyan Communications)

MAY TWP.—See CAMBRIDGE, MN (Midco)

MAYER—NU-Telecom

MAYFIELD TWP.—See McINTOSH, MN (Garden Valley Telephone Co)

MAYNARD—See PAYNESVILLE, MN (Mediacom)

MAZEPPA—Formerly served by US Cable of Coastal Texas LP. No longer in operation

MAZEPPA—See GOODHUE, MN (NU-Telecom. Formerly [MN0208]. This cable system has converted to IPTV)

MCCREA TWP.—See WARREN, MN (Sjoberg's Cable TV Inc)

MCGREGOR (UNINCORPORATED AREAS)—See ROUND LAKE TWP., MN (New Century Communications)

MCGREGOR—SCI Broadband

MCINTOSH—Garden Valley Telephone Co

MCINTOSH—Garden Valley Telephone Co

MEDFORD—See WASECA COUNTY (portions), MN (Midco)

MEDICINE LAKE—See MINNEAPOLIS, MN (Comcast Cable)

MEDINA—See MOUND, MN (Mediacom)

MEIRE GROVE—See MELROSE, MN (Arvig)

MELROSE TWP.—See MELROSE, MN (Arvig)

MELROSE—Charter Communications. Now served by ST. CLOUD, MN [MN0011]

MELROSE—Arvig

MELROSE—See ST. CLOUD, MN (Charter Communications)

MENAHGA—West Central Telephone Assn. This cable system has converted to IPTV. See MENAHGA, MN [MN5130]

MENAHGA—West Central Telephone Assn. This cable system has converted to IPTV

MENDOTA HEIGHTS—See MINNEAPOLIS, MN (Comcast Cable)

MENDOTA—See MINNEAPOLIS, MN (Comcast Cable)

MENTOR—See McINTOSH, MN (Garden Valley Telephone Co)

MENTOR—See McINTOSH, MN (Garden Valley Telephone Co)

MERDOCK—See WILLMAR, MN (Charter Communications)

MIDDLE RIVER—Sjoberg's Cable TV Inc

MIDWAY TWP.—See CLOQUET, MN (Mediacom)

MILACA TWP.—See CAMBRIDGE, MN (Midco)

MILACA—See RICE, MN (Benton Cooperative Telephone)

MILACA—See CAMBRIDGE, MN (Midco)

MILLWOOD TWP.—See MELROSE, MN (Arvig)

MILROY—See WOOD LAKE, MN (Midco)

MILTONA—See PARKERS PRAIRIE, MN (Arvig)

MINDEN TWP.—See ST. CLOUD, MN (Charter Communications)

MINERVA TWP.—See McINTOSH, MN (Garden Valley Telephone Co)

MINNEAPOLIS—Comcast Cable

MINNEISKA—See WINONA, MN (Hiawatha Broadband. Formerly Winona, MN [MN0398]. This cable system has converted to IPTV)

MINNEOTA—See WOOD LAKE, MN (Midco)

MINNESOTA CITY—Hiawatha Broadband. This cable system has converted to IPTV. Now served by WINONA, MN [MN5161]

MINNESOTA CITY—See WINONA, MN (Hiawatha Broadband. Formerly Winona, MN [MN0398]. This cable system has converted to IPTV)

MINNESOTA LAKE—BEVCOMM. This cable system has converted to IPTV. Now served by NEW PRAGUE, MN [MN5366]

MINNESOTA LAKE—See NEW PRAGUE, MN (BEVCOMM. Formerly [MN0337]. This cable system has converted to IPTV)

MINNETONKA BEACH—See MOUND, MN (Mediacom)

MINNETONKA—See MINNEAPOLIS, MN (Comcast Cable)

MINNETRISTA—See MOUND, MN (Mediacom)

MINNIE TWP.—See McINTOSH, MN (Garden Valley Telephone Co)

MISSION TWP.—Formerly served by Crosslake Communications, CROSSLAKE, MN [MN0069]. This cable system has converted to IPTV. Now served by Consolidated Telecommunications Co., RANDALL, MN [MN5026]

MISSION TWP.—See RANDALL, MN (Consolidated Telecommunications Co. Formerly [MN0202]. This cable system has converted to IPTV)

MIZPAH TWP.—See MORSE TWP., MN (Paul Bunyan Communications)

MONTEVIDEO—Charter Communications. Now served by WILLMAR, MN [MN0018]

MONTEVIDEO—See WILLMAR, MN (Charter Communications)

MONTGOMERY—Mediacom. Now served by ST. PETER (formerly Waseca), MN [MN0043]

MONTGOMERY—See ST. PETER, MN (Mediacom)

MONTICELLO—See BUFFALO, MN (Charter Communications)

MONTROSE—Formerly served by Time Warner Cable. Now served by Comcast Cable, MINNEAPOLIS, MN [MN0001]

MONTROSE—See MINNEAPOLIS, MN (Comcast Cable)

MOOSE CREEK TWP.—See McINTOSH, MN (Garden Valley Telephone Co)

MOOSE LAKE TWP.—See CLOQUET, MN (Mediacom)

MOOSE LAKE—Mediacom. Now served by CLOQUET, MO [MN0042]

MOOSE LAKE—See CLOQUET, MN (Mediacom)

MOOSE LAKE—See SOLWAY, MN (Paul Bunyan Communications)

MOOSE RIVER TWP.—See McINTOSH, MN (Garden Valley Telephone Co)

MORA—See CAMBRIDGE, MN (Midco)

MORANVILLE TWP.—See WARROAD, MN (Sjoberg's Cable TV Inc)

MORGAN—See WOOD LAKE, MN (Midco)

MORRIS—Mediacom. Now served by MORRIS, MN [MN0210]

MORRIS—Mediacom

MORRISTOWN—BEVCOMM

MORSE TWP.—Paul Bunyan Communications

MORTON—See FRANKLIN, MN (Mediacom)

MOTLEY—SCI Broadband. Now served by PILLAGER, MN [MN0230]

MOTLEY—See RANDALL, MN (Consolidated Telecommunications Co. Formerly [MN0202]. This cable system has converted to IPTV)

MOTLEY—See PILLAGER, MN (SCI Broadband)

MOUND PRAIRIE—See HOUSTON, MN (AcenTek)

MOUND—Mediacom

MOUNDS VIEW—See MINNEAPOLIS, MN (Comcast Cable)

MOUNT PLEASANT TWP.—See LAKE CITY, MN (Mediacom)

MOUNTAIN IRON—See EVELETH, MN (Mediacom)

MOUNTAIN LAKE—Mediacom. Now served by ST. PETER (formerly Waseca), MN [MN0043]

MOUNTAIN LAKE—See ST. PETER, MN (Mediacom)

MOYLAN TWP.—See McINTOSH, MN (Garden Valley Telephone Co)

MUNSON TWP.—See MELROSE, MN (Arvig)

Minnesota—Cable Community Index

MUNSON TWP.—See CAMBRIDGE, MN (Midco)

NASHWAUK—See GRAND RAPIDS, MN (Mediacom)

NEBISH TWP.—See SOLWAY, MN (Paul Bunyan Communications)

NESSEL TWP.—See CAMBRIDGE, MN (Midco)

NEVIS TWP.—See PERHAM, MN (Arvig)

NEVIS—See PERHAM, MN (Arvig)

NEW ALBIN—See HOUSTON, IA (AcenTek)

NEW AUBURN—Formerly served by North American Communications Corp. This cable system has converted to IPTV. Now served by Jaguar Communications, NEW MARKET, MN [MN5374]

NEW AUBURN—See NEW MARKET, MN (Jaguar Communications)

NEW BRIGHTON—See MINNEAPOLIS, MN (Comcast Cable)

NEW GERMANY—See MAYER, MN (NU-Telecom)

NEW HARTFORD TWP.—See CALEDONIA, MN (Mediacom)

NEW HOPE—See MINNEAPOLIS, MN (Comcast Cable)

NEW LONDON TWP.—See WILLMAR, MN (Charter Communications)

NEW LONDON—See WILLMAR, MN (Charter Communications)

NEW MARKET TWP.—See PRIOR LAKE, MN (Integra Telecom)

NEW MARKET TWP.—See PRIOR LAKE, MN (Mediacom)

NEW MARKET—Formerly served by North American Communications Corp. This cable system has converted to IPTV. Now served by Jaguar Communications. See NEW MARKET, MN [MN5374]

NEW MARKET—Jaguar Communications

NEW MUNICH—See MELROSE, MN (Arvig)

NEW PRAGUE—Formerly served by Time Warner Cable. Now served by Comcast Cable, MINNEAPOLIS, MN [MN0001]

NEW PRAGUE—BEVCOMM. Formerly [MN0337]. This cable system has converted to IPTV

NEW PRAGUE—See MINNEAPOLIS, MN (Comcast Cable)

NEW RICHLAND—See OWATONNA, MN (Jaguar Communications)

NEW RICHLAND—See WASECA COUNTY (portions), MN (Midco)

NEW SCANDIA TWP.—See CAMBRIDGE, MN (Midco)

NEW ULM—Formerly served by Time Warner Cable. Now served by Comcast Cable, MINNEAPOLIS, MN [MN0001]

NEW ULM—NU-Telecom. This cable system has converted to IPTV. See NEW ULM, MN [MN5117]

NEW ULM—See MINNEAPOLIS, MN (Comcast Cable)

NEW ULM—NU-Telecom. Formerly [MN0285]. This cable system has converted to IPTV

NEW YORK MILLS—See PERHAM, MN (Arvig)

NEWFOLDEN—Sjoberg's Cable TV Inc

NEWPORT—See MINNEAPOLIS, MN (Comcast Cable)

NEWTON (TOWN)—See MINNEAPOLIS, WI (Comcast Cable)

NEWTON TWP.—See PERHAM, MN (Arvig)

NICOLLET—Clara City Telephone Co

NIDAROS TWP.—See PERHAM, MN (Arvig)

NIMROD—See MENAHGA, MN (West Central Telephone Assn. This cable system has converted to IPTV)

NININGER TWP.—See CANNON FALLS TWP., MN (Midco)

NISSWA—See BRAINERD, MN (Charter Communications)

NISSWA—See RANDALL, MN (Consolidated Telecommunications Co. Formerly [MN0202]. This cable system has converted to IPTV)

NOKAY LAKE TWP.—See RANDALL, MN (Consolidated Telecommunications Co. Formerly [MN0202]. This cable system has converted to IPTV)

NORCROSS—See BARRETT, MN (Runestone Cable TV)

NORE TWP.—See McINTOSH, MN (Garden Valley Telephone Co)

NORE TWP.—See MORSE TWP., MN (Paul Bunyan Communications)

NORTH BRANCH—See CAMBRIDGE, MN (Midco)

NORTH HUDSON—See MINNEAPOLIS, WI (Comcast Cable)

NORTH MANKATO—See MANKATO, MN (Charter Communications)

NORTH OAKS—See MINNEAPOLIS, MN (Comcast Cable)

NORTH REDWOOD—See FRANKLIN, MN (Mediacom)

NORTH ST. PAUL—See MINNEAPOLIS, MN (Comcast Cable)

NORTH TWP.—See THIEF RIVER FALLS, MN (Sjoberg's Cable TV Inc)

NORTHERN TWP.—See BEMIDJI, MN (Midco)

NORTHERN TWP.—See SOLWAY, MN (Paul Bunyan Communications)

NORTHFIELD—See ROSEMOUNT, MN (Charter Communications)

NORTHFIELD—See NEW MARKET, MN (Jaguar Communications)

NORTHOME—See MORSE TWP., MN (Paul Bunyan Communications)

NORTHROP—Midco

NORWOOD—Mediacom. Now served by MOUND, MN [MN0010]

NORWOOD—See MOUND, MN (Mediacom)

O'BRIEN TWP.—See SOLWAY, MN (Paul Bunyan Communications)

OAK GROVE—See MINNEAPOLIS, MN (Comcast Cable)

OAK LAWN TWP.—See BRAINERD, MN (Charter Communications)

OAK PARK HEIGHTS—See MINNEAPOLIS, MN (Comcast Cable)

OAK TWP.—See MELROSE, MN (Arvig)

OAK VALLEY TWP.—See PERHAM, MN (Arvig)

OAKDALE—See MINNEAPOLIS, MN (Comcast Cable)

OAKPORT—Formerly served by Loretel Cablevision. Now served by Cable One, FARGO, ND [ND0001]

OGEMA—See PERHAM, MN (Arvig)

OGILVIE—See CAMBRIDGE, MN (Midco)

OKABENA—See HERON LAKE, MN (Midco)

OKLEE—Garden Valley Telephone Co. Now served by McINTOSH, MN [MN0105]

OKLEE—See McINTOSH, MN (Garden Valley Telephone Co)

OKLEE—See McINTOSH, MN (Garden Valley Telephone Co)

OLIVER—See DULUTH, WI (Charter Communications)

OLIVIA—Mediacom. Now served by FRANKLIN, MN [MN0057]

OLIVIA—See FRANKLIN, MN (Mediacom)

ONAMIA—SCI Broadband. Now served by ISLE, MN [MN0313]

ONAMIA—See ISLE, MN (SCI Broadband)

ONSTAD TWP.—See McINTOSH, MN (Garden Valley Telephone Co)

ORONO—See MOUND, MN (Mediacom)

ORONOCO TWP.—See ROCHESTER, MN (Charter Communications)

ORONOCO—See PINE ISLAND, MN (BEVCOMM. Formerly [MN0089]. This cable system has converted to IPTV)

ORTONVILLE—Midcontinent Communications. Now served by WATERTOWN, SD [SD0004]

OSAGE TWP.—See PERHAM, MN (Arvig)

OSAKIS—Charter Communications. Now served by ALEXANDRIA, MN [MN0031]

OSAKIS—See PERHAM, MN (Arvig)

OSAKIS—See ALEXANDRIA, MN (Charter Communications)

OSCAR TWP.—See DALTON, MN (Otter Tail Telcom)

OSLO—Midcontinent Communications. Now served by GRAND FORKS, ND [ND0003]

OSSEO—See MINNEAPOLIS, MN (Comcast Cable)

OSSIAN—See HOUSTON, IA (AcenTek)

OSTRANDER—Formerly served by Arvig. No longer on operation

OSTRANDER—See HOUSTON, MN (AcenTek)

OTENEAGEN TWP.—See MORSE TWP., MN (Paul Bunyan Communications)

OTSEGO—See BUFFALO, MN (Charter Communications)

OTTERTAIL PENINSULA TWP.—See SOLWAY, MN (Paul Bunyan Communications)

OTTERTAIL TWP.—See PERHAM, MN (Arvig)

OTTERTAIL—See PERHAM, MN (Arvig)

OTTO TWP.—See PERHAM, MN (Arvig)

OUTING—See RANDALL, MN (Consolidated Telecommunications Co. Formerly [MN0202]. This cable system has converted to IPTV)

OUTING—See EMILY, MN (Emily Cooperative Telephone. Formerly [MS0081]. This cable system has converted to IPTV)

OWATONNA—Charter Communications

OWATONNA—Jaguar Communications

PALMER TWP.—See CAMBRIDGE, MN (Midco)

PARK RAPIDS—Charter Communications. Now served by BRAINERD, MN [MN0022]

PARK RAPIDS—See PERHAM, MN (Arvig)

PARK RAPIDS—See BRAINERD, MN (Charter Communications)

PARKERS PRAIRIE TWP.—See PARKERS PRAIRIE, MN (Arvig)

PARKERS PRAIRIE—Arvig

PARKLAND—See DULUTH, WI (Charter Communications)

PAYNESVILLE—Mediacom. Now served by PAYNESVILLE, MN [MN0125]

PAYNESVILLE—Mediacom

PELICAN LAKE—Formerly served by Loretel Cablevision. Now served by Arvig, PELICAN RAPIDS, MN

Cable Community Index—Minnesota

[MN0265]

PELICAN LAKE—See PELICAN RAPIDS, MN (Arvig)

PELICAN RAPIDS—Formerly served by Loretel Cablevision. Now served by Arvig, PELICAN RAPIDS, MN [MN0265]

PELICAN RAPIDS—Arvig

PELICAN TWP. (CROW WING COUNTY)—See BRAINERD, MN (Charter Communications)

PELICAN TWP.—See PELICAN RAPIDS, MN (Arvig)

PEMBERTON—See ST. PETER, MN (Mediacom)

PENGILLY—SCI Broadband

PENNOCK—See WILLMAR, MN (Charter Communications)

PEQUOT LAKES—Charter Communications. Now served by BRAINERD, MN [MN0022]

PEQUOT LAKES—See BRAINERD, MN (Charter Communications)

PERHAM TWP.—See PERHAM, MN (Arvig)

PERHAM—Arvig

PERRY LAKE TWP.—See BRAINERD, MN (Charter Communications)

PETERSON—Mediacom. Now served by CALEDONIA, MN [MN0086]

PETERSON—See HOUSTON, MN (AcenTek)

PETERSON—See CALEDONIA, MN (Mediacom)

PIERZ—See CAMBRIDGE, MN (Midco)

PIKE BAY TWP.—See PERHAM, MN (Arvig)

PIKE BAY TWP.—See BEMIDJI, MN (Midco)

PIKE BAY TWP.—See SOLWAY, MN (Paul Bunyan Communications)

PIKE CREEK TWP.—See ST. CLOUD, MN (Charter Communications)

PILLAGER—See RANDALL, MN (Consolidated Telecommunications Co. Formerly [MN0202]. This cable system has converted to IPTV)

PILLAGER—SCI Broadband

PINE CITY TWP.—See CAMBRIDGE, MN (Midco)

PINE CITY—See CAMBRIDGE, MN (Midco)

PINE ISLAND—BEVCOMM (formerly Pine Island Telephone Co.) This cable system has converted to IPTV. See PINE ISLAND, MN [MN5365]

PINE ISLAND—BEVCOMM. Formerly [MN0089]. This cable system has converted to IPTV

PINE LAKE TWP. (PORTIONS)—See McINTOSH, MN (Garden Valley Telephone Co)

PINE LAKE TWP.—See PERHAM, MN (Arvig)

PINE LAKE TWP.—See McINTOSH, MN (Garden Valley Telephone Co)

PINE POINT TWP.—See PERHAM, MN (Arvig)

PINE RIVER—See BRAINERD, MN (Charter Communications)

PINE SPRINGS—See MINNEAPOLIS, MN (Comcast Cable)

PIPESTONE—Mediacom. Now served by IVANHOE, MN [MN0189]

PIPESTONE—See ADRIAN, MN (Clarity Telcom)

PIPESTONE—See IVANHOE, MN (Mediacom)

PLAINVIEW—Midcontinent Communications. Now served by CAMBRIDGE, MN [MN0016]

PLAINVIEW—See WINONA, MN (Hiawatha Broadband. Formerly Winona, MN [MN0398]. This cable system has converted to IPTV)

PLAINVIEW—See CAMBRIDGE, MN (Midco)

PLATO—Formerly served by North American Communications Corp. This cable system has converted to IPTV. Now served by Jaguar Communications, NEW MARKET, MN [MN5374]

PLATO—See NEW MARKET, MN (Jaguar Communications)

PLUMMER—See McINTOSH, MN (Garden Valley Telephone Co)

PLUMMER—See McINTOSH, MN (Garden Valley Telephone Co)

PLYMOUTH—See MINNEAPOLIS, MN (Comcast Cable)

POKEGAMA TWP.—See CAMBRIDGE, MN (Midco)

POLK CENTRE TWP.—See McINTOSH, MN (Garden Valley Telephone Co)

POMROY TWP.—See MORSE TWP., MN (Paul Bunyan Communications)

PONEMAH—See MORSE TWP., MN (Paul Bunyan Communications)

POPLAR RIVER TWP.—See McINTOSH, MN (Garden Valley Telephone Co)

POPPLE GROVE TWP.—See PERHAM, MN (Arvig)

POPPLE TWP.—See McINTOSH, MN (Garden Valley Telephone Co)

PORT HOPE TWP.—See BEMIDJI, MN (Midco)

PORT HOPE TWP.—See SOLWAY, MN (Paul Bunyan Communications)

PORTER—See WOOD LAKE, MN (Midco)

PRESCOTT—See MINNEAPOLIS, WI (Comcast Cable)

PRESTON—See CHATFIELD, MN (Mediacom)

PRINCETON—See CAMBRIDGE, MN (Midco)

PRIOR LAKE—Integra Telecom

PRIOR LAKE—Mediacom

PROCTOR—Mediacom. Now served by CLOQUET, MN [MN0042]

PROCTOR—See CLOQUET, MN (Mediacom)

PUPOSKY—See SOLWAY, MN (Paul Bunyan Communications)

QUEEN TWP.—See McINTOSH, MN (Garden Valley Telephone Co)

QUIRING TWP.—See SOLWAY, MN (Paul Bunyan Communications)

RABBIT LAKE TWP.—See BRAINERD, MN (Charter Communications)

RACINE—Arvig. Now served by GRAND MEADOW, MN [MN0168]

RACINE—See GRAND MEADOW, MN (Arvig)

RAMSEY—See MINNEAPOLIS, MN (Comcast Cable)

RANDALL—Consolidated Telecommunications Co. This cable system has converted to IPTV. See RANDALL, MN [MN5026]

RANDALL—Consolidated Telecommunications Co. Formerly [MN0202]. This cable system has converted to IPTV

RANDOLPH TWP.—See CANNON FALLS TWP., MN (Midco)

RANDOLPH—Formerly served by Cannon Valley Cablevision. Now served by Midcontinent Communications, CANNON FALLS TWP., MN [MN0391]

RANDOLPH—See CANNON FALLS TWP., MN (Midco)

RANIER—See INTERNATIONAL FALLS, MN (Midco)

RAVENNA TWP.—See CANNON FALLS TWP., MN (Midco)

RAVENNA—Formerly served by Cannon Valley Cablevision. Now served by Midcontinent Communications, CANNON FALLS TWP., MN [MN0391]

RAYMOND—Clara City Telephone Co

READING—Formerly served by American Telecasting of Minnesota Inc. No longer in operation

READS LANDING—See CAMBRIDGE, MN (Midco)

RED EYE TWP.—West Central Telephone Assn. Formerly served by MENAHGA, MN [MN0112]. This cable system has converted to IPTV. Now served by MENAHGA, MN [MN5130]

RED EYE TWP.—See MENAHGA, MN (West Central Telephone Assn. This cable system has converted to IPTV)

RED LAKE BAND OF CHIPPEWA INDIAN RESERVATION—See SOLWAY, MN (Paul Bunyan Communications)

RED LAKE FALLS TWP.—See McINTOSH, MN (Garden Valley Telephone Co)

RED LAKE FALLS—See McINTOSH, MN (Garden Valley Telephone Co)

RED LAKE FALLS—Sjoberg's Cable TV Inc

RED LAKE TWP.—See RED LAKE FALLS, MN (Sjoberg's Cable TV Inc)

RED ROCK—Formerly served by North American Communications Corp. No longer in operation

RED WING—Charter Communications. Now served by ROSEMOUNT, MN [MN0009]

RED WING—See ROSEMOUNT, MN (Charter Communications)

RED WING—See WINONA, MN (Hiawatha Broadband. Formerly Winona, MN [MN0398]. This cable system has converted to IPTV)

REDWOOD FALLS—See FRANKLIN, MN (Mediacom)

REDWOOD FALLS—See NEW ULM, MN (NU-Telecom. Formerly [MN0285]. This cable system has converted to IPTV)

REINER TWP.—See McINTOSH, MN (Garden Valley Telephone Co)

REIS TWP.—See McINTOSH, MN (Garden Valley Telephone Co)

REMER—Eagle Cablevision Inc

RENVILLE—See WOOD LAKE, MN (Midco)

REVERE—Clara City Telephone Co

RICE (VILLAGE)—See RICE, MN (Benton Cooperative Telephone)

RICE LAKE TWP.—See DULUTH, MN (Charter Communications)

RICE TWP.—See McINTOSH, MN (Garden Valley Telephone Co)

RICE—Benton Cooperative Telephone. IPTV service is no longer planned

RICE—Benton Cooperative Telephone

RICHFIELD—See MINNEAPOLIS, MN (Comcast Cable)

RICHMOND—See MELROSE, MN (Arvig)

RICHMOND—See CAMBRIDGE, MN (Midco)

RICHVILLE—See PERHAM, MN (Arvig)

RICHWOOD TWP.—See PERHAM, MN (Arvig)

RIVER FALLS TWP.—See McINTOSH, MN (Garden Valley Telephone Co)

RIVER FALLS—See MINNEAPOLIS, WI (Comcast Cable)

Minnesota—Cable Community Index

RIVER TWP.—See McINTOSH, MN (Garden Valley Telephone Co)

RIVERTON—See BRAINERD, MN (Charter Communications)

ROBBINSDALE—See MINNEAPOLIS, MN (Comcast Cable)

ROCHESTER—Charter Communications

ROCKFORD—See BUFFALO, MN (Charter Communications)

ROCKSBURY TWP.—See McINTOSH, MN (Garden Valley Telephone Co)

ROCKSBURY TWP.—See THIEF RIVER FALLS, MN (Sjoberg's Cable TV Inc)

ROCKVILLE—See CAMBRIDGE, MN (Midco)

ROGERS—See MINNEAPOLIS, MN (Comcast Cable)

ROLLINGSTONE—Charter Communications. Now served by EAU CLAIRE, WI [WI0011]

ROLLINGSTONE—Hiawatha Broadband. This cable system has converted to IPTV. Now served by WINONA, MN [MN5161]

ROLLINGSTONE—See WINONA, MN (Hiawatha Broadband. Formerly Winona, MN [MN0398]. This cable system has converted to IPTV)

ROLLIS TWP.—See McINTOSH, MN (Garden Valley Telephone Co)

ROOSEVELT TWP.—See SOLWAY, MN (Paul Bunyan Communications)

ROOSEVELT—See McINTOSH, MN (Garden Valley Telephone Co)

ROSCOE—See MELROSE, MN (Arvig)

ROSE CREEK—Formerly served by North American Communications Corp. This cable system has converted to IPTV. Now served by Jaguar Communications, OWATONNA, MN [MN5121]

ROSE CREEK—See OWATONNA, MN (Jaguar Communications)

ROSEAU—Sjoberg's Cable TV Inc

ROSEBUD TWP.—See McINTOSH, MN (Garden Valley Telephone Co)

ROSEMOUNT—Charter Communications

ROSEMOUNT—See CANNON FALLS TWP., MN (Midco)

ROSEVILLE—Comcast Cable. Now served by MINNEAPOLIS, MN [MN0001]

ROSEVILLE—See MINNEAPOLIS, MN (Comcast Cable)

ROTHSAY—See DALTON, MN (Otter Tail Telcom)

ROUND LAKE TWP.—See PERHAM, MN (Arvig)

ROUND LAKE TWP.—New Century Communications

ROUND LAKE—Midco

ROUND PRAIRIE TWP.—See MELROSE, MN (Arvig)

ROYALTON—See CAMBRIDGE, MN (Midco)

RUSH CITY—See CAMBRIDGE, MN (Midco)

RUSH LAKE TWP.—See PERHAM, MN (Arvig)

RUSH LAKE—See CAMBRIDGE, MN (Midco)

RUSHFORD VILLAGE—See CHATFIELD, MN (Mediacom)

RUSHFORD—See HOUSTON, MN (AcenTek)

RUSHFORD—See CHATFIELD, MN (Mediacom)

RUSHMORE—Formerly served by K-Communications Inc. No longer in operation

RUSHMORE—See ADRIAN, MN (Clarity Telcom)

RUSSELL—See WOOD LAKE, MN (Midco)

RUSSIA TWP.—See McINTOSH, MN (Garden Valley Telephone Co)

RUTHTON—Woodstock Communications

RUTLEDGE (village)—Formerly served by New Century Communications. No longer in operation

RUTLEDGE—See SANDSTONE, MN (SCI Broadband)

SABIN—Midcontinent Communications. Now served by WEST FARGO, ND [ND0230]

SACRED HEART—See WOOD LAKE, MN (Midco)

SAGINAW—SCI Broadband

SANBORN—NU-Telecom. This cable system has converted to IPTV. Now served by NEW ULM, MN [MN5117]

SANBORN—See NEW ULM, MN (NU-Telecom. Formerly [MN0285]. This cable system has converted to IPTV)

SAND CREEK TWP.—See MINNEAPOLIS, MN (Comcast Cable)

SAND LAKE TWP.—See MORSE TWP., MN (Paul Bunyan Communications)

SANDERS TWP.—See McINTOSH, MN (Garden Valley Telephone Co)

SANDSTONE—SCI Broadband

SARTELL—See ST. CLOUD, MN (Charter Communications)

SAUK CENTRE TWP.—See SAUK CENTRE, MN (Arvig)

SAUK CENTRE—Formerly served by Charter Communications. No longer in operation

SAUK CENTRE—Arvig

SAUK RAPIDS—See ST. CLOUD, MN (Charter Communications)

SAVAGE—See PRIOR LAKE, MN (Integra Telecom)

SAVAGE—See PRIOR LAKE, MN (Mediacom)

SCAMBLER TWP.—See PELICAN RAPIDS, MN (Arvig)

SCANDIA TWP.—See McINTOSH, MN (Garden Valley Telephone Co)

SCANDIA—See CAMBRIDGE, MN (Midco)

SCANLON—See CLOQUET, MN (Mediacom)

SCHOOLCRAFT TWP.—See SOLWAY, MN (Paul Bunyan Communications)

SEARLES—See NEW ULM, MN (NU-Telecom. Formerly [MN0285]. This cable system has converted to IPTV)

SEBEKA—See MENAHGA, MN (West Central Telephone Assn. This cable system has converted to IPTV)

SHAFER—See CAMBRIDGE, MN (Midco)

SHAKOPEE—Formerly served by Time Warner Cable. Now served by Comcast Cable, MINNEAPOLIS, MN [MN0001]

SHAKOPEE—See MINNEAPOLIS, MN (Comcast Cable)

SHELDON—See HOUSTON, MN (AcenTek)

SHERBURN—See FAIRMONT, MN (Midco)

SHEVLIN TWP.—See McINTOSH, MN (Garden Valley Telephone Co)

SHEVLIN—Garden Valley Telephone Co. This cable system has converted to IPTV. Now served by McINTOSH, MN [MN5241]

SHEVLIN—See McINTOSH, MN (Garden Valley Telephone Co)

SHINGOBEE—See PERHAM, MN (Arvig)

SHOOKS TWP.—See SOLWAY, MN (Paul Bunyan Communications)

SHOREVIEW—See MINNEAPOLIS, MN (Comcast Cable)

SHOREWOOD—See MOUND, MN (Mediacom)

SHOTLEY TWP.—See SOLWAY, MN (Paul Bunyan Communications)

SHULTZ LAKE TWP.—Formerly served by New Century Communications. No longer in operation

SILVER BAY—Mediacom. Now served by CLOQUET, MN [MN0042]

SILVER BAY—See CLOQUET, MN (Mediacom)

SILVER CREEK TWP.—See CLOQUET, MN (Mediacom)

SILVER LAKE—See HUTCHINSON, MN (Mediacom)

SINCLAIR TWP.—See McINTOSH, MN (Garden Valley Telephone Co)

SKYLINE—See MANKATO, MN (Charter Communications)

SLAYTON—Mediacom. Now served by IVANHOE, MN [MN0189]

SLAYTON—See MARSHALL, MN (Clarity Telcom)

SLAYTON—See IVANHOE, MN (Mediacom)

SLEEPY EYE—See FRANKLIN, MN (Mediacom)

SLEEPY EYE—NU-Telecom (formerly Sleepy Eye Telephone). Formerly served by GOODHUE, MN [MN0208]. This cable system has converted to IPTV

SLETTEN TWP. (PORTIONS)—See McINTOSH, MN (Garden Valley Telephone Co)

SLETTEN TWP.—See McINTOSH, MN (Garden Valley Telephone Co)

SMILEY TWP.—See McINTOSH, MN (Garden Valley Telephone Co)

SOLWAY—Paul Bunyan Communications

SOUTH BEND TWP.—See MANKATO, MN (Charter Communications)

SOUTH HARBOR—See ISLE, MN (SCI Broadband)

SOUTH INTERNATIONAL FALLS—See INTERNATIONAL FALLS, MN (Midco)

SOUTH ST. PAUL—See MINNEAPOLIS, MN (Comcast Cable)

SPICER—See WILLMAR, MN (Charter Communications)

SPOONER—See BAUDETTE, MN (Sjoberg's Cable TV Inc)

SPRING CREEK TWP.—See McINTOSH, MN (Garden Valley Telephone Co)

SPRING GROVE—Mediacom. Now served by CALEDONIA, MN [MN0086]

SPRING GROVE—See HOUSTON, MN (AcenTek)

SPRING GROVE—See CALEDONIA, MN (Mediacom)

SPRING HILL TWP.—See MELROSE, MN (Arvig)

SPRING HILL—See MELROSE, MN (Arvig)

SPRING LAKE PARK—See MINNEAPOLIS, MN (Comcast Cable)

SPRING LAKE TWP.—See PRIOR LAKE, MN (Mediacom)

SPRING LAKE—See PRIOR LAKE, MN (Integra Telecom)

SPRING PARK—See MOUND, MN (Mediacom)

SPRING VALLEY—See CHATFIELD, MN (Mediacom)

SPRINGFIELD—Mediacom. Now served by FRANKLIN, MN [MN0057]

Cable Community Index—Minnesota

SPRINGFIELD—NU-Telecom. This cable system has converted to IPTV. Now served by NEW ULM, MN [MN5117]

SPRINGFIELD—See FRANKLIN, MN (Mediacom)

SPRINGFIELD—See NEW ULM, MN (NU-Telecom. Formerly [MN0285]. This cable system has converted to IPTV)

SPRUCE GROVE TWP.—See McINTOSH, MN (Garden Valley Telephone Co)

SPRUCE VALLEY TWP.—See MIDDLE RIVER, MN (Sjoberg's Cable TV Inc)

SQUAW LAKE—See MORSE TWP., MN (Paul Bunyan Communications)

ST. ANTHONY—See MINNEAPOLIS, MN (Comcast Cable)

ST. AUGUSTA—See CAMBRIDGE, MN (Midco)

ST. BONIFACIUS—See MOUND, MN (Mediacom)

ST. CHARLES—Hiawatha Broadband. Formerly [MN0397]. This cable system has converted to IPTV. Now served by WINONA, MN [MN5161]

ST. CHARLES—Hiawatha Broadband. This cable system has converted to IPTV. Now served by WINONA, MN [MN5161]

ST. CHARLES—See WINONA, MN (Hiawatha Broadband. Formerly Winona, MN [MN0398]. This cable system has converted to IPTV)

ST. CHARLES—See CHATFIELD, MN (Mediacom)

ST. CLAIR—See WASECA COUNTY (portions), MN (Midco)

ST. CLOUD—Formerly served by Astound Broadband. No longer in operation

ST. CLOUD—Charter Communications

ST. CROIX—Formerly served by Comcast Cable. No longer in operation

ST. FRANCIS TWP.—See CAMBRIDGE, MN (Midco)

ST. FRANCIS—See CAMBRIDGE, MN (Midco)

ST. HILAIRE—Garden Valley Telephone Co. Now served by McINTOSH, MN [MN0105]

ST. HILAIRE—See McINTOSH, MN (Garden Valley Telephone Co)

ST. HILAIRE—See McINTOSH, MN (Garden Valley Telephone Co)

ST. JAMES—Mediacom. Now served by ST. PETER (formerly Waseca), MN [MN0043]

ST. JAMES—See ST. PETER, MN (Mediacom)

ST. JOHNS TWP.—See WILLMAR, MN (Charter Communications)

ST. JOSEPH TWP.—See ST. CLOUD, MN (Charter Communications)

ST. JOSEPH TWP.—See CAMBRIDGE, MN (Midco)

ST. JOSEPH—Formerly served by Astound Communications. No longer in operation

ST. JOSEPH—See CAMBRIDGE, MN (Midco)

ST. LOUIS PARK—Formerly served by Time Warner Cable. Now served by Comcast Cable, MINNEAPOLIS, MN [MN0001]

ST. LOUIS PARK—See MINNEAPOLIS, MN (Comcast Cable)

ST. MARTIN TWP.—See MELROSE, MN (Arvig)

ST. MARTIN—See MELROSE, MN (Arvig)

ST. MARYS POINT—See MINNEAPOLIS, MN (Comcast Cable)

ST. MICHAEL—See BUFFALO, MN (Charter Communications)

ST. PAUL PARK—See MINNEAPOLIS, MN (Comcast Cable)

ST. PAUL—Comcast Cable. Now served by MINNEAPOLIS, MN [MN0001]

ST. PAUL—Comcast Cable. Now served by MINNEAPOLIS, MN [MN0001]

ST. PAUL—See MINNEAPOLIS, MN (Comcast Cable)

ST. PETER—Mediacom. Now served by ST. PETER (formerly Waseca), MN [MN0043]

ST. PETER—Mediacom

ST. ROSA—See MELROSE, MN (Arvig)

ST. STEPHEN—See CAMBRIDGE, MN (Midco)

ST. WENDEL TWP.—See CAMBRIDGE, MN (Midco)

STACY—Midcontinent Communications. Now served by CAMBRIDGE, MN [MN0016]

STACY—See CAMBRIDGE, MN (Midco)

STANFORD TWP.—See CAMBRIDGE, MN (Midco)

STANTON TWP.—See CANNON FALLS TWP., MN (Midco)

STAPLES—Charter Communications. Now served by BRAINERD, MN [MN0022]

STAPLES—See BRAINERD, MN (Charter Communications)

STAR LAKE TWP.—See PERHAM, MN (Arvig)

STAR TWP.—See McINTOSH, MN (Garden Valley Telephone Co)

STARBUCK—Mediacom. Now served by MORRIS, MN [MN0210]

STARBUCK—See MORRIS, MN (Mediacom)

STEAMBOAT RIVER TWP.—See PERHAM, MN (Arvig)

STEAMBOAT RIVER TWP.—See SOLWAY, MN (Paul Bunyan Communications)

STEENERSON TWP.—See McINTOSH, MN (Garden Valley Telephone Co)

STEPHEN—Wikstrom Cable LLC

STEWART—See HUTCHINSON, MN (Mediacom)

STEWARTVILLE—See ROCHESTER, MN (Charter Communications)

STILLWATER TWP.—See MINNEAPOLIS, MN (Comcast Cable)

STILLWATER—See MINNEAPOLIS, MN (Comcast Cable)

STOCKTON—Formerly served by Midcontinent Communications. Now served by Charter Communications, EAU CLAIRE, WI [WI0011]

STOCKTON—See WINONA, MN (Hiawatha Broadband. Formerly Winona, MN [MN0398]. This cable system has converted to IPTV)

STORDEN—Midco

STOWE PRAIRIE TWP.—See PERHAM, MN (Arvig)

STURGEON LAKE—See CLOQUET, MN (Mediacom)

SUGAR BUSH TWP.—See PERHAM, MN (Arvig)

SUGAR BUSH TWP.—See SOLWAY, MN (Paul Bunyan Communications)

SULLIVAN LAKE—See RANDALL, MN (Consolidated Telecommunications Co. Formerly [MN0202]. This cable system has converted to IPTV)

SUMMIT TWP.—See SOLWAY, MN (Paul Bunyan Communications)

SUNDAL TWP.—See McINTOSH, MN (Garden Valley Telephone Co)

SUNFISH LAKE—See MINNEAPOLIS, MN (Comcast Cable)

SUPERIOR (VILLAGE)—See DULUTH, WI (Charter Communications)

SVERDRUP TWP.—See PERHAM, MN (Arvig)

SWANVILLE—Formerly served by 391 Satellite LLC. No longer in operation

TACONITE—Formerly served by City of Taconite Cable TV. Now served by Mediacom, CALUMET, MN [MN0027]

TACONITE—See CALUMET, MN (Mediacom)

TAUNTON—See WOOD LAKE, MN (Midco)

TAYLOR TWP.—See SOLWAY, MN (Paul Bunyan Communications)

TAYLORS FALLS—Midcontinent Communications. Now served by CAMBRIDGE, MN [MN0016]

TAYLORS FALLS—See CAMBRIDGE, MN (Midco)

TEN LAKE TWP.—See PERHAM, MN (Arvig)

TEN LAKES TWP.—See SOLWAY, MN (Paul Bunyan Communications)

TENSTRIKE—See SOLWAY, MN (Paul Bunyan Communications)

TERREBONNE TWP.—See McINTOSH, MN (Garden Valley Telephone Co)

THIEF RIVER FALLS—Sjoberg's Cable TV Inc

THIRD RIVER TWP.—See MORSE TWP., MN (Paul Bunyan Communications)

THIRD RIVER TWP.—See SOLWAY, MN (Paul Bunyan Communications)

THOMSON—See CLOQUET, MN (Mediacom)

THORPE TWP.—See PERHAM, MN (Arvig)

TINTAH—See BARRETT, MN (Runestone Cable TV)

TOAD LAKE TWP.—See PERHAM, MN (Arvig)

TONKA BAY—See MOUND, MN (Mediacom)

TOWER—Midco. Now served by ELY, MN [MN0060]

TOWER—See ELY, MN (Midco)

TRACY—Charter Communications. Now served by WILLMAR, MN [MN0018]

TRACY—See WILLMAR, MN (Charter Communications)

TRACY—See MARSHALL, MN (Clarity Telcom)

TRAIL—See McINTOSH, MN (Garden Valley Telephone Co)

TRIMONT—Formerly served by Clara City Telephone Co. No longer in operation

TROY—See MINNEAPOLIS, WI (Comcast Cable)

TRUMAN—Formerly served by Clara City Telephone Co. No longer in operation

TURTLE LAKE TWP.—See PERHAM, MN (Arvig)

TURTLE LAKE TWP.—See SOLWAY, MN (Paul Bunyan Communications)

TURTLE RIVER—See BEMIDJI, MN (Midco)

TURTLE RIVER—See SOLWAY, MN (Paul Bunyan Communications)

TURTLE RVER TWP.—See SOLWAY, MN (Paul Bunyan Communications)

TWIN VALLEY—See PERHAM, MN (Arvig)

TWO HARBORS—Mediacom. Now served by CLOQUET, MN [MN0042]

TWO HARBORS—See CLOQUET, MN (Mediacom)

TYLER—See IVANHOE, MN (Mediacom)

Minnesota—Cable Community Index

ULEN TWP.—See PERHAM, MN (Arvig)

ULEN—Formerly served by Loretel Cablevision. Now served by Arvig, PERHAM, MN [MN0050]

ULEN—See PERHAM, MN (Arvig)

UNDERWOOD—See DALTON, MN (Otter Tail Telcom)

URBANK—See PARKERS PRAIRIE, MN (Arvig)

UTICA—See WINONA, MN (Hiawatha Broadband. Formerly Winona, MN [MN0398]. This cable system has converted to IPTV)

VADNAIS HEIGHTS—See MINNEAPOLIS, MN (Comcast Cable)

VALLEY TWP.—See McINTOSH, MN (Garden Valley Telephone Co)

VELDT TWP.—See McINTOSH, MN (Garden Valley Telephone Co)

VERGAS—See PERHAM, MN (Arvig)

VERMILLION TWP.—See CANNON FALLS TWP., MN (Midco)

VERMILLION—See CANNON FALLS TWP., MN (Midco)

VERNDALE—SCI Broadband

VERNDALE—See MENAHGA, MN (West Central Telephone Assn. This cable system has converted to IPTV)

VERNON CENTER—Formerly served by North American Communications Corp. This cable system has converted to IPTV. Now served by Jaguar Communications, OWATONNA, MN [MN5121]

VERNON CENTER—See OWATONNA, MN (Jaguar Communications)

VESELI—See PRIOR LAKE, MN (Mediacom)

VICTORIA—See MOUND, MN (Mediacom)

VIKING—See THIEF RIVER FALLS, MN (Sjoberg's Cable TV Inc)

VIRGINIA—See EVELETH, MN (Mediacom)

WABANICA—See BAUDETTE, MN (Sjoberg's Cable TV Inc)

WABASHA—Hiawatha Broadband. Formerly [MN0399]. This cable system has converted to IPTV. Now served by WINONA, MN [MN5161]

WABASHA—Hiawatha Broadband. This cable system has converted to IPTV. Now served by WINONA, MN [MN5161]

WABASHA—Midco. Now served by CAMBRIDGE, MN [MN0016]

WABASHA—See WINONA, MN (Hiawatha Broadband. Formerly Winona, MN [MN0398]. This cable system has converted to IPTV)

WABASHA—See CAMBRIDGE, MN (Midco)

WABASSO—Clara City Telephone Co

WABEDO TWP.—See PERHAM, MN (Arvig)

WACONIA—See MOUND, MN (Mediacom)

WADENA—Charter Communications. Now served by BRAINERD, MN [MN0022]

WADENA—See BRAINERD, MN (Charter Communications)

WAHKON—See ISLE, MN (SCI Broadband)

WAITE PARK—See ST. CLOUD, MN (Charter Communications)

WAKEFIELD TWP.—See MELROSE, MN (Arvig)

WAKEFIELD TWP.—See CAMBRIDGE, MN (Midco)

WALDEN TWP.—See BRAINERD, MN (Charter Communications)

WALDORF—Formerly served by Dynax Communications Inc. Now served by Mediacom, ST. PETER (formerly Waseca), MN [MN0043]

WALDORF—See ST. PETER, MN (Mediacom)

WALKER—See PERHAM, MN (Arvig)

WALNUT GROVE—Clara City Telephone Co

WALTHAM—See CANNON FALLS, MN (Mediacom)

WANAMINGO—Midco

WARD SPRINGS—See MELROSE, MN (Arvig)

WARREN—Sjoberg's Cable TV Inc

WARROAD—Sjoberg's Cable TV Inc

WARSAW—Formerly served by North American Communications Corp. This cable system has converted to IPTV. Now served by Jaguar Communications, NEW MARKET, MN [MN5374]

WARSAW—See MORRISTOWN, MN (BEVCOMM)

WARSAW—See NEW MARKET, MN (Jaguar Communications)

WASECA COUNTY (PORTIONS)—Midco

WASECA—See OWATONNA, MN (Jaguar Communications)

WASECA—See ST. PETER, MN (Mediacom)

WASHINGTON TWP.—See OWATONNA, MN (Jaguar Communications)

WASKISH—See SOLWAY, MN (Paul Bunyan Communications)

WATERTOWN—See BUFFALO, MN (Charter Communications)

WATERVILLE—See HOUSTON, IA (AcenTek)

WATERVILLE—See WASECA COUNTY (portions), MN (Midco)

WATKINS—See MELROSE, MN (Arvig)

WATSON—Formerly served by Farmers Mutual Telephone. No longer in operation

WAUBUN—See PERHAM, MN (Arvig)

WAVERLY—See MINNEAPOLIS, MN (Comcast Cable)

WAYZATA—See MOUND, MN (Mediacom)

WEBSTER TWP.—See PRIOR LAKE, MN (Mediacom)

WELCOME—Clara City Telephone Co

WELLS TWP.—See NEW MARKET, MN (Jaguar Communications)

WELLS—Mediacom. Now served by ST. PETER (formerly Waseca), MN [MN0043]

WELLS—See NEW PRAGUE, MN (BEVCOMM. Formerly [MN0337]. This cable system has converted to IPTV)

WELLS—See ST. PETER, MN (Mediacom)

WENDELL—See BARRETT, MN (Runestone Cable TV)

WEST CONCORD—See CANNON FALLS, MN (Mediacom)

WEST LAKELAND TWP.—See MINNEAPOLIS, MN (Comcast Cable)

WEST ST. PAUL—See MINNEAPOLIS, MN (Comcast Cable)

WESTBROOK—Formerly served by US Cable of Coastal Texas LP. No longer in operation

WESTBROOK—Westbrook Public Utilities

WHEATON—Mediacom. Now served by APPLETON, MN [MN0106]

WHEATON—See APPLETON, MN (Mediacom)

WHEELER—See BAUDETTE, MN (Sjoberg's Cable TV Inc)

WHIPHOLT—See PERHAM, MN (Arvig)

WHITE BEAR LAKE—See MINNEAPOLIS, MN (Comcast Cable)

WHITE BEAR TWP.—See MINNEAPOLIS, MN (Comcast Cable)

WHITE OAK TWP.—See PERHAM, MN (Arvig)

WHITE ROCK—See GOODHUE, MN (NU-Telecom. Formerly [MN0208]. This cable system has converted to IPTV)

WHITE TWP.—See EVELETH, MN (Mediacom)

WHITELAW—See MINNEAPOLIS, WI (Comcast Cable)

WILKINSON TWP.—See PERHAM, MN (Arvig)

WILKINSON TWP.—See SOLWAY, MN (Paul Bunyan Communications)

WILLERNIE—See MINNEAPOLIS, MN (Comcast Cable)

WILLMAR—Charter Communications

WILLOW RIDGE—See SANDSTONE, MN (SCI Broadband)

WILLOW RIVER—Formerly served by New Century Communications. No longer in operation

WILMONT—Formerly served by K-Communications Inc. No longer in operation

WILSON (TOWN)—See WINONA, MN (Hiawatha Broadband. Formerly Winona, MN [MN0398]. This cable system has converted to IPTV)

WILTON—See BEMIDJI, MN (Midco)

WILTON—See SOLWAY, MN (Paul Bunyan Communications)

WINDERMERE TWP.—See CLOQUET, MN (Mediacom)

WINDOM—Windom Telecomm

WINGER TWP.—See McINTOSH, MN (Garden Valley Telephone Co)

WINGER TWP.—See McINTOSH, MN (Garden Valley Telephone Co)

WINGER—See McINTOSH, MN (Garden Valley Telephone Co)

WINGER—See McINTOSH, MN (Garden Valley Telephone Co)

WINNEBAGO—Mediacom. Now served by ST. PETER (formerly Waseca), MN [MN0043]

WINNEBAGO—See NEW PRAGUE, MN (BEVCOMM. Formerly [MN0337]. This cable system has converted to IPTV)

WINNEBAGO—See ST. PETER, MN (Mediacom)

WINONA—Charter Communications. Now served by EAU CLAIRE, WI [WI0011]

WINONA—Hiawatha Broadband. This cable system has converted to IPTV. Now served by WINONA, MN [MN5161]

WINONA—Hiawatha Broadband. Formerly Winona, MN [MN0398]. This cable system has converted to IPTV

WINSOR TWP.—See McINTOSH, MN (Garden Valley Telephone Co)

WINSTED—See HUTCHINSON, MN (Mediacom)

WINTHROP—See FRANKLIN, MN (Mediacom)

WINTON—See ELY, MN (Midco)

WIRT TWP.—See MORSE TWP., MN (Paul Bunyan Communications)

WOLF LAKE TWP.—See PERHAM, MN (Arvig)

WOLFORD—See BRAINERD, MN (Charter Communications)

WOOD LAKE—Clara City Telephone Co

Cable Community Index—Mississippi

WOOD LAKE—Midco

WOODBURY—See MINNEAPOLIS, MN (Comcast Cable)

WOODLAND—See MOUND, MN (Mediacom)

WOODROW TWP.—See SOLWAY, MN (Paul Bunyan Communications)

WOODSIDE TWP. (PORTIONS)—See McINTOSH, MN (Garden Valley Telephone Co)

WOODSIDE TWP.—See McINTOSH, MN (Garden Valley Telephone Co)

WOODSTOCK—See RUTHTON, MN (Woodstock Communications)

WORTHINGTON—See ADRIAN, MN (Clarity Telcom)

WORTHINGTON—Mediacom

WRENSHALL—Formerly served by New Century Communications. No longer in operation

WYANDOTTE TWP.—See McINTOSH, MN (Garden Valley Telephone Co)

WYKOFF—Formerly served by North American Communications Corp. Now served by Arvig, GRAND MEADOW, MN [MN0168]

WYKOFF—See GRAND MEADOW, MN (Arvig)

WYLIE TWP.—See McINTOSH, MN (Garden Valley Telephone Co)

WYOMING—See CAMBRIDGE, MN (Midco)

YOUNG AMERICA—See MOUND, MN (Mediacom)

YUCATAN—See HOUSTON, MN (AcenTek)

ZEMPLE—See MORSE TWP., MN (Paul Bunyan Communications)

ZIMMERMAN—See CAMBRIDGE, MN (Midco)

ZION TWP.—See MELROSE, MN (Arvig)

ZUMBROTA—See ROCHESTER, MN (Charter Communications)

MISSISSIPPI

ABBEVILLE—See PONTOTOC, MS (MaxxSouth Broadband)

ABERDEEN TWP.—MetroCast Mississippi. Now served by PONTOTOC, MS [MS0045]

ABERDEEN TWP.—See PONTOTOC, MS (MaxxSouth Broadband)

ACKERMAN—Formerly served by Delta Telephone (Telapex). Now served by Franklin Telephone, MEADVILLE, MS [MS5012]

ACKERMAN—See MEADVILLE, MS (Franklin Telephone. Formerly [MS0069]. This cable system has converted to IPTV)

ADAMS COUNTY—See NATCHEZ, MS (Cable One)

ALCORN COUNTY (PORTIONS)—See CORINTH, MS (Comcast Cable)

ALTOONA—See TUPELO, AL (Comcast Cable)

AMORY—MetroCast Mississippi. Now served by PONTOTOC, MS [MS0045]

AMORY—See PONTOTOC, MS (MaxxSouth Broadband)

ANGUILLA—NewWave Communications

ARCOLA—NewWave Communications

ARTESIA—Formerly served by Cable TV Inc. No longer in operation

ARTESIA—Franklin Telephone (Telapex). Now served by MEADVILLE, MS [MS5012]

ARTESIA—See MEADVILLE, MS (Franklin Telephone. Formerly [MS0069]. This cable system has converted to IPTV)

ASHLAND—MetroCast Mississippi. Now served by PONTOTOC, MS [MS0045]

ASHLAND—See PONTOTOC, MS (MaxxSouth Broadband)

ATTALA COUNTY (UNINCORPORATED AREAS)—See KOSCIUSKO, MS (MaxxSouth Broadband)

ATTALA—See TUPELO, AL (Comcast Cable)

BALDWYN—MetroCast Mississippi. Now served by PONTOTOC, MS [MS0045]

BALDWYN—See PONTOTOC, MS (MaxxSouth Broadband)

BARLOW—See MEADVILLE, MS (Franklin Telephone. Formerly [MS0069]. This cable system has converted to IPTV)

BASSFIELD—Alliance Communications

BATESVILLE—See CLARKSDALE, MS (Cable One)

BAY SPRINGS—TEC (formerly Bay Springs Telephone) This cable system has converted to IPTV. See BAY SPRINGS, MS [MS5034]

BAY SPRINGS—TEC (formerly Video Inc.) This cable system has converted to IPTV. See BAY SPRINGS, MS [MS5034]

BAY SPRINGS—TEC. This cable system has converted to IPTV

BAY ST. LOUIS—Mediacom. Now served by WAVELAND, MS [MS0022]

BAY ST. LOUIS—See WAVELAND, MS (Mediacom)

BEAUMONT—Mediacom

BECKER—See PONTOTOC, MS (MaxxSouth Broadband)

BELDEN—See TUPELO, MS (Comcast Cable)

BELMONT—Formerly served by Almega Cable. No longer in operation

BELMONT—MetroCast Mississippi. Now served by PONTOTOC, MS [MS0045]

BELMONT—See PONTOTOC, MS (MaxxSouth Broadband)

BELZONI—Cable TV of Belzoni Inc

BENNDALE—See MEADVILLE, MS (Franklin Telephone. Formerly [MS0069]. This cable system has converted to IPTV)

BENOIT—Formerly served by J & L Cable. No longer in operation

BENTONIA—Formerly served by Comcast Cable. No longer in operation

BIG COVE—See TUPELO, AL (Comcast Cable)

BILOXI—Cable One. Now served by GULFPORT, MS [MS0008]

BILOXI—Formerly served by Prime Time Communications. No longer in operation

BILOXI—See GULFPORT, MS (Cable One)

BISSELL—See TUPELO, MS (Comcast Cable)

BLUE MOUNTAIN—See RIPLEY, MS (Ripley Video Cable Co. Inc)

BOLIVAR COUNTY (PORTIONS)—See CLEVELAND, MS (Cable One)

BOLTON—See JACKSON, MS (Comcast Cable)

BOONEVILLE—MetroCast Mississippi. Now served by PONTOTOC, MS [MS0045]

BOONEVILLE—See PONTOTOC, MS (MaxxSouth Broadband)

BOYLE—See CLEVELAND, MS (Cable One)

BRANDON—See JACKSON, MS (Comcast Cable)

BRAXTON—See MENDENHALL, MS (Bailey Cable TV Inc)

BROOKHAVEN—Cable One

BROOKHAVEN—See MEADVILLE, MS (Franklin Telephone. Formerly [MS0069]. This cable system has converted to IPTV)

BROOKSVILLE—See MACON, MS (Cable TV Inc)

BROOKSVILLE—See MEADVILLE, MS (Franklin Telephone. Formerly [MS0069]. This cable system has converted to IPTV)

BROWNSBORO—See TUPELO, AL (Comcast Cable)

BRUCE—MetroCast Mississippi. Now served by PONTOTOC, MS [MS0045]

BRUCE—See PONTOTOC, MS (MaxxSouth Broadband)

BUCKATUNNA—See WAYNESBORO, MS (NewWave Communications)

BUDE—See MEADVILLE, MS (Franklin Telephone. Formerly [MS0069]. This cable system has converted to IPTV)

BURNSVILLE—Formerly served by Almega Cable. No longer in operation

BURNSVILLE—Formerly served by MetroCast Mississippi. Now served by MaxxSouth Broadband, PONTOTOC, MS [MS0045]

BURNSVILLE—See PONTOTOC, MS (MaxxSouth Broadband)

CALEDONIA—See COLUMBUS, MS (Cable One)

CALHOUN CITY—MetroCast Mississippi. Now served by PONTOTOC, MS [MS0045]

CALHOUN CITY—See PONTOTOC, MS (MaxxSouth Broadband)

CALHOUN—See JACKSON, LA (Comcast Cable)

CANTON—Comcast Cable. Now served by JACKSON, MS [MS0001]

CANTON—See JACKSON, MS (Comcast Cable)

CARRIERRE—Charter Communications. Now served by SLIDELL, LA [LA0182]

CARROLL COUNTY (PORTIONS)—See GREENWOOD, MS (Suddenlink Communications)

CARROLLTON—See GRENADA, MS (Cable One)

CARTHAGE—MaxxSouth Broadband

CARY—Formerly served by J & L Cable. No longer in operation

CENTREVILLE—Bailey Cable TV Inc

CHARLESTON—Cable One. Now served by GRENADA, MS [MS0021]

CHARLESTON—See GRENADA, MS (Cable One)

CHEROKEE COUNTY (PORTIONS)—See TUPELO, AL (Comcast Cable)

CHESTER—See MEADVILLE, MS (Franklin Telephone. Formerly [MS0069]. This cable system has converted to IPTV)

CHICKASAW COUNTY (PORTIONS)—See TUPELO, MS (Comcast Cable)

CHOCTAW COUNTY (PORTIONS)—See MEADVILLE, MS (Franklin Telephone. Formerly [MS0069]. This cable system has converted to IPTV)

CHOCTAW INDIAN RESERVATION—See PHILADELPHIA, MS (MaxxSouth Broadband)

CHUNKY—Formerly served by Zoom Media. No longer in operation

Mississippi—Cable Community Index

CLARKE COUNTY (PORTIONS)—See HATTIESBURG, MS (Comcast Cable)

CLARKSDALE—Cable One

CLAY COUNTY (PORTIONS)—See TUPELO, MS (Comcast Cable)

CLEARY HEIGHTS—See JACKSON, MS (Comcast Cable)

CLEVELAND—Cable One

CLINTON—See JACKSON, MS (Comcast Cable)

CLOVERDALE—See TUPELO, AL (Comcast Cable)

COAHOMA COUNTY—See CLARKSDALE, MS (Cable One)

COAHOMA—Media3

COFFEEVILLE—Formerly served by MetroCast Mississippi. Now served by MaxxSouth Broadband, PONTOTOC, MS [MS0045]

COFFEEVILLE—See PONTOTOC, MS (MaxxSouth Broadband)

COLBERT COUNTY (PORTIONS)—See TUPELO, AL (Comcast Cable)

COLES POINT—Formerly served by Foster Communications Inc. No longer in operation

COLLINS—Media3

COLUMBIA—Media3

COLUMBUS AFB—See COLUMBUS, MS (Cable One)

COLUMBUS—Cable One

CONCORDIA PARISH (PORTIONS)—See NATCHEZ, LA (Cable One)

COPIAH COUNTY—See CRYSTAL SPRINGS, MS (Bailey Cable TV Inc)

CORINTH—Formerly served by Zoom Media. No longer in operation

CORINTH—Comcast Cable

COTTONDALE (TUSCALOOSA COUNTY)—See TUPELO, AL (Comcast Cable)

COURTLAND—See CLARKSDALE, MS (Cable One)

COVINGTON COUNTY (PORTIONS)—See COLLINS, MS (Media3)

CRAWFORD—Formerly served by Cable TV Inc. No longer in operation

CRAWFORD—See MEADVILLE, MS (Franklin Telephone. Formerly [MS0069]. This cable system has converted to IPTV)

CROSBY—Franklin Telephone (Telapex). This cable system has converted to IPTV. Now served by MEADVILLE, MS [MS5012]

CROSBY—See MEADVILLE, MS (Franklin Telephone. Formerly [MS0069]. This cable system has converted to IPTV)

CROWDER—Alliance Communications

CRYSTAL SPRINGS—Telepak Networks (Telapex). Now served by MEADVILLE, MS [MS5012]

CRYSTAL SPRINGS—Bailey Cable TV Inc

CRYSTAL SPRINGS—See MEADVILLE, MS (Franklin Telephone. Formerly [MS0069]. This cable system has converted to IPTV)

D'IBERVILLE—See GULFPORT, MS (Cable One)

D'LO—See MENDENHALL, MS (Bailey Cable TV Inc)

DE KALB—Formerly served by Zoom Media. No longer in operation

DECATUR—Formerly served by Mediacom. Now served by MaxxSouth Broadband, PONTOTOC, MS [MS0045]

DECATUR—See PONTOTOC, MS (MaxxSouth Broadband)

DEERFIELD—See JACKSON, MS (Comcast Cable)

DENNIS—See PONTOTOC, MS (MaxxSouth Broadband)

DERMA—See PONTOTOC, MS (MaxxSouth Broadband)

DIAMONDHEAD—See GULFPORT, MS (Cable One)

DREW—See CLEVELAND, MS (Cable One)

DUCK HILL—See GRENADA, MS (Cable One)

DUNCAN—See CLARKSDALE, MS (Cable One)

DURANT—See GRENADA, MS (Cable One)

EAGLE LAKE—Franklin Telephone (Telapex). This cable system has converted to IPTV. Now served by MEADVILLE, MS [MS5012]

EAGLE LAKE—See MEADVILLE, MS (Franklin Telephone. Formerly [MS0069]. This cable system has converted to IPTV)

ECRU—See PONTOTOC, MS (MaxxSouth Broadband)

EDDICETON—See MEADVILLE, MS (Franklin Telephone. Formerly [MS0069]. This cable system has converted to IPTV)

EDWARDS—See JACKSON, MS (Comcast Cable)

ELLISVILLE—See HATTIESBURG, MS (Comcast Cable)

ENTERPRISE—See QUITMAN, MS (NewWave Communications)

ESCATAWPA—See GULFPORT, MS (Cable One)

ETOWAH COUNTY (PORTIONS)—See TUPELO, AL (Comcast Cable)

EUPORA—Cable TV Inc

EVERGREEN—Formerly served by SouthTel Communications L.P. No longer in operation

FANNIN—See JACKSON, MS (Comcast Cable)

FARMINGTON—See CORINTH, MS (Comcast Cable)

FAYETTE—Formerly served by Almega Cable. No longer in operation

FLORA—Franklin Telephone (Telapex). This cable system has converted to IPTV. See FLORA, MS [MS5019]

FLORA—Franklin Telephone (Telapex). Formerly [MS0148]. This cable system has converted to IPTV

FLORENCE—See TUPELO, AL (Comcast Cable)

FLORENCE—See JACKSON, MS (Comcast Cable)

FLOWOOD—See JACKSON, MS (Comcast Cable)

FOREST—MaxxSouth Broadband

FORREST COUNTY (PORTIONS)—See HATTIESBURG, MS (Comcast Cable)

FOXWORTH—See COLUMBIA, MS (Media3)

FRANKLIN COUNTY (PORTIONS)—See MEADVILLE, MS (Franklin Telephone. Formerly [MS0069]. This cable system has converted to IPTV)

FRANKLIN CREEK—Formerly served by CableSouth Inc. No longer in operation

FRIARS POINT—See COAHOMA, MS (Media3)

FULTON—Comcast Cable. Now served by TUPELO, MS [MS0009]

FULTON—See TUPELO, MS (Comcast Cable)

GADSDEN—See TUPELO, AL (Comcast Cable)

GAUTIER—See GULFPORT, MS (Cable One)

GEORGE COUNTY—See LUCEDALE, MS (Mediacom)

GLEN—See CORINTH, MS (Comcast Cable)

GLENCOE—See TUPELO, AL (Comcast Cable)

GLOSTER—Bailey Cable TV Inc

GOLDEN—See PONTOTOC, MS (MaxxSouth Broadband)

GOODMAN—See GRENADA, MS (Cable One)

GREENVILLE—Suddenlink Communications

GREENWOOD—Suddenlink Communications

GRENADA COUNTY—See GRENADA, MS (Cable One)

GRENADA—Cable One

GULFPORT—Cable One

GUNNISON—Formerly served by J & L Cable. No longer in operation

GUNTOWN—See PONTOTOC, MS (MaxxSouth Broadband)

GUYS—See CORINTH, TN (Comcast Cable)

HAMILTON—See COLUMBUS, MS (Cable One)

HAMPTON COVE—See TUPELO, AL (Comcast Cable)

HANCOCK COUNTY (PORTIONS)—See GULFPORT, MS (Cable One)

HANCOCK COUNTY (PORTIONS)—See WAVELAND, MS (Mediacom)

HARRISON COUNTY (PORTIONS)—See GULFPORT, MS (Cable One)

HATLEY—See PONTOTOC, MS (MaxxSouth Broadband)

HATTIESBURG—Comcast Cable

HAWK PRIDE MOUNTAIN—See TUPELO, AL (Comcast Cable)

HAZELHURST—See MEADVILLE, MS (Franklin Telephone. Formerly [MS0069]. This cable system has converted to IPTV)

HAZLEHURST—Bailey Cable TV Inc

HEIDELBERG—See HATTIESBURG, MS (Comcast Cable)

HERMANVILLE—See MEADVILLE, MS (Franklin Telephone. Formerly [MS0069]. This cable system has converted to IPTV)

HICKORY FLAT—Formerly served by MetroCast Mississippi. Now served by MaxxSouth Broadband, PONTOTOC, MS [MS0045]

HICKORY FLAT—See PONTOTOC, MS (MaxxSouth Broadband)

HINDS COUNTY (PORTIONS)—See JACKSON, MS (Comcast Cable)

HOKES BLUFF—See TUPELO, AL (Comcast Cable)

HOLLANDALE—NewWave Communications

HOLLY BLUFF—See MEADVILLE, MS (Franklin Telephone. Formerly [MS0069]. This cable system has converted to IPTV)

HOLLY SPRINGS—Formerly served by MetroCast Mississippi. Now served by MaxxSouth Broadband, PONTOTOC, MS [MS0045]

HOLLY SPRINGS—See PONTOTOC, MS (MaxxSouth Broadband)

HOLT—See TUPELO, AL (Comcast Cable)

Cable Community Index—Mississippi

HOUSTON—Formerly served by MetroCast Mississippi. Now served by MaxxSouth Broadband, PONTOTOC, MS [MS0045]

HOUSTON—See PONTOTOC, MS (MaxxSouth Broadband)

HUMPHREY'S COUNTY (PORTIONS)—See MEADVILLE, MS (Franklin Telephone. Formerly [MS0069]. This cable system has converted to IPTV)

HUNTSVILLE—See TUPELO, AL (Comcast Cable)

INDIANOLA—Formerly served by Adelphia Communications. Now served by Suddenlink Communications, GREENWOOD, MS [MS0151]

INDIANOLA—See GREENWOOD, MS (Suddenlink Communications)

INGOMAR—See PONTOTOC, MS (MaxxSouth Broadband)

INVERNESS—Franklin Telephone (Telapex). Formerly [MS0080]. This cable system has converted to IPTV. Now served by MEADVILLE, MS [MS5012]

INVERNESS—See MEADVILLE, MS (Franklin Telephone. Formerly [MS0069]. This cable system has converted to IPTV)

ISOLA-INVERNESS—Franklin Telephone (Telapex). This cable system has converted to IPTV. Now served by MEADVILLE, MS [MS5012]

ISOLA—Delta Telephone (Telapex). Formerly [MS0080]. This cable system has converted to IPTV. Now served by MEADVILLE, MS [MS5012]

ISOLA—See MEADVILLE, MS (Franklin Telephone. Formerly [MS0069]. This cable system has converted to IPTV)

ITAWAMBA COUNTY (PORTIONS)—See TUPELO, MS (Comcast Cable)

ITTA BENA—Cable One. Now served by GRENADA, MS [MS0021]

ITTA BENA—See GRENADA, MS (Cable One)

IUKA—MetroCast Mississippi. Now served by PONTOTOC, MS [MS0045]

IUKA—See PONTOTOC, MS (MaxxSouth Broadband)

JACKSON COUNTY (PORTIONS)—See GULFPORT, MS (Cable One)

JACKSON—Comcast Cable

JANICE—See MEADVILLE, MS (Franklin Telephone. Formerly [MS0069]. This cable system has converted to IPTV)

JASPER COUNTY (PORTIONS)—See HATTIESBURG, MS (Comcast Cable)

JEFFERSON COUNTY (PORTIONS)—See TUPELO, AL (Comcast Cable)

JOHNS—See JACKSON, MS (Comcast Cable)

JONES COUNTY (PORTIONS)—See HATTIESBURG, MS (Comcast Cable)

JONESTOWN—See COAHOMA, MS (Media3)

JUMPERTOWN—Formerly served by Vista III Media. Now served by MaxxSouth Broadband, PONTOTOC, MS [MS0045]

JUMPERTOWN—See PONTOTOC, MS (MaxxSouth Broadband)

KEESLER AFB—See GULFPORT, MS (Cable One)

KILMICHAEL—See GRENADA, MS (Cable One)

KILN—Formerly served by Trust Cable. No longer in operation

KOSCIUSKO—MaxxSouth Broadband

KOSSUTH—Formerly served by Zoom Media. No longer in operation

LAFAYETTE COUNTY (UNINCORPORATED AREAS)—See PONTOTOC, MS (MaxxSouth Broadband)

LAKE RIDGELEA—See JACKSON, MS (Comcast Cable)

LAKE—Formerly served by Zoom Media. No longer in operation

LAKESHORE—See JACKSON, LA (Comcast Cable)

LAKEVIEW—See TUPELO, AL (Comcast Cable)

LAMAR COUNTY (PORTIONS)—See HATTIESBURG, MS (Comcast Cable)

LAMBERT—See CLARKSDALE, MS (Cable One)

LAUDERDALE COUNTY (PORTIONS)—See TUPELO, AL (Comcast Cable)

LAUDERDALE COUNTY (PORTIONS)—See HATTIESBURG, MS (Comcast Cable)

LAUDERDALE—Comcast Cable. Now served by HATTIESBURG, MS [MS0005]

LAUDERDALE—See HATTIESBURG, MS (Comcast Cable)

LAUREL—Comcast Cable. Now served by HATTIESBURG, MS [MS0005]

LAUREL—See HATTIESBURG, MS (Comcast Cable)

LAUREL—See BAY SPRINGS, MS (TEC. This cable system has converted to IPTV)

LAWRENCE—See MEADVILLE, MS (Franklin Telephone. Formerly [MS0069]. This cable system has converted to IPTV)

LEAKE COUNTY (PORTIONS)—See CARTHAGE, MS (MaxxSouth Broadband)

LEAKESVILLE—Alliance Communications

LEE COUNTY (PORTIONS)—See TUPELO, MS (Comcast Cable)

LEE COUNTY (UNINCORPORATED AREAS)—See PONTOTOC, MS (MaxxSouth Broadband)

LEFLORE COUNTY—See GRENADA, MS (Cable One)

LEFLORE COUNTY—See GREENWOOD, MS (Suddenlink Communications)

LELAND—NewWave Communications

LEXINGTON—Formerly served by CableSouth Media. Now served by Cable One, GRENADA, MS [MS0021]

LEXINGTON—See GRENADA, MS (Cable One)

LIBERTY—Bailey Cable TV Inc

LINCOLN COUNTY (PORTIONS)—See BROOKHAVEN, MS (Cable One)

LONG BEACH—See GULFPORT, MS (Cable One)

LOST RABBIT—See FLORA, MS (Franklin Telephone (Telapex). Formerly [MS0148]. This cable system has converted to IPTV)

LOUIN—See BAY SPRINGS, MS (TEC. This cable system has converted to IPTV)

LOUISE—Franklin Telephone (Telapex). This cable system has converted to IPTV. Now served by MEADVILLE, MS [MS5012]

LOUISE—Franklin Telephone (Telapex). This cable system has converted to IPTV. Now served by MEADVILLE, MS [MS5012]

LOUISE—See MEADVILLE, MS (Franklin Telephone. Formerly [MS0069]. This cable system has converted to IPTV)

LOUISVILLE—Formerly served by Mediacom. Now served by MaxxSouth Broadband, PONTOTOC, MS [MS0045]

LOUISVILLE—See PONTOTOC, MS (MaxxSouth Broadband)

LOWNDES COUNTY—See COLUMBUS, MS (Cable One)

LUCEDALE—Mediacom

LULA—See COAHOMA, MS (Media3)

LUMBERTON—Media3

LYON—See CLARKSDALE, MS (Cable One)

MABEN—Formerly served by MetroCast Mississippi. Now served by MaxxSouth Broadband, PONTOTOC, MS [MS0045]

MABEN—See PONTOTOC, MS (MaxxSouth Broadband)

MACEDONIA—Formerly served by Zoom Media. No longer in operation

MACON—Cable TV Inc

MADISON COUNTY (PORTIONS)—See TUPELO, AL (Comcast Cable)

MADISON COUNTY (PORTIONS)—See JACKSON, MS (Comcast Cable)

MADISON—See TUPELO, AL (Comcast Cable)

MADISON—See JACKSON, MS (Comcast Cable)

MAGEE—Bailey Cable TV Inc

MAGNOLIA—See BROOKHAVEN, MS (Cable One)

MANATACHIE—See TUPELO, MS (Comcast Cable)

MARIETTA—See TUPELO, MS (Comcast Cable)

MARION COUNTY (PORTIONS)—See COLUMBIA, MS (Media3)

MARION—See HATTIESBURG, MS (Comcast Cable)

MARKS—See CLARKSDALE, MS (Cable One)

MATHISTON—See PONTOTOC, MS (MaxxSouth Broadband)

MAYERSVILLE—Formerly served by J & L Cable. No longer in operation

MCADAMS—See KOSCIUSKO, MS (MaxxSouth Broadband)

MCCOMB—See BROOKHAVEN, MS (Cable One)

MCLAIN—See MEADVILLE, MS (Franklin Telephone. Formerly [MS0069]. This cable system has converted to IPTV)

MCLAURIN—Formerly served by Home Cable Entertainment. No longer in operation

MCNAIRY COUNTY (PORTIONS)—See CORINTH, TN (Comcast Cable)

MEADVILLE-BUDE—Franklin Telephone (Telapex). This cable system has converted to IPTV. Now served by MEADVILLE, MS [MS5012]

MEADVILLE—Franklin Telephone. Formerly [MS0069]. This cable system has converted to IPTV

MENDENHALL—Bailey Cable TV Inc

MERIDIAN NAVAL AIR STATION—Media3

MERIDIAN—Comcast Cable. Now served by HATTIESBURG, MS [MS0005]

MERIDIAN—See HATTIESBURG, MS (Comcast Cable)

MERIDIANVILLE—See TUPELO, AL (Comcast Cable)

MERIGOLD—See CLEVELAND, MS (Cable One)

METCALFE—See GREENVILLE, MS (Suddenlink Communications)

MICHIE—See CORINTH, TN (Comcast Cable)

Mississippi—Cable Community Index

MONROE—See JACKSON, LA (Comcast Cable)

MONTGOMERY COUNTY (PORTIONS)—See GRENADA, MS (Cable One)

MONTICELLO—Formerly served by Zoom Media. No longer in operation

MOOREVILLE—Formerly served by Foster Communications Inc. No longer in operation

MOOREVILLE—Formerly served by SouthTel Communications LP. No longer in operation

MOOREVILLE—See TUPELO, MS (Comcast Cable)

MOORHEAD—See GREENWOOD, MS (Suddenlink Communications)

MORTON—See FOREST, MS (MaxxSouth Broadband)

MOSS POINT—See GULFPORT, MS (Cable One)

MOUND BAYOU—Formerly served by Galaxy Cablevision. Now served by Cable One, CLEVELAND, MS [MS0019]

MOUND BAYOU—See CLEVELAND, MS (Cable One)

MOUNT OLIVE—See MENDENHALL, MS (Bailey Cable TV Inc)

MUSCLE SHOALS—See TUPELO, AL (Comcast Cable)

MYRTLE—See PONTOTOC, MS (MaxxSouth Broadband)

NATCHEZ—Cable One

NESHOBA COUNTY (UNINCORPORATED AREAS)—See PHILADELPHIA, MS (MaxxSouth Broadband)

NETTLETON—Formerly served by MetroCast Mississippi. Now served by MaxxSouth Broadband, PONTOTOC, MS [MS0045]

NETTLETON—See PONTOTOC, MS (MaxxSouth Broadband)

NEW ALBANY—Formerly served by MetroCast Mississippi. Now served by MaxxSouth Broadband, PONTOTOC, MS [MS0045]

NEW ALBANY—See PONTOTOC, MS (MaxxSouth Broadband)

NEW AUGUSTA—Franklin Telephone (Telapex). This cable system has converted to IPTV. Now served by MEADVILLE, MS [MS5012]

NEW AUGUSTA—Telapex. This cable system has converted to IPTV. Now served by Franklin Telephone (Telapex), MEADVILLE, MS [MS5012]

NEW AUGUSTA—See MEADVILLE, MS (Franklin Telephone. Formerly [MS0069]. This cable system has converted to IPTV)

NEW HEBRON—Franklin Telephone (Telapex). This cable system has converted to IPTV. Now served by MEADVILLE, MS [MS5012]

NEW HEBRON—Franklin Telephone (Telapex). This cable system has converted to IPTV. Now served by MEADVILLE, MS [MS5012]

NEW HEBRON—See MEADVILLE, MS (Franklin Telephone. Formerly [MS0069]. This cable system has converted to IPTV)

NEW HOPE—See COLUMBUS, MS (Cable One)

NEW SIGHT—See BROOKHAVEN, MS (Cable One)

NEWTON—Formerly served by MetroCast Mississippi. Now served by MaxxSouth Broadband, PONTOTOC, MS [MS0045]

NEWTON—See PONTOTOC, MS (MaxxSouth Broadband)

NORTH CARROLLTON—See GRENADA, MS (Cable One)

NORTHPORT—See TUPELO, AL (Comcast Cable)

NOXAPATER—See PONTOTOC, MS (MaxxSouth Broadband)

OAKLAND—Formerly served by L & J Cable. No longer in operation

OCEAN SPRINGS—See GULFPORT, MS (Cable One)

OCEAN SPRINGS—See ST. ANDREWS, MS (Mediacom)

OKOLONA—See TUPELO, MS (Comcast Cable)

OKTIBBEHA COUNTY (UNINCORPORATED AREAS)—See PONTOTOC, MS (MaxxSouth Broadband)

OKTIBBEHA COUNTY—Dixie Cablevision Inc

OSYKA—Formerly served by Almega Cable. No longer in operation

OUACHITA PARISH (NORTHERN PORTION)—See JACKSON, LA (Comcast Cable)

OWENS CROSS ROADS—See TUPELO, AL (Comcast Cable)

OXFORD—Formerly served by MetroCast Mississippi. Now served by MaxxSouth Broadband, PONTOTOC, MS [MS0045]

OXFORD—See PONTOTOC, MS (MaxxSouth Broadband)

PACE—See CLEVELAND, MS (Cable One)

PACHUTA—Formerly served by Galaxy Cablevision. No longer in operation

PACHUTA—See HATTIESBURG, MS (Comcast Cable)

PANOLA COUNTY (PORTIONS)—See CLARKSDALE, MS (Cable One)

PASCAGOULA—Cable One. Now served by GULFPORT, MS [MS0008]

PASCAGOULA—See GULFPORT, MS (Cable One)

PASS CHRISTIAN—See GULFPORT, MS (Cable One)

PATTISION—See MEADVILLE, MS (Franklin Telephone. Formerly [MS0069]. This cable system has converted to IPTV)

PAULDING—Comcast Cable. Now served by HATTIESBURG, MS [MS0005]

PAULDING—See HATTIESBURG, MS (Comcast Cable)

PEARL—Comcast Cable. Now served by JACKSON, MS [MS0001]

PEARL—See JACKSON, MS (Comcast Cable)

PEARLINGTON—Mediacom. Now served by WAVELAND, MS [MS0022]

PEARLINGTON—See WAVELAND, MS (Mediacom)

PELAHATCHIE—See JACKSON, MS (Comcast Cable)

PETAL—See HATTIESBURG, MS (Comcast Cable)

PHILADELPHIA—MaxxSouth Broadband

PICAYUNE—Charter Communications. Now served by SLIDELL, LA [LA0182]

PICKENS—See GRENADA, MS (Cable One)

PIKE COUNTY—See BROOKHAVEN, MS (Cable One)

PITTSBORO—See PONTOTOC, MS (MaxxSouth Broadband)

PLANTERSVILLE—See TUPELO, MS (Comcast Cable)

PONTOTOC COUNTY (PORTIONS)—See TUPELO, MS (Comcast Cable)

PONTOTOC—Formerly served by Zoom Media. No longer in operation

PONTOTOC—MaxxSouth Broadband

POPE—See CLARKSDALE, MS (Cable One)

POPLARVILLE—Media3

PORT GIBSON—Bailey Cable TV Inc

POTTS CAMP—Formerly served by MetroCast Mississippi. Now served by MaxxSouth Broadband, PONTOTOC, MS [MS0045]

POTTS CAMP—See PONTOTOC, MS (MaxxSouth Broadband)

PRENTISS COUNTY (PORTIONS)—See TUPELO, MS (Comcast Cable)

PRENTISS—Formerly served by Zoom Media. No longer in operation

PUCKETT—Comcast Cable. Now served by JACKSON, MS [MS0001]

PUCKETT—See JACKSON, MS (Comcast Cable)

PURVIS—See HATTIESBURG, MS (Comcast Cable)

QUITMAN COUNTY (PORTIONS)—See CLARKSDALE, MS (Cable One)

QUITMAN—NewWave Communications

RAINBOW CITY—See TUPELO, AL (Comcast Cable)

RALEIGH—MaxxSouth Broadband

RANKIN COUNTY (PORTIONS)—See JACKSON, MS (Comcast Cable)

RANKIN—See JACKSON, MS (Comcast Cable)

RAYMOND—See JACKSON, MS (Comcast Cable)

RED BAY—See PONTOTOC, AL (MaxxSouth Broadband)

REECE CITY—See TUPELO, AL (Comcast Cable)

RENOVA—See CLEVELAND, MS (Cable One)

RICHLAND—See JACKSON, MS (Comcast Cable)

RICHTON—Alliance Communications

RICHWOOD—See JACKSON, LA (Comcast Cable)

RIDGELAND—See JACKSON, MS (Comcast Cable)

RIDGEVILLE—See TUPELO, AL (Comcast Cable)

RIENZI—Formerly served by Zoom Media. No longer in operation

RIPLEY—Ripley Video Cable Co. Inc

ROLLING FORK—RF Cable LLC

ROSEDALE—Cablevision of Rosedale

ROXIE—Franklin Telephone (Telapex). This cable system has converted to IPTV. Now served by MEADVILLE, MS [MS5012]

ROXIE—See MEADVILLE, MS (Franklin Telephone. Formerly [MS0069]. This cable system has converted to IPTV)

RULEVILLE—See CLEVELAND, MS (Cable One)

RURAL HILL—See COLUMBUS, MS (Cable One)

RUSSELL—See HATTIESBURG, MS (Comcast Cable)

SALTILLO—See TUPELO, MS (Comcast Cable)

SALTILLO—See PONTOTOC, MS (MaxxSouth Broadband)

SANDERSVILLE—See HATTIESBURG, MS (Comcast Cable)

SANFORD—Formerly served by Home Cable Entertainment. No longer in operation

SCOOBA—Cable TV Inc

SCOTT COUNTY (UNINCORPORATED AREAS)—See FOREST, MS (MaxxSouth Broadband)

SEMINARY—Formerly served by Home Cable Entertainment. No longer in operation

SHANNON—See PONTOTOC, MS (MaxxSouth Broadband)

SHAW (PORTIONS)—See CLEVELAND, MS (Cable One)

SHEFFIELD—See TUPELO, AL (Comcast Cable)

SHELBY—Formerly served by Galaxy Cablevision. Now served by Cable One, CLEVELAND, MS [MS0019]

SHELBY—See CLEVELAND, MS (Cable One)

SHERMAN—See TUPELO, MS (Comcast Cable)

SHUBUTA—Alliance Communications

SHUQUALAK—See MACON, MS (Cable TV Inc)

SIDON—See GREENWOOD, MS (Suddenlink Communications)

SIMPSON COUNTY—See MENDENHALL, MS (Bailey Cable TV Inc)

SMITHVILLE—See PONTOTOC, MS (MaxxSouth Broadband)

SNOW LAKE SHORES—See PONTOTOC, MS (MaxxSouth Broadband)

SOSO—See BAY SPRINGS, MS (TEC. This cable system has converted to IPTV)

ST. ANDREWS—Mediacom

ST. CLAIR COUNTY (PORTIONS)—See TUPELO, AL (Comcast Cable)

ST. FLORIAN—See TUPELO, AL (Comcast Cable)

STAR—See JACKSON, MS (Comcast Cable)

STARKVILLE—Formerly served by MetroCast Mississippi. Now served by MaxxSouth Broadband, PONTOTOC, MS [MS0045]

STARKVILLE—See PONTOTOC, MS (MaxxSouth Broadband)

STATE LINE—Formerly served by Zoom Media. No longer in operation

STEENS—See COLUMBUS, MS (Cable One)

STONE COUNTY (PORTIONS)—See WAVELAND, MS (Mediacom)

STONEWALL—See QUITMAN, MS (NewWave Communications)

STRINGER—See BAY SPRINGS, MS (TEC. This cable system has converted to IPTV)

SUMMIT—See BROOKHAVEN, MS (Cable One)

SUMNER—Cable One. Now served by GRENADA, MS [MS0021]

SUMNER—See GRENADA, MS (Cable One)

SUMRALL—Media3

SUNFLOWER COUNTY (PORTIONS)—See CLEVELAND, MS (Cable One)

SUNFLOWER COUNTY (PORTIONS)—See MEADVILLE, MS (Franklin Telephone. Formerly [MS0069]. This cable system has converted to IPTV)

SUNFLOWER COUNTY—See GREENWOOD, MS (Suddenlink Communications)

SUNFLOWER—Sledge Cable. This cable system has converted to IPTV. See SUNFLOWER, MS [MS5031]

SUNFLOWER—Sledge Cable. Formerly [MS0195]. This cable system has converted to IPTV

SUNRISE—Formerly served by Home Cable Entertainment. No longer in operation

SWARTZ—See JACKSON, LA (Comcast Cable)

SWIFTWATER—See GREENVILLE, MS (Suddenlink Communications)

TALLAHATCHIE COUNTY—See GRENADA, MS (Cable One)

TAYLORSVILLE—Formerly served by Zoom Media. No longer in operation

TCHULA—See GRENADA, MS (Cable One)

TERRY—Bailey Cable TV Inc

TISHOMINGO COUNTY—See PONTOTOC, MS (MaxxSouth Broadband)

TONEY—See TUPELO, AL (Comcast Cable)

TOOMSUBA—See HATTIESBURG, MS (Comcast Cable)

TREMONT—See TUPELO, MS (Comcast Cable)

TUPELO—Comcast Cable

TUSCALOOSA COUNTY (PORTIONS)—See TUPELO, AL (Comcast Cable)

TUSCALOOSA—See TUPELO, AL (Comcast Cable)

TUSCUMBIA—See TUPELO, AL (Comcast Cable)

TUTWILER—See GRENADA, MS (Cable One)

TYLERTOWN—Media3

UNION (town)—Formerly served by Mediacom. Now served by MaxxSouth Broadband, PONTOTOC, MS [MS0045]

UNION (town)—Formerly served by Mediacom. Now served by MaxxSouth Broadband, PONTOTOC, MS [MS0045]

UNION (TOWN)—See PONTOTOC, MS (MaxxSouth Broadband)

UNION CHURCH—See MEADVILLE, MS (Franklin Telephone. Formerly [MS0069]. This cable system has converted to IPTV)

UNION COUNTY (PORTIONS)—See TUPELO, MS (Comcast Cable)

UNION COUNTY—See PONTOTOC, MS (MaxxSouth Broadband)

UNIVERSITY OF MISSISSIPPI—See PONTOTOC, MS (MaxxSouth Broadband)

VAIDEN—See GRENADA, MS (Cable One)

VAN CLEAVE—See GULFPORT, MS (Cable One)

VARDAMAN—See PONTOTOC, MS (MaxxSouth Broadband)

VERONA—See TUPELO, MS (Comcast Cable)

VICKSBURG—Vicksburg Video Inc

VIDALIA—See NATCHEZ, LA (Cable One)

WALNUT GROVE—See TUPELO, AL (Comcast Cable)

WATER VALLEY—Formerly served by MetroCast Mississippi. Now served by MaxxSouth Broadband, PONTOTOC, MS [MS0045]

WATER VALLEY—See PONTOTOC, MS (MaxxSouth Broadband)

WAVELAND—Mediacom

WAYNESBORO—NewWave Communications

WEBB—See GRENADA, MS (Cable One)

WEBSTER COUNTY—See EUPORA, MS (Cable TV Inc)

WEIR—Delta Telephone (Telapex). This cable system has converted to IPTV. See WEIR, MS [MS5013]

WEIR—Delta Telephone (Telapex). Formerly [MS0126]. This cable system has converted to IPTV

WESSON—See BROOKHAVEN, MS (Cable One)

WEST MONROE—See JACKSON, LA (Comcast Cable)

WEST POINT—See TUPELO, MS (Comcast Cable)

WHEELER—See PONTOTOC, MS (MaxxSouth Broadband)

WIGGINS—Mediacom. Now served by WAVELAND, MS [MS0022]

WIGGINS—See WAVELAND, MS (Mediacom)

WINONA—Cable One. Now served by GRENADA, MS [MS0021]

WINONA—See GRENADA, MS (Cable One)

WINSTON COUNTY—See PONTOTOC, MS (MaxxSouth Broadband)

WINSTONVILLE—Formerly served by J & L Cable. No longer in operation

WOODVILLE—Bailey Cable TV Inc

YAZOO CITY—See GRENADA, MS (Cable One)

MISSOURI

ADAIR COUNTY—See KIRKSVILLE, MO (Cable One)

ADDIEVILLE—See ST. LOUIS, IL (Charter Communications)

ADRIAN—Provincial Cable & Data

ADVANCE—Formerly served by Cebridge Connections. Now served by Semo Communications Corp., ADVANCE, MO [MO0171]

ADVANCE—Semo Communications Corp

AFFTON—See ST. LOUIS, MO (Charter Communications)

AGENCY—See ST. JOSEPH, MO (Suddenlink Communications)

AIRPORT DRIVE VILLAGE—See CARL JUNCTION, MO (Mediacom)

ALBA—Mediacom. Now served by CARL JUNCTION, MO [MO0094]

ALBA—See CARL JUNCTION, MO (Mediacom)

ALBANY—Mediacom. Now served by EXCELSIOR SPRINGS, MO [MO0040]

ALBANY—See EXCELSIOR SPRINGS, MO (Mediacom)

ALBERS—See ST. LOUIS, IL (Charter Communications)

ALMA—See HIGGINSVILLE, MO (Citizens CableVision)

ALORTON—See ST. LOUIS, IL (Charter Communications)

ALTON—Formerly served by Boycom Cablevision Inc. No longer in operation

ALTON—See ST. LOUIS, IL (Charter Communications)

AMAZONIA—Formerly served by CableDirect. No longer in operation

AMSTERDAM—Craw-Kan. Now served by GIRARD, KS [KS0446]

ANDERSON—Mediacom. Now served by DIAMOND, MO [MO0156]

ANDERSON—See DIAMOND, MO (Mediacom)

ANNAPOLIS—Formerly served by Charter Communications. No longer in operation

ANNISTON—See ADVANCE, MO (Semo Communications Corp)

APPLETON CITY—Mediacom

ARCADIA—See ST. LOUIS, MO (Charter Communications)

ARCHIE—Mediacom

ARGYLE—Formerly served by First Cable of Missouri Inc. No longer in operation

Missouri—Cable Community Index

ARMSTRONG—Formerly served by Cebridge Connections. No longer in operation

ARNOLD—See ST. LOUIS, MO (Charter Communications)

ASH GROVE—See EVERTON, MO (Mediacom)

ASHLEY—See ST. LOUIS, IL (Charter Communications)

ATCHISON COUNTY—See ROCK PORT, MO (Rock Port Cablevision)

ATLANTA—Formerly served by CableDirect. No longer in operation

AUDRAIN COUNTY (PORTIONS)—See ST. LOUIS, MO (Charter Communications)

AUNT'S CREEK—See NIXA, MO (Suddenlink Communications)

AURORA—See MONETT, MO (Suddenlink Communications)

AVA—Mediacom. Now served by SEYMOUR, MO [MO0172]

AVA—See SEYMOUR, MO (Mediacom)

AVALON—Green Hills Communications. This cable system has converted to IPTV

AVISTON—See ST. LOUIS, IL (Charter Communications)

AVONDALE—See KANSAS CITY, MO (Time Warner Cable)

BALDWIN PARK—See INDEPENDENCE, MO (Comcast Cable)

BALLWIN—See ST. LOUIS, MO (Charter Communications)

BARING—Formerly served by CableDirect. No longer in operation

BARNARD—Formerly served by CableDirect. No longer in operation

BARNHART—Formerly served by Charter Communications. No longer in operation

BATES CITY—See INDEPENDENCE, MO (Comcast Cable)

BATTLEFIELD—See SPRINGFIELD, MO (Mediacom)

BEAUCOUP—See ST. LOUIS, IL (Charter Communications)

BECKEMEYER—See ST. LOUIS, IL (Charter Communications)

BEL-NOR—See ST. LOUIS, MO (Charter Communications)

BEL-RIDGE—See ST. LOUIS, MO (Charter Communications)

BELL CITY—Semo Communications Corporation. Now served by ADVANCE, MO [MO0171]

BELL CITY—See ADVANCE, MO (Semo Communications Corp)

BELLA VILLA—See ST. LOUIS, MO (Charter Communications)

BELLE—Formerly served by Almega Cable. No longer in operation

BELLERIVE—See ST. LOUIS, MO (Charter Communications)

BELLEVILLE—See ST. LOUIS, IL (Charter Communications)

BELTON—See KANSAS CITY, MO (Time Warner Cable)

BENTON—Charter Communications. Now served by ST. LOUIS, MO [MO0009]

BENTON—See ST. LOUIS, MO (Charter Communications)

BERKELEY—See ST. LOUIS, MO (Charter Communications)

BERNIE—Formerly served by Cebridge Connections. Now served by NewWave Communications, DEXTER, MO [MO0039]

BERNIE—See DEXTER, MO (NewWave Communications)

BETHALTO—See ST. LOUIS, IL (Charter Communications)

BETHANY—Mediacom. Now served by EXCELSIOR SPRINGS, MO [MO0040]

BETHANY—See EXCELSIOR SPRINGS, MO (Mediacom)

BEVERLY HILLS—See ST. LOUIS, MO (Charter Communications)

BEVIER—Chariton Valley Cablevision. Now served by MACON, MO [MO0071]

BEVIER—See MACON, MO (Chariton Valley Cablevision)

BILLINGS—Mediacom. Now served by SEYMOUR, MO [MO0172]

BILLINGS—See SEYMOUR, MO (Mediacom)

BIRCH TREE—Formerly served by Boycom Cablevision Inc. No longer in operation

BISMARCK—Charter Communications. Now served by ST. LOUIS, MO [MO0009]

BISMARCK—See ST. LOUIS, MO (Charter Communications)

BLACK JACK—See ST. LOUIS, MO (Charter Communications)

BLACKBURN—See HIGGINSVILLE, MO (Citizens CableVision)

BLODGETT—See ADVANCE, MO (Semo Communications Corp)

BLOOMFIELD—See DEXTER, MO (NewWave Communications)

BLUE SPRINGS—See INDEPENDENCE, MO (Comcast Cable)

BOGARD—Formerly served by CableDirect. No longer in operation

BOGARD—See AVALON, MO (Green Hills Communications. This cable system has converted to IPTV)

BOLCKOW—Formerly served by CableDirect. No longer in operation

BOLIVAR (TOWN)—Windstream

BONNE TERRE—See ST. LOUIS, MO (Charter Communications)

BONNER SPRINGS—See KANSAS CITY, KS (Time Warner Cable)

BOONE COUNTY (PORTIONS)—See COLUMBIA, MO (Mediacom)

BOONVILLE—Suddenlink Communications

BOSWORTH—Formerly served by CableDirect. No longer in operation

BOURBON—See ST. LOUIS, MO (Charter Communications)

BOWLING GREEN—Formerly served by Crystal Broadband Networks. No longer in operation

BRANSON VIEW ESTATES—See BRANSON, MO (Suddenlink Communications)

BRANSON WEST—See NIXA, MO (Suddenlink Communications)

BRANSON—Suddenlink Communications

BRAYMER—Formerly served by Allegiance Communications. No longer in operation

BRECKENRIDGE HILLS—See ST. LOUIS, MO (Charter Communications)

BRECKENRIDGE—See AVALON, MO (Green Hills Communications. This cable system has converted to IPTV)

BREESE—See ST. LOUIS, IL (Charter Communications)

BRENTWOOD—See ST. LOUIS, MO (Charter Communications)

BRIDGETON TERRACE—See ST. LOUIS, MO (Charter Communications)

BRIDGETON—See ST. LOUIS, MO (Charter Communications)

BROOKFIELD—Suddenlink Communications

BROOKING PARK—See SMITHTON, MO (Provincial Cable & Data)

BROOKLYN HEIGHTS—See CARTHAGE, MO (Suddenlink Communications)

BROWNING—Formerly served by CableDirect. No longer in operation

BROWNWOOD—See ADVANCE, MO (Semo Communications Corp)

BRUNSWICK—Mediacom. Now served by BRUNSWICK (formerly Salisbury), MO [MO0155]

BRUNSWICK—Mediacom

BUCKNER—See INDEPENDENCE, MO (Comcast Cable)

BUFFALO—Provincial Cable & Data

BULL CREEK—See BRANSON, MO (Suddenlink Communications)

BUNCETON—Formerly served by OTELCO. No longer in operation

BUNKER—Formerly served by Cebridge Connections. No longer in operation

BURLINGTON JUNCTION—Formerly served by B & L Technologies LLC. No longer in operation

BUTLER COUNTY (NORTHERN PORTION)—See WAPPAPELLO, MO (Boycom Cablevision Inc)

BUTLER COUNTY (PORTIONS)—See FAIRDEALING, MO (Boycom Cablevision Inc)

BUTLER COUNTY (PORTIONS)—See POPLAR BLUFF, MO (NewWave Communications)

BUTLER—Mediacom

CABOOL—Mediacom. Now served by SEYMOUR, MO [MO0172]

CABOOL—See SEYMOUR, MO (Mediacom)

CAHOKIA—See ST. LOUIS, IL (Charter Communications)

CAINSVILLE—Formerly served by Longview Communications. No longer in operation

CAIRO—Formerly served by Almega Cable. No longer in operation

CALIFORNIA—Formerly served by Crystal Broadband Networks. No longer in operation

CALLAO—See MACON, MO (Chariton Valley Cablevision)

CALLAWAY COUNTY (PORTIONS)—See ST. LOUIS, MO (Charter Communications)

CALLAWAY COUNTY—See JEFFERSON CITY, MO (Mediacom)

CALVERTON PARK—See ST. LOUIS, MO (Charter Communications)

CAMDEN COUNTY—See ST. LOUIS, MO (Charter Communications)

CAMDEN POINT—Formerly served by Allegiance Communications. No longer in operation

CAMDENTON—See ST. LOUIS, MO (Charter Communications)

CAMERON—Mediacom. Now served by EXCELSIOR SPRINGS, MO [MO0040]

CAMERON—See EXCELSIOR SPRINGS, MO (Mediacom)

CAMPBELL—See DEXTER, MO (NewWave Communications)

CANALOU—See ADVANCE, MO (Semo Communications Corp)

CANTON—Formerly served by Westcom. No longer in operation

CAPE GIRARDEAU—Charter Communications. Now served by ST. LOUIS, MO [MO0009]

CAPE GIRARDEAU—See ST. LOUIS, MO (Charter Communications)

CARL JUNCTION—Mediacom

CARLYLE—See ST. LOUIS, IL (Charter Communications)

CARROLLTON—Mediacom

CARTER COUNTY (SOUTHEAST PORTION)—See POPLAR BLUFF, MO (Boycom Cablevision Inc)

Cable Community Index—Missouri

CARTERVILLE—See JOPLIN, MO (Cable One)

CARTHAGE—Suddenlink Communications

CARUTHERSVILLE—Mediacom

CASEYVILLE—See ST. LOUIS, IL (Charter Communications)

CASS COUNTY (northwestern portion)—Formerly served by Cass County Cable. No longer in operation

CASS COUNTY (PORTIONS)—See INDEPENDENCE, MO (Comcast Cable)

CASS COUNTY—Formerly served by Longview Communications. No longer in operation

CASSVILLE—Mediacom

CEDAR HILL LAKES—See ST. LOUIS, MO (Charter Communications)

CEDAR HILL—See ST. LOUIS, MO (Charter Communications)

CENTERTOWN—See COLE COUNTY (portions), MO (Suddenlink Communications)

CENTERVIEW—Formerly served by CableDirect. No longer in operation

CENTRAL CITY—See ST. LOUIS, IL (Charter Communications)

CENTRALIA—Formerly served by US Cable. Now served by Charter Communications, ST. LOUIS, MO [MO0009]

CENTRALIA—See ST. LOUIS, IL (Charter Communications)

CENTRALIA—See ST. LOUIS, MO (Charter Communications)

CENTREVILLE—See ST. LOUIS, IL (Charter Communications)

CHAMOIS—Formerly served by Mid Missouri Broadband. No longer in operation

CHARLACK—See ST. LOUIS, MO (Charter Communications)

CHARLESTON—Charter Communications. Now served by ST. LOUIS, MO [MO0009]

CHARLESTON—See ST. LOUIS, MO (Charter Communications)

CHESTERFIELD—Charter Communications. Now served by ST. LOUIS, MO [MO0009]

CHESTERFIELD—See ST. LOUIS, MO (Charter Communications)

CHILHOWEE—Formerly served by National Cable Inc. No longer in operation

CHILLICOTHE—See AVALON, MO (Green Hills Communications. This cable system has converted to IPTV)

CHILLICOTHE—Zito Media

CHOUTEAU TWP.—See ST. LOUIS, IL (Charter Communications)

CHRISTIAN COUNTY—See NIXA, MO (Suddenlink Communications)

CHULA—Formerly served by CableDirect. No longer in operation

CLARENCE—Milan Interactive Communications

CLARK—See STURGEON, MO (Provincial Cable & Data)

CLARKSBURG—Formerly served by First Cable of Missouri Inc. No longer in operation

CLARKSDALE—Formerly served by CableDirect. No longer in operation

CLARKSON VALLEY—See ST. LOUIS, MO (Charter Communications)

CLARKSVILLE—Formerly served by First Cable of Missouri Inc. No longer in operation

CLARKTON—NewWave Communications. Now served by DEXTER, MO [MO0039]

CLARKTON—See DEXTER, MO (NewWave Communications)

CLAY COUNTY (PORTIONS)—See DEXTER, AR (NewWave Communications)

CLAY COUNTY (PORTIONS)—See KANSAS CITY, MO (Time Warner Cable)

CLAYCOMO—See KANSAS CITY, MO (Time Warner Cable)

CLAYTON—See ST. LOUIS, MO (Charter Communications)

CLEARMONT—Formerly served by Longview Communications. No longer in operation

CLEVER—Formerly served by Suddenlink Communications. No longer in operation

CLEVER—See REPUBLIC, MO (Cable America Corp)

CLIFF VILLAGE—See JOPLIN, MO (Cable One)

CLINTON COUNTY (PORTIONS)—See ST. LOUIS, IL (Charter Communications)

CLINTON—Charter Communications. Now served by ST. LOUIS, MO [MO0009]

CLINTON—See ST. LOUIS, MO (Charter Communications)

COBALT VILLAGE—See ST. LOUIS, MO (Charter Communications)

COFFMAN BEND—Formerly served by Almega Cable. No longer in operation

COLE CAMP—Provincial Cable & Data

COLE COUNTY (PORTIONS)—See JEFFERSON CITY, MO (Mediacom)

COLE COUNTY (PORTIONS)—Suddenlink Communications

COLLINSVILLE—See ST. LOUIS, IL (Charter Communications)

COLUMBIA—Charter Communications. Now served by ST. LOUIS, MO [MO0009]

COLUMBIA—See ST. LOUIS, IL (Charter Communications)

COLUMBIA—See ST. LOUIS, MO (Charter Communications)

COLUMBIA—Mediacom

CONCEPTION JUNCTION—Formerly served by B & L Technologies LLC. No longer in operation

CONCORDIA—See HIGGINSVILLE, MO (Citizens CableVision)

CONWAY—Formerly served by Fidelity Communications. No longer in operation

COOL VALLEY—See ST. LOUIS, MO (Charter Communications)

COOPER COUNTY (PORTIONS)—See BOONVILLE, MO (Suddenlink Communications)

CORDER—See HIGGINSVILLE, MO (Citizens CableVision)

COTTAGE HILLS—See ST. LOUIS, IL (Charter Communications)

COTTLEVILLE—See ST. LOUIS, MO (Charter Communications)

COUNTRY CLUB HILLS—See ST. LOUIS, MO (Charter Communications)

COUNTRY CLUB VILLAGE—See ST. JOSEPH, MO (Suddenlink Communications)

COUNTRY LIFE ACRES—See ST. LOUIS, MO (Charter Communications)

COUNTRYSIDE—See KANSAS CITY, KS (Time Warner Cable)

COWGILL—Green Hills Communications. This cable system has converted to IPTV. Now served by AVALON, MO [MO5156]

COWGILL—See AVALON, MO (Green Hills Communications. This cable system has converted to IPTV)

CRAIG—Formerly served by CableDirect. No longer in operation

CRANE—Mediacom. Now served by SEYMOUR, MO [MO0172]

CRANE—See SEYMOUR, MO (Mediacom)

CRAWFORD COUNTY (PORTIONS)—See ST. LOUIS, MO (Charter Communications)

CRAWFORD COUNTY (PORTIONS)—See PHELPS COUNTY (portions), MO (Fidelity Communications)

CREIGHTON—Formerly served by CableDirect. No longer in operation

CRESTWOOD—See ST. LOUIS, MO (Charter Communications)

CREVE COEUR—See ST. LOUIS, MO (Charter Communications)

CROCKER—Formerly served by Longview Communications. No longer in operation

CRYSTAL CITY—See ST. LOUIS, MO (Charter Communications)

CRYSTAL LAKE PARK—See ST. LOUIS, MO (Charter Communications)

CRYSTAL LAKES—See EXCELSIOR SPRINGS, MO (Mediacom)

CUBA—Formerly served by Charter Communications. No longer in operation

CURRYVILLE—Formerly served by First Cable of Missouri Inc. No longer in operation

DAMIANSVILLE—See ST. LOUIS, IL (Charter Communications)

DARDENNE PRAIRIE—See ST. LOUIS, MO (Charter Communications)

DAWN—See AVALON, MO (Green Hills Communications. This cable system has converted to IPTV)

DE KALB—Formerly served by CableDirect. No longer in operation

DE SOTO—See ST. LOUIS, MO (Charter Communications)

DE SOTO—See KANSAS CITY, KS (Time Warner Cable)

DELLWOOD—See ST. LOUIS, MO (Charter Communications)

DELTA—See ADVANCE, MO (Semo Communications Corp)

DENT COUNTY (PORTIONS)—See PHELPS COUNTY (portions), MO (Fidelity Communications)

DES PERES—See ST. LOUIS, MO (Charter Communications)

DESLOGE—See ST. LOUIS, MO (Charter Communications)

DEXTER—NewWave Communications

DIAMOND—Mediacom. Now served by DIAMOND, MO [MO0156]

DIAMOND—Mediacom

DIXON—Cable America Corp. Now served by ST. ROBERT, MO [MO0023]

DIXON—See ST. ROBERT, MO (Cable America Corp)

DOE RUN—See ST. LOUIS, MO (Charter Communications)

DONIPHAN—Boycom Cablevision Inc

DOOLITTLE—Cable America Corp. Now served by ST. ROBERT, MO [MO0023]

DOOLITTLE—See ST. ROBERT, MO (Cable America Corp)

DOWNING—Formerly served by Longview Communications. No longer in operation

DREXEL—Formerly served by Almega Cable. No longer in operation

DUDLEY—Formerly served by Boycom Cablevision Inc. No longer in operation

DUENWEG—See CARL JUNCTION, MO (Mediacom)

DUNKLIN COUNTY (PORTIONS)—See DEXTER, MO (NewWave Communications)

DUPO—See ST. LOUIS, IL (Charter Communications)

Missouri—Cable Community Index

DUQUESNE—Mediacom. Now served by CARL JUNCTION, MO [MO0094]

DUQUESNE—See CARL JUNCTION, MO (Mediacom)

DURHAM—Formerly served by CableDirect. No longer in operation

EAGLEVILLE—Formerly served by Longview Communications. No longer in operation

EAST ALTON—See ST. LOUIS, IL (Charter Communications)

EAST LYNNE—Formerly served by CableDirect. No longer in operation

EAST PRAIRIE—See ST. LOUIS, MO (Charter Communications)

EAST ST. LOUIS—See ST. LOUIS, IL (Charter Communications)

EASTON—Formerly served by First Cable of Missouri Inc. No longer in operation

EDINA—Formerly served by Charter Communications. No longer in operation

EDMUNDSON—See ST. LOUIS, MO (Charter Communications)

EDWARDSVILLE PARK—See KANSAS CITY, KS (Time Warner Cable)

EDWARDSVILLE—See ST. LOUIS, IL (Charter Communications)

EDWARDSVILLE—See KANSAS CITY, KS (Time Warner Cable)

EL DORADO SPRINGS—Fidelity Communications

ELDON—Charter Communications. Now served by ST. LOUIS, MO [MO0009]

ELDON—See ST. LOUIS, MO (Charter Communications)

ELLINGTON—Formerly served by Boycom Cablevision Inc. No longer in operation

ELLISVILLE—See ST. LOUIS, MO (Charter Communications)

ELLSINORE—See POPLAR BLUFF, MO (Boycom Cablevision Inc)

ELMO—Formerly served by CableDirect. No longer in operation

ELSBERRY—Formerly served by Crystal Broadband Networks. No longer in operation

EMINENCE—Formerly served by Boycom Cablevision Inc. No longer in operation

EMMA—See HIGGINSVILLE, MO (Citizens CableVision)

EOLIA—Formerly served by First Cable of Missouri Inc. No longer in operation

ESSEX—Formerly served by Cebridge Connections. Now served by NewWave Communications, DEXTER, MO [MO0039]

ESSEX—See DEXTER, MO (NewWave Communications)

EUGENE—Formerly served by First Cable of Missouri Inc. No longer in operation

EUREKA—See ST. LOUIS, MO (Charter Communications)

EVERTON—Mediacom

EWING—Formerly served by CableDirect. No longer in operation

EXCELSIOR ESTATES—See EXCELSIOR SPRINGS, MO (Mediacom)

EXCELSIOR SPRINGS—Mediacom

EXETER—See CASSVILLE, MO (Mediacom)

FAIR GROVE—Formerly served by Fidelity Communications. No longer in operation

FAIR PLAY—Formerly served by Cebridge Connections. No longer in operation

FAIRDEALING—Boycom Cablevision Inc

FAIRFAX—See ROCK PORT, MO (Rock Port Cablevision)

FAIRVIEW HEIGHTS—See ST. LOUIS, IL (Charter Communications)

FAIRWAY—See KANSAS CITY, KS (Time Warner Cable)

FARBER—Formerly served by US Cable. Now served by Charter Communications, ST. LOUIS, MO [MO0009]

FARBER—See ST. LOUIS, MO (Charter Communications)

FARMINGTON—Charter Communications. Now served by ST. LOUIS, MO [MO0009]

FARMINGTON—See ST. LOUIS, MO (Charter Communications)

FAUCETT—Formerly served by CableDirect. No longer in operation

FAYETTE—Suddenlink Communications. No longer in operation

FENTON—See ST. LOUIS, MO (Charter Communications)

FERGUSON—Charter Communications. Now served by ST. LOUIS, MO [MO0009]

FERGUSON—See ST. LOUIS, MO (Charter Communications)

FERRELVIEW—See KANSAS CITY, MO (Time Warner Cable)

FESTUS—See ST. LOUIS, MO (Charter Communications)

FIDELITY—See CARTHAGE, MO (Suddenlink Communications)

FISK—Boycom Cablevision Inc. Now served by ELLSINORE, MO [MO0196]

FISK—See POPLAR BLUFF, MO (Boycom Cablevision Inc)

FLAT RIVER—Formerly served by Charter Communications. No longer in operation

FLINT HILL—See ST. LOUIS, MO (Charter Communications)

FLORDELL HILLS—See ST. LOUIS, MO (Charter Communications)

FLORISSANT—See ST. LOUIS, MO (Charter Communications)

FORDLAND—Formerly served by Cebridge Connections. No longer in operation

FOREST CITY—See OREGON, MO (South Holt Cablevision Inc)

FORSYTH—Mediacom. Now served by SEYMOUR, MO [MO0172]

FORSYTH—See SEYMOUR, MO (Mediacom)

FORT LEAVENWORTH—See KANSAS CITY, KS (Time Warner Cable)

FORT LEONARD WOOD—See ST. ROBERT, MO (Cable America Corp)

FOUNTAIN N' LAKES—See ST. LOUIS, MO (Charter Communications)

FRANKFORD—Formerly served by Westcom. No longer in operation

FRANKLIN COUNTY (NORTHEASTERN PORTION)—See ST. LOUIS, MO (Charter Communications)

FRANKLIN COUNTY (PORTIONS)—See PHELPS COUNTY (portions), MO (Fidelity Communications)

FRANKLIN COUNTY (SOUTHWESTERN PORTION)—See ST. LOUIS, MO (Charter Communications)

FREDERICKTOWN (village)—Charter Communications. Now served by ST. LOUIS, MO [MO0009]

FREDERICKTOWN—See ST. LOUIS, MO (Charter Communications)

FREEBURG—Formerly served by CableDirect. No longer in operation

FREEBURG—See ST. LOUIS, IL (Charter Communications)

FREMONT—Formerly served by Cebridge Connections. No longer in operation

FRISBEE—See DEXTER, MO (NewWave Communications)

FRONTENAC—See ST. LOUIS, MO (Charter Communications)

FRUITLAND—See ADVANCE, MO (Semo Communications Corp)

FULTON COUNTY (PORTIONS)—See THAYER, AR (Fidelity Communications)

FULTON—Charter Communications. Now served by ST. LOUIS, MO [MO0009]

FULTON—See ST. LOUIS, MO (Charter Communications)

GAINESVILLE—Formerly served by Almega Cable. No longer in operation

GALENA—Formerly served by Almega Cable. No longer in operation

GALENA—See CARL JUNCTION, KS (Mediacom)

GALLATIN—Formerly served by Longview Communications. No longer in operation

GALT—Formerly served by CableDirect. No longer in operation

GARDEN CITY—Formerly served by Longview Communications. No longer in operation

GARDNER—See KANSAS CITY, KS (Time Warner Cable)

GASCONADE COUNTY (PORTIONS)—See PHELPS COUNTY (portions), MO (Fidelity Communications)

GASCONADE—Formerly served by First Cable of Missouri Inc. No longer in operation

GERALD—Fidelity Communications. Now served by PHELPS COUNTY (portions), MO [MO0475]

GERALD—See PHELPS COUNTY (portions), MO (Fidelity Communications)

GERMANTOWN—See ST. LOUIS, IL (Charter Communications)

GIBSON—See DEXTER, MO (NewWave Communications)

GIDEON—See DEXTER, MO (NewWave Communications)

GILLIAM—See HIGGINSVILLE, MO (Citizens CableVision)

GLADSTONE—See KANSAS CITY, MO (Time Warner Cable)

GLASGOW—Suddenlink Communications. No longer in operation

GLEN CARBON—See ST. LOUIS, IL (Charter Communications)

GLEN ECHO PARK—See ST. LOUIS, MO (Charter Communications)

GLENAIRE—See KANSAS CITY, MO (Time Warner Cable)

GLENDALE—See ST. LOUIS, MO (Charter Communications)

GODFREY—See ST. LOUIS, IL (Charter Communications)

GOLDEN CITY—See EVERTON, MO (Mediacom)

GOODMAN—Mediacom. Now served by DIAMOND, MO [MO0156]

GOODMAN—See DIAMOND, MO (Mediacom)

GOWER—Formerly served by Allegiance Communications. No longer in operation

GRAHAM—See MAITLAND, MO (American Broadband Missouri)

GRAIN VALLEY—See INDEPENDENCE, MO (Comcast Cable)

GRANBY—See DIAMOND, MO (Mediacom)

GRANDIN—See POPLAR BLUFF, MO (Boycom Cablevision Inc)

GRANDVIEW—See KANSAS CITY, MO (Time Warner Cable)

GRANITE CITY—See ST. LOUIS, IL (Charter Communications)

Cable Community Index—Missouri

GRANT CITY—Formerly served by B & L Technologies LLC. No longer in operation

GRANTWOOD VILLAGE—See ST. LOUIS, MO (Charter Communications)

GRAVOIS MILLS—Formerly served by Lake Communications. No longer in operation

GREEN CASTLE—Formerly served by Longview Communications. No longer in operation

GREEN PARK—See ST. LOUIS, MO (Charter Communications)

GREEN RIDGE—Formerly served by CableDirect. No longer in operation

GREENDALE—See ST. LOUIS, MO (Charter Communications)

GREENE COUNTY (PORTIONS)—See SPRINGFIELD, MO (Mediacom)

GREENE COUNTY (PORTIONS)—See DEXTER, AR (NewWave Communications)

GREENE COUNTY (SOUTHWESTERN PORTION)—See REPUBLIC, MO (Cable America Corp)

GREENE COUNTY (UNINCORPORATED AREAS)—See EVERTON, MO (Mediacom)

GREENFIELD—See EVERTON, MO (Mediacom)

GREENTOP—Formerly served by Longview Communications. No longer in operation

GREENVILLE—Formerly served by Almega Cable. No longer in operation

GREENWAY—See DEXTER, AR (NewWave Communications)

GREENWOOD—See INDEPENDENCE, MO (Comcast Cable)

GRUNDY COUNTY (PORTIONS)—See TRENTON, MO (Suddenlink Communications)

HALLSVILLE—Formerly served by Longview Communications. Now served by Provincial Cable & Data, STURGEON, MO [MO0395]

HALLSVILLE—See STURGEON, MO (Provincial Cable & Data)

HAMILTON—Formerly served by Allegiance Communications. No longer in operation

HANLEY HILLS—See ST. LOUIS, MO (Charter Communications)

HANNIBAL—Charter Communications. Now served by ST. LOUIS, MO [MO0009]

HANNIBAL—See ST. LOUIS, MO (Charter Communications)

HARRISBURG—Formerly served by First Cable of Missouri Inc. No longer in operation

HARRISONVILLE—Fidelity Communications

HARTFORD—See ST. LOUIS, IL (Charter Communications)

HARTVILLE—Formerly served by Cebridge Connections. No longer in operation

HAWK POINT—Formerly served by First Cable of Missouri Inc. No longer in operation

HAYTI HEIGHTS—See CARUTHERSVILLE, MO (Mediacom)

HAYTI—See CARUTHERSVILLE, MO (Mediacom)

HAYWOOD CITY—See ADVANCE, MO (Semo Communications Corp)

HAZELWOOD—See ST. LOUIS, MO (Charter Communications)

HENRIETTA—See EXCELSIOR SPRINGS, MO (Mediacom)

HENRY COUNTY—See ST. LOUIS, MO (Charter Communications)

HERCULANEUM—See ST. LOUIS, MO (Charter Communications)

HERMANN—Mediacom

HERMITAGE—See POMME DE TERRE, MO (American Broadband Missouri)

HICKORY COUNTY—See POMME DE TERRE, MO (American Broadband Missouri)

HIGBEE—Formerly served by Longview Communications. No longer in operation

HIGGINSVILLE—Citizens CableVision

HIGH RIDGE—See ST. LOUIS, MO (Charter Communications)

HIGHLAND—See ST. LOUIS, IL (Charter Communications)

HIGHLANDVILLE—See NIXA, MO (Suddenlink Communications)

HIGHWAY DD—Formerly served by Cebridge Connections. Now served by Suddenlink Communications, NIXA, MO [MO0068]

HILLSBORO—See ST. LOUIS, MO (Charter Communications)

HILLSDALE—See ST. LOUIS, MO (Charter Communications)

HOLCOMB—See DEXTER, MO (NewWave Communications)

HOLDEN—Formerly served by Crystal Broadband Networks. No longer in operation

HOLLISTER—See BRANSON, MO (Suddenlink Communications)

HOLT—Formerly served by CableDirect. No longer in operation

HOLTS SUMMIT—Mediacom. Now served by JEFFERSON CITY, MO [MO0020]

HOLTS SUMMIT—See JEFFERSON CITY, MO (Mediacom)

HOMESTEAD VILLAGE—See EXCELSIOR SPRINGS, MO (Mediacom)

HOMESTOWN—See DEXTER, MO (NewWave Communications)

HOPKINS—Formerly served by B & L Technologies LLC. No longer in operation

HORNERSVILLE—Formerly served by Base Cablevision. No longer in operation

HOUSE SPRINGS—See ST. LOUIS, MO (Charter Communications)

HOUSTON LAKE—See KANSAS CITY, MO (Time Warner Cable)

HOUSTON—Formerly served by Houston Cable Inc. Now served by Cable America Corp., ST. ROBERT, MO [MO0023]

HOUSTON—See ST. ROBERT, MO (Cable America Corp)

HOUSTONIA—See HIGGINSVILLE, MO (Citizens CableVision)

HOWARDVILLE—See ST. LOUIS, MO (Charter Communications)

HOWELL COUNTY (PORTIONS)—See WEST PLAINS, MO (Fidelity Communications)

HUMANSVILLE—See POMME DE TERRE, MO (American Broadband Missouri)

HUME—Formerly served by Midwest Cable Inc. No longer in operation

HUNTER—See POPLAR BLUFF, MO (Boycom Cablevision Inc)

HUNTLEIGH—See ST. LOUIS, MO (Charter Communications)

HUNTSVILLE—See ST. LOUIS, MO (Charter Communications)

HURDLAND—Formerly served by CableDirect. No longer in operation

IBERIA—Formerly served by Longview Communications. No longer in operation

IMPERIAL—Charter Communications. Now served by ST. LOUIS, MO [MO0009]

IMPERIAL—See ST. LOUIS, MO (Charter Communications)

INDEPENDENCE—Comcast Cable

INDEPENDENCE—See KANSAS CITY, MO (Time Warner Cable)

INDIAN POINT—See BRANSON, MO (Suddenlink Communications)

IRON MOUNTAIN LAKE—See ST. LOUIS, MO (Charter Communications)

IRONTON—Charter Communications. Now served by ST. LOUIS, MO [MO0009]

IRONTON—See ST. LOUIS, MO (Charter Communications)

IVY BEND—Formerly served by Almega Cable. No longer in operation

JACKSON COUNTY (PORTIONS)—See KANSAS CITY, MO (Time Warner Cable)

JACKSON COUNTY—See INDEPENDENCE, MO (Comcast Cable)

JACKSON—See ST. LOUIS, MO (Charter Communications)

JACKSONVILLE—Formerly served by First Cable of Missouri Inc. No longer in operation

JAMESPORT—Formerly served by CableDirect. No longer in operation

JASPER COUNTY—See CARL JUNCTION, MO (Mediacom)

JASPER—Mediacom. Now served by LIBERAL, MO [MO0187]

JASPER—See LIBERAL, MO (Mediacom)

JEFFERSON CITY—Mediacom

JEFFERSON COUNTY (PORTIONS)—See ST. LOUIS, IL (Charter Communications)

JEFFERSON COUNTY (PORTIONS)—See ST. LOUIS, MO (Charter Communications)

JEFFERSON COUNTY (UNINCORPORATED AREAS)—See ST. LOUIS, MO (Charter Communications)

JENNINGS—See ST. LOUIS, MO (Charter Communications)

JOHN KNOX VILLAGE—See KANSAS CITY, MO (Time Warner Cable)

JOHNSON COUNTY (NORTHEASTERN PORTION)—See KANSAS CITY, KS (Time Warner Cable)

JOHNSON COUNTY (PORTIONS)—See ST. LOUIS, MO (Charter Communications)

JOHNSON COUNTY (PORTIONS)—See INDEPENDENCE, KS (Comcast Cable)

JONESBURG—Formerly served by Charter Communications. No longer in operation

JOPLIN (northwest)—Formerly served by Almega Cable. No longer in operation

JOPLIN—Cable One

JUNCTION CITY—See ST. LOUIS, IL (Charter Communications)

JUNCTION CITY—See ST. LOUIS, MO (Charter Communications)

KAHOKA—Kahoka Cable

KANSAS CITY (PORTIONS)—See INDEPENDENCE, MO (Comcast Cable)

KANSAS CITY (SOUTH OF KAW RIVER)—See KANSAS CITY, KS (Time Warner Cable)

KANSAS CITY—Formerly served by People's Choice TV. No longer in operation

KANSAS CITY—Time Warner Cable

KEARNEY—See KANSAS CITY, MO (Time Warner Cable)

KELSO—See ST. LOUIS, MO (Charter Communications)

Missouri—Cable Community Index

KENNETT—NewWave Communications. Now served by DEXTER, MO [MO0039]

KENNETT—See DEXTER, MO (NewWave Communications)

KEYTESVILLE—Formerly served by Longview Communications. No longer in operation

KIMBERLING CITY—Mediacom. Now served by SEYMOUR, MO [MO0172]

KIMBERLING CITY—See SEYMOUR, MO (Mediacom)

KIMBERLING CITY—See NIXA, MO (Suddenlink Communications)

KIMMSWICK—See ST. LOUIS, MO (Charter Communications)

KING CITY—Formerly served by Longview Communications. No longer in operation

KINGDOM CITY—See ST. LOUIS, MO (Charter Communications)

KINGSTON—Formerly served by First Cable of Missouri Inc. No longer in operation

KINLOCH—Formerly served by Data Cablevision. No longer in operation

KINLOCH—See ST. LOUIS, MO (Charter Communications)

KIRKSVILLE—Cable One

KIRKWOOD—See ST. LOUIS, MO (Charter Communications)

KNOB NOSTER—Charter Communications. Now served by ST. LOUIS, MO [MO0009]

KNOB NOSTER—See ST. LOUIS, MO (Charter Communications)

KNOX CITY—Formerly served by CableDirect. No longer in operation

KNOXVILLE—See AVALON, MO (Green Hills Communications. This cable system has converted to IPTV)

LA BELLE—Formerly served by Westcom. No longer in operation

LA MONTE—Formerly served by Provincial Cable & Data. No longer in operation

LA PLATA—Formerly served by Almega Cable. No longer in operation

LA PLATA—See KIRKSVILLE, MO (Cable One)

LABADIE—See ST. LOUIS, MO (Charter Communications)

LACLEDE COUNTY (PORTIONS)—See PHELPS COUNTY (portions), MO (Fidelity Communications)

LACLEDE—Formerly served by Longview Communications. No longer in operation

LADDONIA—See ST. LOUIS, MO (Charter Communications)

LADUE—See ST. LOUIS, MO (Charter Communications)

LAFAYETTE COUNTY (PORTIONS)—See INDEPENDENCE, MO (Comcast Cable)

LAFE—See DEXTER, AR (NewWave Communications)

LAKE LOTAWANA—See KANSAS CITY, MO (Time Warner Cable)

LAKE LOTAWANO—See INDEPENDENCE, MO (Comcast Cable)

LAKE OF THE FOREST—See KANSAS CITY, KS (Time Warner Cable)

LAKE OZARK—See ST. LOUIS, MO (Charter Communications)

LAKE QUIVERA—See KANSAS CITY, KS (Time Warner Cable)

LAKE SHERWOOD—Cable America Corp

LAKE ST. LOUIS—Charter Communications. Now served by ST. LOUIS, MO [MO0009]

LAKE ST. LOUIS—See ST. LOUIS, MO (Charter Communications)

LAKE TAPAWINGO—See INDEPENDENCE, MO (Comcast Cable)

LAKE VIKING—Formerly served by First Cable of Missouri Inc. No longer in operation

LAKE WAUKOMIS—See KANSAS CITY, MO (Time Warner Cable)

LAKE WINNEBAGO—See INDEPENDENCE, MO (Comcast Cable)

LAKELAND—See ST. LOUIS, MO (Charter Communications)

LAKESHIRE—See ST. LOUIS, MO (Charter Communications)

LAKEVIEW—See NIXA, MO (Suddenlink Communications)

LAMAR HEIGHTS—See LAMAR, MO (Suddenlink Communications)

LAMAR—Suddenlink Communications

LAMBERT—See ST. LOUIS, MO (Charter Communications)

LAMPE—Formerly served by Crystal Broadband Networks. No longer in operation

LANCASTER—Formerly served by Longview Communications. No longer in operation

LANSING—See KANSAS CITY, KS (Time Warner Cable)

LATHROP—Formerly served by Allegiance Communications. No longer in operation

LAURIE—See ST. LOUIS, MO (Charter Communications)

LAWSON—See EXCELSIOR SPRINGS, MO (Mediacom)

LEADINGTON—See ST. LOUIS, MO (Charter Communications)

LEADWOOD—See ST. LOUIS, MO (Charter Communications)

LEAVENWORTH COUNTY (PORTIONS)—See KANSAS CITY, KS (Time Warner Cable)

LEAVENWORTH—See KANSAS CITY, KS (Time Warner Cable)

LEAWOOD—See JOPLIN, MO (Cable One)

LEAWOOD—See KANSAS CITY, KS (Time Warner Cable)

LEBANON—Fidelity Communications. Now served by PHELPS COUNTY (portions), MO [MO0475]

LEBANON—See ST. LOUIS, IL (Charter Communications)

LEBANON—See PHELPS COUNTY (portions), MO (Fidelity Communications)

LEE'S SUMMIT—See KANSAS CITY, MO (Time Warner Cable)

LEEPER—See PIEDMONT, MO (Boycom Cablevision Inc)

LEES SUMMIT—See INDEPENDENCE, MO (Comcast Cable)

LEETON—Formerly served by CableDirect. No longer in operation

LEMAY—See ST. LOUIS, MO (Charter Communications)

LENEXA—See KANSAS CITY, KS (Time Warner Cable)

LESTERVILLE—Formerly served by Almega Cable. No longer in operation

LEXINGTON—Suddenlink Communications

LIBERAL—Mediacom

LIBERTY—See KANSAS CITY, MO (Time Warner Cable)

LICKING—Formerly served by Licking Cable. Now served by Cable America Corp., ST. ROBERT, MO [MO0023]

LICKING—See ST. ROBERT, MO (Cable America Corp)

LILBOURN—See ST. LOUIS, MO (Charter Communications)

LINCOLN COUNTY—See ST. LOUIS, MO (Charter Communications)

LINCOLN—Formerly served by Provincial Cable & Data. No longer in operation

LINN COUNTY (PORTIONS)—See BROOKFIELD, MO (Suddenlink Communications)

LINN CREEK—See ST. LOUIS, MO (Charter Communications)

LINN—Cable America Corp

LIVINGSTON COUNTY (PORTIONS)—See CHILLICOTHE, MO (Zito Media)

LOCH LLOYD—See KANSAS CITY, MO (Time Warner Cable)

LOCK SPRINGS—See AVALON, MO (Green Hills Communications. This cable system has converted to IPTV)

LOCKWOOD—See EVERTON, MO (Mediacom)

LOHMAN—See COLE COUNTY (portions), MO (Suddenlink Communications)

LONE JACK—See KANSAS CITY, MO (Time Warner Cable)

LOOSE CREEK—Formerly served by Mid Missouri Broadband. Now served by Cable America, LINN, MO [MO0411]

LOOSE CREEK—See LINN, MO (Cable America Corp)

LOUISIANA—Charter Communications

LOWRY CITY—Mediacom

LUDLOW—See AVALON, MO (Green Hills Communications. This cable system has converted to IPTV)

MACKENZIE—See ST. LOUIS, MO (Charter Communications)

MACKS CREEK—Formerly served by Almega Cable. No longer in operation

MACON—Chariton Valley Cablevision

MADISON COUNTY (PORTIONS)—See ST. LOUIS, IL (Charter Communications)

MADISON COUNTY—See ST. LOUIS, IL (Charter Communications)

MADISON—Charter Communications. No longer in operation

MADISON—See ST. LOUIS, IL (Charter Communications)

MAITLAND—Formerly served by Holway Telephone Co. Now served by American Broadband Missouri, MAITLAND, MO [MO0473]

MAITLAND—American Broadband Missouri

MALDEN—NewWave Communications. Now served by DEXTER, MO [MO0039]

MALDEN—See DEXTER, MO (NewWave Communications)

MALTA BEND—See HIGGINSVILLE, MO (Citizens CableVision)

MAMMOTH SPRING—See THAYER, AR (Fidelity Communications)

MANCHESTER—See ST. LOUIS, MO (Charter Communications)

MANSFIELD—Mediacom. Now served by SEYMOUR, MO [MO0172]

MANSFIELD—See SEYMOUR, MO (Mediacom)

MAPLEWOOD—See ST. LOUIS, MO (Charter Communications)

MARBLE HILL—Formerly served by Boycom Cablevision Inc. No longer in operation

MARCELINE—Mediacom

MARINE—See ST. LOUIS, IL (Charter Communications)

MARION COUNTY (PORTIONS)—See ST. LOUIS, IL (Charter Communications)

MARIONVILLE—See MONETT, MO (Suddenlink Communications)

MARLBOROUGH—See ST. LOUIS, MO (Charter Communications)

Cable Community Index—Missouri

MARMADUKE—See DEXTER, AR (NewWave Communications)

MARSHALL—Zito Media

MARSHFIELD—Mediacom. Now served by SEYMOUR, MO [MO0172]

MARSHFIELD—See SEYMOUR, MO (Mediacom)

MARSTON—See ST. LOUIS, MO (Charter Communications)

MARTHASVILLE—See LAKE SHERWOOD, MO (Cable America Corp)

MARTINSBURG—See ST. LOUIS, MO (Charter Communications)

MARYLAND HEIGHTS—Cable America Corp

MARYLAND HEIGHTS—See ST. LOUIS, MO (Charter Communications)

MARYVILLE—See ST. LOUIS, IL (Charter Communications)

MARYVILLE—Suddenlink Communications

MASCOUTAH—See ST. LOUIS, IL (Charter Communications)

MATTHEWS—See ADVANCE, MO (Semo Communications Corp)

MAYSVILLE—Formerly served by Allegiance Communications. No longer in operation

MAYVIEW—Formerly served by CableDirect. No longer in operation

MEADVILLE—Formerly served by Longview Communications. No longer in operation

MEHLVILLE—See ST. LOUIS, MO (Charter Communications)

MEMPHIS—Formerly served by Longview Communications. No longer in operation

MERCER—Formerly served by Telnet South LC. No longer in operation

MERRIAM WOODS—See BRANSON, MO (Suddenlink Communications)

MERRIAM—See KANSAS CITY, KS (Time Warner Cable)

META—Formerly served by CableDirect. No longer in operation

MEXICO—Charter Communications. Now served by ST. LOUIS, MO [MO0009]

MEXICO—See ST. LOUIS, MO (Charter Communications)

MIDDLETOWN (town)—Formerly served by First Cable of Missouri Inc. No longer in operation

MILAN—Milan Interactive Communications

MILL SPRING—See PIEDMONT, MO (Boycom Cablevision Inc)

MILLER COUNTY (PORTIONS)—See ST. LOUIS, MO (Charter Communications)

MILLER—See EVERTON, MO (Mediacom)

MILLSTADT (PORTIONS)—See ST. LOUIS, IL (Charter Communications)

MINDENMINES—Formerly served by Cebridge Connections. No longer in operation

MINER—See ST. LOUIS, MO (Charter Communications)

MISSION HILLS—See KANSAS CITY, KS (Time Warner Cable)

MISSION WOODS—See KANSAS CITY, KS (Time Warner Cable)

MISSION—See KANSAS CITY, KS (Time Warner Cable)

MISSIONARY—Formerly served by Crystal Broadband Networks. No longer in operation

MOBERLY—Charter Communications. Now served by ST. LOUIS, MO [MO0009]

MOBERLY—See ST. LOUIS, MO (Charter Communications)

MOKANE—Formerly served by First Cable of Missouri Inc. No longer in operation

MOLINE ACRES—See ST. LOUIS, MO (Charter Communications)

MONETT—Suddenlink Communications

MONROE CITY—Formerly served by US Cable of Coastal Texas LP. Now served by Charter Communications, ST. LOUIS, MO [MO0009]

MONROE CITY—See ST. LOUIS, MO (Charter Communications)

MONROE COUNTY (PORTIONS)—See ST. LOUIS, IL (Charter Communications)

MONTGOMERY CITY—Formerly served by US Cable. Now served by Charter Communications, ST. LOUIS, MO [MO0009]

MONTGOMERY CITY—See ST. LOUIS, MO (Charter Communications)

MONTICELLO—Formerly served by CableDirect. No longer in operation

MOORESVILLE—See AVALON, MO (Green Hills Communications. This cable system has converted to IPTV)

MOREHOUSE COLONY—See ADVANCE, MO (Semo Communications Corp)

MOREHOUSE—See ST. LOUIS, MO (Charter Communications)

MORGAN COUNTY (PORTIONS)—See ST. LOUIS, MO (Charter Communications)

MORLEY—See ADVANCE, MO (Semo Communications Corp)

MORO TWP.—See ST. LOUIS, IL (Charter Communications)

MOSCOW MILLS—See ST. LOUIS, MO (Charter Communications)

MOUND CITY—Rock Port Cablevision

MOUNT VERNON—See ST. LOUIS, IL (Charter Communications)

MOUNT VERNON—See EVERTON, MO (Mediacom)

MOUNTAIN GROVE—Formerly served by Almega Cable. Now served by Cable America Corp., ST. ROBERT, MO [MO0023]

MOUNTAIN GROVE—See ST. ROBERT, MO (Cable America Corp)

MOUNTAIN VIEW—Formerly served by Boycom Cablevision Inc. No longer in operation

MULBERRY—See LIBERAL, KS (Mediacom)

NAMEOKI—See ST. LOUIS, MO (Charter Communications)

NAPOLEON—See LEXINGTON, MO (Suddenlink Communications)

NASHVILLE—See ST. LOUIS, IL (Charter Communications)

NAYLOR—Formerly served by Boycom Cablevision Inc. No longer in operation

NECK CITY—See CARL JUNCTION, MO (Mediacom)

NEOSHO—Suddenlink Communications

NEVADA—Fidelity Communications

NEW BADEN—See ST. LOUIS, IL (Charter Communications)

NEW BLOOMFIELD—Formerly served by Longview Communications. No longer in operation

NEW CAMBRIA—Chariton Valley Cablevision. Now served by MACON, MO [MO0071]

NEW CAMBRIA—See MACON, MO (Chariton Valley Cablevision)

NEW FLORENCE—See ST. LOUIS, MO (Charter Communications)

NEW FRANKLIN—Formerly served by Longview Communications. No longer in operation

NEW HAVEN—Fidelity Communications. Now served by PHELPS COUNTY, MO [MO0045]

NEW HAVEN—See PHELPS COUNTY (portions), MO (Fidelity Communications)

NEW MADRID COUNTY (NORTHERN PORTION)—See ADVANCE, MO (Semo Communications Corp)

NEW MADRID COUNTY (PORTIONS)—See ST. LOUIS, MO (Charter Communications)

NEW MADRID—Charter Communications. Now served by ST. LOUIS, MO [MO0009]

NEW MADRID—See ST. LOUIS, MO (Charter Communications)

NEW MADRID—See DEXTER, MO (NewWave Communications)

NEW MELLE—See LAKE SHERWOOD, MO (Cable America Corp)

NEWBURG—Cable America Corp. Now served by ST. ROBERT, MO [MO0023]

NEWBURG—See ST. ROBERT, MO (Cable America Corp)

NEWTON COUNTY (PORTIONS)—See NEOSHO, MO (Suddenlink Communications)

NEWTON COUNTY—See JOPLIN, MO (Cable One)

NEWTON—Formerly served by Midwest Cable Inc. No longer in operation

NEWTONIA—See DIAMOND, MO (Mediacom)

NIANGUA—Formerly served by Almega Cable. No longer in operation

NIANGUA—Formerly served by Cebridge Connections. No longer in operation

NIXA—Suddenlink Communications

NODAWAY COUNTY (PORTIONS)—See MARYVILLE, MO (Suddenlink Communications)

NOEL—Formerly served by Crystal Broadband Networks. No longer in operation

NORBORNE—Green Hills Communications. This cable system has converted to IPTV. Now served by AVALON, MO [MO5156]

NORBORNE—Mediacom. Now served by EXCELSIOR SPRINGS, MO [MO0040]

NORBORNE—See AVALON, MO (Green Hills Communications. This cable system has converted to IPTV)

NORBORNE—See EXCELSIOR SPRINGS, MO (Mediacom)

NORMANDY—See ST. LOUIS, MO (Charter Communications)

NORTH KANSAS CITY—See KANSAS CITY, MO (Time Warner Cable)

NORTH WARDELL—See DEXTER, MO (NewWave Communications)

NORTHMOOR—See KANSAS CITY, MO (Time Warner Cable)

NORTHSHORE—Formerly served by Almega Cable. No longer in operation

NORTHWEST MISSOURI STATE UNIVERSITY—See MARYVILLE, MO (Suddenlink Communications)

NORTHWOODS—See ST. LOUIS, MO (Charter Communications)

NORWOOD COURT—See ST. LOUIS, MO (Charter Communications)

NORWOOD—Formerly served by Cebridge Connections. No longer in operation

NOVINGER—Formerly served by Longview Communications. No longer in operation

O'FALLON—See ST. LOUIS, IL (Charter Communications)

2017 Edition

Cable Community Index-161

Missouri—Cable Community Index

O'FALLON—See ST. LOUIS, MO (Charter Communications)

OAK GROVE—See INDEPENDENCE, MO (Comcast Cable)

OAKLAND—See ST. LOUIS, MO (Charter Communications)

OAKS VILLAGE—See KANSAS CITY, MO (Time Warner Cable)

OAKVIEW—See KANSAS CITY, MO (Time Warner Cable)

OAKVILLE—See ST. LOUIS, MO (Charter Communications)

OAKWOOD PARK—See KANSAS CITY, MO (Time Warner Cable)

OAKWOOD—See KANSAS CITY, MO (Time Warner Cable)

ODESSA—See INDEPENDENCE, MO (Comcast Cable)

ODIN—See ST. LOUIS, IL (Charter Communications)

OKAWVILLE—See ST. LOUIS, IL (Charter Communications)

OLATHE (PORTIONS)—See KANSAS CITY, KS (Time Warner Cable)

OLATHE—See INDEPENDENCE, KS (Comcast Cable)

OLIVETTE—See ST. LOUIS, MO (Charter Communications)

OLYMPIAN VILLAGE—See ST. LOUIS, MO (Charter Communications)

ORAN—See ST. LOUIS, MO (Charter Communications)

OREGON—South Holt Cablevision Inc

ORONOGO—See CARL JUNCTION, MO (Mediacom)

OSAGE BEACH—Charter Communications. Now served by ST. LOUIS, MO [MO0009]

OSAGE BEACH—See ST. LOUIS, MO (Charter Communications)

OSCEOLA—Mediacom

OTTERVILLE—Formerly served by CableDirect. No longer in operation

OVERLAND PARK—See KANSAS CITY, KS (Time Warner Cable)

OVERLAND—Charter Communications. Now served by ST. LOUIS, MO [MO0009]

OVERLAND—See ST. LOUIS, MO (Charter Communications)

OWENSVILLE—See PHELPS COUNTY (portions), MO (Fidelity Communications)

OXLY—See POPLAR BLUFF, MO (Boycom Cablevision Inc)

OZARK—See NIXA, MO (Suddenlink Communications)

PACIFIC—Charter Communications. Now served by ST. LOUIS, MO [MO0009]

PACIFIC—See ST. LOUIS, MO (Charter Communications)

PAGEDALE—See ST. LOUIS, MO (Charter Communications)

PALMYRA—Formerly served by Cass Cable TV Inc. Now served by Charter Communications, ST. LOUIS, MO [MO0009]

PALMYRA—See ST. LOUIS, MO (Charter Communications)

PARIS—Formerly served by US Cable. Now served by Charter Communications, ST. LOUIS, MO [MO0009]

PARIS—See ST. LOUIS, MO (Charter Communications)

PARK HILLS—See ST. LOUIS, MO (Charter Communications)

PARKVILLE—See KANSAS CITY, MO (Time Warner Cable)

PARKWAY—See ST. LOUIS, MO (Charter Communications)

PARMA—NewWave Communications. Now served by DEXTER, MO [MO0039]

PARMA—See DEXTER, MO (NewWave Communications)

PARNELL—Formerly served by B & L Technologies LLC. No longer in operation

PASADENA HILLS—See ST. LOUIS, MO (Charter Communications)

PASADENA PARK—See ST. LOUIS, MO (Charter Communications)

PATTERSON—See PIEDMONT, MO (Boycom Cablevision Inc)

PECULIAR—See INDEPENDENCE, MO (Comcast Cable)

PEMISCOT COUNTY (PORTIONS)—See DEXTER, MO (NewWave Communications)

PERRY COUNTY (PORTIONS)—See PERRYVILLE, MO (Charter Communications)

PERRY—Formerly served by Charter Communications. No longer in operation

PERRYVILLE—Charter Communications

PETTIS COUNTY (PORTIONS)—See ST. LOUIS, MO (Charter Communications)

PEVELY—See ST. LOUIS, MO (Charter Communications)

PHELPS COUNTY (PORTIONS)—Cable America Corp

PHELPS COUNTY (PORTIONS)—See ST. LOUIS, MO (Charter Communications)

PHELPS COUNTY (PORTIONS)—Fidelity Communications

PIEDMONT—Boycom Cablevision Inc

PIERCE CITY—See MONETT, MO (Suddenlink Communications)

PIGGOTT—See DEXTER, AR (NewWave Communications)

PILOT GROVE—Formerly served by Otelco. No longer in operation

PILOT KNOB—See ST. LOUIS, MO (Charter Communications)

PINE LAWN—See ST. LOUIS, MO (Charter Communications)

PITTSBURG—See POMME DE TERRE, MO (American Broadband Missouri)

PLATTE CITY—See KANSAS CITY, MO (Time Warner Cable)

PLATTE COUNTY (PORTIONS)—See KANSAS CITY, MO (Time Warner Cable)

PLATTE WOODS—See KANSAS CITY, MO (Time Warner Cable)

PLATTSBURG—Formerly served by Allegiance Communications. No longer in operation

PLEASANT HILL—See INDEPENDENCE, MO (Comcast Cable)

PLEASANT HOPE—Formerly served by Fidelity Communications. No longer in operation

PLEASANT VALLEY—See KANSAS CITY, MO (Time Warner Cable)

POCAHONTAS—Semo Communications Corp. Now served by ADVANCE, MO [MO0171]

POCAHONTAS—See ADVANCE, MO (Semo Communications Corp)

POLK COUNTY—See BOLIVAR (town), MO (Windstream)

POLLARD—See DEXTER, AR (NewWave Communications)

POLO—See AVALON, MO (Green Hills Communications. This cable system has converted to IPTV)

POMME DE TERRE—American Broadband Missouri

PONTOON BEACH—See ST. LOUIS, IL (Charter Communications)

POPLAR BLUFF—Boycom Cablevision Inc

POPLAR BLUFF—NewWave Communications

PORTAGE DES SIOUX—Formerly served by Cable America Corp. No longer in operation

PORTAGEVILLE—NewWave Communications. Now served by DEXTER, MO [MO0039]

PORTAGEVILLE—See DEXTER, MO (NewWave Communications)

PORTER MILLS—Formerly served by Lake Communications. No longer in operation

POTOSI—Formerly served by Crystal Broadband Networks. No longer in operation

POWERSITE—Formerly served by Almega Cable. No longer in operation

PRAIRIE VILLAGE—See KANSAS CITY, KS (Time Warner Cable)

PRINCETON—Formerly served by Longview Communications. No longer in operation

PULASKI COUNTY (PORTIONS)—See ST. ROBERT, MO (Cable America Corp)

PURCELL—See CARL JUNCTION, MO (Mediacom)

PURDY—Mediacom. Now served by CASSVILLE, MO [MO0118]

PURDY—See CASSVILLE, MO (Mediacom)

PUXICO—Boycom Cablevision Inc

QULIN—Formerly served by Boycom Cablevision Inc. No longer in operation

RANDOLPH COUNTY (PORTIONS)—See ST. LOUIS, MO (Charter Communications)

RAVENWOOD—Formerly served by B & L Technologies LLC. No longer in operation

RAYMORE—See INDEPENDENCE, MO (Comcast Cable)

RAYTOWN—See INDEPENDENCE, MO (Comcast Cable)

RECTOR—See DEXTER, AR (NewWave Communications)

REDINGS MILL—See JOPLIN, MO (Cable One)

REEDS SPRING—See NIXA, MO (Suddenlink Communications)

RENICK—Formerly served by Charter Communications. No longer in operation

RENICK—Milan Interactive Communications

REPUBLIC—Cable America Corp

RICH HILL—American Broadband Missouri

RICHARDS-GEBAUR AFB—See KANSAS CITY, MO (Time Warner Cable)

RICHLAND—Cable America Corp. Now served by ST. ROBERT, MO [MO0023]

RICHLAND—See ST. ROBERT, MO (Cable America Corp)

RICHMOND HEIGHTS—See ST. LOUIS, MO (Charter Communications)

RICHMOND—Mediacom. Now served by EXCELSIOR SPRINGS, MO [MO0040]

RICHMOND—See EXCELSIOR SPRINGS, MO (Mediacom)

RISCO—See DEXTER, MO (NewWave Communications)

RIVERSIDE—See KANSAS CITY, MO (Time Warner Cable)

RIVERVIEW—See ST. LOUIS, MO (Charter Communications)

ROCK HILL—See ST. LOUIS, MO (Charter Communications)

ROCK PORT—Rock Port Cablevision

ROCKAWAY BEACH—Formerly served by Cox Communications. Now served

Cable Community Index—Missouri

by Suddenlink Communications, BRANSON, MO [MO0038]

ROCKAWAY BEACH—See BRANSON, MO (Suddenlink Communications)

ROCKVILLE—Formerly served by N.W. Communications. No longer in operation

ROELAND PARK—See KANSAS CITY, KS (Time Warner Cable)

ROGERSVILLE—Mediacom. Now served by SEYMOUR, MO [MO0172]

ROGERSVILLE—See SEYMOUR, MO (Mediacom)

ROLLA—Formerly served by Phelps County Cable. Now served by Cable America Corp., PHELPS COUNTY (portions), MO [MO0475]

ROLLA—See PHELPS COUNTY (portions), MO (Cable America Corp)

ROLLA—See PHELPS COUNTY (portions), MO (Fidelity Communications)

ROSEBUD—See PHELPS COUNTY (portions), MO (Fidelity Communications)

ROXANA—See ST. LOUIS, IL (Charter Communications)

RUSSELLVILLE—Formerly served by Longview Communications. No longer in operation

SAGINAW—See JOPLIN, MO (Cable One)

SALEM—Fidelity Communications. Now served by PHELPS COUNTY (portions), MO [MO0475]

SALEM—See ST. LOUIS, IL (Charter Communications)

SALEM—See PHELPS COUNTY (portions), MO (Fidelity Communications)

SALISBURY—See BRUNSWICK, MO (Mediacom)

SANDOVAL—See ST. LOUIS, IL (Charter Communications)

SAPPINGTON—See ST. LOUIS, MO (Charter Communications)

SARCOXIE—Mediacom. Now served by DIAMOND, MO [MO0156]

SARCOXIE—See DIAMOND, MO (Mediacom)

SAVANNAH—See ST. JOSEPH, MO (Suddenlink Communications)

SCHELL CITY—American Broadband Missouri

SCOTT AFB—See ST. LOUIS, IL (Charter Communications)

SCOTT CITY—See ST. LOUIS, MO (Charter Communications)

SCOTT COUNTY (SOUTHERN PORTION)—See ADVANCE, MO (Semo Communications Corp)

SCOTT COUNTY—See ST. LOUIS, MO (Charter Communications)

SEDALIA—Charter Communications. Now served by ST. LOUIS, MO [MO0009]

SEDALIA—See ST. LOUIS, MO (Charter Communications)

SELIGMAN—Formerly served by Allegiance Communications. No longer in operation

SENATH—See DEXTER, MO (NewWave Communications)

SENECA—Formerly served by Crystal Broadband Networks. No longer in operation

SENECA—Formerly served by S-Go Video. IPTV service no longer in operation

SEYMOUR—Mediacom

SHAWNEE—See KANSAS CITY, KS (Time Warner Cable)

SHELBINA—Formerly served by US Cable. Now served by Charter Communications, ST. LOUIS, MO [MO0009]

SHELBINA—See ST. LOUIS, MO (Charter Communications)

SHELBY COUNTY (PORTIONS)—See ST. LOUIS, MO (Charter Communications)

SHELBYVILLE—See ST. LOUIS, MO (Charter Communications)

SHELDON—Formerly served by Cebridge Connections. No longer in operation

SHERIDAN—Formerly served by B & L Technologies LLC. No longer in operation

SHILOH—See ST. LOUIS, IL (Charter Communications)

SHOAL CREEK DRIVE—See JOPLIN, MO (Cable One)

SHREWSBURY—See ST. LOUIS, MO (Charter Communications)

SIBLEY—See INDEPENDENCE, MO (Comcast Cable)

SIKESTON—See ST. LOUIS, MO (Charter Communications)

SILEX—Formerly served by First Cable of Missouri Inc. No longer in operation

SILVER CREEK—See JOPLIN, MO (Cable One)

SKIDMORE—Holway Telephone Co. Now served by MAITLAND, MO [MO0336]

SKIDMORE—See MAITLAND, MO (American Broadband Missouri)

SLATER—See HIGGINSVILLE, MO (Citizens CableVision)

SMITHTON—Provincial Cable & Data

SMITHVILLE—See KANSAS CITY, MO (Time Warner Cable)

SOUTH ROXANA—See ST. LOUIS, IL (Charter Communications)

SPANISH LAKE—See ST. LOUIS, MO (Charter Communications)

SPARTA—Formerly served by Almega Cable. No longer in operation

SPRING CITY—Formerly served by Almega Cable. No longer in operation

SPRINGFIELD—Mediacom

ST. ANN—See ST. LOUIS, MO (Charter Communications)

ST. CHARLES COUNTY (PORTIONS)—See ST. LOUIS, MO (Charter Communications)

ST. CHARLES COUNTY—See LAKE SHERWOOD, MO (Cable America Corp)

ST. CHARLES—Charter Communications. Now served by ST. LOUIS, MO [MO0009]

ST. CHARLES—See ST. LOUIS, MO (Charter Communications)

ST. CLAIR COUNTY (PORTIONS)—See ST. LOUIS, IL (Charter Communications)

ST. CLAIR—Charter Communications. Now served by ST. LOUIS, MO [MO0009]

ST. CLAIR—See ST. LOUIS, MO (Charter Communications)

ST. FRANCIS—See DEXTER, AR (NewWave Communications)

ST. FRANCOIS COUNTY (PORTIONS)—See ST. LOUIS, MO (Charter Communications)

ST. GEORGE—See ST. LOUIS, MO (Charter Communications)

ST. JACOB—See ST. LOUIS, IL (Charter Communications)

ST. JAMES—Charter Communications. Now served by ST. LOUIS, MO [MO0009]

ST. JAMES—See ST. LOUIS, MO (Charter Communications)

ST. JOHN—See ST. LOUIS, MO (Charter Communications)

ST. JOSEPH—Suddenlink Communications

ST. LOUIS COUNTY—See ST. LOUIS, MO (Charter Communications)

ST. LOUIS—Charter Communications. Now served by ST. LOUIS, MO [MO0009]

ST. LOUIS—Formerly served by Sprint Corp. No longer in operation

ST. LOUIS—Charter Communications

ST. MARTINS—See COLE COUNTY (portions), MO (Suddenlink Communications)

ST. PAUL—See ST. LOUIS, MO (Charter Communications)

ST. PETERS—See ST. LOUIS, MO (Charter Communications)

ST. ROBERT—Cable America Corp

ST. THOMAS—Formerly served by First Cable of Missouri Inc. No longer in operation

STANBERRY—Formerly served by Longview Communications. No longer in operation

STARK CITY—See DIAMOND, MO (Mediacom)

STE. GENEVIEVE—Formerly served by Charter Communications. No longer in operation

STE. GENEVIEVE—Formerly served by Charter Communications. No longer in operation

STEELE—NewWave Communications. Now served by DEXTER, MO [MO0039]

STEELE—See DEXTER, MO (NewWave Communications)

STEELVILLE—Charter Communications. Now served by ST. LOUIS, MO [MO0009]

STEELVILLE—See ST. LOUIS, MO (Charter Communications)

STET—See AVALON, MO (Green Hills Communications. This cable system has converted to IPTV)

STOCKTON—Windstream

STODDARD COUNTY (PORTIONS)—See DEXTER, MO (NewWave Communications)

STONE COUNTY (PORTIONS)—See BRANSON, MO (Suddenlink Communications)

STONE COUNTY (PORTIONS)—See NIXA, MO (Suddenlink Communications)

STOTTS CITY—Formerly served by Cebridge Connections. No longer in operation

STOVER—Formerly served by Provincial Cable & Data. No longer in operation

STRAFFORD—Mediacom. Now served by SEYMOUR, MO [MO0172]

STRAFFORD—See SEYMOUR, MO (Mediacom)

STURGEON—Provincial Cable & Data

SUGAR CREEK—See INDEPENDENCE, MO (Comcast Cable)

SULLIVAN—Charter Communications. Now served by ST. LOUIS, MO [MO0009]

SULLIVAN—Charter Communications. Now served by SULLIVAN (formerly WASHINGTON), MO [MO0030]

SULLIVAN—Fidelity Communications. Now served by PHELPS COUNTY (portions), MO [MO0475]

SULLIVAN—See ST. LOUIS, MO (Charter Communications)

SULLIVAN—See PHELPS COUNTY (portions), MO (Fidelity Communications)

SUMMERFIELD—See ST. LOUIS, IL (Charter Communications)

SUMMERSVILLE—Formerly served by Almega Cable. No longer in operation

SUNRISE BEACH—See ST. LOUIS, MO (Charter Communications)

Missouri—Cable Community Index

SUNSET HILLS—See ST. LOUIS, MO (Charter Communications)

SWANSEA—See ST. LOUIS, IL (Charter Communications)

SWEET SPRINGS—See HIGGINSVILLE, MO (Citizens CableVision)

SYCAMORE HILLS—See ST. LOUIS, MO (Charter Communications)

SYRACUSE—Formerly served by First Cable of Missouri Inc. No longer in operation

TALLAPOOSA—See DEXTER, MO (NewWave Communications)

TANEY COUNTY (PORTIONS)—See BRANSON, MO (Suddenlink Communications)

TAOS—Formerly served by Longview Communications. No longer in operation

TARKIO—See ROCK PORT, MO (Rock Port Cablevision)

TERRE DU LAC—Charter Communications. Now served by ST. LOUIS, MO [MO0009]

TERRE DU LAC—See ST. LOUIS, MO (Charter Communications)

THAYER—Fidelity Communications

TIMES BEACH—See ST. LOUIS, MO (Charter Communications)

TINA—Green Hills Communications. This cable system has converted to IPTV. Now served by AVALON, MO [MO5156]

TINA—See AVALON, MO (Green Hills Communications. This cable system has converted to IPTV)

TIPTON—Formerly served by Charter Communications. No longer in operation

TIPTON—Formerly served by Crystal Broadband Networks. No longer in operation

TOWN & COUNTRY—See ST. LOUIS, MO (Charter Communications)

TRACY—See KANSAS CITY, MO (Time Warner Cable)

TRENTON—See ST. LOUIS, IL (Charter Communications)

TRENTON—Suddenlink Communications

TRIMBLE—Formerly served by Time Warner Cable. No longer in operation

TROY—Charter Communications. Now served by ST. LOUIS, MO [MO0009]

TROY—See ST. LOUIS, IL (Charter Communications)

TROY—See ST. LOUIS, MO (Charter Communications)

TRUESDALE—See ST. LOUIS, MO (Charter Communications)

TWIN OAKS—See ST. LOUIS, MO (Charter Communications)

UNION—See ST. LOUIS, MO (Charter Communications)

UNIONVILLE—Unionville Missouri CATV

UNIVERSITY CITY—See ST. LOUIS, MO (Charter Communications)

UNIVERSITY OF MISSOURI—See COLUMBIA, MO (Mediacom)

UPLANDS PARK—See ST. LOUIS, MO (Charter Communications)

URBANA—Formerly served by Cebridge Connections. No longer in operation

URICH—Formerly served by CableDirect. No longer in operation

UTICA (village)—Formerly served by Green Hills Communications Inc. No longer in operation

VALLEY PARK—See ST. LOUIS, MO (Charter Communications)

VAN BUREN—Boycom Cablevision Inc

VANDALIA—Formerly served by Crystal Broadband Networks. No longer in operation

VANDIVER—See ST. LOUIS, MO (Charter Communications)

VANDUSER—See ADVANCE, MO (Semo Communications Corp)

VELDA CITY—See ST. LOUIS, MO (Charter Communications)

VELDA VILLAGE HILLS—See ST. LOUIS, MO (Charter Communications)

VENICE ON THE LAKE—See BRANSON, MO (Suddenlink Communications)

VENICE—See ST. LOUIS, IL (Charter Communications)

VERNON COUNTY (SOUTHWESTERN PORTIONS)—See NEVADA, MO (Fidelity Communications)

VERONA—See MONETT, MO (Suddenlink Communications)

VERSAILLES—Formerly served by Crystal Broadband Networks. No longer in operation

VIBURNUM—Formerly served by Crystal Broadband Networks. No longer in operation

VIENNA—Formerly served by Longview Communications. No longer in operation

VILLA RIDGE—Charter Communications. Now served by ST. LOUIS, MO [MO0009]

VILLA RIDGE—See ST. LOUIS, MO (Charter Communications)

VILLAGE OF FOUR SEASONS—See ST. LOUIS, MO (Charter Communications)

VINITA PARK—See ST. LOUIS, MO (Charter Communications)

VINITA TERRACE—See ST. LOUIS, MO (Charter Communications)

WALNUT GROVE—See EVERTON, MO (Mediacom)

WALNUT HILLS—See ST. LOUIS, MO (Charter Communications)

WAMAC—See ST. LOUIS, IL (Charter Communications)

WAPPAPELLO—Boycom Cablevision Inc

WARDELL—Formerly served by Almega Cable. No longer in operation

WARDELL—See DEXTER, MO (NewWave Communications)

WARDSVILLE—See COLE COUNTY (portions), MO (Suddenlink Communications)

WARREN COUNTY—See LAKE SHERWOOD, MO (Cable America Corp)

WARRENSBURG—Charter Communications. Now served by ST. LOUIS, MO [MO0009]

WARRENSBURG—See ST. LOUIS, MO (Charter Communications)

WARRENTON—Charter Communications. Now served by ST. LOUIS, MO [MO0009]

WARRENTON—See ST. LOUIS, MO (Charter Communications)

WARSAW—Formerly served by Crystal Broadband Networks. No longer in operation

WARSON WOODS—See ST. LOUIS, MO (Charter Communications)

WASHINGTON COUNTY (PORTIONS)—See ST. LOUIS, IL (Charter Communications)

WASHINGTON COUNTY (PORTIONS)—See PHELPS COUNTY (portions), MO (Fidelity Communications)

WASHINGTON—See ST. LOUIS, MO (Charter Communications)

WATERLOO—See ST. LOUIS, IL (Charter Communications)

WAVERLY—See HIGGINSVILLE, MO (Citizens CableVision)

WAYNE COUNTY (PORTIONS)—See PIEDMONT, MO (Boycom Cablevision Inc)

WAYNE COUNTY (SOUTHERN PORTION)—See WAPPAPELLO, MO (Boycom Cablevision Inc)

WAYNESVILLE—See ST. ROBERT, MO (Cable America Corp)

WEATHERBY LAKE—See KANSAS CITY, MO (Time Warner Cable)

WEAUBLEAU—See POMME DE TERRE, MO (American Broadband Missouri)

WEBB CITY—See JOPLIN, MO (Cable One)

WEBSTER GROVES—See ST. LOUIS, MO (Charter Communications)

WELDON SPRING—See ST. LOUIS, MO (Charter Communications)

WELLINGTON—See LEXINGTON, MO (Suddenlink Communications)

WELLSTON—Formerly served by Data Cablevision. No longer in operation

WELLSVILLE—See ST. LOUIS, MO (Charter Communications)

WENTZVILLE—See ST. LOUIS, MO (Charter Communications)

WEST PLAINS—Fidelity Communications

WESTBORO—Formerly served by CableDirect. No longer in operation

WESTON—See KANSAS CITY, MO (Time Warner Cable)

WESTPHALIA—Formerly served by CableDirect. No longer in operation

WESTWOOD HILLS—See KANSAS CITY, KS (Time Warner Cable)

WESTWOOD—See ST. LOUIS, MO (Charter Communications)

WESTWOOD—See KANSAS CITY, KS (Time Warner Cable)

WHEATLAND—See POMME DE TERRE, MO (American Broadband Missouri)

WHEELING—Formerly served by Longview Communications. No longer in operation

WHEELING—See AVALON, MO (Green Hills Communications. This cable system has converted to IPTV)

WHITEMAN AFB—See ST. LOUIS, MO (Charter Communications)

WILBUR PARK—See ST. LOUIS, MO (Charter Communications)

WILDWOOD—See ST. LOUIS, MO (Charter Communications)

WILLARD—See EVERTON, MO (Mediacom)

WILLIAMSVILLE—Formerly served by Almega Cable. No longer in operation

WILLOW SPRINGS—Formerly served by Almega Cable. Now served by Cable America Corp., ST. ROBERT, MO [MO0023]

WILLOW SPRINGS—See ST. ROBERT, MO (Cable America Corp)

WILSON BEND—Formerly served by Almega Cable. No longer in operation

WILSON CITY—See ADVANCE, MO (Semo Communications Corp)

WINCHESTER—See ST. LOUIS, MO (Charter Communications)

WINDSOR—Formerly served by Crystal Broadband Networks. No longer in operation

WINFIELD—Formerly served by Charter Communications. No longer in operation

WINONA—Formerly served by Boycom Cablevision Inc. No longer in operation

WOOD HEIGHTS—See EXCELSIOR SPRINGS, MO (Mediacom)

WOOD RIVER—See ST. LOUIS, IL (Charter Communications)

WOODLAWN—See ST. LOUIS, IL (Charter Communications)

WOODSON TERRACE—See ST. LOUIS, MO (Charter Communications)

Cable Community Index—Montana

WRIGHT CITY—See ST. LOUIS, MO (Charter Communications)

WYACONDA—Formerly served by CableDirect. No longer in operation

WYANDOTTE COUNTY (PORTIONS)—See KANSAS CITY, KS (Time Warner Cable)

WYATT—See ADVANCE, MO (Semo Communications Corp)

MONTANA

ABSAROKEE—Formerly served by USA Communications. No longer in operation

ALBERTON—Formerly served by Optimum. No longer in operation

ANACONDA—Charter Communications

ARLEE—Formerly served by Bresnan Communications. No longer in operation

BAKER—Mid-Rivers Communications

BEAVERHEAD COUNTY (PORTIONS)—See DILLON, MT (Charter Communications)

BELFRY—Formerly served by Belfry Cable TV. No longer in operation

BELGRADE—See BOZEMAN, MT (Charter Communications)

BELT—Formerly served by KLiP Interactive. No longer in operation

BIG FLAT—Formerly served by Bresnan Communications. No longer in operation

BIG SKY RESORT—See BIG SKY, MT (Bulldog Cable)

BIG SKY—Bulldog Cable

BIG TIMBER—Charter Communications

BIGFORK—See KALISPELL, MT (Charter Communications)

BILLINGS (WESTERN PORTION)—USA Communications

BILLINGS—Formerly served by USA Digital TV. No longer in operation

BILLINGS—Charter Communications

BLACK EAGLE—See GREAT FALLS, MT (Charter Communications)

BLACKFEET INDIAN RESERVATION—See CUT BANK, MT (Charter Communications)

BLAINE COUNTY (NORTHERN PORTION)—See CHINOOK, MT (Charter Communications)

BLOOMFIELD—See GLENDIVE, MT (Mid-Rivers Communications)

BONNER—See MISSOULA, MT (Charter Communications)

BOULDER—Charter Communications

BOZEMAN—Charter Communications

BRIDGER—Bridger Cable TV

BROADUS—Skyview TV Inc

BROADWATER COUNTY—See TOWNSEND, MT (Charter Communications)

BROCKWAY—See GLENDIVE, MT (Mid-Rivers Communications)

BUTTE—Charter Communications

CASCADE COUNTY—See GREAT FALLS, MT (Charter Communications)

CASCADE—Charter Communications

CHARLO—Formerly served by KLiP Interactive. No longer in operation

CHESTER—Formerly served by KLiP Interactive. No longer in operation

CHINOOK—Charter Communications

CHOTEAU—3 Rivers Communications

CIRCLE—Mid-Rivers Communications. Now served by GLENDIVE, MT [MT0013]

CIRCLE—See GLENDIVE, MT (Mid-Rivers Communications)

CLANCY—See HELENA, MT (Charter Communications)

CLINTON—See MISSOULA, MT (Charter Communications)

COLSTRIP—USA Communications

COLUMBIA FALLS—See KALISPELL, MT (Charter Communications)

COLUMBUS—Formerly served by Cable Montana. No longer in operation

COLUMBUS—See BILLINGS, MT (Charter Communications)

CONRAD—3 Rivers Communications

CORVALLIS—See HAMILTON, MT (Charter Communications)

CRANE—See SIDNEY (town), MT (Mid-Rivers Communications)

CROW AGENCY—Crow Cable TV

CROW INDIAN RESERVATION—See CROW AGENCY, MT (Crow Cable TV)

CULBERTSON—Formerly served by Bulldog Cable. No longer in operation

CUSTER COUNTY (PORTIONS)—See MILES CITY, MT (Mid-Rivers Communications)

CUT BANK—Charter Communications

DARBY (town)—Formerly served by KLiP Interactive. No longer in operation

DAWSON COUNTY—See GLENDIVE, MT (Mid-Rivers Communications)

DEER LODGE COUNTY—See ANACONDA, MT (Charter Communications)

DEER LODGE—Charter Communications

DILLON—Charter Communications

DRUMMOND—Formerly served by Cowley Telecable. No longer in operation

DUTTON—Formerly served by KLiP Interactive. No longer in operation

EAST HELENA—See HELENA, MT (Charter Communications)

EKALAKA—Mid-Rivers Communications. Now served by BAKER, MT [MT0041]

EKALAKA—See BAKER, MT (Mid-Rivers Communications)

ENNIS—Formerly served by Bulldog Cable. No longer in operation

EUREKA—Tobacco Valley Cable

FAIRVIEW—Mid-Rivers Communications. Now served by SIDNEY (town), MT [MT0018]

FAIRVIEW—See SIDNEY (town), MT (Mid-Rivers Communications)

FALLON—See GLENDIVE, MT (Mid-Rivers Communications)

FERGUS COUNTY—See LEWISTOWN, MT (Mid-Rivers Communications)

FLATHEAD COUNTY—See KALISPELL, MT (Charter Communications)

FLORENCE—See MISSOULA, MT (Charter Communications)

FORSYTH—USA Communications

FORT BENTON—Charter Communications

FOUR CORNERS—Formerly served by Northwestern Communications Corp. No longer in operation

FROMBERG—Formerly served by USA Communications. No longer in operation

GALLATIN COUNTY—See BOZEMAN, MT (Charter Communications)

GARDINER—Formerly served by North Yellowstone Cable TV. No longer in operation

GLACIER COUNTY (PORTIONS)—See CUT BANK, MT (Charter Communications)

GLASGOW—Nemont Communications

GLENDIVE—Mid-Rivers Communications

GRANT CREEK—Formerly served by Charter Communications. No longer in operation

GRASS RANGE—See ROUNDUP, MT (Mid-Rivers Communications)

GREAT FALLS—Charter Communications

HAMILTON—Charter Communications

HARDIN—USA Communications

HARLEM—Charter Communications

HARLOWTON—Mid-Rivers Communications

HAVRE—Charter Communications

HELENA—Charter Communications

HILL COUNTY—See HAVRE, MT (Charter Communications)

HOT SPRINGS—Hot Springs Telephone Co

HYSHAM—Mid-Rivers Communications

JEFFERSON COUNTY (UNINCORPORATED AREAS)—See HELENA, MT (Charter Communications)

JOLIET—Formerly served by USA Communications. No longer in operation

JORDAN—Mid-Rivers Communications

KALISPELL—Charter Communications

LAKE COUNTY—See POLSON, MT (Charter Communications)

LAKESIDE—See KALISPELL, MT (Charter Communications)

LAMBERT—See SIDNEY (town), MT (Mid-Rivers Communications)

LAME DEER—Formerly served by Eagle Cablevision Inc. No longer in operation

LAUREL—Charter Communications. Now served by BILLINGS, MT [MT0001]

LAUREL—See BILLINGS, MT (Charter Communications)

LAVINA—Mid-Rivers Communications. Now served by ROUNDUP, MT [MT0043]

LAVINA—See ROUNDUP, MT (Mid-Rivers Communications)

LEWIS & CLARK COUNTY (PORTIONS)—See HELENA, MT (Charter Communications)

LEWISTOWN—Mid-Rivers Communications

LIBBY—MontanaSky West

LINCOLN COUNTY (PORTIONS)—See LIBBY, MT (MontanaSky West)

LINCOLN—Lincoln Cable TV

LIVINGSTON (TOWN)—Charter Communications

LODGE GRASS—Formerly served by Eagle Cablevision Inc. No longer in operation

LOLO—Formerly served by Bresnan Communications. Now served by Charter Communications, MISSOULA, MT [MT0002]

LOLO—See MISSOULA, MT (Charter Communications)

MALMSTROM AFB—See GREAT FALLS, MT (Charter Communications)

MALTA—Charter Communications

MANHATTAN—Formerly served by Bresnan Communications. Now served by Charter Communications, BOZEMAN, MT [MT0007]

MANHATTAN—See BOZEMAN, MT (Charter Communications)

MARION—Formerly served by Mallard Cablevision. No longer in operation

MELSTONE—Formerly served by Mel-View Cable TV. No longer in operation

MILES CITY—Mid-Rivers Communications

Montana—Cable Community Index

MILLTOWN—Formerly served by Bresnan Communications. Now served by Charter Communications, MISSOULA, MT [MT0002]

MILLTOWN—See MISSOULA, MT (Charter Communications)

MISSOULA COUNTY—See MISSOULA, MT (Charter Communications)

MISSOULA SOUTH—See MISSOULA, MT (Charter Communications)

MISSOULA—Formerly served by Cable Montana. Now served by Charter Communications, MISSOULA, MT [MT0002]

MISSOULA—Charter Communications

MONTANA CITY—See HELENA, MT (Charter Communications)

NINE MILE—Formerly served by Bresnan Communications. No longer in operation

OPPORTUNITY—Formerly served by Western Cable TV. No longer in operation

PABLO—See POLSON, MT (Charter Communications)

PARADISE—Formerly served by KLiP Interactive. No longer in operation

PARK CITY—Formerly served by Optimum. No longer in operation

PARK CITY—See BILLINGS, MT (Charter Communications)

PARK COUNTY—See LIVINGSTON (town), MT (Charter Communications)

PHILIPSBURG—Formerly served by Eagle Cablevision Inc. No longer in operation

PHILLIPS COUNTY (PORTIONS)—See MALTA, MT (Charter Communications)

PLAINS—Access Montana

PLENTYWOOD—Bulldog Cable

POLSON—Charter Communications

PONDERA COUNTY—See CONRAD, MT (3 Rivers Communications)

POPLAR—Bulldog Cable

POWELL COUNTY—See DEER LODGE, MT (Charter Communications)

RAVALLI COUNTY (PORTIONS)—See HAMILTON, MT (Charter Communications)

RAVALLI COUNTY (PORTIONS)—See STEVENSVILLE, MT (Charter Communications)

RED LODGE—Charter Communications

RICHEY—Mid-Rivers Communications. Now served by GLENDIVE, MT [MT0013]

RICHEY—See GLENDIVE, MT (Mid-Rivers Communications)

RICHLAND COUNTY (PORTIONS)—See SIDNEY (town), MT (Mid-Rivers Communications)

RIVERSIDE GREENS—Formerly served by Northwestern Communications Corp. No longer in operation

RONAN—Formerly served by Bresnan Communications. Now served by Charter Communications, POLSON, MT [MT0016]

RONAN—See POLSON, MT (Charter Communications)

ROOSEVELT COUNTY—See WOLF POINT, MT (Nemont Communications)

ROUNDUP—Mid-Rivers Communications

RYEGATE—Mid-Rivers Communications. Now served by ROUNDUP, MT [MT0043]

RYEGATE—See ROUNDUP, MT (Mid-Rivers Communications)

SAVAGE—Mid-Rivers Communications. Now served by SIDNEY (town), MT [MT0018]

SAVAGE—See SIDNEY (town), MT (Mid-Rivers Communications)

SCOBEY—Bulldog Cable

SEELEY LAKE—Access Montana

SHELBY—3 Rivers Communications

SHERIDAN—Formerly served by Ruby Valley Cable Co. Inc. No longer in operation

SIDNEY (TOWN)—Mid-Rivers Communications

SILVER BOW COUNTY—See BUTTE, MT (Charter Communications)

SOMERS—See KALISPELL, MT (Charter Communications)

ST. IGNATIUS—Access Montana

ST. REGIS—Formerly served by KLiP Interactive. No longer in operation

STANFORD—Formerly served by B.E.K. Inc. No longer in operation

STEVENSVILLE—Charter Communications

SUN PRAIRIE—Formerly served by Charter Communications. No longer in operation

SUPERIOR—Access Montana

TERRY—Mid-Rivers Communications. Now served by GLENDIVE, MT [MT0013]

TERRY—See GLENDIVE, MT (Mid-Rivers Communications)

THOMPSON FALLS—Access Montana

TOWNSEND—Charter Communications

TROY—MontanaSky West

TWIN BRIDGES—Formerly served by Twin Bridges Cable TV Inc. No longer in operation

VALIER—Formerly served by KLiP Interactive. No longer in operation

VALLEY COUNTY—See GLASGOW, MT (Nemont Communications)

VICTOR—Formerly served by Bresnan Communications. No longer in operation

WALKERVILLE—See BUTTE, MT (Charter Communications)

WEST YELLOWSTONE—Bulldog Cable

WHITE SULPHUR SPRINGS—Formerly served by Eagle Cablevision Inc. No longer in operation

WHITEFISH—See KALISPELL, MT (Charter Communications)

WHITEHALL—Whitehall Cable TV

WIBAUX—Mid-Rivers Communications

WINNETT—See ROUNDUP, MT (Mid-Rivers Communications)

WOLF POINT—Nemont Communications

YELLOWSTONE COUNTY—See BILLINGS, MT (Charter Communications)

NEBRASKA

ADAMS COUNTY (PORTIONS)—See KEARNEY, NE (Charter Communications)

AINSWORTH—Three River Digital Cable

ALBION (TOWN)—Eagle Communications

ALDA—See KEARNEY, NE (Charter Communications)

ALEXANDRIA—Formerly served by Comstar Cable TV Inc. No longer in operation

ALLEN (village)—CenCom NNTV. This cable system has converted to IPTV. See JACKSON, NE [NE5019]

ALLIANCE—Charter Communications. Now served by SCOTTSBLUFF, NE [NE0008]

ALLIANCE—See SCOTTSBLUFF, NE (Charter Communications)

ALMA—Eagle Communications

AMHERST—See KEARNEY, NE (Charter Communications)

ANSLEY—NCTC Cable. Now served by BURWELL, NE [NE0045]

ANSLEY—See BURWELL, NE (NCTC Cable)

ARAPAHOE—ATC Communications

ARCADIA—NCTC Cable. Now served by BURWELL, NE [NE0045]

ARCADIA—See BURWELL, NE (NCTC Cable)

ARLINGTON—See BLAIR, NE (American Broadband)

ARNOLD—Great Plains Cablevision. Now served by BROKEN BOW, NE [NE0031]

ARNOLD—See BROKEN BOW, NE (Great Plains Communications)

ASHLAND—Charter Communications. Now served by SPRINGFIELD (formerly Plattsmouth), NE [NE0020]

ASHLAND—See SPRINGFIELD, NE (Charter Communications)

ASHTON—NCTC Cable. Now served by BURWELL, NE [NE0045]

ASHTON—See BURWELL, NE (NCTC Cable)

ATKINSON—Formerly served by Fort Randall Cable. No longer in operation

AUBURN—Time Warner Cable. Now served by LINCOLN, NE [NE0002]

AUBURN—See LINCOLN, NE (Time Warner Cable)

AURORA—Mid-State Community TV

AVOCA (town)—Formerly served by CableDirect. No longer in operation

AXTELL—See KEARNEY, NE (Charter Communications)

BANCROFT—Great Plains Communications

BARTLEY—See CAMBRIDGE, NE (PinPoint Communications)

BASSETT—American Broadband

BATTLE CREEK—See NORFOLK, NE (Cable One)

BAYARD—Charter Communications. Now served by SCOTTSBLUFF, NE [NE0008]

BAYARD—See SCOTTSBLUFF, NE (Charter Communications)

BEATRICE—Charter Communications

BEAVER CITY—PinPoint Cable TV. Now served by CAMBRIDGE, NE [NE0269]

BEAVER CITY—See CAMBRIDGE, NE (PinPoint Communications)

BEAVER CROSSING—Formerly served by Zito Media. No longer in operation

BEAVER LAKE—Formerly served by Our Cable. No longer in operation

BEE (village)—Formerly served by TelePartners. No longer in operation

BEEMER—Formerly served by TelePartners. Now served by Cable One, NORFOLK, NE [NE0006]

BEEMER—See NORFOLK, NE (Cable One)

BELDEN—See WAYNE, NE (American Broadband)

BELLEVUE—See OMAHA, NE (CenturyLink Prism. Formerly Qwest [NE0377]. This cable system has converted to IPTV.)

BELLEVUE—See OMAHA, NE (Cox Communications)

BELLWOOD—Eagle Communications

BENEDICT—Formerly served by Galaxy Cablevision. No longer in operation

BENKELMAN—BWTelcom

BENNET—See SYRACUSE, NE (Zito Media)

Cable Community Index—Nebraska

BENNINGTON—Cox Communications. Now served by OMAHA, NE [NE0001]

BENNINGTON—See OMAHA, NE (Cox Communications)

BERTRAND—See KEARNEY, NE (Charter Communications)

BIG SPRINGS—Eagle Communications

BLADEN—See BLUE HILL, NE (Glenwood Telecommunications)

BLAIR—American Broadband

BLOOMFIELD—Great Plains Communications

BLUE HILL—Glenwood Telecommunications

BLUE SPRINGS—See WILBER, NE (Zito Media)

BOELUS—NCTC Cable. Now served by BURWELL, NE [NE0045]

BOELUS—See BURWELL, NE (NCTC Cable)

BOX BUTTE COUNTY (PORTIONS)—See SCOTTSBLUFF, NE (Charter Communications)

BRADSHAW—Zito Media

BRAINARD—Formerly served by Zito Media. No longer in operation

BRIDGEPORT—Charter Communications. Now served by SCOTTSBLUFF, NE [NE0008]

BRIDGEPORT—See SCOTTSBLUFF, NE (Charter Communications)

BRISTOW TWP.—Formerly served by Sky Scan Cable Co. No longer in operation

BROCK—Formerly served by CableDirect. No longer in operation

BROKEN BOW—Great Plains Communications

BRULE—Eagle Communications

BRUNING—See GENEVA, NE (Zito Media)

BRUNSWICK (village)—Formerly served by Sky Scan Cable Co. No longer in operation

BURWELL—NCTC Cable

BUTTE—CenCom NNTV. This cable system has converted to IPTV. See JACKSON, NE [NE5019]

BYRON—Formerly served by Zito Media. No longer in operation

CAIRO—See KEARNEY, NE (Charter Communications)

CALLAWAY—See BROKEN BOW, NE (Great Plains Communications)

CAMBRIDGE—PinPoint Communications

CAMPBELL—See BLUE HILL, NE (Glenwood Telecommunications)

CARROLL—See WAYNE, NE (American Broadband)

CARTER LAKE—See OMAHA, IA (CenturyLink Prism. Formerly Qwest [NE0377]. This cable system has converted to IPTV.)

CARTER LAKE—See OMAHA, IA (Cox Communications)

CASS COUNTY (PORTIONS)—See SPRINGFIELD, NE (Charter Communications)

CASS COUNTY (PORTIONS)—See SYRACUSE, NE (Zito Media)

CEDAR BLUFFS—Formerly served by TelePartners. No longer in operation

CEDAR BLUFFS—See LINCOLN, NE (Time Warner Cable)

CEDAR CREEK—Formerly served by Westcom. No longer in operation

CEDAR RAPIDS—Eagle Communications

CENTER—See BLOOMFIELD, NE (Great Plains Communications)

CENTRAL CITY—Eagle Communications

CERESCO—Zito Media

CHADRON—Great Plains Communications

CHAMBERS—Formerly served by Sky Scan Cable Co. No longer in operation

CHAPMAN—Great Plains Communications

CHAPPELL—PC Telcom. Now served by HOLYOKE, CO [CO0065]

CHASE COUNTY (PORTIONS)—See WAUNETA, NE (BWTelcom)

CHESTER—Zito Media

CHEYENNE COUNTY (PORTIONS)—See SIDNEY (town), NE (Charter Communications)

CLARKS—CenCom Inc.

CLARKSON—Formerly served by TelePartners. No longer in operation

CLATONIA—See WILBER, NE (Zito Media)

CLAY CENTER—Zito Media

CLEARWATER—CenCom NNTV. This cable system has converted to IPTV. See JACKSON, NE [NE5019]

CODY—Formerly served by Midcontinent Communications. No longer in operation

COLERIDGE—CenCom NNTV. This cable system has converted to IPTV. See JACKSON, NE [NE5019]

COLUMBUS (portions)—Formerly served by Sky Scan Cable Co. No longer in operation

COLUMBUS—Time Warner Cable. Now served by LINCOLN, NE [NE0002]

COLUMBUS—Eagle Communications

COLUMBUS—See LINCOLN, NE (Time Warner Cable)

COMSTOCK—Formerly served by Consolidated Cable Inc. No longer in operation

COOK—See SYRACUSE, NE (Zito Media)

CORTLAND—Formerly served by Great Plains Communications. No longer in operation

COUNCIL BLUFFS—See OMAHA, IA (CenturyLink Prism. Formerly Qwest [NE0377]. This cable system has converted to IPTV.)

COUNCIL BLUFFS—See OMAHA, IA (Cox Communications)

COZAD—Charter Communications. Now served by KEARNEY, NE [NE0011]

COZAD—See KEARNEY, NE (Charter Communications)

CRAWFORD—Mobius Communications Co

CREIGHTON—See BLOOMFIELD, NE (Great Plains Communications)

CRESTON—Formerly served by Sky Scan Cable Co. No longer in operation

CRETE—See LINCOLN, NE (Time Warner Cable)

CROFTON—See BLOOMFIELD, NE (Great Plains Communications)

CULBERTSON—PinPoint Cable TV. Now served by CAMBRIDGE, NE [NE0269]

CULBERTSON—See CAMBRIDGE, NE (PinPoint Communications)

CURTIS—Formerly served by Consolidated Cable Inc. No longer in operation

DALTON—Dalton Telephone Co

DANNEBROG—NCTC Cable. Now served by BURWELL, NE [NE0045]

DANNEBROG—See BURWELL, NE (NCTC Cable)

DAVENPORT—See GENEVA, NE (Zito Media)

DAVEY (village)—Formerly served by TelePartners. No longer in operation

DAVID CITY—Time Warner Cable. Now served by LINCOLN, NE [NE0002]

DAVID CITY—See LINCOLN, NE (Time Warner Cable)

DAWSON COUNTY (PORTIONS)—See KEARNEY, NE (Charter Communications)

DAWSON—Formerly served by CableDirect. No longer in operation

DAYKIN—Formerly served by Comstar Cable TV Inc. No longer in operation

DE WITT—See WILBER, NE (Zito Media)

DECATUR—CenCom NNTV. This cable system has converted to IPTV. See JACKSON, NE [NE5019]

DENTON (VILLAGE)—See LINCOLN, NE (Time Warner Cable)

DESHLER—Zito Media

DILLER—Diode Cable

DIX—Formerly served by HunTel Cablevision. Now served by Dalton Telephone Co., DALTON, NE [NE0240]

DIX—See DALTON, NE (Dalton Telephone Co)

DIXON/CONCORD—CenCom NNTV. This cable system has converted to IPTV. See JACKSON, NE [NE5019]

DODGE COUNTY—See LINCOLN, NE (Time Warner Cable)

DODGE—Great Plains Communications. Now served by NORTH BEND, NE [NE0080]

DODGE—See NORTH BEND, NE (Great Plains Communications)

DONIPHAN—Mid-State Community TV

DORCHESTER—See WILBER, NE (Zito Media)

DOUGLAS COUNTY (PORTIONS)—See GRETNA, NE (Zito Media)

DOUGLAS COUNTY (UNINCORPORATED AREAS)—See OMAHA, NE (CenturyLink Prism. Formerly Qwest [NE0377]. This cable system has converted to IPTV.)

DOUGLAS COUNTY—See OMAHA, NE (Cox Communications)

DUBOIS—Formerly served by CableDirect. No longer in operation

DUNCAN—Formerly served by Cable Nebraska. No longer in operation

DUNNING—Formerly served by Consolidated Cable Inc. No longer in operation

DWIGHT (village)—Formerly served by TelePartners. No longer in operation

EAGLE—See SYRACUSE, NE (Zito Media)

EDGAR—See CLAY CENTER, NE (Zito Media)

ELBA—NCTC Cable. Now served by BURWELL, NE [NE0045]

ELBA—See BURWELL, NE (NCTC Cable)

ELGIN—Great Plains Communications

ELKHORN—See OMAHA, NE (Cox Communications)

ELKHORN—See GRETNA, NE (Zito Media)

ELM CREEK—See KEARNEY, NE (Charter Communications)

ELMWOOD—See SYRACUSE, NE (Zito Media)

ELSIE—Elsie Communications. No longer in operation

ELWOOD—See ARAPAHOE, NE (ATC Communications)

EMERSON—See WAYNE, NE (American Broadband)

ENDICOTT—Formerly served by Westcom. No longer in operation

Nebraska—Cable Community Index

EWING—Great Plains Cable TV. Now served by ELGIN, NE [NE0282]

EWING—See ELGIN, NE (Great Plains Communications)

EXETER—See GENEVA, NE (Zito Media)

FAIRBURY—Time Warner Cable. Now served by LINCOLN, NE [NE0002]

FAIRBURY—See LINCOLN, NE (Time Warner Cable)

FAIRFIELD—See CLAY CENTER, NE (Zito Media)

FAIRMONT—See GENEVA, NE (Zito Media)

FALLS CITY—Time Warner Cable. Now served by LINCOLN, NE [NE0002]

FALLS CITY—See LINCOLN, NE (Time Warner Cable)

FARNAM—See ARAPAHOE, NE (ATC Communications)

FARNHAM—Formerly served by Consolidated Cable Inc. No longer in operation

FAWN HEIGHTS—Formerly served by TelePartners. No longer in operation

FILLEY—Formerly served by Comstar Cable TV Inc. No longer in operation

FORT CALHOUN—See BLAIR, NE (American Broadband)

FRANKLIN—Formerly served by PinPoint Cable TV. No longer in operation

FRANKLIN—Eagle Communications

FREMONT—Time Warner Cable. Now served by LINCOLN, NE [NE0002]

FREMONT—See LINCOLN, NE (Time Warner Cable)

FRIEND—See WILBER, NE (Zito Media)

FULLERTON—Eagle Communications

FUNK—Glenwood Telecommunications. Now served by BLUE HILL, NE [NE0093]

FUNK—See BLUE HILL, NE (Glenwood Telecommunications)

GARLAND—Formerly served by Zito Media. No longer in operation

GENEVA—Formerly served by Sprint Corp. No longer in operation

GENEVA—Zito Media

GENOA—Eagle Communications

GERING—See SCOTTSBLUFF, NE (Charter Communications)

GIBBON—See KEARNEY, NE (Charter Communications)

GILTNER—Mid-State Community TV

GINGER COVE—Formerly served by TelePartners. No longer in operation

GLENVIL—Formerly served by Zito Media. No longer in operation

GOEHNER (village)—Formerly served by TelePartners. No longer in operation

GORDON—Great Plains Communications. Now served by CHADRON, NE [NE0024]

GORDON—See CHADRON, NE (Great Plains Communications)

GOTHENBURG—Charter Communications. Now served by KEARNEY, NE [NE0011]

GOTHENBURG—See KEARNEY, NE (Charter Communications)

GRAND ISLAND—Charter Communications. Now served by KEARNEY, NE [NE0011]

GRAND ISLAND—See KEARNEY, NE (Charter Communications)

GRAND ISLAND—Zito Media

GRANT—Great Plains Communications

GREELEY—Center Cable Co

GREENWOOD—Charter Communications. Now served by SPRINGFIELD (formerly Plattsmouth), NE [NE0020]

GREENWOOD—See SPRINGFIELD, NE (Charter Communications)

GRESHAM—Formerly served by Zito Media. No longer in operation

GRETNA—See OMAHA, NE (CenturyLink Prism. Formerly Qwest [NE0377]. This cable system has converted to IPTV.)

GRETNA—See OMAHA, NE (Cox Communications)

GRETNA—Zito Media

GUIDE ROCK—Formerly served by Glenwood Telecommunications. No longer in operation

GURLEY—See DALTON, NE (Dalton Telephone Co)

HADAR—Formerly served by Sky Scan Cable Co. Now served by Cable One, NORFOLK, NE [NE0006]

HADAR—See NORFOLK, NE (Cable One)

HAIGLER—BWTelcom

HALL COUNTY (PORTIONS)—See KEARNEY, NE (Charter Communications)

HALLAM—See WILBER, NE (Zito Media)

HAMPTON—See AURORA, NE (Mid-State Community TV)

HARDY—Formerly served by Diode Cable Co. No longer in operation

HARRISON—WinDBreak Cable

HARTINGTON—Cedarvision

HARVARD—See CLAY CENTER, NE (Zito Media)

HASTINGS—Charter Communications. Now served by KEARNEY, NE [NE0011]

HASTINGS—See KEARNEY, NE (Charter Communications)

HAY SPRINGS—Great Plains Communications. Now served by CHADRON, NE [NE0024]

HAY SPRINGS—See CHADRON, NE (Great Plains Communications)

HAYES CENTER—See GRANT, NE (Great Plains Communications)

HEBRON—Diode Cable

HEMINGFORD—Mobius Communications Co

HENDERSON—Mainstay Cable TV

HERMAN—See BLAIR, NE (American Broadband)

HERSHEY—See SUTHERLAND, NE (Great Plains Communications)

HICKMAN—See WILBER, NE (Zito Media)

HILDRETH—See KEARNEY, NE (Charter Communications)

HOLBROOK—See ARAPAHOE, NE (ATC Communications)

HOLDREGE—Charter Communications. Now served by KEARNEY, NE [NE0011]

HOLDREGE—See KEARNEY, NE (Charter Communications)

HOLSTEIN—See BLUE HILL, NE (Glenwood Telecommunications)

HOMER—Formerly served by HunTel Cablevision. Now served by American Broadband, WAYNE, NE [NE0374]

HOMER—See WAYNE, NE (American Broadband)

HOOPER—WesTel Systems

HORDVILLE—Mid-State Community TV

HOSKINS—See NORFOLK, NE (Cable One)

HOWELLS—Formerly served by TelePartners. No longer in operation

HUBBARD—CenCom NNTV. This cable system has converted to IPTV. See JACKSON, NE [NE5019]

HUMBOLDT—See LINCOLN, NE (Time Warner Cable)

HUMPHREY—Eagle Communications

HYANNIS—Formerly served by Consolidated Cable Inc. No longer in operation

IMPERIAL—See GRANT, NE (Great Plains Communications)

INDIANOLA—PinPoint Cable TV. Now served by CAMBRIDGE, NE [NE0269]

INDIANOLA—See CAMBRIDGE, NE (PinPoint Communications)

INGLEWOOD (VILLAGE)—See LINCOLN, NE (Time Warner Cable)

JANSEN—Formerly served by Diode Cable Co. No longer in operation

JOHNSON LAKE—Charter Communications. Now served by KEARNEY, NE [NE0011]

JOHNSON LAKE—See KEARNEY, NE (Charter Communications)

JOHNSON—See SYRACUSE, NE (Zito Media)

JUNIATA—Charter Communications. Now served by KEARNEY, NE [NE0011]

JUNIATA—See KEARNEY, NE (Charter Communications)

KEARNEY—Charter Communications

KEITH COUNTY (PORTIONS)—See NORTH PLATTE, NE (Charter Communications)

KENESAW—Charter Communications

KENNARD—See BLAIR, NE (American Broadband)

KIMBALL COUNTY (PORTIONS)—See SIDNEY (town), NE (Charter Communications)

KIMBALL—Charter Communications. Now served by SIDNEY (town), NE [NE0021]

KIMBALL—See SIDNEY (town), NE (Charter Communications)

LA VISTA—See OMAHA, NE (CenturyLink Prism. Formerly Qwest [NE0377]. This cable system has converted to IPTV.)

LA VISTA—See OMAHA, NE (Cox Communications)

LAKE CUNNINGHAM—Formerly served by TelePartners. No longer in operation

LAKE MALONEY—Formerly served by Charter Communications. No longer in operation

LAKE VENTURA—Formerly served by Charter Communications. No longer in operation

LAKE WACONDA—Formerly served by Westcom. No longer in operation

LANCASTER COUNTY—See LINCOLN, NE (Time Warner Cable)

LAUREL—American Broadband. Now served by BLAIR, NE [NE0027]

LAWRENCE—See BLUE HILL, NE (Glenwood Telecommunications)

LEIGH—Formerly served by TelePartners. No longer in operation

LEWELLEN—Formerly served by Consolidated Cable Inc. No longer in operation

LEXINGTON—Charter Communications. Now served by KEARNEY, NE [NE0011]

LEXINGTON—See KEARNEY, NE (Charter Communications)

LINCOLN COUNTY (PORTIONS)—See NORTH PLATTE, NE (Charter Communications)

LINCOLN—Formerly served by Sprint Corp. No longer in operation

LINCOLN—Time Warner Cable

LINDSAY—Formerly served by TelePartners. No longer in operation

Cable Community Index—Nebraska

LITCHFIELD—See KEARNEY, NE (Charter Communications)

LOCHLAND—Formerly served by Glenwood Telecommunications. No longer in operation

LODGEPOLE—See DALTON, NE (Dalton Telephone Co)

LONG PINE—See AINSWORTH, NE (Three River Digital Cable)

LOOMIS—See KEARNEY, NE (Charter Communications)

LOUISVILLE—See SPRINGFIELD, NE (Charter Communications)

LOUP CITY—See KEARNEY, NE (Charter Communications)

LYMAN—WinDBreak Cable

LYNCH—Formerly served by TelePartners. No longer in operation

LYONS—American Broadband. Now served by BLAIR, NE [NE0027]

MADISON—See NORFOLK, NE (Cable One)

MADRID—Formerly served by Consolidated Cable Inc. No longer in operation

MALCOLM—Zito Media

MARQUETTE—Mid-State Community TV

MARTINSBURG (village)—CenCom NNTV. This cable system has converted to IPTV. See JACKSON, NE [NE5019]

MASON CITY—NCTC Cable. Now served by BURWELL, NE [NE0045]

MASON CITY—See BURWELL, NE (NCTC Cable)

MAXWELL—Formerly served by Consolidated Cable Inc. No longer in operation

MCCOOK—Great Plains Communications

MCCOOL JUNCTION—See GENEVA, NE (Zito Media)

MEAD—Formerly served by TelePartners. No longer in operation

MEADOW GROVE—Formerly served by USA Communications. No longer in operation

MELBETA—See SCOTTSBLUFF, NE (Charter Communications)

MILFORD—See WILBER, NE (Zito Media)

MILLER (UNINCORPORATED AREAS)—See KEARNEY, NE (Charter Communications)

MILLIGAN—See GENEVA, NE (Zito Media)

MINATARE—Charter Communications. Now served by SCOTTSBLUFF, NE [NE0008]

MINATARE—See SCOTTSBLUFF, NE (Charter Communications)

MINDEN—Charter Communications. Now served by KEARNEY, NE [NE0011]

MINDEN—See KEARNEY, NE (Charter Communications)

MITCHELL—Charter Communications. Now served by SCOTTSBLUFF, NE [NE0008]

MITCHELL—See SCOTTSBLUFF, NE (Charter Communications)

MONROE—Eagle Communications

MORRILL—Charter Communications. Now served by SCOTTSBLUFF, NE [NE0008]

MORRILL—See SCOTTSBLUFF, NE (Charter Communications)

MURDOCK—See SYRACUSE, NE (Zito Media)

MURRAY—See SYRACUSE, NE (Zito Media)

NAPER—Three Rivers Digital Cable (formerly Cable Nebraska). Now served by AINSWORTH, NE [NE0049]

NAPER—See AINSWORTH, NE (Three River Digital Cable)

NEBRASKA CITY—See LINCOLN, NE (Time Warner Cable)

NEHAWKA—Formerly served by Westcom. No longer in operation

NELIGH—See ELGIN, NE (Great Plains Communications)

NELSON—Zito Media

NEMAHA COUNTY (PORTIONS)—See SYRACUSE, NE (Zito Media)

NEWCASTLE—CenCom NNTV. This cable system has converted to IPTV. See JACKSON, NE [NE5019]

NEWMAN GROVE—Eagle Communications

NICKERSON—Formerly served by TelePartners. No longer in operation

NIOBRARA—See BLOOMFIELD, NE (Great Plains Communications)

NORFOLK—Cable One

NORTH BEND—Great Plains Communications

NORTH LOUP—NCTC Cable. Now served by BURWELL, NE [NE0045]

NORTH LOUP—See BURWELL, NE (NCTC Cable)

NORTH PLATTE—Charter Communications

O'NEILL—Three Rivers Digital Cable (formerly Cable Nebraska). Now served by AINSWORTH, NE [NE0049]

O'NEILL—See AINSWORTH, NE (Three River Digital Cable)

OAKDALE—See ELGIN, NE (Great Plains Communications)

OAKLAND—American Broadband. Now served by BLAIR, NE [NE0027]

OBERT/MASKELL—CenCom NNTV. This cable system has converted to IPTV. See JACKSON, NE [NE5019]

OCONTO—Great Plains Cable TV. Now served by BROKEN BOW, NE [NE0031]

OCONTO—See BROKEN BOW, NE (Great Plains Communications)

ODELL—See DILLER, NE (Diode Cable)

ODESSA—See KEARNEY, NE (Charter Communications)

OGALLALA—Charter Communications. Now served by NORTH PLATTE, NE [NE0009]

OGALLALA—See NORTH PLATTE, NE (Charter Communications)

OMAHA (western portion)—CenturyLink (formerly Qwest Choice TV.) This cable system has converted to IPTV. See Omaha, NE [NE5000]

OMAHA—Formerly served by Digital Broadcast Corp. No longer in operation

OMAHA—CenturyLink Prism. Formerly Qwest [NE0377]. This cable system has converted to IPTV.

OMAHA—Cox Communications

ORCHARD—Formerly served by TelePartners. No longer in operation

ORD—Charter Communications. Now served by KEARNEY, NE [NE0011]

ORD—See KEARNEY, NE (Charter Communications)

ORLEANS—Formerly served by PinPoint Cable TV. No longer in operation

OSCEOLA—Eagle Communications

OSHKOSH—WinDBreak Cable

OSMOND—Formerly served by HunTel Cablevision. Now served by American Broadband, WAYNE, NE [NE0374]

OSMOND—See WAYNE, NE (American Broadband)

OTOE—Formerly served by CableDirect. No longer in operation

OVERTON—See KEARNEY, NE (Charter Communications)

OXFORD—PinPoint Cable TV. Now served by CAMBRIDGE, NE [NE0269]

OXFORD—See CAMBRIDGE, NE (PinPoint Communications)

PAGE (village)—Formerly served by Sky Scan Cable Co. No longer in operation

PALISADE—See GRANT, NE (Great Plains Communications)

PALMER—Eagle Communications

PALMYRA—See SYRACUSE, NE (Zito Media)

PAPILLION—See OMAHA, NE (CenturyLink Prism. Formerly Qwest [NE0377]. This cable system has converted to IPTV.)

PAPILLION—See OMAHA, NE (Cox Communications)

PAWNEE CITY—See LINCOLN, NE (Time Warner Cable)

PAXTON—Eagle Communications

PENDER—Formerly served by HunTel Cablevision. Now served by American Broadband, WAYNE, NE [NE0374]

PENDER—See WAYNE, NE (American Broadband)

PERU—Zito Media

PETERSBURG—See ELGIN, NE (Great Plains Communications)

PHILLIPS—See KEARNEY, NE (Charter Communications)

PHILLIPS—See AURORA, NE (Mid-State Community TV)

PICKRELL—Formerly served by Comstar Cable TV Inc. No longer in operation

PIERCE COUNTY (PORTIONS)—See WAYNE, NE (American Broadband)

PIERCE—See NORFOLK, NE (Cable One)

PILGER—Formerly served by Sky Scan Cable Co. Now served by Cable One, NORFOLK, NE [NE0006]

PILGER—See NORFOLK, NE (Cable One)

PLAINVIEW—See BLOOMFIELD, NE (Great Plains Communications)

PLATTE CENTER—Formerly served by TelePartners. No longer in operation

PLATTE CENTER—Eagle Communications

PLATTE COUNTY—See LINCOLN, NE (Time Warner Cable)

PLATTSMOUTH—See SPRINGFIELD, NE (Charter Communications)

PLEASANT DALE—See WILBER, NE (Zito Media)

PLEASANTON—See KEARNEY, NE (Charter Communications)

PLYMOUTH—See WILBER, NE (Zito Media)

POLK—Eagle Communications

PONCA—Great Plains Communications

POTTAWATTAMIE COUNTY (PORTIONS)—See OMAHA, IA (CenturyLink Prism. Formerly Qwest [NE0377]. This cable system has converted to IPTV.)

POTTER—See DALTON, NE (Dalton Telephone Co)

PRAGUE (village)—Formerly served by Westcom. No longer in operation

RALSTON—See OMAHA, NE (CenturyLink Prism. Formerly Qwest [NE0377]. This cable system has converted to IPTV.)

RALSTON—See OMAHA, NE (Cox Communications)

Nebraska—Cable Community Index

RANDOLPH—See NORFOLK, NE (Cable One)

RAVENNA—See KEARNEY, NE (Charter Communications)

RAYMOND—Formerly served by Zito Media. No longer in operation

RED CLOUD—Formerly served by PinPoint Cable TV. No longer in operation

RED CLOUD—Eagle Communications

RED WILLOW COUNTY (PORTIONS)—See McCOOK, NE (Great Plains Communications)

REPUBLICAN CITY—Formerly served by PinPoint Cable TV. No longer in operation

RICHLAND—Formerly served by Eagle Communications. No longer in operation

RISING CITY—Eagle Communications

RIVERDALE (VILLAGE)—See KEARNEY, NE (Charter Communications)

ROCK COUNTY—See BASSETT, NE (American Broadband)

ROSELAND—See BLUE HILL, NE (Glenwood Telecommunications)

RULO—Formerly served by CableDirect. No longer in operation

RUSHVILLE—See CHADRON, NE (Great Plains Communications)

RUSKIN—Formerly served by Diode Cable Co. No longer in operation

SALEM—Formerly served by CableDirect. No longer in operation

SARGENT—NCTC Cable. Now served by BURWELL, NE [NE0045]

SARGENT—See BURWELL, NE (NCTC Cable)

SARPY COUNTY (PORTIONS)—See GRETNA, NE (Zito Media)

SARPY COUNTY (UNINCORPORATED AREAS)—See OMAHA, NE (CenturyLink Prism. Formerly Qwest [NE0377]. This cable system has converted to IPTV.)

SARPY COUNTY (UNINCORPORATED AREAS)—See OMAHA, NE (Cox Communications)

SAUNDERS COUNTY—See LINCOLN, NE (Time Warner Cable)

SCHUYLER—Eagle Communications

SCOTIA—NCTC Cable. Now served by BURWELL, NE [NE0045]

SCOTIA—See BURWELL, NE (NCTC Cable)

SCOTTS BLUFF COUNTY (PORTIONS)—See SCOTTSBLUFF, NE (Charter Communications)

SCOTTSBLUFF—Charter Communications

SCRIBNER—See NORTH BEND, NE (Great Plains Communications)

SEWARD COUNTY—See LINCOLN, NE (Time Warner Cable)

SEWARD—See LINCOLN, NE (Time Warner Cable)

SHELBY—Eagle Communications

SHELTON—See KEARNEY, NE (Charter Communications)

SHICKLEY—See GENEVA, NE (Zito Media)

SHUBERT—Formerly served by CableDirect. No longer in operation

SIDNEY (TOWN)—Charter Communications

SILVER CREEK (VILLAGE)—Eagle Communications

SNYDER—See NORTH BEND, NE (Great Plains Communications)

SPALDING—Eagle Communications

SPENCER—CenCom NNTV. This cable system has converted to IPTV. See JACKSON, NE [NE5019]

SPRINGFIELD (portions)—Formerly served by TelePartners. No longer in operation

SPRINGFIELD—See OMAHA, NE (CenturyLink Prism. Formerly Qwest [NE0377]. This cable system has converted to IPTV.)

SPRINGFIELD—Charter Communications

SPRINGVIEW—See AINSWORTH, NE (Three River Digital Cable)

ST. EDWARD—Eagle Communications

ST. LIBORY—See KEARNEY, NE (Charter Communications)

ST. PAUL—See KEARNEY, NE (Charter Communications)

STAMFORD (town)—Formerly served by PinPoint Cable TV. No longer in operation

STANTON—Stanton Telecom

STAPLEHURST (village)—Formerly served by Zito Media. No longer in operation

STAPLETON—See BROKEN BOW, NE (Great Plains Communications)

STEINAUER—Formerly served by CableDirect. No longer in operation

STELLA (town)—Formerly served by StellaVision. No longer in operation

STERLING—See SYRACUSE, NE (Zito Media)

STRATTON—Peregrine Communications

STROMSBURG—Eagle Communications

STUART—CenCom NNTV. This cable system has converted to IPTV. See JACKSON, NE [NE5019]

SUMNER—See KEARNEY, NE (Charter Communications)

SUPERIOR—Glenwood Telecommunications. Now served by BLUE HILL, NE [NE0093]

SUPERIOR—See BLUE HILL, NE (Glenwood Telecommunications)

SUTHERLAND—Great Plains Communications

SUTTON—See CLAY CENTER, NE (Zito Media)

SWANTON—Formerly served by Comstar Cable TV Inc. No longer in operation

SYRACUSE—Zito Media

TABLE ROCK (VILLAGE)—See LINCOLN, NE (Time Warner Cable)

TALMAGE—Formerly served by Great Plains Communications. No longer in operation

TAYLOR—NCTC Cable. Now served by BURWELL, NE [NE0045]

TAYLOR—See BURWELL, NE (NCTC Cable)

TECUMSEH—See LINCOLN, NE (Time Warner Cable)

TEKAMAH—American Broadband. Now served by BLAIR, NE [NE0027]

TERRYTOWN—See SCOTTSBLUFF, NE (Charter Communications)

TILDEN—See NORFOLK, NE (Cable One)

TOBIAS—Formerly served by CableDirect. No longer in operation

TRENTON—Great Plains Communications

TRUMBULL—Mid-State Community TV

UEHLING—See HOOPER, NE (WesTel Systems)

ULYSSES—Formerly served by Zito Media. No longer in operation

UNADILLA—See SYRACUSE, NE (Zito Media)

UNION—Formerly served by Westcom. No longer in operation

UPLAND—See BLUE HILL, NE (Glenwood Telecommunications)

UTICA—See WACO, NE (Zito Media)

VALENTINE—Three Rivers Digital Cable (formerly Cable Nebraska). Now served by AINSWORTH, NE [NE0049]

VALENTINE—See AINSWORTH, NE (Three River Digital Cable)

VALLEY—See OMAHA, NE (Cox Communications)

VALLEY—See GRETNA, NE (Zito Media)

VALPARAISO—Zito Media

VENANGO—See GRANT, NE (Great Plains Communications)

VERDIGRE—See BLOOMFIELD, NE (Great Plains Communications)

VERDON—Formerly served by CableDirect. No longer in operation

WACO—Zito Media

WAHOO—Charter Communications. Now served by SPRINGFIELD (formerly Plattsmouth), NE [NE0020]

WAHOO—See SPRINGFIELD, NE (Charter Communications)

WAKEFIELD—See WAYNE, NE (American Broadband)

WALLACE—Formerly served by Consolidated Cable Inc. No longer in operation

WALTHILL—Formerly served by HunTel Cablevision. Now served by American Broadband, WAYNE, NE [NE0374]

WALTHILL—See WAYNE, NE (American Broadband)

WASHINGTON (village)—Formerly served by TelePartners. No longer in operation

WASHINGTON COUNTY—See BLAIR, NE (American Broadband)

WATERLOO—See OMAHA, NE (Cox Communications)

WATERLOO—See GRETNA, NE (Zito Media)

WAUNETA—BWTelcom

WAUSA—See BLOOMFIELD, NE (Great Plains Communications)

WAVERLY—See SPRINGFIELD, NE (Charter Communications)

WAYNE—American Broadband

WEEPING WATER—See SYRACUSE, NE (Zito Media)

WEST POINT—See NORFOLK, NE (Cable One)

WESTERN—Zito Media

WESTON (village)—Formerly served by Westcom. No longer in operation

WILBER—Zito Media

WILCOX—See KEARNEY, NE (Charter Communications)

WINNETOON—See BLOOMFIELD, NE (Great Plains Communications)

WINSIDE (village)—Formerly served by Sky Scan Cable Co. No longer in operation

WINSIDE—CenCom NNTV. This cable system has converted to IPTV. See JACKSON, NE [NE5019]

WINSLOW—See HOOPER, NE (WesTel Systems)

WISNER—See NORFOLK, NE (Cable One)

WOLBACH—Great Plains Communications

WOOD RIVER—See KEARNEY, NE (Charter Communications)

WOODCLIFF LAKES—Formerly served by Time Warner Cable. No longer in operation

WOODLAND PARK—See NORFOLK, NE (Cable One)

WYMORE—See WILBER, NE (Zito Media)

WYNOT—Formerly served by CenCom Inc. No longer in operation

WYNOT—See BLOOMFIELD, NE (Great Plains Communications)

YORK—Time Warner Cable. Now served by LINCOLN, NE [NE0002]

YORK—See LINCOLN, NE (Time Warner Cable)

YUTAN—Formerly served by TelePartners. No longer in operation

NEVADA

ALAMO—Rainbow Cable

BATTLE MOUNTAIN—Satview Broadband

BEATTY—Formerly served by Eagle West Communications Inc. No longer in operation

BEAVERDAM—See MESQUITE, AZ (Reliance Connects)

BLUE DIAMOND—Formerly served by Eagle West Communications Inc. No longer in operation

BOULDER CITY (northern portion)—Formerly served by Eagle West Communications Inc. No longer in operation

BOULDER CITY—See LAS VEGAS, NV (Cox Communications)

BUNKERVILLE—See MESQUITE, NV (Reliance Connects)

CALIENTE—Rainbow Cable. Now served by PIOCHE, NV [NV0047]

CALIENTE—See PIOCHE, NV (Rainbow Cable)

CALLVILLE BAY—Formerly served by Eagle West Communications Inc. No longer in operation

CARLIN—Satview Broadband

CARSON CITY—Charter Communications. Now served by RENO, NV [NV0002]

CARSON CITY—Formerly served by Quadravision. No longer in operation

CARSON CITY—See RENO, NV (Charter Communications)

CHURCHILL COUNTY (PORTIONS)—See RENO, NV (Charter Communications)

CLARK COUNTY—See LAS VEGAS, NV (Cox Communications)

CRYSTAL BAY—Formerly served by Charter Communications. No longer in operation

DAYTON—See RENO, NV (Charter Communications)

DOUGLAS COUNTY (PORTIONS)—See RENO, NV (Charter Communications)

EL DORADO COUNTY (PORTIONS)—See RENO, CA (Charter Communications)

ELKO COUNTY (PORTIONS)—See ELKO, NV (Satview Broadband)

ELKO—Satview Broadband

ELY—Beehive Broadband

EMPIRE—Formerly served by United States Gypsum Co. No longer in operation

EUREKA—Beehive Broadband

FALLON STATION—See RENO, NV (Charter Communications)

FALLON—See RENO, NV (Charter Communications)

FERNLEY—Charter Communications. Now served by RENO, NV [NV0002]

FERNLEY—See RENO, NV (Charter Communications)

GARDNERVILLE—Charter Communications. Now served by RENO, NV [NV0002]

GARDNERVILLE—See RENO, NV (Charter Communications)

GLENBROOK—See RENO, NV (Charter Communications)

GOLD HILL—See VIRGINIA CITY, NV (Comstock Community TV Inc)

GOLDFIELD—Formerly served by Eagle West Communications Inc. No longer in operation

GREEN VALLEY—See LAS VEGAS, NV (Cox Communications)

HAWTHORNE—Charter Communications

HENDERSON (portions)—Formerly served by Prime Time Communications. No longer in operation

HENDERSON—See LAS VEGAS, NV (Cox Communications)

HOLBROOK JUNCTION—See TOPAZ LAKE, NV (Satview Broadband)

HUMBOLDT COUNTY (PORTIONS)—See WINNEMUCCA, NV (CalNeva Broadband)

INDIAN SPRINGS AFB—Formerly served by United Cable Management. No longer in operation

INDIAN SPRINGS—Formerly served by United Cable Management. No longer in operation

JACKPOT—Satview Broadband

LAS VEGAS—Formerly served by Sprint Corp. No longer in operation

LAS VEGAS—Cox Communications

LAUGHLIN—Suddenlink Communications

LITTLEFIELD—See MESQUITE, AZ (Reliance Connects)

LOCKWOOD—Charter Communications. Now served by RENO, NV [NV0002]

LOGANDALE—Formerly served by Baja Broadband. No longer in operation

LOVELOCK—Formerly served by Lovelock Cable TV. No longer in operation

LYON COUNTY (NORTHERN PORTION)—See RENO, NV (Charter Communications)

LYON COUNTY (NORTHWESTERN PORTION)—See RENO, NV (Charter Communications)

LYON COUNTY (PORTIONS)—See YERINGTON, NV (Charter Communications)

MCGILL—Beehive Broadband

MESQUITE—Baja Broadband. Now served by ST. GEORGE, UT [UT0007]

MESQUITE—Reliance Connects

MEYERS—See RENO, CA (Charter Communications)

MINDEN—See RENO, NV (Charter Communications)

NELLIS AFB—Formerly served by Bluebird Communications. No longer in operation

NORTH LAKE TAHOE—See RENO, CA (Charter Communications)

NORTH LAS VEGAS—See LAS VEGAS, NV (Cox Communications)

PAHRUMP—Suddenlink Communications

PANACA—See PIOCHE, NV (Rainbow Cable)

PIOCHE—Rainbow Cable. Now served by PIOCHE, NV [NV0047]

PIOCHE—Rainbow Cable

RENO—Formerly served by Quadravision. No longer in operation

RENO—Charter Communications

RUTH—Formerly served by Central Telecom Services (CUTV). No longer in operation

SCENIC—See MESQUITE, AZ (Reliance Connects)

SILVER SPRINGS—Charter Communications. Now served by RENO, NV [NV0002]

SILVER SPRINGS—See RENO, NV (Charter Communications)

SOUTH LAKE TAHOE—See RENO, CA (Charter Communications)

SPARKS—See RENO, NV (Charter Communications)

SPRING CREEK—See ELKO, NV (Satview Broadband)

STATELINE—See RENO, NV (Charter Communications)

STOREY COUNTY (SOUTHERN PORTION)—See RENO, NV (Charter Communications)

TONOPAH—Formerly served by RealStar Communications. No longer in operation

TOPAZ LAKE—Satview Broadband

TOPAZ RANCH ESTATES—See TOPAZ LAKE, NV (Satview Broadband)

VERDI—Formerly served by Suddenlink Communications. No longer in operation

VIRGINIA CITY—Comstock Community TV Inc

WADSWORTH—See RENO, NV (Charter Communications)

WALKER—See TOPAZ LAKE, CA (Satview Broadband)

WASHOE COUNTY—See RENO, NV (Charter Communications)

WELLINGTON—Satview Broadband

WELLS—Satview Broadband

WINNEMUCCA—CalNeva Broadband

YERINGTON—Charter Communications

NEW HAMPSHIRE

ALEXANDRIA—See BELMONT, NH (MetroCast Cablevision)

ALSTEAD—Formerly served by Adelphia Communications. Now served by Comcast Cable, BURLINGTON, VT [VT0001]

ALTON—See BELMONT, NH (MetroCast Cablevision)

ANDOVER (town)—Formerly served by Adelphia Communications. Now served by Comcast Cable, BURLINGTON, VT [VT0001]

ASHLAND—See BERLIN, NH (Time Warner Cable)

ATHOL—See KEENE, MA (Time Warner Cable)

BARNSTEAD—See BELMONT, NH (MetroCast Cablevision)

BARRINGTON—See ROCHESTER, NH (MetroCast Communications)

BATH (village)—Formerly served by Adelphia Communications. Now served by Time Warner Cable, BERLIN, NH [NH0012]

BATH (VILLAGE)—See BERLIN, NH (Time Warner Cable)

BELMONT—MetroCast Cablevision

BERLIN—Time Warner Cable

BETHLEHEM (TOWN)—See BERLIN, NH (Time Warner Cable)

BRADFORD—See WARNER, NH (TDS Cable)

BRIDGEWATER—See BELMONT, NH (MetroCast Cablevision)

BRISTOL—See BELMONT, NH (MetroCast Cablevision)

CAMPTON—Formerly served by Adelphia Communications. Now served by Time Warner Cable, BERLIN, NH [NH0012]

CAMPTON—See BERLIN, NH (Time Warner Cable)

CARROLL—Formerly served by Adelphia Communications. Now served by Time Warner Cable, BERLIN, NH

New Hampshire—Cable Community Index

[NH0012]

CARROLL—See BERLIN, NH (Time Warner Cable)

CENTER HARBOR—See BELMONT, NH (MetroCast Cablevision)

CHESTERFIELD—See SPOFFORD, NH (Argent Communications)

CLAREMONT—Comcast Cable. Now served by BURLINGTON, VT [VT0001]

CONCORD—Comcast Cable. Now served by BOSTON, MA [MA0001]

CONWAY—Time Warner Cable. Now served by PORTLAND, ME [ME0001]

CORNISH—Formerly served by Adelphia Communications. Now served by Comcast Cable, BURLINGTON, VT [VT0001]

DALTON—See BERLIN, NH (Time Warner Cable)

DEERFIELD—See BELMONT, NH (MetroCast Cablevision)

DERRY—Comcast Cable. Now served by BOSTON, MA [MA0001]

DORCHESTER (TOWN)—See BERLIN, NH (Time Warner Cable)

EAST ROCHESTER—See ROCHESTER, NH (MetroCast Communications)

EAST WESTMORELAND—See SPOFFORD, NH (Argent Communications)

EPSOM—See BELMONT, NH (MetroCast Cablevision)

EXETER—Comcast Cable. Now served by BOSTON, MA [MA0001]

FARMINGTON—See ROCHESTER, NH (MetroCast Communications)

FITZWILLIAM—See TROY, NH (Argent Communications)

FRANCONIA—See BERLIN, NH (Time Warner Cable)

FRANKLIN—See BELMONT, NH (MetroCast Cablevision)

FREEDOM (town)—Formerly served by Adelphia Communications. Now served by Time Warner Cable, PORTLAND, ME [ME0001]

GILFORD—See BELMONT, NH (MetroCast Cablevision)

GILMANTON—See BELMONT, NH (MetroCast Cablevision)

GORHAM—See BERLIN, NH (Time Warner Cable)

GRANTHAM—Formerly served by Adelphia Communications. Now served by Comcast Cable, BURLINGTON, VT [VT0001]

GREENVILLE—Formerly served by Adelphia Communications. Now served by Comcast Cable, BOSTON, MA [MA0001]

GROTON (TOWN)—See BERLIN, NH (Time Warner Cable)

GROVETON—See STRATFORD (town), NH (FiberCast Cable)

GROVETON—See BERLIN, NH (Time Warner Cable)

HARRISVILLE (TOWN)—See NELSON (town), NH (FiberCast Cable)

HEBRON—See BELMONT, NH (MetroCast Cablevision)

HILL (town)—Formerly served by Adelphia Communications. Now served by Comcast Cable, BURLINGTON, VT [VT0001]

HINSDALE—Formerly served by Adelphia Communications. No longer in operation

HOLDERNESS (PORTIONS)—See BERLIN, NH (Time Warner Cable)

KEENE—Time Warner Cable

LACONIA—See BELMONT, NH (MetroCast Cablevision)

LANCASTER—See BERLIN, NH (Time Warner Cable)

LEBANON (PORTIONS)—See ROCHESTER, ME (MetroCast Communications)

LEBANON—Comcast Cable. Now served by BURLINGTON, VT [VT0001]

LINCOLN—Formerly served by Adelphia Communications. Now served by Time Warner Cable, BERLIN, NH [NH0012]

LINCOLN—See BERLIN, NH (Time Warner Cable)

LISBON—See BERLIN, NH (Time Warner Cable)

LITTLETON—Time Warner Cable. Now served by BERLIN, NH [NH0012]

LITTLETON—See BERLIN, NH (Time Warner Cable)

LONDONDERRY—Comcast Cable. Now served by BOSTON, MA [MA0001]

MADISON (town)—Formerly served by Adelphia Communications. Now served by Time Warner Cable, PORTLAND, ME [ME0001]

MANCHESTER—Comcast Cable. Now served by BOSTON, MA [MA0001]

MARLBOROUGH—See KEENE, NH (Time Warner Cable)

MARLOW—See STODDARD, NH (FiberCast Cable)

MEREDITH—See BELMONT, NH (MetroCast Cablevision)

MERRIMACK—Formerly served by Adelphia Communications. Now served by Comcast Cable, BOSTON, MA [MA0001]

MILAN (TOWN)—Argent Communications

MILTON MILLS—See ROCHESTER, NH (MetroCast Communications)

MILTON—See ROCHESTER, NH (MetroCast Communications)

MONROE (town)—Formerly served by Adelphia Communications. Now served by Time Warner Cable, BERLIN, NH [NH0012]

MONROE (TOWN)—See BERLIN, NH (Time Warner Cable)

MOULTONBOROUGH (town)—Formerly served by Adelphia Communications. Now served by Time Warner Cable, PORTLAND, ME [ME0001]

NASHUA—Comcast Cable. Now served by BOSTON, MA [MA0001]

NELSON (TOWN)—FiberCast Cable

NEW BOSTON—Formerly served by Adelphia Communications. Now served by Comcast Cable, BOSTON, MA [MA0001]

NEW DURHAM—See BELMONT, NH (MetroCast Cablevision)

NEW HAMPTON—See BELMONT, NH (MetroCast Cablevision)

NEW LONDON—Formerly served by Adelphia Communications. Now served by Comcast Cable, BURLINGTON, VT [VT0001]

NEWBURY—See WARNER, NH (TDS Cable)

NEWPORT—Formerly served by Adelphia Communications. Now served by Comcast Cable, BURLINGTON, VT [VT0001]

NORTH WOODSTOCK—See BERLIN, NH (Time Warner Cable)

NORTHFIELD (TOWN)—See BELMONT, NH (MetroCast Cablevision)

NORTHFIELD—See BELMONT, NH (MetroCast Cablevision)

NORTHUMBERLAND (TOWN)—See BERLIN, NH (Time Warner Cable)

NORTHWOOD—See BELMONT, NH (MetroCast Cablevision)

ORANGE—See KEENE, MA (Time Warner Cable)

PETERBOROUGH—Formerly served by Adelphia Communications. Now served by Comcast Cable, BOSTON, MA [MA0001]

PITTSFIELD—See BELMONT, NH (MetroCast Cablevision)

PLAINFIELD (town)—Formerly served by Adelphia Communications. Now served by Comcast Cable, BURLINGTON, VT [VT0001]

PLYMOUTH—Time Warner Cable. Now served by BERLIN, NH [NH0012]

PLYMOUTH—See BERLIN, NH (Time Warner Cable)

PORTSMOUTH—Comcast Cable. Now served by BOSTON, MA [MA0001]

RANDOLPH—See BERLIN, NH (Time Warner Cable)

RICHMOND (TOWN)—See KEENE, NH (Time Warner Cable)

RINDGE—See TROY, NH (Argent Communications)

ROCHESTER—MetroCast Communications

ROXBURY (TOWN)—See KEENE, NH (Time Warner Cable)

RUMNEY (TOWN)—See BERLIN, NH (Time Warner Cable)

SANBORNTON (TOWN)—See BELMONT, NH (MetroCast Cablevision)

SPOFFORD—Argent Communications

STODDARD—FiberCast Cable

STRAFFORD (TOWN-PORTIONS)—See BELMONT, NH (MetroCast Cablevision)

STRAFFORD (TOWN-PORTIONS)—See ROCHESTER, NH (MetroCast Communications)

STRATFORD (TOWN)—FiberCast Cable

SUGAR HILL (town)—Formerly served by Adelphia Communications. Now served by Time Warner Cable, BERLIN, NH [NH0012]

SUGAR HILL (TOWN)—See BERLIN, NH (Time Warner Cable)

SULLIVAN (TOWN)—See NELSON (town), NH (FiberCast Cable)

SURRY—See KEENE, NH (Time Warner Cable)

SUTTON (TOWN)—See WARNER, NH (TDS Cable)

SWANZEY—See KEENE, NH (Time Warner Cable)

THORNTON—See BERLIN, NH (Time Warner Cable)

TILTON—See BELMONT, NH (MetroCast Cablevision)

TROY—Argent Communications

WAKEFIELD (town)—Formerly served by Adelphia Communications. Now served by Time Warner Cable, PORTLAND, ME [ME0001]

WARNER—TDS Cable

WARREN (TOWN)—See BERLIN, NH (Time Warner Cable)

WENTWORTH (town)—Formerly served by Adelphia Communications. Now served by Time Warner Cable, BERLIN, NH [NH0012]

WENTWORTH (TOWN)—See BERLIN, NH (Time Warner Cable)

Cable Community Index—New Jersey

WEST CHESTERFIELD—See SPOFFORD, NH (Argent Communications)

WEST STEWARTSTOWN—Formerly served by White Mountain Cablevision. No longer in operation

WESTMORELAND—See SPOFFORD, NH (Argent Communications)

WHITEFIELD—See BERLIN, NH (Time Warner Cable)

WOLFEBORO—See BELMONT, NH (MetroCast Cablevision)

WOODSTOCK—See BERLIN, NH (Time Warner Cable)

NEW JERSEY

ABERDEEN TWP.—See RARITAN, NJ (Cablevision)

ABSECON—See AUDUBON, NJ (Comcast Cable)

ALEXANDRIA TWP.—See HUNTERDON COUNTY, NJ (Service Electric Cable TV of Hunterdon Inc.)

ALLAMUCHY TWP.—Cablevision. Now served by MORRIS TWP., NJ [NJ0005]

ALLAMUCHY TWP.—See MORRIS TWP., NJ (Cablevision)

ALLENDALE—See OAKLAND, NJ (Cablevision)

ALLENHURST BOROUGH—See EATONTOWN BOROUGH, NJ (Comcast Cable)

ALLENTOWN—See HAMILTON TWP. (Mercer County), NJ (Cablevision)

ALLOWAY TWP.—See AUDUBON, NJ (Comcast Cable)

ALPHA BORO—See HUNTERDON COUNTY, NJ (Service Electric Cable TV of Hunterdon Inc.)

ALPINE—See OAKLAND, NJ (Cablevision)

AMBLER BOROUGH—See EATONTOWN BOROUGH, PA (Comcast Cable)

AMITY (BUCKS COUNTY)—See EATONTOWN BOROUGH, PA (Comcast Cable)

AMITY—See EATONTOWN BOROUGH, PA (Comcast Cable)

ANDOVER BOROUGH—See SPARTA, NJ (Service Electric Cable Company)

ANDOVER TWP.—See SPARTA, NJ (Service Electric Cable Company)

ASBURY PARK—See AVON-BY-THE-SEA, NJ (Cablevision)

ATLANTIC CITY—Formerly served by OrionVision. No longer in operation

ATLANTIC CITY—See AUDUBON, NJ (Comcast Cable)

ATLANTIC HIGHLANDS BOROUGH—See EATONTOWN BOROUGH, NJ (Comcast Cable)

AUDUBON PARK—See AUDUBON, NJ (Comcast Cable)

AUDUBON—Comcast Cable

AVALON BOROUGH—See AUDUBON, NJ (Comcast Cable)

AVALON—Comcast Cable. Now served by AUDUBON, NJ [NJ0003]

AVALON—Comcast Cable. Now served by AUDUBON, NJ [NJ0003]

AVON-BY-THE-SEA—Cablevision

BALLY—See EATONTOWN BOROUGH, PA (Comcast Cable)

BARNEGAT LIGHT BOROUGH—See AUDUBON, NJ (Comcast Cable)

BARNEGAT TWP.—See AUDUBON, NJ (Comcast Cable)

BARRINGTON—See AUDUBON, NJ (Comcast Cable)

BASS RIVER—See AUDUBON, NJ (Comcast Cable)

BAY HEAD—See EATONTOWN BOROUGH, NJ (Comcast Cable)

BAYONNE—Cablevision

BEACH HAVEN BOROUGH—See AUDUBON, NJ (Comcast Cable)

BEACHWOOD BOROUGH—See AUDUBON, NJ (Comcast Cable)

BECHTELSVILLE—See EATONTOWN BOROUGH, PA (Comcast Cable)

BEDMINSTER (PORTIONS)—See RARITAN, NJ (Cablevision)

BEDMINSTER TWP.—See EATONTOWN BOROUGH, PA (Comcast Cable)

BEDMINSTER—See EATONTOWN BOROUGH, NJ (Comcast Cable)

BELLEVILLE TWP.—See WEST ORANGE TWP., NJ (Comcast Cable)

BELLMAWR—See AUDUBON, NJ (Comcast Cable)

BELMAR—See AVON-BY-THE-SEA, NJ (Cablevision)

BELVIDERE—See WEST ORANGE TWP., NJ (Comcast Cable)

BENSALEM—See EATONTOWN BOROUGH, PA (Comcast Cable)

BERGENFIELD—Cablevision

BERKELEY HEIGHTS TWP.—See WEST ORANGE TWP., NJ (Comcast Cable)

BERKELEY TWP.—See SEASIDE HEIGHTS, NJ (Cablevision)

BERKELEY TWP.—See AUDUBON, NJ (Comcast Cable)

BERLIN BOROUGH—See AUDUBON, NJ (Comcast Cable)

BERNARDS TWP.—See RARITAN, NJ (Cablevision)

BERNARDSVILLE—See EATONTOWN BOROUGH, NJ (Comcast Cable)

BETHLEHEM TWP.—See EATONTOWN BOROUGH, NJ (Comcast Cable)

BEVERLY—See AUDUBON, NJ (Comcast Cable)

BLAIRSTOWN TWP.—See SPARTA, NJ (Service Electric Cable Company)

BLOOMFIELD TWP.—See WEST ORANGE TWP., NJ (Comcast Cable)

BLOOMINGDALE—See OAKLAND, NJ (Cablevision)

BLOOMSBURY—See HUNTERDON COUNTY, NJ (Service Electric Cable TV of Hunterdon Inc.)

BOGOTA—See OAKLAND, NJ (Cablevision)

BOONTON TWP.—See MORRIS TWP., NJ (Cablevision)

BOONTON—See MORRIS TWP., NJ (Cablevision)

BORDENTOWN TWP.—See AUDUBON, NJ (Comcast Cable)

BORDENTOWN—See AUDUBON, NJ (Comcast Cable)

BOUND BROOK—See RARITAN, NJ (Cablevision)

BOYERTOWN—See EATONTOWN BOROUGH, PA (Comcast Cable)

BRADLEY BEACH—See AVON-BY-THE-SEA, NJ (Cablevision)

BRANCHBURG TWP.—See EATONTOWN BOROUGH, NJ (Comcast Cable)

BRANCHVILLE—See SPARTA, NJ (Service Electric Cable Company)

BRICK TWP.—See EATONTOWN BOROUGH, NJ (Comcast Cable)

BRIDGEPORT—See EATONTOWN BOROUGH, PA (Comcast Cable)

BRIDGETON—See AUDUBON, NJ (Comcast Cable)

BRIDGEWATER—See RARITAN, NJ (Cablevision)

BRIELLE—See AVON-BY-THE-SEA, NJ (Cablevision)

BRIGANTINE—See AUDUBON, NJ (Comcast Cable)

BRISTOL BOROUGH—See EATONTOWN BOROUGH, PA (Comcast Cable)

BRISTOL TWP.—See EATONTOWN BOROUGH, PA (Comcast Cable)

BROOKLAWN BOROUGH—See AUDUBON, NJ (Comcast Cable)

BUCKINGHAM TWP. (BUCKS COUNTY)—See EATONTOWN BOROUGH, PA (Comcast Cable)

BUENA VISTA TWP.—See AUDUBON, NJ (Comcast Cable)

BUENA—See AUDUBON, NJ (Comcast Cable)

BURLINGTON CITY—See AUDUBON, NJ (Comcast Cable)

BURLINGTON COUNTY (PORTIONS)—See AUDUBON, NJ (Comcast Cable)

BURLINGTON COUNTY—Comcast Cable. Now served by AUDUBON, NJ [NJ0003]

BURLINGTON TWP.—See AUDUBON, NJ (Comcast Cable)

BUTLER—See OAKLAND, NJ (Cablevision)

BYRAM TWP.—See SPARTA, NJ (Service Electric Cable Company)

CALDWELL BOROUGH—See WEST ORANGE TWP., NJ (Comcast Cable)

CALIFON—See WEST ORANGE TWP., NJ (Comcast Cable)

CAMDEN—See AUDUBON, NJ (Comcast Cable)

CAPE MAY BOROUGH—See AUDUBON, NJ (Comcast Cable)

CAPE MAY POINT—See AUDUBON, NJ (Comcast Cable)

CAPE MAY—See AUDUBON, NJ (Comcast Cable)

CARLSTADT BOROUGH—Comcast Cable. Now served by WEST ORANGE TWP., NJ [NJ0001]

CARLSTADT—See WEST ORANGE TWP., NJ (Comcast Cable)

CARNEYS POINT—See AUDUBON, NJ (Comcast Cable)

CARTERET—See WEST ORANGE TWP., NJ (Comcast Cable)

CEDAR BONNET—See AUDUBON, NJ (Comcast Cable)

CEDAR GROVE TWP.—See OAKLAND, NJ (Cablevision)

CHALFONT—See EATONTOWN BOROUGH, PA (Comcast Cable)

CHARLESTOWN TWP.—See EATONTOWN BOROUGH, PA (Comcast Cable)

CHATHAM TWP.—See EATONTOWN BOROUGH, NJ (Comcast Cable)

CHATHAM—See MORRIS TWP., NJ (Cablevision)

CHERRY HILL TWP.—See AUDUBON, NJ (Comcast Cable)

CHESILHURST BOROUGH—See AUDUBON, NJ (Comcast Cable)

CHESTER—See EATONTOWN BOROUGH, NJ (Comcast Cable)

CHESTERFIELD TWP.—See AUDUBON, NJ (Comcast Cable)

CINNAMINSON—See AUDUBON, NJ (Comcast Cable)

CLARK TWP.—See WEST ORANGE TWP., NJ (Comcast Cable)

CLAYTON—See AUDUBON, NJ (Comcast Cable)

CLEMENTON—See AUDUBON, NJ (Comcast Cable)

CLIFFSIDE PARK BOROUGH—See FORT LEE BOROUGH, NJ (Time Warner Cable)

CLIFTON—See OAKLAND, NJ (Cablevision)

CLINTON—See EATONTOWN BOROUGH, NJ (Comcast Cable)

CLOSTER—See BERGENFIELD, NJ (Cablevision)

New Jersey—Cable Community Index

COLEBROOKDALE—See EATONTOWN BOROUGH, PA (Comcast Cable)

COLLEGEVILLE—See EATONTOWN BOROUGH, PA (Comcast Cable)

COLLINGSWOOD—See AUDUBON, NJ (Comcast Cable)

COLTS NECK—See FREEHOLD, NJ (Cablevision)

COMMERCIAL TWP.—See AUDUBON, NJ (Comcast Cable)

CONSHOHOCKEN—See EATONTOWN BOROUGH, PA (Comcast Cable)

CORBIN CITY—See AUDUBON, NJ (Comcast Cable)

CRANBURY TWP.—See EATONTOWN BOROUGH, NJ (Comcast Cable)

CRANFORD TWP.—See WEST ORANGE TWP., NJ (Comcast Cable)

CRESSKILL—See BERGENFIELD, NJ (Cablevision)

CRESTWOOD VILLAGE—See AUDUBON, NJ (Comcast Cable)

DEAL BOROUGH—See EATONTOWN BOROUGH, NJ (Comcast Cable)

DEERFIELD TWP.—See AUDUBON, NJ (Comcast Cable)

DELANCO—See AUDUBON, NJ (Comcast Cable)

DELAWARE TWP.—See AUDUBON, NJ (Comcast Cable)

DELAWARE TWP.—See EATONTOWN BOROUGH, NJ (Comcast Cable)

DELRAN TWP.—See AUDUBON, NJ (Comcast Cable)

DEMAREST—See BERGENFIELD, NJ (Cablevision)

DENNIS TWP.—See AUDUBON, NJ (Comcast Cable)

DENVILLE—See MORRIS TWP., NJ (Cablevision)

DEPTFORD TWP.—See AUDUBON, NJ (Comcast Cable)

DOUGLASS (BERKS COUNTY)—See EATONTOWN BOROUGH, PA (Comcast Cable)

DOUGLASS TWP. (MONTGOMERY COUNTY)—See EATONTOWN BOROUGH, PA (Comcast Cable)

DOVER TWP. (PORTIONS)—See SEASIDE HEIGHTS, NJ (Cablevision)

DOVER TWP.—See AUDUBON, NJ (Comcast Cable)

DOVER—See MORRIS TWP., NJ (Cablevision)

DOWNE TWP.—See AUDUBON, NJ (Comcast Cable)

DOYLESTOWN BOROUGH—See EATONTOWN BOROUGH, PA (Comcast Cable)

DOYLESTOWN TWP.—See EATONTOWN BOROUGH, PA (Comcast Cable)

DUBLIN—See EATONTOWN BOROUGH, PA (Comcast Cable)

DUMONT—See BERGENFIELD, NJ (Cablevision)

DUNELLEN—See RARITAN, NJ (Cablevision)

EAGLESWOOD TWP.—See AUDUBON, NJ (Comcast Cable)

EARL TWP. (BERKS COUNTY)—See EATONTOWN BOROUGH, PA (Comcast Cable)

EAST AMWELL TWP.—See EATONTOWN BOROUGH, NJ (Comcast Cable)

EAST BRUNSWICK—See EATONTOWN BOROUGH, NJ (Comcast Cable)

EAST COVENTRY TWP.—See EATONTOWN BOROUGH, PA (Comcast Cable)

EAST GREENVILLE—See EATONTOWN BOROUGH, PA (Comcast Cable)

EAST GREENWICH TWP.—See AUDUBON, NJ (Comcast Cable)

EAST HANOVER TWP.—See MORRIS TWP., NJ (Cablevision)

EAST NEWARK—See WEST ORANGE TWP., NJ (Comcast Cable)

EAST NORRITON—See EATONTOWN BOROUGH, PA (Comcast Cable)

EAST ORANGE—See WEST ORANGE TWP., NJ (Comcast Cable)

EAST PIKELAND TWP.—See EATONTOWN BOROUGH, PA (Comcast Cable)

EAST ROCKHILL TWP.—See EATONTOWN BOROUGH, PA (Comcast Cable)

EAST RUTHERFORD—See WEST ORANGE TWP., NJ (Comcast Cable)

EAST VINCENT TWP.—See EATONTOWN BOROUGH, PA (Comcast Cable)

EAST WINDSOR TWP.—See EATONTOWN BOROUGH, PA (Comcast Cable)

EAST WINDSOR—Comcast Cable. Now served by EATONTOWN BOROUGH, NJ [NJ0009]

EASTAMPTON TWP.—See AUDUBON, NJ (Comcast Cable)

EATONTOWN BOROUGH—Comcast Cable

EDGEWATER BOROUGH—See FORT LEE BOROUGH, NJ (Time Warner Cable)

EDGEWATER PARK—See AUDUBON, NJ (Comcast Cable)

EDISON—See RARITAN, NJ (Cablevision)

EDISON—See WEST ORANGE TWP., NJ (Comcast Cable)

EGG HARBOR CITY—See AUDUBON, NJ (Comcast Cable)

EGG HARBOR TWP.—See AUDUBON, NJ (Comcast Cable)

ELIZABETH—Cablevision

ELK TWP.—See AUDUBON, NJ (Comcast Cable)

ELMER BOROUGH—See AUDUBON, NJ (Comcast Cable)

ELMWOOD PARK—See OAKLAND, NJ (Cablevision)

ELSINBORO TWP.—See AUDUBON, NJ (Comcast Cable)

EMERSON—See BERGENFIELD, NJ (Cablevision)

ENGLEWOOD CLIFFS BOROUGH—See FORT LEE BOROUGH, NJ (Time Warner Cable)

ENGLEWOOD—See FORT LEE BOROUGH, NJ (Time Warner Cable)

ENGLISHTOWN—See FREEHOLD, NJ (Cablevision)

ESSEX FELLS BOROUGH—See WEST ORANGE TWP., NJ (Comcast Cable)

EVESHAM TWP.—See AUDUBON, NJ (Comcast Cable)

EWING—See EATONTOWN BOROUGH, NJ (Comcast Cable)

FAIR HAVEN BOROUGH—See EATONTOWN BOROUGH, NJ (Comcast Cable)

FAIR LAWN—See BERGENFIELD, NJ (Cablevision)

FAIRFIELD TWP. (CUMBERLAND COUNTY)—See AUDUBON, NJ (Comcast Cable)

FAIRFIELD TWP. (ESSEX COUNTY)—See WEST ORANGE TWP., NJ (Comcast Cable)

FAIRVIEW BOROUGH—See FORT LEE BOROUGH, NJ (Time Warner Cable)

FALLS TWP. (BUCKS COUNTY)—See EATONTOWN BOROUGH, PA (Comcast Cable)

FANWOOD—See WEST ORANGE TWP., NJ (Comcast Cable)

FAR HILLS BOROUGH—See EATONTOWN BOROUGH, NJ (Comcast Cable)

FARMINGDALE—See AVON-BY-THE-SEA, NJ (Cablevision)

FIELDSBORO—See AUDUBON, NJ (Comcast Cable)

FLEMINGTON—See EATONTOWN BOROUGH, NJ (Comcast Cable)

FLORENCE TWP.—See AUDUBON, NJ (Comcast Cable)

FLORHAM PARK—See MORRIS TWP., NJ (Cablevision)

FOLSOM BOROUGH—See AUDUBON, NJ (Comcast Cable)

FORT DIX—See AUDUBON, NJ (Comcast Cable)

FORT LEE BOROUGH—Time Warner Cable

FORT MONMOUTH—See EATONTOWN BOROUGH, NJ (Comcast Cable)

FRANCONIA—See EATONTOWN BOROUGH, PA (Comcast Cable)

FRANKFORD TWP.—See SPARTA, NJ (Service Electric Cable Company)

FRANKLIN (HUNTERDON COUNTY)—See WEST ORANGE TWP., NJ (Comcast Cable)

FRANKLIN LAKES—See OAKLAND, NJ (Cablevision)

FRANKLIN PARK—See EATONTOWN BOROUGH, NJ (Comcast Cable)

FRANKLIN TWP. (GLOUCESTER COUNTY)—See AUDUBON, NJ (Comcast Cable)

FRANKLIN TWP. (HUNTERDON COUNTY)—See EATONTOWN BOROUGH, NJ (Comcast Cable)

FRANKLIN TWP. (SOMERSET COUNTY)—See EATONTOWN BOROUGH, NJ (Comcast Cable)

FRANKLIN—See SPARTA, NJ (Service Electric Cable Company)

FREDON—See SPARTA, NJ (Service Electric Cable Company)

FREEHOLD BOROUGH—See EATONTOWN BOROUGH, NJ (Comcast Cable)

FREEHOLD TWP.—See FREEHOLD, NJ (Cablevision)

FREEHOLD—Cablevision

FRELINGHYUSEN TWP.—See SPARTA, NJ (Service Electric Cable Company)

FRENCHTOWN BORO—See HUNTERDON COUNTY, NJ (Service Electric Cable TV of Hunterdon Inc.)

GALLOWAY TWP.—See AUDUBON, NJ (Comcast Cable)

GARFIELD—See OAKLAND, NJ (Cablevision)

GARWOOD BOROUGH—See WEST ORANGE TWP., NJ (Comcast Cable)

GIBBSBORO—See AUDUBON, NJ (Comcast Cable)

GLASSBORO—See AUDUBON, NJ (Comcast Cable)

GLEN GARDNER—See WEST ORANGE TWP., NJ (Comcast Cable)

GLEN RIDGE TWP.—See WEST ORANGE TWP., NJ (Comcast Cable)

GLEN ROCK—See OAKLAND, NJ (Cablevision)

GLOUCESTER COUNTY (PORTIONS)—See AUDUBON, NJ (Comcast Cable)

GLOUCESTER COUNTY—Comcast Cable. Now served by AUDUBON, NJ [NJ0003]

GLOUCESTER TWP.—See AUDUBON, NJ (Comcast Cable)

GLOUCESTER—See AUDUBON, NJ (Comcast Cable)

GREEN BROOK—See RARITAN, NJ (Cablevision)

Cable Community Index—New Jersey

GREEN LANE—See EATONTOWN BOROUGH, PA (Comcast Cable)

GREEN TWP.—See SPARTA, NJ (Service Electric Cable Company)

GREENWICH TWP.—See HUNTERDON COUNTY, NJ (Service Electric Cable TV of Hunterdon Inc.)

GREENWICH—See AUDUBON, NJ (Comcast Cable)

GUTTENBERG (TOWN)—See FORT LEE BOROUGH, NJ (Time Warner Cable)

HACKENSACK—See OAKLAND, NJ (Cablevision)

HACKETTSTOWN—See WEST ORANGE TWP., NJ (Comcast Cable)

HADDON HEIGHTS—See AUDUBON, NJ (Comcast Cable)

HADDON TWP.—See AUDUBON, NJ (Comcast Cable)

HADDONFIELD—See AUDUBON, NJ (Comcast Cable)

HAINESPORT TWP.—See AUDUBON, NJ (Comcast Cable)

HALEDON—See OAKLAND, NJ (Cablevision)

HAMBURG—See SPARTA, NJ (Service Electric Cable Company)

HAMILTON TWP. (MERCER COUNTY)—Cablevision

HAMILTON TWP.—See AUDUBON, NJ (Comcast Cable)

HAMMONTON—See AUDUBON, NJ (Comcast Cable)

HAMPTON TWP.—See SPARTA, NJ (Service Electric Cable Company)

HAMPTON—See WEST ORANGE TWP., NJ (Comcast Cable)

HANOVER TWP.—See MORRIS TWP., NJ (Cablevision)

HARDING TWP.—See EATONTOWN BOROUGH, NJ (Comcast Cable)

HARDWICK TWP.—See SPARTA, NJ (Service Electric Cable Company)

HARDYSTON TWP.—See SPARTA, NJ (Service Electric Cable Company)

HARMONY TWP.—See HUNTERDON COUNTY, NJ (Service Electric Cable TV of Hunterdon Inc.)

HARRINGTON PARK—See BERGENFIELD, NJ (Cablevision)

HARRISON (TOWN)—See WEST ORANGE TWP., NJ (Comcast Cable)

HARRISON TWP. (GLOUCESTER COUNTY)—See AUDUBON, NJ (Comcast Cable)

HARVEY CEDARS BOROUGH—See AUDUBON, NJ (Comcast Cable)

HASBROUCK HEIGHTS—See OAKLAND, NJ (Cablevision)

HATBORO BOROUGH—See EATONTOWN BOROUGH, PA (Comcast Cable)

HATFIELD BOROUGH—See EATONTOWN BOROUGH, PA (Comcast Cable)

HATFIELD TWP.—See EATONTOWN BOROUGH, PA (Comcast Cable)

HAWORTH—See BERGENFIELD, NJ (Cablevision)

HAWTHORNE—See OAKLAND, NJ (Cablevision)

HAZLET TWP.—See EATONTOWN BOROUGH, NJ (Comcast Cable)

HELMETTA—See EATONTOWN BOROUGH, NJ (Comcast Cable)

HEREFORD—See EATONTOWN BOROUGH, PA (Comcast Cable)

HI-NELLA—See AUDUBON, NJ (Comcast Cable)

HIGH BRIDGE—See WEST ORANGE TWP., NJ (Comcast Cable)

HIGHLAND PARK—See RARITAN, NJ (Cablevision)

HIGHLANDS BOROUGH—See EATONTOWN BOROUGH, NJ (Comcast Cable)

HIGHTSTOWN—See EATONTOWN BOROUGH, NJ (Comcast Cable)

HILLSBOROUGH—Comcast Cable. Now served by EATONTOWN BOROUGH, NJ [NJ0009]

HILLSBOROUGH—See EATONTOWN BOROUGH, NJ (Comcast Cable)

HILLSDALE—See BERGENFIELD, NJ (Cablevision)

HILLSIDE TWP.—See WEST ORANGE TWP., NJ (Comcast Cable)

HILLTOWN TWP.—See EATONTOWN BOROUGH, PA (Comcast Cable)

HO-HO-KUS—See OAKLAND, NJ (Cablevision)

HOBOKEN—Cablevision

HOLLAND TWP.—See HUNTERDON COUNTY, NJ (Service Electric Cable TV of Hunterdon Inc.)

HOLMDEL TWP.—See EATONTOWN BOROUGH, NJ (Comcast Cable)

HOPATCONG—See MORRIS TWP., NJ (Cablevision)

HOPE—See SPARTA, NJ (Service Electric Cable Company)

HOPEWELL TWP. (CUMBERLAND COUNTY)—See AUDUBON, NJ (Comcast Cable)

HOPEWELL—See AUDUBON, NJ (Comcast Cable)

HORSHAM TWP.—See EATONTOWN BOROUGH, PA (Comcast Cable)

HOWELL TWP.—See FREEHOLD, NJ (Cablevision)

HOWELL—See FREEHOLD, NJ (Cablevision)

HULMEVILLE—See EATONTOWN BOROUGH, PA (Comcast Cable)

HUNTERDON COUNTY—Service Electric Cable TV of Hunterdon Inc.

INDEPENDENCE TWP.—See WEST ORANGE TWP., NJ (Comcast Cable)

INTERLAKEN—See AVON-BY-THE-SEA, NJ (Cablevision)

IRVINGTON TWP.—See WEST ORANGE TWP., NJ (Comcast Cable)

ISLAND HEIGHTS BOROUGH—See AUDUBON, NJ (Comcast Cable)

IVYLAND—See EATONTOWN BOROUGH, PA (Comcast Cable)

JACKSON TWP.—See FREEHOLD, NJ (Cablevision)

JACKSON—See FREEHOLD, NJ (Cablevision)

JAMESBURG—See EATONTOWN BOROUGH, NJ (Comcast Cable)

JEFFERSON TWP.—See MORRIS TWP., NJ (Cablevision)

JEFFERSON TWP.—See SPARTA, NJ (Service Electric Cable Company)

JERSEY CITY—Comcast Cable. Now served by WEST ORANGE TWP., NJ [NJ0001]

JERSEY CITY—See WEST ORANGE TWP., NJ (Comcast Cable)

KEANSBURG—See RARITAN, NJ (Cablevision)

KEARNY—See WEST ORANGE TWP., NJ (Comcast Cable)

KENILWORTH BOROUGH—See WEST ORANGE TWP., NJ (Comcast Cable)

KEYPORT—See RARITAN, NJ (Cablevision)

KING OF PRUSSIA—See EATONTOWN BOROUGH, PA (Comcast Cable)

KINGWOOD TWP.—See HUNTERDON COUNTY, NJ (Service Electric Cable TV of Hunterdon Inc.)

KINNELON—See OAKLAND, NJ (Cablevision)

KNOWLTON—See SPARTA, NJ (Service Electric Cable Company)

LACEY TWP.—See AUDUBON, NJ (Comcast Cable)

LAFAYETTE TWP.—See SPARTA, NJ (Service Electric Cable Company)

LAKE COMO—See AVON-BY-THE-SEA, NJ (Cablevision)

LAKEHURST BOROUGH—See AUDUBON, NJ (Comcast Cable)

LAKEWOOD TWP.—See FREEHOLD, NJ (Cablevision)

LAKEWOOD—See FREEHOLD, NJ (Cablevision)

LAMBERTVILLE—Comcast Cable. Now served by EATONTOWN BOROUGH, NJ [NJ0009]

LAMBERTVILLE—See EATONTOWN BOROUGH, NJ (Comcast Cable)

LANGHORNE BOROUGH—See EATONTOWN BOROUGH, PA (Comcast Cable)

LANGHORNE MANOR BOROUGH—See EATONTOWN BOROUGH, PA (Comcast Cable)

LANSDALE (BOROUGH)—See EATONTOWN BOROUGH, PA (Comcast Cable)

LAUREL LAKE—See AUDUBON, NJ (Comcast Cable)

LAUREL SPRINGS—See AUDUBON, NJ (Comcast Cable)

LAVALLETTE—See SEASIDE HEIGHTS, NJ (Cablevision)

LAWNSIDE—See AUDUBON, NJ (Comcast Cable)

LAWRENCE TWP. (CUMBERLAND COUNTY)—See AUDUBON, NJ (Comcast Cable)

LAWRENCE—See EATONTOWN BOROUGH, NJ (Comcast Cable)

LAWRENCEVILLE—See EATONTOWN BOROUGH, NJ (Comcast Cable)

LEBANON BOROUGH—See EATONTOWN BOROUGH, NJ (Comcast Cable)

LEBANON—See WEST ORANGE TWP., NJ (Comcast Cable)

LEONIA BOROUGH—See FORT LEE BOROUGH, NJ (Time Warner Cable)

LIBERTY TWP.—See WEST ORANGE TWP., NJ (Comcast Cable)

LIMERICK—See EATONTOWN BOROUGH, PA (Comcast Cable)

LINCOLN PARK—See OAKLAND, NJ (Cablevision)

LINDEN—See WEST ORANGE TWP., NJ (Comcast Cable)

LINDENWOLD—See AUDUBON, NJ (Comcast Cable)

LINWOOD—See AUDUBON, NJ (Comcast Cable)

LITTLE EGG HARBOR TWP.—See AUDUBON, NJ (Comcast Cable)

LITTLE FALLS TWP.—See OAKLAND, NJ (Cablevision)

LITTLE FERRY BOROUGH—See FORT LEE BOROUGH, NJ (Time Warner Cable)

LITTLE SILVER BOROUGH—See EATONTOWN BOROUGH, NJ (Comcast Cable)

LIVINGSTON TWP.—See WEST ORANGE TWP., NJ (Comcast Cable)

LOCH ARBOUR (VILLAGE)—See EATONTOWN BOROUGH, NJ (Comcast Cable)

LODI—See OAKLAND, NJ (Cablevision)

LOGAN TWP.—See AUDUBON, NJ (Comcast Cable)

LONG BEACH TWP.—Comcast Cable. Now served by AUDUBON, NJ [NJ0003]

LONG BEACH TWP.—See AUDUBON, NJ (Comcast Cable)

New Jersey—Cable Community Index

LONG BRANCH—See EATONTOWN BOROUGH, NJ (Comcast Cable)

LONG HILL TWP.—See EATONTOWN BOROUGH, NJ (Comcast Cable)

LONG HILL—Comcast Cable. Now served by EATONTOWN BOROUGH, NJ [NJ0009]

LONGPORT—See AUDUBON, NJ (Comcast Cable)

LOPATCONG TWP.—See HUNTERDON COUNTY, NJ (Service Electric Cable TV of Hunterdon Inc.)

LOWER ALLOWAYS CREEK TWP.—See AUDUBON, NJ (Comcast Cable)

LOWER FREDERICK—See EATONTOWN BOROUGH, PA (Comcast Cable)

LOWER GWYNEDD TWP. (MONTGOMERY COUNTY)—See EATONTOWN BOROUGH, PA (Comcast Cable)

LOWER MAKEFIELD TWP.—See EATONTOWN BOROUGH, PA (Comcast Cable)

LOWER POTTSGROVE TWP.—See EATONTOWN BOROUGH, PA (Comcast Cable)

LOWER PROVIDENCE TWP.—See EATONTOWN BOROUGH, PA (Comcast Cable)

LOWER SALFORD—See EATONTOWN BOROUGH, PA (Comcast Cable)

LOWER SOUTHAMPTON—See EATONTOWN BOROUGH, PA (Comcast Cable)

LOWER TWP.—See AUDUBON, NJ (Comcast Cable)

LUMBERTON—See AUDUBON, NJ (Comcast Cable)

LYNDHURST—See WEST ORANGE TWP., NJ (Comcast Cable)

MADISON—See MORRIS TWP., NJ (Cablevision)

MAGNOLIA—See AUDUBON, NJ (Comcast Cable)

MANAHAWKIN—See EATONTOWN BOROUGH, NJ (Comcast Cable)

MANALAPAN TWP.—See FREEHOLD, NJ (Cablevision)

MANASQUAN—See AVON-BY-THE-SEA, NJ (Cablevision)

MANCHESTER TWP.—See EATONTOWN BOROUGH, NJ (Comcast Cable)

MANNINGTON TWP.—See AUDUBON, NJ (Comcast Cable)

MANSFIELD TWP. (BURLINGTON COUNTY)—See AUDUBON, NJ (Comcast Cable)

MANSFIELD TWP. (WARREN COUNTY)—See WEST ORANGE TWP., NJ (Comcast Cable)

MANTOLOKING—See EATONTOWN BOROUGH, NJ (Comcast Cable)

MANTUA TWP.—See AUDUBON, NJ (Comcast Cable)

MANVILLE—See RARITAN, NJ (Cablevision)

MAPLE SHADE TWP.—See AUDUBON, NJ (Comcast Cable)

MAPLE SHADE—Comcast Cable. Now served by AUDUBON, NJ [NJ0003]

MAPLE SHADE—See AUDUBON, NJ (Comcast Cable)

MAPLEWOOD TWP.—See WEST ORANGE TWP., NJ (Comcast Cable)

MARGATE CITY—See AUDUBON, NJ (Comcast Cable)

MARLBORO TWP.—See FREEHOLD, NJ (Cablevision)

MARLBOROUGH TWP.—See EATONTOWN BOROUGH, PA (Comcast Cable)

MATAWAN—See RARITAN, NJ (Cablevision)

MAURICE RIVER—See AUDUBON, NJ (Comcast Cable)

MAYWOOD—See OAKLAND, NJ (Cablevision)

MCGUIRE AFB—See AUDUBON, NJ (Comcast Cable)

MEDFORD LAKES—See AUDUBON, NJ (Comcast Cable)

MEDFORD TWP.—See AUDUBON, NJ (Comcast Cable)

MENDHAM—See EATONTOWN BOROUGH, NJ (Comcast Cable)

MERCHANTVILLE—See AUDUBON, NJ (Comcast Cable)

METUCHEN—See RARITAN, NJ (Cablevision)

MIDDLE TWP.—See AUDUBON, NJ (Comcast Cable)

MIDDLESEX—See RARITAN, NJ (Cablevision)

MIDDLETOWN TWP. (BUCKS COUNTY)—See EATONTOWN BOROUGH, PA (Comcast Cable)

MIDDLETOWN TWP.—See EATONTOWN BOROUGH, NJ (Comcast Cable)

MIDLAND PARK—See OAKLAND, NJ (Cablevision)

MILFORD BORO—See HUNTERDON COUNTY, NJ (Service Electric Cable TV of Hunterdon Inc.)

MILFORD SQUARE—See EATONTOWN BOROUGH, PA (Comcast Cable)

MILLBURN TWP.—See WEST ORANGE TWP., NJ (Comcast Cable)

MILLINGTON—See EATONTOWN BOROUGH, NJ (Comcast Cable)

MILLSTONE TWP.—Cablevision Systems Corp. Now served by FREEHOLD, NJ [NJ0063]

MILLSTONE TWP.—See FREEHOLD, NJ (Cablevision)

MILLSTONE—See EATONTOWN BOROUGH, NJ (Comcast Cable)

MILLTOWN—See RARITAN, NJ (Cablevision)

MILLVILLE—See AUDUBON, NJ (Comcast Cable)

MINE HILL TWP.—See MORRIS TWP., NJ (Cablevision)

MONMOUTH BEACH BOROUGH—See EATONTOWN BOROUGH, NJ (Comcast Cable)

MONMOUTH COUNTY (PORTIONS)—See AVON-BY-THE-SEA, NJ (Cablevision)

MONROE TWP. (GLOUCESTER COUNTY)—See AUDUBON, NJ (Comcast Cable)

MONROE TWP.—See EATONTOWN BOROUGH, NJ (Comcast Cable)

MONTCLAIR TWP.—See WEST ORANGE TWP., NJ (Comcast Cable)

MONTGOMERY TWP.—See EATONTOWN BOROUGH, NJ (Comcast Cable)

MONTVILLE TWP. (NORTHEASTERN PORTION)—See OAKLAND, NJ (Cablevision)

MONTVILLE TWP.—See MORRIS TWP., NJ (Cablevision)

MOONACHIE BOROUGH—See FORT LEE BOROUGH, NJ (Time Warner Cable)

MOORESTOWN TWP.—See AUDUBON, NJ (Comcast Cable)

MORRIS PLAINS—See MORRIS TWP., NJ (Cablevision)

MORRIS TWP.—Cablevision

MORRISTOWN—See MORRIS TWP., NJ (Cablevision)

MORRISVILLE—See EATONTOWN BOROUGH, PA (Comcast Cable)

MOUNT ARLINGTON—See MORRIS TWP., NJ (Cablevision)

MOUNT EPHRAIM BOROUGH—See AUDUBON, NJ (Comcast Cable)

MOUNT HOLLY TWP.—See AUDUBON, NJ (Comcast Cable)

MOUNT LAUREL TWP.—See AUDUBON, NJ (Comcast Cable)

MOUNT OLIVE TWP.—See MORRIS TWP., NJ (Cablevision)

MOUNT OLIVE—See WEST ORANGE TWP., NJ (Comcast Cable)

MOUNTAIN LAKES—See MORRIS TWP., NJ (Cablevision)

MOUNTAINSIDE BOROUGH—See WEST ORANGE TWP., NJ (Comcast Cable)

MULLICA TWP.—See AUDUBON, NJ (Comcast Cable)

NATIONAL PARK—See AUDUBON, NJ (Comcast Cable)

NEPTUNE TWP.—See AVON-BY-THE-SEA, NJ (Cablevision)

NEPTUNE—See AVON-BY-THE-SEA, NJ (Cablevision)

NETCONG—See MORRIS TWP., NJ (Cablevision)

NEW BRITAIN BOROUGH—See EATONTOWN BOROUGH, PA (Comcast Cable)

NEW BRITAIN TWP.—See EATONTOWN BOROUGH, PA (Comcast Cable)

NEW BRUNSWICK—See RARITAN, NJ (Cablevision)

NEW HANOVER (MONTGOMERY COUNTY)—See EATONTOWN BOROUGH, PA (Comcast Cable)

NEW HANOVER TWP.—See AUDUBON, NJ (Comcast Cable)

NEW HOPE (BUCKS COUNTY)—See EATONTOWN BOROUGH, PA (Comcast Cable)

NEW MILFORD—See BERGENFIELD, NJ (Cablevision)

NEW PROVIDENCE—See WEST ORANGE TWP., NJ (Comcast Cable)

NEWARK—Cablevision

NEWFIELD—See AUDUBON, NJ (Comcast Cable)

NEWTON—See SPARTA, NJ (Service Electric Cable Company)

NEWTOWN BOROUGH—See EATONTOWN BOROUGH, PA (Comcast Cable)

NEWTOWN TWP. (BUCKS COUNTY)—See EATONTOWN BOROUGH, PA (Comcast Cable)

NORRISTOWN—See EATONTOWN BOROUGH, PA (Comcast Cable)

NORTH ARLINGTON—See WEST ORANGE TWP., NJ (Comcast Cable)

NORTH BERGEN—See HOBOKEN, NJ (Cablevision)

NORTH BRUNSWICK TWP.—See RARITAN, NJ (Cablevision)

NORTH CALDWELL—See OAKLAND, NJ (Cablevision)

NORTH COVENTRY TWP.—See EATONTOWN BOROUGH, PA (Comcast Cable)

NORTH HALEDON—See OAKLAND, NJ (Cablevision)

NORTH HANOVER TWP.—See AUDUBON, NJ (Comcast Cable)

NORTH PLAINFIELD—See WEST ORANGE TWP., NJ (Comcast Cable)

NORTH WILDWOOD—See AUDUBON, NJ (Comcast Cable)

NORTHAMPTON—See EATONTOWN BOROUGH, PA (Comcast Cable)

NORTHFIELD—See AUDUBON, NJ (Comcast Cable)

NORTHVALE—See BERGENFIELD, NJ (Cablevision)

NORWOOD—See BERGENFIELD, NJ (Cablevision)

NUTLEY TWP.—See OAKLAND, NJ (Cablevision)

Cable Community Index—New Jersey

OAKLAND—Cablevision

OAKLYN—See AUDUBON, NJ (Comcast Cable)

OCEAN BEACH—See AVON-BY-THE-SEA, NJ (Cablevision)

OCEAN CITY—See AUDUBON, NJ (Comcast Cable)

OCEAN COUNTY (PORTIONS)—See EATONTOWN BOROUGH, NJ (Comcast Cable)

OCEAN COUNTY—Comcast Cable. Now served by EATONTOWN BOROUGH, NJ [NJ0009]

OCEAN GATE BOROUGH—See AUDUBON, NJ (Comcast Cable)

OCEAN TWP.—See AVON-BY-THE-SEA, NJ (Cablevision)

OCEAN TWP.—See AUDUBON, NJ (Comcast Cable)

OCEANPORT BOROUGH—See EATONTOWN BOROUGH, NJ (Comcast Cable)

OGDENSBURG—See SPARTA, NJ (Service Electric Cable Company)

OLD BRIDGE—See RARITAN, NJ (Cablevision)

OLD TAPPAN—See BERGENFIELD, NJ (Cablevision)

OLDMANS TWP.—See AUDUBON, NJ (Comcast Cable)

OLEY TWP.—See EATONTOWN BOROUGH, PA (Comcast Cable)

OLEY—See EATONTOWN BOROUGH, PA (Comcast Cable)

ORADELL—See BERGENFIELD, NJ (Cablevision)

ORANGE—See WEST ORANGE TWP., NJ (Comcast Cable)

OXFORD—See WEST ORANGE TWP., NJ (Comcast Cable)

PALISADES PARK—See FORT LEE BOROUGH, NJ (Time Warner Cable)

PALMYRA—See AUDUBON, NJ (Comcast Cable)

PARAMUS—Cablevision. Now served by BERGENFIELD, NJ [NJ0013]

PARAMUS—See BERGENFIELD, NJ (Cablevision)

PARK RIDGE—See OAKLAND, NJ (Cablevision)

PARSIPPANY-TROY HILLS TWP.—See MORRIS TWP., NJ (Cablevision)

PARSIPPANY—See MORRIS TWP., NJ (Cablevision)

PASSAIC—See OAKLAND, NJ (Cablevision)

PATERSON—Cablevision

PAULSBORO—See AUDUBON, NJ (Comcast Cable)

PEAPACK-GLADSTONE—See EATONTOWN BOROUGH, NJ (Comcast Cable)

PEMBERTON BOROUGH—See AUDUBON, NJ (Comcast Cable)

PEMBERTON TWP.—See AUDUBON, NJ (Comcast Cable)

PENNDEL BOROUGH—See EATONTOWN BOROUGH, PA (Comcast Cable)

PENNINGTON BOROUGH—See EATONTOWN BOROUGH, NJ (Comcast Cable)

PENNS GROVE—See AUDUBON, NJ (Comcast Cable)

PENNSAUKEN TWP.—See AUDUBON, NJ (Comcast Cable)

PENNSBURG—See EATONTOWN BOROUGH, PA (Comcast Cable)

PENNSVILLE TWP.—See AUDUBON, NJ (Comcast Cable)

PEQUANNOCK TWP.—See OAKLAND, NJ (Cablevision)

PERKASIE—See EATONTOWN BOROUGH, PA (Comcast Cable)

PERKIOMEN—See EATONTOWN BOROUGH, PA (Comcast Cable)

PERTH AMBOY—See WEST ORANGE TWP., NJ (Comcast Cable)

PHILLIPSBURG—Service Electric Cable TV of Hunterdon Inc. Now served by HUNTERDON COUNTY, NJ [NJ0067]

PHILLIPSBURG—See HUNTERDON COUNTY, NJ (Service Electric Cable TV of Hunterdon Inc.)

PHOENIXVILLE—See EATONTOWN BOROUGH, PA (Comcast Cable)

PICATINNY ARSENAL—See MORRIS TWP., NJ (Cablevision)

PILESGROVE TWP.—See AUDUBON, NJ (Comcast Cable)

PINE BEACH BOROUGH—See AUDUBON, NJ (Comcast Cable)

PINE HILL—See AUDUBON, NJ (Comcast Cable)

PINE VALLEY—See AUDUBON, NJ (Comcast Cable)

PISCATAWAY—See RARITAN, NJ (Cablevision)

PISCATAWAY—See WEST ORANGE TWP., NJ (Comcast Cable)

PITMAN—See AUDUBON, NJ (Comcast Cable)

PITTSGROVE TWP.—See AUDUBON, NJ (Comcast Cable)

PLAINFIELD—Comcast Cable. Now served by WEST ORANGE TWP., NJ [NJ0001]

PLAINFIELD—See WEST ORANGE TWP., NJ (Comcast Cable)

PLAINSBORO—See EATONTOWN BOROUGH, NJ (Comcast Cable)

PLEASANTVILLE—Comcast Cable. Now served by AUDUBON, NJ [NJ0003]

PLEASANTVILLE—See AUDUBON, NJ (Comcast Cable)

PLUMSTEAD—See EATONTOWN BOROUGH, PA (Comcast Cable)

PLUMSTED TWP.—See AUDUBON, NJ (Comcast Cable)

PLYMOUTH TWP. (MONTGOMERY COUNTY)—See EATONTOWN BOROUGH, PA (Comcast Cable)

POHATCONG TWP.—See HUNTERDON COUNTY, NJ (Service Electric Cable TV of Hunterdon Inc.)

POINT PLEASANT BEACH—See EATONTOWN BOROUGH, NJ (Comcast Cable)

POINT PLEASANT—See EATONTOWN BOROUGH, NJ (Comcast Cable)

POMPTON LAKES—See OAKLAND, NJ (Cablevision)

PORT MURRAY—Comcast Cable. Now served by WEST ORANGE TWP., NJ [NJ0001]

PORT MURRAY—See WEST ORANGE TWP., NJ (Comcast Cable)

PORT REPUBLIC—See AUDUBON, NJ (Comcast Cable)

POTTSTOWN—See EATONTOWN BOROUGH, PA (Comcast Cable)

PRINCETON BOROUGH—See EATONTOWN BOROUGH, NJ (Comcast Cable)

PRINCETON JUNCTION—See EATONTOWN BOROUGH, NJ (Comcast Cable)

PRINCETON TWP.—See EATONTOWN BOROUGH, NJ (Comcast Cable)

PRINCETON—Comcast Cable. Now served by EATONTOWN BOROUGH, NJ [NJ0009]

PROSPECT PARK—See OAKLAND, NJ (Cablevision)

QUAKERTOWN—See EATONTOWN BOROUGH, PA (Comcast Cable)

QUINTON TWP.—See AUDUBON, NJ (Comcast Cable)

RAHWAY—See WEST ORANGE TWP., NJ (Comcast Cable)

RAMSEY—See OAKLAND, NJ (Cablevision)

RANDOLPH TWP.—See MORRIS TWP., NJ (Cablevision)

RARITAN TWP.—See EATONTOWN BOROUGH, NJ (Comcast Cable)

RARITAN—Cablevision

READINGTON TWP.—See EATONTOWN BOROUGH, NJ (Comcast Cable)

RED BANK BOROUGH—See EATONTOWN BOROUGH, NJ (Comcast Cable)

RED HILL—See EATONTOWN BOROUGH, PA (Comcast Cable)

RICHLANDTOWN—See EATONTOWN BOROUGH, PA (Comcast Cable)

RIDGEFIELD BOROUGH—See FORT LEE BOROUGH, NJ (Time Warner Cable)

RIDGEFIELD PARK (VILLAGE)—See FORT LEE BOROUGH, NJ (Time Warner Cable)

RIDGEWOOD—See OAKLAND, NJ (Cablevision)

RINGWOOD—See OAKLAND, NJ (Cablevision)

RIVER EDGE—See OAKLAND, NJ (Cablevision)

RIVER VALE TWP.—See BERGENFIELD, NJ (Cablevision)

RIVERDALE—See OAKLAND, NJ (Cablevision)

RIVERSIDE—See AUDUBON, NJ (Comcast Cable)

RIVERTON—See AUDUBON, NJ (Comcast Cable)

ROCHELLE PARK—See OAKLAND, NJ (Cablevision)

ROCKAWAY TWP.—See MORRIS TWP., NJ (Cablevision)

ROCKAWAY—See MORRIS TWP., NJ (Cablevision)

ROCKLEIGH—See BERGENFIELD, NJ (Cablevision)

ROCKY HILL BOROUGH—See EATONTOWN BOROUGH, NJ (Comcast Cable)

ROOSEVELT—See EATONTOWN BOROUGH, NJ (Comcast Cable)

ROSELAND BOROUGH—See WEST ORANGE TWP., NJ (Comcast Cable)

ROSELLE BOROUGH—See WEST ORANGE TWP., NJ (Comcast Cable)

ROSELLE PARK BOROUGH—See WEST ORANGE TWP., NJ (Comcast Cable)

ROXBURY TWP.—See MORRIS TWP., NJ (Cablevision)

ROYERSFORD—See EATONTOWN BOROUGH, PA (Comcast Cable)

RUMSON BOROUGH—See EATONTOWN BOROUGH, NJ (Comcast Cable)

RUNNEMEDE—See AUDUBON, NJ (Comcast Cable)

RUTHERFORD—See WEST ORANGE TWP., NJ (Comcast Cable)

SADDLE BROOK TWP.—See OAKLAND, NJ (Cablevision)

SADDLE RIVER—See BERGENFIELD, NJ (Cablevision)

SALEM—See AUDUBON, NJ (Comcast Cable)

SALFORD—See EATONTOWN BOROUGH, PA (Comcast Cable)

SANDYSTON TWP.—See SPARTA, NJ (Service Electric Cable Company)

SAYREVILLE—See RARITAN, NJ (Cablevision)

SCHWENKSVILLE—See EATONTOWN BOROUGH, PA (Comcast Cable)

New Jersey—Cable Community Index

SCOTCH PLAINS TWP.—See WEST ORANGE TWP., NJ (Comcast Cable)

SEA BRIGHT BOROUGH—See EATONTOWN BOROUGH, NJ (Comcast Cable)

SEA GIRT—See AVON-BY-THE-SEA, NJ (Cablevision)

SEA ISLE CITY—See AUDUBON, NJ (Comcast Cable)

SEASIDE HEIGHTS—Cablevision

SEASIDE PARK—See SEASIDE HEIGHTS, NJ (Cablevision)

SEAVIEW HARBOR—See AUDUBON, NJ (Comcast Cable)

SECAUCUS (TOWN)—See WEST ORANGE TWP., NJ (Comcast Cable)

SELLERSVILLE—See EATONTOWN BOROUGH, PA (Comcast Cable)

SHAMONG TWP.—See AUDUBON, NJ (Comcast Cable)

SHILOH BOROUGH—See AUDUBON, NJ (Comcast Cable)

SHIP BOTTOM BOROUGH—See AUDUBON, NJ (Comcast Cable)

SHORT HILLS—See WEST ORANGE TWP., NJ (Comcast Cable)

SHREWSBURY BOROUGH—See EATONTOWN BOROUGH, NJ (Comcast Cable)

SHREWSBURY TWP.—See EATONTOWN BOROUGH, NJ (Comcast Cable)

SILVERDALE—See EATONTOWN BOROUGH, PA (Comcast Cable)

SKIPPACK—See EATONTOWN BOROUGH, PA (Comcast Cable)

SOLEBURY—See EATONTOWN BOROUGH, PA (Comcast Cable)

SOMERDALE—See AUDUBON, NJ (Comcast Cable)

SOMERS POINT—See AUDUBON, NJ (Comcast Cable)

SOMERVILLE—See RARITAN, NJ (Cablevision)

SOUDERTON—See EATONTOWN BOROUGH, PA (Comcast Cable)

SOUTH AMBOY—See RARITAN, NJ (Cablevision)

SOUTH BOUND BROOK—See RARITAN, NJ (Cablevision)

SOUTH BRUNSWICK TWP.—See EATONTOWN BOROUGH, NJ (Comcast Cable)

SOUTH COVENTRY TWP.—See EATONTOWN BOROUGH, PA (Comcast Cable)

SOUTH HACKENSACK TWP.—See OAKLAND, NJ (Cablevision)

SOUTH HARRISON TWP.—See AUDUBON, NJ (Comcast Cable)

SOUTH ORANGE TWP.—See NEWARK, NJ (Cablevision)

SOUTH PLAINFIELD—See WEST ORANGE TWP., NJ (Comcast Cable)

SOUTH RIVER BOROUGH—See WEST ORANGE TWP., NJ (Comcast Cable)

SOUTH TOMS RIVER BOROUGH—See AUDUBON, NJ (Comcast Cable)

SOUTHAMPTON TWP.—See AUDUBON, NJ (Comcast Cable)

SPARTA TWP.—See SPARTA, NJ (Service Electric Cable Company)

SPARTA—Service Electric Cable Company

SPOTSWOOD—See EATONTOWN BOROUGH, NJ (Comcast Cable)

SPRING CITY—See EATONTOWN BOROUGH, PA (Comcast Cable)

SPRING LAKE HEIGHTS—See AVON-BY-THE-SEA, NJ (Cablevision)

SPRING LAKE—See AVON-BY-THE-SEA, NJ (Cablevision)

SPRINGFIELD TWP. (BURLINGTON COUNTY)—See AUDUBON, NJ (Comcast Cable)

SPRINGFIELD TWP. (DELAWARE COUNTY)—See EATONTOWN BOROUGH, PA (Comcast Cable)

SPRINGFIELD TWP. (UNION COUNTY)—See WEST ORANGE TWP., NJ (Comcast Cable)

STANHOPE—See MORRIS TWP., NJ (Cablevision)

STILLWATER TWP.—See SPARTA, NJ (Service Electric Cable Company)

STOCKTON BOROUGH—See EATONTOWN BOROUGH, NJ (Comcast Cable)

STONE HARBOR BOROUGH—See AUDUBON, NJ (Comcast Cable)

STRATFORD—See AUDUBON, NJ (Comcast Cable)

SUMMIT—See WEST ORANGE TWP., NJ (Comcast Cable)

SURF CITY BOROUGH—See AUDUBON, NJ (Comcast Cable)

SUSSEX—See SPARTA, NJ (Service Electric Cable Company)

SWAINTON—See AUDUBON, NJ (Comcast Cable)

SWEDESBORO—See AUDUBON, NJ (Comcast Cable)

TABERNACLE TWP.—See AUDUBON, NJ (Comcast Cable)

TAVISTOCK—See AUDUBON, NJ (Comcast Cable)

TEANECK—See OAKLAND, NJ (Cablevision)

TELFORD—See EATONTOWN BOROUGH, PA (Comcast Cable)

TENAFLY—See BERGENFIELD, NJ (Cablevision)

TETERBORO BOROUGH—See FORT LEE BOROUGH, NJ (Time Warner Cable)

TEWKSBURY TWP.—See EATONTOWN BOROUGH, NJ (Comcast Cable)

TINICUM TWP. (DELAWARE COUNTY)—See EATONTOWN BOROUGH, PA (Comcast Cable)

TINTON FALLS BOROUGH—See EATONTOWN BOROUGH, NJ (Comcast Cable)

TITUSVILLE—See AUDUBON, NJ (Comcast Cable)

TOMS RIVER—Comcast Cable. Now served by AUDUBON, NJ [NJ0003]

TOTOWA—See OAKLAND, NJ (Cablevision)

TOWAMENCIN TWP.—See EATONTOWN BOROUGH, PA (Comcast Cable)

TRAPPE—See EATONTOWN BOROUGH, PA (Comcast Cable)

TRENTON—Comcast Cable. Now served by AUDUBON, NJ [NJ0003]

TRENTON—See EATONTOWN BOROUGH, NJ (Comcast Cable)

TRUMBAUERSVILLE—See EATONTOWN BOROUGH, PA (Comcast Cable)

TUCKERTON BOROUGH—See EATONTOWN BOROUGH, NJ (Comcast Cable)

TULLYTOWN—See EATONTOWN BOROUGH, PA (Comcast Cable)

UNION BEACH—See RARITAN, NJ (Cablevision)

UNION CITY—See HOBOKEN, NJ (Cablevision)

UNION TWP.—See EATONTOWN BOROUGH, NJ (Comcast Cable)

UNION TWP.—See WEST ORANGE TWP., NJ (Comcast Cable)

UPPER DEERFIELD TWP.—See AUDUBON, NJ (Comcast Cable)

UPPER DUBLIN—See EATONTOWN BOROUGH, PA (Comcast Cable)

UPPER FREDERICK TWP.—See EATONTOWN BOROUGH, PA (Comcast Cable)

UPPER FREEHOLD TWP.—See FREEHOLD, NJ (Cablevision)

UPPER GWYNEDD TWP.—See EATONTOWN BOROUGH, PA (Comcast Cable)

UPPER HANOVER TWP.—See EATONTOWN BOROUGH, PA (Comcast Cable)

UPPER MAKEFIELD TWP.—See EATONTOWN BOROUGH, PA (Comcast Cable)

UPPER MERION TWP.—See EATONTOWN BOROUGH, PA (Comcast Cable)

UPPER PITTSGROVE TWP.—See AUDUBON, NJ (Comcast Cable)

UPPER POTTSGROVE—See EATONTOWN BOROUGH, PA (Comcast Cable)

UPPER PROVIDENCE (DELAWARE COUNTY)—See EATONTOWN BOROUGH, PA (Comcast Cable)

UPPER SADDLE RIVER—See OAKLAND, NJ (Cablevision)

UPPER SALFORD—See EATONTOWN BOROUGH, PA (Comcast Cable)

UPPER SOUTHAMPTON—See EATONTOWN BOROUGH, PA (Comcast Cable)

UPPER TWP.—See AUDUBON, NJ (Comcast Cable)

VENTNOR CITY—See AUDUBON, NJ (Comcast Cable)

VERNON TWP.—See SPARTA, NJ (Service Electric Cable Company)

VERONA TWP.—See WEST ORANGE TWP., NJ (Comcast Cable)

VICTORY GARDENS—See MORRIS TWP., NJ (Cablevision)

VINELAND—Comcast Cable. Now served by AUDUBON, NJ [NJ0003]

VINELAND—See AUDUBON, NJ (Comcast Cable)

VOORHEES TWP.—See AUDUBON, NJ (Comcast Cable)

WALDWICK—See OAKLAND, NJ (Cablevision)

WALL TWP.—See AVON-BY-THE-SEA, NJ (Cablevision)

WALL—See AVON-BY-THE-SEA, NJ (Cablevision)

WALLINGTON—See WEST ORANGE TWP., NJ (Comcast Cable)

WANAQUE—See OAKLAND, NJ (Cablevision)

WANTAGE TWP.—See SPARTA, NJ (Service Electric Cable Company)

WARMINSTER—See EATONTOWN BOROUGH, PA (Comcast Cable)

WARREN TWP.—See RARITAN, NJ (Cablevision)

WARRINGTON TWP. (BUCKS COUNTY)—See EATONTOWN BOROUGH, PA (Comcast Cable)

WARWICK TWP. (BUCKS COUNTY)—See EATONTOWN BOROUGH, PA (Comcast Cable)

WASHINGTON BOROUGH—See WEST ORANGE TWP., NJ (Comcast Cable)

WASHINGTON TWP. (BERGEN COUNTY)—See OAKLAND, NJ (Cablevision)

WASHINGTON TWP. (GLOUCESTER COUNTY)—See AUDUBON, NJ (Comcast Cable)

WASHINGTON TWP. (MERCER COUNTY)—See HAMILTON TWP. (Mercer County), NJ (Cablevision)

WASHINGTON TWP. (MORRIS COUNTY)—See WEST ORANGE TWP., NJ (Comcast Cable)

Cable Community Index—New Mexico

WASHINGTON TWP. (WARREN COUNTY)—See WEST ORANGE TWP., NJ (Comcast Cable)

WASHINGTON—See EATONTOWN BOROUGH, PA (Comcast Cable)

WATCHUNG—See RARITAN, NJ (Cablevision)

WATERFORD TWP.—See AUDUBON, NJ (Comcast Cable)

WAYNE—See OAKLAND, NJ (Cablevision)

WEEHAWKEN—See HOBOKEN, NJ (Cablevision)

WENONAH—See AUDUBON, NJ (Comcast Cable)

WEST AMWELL TWP.—See AUDUBON, NJ (Comcast Cable)

WEST BERLIN—See AUDUBON, NJ (Comcast Cable)

WEST CALDWELL TWP.—See WEST ORANGE TWP., NJ (Comcast Cable)

WEST CAPE MAY BOROUGH—See AUDUBON, NJ (Comcast Cable)

WEST CONSHOHOCKEN—See EATONTOWN BOROUGH, PA (Comcast Cable)

WEST DEPTFORD TWP.—See AUDUBON, NJ (Comcast Cable)

WEST LONG BRANCH—See EATONTOWN BOROUGH, PA (Comcast Cable)

WEST NEW YORK—See HOBOKEN, NJ (Cablevision)

WEST NORRITON—See EATONTOWN BOROUGH, PA (Comcast Cable)

WEST ORANGE TWP.—Comcast Cable

WEST PATERSON—See OAKLAND, NJ (Cablevision)

WEST POTTSGROVE—See EATONTOWN BOROUGH, PA (Comcast Cable)

WEST ROCKHILL TWP.—See EATONTOWN BOROUGH, PA (Comcast Cable)

WEST TRENTON—See AUDUBON, NJ (Comcast Cable)

WEST WILDWOOD BOROUGH—See AUDUBON, NJ (Comcast Cable)

WEST WINDSOR TWP.—See EATONTOWN BOROUGH, NJ (Comcast Cable)

WESTAMPTON TWP.—See AUDUBON, NJ (Comcast Cable)

WESTFIELD (TOWN)—See WEST ORANGE TWP., NJ (Comcast Cable)

WESTVILLE—See AUDUBON, NJ (Comcast Cable)

WESTWOOD—See OAKLAND, NJ (Cablevision)

WEYMOUTH CITY—See AUDUBON, NJ (Comcast Cable)

WHARTON—See MORRIS TWP., NJ (Cablevision)

WHITE TWP.—See WEST ORANGE TWP., NJ (Comcast Cable)

WHITEMARSH TWP.—See EATONTOWN BOROUGH, PA (Comcast Cable)

WHITPAIN TWP.—See EATONTOWN BOROUGH, PA (Comcast Cable)

WILDWOOD CREST BOROUGH—See AUDUBON, NJ (Comcast Cable)

WILDWOOD—Comcast Cable. Now served by AUDUBON, NJ [NJ0003]

WILDWOOD—See AUDUBON, NJ (Comcast Cable)

WILLINGBORO—See AUDUBON, NJ (Comcast Cable)

WINFIELD TWP.—See WEST ORANGE TWP., NJ (Comcast Cable)

WINSLOW TWP.—See AUDUBON, NJ (Comcast Cable)

WOOD-RIDGE—See OAKLAND, NJ (Cablevision)

WOODBINE—See AUDUBON, NJ (Comcast Cable)

WOODBRIDGE TWP.—See WEST ORANGE TWP., NJ (Comcast Cable)

WOODBURY HEIGHTS—See AUDUBON, NJ (Comcast Cable)

WOODBURY—See AUDUBON, NJ (Comcast Cable)

WOODCLIFF LAKE—See BERGENFIELD, NJ (Cablevision)

WOODLAND TWP.—See AUDUBON, NJ (Comcast Cable)

WOODLYNNE—See AUDUBON, NJ (Comcast Cable)

WOODSTOWN BOROUGH—See AUDUBON, NJ (Comcast Cable)

WOOLWICH TWP.—See AUDUBON, NJ (Comcast Cable)

WORCESTER TWP. (MONTGOMERY COUNTY)—See EATONTOWN BOROUGH, PA (Comcast Cable)

WRIGHTSTOWN—See AUDUBON, NJ (Comcast Cable)

WRIGHTSTOWN—See EATONTOWN BOROUGH, PA (Comcast Cable)

WYCKOFF—See OAKLAND, NJ (Cablevision)

YARDLEY BOROUGH—See EATONTOWN BOROUGH, PA (Comcast Cable)

NEW MEXICO

ALAMOGORDO—Baja Broadband

ALBUQUERQUE—Formerly served by Multimedia Development Corp. No longer in operation

ALBUQUERQUE—Comcast Cable

ALTO—See RUIDOSO, NM (Baja Broadband)

ANGEL FIRE (UNINCORPORATED AREAS)—See ANGEL FIRE (village), NM (Comcast Cable)

ANGEL FIRE (VILLAGE)—Comcast Cable

ARTESIA—PVT

AZTEC—See ALBUQUERQUE, NM (Comcast Cable)

BAYARD—See ALBUQUERQUE, NM (Comcast Cable)

BELEN—See ALBUQUERQUE, NM (Comcast Cable)

BERNALILLO COUNTY (PORTIONS)—See ALBUQUERQUE, NM (Comcast Cable)

BERNALILLO—See ALBUQUERQUE, NM (Comcast Cable)

BLOOMFIELD—See ALBUQUERQUE, NM (Comcast Cable)

BLUEWATER—See GRANTS, NM (Comcast Cable)

BOLES ACRES—See ALAMOGORDO, NM (Baja Broadband)

BOSQUE FARMS—See ALBUQUERQUE, NM (Comcast Cable)

BRAZOS—Formerly served by US Cable of Coastal Texas LP. No longer in operation

CANNON AFB—See CLOVIS, NM (Suddenlink Communications)

CAPITAN—See RUIDOSO, NM (Baja Broadband)

CARLSBAD—Baja Broadband

CARRIZOZO—Baja Broadband

CERRO—See QUESTA, NM (Comcast Cable)

CHAMA—Satview Broadband

CHAPARRAL—Chaparral Cable Company

CHAVES COUNTY—See ROSWELL, NM (Cable One)

CIBOLA COUNTY (PORTIONS)—See GRANTS, NM (Comcast Cable)

CIMARRON—Comcast Cable

CLAYTON (town)—Formerly served by Baja Broadband. No longer in operation

CLOUDCROFT—PVT Cable Services. Now served by ARTESIA, NM [NM0016]

CLOUDCROFT—See ARTESIA, NM (PVT)

CLOVIS—Suddenlink Communications

CORRALES—See ALBUQUERQUE, NM (Comcast Cable)

CROWNPOINT—Formerly served by Crownpoint Cable TV Inc. No longer in operation

CUBA—Formerly served by Sun Valley Cable Inc. No longer in operation

DEMING—Comcast Cable

DEXTER—See ARTESIA, NM (PVT)

DIXON—Satview Broadband

DONA ANA COUNTY (PORTIONS)—See HATCH, NM (Comcast Cable)

DONA ANA—See ALBUQUERQUE, NM (Comcast Cable)

EDDY COUNTY (PORTIONS)—See ARTESIA, NM (PVT)

EDDY COUNTY (SOUTHERN PORTIONS)—See CARLSBAD, NM (Baja Broadband)

EDGEWOOD—See ALBUQUERQUE, NM (Comcast Cable)

EL PRADO—See TAOS, NM (Comcast Cable)

ELDORADO—See ALBUQUERQUE, NM (Comcast Cable)

ELEPHANT BUTTE—See TRUTH OR CONSEQUENCES, NM (Baja Broadband)

ELEPHANT BUTTE—PVT

ESPANOLA—Satview Broadband

ESTANCIA—Formerly served by Chamisa Futurevision. No longer in operation

EUNICE—Formerly served by US Cable of Coastal Texas LP. Now served by Baja Broadband, LEA COUNTY (southern portion), NM [NM0006]

EUNICE—See LEA COUNTY (southern portion), NM (Baja Broadband)

FARMINGTON—Comcast Cable. Now served by ALBUQUERQUE, NM [NM0001]

FARMINGTON—See ALBUQUERQUE, NM (Comcast Cable)

FARWELL—See CLOVIS, TX (Suddenlink Communications)

FORT SUMNER—Formerly served by Reach Broadband. No longer in operation

FOUR HILLS—Formerly served by JRC Telecommunications. No longer in operation

GALLUP—Comcast Cable

GAMERCO—See GALLUP, NM (Comcast Cable)

GRANT COUNTY (PORTIONS)—See ALBUQUERQUE, NM (Comcast Cable)

GRANTS—Comcast Cable

HAGERMAN—See ARTESIA, NM (PVT)

HATCH—Comcast Cable

HIGH ROLLS MOUNTAIN PARK—Formerly served by Baja Broadband. No longer in operation

HOBBS—See LEA COUNTY (southern portion), NM (Baja Broadband)

HOLLOMAN AFB—See ALAMOGORDO, NM (Baja Broadband)

HURLEY (TOWN)—See ALBUQUERQUE, NM (Comcast Cable)

ISLETA—See ALBUQUERQUE, NM (Comcast Cable)

JAL—Baja Broadband

New Mexico—Cable Community Index

KIRTLAND AFB—See ALBUQUERQUE, NM (Comcast Cable)

KIRTLAND—See ALBUQUERQUE, NM (Comcast Cable)

LA LUZ—See ALAMOGORDO, NM (Baja Broadband)

LA MESA—Formerly served by Windjammer Cable. No longer in operation

LAS CRUCES—Comcast Cable. Now served by ALBUQUERQUE, NM [NM0001]

LAS CRUCES—Formerly served by Santa Fe Wireless Cable TV. No longer in operation

LAS CRUCES—See ALBUQUERQUE, NM (Comcast Cable)

LAS VEGAS—Comcast Cable

LEA COUNTY (PORTIONS)—See LOVINGTON, NM (Baja Broadband)

LEA COUNTY (SOUTHERN PORTION)—Baja Broadband

LINCOLN—See RUIDOSO, NM (Baja Broadband)

LOGAN—Formerly served by Baja Broadband. No longer in operation

LORDSBURG—Formerly served by City TV Cable. No longer in operation

LOS ALAMOS—Comcast Cable

LOS LUNAS—Comcast Cable. Now served by ALBUQUERQUE, NM [NM0001]

LOS LUNAS—See ALBUQUERQUE, NM (Comcast Cable)

LOS OJOS—Formerly served by US Cable of Coastal Texas LP. No longer in operation

LOS RANCHOS DE ALBUQUERQUE—See ALBUQUERQUE, NM (Comcast Cable)

LOVING—See CARLSBAD, NM (Baja Broadband)

LOVINGTON—Baja Broadband

LUNA COUNTY (PORTIONS)—See DEMING, NM (Comcast Cable)

MAXWELL—Formerly served by Rocky Mountain Cable. No longer in operation

MELROSE—Formerly served by Rapid Cable. No longer in operation

MESILLA—See ALBUQUERQUE, NM (Comcast Cable)

MILAN—See GRANTS, NM (Comcast Cable)

MORA—Formerly served by Rocky Mountain Cable. No longer in operation

MORIARTY—See ALBUQUERQUE, NM (Comcast Cable)

MOUNTAINAIR—Formerly served by Chamisa Futurevision. No longer in operation

NAVAJO—Formerly served by Frontier Communications. No longer in operation

OTERO COUNTY (PORTIONS)—See ALAMOGORDO, NM (Baja Broadband)

PECOS—Comcast Cable

PENASCO—Satview Broadband

PERALTA—See ALBUQUERQUE, NM (Comcast Cable)

PICURIS—See PENASCO, NM (Satview Broadband)

PLACITAS—See ALBUQUERQUE, NM (Comcast Cable)

PLAYAS—Formerly served by Playas CATV. No longer in operation

POJOAQUE—Formerly served by Comcast Cable. No longer in operation

PORTALES—Comcast Cable

QUAY COUNTY (PORTIONS)—See TUCUMCARI, NM (Comcast Cable)

QUESTA—Comcast Cable

RAMAH—Formerly served by Navajo Communications. No longer in operation

RANCHOS DE TAOS—See TAOS, NM (Comcast Cable)

RATON—Comcast Cable

RED RIVER—Comcast Cable

RESERVE TWP.—Formerly served by Eagle West Communications Inc. No longer in operation

RIO ARRIBA COUNTY—See CHAMA, NM (Satview Broadband)

RIO ARRIBA—See ESPANOLA, NM (Satview Broadband)

RIO RANCHO—Cable One

ROOSEVELT COUNTY (PORTIONS)—See PORTALES, NM (Comcast Cable)

ROSWELL—Formerly served by Microwave Communication Services. No longer in operation

ROSWELL—Cable One

RUIDOSO DOWNS—See RUIDOSO, NM (Baja Broadband)

RUIDOSO—Baja Broadband

SAN ANTONIO—Formerly served by Sun Valley Cable Inc. No longer in operation

SAN JON—Formerly served by Elk River TV Cable Co. No longer in operation

SAN JUAN COUNTY (PORTIONS)—See ALBUQUERQUE, NM (Comcast Cable)

SAN JUAN PUEBLO—See ESPANOLA, NM (Satview Broadband)

SAN MIGUEL COUNTY (PORTIONS)—See LAS VEGAS, NM (Comcast Cable)

SAN MIGUEL COUNTY (PORTIONS)—See PECOS, NM (Comcast Cable)

SAN RAFAEL—See GRANTS, NM (Comcast Cable)

SANDOVAL COUNTY (PORTIONS)—See RIO RANCHO, NM (Cable One)

SANDOVAL COUNTY (PORTIONS)—See ALBUQUERQUE, NM (Comcast Cable)

SANTA BARBARA—Formerly served by JRC Telecommunications. No longer in operation

SANTA CLARA (VILLAGE)—See ALBUQUERQUE, NM (Comcast Cable)

SANTA CLARA INDIAN RESERVATION—Formerly served by Baja Broadband. Now served by Satview Broadband, ESPANOLA, NM [NM0014]

SANTA CLARA INDIAN RESERVATION—See ESPANOLA, NM (Satview Broadband)

SANTA FE COUNTY (PORTIONS)—See ALBUQUERQUE, NM (Comcast Cable)

SANTA FE—Comcast Cable. Now served by ALBUQUERQUE, NM [NM0001]

SANTA FE—Formerly served by Santa Fe Wireless Cable TV. No longer in operation

SANTA FE—See ALBUQUERQUE, NM (Comcast Cable)

SANTA FE—See ESPANOLA, NM (Satview Broadband)

SANTA ROSA—Reach Broadband

SHIPROCK—Formerly served by Frontier Communications. No longer in operation

SIERRA COUNTY (UNINCORPORATED AREAS)—See TRUTH OR CONSEQUENCES, NM (Baja Broadband)

SILVER CITY (UNINCORPORATED AREAS)—See ALBUQUERQUE, NM (Comcast Cable)

SILVER CITY—Comcast Cable. Now served by ALBUQUERQUE, NM [NM0001]

SILVER CITY—See ALBUQUERQUE, NM (Comcast Cable)

SOCORRO—Baja Broadband

SOUTH SANTA FE—See ALBUQUERQUE, NM (Comcast Cable)

SPRINGER—Comcast Cable

TAOS COUNTY (PORTIONS)—See RED RIVER, NM (Comcast Cable)

TAOS COUNTY (PORTIONS)—See TAOS, NM (Comcast Cable)

TAOS—Comcast Cable

TATUM—Formerly served by Rapid Cable. No longer in operation

TEUSQUE PUEBLO—See ALBUQUERQUE, NM (Comcast Cable)

TEUSQUE—See ALBUQUERQUE, NM (Comcast Cable)

TEXICO—See CLOVIS, NM (Suddenlink Communications)

THOREAU—Formerly served by Comcast Cable. No longer in operation

TIJERAS—See ALBUQUERQUE, NM (Comcast Cable)

TOHATCHI—Formerly served by Frontier Communications. No longer in operation

TRUTH OR CONSEQUENCES—Baja Broadband

TUCUMCARI—Comcast Cable

TULAROSA—See ALAMOGORDO, NM (Baja Broadband)

TWIN FORKS—PVT Cable Services. Now served by ARTESIA, NM [NM0016]

TWIN FORKS—See ARTESIA, NM (PVT)

TYRONE—See ALBUQUERQUE, NM (Comcast Cable)

VALENCIA COUNTY (PORTIONS)—See GRANTS, NM (Comcast Cable)

VAUGHN—Formerly served by Cebridge Connections. No longer in operation

WAGON MOUND—Formerly served by Rocky Mountain Cable. No longer in operation

WHITE ROCK—See LOS ALAMOS, NM (Comcast Cable)

WHITE SANDS—See ALBUQUERQUE, NM (Comcast Cable)

WILLIAMSBURG—See TRUTH OR CONSEQUENCES, NM (Baja Broadband)

YAH-TA-HEY—Formerly served by Frontier Communications. No longer in operation

ZUNI—Formerly served by Frontier Communications. No longer in operation

NEW YORK

ADAMS (town)—Formerly served by Time Warner Cable. No longer in operation

ADAMS (TOWN)—See DEWITT, NY (Time Warner Cable)

ADAMS (VILLAGE)—See DEWITT, NY (Time Warner Cable)

ADAMS CENTER—See DEWITT, NY (Time Warner Cable)

ADDISON (TOWN)—See DEWITT, NY (Time Warner Cable)

ADDISON (VILLAGE)—See DEWITT, NY (Time Warner Cable)

AFTON (TOWN)—See DEWITT, NY (Time Warner Cable)

AFTON (VILLAGE)—See DEWITT, NY (Time Warner Cable)

AFTON—Adams Cable Service

AIRMONT (VILLAGE)—See ROCKLAND, NY (Cablevision)

AKRON (VILLAGE)—See BUFFALO, NY (Time Warner Cable)

ALABAMA (TOWN)—See BUFFALO, NY (Time Warner Cable)

Cable Community Index—New York

ALBANY—Time Warner Cable

ALBION (town)—Time Warner Cable. Now served by BUFFALO (formerly Lackawanna), NY [NY0216]

ALBION (TOWN)—See BUFFALO, NY (Time Warner Cable)

ALBION (VILLAGE)—See BUFFALO, NY (Time Warner Cable)

ALBION CENTER (TOWN)—See DEWITT, NY (Time Warner Cable)

ALDEN (town)—Time Warner Cable. Now served by BUFFALO (formerly Lackawanna), NY [NY0216]

ALDEN (TOWN)—See BUFFALO, NY (Time Warner Cable)

ALDEN (VILLAGE)—See BUFFALO, NY (Time Warner Cable)

ALEXANDER (TOWN)—See BUFFALO, NY (Time Warner Cable)

ALEXANDER (VILLAGE)—See BUFFALO, NY (Time Warner Cable)

ALEXANDRIA (TOWN)—See DEWITT, NY (Time Warner Cable)

ALEXANDRIA BAY—Castle Cable TV

ALFRED (TOWN)—See DEWITT, NY (Time Warner Cable)

ALFRED (VILLAGE)—See DEWITT, NY (Time Warner Cable)

ALFRED—Formerly served by Alfred Cable System Inc. No longer in operation

ALLEGANY (TOWN)—See BUFFALO, NY (Time Warner Cable)

ALLEGANY (VILLAGE)—See BUFFALO, NY (Time Warner Cable)

ALMA (TOWN)—See DEWITT, NY (Time Warner Cable)

ALMOND (TOWN)—See DEWITT, NY (Time Warner Cable)

ALMOND (VILLAGE)—See DEWITT, NY (Time Warner Cable)

ALPLAUS—See ALBANY, NY (Time Warner Cable)

ALTAMONT (VILLAGE)—See ALBANY, NY (Time Warner Cable)

ALTMAR (VILLAGE)—See DEWITT, NY (Time Warner Cable)

ALTONA (TOWN)—See DEWITT, NY (Time Warner Cable)

AMBOY—See DEWITT, NY (Time Warner Cable)

AMENIA (TOWN)—See WAPPINGERS FALLS, NY (Cablevision)

AMES (VILLAGE)—See ALBANY, NY (Time Warner Cable)

AMHERST (TOWN)—See BUFFALO, NY (Time Warner Cable)

AMITY (TOWN)—See BUFFALO, NY (Time Warner Cable)

AMITYVILLE—Cablevision

AMSTERDAM (TOWN)—See ALBANY, NY (Time Warner Cable)

AMSTERDAM—Time Warner Cable. Now served by ALBANY, NY [NY0014]

AMSTERDAM—See ALBANY, NY (Time Warner Cable)

ANCRAM (TOWN)—See CHATHAM, NY (Charter Communications)

ANDES—MTC Cable. Now served by MARGARETVILLE, NY [NY0155]

ANDES—See MARGARETVILLE, NY (MTC Cable)

ANDES—See BETHEL (town), NY (Time Warner Cable)

ANDOVER (TOWN)—See BUFFALO, NY (Time Warner Cable)

ANDOVER (VILLAGE)—See BUFFALO, NY (Time Warner Cable)

ANGELICA (town)—Time Warner Cable. Now served by DEWITT, NY [NY0013]

ANGELICA (TOWN)—See DEWITT, NY (Time Warner Cable)

ANGELICA (VILLAGE)—See DEWITT, NY (Time Warner Cable)

ANGOLA—See BUFFALO, NY (Time Warner Cable)

ANNSVILLE (TOWN)—See DEWITT, NY (Time Warner Cable)

ANTWERP (TOWN)—See DEWITT, NY (Time Warner Cable)

ANTWERP (VILLAGE)—See DEWITT, NY (Time Warner Cable)

APULIA STATION—See DEWITT, NY (Time Warner Cable)

ARCADE (TOWN)—See BUFFALO, NY (Time Warner Cable)

ARCADE (VILLAGE)—See BUFFALO, NY (Time Warner Cable)

ARCADIA (TOWN)—See BUFFALO, NY (Time Warner Cable)

ARDSLEY—See MAMARONECK, NY (Cablevision)

ARGYLE (TOWN)—See ALBANY, NY (Time Warner Cable)

ARGYLE (VILLAGE)—See ALBANY, NY (Time Warner Cable)

ARGYLE—Time Warner Cable. Now served by ALBANY, NY [NY0014]

ARKPORT (VILLAGE)—See DEWITT, NY (Time Warner Cable)

ARKVILLE—See MARGARETVILLE, NY (MTC Cable)

ASHAROKEN—See AMITYVILLE, NY (Cablevision)

ASHLAND (TOWN) (GREENE COUNTY)—See WINDHAM, NY (Mid-Hudson Cablevision Inc.)

ASHLAND (TOWN)—See DEWITT, NY (Time Warner Cable)

ASTORIA—See NEW YORK CITY, NY (RCN. Formerly served by MANHATTAN, NY [NY0282]. This cable system has converted to IPTV)

ASTORIA—See MANHATTAN, NY (Time Warner Cable)

ATHENS (TOWN)—See CATSKILL, NY (Mid-Hudson Cablevision Inc.)

ATHENS (VILLAGE)—See CATSKILL, NY (Mid-Hudson Cablevision Inc.)

ATHENS BOROUGH—See DEWITT, PA (Time Warner Cable)

ATHENS TWP.—See DEWITT, PA (Time Warner Cable)

ATLANTIC BEACH—See AMITYVILLE, NY (Cablevision)

ATTICA (TOWN)—See BUFFALO, NY (Time Warner Cable)

ATTICA (VILLAGE)—See BUFFALO, NY (Time Warner Cable)

AU SABLE (TOWN)—See PLATTSBURGH, NY (Charter Communications)

AUBURN—Time Warner Cable. Now served by DEWITT, NY [NY0013]

AUBURN—See DEWITT, NY (Time Warner Cable)

AUGUSTA (town)—Formerly served by Chain Lakes Cablevision. Now served by Time Warner Cable, DEWITT, NY [NY0013]

AUGUSTA (TOWN)—See DEWITT, NY (Time Warner Cable)

AURELIUS (TOWN)—See BUFFALO, NY (Time Warner Cable)

AURORA (TOWN)—See BUFFALO, NY (Time Warner Cable)

AURORA (VILLAGE)—See BUFFALO, NY (Time Warner Cable)

AUSTERLITZ (TOWN)—See CHATHAM, NY (Charter Communications)

AVA (TOWN)—See DEWITT, NY (Time Warner Cable)

AVERILL PARK—See ALBANY, NY (Time Warner Cable)

AVOCA (town)—Time Warner Cable. Now served by DEWITT, NY [NY0013]

AVOCA (TOWN)—See DEWITT, NY (Time Warner Cable)

AVOCA (VILLAGE)—See DEWITT, NY (Time Warner Cable)

AVON (TOWN)—See BUFFALO, NY (Time Warner Cable)

AVON (VILLAGE)—See BUFFALO, NY (Time Warner Cable)

BABYLON (VILLAGE)—See AMITYVILLE, NY (Cablevision)

BABYLON—See AMITYVILLE, NY (Cablevision)

BAINBRIDGE (TOWN)—See DEWITT, NY (Time Warner Cable)

BAINBRIDGE (VILLAGE)—See DEWITT, NY (Time Warner Cable)

BAINBRIDGE—Time Warner Cable. Now served by DEWITT, NY [NY0013]

BALDWINSVILLE (VILLAGE)—See DEWITT, NY (Time Warner Cable)

BALDWINSVILLE—Time Warner Cable. Now served by DEWITT, NY [NY0013]

BALLSTON (TOWN)—See ALBANY, NY (Time Warner Cable)

BALLSTON LAKE—See ALBANY, NY (Time Warner Cable)

BALLSTON SPA (VILLAGE)—See ALBANY, NY (Time Warner Cable)

BANGOR (TOWN)—See DEWITT, NY (Time Warner Cable)

BARKER (TOWN)—See DEWITT, NY (Time Warner Cable)

BARKER (VILLAGE)—See BUFFALO, NY (Time Warner Cable)

BARNEVELD (VILLAGE)—See DEWITT, NY (Time Warner Cable)

BARRE (TOWN)—See BUFFALO, NY (Time Warner Cable)

BARRINGTON (TOWN)—See BUFFALO, NY (Time Warner Cable)

BARRYVILLE—See BETHEL (town), NY (Time Warner Cable)

BARTON (TOWN)—See SPENCER, NY (Haefele TV Inc)

BARTON (TOWN)—See DEWITT, NY (Time Warner Cable)

BATAVIA (TOWN)—See BUFFALO, NY (Time Warner Cable)

BATAVIA—Time Warner Cable. Now served by BUFFALO (formerly Lackawanna), NY [NY0216]

BATAVIA—See BUFFALO, NY (Time Warner Cable)

BATH (town)—Time Warner Cable. Now served by DEWITT, NY [NY0013]

BATH (TOWN)—See DEWITT, NY (Time Warner Cable)

BATH (VILLAGE)—See DEWITT, NY (Time Warner Cable)

BAXTER ESTATES—See AMITYVILLE, NY (Cablevision)

BAYSIDE—See MANHATTAN, NY (Time Warner Cable)

BAYVILLE—See AMITYVILLE, NY (Cablevision)

BEACON—See WAPPINGERS FALLS, NY (Cablevision)

BEDFORD HILLS—See OSSINING, NY (Cablevision)

BEDFORD—See YORKTOWN, NY (Cablevision)

BEECHHURST—See MANHATTAN, NY (Time Warner Cable)

BEEKMANTOWN—See PLATTSBURGH, NY (Charter Communications)

BELFAST (TOWN)—See DEWITT, NY (Time Warner Cable)

BELLE TERRE—See SUFFOLK COUNTY, NY (Cablevision)

New York—Cable Community Index

BELLEROSE (NASSAU COUNTY)—See AMITYVILLE, NY (Cablevision)

BELLEROSE (QUEENS COUNTY)—See MANHATTAN, NY (Time Warner Cable)

BELLEVILLE—See DEWITT, NY (Time Warner Cable)

BELLPORT—See BROOKHAVEN, NY (Cablevision)

BELMONT (VILLAGE)—See BUFFALO, NY (Time Warner Cable)

BEMUS POINT (VILLAGE)—See JAMESTOWN, NY (Time Warner Cable)

BENNINGTON (TOWN)—See BUFFALO, NY (Time Warner Cable)

BENTON (TOWN)—See BUFFALO, NY (Time Warner Cable)

BERGEN (TOWN)—See BUFFALO, NY (Time Warner Cable)

BERGEN (VILLAGE)—See BUFFALO, NY (Time Warner Cable)

BERKSHIRE (TOWN)—See BERKSHIRE, NY (Haefele TV Inc)

BERKSHIRE—Haefele TV Inc

BERLIN (town)—Charter Communications. Now served by CHATHAM, NY [NY0088]

BERLIN (TOWN)—See CHATHAM, NY (Charter Communications)

BERNE (TOWN)—See ALBANY, NY (Time Warner Cable)

BETHANY (TOWN)—See BUFFALO, NY (Time Warner Cable)

BETHEL (TOWN)—Time Warner Cable

BETHLEHEM (TOWN)—See CATSKILL, NY (Mid-Hudson Cablevision Inc.)

BETHLEHEM (TOWN)—See ALBANY, NY (Time Warner Cable)

BIG FLATS (TOWN)—See DEWITT, NY (Time Warner Cable)

BIG INDIAN—See BETHEL (town), NY (Time Warner Cable)

BINGHAMTON (TOWN)—See DEWITT, NY (Time Warner Cable)

BINGHAMTON—Time Warner Cable. Now served by DEWITT, NY [NY0013]

BINGHAMTON—See DEWITT, NY (Time Warner Cable)

BLACK BROOK (TOWN)—See PLATTSBURGH, NY (Charter Communications)

BLACK RIVER (VILLAGE)—See DEWITT, NY (Time Warner Cable)

BLASDELL (VILLAGE)—See BUFFALO, NY (Time Warner Cable)

BLEECKER (TOWN)—See ALBANY, NY (Time Warner Cable)

BLENHEIM—MidTel Cable TV

BLOOMFIELD (VILLAGE)—See BUFFALO, NY (Time Warner Cable)

BLOOMING GROVE (TOWN)—See BETHEL (town), NY (Time Warner Cable)

BLOOMING GROVE—See WAPPINGERS FALLS, NY (Cablevision)

BLOOMINGBURG (VILLAGE)—See BETHEL (town), NY (Time Warner Cable)

BLOOMINGDALE—See DEWITT, NY (Time Warner Cable)

BLOOMINGTON—See BETHEL (town), NY (Time Warner Cable)

BLOOMVILLE—DTC Cable

BOICEVILLE—See BETHEL (town), NY (Time Warner Cable)

BOLIVAR (town)—Time Warner Cable. Now served by DEWITT, NY [NY0013]

BOLIVAR (TOWN)—See DEWITT, NY (Time Warner Cable)

BOLIVAR (VILLAGE)—See DEWITT, NY (Time Warner Cable)

BOLTON (TOWN)—See ALBANY, NY (Time Warner Cable)

BOMBAY (TOWN)—See DEWITT, NY (Time Warner Cable)

BOONVILLE (TOWN)—See DEWITT, NY (Time Warner Cable)

BOONVILLE (VILLAGE)—See DEWITT, NY (Time Warner Cable)

BOSTON (TOWN)—See BUFFALO, NY (Time Warner Cable)

BOVINA (town)—DTC Cable. This cable system has converted to IPTV. See BOVINA (town), NY [NY5382]

BOVINA (TOWN)—DTC Cable. Formerly [NY0284]. This cable system has converted to IPTV

BRADFORD (TOWN)—See BURDETT, NY (Haefele TV Inc)

BRANCHPORT—See BUFFALO, NY (Time Warner Cable)

BRANT (TOWN)—See BUFFALO, NY (Time Warner Cable)

BRASHER (TOWN)—See DEWITT, NY (Time Warner Cable)

BRIARCLIFF MANOR—See OSSINING, NY (Cablevision)

BRIDGEWATER (TOWN)—See DEWITT, NY (Time Warner Cable)

BRIDGEWATER (VILLAGE)—See DEWITT, NY (Time Warner Cable)

BRIDGEWATER TWP.—See DEWITT, PA (Time Warner Cable)

BRIGHTON (TOWN)—See DEWITT, NY (Time Warner Cable)

BRIGHTON BEACH—See NEW YORK CITY, NY (RCN. Formerly served by MANHATTAN, NY [NY0282]. This cable system has converted to IPTV)

BRIGHTWATERS—See SUFFOLK COUNTY, NY (Cablevision)

BRISTOL (TOWN)—See BUFFALO, NY (Time Warner Cable)

BROADALBIN (TOWN)—See ALBANY, NY (Time Warner Cable)

BROADALBIN (VILLAGE)—See ALBANY, NY (Time Warner Cable)

BROCKPORT (VILLAGE)—See BUFFALO, NY (Time Warner Cable)

BROCTON (VILLAGE)—See JAMESTOWN, NY (Time Warner Cable)

BRONX—Cablevision

BRONXVILLE—See MAMARONECK, NY (Cablevision)

BROOKFIELD (TOWN)—See DEWITT, NY (Time Warner Cable)

BROOKHAVEN—Cablevision Systems Corp. Now served by BROOKHAVEN, NY [NY0290]

BROOKHAVEN—Cablevision

BROOKLYN HEIGHTS—See MANHATTAN, NY (Time Warner Cable)

BROOKLYN—Formerly served by Cellularvision of New York. No longer in operation

BROOKLYN—Cablevision

BROOKLYN—See NEW YORK CITY, NY (RCN. Formerly served by MANHATTAN, NY [NY0282]. This cable system has converted to IPTV)

BROOKLYN—See MANHATTAN, NY (Time Warner Cable)

BROOKVILLE (VILLAGE)—See AMITYVILLE, NY (Cablevision)

BROOME—See BLENHEIM, NY (MidTel Cable TV)

BROWNVILLE (TOWN)—See DEWITT, NY (Time Warner Cable)

BROWNVILLE (VILLAGE)—See DEWITT, NY (Time Warner Cable)

BRUNSWICK (TOWN)—See ALBANY, NY (Time Warner Cable)

BRUSHTON (VILLAGE)—See DEWITT, NY (Time Warner Cable)

BRUTUS (TOWN)—See DEWITT, NY (Time Warner Cable)

BUCHANAN—See OSSINING, NY (Cablevision)

BUFFALO—Time Warner Cable. Now served by BUFFALO, NY [NY0216]

BUFFALO—Time Warner Cable

BURDETT (VILLAGE)—See BURDETT, NY (Haefele TV Inc)

BURDETT—Haefele TV Inc

BURKE (TOWN)—See DEWITT, NY (Time Warner Cable)

BURKE (VILLAGE)—See DEWITT, NY (Time Warner Cable)

BURLINGTON (town)—Formerly served by Chain Lakes Cablevision. Now served by Time Warner Cable, DEWITT, NY [NY0013]

BURLINGTON (TOWN)—See DEWITT, NY (Time Warner Cable)

BURNS (TOWN)—See DEWITT, NY (Time Warner Cable)

BURNT HILLS—See ALBANY, NY (Time Warner Cable)

BUSTI (TOWN)—See JAMESTOWN, NY (Time Warner Cable)

BUTLER (TOWN)—See BUFFALO, NY (Time Warner Cable)

BUTTERNUTS (TOWN)—See DEWITT, NY (Time Warner Cable)

BYRON (TOWN)—See BUFFALO, NY (Time Warner Cable)

CADOSIA—See HANCOCK, NY (Hancock Video)

CAIRO (TOWN)—See CATSKILL, NY (Mid-Hudson Cablevision Inc.)

CAIRO—See BETHEL (town), NY (Time Warner Cable)

CALEDONIA (TOWN)—See BUFFALO, NY (Time Warner Cable)

CALEDONIA (VILLAGE)—See BUFFALO, NY (Time Warner Cable)

CALLICOON (TOWN)—See BETHEL (town), NY (Time Warner Cable)

CAMBRIA (TOWN)—See BUFFALO, NY (Time Warner Cable)

CAMBRIA HEIGHTS—See MANHATTAN, NY (Time Warner Cable)

CAMBRIDGE (TOWN)—See ALBANY, NY (Time Warner Cable)

CAMBRIDGE (VILLAGE)—See ALBANY, NY (Time Warner Cable)

CAMDEN (TOWN)—See DEWITT, NY (Time Warner Cable)

CAMDEN (VILLAGE)—See DEWITT, NY (Time Warner Cable)

CAMERON—See DEWITT, NY (Time Warner Cable)

CAMILLUS (TOWN)—See DEWITT, NY (Time Warner Cable)

CAMILLUS (VILLAGE)—See DEWITT, NY (Time Warner Cable)

CAMPBELL (TOWN)—See DEWITT, NY (Time Warner Cable)

CANAAN (TOWN)—See CHATHAM, NY (Charter Communications)

CANADICE (TOWN)—See BUFFALO, NY (Time Warner Cable)

CANAJOHARIE (TOWN)—See ALBANY, NY (Time Warner Cable)

CANAJOHARIE (village)—Time Warner Cable. Now served by ALBANY, NY [NY0014]

CANAJOHARIE (VILLAGE)—See ALBANY, NY (Time Warner Cable)

CANANDAIGUA (TOWN)—See BUFFALO, NY (Time Warner Cable)

CANANDAIGUA—See BUFFALO, NY (Time Warner Cable)

CANASERAGA (VILLAGE)—See DEWITT, NY (Time Warner Cable)

Cable Community Index—New York

CANASTOTA (VILLAGE)—See DEWITT, NY (Time Warner Cable)

CANDOR (PORTIONS)—See BERKSHIRE, NY (Haefele TV Inc)

CANDOR (PORTIONS)—See SPENCER, NY (Haefele TV Inc)

CANDOR (TOWN)—See DEWITT, NY (Time Warner Cable)

CANDOR (VILLAGE)—See DEWITT, NY (Time Warner Cable)

CANEADEA (TOWN)—See BUFFALO, NY (Time Warner Cable)

CANISTEO (TOWN)—See DEWITT, NY (Time Warner Cable)

CANISTEO (VILLAGE)—See DEWITT, NY (Time Warner Cable)

CANTON (TOWN)—See DEWITT, NY (Time Warner Cable)

CANTON (VILLAGE)—See DEWITT, NY (Time Warner Cable)

CAPE VINCENT (TOWN)—See DEWITT, NY (Time Warner Cable)

CAPE VINCENT (VILLAGE)—See DEWITT, NY (Time Warner Cable)

CARLTON (TOWN)—See BUFFALO, NY (Time Warner Cable)

CARMEL—Comcast Cable. Now served by NEW BRITAIN, CT [CT0037]

CAROGA (TOWN)—See ALBANY, NY (Time Warner Cable)

CAROLINE (TOWN)—See BERKSHIRE, NY (Haefele TV Inc)

CAROLINE (TOWN)—See DEWITT, NY (Time Warner Cable)

CARROLL (TOWN)—See JAMESTOWN, NY (Time Warner Cable)

CASSADAGA (VILLAGE)—See JAMESTOWN, NY (Time Warner Cable)

CASTILE (TOWN)—See BUFFALO, NY (Time Warner Cable)

CASTILE (VILLAGE)—See BUFFALO, NY (Time Warner Cable)

CASTLETON (VILLAGE)—See ALBANY, NY (Time Warner Cable)

CASTORLAND (VILLAGE)—See DEWITT, NY (Time Warner Cable)

CATHARINE (TOWN)—See ENFIELD, NY (Haefele TV Inc)

CATLIN (TOWN)—See DEWITT, NY (Time Warner Cable)

CATO (town)—Formerly served by Time Warner Cable. Now served by Time Warner Cable, DEWITT, NY [NY0013]

CATO (TOWN)—See DEWITT, NY (Time Warner Cable)

CATO (VILLAGE)—See DEWITT, NY (Time Warner Cable)

CATON (TOWN)—See DEWITT, NY (Time Warner Cable)

CATSKILL (TOWN)—See CATSKILL, NY (Mid-Hudson Cablevision Inc.)

CATSKILL (TOWN)—See BETHEL (town), NY (Time Warner Cable)

CATSKILL (VILLAGE)—See CATSKILL, NY (Mid-Hudson Cablevision Inc.)

CATSKILL—Mid-Hudson Cablevision Inc.

CATTARAUGUS (VILLAGE)—See BUFFALO, NY (Time Warner Cable)

CAYUGA (VILLAGE)—See BUFFALO, NY (Time Warner Cable)

CAYUGA HEIGHTS (VILLAGE)—See DEWITT, NY (Time Warner Cable)

CAYUTA (TOWN)—See SPENCER, NY (Haefele TV Inc)

CAZENOVIA (TOWN)—See DEWITT, NY (Time Warner Cable)

CAZENOVIA (VILLAGE)—See DEWITT, NY (Time Warner Cable)

CEDARHURST—See AMITYVILLE, NY (Cablevision)

CELORON (VILLAGE)—See JAMESTOWN, NY (Time Warner Cable)

CENTRAL SQUARE (village)—Time Warner Cable. Now served by DEWITT, NY [NY0013]

CENTRAL SQUARE (VILLAGE)—See DEWITT, NY (Time Warner Cable)

CENTRE ISLAND—See AMITYVILLE, NY (Cablevision)

CERES TWP.—See BUFFALO, PA (Time Warner Cable)

CERES TWP.—See DEWITT, PA (Time Warner Cable)

CHAFFEE (TOWN)—See BUFFALO, NY (Time Warner Cable)

CHAMPION (TOWN)—See DEWITT, NY (Time Warner Cable)

CHAMPLAIN (town)—Time Warner Cable. Now served by DEWITT, NY [NY0013]

CHAMPLAIN (TOWN)—See DEWITT, NY (Time Warner Cable)

CHAMPLAIN (VILLAGE)—See DEWITT, NY (Time Warner Cable)

CHARLTON (TOWN)—See ALBANY, NY (Time Warner Cable)

CHATEAUGAY (TOWN)—See DEWITT, NY (Time Warner Cable)

CHATEAUGAY (VILLAGE)—See DEWITT, NY (Time Warner Cable)

CHATHAM—Charter Communications

CHAUMONT (VILLAGE)—See DEWITT, NY (Time Warner Cable)

CHAUTAUQUA (TOWN)—See BUFFALO, NY (Time Warner Cable)

CHAZY (TOWN)—See DEWITT, NY (Time Warner Cable)

CHEEKTOWAGA (TOWN)—See BUFFALO, NY (Time Warner Cable)

CHEMUNG (TOWN)—See DEWITT, NY (Time Warner Cable)

CHENANGO (TOWN)—See DEWITT, NY (Time Warner Cable)

CHERRY CREEK (VILLAGE)—See JAMESTOWN, NY (Time Warner Cable)

CHERRY VALLEY (TOWN)—See ALBANY, NY (Time Warner Cable)

CHERRY VALLEY (VILLAGE)—See ALBANY, NY (Time Warner Cable)

CHESTER (TOWN) (ORANGE COUNTY)—See WARWICK, NY (Cablevision)

CHESTER (TOWN)—See ALBANY, NY (Time Warner Cable)

CHESTER (VILLAGE)—See WARWICK, NY (Cablevision)

CHESTER (VILLAGE)—See BETHEL (town), NY (Time Warner Cable)

CHESTERFIELD (TOWN)—See PLATTSBURGH, NY (Charter Communications)

CHESTNUT RIDGE—See ROCKLAND, NY (Cablevision)

CHICHESTER—See BETHEL (town), NY (Time Warner Cable)

CHILI (TOWN)—See BUFFALO, NY (Time Warner Cable)

CHITTENANGO (VILLAGE)—See DEWITT, NY (Time Warner Cable)

CHOCONUT TWP.—See DEWITT, PA (Time Warner Cable)

CHURCHVILLE (VILLAGE)—See BUFFALO, NY (Time Warner Cable)

CICERO (TOWN)—See DEWITT, NY (Time Warner Cable)

CINCINNATUS (TOWN)—See DEWITT, NY (Time Warner Cable)

CINCINNATUS—Formerly served by Chain Lakes Cablevision. Now served by Time Warner Cable, DEWITT, NY [NY0013]

CLARENCE (TOWN)—See BUFFALO, NY (Time Warner Cable)

CLARENDON (TOWN)—See BUFFALO, NY (Time Warner Cable)

CLARKSON (TOWN)—See BUFFALO, NY (Time Warner Cable)

CLARKSTOWN—See ROCKLAND, NY (Cablevision)

CLARKSVILLE (TOWN)—See DEWITT, NY (Time Warner Cable)

CLAVERACK—See CATSKILL, NY (Mid-Hudson Cablevision Inc.)

CLAY (TOWN)—See DEWITT, NY (Time Warner Cable)

CLAYTON (TOWN)—See DEWITT, NY (Time Warner Cable)

CLAYTON (VILLAGE)—See DEWITT, NY (Time Warner Cable)

CLAYVILLE (VILLAGE)—See DEWITT, NY (Time Warner Cable)

CLERMONT—See GERMANTOWN, NY (GTel. This cable system has converted to IPTV)

CLEVELAND (VILLAGE)—See DEWITT, NY (Time Warner Cable)

CLIFTON PARK (TOWN)—See ALBANY, NY (Time Warner Cable)

CLIFTON SPRINGS (VILLAGE)—See BUFFALO, NY (Time Warner Cable)

CLINTON (TOWN)—See WAPPINGERS FALLS, NY (Cablevision)

CLINTON (VILLAGE)—See DEWITT, NY (Time Warner Cable)

CLINTON COUNTY (PORTIONS)—See PLATTSBURGH, NY (Charter Communications)

CLYDE (VILLAGE)—See BUFFALO, NY (Time Warner Cable)

CLYMER (town)—Time Warner Cable. Now served by JAMESTOWN, NY [NY0030]

CLYMER (TOWN)—See JAMESTOWN, NY (Time Warner Cable)

COBLESKILL (town)—Time Warner Cable. Now served by ALBANY, NY [NY0014]

COBLESKILL (TOWN)—See ALBANY, NY (Time Warner Cable)

COBLESKILL (VILLAGE)—See ALBANY, NY (Time Warner Cable)

COCHECTON—See BETHEL (town), NY (Time Warner Cable)

COEYMANS (TOWN)—See ALBANY, NY (Time Warner Cable)

COEYMANS—See CATSKILL, NY (Mid-Hudson Cablevision Inc.)

COHOCTON (town)—Time Warner Cable. Now served by DEWITT, NY [NY0013]

COHOCTON (TOWN)—See DEWITT, NY (Time Warner Cable)

COHOCTON (VILLAGE)—See DEWITT, NY (Time Warner Cable)

COHOES—See ALBANY, NY (Time Warner Cable)

COLCHESTER TWP.—See BETHEL (town), NY (Time Warner Cable)

COLCHESTER—See MARGARETVILLE, NY (MTC Cable)

COLD BROOK (VILLAGE)—See DEWITT, NY (Time Warner Cable)

COLD SPRING—See WAPPINGERS FALLS, NY (Cablevision)

COLDEN—See BUFFALO, NY (Time Warner Cable)

COLDSPRING (TOWN)—See BUFFALO, NY (Time Warner Cable)

COLESVILLE—See AFTON, NY (Adams Cable Service)

COLLEGE POINT—See MANHATTAN, NY (Time Warner Cable)

COLLINS (TOWN)—See BUFFALO, NY (Time Warner Cable)

COLONIE (TOWN)—See ALBANY, NY (Time Warner Cable)

New York—Cable Community Index

COLONIE (VILLAGE)—See ALBANY, NY (Time Warner Cable)

COLTON (TOWN)—See DEWITT, NY (Time Warner Cable)

COLUMBIA (TOWN)—See DEWITT, NY (Time Warner Cable)

COLUMBIAVILLE—See CATSKILL, NY (Mid-Hudson Cablevision Inc.)

COLUMBUS (TOWN)—See DEWITT, NY (Time Warner Cable)

CONCORD (TOWN)—See BUFFALO, NY (Time Warner Cable)

CONESUS (TOWN)—See BUFFALO, NY (Time Warner Cable)

CONESVILLE—See MARGARETVILLE, NY (MTC Cable)

CONEWANGO (TOWN)—See BUFFALO, NY (Time Warner Cable)

CONKLIN (TOWN)—See DEWITT, NY (Time Warner Cable)

CONSTABLE (TOWN)—See DEWITT, NY (Time Warner Cable)

CONSTABLEVILLE (VILLAGE)—See DEWITT, NY (Time Warner Cable)

CONSTANTIA (town)—Time Warner Cable. Now served by DEWITT, NY [NY0013]

CONSTANTIA (TOWN)—See DEWITT, NY (Time Warner Cable)

COOPERSTOWN (village)—Time Warner Cable. Now served by DEWITT, NY [NY0013]

COOPERSTOWN (VILLAGE)—See DEWITT, NY (Time Warner Cable)

COPAKE (TOWN)—See CHATHAM, NY (Charter Communications)

COPENHAGEN (VILLAGE)—See DEWITT, NY (Time Warner Cable)

CORFU (VILLAGE)—See BUFFALO, NY (Time Warner Cable)

CORINTH (TOWN)—See ALBANY, NY (Time Warner Cable)

CORINTH (VILLAGE)—See ALBANY, NY (Time Warner Cable)

CORNING (TOWN)—See DEWITT, NY (Time Warner Cable)

CORNING—See DEWITT, NY (Time Warner Cable)

CORNWALL (TOWN)—See BETHEL (town), NY (Time Warner Cable)

CORNWALL-ON-HUDSON (VILLAGE)—See BETHEL (town), NY (Time Warner Cable)

CORONA—See NEW YORK CITY, NY (RCN. Formerly served by MANHATTAN, NY [NY0282]. This cable system has converted to IPTV)

CORONA—See MANHATTAN, NY (Time Warner Cable)

CORTLAND—Time Warner Cable. Now served by DEWITT, NY [NY0013]

CORTLAND—See DEWITT, NY (Time Warner Cable)

CORTLANDT—See OSSINING, NY (Cablevision)

CORTLANDVILLE (TOWN)—See DEWITT, NY (Time Warner Cable)

COTTEKILL—See BETHEL (town), NY (Time Warner Cable)

COVE NECK—See AMITYVILLE, NY (Cablevision)

COVENTRY (TOWN)—See DEWITT, NY (Time Warner Cable)

COVERT (TOWN)—See BUFFALO, NY (Time Warner Cable)

COVERT (TOWN)—See DEWITT, NY (Time Warner Cable)

COVINGTON (TOWN)—See BUFFALO, NY (Time Warner Cable)

COXSACKIE (TOWN)—See CATSKILL, NY (Mid-Hudson Cablevision Inc.)

COXSACKIE (VILLAGE)—See CATSKILL, NY (Mid-Hudson Cablevision Inc.)

CRAWFORD (TOWN)—See BETHEL (town), NY (Time Warner Cable)

CROGHAN (TOWN)—See DEWITT, NY (Time Warner Cable)

CROGHAN (VILLAGE)—See DEWITT, NY (Time Warner Cable)

CROTON-ON-HUDSON—See OSSINING, NY (Cablevision)

CROWN POINT (TOWN)—See ALBANY, NY (Time Warner Cable)

CUBA (TOWN)—See BUFFALO, NY (Time Warner Cable)

CUBA (VILLAGE)—See BUFFALO, NY (Time Warner Cable)

CUYLER (TOWN)—See DEWITT, NY (Time Warner Cable)

CUYLER—Formerly served by Chain Lakes Cablevision. Now served by Time Warner Cable, DEWITT, NY [NY0013]

DANBY (TOWN)—See DEWITT, NY (Time Warner Cable)

DANNEMORA (VILLAGE)—See PLATTSBURGH, NY (Charter Communications)

DANSVILLE (town)—Time Warner Cable. Now served by DEWITT, NY [NY0013]

DANSVILLE (TOWN)—See DEWITT, NY (Time Warner Cable)

DANSVILLE (VILLAGE)—See DEWITT, NY (Time Warner Cable)

DANUBE (TOWN)—See DEWITT, NY (Time Warner Cable)

DARIEN (TOWN)—See BUFFALO, NY (Time Warner Cable)

DAVENPORT (TOWN)—See DEWITT, NY (Time Warner Cable)

DAY (TOWN)—See ALBANY, NY (Time Warner Cable)

DE KALB (TOWN)—See DEWITT, NY (Time Warner Cable)

DE RUYTER—Formerly served by Chain Lakes Cablevision. No longer in operation

DEANSBORO—See DEWITT, NY (Time Warner Cable)

DECATUR (TOWN)—See DEWITT, NY (Time Warner Cable)

DEERFIELD TWP.—See DEWITT, PA (Time Warner Cable)

DEERFIELD—See DEWITT, NY (Time Warner Cable)

DEERPARK (TOWN)—See BETHEL (town), NY (Time Warner Cable)

DEFERIET (VILLAGE)—See DEWITT, NY (Time Warner Cable)

DEFREESTVILLE—See ALBANY, NY (Time Warner Cable)

DELANCEY—See HAMDEN, NY (DTC Cable. Formerly [NY0223]. This cable system has converted to IPTV)

DELANSON (VILLAGE)—See ALBANY, NY (Time Warner Cable)

DELAWARE (TOWN)—See BETHEL (town), NY (Time Warner Cable)

DELEVAN (VILLAGE)—See BUFFALO, NY (Time Warner Cable)

DELHI (town)—DTC Cable. This cable system has converted to IPTV. Now served by DELHI (village), NY [NY5141]

DELHI (town)—Time Warner Cable. Now served by DEWITT, NY [NY0013]

DELHI (TOWN)—See DELHI (village), NY (DTC Cable. Formerly [NY0140]. This cable system has converted to IPTV)

DELHI (TOWN)—See DEWITT, NY (Time Warner Cable)

DELHI (VILLAGE)—DTC Cable. Formerly [NY0140]. This cable system has converted to IPTV

DELHI (VILLAGE)—See DEWITT, NY (Time Warner Cable)

DELMAR—See ALBANY, NY (Time Warner Cable)

DENMARK (TOWN)—See DEWITT, NY (Time Warner Cable)

DENNING—See BETHEL (town), NY (Time Warner Cable)

DENVER—See BETHEL (town), NY (Time Warner Cable)

DEPEW—See BUFFALO, NY (Time Warner Cable)

DEPOSIT—Adams Cable Service. Now served by AFTON, NY [NY0100]

DEPOSIT—See AFTON, NY (Adams Cable Service)

DERING HARBOR—See RIVERHEAD, NY (Cablevision)

DERUYTER (TOWN)—See DEWITT, NY (Time Warner Cable)

DERUYTER (VILLAGE)—See DEWITT, NY (Time Warner Cable)

DEWITT—Time Warner Cable

DEXTER (VILLAGE)—See DEWITT, NY (Time Warner Cable)

DIANA (TOWN)—See DEWITT, NY (Time Warner Cable)

DICKINSON (TOWN)—See DEWITT, NY (Time Warner Cable)

DIMOCK TWP.—See DEWITT, PA (Time Warner Cable)

DIX—See DEWITT, NY (Time Warner Cable)

DOBBS FERRY—See MAMARONECK, NY (Cablevision)

DOLGEVILLE (VILLAGE)—See DEWITT, NY (Time Warner Cable)

DOUGLASTON—See MANHATTAN, NY (Time Warner Cable)

DOVER (TOWN)—See WAPPINGERS FALLS, NY (Cablevision)

DOVER PLAINS—Cablevision

DOWNSVILLE—Formerly served by Downsville Community Antenna. No longer in operation

DOWNSVILLE—See MARGARETVILLE, NY (MTC Cable)

DRESDEN (village)—Time Warner Cable. Now served by BUFFALO (formerly Lackawanna), NY [NY0216]

DRESDEN (VILLAGE)—See BUFFALO, NY (Time Warner Cable)

DRYDEN (TOWN)—See DEWITT, NY (Time Warner Cable)

DRYDEN (VILLAGE)—See DEWITT, NY (Time Warner Cable)

DUANESBURG—See ALBANY, NY (Time Warner Cable)

DUNDEE (village)—Time Warner Cable. Now served by DEWITT, NY [NY0013]

DUNDEE (VILLAGE)—See DEWITT, NY (Time Warner Cable)

DUNKIRK (TOWN)—See BUFFALO, NY (Time Warner Cable)

DUNKIRK—Time Warner Cable. Now served by BUFFALO (formerly Lackawanna), NY [NY0216]

DUNKIRK—See BUFFALO, NY (Time Warner Cable)

DURHAM—See WINDHAM, NY (Mid-Hudson Cablevision Inc.)

EAGLE (TOWN)—See BUFFALO, NY (Time Warner Cable)

EAGLE BAY—See DEWITT, NY (Time Warner Cable)

EARLVILLE (VILLAGE)—See DEWITT, NY (Time Warner Cable)

EAST AURORA (VILLAGE)—See BUFFALO, NY (Time Warner Cable)

EAST BLOOMFIELD (TOWN)—See BUFFALO, NY (Time Warner Cable)

Cable Community Index—New York

EAST BRANCH—See HANCOCK, NY (Hancock Video)

EAST CARTHAGE (VILLAGE)—See DEWITT, NY (Time Warner Cable)

EAST CONCORD TWP.—See BUFFALO, NY (Time Warner Cable)

EAST ELMHURST—See NEW YORK CITY, NY (RCN. Formerly served by MANHATTAN, NY [NY0282]. This cable system has converted to IPTV)

EAST ELMHURST—See MANHATTAN, NY (Time Warner Cable)

EAST FISHKILL—See WAPPINGERS FALLS, NY (Cablevision)

EAST GREENBUSH (TOWN)—See ALBANY, NY (Time Warner Cable)

EAST HAMPTON—Formerly served by Cablevision Systems Corp. Now served by Optimum, RIVERHEAD, NY [NY0024]

EAST HAMPTON—See RIVERHEAD, NY (Cablevision)

EAST HILLS—See AMITYVILLE, NY (Cablevision)

EAST RANDOLPH (VILLAGE)—See BUFFALO, NY (Time Warner Cable)

EAST ROCHESTER (VILLAGE)—See BUFFALO, NY (Time Warner Cable)

EAST ROCKAWAY—See AMITYVILLE, NY (Cablevision)

EAST SYRACUSE (VILLAGE)—See DEWITT, NY (Time Warner Cable)

EAST WILLISTON—See AMITYVILLE, NY (Cablevision)

EASTCHESTER—See MAMARONECK, NY (Cablevision)

EASTON (TOWN)—See ALBANY, NY (Time Warner Cable)

EATON (TOWN)—See DEWITT, NY (Time Warner Cable)

EDEN (TOWN)—See BUFFALO, NY (Time Warner Cable)

EDINBURG (town)—Formerly served by Adelphia Communications. Now served by Time Warner Cable, ALBANY, NY [NY0014]

EDINBURG (TOWN)—See ALBANY, NY (Time Warner Cable)

EDMESTON (TOWN)—See DEWITT, NY (Time Warner Cable)

ELBA (TOWN)—See BUFFALO, NY (Time Warner Cable)

ELBA (VILLAGE)—See BUFFALO, NY (Time Warner Cable)

ELBRIDGE (TOWN)—See DEWITT, NY (Time Warner Cable)

ELBRIDGE (VILLAGE)—See DEWITT, NY (Time Warner Cable)

ELDRED BOROUGH—See BUFFALO, PA (Time Warner Cable)

ELDRED TWP.—See BUFFALO, PA (Time Warner Cable)

ELDRED—See BETHEL (town), NY (Time Warner Cable)

ELIZABETHTOWN—See PLATTSBURGH, NY (Charter Communications)

ELKLAND—See DEWITT, PA (Time Warner Cable)

ELLENBURG (TOWN)—See DEWITT, NY (Time Warner Cable)

ELLENVILLE (town)—Time Warner Cable. Now served by BETHEL (town), NY [NY0231]

ELLENVILLE (TOWN)—See BETHEL (town), NY (Time Warner Cable)

ELLERY (TOWN)—See JAMESTOWN, NY (Time Warner Cable)

ELLICOTT (TOWN)—See JAMESTOWN, NY (Time Warner Cable)

ELLICOTTVILLE (TOWN)—See BUFFALO, NY (Time Warner Cable)

ELLICOTTVILLE (VILLAGE)—See BUFFALO, NY (Time Warner Cable)

ELLINGTON (TOWN)—See JAMESTOWN, NY (Time Warner Cable)

ELLISBURG (TOWN)—See DEWITT, NY (Time Warner Cable)

ELLISBURG (VILLAGE)—See DEWITT, NY (Time Warner Cable)

ELMA (TOWN)—See BUFFALO, NY (Time Warner Cable)

ELMHURST—See NEW YORK CITY, NY (RCN. Formerly served by MANHATTAN, NY [NY0282]. This cable system has converted to IPTV)

ELMIRA (TOWN)—See DEWITT, NY (Time Warner Cable)

ELMIRA HEIGHTS (VILLAGE)—See DEWITT, NY (Time Warner Cable)

ELMIRA/CORNING—Time Warner Cable. Now served by DEWITT, NY [NY0013]

ELMIRA—Time Warner Cable. Now served by DEWITT, NY [NY0013]

ELMIRA—See DEWITT, NY (Time Warner Cable)

ELMSFORD—See MAMARONECK, NY (Cablevision)

ENDICOTT (VILLAGE)—See DEWITT, NY (Time Warner Cable)

ENFIELD (TOWN)—See ENFIELD, NY (Haefele TV Inc)

ENFIELD—Haefele TV Inc

ERIN (TOWN)—See DEWITT, NY (Time Warner Cable)

ERWIN (TOWN)—See DEWITT, NY (Time Warner Cable)

ESOPUS (TOWN)—See BETHEL (town), NY (Time Warner Cable)

ESOPUS—See WAPPINGERS FALLS, NY (Cablevision)

ESPERANCE (TOWN)—See ALBANY, NY (Time Warner Cable)

ESPERANCE (VILLAGE)—See ALBANY, NY (Time Warner Cable)

ESSEX—See WILLSBORO (town), NY (Cable Communications of Willsboro)

ESSEX—See PLATTSBURGH, NY (Charter Communications)

EVANS (TOWN)—See BUFFALO, NY (Time Warner Cable)

EVANS MILLS (VILLAGE)—See DEWITT, NY (Time Warner Cable)

EXETER (TOWN)—See DEWITT, NY (Time Warner Cable)

FABIUS (TOWN)—See DEWITT, NY (Time Warner Cable)

FABIUS (VILLAGE)—See DEWITT, NY (Time Warner Cable)

FAIR HAVEN (VILLAGE)—See DEWITT, NY (Time Warner Cable)

FAIRFIELD (TOWN)—See DEWITT, NY (Time Warner Cable)

FAIRPORT (VILLAGE)—See BUFFALO, NY (Time Warner Cable)

FALCONER (VILLAGE)—See JAMESTOWN, NY (Time Warner Cable)

FALLSBURG (TOWN)—See BETHEL (town), NY (Time Warner Cable)

FARMINGDALE—See AMITYVILLE, NY (Cablevision)

FARMINGTON (TOWN)—See BUFFALO, NY (Time Warner Cable)

FARNHAM (VILLAGE)—See BUFFALO, NY (Time Warner Cable)

FAYETTE (TOWN)—See BUFFALO, NY (Time Warner Cable)

FAYETTEVILLE (VILLAGE)—See DEWITT, NY (Time Warner Cable)

FENNER (TOWN)—See DEWITT, NY (Time Warner Cable)

FENTON (TOWN)—See DEWITT, NY (Time Warner Cable)

FILLMORE—See BUFFALO, NY (Time Warner Cable)

FISHKILL (VILLAGE)—See WAPPINGERS FALLS, NY (Cablevision)

FISHS EDDY—See HANCOCK, NY (Hancock Video)

FLEISCHMANNS—See MARGARETVILLE, NY (MTC Cable)

FLEISCHMANNS—See BETHEL (town), NY (Time Warner Cable)

FLEMING (TOWN)—See DEWITT, NY (Time Warner Cable)

FLORAL PARK—See AMITYVILLE, NY (Cablevision)

FLORAL PARK—See MANHATTAN, NY (Time Warner Cable)

FLORIDA (TOWN)—See ALBANY, NY (Time Warner Cable)

FLORIDA (VILLAGE)—See WARWICK, NY (Cablevision)

FLOWER HILL—See AMITYVILLE, NY (Cablevision)

FLOYD (TOWN)—See DEWITT, NY (Time Warner Cable)

FLUSHING—See NEW YORK CITY, NY (RCN. Formerly served by MANHATTAN, NY [NY0282]. This cable system has converted to IPTV)

FLUSHING—See MANHATTAN, NY (Time Warner Cable)

FONDA (VILLAGE)—See ALBANY, NY (Time Warner Cable)

FOREST HILLS—See NEW YORK CITY, NY (RCN. Formerly served by MANHATTAN, NY [NY0282]. This cable system has converted to IPTV)

FOREST HILLS—See MANHATTAN, NY (Time Warner Cable)

FORESTBURGH (TOWN)—See BETHEL (town), NY (Time Warner Cable)

FORESTPORT (town)—Time Warner Cable. Now served by DEWITT, NY [NY0013]

FORESTPORT (TOWN)—See DEWITT, NY (Time Warner Cable)

FORESTVILLE (VILLAGE)—See BUFFALO, NY (Time Warner Cable)

FORT ANN (TOWN)—See ALBANY, NY (Time Warner Cable)

FORT ANN (VILLAGE)—See ALBANY, NY (Time Warner Cable)

FORT COVINGTON (TOWN)—See DEWITT, NY (Time Warner Cable)

FORT DRUM—See DEWITT, NY (Time Warner Cable)

FORT EDWARD (TOWN)—See ALBANY, NY (Time Warner Cable)

FORT EDWARD (VILLAGE)—See ALBANY, NY (Time Warner Cable)

FORT JOHNSON (VILLAGE)—See ALBANY, NY (Time Warner Cable)

FORT PLAIN (VILLAGE)—See ALBANY, NY (Time Warner Cable)

FOWLER (TOWN)—See DEWITT, NY (Time Warner Cable)

FRANKFORT (TOWN)—See DEWITT, NY (Time Warner Cable)

FRANKFORT (VILLAGE)—See DEWITT, NY (Time Warner Cable)

FRANKLIN (TOWN)—See DEWITT, NY (Time Warner Cable)

FRANKLIN (VILLAGE)—See DEWITT, NY (Time Warner Cable)

FRANKLIN TWP.—See DEWITT, PA (Time Warner Cable)

FRANKLINVILLE (TOWN)—See BUFFALO, NY (Time Warner Cable)

FRANKLINVILLE (VILLAGE)—See BUFFALO, NY (Time Warner Cable)

FRASER—See DELHI (village), NY (DTC Cable. Formerly [NY0140]. This cable system has converted to IPTV)

New York—Cable Community Index

FREDONIA (village)—Time Warner Cable. Now served by JAMESTOWN, NY [NY0030]

FREDONIA (VILLAGE)—See JAMESTOWN, NY (Time Warner Cable)

FREEDOM (TOWN)—See BUFFALO, NY (Time Warner Cable)

FREEPORT—See AMITYVILLE, NY (Cablevision)

FREEVILLE (VILLAGE)—See DEWITT, NY (Time Warner Cable)

FREMONT (TOWN) (STEUBEN COUNTY)—See DEWITT, NY (Time Warner Cable)

FREMONT (TOWN) (SULLIVAN COUNTY)—See BETHEL (town), NY (Time Warner Cable)

FRENCH CREEK (TOWN)—See JAMESTOWN, NY (Time Warner Cable)

FRESH MEADOWS—See NEW YORK CITY, NY (RCN. Formerly served by MANHATTAN, NY [NY0282]. This cable system has converted to IPTV.

FRESH MEADOWS—See MANHATTAN, NY (Time Warner Cable)

FRIENDSHIP (town)—Time Warner Cable. Now served by DEWITT, NY [NY0013]

FRIENDSHIP (TOWN)—See DEWITT, NY (Time Warner Cable)

FULTON (TOWN)—See ALBANY, NY (Time Warner Cable)

FULTON—Time Warner Cable. Now served by DEWITT, NY [NY0013]

FULTON—See BLENHEIM, NY (MidTel Cable TV)

FULTON—See DEWITT, NY (Time Warner Cable)

FULTONVILLE (VILLAGE)—See ALBANY, NY (Time Warner Cable)

GAINES (TOWN)—See BUFFALO, NY (Time Warner Cable)

GAINESVILLE (TOWN)—See BUFFALO, NY (Time Warner Cable)

GAINESVILLE (VILLAGE)—See BUFFALO, NY (Time Warner Cable)

GALEN (TOWN)—See BUFFALO, NY (Time Warner Cable)

GALLATIN—See CATSKILL, NY (Mid-Hudson Cablevision Inc.)

GALWAY (TOWN)—See ALBANY, NY (Time Warner Cable)

GALWAY (VILLAGE)—See ALBANY, NY (Time Warner Cable)

GARDEN CITY—See AMITYVILLE, NY (Cablevision)

GARDINER (TOWN)—See BETHEL (town), NY (Time Warner Cable)

GARRATTSVILLE—See DEWITT, NY (Time Warner Cable)

GATES (TOWN)—See BUFFALO, NY (Time Warner Cable)

GEDDES (TOWN)—See DEWITT, NY (Time Warner Cable)

GENESEE (TOWN)—See DEWITT, NY (Time Warner Cable)

GENESEE FALLS (TOWN)—See BUFFALO, NY (Time Warner Cable)

GENESEO (TOWN)—See BUFFALO, NY (Time Warner Cable)

GENESEO (VILLAGE)—See BUFFALO, NY (Time Warner Cable)

GENEVA (TOWN)—See BUFFALO, NY (Time Warner Cable)

GENEVA—Time Warner Cable. Now served by BUFFALO (formerly Lackawanna), NY [NY0216]

GENEVA—See BUFFALO, NY (Time Warner Cable)

GENOA TWP.—See MORAVIA, NY (Southern Cayuga County Cablevision)

GEORGETOWN (TOWN)—See DEWITT, NY (Time Warner Cable)

GERMAN FLATTS (TOWN)—See DEWITT, NY (Time Warner Cable)

GERMANTOWN—GTel. This cable system has converted to IPTV. See GERMANTOWN, NY [NY5178]

GERMANTOWN—GTel. This cable system has converted to IPTV

GERRY (TOWN)—See JAMESTOWN, NY (Time Warner Cable)

GHENT (TOWN)—See CHATHAM, NY (Charter Communications)

GILBERTSVILLE (VILLAGE)—See DEWITT, NY (Time Warner Cable)

GILBOA—See MARGARETVILLE, NY (MTC Cable)

GLEN (TOWN)—See ALBANY, NY (Time Warner Cable)

GLEN COVE—See AMITYVILLE, NY (Cablevision)

GLEN OAKS—See MANHATTAN, NY (Time Warner Cable)

GLEN PARK (VILLAGE)—See DEWITT, NY (Time Warner Cable)

GLEN SPEY—See BETHEL (town), NY (Time Warner Cable)

GLENDALE—See MANHATTAN, NY (Time Warner Cable)

GLENFIELD—See DEWITT, NY (Time Warner Cable)

GLENS FALLS—Time Warner Cable. Now served by ALBANY, NY [NY0014]

GLENS FALLS—See ALBANY, NY (Time Warner Cable)

GLENVILLE (TOWN)—See ALBANY, NY (Time Warner Cable)

GLOVERSVILLE—See ALBANY, NY (Time Warner Cable)

GORHAM (TOWN)—See BUFFALO, NY (Time Warner Cable)

GOSHEN (TOWN)—See BETHEL (town), NY (Time Warner Cable)

GOSHEN (VILLAGE)—See BETHEL (town), NY (Time Warner Cable)

GOUVERNEUR (TOWN)—See DEWITT, NY (Time Warner Cable)

GOUVERNEUR (VILLAGE)—See DEWITT, NY (Time Warner Cable)

GOWANDA (VILLAGE)—See BUFFALO, NY (Time Warner Cable)

GRAHAMSVILLE (TOWN)—See BETHEL (town), NY (Time Warner Cable)

GRANBY (TOWN)—See DEWITT, NY (Time Warner Cable)

GRAND GORGE—See BETHEL (town), NY (Time Warner Cable)

GRAND ISLAND (TOWN)—See BUFFALO, NY (Time Warner Cable)

GRAND VIEW-ON-HUDSON—See ROCKLAND, NY (Cablevision)

GRANVILLE (TOWN)—See ALBANY, NY (Time Warner Cable)

GREAT NECK ESTATES—See AMITYVILLE, NY (Cablevision)

GREAT NECK PLAZA (VILLAGE)—See AMITYVILLE, NY (Cablevision)

GREAT NECK—See AMITYVILLE, NY (Cablevision)

GREAT VALLEY (TOWN)—See BUFFALO, NY (Time Warner Cable)

GREAT VALLEY—See SALAMANCA, NY (Atlantic Broadband)

GREECE (TOWN)—See BUFFALO, NY (Time Warner Cable)

GREEN ISLAND (VILLAGE)—See ALBANY, NY (Time Warner Cable)

GREENBURGH—See MAMARONECK, NY (Cablevision)

GREENE (town)—Time Warner Cable. Now served by DEWITT, NY [NY0013]

GREENE (TOWN)—See SMITHVILLE, NY (Haefele TV Inc)

GREENE (TOWN)—See DEWITT, NY (Time Warner Cable)

GREENE (VILLAGE)—See DEWITT, NY (Time Warner Cable)

GREENFIELD (TOWN)—See ALBANY, NY (Time Warner Cable)

GREENPORT (COLUMBIA COUNTY)—See CATSKILL, NY (Mid-Hudson Cablevision Inc.)

GREENPORT—See RIVERHEAD, NY (Cablevision)

GREENVILLE—See WARWICK, NY (Cablevision)

GREENVILLE—See CATSKILL, NY (Mid-Hudson Cablevision Inc.)

GREENWICH (TOWN)—See ALBANY, NY (Time Warner Cable)

GREENWICH (VILLAGE)—See ALBANY, NY (Time Warner Cable)

GREENWOOD LAKE (VILLAGE)—See WARWICK, NY (Cablevision)

GREENWOOD LAKE—See WARWICK, NY (Cablevision)

GREIG (town)—Time Warner Cable. Now served by DEWITT, NY [NY0013]

GREIG (TOWN)—See DEWITT, NY (Time Warner Cable)

GRIFFISS AFB—See DEWITT, NY (Time Warner Cable)

GROTON (TOWN)—See DEWITT, NY (Time Warner Cable)

GROTON (VILLAGE)—See DEWITT, NY (Time Warner Cable)

GROVELAND (PORTIONS)—See BUFFALO, NY (Time Warner Cable)

GROVELAND (PORTIONS)—See DEWITT, NY (Time Warner Cable)

GUILDERLAND (TOWN)—See ALBANY, NY (Time Warner Cable)

GUILFORD (TOWN)—See DEWITT, NY (Time Warner Cable)

HADLEY (TOWN)—See ALBANY, NY (Time Warner Cable)

HAGAMAN (VILLAGE)—See ALBANY, NY (Time Warner Cable)

HAGUE (TOWN)—See ALBANY, NY (Time Warner Cable)

HALCOTT—See MARGARETVILLE, NY (MTC Cable)

HALFMOON (TOWN)—See ALBANY, NY (Time Warner Cable)

HAMBURG (TOWN)—See BUFFALO, NY (Time Warner Cable)

HAMBURG (VILLAGE)—See BUFFALO, NY (Time Warner Cable)

HAMDEN—DTC Cable. This cable system has converted to IPTV. See HAMDEN, NY [NY5383]

HAMDEN—DTC Cable. Formerly [NY0223]. This cable system has converted to IPTV

HAMDEN—See DEWITT, NY (Time Warner Cable)

HAMILTON (TOWN)—See DEWITT, NY (Time Warner Cable)

HAMILTON (VILLAGE)—See DEWITT, NY (Time Warner Cable)

HAMLIN (TOWN)—See BUFFALO, NY (Time Warner Cable)

HAMMOND (TOWN)—Citizens Cablevision. Formerly [NY0289]. This cable system has converted to IPTV

HAMMOND—Citizens Cablevision. This cable system has converted to IPTV. See HAMMOND (town), NY [NY5403]

HAMMONDSPORT (VILLAGE)—See BUFFALO, NY (Time Warner Cable)

HAMPTON (TOWN)—See ALBANY, NY (Time Warner Cable)

HAMPTONBURGH (TOWN)—See BETHEL (town), NY (Time Warner Cable)

HANCOCK FIELD AFB—See DEWITT, NY (Time Warner Cable)

Cable Community Index—New York

HANCOCK TWP.—See HANCOCK, NY (Hancock Video)

HANCOCK—Hancock Video

HANNIBAL (TOWN)—See DEWITT, NY (Time Warner Cable)

HANNIBAL (VILLAGE)—See DEWITT, NY (Time Warner Cable)

HANOVER (TOWN)—See BUFFALO, NY (Time Warner Cable)

HARDENBURGH—See BETHEL (town), NY (Time Warner Cable)

HARFORD (TOWN)—See BERKSHIRE, NY (Haefele TV Inc)

HARLEM—See NEW YORK CITY, NY (RCN. Formerly served by MANHATTAN, NY [NY0282]. This cable system has converted to IPTV)

HARMONY (TOWN)—See JAMESTOWN, NY (Time Warner Cable)

HARPERSFIELD (TOWN)—See DEWITT, NY (Time Warner Cable)

HARRIETSTOWN (TOWN)—See DEWITT, NY (Time Warner Cable)

HARRIMAN—See WAPPINGERS FALLS, NY (Cablevision)

HARRISON—See PORT CHESTER, NY (Cablevision)

HARRISVILLE (TOWN)—See DEWITT, NY (Time Warner Cable)

HARTFORD (town)—Time Warner Cable. Now served by ALBANY, NY [NY0014]

HARTFORD (TOWN)—See ALBANY, NY (Time Warner Cable)

HARTLAND (TOWN)—See BUFFALO, NY (Time Warner Cable)

HARTSVILLE (TOWN)—See DEWITT, NY (Time Warner Cable)

HARTWICK (TOWN)—See DEWITT, NY (Time Warner Cable)

HASTINGS (TOWN)—See DEWITT, NY (Time Warner Cable)

HASTINGS-ON-HUDSON—See MAMARONECK, NY (Cablevision)

HAVERSTRAW—See OSSINING, NY (Cablevision)

HEAD OF THE HARBOR—See SUFFOLK COUNTY, NY (Cablevision)

HECTOR (TOWN - PORTIONS)—See BURDETT, NY (Haefele TV Inc)

HECTOR (TOWN - PORTIONS)—See ENFIELD, NY (Haefele TV Inc)

HELMUTH (TOWN)—See BUFFALO, NY (Time Warner Cable)

HEMPSTEAD (VILLAGE)—See AMITYVILLE, NY (Cablevision)

HENDERSON (town)—Time Warner Cable. Now served by DEWITT, NY [NY0013]

HENDERSON (TOWN)—See DEWITT, NY (Time Warner Cable)

HENRIETTA (TOWN)—See BUFFALO, NY (Time Warner Cable)

HERKIMER (TOWN)—See DEWITT, NY (Time Warner Cable)

HERKIMER (VILLAGE)—See DEWITT, NY (Time Warner Cable)

HERMON (VILLAGE)—See DEWITT, NY (Time Warner Cable)

HERRINGS (VILLAGE)—See DEWITT, NY (Time Warner Cable)

HEUVELTON (VILLAGE)—See DEWITT, NY (Time Warner Cable)

HEWLETT BAY PARK—See AMITYVILLE, NY (Cablevision)

HEWLETT HARBOR—See AMITYVILLE, NY (Cablevision)

HEWLETT NECK—See AMITYVILLE, NY (Cablevision)

HIGH FALLS—See BETHEL (town), NY (Time Warner Cable)

HIGHLAND (TOWN)—See BETHEL (town), NY (Time Warner Cable)

HIGHLAND FALLS (village)—Time Warner Cable. Now served by BETHEL (town), NY [NY0231]

HIGHLAND FALLS (VILLAGE)—See BETHEL (town), NY (Time Warner Cable)

HILLBURN—See ROCKLAND, NY (Cablevision)

HILLSDALE (TOWN)—See CHATHAM, NY (Charter Communications)

HILTON (VILLAGE)—See BUFFALO, NY (Time Warner Cable)

HINSDALE (TOWN)—See BUFFALO, NY (Time Warner Cable)

HINSDALE—See CHATHAM, MA (Charter Communications)

HOBART (VILLAGE)—See DEWITT, NY (Time Warner Cable)

HOLLAND (TOWN)—See BUFFALO, NY (Time Warner Cable)

HOLLAND PATENT (VILLAGE)—See DEWITT, NY (Time Warner Cable)

HOLLEY (VILLAGE)—See BUFFALO, NY (Time Warner Cable)

HOLLIS—See MANHATTAN, NY (Time Warner Cable)

HOMER (TOWN)—See DEWITT, NY (Time Warner Cable)

HOMER (VILLAGE)—See DEWITT, NY (Time Warner Cable)

HONEOYE FALLS (VILLAGE)—See BUFFALO, NY (Time Warner Cable)

HONEOYE—See BUFFALO, NY (Time Warner Cable)

HOOSICK (TOWN)—See ALBANY, NY (Time Warner Cable)

HOOSICK FALLS (VILLAGE)—See ALBANY, NY (Time Warner Cable)

HOPEWELL (TOWN)—See BUFFALO, NY (Time Warner Cable)

HOPKINTON (TOWN)—See DEWITT, NY (Time Warner Cable)

HORICON (TOWN)—See ALBANY, NY (Time Warner Cable)

HORNBY (TOWN)—See DEWITT, NY (Time Warner Cable)

HORNELL—Time Warner Cable. Now served by DEWITT, NY [NY0013]

HORNELL—See DEWITT, NY (Time Warner Cable)

HORNELLSVILLE (TOWN)—See DEWITT, NY (Time Warner Cable)

HORSEHEADS (TOWN)—See DEWITT, NY (Time Warner Cable)

HORSEHEADS (VILLAGE)—See DEWITT, NY (Time Warner Cable)

HORTONVILLE—See BETHEL (town), NY (Time Warner Cable)

HOUNSFIELD (TOWN)—See DEWITT, NY (Time Warner Cable)

HOWARD BEACH—See MANHATTAN, NY (Time Warner Cable)

HUDSON FALLS (VILLAGE)—See ALBANY, NY (Time Warner Cable)

HUDSON VALLEY—See BETHEL (town), NY (Time Warner Cable)

HUDSON—See CATSKILL, NY (Mid-Hudson Cablevision Inc.)

HUME (TOWN)—See BUFFALO, NY (Time Warner Cable)

HUNTER (town)—Time Warner Cable. Now served by BETHEL (town), NY [NY0231]

HUNTER (TOWN)—See BETHEL (town), NY (Time Warner Cable)

HUNTER (VILLAGE)—See BETHEL (town), NY (Time Warner Cable)

HUNTINGTON BAY—See AMITYVILLE, NY (Cablevision)

HUNTINGTON STATION—See AMITYVILLE, NY (Cablevision)

HUNTINGTON—See AMITYVILLE, NY (Cablevision)

HURLEY (TOWN)—See BETHEL (town), NY (Time Warner Cable)

HURON (TOWN)—See BUFFALO, NY (Time Warner Cable)

HYDE PARK—See WAPPINGERS FALLS, NY (Cablevision)

ILION (village)—Time Warner Cable. Now served by DEWITT, NY [NY0013]

ILION (VILLAGE)—See DEWITT, NY (Time Warner Cable)

INDIAN LAKE (TOWN)—Hamilton County Cable TV Inc

INDIAN RIVER—See DEWITT, NY (Time Warner Cable)

INGRAHAM—See DEWITT, NY (Time Warner Cable)

INLET (TOWN)—See DEWITT, NY (Time Warner Cable)

INTERLAKEN (VILLAGE)—See BUFFALO, NY (Time Warner Cable)

IRA (TOWN)—See DEWITT, NY (Time Warner Cable)

IRONDEQUOIT (TOWN)—See BUFFALO, NY (Time Warner Cable)

IRVINGTON (VILLAGE)—See MAMARONECK, NY (Cablevision)

ISCHUA (TOWN)—See BUFFALO, NY (Time Warner Cable)

ISLAND PARK—See AMITYVILLE, NY (Cablevision)

ISLANDIA—See SUFFOLK COUNTY, NY (Cablevision)

ISLIP—Cablevision. Now served by SUFFOLK COUNTY, NY [NY0006]

ISLIP—See SUFFOLK COUNTY, NY (Cablevision)

ITALY (TOWN)—See BUFFALO, NY (Time Warner Cable)

ITHACA (TOWN)—See DEWITT, NY (Time Warner Cable)

ITHACA—Time Warner Cable. Now served by DEWITT, NY [NY0013]

ITHACA—See DEWITT, NY (Time Warner Cable)

JACKSON (TOWN)—See ALBANY, NY (Time Warner Cable)

JACKSON HEIGHTS—See NEW YORK CITY, NY (RCN. Formerly served by MANHATTAN, NY [NY0282]. This cable system has converted to IPTV)

JACKSON HEIGHTS—See MANHATTAN, NY (Time Warner Cable)

JAMAICA—See NEW YORK CITY, NY (RCN. Formerly served by MANHATTAN, NY [NY0282]. This cable system has converted to IPTV)

JAMAICA—See MANHATTAN, NY (Time Warner Cable)

JAMESTOWN—Time Warner Cable

JASPER (town)—Time Warner Cable. Now served by DEWITT, NY [NY0013]

JASPER (TOWN)—See DEWITT, NY (Time Warner Cable)

JAVA (TOWN)—See BUFFALO, NY (Time Warner Cable)

JAY—See PLATTSBURGH, NY (Charter Communications)

JEFFERSON (TOWN)—See DEWITT, NY (Time Warner Cable)

JEFFERSONVILLE (VILLAGE)—See BETHEL (town), NY (Time Warner Cable)

JERUSALEM (TOWN)—See BUFFALO, NY (Time Warner Cable)

JEWETT (TOWN)—See BETHEL (town), NY (Time Warner Cable)

JOHNSBURG (TOWN)—Hamilton County Cable TV Inc

JOHNSON CITY (VILLAGE)—See DEWITT, NY (Time Warner Cable)

New York—Cable Community Index

JOHNSTOWN (city)—Time Warner Cable. Now served by ALBANY, NY [NY0014]

JOHNSTOWN (CITY)—See ALBANY, NY (Time Warner Cable)

JOHNSTOWN (TOWN)—See ALBANY, NY (Time Warner Cable)

JORDAN (VILLAGE)—See DEWITT, NY (Time Warner Cable)

JUNIUS—See BUFFALO, NY (Time Warner Cable)

KEENE (TOWN)—See KEENE VALLEY, NY (Keene Valley Video Inc)

KEENE VALLEY—Keene Valley Video Inc

KEESEVILLE (VILLAGE)—See PLATTSBURGH, NY (Charter Communications)

KENDALL (TOWN)—See BUFFALO, NY (Time Warner Cable)

KENMORE (VILLAGE)—See BUFFALO, NY (Time Warner Cable)

KENSINGTON (VILLAGE)—See AMITYVILLE, NY (Cablevision)

KENT—See WAPPINGERS FALLS, NY (Cablevision)

KEW GARDEN HILLS—See MANHATTAN, NY (Time Warner Cable)

KEW GARDENS—See NEW YORK CITY, NY (RCN. Formerly served by MANHATTAN, NY [NY0282]. This cable system has converted to IPTV)

KIANTONE (TOWN)—See JAMESTOWN, NY (Time Warner Cable)

KILLAWOG—See DEWITT, NY (Time Warner Cable)

KINDERHOOK (TOWN)—See ALBANY, NY (Time Warner Cable)

KINDERHOOK (VILLAGE)—See ALBANY, NY (Time Warner Cable)

KINDERHOOK—Berkshire Cable Corporation

KING FERRY—See MORAVIA, NY (Southern Cayuga County Cablevision)

KINGS COUNTY—See BROOKLYN, NY (Cablevision)

KINGS POINT—See AMITYVILLE, NY (Cablevision)

KINGSBURY (TOWN)—See ALBANY, NY (Time Warner Cable)

KINGSTON (TOWN)—See BETHEL (town), NY (Time Warner Cable)

KINGSTON—Time Warner Cable. Now served by BETHEL (town), NY [NY0231]

KINGSTON—See BETHEL (town), NY (Time Warner Cable)

KIRKLAND (TOWN)—See DEWITT, NY (Time Warner Cable)

KIRKWOOD (TOWN)—See DEWITT, NY (Time Warner Cable)

KIRKWOOD—See AFTON, NY (Adams Cable Service)

KNOX (TOWN)—See ALBANY, NY (Time Warner Cable)

KORTRIGHT (TOWN)—See DEWITT, NY (Time Warner Cable)

KORTRIGHT—See BLOOMVILLE, NY (DTC Cable)

LA GRANGE (TOWN)—See BETHEL (town), NY (Time Warner Cable)

LA GRANGE—See WAPPINGERS FALLS, NY (Cablevision)

LACKAWANNA—See BUFFALO, NY (Time Warner Cable)

LACONA (VILLAGE)—See DEWITT, NY (Time Warner Cable)

LAFAYETTE (TOWN)—See DEWITT, NY (Time Warner Cable)

LAKE COMO (VILLAGE)—See HANCOCK, PA (Hancock Video)

LAKE GEORGE (TOWN)—See ALBANY, NY (Time Warner Cable)

LAKE GEORGE (VILLAGE)—See ALBANY, NY (Time Warner Cable)

LAKE GROVE (VILLAGE)—See BROOKHAVEN, NY (Cablevision)

LAKE LUZERNE (TOWN)—See ALBANY, NY (Time Warner Cable)

LAKE PLACID (VILLAGE)—See DEWITT, NY (Time Warner Cable)

LAKE SUCCESS (VILLAGE)—See AMITYVILLE, NY (Cablevision)

LAKEWOOD (VILLAGE)—See JAMESTOWN, NY (Time Warner Cable)

LAKEWOOD—See HANCOCK, PA (Hancock Video)

LANCASTER (town)—Time Warner Cable. Now served by BUFFALO, NY [NY0216]

LANCASTER (TOWN)—See BUFFALO, NY (Time Warner Cable)

LANCASTER (VILLAGE)—See BUFFALO, NY (Time Warner Cable)

LANESBOROUGH—See CHATHAM, MA (Charter Communications)

LANSING (TOWN)—See DEWITT, NY (Time Warner Cable)

LANSING (VILLAGE)—See DEWITT, NY (Time Warner Cable)

LARCHMONT (VILLAGE)—See MAMARONECK, NY (Cablevision)

LATTINGTOWN—See AMITYVILLE, NY (Cablevision)

LAUREL HOLLOW—See AMITYVILLE, NY (Cablevision)

LAURELTON—See MANHATTAN, NY (Time Warner Cable)

LAURENS (TOWN)—See DEWITT, NY (Time Warner Cable)

LAURENS (VILLAGE)—See DEWITT, NY (Time Warner Cable)

LAWRENCE (TOWN)—See DEWITT, NY (Time Warner Cable)

LAWRENCE TWP.—See DEWITT, PA (Time Warner Cable)

LAWRENCE—See AMITYVILLE, NY (Cablevision)

LAWRENCEVILLE BOROUGH—See DEWITT, PA (Time Warner Cable)

LAWTONS (TOWN)—See BUFFALO, NY (Time Warner Cable)

LE RAY (TOWN)—See DEWITT, NY (Time Warner Cable)

LE ROY (TOWN)—See BUFFALO, NY (Time Warner Cable)

LE ROY (VILLAGE)—See BUFFALO, NY (Time Warner Cable)

LEBANON (TOWN)—See DEWITT, NY (Time Warner Cable)

LEDYARD (TOWN)—See BUFFALO, NY (Time Warner Cable)

LEE (TOWN)—See DEWITT, NY (Time Warner Cable)

LEICESTER (TOWN)—See BUFFALO, NY (Time Warner Cable)

LEICESTER (VILLAGE)—See BUFFALO, NY (Time Warner Cable)

LENOX (TOWN)—See DEWITT, NY (Time Warner Cable)

LEWIS (TOWN)—See DEWITT, NY (Time Warner Cable)

LEWIS—See PLATTSBURGH, NY (Charter Communications)

LEWISBORO—See YORKTOWN, NY (Cablevision)

LEWISTON (TOWN)—See BUFFALO, NY (Time Warner Cable)

LEWISTON (VILLAGE)—See BUFFALO, NY (Time Warner Cable)

LEXINGTON—See BETHEL (town), NY (Time Warner Cable)

LEYDEN (TOWN)—See DEWITT, NY (Time Warner Cable)

LIBERTY (TOWN)—See BETHEL (town), NY (Time Warner Cable)

LIBERTY (VILLAGE)—See BETHEL (town), NY (Time Warner Cable)

LIBERTY TWP.—See DEWITT, PA (Time Warner Cable)

LIMA (TOWN)—See BUFFALO, NY (Time Warner Cable)

LIMA (VILLAGE)—See BUFFALO, NY (Time Warner Cable)

LIMESTONE—Atlantic Broadband. Now served by BRADFORD, PA [PA0085]

LINCOLN (TOWN)—See DEWITT, NY (Time Warner Cable)

LINDEN HILL—See MANHATTAN, NY (Time Warner Cable)

LINDENHURST—See AMITYVILLE, NY (Cablevision)

LINDLEY (TOWN)—See DEWITT, NY (Time Warner Cable)

LISBON (TOWN)—See DEWITT, NY (Time Warner Cable)

LISLE (TOWN)—See DEWITT, NY (Time Warner Cable)

LISLE (VILLAGE)—See DEWITT, NY (Time Warner Cable)

LITCHFIELD (TOWN)—See DEWITT, NY (Time Warner Cable)

LITCHFIELD TWP.—See DEWITT, PA (Time Warner Cable)

LITTLE FALLS (TOWN)—See DEWITT, NY (Time Warner Cable)

LITTLE FALLS—See DEWITT, NY (Time Warner Cable)

LITTLE NECK—See MANHATTAN, NY (Time Warner Cable)

LITTLE VALLEY (TOWN)—See SALAMANCA, NY (Atlantic Broadband)

LITTLE VALLEY (VILLAGE)—See SALAMANCA, NY (Atlantic Broadband)

LIVERPOOL (VILLAGE)—See DEWITT, NY (Time Warner Cable)

LIVINGSTON (TOWN)—See CATSKILL, NY (Mid-Hudson Cablevision Inc.)

LIVONIA (TOWN)—See BUFFALO, NY (Time Warner Cable)

LIVONIA (VILLAGE)—See BUFFALO, NY (Time Warner Cable)

LLOYD (TOWN)—See BETHEL (town), NY (Time Warner Cable)

LLOYD HARBOR—See AMITYVILLE, NY (Cablevision)

LLOYD—See WAPPINGERS FALLS, NY (Cablevision)

LOCKE TWP.—See MORAVIA, NY (Southern Cayuga County Cablevision)

LOCKPORT (TOWN)—See BUFFALO, NY (Time Warner Cable)

LOCKPORT—See BUFFALO, NY (Time Warner Cable)

LODI (TOWN)—See BUFFALO, NY (Time Warner Cable)

LODI (VILLAGE)—See BUFFALO, NY (Time Warner Cable)

LONG BEACH—See AMITYVILLE, NY (Cablevision)

LONG ISLAND CITY—See NEW YORK CITY, NY (RCN. Formerly served by MANHATTAN, NY [NY0282]. This cable system has converted to IPTV)

LONG ISLAND CITY—See MANHATTAN, NY (Time Warner Cable)

LONG LAKE—C H Comm LLC

LORRAINE (TOWN)—See DEWITT, NY (Time Warner Cable)

LOUISVILLE (TOWN)—See DEWITT, NY (Time Warner Cable)

LOWVILLE (TOWN)—See DEWITT, NY (Time Warner Cable)

LOWVILLE (VILLAGE)—See DEWITT, NY (Time Warner Cable)

Cable Community Index—New York

LUMBERLAND (TOWN)—See BETHEL (town), NY (Time Warner Cable)

LYME (TOWN)—See DEWITT, NY (Time Warner Cable)

LYNBROOK—Cablevision Systems Corp. Now served by AMITYVILLE, NY [NY0001]

LYNBROOK—See AMITYVILLE, NY (Cablevision)

LYNDONVILLE (VILLAGE)—See BUFFALO, NY (Time Warner Cable)

LYONS (TOWN)—See BUFFALO, NY (Time Warner Cable)

LYONS (VILLAGE)—See BUFFALO, NY (Time Warner Cable)

LYONS FALLS (VILLAGE)—See DEWITT, NY (Time Warner Cable)

LYONSDALE (TOWN)—See DEWITT, NY (Time Warner Cable)

LYSANDER (TOWN)—See DEWITT, NY (Time Warner Cable)

MACEDON (TOWN)—See BUFFALO, NY (Time Warner Cable)

MACEDON (VILLAGE)—See BUFFALO, NY (Time Warner Cable)

MACHIAS (TOWN)—See BUFFALO, NY (Time Warner Cable)

MADISON (TOWN)—See DEWITT, NY (Time Warner Cable)

MADISON (VILLAGE)—See DEWITT, NY (Time Warner Cable)

MADRID (TOWN)—See DEWITT, NY (Time Warner Cable)

MAHWAH TWP.—See ROCKLAND, NJ (Cablevision)

MAINE (TOWN)—See DEWITT, NY (Time Warner Cable)

MALBA—See MANHATTAN, NY (Time Warner Cable)

MALONE (town)—Time Warner Cable. Now served by DEWITT, NY [NY0013]

MALONE (TOWN)—See DEWITT, NY (Time Warner Cable)

MALONE (VILLAGE)—See DEWITT, NY (Time Warner Cable)

MALTA (TOWN)—See ALBANY, NY (Time Warner Cable)

MALVERNE—See AMITYVILLE, NY (Cablevision)

MAMAKATING (TOWN)—See BETHEL (town), NY (Time Warner Cable)

MAMARONECK—Cablevision

MANCHESTER (TOWN)—See BUFFALO, NY (Time Warner Cable)

MANCHESTER (VILLAGE)—See BUFFALO, NY (Time Warner Cable)

MANDANA—See DEWITT, NY (Time Warner Cable)

MANHASSET—See AMITYVILLE, NY (Cablevision)

MANHATTAN—RCN Corp. This cable system has converted to IPTV. See NEW YORK CITY, NY [NY5312]

MANHATTAN—See NEW YORK CITY, NY (RCN. Formerly served by MANHATTAN, NY [NY0282]. This cable system has converted to IPTV)

MANHATTAN—Time Warner Cable

MANHEIM (TOWN)—See DEWITT, NY (Time Warner Cable)

MANILUS (TOWN)—See DEWITT, NY (Time Warner Cable)

MANLIUS (VILLAGE)—See DEWITT, NY (Time Warner Cable)

MANNSVILLE (VILLAGE)—See DEWITT, NY (Time Warner Cable)

MANORHAVEN—See AMITYVILLE, NY (Cablevision)

MANSFIELD (TOWN)—See BUFFALO, NY (Time Warner Cable)

MAPLE SPRINGS—See JAMESTOWN, NY (Time Warner Cable)

MARATHON (TOWN)—See DEWITT, NY (Time Warner Cable)

MARATHON (VILLAGE)—See DEWITT, NY (Time Warner Cable)

MARBLETOWN (TOWN)—See BETHEL (town), NY (Time Warner Cable)

MARCELLUS (TOWN)—See DEWITT, NY (Time Warner Cable)

MARCELLUS (VILLAGE)—See DEWITT, NY (Time Warner Cable)

MARCY (TOWN)—See DEWITT, NY (Time Warner Cable)

MARCY—See DEWITT, NY (Time Warner Cable)

MARGARETVILLE—MTC Cable

MARIAVILLE—See ALBANY, NY (Time Warner Cable)

MARILLA (TOWN)—See BUFFALO, NY (Time Warner Cable)

MARION (TOWN)—See BUFFALO, NY (Time Warner Cable)

MARLBORO (TOWN)—See BETHEL (town), NY (Time Warner Cable)

MARLBORO—See WAPPINGERS FALLS, NY (Cablevision)

MARSHALL (TOWN)—See DEWITT, NY (Time Warner Cable)

MARTINSBURG (TOWN)—See DEWITT, NY (Time Warner Cable)

MARYLAND (TOWN)—See DEWITT, NY (Time Warner Cable)

MASONVILLE (TOWN)—See DEWITT, NY (Time Warner Cable)

MASPETH—See NEW YORK CITY, NY (RCN. Formerly served by MANHATTAN, NY [NY0282]. This cable system has converted to IPTV)

MASPETH—See MANHATTAN, NY (Time Warner Cable)

MASSAPEQUA PARK—See AMITYVILLE, NY (Cablevision)

MASSAPEQUA—See AMITYVILLE, NY (Cablevision)

MASSENA (VILLAGE)—See DEWITT, NY (Time Warner Cable)

MASSENA—Time Warner Cable. Now served by DEWITT, NY [NY0013]

MASSENA—See DEWITT, NY (Time Warner Cable)

MATAMORAS—See WARWICK, PA (Cablevision)

MATINECOCK—See AMITYVILLE, NY (Cablevision)

MAYBROOK (VILLAGE)—See BETHEL (town), NY (Time Warner Cable)

MAYFIELD (TOWN)—See ALBANY, NY (Time Warner Cable)

MAYFIELD (VILLAGE)—See ALBANY, NY (Time Warner Cable)

MAYFIELD—See ALBANY, NY (Time Warner Cable)

MAYVILLE (VILLAGE)—See BUFFALO, NY (Time Warner Cable)

McDONOUGH—Formerly served by Haefele TV Inc. No longer in operation

MCGRAW (VILLAGE)—See DEWITT, NY (Time Warner Cable)

MECHANICVILLE—See ALBANY, NY (Time Warner Cable)

MEDINA (VILLAGE)—See BUFFALO, NY (Time Warner Cable)

MENANDS (VILLAGE)—See ALBANY, NY (Time Warner Cable)

MENDON (TOWN)—See BUFFALO, NY (Time Warner Cable)

MENTZ (TOWN)—See DEWITT, NY (Time Warner Cable)

MEREDITH (TOWN)—See DEWITT, NY (Time Warner Cable)

MERIDIAN (VILLAGE)—See DEWITT, NY (Time Warner Cable)

MEXICO (TOWN)—See DEWITT, NY (Time Warner Cable)

MEXICO (VILLAGE)—See DEWITT, NY (Time Warner Cable)

MIDDLE GRANVILLE—See ALBANY, NY (Time Warner Cable)

MIDDLE VILLAGE—See NEW YORK CITY, NY (RCN. Formerly served by MANHATTAN, NY [NY0282]. This cable system has converted to IPTV)

MIDDLE VILLAGE—See MANHATTAN, NY (Time Warner Cable)

MIDDLEBURG (VILLAGE)—See BLENHEIM, NY (MidTel Cable TV)

MIDDLEBURGH (TOWN)—See BLENHEIM, NY (MidTel Cable TV)

MIDDLEBURGH (TOWN)—See ALBANY, NY (Time Warner Cable)

MIDDLEBURGH (VILLAGE)—See ALBANY, NY (Time Warner Cable)

MIDDLEBURY (TOWN)—See BUFFALO, NY (Time Warner Cable)

MIDDLEFIELD (TOWN)—See DEWITT, NY (Time Warner Cable)

MIDDLEPORT (VILLAGE)—See BUFFALO, NY (Time Warner Cable)

MIDDLESEX (TOWN)—See BUFFALO, NY (Time Warner Cable)

MIDDLETOWN—See MARGARETVILLE, NY (MTC Cable)

MIDDLETOWN—See BETHEL (town), NY (Time Warner Cable)

MIDDLEVILLE (VILLAGE)—See DEWITT, NY (Time Warner Cable)

MILAN—See WAPPINGERS FALLS, NY (Cablevision)

MILFORD (TOWN)—See DEWITT, NY (Time Warner Cable)

MILFORD (VILLAGE)—See DEWITT, NY (Time Warner Cable)

MILL NECK—See AMITYVILLE, NY (Cablevision)

MILLBROOK—See WAPPINGERS FALLS, NY (Cablevision)

MILLERTON—See WAPPINGERS FALLS, NY (Cablevision)

MILLPORT (VILLAGE)—See DEWITT, NY (Time Warner Cable)

MILO (TOWN)—See BURDETT, NY (Haefele TV Inc)

MILO (TOWN)—See BUFFALO, NY (Time Warner Cable)

MILTON (TOWN)—See ALBANY, NY (Time Warner Cable)

MINA (TOWN)—See JAMESTOWN, NY (Time Warner Cable)

MINDEN (TOWN)—See ALBANY, NY (Time Warner Cable)

MINEOLA—See AMITYVILLE, NY (Cablevision)

MINERVA (TOWN)—C H Comm LLC

MINETTO (TOWN)—See DEWITT, NY (Time Warner Cable)

MINISINK—Cablevision. Now served by WARWICK, NY [NY0045]

MINISINK—See WARWICK, NY (Cablevision)

MINOA (VILLAGE)—See DEWITT, NY (Time Warner Cable)

MOHAWK (TOWN)—See ALBANY, NY (Time Warner Cable)

MOHAWK (VILLAGE)—See DEWITT, NY (Time Warner Cable)

MOIRA (TOWN)—See DEWITT, NY (Time Warner Cable)

MONROE (VILLAGE)—See WAPPINGERS FALLS, NY (Cablevision)

MONTAGUE TWP.—See WARWICK, NJ (Cablevision)

MONTEBELLO—See ROCKLAND, NY (Cablevision)

MONTGOMERY (TOWN)—See BETHEL (town), NY (Time Warner Cable)

New York—Cable Community Index

MONTGOMERY (VILLAGE)—See BETHEL (town), NY (Time Warner Cable)

MONTICELLO (VILLAGE)—See BETHEL (town), NY (Time Warner Cable)

MONTOUR (TOWN)—See BUFFALO, NY (Time Warner Cable)

MONTOUR FALLS (VILLAGE)—See BUFFALO, NY (Time Warner Cable)

MONTROSE BOROUGH—See DEWITT, PA (Time Warner Cable)

MONTVALE—See ROCKLAND, NJ (Cablevision)

MOOERS (TOWN)—See DEWITT, NY (Time Warner Cable)

MOOERS (VILLAGE)—See DEWITT, NY (Time Warner Cable)

MORAVIA (VILLAGE)—See MORAVIA, NY (Southern Cayuga County Cablevision)

MORAVIA—Southern Cayuga County Cablevision

MOREAU (TOWN)—See ALBANY, NY (Time Warner Cable)

MORIAH (TOWN)—See ALBANY, NY (Time Warner Cable)

MORRIS (town)—Time Warner Cable. Now served by DEWITT, NY [NY0013]

MORRIS (TOWN)—See DEWITT, NY (Time Warner Cable)

MORRIS (VILLAGE)—See DEWITT, NY (Time Warner Cable)

MORRISTOWN (TOWN)—See DEWITT, NY (Time Warner Cable)

MORRISTOWN (VILLAGE)—See DEWITT, NY (Time Warner Cable)

MORRISVILLE (VILLAGE)—See DEWITT, NY (Time Warner Cable)

MOUNT HOPE (TOWN)—See BETHEL (town), NY (Time Warner Cable)

MOUNT KISCO—Cablevision. Now served by YORKTOWN, NY [NY0050]

MOUNT KISCO—See YORKTOWN, NY (Cablevision)

MOUNT MORRIS (TOWN)—See BUFFALO, NY (Time Warner Cable)

MOUNT MORRIS (VILLAGE)—See BUFFALO, NY (Time Warner Cable)

MOUNT PLEASANT (WESTCHESTER COUNTY)—See OSSINING, NY (Cablevision)

MOUNT TREMPER—Time Warner Cable. Now served by BETHEL (town), NY [NY0231]

MOUNT TREMPER—See BETHEL (town), NY (Time Warner Cable)

MOUNT UPTON—See DEWITT, NY (Time Warner Cable)

MOUNT VERNON—Time Warner Cable

MUNNSVILLE (VILLAGE)—See DEWITT, NY (Time Warner Cable)

MUNSEY PARK (VILLAGE)—See AMITYVILLE, NY (Cablevision)

MURRAY (TOWN)—See BUFFALO, NY (Time Warner Cable)

MUTTONTOWN—See AMITYVILLE, NY (Cablevision)

NANTICOKE (TOWN)—See DEWITT, NY (Time Warner Cable)

NANUET—See ROCKLAND, NY (Cablevision)

NAPANOCH—See BETHEL (town), NY (Time Warner Cable)

NAPLES (town)—Time Warner Cable. Now served by BUFFALO (formerly Lackawanna), NY [NY0216]

NAPLES (TOWN)—See BUFFALO, NY (Time Warner Cable)

NAPLES (VILLAGE)—See BUFFALO, NY (Time Warner Cable)

NARROWSBURG—See BETHEL (town), NY (Time Warner Cable)

NASSAU (TOWN)—See ALBANY, NY (Time Warner Cable)

NASSAU (VILLAGE)—See ALBANY, NY (Time Warner Cable)

NELLISTON (VILLAGE)—See ALBANY, NY (Time Warner Cable)

NELSON (TOWN)—See DEWITT, NY (Time Warner Cable)

NELSON TWP.—See DEWITT, PA (Time Warner Cable)

NELSONVILLE—See WAPPINGERS FALLS, NY (Cablevision)

NEVERSINK (TOWN)—See BETHEL (town), NY (Time Warner Cable)

NEW ALBION (TOWN)—See BUFFALO, NY (Time Warner Cable)

NEW BALTIMORE—See CATSKILL, NY (Mid-Hudson Cablevision Inc.)

NEW BERLIN (town)—Time Warner Cable. Now served by DEWITT, NY [NY0013]

NEW BERLIN (TOWN)—See DEWITT, NY (Time Warner Cable)

NEW BERLIN (VILLAGE)—See DEWITT, NY (Time Warner Cable)

NEW BREMEN (TOWN)—See DEWITT, NY (Time Warner Cable)

NEW CASTLE—See OSSINING, NY (Cablevision)

NEW HARTFORD (TOWN)—See DEWITT, NY (Time Warner Cable)

NEW HARTFORD (VILLAGE)—See DEWITT, NY (Time Warner Cable)

NEW HAVEN (TOWN)—See DEWITT, NY (Time Warner Cable)

NEW HAVEN (VILLAGE)—See DEWITT, NY (Time Warner Cable)

NEW HEMPSTEAD—See ROCKLAND, NY (Cablevision)

NEW HYDE PARK—See AMITYVILLE, NY (Cablevision)

NEW LEBANON (TOWN)—See CHATHAM, NY (Charter Communications)

NEW LISBON (TOWN)—See DEWITT, NY (Time Warner Cable)

NEW PALTZ (TOWN)—See BETHEL (town), NY (Time Warner Cable)

NEW PALTZ (village)—Time Warner Cable. Now served by BETHEL (town), NY [NY0231]

NEW PALTZ (VILLAGE)—See BETHEL (town), NY (Time Warner Cable)

NEW ROCHELLE—See MAMARONECK, NY (Cablevision)

NEW SCOTLAND (TOWN)—See ALBANY, NY (Time Warner Cable)

NEW WINDSOR (TOWN)—See BETHEL (town), NY (Time Warner Cable)

NEW YORK CITY—RCN. Formerly served by MANHATTAN, NY [NY0282]. This cable system has converted to IPTV

NEW YORK MILLS (VILLAGE)—See DEWITT, NY (Time Warner Cable)

NEW YORK—See MANHATTAN, NY (Time Warner Cable)

NEWARK (VILLAGE)—See BUFFALO, NY (Time Warner Cable)

NEWARK VALLEY (town)—Time Warner Binghamton. Now served by DEWITT, NY [NY0013]

NEWARK VALLEY (TOWN)—See BERKSHIRE, NY (Haefele TV Inc)

NEWARK VALLEY (TOWN)—See DEWITT, NY (Time Warner Cable)

NEWARK VALLEY (VILLAGE)—See DEWITT, NY (Time Warner Cable)

NEWBURGH (TOWN)—See BETHEL (town), NY (Time Warner Cable)

NEWBURGH—Time Warner Cable. Now served by BETHEL (town), NY [NY0231]

NEWBURGH—See BETHEL (town), NY (Time Warner Cable)

NEWCOMB—Formerly served by C H Comm LLC. No longer in operation

NEWFANE (TOWN)—See BUFFALO, NY (Time Warner Cable)

NEWFIELD (TOWN)—See DEWITT, NY (Time Warner Cable)

NEWPORT (TOWN)—See DEWITT, NY (Time Warner Cable)

NEWPORT (VILLAGE)—See DEWITT, NY (Time Warner Cable)

NEWSTEAD (TOWN)—See BUFFALO, NY (Time Warner Cable)

NIAGARA (TOWN)—See BUFFALO, NY (Time Warner Cable)

NIAGARA FALLS—Time Warner Cable. Now served by BUFFALO (formerly Lackawanna), NY [NY0216]

NIAGARA FALLS—See BUFFALO, NY (Time Warner Cable)

NICHOLS (TOWN)—See DEWITT, NY (Time Warner Cable)

NICHOLS (VILLAGE)—See DEWITT, NY (Time Warner Cable)

NILES (TOWN)—See DEWITT, NY (Time Warner Cable)

NISKAYUNA (TOWN)—See ALBANY, NY (Time Warner Cable)

NISSEQUOGUE—See SUFFOLK COUNTY, NY (Cablevision)

NIVERVILLE—See KINDERHOOK, NY (Berkshire Cable Corporation)

NORFOLK (TOWN)—See DEWITT, NY (Time Warner Cable)

NORTH BRANCH—See BETHEL (town), NY (Time Warner Cable)

NORTH CASTLE—See YORKTOWN, NY (Cablevision)

NORTH COLLINS (TOWN)—See BUFFALO, NY (Time Warner Cable)

NORTH COLLINS (VILLAGE)—See BUFFALO, NY (Time Warner Cable)

NORTH DANSVILLE (TOWN)—See DEWITT, NY (Time Warner Cable)

NORTH EAST (TOWN)—See WAPPINGERS FALLS, NY (Cablevision)

NORTH ELBA (TOWN)—See DEWITT, NY (Time Warner Cable)

NORTH GREENBUSH (TOWN)—See ALBANY, NY (Time Warner Cable)

NORTH HARMONY (TOWN)—See JAMESTOWN, NY (Time Warner Cable)

NORTH HAVEN—See RIVERHEAD, NY (Cablevision)

NORTH HEMPSTEAD—See AMITYVILLE, NY (Cablevision)

NORTH HILLS (VILLAGE)—See AMITYVILLE, NY (Cablevision)

NORTH HORNELL (VILLAGE)—See DEWITT, NY (Time Warner Cable)

NORTH NORWICH (TOWN)—See DEWITT, NY (Time Warner Cable)

NORTH PITCHER—See DEWITT, NY (Time Warner Cable)

NORTH SALEM—Formerly served by Cablevision Systems Corp. Now served by Optimum, YORKTOWN, NY [NY0050]

NORTH SALEM—See YORKTOWN, NY (Cablevision)

NORTH SYRACUSE (VILLAGE)—See DEWITT, NY (Time Warner Cable)

NORTH TARRYTOWN—See OSSINING, NY (Cablevision)

NORTH TONAWANDA—See BUFFALO, NY (Time Warner Cable)

NORTHAMPTON (TOWN)—See ALBANY, NY (Time Warner Cable)

NORTHPORT—See AMITYVILLE, NY (Cablevision)

NORTHUMBERLAND (TOWN)—See ALBANY, NY (Time Warner Cable)

Cable Community Index—New York

NORTHVILLE (VILLAGE)—See ALBANY, NY (Time Warner Cable)

NORTHVILLE—Formerly served by Adelphia Communications. Now served by Time Warner Cable, ALBANY, NY [NY0014]

NORWICH (town)—Time Warner Cable. Now served by DEWITT, NY [NY0013]

NORWICH (TOWN)—See DEWITT, NY (Time Warner Cable)

NORWICH—See DEWITT, NY (Time Warner Cable)

NORWOOD (VILLAGE)—See DEWITT, NY (Time Warner Cable)

NUNDA (TOWN)—See BUFFALO, NY (Time Warner Cable)

NUNDA (VILLAGE)—See BUFFALO, NY (Time Warner Cable)

NYACK—See ROCKLAND, NY (Cablevision)

OAKFIELD (TOWN)—See BUFFALO, NY (Time Warner Cable)

OAKFIELD (VILLAGE)—See BUFFALO, NY (Time Warner Cable)

OAKLAND GARDENS—See NEW YORK CITY, NY (RCN. Formerly served by MANHATTAN, NY [NY0282]. This cable system has converted to IPTV)

OAKLAND GARDENS—See MANHATTAN, NY (Time Warner Cable)

ODESSA (VILLAGE)—See BUFFALO, NY (Time Warner Cable)

OGDEN (TOWN)—See BUFFALO, NY (Time Warner Cable)

OGDENSBURG—Time Warner Cable. Now served by DEWITT, NY [NY0013]

OGDENSBURG—See DEWITT, NY (Time Warner Cable)

OLD BROOKVILLE—See AMITYVILLE, NY (Cablevision)

OLD FIELD—See SUFFOLK COUNTY, NY (Cablevision)

OLD FORGE—Formerly served by Adelphia Communications. No longer in operation

OLD WESTBURY—See AMITYVILLE, NY (Cablevision)

OLEAN (TOWN)—See BUFFALO, NY (Time Warner Cable)

OLEAN—Time Warner Cable. Now served by BUFFALO (formerly Lackawanna), NY [NY0216]

OLEAN—See BUFFALO, NY (Time Warner Cable)

OLIVE (town)—Time Warner Cable. Now served by BETHEL (town), NY [NY0231]

OLIVE (TOWN)—See BETHEL (town), NY (Time Warner Cable)

OLIVEREA—See BETHEL (town), NY (Time Warner Cable)

ONEIDA CASTLE (VILLAGE)—See DEWITT, NY (Time Warner Cable)

ONEIDA—Time Warner Cable. Now served by DEWITT, NY [NY0013]

ONEIDA—See DEWITT, NY (Time Warner Cable)

ONEONTA (TOWN)—See DEWITT, NY (Time Warner Cable)

ONEONTA—Time Warner Cable. Now served by DEWITT, NY [NY0013]

ONEONTA—See DEWITT, NY (Time Warner Cable)

ONONDAGA (TOWN)—See DEWITT, NY (Time Warner Cable)

ONTARIO (TOWN)—See BUFFALO, NY (Time Warner Cable)

ORANGE (TOWN)—See BURDETT, NY (Haefele TV Inc)

ORANGETOWN (TOWN)—See ROCKLAND, NY (Cablevision)

ORANGEVILLE (TOWN)—See BUFFALO, NY (Time Warner Cable)

ORCHARD PARK (TOWN)—See BUFFALO, NY (Time Warner Cable)

ORCHARD PARK (VILLAGE)—See BUFFALO, NY (Time Warner Cable)

ORISKANY (VILLAGE)—See DEWITT, NY (Time Warner Cable)

ORISKANY FALLS (VILLAGE)—See DEWITT, NY (Time Warner Cable)

ORLEANS (TOWN)—See DEWITT, NY (Time Warner Cable)

ORWELL (TOWN)—See DEWITT, NY (Time Warner Cable)

OSCEOLA TWP.—See DEWITT, PA (Time Warner Cable)

OSSINING—Cablevision

OSWEGATCHIE (TOWN)—See DEWITT, NY (Time Warner Cable)

OSWEGO (TOWN)—See DEWITT, NY (Time Warner Cable)

OSWEGO—Time Warner Cable. Now served by DEWITT, NY [NY0013]

OSWEGO—See DEWITT, NY (Time Warner Cable)

OTEGO (TOWN)—See DEWITT, NY (Time Warner Cable)

OTEGO (VILLAGE)—See DEWITT, NY (Time Warner Cable)

OTISCO (TOWN)—See DEWITT, NY (Time Warner Cable)

OTISVILLE (VILLAGE)—See BETHEL (town), NY (Time Warner Cable)

OTSEGO (TOWN)—See DEWITT, NY (Time Warner Cable)

OTSELIC (TOWN)—See DEWITT, NY (Time Warner Cable)

OTSELIC—Formerly served by Chain Lakes Cablevision. Now served by Time Warner Cable, DEWITT, NY [NY0013]

OVID (TOWN)—See BUFFALO, NY (Time Warner Cable)

OVID (VILLAGE)—See BUFFALO, NY (Time Warner Cable)

OWASCO (TOWN)—See DEWITT, NY (Time Warner Cable)

OWEGO (TOWN)—See DEWITT, NY (Time Warner Cable)

OWEGO (village)—Time Warner Cable. Now served by DEWITT, NY [NY0013]

OWEGO (VILLAGE)—See DEWITT, NY (Time Warner Cable)

OXFORD (town)—Time Warner Cable. Now served by DEWITT, NY [NY0013]

OXFORD (TOWN)—See DEWITT, NY (Time Warner Cable)

OXFORD (VILLAGE)—See DEWITT, NY (Time Warner Cable)

OYSTER BAY COVE—See AMITYVILLE, NY (Cablevision)

OYSTER BAY—See AMITYVILLE, NY (Cablevision)

OZONE PARK—See MANHATTAN, NY (Time Warner Cable)

PAINTED POST (VILLAGE)—See DEWITT, NY (Time Warner Cable)

PALATINE (TOWN)—See ALBANY, NY (Time Warner Cable)

PALATINE BRIDGE (TOWN)—See ALBANY, NY (Time Warner Cable)

PALERMO (TOWN)—See DEWITT, NY (Time Warner Cable)

PALMYRA (TOWN)—See BUFFALO, NY (Time Warner Cable)

PALMYRA (VILLAGE)—See BUFFALO, NY (Time Warner Cable)

PAMELIA (TOWN)—See DEWITT, NY (Time Warner Cable)

PANAMA (VILLAGE)—See JAMESTOWN, NY (Time Warner Cable)

PARIS (TOWN)—See DEWITT, NY (Time Warner Cable)

PARISH (TOWN)—See DEWITT, NY (Time Warner Cable)

PARISH (VILLAGE)—See DEWITT, NY (Time Warner Cable)

PARISHVILLE (TOWN)—See DEWITT, NY (Time Warner Cable)

PARMA (TOWN)—See BUFFALO, NY (Time Warner Cable)

PATCHOGUE (VILLAGE)—See BROOKHAVEN, NY (Cablevision)

PAVILION (TOWN)—See BUFFALO, NY (Time Warner Cable)

PEEKSKILL—See OSSINING, NY (Cablevision)

PELHAM MANOR—See MAMARONECK, NY (Cablevision)

PELHAM—See MAMARONECK, NY (Cablevision)

PEMBROKE (TOWN)—See BUFFALO, NY (Time Warner Cable)

PENDLETON (TOWN)—See BUFFALO, NY (Time Warner Cable)

PENFIELD (TOWN)—See BUFFALO, NY (Time Warner Cable)

PENN YAN (village)—Time Warner Cable. Now served by BUFFALO (formerly Lackawanna), NY [NY0216]

PENN YAN (VILLAGE)—See BUFFALO, NY (Time Warner Cable)

PENNELLVILLE—See DEWITT, NY (Time Warner Cable)

PERINTON (TOWN)—See BUFFALO, NY (Time Warner Cable)

PERKINSVILLE—See DEWITT, NY (Time Warner Cable)

PERRY (TOWN)—See BUFFALO, NY (Time Warner Cable)

PERRY (VILLAGE)—See BUFFALO, NY (Time Warner Cable)

PERRYSBURG (TOWN)—See BUFFALO, NY (Time Warner Cable)

PERRYSBURG (VILLAGE)—See BUFFALO, NY (Time Warner Cable)

PERSIA (TOWN)—See BUFFALO, NY (Time Warner Cable)

PERTH (TOWN)—See ALBANY, NY (Time Warner Cable)

PERU (TOWN)—See PLATTSBURGH, NY (Charter Communications)

PETERBORO—Formerly served by Chain Lakes Cablevision. Now served by Time Warner Cable, DEWITT, NY [NY0013]

PETERBORO—See DEWITT, NY (Time Warner Cable)

PETERSBURG—See CHATHAM, NY (Charter Communications)

PHARSALIA (TOWN)—See DEWITT, NY (Time Warner Cable)

PHELPS (TOWN)—See BUFFALO, NY (Time Warner Cable)

PHELPS (VILLAGE)—See BUFFALO, NY (Time Warner Cable)

PHILADELPHIA (TOWN)—See DEWITT, NY (Time Warner Cable)

PHILADELPHIA (VILLAGE)—See DEWITT, NY (Time Warner Cable)

PHILIPSTOWN—See OSSINING, NY (Cablevision)

PHILMONT—See CATSKILL, NY (Mid-Hudson Cablevision Inc.)

PHOENICIA—Time Warner Cable. Now served by BETHEL (town), NY [NY0231]

PHOENICIA—See BETHEL (town), NY (Time Warner Cable)

PHOENIX (VILLAGE)—See DEWITT, NY (Time Warner Cable)

PIERMONT—See ROCKLAND, NY (Cablevision)

PIERREPONT (TOWN)—See DEWITT, NY (Time Warner Cable)

New York—Cable Community Index

PIERREPONT MANOR—See DEWITT, NY (Time Warner Cable)

PIKE (TOWN)—See BUFFALO, NY (Time Warner Cable)

PIKE (VILLAGE)—See BUFFALO, NY (Time Warner Cable)

PINE HILL—Formerly served by Time Warner Cable. No longer in operation

PINE PLAINS (TOWN)—See WAPPINGERS FALLS, NY (Cablevision)

PITCAIRN (TOWN)—See DEWITT, NY (Time Warner Cable)

PITCHER (TOWN)—See DEWITT, NY (Time Warner Cable)

PITTSFIELD (TOWN)—See DEWITT, NY (Time Warner Cable)

PITTSFORD (TOWN)—See BUFFALO, NY (Time Warner Cable)

PITTSFORD (VILLAGE)—See BUFFALO, NY (Time Warner Cable)

PITTSTOWN (TOWN)—See ALBANY, NY (Time Warner Cable)

PLAINEDGE—See AMITYVILLE, NY (Cablevision)

PLAINFIELD (TOWN)—See DEWITT, NY (Time Warner Cable)

PLAINVIEW—See AMITYVILLE, NY (Cablevision)

PLANDOME (VILLAGE)—See AMITYVILLE, NY (Cablevision)

PLANDOME HEIGHTS (VILLAGE)—See AMITYVILLE, NY (Cablevision)

PLANDOME MANOR—See AMITYVILLE, NY (Cablevision)

PLATTEKILL (TOWN)—See BETHEL (town), NY (Time Warner Cable)

PLATTEKILL—See WAPPINGERS FALLS, NY (Cablevision)

PLATTSBURGH—Charter Communications

PLEASANT VALLEY (TOWN)—See BETHEL (town), NY (Time Warner Cable)

PLEASANTVILLE—See OSSINING, NY (Cablevision)

PLYMOUTH (TOWN)—See DEWITT, NY (Time Warner Cable)

POESTENKILL (TOWN)—See ALBANY, NY (Time Warner Cable)

POLAND (TOWN)—See JAMESTOWN, NY (Time Warner Cable)

POLAND (VILLAGE)—See DEWITT, NY (Time Warner Cable)

POMFRET (PORTIONS)—See BUFFALO, NY (Time Warner Cable)

POMFRET (PORTIONS)—See JAMESTOWN, NY (Time Warner Cable)

POMONA—See OSSINING, NY (Cablevision)

POMONOK—See MANHATTAN, NY (Time Warner Cable)

POMPEY (TOWN)—See DEWITT, NY (Time Warner Cable)

POND EDDY—See BETHEL (town), NY (Time Warner Cable)

POQUOTT (VILLAGE)—See BROOKHAVEN, NY (Cablevision)

PORT BYRON (VILLAGE)—See DEWITT, NY (Time Warner Cable)

PORT CHESTER—Cablevision

PORT DICKINSON (VILLAGE)—See DEWITT, NY (Time Warner Cable)

PORT HENRY (village)—Time Warner Cable. Now served by ALBANY, NY [NY0014]

PORT HENRY (VILLAGE)—See ALBANY, NY (Time Warner Cable)

PORT JEFFERSON—See SUFFOLK COUNTY, NY (Cablevision)

PORT JERVIS—Time Warner Cable. Now served by BETHEL (town), NY [NY0231]

PORT JERVIS—See BETHEL (town), NY (Time Warner Cable)

PORT LEYDEN (VILLAGE)—See DEWITT, NY (Time Warner Cable)

PORT WASHINGTON—See AMITYVILLE, NY (Cablevision)

PORTAGE (TOWN)—See BUFFALO, NY (Time Warner Cable)

PORTER—See BUFFALO, NY (Time Warner Cable)

PORTLAND (PORTIONS)—See BUFFALO, NY (Time Warner Cable)

PORTLAND (PORTIONS)—See JAMESTOWN, NY (Time Warner Cable)

PORTVILLE (TOWN)—See BUFFALO, NY (Time Warner Cable)

PORTVILLE (VILLAGE)—See BUFFALO, NY (Time Warner Cable)

POTSDAM (town)—Time Warner Cable. Now served by DEWITT, NY [NY0013]

POTSDAM (TOWN)—See DEWITT, NY (Time Warner Cable)

POTSDAM (VILLAGE)—See DEWITT, NY (Time Warner Cable)

POUGHKEEPSIE (TOWN)—See BETHEL (town), NY (Time Warner Cable)

POUGHKEEPSIE—Time Warner Cable. Now served by BETHEL (town), NY [NY0231]

POUGHKEEPSIE—See WAPPINGERS FALLS, NY (Cablevision)

POUGHKEEPSIE—See BETHEL (town), NY (Time Warner Cable)

POUND RIDGE—See YORKTOWN, NY (Cablevision)

PRATTS HOLLOW—See DEWITT, NY (Time Warner Cable)

PRATTSBURGH (TOWN)—See BUFFALO, NY (Time Warner Cable)

PRATTSVILLE (TOWN)—See WINDHAM, NY (Mid-Hudson Cablevision Inc.)

PREBLE (TOWN)—See DEWITT, NY (Time Warner Cable)

PRESTON PARK (VILLAGE)—See HANCOCK, PA (Hancock Video)

PRINCETOWN (town)—Formerly served by Princetown Cable Co. Now served by Time Warner Cable, ALBANY, NY [NY0151]

PRINCETOWN (TOWN)—See ALBANY, NY (Time Warner Cable)

PRINCETOWN—See ALBANY, NY (Time Warner Cable)

PROSPECT (VILLAGE)—See DEWITT, NY (Time Warner Cable)

PROVIDENCE (TOWN)—See ALBANY, NY (Time Warner Cable)

PULASKI (VILLAGE)—See DEWITT, NY (Time Warner Cable)

PULTENEY (TOWN)—See BUFFALO, NY (Time Warner Cable)

PUTNAM (TOWN)—See ALBANY, NY (Time Warner Cable)

PUTNAM VALLEY—See YORKTOWN, NY (Cablevision)

QUEENS VILLAGE—See MANHATTAN, NY (Time Warner Cable)

QUEENS—RCN Corp. This cable system has converted to IPTV. See NEW YORK CITY, NY [NY5312]

QUEENS—See NEW YORK CITY, NY (RCN. Formerly served by MANHATTAN, NY [NY0282]. This cable system has converted to IPTV)

QUEENS—See MANHATTAN, NY (Time Warner Cable)

QUEENSBURY (TOWN)—See ALBANY, NY (Time Warner Cable)

QUEENSBURY—Formerly served by Adelphia Communications. No longer in operation

QUOGUE—See RIVERHEAD, NY (Cablevision)

RAMAPO (town)—Now served by Cablevision, ROCKLAND, NY [NY0017]

RAMAPO (TOWN)—See OSSINING, NY (Cablevision)

RAMAPO CORRIDOR—See ROCKLAND, NY (Cablevision)

RAMAPO—See ROCKLAND, NY (Cablevision)

RANDOLPH (TOWN)—See BUFFALO, NY (Time Warner Cable)

RANDOLPH (VILLAGE)—See BUFFALO, NY (Time Warner Cable)

RANSOMVILLE—See BUFFALO, NY (Time Warner Cable)

RATHBONE—See DEWITT, NY (Time Warner Cable)

RAVENA (VILLAGE)—See CATSKILL, NY (Mid-Hudson Cablevision Inc.)

READING (TOWN)—See BUFFALO, NY (Time Warner Cable)

READING—See BURDETT, NY (Haefele TV Inc)

RED CREEK (VILLAGE)—See BUFFALO, NY (Time Warner Cable)

RED HOOK (TOWN)—See BETHEL (town), NY (Time Warner Cable)

RED HOOK (VILLAGE)—See BETHEL (town), NY (Time Warner Cable)

REGO PARK—See NEW YORK CITY, NY (RCN. Formerly served by MANHATTAN, NY [NY0282]. This cable system has converted to IPTV)

REGO PARK—See MANHATTAN, NY (Time Warner Cable)

REMSEN (TOWN)—See DEWITT, NY (Time Warner Cable)

REMSEN (VILLAGE)—See DEWITT, NY (Time Warner Cable)

RENSSELAER (town)—Time Warner Cable. Now served by ALBANY, NY [NY0014]

RENSSELAER (TOWN)—See ALBANY, NY (Time Warner Cable)

RENSSELAER FALLS (VILLAGE)—See DEWITT, NY (Time Warner Cable)

RENSSELAERVILLE—See WINDHAM, NY (Mid-Hudson Cablevision Inc.)

RHINEBECK (town)—Time Warner Cable. Now served by BETHEL (town), NY [NY0231]

RHINEBECK (TOWN)—See BETHEL (town), NY (Time Warner Cable)

RHINEBECK (VILLAGE)—See BETHEL (town), NY (Time Warner Cable)

RHINECLIFF—See BETHEL (town), NY (Time Warner Cable)

RICHBURG (VILLAGE)—See DEWITT, NY (Time Warner Cable)

RICHFIELD (TOWN)—See DEWITT, NY (Time Warner Cable)

RICHFIELD SPRINGS (VILLAGE)—See DEWITT, NY (Time Warner Cable)

RICHFORD (TOWN)—See BERKSHIRE, NY (Haefele TV Inc)

RICHLAND (TOWN)—See DEWITT, NY (Time Warner Cable)

RICHMOND (TOWN)—See BUFFALO, NY (Time Warner Cable)

RICHMOND HILL—See MANHATTAN, NY (Time Warner Cable)

RICHMONDVILLE (TOWN)—See ALBANY, NY (Time Warner Cable)

RICHMONDVILLE (VILLAGE)—See ALBANY, NY (Time Warner Cable)

RICHVILLE (VILLAGE)—See DEWITT, NY (Time Warner Cable)

RIDGEWAY (TOWN)—See BUFFALO, NY (Time Warner Cable)

RIDGEWOOD—See MANHATTAN, NY (Time Warner Cable)

RIGA (TOWN)—See BUFFALO, NY (Time Warner Cable)

Cable Community Index—New York

RIPLEY (TOWN)—See BUFFALO, NY (Time Warner Cable)

RIVERHEAD—Cablevision

RIVERSIDE (VILLAGE)—See DEWITT, NY (Time Warner Cable)

ROCHESTER (TOWN)—See BETHEL (town), NY (Time Warner Cable)

ROCHESTER—Time Warner Cable. Now served by BUFFALO (formerly Lackawanna), NY [NY0216]

ROCHESTER—See BUFFALO, NY (Time Warner Cable)

ROCKAWAY BEACH—See MANHATTAN, NY (Time Warner Cable)

ROCKAWAY PARK—See MANHATTAN, NY (Time Warner Cable)

ROCKAWAY POINT—See MANHATTAN, NY (Time Warner Cable)

ROCKDALE—See DEWITT, NY (Time Warner Cable)

ROCKLAND (TOWN)—See BETHEL (town), NY (Time Warner Cable)

ROCKLAND COUNTY (UNINCORPORATED AREAS)—See ROCKLAND, NY (Cablevision)

ROCKLAND—Cablevision

ROCKVILLE CENTRE—See AMITYVILLE, NY (Cablevision)

RODMAN (TOWN)—See DEWITT, NY (Time Warner Cable)

ROME—Time Warner Cable. Now served by DEWITT, NY [NY0013]

ROME—See DEWITT, NY (Time Warner Cable)

ROMULUS (TOWN)—See BUFFALO, NY (Time Warner Cable)

ROOSEVELT ISLAND—See MANHATTAN, NY (Time Warner Cable)

ROOT (TOWN)—See ALBANY, NY (Time Warner Cable)

ROSE (TOWN)—See BUFFALO, NY (Time Warner Cable)

ROSEDALE—See MANHATTAN, NY (Time Warner Cable)

ROSENDALE (town)—Time Warner Cable. Now served by BETHEL (town), NY [NY0231]

ROSENDALE (TOWN)—See BETHEL (town), NY (Time Warner Cable)

ROSLYN ESTATES—See AMITYVILLE, NY (Cablevision)

ROSLYN HARBOR (VILLAGE)—See AMITYVILLE, NY (Cablevision)

ROSLYN—See AMITYVILLE, NY (Cablevision)

ROTTERDAM (PORTIONS)—See ALBANY, NY (Time Warner Cable)

ROTTERDAM (TOWN)—See ALBANY, NY (Time Warner Cable)

ROUND LAKE (VILLAGE)—See ALBANY, NY (Time Warner Cable)

ROUSES POINT (VILLAGE)—See DEWITT, NY (Time Warner Cable)

ROXBURY—See WINDHAM, NY (Mid-Hudson Cablevision Inc.)

ROXBURY—See MARGARETVILLE, NY (MTC Cable)

ROYALTON (TOWN)—See BUFFALO, NY (Time Warner Cable)

RUSH (TOWN)—See BUFFALO, NY (Time Warner Cable)

RUSHVILLE (VILLAGE) (ONTARIO COUNTY)—See BUFFALO, NY (Time Warner Cable)

RUSHVILLE (VILLAGE) (YATES COUNTY)—See BUFFALO, NY (Time Warner Cable)

RUSSELL (TOWN)—See DEWITT, NY (Time Warner Cable)

RUSSELL GARDENS (VILLAGE)—See AMITYVILLE, NY (Cablevision)

RUSSIA (TOWN)—See DEWITT, NY (Time Warner Cable)

RUTLAND (TOWN)—See DEWITT, NY (Time Warner Cable)

RYE (CITY)—See MAMARONECK, NY (Cablevision)

RYE BROOK (VILLAGE)—See MAMARONECK, NY (Cablevision)

SACKETS HARBOR (VILLAGE)—See DEWITT, NY (Time Warner Cable)

SADDLE ROCK (VILLAGE)—See AMITYVILLE, NY (Cablevision)

SAG HARBOR—See RIVERHEAD, NY (Cablevision)

SAGAPONACK—See RIVERHEAD, NY (Cablevision)

SALAMANCA (TOWN)—See SALAMANCA, NY (Atlantic Broadband)

SALAMANCA—Atlantic Broadband

SALEM (TOWN)—See ALBANY, NY (Time Warner Cable)

SALEM (VILLAGE)—See ALBANY, NY (Time Warner Cable)

SALINA (TOWN)—See DEWITT, NY (Time Warner Cable)

SALISBURY (TOWN)—See DEWITT, NY (Time Warner Cable)

SANBORN—See BUFFALO, NY (Time Warner Cable)

SAND LAKE (TOWN)—See ALBANY, NY (Time Warner Cable)

SANDS POINT—See AMITYVILLE, NY (Cablevision)

SANDUSKY (TOWN)—See BUFFALO, NY (Time Warner Cable)

SANDY CREEK (TOWN)—See DEWITT, NY (Time Warner Cable)

SANDY CREEK (VILLAGE)—See DEWITT, NY (Time Warner Cable)

SANDYSTON TWP.—See WARWICK, NJ (Cablevision)

SANFORD—See AFTON, NY (Adams Cable Service)

SANGERFIELD (TOWN)—See DEWITT, NY (Time Warner Cable)

SANTA CLARA (TOWN)—See DEWITT, NY (Time Warner Cable)

SARANAC (TOWN)—See PLATTSBURGH, NY (Charter Communications)

SARANAC LAKE (village)—Time Warner Cable. Now served by DEWITT, NY [NY0013]

Saranac Lake (village)—See SARANAC LAKE (village), NY (Time Warner Cable. Now served by DEWITT, NY [NY0013])

SARANAC LAKE (VILLAGE)—See DEWITT, NY (Time Warner Cable)

SARATOGA (TOWN)—See ALBANY, NY (Time Warner Cable)

SARATOGA SPRINGS—Time Warner Cable. Now served by ALBANY, NY [NY0014]

SARATOGA SPRINGS—See ALBANY, NY (Time Warner Cable)

SARDINIA (TOWN)—See BUFFALO, NY (Time Warner Cable)

SAUGERTIES (town)—Time Warner Cable. Now served by BETHEL (town), NY [NY0231]

SAUGERTIES (TOWN)—See BETHEL (town), NY (Time Warner Cable)

SAUGERTIES (VILLAGE)—See BETHEL (town), NY (Time Warner Cable)

SAVANNAH (TOWN)—See BUFFALO, NY (Time Warner Cable)

SAVONA (VILLAGE)—See DEWITT, NY (Time Warner Cable)

SAYRE BOROUGH—See DEWITT, PA (Time Warner Cable)

SCARSDALE—See MAMARONECK, NY (Cablevision)

SCHAGHTICOKE (TOWN)—See ALBANY, NY (Time Warner Cable)

SCHAGHTICOKE (VILLAGE)—See ALBANY, NY (Time Warner Cable)

SCHENECTADY—Time Warner Cable. Now served by ALBANY, NY [NY0014]

SCHENECTADY—See ALBANY, NY (Time Warner Cable)

SCHODACK (TOWN)—See ALBANY, NY (Time Warner Cable)

SCHOHARIE (TOWN)—See BLENHEIM, NY (MidTel Cable TV)

SCHOHARIE (TOWN)—See ALBANY, NY (Time Warner Cable)

SCHOHARIE (VILLAGE)—See BLENHEIM, NY (MidTel Cable TV)

SCHOHARIE (VILLAGE)—See ALBANY, NY (Time Warner Cable)

SCHROEPPEL (town)—Time Warner Cable. Now served by DEWITT, NY [NY0013]

SCHROEPPEL (TOWN)—See DEWITT, NY (Time Warner Cable)

SCHROON (town)—Time Warner Cable. Now served by ALBANY, NY [NY0014]

SCHROON (TOWN)—See ALBANY, NY (Time Warner Cable)

SCHROON LAKE—See ALBANY, NY (Time Warner Cable)

SCHUYLER (TOWN)—See DEWITT, NY (Time Warner Cable)

SCHUYLER FALLS (TOWN)—See PLATTSBURGH, NY (Charter Communications)

SCHUYLERVILLE (VILLAGE)—See ALBANY, NY (Time Warner Cable)

SCIO (PORTIONS)—See BUFFALO, NY (Time Warner Cable)

SCIO (PORTIONS)—See DEWITT, NY (Time Warner Cable)

SCIOTA—See DEWITT, PA (Time Warner Cable)

SCOTIA (VILLAGE)—See ALBANY, NY (Time Warner Cable)

SCOTT (TOWN)—See DEWITT, NY (Time Warner Cable)

SCOTTSVILLE (VILLAGE)—See BUFFALO, NY (Time Warner Cable)

SCRIBA (TOWN)—See DEWITT, NY (Time Warner Cable)

SEA CLIFF—See AMITYVILLE, NY (Cablevision)

SEAFORD—See AMITYVILLE, NY (Cablevision)

SEMPRONIUS (TOWN)—See DEWITT, NY (Time Warner Cable)

SENECA (TOWN)—See BUFFALO, NY (Time Warner Cable)

SENECA FALLS (TOWN)—See BUFFALO, NY (Time Warner Cable)

SENECA FALLS (VILLAGE)—See BUFFALO, NY (Time Warner Cable)

SENNETT (TOWN)—See DEWITT, NY (Time Warner Cable)

SEWARD (TOWN)—See ALBANY, NY (Time Warner Cable)

SHANDAKEN (TOWN)—See BETHEL (town), NY (Time Warner Cable)

SHARON (TOWN)—See ALBANY, NY (Time Warner Cable)

SHARON SPRINGS (VILLAGE)—See ALBANY, NY (Time Warner Cable)

SHAWANGUNK (TOWN)—See BETHEL (town), NY (Time Warner Cable)

SHELBY (TOWN)—See BUFFALO, NY (Time Warner Cable)

SHELDON (TOWN)—See BUFFALO, NY (Time Warner Cable)

SHELTER ISLAND—See RIVERHEAD, NY (Cablevision)

SHERBURNE (TOWN)—See DEWITT, NY (Time Warner Cable)

New York—Cable Community Index

SHERBURNE (VILLAGE)—See DEWITT, NY (Time Warner Cable)

SHERIDAN (TOWN)—See BUFFALO, NY (Time Warner Cable)

SHERMAN (TOWN)—See BUFFALO, NY (Time Warner Cable)

SHERMAN (VILLAGE)—See BUFFALO, NY (Time Warner Cable)

SHERRILL—See DEWITT, NY (Time Warner Cable)

SHINGLEHOUSE—See DEWITT, PA (Time Warner Cable)

SHOKAN—See BETHEL (town), NY (Time Warner Cable)

SHOREHAM—See SUFFOLK COUNTY, NY (Cablevision)

SHORTSVILLE (VILLAGE)—See BUFFALO, NY (Time Warner Cable)

SIDNEY (town)—Time Warner Cable. Now served by DEWITT, NY [NY0013]

SIDNEY (TOWN)—See DEWITT, NY (Time Warner Cable)

SIDNEY (VILLAGE)—See DEWITT, NY (Time Warner Cable)

SILVER CREEK (village)—Time Warner Cable. Now served by BUFFALO (formerly Lackawanna), NY [NY0216]

SILVER CREEK (VILLAGE)—See BUFFALO, NY (Time Warner Cable)

SILVER LAKE TWP.—See DEWITT, PA (Time Warner Cable)

SILVER SPRINGS (VILLAGE)—See BUFFALO, NY (Time Warner Cable)

SINCLAIRVILLE (VILLAGE)—See JAMESTOWN, NY (Time Warner Cable)

SKANEATELES (TOWN)—See DEWITT, NY (Time Warner Cable)

SKANEATELES (VILLAGE)—See DEWITT, NY (Time Warner Cable)

SLEEPY HOLLOW—See OSSINING, NY (Cablevision)

SLOAN (VILLAGE)—See BUFFALO, NY (Time Warner Cable)

SLOATSBURG—See ROCKLAND, NY (Cablevision)

SMITHBORO—See SPENCER, NY (Haefele TV Inc)

SMITHFIELD (TOWN)—See DEWITT, NY (Time Warner Cable)

SMITHTOWN—See SUFFOLK COUNTY, NY (Cablevision)

SMITHVILLE—Haefele TV Inc

SMYRNA (TOWN)—See DEWITT, NY (Time Warner Cable)

SMYRNA (VILLAGE)—See DEWITT, NY (Time Warner Cable)

SODUS (TOWN)—See BUFFALO, NY (Time Warner Cable)

SODUS (VILLAGE)—See BUFFALO, NY (Time Warner Cable)

SODUS POINT (VILLAGE)—See BUFFALO, NY (Time Warner Cable)

SOLVAY (VILLAGE)—See DEWITT, NY (Time Warner Cable)

SOMERS—See YORKTOWN, NY (Cablevision)

SOMERSET (TOWN)—See BUFFALO, NY (Time Warner Cable)

SOUTH BLOOMING GROVE—See WAPPINGERS FALLS, NY (Cablevision)

SOUTH BRISTOL (TOWN)—See BUFFALO, NY (Time Warner Cable)

SOUTH CORNING (VILLAGE)—See DEWITT, NY (Time Warner Cable)

SOUTH DAYTON (VILLAGE)—See JAMESTOWN, NY (Time Warner Cable)

SOUTH FLORAL PARK—See AMITYVILLE, NY (Cablevision)

SOUTH GLENS FALLS (VILLAGE)—See ALBANY, NY (Time Warner Cable)

SOUTH NYACK—See ROCKLAND, NY (Cablevision)

SOUTH WAVERLY—See DEWITT, PA (Time Warner Cable)

SOUTHAMPTON (VILLAGE)—See RIVERHEAD, NY (Cablevision)

SOUTHAMPTON—See RIVERHEAD, NY (Cablevision)

SOUTHOLD—See RIVERHEAD, NY (Cablevision)

SOUTHPORT (TOWN)—See DEWITT, NY (Time Warner Cable)

SPAFFORD (TOWN)—See DEWITT, NY (Time Warner Cable)

SPARTA (TOWN)—See DEWITT, NY (Time Warner Cable)

SPENCER (TOWN)—See SPENCER, NY (Haefele TV Inc)

SPENCER—Haefele TV Inc

SPENCERPORT (VILLAGE)—See BUFFALO, NY (Time Warner Cable)

SPRING VALLEY—See ROCKLAND, NY (Cablevision)

SPRINGFIELD (TOWN)—See DEWITT, NY (Time Warner Cable)

SPRINGFIELD GARDENS—See MANHATTAN, NY (Time Warner Cable)

SPRINGPORT (TOWN)—See BUFFALO, NY (Time Warner Cable)

SPRINGVILLE (village)—Time Warner Cable. Now served by BUFFALO, NY [NY0216]

SPRINGVILLE (VILLAGE)—See BUFFALO, NY (Time Warner Cable)

SPRINGVILLE TWP.—See DEWITT, PA (Time Warner Cable)

SPRINGWATER (TOWN)—See DEWITT, NY (Time Warner Cable)

ST. ARMAND (TOWN)—See DEWITT, NY (Time Warner Cable)

ST. JOHNSVILLE (TOWN)—See ALBANY, NY (Time Warner Cable)

ST. JOHNSVILLE (VILLAGE)—See ALBANY, NY (Time Warner Cable)

STAFFORD (TOWN)—See BUFFALO, NY (Time Warner Cable)

STAMFORD (town)—Time Warner Cable. Now served by DEWITT, NY [NY0013]

STAMFORD (TOWN)—See DEWITT, NY (Time Warner Cable)

STAMFORD (VILLAGE)—See DEWITT, NY (Time Warner Cable)

STANFORD (TOWN)—See WAPPINGERS FALLS, NY (Cablevision)

STARK—See DEWITT, NY (Time Warner Cable)

STARKEY (TOWN)—See DEWITT, NY (Time Warner Cable)

STARLIGHT (VILLAGE)—See HANCOCK, PA (Hancock Video)

STATEN ISLAND—Time Warner Cable

STERLING (TOWN)—See DEWITT, NY (Time Warner Cable)

STEWART MANOR—See AMITYVILLE, NY (Cablevision)

STILLWATER (TOWN)—See ALBANY, NY (Time Warner Cable)

STILLWATER (VILLAGE)—See ALBANY, NY (Time Warner Cable)

STOCKBRIDGE (TOWN)—See DEWITT, NY (Time Warner Cable)

STOCKHOLM (TOWN)—See DEWITT, NY (Time Warner Cable)

STOCKPORT (TOWN)—See CATSKILL, NY (Mid-Hudson Cablevision Inc.)

STOCKPORT—See CATSKILL, NY (Mid-Hudson Cablevision Inc.)

STOCKTON (TOWN)—See JAMESTOWN, NY (Time Warner Cable)

STONE RIDGE—See BETHEL (town), NY (Time Warner Cable)

STONY POINT—See OSSINING, NY (Cablevision)

STOTTVILLE—See CATSKILL, NY (Mid-Hudson Cablevision Inc.)

STUYVESANT (TOWN)—See ALBANY, NY (Time Warner Cable)

STUYVESANT FALLS—See KINDERHOOK, NY (Berkshire Cable Corporation)

STUYVESANT—See KINDERHOOK, NY (Berkshire Cable Corporation)

SUFFERN—See ROCKLAND, NY (Cablevision)

SUFFOLK COUNTY—Cablevision

SULLIVAN (town)—Time Warner Cable. Now served by DEWITT, NY [NY0013]

SULLIVAN (TOWN)—See DEWITT, NY (Time Warner Cable)

SULLIVAN COUNTY (PORTIONS)—See BETHEL (town), NY (Time Warner Cable)

SULLIVAN COUNTY—Time Warner Cable. Now served by BETHEL (town), NY [NY0231]

SUMMIT (town)—Formerly served by C H Comm LLC. No longer in operation

SUMMIT—See BLENHEIM, NY (MidTel Cable TV)

SUMMITT (TOWN)—See DEWITT, NY (Time Warner Cable)

SUNNYSIDE—See NEW YORK CITY, NY (RCN. Formerly served by MANHATTAN, NY [NY0282]. This cable system has converted to IPTV)

SWEDEN (TOWN)—See BUFFALO, NY (Time Warner Cable)

SYLVAN BEACH (VILLAGE)—See DEWITT, NY (Time Warner Cable)

SYRACUSE—Time Warner Cable. Now served by DEWITT, NY [NY0013]

SYRACUSE—See DEWITT, NY (Time Warner Cable)

TAGHKANIC—See CATSKILL, NY (Mid-Hudson Cablevision Inc.)

TANNERSVILLE (VILLAGE)—See BETHEL (town), NY (Time Warner Cable)

TARRYTOWN—See OSSINING, NY (Cablevision)

TAYLOR (TOWN)—See DEWITT, NY (Time Warner Cable)

THENDARA—See DEWITT, NY (Time Warner Cable)

THERESA (TOWN)—See DEWITT, NY (Time Warner Cable)

THERESA (VILLAGE)—See DEWITT, NY (Time Warner Cable)

THOMASTON (VILLAGE)—See AMITYVILLE, NY (Cablevision)

THOMPSON (TOWN)—See BETHEL (town), NY (Time Warner Cable)

THROOP (TOWN)—See DEWITT, NY (Time Warner Cable)

THURSTON (TOWN)—See DEWITT, NY (Time Warner Cable)

TICONDEROGA (TOWN)—See ALBANY, NY (Time Warner Cable)

TILLSON—See BETHEL (town), NY (Time Warner Cable)

TIOGA (TOWN)—See DEWITT, NY (Time Warner Cable)

TIOGA BOROUGH—See DEWITT, PA (Time Warner Cable)

TIOGA—See SPENCER, NY (Haefele TV Inc)

TIVOLI (VILLAGE)—See BETHEL (town), NY (Time Warner Cable)

TOMPKINS (TOWN)—See HANCOCK, NY (Hancock Video)

TOMPKINS COUNTY—Formerly served by Time Warner Cable. No longer in operation

TONAWANDA (TOWN)—See BUFFALO, NY (Time Warner Cable)

Cable Community Index—New York

TONAWANDA—See BUFFALO, NY (Time Warner Cable)

TORREY—See BUFFALO, NY (Time Warner Cable)

TRENTON (TOWN)—See DEWITT, NY (Time Warner Cable)

TRIANGLE (TOWN)—See DEWITT, NY (Time Warner Cable)

TROUPSBURG (town)—Time Warner Cable. Now served by DEWITT, NY [NY0013]

TROUPSBURG (TOWN)—See DEWITT, NY (Time Warner Cable)

TROY—Time Warner Cable. Now served by ALBANY, NY [NY0014]

TROY—See ALBANY, NY (Time Warner Cable)

TRUMANSBURG (VILLAGE)—See DEWITT, NY (Time Warner Cable)

TRUXTON (TOWN)—See DEWITT, NY (Time Warner Cable)

TUCKAHOE—See MAMARONECK, NY (Cablevision)

TULLY (TOWN)—See DEWITT, NY (Time Warner Cable)

TULLY (VILLAGE)—See DEWITT, NY (Time Warner Cable)

TUPPER LAKE (TOWN)—See DEWITT, NY (Time Warner Cable)

TUPPER LAKE (VILLAGE)—See DEWITT, NY (Time Warner Cable)

TURIN (town)—Formerly served by Turin Cable TV. Now served by Time Warner Cable, DEWITT, NY [NY0013]

TURIN (TOWN)—See DEWITT, NY (Time Warner Cable)

TURIN (VILLAGE)—See DEWITT, NY (Time Warner Cable)

TUSCARORA (TOWN)—See DEWITT, NY (Time Warner Cable)

TUSTEN (TOWN)—See BETHEL (town), NY (Time Warner Cable)

TUSTEN—Time Warner Cable. Now served by BETHEL (town), NY [NY0231]

TUXEDO PARK—See ROCKLAND, NY (Cablevision)

TUXEDO—See ROCKLAND, NY (Cablevision)

TYRONE (TOWN)—See BUFFALO, NY (Time Warner Cable)

ULSTER (TOWN)—See BETHEL (town), NY (Time Warner Cable)

ULSTER TWP.—See DEWITT, PA (Time Warner Cable)

ULYSSES (TOWN)—See DEWITT, NY (Time Warner Cable)

ULYSSES BOROUGH—See BUFFALO, PA (Time Warner Cable)

UNADILLA (TOWN)—See DEWITT, NY (Time Warner Cable)

UNADILLA (VILLAGE)—See DEWITT, NY (Time Warner Cable)

UNION (TOWN)—See DEWITT, NY (Time Warner Cable)

UNION SPRINGS (VILLAGE)—See BUFFALO, NY (Time Warner Cable)

UNION VALE (TOWN)—See WAPPINGERS FALLS, NY (Cablevision)

UNIONVILLE—See WARWICK, NY (Cablevision)

UPPER BROOKVILLE—See AMITYVILLE, NY (Cablevision)

UPPER NYACK—See ROCKLAND, NY (Cablevision)

URBANA (TOWN)—See BUFFALO, NY (Time Warner Cable)

UTICA—Time Warner Cable. Now served by DEWITT, NY [NY0013]

UTICA—See DEWITT, NY (Time Warner Cable)

UTOPIA—See MANHATTAN, NY (Time Warner Cable)

VALATIE (VILLAGE)—See KINDERHOOK, NY (Berkshire Cable Corporation)

VALATIE (VILLAGE)—See ALBANY, NY (Time Warner Cable)

VALLEY FALLS (VILLAGE)—See ALBANY, NY (Time Warner Cable)

VALLEY STREAM—See AMITYVILLE, NY (Cablevision)

VAN BUREN (TOWN)—See DEWITT, NY (Time Warner Cable)

VAN ETTEN (VILLAGE)—See SPENCER, NY (Haefele TV Inc)

VARICK (TOWN)—See BUFFALO, NY (Time Warner Cable)

VERBANK—See DOVER PLAINS, NY (Cablevision)

VERMONTVILLE—See DEWITT, NY (Time Warner Cable)

VERNON (TOWN)—See DEWITT, NY (Time Warner Cable)

VERNON (VILLAGE)—See DEWITT, NY (Time Warner Cable)

VERONA (TOWN)—See DEWITT, NY (Time Warner Cable)

VESTAL (TOWN)—See DEWITT, NY (Time Warner Cable)

VETERAN (TOWN)—See DEWITT, NY (Time Warner Cable)

VICTOR (TOWN)—See BUFFALO, NY (Time Warner Cable)

VICTOR (VILLAGE)—See BUFFALO, NY (Time Warner Cable)

VICTORY MILLS (VILLAGE)—See ALBANY, NY (Time Warner Cable)

VIENNA (TOWN)—See DEWITT, NY (Time Warner Cable)

VILLAGE OF THE BRANCH—See SUFFOLK COUNTY, NY (Cablevision)

VILLENOVA (TOWN)—See JAMESTOWN, NY (Time Warner Cable)

VIRGIL (TOWN)—See BERKSHIRE, NY (Haefele TV Inc)

VIRGIL (TOWN)—See DEWITT, NY (Time Warner Cable)

VOLNEY (TOWN)—See DEWITT, NY (Time Warner Cable)

VOORHEESVILLE (VILLAGE)—See ALBANY, NY (Time Warner Cable)

WADDINGTON (TOWN)—See DEWITT, NY (Time Warner Cable)

WADDINGTON (VILLAGE)—See DEWITT, NY (Time Warner Cable)

WALDEN (village)—Time Warner Cable. Now served by BETHEL (town), NY [NY0231]

WALDEN (VILLAGE)—See BETHEL (town), NY (Time Warner Cable)

WALES (TOWN)—See BUFFALO, NY (Time Warner Cable)

WALLKILL (TOWN)—See BETHEL (town), NY (Time Warner Cable)

WALTON (TOWN)—See DEWITT, NY (Time Warner Cable)

WALTON (village)—Time Warner Cable. Now served by DEWITT, NY [NY0013]

WALTON (VILLAGE)—See DEWITT, NY (Time Warner Cable)

WALWORTH (TOWN)—See BUFFALO, NY (Time Warner Cable)

WAMPSVILLE (VILLAGE)—See DEWITT, NY (Time Warner Cable)

WAPPINGER (TOWN)—See WAPPINGERS FALLS, NY (Cablevision)

WAPPINGERS FALLS—Cablevision

WARREN—See DEWITT, NY (Time Warner Cable)

WARRENSBURG (TOWN)—See ALBANY, NY (Time Warner Cable)

WARSAW (TOWN)—See BUFFALO, NY (Time Warner Cable)

WARSAW (village)—Time Warner Cable. Now served by BUFFALO (formerly Lackawanna), NY [NY0216]

WARSAW (VILLAGE)—See BUFFALO, NY (Time Warner Cable)

WARWICK (VILLAGE)—See WARWICK, NY (Cablevision)

WARWICK TWP.—See WARWICK, NY (Cablevision)

WARWICK—Formerly served by Alteva (formerly WVT). No longer in operation

WARWICK—Cablevision

WASHINGTON (TOWN)—See WAPPINGERS FALLS, NY (Cablevision)

WASHINGTONVILLE (village)—Time Warner Cable. Now served by BETHEL (town), NY [NY0231]

WASHINGTONVILLE (VILLAGE)—See BETHEL (town), NY (Time Warner Cable)

WATERFORD (TOWN)—See ALBANY, NY (Time Warner Cable)

WATERFORD (VILLAGE)—See ALBANY, NY (Time Warner Cable)

WATERLOO (TOWN)—See BUFFALO, NY (Time Warner Cable)

WATERLOO (VILLAGE)—See BUFFALO, NY (Time Warner Cable)

WATERTOWN (TOWN)—See DEWITT, NY (Time Warner Cable)

WATERTOWN—Time Warner Cable. Now served by DEWITT, NY [NY0013]

WATERTOWN—Time Warner Cable. Now served by DEWITT, NY [NY0013]

WATERTOWN—See DEWITT, NY (Time Warner Cable)

WATERVILLE (VILLAGE)—See DEWITT, NY (Time Warner Cable)

WATERVLIET ARSENAL—See ALBANY, NY (Time Warner Cable)

WATERVLIET—See ALBANY, NY (Time Warner Cable)

WATKINS GLEN (VILLAGE)—See DEWITT, NY (Time Warner Cable)

WATSON (TOWN)—See DEWITT, NY (Time Warner Cable)

WAVERLY (TOWN)—See DEWITT, NY (Time Warner Cable)

WAVERLY (VILLAGE)—See DEWITT, NY (Time Warner Cable)

WAWARSING (TOWN)—See BETHEL (town), NY (Time Warner Cable)

WAWAYANDA (TOWN)—See BETHEL (town), NY (Time Warner Cable)

WAYLAND (TOWN)—See DEWITT, NY (Time Warner Cable)

WAYLAND (VILLAGE)—See DEWITT, NY (Time Warner Cable)

WAYNE (TOWN)—See BUFFALO, NY (Time Warner Cable)

WAYNE TWP. (ERIE COUNTY)—See JAMESTOWN, PA (Time Warner Cable)

WEBB (TOWN)—See DEWITT, NY (Time Warner Cable)

WEBSTER (TOWN)—See BUFFALO, NY (Time Warner Cable)

WEBSTER (VILLAGE)—See BUFFALO, NY (Time Warner Cable)

WEEDSPORT (VILLAGE)—See DEWITT, NY (Time Warner Cable)

WELLESLEY ISLAND—Time Warner Cable. Now served by DEWITT, NY [NY0013]

WELLESLEY ISLAND—See DEWITT, NY (Time Warner Cable)

WELLS—Hamilton County Cable TV Inc

WELLSBURG (VILLAGE)—See DEWITT, NY (Time Warner Cable)

WELLSVILLE (town)—Time Warner Cable. Now served by BUFFALO, NY [NY0216]

WELLSVILLE (TOWN)—See BUFFALO, NY (Time Warner Cable)

New York—Cable Community Index

WELLSVILLE (VILLAGE)—See BUFFALO, NY (Time Warner Cable)

WESLEY HILLS—See ROCKLAND, NY (Cablevision)

WEST BLOOMFIELD (TOWN)—See BUFFALO, NY (Time Warner Cable)

WEST CARTHAGE (VILLAGE)—See DEWITT, NY (Time Warner Cable)

WEST CHAZY—See DEWITT, NY (Time Warner Cable)

WEST HAMPTON DUNES—See RIVERHEAD, NY (Cablevision)

WEST HAVERSTRAW—See OSSINING, NY (Cablevision)

WEST HURLEY (TOWN)—See BETHEL (town), NY (Time Warner Cable)

WEST LEYDEN—See DEWITT, NY (Time Warner Cable)

WEST MILFORD—See WARWICK, NJ (Cablevision)

WEST MONROE (TOWN)—See DEWITT, NY (Time Warner Cable)

WEST NYACK—See ROCKLAND, NY (Cablevision)

WEST POINT MILITARY ACADEMY—See BETHEL (town), NY (Time Warner Cable)

WEST POINT—See BETHEL (town), NY (Time Warner Cable)

WEST SENECA (TOWN)—See BUFFALO, NY (Time Warner Cable)

WEST SHOKAN—See BETHEL (town), NY (Time Warner Cable)

WEST SPARTA (TOWN)—See DEWITT, NY (Time Warner Cable)

WEST STOCKBRIDGE—See CHATHAM, MA (Charter Communications)

WEST TURIN (TOWN)—See DEWITT, NY (Time Warner Cable)

WEST WINFIELD (VILLAGE)—See DEWITT, NY (Time Warner Cable)

WESTBURY—See AMITYVILLE, NY (Cablevision)

WESTERLO—See CATSKILL, NY (Mid-Hudson Cablevision Inc.)

WESTERN (TOWN)—See DEWITT, NY (Time Warner Cable)

WESTFALL TWP.—See WARWICK, PA (Cablevision)

WESTFIELD (town)—Time Warner Cable. Now served by BUFFALO (formerly Lackawanna), NY [NY0216]

WESTFIELD (TOWN)—See BUFFALO, NY (Time Warner Cable)

WESTFIELD (VILLAGE)—See BUFFALO, NY (Time Warner Cable)

WESTHAMPTON BEACH—See RIVERHEAD, NY (Cablevision)

WESTHAMPTON—See RIVERHEAD, NY (Cablevision)

WESTMORELAND (TOWN)—See DEWITT, NY (Time Warner Cable)

WESTPORT (TOWN)—See PLATTSBURGH, NY (Charter Communications)

WESTVILLE (TOWN)—See DEWITT, NY (Time Warner Cable)

WHEATFIELD (TOWN)—See BUFFALO, NY (Time Warner Cable)

WHEATLAND (TOWN)—See BUFFALO, NY (Time Warner Cable)

WHEELER (PORTIONS)—See BUFFALO, NY (Time Warner Cable)

WHEELER (PORTIONS)—See DEWITT, NY (Time Warner Cable)

WHITE PLAINS—See MAMARONECK, NY (Cablevision)

WHITEHALL (town)—Time Warner Cable. Now served by ALBANY, NY [NY0014]

WHITEHALL (TOWN)—See ALBANY, NY (Time Warner Cable)

WHITEHALL (VILLAGE)—See ALBANY, NY (Time Warner Cable)

WHITESBORO—See DEWITT, NY (Time Warner Cable)

WHITESTONE—See MANHATTAN, NY (Time Warner Cable)

WHITESTOWN (TOWN)—See DEWITT, NY (Time Warner Cable)

WHITESTOWN (VILLAGE)—See DEWITT, NY (Time Warner Cable)

WHITESVILLE—Formerly served by Fitzgerald Cable TV. No longer in operation

WHITNEY POINT (village)—Time Warner Cable. Now served by DEWITT, NY [NY0013]

WHITNEY POINT (VILLAGE)—See DEWITT, NY (Time Warner Cable)

WILLET (TOWN)—See DEWITT, NY (Time Warner Cable)

WILLIAMSON (TOWN)—See BUFFALO, NY (Time Warner Cable)

WILLIAMSVILLE (VILLAGE)—See BUFFALO, NY (Time Warner Cable)

WILLING (TOWN)—See BUFFALO, NY (Time Warner Cable)

WILLISTON PARK—See AMITYVILLE, NY (Cablevision)

WILLSBORO (TOWN)—Cable Communications of Willsboro

WILMINGTON—See PLATTSBURGH, NY (Charter Communications)

WILNA (TOWN)—See DEWITT, NY (Time Warner Cable)

WILSON (TOWN)—See BUFFALO, NY (Time Warner Cable)

WILSON (VILLAGE)—See BUFFALO, NY (Time Warner Cable)

WILTON (TOWN)—See ALBANY, NY (Time Warner Cable)

WINDHAM—Mid-Hudson Cablevision Inc.

WINDSOR (TOWN)—See AFTON, NY (Adams Cable Service)

WINFIELD (TOWN)—See DEWITT, NY (Time Warner Cable)

WINGDALE—See DOVER PLAINS, NY (Cablevision)

WIRT (TOWN)—See DEWITT, NY (Time Warner Cable)

WOLCOTT (TOWN)—See BUFFALO, NY (Time Warner Cable)

WOLCOTT (TOWN)—See DEWITT, NY (Time Warner Cable)

WOLCOTT (VILLAGE)—See BUFFALO, NY (Time Warner Cable)

WOODBURY—See WAPPINGERS FALLS, NY (Cablevision)

WOODHULL (town)—Time Warner Cable. Now served by DEWITT, NY [NY0013]

WOODHULL (TOWN)—See DEWITT, NY (Time Warner Cable)

WOODRIDGE (village)—Time Warner Cable. Now served by BETHEL (town), NY [NY0231]

WOODRIDGE (VILLAGE)—See BETHEL (town), NY (Time Warner Cable)

WOODSBURGH—See AMITYVILLE, NY (Cablevision)

WOODSIDE—See NEW YORK CITY, NY (RCN. Formerly served by MANHATTAN, NY [NY0282]. This cable system has converted to IPTV)

WOODSIDE—See MANHATTAN, NY (Time Warner Cable)

WOODSTOCK (town)—Time Warner Cable. Now served by BETHEL (town), NY [NY0231]

WOODSTOCK (TOWN)—See BETHEL (town), NY (Time Warner Cable)

WORCESTER (TOWN)—See DEWITT, NY (Time Warner Cable)

WRIGHT (TOWN)—See ALBANY, NY (Time Warner Cable)

WURTSBORO (VILLAGE)—See BETHEL (town), NY (Time Warner Cable)

WYOMING—See BUFFALO, NY (Time Warner Cable)

YATES (TOWN)—See BUFFALO, NY (Time Warner Cable)

YONKERS—Cablevision

YORK (TOWN)—See BUFFALO, NY (Time Warner Cable)

YORKSHIRE (TOWN)—See BUFFALO, NY (Time Warner Cable)

YORKTOWN—Cablevision

YORKVILLE (VILLAGE)—See DEWITT, NY (Time Warner Cable)

YOUNGSTOWN (VILLAGE)—See BUFFALO, NY (Time Warner Cable)

YULAN—See BETHEL (town), NY (Time Warner Cable)

NORTH CAROLINA

ABERDEEN (TOWN)—See RALEIGH, NC (Time Warner Cable)

AHOSKIE (TOWN)—See MURFREESBORO, NC (Time Warner Cable)

AHOSKIE—Formerly served by Adelphia Communications. Now served by Time Warner Cable, MURFREESBORO, NC [NC0144]

ALAMANCE (VILLAGE)—See GREENSBORO, NC (Time Warner Cable)

ALAMANCE COUNTY—See GREENSBORO, NC (Time Warner Cable)

ALBEMARLE—Time Warner Cable. Now served by CHARLOTTE, NC [NC0001]

ALBEMARLE—See CHARLOTTE, NC (Time Warner Cable)

ALEXANDER COUNTY—See HICKORY, NC (Charter Communications)

ALLEGHANY COUNTY (PORTIONS)—See HICKORY, NC (Charter Communications)

ALLIANCE (TOWN)—See JACKSONVILLE, NC (Time Warner Cable)

ANDERSON CREEK TWP.—Charter Communications. Now served by ANGIER, NC [NC0194]

ANDERSON CREEK TWP.—See ANGIER, NC (Charter Communications)

ANDREWS—Formerly served by Cable TV of Andrews. Now served by Cable TV of Cherokee County, ANDREWS, NC [NC0254]

ANDREWS—Cable TV of Cherokee County

ANGIER—Charter Communications

ANSON COUNTY—See CHARLOTTE, NC (Time Warner Cable)

ANSONVILLE—See CHARLOTTE, NC (Time Warner Cable)

APEX (TOWN)—See RALEIGH, NC (Time Warner Cable)

ARAPAHOE (TOWN)—See JACKSONVILLE, NC (Time Warner Cable)

ARCHDALE—See GREENSBORO, NC (Time Warner Cable)

ARCHER LODGE—See RALEIGH, NC (Time Warner Cable)

ARROWHEAD BEACH—Mediacom. Now served by EDENTON, NC [NC0076]

ARROWHEAD BEACH—See EDENTON, NC (Mediacom)

ASHE COUNTY (PORTIONS)—See WEST JEFFERSON, NC (Morris Broadband)

ASHE COUNTY—See HICKORY, NC (Charter Communications)

ASHEBORO—Time Warner Cable. Now served by GREENSBORO, NC [NC0006]

Cable Community Index—North Carolina

ASHEBORO—See GREENSBORO, NC (Time Warner Cable)

ASHEVILLE—Charter Communications

ATLANTIC BEACH (TOWN)—See JACKSONVILLE, NC (Time Warner Cable)

AULANDER (TOWN)—See MURFREESBORO, NC (Time Warner Cable)

AULANDER—Formerly served by Adelphia Communications. Now served by Time Warner Cable, MURFREESBORO, NC [NC0144]

AURORA (TOWN)—See JACKSONVILLE, NC (Time Warner Cable)

AUTRYVILLE—See RALEIGH, NC (Time Warner Cable)

AVERY COUNTY—See HICKORY, NC (Charter Communications)

AVON—See BUXTON, NC (Charter Communications)

AYDEN—See GREENVILLE, NC (Suddenlink Communications)

BADIN LAKE—See LIBERTY, NC (Randolph Telephone. Formerly [NC0258]. This cable system has converted to IPTV.)

BADIN—See CHARLOTTE, NC (Time Warner Cable)

BAILEY—Time Warner Cable. Now served by RALEIGH, NC [NC0003]

BAILEY—See RALEIGH, NC (Time Warner Cable)

BAKERSVILLE—See HICKORY, NC (Charter Communications)

BALD HEAD ISLAND—Tele-Media

BANNER ELK—See HICKORY, NC (Charter Communications)

BATH (TOWN)—Red's TV Cable Inc

BAYBORO (TOWN)—See JACKSONVILLE, NC (Time Warner Cable)

BEACON RIDGE (TOWN)—See RALEIGH, NC (Time Warner Cable)

BEARGRASS—See MARTIN COUNTY (central portion), NC (Suddenlink Communications)

BEAUFORT (TOWN)—See JACKSONVILLE, NC (Time Warner Cable)

BEAUFORT COUNTY (PORTIONS)—See WASHINGTON (portions), NC (Suddenlink Communications)

BEAUFORT COUNTY (UNINCORPORATED AREAS)—See BATH (town), NC (Red's TV Cable Inc)

BEAUFORT COUNTY—See JACKSONVILLE, NC (Time Warner Cable)

BEAVERDAM—See HALLS TWP., NC (StarVision)

BEECH MOUNTAIN—See HICKORY, NC (Charter Communications)

BELHAVEN—Belhaven Cable TV

BELHAVEN—TriCounty Telecom

BELMONT—See CHARLOTTE, NC (Time Warner Cable)

BELWOOD—See CHARLOTTE, NC (Time Warner Cable)

BENNETT—See LIBERTY, NC (Randolph Telephone. Formerly [NC0258]. This cable system has converted to IPTV.)

BENSON—Charter Communications. Now served by ANGIER, NC [NC0194]

BENSON—See ANGIER, NC (Charter Communications)

BERMUDA RUN (TOWN)—See GREENSBORO, NC (Time Warner Cable)

BERTIE COUNTY (EASTERN PORTION)—See COLERAIN, NC (Mediacom)

BERTIE COUNTY (PORTIONS)—See MURFREESBORO, NC (Time Warner Cable)

BERTIE COUNTY (WESTERN PORTION)—See CONWAY, NC (Mediacom)

BESSEMER CITY—See CHARLOTTE, NC (Time Warner Cable)

BETHANIA (TOWN)—See GREENSBORO, NC (Time Warner Cable)

BETHEL—See MARTIN COUNTY (central portion), NC (Suddenlink Communications)

BEULAVILLE—See ANGIER, NC (Charter Communications)

BILTMORE FOREST—See ASHEVILLE, NC (Charter Communications)

BISCOE (TOWN)—See GREENSBORO, NC (Time Warner Cable)

BLACK CREEK (TOWN)—See RALEIGH, NC (Time Warner Cable)

BLACK MOUNTAIN—Formerly served by Tri-Star Communications. No longer in operation

BLACK MOUNTAIN—See ASHEVILLE, NC (Charter Communications)

BLADEN COUNTY (PORTIONS)—See WILMINGTON, NC (Time Warner Cable)

BLADENBORO (TOWN)—See WILMINGTON, NC (Time Warner Cable)

BLOWING ROCK—See HICKORY, NC (Charter Communications)

BOGUE—See JACKSONVILLE, NC (Time Warner Cable)

BOILING SPRINGS—See CHARLOTTE, NC (Time Warner Cable)

BOLIVIA—See SHALLOTTE, NC (ATMC. Formerly [NC0050]. This cable system has converted to IPTV.)

BOLLING SPRING LAKES (TOWN)—See WILMINGTON, NC (Time Warner Cable)

BOLTON (TOWN)—See WILMINGTON,

BOONE—Charter Communications. Now served by HICKORY, NC [NC0009]

BOONE—See HICKORY, NC (Charter Communications)

BOONEVILLE (TOWN)—See GREENSBORO, NC (Time Warner Cable)

BOSTIC—See FOREST CITY, NC (Northland Cable Television)

BREVARD—Comporium Communications

BRICK LANDING—See SHALLOTTE, NC (ATMC. Formerly [NC0050]. This cable system has converted to IPTV)

BRIDGETON—See NEW BERN, NC (Suddenlink Communications)

BROADWAY—See ANGIER, NC (Charter Communications)

BROOKFORD—See HICKORY, NC (Charter Communications)

BRUNSWICK (TOWN)—See WILMINGTON, NC (Time Warner Cable)

BRUNSWICK COUNTY (PORTIONS)—See SHALLOTTE, NC (ATMC. Formerly [NC0050]. This cable system has converted to IPTV)

BRUNSWICK COUNTY (PORTIONS)—See WILMINGTON, NC (Time Warner Cable)

BRUNSWICK COUNTY (UNINCORPORATED AREAS)—See SHALLOTTE, NC (ATMC. Formerly [NC0050]. This cable system has converted to IPTV)

BRYSON CITY—Zito Media

BUNCOMBE COUNTY (northern portion)—Charter Communications. Now served by ASHEVILLE, NC [NC0012]

BUNCOMBE COUNTY (NORTHERN PORTION)—See ASHEVILLE, NC (Charter Communications)

BUNN (TOWN)—See RALEIGH, NC (Time Warner Cable)

BUNN—Formerly served by Adelphia Communications. Now served by Time Warner Cable, RALEIGH, NC [NC0003]

BUNNLEVEL—Formerly served by Carolina Cable Partnership. No longer in operation

BURGAW (TOWN)—See WILMINGTON, NC (Time Warner Cable)

BURKE COUNTY—Charter Communications. Now served by HICKORY, NC [NC0009]

BURKE COUNTY—See HICKORY, NC (Charter Communications)

BURLINGTON—Time Warner Cable. Now served by GREENSBORO, NC [NC0006]

BURLINGTON—See GREENSBORO, NC (Time Warner Cable)

BURNSVILLE—Charter Communications. Now served by HICKORY, NC [NC0009]

BURNSVILLE—See HICKORY, NC (Charter Communications)

BURNSVILLE—Country Cablevision Inc

BUTNER (TOWN)—See RALEIGH, NC (Time Warner Cable)

BUXTON—Charter Communications. Now served by BUXTON, NC [NC0118]

BUXTON—Charter Communications

CABARRUS COUNTY—See CHARLOTTE, NC (Time Warner Cable)

CAJAH'S MOUNTAIN—See HICKORY, NC (Charter Communications)

CALABASH—See SHALLOTTE, NC (ATMC. Formerly [NC0050]. This cable system has converted to IPTV)

CALDWELL COUNTY—See HICKORY, NC (Charter Communications)

CALYPSO—See ANGIER, NC (Charter Communications)

CAMDEN COUNTY—Mediacom. Now served by CURRITUCK, NC [NC0083]

CAMDEN COUNTY—See CURRITUCK, NC (Mediacom)

CAMDEN—See CURRITUCK, NC (Mediacom)

CAMERON—See ANGIER, NC (Charter Communications)

CAMP LEACH—See BELHAVEN, NC (TriCounty Telecom)

CAMP LEJEUNE—Charter Communications. Now served by ANGIER, NC [NC0194]

CAMP LEJEUNE—See ANGIER, NC (Charter Communications)

CAMP WESLEY—Time Warner Cable. Now served by CHARLOTTE, NC [NC0001]

CAMP WESLEY—See CHARLOTTE, NC (Time Warner Cable)

CANDOR—See GREENSBORO, NC (Time Warner Cable)

CANTON—See ASHEVILLE, NC (Charter Communications)

CAPE CARTERET (TOWN)—See JACKSONVILLE, NC (Time Warner Cable)

CAROLINA BEACH—Charter Communications. Now served by ANGIER, NC [NC0194]

CAROLINA BEACH—See ANGIER, NC (Charter Communications)

CAROLINA SHORES—See SHALLOTTE, NC (ATMC. Formerly [NC0050]. This cable system has converted to IPTV)

CARRBORO—Time Warner Cable. Now served by RALEIGH, NC [NC0003]

CARRBORO—See RALEIGH, NC (Time Warner Cable)

CARROLL COUNTY (PORTIONS)—See GREENSBORO, VA (Time Warner Cable)

North Carolina—Cable Community Index

CARROLL—See GREENSBORO, NC (Time Warner Cable)

CARTER COUNTY—See HICKORY, TN (Charter Communications)

CARTERET COUNTY—See JACKSONVILLE, NC (Time Warner Cable)

CARTHAGE (TOWN)—See RALEIGH, NC (Time Warner Cable)

CARY (TOWN)—See RALEIGH, NC (Time Warner Cable)

CARY—Time Warner Cable. Now served by RALEIGH, NC [NC0003]

CASAR—See CHARLOTTE, NC (Time Warner Cable)

CASTALIA—See NASH COUNTY, NC (Crystal Broadband Networks)

CASWELL BEACH (TOWN)—See WILMINGTON, NC (Time Warner Cable)

CASWELL COUNTY (PORTIONS)—See ROXBORO, NC (Charter Communications)

CASWELL COUNTY (PORTIONS)—See GREENSBORO, NC (Time Warner Cable)

CATAWBA (NORTHERN PORTION)—See HICKORY, NC (Charter Communications)

CATAWBA COUNTY—See HICKORY, NC (Charter Communications)

CEDAR ISLAND—Time Warner Cable. Now served by JACKSONVILLE, NC [NC0025]

CEDAR ISLAND—See JACKSONVILLE, NC (Time Warner Cable)

CEDAR POINT (TOWN)—See JACKSONVILLE, NC (Time Warner Cable)

CEDAR ROCK—See HICKORY, NC (Charter Communications)

CHADBOURN (TOWN)—See WILMINGTON, NC (Time Warner Cable)

CHAPEL HILL—Time Warner Cable. Now served by RALEIGH, NC [NC0003]

CHAPEL HILL—See RALEIGH, NC (Time Warner Cable)

CHARLOTTE—Time Warner Cable

CHATHAM COUNTY (UNINCORPORATED AREAS)—See ANGIER, NC (Charter Communications)

CHATHAM COUNTY—See RALEIGH, NC (Time Warner Cable)

CHEROKEE COUNTY (PORTIONS)—See MURPHY, NC (Cable TV of Cherokee County)

CHEROKEE INDIAN RESERVATION—Cherokee Cablevision

CHERRY POINT (TOWN)—See JACKSONVILLE, NC (Time Warner Cable)

CHERRY POINT—Time Warner Cable. Now served by JACKSONVILLE, NC [NC0025]

CHERRYVILLE—See CHARLOTTE, NC (Time Warner Cable)

CHIMNEY ROCK—See FOREST CITY, NC (Northland Cable Television)

CHINA GROVE—See CHARLOTTE, NC (Time Warner Cable)

CHINQUAPIN—Formerly served by Charter Communications. No longer in operation

CHOCOWINITY—See WASHINGTON (portions), NC (Suddenlink Communications)

CHOWAN BEACH—See EDENTON, NC (Mediacom)

CHOWAN COUNTY—See EDENTON, NC (Mediacom)

CHURCHLAND—Piedmont Communications Services, Inc

CLAREMONT—See HICKORY, NC (Charter Communications)

CLARKTON (TOWN)—See WILMINGTON, NC (Time Warner Cable)

CLAYTON (TOWN)—See RALEIGH, NC (Time Warner Cable)

CLEMMONS (VILLAGE)—See GREENSBORO, NC (Time Warner Cable)

CLEVELAND COUNTY—See CHARLOTTE, NC (Time Warner Cable)

CLEVELAND—See CHARLOTTE, NC (Time Warner Cable)

CLINTON—See HALLS TWP., NC (StarVision)

CLOVER—See CHARLOTTE, SC (Time Warner Cable)

CLYDE—See ASHEVILLE, NC (Charter Communications)

COATS—See ANGIER, NC (Charter Communications)

COFIELD (VILLAGE)—See MURFREESBORO, NC (Time Warner Cable)

COLERAIN—Mediacom

COLERIDGE—See LIBERTY, NC (Randolph Telephone. Formerly [NC0258]. This cable system has converted to IPTV.)

COLINGTON—See KILL DEVIL HILLS, NC (Charter Communications)

COLUMBIA—Mediacom. Now served by PLYMOUTH (town), NC [NC0085]

COLUMBIA—See PLYMOUTH (town), NC (Mediacom)

COLUMBUS COUNTY (central portion)—Formerly served by Carolina Cable Partnership. No longer in operation

COLUMBUS COUNTY (unincorporated areas)—Time Warner Cable. Now served by WILMINGTON, NC [NC0007]

COLUMBUS COUNTY—See WILMINGTON, NC (Time Warner Cable)

CONCORD—See CHARLOTTE, NC (Time Warner Cable)

CONETOE—See ROCKY MOUNT, NC (Suddenlink Communications)

CONNELLY SPRINGS—See HICKORY, NC (Charter Communications)

CONOVER—See HICKORY, NC (Charter Communications)

CONWAY—Mediacom. Now served by CONWAY (formerly Rich Square), NC [NC0115]

CONWAY—Mediacom

COOLEEMEE (TOWN)—See GREENSBORO, NC (Time Warner Cable)

COOLEEMEE—See FARMINGTON, NC (Yadtel)

CORNELIUS—See MOORESVILLE, NC (MI-Connection)

CORNELIUS—See CHARLOTTE, NC (Time Warner Cable)

COROLLA—Charter Communications. Now served by KILL DEVIL HILLS, NC [NC0256]

COROLLA—See KILL DEVIL HILLS, NC (Charter Communications)

CRAMERTON—See CHARLOTTE, NC (Time Warner Cable)

CRAVEN COUNTY—See NEW BERN, NC (Suddenlink Communications)

CRAVEN COUNTY—See JACKSONVILLE, NC (Time Warner Cable)

CRAVEN—Formerly served by Time Warner Cable. No longer in operation

CREEDMOOR (TOWN)—See RALEIGH, NC (Time Warner Cable)

CRESTON (SOUTHERN PORTION)—Zito Media

CRESWELL—See PLYMOUTH (town), NC (Mediacom)

CROSSNORE—See HICKORY, NC (Charter Communications)

CRUSO—Carolina Mountain Cable. Now served by HAYWOOD COUNTY (portions), NC [NC0127]

CRUSO—See HAYWOOD COUNTY (portions), NC (Carolina Mountain Cablevision Inc)

CUMBERLAND COUNTY—See RALEIGH, NC (Time Warner Cable)

CURRITUCK COUNTY (SOUTHERN PORTION)—See CURRITUCK, NC (Mediacom)

CURRITUCK—Mediacom

DALLAS—See HICKORY, NC (Charter Communications)

DALLAS—See CHARLOTTE, NC (Time Warner Cable)

DANA—See HENDERSONVILLE, NC (Morris Broadband)

DANBURY (TOWN)—See GREENSBORO, NC (Time Warner Cable)

DARE COUNTY (PORTIONS)—See BUXTON, NC (Charter Communications)

DARE COUNTY (PORTIONS)—See KILL DEVIL HILLS, NC (Charter Communications)

DAVIDSON COUNTY (WESTERN PORTION)—See CHURCHLAND, NC (Piedmont Communications Services, Inc)

DAVIDSON COUNTY—Time Warner Cable. Now served by GREENSBORO, NC [NC0006]

DAVIDSON COUNTY—See GREENSBORO, NC (Time Warner Cable)

DAVIDSON—See MOORESVILLE, NC (MI-Connection)

DAVIDSON—See CHARLOTTE, NC (Time Warner Cable)

DAVIE COUNTY (PORTIONS)—See GREENSBORO, NC (Time Warner Cable)

DAVIE COUNTY (PORTIONS)—See FARMINGTON, NC (Yadtel)

DENTON (TOWN)—See GREENSBORO, NC (Time Warner Cable)

DENTON—See LEXINGTON, NC (Windstream)

DILLSBORO—See HENDERSONVILLE, NC (Morris Broadband)

DOBBINS HEIGHTS—See CHARLOTTE, NC (Time Warner Cable)

DOBSON (TOWN)—See GREENSBORO, NC (Time Warner Cable)

DOBSON—Time Warner Cable. Now served by GREENSBORO, NC [NC0006]

DORTCHES—See NASH COUNTY, NC (Crystal Broadband Networks)

DOUGLAS CROSSROADS—See BELHAVEN, NC (TriCounty Telecom)

DOVER—Formerly served by Johnston County Cable LP. No longer in operation

DREXEL—See HICKORY, NC (Charter Communications)

DUBLIN (TOWN)—See WILMINGTON, NC (Time Warner Cable)

DUCK—See KILL DEVIL HILLS, NC (Charter Communications)

DUNCAN—Formerly served by Carolina Cable Partnership. No longer in operation

DUNN—See ANGIER, NC (Charter Communications)

DUNN—See RALEIGH, NC (Time Warner Cable)

DUPLIN COUNTY (PORTIONS)—See JACKSONVILLE, NC (Time Warner Cable)

DUPLIN COUNTY—See ANGIER, NC (Charter Communications)

DURHAM COUNTY—See RALEIGH, NC (Time Warner Cable)

DURHAM—Time Warner Cable. Now served by RALEIGH, NC [NC0003]

Cable Community Index—North Carolina

DURHAM—See RALEIGH, NC (Time Warner Cable)

DYSARTSVILLE TWP.—See HENDERSONVILLE, NC (Morris Broadband)

EARL—See CHARLOTTE, NC (Time Warner Cable)

EAST ARCADIA (TOWN)—See WILMINGTON, NC (Time Warner Cable)

EAST BEND (TOWN)—See GREENSBORO, NC (Time Warner Cable)

EAST FLAT ROCK—See HENDERSONVILLE, NC (Morris Broadband)

EAST SPENCER—See CHARLOTTE, NC (Time Warner Cable)

EASTOVER—See RALEIGH, NC (Time Warner Cable)

EDEN (TOWN)—See GREENSBORO, NC (Time Warner Cable)

EDENTON—Mediacom

EDGECOMBE COUNTY (EASTERN PORTION)—See ROCKY MOUNT, NC (Suddenlink Communications)

EDGECOMBE COUNTY (PORTIONS)—See MID LAKES TRAILER PARK, NC (Crystal Broadband Networks)

EDGECOMBE COUNTY (PORTIONS)—See NASH COUNTY, NC (Crystal Broadband Networks)

EDGECOMBE COUNTY (PORTIONS)—See OAK CITY, NC (Crystal Broadband Networks)

EDGECOMBE COUNTY (PORTIONS)—See PINETOPS, NC (Crystal Broadband Networks)

EDGECOMBE COUNTY (PORTIONS)—See WHITAKERS, NC (Crystal Broadband Networks)

ELIZABETH CITY—Time Warner Cable

ELIZABETHTOWN—Time Warner Cable. Now served by WILMINGTON, NC [NC0007]

ELIZABETHTOWN—See WILMINGTON, NC (Time Warner Cable)

ELK PARK—See HICKORY, NC (Charter Communications)

ELKIN (TOWN)—See GREENSBORO, NC (Time Warner Cable)

ELKIN—Time Warner Cable. Now served by GREENSBORO, NC [NC0006]

ELLENBORO—See FOREST CITY, NC (Northland Cable Television)

ELLERBE—See CHARLOTTE, NC (Time Warner Cable)

ELM CITY—See RALEIGH, NC (Time Warner Cable)

ELON (TOWN)—See GREENSBORO, NC (Time Warner Cable)

EMERALD ISLE (TOWN)—See JACKSONVILLE, NC (Time Warner Cable)

ENFIELD—Suddenlink Communications. Now served by ROCKY MOUNT, NC [NC0016]

ENFIELD—See ROCKY MOUNT, NC (Suddenlink Communications)

ERWIN (TOWN)—See RALEIGH, NC (Time Warner Cable)

ERWIN—See ANGIER, NC (Charter Communications)

EUREKA—See RALEIGH, NC (Time Warner Cable)

EVERETTS—See MARTIN COUNTY (central portion), NC (Suddenlink Communications)

FAIR BLUFF—Formerly served by MIM Cable. No longer in operation

FAIRMONT (TOWN)—See RALEIGH, NC (Time Warner Cable)

FAIRVIEW (TOWN)—See CHARLOTTE, NC (Time Warner Cable)

FAISON—Charter Communications. Now served by ANGIER, NC [NC0194]

FAISON—See ANGIER, NC (Charter Communications)

FAITH—See CHARLOTTE, NC (Time Warner Cable)

FALCON—See RALEIGH, NC (Time Warner Cable)

FALLSTON—See CHARLOTTE, NC (Time Warner Cable)

FARMER—See LIBERTY, NC (Randolph Telephone. Formerly [NC0258]. This cable system has converted to IPTV.)

FARMINGTON—Yadtel

FARMVILLE—Time Warner Cable

FAYETTEVILLE—Time Warner Cable. Now served by RALEIGH, NC [NC0003]

FAYETTEVILLE—See RALEIGH, NC (Time Warner Cable)

FLAT ROCK—See HENDERSONVILLE, NC (Morris Broadband)

FLETCHER—See ASHEVILLE, NC (Charter Communications)

FLETCHER—See HENDERSONVILLE, NC (Morris Broadband)

FOREST CITY—Northland Cable Television

FOREST HILLS—See HENDERSONVILLE, NC (Morris Broadband)

FORSYTH COUNTY—See GREENSBORO, NC (Time Warner Cable)

FORT BRAGG—See RALEIGH, NC (Time Warner Cable)

FORT FISHER AFB—See ANGIER, NC (Charter Communications)

FORT MILL—See CHARLOTTE, SC (Time Warner Cable)

FOUNTAIN—Formerly served by Vital Communications. No longer in operation

FOUR OAKS (TOWN)—See RALEIGH, NC (Time Warner Cable)

FOXFIRE (VILLAGE)—See RALEIGH, NC (Time Warner Cable)

FRANKLIN COUNTY (PORTIONS)—See RALEIGH, NC (Time Warner Cable)

FRANKLIN/SYLVA—Morris Broadband. Now served by HENDERSONVILLE, NC [NC0033]

FRANKLIN—See HENDERSONVILLE, NC (Morris Broadband)

FRANKLINTON (TOWN)—See RALEIGH, NC (Time Warner Cable)

FRANKLINVILLE (TOWN)—See GREENSBORO, NC (Time Warner Cable)

FREMONT (TOWN)—See RALEIGH, NC (Time Warner Cable)

FRISCO—See BUXTON, NC (Charter Communications)

FUQUAY-VARINA (TOWN)—See RALEIGH, NC (Time Warner Cable)

GARLAND—See HALLS TWP., NC (StarVision)

GARNER (TOWN)—See RALEIGH, NC (Time Warner Cable)

GARYSBURG—See ROANOKE RAPIDS, NC (Charter Communications)

GASTON COUNTY—See HICKORY, NC (Charter Communications)

GASTON COUNTY—See CHARLOTTE, NC (Time Warner Cable)

GASTON—See ROANOKE RAPIDS, NC (Charter Communications)

GASTONIA—Time Warner Cable. Now served by CHARLOTTE, NC [NC0001]

GASTONIA—See CHARLOTTE, NC (Time Warner Cable)

GATES COUNTY (portions)—Charter Communications. Now served by SUFFOLK, VA [VA0025]

GIBSONVILLE—See GREENSBORO, NC (Time Warner Cable)

GILKEY TWP.—See FOREST CITY, NC (Northland Cable Television)

GLEN ALPINE—See HICKORY, NC (Charter Communications)

GLENWOOD—See HENDERSONVILLE, NC (Morris Broadband)

GODWIN (TOWN)—See RALEIGH, NC (Time Warner Cable)

GOLD HILL—Time Warner Cable. Now served by CHARLOTTE, NC [NC0001]

GOLD HILL—See CHARLOTTE, NC (Time Warner Cable)

GOLDSBORO—Time Warner Cable. Now served by RALEIGH, NC [NC0003]

GOLDSBORO—See RALEIGH, NC (Time Warner Cable)

GOLDSTON—Formerly served by Main Street Broadband. No longer in operation

GRAHAM COUNTY (CENTRAL PORTION)—See ROBBINSVILLE, NC (Zito Media)

GRAHAM—See GREENSBORO, NC (Time Warner Cable)

GRANITE FALLS—See HICKORY, NC (Charter Communications)

GRANITE QUARRY—See CHARLOTTE, NC (Time Warner Cable)

GRANTSBORO (TOWN)—See JACKSONVILLE, NC (Time Warner Cable)

GRANVILLE COUNTY (PORTIONS)—See RALEIGH, NC (Time Warner Cable)

GREEN LEVEL (TOWN)—See GREENSBORO, NC (Time Warner Cable)

GREENE COUNTY (PORTIONS)—See SNOW HILL, NC (MediaCast)

GREENSBORO—Time Warner Cable

GREENVILLE—Suddenlink Communications

GRIFTON—See SNOW HILL, NC (MediaCast)

GRIMESLAND—See GREENVILLE, NC (Suddenlink Communications)

GROVER—See CHARLOTTE, NC (Time Warner Cable)

GUILFORD COUNTY—See GREENSBORO, NC (Time Warner Cable)

HALIFAX COUNTY (PORTIONS)—See OAK CITY, NC (Crystal Broadband Networks)

HALIFAX COUNTY (PORTIONS)—See ROCKY MOUNT, NC (Suddenlink Communications)

HALIFAX COUNTY (PORTIONS)—See RALEIGH, NC (Time Warner Cable)

HALIFAX COUNTY—See ROANOKE RAPIDS, NC (Charter Communications)

HALIFAX—Crystal Broadband Networks. Now served by WHITAKERS, NC [NC0164]

HALIFAX—See WHITAKERS, NC (Crystal Broadband Networks)

HALLS TWP.—StarVision

HAMILTON—See OAK CITY, NC (Crystal Broadband Networks)

HAMLET—See CHARLOTTE, NC (Time Warner Cable)

HARKERS ISLAND—See JACKSONVILLE, NC (Time Warner Cable)

HARMONY—See CHARLOTTE, NC (Time Warner Cable)

HARMONY—See FARMINGTON, NC (Yadtel)

HARNETT COUNTY (PORTIONS)—See ANGIER, NC (Charter Communications)

HARRIS—Northland Cable Television. Now served by FOREST CITY, NC [NC0054]

HARRIS—See FOREST CITY, NC (Northland Cable Television)

HARRISBURG—See CHARLOTTE, NC (Time Warner Cable)

North Carolina—Cable Community Index

HASSEL—See OAK CITY, NC (Crystal Broadband Networks)

HATTERAS—See BUXTON, NC (Charter Communications)

HAVELOCK—See JACKSONVILLE, NC (Time Warner Cable)

HAW RIVER (TOWN)—See GREENSBORO, NC (Time Warner Cable)

HAYWOOD COUNTY (PORTIONS)—Carolina Mountain Cablevision Inc

HAYWOOD COUNTY—See ASHEVILLE, NC (Charter Communications)

HEMBY BRIDGE—See CHARLOTTE, NC (Time Warner Cable)

HENDERSON (portions)—Time Warner Cable. Now served by RALEIGH, NC [NC0003]

HENDERSON COUNTY (NORTHEASTERN PORTION)—See FOREST CITY, NC (Northland Cable Television)

HENDERSON COUNTY—See HENDERSONVILLE, NC (Morris Broadband)

HENDERSON—See RALEIGH, NC (Time Warner Cable)

HENDERSONVILLE—Morris Broadband

HERTFORD COUNTY (PORTIONS)—See MURFREESBORO, NC (Time Warner Cable)

HERTFORD—See EDENTON, NC (Mediacom)

HICKORY—Charter Communications

HIGH FALLS—See LIBERTY, NC (Randolph Telephone. Formerly [NC0258]. This cable system has converted to IPTV.)

HIGH POINT—Time Warner Cable. Now served by GREENSBORO, NC [NC0006]

HIGH POINT—See GREENSBORO, NC (Time Warner Cable)

HIGH POINT—See LEXINGTON, NC (Windstream)

HIGH SHOALS—See HICKORY, NC (Charter Communications)

HIGHLANDS—Northland Cable Television

HILDEBRAN—See HICKORY, NC (Charter Communications)

HILLSBOROUGH (TOWN)—See RALEIGH, NC (Time Warner Cable)

HOBGOOD—See OAK CITY, NC (Crystal Broadband Networks)

HOFFMAN—See CHARLOTTE, NC (Time Warner Cable)

HOKE COUNTY (PORTIONS)—See RALEIGH, NC (Time Warner Cable)

HOLDEN BEACH (TOWN)—See WILMINGTON, NC (Time Warner Cable)

HOLDEN BEACH—See SHALLOTTE, NC (ATMC. Formerly [NC0050]. This cable system has converted to IPTV.)

HOLDEN BEACH—See WILMINGTON, NC (Time Warner Cable)

HOLLISTER—Crystal Broadband Networks

HOLLY RIDGE—Charter Communications. Now served by ANGIER, NC [NC0194]

HOLLY RIDGE—See ANGIER, NC (Charter Communications)

HOLLY SPRINGS (TOWN)—See RALEIGH, NC (Time Warner Cable)

HONEYCUTT TWP.—See HALLS TWP., NC (StarVision)

HOOKERTON—See SNOW HILL, NC (MediaCast)

HOPE MILLS (TOWN)—See RALEIGH, NC (Time Warner Cable)

HUDSON—See HICKORY, NC (Charter Communications)

HUNTERSVILLE—See CHARLOTTE, NC (Time Warner Cable)

HYDE COUNTY (PORTIONS)—See BELHAVEN, NC (TriCounty Telecom)

INDIAN BEACH (TOWN)—See JACKSONVILLE, NC (Time Warner Cable)

INDIAN TRAIL—See CHARLOTTE, NC (Time Warner Cable)

IREDELL COUNTY (PORTIONS)—See FARMINGTON, NC (Yadtel)

IREDELL COUNTY—See CHARLOTTE, NC (Time Warner Cable)

IRON DUFF—Formerly served by Carolina Mountain Cable. No longer in operation

JACKSON COUNTY (PORTIONS)—See HIGHLANDS, NC (Northland Cable Television)

JACKSON COUNTY (UNINCORPORATED AREAS)—See HENDERSONVILLE, NC (Morris Broadband)

JACKSON CREEK—See LIBERTY, NC (Randolph Telephone. Formerly [NC0258]. This cable system has converted to IPTV.)

JACKSON—See CONWAY, NC (Mediacom)

JACKSONVILLE—Time Warner Cable

JAMESTOWN (TOWN)—See GREENSBORO, NC (Time Warner Cable)

JAMESVILLE—See PLYMOUTH (town), NC (Mediacom)

JEFFERSON—See WEST JEFFERSON, NC (Morris Broadband)

JOHNSON COUNTY (PORTIONS)—See HICKORY, TN (Charter Communications)

JOHNSTON COUNTY (PORTIONS)—See ANGIER, NC (Charter Communications)

JOHNSTON COUNTY (PORTIONS)—See KENLY, NC (Charter Communications)

JOHNSTON COUNTY (PORTIONS)—See RALEIGH, NC (Time Warner Cable)

JONES COUNTY (PORTIONS)—See JACKSONVILLE, NC (Time Warner Cable)

JONESVILLE (TOWN)—See GREENSBORO, NC (Time Warner Cable)

KANNAPOLIS—Time Warner Cable. Now served by CHARLOTTE, NC [NC0001]

KANNAPOLIS—See CHARLOTTE, NC (Time Warner Cable)

KELFORD—See CONWAY, NC (Mediacom)

KENANSVILLE—See ANGIER, NC (Charter Communications)

KENLY—Charter Communications

KERNERSVILLE (TOWN)—See GREENSBORO, NC (Time Warner Cable)

KILL DEVIL HILLS—Charter Communications

KING—Time Warner Cable. Now served by GREENSBORO, NC [NC0006]

KING—See GREENSBORO, NC (Time Warner Cable)

KINGS MOUNTAIN—See CHARLOTTE, NC (Time Warner Cable)

KINGSTOWN—See CHARLOTTE, NC (Time Warner Cable)

KINSTON—Suddenlink Communications

KITTRELL (VILLAGE)—See RALEIGH, NC (Time Warner Cable)

KITTY HAWK—See KILL DEVIL HILLS, NC (Charter Communications)

KNIGHTDALE (TOWN)—See RALEIGH, NC (Time Warner Cable)

KURE BEACH—See ANGIER, NC (Charter Communications)

LA GRANGE—See KINSTON, NC (Suddenlink Communications)

LAKE GASTON—Time Warner Cable. Now served by MURFREESBORO, NC [NC0144]

LAKE GASTON—See MURFREESBORO, NC (Time Warner Cable)

LAKE LURE—See FOREST CITY, NC (Northland Cable Television)

LAKE NORMAN—Formerly served by MI-Connection. No longer in operation

LAKE PARK—See CHARLOTTE, NC (Time Warner Cable)

LAKE TOXAWAY—Comporium Communications. Now served by BREVARD, NC [NC0053]

LAKE TOXAWAY—See BREVARD, NC (Comporium Communications)

LAKE WACCAMAW—Time Warner Cable. Now served by WILMINGTON, NC [NC0007]

LAKE WACCAMAW—See WILMINGTON, NC (Time Warner Cable)

LANCASTER COUNTY (PORTIONS)—See CHARLOTTE, SC (Time Warner Cable)

LANDIS—See CHARLOTTE, NC (Time Warner Cable)

LANSING—Formerly served by Mediacom. Now served by Morris Broadband, WEST JEFFERSON, NC [NC0098]

LANSING—See WEST JEFFERSON, NC (Morris Broadband)

LATTIMORE—See CHARLOTTE, NC (Time Warner Cable)

LAUREL PARK—See HENDERSONVILLE, NC (Morris Broadband)

LAURINBURG—Time Warner Cable. Now served by COLUMBIA, SC [SC0002]

LAWNDALE—See CHARLOTTE, NC (Time Warner Cable)

LEE COUNTY (PORTIONS)—See ANGIER, NC (Charter Communications)

LELAND (TOWN)—See WILMINGTON, NC (Time Warner Cable)

LENOIR COUNTY (PORTIONS)—See SNOW HILL, NC (MediaCast)

LENOIR COUNTY (PORTIONS)—See KINSTON, NC (Suddenlink Communications)

LENOIR COUNTY—See JACKSONVILLE, NC (Time Warner Cable)

LENOIR—See HICKORY, NC (Charter Communications)

LEWISTON—See CONWAY, NC (Mediacom)

LEWISVILLE (TOWN)—See GREENSBORO, NC (Time Warner Cable)

LEXINGTON (TOWN)—See GREENSBORO, NC (Time Warner Cable)

LEXINGTON—Windstream

LIBERTY (ALAMANCE COUNTY)—See LIBERTY, NC (Randolph Telephone. Formerly [NC0258]. This cable system has converted to IPTV.)

LIBERTY (RANDOLPH COUNTY)—See LIBERTY, NC (Randolph Telephone. Formerly [NC0258]. This cable system has converted to IPTV.)

LIBERTY (TOWN)—See LIBERTY, NC (Randolph Telephone. Formerly [NC0258]. This cable system has converted to IPTV.)

LIBERTY—Randolph Telephone. This cable system has converted to IPTV. See LIBERTY, NC [NC5022]

LIBERTY—Randolph Telephone. Formerly [NC0258]. This cable system has converted to IPTV.

LIBERTY—See GREENSBORO, NC (Time Warner Cable)

LILESVILLE—See CHARLOTTE, NC (Time Warner Cable)

LILLINGTON—See ANGIER, NC (Charter Communications)

Cable Community Index—North Carolina

LINCOLN COUNTY—See HICKORY, NC (Charter Communications)

LINCOLNTON—See HICKORY, NC (Charter Communications)

LINDEN—See RALEIGH, NC (Time Warner Cable)

LINWOOD—See LEXINGTON, NC (Windstream)

LITTLE SWITZERLAND—See BURNSVILLE, NC (Country Cablevision Inc)

LITTLETON—Time Warner Cable. Now served by RALEIGH, NC [NC0003]

LITTLETON—See RALEIGH, NC (Time Warner Cable)

LOCUST—See CHARLOTTE, NC (Time Warner Cable)

LONG BEACH (TOWN)—See WILMINGTON, NC (Time Warner Cable)

LONGVIEW—See HICKORY, NC (Charter Communications)

LONGWOOD—See SHALLOTTE, NC (ATMC. Formerly [NC0050]. This cable system has converted to IPTV)

LOUISBURG—See RALEIGH, NC (Time Warner Cable)

LOWELL—See CHARLOTTE, NC (Time Warner Cable)

LUCAMA—See KENLY, NC (Charter Communications)

LUMBER BRIDGE (TOWN)—See RALEIGH, NC (Time Warner Cable)

LUMBERTON—Time Warner Cable. Now served by RALEIGH, NC [NC0003]

LUMBERTON—See RALEIGH, NC (Time Warner Cable)

MACCLESFIELD—See PINETOPS, NC (Crystal Broadband Networks)

MACON COUNTY (EASTERN PORTION)—See HIGHLANDS, NC (Northland Cable Television)

MACON COUNTY—See HENDERSONVILLE, NC (Morris Broadband)

MADISON COUNTY—See BURNSVILLE, NC (Country Cablevision Inc)

MADISON—See GREENSBORO, NC (Time Warner Cable)

MAGGIE VALLEY—See ASHEVILLE, NC (Charter Communications)

MAGNOLIA—See ANGIER, NC (Charter Communications)

MAIDEN—See HICKORY, NC (Charter Communications)

MANNS HARBOR—See KILL DEVIL HILLS, NC (Charter Communications)

MANTEO—See KILL DEVIL HILLS, NC (Charter Communications)

MARION—Charter Communications. Now served by ASHEVILLE, NC [NC0012]

MARION—See ASHEVILLE, NC (Charter Communications)

MARS HILL—See ASHEVILLE, NC (Charter Communications)

MARSHALL—See ASHEVILLE, NC (Charter Communications)

MARSHVILLE—See CHARLOTTE, NC (Time Warner Cable)

MARTIN COUNTY (CENTRAL PORTION)—Suddenlink Communications

MARTIN COUNTY (PORTIONS)—See PLYMOUTH (town), NC (Mediacom)

MARTIN COUNTY (UNINCORPORATED AREAS)—See OAK CITY, NC (Crystal Broadband Networks)

MARVIN (VILLAGE)—See CHARLOTTE, NC (Time Warner Cable)

MATTHEWS—See CHARLOTTE, NC (Time Warner Cable)

MAURY—See SNOW HILL, NC (MediaCast)

MAYODAN—See GREENSBORO, NC (Time Warner Cable)

MAYSVILLE (TOWN)—See JACKSONVILLE, NC (Time Warner Cable)

MCADENVILLE—See CHARLOTTE, NC (Time Warner Cable)

MCBEE—See CHARLOTTE, SC (Time Warner Cable)

MCDOWELL COUNTY (CENTRAL PORTION)—See ASHEVILLE, NC (Charter Communications)

MEBANE—Time Warner Cable. Now served by GREENSBORO, NC [NC0006]

MEBANE—See GREENSBORO, NC (Time Warner Cable)

MECKLENBURG COUNTY (UNINCORPORATED AREAS)—See MOORESVILLE, NC (MI-Connection)

MECKLENBURG COUNTY (UNINCORPORATED AREAS)—See CHARLOTTE, NC (Time Warner Cable)

MERRY HILL—See COLERAIN, NC (Mediacom)

MESIC (TOWN)—See JACKSONVILLE, NC (Time Warner Cable)

MICRO—See KENLY, NC (Charter Communications)

MID LAKES TRAILER PARK—Crystal Broadband Networks

MIDDLEBURG (TOWN)—See RALEIGH, NC (Time Warner Cable)

MIDDLESEX (TOWN)—See RALEIGH, NC (Time Warner Cable)

MIDLAND—See CHARLOTTE, NC (Time Warner Cable)

MIDWAY—See GREENSBORO, NC (Time Warner Cable)

MILLS RIVER—See HENDERSONVILLE, NC (Morris Broadband)

MILTON—See ROXBORO, NC (Charter Communications)

MILWAUKEE—See CONWAY, NC (Mediacom)

MINERAL SPRINGS (TOWN)—See CHARLOTTE, NC (Time Warner Cable)

MINGO—See HALLS TWP., NC (StarVision)

MINNESOTT (TOWN)—See JACKSONVILLE, NC (Time Warner Cable)

MINT HILL—See CHARLOTTE, NC (Time Warner Cable)

MISENHEIMER—See CHARLOTTE, NC (Time Warner Cable)

MITCHELL COUNTY (PORTIONS)—See HICKORY, NC (Charter Communications)

MITCHELL COUNTY—See BURNSVILLE, NC (Country Cablevision Inc)

MOCKSVILLE (TOWN)—See GREENSBORO, NC (Time Warner Cable)

MOCKSVILLE—Time Warner Cable. Now served by GREENSBORO, NC [NC0006]

MOCKSVILLE—See FARMINGTON, NC (Yadtel)

MOMEYER—See RALEIGH, NC (Time Warner Cable)

MONROE—Time Warner Cable. Now served by CHARLOTTE, NC [NC0001]

MONROE—See CHARLOTTE, NC (Time Warner Cable)

MONTGOMERY COUNTY (PORTIONS)—See CHARLOTTE, NC (Time Warner Cable)

MONTREAT—See ASHEVILLE, NC (Charter Communications)

MOORE COUNTY (PORTIONS)—See ANGIER, NC (Charter Communications)

MOORE COUNTY (PORTIONS)—See RALEIGH, NC (Time Warner Cable)

MOORESBORO—See CHARLOTTE, NC (Time Warner Cable)

MOORESVILLE—MI-Connection

MOORESVILLE—See CHARLOTTE, NC (Time Warner Cable)

MOREHEAD CITY—See JACKSONVILLE, NC (Time Warner Cable)

MORGANTON—CoMPAS-City of Morganton Public Antenna System

MORRISVILLE (TOWN)—See RALEIGH, NC (Time Warner Cable)

MORVEN—Formerly served by WFL Cable Television Associates Inc. No longer in operation

MOUNT AIRY—Time Warner Cable. Now served by GREENSBORO, NC [NC0006]

MOUNT AIRY—See GREENSBORO, NC (Time Warner Cable)

MOUNT GILEAD—See CHARLOTTE, NC (Time Warner Cable)

MOUNT HOLLY—See CHARLOTTE, NC (Time Warner Cable)

MOUNT OLIVE (TOWN)—See RALEIGH, NC (Time Warner Cable)

MOUNT PLEASANT—See CHARLOTTE, NC (Time Warner Cable)

MOUNTAIN CITY—See HICKORY, TN (Charter Communications)

MURFREESBORO—Time Warner Cable

MURPHY—Cable TV of Cherokee County

NAGS HEAD—See KILL DEVIL HILLS, NC (Charter Communications)

NASH COUNTY (PORTIONS)—See WHITAKERS, NC (Crystal Broadband Networks)

NASH COUNTY—Crystal Broadband Networks

NASH COUNTY—See ROCKY MOUNT, NC (Suddenlink Communications)

NASH COUNTY—See RALEIGH, NC (Time Warner Cable)

NASHVILLE—See ROCKY MOUNT, NC (Suddenlink Communications)

NAVASSA (TOWN)—See WILMINGTON, NC (Time Warner Cable)

NEBO—Morris Broadband. Now served by HENDERSONVILLE, NC [NC0033]

NEBO—See HENDERSONVILLE, NC (Morris Broadband)

NEW BERN—Suddenlink Communications

NEW HANOVER COUNTY (UNINCORPORATED AREAS)—See ANGIER, NC (Charter Communications)

NEW HANOVER COUNTY—See WILMINGTON, NC (Time Warner Cable)

NEW LONDON—See CHARLOTTE, NC (Time Warner Cable)

NEWLAND—See HICKORY, NC (Charter Communications)

NEWPORT (TOWN)—See JACKSONVILLE, NC (Time Warner Cable)

NEWPORT—Time Warner Cable. Now served by JACKSONVILLE, NC [NC0025]

NEWTON GROVE—Charter Communications. Now served by ANGIER, NC [NC0194]

NEWTON GROVE—See ANGIER, NC (Charter Communications)

NEWTON—See HICKORY, NC (Charter Communications)

NORLINA—See RALEIGH, NC (Time Warner Cable)

NORTH HICKORY—See HICKORY, NC (Charter Communications)

NORTH TOPSAIL BEACH—See ANGIER, NC (Charter Communications)

NORTH WILKESBORO—Charter Communications. Now served by HICKORY, NC [NC0009]

2017 Edition

North Carolina—Cable Community Index

NORTH WILKESBORO—See HICKORY, NC (Charter Communications)

NORTHAMPTON COUNTY (PORTIONS)—See CONWAY, NC (Mediacom)

NORTHAMPTON COUNTY (PORTIONS)—See RALEIGH, NC (Time Warner Cable)

NORTHAMPTON COUNTY—See ROANOKE RAPIDS, NC (Charter Communications)

NORTHWEST (TOWN)—See WILMINGTON, NC (Time Warner Cable)

NORWOOD—See CHARLOTTE, NC (Time Warner Cable)

OAK CITY—Crystal Broadband Networks

OAK ISLAND—See WILMINGTON, NC (Time Warner Cable)

OAK RIDGE (TOWN)—See GREENSBORO, NC (Time Warner Cable)

OAKBORO—See CHARLOTTE, NC (Time Warner Cable)

OCEAN ISLE BEACH (TOWN)—See WILMINGTON, NC (Time Warner Cable)

OCEAN ISLE BEACH/BRICK LANDING—Formerly served by Tele-Media. Now served by Time Warner Cable, WILMINGTON, NC [NC0007]

OCEAN ISLE BEACH—See SHALLOTTE, NC (ATMC. Formerly [NC0050]. This cable system has converted to IPTV.)

OCRACOKE—Belhaven Cable TV

OLD FORT—See ASHEVILLE, NC (Charter Communications)

OLDE POINTE—Formerly served by Charter Communications. No longer in operation

ONSLOW COUNTY—See ANGIER, NC (Charter Communications)

ONSLOW COUNTY—See JACKSONVILLE, NC (Time Warner Cable)

ORANGE COUNTY—See RALEIGH, NC (Time Warner Cable)

ORIENTAL—See JACKSONVILLE, NC (Time Warner Cable)

ORRUM—Formerly served by Carolina Cable Partnership. No longer in operation

OSSIPEE (TOWN)—See GREENSBORO, NC (Time Warner Cable)

OXFORD—See RALEIGH, NC (Time Warner Cable)

PAMLICO BEACH—See BELHAVEN, NC (TriCounty Telecom)

PAMLICO COUNTY—Time Warner Cable. Now served by JACKSONVILLE, NC [NC0025]

PAMLICO COUNTY—See JACKSONVILLE, NC (Time Warner Cable)

PANTEGO—See BELHAVEN, NC (Tri-County Telecom)

PARKTON (TOWN)—See RALEIGH, NC (Time Warner Cable)

PARMELE—See MARTIN COUNTY (central portion), NC (Suddenlink Communications)

PASQUOTANK COUNTY—See ELIZABETH CITY, NC (Time Warner Cable)

PATRICK—See CHARLOTTE, SC (Time Warner Cable)

PATTERSON SPRINGS—See CHARLOTTE, NC (Time Warner Cable)

PELETIER—See JACKSONVILLE, NC (Time Warner Cable)

PEMBROKE (TOWN)—See RALEIGH, NC (Time Warner Cable)

PEMBROKE—Formerly served by Carolina Cable Partnership. No longer in operation

PENDER COUNTY (PORTIONS)—See ANGIER, NC (Charter Communications)

PENDER COUNTY—See WILMINGTON, NC (Time Warner Cable)

PERQUIMANS COUNTY—See EDENTON, NC (Mediacom)

PERSON COUNTY (PORTIONS)—See ROXBORO, NC (Charter Communications)

PIKE ROAD—See BELHAVEN, NC (Tri-County Telecom)

PIKEVILLE (TOWN)—See RALEIGH, NC (Time Warner Cable)

PILOT MOUNTAIN (TOWN)—See GREENSBORO, NC (Time Warner Cable)

PINE KNOLL SHORES (TOWN)—See JACKSONVILLE, NC (Time Warner Cable)

PINE LEVEL (TOWN)—See RALEIGH, NC (Time Warner Cable)

PINEBLUFF (TOWN)—See RALEIGH, NC (Time Warner Cable)

PINEHURST (TOWN)—See RALEIGH, NC (Time Warner Cable)

PINETOPS—Crystal Broadband Networks

PINETOWN—See BELHAVEN, NC (Tri-County Telecom)

PINEVILLE—See CHARLOTTE, NC (Time Warner Cable)

PINEWILD (TOWN)—See RALEIGH, NC (Time Warner Cable)

PINK HILL—Time Warner Cable. Now served by JACKSONVILLE, NC [NC0025]

PINK HILL—See JACKSONVILLE, NC (Time Warner Cable)

PISGAH FOREST—See BREVARD, NC (Comporium Communications)

PISGAH—See LIBERTY, NC (Randolph Telephone. Formerly [NC0258]. This cable system has converted to IPTV.)

PITT COUNTY (PORTIONS)—See SNOW HILL, NC (MediaCast)

PITT COUNTY—See GREENVILLE, NC (Suddenlink Communications)

PITT COUNTY—See FARMVILLE, NC (Time Warner Cable)

PITTSBORO (TOWN)—See RALEIGH, NC (Time Warner Cable)

PLEASANT GARDEN (TOWN)—See GREENSBORO, NC (Time Warner Cable)

PLYMOUTH (TOWN)—Mediacom

POLK COUNTY (NORTHERN PORTION)—See FOREST CITY, NC (Northland Cable Television)

POLKVILLE—See CHARLOTTE, NC (Time Warner Cable)

POLLOCKSVILLE (TOWN)—See JACKSONVILLE, NC (Time Warner Cable)

POPE AFB—See RALEIGH, NC (Time Warner Cable)

POWELLSVILLE—Mediacom. Now served by COLERAIN, NC [NC0255]

POWELLSVILLE—See COLERAIN, NC (Mediacom)

PRINCETON—Formerly served by Southern Cablevision. Now served by Charter Communications, KENLY, NC [NC0148]

PRINCETON—See KENLY, NC (Charter Communications)

PRINCETON—See RALEIGH, NC (Time Warner Cable)

PRINCEVILLE—See ROCKY MOUNT, NC (Suddenlink Communications)

QUALLA—See CHEROKEE INDIAN RESERVATION, NC (Cherokee Cablevision)

RAEFORD (TOWN)—See RALEIGH, NC (Time Warner Cable)

RAEFORD—Time Warner Cable. Now served by RALEIGH, NC [NC0003]

RALEIGH—Time Warner Cable

RAMSEUR (TOWN)—See GREENSBORO, NC (Time Warner Cable)

RANDLEMAN—See GREENSBORO, NC (Time Warner Cable)

RANDOLPH COUNTY (PORTIONS)—See LIBERTY, NC (Randolph Telephone. Formerly [NC0258]. This cable system has converted to IPTV.)

RANDOLPH COUNTY (PORTIONS)—See GREENSBORO, NC (Time Warner Cable)

RANGER—Formerly served by Cable TV of Cherokee County. No longer in operation

RANLO—See CHARLOTTE, NC (Time Warner Cable)

RED CROSS—See CHARLOTTE, NC (Time Warner Cable)

RED OAK—See NASH COUNTY, NC (Crystal Broadband Networks)

RED OAK—See ROCKY MOUNT, NC (Suddenlink Communications)

RED SPRINGS (TOWN)—See RALEIGH, NC (Time Warner Cable)

REEDS CROSS ROADS—See CHURCHLAND, NC (Piedmont Communications Services, Inc)

REIDSVILLE—Time Warner Cable. Now served by GREENSBORO, NC [NC0006]

REIDSVILLE—See GREENSBORO, NC (Time Warner Cable)

RENNERT (TOWN)—See RALEIGH, NC (Time Warner Cable)

RHODHISS—See HICKORY, NC (Charter Communications)

RICH SQUARE—See CONWAY, NC (Mediacom)

RICHFIELD—See CHARLOTTE, NC (Time Warner Cable)

RICHLANDS—See ANGIER, NC (Charter Communications)

RICHMOND COUNTY—See CHARLOTTE, NC (Time Warner Cable)

RIEGELWOOD—Time Warner Cable. Now served by WILMINGTON, NC [NC0007]

RIEGELWOOD—See WILMINGTON, NC (Time Warner Cable)

RIVER BEND—See NEW BERN, NC (Suddenlink Communications)

ROANOKE RAPIDS—Charter Communications

ROARING FORK—Formerly served by Almega Cable. No longer in operation

ROARING GAP—See HICKORY, NC (Charter Communications)

ROBBINS—Formerly served by Vital Communications. No longer in operation

ROBBINSVILLE—Zito Media

ROBERSONVILLE—See MARTIN COUNTY (central portion), NC (Suddenlink Communications)

ROBESON COUNTY (PORTIONS)—See RALEIGH, NC (Time Warner Cable)

ROBESON COUNTY (western portion)—Formerly served by Carolina Cable Partnership. No longer in operation

ROCKFISH—See HALLS TWP., NC (StarVision)

ROCKINGHAM COUNTY (PORTIONS)—See GREENSBORO, NC (Time Warner Cable)

ROCKINGHAM—Time Warner Cable. Now served by CHARLOTTE, NC [NC0001]

ROCKINGHAM—See CHARLOTTE, NC (Time Warner Cable)

Cable Community Index—North Carolina

ROCKWELL—See CHARLOTTE, NC (Time Warner Cable)

ROCKY MOUNT—Suddenlink Communications

RODANTHE—See BUXTON, NC (Charter Communications)

ROLESVILLE (TOWN)—See RALEIGH, NC (Time Warner Cable)

RONDA—See HICKORY, NC (Charter Communications)

ROPER—See PLYMOUTH (town), NC (Mediacom)

ROSE HILL—See ANGIER, NC (Charter Communications)

ROSEBORO—StarVision. Now served by HALLS TWP., NC [NC0070]

ROSEBORO—See HALLS TWP., NC (StarVision)

ROSMAN—See BREVARD, NC (Comporium Communications)

ROWAN COUNTY—See CHARLOTTE, NC (Time Warner Cable)

ROWLAND—Time Warner Cable. Now served by COLUMBIA, SC [SC0002]

ROXBORO—Charter Communications

ROXOBEL—See CONWAY, NC (Mediacom)

RURAL HALL (TOWN)—See GREENSBORO, NC (Time Warner Cable)

RUTH—See FOREST CITY, NC (Northland Cable Television)

RUTHERFORD COLLEGE—See HICKORY, NC (Charter Communications)

RUTHERFORD COUNTY (PORTIONS)—See FOREST CITY, NC (Northland Cable Television)

RUTHERFORDTON—See FOREST CITY, NC (Northland Cable Television)

SALEMBURG—See HALLS TWP., NC (StarVision)

SALISBURY—Time Warner Cable. Now served by CHARLOTTE, NC [NC0001]

SALISBURY—See CHARLOTTE, NC (Time Warner Cable)

SALVO—See BUXTON, NC (Charter Communications)

SAMPSON COUNTY—See HALLS TWP., NC (StarVision)

SANDY CREEK (TOWN)—See WILMINGTON, NC (Time Warner Cable)

SANDY MUSH—See FOREST CITY, NC (Northland Cable Television)

SANFORD—Charter Communications. Now served by ANGIER, NC [NC0194]

SANFORD—See ANGIER, NC (Charter Communications)

SANTEETLAH—See ROBBINSVILLE, NC (Zito Media)

SANTREE MOBILE HOME PARK—Formerly served by Adelphia Communications. No longer in operation

SAPPHIRE VALLEY—See HIGHLANDS, NC (Northland Cable Television)

SARATOGA (TOWN)—See RALEIGH, NC (Time Warner Cable)

SAWMILLS—See HICKORY, NC (Charter Communications)

SCOTLAND NECK—Suddenlink Communications. Now served by ROCKY MOUNT, NC [NC0016]

SCOTLAND NECK—See ROCKY MOUNT, NC (Suddenlink Communications)

SEABOARD—See CONWAY, NC (Mediacom)

SEAGROVE (TOWN)—See GREENSBORO, NC (Time Warner Cable)

SEDALIA—See GREENSBORO, NC (Time Warner Cable)

SELMA (TOWN)—See RALEIGH, NC (Time Warner Cable)

SELMA/GARNER—Time Warner Cable. Now served by RALEIGH, NC [NC0003]

SEVEN DEVILS—See HICKORY, NC (Charter Communications)

SEVEN LAKES (TOWN)—See RALEIGH, NC (Time Warner Cable)

SEVERN—See CONWAY, NC (Mediacom)

SEYMOUR JOHNSON AFB—See RALEIGH, NC (Time Warner Cable)

SHALLOTTE—ATMC. This cable system has converted to IPTV. See SHALLOTTE, NC [NC5004]

SHALLOTTE—ATMC. Formerly [NC0050]. This cable system has converted to IPTV

SHARPSBURG—See ROCKY MOUNT, NC (Suddenlink Communications)

SHELBY—Time Warner Cable. Now served by CHARLOTTE, NC [NC0001]

SHELBY—See CHARLOTTE, NC (Time Warner Cable)

SILER CITY—See ANGIER, NC (Charter Communications)

SIMPSON—Suddenlink Communications. Now served by GREENVILLE, NC [NC0014]

SIMPSON—See GREENVILLE, NC (Suddenlink Communications)

SIMS (TOWN)—See RALEIGH, NC (Time Warner Cable)

SMITHFIELD (TOWN)—See RALEIGH, NC (Time Warner Cable)

SMITHFIELD—Formerly served by Johnston County Cable L.P. Now served by Time Warner Cable, RALEIGH, NC [NC0003]

SMITHTON—See BELHAVEN, NC (Tri-County Telecom)

SNEADS FERRY—See ANGIER, NC (Charter Communications)

SNOW HILL—MediaCast

SOUTH MILLS—See CURRITUCK, NC (Mediacom)

SOUTHERN PINES (TOWN)—See RALEIGH, NC (Time Warner Cable)

SOUTHERN PINES—Time Warner Cable. Now served by RALEIGH, NC [NC0003]

SOUTHERN SHORES—See KILL DEVIL HILLS, NC (Charter Communications)

SOUTHPORT (TOWN)—See WILMINGTON, NC (Time Warner Cable)

SPARTA—Alleghany Cablevision Inc

SPENCER MOUNTAIN—See CHARLOTTE, NC (Time Warner Cable)

SPENCER—See CHARLOTTE, NC (Time Warner Cable)

SPINDALE—See FOREST CITY, NC (Northland Cable Television)

SPRING HOPE (TOWN)—See RALEIGH, NC (Time Warner Cable)

SPRING HOPE—Time Warner Cable. Now served by RALEIGH, NC [NC0003]

SPRING LAKE (TOWN)—See RALEIGH, NC (Time Warner Cable)

SPRUCE PINE—See HICKORY, NC (Charter Communications)

SPRUCE PINE—See BURNSVILLE, NC (Country Cablevision Inc)

ST. HELENA (TOWN)—See WILMINGTON, NC (Time Warner Cable)

ST. JAMES (TOWN)—See WILMINGTON, NC (Time Warner Cable)

ST. PAULS (TOWN)—See RALEIGH, NC (Time Warner Cable)

STALEY—See LIBERTY, NC (Randolph Telephone. Formerly [NC0258]. This cable system has converted to IPTV.)

STALLINGS—See CHARLOTTE, NC (Time Warner Cable)

STANFIELD—See CHARLOTTE, NC (Time Warner Cable)

STANLEY—See CHARLOTTE, NC (Time Warner Cable)

STANLY COUNTY—See CHARLOTTE, NC (Time Warner Cable)

STANTONSBURG (TOWN)—See RALEIGH, NC (Time Warner Cable)

STAR (TOWN)—See GREENSBORO, NC (Time Warner Cable)

STATESVILLE—Formerly served by Adelphia Communications. No longer in operation

STATESVILLE—Time Warner Cable. Now served by CHARLOTTE, NC [NC0001]

STATESVILLE—See CHARLOTTE, NC (Time Warner Cable)

STEDMAN (TOWN)—See RALEIGH, NC (Time Warner Cable)

STEM—See RALEIGH, NC (Time Warner Cable)

STOKES COUNTY (PORTIONS)—See GREENSBORO, NC (Time Warner Cable)

STOKESDALE (TOWN)—See GREENSBORO, NC (Time Warner Cable)

STONEVILLE—See GREENSBORO, NC (Time Warner Cable)

STONEWALL—See JACKSONVILLE, NC (Time Warner Cable)

STOVALL (TOWN)—See RALEIGH, NC (Time Warner Cable)

STUMPY POINT—See KILL DEVIL HILLS, NC (Charter Communications)

SUGAR MOUNTAIN—See HICKORY, NC (Charter Communications)

SUMMERFIELD (TOWN)—See GREENSBORO, NC (Time Warner Cable)

SUNSET BEACH—See SHALLOTTE, NC (ATMC. Formerly [NC0050]. This cable system has converted to IPTV)

SUNSET HARBOR—Formerly served by Tele-Media. Now served by ATMC, SHALLOTTE, NC [NC5004]

SUNSET HARBOR—See SHALLOTTE, NC (ATMC. Formerly [NC0050]. This cable system has converted to IPTV)

SUPPLY—Formerly served by Tele-Media. Now served by ATMC, SHALLOTTE, NC [NC5004]

SUPPLY—See SHALLOTTE, NC (ATMC. Formerly [NC0050]. This cable system has converted to IPTV)

SURF CITY—See ANGIER, NC (Charter Communications)

SURRY COUNTY—See GREENSBORO, NC (Time Warner Cable)

SWAIN COUNTY (PORTIONS)—See BRYSON CITY, NC (Zito Media)

SWANSBORO (TOWN)—See JACKSONVILLE, NC (Time Warner Cable)

SWEPSONVILLE (TOWN)—See GREENSBORO, NC (Time Warner Cable)

SYLVA—Formerly served by Mediacom. Now served by Morris Broadband, HENDERSONVILLE, NC [NC0033]

SYLVA—See HENDERSONVILLE, NC (Morris Broadband)

TABOR CITY (TOWN)—See WILMINGTON, NC (Time Warner Cable)

TABOR CITY—See SHALLOTTE, NC (ATMC. Formerly [NC0050]. This cable system has converted to IPTV)

TAR HEEL—See HALLS TWP., NC (StarVision)

TARBORO—See ROCKY MOUNT, NC (Suddenlink Communications)

TAYLORSVILLE—See HICKORY, NC (Charter Communications)

TAYLORTOWN (TOWN)—See RALEIGH, NC (Time Warner Cable)

TERRA CEIA—See BELHAVEN, NC (Tri-County Telecom)

North Carolina—Cable Community Index

THOMASVILLE—See GREENSBORO, NC (Time Warner Cable)

THOMASVILLE—See LEXINGTON, NC (Windstream)

THURMOND—See HICKORY, NC (Charter Communications)

TOBACCOVILLE (VILLAGE)—See GREENSBORO, NC (Time Warner Cable)

TOPSAIL BEACH—See ANGIER, NC (Charter Communications)

TRADE—See HICKORY, TN (Charter Communications)

TRANSYLVANIA COUNTY—See BREVARD, NC (Comporium Communications)

TRENT WOODS—See NEW BERN, NC (Suddenlink Communications)

TRINITY—See GREENSBORO, NC (Time Warner Cable)

TROUTMAN—See CHARLOTTE, NC (Time Warner Cable)

TROY—Charter Communications

TRYON—Charter Communications. Now served by SPARTANBURG, SC [SC0003]

TURKEY—See HALLS TWP., NC (StarVision)

TYRO—See CHURCHLAND, NC (Piedmont Communications Services, Inc)

TYRRELL COUNTY (PORTIONS)—See PLYMOUTH (town), NC (Mediacom)

UNION COUNTY—See CHARLOTTE, NC (Time Warner Cable)

UNIONVILLE (TOWN)—See CHARLOTTE, NC (Time Warner Cable)

VALDESE—See HICKORY, NC (Charter Communications)

VALE—See HICKORY, NC (Charter Communications)

VANCE COUNTY—See RALEIGH, NC (Time Warner Cable)

VANCEBORO—See NEW BERN, NC (Suddenlink Communications)

VANDEMERE—See JACKSONVILLE, NC (Time Warner Cable)

VARNAMTOWN—See SHALLOTTE, NC (ATMC. Formerly [NC0050]. This cable system has converted to IPTV)

VASS—Charter Communications. Now served by ANGIER, NC [NC0194]

VASS—See ANGIER, NC (Charter Communications)

WACO—See CHARLOTTE, NC (Time Warner Cable)

WADE (TOWN)—See RALEIGH, NC (Time Warner Cable)

WADESBORO—Time Warner Cable. Now served by CHARLOTTE, NC [NC0001]

WADESBORO—See CHARLOTTE, NC (Time Warner Cable)

WAGRAM—Formerly served by Wagram Cable TV. No longer in operation

WAKE COUNTY (PORTIONS)—See RALEIGH, NC (Time Warner Cable)

WAKE FOREST—See RALEIGH, NC (Time Warner Cable)

WALKERTOWN (TOWN)—See GREENSBORO, NC (Time Warner Cable)

WALLACE—See ANGIER, NC (Charter Communications)

WALLBURG (TOWN)—See GREENSBORO, NC (Time Warner Cable)

WALNUT COVE (TOWN)—See GREENSBORO, NC (Time Warner Cable)

WALNUT CREEK—See KINSTON, NC (Suddenlink Communications)

WALSTONBURG—See SNOW HILL, NC (MediaCast)

WANCHESE—See KILL DEVIL HILLS, NC (Charter Communications)

WARREN COUNTY (PORTIONS)—See RALEIGH, NC (Time Warner Cable)

WARRENTON—See RALEIGH, NC (Time Warner Cable)

WARSAW—Charter Communications. Now served by ANGIER, NC [NC0194]

WARSAW—See ANGIER, NC (Charter Communications)

WASHINGTON (PORTIONS)—Suddenlink Communications

WASHINGTON COUNTY—See PLYMOUTH (town), NC (Mediacom)

WASHINGTON PARK—See WASHINGTON (portions), NC (Suddenlink Communications)

WATAUGA COUNTY—See HICKORY, NC (Charter Communications)

WATHA (TOWN)—See WILMINGTON, NC (Time Warner Cable)

WAVES—See BUXTON, NC (Charter Communications)

WAXHAW—See CHARLOTTE, NC (Time Warner Cable)

WAYNE COUNTY (northern portion)—Time Warner Cable. Now served by RALEIGH, NC [NC0003]

WAYNE COUNTY (PORTIONS)—See KINSTON, NC (Suddenlink Communications)

WAYNE COUNTY—See RALEIGH, NC (Time Warner Cable)

WAYNESVILLE—Charter Communications. Now served by ASHEVILLE, NC [NC0012]

WAYNESVILLE—See HAYWOOD COUNTY (portions), NC (Carolina Mountain Cablevision Inc)

WAYNESVILLE—See ASHEVILLE, NC (Charter Communications)

WEAVERVILLE—See ASHEVILLE, NC (Charter Communications)

WEBSTER—See HENDERSONVILLE, NC (Morris Broadband)

WEDDINGTON—See CHARLOTTE, NC (Time Warner Cable)

WELCOME—See LEXINGTON, NC (Windstream)

WELDON—See ROANOKE RAPIDS, NC (Charter Communications)

WENDELL (TOWN)—See RALEIGH, NC (Time Warner Cable)

WENTWORTH (TOWN)—See GREENSBORO, NC (Time Warner Cable)

WESLEY CHAPEL—See CHARLOTTE, NC (Time Warner Cable)

WEST END (TOWN)—See RALEIGH, NC (Time Warner Cable)

WEST JEFFERSON—Morris Broadband

WESTERN PRONG TWP.—See HALLS TWP., NC (StarVision)

WHISPERING PINES—See ANGIER, NC (Charter Communications)

WHITAKERS—Crystal Broadband Networks

WHITE LAKE (TOWN)—See WILMINGTON, NC (Time Warner Cable)

WHITE PLAINS—See GREENSBORO, NC (Time Warner Cable)

WHITE POST—See BELHAVEN, NC (Tri-County Telecom)

WHITEVILLE—Time Warner Cable. Now served by WILMINGTON, NC [NC0007]

WHITEVILLE—See SHALLOTTE, NC (ATMC. Formerly [NC0050]. This cable system has converted to IPTV)

WHITEVILLE—See WILMINGTON, NC (Time Warner Cable)

WHITSETT (TOWN)—See GREENSBORO, NC (Time Warner Cable)

WILKES COUNTY (PORTIONS)—See HICKORY, NC (Charter Communications)

WILKES COUNTY—See GREENSBORO, NC (Time Warner Cable)

WILKESBORO—See HICKORY, NC (Charter Communications)

WILLIAMSTON—See MARTIN COUNTY (central portion), NC (Suddenlink Communications)

WILMINGTON—Formerly served by Microwave Communication Services. No longer in operation

WILMINGTON—Time Warner Cable

WILSON (TOWN)—See RALEIGH, NC (Time Warner Cable)

WILSON COUNTY—See RALEIGH, NC (Time Warner Cable)

WILSON—Time Warner Cable. Now served by RALEIGH, NC [NC0003]

WINDSOR—Mediacom. Now served by COLERAIN, NC [NC0255]

WINDSOR—See COLERAIN, NC (Mediacom)

WINFALL—See EDENTON, NC (Mediacom)

WINGATE—See CHARLOTTE, NC (Time Warner Cable)

WINSTON-SALEM—Time Warner Cable. Now served by GREENSBORO, NC [NC0006]

WINSTON-SALEM—See GREENSBORO, NC (Time Warner Cable)

WINTERVILLE—See GREENVILLE, NC (Suddenlink Communications)

WINTON (TOWN)—See MURFREESBORO, NC (Time Warner Cable)

WOODFIN—See ASHEVILLE, NC (Charter Communications)

WOODLAND—See CONWAY, NC (Mediacom)

WRIGHTSVILLE BEACH (TOWN)—See WILMINGTON, NC (Time Warner Cable)

YADKIN COUNTY (PORTIONS)—See FARMINGTON, NC (Yadtel)

YADKIN COUNTY—See GREENSBORO, NC (Time Warner Cable)

YADKINVILLE (TOWN)—See GREENSBORO, NC (Time Warner Cable)

YADKINVILLE—See FARMINGTON, NC (Yadtel)

YANCEY COUNTY (PORTIONS)—See HICKORY, NC (Charter Communications)

YANCEY COUNTY—See BURNSVILLE, NC (Country Cablevision Inc)

YAUPON BEACH (TOWN)—See WILMINGTON, NC (Time Warner Cable)

YORK COUNTY (PORTIONS)—See CHARLOTTE, SC (Time Warner Cable)

YORK—See CHARLOTTE, SC (Time Warner Cable)

YOUNGSVILLE (TOWN)—See RALEIGH, NC (Time Warner Cable)

ZEBULON (TOWN)—See RALEIGH, NC (Time Warner Cable)

NORTH DAKOTA

ADAMS—See PARK RIVER, ND (Polar Cablevision. Formerly [ND0026]. This cable system has converted to IPTV)

ALEXANDER (PORTIONS)—See PARSHALL (portions), ND (RTC)

ALSEN—See MUNICH, ND (United Communications. Formerly [ND0091]. This cable system has converted to IPTV)

ANAMOOSE—See MINOT, ND (Midco)

ANETA—See COOPERSTOWN (village), ND (Midco)

ANTLER—See VELVA, ND (SRT Communications)

ARNEGARD (PORTIONS)—See PARSHALL (portions), ND (RTC)

Cable Community Index—North Dakota

ARTHUR—See PARK RIVER, ND (Polar Cablevision. Formerly [ND0026]. This cable system has converted to IPTV)

ARVILLA—Formerly served by Midcontinent Communications. No longer in operation

ASHLEY—See OAKES, ND (DRN. Formerly [ND0226]. This cable system has converted to IPTV)

BEACH—Formerly served by Midcontinent Connunications. No longer in operation

BEACH—Beach Cable TV

BELFIELD—See REGENT, ND (Consolidated Cable Vision. Formerly [ND0201]. This cable system has converted to IPTV)

BELFIELD—See SOUTH HEART, ND (Midco)

BERTHOLD—SRT Communications. Now served by VELVA, ND [ND0059]

BERTHOLD—See VELVA, ND (SRT Communications)

BEULAH—Midco

BINFORD—See COOPERSTOWN (village), ND (Midco)

BISBEE—See DEVILS LAKE, ND (Midco)

BISBEE—See MUNICH, ND (United Communications. Formerly [ND0091]. This cable system has converted to IPTV)

BISMARCK—Midco

BORDULAC—See JAMESTOWN, ND (DCT. This cable system has converted to IPTV)

BOTTINEAU—See MINOT, ND (Midco)

BOTTINEAU—See MUNICH, ND (United Communications. Formerly [ND0091]. This cable system has converted to IPTV)

BOWBELLS—See RAY, ND (Northwest Communications Coop)

BOWDON—DCT. This cable system has converted to IPTV. Now served by JAMESTOWN, ND [ND5005]

BOWDON—See JAMESTOWN, ND (DCT. This cable system has converted to IPTV)

BOWMAN—See REGENT, ND (Consolidated Cable Vision. Formerly [ND0201]. This cable system has converted to IPTV)

BOWMAN—Midco

BRECKENRIDGE—See WAHPETON, MN (Midco)

BRIARWOOD—See FARGO, ND (Cable One)

BROCKET—See PARK RIVER, ND (Polar Cablevision. Formerly [ND0026]. This cable system has converted to IPTV)

BUFFALO—See WEST FARGO, ND (Midco)

BURLINGTON—See MINOT, ND (Midco)

BUTTE—See VELVA, ND (SRT Communications)

BUXTON—See GRAND FORKS, ND (Midco)

CALIO—See MUNICH, ND (United Communications. Formerly [ND0091]. This cable system has converted to IPTV)

CALVIN—See MUNICH, ND (United Communications. Formerly [ND0091]. This cable system has converted to IPTV)

CANDO—See DEVILS LAKE, ND (Midco)

CARPIO—SRT Communications. Now served by VELVA, ND [ND0059]

CARPIO—See VELVA, ND (SRT Communications)

CARRINGTON—Midcontinent Communications. Now served by COOPERSTOWN (village), ND [ND0054]

CARRINGTON—See JAMESTOWN, ND (DCT. This cable system has converted to IPTV)

CARRINGTON—See COOPERSTOWN (village), ND (Midco)

CARSON—Formerly served by Northland Communications. No longer in operation

CASS COUNTY (PORTIONS)—See FARGO, ND (Cable One)

CASSELTON—Midcontinent Communications. Now served by WEST FARGO, ND [ND0230]

CASSELTON—See WEST FARGO, ND (Midco)

CAVALIER AIR FORCE STATION—See PARK RIVER, ND (Polar Cablevision. Formerly [ND0026]. This cable system has converted to IPTV)

CAVALIER COUNTY (PORTIONS)—United Communications

CAVALIER—See PARK RIVER, ND (Polar Cablevision. Formerly [ND0026]. This cable system has converted to IPTV)

CENTER—See BEULAH, ND (Midco)

CLEVELAND—DCT. This cable system has converted to IPTV. Now served by JAMESTOWN, ND [ND5005]

CLEVELAND—See JAMESTOWN, ND (DCT. This cable system has converted to IPTV)

COGSWELL—See OAKES, ND (DRN. Formerly [ND0226]. This cable system has converted to IPTV)

COLUMBUS—See RAY, ND (Northwest Communications Coop)

COOPERSTOWN (VILLAGE)—Midco

CRETE—See OAKES, ND (DRN. Formerly [ND0226]. This cable system has converted to IPTV)

CROOKSTON—See GRAND FORKS, MN (Midco)

CROSBY—See RAY, ND (Northwest Communications Coop)

CRYSTAL—See PARK RIVER, ND (Polar Cablevision. Formerly [ND0026]. This cable system has converted to IPTV)

DEERING—See VELVA, ND (SRT Communications)

DES LACS—See VELVA, ND (SRT Communications)

DEVILS LAKE—Midco

DICKEY—See OAKES, ND (DRN. Formerly [ND0226]. This cable system has converted to IPTV)

DICKINSON—Consolidated Telecom

DICKINSON—See SOUTH HEART, ND (Midco)

DILWORTH—See FARGO, MN (Cable One)

DILWORTH—See WEST FARGO, MN (Midco)

DODGE—See REGENT, ND (Consolidated Cable Vision. Formerly [ND0201]. This cable system has converted to IPTV)

DODGE—See BEULAH, ND (Midco)

DONNYBROOK—See VELVA, ND (SRT Communications)

DOUGLAS (PORTIONS)—See PARSHALL (portions), ND (RTC)

DRAKE—See MINOT, ND (Midco)

DRAYTON—See GRAND FORKS, ND (Midco)

DUNN CENTER—Formerly served by Eagle Cablevision Inc. No longer in operation

DUNN CENTER—See REGENT, ND (Consolidated Cable Vision. Formerly [ND0201]. This cable system has converted to IPTV)

DUNSEITH—See MINOT, ND (Midco)

DUNSEITH—See MUNICH, ND (United Communications. Formerly [ND0091]. This cable system has converted to IPTV)

EAST GRAND FORKS—See GRAND FORKS, MN (Midco)

EDGELEY—DRN. This cable system has converted to IPTV. Now served by OAKES, ND [ND5032]

EDGELEY—See OAKES, ND (DRN. Formerly [ND0226]. This cable system has converted to IPTV)

EDINBURG—See PARK RIVER, ND (Polar Cablevision. Formerly [ND0026]. This cable system has converted to IPTV)

EDMORE—See DEVILS LAKE, ND (Midco)

EDMUNDS—See JAMESTOWN, ND (DCT. This cable system has converted to IPTV)

EGELAND—See MUNICH, ND (United Communications. Formerly [ND0091]. This cable system has converted to IPTV)

ELGIN—Formerly served by Northland Communications. No longer in operation

ELLENDALE—See OAKES, ND (DRN. Formerly [ND0226]. This cable system has converted to IPTV)

EMERADO—See GRAND FORKS, ND (Midco)

ENDERLIN—MLGC. This cable system has converted to IPTV. Now served by ENDERLIN, ND [ND5000]

ENDERLIN—MLGC. Formerly [ND0222]. This cable system has converted to IPTV

ESMOND—Formerly served by Midco. No longer in operation

FAIRMOUNT—See WAHPETON, ND (Midco)

FARGO—Cable One

FARGO—See WEST FARGO, ND (Midco)

FESSENDEN—See MINOT, ND (Midco)

FINLEY—MLGC. This cable system has converted to IPTV. Now served by ENDERLIN, ND [ND5000]

FINLEY—See ENDERLIN, ND (MLGC. Formerly [ND0222]. This cable system has converted to IPTV)

FLASHER—Formerly served by Flasher Cablevision Inc. No longer in operation

FLAXTON—See RAY, ND (Northwest Communications Coop)

FORBES—See OAKES, ND (DRN. Formerly [ND0226]. This cable system has converted to IPTV)

FORDVILLE—See PARK RIVER, ND (Polar Cablevision. Formerly [ND0026]. This cable system has converted to IPTV)

FOREST RIVER—Formerly served by Midcontinent Communications. No longer in operation

FORMAN—DRN. This cable system has converted to IPTV. Now served by OAKES, ND [ND5032]

FORMAN—See OAKES, ND (DRN. Formerly [ND0226]. This cable system has converted to IPTV)

FORT RANSOM—See OAKES, ND (DRN. Formerly [ND0226]. This cable system has converted to IPTV)

FREDONIA—See OAKES, ND (DRN. Formerly [ND0226]. This cable system has converted to IPTV)

North Dakota—Cable Community Index

FRONTIER—See FARGO, ND (Cable One)

FRONTIER—See WEST FARGO, ND (Midco)

FULLERTON—See OAKES, ND (DRN. Formerly [ND0226]. This cable system has converted to IPTV)

GACKLE—Formerly served by Midcontinent Communications. No longer in operation

GACKLE—See JAMESTOWN, ND (DCT. This cable system has converted to IPTV)

GALESBURG—See GRAND FORKS, ND (Midco)

GARRISON (PORTIONS)—See PARSHALL (portions), ND (RTC)

GARRISON—RTC. Now served by PARSHALL, ND [ND0020]

GILBY—Formerly served by Midcontinent Communications. No longer in operation

GILBY—See PARK RIVER, ND (Polar Cablevision. Formerly [ND0026]. This cable system has converted to IPTV)

GLADSTONE—See BEULAH, ND (Midco)

GLEN ULLIN—See BISMARCK, ND (Midco)

GLENBURN—See MINOT, ND (Midco)

GLENFIELD—Formerly served by Dakota Central Telecommunications. Now served by GLENFIELD, ND [ND0130]

GLENFIELD—DCTV

GOLDEN VALLEY—See BEULAH, ND (Midco)

GOODRICH—See MCCLUSKY, ND (Midco)

GRACE CITY—See JAMESTOWN, ND (DCT. This cable system has converted to IPTV)

GRAFTON—Midcontinent Communications. Now served by GRAND FORKS, ND [ND0003]

GRAFTON—See GRAND FORKS, ND (Midco)

GRAND FORKS AFB—See GRAND FORKS, ND (Midco)

GRAND FORKS—Formerly served by Microwave Communication Services. No longer in operation

GRAND FORKS—Midco

GRANDIN—See GRAND FORKS, ND (Midco)

GRANVILLE—SRT Communications. Now served by VELVA, ND [ND0059]

GRANVILLE—See VELVA, ND (SRT Communications)

GRENORA—See RAY, ND (Northwest Communications Coop)

GUELPH—See OAKES, ND (DRN. Formerly [ND0226]. This cable system has converted to IPTV)

GWINNER—DRN. This cable system has converted to IPTV. Now served by OAKES, ND [ND5032]

GWINNER—See OAKES, ND (DRN. Formerly [ND0226]. This cable system has converted to IPTV)

HALLIDAY—See REGENT, ND (Consolidated Cable Vision. Formerly [ND0201]. This cable system has converted to IPTV)

HALLIDAY—See BEULAH, ND (Midco)

HANKINSON—Midco. Now served by WAHPETON, ND [ND0007]

HANKINSON—See WAHPETON, ND (Midco)

HANNAFORD—See COOPERSTOWN (village), ND (Midco)

HARVEY—Midco. Now served by MINOT, ND [ND0004]

HARVEY—See MINOT, ND (Midco)

HARWOOD—See WEST FARGO, ND (Midco)

HATTON—See GRAND FORKS, ND (Midco)

HAVANA—See OAKES, ND (DRN. Formerly [ND0226]. This cable system has converted to IPTV)

HAZEN—See BEULAH, ND (Midco)

HEBRON—See BISMARCK, ND (Midco)

HENSEL—See PARK RIVER, ND (Polar Cablevision. Formerly [ND0026]. This cable system has converted to IPTV)

HETTINGER—See REGENT, ND (Consolidated Cable Vision. Formerly [ND0201]. This cable system has converted to IPTV)

HETTINGER—See BOWMAN, ND (Midco)

HILLSBORO—See GRAND FORKS, ND (Midco)

HOOPLE—See PARK RIVER, ND (Polar Cablevision. Formerly [ND0026]. This cable system has converted to IPTV)

HOPE—See COOPERSTOWN (village), ND (Midco)

HORACE—See FARGO, ND (Cable One)

HORACE—See WEST FARGO, ND (Midco)

HUNTER—See PARK RIVER, ND (Polar Cablevision. Formerly [ND0026]. This cable system has converted to IPTV)

HURDSFIELD—See JAMESTOWN, ND (DCT. This cable system has converted to IPTV)

INKSTER—See PARK RIVER, ND (Polar Cablevision. Formerly [ND0026]. This cable system has converted to IPTV)

JAMESTOWN—Cable Services Inc

JAMESTOWN—DCT. This cable system has converted to IPTV

JUD—See OAKES, ND (DRN. Formerly [ND0226]. This cable system has converted to IPTV)

KARLSRUHE—See VELVA, ND (SRT Communications)

KATHRYN—See OAKES, ND (DRN. Formerly [ND0226]. This cable system has converted to IPTV)

KEENE (PORTIONS)—See PARSHALL (portions), ND (RTC)

KENMARE (PORTIONS)—See PARSHALL (portions), ND (RTC)

KENMARE—RTC. Now served by PARSHALL, ND [ND0020]

KENSAL—See JAMESTOWN, ND (DCT. This cable system has converted to IPTV)

KENSAL—See COOPERSTOWN (village), ND (Midco)

KILLDEER—See REGENT, ND (Consolidated Cable Vision. Formerly [ND0201]. This cable system has converted to IPTV)

KILLDEER—See BEULAH, ND (Midco)

KINDRED—MLGC. Now served by ENDERLIN, ND [ND5000]

KINDRED—See ENDERLIN, ND (MLGC. Formerly [ND0222]. This cable system has converted to IPTV)

KRAMER—See MUNICH, ND (United Communications. Formerly [ND0091]. This cable system has converted to IPTV)

KULM—Formerly served by Cable Services Inc. No longer in operation

KULM—See OAKES, ND (DRN. Formerly [ND0226]. This cable system has converted to IPTV)

LA MOURE—Formerly served by Midcontinent Communications. No longer in operation

LAKOTA—Polar Cablevision. This cable system has converted to IPTV. Now served by PARK RIVER, ND [ND5106]

LAKOTA—See PARK RIVER, ND (Polar Cablevision. Formerly [ND0026]. This cable system has converted to IPTV)

LAMOURE—See OAKES, ND (DRN. Formerly [ND0226]. This cable system has converted to IPTV)

LANGDON—Midcontinent Communications. Now served by DEVILS LAKE, ND [ND0009]

LANGDON—See DEVILS LAKE, ND (Midco)

LANGDON—See MUNICH, ND (United Communications. Formerly [ND0091]. This cable system has converted to IPTV)

LANSFORD—See MINOT, ND (Midco)

LARIMORE—Midcontinent Communications. Now served by GRAND FORKS, ND [ND0003]

LARIMORE—See GRAND FORKS, ND (Midco)

LEEDS—Midco

LEONARD—See WEST FARGO, ND (Midco)

LIDGERWOOD—See WAHPETON, ND (Midco)

LIGNITE—See RAY, ND (Northwest Communications Coop)

LINCOLN—See BISMARCK, ND (Midco)

LINTON—See STEELE, ND (Steele Cablevision)

LISBON (VILLAGE)—Formerly served by Cable Services Inc. No longer in operation

LISBON—DRN. This cable system has converted to IPTV. Now served by OAKES, ND [ND5032]

LISBON—See OAKES, ND (DRN. Formerly [ND0226]. This cable system has converted to IPTV)

LITCHVILLE—DRN. This cable system has converted to IPTV. Now served by OAKES, ND [ND5032]

LITCHVILLE—See OAKES, ND (DRN. Formerly [ND0226]. This cable system has converted to IPTV)

MADDOCK—Maddock Cable TV

MAKOTI (PORTIONS)—See PARSHALL (portions), ND (RTC)

MANDAN—See BISMARCK, ND (Midco)

MANDAREE (PORTIONS)—See PARSHALL (portions), ND (RTC)

MANVEL—Midcontinent Communications. Now served by GRAND FORKS, ND [ND0003]

MANVEL—See GRAND FORKS, ND (Midco)

MAPLETON—See WEST FARGO, ND (Midco)

MARION—DRN. This cable system has converted to IPTV. Now served by OAKES, ND [ND5032]

MARION—See OAKES, ND (DRN. Formerly [ND0226]. This cable system has converted to IPTV)

MARMARTH—See REGENT, ND (Consolidated Cable Vision. Formerly [ND0201]. This cable system has converted to IPTV)

MAX (PORTIONS)—See PARSHALL (portions), ND (RTC)

MAX—RTC. Now served by PARSHALL, ND [ND0020]

MAXBASS—See VELVA, ND (SRT Communications)

MAYVILLE—See GRAND FORKS, ND (Midco)

MAYVILLE—See PARK RIVER, ND (Polar Cablevision. Formerly [ND0026]. This cable system has converted to IPTV)

Cable Community Index—North Dakota

MCCLUSKY—Midco

MEDINA—Formerly served by Cable Services Inc. No longer in operation

MEDINA—See JAMESTOWN, ND (DCT. This cable system has converted to IPTV)

MERRICOURT—See OAKES, ND (DRN. Formerly [ND0226]. This cable system has converted to IPTV)

METIGOSHE—SRT Communications. Now served by VELVA, ND [ND0059]

METIGOSHE—See VELVA, ND (SRT Communications)

MICHIGAN—See PARK RIVER, ND (Polar Cablevision. Formerly [ND0026]. This cable system has converted to IPTV)

MILNOR—Formerly served by Dickey Rural Networks. No longer in operation

MILNOR—See OAKES, ND (DRN. Formerly [ND0226]. This cable system has converted to IPTV)

MILTON—See MUNICH, ND (United Communications. Formerly [ND0091]. This cable system has converted to IPTV)

MINNEWAUKAN—Midco

MINOT AFB—See MINOT, ND (Midco)

MINOT—Formerly served by Microwave Communication Services. No longer in operation

MINOT—Formerly served by Vision Systems. No longer in operation

MINOT—Midco

MINTO—Midcontinent Communications. Now served by GRAND FORKS, ND [ND0003]

MINTO—See GRAND FORKS, ND (Midco)

MOHALL—See MINOT, ND (Midco)

MONTPELIER—See JAMESTOWN, ND (DCT. This cable system has converted to IPTV)

MOORHEAD—See FARGO, MN (Cable One)

MOORHEAD—See WEST FARGO, MN (Midco)

MOTT—See REGENT, ND (Consolidated Cable Vision. Formerly [ND0201]. This cable system has converted to IPTV)

MOTT—Midco

MOUNTAIN—See PARK RIVER, ND (Polar Cablevision. Formerly [ND0026]. This cable system has converted to IPTV)

MUNICH—United Communications. This cable system has converted to IPTV. See MUNICH, ND [ND5154]

MUNICH—United Communications. Formerly [ND0091]. This cable system has converted to IPTV

NECHE—See PARK RIVER, ND (Polar Cablevision. Formerly [ND0026]. This cable system has converted to IPTV)

NEW ENGLAND—Formerly served by New England Cablevision Inc. No longer in operation

NEW ENGLAND—See REGENT, ND (Consolidated Cable Vision. Formerly [ND0201]. This cable system has converted to IPTV)

NEW LEIPZIG—Formerly served by Northland Communications. No longer in operation

NEW ROCKFORD—See COOPERSTOWN (village), ND (Midco)

NEW SALEM—See BISMARCK, ND (Midco)

NEW TOWN (PORTIONS)—See PARSHALL (portions), ND (RTC)

NEWBURG—SRT Communications. Now served by VELVA, ND [ND0059]

NEWBURG—See VELVA, ND (SRT Communications)

NIAGARA—See PARK RIVER, ND (Polar Cablevision. Formerly [ND0026]. This cable system has converted to IPTV)

NOONAN—See RAY, ND (Northwest Communications Coop)

NORTHWOOD—MLGC. This cable system has converted to IPTV. Now served by ENDERLIN, ND [ND5000]

NORTHWOOD—See ENDERLIN, ND (MLGC. Formerly [ND0222]. This cable system has converted to IPTV)

OAKES—DRN. This cable system has converted to IPTV. Now served by OAKES, ND [ND5032]

OAKES—Formerly served by Cable Services Inc. No longer in operation

OAKES—DRN. Formerly [ND0226]. This cable system has converted to IPTV

OAKPORT TWP.—See WEST FARGO, MN (Midco)

OAKPORT—See FARGO, MN (Cable One)

OSLO—See GRAND FORKS, MN (Midco)

OSNABROCK—See MUNICH, ND (United Communications. Formerly [ND0091]. This cable system has converted to IPTV)

OXBOW—See WEST FARGO, ND (Midco)

PAGE—See COOPERSTOWN (village), ND (Midco)

PARK RIVER—Polar Cablevision. This cable system has converted to IPTV. Now served by PARK RIVER, ND [ND5106]

PARK RIVER—Polar Cablevision. Formerly [ND0026]. This cable system has converted to IPTV

PARSHALL (PORTIONS)—RTC

PEMBINA—Polar Cablevision. This cable system has converted to IPTV. Now served by PARK RIVER, ND [ND5106]

PEMBINA—See PARK RIVER, ND (Polar Cablevision. Formerly [ND0026]. This cable system has converted to IPTV)

PETERSBURG—See PARK RIVER, ND (Polar Cablevision. Formerly [ND0026]. This cable system has converted to IPTV)

PICK CITY—See BEULAH, ND (Midco)

PISEK—See PARK RIVER, ND (Polar Cablevision. Formerly [ND0026]. This cable system has converted to IPTV)

PLAZA (PORTIONS)—See PARSHALL (portions), ND (RTC)

PORTAL—See STANLEY, ND (Midstate Telephone & Communications)

PORTLAND—See GRAND FORKS, ND (Midco)

PORTLAND—See PARK RIVER, ND (Polar Cablevision. Formerly [ND0026]. This cable system has converted to IPTV)

POWERS LAKE—See RAY, ND (Northwest Communications Coop)

PRAIRIE ROSE—See FARGO, ND (Cable One)

RAY—Northwest Communications Coop

REED—See FARGO, ND (Cable One)

REEDER—See REGENT, ND (Consolidated Cable Vision. Formerly [ND0201]. This cable system has converted to IPTV)

REEDER—See BOWMAN, ND (Midco)

REGENT—Consolidated Cable Vision. This cable system has converted to IPTV. See REGENT, ND [ND5109]

REGENT—Consolidated Cable Vision. Formerly [ND0201]. This cable system has converted to IPTV

REILE'S ACRES—See FARGO, ND (Cable One)

REILE'S ACRES—See WEST FARGO, ND (Midco)

REYNOLDS—See GRAND FORKS, ND (Midco)

RHAME—See REGENT, ND (Consolidated Cable Vision. Formerly [ND0201]. This cable system has converted to IPTV)

RHAME—See BOWMAN, ND (Midco)

RICHARDTON—See REGENT, ND (Consolidated Cable Vision. Formerly [ND0201]. This cable system has converted to IPTV)

RICHARDTON—See BEULAH, ND (Midco)

RIVERDALE—See BEULAH, ND (Midco)

ROCK LAKE—See MUNICH, ND (United Communications. Formerly [ND0091]. This cable system has converted to IPTV)

ROLETTE—Midco. Now served by MINOT, ND [ND0004]

ROLETTE—See MINOT, ND (Midco)

ROLETTE—See MUNICH, ND (United Communications. Formerly [ND0091]. This cable system has converted to IPTV)

ROLLA—See MINOT, ND (Midco)

ROLLA—See MUNICH, ND (United Communications. Formerly [ND0091]. This cable system has converted to IPTV)

ROSS (PORTIONS)—See PARSHALL (portions), ND (RTC)

ROUND PRAIRIE TWP.—See RAY, ND (Northwest Communications Coop)

RUGBY—Midcontinent Communications. Now served by MINOT, ND [ND0004]

RUGBY—See MINOT, ND (Midco)

RUTHVILLE—See MINOT, ND (Midco)

RUTLAND—See OAKES, ND (DRN. Formerly [ND0226]. This cable system has converted to IPTV)

RYDER (PORTIONS)—See PARSHALL (portions), ND (RTC)

SABIN—See WEST FARGO, MN (Midco)

SANBORN—Formerly served by Cable Services Inc. No longer in operation

SARLES—See MUNICH, ND (United Communications. Formerly [ND0091]. This cable system has converted to IPTV)

SAWYER—Formerly served by Sawyer CATV. No longer in operation

SAWYER—See VELVA, ND (SRT Communications)

SCRANTON—See REGENT, ND (Consolidated Cable Vision. Formerly [ND0201]. This cable system has converted to IPTV)

SCRANTON—See BOWMAN, ND (Midco)

SELFRIDGE—Formerly served by West River Cable Television. No longer in operation

SHELDON—See ENDERLIN, ND (MLGC. Formerly [ND0222]. This cable system has converted to IPTV)

SHERWOOD—SRT Communications. Now served by VELVA, ND [ND0059]

North Dakota—Cable Community Index

SHERWOOD—See VELVA, ND (SRT Communications)

SHEYENNE—See GLENFIELD, ND (DCTV)

SOLEN—Formerly served by Midcontinent Communications. No longer in operation

SOURIS—United Communications. This cable system has converted to IPTV. Now served by MUNICH, ND [ND5154]

SOURIS—See MUNICH, ND (United Communications. Formerly [ND0091]. This cable system has converted to IPTV)

SOUTH HEART—See REGENT, ND (Consolidated Cable Vision. Formerly [ND0201]. This cable system has converted to IPTV)

SOUTH HEART—Midco

SQUAW GAP (PORTIONS)—See PARSHALL (portions), ND (RTC)

ST. JOHN—See MINOT, ND (Midco)

ST. JOHN—See MUNICH, ND (United Communications. Formerly [ND0091]. This cable system has converted to IPTV)

ST. THOMAS—See PARK RIVER, ND (Polar Cablevision. Formerly [ND0026]. This cable system has converted to IPTV)

STANLEY—Midstate Telephone & Communications

STANTON—See BEULAH, ND (Midco)

STARKWEATHER—See DEVILS LAKE, ND (Midco)

STEELE—Steele Cablevision

STREETER—See JAMESTOWN, ND (DCT. This cable system has converted to IPTV)

SURREY—See MINOT, ND (Midco)

SYKESTON—DCT. This cable system has converted to IPTV. Now served by JAMESTOWN, ND [ND5005]

SYKESTON—See JAMESTOWN, ND (DCT. This cable system has converted to IPTV)

TAYLOR—Consolidated Cable Vision. This cable system has converted to IPTV. See REGENT, ND [ND5109]

TAYLOR—See REGENT, ND (Consolidated Cable Vision. Formerly [ND0201]. This cable system has converted to IPTV)

THOMPSON—See GRAND FORKS, ND (Midco)

TIOGA—See RAY, ND (Northwest Communications Coop)

TOLLEY—See VELVA, ND (SRT Communications)

TOWNER COUNTY (PORTIONS)—United Communications

TOWNER—See MINOT, ND (Midco)

TURTLE LAKE—See BEULAH, ND (Midco)

UNDERWOOD—See BEULAH, ND (Midco)

UPHAM—Formerly served by RAE Cable. Now served by SRT Communications, VELVA, ND [ND0059]

UPHAM—See VELVA, ND (SRT Communications)

VALLEY CITY—Cable Services Inc

VELVA—SRT Communications

VENTURIA—See OAKES, ND (DRN. Formerly [ND0226]. This cable system has converted to IPTV)

VERONA—See OAKES, ND (DRN. Formerly [ND0226]. This cable system has converted to IPTV)

WAHPETON—Midco

WALES—See MUNICH, ND (United Communications. Formerly [ND0091]. This cable system has converted to IPTV)

WALHALLA—See DEVILS LAKE, ND (Midco)

WALHALLA—See MUNICH, ND (United Communications. Formerly [ND0091]. This cable system has converted to IPTV)

WARD COUNTY (PORTIONS)—See MINOT, ND (Midco)

WASHBURN—See BISMARCK, ND (Midco)

WATFORD CITY (PORTIONS)—See PARSHALL (portions), ND (RTC)

WATFORD CITY—RTC. Now served by PARHSALL, ND [ND0020]

WEST FARGO—See FARGO, ND (Cable One)

WEST FARGO—Midco

WESTHOPE—SRT Communications. Now served by VELVA, ND [ND0059]

WESTHOPE—See VELVA, ND (SRT Communications)

WHITE EARTH (PORTIONS)—See PARSHALL (portions), ND (RTC)

WHITE SHIELD (PORTIONS)—See PARSHALL (portions), ND (RTC)

WILDROSE—See RAY, ND (Northwest Communications Coop)

WILLISTON TWP. (PORTIONS)—See WILLISTON, ND (Midco)

WILLISTON—Midco

WILLOW CITY—See MINOT, ND (Midco)

WILLOW CITY—See MUNICH, ND (United Communications. Formerly [ND0091]. This cable system has converted to IPTV)

WILTON—See STEELE, ND (Steele Cablevision)

WIMBLEDON—See JAMESTOWN, ND (DCT. This cable system has converted to IPTV)

WIMBLEDON—See COOPERSTOWN (village), ND (Midco)

WING—See STEELE, ND (Steele Cablevision)

WISHEK—Formerly served by Midcontinent Communications. No longer in operation

WISHEK—See STEELE, ND (Steele Cablevision)

WOODWORTH—DCT. This cable system has converted to IPTV. Now served by JAMESTOWN, ND [ND5005]

WOODWORTH—See JAMESTOWN, ND (DCT. This cable system has converted to IPTV)

WYNDMERE—Formerly served by Dickey Rural Networks. No longer in operation

YPSILANTI—DCT. This cable system has converted to IPTV. Now served by JAMESTOWN, ND [ND5005]

YPSILANTI—See JAMESTOWN, ND (DCT. This cable system has converted to IPTV)

ZAP—See BEULAH, ND (Midco)

OHIO

ABERDEEN (VILLAGE)—See AMBERLEY (village), OH (Time Warner Cable)

ADA—Time Warner Cable. Now served by COLUMBUS, OH [OH0002]

ADA—See COLUMBUS, OH (Time Warner Cable)

ADAMS TWP. (CHAMPAIGN COUNTY)—See AMBERLEY (village), OH (Time Warner Cable)

ADAMS TWP. (CLINTON COUNTY)—See AMBERLEY (village), OH (Time Warner Cable)

ADAMS TWP. (DARKE COUNTY)—See AMBERLEY (village), OH (Time Warner Cable)

ADAMS TWP. (DARKE COUNTY)—See VERSAILLES, OH (Time Warner Cable)

ADAMS TWP. (GUERNSEY COUNTY)—See CAMBRIDGE, OH (Time Warner Cable)

ADAMS TWP. (SENECA COUNTY)—See TIFFIN, OH (Time Warner Cable)

ADAMS TWP.—See RIDGEVILLE CORNERS, OH (RTEC Communications)

ADAMSVILLE (VILLAGE)—See COLUMBUS, OH (Time Warner Cable)

ADDYSTON (VILLAGE)—See LEBANON, OH (Cincinnati Bell Fioptics TV. This cable system has converted to IPTV)

ADDYSTON (VILLAGE)—See AMBERLEY (village), OH (Time Warner Cable)

ADELPHI—See CHILLICOTHE, OH (Time Warner Cable)

ADENA—Comcast Cable. Now served by WHEELING, WV [WV0004]

AKRON—Time Warner Cable. Now served by CLEVELAND (formerly Cleveland Heights), OH [OH0006]

AKRON—See CLEVELAND, OH (Time Warner Cable)

ALBANY—Time Warner Cable. Now served by JACKSON, OH [OH0098]

ALBANY—See JACKSON, OH (Time Warner Cable)

ALBION BOROUGH—See CLEVELAND, PA (Time Warner Cable)

ALEXANDER TWP.—See COLUMBUS, OH (Time Warner Cable)

ALEXANDER TWP.—See SCIPIO TWP. (Meigs County), OH (Time Warner Cable)

ALEXANDRIA (VILLAGE)—See COLUMBUS, OH (Time Warner Cable)

ALEXANDRIA—See LEBANON, KY (Cincinnati Bell Fioptics TV. This cable system has converted to IPTV)

ALGER—See COLUMBUS, OH (Time Warner Cable)

ALLEN TWP. (DARKE COUNTY)—See AMBERLEY (village), OH (Time Warner Cable)

ALLEN TWP. (HANCOCK COUNTY)—See TIFFIN, OH (Time Warner Cable)

ALLEN TWP. (OTTAWA COUNTY)—See TOLEDO, OH (Buckeye Broadband)

ALLEN TWP. (OTTAWA COUNTY)—See TIFFIN, OH (Time Warner Cable)

ALLIANCE—See CLEVELAND, OH (Time Warner Cable)

AMANDA TWP. (FAIRFIELD COUNTY)—See COLUMBUS, OH (Time Warner Cable)

AMANDA TWP. (FAIRFIELD COUNTY)—See OAKLAND, OH (Time Warner Cable)

AMANDA TWP. (HANCOCK COUNTY)—See TIFFIN, OH (Time Warner Cable)

AMANDA TWP.—See TIFFIN, OH (Time Warner Cable)

AMBERLEY (VILLAGE)—See LEBANON, OH (Cincinnati Bell Fioptics TV. This cable system has converted to IPTV)

AMBERLEY (VILLAGE)—Time Warner Cable

AMBOY TWP.—See TIFFIN, OH (Time Warner Cable)

AMELIA (VILLAGE)—See LEBANON, OH (Cincinnati Bell Fioptics TV. This cable system has converted to IPTV)

AMELIA (VILLAGE)—See AMBERLEY (village), OH (Time Warner Cable)

Cable Community Index—Ohio

AMELIA—Formerly served by Adelphia Communications. No longer in operation

AMERICAN TWP. (ALLEN COUNTY)—See TIFFIN, OH (Time Warner Cable)

AMES TWP.—See NELSONVILLE, OH (Nelsonville TV Cable)

AMESVILLE—Formerly served by Riley Video Services. No longer in operation

AMHERST TWP.—See CLEVELAND, OH (Time Warner Cable)

AMHERST—See CLEVELAND, OH (Time Warner Cable)

AMSTERDAM—Crystal Broadband Networks

ANDERSON TWP. (HAMILTON COUNTY)—See AMBERLEY (village), OH (Time Warner Cable)

ANDERSON TWP.—See LEBANON, OH (Cincinnati Bell Fioptics TV. This cable system has converted to IPTV)

ANDOVER TWP. (PORTIONS)—See VERNON TWP. (Trumbull County), OH (Armstrong Cable Services)

ANDOVER—Formerly served by Cebridge Connections. Now served by Armstrong Cable Services, ZELIENOPLE, PA [PA0053]

ANNA (VILLAGE)—See AMBERLEY (village), OH (Time Warner Cable)

ANNA—See NEW KNOXVILLE, OH (NKTelco)

ANSONIA (VILLAGE)—See AMBERLEY (village), OH (Time Warner Cable)

ANTRIM TWP.—See TIFFIN, OH (Time Warner Cable)

ANTWERP—See HICKSVILLE, OH (Mediacom)

APPLE CREEK—See WOOSTER, OH (MCTV)

AQUILLA (VILLAGE)—See CLEVELAND, OH (Time Warner Cable)

ARCADIA (VILLAGE)—See TIFFIN, OH (Time Warner Cable)

ARCANUM (VILLAGE)—See AMBERLEY (village), OH (Time Warner Cable)

ARCHBOLD—See RIDGEVILLE CORNERS, OH (RTEC Communications)

ARCHBOLD—See TIFFIN, OH (Time Warner Cable)

ARLINGTON (VILLAGE)—See TIFFIN, OH (Time Warner Cable)

ARLINGTON HEIGHTS (VILLAGE)—See LEBANON, OH (Cincinnati Bell Fioptics TV. This cable system has converted to IPTV)

ARLINGTON HEIGHTS (VILLAGE)—See AMBERLEY (village), OH (Time Warner Cable)

ASHLAND—Armstrong Cable Services. Now served by ZELIENOPLE, PA [PA0053]

ASHLAND—See CLEVELAND, OH (Time Warner Cable)

ASHLEY (VILLAGE)—See COLUMBUS, OH (Time Warner Cable)

ASHLEY CORNER—Time Warner Cable

ASHTABULA COUNTY (EASTERN PORTION)—See DENMARK TWP., OH (Zito Media)

ASHTABULA COUNTY (PORTIONS)—See ROCK CREEK, OH (Zito Media)

ASHTABULA TWP. (ASHTABULA COUNTY)—See CLEVELAND, OH (Time Warner Cable)

ASHTABULA—Time Warner Cable. Now served by CLEVELAND (formerly Cleveland Heights), OH [OH0006]

ASHTABULA—See CLEVELAND, OH (Time Warner Cable)

ASHVILLE (VILLAGE)—See COLUMBUS, OH (Time Warner Cable)

ATHENS COUNTY—See NELSONVILLE, OH (Nelsonville TV Cable)

ATHENS TWP. (ATHENS COUNTY)—See COLUMBUS, OH (Time Warner Cable)

ATHENS—Time Warner Cable. Now served by COLUMBUS, OH [OH0002]

ATHENS—Time Warner Cable

ATHENS—See COLUMBUS, OH (Time Warner Cable)

ATTICA (village)—Time Warner Cable. Now served by TIFFIN (formerly Fostoria), OH [OH0050]

ATTICA (VILLAGE)—See TIFFIN, OH (Time Warner Cable)

ATWATER TWP.—Time Warner Cable. Now served by CLEVELAND (formerly Cleveland Heights), OH [OH0006]

ATWATER TWP.—See CLEVELAND, OH (Time Warner Cable)

AUBURN TWP.—Formerly served by Cebridge Connections. Now served by Suddenlink Communications, NELSON TWP., OH [OH0160]

AUBURN TWP.—See NELSON TWP., OH (Suddenlink Communications)

AUBURN TWP.—See CLEVELAND, OH (Time Warner Cable)

AUGLAIZE COUNTY (PORTIONS)—See TIFFIN, OH (Time Warner Cable)

AUGLAIZE TWP.—See DEFIANCE, OH (Time Warner Cable)

AURELIUS TWP.—See WARNER, OH (Zito Media)

AURORA—See CLEVELAND, OH (Time Warner Cable)

AUSTINBURG TWP.—See CLEVELAND, OH (Time Warner Cable)

AUSTINBURG TWP.—See ROCK CREEK, OH (Zito Media)

AVA—Formerly served by Cebridge Connections. No longer in operation

AVON LAKE—See CLEVELAND, OH (Time Warner Cable)

AVON LAKE—See BEREA, OH (WOW! Internet, Cable & Phone)

AVON—See CLEVELAND, OH (Time Warner Cable)

BAILEY LAKES—See CLEVELAND, OH (Time Warner Cable)

BAINBRIDGE TWP.—See NELSON TWP., OH (Suddenlink Communications)

BAINBRIDGE TWP.—See CLEVELAND, OH (Time Warner Cable)

BAINBRIDGE—Time Warner Cable

BAIRDSTOWN (VILLAGE)—See TIFFIN, OH (Time Warner Cable)

BALLVILLE TWP.—See TIFFIN, OH (Time Warner Cable)

BALTIC (VILLAGE)—See CLEVELAND, OH (Time Warner Cable)

BALTIMORE (village)—Time Warner Cable. Now served by COLUMBUS, OH [OH0002]

BALTIMORE (VILLAGE)—See COLUMBUS, OH (Time Warner Cable)

BARBERTON—See CLEVELAND, OH (Time Warner Cable)

BARLOW TWP.—See BEVERLY, OH (Time Warner Cable)

BARNHILL (VILLAGE)—See CLEVELAND, OH (Time Warner Cable)

BARTLOW TWP.—See DESHLER, OH (Time Warner Cable)

BARTON—Powhatan Point Cable Co

BASCOM—BTC Multimedia

BATAVIA (VILLAGE)—See LEBANON, OH (Cincinnati Bell Fioptics TV. This cable system has converted to IPTV)

BATAVIA (VILLAGE)—See AMBERLEY (village), OH (Time Warner Cable)

BATAVIA TWP.—See LEBANON, OH (Cincinnati Bell Fioptics TV. This cable system has converted to IPTV)

BATAVIA TWP.—See AMBERLEY (village), OH (Time Warner Cable)

BATH TWP. (ALLEN COUNTY)—See TIFFIN, OH (Time Warner Cable)

BATH TWP. (GREEN COUNTY)—See AMBERLEY (village), OH (Time Warner Cable)

BATH TWP. (SUMMIT COUNTY)—See CLEVELAND, OH (Time Warner Cable)

BAUGHMAN TWP.—See MASSILLON, OH (MCTV)

BAY TWP. (OTTAWA COUNTY)—See PORT CLINTON, OH (Time Warner Cable)

BAY VIEW—See TOLEDO, OH (Buckeye Broadband)

BAY VILLAGE—See CLEVELAND, OH (Time Warner Cable)

BAY VILLAGE—See BEREA, OH (WOW! Internet, Cable & Phone)

BAZETTA TWP.—Formerly served by Comcast Cable. Now served by Time Warner Cable, CLEVELAND, OH [OH0006]

BAZETTA TWP.—See CLEVELAND, OH (Time Warner Cable)

BEACH CITY (VILLAGE)—See CLEVELAND, OH (Time Warner Cable)

BEACHWOOD—See CLEVELAND, OH (Time Warner Cable)

BEARFIELD TWP.—See COLUMBUS, OH (Time Warner Cable)

BEAVER (VILLAGE)—See JACKSON, OH (Time Warner Cable)

BEAVER TWP.—See JACKSON, OH (Time Warner Cable)

BEAVERCREEK TWP.—See AMBERLEY (village), OH (Time Warner Cable)

BEAVERCREEK—See AMBERLEY (village), OH (Time Warner Cable)

BEAVERDAM (VILLAGE)—See TIFFIN, OH (Time Warner Cable)

BEDFORD HEIGHTS—See CLEVELAND, OH (Time Warner Cable)

BEDFORD TWP.—See TOLEDO, MI (Buckeye Broadband)

BEDFORD TWP.—See SCIPIO TWP. (Meigs County), OH (Time Warner Cable)

BEDFORD—See CLEVELAND, OH (Time Warner Cable)

BELLBROOK—See AMBERLEY (village), OH (Time Warner Cable)

BELLE CENTER (VILLAGE)—See COLUMBUS, OH (Time Warner Cable)

BELLE VALLEY—See CALDWELL, OH (Time Warner Cable)

BELLEFONTAINE—Time Warner Cable. Now served by TIFFIN, OH [OH0050]

BELLEFONTAINE—See URBANA, OH (CT Communications. Formerly [OH0443]. This cable system has converted to IPTV)

BELLEFONTAINE—See TIFFIN, OH (Time Warner Cable)

BELLEVUE—Time Warner Cable. Now served by TIFFIN (formerly Fostoria), OH [OH0050]

BELLEVUE—See LEBANON, KY (Cincinnati Bell Fioptics TV. This cable system has converted to IPTV)

BELLEVUE—See TIFFIN, OH (Time Warner Cable)

BELLVILLE (VILLAGE)—See CLEVELAND, OH (Time Warner Cable)

BELOIT (VILLAGE)—See CLEVELAND, OH (Time Warner Cable)

BELPRE TWP. (WASHINGTON COUNTY)—See BEVERLY, OH (Time Warner Cable)

BENNINGTON—See NEWARK, OH (Time Warner Cable)

Ohio—Cable Community Index

BENTLEYVILLE (VILLAGE)—See CLEVELAND, OH (Time Warner Cable)

BENTON RIDGE—Watch Communications

BENTON TWP. (OTTAWA COUNTY)—See PORT CLINTON, OH (Time Warner Cable)

BENTON TWP. (PIKE COUNTY)—See CHILLICOTHE, OH (Time Warner Cable)

BEREA—See PARMA, OH (Cox Communications)

BEREA—See CLEVELAND, OH (Time Warner Cable)

BEREA—WOW! Internet, Cable & Phone

BERGHOLZ—See AMSTERDAM, OH (Crystal Broadband Networks)

BERKEY—See TOLEDO, OH (Buckeye Broadband)

BERKSHIRE TWP. (DELAWARE COUNTY)—See COLUMBUS, OH (Time Warner Cable)

BERKSHIRE TWP.—See COLUMBUS, OH (Time Warner Cable)

BERLIN HEIGHTS (VILLAGE)—See CLEVELAND, OH (Time Warner Cable)

BERLIN TWP. (ERIE COUNTY)—See TOLEDO, OH (Buckeye Broadband)

BERLIN TWP. (ERIE COUNTY)—See CLEVELAND, OH (Time Warner Cable)

BERLIN TWP. (HOLMES COUNTY)—See CLEVELAND, OH (Time Warner Cable)

BERLIN TWP. (Mahoning County)—Armstrong Cable Services. Now served by ZELIENOPLE, PA [PA0053]

BERNE TWP.—See COLUMBUS, OH (Time Warner Cable)

BESSEMER—See NEW MIDDLETOWN, PA (Comcast Cable)

BETHEL (VILLAGE)—See LEBANON, OH (Cincinnati Bell Fioptics TV. This cable system has converted to IPTV)

BETHEL (VILLAGE)—See AMBERLEY (village), OH (Time Warner Cable)

BETHEL TWP. (CLARK COUNTY)—See AMBERLEY (village), OH (Time Warner Cable)

BETHEL TWP. (MIAMI COUNTY)—See AMBERLEY (village), OH (Time Warner Cable)

BETHLEHEM TWP. (STARK COUNTY)—See MASSILLON, OH (MCTV)

BETHLEHEM TWP. (STARK COUNTY)—See CLEVELAND, OH (Time Warner Cable)

BETTSVILLE (village)—Time Warner Cable. Now served by TIFFIN (formerly Fostoria), OH [OH0050]

BETTSVILLE (VILLAGE)—See TIFFIN, OH (Time Warner Cable)

BEVERLY—Time Warner Cable

BEXLEY—See COLUMBUS, OH (Time Warner Cable)

BEXLEY—See COLUMBUS, OH (WOW! Internet, Cable & Phone)

BIG ISLAND TWP.—Time Warner Cable. Now served by COLUMBUS, OH [OH0002]

BIG ISLAND TWP.—See COLUMBUS, OH (Time Warner Cable)

BIG PRAIRIE (VILLAGE)—See CLEVELAND, OH (Time Warner Cable)

BIG SPRING TWP.—See TIFFIN, OH (Time Warner Cable)

BIGLICK TWP.—See TIFFIN, OH (Time Warner Cable)

BLAKESLEE—See TIFFIN, OH (Time Warner Cable)

BLANCHARD TWP. (HANCOCK COUNTY)—See TIFFIN, OH (Time Warner Cable)

BLANCHARD TWP. (HANCOCK COUNTY)—See BENTON RIDGE, OH (Watch Communications)

BLANCHARD TWP. (PUTNAM COUNTY)—See TIFFIN, OH (Time Warner Cable)

BLANCHESTER (VILLAGE)—See AMBERLEY (village), OH (Time Warner Cable)

BLENDON TWP. (FRANKLIN COUNTY)—See COLUMBUS, OH (Time Warner Cable)

BLENDON TWP.—See COLUMBUS, OH (WOW! Internet, Cable & Phone)

BLOOM TWP. (FAIRFIELD COUNTY)—See COLUMBUS, OH (Time Warner Cable)

BLOOM TWP. (SCIOTO COUNTY)—See PORTSMOUTH, OH (Time Warner Cable)

BLOOM TWP. (SENECA COUNTY)—See TIFFIN, OH (Time Warner Cable)

BLOOM TWP. (WOOD COUNTY)—See TIFFIN, OH (Time Warner Cable)

BLOOMDALE (VILLAGE)—See TIFFIN, OH (Time Warner Cable)

BLOOMINGBURG—See WASHINGTON COURT HOUSE, OH (Time Warner Cable)

BLOOMINGDALE—Suddenlink Communications

BLOOMVILLE (VILLAGE)—See TIFFIN, OH (Time Warner Cable)

BLUE ASH—See LEBANON, OH (Cincinnati Bell Fioptics TV. This cable system has converted to IPTV)

BLUE ASH—See AMBERLEY (village), OH (Time Warner Cable)

BLUE ROCK—See COLUMBUS, OH (Time Warner Cable)

BLUE WATER MANOR—See NELSON TWP., OH (Suddenlink Communications)

BLUFFTON (village)—Time Warner Cable. Now served by TIFFIN, OH [OH0050]

BLUFFTON (VILLAGE)—See TIFFIN, OH (Time Warner Cable)

BOARDMAN TWP.—Armstrong Cable Services. Now served by ZELIENOPLE, PA [PA0053]

BOKES CREEK TWP.—See COLUMBUS, OH (Time Warner Cable)

BOLIVAR (town)—Time Warner Cable. Now served by CLEVELAND (formerly Cleveland Heights), OH [OH0006]

BOLIVAR—See CLEVELAND, OH (Time Warner Cable)

BOSTON HEIGHTS (VILLAGE)—See CLEVELAND, OH (Time Warner Cable)

BOSTON TWP.—See CLEVELAND, OH (Time Warner Cable)

BOTKINS (VILLAGE)—See AMBERLEY (village), OH (Time Warner Cable)

BOTKINS—See NEW KNOXVILLE, OH (NKTelco)

BOURNEVILLE—See BAINBRIDGE, OH (Time Warner Cable)

BOWERSTON (RURAL PORTIONS)—See BOWERSTON, OH (Time Warner Cable)

BOWERSTON—Time Warner Cable

BOWLING GREEN TWP. (LICKING COUNTY)—See COLUMBUS, OH (Time Warner Cable)

BOWLING GREEN TWP. (MUSKINGUM COUNTY)—See COLUMBUS, OH (Time Warner Cable)

BOWLING GREEN—Time Warner Cable. Now served by TIFFIN (formerly Fostoria), OH [OH0050]

BOWLING GREEN—See TIFFIN, OH (Time Warner Cable)

BRACEVILLE TWP.—See NELSON TWP., OH (Suddenlink Communications)

BRACEVILLE TWP.—See CLEVELAND, OH (Time Warner Cable)

BRADFORD (VILLAGE) (DARKE COUNTY)—See AMBERLEY (village), OH (Time Warner Cable)

BRADFORD (VILLAGE) (MIAMI COUNTY)—See AMBERLEY (village), OH (Time Warner Cable)

BRADNER (VILLAGE)—See TIFFIN, OH (Time Warner Cable)

BRADY LAKE (VILLAGE)—See CLEVELAND, OH (Time Warner Cable)

BRADY TWP. (WILLIAMS COUNTY)—See TIFFIN, OH (Time Warner Cable)

BRATENAHL (VILLAGE)—See CLEVELAND, OH (Time Warner Cable)

BRATENAHL—See EAST CLEVELAND, OH (East Cleveland Cable TV & Communications LLC)

BRECKSVILLE—See CLEVELAND, OH (Time Warner Cable)

BRECKSVILLE—See BEREA, OH (WOW! Internet, Cable & Phone)

BREMAN (VILLAGE)—See COLUMBUS, OH (Time Warner Cable)

BREWSTER—See MASSILLON, OH (MCTV)

BREWSTER—See CLEVELAND, OH (Time Warner Cable)

BRIARWOOD BEACH (VILLAGE)—See CLEVELAND, OH (Time Warner Cable)

BRICE—See COLUMBUS, OH (Time Warner Cable)

BRICE—See COLUMBUS, OH (WOW! Internet, Cable & Phone)

BRIMFIELD TWP.—See CLEVELAND, OH (Time Warner Cable)

BRISTOL TWP. (TRUMBULL COUNTY)—See CLEVELAND, OH (Time Warner Cable)

BROADVIEW HEIGHTS—See PARMA, OH (Cox Communications)

BRONSON TWP.—See CLEVELAND, OH (Time Warner Cable)

BROOK PARK—See CLEVELAND, OH (Time Warner Cable)

BROOK PARK—See BEREA, OH (WOW! Internet, Cable & Phone)

BROOKFIELD TWP. (Trumbull County)—Formerly served by Northeast Cable TV. No longer in operation

BROOKFIELD TWP.—See CLEVELAND, OH (Time Warner Cable)

BROOKLYN HEIGHTS—See PARMA, OH (Cox Communications)

BROOKLYN—See CLEVELAND, OH (Time Warner Cable)

BROOKLYN—See BEREA, OH (WOW! Internet, Cable & Phone)

BROOKVILLE (VILLAGE)—See AMBERLEY (village), OH (Time Warner Cable)

BROOKVILLE—See LEBANON, IN (Cincinnati Bell Fioptics TV. This cable system has converted to IPTV)

BROUGHTON—Watch Communications

BROWN TWP. (CARROLL COUNTY)—See CLEVELAND, OH (Time Warner Cable)

BROWN TWP. (DARKE COUNTY)—See AMBERLEY (village), OH (Time Warner Cable)

BROWN TWP. (DELAWARE COUNTY)—See COLUMBUS, OH (Time Warner Cable)

BROWN TWP. (FRANKLIN COUNTY)—See COLUMBUS, OH (Time Warner Cable)

BROWN TWP. (MIAMI COUNTY)—See AMBERLEY (village), OH (Time Warner Cable)

BROWN TWP.—See SUBURBANS MOTOR HOME PARK, OH (Time Warner Cable)

BROWNHELM (TOWN)—See CLEVELAND, OH (Time Warner Cable)

Cable Community Index—Ohio

BROWNHELM TWP.—See WELLINGTON, OH (GLW Broadband)

BRUNSWICK HILLS—See CLEVELAND, OH (Time Warner Cable)

BRUNSWICK—Time Warner Cable. Now served by CLEVELAND (formerly Cleveland Heights), OH [OH0006]

BRUNSWICK—See CLEVELAND, OH (Time Warner Cable)

BRUSH CREEK TWP.—See COLUMBUS, OH (Time Warner Cable)

BRYAN—Time Warner Cable. Now served by TIFFIN (formerly Fostoria), OH [OH0050]

BRYAN—Bryan Municipal Utilities

BRYAN—See TIFFIN, OH (Time Warner Cable)

BUCHTEL—See NELSONVILLE, OH (Nelsonville TV Cable)

BUCK TWP. (HARDIN COUNTY)—See COLUMBUS, OH (Time Warner Cable)

BUCKEYE LAKE—See NEWARK, OH (Time Warner Cable)

BUCKLAND (VILLAGE)—See TIFFIN, OH (Time Warner Cable)

BUCKSKIN TWP.—See CHILLICOTHE, OH (Time Warner Cable)

BUCYRUS TWP.—See COLUMBUS, OH (Time Warner Cable)

BUCYRUS—Time Warner Cable. Now served by COLUMBUS, OH [OH0002]

BUCYRUS—See COLUMBUS, OH (Time Warner Cable)

BUFFALO—See SENECAVILLE, OH (Suddenlink Communications)

BURBANK (VILLAGE)—See CLEVELAND, OH (Time Warner Cable)

BURGOON (VILLAGE)—See TIFFIN, OH (Time Warner Cable)

BURKETSVILLE (VILLAGE) (DARKE COUNTY)—See AMBERLEY (village), OH (Time Warner Cable)

BURKETSVILLE (VILLAGE) (MERCER COUNTY)—See AMBERLEY (village), OH (Time Warner Cable)

BURLINGTON TWP.—See COLUMBUS, OH (Time Warner Cable)

BURTON (VILLAGE)—See CLEVELAND, OH (Time Warner Cable)

BURTON TWP.—See NELSON TWP., OH (Suddenlink Communications)

BURTON TWP.—See CLEVELAND, OH (Time Warner Cable)

BUSHCREEK TWP. (MUSKINGUM COUNTY)—See COLUMBUS, OH (Time Warner Cable)

BUTLER COUNTY (PORTIONS)—See AMBERLEY (village), OH (Time Warner Cable)

BUTLER TWP. (COLUMBIANA COUNTY)—See CLEVELAND, OH (Time Warner Cable)

BUTLER TWP. (DARKE COUNTY)—See AMBERLEY (village), OH (Time Warner Cable)

BUTLER TWP. (MERCER COUNTY)—See TIFFIN, OH (Time Warner Cable)

BUTLER TWP. (MONTGOMERY COUNTY)—See AMBERLEY (village), OH (Time Warner Cable)

BUTLERVILLE (VILLAGE)—See LEBANON, OH (Cincinnati Bell Fioptics TV. This cable system has converted to IPTV)

BUTLERVILLE (VILLAGE)—See AMBERLEY (village), OH (Time Warner Cable)

BYESVILLE—See SENECAVILLE, OH (Suddenlink Communications)

BYESVILLE—See NEWARK, OH (Time Warner Cable)

CADIZ—Time Warner Cable

CAIRO (VILLAGE)—See TIFFIN, OH (Time Warner Cable)

CALDWELL (RURAL PORTIONS)—See CALDWELL, OH (Time Warner Cable)

CALDWELL—Time Warner Cable

CALEDONIA—Time Warner Cable. Now served by MARION, OH [OH0040]

CALEDONIA—See MARION, OH (Time Warner Cable)

CALIFORNIA—See LEBANON, KY (Cincinnati Bell Fioptics TV. This cable system has converted to IPTV)

CAMBRIDGE TWP. (GUERNSEY COUNTY)—See CAMBRIDGE, OH (Time Warner Cable)

CAMBRIDGE—Time Warner Cable

CAMDEN (VILLAGE)—See AMBERLEY (village), OH (Time Warner Cable)

CAMDEN TWP.—See WELLINGTON, OH (GLW Broadband)

CAMERON—Formerly served by Cebridge Connections. No longer in operation

CANAAN TWP. (ATHENS COUNTY)—See ATHENS, OH (Time Warner Cable)

CANAAN TWP. (ATHENS COUNTY)—See COLUMBUS, OH (Time Warner Cable)

CANAAN TWP. (Madison County)—Time Warner Cable. Now served by SUBURBANS MOTOR HOME PARK, OH [OH0452]

CANAAN TWP. (MADISON COUNTY)—See SUBURBANS MOTOR HOME PARK, OH (Time Warner Cable)

CANAAN TWP. (WAYNE COUNTY)—See WOOSTER, OH (MCTV)

CANAAN TWP. (WAYNE COUNTY)—See CLEVELAND, OH (Time Warner Cable)

CANAL FULTON—See MASSILLON, OH (MCTV)

CANAL FULTON—See CLEVELAND, OH (Time Warner Cable)

CANAL WINCHESTER—See COLUMBUS, OH (Time Warner Cable)

CANAL WINCHESTER—See COLUMBUS, OH (WOW! Internet, Cable & Phone)

CANTON TWP.—See CLEVELAND, OH (Time Warner Cable)

CANTON—Time Warner Cable. Now served by CLEVELAND (formerly Cleveland Heights), OH [OH0006]

CANTON—See CLEVELAND, OH (Time Warner Cable)

CARBON HILL—See NELSONVILLE, OH (Nelsonville TV Cable)

CARDINGTON (VILLAGE)—See COLUMBUS, OH (Time Warner Cable)

CARDINGTON TWP.—See COLUMBUS, OH (Time Warner Cable)

CAREY—Time Warner Cable. Now served by TIFFIN (formerly Fostoria), OH [OH0050]

CAREY—See TIFFIN, OH (Time Warner Cable)

CARLISLE (VILLAGE) (MONTGOMERY COUNTY)—See LEBANON, OH (Cincinnati Bell Fioptics TV. This cable system has converted to IPTV)

CARLISLE (VILLAGE) (WARREN COUNTY)—See LEBANON, OH (Cincinnati Bell Fioptics TV. This cable system has converted to IPTV)

CARLISLE TWP.—See CLEVELAND, OH (Time Warner Cable)

CARLISLE—See AMBERLEY (village), OH (Time Warner Cable)

CARROLL (VILLAGE)—See COLUMBUS, OH (Time Warner Cable)

CARROLL TWP. (OTTAWA COUNTY)—See PORT CLINTON, OH (Time Warner Cable)

CARROLLTON (village)—Time Warner Cable. Now served by CLEVELAND (formerly Cleveland Heights), OH [OH0006]

CARROLLTON (VILLAGE)—See CLEVELAND, OH (Time Warner Cable)

CASS TWP. (HANCOCK COUNTY)—See TIFFIN, OH (Time Warner Cable)

CASS TWP. (MUSKINGUM COUNTY)—See CLEVELAND, OH (Time Warner Cable)

CASS TWP. (MUSKINGUM COUNTY)—See COLUMBUS, OH (Time Warner Cable)

CASSTOWN (VILLAGE)—See AMBERLEY (village), OH (Time Warner Cable)

CASTALIA—See TOLEDO, OH (Buckeye Broadband)

CASTINE (VILLAGE)—See AMBERLEY (village), OH (Time Warner Cable)

CATAWBA (VILLAGE)—See AMBERLEY (village), OH (Time Warner Cable)

CATAWBA ISLAND TWP. (OTTAWA COUNTY)—See PORT CLINTON, OH (Time Warner Cable)

CECIL—See PAULDING, OH (Time Warner Cable)

CEDAR GROVE—See LEBANON, IN (Cincinnati Bell Fioptics TV. This cable system has converted to IPTV)

CEDARVILLE (VILLAGE)—See AMBERLEY (village), OH (Time Warner Cable)

CEDARVILLE TWP.—See AMBERLEY (village), OH (Time Warner Cable)

CELINA—Time Warner Cable. Now served by TIFFIN (formerly Fostoria), OH [OH0050]

CELINA—See TIFFIN, OH (Time Warner Cable)

CENTER TWP. (COLUMBIANA COUNTY)—See CLEVELAND, OH (Time Warner Cable)

CENTER TWP. (GUERNSEY COUNTY)—See SENECAVILLE, OH (Suddenlink Communications)

CENTER TWP. (GUERNSEY COUNTY)—See CAMBRIDGE, OH (Time Warner Cable)

CENTER TWP. (MONROE COUNTY)—See WOODSFIELD, OH (City of Woodsfield)

CENTER TWP. (WILLIAMS COUNTY)—See TIFFIN, OH (Time Warner Cable)

CENTER TWP. (WOOD COUNTY)—See TIFFIN, OH (Time Warner Cable)

CENTERBURG (VILLAGE)—See COLUMBUS, OH (Time Warner Cable)

CENTERVILLE—See AMBERLEY (village), OH (Time Warner Cable)

CHAGRIN FALLS (TWP.)—See CLEVELAND, OH (Time Warner Cable)

CHAGRIN FALLS (VILLAGE)—See CLEVELAND, OH (Time Warner Cable)

CHAMPION TWP.—See CLEVELAND, OH (Time Warner Cable)

CHANDLERSVILLE—Time Warner Cable. Now served by COLUMBUS, OH [OH0002]

CHANDLERSVILLE—See COLUMBUS, OH (Time Warner Cable)

CHARDON TWP.—See CLEVELAND, OH (Time Warner Cable)

CHARDON—See CLEVELAND, OH (Time Warner Cable)

CHARLESTOWN TWP.—See CLEVELAND, OH (Time Warner Cable)

CHATFIELD TWP.—See TIFFIN, OH (Time Warner Cable)

CHATHAM TWP.—See CLEVELAND, OH (Time Warner Cable)

CHAUNCEY—See NELSONVILLE, OH (Nelsonville TV Cable)

Ohio—Cable Community Index

CHERRY FORK (VILLAGE)—See AMBERLEY (village), OH (Time Warner Cable)

CHERRY GROVE—See LEBANON, OH (Cincinnati Bell Fioptics TV. This cable system has converted to IPTV)

CHESTER TWP. (GEAUGA COUNTY)—See CLEVELAND, OH (Time Warner Cable)

CHESTER TWP. (MEIGS COUNTY)—See BEVERLY, OH (Time Warner Cable)

CHESTER TWP. (WAYNE COUNTY)—See WOOSTER, OH (MCTV)

CHESTERVILLE (VILLAGE)—See COLUMBUS, OH (Time Warner Cable)

CHEVIOT—See LEBANON, OH (Cincinnati Bell Fioptics TV. This cable system has converted to IPTV)

CHEVIOT—See AMBERLEY (village), OH (Time Warner Cable)

CHICKASAW—See TIFFIN, OH (Time Warner Cable)

CHILLICOTHE—Time Warner Cable

CHILO (VILLAGE)—See AMBERLEY (village), OH (Time Warner Cable)

CHIPPEWA LAKE TWP.—See CLEVELAND, OH (Time Warner Cable)

CHIPPEWA TWP.—Time Warner Cable. Now served by CLEVELAND (formerly Cleveland Heights), OH [OH0006]

CHIPPEWA TWP.—See DOYLESTOWN, OH (Doylestown Communications)

CHIPPEWA TWP.—See CLEVELAND, OH (Time Warner Cable)

CHRISTIANSBURG (VILLAGE)—See AMBERLEY (village), OH (Time Warner Cable)

CINCINNATI—See LEBANON, OH (Cincinnati Bell Fioptics TV. This cable system has converted to IPTV)

CINCINNATI—See AMBERLEY (village), OH (Time Warner Cable)

CIRCLEVILLE TWP.—See OAKLAND, OH (Time Warner Cable)

CIRCLEVILLE—Time Warner Cable. Now served by COLUMBUS, OH [OH0002]

CIRCLEVILLE—Time Warner Cable. Now served by COLUMBUS, OH [OH0002]

CIRCLEVILLE—See COLUMBUS, OH (Time Warner Cable)

CLAIBORNE TWP.—See COLUMBUS, OH (Time Warner Cable)

CLARIDON TWP. (GEAUGA COUNTY)—See CLEVELAND, OH (Time Warner Cable)

CLARIDON TWP. (MARION COUNTY)—See MARION, OH (Time Warner Cable)

CLARIDON—See THOMPSON TWP. (Geauga County), OH (Zito Media)

CLARINGTON—See HANNIBAL, OH (Crystal Broadband Networks)

CLARK BOROUGH—See CLEVELAND, PA (Time Warner Cable)

CLARK TWP. (BROWN COUNTY)—See AMBERLEY (village), OH (Time Warner Cable)

CLARK TWP. (CLINTON COUNTY)—See AMBERLEY (village), OH (Time Warner Cable)

CLARK TWP.—See LEBANON, OH (Cincinnati Bell Fioptics TV. This cable system has converted to IPTV)

CLARKSBURG—See WEST BELLAIRE, OH (Bellaire Television Cable Co)

CLARKSBURG—See NEW HOLLAND, OH (Time Warner Cable)

CLARKSFIELD TWP.—See CLEVELAND, OH (Time Warner Cable)

CLAY CENTER (VILLAGE)—See TIFFIN, OH (Time Warner Cable)

CLAY CENTER/GIBSONBURG—Time Warner Cable. Now served by TIFFIN (formerly Fostoria), OH [OH0050]

CLAY TWP. (AUGLAIZE COUNTY)—See TIFFIN, OH (Time Warner Cable)

CLAY TWP. (MONTGOMERY COUNTY)—See AMBERLEY (village), OH (Time Warner Cable)

CLAY TWP. (OTTAWA COUNTY)—See TIFFIN, OH (Time Warner Cable)

CLAY TWP. (SCIOTO COUNTY)—See PORTSMOUTH, OH (Time Warner Cable)

CLAYTON (VILLAGE)—See AMBERLEY (village), OH (Time Warner Cable)

CLAYTON TWP.—See COLUMBUS, OH (Time Warner Cable)

CLEAR CREEK TWP. (FAIRFIELD COUNTY)—See OAKLAND, OH (Time Warner Cable)

CLEARCREEK TWP. (FAIRFIELD COUNTY)—See AMBERLEY (village), OH (Time Warner Cable)

CLEARCREEK TWP.—See LEBANON, OH (Cincinnati Bell Fioptics TV. This cable system has converted to IPTV)

CLEARCREEK TWP.—See COLUMBUS, OH (Time Warner Cable)

CLEVELAND HEIGHTS (PORTIONS)—See BEREA, OH (WOW! Internet, Cable & Phone)

CLEVELAND HEIGHTS—See CLEVELAND, OH (Time Warner Cable)

CLEVELAND—Time Warner Cable. Now served by CLEVELAND (formerly Cleveland Heights), OH [OH0006]

CLEVELAND—Time Warner Cable

CLEVELAND—See BEREA, OH (WOW! Internet, Cable & Phone)

CLEVES (VILLAGE)—See AMBERLEY (village), OH (Time Warner Cable)

CLEVES—See LEBANON, OH (Cincinnati Bell Fioptics TV. This cable system has converted to IPTV)

CLIFTON (VILLAGE) (CLARK COUNTY)—See AMBERLEY (village), OH (Time Warner Cable)

CLIFTON (VILLAGE) (GREENE COUNTY)—See AMBERLEY (village), OH (Time Warner Cable)

CLINTON TWP. (FRANKLIN COUNTY)—See COLUMBUS, OH (Time Warner Cable)

CLINTON TWP. (FULTON COUNTY)—See TIFFIN, OH (Time Warner Cable)

CLINTON TWP. (KNOX COUNTY)—See COLUMBUS, OH (Time Warner Cable)

CLINTON TWP. (SENECA COUNTY)—See TIFFIN, OH (Time Warner Cable)

CLINTON TWP. (SHELBY COUNTY)—See AMBERLEY (village), OH (Time Warner Cable)

CLINTON TWP. (WAYNE COUNTY)—See WOOSTER, OH (MCTV)

CLINTON TWP.—See COLUMBUS, OH (WOW! Internet, Cable & Phone)

CLINTON—See CLEVELAND, OH (Time Warner Cable)

CLOVERDALE—See OTTOVILLE, OH (OTEC Communication Co.)

CLYDE—See TIFFIN, OH (Time Warner Cable)

COAL TWP. (JACKSON COUNTY)—See CHILLICOTHE, OH (Time Warner Cable)

COAL TWP. (PERRY COUNTY)—See CORNING, OH (Zito Media)

COALTON—See JACKSON, OH (Time Warner Cable)

COITSVILLE TWP.—Armstrong Cable Services. Now served by ZELIENOPLE, PA [PA0053]

COITSVILLE TWP.—See CLEVELAND, OH (Time Warner Cable)

COLD SPRING—See LEBANON, KY (Cincinnati Bell Fioptics TV. This cable system has converted to IPTV)

COLDWATER—See ST. HENRY, OH (NKTelco)

COLDWATER—See TIFFIN, OH (Time Warner Cable)

COLEBROOK—See ORWELL, OH (Orwell Communications)

COLERAIN TWP. (HAMILTON COUNTY)—See AMBERLEY (village), OH (Time Warner Cable)

COLERAIN TWP. (ROSS COUNTY)—See AMBERLEY (village), OH (Time Warner Cable)

COLERAIN TWP.—See LEBANON, OH (Cincinnati Bell Fioptics TV. This cable system has converted to IPTV)

COLLEGE CORNER (VILLAGE) (BUTLER COUNTY)—See AMBERLEY (village), OH (Time Warner Cable)

COLLEGE CORNER (VILLAGE) (PREBLE COUNTY)—See AMBERLEY (village), OH (Time Warner Cable)

COLLEGE TWP.—See COLUMBUS, OH (Time Warner Cable)

COLLINSVILLE—Formerly served by Time Warner Cable. No longer in operation

COLUMBIA TWP. (HAMILTON COUNTY)—See AMBERLEY (village), OH (Time Warner Cable)

COLUMBIA TWP. (LORAIN COUNTY)—See CLEVELAND, OH (Time Warner Cable)

COLUMBIA TWP.—See LEBANON, OH (Cincinnati Bell Fioptics TV. This cable system has converted to IPTV)

COLUMBIANA—See NEW MIDDLETOWN, OH (Comcast Cable)

COLUMBUS GROVE (VILLAGE)—FairPoint Communications

COLUMBUS GROVE (VILLAGE)—See TIFFIN, OH (Time Warner Cable)

COLUMBUS TWP.—See CLEVELAND, PA (Time Warner Cable)

COLUMBUS—Formerly served by Sprint Corp. No longer in operation

COLUMBUS—Time Warner Cable. Now served by COLUMBUS, OH [OH0002]

COLUMBUS—See LEBANON, OH (Cincinnati Bell Fioptics TV. This cable system has converted to IPTV)

COLUMBUS—Time Warner Cable

COLUMBUS—WOW! Internet, Cable & Phone

COMMERCIAL POINT—Time Warner Cable

CONCORD TWP. (CHAMPAIGN COUNTY)—See AMBERLEY (village), OH (Time Warner Cable)

CONCORD TWP. (DELAWARE COUNTY)—See COLUMBUS, OH (Time Warner Cable)

CONCORD TWP. (ERIE COUNTY)—See CLEVELAND, PA (Time Warner Cable)

CONCORD TWP. (FAYETTE COUNTY)—See WASHINGTON COURT HOUSE, OH (Time Warner Cable)

CONCORD TWP. (Lake County)—Time Warner Cable. Now served by CLEVELAND (formerly Cleveland Heights), OH [OH0006]

CONCORD TWP. (LAKE COUNTY)—See CLEVELAND, OH (Time Warner Cable)

CONCORD TWP. (ROSS COUNTY)—See CHILLICOTHE, OH (Time Warner Cable)

CONESVILLE—See COSHOCTON, OH (Time Warner Cable)

CONGRESS TWP. (Wayne County)—Time Warner Cable. Now served by CLEVELAND (formerly Cleveland Heights), OH [OH0006]

CONGRESS TWP. (WAYNE COUNTY)—See CLEVELAND, OH (Time Warner Cable)

CONGRESS TWP.—See WOOSTER, OH (MCTV)

CONNEAUT TWP.—See CLEVELAND, PA (Time Warner Cable)

CONNEAUT—See CLEVELAND, OH (Time Warner Cable)

CONNEAUTVILLE BOROUGH—See CLEVELAND, PA (Time Warner Cable)

CONNEAUTVILLE—See CLEVELAND, PA (Time Warner Cable)

CONTINENTAL—See LEIPSIC, OH (Orwell Communications)

CONVOY—NewWave Communications. Now served by MONROEVILLE, IN [IN0358]

COOLVILLE—See BEVERLY, OH (Time Warner Cable)

COPLEY TWP.—See CLEVELAND, OH (Time Warner Cable)

CORNING—Zito Media

CORRY—See CLEVELAND, PA (Time Warner Cable)

CORTLAND (VILLAGE)—See CLEVELAND, OH (Time Warner Cable)

CORWIN (VILLAGE)—See LEBANON, OH (Cincinnati Bell Fioptics TV. This cable system has converted to IPTV)

CORWIN (VILLAGE)—See AMBERLEY (village), OH (Time Warner Cable)

COSHOCTON COUNTY (PORTIONS)—See COSHOCTON, OH (Time Warner Cable)

COSHOCTON—Time Warner Cable

COSTONIA—See TORONTO, OH (Jefferson County Cable Inc)

COUNTRYSIDE MOBILE HOME PARK—See SUBURBANS MOTOR HOME PARK, OH (Time Warner Cable)

COVENTRY TWP.—See CLEVELAND, OH (Time Warner Cable)

COVINGTON (VILLAGE)—See AMBERLEY (village), OH (Time Warner Cable)

COVINGTON—See LEBANON, KY (Cincinnati Bell Fioptics TV. This cable system has converted to IPTV)

CRAIG BEACH (village)—Time Warner Cable. Now served by CLEVELAND (formerly Cleveland Heights), OH [OH0006]

CRAIG BEACH (VILLAGE)—See CLEVELAND, OH (Time Warner Cable)

CRANBERRY PRAIRIE—See TIFFIN, OH (Time Warner Cable)

CRANBERRY TWP.—See TIFFIN, OH (Time Warner Cable)

CRANE TWP. (PAULDING COUNTY)—See PAULDING, OH (Time Warner Cable)

CRANE TWP. (WYANDOT COUNTY)—See TIFFIN, OH (Time Warner Cable)

CRANESVILLE BOROUGH—See CLEVELAND, PA (Time Warner Cable)

CRAWFORD TWP. (WYANDOT COUNTY)—See TIFFIN, OH (Time Warner Cable)

CRESCENT SPRINGS—See LEBANON, KY (Cincinnati Bell Fioptics TV. This cable system has converted to IPTV)

CRESCENT—See BARTON, OH (Powhatan Point Cable Co)

CRESTLINE (VILLAGE)—See COLUMBUS, OH (Time Warner Cable)

CRESTON (VILLAGE)—See CLEVELAND, OH (Time Warner Cable)

CRESTVIEW HILLS—See LEBANON, KY (Cincinnati Bell Fioptics TV. This cable system has converted to IPTV)

CRESTVIEW—See LEBANON, KY (Cincinnati Bell Fioptics TV. This cable system has converted to IPTV)

CRIDERSVILLE (village)—Time Warner Cable. Now served by TIFFIN, OH [OH0050]

CRIDERSVILLE (VILLAGE)—See TIFFIN, OH (Time Warner Cable)

CRIDERSVILLE—See WAPAKONETA CITY, OH (TSC Communications)

CROOKSVILLE (village)—Time Warner Cable. Now served by COLUMBUS, OH [OH0002]

CROOKSVILLE (VILLAGE)—See COLUMBUS, OH (Time Warner Cable)

CROSBY TWP. (HAMILTON COUNTY)—See AMBERLEY (village), OH (Time Warner Cable)

CROSBY TWP.—See LEBANON, OH (Cincinnati Bell Fioptics TV. This cable system has converted to IPTV)

CROTON (VILLAGE)—See COLUMBUS, OH (Time Warner Cable)

CROWN CITY—Formerly served by Vital Communications. Now served by Armstrong Cable Services, ZELIENOPLE, PA [PA0053]

CRYSTAL LAKE MOBILE HOME PARK—Formerly served by Time Warner Cable. No longer in operation

CUMBERLAND—Formerly served by Almega Cable. No longer in operation

CUMBERLAND—See NEWARK, OH (Time Warner Cable)

CURTICE (LUCAS COUNTY)—See TIFFIN, OH (Time Warner Cable)

CURTICE (OTTAWA COUNTY)—See TIFFIN, OH (Time Warner Cable)

CUSTAR (VILLAGE)—See TIFFIN, OH (Time Warner Cable)

CUYAHOGA FALLS—See CLEVELAND, OH (Time Warner Cable)

CUYAHOGA HEIGHTS (VILLAGE)—See CLEVELAND, OH (Time Warner Cable)

CUYAHOGA HEIGHTS—See BEREA, OH (WOW! Internet, Cable & Phone)

CYGNET (VILLAGE)—See TIFFIN, OH (Time Warner Cable)

CYNTHIAN TWP.—See TIFFIN, OH (Time Warner Cable)

DAMASCUS TWP.—See TIFFIN, OH (Time Warner Cable)

DANBURY TWP. (OTTAWA COUNTY)—See PORT CLINTON, OH (Time Warner Cable)

DANVILLE (VILLAGE)—See COLUMBUS, OH (Time Warner Cable)

DARBY TWP. (MADISON COUNTY)—See COLUMBUS, OH (Time Warner Cable)

DARBY TWP. (PICKAWAY COUNTY)—See COLUMBUS, OH (Time Warner Cable)

DARBY TWP. (PICKAWAY COUNTY)—See COMMERCIAL POINT, OH (Time Warner Cable)

DARBY TWP. (UNION COUNTY)—See COLUMBUS, OH (Time Warner Cable)

DARBY—See SUBURBANS MOTOR HOME PARK, OH (Time Warner Cable)

DARBYVILLE—See COMMERCIAL POINT, OH (Time Warner Cable)

DAYTON—See LEBANON, KY (Cincinnati Bell Fioptics TV. This cable system has converted to IPTV)

DAYTON—See AMBERLEY (village), OH (Time Warner Cable)

DE GRAFF (VILLAGE)—See AMBERLEY (village), OH (Time Warner Cable)

DECATUR TWP. (WASHINGTON COUNTY)—See BEVERLY, OH (Time Warner Cable)

DEER CREEK TWP.—See COLUMBUS, OH (Time Warner Cable)

DEER PARK—See LEBANON, OH (Cincinnati Bell Fioptics TV. This cable system has converted to IPTV)

DEER PARK—See AMBERLEY (village), OH (Time Warner Cable)

DEERFIELD TWP. (PORTAGE COUNTY)—See CLEVELAND, OH (Time Warner Cable)

DEERFIELD TWP. (ROSS COUNTY)—See CHILLICOTHE, OH (Time Warner Cable)

DEERFIELD TWP. (WARREN COUNTY)—See AMBERLEY (village), OH (Time Warner Cable)

DEERFIELD TWP.—See LEBANON, OH (Cincinnati Bell Fioptics TV. This cable system has converted to IPTV)

DEFIANCE TWP.—See DEFIANCE, OH (Time Warner Cable)

DEFIANCE—Arthur Mutual Telephone. This cable system has converted to IPTV. See DEFIANCE, OH [OH5222]

DEFIANCE—Arthur Mutual Telephone. Formerly [OH0455]. This cable system has converted to IPTV

DEFIANCE—Time Warner Cable

DELAWARE TWP. (DELAWARE COUNTY)—See COLUMBUS, OH (Time Warner Cable)

DELAWARE TWP. (HANCOCK COUNTY)—See TIFFIN, OH (Time Warner Cable)

DELAWARE TWP. (MERCER COUNTY)—See CLEVELAND, PA (Time Warner Cable)

DELAWARE—See COLUMBUS, OH (Time Warner Cable)

DELHI TWP.—Formerly served by Adelphia Communications. No longer in operation

DELHI TWP.—See LEBANON, OH (Cincinnati Bell Fioptics TV. This cable system has converted to IPTV)

DELHI TWP.—See AMBERLEY (village), OH (Time Warner Cable)

DELLROY (VILLAGE)—See CLEVELAND, OH (Time Warner Cable)

DELLROY—Time Warner Cable. Now served by CLEVELAND (formerly Cleveland Heights), OH [OH0006]

DELPHOS—Time Warner Cable. Now served by TIFFIN, OH [OH0050]

DELPHOS—See TIFFIN, OH (Time Warner Cable)

DELTA—See TIFFIN, OH (Time Warner Cable)

DENMARK TWP.—Zito Media

DENNISON (VILLAGE)—See CLEVELAND, OH (Time Warner Cable)

DERWENT—See SENECAVILLE, OH (Suddenlink Communications)

DESHLER—Time Warner Cable

DEXTER CITY—See WARNER, OH (Zito Media)

DINSMORE TWP.—See AMBERLEY (village), OH (Time Warner Cable)

DODSON TWP.—See AMBERLEY (village), OH (Time Warner Cable)

DONNELSVILLE (VILLAGE)—See AMBERLEY (village), OH (Time Warner Cable)

DORSET TWP.—See DENMARK TWP., OH (Zito Media)

DOVER (TUSCARAWAS COUNTY)—See CLEVELAND, OH (Time Warner Cable)

DOVER TWP. (FULTON COUNTY)—See TIFFIN, OH (Time Warner Cable)

DOVER TWP. (TUSCARAWAS COUNTY)—See CLEVELAND, OH (Time Warner Cable)

DOVER TWP. (UNION COUNTY)—See COLUMBUS, OH (Time Warner Cable)

DOVER TWP.—See NELSONVILLE, OH (Nelsonville TV Cable)

DOYLESTOWN (VILLAGE)—See CLEVELAND, OH (Time Warner Cable)

DOYLESTOWN—Doylestown Communications

DRESDEN (village)—Time Warner Cable. Now served by COLUMBUS, OH [OH0002]

Ohio—Cable Community Index

DRESDEN (VILLAGE)—See COLUMBUS, OH (Time Warner Cable)

DUBLIN (DELAWARE COUNTY)—See COLUMBUS, OH (Time Warner Cable)

DUBLIN (FRANKLIN COUNTY)—See COLUMBUS, OH (Time Warner Cable)

DUBLIN (UNION COUNTY)—See SUBURBANS MOTOR HOME PARK, OH (Time Warner Cable)

DUBLIN—See COLUMBUS, OH (WOW! Internet, Cable & Phone)

DUCHOUQUET TWP.—See TIFFIN, OH (Time Warner Cable)

DUCHOUQUET TWP.—See WAPAKONETA CITY, OH (TSC Communications)

DUDLEY—See WARNER, OH (Zito Media)

DUNBRIDGE—See TIFFIN, OH (Time Warner Cable)

DUNCAN FALLS—See COLUMBUS, OH (Time Warner Cable)

DUNDAS—See JACKSON, OH (Time Warner Cable)

DUNHAM TWP.—See BEVERLY, OH (Time Warner Cable)

DUNKIRK—Time Warner Cable. Now served by COLUMBUS, OH [OH0002]

DUNKIRK—See COLUMBUS, OH (Time Warner Cable)

DUPONT—See OTTOVILLE, OH (OTEC Communication Co.)

EAGLE TWP. (HANCOCK COUNTY)—See TIFFIN, OH (Time Warner Cable)

EAGLEPORT—See BEVERLY, OH (Time Warner Cable)

EAST CANTON (VILLAGE)—See CLEVELAND, OH (Time Warner Cable)

EAST CLEVELAND—East Cleveland Cable TV & Communications LLC

EAST CLEVELAND—See CLEVELAND, OH (Time Warner Cable)

EAST LIBERTY—See COLUMBUS, OH (Time Warner Cable)

EAST LIVERPOOL—Comcast Cable. Now served by NEW MIDDLETOWN, OH [OH0145]

EAST LIVERPOOL—See NEW MIDDLETOWN, OH (Comcast Cable)

EAST PALESTINE—Comcast Cable. Now served by NEW MIDDLETOWN, OH [OH0145]

EAST PALESTINE—See NEW MIDDLETOWN, OH (Comcast Cable)

EAST SPARTA (VILLAGE)—See CLEVELAND, OH (Time Warner Cable)

EAST UNION TWP. (WAYNE COUNTY)—See WOOSTER, OH (MCTV)

EASTLAKE—See CLEVELAND, OH (Time Warner Cable)

EATON (PREBLE COUNTY)—See AMBERLEY (village), OH (Time Warner Cable)

EATON TWP. (LORAIN COUNTY)—See WELLINGTON, OH (GLW Broadband)

EATON TWP.—See CLEVELAND, OH (Time Warner Cable)

EATON—Time Warner Cable. Now served by AMBERLEY (village), OH [OH0001]

EDEN TWP. (SENECA COUNTY)—See TIFFIN, OH (Time Warner Cable)

EDEN TWP. (WYANDOT COUNTY)—See TIFFIN, OH (Time Warner Cable)

EDEN TWP.—See NEWARK, OH (Time Warner Cable)

EDGERTON (VILLAGE)—See TIFFIN, OH (Time Warner Cable)

EDGEWOOD—See LEBANON, KY (Cincinnati Bell Fioptics TV. This cable system has converted to IPTV)

EDINBURG TWP.—See CLEVELAND, OH (Time Warner Cable)

EDISON (VILLAGE)—See COLUMBUS, OH (Time Warner Cable)

EDON—Formerly served by Vital Communications. No longer in operation

EDON—See TIFFIN, OH (Time Warner Cable)

ELBA—See WARNER, OH (Zito Media)

ELDORADO (VILLAGE)—See AMBERLEY (village), OH (Time Warner Cable)

ELGIN BOROUGH—See CLEVELAND, PA (Time Warner Cable)

ELIDA (VILLAGE)—See TIFFIN, OH (Time Warner Cable)

ELIZABETH TWP. (MIAMI COUNTY)—See AMBERLEY (village), OH (Time Warner Cable)

ELK CREEK TWP.—See CLEVELAND, PA (Time Warner Cable)

ELK TWP. (VINTON COUNTY)—See CHILLICOTHE, OH (Time Warner Cable)

ELMORE (VILLAGE)—See TIFFIN, OH (Time Warner Cable)

ELMWOOD PLACE (VILLAGE)—See LEBANON, OH (Cincinnati Bell Fioptics TV. This cable system has converted to IPTV)

ELMWOOD PLACE (VILLAGE)—See AMBERLEY (village), OH (Time Warner Cable)

ELSMERE—See LEBANON, KY (Cincinnati Bell Fioptics TV. This cable system has converted to IPTV)

ELYRIA TWP. (LORAIN COUNTY)—See CLEVELAND, OH (Time Warner Cable)

ELYRIA—Time Warner Cable. Now served by CLEVELAND (formerly Cleveland Heights), OH [OH0006]

ELYRIA—See CLEVELAND, OH (Time Warner Cable)

EMERALD TWP.—See PAULDING, OH (Time Warner Cable)

EMPIRE—Jefferson County Cable Inc

ENGLEWOOD—See AMBERLEY (village), OH (Time Warner Cable)

ENOCH TWP.—See NEWARK, OH (Time Warner Cable)

ENON (VILLAGE)—See AMBERLEY (village), OH (Time Warner Cable)

ENTERPRISE—See LOGAN, OH (Time Warner Cable)

ERIE TWP. (OTTAWA COUNTY)—See PORT CLINTON, OH (Time Warner Cable)

ERLANGER—See LEBANON, KY (Cincinnati Bell Fioptics TV. This cable system has converted to IPTV)

ETNA TWP. (LICKING COUNTY)—See COLUMBUS, OH (Time Warner Cable)

ETNA TWP.—See COLUMBUS, OH (Time Warner Cable)

EUCLID—See CLEVELAND, OH (Time Warner Cable)

EUREKA—Formerly served by Vital Communications. No longer in operation

EVENDALE (VILLAGE)—See LEBANON, OH (Cincinnati Bell Fioptics TV. This cable system has converted to IPTV)

EVENDALE (VILLAGE)—See AMBERLEY (village), OH (Time Warner Cable)

FAIRBORN—Time Warner Cable. Now served by AMBERLEY (village), OH [OH0001]

FAIRBORN—See AMBERLEY (village), OH (Time Warner Cable)

FAIRFAX (VILLAGE)—See LEBANON, OH (Cincinnati Bell Fioptics TV. This cable system has converted to IPTV)

FAIRFAX (VILLAGE)—See AMBERLEY (village), OH (Time Warner Cable)

FAIRFIELD (Butler County)—Formerly served by Adelphia Communications. Now served by Time Warner Cable, AMBERLEY (village), OH [OH0001]

FAIRFIELD (BUTLER COUNTY)—See LEBANON, OH (Cincinnati Bell Fioptics TV. This cable system has converted to IPTV)

FAIRFIELD (BUTLER COUNTY)—See AMBERLEY (village), OH (Time Warner Cable)

FAIRFIELD (HAMILTON COUNTY)—See LEBANON, OH (Cincinnati Bell Fioptics TV. This cable system has converted to IPTV)

FAIRFIELD BEACH (VILLAGE)—See COLUMBUS, OH (Time Warner Cable)

FAIRFIELD TWP. (BUTLER COUNTY)—See AMBERLEY (village), OH (Time Warner Cable)

FAIRFIELD TWP. (HIGHLAND COUNTY)—See AMBERLEY (village), OH (Time Warner Cable)

FAIRFIELD TWP. (HURON COUNTY)—See CLEVELAND, OH (Time Warner Cable)

FAIRFIELD TWP.—See LEBANON, OH (Cincinnati Bell Fioptics TV. This cable system has converted to IPTV)

FAIRFIELD—See NEW MIDDLETOWN, OH (Comcast Cable)

FAIRFIELD—See SUBURBANS MOTOR HOME PARK, OH (Time Warner Cable)

FAIRLAWN—See CLEVELAND, OH (Time Warner Cable)

FAIRPOINT HARBOR (VILLAGE)—See CLEVELAND, OH (Time Warner Cable)

FAIRVIEW (ERIE COUNTY)—See CLEVELAND, PA (Time Warner Cable)

FAIRVIEW PARK—See PARMA, OH (Cox Communications)

FAIRVIEW PARK—See BEREA, OH (WOW! Internet, Cable & Phone)

FALLS TWP. (HOCKING COUNTY)—See COLUMBUS, OH (Time Warner Cable)

FALLSBURY TWP.—See NEWARK, OH (Time Warner Cable)

FARMERSVILLE (VILLAGE)—See AMBERLEY (village), OH (Time Warner Cable)

FARMINGTON (VILLAGE)—See CLEVELAND, OH (Time Warner Cable)

FARMINGTON—See NELSON TWP., OH (Suddenlink Communications)

FARRELL—See CLEVELAND, PA (Time Warner Cable)

FAYETTE—Formerly served by Adelphia Communications. Now served by Time Warner Cable, TIFFIN, OH [OH0050]

FAYETTE—See TIFFIN, OH (Time Warner Cable)

FAYETTEVILLE (VILLAGE)—See AMBERLEY (village), OH (Time Warner Cable)

FELICITY (VILLAGE)—See AMBERLEY (village), OH (Time Warner Cable)

FINDLAY—Time Warner Cable. Now served by TIFFIN (formerly Fostoria), OH [OH0050]

FINDLAY—See TIFFIN, OH (Time Warner Cable)

FIREBRICK—See PORTSMOUTH, OH (Time Warner Cable)

FITCHVILLE TWP.—See CLEVELAND, OH (Time Warner Cable)

FLATROCK TWP.—See TIFFIN, OH (Time Warner Cable)

FLETCHER (VILLAGE)—See AMBERLEY (village), OH (Time Warner Cable)

FLORENCE TWP. (ERIE COUNTY)—See CLEVELAND, OH (Time Warner Cable)

Cable Community Index—Ohio

FLORENCE—See LEBANON, KY (Cincinnati Bell Fioptics TV. This cable system has converted to IPTV)

FLORIDA—See TIFFIN, OH (Time Warner Cable)

FLUSHING—Comcast Cable. Now served by WHEELING, WV [WV0004]

FOREST (village)—Time Warner Cable. Now served by COLUMBUS, OH [OH0002]

FOREST (VILLAGE)—See COLUMBUS, OH (Time Warner Cable)

FOREST PARK—See LEBANON, OH (Cincinnati Bell Fioptics TV. This cable system has converted to IPTV)

FOREST PARK—See AMBERLEY (village), OH (Time Warner Cable)

FORT JENNINGS—FJ Communications

FORT LORAMIE—See NEW KNOXVILLE, OH (NKTelco)

FORT LORAMIE—See TIFFIN, OH (Time Warner Cable)

FORT MITCHELL—See LEBANON, KY (Cincinnati Bell Fioptics TV. This cable system has converted to IPTV)

FORT RECOVERY—Comcast Cable. Now served by HENDRICKS COUNTY (portions), IN [IN0001]

FORT SENECA—See TIFFIN, OH (Time Warner Cable)

FORT SHAWNEE (VILLAGE)—See TIFFIN, OH (Time Warner Cable)

FORT THOMAS—See LEBANON, KY (Cincinnati Bell Fioptics TV. This cable system has converted to IPTV)

FORT WRIGHT—See LEBANON, KY (Cincinnati Bell Fioptics TV. This cable system has converted to IPTV)

FOSTORIA (HANCOCK COUNTY)—See TIFFIN, OH (Time Warner Cable)

FOSTORIA (SENECA COUNTY)—See TIFFIN, OH (Time Warner Cable)

FOSTORIA (WOOD COUNTY)—See TIFFIN, OH (Time Warner Cable)

FOSTORIA—See BASCOM, OH (BTC Multimedia)

FOWLER TWP.—See CLEVELAND, OH (Time Warner Cable)

FRANKFORT—Formerly served by Adelphia Communications. Now served by Time Warner Cable, CHILLICOTHE, OH [OH0033]

FRANKFORT—See CHILLICOTHE, OH (Time Warner Cable)

FRANKLIN (VILLAGE)—See LEBANON, OH (Cincinnati Bell Fioptics TV. This cable system has converted to IPTV)

FRANKLIN (WARREN COUNTY)—See AMBERLEY (village), OH (Time Warner Cable)

FRANKLIN COUNTY (PORTIONS)—See COMMERCIAL POINT, OH (Time Warner Cable)

FRANKLIN FURNACE—Formerly served by Adelphia Communications. Now served by Time Warner Cable, ASHLAND, KY [KY0326]

FRANKLIN TWP. (ADAMS COUNTY)—See AMBERLEY (village), OH (Time Warner Cable)

FRANKLIN TWP. (CLERMONT COUNTY)—See AMBERLEY (village), OH (Time Warner Cable)

FRANKLIN TWP. (COSHOCTON COUNTY)—See CLEVELAND, OH (Time Warner Cable)

FRANKLIN TWP. (FRANKIN COUNTY)—See COLUMBUS, OH (Time Warner Cable)

FRANKLIN TWP. (LICKING COUNTY)—See NEWARK, OH (Time Warner Cable)

FRANKLIN TWP. (MERCER COUNTY)—See TIFFIN, OH (Time Warner Cable)

FRANKLIN TWP. (PORTAGE COUNTY)—See CLEVELAND, OH (Time Warner Cable)

FRANKLIN TWP. (ROSS COUNTY)—See CHILLICOTHE, OH (Time Warner Cable)

FRANKLIN TWP. (SHELBY COUNTY)—See AMBERLEY (village), OH (Time Warner Cable)

FRANKLIN TWP. (WARREN COUNTY)—See AMBERLEY (village), OH (Time Warner Cable)

FRANKLIN TWP. (WAYNE COUNTY)—See WOOSTER, OH (MCTV)

FRANKLIN TWP.—See LEBANON, OH (Cincinnati Bell Fioptics TV. This cable system has converted to IPTV)

FRANKLIN TWP.—See COLUMBUS, OH (WOW! Internet, Cable & Phone)

FRAZEYBURG (village)—Time Warner Cable. Now served by COLUMBUS, OH [OH0002]

FRAZEYBURG (VILLAGE)—See COLUMBUS, OH (Time Warner Cable)

FREDERICKSBURG (VILLAGE) (WAYNE COUNTY)—See CLEVELAND, OH (Time Warner Cable)

FREDERICKTOWN (village)—Time Warner Cable. Now served by COLUMBUS, OH [OH0002]

FREDERICKTOWN (VILLAGE)—See COLUMBUS, OH (Time Warner Cable)

FREDONIA BOROUGH—See CLEVELAND, PA (Time Warner Cable)

FREEDOM TWP. (PORTAGE COUNTY)—See NELSON TWP., OH (Suddenlink Communications)

FREEDOM TWP. (WOOD COUNTY)—See TIFFIN, OH (Time Warner Cable)

FREEDOM TWP.—See RIDGEVILLE CORNERS, OH (RTEC Communications)

FREEPORT TWP.—Formerly served by Vital Communications. No longer in operation

FREMONT—Time Warner Cable. Now served by TIFFIN (formerly Fostoria), OH [OH0050]

FREMONT—See TIFFIN, OH (Time Warner Cable)

FRIENDSHIP—Time Warner Cable. Now served by PORTSMOUTH, OH [OH0035]

FRIENDSHIP—See PORTSMOUTH, OH (Time Warner Cable)

FT. SHAWNEE—See WAPAKONETA CITY, OH (TSC Communications)

FULTON (VILLAGE)—See COLUMBUS, OH (Time Warner Cable)

FULTON TWP.—Formerly served by Adelphia Communications. Now served by Time Warner Cable, TIFFIN, OH [OH0050]

FULTON TWP.—See TIFFIN, OH (Time Warner Cable)

FULTONHAM (VILLAGE)—See COLUMBUS, OH (Time Warner Cable)

GAHANNA (FRANKLIN COUNTY)—See COLUMBUS, OH (Time Warner Cable)

GAHANNA—See COLUMBUS, OH (Time Warner Cable)

GAHANNA—See COLUMBUS, OH (WOW! Internet, Cable & Phone)

GALENA (VILLAGE)—See COLUMBUS, OH (Time Warner Cable)

GALION—Time Warner Cable. Now served by COLUMBUS, OH [OH0002]

GALION—See COLUMBUS, OH (Time Warner Cable)

GALLIPOLIS—Zito Media

GAMBIER (VILLAGE)—See COLUMBUS, OH (Time Warner Cable)

GARFIELD HEIGHTS—See CLEVELAND, OH (Time Warner Cable)

GARFIELD HEIGHTS—See BEREA, OH (WOW! Internet, Cable & Phone)

GARRETTSVILLE (VILLAGE)—See CLEVELAND, OH (Time Warner Cable)

GASPER TWP.—See AMBERLEY (village), OH (Time Warner Cable)

GATES MILLS (VILLAGE)—See CLEVELAND, OH (Time Warner Cable)

GEAUGA COUNTY (PORTIONS)—See NELSON TWP, OH (Suddenlink Communications)

GENEVA (ASHTABULA COUNTY)—See CLEVELAND, OH (Time Warner Cable)

GENEVA TWP.—See CLEVELAND, OH (Time Warner Cable)

GENEVA-ON-THE-LAKE (VILLAGE)—See CLEVELAND, OH (Time Warner Cable)

GENOA (VILLAGE)—See TIFFIN, OH (Time Warner Cable)

GENOA TWP. (DELAWARE COUNTY)—See COLUMBUS, OH (Time Warner Cable)

GENOA TWP.—See COLUMBUS, OH (WOW! Internet, Cable & Phone)

GEORGETOWN (VILLAGE)—See AMBERLEY (village), OH (Time Warner Cable)

GERMAN (VILLAGE)—See BLOOMINGDALE, OH (Suddenlink Communications)

GERMAN TWP. (AUGLAIZE COUNTY)—See TIFFIN, OH (Time Warner Cable)

GERMAN TWP. (CLARK COUNTY)—See AMBERLEY (village), OH (Time Warner Cable)

GERMAN TWP. (FULTON COUNTY)—See TIFFIN, OH (Time Warner Cable)

GERMAN TWP. (MONTGOMERY COUNTY)—See AMBERLEY (village), OH (Time Warner Cable)

GERMAN TWP.—See RIDGEVILLE CORNERS, OH (RTEC Communications)

GERMANTOWN (town)—Time Warner Cable. Now served by AMBERLEY (village), OH [OH0001]

GERMANTOWN (TOWN)—See AMBERLEY (village), OH (Time Warner Cable)

GETTYSBURG (VILLAGE)—See AMBERLEY (village), OH (Time Warner Cable)

GIBSONBURG (VILLAGE)—See TIFFIN, OH (Time Warner Cable)

GILBOA—See LEIPSIC, OH (Orwell Communications)

GILEAD TWP.—See COLUMBUS, OH (Time Warner Cable)

GIRARD BOROUGH—See CLEVELAND, PA (Time Warner Cable)

GIRARD TWP. (ERIE COUNTY)—See CLEVELAND, PA (Time Warner Cable)

GIRARD—See CLEVELAND, OH (Time Warner Cable)

GLANDORF (VILLAGE)—See TIFFIN, OH (Time Warner Cable)

GLENCOE—Formerly served by Comcast Cable. No longer in operation

GLENCOE—See WEST BELLAIRE, OH (Bellaire Television Cable Co)

GLENDALE (VILLAGE)—See LEBANON, OH (Cincinnati Bell Fioptics TV. This cable system has converted to IPTV)

GLENDALE (VILLAGE)—See AMBERLEY (village), OH (Time Warner Cable)

GLENDALE—See LEBANON, OH (Cincinnati Bell Fioptics TV. This cable system has converted to IPTV)

GLENFORD—See COLUMBUS, OH (Time Warner Cable)

GLENMONT (VILLAGE)—See CLEVELAND, OH (Time Warner Cable)

GLENMONT—Time Warner Cable. Now served by CLEVELAND (formerly Cleveland Heights), OH [OH0006]

Ohio—Cable Community Index

GLENWILLOW (VILLAGE)—See CLEVELAND, OH (Time Warner Cable)

GLORIA GLENS (VILLAGE)—See CLEVELAND, OH (Time Warner Cable)

GLOUSTER—See NELSONVILLE, OH (Nelsonville TV Cable)

GNADENHUTTEN (VILLAGE)—See CLEVELAND, OH (Time Warner Cable)

GOLF MANOR (VILLAGE)—See LEBANON, OH (Cincinnati Bell Fioptics TV. This cable system has converted to IPTV)

GOLF MANOR (VILLAGE)—See AMBERLEY (village), OH (Time Warner Cable)

GOOD HOPE TWP.—See LOGAN, OH (Time Warner Cable)

GORDON (VILLAGE)—See WEST BELLAIRE, OH (Bellaire Television Cable Co)

GORDON (VILLAGE)—See AMBERLEY (village), OH (Time Warner Cable)

GORHAM TWP.—See TIFFIN, OH (Time Warner Cable)

GOSHEN TWP. (AUGLAIZE COUNTY)—See TIFFIN, OH (Time Warner Cable)

GOSHEN TWP. (Clermont County)—Tiime Warner Cable. Now served by AMBERLEY (village), OH [OH0001]

GOSHEN TWP. (CLERMONT COUNTY)—See AMBERLEY (village), OH (Time Warner Cable)

GOSHEN TWP.—See LEBANON, OH (Cincinnati Bell Fioptics TV. This cable system has converted to IPTV)

GOSHEN TWP.—See CLEVELAND, OH (Time Warner Cable)

GRAFTON—Formerly served by Grafton Cable Communications. Now served by GLW Broadband, WELLINGTON, OH [OH0189]

GRAFTON—See WELLINGTON, OH (GLW Broadband)

GRAND PRAIRIE TWP.—See MARION, OH (Time Warner Cable)

GRAND RAPIDS TWP.—See TIFFIN, OH (Time Warner Cable)

GRAND RAPIDS—See TIFFIN, OH (Time Warner Cable)

GRAND RIVER (VILLAGE)—See CLEVELAND, OH (Time Warner Cable)

GRANDVIEW HEIGHTS—See COLUMBUS, OH (Time Warner Cable)

GRANDVIEW HEIGHTS—See COLUMBUS, OH (WOW! Internet, Cable & Phone)

GRANDVIEW TWP.—See HANNIBAL, OH (Crystal Broadband Networks)

GRANGER TWP.—See CLEVELAND, OH (Time Warner Cable)

GRANVILLE (VILLAGE)—See COLUMBUS, OH (Time Warner Cable)

GRANVILLE TWP. (LICKING COUNTY)—See NEWARK, OH (Time Warner Cable)

GRANVILLE TWP. (MERCER COUNTY)—See TIFFIN, OH (Time Warner Cable)

GRANVILLE—See NEWARK, OH (Time Warner Cable)

GRATIOT (VILLAGE)—See COLUMBUS, OH (Time Warner Cable)

GRATIS (VILLAGE)—See AMBERLEY (village), OH (Time Warner Cable)

GRATIS TWP.—See AMBERLEY (village), OH (Time Warner Cable)

GREEN CAMP (VILLAGE)—See COLUMBUS, OH (Time Warner Cable)

GREEN CREEK TWP. (SANDUSKY COUNTY)—See TIFFIN, OH (Time Warner Cable)

GREEN MEADOWS MOBILE HOME PARK—See SUBURBANS MOTOR HOME PARK, OH (Time Warner Cable)

GREEN MEADOWS—Formerly served by Time Warner Cable. No longer in operation

GREEN SPRINGS (VILLAGE) (SANDUSKY COUNTY)—See TIFFIN, OH (Time Warner Cable)

GREEN SPRINGS (VILLAGE) (SENECA COUNTY)—See TIFFIN, OH (Time Warner Cable)

GREEN TWP. (BROWN COUNTY)—See AMBERLEY (village), OH (Time Warner Cable)

GREEN TWP. (CLARK COUNTY)—See AMBERLEY (village), OH (Time Warner Cable)

GREEN TWP. (CLINTON COUNTY)—See AMBERLEY (village), OH (Time Warner Cable)

GREEN TWP. (GALLIA COUNTY)—See GALLIPOLIS, OH (Zito Media)

GREEN TWP. (Hamilton County)—Time Warner Cable. Now served by AMBERLEY (village), OH [OH0001]

GREEN TWP. (HAMILTON COUNTY)—See AMBERLEY (village), OH (Time Warner Cable)

GREEN TWP. (MAHONING COUNTY)—See CLEVELAND, OH (Time Warner Cable)

GREEN TWP. (SHELBY COUNTY)—See AMBERLEY (village), OH (Time Warner Cable)

GREEN TWP. (WAYNE COUNTY)—See WOOSTER, OH (MCTV)

GREEN TWP.—See LEBANON, OH (Cincinnati Bell Fioptics TV. This cable system has converted to IPTV)

GREEN TWP.—See NELSONVILLE, OH (Nelsonville TV Cable)

GREEN TWP.—See CHILLICOTHE, OH (Time Warner Cable)

GREEN—Time Warner Cable. Now served by CLEVELAND (formerly Cleveland Heights), OH [OH0006]

GREEN—See MASSILLON, OH (MCTV)

GREEN—See CLEVELAND, OH (Time Warner Cable)

GREENE TWP. (ERIE COUNTY)—See CLEVELAND, PA (Time Warner Cable)

GREENFIELD ESTATES—Formerly served by World Cable. No longer in operation

GREENFIELD ESTATES—See CLEVELAND, OH (Time Warner Cable)

GREENFIELD TWP. (FAIRFIELD COUNTY)—See COLUMBUS, OH (Time Warner Cable)

GREENFIELD TWP. (HURON COUNTY)—See CLEVELAND, OH (Time Warner Cable)

GREENFIELD—Formerly served by Adelphia Communications. Now served by Time Warner Cable, COLUMBUS, OH [OH0002]

GREENFIELD—See WASHINGTON COURT HOUSE, OH (Time Warner Cable)

GREENHILLS (VILLAGE)—See LEBANON, OH (Cincinnati Bell Fioptics TV. This cable system has converted to IPTV)

GREENHILLS (VILLAGE)—See AMBERLEY (village), OH (Time Warner Cable)

GREENSBURG TWP.—See KALIDA, OH (Kalida Telephone Co)

GREENUP COUNTY (PORTION)—See PORTSMOUTH, KY (Time Warner Cable)

GREENVILLE (TOWN)—See AMBERLEY (village), OH (Time Warner Cable)

GREENVILLE BOROUGH—See CLEVELAND, PA (Time Warner Cable)

GREENVILLE—Time Warner Cable. Now served by AMBERLEY (village), OH [OH0001]

GREENWICH (VILLAGE)—See CLEVELAND, OH (Time Warner Cable)

GREENWOOD (village)—Formerly served by Adelphia Communications. No longer in operation

GROTON TWP. (ERIE COUNTY)—See TOLEDO, OH (Buckeye Broadband)

GROTON TWP.—See TIFFIN, OH (Time Warner Cable)

GROVE CITY—See COLUMBUS, OH (Time Warner Cable)

GROVE CITY—See COLUMBUS, OH (WOW! Internet, Cable & Phone)

GROVEPORT (VILLAGE)—See COLUMBUS, OH (Time Warner Cable)

GROVER HILL—See OTTOVILLE, OH (OTEC Communication Co.)

GUERNSEY COUNTY (portions)—Formerly served by Time Warner Cable. No longer in operation

GUILFORD LAKE—Formerly served by Time Warner Cable. No longer in operation

GUILFORD TWP.—See CLEVELAND, OH (Time Warner Cable)

GUILFORD—See LEBANON, IN (Cincinnati Bell Fioptics TV. This cable system has converted to IPTV)

GUYSVILLE—Formerly served by Adelphia Communications. Now served by Time Warner Cable, BEVERLY, OH [OH0175]

GUYSVILLE—See BEVERLY, OH (Time Warner Cable)

HALE TWP.—See COLUMBUS, OH (Time Warner Cable)

HALLSVILLE—See CHILLICOTHE, OH (Time Warner Cable)

HAMBDEN TWP. (GEAUGA COUNTY)—See THOMPSON TWP. (Geauga County), OH (Zito Media)

HAMBDEN TWP.—See CLEVELAND, OH (Time Warner Cable)

HAMDEN—See JACKSON, OH (Time Warner Cable)

HAMER TWP.—See AMBERLEY (village), OH (Time Warner Cable)

HAMERSVILLE (VILLAGE)—See AMBERLEY (village), OH (Time Warner Cable)

HAMILTON TWP. (BUTLER COUNTY)—See LEBANON, OH (Cincinnati Bell Fioptics TV. This cable system has converted to IPTV)

HAMILTON TWP. (FRANKLIN COUNTY)—See COLUMBUS, OH (Time Warner Cable)

HAMILTON TWP. (WARREN COUNTY)—See LEBANON, OH (Cincinnati Bell Fioptics TV. This cable system has converted to IPTV)

HAMILTON—Time Warner Cable. Now served by AMBERLEY (village), OH [OH0001]

HAMILTON—See LEBANON, OH (Cincinnati Bell Fioptics TV. This cable system has converted to IPTV)

HAMILTON—See AMBERLEY (village), OH (Time Warner Cable)

HAMLER—See DESHLER, OH (Time Warner Cable)

HAMMONDSVILLE—See NEW MIDDLETOWN, OH (Comcast Cable)

HANNIBAL—Crystal Broadband Networks

HANOVER TWP. (COLUMBIANA COUNTY)—See CLEVELAND, OH (Time Warner Cable)

HANOVER TWP. (LICKING COUNTY)—See NEWARK, OH (Time Warner Cable)

Cable Community Index—Ohio

HANOVER TWP.—See LEBANON, OH (Cincinnati Bell Fioptics TV. This cable system has converted to IPTV)

HANOVER—See NEWARK, OH (Time Warner Cable)

HANOVERTON (VILLAGE)—See CLEVELAND, OH (Time Warner Cable)

HARBOR HILLS (VILLAGE)—See COLUMBUS, OH (Time Warner Cable)

HARBOR VIEW—See TOLEDO, OH (Buckeye Broadband)

HARBORCREEK TWP.—See CLEVELAND, PA (Time Warner Cable)

HARDING TWP.—See TIFFIN, OH (Time Warner Cable)

HARDY TWP.—See CLEVELAND, OH (Time Warner Cable)

HARLAN TWP.—See LEBANON, OH (Cincinnati Bell Fioptics TV. This cable system has converted to IPTV)

HARLAN TWP.—See AMBERLEY (village), OH (Time Warner Cable)

HARLEM TWP. (DELAWARE COUNTY)—See COLUMBUS, OH (Time Warner Cable)

HARMON—See MASSILLON, OH (MCTV)

HARMONY TWP. (CLARK COUNTY)—See AMBERLEY (village), OH (Time Warner Cable)

HARPERSFIELD TWP.—See CLEVELAND, OH (Time Warner Cable)

HARPSTER (VILLAGE)—See TIFFIN, OH (Time Warner Cable)

HARRIS TWP.—See TIFFIN, OH (Time Warner Cable)

HARRISBURG (VILLAGE)—See COLUMBUS, OH (Time Warner Cable)

HARRISBURG—See COLUMBUS, OH (Time Warner Cable)

HARRISON (VILLAGE)—See AMBERLEY (village), OH (Time Warner Cable)

HARRISON TWP. (Carroll County)—Time Warner Cable. Now served by CLEVELAND (formerly Cleveland Heights), OH [OH0006]

HARRISON TWP. (CARROLL COUNTY)—See CLEVELAND, OH (Time Warner Cable)

HARRISON TWP. (CHAMPAIGN COUNTY)—See AMBERLEY (village), OH (Time Warner Cable)

HARRISON TWP. (DARKE COUNTY)—See AMBERLEY (village), OH (Time Warner Cable)

HARRISON TWP. (HAMILTON COUNTY)—See AMBERLEY (village), OH (Time Warner Cable)

HARRISON TWP. (HENRY COUNTY)—See TIFFIN, OH (Time Warner Cable)

HARRISON TWP. (LICKING COUNTY)—See COLUMBUS, OH (Time Warner Cable)

HARRISON TWP. (MONTGOMERY COUNTY)—See AMBERLEY (village), OH (Time Warner Cable)

HARRISON TWP. (PICKAWAY COUNTY)—See COLUMBUS, OH (Time Warner Cable)

HARRISON TWP. (PREBLE COUNTY)—See AMBERLEY (village), OH (Time Warner Cable)

HARRISON TWP. (ROSS COUNTY)—See CHILLICOTHE, OH (Time Warner Cable)

HARRISON TWP.—See LEBANON, OH (Cincinnati Bell Fioptics TV. This cable system has converted to IPTV)

HARRISON—See LEBANON, IN (Cincinnati Bell Fioptics TV. This cable system has converted to IPTV)

HARRISON—See PORTSMOUTH, OH (Time Warner Cable)

HARRISVILLE TWP.—See CLEVELAND, OH (Time Warner Cable)

HARROD (VILLAGE)—See TIFFIN, OH (Time Warner Cable)

HARTFORD (VILLAGE)—See COLUMBUS, OH (Time Warner Cable)

HARTFORD TWP. (LICKING COUNTY)—See COLUMBUS, OH (Time Warner Cable)

HARTFORD TWP. (TRUMBULL COUNTY)—See CLEVELAND, OH (Time Warner Cable)

HARTLAND TWP.—See CLEVELAND, OH (Time Warner Cable)

HARTSGROVE—See THOMPSON TWP. (Geauga County), OH (Zito Media)

HARTVILLE (VILLAGE)—See CLEVELAND, OH (Time Warner Cable)

HASKINS TWP.—See TIFFIN, OH (Time Warner Cable)

HAVILAND—See TIFFIN, OH (Time Warner Cable)

HAYDEN HEIGHTS MHP—See COLUMBUS, OH (Time Warner Cable)

HAYDEN HEIGHTS—Formerly served by Time Warner Cable. No longer in operation

HAYDENVILLE—See NELSONVILLE, OH (Nelsonville TV Cable)

HEATH (LICKING COUNTY)—See NEWARK, OH (Time Warner Cable)

HEBRON—See NEWARK, OH (Time Warner Cable)

HELENA (VILLAGE)—See TIFFIN, OH (Time Warner Cable)

HEMLOCK—See CORNING, OH (Zito Media)

HEMPFIELD TWP. (MERCER COUNTY)—See CLEVELAND, PA (Time Warner Cable)

HENRIETTA TWP.—See WELLINGTON, OH (GLW Broadband)

HENRY TWP. (WOOD COUNTY)—See TIFFIN, OH (Time Warner Cable)

HERMITAGE—See CLEVELAND, PA (Time Warner Cable)

HICKSVILLE—Mediacom

HIDE-A-WAY HILLS—Time Warner Cable. Now served by COLUMBUS, OH [OH0002]

HIDE-A-WAY HILLS—See COLUMBUS, OH (Time Warner Cable)

HIGGINSPORT (VILLAGE)—See AMBERLEY (village), OH (Time Warner Cable)

HIGHLAND HEIGHTS—See LEBANON, KY (Cincinnati Bell Fioptics TV. This cable system has converted to IPTV)

HIGHLAND HEIGHTS—See CLEVELAND, OH (Time Warner Cable)

HIGHLAND TWP.—See DEFIANCE, OH (Time Warner Cable)

HIGHLAND—See AMBERLEY (village), OH (Time Warner Cable)

HILLIAR TWP. (KNOX COUNTY)—See COLUMBUS, OH (Time Warner Cable)

HILLIARD—See COLUMBUS, OH (Time Warner Cable)

HILLIARD—See COLUMBUS, OH (WOW! Internet, Cable & Phone)

HILLS & DALES (VILLAGE)—See CLEVELAND, OH (Time Warner Cable)

HILLSBORO—Time Warner Cable. Now served by AMBERLEY (village), OH [OH0001]

HILLSBORO—See AMBERLEY (village), OH (Time Warner Cable)

HINCKLEY TWP.—See CLEVELAND, OH (Time Warner Cable)

HIRAM (VILLAGE)—See CLEVELAND, OH (Time Warner Cable)

HIRAM TWP.—See CLEVELAND, OH (Time Warner Cable)

HOAGLIN TWP.—See OTTOVILLE, OH (OTEC Communication Co.)

HOAGLIN TWP.—See TIFFIN, OH (Time Warner Cable)

HOCKING COUNTY—See CORNING, OH (Zito Media)

HOCKING TWP.—See OAKLAND, OH (Time Warner Cable)

HOCKINGPORT—See BEVERLY, OH (Time Warner Cable)

HOLGATE—See DESHLER, OH (Time Warner Cable)

HOLLAND—See TOLEDO, OH (Buckeye Broadband)

HOLLAND—See COLUMBUS, OH (Time Warner Cable)

HOLLANSBURG (VILLAGE)—See AMBERLEY (village), OH (Time Warner Cable)

HOLMES TWP.—See COLUMBUS, OH (Time Warner Cable)

HOLMESVILLE (VILLAGE)—See CLEVELAND, OH (Time Warner Cable)

HOMER TWP.—See NELSONVILLE, OH (Nelsonville TV Cable)

HOMER TWP.—See COLUMBUS, OH (Time Warner Cable)

HOPEDALE—Time Warner Cable

HOPEWELL TWP. (LICKING COUNTY)—See COLUMBUS, OH (Time Warner Cable)

HOPEWELL TWP. (MERCER COUNTY)—See TIFFIN, OH (Time Warner Cable)

HOPEWELL TWP. (MUSKINGUM COUNTY)—See COLUMBUS, OH (Time Warner Cable)

HOPEWELL TWP. (SENECA COUNTY)—See TIFFIN, OH (Time Warner Cable)

HOWARD TWP.—See COLUMBUS, OH (Time Warner Cable)

HOWARD—Formerly served by Time Warner Cable. No longer in operation

HOWLAND TWP.—See CLEVELAND, OH (Time Warner Cable)

HUBBARD TWP. (Trumbull County)—Formerly served by Northeast Cable TV. No longer in operation

HUBBARD TWP.—See CLEVELAND, OH (Time Warner Cable)

HUBBARD—See CLEVELAND, OH (Time Warner Cable)

HUBER HEIGHTS—See AMBERLEY (village), OH (Time Warner Cable)

HUDSON—See CLEVELAND, OH (Time Warner Cable)

HUNTING VALLEY (VILLAGE)—See CLEVELAND, OH (Time Warner Cable)

HUNTINGTON TWP. (ROSS COUNTY)—See CHILLICOTHE, OH (Time Warner Cable)

HUNTINGTON TWP.—Formerly served by Adelphia Communications. Now served by Time Warner Cable, CHILLICOTHE, OH [OH0033]

HUNTSBURG TWP.—See THOMPSON TWP. (Geauga County), OH (Zito Media)

HUNTSVILLE (VILLAGE)—See TIFFIN, OH (Time Warner Cable)

HURON TWP. (ERIE COUNTY)—See TOLEDO, OH (Buckeye Broadband)

HURON—See TOLEDO, OH (Buckeye Broadband)

IDA—See TOLEDO, MI (Buckeye Broadband)

INDEPENDENCE—See LEBANON, KY (Cincinnati Bell Fioptics TV. This cable system has converted to IPTV)

INDEPENDENCE—See PARMA, OH (Cox Communications)

INDEPENDENCE—See CLEVELAND, OH (Time Warner Cable)

Ohio—Cable Community Index

INDEPENDENCE—See BEREA, OH (WOW! Internet, Cable & Phone)

INDIAN HILL (VILLAGE)—See AMBERLEY (village), OH (Time Warner Cable)

INDIAN HILL—See LEBANON, OH (Cincinnati Bell Fioptics TV. This cable system has converted to IPTV)

IRONDALE—Comcast Cable. Now served by NEW MIDDLETOWN, OH [OH0145]

IRONDALE—See NEW MIDDLETOWN, OH (Comcast Cable)

IRONTON—Formerly served by Comcast Cable. No longer in operation

ISLAND CREEK TWP. (JEFFERSON COUNTY)—See KNOX TWP. (Jefferson County), OH (Suddenlink Communications)

ISRAEL TWP.—See AMBERLEY (village), OH (Time Warner Cable)

ITHACA (VILLAGE)—See AMBERLEY (village), OH (Time Warner Cable)

JACKSON CENTER (VILLAGE)—See AMBERLEY (village), OH (Time Warner Cable)

JACKSON TWP. (ALLEN COUNTY)—See TIFFIN, OH (Time Warner Cable)

JACKSON TWP. (AUGLAIZE COUNTY)—See TIFFIN, OH (Time Warner Cable)

JACKSON TWP. (CHAMPAIGN COUNTY)—See AMBERLEY (village), OH (Time Warner Cable)

JACKSON TWP. (CLERMONT CITY)—See AMBERLEY (village), OH (Time Warner Cable)

JACKSON TWP. (COSCHOCTON COUNTY)—See COLUMBUS, OH (Time Warner Cable)

JACKSON TWP. (CRAWFORD COUNTY)—See TIFFIN, OH (Time Warner Cable)

JACKSON TWP. (DARKE COUNTY)—See AMBERLEY (village), OH (Time Warner Cable)

JACKSON TWP. (FRANKLIN COUNTY)—See COLUMBUS, OH (Time Warner Cable)

JACKSON TWP. (GUERNSEY COUNTY)—See SENECAVILLE, OH (Suddenlink Communications)

JACKSON TWP. (HANCOCK COUNTY)—See TIFFIN, OH (Time Warner Cable)

JACKSON TWP. (JACKSON COUNTY)—See CHILLICOTHE, OH (Time Warner Cable)

JACKSON TWP. (KNOX COUNTY)—See COLUMBUS, OH (Time Warner Cable)

JACKSON TWP. (MONTGOMERY COUNTY)—See AMBERLEY (village), OH (Time Warner Cable)

JACKSON TWP. (MUSKINGUM COUNTY)—See COLUMBUS, OH (Time Warner Cable)

JACKSON TWP. (NOBLE COUNTY)—See WARNER, OH (Zito Media)

JACKSON TWP. (PAULDING COUNTY)—See PAULDING, OH (Time Warner Cable)

JACKSON TWP. (PERRY COUNTY)—See COLUMBUS, OH (Time Warner Cable)

JACKSON TWP. (PICKAWAY COUNTY)—See COMMERCIAL POINT, OH (Time Warner Cable)

JACKSON TWP. (PREBLE CITY)—See AMBERLEY (village), OH (Time Warner Cable)

JACKSON TWP. (PUTNAM COUNTY)—See KALIDA, OH (Kalida Telephone Co)

JACKSON TWP. (PUTNAM COUNTY)—See OTTOVILLE, OH (OTEC Communication Co.)

JACKSON TWP. (SANDUSKY COUNTY)—See TIFFIN, OH (Time Warner Cable)

JACKSON TWP. (STARK COUNTY)—See MASSILLON, OH (MCTV)

JACKSON TWP. (STARK COUNTY)—See CLEVELAND, OH (Time Warner Cable)

JACKSON TWP. (VAN WERT COUNTY)—See OTTOVILLE, OH (OTEC Communication Co.)

JACKSON TWP.—See LEBANON, OH (Cincinnati Bell Fioptics TV. This cable system has converted to IPTV)

JACKSON TWP.—See FORT JENNINGS, OH (FJ Communications)

JACKSON TWP.—See COLUMBUS, OH (WOW! Internet, Cable & Phone)

JACKSON—Time Warner Cable

JACKSONBURG (VILLAGE)—See AMBERLEY (village), OH (Time Warner Cable)

JACKSONVILLE—See NELSONVILLE, OH (Nelsonville TV Cable)

JAMESTOWN (VILLAGE)—See AMBERLEY (village), OH (Time Warner Cable)

JASPER (town)—Time Warner Cable. Now served by CHILLICOTHE, OH [OH0033]

JASPER (TOWN)—See CHILLICOTHE, OH (Time Warner Cable)

JASPER TWP.—See WASHINGTON COURT HOUSE, OH (Time Warner Cable)

JEFFERSON (VILLAGE)—See CLEVELAND, OH (Time Warner Cable)

JEFFERSON COUNTY (PORTIONS)—See EMPIRE, OH (Jefferson County Cable Inc)

JEFFERSON COUNTY (PORTIONS)—See TORONTO, OH (Jefferson County Cable Inc)

JEFFERSON TWP. (ASHTABULA COUNTY)—See CLEVELAND, OH (Time Warner Cable)

JEFFERSON TWP. (ASHTABULA COUNTY)—See DENMARK TWP., OH (Zito Media)

JEFFERSON TWP. (CLINTON COUNTY)—See AMBERLEY (village), OH (Time Warner Cable)

JEFFERSON TWP. (FAYETTE COUNTY)—See WASHINGTON COURT HOUSE, OH (Time Warner Cable)

JEFFERSON TWP. (FRANKLIN COUNTY)—See COLUMBUS, OH (Time Warner Cable)

JEFFERSON TWP. (MADISON COUNTY)—See COLUMBUS, OH (Time Warner Cable)

JEFFERSON TWP. (MADISON COUNTY)—See SUBURBANS MOTOR HOME PARK, OH (Time Warner Cable)

JEFFERSON TWP. (MERCER COUNTY)—See TIFFIN, OH (Time Warner Cable)

JEFFERSON TWP. (MONTGOMERY COUNTY)—See AMBERLEY (village), OH (Time Warner Cable)

JEFFERSON TWP. (MUSKINGUM COUNTY)—See CLEVELAND, OH (Time Warner Cable)

JEFFERSON TWP. (PREBLE COUNTY)—See AMBERLEY (village), OH (Time Warner Cable)

JEFFERSON TWP. (ROSS COUNTY)—See CHILLICOTHE, OH (Time Warner Cable)

JEFFERSON TWP. (WILLIAMS COUNTY)—See TIFFIN, OH (Time Warner Cable)

JEFFERSON TWP.—See CLEVELAND, PA (Time Warner Cable)

JEFFERSON—See PORTSMOUTH, OH (Time Warner Cable)

JEFFERSONVILLE—See WASHINGTON COURT HOUSE, OH (Time Warner Cable)

JENERA (VILLAGE)—See TIFFIN, OH (Time Warner Cable)

JENNINGS TWP. (PUTNAM COUNTY)—See KALIDA, OH (Kalida Telephone Co)

JENNINGS TWP. (PUTNAM COUNTY)—See OTTOVILLE, OH (OTEC Communication Co.)

JENNINGS TWP.—See FORT JENNINGS, OH (FJ Communications)

JENNINGS TWP.—See TIFFIN, OH (Time Warner Cable)

JEROME TWP.—See COLUMBUS, OH (Time Warner Cable)

JEROME—See SUBURBANS MOTOR HOME PARK, OH (Time Warner Cable)

JEROMESVILLE (village)—Time Warner Cable. Now served by CLEVELAND (formerly Cleveland Heights), OH [OH0006]

JEROMESVILLE (VILLAGE)—See CLEVELAND, OH (Time Warner Cable)

JERRY CITY (VILLAGE)—See TIFFIN, OH (Time Warner Cable)

JERSEY TWP.—See COLUMBUS, OH (Time Warner Cable)

JERUSALEM TWP.—See TIFFIN, OH (Time Warner Cable)

JEWETT—Time Warner Cable

JOHNSON TWP. (CHAMPAIGN COUNTY)—See AMBERLEY (village), OH (Time Warner Cable)

JOHNSTON TWP. (TRUMBULL COUNTY)—See CLEVELAND, OH (Time Warner Cable)

JOHNSTOWN (VILLAGE)—See COLUMBUS, OH (Time Warner Cable)

JUNCTION CITY—See COLUMBUS, OH (Time Warner Cable)

KALIDA—Kalida Telephone Co

KEENE TWP.—See COSHOCTON, OH (Time Warner Cable)

KELSO TWP.—See LEBANON, IN (Cincinnati Bell Fioptics TV. This cable system has converted to IPTV)

KENT—Time Warner Cable. Now served by CLEVELAND (formerly Cleveland Heights), OH [OH0006]

KENT—See CLEVELAND, OH (Time Warner Cable)

KENTON—Time Warner Cable. Now served by COLUMBUS, OH [OH0002]

KENTON—See COLUMBUS, OH (Time Warner Cable)

KETTERING—Time Warner Cable. Now served by AMBERLEY (village), OH [OH0001]

KETTERING—See AMBERLEY (village), OH (Time Warner Cable)

KETTLERSVILLE—See TIFFIN, OH (Time Warner Cable)

KEY—Formerly served by Comcast Cable. No longer in operation

KILLBUCK (VILLAGE)—See CLEVELAND, OH (Time Warner Cable)

KIMBOLTON—See CAMBRIDGE, OH (Time Warner Cable)

KINGSTON TWP.—See COLUMBUS, OH (Time Warner Cable)

KINGSTON—Formerly served by Adelphia Communications. Now served by Time Warner Cable, CHILLICOTHE, OH [OH0033]

KINGSTON—See CHILLICOTHE, OH (Time Warner Cable)

KINGSVILLE TWP.—See CLEVELAND, OH (Time Warner Cable)

KINSMAN—Formerly served by Cebridge Connections. Now served by Armstrong Cable Services, VERNON

Cable Community Index—Ohio

TWP., OH [OH0246]

KINSMAN—See VERNON TWP. (Trumbull County), OH (Armstrong Cable Services)

KIPTON (VILLAGE)—See WELLINGTON, OH (GLW Broadband)

KIPTON—See CLEVELAND, OH (Time Warner Cable)

KIRKERSVILLE (village)—Time Warner Cable. Now served by COLUMBUS, OH [OH0002]

KIRKERSVILLE (VILLAGE)—See COLUMBUS, OH (Time Warner Cable)

KIRTLAND HILLS (VILLAGE)—See CLEVELAND, OH (Time Warner Cable)

KIRTLAND—See CLEVELAND, OH (Time Warner Cable)

KNOX TWP. (COLUMBIANA COUNTY)—See CLEVELAND, OH (Time Warner Cable)

KNOX TWP. (JEFFERSON COUNTY)—Suddenlink Communications

LA RUE (village)—Time Warner Cable. Now served by COLUMBUS, OH [OH0002]

LA RUE (VILLAGE)—See COLUMBUS, OH (Time Warner Cable)

LACKAWONNOCK TWP.—See CLEVELAND, PA (Time Warner Cable)

LAFAYETTE (VILLAGE)—See TIFFIN, OH (Time Warner Cable)

LAFAYETTE TWP. (COSHOCTON COUNTY)—See CLEVELAND, OH (Time Warner Cable)

LAGRANGE (VILLAGE)—See WELLINGTON, OH (GLW Broadband)

LAGRANGE TWP.—See WELLINGTON, OH (GLW Broadband)

LAGRANGE—See WELLINGTON, OH (GLW Broadband)

LAKE BUCKHORN—See CLEVELAND, OH (Time Warner Cable)

LAKE CITY BOROUGH—See CLEVELAND, PA (Time Warner Cable)

LAKE TWP. (STARK COUNTY)—See CLEVELAND, OH (Time Warner Cable)

LAKE TWP. (WOOD COUNTY)—See TIFFIN, OH (Time Warner Cable)

LAKELINE (VILLAGE)—See CLEVELAND, OH (Time Warner Cable)

LAKEMORE TWP.—See CLEVELAND, OH (Time Warner Cable)

LAKESIDE PARK—See LEBANON, KY (Cincinnati Bell Fioptics TV. This cable system has converted to IPTV)

LAKEVILLE (VILLAGE)—See CLEVELAND, OH (Time Warner Cable)

LAKEWOOD (CUYAHOGA COUNTY)—See PARMA, OH (Cox Communications)

LAKEWOOD—See CLEVELAND, OH (Time Warner Cable)

LANCASTER—Time Warner Cable. Now served by COLUMBUS, OH [OH0002]

LANCASTER—See COLUMBUS, OH (Time Warner Cable)

LANIER TWP.—See AMBERLEY (village), OH (Time Warner Cable)

LATTY TWP.—See OTTOVILLE, OH (OTEC Communication Co.)

LATTY—See PAULDING, OH (Time Warner Cable)

LAURA (VILLAGE)—See AMBERLEY (village), OH (Time Warner Cable)

LAURELVILLE—See CHILLICOTHE, OH (Time Warner Cable)

LAWRENCE PARK TWP.—See CLEVELAND, PA (Time Warner Cable)

LAWRENCE TWP. (STARK COUNTY)—See MASSILLON, OH (MCTV)

LAWRENCE TWP. (STARK COUNTY)—See CLEVELAND, OH (Time Warner Cable)

LAWRENCE TWP. (TUSCARAWAS COUNTY)—See CLEVELAND, OH (Time Warner Cable)

LAWRENCEBURG—See LEBANON, IN (Cincinnati Bell Fioptics TV. This cable system has converted to IPTV)

LAWRENCEVILLE (VILLAGE)—See AMBERLEY (village), OH (Time Warner Cable)

LEBANON—Cincinnati Bell. This cable system has converted to IPTV. See LEBANON, OH [OH5053]

LEBANON—Formerly served by Adelphia Communications. Now served by Time Warner Cable, AMBERLEY (village), OH [OH0001]

LEBANON—Cincinnati Bell Fioptics TV. This cable system has converted to IPTV

LEBANON—See AMBERLEY (village), OH (Time Warner Cable)

LEE TWP. (ATHENS COUNTY)—See ATHENS, OH (Time Warner Cable)

LEE TWP. (CARROLL COUNTY)—See CLEVELAND, OH (Time Warner Cable)

LEE TWP. (MONROE COUNTY)—See HANNIBAL, OH (Crystal Broadband Networks)

LEESBURG (village)—Time Warner Cable. Now served by AMBERLEY (village), OH [OH0001]

LEESBURG (VILLAGE)—See AMBERLEY (village), OH (Time Warner Cable)

LEESBURG TWP.—See COLUMBUS, OH (Time Warner Cable)

LEESVILLE—See BOWERSTON, OH (Time Warner Cable)

LEETONIA—See NEW MIDDLETOWN, OH (Comcast Cable)

LEIPSIC—Orwell Communications

LEMON TWP.—See LEBANON, OH (Cincinnati Bell Fioptics TV. This cable system has converted to IPTV)

LEMON TWP.—See AMBERLEY (village), OH (Time Warner Cable)

LENOX TWP.—See CLEVELAND, OH (Time Warner Cable)

LEROY TWP. (LAKE COUNTY)—See CLEVELAND, OH (Time Warner Cable)

LEROY TWP. (LAKE COUNTY)—See THOMPSON TWP. (Geauga County), OH (Zito Media)

LEWIS COUNTY (PORTIONS)—See PORTSMOUTH, KY (Time Warner Cable)

LEWIS TWP.—See AMBERLEY (village), OH (Time Warner Cable)

LEWISBURG (VILLAGE)—See AMBERLEY (village), OH (Time Warner Cable)

LEWISVILLE—See WOODSFIELD, OH (City of Woodsfield)

LEXINGTON (VILLAGE)—See CLEVELAND, OH (Time Warner Cable)

LEXINGTON TWP.—See CLEVELAND, OH (Time Warner Cable)

LIBERTY CENTER—See TIFFIN, OH (Time Warner Cable)

LIBERTY TWP. (ADAMS COUNTY)—See AMBERLEY (village), OH (Time Warner Cable)

LIBERTY TWP. (Butler County)—Time Warner Cable. Now served by AMBERLEY (village), OH [OH0001]

LIBERTY TWP. (BUTLER COUNTY)—See AMBERLEY (village), OH (Time Warner Cable)

LIBERTY TWP. (DARKE COUNTY)—See AMBERLEY (village), OH (Time Warner Cable)

LIBERTY TWP. (DELAWARE COUNTY)—See COLUMBUS, OH (Time Warner Cable)

LIBERTY TWP. (FAIRFIELD COUNTY)—See COLUMBUS, OH (Time Warner Cable)

LIBERTY TWP. (GUERNSEY COUNTY)—See CAMBRIDGE, OH (Time Warner Cable)

LIBERTY TWP. (HANCOCK COUNTY)—See TIFFIN, OH (Time Warner Cable)

LIBERTY TWP. (HANCOCK COUNTY)—See BENTON RIDGE, OH (Watch Communications)

LIBERTY TWP. (HARDIN COUNTY)—See COLUMBUS, OH (Time Warner Cable)

LIBERTY TWP. (HENRY COUNTY)—See TIFFIN, OH (Time Warner Cable)

LIBERTY TWP. (HIGHLAND COUNTY)—See AMBERLEY (village), OH (Time Warner Cable)

LIBERTY TWP. (JACKSON COUNTY)—See JACKSON, OH (Time Warner Cable)

LIBERTY TWP. (KNOX COUNTY)—See COLUMBUS, OH (Time Warner Cable)

LIBERTY TWP. (LICKING COUNTY)—See NEWARK, OH (Time Warner Cable)

LIBERTY TWP. (LOGAN COUNTY)—See AMBERLEY (village), OH (Time Warner Cable)

LIBERTY TWP. (ROSS COUNTY)—See CHILLICOTHE, OH (Time Warner Cable)

LIBERTY TWP. (SENECA COUNTY)—See TIFFIN, OH (Time Warner Cable)

LIBERTY TWP. (TRUMBULL COUNTY)—See CLEVELAND, OH (Time Warner Cable)

LIBERTY TWP. (UNION COUNTY)—See COLUMBUS, OH (Time Warner Cable)

LIBERTY TWP. (VAN WERT COUNTY)—See VAN WERT, OH (Time Warner Cable)

LIBERTY TWP.—See LEBANON, OH (Cincinnati Bell Fioptics TV. This cable system has converted to IPTV)

LICK TWP. (JACKSON COUNTY)—See JACKSON, OH (Time Warner Cable)

LICKING COUNTY (PORTIONS)—See NEWARK, OH (Time Warner Cable)

LICKING COUNTY—Time Warner Cable. Now served by NEWARK, OH [OH0019]

LICKING TWP. (LICKING COUNTY)—See COLUMBUS, OH (Time Warner Cable)

LICKING TWP. (LICKING COUNTY)—See NEWARK, OH (Time Warner Cable)

LICKING TWP. (MUSKINGUM COUNTY)—See COLUMBUS, OH (Time Warner Cable)

LIMA—Time Warner Cable. Now served by TIFFIN (formerly Fostoria), OH [OH0050]

LIMA—See TIFFIN, OH (Time Warner Cable)

LIMAVILLE (VILLAGE)—See CLEVELAND, OH (Time Warner Cable)

LINCOLN HEIGHTS (VILLAGE)—See LEBANON, OH (Cincinnati Bell Fioptics TV. This cable system has converted to IPTV)

LINCOLN HEIGHTS (VILLAGE)—See AMBERLEY (village), OH (Time Warner Cable)

LINDSEY (village)—Time Warner Cable. Now served by TIFFIN (formerly Fostoria), OH [OH0050]

LINDSEY (VILLAGE)—See TIFFIN, OH (Time Warner Cable)

LINNDALE (VILLAGE)—See CLEVELAND, OH (Time Warner Cable)

LINNDALE—See BEREA, OH (WOW! Internet, Cable & Phone)

LINTON TWP.—See COLUMBUS, OH (Time Warner Cable)

Ohio—Cable Community Index

LISBON (village)—Time Warner Cable. Now served by CLEVELAND (formerly Cleveland Heights), OH [OH0006]

LISBON (VILLAGE)—See CLEVELAND, OH (Time Warner Cable)

LITHOPOLIS—See COLUMBUS, OH (Time Warner Cable)

LIVERPOOL TWP.—See NEW MIDDLETOWN, OH (Comcast Cable)

LOCKBOURNE VILLAGE—See COLUMBUS, OH (Time Warner Cable)

LOCKINGTON (VILLAGE)—See AMBERLEY (village), OH (Time Warner Cable)

LOCKLAND (VILLAGE)—See LEBANON, OH (Cincinnati Bell Fioptics TV. This cable system has converted to IPTV)

LOCKLAND—See AMBERLEY (village), OH (Time Warner Cable)

LODI (village)—Time Warner Cable. Now served by CLEVELAND (formerly Cleveland Heights), OH [OH0006]

LODI (VILLAGE)—See CLEVELAND, OH (Time Warner Cable)

LOGAN (RURAL PORTIONS)—See LOGAN, OH (Time Warner Cable)

LOGAN COUNTY (PORTIONS)—See AMBERLEY (village), OH (Time Warner Cable)

LOGAN TWP.—See TIFFIN, OH (Time Warner Cable)

LOGAN—See LEBANON, IN (Cincinnati Bell Fioptics TV. This cable system has converted to IPTV)

LOGAN—Time Warner Cable

LONDON—Time Warner Cable. Now served by SUBURBANS MOTOR HOME PARK, OH [OH0452]

LONDON—See SUBURBANS MOTOR HOME PARK, OH (Time Warner Cable)

LORAIN—Time Warner Cable. Now served by CLEVELAND (formerly Cleveland Heights), OH [OH0006]

LORAIN—See CLEVELAND, OH (Time Warner Cable)

LORAMIE TWP.—See VERSAILLES, OH (Time Warner Cable)

LORDSTOWN TWP.—See CLEVELAND, OH (Time Warner Cable)

LORE CITY—See SENECAVILLE, OH (Suddenlink Communications)

LOST PENINSULA—See TOLEDO, MI (Buckeye Broadband)

LOSTCREEK TWP.—See AMBERLEY (village), OH (Time Warner Cable)

LOUDON TWP. (CARROLL COUNTY)—See CLEVELAND, OH (Time Warner Cable)

LOUDON TWP. (SENECA COUNTY)—See TIFFIN, OH (Time Warner Cable)

LOUDON TWP.—See AMSTERDAM, OH (Crystal Broadband Networks)

LOUDONVILLE (ASHLAND COUNTY)—See CLEVELAND, OH (Time Warner Cable)

LOUDONVILLE—Time Warner Cable. Now served by CLEVELAND (formerly Cleveland Heights), OH [OH0006]

LOUISVILLE—See CLEVELAND, OH (Time Warner Cable)

LOVELAND (CLERMONT COUNTY)—See LEBANON, OH (Cincinnati Bell Fioptics TV. This cable system has converted to IPTV)

LOVELAND (CLERMONT COUNTY)—See AMBERLEY (village), OH (Time Warner Cable)

LOVELAND (HAMILTON COUNTY)—See LEBANON, OH (Cincinnati Bell Fioptics TV. This cable system has converted to IPTV)

LOVELAND (HAMILTON COUNTY)—See AMBERLEY (village), OH (Time Warner Cable)

LOVELAND (WARREN COUNTY)—See LEBANON, OH (Cincinnati Bell Fioptics TV. This cable system has converted to IPTV)

LOVELAND (WARREN COUNTY)—See AMBERLEY (village), OH (Time Warner Cable)

LOWELL—Lowell Community TV Corp

LOWELLVILLE (VILLAGE)—See CLEVELAND, OH (Time Warner Cable)

LOWER SALEM—See WARNER, OH (Zito Media)

LUCAS (VILLAGE)—See CLEVELAND, OH (Time Warner Cable)

LUCASVILLE—Time Warner Cable. Now served by PORTSMOUTH, OH [OH0035]

LUCASVILLE—See PORTSMOUTH, OH (Time Warner Cable)

LUCKEY—Time Warner Cable. Now served by TIFFIN, OH [OH0050]

LUCKEY—See TIFFIN, OH (Time Warner Cable)

LUDLOW FALLS (VILLAGE)—See AMBERLEY (village), OH (Time Warner Cable)

LUDLOW—See LEBANON, KY (Cincinnati Bell Fioptics TV. This cable system has converted to IPTV)

LUNDYS LANE—See CLEVELAND, PA (Time Warner Cable)

LYKENS TWP.—See COLUMBUS, OH (Time Warner Cable)

LYME TWP.—See TIFFIN, OH (Time Warner Cable)

LYNCHBURG (village)—Time Warner Cable. Now served by AMBERLEY (village), OH [OH0001]

LYNCHBURG (VILLAGE)—See AMBERLEY (village), OH (Time Warner Cable)

LYNDHURST (VILLAGE)—See CLEVELAND, OH (Time Warner Cable)

LYONS—See TIFFIN, OH (Time Warner Cable)

MACEDONIA—Time Warner Cable. Now served by CLEVELAND (formerly Cleveland Heights), OH [OH0006]

MACEDONIA—See CLEVELAND, OH (Time Warner Cable)

MACKSBURG—See WARNER, OH (Zito Media)

MAD RIVER TWP. (CHAMPAIGN COUNTY)—See AMBERLEY (village), OH (Time Warner Cable)

MAD RIVER TWP. (CLARK COUNTY)—See AMBERLEY (village), OH (Time Warner Cable)

MADEIRA—See LEBANON, OH (Cincinnati Bell Fioptics TV. This cable system has converted to IPTV)

MADEIRA—See AMBERLEY (village), OH (Time Warner Cable)

MADISON (VILLAGE)—See CLEVELAND, OH (Time Warner Cable)

MADISON TWP. (BUTLER COUNTY)—See AMBERLEY (village), OH (Time Warner Cable)

MADISON TWP. (CLARK COUNTY)—See AMBERLEY (village), OH (Time Warner Cable)

MADISON TWP. (COLUMBIANA COUNTY)—See NEW MIDDLETOWN, OH (Comcast Cable)

MADISON TWP. (FRANKLIN COUNTY)—See COLUMBUS, OH (Time Warner Cable)

MADISON TWP. (HANCOCK COUNTY)—See TIFFIN, OH (Time Warner Cable)

MADISON TWP. (HIGHLAND COUNTY)—See AMBERLEY (village), OH (Time Warner Cable)

MADISON TWP. (HIGHLAND COUNTY)—See WASHINGTON COURT HOUSE, OH (Time Warner Cable)

MADISON TWP. (JACKSON COUNTY)—See JACKSON, OH (Time Warner Cable)

MADISON TWP. (LAKE COUNTY)—See CLEVELAND, OH (Time Warner Cable)

MADISON TWP. (LICKING COUNTY)—See NEWARK, OH (Time Warner Cable)

MADISON TWP. (MONTGOMERY COUNTY)—See AMBERLEY (village), OH (Time Warner Cable)

MADISON TWP. (MUSKINGUM COUNTY)—See CLEVELAND, OH (Time Warner Cable)

MADISON TWP. (PICKAWAY COUNTY)—See COLUMBUS, OH (Time Warner Cable)

MADISON TWP. (SANDUSKY COUNTY)—See TIFFIN, OH (Time Warner Cable)

MADISON TWP. (VINTON COUNTY)—See PORTSMOUTH, OH (Time Warner Cable)

MADISON TWP.—See COLUMBUS, OH (WOW! Internet, Cable & Phone)

MAGNETIC SPRINGS (VILLAGE)—See COLUMBUS, OH (Time Warner Cable)

MAGNOLIA (VILLAGE) (CARROLL COUNTY)—See CLEVELAND, OH (Time Warner Cable)

MAGNOLIA (VILLAGE) (STARK COUNTY)—See CLEVELAND, OH (Time Warner Cable)

MAHONING TWP. (LAWRENCE COUNTY)—See NEW MIDDLETOWN, PA (Comcast Cable)

MAINEVILLE (VILLAGE)—See LEBANON, OH (Cincinnati Bell Fioptics TV. This cable system has converted to IPTV)

MAINEVILLE (VILLAGE)—See AMBERLEY (village), OH (Time Warner Cable)

MALAGA TWP.—Formerly served by Richards TV Cable. No longer in operation

MALINTA—See TIFFIN, OH (Time Warner Cable)

MALTA—See BEVERLY, OH (Time Warner Cable)

MALVERN (VILLAGE)—See CLEVELAND, OH (Time Warner Cable)

MANCHESTER (VILLAGE)—See AMBERLEY (village), OH (Time Warner Cable)

MANCHESTER—Formerly served by Adelphia Communications. Now served by Time Warner Cable, AMBERLEY (village), OH [OH0001]

MANSFIELD—Time Warner Cable. Now served by CLEVELAND (formerly Cleveland Heights), OH [OH0006]

MANSFIELD—See CLEVELAND, OH (Time Warner Cable)

MANTUA (VILLAGE)—See CLEVELAND, OH (Time Warner Cable)

MANTUA TWP.—Time Warner Cable. Now served by CLEVELAND (formerly Cleveland Heights), OH [OH0006]

MANTUA TWP.—See CLEVELAND, OH (Time Warner Cable)

MAPLE HEIGHTS—See CLEVELAND, OH (Time Warner Cable)

MAPLE HEIGHTS—See BEREA, OH (WOW! Internet, Cable & Phone)

MARBLE CLIFF (VILLAGE)—See COLUMBUS, OH (Time Warner Cable)

MARBLE CLIFF—See COLUMBUS, OH (WOW! Internet, Cable & Phone)

MARBLEHEAD—See PORT CLINTON, OH (Time Warner Cable)

MARENGO (VILLAGE)—See COLUMBUS, OH (Time Warner Cable)

Cable Community Index—Ohio

MARGARETTA TWP.—Time Warner Cable. Now served by CLEVELAND (formerly Cleveland Heights), OH [OH0006]

MARGARETTA TWP.—See TOLEDO, OH (Buckeye Broadband)

MARGARETTA TWP.—See CLEVELAND, OH (Time Warner Cable)

MARIEMONT (VILLAGE)—See LEBANON, OH (Cincinnati Bell Fioptics TV. This cable system has converted to IPTV)

MARIEMONT (VILLAGE)—See AMBERLEY (village), OH (Time Warner Cable)

MARIETTA—Formerly served by Charter Communications. Now served by Suddenlink Communications, PARKERSBURG, WV [WV0003]

MARION TWP. (ALLEN COUNTY)—See TIFFIN, OH (Time Warner Cable)

MARION TWP. (CLINTON COUNTY)—See AMBERLEY (village), OH (Time Warner Cable)

MARION TWP. (FAYETTE COUNTY)—See WASHINGTON COURT HOUSE, OH (Time Warner Cable)

MARION TWP. (HANCOCK COUNTY)—See TIFFIN, OH (Time Warner Cable)

MARION TWP. (HENRY COUNTY)—See DESHLER, OH (Time Warner Cable)

MARION TWP. (HOCKING COUNTY)—See COLUMBUS, OH (Time Warner Cable)

MARION TWP. (MARION COUNTY)—See MARION, OH (Time Warner Cable)

MARION TWP. (MERCER COUNTY)—See TIFFIN, OH (Time Warner Cable)

MARION TWP. (PIKE COUNTY)—See JACKSON, OH (Time Warner Cable)

MARION TWP.—See FORT JENNINGS, OH (FJ Communications)

MARION—Time Warner Cable

MARION—See TIFFIN, OH (Time Warner Cable)

MARLBORO TWP. (STARK COUNTY)—See CLEVELAND, OH (Time Warner Cable)

MARSEILLES (VILLAGE)—See TIFFIN, OH (Time Warner Cable)

MARSHALL TWP. (CLINTON COUNTY)—See AMBERLEY (village), OH (Time Warner Cable)

MARSHALLVILLE—See DOYLESTOWN, OH (Doylestown Communications)

MARTINS FERRY—Comcast Cable. Now served by WHEELING, WV [WV0004]

MARTINSBURG (village)—Formerly served by National Cable Inc. No longer in operation

MARTINSBURG (VILLAGE)—See COLUMBUS, OH (Time Warner Cable)

MARTINSVILLE (VILLAGE)—See AMBERLEY (village), OH (Time Warner Cable)

MARY ANN TWP.—See NEWARK, OH (Time Warner Cable)

MARYSVILLE—Time Warner Cable. Now served by SUBURBANS MOTOR HOME PARK, OH [OH0452]

MARYSVILLE—See SUBURBANS MOTOR HOME PARK, OH (Time Warner Cable)

MASON—See LEBANON, KY (Cincinnati Bell Fioptics TV. This cable system has converted to IPTV)

MASON—See LEBANON, OH (Cincinnati Bell Fioptics TV. This cable system has converted to IPTV)

MASON—See AMBERLEY (village), OH (Time Warner Cable)

MASSILLON—MCTV

MASSILLON—See CLEVELAND, OH (Time Warner Cable)

MAUMEE—See TOLEDO, OH (Buckeye Broadband)

MAUMEE—See COLUMBUS, OH (Time Warner Cable)

MAYFIELD HEIGHTS—See CLEVELAND, OH (Time Warner Cable)

MAYFIELD VILLAGE—See CLEVELAND, OH (Time Warner Cable)

MAYNARD—See BARTON, OH (Powhatan Point Cable Co)

MCARTHUR—See JACKSON, OH (Time Warner Cable)

MCCLURE (VILLAGE)—See TIFFIN, OH (Time Warner Cable)

MCCOMB (VILLAGE)—See TIFFIN, OH (Time Warner Cable)

McCONNELSVILLE—Formerly served by Adelphia Communications. Now served by Time Warner Cable, BEVERLY, OH [OH0175]

MCCONNELSVILLE—See BEVERLY, OH (Time Warner Cable)

MCGUFFEY—See COLUMBUS, OH (Time Warner Cable)

MCKEAN BOROUGH—See CLEVELAND, PA (Time Warner Cable)

MCKEAN TWP. (ERIE COUNTY)—See CLEVELAND, PA (Time Warner Cable)

MCKEAN TWP.—See NEWARK, OH (Time Warner Cable)

MCLEAN (SHELBY COUNTY)—See TIFFIN, OH (Time Warner Cable)

MECCA TWP.—See CLEVELAND, OH (Time Warner Cable)

MECHANICSBURG (VILLAGE)—See AMBERLEY (village), OH (Time Warner Cable)

MEDINA—Armstrong Cable Services. Now served by ZELIENOPLE, PA [PA0053]

MEDINA—See CLEVELAND, OH (Time Warner Cable)

MEIGS TWP. (ADAMS COUNTY)—See AMBERLEY (village), OH (Time Warner Cable)

MELBOURNE—See LEBANON, KY (Cincinnati Bell Fioptics TV. This cable system has converted to IPTV)

MELROSE—See LEIPSIC, OH (Orwell Communications)

MENDON (VILLAGE)—See TIFFIN, OH (Time Warner Cable)

MENTOR-ON-THE-LAKE—See CLEVELAND, OH (Time Warner Cable)

MENTOR—Time Warner Cable. Now served by CLEVELAND (formerly Cleveland Heights), OH [OH0006]

MENTOR—See LEBANON, KY (Cincinnati Bell Fioptics TV. This cable system has converted to IPTV)

MENTOR—See CLEVELAND, OH (Time Warner Cable)

MERCER COUNTY (PORTIONS)—See CLEVELAND, PA (Time Warner Cable)

METAMORA—Formerly served by Adelphia Communications. Now served by Time Warner Cable, TIFFIN, OH [OH0050]

METAMORA—See TIFFIN, OH (Time Warner Cable)

MEYERS LAKE (VILLAGE)—See CLEVELAND, OH (Time Warner Cable)

MIAMI TWP. (CLERMONT COUNTY)—See AMBERLEY (village), OH (Time Warner Cable)

MIAMI TWP. (GREENE COUNTY)—See AMBERLEY (village), OH (Time Warner Cable)

MIAMI TWP. (HAMILTON COUNTY)—See AMBERLEY (village), OH (Time Warner Cable)

MIAMI TWP. (MONTGOMERY COUNTY)—See AMBERLEY (village), OH (Time Warner Cable)

MIAMI TWP.—See LEBANON, OH (Cincinnati Bell Fioptics TV. This cable system has converted to IPTV)

MIAMISBURG—See AMBERLEY (village), OH (Time Warner Cable)

MIDDLE POINT (VILLAGE)—See TIFFIN, OH (Time Warner Cable)

MIDDLEBURG (Noble County)—Formerly served by Cebridge Connections. No longer in operation

MIDDLEBURG HEIGHTS—See CLEVELAND, OH (Time Warner Cable)

MIDDLEBURG HEIGHTS—See BEREA, OH (WOW! Internet, Cable & Phone)

MIDDLEBURG—See COLUMBUS, OH (Time Warner Cable)

MIDDLEBURY TWP.—See COLUMBUS, OH (Time Warner Cable)

MIDDLEFIELD (VILLAGE)—See CLEVELAND, OH (Time Warner Cable)

MIDDLEFIELD TWP.—See NELSON TWP., OH (Suddenlink Communications)

MIDDLEFIELD TWP.—See CLEVELAND, OH (Time Warner Cable)

MIDDLETON TWP. (WOOD COUNTY)—See TIFFIN, OH (Time Warner Cable)

MIDDLETON TWP.—See TOLEDO, OH (Buckeye Broadband)

MIDDLETON TWP.—See TIFFIN, OH (Time Warner Cable)

MIDDLETON—See NEW MIDDLETOWN, OH (Comcast Cable)

MIDDLETOWN (BUTLER COUNTY)—See LEBANON, OH (Cincinnati Bell Fioptics TV. This cable system has converted to IPTV)

MIDDLETOWN (BUTLER COUNTY)—See AMBERLEY (village), OH (Time Warner Cable)

MIDDLETOWN (WARREN COUNTY)—See LEBANON, OH (Cincinnati Bell Fioptics TV. This cable system has converted to IPTV)

MIDDLETOWN (WARREN COUNTY)—See AMBERLEY (village), OH (Time Warner Cable)

MIDDLETOWN—Time Warner Cable. Now served by AMBERLEY (village), OH [OH0001]

MIDLAND (VILLAGE)—See AMBERLEY (village), OH (Time Warner Cable)

MIDVALE (VILLAGE)—See CLEVELAND, OH (Time Warner Cable)

MIDWAY—Time Warner Cable

MIFFLIN (VILLAGE)—See CLEVELAND, OH (Time Warner Cable)

MIFFLIN TWP. (ASHLAND COUNTY)—See CLEVELAND, OH (Time Warner Cable)

MIFFLIN TWP. (FRANKLIN COUNTY)—See COLUMBUS, OH (Time Warner Cable)

MIFFLIN TWP. (PIKE COUNTY)—See CHILLICOTHE, OH (Time Warner Cable)

MIFFLIN TWP. (RICHLAND COUNTY)—See CLEVELAND, OH (Time Warner Cable)

MIFFLIN TWP.—See COLUMBUS, OH (WOW! Internet, Cable & Phone)

MILAN (VILLAGE) (ERIE COUNTY)—See CLEVELAND, OH (Time Warner Cable)

MILAN (VILLAGE) (HURON COUNTY)—See CLEVELAND, OH (Time Warner Cable)

MILAN TWP. (ERIE COUNTY)—See TOLEDO, OH (Buckeye Broadband)

MILAN TWP.—See CLEVELAND, OH (Time Warner Cable)

Ohio—Cable Community Index

MILFORD (CLERMONT COUNTY)—See LEBANON, OH (Cincinnati Bell Fioptics TV. This cable system has converted to IPTV)

MILFORD (CLERMONT COUNTY)—See AMBERLEY (village), OH (Time Warner Cable)

MILFORD (HAMILTON COUNTY)—See LEBANON, OH (Cincinnati Bell Fioptics TV. This cable system has converted to IPTV)

MILFORD (HAMILTON COUNTY)—See AMBERLEY (village), OH (Time Warner Cable)

MILFORD CENTER (VILLAGE)—See COLUMBUS, OH (Time Warner Cable)

MILFORD TWP.—See LEBANON, OH (Cincinnati Bell Fioptics TV. This cable system has converted to IPTV)

MILL TWP.—See CLEVELAND, OH (Time Warner Cable)

MILLBURY TWP.—See TIFFIN, OH (Time Warner Cable)

MILLCREEK TWP. (ERIE COUNTY)—See CLEVELAND, PA (Time Warner Cable)

MILLCREEK TWP.—See SUBURBANS MOTOR HOME PARK, OH (Time Warner Cable)

MILLEDGEVILLE—See CHILLICOTHE, OH (Time Warner Cable)

MILLER CITY—See LEIPSIC, OH (Orwell Communications)

MILLER—See LEBANON, IN (Cincinnati Bell Fioptics TV. This cable system has converted to IPTV)

MILLERSBURG (VILLAGE)—See CLEVELAND, OH (Time Warner Cable)

MILLERSBURG—Time Warner Cable. Now served by CLEVELAND (formerly Cleveland Heights), OH [OH0006]

MILLERSPORT (VILLAGE)—See COLUMBUS, OH (Time Warner Cable)

MILLFIELD—See NELSONVILLE, OH (Nelsonville TV Cable)

MILLVILLE (VILLAGE)—See AMBERLEY (village), OH (Time Warner Cable)

MILLVILLE—See LEBANON, OH (Cincinnati Bell Fioptics TV. This cable system has converted to IPTV)

MILLWOOD TWP.—See SENECAVILLE, OH (Suddenlink Communications)

MILTON CENTER (VILLAGE)—See TIFFIN, OH (Time Warner Cable)

MILTON TWP. (MAHONING COUNTY)—See CLEVELAND, OH (Time Warner Cable)

MINERAL CITY (VILLAGE)—See CLEVELAND, OH (Time Warner Cable)

MINERVA (village)—Time Warner Cable. Now served by CLEVELAND (formerly Cleveland Heights), OH [OH0006]

MINERVA (VILLAGE)—See CLEVELAND, OH (Time Warner Cable)

MINERVA PARK (VILLAGE)—See COLUMBUS, OH (Time Warner Cable)

MINERVA PARK—See COLUMBUS, OH (WOW! Internet, Cable & Phone)

MINFORD—See JACKSON, OH (Time Warner Cable)

MINSTER—Time Warner Cable. Now served by TIFFIN (formerly Fostoria), OH [OH0050]

MINSTER—See NEW KNOXVILLE, OH (NKTelco)

MINSTER—See TIFFIN, OH (Time Warner Cable)

MOGADORE (VILLAGE) (PORTAGE COUNTY)—See CLEVELAND, OH (Time Warner Cable)

MOGADORE (VILLAGE) (SUMMIT COUNTY)—See CLEVELAND, OH (Time Warner Cable)

MONCLOVA TWP. (LUCAS COUNTY)—See TOLEDO, OH (Buckeye Broadband)

MONCLOVA TWP.—See TIFFIN, OH (Time Warner Cable)

MONROE (BUTLER COUNTY)—See LEBANON, OH (Cincinnati Bell Fioptics TV. This cable system has converted to IPTV)

MONROE (WARREN COUNTY)—See LEBANON, OH (Cincinnati Bell Fioptics TV. This cable system has converted to IPTV)

MONROE COUNTY (EASTERN PORTION)—See HANNIBAL, OH (Crystal Broadband Networks)

MONROE TWP. (ALLEN COUNTY)—See TIFFIN, OH (Time Warner Cable)

MONROE TWP. (ASHTABULA COUNTY)—See CLEVELAND, OH (Time Warner Cable)

MONROE TWP. (ASHTABULA COUNTY)—See DENMARK TWP., OH (Zito Media)

MONROE TWP. (CLERMONT COUNTY)—See AMBERLEY (village), OH (Time Warner Cable)

MONROE TWP. (DARKE COUNTY)—See AMBERLEY (village), OH (Time Warner Cable)

MONROE TWP. (GUERNSEY COUNTY)—See CAMBRIDGE, OH (Time Warner Cable)

MONROE TWP. (HENRY COUNTY)—See TIFFIN, OH (Time Warner Cable)

MONROE TWP. (LOGAN COUNTY)—See COLUMBUS, OH (Time Warner Cable)

MONROE TWP. (MADISON COUNTY)—See SUBURBANS MOTOR HOME PARK, OH (Time Warner Cable)

MONROE TWP. (MIAMI COUNTY)—See AMBERLEY (village), OH (Time Warner Cable)

MONROE TWP. (PERRY COUNTY)—See CORNING, OH (Zito Media)

MONROE TWP. (PREBLE COUNTY)—See AMBERLEY (village), OH (Time Warner Cable)

MONROE TWP.—See LEBANON, OH (Cincinnati Bell Fioptics TV. This cable system has converted to IPTV)

MONROE—See AMBERLEY (village), OH (Time Warner Cable)

MONROEVILLE (VILLAGE)—See CLEVELAND, OH (Time Warner Cable)

MONTEREY TWP.—See OTTOVILLE, OH (OTEC Communication Co.)

MONTEZUMA—See ST. HENRY, OH (NKTelco)

MONTEZUMA—See TIFFIN, OH (Time Warner Cable)

MONTGOMERY TWP. (WOOD COUNTY)—See TIFFIN, OH (Time Warner Cable)

MONTGOMERY—See LEBANON, OH (Cincinnati Bell Fioptics TV. This cable system has converted to IPTV)

MONTGOMERY—See AMBERLEY (village), OH (Time Warner Cable)

MONTPELIER (VILLAGE)—See TIFFIN, OH (Time Warner Cable)

MONTVILLE TWP. (MEDINA COUNTY)—See CLEVELAND, OH (Time Warner Cable)

MONTVILLE—See THOMPSON TWP. (Geauga County), OH (Zito Media)

MOOREFIELD TWP.—See AMBERLEY (village), OH (Time Warner Cable)

MORAINE—See AMBERLEY (village), OH (Time Warner Cable)

MORELAND HILLS (VILLAGE)—See CLEVELAND, OH (Time Warner Cable)

MORGAN TWP. (BUTLER COUNTY)—See AMBERLEY (village), OH (Time Warner Cable)

MORGAN TWP. (SCIOTO COUNTY)—See PORTSMOUTH, OH (Time Warner Cable)

MORGAN TWP.—See ROCK CREEK, OH (Zito Media)

MORGAN—See LEBANON, OH (Cincinnati Bell Fioptics TV. This cable system has converted to IPTV)

MORRAL—See MARION, OH (Time Warner Cable)

MORRIS TWP.—See COLUMBUS, OH (Time Warner Cable)

MORROW (VILLAGE)—See LEBANON, OH (Cincinnati Bell Fioptics TV. This cable system has converted to IPTV)

MORROW (VILLAGE)—See AMBERLEY (village), OH (Time Warner Cable)

MORROW—Formerly served by Adelphia Communications. Now served by Time Warner Cable, AMBERLEY (village), OH [OH0001]

MOSCOW (VILLAGE)—See AMBERLEY (village), OH (Time Warner Cable)

MOULTON TWP.—See WAPAKONETA CITY, OH (TSC Communications)

MOUNT BLANCHARD (VILLAGE)—See TIFFIN, OH (Time Warner Cable)

MOUNT CORY (VILLAGE)—See TIFFIN, OH (Time Warner Cable)

MOUNT EATON—MCTV. Now served by WOOSTER, OH [OH0061]

MOUNT EATON—See WOOSTER, OH (MCTV)

MOUNT GILEAD (village)—Time Warner Cable. Now served by COLUMBUS, OH [OH0002]

MOUNT GILEAD (VILLAGE)—See COLUMBUS, OH (Time Warner Cable)

MOUNT HEALTHY—See LEBANON, OH (Cincinnati Bell Fioptics TV. This cable system has converted to IPTV)

MOUNT HEALTHY—See AMBERLEY (village), OH (Time Warner Cable)

MOUNT ORAB (VILLAGE)—See AMBERLEY (village), OH (Time Warner Cable)

MOUNT ORAB—S. Bryer Cable TV Corp

MOUNT PLEASANT TWP.—Formerly served by Community TV Systems Cable Co. Now served by Comcast Cable, WHEELING, WV [WV0004]

MOUNT STERLING (village) (Muskingum County)—Time Warner Cable. Now served by COLUMBUS, OH [OH0002]

MOUNT STERLING (VILLAGE)—See COLUMBUS, OH (Time Warner Cable)

MOUNT VERNON—Time Warner Cable. Now served by COLUMBUS, OH [OH0002]

MOUNT VERNON—See COLUMBUS, OH (Time Warner Cable)

MOUNT VICTORY (VILLAGE)—See COLUMBUS, OH (Time Warner Cable)

MOXAHALA—See CORNING, OH (Zito Media)

MUHLENBERG TWP.—See COMMERCIAL POINT, OH (Time Warner Cable)

MUNROE FALLS (VILLAGE)—See CLEVELAND, OH (Time Warner Cable)

MUNSON TWP.—See CLEVELAND, OH (Time Warner Cable)

MURRAY CITY—Time Warner Cable. Now served by COLUMBUS, OH [OH0002]

Cable Community Index—Ohio

MURRAY CITY—See COLUMBUS, OH (Time Warner Cable)

MUSKINGUM TWP. (MUSKINGUM COUNTY)—See COLUMBUS, OH (Time Warner Cable)

MUTUAL (VILLAGE)—See AMBERLEY (village), OH (Time Warner Cable)

NAEVE TWP.—See AMBERLEY (village), OH (Time Warner Cable)

NAPOLEON TWP.—See RIDGEVILLE CORNERS, OH (RTEC Communications)

NAPOLEON—Time Warner Cable. Now served by TIFFIN (formerly Fostoria), OH [OH0050]

NAPOLEON—See TIFFIN, OH (Time Warner Cable)

NASHPORT—Formerly served by Time Warner Cable. No longer in operation

NASHVILLE (VILLAGE)—See CLEVELAND, OH (Time Warner Cable)

NAVARRE—See MASSILLON, OH (MCTV)

NAVARRE—See CLEVELAND, OH (Time Warner Cable)

NEFFS—See WEST BELLAIRE, OH (Bellaire Television Cable Co)

NELLIE—See NEWARK, OH (Time Warner Cable)

NELSON LEDGES—See CLEVELAND, OH (Time Warner Cable)

NELSON MOBILE HOME PARK—Formerly served by Time Warner Cable. No longer in operation

NELSON TWP.—Suddenlink Communications

NELSON TWP.—See CLEVELAND, OH (Time Warner Cable)

NELSONVILLE—Nelsonville TV Cable

NELSONVILLE—See ATHENS, OH (Time Warner Cable)

NEVADA (VILLAGE)—See TIFFIN, OH (Time Warner Cable)

NEVILLE (VILLAGE)—See AMBERLEY (village), OH (Time Warner Cable)

NEW ALBANY—See COLUMBUS, OH (Time Warner Cable)

NEW ATHENS—Formerly served by Richards TV Cable. No longer in operation

NEW BLOOMINGTON (VILLAGE)—See COLUMBUS, OH (Time Warner Cable)

NEW BOSTON—See PORTSMOUTH, OH (Time Warner Cable)

NEW BREMEN—See NEW KNOXVILLE, OH (NKTelco)

NEW BREMEN—See TIFFIN, OH (Time Warner Cable)

NEW CARLISLE—See AMBERLEY (village), OH (Time Warner Cable)

NEW CONCORD (village)—Time Warner Cable. Now served by COLUMBUS, OH [OH0002]

NEW CONCORD (VILLAGE)—See COLUMBUS, OH (Time Warner Cable)

NEW FRANKLIN (VILLAGE)—See CLEVELAND, OH (Time Warner Cable)

NEW FRANKLIN—See MASSILLON, OH (MCTV)

NEW GARDEN—See CLEVELAND, OH (Time Warner Cable)

NEW HAVEN TWP.—See CLEVELAND, OH (Time Warner Cable)

NEW HOLLAND (FAYETTE COUNTY)—See WASHINGTON COURT HOUSE, OH (Time Warner Cable)

NEW HOLLAND (PICKAWAY COUNTY)—See WASHINGTON COURT HOUSE, OH (Time Warner Cable)

NEW HOLLAND—Time Warner Cable

NEW JASPER TWP.—See AMBERLEY (village), OH (Time Warner Cable)

NEW KNOXVILLE—NKTelco

NEW KNOXVILLE—See TIFFIN, OH (Time Warner Cable)

NEW LEBANON (VILLAGE)—See AMBERLEY (village), OH (Time Warner Cable)

NEW LEXINGTON (PERRY COUNTY)—See CORNING, OH (Zito Media)

NEW LEXINGTON (village)—Time Warner Cable. Now served by COLUMBUS, OH [OH0002]

NEW LEXINGTON (VILLAGE)—See COLUMBUS, OH (Time Warner Cable)

NEW LONDON (village)—Time Warner Cable. Now served by CLEVELAND (formerly Cleveland Heights), OH [OH0006]

NEW LONDON (VILLAGE)—See CLEVELAND, OH (Time Warner Cable)

NEW LONDON TWP.—See CLEVELAND, OH (Time Warner Cable)

NEW MADISON (VILLAGE)—See AMBERLEY (village), OH (Time Warner Cable)

NEW MARKET TWP.—See AMBERLEY (village), OH (Time Warner Cable)

NEW MARSHFIELD—See ATHENS, OH (Time Warner Cable)

NEW MATAMORAS—Formerly served by Adelphia Communications. Now served by Crystal Broadband Networks, HANNIBAL, OH [OH0251]

NEW MATAMORAS—See HANNIBAL, OH (Crystal Broadband Networks)

NEW MIAMI (VILLAGE)—See LEBANON, OH (Cincinnati Bell Fioptics TV. This cable system has converted to IPTV)

NEW MIAMI (VILLAGE)—See AMBERLEY (village), OH (Time Warner Cable)

NEW MIDDLETOWN—Comcast Cable

NEW PARIS (VILLAGE)—See AMBERLEY (village), OH (Time Warner Cable)

NEW PHILADELPHIA—Time Warner Cable. Now served by CLEVELAND (formerly Cleveland Heights), OH [OH0006]

NEW PHILADELPHIA—See CLEVELAND, OH (Time Warner Cable)

NEW RICHMOND (VILLAGE)—See LEBANON, OH (Cincinnati Bell Fioptics TV. This cable system has converted to IPTV)

NEW RICHMOND (VILLAGE)—See AMBERLEY (village), OH (Time Warner Cable)

NEW RIEGEL (VILLAGE)—See TIFFIN, OH (Time Warner Cable)

NEW RIEGEL—See BASCOM, OH (BTC Multimedia)

NEW ROME—See COLUMBUS, OH (WOW! Internet, Cable & Phone)

NEW RUSSIA TWP.—See OBERLIN, OH (Cable Co-op Inc)

NEW RUSSIA TWP.—See CLEVELAND, OH (Time Warner Cable)

NEW STRAITSVILLE—See CORNING, OH (Zito Media)

NEW TRENTON—See LEBANON, IN (Cincinnati Bell Fioptics TV. This cable system has converted to IPTV)

NEW VIENNA (VILLAGE)—See AMBERLEY (village), OH (Time Warner Cable)

NEW WASHINGTON (VILLAGE)—See TIFFIN, OH (Time Warner Cable)

NEW WATERFORD—See NEW MIDDLETOWN, OH (Comcast Cable)

NEW WESTON (VILLAGE)—See AMBERLEY (village), OH (Time Warner Cable)

NEWARK—Time Warner Cable

NEWBERRY TWP.—See NELSON TWP., OH (Suddenlink Communications)

NEWBERRY TWP.—See AMBERLEY (village), OH (Time Warner Cable)

NEWBURGH HEIGHTS (VILLAGE)—See CLEVELAND, OH (Time Warner Cable)

NEWBURY TWP.—See NELSON TWP., OH (Suddenlink Communications)

NEWBURY TWP.—See CLEVELAND, OH (Time Warner Cable)

NEWCOMERSTOWN (VILLAGE)—See CLEVELAND, OH (Time Warner Cable)

NEWPORT—Formerly served by Vital Communications. No longer in operation

NEWPORT—See LEBANON, KY (Cincinnati Bell Fioptics TV. This cable system has converted to IPTV)

NEWTON FALLS—Time Warner Cable. Now served by CLEVELAND (formerly Cleveland Heights), OH [OH0006]

NEWTON FALLS—See CLEVELAND, OH (Time Warner Cable)

NEWTON TWP. (LICKING COUNTY)—See NEWARK, OH (Time Warner Cable)

NEWTON TWP. (MIAMI COUNTY)—See AMBERLEY (village), OH (Time Warner Cable)

NEWTON TWP. (PIKE COUNTY)—See CHILLICOTHE, OH (Time Warner Cable)

NEWTON TWP. (TRUMBULL COUNTY)—See CLEVELAND, OH (Time Warner Cable)

NEWTON TWP.—See NELSON TWP., OH (Suddenlink Communications)

NEWTONSVILLE (VILLAGE)—See LEBANON, OH (Cincinnati Bell Fioptics TV. This cable system has converted to IPTV)

NEWTONSVILLE (VILLAGE)—See AMBERLEY (village), OH (Time Warner Cable)

NEWTOWN (VILLAGE)—See LEBANON, OH (Cincinnati Bell Fioptics TV. This cable system has converted to IPTV)

NEWTOWN (VILLAGE)—See AMBERLEY (village), OH (Time Warner Cable)

NEY—See DEFIANCE, OH (Time Warner Cable)

NILE TWP.—See PORTSMOUTH, OH (Time Warner Cable)

NILES—See CLEVELAND, OH (Time Warner Cable)

NIMISHILLEN TWP.—See CLEVELAND, OH (Time Warner Cable)

NOBLE TWP. (AUGLAIZE COUNTY)—See ST. MARYS TWP., OH (TSC Communications)

NOBLE TWP.—See DEFIANCE, OH (Time Warner Cable)

NORTH BALTIMORE (village)—Time Warner Cable. Now served by TIFFIN (formerly Fostoria), OH [OH0050]

NORTH BALTIMORE—See TIFFIN, OH (Time Warner Cable)

NORTH BEAVER TWP. (LAWRENCE COUNTY)—See NEW MIDDLETOWN, PA (Comcast Cable)

NORTH BEND (VILLAGE)—See LEBANON, OH (Cincinnati Bell Fioptics TV. This cable system has converted to IPTV)

NORTH BEND (VILLAGE)—See AMBERLEY (village), OH (Time Warner Cable)

NORTH BLOOMFIELD TWP.—See ORWELL, OH (Orwell Communications)

NORTH BLOOMFIELD TWP.—See COLUMBUS, OH (Time Warner Cable)

Ohio—Cable Community Index

NORTH CANTON—See CLEVELAND, OH (Time Warner Cable)

NORTH COLLEGE HILL—See LEBANON, OH (Cincinnati Bell Fioptics TV. This cable system has converted to IPTV)

NORTH COLLEGE HILL—See AMBERLEY (village), OH (Time Warner Cable)

NORTH EAST BOROUGH—See CLEVELAND, PA (Time Warner Cable)

NORTH EAST TWP.—See CLEVELAND, PA (Time Warner Cable)

NORTH FAIRFIELD (VILLAGE)—See CLEVELAND, OH (Time Warner Cable)

NORTH HAMPTON (VILLAGE)—See AMBERLEY (village), OH (Time Warner Cable)

NORTH JACKSON (VILLAGE)—See CLEVELAND, OH (Time Warner Cable)

NORTH KINGSVILLE (VILLAGE)—See CLEVELAND, OH (Time Warner Cable)

NORTH LEWISBURG (VILLAGE)—See COLUMBUS, OH (Time Warner Cable)

NORTH OLMSTED—See CLEVELAND, OH (Time Warner Cable)

NORTH OLMSTED—See BEREA, OH (WOW! Internet, Cable & Phone)

NORTH PERRY (VILLAGE)—See CLEVELAND, OH (Time Warner Cable)

NORTH RANDALL (VILLAGE)—See CLEVELAND, OH (Time Warner Cable)

NORTH RIDGEVILLE—See CLEVELAND, OH (Time Warner Cable)

NORTH ROBINSON (VILLAGE)—See COLUMBUS, OH (Time Warner Cable)

NORTH ROYALTON—See CLEVELAND, OH (Time Warner Cable)

NORTH ROYALTON—See BEREA, OH (WOW! Internet, Cable & Phone)

NORTH STAR—See VERSAILLES, OH (Time Warner Cable)

NORTH TWP.—See CLEVELAND, OH (Time Warner Cable)

NORTHFIELD (VILLAGE)—See CLEVELAND, OH (Time Warner Cable)

NORTHFIELD CENTER TWP.—See CLEVELAND, OH (Time Warner Cable)

NORTHWOOD—Time Warner Cable. Now served by TIFFIN, OH [OH0050]

NORTHWOOD—See TOLEDO, OH (Buckeye Broadband)

NORTHWOOD—See TIFFIN, OH (Time Warner Cable)

NORTON—See CLEVELAND, OH (Time Warner Cable)

NORWALK TWP.—See CLEVELAND, OH (Time Warner Cable)

NORWALK—Time Warner Cable. Now served by CLEVELAND (formerly Cleveland Heights), OH [OH0006]

NORWALK—See CLEVELAND, OH (Time Warner Cable)

NORWICH (VILLAGE)—See COLUMBUS, OH (Time Warner Cable)

NORWICH TWP. (FRANKLIN COUNTY)—See SUBURBANS MOTOR HOME PARK, OH (Time Warner Cable)

NORWICH TWP. (HURON COUNTY)—See CLEVELAND, OH (Time Warner Cable)

NORWICH TWP. (Muskingum County)—Time Warner Cable. Now served by COLUMBUS, OH [OH0002]

NORWICH TWP. (MUSKINGUM COUNTY)—See COLUMBUS, OH (Time Warner Cable)

NORWICH TWP.—See COLUMBUS, OH (WOW! Internet, Cable & Phone)

NORWOOD—See LEBANON, OH (Cincinnati Bell Fioptics TV. This cable system has converted to IPTV)

NORWOOD—See AMBERLEY (village), OH (Time Warner Cable)

OAK HARBOR—Time Warner Cable. Now served by PORT CLINTON, OH [OH0060]

OAK HARBOR—See PORT CLINTON, OH (Time Warner Cable)

OAK HILL—Time Warner Cable. Now served by JACKSON, OH [OH0098]

OAK HILL—See JACKSON, OH (Time Warner Cable)

OAK RUN TWP.—See COLUMBUS, OH (Time Warner Cable)

OAKFIELD—See CORNING, OH (Zito Media)

OAKLAND—Time Warner Cable

OAKWOOD (PAULDING COUNTY)—See LEIPSIC, OH (Orwell Communications)

OAKWOOD (VILLAGE)—See CLEVELAND, OH (Time Warner Cable)

OAKWOOD—See AMBERLEY (village), OH (Time Warner Cable)

OBERLIN—Cable Co-op Inc

OBETZ (VILLAGE)—See COLUMBUS, OH (Time Warner Cable)

OBETZ—See COLUMBUS, OH (WOW! Internet, Cable & Phone)

OCTA—See CHILLICOTHE, OH (Time Warner Cable)

OHIO CITY—See VAN WERT, OH (Time Warner Cable)

OHIO TWP. (MONROE COUNTY)—See HANNIBAL, OH (Crystal Broadband Networks)

OHIO TWP.—See LEBANON, OH (Cincinnati Bell Fioptics TV. This cable system has converted to IPTV)

OHIO TWP.—See AMBERLEY (village), OH (Time Warner Cable)

OLD FORT—See TIFFIN, OH (Time Warner Cable)

OLD WASHINGTON—See SENECAVILLE, OH (Suddenlink Communications)

OLIVE TWP. (MEIGS COUNTY)—See BEVERLY, OH (Time Warner Cable)

OLMSTED FALLS—See PARMA, OH (Cox Communications)

OLMSTED TWP.—Formerly served by Olmsted Cable Co. Corp. Now served by Cox Communications, PARMA, OH [OH0009]

OLMSTED TWP.—See PARMA, OH (Cox Communications)

ONTARIO—See CLEVELAND, OH (Time Warner Cable)

ORANGE (VILLAGE)—See CLEVELAND, OH (Time Warner Cable)

ORANGE TWP. (DELAWARE COUNTY)—See COLUMBUS, OH (Time Warner Cable)

ORANGE TWP. (DELAWARE COUNTY)—See COLUMBUS, OH (WOW! Internet, Cable & Phone)

ORANGE TWP. (HANCOCK COUNTY)—See TIFFIN, OH (Time Warner Cable)

ORANGE TWP. (SHELBY COUNTY)—See TIFFIN, OH (Time Warner Cable)

ORANGE TWP.—See AMBERLEY (village), OH (Time Warner Cable)

ORANGEVILLE (VILLAGE)—See CLEVELAND, OH (Time Warner Cable)

OREGON—See TOLEDO, OH (Buckeye Broadband)

OREGON—See TIFFIN, OH (Time Warner Cable)

ORIENT (VILLAGE)—See COLUMBUS, OH (Time Warner Cable)

ORRVILLE—Armstrong Cable Services. Now served by ZELIENOPLE, PA [PA0053]

ORWELL—Orwell Communications

OSGOOD—See VERSAILLES, OH (Time Warner Cable)

OSNABURG TWP.—See CLEVELAND, OH (Time Warner Cable)

OSTRANDER (VILLAGE)—See COLUMBUS, OH (Time Warner Cable)

OTTAWA (VILLAGE)—See TIFFIN, OH (Time Warner Cable)

OTTAWA HILLS—See TOLEDO, OH (Buckeye Broadband)

OTTAWA HILLS—See COLUMBUS, OH (Time Warner Cable)

OTTAWA TWP.—Time Warner Cable. Now served by TIFFIN, OH [OH0050]

OTTAWA TWP.—See TIFFIN, OH (Time Warner Cable)

OTTOVILLE—OTEC Communication Co.

OWENSVILLE (village)—Time Warner Cable. Now served by AMBERLEY (village), OH [OH0001]

OWENSVILLE (VILLAGE)—See LEBANON, OH (Cincinnati Bell Fioptics TV. This cable system has converted to IPTV)

OWENSVILLE (VILLAGE)—See AMBERLEY (village), OH (Time Warner Cable)

OXFORD TWP. (BUTLER COUNTY)—See AMBERLEY (village), OH (Time Warner Cable)

OXFORD TWP. (ERIE COUNTY)—See TOLEDO, OH (Buckeye Broadband)

OXFORD TWP. (ERIE COUNTY)—See CLEVELAND, OH (Time Warner Cable)

OXFORD—Time Warner Cable. Now served by AMBERLEY (village), OH [OH0001]

OXFORD—See AMBERLEY (village), OH (Time Warner Cable)

PAINESVILLE TWP.—See CLEVELAND, OH (Time Warner Cable)

PAINESVILLE—See CLEVELAND, OH (Time Warner Cable)

PAINT TWP. (FAYETTE COUNTY)—See MIDWAY, OH (Time Warner Cable)

PAINT TWP. (FAYETTE COUNTY)—See WASHINGTON COURT HOUSE, OH (Time Warner Cable)

PAINT TWP. (HIGHLAND COUNTY)—See WASHINGTON COURT HOUSE, OH (Time Warner Cable)

PAINT TWP. (MADISON COUNTY)—See MIDWAY, OH (Time Warner Cable)

PAINT TWP. (WAYNE COUNTY)—See WOOSTER, OH (MCTV)

PAINT TWP.—See MASSILLON, OH (MCTV)

PALESTINE (VILLAGE)—See AMBERLEY (village), OH (Time Warner Cable)

PALMYRA TWP.—See NELSON TWP., OH (Suddenlink Communications)

PALMYRA TWP.—See CLEVELAND, OH (Time Warner Cable)

PANDORA—See LEIPSIC, OH (Orwell Communications)

PARIS TWP. (PORTAGE COUNTY)—See NELSON TWP., OH (Suddenlink Communications)

PARIS TWP. (STARK COUNTY)—See CLEVELAND, OH (Time Warner Cable)

PARIS TWP. (UNION COUNTY)—See COLUMBUS, OH (Time Warner Cable)

PARK HILLS—See LEBANON, KY (Cincinnati Bell Fioptics TV. This cable system has converted to IPTV)

PARKMAN TWP.—See NELSON TWP., OH (Suddenlink Communications)

PARKMAN—See NELSON TWP., OH (Suddenlink Communications)

PARMA HEIGHTS—See PARMA, OH (Cox Communications)

PARMA—Cox Communications

PARMA—See CLEVELAND, OH (Time Warner Cable)

Cable Community Index—Ohio

PARRAL (VILLAGE)—See CLEVELAND, OH (Time Warner Cable)

PATASKALA (village)—Time Warner Cable. Now served by COLUMBUS, OH [OH0002]

PATASKALA (VILLAGE)—See COLUMBUS, OH (Time Warner Cable)

PATTERSON (VILLAGE)—See COLUMBUS, OH (Time Warner Cable)

PATTERSON TWP.—See VERSAILLES, OH (Time Warner Cable)

PAULDING TWP. (PAULDING COUNTY)—See PAULDING, OH (Time Warner Cable)

PAULDING—Time Warner Cable

PAXTON TWP.—See CHILLICOTHE, OH (Time Warner Cable)

PAYNE—NewWave Communications. Now served by MONROEVILLE, IN [IN0358]

PEBBLE TWP.—See CHILLICOTHE, OH (Time Warner Cable)

PEDRO—Formerly served by Windjammer Cable. No longer in operation

PEE PEE TWP. (PIKE COUNTY)—See CHILLICOTHE, OH (Time Warner Cable)

PEEBLES (village)—Time Warner Cable. Now served by AMBERLEY (village), OH [OH0001]

PEEBLES (VILLAGE)—See AMBERLEY (village), OH (Time Warner Cable)

PEMBERVILLE—See TIFFIN, OH (Time Warner Cable)

PENFIELD TWP.—See WELLINGTON, OH (GLW Broadband)

PENINSULA (VILLAGE)—See CLEVELAND, OH (Time Warner Cable)

PENN TWP.—See AMBERLEY (village), OH (Time Warner Cable)

PEPPER PIKE—See CLEVELAND, OH (Time Warner Cable)

PERKINS TWP. (ERIE COUNTY)—See TOLEDO, OH (Buckeye Broadband)

PERRY (VILLAGE)—See CLEVELAND, OH (Time Warner Cable)

PERRY COUNTY (PORTIONS)—See COLUMBUS, OH (Time Warner Cable)

PERRY TWP. (ASHLAND COUNTY)—See WOOSTER, OH (MCTV)

PERRY TWP. (ASHLAND COUNTY)—See CLEVELAND, OH (Time Warner Cable)

PERRY TWP. (BROWN COUNTY)—See AMBERLEY (village), OH (Time Warner Cable)

PERRY TWP. (COLUMBIANA COUNTY)—See CLEVELAND, OH (Time Warner Cable)

PERRY TWP. (FAYETTE COUNTY)—See AMBERLEY (village), OH (Time Warner Cable)

PERRY TWP. (FRANKLIN COUNTY)—See COLUMBUS, OH (Time Warner Cable)

PERRY TWP. (LAKE COUNTY)—See CLEVELAND, OH (Time Warner Cable)

PERRY TWP. (LICKING COUNTY)—See NEWARK, OH (Time Warner Cable)

PERRY TWP. (LOGAN COUNTY)—See COLUMBUS, OH (Time Warner Cable)

PERRY TWP. (LOGAN COUNTY)—See TIFFIN, OH (Time Warner Cable)

PERRY TWP. (MONTGOMERY COUNTY)—See AMBERLEY (village), OH (Time Warner Cable)

PERRY TWP. (MUSKINGUM COUNTY)—See CLEVELAND, OH (Time Warner Cable)

PERRY TWP. (PICKAWAY COUNTY)—See COLUMBUS, OH (Time Warner Cable)

PERRY TWP. (PUTNAM COUNTY)—See KALIDA, OH (Kalida Telephone Co)

PERRY TWP. (PUTNAM COUNTY)—See OTTOVILLE, OH (OTEC Communication Co.)

PERRY TWP. (RICHLAND COUNTY)—See CLEVELAND, OH (Time Warner Cable)

PERRY TWP. (SHELBY COUNTY)—See AMBERLEY (village), OH (Time Warner Cable)

PERRY TWP. (STARK COUNTY)—See MASSILLON, OH (MCTV)

PERRY TWP. (WOOD COUNTY)—See TIFFIN, OH (Time Warner Cable)

PERRY TWP.—See COLUMBUS, OH (WOW! Internet, Cable & Phone)

PERRYSBURG TWP.—See TOLEDO, OH (Buckeye Broadband)

PERRYSBURG TWP.—See TIFFIN, OH (Time Warner Cable)

PERRYSBURG—See TIFFIN, OH (Time Warner Cable)

PERRYSVILLE (VILLAGE)—See CLEVELAND, OH (Time Warner Cable)

PERU TWP.—See COLUMBUS, OH (Time Warner Cable)

PETTISVILLE—See TIFFIN, OH (Time Warner Cable)

PHILLIPSBURG (VILLAGE)—See AMBERLEY (village), OH (Time Warner Cable)

PHILO (village)—Time Warner Cable. Now served by COLUMBUS, OH [OH0002]

PHILO (VILLAGE)—See COLUMBUS, OH (Time Warner Cable)

PICKAWAY TWP.—See OAKLAND, OH (Time Warner Cable)

PICKERINGTON—See COLUMBUS, OH (Time Warner Cable)

PICKERINGTON—See COLUMBUS, OH (WOW! Internet, Cable & Phone)

PIERCE TWP.—See LEBANON, OH (Cincinnati Bell Fioptics TV. This cable system has converted to IPTV)

PIERCE TWP.—See AMBERLEY (village), OH (Time Warner Cable)

PIERPONT TWP.—See DENMARK TWP., OH (Zito Media)

PIKE TWP. (BROWN COUNTY)—See AMBERLEY (village), OH (Time Warner Cable)

PIKE TWP. (CLARK COUNTY)—See AMBERLEY (village), OH (Time Warner Cable)

PIKE TWP. (FULTON COUNTY)—See TIFFIN, OH (Time Warner Cable)

PIKE TWP. (MADISON COUNTY)—See SUBURBANS MOTOR HOME PARK, OH (Time Warner Cable)

PIKE TWP. (PERRY COUNTY)—See COLUMBUS, OH (Time Warner Cable)

PIKE TWP. (STARK COUNTY)—See CLEVELAND, OH (Time Warner Cable)

PIKE TWP.—See LEBANON, OH (Cincinnati Bell Fioptics TV. This cable system has converted to IPTV)

PIKETON—Time Warner Cable. Now served by CHILLICOTHE, OH [OH0033]

PIKETON—See CHILLICOTHE, OH (Time Warner Cable)

PINE LAKE TRAILER PARK—Formerly served by Marshall County Cable. No longer in operation

PIONEER—Formerly served by Windjammer Cable. No longer in operation

PIONEER—See TIFFIN, OH (Time Warner Cable)

PIQUA—Formerly served by Time Warner Cable. No longer in operation

PIQUA—See AMBERLEY (village), OH (Time Warner Cable)

PITSBURG (VILLAGE)—See AMBERLEY (village), OH (Time Warner Cable)

PITT TWP.—See TIFFIN, OH (Time Warner Cable)

PITTSFIELD TWP.—See OBERLIN, OH (Cable Co-op Inc)

PITTSFIELD TWP.—See WELLINGTON, OH (GLW Broadband)

PLAIN CITY (VILLAGE)—See COLUMBUS, OH (Time Warner Cable)

PLAIN TWP. (FRANKLIN COUNTY)—See COLUMBUS, OH (Time Warner Cable)

PLAIN TWP. (WAYNE COUNTY)—See WOOSTER, OH (MCTV)

PLAINFIELD (VILLAGE)—See COLUMBUS, OH (Time Warner Cable)

PLATEA BOROUGH—See CLEVELAND, PA (Time Warner Cable)

PLEASANT CITY—See SENECAVILLE, OH (Suddenlink Communications)

PLEASANT HILL (JEFFERSON COUNTY)—See TORONTO, OH (Jefferson County Cable Inc)

PLEASANT HILL (VILLAGE)—See AMBERLEY (village), OH (Time Warner Cable)

PLEASANT PLAIN (VILLAGE)—See LEBANON, OH (Cincinnati Bell Fioptics TV. This cable system has converted to IPTV)

PLEASANT PLAIN (VILLAGE)—See AMBERLEY (village), OH (Time Warner Cable)

PLEASANT TWP. (BROWN COUNTY)—See AMBERLEY (village), OH (Time Warner Cable)

PLEASANT TWP. (CLARK COUNTY)—See AMBERLEY (village), OH (Time Warner Cable)

PLEASANT TWP. (FAIRFIELD COUNTY)—See COLUMBUS, OH (Time Warner Cable)

PLEASANT TWP. (FRANKLIN COUNTY)—See COLUMBUS, OH (Time Warner Cable)

PLEASANT TWP. (HANCOCK COUNTY)—See TIFFIN, OH (Time Warner Cable)

PLEASANT TWP. (HENRY COUNTY)—See DESHLER, OH (Time Warner Cable)

PLEASANT TWP. (KNOX COUNTY)—See COLUMBUS, OH (Time Warner Cable)

PLEASANT TWP. (MADISON COUNTY)—See SUBURBANS MOTOR HOME PARK, OH (Time Warner Cable)

PLEASANT TWP. (MARION COUNTY)—See MARION, OH (Time Warner Cable)

PLEASANT TWP. (PERRY COUNTY)—See COLUMBUS, OH (Time Warner Cable)

PLEASANT TWP. (PERRY COUNTY)—See CORNING, OH (Zito Media)

PLEASANT TWP. (PUTNAM COUNTY)—See VAN WERT, OH (Time Warner Cable)

PLEASANT TWP. (SENECA COUNTY)—See TIFFIN, OH (Time Warner Cable)

PLEASANT TWP. (VAN WERT COUNTY)—See VAN WERT, OH (Time Warner Cable)

PLEASANTVILLE (VILLAGE)—See COLUMBUS, OH (Time Warner Cable)

PLUMWOOD—See MIDWAY, OH (Time Warner Cable)

PLYMOUTH (VILLAGE) (HURON COUNTY)—See CLEVELAND, OH (Time Warner Cable)

PLYMOUTH (VILLAGE) (RICHLAND COUNTY)—See CLEVELAND, OH (Time Warner Cable)

PLYMOUTH TWP. (ASHTABULA COUNTY)—See CLEVELAND, OH (Time Warner Cable)

Ohio—Cable Community Index

PLYMOUTH TWP. (ASHTABULA COUNTY)—See DENMARK TWP., OH (Zito Media)

PLYMOUTH TWP. (RICHLAND COUNTY)—See CLEVELAND, OH (Time Warner Cable)

POLAND TWP.—See CLEVELAND, OH (Time Warner Cable)

POLK (village)—Time Warner Cable. Now served by CLEVELAND (formerly Cleveland Heights), OH [OH0006]

POLK (VILLAGE)—See CLEVELAND, OH (Time Warner Cable)

POLK TWP.—See COLUMBUS, OH (Time Warner Cable)

PONDEROSA MOTOR HOME PARK—See SUBURBANS MOTOR HOME PARK, OH (Time Warner Cable)

PORT CLINTON—Time Warner Cable

PORT JEFFERSON (VILLAGE)—See AMBERLEY (village), OH (Time Warner Cable)

PORT WASHINGTON (VILLAGE)—See CLEVELAND, OH (Time Warner Cable)

PORT WILLIAM—Formerly served by Time Warner Cable. No longer in operation

PORTAGE (VILLAGE)—See TIFFIN, OH (Time Warner Cable)

PORTAGE TWP. (HANCOCK COUNTY)—See TIFFIN, OH (Time Warner Cable)

PORTAGE TWP. (OTTAWA COUNTY)—See PORT CLINTON, OH (Time Warner Cable)

PORTAGE TWP. (WOOD COUNTY)—See TIFFIN, OH (Time Warner Cable)

PORTER TWP. (DELAWARE COUNTY)—See COLUMBUS, OH (Time Warner Cable)

PORTER TWP. (SCIOTO COUNTY)—See PORTSMOUTH, OH (Time Warner Cable)

PORTERFIELD—Formerly served by Adelphia Communications. No longer in operation

PORTERFIELD—See BEVERLY, OH (Time Warner Cable)

PORTSMOUTH—Time Warner Cable

POTSDAM (VILLAGE)—See AMBERLEY (village), OH (Time Warner Cable)

POTTERY ADDITION—See TORONTO, OH (Jefferson County Cable Inc)

POWELL TWP.—See COLUMBUS, OH (Time Warner Cable)

POWHATAN POINT—Powhatan Point Cable Co

PRAIRIE TWP. (FRANKLIN COUNTY)—See COLUMBUS, OH (Time Warner Cable)

PRAIRIE TWP.—See COLUMBUS, OH (WOW! Internet, Cable & Phone)

PROCTORVILLE—Formerly served by Lycom Communications. No longer in operation

PROSPECT (VILLAGE)—See COLUMBUS, OH (Time Warner Cable)

PROSPECT TWP.—See COLUMBUS, OH (Time Warner Cable)

PROSPECT TWP.—See MARION, OH (Time Warner Cable)

PROVIDENCE TWP.—See TIFFIN, OH (Time Warner Cable)

PULASKI TWP. (WILLIAMS COUNTY)—See TIFFIN, OH (Time Warner Cable)

PULASKI TWP.—See BRYAN, OH (Bryan Municipal Utilities)

PUSHETA TWP.—See TIFFIN, OH (Time Warner Cable)

PUSHETA TWP.—See WAPAKONETA CITY, OH (TSC Communications)

PUT-IN-BAY—Time Warner Cable. Now served by CLEVELAND (formerly Cleveland Heights), OH [OH0006]

PUT-IN-BAY—See CLEVELAND, OH (Time Warner Cable)

PYMATUNING STATE PARK—See VERNON TWP. (Trumbull County), OH (Armstrong Cable Services)

PYMATUNING TWP.—See CLEVELAND, PA (Time Warner Cable)

QUAKER CITY—See SENECAVILLE, OH (Suddenlink Communications)

QUINCY (VILLAGE)—See AMBERLEY (village), OH (Time Warner Cable)

RACCOON TWP.—See CHILLICOTHE, OH (Time Warner Cable)

RADNOR TWP.—See COLUMBUS, OH (Time Warner Cable)

RAINSBORO TWP.—See WASHINGTON COURT HOUSE, OH (Time Warner Cable)

RAINSBORO—Formerly served by Adelphia Communications. Now served by Time Warner Cable, WASHINGTON COURT HOUSE, OH [OH0070]

RANDOLPH TWP. (MONTGOMERY COUNTY)—See AMBERLEY (village), OH (Time Warner Cable)

RANDOLPH TWP. (PORTAGE COUNTY)—See CLEVELAND, OH (Time Warner Cable)

RANGE TWP.—See MIDWAY, OH (Time Warner Cable)

RAVENNA TWP.—See CLEVELAND, OH (Time Warner Cable)

RAVENNA—See CLEVELAND, OH (Time Warner Cable)

RAWSON (VILLAGE)—See TIFFIN, OH (Time Warner Cable)

READING TWP.—See COLUMBUS, OH (Time Warner Cable)

READING—See LEBANON, OH (Cincinnati Bell Fioptics TV. This cable system has converted to IPTV)

READING—See AMBERLEY (village), OH (Time Warner Cable)

REED TWP.—See TIFFIN, OH (Time Warner Cable)

REEDSVILLE—See BEVERLY, OH (Time Warner Cable)

REILY TWP.—See LEBANON, OH (Cincinnati Bell Fioptics TV. This cable system has converted to IPTV)

REILY TWP.—See AMBERLEY (village), OH (Time Warner Cable)

REMINDERVILLE (TOWN)—See CLEVELAND, OH (Time Warner Cable)

RENDVILLE—See CORNING, OH (Zito Media)

REPUBLIC (VILLAGE)—See TIFFIN, OH (Time Warner Cable)

REYNOLDSBURG—See COLUMBUS, OH (Time Warner Cable)

REYNOLDSBURG—See COLUMBUS, OH (WOW! Internet, Cable & Phone)

RICE TWP.—See CLEVELAND, OH (Time Warner Cable)

RICH HILL TWP.—See COLUMBUS, OH (Time Warner Cable)

RICHFIELD (VILLAGE)—See CLEVELAND, OH (Time Warner Cable)

RICHFIELD TWP. (LUCAS COUNTY)—See TOLEDO, OH (Buckeye Broadband)

RICHFIELD TWP. (SUMMIT COUNTY)—See CLEVELAND, OH (Time Warner Cable)

RICHLAND TWP. (ALLEN COUNTY)—See TIFFIN, OH (Time Warner Cable)

RICHLAND TWP. (CLINTON COUNTY)—See WASHINGTON COURT HOUSE, OH (Time Warner Cable)

RICHLAND TWP. (DARKE COUNTY)—See AMBERLEY (village), OH (Time Warner Cable)

RICHLAND TWP. (DEFIANCE COUNTY)—See DEFIANCE, OH (Time Warner Cable)

RICHLAND TWP. (FAIRFIELD COUNTY)—See COLUMBUS, OH (Time Warner Cable)

RICHLAND TWP. (GUERNSEY COUNTY)—See SENECAVILLE, OH (Suddenlink Communications)

RICHLAND TWP. (LOGAN COUNTY)—See COLUMBUS, OH (Time Warner Cable)

RICHLAND TWP. (WYANDOT COUNTY)—See COLUMBUS, OH (Time Warner Cable)

RICHLAND TWP.—See RIDGEVILLE CORNERS, OH (RTEC Communications)

RICHLAND TWP.—See CLEVELAND, OH (Time Warner Cable)

RICHMOND DALE—Formerly served by Adelphia Communications. Now served by Time Warner Cable, CHILLICOTHE, OH [OH0033]

RICHMOND DALE—See CHILLICOTHE, OH (Time Warner Cable)

RICHMOND HEIGHTS—See CLEVELAND, OH (Time Warner Cable)

RICHMOND TWP. (HURON COUNTY)—See CLEVELAND, OH (Time Warner Cable)

RICHWOOD (VILLAGE)—See COLUMBUS, OH (Time Warner Cable)

RIDGE TWP. (VAN WERT COUNTY)—See VAN WERT, OH (Time Warner Cable)

RIDGEFIELD TWP.—See CLEVELAND, OH (Time Warner Cable)

RIDGEVILLE CORNERS—RTEC Communications

RIDGEVILLE TWP.—See RIDGEVILLE CORNERS, OH (RTEC Communications)

RIDGEWAY (VILLAGE)—See COLUMBUS, OH (Time Warner Cable)

RIGA TWP.—See TOLEDO, MI (Buckeye Broadband)

RILEY TWP. (SANDUSKY COUNTY)—See TIFFIN, OH (Time Warner Cable)

RIO GRANDE—Time Warner Cable. Now served by CHILLICOTHE, OH [OH0033]

RIO GRANDE—See CHILLICOTHE, OH (Time Warner Cable)

RIPLEY (VILLAGE)—See AMBERLEY (village), OH (Time Warner Cable)

RIPLEY TWP.—See CLEVELAND, OH (Time Warner Cable)

RIPLEY—Formerly served by Adelphia Communications. Now served by Time Warner Cable, AMBERLEY (village), OH [OH0001]

RISING SUN (village)—Time Warner Cable. Now served by TIFFIN (formerly Fostoria), OH [OH0050]

RISING SUN (VILLAGE)—See TIFFIN, OH (Time Warner Cable)

RITTMAN (MEDINA COUNTY)—See CLEVELAND, OH (Time Warner Cable)

RITTMAN (WAYNE COUNTY)—See CLEVELAND, OH (Time Warner Cable)

RITTMAN—See DOYLESTOWN, OH (Doylestown Communications)

RIVERLEA (VILLAGE)—See COLUMBUS, OH (Time Warner Cable)

RIVERLEA—See COLUMBUS, OH (WOW! Internet, Cable & Phone)

RIVERSIDE (Montgomery County)—Time Warner Cable. Now served by AMBERLEY (village), OH [OH0001]

RIVERSIDE—Time Warner Cable. Now served by AMBERLEY (village), OH [OH0001]

RIVERSIDE—See AMBERLEY (village), OH (Time Warner Cable)

ROAMING SHORES—See ROCK CREEK, OH (Zito Media)

Cable Community Index—Ohio

ROBBINS MOBILE HOME PARK—Formerly served by Time Warner Cable. No longer in operation

ROCHESTER (VILLAGE)—See WELLINGTON, OH (GLW Broadband)

ROCHESTER TWP.—See WELLINGTON, OH (GLW Broadband)

ROCK CREEK—Zito Media

ROCKBRIDGE—See LOGAN, OH (Time Warner Cable)

ROCKFORD (village)—Time Warner Cable. Now served by TIFFIN, OH [OH0050]

ROCKFORD (VILLAGE)—See TIFFIN, OH (Time Warner Cable)

ROCKY RIDGE—See PORT CLINTON, OH (Time Warner Cable)

ROCKY RIVER—See PARMA, OH (Cox Communications)

ROGERS (VILLAGE)—See NEW MIDDLETOWN, OH (Comcast Cable)

ROME TWP. (ASHTABULA COUNTY)—See ROCK CREEK, OH (Zito Media)

ROME TWP. (ATHENS COUNTY)—See BEVERLY, OH (Time Warner Cable)

ROME TWP.—See ORWELL, OH (Orwell Communications)

ROOTSTOWN TWP.—See CLEVELAND, OH (Time Warner Cable)

ROSEVILLE (VILLAGE) (MUSKINGUM COUNTY)—See COLUMBUS, OH (Time Warner Cable)

ROSEVILLE (VILLAGE) (PERRY COUNTY)—See COLUMBUS, OH (Time Warner Cable)

ROSEWOOD (VILLAGE)—See AMBERLEY (village), OH (Time Warner Cable)

ROSS TWP. (Butler County)—Formerly served by Adelphia Communications. Now served by Time Warner Cable, AMBERLEY (village), OH [OH0001]

ROSS TWP. (BUTLER COUNTY)—See AMBERLEY (village), OH (Time Warner Cable)

ROSS TWP. (JEFFERSON COUNTY)—See BLOOMINGDALE, OH (Suddenlink Communications)

ROSS TWP.—See LEBANON, OH (Cincinnati Bell Fioptics TV. This cable system has converted to IPTV)

ROSSBURG (VILLAGE)—See AMBERLEY (village), OH (Time Warner Cable)

ROSSFORD—See TOLEDO, OH (Buckeye Broadband)

ROSSFORD—See TIFFIN, OH (Time Warner Cable)

ROSWELL (VILLAGE)—See CLEVELAND, OH (Time Warner Cable)

ROUNDHEAD TWP.—See TIFFIN, OH (Time Warner Cable)

ROWSBURG (VILLAGE)—See CLEVELAND, OH (Time Warner Cable)

ROYALTON TWP.—See TIFFIN, OH (Time Warner Cable)

RUGGLES TWP.—See CLEVELAND, OH (Time Warner Cable)

RUSH CREEK TWP. (FAIRFIELD COUNTY)—See COLUMBUS, OH (Time Warner Cable)

RUSH RUN—See SMITHFIELD, OH (Jefferson County Cable Inc)

RUSH TWP. (CHAMPAIGN COUNTY)—See AMBERLEY (village), OH (Time Warner Cable)

RUSH TWP. (SCIOTO COUNTY)—See PORTSMOUTH, OH (Time Warner Cable)

RUSHCREEK TWP. (LOGAN COUNTY)—See COLUMBUS, OH (Time Warner Cable)

RUSHSYLVANIA (VILLAGE)—See COLUMBUS, OH (Time Warner Cable)

RUSHVILLE (VILLAGE)—See COLUMBUS, OH (Time Warner Cable)

RUSSELL TWP.—See CLEVELAND, OH (Time Warner Cable)

RUSSELLS POINT (VILLAGE)—See TIFFIN, OH (Time Warner Cable)

RUSSELLVILLE (VILLAGE)—See AMBERLEY (village), OH (Time Warner Cable)

RUSSIA—See VERSAILLES, OH (Time Warner Cable)

RUTLAND TWP.—See SCIPIO TWP. (Meigs County), OH (Time Warner Cable)

SABINA—See WASHINGTON COURT HOUSE, OH (Time Warner Cable)

SAGAMORE HILLS TWP.—See CLEVELAND, OH (Time Warner Cable)

SALEM TWP. (CHAMPAIGN COUNTY)—See AMBERLEY (village), OH (Time Warner Cable)

SALEM TWP. (COLUMBIANA COUNTY)—See CLEVELAND, OH (Time Warner Cable)

SALEM TWP. (HIGHLAND COUNTY)—See AMBERLEY (village), OH (Time Warner Cable)

SALEM TWP. (JEFFERSON COUNTY)—See BLOOMINGDALE, OH (Suddenlink Communications)

SALEM TWP. (OTTAWA COUNTY)—See PORT CLINTON, OH (Time Warner Cable)

SALEM TWP. (SHELBY COUNTY)—See AMBERLEY (village), OH (Time Warner Cable)

SALEM TWP. (WARREN COUNTY)—See AMBERLEY (village), OH (Time Warner Cable)

SALEM TWP. (WASHINGTON COUNTY)—See WARNER, OH (Zito Media)

SALEM—Time Warner Cable. Now served by CLEVELAND (formerly Cleveland Heights), OH [OH0006]

SALEM—See NEW MIDDLETOWN, OH (Comcast Cable)

SALEM—See CLEVELAND, OH (Time Warner Cable)

SALESVILLE—See SENECAVILLE, OH (Suddenlink Communications)

SALINE TWP.—See KNOX TWP. (Jefferson County), OH (Suddenlink Communications)

SALINEVILLE—Crystal Broadband Networks

SALISBURY TWP.—See SCIPIO TWP. (Meigs County), OH (Time Warner Cable)

SALT CREEK TWP. (MUSKINGUM COUNTY)—See COLUMBUS, OH (Time Warner Cable)

SALT CREEK TWP.—See MASSILLON, OH (MCTV)

SALT CREEK TWP.—See WOOSTER, OH (MCTV)

SALT CREEK—See COLUMBUS, OH (Time Warner Cable)

SALT LICK TWP.—See CORNING, OH (Zito Media)

SALT ROCK TWP.—See MARION, OH (Time Warner Cable)

SALTCREEK TWP. (PICKAWAY COUNTY)—See OAKLAND, OH (Time Warner Cable)

SANDUSKY TWP. (RICHLAND COUNTY)—See CLEVELAND, OH (Time Warner Cable)

SANDUSKY TWP. (RICHLAND COUNTY)—See COLUMBUS, OH (Time Warner Cable)

SANDUSKY TWP. (SANDUSKY COUNTY)—See PORT CLINTON, OH (Time Warner Cable)

SANDUSKY—Buckeye Cable System Inc. Now served by TOLEDO, OH [OH0004]

SANDUSKY—See TOLEDO, OH (Buckeye Broadband)

SANDY TWP. (STARK COUNTY)—See CLEVELAND, OH (Time Warner Cable)

SANDY TWP. (TUSCARAWAS COUNTY)—See CLEVELAND, OH (Time Warner Cable)

SARAHSVILLE—Formerly served by Cebridge Connections. No longer in operation

SARDINIA—Formerly served by Crystal Broadband Networks. No longer in operation

SARDIS—See HANNIBAL, OH (Crystal Broadband Networks)

SAVANNAH (VILLAGE)—See CLEVELAND, OH (Time Warner Cable)

SAYBROOK TWP. (ASHTABULA COUNTY)—See CLEVELAND, OH (Time Warner Cable)

SCIO—Time Warner Cable

SCIOTO TWP. (PICKAWAY COUNTY)—See COMMERCIAL POINT, OH (Time Warner Cable)

SCIOTO TWP. (ROSS COUNTY)—See CHILLICOTHE, OH (Time Warner Cable)

SCIPIO TWP. (MEIGS COUNTY)—Time Warner Cable

SCIPIO TWP. (SENECA COUNTY)—See TIFFIN, OH (Time Warner Cable)

SCOTT (village)—Formerly served by CableDirect. No longer in operation

SCOTT (VILLAGE)—See TIFFIN, OH (Time Warner Cable)

SCOTT TWP. (BROWN COUNTY)—See AMBERLEY (village), OH (Time Warner Cable)

SCOTT TWP. (SANDUSKY COUNTY)—See TIFFIN, OH (Time Warner Cable)

SEAL TWP.—See CHILLICOTHE, OH (Time Warner Cable)

SEAMAN (village)—Time Warner Cable. Now served by AMBERLEY (village), OH [OH0001]

SEAMAN (VILLAGE)—See AMBERLEY (village), OH (Time Warner Cable)

SEBRING (village)—Time Warner Cable. Now served by CLEVELAND (formerly Cleveland Heights), OH [OH0006]

SEBRING (VILLAGE)—See CLEVELAND, OH (Time Warner Cable)

SENECA TWP. (SENECA COUNTY)—See TIFFIN, OH (Time Warner Cable)

SENECAVILLE—Suddenlink Communications

SEVEN HILLS—See PARMA, OH (Cox Communications)

SEVEN HILLS—See CLEVELAND, OH (Time Warner Cable)

SEVEN MILE (VILLAGE)—See AMBERLEY (village), OH (Time Warner Cable)

SEVEN MILE—See LEBANON, OH (Cincinnati Bell Fioptics TV. This cable system has converted to IPTV)

SEVILLE (VILLAGE)—See CLEVELAND, OH (Time Warner Cable)

SHAKER HEIGHTS—See CLEVELAND, OH (Time Warner Cable)

SHAKER HEIGHTS—See BEREA, OH (WOW! Internet, Cable & Phone)

SHALERSVILLE TWP.—See NELSON TWP., OH (Suddenlink Communications)

SHALERSVILLE TWP.—See CLEVELAND, OH (Time Warner Cable)

SHARON TWP. (FRANKLIN COUNTY)—See COLUMBUS, OH (Time Warner Cable)

SHARON TWP. (MEDINA COUNTY)—See CLEVELAND, OH (Time Warner Cable)

SHARON TWP.—See COLUMBUS, OH (WOW! Internet, Cable & Phone)

Ohio—Cable Community Index

SHARON—See CLEVELAND, PA (Time Warner Cable)

SHARONVILLE (BUTLER COUNTY)—See LEBANON, OH (Cincinnati Bell Fioptics TV. This cable system has converted to IPTV)

SHARONVILLE (BUTLER COUNTY)—See AMBERLEY (village), OH (Time Warner Cable)

SHARONVILLE (HAMILTON COUNTY)—See LEBANON, OH (Cincinnati Bell Fioptics TV. This cable system has converted to IPTV)

SHARONVILLE (HAMILTON COUNTY)—See AMBERLEY (village), OH (Time Warner Cable)

SHARPSVILLE BOROUGH—See CLEVELAND, PA (Time Warner Cable)

SHAWNEE HILLS (VILLAGE)—See COLUMBUS, OH (Time Warner Cable)

SHAWNEE TWP. (ALLEN COUNTY)—See TIFFIN, OH (Time Warner Cable)

SHAWNEE TWP.—See WAPAKONETA CITY, OH (TSC Communications)

SHAWNEE—See CORNING, OH (Zito Media)

SHEFFIELD (VILLAGE)—See CLEVELAND, OH (Time Warner Cable)

SHEFFIELD LAKE—See CLEVELAND, OH (Time Warner Cable)

SHEFFIELD TWP. (ASHTABULA COUNTY)—See CLEVELAND, OH (Time Warner Cable)

SHEFFIELD TWP. (ASHTABULA COUNTY)—See DENMARK TWP., OH (Zito Media)

SHEFFIELD TWP. (LORAIN COUNTY)—See CLEVELAND, OH (Time Warner Cable)

SHELBY—Time Warner Cable. Now served by CLEVELAND (formerly Cleveland Heights), OH [OH0006]

SHELBY—See CLEVELAND, OH (Time Warner Cable)

SHENANGO TWP.—See CLEVELAND, PA (Time Warner Cable)

SHERMAN TWP.—See TIFFIN, OH (Time Warner Cable)

SHERRODSVILLE (VILLAGE)—See CLEVELAND, OH (Time Warner Cable)

SHERWOOD—Shertel Cable. This cable system has converted to IPTV. See SHERWOOD, OH [OH5191]

SHERWOOD—Formerly [OH0365]. This cable system has converted to IPTV

SHILOH (VILLAGE)—See CLEVELAND, OH (Time Warner Cable)

SHREVE (village)—Time Warner Cable. Now served by CLEVELAND (formerly Cleveland Heights), OH [OH0006]

SHREVE (VILLAGE)—See CLEVELAND, OH (Time Warner Cable)

SIDNEY (town)—Time Warner Cable. Now served by AMBERLEY (village), OH [OH0001]

SIDNEY—See AMBERLEY (village), OH (Time Warner Cable)

SILVER GROVE—See LEBANON, KY (Cincinnati Bell Fioptics TV. This cable system has converted to IPTV)

SILVER LAKE (VILLAGE)—See CLEVELAND, OH (Time Warner Cable)

SILVERCREEK TWP.—See AMBERLEY (village), OH (Time Warner Cable)

SILVERTON (VILLAGE)—See LEBANON, OH (Cincinnati Bell Fioptics TV. This cable system has converted to IPTV)

SILVERTON—See AMBERLEY (village), OH (Time Warner Cable)

SMITH TWP. (MAHONING COUNTY)—See CLEVELAND, OH (Time Warner Cable)

SMITHFIELD—Jefferson County Cable Inc

SMITHVILLE—See WOOSTER, OH (MCTV)

SOLON—See CLEVELAND, OH (Time Warner Cable)

SOMERFORD TWP.—See COLUMBUS, OH (Time Warner Cable)

SOMERS TWP.—See AMBERLEY (village), OH (Time Warner Cable)

SOMERSET (village)—Time Warner Cable. Now served by CLEVELAND (formerly Cleveland Heights), OH [OH0006]

SOMERSET (VILLAGE)—See CLEVELAND, OH (Time Warner Cable)

SOMERVILLE (VILLAGE)—See LEBANON, OH (Cincinnati Bell Fioptics TV. This cable system has converted to IPTV)

SOMERVILLE (VILLAGE)—See AMBERLEY (village), OH (Time Warner Cable)

SONORA—See COLUMBUS, OH (Time Warner Cable)

SOUTH AMHERST (VILLAGE)—See CLEVELAND, OH (Time Warner Cable)

SOUTH BLOOMFIELD (VILLAGE)—See COLUMBUS, OH (Time Warner Cable)

SOUTH BLOOMFIELD—See COLUMBUS, OH (Time Warner Cable)

SOUTH CHARLESTON (VILLAGE)—See AMBERLEY (village), OH (Time Warner Cable)

SOUTH EUCLID—See CLEVELAND, OH (Time Warner Cable)

SOUTH EUCLID—See BEREA, OH (WOW! Internet, Cable & Phone)

SOUTH LEBANON (VILLAGE)—See AMBERLEY (village), OH (Time Warner Cable)

SOUTH LEBANON TWP.—See LEBANON, OH (Cincinnati Bell Fioptics TV. This cable system has converted to IPTV)

SOUTH POINT—Armstrong Cable Services. Now served by ZELIENOPLE, PA [PA0053]

SOUTH PYMATUNING TWP.—See CLEVELAND, PA (Time Warner Cable)

SOUTH RUSSELL (VILLAGE)—See CLEVELAND, OH (Time Warner Cable)

SOUTH SALEM—See CHILLICOTHE, OH (Time Warner Cable)

SOUTH SHORE—See PORTSMOUTH, KY (Time Warner Cable)

SOUTH SOLON (VILLAGE)—See AMBERLEY (village), OH (Time Warner Cable)

SOUTH VIENNA (VILLAGE)—See AMBERLEY (village), OH (Time Warner Cable)

SOUTH WEBSTER (SCIOTO COUNTY)—See ASHLEY CORNER, OH (Time Warner Cable)

SOUTH WEBSTER (VILLAGE)—See PORTSMOUTH, OH (Time Warner Cable)

SOUTH ZANESVILLE—See COLUMBUS, OH (Time Warner Cable)

SOUTHGATE—See LEBANON, KY (Cincinnati Bell Fioptics TV. This cable system has converted to IPTV)

SOUTHINGTON TWP.—See CLEVELAND, OH (Time Warner Cable)

SPARTA (VILLAGE)—See COLUMBUS, OH (Time Warner Cable)

SPENCER (VILLAGE)—See CLEVELAND, OH (Time Warner Cable)

SPENCER TWP. (ALLEN COUNTY)—See TIFFIN, OH (Time Warner Cable)

SPENCER TWP. (LUCAS COUNTY)—See TIFFIN, OH (Time Warner Cable)

SPENCER TWP.—See TOLEDO, OH (Buckeye Broadband)

SPENCERVILLE (VILLAGE)—See TIFFIN, OH (Time Warner Cable)

SPRIGG TWP.—See AMBERLEY (village), OH (Time Warner Cable)

SPRING LAKES MOBILE HOME PARK—See CLEVELAND, OH (Time Warner Cable)

SPRING TWP. (CRAWFORD COUNTY)—See CLEVELAND, PA (Time Warner Cable)

SPRING VALLEY (VILLAGE)—See AMBERLEY (village), OH (Time Warner Cable)

SPRING VALLEY TWP.—See AMBERLEY (village), OH (Time Warner Cable)

SPRINGBORO (MONTGOMERY COUNTY)—See LEBANON, OH (Cincinnati Bell Fioptics TV. This cable system has converted to IPTV)

SPRINGBORO (WARREN COUNTY)—See LEBANON, OH (Cincinnati Bell Fioptics TV. This cable system has converted to IPTV)

SPRINGBORO BOROUGH—See CLEVELAND, PA (Time Warner Cable)

SPRINGBORO—See AMBERLEY (village), OH (Time Warner Cable)

SPRINGCREEK TWP.—See AMBERLEY (village), OH (Time Warner Cable)

SPRINGDALE—See LEBANON, OH (Cincinnati Bell Fioptics TV. This cable system has converted to IPTV)

SPRINGDALE—See AMBERLEY (village), OH (Time Warner Cable)

SPRINGFIELD TWP. (CLARK COUNTY)—See AMBERLEY (village), OH (Time Warner Cable)

SPRINGFIELD TWP. (GALLIA COUNTY)—See GALLIPOLIS, OH (Zito Media)

SPRINGFIELD TWP. (HAMILTON COUNTY)—See AMBERLEY (village), OH (Time Warner Cable)

SPRINGFIELD TWP. (JEFFERSON COUNTY)—See BLOOMINGDALE, OH (Suddenlink Communications)

SPRINGFIELD TWP. (LUCAS COUNTY)—See TOLEDO, OH (Buckeye Broadband)

SPRINGFIELD TWP. (LUCAS COUNTY)—See TIFFIN, OH (Time Warner Cable)

SPRINGFIELD TWP. (MUSKINGUM COUNTY)—See COLUMBUS, OH (Time Warner Cable)

SPRINGFIELD TWP. (PORTIONS)—See AMSTERDAM, OH (Crystal Broadband Networks)

SPRINGFIELD TWP. (RICHLAND COUNTY)—See CLEVELAND, OH (Time Warner Cable)

SPRINGFIELD TWP. (ROSS COUNTY)—See CHILLICOTHE, OH (Time Warner Cable)

SPRINGFIELD TWP. (SUMMIT COUNTY)—See CLEVELAND, OH (Time Warner Cable)

SPRINGFIELD TWP.—See LEBANON, IN (Cincinnati Bell Fioptics TV. This cable system has converted to IPTV)

SPRINGFIELD TWP.—See LEBANON, OH (Cincinnati Bell Fioptics TV. This cable system has converted to IPTV)

SPRINGFIELD TWP.—See RIDGEVILLE CORNERS, OH (RTEC Communications)

SPRINGFIELD TWP.—See CLEVELAND, PA (Time Warner Cable)

SPRINGFIELD—Time Warner Cable. Now served by AMBERLEY (village), OH [OH0001]

SPRINGFIELD—See NEW MIDDLETOWN, OH (Comcast Cable)

Cable Community Index—Ohio

SPRINGFIELD—See AMBERLEY (village), OH (Time Warner Cable)

ST. ALBANS TWP. (LICKING COUNTY)—See COLUMBUS, OH (Time Warner Cable)

ST. ALBANS TWP.—See COLUMBUS, OH (Time Warner Cable)

ST. ANTHONY—Formerly served by Wabash Mutual Telephone. No longer in operation

ST. BERNARD (VILLAGE)—See LEBANON, OH (Cincinnati Bell Fioptics TV. This cable system has converted to IPTV)

ST. BERNARD—See AMBERLEY (village), OH (Time Warner Cable)

ST. CLAIR TWP. (COLUMBIANA COUNTY)—See NEW MIDDLETOWN, OH (Comcast Cable)

ST. CLAIR TWP.—See LEBANON, OH (Cincinnati Bell Fioptics TV. This cable system has converted to IPTV)

ST. CLAIR TWP.—See AMBERLEY (village), OH (Time Warner Cable)

ST. CLAIRSVILLE—Comcast Cable. Now served by WHEELING, WV [WV0004]

ST. CLAIRSVILLE—See WEST BELLAIRE, OH (Bellaire Television Cable Co)

ST. HENRY—NKTelco

ST. HENRY—See TIFFIN, OH (Time Warner Cable)

ST. JOE—See WEST BELLAIRE, OH (Bellaire Television Cable Co)

ST. JOSEPH (WILLIAMS COUNTY)—See TIFFIN, OH (Time Warner Cable)

ST. LOUISVILLE—See NEWARK, OH (Time Warner Cable)

ST. MARTIN (VILLAGE)—See AMBERLEY (village), OH (Time Warner Cable)

ST. MARY'S TWP.—See TIFFIN, OH (Time Warner Cable)

ST. MARY'S—Time Warner Cable. Now served by TIFFIN, OH [OH0050]

ST. MARY'S—See TIFFIN, OH (Time Warner Cable)

ST. MARYS TWP.—TSC Communications

ST. MARYS TWP.—See WAPAKONETA CITY, OH (TSC Communications)

ST. MARYS—See WAPAKONETA CITY, OH (TSC Communications)

ST. PARIS (village)—Time Warner Cable. Now served by AMBERLEY (village), OH [OH0001]

ST. PARIS (VILLAGE)—See AMBERLEY (village), OH (Time Warner Cable)

STARR TWP.—See NELSONVILLE, OH (Nelsonville TV Cable)

STAUNTON TWP.—See AMBERLEY (village), OH (Time Warner Cable)

STERLING TWP. (BROWN COUNTY)—See AMBERLEY (village), OH (Time Warner Cable)

STERLING TWP.—See LEBANON, OH (Cincinnati Bell Fioptics TV. This cable system has converted to IPTV)

STERLING—See CLEVELAND, OH (Time Warner Cable)

STEUBENVILLE—Comcast Cable. Now served by WHEELING, WV [WV0004]

STEWART—See BEVERLY, OH (Time Warner Cable)

STEWARTSVILLE—See WEST BELLAIRE, OH (Bellaire Television Cable Co)

STOCKPORT—See BEVERLY, OH (Time Warner Cable)

STOKES TWP. (LOGAN COUNTY)—See TIFFIN, OH (Time Warner Cable)

STONE CREEK VILLAGE—See CLEVELAND, OH (Time Warner Cable)

STONELICK TWP.—See LEBANON, OH (Cincinnati Bell Fioptics TV. This cable system has converted to IPTV)

STONELICK TWP.—See AMBERLEY (village), OH (Time Warner Cable)

STOUTSVILLE (VILLAGE)—See COLUMBUS, OH (Time Warner Cable)

STOW—See CLEVELAND, OH (Time Warner Cable)

STRASBURG (VILLAGE)—See CLEVELAND, OH (Time Warner Cable)

STRATTON—See EMPIRE, OH (Jefferson County Cable Inc)

STREETSBORO—See CLEVELAND, OH (Time Warner Cable)

STRONGSVILLE—See CLEVELAND, OH (Time Warner Cable)

STRONGSVILLE—See BEREA, OH (WOW! Internet, Cable & Phone)

STRUTHERS—Time Warner Cable. Now served by CLEVELAND (formerly Cleveland Heights), OH [OH0006]

STRUTHERS—See CLEVELAND, OH (Time Warner Cable)

STRYKER—See TIFFIN, OH (Time Warner Cable)

SUBURBANS MOTOR HOME PARK—Time Warner Cable

SUFFIELD TWP.—See CLEVELAND, OH (Time Warner Cable)

SUGAR BUSH KNOLLS (VILLAGE)—See CLEVELAND, OH (Time Warner Cable)

SUGAR CREEK TWP. (ALLEN COUNTY)—See TIFFIN, OH (Time Warner Cable)

SUGAR CREEK TWP. (GREENE COUNTY)—See AMBERLEY (village), OH (Time Warner Cable)

SUGAR CREEK TWP. (PUTNAM COUNTY)—See KALIDA, OH (Kalida Telephone Co)

SUGAR CREEK TWP. (PUTNAM COUNTY)—See TIFFIN, OH (Time Warner Cable)

SUGAR CREEK TWP. (STARK COUNTY)—See MASSILLON, OH (MCTV)

SUGAR CREEK TWP. (WAYNE COUNTY)—See WOOSTER, OH (MCTV)

SUGAR CREEK TWP.—See FORT JENNINGS, OH (FJ Communications)

SUGAR GROVE (VILLAGE)—See COLUMBUS, OH (Time Warner Cable)

SUGAR GROVE TWP.—See CLEVELAND, PA (Time Warner Cable)

SUGARCREEK (VILLAGE)—See CLEVELAND, OH (Time Warner Cable)

SULPHUR SPRINGS—See COLUMBUS, OH (Time Warner Cable)

SUMMERFIELD (village)—Formerly served by Almega Cable. No longer in operation

SUMMERFIELD TWP. (MONROE COUNTY)—See TOLEDO, MI (Buckeye Broadband)

SUMMIT TWP. (ERIE COUNTY)—See CLEVELAND, PA (Time Warner Cable)

SUMMIT TWP.—See WOODSFIELD, OH (City of Woodsfield)

SUNBURY (village)—Time Warner Cable. Now served by COLUMBUS, OH [OH0002]

SUNBURY (VILLAGE)—See COLUMBUS, OH (Time Warner Cable)

SUNFISH TWP.—See CHILLICOTHE, OH (Time Warner Cable)

SUPERIOR TWP.—See TIFFIN, OH (Time Warner Cable)

SWAN CREEK TWP.—See TIFFIN, OH (Time Warner Cable)

SWANTON TWP.—See TIFFIN, OH (Time Warner Cable)

SWANTON—See TIFFIN, OH (Time Warner Cable)

SYCAMORE TWP. (HAMILTON COUNTY)—See AMBERLEY (village), OH (Time Warner Cable)

SYCAMORE TWP. (Wyandot County)—Time Warner Cable. Now served by TIFFIN (formerly Fostoria), OH [OH0050]

SYCAMORE TWP. (WYANDOT COUNTY)—See TIFFIN, OH (Time Warner Cable)

SYCAMORE TWP.—See LEBANON, OH (Cincinnati Bell Fioptics TV. This cable system has converted to IPTV)

SYLVANIA TWP. (LUCAS COUNTY)—See TOLEDO, OH (Buckeye Broadband)

SYLVANIA—See TOLEDO, OH (Buckeye Broadband)

SYLVANIA—See COLUMBUS, OH (Time Warner Cable)

SYMMES TWP. (HAMILTON COUNTY)—See AMBERLEY (village), OH (Time Warner Cable)

SYMMES TWP.—See LEBANON, OH (Cincinnati Bell Fioptics TV. This cable system has converted to IPTV)

TALLMADGE—See CLEVELAND, OH (Time Warner Cable)

TARLTON—See OAKLAND, OH (Time Warner Cable)

TATE TWP.—See LEBANON, OH (Cincinnati Bell Fioptics TV. This cable system has converted to IPTV)

TATE TWP.—See AMBERLEY (village), OH (Time Warner Cable)

TAYLOR MILL—See LEBANON, KY (Cincinnati Bell Fioptics TV. This cable system has converted to IPTV)

TAYLOR TWP.—See COLUMBUS, OH (Time Warner Cable)

TAYLORTOWN—See TORONTO, OH (Jefferson County Cable Inc)

TEMPERANCE—See TOLEDO, MI (Buckeye Broadband)

TERRACE PARK (VILLAGE)—See LEBANON, OH (Cincinnati Bell Fioptics TV. This cable system has converted to IPTV)

TERRACE PARK (VILLAGE)—See AMBERLEY (village), OH (Time Warner Cable)

THE PLAINS (VILLAGE)—See COLUMBUS, OH (Time Warner Cable)

THE PLAINS—See NELSONVILLE, OH (Nelsonville TV Cable)

THOMPSON TWP. (GEAUGA COUNTY)—Zito Media

THOMPSON TWP. (SENECA COUNTY)—See TIFFIN, OH (Time Warner Cable)

THORN TWP.—See COLUMBUS, OH (Time Warner Cable)

THORNVILLE (village)—Time Warner Cable. Now served by COLUMBUS, OH [OH0002]

THORNVILLE (VILLAGE)—See COLUMBUS, OH (Time Warner Cable)

THURSTON (VILLAGE)—See COLUMBUS, OH (Time Warner Cable)

TIFFIN TWP. (ADAMS COUNTY)—See AMBERLEY (village), OH (Time Warner Cable)

TIFFIN TWP. (DEFIANCE COUNTY)—See DEFIANCE, OH (Time Warner Cable)

TIFFIN TWP. (DEFIANCE COUNTY)—See TIFFIN, OH (Time Warner Cable)

TIFFIN—See BASCOM, OH (BTC Multimedia)

TIFFIN—Time Warner Cable

TIMBERLAKE (VILLAGE)—See CLEVELAND, OH (Time Warner Cable)

Ohio—Cable Community Index

TIPP CITY—See AMBERLEY (village), OH (Time Warner Cable)

TIRO—See CLEVELAND, OH (Time Warner Cable)

TOLEDO—Formerly served by American Telecasting/WanTV. No longer in operation

TOLEDO—Buckeye Broadband

TOLEDO—See TIFFIN, OH (Time Warner Cable)

TONTOGANY—See TIFFIN, OH (Time Warner Cable)

TORONTO—Jefferson County Cable Inc

TOWNSEND TWP. (HURON COUNTY)—See CLEVELAND, OH (Time Warner Cable)

TOWNSEND TWP. (SANDUSKY COUNTY)—See TIFFIN, OH (Time Warner Cable)

TOWNSEND TWP.—See TOLEDO, OH (Buckeye Broadband)

TREMONT CITY (VILLAGE)—See AMBERLEY (village), OH (Time Warner Cable)

TRENTON TWP.—See COLUMBUS, OH (Time Warner Cable)

TRENTON—See LEBANON, OH (Cincinnati Bell Fioptics TV. This cable system has converted to IPTV)

TRENTON—See AMBERLEY (village), OH (Time Warner Cable)

TRIMBLE—See NELSONVILLE, OH (Nelsonville TV Cable)

TRINWAY—See COLUMBUS, OH (Time Warner Cable)

TROTWOOD—See AMBERLEY (village), OH (Time Warner Cable)

TROY TWP. (DELAWARE COUNTY)—See COLUMBUS, OH (Time Warner Cable)

TROY TWP. (GEAUGA COUNTY)—See NELSON TWP., OH (Suddenlink Communications)

TROY TWP. (RICHLAND COUNTY)—See CLEVELAND, OH (Time Warner Cable)

TROY—Time Warner Cable. Now served by AMBERLEY (village), OH [OH0001]

TROY—See AMBERLEY (village), OH (Time Warner Cable)

TRUMBULL TWP.—See THOMPSON TWP. (Geauga County), OH (Zito Media)

TRURO TWP.—See COLUMBUS, OH (Time Warner Cable)

TUPPERS PLAINS—See BEVERLY, OH (Time Warner Cable)

TURTLE CREEK TWP. (WARREN COUNTY)—See AMBERLEY (village), OH (Time Warner Cable)

TURTLECREEK TWP.—See LEBANON, OH (Cincinnati Bell Fioptics TV. This cable system has converted to IPTV)

TUSCARAWAS (VILLAGE)—See CLEVELAND, OH (Time Warner Cable)

TUSCARAWAS TWP. (STARK COUNTY)—See MASSILLON, OH (MCTV)

TWIN TWP. (DARKE COUNTY)—See AMBERLEY (village), OH (Time Warner Cable)

TWIN TWP. (PREBLE COUNTY)—See AMBERLEY (village), OH (Time Warner Cable)

TWIN TWP. (ROSS COUNTY)—See CHILLICOTHE, OH (Time Warner Cable)

TWINSBURG TWP.—See CLEVELAND, OH (Time Warner Cable)

TWINSBURG—See CLEVELAND, OH (Time Warner Cable)

TYMOCHTEE TWP.—See TIFFIN, OH (Time Warner Cable)

UHRICHSVILLE—See CLEVELAND, OH (Time Warner Cable)

UNION CITY (VILLAGE)—See AMBERLEY (village), OH (Time Warner Cable)

UNION CITY BOROUGH—See CLEVELAND, PA (Time Warner Cable)

UNION CITY—See AMBERLEY (village), IN (Time Warner Cable)

UNION FURNACE—See NELSONVILLE, OH (Nelsonville TV Cable)

UNION TWP. (AUGLAIZE COUNTY)—See WAPAKONETA CITY, OH (TSC Communications)

UNION TWP. (CLERMONT COUNTY)—See LEBANON, OH (Cincinnati Bell Fioptics TV. This cable system has converted to IPTV)

UNION TWP. (CLERMONT COUNTY)—See AMBERLEY (village), OH (Time Warner Cable)

UNION TWP. (CLINTON COUNTY)—See AMBERLEY (village), OH (Time Warner Cable)

UNION TWP. (ERIE COUNTY)—See CLEVELAND, PA (Time Warner Cable)

UNION TWP. (HANCOCK COUNTY)—See TIFFIN, OH (Time Warner Cable)

UNION TWP. (HANCOCK COUNTY)—See BENTON RIDGE, OH (Watch Communications)

UNION TWP. (HIGHLAND COUNTY)—See AMBERLEY (village), OH (Time Warner Cable)

UNION TWP. (KNOX COUNTY)—See COLUMBUS, OH (Time Warner Cable)

UNION TWP. (LICKING COUNTY)—See NEWARK, OH (Time Warner Cable)

UNION TWP. (LOGAN COUNTY)—See COLUMBUS, OH (Time Warner Cable)

UNION TWP. (MADISON COUNTY)—See COLUMBUS, OH (Time Warner Cable)

UNION TWP. (MIAMI COUNTY)—See AMBERLEY (village), OH (Time Warner Cable)

UNION TWP. (MUSKINGUM COUNTY)—See COLUMBUS, OH (Time Warner Cable)

UNION TWP. (PIKE COUNTY)—See JACKSON, OH (Time Warner Cable)

UNION TWP. (PUTNAM COUNTY)—See KALIDA, OH (Kalida Telephone Co)

UNION TWP. (ROSS COUNTY)—See CHILLICOTHE, OH (Time Warner Cable)

UNION TWP. (SCIOTO COUNTY)—See PORTSMOUTH, OH (Time Warner Cable)

UNION TWP. (UNION COUNTY)—See COLUMBUS, OH (Time Warner Cable)

UNION TWP. (VAN WERT COUNTY)—See VAN WERT, OH (Time Warner Cable)

UNION TWP. (WARREN COUNTY)—See LEBANON, OH (Cincinnati Bell Fioptics TV. This cable system has converted to IPTV)

UNION TWP. (WARREN COUNTY)—See AMBERLEY (village), OH (Time Warner Cable)

UNION TWP.—See LEBANON, KY (Cincinnati Bell Fioptics TV. This cable system has converted to IPTV)

UNION—See AMBERLEY (village), OH (Time Warner Cable)

UNIONVILLE CENTER (VILLAGE)—See COLUMBUS, OH (Time Warner Cable)

UNIOPOLIS (VILLAGE)—See TIFFIN, OH (Time Warner Cable)

UNIOPOLIS—See WAPAKONETA CITY, OH (TSC Communications)

UNITY—See NEW MIDDLETOWN, OH (Comcast Cable)

UNIVERSITY HEIGHTS—See CLEVELAND, OH (Time Warner Cable)

UNIVERSITY HEIGHTS—See BEREA, OH (WOW! Internet, Cable & Phone)

UPPER ARLINGTON—See COLUMBUS, OH (Time Warner Cable)

UPPER ARLINGTON—See COLUMBUS, OH (WOW! Internet, Cable & Phone)

UPPER SANDUSKY—Time Warner Cable. Now served by TIFFIN (formerly Fostoria), OH [OH0050]

UPPER SANDUSKY—See TIFFIN, OH (Time Warner Cable)

URBANA TWP.—See AMBERLEY (village), OH (Time Warner Cable)

URBANA—Champaign Telephone Co. This cable system has converted to IPTV. See URBANA, OH [OH5029]

URBANA—Time Warner Cable. Now served by AMBERLEY (village), OH [OH0001]

URBANA—CT Communications. Formerly [OH0443]. This cable system has converted to IPTV

URBANA—See AMBERLEY (village), OH (Time Warner Cable)

URBANCREST (VILLAGE)—See COLUMBUS, OH (Time Warner Cable)

URBANCREST—See COLUMBUS, OH (WOW! Internet, Cable & Phone)

UTICA (VILLAGE)—See COLUMBUS, OH (Time Warner Cable)

VALLEY HI (VILLAGE)—See COLUMBUS, OH (Time Warner Cable)

VALLEY TWP. (GUERNSEY COUNTY)—See SENECAVILLE, OH (Suddenlink Communications)

VALLEY TWP. (SCIOTO COUNTY)—See PORTSMOUTH, OH (Time Warner Cable)

VALLEY VIEW (VILLAGE)—See CLEVELAND, OH (Time Warner Cable)

VALLEY VIEW—See BEREA, OH (WOW! Internet, Cable & Phone)

VALLEYVIEW (VILLAGE)—See COLUMBUS, OH (Time Warner Cable)

VALLEYVIEW—See COLUMBUS, OH (WOW! Internet, Cable & Phone)

VAN BUREN (VILLAGE)—See TIFFIN, OH (Time Warner Cable)

VAN BUREN TWP. (DARKE COUNTY)—See AMBERLEY (village), OH (Time Warner Cable)

VAN BUREN TWP. (HANCOCK COUNTY)—See TIFFIN, OH (Time Warner Cable)

VAN BUREN TWP. (SHELBY COUNTY)—See TIFFIN, OH (Time Warner Cable)

VAN WERT—Time Warner Cable

VANDALIA—Time Warner Cable. Now served by AMBERLEY (village), OH [OH0001]

VANDALIA—See AMBERLEY (village), OH (Time Warner Cable)

VANLUE (VILLAGE)—See TIFFIN, OH (Time Warner Cable)

VENEDOCIA (VILLAGE)—See TIFFIN, OH (Time Warner Cable)

VENICE TWP.—See TIFFIN, OH (Time Warner Cable)

VERMILION TWP.—See CLEVELAND, OH (Time Warner Cable)

VERMILION—See CLEVELAND, OH (Time Warner Cable)

VERNON TWP. (CRAWFORD COUNTY)—See COLUMBUS, OH (Time Warner Cable)

VERNON TWP. (SCIOTO COUNTY)—See PORTSMOUTH, OH (Time Warner Cable)

VERNON TWP. (TRUMBULL COUNTY)—Armstrong Cable Services

VERONA (VILLAGE) (MONTGOMERY COUNTY)—See AMBERLEY (village), OH (Time Warner Cable)

Cable Community Index—Ohio

VERONA (VILLAGE) (PREBLE COUNTY)—See AMBERLEY (village), OH (Time Warner Cable)

VERSAILLES—Time Warner Cable

VICKERY—See TIFFIN, OH (Time Warner Cable)

VIENNA AIR FORCE BASE—See CLEVELAND, OH (Time Warner Cable)

VIENNA TWP.—See CLEVELAND, OH (Time Warner Cable)

VILLA HILLS—See LEBANON, KY (Cincinnati Bell Fioptics TV. This cable system has converted to IPTV)

VINTON (VILLAGE)—See GALLIPOLIS, OH (Zito Media)

VIOLET TWP.—See COLUMBUS, OH (Time Warner Cable)

VIOLET TWP.—See COLUMBUS, OH (WOW! Internet, Cable & Phone)

VIRGINIA TWP.—See NEWARK, OH (Time Warner Cable)

WABASH TWP.—See VERSAILLES, OH (Time Warner Cable)

WADSWORTH TWP.—See CLEVELAND, OH (Time Warner Cable)

WADSWORTH—See CLEVELAND, OH (Time Warner Cable)

WADSWORTH—Wadsworth Cable TV

WAITE HILL (VILLAGE)—See CLEVELAND, OH (Time Warner Cable)

WAKEMAN (VILLAGE)—See CLEVELAND, OH (Time Warner Cable)

WAKEMAN—Time Warner Cable. Now served by CLEVELAND (formerly Cleveland Heights), OH [OH0006]

WAKERMAN TWP.—See CLEVELAND, OH (Time Warner Cable)

WALBRIDGE—See TIFFIN, OH (Time Warner Cable)

WALDO (VILLAGE)—See COLUMBUS, OH (Time Warner Cable)

WALDO TWP.—See COLUMBUS, OH (Time Warner Cable)

WALNUT CREEK TWP.—See CLEVELAND, OH (Time Warner Cable)

WALNUT TWP. (FAIRFIELD COUNTY)—See NEWARK, OH (Time Warner Cable)

WALNUT TWP. (PICKAWAY COUNTY)—See OAKLAND, OH (Time Warner Cable)

WALTON HILLS (VILLAGE)—See CLEVELAND, OH (Time Warner Cable)

WALTON—See LEBANON, KY (Cincinnati Bell Fioptics TV. This cable system has converted to IPTV)

WAPAKONETA CITY—TSC Communications

WAPAKONETA—Time Warner Cable. Now served by TIFFIN, OH [OH0050]

WAPAKONETA—See TIFFIN, OH (Time Warner Cable)

WARD TWP.—See NELSONVILLE, OH (Nelsonville TV Cable)

WARD TWP.—See COLUMBUS, OH (Time Warner Cable)

WARNER—Zito Media

WARREN TWP. (Trumbull County)—Formerly served by Northeast Cable TV. No longer in operation

WARREN TWP. (TRUMBULL COUNTY)—See CLEVELAND, OH (Time Warner Cable)

WARREN—Time Warner Cable. Now served by CLEVELAND (formerly Cleveland Heights), OH [OH0006]

WARREN—See CLEVELAND, OH (Time Warner Cable)

WARRENSVILLE HEIGHTS—See CLEVELAND, OH (Time Warner Cable)

WARRENSVILLE TWP.—See CLEVELAND, OH (Time Warner Cable)

WARSAW—See LEBANON, KY (Cincinnati Bell Fioptics TV. This cable system has converted to IPTV)

WARSAW—See COSHOCTON, OH (Time Warner Cable)

WARWICK TWP.—See CLEVELAND, OH (Time Warner Cable)

WASHINGTON COURT HOUSE—Time Warner Cable

WASHINGTON TWP. (AUGLAIZE COUNTY)—See TIFFIN, OH (Time Warner Cable)

WASHINGTON TWP. (CLERMONT COUNTY)—See AMBERLEY (village), OH (Time Warner Cable)

WASHINGTON TWP. (CLINTON COUNTY)—See AMBERLEY (village), OH (Time Warner Cable)

WASHINGTON TWP. (DARKE COUNTY)—See AMBERLEY (village), OH (Time Warner Cable)

WASHINGTON TWP. (DEFIANCE COUNTY)—See DEFIANCE, OH (Time Warner Cable)

WASHINGTON TWP. (FRANKLIN COUNTY)—See COLUMBUS, OH (Time Warner Cable)

WASHINGTON TWP. (HANCOCK COUNTY)—See TIFFIN, OH (Time Warner Cable)

WASHINGTON TWP. (HARDIN COUNTY)—See SUBURBANS MOTOR HOME PARK, OH (Time Warner Cable)

WASHINGTON TWP. (LICKING COUNTY)—See COLUMBUS, OH (Time Warner Cable)

WASHINGTON TWP. (LUCAS COUNTY)—See TOLEDO, OH (Buckeye Broadband)

WASHINGTON TWP. (MIAMI COUNTY)—See AMBERLEY (village), OH (Time Warner Cable)

WASHINGTON TWP. (MONTGOMERY COUNTY)—See AMBERLEY (village), OH (Time Warner Cable)

WASHINGTON TWP. (MORROW COUNTY)—See COLUMBUS, OH (Time Warner Cable)

WASHINGTON TWP. (MUSKINGUM COUNTY)—See COLUMBUS, OH (Time Warner Cable)

WASHINGTON TWP. (PAULDING COUNTY)—See OTTOVILLE, OH (OTEC Communication Co.)

WASHINGTON TWP. (PICKAWAY COUNTY)—See OAKLAND, OH (Time Warner Cable)

WASHINGTON TWP. (PREBLE COUNTY)—See AMBERLEY (village), OH (Time Warner Cable)

WASHINGTON TWP. (RICHLAND COUNTY)—See CLEVELAND, OH (Time Warner Cable)

WASHINGTON TWP. (SANDUSKY COUNTY)—See TIFFIN, OH (Time Warner Cable)

WASHINGTON TWP. (SCIOTO COUNTY)—See PORTSMOUTH, OH (Time Warner Cable)

WASHINGTON TWP. (SHELBY COUNTY)—See AMBERLEY (village), OH (Time Warner Cable)

WASHINGTON TWP. (STARK COUNTY)—See CLEVELAND, OH (Time Warner Cable)

WASHINGTON TWP. (VAN WERT COUNTY)—See OTTOVILLE, OH (OTEC Communication Co.)

WASHINGTON TWP. (VAN WERT COUNTY)—See TIFFIN, OH (Time Warner Cable)

WASHINGTON TWP. (WOOD COUNTY)—See TIFFIN, OH (Time Warner Cable)

WASHINGTON TWP.—See LEBANON, OH (Cincinnati Bell Fioptics TV. This cable system has converted to IPTV)

WASHINGTON—See TIFFIN, OH (Time Warner Cable)

WASHINGTONVILLE—See NEW MIDDLETOWN, OH (Comcast Cable)

WATERFORD BOROUGH (ERIE COUNTY)—See CLEVELAND, PA (Time Warner Cable)

WATERFORD TWP. (ERIE COUNTY)—See CLEVELAND, PA (Time Warner Cable)

WATERFORD TWP.—See BEVERLY, OH (Time Warner Cable)

WATERLOO TWP.—See ATHENS, OH (Time Warner Cable)

WATERTOWN—See BEVERLY, OH (Time Warner Cable)

WATERVILLE TWP. (LUCAS COUNTY)—See TOLEDO, OH (Buckeye Broadband)

WATERVILLE TWP.—See TIFFIN, OH (Time Warner Cable)

WATERVILLE—Time Warner Cable. Now served by TIFFIN (formerly Fostoria), OH [OH0050]

WATERVILLE—See TOLEDO, OH (Buckeye Broadband)

WATERVILLE—See TIFFIN, OH (Time Warner Cable)

WAUSEON—Time Warner Cable. Now served by TIFFIN, OH [OH0050]

WAUSEON—See TIFFIN, OH (Time Warner Cable)

WAVERLY—Formerly served by Adelphia Communications. Now served by Time Warner Cable, CHILLICOTHE, OH [OH0033]

WAVERLY—See CHILLICOTHE, OH (Time Warner Cable)

WAYNE (VILLAGE)—See TIFFIN, OH (Time Warner Cable)

WAYNE COUNTY (EASTERN PORTION)—See MASSILLON, OH (MCTV)

WAYNE COUNTY (SOUTHEASTERN PORTION)—See WOOSTER, OH (MCTV)

WAYNE LAKES (VILLAGE)—See AMBERLEY (village), OH (Time Warner Cable)

WAYNE TWP. (ASHTABULA COUNTY)—See CLEVELAND, OH (Time Warner Cable)

WAYNE TWP. (AUGLAIZE COUNTY)—See TIFFIN, OH (Time Warner Cable)

WAYNE TWP. (BUTLER COUNTY)—See LEBANON, OH (Cincinnati Bell Fioptics TV. This cable system has converted to IPTV)

WAYNE TWP. (CLERMONT COUNTY)—See AMBERLEY (village), OH (Time Warner Cable)

WAYNE TWP. (FAYETTE COUNTY)—See WASHINGTON COURT HOUSE, OH (Time Warner Cable)

WAYNE TWP. (JEFFERSON COUNTY)—See BLOOMINGDALE, OH (Suddenlink Communications)

WAYNE TWP. (KNOX COUNTY)—See COLUMBUS, OH (Time Warner Cable)

WAYNE TWP. (MUSKINGUM COUNTY)—See COLUMBUS, OH (Time Warner Cable)

WAYNE TWP. (PICKAWAY COUNTY)—See COLUMBUS, OH (Time Warner Cable)

WAYNE TWP. (RANDOLPH COUNTY)—See AMBERLEY (village), IN (Time Warner Cable)

WAYNE TWP. (WARREN COUNTY)—See LEBANON, OH (Cincinnati Bell Fioptics TV. This cable system has converted to IPTV)

Ohio—Cable Community Index

WAYNE TWP. (WARREN COUNTY)—See AMBERLEY (village), OH (Time Warner Cable)

WAYNE TWP. (WAYNE COUNTY)—See WOOSTER, OH (MCTV)

WAYNE TWP.—See VERSAILLES, OH (Time Warner Cable)

WAYNESBURG (VILLAGE)—See CLEVELAND, OH (Time Warner Cable)

WAYNESFIELD (village)—Time Warner Cable. Now served by TIFFIN, OH [OH0050]

WAYNESFIELD (VILLAGE)—See TIFFIN, OH (Time Warner Cable)

WAYNESVILLE (VILLAGE)—See LEBANON, OH (Cincinnati Bell Fioptics TV. This cable system has converted to IPTV)

WAYNESVILLE (VILLAGE)—See AMBERLEY (village), OH (Time Warner Cable)

WEATHERSFIELD TWP.—Formerly served by Northeast Cable TV. No longer in operation

WEATHERSFIELD TWP.—See CLEVELAND, OH (Time Warner Cable)

WEBSTER TWP.—See TIFFIN, OH (Time Warner Cable)

WELLER TWP.—See CLEVELAND, OH (Time Warner Cable)

WELLINGTON (VILLAGE)—See WELLINGTON, OH (GLW Broadband)

WELLINGTON TWP.—See WELLINGTON, OH (GLW Broadband)

WELLINGTON—GLW Broadband

WELLSTON—See JACKSON, OH (Time Warner Cable)

WELLSVILLE—See NEW MIDDLETOWN, OH (Comcast Cable)

WESLEYVILLE BOROUGH—See CLEVELAND, PA (Time Warner Cable)

WEST ALEXANDRIA (VILLAGE)—See AMBERLEY (village), OH (Time Warner Cable)

WEST BELLAIRE—Bellaire Television Cable Co

WEST CARROLLTON—See AMBERLEY (village), OH (Time Warner Cable)

WEST CHESTER TWP. (BUTLER COUNTY)—See AMBERLEY (village), OH (Time Warner Cable)

WEST CHESTER TWP.—See LEBANON, OH (Cincinnati Bell Fioptics TV. This cable system has converted to IPTV)

WEST COLLEGE CORNER (TOWN)—See AMBERLEY (village), IN (Time Warner Cable)

WEST ELKTON (VILLAGE)—See AMBERLEY (village), OH (Time Warner Cable)

WEST FARMINGTON (VILLAGE)—See CLEVELAND, OH (Time Warner Cable)

WEST HARRISON (DEARBORN COUNTY)—See LEBANON, IN (Cincinnati Bell Fioptics TV. This cable system has converted to IPTV)

WEST HARRISON (FRANKLIN COUNTY)—See LEBANON, IN (Cincinnati Bell Fioptics TV. This cable system has converted to IPTV)

WEST HARRISON (TOWN)—See AMBERLEY (village), IN (Time Warner Cable)

WEST JEFFERSON (VILLAGE)—See COLUMBUS, OH (Time Warner Cable)

WEST LAFAYETTE TWP.—Time Warner Cable. Now served by COLUMBUS, OH [OH0002]

WEST LAFAYETTE TWP.—See COLUMBUS, OH (Time Warner Cable)

WEST LEIPSIC (VILLAGE)—See LEIPSIC, OH (Orwell Communications)

WEST LIBERTY (VILLAGE)—See AMBERLEY (village), OH (Time Warner Cable)

WEST LIBERTY—See URBANA, OH (CT Communications. Formerly [OH0443]. This cable system has converted to IPTV)

WEST MANCHESTER (VILLAGE)—See AMBERLEY (village), OH (Time Warner Cable)

WEST MANSFIELD (village)—Time Warner Cable. Now served by COLUMBUS, OH [OH0002]

WEST MANSFIELD (VILLAGE)—See COLUMBUS, OH (Time Warner Cable)

WEST MIDDLESEX BOROUGH—See CLEVELAND, PA (Time Warner Cable)

WEST MILLGROVE (VILLAGE)—See TIFFIN, OH (Time Warner Cable)

WEST MILTON (VILLAGE)—See AMBERLEY (village), OH (Time Warner Cable)

WEST RUSHVILLE (VILLAGE)—See COLUMBUS, OH (Time Warner Cable)

WEST SALEM (VILLAGE)—See CLEVELAND, OH (Time Warner Cable)

WEST SALEM TWP.—See CLEVELAND, PA (Time Warner Cable)

WEST TWP.—See CLEVELAND, OH (Time Warner Cable)

WEST UNION (VILLAGE)—See AMBERLEY (village), OH (Time Warner Cable)

WEST UNION—Time Warner Cable. Now served by AMBERLEY (village), OH [OH0001]

WEST UNITY—See TIFFIN, OH (Time Warner Cable)

WESTERVILLE (DELAWARE COUNTY)—See COLUMBUS, OH (Time Warner Cable)

WESTERVILLE (FRANKLIN COUNTY)—See COLUMBUS, OH (Time Warner Cable)

WESTERVILLE—See COLUMBUS, OH (WOW! Internet, Cable & Phone)

WESTFIELD CENTER—See CLEVELAND, OH (Time Warner Cable)

WESTFIELD TWP.—See CLEVELAND, OH (Time Warner Cable)

WESTLAKE—See CLEVELAND, OH (Time Warner Cable)

WESTLAKE—See BEREA, OH (WOW! Internet, Cable & Phone)

WESTLAND TWP.—See NEWARK, OH (Time Warner Cable)

WESTON (VILLAGE)—See TIFFIN, OH (Time Warner Cable)

WESTON TWP.—See TIFFIN, OH (Time Warner Cable)

WHARTON (VILLAGE)—See COLUMBUS, OH (Time Warner Cable)

WHEATLAND BOROUGH—See CLEVELAND, PA (Time Warner Cable)

WHEELING TWP. (GUERNSEY COUNTY)—See CAMBRIDGE, OH (Time Warner Cable)

WHETSTONE TWP.—See COLUMBUS, OH (Time Warner Cable)

WHIPPLE—See WARNER, OH (Zito Media)

WHITEFORD TWP.—See TOLEDO, MI (Buckeye Broadband)

WHITEFORD—See TOLEDO, MI (Buckeye Broadband)

WHITEHALL—See COLUMBUS, OH (Time Warner Cable)

WHITEHALL—See COLUMBUS, OH (WOW! Internet, Cable & Phone)

WHITEHOUSE—See TIFFIN, OH (Time Warner Cable)

WHITEWATER TWP.—See LEBANON, IN (Cincinnati Bell Fioptics TV. This cable system has converted to IPTV)

WHITEWATER TWP.—See LEBANON, OH (Cincinnati Bell Fioptics TV. This cable system has converted to IPTV)

WHITEWATER TWP.—See AMBERLEY (village), OH (Time Warner Cable)

WICKLIFFE—See CLEVELAND, OH (Time Warner Cable)

WILDER—See LEBANON, KY (Cincinnati Bell Fioptics TV. This cable system has converted to IPTV)

WILLARD—Time Warner Cable. Now served by CLEVELAND (formerly Cleveland Heights), OH [OH0006]

WILLARD—See CLEVELAND, OH (Time Warner Cable)

WILLIAMSBURG (VILLAGE)—See LEBANON, OH (Cincinnati Bell Fioptics TV. This cable system has converted to IPTV)

WILLIAMSBURG (VILLAGE)—See AMBERLEY (village), OH (Time Warner Cable)

WILLIAMSBURG TWP.—See LEBANON, OH (Cincinnati Bell Fioptics TV. This cable system has converted to IPTV)

WILLIAMSBURG TWP.—See AMBERLEY (village), OH (Time Warner Cable)

WILLIAMSFIELD—See VERNON TWP. (Trumbull County), OH (Armstrong Cable Services)

WILLIAMSPORT—See NEW HOLLAND, OH (Time Warner Cable)

WILLISTON—See TIFFIN, OH (Time Warner Cable)

WILLOUGHBY (VILLAGE)—See CLEVELAND, OH (Time Warner Cable)

WILLOUGHBY HILLS—See CLEVELAND, OH (Time Warner Cable)

WILLOWICK—See CLEVELAND, OH (Time Warner Cable)

WILLOWS MOBILE HOME PARK—Time Warner Cable. Now served by CLEVELAND (formerly Cleveland Heights), OH [OH0006]

WILLOWS MOBILE HOME PARK—See CLEVELAND, OH (Time Warner Cable)

WILLS TWP.—See SENECAVILLE, OH (Suddenlink Communications)

WILLSHIRE (VILLAGE)—See TIFFIN, OH (Time Warner Cable)

WILMINGTON TWP.—See CLEVELAND, PA (Time Warner Cable)

WILMINGTON—Time Warner Cable. Now served by AMBERLEY (village), OH [OH0001]

WILMINGTON—See AMBERLEY (village), OH (Time Warner Cable)

WILMOT (VILLAGE)—See CLEVELAND, OH (Time Warner Cable)

WINCHESTER (VILLAGE)—See AMBERLEY (village), OH (Time Warner Cable)

WINCHESTER TWP.—See AMBERLEY (village), OH (Time Warner Cable)

WINDHAM (PORTAGE COUNTY)—See NELSON TWP., OH (Suddenlink Communications)

WINDHAM (VILLAGE)—See CLEVELAND, OH (Time Warner Cable)

WINDHAM TWP.—See NELSON TWP., OH (Suddenlink Communications)

WINDHAM TWP.—See CLEVELAND, OH (Time Warner Cable)

WINDSOR TWP. (MORGAN COUNTY)—See BEVERLY, OH (Time Warner Cable)

WINDSOR—See ORWELL, OH (Orwell Communications)

WINDSOR—See THOMPSON TWP. (Geauga County), OH (Zito Media)

WINESBURG—Formerly served by National Cable Inc. No longer in operation

WINONA—See CLEVELAND, OH (Time Warner Cable)

Cable Community Index—Oklahoma

WOODINGTON (VILLAGE)—See AMBERLEY (village), OH (Time Warner Cable)

WOODLAWN (VILLAGE)—See LEBANON, OH (Cincinnati Bell Fioptics TV. This cable system has converted to IPTV)

WOODLAWN (VILLAGE)—See AMBERLEY (village), OH (Time Warner Cable)

WOODLAWN—See LEBANON, KY (Cincinnati Bell Fioptics TV. This cable system has converted to IPTV)

WOODMERE (VILLAGE)—See CLEVELAND, OH (Time Warner Cable)

WOODSFIELD—City of Woodsfield

WOODSTOCK (VILLAGE)—See AMBERLEY (village), OH (Time Warner Cable)

WOODVILLE TWP.—See TIFFIN, OH (Time Warner Cable)

WOOSTER TWP. (WAYNE COUNTY)—See WOOSTER, OH (MCTV)

WOOSTER—MCTV

WORTHINGTON TWP.—See CLEVELAND, OH (Time Warner Cable)

WORTHINGTON—See COLUMBUS, OH (Time Warner Cable)

WORTHINGTON—See COLUMBUS, OH (WOW! Internet, Cable & Phone)

WREN (VILLAGE)—See TIFFIN, OH (Time Warner Cable)

WRIGHT-PATTERSON AFB—See AMBERLEY (village), OH (Time Warner Cable)

WYOMING—See LEBANON, OH (Cincinnati Bell Fioptics TV. This cable system has converted to IPTV)

WYOMING—See AMBERLEY (village), OH (Time Warner Cable)

XENIA TWP.—See AMBERLEY (village), OH (Time Warner Cable)

XENIA—See AMBERLEY (village), OH (Time Warner Cable)

YANKEE LAKE (VILLAGE)—See CLEVELAND, OH (Time Warner Cable)

YELLOW CREEK—See NEW MIDDLETOWN, OH (Comcast Cable)

YELLOW SPRINGS (VILLAGE)—See AMBERLEY (village), OH (Time Warner Cable)

YELLOW SPRINGS—Time Warner Cable. Now served by AMBERLEY (village), OH [OH0001]

YORK TWP. (FULTON COUNTY)—See TIFFIN, OH (Time Warner Cable)

YORK TWP. (SANDUSKY COUNTY)—See TIFFIN, OH (Time Warner Cable)

YORK TWP.—See NELSONVILLE, OH (Nelsonville TV Cable)

YORK—See TIFFIN, OH (Time Warner Cable)

YORKSHIRE—See VERSAILLES, OH (Time Warner Cable)

YOUNGSTOWN—Formerly served by Northeast Cable TV. No longer in operation

YOUNGSTOWN—Formerly served by Sprint Corp. No longer in operation

YOUNGSTOWN—Time Warner Cable. Now served by CLEVELAND (formerly Cleveland Heights), OH [OH0006]

YOUNGSTOWN—See CLEVELAND, OH (Time Warner Cable)

ZALESKI—See JACKSON, OH (Time Warner Cable)

ZANE TWP. (LOGAN COUNTY)—See COLUMBUS, OH (Time Warner Cable)

ZANESFIELD (VILLAGE)—See TIFFIN, OH (Time Warner Cable)

ZANESVILLE—Time Warner Cable. Now served by COLUMBUS, OH [OH0002]

ZANESVILLE—See COLUMBUS, OH (Time Warner Cable)

ZOAR (VILLAGE)—See CLEVELAND, OH (Time Warner Cable)

OKLAHOMA

ACHILLE—Vyve Broadband

ADA—Cable One

ADAIR—Formerly served by Allegiance Communications. No longer in operation

ADAMS—See GUYMON, OK (PTCI)

AFTON—See KETCHUM, OK (Vyve Broadband)

AGRA—Formerly served by Allegiance Communications. No longer in operation

ALDERSON—See McALESTER, OK (Vyve Broadband)

ALEX—Southern Plains Cable

ALINE (town)—Formerly served by Blue Sky Cable LLC. No longer in operation

ALINE—See KINGFISHER, OK (Pioneer Telephone Coop. Formerly [OK0800]. This cable system has converted to IPTV)

ALLEN (town)—Formerly served by Allegiance Communications. No longer in operation

ALTUS AFB—See ALTUS, OK (Cable One)

ALTUS—Cable One

ALVA—Suddenlink Communications

AMES—Pioneer Telephone Coop. This cable system has converted to IPTV. Now served by KINGFISHER, OK [OK5074]

AMES—See KINGFISHER, OK (Pioneer Telephone Coop. Formerly [OK0800]. This cable system has converted to IPTV)

ANADARKO—Suddenlink Communications

ANTLERS—Alliance Communications

APACHE—See KINGFISHER, OK (Pioneer Telephone Coop. Formerly [OK0800]. This cable system has converted to IPTV)

APACHE—Southern Plains Cable

ARAPAHO—Formerly served by Full Circle Communications. No longer in operation

ARDMORE—Cable One

ARMSTRONG—See DURANT, OK (Vyve Broadband)

ARNETT—Pioneer Telephone Coop. This cable system has converted to IPTV. Now served by KINGFISHER, OK [OK5074]

ARNETT—See KINGFISHER, OK (Pioneer Telephone Coop. Formerly [OK0800]. This cable system has converted to IPTV)

ARPELAR—Vyve Broadband

ASHER—Formerly served by CableDirect. No longer in operation

ATOKA—Formerly served by CommuniComm Services. Now served by Vyve Broadband, COALGATE, OK [OK0120]

ATOKA—See COALGATE, OK (Vyve Broadband)

AVANT—Community Cable & Broadband

BALKO—See GUYMON, OK (PTCI)

BARNSDALL—Community Cable & Broadband. Now served by SKIATOOK, OK [OK0065]

BARNSDALL—See SKIATOOK, OK (Community Cable & Broadband)

BARTLESVILLE—Cable One

BEAVER—PTCI. This cable system has converted to IPTV. Now served by GUYMON, OK [OK5005]

BEAVER—See GUYMON, OK (PTCI)

BECKHAM COUNTY (PORTIONS)—See ELK CITY, OK (Cable One)

BEGGS—Formerly served by Allegiance Communications. No longer in operation

BENNINGTON—Formerly served by Allegiance Communications. No longer in operation

BERNICE—See KETCHUM, OK (Vyve Broadband)

BESSIE—Formerly served by Cebridge Connections. No longer in operation

BETHANY—See OKLAHOMA CITY, OK (Cox Communications)

BETHEL ACRES—See SHAWNEE, OK (Vyve Broadband)

BILLINGS—Formerly served by Cebridge Connections. No longer in operation

BINGER—Formerly served by Cable West. No longer in operation

BIXBY—See TULSA, OK (Cox Communications)

BLACKWELL—Get Real Cable

BLAIR—Formerly served by LakeView Cable. No longer in operation

BLAIR—See ALTUS, OK (Cable One)

BLANCHARD—Pioneer Telephone Coop. This cable system has converted to IPTV. Now served by KINGFISHER, OK [OK5074]

BLANCHARD—See KINGFISHER, OK (Pioneer Telephone Coop. Formerly [OK0800]. This cable system has converted to IPTV)

BLANCHARD—See PURCELL, OK (Suddenlink Communications)

BOISE CITY—PTCI. This cable system has converted to IPTV. Now served by GUYMON, OK [OK5005]

BOISE CITY—See GUYMON, OK (PTCI)

BOKCHITO—See DURANT, OK (Vyve Broadband)

BOOKER—See GUYMON, TX (PTCI)

BOSHOKE—Formerly served by Cebridge Connections. No longer in operation

BOSWELL—Formerly served by Allegiance Communications. No longer in operation

BOYNTON—Formerly served by Allegiance Communications. No longer in operation

BRADLEY—See KINGFISHER, OK (Pioneer Telephone Coop. Formerly [OK0800]. This cable system has converted to IPTV)

BRAGGS—Vyve Broadband

BRECKINRIDGE—Formerly served by Cebridge Connections. No longer in operation

BRISTOW—Vyve Broadband

BROKEN ARROW—See TULSA, OK (Cox Communications)

BROKEN BOW—Broken Bow TV Cable Co. Inc

BRYAN COUNTY (PORTIONS)—See DURANT, OK (Vyve Broadband)

BRYAN'S CORNER—See GUYMON, OK (PTCI)

BUFFALO—Pioneer Telephone Coop. This cable system has converted to IPTV. Now served by KINGFISHER, OK [OK5074]

BUFFALO—See KINGFISHER, OK (Pioneer Telephone Coop. Formerly [OK0800]. This cable system has converted to IPTV)

Oklahoma—Cable Community Index

BUNCOMBE CREEK—See DURANT, OK (Vyve Broadband)

BURNS FLAT—Formerly served by Full Circle Communications. No longer in operation

BUTLER—Formerly served by Basic Cable Services Inc. No longer in operation

BYARS—Formerly served by Cebridge Connections. No longer in operation

BYNG—See ADA, OK (Cable One)

CACHE—See PECAN VALLEY, OK (Vyve Broadband)

CADDO—See DURANT, OK (Vyve Broadband)

CALERA—See DURANT, OK (Vyve Broadband)

CALUMET—Pioneer Telephone Coop. This cable system has converted to IPTV. Now served by KINGFISHER, OK [OK5074]

CALUMET—See KINGFISHER, OK (Pioneer Telephone Coop. Formerly [OK0800]. This cable system has converted to IPTV.

CALVIN—Formerly served by Allegiance Communications. No longer in operation

CAMARGO—Formerly served by Cebridge Connections. No longer in operation

CAMERON—Formerly served by Allegiance Communications. No longer in operation

CANADIAN COUNTY (PORTIONS)—See OKLAHOMA CITY, OK (Cox Communications)

CANADIAN—Lakeland Cable TV Inc

CANEY—Formerly served by Allegiance Communications. No longer in operation

CANTON—Formerly served by Blue Sky Cable LLC. No longer in operation

CANTON—See KINGFISHER, OK (Pioneer Telephone Coop. Formerly [OK0800]. This cable system has converted to IPTV.

CANUTE—Formerly served by Full Circle Communications. No longer in operation

CARMEN—Pioneer Telephone Coop. This cable system has converted to IPTV. Now served by KINGFISHER, OK [OK5074]

CARMEN—See KINGFISHER, OK (Pioneer Telephone Coop. Formerly [OK0800]. This cable system has converted to IPTV.

CARNEGIE—Carnegie Cable

CARNEY—Formerly served by Allegiance Communications. No longer in operation

CARTER COUNTY—See ARDMORE, OK (Cable One)

CARTER—Formerly served by CableDirect. No longer in operation

CARTER—See KINGFISHER, OK (Pioneer Telephone Coop. Formerly [OK0800]. This cable system has converted to IPTV.

CARTWRIGHT—See DURANT, OK (Vyve Broadband)

CASHION—Formerly served by Cebridge Connections. No longer in operation

CATOOSA—Formerly served by Summit Digital. No longer in operation

CATOOSA—See TULSA, OK (Cox Communications)

CEDAR LAKE—See HINTON, OK (Hinton CATV Co)

CEMENT—Southern Plains Cable

CHANDLER—Vyve Broadband

CHATTANOOGA—Formerly served by Southern Plains Cable. No longer in operation

CHECOTAH—See EUFAULA, OK (Vyve Broadband)

CHELSEA—Formerly served by Charter Communications. Now served by Allegiance Communications, KETCHUM, OK [OK0179]

CHELSEA—See KETCHUM, OK (Vyve Broadband)

CHEROKEE—Formerly served by Alliance Communications Network. No longer in operation

CHESTER—See KINGFISHER, OK (Pioneer Telephone Coop. Formerly [OK0800]. This cable system has converted to IPTV.

CHEYENNE—James Mogg TV

CHICKASHA—Suddenlink Communications

CHICKEN CREEK—Formerly served by Eagle Media. No longer in operation

CHOCTAW COUNTY (PORTIONS)—See HUGO, OK (Suddenlink Communications)

CHOCTAW—See OKLAHOMA CITY, OK (Cox Communications)

CHOUTEAU—Formerly served by BCI Broadband. Now served by Allegiance Communications, SALINA, OK [OK0071]

CHOUTEAU—See SALINA, OK (Vyve Broadband)

CLAREMORE—Formerly served by Zoom Media. No longer in operation

CLAREMORE—See TULSA, OK (Cox Communications)

CLAYTON—Formerly served by Allegiance Communications. No longer in operation

CLAYTON—Oklahoma Western Telephone Co

CLEO SPRINGS—Formerly served by Blue Sky Cable LLC. No longer in operation

CLEO SPRINGS—See KINGFISHER, OK (Pioneer Telephone Coop. Formerly [OK0800]. This cable system has converted to IPTV.

CLEVELAND COUNTY (PORTIONS)—See OKLAHOMA CITY, OK (Cox Communications)

CLEVELAND COUNTY (PORTIONS)—See PURCELL, OK (Suddenlink Communications)

CLEVELAND—See MANNFORD, OK (Cim Tel Cable Inc)

CLINTON—See ELK CITY, OK (Cable One)

COALGATE—Vyve Broadband

COLBERT—Formerly served by Mediastream. No longer in operation

COLBERT—See DURANT, OK (Vyve Broadband)

COLCORD—Formerly served by Allegiance Communications. No longer in operation

COLLINSVILLE—Community Cable & Broadband. Now served by SKIATOOK, OK [OK0065]

COLONY—See HINTON, OK (Hinton CATV Co)

COMANCHE (eastern portions)—Formerly served by Vyve Broadband. No longer in operation

COMANCHE COUNTY—See LAWTON (village), OK (Fidelity Communications)

COMANCHE—Pioneer. This cable system has converted to IPTV. Now served by TEMPLE, OK [OK5051]

COMMERCE—See MIAMI, OK (Cable One)

COOKSON—Formerly served by Eagle Media. No longer in operation

COPAN—Community Cable & Broadband

CORDELL—See ELK CITY, OK (Cable One)

CORN—Formerly served by Cable West. No longer in operation

CORNISH—See HEALDTON, OK (Suddenlink Communications)

COTTONWOOD—See COALGATE, OK (Vyve Broadband)

COVINGTON—Pioneer Telephone Coop. This cable system has converted to IPTV. Now served by KINGFISHER, OK [OK5074]

COVINGTON—See KINGFISHER, OK (Pioneer Telephone Coop. Formerly [OK0800]. This cable system has converted to IPTV.

COWETA—See TULSA, OK (Cox Communications)

COYLE—See LANGSTON, OK (Vyve Broadband)

CRAIG COUNTY—See VINITA, OK (Cable One)

CREEK COUNTY (PORTIONS)—See TULSA, OK (Cox Communications)

CRESCENT—Formerly served by Suddenlink Communications. No longer in operation

CRESCENT—See KINGFISHER, OK (Pioneer Telephone Coop. Formerly [OK0800]. This cable system has converted to IPTV.

CROMWELL—Vyve Broadband

CROWDER—Lakeland Cable TV Inc

CUSHING—Suddenlink Communications

CUSTER CITY—Pioneer Telephone Coop. This cable system has converted to IPTV. Now served by KINGFISHER, OK [OK5074]

CUSTER CITY—See KINGFISHER, OK (Pioneer Telephone Coop. Formerly [OK0800]. This cable system has converted to IPTV.

CYRIL—Formerly served by Alliance Communications Network. No longer in operation

CYRIL—See CEMENT, OK (Southern Plains Cable)

DACOMA—Pioneer Telephone Coop. This cable system has converted to IPTV. Now served by KINGFISHER, OK [OK5074]

DACOMA—See KINGFISHER, OK (Pioneer Telephone Coop. Formerly [OK0800]. This cable system has converted to IPTV.

DALE—See SHAWNEE, OK (Vyve Broadband)

DAVENPORT—Vi-Tel LLC

DAVIDSON—Formerly served by CableDirect. No longer in operation

DAVIS—See ADA, OK (Cable One)

DEER CREEK—Formerly served by CableDirect. No longer in operation

DEER CREEK—See KINGFISHER, OK (Pioneer Telephone Coop. Formerly [OK0800]. This cable system has converted to IPTV.

DEL CITY—See OKLAHOMA CITY, OK (Cox Communications)

DELAWARE COUNTY (NORTHERN PORTION)—See GROVE, OK (Suddenlink Communications)

Cable Community Index—Oklahoma

DELAWARE—Formerly served by Allegiance Communications. No longer in operation

DEPEW—Vyve Broadband

DEWAR—See HENRYETTA, OK (Suddenlink Communications)

DEWEY—See BARTLESVILLE, OK (Cable One)

DIBBLE—See KINGFISHER, OK (Pioneer Telephone Coop. Formerly [OK0800]. This cable system has converted to IPTV)

DICKSON—See ARDMORE, OK (Cable One)

DILL CITY—Formerly served by Cable West. No longer in operation

DISNEY—Omni III Cable TV Inc

DOUGLAS—See KINGFISHER, OK (Pioneer Telephone Coop. Formerly [OK0800]. This cable system has converted to IPTV)

DOVER—Pioneer Telephone Coop. This cable system has converted to IPTV. Now served by KINGFISHER, OK [OK5074]

DOVER—See KINGFISHER, OK (Pioneer Telephone Coop. Formerly [OK0800]. This cable system has converted to IPTV)

DRUMMOND—Pioneer Telephone Coop. This cable system has converted to IPTV. Now served by KINGFISHER, OK [OK5074]

DRUMMOND—See KINGFISHER, OK (Pioneer Telephone Coop. Formerly [OK0800]. This cable system has converted to IPTV)

DRUMRIGHT—Suddenlink Communications

DUKE—Formerly served by CableDirect. No longer in operation

DUNCAN—Cable One

DURANT—Vyve Broadband

DUSTIN—Formerly served by Allegiance Communications. No longer in operation

EAGLETOWN—See BROKEN BOW, OK (Broken Bow TV Cable Co. Inc)

EAKLY—Hinton CATV Co. Now served by HINTON, OK [OK0140]

EAKLY—See HINTON, OK (Hinton CATV Co)

EARLSBORO—See SHAWNEE, OK (Vyve Broadband)

EDMOND—See OKLAHOMA CITY, OK (Cox Communications)

EL RENO—See OKLAHOMA CITY, OK (Cox Communications)

ELDORADO—Formerly served by Cable West. No longer in operation

ELGIN—See CEMENT, OK (Southern Plains Cable)

ELK CITY—Cable One

ELK CREEK—Formerly served by Eagle Media. No longer in operation

ENID—Suddenlink Communications

ERICK—Reach Broadband

ERIN SPRINGS—See LINDSAY, OK (Suddenlink Communications)

EUFAULA—Vyve Broadband

FAIRFAX—Cim Tel Cable Inc. Now served by MANNFORD, OK [OK0296]

FAIRFAX—See MANNFORD, OK (Cim Tel Cable Inc)

FAIRLAND—See KETCHUM, OK (Vyve Broadband)

FAIRVIEW—Suddenlink Communications

FARGO—Pioneer Telephone Coop. This cable system has converted to IPTV. Now served by KINGFISHER, OK [OK5074]

FARGO—See KINGFISHER, OK (Pioneer Telephone Coop. Formerly [OK0800]. This cable system has converted to IPTV)

FAY—See KINGFISHER, OK (Pioneer Telephone Coop. Formerly [OK0800]. This cable system has converted to IPTV)

FELT—See GUYMON, OK (PTCI)

FLETCHER—Formerly served by Reach Broadband. No longer in operation

FLETCHER—See CEMENT, OK (Southern Plains Cable)

FLORIS—See GUYMON, OK (PTCI)

FOREST PARK—See OKLAHOMA CITY, OK (Cox Communications)

FORGAN—See GUYMON, OK (PTCI)

FORT COBB—Cable West

FORT GIBSON—Vyve Broadband

FORT SILL—Suddenlink Communications

FORT SUPPLY—Formerly served by CableDirect. No longer in operation

FORT SUPPLY—See KINGFISHER, OK (Pioneer Telephone Coop. Formerly [OK0800]. This cable system has converted to IPTV)

FRANCIS—See ADA, OK (Cable One)

FREDERICK—Cable One. Now served by ALTUS, OK [OK0017]

FREDERICK—See ALTUS, OK (Cable One)

FREEDOM—Formerly served by Pioneer Telephone Coop. No longer in operation

FREEDOM—See KINGFISHER, OK (Pioneer Telephone Coop. Formerly [OK0800]. This cable system has converted to IPTV)

GAGE—See KINGFISHER, OK (Pioneer Telephone Coop. Formerly [OK0800]. This cable system has converted to IPTV)

GANS—Formerly served by Allegiance Communications. No longer in operation

GARBER—Formerly served by Longview Communications. No longer in operation

GARBER—See KINGFISHER, OK (Pioneer Telephone Coop. Formerly [OK0800]. This cable system has converted to IPTV)

GARFIELD COUNTY—See ENID, OK (Suddenlink Communications)

GARVIN COUNTY (UNINCORPORATED AREAS)—See PAULS VALLEY, OK (Suddenlink Communications)

GATE—See GUYMON, OK (PTCI)

GEARY—Formerly served by Cebridge Connections. No longer in operation

GEARY—See KINGFISHER, OK (Pioneer Telephone Coop. Formerly [OK0800]. This cable system has converted to IPTV)

GERONIMO—Formerly served by CableDirect. No longer in operation

GERONIMO—Vyve Broadband

GLENCOE—Formerly served by Allegiance Communications. No longer in operation

GLENPOOL (southern portion)—Formerly served by Titan Broadband Services. No longer in operation

GLENPOOL—See TULSA, OK (Cox Communications)

GOLTRY—Formerly served by Cebridge Connections. No longer in operation

GOODWELL—See GUYMON, OK (PTCI)

GOODWELL—Vyve Broadband

GORE—Vyve Broadband

GOTEBO—Formerly served by Basic Cable Services Inc. No longer in operation

GOULD—See KINGFISHER, OK (Pioneer Telephone Coop. Formerly [OK0800]. This cable system has converted to IPTV)

GRACEMONT—Formerly served by Cable West. No longer in operation

GRADY COUNTY (PORTIONS)—See CHICKASHA, OK (Suddenlink Communications)

GRAND LAKE—See KETCHUM, OK (Vyve Broadband)

GRANDFIELD—Southern Plains Cable

GRANITE—Formerly served by Cable West. No longer in operation

GREER COUNTY (PORTIONS)—See ELK CITY, OK (Cable One)

GROVE—Suddenlink Communications

GROVE—See KETCHUM, OK (Vyve Broadband)

GUTHRIE—See OKLAHOMA CITY, OK (Cox Communications)

GUYMON—PTCI

GUYMON—Vyve Broadband

HAILEYVILLE—Vyve Broadband

HAMMON—Formerly served by Rapid Cable. No longer in operation

HARDESTY—PTCI. This cable system has converted to IPTV. Now served by GUYMON, OK [OK5005]

HARDESTY—PTCI. This cable system has converted to IPTV. Now served by GUYMON, OK [OK5005]

HARDESTY—See GUYMON, OK (PTCI)

HARMON—See KINGFISHER, OK (Pioneer Telephone Coop. Formerly [OK0800]. This cable system has converted to IPTV)

HARRAH—See OKLAHOMA CITY, OK (Cox Communications)

HARTSHORNE—See HAILEYVILLE, OK (Vyve Broadband)

HASKELL COUNTY—See STIGLER, OK (Vyve Broadband)

HASKELL—Formerly served by Allegiance Communications. No longer in operation

HAYWOOD—See ARPELAR, OK (Vyve Broadband)

HEALDTON—Suddenlink Communications

HEAVENER—Suddenlink Communications

HECTORVILLE—Formerly served by Quality Cablevision of Oklahoma Inc. No longer in operation

HELENA—Pioneer Telephone Coop. This cable system has converted to IPTV. Now served by KINGFISHER, OK [OK5074]

HELENA—See KINGFISHER, OK (Pioneer Telephone Coop. Formerly [OK0800]. This cable system has converted to IPTV)

HENNESSEY—Pioneer Telephone Coop. This cable system has converted to IPTV. Now served by KINGFISHER, OK [OK5074]

HENNESSEY—See KINGFISHER, OK (Pioneer Telephone Coop. Formerly [OK0800]. This cable system has converted to IPTV)

Oklahoma—Cable Community Index

HENRYETTA—Suddenlink Communications

HINTON—Hinton CATV Co

HOBART—Cable One. Now served by ELK CITY, OK [OK0032]

HOBART—See ELK CITY, OK (Cable One)

HOCHATOWA—See BROKEN BOW, OK (Broken Bow TV Cable Co. Inc)

HOLDENVILLE—Vyve Broadband

HOLLIS—Pioneer Telephone Coop. This cable system has converted to IPTV. Now served by KINGFISHER, OK [OK5074]

HOLLIS—See KINGFISHER, OK (Pioneer Telephone Coop. Formerly [OK0800]. This cable system has converted to IPTV)

HOMINY—Community Cable & Broadband

HOOKER—PTCI. This cable system has converted to IPTV. Now served by GUYMON, OK [OK5005]

HOOKER—See GUYMON, OK (PTCI)

HOPESTON—See KINGFISHER, OK (Pioneer Telephone Coop. Formerly [OK0800]. This cable system has converted to IPTV)

HOWE—Formerly served by Allegiance Communications. No longer in operation

HUGO—Suddenlink Communications

HULBERT—Vyve Broadband

HUNTER (town)—Formerly served by Pioneer Telephone Coop. No longer in operation

HUNTER—See KINGFISHER, OK (Pioneer Telephone Coop. Formerly [OK0800]. This cable system has converted to IPTV)

HYDRO—See HINTON, OK (Hinton CATV Co)

HYDRO—See WEATHERFORD, OK (Suddenlink Communications)

IDABEL (SHULTZ COMMUNITY)—See BROKEN BOW, OK (Broken Bow TV Cable Co. Inc)

IDABEL—Suddenlink Communications

INDIAHOMA—See PECAN VALLEY, OK (Vyve Broadband)

INDIANOLA—See CANADIAN, OK (Lakeland Cable TV Inc)

INOLA—BCI Broadband. Now served by SALINA, OK [OK0071]

INOLA—See SALINA, OK (Vyve Broadband)

JACKSON COUNTY—See ALTUS, OK (Cable One)

JAY—See DISNEY, OK (Omni III Cable TV Inc)

JENKS—See TULSA, OK (Cox Communications)

JENNINGS—See MANNFORD, OK (Cim Tel Cable Inc)

JET—Formerly served by Cebridge Connections. No longer in operation

JOHNSTON COUNTY (PORTIONS)—See KINGSTON, OK (Vyve Broadband)

JONES—Formerly served by Almega Cable. No longer in operation

KANSAS—Formerly served by Allegiance Communications. No longer in operation

KAW CITY—Formerly served by Community Cablevision Co. No longer in operation

KAY COUNTY (PORTIONS)—See PONCA CITY, OK (Cable One)

KELLYVILLE—Vyve Broadband

KEOTA—Vyve Broadband

KETCHUM—Vyve Broadband

KEYES—See GUYMON, OK (PTCI)

KIEFER—See TULSA, OK (Cox Communications)

KINGFISHER—Pioneer Telephone Coop. This cable system has converted to IPTV. Now served by KINGFISHER, OK [OK5074]

KINGFISHER—Pioneer Telephone Coop. Formerly [OK0800]. This cable system has converted to IPTV

KINGSTON—Formerly served by Allegiance Communications. Now served by Vyve Broadband, KINGSTON (formerly Tishomingo), OK [OK0064]

KINGSTON—Vyve Broadband

KINTA—See QUINTON, OK (Vyve Broadband)

KIOWA COUNTY (PORTIONS)—See ELK CITY, OK (Cable One)

KIOWA—See SAVANNA, OK (Vyve Broadband)

KONAWA—Formerly served by Allegiance Communications. No longer in operation

KREBS—See McALESTER, OK (Vyve Broadband)

KREMLIN—Formerly served by Cebridge Connections. No longer in operation

LAHOMA—Pioneer Telephone Coop. This cable system has converted to IPTV. Now served by KINGFISHER, OK [OK5074]

LAHOMA—See KINGFISHER, OK (Pioneer Telephone Coop. Formerly [OK0800]. This cable system has converted to IPTV)

LAKE ALUMA—See OKLAHOMA CITY, OK (Cox Communications)

LAKE ELLSWORTH—Formerly served by LakeView Cable. No longer in operation

LAKE LAWTONKA—Southern Plains Cable

LAKE TENKILLER—Formerly served by Cox Communications. No longer in operation

LAMONT—Formerly served by Blue Sky Cable LLC. No longer in operation

LAMONT—See KINGFISHER, OK (Pioneer Telephone Coop. Formerly [OK0800]. This cable system has converted to IPTV)

LANGLEY—See KETCHUM, OK (Vyve Broadband)

LANGSTON—Vyve Broadband

LAVERNE—PTCI. This cable system has converted to IPTV. Now served by GUYMON, OK [OK5005]

LAVERNE—See GUYMON, OK (PTCI)

LAWTON (VILLAGE)—Fidelity Communications

LE FLORE COUNTY (PORTIONS)—See HEAVENER, OK (Suddenlink Communications)

LE FLORE COUNTY (PORTIONS)—See POTEAU, OK (Suddenlink Communications)

LE FLORE COUNTY (PORTIONS)—See SPIRO, OK (Suddenlink Communications)

LE FLORE COUNTY (UNINCORPORATED AREAS)—See PANAMA, OK (Vyve Broadband)

LEEDEY—Formerly served by Rapid Cable. No longer in operation

LEXINGTON—See PURCELL, OK (Suddenlink Communications)

LINDSAY—Suddenlink Communications

LOCUST GROVE—See SALINA, OK (Vyve Broadband)

LOGAN COUNTY (PORTIONS)—See OKLAHOMA CITY, OK (Cox Communications)

LONE GROVE—See ARDMORE, OK (Cable One)

LONE WOLF—Formerly served by Cable West. No longer in operation

LONGDALE—Formerly served by LongView Communications. No longer in operation

LONGDALE—See KINGFISHER, OK (Pioneer Telephone Coop. Formerly [OK0800]. This cable system has converted to IPTV)

LONGTOWN—Formerly served by Allegiance Communications. No longer in operation

LOOKEBA—See HINTON, OK (Hinton CATV Co)

LOYAL—See KINGFISHER, OK (Pioneer Telephone Coop. Formerly [OK0800]. This cable system has converted to IPTV)

LUKFATA—See BROKEN BOW, OK (Broken Bow TV Cable Co. Inc)

LUTHER—Formerly served by Allegiance Communications. No longer in operation

MADILL—See ARDMORE, OK (Cable One)

MANGUM—Cable One. Now served by ELK CITY, OK [OK0032]

MANGUM—See ELK CITY, OK (Cable One)

MANNFORD—Cim Tel Cable Inc

MARIETTA—See ARDMORE, OK (Cable One)

MARLAND—Formerly served by Allegiance Communications. No longer in operation

MARLOW—See DUNCAN, OK (Cable One)

MARSHALL COUNTY (NORTHERN PORTION)—See ARDMORE, OK (Cable One)

MARSHALL—Pioneer Telephone Coop. This cable system has converted to IPTV. Now served by KINGFISHER, OK [OK5074]

MARSHALL—See KINGFISHER, OK (Pioneer Telephone Coop. Formerly [OK0800]. This cable system has converted to IPTV)

MARTHA—Formerly served by CableDirect. No longer in operation

MAUD—Formerly served by Allegiance Communications. No longer in operation

MAY—See KINGFISHER, OK (Pioneer Telephone Coop. Formerly [OK0800]. This cable system has converted to IPTV)

MAYES COUNTY (PORTIONS)—See PRYOR, OK (Vyve Broadband)

MAYES COUNTY (WESTERN PORTION)—See ROGERS COUNTY (northern portion), OK (Time Warner Cable)

MAYSVILLE—See PURCELL, OK (Suddenlink Communications)

MCALESTER ARMY AMMUNITION PLANT—See SAVANNA, OK (Vyve Broadband)

MCALESTER—Vyve Broadband

MCCLAIN COUNTY (PORTIONS)—See PURCELL, OK (Suddenlink Communications)

MCCURTAIN COUNTY (PORTIONS)—See BROKEN BOW, OK (Broken Bow TV Cable Co. Inc)

Cable Community Index—Oklahoma

MCCURTAIN COUNTY (PORTIONS)—See IDABEL, OK (Suddenlink Communications)

McCURTAIN—Formerly served by Allegiance Communications. No longer in operation

MCINTOSH COUNTY (PORTIONS)—See EUFAULA, OK (Vyve Broadband)

MCLOUD—See SHAWNEE, OK (Vyve Broadband)

MEDICINE PARK—Southern Plains Cable

MEEKER—See SHAWNEE, OK (Vyve Broadband)

MENO—Formerly served by CableDirect. No longer in operation

MENO—See KINGFISHER, OK (Pioneer Telephone Coop. Formerly [OK0800]. This cable system has converted to IPTV)

MIAMI—Cable One

MIDWEST CITY—See OKLAHOMA CITY, OK (Cox Communications)

MILBURN—Formerly served by Allegiance Communications. No longer in operation

MONKEY ISLAND—See KETCHUM, OK (Vyve Broadband)

MOORE—See OKLAHOMA CITY, OK (Cox Communications)

MOORELAND—Pioneer Telephone Coop. This cable system has converted to IPTV. Now served by KINGFISHER, OK [OK5074]

MOORELAND—See KINGFISHER, OK (Pioneer Telephone Coop. Formerly [OK0800]. This cable system has converted to IPTV)

MOORELAND—See WOODWARD, OK (Suddenlink Communications)

MORRIS (town)—Formerly served by Allegiance Communications. No longer in operation

MORRISON—Formerly served by Allegiance Communications. No longer in operation

MOUNDS—Vyve Broadband

MOUNTAIN PARK—Vyve Broadband

MOUNTAIN VIEW—Mountain View Cable TV

MUSKOGEE COUNTY—See MUSKOGEE, OK (Suddenlink Communications)

MUSKOGEE—Suddenlink Communications

MUSTANG—See OKLAHOMA CITY, OK (Cox Communications)

MUTUAL—See KINGFISHER, OK (Pioneer Telephone Coop. Formerly [OK0800]. This cable system has converted to IPTV)

NASH—Pioneer Telephone Coop. This cable system has converted to IPTV. Now served by KINGFISHER, OK [OK5074]

NASH—See KINGFISHER, OK (Pioneer Telephone Coop. Formerly [OK0800]. This cable system has converted to IPTV)

NEWCASTLE—Pioneer Telephone Coop. This cable system has converted to IPTV. Now served by KINGFISHER, OK [OK5074]

NEWCASTLE—See KINGFISHER, OK (Pioneer Telephone Coop. Formerly [OK0800]. This cable system has converted to IPTV)

NEWKIRK—Vyve Broadband

NICHOLS HILLS—See OKLAHOMA CITY, OK (Cox Communications)

NINNEKAH—Formerly served by Cable West. No longer in operation

NOBLE COUNTY (PORTIONS)—See PERRY, OK (Suddenlink Communications)

NOBLE—Formerly served by Cebridge Connections. Now served by Suddenlink Communications, PURCELL, OK [OK0048]

NOBLE—See PURCELL, OK (Suddenlink Communications)

NORMAN—See OKLAHOMA CITY, OK (Cox Communications)

NORTH ENID—See ENID, OK (Suddenlink Communications)

NORTH MIAMI—See MIAMI, OK (Cable One)

NOWATA COUNTY—See BARTLESVILLE, OK (Cable One)

NOWATA—Cable One. Now served by BARTLESVILLE, OK [OK0010]

NOWATA—See BARTLESVILLE, OK (Cable One)

OAKLAND—See ARDMORE, OK (Cable One)

OAKWOOD—See KINGFISHER, OK (Pioneer Telephone Coop. Formerly [OK0800]. This cable system has converted to IPTV)

OCHELATA—Community Cable & Broadband

OILTON—Community Cable & Broadband. Now served by YALE, OK [OK0141]

OILTON—See YALE, OK (Community Cable & Broadband)

OKARCHE—Pioneer Telephone Coop. This cable system has converted to IPTV. Now served by KINGFISHER, OK [OK5074]

OKARCHE—See KINGFISHER, OK (Pioneer Telephone Coop. Formerly [OK0800]. This cable system has converted to IPTV)

OKAY—BCI Broadband. Now served by FORT GIBSON, OK [OK0090]

OKAY—See FORT GIBSON, OK (Vyve Broadband)

OKEENE—Pioneer Telephone Coop. This cable system has converted to IPTV. Now served by KINGFISHER, OK [OK5074]

OKEENE—See KINGFISHER, OK (Pioneer Telephone Coop. Formerly [OK0800]. This cable system has converted to IPTV)

OKEMAH—Vyve Broadband

OKLAHOMA CITY—Formerly served by WANTV of OKC. No longer in operation

OKLAHOMA CITY—Cox Communications

OKMULGEE COUNTY (CENTRAL PORTION)—See OKMULGEE, OK (Suddenlink Communications)

OKMULGEE COUNTY (PORTIONS)—See HENRYETTA, OK (Suddenlink Communications)

OKMULGEE—Suddenlink Communications

OLUSTEE—Formerly served by Basic Cable Services Inc. No longer in operation

OOLOGAH—Formerly served by Allegiance Communications. No longer in operation

OPTIMA—See GUYMON, OK (PTCI)

ORLANDO—Formerly served by CableDirect. No longer in operation

ORLANDO—See KINGFISHER, OK (Pioneer Telephone Coop. Formerly [OK0800]. This cable system has converted to IPTV)

OSAGE COUNTY (PORTIONS)—See PONCA CITY, OK (Cable One)

OSAGE COUNTY (PORTIONS)—See TULSA, OK (Cox Communications)

OSAGE COUNTY (PORTIONS)—See PAWHUSKA, OK (Vyve Broadband)

OSAGE—See MANNFORD, OK (Cim Tel Cable Inc)

OTTAWA COUNTY—See MIAMI, OK (Cable One)

OWASSO—See TULSA, OK (Cox Communications)

PANAMA—Vyve Broadband

PAOLI—Formerly served by Cebridge Connections. No longer in operation

PARADISE HILL—Formerly served by Eagle Media. No longer in operation

PARK HILL—Formerly served by Eagle Media. No longer in operation

PAULS VALLEY—Suddenlink Communications

PAWHUSKA—Vyve Broadband

PAWNEE—Cim Tel Cable Inc. Now served by MANNFORD, OK [OK0296]

PAWNEE—See MANNFORD, OK (Cim Tel Cable Inc)

PAYNE COUNTY (PORTIONS)—See STILLWATER, OK (Suddenlink Communications)

PECAN VALLEY—Vyve Broadband

PERKINS—See STILLWATER, OK (Suddenlink Communications)

PERRY—Suddenlink Communications

PERRYTON—See GUYMON, TX (PTCI)

PICHER—Formerly served by Mediacom. No longer in operation

PIEDMONT—Formerly served by Almega Cable. No longer in operation

PITTSBURG—See SAVANNA, OK (Vyve Broadband)

PLATTER—See DURANT, OK (Vyve Broadband)

POCASSET—Formerly served by CableDirect. No longer in operation

POCOLA—Cox Communications. Now served by FORT SMITH, AR [AR0003]

PONCA CITY—Cable One

POND CREEK—Pioneer Telephone Coop. This cable system has converted to IPTV. Now served by KINGFISHER, OK [OK5074]

POND CREEK—See KINGFISHER, OK (Pioneer Telephone Coop. Formerly [OK0800]. This cable system has converted to IPTV)

PONTOTOC COUNTY—See ADA, OK (Cable One)

PORTER—Formerly served by Allegiance Communications. No longer in operation

PORUM LANDING—Vyve Broadband

PORUM—Vyve Broadband

POTEAU—Suddenlink Communications

POTTAWATOMIE COUNTY (PORTIONS)—See SHAWNEE, OK (Vyve Broadband)

PRAGUE—See SHAWNEE, OK (Vyve Broadband)

PRESTON—Formerly served by Quality Cablevision of Oklahoma Inc. No longer in operation

PRUE—See MANNFORD, OK (Cim Tel Cable Inc)

PRYOR (outside areas)—Formerly served by Time Warner Cable. No longer in operation

PRYOR—Vyve Broadband

PURCELL—Suddenlink Communications

Oklahoma—Cable Community Index

PUTNAM—See KINGFISHER, OK (Pioneer Telephone Coop. Formerly [OK0800]. This cable system has converted to IPTV)

QUINLAN—See KINGFISHER, OK (Pioneer Telephone Coop. Formerly [OK0800]. This cable system has converted to IPTV)

QUINTON—Vyve Broadband

RALSTON—Formerly served by Allegiance Communications. No longer in operation

RAMONA—Community Cable & Broadband

RANDLETT—Formerly served by Cable Television Inc. No longer in operation

RATTAN—Formerly served by Allegiance Communications. No longer in operation

RAVIA—See KINGSTON, OK (Vyve Broadband)

RED OAK—See WILBURTON, OK (Vyve Broadband)

RED ROCK—Formerly served by Blue Sky Cable LLC. No longer in operation.

RINGLING—See HEALDTON, OK (Suddenlink Communications)

RINGWOOD—Pioneer Telephone Coop. This cable system has converted to IPTV. Now served by KINGFISHER, OK [OK5074]

RINGWOOD—See KINGFISHER, OK (Pioneer Telephone Coop. Formerly [OK0800]. This cable system has converted to IPTV)

RIPLEY—Formerly served by CableDirect. No longer in operation

ROCKY—Formerly served by CableDirect. No longer in operation

ROFF—See ADA, OK (Cable One)

ROGERS COUNTY (NORTHERN PORTION)—Time Warner Cable

ROGERS COUNTY (PORTIONS)—See TULSA, OK (Cox Communications)

ROOSEVELT—Formerly served by Cable West. No longer in operation

RUSH SPRINGS—Formerly served by Reach Broadband. No longer in operation

RUSH SPRINGS—Southern Plains Cable

RYAN—Formerly served by Almega Cable. No longer in operation

SALINA—Vyve Broadband

SALLISAW—Suddenlink Communications

SAND POINT—Formerly served by Allegiance Communications. No longer in operation

SAND SPRINGS—See TULSA, OK (Cox Communications)

SAPULPA—See TULSA, OK (Cox Communications)

SAVANNA—Vyve Broadband

SAYRE—See ELK CITY, OK (Cable One)

SCHULTER—Formerly served by Allegiance Communications. No longer in operation

SEILING—Pioneer Telephone Coop. This cable system has converted to IPTV. Now served by KINGFISHER, OK [OK5074]

SEILING—See KINGFISHER, OK (Pioneer Telephone Coop. Formerly [OK0800]. This cable system has converted to IPTV)

SEMINOLE—Suddenlink Communications

SENTINEL—Formerly served by Cable West. No longer in operation

SENTINEL—See KINGFISHER, OK (Pioneer Telephone Coop. Formerly [OK0800]. This cable system has converted to IPTV)

SHADY POINT—See PANAMA, OK (Vyve Broadband)

SHARON—See KINGFISHER, OK (Pioneer Telephone Coop. Formerly [OK0800]. This cable system has converted to IPTV)

SHATTUCK—Pioneer Telephone Coop. This cable system has converted to IPTV. Now served by KINGFISHER, OK [OK5074]

SHATTUCK—See KINGFISHER, OK (Pioneer Telephone Coop. Formerly [OK0800]. This cable system has converted to IPTV)

SHAWNEE—Vyve Broadband

SHIDLER—Formerly served by Community Cablevision Co. No longer in operation

SKIATOOK—Community Cable & Broadband

SNYDER—Formerly served by LongView Communications. Now served by Vyve Broadband, MOUNTAIN PARK, OK [OK0300]

SNYDER—See MOUNTAIN PARK, OK (Vyve Broadband)

SOPER—Formerly served by Soper Cable TV. No longer in operation

SPAVINAW—See KETCHUM, OK (Vyve Broadband)

SPEARMAN—See GUYMON, TX (PTCI)

SPENCER—See OKLAHOMA CITY, OK (Cox Communications)

SPERRY—See SKIATOOK, OK (Community Cable & Broadband)

SPIRO—Suddenlink Communications

STEPHENS COUNTY (PORTIONS)—See DUNCAN, OK (Cable One)

STERLING—Southern Plains Cable

STIGLER—Vyve Broadband

STILLWATER—Suddenlink Communications

STILWELL—Vyve Broadband

STONEWALL—Formerly served by CommuniComm Services. Now served by Vyve Broadband, COALGATE, OK [OK0120]

STONEWALL—See COALGATE, OK (Vyve Broadband)

STRANG—Formerly served by Allegiance Communications. Now served by Vyve Broadband, KETCHUM, OK [OK0179]

STRANG—See KETCHUM, OK (Vyve Broadband)

STRATFORD—Vyve Broadband

STRINGTOWN—Formerly served by Allegiance Communications. No longer in operation

STROUD—Vyve Broadband

STUART—See ARPELAR, OK (Vyve Broadband)

SULPHUR—See ADA, OK (Cable One)

TAHLEQUAH—Tahlequah Cable TV Inc

TALALA—Formerly served by Quality Cablevision of Oklahoma Inc. No longer in operation

TALIHINA—Formerly served by Allegiance Communications. No longer in operation

TALOGA—Taloga Cable TV

TECUMSEH—See SHAWNEE, OK (Vyve Broadband)

TEMPLE—See WALTERS, OK (Alliance Communications)

TERRAL—Formerly served by Almega Cable. No longer in operation

TEXHOMA—See GUYMON, OK (PTCI)

TEXHOMA—See GUYMON, TX (PTCI)

THE VILLAGE—See OKLAHOMA CITY, OK (Cox Communications)

THOMAS—Pioneer Telephone Coop. This cable system has converted to IPTV. Now served by KINGFISHER, OK [OK5074]

THOMAS—See KINGFISHER, OK (Pioneer Telephone Coop. Formerly [OK0800]. This cable system has converted to IPTV)

TIPTON—Formerly served by LakeView Cable. No longer in operation

TIPTON—See ALTUS, OK (Cable One)

TISHOMINGO—See KINGSTON, OK (Vyve Broadband)

TONKAWA—See PONCA CITY, OK (Cable One)

TRYON—Formerly served by Allegiance Communications. No longer in operation

TULSA (NORTHWESTERN PORTION)—See ROGERS COUNTY (northern portion), OK (Time Warner Cable)

TULSA COUNTY (PORTIONS)—See TULSA, OK (Cox Communications)

TULSA COUNTY (western portion)—Formerly served by Summit Digital. No longer in operation

TULSA—Cox Communications

TUPELO—See COALGATE, OK (Vyve Broadband)

TURPIN—Formerly served by Allegiance Communications. No longer in operation

TURPIN—See GUYMON, OK (PTCI)

TUSHKA—See COALGATE, OK (Vyve Broadband)

TUTTLE—Formerly served by Vidia Communications. No longer in operation

TYRONE—Formerly served by Allegiance Communications. No longer in operation

TYRONE—See GUYMON, OK (PTCI)

UNION CITY—Formerly served by Vidia Communications. No longer in operation

VALLEY BROOK—See OKLAHOMA CITY, OK (Cox Communications)

VALLIANT—Formerly served by Allegiance Communications. No longer in operation

VANCE AFB—See ENID, OK (Suddenlink Communications)

VELMA—Formerly served by Reach Broadband. No longer in operation

VERDEN—Formerly served by Cable West. No longer in operation

VERDIGRIS—Formerly served by Allegiance Communications. No longer in operation

VIAN—Vyve Broadband

VICI—Formerly served by Rapid Cable. No longer in operation

VINITA—Cable One

WAGONER COUNTY (EASTERN PORTION)—See MUSKOGEE, OK (Suddenlink Communications)

WAGONER COUNTY (PORTIONS)—See TULSA, OK (Cox Communications)

WAGONER—See MUSKOGEE, OK (Suddenlink Communications)

WAGONER—Vyve Broadband

WAKITA—Pioneer Telephone Coop. This cable system has converted to IPTV. Now served by KINGFISHER, OK

Cable Community Index—Oregon

[OK5074]

WAKITA—See KINGFISHER, OK (Pioneer Telephone Coop. Formerly [OK0800]. This cable system has converted to IPTV)

WALTERS—Alliance Communications

WANETTE—Formerly served by Cebridge Connections. No longer in operation

WAPANUCKA—Formerly served by Allegiance Communications. No longer in operation

WARNER—Cross Telephone Co

WARR ACRES—See OKLAHOMA CITY, OK (Cox Communications)

WASHINGTON (portions)—Formerly served by Cebridge Connections. No longer in operation

WATONGA—Pioneer Telephone Coop. This cable system has converted to IPTV. Now served by KINGFISHER, OK [OK5074]

WATONGA—See KINGFISHER, OK (Pioneer Telephone Coop. Formerly [OK0800]. This cable system has converted to IPTV)

WAUKOMIS—Formerly served by Adelphia Cable. No longer in operation

WAURIKA—Alliance Communications

WAYNE—See PURCELL, OK (Suddenlink Communications)

WAYNOKA—Formerly served by Waynoka Community TV. No longer in operation

WAYNOKA—See KINGFISHER, OK (Pioneer Telephone Coop. Formerly [OK0800]. This cable system has converted to IPTV)

WEATHERFORD—Suddenlink Communications

WEBBERS FALLS—See GORE, OK (Vyve Broadband)

WELCH—Formerly served by Allegiance Communications. No longer in operation

WELEETKA—Formerly served by Allegiance Communications. No longer in operation

WELLSTON—Formerly served by Allegiance Communications. No longer in operation

WESTPORT—See MANNFORD, OK (Cim Tel Cable Inc)

WESTVILLE—Formerly served by Vyve Broadband. No longer in operation

WETUMKA—Formerly served by Vyve Broadband. No longer in operation

WEWOKA—Suddenlink Communications

WHITE HORN COVE—Formerly served by Lake Area TV Cable. No longer in operation

WHITEFIELD—See STIGLER, OK (Vyve Broadband)

WILBURTON—Vyve Broadband

WILSON—See HEALDTON, OK (Suddenlink Communications)

WISTER—Formerly served by Allegiance Communications. No longer in operation

WOODALL—Formerly served by Eagle Media. No longer in operation

WOODS COUNTY (EASTERN PORTION)—See ALVA, OK (Suddenlink Communications)

WOODWARD—Suddenlink Communications

WRIGHT CITY—Formerly served by Allegiance Communications. No longer in operation

WYANDOTTE—Formerly served by Allegiance Communications. No longer in operation

WYNNEWOOD—See PAULS VALLEY, OK (Suddenlink Communications)

WYNONA—Community Cable & Broadband

YALE—Community Cable & Broadband

YUKON—See OKLAHOMA CITY, OK (Cox Communications)

OREGON

ADAIR VILLAGE—See PORTLAND, OR (Comcast Cable)

ALBANY—See PORTLAND, OR (Comcast Cable)

ALOHA—See PORTLAND, OR (Comcast Cable)

AMITY—See PORTLAND, OR (Comcast Cable)

ARLINGTON—Formerly served by Arlington TV Cooperative Inc. No longer in operation

ASHLAND—Ashland TV. This cable system has converted to IPTV. See ASHLAND, OR [OR5023]

ASHLAND—Ashland TV. Formerly [OR0174]. This cable system has converted to IPTV

ASHLAND—See MEDFORD, OR (Charter Communications)

ASTORIA—Charter Communications

AUMSVILLE—See TURNER, OR (Wave Broadband)

AURORA—See SILVERTON, OR (Wave Broadband)

BANDON—See COOS BAY, OR (Charter Communications)

BANKS—See PORTLAND, OR (Comcast Cable)

BARLOW—See SILVERTON, OR (Wave Broadband)

BAY CITY—See LINCOLN CITY, OR (Charter Communications)

BEAVERCREEK—BCT. This cable system has converted to IPTV. See BEAVERCREEK, OR [OR5024]

BEAVERCREEK—BCT. Formerly [OR0167]. This cable system has converted to IPTV

BEAVERTON—Comcast Cable. Now served by PORTLAND, OR [OR0001]

BEAVERTON—See PORTLAND, OR (Comcast Cable)

BEND—Formerly served by WANTV. No longer in operation

BEND—BendBroadband

BENTON COUNTY (PORTIONS)—See PORTLAND, OR (Comcast Cable)

BINGEN—See THE DALLES, WA (Charter Communications)

BLACK BUTTE RANCH—See BEND, OR (BendBroadband)

BLY—Formerly served by Bly Cable Co. No longer in operation

BOARDMAN—Formerly served by Rapid Cable. No longer in operation

BONANZA—Formerly served by Almega Cable. No longer in operation

BORING—Formerly served by Community Cable Inc. No longer in operation

BROOKINGS—Charter Communications. Now served by CRESCENT CITY, CA [CA0155]

BROOKS—Formerly served by Country Cablevision Ltd. No longer in operation

BROWNSVILLE—Formerly served by Rapid Cable. No longer in operation

BURNS—Charter Communications

BUTTE FALLS—Formerly served by Almega Cable. No longer in operation

CANBY—Wave Broadband. Now served by SILVERTON, OR [OR0047]

CANBY—See SILVERTON, OR (Wave Broadband)

CANNON BEACH—See ASTORIA, OR (Charter Communications)

CANYON CITY—See MOUNT VERNON, OR (Blue Mountain TV Cable Co)

CANYONVILLE—See ROSEBURG, OR (Charter Communications)

CARLTON—See PORTLAND, OR (Comcast Cable)

CASCADE LOCKS—City of Cascade Locks Cable TV

CAVE JUNCTION—Formerly served by Almega Cable. No longer in operation

CENTRAL POINT—See MEDFORD, OR (Charter Communications)

CHILOQUIN—Formerly served by Almega Cable. No longer in operation

CLACKAMAS COUNTY (PORTIONS)—See PORTLAND, OR (Comcast Cable)

CLACKAMAS COUNTY (PORTIONS)—See SANDY, OR (Wave Broadband)

CLACKAMAS COUNTY (PORTIONS)—See SILVERTON, OR (Wave Broadband)

CLACKAMAS COUNTY—See ESTACADA, OR (Reliance Connects)

CLACKAMAS—See SILVERTON, OR (Wave Broadband)

CLATSKANIE—See ASTORIA, OR (Charter Communications)

CLATSOP COUNTY—See ASTORIA, OR (Charter Communications)

CLOVERDALE—See LINCOLN CITY, OR (Charter Communications)

COBURG—See COTTAGE GROVE, OR (Charter Communications)

COLTON—ColtonTel

COLUMBIA CITY—See PORTLAND, OR (Comcast Cable)

COLUMBIA COUNTY (NORTHERN PORTION)—See ASTORIA, OR (Charter Communications)

CONDON—J & N Cable

COOS BAY—Charter Communications

COOS COUNTY (NORTHERN PORTION)—See COOS BAY, OR (Charter Communications)

COQUILLE—See COOS BAY, OR (Charter Communications)

CORBETT—See ESTACADA, OR (Reliance Connects)

CORNELIUS—See PORTLAND, OR (Comcast Cable)

CORVALLIS—Comcast Cable. Now served by PORTLAND, OR [OR0001]

CORVALLIS—See PORTLAND, OR (Comcast Cable)

COTTAGE GROVE—Charter Communications

COVE—Formerly served by Almega Cable. No longer in operation

CRESWELL—See COTTAGE GROVE, OR (Charter Communications)

CULVER—See MADRAS, OR (Crestview Cable TV)

CURRY COUNTY (PORTIONS)—See SUNRIVER, OR (BendBroadband)

DALLAS—Charter Communications

DALLESPORT—See THE DALLES, WA (Charter Communications)

DAYTON—See PORTLAND, OR (Comcast Cable)

DAYVILLE—Formerly served by Blue Mountain TV Cable Co. No longer in operation

DEER ISLAND—See PORTLAND, OR (Comcast Cable)

DEPOE BAY—Wave Broadband

DESCHUTES COUNTY (UNINCORPORATED AREAS)—See BEND, OR (BendBroadband)

2017 Edition

Cable Community Index-239

Oregon—Cable Community Index

DILLARD—See ROSEBURG, OR (Charter Communications)

DONALD—See SILVERTON, OR (Wave Broadband)

DOUGLAS COUNTY (NORTHERN PORTION)—See COTTAGE GROVE, OR (Charter Communications)

DOUGLAS COUNTY (PORTIONS)—See COOS BAY, OR (Charter Communications)

DOUGLAS COUNTY (PORTIONS)—See ROSEBURG, OR (Charter Communications)

DRAIN—See COTTAGE GROVE, OR (Charter Communications)

DUFUR—Northstate Cablevision

DUNDEE—See PORTLAND, OR (Comcast Cable)

DUNES CITY—See FLORENCE, OR (Charter Communications)

DURHAM—See PORTLAND, OR (Comcast Cable)

EAGLE CREEK—See ESTACADA, OR (Reliance Connects)

EAGLE POINT—See MEDFORD, OR (Charter Communications)

ELGIN—Elgin TV Assn. Inc

ENTERPRISE—Crystal Broadband Networks

ESTACADA—Reliance Connects

EUGENE—Comcast Cable. Now served by PORTLAND, OR [OR0001]

EUGENE—See PORTLAND, OR (Comcast Cable)

FAIRVIEW—See PORTLAND, OR (Comcast Cable)

FALLS CITY—See DALLAS, OR (Charter Communications)

FLORENCE—Charter Communications

FOREST GROVE—See PORTLAND, OR (Comcast Cable)

FOSSIL—Fossil Community TV Inc.

GARDINER—See COOS BAY, OR (Charter Communications)

GARIBALDI—See LINCOLN CITY, OR (Charter Communications)

GASTON—See PORTLAND, OR (Comcast Cable)

GATES—See TURNER, OR (Wave Broadband)

GEARHART—See ASTORIA, OR (Charter Communications)

GERVAIS—See SILVERTON, OR (Wave Broadband)

GILCHRIST—Formerly served by Country Cablevision Ltd. No longer in operation

GLADSTONE—See PORTLAND, OR (Comcast Cable)

GLENDALE—Formerly served by Almega Cable. No longer in operation

GLIDE—Formerly served by Glide Cablevision. No longer in operation

GOLD BEACH—Charter Communications. Now served by CRESCENT CITY, CA [CA0155]

GOLD HILL—See MEDFORD, OR (Charter Communications)

GOVERNMENT CAMP—CharlieVision

GRAND RONDE—See SILVERTON, OR (Wave Broadband)

GRANTS PASS—Charter Communications. Now served by MEDFORD, OR [OR0006]

GRANTS PASS—See MEDFORD, OR (Charter Communications)

GREEN ACRES—Greenacres TV Cable

GRESHAM—See PORTLAND, OR (Comcast Cable)

HAINES—Formerly served by Almega Cable. No longer in operation

HALFWAY—Formerly served by Charter Communications. No longer in operation

HALSEY—Roome Telecommunications Inc. No longer in operation

HAMMOND—See ASTORIA, OR (Charter Communications)

HAPPY VALLEY—See PORTLAND, OR (Comcast Cable)

HARNEY COUNTY (PORTIONS)—See BURNS, OR (Charter Communications)

HARRISBURG—See PORTLAND, OR (Comcast Cable)

HAUSER—See COOS BAY, OR (Charter Communications)

HAYDEN ISLAND—See PORTLAND, OR (Comcast Cable)

HELIX—Formerly served by Helix Communications. No longer in operation

HEPPNER—Heppner TV Inc

HILLSBORO—See PORTLAND, OR (Comcast Cable)

HINES—See BURNS, OR (Charter Communications)

HOOD RIVER COUNTY—See THE DALLES, OR (Charter Communications)

HOOD RIVER—See THE DALLES, OR (Charter Communications)

HUBBARD—See SILVERTON, OR (Wave Broadband)

IDANHA—Formerly served by Wave Broadband. No longer in operation

ILWACO—See ASTORIA, WA (Charter Communications)

IMBLER—Formerly served by Almega Cable. No longer in operation

INDEPENDENCE—See DALLAS, OR (Charter Communications)

IONE—Formerly served by Ione TV Co-op. Now served by Heppner TV Inc., HEPPNER, OR [OR0077]

IONE—See HEPPNER, OR (Heppner TV Inc)

ISLAND CITY—See LA GRANDE, OR (Charter Communications)

JACKSON COUNTY—See MEDFORD, OR (Charter Communications)

JACKSONVILLE—See MEDFORD, OR (Charter Communications)

JEFFERSON—See DALLAS, OR (Charter Communications)

JOHN DAY—See MOUNT VERNON, OR (Blue Mountain TV Cable Co)

JOHNSON CITY—See PORTLAND, OR (Comcast Cable)

JOSEPH—See ENTERPRISE, OR (Crystal Broadband Networks)

JOSEPHINE COUNTY (PORTIONS)—See MEDFORD, OR (Charter Communications)

JUNCTION CITY—See PORTLAND, OR (Comcast Cable)

KEIZER—See PORTLAND, OR (Comcast Cable)

KING CITY—See PORTLAND, OR (Comcast Cable)

KLAMATH COUNTY (UNINCORPORATED AREAS)—See KLAMATH FALLS, OR (Charter Communications)

KLAMATH FALLS—Charter Communications

KLICKITAT COUNTY (PORTIONS)—See THE DALLES, WA (Charter Communications)

KLICKITAT—See THE DALLES, WA (Charter Communications)

KNAPPA—Formerly served by Rapid Cable. No longer in operation

LA GRANDE—Charter Communications

LA PINE—Crestview Cable TV

LACOMB—Formerly served by Wave Broadband. No longer in operation

LAFAYETTE—See PORTLAND, OR (Comcast Cable)

LAKE COUNTY (PORTIONS)—See LAKEVIEW, OR (Charter Communications)

LAKE OSWEGO—See PORTLAND, OR (Comcast Cable)

LAKESIDE—See COOS BAY, OR (Charter Communications)

LAKEVIEW—Charter Communications

LANE COUNTY (PORTIONS)—See COTTAGE GROVE, OR (Charter Communications)

LANE COUNTY (PORTIONS)—See FLORENCE, OR (Charter Communications)

LANE COUNTY (PORTIONS)—See PORTLAND, OR (Comcast Cable)

LEBANON—Comcast Cable. Now served by PORTLAND, OR [OR0001]

LEBANON—See PORTLAND, OR (Comcast Cable)

LEXINGTON—See HEPPNER, OR (Heppner TV Inc)

LINCOLN BEACH—See DEPOE BAY, OR (Wave Broadband)

LINCOLN CITY—Charter Communications

LINCOLN COUNTY (PORTIONS)—See WALDPORT, OR (Alsea River Cable Co)

LINCOLN COUNTY (PORTIONS)—See LINCOLN CITY, OR (Charter Communications)

LINCOLN COUNTY (PORTIONS)—See DEPOE BAY, OR (Wave Broadband)

LINN COUNTY (WESTERN PORTION)—See PORTLAND, OR (Comcast Cable)

LITTLE ALBANY—See WALDPORT, OR (Alsea River Cable Co)

LONG BEACH—See ASTORIA, WA (Charter Communications)

LOSTINE—See ENTERPRISE, OR (Crystal Broadband Networks)

LOWELL—See COTTAGE GROVE, OR (Charter Communications)

LYONS—See TURNER, OR (Wave Broadband)

MACLEAY—Formerly served by Country Cablevision Ltd. No longer in operation

MADRAS—Crestview Cable TV

MALIN—Formerly served by Almega Cable. No longer in operation

MANZANITA—See LINCOLN CITY, OR (Charter Communications)

MAPLETON—Formerly served by Rapid Communications. No longer in operation

MARION COUNTY (PORTIONS)—See PORTLAND, OR (Comcast Cable)

MARION COUNTY (PORTIONS)—See SILVERTON, OR (Wave Broadband)

MARION COUNTY (SOUTHWESTERN PORTION)—See DALLAS, OR (Charter Communications)

MAYWOOD PARK—See PORTLAND, OR (Comcast Cable)

MCMINNVILLE—See PORTLAND, OR (Comcast Cable)

MEDFORD—Charter Communications

MEHAMA—See TURNER, OR (Wave Broadband)

MERRILL—Formerly served by Almega Cable. No longer in operation

METOLIUS—See MADRAS, OR (Crestview Cable TV)

MILL CITY—See TURNER, OR (Wave Broadband)

MILLERSBURG—See PORTLAND, OR (Comcast Cable)

Cable Community Index—Oregon

MILTON-FREEWATER—Charter Communications. Now served by KEN-NEWICK, WA [WA0008]

MILWAUKIE—Comcast Cable. Now served by PORTLAND, OR [OR0001]

MILWAUKIE—See PORTLAND, OR (Comcast Cable)

MOLALLA—See SILVERTON, OR (Wave Broadband)

MONMOUTH—See DALLAS, OR (Charter Communications)

MONROE—Monroe Telephone Co. This cable system has converted to IPTV. See MONROE, OR [OR5001]

MONROE—Monroe Telephone. Formerly [OR0105]. This cable system has converted to IPTV

MORO—J & N Cable

MOUNT ANGEL—See SILVERTON, OR (Wave Broadband)

MOUNT HOOD—See PARKDALE, OR (Valley TV Co-op Inc)

MOUNT VERNON—Blue Mountain TV Cable Co

MULINO—See BEAVERCREEK, OR (BCT. Formerly [OR0167]. This cable system has converted to IPTV)

MULTNOMAH COUNTY (PORTIONS)—See PORTLAND, OR (Comcast Cable)

MYRTLE CREEK—Charter Communications. Now served by ROSEBURG, OR [OR0016]

MYRTLE CREEK—See ROSEBURG, OR (Charter Communications)

MYRTLE POINT—See COOS BAY, OR (Charter Communications)

NAHCOTTA—See ASTORIA, WA (Charter Communications)

NASELLE—See ASTORIA, WA (Charter Communications)

NEHALEM—See LINCOLN CITY, OR (Charter Communications)

NETARTS—See LINCOLN CITY, OR (Charter Communications)

NEW BRIDGE—See RICHLAND, OR (Eagle Valley Communications)

NEWBERG—Comcast Cable. Now served by PORTLAND, OR [OR0001]

NEWBERG—See PORTLAND, OR (Comcast Cable)

NEWPORT—See LINCOLN CITY, OR (Charter Communications)

NORTH BEND—See COOS BAY, OR (Charter Communications)

NORTH PLAINS—See PORTLAND, OR (Comcast Cable)

NORTH POWDER—Formerly served by Almega Cable. No longer in operation

OAKLAND—See ROSEBURG, OR (Charter Communications)

OAKRIDGE—See COTTAGE GROVE, OR (Charter Communications)

OCEAN PARK—See ASTORIA, WA (Charter Communications)

ODELL—Valley TV Co-op Inc

OREGON CITY (UNINCORPORATED AREAS)—Clear Creek Telephone & TeleVision

OREGON CITY—See BEAVERCREEK, OR (BCT. Formerly [OR0167]. This cable system has converted to IPTV)

OREGON CITY—See PORTLAND, OR (Comcast Cable)

OTIS—Formerly served by Wave Broadband. No longer in operation

OYSTERVILLE—See ASTORIA, WA (Charter Communications)

PACIFIC COUNTY—See ASTORIA, WA (Charter Communications)

PARKDALE—Valley TV Co-op Inc

PENDLETON—Charter Communications. Now served by KENNEWICK, WA [WA0008]

PHILOMATH—See PORTLAND, OR (Comcast Cable)

PHOENIX—See MEDFORD, OR (Charter Communications)

POLK COUNTY (PORTIONS)—See DALLAS, OR (Charter Communications)

POLK COUNTY (PORTIONS)—See PORTLAND, OR (Comcast Cable)

PORT ORFORD—See COOS BAY, OR (Charter Communications)

PORTLAND (western portion)—Comcast Cable. Now served by PORTLAND, OR [OR0001]

PORTLAND—Comcast Cable

POWERS—Formerly served by Charter Communications. No longer in operation

PRAIRIE CITY—Blue Mountain TV Cable Co. Now served by MOUNT VERNON, OR [OR0061]

PRAIRIE CITY—See MOUNT VERNON, OR (Blue Mountain TV Cable Co)

PRINEVILLE—Formerly served by Central Vision. No longer in operation

PRINEVILLE—Crestview Cable TV

PROSPECT—Formerly served by Almega Cable. No longer in operation

RAINIER—J & N Cable

REDLAND—See OREGON CITY (unincorporated areas), OR (Clear Creek Telephone & TeleVision)

REDMOND—Formerly served by Central Vision. No longer in operation

REDMOND—See BEND, OR (BendBroadband)

REEDSPORT—See COOS BAY, OR (Charter Communications)

RICHLAND—Eagle Valley Communications

RIDDLE—See ROSEBURG, OR (Charter Communications)

RIVERGROVE—See PORTLAND, OR (Comcast Cable)

ROCKAWAY BEACH—See LINCOLN CITY, OR (Charter Communications)

ROGUE RIVER—See MEDFORD, OR (Charter Communications)

ROSE LODGE—Formerly served by Wave Broadband. No longer in operation

ROSEBURG—Charter Communications

SALEM (southeastern portion)—Formerly served by Mill Creek Cable TV Inc. No longer in operation

SALEM—Comcast Cable. Now served by PORTLAND, OR [OR0001]

SALEM—See PORTLAND, OR (Comcast Cable)

SALMON RIVER—See DEPOE BAY, OR (Wave Broadband)

SANDY—Wave Broadband

SCAPPOOSE—See PORTLAND, OR (Comcast Cable)

SCIO—Scio Cablevision Inc

SEASIDE—See ASTORIA, OR (Charter Communications)

SEAVIEW—See ASTORIA, WA (Charter Communications)

SENECA—Blue Mountain TV Cable Co. Now served by MOUNT VERNON, OR [OR0061]

SENECA—See MOUNT VERNON, OR (Blue Mountain TV Cable Co)

SHADY COVE—Formerly served by Almega Cable. No longer in operation

SHERIDAN—Wave Broadband. Now served by SILVERTON, OR [OR0047]

SHERIDAN—See SILVERTON, OR (Wave Broadband)

SHERWOOD—See PORTLAND, OR (Comcast Cable)

SILETZ RIVER—See DEPOE BAY, OR (Wave Broadband)

SILETZ—Formerly served by Millennium Digital Media. Now served by Wave Broadband, DEPOE BAY, OR [OR0134]

SILETZ—See DEPOE BAY, OR (Wave Broadband)

SILVERTON—Wave Broadband

SISTERS—See BEND, OR (BendBroadband)

SODAVILLE—See PORTLAND, OR (Comcast Cable)

SOUTH BEACH—Formerly served by Millennium Digital Media. Now served by Wave Broadband, DEPOE BAY, OR [OR0134]

SOUTH BEACH—See DEPOE BAY, OR (Wave Broadband)

SOUTH SALEM—Formerly served by Country Cablevision Ltd. No longer in operation

SPRING RIVER—See SUNRIVER, OR (BendBroadband)

SPRINGFIELD—See PORTLAND, OR (Comcast Cable)

ST. HELENS—Comcast Cable. Now served by PORTLAND, OR [OR0001]

ST. HELENS—See PORTLAND, OR (Comcast Cable)

ST. PAUL (town)—Formerly served by St. Paul Cooperative Telephone Assoc. No longer in operation

STAYTON—See TURNER, OR (Wave Broadband)

SUBLIMITY—See SILVERTON, OR (Wave Broadband)

SUMPTER—Formerly served by Almega Cable. No longer in operation

SUNRIVER—BendBroadband

SUTHERLIN—See ROSEBURG, OR (Charter Communications)

SWEET HOME—See PORTLAND, OR (Comcast Cable)

TALENT—See MEDFORD, OR (Charter Communications)

TANGENT—See PORTLAND, OR (Comcast Cable)

TERREBONNE—See BEND, OR (BendBroadband)

THE DALLES—Charter Communications

TIDEWATER—See WALDPORT, OR (Alsea River Cable Co)

TIGARD—See PORTLAND, OR (Comcast Cable)

TILLAMOOK COUNTY (PORTIONS)—See LINCOLN CITY, OR (Charter Communications)

TILLAMOOK—See LINCOLN CITY, OR (Charter Communications)

TOLEDO—See LINCOLN CITY, OR (Charter Communications)

TRI-CITY—See ROSEBURG, OR (Charter Communications)

TROUTDALE—See PORTLAND, OR (Comcast Cable)

TUALATIN—See PORTLAND, OR (Comcast Cable)

TURNER—Wave Broadband

TYGH VALLEY—Formerly served by J & N Cable. No longer in operation

UMATILLA—Formerly served by Rapid Cable. No longer in operation

UNION COUNTY—See LA GRANDE, OR (Charter Communications)

UNION—See LA GRANDE, OR (Charter Communications)

VENETA—See COTTAGE GROVE, OR (Charter Communications)

VERNONIA—Vernonia CATV Inc.

WALDPORT—Alsea River Cable Co

Oregon—Cable Community Index

WALDPORT—See LINCOLN CITY, OR (Charter Communications)

WALLOWA LAKE—See ENTERPRISE, OR (Crystal Broadband Networks)

WALLOWA—See ENTERPRISE, OR (Crystal Broadband Networks)

WARM SPRINGS—Formerly served by American Telecasting of America Inc. No longer in operation

WARREN—See PORTLAND, OR (Comcast Cable)

WARRENTON—See ASTORIA, OR (Charter Communications)

WASCO COUNTY—See THE DALLES, OR (Charter Communications)

WASCO—Formerly served by J & N Cable. No longer in operation

WASHINGTON COUNTY (PORTIONS)—See PORTLAND, OR (Comcast Cable)

WATERLOO—See PORTLAND, OR (Comcast Cable)

WEMME—See SANDY, OR (Wave Broadband)

WEST LINN—See PORTLAND, OR (Comcast Cable)

WESTFIR—See COTTAGE GROVE, OR (Charter Communications)

WESTON—Formerly served by Rapid Cable. No longer in operation

WESTPORT—Formerly served by Almega Cable. No longer in operation

WESTWOOD VILLAGE—See WALDPORT, OR (Alsea River Cable Co)

WHEELER—See LINCOLN CITY, OR (Charter Communications)

WHITE SALMON—See THE DALLES, WA (Charter Communications)

WILLAMINA—See SILVERTON, OR (Wave Broadband)

WILSONVILLE—See PORTLAND, OR (Comcast Cable)

WINCHESTER BAY—See COOS BAY, OR (Charter Communications)

WINSTON—See ROSEBURG, OR (Charter Communications)

WOOD VILLAGE—See PORTLAND, OR (Comcast Cable)

WOODBURN—Wave Broadband. Now served by SILVERTON, OR [OR0047]

WOODBURN—See SILVERTON, OR (Wave Broadband)

YACHATS—See LINCOLN CITY, OR (Charter Communications)

YAMHILL—See PORTLAND, OR (Comcast Cable)

PENNSYLVANIA

AARONSBURG—See MILLHEIM, PA (Millheim TV Transmission Co.)

ABBOTTSTOWN—See HARRISBURG, PA (Comcast Cable)

ABINGTON TWP. (MONTGOMERY COUNTY)—See HARRISBURG, PA (Comcast Cable)

ACCIDENT (UNINCORPORATED AREAS)—See ADDISON TWP. (southern portion), MD (Somerfield Cable TV Co)

ACCIDENT—See BLAIRSVILLE, MD (Comcast Cable)

ACME—See MAMMOTH, PA (Citizens Telecom. Formerly [PA0400]. This cable system has converted to IPTV)

ACME—See SALTLICK TWP., PA (Laurel Highland Total Communications)

ADAMS COUNTY (PORTIONS)—See HARRISBURG, PA (Comcast Cable)

ADAMS TWP. (BUTLER COUNTY)—See ZELIENOPLE, PA (Armstrong Cable Services)

ADAMS TWP. (Cambria County)—Comcast Cable. Now served by BLAIRSVILLE, PA [PA0320]

ADAMS TWP. (CAMBRIA COUNTY)—See BLAIRSVILLE, PA (Comcast Cable)

ADAMSBURG—See GREENSBURG, PA (Comcast Cable)

ADAMSTOWN—See EPHRATA, PA (Blue Ridge Communications)

ADDISON TWP. (SOUTHERN PORTION)—Somerfield Cable TV Co

ADDISON—See ADDISON TWP. (southern portion), PA (Somerfield Cable TV Co)

AKRON—See EPHRATA, PA (Blue Ridge Communications)

ALBA—See CANTON, PA (Zito Media)

ALBANY TWP.—See TUNKHANNOCK, PA (Blue Ridge Communications)

ALBRIGHTSVILLE—See LEHIGHTON, PA (Blue Ridge Communications)

ALBURTIS—See ALLENTOWN, PA (RCN. Formerly served by NORTHAMPTON BOROUGH, PA [PA0008]. This cable system has converted to IPTV)

ALBURTIS—See ALLENTOWN, PA (Service Electric Cable TV & Communications)

ALDAN—Comcast Cable. Now served by PHILADELPHIA, PA [PA0005]

ALDAN—See PHILADELPHIA, PA (Comcast Cable)

ALEXANDRIA BOROUGH—See HARRISBURG, PA (Comcast Cable)

ALIQUIPPA—See PITTSBURGH, PA (Comcast Cable)

ALLEGHENY TWP. (BLAIR COUNTY)—See ALTOONA, PA (Atlantic Broadband)

ALLEGHENY TWP. (CAMBRIA COUNTY)—See BLAIRSVILLE, PA (Comcast Cable)

ALLEGHENY TWP. (SOMERSET COUNTY)—See BLAIRSVILLE, PA (Comcast Cable)

ALLEGHENY TWP. (VENANGO COUNTY)—See ZELIENOPLE, PA (Armstrong Cable Services)

ALLEGHENY TWP. (WESTMORELAND COUNTY)—See BLAIRSVILLE, PA (Comcast Cable)

ALLEN TWP.—See LEHIGHTON, PA (Blue Ridge Communications)

ALLEN TWP.—See ALLENTOWN, PA (RCN. Formerly served by NORTHAMPTON BOROUGH, PA [PA0008]. This cable system has converted to IPTV)

ALLEN TWP.—See ALLENTOWN, PA (Service Electric Cable TV & Communications)

ALLENPORT—See ZELIENOPLE, PA (Armstrong Cable Services)

ALLENSVILLE—Formerly served by Valley Cable Systems. No longer in operation

ALLENTOWN—RCN. Formerly served by NORTHAMPTON BOROUGH, PA [PA0008]. This cable system has converted to IPTV

ALLENTOWN—Service Electric Cable TV & Communications

ALLIS HOLLOW—See ROME, PA (Beaver Valley Cable Co)

ALLISON TWP.—See HARRISBURG, PA (Comcast Cable)

ALSACE TWP.—See HARRISBURG, PA (Comcast Cable)

ALTOONA—Atlantic Broadband

ALUM BANK—See BLAIRSVILLE, PA (Comcast Cable)

AMBRIDGE—See PITTSBURGH, PA (Comcast Cable)

AMITY TWP. (BERKS COUNTY)—See BIRDSBORO, PA (Service Electric Cablevision)

AMWELL TWP.—See NORTH BETHLEHEM TWP., PA (Bentleyville Communications)

AMWELL TWP.—See PITTSBURGH, PA (Comcast Cable)

ANDOVER VILLAGE—See ZELIENOPLE, OH (Armstrong Cable Services)

ANDOVER—See ZELIENOPLE, OH (Armstrong Cable Services)

ANNIN TWP.—See COUDERSPORT, PA (Zito Media)

ANNVILLE—See HARRISBURG, PA (Comcast Cable)

ANTHONY TWP.—See HARRISBURG, PA (Comcast Cable)

ANTIS TWP.—See ALTOONA, PA (Atlantic Broadband)

ANTRIM TWP.—See HARRISBURG, PA (Comcast Cable)

APOLLO BOROUGH—See PITTSBURGH, PA (Comcast Cable)

APPLEWOLD—See BLAIRSVILLE, PA (Comcast Cable)

ARARAT TWP.—See THOMPSON TWP., PA (Adams Cable Service)

ARCHBALD BOROUGH—See HARRISBURG, PA (Comcast Cable)

ARDEN—See PHILADELPHIA, DE (Comcast Cable)

ARDENCROFT—See PHILADELPHIA, DE (Comcast Cable)

ARDENTOWN—See PHILADELPHIA, DE (Comcast Cable)

ARENDTSVILLE—See HARRISBURG, PA (Comcast Cable)

ARISTES—See SUNBURY (village), PA (Service Electric Cablevision)

ARMAGH—Comcast Cable. Now served by BLAIRSVILLE, PA [PA0320]

ARMAGH—See BLAIRSVILLE, PA (Comcast Cable)

ARMAGH—See HARRISBURG, PA (Comcast Cable)

ARMSTRONG TWP. (INDIANA COUNTY)—See BLAIRSVILLE, PA (Comcast Cable)

ARMSTRONG TWP. (LYCOMING COUNTY)—See HARRISBURG, PA (Comcast Cable)

ARNOLD—See PITTSBURGH, PA (Comcast Cable)

ARNOT—Blue Ridge Communications. Now served by MANSFIELD, PA [PA0421]

ARNOT—See MANSFIELD, PA (Blue Ridge Communications)

ARONA—See GREENSBURG, PA (Comcast Cable)

ASHLAND TWP.—See SHIPPENVILLE, PA (Atlantic Broadband)

ASHLAND—See ZELIENOPLE, OH (Armstrong Cable Services)

ASHLAND—See SOUTH CREEK TWP., NY (Blue Ridge Communications)

ASHLAND—See HAZLETON, PA (Service Electric Cablevision)

ASHLEY—See WILKES-BARRE, PA (Service Electric Cable Company)

ASHVILLE BOROUGH—See BLAIRSVILLE, PA (Comcast Cable)

ASPINWALL—See PITTSBURGH, PA (Comcast Cable)

ASTON TWP.—See PHILADELPHIA, PA (Comcast Cable)

ASYLUM TWP.—See HARRISBURG, PA (Comcast Cable)

ATGLEN—See PHILADELPHIA, PA (Comcast Cable)

ATHALIA—See ZELIENOPLE, OH (Armstrong Cable Services)

Cable Community Index—Pennsylvania

AUBURN—Comcast Cable. Now served by HARRISBURG, PA [PA0009]

AUBURN—See HARRISBURG, PA (Comcast Cable)

AULTMAN—Formerly served by Adelphia Communications. No longer in operation

AUSTIN BOROUGH—See COUDERSPORT, PA (Zito Media)

AUSTINTOWN TWP.—See ZELIENOPLE, OH (Armstrong Cable Services)

AUSTINVILLE—See TROY, PA (Blue Ridge Communications)

AVALON—See PITTSBURGH, PA (Comcast Cable)

AVELLA—Blue Devil Cable TV Inc. Now served by BURGETTSTOWN, PA [PA0323]

AVELLA—See BURGETTSTOWN, PA (Blue Devil Cable TV Inc)

AVIS—See HARRISBURG, PA (Comcast Cable)

AVOCA—See HARRISBURG, PA (Comcast Cable)

AVONDALE BOROUGH—See PHILADELPHIA, PA (Comcast Cable)

AVONMORE—See PITTSBURGH, PA (Comcast Cable)

AYR TWP.—See HARRISBURG, PA (Comcast Cable)

BADEN—See PITTSBURGH, PA (Comcast Cable)

BAGGALEY—See MAMMOTH, PA (Citizens Telecom. Formerly [PA0400]. This cable system has converted to IPTV)

BALD EAGLE TWP. (CLINTON COUNTY)—See HARRISBURG, PA (Comcast Cable)

BALDWIN—See PITTSBURGH, PA (Comcast Cable)

BANGOR BORO—See ALLENTOWN, PA (Service Electric Cable TV & Communications)

BANGOR BOROUGH—See ALLENTOWN, PA (RCN. Formerly served by NORTHAMPTON BOROUGH, PA [PA0008]. This cable system has converted to IPTV)

BANKS TWP. (CARBON COUNTY)—See HAZLETON, PA (Service Electric Cablevision)

BANKS TWP.—See BLAIRSVILLE, PA (Comcast Cable)

BARBOURS—See ELDRED TWP., PA (Herr Cable Co)

BARKEYVILLE—See ZELIENOPLE, PA (Armstrong Cable Services)

BARNES—See SHEFFIELD, PA (WestPA.net Inc)

BARR TWP.—See BLAIRSVILLE, PA (Comcast Cable)

BARREE TWP.—See McALEVYS FORT, PA (Atlantic Broadband)

BARRETT TWP.—See STROUDSBURG, PA (Blue Ridge Communications)

BARRY TWP.—See HAZLETON, PA (Service Electric Cablevision)

BART TWP.—See HARRISBURG, PA (Comcast Cable)

BASTRESS TWP.—Formerly served by Bastress TV Cable Association. No longer in operation

BASTRESS TWP.—See HARRISBURG, PA (Comcast Cable)

BATH BORO—See ALLENTOWN, PA (Service Electric Cable TV & Communications)

BATH—See ALLENTOWN, PA (RCN. Formerly served by NORTHAMPTON BOROUGH, PA [PA0008]. This cable system has converted to IPTV)

BAUGHMAN TWP.—See ZELIENOPLE, OH (Armstrong Cable Services)

BEACH HAVEN—See BERWICK, PA (MetroCast Communications)

BEACH LAKE—Blue Ridge Communications

BEALLSVILLE—See UNIONTOWN, PA (Atlantic Broadband)

BEAR CREEK TWP.—See WEATHERLY, PA (MetroCast Communications)

BEAR CREEK TWP.—See WILKES-BARRE, PA (Service Electric Cable Company)

BEAVER FALLS—Comcast Cable. Now served by PITTSBURGH, PA [PA0001]

BEAVER FALLS—See PITTSBURGH, PA (Comcast Cable)

BEAVER MEADOWS—See HAZLETON, PA (Service Electric Cablevision)

BEAVER SPRINGS—Formerly served by Service Electric Cable TV & Communications. No longer in operation

BEAVER TWP. (CLARION COUNTY)—See SHIPPENVILLE, PA (Atlantic Broadband)

BEAVER TWP. (JEFFERSON COUNTY)—See PUNXSUTAWNEY, PA (Comcast Cable)

BEAVER TWP. (SNYDER COUNTY)—See SUNBURY (village), PA (Service Electric Cablevision)

BEAVER TWP.—See ZELIENOPLE, OH (Armstrong Cable Services)

BEAVER VALLEY—Formerly served by Comcast Cable. No longer in operation

BEAVER—See PITTSBURGH, PA (Comcast Cable)

BEAVERTOWN BOROUGH—See SUNBURY (village), PA (Service Electric Cablevision)

BEAVERTOWN—Formerly served by Nittany Media Inc. No longer in operation

BECCARIA TWP.—See BLAIRSVILLE, PA (Comcast Cable)

BEDFORD TWP.—See BLAIRSVILLE, PA (Comcast Cable)

BEDFORD—Comcast Cable. Now served by BLAIRSVILLE, PA [PA0320]

BEDFORD—See BLAIRSVILLE, PA (Comcast Cable)

BEECH CREEK BOROUGH—See HARRISBURG, PA (Comcast Cable)

BEECH CREEK TWP.—See HARRISBURG, PA (Comcast Cable)

BELFAST—See ALLENTOWN, PA (RCN. Formerly served by NORTHAMPTON BOROUGH, PA [PA0008]. This cable system has converted to IPTV)

BELL ACRES—See PITTSBURGH, PA (Comcast Cable)

BELL TWP. (CLEARFIELD COUNTY)—See PUNXSUTAWNEY, PA (Comcast Cable)

BELL TWP. (JEFFERSON COUNTY)—See PUNXSUTAWNEY, PA (Comcast Cable)

BELL TWP. (WESTMORELAND COUNTY)—See BLAIRSVILLE, PA (Comcast Cable)

BELLE VERNON—See PITTSBURGH, PA (Comcast Cable)

BELLEFONTE BOROUGH—See HARRISBURG, PA (Comcast Cable)

BELLEFONTE—See PHILADELPHIA, DE (Comcast Cable)

BELLEVILLE—Zampelli Electronics

BELLEVUE—See PITTSBURGH, PA (Comcast Cable)

BELLWOOD—See ALTOONA, PA (Atlantic Broadband)

BEN AVON HEIGHTS—See PITTSBURGH, PA (Comcast Cable)

BEN AVON—See PITTSBURGH, PA (Comcast Cable)

BENDERSVILLE—See HARRISBURG, PA (Comcast Cable)

BENNER TWP.—See HARRISBURG, PA (Comcast Cable)

BENSALEM—Comcast Cable. Now served by EATONTOWN BOROUGH, NJ [NJ0009]

BENSON—See JOHNSTOWN, PA (Atlantic Broadband)

BENTLEY CREEK—Blue Ridge Communications

BENTLEYVILLE—See UNIONTOWN, PA (Atlantic Broadband)

BENTLEYVILLE—See NORTH BETHLEHEM TWP., PA (Bentleyville Communications)

BENTON TWP. (LACKAWANNA COUNTY)—See HARRISBURG, PA (Comcast Cable)

BENTON—See BERWICK, PA (MetroCast Communications)

BENZINGER TWP.—See ST. MARY'S, PA (Zito Media)

BERLIN BOROUGH—See BLAIRSVILLE, PA (Comcast Cable)

BERLIN TWP. (MAHONING COUNTY)—See ZELIENOPLE, OH (Armstrong Cable Services)

BERLIN TWP. (WAYNE COUNTY)—See MILFORD, PA (Blue Ridge Communications)

BERN TWP. (BERKS COUNTY)—See HARRISBURG, PA (Comcast Cable)

BERN TWP.—See HARRISBURG, PA (Comcast Cable)

BERNVILLE—See HARRISBURG, PA (Comcast Cable)

BERRYSBURG—See HARRISBURG, PA (Comcast Cable)

BERWICK TWP. (ADAMS COUNTY)—See HARRISBURG, PA (Comcast Cable)

BERWICK—MetroCast Communications

BETHANY—See MILFORD, PA (Blue Ridge Communications)

BETHEL (BERKS COUNTY)—See HARRISBURG, PA (Comcast Cable)

BETHEL TWP. (ARMSTRONG COUNTY)—See BLAIRSVILLE, PA (Comcast Cable)

BETHEL TWP. (DELAWARE COUNTY)—See PHILADELPHIA, PA (Comcast Cable)

BETHEL TWP. (LEBANON COUNTY)—See HARRISBURG, PA (Comcast Cable)

BETHEL—Comcast Cable. Now served by PITTSBURGH, PA [PA0001]

BETHEL—See PITTSBURGH, PA (Comcast Cable)

BETHLEHEM TWP.—See ALLENTOWN, PA (RCN. Formerly served by NORTHAMPTON BOROUGH, PA [PA0008]. This cable system has converted to IPTV)

BETHLEHEM TWP.—See ALLENTOWN, PA (Service Electric Cable TV & Communications)

BETHLEHEM—See ALLENTOWN, PA (RCN. Formerly served by NORTHAMPTON BOROUGH, PA [PA0008]. This cable system has converted to IPTV)

BETHLEHEM—See ALLENTOWN, PA (Service Electric Cable TV & Communications)

BEVERLY HILLS—See RIDLEY PARK, PA (RCN. Formerly served by PHILADELPHIA (suburbs), PA [PA0447]. This cable system has converted to IPTV)

BIG BEAVER TWP.—See PITTSBURGH, PA (Comcast Cable)

Pennsylvania—Cable Community Index

BIG BEAVER—See ZELIENOPLE, PA (Armstrong Cable Services)

BIG POND—Formerly served by Barrett's TV Cable System. No longer in operation

BIG RUN—See PUNXSUTAWNEY, PA (Comcast Cable)

BIGLER TWP.—Comcast Cable. Now served by HARRISBURG, PA [PA0009]

BIGLER TWP.—See HARRISBURG, PA (Comcast Cable)

BIGLERVILLE—See HARRISBURG, PA (Comcast Cable)

BIRDSBORO—Service Electric Cablevision

BIRMINGHAM BOROUGH—See ALTOONA, PA (Atlantic Broadband)

BIRMINGHAM TWP.—See PHILADELPHIA, PA (Comcast Cable)

BLACK CREEK TWP.—See BERWICK, PA (MetroCast Communications)

BLACK LICK TWP.—See BLAIRSVILLE, PA (Comcast Cable)

BLACK TWP.—See BLAIRSVILLE, PA (Comcast Cable)

BLACKLICK TWP.—See BLAIRSVILLE, PA (Comcast Cable)

BLACKSVILLE—See BRAVE, WV (Zito Media)

BLAIR TWP. (BLAIR COUNTY)—See ALTOONA, PA (Atlantic Broadband)

BLAIRS MILLS—See DOYLESBURG, PA (Valley Cable Systems)

BLAIRSVILLE—Comcast Cable

BLAKELY BOROUGH—See HARRISBURG, PA (Comcast Cable)

BLAKESLEE—See WEATHERLY, PA (MetroCast Communications)

BLAWNOX BOROUGH—See PITTSBURGH, PA (Comcast Cable)

BLOOM TWP.—See CLEARFIELD, PA (Atlantic Broadband)

BLOOMFIELD TWP.—See ALTOONA, PA (Atlantic Broadband)

BLOOMFIELD TWP.—See CANADOHTA LAKE, PA (Master Vision)

BLOOMING GROVE TWP. (RICHLAND COUNTY)—See ZELIENOPLE, OH (Armstrong Cable Services)

BLOOMING VALLEY—See ZELIENOPLE, PA (Armstrong Cable Services)

BLOOMSBURG—Service Electric Cable TV & Communications. Now served by SUNBURY (village), PA [PA0029]

BLOOMSBURG—See SUNBURY (village), PA (Service Electric Cablevision)

BLOSERVILLE—Kuhn Communications

BLOSS—See MANSFIELD, PA (Blue Ridge Communications)

BLOSSBURG—Formerly served by Williamson Road TV Co. Inc. No longer in operation

BLOSSBURG—See MANSFIELD, PA (Blue Ridge Communications)

BLUE BALL—See HARRISBURG, PA (Comcast Cable)

BLYTHE TWP.—See WEATHERLY, PA (MetroCast Communications)

BLYTHE TWP.—See HAZLETON, PA (Service Electric Cablevision)

BOARDMAN TWP.—See ZELIENOPLE, OH (Armstrong Cable Services)

BOBTOWN—See UNIONTOWN, PA (Atlantic Broadband)

BOGGS TWP. (ARMSTRONG COUNTY)—See BLAIRSVILLE, PA (Comcast Cable)

BOGGS TWP. (CENTRE COUNTY)—See HARRISBURG, PA (Comcast Cable)

BOGGS TWP. (CLEARFIELD COUNTY)—See CLEARFIELD, PA (Atlantic Broadband)

BOGGS TWP. (CLEARFIELD COUNTY)—See HARRISBURG, PA (Comcast Cable)

BOGGS TWP. (CLEARFIELD COUNTY)—See SNOW SHOE, PA (Tele-Media)

BOHEMIA—See MILFORD, PA (Blue Ridge Communications)

BOLIVAR BOROUGH—See BLAIRSVILLE, PA (Comcast Cable)

BONNEAUVILLE—See HARRISBURG, PA (Comcast Cable)

BOONE COUNTY (PORTIONS)—See ZELIENOPLE, WV (Armstrong Cable Services)

BOSWELL BOROUGH—See BLAIRSVILLE, PA (Comcast Cable)

BOWMANSTOWN—See LEHIGHTON, PA (Blue Ridge Communications)

BOYD COUNTY (PORTIONS)—See ZELIENOPLE, KY (Armstrong Cable Services)

BOYERS—Formerly served by Cebridge Connections. Now served by Armstrong Cable Services, ZELIENOPLE, PA [PA0053]

BOYERS—See ZELIENOPLE, PA (Armstrong Cable Services)

BRACKENRIDGE BOROUGH—See PITTSBURGH, PA (Comcast Cable)

BRADDOCK BOROUGH—See PITTSBURGH, PA (Comcast Cable)

BRADDOCK HILLS—See PITTSBURGH, PA (Comcast Cable)

BRADFORD COUNTY—See BENTLEY CREEK, PA (Blue Ridge Communications)

BRADFORD TWP. (CLEARFIELD COUNTY)—See CLEARFIELD, PA (Atlantic Broadband)

BRADFORD TWP. (MCKEAN COUNTY)—See BRADFORD, PA (Atlantic Broadband)

BRADFORD WOODS—See ZELIENOPLE, PA (Armstrong Cable Services)

BRADFORD—Atlantic Broadband

BRADY TWP. (BUTLER COUNTY)—See ZELIENOPLE, PA (Armstrong Cable Services)

BRADY TWP. (CLEARFIELD COUNTY)—See PUNXSUTAWNEY, PA (Comcast Cable)

BRADY TWP. (HUNTINGDON COUNTY)—See HARRISBURG, PA (Comcast Cable)

BRADY TWP. (LYCOMING COUNTY)—See HARRISBURG, PA (Comcast Cable)

BRADY TWP.—See ZELIENOPLE, PA (Armstrong Cable Services)

BRADYS BEND TWP.—See ZELIENOPLE, PA (Armstrong Cable Services)

BRAINTRIM TWP.—See TUNKHANNOCK, PA (Blue Ridge Communications)

BRANCH TWP.—See HARRISBURG, PA (Comcast Cable)

BRANCH TWP.—See CASS TWP. (Schuylkill County), PA (J. B. Cable)

BRATTON TWP.—See MIFFLINTOWN, PA (Nittany Media Inc.)

BRAVE—Zito Media

BRECKNOCK TWP. (BERKS COUNTY)—See BIRDSBORO, PA (Service Electric Cablevision)

BRECKNOCK TWP. (LANCASTER COUNTY)—See EPHRATA, PA (Blue Ridge Communications)

BRECKNOCK TWP. (LANCASTER COUNTY)—See HARRISBURG, PA (Comcast Cable)

BREINIGSVILLE—See ALLENTOWN, PA (RCN. Formerly served by NORTHAMPTON BOROUGH, PA [PA0008]. This cable system has converted to IPTV)

BRENTWOOD—See PITTSBURGH, PA (Comcast Cable)

BRIAR CREEK—See BERWICK, PA (MetroCast Communications)

BRIDGETON TWP.—See ALLENTOWN, PA (Service Electric Cable TV & Communications)

BRIDGEVILLE—See PITTSBURGH, PA (Comcast Cable)

BRIDGEWATER—See PITTSBURGH, PA (Comcast Cable)

BRIGHTON TWP.—See ZELIENOPLE, OH (Armstrong Cable Services)

BRIGHTON TWP.—See PITTSBURGH, PA (Comcast Cable)

BRISBIN BOROUGH—See HARRISBURG, PA (Comcast Cable)

BROAD TOP CITY—Formerly served by Adelphia Communications. Now served by Comcast Cable, HARRISBURG, PA [PA0009]

BROAD TOP CITY—See HARRISBURG, PA (Comcast Cable)

BROAD TOP TWP.—See HARRISBURG, PA (Comcast Cable)

BROCKTON—See WEATHERLY, PA (MetroCast Communications)

BROCKWAY—Brockway TV Inc

BROKENSTRAW TWP.—See ZELIENOPLE, PA (Armstrong Cable Services)

BROKENSTRAW TWP.—See YOUNGSVILLE, PA (Youngsville TV Corp)

BROOKHAVEN—See PHILADELPHIA, PA (Comcast Cable)

BROOKLYN TWP.—See THOMPSON TWP., PA (Adams Cable Service)

BROOKVILLE BOROUGH—See PUNXSUTAWNEY, PA (Comcast Cable)

BROOKVILLE—See PUNXSUTAWNEY, PA (Comcast Cable)

BROTHERSVALLEY TWP.—Comcast Cable. Now served by BLAIRSVILLE, PA [PA0320]

BROTHERSVALLEY TWP.—See BLAIRSVILLE, PA (Comcast Cable)

BROWN TWP. (MIFFLIN COUNTY)—See HARRISBURG, PA (Comcast Cable)

BROWNDALE—See CARBONDALE TWP. (Lackawanna County), PA (Adams Cable Service)

BROWNSTOWN (CAMBRIA COUNTY)—See JOHNSTOWN, PA (Atlantic Broadband)

BROWNSVILLE—See UNIONTOWN, PA (Atlantic Broadband)

BRUCETON MILLS—See GREENSBURG, WV (Comcast Cable)

BRUIN—See ZELIENOPLE, PA (Armstrong Cable Services)

BRUNSWICK HILLS TWP.—See ZELIENOPLE, OH (Armstrong Cable Services)

BRUSH VALLEY TWP.—Formerly served by Brush Valley Cablevision. No longer in operation

BUCK HILL FALLS—See STROUDSBURG, PA (Blue Ridge Communications)

BUCK TWP.—See WILKES-BARRE, PA (Service Electric Cable Company)

BUFFALO TWP. (BUTLER COUNTY)—See ZELIENOPLE, PA (Armstrong Cable Services)

BUFFALO TWP. (BUTLER COUNTY)—See PITTSBURGH, PA (Comcast Cable)

BUFFALO TWP. (PERRY COUNTY)—See HARRISBURG, PA (Comcast Cable)

Cable Community Index—Pennsylvania

BUFFALO TWP. (UNION COUNTY)—See MIFFLINBURG, PA (Atlantic Broadband)

BUFFALO TWP. (UNION COUNTY)—See SUNBURY (village), PA (Service Electric Cablevision)

BUFFALO TWP. (WASHINGTON COUNTY)—See PITTSBURGH, PA (Comcast Cable)

BUFFALO TWP.—Formerly served by D&E Communications/Windstream. IPTV service no longer in operation

BUFFINGTON TWP.—See BLAIRSVILLE, PA (Comcast Cable)

BULLSKIN TWP.—See ZELIENOPLE, PA (Armstrong Cable Services)

BURGETTSTOWN—Blue Devil Cable TV Inc

BURLINGTON BOROUGH—See TROY, PA (Blue Ridge Communications)

BURLINGTON—See TROY, PA (Blue Ridge Communications)

BURNHAM BOROUGH—See HARRISBURG, PA (Comcast Cable)

BURNSIDE (CLEARFIELD COUNTY)—See SNOW SHOE, PA (Tele-Media)

BURNSIDE TWP. (CLEARFIELD COUNTY)—See BLAIRSVILLE, PA (Comcast Cable)

BURNSIDE—See PUNXSUTAWNEY, PA (Comcast Cable)

BURRELL TWP. (ARMSTRONG COUNTY)—See BLAIRSVILLE, PA (Comcast Cable)

BURRELL TWP. (INDIANA COUNTY)—See BLAIRSVILLE, PA (Comcast Cable)

BUSHKILL TWP.—See ALLENTOWN, PA (Service Electric Cable TV & Communications)

BUTLER TWP. (ADAMS COUNTY)—See HARRISBURG, PA (Comcast Cable)

BUTLER TWP. (BUTLER COUNTY)—See ZELIENOPLE, PA (Armstrong Cable Services)

BUTLER TWP. (LUZERNE COUNTY)—See HAZLETON, PA (Service Electric Cablevision)

BUTLER TWP. (RICHLAND COUNTY)—See ZELIENOPLE, OH (Armstrong Cable Services)

BUTLER—Armstrong Cable Services. Now served by ZELIENOPLE, PA [PA0053]

BUTLER—See ZELIENOPLE, PA (Armstrong Cable Services)

CADOGAN—See BLAIRSVILLE, PA (Comcast Cable)

CAERNARVON TWP. (BERKS COUNTY)—See BIRDSBORO, PA (Service Electric Cablevision)

CAERNARVON TWP. (LANCASTER COUNTY)—See EPHRATA, PA (Blue Ridge Communications)

CAERNARVON TWP. (LANCASTER COUNTY)—See HARRISBURG, PA (Comcast Cable)

CAERNARVON TWP. (LANCASTER COUNTY)—See BIRDSBORO, PA (Service Electric Cablevision)

CALEDONIA—See WEEDVILLE, PA (Zito Media)

CALIFORNIA—Armstrong Cable Services. Now served by ZELIENOPLE, PA [PA0053]

CALIFORNIA—See ZELIENOPLE, PA (Armstrong Cable Services)

CALLENSBURG—Formerly served by Cebridge Connections. Now served by Armstrong Cable Services, BUTLER, PA [PA0044]

CALLENSBURG—See ZELIENOPLE, PA (Armstrong Cable Services)

CALLERY—See ZELIENOPLE, PA (Armstrong Cable Services)

CALN TWP.—See PHILADELPHIA, PA (Comcast Cable)

CAMBRIA TWP.—See BLAIRSVILLE, PA (Comcast Cable)

CAMBRIDGE SPRINGS—See EDINBORO, PA (Coaxial Cable TV Corp)

CAMBRIDGE TWP. (CRAWFORD COUNTY)—See EDINBORO, PA (Coaxial Cable TV Corp)

CAMP HILL CORRECTIONAL INSTITUTE—Formerly served by Suddenlink Communications. No longer in operation

CAMP HILL—See HARRISBURG, PA (Comcast Cable)

CAMPBELL—See ZELIENOPLE, OH (Armstrong Cable Services)

CAMPTOWN—See TUNKHANNOCK, PA (Blue Ridge Communications)

CANAAN TWP. (WAYNE COUNTY)—See CARBONDALE TWP. (Lackawanna County), PA (Adams Cable Service)

CANADOHTA LAKE—Master Vision

CANFIELD TWP.—See ZELIENOPLE, OH (Armstrong Cable Services)

CANFIELD—See ZELIENOPLE, OH (Armstrong Cable Services)

CANOE CREEK—Atlantic Broadband. Now served by ALTOONA, PA [PA0018]

CANOE CREEK—See ALTOONA, PA (Atlantic Broadband)

CANOE TWP.—See PUNXSUTAWNEY, PA (Comcast Cable)

CANONSBURG—Comcast Cable. Now served by PITTSBURGH, PA [PA0001]

CANONSBURG—See PITTSBURGH, PA (Comcast Cable)

CANTON TWP. (BRADFORD COUNTY)—See CANTON, PA (Zito Media)

CANTON—Zito Media

CARBON TWP.—See HARRISBURG, PA (Comcast Cable)

CARBONDALE TWP. (LACKAWANNA COUNTY)—Adams Cable Service

CARBONDALE—See CARBONDALE TWP. (Lackawanna County), PA (Adams Cable Service)

CARLISLE BARRACKS—See HARRISBURG, PA (Comcast Cable)

CARLISLE—Comcast Cable. Now served by HARRISBURG, PA [PA0009]

CARLISLE—See HARRISBURG, PA (Comcast Cable)

CARMICHAELS—See UNIONTOWN, PA (Atlantic Broadband)

CARNEGIE—Comcast Cable. Now served by PITTSBURGH, PA [PA0001]

CARNEGIE—See PITTSBURGH, PA (Comcast Cable)

CARROLL TWP. (PERRY COUNTY)—See NEWBERRY TWP., PA (Blue Ridge Communications)

CARROLL TWP. (PERRY COUNTY)—See HARRISBURG, PA (Comcast Cable)

CARROLL TWP. (WASHINGTON COUNTY)—See PITTSBURGH, PA (Comcast Cable)

CARROLL TWP. (YORK COUNTY)—See HARRISBURG, PA (Comcast Cable)

CARROLL VALLEY—See HARRISBURG, PA (Comcast Cable)

CARROLLTON (TOWN)—See BRADFORD, NY (Atlantic Broadband)

CARROLLTOWN BOROUGH—Formerly served by Adelphia Communications. Now served by Comcast Cable, BLAIRSVILLE, PA [PA0320]

CARROLLTOWN BOROUGH—See BLAIRSVILLE, PA (Comcast Cable)

CARROLLTOWN—Formerly served by Adelphia Communications. Now served by Comcast Cable, BLAIRSVILLE, PA [PA0320]

CASCADE—See HARRISBURG, MD (Comcast Cable)

CASS TWP. (HUNTINGDON COUNTY)—See ALTOONA, PA (Atlantic Broadband)

CASS TWP. (SCHUYLKILL COUNTY)—See HARRISBURG, PA (Comcast Cable)

CASS TWP. (SCHUYLKILL COUNTY)—J. B. Cable

CASSANDRA BOROUGH—See BLAIRSVILLE, PA (Comcast Cable)

CASSVILLE—See ALTOONA, PA (Atlantic Broadband)

CASTANEA—See HARRISBURG, PA (Comcast Cable)

CASTLE SHANNON—Comcast Cable. Now served by PITTSBURGH, PA [PA0001]

CASTLE SHANNON—See PITTSBURGH, PA (Comcast Cable)

CATASAUQUA BORO—See ALLENTOWN, PA (Service Electric Cable TV & Communications)

CATASAUQUA—See ALLENTOWN, PA (RCN. Formerly served by NORTHAMPTON BOROUGH, PA [PA0008]. This cable system has converted to IPTV)

CATAWISSA BOROUGH—See SUNBURY (village), PA (Service Electric Cablevision)

CATAWISSA TWP.—See SUNBURY (village), PA (Service Electric Cablevision)

CATHERINE TWP.—See ALTOONA, PA (Atlantic Broadband)

CATHERINE TWP.—See HARRISBURG, PA (Comcast Cable)

CATLETTSBURG—See ZELIENOPLE, KY (Armstrong Cable Services)

CATLIN HOLLOW—See MANSFIELD, PA (Blue Ridge Communications)

CECIL—See PITTSBURGH, PA (Comcast Cable)

CEMENTON—See ALLENTOWN, PA (RCN. Formerly served by NORTHAMPTON BOROUGH, PA [PA0008]. This cable system has converted to IPTV)

CENTER CITY—See ALLENTOWN, PA (RCN. Formerly served by NORTHAMPTON BOROUGH, PA [PA0008]. This cable system has converted to IPTV)

CENTER TWP. (BEAVER COUNTY)—See PITTSBURGH, PA (Comcast Cable)

CENTER TWP. (BUTLER COUNTY)—See ZELIENOPLE, PA (Armstrong Cable Services)

CENTER TWP. (INDIANA COUNTY)—See BLAIRSVILLE, PA (Comcast Cable)

CENTER TWP. (PERRY COUNTY)—See MIFFLINTOWN, PA (Nittany Media Inc.)

CENTER TWP. (SNYDER COUNTY)—See HARRISBURG, PA (Comcast Cable)

CENTER TWP. (SNYDER COUNTY)—See SUNBURY (village), PA (Service Electric Cablevision)

CENTER VALLEY—See ALLENTOWN, PA (RCN. Formerly served by NORTHAMPTON BOROUGH, PA [PA0008]. This cable system has converted to IPTV)

CENTERPORT—See HARRISBURG, PA (Comcast Cable)

Pennsylvania—Cable Community Index

CENTERVILLE (BRADFORD COUNTY)—See BENTLEY CREEK, PA (Blue Ridge Communications)

CENTERVILLE—See ZELIENOPLE, PA (Armstrong Cable Services)

CENTERVILLE—See UNIONTOWN, PA (Atlantic Broadband)

CENTRAL CITY BOROUGH—See BLAIRSVILLE, PA (Comcast Cable)

CENTRALIA—See HAZLETON, PA (Service Electric Cablevision)

CENTRE HALL BOROUGH—See HARRISBURG, PA (Comcast Cable)

CENTRE TWP. (SNYDER COUNTY)—See SUNBURY (village), PA (Service Electric Cablevision)

CENTRE TWP.—See HARRISBURG, PA (Comcast Cable)

CEREDO—See ZELIENOPLE, WV (Armstrong Cable Services)

CETRONIA—See ALLENTOWN, PA (RCN. Formerly served by NORTHAMPTON BOROUGH, PA [PA0008]. This cable system has converted to IPTV)

CHADDS FORD TWP.—See PHILADELPHIA, PA (Comcast Cable)

CHALFANT—See PITTSBURGH, PA (Comcast Cable)

CHAMBERSBURG—See HARRISBURG, PA (Comcast Cable)

CHAMPION—See SALTLICK TWP., PA (Laurel Highland Total Communications)

CHANCEFORD—See HARRISBURG, PA (Comcast Cable)

CHAPMAN BORO—See ALLENTOWN, PA (Service Electric Cable TV & Communications)

CHAPMAN TWP. (CLINTON COUNTY)—See HARRISBURG, PA (Comcast Cable)

CHARLEROI—See PITTSBURGH, PA (Comcast Cable)

CHARLESTON TWP.—See MANSFIELD, PA (Blue Ridge Communications)

CHARTIERS TWP.—See PITTSBURGH, PA (Comcast Cable)

CHEMUNG—See SOUTH CREEK TWP., NY (Blue Ridge Communications)

CHERRY RIDGE TWP. (WAYNE COUNTY)—See MILFORD, PA (Blue Ridge Communications)

CHERRY TREE BOROUGH—See BLAIRSVILLE, PA (Comcast Cable)

CHERRY TWP. (SULLIVAN COUNTY)—See TUNKHANNOCK, PA (Blue Ridge Communications)

CHERRY TWP.—See ZELIENOPLE, PA (Armstrong Cable Services)

CHERRYHILL TWP.—See BLAIRSVILLE, PA (Comcast Cable)

CHERRYVILLE—See ALLENTOWN, PA (RCN. Formerly served by NORTHAMPTON BOROUGH, PA [PA0008]. This cable system has converted to IPTV)

CHESAPEAKE—See ZELIENOPLE, OH (Armstrong Cable Services)

CHESTER HEIGHTS—See PHILADELPHIA, PA (Comcast Cable)

CHESTER HILL BOROUGH—See HARRISBURG, PA (Comcast Cable)

CHESTER TWP.—See PHILADELPHIA, PA (Comcast Cable)

CHESTER—See PHILADELPHIA, PA (Comcast Cable)

CHESTNUT RIDGE—See PITTSBURGH, PA (Comcast Cable)

CHESTNUTHILL TWP.—See STROUDSBURG, PA (Blue Ridge Communications)

CHESTNUTHILL TWP.—See WEATHERLY, PA (MetroCast Communications)

CHESWICK BOROUGH—See PITTSBURGH, PA (Comcast Cable)

CHICORA—Armstrong Cable Services. Now served by ZELIENOPLE, PA [PA0053]

CHICORA—See ZELIENOPLE, PA (Armstrong Cable Services)

CHINCHILLA—See HARRISBURG, PA (Comcast Cable)

CHIPPEWA TWP.—See PITTSBURGH, PA (Comcast Cable)

CHRISTIANA—See HARRISBURG, PA (Comcast Cable)

CHURCHILL BOROUGH—See PITTSBURGH, PA (Comcast Cable)

CLAIRTON—See PITTSBURGH, PA (Comcast Cable)

CLARENDON HEIGHTS—See CLARENDON, PA (Clarendon TV Association)

CLARENDON—Clarendon TV Association

CLARION BOROUGH—Comcast Cable. Now served by OIL CITY, PA [PA0086]

CLARION BOROUGH—See OIL CITY, PA (Comcast Cable)

CLARION COUNTY (PORTIONS)—See SHIPPENVILLE, PA (Atlantic Broadband)

CLARION TWP.—See OIL CITY, PA (Comcast Cable)

CLARKS GREEN BOROUGH—See HARRISBURG, PA (Comcast Cable)

CLARKS SUMMIT BOROUGH—See HARRISBURG, PA (Comcast Cable)

CLARKSBURG—See BLAIRSVILLE, PA (Comcast Cable)

CLARKSVILLE—See UNIONTOWN, PA (Atlantic Broadband)

CLAY (LANCASTER COUNTY)—See HARRISBURG, PA (Comcast Cable)

CLAY TWP. (HUNTINGDON COUNTY)—See ALTOONA, PA (Atlantic Broadband)

CLAY TWP. (LANCASTER COUNTY)—See ZELIENOPLE, PA (Armstrong Cable Services)

CLAY TWP. (LANCASTER COUNTY)—See EPHRATA, PA (Blue Ridge Communications)

CLAYSBURG—See ALTOONA, PA (Atlantic Broadband)

CLAYSVILLE BOROUGH—See PITTSBURGH, PA (Comcast Cable)

CLAYSVILLE—Formerly served by Blue Devil Cable TV Inc. No longer in operation

CLEAR CREEK TWP.—See ZELIENOPLE, OH (Armstrong Cable Services)

CLEARFIELD TWP.—See ZELIENOPLE, PA (Armstrong Cable Services)

CLEARFIELD TWP.—See BLAIRSVILLE, PA (Comcast Cable)

CLEARFIELD—Atlantic Broadband

CLEONA—See HARRISBURG, PA (Comcast Cable)

CLEVELAND TWP.—See SUNBURY (village), PA (Service Electric Cablevision)

CLIFFORD TWP. (SUSQUEHANNA COUNTY)—See CARBONDALE TWP. (Lackawanna County), PA (Adams Cable Service)

CLIFFORD—See CARBONDALE TWP. (Lackawanna County), PA (Adams Cable Service)

CLIFTON HEIGHTS—See PHILADELPHIA, PA (Comcast Cable)

CLIFTON HEIGHTS—See RIDLEY PARK, PA (RCN. Formerly served by PHILADELPHIA (suburbs), PA [PA0447]. This cable system has converted to IPTV)

CLIFTON TWP.—See MILFORD, PA (Blue Ridge Communications)

CLINTON TWP. (BUTLER COUNTY)—See ZELIENOPLE, PA (Armstrong Cable Services)

CLINTON TWP. (LYCOMING COUNTY)—See HARRISBURG, PA (Comcast Cable)

CLINTON TWP. (VENANGO COUNTY)—See ZELIENOPLE, PA (Armstrong Cable Services)

CLINTON TWP. (WAYNE COUNTY)—See CARBONDALE TWP. (Lackawanna County), PA (Adams Cable Service)

CLINTON TWP.—See PITTSBURGH, PA (Comcast Cable)

CLINTONVILLE—Armstrong Cable Services. Now served by ZELIENOPLE, PA [PA0053]

CLINTONVILLE—See ZELIENOPLE, PA (Armstrong Cable Services)

CLOVER TWP.—See PUNXSUTAWNEY, PA (Comcast Cable)

CLYMER BOROUGH—See BLAIRSVILLE, PA (Comcast Cable)

COAL CENTER—See ZELIENOPLE, PA (Armstrong Cable Services)

COAL TWP. (NORTHUMBERLAND COUNTY)—See SUNBURY (village), PA (Service Electric Cablevision)

COAL—See SUNBURY (village), PA (Service Electric Cablevision)

COALDALE BOROUGH (SCHUYLKILL COUNTY)—See HARRISBURG, PA (Comcast Cable)

COALDALE—See LEHIGHTON, PA (Blue Ridge Communications)

COALMONT BOROUGH—See HARRISBURG, PA (Comcast Cable)

COALPORT—Comcast Cable. Now served by BLAIRSVILLE, PA [PA0320]

COALPORT—See BLAIRSVILLE, PA (Comcast Cable)

COATESVILLE—Comcast Cable. Now served by PHILADELPHIA, PA [PA0005]

COATESVILLE—See PHILADELPHIA, PA (Comcast Cable)

COBBS CREEK—See RIDLEY PARK, PA (RCN. Formerly served by PHILADELPHIA (suburbs), PA [PA0447]. This cable system has converted to IPTV)

COBURN—See MILLHEIM, PA (Millheim TV Transmission Co.)

COCHRANTON—See ZELIENOPLE, PA (Armstrong Cable Services)

COGAN STATION—Zito Media

COITSVILLE TWP.—See ZELIENOPLE, OH (Armstrong Cable Services)

COKEBURG—See UNIONTOWN, PA (Atlantic Broadband)

COLEBROOK—See HARRISBURG, PA (Comcast Cable)

COLERAIN TWP. (BEDFORD COUNTY)—See BLAIRSVILLE, PA (Comcast Cable)

COLLEGE HILL—See ALLENTOWN, PA (RCN. Formerly served by NORTHAMPTON BOROUGH, PA [PA0008]. This cable system has converted to IPTV)

COLLEGE TWP. (CENTRE COUNTY)—See HARRISBURG, PA (Comcast Cable)

COLLEY TWP. (SULLIVAN COUNTY)—See TUNKHANNOCK, PA (Blue Ridge Communications)

COLLIER TWP.—See PITTSBURGH, PA (Comcast Cable)

COLLINGDALE—See PHILADELPHIA, PA (Comcast Cable)

COLLINGDALE—See ALLENTOWN, PA (RCN. Formerly served by

Cable Community Index—Pennsylvania

NORTHAMPTON BOROUGH, PA [PA0008]. This cable system has converted to IPTV)

COLUMBIA CROSSROADS—See TROY, PA (Blue Ridge Communications)

COLUMBIA TWP. (BRADFORD COUNT)—See EAST SMITHFIELD, PA (North Penn Video)

COLUMBIA TWP. (BRADFORD COUNTY)—See TROY, PA (Blue Ridge Communications)

COLUMBIA—See HARRISBURG, PA (Comcast Cable)

COLWYN—See PHILADELPHIA, PA (Comcast Cable)

COLWYN—See ALLENTOWN, PA (RCN. Formerly served by NORTHAMPTON BOROUGH, PA [PA0008]. This cable system has converted to IPTV)

COMMODORE (INDIANA COUNTY)—See BLAIRSVILLE, PA (Comcast Cable)

CONCORD TWP. (BUTLER COUNTY)—See ZELIENOPLE, PA (Armstrong Cable Services)

CONCORD TWP. (DELAWARE COUNTY)—See PHILADELPHIA, PA (Comcast Cable)

CONCORDVILLE—See PHILADELPHIA, PA (Comcast Cable)

CONEMAUGH TWP. (CAMBRIA COUNTY)—See JOHNSTOWN, PA (Atlantic Broadband)

CONEMAUGH TWP. (INDIANA COUNTY)—See BLAIRSVILLE, PA (Comcast Cable)

CONEMAUGH TWP. (SOMERSET COUNTY)—See JOHNSTOWN, PA (Atlantic Broadband)

CONEMAUGH—See BLAIRSVILLE, PA (Comcast Cable)

CONESTOGA (LANCASTER COUNTY)—See HARRISBURG, PA (Comcast Cable)

CONEWAGO TWP. (ADAMS COUNTY)—See HARRISBURG, PA (Comcast Cable)

CONEWAGO TWP. (DAUPHIN COUNTY)—See HARRISBURG, PA (Comcast Cable)

CONEWANGO TWP. (WARREN COUNTY)—See WARREN, PA (Atlantic Broadband)

CONFLUENCE—See GREENSBURG, PA (Comcast Cable)

CONNEAUT LAKE—See ZELIENOPLE, PA (Armstrong Cable Services)

CONNELLSVILLE TWP. (FAYETTE COUNTY)—See ZELIENOPLE, PA (Armstrong Cable Services)

CONNELLSVILLE—Armstrong Cable Services. Now served by ZELIENOPLE, PA [PA0053]

CONNELLSVILLE—See ZELIENOPLE, PA (Armstrong Cable Services)

CONNELLSVILLE—See SALTLICK TWP., PA (Laurel Highland Total Communications)

CONNOQUENESSING BOROUGH—See ZELIENOPLE, PA (Armstrong Cable Services)

CONNOQUENESSING TWP. (BUTLER COUNTY)—See ZELIENOPLE, PA (Armstrong Cable Services)

CONOY TWP.—See HARRISBURG, PA (Comcast Cable)

CONWAY—See PITTSBURGH, PA (Comcast Cable)

CONYNGHAM BOROUGH—See HAZLETON, PA (Service Electric Cablevision)

CONYNGHAM—See BERWICK, PA (MetroCast Communications)

COOK TWP.—See SALTLICK TWP., PA (Laurel Highland Total Communications)

COOLBAUGH TWP.—See MILFORD, PA (Blue Ridge Communications)

COOLSPRING TWP. (PORTIONS)—See ZELIENOPLE, PA (Armstrong Cable Services)

COOPER TWP. (CLEARFIELD COUNTY)—See SNOW SHOE, PA (Tele-Media)

COOPER TWP. (MONTOUR COUNTY)—See SUNBURY (village), PA (Service Electric Cablevision)

COOPER TWP.—See SNOW SHOE, PA (Tele-Media)

COOPERSBURG BORO—See ALLENTOWN, PA (Service Electric Cable TV & Communications)

COOPERSBURG—See ALLENTOWN, PA (RCN. Formerly served by NORTHAMPTON BOROUGH, PA [PA0008]. This cable system has converted to IPTV)

COOPERSTOWN—Formerly served by Cebridge Connections. Now served by Armstrong Cable Services, ZELIENOPLE, PA [PA0053]

COOPERSTOWN—See ZELIENOPLE, PA (Armstrong Cable Services)

COPLAY BORO—See ALLENTOWN, PA (Service Electric Cable TV & Communications)

COPLAY—See ALLENTOWN, PA (RCN. Formerly served by NORTHAMPTON BOROUGH, PA [PA0008]. This cable system has converted to IPTV)

CORAOPOLIS—Comcast Cable. Now served by PITTSBURGH, PA [PA0001]

CORAOPOLIS—See PITTSBURGH, PA (Comcast Cable)

CORNPLANTER TWP. (VENANGO COUNTY)—See ZELIENOPLE, PA (Armstrong Cable Services)

CORNPLANTER TWP. (VENANGO COUNTY)—See OIL CITY, PA (Comcast Cable)

CORNWALL—See HARRISBURG, PA (Comcast Cable)

CORRY—Time Warner Cable. Now served by CLEVELAND (formerly Cleveland Heights), OH [OH0006]

CORSICA BOROUGH—See PUNXSUTAWNEY, PA (Comcast Cable)

COUDERSPORT—Zito Media

COURTDALE—See WILKES-BARRE, PA (Service Electric Cable Company)

COVINGTON TWP. (CLEARFIELD COUNTY)—See HARRISBURG, PA (Comcast Cable)

COVINGTON TWP. (CLEARFIELD COUNTY)—See SNOW SHOE, PA (Tele-Media)

COVINGTON TWP.—See MANSFIELD, PA (Blue Ridge Communications)

COWANSHANNOCK TWP.—See BLAIRSVILLE, PA (Comcast Cable)

CRAFTON—See PITTSBURGH, PA (Comcast Cable)

CRANBERRY (VENANGO COUNTY)—See FRANKLIN (Venango County), PA (Time Warner Cable)

CRANBERRY TWP. (BUTLER COUNTY)—See ZELIENOPLE, PA (Armstrong Cable Services)

CRANBERRY TWP. (VENANGO COUNTY)—See OIL CITY, PA (Comcast Cable)

CRAWFORD TWP.—See HARRISBURG, PA (Comcast Cable)

CREEKSIDE—See BLAIRSVILLE, PA (Comcast Cable)

CRESCENT TWP.—See PITTSBURGH, PA (Comcast Cable)

CRESSON TWP.—See BLAIRSVILLE, PA (Comcast Cable)

CRESSON—Comcast Cable. Now served by BLAIRSVILLE, PA [PA0320]

CRESSON—See BLAIRSVILLE, PA (Comcast Cable)

CRESSONA—See HARRISBURG, PA (Comcast Cable)

CROSBY—Formerly served by GMP-County Cable. No longer in operation

CROWN CITY—See ZELIENOPLE, OH (Armstrong Cable Services)

CROYLE TWP.—See BLAIRSVILLE, PA (Comcast Cable)

CRUCIBLE—See UNIONTOWN, PA (Atlantic Broadband)

CRUM LYNNE—See RIDLEY PARK, PA (RCN. Formerly served by PHILADELPHIA (suburbs), PA [PA0447]. This cable system has converted to IPTV)

CUDDY—See PITTSBURGH, PA (Comcast Cable)

CUMBERLAND TWP. (ADAMS COUNTY)—See HARRISBURG, PA (Comcast Cable)

CUMBERLAND TWP. (GREENE COUNTY)—See UNIONTOWN, PA (Atlantic Broadband)

CUMBOLA—See WEATHERLY, PA (MetroCast Communications)

CUMMINGS TWP.—See HARRISBURG, PA (Comcast Cable)

CUMRU TWP.—See HARRISBURG, PA (Comcast Cable)

CUMRU—See BIRDSBORO, PA (Service Electric Cablevision)

CURTIN TWP.—Formerly served by Adelphia Communications. Now served by Comcast Cable, HARRISBURG, PA [PA0009]

CURTIN TWP.—See HARRISBURG, PA (Comcast Cable)

CURWENSVILLE (CLEARFIELD COUNTY)—See CLEARFIELD, PA (Atlantic Broadband)

DAGUSCAHONDA—See ST. MARY'S, PA (Zito Media)

DAISYTOWN (CAMBRIA COUNTY)—See JOHNSTOWN, PA (Atlantic Broadband)

DALE (CAMBRIA COUNTY)—See JOHNSTOWN, PA (Atlantic Broadband)

DALLAS CORRECTIONAL INSTITUTE—Formerly served by Suddenlink Communications. No longer in operation

DALLAS TWP.—See TUNKHANNOCK, PA (Blue Ridge Communications)

DALLAS TWP.—See HARRISBURG, PA (Comcast Cable)

DALLAS—Comcast Cable. Now served by HARRISBURG, PA [PA0009]

DALLAS—See TUNKHANNOCK, PA (Blue Ridge Communications)

DALLAS—See HARRISBURG, PA (Comcast Cable)

DALLASTOWN—See HARRISBURG, PA (Comcast Cable)

DALMATIA—See HARRISBURG, PA (Comcast Cable)

DALTON BOROUGH—See HARRISBURG, PA (Comcast Cable)

DALTON—See ZELIENOPLE, OH (Armstrong Cable Services)

DAMASCUS TWP.—See MILFORD, PA (Blue Ridge Communications)

DANIELSVILLE—See ALLENTOWN, PA (RCN. Formerly served by NORTHAMPTON BOROUGH, PA [PA0008]. This cable system has converted to IPTV)

DANVILLE—CATV Service Inc

DARBY BOROUGH—See PHILADELPHIA, PA (Comcast Cable)

DARBY TWP.—See PHILADELPHIA, PA (Comcast Cable)

2017 Edition   Cable Community Index-247

Pennsylvania—Cable Community Index

DARBY TWP.—See RIDLEY PARK, PA (RCN. Formerly served by PHILADELPHIA (suburbs), PA [PA0447]. This cable system has converted to IPTV)

DARBY—See RIDLEY PARK, PA (RCN. Formerly served by PHILADELPHIA (suburbs), PA [PA0447]. This cable system has converted to IPTV)

DARLINGTON BOROUGH—See PITTSBURGH, PA (Comcast Cable)

DARLINGTON TWP. (Beaver County)—Comcast Cable. Now served by PITTSBURGH, PA [PA0001]

DARLINGTON TWP. (BEAVER COUNTY)—See PITTSBURGH, PA (Comcast Cable)

DAUGHERTY TWP.—See ZELIENOPLE, PA (Armstrong Cable Services)

DAUGHERTY TWP.—See PITTSBURGH, PA (Comcast Cable)

DAUPHIN BOROUGH—See HARRISBURG, PA (Comcast Cable)

DAVIDSON TWP.—See MUNCY VALLEY, PA (Blue Ridge Communications)

DAWSON—See UNIONTOWN, PA (Atlantic Broadband)

DAYBROOK—See BRAVE, WV (Zito Media)

DAYTON BOROUGH—See BLAIRSVILLE, PA (Comcast Cable)

DEAN TWP. (CAMBRIA COUNTY)—See BLAIRSVILLE, PA (Comcast Cable)

DECATUR TWP. (MIFFLIN COUNTY)—See HARRISBURG, PA (Comcast Cable)

DECATUR—See DERRY/DECATUR, PA (Atlantic Broadband)

DEEMSTON—See UNIONTOWN, PA (Atlantic Broadband)

DEER CREEK TWP. (MERCER COUNTY)—See ZELIENOPLE, PA (Armstrong Cable Services)

DEER LAKE BOROUGH (SCHUYLKILL COUNTY)—See HARRISBURG, PA (Comcast Cable)

DEERFIELD TWP. (WARREN COUNTY)—See ZELIENOPLE, PA (Armstrong Cable Services)

DELANO—See HAZLETON, PA (Service Electric Cablevision)

DELAWARE TWP. (JUNIATA COUNTY)—See MIFFLINTOWN, PA (Nittany Media Inc.)

DELAWARE TWP. (NORTHUMBERLAND COUNTY)—See HARRISBURG, PA (Comcast Cable)

DELAWARE TWP. (NORTHUMBERLAND COUNTY)—See SUNBURY (village), PA (Service Electric Cablevision)

DELAWARE WATER GAP—See STROUDSBURG, PA (Blue Ridge Communications)

DELMAR TWP.—See MANSFIELD, PA (Blue Ridge Communications)

DELMONT BOROUGH—See BLAIRSVILLE, PA (Comcast Cable)

DENNISON TWP.—See WEATHERLY, PA (MetroCast Communications)

DENVER—See EPHRATA, PA (Blue Ridge Communications)

DERRY BOROUGH—See BLAIRSVILLE, PA (Comcast Cable)

DERRY TWP. (DAUPHIN COUNTY)—See HARRISBURG, PA (Comcast Cable)

DERRY TWP. (MIFFLIN COUNTY)—See HARRISBURG, PA (Comcast Cable)

DERRY TWP. (MONTOUR COUNTY)—See SUNBURY (village), PA (Service Electric Cablevision)

DERRY TWP. (WESTMORELAND COUNTY)—See BLAIRSVILLE, PA (Comcast Cable)

DERRY/DECATUR—Atlantic Broadband

DERRY—See BLAIRSVILLE, PA (Comcast Cable)

DERRY—See GREENSBURG, PA (Comcast Cable)

DICKINSON TWP. (CUMBERLAND COUNTY)—See HARRISBURG, PA (Comcast Cable)

DICKSON CITY—See HARRISBURG, PA (Comcast Cable)

DILLSBURG—Formerly served by Adelphia Communications. Now served by Comcast Cable, HARRISBURG, PA [PA0009]

DILLSBURG—See HARRISBURG, PA (Comcast Cable)

DINGMAN TWP.—See MILFORD, PA (Blue Ridge Communications)

DISTRICT TWP.—See BIRDSBORO, PA (Service Electric Cablevision)

DIXONVILLE (INDIANA COUNTY)—See BLAIRSVILLE, PA (Comcast Cable)

DONEGAL TWP. (BUTLER COUNTY)—See ZELIENOPLE, PA (Armstrong Cable Services)

DONEGAL TWP. (WASHINGTON COUNTY)—See PITTSBURGH, PA (Comcast Cable)

DONEGAL TWP. (WESTMORELAND COUNTY)—See ZELIENOPLE, PA (Armstrong Cable Services)

DONEGAL TWP. (WESTMORELAND COUNTY)—See SALTLICK TWP., PA (Laurel Highland Total Communications)

DONEGAL—See SALTLICK TWP., PA (Laurel Highland Total Communications)

DONORA—See PITTSBURGH, PA (Comcast Cable)

DORMONT—See PITTSBURGH, PA (Comcast Cable)

DORNEYVILLE—See ALLENTOWN, PA (RCN. Formerly served by NORTHAMPTON BOROUGH, PA [PA0008]. This cable system has converted to IPTV)

DORRANCE TWP.—See HAZLETON, PA (Service Electric Cablevision)

DORRANCE—See BERWICK, PA (MetroCast Communications)

DOVER BOROUGH—See HARRISBURG, PA (Comcast Cable)

DOVER TWP.—See HARRISBURG, PA (Comcast Cable)

DOWNINGTOWN BOROUGH—See PHILADELPHIA, PA (Comcast Cable)

DOYLESBURG—Valley Cable Systems

DRAVOSBURG—See PITTSBURGH, PA (Comcast Cable)

DREHER TWP.—See MILFORD, PA (Blue Ridge Communications)

DREXEL HILL—See RIDLEY PARK, PA (RCN. Formerly served by PHILADELPHIA (suburbs), PA [PA0447]. This cable system has converted to IPTV)

DRUMORE TWP.—See HARRISBURG, PA (Comcast Cable)

DU BOIS—Formerly served by Adelphia Communications. Now served by Comcast Cable, PUNXSUTAWNEY, PA [PA0397]

DU BOIS—See PUNXSUTAWNEY, PA (Comcast Cable)

DUBLIN TWP. (HUNTINGDON COUNTY)—See HARRISBURG, PA (Comcast Cable)

DUBLIN TWP. (HUNTINGDON COUNTY)—See SHADE GAP, PA (Shade Gap TV Assn)

DUBOISTOWN BOROUGH—See HARRISBURG, PA (Comcast Cable)

DUDLEY BOROUGH—See HARRISBURG, PA (Comcast Cable)

DUKE CENTER—See PUNXSUTAWNEY, PA (Comcast Cable)

DUNBAR TWP.—See ZELIENOPLE, PA (Armstrong Cable Services)

DUNBAR—See ZELIENOPLE, PA (Armstrong Cable Services)

DUNCAN TWP.—See MANSFIELD, PA (Blue Ridge Communications)

DUNCANNON—Blue Ridge Communications. Now served by NEWBERRY TWP., PA [PA0105]

DUNCANNON—See NEWBERRY TWP., PA (Blue Ridge Communications)

DUNCANSVILLE—See ALTOONA, PA (Atlantic Broadband)

DUNKARD TWP.—See UNIONTOWN, PA (Atlantic Broadband)

DUNLEVY—See ZELIENOPLE, PA (Armstrong Cable Services)

DUNMORE BOROUGH—Comcast Cable. Now served by HARRISBURG, PA [PA0009]

DUNMORE BOROUGH—See HARRISBURG, PA (Comcast Cable)

DUNNSTABLE TWP.—See HARRISBURG, PA (Comcast Cable)

DUPONT BOROUGH—See HARRISBURG, PA (Comcast Cable)

DUQUESNE—See PITTSBURGH, PA (Comcast Cable)

DURHAM TWP.—See ALLENTOWN, PA (Service Electric Cable TV & Communications)

DURYEA BOROUGH—See HARRISBURG, PA (Comcast Cable)

DUSHORE—Blue Ridge Communications. Now served by TUNKHANNOCK, PA [PA0367]

DUSHORE—See TUNKHANNOCK, PA (Blue Ridge Communications)

DYBERRY TWP.—See MILFORD, PA (Blue Ridge Communications)

EAGLES MERE BOROUGH—See HARRISBURG, PA (Comcast Cable)

EARL TWP. (LANCASTER COUNTY)—See EPHRATA, PA (Blue Ridge Communications)

EARL TWP. (LANCASTER COUNTY)—See HARRISBURG, PA (Comcast Cable)

EARL TWP. (LANCASTER COUNTY)—See BIRDSBORO, PA (Service Electric Cablevision)

EAST ALLEN TWP.—See ALLENTOWN, PA (RCN. Formerly served by NORTHAMPTON BOROUGH, PA [PA0008]. This cable system has converted to IPTV)

EAST ALLEN TWP.—See ALLENTOWN, PA (Service Electric Cable TV & Communications)

EAST BANGOR BORO—See ALLENTOWN, PA (Service Electric Cable TV & Communications)

EAST BANGOR—See ALLENTOWN, PA (RCN. Formerly served by NORTHAMPTON BOROUGH, PA [PA0008]. This cable system has converted to IPTV)

EAST BERLIN (ADAMS COUNTY)—See HARRISBURG, PA (Comcast Cable)

EAST BETHLEHEM TWP. (WASHINGTON COUNTY)—See UNIONTOWN, PA (Atlantic Broadband)

EAST BRADFORD TWP.—See PHILADELPHIA, PA (Comcast Cable)

EAST BRADY—See ZELIENOPLE, PA (Armstrong Cable Services)

EAST BRANDYWINE TWP.—See PHILADELPHIA, PA (Comcast Cable)

EAST BRUNSWICK TWP.—See HAZLETON, PA (Service Electric Cablevision)

Cable Community Index—Pennsylvania

EAST BUFFALO TWP.—Formerly served by D&E Communications/Windstream. IPTV service no longer in operation

EAST BUFFALO TWP.—See DANVILLE, PA (CATV Service Inc)

EAST BUFFALO TWP.—See SUNBURY (village), PA (Service Electric Cablevision)

EAST BUTLER—See ZELIENOPLE, PA (Armstrong Cable Services)

EAST CALN TWP.—See PHILADELPHIA, PA (Comcast Cable)

EAST CAMERON TWP.—See SUNBURY (village), PA (Service Electric Cablevision)

EAST CANTON—See CANTON, PA (Zito Media)

EAST CARROLL TWP.—See BLAIRSVILLE, PA (Comcast Cable)

EAST CHILLISQUAQUE TWP.—See SUNBURY (village), PA (Service Electric Cablevision)

EAST COCALICO TWP.—See EPHRATA, PA (Blue Ridge Communications)

EAST CONEMAUGH BOROUGH—See BLAIRSVILLE, PA (Comcast Cable)

EAST CONEMAUGH—Formerly served by Adelphia Communications. Now served by Comcast Cable, BLAIRSVILLE, PA [PA0320]

EAST CONEMAUGH—See BLAIRSVILLE, PA (Comcast Cable)

EAST DEER TWP.—See PITTSBURGH, PA (Comcast Cable)

EAST DONEGAL TWP.—See HARRISBURG, PA (Comcast Cable)

EAST DRUMORE TWP.—See HARRISBURG, PA (Comcast Cable)

EAST EARL TWP. (PORTIONS)—See EPHRATA, PA (Blue Ridge Communications)

EAST EARL TWP.—See HARRISBURG, PA (Comcast Cable)

EAST FALLOWFIELD TWP. (CHESTER COUNTY)—See PHILADELPHIA, PA (Comcast Cable)

EAST FRANKLIN TWP.—See BLAIRSVILLE, PA (Comcast Cable)

EAST GOSHEN TWP.—See PHILADELPHIA, PA (Comcast Cable)

EAST HANOVER TWP. (DAUPHIN COUNTY)—See HARRISBURG, PA (Comcast Cable)

EAST HANOVER TWP. (LEBANON COUNTY)—See HARRISBURG, PA (Comcast Cable)

EAST HANOVER TWP. (LEBANON COUNTY)—See FORT INDIANTOWN GAP, PA (Gap Cable TV Inc)

EAST HEMPFIELD TWP.—See HARRISBURG, PA (Comcast Cable)

EAST HUNTINGDON TWP.—See ZELIENOPLE, PA (Armstrong Cable Services)

EAST HUNTINGDON TWP.—See GREENSBURG, PA (Comcast Cable)

EAST LACKAWANNOCK TWP. (PORTIONS)—See ZELIENOPLE, PA (Armstrong Cable Services)

EAST LAMPETER TWP.—See HARRISBURG, PA (Comcast Cable)

EAST LANSDOWNE—See PHILADELPHIA, PA (Comcast Cable)

EAST LANSDOWNE—See RIDLEY PARK, PA (RCN. Formerly served by PHILADELPHIA (suburbs), PA [PA0447]. This cable system has converted to IPTV)

EAST MANCHESTER TWP.—See HARRISBURG, PA (Comcast Cable)

EAST MARLBOROUGH TWP.—See PHILADELPHIA, PA (Comcast Cable)

EAST MCKEESPORT BOROUGH—See PITTSBURGH, PA (Comcast Cable)

EAST NANTMEAL TWP.—See BIRDSBORO, PA (Service Electric Cablevision)

EAST NORWEGIAN TWP.—See HARRISBURG, PA (Comcast Cable)

EAST NORWEGIAN TWP.—See HAZLETON, PA (Service Electric Cablevision)

EAST PENN TWP.—See LEHIGHTON, PA (Blue Ridge Communications)

EAST PENNSBORO TWP.—See HARRISBURG, PA (Comcast Cable)

EAST PETERSBURG—See HARRISBURG, PA (Comcast Cable)

EAST PITTSBURGH BOROUGH—See PITTSBURGH, PA (Comcast Cable)

EAST PROSPECT—See HARRISBURG, PA (Comcast Cable)

EAST PROVIDENCE TWP.—See BLAIRSVILLE, PA (Comcast Cable)

EAST ROCHESTER—See PITTSBURGH, PA (Comcast Cable)

EAST SIDE—See WEATHERLY, PA (MetroCast Communications)

EAST SMITHFIELD—North Penn Video

EAST ST. CLAIR TWP. (BEDFORD COUNTY)—See NEW ENTERPRISE, PA (Atlantic Broadband)

EAST ST. CLAIR TWP. (BEDFORD COUNTY)—See BLAIRSVILLE, PA (Comcast Cable)

EAST STROUDSBURG—See STROUDSBURG, PA (Blue Ridge Communications)

EAST TAYLOR TWP.—See JOHNSTOWN, PA (Atlantic Broadband)

EAST TEXAS—See ALLENTOWN, PA (RCN. Formerly served by NORTHAMPTON BOROUGH, PA [PA0008]. This cable system has converted to IPTV)

EAST TROY—See TROY, PA (Blue Ridge Communications)

EAST UNION TWP.—See ZELIENOPLE, OH (Armstrong Cable Services)

EAST UNION TWP.—See HAZLETON, PA (Service Electric Cablevision)

EAST VANDERGRIFT BOROUGH—See PITTSBURGH, PA (Comcast Cable)

EAST WASHINGTON—See PITTSBURGH, PA (Comcast Cable)

EAST WATERFORD—Formerly served by Valley Cable Systems. No longer in operation

EAST WHEATFIELD TWP.—See BLAIRSVILLE, PA (Comcast Cable)

EAST WHITELAND TWP.—See PHILADELPHIA, PA (Comcast Cable)

EASTON—Service Electric Cable TV & Communications. Now served by ALLENTOWN, PA [PA0006]

EASTON—See ALLENTOWN, PA (RCN. Formerly served by NORTHAMPTON BOROUGH, PA [PA0008]. This cable system has converted to IPTV)

EASTON—See ALLENTOWN, PA (Service Electric Cable TV & Communications)

EASTTOWN TWP.—See PHILADELPHIA, PA (Comcast Cable)

EASTVALE BOROUGH—See PITTSBURGH, PA (Comcast Cable)

EASTVALE—See PITTSBURGH, PA (Comcast Cable)

EASTVILLE—Formerly served by Eastville TV Cable. No longer in operation

EATON TWP.—See TUNKHANNOCK, PA (Blue Ridge Communications)

EATONVILLE—See TUNKHANNOCK, PA (Blue Ridge Communications)

EAU CLAIRE—Formerly served by Cebridge Connections. Now served by Armstrong Cable Services. ZELIENOPLE, PA [PA0053]

EAU CLAIRE—See ZELIENOPLE, PA (Armstrong Cable Services)

EBENSBURG BOROUGH—See BLAIRSVILLE, PA (Comcast Cable)

EBENSBURG—See BLAIRSVILLE, PA (Comcast Cable)

ECONOMY—See PITTSBURGH, PA (Comcast Cable)

EDDYSTONE (DELAWARE COUNTY)—See PHILADELPHIA, PA (Comcast Cable)

EDDYSTONE—See RIDLEY PARK, PA (RCN. Formerly served by PHILADELPHIA (suburbs), PA [PA0447]. This cable system has converted to IPTV)

EDEN—See HARRISBURG, PA (Comcast Cable)

EDGEMONT TWP.—See PHILADELPHIA, PA (Comcast Cable)

EDGEWOOD—See PITTSBURGH, PA (Comcast Cable)

EDGEWORTH—See PITTSBURGH, PA (Comcast Cable)

EDINBORO—Coaxial Cable TV Corp

EDWARDSVILLE—See HARRISBURG, PA (Comcast Cable)

EGYPT—See ALLENTOWN, PA (RCN. Formerly served by NORTHAMPTON BOROUGH, PA [PA0008]. This cable system has converted to IPTV)

EHRENFELD BOROUGH—See BLAIRSVILLE, PA (Comcast Cable)

ELCO—See ZELIENOPLE, PA (Armstrong Cable Services)

ELDER TWP.—See BLAIRSVILLE, PA (Comcast Cable)

ELDERTON BOROUGH—Comcast Cable. Now served by BLAIRSVILLE, PA [PA0320]

ELDERTON BOROUGH—See BLAIRSVILLE, PA (Comcast Cable)

ELDRED TWP. (JEFFERSON COUNTY)—See PUNXSUTAWNEY, PA (Comcast Cable)

ELDRED TWP. (MCKEAN COUNTY)—See PUNXSUTAWNEY, PA (Comcast Cable)

ELDRED TWP. (MONROE COUNTY)—See LEHIGHTON, PA (Blue Ridge Communications)

ELDRED TWP.—Herr Cable Co

ELIZABETH BOROUGH—See PITTSBURGH, PA (Comcast Cable)

ELIZABETH TWP. (LANCASTER COUNTY)—See EPHRATA, PA (Blue Ridge Communications)

ELIZABETH TWP. (LANCASTER COUNTY)—See HARRISBURG, PA (Comcast Cable)

ELIZABETH TWP.—See PITTSBURGH, PA (Comcast Cable)

ELIZABETHTOWN—Comcast Cable. Now served by HARRISBURG, PA [PA0009]

ELIZABETHTOWN—See HARRISBURG, PA (Comcast Cable)

ELIZABETHVILLE—See HARRISBURG, PA (Comcast Cable)

ELK TWP. (CLARION COUNTY)—See SHIPPENVILLE, PA (Atlantic Broadband)

ELKLAND—Time Warner Cable. Now served by DEWITT, NY [NY0013]

ELLPORT—See ZELIENOPLE, PA (Armstrong Cable Services)

ELLSWORTH TWP.—See ZELIENOPLE, OH (Armstrong Cable Services)

ELLSWORTH—See UNIONTOWN, PA (Atlantic Broadband)

Pennsylvania—Cable Community Index

ELLSWORTH—See NORTH BETHLEHEM TWP., PA (Bentleyville Communications)

ELLWOOD CITY—See ZELIENOPLE, PA (Armstrong Cable Services)

ELMHURST TWP.—See HARRISBURG, PA (Comcast Cable)

ELSMERE—See PHILADELPHIA, DE (Comcast Cable)

ELVERSON BOROUGH—See BIRDSBORO, PA (Service Electric Cablevision)

ELYSBURG—See SUNBURY (village), PA (Service Electric Cablevision)

EMLENTON BOROUGH—See OIL CITY, PA (Comcast Cable)

EMMAUS—Service Electric Cable TV & Communications. Now served by ALLENTOWN, PA [PA0006]

EMMAUS—See ALLENTOWN, PA (RCN. Formerly served by NORTHAMPTON BOROUGH, PA [PA0008]. This cable system has converted to IPTV)

EMMAUS—See ALLENTOWN, PA (Service Electric Cable TV & Communications)

EMPORIUM—See COUDERSPORT, PA (Zito Media)

EMSWORTH—See PITTSBURGH, PA (Comcast Cable)

ENON VALLEY BOROUGH—See PITTSBURGH, PA (Comcast Cable)

EPHRATA TWP. (LANCASTER COUNTY)—See EPHRATA, PA (Blue Ridge Communications)

EPHRATA—Blue Ridge Communications

ERIE—Time Warner Cable

ERNEST BOROUGH—See BLAIRSVILLE, PA (Comcast Cable)

ESSINGTON—See RIDLEY PARK, PA (RCN. Formerly served by PHILADELPHIA (suburbs), PA [PA0447]. This cable system has converted to IPTV)

ETNA—See PITTSBURGH, PA (Comcast Cable)

EULALIA TWP.—See COUDERSPORT, PA (Zito Media)

EVANS CITY—See ZELIENOPLE, PA (Armstrong Cable Services)

EVERETT BOROUGH—See BLAIRSVILLE, PA (Comcast Cable)

EVERSON—See ZELIENOPLE, PA (Armstrong Cable Services)

EXETER BOROUGH—See HARRISBURG, PA (Comcast Cable)

EXETER TWP. (BERKS COUNTY)—See BIRDSBORO, PA (Service Electric Cablevision)

EXETER TWP. (LUZERNE COUNTY)—See HARRISBURG, PA (Comcast Cable)

EXETER TWP. (WYOMING COUNTY)—See HARRISBURG, PA (Comcast Cable)

EXETER TWP.—See HARRISBURG, PA (Comcast Cable)

EXPORT BOROUGH—See BLAIRSVILLE, PA (Comcast Cable)

FACTORYVILLE BOROUGH—See HARRISBURG, PA (Comcast Cable)

FAIRCHANCE—See UNIONTOWN, PA (Atlantic Broadband)

FAIRFIELD TWP. (LYCOMING COUNTY)—See HARRISBURG, PA (Comcast Cable)

FAIRFIELD TWP. (LYCOMING COUNTY)—See ELDRED TWP., PA (Herr Cable Co)

FAIRFIELD TWP. (WESTMORELAND COUNTY)—See BLAIRSVILLE, PA (Comcast Cable)

FAIRFIELD—See HARRISBURG, PA (Comcast Cable)

FAIRFIELD—See BRAVE, WV (Zito Media)

FAIRVIEW TWP. (YORK COUNTY)—See HARRISBURG, PA (Comcast Cable)

FAIRMOUNT CITY—See PUNXSUTAWNEY, PA (Comcast Cable)

FAIRVIEW BOROUGH—See ZELIENOPLE, PA (Armstrong Cable Services)

FAIRVIEW TWP. (BUTLER COUNTY)—See ZELIENOPLE, PA (Armstrong Cable Services)

FAIRVIEW TWP. (LUZERNE COUNTY)—See WILKES-BARRE, PA (Service Electric Cable Company)

FAIRVIEW TWP. (YORK COUNTY)—See NEWBERRY TWP., PA (Blue Ridge Communications)

FALLOWFIELD TWP.—See NORTH BETHLEHEM TWP., PA (Bentleyville Communications)

FALLOWFIELD TWP.—See PITTSBURGH, PA (Comcast Cable)

FALLS CREEK BOROUGH—See PUNXSUTAWNEY, PA (Comcast Cable)

FALLS TWP. (WYOMING COUNTY)—See TUNKHANNOCK, PA (Blue Ridge Communications)

FALLSTON BOROUGH—See PITTSBURGH, PA (Comcast Cable)

FALLSTON—See PITTSBURGH, PA (Comcast Cable)

FANNETT TWP. (FRANKLIN COUNTY)—See DOYLESBURG, PA (Valley Cable Systems)

FANNETTSBURG—Formerly served by Fannettsburg Cable TV Co. No longer in operation

FARMINGTON TWP. (CLARION COUNTY)—See ZELIENOPLE, PA (Armstrong Cable Services)

FASSETT—See BENTLEY CREEK, PA (Blue Ridge Communications)

FAWN GROVE—Formerly served by Armstrong Cable Services. No longer in operation

FAWN TWP. (ALLEGHENY COUNTY)—See PITTSBURGH, PA (Comcast Cable)

FAYETTE CITY (FAYETTE COUNTY)—See UNIONTOWN, PA (Atlantic Broadband)

FAYETTE TWP.—See ZELIENOPLE, OH (Armstrong Cable Services)

FAYETTE TWP.—See MIFFLINTOWN, PA (Nittany Media Inc.)

FELL TWP.—See CARBONDALE TWP. (Lackawanna County), PA (Adams Cable Service)

FELTON—See HARRISBURG, PA (Comcast Cable)

FERGUSON TWP.—See HARRISBURG, PA (Comcast Cable)

FERMANAGH TWP.—See MIFFLINTOWN, PA (Nittany Media Inc.)

FERNDALE (CAMBRIA COUNTY)—See JOHNSTOWN, PA (Atlantic Broadband)

FINDLAY TWP. (ALLEGHENY COUNTY)—See PITTSBURGH, PA (Comcast Cable)

FINDLEY TWP. (MERCER COUNTY)—See ZELIENOPLE, PA (Armstrong Cable Services)

FINLEYVILLE—See PITTSBURGH, PA (Comcast Cable)

FLATWOODS—See ZELIENOPLE, KY (Armstrong Cable Services)

FLEETWOOD—See BIRDSBORO, PA (Service Electric Cablevision)

FLEMING BOROUGH—See UNION TWP. (Centre County), PA (Country Cable)

FLEMINGTON—See HARRISBURG, PA (Comcast Cable)

FLORENCE—See PITTSBURGH, PA (Comcast Cable)

FOGLESVILLE—See ALLENTOWN, PA (RCN. Formerly served by NORTHAMPTON BOROUGH, PA [PA0008]. This cable system has converted to IPTV)

FOLCROFT—See PHILADELPHIA, PA (Comcast Cable)

FOLCROFT—See RIDLEY PARK, PA (RCN. Formerly served by PHILADELPHIA (suburbs), PA [PA0447]. This cable system has converted to IPTV)

FOLSOM—See RIDLEY PARK, PA (RCN. Formerly served by PHILADELPHIA (suburbs), PA [PA0447]. This cable system has converted to IPTV)

FORD CITY—See BLAIRSVILLE, PA (Comcast Cable)

FORD CLIFF—See BLAIRSVILLE, PA (Comcast Cable)

FOREST CITY—Adams Cable Service. Now served by CARBONDALE TWP. (Lackawanna County), PA [PA0067]

FOREST CITY—See CARBONDALE TWP. (Lackawanna County), PA (Adams Cable Service)

FOREST HILLS—See PITTSBURGH, PA (Comcast Cable)

FORKS TWP.—See ALLENTOWN, PA (RCN. Formerly served by NORTHAMPTON BOROUGH, PA [PA0008]. This cable system has converted to IPTV)

FORKS TWP.—See ALLENTOWN, PA (Service Electric Cable TV & Communications)

FORKSTON TWP.—See TUNKHANNOCK, PA (Blue Ridge Communications)

FORT INDIANTOWN GAP—Gap Cable TV Inc

FORT LOUDON—Comcast Cable. Now served by HARRISBURG, PA [PA0009]

FORT LOUDON—See HARRISBURG, PA (Comcast Cable)

FORTY FORT—See HARRISBURG, PA (Comcast Cable)

FORWARD TWP. (ALLEGHENY COUNTY)—See PITTSBURGH, PA (Comcast Cable)

FORWARD TWP.—See ZELIENOPLE, PA (Armstrong Cable Services)

FORWARD—See ZELIENOPLE, PA (Armstrong Cable Services)

FOSTER TWP. (LUZERNE COUNTY)—See WEATHERLY, PA (MetroCast Communications)

FOSTER TWP. (LUZERNE COUNTY)—See HAZLETON, PA (Service Electric Cablevision)

FOSTER TWP. (MCKEAN COUNTY)—See BRADFORD, PA (Atlantic Broadband)

FOSTER TWP. (MCKEAN COUNTY)—See PUNXSUTAWNEY, PA (Comcast Cable)

FOSTER TWP. (SCHUYLKILL COUNTY)—See CASS TWP. (Schuylkill County), PA (J. B. Cable)

FOUNTAIN HILL BORO—See ALLENTOWN, PA (Service Electric Cable TV & Communications)

FOUNTAIN HILL BOROUGH—See ALLENTOWN, PA (RCN. Formerly served by NORTHAMPTON BOROUGH, PA [PA0008]. This cable system has converted to IPTV)

FOX CHAPEL—See PITTSBURGH, PA (Comcast Cable)

FOX TWP. (ELK COUNTY)—See ST. MARY'S, PA (Zito Media)

FOXBURG BOROUGH—See OIL CITY, PA (Comcast Cable)

Cable Community Index—Pennsylvania

FRACKVILLE—See HAZLETON, PA (Service Electric Cablevision)

FRAILEY TWP.—See TREMONT, PA (Wire Television Corp)

FRANKLIN (CAMBRIA COUNTY)—See JOHNSTOWN, PA (Atlantic Broadband)

FRANKLIN (VENANGO COUNTY)—See ZELIENOPLE, PA (Armstrong Cable Services)

FRANKLIN (VENANGO COUNTY)—Time Warner Cable

FRANKLIN PARK—See PITTSBURGH, PA (Comcast Cable)

FRANKLIN TWP. (ADAMS COUNTY)—See HARRISBURG, PA (Comcast Cable)

FRANKLIN TWP. (BEAVER COUNTY)—See ZELIENOPLE, PA (Armstrong Cable Services)

FRANKLIN TWP. (BUTLER COUNTY)—See ZELIENOPLE, PA (Armstrong Cable Services)

FRANKLIN TWP. (CARBON COUNTY)—See LEHIGHTON, PA (Blue Ridge Communications)

FRANKLIN TWP. (CHESTER COUNTY)—See PHILADELPHIA, PA (Comcast Cable)

FRANKLIN TWP. (COLUMBIA COUNTY)—See SUNBURY (village), PA (Service Electric Cablevision)

FRANKLIN TWP. (ERIE COUNTY)—See EDINBORO, PA (Coaxial Cable TV Corp)

FRANKLIN TWP. (FAYETTE COUNTY)—See ZELIENOPLE, PA (Armstrong Cable Services)

FRANKLIN TWP. (HUNTINGDON COUNTY)—See HARRISBURG, PA (Comcast Cable)

FRANKLIN TWP. (LUZERNE COUNTY)—See HARRISBURG, PA (Comcast Cable)

FRANKLIN TWP. (NORTHUMBERLAND COUNTY)—See SUNBURY (village), PA (Service Electric Cablevision)

FRANKLIN TWP. (SNYDER COUNTY)—See SUNBURY (village), PA (Service Electric Cablevision)

FRANKLIN TWP.—See PITTSBURGH, PA (Comcast Cable)

FRANKLINDALE TWP.—See TROY, PA (Blue Ridge Communications)

FRANKLINTOWN—See HARRISBURG, PA (Comcast Cable)

FRANKSTOWN TWP. (BLAIR COUNTY)—See ALTOONA, PA (Atlantic Broadband)

FRANKSTOWN TWP.—See ALTOONA, PA (Atlantic Broadband)

FRANKSTOWN—See ALTOONA, PA (Atlantic Broadband)

FRAZER TWP.—See PITTSBURGH, PA (Comcast Cable)

FREDERICK COUNTY (PORTIONS)—See HARRISBURG, MD (Comcast Cable)

FREEBURG—See SUNBURY (village), PA (Service Electric Cablevision)

FREEDOM TWP. (ADAMS COUNTY)—See HARRISBURG, PA (Comcast Cable)

FREEDOM TWP. (BLAIR COUNTY)—See ALTOONA, PA (Atlantic Broadband)

FREEDOM—See PITTSBURGH, PA (Comcast Cable)

FREELAND—See HAZLETON, PA (Service Electric Cablevision)

FREEMANSBURG BORO—See ALLENTOWN, PA (Service Electric Cable TV & Communications)

FREEMANSBURG BOROUGH—See ALLENTOWN, PA (RCN. Formerly served by NORTHAMPTON BOROUGH, PA [PA0008]. This cable system has converted to IPTV)

FREEPORT—Formerly served by Adelphia Communications. Now served by Comcast Cable, BLAIRSVILLE, PA [PA0320]

FREEPORT—See BLAIRSVILLE, PA (Comcast Cable)

FRENCHCREEK TWP. (VENANGO COUNTY)—See FRANKLIN (Venango County), PA (Time Warner Cable)

FRIEDENSBURG—See HARRISBURG, PA (Comcast Cable)

FRIENDSVILLE (UNINCORPORATED AREAS)—See ADDISON TWP. (southern portion), MD (Somerfield Cable TV Co)

FRIENDSVILLE—See BLAIRSVILLE, MD (Comcast Cable)

FULTON TWP.—See HARRISBURG, PA (Comcast Cable)

GAINES TWP.—See MANSFIELD, PA (Blue Ridge Communications)

GAINES—Formerly served by Gaines-Watrous TV Inc. No longer in operation

GALETON—Blue Ridge Communications. Now served by MANSFIELD, PA [PA0421]

GALETON—See MANSFIELD, PA (Blue Ridge Communications)

GALLITZIN BOROUGH—See BLAIRSVILLE, PA (Comcast Cable)

GALLITZIN TWP.—See BLAIRSVILLE, PA (Comcast Cable)

GALLITZIN—See ALTOONA, PA (Atlantic Broadband)

GAP—See HARRISBURG, PA (Comcast Cable)

GARLAND—Formerly served by Cebridge Connections. No longer in operation

GARRETT COUNTY (PORTIONS)—See ADDISON TWP. (southern portion), MD (Somerfield Cable TV Co)

GARRETT—See BLAIRSVILLE, PA (Comcast Cable)

GASKILL TWP.—See PUNXSUTAWNEY, PA (Comcast Cable)

GEISTOWN—See JOHNSTOWN, PA (Atlantic Broadband)

GENESEE TWP.—See COUDERSPORT, PA (Zito Media)

GENESEE—See OSWAYO, PA (Zito Media)

GEORGES TWP. (FAYETTE COUNTY)—See UNIONTOWN, PA (Atlantic Broadband)

GEORGETOWN BOROUGH—See PITTSBURGH, PA (Comcast Cable)

GERMAN TWP. (FAYETTE COUNTY)—See UNIONTOWN, PA (Atlantic Broadband)

GERMANSVILLE—See ALLENTOWN, PA (RCN. Formerly served by NORTHAMPTON BOROUGH, PA [PA0008]. This cable system has converted to IPTV)

GERMANY TWP.—See HARRISBURG, PA (Comcast Cable)

GETTYSBURG—Comcast Cable. Now served by HARRISBURG, PA [PA0009]

GETTYSBURG—See HARRISBURG, PA (Comcast Cable)

GIBSON TWP.—See COUDERSPORT, PA (Zito Media)

GILBERTON—See HAZLETON, PA (Service Electric Cablevision)

GILPIN TWP.—See BLAIRSVILLE, PA (Comcast Cable)

GILPIN—See BLAIRSVILLE, PA (Comcast Cable)

GIRARD TWP.—See SNOW SHOE, PA (Tele-Media)

GIRARDVILLE—See HAZLETON, PA (Service Electric Cablevision)

GLADE TWP. (WARREN COUNTY)—See WARREN, PA (Atlantic Broadband)

GLASGOW—See PITTSBURGH, PA (Comcast Cable)

GLASSPORT—See PITTSBURGH, PA (Comcast Cable)

GLASSWORKS—See UNIONTOWN, PA (Atlantic Broadband)

GLEN CAMPBELL—See BLAIRSVILLE, PA (Comcast Cable)

GLEN HOPE BOROUGH—See BLAIRSVILLE, PA (Comcast Cable)

GLEN IRON—See MIFFLINBURG, PA (Atlantic Broadband)

GLEN ROCK BOROUGH—See HARRISBURG, PA (Comcast Cable)

GLEN ROCK—Formerly served by Adelphia Communications. Now served by Comcast Cable, HARRISBURG, PA [PA0009]

GLENBURN TWP.—See HARRISBURG, PA (Comcast Cable)

GLENDALE (CLEARFIELD COUNTY)—See BLAIRSVILLE, PA (Comcast Cable)

GLENDON—See ALLENTOWN, PA (RCN. Formerly served by NORTHAMPTON BOROUGH, PA [PA0008]. This cable system has converted to IPTV)

GLENDON—See ALLENTOWN, PA (Service Electric Cable TV & Communications)

GLENFIELD—See PITTSBURGH, PA (Comcast Cable)

GLENOLDEN—See PHILADELPHIA, PA (Comcast Cable)

GLENOLDEN—See RIDLEY PARK, PA (RCN. Formerly served by PHILADELPHIA (suburbs), PA [PA0447]. This cable system has converted to IPTV)

GOLDSBORO—See HARRISBURG, PA (Comcast Cable)

GORDON—See HAZLETON, PA (Service Electric Cablevision)

GOSHEN—See ZELIENOPLE, OH (Armstrong Cable Services)

GOULDSBORO—See MILFORD, PA (Blue Ridge Communications)

GRAFTON TWP.—See ZELIENOPLE, OH (Armstrong Cable Services)

GRAHAM TWP.—Tele-Media. Now served by SNOW SHOE, PA [PA0188]

GRAHAM TWP.—See SNOW SHOE, PA (Tele-Media)

GRAMPIAN—Atlantic Broadband. Now served by CLEARFIELD, PA [PA0084]

GRAMPIAN—See CLEARFIELD, PA (Atlantic Broadband)

GRANGER TWP.—See ZELIENOPLE, OH (Armstrong Cable Services)

GRANTSVILLE (UNINCORPORATED AREAS)—See ADDISON TWP. (southern portion), MD (Somerfield Cable TV Co)

GRANTSVILLE—See BLAIRSVILLE, MD (Comcast Cable)

GRANVILLE TWP. (BRADFORD COUNTY)—See TROY, PA (Blue Ridge Communications)

GRANVILLE TWP.—Nittany Media Inc. Now served by MIFFLINTOWN, PA [PA0365]

GRANVILLE TWP.—See MIFFLINTOWN, PA (Nittany Media Inc.)

GRANVILLE—See HARRISBURG, PA (Comcast Cable)

GRATZ—See HARRISBURG, PA (Comcast Cable)

Pennsylvania—Cable Community Index

GRATZTOWN—See PITTSBURGH, PA (Comcast Cable)

GREAT BEND BOROUGH—See THOMPSON TWP., PA (Adams Cable Service)

GREAT BEND TWP.—See THOMPSON TWP., PA (Adams Cable Service)

GREAT BEND—See THOMPSON TWP., PA (Adams Cable Service)

GREEN TREE—See PITTSBURGH, PA (Comcast Cable)

GREEN TWP. (Indiana County)—Formerly served by Adelphia Communications. Now served by Comcast Cable, BLAIRSVILLE, PA [PA0320]

GREEN TWP. (INDIANA COUNTY)—See BLAIRSVILLE, PA (Comcast Cable)

GREEN TWP. (MAHONING COUNTY)—See ZELIENOPLE, OH (Armstrong Cable Services)

GREEN TWP. (WAYNE COUNTY)—See ZELIENOPLE, OH (Armstrong Cable Services)

GREENAWALDS—See ALLENTOWN, PA (RCN. Formerly served by NORTHAMPTON BOROUGH, PA [PA0008]. This cable system has converted to IPTV)

GREENBURR—Formerly served by Greenburr TV Cable. No longer in operation

GREENCASTLE BOROUGH—See HARRISBURG, PA (Comcast Cable)

GREENE COUNTY (PORTIONS)—See UNIONTOWN, PA (Atlantic Broadband)

GREENE COUNTY—Formerly served by DuCom Cable TV. No longer in operation

GREENE TWP. (BEAVER COUNTY)—See PITTSBURGH, PA (Comcast Cable)

GREENE TWP. (CLINTON COUNTY)—See HARRISBURG, PA (Comcast Cable)

GREENE TWP. (FRANKLIN COUNTY)—See HARRISBURG, PA (Comcast Cable)

GREENE TWP. (GREENE COUNTY)—See UNIONTOWN, PA (Atlantic Broadband)

GREENE TWP. (PIKE COUNTY)—See MILFORD, PA (Blue Ridge Communications)

GREENFIELD TWP. (BLAIR COUNTY)—See ALTOONA, PA (Atlantic Broadband)

GREENFIELD TWP. (LACKAWANNA COUNTY)—See CARBONDALE TWP. (Lackawanna County), PA (Adams Cable Service)

GREENSBORO—See UNIONTOWN, PA (Atlantic Broadband)

GREENSBURG—Comcast Cable

GREENTOWN—Formerly served by Blue Ridge Communications. No longer in operation

GREENUP COUNTY (EASTERN PORTION)—See ZELIENOPLE, KY (Armstrong Cable Services)

GREENUP—See ZELIENOPLE, KY (Armstrong Cable Services)

GREENVILLE BOROUGH—Time Warner Cable. Now served by CLEVELAND (formerly Cleveland Heights), OH [OH0006]

GREENWICH TWP.—See HARRISBURG, PA (Comcast Cable)

GREENWICH TWP.—See ALLENTOWN, PA (Service Electric Cable TV & Communications)

GREENWOOD TWP. (CLEARFIELD COUNTY)—See CLEARFIELD, PA (Atlantic Broadband)

GREENWOOD TWP. (JUNIATA COUNTY)—See MIFFLINTOWN, PA (Nittany Media Inc.)

GREENWOOD TWP. (PERRY COUNTY)—See HARRISBURG, PA (Comcast Cable)

GREENWOOD TWP.—See BERWICK, PA (MetroCast Communications)

GREGG TWP. (UNION COUNTY)—See HARRISBURG, PA (Comcast Cable)

GREGG TWP. (UNION COUNTY)—See SUNBURY (village), PA (Service Electric Cablevision)

GROVE CITY—Armstrong Cable Services. Now served by ZELIENOPLE, PA [PA0053]

GROVE CITY—See ZELIENOPLE, PA (Armstrong Cable Services)

GROVER—See CANTON, PA (Zito Media)

GUILFORD TWP.—See HARRISBURG, PA (Comcast Cable)

GULICH TWP.—See HARRISBURG, PA (Comcast Cable)

GUYAN TWP.—See ZELIENOPLE, OH (Armstrong Cable Services)

GUYS MILLS—See ZELIENOPLE, PA (Armstrong Cable Services)

HALFMOON TWP.—See HARRISBURG, PA (Comcast Cable)

HALIFAX BOROUGH—See HARRISBURG, PA (Comcast Cable)

HALIFAX TWP.—See HARRISBURG, PA (Comcast Cable)

HALLAM BOROUGH—See HARRISBURG, PA (Comcast Cable)

HALLSTEAD BOROUGH—See THOMPSON TWP., PA (Adams Cable Service)

HAMBURG—Comcast Cable. Now served by HARRISBURG, PA [PA0009]

HAMBURG—See HARRISBURG, PA (Comcast Cable)

HAMILTON TWP. (ADAMS COUNTY)—See HARRISBURG, PA (Comcast Cable)

HAMILTON TWP. (FRANKLIN COUNTY)—See HARRISBURG, PA (Comcast Cable)

HAMILTON TWP. (MONROE COUNTY)—See STROUDSBURG, PA (Blue Ridge Communications)

HAMILTONBAN TWP.—See HARRISBURG, PA (Comcast Cable)

HAMLIN TWP.—See PUNXSUTAWNEY, PA (Comcast Cable)

HAMPDEN TWP. (CUMBERLAND COUNTY)—See HARRISBURG, PA (Comcast Cable)

HAMPTON TWP. (ALLEGHENY COUNTY)—See ZELIENOPLE, PA (Armstrong Cable Services)

HAMPTON TWP.—Comcast Cable. Now served by PITTSBURGH, PA [PA0001]

HAMPTON TWP.—See PITTSBURGH, PA (Comcast Cable)

HANOVER BOROUGH—See HARRISBURG, PA (Comcast Cable)

HANOVER TWP. (BEAVER COUNTY)—See PITTSBURGH, PA (Comcast Cable)

HANOVER TWP. (LEHIGH COUNTY)—See ALLENTOWN, PA (RCN. Formerly served by NORTHAMPTON BOROUGH, PA [PA0008]. This cable system has converted to IPTV)

HANOVER TWP. (LUZERNE COUNTY)—See WILKES-BARRE, PA (Service Electric Cable Company)

HANOVER TWP. (NORTHAMPTON COUNTY)—See ALLENTOWN, PA (RCN. Formerly served by NORTHAMPTON BOROUGH, PA [PA0008]. This cable system has converted to IPTV)

HANOVER TWP. (WASHINGTON COUNTY)—See PITTSBURGH, PA (Comcast Cable)

HANOVER TWP.—See ALLENTOWN, PA (Service Electric Cable TV & Communications)

HARBORCREEK TWP.—Time Warner Cable. Now served by CLEVELAND (formerly Cleveland Heights), OH [OH0006]

HARFORD—See THOMPSON TWP., PA (Adams Cable Service)

HARMAR TWP.—See PITTSBURGH, PA (Comcast Cable)

HARMONY TWP.—See THOMPSON TWP., PA (Adams Cable Service)

HARMONY TWP.—See PITTSBURGH, PA (Comcast Cable)

HARMONY—See ZELIENOPLE, PA (Armstrong Cable Services)

HARRIS TWP. (CENTRE COUNTY)—See HARRISBURG, PA (Comcast Cable)

HARRISBURG—Formerly served by Gap Cable TV. No longer in operation

HARRISBURG—Comcast Cable

HARRISON TWP. (ALLEGHENY COUNTY)—See PITTSBURGH, PA (Comcast Cable)

HARRISON TWP. (BEDFORD COUNTY)—See BLAIRSVILLE, PA (Comcast Cable)

HARRISON TWP. (BEDFORD COUNTY)—See LONDONDERRY TWP. (Bedford County), PA (Leap Cable TV)

HARRISON VALLEY—Zito Media

HARRISVILLE—See ZELIENOPLE, PA (Armstrong Cable Services)

HARTLETON—See MIFFLINBURG, PA (Atlantic Broadband)

HARTLETON—See STATE COLLEGE, PA (Windstream (formerly D&E Communications). New IPTV service no longer available)

HARTLEY TWP.—Formerly served by D&E Communications/Windstream. IPTV service no longer in operation

HARTLEY TWP.—See MIFFLINBURG, PA (Atlantic Broadband)

HARTSLOG—Formerly served by Milestone Communications LP. No longer in operation

HARVEYS LAKE BOROUGH—See HARRISBURG, PA (Comcast Cable)

HASTINGS BOROUGH—See BLAIRSVILLE, PA (Comcast Cable)

HAVERFORD TWP.—See PHILADELPHIA, PA (Comcast Cable)

HAVERTOWN—See RIDLEY PARK, PA (RCN. Formerly served by PHILADELPHIA (suburbs), PA [PA0447]. This cable system has converted to IPTV)

HAWLEY—Blue Ridge Communications. Now served by MILFORD, PA [PA0369]

HAWLEY—See MILFORD, PA (Blue Ridge Communications)

HAWTHORN—See PUNXSUTAWNEY, PA (Comcast Cable)

HAYCOCK TWP.—See ALLENTOWN, PA (Service Electric Cable TV & Communications)

HAYESVILLE—See ZELIENOPLE, OH (Armstrong Cable Services)

HAYSVILLE—See PITTSBURGH, PA (Comcast Cable)

HAZEN—Zito Media

HAZLE TWP.—See HAZLETON, PA (Service Electric Cablevision)

HAZLETON—Service Electric Cablevision

HEBRON TWP.—See COUDERSPORT, PA (Zito Media)

Cable Community Index—Pennsylvania

HECLA—See MAMMOTH, PA (Citizens Telecom. Formerly [PA0400]. This cable system has converted to IPTV)

HEGINS TWP.—See HARRISBURG, PA (Comcast Cable)

HEIDELBERG TWP. (BERKS COUNTY)—See HARRISBURG, PA (Comcast Cable)

HEIDELBERG TWP. (LEBANON COUNTY)—See HARRISBURG, PA (Comcast Cable)

HEIDELBERG TWP. (LEHIGH COUNTY)—See LEHIGHTON, PA (Blue Ridge Communications)

HEIDELBERG TWP. (YORK COUNTY)—See HARRISBURG, PA (Comcast Cable)

HEIDELBERG—See PITTSBURGH, PA (Comcast Cable)

HELLAM TWP. (YORK COUNTY)—See HARRISBURG, PA (Comcast Cable)

HELLAM—See HARRISBURG, PA (Comcast Cable)

HELLERTOWN BORO—See ALLENTOWN, PA (Service Electric Cable TV & Communications)

HELLERTOWN—See ALLENTOWN, PA (RCN. Formerly served by NORTHAMPTON BOROUGH, PA [PA0008]. This cable system has converted to IPTV)

HEMLOCK FARMS DEVELOPMENT—Blue Ridge Communications. Now served by MILFORD, PA [PA0369]

HEMLOCK FARMS DEVELOPMENT—See MILFORD, PA (Blue Ridge Communications)

HEMLOCK TWP.—See SUNBURY (village), PA (Service Electric Cablevision)

HEMPFIELD TWP. (WESTMORELAND COUNTY)—See GREENSBURG, PA (Comcast Cable)

HENDERSON TWP. (HUNTINGDON COUNTY)—See HARRISBURG, PA (Comcast Cable)

HENDERSON TWP. (JEFFERSON COUNTY)—See PUNXSUTAWNEY, PA (Comcast Cable)

HENRY CLAY TWP.—See GREENSBURG, PA (Comcast Cable)

HEPBURN TWP.—See HARRISBURG, PA (Comcast Cable)

HEPBURNVILLE—See COGAN STATION, PA (Zito Media)

HEREFORD TWP. (BERKS COUNTY)—See ALLENTOWN, PA (Service Electric Cable TV & Communications)

HERNDON—Formerly served by Pike's Peak TV Association. No longer in operation

HERNDON—See SUNBURY (village), PA (Service Electric Cablevision)

HERSHEY—Comcast Cable. Now served by HARRISBURG, PA [PA0009]

HERSHEY—See HARRISBURG, PA (Comcast Cable)

HICKORY TWP. (LAWRENCE COUNTY)—See HARRISBURG, PA (Comcast Cable)

HIGHLAND TWP. (ADAMS COUNTY)—See HARRISBURG, PA (Comcast Cable)

HIGHLAND TWP. (ELK COUNTY)—See PUNXSUTAWNEY, PA (Comcast Cable)

HIGHSPIRE BOROUGH—See HARRISBURG, PA (Comcast Cable)

HILLSGROVE—See ELDRED TWP., PA (Herr Cable Co)

HOKENDAUQUA—See ALLENTOWN, PA (RCN. Formerly served by NORTHAMPTON BOROUGH, PA [PA0008]. This cable system has converted to IPTV)

HOLLAND—Formerly served by Comcast Cable. No longer in operation

HOLLIDAYSBURG—See ALTOONA, PA (Atlantic Broadband)

HOLMES—See RIDLEY PARK, PA (RCN. Formerly served by PHILADELPHIA (suburbs), PA [PA0447]. This cable system has converted to IPTV)

HOMER CITY—See BLAIRSVILLE, PA (Comcast Cable)

HOMESTEAD—See PITTSBURGH, PA (Comcast Cable)

HOMEWOOD—See ZELIENOPLE, PA (Armstrong Cable Services)

HONESDALE—Blue Ridge Communications. Now served by MILFORD, PA [PA0369]

HONESDALE—See MILFORD, PA (Blue Ridge Communications)

HONEY BROOK BOROUGH—See BIRDSBORO, PA (Service Electric Cablevision)

HONEY BROOK—See PHILADELPHIA, PA (Comcast Cable)

HONEY GROVE—Formerly served by Nittany Media. No longer in operation

HONEYBROOK TWP. (CHESTER COUNTY)—See BIRDSBORO, PA (Service Electric Cablevision)

HOOKSTOWN BOROUGH—See PITTSBURGH, PA (Comcast Cable)

HOOVERSVILLE BOROUGH—See BLAIRSVILLE, PA (Comcast Cable)

HOP BOTTOM—See THOMPSON TWP., PA (Adams Cable Service)

HOPEWELL BOROUGH—See HARRISBURG, PA (Comcast Cable)

HOPEWELL TWP. (BEAVER COUNTY)—See PITTSBURGH, PA (Comcast Cable)

HOPEWELL TWP. (BEDFORD COUNTY)—See BLAIRSVILLE, PA (Comcast Cable)

HOPEWELL TWP. (BEDFORD COUNTY)—See HARRISBURG, PA (Comcast Cable)

HOPEWELL TWP.—See NEWBURG, PA (Kuhn Communications)

HOPWOOD—See UNIONTOWN, PA (Atlantic Broadband)

HORNBROOK—See ROME, PA (Beaver Valley Cable Co)

HORTON TWP. (ELK COUNTY)—See BROCKWAY, PA (Brockway TV Inc)

HORTON TWP. (ELK COUNTY)—See PUNXSUTAWNEY, PA (Comcast Cable)

HOSTETTER—See MAMMOTH, PA (Citizens Telecom. Formerly [PA0400]. This cable system has converted to IPTV)

HOUSTON—See PITTSBURGH, PA (Comcast Cable)

HOUTZDALE—See HARRISBURG, PA (Comcast Cable)

HOVEY TWP.—See OIL CITY, PA (Comcast Cable)

HOWARD BOROUGH—See HARRISBURG, PA (Comcast Cable)

HOWARD TWP.—See HARRISBURG, PA (Comcast Cable)

HOWE TWP.—See HARRISBURG, PA (Comcast Cable)

HUBBARD TWP. (TRUMBULL COUNTY)—See ZELIENOPLE, OH (Armstrong Cable Services)

HUBLERSBURG—See ZION, PA (TeleMedia)

HUBLEY TWP.—See HARRISBURG, PA (Comcast Cable)

HUGHESTOWN BOROUGH—See HARRISBURG, PA (Comcast Cable)

HUGHESVILLE BOROUGH—See HARRISBURG, PA (Comcast Cable)

HUMMELSTOWN BOROUGH—See HARRISBURG, PA (Comcast Cable)

HUMPHREYS—See MAMMOTH, PA (Citizens Telecom. Formerly [PA0400]. This cable system has converted to IPTV)

HUNKER—See GREENSBURG, PA (Comcast Cable)

HUNKER—See SALTLICK TWP., PA (Laurel Highland Total Communications)

HUNLOCK CREEK—See TUNKHANNOCK, PA (Blue Ridge Communications)

HUNLOCK CREEK—See BERWICK, PA (MetroCast Communications)

HUNTINGDON TWP. (ADAMS COUNTY)—See HARRISBURG, PA (Comcast Cable)

HUNTINGDON—Comcast Cable. Now served by HARRISBURG, PA [PA0009]

HUNTINGTON TWP. (Luzerne County)—Formerly served by Comcast Cable. No longer in operation

HUNTINGTON TWP. (LUZERNE COUNTY)—See TUNKHANNOCK, PA (Blue Ridge Communications)

HUSTON TWP. (BLAIR COUNTY)—See ALTOONA, PA (Atlantic Broadband)

HUSTON TWP. (CENTRE COUNTY)—See UNION TWP. (Centre County), PA (Country Cable)

HUSTON TWP. (CLEARFIELD COUNTY)—See TREASURE LAKE, PA (Zito Media)

HUSTON—See ALTOONA, PA (Atlantic Broadband)

HYDE PARK BOROUGH—See PITTSBURGH, PA (Comcast Cable)

HYDETOWN—See ZELIENOPLE, PA (Armstrong Cable Services)

HYNDMAN BOROUGH—Formerly served by Adelphia Communications. Now served by Comcast Cable, BLAIRSVILLE, PA [PA0320]

HYNDMAN BOROUGH—See BLAIRSVILLE, PA (Comcast Cable)

ICKESBURG—Nittany Media Inc. Now served by MIFFLINTOWN, PA [PA0365]

ICKESBURG—See MIFFLINTOWN, PA (Nittany Media Inc.)

INDEPENDENCE TWP.—See PITTSBURGH, PA (Comcast Cable)

INDIAN CREEK—See SALTLICK TWP., PA (Laurel Highland Total Communications)

INDIAN HEAD—See SALTLICK TWP., PA (Laurel Highland Total Communications)

INDIAN LAKE BOROUGH—See BLAIRSVILLE, PA (Comcast Cable)

INDIANA TWP.—Formerly served by Adelphia Communications. Now served by Comcast Cable, BLAIRSVILLE, PA [PA0320]

INDIANA TWP.—See BLAIRSVILLE, PA (Comcast Cable)

INDUSTRY—See PITTSBURGH, PA (Comcast Cable)

INGRAM—See PITTSBURGH, PA (Comcast Cable)

IRVINE—See YOUNGSVILLE, PA (Youngsville TV Corp)

IRVONA BOROUGH—See BLAIRSVILLE, PA (Comcast Cable)

IRWIN TWP. (VENANGO COUNTY)—See ZELIENOPLE, PA (Armstrong Cable Services)

IRWIN—See GREENSBURG, PA (Comcast Cable)

ISABELLA—See UNIONTOWN, PA (Atlantic Broadband)

Pennsylvania—Cable Community Index

JACKSON CENTER—See ZELIENOPLE, PA (Armstrong Cable Services)

JACKSON TWP. (BUTLER COUNTY)—See ZELIENOPLE, PA (Armstrong Cable Services)

JACKSON TWP. (BUTLER COUNTY)—See EAST SMITHFIELD, PA (North Penn Video)

JACKSON TWP. (CAMBRIA COUNTY)—See JOHNSTOWN, PA (Atlantic Broadband)

JACKSON TWP. (CAMBRIA COUNTY)—See BLAIRSVILLE, PA (Comcast Cable)

JACKSON TWP. (COLUMBIA COUNTY)—See BERWICK, PA (MetroCast Communications)

JACKSON TWP. (DAUPHIN COUNTY)—See HARRISBURG, PA (Comcast Cable)

JACKSON TWP. (HUNTINGDON COUNTY)—See McALEVYS FORT, PA (Atlantic Broadband)

JACKSON TWP. (LEBANON COUNTY)—See HARRISBURG, PA (Comcast Cable)

JACKSON TWP. (MAHONING COUNTY)—See ZELIENOPLE, OH (Armstrong Cable Services)

JACKSON TWP. (MONROE COUNTY)—See STROUDSBURG, PA (Blue Ridge Communications)

JACKSON TWP. (NORTHUMBERLAND COUNTY)—See SUNBURY (village), PA (Service Electric Cablevision)

JACKSON TWP. (SNYDER COUNTY)—See SUNBURY (village), PA (Service Electric Cablevision)

JACKSON TWP. (TIOGA COUNTY)—Blue Ridge Communications

JACKSON TWP. (VENANGO COUNTY)—See FRANKLIN (Venango County), PA (Time Warner Cable)

JACKSON TWP. (YORK COUNTY)—See HARRISBURG, PA (Comcast Cable)

JACKSON TWP.—See THOMPSON TWP., PA (Adams Cable Service)

JACOBSBURG—See ALLENTOWN, PA (RCN. Formerly served by NORTHAMPTON BOROUGH, PA [PA0008]. This cable system has converted to IPTV)

JACOBUS—See HARRISBURG, PA (Comcast Cable)

JAMES CITY—See PUNXSUTAWNEY, PA (Comcast Cable)

JAMESTOWN—Formerly served by Cebridge Connections. Now served by Armstrong Cable Services, ZELIENOPLE, PA [PA0053]

JAMESTOWN—See ZELIENOPLE, PA (Armstrong Cable Services)

JAMISON—Formerly served by Comcast Cable. No longer in operation

JAY TWP.—See ST. MARY'S, PA (Zito Media)

JEDDO BOROUGH—See HAZLETON, PA (Service Electric Cablevision)

JEFFERSON (GREENE COUNTY)—See UNIONTOWN, PA (Atlantic Broadband)

JEFFERSON TWP. (BERKS COUNTY)—See HARRISBURG, PA (Comcast Cable)

JEFFERSON TWP. (DAUPHIN COUNTY)—See HARRISBURG, PA (Comcast Cable)

JEFFERSON TWP. (FAYETTE COUNTY)—See ZELIENOPLE, PA (Armstrong Cable Services)

JEFFERSON TWP. (LACKAWANNA COUNTY)—See CARBONDALE TWP. (Lackawanna County), PA (Adams Cable Service)

JEFFERSON TWP. (LACKAWANNA COUNTY)—See HARRISBURG, PA (Comcast Cable)

JEFFERSON—See PITTSBURGH, PA (Comcast Cable)

JENKINS BOROUGH—See HARRISBURG, PA (Comcast Cable)

JENNER TWP. (SOMERSET COUNTY)—See JOHNSTOWN, PA (Atlantic Broadband)

JENNER TWP.—See BLAIRSVILLE, PA (Comcast Cable)

JENNERSTOWN BOROUGH—See BLAIRSVILLE, PA (Comcast Cable)

JERMYN—See CARBONDALE TWP. (Lackawanna County), PA (Adams Cable Service)

JEROME—See JOHNSTOWN, PA (Atlantic Broadband)

JERSEY SHORE—See HARRISBURG, PA (Comcast Cable)

JESSUP BOROUGH—See HARRISBURG, PA (Comcast Cable)

JIM THORPE—See LEHIGHTON, PA (Blue Ridge Communications)

JOHNSONBURG—Johnsonburg Community TV Co

JOHNSONBURG—Zito Media

JOHNSTOWN—Atlantic Broadband

JONES MILLS—See SALTLICK TWP., PA (Laurel Highland Total Communications)

JONES TWP.—See WILCOX, PA (Zito Media)

JONESTOWN (LEBANON COUNTY)—See HARRISBURG, PA (Comcast Cable)

JORDAN CREEK—See ALLENTOWN, PA (RCN. Formerly served by NORTHAMPTON BOROUGH, PA [PA0008]. This cable system has converted to IPTV)

JORDAN TWP.—See SUNBURY (village), PA (Service Electric Cablevision)

JUNIATA TERRACE—See HARRISBURG, PA (Comcast Cable)

JUNIATA TWP. (BLAIR COUNTY)—See ALTOONA, PA (Atlantic Broadband)

JUNIATA TWP. (PERRY COUNTY)—See HARRISBURG, PA (Comcast Cable)

JUNIATA TWP. (PORTIONS, HUNTINGDON COUNTY)—See BLAIRSVILLE, PA (Comcast Cable)

JUNIATA TWP. (PORTIONS, HUNTINGDON COUNTY)—See HARRISBURG, PA (Comcast Cable)

KANE—Comcast Cable. Now served by PUNXSUTAWNEY, PA [PA0397]

KANE—See PUNXSUTAWNEY, PA (Comcast Cable)

KARNS CITY—See ZELIENOPLE, PA (Armstrong Cable Services)

KARTHAUS TWP.—See SNOW SHOE, PA (Tele-Media)

KASKA—See WEATHERLY, PA (MetroCast Communications)

KEATING TWP. (McKEAN COUNTY)—See PUNXSUTAWNEY, PA (Comcast Cable)

KECKSBURG—See MAMMOTH, PA (Citizens Telecom. Formerly [PA0400]. This cable system has converted to IPTV)

KEISTERVILLE—See UNIONTOWN, PA (Atlantic Broadband)

KELLETTVILLE—Formerly served by Cebridge Connections. No longer in operation

KELLY TWP. (UNION COUNTY)—See DANVILLE, PA (CATV Service Inc)

KELLY TWP.—Formerly served by D&E Communications/Windstream. IPTV service no longer in operation

KELLY TWP.—See SUNBURY (village), PA (Service Electric Cablevision)

KENHORST—See HARRISBURG, PA (Comcast Cable)

KENNEDY—See PITTSBURGH, PA (Comcast Cable)

KENNEDYVILLE—See MANSFIELD, PA (Blue Ridge Communications)

KENNETT SQUARE BOROUGH—Comcast Cable. Now served by PHILADELPHIA, PA [PA0005]

KENNETT SQUARE BOROUGH—See PHILADELPHIA, PA (Comcast Cable)

KENNETT TWP.—See PHILADELPHIA, PA (Comcast Cable)

KENOVA—See ZELIENOPLE, WV (Armstrong Cable Services)

KERSEY—See ST. MARY'S, PA (Zito Media)

KIDDER TWP. (CARBON COUNTY)—See LEHIGHTON, PA (Blue Ridge Communications)

KIDDER TWP.—See WEATHERLY, PA (MetroCast Communications)

KILBUCK—See PITTSBURGH, PA (Comcast Cable)

KIMMELL TWP.—See ALTOONA, PA (Atlantic Broadband)

KING OF PRUSSIA—Comcast Cable. Now served by EATONTOWN BOROUGH, NJ [NJ0009]

KING TWP.—See NEW ENTERPRISE, PA (Atlantic Broadband)

KINGSTON (LUZERNE COUNTY)—See WILKES-BARRE, PA (Service Electric Cable Company)

KINGSTON—See HARRISBURG, PA (Comcast Cable)

KINZERS—See HARRISBURG, PA (Comcast Cable)

KISKIMINETAS TWP.—Comcast Cable. Now served by BLAIRSVILLE, PA [PA0320]

KISKIMINETAS TWP.—See BLAIRSVILLE, PA (Comcast Cable)

KISTLER BOROUGH—See HARRISBURG, PA (Comcast Cable)

KITTANNING BOROUGH—See BLAIRSVILLE, PA (Comcast Cable)

KITTANNING TWP.—See BLAIRSVILLE, PA (Comcast Cable)

KITTANNING—Comcast Cable. Now served by BLAIRSVILLE, PA [PA0320]

KLECKNERSVILLE—See ALLENTOWN, PA (RCN. Formerly served by NORTHAMPTON BOROUGH, PA [PA0008]. This cable system has converted to IPTV)

KLINE TWP.—See HAZLETON, PA (Service Electric Cablevision)

KNOX TWP. (CLARION COUNTY)—See SHIPPENVILLE, PA (Atlantic Broadband)

KNOX TWP. (CLARION COUNTY)—See PUNXSUTAWNEY, PA (Comcast Cable)

KNOX TWP. (JEFFERSON COUNTY)—See PUNXSUTAWNEY, PA (Comcast Cable)

KNOX TWP.—See CLEARFIELD, PA (Atlantic Broadband)

KNOX—See SHIPPENVILLE, PA (Atlantic Broadband)

KOPPEL—See ZELIENOPLE, PA (Armstrong Cable Services)

KREAMER—See SUNBURY (village), PA (Service Electric Cablevision)

KUHNSVILLE—See ALLENTOWN, PA (RCN. Formerly served by NORTHAMPTON BOROUGH, PA [PA0008]. This cable system has converted to IPTV)

KULPMONT (NORTHUMBERLAND COUNTY)—See SUNBURY (village), PA (Service Electric Cablevision)

KUNKLE—See TUNKHANNOCK, PA (Blue Ridge Communications)

KUTZTOWN—Hometown Utilicom. This cable system has converted to IPTV. See KUTZTOWN, PA [PA5144]

KUTZTOWN—Home Net. Formerly [PA0452]. This cable system has converted to IPTV

KUTZTOWN—See BIRDSBORO, PA (Service Electric Cablevision)

KYLERTOWN—Formerly served by Tele-Media. No longer in operation

LA BELLE—See UNIONTOWN, PA (Atlantic Broadband)

LA PLUME TWP.—See HARRISBURG, PA (Comcast Cable)

LA PORTE BOROUGH—See HARRISBURG, PA (Comcast Cable)

LACEYVILLE—See TUNKHANNOCK, PA (Blue Ridge Communications)

LACKAWAXEN TWP.—See MILFORD, PA (Blue Ridge Communications)

LAFAYETTE TWP. (PORTIONS)—See ZELIENOPLE, OH (Armstrong Cable Services)

LAFAYETTE TWP.—See BRADFORD, PA (Atlantic Broadband)

LAFLIN BOROUGH—See HARRISBURG, PA (Comcast Cable)

LAIRDSVILLE—Formerly served by Ralph Herr TV. No longer in operation

LAKE CAREY—See TUNKHANNOCK, PA (Blue Ridge Communications)

LAKE HARMONY—See WEATHERLY, PA (MetroCast Communications)

LAKE TWP. (LUZERNE COUNTY)—See TUNKHANNOCK, PA (Blue Ridge Communications)

LAKE TWP. (WAYNE COUNTY)—See CARBONDALE TWP. (Lackawanna County), PA (Adams Cable Service)

LAKE WINOLA—See TUNKHANNOCK, PA (Blue Ridge Communications)

LAKEWOOD—Hancock Video. Now served by HANCOCK, NY [NY0147]

LAMAR TWP. (CLINTON COUNTY)—See HARRISBURG, PA (Comcast Cable)

LAMBS CREEK—See MANSFIELD, PA (Blue Ridge Communications)

LANCASTER (LANCASTER COUNTY)—See HARRISBURG, PA (Comcast Cable)

LANCASTER TWP. (BUTLER COUNTY)—See ZELIENOPLE, PA (Armstrong Cable Services)

LANCASTER—Comcast Cable. Now served by HARRISBURG, PA [PA0009]

LANDINGVILLE—See HARRISBURG, PA (Comcast Cable)

LANDISBURG—Kuhn Communications

LANESBORO—See THOMPSON TWP., PA (Adams Cable Service)

LANSDALE—Comcast Cable. Now served by EATONTOWN BOROUGH, NJ [NJ0009]

LANSDOWNE—See PHILADELPHIA, PA (Comcast Cable)

LANSDOWNE—See RIDLEY PARK, PA (RCN. Formerly served by PHILADELPHIA (suburbs), PA [PA0447]. This cable system has converted to IPTV)

LANSFORD—See LEHIGHTON, PA (Blue Ridge Communications)

LAPORTE TWP. (SULLIVAN COUNTY)—See HARRISBURG, PA (Comcast Cable)

LAPORTE TWP.—Comcast Cable. Now served by HARRISBURG, PA [PA0009]

LARKSVILLE—See BERWICK, PA (MetroCast Communications)

LATHROP TWP.—See THOMPSON TWP., PA (Adams Cable Service)

LATIMORE TWP.—See HARRISBURG, PA (Comcast Cable)

LATROBE—Comcast Cable. Now served by BLAIRSVILLE, PA [PA0320]

LATROBE—See BLAIRSVILLE, PA (Comcast Cable)

LAUREL MOUNTAIN PARK—See BLAIRSVILLE, PA (Comcast Cable)

LAUREL RUN—See WILKES-BARRE, PA (Service Electric Cable Company)

LAURELDALE—See HARRISBURG, PA (Comcast Cable)

LAURELTON—Formerly served by D&E Communications. No longer in operation

LAURELTON—See MIFFLINBURG, PA (Atlantic Broadband)

LAURELVILLE—See MAMMOTH, PA (Citizens Telecom. Formerly [PA0400]. This cable system has converted to IPTV)

LAURYS STATION—See ALLENTOWN, PA (RCN. Formerly served by NORTHAMPTON BOROUGH, PA [PA0008]. This cable system has converted to IPTV)

LAUSANNE TWP—See WEATHERLY, PA (MetroCast Communications)

LAWRENCE COUNTY (SOUTHERN PORTION)—See ZELIENOPLE, PA (Armstrong Cable Services)

LAWRENCE TWP. (CLEARFIELD COUNTY)—See CLEARFIELD, PA (Atlantic Broadband)

LAWRENCEVILLE—Formerly served by Time Warner Cable. No longer in operation

LAWSON HEIGHTS—See MAMMOTH, PA (Citizens Telecom. Formerly [PA0400]. This cable system has converted to IPTV)

LE RAYSVILLE BOROUGH—See ROME, PA (Beaver Valley Cable Co)

LE RAYSVILLE—See ROME, PA (Beaver Valley Cable Co)

LEACOCK TWP.—See HARRISBURG, PA (Comcast Cable)

LEBANON—Comcast Cable. Now served by HARRISBURG, PA [PA0009]

LEBANON—See HARRISBURG, PA (Comcast Cable)

LEBOEUF TWP.—See EDINBORO, PA (Coaxial Cable TV Corp)

LEECHBURG BOROUGH—See PITTSBURGH, PA (Comcast Cable)

LEEPER—See ZELIENOPLE, PA (Armstrong Cable Services)

LEESPORT—See HARRISBURG, PA (Comcast Cable)

LEET TWP.—See PITTSBURGH, PA (Comcast Cable)

LEETSDALE—See PITTSBURGH, PA (Comcast Cable)

LEHIGH TWP. (CARBON COUNTY)—See WEATHERLY, PA (MetroCast Communications)

LEHIGH TWP. (NORTHAMPTON COUNTY)—See LEHIGHTON, PA (Blue Ridge Communications)

LEHIGH TWP.—See ALLENTOWN, PA (RCN. Formerly served by NORTHAMPTON BOROUGH, PA [PA0008]. This cable system has converted to IPTV)

LEHIGH VALLEY—See ALLENTOWN, PA (RCN. Formerly served by NORTHAMPTON BOROUGH, PA [PA0008]. This cable system has converted to IPTV)

LEHIGH VALLEY—See ALLENTOWN, PA (Service Electric Cable TV & Communications)

LEHIGHTON—Blue Ridge Communications

LEHMAN TWP. (LUZERNE COUNTY)—See HARRISBURG, PA (Comcast Cable)

LEHMAN TWP. (PIKE COUNTY)—See STROUDSBURG, PA (Blue Ridge Communications)

LEMON TWP.—See TUNKHANNOCK, PA (Blue Ridge Communications)

LEMOYNE BOROUGH—See HARRISBURG, PA (Comcast Cable)

LENHARTSVILLE—See HARRISBURG, PA (Comcast Cable)

LEOLA—See HARRISBURG, PA (Comcast Cable)

LEROY TWP.—Blue Ridge Communications. Now served by TROY, PA [PA0165]

LEROY TWP.—See TROY, PA (Blue Ridge Communications)

LETTERKENNY TWP. (FRANKLIN COUNTY)—See HARRISBURG, PA (Comcast Cable)

LEVITTOWN—Formerly served by Comcast Cable. No longer in operation

LEWIS RUN—See BRADFORD, PA (Atlantic Broadband)

LEWIS TWP. (NORTHUMBERLAND COUNTY)—See SUNBURY (village), PA (Service Electric Cablevision)

LEWIS TWP. (UNION COUNTY)—See MIFFLINBURG, PA (Atlantic Broadband)

LEWIS TWP.—Comcast Cable. Now served by HARRISBURG, PA [PA0009]

LEWIS TWP.—Formerly served by D&E Communications/Windstream. IPTV service no longer in operation

LEWIS TWP.—See HARRISBURG, PA (Comcast Cable)

LEWISBERRY—See NEWBERRY TWP., PA (Blue Ridge Communications)

LEWISBURG—Formerly served by Lewisburg CATV. Now served by CATV Service Inc., DANVILLE, PA [PA0054]

LEWISBURG—Windstream (formerly D&E Communications.) This cable system has converted to IPTV. Now served by STATE COLLEGE, PA [PA5280]

LEWISBURG—See DANVILLE, PA (CATV Service Inc)

LEWISBURG—See SUNBURY (village), PA (Service Electric Cablevision)

LEWISBURG—See STATE COLLEGE, PA (Windstream (formerly D&E Communications). New IPTV service no longer available)

LEWISTOWN—Comcast Cable. Now served by HARRISBURG, PA [PA0009]

LEWISTOWN—See DERRY/DECATUR, PA (Atlantic Broadband)

LEWISTOWN—See HARRISBURG, PA (Comcast Cable)

LEWISTOWN—See MIFFLINTOWN, PA (Nittany Media Inc.)

LIBERTY TWP. (ADAMS COUNTY)—See HARRISBURG, PA (Comcast Cable)

LIBERTY TWP. (BEDFORD COUNTY)—See HARRISBURG, PA (Comcast Cable)

LIBERTY TWP. (CENTRE COUNTY)—See HARRISBURG, PA (Comcast Cable)

LIBERTY TWP. (MCKEAN COUNTY)—See COUDERSPORT, PA (Zito Media)

LIBERTY TWP. (MERCER COUNTY)—See ZELIENOPLE, PA (Armstrong Cable Services)

Pennsylvania—Cable Community Index

LIBERTY TWP. (MONTOUR COUNTY)—See DANVILLE, PA (CATV Service Inc)

LIBERTY TWP. (MONTOUR COUNTY)—See SUNBURY (village), PA (Service Electric Cablevision)

LIBERTY—Blue Ridge Communications. Now served by MANSFIELD, PA [PA0421]

LIBERTY—See MANSFIELD, PA (Blue Ridge Communications)

LIBERTY—See PITTSBURGH, PA (Comcast Cable)

LIGONIER BOROUGH—See BLAIRSVILLE, PA (Comcast Cable)

LIGONIER BOROUGH—See SALTLICK TWP., PA (Laurel Highland Total Communications)

LIGONIER TWP.—See BLAIRSVILLE, PA (Comcast Cable)

LIGONIER—Formerly served by Adelphia Communications. Now served by Comcast Cable, BLAIRSVILLE, PA [PA0320]

LILLY BOROUGH—See BLAIRSVILLE, PA (Comcast Cable)

LIMESTONE TWP. (CLARION COUNTY)—See SHIPPENVILLE, PA (Atlantic Broadband)

LIMESTONE TWP. (CLARION COUNTY)—See PUNXSUTAWNEY, PA (Comcast Cable)

LIMESTONE TWP. (Lycoming County)—Comcast Cable. Now served by HARRISBURG, PA [PA0009]

LIMESTONE TWP. (LYCOMING COUNTY)—See HARRISBURG, PA (Comcast Cable)

LIMESTONE TWP. (MONTOUR COUNTY)—See DANVILLE, PA (CATV Service Inc)

LIMESTONE TWP. (MONTOUR COUNTY)—See HARRISBURG, PA (Comcast Cable)

LIMESTONE TWP. (UNION COUNTY)—See MIFFLINBURG, PA (Atlantic Broadband)

LIMESTONE TWP. (UNION COUNTY)—See SUNBURY (village), PA (Service Electric Cablevision)

LIMESTONE TWP. (WARREN COUNTY)—See ZELIENOPLE, PA (Armstrong Cable Services)

LIMESTONE TWP.—Formerly served by D&E Communications/Windstream. IPTV service no longer in operation

LIMESTONE—Atlantic Broadband. Now served by MIFFLINBURG, PA [PA0131]

LIMESTONE—See BRADFORD, NY (Atlantic Broadband)

LIMESTONE—See MIFFLINBURG, PA (Atlantic Broadband)

LINCOLN TWP. (BEDFORD COUNTY)—See HARRISBURG, PA (Comcast Cable)

LINCOLN TWP.—See BLAIRSVILLE, PA (Comcast Cable)

LINCOLN—See PITTSBURGH, PA (Comcast Cable)

LINESVILLE—Formerly served by Cebridge Connections. No longer in operation

LITCHFIELD TWP. (PORTIONS)—See ZELIENOPLE, OH (Armstrong Cable Services)

LITITZ—See EPHRATA, PA (Blue Ridge Communications)

LITTLE BRITAIN—See HARRISBURG, PA (Comcast Cable)

LITTLE MAHANOY TWP.—See SUNBURY (village), PA (Service Electric Cablevision)

LITTLE MEADOWS BOROUGH—See ROME, PA (Beaver Valley Cable Co)

LITTLE MEADOWS—See ROME, PA (Beaver Valley Cable Co)

LITTLESTOWN—See HARRISBURG, PA (Comcast Cable)

LIVERPOOL TWP.—See ZELIENOPLE, OH (Armstrong Cable Services)

LIVERPOOL TWP.—See HARRISBURG, PA (Comcast Cable)

LIVERPOOL—Zampelli Electronics

LLEWELLYN—See HARRISBURG, PA (Comcast Cable)

LOCK HAVEN—Comcast Cable. Now served by HARRISBURG, PA [PA0009]

LOCK HAVEN—See HARRISBURG, PA (Comcast Cable)

LOCUST TWP.—See SUNBURY (village), PA (Service Electric Cablevision)

LOGAN TWP. (BLAIR COUNTY)—See ALTOONA, PA (Atlantic Broadband)

LOGAN TWP. (HUNTINGDON COUNTY)—See HARRISBURG, PA (Comcast Cable)

LOGANTON BOROUGH—See HARRISBURG, PA (Comcast Cable)

LOGANTON—Formerly served by TV Cable Associates Inc. No longer in operation

LOGANVILLE—See HARRISBURG, PA (Comcast Cable)

LONDON BRITAIN TWP.—See PHILADELPHIA, PA (Comcast Cable)

LONDON GROVE TWP.—See PHILADELPHIA, PA (Comcast Cable)

LONDONDERRY TWP. (BEDFORD COUNTY)—See BLAIRSVILLE, PA (Comcast Cable)

LONDONDERRY TWP. (BEDFORD COUNTY)—Leap Cable TV

LONG BRANCH—See ZELIENOPLE, PA (Armstrong Cable Services)

LONGSWAMP TWP. (PORTIONS)—See ALLENTOWN, PA (Service Electric Cable TV & Communications)

LONGSWAMP TWP. (PORTIONS)—See BIRDSBORO, PA (Service Electric Cablevision)

LOOMIS LAKE—Formerly served by Adams Cable Service. No longer in operation

LORAIN—See JOHNSTOWN, PA (Atlantic Broadband)

LORETTO BOROUGH—See BLAIRSVILLE, PA (Comcast Cable)

LOWBER—See PITTSBURGH, PA (Comcast Cable)

LOWER ALLEN TWP.—See HARRISBURG, PA (Comcast Cable)

LOWER ALSACE TWP.—See HARRISBURG, PA (Comcast Cable)

LOWER BURRELL—See PITTSBURGH, PA (Comcast Cable)

LOWER CHICHESTER TWP.—See PHILADELPHIA, PA (Comcast Cable)

LOWER FRANKFORD TWP.—See HARRISBURG, PA (Comcast Cable)

LOWER HEIDELBERG TWP.—See HARRISBURG, PA (Comcast Cable)

LOWER MACUNGIE TWP.—See ALLENTOWN, PA (RCN. Formerly served by NORTHAMPTON BOROUGH, PA [PA0008]. This cable system has converted to IPTV)

LOWER MACUNGIE TWP.—See ALLENTOWN, PA (Service Electric Cable TV & Communications)

LOWER MAHANOY TWP.—See HARRISBURG, PA (Comcast Cable)

LOWER MAHANOY TWP.—See SUNBURY (village), PA (Service Electric Cablevision)

LOWER MERION TWP.—Comcast Cable. Now served by PHILADELPHIA, PA [PA0005]

LOWER MERION TWP.—See PHILADELPHIA, PA (Comcast Cable)

LOWER MIFFLIN TWP.—See HARRISBURG, PA (Comcast Cable)

LOWER MILFORD TWP.—See ALLENTOWN, PA (Service Electric Cable TV & Communications)

LOWER MORELAND TWP.—See PHILADELPHIA, PA (Comcast Cable)

LOWER MOUNT BETHEL TWP.—See ALLENTOWN, PA (Service Electric Cable TV & Communications)

LOWER NAZARETH TWP.—See ALLENTOWN, PA (RCN. Formerly served by NORTHAMPTON BOROUGH, PA [PA0008]. This cable system has converted to IPTV)

LOWER NAZARETH TWP.—See ALLENTOWN, PA (Service Electric Cable TV & Communications)

LOWER OXFORD TWP.—Armstrong Cable Services. Now served by ABINGDON, MD [MD0019]

LOWER PAXTON TWP.—See HARRISBURG, PA (Comcast Cable)

LOWER SAUCON TWP.—See ALLENTOWN, PA (RCN. Formerly served by NORTHAMPTON BOROUGH, PA [PA0008]. This cable system has converted to IPTV)

LOWER SAUCON TWP.—See ALLENTOWN, PA (Service Electric Cable TV & Communications)

LOWER SWATARA TWP.—See HARRISBURG, PA (Comcast Cable)

LOWER TOWAMENSING TWP.—See LEHIGHTON, PA (Blue Ridge Communications)

LOWER TURKEYFOOT TWP.—See GREENSBURG, PA (Comcast Cable)

LOWER TYRONE TWP.—See UNIONTOWN, PA (Atlantic Broadband)

LOWER WINDSOR TWP.—See HARRISBURG, PA (Comcast Cable)

LOWER YODER TWP.—See JOHNSTOWN, PA (Atlantic Broadband)

LOWHILL TWP.—See ALLENTOWN, PA (RCN. Formerly served by NORTHAMPTON BOROUGH, PA [PA0008]. This cable system has converted to IPTV)

LOWHILL TWP.—See ALLENTOWN, PA (Service Electric Cable TV & Communications)

LOYALHANNA TWP.—See BLAIRSVILLE, PA (Comcast Cable)

LOYALHANNA—See BLAIRSVILLE, PA (Comcast Cable)

LOYALSOCK TWP.—See HARRISBURG, PA (Comcast Cable)

LUDLOW—See SHEFFIELD, PA (WestPA.net Inc)

LUMBER TWP. (CAMERON COUNTY)—See COUDERSPORT, PA (Zito Media)

LUZERNE TWP.—See UNIONTOWN, PA (Atlantic Broadband)

LUZERNE—See HARRISBURG, PA (Comcast Cable)

LYCOMING TWP.—See HARRISBURG, PA (Comcast Cable)

LYKENS BOROUGH—Comcast Cable. Now served by HARRISBURG, PA [PA0009]

LYKENS BOROUGH—See HARRISBURG, PA (Comcast Cable)

LYKENS TWP.—See HARRISBURG, PA (Comcast Cable)

LYNN TWP. (LEHIGH COUNTY)—See LEHIGHTON, PA (Blue Ridge Communications)

LYNN TWP.—See ALLENTOWN, PA (Service Electric Cable TV & Communications)

Cable Community Index—Pennsylvania

LYON STATION—See BIRDSBORO, PA (Service Electric Cablevision)

MACUNGIE—See ALLENTOWN, PA (RCN. Formerly served by NORTHAMPTON BOROUGH, PA [PA0008]. This cable system has converted to IPTV)

MACUNGIE—See ALLENTOWN, PA (Service Electric Cable TV & Communications)

MADISON TWP. (ARMSTRONG COUNTY)—See BLAIRSVILLE, PA (Comcast Cable)

MADISON TWP. (COLUMBIA COUNTY)—See HARRISBURG, PA (Comcast Cable)

MADISON TWP. (LACKAWANNA COUNTY)—See CARBONDALE TWP. (Lackawanna County), PA (Adams Cable Service)

MADISON TWP. (LACKAWANNA COUNTY)—See HARRISBURG, PA (Comcast Cable)

MADISON TWP.—See OIL CITY, PA (Comcast Cable)

MADISON—See GREENSBURG, PA (Comcast Cable)

MAHAFFEY—Formerly served by Adelphia Communications. Now served by Comcast Cable, PUNXSUTAWNEY, PA [PA0397]

MAHAFFEY—See PUNXSUTAWNEY, PA (Comcast Cable)

MAHANOY CITY—Service Electric Cable Company. Now served by HAZLETON, PA [PA0050]

MAHANOY CITY—See HAZLETON, PA (Service Electric Cablevision)

MAHANOY TWP.—See HAZLETON, PA (Service Electric Cablevision)

MAHONING COUNTY (PORTIONS)—See ZELIENOPLE, OH (Armstrong Cable Services)

MAHONING TWP. (ARMSTRONG COUNTY)—See BLAIRSVILLE, PA (Comcast Cable)

MAHONING TWP. (CARBON COUNTY)—See LEHIGHTON, PA (Blue Ridge Communications)

MAHONING TWP. (LAWRENCE COUNTY)—See HARRISBURG, PA (Comcast Cable)

MAHONING TWP. (MONTOUR COUNTY)—See DANVILLE, PA (CATV Service Inc)

MAHONING TWP. (MONTOUR COUNTY)—See SUNBURY (village), PA (Service Electric Cablevision)

MAIDENCREEK TWP.—See HARRISBURG, PA (Comcast Cable)

MAIDENCREEK TWP.—See BIRDSBORO, PA (Service Electric Cablevision)

MAIDENCREEK—See BIRDSBORO, PA (Service Electric Cablevision)

MAIN TWP.—See SUNBURY (village), PA (Service Electric Cablevision)

MAINESBURG—See MANSFIELD, PA (Blue Ridge Communications)

MALVERN—Comcast Cable. Now served by PHILADELPHIA, PA [PA0005]

MALVERN—See PHILADELPHIA, PA (Comcast Cable)

MAMMOTH—Citizens Cable Communications. This cable system has converted to IPTV. See MAMMOTH, PA [PA5000]

MAMMOTH—Citizens Telecom. Formerly [PA0400]. This cable system has converted to IPTV

MANCHESTER BOROUGH—See HARRISBURG, PA (Comcast Cable)

MANCHESTER TWP. (YORK COUNTY)—See HARRISBURG, PA (Comcast Cable)

MANHEIM TWP. (YORK COUNTY)—See HARRISBURG, PA (Comcast Cable)

MANHEIM—See EPHRATA, PA (Blue Ridge Communications)

MANHEIM—See HARRISBURG, PA (Comcast Cable)

MANNS CHOICE BOROUGH—See BLAIRSVILLE, PA (Comcast Cable)

MANOR (PORTIONS, WESTMORELAND COUNTY)—See BLAIRSVILLE, PA (Comcast Cable)

MANOR (PORTIONS, WESTMORELAND COUNTY)—See HARRISBURG, PA (Comcast Cable)

MANOR TWP. (ARMSTRONG COUNTY)—See BLAIRSVILLE, PA (Comcast Cable)

MANOR—See GREENSBURG, PA (Comcast Cable)

MANORVILLE—See BLAIRSVILLE, PA (Comcast Cable)

MANSFIELD—Blue Ridge Communications

MAPLETON—See ALTOONA, PA (Atlantic Broadband)

MAPLETOWN—See UNIONTOWN, PA (Atlantic Broadband)

MARCUS HOOK—See PHILADELPHIA, PA (Comcast Cable)

MARGUERITE—See MAMMOTH, PA (Citizens Telecom. Formerly [PA0400]. This cable system has converted to IPTV)

MARIANNA—See UNIONTOWN, PA (Atlantic Broadband)

MARIENVILLE—Formerly served by Armstrong Cable Services. No longer in operation

MARIETTA—See HARRISBURG, PA (Comcast Cable)

MARION CENTER—See BLAIRSVILLE, PA (Comcast Cable)

MARION HEIGHTS—See SUNBURY (village), PA (Service Electric Cablevision)

MARION TWP. (BERKS COUNTY)—See HARRISBURG, PA (Comcast Cable)

MARION TWP. (BUTLER COUNTY)—See ZELIENOPLE, PA (Armstrong Cable Services)

MARION TWP. (CENTRE COUNTY)—See HARRISBURG, PA (Comcast Cable)

MARION TWP. (CENTRE COUNTY)—See ZION, PA (Tele-Media)

MARKLESBURG BOROUGH—See HARRISBURG, PA (Comcast Cable)

MARKLEYSBURG—Comcast Cable. Now served by GREENSBURG, PA [PA0015]

MARKLEYSBURG—See GREENSBURG, PA (Comcast Cable)

MARPLE TWP.—See PHILADELPHIA, PA (Comcast Cable)

MARS—See ZELIENOPLE, PA (Armstrong Cable Services)

MARSHALL TWP.—See ZELIENOPLE, PA (Armstrong Cable Services)

MARSHALLVILLE—See ZELIENOPLE, OH (Armstrong Cable Services)

MARTIC TWP.—See HARRISBURG, PA (Comcast Cable)

MARTINSBURG—See ALTOONA, PA (Atlantic Broadband)

MARY D—See WEATHERLY, PA (MetroCast Communications)

MARYSVILLE—See HARRISBURG, PA (Comcast Cable)

MASONTOWN—See UNIONTOWN, PA (Atlantic Broadband)

MATAMORAS—Cablevision. Now served by WARWICK, NY [NY0045]

MATTAWANA—See McVEYTOWN, PA (Zampelli Electronics)

MAXATAWNY TWP.—See BIRDSBORO, PA (Service Electric Cablevision)

MAYBERRY TWP. (MONTOUR COUNTY)—See DANVILLE, PA (CATV Service Inc)

MAYFIELD—See CARBONDALE TWP. (Lackawanna County), PA (Adams Cable Service)

MAYTOWN—See HARRISBURG, PA (Comcast Cable)

MCADOO BOROUGH—See HAZLETON, PA (Service Electric Cablevision)

MCALEVYS FORT—Atlantic Broadband

MCALISTERVILLE—See MIFFLINTOWN, PA (Nittany Media Inc.)

MCCALMONT TWP.—See PUNXSUTAWNEY, PA (Comcast Cable)

MCCANDLESS—See PITTSBURGH, PA (Comcast Cable)

MCCLURE—Nittany Media Inc.

McCONNELLSBURG BOROUGH—Comcast Cable. Now served by HARRISBURG, PA [PA0009]

MCCONNELLSBURG BOROUGH—See HARRISBURG, PA (Comcast Cable)

MCDONALD (VILLAGE)—See ZELIENOPLE, OH (Armstrong Cable Services)

MCDONALD—See PITTSBURGH, PA (Comcast Cable)

MCEWENSVILLE—See DANVILLE, PA (CATV Service Inc)

MCEWENSVILLE—See SUNBURY (village), PA (Service Electric Cablevision)

MCHENRY—See BLAIRSVILLE, MD (Comcast Cable)

MCKEES ROCKS—See PITTSBURGH, PA (Comcast Cable)

MCKEESPORT—See PITTSBURGH, PA (Comcast Cable)

MCSHERRYSTOWN—See HARRISBURG, PA (Comcast Cable)

MCVEYTOWN—Zampelli Electronics

MEAD TWP. (WARREN COUNTY)—See WARREN, PA (Atlantic Broadband)

MEADVILLE—Armstrong Cable Services. Now served by ZELIENOPLE, PA [PA0053]

MEADVILLE—See ZELIENOPLE, PA (Armstrong Cable Services)

MECHANICSBURG—See HARRISBURG, PA (Comcast Cable)

MECHANICSVILLE (SCHUYLKILL COUNTY)—See HARRISBURG, PA (Comcast Cable)

MEDIA BOROUGH—See PHILADELPHIA, PA (Comcast Cable)

MEDINA TWP.—See ZELIENOPLE, OH (Armstrong Cable Services)

MEDINA—See ZELIENOPLE, OH (Armstrong Cable Services)

MEHOOPANY—See TUNKHANNOCK, PA (Blue Ridge Communications)

MELCROFT—See SALTLICK TWP., PA (Laurel Highland Total Communications)

MENALLEN TWP. (FAYETTE COUNTY)—See UNIONTOWN, PA (Atlantic Broadband)

MENALLEN TWP.—See HARRISBURG, PA (Comcast Cable)

MERCER COUNTY (portions)—Time Warner Cable. Now served by CLEVELAND (formerly Cleveland Heights), OH [OH0006]

MERCER TWP. (PORTIONS)—See ZELIENOPLE, PA (Armstrong Cable Services)

MERCER—See ZELIENOPLE, PA (Armstrong Cable Services)

Pennsylvania—Cable Community Index

MERCERSBURG BOROUGH—See HARRISBURG, PA (Comcast Cable)

MERTZTOWN—See RIDLEY PARK, PA (RCN. Formerly served by PHILADELPHIA (suburbs), PA [PA0447]. This cable system has converted to IPTV)

MESHOPPEN BOROUGH—See TUNKHANNOCK, PA (Blue Ridge Communications)

MESHOPPEN TWP.—See TUNKHANNOCK, PA (Blue Ridge Communications)

MESHOPPEN—See TUNKHANNOCK, PA (Blue Ridge Communications)

METAL TWP.—See HARRISBURG, PA (Comcast Cable)

METAL TWP.—Valley Cable Systems

MEYERSDALE—Comcast Cable. Now served by BLAIRSVILLE, PA [PA0320]

MEYERSDALE—See BLAIRSVILLE, PA (Comcast Cable)

MIDDLE PAXTON—See HARRISBURG, PA (Comcast Cable)

MIDDLE SMITHFIELD TWP.—See STROUDSBURG, PA (Blue Ridge Communications)

MIDDLE SMITHFIELD—See STROUDSBURG, PA (Blue Ridge Communications)

MIDDLE TAYLOR TWP.—See JOHNSTOWN, PA (Atlantic Broadband)

MIDDLEBURG BOROUGH—See SUNBURY (village), PA (Service Electric Cablevision)

MIDDLEBURG—See SUNBURY (village), PA (Service Electric Cablevision)

MIDDLEBURY—See MANSFIELD, PA (Blue Ridge Communications)

MIDDLECREEK TWP. (LEBANON COUNTY)—See HARRISBURG, PA (Comcast Cable)

MIDDLECREEK TWP.—See SUNBURY (village), PA (Service Electric Cablevision)

MIDDLEPORT—See WEATHERLY, PA (MetroCast Communications)

MIDDLESEX TWP. (CUMBERLAND COUNTY)—See HARRISBURG, PA (Comcast Cable)

MIDDLESEX TWP.—See ZELIENOPLE, PA (Armstrong Cable Services)

MIDDLESEX—See HARRISBURG, PA (Comcast Cable)

MIDDLETON TWP.—See HARRISBURG, PA (Comcast Cable)

MIDDLETOWN (DAUPHIN COUNTY)—See HARRISBURG, PA (Comcast Cable)

MIDDLETOWN TWP.—See PHILADELPHIA, PA (Comcast Cable)

MIDLAND—Comcast Cable. Now served by PITTSBURGH, PA [PA0001]

MIDLAND—See PITTSBURGH, PA (Comcast Cable)

MIDWAY BOROUGH—Formerly served by Adelphia Communications. Now served by Comcast Cable, PITTSBURGH, PA [PA0001]

MIDWAY BOROUGH—See PITTSBURGH, PA (Comcast Cable)

MIFFLIN TWP. (ASHLAND COUNTY)—See ZELIENOPLE, OH (Armstrong Cable Services)

MIFFLIN TWP. (DAUPHIN COUNTY)—See HARRISBURG, PA (Comcast Cable)

MIFFLIN TWP. (LYCOMING COUNTY)—See HARRISBURG, PA (Comcast Cable)

MIFFLIN TWP.—See BERWICK, PA (MetroCast Communications)

MIFFLIN—See MIFFLINTOWN, PA (Nittany Media Inc.)

MIFFLINBURG—Atlantic Broadband

MIFFLINBURG—See STATE COLLEGE, PA (Windstream (formerly D&E Communications). New IPTV service no longer available)

MIFFLINTOWN—Nittany Media Inc. Now served by MIFFLINTOWN (formerly Lewistown), PA [PA0365]

MIFFLINTOWN—Nittany Media Inc.

MILESBURG—See HARRISBURG, PA (Comcast Cable)

MILFORD TWP. (PIKE COUNTY)—See MILFORD, PA (Blue Ridge Communications)

MILFORD TWP. (SOMERSET COUNTY)—See BLAIRSVILLE, PA (Comcast Cable)

MILFORD TWP.—See MIFFLINTOWN, PA (Nittany Media Inc.)

MILFORD TWP.—See ALLENTOWN, PA (Service Electric Cable TV & Communications)

MILFORD—Blue Ridge Communications

MILL CREEK BOROUGH—See HARRISBURG, PA (Comcast Cable)

MILL HALL BOROUGH—See HARRISBURG, PA (Comcast Cable)

MILL RUN—See SALTLICK TWP., PA (Laurel Highland Total Communications)

MILL VILLAGE—Formerly served by Cebridge Connections. Now served by Armstrong Cable Services, ZELIENOPLE, PA [PA0053]

MILL VILLAGE—See ZELIENOPLE, PA (Armstrong Cable Services)

MILLBOURNE—See PHILADELPHIA, PA (Comcast Cable)

MILLBOURNE—See RIDLEY PARK, PA (RCN. Formerly served by PHILADELPHIA (suburbs), PA [PA0447]. This cable system has converted to IPTV)

MILLER TWP. (HUNTINGDON COUNTY)—See HARRISBURG, PA (Comcast Cable)

MILLER TWP. (PERRY COUNTY)—See NEWBERRY TWP., PA (Blue Ridge Communications)

MILLERSBURG BOROUGH—Comcast Cable. Now served by HARRISBURG, PA [PA0009]

MILLERSBURG BOROUGH—See HARRISBURG, PA (Comcast Cable)

MILLERSTOWN—See HARRISBURG, PA (Comcast Cable)

MILLERSVILLE—See HARRISBURG, PA (Comcast Cable)

MILLHEIM—Millheim TV Transmission Co.

MILLMONT—Formerly served by D&E Communications. No longer in operation

MILLVALE—See PITTSBURGH, PA (Comcast Cable)

MILLVILLE—See BERWICK, PA (MetroCast Communications)

MILROY—See HARRISBURG, PA (Comcast Cable)

MILTON TWP. (ASHLAND COUNTY)—See ZELIENOPLE, OH (Armstrong Cable Services)

MILTON TWP. (MAHONING COUNTY)—See ZELIENOPLE, OH (Armstrong Cable Services)

MILTON—See DANVILLE, PA (CATV Service Inc)

MILTON—See SUNBURY (village), PA (Service Electric Cablevision)

MILTON—See STATE COLLEGE, PA (Windstream (formerly D&E Communications). New IPTV service no longer available)

MINERAL TWP.—See FRANKLIN (Venango County), PA (Time Warner Cable)

MINERSVILLE—See HARRISBURG, PA (Comcast Cable)

MINGOVILLE—See ZION, PA (TeleMedia)

MINTON TWP. (WAYNE COUNTY)—See ZELIENOPLE, OH (Armstrong Cable Services)

MODENA BOROUGH—See PHILADELPHIA, PA (Comcast Cable)

MOHNTON—See HARRISBURG, PA (Comcast Cable)

MONACA—See PITTSBURGH, PA (Comcast Cable)

MONESSEN—See PITTSBURGH, PA (Comcast Cable)

MONONGAHELA TWP.—See UNIONTOWN, PA (Atlantic Broadband)

MONONGAHELA—See PITTSBURGH, PA (Comcast Cable)

MONONGALIA COUNTY (PORTIONS)—See UNIONTOWN, WV (Atlantic Broadband)

MONROE COUNTY (PORTIONS)—See WEATHERLY, PA (MetroCast Communications)

MONROE TWP. (BRADFORD COUNTY)—See TROY, PA (Blue Ridge Communications)

MONROE TWP. (BRADFORD COUNTY)—See HARRISBURG, PA (Comcast Cable)

MONROE TWP. (CLARION COUNTY)—See SHIPPENVILLE, PA (Atlantic Broadband)

MONROE TWP. (CLARION COUNTY)—See OIL CITY, PA (Comcast Cable)

MONROE TWP. (CUMBERLAND COUNTY)—See HARRISBURG, PA (Comcast Cable)

MONROE TWP. (JUNIATA COUNTY)—See MIFFLINTOWN, PA (Nittany Media Inc.)

MONROE TWP. (SNYDER COUNTY)—See SUNBURY (village), PA (Service Electric Cablevision)

MONROE TWP.—See TUNKHANNOCK, PA (Blue Ridge Communications)

MONROE—See MOUNT PLEASANT MILLS, PA (Zampelli Electronics)

MONROETON—See HARRISBURG, PA (Comcast Cable)

MONROEVILLE—Comcast Cable. Now served by PITTSBURGH, PA [PA0001]

MONROEVILLE—See PITTSBURGH, PA (Comcast Cable)

MONT ALTO BOROUGH—See HARRISBURG, PA (Comcast Cable)

MONTGOMERY TWP. (ASHLAND COUNTY)—See ZELIENOPLE, OH (Armstrong Cable Services)

MONTGOMERY TWP. (FRANKLIN COUNTY)—See HARRISBURG, PA (Comcast Cable)

MONTGOMERY TWP. (INDIANA COUNTY)—See BLAIRSVILLE, PA (Comcast Cable)

MONTGOMERY TWP. (Lycoming County)—Comcast Cable. Now served by HARRISBURG, PA [PA0009]

MONTGOMERY TWP. (LYCOMING COUNTY)—See HARRISBURG, PA (Comcast Cable)

MONTOUR COUNTY—See DANVILLE, PA (CATV Service Inc)

MONTOUR TWP. (COLUMBIA COUNTY)—See SUNBURY (village), PA (Service Electric Cablevision)

MONTOURSVILLE BOROUGH—See HARRISBURG, PA (Comcast Cable)

MONTROSE BOROUGH—Time Warner Cable. Now served by DEWITT, NY [NY0013]

Cable Community Index—Pennsylvania

MONTVILLE TWP.—See ZELIENOPLE, OH (Armstrong Cable Services)

MONUMENT—Formerly served by Monument TV. No longer in operation

MOON—See PITTSBURGH, PA (Comcast Cable)

MOORE TWP.—See RIDLEY PARK, PA (RCN. Formerly served by PHILADELPHIA (suburbs), PA [PA0447]. This cable system has converted to IPTV)

MOORE TWP.—See ALLENTOWN, PA (Service Electric Cable TV & Communications)

MOORESVILLE—See BRAVE, WV (Zito Media)

MOOSIC—See HARRISBURG, PA (Comcast Cable)

MORGAN TWP.—See UNIONTOWN, PA (Atlantic Broadband)

MORRIS TWP.—See HARRISBURG, PA (Comcast Cable)

MORRIS—See PITTSBURGH, PA (Comcast Cable)

MORRISDALE—See SNOW SHOE, PA (Tele-Media)

MORTON (DELAWARE COUNTY)—See PHILADELPHIA, PA (Comcast Cable)

MORTON—See RIDLEY PARK, PA (RCN. Formerly served by PHILADELPHIA (suburbs), PA [PA0447]. This cable system has converted to IPTV)

MOSCOW BOROUGH—See HARRISBURG, PA (Comcast Cable)

MOUNT CARBON—See HARRISBURG, PA (Comcast Cable)

MOUNT CARMEL BOROUGH—See SUNBURY (village), PA (Service Electric Cablevision)

MOUNT CARMEL TWP. (NORTHUMBERLAND COUNTY)—See SUNBURY (village), PA (Service Electric Cablevision)

MOUNT GRETNA—See HARRISBURG, PA (Comcast Cable)

MOUNT HOLLY SPRINGS—See HARRISBURG, PA (Comcast Cable)

MOUNT JEWETT BOROUGH—See PUNXSUTAWNEY, PA (Comcast Cable)

MOUNT JOY BOROUGH—See HARRISBURG, PA (Comcast Cable)

MOUNT JOY TWP. (ADAMS COUNTY)—See HARRISBURG, PA (Comcast Cable)

MOUNT JOY TWP. (LANCASTER COUNTY)—See HARRISBURG, PA (Comcast Cable)

MOUNT LEBANON—See PITTSBURGH, PA (Comcast Cable)

MOUNT MORRIS—Comcast Cable. Now served by PITTSBURGH, PA [PA0001]

MOUNT MORRIS—See PITTSBURGH, PA (Comcast Cable)

MOUNT OLIVER—Formerly served by Mount Oliver TV Cable/Adelphia Cable. Now served by Comcast Cable, PITTSBURGH, PA [PA0001]

MOUNT OLIVER—See PITTSBURGH, PA (Comcast Cable)

MOUNT PENN—See HARRISBURG, PA (Comcast Cable)

MOUNT PLEASANT (ADAMS COUNTY)—See HARRISBURG, PA (Comcast Cable)

MOUNT PLEASANT MILLS—Zampelli Electronics

MOUNT PLEASANT TWP. (COLUMBIA COUNTY)—See SUNBURY (village), PA (Service Electric Cablevision)

MOUNT PLEASANT TWP. (WAYNE COUNTY)—See CARBONDALE TWP. (Lackawanna County), PA (Adams Cable Service)

MOUNT PLEASANT TWP. (WESTMORELAND COUNTY)—See ZELIENOPLE, PA (Armstrong Cable Services)

MOUNT PLEASANT TWP.—See PITTSBURGH, PA (Comcast Cable)

MOUNT PLEASANT—See ZELIENOPLE, PA (Armstrong Cable Services)

MOUNT PLEASANT—See PITTSBURGH, PA (Comcast Cable)

MOUNT POCONO—See STROUDSBURG, PA (Blue Ridge Communications)

MOUNT UNION BOROUGH—See HARRISBURG, PA (Comcast Cable)

MOUNT WOLF—See HARRISBURG, PA (Comcast Cable)

MOUNTAIN TOP—See WILKES-BARRE, PA (Service Electric Cable Company)

MOUNTAINVILLE—See ALLENTOWN, PA (RCN. Formerly served by NORTHAMPTON BOROUGH, PA [PA0008]. This cable system has converted to IPTV)

MOUNTVILLE—See HARRISBURG, PA (Comcast Cable)

MUDDYCREEK TWP.—See ZELIENOPLE, PA (Armstrong Cable Services)

MUHLENBERG (BERKS COUNTY)—See HARRISBURG, PA (Comcast Cable)

MUNCY BOROUGH—See HARRISBURG, PA (Comcast Cable)

MUNCY CREEK TWP.—See HARRISBURG, PA (Comcast Cable)

MUNCY TWP.—See HARRISBURG, PA (Comcast Cable)

MUNCY VALLEY—Blue Ridge Communications

MUNHALL—See PITTSBURGH, PA (Comcast Cable)

MURRYSVILLE (MUNICIPALITY)—See BLAIRSVILLE, PA (Comcast Cable)

MURRYSVILLE—Formerly served by Adelphia Communications. No longer in operation

MUTUAL—See MAMMOTH, PA (Citizens Telecom. Formerly [PA0400]. This cable system has converted to IPTV)

MYERSTOWN—See HARRISBURG, PA (Comcast Cable)

NANTICOKE—See HARRISBURG, PA (Comcast Cable)

NANTY GLO—Formerly served by Adelphia Communications. Now served by Comcast Cable, BLAIRSVILLE, PA [PA0320]

NANTY GLO—See BLAIRSVILLE, PA (Comcast Cable)

NAPIER TWP. (BEDFORD COUNTY)—See BLAIRSVILLE, PA (Comcast Cable)

NARBERTH BOROUGH—See PHILADELPHIA, PA (Comcast Cable)

NARVON—See HARRISBURG, PA (Comcast Cable)

NAZARETH BORO—See ALLENTOWN, PA (Service Electric Cable TV & Communications)

NAZARETH—See ALLENTOWN, PA (RCN. Formerly served by NORTHAMPTON BOROUGH, PA [PA0008]. This cable system has converted to IPTV)

NEELYTON—Formerly served by Valley Cable Systems. No longer in operation

NEMACOLIN—See UNIONTOWN, PA (Atlantic Broadband)

NESCOPECK—See BERWICK, PA (MetroCast Communications)

NESHANNOCK TWP.—See HARRISBURG, PA (Comcast Cable)

NESQUEHONING—See LEHIGHTON, PA (Blue Ridge Communications)

NETHER PROVIDENCE TWP.—See PHILADELPHIA, PA (Comcast Cable)

NEVILLE TWP.—See PITTSBURGH, PA (Comcast Cable)

NEW ALBANY—See TUNKHANNOCK, PA (Blue Ridge Communications)

NEW ALEXANDRIA—See GREENSBURG, PA (Comcast Cable)

NEW BALTIMORE BOROUGH (SOMERSET COUNTY)—See BLAIRSVILLE, PA (Comcast Cable)

NEW BALTIMORE—Comcast Cable. Now served by BLAIRSVILLE, PA [PA0320]

NEW BEAVER BOROUGH—See PITTSBURGH, PA (Comcast Cable)

NEW BEAVER—See ZELIENOPLE, PA (Armstrong Cable Services)

NEW BERLIN—Formerly served by D&E Communications/Windstream. IPTV service no longer in operation

NEW BERLIN—See SUNBURY (village), PA (Service Electric Cablevision)

NEW BETHLEHEM—Formerly served by Adelphia Communications. Now served by Comcast Cable, PUNXSUTAWNEY, PA [PA0397]

NEW BETHLEHEM—See PUNXSUTAWNEY, PA (Comcast Cable)

NEW BLOOMFIELD—Nittany Media Inc. Now served by MIFFLINTOWN, PA [PA0365]

NEW BLOOMFIELD—See MIFFLINTOWN, PA (Nittany Media Inc.)

NEW BRIGHTON BOROUGH—See PITTSBURGH, PA (Comcast Cable)

NEW BRIGHTON—See PITTSBURGH, PA (Comcast Cable)

NEW BUFFALO—See NEWBERRY TWP., PA (Blue Ridge Communications)

NEW CASTLE COUNTY (PORTIONS)—See PHILADELPHIA, DE (Comcast Cable)

NEW CASTLE TWP. (SCHUYLKILL COUNTY)—See HARRISBURG, PA (Comcast Cable)

NEW CASTLE TWP.—See HAZLETON, PA (Service Electric Cablevision)

NEW CASTLE—Comcast Cable. Now served by HARRISBURG, PA [PA0009]

NEW CASTLE—See PHILADELPHIA, DE (Comcast Cable)

NEW CASTLE—See HARRISBURG, PA (Comcast Cable)

NEW COLUMBIA—Formerly served by D&E Communications. No longer in operation

NEW CUMBERLAND—See HARRISBURG, PA (Comcast Cable)

NEW EAGLE—See PITTSBURGH, PA (Comcast Cable)

NEW ENTERPRISE—Atlantic Broadband

NEW FLORENCE BOROUGH—See BLAIRSVILLE, PA (Comcast Cable)

NEW FREEDOM—See HARRISBURG, PA (Comcast Cable)

NEW GALILEE BOROUGH—See PITTSBURGH, PA (Comcast Cable)

NEW GARDEN TWP.—See PHILADELPHIA, PA (Comcast Cable)

NEW GRENADA—See WATERFALL, PA (Waterfall Community TV)

NEW HOLLAND—See HARRISBURG, PA (Comcast Cable)

NEW KENSINGTON—See PITTSBURGH, PA (Comcast Cable)

NEW LONDON TWP.—See PHILADELPHIA, PA (Comcast Cable)

Pennsylvania—Cable Community Index

NEW MILFORD BOROUGH—See THOMPSON TWP., PA (Adams Cable Service)

NEW MILFORD TWP.—Adams Cable Service. Now served by THOMPSON TWP., PA [PA0414]

NEW MILFORD TWP.—See THOMPSON TWP., PA (Adams Cable Service)

NEW OXFORD—See HARRISBURG, PA (Comcast Cable)

NEW PARIS BOROUGH—See BLAIRSVILLE, PA (Comcast Cable)

NEW PHILADELPHIA—See WEATHERLY, PA (MetroCast Communications)

NEW RINGGOLD—See HAZLETON, PA (Service Electric Cablevision)

NEW SEWICKLEY TWP.—See ZELIENOPLE, PA (Armstrong Cable Services)

NEW SEWICKLEY TWP.—See PITTSBURGH, PA (Comcast Cable)

NEW STANTON—See GREENSBURG, PA (Comcast Cable)

NEW STANTON—See SALTLICK TWP., PA (Laurel Highland Total Communications)

NEW TRIPOLI—See ALLENTOWN, PA (RCN. Formerly served by NORTHAMPTON BOROUGH, PA [PA0008]. This cable system has converted to IPTV)

NEW VERNON TWP.—See ZELIENOPLE, PA (Armstrong Cable Services)

NEW WILMINGTON—Armstrong Cable Services. Now served by ZELIENOPLE, PA [PA0053]

NEW WILMINGTON—See ZELIENOPLE, PA (Armstrong Cable Services)

NEWARK—See PHILADELPHIA, DE (Comcast Cable)

NEWBERRY TWP.—Blue Ridge Communications

NEWBERRY TWP.—See HARRISBURG, PA (Comcast Cable)

NEWBURG—Kuhn Communications

NEWELL—See ZELIENOPLE, PA (Armstrong Cable Services)

NEWPORT BOROUGH—Comcast Cable. Now served by HARRISBURG, PA [PA0009]

NEWPORT BOROUGH—See HARRISBURG, PA (Comcast Cable)

NEWPORT TWP.—See BERWICK, PA (MetroCast Communications)

NEWPORT—See PHILADELPHIA, DE (Comcast Cable)

NEWRY—See ALTOONA, PA (Atlantic Broadband)

NEWTON HAMILTON—See HARRISBURG, PA (Comcast Cable)

NEWTON TWP. (LACKAWANNA COUNTY)—See TUNKHANNOCK, PA (Blue Ridge Communications)

NEWTON TWP. (LACKAWANNA COUNTY)—See HARRISBURG, PA (Comcast Cable)

NEWTOWN BOROUGH—Comcast Cable. Now served by EATONTOWN BOROUGH, NJ [NJ0009]

NEWTOWN TWP.—See PHILADELPHIA, PA (Comcast Cable)

NEWVILLE BOROUGH—See HARRISBURG, PA (Comcast Cable)

NICHOLSON BOROUGH—See HARRISBURG, PA (Comcast Cable)

NICHOLSON TWP. (FAYETTE COUNTY)—See UNIONTOWN, PA (Atlantic Broadband)

NICHOLSON TWP.—See HARRISBURG, PA (Comcast Cable)

NINEVAH—See SHIPPENVILLE, PA (Atlantic Broadband)

NIPPENOSE TWP.—See HARRISBURG, PA (Comcast Cable)

NOCKAMIXON TWP.—See ALLENTOWN, PA (Service Electric Cable TV & Communications)

NORMALVILLE—See SALTLICK TWP., PA (Laurel Highland Total Communications)

NORRISTOWN—Comcast Cable. Now served by EATONTOWN BOROUGH, NJ [NJ0009]

NORTH ABINGTON TWP.—See HARRISBURG, PA (Comcast Cable)

NORTH ANNVILLE TWP.—See HARRISBURG, PA (Comcast Cable)

NORTH APOLLO—See BLAIRSVILLE, PA (Comcast Cable)

NORTH BEAVER TWP. (LAWRENCE COUNTY)—See ZELIENOPLE, PA (Armstrong Cable Services)

NORTH BELLE VERNON—See PITTSBURGH, PA (Comcast Cable)

NORTH BEND—See HARRISBURG, PA (Comcast Cable)

NORTH BETHLEHEM TWP. (PORTIONS)—See UNIONTOWN, PA (Atlantic Broadband)

NORTH BETHLEHEM TWP.—Bentleyville Communications

NORTH BRADDOCK BOROUGH—See PITTSBURGH, PA (Comcast Cable)

NORTH BUFFALO—See BLAIRSVILLE, PA (Comcast Cable)

NORTH CATASAUQUA BORO—See ALLENTOWN, PA (Service Electric Cable TV & Communications)

NORTH CATASAUQUA BOROUGH—See ALLENTOWN, PA (RCN. Formerly served by NORTHAMPTON BOROUGH, PA [PA0008]. This cable system has converted to IPTV)

NORTH CENTRE (PORTIONS)—See SUNBURY (village), PA (Service Electric Cablevision)

NORTH CENTRE TWP.—See BERWICK, PA (MetroCast Communications)

NORTH CHARLEROI—See PITTSBURGH, PA (Comcast Cable)

NORTH CLARION—Armstrong Cable Services. Now served by ZELIENOPLE, PA [PA0053]

NORTH CLARION—See ZELIENOPLE, PA (Armstrong Cable Services)

NORTH CODORUS TWP.—See HARRISBURG, PA (Comcast Cable)

NORTH CORNWALL—See HARRISBURG, PA (Comcast Cable)

NORTH FAYETTE TWP.—See PITTSBURGH, PA (Comcast Cable)

NORTH FRANKLIN TWP.—See PITTSBURGH, PA (Comcast Cable)

NORTH HEIDELBERG—See HARRISBURG, PA (Comcast Cable)

NORTH HUNTINGDON TWP. (PORTIONS)—See GREENSBURG, PA (Comcast Cable)

NORTH HUNTINGDON TWP.—See PITTSBURGH, PA (Comcast Cable)

NORTH IRWIN—See GREENSBURG, PA (Comcast Cable)

NORTH LEBANON TWP.—See HARRISBURG, PA (Comcast Cable)

NORTH LONDONDERRY TWP.—See HARRISBURG, PA (Comcast Cable)

NORTH MANHEIM TWP.—See HARRISBURG, PA (Comcast Cable)

NORTH MIDDLETON TWP.—See HARRISBURG, PA (Comcast Cable)

NORTH ORWELL—See ROME, PA (Beaver Valley Cable Co)

NORTH ROME—See ROME, PA (Beaver Valley Cable Co)

NORTH SEWICKLEY TWP.—See ZELIENOPLE, PA (Armstrong Cable Services)

NORTH STABANE—See PITTSBURGH, PA (Comcast Cable)

NORTH TOWANDA—See HARRISBURG, PA (Comcast Cable)

NORTH UNION TWP. (SCHUYLKILL COUNTY)—See BERWICK, PA (MetroCast Communications)

NORTH UNION TWP.—See ZELIENOPLE, PA (Armstrong Cable Services)

NORTH UNION TWP.—See UNIONTOWN, PA (Atlantic Broadband)

NORTH VERSAILLES TWP.—See PITTSBURGH, PA (Comcast Cable)

NORTH WHITEHALL TWP.—See LEHIGHTON, PA (Blue Ridge Communications)

NORTH WHITEHALL TWP.—See ALLENTOWN, PA (RCN. Formerly served by NORTHAMPTON BOROUGH, PA [PA0008]. This cable system has converted to IPTV)

NORTH WHITEHALL TWP.—See ALLENTOWN, PA (Service Electric Cable TV & Communications)

NORTH WOODBURY TWP.—See ALTOONA, PA (Atlantic Broadband)

NORTH YORK—See HARRISBURG, PA (Comcast Cable)

NORTHAMPTON COUNTY (PORTIONS)—See ALLENTOWN, PA (Service Electric Cable TV & Communications)

NORTHAMPTON—RCN Corp. This cable system has converted to IPTV. See ALLENTOWN, PA [PA5201]

NORTHAMPTON—See ALLENTOWN, PA (RCN. Formerly served by NORTHAMPTON BOROUGH, PA [PA0008]. This cable system has converted to IPTV)

NORTHERN CAMBRIA—See BLAIRSVILLE, PA (Comcast Cable)

NORTHMORELAND TWP.—See HARRISBURG, PA (Comcast Cable)

NORTHUMBERLAND—See SUNBURY (village), PA (Service Electric Cablevision)

NORVELT—See MAMMOTH, PA (Citizens Telecom. Formerly [PA0400]. This cable system has converted to IPTV)

NORWEGIAN TWP.—See HARRISBURG, PA (Comcast Cable)

NORWEGIAN TWP.—See HAZLETON, PA (Service Electric Cablevision)

NORWOOD—See PHILADELPHIA, PA (Comcast Cable)

NORWOOD—See RIDLEY PARK, PA (RCN. Formerly served by PHILADELPHIA (suburbs), PA [PA0447]. This cable system has converted to IPTV)

NOTTINGHAM TWP.—See PITTSBURGH, PA (Comcast Cable)

NOTTINGHAM—See PITTSBURGH, PA (Comcast Cable)

NOXEN—See TUNKHANNOCK, PA (Blue Ridge Communications)

NOYES TWP.—See HARRISBURG, PA (Comcast Cable)

NUANGOLA—See BERWICK, PA (MetroCast Communications)

O'HARA TWP.—See PITTSBURGH, PA (Comcast Cable)

OAK RIDGE—See PUNXSUTAWNEY, PA (Comcast Cable)

OAKDALE—See PITTSBURGH, PA (Comcast Cable)

OAKLAND BOROUGH—See THOMPSON TWP., PA (Adams Cable Service)

OAKLAND TWP. (BUTLER COUNTY)—See ZELIENOPLE, PA (Armstrong Cable Services)

Cable Community Index—Pennsylvania

OAKLAND TWP. (VENANGO COUNTY)—See FRANKLIN (Venango County), PA (Time Warner Cable)

OAKLAND TWP.—See THOMPSON TWP., PA (Adams Cable Service)

OAKLAND TWP.—See OIL CITY, PA (Comcast Cable)

OAKMONT BOROUGH—See PITTSBURGH, PA (Comcast Cable)

OGLE TWP.—See BLAIRSVILLE, PA (Comcast Cable)

OHIO TWP.—See PITTSBURGH, PA (Comcast Cable)

OHIOPYLE—See GREENSBURG, PA (Comcast Cable)

OHIOVILLE—See PITTSBURGH, PA (Comcast Cable)

OIL CITY—Comcast Cable

OKLAHOMA BOROUGH—See PITTSBURGH, PA (Comcast Cable)

OLD FORGE—See HARRISBURG, PA (Comcast Cable)

OLD LYCOMING TWP.—See HARRISBURG, PA (Comcast Cable)

OLD PORT—Nittany Media Inc. Now served by MIFFLINTOWN, PA [PA0365]

OLD PORT—See MIFFLINTOWN, PA (Nittany Media Inc.)

OLEY—See BIRDSBORO, PA (Service Electric Cablevision)

OLIVER TWP. (JEFFERSON COUNTY)—See PUNXSUTAWNEY, PA (Comcast Cable)

OLIVER TWP. (PERRY COUNTY)—See HARRISBURG, PA (Comcast Cable)

OLIVER TWP.—See MIFFLINTOWN, PA (Nittany Media Inc.)

OLYPHANT BOROUGH—See HARRISBURG, PA (Comcast Cable)

ONEIDA TWP.—See HARRISBURG, PA (Comcast Cable)

ONTELAUNEE—See HARRISBURG, PA (Comcast Cable)

ORANGE TWP. (ASHLAND COUNTY)—See ZELIENOPLE, OH (Armstrong Cable Services)

ORANGE TWP. (COLUMBIA COUNTY)—See SUNBURY (village), PA (Service Electric Cablevision)

ORANGE TWP.—See BERWICK, PA (MetroCast Communications)

ORANGEVILLE—See BERWICK, PA (MetroCast Communications)

OREFIELD—See ALLENTOWN, PA (RCN. Formerly served by NORTHAMPTON BOROUGH, PA [PA0008]. This cable system has converted to IPTV)

ORRSTOWN—Kuhn Communications

ORRVILLE—See ZELIENOPLE, OH (Armstrong Cable Services)

ORVISTON—Formerly served by Orviston TV. No longer in operation

ORWIGSBURG—See HARRISBURG, PA (Comcast Cable)

OSBORNE—See PITTSBURGH, PA (Comcast Cable)

OSCEOLA MILLS BOROUGH—See HARRISBURG, PA (Comcast Cable)

OSWAYO—Zito Media

OTTO TWP.—See PUNXSUTAWNEY, PA (Comcast Cable)

OVERFIELD TWP.—See TUNKHANNOCK, PA (Blue Ridge Communications)

OXFORD TWP.—See HARRISBURG, PA (Comcast Cable)

PACKER TWP.—See WEATHERLY, PA (MetroCast Communications)

PAINT BOROUGH—See BLAIRSVILLE, PA (Comcast Cable)

PAINT TWP. (CLARION COUNTY)—See SHIPPENVILLE, PA (Atlantic Broadband)

PAINT TWP. (SOMERSET COUNTY)—See JOHNSTOWN, PA (Atlantic Broadband)

PAINT TWP. (SOMERSET COUNTY)—See BLAIRSVILLE, PA (Comcast Cable)

PALMER TWP.—See ALLENTOWN, PA (RCN. Formerly served by NORTHAMPTON BOROUGH, PA [PA0008]. This cable system has converted to IPTV)

PALMER TWP.—See ALLENTOWN, PA (Service Electric Cable TV & Communications)

PALMERTON—See LEHIGHTON, PA (Blue Ridge Communications)

PALMYRA BOROUGH—See HARRISBURG, PA (Comcast Cable)

PALMYRA TWP. (PIKE COUNTY)—See MILFORD, PA (Blue Ridge Communications)

PALMYRA TWP. (WAYNE COUNTY)—See MILFORD, PA (Blue Ridge Communications)

PALO ALTO—See POTTSVILLE, PA (Wire Television Corp)

PARADISE TWP. (LANCASTER COUNTY)—See HARRISBURG, PA (Comcast Cable)

PARADISE TWP. (MONROE COUNTY)—See STROUDSBURG, PA (Blue Ridge Communications)

PARADISE TWP. (YORK COUNTY)—See HARRISBURG, PA (Comcast Cable)

PARKER TWP.—See ZELIENOPLE, PA (Armstrong Cable Services)

PARKER TWP.—See OIL CITY, PA (Comcast Cable)

PARKER—See OIL CITY, PA (Comcast Cable)

PARKESBURG BOROUGH—See PHILADELPHIA, PA (Comcast Cable)

PARKS TWP.—Comcast Cable. Now served by BLAIRSVILLE, PA [PA0320]

PARKS TWP.—See BLAIRSVILLE, PA (Comcast Cable)

PARKSIDE—See PHILADELPHIA, PA (Comcast Cable)

PARRYVILLE—See LEHIGHTON, PA (Blue Ridge Communications)

PATTERSON HEIGHTS BOROUGH—See PITTSBURGH, PA (Comcast Cable)

PATTERSON HEIGHTS—See PITTSBURGH, PA (Comcast Cable)

PATTERSON TWP.—See PITTSBURGH, PA (Comcast Cable)

PATTERSON—See PITTSBURGH, PA (Comcast Cable)

PATTON BOROUGH—See BLAIRSVILLE, PA (Comcast Cable)

PATTON TWP.—See HARRISBURG, PA (Comcast Cable)

PAUPACK TWP. (WAYNE COUNTY)—See CARBONDALE TWP. (Lackawanna County), PA (Adams Cable Service)

PAUPACK TWP. (WAYNE COUNTY)—See MILFORD, PA (Blue Ridge Communications)

PAVIA TWP.—See ALTOONA, PA (Atlantic Broadband)

PAXINOS—See SUNBURY (village), PA (Service Electric Cablevision)

PAXTANG—See HARRISBURG, PA (Comcast Cable)

PAXTONVILLE—See SUNBURY (village), PA (Service Electric Cablevision)

PECKVILLE—See HARRISBURG, PA (Comcast Cable)

PEN ARGYL BORO—See ALLENTOWN, PA (Service Electric Cable TV & Communications)

PEN ARGYL—See ALLENTOWN, PA (RCN. Formerly served by NORTHAMPTON BOROUGH, PA [PA0008]. This cable system has converted to IPTV)

PENBROOK BOROUGH—See HARRISBURG, PA (Comcast Cable)

PENFIELD—See TREASURE LAKE, PA (Zito Media)

PENN BOROUGH—See GREENSBURG, PA (Comcast Cable)

PENN FOREST TWP.—See LEHIGHTON, PA (Blue Ridge Communications)

PENN HILLS—Comcast Cable. Now served by PITTSBURGH, PA [PA0001]

PENN HILLS—See PITTSBURGH, PA (Comcast Cable)

PENN LAKE PARK (BOROUGH)—See WEATHERLY, PA (MetroCast Communications)

PENN TWP. (BERKS COUNTY)—See HARRISBURG, PA (Comcast Cable)

PENN TWP. (BUTLER COUNTY)—See ZELIENOPLE, PA (Armstrong Cable Services)

PENN TWP. (CHESTER COUNTY)—See PHILADELPHIA, PA (Comcast Cable)

PENN TWP. (CUMBERLAND COUNTY)—See HARRISBURG, PA (Comcast Cable)

PENN TWP. (HUNTINGDON COUNTY)—See HARRISBURG, PA (Comcast Cable)

PENN TWP. (LANCASTER COUNTY)—See EPHRATA, PA (Blue Ridge Communications)

PENN TWP. (LYCOMING COUNTY)—See HARRISBURG, PA (Comcast Cable)

PENN TWP. (PERRY COUNTY)—See NEWBERRY TWP., PA (Blue Ridge Communications)

PENN TWP. (SNYDER COUNTY)—See SUNBURY (village), PA (Service Electric Cablevision)

PENN TWP. (WESTMORELAND COUNTY)—See BLAIRSVILLE, PA (Comcast Cable)

PENN TWP. (WESTMORELAND COUNTY)—See GREENSBURG, PA (Comcast Cable)

PENN TWP. (YORK COUNTY)—See HARRISBURG, PA (Comcast Cable)

PENN TWP.—See CLEARFIELD, PA (Atlantic Broadband)

PENNS CREEK—See SUNBURY (village), PA (Service Electric Cablevision)

PENNSBORO—See ZELIENOPLE, WV (Armstrong Cable Services)

PENNSBURY TWP.—See PHILADELPHIA, PA (Comcast Cable)

PENNSBURY VILLAGE—See PITTSBURGH, PA (Comcast Cable)

PENTRESS—See BRAVE, WV (Zito Media)

PEQUEA (LANCASTER COUNTY)—See HARRISBURG, PA (Comcast Cable)

PERRY (BERKS COUNTY)—See HARRISBURG, PA (Comcast Cable)

PERRY COUNTY (PORTIONS)—See LANDISBURG, PA (Kuhn Communications)

PERRY TWP. (CLARION COUNTY)—See OIL CITY, PA (Comcast Cable)

PERRY TWP. (FAYETTE COUNTY)—See UNIONTOWN, PA (Atlantic Broadband)

PERRY TWP. (JEFFERSON COUNTY)—See PUNXSUTAWNEY, PA (Comcast Cable)

PERRY TWP. (LAWRENCE COUNTY)—See ZELIENOPLE, OH (Armstrong Cable Services)

Pennsylvania—Cable Community Index

PERRY TWP. (LAWRENCE COUNTY)—See ZELIENOPLE, PA (Armstrong Cable Services)

PERRY TWP. (LAWRENCE COUNTY)—See PITTSBURGH, PA (Comcast Cable)

PERRY TWP. (MERCER COUNTY)—See ZELIENOPLE, PA (Armstrong Cable Services)

PERRYOPOLIS—See UNIONTOWN, PA (Atlantic Broadband)

PERRYVILLE—See COGAN STATION, PA (Zito Media)

PETERS TWP. (FRANKLIN COUNTY)—See HARRISBURG, PA (Comcast Cable)

PETERS TWP.—See PITTSBURGH, PA (Comcast Cable)

PETERSBURG BOROUGH—See HARRISBURG, PA (Comcast Cable)

PETROLIA—See ZELIENOPLE, PA (Armstrong Cable Services)

PHILADELPHIA (Area 1)—Comcast Cable. Now served by PHILADELPHIA, PA [PA0005]

PHILADELPHIA (Area 2)—Comcast Cable. Now served by PHILADELPHIA, PA [PA0005]

PHILADELPHIA (suburbs)—RCN Corp. This cable system has converted to IPTV. See ALLENTOWN, PA [PA5201]

PHILADELPHIA (SUBURBS)—See ALLENTOWN, PA (RCN. Formerly served by NORTHAMPTON BOROUGH, PA [PA0008]. This cable system has converted to IPTV)

PHILADELPHIA—Comcast Cable

PHILIPSBURG BOROUGH—Comcast Cable. Now served by HARRISBURG, PA [PA0009]

PHILIPSBURG BOROUGH—See HARRISBURG, PA (Comcast Cable)

PIATT TWP.—See HARRISBURG, PA (Comcast Cable)

PICTURE ROCKS BOROUGH—See HARRISBURG, PA (Comcast Cable)

PIKE TWP. (CLEARFIELD COUNTY)—See CLEARFIELD, PA (Atlantic Broadband)

PIKE TWP. (POTTER COUNTY)—See MANSFIELD, PA (Blue Ridge Communications)

PIKE TWP.—See BIRDSBORO, PA (Service Electric Cablevision)

PILLOW—See HARRISBURG, PA (Comcast Cable)

PINE CREEK TWP. (JEFFERSON COUNTY)—See PUNXSUTAWNEY, PA (Comcast Cable)

PINE CREEK TWP.—See HARRISBURG, PA (Comcast Cable)

PINE GROVE BOROUGH—See HARRISBURG, PA (Comcast Cable)

PINE GROVE TWP. (SCHUYLKILL COUNTY)—See HARRISBURG, PA (Comcast Cable)

PINE GROVE TWP. (WARREN COUNTY)—See WARREN, PA (Atlantic Broadband)

PINE TWP. (ALLEGHENY COUNTY)—See ZELIENOPLE, PA (Armstrong Cable Services)

PINE TWP. (ARMSTRONG COUNTY)—See BLAIRSVILLE, PA (Comcast Cable)

PINE TWP. (BUTLER COUNTY)—See ZELIENOPLE, PA (Armstrong Cable Services)

PINE TWP. (INDIANA COUNTY)—See BLAIRSVILLE, PA (Comcast Cable)

PINE TWP. (MERCER COUNTY)—See ZELIENOPLE, PA (Armstrong Cable Services)

PINECREEK—See HAZEN, PA (Zito Media)

PINEY TWP.—See OIL CITY, PA (Comcast Cable)

PINEY—See SHIPPENVILLE, PA (Atlantic Broadband)

PINOAK—Formerly served by Armstrong Cable Services. No longer in operation

PITCAIRN—Pitcairn Community Cable System

PITTSBURGH—Comcast Cable

PITTSFIELD—See YOUNGSVILLE, PA (Youngsville TV Corp)

PITTSTON BOROUGH—See HARRISBURG, PA (Comcast Cable)

PITTSTON—See HARRISBURG, PA (Comcast Cable)

PLAIN GROVE TWP.—See ZELIENOPLE, PA (Armstrong Cable Services)

PLAIN GROVE TWP.—See HARRISBURG, PA (Comcast Cable)

PLAINFIELD TWP.—See ALLENTOWN, PA (RCN. Formerly served by NORTHAMPTON BOROUGH, PA [PA0008]. This cable system has converted to IPTV)

PLAINFIELD TWP.—See ALLENTOWN, PA (Service Electric Cable TV & Communications)

PLAINS—See HARRISBURG, PA (Comcast Cable)

PLEASANT HILLS BOROUGH—See PITTSBURGH, PA (Comcast Cable)

PLEASANT TWP. (WARREN COUNTY)—See WARREN, PA (Atlantic Broadband)

PLEASANT TWP.—See ZELIENOPLE, PA (Armstrong Cable Services)

PLEASANT UNITY—See MAMMOTH, PA (Citizens Telecom. Formerly [PA0400]. This cable system has converted to IPTV)

PLEASANTVILLE—See ZELIENOPLE, PA (Armstrong Cable Services)

PLUM BOROUGH—See BLAIRSVILLE, PA (Comcast Cable)

PLUM—Comcast Cable. Now served by BLAIRSVILLE, PA [PA0320]

PLUMCREEK TWP.—See BLAIRSVILLE, PA (Comcast Cable)

PLUMER—Formerly served by Cebridge Connections. No longer in operation

PLUMVILLE BOROUGH—See BLAIRSVILLE, PA (Comcast Cable)

PLUNKETTS CREEK TWP.—See ELDRED TWP., PA (Herr Cable Co)

PLYMOUTH TWP. (LUZERNE COUNTY)—See BERWICK, PA (MetroCast Communications)

PLYMOUTH—See HARRISBURG, PA (Comcast Cable)

POCONO LAKE—See STROUDSBURG, PA (Blue Ridge Communications)

POCONO TWP.—See STROUDSBURG, PA (Blue Ridge Communications)

POCOPSON TWP.—See PHILADELPHIA, PA (Comcast Cable)

POINT MARION—See UNIONTOWN, PA (Atlantic Broadband)

POINT TWP. (NORTHUMBERLAND COUNTY)—See SUNBURY (village), PA (Service Electric Cablevision)

POLAND TWP.—See ZELIENOPLE, OH (Armstrong Cable Services)

POLAND—See ZELIENOPLE, OH (Armstrong Cable Services)

POLK BOROUGH—See FRANKLIN (Venango County), PA (Time Warner Cable)

POLK TWP. (JEFFERSON COUNTY)—See HAZEN, PA (Zito Media)

POLK TWP. (MONROE COUNTY)—See STROUDSBURG, PA (Blue Ridge Communications)

PORT ALLEGANY—See COUDERSPORT, PA (Zito Media)

PORT CARBON—See POTTSVILLE, PA (Wire Television Corp)

PORT CLINTON—See HARRISBURG, PA (Comcast Cable)

PORT MATILDA—See HARRISBURG, PA (Comcast Cable)

PORT ROYAL—Nittany Media Inc. Now served by MIFFLINTOWN, PA [PA0365]

PORT ROYAL—See MIFFLINTOWN, PA (Nittany Media Inc.)

PORT TREVORTON—See MOUNT PLEASANT MILLS, PA (Zampelli Electronics)

PORT VUE—See PITTSBURGH, PA (Comcast Cable)

PORTAGE BOROUGH—See BLAIRSVILLE, PA (Comcast Cable)

PORTAGE TWP. (CAMBRIA COUNTY)—See BLAIRSVILLE, PA (Comcast Cable)

PORTAGE TWP. (POTTER TWP.)—See COUDERSPORT, PA (Zito Media)

PORTAGE—Formerly served by Adelphia Communications. Now served by Comcast Cable, BLAIRSVILLE, PA [PA0320]

PORTER TWP. (CLARION COUNTY)—See SHIPPENVILLE, PA (Atlantic Broadband)

PORTER TWP. (CLINTON COUNTY)—See HARRISBURG, PA (Comcast Cable)

PORTER TWP. (HUNTINGDON COUNTY)—See HARRISBURG, PA (Comcast Cable)

PORTER TWP. (LYCOMING COUNTY)—See HARRISBURG, PA (Comcast Cable)

PORTER TWP. (PIKE COUNTY)—See MILFORD, PA (Blue Ridge Communications)

PORTER TWP. (SCHUYLKILL COUNTY)—See HARRISBURG, PA (Comcast Cable)

PORTER—See PUNXSUTAWNEY, PA (Comcast Cable)

PORTERSVILLE—See ZELIENOPLE, PA (Armstrong Cable Services)

PORTLAND BORO—See ALLENTOWN, PA (Service Electric Cable TV & Communications)

POTTER TWP. (BEAVER COUNTY)—See PITTSBURGH, PA (Comcast Cable)

POTTER TWP. (CENTRE COUNTY)—See HARRISBURG, PA (Comcast Cable)

POTTERVILLE—See ROME, PA (Beaver Valley Cable Co)

POTTSTOWN—Comcast Cable. Now served by EATONTOWN BOROUGH, NJ [NJ0009]

POTTSVILLE—Comcast Cable. Now served by HARRISBURG, PA [PA0009]

POTTSVILLE—See HARRISBURG, PA (Comcast Cable)

POTTSVILLE—Wire Television Corp

POWELL TWP.—See TROY, PA (Blue Ridge Communications)

POWELL—See TROY, PA (Blue Ridge Communications)

PRESTO—See PITTSBURGH, PA (Comcast Cable)

PRESTON COUNTY (PORTIONS)—See GREENSBURG, WV (Comcast Cable)

PRESTON TWP.—See THOMPSON TWP., PA (Adams Cable Service)

PRICE TWP. (MONROE COUNTY)—See STROUDSBURG, PA (Blue Ridge Communications)

PRIMOS—See RIDLEY PARK, PA (RCN. Formerly served by PHILADELPHIA (suburbs), PA [PA0447]. This cable

Cable Community Index—Pennsylvania

system has converted to IPTV)

PRIMROSE—See CASS TWP. (Schuylkill County), PA (J. B. Cable)

PRINGLE—See WILKES-BARRE, PA (Service Electric Cable Company)

PROCTORVILLE—See ZELIENOPLE, OH (Armstrong Cable Services)

PROMPTON—See CARBONDALE TWP. (Lackawanna County), PA (Adams Cable Service)

PROSPECT PARK—See PHILADELPHIA, PA (Comcast Cable)

PROSPECT PARK—See RIDLEY PARK, PA (RCN. Formerly served by PHILADELPHIA (suburbs), PA [PA0447]. This cable system has converted to IPTV)

PROSPECT—See ZELIENOPLE, PA (Armstrong Cable Services)

PROVIDENCE TWP.—See HARRISBURG, PA (Comcast Cable)

PULASKI TWP. (LAWRENCE COUNTY)—See HARRISBURG, PA (Comcast Cable)

PULASKI TWP.—See PITTSBURGH, PA (Comcast Cable)

PULASKI—Comcast Cable. Now served by PITTSBURGH, PA [PA0001]

PULASKI—See PITTSBURGH, PA (Comcast Cable)

PUNXSUTAWNEY—Comcast Cable

PUTNAM TWP.—See MANSFIELD, PA (Blue Ridge Communications)

QUARRYVILLE—See HARRISBURG, PA (Comcast Cable)

QUEMAHONING TWP. (SOMERSET COUNTY)—See JOHNSTOWN, PA (Atlantic Broadband)

QUEMAHONING TWP. (SOMERSET COUNTY)—See BLAIRSVILLE, PA (Comcast Cable)

QUIGGLEVILLE—See COGAN STATION, PA (Zito Media)

QUINCY TWP.—See HARRISBURG, PA (Comcast Cable)

RACCOON TWP.—See PITTSBURGH, PA (Comcast Cable)

RADNOR—See PHILADELPHIA, PA (Comcast Cable)

RAILROAD—See HARRISBURG, PA (Comcast Cable)

RAINSBURG BOROUGH—See BLAIRSVILLE, PA (Comcast Cable)

RALPHO TWP.—See SUNBURY (village), PA (Service Electric Cablevision)

RALSTON—Zito Media

RAMEY BOROUGH—See HARRISBURG, PA (Comcast Cable)

RANKIN BOROUGH—See PITTSBURGH, PA (Comcast Cable)

RANSOM TWP.—See HARRISBURG, PA (Comcast Cable)

RAPHO TWP. (LANCASTER COUNTY)—See EPHRATA, PA (Blue Ridge Communications)

RAPHO TWP. (LANCASTER COUNTY)—See HARRISBURG, PA (Comcast Cable)

RAYBURN TWP.—See BLAIRSVILLE, PA (Comcast Cable)

RAYNE TWP.—Formerly served by Satterlee Leasing Inc. No longer in operation

RAYNE TWP.—See BLAIRSVILLE, PA (Comcast Cable)

READE TWP. (CAMBRIA COUNTY)—See BLAIRSVILLE, PA (Comcast Cable)

READING TWP.—See HARRISBURG, PA (Comcast Cable)

READING—Comcast Cable. Now served by HARRISBURG, PA [PA0009]

READING—Formerly served by Digital Wireless Systems. No longer in operation

READING—See HARRISBURG, PA (Comcast Cable)

RECTOR—See SALTLICK TWP., PA (Laurel Highland Total Communications)

RED LION BOROUGH—See HARRISBURG, PA (Comcast Cable)

REDBANK TWP. (CLARION COUNTY)—See SHIPPENVILLE, PA (Atlantic Broadband)

REDBANK TWP. (CLARION COUNTY)—See PUNXSUTAWNEY, PA (Comcast Cable)

REDSTONE TWP. (FAYETTE COUNTY)—See UNIONTOWN, PA (Atlantic Broadband)

REED TWP. (PERRY COUNTY)—See NEWBERRY TWP., PA (Blue Ridge Communications)

REED TWP.—See HARRISBURG, PA (Comcast Cable)

REEDSVILLE—Comcast Cable. Now served by HARRISBURG, PA [PA0009]

REEDSVILLE—See HARRISBURG, PA (Comcast Cable)

REILLY TWP.—See CASS TWP. (Schuylkill County), PA (J. B. Cable)

RENO—Time Warner Cable. Now served by FRANKLIN (Venango County), PA [PA0100]

RENO—See FRANKLIN (Venango County), PA (Time Warner Cable)

RENOVO BOROUGH—See HARRISBURG, PA (Comcast Cable)

RESERVE TWP. (ALLEGHENY COUNTY)—See PITTSBURGH, PA (Comcast Cable)

RETREAT CORRECTIONAL INSTITUTION—Formerly served by Suddenlink Communications. No longer in operation

REYNOLDS—See LEHIGHTON, PA (Blue Ridge Communications)

REYNOLDSVILLE—See PUNXSUTAWNEY, PA (Comcast Cable)

RICE TWP.—See BERWICK, PA (MetroCast Communications)

RICE TWP.—See WILKES-BARRE, PA (Service Electric Cable Company)

RICES LANDING—See UNIONTOWN, PA (Atlantic Broadband)

RICHFIELD—Formerly served by Zampelli Electronics. No longer in operation

RICHFIELD—See MIFFLINTOWN, PA (Nittany Media Inc.)

RICHLAND (LEBANON COUNTY)—See HARRISBURG, PA (Comcast Cable)

RICHLAND TWP. (ALLEGHENY COUNTY)—See ZELIENOPLE, PA (Armstrong Cable Services)

RICHLAND TWP. (ALLEGHENY COUNTY)—See PITTSBURGH, PA (Comcast Cable)

RICHLAND TWP. (CAMBRIA COUNTY)—See JOHNSTOWN, PA (Atlantic Broadband)

RICHLAND TWP. (CLARION COUNTY)—See OIL CITY, PA (Comcast Cable)

RICHLAND TWP. (VENANGO COUNTY)—See OIL CITY, PA (Comcast Cable)

RICHLAND TWP.—See ALLENTOWN, PA (Service Electric Cable TV & Communications)

RICHMOND TWP. (CRAWFORD COUNTY)—See EDINBORO, PA (Coaxial Cable TV Corp)

RICHMOND TWP.—See MANSFIELD, PA (Blue Ridge Communications)

RICHMOND TWP.—See BIRDSBORO, PA (Service Electric Cablevision)

RICHMONDALE VILLAGE—See CARBONDALE TWP. (Lackawanna County), PA (Adams Cable Service)

RIDGEBURY TWP.—See SOUTH CREEK TWP., PA (Blue Ridge Communications)

RIDGEBURY TWP.—See TROY, PA (Blue Ridge Communications)

RIDGEWAY TWP.—See ST. MARY'S, PA (Zito Media)

RIDGWAY BOROUGH—Formerly served by Adelphia Communications. Now served by Comcast Cable, PUNXSUTAWNEY, PA [PA0397]

RIDGWAY BOROUGH—See PUNXSUTAWNEY, PA (Comcast Cable)

RIDGWAY TWP.—See PUNXSUTAWNEY, PA (Comcast Cable)

RIDLEY PARK (DELAWARE COUNTY)—See PHILADELPHIA, PA (Comcast Cable)

RIDLEY PARK—RCN. Formerly served by PHILADELPHIA (suburbs), PA [PA0447]. This cable system has converted to IPTV

RIDLEY TWP.—See PHILADELPHIA, PA (Comcast Cable)

RIDLEY TWP.—See RIDLEY PARK, PA (RCN. Formerly served by PHILADELPHIA (suburbs), PA [PA0447]. This cable system has converted to IPTV)

RIEGELSVILLE BORO—See ALLENTOWN, PA (Service Electric Cable TV & Communications)

RIEGLESVILLE—See ALLENTOWN, PA (RCN. Formerly served by NORTHAMPTON BOROUGH, PA [PA0008]. This cable system has converted to IPTV)

RIMERSBURG—See OIL CITY, PA (Comcast Cable)

RINGGOLD TWP.—See PUNXSUTAWNEY, PA (Comcast Cable)

RINGTOWN—See HAZLETON, PA (Service Electric Cablevision)

RIVERSIDE (NORTHUMBERLAND COUNTY)—See DANVILLE, PA (CATV Service Inc)

RIVERSIDE—See SUNBURY (village), PA (Service Electric Cablevision)

RIXFORD—See PUNXSUTAWNEY, PA (Comcast Cable)

ROARING BRANCH—See RALSTON, PA (Zito Media)

ROARING BROOK TWP.—See HARRISBURG, PA (Comcast Cable)

ROARING CREEK TWP.—See SUNBURY (village), PA (Service Electric Cablevision)

ROARING SPRING—See ALTOONA, PA (Atlantic Broadband)

ROBESON TWP.—See BIRDSBORO, PA (Service Electric Cablevision)

ROBESONIA—See HARRISBURG, PA (Comcast Cable)

ROBINSON TWP. (Allegheny County)—Formerly served by Comcast Cable. No longer in operation

ROBINSON TWP. (WASHINGTON COUNTY)—See PITTSBURGH, PA (Comcast Cable)

ROBINSON—See PITTSBURGH, PA (Comcast Cable)

ROCHESTER TWP.—Comcast Cable. Now served by PITTSBURGH, PA [PA0001]

ROCHESTER TWP.—See PITTSBURGH, PA (Comcast Cable)

ROCHESTER—See PITTSBURGH, PA (Comcast Cable)

ROCKDALE TWP. (CRAWFORD COUNTY)—See EDINBORO, PA (Coaxial Cable TV Corp)

Pennsylvania—Cable Community Index

ROCKEFELLER TWP.—See SUNBURY (village), PA (Service Electric Cablevision)

ROCKLAND TWP. (VENANGO COUNTY)—See ZELIENOPLE, PA (Armstrong Cable Services)

ROCKLAND TWP.—See BIRDSBORO, PA (Service Electric Cablevision)

ROCKMERE—Formerly served by Cebridge Connections. Now served by Armstrong Cable Services, ZELIENOPLE, PA [PA0053]

ROCKMERE—See ZELIENOPLE, PA (Armstrong Cable Services)

ROCKWOOD—Formerly served by Adelphia Communications. Now served by Comcast Cable, BLAIRSVILLE, PA [PA0320]

ROCKWOOD—See BLAIRSVILLE, PA (Comcast Cable)

ROME BOROUGH—See ROME, PA (Beaver Valley Cable Co)

ROME TWP. (LAWRENCE COUNTY)—See ZELIENOPLE, OH (Armstrong Cable Services)

ROME—Beaver Valley Cable Co

ROSCOE—See ZELIENOPLE, PA (Armstrong Cable Services)

ROSE TWP.—Formerly served by Adelphia Communications. Now served by Comcast Cable, PUNXSUTAWNEY, PA [PA0397]

ROSE TWP.—See PUNXSUTAWNEY, PA (Comcast Cable)

ROSE VALLEY—See PHILADELPHIA, PA (Comcast Cable)

ROSETO BORO—See ALLENTOWN, PA (Service Electric Cable TV & Communications)

ROSETO—See ALLENTOWN, PA (RCN. Formerly served by NORTHAMPTON BOROUGH, PA [PA0008]. This cable system has converted to IPTV)

ROSEVILLE—See JACKSON TWP. (Tioga County), PA (Blue Ridge Communications)

ROSEVILLE—See EAST SMITHFIELD, PA (North Penn Video)

ROSS TWP. (Allegheny County)—Comcast Cable. Now served by PITTSBURGH, PA [PA0001]

ROSS TWP. (ALLEGHENY COUNTY)—See PITTSBURGH, PA (Comcast Cable)

ROSS TWP. (MONROE COUNTY)—See STROUDSBURG, PA (Blue Ridge Communications)

ROSSITER—See PUNXSUTAWNEY, PA (Comcast Cable)

ROSSLYN FARMS—See PITTSBURGH, PA (Comcast Cable)

ROSTRAVER (WESTMORELAND COUNTY)—See UNIONTOWN, PA (Atlantic Broadband)

ROSTRAVER TWP.—See PITTSBURGH, PA (Comcast Cable)

ROSTRAVER—See PITTSBURGH, PA (Comcast Cable)

ROULETTE TWP.—See COUDERSPORT, PA (Zito Media)

ROUSEVILLE BOROUGH—See OIL CITY, PA (Comcast Cable)

ROUZERVILLE—See HARRISBURG, PA (Comcast Cable)

ROYALTON BOROUGH—See HARRISBURG, PA (Comcast Cable)

RUFFSDALE—See SALTLICK TWP., PA (Laurel Highland Total Communications)

RURAL VALLEY BOROUGH—See BLAIRSVILLE, PA (Comcast Cable)

RURAL VALLEY—Comcast Cable. Now served by BLAIRSVILLE, PA [PA0320]

RUSCOMBMANOR TWP.—See HARRISBURG, PA (Comcast Cable)

RUSCOMBMANOR TWP.—See BIRDSBORO, PA (Service Electric Cablevision)

RUSH TWP. (CENTRE COUNTY)—See HARRISBURG, PA (Comcast Cable)

RUSH TWP. (SCHUYLKILL COUNTY)—See HARRISBURG, PA (Comcast Cable)

RUSH TWP. (SCHUYLKILL COUNTY)—See HAZLETON, PA (Service Electric Cablevision)

RUSH TWP.—See LEHIGHTON, PA (Blue Ridge Communications)

RUTLAND TWP.—See JACKSON TWP. (Tioga County), PA (Blue Ridge Communications)

RUTLAND TWP.—See EAST SMITHFIELD, PA (North Penn Video)

RUTLEDGE—See PHILADELPHIA, PA (Comcast Cable)

RUTLEDGE—See RIDLEY PARK, PA (RCN. Formerly served by PHILADELPHIA (suburbs), PA [PA0447]. This cable system has converted to IPTV)

RYAN TWP.—See HAZLETON, PA (Service Electric Cablevision)

RYE TWP.—See NEWBERRY TWP., PA (Blue Ridge Communications)

RYE TWP.—See HARRISBURG, PA (Comcast Cable)

SABULA—Zito Media

SADSBURY TWP. (CHESTER COUNTY)—See PHILADELPHIA, PA (Comcast Cable)

SADSBURY TWP. (LANCASTER COUNTY)—See HARRISBURG, PA (Comcast Cable)

SAEGERTOWN—See ZELIENOPLE, PA (Armstrong Cable Services)

SALEM TWP. (CLARION COUNTY)—See SHIPPENVILLE, PA (Atlantic Broadband)

SALEM TWP. (LUZERNE COUNTY)—See BERWICK, PA (MetroCast Communications)

SALEM TWP. (WAYNE COUNTY)—See CARBONDALE TWP. (Lackawanna County), PA (Adams Cable Service)

SALEM TWP. (WESTMORELAND COUNTY)—See BLAIRSVILLE, PA (Comcast Cable)

SALEM TWP. (WESTMORELAND COUNTY)—See GREENSBURG, PA (Comcast Cable)

SALISBURY TWP. (LANCASTER COUNTY)—See HARRISBURG, PA (Comcast Cable)

SALISBURY TWP.—See ALLENTOWN, PA (RCN. Formerly served by NORTHAMPTON BOROUGH, PA [PA0008]. This cable system has converted to IPTV)

SALISBURY TWP.—See ALLENTOWN, PA (Service Electric Cable TV & Communications)

SALLADASBURG BOROUGH—See HARRISBURG, PA (Comcast Cable)

SALTILLO—See ALTOONA, PA (Atlantic Broadband)

SALTILLO—Saltillo TV Cable Corp

SALTLICK TWP.—Laurel Highland Total Communications

SALTSBURG—See PITTSBURGH, PA (Comcast Cable)

SANDY CREEK TWP. (MERCER COUNTY)—See ZELIENOPLE, PA (Armstrong Cable Services)

SANDY CREEK TWP. (VENANGO COUNTY)—See FRANKLIN (Venango County), PA (Time Warner Cable)

SANDY LAKE TWP.—See ZELIENOPLE, PA (Armstrong Cable Services)

SANDY LAKE—Formerly served by Cebridge Connections. Now served by Armstrong Cable Services, ZELIENOPLE, PA [PA0053]

SANDY LAKE—See ZELIENOPLE, PA (Armstrong Cable Services)

SANDY TWP. (Clearfield County)—Formerly served by Satterlee Leasing Inc. No longer in operation

SANDY TWP.—See BROCKWAY, PA (Brockway TV Inc)

SANDY TWP.—See PUNXSUTAWNEY, PA (Comcast Cable)

SANDY—See TREASURE LAKE, PA (Zito Media)

SANKERTOWN BOROUGH—See BLAIRSVILLE, PA (Comcast Cable)

SAUCON VALLEY—See ALLENTOWN, PA (RCN. Formerly served by NORTHAMPTON BOROUGH, PA [PA0008]. This cable system has converted to IPTV)

SAVILLE TWP.—See MIFFLINTOWN, PA (Nittany Media Inc.)

SAXONBURG—See ZELIENOPLE, PA (Armstrong Cable Services)

SAXTON BOROUGH—See HARRISBURG, PA (Comcast Cable)

SAYBROOK—See SHEFFIELD, PA (WestPA.net Inc)

SAYRE BOROUGH—Time Warner Cable. Now served by DEWITT, NY [NY0013]

SCALP LEVEL BOROUGH—See BLAIRSVILLE, PA (Comcast Cable)

SCHELLSBURG BOROUGH—See BLAIRSVILLE, PA (Comcast Cable)

SCHNECKSVILLE—See ALLENTOWN, PA (RCN. Formerly served by NORTHAMPTON BOROUGH, PA [PA0008]. This cable system has converted to IPTV)

SCHUYLKILL COUNTY (PORTIONS)—See WEATHERLY, PA (MetroCast Communications)

SCHUYLKILL COUNTY (PORTIONS)—See HAZLETON, PA (Service Electric Cablevision)

SCHUYLKILL HAVEN—See HARRISBURG, PA (Comcast Cable)

SCHUYLKILL TWP.—Formerly served by MetroCast Communications. No longer in operation

SCOTT TWP. (ALLEGHENY TWP.)—See PITTSBURGH, PA (Comcast Cable)

SCOTT TWP. (COLUMBIA COUNTY)—See SUNBURY (village), PA (Service Electric Cablevision)

SCOTT TWP. (LACKAWANNA COUNTY)—See HARRISBURG, PA (Comcast Cable)

SCOTT TWP. (LAWRENCE COUNTY)—See HARRISBURG, PA (Comcast Cable)

SCOTT TWP. (WAYNE COUNTY)—See CARBONDALE TWP. (Lackawanna County), PA (Adams Cable Service)

SCOTTDALE—See ZELIENOPLE, PA (Armstrong Cable Services)

SCRANTON—Comcast Cable. Now served by HARRISBURG, PA [PA0009]

SCRANTON—See HARRISBURG, PA (Comcast Cable)

SECANE—See RIDLEY PARK, PA (RCN. Formerly served by PHILADELPHIA (suburbs), PA [PA0447]. This cable system has converted to IPTV)

SELINSGROVE—See SUNBURY (village), PA (Service Electric Cablevision)

SELLERSVILLE—Comcast Cable. Now served by EATONTOWN BOROUGH, NJ [NJ0009]

Cable Community Index—Pennsylvania

SELTZER—See HARRISBURG, PA (Comcast Cable)

SEVEN FIELDS—See ZELIENOPLE, PA (Armstrong Cable Services)

SEVEN VALLEYS—See HARRISBURG, PA (Comcast Cable)

SEWARD BOROUGH—See BLAIRSVILLE, PA (Comcast Cable)

SEWICKLEY (PORTIONS)—See GREENSBURG, PA (Comcast Cable)

SEWICKLEY (PORTIONS)—See PITTSBURGH, PA (Comcast Cable)

SEWICKLEY HEIGHTS BOROUGH—See PITTSBURGH, PA (Comcast Cable)

SEWICKLEY HILLS—See PITTSBURGH, PA (Comcast Cable)

SHADE GAP—Shade Gap TV Assn

SHADE TWP. (SOMERSET COUNTY)—See BLAIRSVILLE, PA (Comcast Cable)

SHADY GROVE—See HARRISBURG, PA (Comcast Cable)

SHALER TWP.—See PITTSBURGH, PA (Comcast Cable)

SHALER—See PITTSBURGH, PA (Comcast Cable)

SHAMOKIN DAM—See SUNBURY (village), PA (Service Electric Cablevision)

SHAMOKIN TWP.—See SUNBURY (village), PA (Service Electric Cablevision)

SHAMOKIN—See SUNBURY (village), PA (Service Electric Cablevision)

SHANKSVILLE BOROUGH—See BLAIRSVILLE, PA (Comcast Cable)

SHARON HILL—See PHILADELPHIA, PA (Comcast Cable)

SHARON HILL—See RIDLEY PARK, PA (RCN. Formerly served by PHILADELPHIA (suburbs), PA [PA0447]. This cable system has converted to IPTV)

SHARON—Time Warner Cable. Now served by CLEVELAND (formerly Cleveland Heights), OH [OH0006]

SHARPSBURG—See PITTSBURGH, PA (Comcast Cable)

SHARTLESVILLE—See HARRISBURG, PA (Comcast Cable)

SHEAKLEYVILLE TWP.—See ZELIENOPLE, PA (Armstrong Cable Services)

SHEAKLEYVILLE—See ZELIENOPLE, PA (Armstrong Cable Services)

SHEFFIELD—WestPA.net Inc. Now served by SHEFFIELD, PA [PA0473]

SHEFFIELD—WestPA.net Inc

SHELOCTA BOROUGH—See BLAIRSVILLE, PA (Comcast Cable)

SHENANDOAH—Service Electric Cablevision. Now served by HAZLETON, PA [PA0050]

SHENANDOAH—See HAZLETON, PA (Service Electric Cablevision)

SHENANGO TWP. (LAWRENCE COUNTY)—See HARRISBURG, PA (Comcast Cable)

SHERMANS DALE—See HARRISBURG, PA (Comcast Cable)

SHESHEQUIN TWP.—See ROME, PA (Beaver Valley Cable Co)

SHICKSHINNY—See BERWICK, PA (MetroCast Communications)

SHILLINGTON—See HARRISBURG, PA (Comcast Cable)

SHIPPEN TWP. (CAMERON COUNTY)—See COUDERSPORT, PA (Zito Media)

SHIPPEN TWP. (TIOGA COUNTY)—See MANSFIELD, PA (Blue Ridge Communications)

SHIPPEN—See COUDERSPORT, PA (Zito Media)

SHIPPENSBURG TWP.—See HARRISBURG, PA (Comcast Cable)

SHIPPENSBURG—Comcast Cable. Now served by HARRISBURG, PA [PA0009]

SHIPPENSBURG—See HARRISBURG, PA (Comcast Cable)

SHIPPENVILLE—Atlantic Broadband. Now served by SHIPPENVILLE, PA [PA0387]

SHIPPENVILLE—Atlantic Broadband

SHIPPINGPORT BOROUGH—Comcast Cable. Now served by PITTSBURGH, PA [PA0001]

SHIPPINGPORT BOROUGH—See PITTSBURGH, PA (Comcast Cable)

SHIREMANSTOWN—See HARRISBURG, PA (Comcast Cable)

SHIRLEY TWP.—Formerly served by Adelphia Communications. Now served by Comcast Cable, HARRISBURG, PA [PA0009]

SHIRLEY TWP.—See HARRISBURG, PA (Comcast Cable)

SHIRLEYSBURG BOROUGH—See HARRISBURG, PA (Comcast Cable)

SHOEMAKERSVILLE—See HARRISBURG, PA (Comcast Cable)

SHOHOLA TWP.—See MILFORD, PA (Blue Ridge Communications)

SHREWSBURY TWP. (LYCOMING COUNTY)—See HARRISBURG, PA (Comcast Cable)

SHREWSBURY TWP. (SULLIVAN COUNTY)—See HARRISBURG, PA (Comcast Cable)

SHREWSBURY—See HARRISBURG, PA (Comcast Cable)

SILVER SPRING TWP.—See HARRISBURG, PA (Comcast Cable)

SINKING SPRING—See HARRISBURG, PA (Comcast Cable)

SIX MILE RUN—Six Mile Run TV Assn.

SLATINGTON—See LEHIGHTON, PA (Blue Ridge Communications)

SLATINGTON—See ALLENTOWN, PA (RCN. Formerly served by NORTHAMPTON BOROUGH, PA [PA0008]. This cable system has converted to IPTV)

SLIGO—See OIL CITY, PA (Comcast Cable)

SLIPPERY ROCK (BUTLER COUNTY)—See ZELIENOPLE, PA (Armstrong Cable Services)

SLIPPERY ROCK TWP. (BUTLER COUNTY)—See ZELIENOPLE, PA (Armstrong Cable Services)

SLIPPERY ROCK TWP. (LAWRENCE COUNTY)—See ZELIENOPLE, PA (Armstrong Cable Services)

SLOCUM TWP.—See BERWICK, PA (MetroCast Communications)

SMETHPORT—Comcast Cable. Now served by PUNXSUTAWNEY, PA [PA0397]

SMETHPORT—See PUNXSUTAWNEY, PA (Comcast Cable)

SMITH TWP. (MAHONING COUNTY)—See ZELIENOPLE, OH (Armstrong Cable Services)

SMITH TWP. (WASHINGTON COUNTY)—See PITTSBURGH, PA (Comcast Cable)

SMITH TWP.—See BURGETTSTOWN, PA (Blue Devil Cable TV Inc)

SMITHFIELD TWP. (HUNTINGDON COUNTY)—See HARRISBURG, PA (Comcast Cable)

SMITHFIELD TWP. (MONROE COUNTY)—See STROUDSBURG, PA (Blue Ridge Communications)

SMITHFIELD—See UNIONTOWN, PA (Atlantic Broadband)

SMITHTON—See UNIONTOWN, PA (Atlantic Broadband)

SMOCK (PORTIONS)—See UNIONTOWN, PA (Atlantic Broadband)

SNAKE SPRING VALLEY TWP.—See BLAIRSVILLE, PA (Comcast Cable)

SNOW SHOE—Tele-Media

SNYDER TWP. (BLAIR COUNTY)—See HARRISBURG, PA (Comcast Cable)

SNYDER TWP. (JEFFERSON COUNTY)—See BROCKWAY, PA (Brockway TV Inc)

SNYDER TWP. (JEFFERSON COUNTY)—See PUNXSUTAWNEY, PA (Comcast Cable)

SNYDER TWP.—See HAZEN, PA (Zito Media)

SNYDER—See ALTOONA, PA (Atlantic Broadband)

SNYDERTOWN (NORTHUMBERLAND COUNTY)—See SUNBURY (village), PA (Service Electric Cablevision)

SOMERSET BOROUGH—See BLAIRSVILLE, PA (Comcast Cable)

SOMERSET COUNTY (PORTIONS)—See ZELIENOPLE, PA (Armstrong Cable Services)

SOMERSET TWP. (SOMERSET COUNTY)—See ZELIENOPLE, PA (Armstrong Cable Services)

SOMERSET TWP. (SOMERSET COUNTY)—See BLAIRSVILLE, PA (Comcast Cable)

SOMERSET TWP. (WASHINGTON COUNTY)—See UNIONTOWN, PA (Atlantic Broadband)

SOMERSET TWP. (WASHINGTON COUNTY)—See NORTH BETHLEHEM TWP., PA (Bentleyville Communications)

SOMERSET TWP.—Formerly served by Adelphia Communications. Now served by Comcast Cable, BLAIRSVILLE, PA [PA0320]

SOMERSET—Formerly served by Cebridge Connections. Now served by Armstrong Cable Services, ZELIENOPLE, PA [PA0053]

SOMERSET—See ZELIENOPLE, PA (Armstrong Cable Services)

SOMERSET—See PITTSBURGH, PA (Comcast Cable)

SOUTH ABINGTON TWP.—See HARRISBURG, PA (Comcast Cable)

SOUTH ANNVILLE TWP.—See HARRISBURG, PA (Comcast Cable)

SOUTH BEAVER TWP.—See PITTSBURGH, PA (Comcast Cable)

SOUTH BEND TWP.—See BLAIRSVILLE, PA (Comcast Cable)

SOUTH BETHLEHEM—See PUNXSUTAWNEY, PA (Comcast Cable)

SOUTH BUFFALO TWP.—Formerly served by South Buffalo Cablevision. Now served by Comcast Cable, BLAIRSVILLE, PA [PA0320]

SOUTH BUFFALO TWP.—See BLAIRSVILLE, PA (Comcast Cable)

SOUTH CANAAN TWP.—See CARBONDALE TWP. (Lackawanna County), PA (Adams Cable Service)

SOUTH CENTRE TWP. (COLUMBIA COUNTY)—See SUNBURY (village), PA (Service Electric Cablevision)

SOUTH CENTRE TWP.—See BERWICK, PA (MetroCast Communications)

SOUTH COATESVILLE BOROUGH—See PHILADELPHIA, PA (Comcast Cable)

SOUTH CREEK TWP.—Blue Ridge Communications

SOUTH CREEK TWP.—See TROY, PA (Blue Ridge Communications)

Pennsylvania—Cable Community Index

SOUTH CREEK TWP.—See EAST SMITHFIELD, PA (North Penn Video)

SOUTH FAYETTE TWP.—See PITTSBURGH, PA (Comcast Cable)

SOUTH FORK BOROUGH—See BLAIRSVILLE, PA (Comcast Cable)

SOUTH FORK—Formerly served by Adelphia Communications. Now served by Comcast Cable, BLAIRSVILLE, PA [PA0320]

SOUTH FRANKLIN TWP.—See PITTSBURGH, PA (Comcast Cable)

SOUTH GREENSBURG—See GREENSBURG, PA (Comcast Cable)

SOUTH HANOVER TWP.—See HARRISBURG, PA (Comcast Cable)

SOUTH HEIDELBERG TWP. (BERKS COUNTY)—See EPHRATA, PA (Blue Ridge Communications)

SOUTH HEIDELBERG TWP.—See HARRISBURG, PA (Comcast Cable)

SOUTH HEIGHTS—See PITTSBURGH, PA (Comcast Cable)

SOUTH HUNTINGDON TWP.—See ZELIENOPLE, PA (Armstrong Cable Services)

SOUTH HUNTINGDON TWP.—See UNIONTOWN, PA (Atlantic Broadband)

SOUTH HUNTINGDON TWP.—See GREENSBURG, PA (Comcast Cable)

SOUTH LEBANON—See HARRISBURG, PA (Comcast Cable)

SOUTH LONDONDERRY TWP.—See HARRISBURG, PA (Comcast Cable)

SOUTH MAHONING TWP.—See BLAIRSVILLE, PA (Comcast Cable)

SOUTH MANHEIM TWP.—See HARRISBURG, PA (Comcast Cable)

SOUTH MIDDLETON TWP.—See HARRISBURG, PA (Comcast Cable)

SOUTH MOUNTAIN—See ALLENTOWN, PA (RCN. Formerly served by NORTHAMPTON BOROUGH, PA [PA0008]. This cable system has converted to IPTV)

SOUTH NEW CASTLE BOROUGH—See HARRISBURG, PA (Comcast Cable)

SOUTH PARK—See PITTSBURGH, PA (Comcast Cable)

SOUTH PHILIPSBURG BOROUGH—See HARRISBURG, PA (Comcast Cable)

SOUTH POINT—See ZELIENOPLE, OH (Armstrong Cable Services)

SOUTH RENOVO—See HARRISBURG, PA (Comcast Cable)

SOUTH SHENANGO TWP.—See ZELIENOPLE, PA (Armstrong Cable Services)

SOUTH STRABANE TWP.—See NORTH BETHLEHEM TWP., PA (Bentleyville Communications)

SOUTH STRABANE TWP.—See PITTSBURGH, PA (Comcast Cable)

SOUTH UNION TWP.—See UNIONTOWN, PA (Atlantic Broadband)

SOUTH VERSAILLES TWP. (PORTIONS)—See GREENSBURG, PA (Comcast Cable)

SOUTH VERSAILLES—See GREENSBURG, PA (Comcast Cable)

SOUTH WHITEHALL TWP.—See ALLENTOWN, PA (RCN. Formerly served by NORTHAMPTON BOROUGH, PA [PA0008]. This cable system has converted to IPTV)

SOUTH WHITEHALL TWP.—See ALLENTOWN, PA (Service Electric Cable TV & Communications)

SOUTH WILLIAMSPORT—See HARRISBURG, PA (Comcast Cable)

SOUTH WOODBURY TWP.—See NEW ENTERPRISE, PA (Atlantic Broadband)

SOUTHAMPTON TWP. (FRANKLIN COUNTY)—See HARRISBURG, PA (Comcast Cable)

SOUTHAMPTON TWP.—See HARRISBURG, PA (Comcast Cable)

SOUTHMONT—See JOHNSTOWN, PA (Atlantic Broadband)

SOUTHWEST GREENSBURG—See GREENSBURG, PA (Comcast Cable)

SOUTHWEST TWP.—See ZELIENOPLE, PA (Armstrong Cable Services)

SPARTA TWP. (CRAWFORD COUNTY)—See SPARTANSBURG, PA (Zito Media)

SPARTANSBURG—Zito Media

SPEERS—See PITTSBURGH, PA (Comcast Cable)

SPRAGGS (GREENE COUNTY)—See BRAVE, PA (Zito Media)

SPRING GARDEN TWP.—See HARRISBURG, PA (Comcast Cable)

SPRING GROVE—See HARRISBURG, PA (Comcast Cable)

SPRING MILLS—Formerly served by Spring Mills TV Co. Now served by Millheim TV Transmission Co., MILLHEIM, PA [PA0216]

SPRING MILLS—See MILLHEIM, PA (Millheim TV Transmission Co.)

SPRING TWP. (BERKS COUNTY)—See EPHRATA, PA (Blue Ridge Communications)

SPRING TWP. (BERKS COUNTY)—See HARRISBURG, PA (Comcast Cable)

SPRING TWP. (CENTRE COUNTY)—See HARRISBURG, PA (Comcast Cable)

SPRING TWP. (CENTRE COUNTY)—See ZION, PA (Tele-Media)

SPRING TWP. (Crawford County)—Formerly served by Adelphia Communications. Now served by Time Warner Cable, CLEVELAND, OH [OH0006]

SPRING TWP. (PERRY COUNTY)—See HARRISBURG, PA (Comcast Cable)

SPRING TWP. (SNYDER COUNTY)—See SUNBURY (village), PA (Service Electric Cablevision)

SPRINGBROOK TWP. (LACKAWANNA COUNTY)—See HARRISBURG, PA (Comcast Cable)

SPRINGDALE BOROUGH—See PITTSBURGH, PA (Comcast Cable)

SPRINGDALE TWP.—See PITTSBURGH, PA (Comcast Cable)

SPRINGETTSBURY TWP.—See HARRISBURG, PA (Comcast Cable)

SPRINGFIELD TWP. (BRADFORD COUNTY)—See TROY, PA (Blue Ridge Communications)

SPRINGFIELD TWP. (MAHONING COUNTY)—See ZELIENOPLE, OH (Armstrong Cable Services)

SPRINGFIELD TWP. (MERCER COUNTY)—See ZELIENOPLE, PA (Armstrong Cable Services)

SPRINGFIELD TWP.—See HARRISBURG, PA (Comcast Cable)

SPRINGFIELD TWP.—See ALLENTOWN, PA (Service Electric Cable TV & Communications)

SPRINGFIELD—See PHILADELPHIA, PA (Comcast Cable)

SPRINGFIELD—See RIDLEY PARK, PA (RCN. Formerly served by PHILADELPHIA (suburbs), PA [PA0447]. This cable system has converted to IPTV)

SPRINGHILL TWP. (FAYETTE COUNTY)—See UNIONTOWN, PA (Atlantic Broadband)

SPRINGHILL TWP. (GREENE COUNTY)—See UNIONTOWN, PA (Atlantic Broadband)

SPRUCE CREEK TWP.—Atlantic Broadband. Now served by ALTOONA, PA [PA0018]

SPRUCE CREEK TWP.—See ALTOONA, PA (Atlantic Broadband)

ST. CLAIR (SCHUYLKILL COUNTY)—See HAZLETON, PA (Service Electric Cablevision)

ST. CLAIR TWP.—See BLAIRSVILLE, PA (Comcast Cable)

ST. CLAIRSVILLE—See NEW ENTERPRISE, PA (Atlantic Broadband)

ST. LAWRENCE—See BIRDSBORO, PA (Service Electric Cablevision)

ST. MARY'S—Zito Media

ST. PETERSBURG BOROUGH—See OIL CITY, PA (Comcast Cable)

ST. THOMAS TWP.—See HARRISBURG, PA (Comcast Cable)

STAHLSTOWN—See SALTLICK TWP., PA (Laurel Highland Total Communications)

STARRUCCA BOROUGH—See THOMPSON TWP., PA (Adams Cable Service)

STATE COLLEGE—Comcast Cable. Now served by HARRISBURG, PA [PA0009]

STATE COLLEGE—Windstream (formerly D&E Communications.) This cable system has converted to IPTV. Now served by STATE COLLEGE, PA [PA5280]

STATE COLLEGE—See HARRISBURG, PA (Comcast Cable)

STATE COLLEGE—Windstream (formerly D&E Communications). New IPTV service no longer available

STATE LINE—See HARRISBURG, PA (Comcast Cable)

STEELTON—See HARRISBURG, PA (Comcast Cable)

STERLING—See CARBONDALE TWP. (Lackawanna County), PA (Adams Cable Service)

STILLWATER—See BERWICK, PA (MetroCast Communications)

STOCKDALE—See ZELIENOPLE, PA (Armstrong Cable Services)

STOCKERTOWN—See ALLENTOWN, PA (RCN. Formerly served by NORTHAMPTON BOROUGH, PA [PA0008]. This cable system has converted to IPTV)

STOCKERTOWN—See ALLENTOWN, PA (Service Electric Cable TV & Communications)

STONEBORO—See ZELIENOPLE, PA (Armstrong Cable Services)

STONEHAM—See CLARENDON, PA (Clarendon TV Association)

STONYCREEK TWP. (CAMBRIA COUNTY)—See JOHNSTOWN, PA (Atlantic Broadband)

STONYCREEK TWP. (SOMERSET COUNTY)—See BLAIRSVILLE, PA (Comcast Cable)

STOWE TWP. (ALLEGHENY COUNTY)—See PITTSBURGH, PA (Comcast Cable)

STOYSTOWN BOROUGH—See BLAIRSVILLE, PA (Comcast Cable)

STRABAN TWP.—See HARRISBURG, PA (Comcast Cable)

STRASBURG BOROUGH—See HARRISBURG, PA (Comcast Cable)

STRASBURG TWP.—See HARRISBURG, PA (Comcast Cable)

STRATTANVILLE BOROUGH—See OIL CITY, PA (Comcast Cable)

STRAUSSTOWN—See HARRISBURG, PA (Comcast Cable)

STRONG—See SUNBURY (village), PA (Service Electric Cablevision)

STROUD TWP. (MONROE COUNTY)—See STROUDSBURG, PA (Blue Ridge Communications)

Cable Community Index—Pennsylvania

STROUDSBURG—Blue Ridge Communications

SUGAR CREEK TWP. (WAYNE COUNTY)—See ZELIENOPLE, OH (Armstrong Cable Services)

SUGAR GROVE—Formerly served by Atlantic Broadband. Now served by WARREN, PA [PA0090]

SUGAR GROVE—See WARREN, PA (Atlantic Broadband)

SUGAR NOTCH—See WILKES-BARRE, PA (Service Electric Cable Company)

SUGARCREEK (VENANGO COUNTY)—See ZELIENOPLE, PA (Armstrong Cable Services)

SUGARCREEK (VENANGO COUNTY)—See FRANKLIN (Venango County), PA (Time Warner Cable)

SUGARCREEK BOROUGH—See OIL CITY, PA (Comcast Cable)

SUGARCREEK TWP. (ARMSTRONG COUNTY)—See ZELIENOPLE, PA (Armstrong Cable Services)

SUGARCREEK TWP.—See BLAIRSVILLE, PA (Comcast Cable)

SUGARLOAF TWP.—MetroCast Communications. Now served by BERWICK, PA [PA0094]

SUGARLOAF TWP.—See BERWICK, PA (MetroCast Communications)

SUGARLOAF TWP.—See HAZLETON, PA (Service Electric Cablevision)

SUGARLOAF—See BERWICK, PA (MetroCast Communications)

SULLIVAN TWP.—See ZELIENOPLE, OH (Armstrong Cable Services)

SULLIVAN TWP.—See MANSFIELD, PA (Blue Ridge Communications)

SULLIVAN TWP.—See EAST SMITHFIELD, PA (North Penn Video)

SUMMERHILL BOROUGH—See BLAIRSVILLE, PA (Comcast Cable)

SUMMERHILL TWP.—See BLAIRSVILLE, PA (Comcast Cable)

SUMMERVILLE BOROUGH—See PUNXSUTAWNEY, PA (Comcast Cable)

SUMMERVILLE—Formerly served by Adelphia Communications. Now served by Comcast Cable, PUNXSUTAWNEY, PA [PA0397]

SUMMIT HILL—See LEHIGHTON, PA (Blue Ridge Communications)

SUMMIT TWP. (BUTLER COUNTY)—See ZELIENOPLE, PA (Armstrong Cable Services)

SUNBURY (VILLAGE)—Service Electric Cablevision

SUSQUEHANNA DEPOT BOROUGH—See THOMPSON TWP., PA (Adams Cable Service)

SUSQUEHANNA TWP. (CAMBRIA COUNTY)—See BLAIRSVILLE, PA (Comcast Cable)

SUSQUEHANNA TWP. (DAUPHIN COUNTY)—See HARRISBURG, PA (Comcast Cable)

SUSQUEHANNA TWP. (JUNIATA COUNTY)—See HARRISBURG, PA (Comcast Cable)

SUSQUEHANNA TWP. (LYCOMING COUNTY)—See HARRISBURG, PA (Comcast Cable)

SUTERSVILLE—See PITTSBURGH, PA (Comcast Cable)

SWARTHMORE—See PHILADELPHIA, PA (Comcast Cable)

SWARTHMORE—See RIDLEY PARK, PA (RCN. Formerly served by PHILADELPHIA (suburbs), PA [PA0447]. This cable system has converted to IPTV)

SWATARA TWP. (DAUPHIN COUNTY)—See HARRISBURG, PA (Comcast Cable)

SWATARA TWP. (LEBANON COUNTY)—See HARRISBURG, PA (Comcast Cable)

SWATARA—See HARRISBURG, PA (Comcast Cable)

SWEDEN VALLEY—See COUDERSPORT, PA (Zito Media)

SWEET VALLEY—See TUNKHANNOCK, PA (Blue Ridge Communications)

SWENGEL—Formerly served by D&E Communications. No longer in operation

SWENGEL—See MIFFLINBURG, PA (Atlantic Broadband)

SWISSVALE BOROUGH—See PITTSBURGH, PA (Comcast Cable)

SWOYERSVILLE—See HARRISBURG, PA (Comcast Cable)

SYKESVILLE—See PUNXSUTAWNEY, PA (Comcast Cable)

SYLVANIA BOROUGH—See TROY, PA (Blue Ridge Communications)

SYLVANIA—See TROY, PA (Blue Ridge Communications)

TAMAQUA—See WEATHERLY, PA (MetroCast Communications)

TAMAQUA—See HAZLETON, PA (Service Electric Cablevision)

TARENTUM BOROUGH—Comcast Cable. Now served by PITTSBURGH, PA [PA0001]

TARENTUM BOROUGH—See PITTSBURGH, PA (Comcast Cable)

TATAMY BORO—See ALLENTOWN, PA (Service Electric Cable TV & Communications)

TATAMY—See ALLENTOWN, PA (RCN. Formerly served by NORTHAMPTON BOROUGH, PA [PA0008]. This cable system has converted to IPTV)

TAYLOR TWP. (BLAIR COUNTY)—See ALTOONA, PA (Atlantic Broadband)

TAYLOR TWP. (CENTRE COUNTY)—See HARRISBURG, PA (Comcast Cable)

TAYLOR TWP. (LAWRENCE COUNTY)—See ZELIENOPLE, PA (Armstrong Cable Services)

TAYLOR—See HARRISBURG, PA (Comcast Cable)

TELL TWP.—See DOYLESBURG, PA (Valley Cable Systems)

TEMPLE—See HARRISBURG, PA (Comcast Cable)

TERRE HILL—See EPHRATA, PA (Blue Ridge Communications)

TERRY TWP.—See TUNKHANNOCK, PA (Blue Ridge Communications)

TEXAS TWP. (WAYNE COUNTY)—See MILFORD, PA (Blue Ridge Communications)

TEXAS TWP.—See CARBONDALE TWP. (Lackawanna County), PA (Adams Cable Service)

THOMPSON BOROUGH—See THOMPSON TWP., PA (Adams Cable Service)

THOMPSON TWP.—Adams Cable Service

THOMPSONTOWN—Nittany Media Inc. Now served by MIFFLINTOWN, PA [PA0365]

THOMPSONTOWN—See MIFFLINTOWN, PA (Nittany Media Inc.)

THORNBURG—See PITTSBURGH, PA (Comcast Cable)

THORNBURY TWP. (CHESTER COUNTY)—See PHILADELPHIA, PA (Comcast Cable)

THORNBURY TWP. (DELAWARE COUNTY)—See PHILADELPHIA, PA (Comcast Cable)

THREE SPRINGS—Atlantic Broadband. Now served by ALTOONA, PA [PA0018]

THREE SPRINGS—See ALTOONA, PA (Atlantic Broadband)

THROOP—See HARRISBURG, PA (Comcast Cable)

TIDIOUTE—Formerly served by Cebridge Connections. No longer in operation

TIDIOUTE—See ZELIENOPLE, PA (Armstrong Cable Services)

TILDEN TWP.—See HARRISBURG, PA (Comcast Cable)

TIMBLIN—Formerly served by Adelphia Communications. Now served by Comcast Cable, PUNXSUTAWNEY, PA [PA0397]

TIMBLIN—See PUNXSUTAWNEY, PA (Comcast Cable)

TINICUM TWP.—See PHILADELPHIA, PA (Comcast Cable)

TINICUM TWP.—See ALLENTOWN, PA (Service Electric Cable TV & Communications)

TINICUM—See RIDLEY PARK, PA (RCN. Formerly served by PHILADELPHIA (suburbs), PA [PA0447]. This cable system has converted to IPTV)

TIONA—See SHEFFIELD, PA (WestPA.net Inc)

TIONESTA TWP.—See ZELIENOPLE, PA (Armstrong Cable Services)

TIONESTA—See ZELIENOPLE, PA (Armstrong Cable Services)

TITUSVILLE—Armstrong Cable Services. Now served by ZELIENOPLE, PA [PA0053]

TITUSVILLE—Formerly served by Cebridge Connections. Now served by Armstrong Cable Services, ZELIENOPLE, PA [PA0053]

TITUSVILLE—See ZELIENOPLE, PA (Armstrong Cable Services)

TOBY TWP.—Formerly served by Adelphia Communications. Now served by Comcast Cable, OIL CITY, PA [PA0086]

TOBY TWP.—See OIL CITY, PA (Comcast Cable)

TOBYHANNA TWP. (MONROE COUNTY)—See STROUDSBURG, PA (Blue Ridge Communications)

TOBYHANNA TWP.—See WEATHERLY, PA (MetroCast Communications)

TODD TWP. (FULTON COUNTY)—See HARRISBURG, PA (Comcast Cable)

TODD TWP. (HUNTINGDON COUNTY)—See ALTOONA, PA (Atlantic Broadband)

TODD TWP. (HUNTINGDON COUNTY)—See HARRISBURG, PA (Comcast Cable)

TOPTON—See BIRDSBORO, PA (Service Electric Cablevision)

TOWAMENSING TWP.—See LEHIGHTON, PA (Blue Ridge Communications)

TOWANDA BOROUGH—Comcast Cable. Now served by HARRISBURG, PA [PA0009]

TOWANDA BOROUGH—See HARRISBURG, PA (Comcast Cable)

TOWANDA TWP.—See HARRISBURG, PA (Comcast Cable)

TOWER CITY—See HARRISBURG, PA (Comcast Cable)

TOWNVILLE—Formerly served by Cebridge Connections. Now served by Armstrong Cable Services, ZELIENOPLE, PA [PA0053]

TOWNVILLE—See ZELIENOPLE, PA (Armstrong Cable Services)

TOWNVILLE—See EDINBORO, PA (Coaxial Cable TV Corp)

TRAFFORD BOROUGH—See PITTSBURGH, PA (Comcast Cable)

Pennsylvania—Cable Community Index

TRAINER—See PHILADELPHIA, PA (Comcast Cable)

TRAPPE—Comcast Cable. Now served by EATONTOWN BOROUGH, NJ [NJ0009]

TREASURE LAKE—Zito Media

TREDYFFRIN TWP.—See PHILADELPHIA, PA (Comcast Cable)

TREESDALE—See ZELIENOPLE, PA (Armstrong Cable Services)

TREICHLERS—See ALLENTOWN, PA (RCN. Formerly served by NORTHAMPTON BOROUGH, PA [PA0008]. This cable system has converted to IPTV)

TREMONT TWP.—See HARRISBURG, PA (Comcast Cable)

TREMONT—Wire Television Corp

TREXLERTOWN—See ALLENTOWN, PA (RCN. Formerly served by NORTHAMPTON BOROUGH, PA [PA0008]. This cable system has converted to IPTV)

TRIUMPH TWP.—See ZELIENOPLE, PA (Armstrong Cable Services)

TROUT RUN—See COGAN STATION, PA (Zito Media)

TROUTVILLE BOROUGH—See PUNXSUTAWNEY, PA (Comcast Cable)

TROY TWP. (ASHLAND COUNTY)—See ZELIENOPLE, OH (Armstrong Cable Services)

TROY TWP.—See TROY, PA (Blue Ridge Communications)

TROY TWP.—See EAST SMITHFIELD, PA (North Penn Video)

TROY—Blue Ridge Communications

TULPEHOCKEN TWP.—See HARRISBURG, PA (Comcast Cable)

TUNKHANNOCK TWP. (WYOMING COUNTY)—See TUNKHANNOCK, PA (Blue Ridge Communications)

TUNKHANNOCK TWP.—See WEATHERLY, PA (MetroCast Communications)

TUNKHANNOCK—Blue Ridge Communications

TUNNELHILL BOROUGH—See BLAIRSVILLE, PA (Comcast Cable)

TURBETT TWP.—See MIFFLINTOWN, PA (Nittany Media Inc.)

TURBOT TWP. (NORTHUMBERLAND COUNTY)—See HARRISBURG, PA (Comcast Cable)

TURBOT TWP.—See DANVILLE, PA (CATV Service Inc)

TURBOT TWP.—See SUNBURY (village), PA (Service Electric Cablevision)

TURBOTVILLE—See DANVILLE, PA (CATV Service Inc)

TURBOTVILLE—See SUNBURY (village), PA (Service Electric Cablevision)

TURTLE CREEK BOROUGH—See PITTSBURGH, PA (Comcast Cable)

TUSCARORA TWP. (BRADFORD COUNTY)—See TUNKHANNOCK, PA (Blue Ridge Communications)

TUSCARORA TWP. (PERRY COUNTY)—See HARRISBURG, PA (Comcast Cable)

TUSCARORA—See WEATHERLY, PA (MetroCast Communications)

TWILIGHT—See PITTSBURGH, PA (Comcast Cable)

TYLERSVILLE—Tylersville Community TV Cable Assoc

TYRONE BOROUGH—See HARRISBURG, PA (Comcast Cable)

TYRONE TWP. (BLAIR COUNTY)—See ALTOONA, PA (Atlantic Broadband)

TYRONE TWP.—See HARRISBURG, PA (Comcast Cable)

TYRONE—Formerly served by Adelphia Communications. Now served by Comcast Cable, HARRISBURG, PA [PA0009]

TYRONE—See ALTOONA, PA (Atlantic Broadband)

ULSTER TWP.—See EAST SMITHFIELD, PA (North Penn Video)

ULSTER—See ROME, PA (Beaver Valley Cable Co)

ULYSSES BOROUGH—Time Warner Cable. Now served by BUFFALO, NY [NY0216]

ULYSSES—See HARRISON VALLEY, PA (Zito Media)

UNION COUNTY (PORTIONS)—See MIFFLINBURG, PA (Atlantic Broadband)

UNION TWP. (ADAMS COUNTY)—See HARRISBURG, PA (Comcast Cable)

UNION TWP. (BERKS COUNTY)—See BIRDSBORO, PA (Service Electric Cablevision)

UNION TWP. (CENTRE COUNTY)—Country Cable

UNION TWP. (CLEARFIELD COUNTY)—See PUNXSUTAWNEY, PA (Comcast Cable)

UNION TWP. (Huntingdon County)—Formerly served by Atlantic Broadband. No longer in operation

UNION TWP. (HUNTINGTON COUNTY)—See HARRISBURG, PA (Comcast Cable)

UNION TWP. (JEFFERSON COUNTY)—See PUNXSUTAWNEY, PA (Comcast Cable)

UNION TWP. (LAWRENCE COUNTY)—See ZELIENOPLE, OH (Armstrong Cable Services)

UNION TWP. (LAWRENCE COUNTY)—See HARRISBURG, PA (Comcast Cable)

UNION TWP. (LEBANON COUNTY)—See HARRISBURG, PA (Comcast Cable)

UNION TWP. (LEBANON COUNTY)—See FORT INDIANTOWN GAP, PA (Gap Cable TV Inc)

UNION TWP. (LUZERNE COUNTY)—See BERWICK, PA (MetroCast Communications)

UNION TWP. (SCHUYLKILL COUNTY)—See HAZLETON, PA (Service Electric Cablevision)

UNION TWP. (Union County)—Formerly served by D&E Communications/Windstream. IPTV service no longer in operation

UNION TWP. (UNION COUNTY)—See SUNBURY (village), PA (Service Electric Cablevision)

UNION TWP. (WASHINGTON COUNTY)—See PITTSBURGH, PA (Comcast Cable)

UNION TWP.—See TUNKHANNOCK, PA (Blue Ridge Communications)

UNIONDALE—See CARBONDALE TWP. (Lackawanna County), PA (Adams Cable Service)

UNIONTOWN—Atlantic Broadband

UNITED—See MAMMOTH, PA (Citizens Telecom. Formerly [PA0400]. This cable system has converted to IPTV)

UNITY TWP. (WESTMORELAND COUNTY)—See GREENSBURG, PA (Comcast Cable)

UNITY TWP.—See BLAIRSVILLE, PA (Comcast Cable)

UPLAND—See PHILADELPHIA, PA (Comcast Cable)

UPPER ALLEN TWP.—See HARRISBURG, PA (Comcast Cable)

UPPER AUGUSTA TWP.—See SUNBURY (village), PA (Service Electric Cablevision)

UPPER BERN TWP.—See HARRISBURG, PA (Comcast Cable)

UPPER BURRELL TWP.—See BLAIRSVILLE, PA (Comcast Cable)

UPPER CHICHESTER TWP.—See PHILADELPHIA, PA (Comcast Cable)

UPPER DARBY—See PHILADELPHIA, PA (Comcast Cable)

UPPER DARBY—See RIDLEY PARK, PA (RCN. Formerly served by PHILADELPHIA (suburbs), PA [PA0447]. This cable system has converted to IPTV)

UPPER LEACOCK TWP.—See HARRISBURG, PA (Comcast Cable)

UPPER MACUNGIE TWP.—See ALLENTOWN, PA (RCN. Formerly served by NORTHAMPTON BOROUGH, PA [PA0008]. This cable system has converted to IPTV)

UPPER MACUNGIE TWP.—See ALLENTOWN, PA (Service Electric Cable TV & Communications)

UPPER MAHANOY TWP.—See SUNBURY (village), PA (Service Electric Cablevision)

UPPER MAHANTANGO TWP.—See HARRISBURG, PA (Comcast Cable)

UPPER MILFORD TWP.—See ALLENTOWN, PA (Service Electric Cable TV & Communications)

UPPER MORELAND TWP.—See PHILADELPHIA, PA (Comcast Cable)

UPPER MOUNT BETHEL TWP.—See ALLENTOWN, PA (Service Electric Cable TV & Communications)

UPPER NAZARETH TWP.—See ALLENTOWN, PA (RCN. Formerly served by NORTHAMPTON BOROUGH, PA [PA0008]. This cable system has converted to IPTV)

UPPER NAZARETH TWP.—See ALLENTOWN, PA (Service Electric Cable TV & Communications)

UPPER OXFORD TWP.—See PHILADELPHIA, PA (Comcast Cable)

UPPER PAXTON TWP. (DAUPHIN COUNTY)—See HARRISBURG, PA (Comcast Cable)

UPPER PROVIDENCE—See PHILADELPHIA, PA (Comcast Cable)

UPPER SAUCON TWP.—See ALLENTOWN, PA (RCN. Formerly served by NORTHAMPTON BOROUGH, PA [PA0008]. This cable system has converted to IPTV)

UPPER SAUCON TWP.—See ALLENTOWN, PA (Service Electric Cable TV & Communications)

UPPER ST. CLAIR TWP.—See PITTSBURGH, PA (Comcast Cable)

UPPER TULPEHOCKEN TWP.—See HARRISBURG, PA (Comcast Cable)

UPPER UWCHLAN TWP.—See PHILADELPHIA, PA (Comcast Cable)

UPPER YODER TWP.—See JOHNSTOWN, PA (Atlantic Broadband)

URSINA BOROUGH—See GREENSBURG, PA (Comcast Cable)

UTICA—See ZELIENOPLE, PA (Armstrong Cable Services)

UWCHLAN TWP.—See PHILADELPHIA, PA (Comcast Cable)

VALENCIA—See ZELIENOPLE, PA (Armstrong Cable Services)

VALLEY TWP. (ARMSTRONG COUNTY)—See BLAIRSVILLE, PA (Comcast Cable)

VALLEY TWP. (CHESTER COUNTY)—See PHILADELPHIA, PA (Comcast Cable)

VALLEY TWP. (MONTOUR COUNTY)—See DANVILLE, PA (CATV Service Inc)

Cable Community Index—Pennsylvania

VANDERBILT—See ZELIENOPLE, PA (Armstrong Cable Services)

VANDERGRIFT BOROUGH—See PITTSBURGH, PA (Comcast Cable)

VANDLING BOROUGH—See CARBONDALE TWP. (Lackawanna County), PA (Adams Cable Service)

VANPORT—See PITTSBURGH, PA (Comcast Cable)

VENANGO TWP. (BUTLER COUNTY)—See ZELIENOPLE, PA (Armstrong Cable Services)

VENANGO TWP. (CRAWFORD COUNTY)—See EDINBORO, PA (Coaxial Cable TV Corp)

VENANGO—See EDINBORO, PA (Coaxial Cable TV Corp)

VERONA BOROUGH—See PITTSBURGH, PA (Comcast Cable)

VERSAILLES—See PITTSBURGH, PA (Comcast Cable)

VICKSBURG—Formerly served by D&E Communications. No longer in operation

VINTONDALE BOROUGH—See BLAIRSVILLE, PA (Comcast Cable)

VOLANT BOROUGH—See ZELIENOPLE, PA (Armstrong Cable Services)

WADESTOWN—See BRAVE, WV (Zito Media)

WALKER TWP. (CENTRE COUNTY)—See HARRISBURG, PA (Comcast Cable)

WALKER TWP. (CENTRE COUNTY)—See ZION, PA (Tele-Media)

WALKER TWP. (HUNTINGDON COUNTY)—See HARRISBURG, PA (Comcast Cable)

WALKER TWP. (NORTHUMBERLAND COUNTY)—See HAZLETON, PA (Service Electric Cablevision)

WALKER TWP. (SCHUYLKILL COUNTY)—See LEHIGHTON, PA (Blue Ridge Communications)

WALKER—See SNOW SHOE, PA (Tele-Media)

WALL—See PITTSBURGH, PA (Comcast Cable)

WALLACE TWP.—See PHILADELPHIA, PA (Comcast Cable)

WALLACETON—See SNOW SHOE, PA (Tele-Media)

WALNUT BOTTOM—Kuhn Communications

WALNUT GROVE (YORK COUNTY)—See HARRISBURG, PA (Comcast Cable)

WALNUT—Formerly served by Penn CATV of Walnut. No longer in operation

WALNUTPORT—See LEHIGHTON, PA (Blue Ridge Communications)

WALNUTPORT—See ALLENTOWN, PA (RCN. Formerly served by NORTHAMPTON BOROUGH, PA [PA0008]. This cable system has converted to IPTV)

WAMPUM—See ZELIENOPLE, PA (Armstrong Cable Services)

WANA—See BRAVE, WV (Zito Media)

WAPWALLOPEN—See BERWICK, PA (MetroCast Communications)

WARD TWP.—See CANTON, PA (Zito Media)

WARREN CENTER TWP.—See ROME, PA (Beaver Valley Cable Co)

WARREN COUNTY—See WARREN, PA (Atlantic Broadband)

WARREN—Atlantic Broadband

WARRENSVILLE—See ELDRED TWP., PA (Herr Cable Co)

WARRINGTON TWP. (YORK COUNTY)—See NEWBERRY TWP., PA (Blue Ridge Communications)

WARRINGTON TWP.—See HARRISBURG, PA (Comcast Cable)

WARRIOR RUN BOROUGH—See WILKES-BARRE, PA (Service Electric Cable Company)

WARRIORS MARK—Atlantic Broadband. Now served by ALTOONA, PA [PA0018]

WARRIORS MARK—See ALTOONA, PA (Atlantic Broadband)

WARSAW TWP.—See HAZEN, PA (Zito Media)

WARWICK TWP. (BERKS COUNTY)—See BIRDSBORO, PA (Service Electric Cablevision)

WARWICK TWP. (CHESTER COUNTY)—See BIRDSBORO, PA (Service Electric Cablevision)

WARWICK TWP. (LANCASTER COUNTY)—See EPHRATA, PA (Blue Ridge Communications)

WARWICK—See BIRDSBORO, PA (Service Electric Cablevision)

WASHINGTON COUNTY (PORTIONS)—See HARRISBURG, MD (Comcast Cable)

WASHINGTON TWP. (ARMSTRONG COUNTY)—See BLAIRSVILLE, PA (Comcast Cable)

WASHINGTON TWP. (BUTLER COUNTY)—See ZELIENOPLE, PA (Armstrong Cable Services)

WASHINGTON TWP. (BUTLER COUNTY)—See HARRISBURG, PA (Comcast Cable)

WASHINGTON TWP. (CAMBRIA COUNTY)—See BLAIRSVILLE, PA (Comcast Cable)

WASHINGTON TWP. (CARBON COUNTY)—See LEHIGHTON, PA (Blue Ridge Communications)

WASHINGTON TWP. (CLARION COUNTY)—See ZELIENOPLE, PA (Armstrong Cable Services)

WASHINGTON TWP. (DAUPHIN COUNTY)—See HARRISBURG, PA (Comcast Cable)

WASHINGTON TWP. (ERIE COUNTY)—See EDINBORO, PA (Coaxial Cable TV Corp)

WASHINGTON TWP. (FAYETTE COUNTY)—See UNIONTOWN, PA (Atlantic Broadband)

WASHINGTON TWP. (FRANKLIN COUNTY)—See HARRISBURG, PA (Comcast Cable)

WASHINGTON TWP. (JEFFERSON COUNTY)—See BROCKWAY, PA (Brockway TV Inc)

WASHINGTON TWP. (JEFFERSON COUNTY)—See PUNXSUTAWNEY, PA (Comcast Cable)

WASHINGTON TWP. (JEFFERSON COUNTY)—See HAZEN, PA (Zito Media)

WASHINGTON TWP. (LAWRENCE COUNTY)—See ZELIENOPLE, PA (Armstrong Cable Services)

WASHINGTON TWP. (LYCOMING COUNTY)—See HARRISBURG, PA (Comcast Cable)

WASHINGTON TWP. (NORTHUMBERLAND COUNTY)—See SUNBURY (village), PA (Service Electric Cablevision)

WASHINGTON TWP. (SCHUYLKILL COUNTY)—See HARRISBURG, PA (Comcast Cable)

WASHINGTON TWP. (SNYDER COUNTY)—See SUNBURY (village), PA (Service Electric Cablevision)

WASHINGTON TWP. (WESTMORELAND COUNTY)—See BLAIRSVILLE, PA (Comcast Cable)

WASHINGTON TWP. (WYOMING COUNTY)—See TUNKHANNOCK, PA (Blue Ridge Communications)

WASHINGTON TWP. (YORK COUNTY)—See HARRISBURG, PA (Comcast Cable)

WASHINGTON TWP.—See ALLENTOWN, PA (RCN. Formerly served by NORTHAMPTON BOROUGH, PA [PA0008]. This cable system has converted to IPTV)

WASHINGTON TWP.—See ALLENTOWN, PA (Service Electric Cable TV & Communications)

WASHINGTON—Comcast Cable. Now served by PITTSBURGH, PA [PA0001]

WASHINGTON—See BLAIRSVILLE, PA (Comcast Cable)

WASHINGTON—See PITTSBURGH, PA (Comcast Cable)

WASHINGTONVILLE—See DANVILLE, PA (CATV Service Inc)

WASHINGTONVILLE—See SUNBURY (village), PA (Service Electric Cablevision)

WATERFALL—Waterfall Community TV

WATSON TWP.—See ZELIENOPLE, PA (Armstrong Cable Services)

WATSON TWP.—See HARRISBURG, PA (Comcast Cable)

WATSONTOWN—See DANVILLE, PA (CATV Service Inc)

WATSONTOWN—See SUNBURY (village), PA (Service Electric Cablevision)

WATTS TWP.—See NEWBERRY TWP., PA (Blue Ridge Communications)

WATTSBURG—Formerly served by Cebridge Connections. Now served by Armstrong Cable Services, ZELIENOPLE, PA [PA0053]

WATTSBURG—See ZELIENOPLE, PA (Armstrong Cable Services)

WAYMART—See CARBONDALE TWP. (Lackawanna County), PA (Adams Cable Service)

WAYNE COUNTY (NORTHERN PORTION)—See ZELIENOPLE, WV (Armstrong Cable Services)

WAYNE TWP. (CLINTON COUNTY)—See HARRISBURG, PA (Comcast Cable)

WAYNE TWP. (DAUPHIN COUNTY)—See HARRISBURG, PA (Comcast Cable)

WAYNE TWP. (LAWRENCE COUNTY)—See ZELIENOPLE, PA (Armstrong Cable Services)

WAYNE TWP. (LAWRENCE COUNTY)—See HARRISBURG, PA (Comcast Cable)

WAYNE TWP. (MIFFLIN COUNTY)—See HARRISBURG, PA (Comcast Cable)

WAYNE TWP. (SCHUYLKILL COUNTY)—See HARRISBURG, PA (Comcast Cable)

WAYNE TWP.—See BRAVE, PA (Zito Media)

WAYNESBORO—See HARRISBURG, PA (Comcast Cable)

WAYNESBURG BOROUGH—Comcast Cable. Now served by PITTSBURGH, PA [PA0001]

WAYNESBURG BOROUGH—See PITTSBURGH, PA (Comcast Cable)

WEATHERLY—MetroCast Communications

WEATHERSFIELD TWP. (TRUMBULL COUNTY)—See ZELIENOPLE, OH (Armstrong Cable Services)

WEEDVILLE—Zito Media

WEIKERT—See MIFFLINBURG, PA (Atlantic Broadband)

WEISENBERG TWP.—See ALLENTOWN, PA (Service Electric Cable TV & Communications)

WEISSPORT—See LEHIGHTON, PA (Blue Ridge Communications)

Pennsylvania—Cable Community Index

WELDBANK—See SHEFFIELD, PA (WestPA.net Inc)

WELLER TWP. (RICHLAND COUNTY)—See ZELIENOPLE, OH (Armstrong Cable Services)

WELLS TANNERY—See WATERFALL, PA (Waterfall Community TV)

WELLS TWP. (BRADFORD COUNTY)—See JACKSON TWP. (Tioga County), PA (Blue Ridge Communications)

WELLS TWP.—See HARRISBURG, PA (Comcast Cable)

WELLS TWP.—See EAST SMITHFIELD, PA (North Penn Video)

WELLSBORO—See MANSFIELD, PA (Blue Ridge Communications)

WELLSVILLE—See NEWBERRY TWP., PA (Blue Ridge Communications)

WERNERSVILLE—See HARRISBURG, PA (Comcast Cable)

WESCOSVILLE—See ALLENTOWN, PA (RCN. Formerly served by NORTHAMPTON BOROUGH, PA [PA0008]. This cable system has converted to IPTV)

WEST ALEXANDER—Comcast Cable. Now served by PITTSBURGH, PA [PA0001]

WEST ALEXANDER—See PITTSBURGH, PA (Comcast Cable)

WEST BEAVER TWP.—See McCLURE, PA (Nittany Media Inc.)

WEST BETHLEHEM TWP.—See UNIONTOWN, PA (Atlantic Broadband)

WEST BRADFORD TWP.—See PHILADELPHIA, PA (Comcast Cable)

WEST BRANCH TWP. (POTTER COUNTY)—See MANSFIELD, PA (Blue Ridge Communications)

WEST BRANDYWINE TWP.—See PHILADELPHIA, PA (Comcast Cable)

WEST BROWNSVILLE—See ZELIENOPLE, PA (Armstrong Cable Services)

WEST BRUNSWICK TWP.—See HARRISBURG, PA (Comcast Cable)

WEST BUFFALO TWP. (PORTIONS)—See MIFFLINBURG, PA (Atlantic Broadband)

WEST BUFFALO TWP.—Formerly served by D&E Communications/Windstream. IPTV service no longer in operation

WEST BURLINGTON TWP.—Formerly served by Barrett's TV Cable System. No longer in operation

WEST BURLINGTON TWP.—See TROY, PA (Blue Ridge Communications)

WEST CALN TWP.—See PHILADELPHIA, PA (Comcast Cable)

WEST CAMERON TWP.—See SUNBURY (village), PA (Service Electric Cablevision)

WEST CARROLL TWP.—See BLAIRSVILLE, PA (Comcast Cable)

WEST CHESTER BOROUGH—See PHILADELPHIA, PA (Comcast Cable)

WEST CHILLISQUAQUE TWP. (PORTIONS)—See DANVILLE, PA (CATV Service Inc)

WEST CHILLISQUAQUE TWP.—Formerly served by D&E Communications/Windstream. IPTV service no longer in operation

WEST CHILLISQUAQUE TWP.—See SUNBURY (village), PA (Service Electric Cablevision)

WEST COCALICO TWP.—See EPHRATA, PA (Blue Ridge Communications)

WEST COCALICO TWP.—See HARRISBURG, PA (Comcast Cable)

WEST CORNWALL TWP.—See HARRISBURG, PA (Comcast Cable)

WEST DEER TWP. (PORTIONS)—See ZELIENOPLE, PA (Armstrong Cable Services)

WEST DEER TWP.—Comcast Cable. Now served by PITTSBURGH, PA [PA0001]

WEST DEER TWP.—See PITTSBURGH, PA (Comcast Cable)

WEST DONEGAL TWP.—See HARRISBURG, PA (Comcast Cable)

WEST EARL TWP. (NORTHERN PORTION)—See EPHRATA, PA (Blue Ridge Communications)

WEST EARL TWP.—See HARRISBURG, PA (Comcast Cable)

WEST EASTON BOROUGH—See ALLENTOWN, PA (RCN. Formerly served by NORTHAMPTON BOROUGH, PA [PA0008]. This cable system has converted to IPTV)

WEST EASTON—See ALLENTOWN, PA (Service Electric Cable TV & Communications)

WEST ELIZABETH—See PITTSBURGH, PA (Comcast Cable)

WEST FAIRVIEW—See HARRISBURG, PA (Comcast Cable)

WEST FRANKLIN TWP.—See ZELIENOPLE, PA (Armstrong Cable Services)

WEST FRANKLIN TWP.—See BLAIRSVILLE, PA (Comcast Cable)

WEST GOSHEN TWP.—See PHILADELPHIA, PA (Comcast Cable)

WEST GROVE BOROUGH—See PHILADELPHIA, PA (Comcast Cable)

WEST HANOVER TWP. (DAUPHIN COUNTY)—See HARRISBURG, PA (Comcast Cable)

WEST HAZLETON BOROUGH—See HAZLETON, PA (Service Electric Cablevision)

WEST HEMLOCK TWP.—See DANVILLE, PA (CATV Service Inc)

WEST HEMLOCK TWP.—See SUNBURY (village), PA (Service Electric Cablevision)

WEST HEMPFIELD TWP. (LANCASTER COUNTY)—See HARRISBURG, PA (Comcast Cable)

WEST HOMESTEAD—See PITTSBURGH, PA (Comcast Cable)

WEST KITTANNING—See BLAIRSVILLE, PA (Comcast Cable)

WEST LAMPETER TWP.—See HARRISBURG, PA (Comcast Cable)

WEST LAWN—See HARRISBURG, PA (Comcast Cable)

WEST LEBANON—See HARRISBURG, PA (Comcast Cable)

WEST LEECHBURG BOROUGH—See PITTSBURGH, PA (Comcast Cable)

WEST LIBERTY—See ZELIENOPLE, PA (Armstrong Cable Services)

WEST MAHANOY TWP.—See HAZLETON, PA (Service Electric Cablevision)

WEST MAHANOY—See HAZLETON, PA (Service Electric Cablevision)

WEST MANCHESTER TWP.—See HARRISBURG, PA (Comcast Cable)

WEST MANHEIM—See HARRISBURG, PA (Comcast Cable)

WEST MAYFIELD BOROUGH—See PITTSBURGH, PA (Comcast Cable)

WEST MAYFIELD—See PITTSBURGH, PA (Comcast Cable)

WEST MEAD TWP.—See ZELIENOPLE, PA (Armstrong Cable Services)

WEST MIFFLIN—Formerly served by Adelphia Communications. Now served by Comcast Cable, PITTSBURGH, PA [PA0001]

WEST MIFFLIN—See PITTSBURGH, PA (Comcast Cable)

WEST NANTICOKE—See BERWICK, PA (MetroCast Communications)

WEST NANTMEAL TWP.—See PHILADELPHIA, PA (Comcast Cable)

WEST NEWTON—Formerly served by Adelphia Communications. Now served by Comcast Cable, PITTSBURGH, PA [PA0001]

WEST NEWTON—See PITTSBURGH, PA (Comcast Cable)

WEST NEWTON—See SALTLICK TWP., PA (Laurel Highland Total Communications)

WEST PENN TWP. (NORTHWESTERN PORTION)—See HAZLETON, PA (Service Electric Cablevision)

WEST PENN TWP. (SOUTHEASTERN PORTION)—See LEHIGHTON, PA (Blue Ridge Communications)

WEST PENNSBORO TWP. (CUMBERLAND COUNTY)—See HARRISBURG, PA (Comcast Cable)

WEST PERRY TWP.—See MIFFLINTOWN, PA (Nittany Media Inc.)

WEST PERRY TWP.—See MOUNT PLEASANT MILLS, PA (Zampelli Electronics)

WEST PIKE RUN TWP.—See ZELIENOPLE, PA (Armstrong Cable Services)

WEST PIKE RUN TWP.—See UNIONTOWN, PA (Atlantic Broadband)

WEST PIKELAND TWP.—See PHILADELPHIA, PA (Comcast Cable)

WEST PITTSTON BOROUGH—See HARRISBURG, PA (Comcast Cable)

WEST PROVIDENCE TWP.—See BLAIRSVILLE, PA (Comcast Cable)

WEST READING—See HARRISBURG, PA (Comcast Cable)

WEST SADSBURY TWP.—See PHILADELPHIA, PA (Comcast Cable)

WEST ST. CLAIR TWP.—See BLAIRSVILLE, PA (Comcast Cable)

WEST SUNBURY—See ZELIENOPLE, PA (Armstrong Cable Services)

WEST TAYLOR TWP.—See JOHNSTOWN, PA (Atlantic Broadband)

WEST TWP.—See McALEVYS FORT, PA (Atlantic Broadband)

WEST UNION—See ZELIENOPLE, WV (Armstrong Cable Services)

WEST VIEW—See PITTSBURGH, PA (Comcast Cable)

WEST VINCENT TWP.—See PHILADELPHIA, PA (Comcast Cable)

WEST WHEATFIELD TWP.—See BLAIRSVILLE, PA (Comcast Cable)

WEST WHITELAND TWP.—See PHILADELPHIA, PA (Comcast Cable)

WEST WYOMING BOROUGH—See HARRISBURG, PA (Comcast Cable)

WEST YORK—See HARRISBURG, PA (Comcast Cable)

WESTBROOK PARK—See ALLENTOWN, PA (RCN. Formerly served by NORTHAMPTON BOROUGH, PA [PA0008]. This cable system has converted to IPTV)

WESTFIELD TWP.—See WESTFIELD, PA (Westfield Community Antenna)

WESTFIELD—Westfield Community Antenna

WESTFIELD—See HARRISON VALLEY, PA (Zito Media)

WESTLINE—Formerly served by Keystone Wilcox Cable TV Inc. No longer in operation

WESTMONT (CAMBRIA COUNTY)—See JOHNSTOWN, PA (Atlantic Broadband)

WESTOVER—See PUNXSUTAWNEY, PA (Comcast Cable)

Cable Community Index—Pennsylvania

WESTTOWN TWP.—See PHILADELPHIA, PA (Comcast Cable)

WETMORE TWP.—See PUNXSUTAWNEY, PA (Comcast Cable)

WHEATFIELD TWP.—See NEWBERRY TWP., PA (Blue Ridge Communications)

WHITAKER—See PITTSBURGH, PA (Comcast Cable)

WHITE DEER TWP.—Formerly served by D&E Communications/Windstream. IPTV service no longer in operation

WHITE DEER TWP.—See DANVILLE, PA (CATV Service Inc)

WHITE HAVEN—See WEATHERLY, PA (MetroCast Communications)

WHITE OAK (PORTIONS)—See GREENSBURG, PA (Comcast Cable)

WHITE OAK (PORTIONS)—See PITTSBURGH, PA (Comcast Cable)

WHITE TWP. (BEAVER COUNTY)—See PITTSBURGH, PA (Comcast Cable)

WHITE TWP. (CAMBRIA COUNTY)—See BLAIRSVILLE, PA (Comcast Cable)

WHITE TWP. (INDIANA COUNTY)—See BLAIRSVILLE, PA (Comcast Cable)

WHITE—See SALTLICK TWP., PA (Laurel Highland Total Communications)

WHITEHALL TWP.—See ALLENTOWN, PA (Service Electric Cable TV & Communications)

WHITEHALL—See PITTSBURGH, PA (Comcast Cable)

WHITEHALL—See ALLENTOWN, PA (RCN. Formerly served by NORTHAMPTON BOROUGH, PA [PA0008]. This cable system has converted to IPTV)

WHITNEY—See MAMMOTH, PA (Citizens Telecom. Formerly [PA0400]. This cable system has converted to IPTV)

WICONISCO—See HARRISBURG, PA (Comcast Cable)

WILCOX—Zito Media

WILKES-BARRE TWP.—See WILKES-BARRE, PA (Service Electric Cable Company)

WILKES-BARRE—Service Electric Cable Company

WILKINS TWP.—See PITTSBURGH, PA (Comcast Cable)

WILKINSBURG—See PITTSBURGH, PA (Comcast Cable)

WILLIAMS TWP. (DAUPHIN COUNTY)—See HARRISBURG, PA (Comcast Cable)

WILLIAMS TWP.—Formerly served by NORTHAMPTON BOROUGH, PA [PA0008]. RCN. This cable system has converted to IPTV. Now served by ALLENTOWN, PA [PA5201]

WILLIAMS TWP.—See ALLENTOWN, PA (RCN. Formerly served by NORTHAMPTON BOROUGH, PA [PA0008]. This cable system has converted to IPTV)

WILLIAMS TWP.—See ALLENTOWN, PA (Service Electric Cable TV & Communications)

WILLIAMSBURG (Blair County)—Formerly served by Adelphia Communications. No longer in operation

WILLIAMSBURG BOROUGH—See HARRISBURG, PA (Comcast Cable)

WILLIAMSPORT BOROUGH—See HARRISBURG, PA (Comcast Cable)

WILLIAMSPORT—Comcast Cable. Now served by HARRISBURG, PA [PA0009]

WILLIAMSTOWN (DAUPHIN COUNTY)—See HARRISBURG, PA (Comcast Cable)

WILLISTOWN TWP.—See PHILADELPHIA, PA (Comcast Cable)

WILLOW GROVE—Formerly served by Comcast Cable. No longer in operation

WILMERDING—See PITTSBURGH, PA (Comcast Cable)

WILMINGTON TWP. (LAWRENCE COUNTY)—See HARRISBURG, PA (Comcast Cable)

WILMINGTON—See PHILADELPHIA, DE (Comcast Cable)

WILMORE BOROUGH—See BLAIRSVILLE, PA (Comcast Cable)

WILMOT TWP.—See TUNKHANNOCK, PA (Blue Ridge Communications)

WILSON—See ALLENTOWN, PA (RCN. Formerly served by NORTHAMPTON BOROUGH, PA [PA0008]. This cable system has converted to IPTV)

WILSON—See ALLENTOWN, PA (Service Electric Cable TV & Communications)

WIND GAP BORO—See ALLENTOWN, PA (Service Electric Cable TV & Communications)

WIND GAP—See ALLENTOWN, PA (RCN. Formerly served by NORTHAMPTON BOROUGH, PA [PA0008]. This cable system has converted to IPTV)

WINDBER BOROUGH—See BLAIRSVILLE, PA (Comcast Cable)

WINDHAM TWP.—See TUNKHANNOCK, PA (Blue Ridge Communications)

WINDSOR BOROUGH—See HARRISBURG, PA (Comcast Cable)

WINDSOR TWP. (LAWRENCE COUNTY)—See ZELIENOPLE, OH (Armstrong Cable Services)

WINDSOR TWP.—See HARRISBURG, PA (Comcast Cable)

WINDSOR—See HARRISBURG, PA (Comcast Cable)

WINFIELD TWP.—See ZELIENOPLE, PA (Armstrong Cable Services)

WINFIELD—Formerly served by D&E Communications. No longer in operation

WINSLOW TWP.—See PUNXSUTAWNEY, PA (Comcast Cable)

WOLF CREEK TWP.—See ZELIENOPLE, PA (Armstrong Cable Services)

WOLF TWP.—See HARRISBURG, PA (Comcast Cable)

WOMELSDORF—See HARRISBURG, PA (Comcast Cable)

WOOD TWP.—See HARRISBURG, PA (Comcast Cable)

WOODBURY TWP. (BEDFORD COUNTY)—See ALTOONA, PA (Atlantic Broadband)

WOODBURY TWP. (BLAIR COUNTY)—See ALTOONA, PA (Atlantic Broadband)

WOODBURY TWP.—See HARRISBURG, PA (Comcast Cable)

WOODBURY—Atlantic Broadband. Now served by ALTOONA, PA [PA0018]

WOODBURY—See ALTOONA, PA (Atlantic Broadband)

WOODCOCK BOROUGH—See EDINBORO, PA (Coaxial Cable TV Corp)

WOODLYN—See RIDLEY PARK, PA (RCN. Formerly served by PHILADELPHIA (suburbs), PA [PA0447]. This cable system has converted to IPTV)

WOODWARD TWP. (LYCOMING COUNTY)—See HARRISBURG, PA (Comcast Cable)

WORMLEYSBURG BOROUGH—See HARRISBURG, PA (Comcast Cable)

WORTH TWP.—See ZELIENOPLE, PA (Armstrong Cable Services)

WORTH TWP.—See HARRISBURG, PA (Comcast Cable)

WORTHINGTON—See BLAIRSVILLE, PA (Comcast Cable)

WORTHVILLE—See PUNXSUTAWNEY, PA (Comcast Cable)

WRIGHT TWP.—See WILKES-BARRE, PA (Service Electric Cable Company)

WRIGHTSVILLE—See HARRISBURG, PA (Comcast Cable)

WURTLAND—See ZELIENOPLE, KY (Armstrong Cable Services)

WYALUSING BOROUGH—See TUNKHANNOCK, PA (Blue Ridge Communications)

WYALUSING TWP.—See TUNKHANNOCK, PA (Blue Ridge Communications)

WYANO—See SALTLICK TWP., PA (Laurel Highland Total Communications)

WYOMING COUNTY—See TUNKHANNOCK, PA (Blue Ridge Communications)

WYOMING—See HARRISBURG, PA (Comcast Cable)

WYOMISSING HILLS—See HARRISBURG, PA (Comcast Cable)

WYOMISSING—See HARRISBURG, PA (Comcast Cable)

WYSOX TWP.—See HARRISBURG, PA (Comcast Cable)

YATESVILLE BOROUGH—See HARRISBURG, PA (Comcast Cable)

YEADON—See PHILADELPHIA, PA (Comcast Cable)

YEADON—See ALLENTOWN, PA (RCN. Formerly served by NORTHAMPTON BOROUGH, PA [PA0008]. This cable system has converted to IPTV)

YOE BOROUGH—See HARRISBURG, PA (Comcast Cable)

YORK HAVEN BOROUGH—See HARRISBURG, PA (Comcast Cable)

YORK SPRINGS BOROUGH—See HARRISBURG, PA (Comcast Cable)

YORK TWP.—See ZELIENOPLE, OH (Armstrong Cable Services)

YORK—Comcast Cable. Now served by HARRISBURG, PA [PA0009]

YORK—See HARRISBURG, PA (Comcast Cable)

YORKANA BOROUGH—See HARRISBURG, PA (Comcast Cable)

YOUNG TWP. (INDIANA COUNTY)—See BLAIRSVILLE, PA (Comcast Cable)

YOUNG TWP. (JEFFERSON COUNTY)—See BLAIRSVILLE, PA (Comcast Cable)

YOUNG TWP. (JEFFERSON COUNTY)—See PUNXSUTAWNEY, PA (Comcast Cable)

YOUNGSTOWN—See MAMMOTH, PA (Citizens Telecom. Formerly [PA0400]. This cable system has converted to IPTV)

YOUNGSTOWN—See BLAIRSVILLE, PA (Comcast Cable)

YOUNGSVILLE—Youngsville TV Corp

YOUNGWOOD—See GREENSBURG, PA (Comcast Cable)

YUKON—See SALTLICK TWP., PA (Laurel Highland Total Communications)

ZELIENOPLE—Armstrong Cable Services

ZERBE TWP.—See SUNBURY (village), PA (Service Electric Cablevision)

ZERBE—See TREMONT, PA (Wire Television Corp)

Pennsylvania—Cable Community Index

ZION—Tele-Media

ZULINGER—See HARRISBURG, PA (Comcast Cable)

PUERTO RICO

ADJUNTAS—See PONCE, PR (Choice Cable)

AGUADA—See MAYAGUEZ, PR (Choice Cable)

AGUADILLA—See MAYAGUEZ, PR (Choice Cable)

AGUAS BUENAS—See CAGUAS, PR (Liberty Cablevision)

AIBONITO—See CAGUAS, PR (Liberty Cablevision)

ANASCO—See MAYAGUEZ, PR (Choice Cable)

ARECIBO—See CIALES, PR (Liberty Cablevision)

ARROYO—See PONCE, PR (Choice Cable)

BARCELONETA—See LUQUILLO, PR (Liberty Cablevision)

BARRANQUITAS—See CAGUAS, PR (Liberty Cablevision)

BAYAMON—Liberty Cablevision

CABA ROJO—See MAYAGUEZ, PR (Choice Cable)

CAGUAS—Liberty Cablevision

CAGUAS—See LUQUILLO, PR (Liberty Cablevision)

CAMUY—See LUQUILLO, PR (Liberty Cablevision)

CANOVANAS—See LUQUILLO, PR (Liberty Cablevision)

CAROLINA—See BAYAMON, PR (Liberty Cablevision)

CATANO—See BAYAMON, PR (Liberty Cablevision)

CAYEY—See CAGUAS, PR (Liberty Cablevision)

CEIBA NAVAL BASE—Formerly served by Americable International. No longer in operation

CEIBA—See LUQUILLO, PR (Liberty Cablevision)

CIALES—Liberty Cablevision

CIDRA—See CAGUAS, PR (Liberty Cablevision)

COAMO—See PONCE, PR (Choice Cable)

COMERIO—See CAGUAS, PR (Liberty Cablevision)

COROZAL—See CIALES, PR (Liberty Cablevision)

DORADO—See LUQUILLO, PR (Liberty Cablevision)

FAJARDO—See LUQUILLO, PR (Liberty Cablevision)

FLORIDA—See CIALES, PR (Liberty Cablevision)

GUANICA—See PONCE, PR (Choice Cable)

GUAYAMA—See PONCE, PR (Choice Cable)

GUAYANILLA—See PONCE, PR (Choice Cable)

GUAYNABO—See BAYAMON, PR (Liberty Cablevision)

GURABO—See CAGUAS, PR (Liberty Cablevision)

HATILLO—See LUQUILLO, PR (Liberty Cablevision)

HORMIGUEROS—See MAYAGUEZ, PR (Choice Cable)

HUMACAO—See CAGUAS, PR (Liberty Cablevision)

ISABELA—See MAYAGUEZ, PR (Choice Cable)

JAYUYA—See PONCE, PR (Choice Cable)

JUANA DIAZ—See PONCE, PR (Choice Cable)

JUNCOS—See CAGUAS, PR (Liberty Cablevision)

LAJAS—See MAYAGUEZ, PR (Choice Cable)

LARES—See CIALES, PR (Liberty Cablevision)

LAS MARIAS—See MAYAGUEZ, PR (Choice Cable)

LAS PIEDRAS—See CAGUAS, PR (Liberty Cablevision)

LEVITTOWN—Liberty Cablevision. Now served by LUQUILLO, PR [PR0003]

LEVITTOWN—See LUQUILLO, PR (Liberty Cablevision)

LOIZA—See LUQUILLO, PR (Liberty Cablevision)

LUQUILLO—Liberty Cablevision

MANATI—See LUQUILLO, PR (Liberty Cablevision)

MARICAO—See PONCE, PR (Choice Cable)

MAUNABO—See PONCE, PR (Choice Cable)

MAYAGUEZ—Choice Cable

MERCEDITA—Formerly served by Centennial de Puerto Rico. Now served by Choice Cable, PONCE, PR [PR0008]

MERCEDITA—See PONCE, PR (Choice Cable)

MOCA—See MAYAGUEZ, PR (Choice Cable)

MOROVIS—See CIALES, PR (Liberty Cablevision)

NAGUABO—See LUQUILLO, PR (Liberty Cablevision)

NARANJITO—See CAGUAS, PR (Liberty Cablevision)

OROCOVIS—See CIALES, PR (Liberty Cablevision)

PATILLAS—See PONCE, PR (Choice Cable)

PENUELAS—See PONCE, PR (Choice Cable)

PLAYA DE PONCE—See PONCE, PR (Choice Cable)

PONCE—Choice Cable

QUEBRADILLAS—See MAYAGUEZ, PR (Choice Cable)

RINCON—See MAYAGUEZ, PR (Choice Cable)

RIO GRANDE—See LUQUILLO, PR (Liberty Cablevision)

SABANNA GRANDE—See MAYAGUEZ, PR (Choice Cable)

SALINAS—See PONCE, PR (Choice Cable)

SAN GERMAN—See PONCE, PR (Choice Cable)

SAN JUAN—Liberty Cablevision. Now served by BAYAMON, PR [PR0002]

SAN JUAN—See BAYAMON, PR (Liberty Cablevision)

SAN LORENZO—See LUQUILLO, PR (Liberty Cablevision)

SAN SEBASTION—See CIALES, PR (Liberty Cablevision)

SANTA ISABEL—See PONCE, PR (Choice Cable)

TALLABOA—See PONCE, PR (Choice Cable)

TOA ALTA—See BAYAMON, PR (Liberty Cablevision)

TOA BAJA—See BAYAMON, PR (Liberty Cablevision)

TRUJILLO ALTO—See BAYAMON, PR (Liberty Cablevision)

UTUADO—See CIALES, PR (Liberty Cablevision)

VEGA ALTA—See LUQUILLO, PR (Liberty Cablevision)

VEGA BAJA—See LUQUILLO, PR (Liberty Cablevision)

VILLALBA—See PONCE, PR (Choice Cable)

YABUCOA—See CAGUAS, PR (Liberty Cablevision)

YAUCO—See PONCE, PR (Choice Cable)

RHODE ISLAND

BARRINGTON—See WEST WARWICK, RI (Cox Communications)

BARRINGTON—See WARREN, RI (Full Channel Inc)

BRADFORD—See WEST WARWICK, RI (Cox Communications)

BRISTOL COUNTY (PORTIONS)—See WARREN, RI (Full Channel Inc)

BRISTOL COUNTY—See WEST WARWICK, RI (Cox Communications)

BRISTOL—See WEST WARWICK, RI (Cox Communications)

BURRILLVILLE (town)—Cox Communications. Now served by WEST WARWICK, RI [RI0001]

BURRILLVILLE (TOWN)—See WEST WARWICK, RI (Cox Communications)

CENTRAL FALLS—See WEST WARWICK, RI (Cox Communications)

CHARLESTOWN—See WEST WARWICK, RI (Cox Communications)

COVENTRY—See WEST WARWICK, RI (Cox Communications)

CRANSTON—Cox Communications. Now served by WEST WARWICK, RI [RI0001]

CRANSTON—See WEST WARWICK, RI (Cox Communications)

CUMBERLAND—See WEST WARWICK, RI (Cox Communications)

EAST GREENWICH—See WEST WARWICK, RI (Cox Communications)

EAST PROVIDENCE—See WEST WARWICK, RI (Cox Communications)

EXETER (TOWN)—See WEST WARWICK, RI (Cox Communications)

FOSTER—See WEST WARWICK, RI (Cox Communications)

GLOCESTER (TOWN)—See WEST WARWICK, RI (Cox Communications)

HOPKINTON—See WEST WARWICK, RI (Cox Communications)

JAMESTOWN—See WEST WARWICK, RI (Cox Communications)

JOHNSTON—See WEST WARWICK, RI (Cox Communications)

LINCOLN—See WEST WARWICK, RI (Cox Communications)

LITTLE COMPTON—See WEST WARWICK, RI (Cox Communications)

MIDDLETOWN—See WEST WARWICK, RI (Cox Communications)

NARRAGANSETT—See WEST WARWICK, RI (Cox Communications)

NEW SHOREHAM—Formerly served by Block Island Cable TV. No longer in operation

NEWPORT & LINCOLN—Cox Communications. Now served by WEST WARWICK, RI [RI0001]

NEWPORT COUNTY—See WEST WARWICK, RI (Cox Communications)

NEWPORT NAVAL BASE—See WEST WARWICK, RI (Cox Communications)

NEWPORT—Cox Communications. Now served by WEST WARWICK, RI [RI0001]

NEWPORT—See WEST WARWICK, RI (Cox Communications)

NORTH KINGSTOWN—See WEST WARWICK, RI (Cox Communications)

Cable Community Index—South Carolina

NORTH PROVIDENCE—See WEST WARWICK, RI (Cox Communications)

NORTH SMITHFIELD—See WEST WARWICK, RI (Cox Communications)

PAWTUCKET—See WEST WARWICK, RI (Cox Communications)

PROVIDENCE COUNTY—See WEST WARWICK, RI (Cox Communications)

PROVIDENCE—See WEST WARWICK, RI (Cox Communications)

RICHMOND—See WEST WARWICK, RI (Cox Communications)

SCITUATE (TOWN)—See WEST WARWICK, RI (Cox Communications)

SMITHFIELD—See WEST WARWICK, RI (Cox Communications)

SOUTH KINGSTOWN—See WEST WARWICK, RI (Cox Communications)

TIVERTON—See WEST WARWICK, RI (Cox Communications)

WARREN—Full Channel Inc

WARWICK—See WEST WARWICK, RI (Cox Communications)

WEST GREENWICH—See WEST WARWICK, RI (Cox Communications)

WEST WARWICK—Cox Communications

WESTERLY—Cox Communications. Now served by WEST WARWICK, RI [RI0001]

WESTERLY—See WEST WARWICK, RI (Cox Communications)

WOONSOCKET—See WEST WARWICK, RI (Cox Communications)

SOUTH CAROLINA

ABBEVILLE COUNTY (PORTIONS)—See SPARTANBURG, SC (Charter Communications)

ABBEVILLE COUNTY (UNINCORPORATED AREAS)—See GREENWOOD, SC (Northland Cable Television)

ABBEVILLE—Charter Communications. Now served by SPARTANBURG, SC [SC0003]

ABBEVILLE—See SPARTANBURG, SC (Charter Communications)

ADAMS RUN—See NORTH CHARLESTON, SC (Comcast Cable)

AIKEN COUNTY (PORTIONS)—See GILBERT, SC (Comporium Cable)

AIKEN—Atlantic Broadband

ALLENDALE COUNTY—See ALLENDALE, SC (Atlantic Broadband)

ALLENDALE—Atlantic Broadband

ANCHOR POINT—Formerly served by Charter Communications. No longer in operation

ANDERSON COUNTY (PORTIONS)—See SPARTANBURG, SC (Charter Communications)

ANDERSON—Charter Communications. Now served by SPARTANBURG, SC [SC0003]

ANDERSON—See SPARTANBURG, SC (Charter Communications)

ANDREWS—See TURBEVILLE, SC (FTC. Formerly [SC0085]. This cable system has converted to IPTV)

ANDREWS—See COLUMBIA, SC (Time Warner Cable)

ARCADIA LAKES—See COLUMBIA, SC (Time Warner Cable)

ATLANTIC BEACH—See COLUMBIA, SC (Time Warner Cable)

AWENDAW—Formerly served by US Cable of Coastal Texas LP. Now served by Comcast Cable, NORTH CHARLESTON, SC [SC0001]

AWENDAW—See NORTH CHARLESTON, SC (Comcast Cable)

AYNOR—See HOMEWOOD, SC (Horry Telephone Coop)

BAMBERG COUNTY—See BAMBERG, SC (Atlantic Broadband)

BAMBERG—Atlantic Broadband

BARNWELL COUNTY—See BARNWELL, SC (Atlantic Broadband)

BARNWELL—Atlantic Broadband

BATESBURG—See COLUMBIA, SC (Time Warner Cable)

BEAUFORT COUNTY (PORTIONS)—See NORTH CHARLESTON, SC (Comcast Cable)

BEAUFORT COUNTY (SOUTHERN PORTION)—See BLUFFTON (village), SC (Hargray)

BEAUFORT COUNTY—See HILTON HEAD ISLAND, SC (Time Warner Cable)

BEAUFORT USMC AIR STATION—Comcast Cable

BEAUFORT—See LADY'S ISLAND, SC (Comcast Cable)

BELTON—Charter Communications. Now served by SPARTANBURG, SC [SC0003]

BELTON—See SPARTANBURG, SC (Charter Communications)

BENNETTSVILLE—MetroCast Communications

BERKELEY COUNTY (PORTIONS)—See NORTH CHARLESTON, SC (Comcast Cable)

BERKELEY COUNTY (PORTIONS)—See COLUMBIA, SC (Time Warner Cable)

BERKELEY COUNTY (PORTIONS)—See CHARLESTON, SC (WOW! Internet, Cable & Phone)

BERKELEY COUNTY (UNINCORPORATED AREAS)—See DANIEL ISLAND, SC (Home Telecom)

BETHUNE—Formerly served by Pine Tree Cablevision. No longer in operation

BETHUNE—Sandhill Telephone Cooperative

BISHOPVILLE—Time Warner Cable. Now served by COLUMBIA, SC [SC0002]

BISHOPVILLE—See TURBEVILLE, SC (FTC. Formerly [SC0085]. This cable system has converted to IPTV)

BISHOPVILLE—See COLUMBIA, SC (Time Warner Cable)

BLACKSBURG—See SPARTANBURG, SC (Charter Communications)

BLACKVILLE—See BARNWELL, SC (Atlantic Broadband)

BLUFFTON (village)—Hargray. Now served by BLUFFTON (village), SC [SC0020]

BLUFFTON (VILLAGE)—Hargray

BLUFFTON—See HILTON HEAD ISLAND, SC (Time Warner Cable)

BLYTHEWOOD—See COLUMBIA, SC (Time Warner Cable)

BONNEAU—See DANIEL ISLAND, SC (Home Telecom)

BOWMAN—Formerly served by Almega Cable. No longer in operation

BRIARCLIFF ACRES—Formerly served by Cablevision Industries Inc. Now served by Time Warner Cable, COLUMBIA, SC [SC0002]

BRIARCLIFF ACRES—See COLUMBIA, SC (Time Warner Cable)

BRISSEY ROCK—Formerly served by KLiP Interactive. No longer in operation

BROWNS FERRY—Time Warner Cable. Now served by COLUMBIA, SC [SC0002]

BROWNS FERRY—See COLUMBIA, SC (Time Warner Cable)

BRUNSON—See NORTH CHARLESTON, SC (Comcast Cable)

BUCKSPORT—See HOMEWOOD, SC (Horry Telephone Coop)

BUFFALO—See SPARTANBURG, SC (Charter Communications)

BURNETTOWN—See AIKEN, SC (Atlantic Broadband)

CALHOUN COUNTY (PORTIONS)—See COLUMBIA, SC (Time Warner Cable)

CALHOUN FALLS—Comcast Cable. Now served by ELBERTON, GA [GA0192]

CALLAWASSIE ISLAND—See BLUFFTON (village), SC (Hargray)

CAMDEN—TruVista Communications

CAMERON—Formerly served by Almega Cable. No longer in operation

CAMPOBELLO—See SPARTANBURG, SC (Charter Communications)

CASSATT—See CAMDEN, SC (TruVista Communications)

CAYCE—See COLUMBIA, SC (Time Warner Cable)

CENTRAL PACOLET—See SPARTANBURG, SC (Charter Communications)

CENTRAL—See SENECA, SC (Northland Cable Television)

CHAPIN—See COLUMBIA, SC (Time Warner Cable)

CHARLESTON AIR FORCE BASE—See NORTH CHARLESTON, SC (Comcast Cable)

CHARLESTON COUNTY (NORTHERN PORTION)—See NORTH CHARLESTON, SC (Comcast Cable)

CHARLESTON NAVAL BASE—See NORTH CHARLESTON, SC (Comcast Cable)

CHARLESTON—See COLUMBIA, SC (Time Warner Cable)

CHARLESTON—WOW! Internet, Cable & Phone

CHERAW—Time Warner Cable. Now served by COLUMBIA, SC [SC0002]

CHERAW—See COLUMBIA, SC (Time Warner Cable)

CHEROKEE COUNTY (UNINCORPORATED AREAS)—See SPARTANBURG, SC (Charter Communications)

CHESNEE—See SPARTANBURG, SC (Charter Communications)

CHESTER COUNTY (UNINCORPORATED AREAS)—See SPARTANBURG, SC (Charter Communications)

CHESTER COUNTY (UNINCORPORATED AREAS)—See ROCK HILL, SC (Comporium Communications)

CHESTER COUNTY (UNINCORPORATED AREAS)—See CHESTER, SC (TruVista Communications)

CHESTER—TruVista Communications

CHESTERFIELD (town)—Formerly served by NewWave Communications. This cable system has converted to IPTV. Now served by Sandhill Telephone Coop., BETHUNE, SC [SC5035]

CHESTERFIELD COUNTY—See COLUMBIA, SC (Time Warner Cable)

CHESTERFIELD—See BETHUNE, SC (Sandhill Telephone Cooperative)

CLARENDON COUNTY (PORTIONS)—See TURBEVILLE, SC (FTC. Formerly [SC0085]. This cable system has converted to IPTV)

CLARENDON COUNTY—See COLUMBIA, SC (Time Warner Cable)

CLEMSON—See SENECA, SC (Northland Cable Television)

CLINTON—See SPARTANBURG, SC (Charter Communications)

CLIO—See BENNETTSVILLE, SC (MetroCast Communications)

COLUMBIA—Time Warner Cable

South Carolina—Cable Community Index

COLUMBUS—See SPARTANBURG, NC (Charter Communications)

CONWAY—See HOMEWOOD, SC (Horry Telephone Coop)

CONWAY—See COLUMBIA, SC (Time Warner Cable)

CORDOVA—See COLUMBIA, SC (Time Warner Cable)

COTTAGEVILLE—Formerly served by Pine Tree Cablevision. No longer in operation

COWARD—See TURBEVILLE, SC (FTC. Formerly [SC0085]. This cable system has converted to IPTV)

COWPENS—See SPARTANBURG, SC (Charter Communications)

CROSS HILL—Formerly served by KLiP Interactive. No longer in operation

CROSS—Formerly served by Pine Tree Cablevision. No longer in operation

CROSS—See DANIEL ISLAND, SC (Home Telecom)

DANIEL ISLAND—Home Telecom

DARLINGTON COUNTY—See COLUMBIA, SC (Time Warner Cable)

DARLINGTON—See COLUMBIA, SC (Time Warner Cable)

DATAW ISLAND—See LADY'S ISLAND, SC (Comcast Cable)

DAUFUSKIE ISLAND—Resorts Cable TV

DEBORDIEU COLONY—Formerly served by Time Warner Cable. No longer in operation

DENMARK—See BAMBERG, SC (Atlantic Broadband)

DILLON COUNTY—See COLUMBIA, SC (Time Warner Cable)

DILLON—Formerly served by Adelphia Communications. Now served by Time Warner Cable, COLUMBIA, SC [SC0002]

DILLON—See COLUMBIA, SC (Time Warner Cable)

DONALDS—See SPARTANBURG, SC (Charter Communications)

DORCHESTER COUNTY (PORTIONS)—See COLUMBIA, SC (Time Warner Cable)

DUE WEST—See SPARTANBURG, SC (Charter Communications)

DUNCAN—See SPARTANBURG, SC (Charter Communications)

EASLEY—See SPARTANBURG, SC (Charter Communications)

EAST LAURINBURG—See COLUMBIA, NC (Time Warner Cable)

EASTOVER—See COLUMBIA, SC (Time Warner Cable)

EBENEZER—See SPARTANBURG, SC (Charter Communications)

EDGEFIELD COUNTY (PORTIONS)—See EDGEFIELD, SC (Northland Communications)

EDGEFIELD—Northland Communications

EDISTO BEACH—See NORTH CHARLESTON, SC (Comcast Cable)

EHRHARDT—Formerly served by Almega Cable. No longer in operation

ELGIN—See COLUMBIA, SC (Time Warner Cable)

ELKO—See BARNWELL, SC (Atlantic Broadband)

ELLOREE—Formerly served by Pine Tree Cablevision. No longer in operation

ENOREE—See SPARTANBURG, SC (Charter Communications)

ESTILL—Hargray. Now served by BLUFFTON (village), SC [SC0020]

ESTILL—See BLUFFTON (village), SC (Hargray)

FAIRFAX—See ALLENDALE, SC (Atlantic Broadband)

FAIRFIELD COUNTY (NORTHERN PORTION)—See ROCK HILL, SC (Comporium Communications)

FAIRFIELD COUNTY (PORTIONS)—See WINNSBORO, SC (Fairfield Communications)

FIVE POINTS—Northland Cable Television. Now served by SENECA, SC [SC0019]

FIVE POINTS—See SENECA, SC (Northland Cable Television)

FLORENCE COUNTY (PORTIONS)—See TURBEVILLE, SC (FTC. Formerly [SC0085]. This cable system has converted to IPTV)

FLORENCE COUNTY—See COLUMBIA, SC (Time Warner Cable)

FLORENCE—Time Warner Cable. Now served by COLUMBIA, SC [SC0002]

FLORENCE—See COLUMBIA, SC (Time Warner Cable)

FOLLY BEACH—Formerly served by US Cable of Coastal Texas LP. Now served by Comcast Cable, NORTH CHARLESTON, SC [SC0001]

FOLLY BEACH—See NORTH CHARLESTON, SC (Comcast Cable)

FOREST ACRES—See COLUMBIA, SC (Time Warner Cable)

FORT JACKSON—See COLUMBIA, SC (Time Warner Cable)

FORT LAWN—See ROCK HILL, SC (Comporium Communications)

FORT MILL—Comporium Communications. Now served by ROCK HILL, SC [SC0138]

FORT MILL—See ROCK HILL, SC (Comporium Communications)

FOUNTAIN INN—See SPARTANBURG, SC (Charter Communications)

FRIPP ISLAND—See LADY'S ISLAND, SC (Comcast Cable)

GAFFNEY—Charter Communications. Now served by SPARTANBURG, SC [SC0003]

GAFFNEY—See SPARTANBURG, SC (Charter Communications)

GASTON—Formerly served by Pine Tree Cablevision. No longer in operation

GEORGETOWN COUNTY (PORTIONS)—See TURBEVILLE, SC (FTC. Formerly [SC0085]. This cable system has converted to IPTV)

GEORGETOWN COUNTY (PORTIONS)—See HOMEWOOD, SC (Horry Telephone Coop)

GEORGETOWN COUNTY (PORTIONS)—See GEORGETOWN, SC (Southern Coastal Cable)

GEORGETOWN COUNTY—See COLUMBIA, SC (Time Warner Cable)

GEORGETOWN—Southern Coastal Cable

GEORGETOWN—See COLUMBIA, SC (Time Warner Cable)

GEORGIA STATE PRISON—See BLUFFTON (village), GA (Hargray)

GIBSON—See COLUMBIA, NC (Time Warner Cable)

GILBERT—Comporium Cable

GLOVERVILLE—See AIKEN, SC (Atlantic Broadband)

GOOSE CREEK—See NORTH CHARLESTON, SC (Comcast Cable)

GOOSE CREEK—See DANIEL ISLAND, SC (Home Telecom)

GOOSE CREEK—See COLUMBIA, SC (Time Warner Cable)

GRAY COURT—Charter Communications. Now served by SPARTANBURG, SC [SC0003]

GRAY COURT—See SPARTANBURG, SC (Charter Communications)

GREAT FALLS—See ROCK HILL, SC (Comporium Communications)

GREAT FALLS—See CHESTER, SC (TruVista Communications)

GREELEYVILLE—See TURBEVILLE, SC (FTC. Formerly [SC0085]. This cable system has converted to IPTV)

GREELEYVILLE—See COLUMBIA, SC (Time Warner Cable)

GREENVILLE COUNTY—Formerly served by KLiP Interactive. No longer in operation

GREENVILLE COUNTY—See SPARTANBURG, SC (Charter Communications)

GREENWOOD COUNTY—See GREENWOOD, SC (Northland Cable Television)

GREENWOOD—Northland Cable Television

GREER—Charter Communications. Now served by SPARTANBURG, SC [SC0003]

GREER—See SPARTANBURG, SC (Charter Communications)

HAMPTON COUNTY (PORTIONS)—See NORTH CHARLESTON, SC (Comcast Cable)

HAMPTON—Comcast Cable. Now served by NORTH CHARLESTON, SC [SC0001]

HAMPTON—See NORTH CHARLESTON, SC (Comcast Cable)

HANAHAN—See NORTH CHARLESTON, SC (Comcast Cable)

HANAHAN—See CHARLESTON, SC (WOW! Internet, Cable & Phone)

HARBISON—See COLUMBIA, SC (Time Warner Cable)

HARDEEVILLE—Hargray. Now served by BLUFFTON (village), SC [SC0020]

HARDEEVILLE—See BLUFFTON (village), SC (Hargray)

HARDEEVILLE—See HILTON HEAD ISLAND, SC (Time Warner Cable)

HARLEYVILLE—See DANIEL ISLAND, SC (Home Telecom)

HARTSVILLE—Time Warner Cable. Now served by COLUMBIA, SC [SC0002]

HARTSVILLE—See COLUMBIA, SC (Time Warner Cable)

HARTWELL VILLAS—Formerly served by Charter Communications. No longer in operation

HEATH SPRINGS—See ROCK HILL, SC (Comporium Communications)

HEMINGWAY—See COLUMBIA, SC (Time Warner Cable)

HICKORY GROVE—See ROCK HILL, SC (Comporium Communications)

HILDA—Formerly served by Pine Tree Cablevision. No longer in operation

HILTON HEAD ISLAND—Hargray

HILTON HEAD ISLAND—See BLUFFTON (village), SC (Hargray)

HILTON HEAD ISLAND—Time Warner Cable

HODGES—See GREENWOOD, SC (Northland Cable Television)

HOLLY HILL—Formerly served by Almega Cable. No longer in operation

HOLLYWOOD—Formerly served by US Cable of Coastal Texas LP. Now served by Comcast Cable, NORTH CHARLESTON, SC [SC0001]

HOLLYWOOD—See NORTH CHARLESTON, SC (Comcast Cable)

HOMEWOOD—Horry Telephone Coop

HOPKINS—Formerly served by Pine Tree Cablevision. No longer in operation

Cable Community Index—South Carolina

HORNEA PATH—See SPARTANBURG, SC (Charter Communications)

HORRY COUNTY (PORTIONS)—See HOMEWOOD, SC (Horry Telephone Coop)

HORRY COUNTY—See COLUMBIA, SC (Time Warner Cable)

HUNLEY PARK—See NORTH CHARLESTON, SC (Comcast Cable)

INMAN—See SPARTANBURG, SC (Charter Communications)

IRMO—See COLUMBIA, SC (Time Warner Cable)

ISLE OF PALMS—See NORTH CHARLESTON, SC (Comcast Cable)

IVA—Charter Communications. Now served by SPARTANBURG, SC [SC0003]

IVA—See SPARTANBURG, SC (Charter Communications)

JACKSON—See AIKEN, SC (Atlantic Broadband)

JAMES ISLAND—See NORTH CHARLESTON, SC (Comcast Cable)

JASPER COUNTY (PORTIONS)—See NORTH CHARLESTON, SC (Comcast Cable)

JASPER COUNTY (PORTIONS)—See HILTON HEAD ISLAND, SC (Time Warner Cable)

JEFFERSON—Formerly served by Pine Tree Cablevision. No longer in operation

JEFFERSON—See BETHUNE, SC (Sandhill Telephone Cooperative)

JOHNS ISLAND—Formerly served by US Cable of Coastal Texas LP. Now served by Comcast Cable, NORTH CHARLESTON, SC [SC0001]

JOHNS ISLAND—See NORTH CHARLESTON, SC (Comcast Cable)

JOHNSONVILLE—Time Warner Cable. Now served by COLUMBIA, SC [SC0002]

JOHNSONVILLE—See COLUMBIA, SC (Time Warner Cable)

JOHNSTON—See EDGEFIELD, SC (Northland Communications)

JONESVILLE—See SPARTANBURG, SC (Charter Communications)

KEOWEE KEY—See SPARTANBURG, SC (Charter Communications)

KERSHAW COUNTY (PORTIONS)—See COLUMBIA, SC (Time Warner Cable)

KERSHAW COUNTY—See CAMDEN, SC (TruVista Communications)

KERSHAW—See ROCK HILL, SC (Comporium Communications)

KIAWAH ISLAND—See NORTH CHARLESTON, SC (Comcast Cable)

KINGSTREE—See TURBEVILLE, SC (FTC. Formerly [SC0085]. This cable system has converted to IPTV)

KINGSTREE—See COLUMBIA, SC (Time Warner Cable)

LADSON—See CHARLESTON, SC (WOW! Internet, Cable & Phone)

LADY'S ISLAND—Comcast Cable

LAKE CITY—Time Warner Cable. Now served by COLUMBIA, SC [SC0002]

LAKE CITY—See TURBEVILLE, SC (FTC. Formerly [SC0085]. This cable system has converted to IPTV)

LAKE CITY—See COLUMBIA, SC (Time Warner Cable)

LAKE MURRAY—See GILBERT, SC (Comporium Cable)

LAKE MURRAY—See COLUMBIA, SC (Time Warner Cable)

LAKE VIEW—Time Warner Cable. Now served by COLUMBIA, SC [SC0002]

LAKE VIEW—See COLUMBIA, SC (Time Warner Cable)

LAKE WYLIE WOODS—See ROCK HILL, SC (Comporium Communications)

LAMAR—Formerly served by Pine Tree Cablevision. No longer in operation

LANCASTER COUNTY (PORTIONS)—See ROCK HILL, SC (Comporium Communications)

LANCASTER—Comporium Communications. Now served by ROCK HILL, SC [SC0138]

LANCASTER—See ROCK HILL, SC (Comporium Communications)

LANDRAN—See SPARTANBURG, NC (Charter Communications)

LANDRUM—See SPARTANBURG, SC (Charter Communications)

LANE—Time Warner Cable. Now served by COLUMBIA, SC [SC0002]

LANE—See TURBEVILLE, SC (FTC. Formerly [SC0085]. This cable system has converted to IPTV)

LANE—See COLUMBIA, SC (Time Warner Cable)

LANGLEY—See AIKEN, SC (Atlantic Broadband)

LATTA—See COLUMBIA, SC (Time Warner Cable)

LAURENS COUNTY (PORTIONS)—See SPARTANBURG, SC (Charter Communications)

LAURENS COUNTY (PORTIONS)—See GREENWOOD, SC (Northland Cable Television)

LAURENS—Charter Communications. Now served by SPARTANBURG, SC [SC0003]

LAURENS—See SPARTANBURG, SC (Charter Communications)

LAURINBURG—See COLUMBIA, NC (Time Warner Cable)

LEE COUNTY (PORTIONS)—See TURBEVILLE, SC (FTC. Formerly [SC0085]. This cable system has converted to IPTV)

LEE COUNTY—See COLUMBIA, SC (Time Warner Cable)

LEESVILLE—See COLUMBIA, SC (Time Warner Cable)

LEXINGTON COUNTY (NORTHWESTERN PORTION)—See GILBERT, SC (Comporium Cable)

LEXINGTON COUNTY—See COLUMBIA, SC (Time Warner Cable)

LEXINGTON—See COLUMBIA, SC (Time Warner Cable)

LIBERTY—See SENECA, SC (Northland Cable Television)

LINCOLNVILLE—See COLUMBIA, SC (Time Warner Cable)

LINCOLNVILLE—See CHARLESTON, SC (WOW! Internet, Cable & Phone)

LITTLE MOUNTAIN—See COLUMBIA, SC (Time Warner Cable)

LITTLE RIVER—Formerly served by Time Warner Cable. No longer in operation

LITTLE RIVER—See HOMEWOOD, SC (Horry Telephone Coop)

LOCKHART—Charter Communications. Now served by SPARTANBURG, SC [SC0003]

LOCKHART—See SPARTANBURG, SC (Charter Communications)

LONGS—See HOMEWOOD, SC (Horry Telephone Coop)

LORIS—See HOMEWOOD, SC (Horry Telephone Coop)

LUGOFF—Formerly served by Pine Tree Cablevision. No longer in operation

LUGOFF—See CAMDEN, SC (TruVista Communications)

LYMAN—See SPARTANBURG, SC (Charter Communications)

LYNCHBURG—See TURBEVILLE, SC (FTC. Formerly [SC0085]. This cable system has converted to IPTV)

MACEDONIA—See DANIEL ISLAND, SC (Home Telecom)

MANNING—See TURBEVILLE, SC (FTC. Formerly [SC0085]. This cable system has converted to IPTV)

MANNING—See COLUMBIA, SC (Time Warner Cable)

MARION COUNTY—See COLUMBIA, SC (Time Warner Cable)

MARION—See COLUMBIA, SC (Time Warner Cable)

MARLBORO COUNTY—See BENNETTSVILLE, SC (MetroCast Communications)

MAULDIN—See SPARTANBURG, SC (Charter Communications)

MAXTON—See COLUMBIA, NC (Time Warner Cable)

MAYESVILLE—See TURBEVILLE, SC (FTC. Formerly [SC0085]. This cable system has converted to IPTV)

MAYESVILLE—See COLUMBIA, SC (Time Warner Cable)

MCBEE—See BETHUNE, SC (Sandhill Telephone Cooperative)

McCLELLANVILLE—Formerly served by Allegiance Communications. No longer in operation

MCCOLL—See BENNETTSVILLE, SC (MetroCast Communications)

McCORMICK COUNTY—Formerly served by KLiP Interactive. No longer in operation

McCORMICK—Formerly served by McCormick Cable. No longer in operation

MEGGETT—See NORTH CHARLESTON, SC (Comcast Cable)

MONCKS CORNER—See DANIEL ISLAND, SC (Home Telecom)

MONCKS CORNER—See COLUMBIA, SC (Time Warner Cable)

MONETTA—See GILBERT, SC (Comporium Cable)

MOUNT PLEASANT—Comcast Cable. Now served by NORTH CHARLESTON, SC [SC0001]

MOUNT PLEASANT—See NORTH CHARLESTON, SC (Comcast Cable)

MOUNT PLEASANT—See CHARLESTON, SC (WOW! Internet, Cable & Phone)

MULLINS—Time Warner Cable. Now served by COLUMBIA, SC [SC0002]

MULLINS—See COLUMBIA, SC (Time Warner Cable)

MURRELLS INLET—See HOMEWOOD, SC (Horry Telephone Coop)

MYRTLE BEACH—Time Warner Cable. Now served by COLUMBIA, SC [SC0002]

MYRTLE BEACH—See HOMEWOOD, SC (Horry Telephone Coop)

MYRTLE BEACH—See COLUMBIA, SC (Time Warner Cable)

NEW ELLENTON—See AIKEN, SC (Atlantic Broadband)

NEWBERRY COUNTY (PORTIONS)—See SPARTANBURG, SC (Charter Communications)

NEWBERRY COUNTY (PORTIONS)—See NEWBERRY, SC (Comcast Cable)

NEWBERRY COUNTY (PORTIONS)—See COLUMBIA, SC (Time Warner Cable)

NEWBERRY—See SPARTANBURG, SC (Charter Communications)

NEWBERRY—Comcast Cable

NICHOLS—See COLUMBIA, SC (Time Warner Cable)

NINETY-SIX—See GREENWOOD, SC (Northland Cable Television)

South Carolina—Cable Community Index

NORRIS—See SENECA, SC (Northland Cable Television)

NORTH CHARLESTON (PORTIONS)—See DANIEL ISLAND, SC (Home Telecom)

NORTH CHARLESTON—Comcast Cable

NORTH CHARLESTON—See COLUMBIA, SC (Time Warner Cable)

NORTH CHARLESTON—See CHARLESTON, SC (WOW! Internet, Cable & Phone)

NORTH MYRTLE BEACH (PORTIONS)—See HOMEWOOD, SC (Horry Telephone Coop)

NORTH MYRTLE BEACH—See COLUMBIA, SC (Time Warner Cable)

NORTH STONE—See COLUMBIA, SC (Time Warner Cable)

NORTH—Formerly served by Pine Tree Cablevision. No longer in operation

NORWAY—Formerly served by Almega Cable. No longer in operation

OCONEE COUNTY (PORTIONS)—See SENECA, SC (Northland Cable Television)

OCONEE COUNTY (UNINCORPORATED AREAS)—See SPARTANBURG, SC (Charter Communications)

OKATIE—See BLUFFTON (village), SC (Hargray)

OLANTA—See TURBEVILLE, SC (FTC. Formerly [SC0085]. This cable system has converted to IPTV)

ORANGEBURG COUNTY (PORTIONS)—See COLUMBIA, SC (Time Warner Cable)

ORANGEBURG—See COLUMBIA, SC (Time Warner Cable)

PACOLET MILLS—See SPARTANBURG, SC (Charter Communications)

PACOLET—See SPARTANBURG, SC (Charter Communications)

PAGELAND—Formerly served by NewWave Communications. This cable system has converted to IPTV. Now served by Sandhill Telephone Coop., BETHUNE, SC [SC5035]

PAGELAND—See BETHUNE, SC (Sandhill Telephone Cooperative)

PAMPLICO—See COLUMBIA, SC (Time Warner Cable)

PATRICK—See BETHUNE, SC (Sandhill Telephone Cooperative)

PAWLEY'S ISLAND—See COLUMBIA, SC (Time Warner Cable)

PAXVILLE—See TURBEVILLE, SC (FTC. Formerly [SC0085]. This cable system has converted to IPTV)

PAXVILLE—See COLUMBIA, SC (Time Warner Cable)

PELION—See COLUMBIA, SC (Time Warner Cable)

PENDLETON—See SENECA, SC (Northland Cable Television)

PICKENS COUNTY (PORTIONS)—See SPARTANBURG, SC (Charter Communications)

PICKENS COUNTY—See SENECA, SC (Northland Cable Television)

PICKENS—Charter Communications. Now served by SPARTANBURG, SC [SC0003]

PICKENS—See SPARTANBURG, SC (Charter Communications)

PICKENS—See SENECA, SC (Northland Cable Television)

PIMLICO—See DANIEL ISLAND, SC (Home Telecom)

PINERIDGE—See COLUMBIA, SC (Time Warner Cable)

PINEWOOD—See TURBEVILLE, SC (FTC. Formerly [SC0085]. This cable system has converted to IPTV)

PINEWOOD—See COLUMBIA, SC (Time Warner Cable)

PINOPOLIS—See DANIEL ISLAND, SC (Home Telecom)

POOLER—See BLUFFTON (village), GA (Hargray)

PROSPERITY—See NEWBERRY, SC (Comcast Cable)

QUINBY—See COLUMBIA, SC (Time Warner Cable)

RAVENEL—See NORTH CHARLESTON, SC (Comcast Cable)

RAVENWOOD—See COLUMBIA, SC (Time Warner Cable)

REGENT PARK—Formerly served by Comporium Communications. No longer in operation

REIDSVILLE—See BLUFFTON (village), GA (Hargray)

REIDVILLE—See SPARTANBURG, SC (Charter Communications)

RICHBURG—See ROCK HILL, SC (Comporium Communications)

RICHBURG—See CHESTER, SC (TruVista Communications)

RICHLAND COUNTY—See COLUMBIA, SC (Time Warner Cable)

RIDGE SPRING—See GILBERT, SC (Comporium Cable)

RIDGELAND—Hargray. Now served by BLUFFTON (village), SC [SC0020]

RIDGELAND—See BLUFFTON (village), SC (Hargray)

RIDGEVILLE—Time Warner Cable. Now served by COLUMBIA, SC [SC0002]

RIDGEVILLE—See COLUMBIA, SC (Time Warner Cable)

RIDGEWAY—TruVista Communications. Now served by WINNSBORO, SC [SC0048]

RIDGEWAY—See WINNSBORO, SC (Fairfield Communications)

RIVER HILLS—See ROCK HILL, SC (Comporium Communications)

ROBESON COUNTY (PORTIONS)—See COLUMBIA, NC (Time Warner Cable)

ROCK HILL—Comporium Communications

ROCKVILLE—See NORTH CHARLESTON, SC (Comcast Cable)

ROWESVILLE—Formerly served by Almega Cable. No longer in operation

ROWLAND—See COLUMBIA, NC (Time Warner Cable)

RUBY—See BETHUNE, SC (Sandhill Telephone Cooperative)

SALEM—Charter Communications. Now served by SPARTANBURG, SC [SC0003]

SALEM—See SPARTANBURG, SC (Charter Communications)

SALUDA COUNTY (EASTERN PORTION)—See GILBERT, SC (Comporium Cable)

SALUDA COUNTY (PORTIONS)—See SALUDA, SC (Northland Communications)

SALUDA COUNTY (PORTIONS)—See COLUMBIA, SC (Time Warner Cable)

SALUDA—See SPARTANBURG, NC (Charter Communications)

SALUDA—Northland Communications

SAMPIT—Time Warner Cable. Now served by COLUMBIA, SC [SC0002]

SAMPIT—See COLUMBIA, SC (Time Warner Cable)

SANTEE CIRCLE—See DANIEL ISLAND, SC (Home Telecom)

SANTEE—Formerly served by Almega Cable. No longer in operation

SAVANNAH—See BLUFFTON (village), GA (Hargray)

SCOTLAND COUNTY—See COLUMBIA, NC (Time Warner Cable)

SCRANTON—See TURBEVILLE, SC (FTC. Formerly [SC0085]. This cable system has converted to IPTV)

SCRANTON—See COLUMBIA, SC (Time Warner Cable)

SEABROOK ISLAND—See NORTH CHARLESTON, SC (Comcast Cable)

SENECA—Northland Cable Television

SHARON—See ROCK HILL, SC (Comporium Communications)

SHAW AFB—See COLUMBIA, SC (Time Warner Cable)

SIMPSONVILLE—See SPARTANBURG, SC (Charter Communications)

SIX MILE—See SENECA, SC (Northland Cable Television)

SNELLING—See BARNWELL, SC (Atlantic Broadband)

SOCASTEE—See HOMEWOOD, SC (Horry Telephone Coop)

SOCIETY HILL—See COLUMBIA, SC (Time Warner Cable)

SOUTH CONGAREE—See COLUMBIA, SC (Time Warner Cable)

SPARTANBURG COUNTY—See SPARTANBURG, SC (Charter Communications)

SPARTANBURG—Charter Communications. Now served by SPARTANBURG, SC [SC0003]

SPARTANBURG—Charter Communications

SPRINGDALE—See COLUMBIA, SC (Time Warner Cable)

SPRINGFIELD—Formerly served by Almega Cable. No longer in operation

ST. GEORGE—Formerly served by Almega Cable. No longer in operation

ST. HELENA ISLAND—See LADY'S ISLAND, SC (Comcast Cable)

ST. MATTHEWS—See COLUMBIA, SC (Time Warner Cable)

ST. STEPHEN—Formerly served by Pine Tree Cablevision. No longer in operation

ST. STEPHEN—See DANIEL ISLAND, SC (Home Telecom)

STARR—See SPARTANBURG, SC (Charter Communications)

SULLIVAN'S ISLAND—See NORTH CHARLESTON, SC (Comcast Cable)

SUMMERTON—Time Warner Cable. Now served by COLUMBIA, SC [SC0002]

SUMMERTON—See TURBEVILLE, SC (FTC. Formerly [SC0085]. This cable system has converted to IPTV)

SUMMERTON—See COLUMBIA, SC (Time Warner Cable)

SUMMERVILLE—Time Warner Cable. Now served by COLUMBIA, SC [SC0002]

SUMMERVILLE—See NORTH CHARLESTON, SC (Comcast Cable)

SUMMERVILLE—See DANIEL ISLAND, SC (Home Telecom)

SUMMERVILLE—See COLUMBIA, SC (Time Warner Cable)

SUMMERVILLE—See CHARLESTON, SC (WOW! Internet, Cable & Phone)

SUMMIT—See GILBERT, SC (Comporium Cable)

SUMTER COUNTY (PORTIONS)—See TURBEVILLE, SC (FTC. Formerly [SC0085]. This cable system has converted to IPTV)

SUMTER COUNTY—See COLUMBIA, SC (Time Warner Cable)

SUMTER—See TURBEVILLE, SC (FTC. Formerly [SC0085]. This cable system has converted to IPTV)

SUMTER—See COLUMBIA, SC (Time Warner Cable)

Cable Community Index—South Dakota

SUN CITY—Hargray. This system has converted to IPTV. Now served by HILTON HEAD ISLAND, SC [SC5000]

SUN CITY—See HILTON HEAD ISLAND, SC (Hargray)

SUN CITY—See HILTON HEAD ISLAND, SC (Time Warner Cable)

SURFSIDE BEACH—Time Warner Cable. Now served by COLUMBIA, SC [SC0002]

SURFSIDE BEACH—See COLUMBIA, SC (Time Warner Cable)

SWANSEA—Formerly served by Pine Tree Cablevision. No longer in operation

SWANSEA—See GILBERT, SC (Comporium Cable)

TATTNALL COUNTY (PORTIONS)—See BLUFFTON (village), GA (Hargray)

TATUM—See BENNETTSVILLE, SC (MetroCast Communications)

TEGA CAY—See ROCK HILL, SC (Comporium Communications)

THE SUMMIT—Formerly served by Adelphia Communications. No longer in operation

TIMMONSVILLE—See COLUMBIA, SC (Time Warner Cable)

TRAVELERS REST—Charter Communications. Now served by SPARTANBURG, SC [SC0003]

TRAVELERS REST—See SPARTANBURG, SC (Charter Communications)

TRYON—See SPARTANBURG, NC (Charter Communications)

TURBEVILLE—FTC. This cable system has converted to IPTV. See TURBEVILLE, SC [SC5026]

TURBEVILLE—FTC. Formerly [SC0085]. This cable system has converted to IPTV

UNION COUNTY (PORTIONS)—See SPARTANBURG, SC (Charter Communications)

UNION—Charter Communications. Now served by SPARTANBURG, SC [SC0003]

UNION—See SPARTANBURG, SC (Charter Communications)

VARNVILLE—See NORTH CHARLESTON, SC (Comcast Cable)

WADMALAW ISLAND—See NORTH CHARLESTON, SC (Comcast Cable)

WAGENER—Formerly served by Pine Tree Cablevision. No longer in operation

WALHALLA—See SENECA, SC (Northland Cable Television)

WALTERBORO—Comcast Cable. Now served by NORTH CHARLESTON, SC [SC0001]

WALTERBORO—See NORTH CHARLESTON, SC (Comcast Cable)

WAMPEE—See HOMEWOOD, SC (Horry Telephone Coop)

WARE SHOALS—See GREENWOOD, SC (Northland Cable Television)

WELLFORD—See SPARTANBURG, SC (Charter Communications)

WEST COLUMBIA—See COLUMBIA, SC (Time Warner Cable)

WEST PELZER—Charter Communications. Now served by SPARTANBURG, SC [SC0003]

WEST PELZER—See SPARTANBURG, SC (Charter Communications)

WEST UNION—See SENECA, SC (Northland Cable Television)

WESTMINSTER—See SENECA, SC (Northland Cable Television)

WHITESVILLE—See DANIEL ISLAND, SC (Home Telecom)

WHITMIRE—Charter Communications. Now served by SPARTANBURG, SC [SC0003]

WHITMIRE—See SPARTANBURG, SC (Charter Communications)

WILD DUNES—Comcast Cable. Now served by NORTH CHARLESTON, SC [SC0001]

WILD DUNES—See NORTH CHARLESTON, SC (Comcast Cable)

WILLIAMSBURG COUNTY (PORTIONS)—See TURBEVILLE, SC (FTC. Formerly [SC0085]. This cable system has converted to IPTV)

WILLIAMSBURG COUNTY—See COLUMBIA, SC (Time Warner Cable)

WILLIAMSTON—Charter Communications. Now served by SPARTANBURG, SC [SC0003]

WILLIAMSTON—See SPARTANBURG, SC (Charter Communications)

WILLISTON—See BARNWELL, SC (Atlantic Broadband)

WINNSBORO—Fairfield Communications

WOODRUFF—See SPARTANBURG, SC (Charter Communications)

YEMASSEE—See NORTH CHARLESTON, SC (Comcast Cable)

YORK COUNTY—See ROCK HILL, SC (Comporium Communications)

YORK—See ROCK HILL, SC (Comporium Communications)

SOUTH DAKOTA

ABERDEEN TWP.—Formerly served by ITC. No longer in operation

ABERDEEN—Midco

AGAR—See GETTYSBURG, SD (Venture Communications. Formerly [SD0036]. This cable system has converted to IPTV)

AKASKA—See GETTYSBURG, SD (Venture Communications. Formerly [SD0036]. This cable system has converted to IPTV)

ALCESTER—See GARRETSON, SD (Alliance Communications)

ALCESTER—See VIBORG, SD (Clarity Telcom)

ALEXANDRIA—TrioTel Communications Inc. This cable system has converted to IPTV. Now served by SALEM, SD [SD5106]

ALEXANDRIA—See SALEM, SD (TrioTel Communications Inc)

ALPENA (TOWN)—See WOONSOCKET, SD (Santel Communications. Formerly [SD0096]. This cable system has converted to IPTV)

ALTAMONT—See CLEAR LAKE, SD (ITC. Formerly [SD0047]. This cable system has converted to IPTV)

AMHERST—See BRITTON, SD (Venture Communications. This cable system has converted to IPTV)

ANDOVER—See GROTON, SD (James Valley Telecommunications. Formerly [SD0030]. This cable system has converted to IPTV)

ANTELOPE—See WINNER, SD (Golden West Telecommunications)

ARLINGTON—See BROOKINGS, SD (Mediacom)

ARMOUR—Golden West Telecommunications. Now served by FREEMAN, SD [SD0038]

ARMOUR—See FREEMAN, SD (Golden West Telecommunications)

ARTESIAN—See WOONSOCKET, SD (Santel Communications. Formerly [SD0096]. This cable system has converted to IPTV)

ASHTON—Formerly served by Midcontinent Communications. No longer in operation

ASTORIA—Formerly served by Satellite Cable Services Inc. This cable system has converted to IPTV. Now served by ITC, CLEAR LAKE, SD [SD5042]

ASTORIA—See CLEAR LAKE, SD (ITC. Formerly [SD0047]. This cable system has converted to IPTV)

AURORA—See CLEAR LAKE, SD (ITC. Formerly [SD0047]. This cable system has converted to IPTV)

AURORA—See BROOKINGS, SD (Mediacom)

AVON—Golden West Telecommunications. Now served by FREEMAN, SD [SD0038]

AVON—See FREEMAN, SD (Golden West Telecommunications)

BALTIC—See GARRETSON, SD (Alliance Communications)

BALTIC—See SIOUX FALLS, SD (Midco)

BATH—See ABERDEEN, SD (Midco)

BEADLE COUNTY (PORTIONS)—See HURON, SD (Midco)

BELLE FOURCHE—See RAPID CITY, SD (Clarity Telcom)

BELLE FOURCHE—See RAPID CITY, SD (Midco)

BERESFORD—Beresford Cablevision Inc

BIG STONE CITY—See WATERTOWN, MN (Midco)

BIG STONE TWP.—See WATERTOWN, MN (Midco)

BISON—West River Cable Television

BLACK HAWK—See RAPID CITY, SD (Clarity Telcom)

BLACK HAWK—See RAPID CITY, SD (Midco)

BLUNT—See HIGHMORE, SD (Venture Communications. This cable system has converted to IPTV.)

BONESTEEL—See WINNER, SD (Golden West Telecommunications)

BOULDER CANYON—Midco. Now served by RAPID CITY, SD [SD0002]

BOULDER CANYON—See RAPID CITY, SD (Midco)

BOWDLE (RURAL)—See GETTYSBURG, SD (Venture Communications. Formerly [SD0036]. This cable system has converted to IPTV)

BOWDLE—See ABERDEEN, SD (Midco)

BOX ELDER—See RAPID CITY, SD (Clarity Telcom)

BOX ELDER—See RAPID CITY, SD (Midco)

BRADLEY—See CLEAR LAKE, SD (ITC. Formerly [SD0047]. This cable system has converted to IPTV)

BRANDON—See GARRETSON, SD (Alliance Communications)

BRANDON—See SIOUX FALLS, SD (Midco)

BRANDT—See CLEAR LAKE, SD (ITC. Formerly [SD0047]. This cable system has converted to IPTV)

BRENTFORD—See GROTON, SD (James Valley Telecommunications. Formerly [SD0030]. This cable system has converted to IPTV)

BRIDGEWATER—See FREEMAN, SD (Golden West Telecommunications)

BRISTOL—See ABERDEEN, SD (Midco)

BRITTON—Venture Communications. This cable system has converted to IPTV. See BRITTON, SD [SD5099]

BRITTON—Venture Communications. This cable system has converted to IPTV

South Dakota—Cable Community Index

BROOKINGS—See CLEAR LAKE, SD (ITC. Formerly [SD0047]. This cable system has converted to IPTV)

BROOKINGS—Mediacom

BROWN COUNTY—See ABERDEEN, SD (Midco)

BRUCE—Mediacom. Now served by BROOKINGS, SD [SD0005]

BRUCE—See BROOKINGS, SD (Mediacom)

BRYANT—Formerly served by Satellite Cable Services Inc. This cable system has converted to IPTV. Now served by ITC, CLEAR LAKE, SD [SD5042]

BRYANT—See CLEAR LAKE, SD (ITC. Formerly [SD0047]. This cable system has converted to IPTV)

BUFFALO GAP—See CUSTER, SD (Golden West Telecommunications)

BUFFALO—Formerly served by West River Cable Television. No longer in operation

BUFFALO—See BISON, SD (West River Cable Television)

BURKE—Golden West Telecommunications. Now served by WINNER, SD [SD0021]

BURKE—See WINNER, SD (Golden West Telecommunications)

BUSHNELL—See CLEAR LAKE, SD (ITC. Formerly [SD0047]. This cable system has converted to IPTV)

CANISTOTA—See FREEMAN, SD (Golden West Telecommunications)

CANOVA—See SALEM, SD (TrioTel Communications Inc)

CANTON (PORTIONS)—See VIBORG, SD (Clarity Telcom)

CANTON—See SIOUX FALLS, SD (Midco)

CARTHAGE—Alliance Communications. This cable system has converted to IPTV. Now served by HOWARD, SD [SD5082]

CARTHAGE—See HOWARD, SD (Alliance Communications. Formerly [SD0052]. This cable system has converted to IPTV)

CASTLEWOOD—Mediacom. Now served by BROOKINGS, SD [SD0005]

CASTLEWOOD—See CLEAR LAKE, SD (ITC. Formerly [SD0047]. This cable system has converted to IPTV)

CASTLEWOOD—See BROOKINGS, SD (Mediacom)

CAVOUR—Formerly served by Midcontinent Communications. No longer in operation

CENTERVILLE—See VIBORG, SD (Clarity Telcom)

CENTRAL CITY—See RAPID CITY, SD (Midco)

CHAMBERLAIN—See WHITE LAKE, SD (Midstate Communications)

CHANCELLOR—See VIBORG, SD (Clarity Telcom)

CHELSEA—See GROTON, SD (James Valley Telecommunications. Formerly [SD0030]. This cable system has converted to IPTV)

CHERRY CREEK—Formerly served by Cheyenne River Sioux Tribe Telephone Authority. No longer in operation

CHESTER—Formerly served by Satellite Cable Services Inc. This cable system has converted to IPTV. Now served by ITC, CLEAR LAKE, SD [SD5042]

CHESTER—See CLEAR LAKE, SD (ITC. Formerly [SD0047]. This cable system has converted to IPTV)

CLAIRE CITY—See NEW EFFINGTON, SD (RC Technologies. Formerly [SD018]. This cable system has converted to IPTV)

CLAREMONT—See GROTON, SD (James Valley Telecommunications. Formerly [SD0030]. This cable system has converted to IPTV)

CLARK—Formerly served by Satellite Cable Services Inc. This cable system has converted to IPTV. Now served by ITC, CLEAR LAKE, SD [SD5042]

CLARK—See CLEAR LAKE, SD (ITC. Formerly [SD0047]. This cable system has converted to IPTV)

CLEAR LAKE—Formerly served by HD Electric Cooperative. No longer in operation

CLEAR LAKE—ITC. This cable system has converted to IPTV. See CLEAR LAKE, SD [SD5042]

CLEAR LAKE—ITC. Formerly [SD0047]. This cable system has converted to IPTV

CODINGTON COUNTY (PORTIONS)—See WATERTOWN, SD (Midco)

COLMAN—Clarity Telcom. Now served by VIBORG, SD [SD0071]

COLMAN—Mediacom. Now served by BROOKINGS, SD [SD0005]

COLMAN—See VIBORG, SD (Clarity Telcom)

COLMAN—See BROOKINGS, SD (Mediacom)

COLOME—See WINNER, SD (Golden West Telecommunications)

COLTON—See SIOUX FALLS, SD (Midco)

COLUMBIA—See GROTON, SD (James Valley Telecommunications. Formerly [SD0030]. This cable system has converted to IPTV)

CONDE—Formerly served by Satellite Cable Services Inc. This cable system has converted to IPTV. Now served by James Valley Telecommunications, GROTON, SD [SD5005]

CONDE—See GROTON, SD (James Valley Telecommunications. Formerly [SD0030]. This cable system has converted to IPTV)

CORSICA—Golden West Telecommunications. Now served by FREEMAN, SD [SD0038]

CORSICA—See FREEMAN, SD (Golden West Telecommunications)

CORSON—See GARRETSON, SD (Alliance Communications)

COUNTRYSIDE MOBILE HOME PARK—See RAPID CITY, SD (Midco)

CRESBARD—Venture Communications. This cable system has converted to IPTV. See CRESBARD, SD [SD5104]

CRESBARD—Venture Communications. Formerly [SD0245]. This cable system has converted to IPTV

CROCKER—See CLEAR LAKE, SD (ITC. Formerly [SD0047]. This cable system has converted to IPTV)

CROOKS—See GARRETSON, SD (Alliance Communications)

CROOKS—See SIOUX FALLS, SD (Midco)

CUSTER COUNTY (UNINCORPORATED AREAS)—See CUSTER, SD (Golden West Telecommunications)

CUSTER—Golden West Telecommunications

DAKOTA DUNES—Long Lines. Now served by SALIX, IA [IA0510]

DE SMET—See BROOKINGS, SD (Mediacom)

DEADWOOD—See RAPID CITY, SD (Clarity Telecom)

DEADWOOD—See RAPID CITY, SD (Midco)

DELL RAPIDS—Golden West Telecommunications

DELMONT—Midstate Communications. Now served by WHITE LAKE, SD [SD0026]

DELMONT—See WHITE LAKE, SD (Midstate Communications)

DOLAND—See ABERDEEN, SD (Midco)

DUPREE—See EAGLE BUTTE, SD (CRST Telephone Authority. Formerly [SD0164]. This cable system has converted to IPTV)

EAGLE BUTTE—Cheyenne River Sioux Tribe Telephone. This cable system has converted to IPTV. See EAGLE BUTTE, SD [SD5048]

EAGLE BUTTE—CRST Telephone Authority. Formerly [SD0164]. This cable system has converted to IPTV

EDEN—Venture Communications Co-operative. This cable system has converted to IPTV. Now served by BRITTON, SD [SD5099]

EDEN—See BRITTON, SD (Venture Communications. This cable system has converted to IPTV)

EDGEMONT—Golden West Telecommunications. Now served by CUSTER, SD [SD0034]

EDGEMONT—See CUSTER, SD (Golden West Telecommunications)

EGAN—See BROOKINGS, SD (Mediacom)

ELK POINT—See VIBORG, SD (Clarity Telcom)

ELKTON—See CLEAR LAKE, MN (ITC. Formerly [SD0047]. This cable system has converted to IPTV)

ELKTON—See CLEAR LAKE, SD (ITC. Formerly [SD0047]. This cable system has converted to IPTV)

ELKTON—See BROOKINGS, SD (Mediacom)

ELLSWORTH AFB—See RAPID CITY, SD (Midco)

EMERY—TrioTel Communications Inc. This system has converted to IPTV. Now served by SALEM, SD [SD5106]

EMERY—See SALEM, SD (TrioTel Communications Inc)

ESTELLINE—Mediacom. Now served by BROOKINGS, SD [SD0005]

ESTELLINE—See CLEAR LAKE, SD (ITC. Formerly [SD0047]. This cable system has converted to IPTV)

ESTELLINE—See BROOKINGS, SD (Mediacom)

ETHAN—Santel Communications. Now served by WOONSOCKET, SD [SD5020]

ETHAN—Santel Communications. This cable system has converted to IPTV. Now served by WOONSOCKET, SD [SD5020]

ETHAN—See WOONSOCKET, SD (Santel Communications. Formerly [SD0096]. This cable system has converted to IPTV)

EUREKA—Valley Telecommunications Coop. Assn. This cable system has converted to IPTV. Now served by HERREID, SD [SD5032]

EUREKA—Valley Telecommunications Coop. Assn. This cable system has converted to IPTV. Now served by HERREID, SD [SD5032]

EUREKA—See HERREID, SD (Valley Telecommunications Coop. Assn. Formerly [SD0091]. This cable system has converted to IPTV)

Cable Community Index—South Dakota

EVERGREEN HOUSING—See PINE RIDGE, SD (Golden West Telecommunications)

FAIRFAX—Golden West Telecommunications. Now served by WINNER, SD [SD0021]

FAIRFAX—See WINNER, SD (Golden West Telecommunications)

FAITH—West River Cable Television

FALL RIVER COUNTY—See CUSTER, SD (Golden West Telecommunications)

FAULKTON—Venture Communications. This cable system has converted to IPTV. See FAULKTON, SD [SD5103]

FAULKTON—Venture Communications. Formerly [SD0170]. This cable system has converted to IPTV

FERNEY—See GROTON, SD (James Valley Telecommunications. Formerly [SD0030]. This cable system has converted to IPTV)

FLANDREAU—See VIBORG, SD (Clarity Telcom)

FLANDREAU—See BROOKINGS, SD (Mediacom)

FLORENCE—Formerly served by Satellite Cable Services Inc. This cable system has converted to IPTV. Now served by ITC, CLEAR LAKE, SD [SD5042]

FLORENCE—See CLEAR LAKE, SD (ITC. Formerly [SD0047]. This cable system has converted to IPTV)

FORT PIERRE—Midco

FRANKFORT—James Valley Telecommunications. This cable system has converted to IPTV. Now served by GROTON, SD [SD5005]

FRANKFORT—See GROTON, SD (James Valley Telecommunications. Formerly [SD0030]. This cable system has converted to IPTV)

FREDERICK—See ABERDEEN, SD (Midco)

FREEMAN—Golden West Telecommunications

GARRETSON—Alliance Communications

GARY—Formerly served by Satellite Cable Services Inc. Now served by ITC, CLEAR LAKE, SD [SD5042]

GARY—See CLEAR LAKE, SD (ITC. Formerly [SD0047]. This cable system has converted to IPTV)

GAYVILLE—See VIBORG, SD (Clarity Telcom)

GAYVILLE—See YANKTON, SD (Midco)

GEDDES—Midstate Communications. Now served by WHITE LAKE, SD [SD0026]

GEDDES—See WHITE LAKE, SD (Midstate Communications)

GETTYSBURG—Venture Communications. This cable system has converted to IPTV. See GETTYSBURG, SD [SD5023]

GETTYSBURG—Venture Communications. Formerly [SD0036]. This cable system has converted to IPTV

GLENHAM—Valley Telecommunications Coop. Assn. This cable system has converted to IPTV. Now served by HERREID, SD [SD5032]

GLENHAM—Valley Telecommunications Coop. Assn. This cable system has converted to IPTV. Now served by HERREID, SD [SD5032]

GLENHAM—See HERREID, SD (Valley Telecommunications Coop. Assn. Formerly [SD0091]. This cable system has converted to IPTV)

GOODWIN—See CLEAR LAKE, SD (ITC. Formerly [SD0047]. This cable system has converted to IPTV)

GRANT COUNTY (PORTIONS)—See WATERTOWN, SD (Midco)

GREGORY—Golden West Telecommunications. Now served by WINNER, SD [SD0021]

GREGORY—See WINNER, SD (Golden West Telecommunications)

GRENVILLE—See SISSETON, SD (Venture Communications. Formerly [SD0023]. This cable system has converted to IPTV)

GROTON—James Valley Telecommunications. This cable system has converted to IPTV. Now served by GROTON, SD [SD5005]

GROTON—James Valley Telecommunications. Formerly [SD0030]. This cable system has converted to IPTV

HARRISBURG—See VIBORG, SD (Clarity Telcom)

HARRISBURG—See SIOUX FALLS, SD (Midco)

HARROLD—See HIGHMORE, SD (Venture Communications. This cable system has converted to IPTV.)

HART RANCH—Midco. Now served by RAPID CITY, SD [SD0002]

HART RANCH—See RAPID CITY, SD (Midco)

HARTFORD—Golden West Telecommunications. Now served by DELL RAPIDS, SD [SD0028]

HARTFORD—See DELL RAPIDS, SD (Golden West Telecommunications)

HAYTI—Mediacom. Now served by BROOKINGS, SD [SD0005]

HAYTI—See CLEAR LAKE, SD (ITC. Formerly [SD0047]. This cable system has converted to IPTV)

HAYTI—See BROOKINGS, SD (Mediacom)

HECLA—See GROTON, SD (James Valley Telecommunications. Formerly [SD0030]. This cable system has converted to IPTV)

HENDRICKS—See CLEAR LAKE, MN (ITC. Formerly [SD0047]. This cable system has converted to IPTV)

HENRY—Formerly served by Satellite Cable Services Inc. Now served by ITC, CLEAR LAKE, SD [SD5042]

HENRY—See CLEAR LAKE, SD (ITC. Formerly [SD0047]. This cable system has converted to IPTV)

HERREID—Valley Telecommunications Coop. Assn. This cable system has converted to IPTV. Now served by HERREID, SD [SD5032]

HERREID—Valley Telecommunications Coop. Assn. Formerly [SD0091]. This cable system has converted to IPTV

HIGHMORE—Venture Communications. This cable system has converted to IPTV.

HILL CITY—Golden West Telecommunications. Now served by CUSTER, SD [SD0034]

HILL CITY—See CUSTER, SD (Golden West Telecommunications)

HILLS—See GARRETSON, MN (Alliance Communications)

HITCHCOCK—See HIGHMORE, SD (Venture Communications. This cable system has converted to IPTV.)

HOLABIRD—See HIGHMORE, SD (Venture Communications. This cable system has converted to IPTV.)

HORSE CREEK—See PINE RIDGE, SD (Golden West Telecommunications)

HOSMER—Valley Telecommunications Coop. Assn. This cable system has converted to IPTV. Now served by HERREID, SD [SD5032]

HOSMER—See HERREID, SD (Valley Telecommunications Coop. Assn. Formerly [SD0091]. This cable system has converted to IPTV)

HOT SPRINGS—Golden West Telecommunications. Now served by CUSTER, SD [SD0034]

HOT SPRINGS—See CUSTER, SD (Golden West Telecommunications)

HOUGHTON—See GROTON, SD (James Valley Telecommunications. Formerly [SD0030]. This cable system has converted to IPTV)

HOVEN—Venture Communications Cooperative. This cable system has converted to IPTV. Now served by HIGHMORE, SD [SD5022]

HOVEN—See HIGHMORE, SD (Venture Communications. This cable system has converted to IPTV.)

HOWARD—Alliance Communications. This cable system has converted to IPTV. See HOWARD, SD [SD5082]

HOWARD—Alliance Communications. Formerly [SD0052]. This cable system has converted to IPTV

HUDSON—Alliance Communications. Now served by GARRETSON, SD [SD0016]

HUDSON—Formerly served by Sioux Valley Wireless. Now served by Alliance Communications, GARRETSON, SD [SD0016]

HUDSON—See GARRETSON, SD (Alliance Communications)

HUMBOLDT—See DELL RAPIDS, SD (Golden West Telecommunications)

HUMBOLDT—See SIOUX FALLS, SD (Midco)

HURLEY—See VIBORG, SD (Clarity Telcom)

HURON—Midco

INWOOD—See GARRETSON, IA (Alliance Communications)

IPSWICH—See ABERDEEN, SD (Midco)

IRENE—See VIBORG, SD (Clarity Telcom)

IROQUOIS—Formerly served by Midcontinent Communications. No longer in operation

JAVA (RURAL)—See GETTYSBURG, SD (Venture Communications. Formerly [SD0036]. This cable system has converted to IPTV)

JAVA—See ABERDEEN, SD (Midco)

JEFFERSON—Formerly served by Jefferson Satellite Telecommunications Inc. Now served by Long Lines, SALIX, IA [IA0510]

KADOKA—See WALL, SD (Golden West Telecommunications)

KENNEBEC—Kennebec Telephone Co. Inc

KIMBALL—Midstate Communications. Now served by WHITE LAKE, SD [SD0026]

KIMBALL—See WHITE LAKE, SD (Midstate Communications)

KYLE—See PINE RIDGE, SD (Golden West Telecommunications)

LA BOLT—See CLEAR LAKE, SD (ITC. Formerly [SD0047]. This cable system has converted to IPTV)

LAKE ANDES—Formerly served by Satellite Cable Services Inc. Now served by Fort Randall Cable, TRIPP, SD [SD0087]

LAKE ANDES—See TRIPP, SD (Fort Randall Cable)

South Dakota—Cable Community Index

LAKE BENTON—See CLEAR LAKE, SD (ITC. Formerly [SD0047]. This cable system has converted to IPTV)

LAKE CITY—See BRITTON, SD (Venture Communications. This cable system has converted to IPTV)

LAKE NORDEN—Mediacom. Now served by BROOKINGS, SD [SD0005]

LAKE NORDEN—See CLEAR LAKE, SD (ITC. Formerly [SD0047]. This cable system has converted to IPTV)

LAKE NORDEN—See BROOKINGS, SD (Mediacom)

LAKE PRESTON—See BROOKINGS, SD (Mediacom)

LAKESIDE—See VIBORG, IA (Clarity Telcom)

LANE—See WESSINGTON SPRINGS, SD (Venture Communications. Formerly [SD0051]. This cable system has converted to IPTV)

LANGFORD—Venture Communications Cooperative. This cable system has converted to IPTV. Now served by BRITTON, SD [SD5099]

LANGFORD—See BRITTON, SD (Venture Communications. This cable system has converted to IPTV)

LARCHWOOD—See GARRETSON, IA (Alliance Communications)

LAWRENCE COUNTY (NORTHERN PORTION)—See RAPID CITY, SD (Midco)

LAWRENCE COUNTY (PORTIONS)—See RAPID CITY, SD (Clarity Telcom)

LEAD—See RAPID CITY, SD (Clarity Telcom)

LEAD—See RAPID CITY, SD (Midco)

LEBANON—See GETTYSBURG, SD (Venture Communications. Formerly [SD0036]. This cable system has converted to IPTV)

LEMMON—West River Cable Television. Now served by BISON, SD [SD0103]

LEMMON—See BISON, SD (West River Cable Television)

LENNOX—See VIBORG, SD (Clarity Telcom)

LENNOX—See SIOUX FALLS, SD (Midco)

LEOLA—Valley Telecommunications Coop. Assn. This cable system has converted to IPTV. Now served by HERREID, SD [SD5032]

LEOLA—Valley Telecommunications Coop. Assn. This cable system has converted to IPTV. Now served by HERREID, SD [SD5032]

LEOLA—See HERREID, SD (Valley Telecommunications Coop. Assn. Formerly [SD0091]. This cable system has converted to IPTV)

LETCHER—Santel Communications. Now served by WOONSOCKET, SD [SD5020]

LETCHER—See WOONSOCKET, SD (Santel Communications. Formerly [SD0096]. This cable system has converted to IPTV)

LOWER BRULE—Golden West Telecommunications. Now served by WINNER, SD [SD0021]

LOWER BRULE—See WINNER, SD (Golden West Telecommunications)

MADISON—See VIBORG, SD (Clarity Telcom)

MADISON—See SIOUX FALLS, SD (Midco)

MANDERSON—See PINE RIDGE, SD (Golden West Telecommunications)

MANSFIELD—See GROTON, SD (James Valley Telecommunications. Formerly [SD0030]. This cable system has converted to IPTV)

MARION—See FREEMAN, SD (Golden West Telecommunications)

MARTIN—See PINE RIDGE, SD (Golden West Telecommunications)

McINTOSH—West River Cable Television. Now served by BISON, SD [SD0103]

MCINTOSH—See BISON, SD (West River Cable Television)

MCLAUGHLIN—Formerly served by West River Cable Television. No longer in operation

MEADE COUNTY (PORTIONS)—See RAPID CITY, SD (Clarity Telcom)

MEADE COUNTY (WESTERN PORTION)—See RAPID CITY, SD (Midco)

MECKLING—See YANKTON, SD (Midco)

MELLETTE—Formerly served by Satellite Cable Services Inc. This cable system has converted to IPTV. Now served by James Valley Telecommunications, GROTON, SD [SD5005]

MELLETTE—See GROTON, SD (James Valley Telecommunications. Formerly [SD0030]. This cable system has converted to IPTV)

MENNO—See FREEMAN, SD (Golden West Telecommunications)

MIDLAND—See WALL, SD (Golden West Telecommunications)

MILBANK—See CLEAR LAKE, SD (ITC. Formerly [SD0047]. This cable system has converted to IPTV)

MILBANK—See WATERTOWN, SD (Midco)

MILLER—See HURON, SD (Midco)

MINA—See ABERDEEN, SD (Midco)

MINNEHAHA COUNTY—See DELL RAPIDS, SD (Golden West Telecommunications)

MISSION TWP.—Golden West Telecommunications. Now served by WINNER, SD [SD0021]

MISSION TWP.—See WINNER, SD (Golden West Telecommunications)

MITCHELL—Mitchell Telecom. This cable system has converted to IPTV. See MITCHELL, SD [SD5105]

MITCHELL—Midco

MITCHELL—Mitchell Telecom. Formerly [SD0256]. This cable system has converted to IPTV

MOBRIDGE—Midcontinent Communications. Now served by ABERDEEN, SD [SD0003]

MOBRIDGE—See ABERDEEN, SD (Midco)

MONROE—Formerly served by Sioux Valley Wireless. No longer in operation

MONTROSE—Golden West Telecommunications. Now served by DELL RAPIDS, SD [SD0028]

MONTROSE—See DELL RAPIDS, SD (Golden West Telecommunications)

MOUND CITY—Valley Telecommunications Coop. Assn. This cable system has converted to IPTV. Now served by HERREID, SD [SD5032]

MOUND CITY—See HERREID, SD (Valley Telecommunications Coop. Assn. Formerly [SD0091]. This cable system has converted to IPTV)

MOUNT VERNON—Santel Communications. This cable system has converted to IPTV. Now served by WOONSOCKET, SD [SD5020]

MOUNT VERNON—Santel Communications. This cable system has converted to IPTV. Now served by WOONSOCKET, SD [SD5020]

MOUNT VERNON—See WOONSOCKET, SD (Santel Communications. Formerly [SD0096]. This cable system has converted to IPTV)

MURDO—See WINNER, SD (Golden West Telecommunications)

NEW EFFINGTON—RC Technologies. This cable system has converted to IPTV. See NEW EFFINGTON, SD [SD5064]

NEW EFFINGTON—RC Technologies. Formerly [SD018]. This cable system has converted to IPTV

NEW UNDERWOOD—See WALL, SD (Golden West Telecommunications)

NEWELL—Formerly served by West River Cable Television. No longer in operation

NEWELL—See BISON, SD (West River Cable Television)

NORTHVILLE—See GROTON, SD (James Valley Telecommunications. Formerly [SD0030]. This cable system has converted to IPTV)

NUNDA—See CLEAR LAKE, SD (ITC. Formerly [SD0047]. This cable system has converted to IPTV)

OACOMA—Midstate Communications. Now served by WHITE LAKE, SD [SD0026]

OACOMA—See WHITE LAKE, SD (Midstate Communications)

OELRICHS—Golden West Telecommunications. Now served by CUSTER, SD [SD0034]

OELRICHS—See CUSTER, SD (Golden West Telecommunications)

OLDHAM—Alliance Communications. This cable system has converted to IPTV. Now served by HOWARD, SD [SD5082]

OLDHAM—See HOWARD, SD (Alliance Communications. Formerly [SD0052]. This cable system has converted to IPTV)

ONAKA—See HIGHMORE, SD (Venture Communications. This cable system has converted to IPTV.)

ONIDA—Venture Communications. This cable system has converted to IPTV. See ONIDA, SD [SD5024]

ONIDA—Venture Communications. Formerly [SD0092]. This cable system has converted to IPTV

ORIENT—See FAULKTON, SD (Venture Communications. Formerly [SD0170]. This cable system has converted to IPTV)

ORTONVILLE TWP.—See WATERTOWN, MN (Midco)

ORTONVILLE—See WATERTOWN, MN (Midco)

PARKER—See VIBORG, SD (Clarity Telcom)

PARKSTON—Santel Communications. This cable system has converted to IPTV. Now served by WOONSOCKET, SD [SD5020]

PARKSTON—See TRIPP, SD (Fort Randall Cable)

PARKSTON—See WOONSOCKET, SD (Santel Communications. Formerly [SD0096]. This cable system has converted to IPTV)

PENNINGTON COUNTY (PORTIONS)—See RAPID CITY, SD (Clarity Telcom)

Cable Community Index—South Dakota

PENNINGTON COUNTY (PORTIONS)—See RAPID CITY, SD (Midco)

PHILIP—See WALL, SD (Golden West Telecommunications)

PICKSTOWN—Formerly served by Satellite Cable Services Inc. Now served by Fort Randall Cable, TRIPP, SD [SD0087]

PICKSTOWN—See TRIPP, SD (Fort Randall Cable)

PIEDMONT—See RAPID CITY, SD (Clarity Telecom)

PIEDMONT—See RAPID CITY, SD (Midco)

PIERPONT—Venture Communications Cooperative. This cable system has converted to IPTV. Now served by BRITTON, SD [SD5099]

PIERPONT—See BRITTON, SD (Venture Communications. This cable system has converted to IPTV)

PIERRE—See FORT PIERRE, SD (Midco)

PINE RIDGE—Golden West Telecommunications

PLANKINTON—Golden West Telecommunications. Now served by FREEMAN, SD [SD0038]

PLANKINTON—See FREEMAN, SD (Golden West Telecommunications)

PLATTE—Midstate Communications. Now served by WHITE LAKE, SD [SD0026]

PLATTE—See WHITE LAKE, SD (Midstate Communications)

POLLOCK—Formerly served by Valley Cable & Satellite Communications Inc. This cable system has converted to IPTV. Now served by Valley Telecommunications Coop. Assn., HERREID, SD [SD5032]

POLLOCK—Valley Telecommunications Coop. Assn. This cable system has converted to IPTV. Now served by HERREID, SD [SD5032]

POLLOCK—See HERREID, SD (Valley Telecommunications Coop. Assn. Formerly [SD0091]. This cable system has converted to IPTV)

PRAIRIE ACRES ESTATES—Formerly served by Midcontinent Communications. No longer in operation

PRAIRIEWOOD (village)—Midcontinent Communications. Now served by ABERDEEN, SD [SD0003]

PRAIRIEWOOD (VILLAGE)—See ABERDEEN, SD (Midco)

PRESHO—See KENNEBEC, SD (Kennebec Telephone Co. Inc)

PUKWANA—See WHITE LAKE, SD (Midstate Communications)

RAMONA—Alliance Communications. This cable system has converted to IPTV. See HOWARD, SD [SD5082]

RAMONA—See HOWARD, SD (Alliance Communications. Formerly [SD0052]. This cable system has converted to IPTV)

RAPID CITY—Formerly served by USA Digital TV. No longer in operation

RAPID CITY—Clarity Telecom

RAPID CITY—Midco

RAYMOND—Formerly served by Satellite Cable Services Inc. Now served by ITC, CLEAR LAKE, SD [SD5042]

RAYMOND—See CLEAR LAKE, SD (ITC. Formerly [SD0047]. This cable system has converted to IPTV)

REDFIELD—Formerly served by Spink Electric. No longer in operation

REDFIELD—See GROTON, SD (James Valley Telecommunications. Formerly [SD0030]. This cable system has converted to IPTV)

REDFIELD—See ABERDEEN, SD (Midco)

REE HEIGHTS—See HIGHMORE, SD (Venture Communications. This cable system has converted to IPTV.)

RELIANCE—Golden West Telecommunications. Now served by WINNER, SD [SD0021]

RELIANCE—See WINNER, SD (Golden West Telecommunications)

RENNER—See SIOUX FALLS, SD (Midco)

REVILLO—See CLEAR LAKE, SD (ITC. Formerly [SD0047]. This cable system has converted to IPTV)

RIMROCK—Formerly served by Midco. No longer in operation

ROSCOE (RURAL)—See GETTYSBURG, SD (Venture Communications. Formerly [SD0036]. This cable system has converted to IPTV)

ROSCOE—See ABERDEEN, SD (Midco)

ROSEBUD—Golden West Telecommunications. Now served by WINNER, SD [SD0021]

ROSEBUD—See WINNER, SD (Golden West Telecommunications)

ROSHOLT—Venture Communications. This cable system has converted to IPTV. See ROSHOLT, SD [SD5100]

ROSHOLT—Venture Communications. Formerly [SD0115]. This cable system has converted to IPTV

ROSLYN (RURAL)—See SISSETON, SD (Venture Communications. Formerly [SD0023]. This cable system has converted to IPTV)

ROSLYN—See ABERDEEN, SD (Midco)

RUTLAND—See CLEAR LAKE, SD (ITC. Formerly [SD0047]. This cable system has converted to IPTV)

SALEM—TrioTel Communications Inc

SCOTLAND—See FREEMAN, SD (Golden West Telecommunications)

SELBY (RURAL)—See GETTYSBURG, SD (Venture Communications. Formerly [SD0036]. This cable system has converted to IPTV)

SELBY—See ABERDEEN, SD (Midco)

SENECA—See HIGHMORE, SD (Venture Communications. This cable system has converted to IPTV.)

SHERMAN—See GARRETSON, SD (Alliance Communications)

SHINDLER—See SIOUX FALLS, SD (Midco)

SINAI—See CLEAR LAKE, SD (ITC. Formerly [SD0047]. This cable system has converted to IPTV)

SIOUX CITY (NORTHERN PORTION)—See VIBORG, IA (Clarity Telcom)

SIOUX FALLS—Midco

SISSETON—Venture Communications. This cable system has converted to IPTV. See SISSETON, SD [SD5101]

SISSETON—Venture Communications. Formerly [SD0023]. This cable system has converted to IPTV

SOUTH SHORE—See CLEAR LAKE, SD (ITC. Formerly [SD0047]. This cable system has converted to IPTV)

SPEARFISH—Midco. Now served by RAPID CITY, SD [SD0002]

SPEARFISH—See RAPID CITY, SD (Clarity Telecom)

SPEARFISH—See RAPID CITY, SD (Midco)

SPENCER—See SALEM, SD (TrioTel Communications Inc)

SPRINGFIELD—Golden West Telecommunications. Now served by FREEMAN, SD [SD0038]

SPRINGFIELD—See FREEMAN, SD (Golden West Telecommunications)

ST. FRANCIS—Golden West Telecommunications. Now served by WINNER, SD [SD0021]

ST. FRANCIS—See WINNER, SD (Golden West Telecommunications)

ST. LAWRENCE—See HURON, SD (Midco)

STANDBURG—See CLEAR LAKE, SD (ITC. Formerly [SD0047]. This cable system has converted to IPTV)

STEPHAN—See HIGHMORE, SD (Venture Communications. This cable system has converted to IPTV.)

STICKNEY—See WHITE LAKE, SD (Midstate Communications)

STOCKHOLM—See CLEAR LAKE, SD (ITC. Formerly [SD0047]. This cable system has converted to IPTV)

STORM LAKE—See VIBORG, IA (Clarity Telcom)

STRATFORD—See GROTON, SD (James Valley Telecommunications. Formerly [SD0030]. This cable system has converted to IPTV)

STURGIS—See RAPID CITY, SD (Clarity Telecom)

STURGIS—See RAPID CITY, SD (Midco)

SUMMERSET—See RAPID CITY, SD (Clarity Telecom)

SUMMERSET—See RAPID CITY, SD (Midco)

SUMMIT—Formerly served by Satellite Cable Services Inc. This cable system has converted to IPV. Now served by RC Technologies, SUMMIT, SD [SD5073]

SUMMIT—RC Technologies. Formerly [SD0207]. This cable system has converted to IPTV

TABOR—Formerly served by Satellite Cable Services Inc. Now served by Fort Randall Cable, TRIPP, SD [SD0087]

TABOR—See TRIPP, SD (Fort Randall Cable)

TAKINI—Formerly served by Cheyenne River Sioux Tribe Telephone Authority. No longer in operation

TEA—See VIBORG, SD (Clarity Telcom)

TEA—See SIOUX FALLS, SD (Midco)

TIMBER LAKE—Formerly served by West River Cable Television. No longer in operation

TOLSTOY—See HIGHMORE, SD (Venture Communications. This cable system has converted to IPTV.)

TORONTO—Formerly served by Satellite Cable Services Inc. Now served by ITC, CLEAR LAKE, SD [SD5042]

TORONTO—See CLEAR LAKE, SD (ITC. Formerly [SD0047]. This cable system has converted to IPTV)

TRENT—Golden West Telecommunications. Now served by DELL RAPIDS, SD [SD0028]

TRENT—See DELL RAPIDS, SD (Golden West Telecommunications)

TRIPP—Santel Communications. This cable system has converted to IPTV. Now served by WOONSOCKET, SD [SD5020]

TRIPP—Fort Randall Cable

TRIPP—See WOONSOCKET, SD (Santel Communications. Formerly [SD0096]. This cable system has converted to IPTV

South Dakota—Cable Community Index

TULARE—See HIGHMORE, SD (Venture Communications. This cable system has converted to IPTV.)

TURTON—See GROTON, SD (James Valley Telecommunications. Formerly [SD0030]. This cable system has converted to IPTV)

TYNDALL—Formerly served by Satellite Cable Services Inc. Now served by Fort Randall Cable, TRIPP, SD [SD0087]

TYNDALL—See TRIPP, SD (Fort Randall Cable)

VALLEY SPRINGS—Alliance Communications. Now served by GARRETSON, SD [SD0016]

VALLEY SPRINGS—See GARRETSON, SD (Alliance Communications)

VEBLEN—See NEW EFFINGTON, SD (RC Technologies. Formerly [SD018]. This cable system has converted to IPTV)

VERMILLION—Formerly served by Mediacom. Now served by Midco, YANKTON, SD [SD0009]

VERMILLION—See YANKTON, SD (Midco)

VIBORG—Clarity Telcom

VOLGA—See BROOKINGS, SD (Mediacom)

WAGNER—Formerly served by Satellite Cable Services Inc. Now served by Fort Randall Cable, TRIPP, SD [SD0087]

WAGNER—See TRIPP, SD (Fort Randall Cable)

WAKONDA—See VIBORG, SD (Clarity Telcom)

WALL—Golden West Telecommunications

WALWORTH COUNTY (PORTIONS)—See ABERDEEN, SD (Midco)

WANBLEE—See PINE RIDGE, SD (Golden West Telecommunications)

WARD—See CLEAR LAKE, SD (ITC. Formerly [SD0047]. This cable system has converted to IPTV)

WARNER—See ABERDEEN, SD (Midco)

WATERTOWN—Clarity Telcom. Now served by VIBORG, SD [SD0071]

WATERTOWN—See VIBORG, SD (Clarity Telcom)

WATERTOWN—Midco

WAUBAY—See CLEAR LAKE, SD (ITC. Formerly [SD0047]. This cable system has converted to IPTV)

WAUBAY—See ABERDEEN, SD (Midco)

WEBSTER—See CLEAR LAKE, SD (ITC. Formerly [SD0047]. This cable system has converted to IPTV)

WEBSTER—See ABERDEEN, SD (Midco)

WENTWORTH—Formerly served by Satellite Cable Services Inc. Now served by ITC, CLEAR LAKE, SD [SD5042]

WENTWORTH—See CLEAR LAKE, SD (ITC. Formerly [SD0047]. This cable system has converted to IPTV)

WESSINGTON SPRINGS—Venture Communications. This cable system has converted to IPTV. See WESSINGTON SPRINGS, SD [SD5102]

WESSINGTON SPRINGS—Venture Communications. Formerly [SD0051]. This cable system has converted to IPTV

WESSINGTON—Venture Communications. This cable system has converted to IPTV. Now served by HIGHMORE, SD [SD5022]

WESSINGTON—Venture Communications. This cable system has converted to IPTV. Now served by HIGHMORE, SD [SD5022]

WESSINGTON—See HIGHMORE, SD (Venture Communications. This cable system has converted to IPTV.)

WEST WHITLOCK—Formerly served by Western Telephone Company. No longer in operation

WHITE LAKE—Midstate Communications

WHITE RIVER—See WINNER, SD (Golden West Telecommunications)

WHITE—Mediacom. Now served by BROOKINGS, SD [SD0005]

WHITE—See CLEAR LAKE, SD (ITC. Formerly [SD0047]. This cable system has converted to IPTV)

WHITE—See BROOKINGS, SD (Mediacom)

WHITEWOOD—Midcontinent Communications. Now served by RAPID CITY, SD [SD0002]

WHITEWOOD—See RAPID CITY, SD (Clarity Telcom)

WHITEWOOD—See RAPID CITY, SD (Midco)

WILLOW LAKE—Formerly served by Satellite Cable Services Inc. Now served by ITC, CLEAR LAKE, SD [SD5042]

WILLOW LAKE—See CLEAR LAKE, SD (ITC. Formerly [SD0047]. This cable system has converted to IPTV)

WILMOT—RC Technologies. This cable system has converted to IPTV. Now served by NEW EFFINGTON, SD [SD5067]

WILMOT—RC Technologies. This cable system has converted to IPTV. See NEW EFFINGTON, SD [SD5067]

WILMOT—See NEW EFFINGTON, SD (RC Technologies. Formerly [SD018]. This cable system has converted to IPTV)

WINFRED—See SALEM, SD (TrioTel Communications Inc)

WINNER—Golden West Telecommunications

WOLSEY—Santel Communications. This cable system has converted to IPTV. Now served by WOONSOCKET, SD [SD5020]

WOLSEY—See HURON, SD (Midco)

WOLSEY—See WOONSOCKET, SD (Santel Communications. Formerly [SD0096]. This cable system has converted to IPTV)

WOONSOCKET—Santel Communications. This cable system has converted to IPTV. Now served by WOONSOCKET, SD [SD5020]

WOONSOCKET—Santel Communications. Formerly [SD0096]. This cable system has converted to IPTV

WORTHING—See VIBORG, SD (Clarity Telcom)

YALE—Formerly served by Midcontinent Communications. No longer in operation

YANKTON—See VIBORG, SD (Clarity Telcom)

YANKTON—Midco

TENNESSEE

ABINGDON—See KNOXVILLE, VA (Comcast Cable)

ADAMS—See NASHVILLE, TN (Comcast Cable)

ADAMSVILLE—See JACKSON CITY, TN (Charter Communications)

ALAMO—See JACKSON CITY, TN (Charter Communications)

ALCOA—Charter Communications

ALCORN—See MEMPHIS, MS (Comcast Cable)

ALEXANDRIA—See LEBANON, TN (Charter Communications)

ALGOOD—See COOKEVILLE, TN (Charter Communications)

ALLARDT—See KNOXVILLE, TN (Comcast Cable)

ALTAMONT—Charter Communications. Now served by MANCHESTER, TN [TN0032]

ALTAMONT—See MANCHESTER, TN (Charter Communications)

ANDERSON COUNTY (PORTIONS)—See KNOXVILLE, TN (Comcast Cable)

APISON—See CHATTANOOGA, TN (EPB)

APPALACHIA (TOWN)—See KNOXVILLE, VA (Comcast Cable)

ARLINGTON—See MEMPHIS, TN (Comcast Cable)

ARRINGTON—See NASHVILLE, TN (Comcast Cable)

ARTHUR—See NEW TAZEWELL, TN (Vyve Broadband)

ASHLAND CITY—Comcast Cable. Now served by NASHVILLE, TN [TN0002]

ASHLAND CITY—See CLARKSVILLE, TN (Charter Communications)

ASHLAND CITY—See NASHVILLE, TN (Comcast Cable)

ATHENS—Comcast Cable. Now served by KNOXVILLE, TN [TN0004]

ATHENS—See KNOXVILLE, TN (Comcast Cable)

ATKINS—See KNOXVILLE, VA (Comcast Cable)

ATOKA—See MILLINGTON, TN (Millington CATV)

ATWOOD—See JACKSON CITY, TN (Charter Communications)

BAILEYTON—See KNOXVILLE, TN (Comcast Cable)

BAKEWELL—See CHATTANOOGA, TN (EPB)

BANEBERRY—See MORRISTOWN, TN (Charter Communications)

BARTLETT—See MEMPHIS, TN (Comcast Cable)

BAXTER—See COOKEVILLE, TN (Charter Communications)

BEAN STATION—See MORRISTOWN, TN (Charter Communications)

BEDFORD COUNTY (PORTIONS)—See COLUMBIA, TN (Charter Communications)

BEDFORD COUNTY (PORTIONS)—See MANCHESTER, TN (Charter Communications)

BEERSHEBA SPRINGS—See MANCHESTER, TN (Charter Communications)

BELFAST—See COLUMBIA, TN (Charter Communications)

BELL BUCKLE—See MANCHESTER, TN (Charter Communications)

BELLS—See JACKSON CITY, TN (Charter Communications)

BEN HUR—See KNOXVILLE, VA (Comcast Cable)

BENTON COUNTY (PORTIONS)—Benton County Cable

BENTON—Comcast Cable. Now served by KNOXVILLE, TN [TN0004]

BENTON—See KNOXVILLE, TN (Comcast Cable)

BETHEL SPRINGS—See JACKSON CITY, TN (Charter Communications)

Cable Community Index—Tennessee

BIG SANDY—See BENTON COUNTY (portions), TN (Benton County Cable)

BIG STONE GAP (TOWN)—See KNOXVILLE, VA (Comcast Cable)

BLAINE—See KNOXVILLE, TN (Comcast Cable)

BLEDSOE COUNTY (PORTIONS)—See PIKEVILLE, TN (Bledsoe Telephone Coop)

BLOUNT COUNTY (PORTIONS)—See ALCOA, TN (Charter Communications)

BLOUNT COUNTY (PORTIONS)—See KNOXVILLE, TN (Comcast Cable)

BLUFF CITY—See KINGSPORT, TN (Charter Communications)

BOLIVAR (TOWN)—Time Warner Cable

BON AQUA—See NASHVILLE, TN (Comcast Cable)

BRADEN—See MEMPHIS, TN (Comcast Cable)

BRADFORD—Formerly served by NewWave Communications. Now served by Time Warner Cable, MAYFIELD, KY [KY0037]

BRADLEY COUNTY—See CLEVELAND, TN (Charter Communications)

BRENTWOOD—See NASHVILLE, TN (Comcast Cable)

BRIDGEPORT—See JASPER, AL (Charter Communications)

BRIGHTON—See MEMPHIS, TN (Comcast Cable)

BRISTOL—Charter Communications. Now served by KINGSPORT, TN [TN0007]

BRISTOL—BTES

BRISTOL—BTES

BRISTOL—See KINGSPORT, TN (Charter Communications)

BRISTOL—See KINGSPORT, VA (Charter Communications)

BRISTOL—See KNOXVILLE, TN (Comcast Cable)

BROWNSVILLE—Time Warner Cable

BRUCETON—See JACKSON CITY, TN (Charter Communications)

BRUSH CREEK—See NASHVILLE, TN (Comcast Cable)

BULLS GAP—See KNOXVILLE, TN (Comcast Cable)

BURLISON—See MEMPHIS, TN (Comcast Cable)

BURNS—See NASHVILLE, TN (Comcast Cable)

BURSON PLACE—See KNOXVILLE, VA (Comcast Cable)

BYBEE—See KNOXVILLE, TN (Comcast Cable)

BYHALIA—See MEMPHIS, MS (Comcast Cable)

BYRDSTOWN—Celina Cable

CALHOUN—Charter Communications. Now served by CLEVELAND, TN [TN0013]

CALHOUN—See CLEVELAND, TN (Charter Communications)

CAMDEN—See JACKSON CITY, TN (Charter Communications)

CAMPBELL COUNTY (PORTIONS)—See JELLICO, TN (Access Cable Television Inc)

CAMPBELL COUNTY (PORTIONS)—See KNOXVILLE, TN (Comcast Cable)

CANNON COUNTY (PORTIONS)—See NASHVILLE, TN (Comcast Cable)

CARROLL COUNTY (PORTIONS)—See KNOXVILLE, VA (Comcast Cable)

CARTER COUNTY (PORTIONS)—See KINGSPORT, TN (Charter Communications)

CARTER COUNTY (PORTIONS)—See KNOXVILLE, TN (Comcast Cable)

CARTER COUNTY (PORTIONS)—Zito Media

CARTHAGE—Comcast Cable. Now served by NASHVILLE, TN [TN0002]

CARTHAGE—See NASHVILLE, TN (Comcast Cable)

CARYVILLE—See KNOXVILLE, TN (Comcast Cable)

CATOOSA COUNTY (PORTIONS)—See KNOXVILLE, GA (Comcast Cable)

CATOOSA COUNTY (PORTIONS)—See CHATTANOOGA, GA (EPB)

CEDAR HILL—See NASHVILLE, TN (Comcast Cable)

CELINA—Celina Cable

CENTERTOWN—See MANCHESTER, TN (Charter Communications)

CENTERVILLE—Charter Communications. Now served by COLUMBIA, TN [TN0017]

CENTERVILLE—See COLUMBIA, TN (Charter Communications)

CHAPEL HILL—Formerly served by Small Town Cable. No longer in operation

CHARLESTON—See CLEVELAND, TN (Charter Communications)

CHARLOTTE HALL—See NASHVILLE, TN (Comcast Cable)

CHATTANOOGA—Comcast Cable. Now served by KNOXVILLE, TN [TN0004]

CHATTANOOGA—See KNOXVILLE, TN (Comcast Cable)

CHATTANOOGA—EPB

CHEATHAM COUNTY (PORTIONS)—See CLARKSVILLE, TN (Charter Communications)

CHEATHAM COUNTY (PORTIONS)—See NASHVILLE, TN (Comcast Cable)

CHESTER COUNTY (PORTIONS)—See JACKSON CITY, TN (Charter Communications)

CHICKAMAUGA—See KNOXVILLE, GA (Comcast Cable)

CHILHOWIE—See KNOXVILLE, VA (Comcast Cable)

CHUCKEY—See KNOXVILLE, TN (Comcast Cable)

CHURCH HILL—See KINGSPORT, TN (Charter Communications)

CLAIBORNE COUNTY (PORTIONS)—See NEW TAZEWELL, TN (Vyve Broadband)

CLARKRANGE—See KNOXVILLE, TN (Comcast Cable)

CLARKSBURG—See JACKSON CITY, TN (Charter Communications)

CLARKSVILLE—Formerly served by Virginia Communications Inc. No longer in operation

CLARKSVILLE—Charter Communications

CLAXTON—See KNOXVILLE, TN (Comcast Cable)

CLAY COUNTY (UNINCORPORATED AREAS)—See CELINA, TN (Celina Cable)

CLEVELAND—Charter Communications

CLIFTON—Charter Communications. Now served by JACKSON CITY, TN [TN0008]

CLIFTON—See JACKSON CITY, TN (Charter Communications)

CLINTON—See KNOXVILLE, TN (Comcast Cable)

CLINTWOOD (TOWN)—See KNOXVILLE, VA (Comcast Cable)

COALFIELD—See KNOXVILLE, TN (Comcast Cable)

COALMONT—See MANCHESTER, TN (Charter Communications)

COBBLY NOB—Comcast Cable. Now served by KNOXVILLE, TN [TN0004]

COBBLY NOB—See KNOXVILLE, TN (Comcast Cable)

COCKE COUNTY (PORTIONS)—See KNOXVILLE, TN (Comcast Cable)

COCKE COUNTY—See MORRISTOWN, TN (Charter Communications)

COEBURN (TOWN)—See KNOXVILLE, VA (Comcast Cable)

COFFEE COUNTY (PORTIONS)—See MANCHESTER, TN (Charter Communications)

COLDWATER—See MEMPHIS, MS (Comcast Cable)

COLLEGEDALE—See KNOXVILLE, TN (Comcast Cable)

COLLEGEDALE—See CHATTANOOGA, TN (EPB)

COLLIERVILLE—See MEMPHIS, TN (Comcast Cable)

COLLINWOOD—See JACKSON CITY, TN (Charter Communications)

COLUMBIA—Charter Communications

COLUMBIA—CPWS Broadband

COMO—See MEMPHIS, MS (Comcast Cable)

COOKEVILLE—Charter Communications

COOPERTOWN—See CLARKSVILLE, TN (Charter Communications)

CORNERSVILLE—Formerly served by Small Town Cable. No longer in operation

COSBY—See KNOXVILLE, TN (Comcast Cable)

COTTONTOWN—See NASHVILLE, TN (Comcast Cable)

COUNCE—Pickwick Cablevision

COVINGTON—Comcast Cable. Now served by MEMPHIS, TN [TN0001]

COVINGTON—See MEMPHIS, TN (Comcast Cable)

COWAN—See NASHVILLE, TN (Comcast Cable)

CRAB ORCHARD—See CUMBERLAND COUNTY, TN (Spirit Broadband)

CRENSHAW—See MEMPHIS, MS (Comcast Cable)

CRITTENDEN COUNTY (PORTIONS)—See MEMPHIS, AR (Comcast Cable)

CROCKETT COUNTY (PORTIONS)—See JACKSON CITY, TN (Charter Communications)

CROSS PLAINS—See NASHVILLE, TN (Comcast Cable)

CROSSVILLE—Charter Communications

CROSSVILLE—See KNOXVILLE, TN (Comcast Cable)

CROSSVILLE—See CUMBERLAND COUNTY, TN (Spirit Broadband)

CRUMP—See JACKSON CITY, TN (Charter Communications)

CUMBERLAND COUNTY (PORTIONS)—See PIKEVILLE, TN (Bledsoe Telephone Coop)

CUMBERLAND COUNTY (PORTIONS)—See KNOXVILLE, TN (Comcast Cable)

CUMBERLAND COUNTY—See CROSSVILLE, TN (Charter Communications)

CUMBERLAND COUNTY—Spirit Broadband

CUMBERLAND FURNACE—See NASHVILLE, TN (Comcast Cable)

CUMBERLAND GAP—See NEW TAZEWELL, TN (Vyve Broadband)

DADE COUNTY (PORTIONS)—See KNOXVILLE, GA (Comcast Cable)

DADE COUNTY (PORTIONS)—See CHATTANOOGA, GA (EPB)

DANDRIDGE—See MORRISTOWN, TN (Charter Communications)

DANDRIDGE—Haywood Cablevision

Tennessee—Cable Community Index

DAVIDSON COUNTY (PORTIONS)—See NASHVILLE, TN (Comcast Cable)

DAYTON—Charter Communications. Now served by CLEVELAND, TN [TN0013]

DAYTON—See CLEVELAND, TN (Charter Communications)

DECATUR COUNTY (PORTIONS)—See JACKSON CITY, TN (Charter Communications)

DECATUR—Charter Communications. Now served by CLEVELAND, TN [TN0013]

DECATUR—See CLEVELAND, TN (Charter Communications)

DECATURVILLE—See JACKSON CITY, TN (Charter Communications)

DECHERD—See NASHVILLE, TN (Comcast Cable)

DEER LODGE—See KNOXVILLE, TN (Comcast Cable)

DEKALB COUNTY (PORTIONS)—See LEBANON, TN (Charter Communications)

DEKALB COUNTY (PORTIONS)—See NASHVILLE, TN (Comcast Cable)

DELANO—See KNOXVILLE, TN (Comcast Cable)

DESOTO COUNTY (PORTIONS)—See MEMPHIS, MS (Comcast Cable)

DICKENSON COUNTY (PORTIONS)—See KNOXVILLE, VA (Comcast Cable)

DICKSON COUNTY (PORTIONS)—See NASHVILLE, TN (Comcast Cable)

DICKSON—See NASHVILLE, TN (Comcast Cable)

DOVER—Mediacom. Now served by TRENTON, KY [KY0101]

DOWELLTOWN—See LEBANON, TN (Charter Communications)

DOWELLTOWN—See NASHVILLE, TN (Comcast Cable)

DOYLE—See COOKEVILLE, TN (Charter Communications)

DRESDEN (village)—Formerly served by Dresden Cable Inc. No longer in operation

DUFFIELD (TOWN)—See KNOXVILLE, VA (Comcast Cable)

DUNLAP—Bledsoe Telephone Coop. Now served by PIKEVILLE, TN [TN0158]

DUNLAP—See PIKEVILLE, TN (Bledsoe Telephone Coop)

DUNLAP—See ORME, TN (BlueBridge Media)

DYER COUNTY—See DYERSBURG, TN (Cable One)

DYER—Time Warner Cable. Now served by MAYFIELD, KY [KY0037]

DYERSBURG—Cable One

EAGLEVILLE—Formerly served by Small Town Cable. No longer in operation

EARLE—See MEMPHIS, AR (Comcast Cable)

EAST RIDGE—See KNOXVILLE, TN (Comcast Cable)

EAST RIDGE—See CHATTANOOGA, TN (EPB)

ELIZABETHTON—Charter Communications. Now served by KINGSPORT, TN [TN0007]

ELIZABETHTON—See KINGSPORT, TN (Charter Communications)

ELMWOOD—See NASHVILLE, TN (Comcast Cable)

EMBREEVILLE—See KNOXVILLE, TN (Comcast Cable)

ENGLEWOOD—See KNOXVILLE, TN (Comcast Cable)

ERIN—Peoples CATV Inc

ERWIN—See KNOXVILLE, TN (Comcast Cable)

ESTILL SPRINGS—See NASHVILLE, TN (Comcast Cable)

ETOWAH—See KNOXVILLE, TN (Comcast Cable)

EVA—See BENTON COUNTY (portions), TN (Benton County Cable)

FAIRFIELD GLADE—Comcast Cable. Now served by KNOXVILLE, TN [TN0004]

FAIRFIELD GLADE—See KNOXVILLE, TN (Comcast Cable)

FAIRVIEW—See NASHVILLE, TN (Comcast Cable)

FALL BRANCH—See KNOXVILLE, TN (Comcast Cable)

FARRAGUT—See ALCOA, TN (Charter Communications)

FAYETTE COUNTY (PORTIONS)—See MEMPHIS, TN (Comcast Cable)

FAYETTEVILLE—Charter Communications. Now served by MANCHESTER, TN [TN0032]

FAYETTEVILLE—See MANCHESTER, TN (Charter Communications)

FAYETTEVILLE—Fayette Public Utilities

FENTRESS COUNTY (PORTIONS)—See KNOXVILLE, TN (Comcast Cable)

FLINTSTONE—See CHATTANOOGA, GA (EPB)

FLINTVILLE—Charter Communications. Now served by MANCHESTER, TN [TN0032]

FLINTVILLE—See MANCHESTER, TN (Charter Communications)

FORT CAMPBELL—See NASHVILLE, KY (Comcast Cable)

FORT OGLETHORPE—See KNOXVILLE, GA (Comcast Cable)

FRANKLIN COUNTY (PORTIONS)—See MANCHESTER, TN (Charter Communications)

FRANKLIN COUNTY (PORTIONS)—See NASHVILLE, TN (Comcast Cable)

FRANKLIN—See NASHVILLE, KY (Comcast Cable)

FRANKLIN—See NASHVILLE, TN (Comcast Cable)

FRIENDSHIP—Cable One

FRIENDSVILLE (town)—Comcast Cable. Now served by KNOXVILLE, TN [TN0004]

FRIENDSVILLE (TOWN)—See KNOXVILLE, TN (Comcast Cable)

FRIES (TOWN)—See KNOXVILLE, VA (Comcast Cable)

GADSDEN—See JACKSON CITY, TN (Charter Communications)

GAINESBORO—Gainesboro CATV Inc.

GALAX—See KNOXVILLE, VA (Comcast Cable)

GALLATIN—See NASHVILLE, TN (Comcast Cable)

GALLAWAY—See MEMPHIS, TN (Comcast Cable)

GARLAND—See MEMPHIS, TN (Comcast Cable)

GATES—See BROWNSVILLE, TN (Time Warner Cable)

GATLINBURG—Charter Communications. Now served by ALCOA, TN [TN0151]

GATLINBURG—See ALCOA, TN (Charter Communications)

GATLINBURG—See KNOXVILLE, TN (Comcast Cable)

GERMANTOWN—See MEMPHIS, TN (Comcast Cable)

GIBSON COUNTY (PORTIONS)—See JACKSON CITY, TN (Charter Communications)

GIBSON—See JACKSON CITY, TN (Charter Communications)

GILES COUNTY (PORTIONS)—See COLUMBIA, TN (Charter Communications)

GILT EDGE—See MEMPHIS, TN (Comcast Cable)

GLADE SPRING—See KNOXVILLE, VA (Comcast Cable)

GLEASON—See JACKSON CITY, TN (Charter Communications)

GOODLETTSVILLE—See NASHVILLE, TN (Comcast Cable)

GORDONSVILLE—See LEBANON, TN (Charter Communications)

GRAINGER COUNTY (NORTHEASTERN PORTION)—See MORRISTOWN, TN (Charter Communications)

GRAND JUNCTION—See MEMPHIS, TN (Comcast Cable)

GRAY—Comcast Cable. Now served by KNOXVILLE, TN [TN0004]

GRAY—See KNOXVILLE, TN (Comcast Cable)

GRAYSON COUNTY (PORTIONS)—See KNOXVILLE, VA (Comcast Cable)

GRAYSVILLE—See CLEVELAND, TN (Charter Communications)

GRAYSVILLE—See CHATTANOOGA, TN (EPB)

GREENBACK (TOWN)—See KNOXVILLE, TN (Comcast Cable)

GREENBRIER—See NASHVILLE, TN (Comcast Cable)

GREENE COUNTY (PORTIONS)—See KNOXVILLE, TN (Comcast Cable)

GREENFIELD—See JACKSON CITY, TN (Charter Communications)

GREENVILLE—Comcast Cable. Now served by KNOXVILLE, TN [TN0004]

GREENVILLE—See KNOXVILLE, TN (Comcast Cable)

GRIMSLEY—Comcast Cable. Now served by KNOXVILLE, TN [TN0004]

GRIMSLEY—See KNOXVILLE, TN (Comcast Cable)

GRUETLI-LAAGER—See MANCHESTER, TN (Charter Communications)

GRUNDY COUNTY (PORTIONS)—See MANCHESTER, TN (Charter Communications)

GUILD—See CHATTANOOGA, TN (EPB)

HALLS—See BROWNSVILLE, TN (Time Warner Cable)

HAMBLEN COUNTY (PORTIONS)—See KNOXVILLE, TN (Comcast Cable)

HAMBLEN COUNTY—See MORRISTOWN, TN (Charter Communications)

HAMILTON COUNTY (PORTIONS)—See PIKEVILLE, TN (Bledsoe Telephone Coop)

HAMILTON COUNTY (PORTIONS)—See KNOXVILLE, TN (Comcast Cable)

HAMILTON COUNTY (PORTIONS)—See CHATTANOOGA, TN (EPB)

HAMPTON—See KNOXVILLE, TN (Comcast Cable)

HARDEMAN COUNTY (PORTIONS)—See MEMPHIS, TN (Comcast Cable)

HARDEMAN COUNTY (PORTIONS)—See BOLIVAR (town), TN (Time Warner Cable)

HARDIN COUNTY (PORTIONS)—See JACKSON CITY, TN (Charter Communications)

HARDIN COUNTY (PORTIONS)—See COUNCE, TN (Pickwick Cablevision)

HARRIMAN—Comcast Cable. Now served by KNOXVILLE, TN [TN0004]

HARRIMAN—See KNOXVILLE, TN (Comcast Cable)

HARRISON—See CHATTANOOGA, TN (EPB)

HARROGATE—See NEW TAZEWELL, TN (Vyve Broadband)

284-Cable Community Index

TV & Cable Factbook No. 85

Cable Community Index—Tennessee

HARTSVILLE—Comcast Cable. Now served by NASHVILLE, TN [TN0002]

HARTSVILLE—See NASHVILLE, TN (Comcast Cable)

HAWKINS COUNTY (CENTRAL PORTION)—See ROGERSVILLE, TN (Middle Tennessee Broadband)

HAWKINS COUNTY (PORTIONS)—See KNOXVILLE, TN (Comcast Cable)

HAWKINS COUNTY—See KINGSPORT, TN (Charter Communications)

HAYWOOD COUNTY (PORTIONS)—See MEMPHIS, TN (Comcast Cable)

HAYWOOD COUNTY (PORTIONS)—See BROWNSVILLE, TN (Time Warner Cable)

HELENWOOD—See KNOXVILLE, TN (Comcast Cable)

HENDERSON COUNTY—See JACKSON CITY, TN (Charter Communications)

HENDERSON—Charter Communications. Now served by JACKSON CITY, TN [TN0008]

HENDERSON—See JACKSON CITY, TN (Charter Communications)

HENDERSONVILLE—See NASHVILLE, TN (Comcast Cable)

HENNING—See BROWNSVILLE, TN (Time Warner Cable)

HENRY COUNTY (UNINCORPORATED AREAS)—See JACKSON CITY, TN (Charter Communications)

HENRY—Peoples CATV Inc. Now served by ERIN, TN [TN0083]

HENRY—See ERIN, TN (Peoples CATV Inc)

HERMITAGE—See NASHVILLE, TN (Comcast Cable)

HERNANDO—See MEMPHIS, MS (Comcast Cable)

HICKMAN COUNTY (PORTIONS)—See NASHVILLE, TN (Comcast Cable)

HILLSVILLE (TOWN)—See KNOXVILLE, VA (Comcast Cable)

HIXSON—See CHATTANOOGA, TN (EPB)

HOHENWALD—Charter Communications. Now served by COLUMBIA, TN [TN0017]

HOHENWALD—See COLUMBIA, TN (Charter Communications)

HOLLOW ROCK—See JACKSON CITY, TN (Charter Communications)

HORN LAKE—See MEMPHIS, MS (Comcast Cable)

HUMBOLDT—Click1.Net

HUMPHREYS COUNTY (PORTIONS)—See NASHVILLE, TN (Comcast Cable)

HUNTINGDON—See JACKSON CITY, TN (Charter Communications)

HUNTLAND—Mediacom

HUNTSVILLE—Comcast Cable. Now served by KNOXVILLE, TN [TN0004]

HUNTSVILLE—See KNOXVILLE, TN (Comcast Cable)

INDEPENDENCE (TOWN)—See KNOXVILLE, VA (Comcast Cable)

IRON CITY—See COLUMBIA, TN (Charter Communications)

JACKSBORO—See KNOXVILLE, TN (Comcast Cable)

JACKSON CITY—Charter Communications

JACKSON COUNTY (PORTIONS)—See GAINESBORO, TN (Gainesboro CATV Inc.)

JAMESTOWN—Comcast Cable. Now served by KNOXVILLE, TN [TN0004]

JAMESTOWN—See KNOXVILLE, TN (Comcast Cable)

JASPER—See ORME, TN (BlueBridge Media)

JASPER—Charter Communications

JEFFERSON CITY—See MORRISTOWN, TN (Charter Communications)

JEFFERSON COUNTY (PORTIONS)—See KNOXVILLE, TN (Comcast Cable)

JEFFERSON COUNTY—See MORRISTOWN, TN (Charter Communications)

JELLICO—Access Cable Television Inc

JOELTON—See NASHVILLE, TN (Comcast Cable)

JOHNSON CITY—Charter Communications. Now served by KINGSPORT, TN [TN0007]

JOHNSON CITY—See KINGSPORT, TN (Charter Communications)

JOHNSON CITY—See KNOXVILLE, TN (Comcast Cable)

JONESBOROUGH—See KNOXVILLE, TN (Comcast Cable)

JONESVILLE (TOWN)—See KNOXVILLE, VA (Comcast Cable)

KIMBALL—See ORME, TN (BlueBridge Media)

KIMBALL—See JASPER, TN (Charter Communications)

KINGSPORT—Charter Communications

KINGSTON SPRINGS—See NASHVILLE, TN (Comcast Cable)

KINGSTON—See TEN MILE, TN (Charter Communications)

KINGSTON—See KNOXVILLE, TN (Comcast Cable)

KNOX COUNTY (PORTIONS)—See ALCOA, TN (Charter Communications)

KNOX COUNTY (PORTIONS)—See KNOXVILLE, TN (Comcast Cable)

KNOXVILLE—Formerly served by Tennessee Wireless Inc. No longer in operation

KNOXVILLE—Comcast Cable

KNOXVILLE—WOW! Internet, Cable & Phone

KODAK—Comcast Cable. Now served by KNOXVILLE, TN [TN0004]

KODAK—See KNOXVILLE, TN (Comcast Cable)

LA FOLLETTE—Comcast Cable. Now served by KNOXVILLE, TN [TN0004]

LA FOLLETTE—See KNOXVILLE, TN (Comcast Cable)

LA GRANGE—See MEMPHIS, TN (Comcast Cable)

LA VERGNE—See NASHVILLE, TN (Comcast Cable)

LAFAYETTE—Comcast Cable. Now served by NASHVILLE, TN [TN0002]

LAFAYETTE—See KNOXVILLE, GA (Comcast Cable)

LAFAYETTE—See NASHVILLE, TN (Comcast Cable)

LAKE CITY—See KNOXVILLE, TN (Comcast Cable)

LAKE TANSI—See CROSSVILLE, TN (Charter Communications)

LAKELAND—See MEMPHIS, TN (Comcast Cable)

LAKESITE—See KNOXVILLE, TN (Comcast Cable)

LAKESITE—See CHATTANOOGA, TN (EPB)

LANCING—See KNOXVILLE, TN (Comcast Cable)

LAUDERDALE COUNTY (PORTIONS)—See COLUMBIA, AL (Charter Communications)

LAUDERDALE COUNTY (UNINCORPORATED AREAS)—See BROWNSVILLE, TN (Time Warner Cable)

LAUREL BLOOMERY—Formerly served by Charter Communications. No longer in operation

LAWRENCE COUNTY (PORTIONS)—See COLUMBIA, TN (Charter Communications)

LAWRENCEBURG—Charter Communications. Now served by COLUMBIA, TN [TN0017]

LAWRENCEBURG—See COLUMBIA, TN (Charter Communications)

LEBANON—Charter Communications

LEBANON—See NASHVILLE, TN (Comcast Cable)

LEE COUNTY (PORTIONS)—See KNOXVILLE, VA (Comcast Cable)

LENOIR CITY—See ALCOA, TN (Charter Communications)

LEWIS COUNTY (PORTIONS)—See COLUMBIA, TN (Charter Communications)

LEWISBURG—Charter Communications. Now served by COLUMBIA, TN [TN0017]

LEWISBURG—See COLUMBIA, TN (Charter Communications)

LEXINGTON—Charter Communications. Now served by JACKSON CITY, TN [TN0008]

LEXINGTON—See JACKSON CITY, TN (Charter Communications)

LIBERTY—See LEBANON, TN (Charter Communications)

LINCOLN COUNTY (PORTIONS)—See MANCHESTER, TN (Charter Communications)

LINCOLN COUNTY (PORTIONS)—See FAYETTEVILLE, TN (Fayette Public Utilities)

LINDEN—Formerly served by Two Rivers Media. No longer in operation

LIVINGSTON—See CELINA, TN (Celina Cable)

LIVINGSTON—Comcast Cable

LOBELVILLE—Formerly served by Two Rivers Media. No longer in operation

LONE MOUNTAIN—See NEW TAZEWELL, TN (Vyve Broadband)

LOOKOUT MOUNTAIN—See KNOXVILLE, GA (Comcast Cable)

LOOKOUT MOUNTAIN—See KNOXVILLE, TN (Comcast Cable)

LOOKOUT MOUNTAIN—See CHATTANOOGA, GA (EPB)

LOOKOUT MOUNTAIN—See CHATTANOOGA, TN (EPB)

LORETTO—Charter Communications. Now served by COLUMBIA, TN [TN0017]

LORETTO—See COLUMBIA, TN (Charter Communications)

LOUDON COUNTY (PORTIONS)—See ALCOA, TN (Charter Communications)

LOUDON COUNTY (PORTIONS)—See KNOXVILLE, TN (Comcast Cable)

LOUDON—Charter Communications. Now served by ALCOA, TN [TN0151]

LOUDON—See ALCOA, TN (Charter Communications)

LOUISVILLE—See ALCOA, TN (Charter Communications)

LOUISVILLE—See KNOXVILLE, TN (Comcast Cable)

LUPTON CITY—See CHATTANOOGA, TN (EPB)

LUTTRELL—See KNOXVILLE, TN (Comcast Cable)

LYLES—See NASHVILLE, TN (Comcast Cable)

LYNCHBURG—Comcast Cable. Now served by NASHVILLE, TN [TN0002]

LYNCHBURG—See NASHVILLE, TN (Comcast Cable)

LYNNVILLE—Formerly served by Small Town Cable. No longer in operation

MACON COUNTY (PORTIONS)—See NASHVILLE, TN (Comcast Cable)

Tennessee—Cable Community Index

MADISON COUNTY (PORTIONS)—See JACKSON CITY, TN (Charter Communications)

MADISONVILLE—Charter Communications. Now served by ALCOA, TN [TN0151]

MADISONVILLE—See ALCOA, TN (Charter Communications)

MANCHESTER—Charter Communications

MARION (TOWN)—See KNOXVILLE, VA (Comcast Cable)

MARION COUNTY (PORTIONS)—See KNOXVILLE, TN (Comcast Cable)

MARION COUNTY (PORTIONS)—See CHATTANOOGA, GA (EPB)

MARION COUNTY—See JASPER, TN (Charter Communications)

MARION—See MEMPHIS, AR (Comcast Cable)

MARSHALL COUNTY (PORTIONS)—See COLUMBIA, TN (Charter Communications)

MARSHALL COUNTY (PORTIONS)—See MEMPHIS, MS (Comcast Cable)

MARTIN—Charter Communications. Now served by JACKSON CITY, TN [TN0008]

MARTIN—See JACKSON CITY, TN (Charter Communications)

MARYVILLE—See ALCOA, TN (Charter Communications)

MASON—See MEMPHIS, TN (Comcast Cable)

MAURY CITY—See JACKSON CITY, TN (Charter Communications)

MAURY COUNTY (PORTIONS)—See COLUMBIA, TN (Charter Communications)

MAYNARDVILLE—Comcast. Now served by KNOXVILLE, TN [TN0004]

MAYNARDVILLE—See KNOXVILLE, TN (Comcast Cable)

MCDONALD—See CHATTANOOGA, TN (EPB)

MCEWEN—Charter Communications

McKENZIE—Charter Communications. Now served by JACKSON CITY, TN [TN0008]

MCKENZIE—See JACKSON CITY, TN (Charter Communications)

MCLEMORESVILLE—See JACKSON CITY, TN (Charter Communications)

MCMINN COUNTY (PORTIONS)—See KNOXVILLE, TN (Comcast Cable)

MCMINN COUNTY—See CLEVELAND, TN (Charter Communications)

MCMINNVILLE—See MANCHESTER, TN (Charter Communications)

MCNAIRY COUNTY (PORTIONS)—See JACKSON CITY, TN (Charter Communications)

MCNAIRY—See JACKSON CITY, TN (Charter Communications)

MEADOWVIEW—See KNOXVILLE, TN (Comcast Cable)

MEDINA—See HUMBOLDT, TN (Click1.Net)

MEMPHIS—Comcast Cable

MIDDLETON—See MEMPHIS, TN (Comcast Cable)

MIDTOWN—See KNOXVILLE, TN (Comcast Cable)

MIDWAY—See KNOXVILLE, TN (Comcast Cable)

MILAN—See JACKSON CITY, TN (Charter Communications)

MILLEDGEVILLE—See JACKSON CITY, TN (Charter Communications)

MILLERSVILLE—See NASHVILLE, TN (Comcast Cable)

MILLINGTON—Millington CATV

MINOR HILL—Formerly served by Small Town Cable. No longer in operation

MITCHELLVILLE—See NASHVILLE, TN (Comcast Cable)

MONROE COUNTY (PORTIONS)—See ALCOA, TN (Charter Communications)

MONROE—See KNOXVILLE, TN (Comcast Cable)

MONTEAGLE—Charter Communications. Now served by MANCHESTER, TN [TN0032]

MONTEAGLE—See MANCHESTER, TN (Charter Communications)

MONTEREY—See COOKEVILLE, TN (Charter Communications)

MONTGOMERY COUNTY (portions)—Charter Communications. Now served by CLARKSVILLE, TN [TN0009]

MONTGOMERY COUNTY (PORTIONS)—See CLARKSVILLE, TN (Charter Communications)

MOORE COUNTY (PORTIONS)—See MANCHESTER, TN (Charter Communications)

MORGAN COUNTY (PORTIONS)—See KNOXVILLE, TN (Comcast Cable)

MORRISON—See MANCHESTER, TN (Charter Communications)

MORRISTOWN—Charter Communications

MOSCOW—See MEMPHIS, TN (Comcast Cable)

MOSHEIM—See KNOXVILLE, TN (Comcast Cable)

MOUNT CARMEL—See KINGSPORT, TN (Charter Communications)

MOUNT JULIET—See NASHVILLE, TN (Comcast Cable)

MOUNT PLEASANT—See COLUMBIA, TN (Charter Communications)

MOUNTAIN CITY—Charter Communications. Now served by HICKORY, NC [NC0009]

MUNFORD—See MILLINGTON, TN (Millington CATV)

MURFREESBORO—See NASHVILLE, TN (Comcast Cable)

NASHVILLE—Comcast Cable

NEW DEAL—See NASHVILLE, TN (Comcast Cable)

NEW HOPE—See JASPER, TN (Charter Communications)

NEW MARKET—See MORRISTOWN, TN (Charter Communications)

NEW TAZEWELL—Vyve Broadband

NEWBERN—Charter Communications. Now served by JACKSON CITY, TN [TN0008]

NEWBERN—Charter Communications. Now served by JACKSON CITY, TN [TN0008]

NEWBERN—See JACKSON CITY, TN (Charter Communications)

NEWPORT—See MORRISTOWN, TN (Charter Communications)

NEWPORT—See KNOXVILLE, TN (Comcast Cable)

NEWPORT—Haywood Cablevision

NIOTA—See KNOXVILLE, TN (Comcast Cable)

NOLENSVILLE—See NASHVILLE, TN (Comcast Cable)

NORRIS—Comcast Cable. Now served by KNOXVILLE, TN [TN0004]

NORRIS—See KNOXVILLE, TN (Comcast Cable)

NORTHAVEN—See MILLINGTON, TN (Millington CATV)

NORTON—See KNOXVILLE, VA (Comcast Cable)

OAK RIDGE—Comcast Cable. Now served by KNOXVILLE, TN [TN0004]

OAK RIDGE—See KNOXVILLE, TN (Comcast Cable)

OAKDALE—See KNOXVILLE, TN (Comcast Cable)

OAKLAND—See MEMPHIS, TN (Comcast Cable)

OBION COUNTY (UNINCORPORATED AREAS)—See JACKSON CITY, TN (Charter Communications)

OBION—See JACKSON CITY, TN (Charter Communications)

OCOEE—See KNOXVILLE, TN (Comcast Cable)

OLD HICKORY—See NASHVILLE, TN (Comcast Cable)

OLDFORT—See KNOXVILLE, TN (Comcast Cable)

OLIVE BRANCH—See MEMPHIS, MS (Comcast Cable)

OLIVER SPRINGS—See KNOXVILLE, TN (Comcast Cable)

ONEIDA—See KNOXVILLE, TN (Comcast Cable)

OOLTEWAH—See CHATTANOOGA, TN (EPB)

ORLINDA—See NASHVILLE, TN (Comcast Cable)

ORME—BlueBridge Media

OVERTON COUNTY (PORTIONS)—Overton County Cable

PALMER—See MANCHESTER, TN (Charter Communications)

PARIS—Charter Communications. Now served by JACKSON CITY, TN [TN0008]

PARIS—See JACKSON CITY, TN (Charter Communications)

PARKIN—See MEMPHIS, AR (Comcast Cable)

PARROTTSVILLE—See KNOXVILLE, TN (Comcast Cable)

PARSONS—Charter Communications. Now served by JACKSON CITY, TN [TN0008]

PARSONS—See JACKSON CITY, TN (Charter Communications)

PEGRAM—See NASHVILLE, TN (Comcast Cable)

PENNINGTON GAP (TOWN)—See KNOXVILLE, VA (Comcast Cable)

PETROS—See KNOXVILLE, TN (Comcast Cable)

PHILADELPHIA—See ALCOA, TN (Charter Communications)

PICKETT COUNTY—See BYRDSTOWN, TN (Celina Cable)

PICKWICK DAM—See COUNCE, TN (Pickwick Cablevision)

PIGEON FORGE—See ALCOA, TN (Charter Communications)

PIGEON FORGE—See KNOXVILLE, TN (Comcast Cable)

PIKEVILLE—Bledsoe Telephone Coop

PINEY FLATS—See KINGSPORT, TN (Charter Communications)

PIPERTON—See MEMPHIS, TN (Comcast Cable)

PITTMAN CENTER—See KNOXVILLE, TN (Comcast Cable)

PLEASANT HILL—See CUMBERLAND COUNTY, TN (Spirit Broadband)

PLEASANT VIEW—See CLARKSVILLE, TN (Charter Communications)

POLK COUNTY (PORTIONS)—See KNOXVILLE, TN (Comcast Cable)

PORTLAND—Comcast Cable. Now served by NASHVILLE, TN [TN0002]

PORTLAND—See NASHVILLE, TN (Comcast Cable)

POWELL—See KNOXVILLE, TN (Comcast Cable)

PULASKI—Charter Communications. Now served by COLUMBIA, TN [TN0017]

Cable Community Index—Tennessee

PULASKI—See COLUMBIA, TN (Charter Communications)

PUTNAM COUNTY (PORTIONS)—See COOKEVILLE, TN (Charter Communications)

READYVILLE—See NASHVILLE, TN (Comcast Cable)

RED BANK—See KNOXVILLE, TN (Comcast Cable)

RED BANK—See CHATTANOOGA, TN (EPB)

RED BOILING SPRINGS—Formerly served by Celina Cable. This cable system has converted to IPTV. Now served by NCTC, SCOTTSVILLE, KY [KY5016]

REDDY CREEK—See KINGSPORT, TN (Charter Communications)

RHEA COUNTY (PORTIONS)—See CLEVELAND, TN (Charter Communications)

RHEA COUNTY—See SPRING CITY, TN (Spring City Cable TV Inc)

RICEVILLE—See KNOXVILLE, TN (Comcast Cable)

RIDGESIDE—See KNOXVILLE, TN (Comcast Cable)

RIDGESIDE—See CHATTANOOGA, TN (EPB)

RIDGETOP—See NASHVILLE, TN (Comcast Cable)

RIPLEY—Formerly served by NewWave Communications. Now served by Time Warner Cable, BROWNSVILLE, TN [TN0054]

RIPLEY—See BROWNSVILLE, TN (Time Warner Cable)

RIVES—See JACKSON CITY, TN (Charter Communications)

ROANE COUNTY (PORTIONS)—See KNOXVILLE, TN (Comcast Cable)

ROBERTSON COUNTY (PORTIONS)—See CLARKSVILLE, TN (Charter Communications)

ROBERTSON COUNTY (PORTIONS)—See NASHVILLE, TN (Comcast Cable)

ROBINSONVILLE—See MEMPHIS, MS (Comcast Cable)

ROCKFORD—See KNOXVILLE, TN (Comcast Cable)

ROCKWOOD—See KNOXVILLE, TN (Comcast Cable)

ROGERSVILLE—Charter Communications. Now served by KINGSPORT, TN [TN0007]

ROGERSVILLE—See KINGSPORT, TN (Charter Communications)

ROGERSVILLE—Middle Tennessee Broadband

ROSSVILLE—See KNOXVILLE, GA (Comcast Cable)

ROSSVILLE—See MEMPHIS, TN (Comcast Cable)

ROSSVILLE—See CHATTANOOGA, GA (EPB)

RUSSELLVILLE—See KNOXVILLE, TN (Comcast Cable)

RUTHERFORD COUNTY (PORTIONS)—See NASHVILLE, TN (Comcast Cable)

RUTLEDGE—See MORRISTOWN, TN (Charter Communications)

SALE CREEK—See CHATTANOOGA, TN (EPB)

SALTILLO—See JACKSON CITY, TN (Charter Communications)

SALTVILLE—See KNOXVILLE, VA (Comcast Cable)

SARDIS—See MEMPHIS, MS (Comcast Cable)

SAULSBURY—See MEMPHIS, TN (Comcast Cable)

SAVANNAH—Charter Communications. Now served by JACKSON CITY, TN [TN0008]

SAVANNAH—See JACKSON CITY, TN (Charter Communications)

SCOTT COUNTY (PORTIONS)—See KINGSPORT, VA (Charter Communications)

SCOTT COUNTY (PORTIONS)—See KNOXVILLE, TN (Comcast Cable)

SELMER—Charter Communications. Now served by JACKSON CITY, TN [TN0008]

SELMER—See JACKSON CITY, TN (Charter Communications)

SENATOBIA—See MEMPHIS, MS (Comcast Cable)

SEQUATCHIE COUNTY (PORTIONS)—See PIKEVILLE, TN (Bledsoe Telephone Coop)

SEQUATCHIE COUNTY (PORTIONS)—See ORME, TN (BlueBridge Media)

SEQUATCHIE COUNTY (PORTIONS)—See KNOXVILLE, TN (Comcast Cable)

SEVEN MILE FORD—See KNOXVILLE, VA (Comcast Cable)

SEVIER COUNTY (PORTIONS)—See ALCOA, TN (Charter Communications)

SEVIER COUNTY (PORTIONS)—See KNOXVILLE, TN (Comcast Cable)

SEVIERVILLE—See ALCOA, TN (Charter Communications)

SEVIERVILLE—See KNOXVILLE, TN (Comcast Cable)

SEWANEE—See MANCHESTER, TN (Charter Communications)

SEYMOUR—See ALCOA, TN (Charter Communications)

SHARON—See JACKSON CITY, TN (Charter Communications)

SHAWANEE—See NEW TAZEWELL, TN (Vyve Broadband)

SHELBY COUNTY (PORTIONS)—See MEMPHIS, TN (Comcast Cable)

SHELBY COUNTY (PORTIONS)—See MILLINGTON, TN (Millington CATV)

SHELBYVILLE (PORTIONS)—See COLUMBIA, TN (Charter Communications)

SHELBYVILLE (PORTIONS)—See MANCHESTER, TN (Charter Communications)

SIGNAL MOUNTAIN—See KNOXVILLE, TN (Comcast Cable)

SIGNAL MOUNTAIN—See CHATTANOOGA, TN (EPB)

SIMERLY CREEK—See CARTER COUNTY (portions), TN (Zito Media)

SIMPSON COUNTY (PORTIONS)—See NASHVILLE, KY (Comcast Cable)

SLAYDEN—See NASHVILLE, TN (Comcast Cable)

SLEDGE—See MEMPHIS, MS (Comcast Cable)

SMITH COUNTY (UNINCORPORATED AREAS)—See LEBANON, TN (Charter Communications)

SMITHVILLE—Comcast Cable. Now served by NASHVILLE, TN [TN0002]

SMITHVILLE—See NASHVILLE, TN (Comcast Cable)

SMYRNA—See NASHVILLE, TN (Comcast Cable)

SMYTH COUNTY (PORTIONS)—See KNOXVILLE, VA (Comcast Cable)

SNEEDVILLE—Zito Media

SODDY DAISY—See KNOXVILLE, TN (Comcast Cable)

SODDY DAISY—See CHATTANOOGA, TN (EPB)

SOMERVILLE—See MEMPHIS, TN (Comcast Cable)

SOUTH CARTHAGE—See NASHVILLE, TN (Comcast Cable)

SOUTH FULTON—Time Warner Cable. Now served by MAYFIELD, KY [KY0037]

SOUTH PITTSBURG—See ORME, TN (BlueBridge Media)

SOUTH PITTSBURG—See JASPER, TN (Charter Communications)

SOUTHAVEN—See MEMPHIS, MS (Comcast Cable)

SPARTA—See COOKEVILLE, TN (Charter Communications)

SPEEDWELL—See NEW TAZEWELL, TN (Vyve Broadband)

SPENCER—See MANCHESTER, TN (Charter Communications)

SPRING CITY—Spring City Cable TV Inc

SPRING HILL—See COLUMBIA, TN (Charter Communications)

SPRINGFIELD—See NASHVILLE, TN (Comcast Cable)

ST. JOSEPH—See COLUMBIA, TN (Charter Communications)

STANTON—See MEMPHIS, TN (Comcast Cable)

STEVENSON—See JASPER, AL (Charter Communications)

STONEY CREEK—Charter Communications. Now served by KINGSPORT, TN [TN0007]

STONEY CREEK—See KINGSPORT, TN (Charter Communications)

SUGAR GROVE—See KNOXVILLE, VA (Comcast Cable)

SULLIVAN COUNTY (PORTIONS)—See KNOXVILLE, TN (Comcast Cable)

SULLIVAN COUNTY—See KINGSPORT, TN (Charter Communications)

SUMMERTOWN—Formerly served by Small Town Cable. No longer in operation

SUMNER COUNTY (PORTIONS)—See NASHVILLE, TN (Comcast Cable)

SUNBRIGHT—See KNOXVILLE, TN (Comcast Cable)

SUNSET—See MEMPHIS, AR (Comcast Cable)

SURGOINSVILLE—See ROGERSVILLE, TN (Middle Tennessee Broadband)

SWEETWATER—See ALCOA, TN (Charter Communications)

TALBOTT—Haywood Cablevision

TATE COUNTY (PORTIONS)—See MEMPHIS, MS (Comcast Cable)

TAZEWELL—See NEW TAZEWELL, TN (Vyve Broadband)

TELCO VILLAGE—See ALCOA, TN (Charter Communications)

TELLICO PLAINS—See KNOXVILLE, TN (Comcast Cable)

TEMPLE HILLS—See NASHVILLE, TN (Comcast Cable)

TEN MILE—Charter Communications

TENNESSEE CITY—See NASHVILLE, TN (Comcast Cable)

TENNESSEE RIDGE—See ERIN, TN (Peoples CATV Inc)

THOMPSON'S STATION—See COLUMBIA, TN (Charter Communications)

TIPPAH COUNTY (PORTIONS)—See MEMPHIS, MS (Comcast Cable)

TIPTON COUNTY (PORTIONS)—See MEMPHIS, TN (Comcast Cable)

TIPTON COUNTY (PORTIONS)—See MILLINGTON, TN (Millington CATV)

TIPTONVILLE—Time Warner Cable. Now served by MAYFIELD, KY [KY0037]

TOWNSEND—See KNOXVILLE, TN (Comcast Cable)

TRACY CITY—See MANCHESTER, TN (Charter Communications)

TRENTON—See JASPER, GA (Charter Communications)

Tennessee—Cable Community Index

TRENTON—Trenton TV Cable Co

TREZEVANT—See JACKSON CITY, TN (Charter Communications)

TRIMBLE—See JACKSON CITY, TN (Charter Communications)

TROY—See JACKSON CITY, TN (Charter Communications)

TULLAHOMA—See MANCHESTER, TN (Charter Communications)

TUNICA COUNTY (PORTIONS)—See MEMPHIS, MS (Comcast Cable)

TUNICA—See MEMPHIS, MS (Comcast Cable)

TURTLETOWN—Ellijay Telephone Co. No longer in operation

TUSCULUM—See KNOXVILLE, TN (Comcast Cable)

UNICOI COUNTY (PORTIONS)—See CARTER COUNTY (portions), TN (Zito Media)

UNICOI—Zito Media. Now served by CARTER COUNTY (portions), TN [TN0105]

UNICOI—See KNOXVILLE, TN (Comcast Cable)

UNICOI—See CARTER COUNTY (portions), TN (Zito Media)

UNION CITY—Formerly served by MetroVision. No longer in operation

UNION CITY—See JACKSON CITY, TN (Charter Communications)

UNION COUNTY (PORTIONS)—See KNOXVILLE, TN (Comcast Cable)

VAN BUREN COUNTY (PORTIONS)—See PIKEVILLE, TN (Bledsoe Telephone Coop)

VAN BUREN COUNTY (PORTIONS)—See MANCHESTER, TN (Charter Communications)

VANLEER—See NASHVILLE, TN (Comcast Cable)

VIOLA—See MANCHESTER, TN (Charter Communications)

VONORE—Comcast Cable. Now served by KNOXVILLE, TN [TN0004]

VONORE—See KNOXVILLE, TN (Comcast Cable)

WALDEN CREEK—Comcast Cable. Now served by KNOXVILLE, TN [TN0004]

WALDEN CREEK—See KNOXVILLE, TN (Comcast Cable)

WALDEN—See KNOXVILLE, TN (Comcast Cable)

WALDEN—See CHATTANOOGA, TN (EPB)

WALKER COUNTY (PORTIONS)—See KNOXVILLE, GA (Comcast Cable)

WALKER COUNTY (PORTIONS)—See CHATTANOOGA, GA (EPB)

WALKER—See KNOXVILLE, GA (Comcast Cable)

WALLS—See MEMPHIS, MS (Comcast Cable)

WALNUT—See MEMPHIS, MS (Comcast Cable)

WARREN COUNTY (PORTIONS)—See MANCHESTER, TN (Charter Communications)

WARTBURG—Comcast Cable. Now served by KNOXVILLE, TN [TN0004]

WARTBURG—See KNOXVILLE, TN (Comcast Cable)

WARTRACE—See MANCHESTER, TN (Charter Communications)

WASHINGTON COUNTY (PORTIONS)—See KINGSPORT, VA (Charter Communications)

WASHINGTON COUNTY (PORTIONS)—See KNOXVILLE, TN (Comcast Cable)

WATERTOWN—See LEBANON, TN (Charter Communications)

WAUTAUGA—See KINGSPORT, TN (Charter Communications)

WAVERLY—Comcast Cable. Now served by NASHVILLE, TN [TN0002]

WAVERLY—See NASHVILLE, TN (Comcast Cable)

WAYNE COUNTY (PORTIONS)—See JACKSON CITY, TN (Charter Communications)

WAYNESBORO—Charter Communications. Now served by JACKSON CITY, TN [TN0008]

WAYNESBORO—See JACKSON CITY, TN (Charter Communications)

WEARS VALLEY—See KNOXVILLE, TN (Comcast Cable)

WEST MEMPHIS—See MEMPHIS, AR (Comcast Cable)

WESTMORELAND—Comcast Cable. Now served by NASHVILLE, TN [TN0002]

WESTMORELAND—See NASHVILLE, TN (Comcast Cable)

WESTPOINT—Charter Communications. Now served by COLUMBIA, TN [TN0017]

WESTPOINT—See COLUMBIA, TN (Charter Communications)

WHITE BLUFF—See NASHVILLE, TN (Comcast Cable)

WHITE COUNTY (PORTIONS)—See COOKEVILLE, TN (Charter Communications)

WHITE HOUSE—Comcast Cable. Now served by NASHVILLE, TN [TN0002]

WHITE HOUSE—See NASHVILLE, TN (Comcast Cable)

WHITE PINE—See MORRISTOWN, TN (Charter Communications)

WHITES CREEK—See NASHVILLE, TN (Comcast Cable)

WHITESBURG—Formerly served by Adelphia Communications. Now served by Comcast Cable, KNOXVILLE, TN [TN0004]

WHITESBURG—See KNOXVILLE, TN (Comcast Cable)

WHITESIDE—See CHATTANOOGA, TN (EPB)

WHITEVILLE—See MEMPHIS, TN (Comcast Cable)

WHITLEY COUNTY (SOUTHERN PORTION)—See JELLICO, KY (Access Cable Television Inc)

WHITWELL—See ORME, TN (BlueBridge Media)

WHITWELL—See JASPER, TN (Charter Communications)

WILDWOOD—See CHATTANOOGA, GA (EPB)

WILLIAMSBURG—See NASHVILLE, TN (Comcast Cable)

WILLIAMSON COUNTY (PORTIONS)—See COLUMBIA, TN (Charter Communications)

WILLIAMSON COUNTY (PORTIONS)—See NASHVILLE, TN (Comcast Cable)

WILLISTON—See MEMPHIS, TN (Comcast Cable)

WILSON COUNTY (PORTIONS)—See LEBANON, TN (Charter Communications)

WILSON COUNTY (PORTIONS)—See NASHVILLE, TN (Comcast Cable)

WINCHESTER—Comcast Cable. Now served by NASHVILLE, TN [TN0002]

WINCHESTER—See NASHVILLE, TN (Comcast Cable)

WINFIELD—See KNOXVILLE, TN (Comcast Cable)

WISE (TOWN)—See KNOXVILLE, VA (Comcast Cable)

WISE COUNTY (TOWN)—See KNOXVILLE, VA (Comcast Cable)

WOODBURY—Comcast Cable. Now served by NASHVILLE, TN [TN0002]

WOODBURY—See NASHVILLE, TN (Comcast Cable)

WOODLAND MILLS—See JACKSON CITY, TN (Charter Communications)

WRIGLEY—See NASHVILLE, TN (Comcast Cable)

TEXAS

ABERNATHY—NTS Communications. This cable system has converted to IPTV. See ABERNATHY, TX [TX5542]

ABERNATHY—NTS Communications. Formerly [TX0388]. This cable system has converted to IPTV

ABILENE—Suddenlink Communications

ACE—Formerly served by Jones Broadcasting. No longer in operation

ACKERLY—Formerly served by National Cable Inc. No longer in operation

ADDISON (TOWN)—See DALLAS, TX (Time Warner Cable)

ADDISON—See CARROLLTON, TX (Charter Communications)

ADKINS—Formerly served by Almega Cable. No longer in operation

ADRIAN—Formerly served by Sunset Cablevision. No longer in operation

ALAMO HEIGHTS—See SAN ANTONIO, TX (Grande Communications)

ALAMO HEIGHTS—See SAN ANTONIO, TX (Time Warner Cable)

ALAMO—See PHARR, TX (Time Warner Cable)

ALBA—Formerly served by Almega Cable. No longer in operation

ALBANY—Suddenlink Communications

ALGOA—Formerly served by Almega Cable. No longer in operation

ALICE—Time Warner Cable. Now served by CORPUS CHRISTI, TX [TX0010]

ALICE—See CORPUS CHRISTI, TX (Time Warner Cable)

ALLEN—Time Warner Cable. Now served by DALLAS, TX [TX0003]

ALLEN—See DALLAS (northwest suburbs), TX (Grande Communications)

ALLEN—See DALLAS, TX (Time Warner Cable)

ALLENDALE—Formerly served by Ccbridge Connections. No longer in operation

ALMA—See MIDLOTHIAN, TX (Charter Communications)

ALPINE—Baja Broadband

ALTO—Formerly served by Almega Cable. No longer in operation

ALTON—Time Warner Cable. Now served by PHARR, TX [TX0017]

ALTON—See PHARR, TX (Time Warner Cable)

ALUM CREEK—Formerly served by Time Warner Cable. No longer in operation

ALVARADO—Formerly served by Almega Cable. No longer in operation

ALVIN—See HOUSTON, TX (Comcast Cable)

ALVORD—See DECATUR, TX (Vyve Broadband)

AMARILLO—Suddenlink Communications

AMHERST—See MULESHOE, TX (Reach Broadband)

ANAHUAC—Formerly served by Carrell Communications. No longer in operation

ANDERSON COUNTY (UNINCORPORATED AREAS)—See TYLER, TX (Suddenlink Communications)

ANDERSON COUNTY—See PALESTINE, TX (Zito Media)

Cable Community Index—Texas

ANDERSON—Formerly served by National Cable Inc. No longer in operation

ANDREWS COUNTY—See ANDREWS, TX (Suddenlink Communications)

ANDREWS—Suddenlink Communications

ANGELINA COUNTY—See LUFKIN, TX (Suddenlink Communications)

ANGLETON—NewWave Communications

ANNA—Suddenlink Communications. Now served by PILOT POINT, TX [TX0286]

ANNA—See PILOT POINT, TX (Suddenlink Communications)

ANNONA—See CLARKSVILLE, TX (Suddenlink Communications)

ANSON—Suddenlink Communications

ANTHONY—See EL PASO, NM (Time Warner Cable)

ANTHONY—See EL PASO, TX (Time Warner Cable)

ANTON—Formerly served by NTS Communications. No longer in operation.

APPLEBY—See NACOGDOCHES, TX (Suddenlink Communications)

APRIL SOUND SUBDIVISION—See KINGWOOD, TX (Suddenlink Communications)

AQUA DULCE—See CORPUS CHRISTI, TX (Time Warner Cable)

AQUA VISTA—Formerly served by Cebridge Connections. No longer in operation

ARANSAS COUNTY (PORTIONS)—See ARANSAS PASS, TX (Cable One)

ARANSAS COUNTY (PORTIONS)—See ROCKPORT, TX (Time Warner Cable)

ARANSAS PASS—Cable One

ARCHER CITY—Time Warner Cable. Now served by WICHITA FALLS, TX [TX0026]

ARCHER CITY—See WICHITA FALLS, TX (Time Warner Cable)

ARCOLA—Formerly served by Almega Cable. No longer in operation

ARGYLE—Formerly served by SouthTel Communications LP. No longer in operation

ARGYLE—See DALLAS (northwest suburbs), TX (Grande Communications)

ARLINGTON—Time Warner Cable. Now served by DALLAS, TX [TX0003]

ARLINGTON—See DALLAS (northwest suburbs), TX (Grande Communications)

ARLINGTON—See DALLAS, TX (Time Warner Cable)

ARNETT—See WOODROW, TX (South Plains Telephone Cooperative)

ARP—Formerly served by Zoom Media. No longer in operation

ASHERTON—Time Warner Cable. Now served by CRYSTAL CITY, TX [TX0147]

ASHERTON—See CRYSTAL CITY, TX (Time Warner Cable)

ASPERMONT—Formerly served by Alliance Communications Network. No longer in operation

ATASCOSA COUNTY (PORTIONS)—See PLEASANTON, TX (CommZoom)

ATASCOSA COUNTY (PORTIONS)—See SAN ANTONIO, TX (Time Warner Cable)

ATASCOSA COUNTY—See JOURDANTON, TX (Alliance Communications)

ATASCOSA—Formerly served by Almega Cable. No longer in operation

ATHENS—Suddenlink Communications

ATLANTA—Fidelity Communications

AUBREY—See PILOT POINT, TX (Suddenlink Communications)

AUSTIN (portions)—Grande Communications. Now served by AUSTIN, TX [TX0989]

AUSTIN—Grande Communications

AUSTIN—Time Warner Cable

AVERY—See CLARKSVILLE, TX (Suddenlink Communications)

AVINGER—Formerly served by Almega Cable. No longer in operation

AZLE—See FORT WORTH (northern portions), TX (Charter Communications)

AZTEC—Formerly served by Cebridge Connections. No longer in operation

BACLIFF—See HOUSTON, TX (Comcast Cable)

BAILEY'S PRAIRIE—See ANGLETON, TX (NewWave Communications)

BAIRD—Formerly served by Brownwood TV Cable Service Inc. No longer in operation

BALCH SPRINGS—See TERRELL, TX (Suddenlink Communications)

BALCONES HEIGHTS—See SAN ANTONIO, TX (Grande Communications)

BALCONES HEIGHTS—See SAN ANTONIO, TX (Time Warner Cable)

BALLINGER—Vyve Broadband

BALMORHEA—Mountain Zone TV

BANDERA—CommZoom

BANQUETE—See CORPUS CHRISTI, TX (Time Warner Cable)

BARSTOW—Formerly served by Almega Cable. No longer in operation

BARTLETT—Reveille Broadband

BASTROP COUNTY (PORTIONS)—See LOST PINES, TX (Suddenlink Communications)

BASTROP COUNTY (PORTIONS)—See AUSTIN, TX (Time Warner Cable)

BASTROP—See AUSTIN, TX (Time Warner Cable)

BATESVILLE—Formerly served by Almega Cable. No longer in operation

BAY CITY—NewWave Communications. Now served by WHARTON, TX [TX0171]

BAY CITY—See WHARTON, TX (NewWave Communications)

BAYOU VISTA—See HOUSTON, TX (Comcast Cable)

BAYTOWN—See HOUSTON, TX (Comcast Cable)

BAYTOWN—See MONT BELVIEU, TX (Suddenlink Communications)

BEACH CITY—Formerly served by Carrell Communications. No longer in operation

BEAR CREEK—See HOUSTON, TX (Comcast Cable)

BEAUMONT COLONY—Formerly served by Carrell Communications. No longer in operation

BEAUMONT—See PORT ARTHUR, TX (Time Warner Cable)

BECKVILLE—See LAKE CHEROKEE, TX (Alliance Communications)

BEDFORD—Time Warner Cable. Now served by DALLAS, TX [TX0003]

BEDFORD—See DALLAS, TX (Time Warner Cable)

BEDIAS—Formerly served by Almega Cable. No longer in operation

BEE CAVE—See AUSTIN, TX (Time Warner Cable)

BEE COUNTY (PORTIONS)—See CORPUS CHRISTI, TX (Time Warner Cable)

BEEVILLE—Time Warner Cable. Now served by CORPUS CHRISTI, TX [TX0010]

BEEVILLE—See CORPUS CHRISTI, TX (Time Warner Cable)

BELL COUNTY (PORTIONS)—See AUSTIN, TX (Time Warner Cable)

BELLAIRE—See HOUSTON, TX (Comcast Cable)

BELLEVUE—Formerly served by Cebridge Connections. No longer in operation

BELLMEAD—See WACO, TX (Grande Communications)

BELLMEAD—See AUSTIN, TX (Time Warner Cable)

BELLS—See SHERMAN, TX (Cable One)

BELLVILLE—See SEALY, TX (NewWave Communications)

BELTON—See AUSTIN, TX (Time Warner Cable)

BEN BOLT—Formerly served by National Cable Inc. Now served by Time Warner Cable, CORPUS CHRISTI, TX [TX0010]

BEN BOLT—See CORPUS CHRISTI, TX (Time Warner Cable)

BEN WHEELER—Formerly served by Zoom Media. No longer in operation

BENAVIDES—Time Warner Cable. Now served by CORPUS CHRISTI, TX [TX0010]

BENAVIDES—See CORPUS CHRISTI, TX (Time Warner Cable)

BENBROOK—See FORT WORTH (northern portions), TX (Charter Communications)

BENJAMIN—Formerly served by Jayroc Cablevision. No longer in operation

BENTSEN GROVE—Formerly served by CableDirect. No longer in operation

BERRYVILLE—See TYLER, TX (Suddenlink Communications)

BERTRAM—See AUSTIN, TX (Time Warner Cable)

BEVERLY HILLS—See WACO, TX (Grande Communications)

BEVERLY HILLS—See AUSTIN, TX (Time Warner Cable)

BEVIL OAKS—See SOUR LAKE, TX (NewWave Communications)

BEXAR COUNTY (PORTIONS)—See SAN ANTONIO, TX (Time Warner Cable)

BIG LAKE—Suddenlink Communications

BIG SANDY—See HAWKINS, TX (Suddenlink Communications)

BIG SPRING—Suddenlink Communications

BIG WELLS—Formerly served by Almega Cable. No longer in operation

BIGGS AIRFIELD—See EL PASO, TX (Time Warner Cable)

BIRCH CREEK—Reveille Broadband

BISHOP—Time Warner Cable. Now served by CORPUS CHRISTI, TX [TX0010]

BISHOP—See CORPUS CHRISTI, TX (Time Warner Cable)

BLACKWELL—NewWave Communications

BLANCO—Formerly served by Zoom Media. No longer in operation

BLANCO—See BOERNE, TX (GVTC Communications. Formerly [TX0315]. This cable system has converted to IPTV)

BLANKET—Formerly served by National Cable Inc. No longer in operation

BLESSING—Formerly served by Bay City Cablevision. Now served by NewWave Communications, WHARTON, TX [TX0171]

Texas—Cable Community Index

BLESSING—See WHARTON, TX (NewWave Communications)

BLOOMING GROVE—Formerly served by Almega Cable. No longer in operation

BLOOMINGTON—Formerly served by Almega Cable. No longer in operation

BLOSSOM—See CLARKSVILLE, TX (Suddenlink Communications)

BLUE MOUND—See FORT WORTH (northern portions), TX (Charter Communications)

BOERNE (portions)—GVTC Communications. Formerly [TX0315]. This cable system has converted to IPTV. See BOERNE (portions) [TX5465]

BOERNE—GVTC Communications. Formerly [TX0315]. This cable system has converted to IPTV

BOERNE—See SAN ANTONIO, TX (Time Warner Cable)

BOGATA—See CLARKSVILLE, TX (Suddenlink Communications)

BOLING—Formerly served by Cebridge Connections. No longer in operation

BONHAM—See SHERMAN, TX (Cable One)

BOOKER—PTCI. This cable system has converted to IPTV. Now served by GUYMON, OK [OK5005]

BORDERLAND—See EL PASO, TX (Time Warner Cable)

BORGER—Cable One

BOWIE COUNTY (PORTIONS)—See TEXARKANA, TX (Cable One)

BOWIE COUNTY (PORTIONS)—See NEW BOSTON, TX (Vyve Broadband)

BOWIE COUNTY—See TEXARKANA, TX (Cable One)

BOWIE—Vyve Broadband

BOYD—Formerly served by SouthTel Communications LP. No longer in operation

BOYS RANCH—See DALHART, TX (XIT Communications. Formerly [TX1023]. This cable system has converted to IPTV)

BRACKETTVILLE—Formerly served by Almega Cable. No longer in operation

BRADY—Formerly served by Central Texas Communications. No longer in operation

BRADY—Suddenlink Communications

BRAZORIA COUNTY (PORTIONS)—See HOUSTON, TX (Comcast Cable)

BRAZORIA COUNTY (UNINCORPORATED AREAS)—See WHARTON, TX (NewWave Communications)

BRAZORIA—Formerly served by Suddenlink Communications. No longer in operation

BRAZORIA—Coastal Link Communications

BRAZOS COUNTY (UNINCORPORATED AREAS)—See BRYAN, TX (Suddenlink Communications)

BRECKENRIDGE—Suddenlink Communications

BREMOND—Zito Media

BRENHAM—Suddenlink Communications

BREWSTER COUNTY (PORTIONS)—See ALPINE, TX (Baja Broadband)

BRIARCLIFF—See AUSTIN, TX (Time Warner Cable)

BRIDGE CITY—Time Warner Cable. Now served by PORT ARTHUR (formerly Beaumont), TX [TX0022]

BRIDGE CITY—See PORT ARTHUR, TX (Time Warner Cable)

BRIDGEPORT—See DECATUR, TX (Vyve Broadband)

BRONTE—See ROBERT LEE, TX (NewWave Communications)

BROOKELAND—Formerly served by Cebridge Connections. No longer in operation

BROOKS AFB—See SAN ANTONIO, TX (Time Warner Cable)

BROOKS COUNTY (PORTIONS)—See CORPUS CHRISTI, TX (Time Warner Cable)

BROOKSHIRE—Formerly served by Northland Cable Television. No longer in operation

BROOKSIDE VILLAGE—See HOUSTON, TX (Comcast Cable)

BROWNFIELD—NTS Communications. This cable system has converted to IPTV. Now served by WOLFFORTH, TX [TX5540]

BROWNFIELD—See WOLFFORTH, TX (NTS Communications)

BROWNSVILLE—Time Warner Cable. Now served by PHARR, TX [TX0017]

BROWNSVILLE—See PHARR, TX (Time Warner Cable)

BROWNWOOD—Formerly served by Brownwood TV Cable Service Inc. No longer in operation

BRUCEVILLE-EDDY—See AUSTIN, TX (Time Warner Cable)

BRUNI—Formerly served by Windjammer Cable. No longer in operation

BRYAN—Suddenlink Communications

BRYSON—Vyve Broadband

BUCKHOLTS—Formerly served by National Cable Inc. No longer in operation

BUDA (portions)—Grande Communications. Now served by AUSTIN, TX [TX0989]

BUDA—See AUSTIN, TX (Time Warner Cable)

BUFFALO GAP—See TUSCOLA, TX (NewWave Communications)

BUFFALO SPRINGS LAKE—Formerly served by Almega Cable. No longer in operation

BUFFALO—Formerly served by Northland Cable Television. No longer in operation

BULLARD—See TYLER, TX (Suddenlink Communications)

BULVERDE—See BOERNE, TX (GVTC Communications. Formerly [TX0315]. This cable system has converted to IPTV)

BULVERDE—See SAN ANTONIO, TX (Time Warner Cable)

BUNA—Formerly served by Cable Plus Inc. No longer in operation

BUNKER HILL (VILLAGE)—See HOUSTON, TX (Comcast Cable)

BURKBURNETT—Suddenlink Communications

BURKE—See LUFKIN, TX (Suddenlink Communications)

BURLESON COUNTY (PORTIONS)—See LYONS, TX (Reveille Broadband)

BURLESON—Pathway. This cable system has converted to IPTV. Now served by BURLESON, TX [TX5530]

BURLESON—See FORT WORTH (northern portions), TX (Charter Communications)

BURLESON—Pathway. Formerly [TX0103]. This cable system has converted to IPTV

BURNET—See MARBLE FALLS, TX (Northland Cable Television)

BURNET—See AUSTIN, TX (Time Warner Cable)

BURTON—Formerly served by Reveille Broadband. No longer in operation

BYERS—Formerly served by Byers-Petrolia Cable TV/North Texas Telephone Co. No longer in operation

CACTUS—Formerly served by Elk River TV Cable Co. No longer in operation

CADDO PEAK—North Texas Broadband

CALDWELL COUNTY (PORTIONS)—See AUSTIN, TX (Time Warner Cable)

CALDWELL—Suddenlink Communications

CALHOUN COUNTY—See PORT LAVACA, TX (Cable One)

CALVERT—Zito Media

CAMERON COUNTY (PORTIONS)—See PHARR, TX (Time Warner Cable)

CAMERON COUNTY (southern portion)—Formerly served by Ridgewood Cablevision. No longer in operation

CAMERON—Zito Media

CAMP COUNTY (PORTIONS)—See PITTSBURG, TX (Suddenlink Communications)

CAMP WOODS—Formerly served by Cebridge Connections. No longer in operation

CAMPBELL—Formerly served by CableSouth Inc. No longer in operation

CANADIAN—Suddenlink Communications

CANEY CITY—See ATHENS, TX (Suddenlink Communications)

CANTON—East Texas Cable Co

CANUTILLO—See EL PASO, TX (Time Warner Cable)

CANYON LAKE—GVTC. This cable system has converted to IPTV. Now served by BOERNE, TX [TX5465]

CANYON LAKE—See BOERNE, TX (GVTC Communications. Formerly [TX0315]. This cable system has converted to IPTV)

CANYON LAKE—See SAN ANTONIO, TX (Time Warner Cable)

CANYON—See AMARILLO, TX (Suddenlink Communications)

CARLSBAD—Formerly served by Cebridge Connections. No longer in operation

CARMINE—Formerly served by Reveille Broadband. No longer in operation

CAROLINA COVE—Formerly served by Cablevision of Walker County. No longer in operation

CARRIZO SPRINGS—See CRYSTAL CITY, TX (Time Warner Cable)

CARROLLTON—Charter Communications

CARROLLTON—See DALLAS (northwest suburbs), TX (Grande Communications)

CARROLLTON—See DALLAS, TX (Time Warner Cable)

CARTHAGE—Fidelity Communications

CASON—See DAINGERFIELD, TX (Suddenlink Communications)

CASS COUNTY (PORTIONS)—See ATLANTA, TX (Fidelity Communications)

CASS COUNTY (PORTIONS)—See DAINGERFIELD, TX (Suddenlink Communications)

CASTLE HILLS—See SAN ANTONIO, TX (Grande Communications)

CASTLE HILLS—See SAN ANTONIO, TX (Time Warner Cable)

CASTROVILLE—Formerly served by Charter Communications. Now served by CommZoom, HONDO, TX [TX0218]

CASTROVILLE—See HONDO, TX (CommZoom)

CEDAR CREEK—Formerly served by Trust Cable. No longer in operation

CEDAR HILL—See DALLAS, TX (Time Warner Cable)

Cable Community Index—Texas

CEDAR PARK—See AUSTIN, TX (Grande Communications)

CEDAR PARK—See AUSTIN, TX (Time Warner Cable)

CEDAR SPRINGS—Formerly served by Cebridge Connections. No longer in operation

CEDAR VALLEY—See AUSTIN, TX (Time Warner Cable)

CELINA—See PILOT POINT, TX (Suddenlink Communications)

CENTER POINT—Formerly served by Almega Cable. No longer in operation

CENTER—Suddenlink Communications

CENTERVILLE—Formerly served by Almega Cable. No longer in operation

CENTRAL—Formerly served by Almega Cable. No longer in operation

CHAMBERS COUNTY (PORTIONS)—See HOUSTON, TX (Comcast Cable)

CHAMBERS COUNTY (PORTIONS)—See PORT ARTHUR, TX (Time Warner Cable)

CHAMBERS COUNTY (WESTERN PORTION)—See MONT BELVIEU, TX (Suddenlink Communications)

CHANDLER—See TYLER, TX (Suddenlink Communications)

CHANNELVIEW—See HOUSTON, TX (Comcast Cable)

CHANNING—Formerly served by Sunset Cablevision. No longer in operation

CHANNING—See DALHART, TX (XIT Communications. Formerly [TX1023]. This cable system has converted to IPTV)

CHAPPELL HILL—Formerly served by Reveille Broadband. No longer in operation

CHARLOTTE—Formerly served by Zoom Media. No longer in operation

CHEEK—Formerly served by Cebridge Connections. No longer in operation

CHEROKEE COUNTY (northern portions)—Formerly served by Reach Broadband. No longer in operation

CHEROKEE COUNTY (PORTIONS)—See RUSK, TX (Suddenlink Communications)

CHEROKEE COUNTY—See JACKSONVILLE, TX (Suddenlink Communications)

CHESTER—Formerly served by Cebridge Connections. No longer in operation

CHICO—See DECATUR, TX (Vyve Broadband)

CHILDRESS—Formerly served by Cebridge Connections. Now served by Suddenlink Communications, WELLINGTON, TX [TX0313]

CHILDRESS—See WELLINGTON, TX (Suddenlink Communications)

CHILLICOTHE—Formerly served by Almega Cable. No longer in operation

CHILTON—Formerly served by Galaxy Cablevision. No longer in operation

CHINA GROVE—See SAN ANTONIO, TX (Time Warner Cable)

CHINA SPRING—See AUSTIN, TX (Time Warner Cable)

CHINA—Formerly served by CMA Cablevision. No longer in operation

CHINA—See SOUR LAKE, TX (NewWave Communications)

CHRISTOVAL—Formerly served by Almega Cable. No longer in operation

CIBOLO CREEK (BEXAR)—See SAN ANTONIO, TX (Time Warner Cable)

CIBOLO—See SAN ANTONIO, TX (Time Warner Cable)

CISCO—See EASTLAND, TX (Suddenlink Communications)

CITY BY THE SEA—See ARANSAS PASS, TX (Cable One)

CLARENDON—Suddenlink Communications

CLARKSVILLE CITY—See GLADEWATER, TX (Suddenlink Communications)

CLARKSVILLE—Suddenlink Communications

CLAUDE—Formerly served by Almega Cable. No longer in operation

CLEAR LAKE SHORES—See HOUSTON, TX (Comcast Cable)

CLEBURNE—Charter Communications. Now served by FORT WORTH (northern portions), TX [TX0008]

CLEBURNE—See FORT WORTH (northern portions), TX (Charter Communications)

CLEVELAND—NewWave Communications

CLIFTON—LynnStar Communications

CLINT—See EL PASO, TX (Time Warner Cable)

CLUTE—See HOUSTON, TX (Comcast Cable)

COAHOMA—See BIG SPRING, TX (Suddenlink Communications)

COAHOMA—See STANTON, TX (WesTex. Formerly [TX1031]. This cable system has converted to IPTV)

COCHRAN COUNTY (PORTIONS)—See WOLFFORTH, TX (NTS Communications)

COCKRELL HILL—See DALLAS, TX (Time Warner Cable)

COKE COUNTY (PORTIONS)—See ROBERT LEE, TX (NewWave Communications)

COLDSPRING—See ONALASKA, TX (Suddenlink Communications)

COLEMAN COUNTY—Formerly served by Coleman County Telecommunications. No longer in operation

COLEMAN—LynnStar Communications

COLETO CREEK—Formerly served by National Cable Inc. No longer in operation

COLLEGE STATION—See BRYAN, TX (Suddenlink Communications)

COLLEYVILLE—See DALLAS, TX (Time Warner Cable)

COLLIN COUNTY (PORTIONS)—See TERRELL, TX (Suddenlink Communications)

COLLIN COUNTY (PORTIONS)—See DALLAS, TX (Time Warner Cable)

COLLINGSWORTH COUNTY—See WELLINGTON, TX (Suddenlink Communications)

COLLINSVILLE—See VALLEY VIEW, TX (Nortex Communications)

COLMESNEIL—Formerly served by Carrell Communications. No longer in operation

COLORADO CITY—NTS Communications. This cable system has converted to IPTV. See COLORADO CITY, TX [TX5543]

COLORADO CITY—NTS Communications. Formerly [TX0172]. This cable system has converted to IPTV

COLORADO COUNTY (PORTIONS)—See COLUMBUS, TX (Time Warner Cable)

COLUMBIA LAKES—See WHARTON, TX (NewWave Communications)

COLUMBUS—Time Warner Cable

COMAL COUNTY (PORTIONS)—See SAN ANTONIO, TX (Time Warner Cable)

COMANCHE—LynnStar Communications

COMBES—See PHARR, TX (Time Warner Cable)

COMBINE—Formerly served by Charter Communications. No longer in operation

COMFORT—Formerly served by Cebridge Connections. No longer in operation

COMFORT—CommZoom

COMMERCE—See GREENVILLE, TX (Time Warner Cable)

COMO—See SULPHUR SPRINGS, TX (Suddenlink Communications)

CONCHO COUNTY (PORTIONS)—See EDEN, TX (LynnStar Communications)

CONE—See WOODROW, TX (South Plains Telephone Cooperative)

CONROE WEST—Formerly served by Suddenlink Communications. No longer in operation

CONROE—See HOUSTON, TX (Comcast Cable)

CONROE—Suddenlink Communications

CONVERSE—See SAN ANTONIO, TX (Time Warner Cable)

COOKE COUNTY—See GAINESVILLE, TX (Suddenlink Communications)

COOLIDGE—Formerly served by Northland Cable Television. No longer in operation

COOPER—Alliance Communications

COPPELL—See DALLAS, TX (Time Warner Cable)

COPPERAS COVE—See AUSTIN, TX (Time Warner Cable)

CORINTH—See DENTON, TX (Charter Communications)

CORINTH—See DALLAS (northwest suburbs), TX (Grande Communications)

CORPUS CHRISTI NAVAL AIR STATION—See CORPUS CHRISTI, TX (Time Warner Cable)

CORPUS CHRISTI—Grande Communications

CORPUS CHRISTI—Time Warner Cable

CORRIGAN—Telecom Cable

CORSICANA—Northland Cable Television

CORYELL COUNTY (PORTIONS)—See AUSTIN, TX (Time Warner Cable)

COTTON CENTER—See WOODROW, TX (South Plains Telephone Cooperative)

COTTONWOOD SHORES—See MARBLE FALLS, TX (Northland Cable Television)

COTULLA—Time Warner Cable. Now served by DILLEY (formerly Pearsall), TX [TX0196]

COTULLA—See DILLEY, TX (Time Warner Cable)

COUNTRY CLUB SHORES—Formerly served by CableSouth Inc. No longer in operation

COUNTRY HAVEN—Formerly served by Cebridge Connections. No longer in operation

CRANDALL—Formerly served by Almega Cable. No longer in operation

CRANE COUNTY (PORTIONS)—See CRANE, TX (Suddenlink Communications)

CRANE—Suddenlink Communications

CRANFILLS GAP—Formerly served by National Cable Inc. No longer in operation

CRAWFORD—Zito Media

CROCKETT—Northland Cable Television

CROSBY—See HOUSTON, TX (Comcast Cable)

CROSBYTON—Reach Broadband

Texas—Cable Community Index

CROWELL—Formerly served by Alliance Communications. No longer in operation

CROWLEY—See FORT WORTH (northern portions), TX (Charter Communications)

CRYSTAL BEACH—Formerly served by Rapid Cable. No longer in operation

CRYSTAL CITY—Time Warner Cable

CUERO—Time Warner Cable. Now served by GONZALES, TX [TX0209]

CUERO—See GONZALES, TX (Time Warner Cable)

CUMBY—Formerly served by Cebridge Connections. No longer in operation

CUSHING—Formerly served by Almega Cable. No longer in operation

CUT AND SHOOT—Formerly served by Northland Cable Television. No longer in operation

CYPRESS TRAILS—See HOUSTON, TX (Comcast Cable)

CYPRESS—Formerly served by Almega Cable. No longer in operation

CYPRESS—See HOUSTON, TX (EnTouch Systems Inc)

DAINGERFIELD—Suddenlink Communications

DALHART—XIT Communications. This cable system has converted to IPTV. See DALHART, TX [TX5049]

DALHART—Vyve Broadband

DALHART—XIT Communications. Formerly [TX1023]. This cable system has converted to IPTV

DALLAM COUNTY—See DALHART, TX (Vyve Broadband)

DALLAS (NORTHWEST SUBURBS)—Grande Communications

DALLAS COUNTY (PORTIONS)—See TERRELL, TX (Suddenlink Communications)

DALLAS COUNTY—See DALLAS, TX (Time Warner Cable)

DALLAS—Time Warner Cable

DALWORTHINGTON GARDENS (TOWN)—See DALLAS, TX (Time Warner Cable)

DANBURY—See ANGLETON, TX (NewWave Communications)

DARROUZETT—Formerly served by Panhandle Telephone Coop. Inc. No longer in operation

DAWSON COUNTY (UNINCORPORATED AREAS)—See LAMESA, TX (Northland Cable Television)

DAYTON—See HOUSTON, TX (Comcast Cable)

DE KALB—Formerly served by BCI Broadband. Now served by Vyve Broadband, NEW BOSTON, TX [TX0204]

DE KALB—See NEW BOSTON, TX (Vyve Broadband)

DE LEON—Reach Broadband

DE SOTO—Time Warner Cable. Now served by DALLAS, TX [TX0003]

DE SOTO—See DALLAS, TX (Time Warner Cable)

DECATUR—Vyve Broadband

DEER PARK—See HOUSTON, TX (Comcast Cable)

DEL RIO—Time Warner Cable

DELTA COUNTY (PORTIONS)—See COOPER, TX (Alliance Communications)

DENISON—See SHERMAN, TX (Cable One)

DENTON COUNTY (PORTIONS)—See DALLAS, TX (Time Warner Cable)

DENTON—Charter Communications

DENTON—See DALLAS (northwest suburbs), TX (Grande Communications)

DENVER CITY—See SEMINOLE, TX (Baja Broadband)

DEPORT—See CLARKSVILLE, TX (Suddenlink Communications)

DETROIT—See CLARKSVILLE, TX (Suddenlink Communications)

DEVINE—CommZoom

DEWITT COUNTY (PORTIONS)—See GONZALES, TX (Time Warner Cable)

DIANA—Formerly served by Almega Cable. No longer in operation

DIBOLL—See LUFKIN, TX (Suddenlink Communications)

DICKENS—Formerly served by Almega Cable. No longer in operation

DICKINSON—See HOUSTON, TX (Comcast Cable)

DILLEY—Time Warner Cable. Now served by DILLEY (formerly Pearsall), TX [TX0196]

DILLEY—Time Warner Cable

DIME BOX—Formerly served by Reveille Broadband. No longer in operation

DIMMIT COUNTY (PORTIONS)—See CRYSTAL CITY, TX (Time Warner Cable)

DIMMITT—Suddenlink Communications

DIXIE—Formerly served by Northland Communications. No longer in operation

DONA ANA COUNTY (PORTIONS)—See EL PASO, NM (Time Warner Cable)

DONNA—See PHARR, TX (Time Warner Cable)

DOUBLE OAK (TOWN)—See DALLAS, TX (Time Warner Cable)

DRIFTWOOD—See AUSTIN, TX (Time Warner Cable)

DRIPPING SPRINGS—See AUSTIN, TX (Time Warner Cable)

DRISCOLL—Time Warner Cable. Now served by CORPUS CHRISTI, TX [TX0010]

DRISCOLL—See CORPUS CHRISTI, TX (Time Warner Cable)

DUBLIN—Northland Cable Television. Now served by STEPHENVILLE, TX [TX0098]

DUBLIN—See STEPHENVILLE, TX (Northland Cable Television)

DUMAS—See BORGER, TX (Cable One)

DUNCANVILLE—Charter Communications

DUVAL COUNTY (NORTHERN PORTION)—See FREER, TX (Alliance Communications)

DUVAL COUNTY (PORTIONS)—See CORPUS CHRISTI, TX (Time Warner Cable)

DYESS AFB—See ABILENE, TX (Suddenlink Communications)

EAGLE LAKE—Time Warner Cable. Now served by COLUMBUS, TX [TX0257]

EAGLE LAKE—See COLUMBUS, TX (Time Warner Cable)

EAGLE PASS—Time Warner Cable

EARTH—See MULESHOE, TX (Reach Broadband)

EAST MOUNTAIN—Formerly served by Gilmer Cable. No longer in operation

EASTLAND COUNTY—See EASTLAND, TX (Suddenlink Communications)

EASTLAND—Suddenlink Communications

EASTON—See LAKE CHEROKEE, TX (Alliance Communications)

ECTOR COUNTY (PORTIONS)—Ridgewood Cablevision

ECTOR COUNTY—See ODESSA, TX (Cable One)

ECTOR—TV Cable of Grayson County

EDCOUCH—Time Warner Cable. Now served by PHARR, TX [TX0017]

EDCOUCH—See PHARR, TX (Time Warner Cable)

EDEN—LynnStar Communications

EDGECLIFF VILLAGE—See FORT WORTH (northern portions), TX (Charter Communications)

EDINBURG—See PHARR, TX (Time Warner Cable)

EDMONDSON—See WOODROW, TX (South Plains Telephone Cooperative)

EDNA—NewWave Communications. Now served by WHARTON, TX [TX0171]

EDNA—See WHARTON, TX (NewWave Communications)

EGAN COUNTY (PORTIONS)—See EGAN, TX (North Texas Broadband)

EGAN—North Texas Broadband

EL CAMPO—NewWave Communications. Now served by WHARTON, TX [TX0171]

EL CAMPO—See WHARTON, TX (NewWave Communications)

EL CENIZO—See LAREDO, TX (Time Warner Cable)

EL LAGO—See HOUSTON, TX (Comcast Cable)

EL PASO COUNTY—See EL PASO, TX (Time Warner Cable)

EL PASO—Time Warner Cable

ELDORADO—Formerly served by Reach Broadband. No longer in operation

ELECTRA—Suddenlink Communications

ELGIN—See AUSTIN, TX (Time Warner Cable)

ELKHART—See PALESTINE, TX (Zito Media)

ELKINS LAKE—See HUNTSVILLE, TX (Suddenlink Communications)

ELLINGER—Formerly served by National Cable Inc. No longer in operation

ELLIS COUNTY (PORTIONS)—See MIDLOTHIAN, TX (Charter Communications)

ELM MOTT—See AUSTIN, TX (Time Warner Cable)

ELMENDORF—See SAN ANTONIO, TX (Time Warner Cable)

ELMO—Formerly served by Almega Cable. No longer in operation

ELSA—See PHARR, TX (Time Warner Cable)

EMORY—Formerly served by Alliance Communications Network. No longer in operation

ENCHANTED OAKS—See ATHENS, TX (Suddenlink Communications)

ENCINAL—Formerly served by Telecom Cable. No longer in operation

ENCLAVE AT PAVILLION—See HOUSTON, TX (Comcast Cable)

ENNIS—Charter Communications. Now served by MIDLOTHIAN, TX [TX0122]

ENNIS—See MIDLOTHIAN, TX (Charter Communications)

ESCOBARES—See PHARR, TX (Time Warner Cable)

EULESS (VILLAGE)—See DALLAS, TX (Time Warner Cable)

EVANT—Formerly served by Almega Cable. No longer in operation

EVERMAN—See FORT WORTH (northern portions), TX (Charter Communications)

FABENS—See EL PASO, TX (Time Warner Cable)

FAIR OAKS RANCH (BEXAR COUNTY)—See SAN ANTONIO, TX (Time Warner Cable)

Cable Community Index—Texas

FAIR OAKS RANCH (COMAL COUNTY)—See SAN ANTONIO, TX (Time Warner Cable)

FAIR OAKS RANCH (KENDALL COUNTY)—See SAN ANTONIO, TX (Time Warner Cable)

FAIR OAKS RANCH—See BOERNE, TX (GVTC Communications. Formerly [TX0315]. This cable system has converted to IPTV)

FAIRFIELD—Northland Cable Television

FAIRVIEW (TOWN)—See DALLAS, TX (Time Warner Cable)

FAIRVIEW—See DALLAS (northwest suburbs), TX (Grande Communications)

FAIRVIEW—See TERRELL, TX (Suddenlink Communications)

FALFURRIAS—Time Warner Cable. Now served by CORPUS CHRISTI, TX [TX0010]

FALFURRIAS—See CORPUS CHRISTI, TX (Time Warner Cable)

FANNETT—Formerly served by Almega Cable. No longer in operation

FANNIN COUNTY (PORTIONS)—See SHERMAN, TX (Cable One)

FARMERS BRANCH—See DALLAS, TX (Time Warner Cable)

FARMERSVILLE—Time Warner Cable. Now served by DALLAS, TX [TX0003]

FARMERSVILLE—See DALLAS, TX (Time Warner Cable)

FATE—See TERRELL, TX (Suddenlink Communications)

FAYETTEVILLE—Formerly served by Grisham TV Cable Co. No longer in operation

FENTRESS—Formerly served by National Cable Inc. No longer in operation

FIELDTON—See WOODROW, TX (South Plains Telephone Cooperative)

FLAT—Formerly served by National Cable Inc. No longer in operation

FLATONIA—Formerly served by Almega Cable. No longer in operation

FLEETWOOD OAKS—See HOUSTON, TX (Comcast Cable)

FLEETWOOD—See HOUSTON, TX (Comcast Cable)

FLINT (UNINCORPORATED AREAS)—See TYLER, TX (Suddenlink Communications)

FLORENCE—Formerly served by Windjammer Cable. No longer in operation

FLORESVILLE—Formerly served by Clear Vu Cable. No longer in operation

FLORESVILLE—See SAN ANTONIO, TX (Time Warner Cable)

FLOWER MOUND (TOWN)—See DALLAS, TX (Time Warner Cable)

FLOWER MOUND—Time Warner Cable. Now served by DALLAS, TX [TX0003]

FLOWER MOUND—See DALLAS (northwest suburbs), TX (Grande Communications)

FLOYDADA—Suddenlink Communications. Now served by PLAINVIEW, TX [TX0076]

FLOYDADA—See PLAINVIEW, TX (Suddenlink Communications)

FOLLETT—Formerly served by Panhandle Telephone Coop. Inc. No longer in operation

FOREST BEND—See HOUSTON, TX (Comcast Cable)

FOREST GROVE—See TERRELL, TX (Suddenlink Communications)

FOREST HILL—See FORT WORTH (northern portions), TX (Charter Communications)

FORNEY—See TERRELL, TX (Suddenlink Communications)

FORSAN—Formerly served by National Cable Inc. No longer in operation

FORT BEND COUNTY (portions)—Formerly served by Rapid Cable. Now served by Comcast Cable, HOUSTON, TX [TX0001]

FORT BEND COUNTY (PORTIONS)—See HOUSTON, TX (Comcast Cable)

FORT BEND COUNTY (PORTIONS)—See HOUSTON, TX (Phonoscope Ltd)

FORT BLISS—See EL PASO, TX (Time Warner Cable)

FORT DAVIS—Mountain Zone TV

FORT GATES—See GATESVILLE, TX (Suddenlink Communications)

FORT HOOD—See AUSTIN, TX (Time Warner Cable)

FORT SAM HOUSTON—See SAN ANTONIO, TX (Time Warner Cable)

FORT STOCKTON—Baja Broadband

FORT WORTH (NORTHERN PORTIONS)—Charter Communications

FORT WORTH NAVAL AIR STATION—See FORT WORTH (northern portions), TX (Charter Communications)

FORT WORTH—See KELLER, TX (Millennium Telcom)

FOUKE—See TEXARKANA, AR (Cable One)

FRANKLIN COUNTY (PORTIONS)—See MOUNT VERNON, TX (Suddenlink Communications)

FRANKLIN—Zito Media

FRANKSTON—See TYLER, TX (Suddenlink Communications)

FREDERICKSBURG—Time Warner Cable. Now served by AUSTIN, TX [TX0005]

FREDERICKSBURG—See AUSTIN, TX (Time Warner Cable)

FREEPORT—See HOUSTON, TX (Comcast Cable)

FREER—Alliance Communications

FRIENDSHIP—See WOLFFORTH, TX (NTS Communications)

FRIENDSWOOD—See HOUSTON, TX (Comcast Cable)

FRIO COUNTY (PORTIONS)—See DILLEY, TX (Time Warner Cable)

FRIONA—Formerly served by Reach Broadband. No longer in operation

FRISCO (TOWN) (COLLIN COUNTY)—See DALLAS, TX (Time Warner Cable)

FRISCO (TOWN) (DENTON COUNTY)—See DALLAS, TX (Time Warner Cable)

FRISCO—See DALLAS (northwest suburbs), TX (Grande Communications)

FRITCH—See BORGER, TX (Cable One)

FRONTON—See PHARR, TX (Time Warner Cable)

FRUITVALE—Formerly served by Almega Cable. No longer in operation

FULLER SPRINGS—See LUFKIN, TX (Suddenlink Communications)

FULSHEAR—See HOUSTON, TX (Comcast Cable)

FULTON—See ROCKPORT, TX (Time Warner Cable)

GAINES COUNTY (PORTIONS)—See SEMINOLE, TX (Baja Broadband)

GAINESVILLE—Suddenlink Communications

GALENA PARK—See HOUSTON, TX (Comcast Cable)

GALVESTON COUNTY (PORTIONS)—See HOUSTON, TX (Comcast Cable)

GALVESTON—See HOUSTON, TX (Comcast Cable)

GANADO—NewWave Communications. Now served by WHARTON, TX [TX0171]

GANADO—See WHARTON, TX (NewWave Communications)

GARCENO—See PHARR, TX (Time Warner Cable)

GARCIASVILLE—See PHARR, TX (Time Warner Cable)

GARDEN CITY—Formerly served by National Cable Inc. No longer in operation

GARDEN RIDGE—See SAN ANTONIO, TX (Time Warner Cable)

GARDENDALE—Formerly served by Cebridge Connections. No longer in operation

GARLAND—Time Warner Cable. Now served by DALLAS, TX [TX0003]

GARLAND—See DALLAS, TX (Time Warner Cable)

GARRETT—See MIDLOTHIAN, TX (Charter Communications)

GARRISON—Formerly served by Almega Cable. No longer in operation

GARWOOD—Formerly served by National Cable Inc. No longer in operation

GARY—Formerly served by Almega Cable. No longer in operation

GATESVILLE—Suddenlink Communications

GAUSE—Formerly served by National Cable Inc. No longer in operation

GEORGE WEST—Time Warner Cable

GEORGETOWN—Suddenlink Communications

GERONIMO—See SAN ANTONIO, TX (Time Warner Cable)

GIDDINGS—See LA GRANGE, TX (NewWave Communications)

GILLESPIE COUNTY (PORTIONS)—See AUSTIN, TX (Time Warner Cable)

GILMER—Formerly served by Gilmer Cable. No longer in operation

GLADEWATER (PORTIONS)—See HAWKINS, TX (Suddenlink Communications)

GLADEWATER—Suddenlink Communications

GLEN ROSE—Formerly served by Glen Rose CATV. No longer in operation

GLEN ROSE—See FORT WORTH (northern portions), TX (Charter Communications)

GLENN HEIGHTS—See MIDLOTHIAN, TX (Charter Communications)

GODLEY—Formerly served by Almega Cable. No longer in operation

GOLDEN—Formerly served by Almega Cable. No longer in operation

GOLDSMITH—Formerly served by Cebridge Connections. No longer in operation

GOLDTHWAITE—Formerly served by Almega Cable. No longer in operation

GOLDTHWAITE—Formerly served by Central Texas Communications. No longer in operation

GOLIAD—CommZoom

GOLINDA—Formerly served by National Cable Inc. No longer in operation

GONZALES COUNTY (PORTIONS)—See GONZALES, TX (Time Warner Cable)

GONZALES—See BOERNE, TX (GVTC Communications. Formerly [TX0315]. This cable system has converted to IPTV)

GONZALES—Time Warner Cable

GOODFELLOW AFB—See SAN ANGELO, TX (Suddenlink Communications)

GOODRICH—Livingston Communications (formerly Versalink). This cable system has converted to IPTV. See

Texas—Cable Community Index

GOODRICH, TX [TX5565]

GOODRICH—Livingston Communications (formerly Versalink). This cable system has converted to IPTV

GORDON—Formerly served by Mallard Cablevision. No longer in operation

GORDONVILLE—TV Cable of Grayson County

GOREE—Formerly served by Jayroc Cablevision. No longer in operation

GORMAN—Reach Broadband

GRAFORD—Vyve Broadband

GRAHAM—Zito Media

GRANADA HILLS (PORTIONS)—See AUSTIN, TX (Time Warner Cable)

GRANADA HILLS—Time Warner Cable. Now served by AUSTIN, TX [TX0005]

GRANBURY—Charter Communications. Now served by FORT WORTH (northern portions), TX [TX0008]

GRANBURY—See FORT WORTH (northern portions), TX (Charter Communications)

GRAND PRAIRIE—Time Warner Cable. Now served by DALLAS, TX [TX0003]

GRAND PRAIRIE—See DALLAS, TX (Time Warner Cable)

GRAND SALINE—See MINEOLA, TX (Suddenlink Communications)

GRANDFALLS—Formerly served by Almega Cable. No longer in operation

GRANGER—See BARTLETT, TX (Reveille Broadband)

GRANITE SHOALS—See MARBLE FALLS, TX (Northland Cable Television)

GRAPE CREEK—NewWave Communications

GRAPELAND—Suddenlink Communications

GRAPEVINE—See DALLAS, TX (Time Warner Cable)

GRAYSON COUNTY (NORTHERN PORTION)—See SHERMAN, TX (Cable One)

GRAYSON COUNTY (PORTIONS)—See WHITESBORO, TX (Suddenlink Communications)

GRAYSON COUNTY—TV Cable of Grayson County

GREENVILLE (RURAL AREAS)—See GREENVILLE, TX (Time Warner Cable)

GREENVILLE—GEUS

GREENVILLE—Time Warner Cable

GREENWOOD—Ridgewood Cablevision

GREGG COUNTY (PORTIONS)—See HAWKINS, TX (Suddenlink Communications)

GREGG COUNTY (UNINCORPORATED AREAS)—See LAKE CHEROKEE, TX (Alliance Communications)

GREGORY—See ARANSAS PASS, TX (Cable One)

GRESHAM (UNINCORPORATED AREAS)—See TYLER, TX (Suddenlink Communications)

GREY FOREST—See SAN ANTONIO, TX (Time Warner Cable)

GRIMES COUNTY (PORTIONS)—See BRENHAM, TX (Suddenlink Communications)

GROESBECK—See MEXIA, TX (Northland Cable Television)

GROOM—Formerly served by Almega Cable. No longer in operation

GROVES—See PORT ARTHUR, TX (Time Warner Cable)

GROVETON—Formerly served by Almega Cable. No longer in operation

GRUVER—Formerly served by Elk River TV Cable Co. No longer in operation

GUADALUPE COUNTY—See SAN ANTONIO, TX (Time Warner Cable)

GUN BARREL CITY—Suddenlink Communications. Now served by ATHENS, TX [TX0711]

GUN BARREL CITY—See ATHENS, TX (Suddenlink Communications)

GUNTER—See PILOT POINT, TX (Suddenlink Communications)

GUSTINE—Formerly served by Cable Unlimited. No longer in operation

GUY—Formerly served by Cebridge Connections. No longer in operation

HALE CENTER—NTS Communications. This cable system has converted to IPTV. See HALE CENTER, TX [TX5544]

HALE CENTER—NTS Communications. Formerly [TX0402]. This cable system has converted to IPTV

HALE COUNTY—See PLAINVIEW, TX (Suddenlink Communications)

HALL COUNTY (PORTIONS)—See MEMPHIS, TX (Reach Broadband)

HALLETTSVILLE—See LA GRANGE, TX (NewWave Communications)

HALLSVILLE—See MARSHALL, TX (Fidelity Communications)

HALTOM CITY—See FORT WORTH (northern portions), TX (Charter Communications)

HAMILTON—Northland Cable Television

HAMLIN—Suddenlink Communications

HAPPY COUNTRY HOMES—See TERRELL, TX (Suddenlink Communications)

HAPPY—Formerly served by Almega Cable. No longer in operation

HARBOR POINT—Formerly served by CableSouth Inc. No longer in operation

HARDIN COUNTY (PORTIONS)—See PORT ARTHUR, TX (Time Warner Cable)

HARKER HEIGHTS—See AUSTIN, TX (Time Warner Cable)

HARLINGEN—Time Warner Cable. Now served by PHARR, TX [TX0017]

HARLINGEN—See PHARR, TX (Time Warner Cable)

HARPER—Formerly served by Cable Comm Ltd. No longer in operation

HARRIS COUNTY (northern portion)—Charter Communications. Now served by MONTGOMERY COUNTY (portions), TX [TX0044]

HARRIS COUNTY (NORTHERN PORTION)—See MONTGOMERY COUNTY (portions), TX (Charter Communications)

HARRIS COUNTY (portions)—Comcast Cable. Now served by HOUSTON, TX [TX0001]

HARRIS COUNTY (PORTIONS)—See HOUSTON, TX (Comcast Cable)

HARRIS COUNTY (PORTIONS)—See HOUSTON, TX (En-Touch Systems Inc)

HARRIS COUNTY (SOUTHEASTERN PORTION)—See MONT BELVIEU, TX (Suddenlink Communications)

HARRIS COUNTY—See HOUSTON, TX (Comcast Cable)

HARRISON COUNTY (PORTIONS)—See MARSHALL, TX (Fidelity Communications)

HART—Reach Broadband

HARTLEY—See DALHART, TX (XIT Communications. Formerly [TX1023]. This cable system has converted to IPTV)

HASKELL—Formerly served by Alliance Communications. Now served by WesTex Telephone Cooperative

HASLET—See FORT WORTH (northern portions), TX (Charter Communications)

HASLET—See KELLER, TX (Millennium Telcom)

HASSE—Formerly served by Cable Unlimited. No longer in operation

HAWKINS—Suddenlink Communications

HAWLEY—Formerly served by Jayroc Cablevision. No longer in operation

HAYS COUNTY (NORTHEASTERN PORTION)—See SAN MARCOS, TX (Time Warner Cable)

HAYS—See AUSTIN, TX (Time Warner Cable)

HEARNE—Suddenlink Communications

HEATH—See TERRELL, TX (Suddenlink Communications)

HEBBRONVILLE—Alliance Communications

HEBRON—See DALLAS, TX (Time Warner Cable)

HEDLEY—Formerly served by Almega Cable. No longer in operation

HEDWIG VILLAGE—See HOUSTON, TX (Comcast Cable)

HEIGHTS (unincorporated areas)—Formerly served by Almega Cable. No longer in operation

HELOTES—See SAN ANTONIO, TX (Time Warner Cable)

HEMPHILL COUNTY (PORTIONS)—See CANADIAN, TX (Suddenlink Communications)

HEMPHILL—Formerly served by Almega Cable. No longer in operation

HEMPSTEAD—NewWave Communications

HENDERSON COUNTY (PORTIONS)—See ATHENS, TX (Suddenlink Communications)

HENDERSON—Suddenlink Communications

HENRIETTA—Suddenlink Communications

HEREFORD—WT Services (formerly XIT)

HERMLEIGH—See SNYDER, TX (Suddenlink Communications)

HEWITT—See WACO, TX (Grande Communications)

HEWITT—See AUSTIN, TX (Time Warner Cable)

HICKORY CREEK—See DENTON, TX (Charter Communications)

HICO—Formerly served by Northland Cable Television. No longer in operation

HIDALGO COUNTY (PORTIONS)—See PHARR, TX (Time Warner Cable)

HIDALGO—Time Warner Cable. Now served by PHARR, TX [TX0017]

HIDALGO—See PHARR, TX (Time Warner Cable)

HIDEAWAY—See MINEOLA, TX (Suddenlink Communications)

HIGGINS—Formerly served by Almega Cable. No longer in operation

HIGHLAND HAVEN—See MARBLE FALLS, TX (Northland Cable Television)

HIGHLAND PARK—See UNIVERSITY PARK, TX (Charter Communications)

HIGHLAND RANGE—Formerly served by Highland Cable. No longer in operation

HIGHLAND VILLAGE—See DALLAS, TX (Time Warner Cable)

HIGHLANDS—See HOUSTON, TX (Comcast Cable)

Cable Community Index—Texas

HILL COUNTRY VILLAGE—See SAN ANTONIO, TX (Time Warner Cable)

HILL COUNTY (PORTIONS)—See HILLSBORO, TX (Northland Cable Television)

HILLCREST VILLAGE—See HOUSTON, TX (Comcast Cable)

HILLSBORO—Northland Cable Television

HILLSHIRE VILLAGE—See HOUSTON, TX (Comcast Cable)

HITCHCOCK—See HOUSTON, TX (Comcast Cable)

HOLIDAY LAKES—Formerly served by Cebridge Connections. No longer in operation

HOLLAND—See AUSTIN, TX (Time Warner Cable)

HOLLIDAY—Time Warner Cable. Now served by WICHITA FALLS, TX [TX0026]

HOLLIDAY—See WICHITA FALLS, TX (Time Warner Cable)

HOLLYWOOD PARK—See SAN ANTONIO, TX (Time Warner Cable)

HOMER—Formerly served by Almega Cable. No longer in operation

HOMESTEAD HOMES—See EL PASO, TX (Time Warner Cable)

HONDO—CommZoom

HONEY GROVE—Formerly served by Suddenlink Communications. No longer in operation

HOOD COUNTY (PORTIONS)—See FORT WORTH (northern portions), TX (Charter Communications)

HOOKS—Allegiance Communications. Now served by NEW BOSTON, TX [TX0204]

HOOKS—See NEW BOSTON, TX (Vyve Broadband)

HOPEWELL—See PARIS, TX (Suddenlink Communications)

HOPKINS COUNTY (PORTIONS)—See SULPHUR SPRINGS, TX (Suddenlink Communications)

HORIZON CITY—See EL PASO, TX (Time Warner Cable)

HORSESHOE BAY—See MARBLE FALLS, TX (Northland Cable Television)

HORSESHOE BAY—See AUSTIN, TX (Time Warner Cable)

HOUSTON COUNTY (PORTIONS)—See CROCKETT, TX (Northland Cable Television)

HOUSTON—Formerly served by Sprint Corp. No longer in operation

HOUSTON—Formerly served by Wavevision/TVMAX. No longer in operation

HOUSTON—Comcast Cable

HOUSTON—En-Touch Systems Inc

HOUSTON—Phonoscope Ltd

HOWARD COUNTY—See BIG SPRING, TX (Suddenlink Communications)

HOWARDWICK—Formerly served by Almega Cable. No longer in operation

HOWE—See SHERMAN, TX (Cable One)

HUBBARD—Formerly served by Almega Cable. No longer in operation

HUDSON—Suddenlink Communications. Now served by LUFKIN, TX [TX0051]

HUDSON—See LUFKIN, TX (Suddenlink Communications)

HUFFMAN—See KINGWOOD, TX (Suddenlink Communications)

HUGHES SPRINGS—See DAINGERFIELD, TX (Suddenlink Communications)

HULL—Formerly served by Carrell Communications. No longer in operation

HUMBLE—See HOUSTON, TX (Comcast Cable)

HUNT COUNTY (PORTIONS)—See DALLAS, TX (Time Warner Cable)

HUNT—See INGRAM, TX (Suddenlink Communications)

HUNTER CREEK VILLAGE—See HOUSTON, TX (Comcast Cable)

HUNTINGTON—Vyve Broadband

HUNTSVILLE—Suddenlink Communications

HURST—See FORT WORTH (northern portions), TX (Charter Communications)

HUTCHINS—See DALLAS, TX (Time Warner Cable)

HUTTO—See AUSTIN, TX (Time Warner Cable)

IDALOU—NTS Communications. This cable system has converted to IPTV. See IDALOU, TX [TX5554]

IDALOU—NTS Communications. Formerly [TX0406]. This cable system has converted to IPTV

IMPERIAL—Formerly served by Cebridge Connections. No longer in operation

INDIAN HILLS—See BOERNE, TX (GVTC Communications. Formerly [TX0315]. This cable system has converted to IPTV)

INDIAN LAKE—See PHARR, TX (Time Warner Cable)

INDIAN SHORE—See KINGWOOD, TX (Suddenlink Communications)

INDIAN SPRINGS—Formerly served by Cebridge Connections. No longer in operation

INGLESIDE ON THE BAY—See ARANSAS PASS, TX (Cable One)

INGLESIDE—See ARANSAS PASS, TX (Cable One)

INGRAM—Suddenlink Communications

IOLA—Formerly served by National Cable Inc. No longer in operation

IOWA PARK—Formerly served by Cebridge Connections. Now served by Suddenlink Communications, BURKBURNETT, TX [TX0154]

IOWA PARK—See BURKBURNETT, TX (Suddenlink Communications)

IRAAN—LynnStar Communications

IRVING—Time Warner Cable. Now served by DALLAS, TX [TX0003]

IRVING—See DALLAS, TX (Time Warner Cable)

ITALY—Formerly served by Almega Cable. No longer in operation

JACINTO CITY—See HOUSTON, TX (Comcast Cable)

JACKSBORO—Vyve Broadband

JACKSON COUNTY (UNINCORPORATED AREAS)—See WHARTON, TX (NewWave Communications)

JACKSON'S LANDING (UNINCORPORATED ARESAS)—See TYLER, TX (Suddenlink Communications)

JACKSONVILLE—Suddenlink Communications

JAMAICA BEACH (VILLAGE)—See HOUSTON, TX (Comcast Cable)

JARRELL—Suddenlink Communications

JASPER—NewWave Communications

JAYTON—Formerly served by Jayroc Cablevision. No longer in operation

JEFFERSON—See MARSHALL, TX (Fidelity Communications)

JERSEY VILLAGE—See HOUSTON, TX (Comcast Cable)

JEWETT—Formerly served by Northland Cable Television. No longer in operation

JIM WELLS COUNTY (PORTIONS)—See CORPUS CHRISTI, TX (Time Warner Cable)

JOAQUIN—NewWave Communications. Now served by LOGANSPORT, LA [LA0096]

JOHNSON CITY—Formerly served by Almega Cable. No longer in operation

JOHNSON COUNTY (PORTIONS)—See CADDO PEAK, TX (North Texas Broadband)

JONES COUNTY (PORTIONS)—See ANSON, TX (Suddenlink Communications)

JONES COUNTY (PORTIONS)—See HAMLIN, TX (Suddenlink Communications)

JONES CREEK—See BRAZORIA, TX (Coastal Link Communications)

JONESTOWN—See AUSTIN, TX (Time Warner Cable)

JOSEPHINE—Formerly served by Almega Cable. No longer in operation

JOSHUA—Pathway. This cable system has converted to IPTV. Now served by BURLESON, TX [TX5530]

JOSHUA—Pathway. This cable system has converted to IPTV. Now served by BURLESON, TX [TX5530]

JOSHUA—See BURLESON, TX (Pathway. Formerly [TX0103]. This cable system has converted to IPTV)

JOURDANTON—Alliance Communications

JUNCTION—Suddenlink Communications

KARNES CITY—See KENEDY, TX (CommZoom)

KATY (southern portion)—Formerly served by Cebridge Connections. No longer in operation

KATY—See HOUSTON, TX (Comcast Cable)

KATY—See HOUSTON, TX (En-Touch Systems Inc)

KAUFMAN COUNTY—See TERRELL, TX (Suddenlink Communications)

KAUFMAN—Suddenlink Communications

KELLER—See FORT WORTH (northern portions), TX (Charter Communications)

KELLER—Millennium Telcom

KELLY AFB—See SAN ANTONIO, TX (Time Warner Cable)

KEMAH—See HOUSTON, TX (Comcast Cable)

KEMPNER—Formerly served by National Cable Inc. No longer in operation

KEMPNER—See AUSTIN, TX (Time Warner Cable)

KENDALL COUNTY (PORTIONS)—See SAN ANTONIO, TX (Time Warner Cable)

KENEDY—CommZoom

KENEFICK—Formerly served by Carrell Communications. No longer in operation

KENNEDALE—See FORT WORTH (northern portions), TX (Charter Communications)

KERENS—Formerly served by Northland Cable Television. No longer in operation

KERMIT—Suddenlink Communications

KERR COUNTY (PORTIONS)—See INGRAM, TX (Suddenlink Communications)

KERR COUNTY (PORTIONS)—See KERRVILLE, TX (Time Warner Cable)

KERRVILLE—Time Warner Cable

KILGORE—Formerly served by Almega Cable. Now served by LONGVIEW, TX [TX0033]

Texas—Cable Community Index

KILGORE—Kilgore Cable TV Co. Now served by LONGVIEW, TX [TX0033]

KILGORE—See LONGVIEW, TX (Longview Cable Television)

KILLEEN—Time Warner Cable. Now served by AUSTIN, TX [TX0005]

KILLEEN—See AUSTIN, TX (Time Warner Cable)

KIMBLE COUNTY (PORTIONS)—See JUNCTION, TX (Suddenlink Communications)

KINGSLAND—See MARBLE FALLS, TX (Northland Cable Television)

KINGSVILLE—NewWave Communications

KINGWOOD—Suddenlink Communications

KIRBY—See SAN ANTONIO, TX (Grande Communications)

KIRBY—See SAN ANTONIO, TX (Time Warner Cable)

KIRBYVILLE—Formerly served by CommuniComm Services. No longer in operation

KNIPPA—See UVALDE, TX (Time Warner Cable)

KNOLLWOOD—See SHERMAN, TX (Cable One)

KNOX CITY—Formerly served by Alliance Communications. No longer In operation

KOSSE—Formerly served by Almega Cable. No longer in operation

KOUNTZE—Time Warner Cable. Now served by PORT ARTHUR (formerly Beaumont), TX [TX0022]

KOUNTZE—See PORT ARTHUR, TX (Time Warner Cable)

KRESS—Formerly served by Almega Cable. No longer in operation

KRUGERVILLE—See PILOT POINT, TX (Suddenlink Communications)

KRUM—Suddenlink Communications

KYLE—See AUSTIN, TX (Time Warner Cable)

LA COSTE—See SAN ANTONIO, TX (Time Warner Cable)

LA FERIA—See PHARR, TX (Time Warner Cable)

LA GRANGE—NewWave Communications

LA GRULLA—Time Warner Cable. Now served by PHARR, TX [TX0017]

LA GRULLA—See PHARR, TX (Time Warner Cable)

LA JOYA—See PHARR, TX (Time Warner Cable)

LA MARQUE—See HOUSTON, TX (Comcast Cable)

LA PORTE—See HOUSTON, TX (Comcast Cable)

LA PRYOR—Formerly served by Almega Cable. No longer in operation

LA ROSITA—See PHARR, TX (Time Warner Cable)

LA SALLE COUNTY (PORTIONS)—See DILLEY, TX (Time Warner Cable)

LA UNION—See EL PASO, NM (Time Warner Cable)

LA VERNIA—CommZoom

LA VILLA—See PHARR, TX (Time Warner Cable)

LACKLAND AFB—See SAN ANTONIO, TX (Time Warner Cable)

LACY LAKEVIEW—See WACO, TX (Grande Communications)

LACY-LAKEVIEW—See AUSTIN, TX (Time Warner Cable)

LAGO VISTA—See AUSTIN, TX (Time Warner Cable)

LAGUNA HEIGHTS—See PHARR, TX (Time Warner Cable)

LAGUNA VISTA—See PHARR, TX (Time Warner Cable)

LAKE ARROWHEAD—Formerly served by Buford Media Group. No longer in operation

LAKE BRIDGEPORT—See DECATUR, TX (Vyve Broadband)

LAKE BROWNWOOD—Formerly served by National Cable Inc. No longer in operation

LAKE BUCHANAN—Formerly served by Northland Cable Television. No longer in operation

LAKE CHEROKEE—Alliance Communications

LAKE CITY—See CORPUS CHRISTI, TX (Time Warner Cable)

LAKE CONROE EAST—See KINGWOOD, TX (Suddenlink Communications)

LAKE DALLAS—See DENTON, TX (Charter Communications)

LAKE DALLAS—See DALLAS (northwest suburbs), TX (Grande Communications)

LAKE GRAHAM—Westlake Cable

LAKE HILLS—Formerly served by Zoom Media. No longer in operation

LAKE JACKSON—See HOUSTON, TX (Comcast Cable)

LAKE KIOWA—See VALLEY VIEW, TX (Nortex Communications)

LAKE L.B. JOHNSON—See MARBLE FALLS, TX (Northland Cable Television)

LAKE MEXIA—See MEXIA, TX (Northland Cable Television)

LAKE PALESTINE EAST—Suddenlink Communications. Now served by TYLER, TX [TX0027]

LAKE PALESTINE EAST—See TYLER, TX (Suddenlink Communications)

LAKE PALESTINE WEST—Suddenlink Communications. Now served by TYLER, TX [TX0027]

LAKE PALESTINE WEST—See TYLER, TX (Suddenlink Communications)

LAKE TANGLEWOOD—See AMARILLO, TX (Suddenlink Communications)

LAKE THUNDERBIRD ESTATES—See SMITHVILLE, TX (Reveille Broadband)

LAKE TYLER—See TYLER, TX (Suddenlink Communications)

LAKE WHITNEY—See WHITNEY, TX (LynnStar Communications)

LAKE WORTH—See FORT WORTH (northern portions), TX (Charter Communications)

LAKEPORT—See LAKE CHEROKEE, TX (Alliance Communications)

LAKESIDE CITY—See WICHITA FALLS, TX (Time Warner Cable)

LAKESIDE—See FORT WORTH (northern portions), TX (Charter Communications)

LAKESIDE—See CORPUS CHRISTI, TX (Time Warner Cable)

LAKEWAY—See AUSTIN, TX (Time Warner Cable)

LAKEWOOD VILLAGE—See PILOT POINT, TX (Suddenlink Communications)

LAMAR COUNTY (PORTIONS)—See CLARKSVILLE, TX (Suddenlink Communications)

LAMAR COUNTY (UNINCORPORATED AREAS)—See PARIS, TX (Suddenlink Communications)

LAMESA—Northland Cable Television

LAMESA—See WOLFFORTH, TX (NTS Communications)

LAMPASAS COUNTY (PORTIONS)—See AUSTIN, TX (Time Warner Cable)

LAMPASAS COUNTY—See LAMPASAS, TX (Suddenlink Communications)

LAMPASAS—Suddenlink Communications

LANCASTER—See DALLAS, TX (Time Warner Cable)

LANEVILLE—Formerly served by Cebridge Connections. No longer in operation

LANSING—Formerly served by Zoom Media. No longer in operation

LANTANNA—See DALLAS (northwest suburbs), TX (Grande Communications)

LAREDO—Time Warner Cable

LAS GALLINAS—Formerly served by Almega Cable. No longer in operation

LAS MILPAS—See PHARR, TX (Time Warner Cable)

LATEXO—See GRAPELAND, TX (Suddenlink Communications)

LAUGHLIN AFB—See DEL RIO, TX (Time Warner Cable)

LAVACA COUNTY (PORTIONS)—See GONZALES, TX (Time Warner Cable)

LEAGUE CITY—See HOUSTON, TX (Comcast Cable)

LEANDER—See AUSTIN, TX (Grande Communications)

LEANDER—Suddenlink Communications

LEANDER—See AUSTIN, TX (Time Warner Cable)

LEARY—See TEXARKANA, TX (Cable One)

LEFORS—Formerly served by Almega Cable. No longer in operation

LEON SPRINGS—See SAN ANTONIO, TX (Time Warner Cable)

LEON VALLEY—See SAN ANTONIO, TX (Time Warner Cable)

LEONA—Formerly served by Charter Communications. No longer in operation

LEONARD—Formerly served by Zoom Media. No longer in operation

LEVELLAND—NTS Communications. This cable system has converted to IPTV. Now served by WOLFFORTH, TX [TX5540]

LEVELLAND—See WOLFFORTH, TX (NTS Communications)

LEWISVILLE—See DALLAS (northwest suburbs), TX (Grande Communications)

LEWISVILLE—See DALLAS, TX (Time Warner Cable)

LEXINGTON—Reveille Broadband

LIBERTY CITY—See GLADEWATER, TX (Suddenlink Communications)

LIBERTY COUNTY (PORTIONS)—See HOUSTON, TX (Comcast Cable)

LIBERTY COUNTY (SOUTHEASTERN PORTION)—See MONT BELVIEU, TX (Suddenlink Communications)

LIBERTY HILL—See AUSTIN, TX (Time Warner Cable)

LIBERTY—Formerly served by Time Warner Cable. Now served by Comcast Cable, HOUSTON, TX [TX0001]

LIBERTY—See HOUSTON, TX (Comcast Cable)

LINDALE—See MINEOLA, TX (Suddenlink Communications)

LINDEN—Formerly served by Reach Broadband. No longer in operation

LINDSAY—See VALLEY VIEW, TX (Nortex Communications)

LIPAN—Formerly served by Almega Cable. No longer in operation

LITTLE ELM—See DALLAS (northwest suburbs), TX (Grande Communications)

LITTLE ELM—See PILOT POINT, TX (Suddenlink Communications)

LITTLE RIVER-ACADEMY—Grande Communications

296-Cable Community Index

TV & Cable Factbook No. 85

Cable Community Index—Texas

LITTLEFIELD—See WOLFFORTH, TX (NTS Communications)

LIVE OAK—See SAN ANTONIO, TX (Time Warner Cable)

LIVERPOOL—Formerly served by Almega Cable. No longer in operation

LIVINGSTON—Formerly served by Suddenlink Communications. No longer in operation

LLANO—Northland Cable Television

LOCKHART—Time Warner Cable. Now served by SAN MARCOS, TX [TX0849]

LOCKHART—See SAN MARCOS, TX (Time Warner Cable)

LOCKNEY—Reach Broadband

LOG CABIN—See ATHENS, TX (Suddenlink Communications)

LOLITA—Formerly served by Clearview Cable. No longer in operation

LOMETA—Formerly served by Almega Cable. No longer in operation

LONE STAR—See DAINGERFIELD, TX (Suddenlink Communications)

LONGVIEW—Longview Cable Television

LOOP—Formerly served by National Cable Inc. No longer in operation

LOPEZVILLE—See PHARR, TX (Time Warner Cable)

LORAINE (town)—Formerly served by Almega Cable. No longer in operation

LORENA—Time Warner Cable. Now served by AUSTIN, TX [TX0005]

LORENA—See AUSTIN, TX (Time Warner Cable)

LORENZO—Formerly served by Almega Cable. No longer in operation

LOS BARRERAS—See PHARR, TX (Time Warner Cable)

LOS FRESNOS—Time Warner Cable. Now served by PHARR, TX [TX0017]

LOS FRESNOS—See PHARR, TX (Time Warner Cable)

LOS SAENZ—See PHARR, TX (Time Warner Cable)

LOST PINES—Suddenlink Communications

LOTT—Zito Media

LOUISE—NewWave Communications. Now served by WHARTON, TX [TX0171]

LOUISE—See WHARTON, TX (NewWave Communications)

LOVELADY—Formerly served by Almega Cable. No longer in operation

LOWRY CROSSING—Suddenlink Communications. Now served by TERRELL, TX [TX0920]

LOWRY CROSSING—See TERRELL, TX (Suddenlink Communications)

LUBBOCK COUNTY (southeastern portion)—Formerly served by Almega Cable. No longer in operation

LUBBOCK—NTS Communications. This cable system has converted to IPTV. Now served by WOLFFORTH, TX [TX5540]

LUBBOCK—See WOLFFORTH, TX (NTS Communications)

LUBBOCK—Suddenlink Communications

LUCAS—Suddenlink Communications. Now served by TERRELL, TX [TX0920]

LUCAS—See DALLAS (northwest suburbs), TX (Grande Communications)

LUCAS—See TERRELL, TX (Suddenlink Communications)

LUEDERS—Formerly served by Jayroc Cablevision. No longer in operation

LUFKIN—Suddenlink Communications

LULING—Time Warner Cable. Now served by SAN MARCOS, TX [TX0849]

LULING—See SAN MARCOS, TX (Time Warner Cable)

LUMBERTON—See PORT ARTHUR, TX (Time Warner Cable)

LYFORD—See PHARR, TX (Time Warner Cable)

LYONS—Reveille Broadband

LYTLE—See DEVINE, TX (CommZoom)

MABANK—See ATHENS, TX (Suddenlink Communications)

MADISON COUNTY—See MADISONVILLE, TX (Northland Cable Television)

MADISONVILLE—Northland Cable Television

MAGNOLIA—Formerly served by Versalink Media. No longer in operation

MAGNOLIA—See HOUSTON, TX (Comcast Cable)

MALAKOFF—Formerly served by Northland Cable Television. Now served by Suddenlink Communications, ATHENS, TX [TX0711]

MALAKOFF—See ATHENS, TX (Suddenlink Communications)

MANOR—Formerly served by Almega Cable. No longer in operation

MANOR—See AUSTIN, TX (Time Warner Cable)

MANSFIELD—See FORT WORTH (northern portions), TX (Charter Communications)

MANVEL—NewWave Communications. Now served by WHARTON, TX [TX0171]

MANVEL—See WHARTON, TX (NewWave Communications)

MARATHON—Mountain Zone TV

MARBLE FALLS—Northland Cable Television

MARBLE FALLS—See AUSTIN, TX (Time Warner Cable)

MARFA—Marfa TV Cable Co. Inc

MARION COUNTY (PORTIONS)—See MARSHALL, TX (Fidelity Communications)

MARION—See SAN ANTONIO, TX (Time Warner Cable)

MARKHAM—See WHARTON, TX (NewWave Communications)

MARLIN—Northland Cable Television

MARSHALL—Fidelity Communications

MART—LynnStar Communications

MARTINDALE—See SAN MARCOS, TX (Time Warner Cable)

MASON COUNTY (PORTIONS)—See MASON, TX (LynnStar Communications)

MASON—LynnStar Communications

MATADOR (TOWN)—Reach Broadband

MATAGORDA COUNTY (UNINCORPORATED AREAS)—See WHARTON, TX (NewWave Communications)

MATHIS—Time Warner Cable. Now served by CORPUS CHRISTI, TX [TX0010]

MATHIS—See CORPUS CHRISTI, TX (Time Warner Cable)

MAUD—BCI Broadband. Now served by NEW BOSTON, TX [TX0204]

MAUD—See NEW BOSTON, TX (Vyve Broadband)

MAURICEVILLE—Formerly served by Cebridge Connections. No longer in operation

MAVERICK COUNTY (PORTIONS)—See EAGLE PASS, TX (Time Warner Cable)

MAXWELL—See SAN MARCOS, TX (Time Warner Cable)

MAY—Formerly served by Cable Unlimited. No longer in operation

MCADOO—See WOODROW, TX (South Plains Telephone Cooperative)

MCALLEN—See PHARR, TX (Time Warner Cable)

MCCAMEY—Reach Broadband

MCCLENDON-CHISOLM—See TERRELL, TX (Suddenlink Communications)

MCCULLOCH COUNTY (PORTIONS)—See BRADY, TX (Suddenlink Communications)

MCDADE—See AUSTIN, TX (Time Warner Cable)

MCGREGOR—See AUSTIN, TX (Time Warner Cable)

MCKINNEY—See DALLAS (northwest suburbs), TX (Grande Communications)

MCKINNEY—See DALLAS, TX (Time Warner Cable)

MCLENNAN COUNTY (PORTIONS)—See AUSTIN, TX (Time Warner Cable)

MEADOW—See WOLFFORTH, TX (NTS Communications)

MEADOWLAKES—See MARBLE FALLS, TX (Northland Cable Television)

MEADOWS PLACE—See HOUSTON, TX (Comcast Cable)

MEDINA COUNTY (PORTIONS)—See DEVINE, TX (CommZoom)

MEDINA COUNTY (PORTIONS)—See HONDO, TX (CommZoom)

MEDINA COUNTY (PORTIONS)—See SAN ANTONIO, TX (Time Warner Cable)

MEDINA—Formerly served by Medina Cable Ltd. No longer in operation

MELISSA—See PILOT POINT, TX (Suddenlink Communications)

MEMPHIS—Reach Broadband

MENARD COUNTY (PORTIONS)—See MENARD, TX (LynnStar Communications)

MENARD—LynnStar Communications

MERCEDES—See PHARR, TX (Time Warner Cable)

MERIDIAN—Formerly served by Almega Cable. No longer in operation

MERKEL—NewWave Communications

MERTZON—Formerly served by Reach Broadband. No longer in operation

MESQUITE—See DALLAS, TX (Time Warner Cable)

MEXIA—Northland Cable Television

MEYERLAND—See HOUSTON, TX (Comcast Cable)

MIAMI—Formerly served by Elk River TV Cable Co. No longer in operation

MIDLAND COUNTY (PORTIONS)—See MIDLAND, TX (Suddenlink Communications)

MIDLAND—See ODESSA, TX (Grande Communications)

MIDLAND—Suddenlink Communications

MIDLOTHIAN—Charter Communications

MIDWAY—Formerly served by Almega Cable. No longer in operation

MILAM COUNTY (PORTIONS)—See CAMERON, TX (Zito Media)

MILES—Formerly served by Allegiance Communications. No longer in operation

MILLER COUNTY (PORTIONS)—See TEXARKANA, AR (Cable One)

MILLSAP—Formerly served by Mallard Cablevision. No longer in operation

MINEOLA—Suddenlink Communications

MINERAL WELLS—Suddenlink Communications

Texas—Cable Community Index

MISSION—See PHARR, TX (Time Warner Cable)

MISSOURI CITY—See HOUSTON, TX (Comcast Cable)

MISSOURI CITY—See HOUSTON, TX (En-Touch Systems Inc)

MOBILE CITY—See TERRELL, TX (Suddenlink Communications)

MONAHANS—Suddenlink Communications

MONT BELVIEU—Suddenlink Communications

MONTAGUE—Formerly served by Cebridge Connections. No longer in operation

MONTGOMERY COUNTY (PORTIONS)—Charter Communications

MONTGOMERY COUNTY (PORTIONS)—See HOUSTON, TX (Comcast Cable)

MONTGOMERY COUNTY (PORTIONS)—See KINGWOOD, TX (Suddenlink Communications)

MONTGOMERY COUNTY (unincorporated areas)—Formerly served by Versalink Media. No longer in operation

MONTGOMERY COUNTY—See CONROE, TX (Suddenlink Communications)

MONTGOMERY COUNTY—See KINGWOOD, TX (Suddenlink Communications)

MONTGOMERY—See KINGWOOD, TX (Suddenlink Communications)

MOODY—Grande Communications

MORAN—Formerly served by Jayroc Cablevision. No longer in operation

MORGAN'S POINT RESORT—Grande Communications

MORGANS POINT—See HOUSTON, TX (Comcast Cable)

MORRIS COUNTY—See DAINGERFIELD, TX (Suddenlink Communications)

MORTON—See WOLFFORTH, TX (NTS Communications)

MOSS BLUFF—Formerly served by Carrell Communications. No longer in operation

MOULTON—Formerly served by National Cable Inc. No longer in operation

MOUND—Formerly served by National Cable Inc. No longer in operation

MOUNT ENTERPRISE—Formerly served by Cebridge Connections. No longer in operation

MOUNT PLEASANT—Suddenlink Communications

MOUNT VERNON—Suddenlink Communications

MOUNTAIN CITY—See AUSTIN, TX (Time Warner Cable)

MUENSTER—See VALLEY VIEW, TX (Nortex Communications)

MULESHOE—Reach Broadband

MUNDAY—Formerly served by Alliance Communications. Now served by WesTex Telephone Cooperative

MURPHY—See DALLAS, TX (Time Warner Cable)

MUSTANG RIDGE—Formerly served by Almega Cable. No longer in operation

MUSTANG RIDGE—See AUSTIN, TX (Time Warner Cable)

MYRTLE SPRINGS—Formerly served by Cebridge Connections. No longer in operation

NACOGDOCHES COUNTY—See NACOGDOCHES, TX (Suddenlink Communications)

NACOGDOCHES—Suddenlink Communications

NAPLES (town)—Formerly served by Alliance Communications Network. No longer in operation

NASH—See TEXARKANA, TX (Cable One)

NASSAU BAY—See HOUSTON, TX (Comcast Cable)

NATALIA—See DEVINE, TX (CommZoom)

NAVAL AIR STATION KINGSVILLE—See KINGSVILLE, TX (NewWave Communications)

NAVARRO COUNTY (PORTIONS)—See CORSICANA, TX (Northland Cable Television)

NAVASOTA—Suddenlink Communications. Now served by BRENHAM, TX [TX0124]

NAVASOTA—See BRENHAM, TX (Suddenlink Communications)

NAZARETH—Formerly served by Elk River TV Cable Co. No longer in operation

NEDERLAND—See PORT ARTHUR, TX (Time Warner Cable)

NEEDVILLE—See HOUSTON, TX (Comcast Cable)

NEW BOSTON—Vyve Broadband

NEW BRAUNFELS—See SAN MARCOS, TX (Grande Communications)

NEW BRAUNFELS—See SAN ANTONIO, TX (Time Warner Cable)

NEW CANEY—Formerly served by Suddenlink Communications. No longer in operation

NEW CHAPEL HILL—See TYLER, TX (Suddenlink Communications)

NEW DEAL—See WOLFFORTH, TX (NTS Communications)

NEW HOPE—See TERRELL, TX (Suddenlink Communications)

NEW SUMMERFIELD—Formerly served by Almega Cable. No longer in operation

NEW ULM—Formerly served by National Cable Inc. No longer in operation

NEW WAVERLY—Cablevision of Walker County

NEWCASTLE—Zito Media

NIEDERWALD—See AUSTIN, TX (Time Warner Cable)

NIXON—Formerly served by Almega Cable. No longer in operation

NOCONA—Suddenlink Communications

NOLAN COUNTY (NORTHERN PORTION)—See SWEETWATER, TX (Suddenlink Communications)

NOLANVILLE—See AUSTIN, TX (Time Warner Cable)

NOME—Formerly served by Carrell Communications. No longer in operation

NOONDAY—See TYLER, TX (Suddenlink Communications)

NORDHEIM—Formerly served by National Cable Inc. No longer in operation

NORMANGEE—Formerly served by Almega Cable. No longer in operation

NORTH CLEVELAND—See CLEVELAND, TX (NewWave Communications)

NORTH RICHLAND HILLS—See FORT WORTH (northern portions), TX (Charter Communications)

NORTH SILSBEE—Formerly served by Carrell Communications. No longer in operation

NORTH ZULCH—Formerly served by Almega Cable. No longer in operation

NORTHCLIFF—See SAN ANTONIO, TX (Time Warner Cable)

NORTHLAKE—See FORT WORTH (northern portions), TX (Charter Communications)

NUECES COUNTY—See CORPUS CHRISTI, TX (Time Warner Cable)

NURSERY—Formerly served by National Cable Inc. No longer in operation

O'DONNELL—NTS Communications. This cable system has converted to IPTV. See O'DONNELL, TZ [TX5556]

O'DONNELL—NTS Communications. Formerly [TX0496]. This cable system has converted to IPTV

OAK GROVE—See KAUFMAN, TX (Suddenlink Communications)

OAK LEAF—See MIDLOTHIAN, TX (Charter Communications)

OAK POINT—See PILOT POINT, TX (Suddenlink Communications)

OAK RIDGE NORTH—See MONTGOMERY COUNTY (portions), TX (Charter Communications)

OAK RIDGE—See GAINESVILLE, TX (Suddenlink Communications)

OAK RIDGE—See TERRELL, TX (Suddenlink Communications)

OAK TRAIL SHORES—See FORT WORTH (northern portions), TX (Charter Communications)

OAKWOOD—Formerly served by Charter Communications. No longer in operation

ODEM—See CORPUS CHRISTI, TX (Time Warner Cable)

ODESSA—Cable One

ODESSA—Grande Communications

OILTON—Formerly served by Windjammer Cable. No longer in operation

OKLAHOMA—Suddenlink Communications. Now served by KINGWOOD, TX [TX0052]

OKLAHOMA—See KINGWOOD, TX (Suddenlink Communications)

OLD RIVER-WINFREE—See MONT BELVIEU, TX (Suddenlink Communications)

OLDEN—See EASTLAND, TX (Suddenlink Communications)

OLMITO—See PHARR, TX (Time Warner Cable)

OLMOS PARK—See SAN ANTONIO, TX (Grande Communications)

OLMOS PARK—See SAN ANTONIO, TX (Time Warner Cable)

OLNEY—Suddenlink Communications

OLTON—NTS Communications. This cable system has converted to IPTV. See OLTON, TX [TX5557]

OLTON—NTS Communications. Formerly [TX0387]. This cable system has converted to IPTV

ONALASKA—Suddenlink Communications

ORANGE COUNTY (PORTIONS)—See PORT ARTHUR, TX (Time Warner Cable)

ORANGE GROVE—Time Warner Cable. Now served by CORPUS CHRISTI, TX [TX0010]

ORANGE GROVE—See CORPUS CHRISTI, TX (Time Warner Cable)

ORANGE—Time Warner Cable. Now served by PORT ARTHUR (formerly Beaumont), TX [TX0022]

ORANGE—See PORT ARTHUR, TX (Time Warner Cable)

ORE CITY—Formerly served by Rapid Communications. No longer in operation

OVILLA—See MIDLOTHIAN, TX (Charter Communications)

OWENTOWN—See HAWKINS, TX (Suddenlink Communications)

OYSTER CREEK—Formerly served by Almega Cable. No longer in operation

Cable Community Index—Texas

OYSTER CREEK—Telecom Cable

OZONA—Circle Bar Cable TV Inc

PADUCAH (TOWN)—Suddenlink Communications

PALACIOS—NewWave Communications. Now served by WHARTON, TX [TX0171]

PALACIOS—See WHARTON, TX (NewWave Communications)

PALESTINE—Zito Media

PALM HARBOR RV PARK—See ARANSAS PASS, TX (Cable One)

PALM PARK—See SAN ANTONIO, TX (Time Warner Cable)

PALM VALLEY—See PHARR, TX (Time Warner Cable)

PALMER—See MIDLOTHIAN, TX (Charter Communications)

PALMHURST—See PHARR, TX (Time Warner Cable)

PALMVIEW—See PHARR, TX (Time Warner Cable)

PALO PINTO COUNTY (PORTIONS)—See MINERAL WELLS, TX (Suddenlink Communications)

PALO PINTO—Formerly served by Mallard Cablevision. No longer in operation

PAMPA—See BORGER, TX (Cable One)

PANHANDLE—See BORGER, TX (Cable One)

PANOLA COUNTY (UNINCORPORATED AREAS)—See LAKE CHEROKEE, TX (Alliance Communications)

PANORAMA VILLAGE—See CONROE, TX (Suddenlink Communications)

PANTEGO (VILLAGE)—See DALLAS, TX (Time Warner Cable)

PARADISE—Formerly served by CableSouth Inc. No longer in operation

PARIS—Suddenlink Communications

PARKER COUNTY (PORTIONS)—See FORT WORTH (northern portions), TX (Charter Communications)

PARKER—See DALLAS, TX (Time Warner Cable)

PARKWAY VILLAGE—Formerly served by Time Warner Cable. No longer in operation

PASADENA—See HOUSTON, TX (Comcast Cable)

PATTON VILLAGE—See KINGWOOD, TX (Suddenlink Communications)

PAYNE SPRINGS—See ATHENS, TX (Suddenlink Communications)

PEARLAND—See HOUSTON, TX (Comcast Cable)

PEARLAND—See WHARTON, TX (NewWave Communications)

PEARSALL—See DILLEY, TX (Time Warner Cable)

PECAN HILL—See MIDLOTHIAN, TX (Charter Communications)

PECOS—Suddenlink Communications

PELICAN BAY—Formerly served by SouthTel Communications LP. No longer in operation

PENITAS—See PHARR, TX (Time Warner Cable)

PERRIN—Formerly served by Mallard Cablevision. No longer in operation

PERRYTON—Vyve Broadband

PETERSBURG—Formerly served by Almega Cable. No longer in operation

PETTIT—See WOODROW, TX (South Plains Telephone Cooperative)

PETTUS—Formerly served by National Cable Inc. No longer in operation

PFLUGERVILLE (TRAVIS COUNTY)—See AUSTIN, TX (Time Warner Cable)

PFLUGERVILLE (WILLIAMSON COUNTY)—See AUSTIN, TX (Time Warner Cable)

PFLUGERVILLE—See AUSTIN, TX (Grande Communications)

PFLUGERVILLE—Suddenlink Communications

PHARR—Time Warner Cable

PILOT POINT—Suddenlink Communications

PINE FOREST—See PORT ARTHUR, TX (Time Warner Cable)

PINEHURST—See PORT ARTHUR, TX (Time Warner Cable)

PINEY POINT—See HOUSTON, TX (Comcast Cable)

PITTSBURG—Suddenlink Communications

PLACEDO—Formerly served by National Cable Inc. No longer in operation

PLAINS—Formerly served by Almega Cable. No longer in operation

PLAINVIEW—Suddenlink Communications

PLANO—Time Warner Cable. Now served by DALLAS, TX [TX0003]

PLANO—See DALLAS (northwest suburbs), TX (Grande Communications)

PLANO—See DALLAS, TX (Time Warner Cable)

PLEAK—Formerly served by Almega Cable. No longer in operation

PLEASANT VALLEY—Formerly served by CableDirect. No longer in operation

PLEASANTON—CommZoom

PLUM GROVE—Formerly served by Carrell Communications. No longer in operation

POINT BLANK—See ONALASKA, TX (Suddenlink Communications)

POINT COMFORT—See PORT LAVACA, TX (Cable One)

POINT VENTURE—See AUSTIN, TX (Time Warner Cable)

POLK COUNTY (PORTIONS)—See LUFKIN, TX (Suddenlink Communications)

PONDER—Formerly served by SouthTel Communications LP. No longer in operation

PORT ACRES—See PORT ARTHUR, TX (Time Warner Cable)

PORT ARANSAS—Formerly served by Charter Communications. Now served by Time Warner Cable, ROCKPORT, TX [TX0116]

PORT ARANSAS—See ROCKPORT, TX (Time Warner Cable)

PORT ARTHUR—Time Warner Cable. Now served by PORT ARTHUR (formerly Beaumont), TX [TX0022]

PORT ARTHUR—Time Warner Cable

PORT ISABEL—Time Warner Cable. Now served by PHARR, TX [TX0017]

PORT ISABEL—See PHARR, TX (Time Warner Cable)

PORT LAVACA—Cable One

PORT NECHES—See PORT ARTHUR, TX (Time Warner Cable)

PORT O'CONNOR—Time Warner Cable. Now served by SEADRIFT, TX [TX0433]

PORT O'CONNOR—See SEADRIFT, TX (Time Warner Cable)

PORTER (PORTIONS)—See KINGWOOD, TX (Suddenlink Communications)

PORTER HEIGHTS (UNINCORPORATED AREAS)—See KINGWOOD, TX (Suddenlink Communications)

PORTER—Suddenklink Communications. Now served by KINGWOOD, TX [TX0052]

PORTER—See KINGWOOD, TX (Suddenlink Communications)

PORTLAND—Formerly served by Charter Communications. Now served by Time Warner Cable, ROCKPORT, TX [TX0116]

PORTLAND—See ROCKPORT, TX (Time Warner Cable)

POSSUM KINGDOM LAKE—Vyve Broadband

POST—Suddenlink Communications. Now served by LUBBOCK, TX [TX0012]

POST—See LUBBOCK, TX (Suddenlink Communications)

POTEET—See JOURDANTON, TX (Alliance Communications)

POTOSI—Formerly served by Jayroc Cablevision. No longer in operation

POTTSBORO—TV Cable of Grayson County

POTTSBORO—See PRESTON PENINSULA, TX (Vyve Broadband)

POWDERLY—Formerly served by Almega Cable. No longer in operation

PRAIRIE VIEW—Suddenlink Communications

PREMONT—Time Warner Cable. Now served by CORPUS CHRISTI, TX [TX0010]

PREMONT—See CORPUS CHRISTI, TX (Time Warner Cable)

PRESIDIO—Presidio TV Cable

PRESTON PENINSULA—Vyve Broadband

PRICE—Formerly served by Almega Cable. No longer in operation

PRIMERA—See PHARR, TX (Time Warner Cable)

PRINCETON—See DALLAS, TX (Time Warner Cable)

PROGRESO—Formerly served by CableDirect. No longer in operation

PROSPER—See PILOT POINT, TX (Suddenlink Communications)

QUANAH—Suddenlink Communications

QUEEN CITY—See ATLANTA, TX (Fidelity Communications)

QUEMADO—Time Warner Cable. Now served by EAGLE PASS, TX [TX0067]

QUEMADO—See EAGLE PASS, TX (Time Warner Cable)

QUINLAN—Formerly served by Zoom Media. No longer in operation

QUITAQUE—Formerly served by Almega Cable. No longer in operation

QUITMAN—See MINEOLA, TX (Suddenlink Communications)

RALLS—Reach Broadband

RANCHO VIEJO—See PHARR, TX (Time Warner Cable)

RANDOLPH AFB—See SAN ANTONIO, TX (Time Warner Cable)

RANGER—See EASTLAND, TX (Suddenlink Communications)

RANKIN—LynnStar Communications

RAVENNA—See SHERMAN, TX (Cable One)

RAYFORD FOREST—See MONTGOMERY COUNTY (portions), TX (Charter Communications)

RAYMONDVILLE—Time Warner Cable. Now served by PHARR, TX [TX0017]

RAYMONDVILLE—See PHARR, TX (Time Warner Cable)

RAYWOOD—Formerly served by Cebridge Connections. No longer in operation

REALITOS—Formerly served by National Cable Inc. No longer in operation

RED ACKERS—See TYLER, TX (Suddenlink Communications)

Texas—Cable Community Index

RED LICK—See TEXARKANA, TX (Cable One)

RED OAK—See MIDLOTHIAN, TX (Charter Communications)

RED RIVER ARMY DEPOT—See NEW BOSTON, TX (Vyve Broadband)

REDWATER—Cable One. Now served by TEXARKANA, TX [TX0031]

REDWATER—See TEXARKANA, TX (Cable One)

REESE AFB—See WOLFFORTH, TX (NTS Communications)

REEVES COUNTY (PORTIONS)—See PECOS, TX (Suddenlink Communications)

REFUGIO—Time Warner Cable. Now served by CORPUS CHRISTI, TX [TX0010]

REFUGIO—See CORPUS CHRISTI, TX (Time Warner Cable)

REKLAW—Formerly served by Almega Cable. No longer in operation

RENO (LAMAR COUNTY)—See PARIS, TX (Suddenlink Communications)

RENO (Parker County)—Formerly served by Almega Cable. No longer in operation

RICARDO—Formerly served by Riviera Cable TV. No longer in operation

RICHARDSON—See DALLAS, TX (Time Warner Cable)

RICHLAND HILLS—See FORT WORTH (northern portions), TX (Charter Communications)

RICHLAND SPRINGS—Formerly served by Almega Cable. No longer in operation

RICHMOND—See HOUSTON, TX (Comcast Cable)

RICHMOND—See HOUSTON, TX (EnTouch Systems Inc)

RICHMOND—See HOUSTON, TX (Phonoscope Ltd)

RICHWOOD—See HOUSTON, TX (Comcast Cable)

RIESEL—Formerly served by Cabletex Systems Inc. No longer in operation

RIO BRAVO—See LAREDO, TX (Time Warner Cable)

RIO DEL SOL—See PHARR, TX (Time Warner Cable)

RIO GRANDE CITY—Time Warner Cable. Now served by PHARR, TX [TX0017]

RIO GRANDE CITY—See PHARR, TX (Time Warner Cable)

RIO HONDO—See PHARR, TX (Time Warner Cable)

RIO VISTA—Formerly served by National Cable Inc. No longer in operation

RISING STAR—Formerly served by Brownwood TV Cable Service Inc. No longer in operation

RIVER OAKS—Charter Communications. Now served by FORT WORTH (northern portions), TX [TX0008]

RIVER OAKS—See FORT WORTH (northern portions), TX (Charter Communications)

RIVERSIDE—Formerly served by Almega Cable. No longer in operation

RIVIERA—Formerly served by Riviera Cable TV. No longer in operation

ROANOKE—See FORT WORTH (northern portions), TX (Charter Communications)

ROANOKE—See DALLAS (northwest suburbs), TX (Grande Communications)

ROARING SPRINGS (town)—Formerly served by Almega Cable. No longer in operation

ROBERT LEE—NewWave Communications

ROBERTSON COUNTY (PORTIONS)—See HEARNE, TX (Suddenlink Communications)

ROBINSON—See WACO, TX (Grande Communications)

ROBINSON—See AUSTIN, TX (Time Warner Cable)

ROBSTOWN—See CORPUS CHRISTI, TX (Time Warner Cable)

ROBY—Formerly served by Almega Cable. No longer in operation

ROCHESTER—Formerly served by Jayroc Cablevision. No longer in operation

ROCKDALE—Suddenlink Communications

ROCKPORT—Time Warner Cable

ROCKSPRINGS—Formerly served by Almega Cable. No longer in operation

ROCKWALL COUNTY (PORTIONS)—See TERRELL, TX (Suddenlink Communications)

ROCKWALL—Charter Communications

ROGERS—Grande Communications

ROLLING HILLS—See AMARILLO, TX (Suddenlink Communications)

ROLLINGWOOD—See AUSTIN, TX (Time Warner Cable)

ROMA—Time Warner Cable. Now served by PHARR, TX [TX0017]

ROMA—See PHARR, TX (Time Warner Cable)

ROMAN FOREST—See KINGWOOD, TX (Suddenlink Communications)

ROPESVILLE—See WOLFFORTH, TX (NTS Communications)

ROSCOE—NewWave Communications

ROSE CITY—Formerly served by Cebridge Connections. No longer in operation

ROSE HILL ACRES—See PORT ARTHUR, TX (Time Warner Cable)

ROSEBUD—Formerly served by DMS Cable. No longer in operation

ROSENBERG—See HOUSTON, TX (Comcast Cable)

ROSENBERG—See HOUSTON, TX (Phonoscope Ltd)

ROSHARON—See HOUSTON, TX (EnTouch Systems Inc)

ROTAN—Suddenlink Communications

ROUND ROCK (portions)—Grande Communications. Now served by AUSTIN, TX [TX0989]

ROUND ROCK—See AUSTIN, TX (Grande Communications)

ROUND ROCK—See AUSTIN, TX (Time Warner Cable)

ROWLETT—See DALLAS, TX (Time Warner Cable)

ROXTON—See PARIS, TX (Suddenlink Communications)

ROYSE CITY—Suddenlink Communications. Now served by TERRELL, TX [TX0920]

ROYSE CITY—See TERRELL, TX (Suddenlink Communications)

RULE—Formerly served by Alliance Communications. No longer in operation

RUNAWAY BAY—See DECATUR, TX (Vyve Broadband)

RUNGE—Formerly served by Almega Cable. No longer in operation

RUSK COUNTY (UNINCORPORATED AREAS)—See LAKE CHEROKEE, TX (Alliance Communications)

RUSK COUNTY—See HENDERSON, TX (Suddenlink Communications)

RUSK—Suddenlink Communications

SABINAL—Formerly served by Almega Cable. No longer in operation

SABINE PASS—See PORT ARTHUR, TX (Time Warner Cable)

SACHSE—See DALLAS, TX (Time Warner Cable)

SADLER—See WHITESBORO, TX (Suddenlink Communications)

SAGINAW—See FORT WORTH (northern portions), TX (Charter Communications)

SALADO—Grande Communications

SAN ANGELO—Formerly served by C & W Enterprises Inc. No longer in operation

SAN ANGELO—Suddenlink Communications

SAN ANTONIO (portions)—Grande Communications. Now served by SAN ANTONIO, TX [TX0990]

SAN ANTONIO—Grande Communications

SAN ANTONIO—Time Warner Cable

SAN AUGUSTINE—Formerly served by Cebridge Connections. Now served by Suddenlink Communications, CENTER, TX [TX0192]

SAN AUGUSTINE—See CENTER, TX (Suddenlink Communications)

SAN BENITO—See PHARR, TX (Time Warner Cable)

SAN CARLOS—Formerly served by CableDirect. No longer in operation

SAN DIEGO (DUVAL COUNTY)—See CORPUS CHRISTI, TX (Time Warner Cable)

SAN DIEGO (JIM WELLS COUNTY)—See CORPUS CHRISTI, TX (Time Warner Cable)

SAN ELIZARIO—See EL PASO, TX (Time Warner Cable)

SAN JACINTO COUNTY (PORTIONS)—See WATERWOOD, TX (Cablevision of Walker County)

SAN JUAN (HIDALGO COUNTY)—See PHARR, TX (Time Warner Cable)

SAN LEANNA—See AUSTIN, TX (Time Warner Cable)

SAN LEON—Formerly served by Almega Cable. No longer in operation

SAN MARCOS—Grande Communications

SAN MARCOS—Time Warner Cable

SAN PATRICIO COUNTY—Time Warner Cable. Now served by CORPUS CHRISTI, TX [TX0010]

SAN PATRICIO COUNTY—See ARANSAS PASS, TX (Cable One)

SAN PATRICIO COUNTY—See CORPUS CHRISTI, TX (Time Warner Cable)

SAN PATRICIO—See CORPUS CHRISTI, TX (Time Warner Cable)

SAN SABA—Central Texas Communications

SAN SABA—Suddenlink Communications

SAN YGNACIO—Time Warner Cable. Now served by LAREDO, TX [TX0029]

SAN YGNACIO—See LAREDO, TX (Time Warner Cable)

SANCTUARY—See FORT WORTH (northern portions), TX (Charter Communications)

SANDERSON—Mountain Zone TV

SANDIA—Formerly served by National Cable Inc. No longer in operation

SANGER—See PILOT POINT, TX (Suddenlink Communications)

SANSOM PARK—See FORT WORTH (northern portions), TX (Charter Communications)

SANTA ANNA—Formerly served by Brownwood TV Cable Service Inc. No longer in operation

Cable Community Index—Texas

SANTA CRUZ—See PHARR, TX (Time Warner Cable)

SANTA FE (unincorporated areas)—Formerly served by Almega Cable. No longer in operation

SANTA FE—See HOUSTON, TX (Comcast Cable)

SANTA ROSA—See PHARR, TX (Time Warner Cable)

SANTA TERESA—See EL PASO, NM (Time Warner Cable)

SARGENT—Formerly served by Almega Cable. No longer in operation

SAVOY—See SHERMAN, TX (Cable One)

SCENIC OAKS—See SAN ANTONIO, TX (Time Warner Cable)

SCHERTZ—See SAN ANTONIO, TX (Time Warner Cable)

SCHULENBURG—See LA GRANGE, TX (NewWave Communications)

SCURRY COUNTY (PORTIONS)—See SNYDER, TX (Suddenlink Communications)

SEABROOK—See HOUSTON, TX (Comcast Cable)

SEADRIFT—Time Warner Cable

SEAGOVILLE—See TERRELL, TX (Suddenlink Communications)

SEAGRAVES—See SEMINOLE, TX (Baja Broadband)

SEALY—NewWave Communications. Now served by SEALY (formerly Bellville), TX [TX0292]

SEALY—NewWave Communications

SEBASTIAN—Formerly served by Fiesta Cable. No longer in operation

SEGUIN—See SAN ANTONIO, TX (Time Warner Cable)

SELMA—See SAN ANTONIO, TX (Time Warner Cable)

SEMINOLE—Baja Broadband

SEVEN POINTS (northern portion)—Formerly served by Trust Cable. No longer in operation

SEVEN POINTS (SOUTHERN PORTION)—See ATHENS, TX (Suddenlink Communications)

SEYMOUR—Suddenlink Communications

SHADY SHORES—See DENTON, TX (Charter Communications)

SHALLOWATER—See WOLFFORTH, TX (NTS Communications)

SHALLOWATER—See LUBBOCK, TX (Suddenlink Communications)

SHAMROCK—Suddenlink Communications

SHAVANO PARK—See SAN ANTONIO, TX (Time Warner Cable)

SHEFFIELD—Formerly served by Ector Cable. No longer in operation

SHENANDOAH (UNINCORPORATED AREAS)—See HOUSTON, TX (Comcast Cable)

SHENANDOAH—See MONTGOMERY COUNTY (portions), TX (Charter Communications)

SHEPHERD—See ONALASKA, TX (Suddenlink Communications)

SHEPPARD AFB—See WICHITA FALLS, TX (Time Warner Cable)

SHERIDAN—Formerly served by National Cable Inc. No longer in operation

SHERMAN—Cable One

SHERWOOD SHORES—See GORDONVILLE, TX (TV Cable of Grayson County)

SHINER—Formerly served by Almega Cable. No longer in operation

SHOREACRES—See HOUSTON, TX (Comcast Cable)

SIERRA BLANCA—Formerly served by Sierra Cable TV. No longer in operation

SILSBEE—Time Warner Cable. Now served by PORT ARTHUR (formerly Beaumont), TX [TX0022]

SILSBEE—See PORT ARTHUR, TX (Time Warner Cable)

SILVERTON—Formerly served by Reach Broadband. No longer in operation

SINTON—Formerly served by Charter Communications. Now served by Time Warner Cable, ROCKPORT, TX [TX0116]

SINTON—See ROCKPORT, TX (Time Warner Cable)

SKELLYTOWN—Formerly served by Almega Cable. No longer in operation

SKIDMORE—See CORPUS CHRISTI, TX (Time Warner Cable)

SLATON—Formerly served by NTS Communications. This cable system has converted to IPTV. Now served by WOLFFORTH, TX [TX5540]

SLATON—See WOLFFORTH, TX (NTS Communications)

SMILEY—Formerly served by National Cable Inc. No longer in operation

SMITH (UNINCORPORATED AREAS)—See TYLER, TX (Suddenlink Communications)

SMITH COUNTY (PORTIONS)—East Texas Cable Co.

SMITH COUNTY (PORTIONS)—See HAWKINS, TX (Suddenlink Communications)

SMITH COUNTY—See MINEOLA, TX (Suddenlink Communications)

SMITH COUNTY—See TYLER, TX (Suddenlink Communications)

SMITHVILLE—Reveille Broadband

SMITHVILLE—See AUSTIN, TX (Time Warner Cable)

SMYER—See WOLFFORTH, TX (NTS Communications)

SNOOK—Formerly served by National Cable Inc. No longer in operation

SNYDER—Formerly served by Snyder Microwave Communications LC. No longer in operation

SNYDER—Suddenlink Communications

SOCORRO—See EL PASO, TX (Time Warner Cable)

SOMERSET—See SAN ANTONIO, TX (Time Warner Cable)

SOMERVELL COUNTY (PORTIONS)—See FORT WORTH (northern portions), TX (Charter Communications)

SOMERVILLE—See LYONS, TX (Reveille Broadband)

SONORA—Suddenlink Communications

SOUR LAKE—NewWave Communications

SOUTH HOUSTON—See HOUSTON, TX (Comcast Cable)

SOUTH MOUNTAIN—See GATESVILLE, TX (Suddenlink Communications)

SOUTH PADRE ISLAND—See PHARR, TX (Time Warner Cable)

SOUTH PORT ARTHUR—See PORT ARTHUR, TX (Time Warner Cable)

SOUTH SHORES—Formerly served by Cable Unlimited. No longer in operation

SOUTH SILSBEE—Formerly served by Cebridge Connections. No longer in operation

SOUTHLAKE—See FORT WORTH (northern portions), TX (Charter Communications)

SOUTHLAKE—See KELLER, TX (Millennium Telcom)

SOUTHMAYD—See POTTSBORO, TX (TV Cable of Grayson County)

SOUTHSIDE PLACE—See HOUSTON, TX (Comcast Cable)

SPEARMAN—PTCI. This cable system has converted to IPTV. Now served by GUYMON, OK [OK5005]

SPICEWOOD BEACH—Formerly served by Charter Communications. No longer in operation

SPICEWOOD—See AUSTIN, TX (Time Warner Cable)

SPLENDORA—Formerly served by Almega Cable. No longer in operation

SPLENDORA—See KINGWOOD, TX (Suddenlink Communications)

SPRING VALLEY—See HOUSTON, TX (Comcast Cable)

SPRING—See MONTGOMERY COUNTY (portions), TX (Charter Communications)

SPRING—See HOUSTON, TX (Comcast Cable)

SPRING—See HOUSTON, TX (En-Touch Systems Inc)

SPRINGTOWN—Vyve Broadband

SPUR—Formerly served by Almega Cable. No longer in operation

SPURGER—Formerly served by Carrell Communications. No longer in operation

ST. FRANCIS VILLAGE—Formerly served by National Cable Inc. No longer in operation

ST. JO—Formerly served by Rapid Cable. Now served by Nortex Communications, VALLEY VIEW, TX [TX0792]

ST. JO—See VALLEY VIEW, TX (Nortex Communications)

ST. PAUL—See DALLAS, TX (Time Warner Cable)

STAFFORD—See HOUSTON, TX (Comcast Cable)

STAMFORD—Formerly served by Alliance Communications. Now served by WesTex Telephone Cooperative

STANTON—Formerly served by Almega Cable. No longer in operation

STANTON—WesTex Telecom. This cable system has converted to IPTV. See STANTON, TX [TX5564]

STANTON—WesTex. Formerly [TX1031]. This cable system has converted to IPTV

STAPLES—See SAN MARCOS, TX (Time Warner Cable)

STAR HARBOR—See ATHENS, TX (Suddenlink Communications)

STARR COUNTY (PORTIONS)—See PHARR, TX (Time Warner Cable)

STEPHENVILLE—Northland Cable Television

STERLING CITY—Formerly served by Reach Broadband. No longer in operation

STINNETT—See BORGER, TX (Cable One)

STOCKDALE—Formerly served by Windjammer Cable. No longer in operation

STONY POINT—Formerly served by Almega Cable. No longer in operation

STOWELL—See WINNIE, TX (Time Warner Cable)

STRATFORD—Formerly served by Almega Cable. No longer in operation

STRATFORD—See DALHART, TX (XIT Communications. Formerly [TX1023]. This cable system has converted to IPTV)

STRAWN—Formerly served by Strawn TV Cable Inc. No longer in operation

SUDAN—See MULESHOE, TX (Reach Broadband)

Texas—Cable Community Index

SUGAR LAND—See HOUSTON, TX (Comcast Cable)

SUGAR LAND—See HOUSTON, TX (En-Touch Systems Inc)

SULLIVAN CITY—Time Warner Cable. Now served by PHARR, TX [TX0017]

SULLIVAN CITY—See PHARR, TX (Time Warner Cable)

SULPHUR SPRINGS—Suddenlink Communications

SUNDOWN—Formerly served by Almega Cable. No longer in operation

SUNLAND PARK—See EL PASO, NM (Time Warner Cable)

SUNNYVALE (TOWN)—See DALLAS, TX (Time Warner Cable)

SUNRAY—See BORGER, TX (Cable One)

SUNRISE BEACH—See MARBLE FALLS, TX (Northland Cable Television)

SUNSET VALLEY—See AUSTIN, TX (Grande Communications)

SUNSET VALLEY—See AUSTIN, TX (Time Warner Cable)

SUTTON COUNTY (PORTIONS)—See SONORA, TX (Suddenlink Communications)

SWEENY—NewWave Communications. Now served by WHARTON, TX [TX0171]

SWEENY—See WHARTON, TX (NewWave Communications)

SWEETWATER—Suddenlink Communications

TAFT—See ARANSAS PASS, TX (Cable One)

TAHOKA—NTS Communications. This cable system has converted to IPTV. See TAHOKA, TX [TX5558]

TAHOKA—NTS Communications. Formerly [TX0322]. This cable system has converted to IPTV

TALCO—See CLARKSVILLE, TX (Suddenlink Communications)

TALTY—See TERRELL, TX (Suddenlink Communications)

TAPATIO SPRINGS—See BOERNE, TX (GVTC Communications. Formerly [TX0315]. This cable system has converted to IPTV)

TARKINGTON PRAIRIE—Formerly served by Jones Broadcasting. No longer in operation

TARRANT COUNTY (PORTIONS)—See KELLER, TX (Millennium Telcom)

TARRANT COUNTY (PORTIONS)—See CADDO PEAK, TX (North Texas Broadband)

TATUM—See LAKE CHEROKEE, TX (Alliance Communications)

TAYLOR COUNTY (NORTHERN PORTION)—See ABILENE, TX (Suddenlink Communications)

TAYLOR LAKE VILLAGE—See HOUSTON, TX (Comcast Cable)

TAYLOR—See AUSTIN, TX (Time Warner Cable)

TEAGUE—See FAIRFIELD, TX (Northland Cable Television)

TEHUACANA—See MEXIA, TX (Northland Cable Television)

TEMPLE—Grande Communications

TEMPLE—See AUSTIN, TX (Time Warner Cable)

TENAHA—Formerly served by Almega Cable. No longer in operation

TERRELL HILLS—See SAN ANTONIO, TX (Grande Communications)

TERRELL HILLS—See SAN ANTONIO, TX (Time Warner Cable)

TERRELL—Suddenlink Communications

TEXARKANA—See TEXARKANA, AR (Cable One)

TEXARKANA—Cable One

TEXAS CITY—See HOUSTON, TX (Comcast Cable)

TEXHOMA—PTCI. This cable system has converted to IPTV. Now served by GUYMON, OK [OK5005]

TEXLINE—Formerly served by Baja Broadband. No longer in operation

TEXLINE—See DALHART, TX (XIT Communications. Formerly [TX1023]. This cable system has converted to IPTV)

THE COLONY—See DALLAS, TX (Time Warner Cable)

THE HILLS—See AUSTIN, TX (Time Warner Cable)

THE WOODLANDS—See HOUSTON, TX (Comcast Cable)

THORNDALE—See AUSTIN, TX (Time Warner Cable)

THORNTON—Formerly served by National Cable Inc. No longer in operation

THORNTONVILLE—See MONAHANS, TX (Suddenlink Communications)

THRALL—See AUSTIN, TX (Time Warner Cable)

THREE RIVERS—CommZoom

THROCKMORTON—Throckmorton Cablevision

THUNDERBIRD BAY—Formerly served by Cable Unlimited. No longer in operation

TIKI ISLAND (VILLAGE)—See HOUSTON, TX (Comcast Cable)

TILDEN—Formerly served by Almega Cable. No longer in operation

TIMPSON—Formerly served by Almega Cable. No longer in operation

TIOGA—See PILOT POINT, TX (Suddenlink Communications)

TITUS COUNTY (PORTIONS)—See MOUNT PLEASANT, TX (Suddenlink Communications)

TOCO—See PARIS, TX (Suddenlink Communications)

TOLAR—Formerly served by Charter Communications. No longer in operation

TOLEDO VILLAGE—Formerly served by Carrell Communications. No longer in operation

TOM BEAN—See SHERMAN, TX (Cable One)

TOM GREEN COUNTY (PORTIONS)—See ROBERT LEE, TX (NewWave Communications)

TOMBALL—See HOUSTON, TX (Comcast Cable)

TOOL—See ATHENS, TX (Suddenlink Communications)

TRAVIS COUNTY (PORTIONS)—See PFLUGERVILLE, TX (Suddenlink Communications)

TRAVIS COUNTY (PORTIONS)—See AUSTIN, TX (Time Warner Cable)

TRENT—Formerly served by Jayroc Cablevision. No longer in operation

TRINIDAD—See ATHENS, TX (Suddenlink Communications)

TRINITY—Formerly served by Cebridge Connections. Now served by Suddenlink Communications, ONALASKA, TX [TX0851]

TRINITY—See ONALASKA, TX (Suddenlink Communications)

TROPHY CLUB—See FORT WORTH (northern portions), TX (Charter Communications)

TROY—Grande Communications

TULETA—Formerly served by National Cable Inc. No longer in operation

TULIA—Suddenlink Communications. Now served by AMARILLO, TX [TX0014]

TULIA—See AMARILLO, TX (Suddenlink Communications)

TURKEY—Formerly served by Elk River TV Cable Co. No longer in operation

TUSCOLA—NewWave Communications

TYE—See ABILENE, TX (Suddenlink Communications)

TYLER—Suddenlink Communications

TYNAN—See CORPUS CHRISTI, TX (Time Warner Cable)

UHLAND (CALDWELL COUNTY)—See AUSTIN, TX (Time Warner Cable)

UHLAND (HAYS COUNTY)—See AUSTIN, TX (Time Warner Cable)

UNION GROVE—See GLADEWATER, TX (Suddenlink Communications)

UNIVERSAL CITY—See SAN ANTONIO, TX (Grande Communications)

UNIVERSAL CITY—See SAN ANTONIO, TX (Time Warner Cable)

UNIVERSITY PARK—Charter Communications

UVALDE COUNTY (PORTIONS)—See UVALDE, TX (Time Warner Cable)

UVALDE—Time Warner Cable

VADO—See EL PASO, NM (Time Warner Cable)

VAL VERDE COUNTY (PORTIONS)—See DEL RIO, TX (Time Warner Cable)

VALENTINE—Formerly served by Valentine TV Cable. No longer in operation

VALLEY MILLS—LynnStar Communications

VALLEY VIEW—Nortex Communications

VAN ALSTYNE—See SHERMAN, TX (Cable One)

VAN HORN—Reach Broadband

VAN VLECK—See WHARTON, TX (NewWave Communications)

VAN ZANDT COUNTY—See MINEOLA, TX (Suddenlink Communications)

VEGA—XIT Communications. This cable system has converted to IPTV. See VEGA, TX [TX5081]

VEGA—XIT Communications. Formerly [TX0868]. This cable system has converted to IPTV

VERNON—Suddenlink Communications

VICTORIA COUNTY (UNINCORPORATED AREAS)—See VICTORIA, TX (Suddenlink Communications)

VICTORIA—Suddenlink Communications

VIDOR (southern portion)—Formerly served by Cebridge Connections. No longer in operation

VIDOR—Time Warner Cable. Now served by PORT ARTHUR (formerly Beaumont), TX [TX0022]

VIDOR—See PORT ARTHUR, TX (Time Warner Cable)

VINTON—See EL PASO, TX (Time Warner Cable)

VOLENTE—See AUSTIN, TX (Time Warner Cable)

WACO—Time Warner Cable. Now served by AUSTIN, TX [TX0005]

WACO—Grande Communications

WACO—See AUSTIN, TX (Time Warner Cable)

WAELDER—Formerly served by National Cable Inc. No longer in operation

WAKE VILLAGE—See TEXARKANA, TX (Cable One)

WALDEN (village)—Suddenlink Communications. Now served by KINGWOOD, TX [TX0052]

WALDEN (VILLAGE)—See KINGWOOD, TX (Suddenlink Communications)

Cable Community Index—Utah

WALKER COUNTY—See HUNTSVILLE, TX (Suddenlink Communications)

WALLER—See PRAIRIE VIEW, TX (Suddenlink Communications)

WALLIS—Formerly served by Rapid Cable. No longer in operation

WALNUT SPRINGS—Formerly served by National Cable Inc. No longer in operation

WARD COUNTY—See MONAHANS, TX (Suddenlink Communications)

WARREN CITY—See GLADEWATER, TX (Suddenlink Communications)

WASHINGTON COUNTY (PORTIONS)—See BRENHAM, TX (Suddenlink Communications)

WATAUGA—See FORT WORTH (northern portions), TX (Charter Communications)

WATERWOOD—Cablevision of Walker County

WAUTAGA—See KELLER, TX (Millennium Telcom)

WAXAHACHIE—See MIDLOTHIAN, TX (Charter Communications)

WEATHERFORD—Charter Communications. Now served by FORT WORTH (northern portions), TX [TX0008]

WEATHERFORD—See FORT WORTH (northern portions), TX (Charter Communications)

WEBB COUNTY (PORTIONS)—See LAREDO, TX (Time Warner Cable)

WEBSTER—See HOUSTON, TX (Comcast Cable)

WEIMAR—See LA GRANGE, TX (NewWave Communications)

WEINERT—Formerly served by Jayroc Cablevision. No longer in operation

WELCH—Formerly served by National Cable Inc. No longer in operation

WELLINGTON—Suddenlink Communications

WELLMAN—Formerly served by National Cable Inc. No longer in operation

WELLS—Formerly served by Cebridge Connections. No longer in operation

WESLACO—Time Warner Cable. Now served by PHARR, TX [TX0017]

WESLACO—See PHARR, TX (Time Warner Cable)

WEST COLUMBIA—NewWave Communications. Now served by WHARTON, TX [TX0171]

WEST COLUMBIA—See WHARTON, TX (NewWave Communications)

WEST GRAYSON COUNTY—TV Cable of Grayson County. Now served by GRAYSON COUNTY, TX [TX1014]

WEST LAKE HILLS—See AUSTIN, TX (Time Warner Cable)

WEST ODESSA—Reach Broadband

WEST ORANGE—See PORT ARTHUR, TX (Time Warner Cable)

WEST UNIVERSITY PLACE—See HOUSTON, TX (Comcast Cable)

WEST—LynnStar Communications

WESTBROOK—Formerly served by National Cable Inc. No longer in operation

WESTHOFF—Formerly served by National Cable Inc. No longer in operation

WESTLAKE HILLS—See AUSTIN, TX (Grande Communications)

WESTLAKE—See FORT WORTH (northern portions), TX (Charter Communications)

WESTLAKE—See KELLER, TX (Millennium Telcom)

WESTON LAKES—Telecom Cable

WESTOVER HILLS—See FORT WORTH (northern portions), TX (Charter Communications)

WESTWAY—See EL PASO, TX (Time Warner Cable)

WESTWORTH VILLAGE—See FORT WORTH (northern portions), TX (Charter Communications)

WHARTON COUNTY (UNINCORPORATED AREAS)—See WHARTON, TX (NewWave Communications)

WHARTON—NewWave Communications

WHEELER—Formerly served by Elk River TV Cable Co. No longer in operation

WHITE DEER—See BORGER, TX (Cable One)

WHITE OAK—See GLADEWATER, TX (Suddenlink Communications)

WHITE SETTLEMENT—See FORT WORTH (northern portions), TX (Charter Communications)

WHITEFACE—Formerly served by Cebridge Connections. No longer in operation

WHITEHOUSE—See TYLER, TX (Suddenlink Communications)

WHITESBORO—Suddenlink Communications

WHITEWRIGHT—See SHERMAN, TX (Cable One)

WHITHARRAL—See WOLFFORTH, TX (NTS Communications)

WHITNEY—LynnStar Communications

WICHITA COUNTY (PORTIONS)—See WICHITA FALLS, TX (Time Warner Cable)

WICHITA FALLS—Time Warner Cable

WICKETT—Formerly served by Almega Cable. No longer in operation

WILDWOOD—Formerly served by Daybreak Communications. No longer in operation

WILLACY COUNTY (PORTIONS)—See PHARR, TX (Time Warner Cable)

WILLIAMSON COUNTY (PORTIONS)—See AUSTIN, TX (Time Warner Cable)

WILLIS—See CONROE, TX (Suddenlink Communications)

WILLOW PARK—Formerly served by Mallard Cablevision. No longer in operation

WILLS POINT—Formerly served by Zoom Media. No longer in operation

WILMER—Formerly served by Metro Cable. No longer in operation

WILSON COUNTY (PORTIONS)—See SAN ANTONIO, TX (Time Warner Cable)

WILSON—Formerly served by Charter Communications. No longer in operation

WIMBERLEY—See SAN MARCOS, TX (Time Warner Cable)

WINDCREST (PORTIONS)—See SAN ANTONIO, TX (Grande Communications)

WINDCREST (PORTIONS)—See SAN MARCOS, TX (Grande Communications)

WINDCREST—See SAN ANTONIO, TX (Time Warner Cable)

WINFIELD—See MOUNT PLEASANT, TX (Suddenlink Communications)

WINK—Formerly served by Almega Cable. No longer in operation

WINKLER COUNTY (PORTIONS)—See KERMIT, TX (Suddenlink Communications)

WINNIE—Time Warner Cable

WINNSBORO—Suddenlink Communications

WINONA—See HAWKINS, TX (Suddenlink Communications)

WINTERS—Vyve Broadband

WODEN—Formerly served by Almega Cable. No longer in operation

WOLFE CITY—Formerly served by Zoom Media. No longer in operation

WOLFFORTH—NTS Communications

WOLFFORTH—See LUBBOCK, TX (Suddenlink Communications)

WOOD COUNTY (PORTIONS)—See HAWKINS, TX (Suddenlink Communications)

WOOD COUNTY (PORTIONS)—See WINNSBORO, TX (Suddenlink Communications)

WOOD COUNTY—See MINEOLA, TX (Suddenlink Communications)

WOODBRANCH VILLAGE—See KINGWOOD, TX (Suddenlink Communications)

WOODCREEK—See SAN MARCOS, TX (Time Warner Cable)

WOODLOCH—See MONTGOMERY COUNTY (portions), TX (Charter Communications)

WOODROW—Suddenlink Communications. Now served by LUBBOCK, TX [TX0012]

WOODROW—South Plains Telephone Cooperative

WOODROW—See LUBBOCK, TX (Suddenlink Communications)

WOODSBORO—See CORPUS CHRISTI, TX (Time Warner Cable)

WOODVILLE—NewWave Communications

WOODWAY—See WACO, TX (Grande Communications)

WOODWAY—See AUSTIN, TX (Time Warner Cable)

WORTHAM—Formerly served by Northland Cable Television. No longer in operation

WYLIE—Time Warner Cable. Now served by DALLAS, TX [TX0003]

WYLIE—See DALLAS, TX (Time Warner Cable)

YOAKUM COUNTY (PORTIONS)—See SEMINOLE, TX (Baja Broadband)

YOAKUM—Time Warner Cable. Now served by GONZALES, TX [TX0209]

YOAKUM—See GONZALES, TX (Time Warner Cable)

YORKTOWN—Formerly served by Almega Cable. No longer in operation

YOUNG COUNTY (PORTIONS)—See OLNEY, TX (Suddenlink Communications)

YOUNG COUNTY—See GRAHAM, TX (Zito Media)

ZAPATA—Time Warner Cable. Now served by LAREDO, TX [TX0029]

ZAPATA—See LAREDO, TX (Time Warner Cable)

ZAVALA COUNTY (PORTIONS)—See CRYSTAL CITY, TX (Time Warner Cable)

ZAVALLA—Formerly served by Almega Cable. No longer in operation

ZION HILL—Formerly served by National Cable Inc. No longer in operation

UTAH

ALPINE—See SALT LAKE CITY, UT (Comcast Cable)

AMERICAN FORK—See SALT LAKE CITY, UT (Comcast Cable)

ANNABELLA—See CENTRAL, UT (CentraCom)

AURORA—See SALINA, UT (CentraCom)

AUSTIN—See CENTRAL, UT (CentraCom)

AXTELL—See CENTERFIELD, UT (CentraCom)

Utah—Cable Community Index

BEAR RIVER CITY—See SALT LAKE CITY, UT (Comcast Cable)

BEAVER—South Central Communications. Now served by ENOCH, UT [UT0071]

BEAVER—See ENOCH, UT (South Central Communications)

BICKNELL—See LYMAN, UT (South Central Communications)

BLANDING—Emery Telcom. Now served by EMERY, UT [UT0098]

BLANDING—See EMERY, UT (Emery Telecom)

BLUFFDALE—See SALT LAKE CITY, UT (Comcast Cable)

BOUNTIFUL—See SALT LAKE CITY, UT (Comcast Cable)

BOX ELDER COUNTY (PORTIONS)—See SALT LAKE CITY, UT (Comcast Cable)

BRIAN HEAD—South Central Communications. Now served by ENOCH, UT [UT0071]

BRIAN HEAD—See ENOCH, UT (South Central Communications)

BRIGHAM CITY—Comcast Cable. Now served by SALT LAKE CITY, UT [UT0001]

BRIGHAM CITY—Formerly served by Connected Lyfe. No longer in operation

BRIGHAM CITY—See SALT LAKE CITY, UT (Comcast Cable)

BRYCE—See PANGUITCH, UT (South Central Communications)

BUNKERVILLE—See ST. GEORGE, NV (Baja Broadband)

CACHE COUNTY (PORTIONS)—See SALT LAKE CITY, UT (Comcast Cable)

CASTLE DALE—Emery Telcom. Now served by EMERY, UT [UT0098]

CASTLE DALE—See EMERY, UT (Emery Telecom)

CEDAR CITY—Formerly served by Connected Lyfe. No longer in operation

CEDAR CITY—Baja Broadband

CEDAR HILLS—Formerly served by Connected Lyfe. No longer in operation

CEDAR HILLS—See SALT LAKE CITY, UT (Comcast Cable)

CENTERFIELD—CentraCom

CENTERVILLE—Formerly served by Connected Lyfe. No longer in operation

CENTERVILLE—See SALT LAKE CITY, UT (Comcast Cable)

CENTRAL—CentraCom

CIRCLEVILLE—See PANGUITCH, UT (South Central Communications)

CLARKSTON—See SALT LAKE CITY, UT (Comcast Cable)

CLAWSON—See EMERY, UT (Emery Telecom)

CLEARFIELD—See SALT LAKE CITY, UT (Comcast Cable)

CLEVELAND—Emery Telcom. Now served by EMERY, UT [UT0098]

CLEVELAND—See EMERY, UT (Emery Telecom)

CLINTON—See SALT LAKE CITY, UT (Comcast Cable)

COALVILLE—Formerly served by Comcast Cable. No longer in operation

COALVILLE—See OAKLEY, UT (All West Communications. Formerly served by Kamas, UT [UT0053]. This cable system has converted to IPTV)

COKEVILLE—See OAKLEY, WY (All West Communications. Formerly served by Kamas, UT [UT0053]. This cable system has converted to IPTV)

CORINNE—See SALT LAKE CITY, UT (Comcast Cable)

CORNISH—See SALT LAKE CITY, UT (Comcast Cable)

DAVIS COUNTY (PORTIONS)—See SALT LAKE CITY, UT (Comcast Cable)

DAVIS—See SALT LAKE CITY, UT (Comcast Cable)

DEER MOUNTAIN—See OAKLEY, UT (All West Communications. Formerly served by Kamas, UT [UT0053]. This cable system has converted to IPTV)

DELTA—CentraCom

DEWEYVILLE—See SALT LAKE CITY, UT (Comcast Cable)

DRAPER—See SALT LAKE CITY, UT (Comcast Cable)

DUCHESNE—Strata Networks

DUGWAY AFB—CentraCom

EAST CARBON—Emery Telcom. Now served by EMERY, UT [UT0098]

EAST CARBON—See EMERY, UT (Emery Telecom)

ECHO—See OAKLEY, UT (All West Communications. Formerly served by Kamas, UT [UT0053]. This cable system has converted to IPTV)

EDEN—See HUNTSVILLE, UT (HLS Communications)

ELK RIDGE—See SALT LAKE CITY, UT (Comcast Cable)

ELMO—See EMERY, UT (Emery Telecom)

ELSINORE—See CENTRAL, UT (CentraCom)

EMERY—Emery Telecom

ENOCH—South Central Communications

ENTERPRISE—South Central Communications

EPHRAIM—CentraCom

ESCALANTE—South Central Communications. Now served by PANGUITCH, UT [UT0043]

ESCALANTE—See PANGUITCH, UT (South Central Communications)

EUREKA—CentraCom. Now served by SANTAQUIN, UT [UT0041]

EUREKA—See SANTAQUIN, UT (CentraCom)

EVANSTON—See OAKLEY, UT (All West Communications. Formerly served by Kamas, UT [UT0053]. This cable system has converted to IPTV)

FAIRVIEW—See MOUNT PLEASANT, UT (CentraCom)

FARMINGTON—Comcast Cable. Now served by SALT LAKE CITY, UT [UT0001]

FARMINGTON—See SALT LAKE CITY, UT (Comcast Cable)

FARR WEST—See SALT LAKE CITY, UT (Comcast Cable)

FERRON—Emery Telcom. Now served by EMERY, UT [UT0098]

FERRON—See EMERY, UT (Emery Telecom)

FIELDING—Comcast Cable. Now served by TREMONTON, UT [UT0096]

FIELDING—See SALT LAKE CITY, UT (Comcast Cable)

FILLMORE—CentraCom

FOUNTAIN GREEN—See MORONI, UT (CentraCom)

FRANCIS—See OAKLEY, UT (All West Communications. Formerly served by Kamas, UT [UT0053]. This cable system has converted to IPTV)

FRANKLIN COUNTY (PORTIONS)—See SALT LAKE CITY, ID (Comcast Cable)

FRANKLIN—See SALT LAKE CITY, ID (Comcast Cable)

FREDONIA—See PANGUITCH, AZ (South Central Communications)

FRUIT HEIGHTS—See SALT LAKE CITY, UT (Comcast Cable)

GARLAND—See SALT LAKE CITY, UT (Comcast Cable)

GLENWOOD—CentraCom. Now served by CENTRAL, UT [UT0070]

GLENWOOD—See CENTRAL, UT (CentraCom)

GOSHEN—CentraCom. Now served by SANTAQUIN, UT [UT0041]

GOSHEN—See SANTAQUIN, UT (CentraCom)

GRANTSVILLE—See SALT LAKE CITY, UT (Comcast Cable)

GREEN RIVER—Emery Telcom. Now served by EMERY, UT [UT0098]

GREEN RIVER—See EMERY, UT (Emery Telecom)

GUNNISON—See CENTERFIELD, UT (CentraCom)

HARRISVILLE—See SALT LAKE CITY, UT (Comcast Cable)

HEBER (PORTIONS)—See OAKLEY, UT (All West Communications. Formerly served by Kamas, UT [UT0053]. This cable system has converted to IPTV)

HEBER CITY—Comcast Cable. Now served by SALT LAKE CITY, UT [UT0001]

HEBER CITY—See SALT LAKE CITY, UT (Comcast Cable)

HELPER—See EMERY, UT (Emery Telecom)

HENEFER—See OAKLEY, UT (All West Communications. Formerly served by Kamas, UT [UT0053]. This cable system has converted to IPTV)

HERRIMAN—See SALT LAKE CITY, UT (Comcast Cable)

HIGHLAND—See SALT LAKE CITY, UT (Comcast Cable)

HILL AFB—See SALT LAKE CITY, UT (Comcast Cable)

HINCKLEY—See DELTA, UT (CentraCom)

HOLDEN—See FILLMORE, UT (CentraCom)

HOLLADAY—See SALT LAKE CITY, UT (Comcast Cable)

HONEYVILLE—See SALT LAKE CITY, UT (Comcast Cable)

HOOPER—See SALT LAKE CITY, UT (Comcast Cable)

HOYTSVILLE—See OAKLEY, UT (All West Communications. Formerly served by Kamas, UT [UT0053]. This cable system has converted to IPTV)

HUNTINGTON—See EMERY, UT (Emery Telecom)

HUNTSVILLE—HLS Communications

HURRICANE—Formerly served by Charter Communications. Now served by Baja Broadband, ST. GEORGE, UT [UT0007]

HURRICANE—See ST. GEORGE, UT (Baja Broadband)

HYDE PARK—See SALT LAKE CITY, UT (Comcast Cable)

HYRUM—See SALT LAKE CITY, UT (Comcast Cable)

IRON COUNTY (PORTIONS)—See CEDAR CITY, UT (Baja Broadband)

IVINS—See ST. GEORGE, UT (Baja Broadband)

KAMAS—All West Communications. This cable system has converted to IPTV. See OAKLEY, UT [UT5034]

Cable Community Index—Utah

KAMAS—See OAKLEY, UT (All West Communications. Formerly served by Kamas, UT [UT0053]. This cable system has converted to IPTV)

KANAB—South Central Communications. Now served by PANGUITCH, UT [UT0043]

KANAB—See PANGUITCH, UT (South Central Communications)

KANARRAVILLE—Formerly served by South Central Communications. No longer in operation

KAYSVILLE—See SALT LAKE CITY, UT (Comcast Cable)

KENILWORTH—See EMERY, UT (Emery Telecom)

LA VERKIN—See ST. GEORGE, UT (Baja Broadband)

LAYTON—Formerly served by Connected Lyfe. No longer in operation

LAYTON—See SALT LAKE CITY, UT (Comcast Cable)

LEEDS—See ST. GEORGE, UT (Baja Broadband)

LEHI—See SALT LAKE CITY, UT (Comcast Cable)

LEWISTON—See SALT LAKE CITY, UT (Comcast Cable)

LINDON—Formerly served by Connected Lyfe. No longer in operation

LINDON—Formerly served by Nuvont Communications. IPTV service no longer in operation

LINDON—See SALT LAKE CITY, UT (Comcast Cable)

LOA—See LYMAN, UT (South Central Communications)

LOGAN—Comcast Cable. Now served by SALT LAKE CITY, UT [UT0001]

LOGAN—See SALT LAKE CITY, UT (Comcast Cable)

LYMAN—South Central Communications

LYNNDYL—See DELTA, UT (CentraCom)

MAESER—See DUCHESNE, UT (Strata Networks)

MANILA—Formerly served by Myvocom. No longer in operation

MANTI—See EPHRAIM, UT (CentraCom)

MAPLETON—See SALT LAKE CITY, UT (Comcast Cable)

MARION—See OAKLEY, UT (All West Communications. Formerly served by Kamas, UT [UT0053]. This cable system has converted to IPTV)

MAYFIELD—CentraCom. Now served by CENTRAL, UT [UT0070]

MAYFIELD—See CENTRAL, UT (CentraCom)

MENDON—See SALT LAKE CITY, UT (Comcast Cable)

MESQUITE—See ST. GEORGE, NV (Baja Broadband)

MIDVALE—Formerly served by Connected Lyfe. No longer in operation

MIDVALE—Formerly served by Nuvont Communications. IPTV service no longer in operation

MIDVALE—See SALT LAKE CITY, UT (Comcast Cable)

MIDWAY—See SALT LAKE CITY, UT (Comcast Cable)

MILFORD—South Central Communications

MILLVILLE—See SALT LAKE CITY, UT (Comcast Cable)

MINERSVILLE—South Central Communications. Now served by ENOCH, UT [UT0071]

MINERSVILLE—See ENOCH, UT (South Central Communications)

MOAB—Emery Telcom. Now served by EMERY, UT [UT0098]

MOAB—See EMERY, UT (Emery Telecom)

MOHAVE—See ST. GEORGE, AZ (Baja Broadband)

MONA—CentraCom. Now served by SANTAQUIN, UT [UT0041]

MONA—See SANTAQUIN, UT (CentraCom)

MONROE—See CENTRAL, UT (CentraCom)

MONTICELLO—Emery Telcom. Now served by EMERY, UT [UT0098]

MONTICELLO—See EMERY, UT (Emery Telecom)

MORGAN CITY—Formerly served by Comcast Cable. No longer in operation

MORGAN COUNTY (portions)—Formerly served by Comcast Cable. No longer in operation

MORONI—CentraCom

MOUNT PLEASANT—CentraCom

MURRAY—Formerly served by Connected Lyfe. No longer in operation

MURRAY—Formerly served by Nuvont Communications. IPTV service no longer in operation

MURRAY—See SALT LAKE CITY, UT (Comcast Cable)

NAPLES—See DUCHESNE, UT (Strata Networks)

NEPHI—CentraCom

NEW HARMONY—Formerly served by South Central Communications. No longer in operation

NEWTON—See SALT LAKE CITY, UT (Comcast Cable)

NIBLEY—See SALT LAKE CITY, UT (Comcast Cable)

NORTH LOGAN—See SALT LAKE CITY, UT (Comcast Cable)

NORTH OGDEN—See SALT LAKE CITY, UT (Comcast Cable)

NORTH SALT LAKE—See SALT LAKE CITY, UT (Comcast Cable)

OAKLEY—All West Communications. Formerly served by Kamas, UT [UT0053]. This cable system has converted to IPTV

Ogden—Comcast Cable. Now served by SALT LAKE CITY, UT [UT0001]

OGDEN—See SALT LAKE CITY, UT (Comcast Cable)

ORANGEVILLE—See EMERY, UT (Emery Telecom)

OREM—Formerly served by Connected Lyfe. No longer in operation

OREM—Formerly served by Nuvont Communications. IPTV service no longer in operation

OREM—See SALT LAKE CITY, UT (Comcast Cable)

PANGUITCH (portions)—South Central Communications. Now served by PANGUITCH, UT [UT0043]

PANGUITCH—South Central Communications

PARADISE—See SALT LAKE CITY, UT (Comcast Cable)

PARAGONAH—South Central Communications. Now served by ENOCH, UT [UT0071]

PARAGONAH—See ENOCH, UT (South Central Communications)

PARK CITY—Comcast Cable. Now served by SALT LAKE CITY, UT [UT0001]

PARK CITY—See SALT LAKE CITY, UT (Comcast Cable)

PAROWAN—South Central Communications. Now served by ENOCH, UT [UT0071]

PAROWAN—See ENOCH, UT (South Central Communications)

PAYSON (town)—Formerly served by Nuvont Communications. IPTV service no longer in operation

PAYSON—Formerly served by Connected Lyfe. No longer in operation

PAYSON—See SALT LAKE CITY, UT (Comcast Cable)

PEOA—See OAKLEY, UT (All West Communications. Formerly served by Kamas, UT [UT0053]. This cable system has converted to IPTV)

PERRY—Formerly served by Connected Lyfe. No longer in operation

PERRY—See SALT LAKE CITY, UT (Comcast Cable)

PLAIN CITY—See SALT LAKE CITY, UT (Comcast Cable)

PLEASANT GROVE—Comcast Cable. Now served by SALT LAKE CITY, UT [UT0001]

PLEASANT GROVE—See SALT LAKE CITY, UT (Comcast Cable)

PLEASANT VIEW—See SALT LAKE CITY, UT (Comcast Cable)

PLYMOUTH—See SALT LAKE CITY, UT (Comcast Cable)

PRICE—Emery Telcom. Now served by EMERY, UT [UT0098]

PRICE—See EMERY, UT (Emery Telecom)

PROMONTORY—See OAKLEY, UT (All West Communications. Formerly served by Kamas, UT [UT0053]. This cable system has converted to IPTV)

PROVIDENCE—See SALT LAKE CITY, UT (Comcast Cable)

PROVO—Comcast Cable. Now served by SALT LAKE CITY, UT [UT0001]

PROVO—Formerly served by Nuvont Communications. IPTV service no longer in operation

PROVO—Formerly served by Provo Cable. No longer in operation

PROVO—See SALT LAKE CITY, UT (Comcast Cable)

RANDOLPH TWP.—All West Communications. This cable system has converted to IPTV. See OAKLEY, UT [UT5034]

RANDOLPH TWP.—See OAKLEY, UT (All West Communications. Formerly served by Kamas, UT [UT0053]. This cable system has converted to IPTV)

REDMOND—See SALINA, UT (CentraCom)

RICHFIELD—CentraCom

RICHMOND—Comcast Cable. Now served by SALT LAKE CITY, UT [UT0001]

RICHMOND—See SALT LAKE CITY, UT (Comcast Cable)

RIVER HEIGHTS—See SALT LAKE CITY, UT (Comcast Cable)

RIVERDALE—Comcast Cable. Now served by SALT LAKE CITY, UT [UT0001]

RIVERDALE—See SALT LAKE CITY, UT (Comcast Cable)

RIVERTON—Formerly served by Connected Lyfe. No longer in operation

RIVERTON—See SALT LAKE CITY, UT (Comcast Cable)

ROCKVILLE—Formerly served by Baja Broadband. No longer in operation

ROOSEVELT—Strata Networks. Now served by DUCHESNE, UT [UT0052]

ROOSEVELT—See DUCHESNE, UT (Strata Networks)

2017 Edition

Utah—Cable Community Index

ROY—See SALT LAKE CITY, UT (Comcast Cable)

SALEM—Comcast Cable. Now served by PROVO, UT [UT0005]

SALEM—See SALT LAKE CITY, UT (Comcast Cable)

SALINA—CentraCom

SALT LAKE CITY—Formerly served by TechnoVision Inc. No longer in operation

SALT LAKE CITY—See SOUTH JORDAN, UT (CenturyLink Prism (formerly Qwest). This cable system has converted to IPTV)

SALT LAKE CITY—Comcast Cable

SALT LAKE COUNTY (PORTIONS)—See SALT LAKE CITY, UT (Comcast Cable)

SANDY—Comcast Cable. Now served by SALT LAKE CITY, UT [UT0001]

SANDY—See SALT LAKE CITY, UT (Comcast Cable)

SANPETE COUNTY (PORTIONS)—See MOUNT PLEASANT, UT (CentraCom)

SANTA CLARA—See ST. GEORGE, UT (Baja Broadband)

SANTAQUIN—CentraCom

SARATOGA SPRINGS—See SALT LAKE CITY, UT (Comcast Cable)

SCIPIO—See FILLMORE, UT (CentraCom)

SEVIER COUNTY—See SALINA, UT (CentraCom)

SIGURD—See SALINA, UT (CentraCom)

SMITHFIELD—See SALT LAKE CITY, UT (Comcast Cable)

SOUTH JORDAN—Formerly served by Qwest Choice TV. This cable system has converted to IPTV. Now served by Centurylink, SOUTH JORDAN, UT [UT5021]

SOUTH JORDAN—CenturyLink Prism (formerly Qwest). This cable system has converted to IPTV

SOUTH JORDAN—See SALT LAKE CITY, UT (Comcast Cable)

SOUTH OGDEN—See SALT LAKE CITY, UT (Comcast Cable)

SOUTH SALT LAKE CITY—See SALT LAKE CITY, UT (Comcast Cable)

SOUTH WEBER—See SALT LAKE CITY, UT (Comcast Cable)

SPANISH FORK CITY—See SALT LAKE CITY, UT (Comcast Cable)

SPANISH FORK—Spanish Fork Community Network

SPRING CITY—See MOUNT PLEASANT, UT (CentraCom)

SPRING LAKE—See SALT LAKE CITY, UT (Comcast Cable)

SPRINGVILLE—Comcast Cable. Now served by SALT LAKE CITY, UT [UT0001]

SPRINGVILLE—See SALT LAKE CITY, UT (Comcast Cable)

ST. GEORGE—Formerly served by Prime Time Communications. No longer in operation

ST. GEORGE—Baja Broadband

STANSBURY PARK—Comcast Cable. Now served by SALT LAKE CITY, UT [UT0001]

STANSBURY PARK—See SALT LAKE CITY, UT (Comcast Cable)

SUMMIT COUNTY (PORTIONS)—See SALT LAKE CITY, UT (Comcast Cable)

SUNNYSIDE—See EMERY, UT (Emery Telecom)

SUNSET—See SALT LAKE CITY, UT (Comcast Cable)

SYRACUSE—See SALT LAKE CITY, UT (Comcast Cable)

TAYLORSVILLE—See SALT LAKE CITY, UT (Comcast Cable)

TIMBER LAKES—See OAKLEY, UT (All West Communications. Formerly served by Kamas, UT [UT0053]. This cable system has converted to IPTV)

TOOELE—Comcast Cable. Now served by STANSBURY PARK, UT [UT0093]

TOOELE—See SALT LAKE CITY, UT (Comcast Cable)

TOQUERVILLE—See ST. GEORGE, UT (Baja Broadband)

TREMENTON—Formerly served by Connected Lyfe. No longer in operation

TREMONTON—Comcast Cable. Now served by SALT LAKE CITY, UT [UT0001]

TREMONTON—See SALT LAKE CITY, UT (Comcast Cable)

TROPIC—See PANGUITCH, UT (South Central Communications)

TUHAYE—See OAKLEY, UT (All West Communications. Formerly served by Kamas, UT [UT0053]. This cable system has converted to IPTV)

UINTA COUNTY (PORTIONS)—See OAKLEY, WY (All West Communications. Formerly served by Kamas, UT [UT0053]. This cable system has converted to IPTV)

UINTAH CITY—See SALT LAKE CITY, UT (Comcast Cable)

UINTAH COUNTY—See DUCHESNE, UT (Strata Networks)

UTAH COUNTY (PORTIONS)—See SANTAQUIN, UT (CentraCom)

UTAH COUNTY (PORTIONS)—See SALT LAKE CITY, UT (Comcast Cable)

VERNAL—Formerly served by Bresnan Communications. No longer in operation

VERNAL—See DUCHESNE, UT (Strata Networks)

VINEYARD—Formerly served by Connected Lyfe. No longer in operation

WANSHIP—See OAKLEY, UT (All West Communications. Formerly served by Kamas, UT [UT0053]. This cable system has converted to IPTV)

WASATCH COUNTY (PORTIONS)—See SALT LAKE CITY, UT (Comcast Cable)

WASHINGTON COUNTY (PORTIONS)—See ST. GEORGE, UT (Baja Broadband)

WASHINGTON TERRACE—See SALT LAKE CITY, UT (Comcast Cable)

WASHINGTON—Formerly served by Connected Lyfe. No longer in operation

WASHINGTON—See ST. GEORGE, UT (Baja Broadband)

WEBER COUNTY (PORTIONS)—See SALT LAKE CITY, UT (Comcast Cable)

WELLINGTON—See EMERY, UT (Emery Telecom)

WELLSVILLE—See SALT LAKE CITY, UT (Comcast Cable)

WENDOVER—Formerly served by Precis Communications. Now served by CentraCom, WENDOVER, NV [NV0054]

WENDOVER—CentraCom

WEST BOUNTIFUL—See SALT LAKE CITY, UT (Comcast Cable)

WEST HAVEN—See SALT LAKE CITY, UT (Comcast Cable)

WEST JORDAN—See SALT LAKE CITY, UT (Comcast Cable)

WEST POINT—See SALT LAKE CITY, UT (Comcast Cable)

WEST VALLEY CITY—Formerly served by Connected Lyfe. No longer in operation

WEST VALLEY CITY—Formerly served by Nuvont Communications. IPTV service no longer in operation

WEST VALLEY CITY—See SALT LAKE CITY, UT (Comcast Cable)

WEST WENDOVER—See WENDOVER, NV (CentraCom)

WILLARD—See SALT LAKE CITY, UT (Comcast Cable)

WINCHESTER—Formerly served by South Central Communications. No longer in operation

WOODLAND—See OAKLEY, UT (All West Communications. Formerly served by Kamas, UT [UT0053]. This cable system has converted to IPTV)

WOODRUFF—See OAKLEY, UT (All West Communications. Formerly served by Kamas, UT [UT0053]. This cable system has converted to IPTV)

WOODS CROSS—See SALT LAKE CITY, UT (Comcast Cable)

VERMONT

AGAWAM—See BURLINGTON, MA (Comcast Cable)

ALSTEAD—See BURLINGTON, NH (Comcast Cable)

AMHERST—See BURLINGTON, MA (Comcast Cable)

ANDOVER—See BURLINGTON, NH (Comcast Cable)

ARLINGTON—See BURLINGTON, VT (Comcast Cable)

ASCUTNEY—See BURLINGTON, VT (Comcast Cable)

ATHENS—See BURLINGTON, VT (Comcast Cable)

BAKERSFIELD—See BURLINGTON, VT (Comcast Cable)

BARNET—See ST. JOHNSBURY, VT (Charter Communications)

BARRE—Charter Communications. Now served by DANVILLE (town) (formerly St. Johnsbury), VT [VT0009]

BARRE—See ST. JOHNSBURY, VT (Charter Communications)

BARTON—See BURLINGTON, VT (Comcast Cable)

BATH—See ST. JOHNSBURY, NH (Charter Communications)

BELLOWS FALLS—See BURLINGTON, VT (Comcast Cable)

BENNINGTON—Comcast Cable. Now served by BURLINGTON, VT [VT0001]

BENNINGTON—See BURLINGTON, VT (Comcast Cable)

BERKSHIRE—See BURLINGTON, VT (Comcast Cable)

BERLIN—Comcast Cable. Now served by BURLINGTON, VT [VT0001]

BERLIN—See ST. JOHNSBURY, VT (Charter Communications)

BERLIN—See BURLINGTON, VT (Comcast Cable)

BERLIN—See NORTHFIELD (village), VT (Trans-Video Inc)

BERNARDSTON—See BURLINGTON, MA (Comcast Cable)

BETHEL—See BURLINGTON, VT (Comcast Cable)

BLOOMFIELD TWP.—Formerly served by Adelphia Communications. No longer in operation

BOLTON—See WAITSFIELD, VT (Waitsfield Cable Co)

BOMOSEEN—See BURLINGTON, VT (Comcast Cable)

BONDVILLE—See BURLINGTON, VT (Comcast Cable)

Cable Community Index—Vermont

BRADFORD—Charter Communications. Now served by DANVILLE (town) (formerly St. Johnsbury), VT [VT0009]

BRADFORD—See ST. JOHNSBURY, VT (Charter Communications)

BRAINTREE—Formerly served by Adelphia Cable-Berlin. Now served by BURLINGTON, VT [VT0001]

BRAINTREE—See BURLINGTON, VT (Comcast Cable)

BRANDON—See BURLINGTON, VT (Comcast Cable)

BRATTLEBORO—Comcast Cable. Now served by BURLINGTON, VT [VT0001]

BRATTLEBORO—See BURLINGTON, VT (Comcast Cable)

BRIDGEWATER—See BURLINGTON, VT (Comcast Cable)

BRIGHTON—See BURLINGTON, VT (Comcast Cable)

BRISTOL—See BURLINGTON, VT (Comcast Cable)

BROMLEY—See BURLINGTON, VT (Comcast Cable)

BROOKFIELD—See BURLINGTON, VT (Comcast Cable)

BROWNINGTON—See BURLINGTON, VT (Comcast Cable)

BUCKLAND—See BURLINGTON, MA (Comcast Cable)

BURLINGTON—Comcast Cable

CALAIS—See BURLINGTON, VT (Comcast Cable)

CAMBRIDGE JUNCTION—See JEFFERSONVILLE, VT (Jeffersonville Cable TV Corp)

CAMBRIDGE—See JEFFERSONVILLE, VT (Jeffersonville Cable TV Corp)

CAMBRIDGEPORT—See BURLINGTON, VT (Comcast Cable)

CANAAN—See BURLINGTON, NH (Comcast Cable)

CASTLETON—See BURLINGTON, VT (Comcast Cable)

CAVENDISH—See BURLINGTON, VT (Comcast Cable)

CENTER RUTLAND—See BURLINGTON, VT (Comcast Cable)

CHARLESTON—Comcast Cable. Now served by BURLINGTON, VT [VT0001]

CHARLESTON—See BURLINGTON, VT (Comcast Cable)

CHARLESTOWN—See BURLINGTON, NH (Comcast Cable)

CHARLOTTE—See BURLINGTON, VT (Comcast Cable)

CHELSEA—Charter Communications. Now served by DANVILLE (town) (formerly St. Johnsbury), VT [VT0009]

CHELSEA—See ST. JOHNSBURY, VT (Charter Communications)

CHESTER DEPOT—See BURLINGTON, VT (Comcast Cable)

CHESTER—See BURLINGTON, MA (Comcast Cable)

CHESTER—See BURLINGTON, VT (Comcast Cable)

CHITTENDEN—See BURLINGTON, VT (Comcast Cable)

CLAREMONT—See BURLINGTON, NH (Comcast Cable)

CLARENDON—See BURLINGTON, VT (Comcast Cable)

COLCHESTER—See BURLINGTON, VT (Comcast Cable)

CONCORD—See ST. JOHNSBURY, VT (Charter Communications)

CONWAY—See BURLINGTON, MA (Comcast Cable)

CORNISH (TOWN)—See BURLINGTON, NH (Comcast Cable)

CORNISH FLAT—See BURLINGTON, NH (Comcast Cable)

COVENTRY TWP.—Formerly served by Adelphia Communications. No longer in operation

COVENTRY—See BURLINGTON, VT (Comcast Cable)

DANBURY (TOWN)—See BURLINGTON, NH (Comcast Cable)

DANBY—See BURLINGTON, VT (Comcast Cable)

DANVILLE (TOWN)—See ST. JOHNSBURY, VT (Charter Communications)

DEERFIELD—See BURLINGTON, MA (Comcast Cable)

DERBY LINE—See BURLINGTON, VT (Comcast Cable)

DERBY—Comcast Cable. Now served by BURLINGTON, VT [VT0001]

DERBY—See BURLINGTON, VT (Comcast Cable)

DORSET—See BURLINGTON, VT (Comcast Cable)

DREWSVILLE—See BURLINGTON, NH (Comcast Cable)

DUXBURY—See BURLINGTON, VT (Comcast Cable)

DUXBURY—See WAITSFIELD, VT (Waitsfield Cable Co)

EAST BARRE—See ST. JOHNSBURY, VT (Charter Communications)

EAST BURKE—See ST. JOHNSBURY, VT (Charter Communications)

EAST CORINTH—Formerly served by Olsen TV. No longer in operation

EAST FAIRFIELD—See BURLINGTON, VT (Comcast Cable)

EAST MONTPELIER—See ST. JOHNSBURY, VT (Charter Communications)

EAST MONTPELIER—See BURLINGTON, VT (Comcast Cable)

EAST RYEGATE—See ST. JOHNSBURY, VT (Charter Communications)

EAST ST. JOHNSBURY—See ST. JOHNSBURY, VT (Charter Communications)

ENFIELD—See BURLINGTON, NH (Comcast Cable)

ENOSBURG FALLS—Comcast Cable. Now served by BURLINGTON, VT [VT0001]

ENOSBURG FALLS—See BURLINGTON, VT (Comcast Cable)

ENOSBURG—See BURLINGTON, VT (Comcast Cable)

ERVING—See BURLINGTON, MA (Comcast Cable)

ESSEX CENTER—See BURLINGTON, VT (Comcast Cable)

ESSEX JUNCTION—See BURLINGTON, VT (Comcast Cable)

FAIR HAVEN—See BURLINGTON, VT (Comcast Cable)

FAIRFAX—See BURLINGTON, VT (Comcast Cable)

FAIRFIELD—See BURLINGTON, VT (Comcast Cable)

FAYSTON—See WAITSFIELD, VT (Waitsfield Cable Co)

FERRISBURG—See BURLINGTON, VT (Comcast Cable)

FOREST DALE—See BURLINGTON, VT (Comcast Cable)

GEORGIA—See BURLINGTON, VT (Comcast Cable)

GILL—See BURLINGTON, MA (Comcast Cable)

GILSUM—See BURLINGTON, NH (Comcast Cable)

GLOVER—See BURLINGTON, VT (Comcast Cable)

GRAFTON—See BURLINGTON, VT (Comcast Cable)

GRANBY—See BURLINGTON, MA (Comcast Cable)

GRAND ISLE—See BURLINGTON, VT (Comcast Cable)

GRANITEVILLE—See ST. JOHNSBURY, VT (Charter Communications)

GRANTHAM—See BURLINGTON, NH (Comcast Cable)

GRANVILLE—See BURLINGTON, MA (Comcast Cable)

GREENFIELD—See BURLINGTON, MA (Comcast Cable)

GREENSBORO—See BURLINGTON, VT (Comcast Cable)

GROTON—See ST. JOHNSBURY, VT (Charter Communications)

GUILFORD—See BURLINGTON, VT (Comcast Cable)

HANOVER—See BURLINGTON, NH (Comcast Cable)

HARDWICK—See BURLINGTON, MA (Comcast Cable)

HARDWICK—See BURLINGTON, VT (Comcast Cable)

HARTFORD—See BURLINGTON, VT (Comcast Cable)

HARTLAND—See BURLINGTON, VT (Comcast Cable)

HATFIELD—See BURLINGTON, MA (Comcast Cable)

HAVERHILL—See ST. JOHNSBURY, NH (Charter Communications)

HIGHGATE CENTER—See BURLINGTON, VT (Comcast Cable)

HILL—See BURLINGTON, NH (Comcast Cable)

HINESBURG—See BURLINGTON, VT (Comcast Cable)

HINSDALE—See BURLINGTON, NH (Comcast Cable)

HOLLAND—See BURLINGTON, VT (Comcast Cable)

HOLYOKE—See BURLINGTON, MA (Comcast Cable)

HUBBARDTON—See BURLINGTON, VT (Comcast Cable)

HUNTINGTON—See BURLINGTON, MA (Comcast Cable)

HUNTINGTON—See BURLINGTON, VT (Comcast Cable)

HYDE PARK—See BURLINGTON, VT (Comcast Cable)

IRA—See BURLINGTON, VT (Comcast Cable)

IRASBURG TWP.—Formerly served by Adelphia Communications. No longer in operation

IRASBURG—See BURLINGTON, VT (Comcast Cable)

ISLAND POND—See BURLINGTON, VT (Comcast Cable)

JACKSONVILLE—Formerly served by Area Telecable. No longer in operation

JAMAICA TWP.—Southern Vermont Cable Co. Now served by PUTNEY, VT [VT0067]

JAMAICA—See BURLINGTON, VT (Comcast Cable)

JAY—See BURLINGTON, VT (Comcast Cable)

JEFFERSONVILLE—Jeffersonville Cable TV Corp

JERICHO—See BURLINGTON, VT (Comcast Cable)

JOHNSON—See BURLINGTON, VT (Comcast Cable)

KILLINGTON—See BURLINGTON, VT (Comcast Cable)

LANGDON—See BURLINGTON, NH (Comcast Cable)

LEBANON—See BURLINGTON, NH (Comcast Cable)

LEICESTER—See BURLINGTON, VT (Comcast Cable)

Vermont—Cable Community Index

LINCOLN—See BURLINGTON, VT (Comcast Cable)

LONDONDERRY—See BURLINGTON, VT (Comcast Cable)

LONGMEADOW—See BURLINGTON, MA (Comcast Cable)

LUDLOW—See BURLINGTON, VT (Comcast Cable)

LYNDON CENTER—See ST. JOHNSBURY, VT (Charter Communications)

LYNDON CORNERS—See ST. JOHNSBURY, VT (Charter Communications)

LYNDON—See ST. JOHNSBURY, VT (Charter Communications)

LYNDONVILLE—See ST. JOHNSBURY, VT (Charter Communications)

MANCHESTER CENTER—See BURLINGTON, VT (Comcast Cable)

MANCHESTER—Formerly served by Adelphia Communications. Now served by Comcast, BURLINGTON, VT [VT0001]

MANCHESTER—See BURLINGTON, VT (Comcast Cable)

MARSHFIELD—See ST. JOHNSBURY, VT (Charter Communications)

MCINDOE FALLS—See ST. JOHNSBURY, VT (Charter Communications)

MENDON—See BURLINGTON, VT (Comcast Cable)

MIDDLEBURY—See BURLINGTON, VT (Comcast Cable)

MIDDLESEX—See BURLINGTON, VT (Comcast Cable)

MIDDLETOWN SPRINGS—See BURLINGTON, VT (Comcast Cable)

MILTON—See BURLINGTON, VT (Comcast Cable)

MONKTON BORO—See BURLINGTON, VT (Comcast Cable)

MONSON—See BURLINGTON, MA (Comcast Cable)

MONTAGUE—See BURLINGTON, MA (Comcast Cable)

MONTGOMERY—See BURLINGTON, VT (Comcast Cable)

MONTPELIER—Comcast Cable. Now served by BURLINGTON, VT [VT0001]

MONTPELIER—See BURLINGTON, VT (Comcast Cable)

MORETOWN—See BURLINGTON, VT (Comcast Cable)

MORETOWN—See WAITSFIELD, VT (Waitsfield Cable Co)

MORGAN—See BURLINGTON, VT (Comcast Cable)

MORRISTOWN—See BURLINGTON, VT (Comcast Cable)

MORRISVILLE—See BURLINGTON, VT (Comcast Cable)

MOUNT ASCUTNEY—Formerly served by New England Wireless Inc. No longer in operation

MOUNT HOLLY—See BURLINGTON, VT (Comcast Cable)

MOUNT TABOR—See BURLINGTON, VT (Comcast Cable)

NEW HAVEN—See BURLINGTON, VT (Comcast Cable)

NEW LONDON—See BURLINGTON, NH (Comcast Cable)

NEWBURY—See ST. JOHNSBURY, VT (Charter Communications)

NEWFANE—Southern Vermont Cable Co

NEWPORT CENTER—See BURLINGTON, VT (Comcast Cable)

NEWPORT—See BURLINGTON, NH (Comcast Cable)

NEWPORT—See BURLINGTON, VT (Comcast Cable)

NORTH BENNINGTON—See BURLINGTON, VT (Comcast Cable)

NORTH FERRISBURG—See BURLINGTON, VT (Comcast Cable)

NORTH HARTLAND—See BURLINGTON, VT (Comcast Cable)

NORTH HAVERHILL—See ST. JOHNSBURY, NH (Charter Communications)

NORTH HERO—See BURLINGTON, VT (Comcast Cable)

NORTH TROY—See BURLINGTON, VT (Comcast Cable)

NORTH WALPOLE—See BURLINGTON, NH (Comcast Cable)

NORTHAMPTON—See BURLINGTON, MA (Comcast Cable)

NORTHFIELD (TOWN)—See NORTHFIELD (village), VT (Trans-Video Inc)

NORTHFIELD (VILLAGE)—Trans-Video Inc

NORTHFIELD—See BURLINGTON, MA (Comcast Cable)

NORWICH—See BURLINGTON, VT (Comcast Cable)

OLD BENNINGTON—See BURLINGTON, VT (Comcast Cable)

ORLEANS—See BURLINGTON, VT (Comcast Cable)

PALMER—See BURLINGTON, MA (Comcast Cable)

PASSUMPSIC—See ST. JOHNSBURY, VT (Charter Communications)

PAWLET—See BURLINGTON, VT (Comcast Cable)

PEACHAM—See ST. JOHNSBURY, VT (Charter Communications)

PELHAM—See BURLINGTON, MA (Comcast Cable)

PERKINSVILLE—See BURLINGTON, VT (Comcast Cable)

PIERMONT—See ST. JOHNSBURY, NH (Charter Communications)

PIKE—See ST. JOHNSBURY, NH (Charter Communications)

PITTSFORD—See BURLINGTON, VT (Comcast Cable)

PLAINFIELD (TOWN)—See BURLINGTON, NH (Comcast Cable)

PLAINFIELD—See ST. JOHNSBURY, VT (Charter Communications)

PLAINFIELD—See BURLINGTON, VT (Comcast Cable)

PLYMOUTH—See BURLINGTON, VT (Comcast Cable)

POULTNEY—See BURLINGTON, VT (Comcast Cable)

POWNAL—See BURLINGTON, VT (Comcast Cable)

PROCTOR—See BURLINGTON, VT (Comcast Cable)

PROCTORSVILLE—See BURLINGTON, VT (Comcast Cable)

PUTNEY—Southern Vermont Cable Co

RANDOLPH—See BURLINGTON, VT (Comcast Cable)

READING—See BURLINGTON, VT (Comcast Cable)

RICHFORD—See BURLINGTON, VT (Comcast Cable)

RICHMOND—Formerly served by Adelphia Communications. Now served by Comcast Cable, BURLINGTON, VT [VT0001]

RICHMOND—See BURLINGTON, VT (Comcast Cable)

RIVERTON—See NORTHFIELD (village), VT (Trans-Video Inc)

ROCHESTER—Formerly served by Adelphia Communications. Now served by Comcast Cable, BURLINGTON, VT [VT0001]

ROCHESTER—See BURLINGTON, VT (Comcast Cable)

ROCKINGHAM—See BURLINGTON, VT (Comcast Cable)

RUPERT—See BURLINGTON, VT (Comcast Cable)

RUTLAND—Comcast Cable. Now served by BURLINGTON, VT [VT0001]

RUTLAND—Formerly served by Satellite Signals of New England. No longer in operation

RUTLAND—See BURLINGTON, VT (Comcast Cable)

SALISBURY (TOWN)—See BURLINGTON, NH (Comcast Cable)

SAXTONS RIVER—See BURLINGTON, VT (Comcast Cable)

SHAFTSBURY—See BURLINGTON, VT (Comcast Cable)

SHEFFIELD—See ST. JOHNSBURY, VT (Charter Communications)

SHELBURNE—See BURLINGTON, MA (Comcast Cable)

SHELBURNE—See BURLINGTON, VT (Comcast Cable)

SHELDON—See BURLINGTON, VT (Comcast Cable)

SHREWSBURY—See BURLINGTON, VT (Comcast Cable)

SMUGGLERS NOTCH—See JEFFERSONVILLE, VT (Jeffersonville Cable TV Corp)

SOUTH BARRE—See ST. JOHNSBURY, VT (Charter Communications)

SOUTH BURLINGTON—See BURLINGTON, VT (Comcast Cable)

SOUTH CHARLESTOWN—See BURLINGTON, NH (Comcast Cable)

SOUTH HADLEY—See BURLINGTON, MA (Comcast Cable)

SOUTH HERO—See BURLINGTON, VT (Comcast Cable)

SOUTH ROYALTON—See ST. JOHNSBURY, VT (Charter Communications)

SOUTH RYEGATE—See ST. JOHNSBURY, VT (Charter Communications)

SOUTHWICK—See BURLINGTON, MA (Comcast Cable)

SPRINGFIELD—Comcast Cable. Now served by BURLINGTON, VT [VT0001]

SPRINGFIELD—See BURLINGTON, MA (Comcast Cable)

SPRINGFIELD—See BURLINGTON, VT (Comcast Cable)

ST. ALBANS (TOWN)—See BURLINGTON, VT (Comcast Cable)

ST. ALBANS—See BURLINGTON, VT (Comcast Cable)

ST. GEORGE (TOWN)—See BURLINGTON, VT (Comcast Cable)

ST. JOHNSBURY CENTER—See ST. JOHNSBURY, VT (Charter Communications)

ST. JOHNSBURY—Charter Communications

STARKSBORO TWP.—See BURLINGTON, VT (Comcast Cable)

STOWE—Stowe Cablevision Inc

STRATTON—See BURLINGTON, VT (Comcast Cable)

SUNAPEE—See BURLINGTON, NH (Comcast Cable)

SUNDERLAND—See BURLINGTON, MA (Comcast Cable)

SUNDERLAND—See BURLINGTON, VT (Comcast Cable)

SUTTON—See ST. JOHNSBURY, VT (Charter Communications)

SWANTON (VILLAGE)—See BURLINGTON, VT (Comcast Cable)

SWANTON—See BURLINGTON, VT (Comcast Cable)

TAFTSVILLE—See BURLINGTON, VT (Comcast Cable)

Cable Community Index—Virginia

TINMOUTH—See BURLINGTON, VT (Comcast Cable)

TOWNSHEND—Southern Vermont Cable Co

TROY—See BURLINGTON, VT (Comcast Cable)

TYSON—See BURLINGTON, VT (Comcast Cable)

UNDERHILL (TOWN)—See BURLINGTON, VT (Comcast Cable)

VERGENNES—See BURLINGTON, VT (Comcast Cable)

VERNON—See BURLINGTON, VT (Comcast Cable)

WAITSFIELD—Waitsfield Cable Co

WALDEN—See BURLINGTON, VT (Comcast Cable)

WALLINGFORD—See BURLINGTON, VT (Comcast Cable)

WALPOLE—See BURLINGTON, NH (Comcast Cable)

WALTHAM (TOWN)—See BURLINGTON, VT (Comcast Cable)

WARDSBORO TWP.—See WILMINGTON, VT (Duncan Cable TV Service)

WARE—See BURLINGTON, MA (Comcast Cable)

WARREN—See BURLINGTON, MA (Comcast Cable)

WARREN—See WAITSFIELD, VT (Waitsfield Cable Co)

WASHINGTON (TOWN)—See ST. JOHNSBURY, VT (Charter Communications)

WASHINGTON COUNTY (PORTIONS)—See WAITSFIELD, VT (Waitsfield Cable Co)

WATERBURY—See BURLINGTON, VT (Comcast Cable)

WATERFORD—See ST. JOHNSBURY, VT (Charter Communications)

WEATHERSFIELD (TOWN)—See BURLINGTON, VT (Comcast Cable)

WELLS RIVER—See ST. JOHNSBURY, VT (Charter Communications)

WELLS—See BURLINGTON, VT (Comcast Cable)

WEST BURKE—See ST. JOHNSBURY, VT (Charter Communications)

WEST CHESTERFIELD—See BURLINGTON, NH (Comcast Cable)

WEST DOVER—Duncan Cable TV (formerly Area Telecable). Now served by WILMINGTON, VT [VT0017]

WEST DOVER—See WILMINGTON, VT (Duncan Cable TV Service)

WEST LEBANON—See BURLINGTON, NH (Comcast Cable)

WEST PAWLET—See BURLINGTON, VT (Comcast Cable)

WEST RUTLAND—See BURLINGTON, VT (Comcast Cable)

WEST SPRINGFIELD—See BURLINGTON, MA (Comcast Cable)

WEST TOWNSHEND—See TOWNSHEND, VT (Southern Vermont Cable Co)

WESTFIELD—See BURLINGTON, MA (Comcast Cable)

WESTFIELD—See BURLINGTON, VT (Comcast Cable)

WESTFORD—See BURLINGTON, VT (Comcast Cable)

WESTHAMPTON—See BURLINGTON, MA (Comcast Cable)

WESTMINSTER—See BURLINGTON, VT (Comcast Cable)

WESTON—See BURLINGTON, VT (Comcast Cable)

WEYBRIDGE—See BURLINGTON, VT (Comcast Cable)

WHATELY—See BURLINGTON, MA (Comcast Cable)

WHITE RIVER JUNCTION—See BURLINGTON, VT (Comcast Cable)

WHITINGHAM—Formerly served by Area Telecable. No longer in operation

WILDER—See BURLINGTON, VT (Comcast Cable)

WILLIAMSBURG—See BURLINGTON, MA (Comcast Cable)

WILLIAMSTOWN (portions)—Formerly served by North Valley Cable Systems Inc. No longer in operation

WILLIAMSTOWN—See ST. JOHNSBURY, VT (Charter Communications)

WILLISTON—See BURLINGTON, VT (Comcast Cable)

WILMINGTON—Duncan Cable TV Service

WILMOT—See BURLINGTON, NH (Comcast Cable)

WINCHESTER—See BURLINGTON, NH (Comcast Cable)

WINDSOR—See BURLINGTON, VT (Comcast Cable)

WINHALL—See BURLINGTON, VT (Comcast Cable)

WINOOSKI—See BURLINGTON, VT (Comcast Cable)

WOODBURY—See BURLINGTON, VT (Comcast Cable)

WOODFORD—See BURLINGTON, VT (Comcast Cable)

WOODSTOCK—See BURLINGTON, VT (Comcast Cable)

WOODSVILLE—See ST. JOHNSBURY, NH (Charter Communications)

WORCESTER—See BURLINGTON, VT (Comcast Cable)

VIRGINIA

ABINGDON (TOWN)—See BRISTOL, VA (BVU OptiNet. Formerly [VA0190]. This cable system has converted to IPTV)

ACCOMAC—See ONANCOCK, VA (Charter Communications)

ACCOMACK COUNTY—See ONANCOCK, VA (Charter Communications)

ALBERTA—See LAWRENCEVILLE, VA (Shentel)

ALEXANDRIA (PORTIONS)—See FAIRFAX COUNTY, VA (Cox Communications)

ALEXANDRIA—Comcast Cable. Now served by PRINCE WILLIAM COUNTY (portions), VA [VA0148]

ALLEGHANY COUNTY—See COVINGTON, VA (Shentel)

ALTA VISTA—See RUSTBURG, VA (Shentel)

ALTAVISTA—Formerly served by Adelphia Communications. Now served by Comcast Cable, DANVILLE, VA [VA0012]

ALTAVISTA—See CHARLOTTESVILLE, VA (Comcast Cable)

AMELIA COUNTY (portions)—Comcast Cable. Now served by PETERSBURG, VA [VA0186]

AMELIA COUNTY (PORTIONS)—See PETERSBURG, VA (Comcast Cable)

AMHERST COUNTY (portions)—Comcast Cable. Now served by LYNCHBURG, VA [VA0013]

AMHERST COUNTY (PORTIONS)—See LYNCHBURG, VA (Comcast Cable)

AMHERST—See LYNCHBURG, VA (Comcast Cable)

ANNANDALE—See FAIRFAX COUNTY, VA (Cox Communications)

APPOMATTOX COUNTY (PORTIONS)—See RUSTBURG, VA (Shentel)

APPOMATTOX—Formerly served by Jet Broadband. Now served by Shentel, RUSTBURG, VA [VA0128]

APPOMATTOX—See RUSTBURG, VA (Shentel)

ARLINGTON COUNTY (portions)—Comcast Cable. Now served by PRINCE WILLIAM COUNTY (portions), VA [VA0148]

ASHLAND—See PETERSBURG, VA (Comcast Cable)

ATLANTIC—See ONANCOCK, VA (Charter Communications)

AUGUSTA COUNTY (PORTIONS)—See CHARLOTTESVILLE, VA (Comcast Cable)

AUGUSTA COUNTY (PORTIONS)—See WINTERGREEN, VA (Nelson Cable)

AUSTINVILLE—Formerly served by Citizens Telephone Coop. No longer in operation

AXTON—See BROSVILLE, VA (Chatmoss Cablevision)

BACHELOR'S HALL—See BROSVILLE, VA (Chatmoss Cablevision)

BANCROFT (TOWN)—See PETERSBURG, WV (Comcast Cable)

BANDY—See RICHLANDS (town), VA (Time Warner Cable)

BARBOURSVILLE—See CHARLOTTESVILLE, VA (Comcast Cable)

BARBOURSVILLE—See PETERSBURG, WV (Comcast Cable)

BARREN SPRINGS—Formerly served by Citizens Telephone Coop. No longer in operation

BASTIAN—Formerly served by Almega Cable. No longer in operation

BASYE—See WOODSTOCK, VA (Shentel)

BEALETON—See CHARLOTTESVILLE, VA (Comcast Cable)

BEDFORD COUNTY (NORTHERN PORTION)—See RUSTBURG, VA (Shentel)

BEDFORD COUNTY (PORTIONS)—See CHARLOTTESVILLE, VA (Comcast Cable)

BEDFORD COUNTY (PORTIONS)—See LYNCHBURG, VA (Comcast Cable)

BEDFORD COUNTY (SOUTHWESTERN PORTION)—See ROCKY MOUNT, VA (Shentel)

BEDFORD—Formerly served by Charter Communications. Now served by Shentel, ROCKY MOUNT, VA [VA0196]

BEDFORD—See ROCKY MOUNT, VA (Shentel)

BELFAST MILLS—See ROSEDALE, VA (Cable Plus)

BELLE HAVEN—Charter Communications. Now served by ACCOMAC, VA [VA0158]

BELLE HAVEN—See ONANCOCK, VA (Charter Communications)

BEN HUR—Comcast Cable. Now served by KNOXVILLE, TN [TN0004]

BIG ROCK—See RICHLANDS (town), VA (Time Warner Cable)

BIRCHLEAF—Formerly served by R&S Communications LLC. No longer in operation

BISHOP—Formerly served by Bishop TV Club Inc. Now served by Time Warner Cable, RICHLANDS (town), VA [VA0041]

BISHOP—See RICHLANDS (town), VA (Time Warner Cable)

BLACKSBURG—Comcast Cable. Now served by SALEM, VA [VA0024]

BLACKSBURG—See CHARLOTTESVILLE, VA (Comcast Cable)

Virginia—Cable Community Index

BLACKSTONE—Formerly served by Nesbe Cable TV. Now served by Shentel, CREWE, VA [VA0099]

BLACKSTONE—See CREWE, VA (Shentel)

BLOXOM—See ONANCOCK, VA (Charter Communications)

BLUE RIDGE—See CHARLOTTESVILLE, VA (Comcast Cable)

BOONES MILL—See ROCKY MOUNT, VA (Shentel)

BOTETOURT COUNTY (PORTIONS)—See CHARLOTTESVILLE, VA (Comcast Cable)

BOWLING GREEN—MetroCast. Now served by KING GEORGE, VA [VA0058]

BOWLING GREEN—See KING GEORGE, VA (MetroCast Communications)

BOYDTON—See CHARLOTTESVILLE, VA (Comcast Cable)

BOYKINS—See SUFFOLK, VA (Charter Communications)

BRACEY—See LAKE GASTON, VA (CWA Cable)

BRANCHVILLE—See SUFFOLK, VA (Charter Communications)

BRIDGEWATER—See CHARLOTTESVILLE, VA (Comcast Cable)

BRISTOL—BVU OptiNet. This cable system has converted to IPTV. See BRISTOL, VA [VA5201]

BRISTOL—BVU OptiNet. Formerly [VA0190]. This cable system has converted to IPTV

BRISTOW—See CHARLOTTESVILLE, VA (Comcast Cable)

BROADWAY—See CHARLOTTESVILLE, VA (Comcast Cable)

BROOKNEAL—Comcast Cable. Now served by DANVILLE, VA [VA0012]

BROOKNEAL—See CHARLOTTESVILLE, VA (Comcast Cable)

BROSVILLE—Chatmoss Cablevision

BRUNSWICK COUNTY (PORTIONS)—See LAKE GASTON, VA (CWA Cable)

BRUNSWICK COUNTY—See LAWRENCEVILLE, VA (Shentel)

BUCHANAN COUNTY (PORTIONS)—See RICHLANDS (town), VA (Time Warner Cable)

BUCHANAN—Shentel

BUENA VISTA—Comcast Cable. Now served by CHARLOTTESVILLE, VA [VA0131]

BUENA VISTA—Formerly served by Adelphia Communications. Now served by Comcast Cable, BUENA VISTA, VA [VA0147]

BUENA VISTA—See CHARLOTTESVILLE, VA (Comcast Cable)

BUFFALO (TOWN)—See PETERSBURG, WV (Comcast Cable)

BURGESS—See NORTHUMBERLAND COUNTY, VA (MetroCast Communications)

BURKE—See FAIRFAX COUNTY, VA (Cox Communications)

BURKEVILLE—See CREWE, VA (Shentel)

CABELL COUNTY (PORTIONS)—See PETERSBURG, WV (Comcast Cable)

CALLAGHAN—Formerly served by Clearview TV Cable. No longer in operation

CALLAO—See NORTHUMBERLAND COUNTY, VA (MetroCast Communications)

CAMPBELL COUNTY (PORTIONS)—See LYNCHBURG, VA (Comcast Cable)

CAMPBELL COUNTY (PORTIONS)—See RUSTBURG, VA (Shentel)

CAPE CHARLES—See ONANCOCK, VA (Charter Communications)

CAROLINE COUNTY (PORTIONS)—See CHARLOTTESVILLE, VA (Comcast Cable)

CAROLINE COUNTY (UNINCORPORATED AREAS)—See KING GEORGE, VA (MetroCast Communications)

CAROLINE COUNTY—See KING GEORGE, VA (MetroCast Communications)

CASCADE—See BROSVILLE, VA (Chatmoss Cablevision)

CASTLEWOOD—See LEBANON, VA (Shentel)

CASWELL COUNTY (PORTIONS)—See CHARLOTTESVILLE, NC (Comcast Cable)

CATLETT—See CHARLOTTESVILLE, VA (Comcast Cable)

CEDAR BLUFF (TOWN)—See RICHLANDS (town), VA (Time Warner Cable)

CENTREVILLE—See FAIRFAX COUNTY, VA (Cox Communications)

CHANTILLY—See FAIRFAX COUNTY, VA (Cox Communications)

CHARLES CITY COUNTY (portions)—Formerly served by Comcast Cable. No longer in operation

CHARLES CITY COUNTY (PORTIONS)—See PETERSBURG, VA (Comcast Cable)

CHARLOTTE COUNTY (EASTERN PORTION)—See FARMVILLE, VA (Shentel)

CHARLOTTE COURT HOUSE—See FARMVILLE, VA (Shentel)

CHARLOTTESVILLE—Formerly served by NTELOS. No longer in operation

CHARLOTTESVILLE—Comcast Cable

CHASE CITY—Formerly served by Adelphia Communications. Now served by Comcast Cable, SOUTH HILL, VA [VA0062]

CHASE CITY—See CHARLOTTESVILLE, VA (Comcast Cable)

CHATHAM—See CHARLOTTESVILLE, VA (Comcast Cable)

CHERITON—See ONANCOCK, VA (Charter Communications)

CHESAPEAKE—See VIRGINIA BEACH, VA (Cox Communications)

CHESAPEAKE—Mediacom

CHESTERFIELD COUNTY (PORTIONS)—See PETERSBURG, VA (Comcast Cable)

CHESTERFIELD COUNTY—Formerly served by Comcast Cable. No longer in operation

CHINCOTEAGUE ISLAND—Charter Communications

CHRISTIANSBURG—See CHARLOTTESVILLE, VA (Comcast Cable)

CHRISTIANSBURG—See RADFORD, VA (Shentel)

CLARAVILLE—Formerly served by Adelphia Communications. No longer in operation

CLARION—See RUSTBURG, VA (Shentel)

CLARKSVILLE—Shentel

CLIFTON FORGE—See COVINGTON, VA (Shentel)

CLIFTON—See FAIRFAX COUNTY, VA (Cox Communications)

CLINTWOOD (town)—Formerly served by Adelphia Communications. Now served by Comcast Cable, KNOXVILLE, TN [TN0004]

CLOVERDALE—See CHARLOTTESVILLE, VA (Comcast Cable)

COLONIAL BEACH—MetroCast. Now served by KING GEORGE, VA [VA0058]

COLONIAL BEACH—See KING GEORGE, VA (MetroCast Communications)

COLONIAL HEIGHTS—See PETERSBURG, VA (Comcast Cable)

CONCORD—See RUSTBURG, VA (Shentel)

COURTLAND—See SUFFOLK, VA (Charter Communications)

COVINGTON—Shentel

CRADDOCKVILLE—See ONANCOCK, VA (Charter Communications)

CRAIG COUNTY (PORTIONS)—See NEW CASTLE (town), VA (Citizens Telephone Coop)

CRAIGSVILLE (TOWN)—See CHARLOTTESVILLE, VA (Comcast Cable)

CRAIGSVILLE—Formerly served by Adelphia Communications. Now served by Comcast Cable, STAUNTON, VA [VA0026]

CRAWFORD MANOR—Crawford Manor Cable TV

CREWE—Shentel

CRIMORA—See CHARLOTTESVILLE, VA (Comcast Cable)

CROCKETT—See SPEEDWELL, VA (R&S Communications LLC)

CROZET—Formerly served by Adelphia Communications. Now served by Comcast Cable, CHARLOTTESVILLE, VA [VA0131]

CROZET—See CHARLOTTESVILLE, VA (Comcast Cable)

CULPEPER (town)—Formerly served by Adelphia Communications. Now served by Comcast Cable, CULPEPPER, VA [VA0182]

CULPEPER (TOWN)—See CHARLOTTESVILLE, VA (Comcast Cable)

CULPEPER COUNTY (PORTIONS)—See CHARLOTTESVILLE, VA (Comcast Cable)

CULPEPER—Comcast Cable. Now served by CHARLOTTESVILLE, VA [VA0131]

CULPEPER—See CHARLOTTESVILLE, VA (Comcast Cable)

CUMBERLAND COUNTY (SOUTHWESTERN PORTION)—See FARMVILLE, VA (Shentel)

DAHLGREN—See KING GEORGE, VA (MetroCast Communications)

DALE CITY—See CHARLOTTESVILLE, VA (Comcast Cable)

DALEVILLE—See CHARLOTTESVILLE, VA (Comcast Cable)

DAMASCUS—Zito Media

DANIEL BOONE—See GATE CITY, VA (Scott Telecom & Electronics)

DANTE—See LEBANON, VA (Shentel)

DANVILLE—Comcast Cable. Now served by CHARLOTTESVILLE, VA [VA0131]

DANVILLE—See CHARLOTTESVILLE, VA (Comcast Cable)

DAYTON—See CHARLOTTESVILLE, VA (Comcast Cable)

DELTAVILLE—MetroCast Communications

DILLWYN—Comcast Cable. Now served by PETERSBURG, VA [VA0186]

DILLWYN—See PETERSBURG, VA (Comcast Cable)

DINWIDDIE—See PETERSBURG, VA (Comcast Cable)

DORAN—See RICHLANDS (town), VA (Time Warner Cable)

DRAKES BRANCH—See FARMVILLE, VA (Shentel)

Cable Community Index—Virginia

DRY FORK—See BROSVILLE, VA (Chatmoss Cablevision)

DUBLIN (TOWN)—See CHARLOTTESVILLE, VA (Comcast Cable)

DUFFIELD (town)—Formerly served by Adelphia Communications. Now served by Comcast Cable, KNOXVILLE, TN [TN0004]

DUMFRIES (TOWN)—See CHARLOTTESVILLE, VA (Comcast Cable)

EASTVILLE—See ONANCOCK, VA (Charter Communications)

EDGEHILL—See KING GEORGE, VA (MetroCast Communications)

EDINBURG—See WOODSTOCK, VA (Shentel)

EDWARDSVILLE—See NORTHUMBERLAND COUNTY, VA (MetroCast Communications)

ELEANOR (TOWN)—See PETERSBURG, WV (Comcast Cable)

ELKTON—See CHARLOTTESVILLE, VA (Comcast Cable)

EMPORIA—Comcast Cable. Now served by PETERSBURG, VA [VA0186]

EMPORIA—See PETERSBURG, VA (Comcast Cable)

ESSEX COUNTY (PORTIONS)—See KING GEORGE, VT (MetroCast Communications)

EVINGTON—See RUSTBURG, VA (Shentel)

EWING—Zito Media

EXMORE—See ONANCOCK, VA (Charter Communications)

FAIRFAX COUNTY—Cox Communications

FAIRFAX STATION—See FAIRFAX COUNTY, VA (Cox Communications)

FAIRFAX—See FAIRFAX COUNTY, VA (Cox Communications)

FAIRLAWN—See RADFORD, VA (Shentel)

FALLS CHURCH—RCN. This cable system has converted to IPTV. See WASHINGTON, DC (portions) [DC5001]

FALLS CHURCH—See FAIRFAX COUNTY, VA (Cox Communications)

FARMVILLE—Shentel

FAUQUIER COUNTY—See CHARLOTTESVILLE, VA (Comcast Cable)

FINCASTLE—See CHARLOTTESVILLE, VA (Comcast Cable)

FISHERSVILLE—See CHARLOTTESVILLE, VA (Comcast Cable)

FLOYD COUNTY (PORTIONS)—See FLOYD, VA (Citizens Telephone Coop)

FLOYD—Citizens Telephone Coop

FLUVANNA COUNTY (PORTIONS)—See CHARLOTTESVILLE, VA (Comcast Cable)

FOREST—See RUSTBURG, VA (Shentel)

FORT A.P. HILL—Formerly served by MetroCast Communications. No longer in operation

FORT BELVOIR ARMY BASE—Comcast Cable. Now served by PRINCE WILLIAM COUNTY (portions), VA [VA0148]

FORT BELVOIR ARMY BASE—See CHARLOTTESVILLE, VA (Comcast Cable)

FORT CHISWELL—Citizens Telephone Coop. Now served by FLOYD, VA [VA0104]

FORT CHISWELL—Citizens Telephone Coop. Now served by FLOYD, VA [VA0104]

FORT CHISWELL—See FLOYD, VA (Citizens Telephone Coop)

FORT EUSTIS ARMY BASE—See VIRGINIA BEACH, VA (Cox Communications)

FORT LEE—See PETERSBURG, VA (Comcast Cable)

FORT MONROE—See VIRGINIA BEACH, VA (Cox Communications)

FORT MYER ARMY BASE—See CHARLOTTESVILLE, VA (Comcast Cable)

FORT STORY—See VIRGINIA BEACH, VA (Cox Communications)

FRANKLIN COUNTY—See ROCKY MOUNT, VA (Shentel)

FRANKLIN—Charter Communications. Now served by SUFFOLK, VA [VA0025]

FRANKLIN—See SUFFOLK, VA (Charter Communications)

FREDERICKSBURG—See CHARLOTTESVILLE, VA (Comcast Cable)

FREDERICKSBURG—Cox Communications

FRONT ROYAL—Comcast Cable. Now served by FREDERICK COUNTY (portions), MD [MD0009]

GAINESVILLE—See CHARLOTTESVILLE, VA (Comcast Cable)

GALAX—Comcast Cable. Now served by KNOXVILLE, TN [TN0004]

GARRISONVILLE—See CHARLOTTESVILLE, VA (Comcast Cable)

GATE CITY—Scott Telecom & Electronics

GATES COUNTY (PORTIONS)—See SUFFOLK, NC (Charter Communications)

GATESVILLE—See SUFFOLK, NC (Charter Communications)

GLADE SPRING—Comcast Cable. Now served by KNOXVILLE, TN [TN0004]

GLASGOW—Formerly served by Adelphia Communications. Now served by Comcast Cable, BUENA VISTA, VA [VA0147]

GLASGOW—See CHARLOTTESVILLE, VA (Comcast Cable)

GLOUCESTER COUNTY—Cox Communications. Now served by HAMPTON ROADS (formerly Virginia Beach), VA [VA0002]

GLOUCESTER COUNTY—See VIRGINIA BEACH, VA (Cox Communications)

GOOCHLAND—See PETERSBURG, VA (Comcast Cable)

GOODE—See RUSTBURG, VA (Shentel)

GOODVIEW—See CHARLOTTESVILLE, VA (Comcast Cable)

GORDONSVILLE—Comcast Cable. Now served by CULPEPER, VA [VA0182]

GORDONSVILLE—See CHARLOTTESVILLE, VA (Comcast Cable)

GOSHEN—Comcast Cable. Now served by BUENA VISTA, VA [VA0147]

GOSHEN—See CHARLOTTESVILLE, VA (Comcast Cable)

GRAFTON—See VIRGINIA BEACH, VA (Cox Communications)

GRATTON—See RICHLANDS (town), VA (Time Warner Cable)

GREAT FALLS—See FAIRFAX COUNTY, VA (Cox Communications)

GREENE COUNTY (PORTIONS)—See CHARLOTTESVILLE, VA (Comcast Cable)

GREENSVILLE COUNTY (PORTIONS)—See PETERSBURG, VA (Comcast Cable)

GRETNA—See CHARLOTTESVILLE, VA (Comcast Cable)

GROTTOES—See CHARLOTTESVILLE, VA (Comcast Cable)

GRUNDY (town)—Time Warner Cable. Now served by RICHLANDS (town), VA [VA0041]

GRUNDY (TOWN)—See RICHLANDS (town), VA (Time Warner Cable)

HALIFAX COUNTY (PORTIONS)—See CHARLOTTESVILLE, VA (Comcast Cable)

HALIFAX—See CHARLOTTESVILLE, VA (Comcast Cable)

HALLWOOD—See ONANCOCK, VA (Charter Communications)

HAMPDEN SYDNEY—See FARMVILLE, VA (Shentel)

HAMPTON ROADS—See VIRGINIA BEACH, VA (Cox Communications)

HAMPTON—See VIRGINIA BEACH, VA (Cox Communications)

HANOVER COUNTY (PORTIONS)—See PETERSBURG, VA (Comcast Cable)

HARBORTON—See ONANCOCK, VA (Charter Communications)

HARMAN—See RICHLANDS (town), VA (Time Warner Cable)

HARRISONBURG—Comcast Cable. Now served by CHARLOTTESVILLE, VA [VA0131]

HARRISONBURG—Formerly served by NTELOS. No longer in operation

HARRISONBURG—See CHARLOTTESVILLE, VA (Comcast Cable)

HAYMARKET—See CHARLOTTESVILLE, VA (Comcast Cable)

HAYSI—Formerly served by K & V Cable TV Co. No longer in operation

HEATHSVILLE—See NORTHUMBERLAND COUNTY, VA (MetroCast Communications)

HENRICO COUNTY (PORTIONS)—See PETERSBURG, VA (Comcast Cable)

HENRICO COUNTY—Comcast Cable. Now served by PETERSBURG, VA [VA0186]

HENRY COUNTY (PORTIONS)—See CHARLOTTESVILLE, VA (Comcast Cable)

HERNDON—See FAIRFAX COUNTY, VA (Cox Communications)

HILTONS—See BRISTOL, VA (BVU OptiNet. Formerly [VA0190]. This cable system has converted to IPTV)

HILTONS—See GATE CITY, VA (Scott Telecom & Electronics)

HOMETOWN—See PETERSBURG, WV (Comcast Cable)

HONAKER—See LEBANON, VA (Shentel)

HOPEWELL—See PETERSBURG, VA (Comcast Cable)

HOT SPRINGS—Comcast Cable. Now served by BUENA VISTA, VA [VA0147]

HOT SPRINGS—See CHARLOTTESVILLE, VA (Comcast Cable)

HUDDLESTON—See CHARLOTTESVILLE, VA (Comcast Cable)

HUNTINGTON (CITY)—See PETERSBURG, WV (Comcast Cable)

HUNTINGTON—See PETERSBURG, WV (Comcast Cable)

HURLEY—See RICHLANDS (town), VA (Time Warner Cable)

HURT—Formerly served by Adelphia Communications. Now served by Comcast Cable, DANVILLE, VA [VA0012]

HURT—See CHARLOTTESVILLE, VA (Comcast Cable)

INDEPENDENCE (town)—Formerly served by Adelphia Communications. Now served by Comcast Cable,

Virginia—Cable Community Index

KNOXVILLE, TN [TN0004]

IRON GATE—See COVINGTON, VA (Shentel)

IRVINGTON (TOWN)—See DELTAVILLE, VA (MetroCast Communications)

ISLE OF WIGHT COUNTY—See SUFFOLK, VA (Charter Communications)

IVANHOE—Citizens Telephone Coop. Now served by FORT CHISWELL, VA [VA0066]

IVOR—See SUFFOLK, VA (Charter Communications)

JAMES CITY COUNTY—Cox Communications. Now served by HAMPTON ROADS (formerly Virginia Beach), VA [VA0002]

JAMES CITY COUNTY—See VIRGINIA BEACH, VA (Cox Communications)

JARRATT—CWA Cable

JONESVILLE (town)—Formerly served by CC & S Cable TV. Now served by Comcast Cable, KNOXVILLE, TN [TN0004]

KANAWHA COUNTY (PORTIONS)—See PETERSBURG, WV (Comcast Cable)

KEEN MOUNTAIN—Time Warner Cable. Now served by RICHLANDS (town), VA [VA0041]

KEEN MOUNTAIN—See RICHLANDS (town), VA (Time Warner Cable)

KELLER—See ONANCOCK, VA (Charter Communications)

KENBRIDGE—Shentel. Now served by CREWE, VA [VA0099]

KENBRIDGE—See CREWE, VA (Shentel)

KEYSVILLE—Shentel. Now served by FARMVILLE, VA [VA0050]

KEYSVILLE—See FARMVILLE, VA (Shentel)

KILMARNOCK (TOWN)—See DELTAVILLE, VA (MetroCast Communications)

KING & QUEEN COUNTY (PORTIONS)—See VIRGINIA BEACH, VA (Cox Communications)

KING GEORGE—MetroCast Communications

KING WILLIAM (portions)—Comcast Cable. Now served by PRINCE WILLIAM COUNTY (portions), VA [VA0148]

KING WILLIAM (PORTIONS)—See CHARLOTTESVILLE, VA (Comcast Cable)

KING WILLIAM COUNTY (PORTIONS)—See VIRGINIA BEACH, VA (Cox Communications)

LA CROSSE—See CHARLOTTESVILLE, VA (Comcast Cable)

LACEY SPRING—Formerly served by Adelphia Communications. Now served by Comcast Cable, HARRISONBURG, VA [VA0016]

LACEY SPRING—See CHARLOTTESVILLE, VA (Comcast Cable)

LAKE GASTON—CWA Cable

LAKE MONTICELLO—See CHARLOTTESVILLE, VA (Comcast Cable)

LAKE RIDGE—See CHARLOTTESVILLE, VA (Comcast Cable)

LANCASTER COUNTY—MetroCast Communications. Now served by DELTAVILLE, VA [VA0085]

LANCASTER COUNTY—See DELTAVILLE, VA (MetroCast Communications)

LANEXA—See VIRGINIA BEACH, VA (Cox Communications)

LANGLEY AFB—Cox Communications. Now served by HAMPTON ROADS (formerly Virginia Beach), VA [VA0002]

LANGLEY AFB—See VIRGINIA BEACH, VA (Cox Communications)

LAWRENCEVILLE—Shentel

LEBANON (portions)—Formerly served by Almega Cable. No longer in operation

LEBANON—Shentel

LEE COUNTY (PORTIONS)—See EWING, VA (Zito Media)

LESAGE—See PETERSBURG, WV (Comcast Cable)

LEWISETTA—See NORTHUMBERLAND COUNTY, VA (MetroCast Communications)

LEXINGTON—See CHARLOTTESVILLE, VA (Comcast Cable)

LOCUST GROVE—See CHARLOTTESVILLE, VA (Comcast Cable)

LORTON—See FAIRFAX COUNTY, VA (Cox Communications)

LOTTSBURG—See NORTHUMBERLAND COUNTY, VA (MetroCast Communications)

LOUDOUN COUNTY (portions)—Comcast Cable. Now served by PRINCE WILLIAM COUNTY (portions), VA [VA0148]

LOUISA (TOWN)—See CHARLOTTESVILLE, VA (Comcast Cable)

LOUISA COUNTY (PORTIONS)—See CHARLOTTESVILLE, VA (Comcast Cable)

LOUISA—Comcast Cable. Now served by CHARLOTTESVILLE, VA [VA0131]

LOUISA—See CHARLOTTESVILLE, VA (Comcast Cable)

LOVINGSTON/SHIPMAN—Nelson Cable

LUNENBURG COUNTY (PORTIONS)—See CREWE, VA (Shentel)

LURAY—Comcast Cable. Now served by HARRISONBURG, VA [VA0016]

LURAY—See CHARLOTTESVILLE, VA (Comcast Cable)

LYNCHBURG—Comcast Cable

MADISON COUNTY—See CHARLOTTESVILLE, VA (Comcast Cable)

MADISON—Comcast Cable. Now served by CHARLOTTESVILLE, VA [VA0131]

MADISON—See CHARLOTTESVILLE, VA (Comcast Cable)

MANASSAS PARK—See CHARLOTTESVILLE, VA (Comcast Cable)

MANASSAS—See CHARLOTTESVILLE, VA (Comcast Cable)

MAPPSVILLE—See ONANCOCK, VA (Charter Communications)

MARINE CORPS BASE QUANTICO—See CHARLOTTESVILLE, VA (Comcast Cable)

MARION (town)—Comcast Cable. Now served by KNOXVILLE, TN [TN0004]

MARTINSVILLE—Comcast Cable. Now served by DANVILLE, VA [VA0012]

MARTINSVILLE—See CHARLOTTESVILLE, VA (Comcast Cable)

MATHEWS COUNTY—See MATHEWS, VA (MctroCast Communications)

MATHEWS—MetroCast Communications

MATTAPONI—See VIRGINIA BEACH, VA (Cox Communications)

MAURERTOWN—See WOODSTOCK, VA (Shentel)

MAVISDALE—See RICHLANDS (town), VA (Time Warner Cable)

MAX MEADOWS—Citizens Telephone Coop. Now served by FORT CHISWELL, VA [VA0066]

MAXIE—See RICHLANDS (town), VA (Time Warner Cable)

MCGAHEYSVILLE—See CHARLOTTESVILLE, VA (Comcast Cable)

MCKENNEY—Formerly served by Adelphia Communications. Now served by Comcast Cable, PETERSBURG, VA [VA0186]

MCKENNEY—See PETERSBURG, VA (Comcast Cable)

MCLEAN—See FAIRFAX COUNTY, VA (Cox Communications)

MECKLENBURG COUNTY (PORTIONS)—See LAKE GASTON, VA (CWA Cable)

MECKLENBURG COUNTY (PORTIONS)—See CLARKSVILLE, VA (Shentel)

MECKLENBURG COUNTY—See CHARLOTTESVILLE, VA (Comcast Cable)

MELFA—See ONANCOCK, VA (Charter Communications)

MIDDLESEX COUNTY—See DELTAVILLE, VA (MetroCast Communications)

MINERAL (TOWN)—See CHARLOTTESVILLE, VA (Comcast Cable)

MONETA—See CHARLOTTESVILLE, VA (Comcast Cable)

MONTCLAIR—See CHARLOTTESVILLE, VA (Comcast Cable)

MONTEREY—Formerly served by Highland Communications. No longer in operation

MONTGOMERY COUNTY (PORTIONS)—See CHARLOTTESVILLE, VA (Comcast Cable)

MONTGOMERY COUNTY—See RADFORD, VA (Shentel)

MONTROSS—See KING GEORGE, VA (MetroCast Communications)

MOUNT CLINTON—Formerly served by Adelphia Communications. Now served by Comcast Cable, HARRISONBURG, VA [VA0016]

MOUNT CLINTON—See CHARLOTTESVILLE, VA (Comcast Cable)

MOUNT CRAWFORD—See CHARLOTTESVILLE, VA (Comcast Cable)

MOUNT JACKSON—See WOODSTOCK, VA (Shentel)

MOUNT SIDNEY—See CHARLOTTESVILLE, VA (Comcast Cable)

NASSAWODOX—See ONANCOCK, VA (Charter Communications)

NELSON COUNTY (PORTIONS)—See WINTERGREEN, VA (Nelson Cable)

NEW CASTLE (TOWN)—Citizens Telephone Coop

NEW CHURCH—See ONANCOCK, VA (Charter Communications)

NEW KENT COUNTY (PORTIONS)—See VIRGINIA BEACH, VA (Cox Communications)

NEW KENT—Cox Communications. Now served by HAMPTON ROADS (formerly Virginia Beach), VA [VA0002]

NEW KENT—See VIRGINIA BEACH, VA (Cox Communications)

NEW MARKET—See WOODSTOCK, VA (Shentel)

NEWPORT NEWS—See VIRGINIA BEACH, VA (Cox Communications)

NEWPORT—PemTel

NEWSOMS—See SUFFOLK, VA (Charter Communications)

NICKELSVILLE—Formerly served by Scott Telecom & Electronics. No longer in operation

NICKELSVILLE—See GATE CITY, VA (Scott Telecom & Electronics)

Cable Community Index—Virginia

NITRO (PORTIONS)—See PETERSBURG, WV (Comcast Cable)

NOKESVILLE—See CHARLOTTESVILLE, VA (Comcast Cable)

NORFOLK NAVAL BASE/SOUTHSIDE HAMPTON ROADS—See VIRGINIA BEACH, VA (Cox Communications)

NORFOLK—See VIRGINIA BEACH, VA (Cox Communications)

NORTH TAZEWELL—See RICHLANDS (town), VA (Time Warner Cable)

NORTHAMPTON COUNTY—See ONANCOCK, VA (Charter Communications)

NORTHUMBERLAND COUNTY (PORTIONS)—See DELTAVILLE, VA (MetroCast Communications)

NORTHUMBERLAND COUNTY—MetroCast Communications

NORTON—Comcast Cable. Now served by KNOXVILLE, TN [TN0004]

OAK HALL—See ONANCOCK, VA (Charter Communications)

OAKTON—See FAIRFAX COUNTY, VA (Cox Communications)

OAKWOOD—See RICHLANDS (town), VA (Time Warner Cable)

OCCOQUAN—See CHARLOTTESVILLE, VA (Comcast Cable)

ONANCOCK—Charter Communications

ONLEY—See ONANCOCK, VA (Charter Communications)

OPHELIA—See NORTHUMBERLAND COUNTY, VA (MetroCast Communications)

ORANGE COUNTY (PORTIONS)—See CHARLOTTESVILLE, VA (Comcast Cable)

ORANGE—Comcast Cable. Now served by CULPEPER, VA [VA0182]

ORANGE—See CHARLOTTESVILLE, VA (Comcast Cable)

PAGE COUNTY (PORTIONS)—See CHARLOTTESVILLE, VA (Comcast Cable)

PAINT LICK—See RICHLANDS (town), VA (Time Warner Cable)

PAINTER—See ONANCOCK, VA (Charter Communications)

PALMYRA—Comcast Cable. Now served by CHARLOTTESVILLE, VA [VA0131]

PALMYRA—See CHARLOTTESVILLE, VA (Comcast Cable)

PAMPLIN—See RUSTBURG, VA (Shentel)

PARKSLEY—See ONANCOCK, VA (Charter Communications)

PATRICK COUNTY (PORTIONS)—See CHARLOTTESVILLE, VA (Comcast Cable)

PEARISBURG—Formerly served by Charter Communications. Now served by Suddenlink Communications, BECKLEY, WV [WV0005]

PEMBROKE—See NEWPORT, VA (PemTel)

PENNINGTON GAP (town)—Formerly served by Adelphia Communications. Now served by Comcast Cable, KNOXVILLE, TN [TN0004]

PETERSBURG—Comcast Cable. Now served by PETERSBURG, VA [VA0186]

PETERSBURG—Comcast Cable

PHENIX—See FARMVILLE, VA (Shentel)

PILGRIMS KNOB—See RICHLANDS (town), VA (Time Warner Cable)

POCA (TOWN)—See PETERSBURG, WV (Comcast Cable)

POQUOSON—Cox Communications. Now served by HAMPTON ROADS (formerly Virginia Beach), VA [VA0002]

POQUOSON—See VIRGINIA BEACH, VA (Cox Communications)

PORT ROYAL—See KING GEORGE, VA (MetroCast Communications)

PORTSMOUTH—See VIRGINIA BEACH, VA (Cox Communications)

POUNDING MILL—See RICHLANDS (town), VA (Time Warner Cable)

POWHATAN—Comcast Cable. Now served by PETERSBURG, VA [VA0186]

POWHATAN—See PETERSBURG, VA (Comcast Cable)

PRINCE EDWARD COUNTY (NORTHWESTERN PORTION)—See FARMVILLE, VA (Shentel)

PRINCE GEORGE—Formerly served by Adelphia Communications. Now served by Comcast Cable, PETERSBURG, VA [VA0186]

PRINCE GEORGE—See PETERSBURG, VA (Comcast Cable)

PRINCE WILLIAM COUNTY (portions)—Comcast Cable. Now served by CHARLOTTESVILLE, VA [VA0131]

PRINCE WILLIAM COUNTY (PORTIONS)—See CHARLOTTESVILLE, VA (Comcast Cable)

PROVIDENCE FORGE—See VIRGINIA BEACH, VA (Cox Communications)

PULASKI COUNTY (PORTIONS)—See CHARLOTTESVILLE, VA (Comcast Cable)

PULASKI COUNTY (PORTIONS)—See RADFORD, VA (Shentel)

PULASKI—Comcast Cable. Now served by DANVILLE, VA [VA0012]

PULASKI—See CHARLOTTESVILLE, VA (Comcast Cable)

PUNGOTEAGUE—See ONANCOCK, VA (Charter Communications)

PUTNAM COUNTY (PORTIONS)—See PETERSBURG, WV (Comcast Cable)

QUANTICO (TOWN)—See CHARLOTTESVILLE, VA (Comcast Cable)

QUINTON—See VIRGINIA BEACH, VA (Cox Communications)

RADFORD—Shentel

RAVEN—See RICHLANDS (town), VA (Time Warner Cable)

RED ASH—See RICHLANDS (town), VA (Time Warner Cable)

RED HOUSE—See PETERSBURG, WV (Comcast Cable)

REDWOOD—Formerly served by Suddenlink Communications. No longer in operation

REEDVILLE—See NORTHUMBERLAND COUNTY, VA (MetroCast Communications)

RESTON—Comcast Cable. Now served by PRINCE WILLIAM COUNTY (portions), VA [VA0148]

RESTON—See CHARLOTTESVILLE, VA (Comcast Cable)

RICHLANDS (TOWN)—Time Warner Cable

RICHMOND COUNTY (PORTIONS)—See KING GEORGE, VA (MetroCast Communications)

RICHMOND—Comcast Cable. Now served by PETERSBURG, VA [VA0186]

RICHMOND—Formerly served by CavTel/Windstream. IPTV service no longer in operation

RICHMOND—Formerly served by NTELOS. No longer in operation

RICHMOND—See PETERSBURG, VA (Comcast Cable)

RIDGEWAY—See CHARLOTTESVILLE, VA (Comcast Cable)

RIVER OAKS—Formerly served by Comcast Cable. No longer in operation

ROANOKE COUNTY (PORTIONS)—See CHARLOTTESVILLE, VA (Comcast Cable)

ROANOKE COUNTY—See ROANOKE, VA (Cox Communications)

ROANOKE—Formerly served by NTELOS. No longer in operation

ROANOKE—Cox Communications

ROCKBRIDGE COUNTY (PORTIONS)—See CHARLOTTESVILLE, VA (Comcast Cable)

ROCKFISH—See WINTERGREEN, VA (Nelson Cable)

ROCKINGHAM COUNTY (PORTIONS)—See CHARLOTTESVILLE, VA (Comcast Cable)

ROCKINGHAM—Formerly served by Adelphia Communications. Now served by Comcast Cable, HARRISONBURG, VA [VA0016]

ROCKINGHAM—See CHARLOTTESVILLE, VA (Comcast Cable)

ROCKY MOUNT—Shentel

ROSE HILL—See EWING, VA (Zito Media)

ROSEDALE—Cable Plus

ROYAL CITY—See RICHLANDS (town), VA (Time Warner Cable)

RUCKERSVILLE—Comcast Cable. Now served by CHARLOTTESVILLE, VA [VA0131]

RUCKERSVILLE—See CHARLOTTESVILLE, VA (Comcast Cable)

RURAL RETREAT (PORTIONS)—See SPEEDWELL, VA (R&S Communications LLC)

RURAL RETREAT—Formerly served by Rural Retreat Cable TV Inc. No longer in operation

RURAL RETREAT—See WYTHEVILLE, VA (Shentel)

RUSSELL COUNTY (PORTIONS)—See ROSEDALE, VA (Cable Plus)

RUSSELL COUNTY (PORTIONS)—See RICHLANDS (town), VA (Time Warner Cable)

RUSSELL COUNTY—See LEBANON, VA (Shentel)

RUSTBURG—Shentel

RUTHER GLEN—Comcast Cable. Now served by PRINCE WILLIAM COUNTY (portions), VA [VA0148]

RUTHER GLEN—See CHARLOTTESVILLE, VA (Comcast Cable)

SALEM—Comcast Cable. Now served by CHARLOTTESVILLE, VA [VA0131]

SALEM—See CHARLOTTESVILLE, VA (Comcast Cable)

SALUDA—See DELTAVILLE, VA (MetroCast Communications)

SANDY RIDGE—Scott Telecom & Electronics

SANFORD—See ONANCOCK, VA (Charter Communications)

SAXIS—See ONANCOCK, VA (Charter Communications)

SCOTT DEPOT—See PETERSBURG, WV (Comcast Cable)

SCOTTSVILLE—Nelson Cable. Now served by LOVINGSTON/SHIPMAN, VA [VA0192]

SCOTTSVILLE—See SCOTTSVILLE, VA (Nelson Cable. Now served by LOVINGSTON/SHIPMAN, VA [VA0192])

SCOTTSVILLE—See LOVINGSTON/SHIPMAN, VA (Nelson Cable)

Virginia—Cable Community Index

SEALSTON—See KING GEORGE, VA (MetroCast Communications)

SHACKLEFORDS—See VIRGINIA BEACH, VA (Cox Communications)

SHADYSIDE—See ONANCOCK, VA (Charter Communications)

SHENANDOAH (TOWN)—See CHARLOTTESVILLE, VA (Comcast Cable)

SHENANDOAH COUNTY (PORTIONS)—See CHARLOTTESVILLE, VA (Comcast Cable)

SHENANDOAH COUNTY—See WOODSTOCK, VA (Shentel)

SHENANDOAH—Formerly served by Adelphia Communications. Now served by Comcast Cable, HARRISONBURG, VA [VA0016]

SHIPMAN—See LOVINGSTON/SHIPMAN, VA (Nelson Cable)

SIMMONSVILLE—See NEWPORT, VA (PemTel)

SMITHFIELD—See SUFFOLK, VA (Charter Communications)

SOUTH BOSTON—Comcast Cable. Now served by DANVILLE, VA [VA0012]

SOUTH BOSTON—See CHARLOTTESVILLE, VA (Comcast Cable)

SOUTH HILL—Comcast Cable. Now served by CHARLOTTESVILLE, VA [VA0131]

SOUTH HILL—See CHARLOTTESVILLE, VA (Comcast Cable)

SOUTHAMPTON COUNTY—See SUFFOLK, VA (Charter Communications)

SPEEDWELL—R&S Communications LLC

SPOTSYLVANIA COUNTY (PORTIONS)—See CHARLOTTESVILLE, VA (Comcast Cable)

SPOTSYLVANIA COUNTY—See FREDERICKSBURG, VA (Cox Communications)

SPOTSYLVANIA—Formerly served by Comcast Cable. No longer in operation

SPRINGFIELD—See FAIRFAX COUNTY, VA (Cox Communications)

ST. ALBANS (PORTIONS)—See PETERSBURG, WV (Comcast Cable)

ST. PAUL—See LEBANON, VA (Shentel)

STACY—See RICHLANDS (town), VA (Time Warner Cable)

STAFFORD COUNTY (PORTIONS)—See CHARLOTTESVILLE, VA (Comcast Cable)

STAFFORD COUNTY (SOUTHERN PORTION)—See FREDERICKSBURG, VA (Cox Communications)

STANARDSVILLE—See CHARLOTTESVILLE, VA (Comcast Cable)

STANLEY (TOWN)—See CHARLOTTESVILLE, VA (Comcast Cable)

STANLEYTOWN—See CHARLOTTESVILLE, VA (Comcast Cable)

STAUNTON—Comcast Cable. Now served by CHARLOTTESVILLE, VA [VA0131]

STAUNTON—See CHARLOTTESVILLE, VA (Comcast Cable)

STEELBURG—See RICHLANDS (town), VA (Time Warner Cable)

STRASBURG—See WOODSTOCK, VA (Shentel)

STUART—Comcast Cable. Now served by DANVILLE, VA [VA0012]

STUART—See CHARLOTTESVILLE, VA (Comcast Cable)

STUARTS DRAFT—See CHARLOTTESVILLE, VA (Comcast Cable)

SUFFOLK—Charter Communications

SUSSEX COUNTY—See SUFFOLK, VA (Charter Communications)

SWORDS CREEK—See RICHLANDS (town), VA (Time Warner Cable)

TANGIER ISLAND—Formerly served by Charter Communications. No longer in operation

TAPPAHANNOCK—MetroCast Communications. Now served by KING GEORGE, VA [VA0058]

TAPPAHANNOCK—See KING GEORGE, VA (MetroCast Communications)

TAZEWELL (town)—Formerly served by Adelphia Communications. Now served by Time Warner Cable, RICHLANDS (town), VA [VA0041]

TAZEWELL (TOWN)—See RICHLANDS (town), VA (Time Warner Cable)

TAZEWELL COUNTY (PORTIONS)—See RICHLANDS (town), VA (Time Warner Cable)

TEMPERANCEVILLE—See ONANCOCK, VA (Charter Communications)

THAXTON—See CHARLOTTESVILLE, VA (Comcast Cable)

THE PLAINS—See CHARLOTTESVILLE, VA (Comcast Cable)

TIMBERLAKE—See RUSTBURG, VA (Shentel)

TIMBERVILLE—See CHARLOTTESVILLE, VA (Comcast Cable)

TIPTOP—See RICHLANDS (town), VA (Time Warner Cable)

TOMS BROOK—See WOODSTOCK, VA (Shentel)

TRIANGLE—See CHARLOTTESVILLE, VA (Comcast Cable)

TROUTVILLE—Comcast Cable. Now served by SALEM, VA [VA0024]

TROUTVILLE—See CHARLOTTESVILLE, VA (Comcast Cable)

TUNSTALL (PITTSYLVANIA COUNTY)—See BROSVILLE, VA (Chatmoss Cablevision)

U.S. COAST GUARD 5TH DISTRICT—See VIRGINIA BEACH, VA (Cox Communications)

U.S. COAST GUARD SUPPORT CENTER—See VIRGINIA BEACH, VA (Cox Communications)

URBANNA—See DELTAVILLE, VA (MetroCast Communications)

VANDOLA—See BROSVILLE, VA (Chatmoss Cablevision)

VANSANT—See RICHLANDS (town), VA (Time Warner Cable)

VERONA—See CHARLOTTESVILLE, VA (Comcast Cable)

VICTORIA—Formerly served by Adelphia Communications. Now served by Comcast Cable, SOUTH HILL, VA [VA0062]

VICTORIA—See CHARLOTTESVILLE, VA (Comcast Cable)

VIENNA—See FAIRFAX COUNTY, VA (Cox Communications)

VINTON—See ROANOKE, VA (Cox Communications)

VIRGINIA BEACH—Cox Communications

WACHAPREAGUE—See ONANCOCK, VA (Charter Communications)

WAKEFIELD—See SUFFOLK, VA (Charter Communications)

WALMSLEY—See NORTHUMBERLAND COUNTY, VA (MetroCast Communications)

WARDELL—See RICHLANDS (town), VA (Time Warner Cable)

WARM SPRINGS—See CHARLOTTESVILLE, VA (Comcast Cable)

WARRENTON—Comcast Cable. Now served by PRINCE WILLIAM COUNTY (portions), VA [VA0148]

WARRENTON—See CHARLOTTESVILLE, VA (Comcast Cable)

WARSAW—MetroCast Communications. Now served by KING GEORGE, VA [VA0058]

WARSAW—See KING GEORGE, VA (MetroCast Communications)

WASHINGTON COUNTY (PORTIONS)—See DAMASCUS, VA (Zito Media)

WASHINGTON COUNTY (UNINCORPORATED AREAS)—See BRISTOL, VA (BVU OptiNet. Formerly [VA0190]. This cable system has converted to IPTV)

WATTSVILLE—See ONANCOCK, VA (Charter Communications)

WAVERLY—See SUFFOLK, VA (Charter Communications)

WAYNE COUNTY (PORTIONS)—See PETERSBURG, WV (Comcast Cable)

WAYNESBORO—See CHARLOTTESVILLE, VA (Comcast Cable)

WEBER CITY—See GATE CITY, VA (Scott Telecom & Electronics)

WEST POINT—See VIRGINIA BEACH, VA (Cox Communications)

WESTMORELAND COUNTY (UNINCORPORATED AREAS)—See KING GEORGE, VA (MetroCast Communications)

WESTMORELAND—MetroCast Communications. Now served by KING GEORGE, VA [VA0058]

WESTMORELAND—See KING GEORGE, VA (MetroCast Communications)

WEYERS CAVE—See CHARLOTTESVILLE, VA (Comcast Cable)

WHITE STONE (TOWN)—See DELTAVILLE, VA (MetroCast Communications)

WHITEWOOD—See RICHLANDS (town), VA (Time Warner Cable)

WHITMELL—See BROSVILLE, VA (Chatmoss Cablevision)

WICOMICO CHURCH—See NORTHUMBERLAND COUNTY, VA (MetroCast Communications)

WILLIAMSBURG—Cox Communications. Now served by HAMPTON ROADS (formerly Virginia Beach), VA [VA0002]

WILLIAMSBURG—See VIRGINIA BEACH, VA (Cox Communications)

WINCHESTER—Comcast Cable. Now served by FREDERICK COUNTY (portions), MD [MD0009]

WINDSOR—See SUFFOLK, VA (Charter Communications)

WINFIELD (TOWN)—See PETERSBURG, WV (Comcast Cable)

WINTERGREEN—Nelson Cable

WISE—See LEBANON, VA (Shentel)

WOLFORD—See RICHLANDS (town), VA (Time Warner Cable)

WOODBRIDGE—See CHARLOTTESVILLE, VA (Comcast Cable)

WOODFORD—See CHARLOTTESVILLE, VA (Comcast Cable)

WOODSTOCK—Shentel

WYTHE COUNTY (PORTIONS)—See WYTHEVILLE, VA (Shentel)

WYTHE COUNTY—Citizens Telephone Coop. Now served by FORT CHISWELL, VA [VA0066]

WYTHEVILLE—Shentel

YANCEYVILLE—See CHARLOTTESVILLE, NC (Comcast Cable)

YORK COUNTY—See VIRGINIA BEACH, VA (Cox Communications)

Cable Community Index—Washington

YORKTOWN NAVAL WEAPONS STATION—See VIRGINIA BEACH, VA (Cox Communications)

YORKTOWN—Cox Communications. Now served by HAMPTON ROADS (formerly Virginia Beach), VA [VA0002]

YORKTOWN—See VIRGINIA BEACH, VA (Cox Communications)

YUMA—See GATE CITY, VA (Scott Telecom & Electronics)

WASHINGTON

ABERDEEN TWP.—Comcast Cable. Now served by ABERDEEN, WA [WA0003]

ABERDEEN TWP.—Comcast Cable

ADAMS COUNTY—See OTHELLO, WA (Northland Cable Television)

AIRWAY HEIGHTS—See SPOKANE, WA (Comcast Cable)

ALBION—See PULLMAN, WA (Time Warner Cable)

ALGONA—See SEATTLE, WA (Comcast Cable)

ALLYN (PORTIONS)—See PORT ORCHARD, WA (Wave Broadband)

ALMIRA—Formerly served by Almega Cable. No longer in operation

ANACORTES—See BELLINGHAM, WA (Comcast Cable)

ANDERSON ISLAND—Wave Broadband. Now served by LAKE BAY, WA [WA0201]

ANDERSON ISLAND—See LAKEBAY, WA (Wave Broadband)

ARDEN—See COLVILLE, WA (Charter Communications)

ARLINGTON—Comcast Cable. Now served by SEATTLE, WA [WA0001]

ARLINGTON—See SEATTLE, WA (Comcast Cable)

AUBURN—Comcast Cable. Now served by SEATTLE, WA [WA0001]

AUBURN—See SEATTLE, WA (Comcast Cable)

BAINBRIDGE ISLAND—Comcast Cable. Now served by SEATTLE, WA [WA0001]

BAINBRIDGE ISLAND—See SEATTLE, WA (Comcast Cable)

BANGOR SUBMARINE BASE—See PORT ORCHARD, WA (Wave Broadband)

BATTLE GROUND—See VANCOUVER, WA (Comcast Cable)

BAYVIEW—Wave Broadband. Now served by CAMANO ISLAND, WA [WA0046]

BAYVIEW—See CAMANO ISLAND, WA (Wave Broadband)

BEAUX ARTS VILLAGE—See SEATTLE, WA (Comcast Cable)

BELFAIR—See PORT ORCHARD, WA (Wave Broadband)

BELLEVUE—Comcast Cable. Now served by SEATTLE, WA [WA0001]

BELLEVUE—See SEATTLE, WA (Comcast Cable)

BELLEVUE—See SEATTLE (surrounding areas), WA (Wave Broadband)

BELLINGHAM—Comcast Cable

BELLINGHAM—Wave Broadband

BENTON COUNTY—See KENNEWICK, WA (Charter Communications)

BIG LAKE—Wave Broadband. Now served by CAMANO ISLAND, WA [WA0046]

BIG LAKE—See CAMANO ISLAND, WA (Wave Broadband)

BLACK DIAMOND—See SEATTLE, WA (Comcast Cable)

BLAINE—See BELLINGHAM, WA (Comcast Cable)

BONNER COUNTY (UNINCORPORATED AREAS)—See NEWPORT, ID (Concept Cable)

BONNEY LAKE—See SEATTLE, WA (Comcast Cable)

BOTHELL—See SEATTLE, WA (Comcast Cable)

BREMERTON—Comcast Cable. Now served by SEATTLE, WA [WA0001]

BREMERTON—See SEATTLE, WA (Comcast Cable)

BREMERTON—See PORT ORCHARD, WA (Wave Broadband)

BREWSTER—Formerly served by Wave Broadband. No longer in operation

BRIER—See SEATTLE, WA (Comcast Cable)

BUCKLEY—See SEATTLE, WA (Comcast Cable)

BURIEN—Comcast Cable. Now served by SEATTLE, WA [WA0001]

BURIEN—See SEATTLE, WA (Comcast Cable)

BURLINGTON—Comcast Cable. Now served by BELLINGHAM, WA [WA0011]

BURLINGTON—See BELLINGHAM, WA (Comcast Cable)

CAMANO ISLAND—Wave Broadband

CAMAS—See VANCOUVER, WA (Comcast Cable)

CARBONADO—See SEATTLE, WA (Comcast Cable)

CARNATION—See SEATTLE, WA (Comcast Cable)

CARNATION—See DUVALL, WA (Wave Broadband)

CARSON—Wave Broadband

CASHMERE—See WENATCHEE, WA (Charter Communications)

CASTLE ROCK—See VANCOUVER, WA (Comcast Cable)

CENTRALIA-CHEHALIS—Comcast Cable. Now served by SEATTLE, WA [WA0001]

CENTRALIA—See SEATTLE, WA (Comcast Cable)

CHATTAROY—Formerly served by Almega Cable. No longer in operation

CHEHALIS—See SEATTLE, WA (Comcast Cable)

CHELAN COUNTY—See WENATCHEE, WA (Charter Communications)

CHELAN FALLS—See CHELAN, WA (Wave Broadband)

CHELAN—Wave Broadband

CHENEY—Formerly served by Wave Broadband. No longer in operation

CHENEY—Davis Communications

CHEWELAH—See WENATCHEE, WA (Charter Communications)

CHINOOK PASS—Formerly served by Almega Cable. No longer in operation

CHINOOK—Chinook Progressive Club TV

CLALLAM BAY—Formerly served by Wave Broadband. No longer in operation

CLALLAM COUNTY (UNINCORPORATED AREAS)—See PORT ANGELES, WA (Wave Broadband)

CLARK COUNTY (PORTIONS)—See VANCOUVER, WA (Comcast Cable)

CLARK FORK—See NEWPORT, ID (Concept Cable)

CLE ELUM—R & R Cable

CLINTON—See BELLINGHAM, WA (Comcast Cable)

CLYDE HILL—See SEATTLE, WA (Comcast Cable)

COLFAX—Colfax Cable Co

COLLEGE PLACE—See KENNEWICK, WA (Charter Communications)

COLVILLE—Charter Communications

CONCRETE—Wave Broadband

CONNELL—Northstar Broadband

CONWAY—See CAMANO ISLAND, WA (Wave Broadband)

COSMOPOLIS—See ABERDEEN TWP., WA (Comcast Cable)

COULEE CITY—Formerly served by Almega Cable. No longer in operation

COULEE DAM—Country Cable

COUPEVILLE—Comcast Cable. Now served by BELLINGHAM, WA [WA0011]

COUPEVILLE—See BELLINGHAM, WA (Comcast Cable)

COVINGTON—See SEATTLE, WA (Comcast Cable)

COWICHE—See NACHES, WA (J & N Cable)

COWLITZ COUNTY (PORTIONS)—See VANCOUVER, WA (Comcast Cable)

CRESTON—Formerly served by Wave Broadband. No longer in operation

DARRINGTON—Formerly served by Wave Broadband. No longer in operation

DAVENPORT—Northstar Broadband

DAYTON—Touchet Valley TV Inc

DEER LAKE—See WENATCHEE, WA (Charter Communications)

DEER PARK—Northstar Broadband

DEMING—See BELLINGHAM, WA (Comcast Cable)

DES MOINES—See SEATTLE, WA (Comcast Cable)

DIAMOND LAKE—Northstar Broadband

DIXIE—See KENNEWICK, WA (Charter Communications)

DOUGLAS COUNTY—See WENATCHEE, WA (Charter Communications)

DU PONT—See SEATTLE, WA (Comcast Cable)

DUVALL—Wave Broadband

EAST SEATTLE—See SEATTLE, WA (Comcast Cable)

EAST WENATCHEE—See WENATCHEE, WA (Charter Communications)

EASTON—Formerly served by Wave Broadband. No longer in operation

EATONVILLE—See SEATTLE, WA (Comcast Cable)

EATONVILLE—Rainier Cable

ECHO LAKE/SNOHOMISH—Wave Broadband

ECHO—See KENNEWICK, OR (Charter Communications)

EDGEWOOD—See SEATTLE, WA (Comcast Cable)

EDMONDS—Comcast Cable. Now served by SEATTLE, WA [WA0001]

EDMONDS—See SEATTLE, WA (Comcast Cable)

ELECTRIC CITY—See GRAND COULEE, WA (Charter Communications)

ELLENSBURG—Charter Communications

ELMA—See ABERDEEN TWP., WA (Comcast Cable)

ELMER CITY—See GRAND COULEE, WA (Charter Communications)

ENDICOTT—See ST. JOHN, WA (St. John Cable Co. Inc)

ENTIAT—Wave Broadband. Now served by CHELAN, WA [WA0058]

ENTIAT—See CHELAN, WA (Wave Broadband)

ENUMCLAW—See SEATTLE, WA (Comcast Cable)

EPHRATA—Northland Cable Television

Washington—Cable Community Index

EVERETT NAVAL AIR STATION—See SEATTLE, WA (Comcast Cable)

EVERETT—Comcast Cable. Now served by SEATTLE, WA [WA0001]

EVERETT—See SEATTLE, WA (Comcast Cable)

EVERSON—See BELLINGHAM, WA (Comcast Cable)

FAIRCHILD AFB—Formerly served by Cable Montana. Now served by Comcast Cable, SPOKANE, WA [WA0004]

FAIRCHILD AFB—See SPOKANE, WA (Comcast Cable)

FAIRFIELD—Formerly served by Elk River TV Cable Co. No longer in operation

FALL CITY—See SEATTLE, WA (Comcast Cable)

FEDERAL WAY—See SEATTLE, WA (Comcast Cable)

FERNDALE—See BELLINGHAM, WA (Comcast Cable)

FIFE—See TACOMA, WA (Click! Network)

FIFE—See SEATTLE, WA (Comcast Cable)

FIRCREST—See TACOMA, WA (Click! Network)

FIRCREST—See SEATTLE, WA (Comcast Cable)

FORKS—Formerly served by New Day Broadband. No longer in operation

FORT LEWIS—See SEATTLE, WA (Comcast Cable)

FOUR LAKES—See CHENEY, WA (Davis Communications)

FOX ISLAND—See SEATTLE, WA (Comcast Cable)

FRANKLIN COUNTY—See KENNEWICK, WA (Charter Communications)

FREELAND—Comcast Cable. Now served by SEATTLE, WA [WA0001]

FREELAND—See BELLINGHAM, WA (Comcast Cable)

FRIDAY HARBOR—Zito Media

GARFIELD—Formerly served by Elk River TV Cable Co. No longer in operation

GIG HARBOR—See SEATTLE, WA (Comcast Cable)

GLEED—See NACHES, WA (J & N Cable)

GLENOMA—See RANDLE, WA (Wave Broadband)

GOLDBAR—See SEATTLE, WA (Comcast Cable)

GOLDENDALE—J & N Cable

GRAHAM—See SEATTLE, WA (Comcast Cable)

GRAHAM—See EATONVILLE, WA (Rainier Cable)

GRAND COULEE—Charter Communications

GRANDVIEW—Charter Communications. Now served by YAKIMA, WA [WA0009]

GRANDVIEW—See YAKIMA, WA (Charter Communications)

GRANGER—See YAKIMA, WA (Charter Communications)

GRANITE FALLS—See SEATTLE, WA (Comcast Cable)

GRANT COUNTY (PORTIONS)—See EPHRATA, WA (Northland Cable Television)

GRANT COUNTY (PORTIONS)—See MOSES LAKE, WA (Northland Cable Television)

GRANT COUNTY—See GRAND COULEE, WA (Charter Communications)

GRAYLAND—See ABERDEEN TWP., WA (Comcast Cable)

GRAYS HARBOR COUNTY (PORTIONS)—See ABERDEEN TWP., WA (Comcast Cable)

GRAYS HARBOR COUNTY (PORTIONS)—See ROCHESTER, WA (Comcast Cable)

GRAYS HARBOR COUNTY—See OCEAN SHORES, WA (Coast Communications Co. Inc)

GREENBANK—Wave Broadband. Now served by WHIDBEY ISLAND, WA [WA0186]

GREENBANK—See WHIDBEY ISLAND, WA (Wave Broadband)

GUEMES ISLAND—Formerly served by Index Cable TV Inc. No longer in operation

HAMILTON—See CONCRETE, WA (Wave Broadband)

HANSVILLE—See SEATTLE, WA (Comcast Cable)

HARRINGTON—Formerly served by Elk River TV Cable Co. No longer in operation

HERMISTON—See KENNEWICK, OR (Charter Communications)

HERRON ISLAND—See LAKEBAY, WA (Wave Broadband)

HOLLY—See PORT ORCHARD, WA (Wave Broadband)

HOOD CANAL—Wave Broadband. Now served by PORT ORCHARD, WA [WA0010]

HOOD CANAL—See PORT ORCHARD, WA (Wave Broadband)

HOQUAIM—See ABERDEEN TWP., WA (Comcast Cable)

HUNTS POINT—See SEATTLE, WA (Comcast Cable)

INDEX—Formerly served by Iron Goat Networks LLC. No longer in operation

INDIANOLA—See SEATTLE, WA (Comcast Cable)

IONE—Northstar Broadband

ISLAND COUNTY (PORTIONS)—See BELLINGHAM, WA (Comcast Cable)

ISSAQUAH (SOUTHEASTERN PORTION)—See DUVALL, WA (Wave Broadband)

ISSAQUAH—See SEATTLE, WA (Comcast Cable)

JACKSON PARK—See PORT ORCHARD, WA (Wave Broadband)

KAHLOTUS—Formerly served by Community Cable Service. No longer in operation

KALA POINT—Wave Broadband. Now served by PORT TOWNSEND, WA [WA0027]

KALA POINT—See PORT TOWNSEND, WA (Wave Broadband)

KALAMA—See VANCOUVER, WA (Comcast Cable)

KELSO—See VANCOUVER, WA (Comcast Cable)

KENDALL—See BELLINGHAM, WA (Comcast Cable)

KENMORE—See SEATTLE, WA (Comcast Cable)

KENMORE—See SEATTLE (surrounding areas), WA (Wave Broadband)

KENNEWICK—Charter Communications

KENT—See SEATTLE, WA (Comcast Cable)

KETTLE FALLS—See COLVILLE, WA (Charter Communications)

KEY PENINSULA—See LAKEBAY, WA (Wave Broadband)

KEYPORT NAVAL BASE—See PORT ORCHARD, WA (Wave Broadband)

KEYPORT—See PORT ORCHARD, WA (Wave Broadband)

KING COUNTY (PORTIONS)—See SEATTLE, WA (Comcast Cable)

KING COUNTY (PORTIONS)—See DUVALL, WA (Wave Broadband)

KINGSTON—See SEATTLE, WA (Comcast Cable)

KIRKLAND—See SEATTLE, WA (Comcast Cable)

KITSAP COUNTY (PORTIONS)—See SEATTLE, WA (Comcast Cable)

KITSAP LAKE—See PORT ORCHARD, WA (Wave Broadband)

KITTITAS COUNTY (NORTHERN PORTION)—See CLE ELUM, WA (R & R Cable)

KITTITAS COUNTY (PORTIONS)—See ELLENSBURG, WA (Charter Communications)

KITTITAS COUNTY (PORTIONS)—See ROSLYN, WA (R & R Cable)

KITTITAS—See ELLENSBURG, WA (Charter Communications)

LA CENTER—See VANCOUVER, WA (Comcast Cable)

LA CONNER—Wave Broadband. Now served by CAMANO ISLAND, WA [WA0046]

LA CONNER—See CAMANO ISLAND, WA (Wave Broadband)

LACEY—See SEATTLE, WA (Comcast Cable)

LACROSSE—See ST. JOHN, WA (St. John Cable Co. Inc)

LAKE CLE ELUM—See ROSLYN, WA (R & R Cable)

LAKE FOREST PARK—See SEATTLE, WA (Comcast Cable)

LAKE GOODWIN—Wave Broadband. Now served by CAMANO ISLAND, WA [WA0046]

LAKE MCMURRAY—See CAMANO ISLAND, WA (Wave Broadband)

LAKE ROESIGER—See ECHO LAKE/SNOHOMISH, WA (Wave Broadband)

LAKE SAMISH—See BELLINGHAM, WA (Comcast Cable)

LAKE STEVENS—See SEATTLE, WA (Comcast Cable)

LAKE SYMINGTON—See PORT ORCHARD, WA (Wave Broadband)

LAKEBAY—See SEATTLE, WA (Comcast Cable)

LAKEBAY—Wave Broadband

LAKEWOOD—See TACOMA, WA (Click! Network)

LAKEWOOD—See SEATTLE, WA (Comcast Cable)

LANGLEY—See BELLINGHAM, WA (Comcast Cable)

LATAH COUNTY (PORTIONS)—See PULLMAN, ID (Time Warner Cable)

LEAVENWORTH—See WENATCHEE, WA (Charter Communications)

LEWIS COUNTY (PORTIONS)—See MOSSYROCK, WA (Comcast Cable)

LEWIS COUNTY (PORTIONS)—See SEATTLE, WA (Comcast Cable)

LEWIS COUNTY (PORTIONS)—See WINLOCK, WA (Comcast Cable)

LEWIS COUNTY—See MORTON, WA (Wave Broadband)

LIBERTY LAKE—No longer in operation

LIBERTY LAKE—See SPOKANE, WA (Comcast Cable)

LIND—Northstar Broadband

LONGVIEW—Comcast Cable. Now served by VANCOUVER, WA [WA0005]

LONGVIEW—See VANCOUVER, WA (Comcast Cable)

LOOMIS—Formerly served by JKA Cable Systems. No longer in operation

LOON LAKE—Charter Communications. Now served by WENATCHEE, WA [WA0015]

Cable Community Index—Washington

LOON LAKE—See WENATCHEE, WA (Charter Communications)

LUMMI INDIAN RESERVATION—See BELLINGHAM, WA (Comcast Cable)

LUMMI INDIAN RESERVATION—San Juan Cable & Construction

LUMMI ISLAND—Lummi Island Cable

LYLE—J & N Cable

LYMAN—See CONCRETE, WA (Wave Broadband)

LYNDEN—See BELLINGHAM, WA (Comcast Cable)

LYNWOOD—See SEATTLE, WA (Comcast Cable)

MABTON—See YAKIMA, WA (Charter Communications)

MALAGA—Formerly served by Almega Cable. No longer in operation

MANCHESTER—See PORT ORCHARD, WA (Wave Broadband)

MANSFIELD—Formerly served by Wave Broadband. No longer in operation

MANSON—Formerly served by Millennium Digital Media. Now served by Wave Broadband, CHELAN, WA [WA0058]

MANSON—See CHELAN, WA (Wave Broadband)

MAPLE FALLS—See BELLINGHAM, WA (Comcast Cable)

MAPLE VALLEY—See SEATTLE, WA (Comcast Cable)

MARBLEMOUNT—Formerly served by Wave Broadband. No longer in operation

MARYSVILLE—See SEATTLE, WA (Comcast Cable)

MASON COUNTY (PORTIONS)—See SEATTLE, WA (Comcast Cable)

MASON COUNTY—See PORT ORCHARD, WA (Wave Broadband)

MATTAWA—Formerly served by Almega Cable. No longer in operation

MAXWELTON—Formerly served by Comcast Cable. No longer in operation

McCHORD AFB—See SEATTLE, WA (Comcast Cable)

McCHORD AIR FORCE BASE—Comcast Cable. Now served by SEATTLE, WA [WA0001]

McCLEARY—See ABERDEEN TWP., WA (Comcast Cable)

MCKENNA—See SEATTLE, WA (Comcast Cable)

MEDICAL LAKE—Formerly served by Wave Broadband. No longer in operation

MEDICAL LAKE—See CHENEY, WA (Davis Communications)

MEDINA—See SEATTLE, WA (Comcast Cable)

MERCER ISLAND—See SEATTLE, WA (Comcast Cable)

METALINE FALLS—Northstar Broadband

METALINE—See METALINE FALLS, WA (Northstar Broadband)

MILL CREEK—See SEATTLE, WA (Comcast Cable)

MILLWOOD—See SPOKANE, WA (Comcast Cable)

MILTON-FREEWATER—See KENNEWICK, OR (Charter Communications)

MILTON—See SEATTLE, WA (Comcast Cable)

MINERAL—Comcast Cable

MONROE—See SEATTLE, WA (Comcast Cable)

MONTESANO—Comcast Cable. Now served by ABERDEEN TWP., WA [WA0003]

MONTESANO—See ABERDEEN TWP., WA (Comcast Cable)

MORTON—Wave Broadband

MOSCOW—See PULLMAN, ID (Time Warner Cable)

MOSES LAKE—Northland Cable Television

MOSSYROCK—Comcast Cable

MOUNT VERNON—See BELLINGHAM, WA (Comcast Cable)

MOUNTLAKE TERRACE—See SEATTLE, WA (Comcast Cable)

MOXEE CITY—See YAKIMA, WA (Charter Communications)

MUKITEO—See SEATTLE, WA (Comcast Cable)

NACHES—J & N Cable

NAPAVINE—Wave Broadband

NESPELEM—Formerly served by Country Cable. No longer in operation

NEWCASTLE—See SEATTLE, WA (Comcast Cable)

NEWPORT—Concept Cable

NOOKSACK—See BELLINGHAM, WA (Comcast Cable)

NORMANDY PARK—See SEATTLE, WA (Comcast Cable)

NORTH BEND—See SEATTLE, WA (Comcast Cable)

NORTH BONNEVILLE—Formerly served by North Bonneville Community Cable TV System. No longer in operation

NORTH SHORE—See PORT ORCHARD, WA (Wave Broadband)

NORTHPORT—Formerly served by Almega Cable. No longer in operation

OAK HARBOR—Comcast Cable. Now served by BELLINGHAM, WA [WA0011]

OAK HARBOR—See BELLINGHAM, WA (Comcast Cable)

OAKESDALE—Formerly served by Elk River TV Cable Co. No longer in operation

OAKVILLE—See ROCHESTER, WA (Comcast Cable)

OCEAN SHORES—Coast Communications Co. Inc

ODESSA (TOWN)—Northstar Broadband

OKANOGAN COUNTY (UNINCORPORATED AREAS)—See WENATCHEE, WA (Charter Communications)

OKANOGAN—Charter Communications. Now served by WENATCHEE, WA [WA0015]

OKANOGAN—See WENATCHEE, WA (Charter Communications)

OLDTOWN—See NEWPORT, ID (Concept Cable)

OLYMPIA—Comcast Cable. Now served by SEATTLE, WA [WA0001]

OLYMPIA—See SEATTLE, WA (Comcast Cable)

ORCAS ISLAND—Formerly served by Almega Cable. No longer in operation

ORCAS ISLAND—Mt. Baker Cable

OROVILLE—Charter Communications. Now served by WENATCHEE, WA [WA0015]

OROVILLE—See WENATCHEE, WA (Charter Communications)

ORTING—See SEATTLE, WA (Comcast Cable)

OTHELLO—Northland Cable Television

PACIFIC (GRAYS HARBOR COUNTY)—See ABERDEEN TWP., WA (Comcast Cable)

PACIFIC (KING COUNTY)—See SEATTLE, WA (Comcast Cable)

PACIFIC BEACH—See OCEAN SHORES, WA (Coast Communications Co. Inc)

PACIFIC COUNTY (PORTIONS)—See RAYMOND, WA (Comcast Cable)

PACKWOOD—Wave Broadband

PASCO—See KENNEWICK, WA (Charter Communications)

PE ELL—Formerly served by Wave Broadband. No longer in operation

PEND OREILLE COUNTY—See NEWPORT, WA (Concept Cable)

PENDLETON—See KENNEWICK, OR (Charter Communications)

PIERCE COUNTY (PORTIONS)—See TACOMA, WA (Click! Network)

PIERCE COUNTY (PORTIONS)—See SEATTLE, WA (Comcast Cable)

PIERCE COUNTY (PORTIONS)—See EATONVILLE, WA (Rainier Cable)

POINT ROBERTS—Delta Cable

POMEROY—Formerly served by Almega Cable. No longer in operation

PORT ANGELES—Wave Broadband

PORT HADLOCK—See PORT TOWNSEND, WA (Wave Broadband)

PORT LUDLOW—See PORT TOWNSEND, WA (Wave Broadband)

PORT ORCHARD—See SEATTLE, WA (Comcast Cable)

PORT ORCHARD—Wave Broadband

PORT TOWNSEND—Wave Broadband

POULSBO—See SEATTLE, WA (Comcast Cable)

PRESCOTT—Formerly served by Charter Communications. No longer in operation

PRESTON—See SEATTLE, WA (Comcast Cable)

PRIEST RIVER—See NEWPORT, ID (Concept Cable)

PROSSER—See YAKIMA, WA (Charter Communications)

PUGET SOUND (KING COUNTY)—See SEATTLE, WA (Comcast Cable)

PUGET SOUND (KITSAP COUNTY)—See SEATTLE, WA (Comcast Cable)

PUGET SOUND NAVAL SHIPYARD—See PORT ORCHARD, WA (Wave Broadband)

PULLMAN—Time Warner Cable

PUYALLUP—See SEATTLE, WA (Comcast Cable)

PUYALLUP—See EATONVILLE, WA (Rainier Cable)

QUILCENE—See PORT TOWNSEND, WA (Wave Broadband)

QUINCY—Formerly served by J & N Cable. No longer in operation

RAINIER—See SEATTLE, WA (Comcast Cable)

RANDLE—Wave Broadband

RAYMOND—Comcast Cable

REARDAN—Formerly served by Elk River Cable TV Co. No longer in operation

REDMOND—Comcast Cable. Now served by SEATTLE, WA [WA0001]

REDMOND—See SEATTLE, WA (Comcast Cable)

REDMOND—See DUVALL, WA (Wave Broadband)

RENTON—See SEATTLE, WA (Comcast Cable)

REPUBLIC—Television Assn. of Republic

RICHLAND—See KENNEWICK, WA (Charter Communications)

RIDGEFIELD—See VANCOUVER, WA (Comcast Cable)

RITZVILLE—Northstar Broadband

ROCHESTER—Comcast Cable

Washington—Cable Community Index

ROCK ISLAND—See WENATCHEE, WA (Charter Communications)

RONALD—See ROSLYN, WA (R & R Cable)

ROSALIA—Formerly served by Elk River TV Cable Co. No longer in operation

ROSLYN—R & R Cable

ROY—See SEATTLE, WA (Comcast Cable)

ROYAL CITY—Formerly served by Almega Cable. No longer in operation

RUSTON—Comcast Cable. Now served by SEATTLE, WA [WA0001]

RUSTON—See SEATTLE, WA (Comcast Cable)

RYDERWOOD—Comcast Cable

SAHALEE—See DUVALL, WA (Wave Broadband)

SAMMAMISH—See SEATTLE, WA (Comcast Cable)

SAN JUAN COUNTY (PORTIONS)—See FRIDAY HARBOR, WA (Zito Media)

SEABECK—See PORT ORCHARD, WA (Wave Broadband)

SEATAC—See SEATTLE, WA (Comcast Cable)

SEATTLE (SURROUNDING AREAS)—Wave Broadband

SEATTLE—Formerly served by Sprint Corp. No longer in operation

SEATTLE—Comcast Cable

SEDRO WOOLLEY—See BELLINGHAM, WA (Comcast Cable)

SELAH—See YAKIMA, WA (Charter Communications)

SEQUIM—Wave Broadband. Now served by PORT ANGELES, WA [WA0020]

SEQUIM—See PORT ANGELES, WA (Wave Broadband)

SEVEN LAKES—See CAMANO ISLAND, WA (Wave Broadband)

SHELTER BAY—See CAMANO ISLAND, WA (Wave Broadband)

SHELTON—Comcast Cable. Now served by SEATTLE, WA [WA0001]

SHELTON—See SEATTLE, WA (Comcast Cable)

SHORELINE—See SEATTLE, WA (Comcast Cable)

SILVER LAKE—See SEATTLE, WA (Comcast Cable)

SILVERDALE—See SEATTLE, WA (Comcast Cable)

SILVERDALE—See PORT ORCHARD, WA (Wave Broadband)

SKAGIT COUNTY (PORTIONS)—See BELLINGHAM, WA (Comcast Cable)

SKAGIT COUNTY (PORTIONS)—See CAMANO ISLAND, WA (Wave Broadband)

SKAGIT COUNTY (PORTIONS)—See CONCRETE, WA (Wave Broadband)

SKAGIT—See BELLINGHAM, WA (Comcast Cable)

SKAMANIA COUNTY (PORTIONS)—See CARSON, WA (Wave Broadband)

SKAMOKAWA—Formerly served by Wright Cablevision. No longer in operation

SNOHOMISH COUNTY (NORTHWESTERN PORTION)—See CAMANO ISLAND, WA (Wave Broadband)

SNOHOMISH COUNTY (PORTIONS)—See SEATTLE, WA (Comcast Cable)

SNOHOMISH COUNTY (SOUTHWESTERN PORTIONS)—See ECHO LAKE/SNOHOMISH, WA (Wave Broadband)

SNOHOMISH—See SEATTLE, WA (Comcast Cable)

SNOQUALMIE VALLEY—See DUVALL, WA (Wave Broadband)

SNOQUALMIE—See SEATTLE, WA (Comcast Cable)

SOAP LAKE—See EPHRATA, WA (Northland Cable Television)

SOUTH BEND—See RAYMOND, WA (Comcast Cable)

SOUTH CLE ELUM—See CLE ELUM, WA (R & R Cable)

SOUTH KITSAP—See PORT ORCHARD, WA (Wave Broadband)

SOUTH PRAIRIE—See SEATTLE, WA (Comcast Cable)

SOUTH TACOMA—See SEATTLE, WA (Comcast Cable)

SPANGLE—Formerly served by Elk River TV Cable Co. No longer in operation

SPOKANE COUNTY (PORTIONS)—See SPOKANE, WA (Comcast Cable)

SPOKANE—Formerly served by Video Wave Television. No longer in operation

SPOKANE—Comcast Cable

SPRAGUE—Formerly served by Elk River TV Cable Co. No longer in operation

SPRINGDALE—Formerly served by Elk River TV Cable Co. No longer in operation

ST. JOHN—St. John Cable Co. Inc

STANFIELD—See KENNEWICK, OR (Charter Communications)

STANWOOD—See CAMANO ISLAND, WA (Wave Broadband)

STARBUCK—Formerly served by Charter Communications. No longer in operation

STARTUP—See SEATTLE, WA (Comcast Cable)

STEILACOOM—See SEATTLE, WA (Comcast Cable)

STEVENSON—See CARSON, WA (Wave Broadband)

SUDDEN VALLEY—Comcast Cable. Now served by BELLINGHAM, WA [WA0011]

SUDDEN VALLEY—See BELLINGHAM, WA (Comcast Cable)

SULTAN—See SEATTLE, WA (Comcast Cable)

SUMAS—City of Sumas TV Cable System

SUMNER—See SEATTLE, WA (Comcast Cable)

SUNCREST—Formerly served by TV Max. Now served by Comcast Cable, SPOKANE, WA [WA0004]

SUNCREST—See SPOKANE, WA (Comcast Cable)

SUNNYSIDE—Charter Communications. Now served by YAKIMA, WA [WA0009]

SUNNYSIDE—See YAKIMA, WA (Charter Communications)

SUQUAMISH (UNINCORPORATED AREAS)—See SEATTLE, WA (Comcast Cable)

SWINOMISH INDIAN RESERVATION—See CAMANO ISLAND, WA (Wave Broadband)

TACOMA—Click! Network

TACOMA—See SEATTLE, WA (Comcast Cable)

TAHUYA—See PORT ORCHARD, WA (Wave Broadband)

TEKOA—Northstar Broadband

TENINO—See SEATTLE, WA (Comcast Cable)

THORP—Formerly served by Wave Broadband. No longer in operation

THURSTON COUNTY (PORTIONS)—See SEATTLE, WA (Comcast Cable)

TIETON—See NACHES, WA (J & N Cable)

TOKELAND—See ABERDEEN TWP., WA (Comcast Cable)

TOLEDO—Formerly served by RGA Cable TV. No longer in operation

TOPPENISH—See YAKIMA, WA (Charter Communications)

TOUTLE—See VANCOUVER, WA (Comcast Cable)

TRACYTON—See ABERDEEN TWP., WA (Comcast Cable)

TUKWILA—See SEATTLE, WA (Comcast Cable)

TULALIP INDIAN RESERVATION—Tulalip Tribes Broadband

TURNWATER—See SEATTLE, WA (Comcast Cable)

TWISP—Formerly served by Wave Broadband. No longer in operation

UMATILLA COUNTY (PORTIONS)—See KENNEWICK, OR (Charter Communications)

UNION GAP—See YAKIMA, WA (Charter Communications)

UNION—Hood Canal Communications

UNIVERSITY PLACE—See TACOMA, WA (Click! Network)

UNIVERSITY PLACE—See SEATTLE, WA (Comcast Cable)

UNIVERSITY PLACE—See EATONVILLE, WA (Rainier Cable)

UTSALADY—See CAMANO ISLAND, WA (Wave Broadband)

VADER—Formerly served by Millennium Digital Media. No longer in operation

VANCOUVER—Comcast Cable

VASHON ISLAND—See SEATTLE, WA (Comcast Cable)

WAITSBURG—Charter Communications. Now served by KENNEWICK, WA [WA0008]

WAITSBURG—See KENNEWICK, WA (Charter Communications)

WALLA WALLA COUNTY (PORTIONS)—See KENNEWICK, WA (Charter Communications)

WALLA WALLA COUNTY—See KENNEWICK, WA (Charter Communications)

WALLA WALLA—Charter Communications. Now served by KENNEWICK, WA [WA0008]

WALLA WALLA—See KENNEWICK, WA (Charter Communications)

WAPATO—See YAKIMA, WA (Charter Communications)

WARDEN—Northstar Broadband

WASHOUGAL—See VANCOUVER, WA (Comcast Cable)

WASHTUCNA—Formerly served by Charter Communications. No longer in operation

WATERVILLE—Formerly served by Wave Broadband. No longer in operation

WENATCHEE—Charter Communications

WEST RICHLAND—Charter Communications. Now served by KENNEWICK, WA [WA0008]

WEST RICHLAND—See KENNEWICK, WA (Charter Communications)

WESTPORT—Comcast Cable. Now served by ABERDEEN, WA [WA0003]

WESTPORT—See ABERDEEN TWP., WA (Comcast Cable)

WHATCOM COUNTY (PORTIONS)—See BELLINGHAM, WA (Comcast Cable)

WHATCOM COUNTY (PORTIONS)—See BELLINGHAM, WA (Wave Broadband)

WHATCOM COUNTY (SOUTHERN PORTION)—See CAMANO ISLAND, WA (Wave Broadband)

WHIDBEY ISLAND NAVAL AIR STATION—See BELLINGHAM, WA (Comcast Cable)

WHIDBEY ISLAND—Wave Broadband

WHITMAN COUNTY (PORTIONS)—See PULLMAN, WA (Time Warner Cable)

WILBUR—Formerly served by Northstar Broadband. No longer in operation

WILKESON—See SEATTLE, WA (Comcast Cable)

WILSON CREEK—Formerly served by Almega Cable. No longer in operation

WINLOCK—Comcast Cable

WISHKAH—See ABERDEEN TWP., WA (Comcast Cable)

WISHRAM—Formerly served by J & N Cable. No longer in operation

WOODINVILLE—See SEATTLE, WA (Comcast Cable)

WOODINVILLE—See DUVALL, WA (Wave Broadband)

WOODLAND—See VANCOUVER, WA (Comcast Cable)

WOODS CREEK—See SEATTLE, WA (Comcast Cable)

WOODWAY—See SEATTLE, WA (Comcast Cable)

YACOLT—J & N Cable

YAKIMA COUNTY (PORTIONS)—See YAKIMA, WA (Charter Communications)

YAKIMA COUNTY (UNINCORPORATED AREAS)—See NACHES, WA (J & N Cable)

YAKIMA INDIAN RESERVATION—See YAKIMA, WA (Charter Communications)

YAKIMA—Formerly served by Wireless Broadcasting Systems of Yakima Inc. No longer in operation

YAKIMA—Charter Communications

YARROW POINT—See SEATTLE, WA (Comcast Cable)

YELM—See SEATTLE, WA (Comcast Cable)

ZILLAH—See YAKIMA, WA (Charter Communications)

WEST VIRGINIA

ADAMSVILLE—See SHINNSTON, WV (Suddenlink Communications)

ADDISON TWP.—See PARKERSBURG, OH (Suddenlink Communications)

ADENA—See WHEELING, OH (Comcast Cable)

ADRIAN—See BUCKHANNON, WV (Suddenlink Communications)

AFLEX—See KERMIT, KY (Suddenlink Communications)

ALBRIGHT—See KINGWOOD, WV (Atlantic Broadband)

ALDERSON—Formerly served by Charter Communications. Now served by Suddenlink Communications, BECKLEY, WV [WV0005]

ALDERSON—See BECKLEY, WV (Suddenlink Communications)

ALKOL—See CHARLESTON, WV (Suddenlink Communications)

ALLEGANY COUNTY (PORTIONS)—See KEYSER, MD (Comcast Cable)

ALPOCA (PORTIONS)—See PINEVILLE, WV (Shentel)

ALUM BRIDGE—Shentel. Now served by WESTON, WV [WV0034]

ALUM BRIDGE—See WESTON, WV (Shentel)

ALUM CREEK—See SISSONVILLE, WV (Suddenlink Communications)

AMEAGLE—See BECKLEY, WV (Suddenlink Communications)

AMES HEIGHTS—See SUMMERSVILLE, WV (Shentel)

AMMA—See PARKERSBURG, WV (Suddenlink Communications)

AMONATE—See PINEVILLE, VA (Shentel)

ANAWALT—See PINEVILLE, WV (Shentel)

ANMOORE (TOWN)—See CLARKSBURG, WV (Time Warner Cable)

ANSTED—Shentel. Now served by SUMMERSVILLE, WV [WV0213]

ANSTED—See SUMMERSVILLE, WV (Shentel)

ANTHONY CREEK—Crystal Broadband Networks

APPLE GROVE—Formerly served by Vital Communications. No longer in operation

ARNETT—See CHARLESTON, WV (Suddenlink Communications)

ARNETTSVILLE—Formerly served by Adelphia Communications. No longer in operation

ARTHURDALE—See KINGWOOD, WV (Atlantic Broadband)

ASBURY—Formerly served by Vital Communications. No longer in operation

ATHENS—See BECKLEY, WV (Suddenlink Communications)

AUBURN—Formerly served by Cebridge Connections. No longer in operation

AUGUSTA—Comcast Cable. Now served by KEYSER, WV [WV0020]

AUGUSTA—See KEYSER, WV (Comcast Cable)

BAISDEN—See OMAR, WV (Shentel)

BALD KNOB—See VAN, WV (Shentel)

BALLARD—Formerly served by Vital Communications. No longer in operation

BARBOUR COUNTY (NORTHEASTERN PORTION)—See SHINNSTON, WV (Suddenlink Communications)

BARBOUR COUNTY (PORTIONS)—See PHILIPPI, WV (Philippi Communications System)

BARBOUR COUNTY—See BELINGTON, WV (Shentel)

BARBOURSVILLE—See CHARLESTON, WV (Suddenlink Communications)

BARNABUS—See OMAR, WV (Shentel)

BARNESVILLE—See WHEELING, OH (Comcast Cable)

BARRACKVILLE (TOWN)—See CLARKSBURG, WV (Time Warner Cable)

BARRETT—See VAN, WV (Shentel)

BARTON—See KEYSER, MD (Comcast Cable)

BAXTER—See GRANT TOWN, WV (Atlantic Broadband)

BEAUTY—See KERMIT, KY (Suddenlink Communications)

BECKLEY—Suddenlink Communications

BEECH BOTTOM—Blue Devil Cable TV Inc

BEECH BOTTOM—See WARWOOD, WV (Centre TV Cable)

BEECH CREEK—Shentel

BELINGTON—Shentel

BELLAIRE—See WHEELING, OH (Comcast Cable)

BELLE—See CHARLESTON, WV (Suddenlink Communications)

BELLEVILLE—See WASHINGTON, WV (Community Antenna Service)

BELMONT COUNTY (PORTIONS)—See WHEELING, OH (Comcast Cable)

BELMONT—See PARKERSBURG, WV (Suddenlink Communications)

BELO—See KERMIT, WV (Suddenlink Communications)

BELPRE—See PARKERSBURG, OH (Suddenlink Communications)

BENS CREEK—Formerly served by Charter Communications. Now served by Colane Cable TV Inc., OMAR, WV [WV0191]

BENS CREEK—See OMAR, WV (Shentel)

BENWOOD—See WHEELING, WV (Comcast Cable)

BERGOO—Formerly served by Charter Communications. Now served by Shentel, SUMMERSVILLE, WV [WV0213]

BERGOO—See SUMMERSVILLE, WV (Shentel)

BETHANY—Comcast Cable. Now served by WHEELING, WV [WV0004]

BETHANY—See WHEELING, WV (Comcast Cable)

BETHESDA—See WHEELING, OH (Comcast Cable)

BETHLEHEM—See WHEELING, WV (Comcast Cable)

BETHLEHEM—See SHINNSTON, WV (Suddenlink Communications)

BEVERLY—Suddenlink Communications

BIAS—See KERMIT, WV (Suddenlink Communications)

BICKMORE—See CHARLESTON, WV (Suddenlink Communications)

BIG CREEK—See HAMLIN, WV (Armstrong Cable Services)

BIM—See VAN, WV (Shentel)

BIRCH RIVER—Formerly served by Vital Communications. No longer in operation

BLAINE—See WHEELING, OH (Comcast Cable)

BLAIR—See KERMIT, WV (Suddenlink Communications)

BLAND COUNTY (PORTIONS)—See BLUEFIELD, VA (Comcast Cable)

BLOOMINGTON—See KEYSER, MD (Comcast Cable)

BLUEFIELD—See BLUEFIELD, VA (Comcast Cable)

BLUEFIELD—Comcast Cable

BLUEWELL—See BLUEFIELD, WV (Comcast Cable)

BOAZ—See PARKERSBURG, WV (Suddenlink Communications)

BOB WHITE—See VAN, WV (Shentel)

BOMONT—Formerly served by Vital Communications. No longer in operation

BOOMER—See CHARLESTON, WV (Suddenlink Communications)

BOONE COUNTY (portions)—Armstrong Cable Services. Now served by ZELIENOPLE, PA [PA0053]

BOONE COUNTY (PORTIONS)—See HAMLIN, WV (Armstrong Cable Services)

BOONE COUNTY (PORTIONS)—See VAN, WV (Shentel)

BOONE COUNTY (PORTIONS)—See CHARLESTON, WV (Suddenlink Communications)

BOONE COUNTY—See KERMIT, WV (Suddenlink Communications)

BOOTHSVILLE—See SHINNSTON, WV (Suddenlink Communications)

BRADLEY—See BECKLEY, WV (Suddenlink Communications)

BRADSHAW—See PINEVILLE, WV (Shentel)

BRAMWELL—See BLUEFIELD, WV (Comcast Cable)

BRANCHLAND—See HAMLIN, WV (Armstrong Cable Services)

BRANDYWINE—Formerly served by Brandywine Cablevision. No longer in operation

West Virginia—Cable Community Index

BRAXTON COUNTY (PORTIONS)—See WESTON, WV (Shentel)

BRAXTON COUNTY—See SUMMERSVILLE, WV (Shentel)

BRENTON—See PINEVILLE, WV (Shentel)

BRETZ—See KINGWOOD, WV (Atlantic Broadband)

BRIAR CREEK—See PINEVILLE, WV (Shentel)

BRIDGEPORT—See WHEELING, OH (Comcast Cable)

BRIDGEPORT—See CLARKSBURG, WV (Time Warner Cable)

BRILLIANT—See WHEELING, OH (Comcast Cable)

BRISTOL—See WESTON, WV (Shentel)

BROAD RUN—Shentel. Now served by WESTON, WV [WV0034]

BROAD RUN—See WESTON, WV (Shentel)

BROOKE COUNTY (PORTIONS)—See WHEELING, WV (Comcast Cable)

BROOKHAVEN—Formerly served by Adelphia Communications. No longer in operation

BROOKSIDE—See WHEELING, OH (Comcast Cable)

BROWNSVILLE—See CHARLESTON, WV (Suddenlink Communications)

BROWNTON—See SHINNSTON, WV (Suddenlink Communications)

BRUNO—Shentel

BUCKHANNON—Suddenlink Communications

BUD (PORTIONS)—See PINEVILLE, WV (Shentel)

BUD—Formerly served by Bud-Alpoca TV Cable Club Inc. No longer in operation

BURNSVILLE—Formerly served by Charter Communications. Now served by Shentel, WESTON, WV [WV0034]

BURNSVILLE—See WESTON, WV (Shentel)

BURNWELL—See KERMIT, KY (Suddenlink Communications)

BURTON—See LITTLETON, WV (Zito Media)

CABELL COUNTY (PORTIONS)—See CHARLESTON, WV (Suddenlink Communications)

CABELL COUNTY (UNINCORPORATED AREAS)—See HAMLIN, WV (Armstrong Cable Services)

CAIRO—Formerly served by Almega Cable. No longer in operation

CALHOUN COUNTY (PORTIONS)—See GRANTSVILLE, WV (Shentel)

CAMDEN (TOWN)—See SUMMERSVILLE, WV (Shentel)

CAMDEN ON GAULEY—Formerly served by Charter Communications. Now served by Shentel, SUMMERSVILLE, WV [WV0213]

CAMDEN ON GAULEY—See SUMMERSVILLE, WV (Shentel)

CAMDEN—See WESTON, WV (Shentel)

CAMERON—Zito Media

CAMPBELLS CREEK—See CHARLESTON, WV (Suddenlink Communications)

CANVAS—Formerly served by Econoco Inc. No longer in operation

CAPELS—See PINEVILLE, WV (Shentel)

CAPON BRIDGE—Formerly served by Valley Cable Systems. No longer in operation

CARETTA—See PINEVILLE, WV (Shentel)

CASS—Spruce Knob Seneca Rocks Telephone

CEDAR GROVE—See CHARLESTON, WV (Suddenlink Communications)

CHAPEL—Formerly served by Vital Communications. No longer in operation

CHAPMANVILLE—See HAMLIN, WV (Armstrong Cable Services)

CHAPMANVILLE—See KERMIT, WV (Suddenlink Communications)

CHARLESTON—Suddenlink Communications

CHATTAROY—Formerly served by Charter Communications. Now served by Suddenlink Communications, KERMIT, WV [WV0038]

CHATTAROY—See KERMIT, WV (Suddenlink Communications)

CHAUNCEY—See OMAR, WV (Shentel)

CHELYAN—See CHARLESTON, WV (Suddenlink Communications)

CHESAPEAKE—See CHARLESTON, WV (Suddenlink Communications)

CHESHIRE TWP.—See PARKERSBURG, OH (Suddenlink Communications)

CHESHIRE—See PARKERSBURG, OH (Suddenlink Communications)

CHESTER—Comcast Cable. Now served by WHEELING, WV [WV0004]

CHESTER—See WHEELING, WV (Comcast Cable)

CLARKSBURG—Formerly served by Adelphia Communications. Now served by Comcast Cable, MORGANTOWN, WV [WV0198]

CLARKSBURG—See MORGANTOWN, WV (Comcast Cable)

CLARKSBURG—Time Warner Cable

CLAY (town)—Formerly served by Vital Communications. No longer in operation

CLAY COUNTY (SOUTHERN PORTION)—See CHARLESTON, WV (Suddenlink Communications)

CLEAR FORK—See PINEVILLE, WV (Shentel)

CLEARVIEW—See WHEELING, WV (Comcast Cable)

CLENDENIN—See CHARLESTON, WV (Suddenlink Communications)

COALTON—Formerly served by Country Cable. No longer in operation

COALWOOD—See PINEVILLE, WV (Shentel)

COLCORD—See BECKLEY, WV (Suddenlink Communications)

COLERAIN TWP.—See WHEELING, OH (Comcast Cable)

COLFAX—Formerly served by Comcast Cable. No longer in operation

COLLIERS—Formerly served by Blue Devil Cable TV Inc. No longer in operation

COLLIERS—See WELLSBURG, WV (Blue Devil Cable TV Inc)

CORE—See MORGANTOWN, WV (Comcast Cable)

CORINNE—See PINEVILLE, WV (Shentel)

COSTA—See CHARLESTON, WV (Suddenlink Communications)

COTTAGEVILLE—Community Antenna Service

COTTLE—See SUMMERSVILLE, WV (Shentel)

COVE GAP—See HAMLIN, WV (Armstrong Cable Services)

COVEL—See PINEVILLE, WV (Shentel)

COW CREEK—See OMAR, WV (Shentel)

COWEN—Formerly served by Charter Communications. Now served by Shentel, SUMMERSVILLE, WV [WV0213]

COWEN—See SUMMERSVILLE, WV (Shentel)

CRABTREE—See CHARLESTON, WV (Suddenlink Communications)

CRAIGSVILLE—Shentel. Now served by SUMMERSVILLE, WV [WV0213]

CRAIGSVILLE—See SUMMERSVILLE, WV (Shentel)

CRAWLEY CREEK—Shentel

CROSS CREEK TWP.—See WHEELING, OH (Comcast Cable)

CROSS LANES—See CHARLESTON, WV (Suddenlink Communications)

CROSSROADS—Formerly served by Crossroads TV Cable. No longer in operation

CRUM—See KERMIT, WV (Suddenlink Communications)

CUCUMBER—See PINEVILLE, WV (Shentel)

CURTIN—Formerly served by Charter Communications. Now served by Shentel, SUMMERSVILLE, WV [WV0213]

CURTIN—See SUMMERSVILLE, WV (Shentel)

CYCLONE—See PINEVILLE, WV (Shentel)

DAILEY—See BEVERLY, WV (Suddenlink Communications)

DALLISON—See WASHINGTON, WV (Community Antenna Service)

DANVILLE—See CHARLESTON, WV (Suddenlink Communications)

DAVELLA—See KERMIT, KY (Suddenlink Communications)

DAVIS CREEK—See CHARLESTON, WV (Suddenlink Communications)

DAVIS—Atlantic Broadband

DAVISVILLE—See PARKERSBURG, WV (Suddenlink Communications)

DAVY—See PINEVILLE, WV (Shentel)

DAWSON—Formerly served by Econoco Inc. No longer in operation

DEBORD—See KERMIT, KY (Suddenlink Communications)

DELBARTON—Colane Cable TV Inc. Now served by OMAR, WV [WV0191]

DELBARTON—See OMAR, WV (Shentel)

DENVER—See KINGWOOD, WV (Atlantic Broadband)

DIANA—Formerly served by Country Cable. No longer in operation

DILLONVALE—See WHEELING, OH (Comcast Cable)

DINGESS—Armstrong Utilities Inc. Now served by DINGESS (formerly Harts), WV [WV0270]

DINGESS—Armstrong Cable Services

DIXIE—See CHARLESTON, WV (Suddenlink Communications)

DODDRIDGE COUNTY (NORTHEAST PORTION)—See WESTON, WV (Shentel)

DORCAS—C T & R Cable

DOROTHY—Formerly served by Charter Communications. Now served by Suddenlink Communications, BECKLEY, WV [WV0005]

DOROTHY—See BECKLEY, WV (Suddenlink Communications)

DOTHAN—See SUMMERSVILLE, WV (Shentel)

DRENNEN—Shentel. Now served by SUMMERSVILLE, WV [WV0213]

DRENNEN—See SUMMERSVILLE, WV (Shentel)

DUNBAR—See CHARLESTON, WV (Suddenlink Communications)

DUNLOW—Formerly served by Almega Cable. No longer in operation

DURBIN—Spruce Knob Seneca Rocks Telephone. Now served by CASS, WV [WV0173]

DURBIN—See CASS, WV (Spruce Knob Seneca Rocks Telephone)

EAST BANK—See CHARLESTON, WV (Suddenlink Communications)

EAST DAILEY—See BEVERLY, WV (Suddenlink Communications)

EAST KERMIT—See KERMIT, WV (Suddenlink Communications)

EAST LOVELY—See KERMIT, WV (Suddenlink Communications)

EAST LYNN—See CHARLESTON, WV (Suddenlink Communications)

EASTON—Formerly served by Adelphia Communications. No longer in operation

ECHO—See CHARLESTON, WV (Suddenlink Communications)

ELIZABETH—See PARKERSBURG, WV (Suddenlink Communications)

ELK CREEK—See KERMIT, KY (Suddenlink Communications)

ELKINS—See BEVERLY, WV (Suddenlink Communications)

ELLAMORE—Formerly served by Vital Communications. No longer in operation

ELLENBORO—Formerly served by Charter Communications. Now served by Shentel, WESTON, WV [WV0034]

ELLENBORO—See WESTON, WV (Shentel)

ENON—See SUMMERSVILLE, WV (Shentel)

ENTERPRISE—See SHINNSTON, WV (Suddenlink Communications)

ERIE—See SHINNSTON, WV (Suddenlink Communications)

EUREKA—See PARKERSBURG, WV (Suddenlink Communications)

FAIRMONT—Time Warner Cable. Now served by CLARKSBURG, WV [WV0010]

FAIRMONT—See MORGANTOWN, WV (Comcast Cable)

FAIRMONT—See CLARKSBURG, WV (Time Warner Cable)

FAIRPOINT—See WHEELING, OH (Comcast Cable)

FAIRVIEW—See GRANT TOWN, WV (Atlantic Broadband)

FANROCK—See PINEVILLE, WV (Shentel)

FARMINGTON—See SHINNSTON, WV (Suddenlink Communications)

FAYETTE COUNTY (PORTIONS)—See SUMMERSVILLE, WV (Shentel)

FAYETTE COUNTY (PORTIONS)—See BECKLEY, WV (Suddenlink Communications)

FAYETTEVILLE—See BECKLEY, WV (Suddenlink Communications)

FENWICK—See SUMMERSVILLE, WV (Shentel)

FERRELLSBURG—See HAMLIN, WV (Armstrong Cable Services)

FLAT ROCK—Formerly served by Windjammer Cable. No longer in operation

FLATWOODS—See SUMMERSVILLE, WV (Shentel)

FLEMINGTON—Suddenlink Communications. Now served by SHINNSTON, WV [WV0029]

FLEMINGTON—See SHINNSTON, WV (Suddenlink Communications)

FLOYD COUNTY (PORTIONS)—See KERMIT, KY (Suddenlink Communications)

FLUSHING—See WHEELING, OH (Comcast Cable)

FOLLANSBEE—See WELLSBURG, WV (Blue Devil Cable TV Inc)

FOLLANSBEE—See WHEELING, WV (Comcast Cable)

FOLSOM—Jones TV Cable & Satellite Systems Inc

FOREST HILLS—See KERMIT, KY (Suddenlink Communications)

FORT GAY—See CHARLESTON, WV (Suddenlink Communications)

FOUR STATES—See SHINNSTON, WV (Suddenlink Communications)

FRAME—Formerly served by Vital Communications. No longer in operation

FRAMETOWN—Formerly served by Vital Communications. No longer in operation

FRANKFORD—Formerly served by Clearview TV Cable. No longer in operation

FRANKLIN—Shentel. Now served by PETERSBURG, WV [WV0064]

FRANKLIN—See PETERSBURG, WV (Shentel)

FRENCH CREEK—See BUCKHANNON, WV (Suddenlink Communications)

FRIENDLY—Formerly served by Vital Communications. No longer in operation

FROSTBURG—See KEYSER, MD (Comcast Cable)

GALLIA COUNTY (PORTIONS)—See PARKERSBURG, OH (Suddenlink Communications)

GALLIPOLIS FERRY—See PARKERSBURG, WV (Suddenlink Communications)

GALLIPOLIS—See PARKERSBURG, OH (Suddenlink Communications)

GALLOWAY—See SHINNSTON, WV (Suddenlink Communications)

GANDEEVILLE—Formerly served by Econoco Inc. No longer in operation

GARRETT COUNTY (PORTIONS)—See KEYSER, MD (Comcast Cable)

GARWOOD—See PINEVILLE, WV (Shentel)

GARY—See PINEVILLE, WV (Shentel)

GASSAWAY—Shentel. Now served by SUMMERSVILLE, WV [WV0213]

GASSAWAY—See SUMMERSVILLE, WV (Shentel)

GAULEY BRIDGE—See CHARLESTON, WV (Suddenlink Communications)

GENOA—Formerly served by Lycom Communications. No longer in operation

GILBERT CREEK—See OMAR, WV (Shentel)

GILBERT—Shentel

GILBOA—Shentel. Now served by SUMMERSVILLE, WV [WV0213]

GILBOA—See SUMMERSVILLE, WV (Shentel)

GILES COUNTY (PORTIONS)—See BECKLEY, VA (Suddenlink Communications)

GILMER COUNTY (PORTIONS)—See WESTON, WV (Shentel)

GLASGOW—See CHARLESTON, WV (Suddenlink Communications)

GLEN DALE—Comcast Cable. Now served by WHEELING, WV [WV0004]

GLEN DALE—See WHEELING, WV (Comcast Cable)

GLEN FORK—See PINEVILLE, WV (Shentel)

GLEN JEAN—See SUMMERSVILLE, WV (Shentel)

GLEN LYN—See BECKLEY, VA (Suddenlink Communications)

GLEN ROBBINS—See WHEELING, OH (Comcast Cable)

GLEN ROGERS—See PINEVILLE, WV (Shentel)

GLENHAYES—Formerly served by Lycom Communications. No longer in operation

GLENVILLE—Shentel. Now served by WESTON, WV [WV0034]

GLENVILLE—See WESTON, WV (Shentel)

GOLDTOWN—Formerly served by Econoco Inc. Now served by Suddenlink Communications, PARKERSBURG, WV [WV0003]

GOLDTOWN—See PARKERSBURG, WV (Suddenlink Communications)

GOODY—See KERMIT, KY (Suddenlink Communications)

GORDON—See VAN, WV (Shentel)

GOSHEN TWP. (BELMONT COUNTY)—See WHEELING, OH (Comcast Cable)

GRAFTON—Comcast Cable. Now served by TAYLOR COUNTY (portions), WV [WV0278]

GRAFTON—See MORGANTOWN, WV (Comcast Cable)

GRANT COUNTY (PORTIONS)—See PETERSBURG, WV (Shentel)

GRANT TOWN—Atlantic Broadband

GRANTSVILLE—Shentel

GRANVILLE—See MORGANTOWN, WV (Comcast Cable)

GRAYSVILLE—Formerly served by Vital Communications. No longer in operation

GREEN ACRES—Formerly served by Almega Cable. No longer in operation

GREEN BANK—See CASS, WV (Spruce Knob Seneca Rocks Telephone)

GREEN VALLEY—See BLUEFIELD, WV (Comcast Cable)

GREENBRIER COUNTY (PORTIONS)—See RONCEVERTE, WV (Shentel)

GREENBRIER COUNTY (PORTIONS)—See BECKLEY, WV (Suddenlink Communications)

GREENWOOD—See VAN, WV (Shentel)

GREY EAGLE—See KERMIT, WV (Suddenlink Communications)

GRIFFITHSVILLE—See SISSONVILLE, WV (Suddenlink Communications)

GUTHRIE—See SISSONVILLE, WV (Suddenlink Communications)

GYPSY—See SHINNSTON, WV (Suddenlink Communications)

HADDLETON—See LOW GAP, WV (Shentel)

HAMBLETON—See DAVIS, WV (Atlantic Broadband)

HAMLIN—Armstrong Cable Services

HAMPDEN—Colane Cable TV Inc. Now served by OMAR, WV [WV0191]

HAMPDEN—See OMAR, WV (Shentel)

HANCOCK COUNTY (PORTIONS)—See WHEELING, WV (Comcast Cable)

HANDLEY—See CHARLESTON, WV (Suddenlink Communications)

HANOVER—Shentel

HARDY COUNTY (PORTIONS)—See MOOREFIELD, WV (Hardy Telecommunications)

HARDY—See KERMIT, KY (Suddenlink Communications)

HARMAN—Formerly served by Harman Cable Corp. No longer in operation

HARRISON COUNTY (PORTIONS)—See WESTON, WV (Shentel)

HARRISON COUNTY (PORTIONS)—See BUCKHANNON, WV (Suddenlink Communications)

HARRISON COUNTY (PORTIONS)—See SHINNSTON, WV (Suddenlink Communications)

West Virginia—Cable Community Index

HARRISON COUNTY (PORTIONS)—See CLARKSBURG, WV (Time Warner Cable)

HARRISON COUNTY—See WESTON, WV (Shentel)

HARRISVILLE—Formerly served by Rapid Cable. Now served by Shentel, WESTON, WV [WV0034]

HARRISVILLE—See WHEELING, OH (Comcast Cable)

HARRISVILLE—See WESTON, WV (Shentel)

HARTFORD—See PARKERSBURG, WV (Suddenlink Communications)

HARTS—See HAMLIN, WV (Armstrong Cable Services)

HARVEY—See SUMMERSVILLE, WV (Shentel)

HASTINGS—See PINE GROVE, WV (Zito Media)

HATFIELD—See OMAR, WV (Shentel)

HATFIELD—See KERMIT, KY (Suddenlink Communications)

HAVACO—See PINEVILLE, WV (Shentel)

HAYWOOD—See SHINNSTON, WV (Suddenlink Communications)

HAZELWOOD—See BEVERLY, WV (Suddenlink Communications)

HEMPHILL—See PINEVILLE, WV (Shentel)

HENDERSON—See PARKERSBURG, WV (Suddenlink Communications)

HENDRICKS—See DAVIS, WV (Atlantic Broadband)

HEPZIBAH—See SHINNSTON, WV (Suddenlink Communications)

HERNDON—Shentel. Now served by PINEVILLE, WV [WV0204]

HERNDON—See PINEVILLE, WV (Shentel)

HEWETT—Shentel

HILLSBORO—See MARLINTON (town), WV (Shentel)

HILLTOP—See SUMMERSVILLE, WV (Shentel)

HINTON—Formerly served by Charter Communications. Now served by Suddenlink Communications, BECKLEY, WV [WV0005]

HINTON—See BECKLEY, WV (Suddenlink Communications)

HODE—See KERMIT, KY (Suddenlink Communications)

HODGESVILLE—See BUCKHANNON, WV (Suddenlink Communications)

HOLCOMB—See SUMMERSVILLE, WV (Shentel)

HOLLOWAY—See WHEELING, OH (Comcast Cable)

HOTCHKISS—See PINEVILLE, WV (Shentel)

HUDDY—See KERMIT, KY (Suddenlink Communications)

HUNDRED—See LITTLETON, WV (Zito Media)

HUNTERSVILLE—Milestone Communications LP

HUNTINGTON—Comcast Cable. Now served by PETERSBURG, VA [VA0186]

HURRICANE—See CHARLESTON, WV (Suddenlink Communications)

HUTCHINSON—Formerly served by Comcast Cable. No longer in operation

HUTTONSVILLE—See BEVERLY, WV (Suddenlink Communications)

IAEGER—Shentel. Now served by PINEVILLE, WV [WV0204]

IAEGER—See PINEVILLE, WV (Shentel)

IDAMAY—See SHINNSTON, WV (Suddenlink Communications)

INDEPENDENCE—See KINGWOOD, WV (Atlantic Broadband)

INDORE—See CHARLESTON, WV (Suddenlink Communications)

INDUSTRIAL—See WESTON, WV (Shentel)

INEZ—See KERMIT, KY (Suddenlink Communications)

INGRAM BRANCH—See SUMMERSVILLE, WV (Shentel)

INSTITUTE—See CHARLESTON, WV (Suddenlink Communications)

INWOOD—Formerly served by Adelphia Communications. Now served by Comcast Cable, JEFFERSON COUNTY (portions), WV [WV0016]

ISLAND CREEK TWP.—See WHEELING, OH (Comcast Cable)

ITMANN—See PINEVILLE, WV (Shentel)

JACKSON COUNTY (PORTIONS)—See COTTAGEVILLE, WV (Community Antenna Service)

JACKSON COUNTY (PORTIONS)—See SISSONVILLE, WV (Suddenlink Communications)

JACKSONBURG—See PINE GROVE, WV (Zito Media)

JANE LEW—See WESTON, WV (Shentel)

JEFFERSON COUNTY (portions)—Comcast Cable. Now served by FREDERICK COUNTY (portions), MD [MD0009]

JEFFREY—See HEWETT, WV (Shentel)

JENKINJONES—Formerly served by Obey's TV Cable. No longer in operation

JESSE—See PINEVILLE, WV (Shentel)

JODIE—See CHARLESTON, WV (Suddenlink Communications)

JOHNSON BRANCH—See SUMMERSVILLE, WV (Shentel)

JOHNSON COUNTY (PORTIONS)—See KERMIT, KY (Suddenlink Communications)

JULIAN—See CHARLESTON, WV (Suddenlink Communications)

JUNIOR—See BELINGTON, WV (Shentel)

JUSTICE—See GILBERT, WV (Shentel)

KANAWHA COUNTY (PORTIONS)—See SISSONVILLE, WV (Suddenlink Communications)

KANAWHA COUNTY—See CHARLESTON, WV (Suddenlink Communications)

KENNA—See PARKERSBURG, WV (Suddenlink Communications)

KERMIT—Suddenlink Communications

KEYSER—Comcast Cable

KEYSTONE—See PINEVILLE, WV (Shentel)

KIAHSVILLE—See DINGESS, WV (Armstrong Cable Services)

KIMBALL—Formerly served by Comcast Cable. Now served by Shentel, PINEVILLE, WV [WV0204]

KIMBALL—See PINEVILLE, WV (Shentel)

KINCAID—See SUMMERSVILLE, WV (Shentel)

KINGSTON—See SUMMERSVILLE, WV (Shentel)

KINGWOOD—Atlantic Broadband

KOPPERSTOWN—See PINEVILLE, WV (Shentel)

LAFFERTY—See WHEELING, OH (Comcast Cable)

LAKE—See HEWETT, WV (Shentel)

LANSING—See WHEELING, OH (Comcast Cable)

LANSING—See SUMMERSVILLE, WV (Shentel)

LANSING—See BECKLEY, WV (Suddenlink Communications)

LAUREL CREEK—See KERMIT, WV (Suddenlink Communications)

LAVALETTE—See CHARLESTON, WV (Suddenlink Communications)

LAWRENCE COUNTY (PORTIONS)—See OMAR, KY (Shentel)

LAWRENCE COUNTY (PORTIONS)—See KERMIT, KY (Suddenlink Communications)

LAWRENCEVILLE—See WHEELING, WV (Comcast Cable)

LEFT HAND—Formerly served by Econoco Inc. Now served by Suddenlink Communications, PARKERSBURG, WV [WV0003]

LEFT HAND—See PARKERSBURG, WV (Suddenlink Communications)

LENORE—Formerly served by Charter Communications. Now served by Suddenlink Communications, KERMIT, WV [WV0038]

LENORE—See KERMIT, WV (Suddenlink Communications)

LEON—Formerly served by Vital Communications. No longer in operation

LESTER—See BECKLEY, WV (Suddenlink Communications)

LEWIS COUNTY (NORTHERN PORTION)—See BUCKHANNON, WV (Suddenlink Communications)

LEWIS COUNTY (PORTIONS)—See WESTON, WV (Shentel)

LEWISBURG—Formerly served by Charter Communications. Now served by Suddenlink Communications, BECKLEY, WV [WV0005]

LEWISBURG—See BECKLEY, WV (Suddenlink Communications)

LINCOLN COUNTY (PORTIONS)—See HAMLIN, WV (Armstrong Cable Services)

LINCOLN COUNTY (PORTIONS)—See SISSONVILLE, WV (Suddenlink Communications)

LINN—See WESTON, WV (Shentel)

LITTLE OTTER—Shentel. Now served by SUMMERSVILLE, WV [WV0213]

LITTLE OTTER—See SUMMERSVILLE, WV (Shentel)

LITTLETON—Zito Media

LOCKWOOD—See SUMMERSVILLE, WV (Shentel)

LOGAN COUNTY (PORTIONS)—See DINGESS, WV (Armstrong Cable Services)

LOGAN COUNTY—See KERMIT, WV (Suddenlink Communications)

LOGAN—Formerly served by Charter Communications. Now served by Suddenlink Communications, KERMIT, WV [WV0038]

LOGAN—See KERMIT, WV (Suddenlink Communications)

LONACONING—See KEYSER, MD (Comcast Cable)

LONDON—See CHARLESTON, WV (Suddenlink Communications)

LORENTZ—See BUCKHANNON, WV (Suddenlink Communications)

LOST CREEK—See BUCKHANNON, WV (Suddenlink Communications)

LOUDENDALE—See CHARLESTON, WV (Suddenlink Communications)

LOVELY—See KERMIT, KY (Suddenlink Communications)

LOW GAP—Shentel

Cable Community Index—West Virginia

LUKE—See KEYSER, MD (Comcast Cable)

LUMBERPORT—See SHINNSTON, WV (Suddenlink Communications)

LYBURN—See NEIBERT, WV (Shentel)

MABEN—See PINEVILLE, WV (Shentel)

MABSCOTT—See BECKLEY, WV (Suddenlink Communications)

MADISON—Suddenlink Communications. Now served by CHARLESTON, WV [WV0006]

MADISON—See CHARLESTON, WV (Suddenlink Communications)

MAHER—See KERMIT, WV (Suddenlink Communications)

MAIDSVILLE—See MORGANTOWN, WV (Comcast Cable)

MAITLAND-SUPERIOR—See PINEVILLE, WV (Shentel)

MAN—See KERMIT, WV (Suddenlink Communications)

MANNINGTON—Formerly served by Mannington TV Inc. Now served by Comcast Cable, MORGANTOWN, WV [WV0198]

MANNINGTON—See MORGANTOWN, WV (Comcast Cable)

MARIETTA—See PARKERSBURG, OH (Suddenlink Communications)

MARION COUNTY (PORTIONS)—See GRANT TOWN, WV (Atlantic Broadband)

MARION COUNTY (PORTIONS)—See MORGANTOWN, WV (Comcast Cable)

MARION COUNTY (PORTIONS)—See SHINNSTON, WV (Suddenlink Communications)

MARION COUNTY (PORTIONS)—See CLARKSBURG, WV (Time Warner Cable)

MARLINTON (TOWN)—Shentel

MARMET—See CHARLESTON, WV (Suddenlink Communications)

MARSHALL COUNTY (PORTIONS)—See WHEELING, WV (Comcast Cable)

MARSHALL COUNTY (PORTIONS)—See CAMERON, WV (Zito Media)

MARTIN COUNTY (PORTIONS)—See OMAR, KY (Shentel)

MARTIN COUNTY (PORTIONS)—See KERMIT, KY (Suddenlink Communications)

MARTINS FERRY—See WHEELING, OH (Comcast Cable)

MARTINSBURG—Formerly served by Adelphia Communications. Now served by Comcast Cable, JEFFERSON COUNTY (portions), WV [WV0016]

MASON—See PARKERSBURG, WV (Suddenlink Communications)

MASONTOWN—See KINGWOOD, WV (Atlantic Broadband)

MATEWAN—Formerly served by Charter Communications. No longer in operation

MATOAKA—See BECKLEY, WV (Suddenlink Communications)

MAYSEL—Formerly served by Econoco Inc. No longer in operation

MAYSVILLE—See DORCAS, WV (C T & R Cable)

MCCOOLE—See KEYSER, MD (Comcast Cable)

MCDOWELL COUNTY (PORTIONS)—See PINEVILLE, WV (Shentel)

MCGRAWS—See PINEVILLE, WV (Shentel)

MCMECHEN—See WHEELING, WV (Comcast Cable)

MCWHORTER—See BUCKHANNON, WV (Suddenlink Communications)

MEAD TWP.—See WHEELING, OH (Comcast Cable)

MEADOW BRIDGE—Formerly served by Vital Communications. No longer in operation

MEADOWBROOK—See SHINNSTON, WV (Suddenlink Communications)

MEADOWDALE—Formerly served by Adelphia Communications. No longer in operation

MEIGS COUNTY (PORTIONS)—See PARKERSBURG, OH (Suddenlink Communications)

MERCER COUNTY (PORTIONS)—See BLUEFIELD, WV (Comcast Cable)

MERCER COUNTY (PORTIONS)—See BECKLEY, WV (Suddenlink Communications)

MERRIMAC—See KERMIT, WV (Suddenlink Communications)

MIAMI—See CHARLESTON, WV (Suddenlink Communications)

MICCO—See OMAR, WV (Shentel)

MIDDLEBOURNE—Formerly served by Richards TV Cable. No longer in operation

MIDDLEPORT—See PARKERSBURG, OH (Suddenlink Communications)

MIDKIFF—See DINGESS, WV (Armstrong Cable Services)

MIDLAND—See KEYSER, MD (Comcast Cable)

MIDLOTHIAN—See KEYSER, MD (Comcast Cable)

MILL CREEK—See BEVERLY, WV (Suddenlink Communications)

MILO—See KERMIT, KY (Suddenlink Communications)

MILTON—Suddenlink Communications. Now served by CHARLESTON, WV [WV0006]

MILTON—See CHARLESTON, WV (Suddenlink Communications)

MINEHAHA SPRINGS—See HUNTERSVILLE, WV (Milestone Communications LP)

MINERAL COUNTY (PORTIONS)—See KEYSER, WV (Comcast Cable)

MINERSVILLE—See PARKERSBURG, OH (Suddenlink Communications)

MINGO COUNTY (PORTIONS)—See OMAR, WV (Shentel)

MINGO COUNTY (PORTIONS)—See KERMIT, WV (Suddenlink Communications)

MINGO COUNTY (UNINCORPORATED AREAS)—See DINGESS, WV (Armstrong Cable Services)

MINGO JUNCTION—See WHEELING, OH (Comcast Cable)

MITCHELL HEIGHTS—See KERMIT, WV (Suddenlink Communications)

MONONGAH—Formerly served by Adelphia Communications. Now served by Comcast Cable, TAYLOR COUNTY (portions), WV [WV0278]

MONONGAH—See MORGANTOWN, WV (Comcast Cable)

MONONGALIA COUNTY (PORTIONS)—See GRANT TOWN, WV (Atlantic Broadband)

MONONGALIA COUNTY (PORTIONS)—See MORGANTOWN, WV (Comcast Cable)

MONROE COUNTY—See BECKLEY, WV (Suddenlink Communications)

MONTGOMERY HEIGHTS—See CHARLESTON, WV (Suddenlink Communications)

MONTGOMERY—See CHARLESTON, WV (Suddenlink Communications)

MONTROSE—See BEVERLY, WV (Suddenlink Communications)

MOOREFIELD—Hardy Telecommunications

MORGANTOWN—Comcast Cable

MORRISVALE—See CHARLESTON, WV (Suddenlink Communications)

MOSSY—See SUMMERSVILLE, WV (Shentel)

MOUNDSVILLE—Comcast Cable. Now served by WHEELING, WV [WV0004]

MOUNDSVILLE—See WHEELING, WV (Comcast Cable)

MOUNT ALTO—See PARKERSBURG, WV (Suddenlink Communications)

MOUNT HOPE—See BECKLEY, WV (Suddenlink Communications)

MOUNT LOOKOUT—Formerly served by Econoco Inc. No longer in operation

MOUNT PLEASANT (VILLAGE)—See WHEELING, OH (Comcast Cable)

MOUNT PLEASANT TWP.—See WHEELING, OH (Comcast Cable)

MOUNT PLEASANT—See WHEELING, OH (Comcast Cable)

MOUNT STORM—Formerly served by Almega Cable. No longer in operation

MOUNT ZION—See GRANTSVILLE, WV (Shentel)

MUD RIVER—Shentel

MUDFORK—See KERMIT, WV (Suddenlink Communications)

MULLENS—Formerly served by Jet Broadband. Now served by Shentel, PINEVILLE, WV [WV0204]

MULLENS—See PINEVILLE, WV (Shentel)

MURPHYTOWN—See WASHINGTON, WV (Community Antenna Service)

MYRTLE—See KERMIT, WV (Suddenlink Communications)

NARROWS—See BECKLEY, VA (Suddenlink Communications)

NAUGATUCK—See KERMIT, WV (Suddenlink Communications)

NEBO—Formerly served by Windjammer Cable. No longer in operation

NEFFS—See WHEELING, OH (Comcast Cable)

NEIBERT—Shentel

NETTIE—Formerly served by Vital Communications. No longer in operation

NEW ALEXANDRIA—See WHEELING, OH (Comcast Cable)

NEW CREEK—See KEYSER, WV (Comcast Cable)

NEW CUMBERLAND—Comcast Cable. Now served by STEUBENVILLE, OH [OH0048]

NEW CUMBERLAND—See WHEELING, WV (Comcast Cable)

NEW HAVEN—See PARKERSBURG, WV (Suddenlink Communications)

NEW HOPE—See SUMMERSVILLE, WV (Shentel)

NEW MANCHESTER—See WHEELING, WV (Comcast Cable)

NEW MARTINSVILLE—Formerly served by Charter Communications. Now served by Suddenlink Communications, PARKERSBURG, WV [WV0003]

NEW MARTINSVILLE—See PARKERSBURG, WV (Suddenlink Communications)

NEW RICHMOND—See PINEVILLE, WV (Shentel)

NEWBURG—See KINGWOOD, WV (Atlantic Broadband)

NEWELL—See WHEELING, WV (Comcast Cable)

NEWTON—See PARKERSBURG, WV (Suddenlink Communications)

NICHOLAS COUNTY (PORTIONS)—See CHARLESTON, WV (Suddenlink Communications)

West Virginia—Cable Community Index

NICHOLAS COUNTY—See SUMMERSVILLE, WV (Shentel)

NIMITZ—See BECKLEY, WV (Suddenlink Communications)

NITRO—Formerly served by Charter Communications. Now served by Suddenlink Communications, CHARLESTON, WV [WV0006]

NITRO—See CHARLESTON, WV (Suddenlink Communications)

NOLAN—See KERMIT, WV (Suddenlink Communications)

NORTH HILLS—See PARKERSBURG, WV (Suddenlink Communications)

NORTH PAGE—See SUMMERSVILLE, WV (Shentel)

NORTH WELCH—See PINEVILLE, WV (Shentel)

NORTHFORK—Shentel. Now served by PINEVILLE, WV [WV0204]

NORTHFORK—See PINEVILLE, WV (Shentel)

NORTON—Formerly served by Vital Communications. No longer in operation

NUTTER FORT (TOWN)—See CLARKSBURG, WV (Time Warner Cable)

OAK HILL—Formerly served by Charter Communications. Now served by Suddenlink Communications, BECKLEY, WV [WV0005]

OAK HILL—See BECKLEY, WV (Suddenlink Communications)

OAKVALE—Formerly served by Shentel. No longer in operation

OCEANA—See PINEVILLE, WV (Shentel)

OHIO COUNTY (PORTIONS)—See WHEELING, WV (Comcast Cable)

OMAR—Shentel

OPPY—See KERMIT, KY (Suddenlink Communications)

OSAGE—See MORGANTOWN, WV (Comcast Cable)

OTTAWA—See KERMIT, WV (Suddenlink Communications)

PADEN CITY—See PARKERSBURG, WV (Suddenlink Communications)

PAGE—Shentel. Now served by SUMMERSVILLE, WV [WV0213]

PAGE—See SUMMERSVILLE, WV (Shentel)

PAINT CREEK (PORTIONS)—See CHARLESTON, WV (Suddenlink Communications)

PAINTSVILLE—See KERMIT, KY (Suddenlink Communications)

PANTHER—Formerly served by A & A Communications. No longer in operation

PARCOAL—See SUMMERSVILLE, WV (Shentel)

PARKERSBURG (SOUTHERN PORTION)—See WASHINGTON, WV (Community Antenna Service)

PARKERSBURG—Suddenlink Communications

PARSONS—See DAVIS, WV (Atlantic Broadband)

PAW PAW—Atlantic Broadband

PAX—Formerly served by Charter Communications. Now served by Suddenlink Communications, BECKLEY, WV [WV0005]

PAX—See BECKLEY, WV (Suddenlink Communications)

PEARISBURG—See BECKLEY, VA (Suddenlink Communications)

PEASE TWP. (BELMONT COUNTY)—See WHEELING, OH (Comcast Cable)

PEMBROKE—See BECKLEY, VA (Suddenlink Communications)

PENDLETON COUNTY (PORTIONS)—See PETERSBURG, WV (Shentel)

PENNSBORO—Armstrong Cable Services. Now served by ZELIENOPLE, PA [PA0053]

PETERSBURG—Shentel

PETERSTOWN—Formerly served by Charter Communications. Now served by Suddenlink Communications, BECKLEY, WV [WV0005]

PETERSTOWN—See BECKLEY, WV (Suddenlink Communications)

PHILIPPI—Philippi Communications System

PIEDMONT—See KEYSER, WV (Comcast Cable)

PIERPOINT—See PINEVILLE, WV (Shentel)

PIKE COUNTY (PORTIONS)—See OMAR, KY (Shentel)

PIKE COUNTY (UNINCORPORATED AREAS)—See KERMIT, KY (Suddenlink Communications)

PILGRIM—See KERMIT, KY (Suddenlink Communications)

PINE GROVE—Zito Media

PINEVILLE—Shentel

PIPESTEM—Suddenlink Communications. Now served by BECKLEY, WV [WV0005]

PIPESTEM—See BECKLEY, WV (Suddenlink Communications)

PLEASANT VALLEY—See MORGANTOWN, WV (Comcast Cable)

PLEASANT VALLEY—See CLARKSBURG, WV (Time Warner Cable)

PLEASANTS COUNTY—See PARKERSBURG, WV (Suddenlink Communications)

PLINY—Formerly served by Vital Communications. No longer in operation

POCA—See CHARLESTON, WV (Suddenlink Communications)

POCAHONTAS COUNTY (PORTIONS)—See MARLINTON (town), WV (Shentel)

POCAHONTAS—See BLUEFIELD, VA (Comcast Cable)

POCATALICO—See SISSONVILLE, WV (Suddenlink Communications)

POE—See SUMMERSVILLE, WV (Shentel)

POINT PLEASANT—Formerly served by Charter Communications. Now served by Suddenlink Communications, PARKERSBURG, WV [WV0003]

POINT PLEASANT—See PARKERSBURG, WV (Suddenlink Communications)

POMEROY—See PARKERSBURG, OH (Suddenlink Communications)

POND CREEK—See KERMIT, KY (Suddenlink Communications)

POND GAP—See CHARLESTON, WV (Suddenlink Communications)

PRATT—See CHARLESTON, WV (Suddenlink Communications)

PREMIER—See PINEVILLE, WV (Shentel)

PRENTER—See CHARLESTON, WV (Suddenlink Communications)

PRESTON COUNTY (PORTIONS)—See KINGWOOD, WV (Atlantic Broadband)

PRESTON COUNTY (PORTIONS)—See MORGANTOWN, WV (Comcast Cable)

PRESTONSBURG—See KERMIT, KY (Suddenlink Communications)

PRICETOWN—Formerly served by Cebridge Connections. No longer in operation

PRICHARD—Lycom Communications

PRINCETON—Formerly served by Charter Communications. Now served by Suddenlink Communications, BECKLEY, WV [WV0005]

PRINCETON—See BECKLEY, WV (Suddenlink Communications)

PULLMAN—Formerly served by Cebridge Connections. No longer in operation

PULTNEY TWP.—See WHEELING, OH (Comcast Cable)

PULTNEY—See WHEELING, OH (Comcast Cable)

PURSGLOVE—See MORGANTOWN, WV (Comcast Cable)

PUTNAM COUNTY (PORTIONS)—See CHARLESTON, WV (Suddenlink Communications)

QUICK—Formerly served by Vital Communications. No longer in operation

QUINWOOD—See BECKLEY, WV (Suddenlink Communications)

RACHEL—See MORGANTOWN, WV (Comcast Cable)

RACINE—See PARKERSBURG, OH (Suddenlink Communications)

RACINE—See CHARLESTON, WV (Suddenlink Communications)

RAINELLE—See BECKLEY, WV (Suddenlink Communications)

RALEIGH COUNTY (PORTIONS)—See BECKLEY, WV (Suddenlink Communications)

RALEIGH COUNTY (SOUTHWEST PORTION)—See PINEVILLE, WV (Shentel)

RAND—See CHARLESTON, WV (Suddenlink Communications)

RANDOLPH COUNTY (PORTIONS)—See BEVERLY, WV (Suddenlink Communications)

RANGER—See HAMLIN, WV (Armstrong Cable Services)

RAVENCLIFF—Formerly served by Jet Broadband. Now served by Shentel, PINEVILLE, WV [WV0204]

RAVENCLIFF—See PINEVILLE, WV (Shentel)

RAVENSWOOD—See COTTAGEVILLE, WV (Community Antenna Service)

RAVENSWOOD—See PARKERSBURG, WV (Suddenlink Communications)

RAWL—See KERMIT, WV (Suddenlink Communications)

RAYLAND—See WHEELING, OH (Comcast Cable)

RD NO. 1 TRAILER COURTS—See WARWOOD, WV (Centre TV Cable)

READER—See PINE GROVE, WV (Zito Media)

RED HOUSE—Comcast Cable. Now served by HUNTINGTON, WV [WV0002]

REDSTAR—See SUMMERSVILLE, WV (Shentel)

REEDSVILLE—See KINGWOOD, WV (Atlantic Broadband)

RENO—See PARKERSBURG, OH (Suddenlink Communications)

RENO—See PARKERSBURG, WV (Suddenlink Communications)

RHODELL—See BECKLEY, WV (Suddenlink Communications)

RICH CREEK—See BECKLEY, VA (Suddenlink Communications)

RICHLAND TWP.—See WHEELING, OH (Comcast Cable)

RICHLAND—See WHEELING, OH (Comcast Cable)

RICHMOND TWP.—See WHEELING, OH (Comcast Cable)

RICHWOOD—Shentel. Now served by SUMMERSVILLE, WV [WV0213]

RICHWOOD—See SUMMERSVILLE, WV (Shentel)

Cable Community Index—West Virginia

RIDGEVIEW—See CHARLESTON, WV (Suddenlink Communications)

RIG—C T & R Cable

RIPLEY—See COTTAGEVILLE, WV (Community Antenna Service)

RIPLEY—See PARKERSBURG, WV (Suddenlink Communications)

RIVERFRONT—See KERMIT, KY (Suddenlink Communications)

RIVESVILLE—See MORGANTOWN, WV (Comcast Cable)

ROBSON—Formerly served by Charter Communications. Now served by Suddenlink Communications, CHARLESTON, WV [WV0006]

ROBSON—See CHARLESTON, WV (Suddenlink Communications)

ROCK CAVE—See BUCKHANNON, WV (Suddenlink Communications)

ROCK VIEW—See PINEVILLE, WV (Shentel)

ROCKY GAP—See BLUEFIELD, VA (Comcast Cable)

RONCEVERTE—Shentel

ROSEMONT—See SHINNSTON, WV (Suddenlink Communications)

ROWLESBURG—See MORGANTOWN, WV (Comcast Cable)

RUPERT—Formerly served by Charter Communications. Now served by Suddenlink Communications, BECKLEY, WV [WV0005]

RUPERT—See BECKLEY, WV (Suddenlink Communications)

RUTLAND—See PARKERSBURG, OH (Suddenlink Communications)

SABINE—See PINEVILLE, WV (Shentel)

SALEM COLLEGE—Formerly served by Basco Electronics Inc. No longer in operation

SALEM TWP. (JEFFERSON COUNTY)—See WHEELING, OH (Comcast Cable)

SALEM—Shentel. Now served by WESTON, WV [WV0034]

SALEM—See WESTON, WV (Shentel)

SALT ROCK—Formerly served by Armstrong Cable Services. No longer in operation

SAND FORK—Shentel. Now served by WESTON, WV [WV0034]

SAND FORK—See WESTON, WV (Shentel)

SANDYVILLE—Formerly served by Vital Communications. No longer in operation

SARAH ANN—Colane Cable TV Inc. Now served by OMAR, WV [WV0191]

SARAH ANN—See OMAR, WV (Shentel)

SARDIS—Formerly served by Country Cable. No longer in operation

SAULSVILLE—See PINEVILLE, WV (Shentel)

SCARBRO—Shentel. Now served by SUMMERSVILLE, WV [WV0213]

SCARBRO—See SUMMERSVILLE, WV (Shentel)

SCOTT DEPOT—See CHARLESTON, WV (Suddenlink Communications)

SETH—See CHARLESTON, WV (Suddenlink Communications)

SHADYSIDE—See WHEELING, OH (Comcast Cable)

SHARON HEIGHTS—See OMAR, WV (Shentel)

SHARONDALE—See KERMIT, KY (Suddenlink Communications)

SHINNSTON—Suddenlink Communications

SHORT CREEK TWP.—See WHEELING, OH (Comcast Cable)

SHORT CREEK—See WARWOOD, WV (Centre TV Cable)

SIMPSON—See SHINNSTON, WV (Suddenlink Communications)

SISSONVILLE—Suddenlink Communications

SISTERSVILLE—See PARKERSBURG, WV (Suddenlink Communications)

SIX MILE ROAD—Shentel

SLAB FORK—See PINEVILLE, WV (Shentel)

SMITH TWP.—See WHEELING, OH (Comcast Cable)

SMITHERS—See CHARLESTON, WV (Suddenlink Communications)

SMITHFIELD TWP. (JEFFERSON COUNTY)—See WHEELING, OH (Comcast Cable)

SMITHFIELD—Formerly served by Almega Cable. No longer in operation

SNOWSHOE—Crystal Broadband Networks

SOD—See SISSONVILLE, WV (Suddenlink Communications)

SOPHIA—See BECKLEY, WV (Suddenlink Communications)

SOUTH CHARLESTON—See CHARLESTON, WV (Suddenlink Communications)

SOUTH WILLIAMSON—See KERMIT, KY (Suddenlink Communications)

SPEEDWAY—See BECKLEY, WV (Suddenlink Communications)

SPELTER—See SHINNSTON, WV (Suddenlink Communications)

SPENCER—Formerly served by Charter Communications. Now served by Suddenlink Communications, PARKERSBURG, WV [WV0003]

SPENCER—See PARKERSBURG, WV (Suddenlink Communications)

SPRINGFIELD TWP.—See PARKERSBURG, OH (Suddenlink Communications)

SPRINGFIELD—Comcast Cable. Now served by KEYSER, WV [WV0020]

SPRINGFIELD—See KEYSER, WV (Comcast Cable)

ST. ALBANS—See CHARLESTON, WV (Suddenlink Communications)

ST. CLAIRSVILLE—See WHEELING, OH (Comcast Cable)

ST. MARY'S—Formerly served by Charter Communications. Now served by Suddenlink Communications, PARKERSBURG, WV [WV0003]

ST. MARY'S—See PARKERSBURG, WV (Suddenlink Communications)

STAR CITY—See MORGANTOWN, WV (Comcast Cable)

STEPHENSON—See BECKLEY, WV (Suddenlink Communications)

STEUBENVILLE TWP.—See WHEELING, OH (Comcast Cable)

STEUBENVILLE—See WHEELING, OH (Comcast Cable)

STIRRAT—See OMAR, WV (Shentel)

STONE—See KERMIT, KY (Suddenlink Communications)

STONECOAL—See KERMIT, WV (Suddenlink Communications)

STONEWOOD—See CLARKSBURG, WV (Time Warner Cable)

SUMERCO—See SISSONVILLE, WV (Suddenlink Communications)

SUMMERS COUNTY (UNINCORPORATED AREAS)—See BECKLEY, WV (Suddenlink Communications)

SUMMERSVILLE—Shentel

SUTTON—See SUMMERSVILLE, WV (Shentel)

SWITZER—See OMAR, WV (Shentel)

SYLVESTER—See CHARLESTON, WV (Suddenlink Communications)

SYRACUSE—See PARKERSBURG, OH (Suddenlink Communications)

TALCOTT—Formerly served by Vital Communications. No longer in operation

TAMCLIFF—See GILBERT, WV (Shentel)

TANNER—Formerly served by Vital Communications. No longer in operation

TAYLOR COUNTY (EASTERN PORTION)—See SHINNSTON, WV (Suddenlink Communications)

TAYLOR COUNTY (portions)—Comcast Cable. Now served by MORGANTOWN, WV [WV0198]

TAYLOR COUNTY (PORTIONS)—See MORGANTOWN, WV (Comcast Cable)

TAYLOR COUNTY (PORTIONS)—See CLARKSBURG, WV (Time Warner Cable)

TAZEWELL COUNTY (PORTIONS)—See BLUEFIELD, VA (Comcast Cable)

TERRA ALTA—See KINGWOOD, WV (Atlantic Broadband)

THOMAS—See DAVIS, WV (Atlantic Broadband)

TILTONSVILLE—See WHEELING, OH (Comcast Cable)

TOLER—See KERMIT, KY (Suddenlink Communications)

TOMAHAWK—See KERMIT, KY (Suddenlink Communications)

TORNADO—See SISSONVILLE, WV (Suddenlink Communications)

TRIADELPHIA—See WHEELING, WV (Comcast Cable)

TRIPP—See KERMIT, WV (Suddenlink Communications)

TROY—See WESTON, WV (Shentel)

TUCKER COUNTY (PORTIONS)—See DAVIS, WV (Atlantic Broadband)

TUNNELTON—Formerly served by Community Antenna Service. No longer in operation

TURKEY CREEK—See KERMIT, KY (Suddenlink Communications)

TURTLE CREEK—Colane Cable TV Inc. No longer in operation

TWILIGHT—See VAN, WV (Shentel)

TYLER COUNTY (PORTIONS)—See PARKERSBURG, WV (Suddenlink Communications)

TYLER MOUNTAIN—See SISSONVILLE, WV (Suddenlink Communications)

UNION—Formerly served by Vital Communications. No longer in operation

UPPER TRACT—Formerly served by Cebridge Connections. No longer in operation

UPPERGLADE—See SUMMERSVILLE, WV (Shentel)

UPSHUR COUNTY—See BUCKHANNON, WV (Suddenlink Communications)

VALLEY BEND—See BEVERLY, WV (Suddenlink Communications)

VALLEY GROVE—See WHEELING, WV (Comcast Cable)

VAN—Shentel

VARNEY—Colane Cable TV Inc. Now served by OMAR, WV [WV0191]

VARNEY—See OMAR, WV (Shentel)

VICTOR—See SUMMERSVILLE, WV (Shentel)

VIENNA—See WASHINGTON, WV (Community Antenna Service)

VIENNA—See PARKERSBURG, WV (Suddenlink Communications)

WALKER—See WASHINGTON, WV (Community Antenna Service)

WALKERSVILLE—Formerly served by Almega Cable. No longer in operation

West Virginia—Cable Community Index

WALLACE—See FOLSOM, WV (Jones TV Cable & Satellite Systems Inc)

WALTON—Formerly served by Windjammer Cable. No longer in operation

WAR—Formerly served by Suddenlink Communications. Now served by Shentel, NORTHFORK, WV [WV0045]

WAR—See PINEVILLE, WV (Shentel)

WARDENSVILLE—Formerly served by Valley Cable Systems. No longer in operation

WARDENSVILLE—See MOOREFIELD, WV (Hardy Telecommunications)

WARFIELD—See KERMIT, KY (Suddenlink Communications)

WARREN TWP. (BELMONT COUNTY)—See WHEELING, OH (Comcast Cable)

WARWOOD—Centre TV Cable

WARWOOD—See WHEELING, WV (Comcast Cable)

WASHINGTON—Community Antenna Service

WAVERLY—See PARKERSBURG, WV (Suddenlink Communications)

WAYNE COUNTY (PORTIONS)—See OMAR, WV (Shentel)

WAYNE COUNTY (UNINCORPORATED AREAS)—See PRICHARD, WV (Lycom Communications)

WAYNE COUNTY—See DINGESS, WV (Armstrong Cable Services)

WAYNE—Suddenlink Communications. Now served by CHARLESTON, WV [WV0006]

WAYNE—See HAMLIN, WV (Armstrong Cable Services)

WAYNE—See CHARLESTON, WV (Suddenlink Communications)

WEBSTER COUNTY (PORTIONS)—See SUMMERSVILLE, WV (Shentel)

WEBSTER SPRINGS—Shentel. Now served by SUMMERSVILLE, WV [WV0213]

WEBSTER SPRINGS—See SUMMERSVILLE, WV (Shentel)

WEIRTON—See WHEELING, WV (Comcast Cable)

WELCH—Shentel (formerly Jet Broadband). Now served by PINEVILLE, WV [WV0204]

WELCH—See PINEVILLE, WV (Shentel)

WELLSBURG—Blue Devil Cable TV Inc

WELLSBURG—See WHEELING, WV (Comcast Cable)

WEST HAMLIN—See HAMLIN, WV (Armstrong Cable Services)

WEST LIBERTY (town)—Comcast Cable. Now served by WHEELING, WV [WV0004]

WEST LIBERTY—See WHEELING, WV (Comcast Cable)

WEST LOGAN—See KERMIT, WV (Suddenlink Communications)

WEST MILFORD—Formerly served by Cebridge Connections. Now served by Suddenlink Communications, BUCKHANNON, WV [WV0024]

WEST MILFORD—See BUCKHANNON, WV (Suddenlink Communications)

WEST UNION—Armstrong Cable Services. Now served by ZELIENOPLE, PA [PA0053]

WESTERNPORT—See KEYSER, MD (Comcast Cable)

WESTON—Shentel

WESTOVER—Formerly served by Adelphia Communications. Now served by Comcast Cable, MORGANTOWN, WV [WV0198]

WESTOVER—See MORGANTOWN, WV (Comcast Cable)

WETZEL COUNTY (PORTIONS)—See PARKERSBURG, WV (Suddenlink Communications)

WETZEL COUNTY—See PINE GROVE, WV (Zito Media)

WHARNCLIFFE—Shentel

WHARTON—See VAN, WV (Shentel)

WHEELING TWP.—See WHEELING, OH (Comcast Cable)

WHEELING—Comcast Cable

WHITE SULPHUR SPRINGS—Formerly served by Charter Communications. Now served by Suddenlink Communications, BECKLEY, WV [WV0005]

WHITE SULPHUR SPRINGS—See ANTHONY CREEK, WV (Crystal Broadband Networks)

WHITE SULPHUR SPRINGS—See BECKLEY, WV (Suddenlink Communications)

WHITEHALL—Formerly served by Adelphia Communications. Now served by Comcast Cable, MORGANTOWN, WV [WV0198]

WHITEHALL—See MORGANTOWN, WV (Comcast Cable)

WHITESVILLE—See CHARLESTON, WV (Suddenlink Communications)

WILEYVILLE—Formerly served by Almega Cable. No longer in operation

WILLIAMS MOUNTAIN—See VAN, WV (Shentel)

WILLIAMSON—Formerly served by Charter Communications. Now served by Suddenlink Communications, KERMIT, WV [WV0038]

WILLIAMSON—See KERMIT, WV (Suddenlink Communications)

WILLIAMSTOWN—See WASHINGTON, WV (Community Antenna Service)

WILLIAMSTOWN—See PARKERSBURG, WV (Suddenlink Communications)

WINDSOR HEIGHTS—See WARWOOD, WV (Centre TV Cable)

WINTERSVILLE—See WHEELING, OH (Comcast Cable)

WIRT COUNTY (PORTIONS)—See PARKERSBURG, WV (Suddenlink Communications)

WOLF CREEK—See KERMIT, KY (Suddenlink Communications)

WOOD COUNTY—See PARKERSBURG, WV (Suddenlink Communications)

WORTHINGTON—Formerly served by Adelphia Communications. Now served by Comcast Cable, MORGANTOWN, WV [WV0198]

WORTHINGTON—See MORGANTOWN, WV (Comcast Cable)

WRISTON—See SUMMERSVILLE, WV (Shentel)

WYATT—Formerly served by Country Cable. No longer in operation

WYCO—See BECKLEY, WV (Suddenlink Communications)

WYOMING COUNTY (PORTIONS)—See PINEVILLE, WV (Shentel)

WYOMING COUNTY (PORTIONS)—See BECKLEY, WV (Suddenlink Communications)

WYOMING COUNTY (PORTIONS)—See KERMIT, WV (Suddenlink Communications)

WYOMING COUNTY—See HANOVER, WV (Shentel)

YAWKEY—See SISSONVILLE, WV (Suddenlink Communications)

YORKVILLE—See WHEELING, OH (Comcast Cable)

ZELA—See SUMMERSVILLE, WV (Shentel)

WISCONSIN

ABBOTSFORD—See STEVENS POINT, WI (Charter Communications)

ABRAMS (TOWN)—See APPLETON, WI (Time Warner Cable)

ADAMS (TOWN)—See ADAMS, WI (Charter Communications)

ADAMS TWP.—See EAU CLAIRE, WI (Charter Communications)

ADAMS—Charter Communications

ADELL (VILLAGE)—See MILWAUKEE, WI (Time Warner Cable)

AFTON—See MADISON, WI (Charter Communications)

ALBAN (TOWN)—See AMHERST (village), WI (Tomorrow Valley Video)

ALBANY (TOWN)—See ELMWOOD (village), WI (Video services provided by Celect Communications & available through Bloomer Tel, Bruce Tel, Celect Communications, NextGen & West WI Telcom. Formerly [WI0337]. This cable system has converted to IPTV)

ALBANY TWP.—See ALBANY, WI (Mediacom)

ALBANY—Mediacom

ALBION—See MADISON, WI (Charter Communications)

ALGOMA (TOWN)—See APPLETON, WI (Time Warner Cable)

ALGOMA—See FOND DU LAC, WI (Charter Communications)

ALLOUEZ—See APPLETON, WI (Time Warner Cable)

ALMA CENTER—See WHITEHALL, WI (Western Wisconsin Communications Cooperative)

ALMA—Midco

ALMENA—See SAND CREEK, WI (Mosaic Telecom)

ALMOND—Formerly served by New Century Communications. No longer in operation

ALTOONA—See EAU CLAIRE, WI (Charter Communications)

ALTURA—See EAU CLAIRE, MN (Charter Communications)

AMBERG—Packerland Broadband

AMERY—Northwest Community Communications

AMHERST (TOWN)—See AMHERST (village), WI (Tomorrow Valley Video)

AMHERST (village)—Amherst Telephone. This cable system has converted to IPTV. See AMHERST (village), WI [WI5372]

AMHERST (VILLAGE)—Tomorrow Valley Video

AMHERST JUNCTION (VILLAGE)—See AMHERST (village), WI (Tomorrow Valley Video)

ANGELICA—Formerly served by Packerland Broadband. No longer in operation

ANGELO—See EAU CLAIRE, WI (Charter Communications)

ANIWA (VILLAGE)—See STEVENS POINT, WI (Charter Communications)

ANSON TWP.—See EAU CLAIRE, WI (Charter Communications)

ANTIGO—Charter Communications. Now served by STEVENS POINT, WI [WI0019]

ANTIGO—See STEVENS POINT, WI (Charter Communications)

APPLE RIVER (TOWN)—See LUCK (village), WI (Lakeland Communications)

APPLETON—Time Warner Cable

ARBOR VITAE—See STEVENS POINT, WI (Charter Communications)

ARCADIA—See WHITEHALL, WI (Western Wisconsin Communications Cooperative)

Cable Community Index—Wisconsin

ARENA (VILLAGE)—See MADISON, WI (Charter Communications)

ARGONNE—See STEVENS POINT, WI (Charter Communications)

ARGYLE—Mediacom

ARKANSAW—NTec (formerly Chippewa Valley Cable Co. Inc.)

ARLINGTON—See MADISON, WI (Charter Communications)

ARMENIA—See WISCONSIN RAPIDS, WI (Solarus)

ARPIN (VILLAGE)—See VESPER, WI (Packerland Broadband)

ASHIPPUN (TOWN)—See MILWAUKEE, WI (Time Warner Cable)

ASHLAND—Charter Communications. Now served by EAU CLAIRE, WI [WI0011]

ASHLAND—See EAU CLAIRE, WI (Charter Communications)

ASHWAUBENON—See APPLETON, WI (Time Warner Cable)

ATHENS—See STEVENS POINT, WI (Charter Communications)

ATLANTA (TOWN)—See ELMWOOD (village), WI (Video services provided by Celect Communications & available through Bloomer Tel, Bruce Tel, Celect Communications, NextGen & West WI Telcom. Formerly [WI0337]. This cable system has converted to IPTV)

AUBURN (TOWN)—See ELMWOOD (village), WI (Video services provided by Celect Communications & available through Bloomer Tel, Bruce Tel, Celect Communications, NextGen & West WI Telcom. Formerly [WI0337]. This cable system has converted to IPTV)

AUBURN—See FOND DU LAC, WI (Charter Communications)

AUBURNDALE—Packerland Broadband

AUGUSTA—Packerland Broadband

AUGUSTA—See FALL CREEK, WI (Packerland Broadband)

AURORA (TOWN)—See FOND DU LAC, WI (Charter Communications)

AVOCA—Packerland Broadband

AZTALAN TWP.—See MADISON, WI (Charter Communications)

BAGLEY (VILLAGE)—Dairyland Cable Systems Inc

BALDWIN (TOWN)—See BALDWIN TWP., WI (Baldwin Telecom Inc)

BALDWIN (VILLAGE)—See BALDWIN TWP., WI (Baldwin Telecom Inc)

BALDWIN TWP.—Baldwin Telecom Inc

BALSAM LAKE (VILLAGE)—See LUCK (village), WI (Lakeland Communications)

BALSAM LAKE TWP.—See LUCK (village), WI (Lakeland Communications)

BANCROFT—New Century Communications

BANGOR—See EAU CLAIRE, WI (Charter Communications)

BARABOO (TOWN)—See MADISON, WI (Charter Communications)

BARABOO—See MADISON, WI (Charter Communications)

BARKSDALE (TOWN)—See EAU CLAIRE, WI (Charter Communications)

BARNEVELD—See MADISON, WI (Charter Communications)

BARRE TWP.—See EAU CLAIRE, WI (Charter Communications)

BARRON (TOWN)—See EAU CLAIRE, WI (Charter Communications)

BARRON TWP.—See EAU CLAIRE, WI (Charter Communications)

BARRON—See EAU CLAIRE, WI (Charter Communications)

BARTON (TOWN)—See FOND DU LAC, WI (Charter Communications)

BASS LAKE TWP.—See EAU CLAIRE, WI (Charter Communications)

BAY CITY—Midcontinent Communications. Now served by ELLSWORTH, WI [WI0248]

BAYFIELD—See EAU CLAIRE, WI (Charter Communications)

BAYSIDE (VILLAGE)—See MILWAUKEE, WI (Time Warner Cable)

BEAR CREEK—Charter Communications. Now served by STEVENS POINT, WI [WI0019]

BEAR CREEK—See STEVENS POINT, WI (Charter Communications)

BEAVER DAM—See FOND DU LAC, WI (Charter Communications)

BELGIUM (TOWN)—See MILWAUKEE, WI (Time Warner Cable)

BELL CENTER—Formerly served by Richland-Grant Telephone Co-op. No longer in operation

BELL CENTER—Formerly served by Richland-Grant Telephone Co-op. No longer in operation

BELLE PLAINE—See STEVENS POINT, WI (Charter Communications)

BELLEVILLE (VILLAGE)—See MADISON, WI (Charter Communications)

BELLEVILLE—Charter Communications. Now served by MADISON, WI [WI0002]

BELLEVUE—See APPLETON, WI (Time Warner Cable)

BELMONT TWP.—See PLATTEVILLE, WI (CenturyLink Prism. This cable system has converted to IPTV)

BELMONT—See CUBA CITY, WI (Mediacom)

BELOIT—See MADISON, WI (Charter Communications)

BENTON—See CUBA CITY, WI (Mediacom)

BERGEN—See STEVENS POINT, WI (Charter Communications)

BERLIN—See FOND DU LAC, WI (Charter Communications)

BEVENT—See WITTENBERG, WI (Wittenberg Cable TV)

BIG BEND (TOWN)—See ELMWOOD (village), WI (Video services provided by Celect Communications & available through Bloomer Tel, Bruce Tel, Celect Communications, NextGen & West WI Telcom. Formerly [WI0337]. This cable system has converted to IPTV)

BIG BEND (VILLAGE)—See MILWAUKEE, WI (Time Warner Cable)

BIRCH CREEK (TOWN)—See ELMWOOD (village), WI (Video services provided by Celect Communications & available through Bloomer Tel, Bruce Tel, Celect Communications, NextGen & West WI Telcom. Formerly [WI0337]. This cable system has converted to IPTV)

BIRCHWOOD—See MIKANA, WI (S & K TV Systems)

BIRNAMWOOD—See STEVENS POINT, WI (Charter Communications)

BIRON—See STEVENS POINT, WI (Charter Communications)

BLACK CREEK—See STEVENS POINT, WI (Charter Communications)

BLACK EARTH—See MADISON, WI (Charter Communications)

BLACK RIVER FALLS—Charter Communications. Now served by EAU CLAIRE, WI [WI0011]

BLACK RIVER FALLS—See EAU CLAIRE, WI (Charter Communications)

BLACK WOLF (TOWN)—See FOND DU LAC, WI (Charter Communications)

BLACK WOLF (TOWN)—See APPLETON, WI (Time Warner Cable)

BLAIR—See WHITEHALL, WI (Western Wisconsin Communications Cooperative)

BLANCHARDVILLE—Mediacom

BLOOMER (TOWN)—See ELMWOOD (village), WI (Video services provided by Celect Communications & available through Bloomer Tel, Bruce Tel, Celect Communications, NextGen & West WI Telcom. Formerly [WI0337]. This cable system has converted to IPTV)

BLOOMER—See EAU CLAIRE, WI (Charter Communications)

BLOOMER—See ELMWOOD (village), WI (Video services provided by Celect Communications & available through Bloomer Tel, Bruce Tel, Celect Communications, NextGen & West WI Telcom. Formerly [WI0337]. This cable system has converted to IPTV)

BLOOMFIELD (TOWN)—See MILWAUKEE, WI (Time Warner Cable)

BLOOMING GROVE—See MADISON, WI (Charter Communications)

BLOOMINGDALE—Formerly served by Midwest Cable Inc. No longer in operation

BLOOMINGTON—See LANCASTER, WI (Charter Communications)

BLUE MOUNDS—See MADISON, WI (Charter Communications)

BLUE RIVER (VILLAGE)—Dairyland Cable Systems Inc

BLUFFVIEW MOBILE HOME PARK—Formerly served by HLM Cable Corp. Now served by Merrimac Cable, MERRIMAC, WI [WI0154]

BOAZ (VILLAGE)—Village of Boaz

BONDUEL—Packerland Broadband

BONE LAKE (TOWN)—See LUCK (village), WI (Lakeland Communications)

BORON—See WISCONSIN RAPIDS, WI (Solarus)

BOSCOBEL—Mediacom

BOULDER JUNCTION—Karban TV Systems Inc

BOVINA—See STEVENS POINT, WI (Charter Communications)

BOWLER (VILLAGE)—See STEVENS POINT, WI (Charter Communications)

BOYCEVILLE—Nextgen Communications

BOYCEVILLE—See ELMWOOD (village), WI (Video services provided by Celect Communications & available through Bloomer Tel, Bruce Tel, Celect Communications, NextGen & West WI Telcom. Formerly [WI0337]. This cable system has converted to IPTV)

BOYD/CADOTT—Charter Communications. Now served by EAU CLAIRE, WI [WI0011]

BOYD—See EAU CLAIRE, WI (Charter Communications)

BRADFORD TWP.—See MADISON, WI (Charter Communications)

BRADLEY (TOWN)—See STEVENS POINT, WI (Charter Communications)

BRANDON—See FOND DU LAC, WI (Charter Communications)

BRIDGEPORT (TOWN)—See PRAIRIE DU CHIEN, WI (Mediacom)

BRIGGSVILLE—New Century Communications

BRILLION (TOWN)—See APPLETON, WI (Time Warner Cable)

BRILLION—See FOND DU LAC, WI (Charter Communications)

Wisconsin—Cable Community Index

BRISTOL (TOWN)—See MADISON, WI (Charter Communications)

BRISTOL (TOWN)—See MILWAUKEE, WI (Time Warner Cable)

BROCKWAY TWP.—See EAU CLAIRE, WI (Charter Communications)

BRODHEAD—See MADISON, WI (Charter Communications)

BROKAW—See STEVENS POINT, WI (Charter Communications)

BROOKFIELD—Time Warner Cable. Now served by MILWAUKEE, WI [WI0001]

BROOKFIELD—See MILWAUKEE, WI (Time Warner Cable)

BROOKLYN (TOWN)—See FOND DU LAC, WI (Charter Communications)

BROOKLYN (VILLAGE)—See MADISON, WI (Charter Communications)

BROOKVIEW TRAILER COURT—See VIROQUA, WI (Mediacom)

BROTHERTOWN—See FOND DU LAC, WI (Charter Communications)

BROWN DEER (VILLAGE)—See MILWAUKEE, WI (Time Warner Cable)

BROWNSVILLE—See LOMIRA, WI (Packerland Broadband)

BRUCE (TOWN)—See ELMWOOD (village), WI (Video services provided by Celect Communications & available through Bloomer Tel, Bruce Tel, Celect Communications, NextGen & West WI Telcom. Formerly [WI0337]. This cable system has converted to IPTV)

BRUCE (VILLAGE)—See EAU CLAIRE, WI (Charter Communications)

BRUNSWICK TWP.—See EAU CLAIRE, WI (Charter Communications)

BUCHANAN (TOWN)—See APPLETON, WI (Time Warner Cable)

BUENA VISTA (TOWN)—See MADISON, WI (Charter Communications)

BUENA VISTA (TOWN)—See AMHERST (village), WI (Tomorrow Valley Video)

BURKE—See MADISON, WI (Charter Communications)

BURLINGTON—Time Warner Cable. Now served by MILWAUKEE, WI [WI0001]

BURLINGTON—See MILWAUKEE, WI (Time Warner Cable)

BURNETT (TOWN)—See FOND DU LAC, WI (Charter Communications)

BURNZWICK (TOWN)—See ELMWOOD (village), WI (Video services provided by Celect Communications & available through Bloomer Tel, Bruce Tel, Celect Communications, NextGen & West WI Telcom. Formerly [WI0337]. This cable system has converted to IPTV)

BUTLER (VILLAGE)—See MILWAUKEE, WI (Time Warner Cable)

BUTTE DES MORTS—See FOND DU LAC, WI (Charter Communications)

BUTTERNUT—Packerland Broadband

BUTTERNUT—See FIFIELD, WI (Packerland Broadband)

CADOTT (VILLAGE)—See EAU CLAIRE, WI (Charter Communications)

CADY (TOWN)—See ELMWOOD (village), WI (Video services provided by Celect Communications & available through Bloomer Tel, Bruce Tel, Celect Communications, NextGen & West WI Telcom. Formerly [WI0337]. This cable system has converted to IPTV)

CALAMUS—See FOND DU LAC, WI (Charter Communications)

CALEDONIA (TOWN)—See MERRIMAC, WI (Merrimac Cable)

CALEDONIA (TOWN)—See MILWAUKEE, WI (Time Warner Cable)

CALUMET (TOWN)—See FOND DU LAC, WI (Charter Communications)

CAMBRIA (VILLAGE)—See RANDOLPH, WI (CenturyLink)

CAMBRIA—See MADISON, WI (Charter Communications)

CAMBRIDGE—See MADISON, WI (Charter Communications)

CAMERON (TOWN)—See STEVENS POINT, WI (Charter Communications)

CAMERON—See EAU CLAIRE, WI (Charter Communications)

CAMERON—See SAND CREEK, WI (Mosaic Telecom)

CAMP DOUGLAS—See MAUSTON, WI (Mediacom)

CAMPBELL TWP.—See EAU CLAIRE, WI (Charter Communications)

CAMPBELLSPORT—See FOND DU LAC, WI (Charter Communications)

CARLTON (TOWN)—See FOND DU LAC, WI (Charter Communications)

CARSON—See STEVENS POINT, WI (Charter Communications)

CARSON—See WISCONSIN RAPIDS, WI (Solarus)

CASCADE (VILLAGE)—See MILWAUKEE, WI (Time Warner Cable)

CASCO (TOWN)—See NEW FRANKEN, WI (CenturyLink)

CASCO (VILLAGE)—See NEW FRANKEN, WI (CenturyLink)

CASCO—CenturyLink. Now served by NEW FRANKEN, WI [WI0269]

CASHTON—See VIROQUA, WI (Mediacom)

CASSIAN (TOWN)—See STEVENS POINT, WI (Charter Communications)

CASSVILLE—See LANCASTER, WI (Charter Communications)

CATO (TOWN)—See APPLETON, WI (Time Warner Cable)

CAZENOVIA—Community Antenna System Inc

CECIL—Packerland Broadband

CEDAR GROVE (VILLAGE)—See MILWAUKEE, WI (Time Warner Cable)

CEDARBURG—Time Warner Cable. Now served by MILWAUKEE, WI [WI0001]

CEDARBURG—See MILWAUKEE, WI (Time Warner Cable)

CENTER (TOWN)—See MADISON, WI (Charter Communications)

CENTER—See APPLETON, WI (Time Warner Cable)

CENTURIA—See LUCK (village), WI (Lakeland Communications)

CHARLESTOWN—See FOND DU LAC, WI (Charter Communications)

CHASE—See APPLETON, WI (Time Warner Cable)

CHASEBURG—Mediacom. Now served by STODDARD, WI [WI0161]

CHASEBURG—See STODDARD, WI (Mediacom)

CHESTER—See FOND DU LAC, WI (Charter Communications)

CHETEK (TOWN)—See EAU CLAIRE, WI (Charter Communications)

CHETEK (TOWN)—See ELMWOOD (village), WI (Video services provided by Celect Communications & available through Bloomer Tel, Bruce Tel, Celect Communications, NextGen & West WI Telcom. Formerly [WI0337]. This cable system has converted to IPTV)

CHETEK TWP.—See EAU CLAIRE, WI (Charter Communications)

CHETEK—See EAU CLAIRE, WI (Charter Communications)

CHILTON—See FOND DU LAC, WI (Charter Communications)

CHIPPEWA FALLS—See EAU CLAIRE, WI (Charter Communications)

CHRISTIANA—See MADISON, WI (Charter Communications)

CLARNO TWP.—See MADISON, WI (Charter Communications)

CLAYTON (POLK COUNTY)—See AMERY, WI (Northwest Community Communications)

CLAYTON (WINNEBAGO COUNTY)—See APPLETON, WI (Time Warner Cable)

CLAYTON COUNTY—See PRAIRIE DU CHIEN, IA (Mediacom)

CLAYTON—See BOSCOBEL, IA (Mediacom)

CLEAR LAKE—CLT Communications

CLEVELAND (TOWN)—See ELMWOOD (village), WI (Video services provided by Celect Communications & available through Bloomer Tel, Bruce Tel, Celect Communications, NextGen & West WI Telcom. Formerly [WI0337]. This cable system has converted to IPTV)

CLEVELAND (VILLAGE)—See MILWAUKEE, WI (Time Warner Cable)

CLINTON—See MADISON, WI (Charter Communications)

CLINTONVILLE—Charter Communications. Now served by STEVENS POINT, WI [WI0019]

CLINTONVILLE—See STEVENS POINT, WI (Charter Communications)

CLYMAN—See FOND DU LAC, WI (Charter Communications)

COBB—See MADISON, WI (Charter Communications)

COLBY—See STEVENS POINT, WI (Charter Communications)

COLEMAN—Packerland Broadband

COLFAX (TOWN)—See ELMWOOD (village), WI (Video services provided by Celect Communications & available through Bloomer Tel, Bruce Tel, Celect Communications, NextGen & West WI Telcom. Formerly [WI0337]. This cable system has converted to IPTV)

COLFAX TWP.—See EAU CLAIRE, WI (Charter Communications)

COLOMA—See STEVENS POINT, WI (Charter Communications)

COLUMBUS—See MADISON, WI (Charter Communications)

COMBINED LOCKS—See APPLETON, WI (Time Warner Cable)

CONCORD—See MADISON, WI (Charter Communications)

COOKS VALLEY (TOWN)—See ELMWOOD (village), WI (Video services provided by Celect Communications & available through Bloomer Tel, Bruce Tel, Celect Communications, NextGen & West WI Telcom. Formerly [WI0337]. This cable system has converted to IPTV)

COON VALLEY—Mediacom. Now served by VIROQUA, WI [WI0068]

COON VALLEY—See VIROQUA, WI (Mediacom)

COOPERSTOWN (TOWN)—See FOND DU LAC, WI (Charter Communications)

CORNELL—See EAU CLAIRE, WI (Charter Communications)

COTTAGE GROVE—See MADISON, WI (Charter Communications)

COURTLAND—See RANDOLPH, WI (CenturyLink)

CRANDON—See STEVENS POINT, WI (Charter Communications)

CRAWFORD COUNTY (PORTIONS)—See VIROQUA, WI (Mediacom)

Cable Community Index—Wisconsin

CRAWFORD COUNTY (UNINCORPORATED AREAS)—See PRAIRIE DU CHIEN, WI (Mediacom)

CRESCENT—See STEVENS POINT, WI (Charter Communications)

CRIVITZ—Howard Cable

CROSS PLAINS (VILLAGE)—See MADISON, WI (Charter Communications)

CUBA CITY—Mediacom

CUDAHY—See MILWAUKEE, WI (Time Warner Cable)

CUMBERLAND—See EAU CLAIRE, WI (Charter Communications)

CUSHING—See LUCK (village), WI (Lakeland Communications)

DAKOTA (TOWN)—See STEVENS POINT, WI (Charter Communications)

DALE (TOWN)—See STEVENS POINT, WI (Charter Communications)

DALE—See APPLETON, WI (Time Warner Cable)

DALLAS—See SAND CREEK, WI (Mosaic Telecom)

DALTON—Formerly served by New Century Communications. No longer in operation

DANE (VILLAGE)—See MADISON, WI (Charter Communications)

DARIEN—See MADISON, WI (Charter Communications)

DARIEN—Packerland Broadband

DARLINGTON—See CUBA CITY, WI (Mediacom)

DAYTON (TOWN)—See STEVENS POINT, WI (Charter Communications)

DE FOREST—See MADISON, WI (Charter Communications)

DE PERE—See APPLETON, WI (Time Warner Cable)

DE SOTO—See STODDARD, WI (Mediacom)

DECATUR TWP.—See MADISON, WI (Charter Communications)

DEER PARK—See AMERY, WI (Northwest Community Communications)

DEERFIELD TWP.—See MADISON, WI (Charter Communications)

DEKORRA (TOWN)—See MADISON, WI (Charter Communications)

DELAFIELD (TOWN)—See MILWAUKEE, WI (Time Warner Cable)

DELAVAN—Charter Communications. Now served by MADISON, WI [WI0002]

DELAVAN—See MADISON, WI (Charter Communications)

DELTON—See MADISON, WI (Charter Communications)

DENMARK—See FOND DU LAC, WI (Charter Communications)

DICKEYVILLE—See LANCASTER, WI (Charter Communications)

DODGE COUNTY (portions)—Packerland Broadband. Now served by LOMIRA, WI [WI0345]

DODGE COUNTY (PORTIONS)—See LOMIRA, WI (Packerland Broadband)

DODGEVILLE—See MADISON, WI (Charter Communications)

DORCHESTER—See STEVENS POINT, WI (Charter Communications)

DOUSMAN (VILLAGE)—See MILWAUKEE, WI (Time Warner Cable)

DOVER (TOWN)—See MILWAUKEE, WI (Time Warner Cable)

DOVRE (TOWN)—See ELMWOOD (village), WI (Video services provided by Celect Communications & available through Bloomer Tel, Bruce Tel, Celect Communications, NextGen & West WI Telcom. Formerly [WI0337]. This cable system has converted to IPTV)

DOWNING—See BOYCEVILLE, WI (Nextgen Communications)

DOWNING—See ELMWOOD (village), WI (Video services provided by Celect Communications & available through Bloomer Tel, Bruce Tel, Celect Communications, NextGen & West WI Telcom. Formerly [WI0337]. This cable system has converted to IPTV)

DOWNSVILLE—See EAU CLAIRE, WI (Charter Communications)

DOYLE (TOWN)—See ELMWOOD (village), WI (Video services provided by Celect Communications & available through Bloomer Tel, Bruce Tel, Celect Communications, NextGen & West WI Telcom. Formerly [WI0337]. This cable system has converted to IPTV)

DOYLESTOWN—Formerly served by New Century Communications. No longer in operation

DRAMMEN—See ELMWOOD (village), WI (Video services provided by Celect Communications & available through Bloomer Tel, Bruce Tel, Celect Communications, NextGen & West WI Telcom. Formerly [WI0337]. This cable system has converted to IPTV)

DRESSER (village)—Charter Communications. Now served by EAU CLAIRE, WI [WI0011]

DRESSER (VILLAGE)—See EAU CLAIRE, WI (Charter Communications)

DUNKIRK—See MADISON, WI (Charter Communications)

DUNN (TOWN)—See ELMWOOD (village), WI (Video services provided by Celect Communications & available through Bloomer Tel, Bruce Tel, Celect Communications, NextGen & West WI Telcom. Formerly [WI0337]. This cable system has converted to IPTV)

DUNN—See MADISON, WI (Charter Communications)

DURAND—See ARKANSAW, WI (NTec (formerly Chippewa Valley Cable Co. Inc.))

EAGLE (TOWN)—See MILWAUKEE, WI (Time Warner Cable)

EAGLE POINT—See EAU CLAIRE, WI (Charter Communications)

EAGLE RIVER—Charter Communications. Now served by STEVENS POINT, WI [WI0019]

EAGLE RIVER—See STEVENS POINT, WI (Charter Communications)

EAST TROY (TOWN)—See MILWAUKEE, WI (Time Warner Cable)

EASTMAN (UNINCORPORATED AREAS)—See SENECA (village), WI (Dairyland Cable Systems Inc)

EAU CLAIRE (TOWN)—See ELMWOOD (village), WI (Video services provided by Celect Communications & available through Bloomer Tel, Bruce Tel, Celect Communications, NextGen & West WI Telcom. Formerly [WI0337]. This cable system has converted to IPTV)

EAU CLAIRE—Charter Communications

EAU CLAIRE—See ELMWOOD (village), WI (Video services provided by Celect Communications & available through Bloomer Tel, Bruce Tel, Celect Communications, NextGen & West WI Telcom. Formerly [WI0337]. This cable system has converted to IPTV)

EAU GALLE TWP.—See BALDWIN TWP., WI (Baldwin Telecom Inc)

EDEN (VILLAGE)—See FOND DU LAC, WI (Charter Communications)

EDGAR—See STEVENS POINT, WI (Charter Communications)

EDGERTON—See MADISON, WI (Charter Communications)

EGG HARBOR—See FOND DU LAC, WI (Charter Communications)

EILEEN (TOWN)—See EAU CLAIRE, WI (Charter Communications)

EISENSTEIN (TOWN)—See PHILLIPS, WI (Price County Telephone Co. Formerly [WI0119]. This cable system has converted to IPTV)

EISENSTEIN (VILLAGE)—See EAU CLAIRE, WI (Charter Communications)

EL PASO (TOWN)—See ELMWOOD (village), WI (Video services provided by Celect Communications & available through Bloomer Tel, Bruce Tel, Celect Communications, NextGen & West WI Telcom. Formerly [WI0337]. This cable system has converted to IPTV)

ELAND—See WITTENBERG, WI (Wittenberg Cable TV)

ELBA (TOWN)—See MADISON, WI (Charter Communications)

ELCHO (TOWN)—Packerland Broadband

ELDERDON—See WITTENBERG, WI (Wittenberg Cable TV)

ELDORADO (TOWN)—See FOND DU LAC, WI (Charter Communications)

ELEVA—See WHITEHALL, WI (Western Wisconsin Communications Cooperative)

ELK (TOWN)—See PHILLIPS, WI (Price County Telephone Co. Formerly [WI0119]. This cable system has converted to IPTV)

ELK MOUND (TOWN)—See ELMWOOD (village), WI (Video services provided by Celect Communications & available through Bloomer Tel, Bruce Tel, Celect Communications, NextGen & West WI Telcom. Formerly [WI0337]. This cable system has converted to IPTV)

ELK MOUND (VILLAGE)—See EAU CLAIRE, WI (Charter Communications)

ELKADER—See BOSCOBEL, IA (Mediacom)

ELKHART LAKE (VILLAGE)—See MILWAUKEE, WI (Time Warner Cable)

ELKHORN—See MADISON, WI (Charter Communications)

ELKHORN—See SUGAR CREEK (town), WI (Mediacom)

ELLINGTON—See STEVENS POINT, WI (Charter Communications)

ELLINGTON—See APPLETON, WI (Time Warner Cable)

ELLSWORTH—Midco

ELM GROVE (VILLAGE)—See MILWAUKEE, WI (Time Warner Cable)

ELMWOOD (VILLAGE)—Video services provided by Celect Communications & available through Bloomer Tel, Bruce Tel, Celect Communications, NextGen & West WI Telcom. Formerly [WI0337]. This cable system has converted to IPTV

ELMWOOD PARK (VILLAGE)—See MILWAUKEE, WI (Time Warner Cable)

ELROY—Community Antenna System Inc

EMBARRASS—See STEVENS POINT, WI (Charter Communications)

EMERALD TWP.—See BALDWIN TWP., WI (Baldwin Telecom Inc)

EMERY (TOWN)—See PHILLIPS, WI (Price County Telephone Co. Formerly [WI0119]. This cable system has converted to IPTV)

EMMET—See MADISON, WI (Charter Communications)

Wisconsin—Cable Community Index

EMPIRE (TOWN)—See FOND DU LAC, WI (Charter Communications)

ENDEAVOR—Formerly served by New Century Communications. No longer in operation

ENTERPRISE—Packerland Broadband

EPHRAIM—See FOND DU LAC, WI (Charter Communications)

ERIN TWP.—See BALDWIN TWP, WI (Baldwin Telecom Inc)

ERIN—See FOND DU LAC, WI (Charter Communications)

ETTRICK—See WHITEHALL, WI (Western Wisconsin Communications Cooperative)

EUREKA (TOWN)—See LUCK (village), WI (Lakeland Communications)

EVANSVILLE—See MADISON, WI (Charter Communications)

EVERGREEN VILLAGE MOBILE HOME PARK—See PLATTEVILLE, WI (CenturyLink Prism. This cable system has converted to IPTV)

EXCELSIOR—See MADISON, WI (Charter Communications)

EXELAND—See MIKANA, WI (S & K TV Systems)

EXETER (TOWN) See MADISON, WI (Charter Communications)

FAIRCHILD—See WHITEHALL, WI (Western Wisconsin Communications Cooperative)

FAIRWATER—Formerly served by CenturyTel. No longer in operation

FALL CREEK—Packerland Broadband

FALL RIVER (VILLAGE)—See RANDOLPH, WI (CenturyLink)

FALL RIVER—See MADISON, WI (Charter Communications)

FARMERSVILLE—See LOMIRA, WI (Packerland Broadband)

FARMINGTON (TOWN)—See STEVENS POINT, WI (Charter Communications)

FENNIMORE—Mediacom. Now served by PRAIRIE DU CHIEN, WI [WI0066]

FENNIMORE—See PRAIRIE DU CHIEN, WI (Mediacom)

FERRYVILLE—See STODDARD, WI (Mediacom)

FIFIELD (TOWN)—See PHILLIPS, WI (Price County Telephone Co. Formerly [WI0119]. This cable system has converted to IPTV)

FIFIELD—Packerland Broadband

FISH CREEK—See FOND DU LAC, WI (Charter Communications)

FITCHBURG—See MADISON, WI (Charter Communications)

FLAMBEAU (TOWN)—See EAU CLAIRE, WI (Charter Communications)

FLAMBEAU (TOWN)—See PHILLIPS, WI (Price County Telephone Co. Formerly [WI0119]. This cable system has converted to IPTV)

FOND DU LAC—Charter Communications

FONTANA (VILLAGE)—See MADISON, WI (Charter Communications)

FOOTVILLE—See ORFORDVILLE, WI (Mediacom)

FORESTVILLE (VILLAGE)—See NEW FRANKEN, WI (CenturyLink)

FORT ATKINSON—See MADISON, WI (Charter Communications)

FORT MCCOY—Mediacom

FORT WINNEBAGO—See RANDOLPH, WI (CenturyLink)

FORT WINNEBAGO—See MADISON, WI (Charter Communications)

FOUNTAIN CITY—Charter Communications. Now served by EAU CLAIRE, WI [WI0011]

FOUNTAIN CITY—See EAU CLAIRE, WI (Charter Communications)

FOUNTAIN PRAIRIE—See RANDOLPH, WI (CenturyLink)

FOX LAKE TWP.—See RANDOLPH, WI (CenturyLink)

FOX LAKE—See FOND DU LAC, WI (Charter Communications)

FOX POINT (VILLAGE)—See MILWAUKEE, WI (Time Warner Cable)

FRANCIS CREEK—See FOND DU LAC, WI (Charter Communications)

FRANKLIN—See MILWAUKEE, WI (Time Warner Cable)

FRANZEN (TOWN)—See AMHERST (village), WI (Tomorrow Valley Video)

FREDERIC—See LUCK (village), WI (Lakeland Communications)

FREDONIA (TOWN)—See MILWAUKEE, WI (Time Warner Cable)

FREEDOM—See APPLETON, WI (Time Warner Cable)

FREMONT—Mediacom

FRIENDSHIP (TOWN)—See FOND DU LAC, WI (Charter Communications)

FRIENDSHIP—See ADAMS, WI (Charter Communications)

FRIESLAND—See RANDOLPH, WI (CenturyLink)

FULTON TWP.—See MADISON, WI (Charter Communications)

GALESVILLE—See WHITEHALL, WI (Western Wisconsin Communications Cooperative)

GALLOWAY—See WITTENBERG, WI (Wittenberg Cable TV)

GARNAVILLO—See BOSCOBEL, IA (Mediacom)

GAYS MILLS—See VIROQUA, WI (Mediacom)

GENESEE (TOWN)—See MILWAUKEE, WI (Time Warner Cable)

GENEVA (TOWN)—See MILWAUKEE, WI (Time Warner Cable)

GENOA CITY—Charter Communications. Now served by MADISON, WI [WI0002]

GENOA CITY—See MADISON, WI (Charter Communications)

GENOA—See MADISON, IL (Charter Communications)

GEORGETOWN (TOWN)—See LUCK (village), WI (Lakeland Communications)

GERMANTOWN—See MAUSTON, WI (Mediacom)

GERMANTOWN—See MILWAUKEE, WI (Time Warner Cable)

GIBRALTAR (TOWN)—See FOND DU LAC, WI (Charter Communications)

GIBSON (TOWN)—See FOND DU LAC, WI (Charter Communications)

GILLETT—Packerland Broadband

GILMAN (TOWN)—See ELMWOOD (village), WI (Video services provided by Celect Communications & available through Bloomer Tel, Bruce Tel, Celect Communications, NextGen & West WI Telcom. Formerly [WI0337]. This cable system has converted to IPTV)

GILMAN—Formerly served by S & K TV Systems. No longer in operation

GLENBEULAH (VILLAGE)—See MILWAUKEE, WI (Time Warner Cable)

GLENDALE—See MILWAUKEE, WI (Time Warner Cable)

GLENWOOD CITY—Nextgen Communications

GLIDDEN—Packerland Broadband

GOODMAN—Packerland Broadband

GOODVIEW—See EAU CLAIRE, MN (Charter Communications)

GRAFTON (TOWN)—See MILWAUKEE, WI (Time Warner Cable)

GRAND CHUTE (TOWN)—See APPLETON, WI (Time Warner Cable)

GRAND RAPIDS—See STEVENS POINT, WI (Charter Communications)

GRAND RAPIDS—See WISCONSIN RAPIDS, WI (Solarus)

GRANT (PORTAGE COUNTY)—See STEVENS POINT, WI (Charter Communications)

GRANT (RUSK COUNTY)—See EAU CLAIRE, WI (Charter Communications)

GRANT (TOWN)—See ELMWOOD (village), WI (Video services provided by Celect Communications & available through Bloomer Tel, Bruce Tel, Celect Communications, NextGen & West WI Telcom. Formerly [WI0337]. This cable system has converted to IPTV)

GRANT COUNTY (UNINCORPORATED AREAS)—See BOSCOBEL, WI (Mediacom)

GRANT—See WISCONSIN RAPIDS, WI (Solarus)

GRANTON—See STEVENS POINT, WI (Charter Communications)

GRANTON—New Century Communications

GRANTSBURG—Grantsburg Telcom

GREEN BAY (TOWN)—See NEW FRANKEN, WI (CenturyLink)

GREEN BAY—Formerly served by Sprint Corp. No longer in operation

GREEN BAY—See APPLETON, WI (Time Warner Cable)

GREEN LAKE—See FOND DU LAC, WI (Charter Communications)

GREENBUSH (TOWN)—See MILWAUKEE, WI (Time Warner Cable)

GREENDALE (VILLAGE)—See MILWAUKEE, WI (Time Warner Cable)

GREENFIELD (LA CROSSE COUNTY)—See VIROQUA, WI (Mediacom)

GREENFIELD (Milwaukee County)—Time Warner Cable. Now served by MILWAUKEE, WI [WI0001]

GREENFIELD (TOWN)—See EAU CLAIRE, WI (Charter Communications)

GREENFIELD TWP.—See MADISON, WI (Charter Communications)

GREENFIELD—See MILWAUKEE, WI (Time Warner Cable)

GREENLEAF—Formerly served by CenturyTel. No longer in operation

GREENVILLE (TOWN)—See APPLETON, WI (Time Warner Cable)

GREENWOOD—Packerland Broadband

GRESHAM—See STEVENS POINT, WI (Charter Communications)

GUTTENBERG—See BOSCOBEL, IA (Mediacom)

HACKETT (TOWN)—See PHILLIPS, WI (Price County Telephone Co. Formerly [WI0119]. This cable system has converted to IPTV)

HALES CORNERS (VILLAGE)—See MILWAUKEE, WI (Time Warner Cable)

HALLIE (TOWN)—See ELMWOOD (village), WI (Video services provided by Celect Communications & available through Bloomer Tel, Bruce Tel, Celect Communications, NextGen & West WI Telcom. Formerly [WI0337]. This cable system has converted to IPTV)

HALLIE (VILLAGE)—See ELMWOOD (village), WI (Video services provided by Celect Communications & available through Bloomer Tel, Bruce Tel, Celect Communications, NextGen & West WI Telcom. Formerly [WI0337].

Cable Community Index—Wisconsin

This cable system has converted to IPTV)

HALLIE—See EAU CLAIRE, WI (Charter Communications)

HAMILTON TWP.—See EAU CLAIRE, WI (Charter Communications)

HAMMOND (VILLAGE)—See BALDWIN TWP., WI (Baldwin Telecom Inc)

HAMMOND TWP.—See BALDWIN TWP., WI (Baldwin Telecom Inc)

HANCOCK—See STEVENS POINT, WI (Charter Communications)

HARLEM TWP.—See MADISON, IL (Charter Communications)

HARMONY (TOWN)—See PHILLIPS, WI (Price County Telephone Co. Formerly [WI0119]. This cable system has converted to IPTV)

HARMONY—See MADISON, WI (Charter Communications)

HARPERS FERRY—See BOSCOBEL, IA (Mediacom)

HARRISON (TOWN)—See APPLETON, WI (Time Warner Cable)

HARRISON (TOWN)—See AMHERST (village), WI (Tomorrow Valley Video)

HARTFORD—See FOND DU LAC, WI (Charter Communications)

HARTLAND—See MILWAUKEE, WI (Time Warner Cable)

HARVARD—See MADISON, IL (Charter Communications)

HATLEY (VILLAGE)—See STEVENS POINT, WI (Charter Communications)

HAUGEN—See EAU CLAIRE, WI (Charter Communications)

HAWKINS (VILLAGE)—Packerland Broadband

HAY RIVER (TOWN)—See ELMWOOD (village), WI (Video services provided by Celect Communications & available through Bloomer Tel, Bruce Tel, Celect Communications, NextGen & West WI Telcom. Formerly [WI0337]. This cable system has converted to IPTV)

HAYWARD TWP.—See EAU CLAIRE, WI (Charter Communications)

HAYWARD—Charter Communications. Now served by EAU CLAIRE, WI [WI0011]

HAYWARD—See EAU CLAIRE, WI (Charter Communications)

HAZEL GREEN—See CUBA CITY, WI (Mediacom)

HAZELHURST—See STEVENS POINT, WI (Charter Communications)

HELENVILLE—See MADISON, WI (Charter Communications)

HELVETIA—See MANAWA, WI (Manawa Telecom Video)

HERMAN (TOWN)—See MILWAUKEE, WI (Time Warner Cable)

HEWITT—See AUBURNDALE, WI (Packerland Broadband)

HIGHLAND—See MADISON, WI (Charter Communications)

HILBERT (VILLAGE)—See APPLETON, WI (Time Warner Cable)

HILLSBORO—Community Antenna System Inc

HILLSDALE TWP.—See EAU CLAIRE, MN (Charter Communications)

HIXTON—See WHITEHALL, WI (Western Wisconsin Communications Cooperative)

HOBART—See APPLETON, WI (Time Warner Cable)

HOLCOMBE—S & K TV Systems

HOLLAND (TOWN)—See APPLETON, WI (Time Warner Cable)

HOLLAND (TOWN)—See MILWAUKEE, WI (Time Warner Cable)

HOLLAND TWP.—See EAU CLAIRE, WI (Charter Communications)

HOLLANDALE—Packerland Broadband

HOLMEN—See EAU CLAIRE, WI (Charter Communications)

HOMER—See EAU CLAIRE, MN (Charter Communications)

HORICON—See FOND DU LAC, WI (Charter Communications)

HORTONIA (TOWN)—See STEVENS POINT, WI (Charter Communications)

HORTONVILLE—See STEVENS POINT, WI (Charter Communications)

HOWARD (TOWN)—See ELMWOOD (village), WI (Video services provided by Celect Communications & available through Bloomer Tel, Bruce Tel, Celect Communications, NextGen & West WI Telcom. Formerly [WI0337]. This cable system has converted to IPTV)

HOWARD (VILLAGE)—See APPLETON, WI (Time Warner Cable)

HOWARDS GROVE (VILLAGE)—See MILWAUKEE, WI (Time Warner Cable)

HOWARDS GROVE—Time Warner Cable. Now served by MILWAUKEE, WI [WI0001]

HUBBARD—See FOND DU LAC, WI (Charter Communications)

HUBERTUS—See FOND DU LAC, WI (Charter Communications)

HUDSON (town)—Baldwin Telecom Inc. Now served by BALDWIN (town), WI [WI0079]

HUDSON TWP.—See BALDWIN TWP., WI (Baldwin Telecom Inc)

HULL—See STEVENS POINT, WI (Charter Communications)

HUMBIRD—See WHITEHALL, WI (Western Wisconsin Communications Cooperative)

HUSTISFORD—Charter Communications. Now served by FOND DU LAC, WI [WI0018]

HUSTISFORD—See FOND DU LAC, WI (Charter Communications)

HUSTLER—See MAUSTON, WI (Mediacom)

INDEPENDENCE—See WHITEHALL, WI (Western Wisconsin Communications Cooperative)

INDIANFORD—See MADISON, WI (Charter Communications)

INGALLSTON TWP.—See MARINETTE, MI (Time Warner Cable)

IOLA—Mediacom

IRON RIDGE—See FOND DU LAC, WI (Charter Communications)

IRONTON—Formerly served by Dairyland Cable Systems Inc. No longer in operation

IXONIA (TOWN)—See MILWAUKEE, WI (Time Warner Cable)

JACKSON—See FOND DU LAC, WI (Charter Communications)

JACKSONPORT—See FOND DU LAC, WI (Charter Communications)

JANESVILLE—Charter Communications. Now served by MADISON, WI [WI0002]

JANESVILLE—Formerly served by Wireless Cable Systems Inc. No longer in operation

JANESVILLE—See MADISON, WI (Charter Communications)

JEFFERSON—See MADISON, WI (Charter Communications)

JOHNSON CREEK—See MADISON, WI (Charter Communications)

JUNCTION CITY—Packerland Broadband

JUNEAU COUNTY (UNINCORPORATED AREAS)—See MAUSTON, WI (Mediacom)

JUNEAU—See FOND DU LAC, WI (Charter Communications)

KAUKAUNA (TOWN)—See APPLETON, WI (Time Warner Cable)

KAUKAUNA—See APPLETON, WI (Time Warner Cable)

KEKOSKEE—See LOMIRA, WI (Packerland Broadband)

KELLNERSVILLE—See FOND DU LAC, WI (Charter Communications)

KELLNERSVILLE—New Century Communications

KENDALL—Community Antenna System Inc

KENOSHA—Time Warner Cable. Now served by MILWAUKEE, WI [WI0001]

KENOSHA—See MILWAUKEE, WI (Time Warner Cable)

KEWASKUM—See FOND DU LAC, WI (Charter Communications)

KEWAUNEE—See FOND DU LAC, WI (Charter Communications)

KIEL—See FOND DU LAC, WI (Charter Communications)

KIELER—See LANCASTER, WI (Charter Communications)

KIMBERLY—See APPLETON, WI (Time Warner Cable)

KINGSTON—Formerly served by New Century Communications. No longer in operation

KINGSTON—See MADISON, IL (Charter Communications)

KINGSTON—See FOND DU LAC, WI (Charter Communications)

KNAPP (village)—Formerly served by Baldwin Telecom Inc. No longer in operation

KNAPP (VILLAGE)—See BALDWIN TWP., WI (Baldwin Telecom Inc)

KNOWLES—Packerland Broadband. Now served by LOMIRA, WI [WI0345]

KNOWLES—See LOMIRA, WI (Packerland Broadband)

KOHLER—See FOND DU LAC, WI (Charter Communications)

KOSHKONONG TWP.—See MADISON, WI (Charter Communications)

KOSSUTH (TOWN)—See FOND DU LAC, WI (Charter Communications)

KRAKOW—Packerland Broadband

KRONENWETTER—See STEVENS POINT, WI (Charter Communications)

LA CRESCENT (VILLAGE)—See EAU CLAIRE, MN (Charter Communications)

LA CRESCENT—See EAU CLAIRE, MN (Charter Communications)

LA CROSSE—Charter Communications. Now served by EAU CLAIRE, WI [WI0011]

LA CROSSE—See EAU CLAIRE, WI (Charter Communications)

LA CROSSE—See VIROQUA, WI (Mediacom)

LA FARGE—See VIROQUA, WI (Mediacom)

LA GRANGE TWP.—See EAU CLAIRE, WI (Charter Communications)

LA GRANGE TWP.—See SUGAR CREEK (town), WI (Mediacom)

LA VALLE (VILLAGE)—Packerland Broadband

LAC DU FLAMBEAU—Formerly served by Gauthier Cablevision. No longer in operation

LAC LA BELLE—See MILWAUKEE, WI (Time Warner Cable)

LADYSMITH—Charter Communications. Now served by EAU CLAIRE, WI [WI0011]

Wisconsin—Cable Community Index

LADYSMITH—See EAU CLAIRE, WI (Charter Communications)

LAFAYETTE TWP.—See SUGAR CREEK (town), WI (Mediacom)

LAFAYETTE—See EAU CLAIRE, WI (Charter Communications)

LAKE (TOWN)—See PHILLIPS, WI (Price County Telephone Co. Formerly [WI0119]. This cable system has converted to IPTV)

LAKE DELTON—See MADISON, WI (Charter Communications)

LAKE GENEVA—See MILWAUKEE, WI (Time Warner Cable)

LAKE LUCERNE—Packerland Broadband

LAKE LUCERNE—See ELCHO (town), WI (Packerland Broadband)

LAKE MILLS—See MADISON, WI (Charter Communications)

LAKE NEBAGAMON—Charter Communications. Now served by DULUTH, MN [MN0006]

LAKE TWP.—See EAU CLAIRE, WI (Charter Communications)

LAKETOWN—See LUCK (village), WI (Lakeland Communications)

LAMARTINE—See FOND DU LAC, WI (Charter Communications)

LANARK (TOWN)—See AMHERST (village), WI (Tomorrow Valley Video)

LANCASTER—Charter Communications

LAND O'LAKES—Karban TV Systems Inc

LANNON (VILLAGE)—See MILWAUKEE, WI (Time Warner Cable)

LANSING—See BOSCOBEL, IA (Mediacom)

LAONA—Packerland Broadband

LARRABEE (TOWN)—See STEVENS POINT, WI (Charter Communications)

LAWRENCE (TOWN)—See APPLETON, WI (Time Warner Cable)

LEBANON (TOWN)—See STEVENS POINT, WI (Charter Communications)

LEBANON—See MANAWA, WI (Manawa Telecom Video)

LEDGEVIEW (TOWN)—See APPLETON, WI (Time Warner Cable)

LENA—Packerland Broadband

LEON—See EAU CLAIRE, WI (Charter Communications)

LEROY—See LOMIRA, WI (Packerland Broadband)

LEWISTON—See EAU CLAIRE, MN (Charter Communications)

LEWISTON—See MADISON, WI (Charter Communications)

LIBERTY (TOWN)—See STEVENS POINT, WI (Charter Communications)

LIBERTY (TOWN)—See APPLETON, WI (Time Warner Cable)

LIBERTY GROVE (TOWN)—See FOND DU LAC, WI (Charter Communications)

LIMA (TOWN)—See FOND DU LAC, WI (Charter Communications)

LIMA (TOWN)—See MILWAUKEE, WI (Time Warner Cable)

LINCOLN (TOWN)—See STEVENS POINT, WI (Charter Communications)

LINCOLN TWP.—See WHITEHALL, WI (Western Wisconsin Communications Cooperative)

LINCOLN—See STEVENS POINT, WI (Charter Communications)

LIND (TOWN)—See STEVENS POINT, WI (Charter Communications)

LINDEN—See MADISON, WI (Charter Communications)

LINN (TOWN)—See MILWAUKEE, WI (Time Warner Cable)

LINN TWP.—See MADISON, WI (Charter Communications)

LINWOOD—See STEVENS POINT, WI (Charter Communications)

LINWOOD—See WISCONSIN RAPIDS, WI (Solarus)

LISBON (TOWN)—See FOND DU LAC, WI (Charter Communications)

LISBON (TOWN)—See MILWAUKEE, WI (Time Warner Cable)

LITTLE CHUTE—See APPLETON, WI (Time Warner Cable)

LITTLE SUAMICO—See APPLETON, WI (Time Warner Cable)

LITTLE WOLF—See MANAWA, WI (Manawa Telecom Video)

LIVINGSTON—See MADISON, WI (Charter Communications)

LODI—See MADISON, WI (Charter Communications)

LOGANVILLE (VILLAGE)—Dairyland Cable Systems Inc

LOHRVILLE—See STEVENS POINT, WI (Charter Communications)

LOMIRA—See FOND DU LAC, WI (Charter Communications)

LOMIRA—Packerland Broadband

LONE ROCK—See MADISON, WI (Charter Communications)

LOWELL—See FOND DU LAC, WI (Charter Communications)

LOWVILLE—See RANDOLPH, WI (CenturyLink)

LOYAL—See STEVENS POINT, WI (Charter Communications)

LUCAS (TOWN)—See ELMWOOD (village), WI (Video services provided by Celect Communications & available through Bloomer Tel, Bruce Tel, Celect Communications, NextGen & West WI Telcom. Formerly [WI0337]. This cable system has converted to IPTV)

LUCK (VILLAGE)—Lakeland Communications

LUCK TWP.—See LUCK (village), WI (Lakeland Communications)

LUXEMBURG (TOWN)—See NEW FRANKEN, WI (CenturyLink)

LUXEMBURG (VILLAGE)—See NEW FRANKEN, WI (CenturyLink)

LYNDON (TOWN)—See MILWAUKEE, WI (Time Warner Cable)

LYNDON STATION—See MADISON, WI (Charter Communications)

LYNXVILLE (UNINCORPORATED AREAS)—See SENECA (village), WI (Dairyland Cable Systems Inc)

LYONS (TOWN)—See MILWAUKEE, WI (Time Warner Cable)

MACHESNEY PARK—See MADISON, WI (Charter Communications)

MADISON—Charter Communications

MAINE—See STEVENS POINT, WI (Charter Communications)

MANAWA—Manawa Telecom Video

MANCHESTER TWP.—See MADISON, IL

MANITOWOC (TOWN)—See FOND DU LAC, WI (Charter Communications)

MANITOWOC—Comcast Cable. Now served by MINNEAPOLIS, MN [MN0001]

MAPLE BLUFF (VILLAGE)—See MADISON, WI (Charter Communications)

MAPLE CREEK (TOWN)—See STEVENS POINT, WI (Charter Communications)

MARATHON CITY—See STEVENS POINT, WI (Charter Communications)

MARCELLON—See RANDOLPH, WI (CenturyLink)

MARENGO—See MADISON, IL (Charter Communications)

MARIBEL—See FOND DU LAC, WI (Charter Communications)

MARINETTE—Time Warner Cable

MARION (TOWN)—See STEVENS POINT, WI (Charter Communications)

MARION—See STEVENS POINT, WI (Charter Communications)

MARKESAN—See FOND DU LAC, WI (Charter Communications)

MARQUETTE—See FOND DU LAC, WI (Charter Communications)

MARQUETTE—See BOSCOBEL, IA (Mediacom)

MARQUETTE—New Century Communications

MARSHALL (VIILLAGE)—See MADISON, WI (Charter Communications)

MARSHFIELD (PORTIONS)—See AUBURNDALE, WI (Packerland Broadband)

MARSHFIELD—Charter Communications. Now served by STEVENS POINT, WI [WI0019]

MARSHFIELD—See STEVENS POINT, WI (Charter Communications)

MARTELL (TOWN)—See ELMWOOD (village), WI (Video services provided by Celect Communications & available through Bloomer Tel, Bruce Tel, Celect Communications, NextGen & West WI Telcom. Formerly [WI0337]. This cable system has converted to IPTV)

MATTESON (TOWN)—See STEVENS POINT, WI (Charter Communications)

MATTOON (VILLAGE)—See STEVENS POINT, WI (Charter Communications)

MAUSTON—Mediacom

MAYVILLE—See FOND DU LAC, WI (Charter Communications)

MAZOMANIE TWP.—See MERRIMAC, WI (Merrimac Cable)

MAZOMANIE—Charter Communications. Now served by MADISON, WI [WI0002]

MAZOMANIE—See MADISON, WI (Charter Communications)

MCFARLAND (VILLAGE)—See MADISON, WI (Charter Communications)

MCGREGOR—See BOSCOBEL, IA (Mediacom)

MCMILLAN (TOWN)—See STEVENS POINT, WI (Charter Communications)

MEDARY TWP.—See EAU CLAIRE, WI (Charter Communications)

MEDFORD—Charter Communications. Now served by STEVENS POINT, WI [WI0019]

MEDFORD—See STEVENS POINT, WI (Charter Communications)

MEDINA—See MADISON, WI (Charter Communications)

MEDINA—See APPLETON, WI (Time Warner Cable)

MELLEN—Packerland Broadband

MELROSE—Charter Communications. Now served by EAU CLAIRE, WI [WI0011]

MELROSE—See EAU CLAIRE, WI (Charter Communications)

MELVINA—Formerly served by Midwest Cable Inc. No longer in operation

MENASHA (TOWN)—See APPLETON, WI (Time Warner Cable)

MENOMINEE (TOWN)—See MARINETTE, WI (Time Warner Cable)

MENOMINEE—See MARINETTE, MI (Time Warner Cable)

MENOMONEE FALLS (VILLAGE)—See MILWAUKEE, WI (Time Warner Cable)

MENOMONEE FALLS—Time Warner Cable. Now served by MILWAUKEE, WI [WI0001]

Cable Community Index—Wisconsin

MENOMONIE (TOWN)—See ELMWOOD (village), WI (Video services provided by Celect Communications & available through Bloomer Tel, Bruce Tel, Celect Communications, NextGen & West WI Telcom. Formerly [WI0337]. This cable system has converted to IPTV)

MENOMONIE TWP.—See EAU CLAIRE, WI (Charter Communications)

MENOMONIE—Charter Communications. Now served by EAU CLAIRE, WI [WI0011]

MENOMONIE—See EAU CLAIRE, WI (Charter Communications)

MENOMONIE—See ELMWOOD (village), WI (Video services provided by Celect Communications & available through Bloomer Tel, Bruce Tel, Celect Communications, NextGen & West WI Telcom. Formerly [WI0337]. This cable system has converted to IPTV)

MEQUON—Time Warner Cable. Now served by MILWAUKEE, WI [WI0001]

MEQUON—See MILWAUKEE, WI (Time Warner Cable)

MERCER—Karban TV Systems Inc

MERILLAN—See WHITEHALL, WI (Western Wisconsin Communications Cooperative)

MERRILL—Charter Communications. Now served by STEVENS POINT, WI [WI0019]

MERRILL—See STEVENS POINT, WI (Charter Communications)

MERRIMAC (TOWN)—See MERRIMAC, WI (Merrimac Cable)

MERRIMAC—Merrimac Cable

MERTON (TOWN)—See MILWAUKEE, WI (Time Warner Cable)

MIDDLETON TWP.—See MADISON, WI (Charter Communications)

MIKANA—S & K TV Systems

MILFORD TWP.—See MADISON, WI (Charter Communications)

MILLADORE (TOWN)—New Century Communications

MILLADORE—See STEVENS POINT, WI (Charter Communications)

MILLTOWN (VILLAGE)—See LUCK (village), WI (Lakeland Communications)

MILLTOWN TWP.—See LUCK (village), WI (Lakeland Communications)

MILTON TWP.—See MADISON, WI (Charter Communications)

MILWAUKEE—Time Warner Cable

MINDORO (TOWN)—See EAU CLAIRE, WI (Charter Communications)

MINDORO—Charter Communications. Now served by EAU CLAIRE, WI [WI0011]

MINERAL POINT—See MADISON, WI (Charter Communications)

MINNESOTA CITY—See EAU CLAIRE, MN (Charter Communications)

MINOCQUA—Charter Communications. Now served by STEVENS POINT, WI [WI0019]

MINOCQUA—See STEVENS POINT, WI (Charter Communications)

MINONG—S & K TV Systems

MISHICOT—See FOND DU LAC, WI (Charter Communications)

MONDOVI—See ARKANSAW, WI (NTec (formerly Chippewa Valley Cable Co. Inc.))

MONICO—See STEVENS POINT, WI (Charter Communications)

MONONA—See MADISON, WI (Charter Communications)

MONROE—See MADISON, WI (Charter Communications)

MONTELLO—Charter Communications

MONTFORT—See MADISON, WI (Charter Communications)

MONTICELLO—Mediacom

MONTROSE—See MADISON, WI (Charter Communications)

MOSEL (TOWN)—See MILWAUKEE, WI (Time Warner Cable)

MOSINEE—See STEVENS POINT, WI (Charter Communications)

MOUNT CALVARY—See FOND DU LAC, WI (Charter Communications)

MOUNT HOREB—See MADISON, WI (Charter Communications)

MOUNT PLEASANT (TOWN)—See MILWAUKEE, WI (Time Warner Cable)

MOUNT STERLING (UNINCORPORATED AREAS)—See SENECA (village), WI (Dairyland Cable Systems Inc)

MUKWA (TOWN)—See STEVENS POINT, WI (Charter Communications)

MUKWONAGO (VILLAGE)—See MILWAUKEE, WI (Time Warner Cable)

MURRY (TOWN)—See ELMWOOD (village), WI (Video services provided by Celect Communications & available through Bloomer Tel, Bruce Tel, Celect Communications, NextGen & West WI Telcom. Formerly [WI0337]. This cable system has converted to IPTV)

MUSCODA TWP.—See PRAIRIE DU CHIEN, WI (Mediacom)

MUSCODA—See PRAIRIE DU CHIEN, WI (Mediacom)

MUSKEGO—Time Warner Cable. Now served by MILWAUKEE, WI [WI0001]

MUSKEGO—See MILWAUKEE, WI (Time Warner Cable)

NASAWAPI—See FOND DU LAC, WI (Charter Communications)

NASHOTA (VILLAGE)—See MILWAUKEE, WI (Time Warner Cable)

NECEDAH—See MAUSTON, WI (Mediacom)

NEENAH (TOWN)—See APPLETON, WI (Time Warner Cable)

NEILLSVILLE—See STEVENS POINT, WI (Charter Communications)

NEKIMI (TOWN)—See FOND DU LAC, WI (Charter Communications)

NEKOOSA—See STEVENS POINT, WI (Charter Communications)

NEKOOSA—See WISCONSIN RAPIDS, WI (Solarus)

NELSON—See ALMA, WI (Midco)

NELSONVILLE (VILLAGE)—See AMHERST (village), WI (Tomorrow Valley Video)

NEOSHO—See FOND DU LAC, WI (Charter Communications)

NESHKORO—See STEVENS POINT, WI (Charter Communications)

NEW AUBURN (VILLAGE)—See ELMWOOD (village), WI (Video services provided by Celect Communications & available through Bloomer Tel, Bruce Tel, Celect Communications, NextGen & West WI Telcom. Formerly [WI0337]. This cable system has converted to IPTV)

NEW AUBURN—See EAU CLAIRE, WI (Charter Communications)

NEW BERLIN—Time Warner Cable. Now served by MILWAUKEE, WI [WI0001]

NEW BERLIN—See MILWAUKEE, WI (Time Warner Cable)

NEW FRANKEN—CenturyLink

NEW GLARUS—See MADISON, WI (Charter Communications)

NEW HOLSTEIN—See FOND DU LAC, WI (Charter Communications)

NEW HOPE (TOWN)—See AMHERST (village), WI (Tomorrow Valley Video)

NEW LISBON—See MAUSTON, WI (Mediacom)

NEW LONDON—See STEVENS POINT, WI (Charter Communications)

NEW RICHMOND—Northwest Community Communications

NEWBOLD—See STEVENS POINT, WI (Charter Communications)

NEWBURG (VILLAGE)—See MILWAUKEE, WI (Time Warner Cable)

NEWBURG—Tiime Warner Cable. Now served by MILWAUKEE, WI [WI0001]

NIAGARA—Formerly served by Niagara Community TV Co-op. No longer in operation

NICHOLS—Packerland Broadband

NOKOMIS—See STEVENS POINT, WI (Charter Communications)

NORTH BAY (VILLAGE)—See MILWAUKEE, WI (Time Warner Cable)

NORTH FOND DU LAC—See FOND DU LAC, WI (Charter Communications)

NORTH FREEDOM—Charter Communications. Now served by MADISON, WI [WI0002]

NORTH FREEDOM—See MADISON, WI (Charter Communications)

NORTH PRAIRIE (VILLAGE)—See MILWAUKEE, WI (Time Warner Cable)

NORTH PRAIRIE—Time Warner Cable. Now served by MILWAUKEE, WI [WI0001]

NORTHFIELD—See WHITEHALL, WI (Western Wisconsin Communications Cooperative)

NORWALK—Mediacom. Now served by MAUSTON, WI [WI0084]

NORWALK—See MAUSTON, WI (Mediacom)

NORWAY—See MILWAUKEE, WI (Time Warner Cable)

OAK CREEK—See MILWAUKEE, WI (Time Warner Cable)

OAK GROVE—See FOND DU LAC, WI (Charter Communications)

OAKDALE—See EAU CLAIRE, WI (Charter Communications)

OAKFIELD—See FOND DU LAC, WI (Charter Communications)

OAKLAND TWP.—See MADISON, WI (Charter Communications)

OCONOMOWOC (TOWN)—See MILWAUKEE, WI (Time Warner Cable)

OCONOMOWOC LAKE (VILLAGE)—See MILWAUKEE, WI (Time Warner Cable)

OCONOMOWOC LAKE—Time Warner Cable. Now served by MILWAUKEE, WI [WI0001]

OCONOMOWOC—See MADISON, WI (Charter Communications)

OCONTO COUNTY (PORTIONS)—See APPLETON, WI (Time Warner Cable)

OCONTO FALLS—Formerly served by Oconto Falls Cable TV. Now served by Packerland Broadband, OCONTO FALLS, WI [WI0349]

OCONTO FALLS—Packerland Broadband

OCONTO—Formerly served by Charter Communications. No longer in operation

OGDENSBURG—See MANAWA, WI (Manawa Telecom Video)

OMRO—See FOND DU LAC, WI (Charter Communications)

ONALASKA—Charter Communications. Now served by EAU CLAIRE, WI [WI0011]

ONALASKA—See EAU CLAIRE, WI (Charter Communications)

ONEIDA COUNTY (PORTIONS)—See ELCHO (town), WI (Packerland Broadband)

Wisconsin—Cable Community Index

ONEIDA—See APPLETON, WI (Time Warner Cable)

ONTARIO—Mediacom. Now served by MAUSTON, WI [WI0084]

ONTARIO—See MAUSTON, WI (Mediacom)

OOSTBURG (VILLAGE)—See MILWAUKEE, WI (Time Warner Cable)

OREGON (VILLAGE)—See MADISON, WI (Charter Communications)

ORFORDVILLE—Mediacom

OSBORN—See APPLETON, WI (Time Warner Cable)

OSCEOLA (TOWN)—See EAU CLAIRE, WI (Charter Communications)

OSHKOSH—See FOND DU LAC, WI (Charter Communications)

OSHKOSH—See APPLETON, WI (Time Warner Cable)

OSSEO—See WHITEHALL, WI (Western Wisconsin Communications Cooperative)

OTSEGO—See RANDOLPH, WI (CenturyLink)

OTTAWA (TOWN)—See MILWAUKEE, WI (Time Warner Cable)

OTTER CREEK (TOWN)—See ELMWOOD (village), WI (Video services provided by Celect Communications & available through Bloomer Tel, Bruce Tel, Celect Communications, NextGen & West WI Telcom. Formerly [WI0337]. This cable system has converted to IPTV)

OWEN—See STEVENS POINT, WI (Charter Communications)

OXFORD—New Century Communications

PACIFIC—See RANDOLPH, WI (CenturyLink)

PACIFIC—See MADISON, WI (Charter Communications)

PACKWAUKEE—New Century Communications

PADDOCK LAKE (VILLAGE)—See MILWAUKEE, WI (Time Warner Cable)

PALMYRA—See MADISON, WI (Charter Communications)

PARDEEVILLE (VILLAGE)—See RANDOLPH, WI (CenturyLink)

PARDEEVILLE—See MADISON, WI (Charter Communications)

PARK FALLS—Charter Communications. Now served by EAU CLAIRE, WI [WI0011]

PARK FALLS—See EAU CLAIRE, WI (Charter Communications)

PARK FALLS—See PHILLIPS, WI (Price County Telephone Co. Formerly [WI0119]. This cable system has converted to IPTV)

PARK RIDGE (VILLAGE)—See STEVENS POINT, WI (Charter Communications)

PATCH GROVE—See LANCASTER, WI (Charter Communications)

PELICAN—See STEVENS POINT, WI (Charter Communications)

PEMBINE—Packerland Broadband

PEPIN—Midcontinent Communications. Now served by ALMA, WI [WI0234]

PEPIN—See ALMA, WI (Midco)

PERU (TOWN)—See ELMWOOD (village), WI (Video services provided by Celect Communications & available through Bloomer Tel, Bruce Tel, Celect Communications, NextGen & West WI Telcom. Formerly [WI0337]. This cable system has converted to IPTV)

PESHTIGO (TOWN)—See MARINETTE, WI (Time Warner Cable)

PEWAUKEE (TOWN)—See MILWAUKEE, WI (Time Warner Cable)

PHELPS—See STEVENS POINT, WI (Charter Communications)

PHELPS—Upper Peninsula Communications

PHILLIPS—Price County Telephone Co. This cable system has converted to IPTV. See PHILLPS, WI [WI5049]

PHILLIPS—Price County Telephone Co. Formerly [WI0119]. This cable system has converted to IPTV

PIERCE—See FOND DU LAC, WI (Charter Communications)

PIGEON FALLS—See WHITEHALL, WI (Western Wisconsin Communications Cooperative)

PIGEON—See WHITEHALL, WI (Western Wisconsin Communications Cooperative)

PINE LAKE—See STEVENS POINT, WI (Charter Communications)

PITTSFIELD—See APPLETON, WI (Time Warner Cable)

PITTSVILLE—Packerland Broadband

PLAIN—See MADISON, WI (Charter Communications)

PLAINFIELD—See STEVENS POINT, WI (Charter Communications)

PLATTEVILLE TWP.—See PLATTEVILLE, WI (CenturyLink Prism. This cable system has converted to IPTV)

PLATTEVILLE—CenturyLink Prism. This cable system has converted to IPTV. See PLATTEVILLE, WI [WI5387]

PLATTEVILLE—Formerly served by Mediacom. No longer in operation

PLATTEVILLE—CenturyLink Prism. This cable system has converted to IPTV

PLEASANT PRAIRIE (VILLAGE)—See MILWAUKEE, WI (Time Warner Cable)

PLEASANT SPRINGS TWP.—See MADISON, WI (Charter Communications)

PLOVER (TOWN)—See WISCONSIN RAPIDS, WI (Solarus)

PLOVER (VILLAGE)—See STEVENS POINT, WI (Charter Communications)

PLOVER—See STEVENS POINT, WI (Charter Communications)

PLUM CITY—See ARKANSAW, WI (NTec (formerly Chippewa Valley Cable Co. Inc.))

PLYMOUTH (TOWN)—See MADISON, WI (Charter Communications)

PLYMOUTH—Time Warner Cable. Now served by MILWAUKEE, WI [WI0001]

PLYMOUTH—See MILWAUKEE, WI (Time Warner Cable)

POLK COUNTY (PORTIONS)—See AMERY, WI (Northwest Community Communications)

POLK—See FOND DU LAC, WI (Charter Communications)

PORT EDWARDS (VILLAGE)—See STEVENS POINT, WI (Charter Communications)

PORT EDWARDS—See STEVENS POINT, WI (Charter Communications)

PORT EDWARDS—See WISCONSIN RAPIDS, WI (Solarus)

PORT WASHINGTON—See MILWAUKEE, WI (Time Warner Cable)

PORTAGE—See MADISON, WI (Charter Communications)

PORTERFIELD—See MARINETTE, WI (Time Warner Cable)

PORTLAND TWP.—See MADISON, WI (Charter Communications)

POTOSI—See CUBA CITY, WI (Mediacom)

POTTER—See STEVENS POINT, WI (Charter Communications)

POYNETTE—See MADISON, WI (Charter Communications)

PRAIRIE DU CHIEN—Mediacom

PRAIRIE DU SAC (TOWN)—See MADISON, WI (Charter Communications)

PRAIRIE DU SAC (VILLAGE)—See MERRIMAC, WI (Merrimac Cable)

PRAIRIE DU SAC TWP.—See MERRIMAC, WI (Merrimac Cable)

PRAIRIE FARM—See SAND CREEK, WI (Mosaic Telecom)

PRAIRIE LAKE (TOWN)—See ELMWOOD (village), WI (Video services provided by Celect Communications & available through Bloomer Tel, Bruce Tel, Celect Communications, NextGen & West WI Telcom. Formerly [WI0337]. This cable system has converted to IPTV)

PRAIRIE LAKE—See EAU CLAIRE, WI (Charter Communications)

PRENTICE (TOWN)—See PHILLIPS, WI (Price County Telephone Co. Formerly [WI0119]. This cable system has converted to IPTV)

PRENTICE (VILLAGE)—See PHILLIPS, WI (Price County Telephone Co. Formerly [WI0119]. This cable system has converted to IPTV)

PRENTICE—Packerland Broadband

PRESTON—See ADAMS, WI (Charter Communications)

PRINCETON—See FOND DU LAC, WI (Charter Communications)

PULASKI—Nsight. This cable system has converted to IPTV. See PULASKI, WI [WI5377]

PULASKI—Nsight. Formerly [WI0114]. This cable system has converted to IPTV

RACINE—See MILWAUKEE, WI (Time Warner Cable)

RADISSON—S & K TV Systems. Now served by MIKANA, WI [WI0265]

RADISSON—See MIKANA, WI (S & K TV Systems)

RANDALL (TOWN)—See MILWAUKEE, WI (Time Warner Cable)

RANDOLPH—CenturyLink

RANDOLPH—See FOND DU LAC, WI (Charter Communications)

RANDOM LAKE (village)—Time Warner Cable. Now served by MILWAUKEE, WI [WI0001]

RANDOM LAKE (VILLAGE)—See MILWAUKEE, WI (Time Warner Cable)

RANTOUL (TOWN)—See STEVENS POINT, WI (Charter Communications)

RAYMOND—See MILWAUKEE, WI (Time Warner Cable)

READSTOWN—See VIROQUA, WI (Mediacom)

RED CEDAR (TOWN)—See ELMWOOD (village), WI (Video services provided by Celect Communications & available through Bloomer Tel, Bruce Tel, Celect Communications, NextGen & West WI Telcom. Formerly [WI0337]. This cable system has converted to IPTV)

RED CEDAR TWP.—See EAU CLAIRE, WI (Charter Communications)

RED CLIFF RESERVATION—See EAU CLAIRE, WI (Charter Communications)

RED RIVER (TOWN)—See NEW FRANKEN, WI (CenturyLink)

REDGRANITE—See STEVENS POINT, WI (Charter Communications)

REEDSBURG—See MADISON, WI (Charter Communications)

REEDSVILLE—See APPLETON, WI (Time Warner Cable)

REESEVILLE—See FOND DU LAC, WI (Charter Communications)

REID—See WITTENBERG, WI (Wittenberg Cable TV)

Cable Community Index—Wisconsin

RHINE (TOWN)—See MILWAUKEE, WI (Time Warner Cable)

RHINELANDER—Charter Communications. Now served by STEVENS POINT, WI [WI0019]

RHINELANDER—See STEVENS POINT, WI (Charter Communications)

RIB LAKE—Formerly served by Citizens Communications. No longer in operation

RIB MOUNTAIN—See STEVENS POINT, WI (Charter Communications)

RICE LAKE (TOWN)—See ELMWOOD (village), WI (Video services provided by Celect Communications & available through Bloomer Tel, Bruce Tel, Celect Communications, NextGen & West WI Telcom. Formerly [WI0337]. This cable system has converted to IPTV)

RICE LAKE—Charter Communications. Now served by EAU CLAIRE, WI [WI0011]

RICE LAKE—See EAU CLAIRE, WI (Charter Communications)

RICHFIELD—See FOND DU LAC, WI (Charter Communications)

RICHLAND CENTER—See MADISON, WI (Charter Communications)

RICHLAND CENTER—Richland Center Cable TV

RICHMOND (TOWN)—See STEVENS POINT, WI (Charter Communications)

RICHMOND (VILLAGE)—See MADISON, IL (Charter Communications)

RIDGELAND—See SAND CREEK, WI (Mosaic Telecom)

RIDGEWAY—See MADISON, WI (Charter Communications)

RILEY—See MADISON, IL (Charter Communications)

RINGLE (TOWN)—See STEVENS POINT, WI (Charter Communications)

RIO (VILLAGE)—See RANDOLPH, WI (CenturyLink)

RIPON—See FOND DU LAC, WI (Charter Communications)

RIVER HILLS (VILLAGE)—See MILWAUKEE, WI (Time Warner Cable)

ROBERTS (VILLAGE)—See BALDWIN TWP., WI (Baldwin Telecom Inc)

ROCHESTER (VILLAGE)—See MILWAUKEE, WI (Time Warner Cable)

ROCK CREEK (TOWN)—See ELMWOOD (village), WI (Video services provided by Celect Communications & available through Bloomer Tel, Bruce Tel, Celect Communications, NextGen & West WI Telcom. Formerly [WI0337]. This cable system has converted to IPTV)

ROCK ELM (TOWN)—See ELMWOOD (village), WI (Video services provided by Celect Communications & available through Bloomer Tel, Bruce Tel, Celect Communications, NextGen & West WI Telcom. Formerly [WI0337]. This cable system has converted to IPTV)

ROCK SPRINGS—See MADISON, WI (Charter Communications)

ROCK—See MADISON, WI (Charter Communications)

ROCKLAND (TOWN)—See APPLETON, WI (Time Warner Cable)

ROCKLAND—See EAU CLAIRE, WI (Charter Communications)

ROCKTON (VILLAGE)—See MADISON, IL (Charter Communications)

ROCKTON TWP.—See MADISON, IL (Charter Communications)

ROLLING (TOWN)—See STEVENS POINT, WI (Charter Communications)

ROLLINGSTONE—See EAU CLAIRE, MN (Charter Communications)

ROME TWP.—See WISCONSIN RAPIDS, WI (Solarus)

ROSCOE TWP.—See MADISON, IL (Charter Communications)

ROSENDALE—See FOND DU LAC, WI (Charter Communications)

ROSHOLT (VILLAGE)—See AMHERST (village), WI (Tomorrow Valley Video)

ROSHOLT—Formerly served by New Century Communications. No longer in operation

ROTHSCHILD—See STEVENS POINT, WI (Charter Communications)

ROXBURY TWP.—See MERRIMAC, WI (Merrimac Cable)

ROXBURY—See MADISON, WI (Charter Communications)

ROYALTON (TOWN)—See STEVENS POINT, WI (Charter Communications)

ROYALTON TWP.—See MANAWA, WI (Manawa Telecom Video)

ROZELLVILLE—Formerly served by New Century Communications. No longer in operation

RUBICON—See FOND DU LAC, WI (Charter Communications)

RUDOLPH (TOWN)—See STEVENS POINT, WI (Charter Communications)

RUDOLPH (TOWN)—See WISCONSIN RAPIDS, WI (Solarus)

RUDOLPH (VILLAGE)—See WISCONSIN RAPIDS, WI (Solarus)

RUDOLPH—Charter Communications. Now served by STEVENS POINT, WI [WI0019]

RUDOLPH—See STEVENS POINT, WI (Charter Communications)

RUSK (TOWN)—See ELMWOOD (village), WI (Video services provided by Celect Communications & available through Bloomer Tel, Celect Communications, NextGen & West WI Telcom. Formerly [WI0337]. This cable system has converted to IPTV)

RUTLAND—See MADISON, WI (Charter Communications)

SABIN—Formerly served by Richland-Grant Telephone Co-op. No longer in operation

SALEM (TOWN)—See MILWAUKEE, WI (Time Warner Cable)

SAMPSON (TOWN)—See ELMWOOD (village), WI (Video services provided by Celect Communications & available through Bloomer Tel, Bruce Tel, Celect Communications, NextGen & West WI Telcom. Formerly [WI0337]. This cable system has converted to IPTV)

SAND CREEK—Mosaic Telecom

SAND LAKE TWP.—See EAU CLAIRE, WI (Charter Communications)

SARATOGA—See STEVENS POINT, WI (Charter Communications)

SARATOGA—See WISCONSIN RAPIDS, WI (Solarus)

SAUK CITY—See MADISON, WI (Charter Communications)

SAUK CITY—See MERRIMAC, WI (Merrimac Cable)

SAUKVILLE (VILLAGE)—See MILWAUKEE, WI (Time Warner Cable)

SAXEVILLE—New Century Communications

SCANDINAVIA—See IOLA, WI (Mediacom)

SCHLESWIG (TOWN)—See FOND DU LAC, WI (Charter Communications)

SCHOFIELD—See STEVENS POINT, WI (Charter Communications)

SCOTT (TOWN)—See NEW FRANKEN, WI (CenturyLink)

SCOTT (TOWN)—See MILWAUKEE, WI (Time Warner Cable)

SENECA (VILLAGE)—Dairyland Cable Systems Inc

SENECA—See STEVENS POINT, WI (Charter Communications)

SENECA—See WISCONSIN RAPIDS, WI (Solarus)

SEVASTAPOL—See FOND DU LAC, WI (Charter Communications)

SEYMOUR—See APPLETON, WI (Time Warner Cable)

SHARON (TOWN)—See AMHERST (village), WI (Tomorrow Valley Video)

SHARON (VILLAGE)—See MADISON, WI (Charter Communications)

SHARON—Charter Communications. Now served by MADISON, WI [WI0002]

SHAWANO—See STEVENS POINT, WI (Charter Communications)

SHEBOYGAN FALLS—See FOND DU LAC, WI (Charter Communications)

SHEBOYGAN—Charter Communications. Now served by FOND DU LAC, WI [WI0018]

SHEBOYGAN—See FOND DU LAC, WI (Charter Communications)

SHELBY—See EAU CLAIRE, WI (Charter Communications)

SHELBY—See VIROQUA, WI (Mediacom)

SHELL LAKE—See EAU CLAIRE, WI (Charter Communications)

SHERMAN (TOWN)—See MILWAUKEE, WI (Time Warner Cable)

SHERMAN (TOWN)—See ELMWOOD (village), WI (Video services provided by Celect Communications & available through Bloomer Tel, Bruce Tel, Celect Communications, NextGen & West WI Telcom. Formerly [WI0337]. This cable system has converted to IPTV)

SHERRY—See STEVENS POINT, WI (Charter Communications)

SHERRY—See WISCONSIN RAPIDS, WI (Solarus)

SHERWOOD (VILLAGE)—See APPLETON, WI (Time Warner Cable)

SHIOCTIN—See STEVENS POINT, WI (Charter Communications)

SHOREWOOD (VILLAGE)—See MILWAUKEE, WI (Time Warner Cable)

SHOREWOOD HILLS (VILLAGE)—See MADISON, WI (Charter Communications)

SHULLSBURG—See CUBA CITY, WI (Mediacom)

SIGEL—See WISCONSIN RAPIDS, WI (Solarus)

SILVER LAKE (VILLAGE)—See MILWAUKEE, WI (Time Warner Cable)

SIOUX CREEK (TOWN)—See ELMWOOD (village), WI (Video services provided by Celect Communications & available through Bloomer Tel, Bruce Tel, Celect Communications, NextGen & West WI Telcom. Formerly [WI0337]. This cable system has converted to IPTV)

SIREN—Siren Communications

SISTER BAY—Charter Communications. Now served by FOND DU LAC, WI [WI0018]

SISTER BAY—See FOND DU LAC, WI (Charter Communications)

SLINGER—See FOND DU LAC, WI (Charter Communications)

SOLDIER'S GROVE—See VIROQUA, WI (Mediacom)

SOLON SPRINGS—Northwest Community Communications

SOMERS (TOWN)—See MILWAUKEE, WI (Time Warner Cable)

Wisconsin—Cable Community Index

SOMERSET (village)—Northwest Community Communications. Now served by NEW RICHMOND, WI [WI0077]

SOMERSET (VILLAGE)—See NEW RICHMOND, WI (Northwest Community Communications)

SOUTH BELOIT—See MADISON, IL (Charter Communications)

SOUTH BYRON—See LOMIRA, WI (Packerland Broadband)

SOUTH MILWAUKEE—See MILWAUKEE, WI (Time Warner Cable)

SPARTA—Charter Communications. Now served by EAU CLAIRE, WI [WI0011]

SPARTA—See EAU CLAIRE, WI (Charter Communications)

SPENCER—Charter Communications. Now served by STEVENS POINT, WI [WI0019]

SPENCER—See STEVENS POINT, WI (Charter Communications)

SPOONER—Charter Communications. Now served by EAU CLAIRE, WI [WI0011]

SPOONER—See EAU CLAIRE, WI (Charter Communications)

SPRING GREEN—See MADISON, WI (Charter Communications)

SPRING LAKE (TOWN)—See ELMWOOD (village), WI (Video services provided by Celect Communications & available through Bloomer Tel, Bruce Tel, Celect Communications, NextGen & West WI Telcom. Formerly [WI0337]. This cable system has converted to IPTV)

SPRING PRAIRIE (TOWN)—See MILWAUKEE, WI (Time Warner Cable)

SPRING VALLEY (VILLAGE)—See ELMWOOD (village), WI (Video services provided by Celect Communications & available through Bloomer Tel, Bruce Tel, Celect Communications, NextGen & West WI Telcom. Formerly [WI0337]. This cable system has converted to IPTV)

SPRING VALLEY—Celect Communications. This cable system has converted to IPTV. Now served by ELMWOOD (village), WI [WI5045]

SPRINGBROOK (TOWN)—See ELMWOOD (village), WI (Video services provided by Celect Communications & available through Bloomer Tel, Bruce Tel, Celect Communications, NextGen & West WI Telcom. Formerly [WI0337]. This cable system has converted to IPTV)

SPRINGFIELD (TOWN)—See MADISON, WI (Charter Communications)

SPRINGFIELD (TOWN)—See ELMWOOD (village), WI (Video services provided by Celect Communications & available through Bloomer Tel, Bruce Tel, Celect Communications, NextGen & West WI Telcom. Formerly [WI0337]. This cable system has converted to IPTV)

SPRINGVALE—See RANDOLPH, WI (CenturyLink)

ST. CLOUD—See FOND DU LAC, WI (Charter Communications)

ST. CROIX FALLS (TOWN)—See LUCK (village), WI (Lakeland Communications)

ST. CROIX FALLS (VILLAGE)—See LUCK (village), WI (Lakeland Communications)

ST. CROIX FALLS—See EAU CLAIRE, WI (Charter Communications)

ST. FRANCIS—See MILWAUKEE, WI (Time Warner Cable)

ST. JOSEPH TWP.—Formerly served by Tele-Communications Cable Co. No longer in operation

ST. JOSEPH—See NEW RICHMOND, WI (Northwest Community Communications)

ST. LAWRENCE—See MANAWA, WI (Manawa Telecom Video)

ST. NAZIANZ—See APPLETON, WI (Time Warner Cable)

STANLEY (TOWN)—See ELMWOOD (village), WI (Video services provided by Celect Communications & available through Bloomer Tel, Bruce Tel, Celect Communications, NextGen & West WI Telcom. Formerly [WI0337]. This cable system has converted to IPTV)

STANLEY—See EAU CLAIRE, WI (Charter Communications)

STANTON (TOWN)—See ELMWOOD (village), WI (Video services provided by Celect Communications & available through Bloomer Tel, Bruce Tel, Celect Communications, NextGen & West WI Telcom. Formerly [WI0337]. This cable system has converted to IPTV)

STAR PRAIRIE (TOWN)—See NEW RICHMOND, WI (Northwest Community Communications)

STAR PRAIRIE (VILLAGE)—See NEW RICHMOND, WI (Northwest Community Communications)

STELLA—See STEVENS POINT, WI (Charter Communications)

STERLING (TOWN)—See LUCK (village), WI (Lakeland Communications)

STETSONVILLE—Charter Communications. Now served by STEVENS POINT, WI [WI0019]

STETSONVILLE—See STEVENS POINT, WI (Charter Communications)

STETTIN—See STEVENS POINT, WI (Charter Communications)

STEUBEN—Formerly served by Steuben Community TV System. No longer in operation

STEVENS POINT—Charter Communications

STILES (TOWN)—See APPLETON, WI (Time Warner Cable)

STOCKBRIDGE (TOWN)—See APPLETON, WI (Time Warner Cable)

STOCKBRIDGE (VILLAGE)—See APPLETON, WI (Time Warner Cable)

STOCKTON (TOWN)—See STEVENS POINT, WI (Charter Communications)

STOCKTON (TOWN)—See AMHERST (village), WI (Tomorrow Valley Video)

STOCKTON—See EAU CLAIRE, MN (Charter Communications)

STODDARD—Mediacom

STONE LAKE TWP.—See EAU CLAIRE, WI (Charter Communications)

STOUGHTON—See MADISON, WI (Charter Communications)

STRATFORD—See STEVENS POINT, WI (Charter Communications)

STRICKLAND (TOWN)—See ELMWOOD (village), WI (Video services provided by Celect Communications & available through Bloomer Tel, Bruce Tel, Celect Communications, NextGen & West WI Telcom. Formerly [WI0337]. This cable system has converted to IPTV)

STRUM—See WHITEHALL, WI (Western Wisconsin Communications Cooperative)

STUBBS (TOWN)—See ELMWOOD (village), WI (Video services provided by Celect Communications & available through Bloomer Tel, Bruce Tel, Celect Communications, NextGen & West WI Telcom. Formerly [WI0337]. This cable system has converted to IPTV)

STURGEON BAY—Charter Communications. Now served by FOND DU LAC, WI [WI0018]

STURGEON BAY—See FOND DU LAC, WI (Charter Communications)

STURTEVANT (VILLAGE)—See MILWAUKEE, WI (Time Warner Cable)

SUAMICO—See APPLETON, WI (Time Warner Cable)

SUGAR CAMP—See STEVENS POINT, WI (Charter Communications)

SUGAR CREEK (TOWN)—Mediacom

SULLIVAN (TOWN)—See MILWAUKEE, WI (Time Warner Cable)

SULLIVAN—See MADISON, WI (Charter Communications)

SUMMIT (TOWN)—See MILWAUKEE, WI (Time Warner Cable)

SUMNER (TOWN)—See ELMWOOD (village), WI (Video services provided by Celect Communications & available through Bloomer Tel, Bruce Tel, Celect Communications, NextGen & West WI Telcom. Formerly [WI0337]. This cable system has converted to IPTV)

SUMNER TWP.—See MADISON, WI (Charter Communications)

SUMPTER (TOWN)—See MERRIMAC, WI (Merrimac Cable)

SUN PRAIRIE TWP.—See MADISON, WI (Charter Communications)

SURING—Packerland Broadband

SUSSEX (VILLAGE)—See MILWAUKEE, WI (Time Warner Cable)

TAINTER (TOWN)—See ELMWOOD (village), WI (Video services provided by Celect Communications & available through Bloomer Tel, Bruce Tel, Celect Communications, NextGen & West WI Telcom. Formerly [WI0337]. This cable system has converted to IPTV)

TAINTER TWP.—See EAU CLAIRE, WI (Charter Communications)

TAYCHEEDAH (TOWN)—See FOND DU LAC, WI (Charter Communications)

TAYLOR—See WHITEHALL, WI (Western Wisconsin Communications Cooperative)

TENNYSON—See CUBA CITY, WI (Mediacom)

TEXAS (TOWN)—See STEVENS POINT, WI (Charter Communications)

THERESA—See FOND DU LAC, WI (Charter Communications)

THIENSVILLE—See MILWAUKEE, WI (Time Warner Cable)

THORNAPPLE (TOWN)—See ELMWOOD (village), WI (Video services provided by Celect Communications & available through Bloomer Tel, Bruce Tel, Celect Communications, NextGen & West WI Telcom. Formerly [WI0337]. This cable system has converted to IPTV)

THORP—CenturyLink

THREE LAKES—Karban TV Systems Inc

TIFFANY (TOWN)—See ELMWOOD (village), WI (Video services provided by Celect Communications & available through Bloomer Tel, Bruce Tel, Celect Communications, NextGen & West WI Telcom. Formerly [WI0337]. This cable system has converted to IPTV)

TIGERTON—Wittenberg Cable TV. Now served by WITTENBERG, WI [WI0158]

TIGERTON—See WITTENBERG, WI (Wittenberg Cable TV)

TILDEN (TOWN)—See ELMWOOD (village), WI (Video services provided by Celect Communications & available through Bloomer Tel, Bruce Tel, Celect Communications, NextGen & West WI Telcom. Formerly [WI0337]. This

Cable Community Index—Wisconsin

cable system has converted to IPTV)

TILDEN—See EAU CLAIRE, WI (Charter Communications)

TOMAH—Charter Communications. Now served by EAU CLAIRE, WI [WI0011]

TOMAH—See EAU CLAIRE, WI (Charter Communications)

TOMAHAWK—See STEVENS POINT, WI (Charter Communications)

TONY (VILLAGE)—See EAU CLAIRE, WI (Charter Communications)

TRADE LAKE (TOWN)—See LUCK (village), WI (Lakeland Communications)

TREGO—See MINONG, WI (S & K TV Systems)

TREMPEALEAU COUNTY—See WHITEHALL, WI (Western Wisconsin Communications Cooperative)

TRENTON (TOWN)—See FOND DU LAC, WI (Charter Communications)

TROY (TOWN)—See MILWAUKEE, WI (Time Warner Cable)

TROY TWP.—See BALDWIN TWP., WI (Baldwin Telecom Inc)

TURTLE LAKE—See AMERY, WI (Northwest Community Communications)

TURTLE TWP.—See MADISON, WI (Charter Communications)

TUSTIN—Formerly served by New Century Communications. No longer in operation

TWIN LAKES (VILLAGE)—See MADISON, WI (Charter Communications)

TWIN LAKES—See MILWAUKEE, WI (Time Warner Cable)

TWO CREEKS—See FOND DU LAC, WI (Charter Communications)

TWO RIVERS—Charter Communications. Now served by STEVENS POINT, WI [WI0019]

TWO RIVERS—See STEVENS POINT, WI (Charter Communications)

UNION (TOWN)—See ELMWOOD (village), WI (Video services provided by Celect Communications & available through Bloomer Tel, Bruce Tel, Celect Communications, NextGen & West WI Telcom. Formerly [WI0337]. This cable system has converted to IPTV)

UNION CENTER—See WONEWOC, WI (Packerland Broadband)

UNION GROVE (VILLAGE)—See MILWAUKEE, WI (Time Warner Cable)

UNION TWP. (EAU CLAIRE COUNTY)—See EAU CLAIRE, WI (Charter Communications)

UNION TWP. (ROCK COUNTY)—See MADISON, WI (Charter Communications)

UNION—See MADISON, IL (Charter Communications)

UNION—See MANAWA, WI (Manawa Telecom Video)

UNITY—See STEVENS POINT, WI (Charter Communications)

UPHAM—Packerland Broadband

UTICA (TOWN)—See FOND DU LAC, WI (Charter Communications)

VALDERS—See APPLETON, WI (Time Warner Cable)

VAN DYNE—See FOND DU LAC, WI (Charter Communications)

VANDENBROEK—See APPLETON, WI (Time Warner Cable)

VERNON (TOWN)—See MILWAUKEE, WI (Time Warner Cable)

VERNON COUNTY (PORTIONS)—See VIROQUA, WI (Mediacom)

VERONA (TOWN)—See MADISON, WI (Charter Communications)

VESPER—Packerland Broadband

VIENNA TWP.—See MADISON, WI (Charter Communications)

VINLAND (TOWN)—See APPLETON, WI (Time Warner Cable)

VIOLA—See VIROQUA, WI (Mediacom)

VIROQUA—Mediacom

WABENO—Packerland Broadband

WALDO (VILLAGE)—See MILWAUKEE, WI (Time Warner Cable)

WALES (VILLAGE)—See MILWAUKEE, WI (Time Warner Cable)

WALWORTH (VILLAGE)—See MADISON, WI (Charter Communications)

WARRENS—Charter Communications. Now served by EAU CLAIRE, WI [WI0011]

WARRENS—See EAU CLAIRE, WI (Charter Communications)

WASHBURN—See EAU CLAIRE, WI (Charter Communications)

WASHINGTON (TOWN)—See STEVENS POINT, WI (Charter Communications)

WASHINGTON (TOWN)—See ELMWOOD (village), WI (Video services provided by Celect Communications & available through Bloomer Tel, Bruce Tel, Celect Communications, NextGen & West WI Telcom. Formerly [WI0337]. This cable system has converted to IPTV)

WASHINGTON—See STEVENS POINT, WI (Charter Communications)

WASHINGTON—Packerland Broadband

WATERFORD (TOWN)—See MILWAUKEE, WI (Time Warner Cable)

WATERLOO—See MADISON, WI (Charter Communications)

WATERTOWN TWP.—See MADISON, WI (Charter Communications)

WATERTOWN—See MADISON, WI (Charter Communications)

WATERVILLE (TOWN)—See ELMWOOD (village), WI (Video services provided by Celect Communications & available through Bloomer Tel, Bruce Tel, Celect Communications, NextGen & West WI Telcom. Formerly [WI0337]. This cable system has converted to IPTV)

WAUBEEK (TOWN)—See ELMWOOD (village), WI (Video services provided by Celect Communications & available through Bloomer Tel, Bruce Tel, Celect Communications, NextGen & West WI Telcom. Formerly [WI0337]. This cable system has converted to IPTV)

WAUKECHON (TOWN)—See STEVENS POINT, WI (Charter Communications)

WAUKESHA—See MILWAUKEE, WI (Time Warner Cable)

WAUKON JUNCTION—See BOSCOBEL, IA (Mediacom)

WAUKON—See BOSCOBEL, IA (Mediacom)

WAUNAKEE—See MADISON, WI (Charter Communications)

WAUPACA—See STEVENS POINT, WI (Charter Communications)

WAUPUN—See FOND DU LAC, WI (Charter Communications)

WAUSAU—Charter Communications. Now served by STEVENS POINT, WI [WI0019]

WAUSAU—See STEVENS POINT, WI (Charter Communications)

WAUTOMA (TOWN)—See STEVENS POINT, WI (Charter Communications)

WAUTOMA—Charter Communications. Now served by STEVENS POINT, WI [WI0019]

WAUTOMA—See STEVENS POINT, WI (Charter Communications)

WAUWATOSA—Time Warner Cable. Now served by MILWAUKEE, WI [WI0001]

WAUWATOSA—See MILWAUKEE, WI (Time Warner Cable)

WAUZEKA—Packerland Broadband

WESCOTT (TOWN)—See STEVENS POINT, WI (Charter Communications)

WEST ALLIS—See MILWAUKEE, WI (Time Warner Cable)

WEST BARABOO (VILLAGE)—See MADISON, WI (Charter Communications)

WEST BEND—Charter Communications. Now served by FOND DU LAC, WI [WI0018]

WEST BEND—See FOND DU LAC, WI (Charter Communications)

WEST MILWAUKEE—See MILWAUKEE, WI (Time Warner Cable)

WEST POINT TWP.—See MADISON, WI (Charter Communications)

WEST POINT TWP.—See MERRIMAC, WI (Merrimac Cable)

WEST SALEM—See EAU CLAIRE, WI (Charter Communications)

WEST SWEDEN (TOWN)—See LUCK (village), WI (Lakeland Communications)

WESTBY—See VIROQUA, WI (Mediacom)

WESTFIELD—See STEVENS POINT, WI (Charter Communications)

WESTFORD—See RANDOLPH, WI (CenturyLink)

WESTON (TOWN)—See ELMWOOD (village), WI (Video services provided by Celect Communications & available through Bloomer Tel, Bruce Tel, Celect Communications, NextGen & West WI Telcom. Formerly [WI0337]. This cable system has converted to IPTV)

WESTON—See STEVENS POINT, WI (Charter Communications)

WESTPORT TWP.—See MADISON, WI (Charter Communications)

WEYAUWEGA—See STEVENS POINT, WI (Charter Communications)

WEYERHAEUSER—Formerly served by S & K TV Systems. No longer in operation

WHEATLAND (TOWN)—See MILWAUKEE, WI (Time Warner Cable)

WHEATLAND—See MADISON, WI (Charter Communications)

WHEATON (TOWN)—See ELMWOOD (village), WI (Video services provided by Celect Communications & available through Bloomer Tel, Bruce Tel, Celect Communications, NextGen & West WI Telcom. Formerly [WI0337]. This cable system has converted to IPTV)

WHEATON TWP.—See EAU CLAIRE, WI (Charter Communications)

WHEELER (VILLAGE)—See EAU CLAIRE, WI (Charter Communications)

WHITE LAKE—Packerland Broadband

WHITEFISH BAY (VILLAGE)—See MILWAUKEE, WI (Time Warner Cable)

WHITEHALL—Western Wisconsin Communications Cooperative

WHITEWATER—Charter Communications. Now served by MADISON, WI [WI0002]

WHITEWATER—See MADISON, WI (Charter Communications)

WHITING (VILLAGE)—See STEVENS POINT, WI (Charter Communications)

WILD ROSE—See STEVENS POINT, WI (Charter Communications)

WILKINSON (TOWN)—See ELMWOOD (village), WI (Video services provided by Celect Communications & avail-

Wisconsin—Cable Community Index

able through Bloomer Tel, Bruce Tel, Celect Communications, NextGen & West WI Telcom. Formerly [WI0337]. This cable system has converted to IPTV)

WILLIAMS BAY—See MADISON, WI (Charter Communications)

WILLIAMSTOWN—See FOND DU LAC, WI (Charter Communications)

WILSON (TOWN)—See ELMWOOD (village), WI (Video services provided by Celect Communications & available through Bloomer Tel, Bruce Tel, Celect Communications, NextGen & West WI Telcom. Formerly [WI0337]. This cable system has converted to IPTV)

WILSON (VILLAGE)—See ELMWOOD (village), WI (Video services provided by Celect Communications & available through Bloomer Tel, Bruce Tel, Celect Communications, NextGen & West WI Telcom. Formerly [WI0337]. This cable system has converted to IPTV)

WILSON—See EAU CLAIRE, MN (Charter Communications)

WILSON—See FOND DU LAC, WI (Charter Communications)

WILTON—Mediacom. Now served by MAUSTON, WI [WI0084]

WILTON—See MAUSTON, WI (Mediacom)

WINCHESTER (TOWN)—See APPLETON, WI (Time Warner Cable)

WIND LAKE (TOWN)—See MILWAUKEE, WI (Time Warner Cable)

WIND POINT (VILLAGE)—See MILWAUKEE, WI (Time Warner Cable)

WINDSOR TWP.—See MADISON, WI (Charter Communications)

WINNECONNE (VILLAGE)—See FOND DU LAC, WI (Charter Communications)

WINONA—See EAU CLAIRE, MN (Charter Communications)

WINTER (TOWN)—See PHILLIPS, WI (Price County Telephone Co. Formerly [WI0119]. This cable system has converted to IPTV)

WINTER—See MIKANA, WI (S & K TV Systems)

WISCONSIN DELLS—See MADISON, WI (Charter Communications)

WISCONSIN RAPIDS—Charter Communications. Now served by STEVENS POINT, WI [WI0019]

WISCONSIN RAPIDS—See STEVENS POINT, WI (Charter Communications)

WISCONSIN RAPIDS—Solarus

WITHEE—See STEVENS POINT, WI (Charter Communications)

WITTENBERG—Wittenberg Cable TV

WOLF RIVER—New Century Communications

WONEWOC—Packerland Broadband

WOOD MOHR (TOWN)—See ELMWOOD (village), WI (Video services provided by Celect Communications & available through Bloomer Tel, Bruce Tel, Celect Communications, NextGen & West WI Telcom. Formerly [WI0337]. This cable system has converted to IPTV)

WOODBORO (TOWN)—See STEVENS POINT, WI (Charter Communications)

WOODMAN—Formerly served by Woodman TV Cable System. No longer in operation

WOODRUFF—See STEVENS POINT, WI (Charter Communications)

WOODVILLE (TOWN)—See APPLETON, WI (Time Warner Cable)

WOODVILLE (VILLAGE)—See BALDWIN TWP., WI (Baldwin Telecom Inc)

WORCESTER (TOWN)—See PHILLIPS, WI (Price County Telephone Co. Formerly [WI0119]. This cable system has converted to IPTV)

WRIGHTSTOWN (TOWN)—See APPLETON, WI (Time Warner Cable)

WRIGHTSTOWN (VILLAGE)—See APPLETON, WI (Time Warner Cable)

WYOCENA—See RANDOLPH, WI (CenturyLink)

WYOCENA—See MADISON, WI (Charter Communications)

YORKVILLE (TOWN)—See MILWAUKEE, WI (Time Warner Cable)

WYOMING

AFTON (town)—Formerly served by KLiP Interactive. No longer in operation

ALBANY COUNTY (PORTIONS)—See LARAMIE, WY (Charter Communications)

BAR NUNN—See CASPER, WY (Charter Communications)

BASIN—TCT West Inc. This cable system has converted to IPTV. See BASIN, WY [WY5003]

BASIN—See GREYBULL, WY (Charter Communications)

BASIN—TCT West Inc. This cable system has converted to IPTV

BIG HORN COUNTY—See GREYBULL, WY (Charter Communications)

BUFFALO—Charter Communications

BURLINGTON—TCT West. This cable system has converted to IPTV. Now served by BASIN, WY [WY5033]

BURLINGTON—See BASIN, WY (TCT West Inc. This cable system has converted to IPTV)

BURNS—Formerly served by B & C Cablevision Inc. No longer in operation

BYRON—Formerly served by Byron Cable TV. No longer in operation

BYRON—TCT West. This cable system has converted to IPTV. Now served by BASIN, WY [WY5033]

BYRON—See BASIN, WY (TCT West Inc. This cable system has converted to IPTV)

CAMPBELL COUNTY (PORTIONS)—See GILLETTE, WY (Charter Communications)

CARBON COUNTY (PORTIONS)—See SARATOGA, WY (Vyve Broadband)

CASPER—Charter Communications

CHEYENNE—Charter Communications

CODY—Charter Communications

CODY—See BASIN, WY (TCT West Inc. This cable system has converted to IPTV)

COKEVILLE—All West Communications. This cable system has converted to IPTV. See OAKLEY, UT [UT5034]

CONVERSE COUNTY (PORTIONS)—See DOUGLAS, WY (Vyve Broadband)

COWLEY—Formerly served by Cowley Telecable Inc. No longer in operation

COWLEY—TCT West. This cable system has converted to IPTV. Now served by BASIN, WY [WY5033]

COWLEY—See BASIN, WY (TCT West Inc. This cable system has converted to IPTV)

DAYTON—See RANCHESTER, WY (Tongue River Communications)

DEAVER—See BASIN, WY (TCT West Inc. This cable system has converted to IPTV)

DOUGLAS—Vyve Broadband

DUBOIS—Formerly served by KLiP Interactive. No longer in operation

EAST THERMOPOLIS—See THERMOPOLIS, WY (Charter Communications)

EDGERTON—Formerly served by Tongue River Cable TV Inc. No longer in operation

EMBLEM—TCT West. This cable system has converted to IPTV. Now served by BASIN, WY [WY5033]

EMBLEM—See BASIN, WY (TCT West Inc. This cable system has converted to IPTV)

ENCAMPMENT—See RIVERSIDE, WY (Vyve Broadband)

EVANSTON—All West Communications

EVANSVILLE—See CASPER, WY (Charter Communications)

FORT LARAMIE—See GUERNSEY, WY (WinDBreak Cable)

FRANNIE—TCT West. This cable system has converted to IPTV. Now served by BASIN, WY [WY5033]

FRANNIE—See BASIN, WY (TCT West Inc. This cable system has converted to IPTV)

FREMONT COUNTY (PORTIONS)—See RIVERTON, WY (Charter Communications)

GILLETTE—Charter Communications

GLENDO—Formerly served by CommuniComm Services. No longer in operation

GLENROCK—Vyve Broadband

GOSHEN COUNTY (UNINCORPORATED AREAS)—See TORRINGTON, WY (Vyve Broadband)

GREEN RIVER—Green River Cable TV. Now served by Sweetwater Cable TV, ROCK SPRINGS, WY [WY0004]

GREEN RIVER—See ROCK SPRINGS, WY (Sweetwater Cable TV Co. Inc)

GREYBULL—TCT West. This cable system has converted to IPTV. Now served by BASIN, WY [WY5033]

GREYBULL—Charter Communications

GREYBULL—See BASIN, WY (TCT West Inc. This cable system has converted to IPTV)

GUERNSEY—WinDBreak Cable

HANNA—See SARATOGA, WY (Vyve Broadband)

HARTVILLE—See GUERNSEY, WY (WinDBreak Cable)

HOT SPRINGS COUNTY (PORTIONS)—See THERMOPOLIS, WY (Charter Communications)

HULETT—Formerly served by Tongue River Communications. No longer in operation

HYATTVILLE—TCT West. This cable system has converted to IPTV. Now served by BASIN, WY [WY5033]

HYATTVILLE—See BASIN, WY (TCT West Inc. This cable system has converted to IPTV)

JACKSON (TOWN)—Charter Communications

JOHNSON COUNTY (PORTIONS)—See BUFFALO, WY (Charter Communications)

KEMMERER—Formerly served by KLiP Interactive. No longer in operation

LANDER—Formerly served by Bresnan Communications. Now served by Charter Communications, RIVERTON, WY [WY0059]

LANDER—See RIVERTON, WY (Charter Communications)

LARAMIE COUNTY (PORTIONS)—See CHEYENNE, WY (Charter Communications)

LARAMIE—Charter Communications

LINGLE—See TORRINGTON, WY (Vyve Broadband)

Cable Systems State Index

Alabama	D-15	Nevada	D-500
Alaska	D-37	New Hampshire	D-506
Arizona	D-44	New Jersey	D-510
Arkansas	D-54	New Mexico	D-519
California	D-82	New York	D-529
Colorado	D-111	North Carolina	D-550
Connecticut	D-127	North Dakota	D-568
Delaware	D-132	Ohio	D-577
District of Columbia	D-133	Oklahoma	D-607
Florida	D-134	Oregon	D-637
Georgia	D-151	Pennsylvania	D-648
Hawaii	D-177	Rhode Island	D-683
Idaho	D-179	South Carolina	D-684
Illinois	D-186	South Dakota	D-694
Indiana	D-225	Tennessee	D-705
Iowa	D-240	Texas	D-718
Kansas	D-278	Utah	D-790
Kentucky	D-306	Vermont	D-797
Louisiana	D-333	Virginia	D-801
Maine	D-353	Washington	D-814
Maryland	D-359	West Virginia	D-833
Massachusetts	D-365	Wisconsin	D-848
Michigan	D-370	Wyoming	D-871
Minnesota	D-391	Other U.S. Territories and Possessions	D-881
Mississippi	D-426		
Missouri	D-440	Cable Owners	D-887
Montana	D-464	Cable Community Index	(end of Cable Volume 2)
Nebraska	D-479		

Cable Community Index—Cuba

LOVELL—TCT West Inc. This cable system has converted to IPTV. Now served by BASIN, WY [WY5003]

LOVELL—TCT West. This cable system has converted to IPTV. Now served by BASIN, WY [WY5033]

LOVELL—See BASIN, WY (TCT West Inc. This cable system has converted to IPTV)

LUSK—Vyve Broadband

MAMMOTH HOT SPRINGS—Formerly served by North Yellowstone Cable TV. No longer in operation

MANDERSON—TCT West. This cable system has converted to IPTV. Now served by BASIN, WY [WY5033]

MANDERSON—See BASIN, WY (TCT West Inc. This cable system has converted to IPTV)

MEDICINE BOW—Formerly served by Medicine Bow Cable. No longer in operation

MEETEESE—See BASIN, WY (TCT West Inc. This cable system has converted to IPTV)

MEETEETSE—Formerly served by KLiP Interactive. No longer in operation

MEETEETSE—TCT West. This cable system has converted to IPTV. Now served by BASIN, WY [WY5033]

MILLS—See CASPER, WY (Charter Communications)

MOORCROFT—Tongue River Communications

MOUNTAIN VIEW (NATRONA COUNTY)—See CASPER, WY (Charter Communications)

MOUNTAIN VIEW (UINTA COUNTY)—Union Cable Co

NATRONA COUNTY—See CASPER, WY (Charter Communications)

NEWCASTLE—Charter Communications

NORTH ROCK SPRINGS—See ROCK SPRINGS, WY (Sweetwater Cable TV Co. Inc)

OSAGE—Formerly served by Tongue River Cable TV Inc. No longer in operation

OTTO—TCT West. This cable system has converted to IPTV. Now served by BASIN, WY [WY5033]

OTTO—See BASIN, WY (TCT West Inc. This cable system has converted to IPTV)

PARK COUNTY (PORTIONS)—See CODY, WY (Charter Communications)

PARK COUNTY (PORTIONS)—See POWELL, WY (Charter Communications)

PINE BLUFFS—WinDBreak Cable

PINE HAVEN—Tongue River Communications

PINEDALE—Formerly served by KLiP Interactive. No longer in operation

PLATTE COUNTY (UNINCORPORATED AREAS)—See WHEATLAND, WY (Vyve Broadband)

POWELL—TCT West. This cable system has converted to IPTV. Now served by BASIN, WY [WY5033]

POWELL—Charter Communications

POWELL—See BASIN, WY (TCT West Inc. This cable system has converted to IPTV)

RANCHESTER—Tongue River Communications

RAWLINS—Charter Communications

RELIANCE—See ROCK SPRINGS, WY (Sweetwater Cable TV Co. Inc)

RIVERSIDE—Vyve Broadband

RIVERTON—Charter Communications

ROCK SPRINGS—Sweetwater Cable TV Co. Inc

ROLLING HILLS—See GLENROCK, WY (Vyve Broadband)

SARATOGA—Vyve Broadband

SHELL—TCT West. This cable system has converted to IPTV. Now served by BASIN, WY [WY5033]

SHELL—See BASIN, WY (TCT West Inc. This cable system has converted to IPTV)

SHERIDAN COUNTY (PORTIONS)—See SHERIDAN, WY (Charter Communications)

SHERIDAN—Formerly served by Sprint Corp. No longer in operation

SHERIDAN—Charter Communications

SHOSHONI—Formerly served by Winhill Corp. No longer in operation

SINCLAIR—See RAWLINS, WY (Charter Communications)

STORY—Tongue River Communications

SUNDANCE—Tongue River Communications

SWEETWATER COUNTY (PORTIONS)—See ROCK SPRINGS, WY (Sweetwater Cable TV Co. Inc)

SWEETWATER COUNTY (UNINCORPORATED AREAS)—See ROCK SPRINGS, WY (Sweetwater Cable TV Co. Inc)

TEN SLEEP—TCT West. Now served by BASIN, WY [WY5003]

TEN SLEEP—TCT West. This cable system has converted to IPTV. Now served by BASIN, WY [WY5033]

TEN SLEEP—See BASIN, WY (TCT West Inc. This cable system has converted to IPTV)

TETON COUNTY (PORTIONS)—See JACKSON (town), WY (Charter Communications)

THERMOPOLIS—Charter Communications

TORRINGTON—Vyve Broadband

UINTA COUNTY (PORTIONS)—See EVANSTON, WY (All West Communications)

UPTON—Tongue River Communications

WAMSUTTER—Formerly served by Sweetwater Cable TV Co. Inc. No longer in operation

WARREN AFB—See CHEYENNE, WY (Charter Communications)

WASHAKIE COUNTY (PORTIONS)—See WORLAND, WY (Charter Communications)

WESTON COUNTY (PORTIONS)—See NEWCASTLE, WY (Charter Communications)

WHEATLAND—Vyve Broadband

WORLAND—Charter Communications

WRIGHT—Formerly served by Charter Communications. No longer in operation

WYODAK—Formerly served by Tongue River Cable TV Inc. No longer in operation

GUAM

AGANA HEIGHTS—See AGANA, GU (Docomo Pacific)

AGANA—Docomo Pacific

AGAT—See AGANA, GU (Docomo Pacific)

ASAN-MAINA—See AGANA, GU (Docomo Pacific)

BARRIGADA—See AGANA, GU (Docomo Pacific)

CHALAN PAGO-ORDOT—See AGANA, GU (Docomo Pacific)

DEDEDO—See AGANA, GU (Docomo Pacific)

HAGATNA—See AGANA, GU (Docomo Pacific)

INARAJAN—See AGANA, GU (Docomo Pacific)

MANGILAO—See AGANA, GU (Docomo Pacific)

MERIZO—See AGANA, GU (Docomo Pacific)

MONGMONG-TOTO-MAITE—See AGANA, GU (Docomo Pacific)

PITI—See AGANA, GU (Docomo Pacific)

SANTA RITA—See AGANA, GU (Docomo Pacific)

SINAJANA—See AGANA, GU (Docomo Pacific)

TALOFOFO—See AGANA, GU (Docomo Pacific)

TAMUNING—See AGANA, GU (Docomo Pacific)

UMATAC—See AGANA, GU (Docomo Pacific)

YIGO—See AGANA, GU (Docomo Pacific)

YONA—See AGANA, GU (Docomo Pacific)

MARIANA ISLANDS

ROTA—See SAIPAN, MP (CNMI Cablevision)

SAIPAN—CNMI Cablevision

SINAPALO—CNMI Cablevision

SUSUPE—CNMI Cablevision

TINIAN—See SAIPAN, MP (CNMI Cablevision)

VIRGIN ISLANDS

ST. CROIX—St. Croix Cable TV

ST. JOHN—See ST. THOMAS, VI (Caribbean Communications Corp.)

ST. THOMAS—Caribbean Communications Corp.

CUBA

GUANTANAMO BAY—C H Comm LLC